The Official Museum Directory™ 2010

The 2010 edition of The Official Museum Directory™ is published by National Register Publishing in partnership with the American Association of Museums.

Printed and bound in the United States of America

International Standard Book Number: 978-0-87217-758-1
International Standard Serial Number: 0090-6700
Library of Congress Catalog Card Number: 79-144808

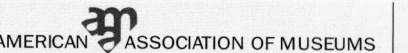

The Official Museum Directory™ 2010

Table of Contents

Key to Symbols:
Accredited Museums [*]
Members of the AAM [M]
Institutional Member of ICOM-US, the U.S. National Committee of the International Council of Museums [I]
Volunteer President [Pres. (V)]
Volunteer Chairman [Chm. (V)]
Traveling Exhibit [(T)]
Telecommunications Device for the Deaf [TDD]
Handicapped Accessible [♿]

The Official Museum Directory™

On behalf of National Register Publishing and the American Association of Museums, we take great pride in presenting the 2010 edition of The Official Museum Directory™. By bringing the full resources of our two organizations and over 125 years of combined experience to bear, we are able to ensure that the OMD is the most comprehensive directory of America's museums, zoos, historic sites, and other related institutions. In this edition you will find a wealth of information on the nation's ever-expanding and influential museum community.

The 2010 Directory contains information on more than 12,200 museums operating in 87 different fields, ranging from fine arts to historic homes, from zoos to science museums. We are pleased to include information on new exhibits along with 1,020 new listings.

In compiling the 2010 edition, we use the same stringent quality control and collection procedures as we have in the past. Each institution receives a copy of its listing for review. Returned listings are scrupulously reviewed and updated by NRP editors. The resulting directory is both current and accurate, with most of the information comin from the museums themselves.

The Official Museum Directory™ is an invaluable source for museum professionals seeking to contact directors and curators, identify unique collections and locate traveling exhibitions. Library patrons and travelers can discover important local cultural centers and identify educational travel destinations. Additionally, the directory contains a series of indexes that provide numerous ways to access museum information and the Products & Services section, which assists in locating suppliers who specialize in the museum field.

This directory is only one example of how the American Association of Museums serves the museum community and the public. We hope The Official Museum Directory™ will prove to be not only an inspiration but also a valuable tool to help you take full advantage of one of American's truly great national resources – our country's diverse community of museums.

Sincerely,

Robert Docherty
Publisher
National Register Publishing
890 Mountain Avenue, Suite 300
New Providence, NJ 07974
(800) 473-7020
www.officialmuseumdirectory.com

Ford W. Bell, DVM
American Association of Museums
1575 Eye Street, NW Suite 400
Washington, DC 20005
(202) 289-1818
www.aam-us.org

About the American Association of Museums

1575 Eye St. N.W.
Suite 400
Washington, DC 20005

Phone: 202-289-1818
Fax: 202-289-6578

E-mail: membership@aam-us.org
Web: www.aam-us.org

AAM History

Founded in 1906, the American Association of Museums (AAM) is dedicated to promoting excellence within the museum community. Through advocacy, professional education, information exchange, accreditation and guidance on current professional standards of performance, AAM assists museum staff, boards and volunteers across the country to better serve the public.

AAM is the only organization representing the entire scope of museums and the professionals and unpaid staff who work for and with them. AAM currently represents more than 23,000 members—20,000 individual museum professionals and volunteers, 3,100 institutions and 300 corporate members. Individual members span the range of museum occupations, including directors, curators, registrars, educators, exhibit designers, public relations officers, development officers, security managers, trustees and volunteers. In addition, every type of museum is represented by AAM's institutional members, including art, history, culturally specific, natural history, science, military, maritime, and children's museums, as well as aquariums, zoos, botanical gardens, arboretums, historic sites and science and technology centers.

Mission of the American Association of Museums

To enhance the value of museums to their communities through leadership, advocacy and service.

What is a Museum?

The AAM Code of Ethics for Museums notes that museums' common denominator is making a "unique contribution to the public by collecting, preserving, and interpreting the things of this world." The code also acknowledges the variety of museums: "Their numbers include both governmental and private museums of anthropology, art history and natural history, aquariums, arboreta, art centers, botanical gardens, children's museums, historic sites, nature centers, planetariums, science and technology centers, and zoos."

About the American Association of Museums

The association is governed by a 21-member board of directors elected by AAM members via a single-slate election process. Board members serve three-year terms; the chair serves for two years and the vice chair serves for one year. The board meets in April or May (in conjunction with the annual meeting), in July and in November. Members are welcome to attend board meetings.

In addition to the board of directors, three councils—the Council of Standing Professional Committees, the Council of Regional Associations and the Council of Affiliates—have input into the board's agenda. A fourth group—AAM Professional Interest Committees—enables individuals and institutions in the field with similar interests to develop professional associations.

Up-to-date contact information for the AAM Board, committees and councils is available at www.aam-us.org.

Council of Standing Professional Committees

AAM's 13 Standing Professional Committees represent specific disciplines within the museum community.

- Committee for Diversity in Museums (provisional) (DIVCOM)
- Committee on Audience Research and Evaluation (CARE)
- Committee on Education (EdCom)
- Committee on Museum Professional Training (COMPT)
- Curators Committee (CurCom)
- Development and Membership Committee (DAM)
- Media and Technology Committee (M&T)
- Museum Association Security Committee (MASC)
- Museum Management Committee (MMC)
- National Association for Museum Exhibition (NAME)
- Public Relations and Marketing Committee (PRAM)
- Registrars Committee (RC-AAM)
- Small Museum Administrators Committee (SMAC)

Council of Regional Associations

The AAM Council of Regional Associations serves as a source of information in policy deliberations that may have an impact beyond AAM's members.

- Association of Midwest Museums (AMM)
- Mid-Atlantic Association of Museums (MAAM)
- Mountain-Plains Museum Association (MPMA)
- New England Museum Association (NEMA)
- Southeastern Museums Conference (SEMC)
- Western Museums Association (WMA)

About the American Association of Museums

Council of Affiliates

The AAM Council of Affiliates serves as a source of information for policy deliberations that may have an impact beyond AAM's members.

- American Association for Museum Volunteers (AAMV)
- American Association for State and Local History (AASLH)
- American Association of Botanical Gardens and Arboreta (APGA)
- American Federation of Arts (AFA)
- American Institute for Conservation of Historic and Artistic Works (AIC)
- American Zoo and Aquarium Association (AZA)
- Association for Living History, Farm and Agricultural Museums (ALHFAM)
- Association of African American Museums (AAAM)
- Association of Art Museum Directors (AAMD)
- Association of Children's Museums (ACM)
- Association of College and University Museums and Galleries (ACUMG)
- Association of Railway Museums (ARM)
- Association of Science Museum Directors (ASMD)
- Association of Science-Technology Centers (ASTC)
- College Art Association (CAA)
- Council for Museum Anthropology (CMA)
- Council of American Jewish Museums (CAJM)
- Council of American Maritime Museums (CAMM)
- International Association of Museum Facility Administrators (IAMFA)
- International Museum Theatre Alliance (IMTAL)
- Museum Computer Network (MCN)
- Museum Store Association (MSA)
- Museum Trustee Association (MTA)
- Natural Science Collections Alliance (NSC)

Professional Interest Committees

AAM Professional Interest Committees enable individuals and institutions that share a common interest or have a common need related to working in the museum field to develop professional associations.

- Alliance for Lesbian and Gay Concerns Professional Interest Committee (ALGC)
- Asian Pacific American Professional Interest Committee Network (ASIAN)
- Historic House Museums Professional Interest Council (HIST_HOUSE)
- Latino Network Professional Interest Committee (LN-PIC)
- Native Americans and Museums Collaboration Network Professional Interest Committee (NATIVE)
- Packing and Crating Information Network Professional Interest Committee (PACIN)
- Professional Interest Committee-Green (PIC-GREEN)
- Traveling Exhibitions Professional Interest Committee (TRAVEL_EXHIBIT)
- Visitor Services Professional Interest Committee (VSPIC)

ICOM-US Board

ICOM-US is the U.S. National Committee of the International Council of Museums (ICOM). ICOM-US advises and assists AAM's participation in programs of international interest, represents museums in the United States within ICOM, and shares ICOM's activities with the U.S. museum field.

AAM Resources

JOIN AAM TODAY!

AAM members enjoy a wide range of resources and services, a number of which are described below. And membership also brings the added benefit of supporting AAM's efforts to provide museums a strong, constructive, effective voice with Congress, policymakers and the media. Help us make the case for museums. Join AAM today, by visiting www.aam-us.org.

Accreditation

www.aam-us.org/accred
202-289-1818
accreditation@aam-us.org

Accreditation provides a museum national recognition that signifies it operates according to the highest and most current professional standards and best practices, and that it fulfills its obligations to the public as put forth in its mission.

The positive public image and credibility resulting from accreditation can attract volunteers, visitors, contributions, loans and traveling exhibitions, and can help museums lobby local and state governments. Internally, the rigorous process builds teamwork within the institution, which emerges from the process with a clearer sense of purpose and understanding of its strengths, goals, priorities and mission.

Information Center

www.aam-us.org/ic
202-289-1818
infocenter@aam-us.org

The Information Center and its online resources provide all AAM members with fast, easy-to-access information that helps museums make informed decisions. Information Center resources on the AAM website provide guidance on museum operations, standards and best practices and emerging issues.

Topics include institutional planning, governance, financial stability, human resources, facilities, risk management and much more. In addition, the Information Center offers customized reference services to AAM institutional member museums, including access to more than 1,000 sample documents from accredited museums.

jobHQ

www.aam-us.org/jobhq

JobHQ allows employers to place classified job advertisements in real time on the AAM website. This online service offers updated job listings 24 hours a day; searchable listings by employer, location, salary range, job category and/or title; and e-mail alerts when new listings appear matching a preferred profile. Employers can post jobs from their desktops and track activity online to measure and report on recruitment advertising, as well as pay for ads online with a credit card. Marketplace and Career Development ads remain in Aviso, AAM's monthly e-newsletter, but employment ads are available only on jobHQ.

AAM Museum Advocacy

www.speakupformuseums.org
202-218-7703
mat@aam-us.org

Every museum professional and supporter can be a museum advocate! At AAM's advocacy website www.speakupformuseums.org you can find your federal and state legislators, learn about issues affecting the museum field, and use AAM's sample letters to contact your legislators with just a few clicks. AAM's Action Alerts and Legislative Updates provide timely information on critical policy issues such as federal funding for museums, tax incentives for charitable giving, and education policies and letting you know when and how to take action with your elected officials. AAM also provides online advocacy training, much of it accessible on the www.speakupformuseums.org website. AAM also coordinates an annual Museums Advocacy Day, bringing together a diverse group of museum professionals and advocates from around the country to take our message about the value of museums to Capitol Hill.

Emerging Museum Professionals

www.aam-us.org/emp

AAM's Emerging Museum Professional program serves the needs of those in the first ten years of their career working for or with museums. The program provides tools and information about networking, finding a mentor, fellowships and affordable professional development opportunities. EMPs can access this information through AAM's EMP website and listserv, as well as at a wide array of events and activities at AAM's Annual Meeting, regional museum association meetings and networking events nationwide.

Museum Assessment Program (MAP)

www.aam-us.org/map
202-289-9118
map@aam-us.org

The Museum Assessment Program (MAP) helps museums pursue excellence through self-study and peer review and is adaptable to museums of all types and sizes. Museums choose from four different assessments based on their needs and resources; the Institutional Assessment is the core assessment focusing on all museum operations, while the Collections Management, Public Dimension and Governance Assessments are particular to those respective functions. All participants receive advice from MAP staff and objective feedback from a qualified AAM Peer Reviewer. MAP participants are nationally recognized for pursuing excellence and can leverage future funding with the results of their assessment efforts. Thanks to support from the Institute of Museum and Library Services, assessments are very affordable. Participation in MAP is non-competitive for eligible museums who apply by the annual application deadline. Please check the MAP website for application details: www.aam-us.org/map.

Museums & Community Collaborations Abroad

www.aam-us.org/mcca
202.289.1818
mcca@aam-us.org

Museums & Community Collaborations Abroad (MCCA) supports museum-based international exchanges in which members of the museums' communities play a leading role in shaping their owncollaborative experience while simultaneously creating new connections with communities abroad. The projects empower citizens to explore, compare, and document their own experiences and to share their perspectives with their peers across the globe. MCCA awardees design their own project structure, can request MCCA grants from $75,000-$150,000, and have 18 months to complete their projects. AAM administers the program, which is funded by the US Department of State Bureau of Educational and Cultural Affairs.

Nazi Era Provenance Internet Portal

www.nepip.org
202-289-9121
eledbetter@aam-us.org

The Nazi-Era Provenance Internet Portal provides a searchable registry of objects in U.S. museum collections that were created before 1946 and changed hands in continental Europe during the Nazi era (1933–45). Designed and managed by AAM, the portal helps U.S. museums fulfill their responsibility under AAM's Recommended Procedures to make Nazi-era provenance information centrally accessible to the public. By joining the portal project, museums can assure members, donors, patrons and the community that they are taking all reasonable steps to make Nazi-era provenance information accessible. Museums participate free of charge and do not have to have completed their World War II-era provenance research to do so.

Peer Review

www.aam-us.org/peer-review
202-289-1818
peer-review@aam-us.org

Peer review for the Museum Assessment Program (MAP) and Accreditation Program is a unique professional development opportunity premised on the idea that professionals who develop and follow standards of excellence in their own everyday work are best equipped to evaluate the work of their colleagues. Peer reviewers consider current standards and best practices as they take an in-depth look at another institution. Eligibility requirements, position description and application information can be found at on the AAM website.

AAM Resources

AAM Professional Development (AAM PD)

www.aam-us.org/profed
seminars@aam-us.org

Launched officially in 1988, AAM PD provides tools to address some of the most critical and relevant issues in the field through online webinars and web conferences (both live and on-demand), podcasts and audio conferences, face-to-face seminars and workshops, and the AAM Career Café™ at the AAM Annual Meeting. AAM PD is committed to providing the highest quality programs to the broadest audience, addressing the AAM goals of leadership, collaboration, and excellence. A range of programs are held throughout the year to meet the needs of museum practitioners at every stage of their career, in all functional areas, and in a wide range of museum types, sizes, budgets and disciplines. In doing so, AAM PD helps individual museum practitioners improve both their technical and interpersonal management and leadership skills (hard and soft skills), thus helping create stronger institutions that can better serve their communities, and ultimately help communicate the value of museums to society in these challenging times and beyond.

For more information, please contact Greg Stevens, Assistant Director for Professional Development at gstevens@aam-us.org.

In 2010, AAM Professional Development will include the following in its menu of offerings:

- Collections Care webinar
- Preservation and Conservation webinar
- Executive Suite Web Conference: Succession Planning and Leadership Transition
- Straight Talk Web Conference: Communication with your board, your staff, your teams
- Preparing for Disaster
- Copyright Web Conference
- Museums Going Green webinar
- Universal Design webinar
- Museum Management Seminar
- Standards and Best Practices for Museums webinar
- Unraveling Accreditation Mysteries webinar
- Museum and School Partnerships webinar
- Managing Board Communications webinar
- Collections Management (in Spanish) webinar
- Podcasts and Audio conferences for all of the above

The Year in Review 2009

By Gretchen Sullivan Sorin
Director and Distinguished Professor
The Cooperstown Graduate Program

Doing more with less and rethinking the museum, its mission and relevance were prominent themes for American museums in 2009. Finding new audiences and keeping old ones, finding new sources of revenue in a difficult economic climate, and generating popular programs in the face of decreasing assets are the greatest challenges for the future. Museums of all disciplines are searching for strategies to remain afloat and to find their footing in the struggling economy. Some institutions, like the Museum of Contemporary Art in Los Angeles survived only through a bailout from a major donor while other institutions tightened their belts, streamlined their staffs and worked hard to reach out to their communities with new programs that stretched their missions and enticed visitors. "People bring museums to life," Pulitzer Prize winning art critic Holland Cotter reminded us in an article in the *New York Times*. And museums are experimenting with all kinds of ideas to boost audience numbers, to respond to the needs

The Philadelphia Museum of Art
Philadelphia, PA

of changing communities, and thereby to find ways to stay alive and lively. "Several of our veteran museums are doing by undoing: loosening up the rigid values and temple-of-art models that shaped them," says Cotter, "and replacing these with a new 'people's museum' model, unsacred in atmosphere, fluid in values, with complicated answers to the question of what museums are."[1]

Museums and the Recession

Dramatically shrinking endowments brought on by the recession led museums across the country to cut staff members, reduce salaries, and to institute hiring freezes and staff furloughs in 2009. The crisis seems to have disproportionately affected large and medium size art and history museums, those most dependent on endowment income. Institutions from the Metropolitan Museum in New York and the Houston Museum of Art in Texas to the Museum of the City of New York and the Milwaukee Public Museum in Wisconsin experienced a significant loss of endowment and a decrease in public funding. Many museums cancelled expensive new exhibitions and extended the run of other shows to avoid the expense of loans and exhibition rental fees. To close budget deficits some institutions also looked for ways to creatively expand the use of their permanent collections while others reduced open hours or CEO compensation. Some are considering mergers. The Brooklyn Museum and the Philadelphia Museum of Art are among those museums that raised their admission prices in an attempt to generate more revenue while other museum professionals debated whether or not museums should charge admission at all.[2] The Las Vegas Museum of Art finally succumbed to what its director, art historian Libby Lumpkin called an "economic Katrina" in the city after several years of trying to remain afloat with a small endowment and a sinking economy.[3]

"Two categories of museums that are really having problems are historic houses and living history museums," commented Elizabeth Merritt, Founding Director of the Center for the Future of Museums. "I think a bunch of them are going to close or they are not going to be museums anymore. They are finding themselves in a situation in which their core function is not matched up to their source of revenue."[4] While declining visitation to historic house museums and living history farms has been a trend for several years, the nation's economic woes have exacerbated the problem. The proliferation of historic houses—there are more than 300 in Philadelphia alone—also contributes to the problem. Hundreds of historic buildings throughout the country, swept up in the patriotic fervor of the bicentennial, were preserved as museums, open to the public with collections of artifacts. There are between 8,000 and 15,000 historic house museums across the country. Now, more than 30 years after the bicentennial many of these buildings are suffering from undercapitalization and deferred maintenance. Often frozen in time with stagnant period rooms and unchanging programs these museums no longer relate to their communities. Reflecting the changing demographics of the United States and the interest in 20th-century history, new historic house museums continue to be added to the mix. Marion Anderson's Philadelphia home as well as her Danbury Connecticut studio and The Dix Hills, New York ranch house belonging to jazz musician John Coltrane are among the newer historic house museums. Concerned about the future of historic house museums, preservationists and museum professionals at the National Trust for Historic Preservation and the American Association for State and Local History have convened summits and sessions at their annual conferences to debate this issue. Both groups envision a future in which successful historic house museums will broaden their missions and go beyond the

1 Holland Cotter, "Museums Look Inward for Their Own Bailouts," *The New York Times*, January 7, 2009.

2 An informal survey conduced by the California Association of Museums resulted in a spirited debated about museums admission fees. 36% of the respondents believed museums should be free. 35% believed they should charge admission fees. California Association of Museums, http://www.calmuseums.org/e-news/poll/2008-08.html accessed, November 10, 2009.

3 Sarah Douglas, "Libby Lumpkin on Leaving Las Vegas," *ARTINFO*, February 27, 2009

4 Elizabeth Merritt, interview with Gretchen Sullivan Sorin, November 10, 2009.

The Farmers' Museum - Cooperstown, NY

"frozen view of the past" to transform themselves into sustainable, community-focused institutions.[5] Many may not survive as museums, as Elizabeth Merritt predicts, and will need to find other ways of protecting their community's architectural heritage, perhaps as Historic New England has done with their Stewardship Program. "Few [historic houses] will ever approach the revered status of Mount Vernon or Monticello," wrote Marian Godfrey of the Pew Charitable Trusts and Barbara Silberman, principal at Heritage Partners Consulting. "As more communities recognize the perilous future facing their historic house museums, more are joining the conversation of conversion, hoping to discover innovative ways to improve the interpretation, access and community involvement of their significant buildings."[6]

Taking a lead from popular farm-based education centers, some history museums are assuming a leadership role developing relevant programming to increase visitation and respond to the interests of their communities. As the recession heated up so too did a passion for gardening, particularly growing vegetables to help families decrease their grocery bills.[7] At the same time, concerns about the environment and the safety of foods have led to a growing movement to eat local and organic foods. Building on this recent craze, Strawbery Banke in Portsmouth, New Hampshire developed a series of public programs linking their historic gardens to sustainable gardening practices. Programs on seed saving, organic gardening, and composting were developed. Future plans include using solar panels in their Victorian hothouse. Similarly, The Farmers' Museum in Cooperstown New York uses their historic barnyard to reconnect people with the source of their food through participatory activities such as milking a cow and learning how to start your own healthy hen house or beehive. "Younger families and visitors have a less precious view of history museums than their parents and grandparents and want very much to be drawn in with hooks to today's issues and their own lives," says D. Stephen Elliott, President and CEO of the New York State

5 From the Pocantico Proclamation, November, 2008, accessed, November 21, 2009 http://www.preservationnation.org/issues/sustainability/additional-resources/Pocantico-Proclamation.pdf

6 Marian Godfrey and Barbara Silberman, "A Model for Historic House Museums," *The Virginian-Pilot*, January 2008, accessed, November 21, 2009.

7 Bruce Horowitz, *USA Today*, "Recession Grows Interest in Seeds, Vegetable Gardening," February 20, 2009.

Historical Association and The Farmers' Museum. "They also enjoy special events and programs that may have looser ties to mission but that entice less seriously committed audiences to come have fun and serendipitously have a museum experience as well. These opportunities abound but require us to be more attuned to different audience segments and more creative in experimenting with and adapting programs and events."[8]

Some museums—particularly children's museums and science museums have actually fared somewhat better than large art and history museums either because of their already smaller budgets or because of less dependence on endowment income and thus limited exposure to the stock market.[9] Science museums willingness to push the boundaries of their missions also helped their bottom lines. To boost visitation, science museums continued to take on tremendously popular but somewhat controversial exhibitions. "Harry Potter: The Exhibition" at the Boston Museum of Science fascinated its young viewers with "authentic" artifacts from the motion picture. Elaborate room settings recreate Hogwarts and Hagrid's hut with props from the motion picture, but critics found it only peripherally related to science.[10] The Houston Museum of Natural Science at Sugarland similarly delighted young visitors with Disney's "Chronicles of Narnia" exhibition composed of fanciful environments that immersed children in the world of the popular books.

Ironically, the sluggish economy may have contributed to an increase in museum visitation in some museums even as other sources of revenue decreased. In the midst of the fiscal crisis, rather than going on vacation many families chose to explore entertainment and cultural resources in their own backyards to save money. Special and family oriented programs boosted visits to these institutions. New York City's Tenement Museum reported a substantial 20% increase in visitation over last year. Free or inexpensive museum entertainment represented good value for cash strapped families. Many museums responded to the decline in the economy by expanding their programming to encourage visitation even as they cut hours and staff.[11]

Don't Close the Rose

Emblematic of the year's economic problems was the situation at Brandeis University, the home institution of the Rose Museum in Waltham, Massachusetts. The University took particularly dramatic steps to address their institutional deficit. Faced with a ten million dollar shortfall resulting from the dip in the stock market and the concurrent drop in their endowment, the university decided to dispose of the art collection housed in their Rose Museum and to close the museum's doors to raise needed cash. University President Jehuda Reinharz's ill conceived decision ignited a firestorm of criticism for the 48-year-old Rose and its important collection of postwar art that includes significant works by such artists as Willem de Kooning, Jasper Johns, Roy Lichtenstein, Andy Warhol, Robert Motherwell, and Richard Serra. As supporters sported buttons and plastered signs on the museum reading such things as "Don't Close the Rose," the museum's director, Michael Rush, donors and supporters, students and the museum professional community mounted loud protests. In an article in the *New York Times*, art critic Roberta Smith called the decision to sell the Rose's collection, "an act of breathtaking stealth and presumption: a raid on a

8 D. Stephen Elliott, interview with Gretchen Sullivan Sorin, November 16, 2009.

9 *Milwaukee Wisconsin Journal Sentinel*, "Milwaukee Public Museum to furlough employees, suspend 401(k) addition," March 5, 2009; Economic Change and the Future of American Museums, Guest blog by James Chung and Susie Wilkening, Reach Advisors http://futureofmuseums.blogspot.com/2009/09/economic-change-and-future-of-american.html, Accessed, November 10, 2009

10 Mark Feeney, "'Harry Potter' & the green machine: Not much science, but exhibit's enchantments will bring in the crowds," *The Boston Globe*, October 24, 2009.

11 Nicole G. Anderson, *Gotham Gazette*, "Museums Struggle to Maintain Programs and Projects," October 2009. http://www.gothamgazette.com/article/arts/20091006/1/3046/Accessed November 8, 2009; *Portland Press Herald*, "Colby art museum a picture of financial health," September 7, 2009.

Rose Art Museum at Brandeis University - Waltham, MA

museum that supports itself, raises its own funds and has consistently planned wisely for its own future without leaning on the university."[12]

In July, three overseers of the Museum, including a member of the founding Rose family filed suit against Brandeis in a Massachusetts court to stop the sale of artwork and the closure of the Rose as a public museum. The court declined the university's request to dismiss the suit. In the future the university will inform the attorney general's office if a decision is made to sell art from the collection. The outcry from donors to the museum and from those both within and outside the Brandeis community stunned the University's administration and ultimately led to the formation of a committee to save the museum and to establish the Future of the Rose Committee, headed by Dr. Jerry Samet, the Chair of the University's Philosophy department.[13] The American Association of Museums immediately weighed in on the controversy expressing the organization's alarm.

"Brandeis University is in fundamental violation of the public trust responsibilities it accepted the day it founded the Rose Museum. Such a sale is also a betrayal of the donors, who generously gave art for the benefit of the students and the public, not for

12 Roberta Smith, "In the Closing of Brandeis Museum, a Stark Statement of Priorities," *New York Times*, February 1, 2009.

13 Future of the Rose Committee http://www.brandeis.edu/provost/adhoc/rose_cmte.html accessed November 6, 2009; *New York Times*, "Outcry Over a Plan to Sell Museum's Holdings," January 27, 2009; *New York Times*, "In the Closing of Brandeis Museum, a Stark Statement of Priorities," February 1, 2009; "Museum Family Denounces Brandeis," March 16, 2009; *Los Angeles Times*, "Rose Art Museum lawsuit recalls the Barnes 'legal theft,'" July 27, 2009; *New York Times*, "Brandeis Pledges Not to Sell Art Donated by Overseers," October 15, 2009; *The Boston Globe*, "Judge refuses to dismiss Brandeis museum lawsuit," October 14, 2009.

paying bills. This is a direct violation of the AAM Code of Ethics for museums," wrote AAM President Ford Bell.[14] The Association of Art Museum Directors (AAMD) also denounced the University's decision.

The controversy over the Rose reflects a larger concern about the use of valuable museum collections as assets that anxious boards may sell to replace a leaking roof or to balance the budget. "Current deaccession concerns are very negative for a process that should actually be a part of sound collections management," commented Historic New England President and CEO Carl Nold. University museums, foundation museums, state government, any museum that has a parent with a different purpose than the museum faces the possibility that the collection will be viewed as a disposable asset in times of economic crisis. Deaccessioning collections is tied to issues of financial stability for these institutions. "The Rose is the most visible manifestation of this problem," Nold noted. "The College Art Association and the Museums Association of New York among other professional organizations are working on the problem of institutions deaccessioning collections to meet financial needs and they are strengthening standards."[15]

A New Internationalism

The recession helped to highlight the changing museum world as a global community with common goals and common values. We are beginning to see ourselves as one large profession across the globe with similar interests and shared concerns from climate change to the standards for protecting collections in a disaster and the concerns of civil rights. "When we did a strategic plan [for the American Association of Museums] five years ago there was a huge battle over anything that was not about American museums," said Carl Nold. "The world has changed so much in that five year period. Museums large and small realize that we live in a global community. We have all struggled across the globe with the economic crisis. There is much to share."[16]

The growing reputation of the museums throughout the world that focus on human rights and promote conversations on issues related to war, slavery, genocide, oppression, and immigration demonstrates the depth of collaboration within the international museum community. With only 9 members when it started in Bellagio, Italy in 1999, the International Coalition of Sites of Conscience now includes 110 museums in 29 countries. Sites as diverse as the Lower East Side Tenement Museum, that with its founding director Ruth Abram organized the first Coalition meeting, to the Tuol Sleng Genocide Museum in Cambodia, Terezin, the Nazi concentration camp in the Czech Republic, and Haskell, the Native American boarding school in Lawrence, Kansas are all a part of the group. The Coalition clearly defines museums as places that embrace their role as forums supporting discussions about contemporary topics like immigration and torture. This responsibility, once considered controversial for history museums, is now mainstream and international.[17]

To assist museums in collaborating across national borders the American Association of Museums undertook a major effort in 2009 to bring "international voices and perspectives into the core" of the organization's publications, their professional development programs, and the AAM annual meeting. At the April 2008 meeting the Board of Directors of the Association formed a Taskforce on International Programs that completed its final report in 2009. Taskforce recommendations include beginning immediately to create a truly international and multicultural conference with the next annual meeting in May 2010 in Los Angeles. The meeting in Houston the following year presents similar opportunities. Both are richly multi-

14 AAM Statement on the Closure of the Rose Museum at Brandeis University, Washington, D.C. January 29, 2009 http://www.aam-us.org/pressreleases.cfm?mode=list&id=153 accessed, November 7, 2009.

15 Carl Nold, interview with Gretchen Sullivan Sorin, November 9, 2009

16 Carl Nold, interview with Gretchen Sullivan Sorin, November 9, 2009.

17 Julia Klein, "1 Part History, 2 Parts Shrine," *The New York Times*, March 19, 2009

cultural cities. To encourage larger numbers of international participants the conference will provide simultaneous translation into multiple languages for a global track of sessions that address mutual opportunities and challenges. Popular AAM publications will be available in languages other than English and the AAM will expand involvement with the International Council of Museums (ICOM).[18]

Crisis as Opportunity

Ultimately, the nation's economic problems may result in some positive effect on American museums. The institutions that will emerge from this crisis after a decade of growth and expansion and now an indeterminate amount of time of economic retraction, will be sleeker, more creative and more responsive to their communities' needs because they have to be. As that audience becomes increasingly diverse it will mean truly diversifying the museum—its staff and visitors—and not simply talking about diversity as we have been doing for the past 25 years. The recession will result in museums being more sensitive to the needs of communities and constituents if they want to survive. We will have to look outward, not inward. Elizabeth Merritt agrees, "museums need to question assumptions about who they are, who they serve, and how they operate. They need to be open to rethinking everything from where they get their funding, to their relationship with their users, to the role of the museum and its curators in organizing and presenting content."[19] Museum Consultant and former Deputy Director of the United States Holocaust Memorial Museum, Elaine Gurian goes even farther on the blog, Museum 3.0 with a post entitled, "Museum as Soup Kitchen." She asks how museums are helping their communities in the current economic hard times. "It is clear to me," she writes, "that museums could be much more helpful and timely by changing hours, job retraining, health care information and all manner of social service." Expanding our community service role may also help museum with their bottom lines.

Now 17 years after the publication of Excellence and Equity—the 1992 statement by the American Association of Museums about what museums are, perhaps it is time for us to consider an expanded statement of purpose. As museums move forward to serve more diverse public audiences they will need excellence—outstanding educational programming, and equity—access for everyone. But this must also be tied to enterprise or entrepreneurship—creative, even transformative, self-sustainability. Museums can no longer depend entirely on public and private philanthropy. They must, instead, depend on their own ingenuity, their business acumen, and the institution's responsiveness to the community's needs. Without losing sight of the core mission—the importance of preserving the collection, as well as doing good and serving everyone, including those who can't afford our sometimes exorbitant admission fees—they must learn to use their own resources and ingenuity to recognize opportunities both to increase revenue and to provide programs that people want.

On February 4, 2009, Republican Senator from Oklahoma Tom Coburn introduced an amendment (Amendment number 175) to the economic stimulus bill that prohibited funds from being allocated to museums. Linking museums and aquaria to other forms of community entertainment, the proposal read:

> "None of the amounts appropriated or otherwise made available by this Act may be used for any casino or other gambling establishment, aquarium, zoo, golf course, swimming pool, stadium, community park, museum, theater, arts center, or highway beautification project, including renovation, remodeling, construction, salaries, furniture, zero-gravity chairs, big screen televisions, beautification, rotating pastel lights, and dry heat saunas."

After considerable political jockeying, a second amendment also proposed by Coburn (S. Amdt.

18 Final Report, Taskforce on International Programs of the American Association of Museums, 2009

19 Elizabeth Merritt, interview with Gretchen Sullivan Sorin, November 2009.

No. 309) and still prohibiting funding of museums, passed the Senate. A joint House-Senate Conference Committee reconciled the legislation passed by the two houses, no longer prohibiting funding for museums or arts centers. Zoos and aquaria, however, continued to be listed among the institutions ineligible for federal stimulus money. Thanks to a massive lobbying effort, the American Association of Museums was able to preserve potential funding for most types of museums. President Obama signed the bill into law on February 17, 2009 at the Denver Museum of Nature and Science.[20]

Coburn's comments and the fight to convince Congress that museums contribute substantially to the national economy and to the lives of American communities suggest that we are simply not doing enough to make legislators aware of the value of museums as educational institutions, places of entertainment, storehouses of our collective national memory and economic engines. We need to do more to show them why museums are essential. We are all part of a collective field that provides service to the nation. We need to stand together, Carl Nold reminds us. "Museums are about stories and Americans love to tell their stories and have their stories repeated and we are not doing enough to explain how important it is to provide cultural and educational experiences to the people of our country."[21]

20 American Association of Museums, Advocacy Website, Speakup for Museums, The Coburn Amendment: An Explanation and Timeline http://www.speakupformuseums.org/docs/Coburn%20Amendment.pdf accessed November 23, 2009.

21 Carl Nold, interview with Gretchen Sullivan Sorin, November 2009.

Institutions by State

ALABAMA

(172 listings)

Aliceville

ALICEVILLE MUSEUM, (M), 104 Broad St., Aliceville, AL 35442-2701. Tel.: 205-373-2363.
E-mail: museum@nctv.com
Web Site: www.cityofaliceville.com
Founded: 1993.
Congressional District: 4
Key Personnel: Exec. Dir., Mary Bess Paluzzi; Pres., J.T. Junkins.
Personnel Profile: Full-Time Paid 1; Part-Time Volunteers 25.
Governing Authority: private; nonprofit organization. Tax-exempt: 501(c)(3).
Museum & Cultural Arts Center.
Collections: history of German POW Camp Aliceville 1942-1945; Coca-Cola exhibit & assembly line equipment 1948-1978; Pickens Co., AL military veterans of all wars.
Activities: films; guided tours; lectures; temporary exhibitions.
Publications: quarterly newsletter, Museum News.
Hours & Admission Prices: Mon.-Fri. 10-4, Sat.-Sun. & holidays by appointment. Adults $4, senior citizens & students $3; discounts to AAM members; members no charge. ♿
Attendance: 2,800 (accurate)
Membership: Individual Adult $25; Family $35; Sponsor $100-$499; Director's $1,000-$4,000; President's $5,000 & up.

Anniston

* **ANNISTON MUSEUM OF NATURAL HISTORY, (M),** 800 Museum Dr., Anniston, AL 36206-2813. Mailing Address: P.O. Box 1587, Anniston, AL 36202-1587. Tel.: 256-237-6766 & 6767. Fax: 256-237-6776.
E-mail: cbragg@annistonmuseum.org
Web Site: www.annistonmuseum.org
Founded: 1930.
Congressional District: 3
Key Personnel: Exec. Dir., Cheryl H. Bragg; Chm. (V), Paula Watkins; Cur. Collections, Daniel Spaulding; Program Mgr., Gina Morey; Dir. Devel., Lindie K. Brown; Mktg. Mgr., Margie Conner; Business Mgr., Regina Cooper; Facilities Mgr., Scott Williamon; Exhibits Mgr., John Parker.
Personnel Profile: Full-Time Paid 23; Part-Time Paid 4; Part-Time Volunteers 125; Interns 2.
Governing Authority: municipal. Parent Institution: City of Anniston. Tax-exempt.
Natural History Museum & Cultural Center.
Collections: North American and African animals & their habitats; birds; William H. Werner natural habitat groups including extinct & endangered species; John B. Lagarde international mammal collection; Egyptian mummies; American Indian culture; anthropology; ethnology; entomology; paleontology; geology.
Research Fields: exhibit evaluation & visitor studies; behavioral studies on red-cockaded woodpecker.
Facilities: 2,000-vol. library of reference books & journals on all subjects related to collections available on premises; multimedia auditorium; exhibition hall; classrooms; nature trails & outdoor lecture-demonstration areas; demonstration wildlife garden & bird of prey trail. Museum-related items for sale.
Activities: permanent & temporary exhibitions; changing exhibit gallery; guided tours; live animal programs; lectures; concerts; trips; classes in art, crafts, music & nature studies; school loan services; outreach programs. Special Events: Anniston Museum Day; Black Heritage Festival; Southeastern Indian Cultural Festival & Herpfest.
Publications: bimonthly newsletter; brochures; exhibit guides; annual report.
Hours & Admission Prices: June-Aug. Mon.-Sat. 10-5, Sun.1-5; Sept.-May Tues.-Fri. 9-5, Sat. 10-5, Sun. 1-5. Adults $5, children 4-17 $4; discounts to groups; members no charge. Closed New Year's Day; Thanksgiving; Christmas. ♿
Attendance: 73,223 (accurate)
Membership: Student $15; Individual $25; Family $35; Contributor $50; Sustainer $100; Business $150; Patron $250; Benefactor $500; Director's Circle $1,000.

BERMAN MUSEUM OF WORLD HISTORY, (M), 840 Museum Dr., Anniston, AL 36206-2813. Mailing Address: P.O. Box 2245, Anniston, AL 36202-2245. Tel.: 256-237-6261. Fax: 256-238-9055.
Web Site: www.bermanmuseum.org
Founded: 1996.
Congressional District: 3
Key Personnel: Dir., Cheryl Bragg; Pres. (V), Gaston O. McGinnis, M.D.; Coord. Business Devel., David Ford; Mgr. Collections, Robert Lindley; Registrar, Matt Muaubauer; Facilities Mgr., Adam Cleveland.
Personnel Profile: Full-Time Paid 4; Part-Time Volunteers 50.
Governing Authority: Tax-exempt.
History Museum.
Collections: over 3,000 world history artifacts; bronzes; paintings; ethnographic material; weapons; historical documents; Asian art including bronze statues of Buddha, religious figures from Tibet & India, Chinese cloisonne, Southeast Asian ritual masks, Japanese bronzes & Korean textiles; WWI & II military artifacts; guns & firearms.
Major Exhibits: Mary Lee Bendolph: Gee's Bead Quilts (T), 11/09-1/15/10.
Hours & Admission Prices: June-Aug. Mon.-Sat. 10-5, Sun. 1-5; Sept.-May Tues.-Sat. 10-5, Sun. 1-5. Adults $5, senior citizens $4, children 4-17 $2.50; discounts to AAA members & active military; children 3 & under and members no charge. Closed New Year's Day; Thanksgiving; Christmas Eve & Day. ♿
Attendance: 12,250 (accurate)
Membership: Individual $15; Family $25; Contributor $50; Sustainer $100; Business $150; Patron $250; Benefactor $500 & up.

Arab

ARAB HISTORIC VILLAGE, 1157 N. Main St., Arab, AL 35016-1071. Tel.: 256-586-3138 & 4225.
Web Site: www.arab-chamber.org
Historic Village Museum.
Collections: local history & culture; period furnishings; personal artifacts; photographs. Historic Buildings: Hunt School, 1935; Rice Church, 1910; Smith's Country Store, 1930; Boyd Homestead, 1890.
Hours & Admission Prices: March-Nov. Thurs.-Fri. 10-3, Sat. 1-4; other times by appointment. No charge.

Athens

ALABAMA VETERANS MUSEUM AND ARCHIVES, 100 Pryor St., Athens, AL 35611-1850. Tel.: 256-771-7578.
Military Museum.
Collections: military artifacts; uniforms; medals; weapons; photographs; books; tapes; newspaper clippings.
Hours & Admission Prices: Tues.-Sat. 9-2; group tours by appointment. No charge; donations accepted.

ALTAR OF THE NEW TESTAMENT AND FOUNDERS HALL, Athens State Univ., 300 N. Beaty St., Athens, AL 35611. Tel.: 800-522-0272; 256-233-8215.
Religious History Museum.
Collections: wood carvings depicting the New Testament.
Hours & Admission Prices: Mon.-Fri. 8-4:30. No charge.

DONNELL HOUSE, 601 1/2 S. Clinton St., Athens, AL 35611. Tel.: 256-232-0743 & 7370.
Historic House Museum: housed in the former home of Rev. Robert Donnell, founder of Cumberland Presbyterian Church; built in 1851. Listed on the National Register of Historic Places.
Collections: family history; period furnishings; personal artifacts; photographs.
Activities: rental facilities; guided tours; special events.
Hours & Admission Prices: Wed. 2-4, Fri. 1-3; other times by appointment.

LIMESTONE COUNTY HISTORY MUSEUM, 101 N. Houston St., Athens, AL 35611-2540. Mailing Address: P.O. Box 82, Athens, AL 35612. Tel.: 256-233-8770.
E-mail: mail@limestonecountyhistoricalsociety.org
Web Site: limestonecountyhistoricalsociety.org
Formerly: Houston Memorial Library and Museum
Founded: 1972.
Key Personnel: Dir., Jackie Leonard; Chm. (V) & Museum Shop Mgr., Rex Lewis.
Personnel Profile: Part-Time Volunteers 3.
Governing Authority: Parent Institution: Limestone County Historical Society. Tax-exempt: 501(c)(3).
History Museum: housed in the former home of George S. Houston, attorney, member of U.S. Senate and Governor of Alabama; built in 1835.
Collections: family history; local artifacts; photographs; Native American; documents; personal artifacts; military; clothing; paintings.
Hours & Admission Prices: Mon.-Fri. 10-5, Sat. 9-12. No charge; donations accepted.
Attendance: 700 (estimated)
Membership: Historical Society: Senior & Student $10; Individual $15; Family $20; Life $300; Patron $500.

Attalla

TIGERS FOR TOMORROW AT UNTAMED MOUNTAIN, 710 County Rd. 345, Attalla, AL 35954. Tel.: 256-524-4150.
Animal Preserve.
Collections: wildlife including cougars; leopards; tigers; lions; wolves.
Activities: tours.
Hours & Admission Prices: Sat.-Sun. 9-4. Adults $10, children 12 & over $9, children 3-11 $5; other times by appointment.

Auburn

JAN DEMPSEY COMMUNITY ARTS CENTER, 222 E. Drake Ave., Auburn, AL 36830-3918. Mailing Address: 307 S. Dean Rd., Auburn, AL 36830-6105. Tel.: 334-501-2963. Fax: 334-501-2964.
E-mail: shand@auburnalabama.org
Web Site: www.auburnalabama.org/arts
Art Museum.
Collections: works by regional artists.
Activities: concerts; theatre productions; lectures; studio art classes; theatre classes; dance classes; special events; traveling exhibitions.
Hours & Admission Prices: Mon.-Fri. 8-5. Closed major holidays. ♿

JULE COLLINS SMITH MUSEUM OF FINE ART, (M), Auburn University, 901 S. College St., Auburn, AL 36849-0001. Tel.: 334-844-1484.
E-mail: jcsm@auburn.edu
Web Site: jcsm.auburn.edu
Key Personnel: Dir., Marilyn Laufer; Asst. Dir., Andy Tennant; Devel. Coord., Cindy Cox; Cur. Education, Scott Bishop Wagoner; Cur., Dennis Harper; Mktg. & Special Events, Colleen Bourdeau; Museum Shop Mgr., Carol Robicheaux; Exec. Sec., Robbin Birmingham; Office Admin., Janice Allen; IT Specialist, Mike Cortez; Cur. Education K-12, Andrew Henley; Preparator, Dan Neil; Graphic Designer, Janet Spivey; Registrar, Danielle Funderburk; Security Chief, Carl Ealy.
Personnel Profile: Full-Time Paid 17; Part-Time Paid 10; Part-Time Volunteers 60; Interns 3.
Governing Authority: university.
Art Museum.
Collections: 19th-21st-century American & European art including paintings, sculpture and works on paper.
Facilities: gardens; restaurant; 120-seat auditorium. Museum-related items for sale.
Activities: special programs; lectures; walking paths; films; musical performances; receptions.
Hours & Admission Prices: Mon.-Fri. 8:30-4:45, Sat. 10-4:45. Adults $5, senior citizens $4; children 17 & under and Auburn University students & faculty no charge. Closed New Year's Day; Easter; Memorial Day; Independence Day; Labor Day; Thanksgiving; Christmas. ♿
Attendance: 30,000 (accurate)

Beatrice

RIKARD'S MILL HISTORICAL PARK, 4116 Hwy. 265 N., Beatrice, AL 36425. Mailing Address: c/o MCHM, P.O. Box 1637, Monroeville, AL 36461-1637. Tel.: 251-575-7433. Fax: 251-575-2513.
E-mail: mchm@frontiernet.net
Web Site: www.tokillamockingbird.com
Founded: 1994.
Congressional District: 1
Key Personnel: C.E.O., Jane Ellen Clark; Chm. (V), Dr. John Grider; Museum Shop Mgr., Stephanie Rogers.
Governing Authority: Parent Institution: Monroe County Heritage Museums. Tax-exempt: 501(c)(3).
History Museum: 1845 restored Grist Mill with water-powered turbine.
Collections: pioneer tools; household & agricultural implements; wagon; cane mill & furnace; blacksmith shop.
Activities: Annual Events: Cane Syrup Making Day in November; Pioneer Days in November.
Hours & Admission Prices: April-Dec. Sat. 9-5. Adults $4, children $2. Closed major holidays. ♿
Attendance: 8,500 (estimated)
Membership: Student $20; Individual $35; Family $45; Star $100; Friend $250; Patron $500; Corporate $750.

Bessemer

BESSEMER HALL OF HISTORY, 1905 Alabama Ave., Bessemer, AL 35020-5009. Tel.: 205-426-1633. Fax: 205-426-1633.
E-mail: bessemerhallofhi@bellsouth.net
Web Site: www.bessemerhallofhistory.com
Founded: 1970.
Congressional District: 7
Key Personnel: Co-Chm., Dr. Merith Byram; Co-Chm. (V), Ray Morris; Pres., Wendell Martin; Vice Pres., Bobby Cooper; Cur., Chris Eiland.
Personnel Profile: Full-Time Paid 1.
Governing Authority: bd. of directors. Tax-exempt: 170(b)(1)(A).
History Museum: housed in the Southern R.R. Depot; built in 1916. Listed on the National Register of Historical Places.
Collections: historical items; photographs; documents of the Bessemer area; Bessemer Indian Mound Site artifacts; mining & industry artifacts & photos of the Bessemer & Birmingham area; vintage clothing; Civil War artifacts; 1,000,000 Pullman Standard Boxcar.
Research Fields: state & county history; dialect & folklore.
Facilities: 200-vol. research library of historical & arts & crafts books and newspapers on DVD from 1888-1920 available on premises.
Activities: guided tours; docent program; inter-museum, permanent & temporary exhibitions.
Hours & Admission Prices: Tues.-Sat. 9-12 & 1-4. No charge; donations accepted. ♿
Attendance: 6,500 (estimated)
Membership: Individual $25; Couple $35; Business/Club $70; Patron $110.

Birmingham

ALABAMA JAZZ HALL OF FAME, 1631 4th Ave. N., Birmingham, AL 35203-1903. Tel.: 205-254-2731. Fax: 205-254-2785.
E-mail: ltucker@jazzhall.com
Web Site: www.jazzhall.com
Key Personnel: Exec. Dir., Leah Tucker; Dir. Education & Community Svcs., Dr. Frank E. Adams, Sr.
Jazz Museum.
Collections: Alabama jazz artists including Nat King Cole, Duke Ellington, Lionel Hampton & Erskine Hawkins; jazz history.
Facilities: theater.
Activities: teachers' workshop; elementary school programs; jazz classes; concerts; jazz workshops; special events.
Hours & Admission Prices: Hall of Fame: Tues.-Sat. 10-5. Guided Tours: Tues.-Wed. & Fri. 10-2, Sat. 1-5. Guided Tour: $3; Self-Guided Tour: $2.
Membership: Solo $35; Combo $50; Big Band $100.

ALABAMA MUSEUM OF THE HEALTH SCIENCES, 1700 University Blvd., Birmingham, AL 35294-0001. Mailing Address: 300 LHL - 1530 3rd Ave., S., Birmingham, AL 35294-0001. Tel.: 205-934-4475. Fax: 205-975-8476.
Web Site: www.uab.edu/historical/museum.htm
Founded: 1981.
Congressional District: 7
Key Personnel: Dir., Michael A. Flannery; Cur., Stefanie Rookis.
Personnel Profile: Full-Time Paid 2.
Governing Authority: public university; nonprofit. Parent Institution: University of Alabama at Birmingham. Tax-exempt: 501(c)(3).
Medical Museum.
Collections: equipment; instruments; history & development of the health sciences; southern medicine.
Facilities: library; educational facilities.
Activities: formal education programs for undergraduate or graduate college students; guided tours; study clubs; temporary & traveling exhibitions.
Publications: newsletter, Treasures.
Hours & Admission Prices: Mon.-Fri. 9-5. No charge. Closed New Year's Day; Martin Luther King Jr. Day; Memorial Day; Independence Day; Labor Day; Thanksgiving & day after; Christmas. ♿
Attendance: 3,000 (estimated)
Membership: Student Associate $10; Contributing Associate $25; Sustaining Associate $100; Sponsoring Associate $500; Patron $1,000 & up.

ALABAMA SPORTS HALL OF FAME, 2150 Richard Arrington Jr. Blvd. N., Birmingham, AL 35203-1102. Mailing Address: P.O. Box 10163, Birmingham, AL 35202-0163. Tel.: 205-323-6665. Fax: 205-252-2212.
Web Site: www.ashof.org
Founded: 1967.
Key Personnel: Dir., Scott Myers
Sports Museum.
Collections: Alabama's sports heritage; over 5,000 sports artifacts; sports legends including Jesse Owens, Hank Aaron, Joe Louis, Willie Mays, Carl Lewis.
Activities: tours; children's outreach program. Museum Sponsors: Induction Banquet; Golf Tournament; Reunion of Winners.
Hours & Admission Prices: Mon.-Sat. 9-5. Adults $5, senior citizens 60 & over $4, students $3; discounts to groups of 10 or more.

ARLINGTON, 331 Cotton Ave., S.W., Birmingham, AL 35211-1465. Tel.: 205-780-5656. Fax: 205-788-0585.
Web Site: www.informationbirmingham.com/arlington/index.htm
Founded: 1953.
Congressional District: 6
Key Personnel: Dir., Daniel F. Brooks.
Personnel Profile: Full-Time Paid 7; Part-Time Paid 1.
Governing Authority: municipal. Tax-exempt: 170(b)(1)(A).
Historic House Museum: housed in the home of Judge William S. Mudd, one of 10 founders of Birmingham; built in 1850.
Collections: period furnishings.
Research Fields: furniture; local history; decorative arts.
Facilities: 50-seat auditorium; dining room. Museum-related gifts for sale.
Activities: guided tours; lectures; films; permanent & loan exhibitions; formally organized education programs for children; docent program.
Publications: brochures.
Hours & Admission Prices: Tues.-Sat. 10-4, Sun. 1-4. Adults $5, students 6-18 $3; discount to groups & AAM members; children under 6 no charge when accompanied by an adult. Closed holidays.
Attendance: 25,000 (estimated)
Membership: Single $7.50; Couple $10.

BIRMINGHAM BOTANICAL GARDENS, 2612 Lane Park Rd., Birmingham, AL 35223-1800. Tel.: 205-414-3900. Fax: 205-414-3966.
Web Site: www.bbgardens.org
Founded: 1962.
Congressional District: 6
Key Personnel: Dir., Frederick R. Spicer, Jr.
Personnel Profile: Full-Time Paid 13; Part-Time Paid 2.
Governing Authority: municipal. Parent Institution: Branch of City of Birmingham, Birmingham Park & Recreation Board, 400 Graymont Ave., W., Birmingham, AL 35204. Tel.: 205-254-2391. Tax-exempt: 170(b)(1)(A).
Botanical Garden & Herbarium.
Collections: Japanese garden; conservatory; rhododendron garden; fern glade; rose garden & southern living garden; bonsai lathe house; orchid & camellia collection; wildflower garden; iris & daylily garden.
Research Fields: plant propagation.
Facilities: 5,000-vol. public library of books relating to plants; botanical garden; 400-seat auditorium; 250-seat lecture hall; 3 classrooms; herbarium, diagnostic & propagation labs. Museum-related items for sale.
Activities: guided tours; lectures; films; broadcast programs; summer workshops for children; free discovery field trips, hand-on adult classes; library activities; docent program.
Publications: newsletters & brochures.
Hours & Admission Prices: Daily sunrise-sunset. No charge; donations accepted. ♿
Attendance: 400,000 (estimated)
Membership: Trillium $45; Hydrangea $60; Magnolia $125; Oak $250; Ambassador $500; President's Circle $1,000.

* **BIRMINGHAM CIVIL RIGHTS INSTITUTE, (M),** 520 Sixteenth St., N., Birmingham, AL 35203-1911. Tel.: 205-328-9696; 866-328-9696 (toll free). Fax: 205-251-6104.
E-mail: bcri@bcri.org
Web Site: www.bcri.org
Founded: 1992.
Congressional District: 7
Key Personnel: Pres. & C.E.O., Dr. Lawrence J. Pijeaux, Jr.; Bd. Chm., Robert Holmes; Vice Pres. Publications & Special Projects, Angela Fisher-Hall; Vice Pres. Finance & Operations, Carol Wells; Vice Pres. Institutional Programs, Priscilla Hancock Cooper; Head Archives, Wayne Coleman; Dir. Oral History, Dr. Horace Huntley; Head Education, Ahmad Ward; Archivist, Laura Anderson; Head Devel., Rhonda Ball; Docent & Volunteer Coord., LaQuita Singleton; Operations Mgr., LeRoy Simmons; Bldg. & Grounds Supt., David W. Davis; Administrative Asst., Nigel Weatherspoon; Network Admin., Michael Holland; Resource Gallery Attendant, Yvonne Williams.
Personnel Profile: Full-Time Paid 28; Part-Time Paid 6; Part-Time Volunteers 160; Interns 3.
Governing Authority: nonprofit. Tax-exempt: 501(c)(3).
History Museum.
Collections: Civil Rights Movement; African American life.
Research Fields: Civil Rights Movement; African American life, history & culture.
Facilities: permanent exhibitions; three meeting rooms; rental space available; archival research area.
Activities: public programs; conferences; workshops; storytelling for children; lectures; school tours; after school programs for students. Museum Sponsors: Annual Juneteenth Festival; King Birthday Celebration & Festival; Kwanzaa Celebration; Women's History Month Celebration.
Publications: newsletter; curriculum guide; exhibition guide; volunteer handbook; activity booklet; BCRI Teacher's Packet designed to acquaint educators with mission of institute.
Hours & Admission Prices: Tues.-Sat. 10-5, Sun. 1-5. Adults $11, senior citizens 65 & over and college students with college ID $5; discount to adult groups of 25 or more; members & children 17 and under no charge. Closed major holidays. ♿
Attendance: 145,000 (accurate)
Membership: Student $15; Senior Citizen $25; Individual $35; Family $70; Friend $120; Supporter $270; Patron $520; Ambassador $1,020; Leadership Circle $2,020; Leadership Silver Circle $5,020; Gold Circle $10,020.

BIRMINGHAM-JEFFERSON HISTORY MUSEUM, 12 Office Park Circle, Ste. 107, Birmingham, AL 35223. Tel.: 205-871-3358.
Web Site: bjhm.org/
Key Personnel: Exec. Dir., Jerry R. Desmond; Cur., Marvin Whiting.
Governing Authority: nonprofit organization. Tax-exempt: 501(c)(3).
History Museum.
Collections: photographs; Birmingham's retail history; personal artifacts;
Hours & Admission Prices: Mon.-Fri. 9-12.

* **BIRMINGHAM MUSEUM OF ART, (M),** 2000 Rev. Abraham Woods Jr. Blvd., Birmingham, AL 35203-2205. Tel.: 205-254-2566, ext. 3900. Fax: 205-254-2714.
E-mail: museum@artsbma.org
Web Site: www.artsbma.org
Founded: 1951.
Congressional District: 6
Key Personnel: Dir., Gail Andrews; Chm., Thomas L. Hamby; Sr. Cur. & Cur. Asian Art, Dr. Donald A. Wood; Deputy Dir., Amy Templeton; Cur. Decorative Arts, Dr. Anne Forschler-Tarrasch; Cur. American Art, Dr. Graham Boettcher; Cur. Modern & Contemporary Art, Ron Platt; Chief Cur. & Cur. European Art, Dr. Jeannine O'Grody; Cur. Arts of Africa & Americas, Emily Hanna; Registrar, Melissa Falkner Mercurio; Chief Security, J.R. Feagins; Graphic Designer, James Williams; Dir. Mktg., Melanie Parker; Dir. Devel., Kendra Quandt; Membership Coord., Charlotte Russ; Librarian, Tatum Preston; Bldg. Supt., Wayne Blount; Designer, Terry Beckham; Facilities Coord., Clint Thorne; Business Mgr., D. Mike McLane; Accountant, Ernest Hudson; Volunteer Coord., Rhonda Hethcox; Museum Shop Mgr., Kristie Allen.
Personnel Profile: Full-Time Paid 80; Part-Time Paid 5; Part-Time Volunteers 500; Interns 5.
Governing Authority: municipal. Parent Institution: City of Birmingham. Tax-exempt: 170(b)(1)(A).
Art Museum.
Collections: European & American paintings, sculpture, decorative arts, photography, works on paper; Native American art; Asian, African & pre-Columbian art; contemporary art.
Research Fields: American & European paintings, sculpture, decorative arts, works on paper, photography; contemporary art; Asian, African, & Native American art.
Facilities: 25,000-vol. library of art history books available on premises; studios; 340-seat auditorium; restaurant; sculpture garden. Museum-related items for sale.
Activities: guided tours; lectures; films; gallery talks; concerts; arts festivals; radio programs; formally organized education programs for children; inter-museum loan, permanent, temporary & traveling exhibitions; mobile art van; art classes for adults & children.
Publications: quarterly newsletter; catalogues of special exhibitions & permanent collections; self-guided tour brochures; teacher packets.
Hours & Admission Prices: Tues.-Sat. 10-5, Sun. 12-5. No charge; donations accepted. Closed major holidays. ♿
Attendance: 193,394 (accurate)
Membership: Student $20; Nonprofit Organization $30; Individual $50; Family $70; Junior Patrons $60; Contributor $125; Fellow $300; Patron $600; Benefactor $1,000; Curator's Circle $2,500; Director's Circle $5,000.

BIRMINGHAM ZOO, 2630 Cahaba Rd., Birmingham, AL 35223-1154. Tel.: 205-879-0409. Fax: 205-879-9426.
Web Site: www.BirminghamZoo.com
Founded: 1955.
Congressional District: 6
Key Personnel: C.E.O. & Dir., Dr. William R. Foster; Mktg. & Public Rels., Beth Parmer.
Personnel Profile: Full-Time Paid 78; Full-Time Volunteers 150; Part-Time Paid 17.
Governing Authority: public/private partnership. Tax-exempt: 501(c)(3).
Zoo.
Collections: over 700 animals representing 250 species including mammals, birds, & reptiles.

Facilities: 1,000-vol. library related to animal study; 122 acres.
Activities: guided tours; lectures; formally organized education programs for children & undergraduate college students; docent program or council.
Publications: quarterly magazine, Animal Tracks.
Hours & Admission Prices: Winter: daily 9-5; Summer: Mon.-Fri. 9-5, Sat.-Sun. 9-7. Adults $12, seniors 65 & up and children 2-12 $7; discounts on Tues., children under 2, AZA members & zoo members no charge. Closed Thanksgiving; Christmas. ♿
Attendance: 450,000 (accurate)
Membership: Individual $30; Individual Plus One $50; Family & Grandparents $75; Family Circle $125; Keeper Club $250; Curator Club $500; Director's Circle $1,000.

DON KRESGE MEMORIAL MUSEUM, 600 N. 18th St., Birmingham, AL 35203-2206. Mailing Address: Alabama Historical Radio Society, P.O. Box 130307, Birmingham, AL 35213. Tel.: 205-822-6759.
Governing Authority: Parent Institution: Alabama Historical Radio Society.
History Museum.
Collections: period radios; radio history & memorabilia; broadcasting history.
Activities: classes; educational programs; special programs.
Hours & Admission Prices: Call for hours.

MCWANE SCIENCE CENTER, 200 19th Street, N., Birmingham, AL 35203-3117. Tel.: 205-714-8300. Fax: 205-714-8400.
E-mail: charris@mcwane.org
Web Site: www.mcwane.org
Founded: 1997.
Congressional District: 6
Key Personnel: C.E.O., Timothy Ritchie; Vice Pres. Devel., Linda Baker; Vice Pres. Exhibits & Creative Svcs., Lamar Smith; Dir. Public Rels., Chandler Bibb.
Personnel Profile: Full-Time Paid 70; Full-Time Volunteers 150; Part-Time Paid 45; Part-Time Volunteers 273.
Governing Authority: nonprofit organization. Parent Institution: Discovery 2000, Inc. Tax-exempt.
Science and Technology Center.
Collections: hands-on participatory exhibits focusing on natural & physical science and paleontology.
Major Exhibits: Itty Bitty Magic City, 1/10-5/10; The Adventures of Mr. Potato Head (T), 5/10-8/10; Magic of Model Trains, 11/10-12/10.
Facilities: 154,200 sq. ft. exhibit space; large screen IMAX dome theater.
Activities: hands-on activities.
Publications: newsletter.
Hours & Admission Prices: June-Aug. Mon.-Fri. 9-6, Sat. 10-6, Sun. 12-6; Sept.-May. Mon.-Fri. 9-5, Sat. 10-6, Sun. 12-6. Parking: General Public $5, members no charge. Museum: adults $11, children $8; members no charge. IMAX DMR Movie: adults $10, children $9. IMAX Film: adults $8.50, children $7.50. Combo: adults $16, children $12. Closed New Year's Day; Easter; Thanksgiving; Christmas Eve & Day. ♿
Attendance: 400,000 (estimated)
Membership: Add-A-Guest $20; Individual Plus $70; Family $90; Family Plus $135; Family Deluxe $160.

ROBERT R. MEYER PLANETARIUM, Birmingham-Southern College, 900 Arkadelphia Rd., Birmingham, AL 35254-0001. Tel.: 205-226-4771 & 4770.
E-mail: rbecker@bsc.edu
Web Site: www.bsc.edu/campus/planetarium
Key Personnel: Planetarium Coord., R. Becker Ingram
Planetarium.
Collections: space science.
Hours & Admission Prices: Public Shows: one Sat. or Sun. per month 2pm; call for additional days. Adults $2, children 12 & under $1; BSC students no charge. Reserved Showings: Mon.-Fri. by appointment. Groups of 10-45 $2 per person. Closed holidays; college breaks.

RUFFNER MOUNTAIN NATURE CENTER, 1214 81st St. S., Birmingham, AL 35206-4599. Tel.: 205-833-8264. Fax: 205-836-3960.
E-mail: info@ruffnermountain.org
Web Site: www.ruffnermountain.org
Founded: 1977.
Governing Authority: nonprofit organization. Tax-exempt: 501(c)(3).
Nature Center.
Collections: native species of plants & animals.
Facilities: nature trails.
Activities: educational programs; weekend activities; hiking; birding; workshops; scout programs.
Hours & Admission Prices: Mon.-Sat. 9-5, Sun. 1-5. No charge; donations accepted. Closed New Year's Day; Thanksgiving; Christmas Eve & Day.

SAMUEL ULLMAN MUSEUM, 2150 15th Ave. S., Birmingham, AL 35205-3920. Mailing Address: UAB International Scholar & Student Svcs., 1400 Univ. Blvd., HUC 250, 1530 3rd Ave. S., Birmingham, AL 35294-0001. Tel.: 205-934-3328.
E-mail: isss@uab.edu
General Museum.
Collections: personal artifacts; life & works of Samuel Ullman.
Hours & Admission Prices: By appointment only. No charge; donations accepted.

SLOSS FURNACES NATIONAL HISTORIC LANDMARK, (M), 20 32nd St. N., Birmingham, AL 35222-1236. Tel.: 205-324-1911. Fax: 205-324-6758.
E-mail: info@slossfurnaces.com
Web Site: www.slossfurnaces.com
Founded: 1983.
Congressional District: 6
Key Personnel: C.E.O., Robert R. Rathburn, Ph.D.; Chm., Robin A. Wade, III; Cur., Paige Wainwright; Cur., Karen Utz; Museum Shop Mgr., Kimbellee Fipps.
Personnel Profile: Full-Time Paid 10; Part-Time Paid 6; Interns 5.
Governing Authority: municipal government. Parent Institution: City of Birmingham. Tax-exempt: 170(b)(1)(A).
Industrial Museum: c.1882-1970 ironmaking plant including blast furnaces, blowing engines, power house, boilers & related buildings.
Collections: machinery; tools; paintings; photographs; oral histories.
Research Fields: history of Sloss-Sheffield Steel & Iron Co.; Birmingham economic, technological & labor history.
Facilities: 400-vol. library on technical works on iron, steel & related industries available for research on premises; works on Alabama & Birmingham history; general works on history of technology & labor; manuscripts related to Sloss-Sheffield Steel & Iron Co.; oral histories; 1,500-seat auditorium. Museum-related items for sale.
Activities: guided tours; lectures; films; concerts; dance recitals; arts festivals; organized education programs for children; artistic metal-casting; docent program; temporary & traveling exhibitions.
Publications: brochures, Sloss Furnaces National Historic Landmark: A Self Guided Tour; The Sloss Story.
Hours & Admission Prices: Tues.-Sat. 10-4, Sun. 12-4. No charge; donations accepted. Closed New Year's Day; Thanksgiving; Christmas. ♿
Attendance: 140,000
Membership: Stove Tender $35; Millwright $60; Patternmaker $150; Furnace Keeper $500; Turn Foreman $1,000; James Withers Sloss Circle $5,000.

SOUTHERN MUSEUM OF FLIGHT, 4343 73rd St. N., Birmingham, AL 35206-3642. Tel.: 205-833-8226. Fax: 205-836-2439.
E-mail: southernmuseumofflight@yahoo.com
Web Site: southernmuseumofflight.org
Founded: 1983.
Congressional District: 10
Key Personnel: Exec. Dir. & Chm., Dr. Jim Griffin; Asst. Dir., Wayne Novy; Education Coord., Deborah Watson Stone; Business Mgr., Daphne Foy; Exhibit Designer, Bruce Lucas; Business Mgr., Glenda McCarroll; Asst. Shop Mgr. & Receptionist, Sherry Greene.
Personnel Profile: Full-Time Paid 7; Part-Time Paid 2; Part-Time Volunteers 35.
Governing Authority: municipal. Parent Institution: City of Birmingham, AL. Subsidiary Institution: Southern Museum of Flight Foundation, Inc. Tax-exempt: 501(c)(3).
Aviation Transportation Museum.
Collections: civilian, experimental & military aircraft; engines; models; aviation memorabilia.
Research Fields: aviation.
Facilities: library of aviation books & periodicals available for research on premises; reading rooms; meeting rooms; restoration workshop. Aviation-related items for sale.
Activities: guided tours; flight simulations; restoration workshops; flight instruction class; aviation-related meetings & clubs.
Publications: quarterly newsletter, monthly newsletter, 99 Neighborhood Associations in Birmingham.
Hours & Admission Prices: Tues.-Sat. 9:30-4:30. Adults $5, seniors & students $4; discounts to groups, AAA & AAM members; members, ASTC members & children 3 & under no charge. ♿
Attendance: 63,247 (accurate)

Membership: Family $45.

Blountsville

FREEMAN CABIN MUSEUM, 71406 Main St., Blountsville, AL 35031. Mailing Address: P.O. Box 232, Blountsville, AL 35031-0232. Tel.: 205-429-2338.
History Museum.
Collections: local history & culture; period furnishings; personal artifacts; photographs.
Activities: special events.
Hours & Admission Prices: 1st Sat. of month.

Brewton

THOMAS E. MCMILLAN MUSEUM, Jefferson Davis College, 220 Alco Dr., Brewton, AL 36426. Mailing Address: P.O. Box 958, Brewton, AL 36427-0958. Tel.: 251-809-1528. Fax: 251-867-1527.
E-mail: museum@jdcc.edu
Web Site: www.museum.jdcc.edu
Founded: 1978.
Congressional District: 11
Key Personnel: Pres. College, Dr. Susan McBride; Museum Coord., Jerry Simmons; Maintenance Supvr., Don Odom.
Personnel Profile: Part-Time Paid 1; Part-Time Volunteers 2.
Governing Authority: state. Parent Institution: Jefferson Davis Community College. Tax-exempt: 170(b)(1)(A).
History Museum: located near the site of 1830 Leigh plantation.
Collections: historical archaeology material & artifacts; Indian artifacts & trading wares; Civil War & 1812-1821 military excavated items; small arm weapons; camp & field equipment; insignias & hardware; early 19th century carpenter & cabinet maker tools; blacksmith tools; railroad memorabilia; 19th century lumbering & turpentining materials; print shop; mid 19th century medical, dental & pharmaceutical instruments; period cameras & photographic accessories; late 1800s & early 1900s household items.
Research Fields: genealogical; historical.
Facilities: over 1,000-vol. library of books & microfilm on local history & genealogy museum methodology and guidelines available for research on premises only; classrooms; reading room.
Activities: guided tours.
Hours & Admission Prices: Tues. & Thurs. 9-3; other times by appointment. No charge; donations accepted. Closed New Year's Eve & Day; Memorial Day; Labor Day; Thanksgiving; Christmas week. ♿
Attendance: 1,000 (estimated)

Bridgeport

BRIDGEPORT TRAIN DEPOT MUSEUM, 114 Soulard Sq., Bridgeport, AL 35740. Tel.: 256-495-4020.
Historic Building.
Collections: local history & culture; railroad artifacts; genealogy; photographs.
Hours & Admission Prices: Thurs.-Fri. 9-1, Sat. 9-3, Sun. 1-5. No charge.

RUSSELL CAVE NATIONAL MONUMENT, 3729 County Rd. 98, Bridgeport, AL 35740-6825. Tel.: 256-495-2672. Fax: 256-495-9220.
E-mail: shelia_reed@nps.gov
Web Site: nps.gov/ruca
Founded: 1961.
Congressional District: 5
Key Personnel: Supt., John Bundy; Park Ranger, Kenna Graham.
Governing Authority: federal. A branch of the National Park Service, U.S. Dept. of Interior, Washington, DC 20240. Tax-exempt.
Archaeology Museum.
Collections: archaeology; geology; Southeastern archaic material; Woodland period, Mississippian period Indians.
Research Fields: archaeology; conservation.
Facilities: 450-vol. library of books & approx. 1,000 slides on archaeology; picnic grounds; nature & hiking trail. Books, slides & museum-related items for sale.
Activities: interpretive talks; demonstration of prehistoric weapons & tools, video; junior ranger program; interpretive slide program in excavation.
Publications: Life at Russell Cave.
Hours & Admission Prices: Daily 8-4:30. No charge; donations accepted. Closed New Year's Day; Thanksgiving; Christmas. ♿
Attendance: 30,000

Calera

HEART OF DIXIE RAILROAD MUSEUM, 1919 Ninth St., Calera, AL 35040. Mailing Address: P.O. Box 727, Calera, AL 35040-0727. Tel.: 205-668-3435. Fax: 205-668-9900.
Web Site: www.heartofdixierrmuseum.org
Founded: 1963.
Congressional District: 6
Key Personnel: Pres., Pittman Owen; Archivist, David Coombs; Treas., James Ketchersid; Museum Shop Mgr., Marie Garner.
Personnel Profile: Full-Time Paid 2; Part-Time Volunteers 40.
Governing Authority: private; nonprofit organization. Subsidiary Institution: Calera & Shelby Railroad. Tax-exempt: 501(c)(3).
Railroad Museum: housed in 1890s wooden railroad station building.
Collections: includes about 50 railroad rolling stock, steam & diesel locomotives, passenger & freight cars, cabooses; demonstration train; emphasis on history of railroads in Alabama; concentration on Louisville & Nashville Railroad & Southern Railway.
Facilities: 700-vol. library of railroad history & technology; 2,000 sq. ft. exhibit space. Museum-related items for sale.
Activities: passenger train rides; guided tours; outdoor exhibits. Annual Events: Rail Fest, Halloween train rides, Santa Claus train rides; Cottontail Express; Polar Express; grandparents special; Day Out With Thomas.
Publications: monthly newsletter, Cinders from the Smokestack.
Hours & Admission Prices: Museum: Tues.-Sat. 9-4. No charge; donations requested. Train Rides: March to mid-Dec. Sat. Adults $12, children $8. Closed major holidays. ♿
Attendance: 40,000 (estimated)
Membership: Family Members $8; Individual $45.

Centre

CHEROKEE COUNTY HISTORICAL MUSEUM, 101 E. Main St., Centre, AL 35960. Tel.: 256-927-7835.
E-mail: museumatcentre@gmail.com
Web Site: www.museumatcentre.com
Founded: 1958.
Key Personnel: Dir., David Crum; Chm. (V), Kurt Duryea.
Personnel Profile: Part-Time Paid 2; Part-Time Volunteers 2.
Governing Authority: Parent Institution: Cherokee County Historical Society, Inc. Tax-exempt.
History Museum.
Collections: county history, art & culture; newspapers; photographs; personal artifacts; vehicles; housewares; Civil War; WWI & II; railroad artifacts; farming; education.
Major Exhibits: Local Artist Gallery, 1/10-12/10.
Publications: monthly newsletter.
Hours & Admission Prices: Tues.-Sat. 8:30-4. Adults $3, seniors over 64 & students $2, children 7-12 $1; discounts to AAM & ICOM members; members and children 6 & under no charge. Closed major holidays.
Attendance: 900 (accurate)
Membership: Senior & Student $11; Individual $15; Family $25; Individual Lifetime $250; Family Lifetime $425.

Chatom

WASHINGTON COUNTY MUSEUM, 443 Court St., Chatom, AL 36518. Mailing Address: P.O. Box 233, Chatom, AL 36518-0233. Tel.: 251-847-3156. Fax: 251-847-3677.
History Museum.
Collections: county history; personal artifacts.
Hours & Admission Prices: Mon.-Fri. 8-4:30; guided tours by appointment. No charge. Closed Christmas Eve & Day.

Clanton

THE WATER COURSE, 2030 7th St. S., Clanton, AL 35045-8759. Tel.: 800-280-4442. Fax: 205-280-4444.
E-mail: ncprater@southernco.com
Web Site: www.alabamapower.com/education
Founded: 1994.
Key Personnel: Dir., Nancy Prater.
Personnel Profile: Full-Time Paid 2.
Governing Authority: Parent Institution: Alabama Power Company.
Environmental Education Center.
Collections: hands-on exhibits; water use, safety & environmental issues.
Activities: interactive exhibits; virtual helicopter tour; virtual hydroelectric generation tour; environmental game show.
Hours & Admission Prices: Tues.-Fri. 9-4; groups of 12 or more by appointment. No charge. Closed major holidays. ♿
Attendance: 10,000 (accurate)

Columbiana

KARL C. HARRISON MUSEUM OF GEORGE WASHINGTON, Mildred B. Harrison Regional Library, 50 Lester St., Columbiana, AL 35051-9477. Tel.: 205-669-8767.
E-mail: info@washingtonmuseum.com
Web Site: www.washingtonmuseum.com
Founded: 1982.
History Museum.
Collections: history of America's first First Family; paintings; personal letters; glassware; silver; jewelry; busts; Martha Washington's prayer book; 1787 Samuel Vaughn sketch of Mt. Vernon grounds; writing instruments & tools from George Washington's survey case; 1710 handwritten will of Colonel Daniel Parke; 18th & 19th century furniture; Minton porcelain; c.1805 walnut games table.
Activities: special programs; outreach activities.
Hours & Admission Prices: Mon.-Fri. 10-3.

Cullman

AVE MARIA GROTTO, 1600 St. Bernard Dr., S.E., Cullman, AL 35055-3057. Tel.: 256-734-4110. Fax: 256-737-8768.
E-mail: info@avemariagrotto.com
Web Site: www.avemariagrotto.com
Founded: 1934.
Congressional District: 4
Key Personnel: Dir., Rev. John O'Donnell, O.S.B.; Museum Shop Mgr., Joyce Nix
Religious History Museum: replicas built by Benedictine Monk, Bro. Joseph Zoettl, O.S.B.
Collections: over 125 miniature reproductions of famous churches, shrines, & buildings.
Facilities: 4-acre park. Grotto gift shop.
Hours & Admission Prices: April-Sept. daily 8-6; Oct.-March daily 8-5. Adults $7, senior citizens $5, children 6-12 $4.50; discounts to groups; children under 6 no charge. Closed New Year's Day; Christmas.

CULLMAN COUNTY MUSEUM, 211 Second Ave., N.E., Cullman, AL 35055-2905. Tel.: 256-739-1258; 800-533-1258. Fax: 256-737-8782.
E-mail: efuller@cullmancity.org
Web Site: www.cullmancountymuseum.com
Founded: 1975.
Congressional District: 4
Key Personnel: Cur., Elaine L. Fuller.
Personnel Profile: Full-Time Paid 1; Part-Time Paid 3; Interns 1.
Governing Authority: museum board of trustees; nonprofit organization. Tax-exempt.
History Museum: housed in replica of 1873 home of Col. John G. Cullman, founder of Cullman.
Collections: historic items relative to Cullman & Cullman County.
Major Exhibits: Nimble Thimble Quilt Show, 11/09-12/09; North Alabama China Painters Guild, 2/10-4/10; Cullman Strawberry Fest, 5/10-6/10.
Facilities: Museum-related items for sale.
Activities: guided tours; lectures; permanent exhibits.
Publications: brochures.
Hours & Admission Prices: Mon.-Fri. 9-4, Sun. 1:30-4:30. Adults $5, seniors $4, children under 12 $3; discounts to groups, AAM, AAA & ICOM members; members no charge. Closed New Year's Day; Independence Day; Thanksgiving; Christmas. ♿
Attendance: 15,000 (estimated)
Membership: Life $50.

CULLMAN DEPOT, 301 1st Ave., N.E., Cullman, AL 35055. Mailing Address: 211 2nd Ave., N.E., Cullman, AL 35055-2905. Tel.: 800-533-1258; 256-739-1258. Fax: 256-737-8782.
Historic Building: listed on the National and State Registers of Historic Places.
Collections: railroad history & artifacts; photographs; period furnishings.
Hours & Admission Prices: Mon.-Fri. 8-4:30. No charge.

EVELYN BURROW MUSEUM, Wallace State Community College, 1315 County Rd. 222, Cullman, AL 35057. Tel.: 256-775-7477.
Art Museum.
Collections: porcelain; art; period furnishings; bronzes; cut glass.
Hours & Admission Prices: Mon.-Fri. 8-4. No charge.

WEISS COTTAGE, 211 2nd Ave., N.E., Cullman, AL 35055-2905. Tel.: 800-533-1258.
Historic House Museum: housed in the former home & medical office of Adam Weiss. Listed on the National Register of Historic Places.
Collections: family history; period furnishings; personal artifacts; photographs.
Hours & Admission Prices: By appointment. No charge.

Danville

JESSE OWENS MEMORIAL PARK AND MUSEUM, 7019 County Rd. 203, Danville, AL 35619-9053. Mailing Address: 174 Co. Rd. 241, Moulton, AL 35650-. Tel.: 256-974-3636.
E-mail: jesseowensinfo@charter.net
Web Site: www.jesseowensmuseum.org
Founded: 1998.
Congressional District: 5
Key Personnel: Chm. (V) & Pres. (V), Kenneth Brackins; Museum Shop Mgr., Nancy Pinion.
Personnel Profile: Part-Time Paid 3.
History Museum.
Collections: photographs, memorabilia & films of Jesse Owens; replica home.
Facilities: welcome center; picnic area.
Hours & Admission Prices: Mon.-Sat. 9-5, Sun. 1:30-5. Admission for groups of 10 or more $2 per person; individuals, small family groups & children under 5 no charge; donations accepted. Closed Thanksgiving; Christmas. ♿
Attendance: 45,000 (estimated)

Daphne

AMERICAN SPORT ART MUSEUM AND ARCHIVES, (M), US Sports Academy, One Academy Dr., Daphne, AL 36526-7055. Tel.: 251-626-3303. Fax: 251-621-2527.
E-mail: asama@ussa.edu
Web Site: www.asama.org
Founded: 1985.
Congressional District: 94
Key Personnel: C.E.O., Dr. Thomas P. Rosandich; Cur., Robert Zimlich; Security, Russ Bennett.
Personnel Profile: Full-Time Paid 1; Part-Time Volunteers 8; Interns 1.
Governing Authority: college; nonprofit organization. Parent Institution: U.S. Sports Academy. Tax-exempt: 501(c)(3).
Art Museum.
Collections: bronze sculptures; original paintings; murals; lithographs; giclees, photography & film; all commemorating the artistry of sport; prints; posters; photographs.
Facilities: 100-seat auditorium; educational facilities. Books & art for sale.
Activities: guided tours; loan, temporary & traveling exhibitions. Annual Events: Sport Artist of the Year Program; Youth Sport Art Competition; Academy's Awards of Sport.
Publications: The Academy; The Sport Journal; The Sport Supplement.
Hours & Admission Prices: Mon.-Fri. 8-4. No charge; donations accepted. ♿
Attendance: 2,000 (estimated)
Membership: Bronze $100; Silver $200; Gold $500.

Dauphin Island

ESTUARIUM, Dauphin Island, AL 36528. Mailing Address: Dauphin Island Sea Lab, 101 Bienville Blvd., Dauphin Island, AL 36528-4603. Tel.: 866-403-4409.
E-mail: rdixon@disl.org
Web Site: estuarium.disl.org
Founded: 1998.
Key Personnel: Exec. Dir., Dr. George Crozier; Mgr., Robert Dixon; Registrar, Sally Brennan; Administrative Asst. to the Dir., Aleada Nicholson; Administrative Asst. Discovery Hall Programs, Denise Keaton; Reservations, Sara Orescan.
Governing Authority: Parent Institution: Dauphin Island Sea Lab. Tax-exempt.
Aquarium.
Collections: plants, animals & other natural resources found in the Estuary.
Hours & Admission Prices: March-Aug. Mon.-Sat. 9-6, Sun. 12-6; Sept.-Feb. Mon.-Sat. 9-5, Sun. 1-5. Adults $7, seniors $6, children 5-18 & students with ID $4; discounts to AAA members, groups, & military. Closed New Year's Day; Easter; Thanksgiving; Christmas. ♿
Attendance: 66,407 (accurate)
Membership: Individual $35; Family $75.

Daviston

HORSESHOE BEND NATIONAL MILITARY PARK, 11288 Horseshoe Bend Rd., Daviston, AL 36256-6524. Tel.: 256-234-7111. Fax: 256-329-9905.
Web Site: www.nps.gov/hobe/
Founded: 1959.
Congressional District: 3

Key Personnel: Administrative Officer, Alice Johnson; Park Ranger-Interpreter, Ove Jensen; Museum Shop Mgr., Tracy Eaves.
Personnel Profile: Full-Time Paid 10; Part-Time Volunteers 8.
Governing Authority: federal. Parent Institution: National Park Service, Washington, DC. Tax-exempt.
Historic Site: Horseshoe Bend Battlefield, location of final battle of the Creek Indian War of 1813-1814.
Collections: Indian artifacts; military artifacts, relics & historic documents of the Creek War & War of 1812.
Research Fields: Creek War of 1813-1814 & War of 1812.
Facilities: 500-vol. library of books on national, regional & local history available for use on premises; visitor center; nature trail; tour road through battlefield. Publications related to Horseshoe Bend, postcards & other items for sale.
Activities: permanent & temporary exhibitions; living history demonstrations; Tennessee Militia demonstrations (musket and cannon firing); Creek & Cherokee cultural demonstrations.
Publications: Horseshoe Bend National Military Park Official Guide & Map.
Hours & Admission Prices: Visitor Center: daily 9-4:30. Grounds: daily 8-5. No charge; donations accepted. Closed New Year's Day; Thanksgiving; Christmas. ♿
Attendance: 111,864 (accurate)

Decatur

THE ART GALLERY, JOHN C. CALHOUN STATE COMMUNITY COLLEGE, 6250 U.S. Hwy. 31 N., Fine Arts Bldg., Decatur, AL 35601. Mailing Address: P.O. Box 2216, Decatur, AL 35609-2216. Tel.: 256-306-2695 & 2699. Fax: 256-306-2889.
E-mail: klv@calhoun.cc.al.us
Web Site: www.calhoun.cc.al.us/
Founded: 1965.
Congressional District: 5
Key Personnel: C.E.O., Kristine Beadle; Chm., William Godsey; Pres., Dr. Marilyn Beck; Dir., Kathryn Vaughn.
Personnel Profile: Full-Time Paid 1; Full-Time Volunteers 2; Part-Time Paid 2.
Governing Authority: state. Parent Institution: Calhoun Community College.
College Art Gallery.
Collections: American & European graphics; student art & photographs.
Research Fields: Computer Art.
Facilities: library; student center; studios.
Activities: exhibitions for students, regional artists & traveling art exhibits.
Publications: exhibit announcements.
Hours & Admission Prices: Mon.-Fri. 9-5. No charge; donations accepted. ♿
Attendance: 3,600 (estimated)

BLUE & GRAY MUSEUM OF NORTH ALABAMA, 723 Bank St., N.W., Decatur, AL 35601. Tel.: 256-350-4018.
Military History Museum.
Collections: Civil War military equipment; guns; swords; rifles; uniforms; personal artifacts.
Hours & Admission Prices: Mon.-Sat. 10-5:30. Adults $5, students $3; pre-school children no charge.

CARNEGIE VISUAL ARTS CENTER, 207 Church St., N.E., Decatur, AL 35601-1847. Tel.: 256-341-0562. Fax: 256-341-0713.
Founded: 2003.
Key Personnel: Exec. Dir., Laura Phillips
Art Center.
Collections: works by local, regional & national artists.
Facilities: rental facilities.
Activities: special events; rental facilties; workshops; educational programs; lectures; temporary exhibitions; art classes.
Hours & Admission Prices: Tues.-Fri. 10-5, 3rd Sat. 10-2.

COOK'S NATURAL SCIENCE MUSEUM, 412 13th St., S.E., Decatur, AL 35601-5916. Tel.: 256-350-9347.
Web Site: www.cookspest.com/museum.html
Science Museum.
Collections: insects; mounted birds & animals; rocks & minerals; sea shells; coral.
Facilities: Museum-related items for sale.
Hours & Admission Prices: Mon.-Sat. 9-12 & 1-5, Sun. 2-5. No charge. Closed New Year's Day; Thanksgiving; Christmas Eve & Day. ♿

PRINCESS THEATRE CENTER FOR THE PERFORMING ARTS, 112 Second Ave., N.E., Decatur, AL 35601. Tel.: 256-350-1745 & 340-1778.
Governing Authority: nonprofit organization. Tax-exempt: 501(c)(3).
Theatre Museum: housed in a former livery stable in 1887, later turned into a silent film & vaudeville playhouse. Listed on the National Register of Historic Places.
Collections: theatre history & performers; photographs; costumes.
Facilities: theatre.
Activities: guided tours.
Hours & Admission Prices: Call for hours & admission prices.

WHEELER NATIONAL WILDLIFE REFUGE, 2700 Refuge Headquarters Rd., Decatur, AL 35603. Tel.: 256-350-6639.
Wildlife Refuge.
Collections: wildlife & their habitats; birds; ducks; fish; reptiles & amphibians.
Facilities: nature trails.
Activities: orientation video; hiking.
Hours & Admission Prices: March-Sept. Tues.-Sat. 9-4; Oct.-Feb. daily 9-5. No charge.

Demopolis

BLUFF HALL ANTEBELLUM HOME AND MUSEUM, Marengo County Historical Soc., 405 N. Commissioners Ave., Demopolis, AL 36732. Mailing Address: P.O. Box 159, Demopolis, AL 36732-0159. Tel.: 334-289-9644 & 0282.
E-mail: marengohistory@bellsouth.net
Founded: 1961.
Congressional District: 7
Personnel Profile: Part-Time Paid 4.
Governing Authority: nonprofit organization. Parent Institution: Marengo County Historical Society. Subsidiary Institution: Bluff Hall. Tax-exempt: 501(c)(3).
History Museum: house built in 1832-1850.
Collections: costumes; history; furnishings.
Research Fields: history.
Facilities: Museum-related & hand-made gifts for sale.
Activities: guided tours; permanent exhibitions.
Publications: semi-annual newsletter.
Hours & Admission Prices: Tues.-Sat. 10-5, Sun. 2-5. Adults $5, college students $4, students 6-18 $3; discounts to groups of 15 or more; members no charge. Closed New Year's Day; Easter; Independence Day; Thanksgiving; Christmas.
Attendance: 2,800 (estimated)
Membership: Junior $5; Individual $15; Couple $25; Contributing $50; Supporting $100; Sustaining $200; Corporate & Business $250; Lifetime $500.

GAINESWOOD, 805 S. Cedar Ave., Demopolis, AL 36732-2915. Tel.: 334-289-4846. Fax: 334-289-4846.
E-mail: gaineswd@bellsouth.net
Web Site: www.preserveala.org
Founded: 1975.
Congressional District: 7
Key Personnel: Site Dir., Eleanor W. Cunningham; Dir. Collections & Interpretation, Bruce M. Lipscombe; Maintenance, Richard Rand.
Personnel Profile: Full-Time Paid 3; Part-Time Volunteers 30.
Governing Authority: state. Affiliated with Alabama State Historical Commission. Tax-exempt.
Historical Building & Site: housed in the former home of Nathan Bryan Whitfield; built between 1843-1861.
Collections: furnishings; 19th-century period pieces.
Research Fields: decorative arts; architecture; history; Whitfield family history; study of family letters.
Activities: guided tours; special programs.
Hours & Admission Prices: Tues.-Fri. 9-4; other times by appointment. Adults $5, youth 6-18 $3; discounts to college students, senior citizens, military, groups & AAA members. Closed state holidays. ♿
Attendance: 2,470 (accurate)
Membership: Friends of Gaineswood $25.

Dora

ALABAMA MINING MUSEUM, 120 East St., Dora, AL 35062-4612. Tel.: 205-648-2442.
Founded: 1982.
Congressional District: 4
Key Personnel: Dir., Bonnie Sue Groves.
Personnel Profile: Full-Time Paid 2; Part-Time Volunteers 12.
Governing Authority: non-profit. Tax-exempt: 501(c)(3).
Mining Museum.
Collections: social, cultural & technological aspects of coal and other types of mining in Alabama. Historic Structures: c.1930 two-story WPA project

building built from hand-cut stone; c.1900 one-room schoolhouse; 1905 steam locomotive, ore car & caboose; c.1900 Oakman, Alabama railroad depot building; c.1930 U.S. post office building known as Kellerman, Alabama U.S. Post Office.
Research Fields: oral history of miners.
Facilities: library with oral history tapes; 55-capacity auditorium. Gifts & museum-related items for sale.
Activities: guided tours; lectures; films; organized education programs; hands-on room for children to learn about coal mining & living conditions; school field trips using one-room school building to simulate life in 1910 classroom.
Publications: quarterly newsletter.
Hours & Admission Prices: Tues.-Fri. 8:30-4, Sat. 10-4; school groups by appointment. No charge; donations accepted. ♿
Attendance: 20,000 (estimated)
Membership: Student $2; Senior Citizen $5; Individual $10; Family $15. Business & Corporation $25.

Dothan

ALABAMA AGRICULTURAL MUSEUM, (M), Landmark Park, U.S. Hwy. 431 N., Dothan, AL 36303. Mailing Address: P.O. Box 6362, Dothan, AL 36302-6362. Tel.: 334-794-3452. Fax: 334-677-7229.
E-mail: parkinfo@landmarkpark.com
Web Site: www.landmarkpark.com
Founded: 1996.
Key Personnel: Exec. Dir., William Holman; Farm Mgr., Sid Brannon; Dir. Public Rels., Laura Vanlandinghma.
Personnel Profile: Full-Time Paid 3.
Governing Authority: state government. Subsidiary Institution: Landmark Park. Tax-exempt.
Agriculture Museum.
Collections: state agriculture from prehistory to 1960s; 1900s farmstead; barn; corn crib; 1920s drug store; general store; church; schoolhouse.
Facilities: 3,000 sq. ft. exhibit space.
Activities: Annual Events: seasonal activities in March & October.
Hours & Admission Prices: Museum: by appointment. No charge. Park: June-July Mon.-Thurs. & Sat. 9-5, Fri. 9-8; Aug.-June Mon.-Sat. 9-5, Sun. 12-6. Adults $4, children $3. Closed state holidays.
Attendance: 10,368 (estimated)

DOTHAN AREA BOTANICAL GARDENS, 5130 Headland Ave., Dothan, AL 36303-7691. Tel.: 334-793-3224. Fax: 334-793-5275.
E-mail: dabg@dabg.com
Web Site: www.dabg.com
Key Personnel: Pres., Martha Yearta; Vice Pres., Tri Burns; Gardener, Johnnie Green; Office Mgr., Janie Edmondson
Botanical Gardens.
Collections: Gardens: rose; herb; southern heirloom; demonstration; butterfly; meditation; windmill; wedding garden; camellia; azalea; daylily; hydrangea; Koi ponds; fern glade.
Hours & Admission Prices: Summer: Mon.-Fri. 7-7; Winter: Mon.-Fri. 7-5. No charge. ♿

LANDMARK PARK, Hwy. 431 N., Dothan, AL 36302. Mailing Address: P.O. Box 6362, Dothan, AL 36302-6362. Tel.: 334-794-3452. Fax: 334-677-7229.
E-mail: parkinfo@landmarkpark.com
Web Site: www.landmarkpark.com
Founded: 1976.
Congressional District: 2
Key Personnel: Exec. Dir., William M. Holman; Program Dir., Dana Peters; Office Mgr., Barbara Spears; Membership Coord., Janis Lepley; Teacher & Naturalist, Sharon Chambers; Historical Farm Mgr., Sidney A. Brannon.
Personnel Profile: Full-Time Paid 6; Part-Time Paid 2.
Governing Authority: nonprofit organization. Parent Institution: Dothan Landmarks Foundation, Inc. Tax-exempt: 501(c)(3).
Living History Museum & Park Complex serving as the Official Museum of Agriculture for the State of Alabama.
Collections: 1890 living history farm includes buildings & artifacts; Alabama wildlife exhibits; astronomy.
Facilities: 500-vol. library on local, state, agricultural history, natural science & astronomy available on the premises; nature center & planetarium; nature trails; 150-seat auditorium; educational facilities; picnic area. Museum-related items for sale.
Activities: guided tours; lectures; films; concerts; arts festivals; organized education programs; docent program; participatory, loan, temporary & traveling exhibitions. Park Sponsors: Folklife Festivals.
Publications: bimonthly newsletter, The Lark.
Hours & Admission Prices: June-July Mon.-Thurs. & Sat. 9-5, Fri. 9-8, Sun. 12-6; Aug.-May Mon.-Sat. 9-5, Sun. 12-6. Adults $4, children 4-15 $3; members & children 3 & under no charge. Closed New Year's Day; Thanksgiving; Christmas. ♿
Attendance: 48,600 (accurate)
Membership: Individual $40; Family $60; Historical $90; Heritage $150; Heirloom $250; Legacy $500.

WIREGRASS MUSEUM OF ART, (M), 126 Museum Ave., Dothan, AL 36303-4802. Mailing Address: P.O. Box 1624, Dothan, AL 36302-1624. Tel.: 334-794-3871. Fax: 334-792-9035.
E-mail: director@wiregrassmuseum.org
Web Site: www.wiregrassmuseum.org
Founded: 1988.
Congressional District: 2
Key Personnel: Pres., Ann Hart; Exec. Dir., Susan Robertson; Dir. Community Rels., Deidre Frith; Dir. Visitor Svcs., Kendall Sirkis.
Personnel Profile: Full-Time Paid 5; Part-Time Paid 6; Part-Time Volunteers 75.
Governing Authority: municipal government. Tax-exempt: 501(c)(3).
Art Museum: housed in 1912 electric plant.
Collections: contemporary & regional art; children's sensory exhibits.
Facilities: 300-vol. library on art instruction & history; educational facilities; conference center; catering kitchen; sculpture garden.
Activities: guided tours; lectures; arts festivals; organized education programs; docent program; participatory & traveling exhibitions.
Publications: bimonthly newsletter, Sketches.
Hours & Admission Prices: Tues.-Sat. 10-5. No charge; donations accepted. ♿
Attendance: 20,000 (accurate)
Membership: Student $20; Individual $35; Family $50; Supporter $100; Bronze $350; Silver $500; Gold $750; Platinum $1,000.

Elberta

BALDWIN COUNTY HERITAGE MUSEUM, (M), 25521 Hwy. 98, Elberta, AL 36530. Mailing Address: P.O. Box 356, Elberta, AL 36530-0356. Tel.: 251-986-8375 & 752-8883. Fax: 251-986-8375.
E-mail: bchm@gulftel.com
Web Site: www.baldwincountyheritagemuseum.com
Founded: 1981.
Congressional District: 4
Key Personnel: Dir., Becky Holliday; Chm. (V), Clark Cathey; Clerk, Tammy Kinney.
Personnel Profile: Part-Time Paid 1; Part-Time Volunteers 31.
Governing Authority: private; nonprofit organization. Tax-exempt.
History Museum.
Collections: county history from Civil War to the Great Depression; farming & forestry tools; ethnic land developments c.1900; personal, recreational & communication artifacts; turpentining; early fishing & shrimping industries; period churches, schools & railroads. Historic Buildings: 1908 church; blacksmith; pole barns; potato shed; school.
Major Exhibits: Odyssey Shipwreck! Treasures of the S.S. Republic, 11/09-12/10; Feed Sack Fashions: A Day in the Life of a Farm Family, 11/09-12/10; Little Red Schoolhouse: Early Education in Baldwin County, 11/09-12/10; Amazing Grace: Churches of Baldwin County, 1/10-12/10.
Research Fields: rural history of Baldwin County c.1900; farming, forestry, turpentining, fishing industry; L&N Railroad.
Facilities: nature trails. Museum-related items for sale.
Activities: Annual Event: Winter Festival in January & December.
Hours & Admission Prices: Wed.-Sat. 10-5, 2nd & 4th Sun. 12-5. No charge. Closed all national & state holidays. ♿
Attendance: 2,500 (estimated)
Membership: Individual $10; Family $15; Friend $50; Sustaining $100; Supporting $500; Patron $1,000; Benefactor $5,000.

Eufaula

SHORTER MANSION MUSEUM, 340 N. Eufaula Ave., Eufaula, AL 36027-1518. Mailing Address: P.O. Box 486, Eufaula, AL 36072-0486. Tel.: 334-687-3793; 888-EUFAULA (383-2852). Fax: 334-687-1836.
E-mail: info@eufaulapilgrimage.com
Web Site: www.eufaulapilgrimage.com
Founded: 1965.
Congressional District: 84
Key Personnel: C.E.O., Douglas Purcell.
Personnel Profile: Full-Time Paid 1; Part-Time Paid 5; Part-Time Volunteers 5.
Governing Authority: society; board of directors. Parent Institution: Eufaula Heritage Association, Inc. Tax-exempt.
Local History Museum: housed in the former home of Eli Sims Shorter II; built in 1884. Listed on the National Register of Historic Places.
Collections: period furnishings; period dresses; textiles; photographs; memoirs

of six Alabama Governors from Barbour County; Adm. Thomas H. Moorer Room; UDC & DAR Collections.
Research Fields: genealogy; historic homes within the city of Eufaula.
Facilities: banquet facilities; meeting rooms.
Activities: group tours by appointment; weddings; receptions. Association sponsors: annual Eufaula Pilgrimage of Historic Homes; co-sponsors periodic heritage seminars.
Publications: reprints, Historic Eufaula; History of Eufaula 1875; Backtracking in Barbour County; Foundation Stone.
Hours & Admission Prices: Mon.-Sat. 10-4; group tours by appointment. Adults $5, children 5-12 $3; discounts to groups, AAM & AAA members; children under 4 no charge. ♿
Attendance: 10,000 (accurate)
Membership: Single $25; Couple $50; Sustaining $100-$249; Patron $250 & up.

Fairhope

EASTERN SHORE ART CENTER, 401 Oak St., Fairhope, AL 36532-2403. Tel.: 251-928-2228. Fax: 251-928-5188.
E-mail: esac@esartcenter.com
Web Site: www.esartcenter.com
Founded: 1958.
Congressional District: 94
Key Personnel: Mng. Dir. & C.E.O., Robin Fitzhugh; Pres. (V), Kate Fisher; Museum Shop Mgr., Jane W. Kittrell.
Personnel Profile: Full-Time Paid 2; Part-Time Paid 3; Part-Time Volunteers 125.
Governing Authority: nonprofit organization. Parent Institution: Bd. of Dirs., Eastern Shore Art Assoc. Tax-exempt.
Art Museum.
Collections: contemporary American paintings.
Facilities: library; five studio-classrooms.
Activities: temporary exhibits; 2 annual outdoor art shows; art classes; workshops; lectures.
Publications: The Artline Newsletter; quarterly class schedule; members directory; book, Painters Paradise.
Hours & Admission Prices: Mon.-Fri. 10-4, Sat. 10-2. No charge; donations accepted. Closed major holidays. ♿
Attendance: 16,000 (estimated)
Membership: Individual $25; Family $40; Business $50; Supporting $100; Patron $200; Benefactor $500; Lifetime $1,500.

Fayette

FAYETTE ART MUSEUM, 530 N. Temple Ave., Fayette, AL 35555-2211. Tel.: 205-932-8727. Fax: 205-932-8727.
E-mail: fam@watvc.com
Founded: 1969.
Congressional District: 7
Key Personnel: Dir. & Cur., Anne Perry-Uhlman.
Personnel Profile: Part-Time Paid 1; Part-Time Volunteers 15.
Governing Authority: municipal; nonprofit. Parent Institution: City of Fayette, AL. Tax-exempt.
Art Museum: housed in c.1930 former school building.
Collections: 3,700 pieces of 20th-century art: 2,700 pieces by Lois Wilson (1905-1980), folk art pieces by Jimmy Lee Sudduth, Benjamin F. Perkins, Sybil Gibson & Fred Webster; well-known folk artists.
Facilities: 365-seat auditorium.
Activities: guided tours; arts festivals; temporary exhibits. Annual Event: Fayette Arts Festival in August.
Hours & Admission Prices: Mon.-Fri. 9-12 & 1-4; other times by appointment. No charge; donations accepted. ♿
Attendance: 40,000 (estimated)

Finchburg

ALABAMA RIVER MUSEUM, Claiborne Lock & Dam, Alabama River (north of Monroeville), Finchburg, AL Mailing Address: c/o MCHM, P.O. Box 1637, Monroeville, AL 36461-1637. Tel.: 251-575-7433. Fax: 251-575-2513.
E-mail: mchm@frontiernet.net
Web Site: www.tokillamockingbird.com
Formerly: River Heritage Museum
Founded: 2000.
Congressional District: 1
Key Personnel: C.E.O., Jane Ellen Clark; Chm. (V), John Grider; Cur., Olivia Rowell; Museum Shop Mgr., Stephanie Rogers.
Personnel Profile: Part-Time Paid 1; Part-Time Volunteers 20.
Governing Authority: Parent Institution: Monroe County Heritage Museums. Tax-exempt: 501(c)(3).
History Museum.
Collections: tools, points & ceremonial from Native Americans of Alabama; Alabama River steamboats artifacts; eocene-age fossils from the Claiborne Bluff.
Activities: Museum Sponsors: Alabama River Festival in March.
Hours & Admission Prices: March-Oct. Sat. 9-4. No charge; donations accepted. ♿
Attendance: 5,000

Florence

CHILDREN'S MUSEUM OF THE SHOALS, 2810 Darby Dr., Florence, AL 35630-1524. Tel.: 256-765-0500.
E-mail: juliasanford.cmos@gmail.com
Web Site: www.shoalschildrensmuseum.org
Founded: 2001.
Governing Authority: Tax-exempt.
Children's Museum.
Collections: hands-on exhibits.
Facilities: Museum-related items for sale.
Activities: educational programs; rental facilities; special events.
Hours & Admission Prices: Thurs.-Sat. 10:30-4:30; groups by appointment. Admission 2 & over $5; discounts to ACM members & groups of 15 or more; children under 2 & members no charge. Closed major holidays. ♿

FRANK LLOYD WRIGHT ROSENBAUM HOUSE, 601 Riverview Dr., Florence, AL 35630-6026. Mailing Address: 217 E. Tuscaloosa St., Florence, AL 35630-4724. Tel.: 256-740-8899.
Web Site: www.wrightinalabama.com
Founded: 1999.
Congressional District: 5
Key Personnel: Dir., Barbara K. Broach.
Personnel Profile: Part-Time Paid 4.
Governing Authority: municipal. Parent Institution: City of Florence. Tax-exempt: 501(c)(3).
Historic House Museum: designed by Frank Lloyd Wright, c.1939.
Collections: Wright-designed furniture; photographs; blueprints; Rosenbaum family artifacts.
Research Fields: Frank Lloyd Wright architecture; construction, restoration & preservation of the Rosenbaum house.
Facilities: Museum-related items for sale.
Activities: guided tours.
Publications: museum brochure.
Hours & Admission Prices: Tues.-Sat. 10-4, Sun. 1-4. Adults $8, senior citizens, students & children $5; discounts to groups of 10 or more. Closed major holidays.
Attendance: 5,000 (estimated)

INDIAN MOUND & MUSEUM, 1028 S. Court St., Florence, AL 35630-6116. Mailing Address: 217 E. Tuscaloosa St., Florence, AL 35630-4724. Tel.: 256-760-6427.
Web Site: www.florenceal.org
Founded: 1968.
Congressional District: 5
Key Personnel: Dir., Barbara K. Broach.
Personnel Profile: Part-Time Paid 3.
Governing Authority: municipal. Parent Institution: City of Florence. Tax-exempt.
History Museum.
Collections: Native American artifacts including points, pottery, axes, belts, shell necklaces & blades from Paleo to historic ages.
Research Fields: Native American history; historic artifacts.
Activities: guided tours.
Publications: museum brochure.
Hours & Admission Prices: Tues.-Sat. 10-4; groups by appointment. Adults $2, students $.50. Closed major holidays. ♿
Attendance: 3,500 (estimated)

KENNEDY-DOUGLASS CENTER FOR THE ARTS, 217 E. Tuscaloosa St., Florence, AL 35630-4724. Tel.: 256-760-6379. Fax: 256-760-6382.
E-mail: bbroach@florenceal.org
Web Site: www.florenceal.org
Founded: 1976.
Congressional District: 5
Key Personnel: Dir., Barbara K. Broach; Program Coord., Mary Nicely; Administrative Asst., Faye Vines.
Personnel Profile: Full-Time Paid 3.
Governing Authority: municipal; nonprofit. Tax-exempt.
Art Council: housed in 1917-18 Kennedy-Douglass House.
Collections: genealogy; historical records; art collections. Historic Houses:

1890 Southall-Moore House; 1915 Wright-Douglass House; 1917-18 Kennedy-Douglass House.
Facilities: library of books available for research on premises; reading room; classrooms. Museum-related items for sale.
Activities: guided tours; lectures; films; gallery talks; concerts; arts festivals; study clubs; formally organized education programs; docent program & council; permanent, temporary & traveling exhibitions.
Hours & Admission Prices: Mon.-Fri. 9-4; other times by appointment. No charge. ♿
Attendance: 12,000 (estimated)

POPE'S TAVERN MUSEUM, 203 Hermitage Dr., Florence, AL 35630-4667. Mailing Address: 217 E. Tuscaloosa St., Florence, AL 35630-4724. Tel.: 256-760-6439.
Web Site: www.florenceal.org
Founded: 1968.
Congressional District: 5
Key Personnel: Cur., Jo Parkhurst.
Personnel Profile: Part-Time Paid 3.
Governing Authority: municipal; City of Florence.
Historic House; housed in a former stagecoach stop, tavern & inn; used as a hospital by Confederate & Union forces.
Collections: colonial period furnishings, relics, & artifacts; Civil War artifacts.
Research Fields: Revolutionary & Civil War Periods; city & county history.
Activities: tours; temporary exhibits; art & craft demonstrations. Museum Sponsors: Frontier Day in June; Open House in December.
Publications: historic brochures.
Hours & Admission Prices: Tues.-Sat. 10-4. Adults $2, children $.50. ♿
Attendance: 2,657 (accurate)

W.C. HANDY HOME MUSEUM AND LIBRARY, 620 W. College St., Florence, AL 35630-5360. Mailing Address: 217 Tuscaloosa St., Florence, AL 35630-4724. Tel.: 256-760-6434. Fax: 256-760-6382.
E-mail: bbroach@florenceal.org
Web Site: www.florenceal.org
Founded: 1968.
Congressional District: 5
Key Personnel: Dir., Barbara K. Broach; Cur., Sandra Ford.
Personnel Profile: Part-Time Paid 2.
Governing Authority: municipal. Parent Institution: City of Florence, Mayor Council. Tax-exempt.
Historic House.
Collections: artifacts; memorabilia related to the life of W.C. Handy.
Research Fields: W.C. Handy papers.
Facilities: library.
Activities: guided tours. Annual Event: W.C. Handy Birthday Celebration in November.
Publications: brochures.
Hours & Admission Prices: Tues.-Sat. 10-4. Adults $2, students $.50. ♿
Attendance: 3,500 (estimated)

Fort Payne

ALABAMA FAN CLUB AND MUSEUM, 101 Glenn Blvd., S.W., Fort Payne, AL 35967-4963. Tel.: 800-557-8223; 256-845-1646. Fax: 256-845-5650.
Country Music Group Museum.
Collections: country music & group history; personal artifacts; photographs.
Facilities: Museum-related items for sale.
Activities: group fan club.
Hours & Admission Prices: Memorial Day to Labor Day daily 9-6; Sept.-May Wed.-Sat. 9-6, Sun. 1-6.

COOK SOUND STUDIOS, 1419 Scenic Rd., Fort Payne, AL 35968. Tel.: 256-845-2286.
Country Music Museum: housed in the studio of Alabama band member, Jeff Cook.
Collections: Jeff Cook's music & life; personal artifacts; photographs.
Hours & Admission Prices: By appointment.

FORT PAYNE DEPOT MUSEUM, 105 5th St., N.E., Fort Payne, AL 35967-2455. Mailing Address: P.O. Box 681420, Fort Payne, AL 35968-1615. Tel.: 256-845-5714.
Web Site: fortpaynedepotmuseum.org
Founded: 1986.
Key Personnel: Chm. (V), Scott Bateman.
Personnel Profile: Full-Time Volunteers 1; Part-Time Paid 2; Part-Time Volunteers 5.
Governing Authority: nonprofit organization.
History Museum: housed in historic Fort Payne railroad depot built by the Alabama Great Southern Railroad in 1891.
Collections: historical documents & artifacts; Indian artifacts; turn of the century clothing; farm equipment; household items; tools & machinery.
Hours & Admission Prices: Mon., Wed. & Fri. 10-12 & 12:30-4. Donations accepted. Closed major holidays.
Attendance: 15,000 (estimated)

Fort Rucker

U.S. ARMY AVIATION MUSEUM, Bldg. 6000, Fort Rucker, AL 36362. Mailing Address: P.O. Box 620610, Fort Rucker, AL 36362-0610. Tel.: 334-255-3036 & 2893. Fax: 334-255-3054.
E-mail: avnmuseum@alanet.com
Web Site: www.armyavnmuseum.org
Founded: 1962.
Congressional District: 2
Key Personnel: Dir., R.S. Maxham; Cur. Collections, Harford Edwards, Jr.; Registrar, Lynne Cosby.
Governing Authority: Army Regulation 870-20. Parent Institution: Center of Military History, Washington, DC. Tax-exempt.
Aviation Technology and Military Museum.
Collections: aircraft, fixed wing and rotary wing; army aviation memorabilia.
Research Fields: army aviation & related activities.
Facilities: library of general & technical Army Aviation books & manuals available to persons performing Army Aviation research.
Activities: scheduled VIP, school & special group tours; permanent & temporary exhibits; classes.
Hours & Admission Prices: Mon.-Sat. 9-4, Sun. 12-4. No charge; donations accepted. Closed New Year's Eve & Day; Thanksgiving; Christmas Eve & Day. ♿
Membership: U.S. Army Aviation Museum Foundation, Inc.: Organization, In Memoriam & Life $100; Distinguished $500; Charter $1,000.

Gadsden

GADSDEN MUSEUM OF ART, (M), 515 Broad St., Gadsden, AL 35901-3719. Tel.: 256-546-7365. Fax: 256-546-7365.
E-mail: museum@cityofgadsen.com
Web Site: gadsdenmuseum.com
Founded: 1965.
Congressional District: 7
Key Personnel: Dir., Steve Temple; Graphics Dir., Dan Hampton.
Personnel Profile: Full-Time Paid 3; Part-Time Paid 1; Interns 3.
Governing Authority: municipal; nonprofit organization. Parent Institution: Gadsden Public Library. Tax-exempt: 170(b)(1)(A).
Art & History Museum.
Collections: paintings in oil, acrylics & watercolors; period artifacts; lithographs; Indian artifacts; china & porcelain; historical decorative arts of Gadsden area.
Facilities: library of fine arts books & slides.
Activities: guided tours; permanent & temporary exhibitions.
Publications: brochure.
Hours & Admission Prices: Mon.-Sat. 10-4, 1st Fri. of month 10-8. No charge; donations accepted. ♿
Attendance: 75,000 (estimated)
Membership: Student & Senior $10; Individual $25; Family $50; Contributing $200-$500; Patron $1,000.

MARY G. HARDIN CENTER FOR CULTURAL ARTS, 501 Broad St., Gadsden, AL 35901-3719. Mailing Address: P.O. Box 1507, Gadsden, AL 35902-1507. Tel.: 256-543-2787. Fax: 256-546-7435.
E-mail: bobwelch@culturalarts.org
Web Site: www.culturalarts.org
Founded: 1987.
Congressional District: 7
Key Personnel: C.E.O. & Exec. Dir., Robert M. Welch; Chm. (V), Charles Hill; Vice Chm., Kay Moore; Financial Dir., Allen Ray; Devel., Membership & Public Rels., Tom Banks; Dir. Children's Museum & Education, Mickey Barrett; School for the Arts, Mike Barrett; Office Mgr., Judy Atkins.
Personnel Profile: Full-Time Paid 12; Part-Time Paid 27; Part-Time Volunteers 110; Interns 1.
Governing Authority: nonprofit organization. Parent Institution: Gadsden Cultural Arts Foundation. Subsidiary Institution: Imagination Place Children's Museum. Tax-exempt: 501(c)(3).
Art Center.
Collections: old postcards of Etowah County, AL.
Research Fields: visitor behavior.
Facilities: library; recital hall; theater; restaurant; meeting rooms; ballet studio.
Activities: guided tours; lectures; concerts; dance recitals; arts festivals; hobby

workshops; organized education programs; docent program; participatory & traveling exhibitions.
Publications: quarterly newsletter, For Arts Sake.
Hours & Admission Prices: Mon.-Sat. 10-8, Sun. 1-5. Imagination Place: Mon.-Sat. 10-6, Sun. 1-5. Adults $6, children $5; discounts to groups & ASTC reciprocal; Tues. & members no charge. Closed New Year's Day; Independence Day; Labor Day; Thanksgiving; Christmas. ♿
Attendance: 120,000 (estimated)
Membership: Individual $50; Family $80.

Gilbertown

CHOCTAW COUNTY HISTORICAL MUSEUM, 40 Melvin Rd., Gilbertown, AL 36908. Mailing Address: P.O. Box 162, Gilbertown, AL 36908-0162. Tel.: 251-843-2501.
Founded: 1987.
Key Personnel: Pres. (V), Earl Ray Mason
History Museum.
Collections: local history & culture; photographs; personal artifacts; period furnishings; war memorabilia; fossils.
Hours & Admission Prices: Call for hours. No charge; donations accepted. ♿
Attendance: 1,200 (estimated)
Membership: Individual $10; Family $15; Lifetime $200.

Grand Bay

EL CAZADOR MUSEUM, 10329 Freeland Ave., Grand Bay, AL 36541-5731. Mailing Address: P.O. Drawer 605, Grand Bay, AL 36541. Tel.: 251-865-0128. Fax: 251-865-3419.
Web Site: www.elcazador.com
History Museum: Spanish Brigantine El Cazador lost at sea in 1784.
Collections: shipwreck artifacts including a breech loading cannon, the ship's bell, bronze sword handles, mint shipment of silver coins; gold artifacts.
Hours & Admission Prices: Thurs.-Sat. 10-4.

Graysville

MERIKS ZOO, 662 Windsor Dr. NE, Graysville, AL 35073-1231.
Key Personnel: Pres., Paul Stein; Exec. Dir., Tillian Smith; Assoc. Dir., Rey Jones; Cur. Mammals & Birds, Shawna Williams; Exhibitions, Jennifer Jackovino; Admin., Stephen Jurcsek; Zoo Keeper, Lynn Harjes.
Personnel Profile: Full-Time Paid 3; Part-Time Paid 5.
Governing Authority: state. Tax-exempt 501(c)(3).
Zoo.
Collections: zoological collection of over 3,000 animals
Research Fields: animal research, reproduction & behavior.
Facilities: 1,000-vol. library of zoo-related books available for use by public; 250-seat theater. Gift-related items for sale.
Activities: guided tours; lectures; films; formally organized education program for children & adults.
Publications: brochures; annual report; pamphlets.
Hours & Admission Prices: Daily 9-6. Adults $15, children 3-16 $10, students with ID & seniors $5; members & children under 3 no charge. Closed New Years Day; Independence Day; Christmas.
Attendance: 10,000 (estimated)
Membership: Individual $15; Associate $25; Director $35.

Greensboro

MAGNOLIA GROVE-HISTORIC HOUSE MUSEUM, 1002 Hobson St., Greensboro, AL 36744-1414. Tel.: 334-624-8618. Fax: 334-624-8618.
E-mail: maggrov2@bellsouth.net
Web Site: www.preserveala.org
Founded: 1943.
Congressional District: 7
Key Personnel: Site Dir., Eleanor W. Cunningham.
Personnel Profile: Full-Time Paid 2; Part-Time Volunteers 5.
Governing Authority: state. Parent Institution: Alabama Historical Commission. Tax-exempt.
Historic House Museum: c.1840 Greek Revival style home built by Isaac Croom. Boyhood home of Rear Admiral Richmond Pearson Hobson, Spanish-American war hero.
Collections: Hobson memorabilia; family furnishings.
Research Fields: historic homes of America, Spanish American War; decorative arts.
Activities: guided tours; educational programs; community events.
Publications: pamphlets
Hours & Admission Prices: House: Tues.-Fri. and 1st & 3rd Sat. 10-4. Grounds: Tues.-Fri. and 1st & 3rd Sat. 10-4, Sun. 1-4. Adults $5, college students $4, children 6-18 $3; discount to AAA, military, seniors & groups. Closed state holidays. ♿
Attendance: 1,763 (accurate)

Gulf Shores

ALABAMA GULF COAST ZOO, 1204 Gulf Shores Pkwy., Gulf Shores, AL 36542-5908. Tel.: 251-968-5732.
E-mail: info@alabamagulfcoastzoo.org
Key Personnel: Dir., Patti Hall.
Governing Authority: Operated By: Zoo Foundation, Inc. Tax-exempt: 501(c)(3).
Zoo.
Collections: over 290 animals including lions, tigers, bears, monkeys & macaws.
Activities: animal shows; petting zoo.
Hours & Admission Prices: Daily 9-4. Adults 12-54 $10, seniors 55 & over $8, children 3-12 $7; children 2 & under no charge. Closed New Year's Day; Thanksgiving; Christmas Eve & Day.

FORT MORGAN MUSEUM, 110 Hwy. 180 W., Gulf Shores, AL 36542-7802. Tel.: 251-540-7202. Fax: 334-540-7665.
E-mail: fortmorgan@centurytel.net
Founded: 1967.
Congressional District: 1
Key Personnel: Dir., Blanton Blankenship; Educational Program Developer, Michael Bailey; Museum Shop Mgr., Peggy McKeithen.
Personnel Profile: Full-Time Paid 7; Part-Time Volunteers 5.
Governing Authority: society. Parent Institution: Alabama Historical Commission, 468 South Perry St., Montgomery, AL 36130-0900. Tax-exempt.
Military History Museum.
Collections: weapons; Civil War artifacts; War of 1812 memorabilia; Spanish American War, World War I & World War II memorabilia.
Research Fields: Civil War; War of 1812; Spanish-American War; Endicott Era.
Facilities: picnic areas; bird sanctuary; concession stand.
Activities: pre-arranged tours. Museum Sponsors: Living History Program June & July.
Publications: brochures; pamphlets.
Hours & Admission Prices: Museum: daily 9-5. Fort & Grounds: March-Oct. daily 8-7, Nov.-Feb. daily 8-5. Adults $5, children 6-18 $3; children under 6 no charge. Closed New Year's Day; Thanksgiving; Christmas. ♿
Attendance: 89,147 (accurate)

GULF SHORES MUSEUM, 244 W. 19th Ave., Gulf Shores, AL 36542. Mailing Address: P.O. Box 299, Gulf Shores, AL 36547-0299. Tel.: 251-968-1473. Fax: 251-968-1175.
E-mail: museum@gulfshoresal.gov
Web Site: www.cityofgulfshores.org
Founded: 1999.
Congressional District: 32
Key Personnel: Chm. (V), May Alanko; Dir. Special Events, Patsy Hollingsworth; Museum Coord., Christie Shannon.
Personnel Profile: Part-Time Paid 1; Part-Time Volunteers 5.
Governing Authority: municipal. Parent Institution: City of Gulf Shores.
History Museum.
Collections: local history from Native American period to present; hurricane weather; shrimping & fishing industry; boat building tools.
Research Fields: history of Gulf Shores.
Facilities: library; 1,200 sq. ft. exhibit space.
Activities: loan, participatory & traveling exhibitions; winter film series. Annual Event: Christmas Open House.
Hours & Admission Prices: Tues.-Fri. 10-12 & 1-5, Sat. 10-2. No charge; donations accepted. Closed New Year's Day; Mardi Gras Day; Memorial Day; Independence Day; Labor Day; Veterans Day; Thanksgiving; Christmas Eve & Day. ♿
Attendance: 4,340 (accurate)

Guntersville

GUNTERSVILLE MUSEUM AND CULTURAL CENTER, 1215 Rayburn Ave., Guntersville, AL 35976-1432. Tel.: 256-571-7597. Fax: 256-571-7584.
E-mail: info@guntersvillemuseum.org
Web Site: guntersvillemuseum.org
History Museum: housed in a former military armory for Company E 167th Infantry Division; built in 1936.
Collections: area history & culture; Native American artifacts; personal artifacts; photographs; paintings.
Hours & Admission Prices: Tues.-Fri. 10-4, Sat.-Sun. 1-4. No charge.

Huntsville

THE ART GALLERIES AT UAH, Dept. of Art & Art History UAH, Robert Hall 313, Huntsville, AL 35899-0001. Tel.: 256-824-6114. Fax: 256-824-6438.
E-mail: art@uah.edu
Web Site: www.uah.edu/colleges/liberal/art
Founded: 1975.
Key Personnel: Printmaking & Design, Brandon Gardner; Acting Dean Sculpture & Drawing, Glenn Dasher; Painting, Kathryn Jill Johnson; Graphic Design, Keith Jones; Art History, Lillian Joyce; Art History, David Stewart; Drawing, Roxie Veasey; Art History, Martha Vines; Staff Asst., Marylyn Coffey; Studio & Gallery Technician, Monique K. Given.
Personnel Profile: Part-Time Paid 1; Part-Time Volunteers 2.
Governing Authority: university. nonprofit organization. Tax-exempt: 170(b)(1)(A).
Union Grove Gallery & Meeting House: housed in 1830s Greek Revival Presbyterian Chapel; University Center Gallery.
Collections: prints.
Activities: lectures; gallery talks; traveling & student exhibitions.
Hours & Admission Prices: Union Grove Gallery (primarily student shows): Mon.-Fri. 12:30-4:30; other times by appointment. Library Gallery (visiting artists): Mon.-Thurs. 8am-12 midnight, Fri. 8-8, Sat. 9-6, Sun. 1-10. ♿
Attendance: 7,000 (estimated)

BURRITT ON THE MOUNTAIN - A LIVING MUSEUM, 3101 Burritt Dr., Huntsville, AL 35801-1142. Tel.: 256-536-2882. Fax: 256-532-1784.
E-mail: bm-recep@ci.hunstville.al.us
Web Site: www.burrittonthemountain.com/
Formerly: Burritt Museum & Park
Founded: 1955.
Congressional District: 5
Key Personnel: Exec. Dir. & C.E.O., Leslie Ecklund; Dir. Operations, Pat Robertson; Exec. Asst., Teresa O'Malley; Bd. Chm. (V), Butch Damson; Bd. Vice-Chm., LeVon Nunn; Cur. & Historic Park Coord., Stephanie Timberlake; Dir. Education, Joan Morehead; Dir. Mktg., Gina Haskins; Museum Shop Mgr., Susan Clements.
Personnel Profile: Full-Time Paid 6; Part-Time Paid 11; Part-Time Volunteers 150.
Governing Authority: municipal government. Tax-exempt: 501(c)(3).
Historic Village & Museum: housed in a 1935 mansion. Listed on the National Register of Historic Places.
Collections: 19th-century rural life in north Alabama & south central Tennessee; local natural history; 1850 & 1900 living history farmsteads; local & nationally renowned artists; textiles.
Research Fields: north Alabama flora & fauna; folk medicines; 19th-century rural lifestyles; Tennessee Valley prehistoric Indian archeology; textiles; rural architecture; Southern decorative arts.
Facilities: research library; picnic area; nature trails; scenic overlook; gazebo; program areas; classrooms. Museum-related items for sale.
Activities: guided tours; lectures; concerts; arts festivals; hobby workshops; docent program; loan & temporary exhibitions; seasonal living history events. Museum Sponsors: Sorghum Festival; Earth Day; Indian Heritage Festival; Earth Camp; Spring Farm Days; Fall Festival; Candlelight Christmas.
Publications: books: Faces; Shadows On The Wall; On Gossamer Threads; brochures.
Hours & Admission Prices: April-Oct. Tues.-Sat. 9-5, Sun 12-5; Nov.-March Tues.-Sat. 10-4, Sun. 12-4. Adults $7, seniors 60 & over and military $6, students 13-17 $5, children 3-12 $4; discounts to local residents and AAM & AAA members; children 2 & under and members no charge. Closed New Year's Day; Thanksgiving; Christmas Eve & Day. ♿
Attendance: 100,000 (estimated)
Membership: Individual $25; Family $50; Piedmont Society $100-$249; Foothill Society $250-$999; Summit Society $1,000 & up.

EARLYWORKS MUSEUMS, (M), 404 Madison St., Huntsville, AL 35801-4203. Tel.: 256-564-8100 & 8124. Fax: 256-564-8151.
E-mail: bart.williams@hsvcity.com
Web Site: www.earlyworks.com
Formerly: Earlyworks Children's Museum
Founded: 1982.
Congressional District: 5
Key Personnel: Exec. Dir., Bart Williams; Dir. Foundation, Dorothy Havens; Dir. Volunteers, Margo Alford; Constitution Village Museum Shop Mgr., Lora McGoldan.
Personnel Profile: Full-Time Paid 16; Part-Time Paid 22; Part-Time Volunteers 250.
Governing Authority: municipal government. Parent Institution: City of Huntsville, AL. Branch Museums: Alabama Constitution Village, 109 Gates Ave., Huntsville, AL 35801; Humphreys-Rodgers House, corner Gates Ave. & Fountain Circle, Huntsville, AL 35801; Historic Huntsville Depot, 320 Church St., Huntsville, AL 35801. Tax-exempt: 170(b)(1)(A).
History Museum.
Collections: Earlyworks Museum: hands-on exhibits; Alabama Constitution Village: living history village & site in 1819; Historic Huntsville Depot: once used as a prison in Civil War; Humphreys-Rogers House: collection house & site for decorative arts exhibits.
Research Fields: history-related fields; social & women's history; domestic life; 19th-century crafts; architectural history; decorative arts; Federal Period; Alabama history & politics.
Facilities: research library; education classrooms; multi-purpose room; facilities available for meetings & receptions. Museum-related items for sale.
Activities: guided interpretive tours; domestic & labor skills demonstrations; special events; lectures; workshops; State History Teachers' Conference; Biscuit's Backyard preschool area; history teams outreach program; hands-on programs; organized education programs; furniture making; spinning; weaving; open hearth cooking; candledipping; printing; soapmaking; fabric dyeing; 19th-century domestic skill interpretation. Seasonal Special Programs: Holiday Open House; Folktales & Gingerbread; Dairy program; lavender & lace; boxcar children's camp; polar express.
Publications: quarterly calendar of events; brochures announcing special programs; video & activity book, The Spirit of the Times; cookbooks, Mrs. Neal's Cookbook; Society Sampler Cookbook.
Hours & Admission Prices: EarlyWorks: Tues.-Sat. 9-4. Village: March-Oct. Tues.-Sat. 10-4; Thanksgiving to Dec. 23 5 pm-9 pm. Depot: March-Dec. Tues.-Sat. 10-4. EarlyWorks: adults $10, senior citizens 55 & over and youth 4-17 $8, children 1-3 $4; discounts to AAM & ACM members; members and children 3 & under no charge. Village & Depot: adults $7, senior citizens & youth 4-17 $6; discounts to AAM & ACM members; members and children 3 & under no charge. Closed New Year's Day; Thanksgiving; Christmas Eve & Day. ♿
Attendance: 150,000 (accurate)
Membership: Individual & Grandparent $55 & $75; Contributing $100 & up; Corporate $100-$5,000.

HOWARD WEEDEN HOUSE MUSEUM, 300 Gates Ave., S.E., Huntsville, AL 35801-3101. Mailing Address: P.O. Box 2239, Huntsville, AL 35804-2239. Tel.: 256-536-7718.
E-mail: weedenhousemuseum@comcast.net
Web Site: www.weedenhousemuseum.com
Founded: 1981.
Key Personnel: Dir., Barbara L. Scott
History Museum: housed in 1819 Federal style home & birthplace of artist & poet, Maria Howard Weeden.
Collections: paintings; personal artifacts; furnishings.
Hours & Admission Prices: Call for hours.

HUNTSVILLE/MADISON COUNTY BOTANICAL GARDEN, 4747 Bob Wallace Ave., Huntsville, AL 35805-3390. Tel.: 256-830-4447. Fax: 256-830-5314.
E-mail: vmhurst@hiwaay.net
Web Site: www.hsvbg.org
Founded: 1988.
Key Personnel: Dir., Paula Steigerwald
Botanical Garden.
Collections: dogwood trail; daylily garden; herb garden; vegetable garden.
Facilities: 112 acres; cafe; nature trail. Museum-related items for sale.
Activities: group tours.
Hours & Admission Prices: May-Sept. Mon.-Wed. & Fri.-Sat. 9-6, Thurs. 9-8, Sun. 12-6; Oct.-April Mon.-Sat. 9-5, Sun. 12-5; groups by appointment. Adults $10, seniors 55 & over and military $8, children 3-18 $5; members and children 2 & under 3 no charge. Closed New Year's Day; Thanksgiving; Christmas.
Attendance: 325,000 (accurate)
Membership: Individual $45; Family $70.

* **HUNTSVILLE MUSEUM OF ART, (M),** 300 Church St., S., Huntsville, AL 35801-4910. Tel.: 256-535-4350. Fax: 256-532-1743.
E-mail: info@hsvmuseum.org
Web Site: www.hsvmuseum.org
Founded: 1970.
Congressional District: 5
Key Personnel: Chm. (V), Oscar Maxwell; Pres. & C.E.O., Clayton Bass; C.F.O., Debbie Higdon; Dir. Curatorial Affairs, Peter J. Baldaia; Dir. Institutional Advancement, Alison Trefry; Registrar, Deborah S. Taylor; Deputy Dir., Carolyn Faraci; Cur. Exhibitions, David Reyes; Museum Academy Dir., Laura Smith; Communications Mgr., Jenny Lane; Facility & Event Mgr., Lil Parton; Security Supvr., Linda Berry.

Personnel Profile: Full-Time Paid 10; Part-Time Paid 11; Part-Time Volunteers 400; Interns 1.
Governing Authority: municipal. Tax-exempt: 501(c)(3).
Art Museum.
Collections: 19th- & 20th-century American Art with an emphasis on Southern art. Contemporary crafts & glass.
Major Exhibits: The Royal Holloway Collection (T), 11/09-1/10; Lowe Collection Highlights, 12/09-2/10; Gala Art Exhibition, 2/10-3/10; Red Clay Survey, 3/10-5/10; Youth Art Month, 3/10-5/10; Encounters: Kathy Chan, 5/10-8/10; Asian Treasures, 7/10-8/10; The Sellars Collection, 6/10-8/10; World of the Pharoahs (T), 10/10-12/10.
Research Fields: 19th- & 20th-century American art; Southern art.
Facilities: 2,000-vol. art research library; 46,000 sq. ft. exhibit space; four meeting rooms; special events area.
Activities: guided tours; films; gallery talks; organized training programs; temporary & traveling exhibitions; special exhibitions; partnership in art program; musical presentations; lectures; museum academy art classes & workshops.
Publications: quarterly newsletter; exhibition catalogues; exhibition brochures.
Hours & Admission Prices: Tues.-Wed. & Fri.-Sat. 10-5, Thurs. 10-8, Sun. 1-5. Adults $7; discounts to groups, seniors over 60, military & students with valid ID; children under 6 & members no charge. Closed some major holidays. ♿
Attendance: 77,652 (accurate)
Membership: Student $20; Individual $35; Family $60; Friend $125; Sponsor $300; Patron $600; Benefactor $1,200; President's Circle $2,500; Silver Circle $5,000; Gold Circle $10,000; Platinum Circle $20,000 & up.

NORTH ALABAMA RAILROAD MUSEUM, 694 Chase Rd., Huntsville, AL 35811-1523. Mailing Address: P.O. Box 4163, Huntsville, AL 35815-4163. Tel.: 256-851-6276.
Founded: 1967.
Key Personnel: Pres. (V), Robert Jackson; Dir., Hugh Dudley; Museum Shop Mgr., Mrs. Terry Lott.
Personnel Profile: Full-Time Volunteers 2; Part-Time Volunteers 40.
Governing Authority: Tax-exempt.
Railroad Museum.
Collections: railcar; restored Railway Post Office car; day coach; Pullman sleeping car; freight & passenger equipment.
Activities: train rides; guided tours; charters; school field trips.
Publications: monthly newsletter; brochures; children's coloring book school program.
Hours & Admission Prices: Daily 9-4; groups by appointment. No charge; donations accepted.
Attendance: 5,000 (estimated)
Membership: Individual $49; Family $56.

SCI-QUEST HANDS-ON SCIENCE CENTER, 102-D Wynn Dr., Huntsville, AL 35805-1957. Tel.: 256-837-0606. Fax: 256-837-4536.
E-mail: information@sci-quest.org
Web Site: www.sci-quest.org
Formerly: The North Alabama Science Center
Key Personnel: C.E.O. & Dir., Cyndy Morgan; Dir. Education, Angela Giles-Moulton; Museum Shop Mgr., Kelly Brown.
Personnel Profile: Full-Time Paid 17; Part-Time Paid 11; Part-Time Volunteers 15; Interns 2.
Science Center.
Collections: hands-on exhibits.
Facilities: 3D high definition immersive theater. Museum-related items for sale.
Activities: hands-on informal science programs; outreach; summer camps; overnight science programs in the science center; birthday party programs.
Hours & Admission Prices: Mon.-Fri. 9-5, Sat. 10-6, Sun. 1-5. Center: adults $9, seniors $8.50, children $8. Visual Vortex Show $3; CineMuse Hi-Def Cinema $2; discount to military. Closed New Year's Day; Thanksgiving; Christmas Eve & Day.
Attendance: 90,722 (accurate)
Membership: Family & Grandparents $75; Extended Family $95; Supporting $115; Patron $500.

THE U.S. SPACE & ROCKET CENTER, One Tranquility Base, Huntsville, AL 35805-3371. Mailing Address: P.O. Box 070015, Huntsville, AL 35807-7015. Tel.: 256-721-7192. Fax: 256-721-7180.
E-mail: ralphb@spacecamp.com
Web Site: www.spacecamp.com
Founded: 1968.
Congressional District: 5
Key Personnel: C.E.O., Larry Capps; Chm., Jim Flynn; C.O.O., Clif Broderick; Exec. Vice Pres., Ralph Bryson; Vice Pres. Aerospace Programs, Michael Flachbart; Vice Pres. Finance, Donnie Claxton; Vice Pres. Human Resources, Vickie Henderson; Cur., Irene Willhite; Dir. Museum Operations, Samantha Peterson; Dir. Retail Sales, Scott Harbour; Vice Pres. Advancement, Brenda Carr; Corporate Donor Rels., Kelly Hatley.
Personnel Profile: Full-Time Paid 156; Part-Time Paid 400; Part-Time Volunteers 84.
Governing Authority: state. Parent Institution: State of Alabama; Alabama Space Science Exhibit Commission. Subsidiary Institution: U.S. Space & Rocket Center Foundation. Tax-exempt.
Aeronautics & Space Museum.
Collections: missiles, rockets, & space hardware from early space history to space shuttle & other future programs; exhibits on utilizing the technology of space; manuscripts; Saturn V; SR-71 Blackbird Jet; Full Stack Space Shuttle, orbiter & solid rocket boosters; Apollo artifacts; Apollo Saturn V; 2 full-scale replicas of Saturn V; Dr. Wernher von Braun's personal artifacts.
Major Exhibits: Star Wars: Where Science Meets the Imagination (T), 6/10-8/10.
Research Fields: history of rocketry development in United States.
Facilities: archives; 200-seat auditorium; 280-seat IMAX(R) theater; 350-seat digital theater; youth recreation area; food court; training center for U.S. Space Camp. Space-related items for sale.
Activities: museum & rocket park tours; permanent, temporary & traveling exhibits; hands-on exhibits; IMAX(R) movies; 4-G SpaceShot(TM) simulator ride; motion-based simulator; home of SPACE CAMP(R) & AVIATION CHALLENGE(R); demonstrations of life on the International Space Station; climbing wall.
Publications: Quest.
Hours & Admission Prices: March-Oct. daily 9-5; Nov.-Feb. see website for hours. Adults $24.95, children 6-12 $19.95; discount to ASTC Passport Program members & AAA members. Closed New Year's Eve & Day; Thanksgiving; Christmas Eve & Day. ♿
Attendance: 509,006 (accurate)
Membership: Pathfinder Individual $50; Pathfinder Family $100; Enterprise Family $145.

VETERANS MEMORIAL MUSEUM, 2060A Airport Rd., Huntsville, AL 35801-5338. Tel.: 256-883-3737. Fax: 256-883-3912.
E-mail: info@memorialmuseum.org
Web Site: www.memorialmuseum.org
Founded: 2001.
Congressional District: 5
Key Personnel: Dir., Randall Withrow.
Personnel Profile: Full-Time Volunteers 3; Part-Time Volunteers 12.
Governing Authority: Parent Institution: Alabama Center of Military History. Tax-exempt.
Military History Museum.
Collections: ground vehicles, wheeled; ground vehicles, tracked; artillery; helicopters; patrol boat; military artifacts from American Revolutionary to present; uniforms; military reference books & documents.
Facilities: 12,000 sq. ft. exhibit space.
Activities: Museum Sponsors: Military Vehicle Preservation Assoc. Rally in May; Veterans Day Open House.
Hours & Admission Prices: Memorial Day to Labor Day Wed.-Sat. 10-5; Sept.-May Wed.-Sat. 10-4; other times by appointment. Adults $5, seniors $4, students $3. Closed New Year's Day; Thanksgiving; Christmas. ♿
Attendance: 2,400 (estimated)

Jacksonville

DR. FRANCIS MEDICAL AND APOTHECARY MUSEUM, 207 Gayle Ave., S.E., Jacksonville, AL 36265-2544. Mailing Address: #16 Public Square W., Ste. 6, Jacksonville, AL 36265-2544. Tel.: 256-435-5091. Fax: 256-435-5410.
E-mail: calhounrsvp@cableone.net
Web Site: www.jacksonville-al.org
Founded: 1968.
Congressional District: 3
Key Personnel: Dir. Reservations, Denise Rucker.
Governing Authority: state. Affiliated with the Alabama State Historical Commission & the General John H. Forney Historical Society.
Medical Museum: housed in 1850 Antebellum office & apothecary of Dr. Francis.
Collections: period furnishings; medical instruments; display cases; books; journals; apothecary artifacts; bottles; desks; other medical & apothecary memorabilia.
Activities: guided tours for school & other groups; loan & permanent exhibitions.
Publications: brochures.
Hours & Admission Prices: By appointment. No charge; donations accepted.
Attendance: 47 (accurate)

Leeds

BARBER VINTAGE MOTORSPORTS MUSEUM, (M), 6030 Barber Motorsports Pkwy., Leeds, AL 35094-3418. Tel.: 205-699-7275. Fax: 205-702-8700.
E-mail: bvmm@barbermuseum.org
Web Site: www.barbermuseum.org
Founded: 1994.
Key Personnel: Dir., Jeff Ray; Museum Shop Mgr., Lee L. Woehle.
Governing Authority: nonprofit. Tax-exempt: 501(c)(3).
Motorsports Museum.
Collections: over 1,200 motorcycles & 60 cars from 20 nations with 200 manufacturers represented; history of motorcycles.
Publications: newsletter, VIN.
Hours & Admission Prices: April-Sept. Mon.-Sat. 10-6, Sun. 12-6; Oct.-March Mon.-Sat. 10-5, Sun. 12-5. Adults $15, children 4-12 $10; discounts to AAA members; children 3 & under no charge. Closed New Year's Day; Easter; Independence Day; Thanksgiving; Christmas Eve & Day. ♿

Lincoln

INTERNATIONAL MOTORSPORTS HALL OF FAME AND MUSEUM, 3198 Speedway Blvd., Lincoln, AL 35096-6327. Mailing Address: P.O. Box 1018, Talladega, AL 35161-1018. Tel.: 256-362-5002. Fax: 256-315-4565.
E-mail: kking@talladegasuperspeedway.com
Web Site: www.motorsportshalloffame.com/index.htm
Founded: 1983.
Key Personnel: Exec. Dir., Rick Humphrey; Mgr. Hall of Fame, Bruce Ramey; Dir. Communications & Mktg., Kristi King.
Personnel Profile: Full-Time Paid 5.
Governing Authority: nonprofit organization.
Motorsports Museum.
Collections: racing vehicles & memorabilia from 1902 to present.
Facilities: 14,000-vol. library. Museum-related items for sale.
Activities: Annual Event: Induction Ceremony in spring.
Hours & Admission Prices: April 4 to Labor Day daily 9-5; groups of 25 or more by appointment; extended hours during race weeks at Talladega Superspeedway. Adults $10, students 7-17 $5; discounts to senior citizens, military, policemen, firemen, AAA & AARP members; children 6 & under no charge. Closed New Year's Day; Thanksgiving; Christmas.
Attendance: 900 (estimated)

Loachapoka

LEE COUNTY HISTORICAL SOCIETY, 6500 Stage Rd., Loachapoka, AL 36865. Mailing Address: P.O. Box 206, Loachapoka, AL 36865-0206. Tel.: 334-887-3007.
E-mail: bigalmccord@bellsouth.net
Founded: 1968.
Key Personnel: Pres., Deborah McCord; Vice Pres., Charles Mitchell.
Personnel Profile: Part-Time Paid 1; Part-Time Volunteers 10; Interns 2.
Governing Authority: nonprofit corporation. Tax-exempt: 501(c)(3).
Historical Society Museum.
Collections: tools, artifacts, documents, books, records, furnishings & equipment belonging to the early settlers of the region.
Research Fields: agricultural; Creek Indians; natural resources of the area; family heirlooms & documents.
Facilities: library of material on music, genealogy, local, state & national history available for use on premises. Books & booklets for sale.
Activities: guided tours. Museum Sponsors: annual Historical Fair.
Publications: quarterly, Trails in History.
Hours & Admission Prices: By appointment only. No charge; donations accepted.
Attendance: 6,500 (estimated)
Membership: Individual $20; Family $30; Friend $50; Patron $100; Benefactor $250.

Marion

ALABAMA WOMEN'S HALL OF FAME, Judson College, Howard Bean Hall, 302 Bibb St., Marion, AL 36756-2504. Tel.: 334-683-5100 & 5156.
E-mail: bmathews@judson.edu
Web Site: www.awhf.org
Founded: 1970.
Key Personnel: Exec. Sec., Bill Mathews
History Museum.
Collections: Alabama women who have made significant contributions to the state & nation including Helen Adams Keller, Julia Strudwick Tutwiler, Amelia Gayle Gorgas, Tallulah Bankhead, and Mildred Westervelt Warner; portraits; photographs; letters; bronze plaques.
Hours & Admission Prices: Call for hours. No charge; donations accepted.

McCalla

IRON & STEEL MUSEUM OF ALABAMA, TANNEHILL IRONWORKS HISTORICAL STATE PARK, 12632 Confederate Pkwy., McCalla, AL 35111-2620. Tel.: 205-477-5711. Fax: 205-477-9400.
E-mail: ironmuseum@bellsouth.net
Web Site: www.Tannehill.org
Founded: 1970.
Congressional District: 7
Key Personnel: C.E.O. & Park Admin., Matt Walker; Museum Dir., Jack R. Bergstresser, Sr., Ph.D.; Chm. (V), Dorman Avery; Business Officer, Margaret Crumpton; Museum Events Coord., Jan Jones; Registrar, Carl Addison.
Personnel Profile: Full-Time Paid 20; Part-Time Paid 50; Part-Time Volunteers 50.
Governing Authority: state; nonprofit. Tax-exempt: 501(c)(3).
Industrial Museum & State Park: located on the c.1839 Tannehill Furnace Site.
Collections: c.1890s agricultural implements; iron working implements; artifacts relating to the iron industry of the 1700s-1850s; home furnishings; restored structures. Historic House & Buildings: 1820-1900 Tannehill Rural Village complex.
Research Fields: history of iron technology; architectural history; local genealogy; anthropology; agricultural history; folk life studies; historical archaeology.
Facilities: 1,000-vol. library of books & periodicals relating to the history of the iron industry, Alabama history & history of the United States available for research on premises only; nature center; reading room; classrooms; learning center; cafeteria. Objects related to Alabama folk life for sale.
Activities: guided tours; lectures; arts festivals; study clubs; hobby workshops; formally organized education programs for children, adults & undergraduate college students; loan, permanent, temporary & traveling exhibitions; archaeological projects.
Publications: newsletter, Tannehill Blast; book, Old Tannehill.
Hours & Admission Prices: Museum: Tues.-Fri. 8:30-4:30, Sat. 9:30-4:30, Sun. 12:30-4:30. Park: daily 7-sunset. Adults $2, children 6-11 and 62 & over $1; chidren 5 & under no charge. ♿
Attendance: 500,000 (accurate)
Membership: Student & Senior Citizen $5; Individual $10; Family $20; Supporting Family $50; Donor $100; Patron $1,000.

Mentone

LOOKOUT MOUNTAIN WILD ANIMAL PARK, 3593 Hwy. 117, Mentone, AL 35984-2929. Tel.: 256-634-8211.
E-mail: doc@lookoutmtnzoo.com
Web Site: lookoutmtnzoo.com
Governing Authority: nonprofit organization.
Zoo.
Collections: animals from around the world including monkeys, parrots, llamas, bengal tigers; black bear; buffalo; lynx.
Activities: feeding, training & playing with animals.
Hours & Admission Prices: Call for hours. Admission $6.

Mobile

BRAGG-MITCHELL MANSION, 1906 Springhill Ave., Mobile, AL 36607-2304. Tel.: 251-471-6364. Fax: 251-478-3800.
E-mail: info@braggmitchellmansion.com
Web Site: braggmitchellmansion.com
Founded: 1987.
Congressional District: 1
Key Personnel: Dir., Lynn Stewart.
Personnel Profile: Full-Time Paid 1; Part-Time Paid 9; Part-Time Volunteers 1.
Governing Authority: private; nonprofit organization. Branch Museum: The Explore Center, 1906 Springhill Ave., Mobile, AL 36607. Tax-exempt: 501(c)(3).
Antebellum Historic Museum.
Collections: furnishings from 1725-1900.
Hours & Admission Prices: Tues.-Fri. 10-4. Adults $5, senior citizens $4.50, students $3; discounts to groups; children under 6 no charge. Closed New Year's Day; Mardi Gras Day; Easter; Memorial Day; Labor Day; Christmas. ♿
Attendance: 3,819 (accurate)

CARLEN HOUSE MUSEUM, 54 N. Carlen St., Mobile, AL 36606-1472. Tel.: 251-470-7768.
Historic House Museum: housed in restored Creole cottage, built in 1842.
Collections: period artifacts & furnishings.
Hours & Admission Prices: Tues.-Sat. 1-5. No charge.

CENTRE FOR THE LIVING ARTS, (M), 250 Conti St., Cathedral Square, Mobile, AL 36602-2714. Tel.: 251-208-5652.
Founded: 1999.
Congressional District: 1
Key Personnel: Dir., Carlos F. Parkman; Chm. (V), Mike Rogers
Performing Arts Center: housed in the Saenger Theatre; built in 1927.
Collections: contemporary visual arts; works by local, regional & national artists.
Major Exhibits: Moving Vehicles, 1/8/10-3/7/10; Opportunistic Architecture: The Works of LTL Architects, 3/12/10-5/9/10; Alan Feltus and Lani Irwin With Sons, Tobias and Joseph, 5/14/10-7/3/10.
Facilities: theater; art center.
Activities: performances; art classes & workshops; temporary exhibits.
Publications: newsletters.
Hours & Admission Prices: Wed.-Sat. 10-5, Sun. 12-5. Gallery: no charge; donations accepted. Opening Receptions: adults $5; members no charge. Closed New Year's Day; Mardi Gras; Memorial Day; Independence Day; Labor Day; Thanksgiving; Christmas. ♿
Attendance: 122,000 (estimated)
Membership: Student $15; Individual $25-$39; Family $40-$74; Friend $75-$99; Sustainer $100-$249; Associate $250-$499; Supporter $500-$999; Partner $1,000-$2,499; Benefactor $2,500 & up.

GULF COAST EXPLOREUM SCIENCE CENTER, 65 Government St., Mobile, AL 36602-3107. Mailing Address: P.O. Box 1968, Mobile, AL 36633-1968. Tel.: 251-208-6870 & 6873. Fax: 251-208-6889.
E-mail: mike@exploreum.com
Web Site: www.exploreum.com
Formerly: Gulf Coast Exploreum Museum of Science
Founded: 1979.
Congressional District: 1
Key Personnel: Asst. Dir., Caroline Etherton; Business Mgr., W. Tyre Smithweck, Jr.; Mktg. Mgr., Hela Sheth.
Personnel Profile: Full-Time Paid 18; Part-Time Paid 32; Interns 2.
Governing Authority: nonprofit organization. Parent Institution: The Explore Center, Inc. Subsidiary Institution: Bragg Mitchel Mansion, Springhill Ave., Mobile, AL. Tax-exempt: 501(c)(3).
Science Center.
Collections: interactive exhibits.
Facilities: 52,000 sq. ft. exhibit space; learning center; IMAX dome theatre. Museum-related items for sale.
Activities: films; organized education programs; overnight program; curriculum boxes for teachers; participatory & traveling exhibitions.
Publications: brochure; newsletter.
Hours & Admission Prices: Mon.-Fri. 9-5, Sat. 10-5, Sun. 12-5. Exhibits: adult $11, youth 13-18 $9.50, child 2-12 $9; discounts to ASTC members; members no charge. Closed Mardi Gras Tuesday; Easter; Thanksgiving; Christmas. ♿
Attendance: 200,000 (accurate)
Membership: Family $100; Explorer $250; Discoverer $500; Odyssey $1,000.

HISTORIC MOBILE PRESERVATION SOCIETY, 350 Oakleigh Place, Mobile, AL 36604-2910. Tel.: 251-432-1281. Fax: 251-432-8843.
E-mail: hmps@bellsouth.net
Web Site: www.historicmobile.org
Founded: 1935.
Congressional District: 1
Key Personnel: Pres., Martha LoCicero, M.D.; Pres.-Elect, Douglas Kearley; 1st Vice Pres., Dora Finley; 2nd Vice Pres., Beth Walmsley; 3rd Vice Pres., Amy Hamilton; Sec., Sally Trufant.
Personnel Profile: Full-Time Paid 3; Full-Time Volunteers 7; Part-Time Paid 5; Part-Time Volunteers 100.
Governing Authority: society. Branch Museum: Oakleigh House. Subsidiary Institution: Oakleigh House Museum. Tax-exempt: 501(c)(3).
Historical Preservation Society & Historic House: 1833, Oakleigh House, an example of the raised type architecture along the Gulf Coast; 1850 Cox-Deasy House.
Collections: archives: local history; Civil War artifacts; photographs; books; maps. Museum Houses: period silver; china; furniture; paintings; costumes; clothing; accessories.
Research Fields: archives.
Facilities: 625-vol. library of books, papers & photographs relating to the Mobile area available in archives building for research on premises. Photographs for sale.
Activities: guided tours; lectures; TV & radio programs; docent programs & council.
Publications: quarterly journal, Landmark Letter; research material & books, Church St. Graveyards; Lost Villages & Ancient Kingdoms; 19th Century Mobile Silver; Mobile: The Life & Times of a Great Southern City; triannual journal, Landmark Letter; Mobile City Directory 1867.
Hours & Admission Prices: Thurs.-Sat. 10-4, Sun. 1-4. Adults $5; discounts to AAM & ICOM members; members no charge. Closed legal holidays; New Year's Eve & Day; Christmas Eve, Day & week. ♿
Attendance: 25,000 (estimated)
Membership: Junior (under 21) $12; Individual $35; Couple $45; Family $55; Contributing $100; Supporting $150; Sustaining $300; Life $1,000.

MOBILE BOTANICAL GARDENS, 5151 Museum Dr., Mobile, AL 36608-1919. Tel.: 251-342-0555.
E-mail: mbg2@bellsouth.net
Web Site: www.mobilebotanicalgardens.org
Formerly: Southern Alabama Botanical & Horticultural Society
Founded: 1974.
Key Personnel: Dir., Marion Drummond; Vice Pres. Bd. Dirs., David Norris.
Personnel Profile: Full-Time Paid 6; Part-Time Volunteers 200.
Botanical Gardens.
Collections: azaleas; camellias; hollies; magnolias; roses; ferns; perennials; herbs; rhododendron; longleaf pine.
Facilities: 100-acre site; nature trails; gardens.
Hours & Admission Prices: Gardens: dawn to dusk. Office: Mon.-Fri. 8-5. No charge; donations accepted.
Membership: Individual $30; Family $40; Affiliate $60; Friend $100; Fellow $250; Patron $500; Benefactor $1,000.

MOBILE MEDICAL MUSEUM, (M), 1664 Springhill Ave., Mobile, AL 36604-1405. Tel.: 251-415-1109. Fax: 251-415-1110.
Web Site: mobilemedicalmuseum.com
Formerly: Eichold Heustis Medical Museum of the South
Founded: 1962.
Congressional District: 101
Key Personnel: Founder & Advisor, Dr. Samuel Eichold, II; Pres. (V), Sally C. Green; Vice Pres., Henry A. Callaway, III, Esq.; Sec., Shirley P. Mull; Treas., Charles S. Jones.
Personnel Profile: Full-Time Volunteers 1; Part-Time Paid 3; Part-Time Volunteers 2.
Governing Authority: community; nonprofit organization. Tax-exempt: 501(c)(3).
Medical History Museum.
Collections: early 1700s medical artifacts; history of the practice of medicine during the past 300 years; Civil War gallery of documents, artifacts, photographs; apothecary; old & rare medical books.
Research Fields: transactions of the state & city medical societies journals and city hospitals journals.
Facilities: 500-vol. medical reference library; 1,000 sq. ft. exhibit space.
Activities: guided tours; loan, temporary exhibits; lecture series. Museum Sponsors: International Museum Day.
Publications: quarterly newsletters.
Hours & Admission Prices: Tues.-Fri. 10-4. Adults $5; discounts to senior citizens; members no charge. Closed federal holidays. ♿
Attendance: 5,000 (estimated)
Membership: Student, Senior Citizen & Retired $15; Individual $35; Family $50; Supporting $100; Sponsor $250; Patron $500; Associate $1,000; Partner $5,000.

* **MOBILE MUSEUM OF ART, (M),** 4850 Museum Dr., Langan Park, Mobile, AL 36608-1917. Tel.: 251-208-5200 & 5203. Fax: 251-208-5201. TDD: 251-208-5200.
Web Site: www.MobileMuseumOfArt.com
Founded: 1964.
Congressional District: 1
Key Personnel: Dir., Tommy McPherson; Deputy Dir., Marlene Buckner; Chief Cur., Paul W. Richelson; Chm. (V), Tammy L. Smith; Cur. Exhibitions, Donan Klooz; Museum Shop Mgr., Loretta Potapenko; Museum Shop Mgr., Sydney Betbeze.
Personnel Profile: Full-Time Paid 46; Part-Time Paid 5; Part-Time Volunteers 98; Interns 3.
Governing Authority: municipal; nonprofit organization. Parent Institution: City of Mobile. Tax-exempt: 501(c)(3).
Art Museum.
Collections: Southern furniture & art; contemporary crafts; European & American paintings & prints; ethnic art; 1930-1940s American paintings; international contemporary glass.
Research Fields: American art 1930s - 1940s; contemporary decorative arts.
Facilities: library.
Activities: guided tours; lectures; films; gallery talks; concerts; arts festivals; formally organized education programs; temporary exhibitions. Gallery Sponsors: urban & rural school art programs.
Publications: quarterly calendar of events; exhibitions catalogues.
Hours & Admission Prices: Mon.-Sat. 10-5, Sun. 1-5. Adults $10, students $6;

discount to AAA, AAM, ICOM & AARP members & SE museums reciprocal program; members no charge. Closed New Year's Day; Thanksgiving; Christmas. ♿
Attendance: 79,711 (accurate)
Membership: Individual $25; Family $35; Sustaining $75; Patron $100; Associate & Business Friend $250; Supporting & Business Associate $500; Benefactor & Corporate Supporting $1,000; Corporate Investor $1,500; Corporate Patron $5,000; Life & Corporate Benefactor $10,000.

THE MUSEUM OF MOBILE, 111 S. Royal St., Mobile, AL 36602-3101. Mailing Address: P.O. Box 2068, Mobile, AL 36652-2068. Tel.: 251-208-7569. Fax: 251-208-7686.
E-mail: museum@cityofmobile.org
Web Site: www.museumofmobile.com
Founded: 1962.
Congressional District: 1
Key Personnel: Dir., David Alsobrook; Chm. (V), Gertrude Baker; Chm. Bd., Tony Kendall; Cur. Exhibits, Jacob Laurence; Cur. Collections, Shea McLean; Cur. History, Todd A. Kreamer; Asst. Dir., Shelia M. Flanagan; Registrar, Shelley Berger; Education, Jennifer Fondren; Research Historican, Chuck Torrey; Special Events, Elyse Marley; Security, Donnie Curtis; Museum Tech, Lori Rockhold; Museum Shop Mgr., Sydney Betbeze.
Personnel Profile: Full-Time Paid 24; Part-Time Paid 10; Part-Time Volunteers 10.
Governing Authority: municipal; nonprofit. Parent Institution: Museum of Mobile. Branch Museums: Phoenix Fire Museum, 203 S. Claiborne St., Mobile, AL; Historic Fort Conde, 150 S. Royal St., Mobile, AL. Tax-exempt.
History Museum.
Collections: Museum of Mobile: French, British & Spanish Colonial history; Indian, African-American & Confederate artifacts; costumes; documents; naval; transportation; silver; glass; ceramics; manuscripts; paintings; engravings; prints; maps; Mardi Gras; steamboat & ship models; carriages; hands-on exhibits. Phoenix Museum: firefighting equipment; fire memorabilia. Ft. Conde colonial period.
Major Exhibits: George Washington Carver (T), 3/29/10-7/4/10.
Research Fields: local & regional history of the Gulf Coast area from 1702.
Facilities: 2,500-vol. library of museum reference books & manuscripts; two classrooms; one discovery room.
Activities: docent program; guided tours; lectures; formal education programs for children; inter-museum loan; permanent & temporary exhibitions; special exhibits.
Publications: books: The Phoenix Volunteer Fire Company of Mobile; Military Buttons of the Gulf Coast; A Voyage to Dauphin Island in 1720; The Journal of Bertet de la Clue; Old Mobile Fort Louis de la Louisiane 1702-1711; Raphael Semmes, Rear Admiral Confederate States Navy; Brigadier General Confederate States Army; Iron Ore to Iron Lace; Confederate & Union Button of the Gulf Coast 1681-1865; Queens of Mardi Gras 1893-1986; newsletter, Timeline.
Hours & Admission Prices: Museum of Mobile: Mon.-Sat. 9-5, Sun. 1-5. Adults $5, seniors 55 & up $4, students $3; discounts to AAM & ICOM members; children under 6 & members no charge. Historic Fort Conde: daily 8-5. No charge; donations accepted. Phoenix Fire Museum: Tues.-Sat. 9-5, Sun. 1-5. Closed New Year's Day; Thanksgiving; Christmas; some city holidays. ♿
Attendance: 82,412 (accurate)
Membership: Student $10; Individual $25; Family $35; Supporting $100; Patron $500; Benefactor $1,000.

THE NATIONAL AFRICAN-AMERICAN ARCHIVES AND MUSEUM, 564 Dr. Martin Luther King Jr. Ave., Mobile, AL 36603-5916.
History Museum: housed in the former Davis Avenue Branch of the Mobile Public Library, the only library for African-Americans from 1932 to the mid-1960s. Listed on the National Register for Historic Places.
Collections: African-American history; cultural heritage; portraits; books; family histories; period artifacts.
Activities: group tours.
Hours & Admission Prices: Mon.-Fri. 8-4, Sat. 10-2, Sun. by appointment.

OAKLEIGH PERIOD HOUSE MUSEUM, 350 Oakleigh Place, Mobile, AL 36604-2910. Tel.: 334-432-1281.
E-mail: oakleighop@aol.com
Historic House Museum.
Collections: period furniture; portraits; silver; china; jewelry; kitchen implements; toys.
Facilities: Museum-related items for sale.
Activities: guided tours. Annual Event: Haunted Oakleigh; Candlelight Christmas at Oakleigh in December.
Hours & Admission Prices: Thurs.-Sat. 10-4, Sun. 1-4. Adults $5; members no charge. Closed legal holidays; Christmas week.

PHOENIX FIRE MUSEUM, 203 S. Claiborne St., Mobile, AL 36602-2322. Tel.: 251-208-7569.
Web Site: www.museumofmobile.com
Key Personnel: Exec. Dir., David Alsobrook
History Museum: housed in the restored home of Phoenix Volunteer Fire Company No. 6.
Collections: Mobile volunteer fire companies history; horse-drawn steam engines; early motorized vehicles.
Hours & Admission Prices: Tues.-Sat. 9-5, Sun. 1-5. No charge.

RICHARDS DAR HOUSE MUSEUM, 256 N. Joachim St., Mobile, AL 36603-6472. Tel.: 251-208-7320.
Founded: 1973.
Congressional District: 1
Key Personnel: Pres. (V), Pamela H. Whiteside; Museum Shop Mgr., Dawes Waibel.
Personnel Profile: Part-Time Paid 4; Part-Time Volunteers 124.
Governing Authority: private; nonprofit organization. Tax-exempt: 501(c)(3).
Historic House: built in 1860.
Collections: furnishings predating 1870.
Activities: Museum Sponsors: decorative arts series, Christmas at the Richards DAR House Museum.
Hours & Admission Prices: Mon.-Fri. 11-3:30, Sat. 10-4, Sun. 1-4. Adults $5, students $2; discounts to groups; children under 6 no charge. Closed New Year's Day; Mardi Gras; Easter; Independence Day; Labor Day; Thanksgiving; Christmas.
Attendance: 3,750 (estimated)

USS ALABAMA BATTLESHIP MEMORIAL PARK, 2703 Battleship Pkwy., Mobile, AL 36601. Mailing Address: P.O. Box 65, Mobile, AL 36601-0065. Tel.: 251-433-2703. Fax: 251-433-2777.
E-mail: btunnell@ussalabama.com
Web Site: www.ussalabama.com
Founded: 1963.
Congressional District: 1
Key Personnel: C.E.O., Bill Tunnell; Museum Shop Mgr., Cherie Daniels.
Personnel Profile: Full-Time Paid 34; Part-Time Paid 4; Part-Time Volunteers 2.
Governing Authority: state commission. Tax-exempt.
Historic Ship & Military Museum.
Collections: 1942 Battleship USS Alabama; 1941 Submarine USS Drum; naval, air force, marine, army & coast guard weapons & equipment; over 20 restored military aircraft; Vietnam-era PBR river patrol boat; original documents, photographs & uniforms; graphics; silver.
Research Fields: military history.
Facilities: picnic area. Gift items for sale.
Activities: self-guided ship tours; overnight youth camping program aboard battleship; flight simulator ride; coastal birding trail stop & kiosk; wildlife observatory.
Publications: semi-annual development newsletter.
Hours & Admission Prices: March-Oct. daily 8-6; Nov.-Feb. daily 8-4. Adults $12, children 6-11 $6; discounts to groups, AARP & AAA members; children under 6 & active duty military personnel no charge. Parking: $2 per vehicle. Closed Christmas. ♿
Attendance: 228,226 (accurate)
Membership: Honorary $25; Individual $50; Family $100; Life $1,000.

Monroeville

MONROE COUNTY HERITAGE MUSEUM, 31 N. Alabama Ave., Monroeville, AL 36460. Mailing Address: P.O. Box 1637, Monroeville, AL 36461-1637. Tel.: 251-575-7433. Fax: 251-575-2513.
E-mail: mchm@frontiernet.net
Web Site: www.tokillamockingbird.com
Founded: 1990.
Congressional District: 1
Key Personnel: Exec. Dir., Jane Ellen Clark; Dir. Education, Dennis Mixon; Public Rels. & Administration, Nathan Carter; Dir. Funding, Stephanie Rogers; Mgr. Rikard's Mill Museum, Robert McMillian; Asst. Dir. Education, Barbara Wilson; Devel. Officer, Gail Deas; Mgr. Alabama River Museum, Olivia Rowell.
Personnel Profile: Full-Time Paid 7; Part-Time Paid 3; Part-Time Volunteers 75.
Governing Authority: county government; nonprofit. Parent Institution: Monroe Co. Museum. Tax-exempt: 501(c)(3).
Historic Building: housed in the 1903 Old Monroe County Courthouse; setting for the film To Kill A Mockingbird.
Collections: 1900-1950s clothing; historical photographs.
Activities: Museum Sponsors: annual production of To Kill a Mockingbird in April & May.

Hours & Admission Prices: Courthouse: Mon.-Fri. 8-4, Sat. 10-2. No charge; donations accepted. Closed major holidays. ♿
Attendance: 25,000 (estimated)
Membership: Student $20; Individual $35; Family $45; Star Family $100; Friend $250; Patron $500; Corporate $750.

Montevallo

ALDRICH COAL MINE MUSEUM, 137 Hwy. 203, Montevallo, AL 35115-7105. Tel.: 205-665-2886.
Key Personnel: Owner, Rose Emfinger; Owner, Henry Emfinger
Coal Mining Museum.
Collections: area history; coal mining industry; photographs; period artifacts; simulated coal mine.
Hours & Admission Prices: Thurs.-Sat. 10-4, Sun. 1-4; other times by appointment. Adults $5, children $3. ♿

THE AMERICAN VILLAGE, 3727 Hwy. 119 S., Montevallo, AL 35115. Mailing Address: P.O. Box 6, Montevallo, AL 35115-0006. Tel.: 205-665-3535; 877-811-1776 (Toll Free). Fax: 205-665-7577.
Web Site: www.americanvillage.org
Key Personnel: Exec. Dir., Tom Walker
History Museum.
Collections: period history; personal artifacts; military weapons & uniforms; photographs.
Facilities: theater. Museum-related items for sale.
Activities: educational programs; special events; rental facilities; group tours.
Hours & Admission Prices: Mon.-Fri. 10-4; other times by appointment. ♿

Montgomery

ALABAMA ARTIST'S GALLERY, Alabama State Council on the Arts, 201 Monroe St., Montgomery, AL 36130-0001. Mailing Address: Alabama State Council on the Arts, 201 Monroe St., Ste. 110, Montgomery, AL 36130-0001. Tel.: 334-242-4076, ext. 250. Fax: 334-240-3269.
E-mail: georgine.clarke@arts.alabama.gov
Web Site: www.arts.state.al.us
Key Personnel: Dir. Alabama State Council on the Arts, Albert B. Head; Dir. Gallery & Mgr. Visual Arts Program, Georgine Clarke
Art Museum.
Collections: works by Alabama artists.
Hours & Admission Prices: Mon.-Fri. 8-5. No charge. Closed state holidays. ♿
Attendance: 5,000

ALABAMA DEPARTMENT OF ARCHIVES & HISTORY, (M), 624 Washington Ave., Montgomery, AL 36130-3003. Mailing Address: P.O. Box 300100, Montgomery, AL 36130-0100. Tel.: 334-353-4712 & 4648. Fax: 334-240-3433. TDD: 334-242-4363.
E-mail: sherrie.hamil@archives.alabama.gov
Web Site: www.archives.alabama.gov
Founded: 1901.
Congressional District: 2
Key Personnel: Dir., Edwin C. Bridges; Volunteer Coord., Genene Nelson; Asst. Dir. Government Records, Tracey Berezansky; Asst. Dir. Public Svcs., Debbie Pendleton; Cur. Education, Sherrie Hamil; Asst. Dir. Administrative Svcs., Steve Murray; Education Specialist, Susan DuBose; Museum Shop Mgr., Allison Gore.
Personnel Profile: Full-Time Paid 49; Part-Time Paid 1; Part-Time Volunteers 105.
Governing Authority: board of trustees. Parent Institution: State of Alabama. Tax-exempt.
History Museum.
Collections: state archives; state & local government records; manuscripts; portraits; artifacts of Alabama history; southeastern Indian artifacts; 19th-century Alabamiana; flags; military artifacts; civil rights photographs.
Research Fields: U.S., southern, & Alabama history, sociology, economics, culture, genealogy, anthropology & archaeology.
Facilities: reference room; auditorium.
Activities: guided tours; permanent & temporary exhibitions; monthly lecture series.
Publications: newsletter, Friends of the Alabama Archives.
Hours & Admission Prices: Museum & Archives: Mon.-Fri. 8:30-4:30. Reference Room: Tues.-Fri. 8:30-4:30. No charge. Closed state holidays. ♿
Attendance: 50,000 (estimated)
Membership: Friends of the Alabama Archives: Individual $25; Corporate $50; Sponsors $100; Sustainer $250; Benefactors $500; Patron $750; Benefactors $1,000.

DEXTER PARSONAGE MUSEUM, 309 S. Jackson St., Montgomery, AL 36104-4407. Tel.: 334-261-3270.
Key Personnel: Pres. (V), Rev. Michael F. Thurman.
Governing Authority: Subsidiary Institution: Dexter Avenue King Memorial Foundation, Inc., P.O. Box 4901., Montgomery, AL. Tax-exempt.
Historic House Museum: housed in the former home of 12 pastors of the Dexter Avenue King Memorial Baptist Church from 1920-1992. Listed on the National Register of Historic Places.
Collections: period furnishings; photographs; religious artifacts.
Facilities: Museum-related items for sale.
Hours & Admission Prices: Tues.-Fri. 10-4, Sat. 10-2. ♿

FIRST WHITE HOUSE OF THE CONFEDERACY, 644 Washington Ave., Montgomery, AL 36130-3057. Mailing Address: P.O. Box 1861, Montgomery, AL 36102-1861. Tel.: 334-242-1861.
Founded: 1900.
Congressional District: 2
Key Personnel: Regent, Mrs. John H. Napier, III; Supvr. Hostesses & Museum Shop Mgr., Eva Newman.
Personnel Profile: Full-Time Paid 2; Full-Time Volunteers 2; Part-Time Paid 1; Part-Time Volunteers 61.
Governing Authority: state; association. Parent Institution: State of Alabama. Subsidiary Institution: White House Association of Alabama. Tax-exempt.
Historic House Museum: 1832-1835 home of Jefferson Davis & his family in 1861 when Montgomery was the capital of the Confederacy.
Collections: Confederate history; furniture & personal property of President Davis; war relics; Civil War Discovery Trail; period furnishings.
Research Fields: Jefferson Davis & family data.
Facilities: library; archives.
Activities: tours by appointment. Museum Sponsors: Jefferson Davis's birthday in June; Robert E. Lee's birthday in January.
Publications: full color booklet, The White House of The Confederacy; no-color monograph, The Struggle to Preserve the First White House of the Confederacy.
Hours & Admission Prices: Mon.-Fri. 8-4:30. No charge; donations accepted. Closed state & federal holidays. ♿
Attendance: 39,525 (accurate)

HANK WILLIAMS MUSEUM, 118 Commerce St., Montgomery, AL 36104-2538. Tel.: 334-262-3600.
E-mail: hankwilliamsmuse@bellsouth.net
Web Site: thehankwilliamsmuseum.com
Founded: 1997.
History Museum.
Collections: personal artifacts including Hank's 1952 Cadillac; suits designed by Nudie; boots; ties; horse saddle; piano; hats; awards; life-size portraits.
Facilities: Museum-related items for sale.
Hours & Admission Prices: Mon.-Fri. 9-4:30, Sat. 10-4, Sun. 1-4. Admission 12 & over $8, children 3-11 $3; discounts to groups, military & AAA; members no charge. ♿

LANDMARKS FOUNDATION/OLD ALABAMA TOWN, 301 Columbus St., Montgomery, AL 36104-2624. Tel.: 334-240-4500; 888-240-1850. Fax: 334-240-4519.
Web Site: www.oldalabamatown.com
Founded: 1967.
Congressional District: 2
Key Personnel: Exec. Dir., Robert McLain; Cur., Carole King; Dir. Education, Florence Giles; Dir. Mktg., Buffy Lockette.
Personnel Profile: Full-Time Paid 10; Part-Time Paid 9; Part-Time Volunteers 5.
Governing Authority: nonprofit organization. Property of the City of Montgomery. Tax-exempt: 501(c)(3).
Historical & Preservation Society: located in Old Alabama Town Reception Center.
Collections: Historical Houses: 1820s Log Cabin; two-room Dogtrot, home of William Lowndes Yancey; 1850s Greek Revival Cottage, home of Mayor Warren S. Reese; 1856 DeWolf-Cooper Cottage; 1857 Davis-Cook House; 1880s Presbyterian Church, built by Black Presbyterians; 1897 Shotgun House, home of Grant & Vinnie Fitzpatrick; 1875 Pintlala Grange Hall; 1892 Doctor's Office; 1850s Ordeman-Shaw Townhouse & Outbuildings; 1900 Corner Grocery; 1900 one-room schoolhouse; 1840s I-House; 1850s columned mansion; 1890s cotton gin; drugstore museum; blacksmith shop; grist mill; print shop.
Research Fields: architectural history; history-related fields.
Facilities: Gifts & museum-related items for sale.
Activities: guided tours; lectures; films; formally organized education programs for children; working crafts people; docent program or council.
Publications: quarterly, Landmarks; book, The Way It Was, 1850-1930:

Photographs of Montgomery & Her Central Alabama Neighbors; tape, Montgomery Landmarks & Driving Tour; A Narrative History of Cotton in Alabama' Boll Weevil Review; Essays on Central Alabama History; Old Alabama Town: An Illustrated Guide.
Hours & Admission Prices: Mon.-Sat. 9-3. Adults $10, students 6-18 $5; discount to groups, AAA & AAM members; children 5 & under and members no charge. Closed New Year's Day; Easter; Thanksgiving; Christmas. ♿
Attendance: 55,000 (estimated)
Membership: Individual $25; Family $40; Contributing $75; Patron $105; Grand Patron $250-$500.

MANN WILDLIFE LEARNING MUSEUM, 325 Vandiver Blvd., Montgomery, AL 36110-1815. Tel.: 334-240-4900. Fax: 334-240-4916.
Web Site: www.mannmuseum.com
Formerly: Montgomery Zoo
Founded: 2000.
Congressional District: 2
Key Personnel: Zoo Dir., Doug Goode; Deputy Zoo Dir., Marcia Woodard; Animal Care Mgr., Lisa Peek; Dir. Concessions, Jimmy Lisenby; Cur. Education, Jennifer Murphy; Mktg. & Public Rels. Mgr., Sarah McKemey; Mgr. Program Svcs., Steven Pierce; Gift Shop Mgr., Debra Stewart.
Personnel Profile: Full-Time Paid 65; Full-Time Volunteers 15; Part-Time Paid 1; Part-Time Volunteers 300.
Governing Authority: municipal. Parent Institution: City of Montgomery. Tax-exempt.
Wildlife Learning Museum
Collections: wildlife.
Research Fields: wild animal medical care.
Facilities: 300-vol. library of scientific & natural history, available for research on premises only; zoological park; nature center.
Activities: guided tours; catered lunches; after hours parties offered; formally organized education programs; docent program or council.
Publications: newsletter, Jungle Drums.
Hours & Admission Prices: Daily 9-5. Zoo: adults $10, seniors 65 & over $9, children 3-12 $7; discounts to groups with two weeks advanced reservation & military; children 2 & under, AAM, AZA & society members no charge. Mann Museum: adults $6, seniors 65 & over $5, children 3-12 $4. Closed New Year's Day; Thanksgiving; Christmas. ♿
Membership: Individual Plus One $35; Family & Grandparent $50; Family/Grandparent Combo $80; Individual Plus One Combo $60; Chimpanzee Club $250; Zebra Club $300; Giraffe Club $500; President's Club $1,000.

* **MONTGOMERY MUSEUM OF FINE ARTS, (M),** One Museum Dr., Montgomery, AL 36117-4600. Mailing Address: P.O. Box 230819, Montgomery, AL 36123-0819. Tel.: 334-240-4333. Fax: 334-240-4384.
E-mail: museum@mmfa.org
Web Site: www.mmfa.org
Founded: 1930.
Congressional District: 2
Key Personnel: Dir., Mark M. Johnson; Deputy Dir., Andrea Carman; Asst. Dir. Operations, Steve Shuemake; Devel. Officer, Courtney Armstrong; Devel. Asst., Jennifer Pope; Dir. Mktg. & Public Rels., Lara Lewis; Cur. Art, Margaret Lynne Ausfeld; Cur. Art, Michael Panhorst; Cur. Art, Shannon Masterson; Cur. Education, Jennifer Beradino; Asst. Cur. Education, Alice Novak; Asst. Cur. Education, Donna Pickens; Registrar, Pamela Bransford; Librarian, Alice Carter; Preparator & Designer, Jeff Dutton; Special Events Coord., Tisha Rhodes; Museum Shop Mgr., Pat Tomberlin.
Personnel Profile: Full-Time Paid 45; Part-Time Paid 11; Part-Time Volunteers 700; Interns 1.
Governing Authority: city; nonprofit organization. Parent Institution: City of Montgomery. Tax-exempt: 501(c)(3).
Art Museum.
Collections: 19th & 20th-century American paintings & sculptures; Old Master paints; southern regional art; decorative arts; studio glass.
Major Exhibits: A Century of Retablos: The Janis and Dennis Lyon Collection of New Mexican Santos (T), 11/09-1/17/10; Edgar Soberon (T), 11/09-1/17/10; Lost Form/Found in Line an Exhibition of Works by Robert Motherwell (T), 4/3/10-6/27/10; Nicola Marschall (T), 4/3/10-6/27/10; Still Life from the Norton (T), 7/3/10-10/10/10.
Research Fields: research in support of permanent collection.
Facilities: 6,000-vol. library; 73,000 sq. ft. of space; 250-seat auditorium; orientation center; ARTWORKS interactive gallery; cafe. Art-related items for sale.
Activities: guided tours; lectures; films; concerts; permanent & temporary exhibitions; children's programs; outreach programs.
Publications: annual report; quarterly magazine; exhibition catalogues; promotional brochures.
Hours & Admission Prices: Tues.-Wed. & Fri.-Sat. 10-5, Thurs. 10-9, Sun. 12-5. No charge; donations accepted. Closed New Year's Day; Veterans Day; Thanksgiving; Christmas. ♿
Attendance: 155,068 (accurate)
Membership: Student $30; Individual $45; Family $60; Contributing $100; Subscribing $150; Supporting $250; Sustaining $500; Sponsoring $800; Benefactor $1,200; Major Benefactor $2,500; Distinguished Benefactor $5,000.

THE MOOSEUM, 201 S. Bainbridge St., Montgomery, AL 36104-4332. Mailing Address: P.O. Box 2499, Montgomery, AL 36102-2499. Tel.: 334-265-1867; 800-622-8853. Fax: 334-834-5326.
E-mail: lwilson@bamabeef.org
Web Site: www.bamabeef.org
Founded: 1995.
Key Personnel: Coord., Lewis Wilson
Children's Museum.
Collections: history of the agriculture & beef cattle industry; hands-on exhibits.
Hours & Admission Prices: Mon.-Fri. 8-12 & 1-4:30 by appointment. No charge. Closed major holidays; special events.

ROSA PARKS LIBRARY AND MUSEUM, 252 Montgomery St., Montgomery, AL 36104-3527. Tel.: 334-241-8661 & 8615.
Personnel Profile: Full-Time Paid 7; Part-Time Paid 2.
Governing Authority: Parent Institution: Troy University. Tax-exempt.
Library & History Museum.
Collections: story of Rosa Parks' life; civil rights history; bus replica; 1955 station wagon; documents.
Major Exhibits: Charly Palmer, 12/09-1/26/10; Faith Ringgold, 4/8/10-6/10/10.
Facilities: 103-seat auditorium.
Hours & Admission Prices: Mon.-Fri. 9-5, Sat. 9-3; groups of 10 or more by appointment. Adults over 12 $5.50, children 12 & under $3.50; discounts to AAA members & Alabama College students. Closed holidays. ♿
Attendance: 50,095 (accurate)

SCOTT & ZELDA FITZGERALD MUSEUM, 919 Felder Ave., Montgomery, AL 36106-1926. Mailing Address: 919 Felder Ave., Apt. B, Montgomery, AL 36106-1927. Tel.: 334-264-4222.
Key Personnel: Exec. Dir., Michael McCreedy
General Museum.
Collections: photographs; manuscripts; Scott's books; Zeldax family memorabilia; portraits; paintings; personal artifacts.
Hours & Admission Prices: Wed.-Fri. 10-2, Sat.-Sun. 1-5. Donations: adults $5, students & seniors $2. Closed major holidays.

W.A. GAYLE PLANETARIUM, 1010 Forest Ave., Montgomery, AL 36106-1115. Tel.: 334-241-4799. Fax: 334-241-2301.
E-mail: rlevans@troy.edu
Web Site: montgomery.troy.edu/planet
Founded: 1968.
Congressional District: 2
Key Personnel: Dir. & Museum Shop Mgr., Rick Evans.
Personnel Profile: Full-Time Paid 2; Part-Time Paid 2.
Governing Authority: municipal & university. Parent Institution: Troy University, Montgomery. Tax-exempt.
Planetarium.
Collections: astronomy; 21 slide projectors.
Facilities: 200-seat theater. Space science & astronomy items for sale.
Activities: lectures; films; formally organized education programs for children; laser light shows.
Hours & Admission Prices: Public Programs: Sun. 2 pm, call for information. School Programs K-12: Mon.-Fri. by reservation only. Public Shows: Mon.-Thurs. 3, Sun. 2. School Programs: adults $3.50, students $2; discounts to members. Public Shows: admission $3.50; discounts to members. ♿
Attendance: 30,000 (accurate)

Moundville

MOUNDVILLE ARCHAEOLOGICAL PARK, AL Hwy. 69, Mound State Pkwy., Moundville, AL 35474. Mailing Address: P.O. Box 66, Moundville, AL 35474-0066. Tel.: 205-371-2234. Fax: 205-371-4180.
E-mail: moundville@bama.ua.edu
Web Site: moundville.ua.edu
Founded: 1939.
Congressional District: 7
Key Personnel: Dir., Bill Bomar; Education Coord., Betsy Irwin; Office Asst., Angela Jones; Museum Shop Mgr., Dorothy Beckham.

Personnel Profile: Full-Time Paid 11; Part-Time Paid 2; Part-Time Volunteers 150.
Governing Authority: public university; nonprofit. Parent Institution: University of Alabama Museums, University of Alabama. Tax-exempt.
Archaeological Site: over two dozen Mississippian mounds and 320-acre park.
Collections: archaeological collections; simulated Indian village with life-sized dioramas.
Research Fields: archaeology.
Facilities: theater; meeting space; conference center; nature trail; campground.
Activities: teaching craft huts; hiking trails. Annual Event: Moundville Native American Festival with living history encampments, artisans & performers in October.
Publications: teacher guides; fact sheets; brochures; special publications.
Hours & Admission Prices: Park: daily 8-dusk. Museum: call for hours. ♿
Attendance: 50,000 (estimated)
Membership: Alabama Natural History Society: Individual $20; Family $30; Associated $50-$249; Contributor $250-$499; Director's Circle $500-$999; Sustainer $1,000 and up.

Normal

STATE BLACK ARCHIVES RESEARCH CENTER AND MUSEUM, James Hembray Wilson Bldg., Alabama A&M University, Normal, AL 35762. Mailing Address: P.O. Box 595, Normal, AL 35762-0595. Tel.: 256-372-5846. Fax: 256-372-5338.
Founded: 1987.
Congressional District: 5
Personnel Profile: Full-Time Paid 2; Part-Time Paid 4; Part-Time Volunteers 2.
Governing Authority: Parent Institution: Alabama A&M University. Tax-exempt.
History Museum.
Collections: African American history & culture; photographs; personal artifacts; uniforms; paintings.
Major Exhibits: Shambala Art Exhibit by Mr. John Moore (T), 1/11/10-3/10; 1915-1935 The New Negro - A Literature & Culture Movement (T), 2/11/10; The Untold Story of The Black West, 2/25/10-3/10; Velma A. Walker Art Collection, 4/10; Buffalo Soldiers: The Ignoble Mission, 4/10-10/10; African American Women: Achievement Against the Odds, 4/10-10/10; Southern Journey: African American Artists of the South (T), 9/10-10/20/10; Kwanzaa Tradition and Creativity, 11/10-12/10.
Activities: permanent & traveling exhibitions.
Hours & Admission Prices: Mon.-Fri. 9-4:30. Adults 12 & over $5, senior citizens $4, children 11 & under $3; discounts to groups; children 5 & under no charge. Closed Martin Luther King Jr. Day; Memorial Day; Independence Day; Labor Day; Thanksgiving; Christmas. ♿
Attendance: 3,000 (accurate)

Northport

THE KENTUCK MUSEUM ASSOCIATION/ART CENTER/FESTIVAL OF THE ARTS, 503 Main Ave., Northport, AL 35476-4483. Tel.: 205-758-1257. Fax: 205-758-1258.
E-mail: kentuck@kentuck.org
Web Site: www.kentuck.org
Founded: 1971.
Congressional District: 6
Key Personnel: Pres. (V), Janet Teer; Treas., A.D. Christian, Jr.; Public Rels., Chandler Kemble.
Personnel Profile: Full-Time Paid 2; Part-Time Paid 2; Part-Time Volunteers 50.
Governing Authority: private; nonprofit organizations. Tax-exempt: 501(c)(3).
Art Museum.
Collections: works by local, regional & national artists.
Facilities: artist studios; courtyard garden. Museum-related items for sale.
Activities: arts festival; children's programs. Annual Events: The Kentuck Festival of the Arts in October; Fine Crafts & Art; folk artists.
Hours & Admission Prices: Mon.-Fri. 9-5, Sat. 10-4:30. No charge. Closed New Year's Day; Memorial Day; Labor Day; Christmas.
Attendance: 35,000 (estimated)
Membership: Individual $30; Family $40; Supporting $100; Contributing $250; Benefactor $500.

RENAISSANCE GALLERY, 431 Main Ave., Northport, AL 35476-5063. Tel.: 205-752-4422.
E-mail: renaissanceartga@bellsouth.net
Web Site: www.renaissanceartgallery.com
Key Personnel: Co Dir., Anne Stickney; Co Dir., Kathy Groshong
Art Gallery.
Collections: works by regional & local artists.
Hours & Admission Prices: Tues.-Sat. 11-4:30, 1st Thurs. of month 9-4:30; other times by appointment. No charge.

Oneonta

BLOUNT COUNTY MEMORIAL MUSEUM, 204 2nd St. N., Oneonta, AL 35121-1740. Mailing Address: P.O. Box 45, Oneonta, AL 35121-0001. Tel.: 205-625-6905.
E-mail: bcmuseum71@yahoo.com
Web Site: www.coveredbridge.org
Founded: 1971.
Key Personnel: Cur. & Museum Shop Mgr., Amy Rhudy.
Governing Authority: Parent Institution: Blount County Historical Society. Tax-exempt.
County History Museum.
Collections: local history; county war veterans; family books & files; arrowheads; sandstone; covered bridge art; maps.
Research Fields: Blount County genealogy.
Publications: quarterly newsletter, Blount County Historical Society.
Hours & Admission Prices: Tues.-Fri. 9-3. No charge; donations accepted. ♿
Attendance: 2,000 (estimated)
Membership: Blount County Historical Society $10.

Opelika

THE MUSEUM OF EAST ALABAMA, 121 S. 9th St., Opelika, AL 36801-4917. Mailing Address: P.O. Box 3085, Opelika, AL 36803-3085. Tel.: 334-749-2751.
E-mail: museum@eastalabama.org
Web Site: www.eastalabama.org
Founded: 1989.
Congressional District: 3
Key Personnel: Pres. (V), Bert Harris; Treas., Mike Martin.
Personnel Profile: Full-Time Paid 1; Part-Time Paid 1; Part-Time Volunteers 100.
Governing Authority: private; nonprofit organization. Tax-exempt: 501(c)(3).
General Museum.
Collections: Roanoke dolls; Camp Opelika (WWII) memorabilia; early 20th-century recording technology (Orr RADIO); agricultural implements; fire fighting tools & trucks; local history artifacts.
Facilities: 5,468 sq. ft. exhibit space.
Activities: docent program; guided tours; lectures; temporary exhibitions.
Hours & Admission Prices: Tues.-Fri. 10-4, Sat. 2-4. No charge; donations accepted. Closed New Year's Day; Memorial Day; Christmas Eve & Day. ♿
Attendance: 1,386 (estimated)
Membership: Student $10; Retired $15; Individual $20; Family $25; Associate $100; Contributor $250; Friend $500; Patron $1,000; Sponsor $2,500; Benefactor $5,000; Charter $10,000; Golden Charter $50,000.

Orange Beach

ORANGE BEACH INDIAN AND SEA MUSEUM, 25850 John Snook Dr., Orange Beach, AL 36561. Mailing Address: P.O. Box 458, Orange Beach, AL 36561-0458. Tel.: 251-981-8545. Fax: 251-981-6053.
Web Site: www.obparksandrec.com
Founded: 1995.
Key Personnel: Museum Guide, Gail Graham
Historic Building: housed in period schoolhouse.
Collections: period artifacts & furnishings; area history.
Hours & Admission Prices: Tues. & Thurs. 9-1; tours by appointment. No charge.

Pelham

ALABAMA WILDLIFE CENTER, Oak Mountain State Park, 100 Terrace Dr., Pelham, AL 35124-4314. Tel.: 205-663-7930. Fax: 205-682-6867.
E-mail: wildlife@awrc.org
Web Site: www.awrc.org
Formerly: The Wildlife Center
Founded: 1977.
Key Personnel: Chm. (V), Richard Esposito; Devel., Janet Byars.
Personnel Profile: Full-Time Paid 3; Part-Time Volunteers 250.
Governing Authority: nonprofit organization. Tax-exempt: 501(c)(3).
Nature & Rehabilitation Center.
Collections: over 2,500 native birds, mammals, & reptiles of over 100 species.
Facilities: nature trails; wildlife rehabilitation center.
Activities: educational programs; information stations program. Annual Events: Migration Celebration in August; Creatures of the Night in October.
Hours & Admission Prices: Daily 9-5. Guided Tours: call for admission prices. Self-Guided Tours: no charge. ♿
Attendance: 10,000 (estimated)
Membership: Annual $35-$1,000.

Prattville

AUTAUGA COUNTY HERITAGE ASSOCIATION, 102 E. Main St., Prattville, AL 36067-3114. Tel.: 334-361-0961. Fax: 334-491-2961.
E-mail: brobmc@gmail.com
Web Site: autaugaheritge.com
Founded: 1976.
History Museum.
Collections: county history & genealogy; personal artifacts; photographs.
Activities: lectures; meetings; special events.
Hours & Admission Prices: Mon.-Fri. 10-4. No charge; donations accepted. Closed Independence Day week; Christmas week.

Scottsboro

SCOTTSBORO & JACKSON HERITAGE CENTER MUSEUM, 208 S. Houston St., Scottsboro, AL 35768-4318. Mailing Address: P.O. Box 53, Scottsboro, AL 35768-0053. Tel.: 256-259-2122. Fax: 256-574-6991.
Founded: 1986.
Key Personnel: Dir., Judi Weaver; Chm. (V), Kelly Goodowens.
Governing Authority: Tax-exempt.
History Museum.
Collections: Jackson County history, customs, traditions & art; Native American artifacts; family histories; public records. Historic Buildings: 1800s log cabin village & furnishings.
Research Fields: family history.
Facilities: library.
Activities: special events; research; traveling exhibits; rental facilities.
Hours & Admission Prices: Mon.-Fri. 11-4; tours by appointment. Adults $3; members no charge. ♿
Attendance: 1,500 (estimated)
Membership: Student & Retired $10; Individual $15; Family $20; Corporate & Business $100; Founding Family & Life $1,000.

Selma

NATIONAL VOTING RIGHTS MUSEUM AND INSTITUTE, 1012 Water Ave., Selma, AL 36701-4617. Mailing Address: P.O. Box 1366, Selma, AL 36702-1366. Tel.: 334-418-0800. Fax: 334-418-0278.
E-mail: info@nationalvotingrightsmuseum.org
Web Site: www.nvrm.org
Founded: 1992.
Congressional District: 7
Key Personnel: C.E.O. & Devel., Joanne Bland; Pres. (V) & Treas., Rose M. Sanders; Interim Dir., Mae Richmond; Chm. (V), C.T. Vivian; Cur., Octavia Vivian; Museum Shop Mgr., Afriye Wekandodis; Security, Sam Walker.
Personnel Profile: Full-Time Paid 2; Full-Time Volunteers 2; Part-Time Paid 3; Part-Time Volunteers 15.
Governing Authority: private; nonprofit organization. Tax-exempt: 501(c)(3).
Historical Museum: housed in the former headquarters of the White Citizen's Council of Alabama; located at the foot of the Edmund Pettus Bridge, the site of Bloody Sunday.
Collections: voting rights data; video tape library of living legends who participated in the Voting Rights Movement & the Selma-Montgomery march.
Facilities: 150-seat auditorium. Museum-related items for sale.
Activities: concerts; children's songs; films; guided tours; lectures; traveling & temporary exhibitions. Annual Event: Jubilee Festival commemorating the historic march across the Edmund Pettus Bridge.
Publications: newsletter, NVRM.
Hours & Admission Prices: Mon.-Fri. 9-12:30 & 1:30-5, Sat. 10-12:30 & 1:30-3, Sun. by appointment only. Adults $6, students $4; discounts to members, groups, AAM & ICOM members. Closed New Year's Day; Memorial Day; Martin Luther King Jr. Day; Christmas. ♿
Attendance: 150,000 (estimated)
Membership: Basic $25; Supporter & Organization $100; Dreamer $500; Mountain Top $1,000.

OLD DEPOT MUSEUM, 4 Martin Luther King St., Selma, AL 36703-3109. Tel.: 334-874-2197. Fax: 334-874-1221.
E-mail: olddepot@wwisp.com
Key Personnel: Dir. & Cur., Jean Martin
History Museum.
Collections: period artifacts; early plantation records; 19th-century doctor's traveling kit; confederate bills.
Hours & Admission Prices: Mon.-Sat. 10-4. Adults $4, seniors $3, college students $2, children $1.

STURDIVANT HALL, 713 Mabry St., Selma, AL 36701-5521. Mailing Address: P.O. Box 1205, Selma, AL 36702-1205. Tel.: 334-872-5626.
E-mail: info@sturdivanthall.com
Web Site: sturdivanthall.com
Founded: 1957.
Congressional District: 7
Key Personnel: Dir., Manera S. Searcy; Co-Dir., Nancy Gantt; Pres., Edie Jones; Museum Shop Mgr., Patty DeBardeleben.
Personnel Profile: Full-Time Paid 2; Part-Time Paid 7; Part-Time Volunteers 2.
Governing Authority: county; municipal. Tax-exempt: 501(c)(3).
Historic House Museum: 1852 Sturdivant Hall.
Collections: furnishings of the antebellum period; Victorian, Chippendale & Hepplewhite furniture; Oriental rugs; china; silver; fine linens; pianos; English chests; oil paintings; dolls.
Research Fields: pertaining to the collections.
Facilities: banquet facilities.
Activities: guided tours; concerts; docent council; permanent exhibitions; rental facilities.
Hours & Admission Prices: Tues.-Sat. 10-4. Adults $5, students $2; discounts to groups of 15 or more; discounts to AAA members; members no charge. Closed major holidays. ♿
Attendance: 17,500 (estimated)
Membership: Single $25; Family $50; Patron & Business $100; Lifetime $1,000.

Summerdale

ALLIGATOR ALLEY, 19950 Hwy. 71, Summerdale, AL 36580. Tel.: 866-99-GATOR; 251-946-BITE.
Web Site: www.gatoralleyfarm.com
Alligator Farm.
Collections: over 150 alligators; ospreys; owls; turtles; bull frogs; amphibians; reptiles.
Facilities: Museum-related items for sale.
Activities: group tours; field trips.
Hours & Admission Prices: Spring & Summer: daily 10-5. Adults $10, children 4-12 $8; children under 3 no charge.

Sylacauga

ISABEL ANDERSON COMER MUSEUM & ARTS CENTER, 711 N. Broadway, Sylacauga, AL 35150-2155. Mailing Address: P.O. Box 245, Sylacauga, AL 35150-0245. Tel.: 256-245-4016. Fax: 256-245-4612.
E-mail: comercenter@bellsouth.net
Web Site: comermuseum.freeservers.com
Founded: 1982.
Congressional District: 3
Key Personnel: Exec. Dir., Donna Rentfrow; Bd. Pres., Don Smith; Asst. Dir., Linda Hatchett.
Personnel Profile: Full-Time Paid 1; Full-Time Volunteers 18; Part-Time Paid 1; Part-Time Volunteers 7.
Governing Authority: private; nonprofit organization. Tax-exempt: 501(c)(3).
History & Art Museum.
Collections: fine art; mixed media; Indian artifacts; marble sculpture; period furnishings; a replica of the Hodges Meteorite & written documentation of the incident; photographs; Jim Nabors' memorabilia; costumes; gold & platinum records.
Facilities: educational facilities. Museum-related items for sale.
Activities: formal educational programs; guided tours; lectures; field trips; art classes.
Publications: quarterly newsletter, The Museum Review.
Hours & Admission Prices: Tues.-Fri. 10-5; other times by appointment. No charge; donations accepted. Closed major holidays. ♿
Attendance: 14,200 (estimated)
Membership: Old Master & Friend $10; Student, Artist & Teacher $20; Individual $30; Family & Couple $50; Supporter $250; Patron $500; Benefactor $1,000.

Theodore

BELLINGRATH GARDENS & HOME, 12401 Bellingrath Gardens Rd., Theodore, AL 36582-8496. Tel.: 251-973-2217, ext. 147. Fax: 251-973-0540.
E-mail: tmcgehee@bellingrath.org
Web Site: www.bellingrath.org
Founded: 1932.
Congressional District: 1
Key Personnel: Exec. Dir., William E. Barrick, Ph.D.; Museum Dir., Thomas C. McGehee.
Personnel Profile: Full-Time Paid 60; Part-Time Paid 20; Part-Time Volunteers 75; Interns 1.
Governing Authority: private association. Parent Institution: Bellingrath Morse Foundation. Tax-exempt.
Botanical Garden & Home.

Collections: Bessie Morse Bellingrath china, silver, European porcelains, period furniture; Edward Marshall Boehm porcelain.
Facilities: 65-acre landscaped gardens; restaurant. Museum-related items for sale.
Activities: guided tours of home; films; permanent exhibitions; video show; videocassettes; scenic riverboat cruises on the Fowl River; educational programs for adults & children in summer. Museum Sponsors: Winter Wednesday programs January & February; Wonderful Wednesdays June & July. Annual Event: Christmas in Lights in December.
Publications: books, Bellingrath Gardens & Home; Mister Bell.
Hours & Admission Prices: Home: daily 9-4. Gardens, Home & River Cruise $27. Gardens & Home: $19. Gardens: $11. Closed Thanksgiving; Christmas. ♿
Attendance: 169,000 (accurate)
Membership: Individual $40; Couple $60; Family $100; Patron $150-$250; Belle Camp Society $500-$2,500.

Troy

JOHNSON CENTER FOR THE ARTS, (M), 300 E. Walnut St., Troy, AL 36081-3539. Mailing Address: P.O. Box 863, Troy, AL 36081-0863. Tel.: 334-670-2287. Fax: 334-808-4025.
Web Site: www.tpcac.org
Formerly: Troy-Pike Cultural Arts Center
Founded: 2000.
Key Personnel: Exec. Dir., Richard Metzger; Chm. (V), Mack Gibson.
Personnel Profile: Full-Time Paid 3; Part-Time Paid 10; Part-Time Volunteers 20.
Governing Authority: nonprofit organization. Tax-exempt: 501(c)(3).
Art Museum.
Collections: works by regional, national & international artists.
Facilities: rental facilities.
Activities: theater; workshops; art classes; concerts; receptions.
Hours & Admission Prices: Tues.-Sat. 10-5, Sun. 1-5. No charge; donations accepted. Closed holidays. ♿
Attendance: 800 (estimated)
Membership: Student $25; Individual $50; Dual $90; Family $100; Associate $250.

PIONEER MUSEUM OF ALABAMA, 248 U.S. 231 N., Troy, AL 36081. Tel.: 334-566-3597.
E-mail: pioneer@troycable.net
Web Site: www.pioneer-museum.org
Formerly: Pike Pioneer Museum
Founded: 1969.
Congressional District: 2
Key Personnel: C.E.O., Jeff Kervin; Dir., Jerry M. Peak.
Personnel Profile: Full-Time Paid 1; Part-Time Paid 4; Part-Time Volunteers 38.
Governing Authority: nonprofit organization. Tax-exempt.
History Museum.
Collections: artifacts related to area history along with social & agricultural history of pioneers in Alabama. Historic Buildings: two pen log house; tenant house; log house; one room school; general store; log church; corn crib; smokehouse; grist mill; train depot.
Research Fields: tenant farming in Alabama; Alabama settlers.
Facilities: 35 acre complex; picnic area; nature trails; amphitheater. Museum-related items for sale.
Activities: self guided & guided tours. Museum Sponsors: Living History weekends.
Publications: brochures; calendar of events; teacher packs.
Hours & Admission Prices: Tues.-Sat. 9-5. Adults $6, seniors 60 & over $5, students $4; discounts to military, AAM & ICOM members; members no charge. Closed major holidays. ♿
Attendance: 10,000 (accurate)
Membership: Individual $20; Family $35; Preserver $50; Sustainer $100; Pioneer $250; Patron $500; Underwriter $1,000.

Tuscaloosa

ALABAMA MUSEUM OF NATURAL HISTORY, (M), Smith Hall, University of Alabama Campus, 427 6th Ave., Tuscaloosa, AL 35487-0001. Mailing Address: Box 870340, Tuscaloosa, AL 35487-0001. Tel.: 205-348-7550 & 7551. Fax: 205-348-9292.
E-mail: natural.history@ua.edu
Web Site: museums.ua.edu
Founded: 1847.
Congressional District: 7
Key Personnel: Exec. Dir., Robert Clouse; Coord. Environmental Education & Programs, Dr. Douglas Phillips; Mgr. Collections, Mary Bade.
Personnel Profile: Full-Time Paid 15; Part-Time Paid 3; Part-Time Volunteers 50; Interns 2.
Governing Authority: university. Parent Institution: The University of Alabama. Subsidiary Institution: University of Alabama Museums. Tax-exempt: 501(c)(3).
Natural History Museum.
Collections: anthropology; archaeology; ichthyology; mineralogy; paleontology; herpetology; botany; mammalogy; ornithology; entomology; ethnology.
Research Fields: anthropology; archaeology; ichthyology; vertebrate paleontology; natural history education; teacher education; protohistoric archaeology (DeSoto).
Activities: guided tours; lectures; permanent & traveling exhibitions; special programs for children; year-round field trips & programs; museum expedition; paleontology research site. Annual Event: Moundville Native American Festival.
Publications: bulletin; field trip guides; brochures; special publications; Bulletin of the Alabama Museum of Natural History.
Hours & Admission Prices: Smith Hall Museum: Mon.-Sat. 10-4:30. Adults $2, children $1; members no charge. Closed university holidays. ♿
Attendance: 32,000 (estimated)
Membership: Alabama River $40; Black Warrior River $100; Cahaba River $250; Coosa River $500; Sipsey River $1,000; Eugene Allen Smith Society $5,000.

BATTLE-FRIEDMAN HOUSE, 1010 Greensboro Ave., Tuscaloosa, AL 35401-2336. Mailing Address: P.O. Box 1665, Tuscaloosa, AL 35403-1665. Tel.: 205-758-6138.
Governing Authority: Operated By: the Tuscaloosa County Preservation Society.
Historic House: built in the early 1800s. Listed on the National Register of Historic Places.
Collections: period furnishings; personal artifacts.
Activities: rental facilities; special events.
Hours & Admission Prices: Tues.-Sat. 10-12 & 1-4. Admission $5; children under 12 no charge. Closed major holidays.

CHILDREN'S HANDS-ON MUSEUM (CHOM), 2213 University Blvd., Tuscaloosa, AL 35401-1541. Tel.: 205-349-4235. Fax: 205-349-4272.
E-mail: info@chomonline.org
Web Site: www.chomonline.org
Founded: 1984.
Congressional District: 7
Key Personnel: Exec. Dir. & Dir. Exhibits, Charlotte Gibson; Visitors Svcs. Coord. & Volunteer Coord., Sherie Giles; Membership Coord., Tricia Wagg.
Personnel Profile: Full-Time Paid 6; Part-Time Paid 3; Part-Time Volunteers 80; Interns 5.
Governing Authority: nonprofit organization. Tax-exempt.
Children's Museum.
Collections: hands-on exhibits dealing with history, science & the arts.
Facilities: interactive exhibit spaces; planetarium. Books & educational toys for sale.
Activities: docent program; directed tours; in-depth programs; special events.
Publications: quarterly newsletter, CHOM News.
Hours & Admission Prices: Mon.-Fri. 9-5, Sat. 10-4. Admission 3 & over $8, seniors 60 & over $6, children 1-3 $5; members & children under one no charge. Closed major holidays. ♿
Attendance: 53,000 (estimated)
Membership: Single Parent & Grandparent $40; Family & General $50; Family Plus $100.

GORGAS HOUSE, Capstone at McCorvy Dr., University of Alabama, Tuscaloosa, AL 35487-0001. Mailing Address: Box 870340, University of Alabama Museums, Tuscaloosa, AL 35487-0001. Tel.: 205-348-5906 & 7550. Fax: 205-348-9292.
Web Site: tour.ua.edu/tourstops/gorgashouse.html
Founded: 1954.
Congressional District: 7
Key Personnel: Cur., Mr. Marion Pearson.
Personnel Profile: Full-Time Paid 1.
Governing Authority: state. Parent Institution: University of Alabama. Subsidiary Institution: University of Alabama Museums. Tax-exempt.
Historic House: built in 1829 as a dining hall for students, home of Josiah & Amelia Gayle Gorgas and family from 1878-1953 & one of four buildings to survive the burning of the campus in 1865 by federal troops.
Collections: 18th & 19th century Spanish silver.
Activities: guided tours, Center for Study of University of Alabama History.
Publications: rack card.
Hours & Admission Prices: Mon.-Fri. 9-4. Closed university holidays. ♿

Attendance: 4,000 (estimated)

JEMISON-VAN DE GRAAFF MANSION, 1305 Greensboro Ave., Tuscaloosa, AL 35401-2840. Mailing Address: P.O. Box 1665, Tuscaloosa, AL 35403-1665. Tel.: 205-758-2906.
Governing Authority: Parent Institution: Tuscaloosa County Preservation Society and the Heritage Commission of Tuscaloosa.
Historic House: housed in the former home of Senator Robert Jemison, Jr.; built in 1862.
Collections: period furnishings; personal artifacts.
Activities: teachers' programs; special events; rental facilities. Museum Sponsors: Christmas Open House in December.
Hours & Admission Prices: Mon.-Fri. 10-5; groups by appointment. No charge.

MURPHY AFRICAN AMERICAN MUSEUM, 2601 W. Paul Bryant Dr., Tuscaloosa, AL 35401-2214. Tel.: 205-758-2861. Fax: 205-758-8163.
Web Site: www.historictuscaloosa.org
Founded: 1985.
Congressional District: 7
Key Personnel: Dir. & Chm. (V), Emma Jean Melton.
Personnel Profile: Part-Time Paid 1; Part-Time Volunteers 15; Interns 3.
Governing Authority: Parent Institution: Tuscaloosa County Preservation Society. Tax-exempt.
History Museum: housed in the home of Tuscaloosa's first licensed black mortician; built c. 1920.
Collections: lifestyle of affluent blacks in the early 1900s; personal artifacts; furnishings; African art.
Hours & Admission Prices: Tues.-Fri. 10-12 & 1-4; tours by appointment.

THE OLD TAVERN MUSEUM, 500 28th Ave.-Capitol Park, Tuscaloosa, AL 35401. Mailing Address: P.O. Box 1665, Tuscaloosa, AL 35403-1665. Tel.: 205-758-2238. Fax: 205-758-8163.
E-mail: tcps1966@bellsouth.net
Web Site: www.historictuscaloosa.org
Founded: 1965.
Congressional District: 6
Key Personnel: Exec. Dir., Susan Haynes.
Personnel Profile: Full-Time Paid 1.
Governing Authority: nonprofit organization. Parent Institution: Tuscaloosa County Preservation Society, P.O. Box 1665, Tuscaloosa 35403. Branch Museums: Battle-Friedman House; Civic & Cultural Center; Strickland House. Tax-exempt: 501(c)(3).
Historic House Museum: 1827 Old Tavern, relocated on Capitol Park, the site of the Capitol Building when Alabama's Capitol was in Tuscaloosa.
Collections: period furnishings & artifacts; folklore.
Activities: guided tours; lectures.
Publications: pamphlet, Preservationist.
Hours & Admission Prices: Tues.-Fri. 10-12 & 1-4 by appointment. No charge; donations accepted.
Attendance: 400 (estimated)
Membership: Student $15; Family $35; Century Club $100; Grand Benefactor & Corporate $500; Life $2,500.

PAUL W. BRYANT MUSEUM, (M), 300 Paul W. Bryant Dr., Tuscaloosa, AL 35487-0001. Mailing Address: Box 870385, Tuscaloosa, AL 35487-0001. Tel.: 205-348-4668; 866-772-2327. Fax: 205-348-8883.
E-mail: bryinfo@bama.ua.edu
Web Site: www.bryant.ua.edu
Founded: 1985.
Congressional District: 7
Key Personnel: Dir., Kenneth Gaddy; Visitor Svcs. Coord., Jan Adams; Cur., Taylor Watson; Collections Asst., Brad Green; Administrative Asst., Clem Gryska; Program Asst., Olivia Arnold; Cashier, Kim Jenkins; Cashier, Esther Cade; Museum Shop Mgr., Sarah Reams; Audio Visual Tech, David Mize.
Personnel Profile: Full-Time Paid 8; Part-Time Paid 3; Part-Time Volunteers 50; Interns 2.
Governing Authority: public university; nonprofit. Parent Institution: University of Alabama. Tax-exempt: 501(c)(3).
Sport Museum.
Collections: books, programs, photographs, newspapers & media guides; game films & audio tapes; sports memorabilia related to University of Alabama athletics & Southeastern Conference sports; over 100 years of Alabama football.
Research Fields: Alabama football; SEC sports; college sports.
Facilities: 7,000 sq. ft. exhibit space; 45-seat theater. Museum-related items for sale.
Activities: guided tours; films; rental facilities.
Publications: brochures; rack cards; souvenir book; newsletter, Circle of Champions; teacher's guide, Punt, Pass & Learn.
Hours & Admission Prices: Daily 9-4; call for holiday hours. Adults $2, senior citizens 60 & over, students and children 6-17 $1; children under 6 & members no charge. Closed major holidays. ♿
Attendance: 40,000 (estimated)
Membership: Circle of Champions: Sideline: Students $15; Locker Room Club: Individual $20; Family $30; Press Box Club $100-$249; Director's Club $250-$499; William Little Club $500-$999; Bryant Gold Club $1,000 & up.

SARAH MOODY GALLERY OF ART, THE UNIVERSITY OF ALABAMA, 103 Garland Hall, Tuscaloosa, AL 35487-0001. Mailing Address: Box 870270, Tuscaloosa, AL 35487. Tel.: 205-348-1890 & 5967 (art dept.). Fax: 205-348-0287.
E-mail: wtdooley@bama.ua.edu
Web Site: art.ua.edu/moody.html
Founded: 1967.
Congressional District: 7
Key Personnel: Dir., Bill Dooley; Exhibitions Coord., Vicki Rial.
Personnel Profile: Full-Time Paid 2; Part-Time Paid 6.
Governing Authority: university. Parent Institution: University of Alabama, Tuscaloosa, AL. Tax-exempt.
Art Gallery.
Collections: primitive art; paintings; drawings; prints; photos; sculpture; crafts.
Facilities: 3,200 sq. ft. gallery.
Activities: lectures; films; gallery talks; temporary & traveling exhibitions.
Publications: extended checklists; exhibition catalogs: In These Islands - South Carolina & Georgia; Cora Cohen: Paintings & Altered X-Rays 1983-1996; Richard Zoellner: The Continuous Quest.
Hours & Admission Prices: Sept.-June Mon.-Wed. & Fri. 9-4:30, Thurs. 9-8; Summer: Mon.-Fri. 10-12 & 2-4. No charge; donations accepted. Closed university holidays. ♿
Attendance: 10,000

STILLMAN ART GALLERY, Stillman College, Cordell Wynn Humanities and Fine Arts Center, Rm. 155B, Tuscaloosa, AL 35403. Mailing Address: P.O. Box 1430, Tuscaloosa, AL 35403-1430. Tel.: 205-248-3404.
Web Site: www.stillman.edu
Art Gallery.
Collections: paintings.
Hours & Admission Prices: Mon.-Fri. 9-5.

UNIVERSITY OF ALABAMA ARBORETUM, 4801 Arboretum Way, Tuscaloosa, AL 35404-5424. Mailing Address: Box 870344, Tuscaloosa, AL 35487-0001. Tel.: 205-553-3278. Fax: 205-553-3728.
E-mail: arbor@bama.ua.edu
Web Site: www.arboretum.ua.edu
Founded: 1958.
Congressional District: 7
Key Personnel: Pres. (V), Julia Hartman; Asst. Dir., Mary Jo Modica; Caretaker, Kenneth Robinson.
Personnel Profile: Full-Time Paid 3; Full-Time Volunteers 1; Part-Time Paid 1; Part-Time Volunteers 25.
Governing Authority: University of Alabama. Tax-exempt.
Arboretum & Botanical Garden.
Collections: native & exotic woody plants; native herbaceous plants.
Research Fields: applied ecological research.
Facilities: classroom; picnic area; conservatory; growing house.
Activities: guided tours; lectures.
Publications: quarterly newsletter, Growings On.
Hours & Admission Prices: Daily 8am to sunset. No charge; donations accepted. Closed New Year's Day; Thanksgiving; Christmas.
Attendance: 7,000 (estimated)
Membership: Seedling (Student) $10; Wildflower $25-$49; Azalea $50-$99; Hydrangea $100-$499; Dogwood $500-$999; Magnolia $1,000-$4,999; Oak $5,000 & up.

WESTERVELT-WARNER MUSEUM OF AMERICAN ART, (M), 8316 Mountbatten Rd., N.E., Tuscaloosa, AL 35406-1118. Tel.: 205-343-4540. Fax: 205-345-1493.
Art Museum.
Collections: paintings; sculptures; period artifacts; portraits.
Hours & Admission Prices: Tues.-Fri. 12-5, Sat. 10-5. Adults $9, seniors 65 & over $8, students 10 years old to college age $7; members no charge. ♿
Attendance: 15,000 (estimated)
Membership: Student $15; Individual $30; Family $50; Pioneer $100; Patron $250; Patriot $500; Founding Father $1,000.

Tuscumbia

ALABAMA MUSIC HALL OF FAME, 617 Hwy. 72 W., Tuscumbia, AL 35674-8711. Mailing Address: P.O. Box 740405, Tuscumbia, AL 35674-7417. Tel.: 256-381-4417; 800-239-2643. Fax: 256-381-1031.
E-mail: info@alamhof.org
Web Site: www.alamhof.org
Founded: 1982.
Key Personnel: Chm., Ralph Burke; Exec. Dir., David A. Johnson; Asst. Dir., Marcia Weems; Sales & Mktg., Dixie Connell; Sec., Ann Thompson.
Personnel Profile: Full-Time Paid 9; Part-Time Paid 1; Part-Time Volunteers 5.
Governing Authority: state; nonprofit. Parent Institution: State of Alabama. Tax-exempt.
Music Museum.
Collections: music archives; instruments; clothing; music memorabilia including achievements & awards.
Research Fields: Southern music.
Facilities: library of Southern music heritage material available to the public; 1,500-seat auditorium; 100-seat theater. Gift items for sale.
Activities: guided tours; lectures; films; concerts; study clubs; organized education programs. Museum Sponsors: Induction Banquet; Annual Concert Series
Publications: quarterly newsletter.
Hours & Admission Prices: May-Oct. Mon.-Sat. 9-5, Sun. 1-5; Nov.-April Mon.-Sat. 9-5. Adults $8, senior citizens & students 13-18 $7, children 6-12 $5; discounts to AAA, AAM & ICOM members and groups of 10 or more; children 5 & under no charge. Closed New Year's Day; Easter; Thanksgiving & day after; Christmas Eve, Day & week. ♿
Attendance: 35,000 (accurate)
Membership: Annual $25.

BELLE MONT MANSION, 1569 Cook Lane, Tuscumbia, AL 35674. Mailing Address: 12280 AL Hwy. 20, Hillsboro, AL 35643-3808. Tel.: 256-381-5052 & 637-8513.
Personnel Profile: Full-Time Paid 3.
Governing Authority: state. Parent Institution: Alabama Historical Commission.
Historic House: built in the early 1800s.
Collections: period furnishings; personal artifacts.
Activities: group tours.
Hours & Admission Prices: By appointment. Adults $4, students, seniors & military $3, children 6-18 $2. Closed state holidays.

IVY GREEN, BIRTHPLACE OF HELEN KELLER, 300 N. Commons St., W., Tuscumbia, AL 35674-1134. Tel.: 256-383-4066. Fax: 256-383-4068.
E-mail: helenkellerbirthplace@comcast.net
Web Site: helenkellerbirthplace.org
Founded: 1952.
Congressional District: 5
Key Personnel: Mgr., Sue Pilkilton.
Personnel Profile: Full-Time Paid 1; Part-Time Paid 8.
Governing Authority: municipal. Tax-exempt: 501(c)(3).
Historic House Museum: 1820, birthplace of Helen Keller; main house, birthplace cottage, kitchen, carriage house, memorial gardens.
Collections: books; objects connected with Helen Keller's life; period furniture.
Facilities: Museum-related items for sale.
Activities: Museum Sponsors: William Gibson's, The Miracle Worker, staged on the grounds of Ivy Green in June & July; Tennessee Valley Art Association Art Show in City Park; Helen Keller Festival & Historic Tour of Homes by Helen Keller Festival Board; musical entertainment & sports events in June.
Publications: brochures.
Hours & Admission Prices: Mon.-Sat. 8:30-4. Adults $6, AAA members & seniors $5, student 5-18 $2; discount to groups; children under 5 no charge. Closed New Year's Day; Easter; Labor Day; Thanksgiving; Christmas Eve, Day & day after. ♿
Attendance: 35,000

TENNESSEE VALLEY ART CENTER, 511 N. Water St., Tuscumbia, AL 35674-1931. Mailing Address: P.O. Box 474, Tuscumbia, AL 35674-0474. Tel.: 256-383-0533. Fax: 256-383-0535.
E-mail: tvaa@comcast.net
Web Site: www.tvaa.net/
Founded: 1962.
Congressional District: 5
Key Personnel: Exec. Dir., Mary Settle Cooney; Asst. Dir., Jim Berryman; Chm. (V), Verna Brennan; Dir. Mktg. & Devel., Kay Brackin; Program Asst., Lori Curtis; Administrative Asst., J.K. Keith McMurtrey.
Personnel Profile: Full-Time Paid 4; Part-Time Volunteers 150.
Governing Authority: nonprofit organization. Parent Institution: Tennessee Valley Art Assn., Tuscumbia, AL. Tax-exempt: 501(c)(3).
Art Center.
Collections: Reynolds collection; Helen Keller Festival fine art & craft collection; U.S. coins; ISOM prints; 3,000 lb. prehistoric petroglyph.
Facilities: performing arts theater; workrooms; classrooms.
Activities: films; gallery talks; visual & performing arts workshops; photography; monthly exhibits; community theatre presentations; children's art work; classes; meetings of community groups; juried exhibitions; formally organized educational programs; inter-museum loan & traveling exhibitions; theatrical productions for children & adults; Helen Keller Festival of art & craft national touring exhibition.
Publications: newsletter.
Hours & Admission Prices: Mon.-Fri. 9-5, Sun. 1-3. Adults $5; members no charge. Closed Easter; Memorial Day; Labor Day; Thanksgiving; Christmas. ♿
Attendance: 60,000 (accurate)
Membership: Student $10; Individual $20; Family (Dual) & Sustaining $30; Family $50; Benefactor $100; Supporter $250; Patron $500.

Tuskegee Institute

TUSKEGEE INSTITUTE NATIONAL HISTORIC SITE, 1212 W. Montgomery Rd., Tuskegee Institute, AL 36088-1923. Mailing Address: P.O. Drawer 10, Tuskegee Institute, AL 36087-0010. Tel.: 334-727-6390, 3200 & 9321. Fax: 334-727-4597 & 1448. TDD: 334-727-3201.
Web Site: www.nps.gov/tuin
Founded: 1941.
Congressional District: 3
Key Personnel: Acting Supt., Catherine Farmer Light; Chief Maintenance, L.H. Howard.
Personnel Profile: Full-Time Paid 3; Part-Time Paid 2; Part-Time Volunteers 12.
Governing Authority: federal. National Park Service, Dept. of the Interior, Southeast Region, Atlanta Federal Center, 1924 Bldg. 100 Alabama St. S.W. Atlanta, GA 30303.
History Museum: The George Washington Carver Museum; 1899 The Oaks, home of Booker T. Washington.
Collections: personal memorabilia & awards associated with Dr. George W. Carver & Booker T. Washington; items pertaining to the growth & development of Tuskegee Institute; natural history collections; paintings; pottery; needle-art; manuscripts; furnishings; products related to Dr. Carver's scientific experimentation. Historic House: 1899 The Oaks.
Facilities: 200-vol. library of African art books available for research on premise; 40-seat auditorium. Books & other museum-related items for sale.
Activities: guided tours; lectures; gallery talks; art & craft demonstrations; inter-museum loan; permanent, temporary & traveling exhibitions; films.
Publications: park brochure; site bulletins.
Hours & Admission Prices: Daily 9-4:30. No charge. Closed New Year's Day; Thanksgiving; Christmas. ♿
Attendance: 490,861 (estimated)

Vance

MERCEDES-BENZ VISITOR CENTER AND MUSEUM, 1 Mercedes Dr., Vance, AL 35490-2900. Tel.: 888-286-8762 (Toll Free); 205-507-2252.
E-mail: webteam@mbusi.com
Web Site: mbusi.com/pages/vc_home.asp
Transportation Museum.
Collections: history of Daimler-Benz; automobile technology.
Activities: tours.
Hours & Admission Prices: Museum & Center: late June to late May Mon.-Fri. 8:30-4:30. Factory Tours: Tues. & Thurs. 9am, 9:15am, 12:30 & 12:45 by appointment. Closed holidays.

Vinemont

CROOKED CREEK CIVIL WAR MUSEUM, 516 County Rd. 1127, Vinemont, AL 35179. Tel.: 256-739-2741.
Military Museum: housed on the site of the Crooked Creek Civil War Battle.
Collections: Civil War history & artifacts; uniforms; photographs; personal artifacts.
Hours & Admission Prices: Daily 9-6.

ECHOTA CHEROKEE INTERPRETIVE CENTER, 630 County Rd. 222, Vinemont, AL 35179. Tel.: 256-734-7337.
Native American History Center.
Collections: Native American history & culture; personal artifacts.
Facilities: 1.5 mile nature trail; outdoor classrooms.
Hours & Admission Prices: Mon.-Wed. 8-4, Thurs. 8-12. No charge.

Waterloo

EDITH NEWMAN CULVER MEMORIAL MUSEUM, 501 Main St., Waterloo, AL 35677. Mailing Address: P.O. Box 251, Waterloo, AL 35677-0251. Tel.: 256-767-6081.
Founded: 1995.
Personnel Profile: Part-Time Paid 1; Part-Time Volunteers 8.
Historic House Museum: built in 1870.
Collections: local history; period furniture; personal artifacts; Civil War; Native American; military.
Activities: Annual Event: Waterloo Heritage Days in May.
Hours & Admission Prices: Summer: Fri.-Sat. 11-5, Sun. 1-4. ♿

Wetumpka

FORT TOULOUSE/JACKSON PARK, 2521 W. Fort Toulouse Rd., Wetumpka, AL 36093-1112. Tel.: 334-567-3002.
E-mail: ftjack1@bellsouth.net
Web Site: www.forttoulouse.com
Key Personnel: Park Dir., Jim Parker; Living History Program Coord. & Archaeologist, Ned Jenkins.
Governing Authority: Parent Institution: Alabama Historical Commission.
Park & Historic Site.
Collections: area history; archaeological artifacts; Native & early American artifacts. Historic Buildings: Fort Jackson; Graves House.
Facilities: 165-acre park; nature trails; picnic area; campground. Museum-related items for sale.
Activities: living history weekends; special events. Park Sponsors: French and Indian Encampment in Spring; Frontier Days in Fall.
Hours & Admission Prices: Park: April-Oct. daily 6am-9pm; Nov.-March daily 8-5. Visitor Center: daily 8-5; groups by appointment. Adults & children over 6 $1, children 6 & under and senior citizens $.50; discounts to groups. Closed New Year's Day; Thanksgiving; Christmas.

Woodville

OLD MACDONALD'S PETTING ZOO, 7826 U.S. Hwy. 72 E., Woodville, AL 35776-6428. Tel.: 256-776-4332.
E-mail: lewissm@hiwaay.net
Web Site: www.oldmacdonaldspettingzoo.com
Zoo.
Collections: farm animals; birds.
Facilities: picnic area. Zoo-related items for sale.
Activities: birthday parties; school field trips; scout troops.
Hours & Admission Prices: March-Aug. Mon.-Fri. 9-2, Sat. 9-4, Sun. 12-4; Sept.-Nov. Thurs.-Fri. 9-2, Sat. 9-4, Sun. 12-4. Admission 2 & over $5; discounts to groups of 12 or more; children under 2 no charge. Closed Mother's Day; Father's Day.

ALASKA

(90 listings)

Anaktuvuk Pass

NORTH SLOPE BOROUGH PLANNING DEPT. - THE SIMON PANEAK MEMORIAL MUSEUM, 341 Mekiana Rd., Anaktuvuk Pass, AK 99721. Mailing Address: P.O. Box 21085, Anaktuvuk Pass, AK 99721-0085. Tel.: 907-661-3413. Fax: 907-661-3414.
E-mail: vera.weber@north-slope.org
Founded: 1986.
Congressional District: 1
Key Personnel: C.E.O., Edward S. Itta; Dir. Planning Dept., Johnny Aiken; Cur., Vera Weber.
Personnel Profile: Full-Time Paid 1; Interns 1.
Governing Authority: municipal. Parent Institution: North Slope Borough Planning Dept. Tax-exempt.
Local History and Ethnographic Museum.
Collections: tools; clothing; skin tent; polar bear; caribou; hunting; fishing; trapping; trading; Nunamiut Eskimo history & traditions.
Research Fields: ethnography; archaeology.
Facilities: research library of Alaskan books, available for public use; educational facilities. Educational materials, local native crafts, gift items & other museum-related items for sale.
Activities: guided tours; formal education programs for children, undergraduate & graduate students; loan exhibits; special events.
Publications: 4 fishing pamphlets; Notes on Nunamiut; Anaktuvuk Mask; Nunamiut Stories, We Hunt to Live; The Silent River; The Hungry Summer; Anaktuvuk Pass, Land of the Nunamiut territoriality among ancient hunters; In a Hungry Country; North Alaska Chronicles: Notes from the End of Time.
Hours & Admission Prices: Mon.-Fri. 8:30-5. Adults $10. Closed New Year's Day; Memorial Day; Seward's Day; Independence Day; Thanksgiving; Christmas. ♿
Attendance: 1,000 (accurate)

Anchorage

ALASKA AVIATION HERITAGE MUSEUM, (M), 4721 Aircraft Dr., Anchorage, AK 99502-1080. Tel.: 907-248-5325. Fax: 907-248-6391.
E-mail: info@alaskaairmuseum.org
Web Site: www.alaskaairmuseum.org
Founded: 1988.
Key Personnel: Exec. Dir., Norm Lagasse; Chm. (V) & Pres. (V), Gail Phillips; Museum Shop Mgr. & Dir. Mktg., Shari Hart.
Personnel Profile: Full-Time Paid 4; Part-Time Paid 2; Part-Time Volunteers 50.
Governing Authority: private; nonprofit organization. Tax-exempt.
Aeronautics Museum.
Collections: 30 aircraft depicting Alaska's role in aviation history.
Research Fields: Lend-Lease aircraft & the men, American & Russian, who flew them; Lockheed Vega for replica construction to recreate Eielson polar flight in 1928; all aspects of Alaskan aviation from 1898 through Alaska's Golden Age of Aviation & World War II; the search for Sigmond Levanevsky, 1937-1994; Russian Lindbergh: disappeared in Polar flight.
Facilities: 25-seat theater; 2 9-seat mini-theaters. Museum-related items for sale.
Activities: films; formal education programs for undergraduate & graduate students affiliated with work study program at University of Alaska-Anchorage; guided tours; hobby workshops; lectures; loan, temporary & traveling exhibitions; training programs for professional museum workers.
Hours & Admission Prices: May 15-Sept. 15 daily 9-5; Sept. 16-May 14 Wed.-Sun. 9-5. Adults $10, seniors 65 & over $8, children 5-12 $6; discounts AAA members; WWII veterans, children under 5 & members no charge. Closed New Year's Day; Thanksgiving; Christmas Eve & Day. ♿
Attendance: 20,000 (accurate)
Membership: Individual $45; Family $60; Polaris $100; Denali $250; Juneau $500; Barrow $1,000; Alaska League $2,500.

ALASKA MASONIC LIBRARY AND MUSEUM, 518 E. 14th Ave., Anchorage, AK 99501. Mailing Address: P.O. Box 200441, Anchorage, AK 99520-0441. Tel.: 907-276-2665.
Library & History Museum.
Collections: books; Freemasonry artifacts; Alaska history & culture; photographs.
Facilities: library of Freemasonry books.
Hours & Admission Prices: Temporarily closed for relocation. ♿

ALASKA MUSEUM OF NATURAL HISTORY, (M), 201 N. Bragaw, Anchorage, AK 99508-1311. Tel.: 907-274-2400.
E-mail: webcontact@alaskamuseum.org
Web Site: www.alaskamuseum.org
Founded: 1992.
Key Personnel: Pres. (V), Kristine Crossen; Vice Pres., Steve Trimble; Sec., Ginny Moore; Treas., Dr. Cindy Schraer; C.E.O. & Dir., Katch Bacheller; Mktg., Janet Oates; Collections Mgr., Phyllys Callina; Exhibits Mgr., Christy Fine; Museum Shop Mgr., Liz Roades.
Personnel Profile: Full-Time Paid 3; Part-Time Paid 2; Part-Time Volunteers 25.
Governing Authority: bd. of dirs. Tax-exempt.
Natural History Museum.
Collections: invertebrate & dinosaur fossils of the Matanuska Formation (Cretaceous period); plant fossils of the Chickaloon Formation (Paleocene period); minerals & rocks of Alaska; large (nonliving) mammals, birds, marine & nonmarine mammal skulls; Gold Rush mining history, tools; metallic minerals exhibits; Alaskan rocks & minerals; dinosaur & invertebrate fossils; plant fossils of the Paleocene & Eocene period; seven large ecosystem dioramas; Gold Rush mining history and tools; metallic minerals; & native artifacts from coastal & interior cultures.
Research Fields: Alaska.
Facilities: Museum-related items for sale.
Activities: lectures; formal education program; natural history field tours.
Publications: quarterly newsletter.
Hours & Admission Prices: Call for hours. Adults $5, children 6-12 $3; discounts to AAM & ICOM members; members & children under 5 no charge. ♿
Attendance: 6,000 (accurate)
Membership: Student & Senior $20; Individual $25, Senior Family $30; Family $50.

ALASKA NATIVE HERITAGE CENTER, (M), 8800 Heritage Center Dr., Anchorage, AK 99504-6100. Tel.: 907-330-8000; 800-315-6608.
Web Site: www.alaskanative.net
Founded: 1999.
Congressional District: 1
Key Personnel: Dir., Jonathon Ross.
Personnel Profile: Full-Time Paid 45; Part-Time Paid 4; Part-Time Volunteers 10; Interns 2.
Governing Authority: private; nonprofit organization. Tax-exempt: 501(c)(3).
Cultural Center.
Collections: native heritage cultures; personal artifacts; photographs.
Facilities: Museum-related items for sale.
Activities: Native dance performances; workshops; tours; demonstrations; videos.
Hours & Admission Prices: Daily 9-5. Adults $24.95, seniors & military $21.15, children 7-16 $15.95; discounts to groups; members and children 6 & under no charge. ♿
Attendance: 118,921 (accurate)
Membership: Jade (Senior) $45; Jade (Individual) $50; Copper (Family) $100; Baleen $250; Ivory $500; Heritage Circle $1,000.

ALASKA ZOO, 4731 O'Malley Rd., Anchorage, AK 99507-6573. Tel.: 907-346-2133. Fax: 907-346-2673.
Web Site: www.alaskazoo.org
Founded: 1969.
Key Personnel: Dir., Patrick S. Lampi; Co Pres., Bill Borchardt; Co Pres., Marnie Brennan.
Personnel Profile: Full-Time Paid 23; Full-Time Volunteers 2; Part-Time Paid 11; Part-Time Volunteers 80; Interns 2.
Governing Authority: Tax-exempt.
Zoo.
Collections: botanical; zoological.
Hours & Admission Prices: May-Sept. daily 9-6; Oct.-April daily 10-5. Adults $10, seniors & military $8, students 3-17 $6; children under 3 & passholders no charge. Closed Thanksgiving; Christmas. ♿
Attendance: 170,000 (accurate)
Membership: Single $40; Family $75; Contributor $250; Benefactor $500.

* **ANCHORAGE MUSEUM,** 625 C St., Anchorage, AK 99501. Tel.: 907-343-6173 (recorded information); 4326 (switchboard). Fax: 907-343-6149.
E-mail: museum@anchoragemuseum.org
Web Site: www.anchoragemuseum.org
Formerly: Anchorage Museum at Rasmuson Center
Founded: 1968.
Key Personnel: Dir. & C.E.O., James Pepper Henry; Dir. Collections Dept., Walter Van Horn; Cur. History & Research, Marilyn Knapp; Dir. Exhibits, David Nicholls; Dir. Education & Public Programs, Paul Perry; Dir. Library & Archives, Kathleen Hertel; Dir. Devel., Cheryl McGrew; Dir. Enterprise, Georgia Blue; Museum Shop Mgr., Mark Weber.
Personnel Profile: Full-Time Paid 26; Part-Time Paid 6; Part-Time Volunteers 400; Interns 1.
Governing Authority: municipality of Anchorage. Tax-exempt: 170(c)(1).
History & Art Museum.
Collections: Alaskan art & artifacts of all periods, archaeological, ethnological, historic & contemporary; archival collection of 400,000 photographs of Alaska; manuscripts; public art.
Research Fields: anthropology, history & art of Alaska.
Facilities: 10,000-vol. library of Alaskan anthropology, history & art, general reference, available for inter-library loan & on premises; 240-seat auditorium; classroom; 12 exhibition galleries; children's gallery & art room; Arctic Studies Center regional office; cafe. Eskimo Aleut, Tlingit, & Athabascan crafts, publications & prints for sale.
Activities: guided tours; lectures; gallery talks; concerts; arts festivals; study clubs; docent program; formally organized art & history education programs for children & adults; regional competitions; community sponsored programs & events; inter-museum loan, permanent, temporary & traveling exhibitions.
Publications: bimonthly newsletter; exhibition catalogs; A Northern Adventure: The Art of Fred Machetanz; Eskimo Drawings; John Hoover: Art and Life; Sydney Laurence, Painter of the North; Spirit of the North: The Art of Eustace Paul Ziegler; Children's Gallery exhibition catalogs; Solo exhibition catalogs; Painting in the North: Alaskan Art in the AMHA; Heaven on Earth: Orthodox Treasures from Siberia and North America; Agayuliyararput (Our Way of Making Prayer): The Living Tradition of Yup'ik Masks.
Hours & Admission Prices: May 11-Sept. 21 daily 9-6; Sept. 22-May 10 Tues.-Sat. 10-6, Sun. 12-6. Adults $8, senior citizens $7; discounts to AAM members; Alaska Museums Assoc., museum members & children under 17 no charge. Closed New Year's Day; Thanksgiving; Christmas. ♿
Attendance: 140,000 (estimated)
Membership: Individual student & senior $30; Individual military $35; Associate & Senior Family $40; Individual Basic $50; Military Family $60; Basic Family $65; Extended Family $75; Sustaining $125; Contributing $250; Benefactor $500; Sponsor $1,000.

FRATERNAL ORDER OF ALASKA STATE TROOPERS MUSEUM, 245 W. 5th Ave., Anchorage, AK 99501-2358. Mailing Address: P.O. Box 100280, Anchorage, AK 99510-0280. Tel.: 800-770-5050; 907-279-5050. Fax: 907-279-5054.
Web Site: www.alaskatroopermuseum.com
Founded: 1990.
Personnel Profile: Full-Time Paid 1; Part-Time Paid 1; Part-Time Volunteers 5.
Governing Authority: Parent Institution: Fraternal Order of Alaska State Troopers (F.O.A.S.T.).
History Museum.
Collections: history of the Alaska State Troopers & law enforcement.
Facilities: Museum-related items for sale.
Activities: youth groups; safety programs; professional seminars; safety presentations.
Publications: quarterly newsletter, Banner.
Hours & Admission Prices: Mon.-Fri. 10-4, Sat. 12-4. No charge; donations accepted. ♿
Attendance: 2,000
Membership: Friends $30; Corporate $500.

HERITAGE LIBRARY MUSEUM, 301 W. Northern Lights Blvd., Ste. 103, Anchorage, AK 99503-2652. Mailing Address: Wells Fargo Historical Services, 420 Montgomery St., MAC-A0101-106, San Francisco, CA 94163-0001. Tel.: 907-265-2834. Fax: 907-265-2860. TDD: 907-267-5678.
Founded: 1968.
Congressional District: 1
Key Personnel: Dir., Beverly Smith; Cur., Tom D. Bennett.
Personnel Profile: Full-Time Paid 1.
Governing Authority: Affiliated with Wells Fargo Bank Alaska.
General Museum.
Collections: Alaskan native ethnology & contemporary crafts; fine arts by Alaskan artists; library of works on Alaskan subjects.
Facilities: 2,500-vol. reference library on Alaskan & Arctic topics available to the public; 3,300 sq. ft. exhibit space.
Activities: guided tours; loan exhibitions; formally organized education programs for children.
Publications: Heritage of Alaska.
Hours & Admission Prices: Mon.-Fri. 12-4. No charge. Closed bank holidays. ♿

THE IMAGINARIUM SCIENCE DISCOVERY CENTER, 737 W. 5th Ave., Ste. G, Anchorage, AK 99501-2129. Tel.: 907-276-3179. Fax: 907-258-4306.
E-mail: info@imaginarium.org
Web Site: www.imaginarium.org
Founded: 1987.
Key Personnel: Exec. Dir., Christopher B. Cable; Dir., SaVina Haywood; Cur. Science, Greg Danner; Pres. (V), Moira Paddock; Treas., Kevin Hemenway; Education, Mia Jackson; Administration, Allison Wieland.
Personnel Profile: Full-Time Paid 13; Full-Time Volunteers 2; Part-Time Paid 8; Part-Time Volunteers 750.
Governing Authority: private; nonprofit organization. Tax-exempt.
Children's Science & Technology Museum.
Collections: Alaska art, history & culture; hands-on exhibits; paintings.
Research Fields: wetlands; red planet Mars; health & wellness; Arctic Ecology.
Facilities: planetarium; Marine touch tanks. Museum-related items for sale.
Activities: formal education programs for children; guided tours; participatory exhibits. Annual Events: Summer Solstice; Kids Day; Trick or Treat Town, a Halloween event.
Publications: quarterly newsletter, The Imaginews; monthly flier.
Hours & Admission Prices: Mon.-Sat. 10-6, Sun. 12-5. Adults $5.50, senior citizens, students & children $5; discounts to AAA & AAM members & groups of 15 or more; members no charge. Closed New Year's Day; Easter; Independence Day; Thanksgiving; Christmas. ♿
Attendance: 100,000 (accurate)
Membership: Individual $50; Family $75; Family Plus $90; Homeschool $105; Associate $110.

MERIKS GALLERY, 9101 Little Creel Dr., Anchorage, AK 99507-3920.
Key Personnel: Pres. & Owner, Paul Davis; Vice Pres., Maria Stein; Conservation, Mark R. Stein, Jr.; Visitor Svcs., Kathleen F. Stein.
Governing Authority: private. nonprofit. Tax-exempt.
Gallery.
Collections: paintings, drawings & prints from local artists.
Facilities: 500-vol. library.

Hours & Admission Prices: Daily 9-5. No charge; donations accepted.
Attendance: 5,000 (estimated)

THE OSCAR ANDERSON HOUSE MUSEUM, 420 M St., (in Elderberry Park), Anchorage, AK 99501-1929. Tel.: 907-274-2336. Fax: 907-274-3600.
Founded: 1982.
Key Personnel: Mgr., Mary A. Flaherty.
Personnel Profile: Part-Time Paid 2; Part-Time Volunteers 10.
Governing Authority: private; nonprofit organization. Parent Institution: Anchorage Historic Properties, Inc., 645 W. Third Ave., Anchorage 99501. Tax-exempt: 501(c)(3).
Historic House: 1915 bungalow style, one and a half story home, the first privately built house in Anchorage.
Collections: focuses on the interpretive period from 1915-1925 depicting the time of the founding of the city of Anchorage; period furnishings; Anderson family artifacts; photos associated with early Anchorage history.
Research Fields: genealogy of the Anderson family; life in Anchorage from 1915-1925.
Facilities: 30-vol. library on local history, museum mgmt. & exhibits; 1,500 sq. ft. exhibit space.
Activities: docent program; formal education programs for children; guided tours; temporary exhibitions. Annual Events: Early Anchorage Summer Celebration including Tent City exhibit, Maypole & Swedish summer festivities; Swedish Christmas Tours in December.
Hours & Admission Prices: By appointment. Adults $3, senior citizens over 65 $2, children 5-12 $1; discounts to AAM & ICOM members and groups.
Attendance: 3,559 (accurate)
Membership: Senior & Student $15; Individual $20; Family $30; Business $50; Benefactor $100.

RUSSIAN ORTHODOX MUSEUM, 605 A St., Anchorage, AK 99501-3623. Tel.: 907-258-7257 & 276-7257. Fax: 907-274-7257.
Religious Museum.
Collections: local Russian Orthodox history; religious artifacts; photographs.
Facilities: Museum-related items for sale.
Hours & Admission Prices: May 15-Sept. 15 Mon.-Fri. 7-5, Sat. 9-4, Sun. 1-4. No charge; donations accepted.

Anvik

ANVIK HISTORICAL SOCIETY AND MUSEUM, Main Rd., Anvik, AK 99558. Mailing Address: P.O. Box 110, Anvik, AK 99558-0110. Tel.: 907-663-6360.
Historical Society Museum.
Collections: Native Athabascan culture & history; photographs; period artifacts; early 20th century trade goods.
Hours & Admission Prices: Summer: by appointment.

Barrow

INUPIAT HERITAGE CENTER, 5421 North Star St., Barrow, AK 99723. Mailing Address: P.O. Box 69, Barrow, AK 99723-0069. Tel.: 907-852-0422. Fax: 907-852-4224.
Web Site: www.nps.gov.inup
Founded: 1999.
Heritage Center.
Collections: Inupiat heritage & history; photographs; personal artifacts.
Facilities: library.
Activities: educational outreach; performances; activities.
Hours & Admission Prices: Mon.-Fri. 8:30-5. ♿

Bethel

YUPIIT PICIRYARAIT MUSEUM, 420 Chief Eddie Hoffman Hwy., Bethel, AK 99559. Mailing Address: P.O. Box 219, Bethel, AK 99559-0219. Tel.: 907-543-1819. Fax: 907-543-1885.
Web Site: www.ypmuseum.org
Founded: 1994.
Governing Authority: Parent Institution: Association of Village Council Presidents.
Regional Tribal Museum.
Collections: clothing; household artifacts; hunting & gathering implements; personal artifacts; Yup'ik, Cup'ik & Dene collections from the Native people who settled the Yukon-Kuskokwim Delta of Alaska.
Facilities: Museum-related items for sale.
Hours & Admission Prices: Tues.-Sat. 12-4. No charge; donations accepted. ♿

Central

THE CENTRAL MUSEUM, 128 Mile Steese Hwy., Central, AK 99730. Mailing Address: P.O. Box 30189, Central, AK 99730-0189. Tel.: 907-520-1893. Fax: 907-520-1893.
Web Site: www.cdhs.us
Founded: 1977.
Congressional District: 4
Key Personnel: Pres. (V) & Public Rels., Al Cook; Treas., Becky Hendrickson; Cur., Julie Cooper; Archivist, Al Cook; Sec. & Museum Shop Mgr., Darae Murphy.
Personnel Profile: Part-Time Paid 1; Part-Time Volunteers 10.
Governing Authority: private; nonprofit organization.
Historical Society & Mining Museum.
Collections: discovery of gold in the central area & living conditions, c.1893; fur trapping.
Facilities: library of old hard-bound novels from early 1900s, a part of Alaskana Collection, available for on-premises use only. Books, Alaskana wild plants, berries, mushrooms, cookbooks, local crafts & gold mining-related items for sale.
Activities: guided tours; study clubs. Annual Event: Christmas Bazaar.
Publications: newsletter.
Hours & Admission Prices: Memorial Day-Labor Day Fri.-Sun. 12-5; tours by appointment. Adults & students $1, children $.50; senior citizens 70 & over and members no charge. ♿
Attendance: 400 (estimated)
Membership: Child $1; Adult $10; Family $15; Business $25.

CIRCLE DISTRICT MUSEUM, 1275 Mile Steese Hwy., Central, AK 99730. Tel.: 907-520-1893.
History Museum.
Collections: mining; local heritage & culture; personal artifacts; photographs.
Hours & Admission Prices: Memorial Day to Labor Day daily 12-5; Winter: by appointment.

Copper Center

GEORGE I. ASHBY MEMORIAL MUSEUM, (M), Mile 101 Old Richardson Hwy., Copper Center Loop Rd., Copper Center, AK 99573. Mailing Address: P.O. Box 84, Copper Center, AK 99573-0084. Tel.: 907-822-5285.
Founded: 1985.
Key Personnel: Chm. (V), Geoff Bleakley; Museum Mgr., Rebecca Nelson; Treas. & Museum Shop Mgr., Barbara Sanders.
Personnel Profile: Part-Time Paid 1; Part-Time Volunteers 20.
Governing Authority: Parent Institution: Copper Valley Historical Society. Tax-exempt.
History Museum.
Collections: concentration on Alaskan history with emphasis on Copper Valley.
Hours & Admission Prices: May 15 to Sept 15 daily 11-5. No charge; donations accepted.
Attendance: 7,735 (accurate)
Membership: Copper Valley Historical Society $15.

Cordova

CORDOVA HISTORICAL MUSEUM, (M), 622 1st St., Cordova, AK 99574. Mailing Address: Box 391, Cordova, AK 99574-0391. Tel.: 907-424-6665. Fax: 907-424-6666.
E-mail: infoservices@cityofcordova.net
Web Site: www.cordovamuseum.org
Founded: 1966.
Key Personnel: Pres. (V), Mike Webber; Vice Pres., Ira Grindle; Dir., Cathy R. Sherman; Treas., Mimi Briggs; Collections Mgr. & Cur., Judy Fulton; Museum Shop Mgr., Sharon Ermold.
Personnel Profile: Full-Time Paid 1; Part-Time Paid 3; Part-Time Volunteers 10.
Governing Authority: municipal; society. Parent Institutions: Cordova Historical Society & City of Cordova. Tax-exempt.
General Museum.
Collections: fishing artifacts; Copper River & Northwestern Railway artifacts; lighthouse lens; Native American (Eyak, Chugach) artifacts; photo archives.
Research Fields: oral history of pioneer Alaskans.
Facilities: library & microfilm of Cordova newspapers, 1906-2008. Books for sale.
Activities: films of old Cordova; gallery talks.
Publications: quarterly newsletter; books, Walking Tour of Cordova; From Fish & Copper: Cordova's Heritage & Buildings; Cordova to Kennecott.
Hours & Admission Prices: Museum: Memorial Day to Labor Day Mon.-Sat. 10-6, Sun. 2-4; Winter: Tues.-Fri. 10-5, Sat. 1-5. Archives: by appointment. No charge; donations accepted. Closed New Year's Day; Independence Day; Christmas. ♿

Attendance: 12,000 (accurate)
Membership: Student $5; Individual $10; Family $25; Life $200.

ILANKA CULTURAL CENTER, 110 Nicholoff Way, Cordova, AK 99574. Mailing Address: P.O. Box 1388, 110 Nicholoff Way, Cordova, AK 99574-1388. Tel.: 907-424-7903. Fax: 907-424-3018.
Cultural Center.
Collections: local native culture, history & art; personal artifacts.
Facilities: Museum-related items for sale.
Activities: classes.
Hours & Admission Prices: Memorial Day to Labor Day Tues. & Thurs.-Fri. 10-5, Wed. 10-6, Sat. 12-4; Sept.-May Tues.-Fri. 10-4.

Delta Junction

SULLIVAN ROADHOUSE HISTORICAL MUSEUM, Mile 267 Richardson Hwy., Delta Junction, AK 99737. Mailing Address: P.O. Box 987, Delta Junction, AK 99737-0987. Tel.: 907-895-5068; 907-895-4415 (seasonal). Fax: 907-895-5141.
E-mail: deltacc@deltachamber.org
Web Site: www.deltachamber.org
Key Personnel: Exec. Dir., Brenda Peterson; Cur. & Project Archaeologist, Jeffrey Durham
Historic House Museum: built in 1905 by John and Florence Sullivan.
Collections: Valdez-Fairbanks Trail history; Alaska history.
Facilities: nature trails.
Activities: nature walks.
Hours & Admission Prices: May-Sept. daily 9-5. No charge; donations accepted.

Denali Park

DENALI NATIONAL PARK AND PRESERVE, Mile Post 237, George Parks Hwy., Denali Park, AK 99755. Mailing Address: P.O. Box 9, Denali Park, AK 99755-0009. Tel.: 907-683-2294. Fax: 907-683-9617. TDD: 907-683-9649.
E-mail: jane_lakeman@nps.gov
Web Site: www.nps.gov/dena
Founded: 1917.
Congressional District: 1
Key Personnel: Park Supt., Paul R. Anderson; Administrative Officer, Julie Wilkerson; Chief Ranger, Peter Armington; Museum Cur., Jane Lakeman.
Personnel Profile: Full-Time Paid 1.
Governing Authority: federal. National Park Service, Alaska Regional Office, 240 W. 5th Ave., Anchorage, AK 99503. Tel. 907-257-2543.
Park Study Collection.
Collections: botany; zoology; geology; history; archaeology; ethnology.
Research Fields: botany; zoology; geology; archaeology.
Facilities: 2,500-vol. library of general reference books available for use on premises; reading room; outdoor museum. Publications for sale.
Activities: traditional park activities.
Publications: Mammals of Mt. McKinley; Sled Dogs of Denali; Denali Bird Finding Guide; A Back Country Companion to Denali National Park; The Denali Road Guide.
Hours & Admission Prices: Mon.-Fri. 8-4:30 & by appointment. ♿

Dillingham

SAMUEL K. FOX MUSEUM, 306 D St. West, Dillingham, AK 99576. Mailing Address: P.O. Box 273, Dillingham, AK 99576-0273. Tel.: 907-842-4831.
E-mail: samfoxmuseum@nushtel.net
Web Site: www.nushtel.com/~dlgchmbr
Founded: 1974.
Congressional District: 16
Key Personnel: Dir., Chm. (V) & Pres. (V), Deb Burton.
Personnel Profile: Part-Time Volunteers 9.
Governing Authority: City of Dillingham, AK. Tax-exempt: 501(c)(3).
Alaskan Native & Indian Museum.
Collections: Southwestern Yup'ik Eskimo arts & crafts; basket weaving; skinsewing; wood, ivory & bone carving; Alaskan culture memorabilia; Aleut, Southwestern Yup'ik, Siberian Yup'ik & Inupiat Eskimo artifacts; historical photographs & prints.
Facilities: library.
Activities: lectures; formally organized education programs for children; loan, permanent, temporary & traveling exhibitions; travel slide show; community workshop.
Hours & Admission Prices: Mon.-Fri. 8-6, Sat. 10-2. No charge; donations accepted. Closed national holidays. ♿
Attendance: 7,500 (estimated)
Membership: Students $3; Adults $15.

Eagle

EAGLE HISTORICAL SOCIETY & MUSEUMS, 3rd & Chamberlain, Eagle, AK 99738. Mailing Address: P.O. Box 23, Eagle, AK 99738-0023. Tel.: 907-547-2325. Fax: 907-547-2325.
E-mail: ehsmus@aptalaska.net
Web Site: eagleak.org
Founded: 1961.
Congressional District: 36
Key Personnel: C.E.O. & Pres. (V), Elva Scott; Dir. & Cur., Jean Turner; Museum Shop Mgr., Betty Borg; Education Cur., Theresa Dean; Bookkeeper, Kristie De Pue.
Personnel Profile: Full-Time Paid 1; Full-Time Volunteers 1; Part-Time Paid 7; Part-Time Volunteers 14.
Governing Authority: bd. of dirs.; nonprofit organization. Parent Institution: Eagle Historical Society. Tax-exempt: 170(b)(1)(A).
Local History Museum: housed in 1900 courthouse; 1898 U.S. Army Mule Barn; 1900-1911 U.S. Army Post Fort Egbert all located in the first city incorporated in interior Alaska.
Collections: archives; photos; maps; court room; machinery; vehicles; tools; documents; living quarters; furniture.
Research Fields: local history from 1890s to present.
Facilities: 1900-1910 restored historic buildings.
Activities: guided tours.
Publications: Jewel On the Yukon: Eagle City; Life in the Northern Army; triannual newsletter.
Hours & Admission Prices: Tour: Memorial Day to Labor Day daily 9am; other times by appointment. Adults $5; members & children under 12 no charge.
Attendance: 6,800 (estimated)
Membership: Single $10; Family $15; Business $25; Sponsoring $100; Life $500.

Eagle River

EAGLE RIVER NATURE CENTER, 32750 Eagle River Rd., Eagle River, AK 99577. Tel.: 907-694-2108. Fax: 907-694-2119.
E-mail: info@ernc.org
Nature Center.
Collections: local natural history & culture; wildlife & their habitats; plants; trees; flowers; ecology; geology.
Facilities: nature trails. Museum-related items for sale.
Activities: hiking; educational programs.
Hours & Admission Prices: May & Sept. Tues.-Sun. 10-5; June-Aug. daily 10-7; Oct.-April Fri.-Sun. 10-5.

Fairbanks

ALASKA HOUSE ART GALLERY, 1003 Cushman St., Fairbanks, AK 99701-4618. Mailing Address: P.O. Box 70501, Fairbanks, AK 99707-0501. Tel.: 907-456-6449.
Key Personnel: Owner, Yolande Fejes; Owner, Ron Veliz
Art Gallery: built in 1939.
Collections: works of Claire Fejes & other Alaskan artists; paintings; drawings; prints; sculpture; carvings; masks; fabric art.
Activities: poetry readings; special events.
Hours & Admission Prices: Summer: call for hours.

DOG MUSHING MUSEUM, 410 Cushman St., Fairbanks, AK 99701-4632. Tel.: 907-456-6874.
Founded: 1987.
Key Personnel: Exec. Dir., Julie Fougeron.
Personnel Profile: Full-Time Paid 2; Part-Time Paid 3.
Governing Authority: Tax-exempt.
History Museum.
Collections: vintage dog sleds; state of the art cold weather gear; Siberian skin clothing; sled dog memorabilia; photo-essay exhibit.
Research Fields: sled dog husbandry; literature research of books, periodicals & newsletters relating to dog mushing.
Facilities: library of Mushing Magazine (complete set), mushing books & miscellaneous periodicals; 1,500 sq. ft. exhibit space; 30-seat theater. Museum-related items for sale.
Activities: theater. Annual Event: autograph signing by Iditarod winners.
Publications: quarterly newsletter.
Hours & Admission Prices: May-Aug. Mon.-Sat. 10-6, Sun. 12-4; Sept.-May Tues.-Sat. 10-6. No charge; donations accepted. Closed all major holidays. ♿
Attendance: 8,000 (estimated)
Membership: Individual $20; Family $50; Business $100; Corporate $500.

FAIRBANKS COMMUNITY MUSEUM, 410 Cushman St., Fairbanks, AK 99701-4632. Tel.: 907-457-3669.
Web Site: www.fairbankscommunitymuseum.com
Key Personnel: Exec. Dir., Diane Fleets.
Personnel Profile: Part-Time Volunteers 8.
Governing Authority: Tax-exempt.
History Museum.
Collections: area history; photographs; mining; dog sleds; Native Alaskans; Fairbanks flood of 1967; Klondike Gold Rush.
Activities: presentations; educational programs.
Hours & Admission Prices: Tues.-Sat. 10-6. No charge; donations accepted. Closed major holidays. ♿

FAIRBANKS ICE MUSEUM, 500 2nd Ave., Fairbanks, AK 99701-4729. Tel.: 907-451-8222.
Historic Building: housed in the Lacey Street Theater; built in 1936.
Collections: ice sculptures; videos.
Activities: ice carvings demonstration.
Hours & Admission Prices: May-Sept. daily 10-8. Shows: 10, 2 & 8. Adult $12, military & seniors $11, children 6-12 $6, children 5 & under $2.

PIONEER AIR MUSEUM, Airport Way & Peger Rd., Fairbanks, AK 99701. Mailing Address: Box 70437, Fairbanks, AK 99707-0437. Tel.: 907-451-0037 & 456-5405. Fax: 907-452-2969.
Web Site: www.akpub.com/akttt/aviat.html
Formerly: Alaskaland Pioneer Air Museum
Founded: 1983.
Congressional District: 4
Key Personnel: Chm. Bd., Mgr. & C.E.O., L.D. (Corky) Corkran.
Personnel Profile: Part-Time Paid 4; Part-Time Volunteers 6.
Governing Authority: Parent Institution: Interior & Arctic Alaska Aeronautical Foundation. Tax-exempt.
Aeronautics Museum.
Collections: aviation artifacts pertaining to the history of interior & Arctic Alaska; aircraft; aircraft remains; engines; pictures; radios; memorabilia of bush pilots & airlines.
Publications: quarterly newsletter.
Hours & Admission Prices: Memorial Day-Labor Day daily 11-9. Families $5, adults $2; members no charge. ♿
Attendance: 13,000 (accurate)
Membership: Regular $20; Associate $50; Life $1,000.

PIONEER MUSEUM & THE BIG STAMPEDE, Pioneer Park, Bldg. #1, 2300 Airport Way, Fairbanks, AK 99701. Mailing Address: P.O. Box 70176, Fairbanks, AK 99707-0176.
Founded: 1964.
Key Personnel: Pres. (V) & Museum Shop Mgr., Joanne Oehring.
Personnel Profile: Part-Time Paid 9; Part-Time Volunteers 45.
Governing Authority: Parent Institution: Pioneers of Alaska Igloos #4 & #8. Tax-exempt.
History Museum.
Collections: photographs; prospecting & mining tools and equipment; telegraphic artifacts; dog sleds; snowshoes; horse-drawn sleds & stages; early aviation artifacts; period Edwardian household furnishings; handmade tools & appliances; medical, engineering, legal & other professional materials; M.C. Rusty Heurlin's paintings of Klondike & Fairbanks Gold Rushes of 1898 & 1903.
Hours & Admission Prices: March-Memorial Day Fri.-Sun. 1-5; late May to Labor Day daily 11-8; Sept. daily 1-5; Nov.-Feb. call for tours. Museum: no charge; donations accepted. Big Stampede Show: Memorial Day to Labor Day. Adults $4, youth 4-12 $2; children under 4 no charge. ♿
Attendance: 16,000 (accurate)

* **UNIVERSITY OF ALASKA MUSEUM OF THE NORTH, (M), (I),** 907 Yukon Dr., Fairbanks, AK 99775-6960. Mailing Address: P.O. Box 756960, Fairbanks, AK 99775-6960. Tel.: 907-474-7505. Fax: 907-474-5469.
E-mail: museum@uaf.edu
Web Site: www.uaf.edu/museum
Founded: 1929.
Congressional District: 1
Key Personnel: Dir., Aldona Jonaitis; Chm. (V), Mike Cook; Asst. to Dir., Andrew Quainton; Operations Mgr., Kevin May; Dir. Devel., Julie Estey; Cur. Archeology, Daniel P. Odess; Cur. Mammalogy, Link E. Olson; Cur. Ornithology, Kevin S. Winker; Cur. Herbarium, Stefanie Ickert-Bond; Cur. Earth Sciences, Patrick Druckenmiller; Cur. Ichthyology, Gordon Haas; Cur. Entomology, Derek Sykes; Dir. Alaska Center for Documentary Film, Leonard J. Kamerling; Cur. Ethnology & History, Molly Lee; Coord. Exhibits & Exhibits Designer, Wanda W. Chin; Coord. Fine Arts, Barry J. McWayne; Coord. Public Education Programs, Laura Conner; Communications Coord., Kerynn Fisher; Visitor Service Mgr., Amy R. Geiger; Museum Shop Mgr., Daniel David.
Personnel Profile: Full-Time Paid 32; Part-Time Paid 53; Part-Time Volunteers 40.
Governing Authority: university. Parent Institution: University of Alaska. Subsidiary Institution: University of Alaska Fairbanks. Tax-exempt: 170(b)(2)(A).
Natural History & Art Museum.
Collections: aquatics; archaeology; birds; botany; earth sciences; ethnology; history; film project; fine arts; herbarium; mammals; fish; insects.
Research Fields: plant ecology & taxonomy; marine invertebrate identification & distribution; Alaskan pre-Cambrian biotas; archeology; ethnohistory; tephrochronology; migratory birds & avian influenza, polar dinosaur population diversity & distribution; mammal diversity & distribution.
Facilities: Books, booklets, postcards & museum-related items for sale.
Activities: guided tours for schools; permanent, temporary & traveling exhibitions.
Publications: annual report; newsletter; exhibit catalogs; informational brochures; research monographs; visitor's guide.
Hours & Admission Prices: May 15 to Sept. 15 daily 9-9; Sept. 16 to May 14 Mon.-Fri. 9-5, Sat.-Sun. 12-5. Adults $10, seniors $9, youth 7-17 $5; children 6 & under, Univ. Alaska students w/ID & members no charge. Closed New Year's Day; Thanksgiving; Christmas. ♿
Attendance: 96,016 (accurate)
Membership: Individual $50; Couple $65; Family $75; Advocate $125; Donor $250; Patron $500.

WICKERSHAM HOUSE MUSEUM (TANANA-YUKON HISTORICAL SOCIETY), 535 2nd Ave., Ste. 201, Fairbanks, AK 99701-4770. Mailing Address: P.O. Box 71336, Fairbanks, AK 99707-1336. Tel.: 907-457-6165. Fax: 907-457-6165.
E-mail: tyhs@polarnet.com
Web Site: www.tyhsonline.org
Founded: 1959.
Congressional District: 1
Key Personnel: C.E.O. & Pres. (V), Renee Blahuta; Chm. (V), Anne Foster; Treas., Elizabeth Cook; Sec., Catherine Williams; Museum Shop Mgr., Lisa Harbo.
Personnel Profile: Full-Time Volunteers 1; Part-Time Paid 5; Part-Time Volunteers 21; Interns 2.
Governing Authority: public; nonprofit. Parent Institution: Tanana-Yukon Historical Society. Tax-exempt: 501(c)(3).
Historical Society Museum: housed in the Wickersham House Museum, home of Judge James Wickersham & the first frame home completed in the rough gold camp which became Fairbanks, AK.
Collections: 1904-1916 Alaska furnishings; photographs; history of interior Alaska following the purchase of Alaska from Russia 1867.
Facilities: Books relating to Alaska history for sale.
Activities: docent program; guided tours; temporary exhibitions. Museum Sponsors: lecture series February-April & September-November. Annual Event: Golden Days Tea honoring the founding of Fairbanks. Preservation Advocacy-Save America's Treasures Grant; Wickersham Day celebrations 1 man play Wickersham of Alaska.
Publications: cookbook, First Catch a Moose; monthly newsletter; Alaska: Saving Our Places; Fairbanks' First Avenue; The History & Preservation of A Streetscape; membership brochure; James Wickersham Brochure; Cold Missions -The Army Air Forces and Ladd Field in WWII.
Hours & Admission Prices: Memorial Day-Labor Day daily 11-9; other times by appointment. No charge; donations accepted. ♿
Attendance: 13,415 (accurate)
Membership: Individual $15; Family $20; Organizations $35; Contributing $100; Life $200.

Girdwood

ALASKA WILDLIFE CONSERVATION CENTER, 79 Seward Hwy., Girdwood, AK 99587. Mailing Address: P.O. Box 949, Girdwood, AK 99587-0949. Tel.: 907-783-2025. Fax: 907-783-2370.
Governing Authority: nonprofit organization. Tax-exempt: 501(c)(3).
Conservation Center.
Collections: bears; moose; bison; elk; deer; caribou; coyotes; foxes; bald eagles; owls; porcupines.
Hours & Admission Prices: Jan. 2-Feb. Sat.-Sun. 10-5; March to mid-May daily 10-6; mid-May to mid-Sept. daily 8-8; mid-Sept. to Jan. 1 daily 10-5. Adults $10, seniors 65 & over and children 4-12 $7.50; children under 4 no charge.

Haines

ALASKA INDIAN ARTS, INC., Historic Bldg. #13, Fort Seward, Haines, AK 99827. Mailing Address: P.O. Box 271, Haines, AK 99827-0271. Tel.: 907-766-2160. Fax: 907-766-2160.
E-mail: mail@alaskaindianarts.com
Web Site: www.alaskaindianarts.com
Founded: 1957.
Key Personnel: C.E.O., Pres. & Exec. Dir., Lee D. Heinmiller; Trustee & Cultural Dir., Charles Jimmie, Sr.; Trustee, John Svenson, Sr.; Art Dir., John Hagen; Design Chief, Greg Horner; Consultant, James Houston; Artist, Clifford Thomas; Museum Shop Mgr., Suzanne McCollum.
Governing Authority: nonprofit organization. Tax-exempt: 501(c)(3).
Indian Living Village Museum.
Collections: Tlinget Indian costumes; Indian art; ethnology. Historic Building: 1904 Fort William H. Seward.
Research Fields: Indian culture; Fort Seward history.
Facilities: 50-vol. library of publications on Northwest Coast Indians available for use on premises; Totem village with tribal house & totem poles. Traditional Indian art items for sale.
Activities: guided tours; dance recitals; permanent exhibitions; slides; educational kits; walking tour.
Hours & Admission Prices: Mon.-Fri. 9-5. No charge; donations accepted. Closed national holidays. ♿

AMERICAN BALD EAGLE FOUNDATION, Corner of 2nd Ave. & Haines Hwy., Haines, AK 99827. Mailing Address: P.O. Box 49, Haines, AK 99827-0049. Tel.: 907-766-3094. Fax: 907-766-3095.
E-mail: info@baldeagles.org
Web Site: www.baldeagles.org
Founded: 1982.
Personnel Profile: Full-Time Volunteers 1; Part-Time Paid 3; Part-Time Volunteers 2; Interns 3.
Governing Authority: nonprofit organization. Tax-exempt.
Natural History Museum.
Collections: over 200 wildlife specimens.
Research Fields: American Bald Eagle.
Facilities: Museum-related items for sale.
Activities: talks; video presentation; live bird presentations, eagles & red tail hawks. Annual Event: Alaska Bald Eagle Festival in November.
Publications: quarterly newsletter.
Hours & Admission Prices: Summer: Mon.-Fri. 9-5, Sat.-Sun. 1-4; Oct.-March by appointment. Adults $5; discounts to active military & senior citizens; members no charge. ♿
Membership: Individual $35; Family $50; Silver $125; Gold $250; Lifetime $1,000.

HAMMER MUSEUM, 108 Main St., Haines, AK 99827. Mailing Address: P.O. Box 702, Haines, AK 99827-0702. Tel.: 907-766-2374.
E-mail: hammermuseum@aptalaska.net
Web Site: www.hammermuseum.org
Founded: 2001.
Personnel Profile: Full-Time Volunteers 1; Part-Time Volunteers 2; Interns 2.
Governing Authority: Tax-exempt: 501(c)(3).
History Museum.
Collections: 1,700 types of hammers representing many different trades & uses from ancient times to present.
Hours & Admission Prices: May-Sept. Mon.-Fri. 10-5. Admission $3.
Attendance: 2,500

* **SHELDON MUSEUM AND CULTURAL CENTER, INC., (M),** 11 Main St., Haines, AK 99827. Mailing Address: P.O. Box 269, Haines, AK 99827-0269. Tel.: 907-766-2366. Fax: 907-766-2368.
E-mail: museumdirector@aptalaska.net
Web Site: sheldonmuseum.org
Founded: 1974.
Congressional District: 1
Key Personnel: Pres. Bd. Trustees (V), Jim Heaton; Dir. & Cur., Jerrie Clarke; Education Coord., Kathy Friedle; Collections & Exhibitions, Karen Meizner; Museum Shop Mgr., Blythe Carter.
Personnel Profile: Full-Time Paid 1; Part-Time Paid 6; Part-Time Volunteers 200.
Governing Authority: bd. of trustees. Subsidiary Institution: Haines Borough. Tax-exempt: 501(c)(3).
History & ethnographic Tlingit Indian Culture museum.
Collections: local pioneer-transportation; mining; local industries; Presbyterian mission; Tlingit & other northwest coast Indian artifacts; some Eskimo/Athabascan; Eldred Rock Lighthouse lens; oral histories.
Research Fields: local & Alaskan history.
Facilities: 1,500-vol. library; archives.
Activities: education programs for school classes; tours for prearranged groups; Tlingits language classes for students & adults; adult educational programs.
Publications: Journey to the Tlingits; Haines-The First Century; Song of the Chilkat People; A Personal Look at the Sheldon Museum & Cultural Center; More Than Gold: Nuggets of Haines History.
Hours & Admission Prices: mid-May to mid-Sept. Mon.-Fri. 10-5, Sat.-Sun. 1-4; call for additional hours. Adults $3; discounts for AAM, Museums Alaska & Chilkat Valley Historical Society members; children under 12 no charge. ♿
Attendance: 13,720 (accurate)
Membership: Sheldon Museum & Cultural Center: Individual $25; Family $50; Sustaining $100; Contributing $250; Benefactor $500; Corporate Sponsor $1,000. Chilkat Valley Historical Society: Individual $12; Family $22; Patron $50; Life $250.

Homer

ALASKA ISLANDS AND OCEAN VISITOR CENTER, 95 Sterling Hwy., Homer, AK 99603-7472. Tel.: 907-235-6961.
Key Personnel: Mgr. Visitor's Center, Marianne Aplin
Marine Wildlife Museum.
Collections: marine wildlife; local history.
Facilities: auditorium; nature trails. Books for sale.
Activities: educational programs.
Hours & Admission Prices: Memorial Day to Labor Day daily 9-6; Sept.-May Tues.-Sat. 10-5. No charge.

BUNNELL STREET GALLERY, 106 W. Bunnell St., Homer, AK 99603-7825. Tel.: 907-235-2662. Fax: 907-235-9427.
Governing Authority: nonprofit organization.
Art Gallery.
Collections: paintings; photographs; sculpture.
Activities: workshops; lectures; concerts.
Hours & Admission Prices: Call for hours.

FIREWEED GALLERY, 475 E. Pioneer Ave., Homer, AK 99603-7622. Tel.: 907-235-3411.
E-mail: art@fireweedgallery.com
Art Gallery.
Collections: contemporary works by Alaskan artists including paintings, sculpture, ceramics, jewelry, & photography.
Activities: special events; traveling exhibitions. Museum Sponsors: Annual Spring Show.
Hours & Admission Prices: Summer: Mon.-Sat. 10-7, Sun. 11-5; Winter: Mon.-Sat. 10:30-5:30.

* **PRATT MUSEUM, (M),** 3779 Bartlett St., Homer, AK 99603-7579. Tel.: 907-235-8635. Fax: 907-235-2764.
E-mail: info@prattmuseum.org
Web Site: www.prattmuseum.org
Founded: 1955.
Congressional District: 7
Key Personnel: C.E.O., Heather Beggs; Pres. (V), Michael Craig; Cur. Collections, Betsy Webb; Dir. Education, Ryjil Christianson; Cur. Exhibits, Holly Cusack-McVeigh; Bldg. Mgr., Neil McArthur; Bookkeeper, Heidi Stage; Museum Shop Mgr., Kim Wylde; Office Mgr., Lisa Forster.
Personnel Profile: Full-Time Paid 8; Part-Time Paid 8; Part-Time Volunteers 50; Interns 5.
Governing Authority: nonprofit organization. Parent Institution: Homer Society of Natural History, Inc. Tax-exempt: 501(c)(3).
General Museum.
Collections: regional Alaskan history, ethnography, archaeology, zoology, herbarium, marine aquarium, botanical garden, art; local art; art of local interest; interpretive nature trail; Homestead Cabin.
Research Fields: local history; anthropology; ornithology; sea mammals.
Facilities: reference library. Museum-related items for sale.
Activities: permanent & special exhibitions; lecture programs; school programs; guided tours; marine aquaria demonstrations; remote controlled cameras in wilderness areas.
Publications: Pratt Museum Newsletter; A History of Kachemak Bay; Rock Paintings of South Coastal Alaska; Homer Historic Building Survey; English Bay & Port Graham Aleutiiq Plantlore; Darkened Waters: A Review of the History, Science & Technology Associated with the Exxon Valdez Oil Spill & Cleanup; Kachemak Bay Bird Watch; A Birder's Guide to the Kenai Peninsula, Alaska.
Hours & Admission Prices: Feb.-April & Oct.-Dec. Tues.-Sun. 12-5; mid-May to mid-Sept. daily 10-6. Family $20, adults $6, seniors $5.50, youths 13-18 $3; discounts to AAM & MAM members; children under 6 & members no charge. ♿
Attendance: 34,300 (accurate)

Membership: Pioneer Club $25 (artist/student/senior); Kittinake Club $50; Octopus Club $100; Wild Rose Club $250; Qayak Club $500; Aurora Club $1,000; Bald Eagle Club $2,500.

Hope

HOPE-SUNRISE HISTORICAL AND MINING MUSEUM, 2nd St., Hope, AK 99605. Mailing Address: P.O. Box 88, Hope, AK 99605-0088. Tel.: 907-782-3740 & 3471.
History Museum.
Collections: photographs; Turnagain Arm Gold Rush of 1896; grader; dog sled; rock crusher; blacksmith bellows; postal boxes. Historic Buildings: mine bunkhouse; blacksmith shop.
Hours & Admission Prices: Memorial Day to Labor Day Fri.-Mon. 12-4. No charge; donations accepted.

Juneau

* **ALASKA STATE MUSEUM, (M),** 395 Whittier, Juneau, AK 99801-1746. Tel.: 907-465-2901. Fax: 907-465-2976.
E-mail: bruce.kato@alaska.gov
Web Site: www.museums.state.ak.us
Founded: 1900.
Congressional District: 4
Key Personnel: Museum Store Mgr., Jeanette Lackey; Friends of the Alaska State Museum Pres., Renee Hughes; Administrative Asst., Debbie McBride; Cur. Collections, Steve Henrikson; Cur. Exhibits, Bob Banghart; Cur. Museum Svcs., Scott Carrlee; Exhibitions Designer, Paul Gardinier; Registrar, Sorrel Goodwin; Mgr. Protection & Visitor Svcs., Lisa Golisek; Asst. Protection & Visitor Svcs., Sara Lee; Supvr. Protection & Visitor Svcs., Mary Irvine; Conservator, Ellen Carrlee.
Personnel Profile: Full-Time Paid 11; Part-Time Paid 3; Part-Time Volunteers 109.
Governing Authority: state. Parent Institution: State of Alaska. Subsidiary Institution: Division of Libraries, Archives & Museums. Branch Museum: Sheldon Jackson Museum, Sitka, AK 99835. Tax-exempt.
General Museum.
Collections: Alaskan history, art, natural history & ethnography; Russian-American; maritime; early industry.
Major Exhibits: Annette Bellamy Solo Exhibition, 2/5/10-3/27/10; Bill Brady Solo Exhibition, 2/5/10-3/27/10; Sue Kraft Solo Exhibition, 4/2/10-10/22/10.
Research Fields: Alaskan history, ethnology, fine art & natural history.
Facilities: library; conservation lab.
Activities: statewide assistance to museums in Alaska; statewide conservation services; grants-in-aid to Alaskan museums; purchase acquisitions program; statewide education services including hands-on loan program to Alaskan schools; general education programs; guided tours; temporary & permanent exhibits; statewide visual arts & traveling exhibits programs.
Publications: educational materials for schools; monographs, concepts; brochures; exhibits books; catalog; museum review.
Hours & Admission Prices: Winter: Tues.-Sat. 10-4; Summer: daily 8:30-5:30. Adults $3 (winter), $5 (summer); discounts to ICOM members; AAM members, children 18 and under & members no charge. Closed holidays. ♿
Attendance: 70,500 (accurate)
Membership: Student & Senior $20; Individual $40; Family $50; Sustaining $125; Corporate $500; Life $1,000.

HOUSE OF WICKERSHAM STATE HISTORICAL SITE, 213 Seventh St., Juneau, AK 99801-1117. Mailing Address: 400 Willoughby Ave., P.O. Box 111017, Juneau, AK 99801-1783. Tel.: 907-586-9001.
Web Site: www.dnr.state.ak.us/parks/units/wickrshm.htm
Founded: 1984.
Personnel Profile: Full-Time Volunteers 1; Part-Time Volunteers 4.
Governing Authority: state government.
Historic House: constructed in 1898 by Frank Hammond, a gold mine superintendent. The house was purchased in 1928 by James Wickersham, a judge & delegate to congress.
Collections: Alaskan memorabilia; native crafts from the Pacific Northwest.
Facilities: 1,000 sq. ft. exhibit space.
Hours & Admission Prices: May-Sept. Tues.-Sat. 10-4, call to confirm. Adults, senior citizens & students $2; children no charge. ♿
Attendance: 1,000 (estimated)

JUNEAU-DOUGLAS CITY MUSEUM, (M), 114 W. 4th St., Juneau, AK 99801-1758. Mailing Address: 155 S. Seward St., Juneau, AK 99801-1332. Tel.: 907-586-3572. Fax: 907-586-4512.
E-mail: jane_lindsey@ci.juneau.ak.us
Web Site: www.juneau.org/parkrec/museum
Founded: 1976.
Congressional District: 1
Key Personnel: Dir., Jane Lindsey; Cur. Collections & Exhibits, Addison E. Field.
Personnel Profile: Full-Time Paid 4; Part-Time Volunteers 35; Interns 2.
Governing Authority: municipal government; county government. Parent Institution: City and Borough of Juneau. Tax-exempt.
Local History & Culture Museum: housed in 1951 library building.
Collections: 1880-1944 gold mining tools & equipment; fine arts; Tlingit Indian culture; pioneer decorative art; pioneer lifeways; archives; photographs; postcards; city documents; mining ruins related to the history and culture of the Juneau-Douglas area.
Research Fields: local history; Auk & Taku Tlingit Indian history; mining history.
Facilities: 525-vol. local history research library & archives; 2,500 sq. ft. exhibit space. Gift items for sale.
Activities: guided tours; lectures; meeting space; organized education programs for children; participatory & temporary exhibits; college student internship placement. Annual Event: historic walking tours May to September.
Publications: quarterly newsletter; trail guide booklet, In the Miners' Footsteps; brochure, Downtown Juneau Walking Guide to historic sites, public art & totem poles.
Hours & Admission Prices: May-Sept. Mon.-Fri. 9-5, Sat.-Sun. 10-5; Oct.-April Tues.-Sat. 10-4; other times by appointment. Summer: adults $4; discounts to AAM, AASLH & Museum Alaska members; children 18 & under no charge. Winter: no charge. Closed Thanksgiving; Christmas. ♿
Attendance: 23,000 (accurate)
Membership: Annual Pass $15.

LAST CHANCE MINING MUSEUM, 1001 Basin Rd., Juneau, AK 99801-1038. Tel.: 907-586-5338.
Key Personnel: Dir., Gary Gillette
Historic Building: listed on the National Register of Historic Places.
Collections: air compressors; gold mining; mining equipment; electric locomotives & rail cars.
Hours & Admission Prices: mid-May to late Sept. daily 9:30-12:30 & 3:30-6:30; other times by appointment. Adults $4. Closed Independence Day.

Kenai

KENAI VISITORS & CULTURAL CENTER, 11471 Kenai Spur Hwy., Kenai, AK 99611-7757. Tel.: 907-283-1991. Fax: 907-283-2230.
E-mail: laura@visitkenai.com
Web Site: www.artskenai.com
Key Personnel: Dir. Prog. and Exhibs., Laura Forbes
History Museum.
Collections: Athabaskan, Aleut & Russian cultural artifacts; homesteading; mining; commercial fishing; oil industry.
Facilities: audiovisual room. Museum-related items for sale.
Activities: films.
Hours & Admission Prices: Mon.-Fri. 9-5, Sat. 11-4. No charge; donations accepted.

Ketchikan

DEER MOUNTAIN TRIBAL HATCHERY AND EAGLE CENTER, 1158 Salmon Rd., Ketchikan, AK 99901-6666. Tel.: 907-228-5278.
Nature Center.
Collections: salmon & their life cycle; eagles; natural, cultural & environmental artifacts; hatchery.
Activities: view Salmon swimming upstream; feed Salmon; Eagle observation area; raptor program.
Hours & Admission Prices: May-Sept. daily 8-4:30. Adults $9; children 12 & under no charge.

SOUTHEAST ALASKA DISCOVERY CENTER, USDA FOREST SERVICE, 50 Main St., Ketchikan, AK 99901-6559. Tel.: 907-228-6220. Fax: 907-228-6234.
History Museum.
Collections: totem poles; rainforest; native fish camp; Southeast Alaska's ecosystems; fishing; mining; timber; tourism.
Activities: audiovisual programs.
Hours & Admission Prices: May-Sept. daily 8-5; Oct.-April Tues.-Fri. 12-4:30, Sat. 10:30-4:30. Summer: $5; Winter: no charge.

TONGASS HISTORICAL MUSEUM, 629 Dock St., Ketchikan, AK 99901-6529. Tel.: 907-225-5600. Fax: 907-225-5602.
E-mail: museumdir@city.ketchikan.ak.us
Web Site: city.ketchikan.ak.us

Founded: 1961.
Congressional District: 1
Key Personnel: Dir., Michael Naab; Administrative Sec., Karla Sunderland; Sr. Cur. Programs, Christopher Hanson; Sr. Cur. Collections, Richard H. Van Cleave; Registrar, Erika Brown; Museum Attendant, Regina Foreman.
Personnel Profile: Full-Time Paid 8; Part-Time Volunteers 14.
Governing Authority: municipal. Parent Institution: City of Ketchikan. Tax-exempt.
General Museum.
Collections: history, art & industry of southern southeast Alaska; Indian artifacts; anthropology; ethnology; manuscripts; archaeology; objects & photos relating to the Tlingit, Haida & Tsimshian cultures; explorer, trader & pioneer history; mining, fishing, logging & marine history.
Research Fields: local area history; industry; fishing; mining; logging; marine; ethnography.
Facilities: reference library of history on Alaska; local history archives.
Activities: lectures; films; inter-museum loan; permanent, temporary & traveling exhibitions; changing exhibits on Alaskan photography, regional art, local history & Alaskan Native arts & crafts; school and special group tours; lecture series.
Publications: quarterly newsletter; descriptive brochures; historical pamphlets.
Hours & Admission Prices: mid-May to Sept. daily. 8-5; Oct. to mid-May Wed.-Fri. 1-5, Sat.-Sun. 1-4. Adults $2; Oct.-April no charge. Closed New Year's Day; Easter; Thanksgiving; Christmas. ♿
Attendance: 30,000 (estimated)

TOTEM HERITAGE CENTER, 601 Deermount, Ketchikan, AK 99901. Mailing Address: 629 Dock St., Ketchikan, AK 99901-6529. Tel.: 907-225-5900. Fax: 907-225-5901.
E-mail: museumdir@city.ketchikan.ak.us
Web Site: city.ketchikan.ak.us
Founded: 1976.
Congressional District: 1
Key Personnel: C.E.O., Michael Naab.
Personnel Profile: Full-Time Paid 8; Part-Time Paid 6.
Governing Authority: municipal. Parent Institution: City of Ketchikan. Tax-exempt.
Anthropology, Ethnology & History Museum; Indian Art Center.
Collections: Alaska Totems; contemporary N.W. Coast Indian art; photographs.
Research Fields: totem poles; Northwest Coast Indian art, culture & history.
Facilities: reference library.
Activities: Native Arts Studies program & certificate of merit in carving/design or textile arts; films, exhibits, guided tours, craft demonstrations, education collection. Lectures; workshops & demonstrations.
Publications: quarterly newsletter; catalogue of native arts classes.
Hours & Admission Prices: mid-May to Sept. daily 8-5; Oct. to mid-May Tues.-Fri. 1-5 & during classes. Adults $5. ♿
Attendance: 60,000 (accurate)

Kodiak

ALUTIIQ MUSEUM AND ARCHAEOLOGICAL REPOSITORY, (M), 215 Mission Rd., Ste. 101, Kodiak, AK 99615-7326. Tel.: 907-486-7004. Fax: 907-486-7048.
E-mail: receptionist@alutiiqmuseum.org
Web Site: www.alutiiqmuseum.org
Founded: 1995.
Congressional District: 1
Key Personnel: Chm. Bd., William Anderson; Vice Chm. Bd., Margaret Roberts; C.E.O., Sven Haakanson, Jr.; Sec., Donene Tweten; Deputy Dir., Amy Steffian; Cur., Patrick Saltonstall; Registrar, Marnie Leist; Businss Mgr., Carol Austerman; Museum Shop Mgr., Sarah Kennedy.
Personnel Profile: Full-Time Paid 6; Part-Time Paid 4; Part-Time Volunteers 20.
Governing Authority: nonprofit organization. Parent Institution: Alutiiq Heritage Foundation. Tax-exempt: 501(c)(3).
Archaeology Museum & Ethnographic.
Collections: archaeological artifacts pertaining to coastal Alaska, with emphasis on Kodiak Archipelago.
Research Fields: archaeological fieldwork; prehistoric & historic periods of Alaska; cultural history of Alutiiq region; Russian Far East.
Facilities: 800-vol. library; 1,600 sq. ft. exhibit space; lab & classrooms. Alaska native arts & crafts, publications and other museum-related items for sale.
Activities: guided tours; lectures; temporary & traveling exhibitions; broadcast programs; docent program; training programs for professional museum workers; school loan services. Annual Events: annual archaeological excavations & surveys.
Publications: quarterly newsletter, Alutiiq Museum Bulletin; occasional papers.
Hours & Admission Prices: Winter: Tues.-Fri. 9-5, Sat. 10:30-4:30; Summer: Mon.-Fri. 9-5, Sat. 10-5. Adults $5; members no charge. ♿
Attendance: 6,500 (estimated)
Membership: Student & Senior Citizen $10; Individual $25; Family $40; Sponsor $100; Benefactor $250; Corporate $5,000.

BARANOV MUSEUM, Erskine House, 101 Marine Way, Kodiak, AK 99615-6307. Mailing Address: Kodiak Historical Society, 101 Marine Way, Kodiak, AK 99615-6307. Tel.: 907-486-5920. Fax: 907-486-3166.
E-mail: baranov@ak.net
Web Site: www.baranovmuseum.org
Founded: 1954.
Congressional District: 1
Key Personnel: Dir., Katie O. Parker; Bd. Pres., Mary Monroe; Archivist, Alice Ryser; Cur. Collections, Ellen Lester.
Personnel Profile: Full-Time Paid 3; Part-Time Paid 4; Part-Time Volunteers 12.
Governing Authority: nonprofit. Parent Institution: Kodiak Historical Society. Tax-exempt: 990(A).
General Museum: housed in c.1800 fur warehouse & offices of Alexander Baranov, chief manager of Russian American Company; after 1867 used by the American Commercial Company; 1911-1948 the W.J. Erskine family home.
Collections: items from the Kodiak & Aleutian Islands; anthropology; archaeology; ethnology; folklore; geology; history; Eskimo artifacts; marine; mineralogy; natural history.
Research Fields: Kodiak & Aleutian Islands archives; World War II; 1912 volcano & 1964 earthquake; grass basket weaving; photographs.
Facilities: rare book library. Russian antiques & handcrafted items for sale.
Activities: guided tours; docent program; videos; school tours.
Publications: quarterly newsletter, The Baranov Quarterly.
Hours & Admission Prices: Summer: Mon.-Sat. 10-4, Sun. 12-4; Winter: Tues.-Sat. 10-3. Adults $3; discounts to AAM, ICOM & Museum Alaska members; members & children under 12 no charge. Closed national holidays. ♿
Attendance: 10,000 (estimated)
Membership: Senior 65 & over $15; Individual $20; Family $25; Supporter $50; Sponsor $100; Patron $250; Benefactor $1,000; Corporate $5,000 & up.

KODIAK MILITARY HISTORY MUSEUM, Fort Abercrombie State Historical Park, 1623 Mill Bay Rd., Kodiak, AK 99615. Mailing Address: 1417B Mill Bay Rd., Kodiak, AK 99615-7505. Tel.: 907-486-7015.
Web Site: www.kodiak.org/museum/museum.html
Key Personnel: Pres., Joe Stevens
Military Museum: housed in the WWII Ready Ammunition bunker at Miller Point; a buried concrete structure built in 1942.
Collections: uniforms; personal artifacts; photographs; artillery; communications equipment.
Facilities: Museum-related items for sale.
Hours & Admission Prices: May & Sept. Sat.-Sun. 1-4; June-Aug. Fri.-Mon. 1-4; other times by appointment. Adults $3; children under 12 no charge.

Metlakatla

DUNCAN COTTAGE MUSEUM, 501 Tait St., Metlakatla, AK 99926. Mailing Address: P.O. Box 8, Metlakatla, AK 99926-0008. Tel.: 907-886-8687. Fax: 907-886-4436.
Web Site: www.metlakatours.net
Founded: 1975.
Key Personnel: Dir. Tourism, Patricia A. Beal.
Personnel Profile: Full-Time Paid 1; Part-Time Paid 1; Part-Time Volunteers 3.
Governing Authority: municipal.
Historic House: 1891 seven room cottage that was home of Father Wm. Duncan, English missionary/teacher of the Tsimpshians of Metlakatla, AK.
Collections: period phonograph, furniture, ring-up wooden telephone; Tsimpshian Bentwood storage box with Tsimpshian designs; ceremonial drum; some 1st edition, technical, theological books; English & Canadian period bibles; magazines; 1800-1900 photographs; paintings; personal artifacts; period furnishings; turn of the century collections of music boxes; medical supplies; educational material; musical instruments.
Research Fields: Metlakatlas' historic origins; Tsimpshian pioneers, clans or crests.
Facilities: library of history books, music, autobiographies of great U.S., Great Britain & Canadian men and women of the past; classrooms. Museum-related items for sale.
Activities: guided tours; formally organized education programs; permanent exhibitions; walking tour.
Publications: Wm. Duncan fact sheet.

Hours & Admission Prices: Mon.-Fri. 8:30-12:30; other times by appointment. Adults $2. ♿
Attendance: 4,000 (estimated)

Nenana

ALFRED STARR NENANA CULTURAL CENTER, 415 Riverfront, Nenana, AK 99760. Mailing Address: P.O. Box 70, Nenana, AK 99760-0070. Tel.: 907-832-5527. Fax: 907-832-5532.
E-mail: nenana1@nenana.net
Web Site: www.nenana.org
Founded: 1997.
Key Personnel: Dir., Alex Ketzler; Asst. Dir., Pamela Coghill
Cultural Center.
Collections: history & culture of Nenana Yukon 800 riverboat racing; dog mushing; beadwork.
Facilities: Museum-related items for sale.
Hours & Admission Prices: Summer: daily 10-6; Winter: by appointment. No charge; donation accepted. ♿

Nome

CARRIE M. MCLAIN MEMORIAL MUSEUM, (M), 223 Front St., Nome, AK 99762. Mailing Address: P.O. Box 53, Nome, AK 99762-0053. Tel.: 907-443-6630. Fax: 907-443-7955.
Web Site: www.nomealaska.org
Key Personnel: Dir., Laura Samuelson
History Museum.
Collections: Eskimo culture & life; Gold Rush; photographs; aviation; Nome history & culture.
Hours & Admission Prices: June-Sept. daily 9:30-5:30; Oct.-May Tues.-Sat. 12-5:30. No charge.

Palmer

COLONY HOUSE MUSEUM - PALMER HISTORICAL SOCIETY, 316 E. Elmwood Ave., Palmer, AK 99645-6621. Mailing Address: P.O. Box 1935, Palmer, AK 99645-1935. Tel.: 907-745-1935.
E-mail: info@palmerhistoricalsociety.org
Web Site: www.palmerhistoricalsociety.org
Historic House Museum: housed in an original Colony Farm House built for the New Deal resettlement in 1935.
Collections: Colony project history; early colonists; period furnishings.
Activities: group tours.
Hours & Admission Prices: Summer: Tues.- Sat. 10-4; Winter: by appointment only.

MUSK OX FARM & MUSEUM, Mile 50 Glenn Hwy., Palmer, AK 99645. Mailing Address: P.O. Box 587, Palmer, AK 99645-0587. Tel.: 907-745-4151. Fax: 907-746-4831.
Farm History Museum.
Collections: musk ox; cows; bulls; calves; farm history.
Facilities: Museum-related items for sale.
Activities: group tours.
Hours & Admission Prices: May & Aug.-Sept. daily 10-6; June-July daily 9-7 other times by appointment. Adults 13-64 $8, seniors 65 & over $7, children 5-12 $6; children 4 & under no charge.

PALMER MUSEUM OF HISTORY AND ART, (M), 723 S. Valley Way, Palmer, AK 99645-6601. Tel.: 907-746-7668.
Web Site: www.palmermuseum.org
Founded: 2005.
Key Personnel: Dir., DeLena Johnson.
Personnel Profile: Full-Time Paid 1; Part-Time Paid 7; Part-Time Volunteers 2.
Governing Authority: nonprofit organization. Tax-exempt: 501(c)(3).
History & Art Museum.
Collections: Greater Palmer regions art & history; Alaska Natives; mining; farming.
Hours & Admission Prices: May-Sept. daily 9-6; Oct.-April Tues.-Fri. 9-1:30. No charge; donations accepted. ♿
Attendance: 35,000 (accurate)
Membership: Senior $10; Individual $15; Family $25; Organization $75; Business $100; Lifetime $200.

Petersburg

CLAUSEN MEMORIAL MUSEUM, (M), 203 Fram St., Petersburg, AK 99833. Mailing Address: P.O. Box 708, Petersburg, AK 99833-0708. Tel.: 907-772-3598. Fax: 907-772-2698.
E-mail: clausenmuseum@aptalaska.net
Web Site: www.clausenmuseum.org
Founded: 1965.
Key Personnel: C.E.O. & Museum Shop Mgr., Sue McCallum; Pres., Beverly Siercks.
Personnel Profile: Full-Time Paid 1; Part-Time Paid 2; Part-Time Volunteers 17.
Governing Authority: bd. of trustees. Tax-exempt.
History Museum.
Collections: reflect the diversity of peoples who have lived in the area, including Tlingit, European & Asian peoples: collections include Tlinget canoe & tools; Cape Decision lightstation lens; Fisk sculpture & fountain; cannery & fishing artifacts.
Activities: winter programs for community & school; temporary exhibits; oral history program; occasional summer programs.
Publications: newsletter; brochure; From Fish Camps to Cold Storages, a brief history of the Petersburg area to 1927; Streets to the Past.
Hours & Admission Prices: Call for hours & special events. Adults $3; Alaska members & members no charge. Closed New Year's Day; Christmas. ♿
Attendance: 5,300 (accurate)
Membership: Senior $10; Basic Individual $25; Basic Family $40; Supporter $100; Contributer $250; Sponsor $500; Lifetime $1,000.

Seward

ALASKA SEALIFE CENTER, 301 Railway Ave., Seward, AK 99664. Mailing Address: P.O. Box 1329, Seward, AK 99664-1329. Tel.: 907-224-6300; 800-224-2525. Fax: 907-224-6320.
Founded: 1998.
Key Personnel: Interim Dir., Ned Smith
Marine Wildlife Center.
Collections: marine wildlife.
Hours & Admission Prices: Summer: Mon.-Thurs. 9-6:30, Fri.-Sun. 8-6:30; Winter: daily 10-5. Adults $20, studlent 12-17 $15, children 4-11 $10; children 3 & under no charge. Closed Thanksgiving; Christmas.

CHUGACH MUSEUM AND INSTITUTE OF HISTORY AND ART, Orca Bldg., 3rd & Washington St., Seward, AK 99503. Mailing Address: 3800 Centerpoint Dr., Ste. 601, Anchorage, AK 99503-5826. Tel.: 907-563-8866, ext. 4151. Fax: 907-563-8402.
E-mail: chugachmuseum@chugach-ak.com
Web Site: www.chugachmuseum.org
Key Personnel: Exec. Dir., Lora Johnson, P.h.D
Culturally Specific.
Collections: history & culture of the Chugach region natives; artwork.
Hours & Admission Prices: By appointment.

QUTEKCAK CULTURE CENTER, 221 Third Ave., Seward, AK 99664. Mailing Address: P.O. Box 1467, Seward, AK 99664-1467. Tel.: 907-224-3118.
Native Heritage Museum.
Collections: Alaska Native culture, arts, & artifacts; paintings; sculpture; personal artifacts.
Facilities: Museum-related items for sale.
Hours & Admission Prices: Call for hours.

SEWARD MUSEUM, 336 3rd Ave., Seward, AK 99664. Mailing Address: P.O. Box 55, Seward, AK 99664-0055. Tel.: 907-224-3902.
Formerly: Resurrection Bay Historical Society Museum
Founded: 1967.
Key Personnel: Dir. & Pres. (V), Lee E. Poleske.
Personnel Profile: Part-Time Paid 1; Part-Time Volunteers 4.
Governing Authority: society; nonprofit organization. Parent Institution: Resurrection Bay Historical Society. Tax-exempt.
Historical Society Museum.
Collections: photographs & artifacts of Seward & Alaska.
Research Fields: local history.
Activities: guided tours; slide tape show on Seward's history.
Hours & Admission Prices: Daily 10-5. Adults $3, children $.50; members no charge. ♿
Attendance: 5,183 (accurate)
Membership: Annual $10; Family $15; Sustaining $25; Benefactor $50; Patron $100.

Sitka

ALASKA RAPTOR CENTER, 1000 Raptor Way, Sitka, AK 99835-9302. Tel.: 800-643-9425.
E-mail: operations.alaskaraptor@alaska.com
Web Site: www.alaskaraptor.org
Key Personnel: Exec. Dir., Debbie Reeder; Avian Cur., Forrest Wentzel

Environmental Conservation Center.
Collections: bald eagles; wild birds.
Facilities: Museum-related items for sale.
Activities: educational programs.
Publications: newsletter.
Hours & Admission Prices: May-Sept. Sun.-Fri. 8-4. Adults $12, children 12 & under $6.
Membership: Individual $45; Family $60.

ISABEL MILLER MUSEUM/SITKA HISTORICAL SOCIETY, (M), 330 Harbor Dr., Sitka, AK 99835-7553. Tel.: 907-747-6455. Fax: 907-747-6588.
Web Site: sitkahistory.org
Founded: 1957.
Congressional District: 3
Key Personnel: Dir., Robert Medinger; Admin., Karen Meizner.
Personnel Profile: Full-Time Volunteers 2; Part-Time Paid 5; Part-Time Volunteers 50.
Governing Authority: nonprofit organization. Parent Institution: Sitka Historical Society. Tax-exempt: 501(c)(3).
General History Museum.
Collections: local artifacts, paintings, manuscripts, documents, photographs & scrapbooks from the pre-Russian period to the present.
Research Fields: historic buildings and locations in the area.
Facilities: 4005-vol. library of books on Alaskan history, including translations in Russian available for research on premises by appointment.
Activities: permanent exhibitions; lectures; tours; newsletter; web exhibitions.
Publications: newsletter; books, Lady Franklin Visits Sitka Alaska, 1870; Streets of Sitka; The Wreck of the Neva; A Sitka Chronology, 1867-1985; From Sitka's Past.
Hours & Admission Prices: May 7-Sept. 22 daily 8-5; Oct.-April Tues.-Sat. 10-4. Summer $1; Winter no charge. ♿
Attendance: 67,415 (accurate)
Membership: Student, Senior Citizen & Non-Resident Associate $20; Individual $35; Family $40; Patron $75; Business & Contributing $100; Sustaining $200; Benefactor $1,000; Life Benefactor $5,000.

RUSSIAN BISHOP'S HOUSE, 201 College Dr., Sitka, AK 99835. Mailing Address: Sitka National Historic Park, 103 Monastary St., Sitka, AK 99835-7617. Tel.: 907-747-6281.
Historic House: the former residence of the Bishop of the Russian Orthodox Church; built in 1842. A National Historic Landmark.
Collections: period furnishings & artifacts.
Hours & Admission Prices: Summer: daily; Winter: by appointment.

SHELDON JACKSON MUSEUM, (M), 104 College Dr., Sitka, AK 99835-7657. Tel.: 907-747-8981. Fax: 907-747-3004.
E-mail: scott.mcadams@alaska.gov
Web Site: www.museums.state.ak.us
Founded: 1887.
Key Personnel: Acting Chief Cur., Glenn Cook; Cur. Collections, Rosemary Carlton; Div. Dir., Linda Thibodeau; Museum Protection & Visitor Svcs. Supvr., Scott McAdams.
Personnel Profile: Full-Time Paid 3; Part-Time Paid 5; Part-Time Volunteers 20.
Governing Authority: state. Parent Institution: State of Alaska. Subsidiary Institution: Div. of Libraries, Archives & Museums. Tax-exempt: 501(c)(3).
Anthropology Museum: housed in the first concrete building built in the territory of Alaska; built in 1895.
Collections: Haida argillite carvings; Eskimo implements, ivory carvings, masks, skin clothing, baskets, kayaks, umiak; Athabaskan birchbark canoes, implements; Tlingit totem poles, shaman charms, baskets, ceremonial equipment & garments.
Research Fields: Tlingit & western Eskimo ethnography & acculturation.
Facilities: Alaskan native arts, crafts, museum-related publications, postcards & lithographs for sale.
Activities: lectures; education programs for undergraduate college students & students K-12; inter-museum loan, permanent & temporary exhibitions; native artist demonstrations.
Publications: booklet, Sheldon Jackson, The Collector; Faces, Voices, & Dreams - Centennial of SJM 1888-1988.
Hours & Admission Prices: mid-May to mid-Sept. daily 9-5; mid-Sept. to mid-May Tues.-Sat. 10-4. Summer: adults $4; Winter: adults $3; AAM members, members with annual pass, children 18 & under no charge. Closed holidays. ♿
Attendance: 28,547 (accurate)
Membership: Student $10; Individual $25; Family $35; Sustaining $60; Contributing $250; Corporate $500.

SITKA NATIONAL HISTORICAL PARK, 106 Metlakatla St., Sitka, AK 99835-7665. Mailing Address: 103 Monastery St., Sitka, AK 99835-7617. Tel.: 907-747-0110. Fax: 907-747-5938.
Web Site: www.nps.gov/sitk
Founded: 1910.
Key Personnel: Supt., Mary Miller; Cur., Sue Thorsen.
Governing Authority: federal. Parent Institution: National Park Service, Dept. of Interior. Tax-exempt: 170(b)(1)(A).
Park Museum & Visitor Center: located near site of 1804 Battle of Sitka, fought between the Tlingit Indians & the Russians.
Collections: spruce root baskets; totem poles; Indian & Russian artifacts; 19th-century period furniture. Historic House: 1842 Russian Bishop's house.
Research Fields: Indian culture; Russian colonization; North Pacific fur trade.
Facilities: 1,000-vol. library on Alaska history available on premises; 50-seat auditorium; 1-mile totem walk.
Activities: self-guided tours; lectures; special programs; classes & demonstrations of traditional Indian arts & crafts.
Publications: continuous folder, Sitka National Historical Park & the Russian Bishop's House Project.
Hours & Admission Prices: Mon.-Sat. 8-5. Summer: $15. Winter: no charge; donations accepted. Closed New Year's Day; Thanksgiving; Christmas. ♿

SOUTHEAST ALASKA INDIAN CULTURAL CENTER, 106 Metlakatla St., Ste. C, Sitka, AK 99835-7665. Tel.: 907-747-8061. Fax: 907-747-8189.
E-mail: seaicc@gci.net
Founded: 1969.
Congressional District: 1
Key Personnel: Mgr., Nancy Douglas; Pres. (V), Kathy Miller.
Personnel Profile: Full-Time Paid 1; Part-Time Paid 5; Interns 1.
Governing Authority: Tax-exempt: 501(c)(3).
Native American Cultural Center.
Collections: Tlingit, Haida, Tsimshean traditional cultural art forms created by contemporary artists.
Research Fields: Tlingit; Haida; Tsimshean.
Activities: demonstrations; classes.
Publications: Celebration of Weavers.
Hours & Admission Prices: May-Sept. daily 8-5; Oct.-April Mon.-Fri. 8-5. No charge; donations accepted. Closed winter holidays. ♿
Attendance: 130,000 (estimated)
Membership: Individual $20; Family $50.

Skagway

CORRINGTON'S MUSEUM OF ALASKAN HISTORY, Broadway & 5th, Skagway, AK 99840. Tel.: 907-983-2579.
Founded: 1976.
Personnel Profile: Full-Time Paid 1; Full-Time Volunteers 1; Part-Time Volunteers 2.
History Museum.
Collections: Alaskan history & culture; personal artifacts; scrimshaw history.
Facilities: Museum-related items for sale.
Hours & Admission Prices: Call for hours. No charge.

KLONDIKE GOLD RUSH NATIONAL HISTORICAL PARK, (M), Second & Broadway, Skagway, AK 99840. Mailing Address: P.O. Box 517, Skagway, AK 99840-0517. Tel.: 907-983-2921 & 9222. Fax: 907-983-9249. TDD: 907-983-2921.
E-mail: Debra_Sanders@nps.gov
Web Site: www.nps.gov/klgo
Founded: 1976.
Key Personnel: Rgnl. Dir., Sue Masic; Park Supt., Susan L. Boudreau; Cur., Debra Sanders.
Personnel Profile: Full-Time Paid 2; Part-Time Paid 1; Part-Time Volunteers 1.
Governing Authority: federal. Parent Institution: Dept. of the Interior. National Park Service, Alaska Regional Office, 240 W. 5th Ave., Anchorage, AK 99501. Tel. 907-644-3480. Tax-exempt.
Park Museum: housed in c.1898 White Pass & Yukon Route Railroad Depot.
Collections: over 200,000 historic archaeology artifacts associated with the Klondike gold rush; over 3,000 copies of historic photographs of the gold rush period; about 1,000 pressed plant specimens; the George & Edna Rapuzzi collection of over 10,000 Klondike Gold Rush & early Skagway artifacts; over 3,000 dried lichen specimens.
Major Exhibits: The George & Edna Rapuzzi Collection, 5/10-9/10.
Research Fields: Klondike gold rush.
Facilities: 900-vol. library of books on Klondike gold rush & Alaskana available for research & study on premises; reading room; 100-seat auditorium.
Activities: guided tours; lectures; films; permanent exhibitions.
Publications: park brochures; archaeological reports; historic structures reports; ethnographic overview and assessment.

Hours & Admission Prices: May-Sept. daily 8-7. Moore House Tour: donations accepted. ♿
Attendance: 800,000 (estimated)

SKAGWAY MUSEUM & ARCHIVES, 700 Spring St., Skagway, AK 99840. Mailing Address: P.O. Box 521, Skagway, AK 99840-0521. Tel.: 907-983-2420. Fax: 907-983-3420.
E-mail: info@skagwaymuseum.org
Web Site: www.skagwaymuseum.org
Founded: 1961.
Congressional District: 4
Key Personnel: Dir., Judith Munns.
Personnel Profile: Full-Time Paid 1; Part-Time Paid 4.
Governing Authority: nonprofit organization. Parent Institution: City of Skagway, AK. Tax-exempt.
History Museum: housed in 1899 McCabe College, built by Methodist Church.
Collections: Alaska pioneer life; Klondike gold rush artifacts & tools; Tlingit artifacts; railroad & transportation history.
Research Fields: gold rush; local history.
Facilities: 812-vol. library.
Activities: permanent & temporary exhibitions.
Publications: brochures; newspapers.
Hours & Admission Prices: May-Sept. Mon.-Fri. 9-5, Sat.-Sun. 1-5; Oct.-April call for hours. Adults $2, students $1; children 12 & under no charge. ♿
Attendance: 38,000 (estimated)

Soldotna

SOLDOTNA HISTORICAL SOCIETY AND MUSEUM, Centennial Park Rd., Soldotna, AK 99669. Mailing Address: P.O. Box 1986, Soldotna, AK 99669-1986. Tel.: 907-262-3832.
Key Personnel: Pres., Margaret Mullen
History Museum: housed in a homesteaders' village.
Collections: local history & culture; wildlife displays.
Activities: lectures.
Hours & Admission Prices: May 15-Sept. 15 Tues.-Sat. 10-4, Sun. 12-4. No charge; donations accepted.

Talkeetna

MUSEUM OF NORTHERN ADVENTURE, Main St., Talkeetna, AK 99676. Tel.: 907-733-3999.
History Museum.
Collections: Alaska history & culture; native masks, totems, baskets, & ivory jewelry; wax figures.
Hours & Admission Prices: Call for hours.

TALKEETNA HISTORICAL SOCIETY AND MUSEUM, First Alley & Village Airstrip, Talkeetna, AK 99676. Mailing Address: P.O. Box 76, Talkeetna, AK 99676-0076. Tel.: 907-733-2487. Fax: 907-733-2484.
E-mail: museum@talkeetnahistoricalsociety.org
Web Site: www.talkeetnahistoricalsociety.org/museum.php
Founded: 1972.
Key Personnel: Pres. (V), John Saily; Cur. & Museum Shop Mgr., Rebecca Nelson; Museum Shop Mgr., Michael Kelly.
Personnel Profile: Part-Time Paid 3; Part-Time Volunteers 2.
Governing Authority: society; nonprofit organization. Tax-exempt.
General Museum: housed in the first school house in Talkeetna. Museum Buildings: The Ole Dahl Cabin; The Three German Bachelor's Cabin & Visitors Information; The Harry Robb Cabin; The Little Red Schoolhouse, Old Railroad Section House & Old Railroad Depot.
Collections: old trading post materials; old tools; mining & trapping equipment; papers & photographs; Alaskan art; Don Sheldon-Ray Genet Memorial display; 144 sq. ft. scale model of Denali with photos by Bradford Washburn; Summit Room, view from the Summit of Denali, two mannequins (climber in modern day gear & clothing compared to Walter Harper, who climbed Denali 1913) standing on the Summit; trapper cabin display; A.R.R. section house & depot.
Research Fields: oral history projects; humanities research & projects; state and local history.
Facilities: library of local history books, documents, photos, scrapbooks & newspapers available for use by requesting xerox copies; reading room. Books & museum-related items for sale.
Activities: films; arts festivals; loan, permanent & traveling exhibitions; tours; special exhibits; in school educational program. Museum Sponsors: Moose Dropping Festival in July; walking history tour of historic sites & buildings in Talkeetna.
Publications: newsletter; brochure; map.
Hours & Admission Prices: Summer: daily 10-6; Winter: by appointment only. Adults $3; members & children under 12 no charge. ♿
Attendance: 15,000 (accurate)
Membership: Senior & Student $10; Standard $25; Contributing $50; Supporting $100.

Trapper Creek

TRAPPER CREEK MUSEUM, Mile 6 W. of Parks Hwy. on Petersville Rd., Trapper Creek, AK 99683. Mailing Address: P.O. Box 13011, Trapper Creek, AK 99683-0011. Tel.: 907-733-2557.
E-mail: trappercreekmuseum@yahoo.com
Web Site: www.trappercreekmuseum.com
Key Personnel: Dir., Kenneth Marsh
History Museum: housed in a log cabin built by the Donaldson family, members of the Michigan 59'ers.
Collections: Alaska's early pioneers including gold miners, fur trappers & homesteaders; personal artifacts; glass bottles; photographs.
Facilities: Museum-related items for sale.
Hours & Admission Prices: Summer: daily 10-4. No charge; donations accepted.

Unalaska

MUSEUM OF THE ALEUTIANS, (M), 314 Salmon Way, Unalaska, AK 99685. Mailing Address: P.O. Box 648, Unalaska, AK 99685-0648. Tel.: 907-581-5150. Fax: 907-581-6682.
E-mail: aleutians@arctic.net
Web Site: www.aleutians.org
Founded: 1997.
Key Personnel: C.E.O. & Dir., Zoya Johnson; Chm. (V), Sharon Svarny-Livingston.
Personnel Profile: Full-Time Paid 4.
Governing Authority: private; nonprofit organization. Tax-exempt.
General Museum.
Collections: archaeological; ethnological; archives; historical items.
Research Fields: archaeology; anthropology.
Facilities: laboratory.
Activities: college credit courses; fundraisers; membership drive & auction; lectures; presentations. Museum Sponsors: Archaeological Field Season - summer dig.
Publications: newsletter, Legacy; store catalog.
Hours & Admission Prices: June-Sept. Tues.-Sat. 9-5, Sun. 11-5; Oct.-May Tues.-Sat. 11-5. Adults $5; discounts to Museum Alaska members; members no charge. Closed New Year's Day; Memorial Day; Independence Day; Thanksgiving; Christmas. ♿
Attendance: 4,036 (accurate)
Membership: Student $5; Individual $25; Family $75; Patron $250; Benefactor $500; Life & Corporate $1,000; Sponsor $5,000.

Valdez

MAXINE & JESSE WHITNEY MUSEUM, (M), 303 Lowe St., Valdez, AK 99686. Tel.: 907-834-1600.
History Museum.
Collections: Native Alaskan art & artifacts; natural history; wildlife mounts; dolls; masks; books; videos; photographs.
Hours & Admission Prices: Summer: daily 9-7; Winter: by appointment. Adults $5, senior citizens & military $4, children under 12 $3.

THE VALDEZ MUSEUM & HISTORICAL ARCHIVE ASSOCIATION, INC., (M), 217 Egan Ave., Valdez, AK 99686-0008. Mailing Address: P.O. Box 8, Valdez, AK 99686-0008. Tel.: 907-835-2764 & 5407. Fax: 907-835-5800.
E-mail: info@valdezmuseum.org
Web Site: www.valdezmuseum.org
Founded: 1976.
Key Personnel: Pres. Bd. Dir., Thomas McAlister; Exec. Dir., Kathryn Hurtley; Cur. Collection & Exhibits, Andrew Goldstein; Public Programs, Administrative Svcs. Mgr., & Store Mgr., Rich Dunkin; Cur. Education, Steve Richardson; Attendant, Tim Harned; Attendant, Doreen Hodges.
Personnel Profile: Full-Time Paid 3; Part-Time Paid 5; Part-Time Volunteers 35; Interns 1.
Governing Authority: Tax-exempt: 501(c)(3).
Local History Museum.
Collections: gold & copper mining artifacts; lighthouse lens; historical artifacts of Valdez & area; aviation & transportation artifacts; firefighting apparatus; 1902 handpumper; 1921 Model T Ford Chemical fire truck; 1907 Ahrens Steam Fire Engine; Pinzon Bar; glaciation; 1964 earthquake photos & information; 1989 Exxon Valdez oil spill.
Major Exhibits: Student Art Show, 1/15/10-2/27/10; Joe Prax - Solo Photo Show, 3/5/10-5/1/10; Celebrating Valdez Artists, 5/7/10-9/11/10; Jean Rene Saunder - Solo Painting Show, 9/16/10-10/30/10; Wildlife by Bob Benda, 11/5/10-1/15/11.

Research Fields: local history.
Facilities: local & regional history archives.
Activities: self-guided tours; permanent & temporary exhibits; local activities.
Publications: quarterly newsletter.
Hours & Admission Prices: Winter: Mon.-Sat. 1-5; Summer: daily 9-5. Adults $6, senior citizens 60 & over $5.50, youth 14-17 $5; discounts to groups; members & children under 13 no charge. Closed New Year's Day; Thanksgiving; Christmas. ♿
Attendance: 20,000 (accurate)
Membership: Fellow $20; Supporter $30; Friend $50; Partner $100; Patron & Business $250; Benefactor $500.

Wasilla

DOROTHY G. PAGE MUSEUM, (M), 323 Main St., Wasilla, AK 99654-7021. Tel.: 907-373-9071. Fax: 907-373-9072.
E-mail: museum@ci.wasilla.ak.us
Web Site: www.cityofwasilla.com/museum
Founded: 1967.
Key Personnel: Cur., Bethany Buckingham; Museum Aide, Margaret Rogers.
Personnel Profile: Full-Time Paid 1; Part-Time Paid 2.
Governing Authority: society; nonprofit organization. Parent Institution: City of Wasilla. Subsidiary Institution: Dorothy G. Page Museum & Visitors Center. Tax-exempt: 501(c)(3).
City of Wasilla Museum: housed in 1931 log Wasilla Community Hall.
Collections: photos, tools, household items & equipment used in the Willow Creek Mining area; historic buildings; Iditarod Trail race history.
Major Exhibits: Iditarod Art Exhibit, 2/26/10-3/26/10; Snoopy as the WWI Flying Ace (T), 7/3/10-8/14/10; 12 x 12 Days of Christmas, 12/5/10-12/24/10.
Research Fields: early settlements of Knik & Wasilla; the Willow Creek Mining area; Iditarod Trail history; Dog Mushing history.
Facilities: historical park.
Activities: guided tours; formally organized education programs for children.
Publications: newsletter.
Hours & Admission Prices: April-Sept. Mon.-Sat. 9-5; Oct.-March Wed.-Fri. 9-5. Adults $3, senior citizens 60 & over $2.50, military $2; discounts to AAM & ICOM members; Historical Society & Museum Alaska members and children 12 & under no charge. Closed New Year's Day; Memorial Day; Independence Day; Labor Day; Thanksgiving; Christmas. ♿
Attendance: 4,702 (accurate)

IDITAROD TRAIL SLED DOG RACE MUSEUM, Mile 2.2 Knik Goose Bay Rd., Wasilla, AK 99654. Mailing Address: P.O. Box 870800, Wasilla, AK 99687-0800. Tel.: 907-376-5155, ext. 108. Fax: 907-373-6998.
Dog Race Museum.
Collections: Iditarod Trail history; photographs; trophies.
Facilities: Museum-related items for sale.
Activities: videos; dog sled rides.
Hours & Admission Prices: mid-May to mid-Sept. daily 8-7; Winter: Mon.-Fri. 8-5.

KNIK MUSEUM, Mile 13.9 Knik Rd., Wasilla, AK 99654. Mailing Address: 300 N. Boundary St., Wasilla, AK 99654-7128. Tel.: 907-376-2005. Fax: 907-373-9072.
E-mail: wasillaknikhistoricalsociety@yahoo.com
Web Site: www.geocities.com/wasillaknikhistoricalsociety/index.html
Key Personnel: Dir., LeRoi Heaven.
Governing Authority: Parent Institution: Wasilla-Knik Historical Society.
History Museum.
Collections: Knik's history & culture; clothing; furniture; period artifacts; Sled Dog Musher's Hall of Fame.
Hours & Admission Prices: June-Sept. 15 Thurs.-Sun. 1-6. Adults $5; members no charge.

MUSEUM OF ALASKA TRANSPORTATION & INDUSTRY, INC., 3800 W. Museum Dr., Wasilla, AK 99654. Mailing Address: P.O. Box 870646, Wasilla, AK 99687-0646. Tel.: 907-376-1211. Fax: 907-376-3082.
Web Site: www.museumofalaska.org/
Founded: 1976.
Key Personnel: Chm. (V), Phil Lockwood.
Personnel Profile: Full-Time Paid 2; Part-Time Paid 2; Part-Time Volunteers 100.
Governing Authority: bd. of trustees; nonprofit organization. Tax-exempt: 501(c)(3).
Alaskan Industrial History & Transportation Museum.
Collections: transportation used in Alaska's history: aircraft; cars; trucks; tractors; railroad rolling stock; fire trucks; boats; snow mobiles; dog sleds; tools & heavy construction equipment also photographs & related materials; railroad memorabilia.
Research Fields: Alaska transportation & Industrial history.
Facilities: 20-acres exhibit area; train yard.
Activities: guided tours; lectures; permanent exhibitions; special events.
Publications: brochures; newsletters.
Hours & Admission Prices: May-Sept. daily 10-5. Adults $8, seniors over 65 & children 3-17 $5; children under 3 & members no charge. ♿
Attendance: 12,000 (estimated)
Membership: Individual $25; Family $35; Sourdough $100; Pioneer $250; Grubstaker $500; Esteemed & Life $1,000; Life Family $1,500.

TRAPPERS FUR INDUSTRY MUSEUM, 5401 E. Mayflower Lane, Wasilla, AK 99654-7817. Tel.: 907-376-5873.
History Museum.
Collections: North American trapping industry & history; paintings; posters; period traps.
Facilities: Museum-related items for sale.
Hours & Admission Prices: Summer: daily 9-6.

Wrangell

NOLAN CENTER MUSEUM, 296 Campbell Dr., Wrangell, AK 99929. Mailing Address: P.O. Box 1050, Wrangell, AK 99929-1050. Tel.: 907-874-3770.
E-mail: museum@wrangell.com
Web Site: www.wrangellalaska.org/museum/index.html
Key Personnel: Dir. & Cur., Dennis Chapman
Natural History Museum.
Collections: Wrangell history; natural history; logging; fishing; Native culture.
Hours & Admission Prices: May-Sept. Mon.-Sat. 10-5; Oct.-April Tues.-Sat. 1-5. Adults $5, seniors $3, children 6-12 $2.

WRANGELL MUSEUM, (M), 296 Campbell Dr., Wrangell, AK 99929. Mailing Address: P.O. Box 1050, Wrangell, AK 99929-1050. Tel.: 907-874-3770. Fax: 907-874-3785.
E-mail: museum@wrangell.com
Web Site: www.wrangell.com
Founded: 1967.
Key Personnel: Dir. & Cur., Dennis Chapman.
Personnel Profile: Full-Time Paid 1; Part-Time Paid 3; Part-Time Volunteers 3.
Governing Authority: city. Tax-exempt.
General Museum.
Collections: Southeast Alaska's native cultures; Wrangell history including flying under Russian, English (Hudson Bay) & American flags; wildlife; garnet ledge; Tlingit/Haida, Gold Rush exploration; early fishing (canneries); fur farming; natural history.
Research Fields: reflects Tlingit, Haida & Russian-American culture; Hudson's Bay; European, Asian & Pacific Islander's impact on area pre- and post-contact; cultural history of Wrangell; geologic, geographic & ethnographic history; Gold Rushes; mining; Sitkine River; fur trade; commercial & industrial history.
Facilities: 2,000 sq. ft. exhibit space; video & viewing area. Museum-related items for sale.
Activities: evening & weekend special events. Museum Sponsors: lecture series January to March.
Publications: Garnet Ledge Brochure; Chief Shakes Island; History of Wrangell.
Hours & Admission Prices: May-Sept. Mon.-Sat. 10-5; Oct.-April Tues.-Fri. 10-4. Family $12, adults $5, seniors 60 & up $3, children 6-12 $2; discounts to groups; Friends of Museum no charge. Closed New Year's Day; Easter; Memorial Day; Independence Day; Labor Day; Thanksgiving; Christmas. ♿
Attendance: 8,237 (accurate)
Membership: Student $5; Individual $10; Family $25.

ARIZONA

(193 listings)

Ajo

ORGAN PIPE CACTUS NATIONAL MONUMENT MUSEUM, 10 Organ Pipe Dr., Ajo, AZ 85321-9626. Tel.: 520-387-6849. Fax: 520-387-7144.
E-mail: orpi_information@nps.gov
Web Site: www.nps.gov/orpi
Founded: 1937.
Congressional District: 2
Key Personnel: C.E.O. & Supt., Kathy Billings.
Governing Authority: federal. Dept. of the Interior, National Park Service. Tax-exempt.
National Monument.

Collections: natural & cultural history specimens; photographs.
Facilities: interpretive-related items for sale.
Activities: interpretive programs including walks, talks; evening amphitheater. Museum Sponsors: programs January to March.
Publications: guide & map.
Hours & Admission Prices: Daily 8-5. Weekly vehicle admission $8; holders of Golden Eagle, Golden Age, Golden Access Passports & children 16 under with adult no charge. Closed holidays April-Dec.
Attendance: 32,000 (estimated)

Apache Junction

SUPERSTITION MOUNTAIN LOST DUTCHMAN MUSEUM, 4087 N. Apache Trail, Apache Junction, AZ 85219-8409. Mailing Address: P.O. Box 3845, Apache Junction, AZ 85217-3845. Tel.: 480-983-4888. Fax: 480-288-6524.
E-mail: smhsgold@aol.com
Web Site: www.superstitionmountainmuseum.org
Founded: 1980.
Congressional District: 6
Key Personnel: Chm. (V), David Carlson; Pres. (V), Rene Lesieutre; Exec. Dir. & Museum Shop Mgr., Kathy Johnson.
Personnel Profile: Full-Time Paid 2; Part-Time Volunteers 20.
Governing Authority: Parent Institution: Superstition Mountain Historical Society. Tax-exempt: 501(c)(3).
History Museum.
Collections: history of Superstition Mountain, Apache Junction & the surrounding region; period artifacts; minerals; mining ore cars; mining equipment; train engines.
Facilities: Elvis Memorial Chapel; The Barn.
Publications: quarterly newsletter, Museum Messenger; annual journal, Superstition Mountain Journal.
Hours & Admission Prices: Daily 9-4. Adults $4, seniors 55 & over $3, students 6-17 $2; discounts to groups; children 5 & under no charge. Closed Thanksgiving; Christmas. ♿
Attendance: 25,000 (estimated)
Membership: Prospector $25; Gold Panner $45; Lifetime $500; Family Lifetime $1,000.

Benson

KARTCHNER CAVERNS & DISCOVERY CENTER, 2980 S. Hwy. 90, Benson, AZ 85602. Mailing Address: P.O. Box 1849, Benson, AZ 85602-1849. Tel.: 520-586-4100.
Natural History Museum.
Collections: local history & culture; natural history; photographs; geology; replica of the cave.
Facilities: amphitheater; nature trails; garden. Museum-related items for sale.
Activities: hiking; picnic area.
Hours & Admission Prices: Daily 7:30-6. Closed Christmas Eve & Day.

Bisbee

BISBEE MINING & HISTORICAL MUSEUM, (M), No. 5 Copper Queen Plaza, Bisbee, AZ 85603. Mailing Address: P.O. Box 14, Bisbee, AZ 85603-0014. Tel.: 520-432-7071 & 7848. Fax: 520-432-7800.
E-mail: carrie@bisbeemuseum.org
Web Site: bisbeemuseum.org
Founded: 1971.
Congressional District: 5
Key Personnel: Chm. (V), Jim Merkel; Dir., Carrie Gustavson; Cur. Collections, Annie Larkins; Office Mgr., Anna Garcia.
Personnel Profile: Full-Time Paid 3; Part-Time Paid 3; Part-Time Volunteers 60.
Governing Authority: nonprofit organization. Parent Institution: Bisbee Council on the Arts & Humanities; Friends of the Warren Ballpark. Subsidiary Institution: Muheim Heritage House. Tax-exempt: 501(3)(c).
History Museum: housed in the Old General Office Building of the Phelps Dodge Corp.; National Registered Landmark, a Smithsonian Affiliate.
Collections: photographs; manuscripts; costumes; mining tools & equipment; household & business artifacts; oral histories; mining artifacts. Historic House: 1905 Muheim House.
Research Fields: history of Bisbee; social history; mining; genealogy; Cochise County & Northern Sonora, Mexico.
Facilities: 1,000-vol. library of social & economic history of Bisbee, Cochise County & Arizona, available for research during regular hours or by appointment; 25,000 historic photograph archive. Gift items for sale.
Activities: school programs; lectures; workshops; slide shows; cultural events; permanent & temporary exhibitions.
Publications: Bisbee Pioneer Homes; Bisbee 1880-1920; The Photographer's View; A Century of Change; Mining Town Trolleys; newsletter; Bisbee: Urban Outpost on the Frontier; Bisbee Historic District Walking Tours; Bisbee Yesterday & Today; Meanwhile Back at the Ranch.
Hours & Admission Prices: Daily 10-4. Adults $7.50, senior citizens 60 & over $6.50, children 3-16 $3; discounts to groups of 10 or more; members & local school groups no charge. Closed New Year's Day; Thanksgiving; Christmas. ♿
Attendance: 21,430 (accurate)
Membership: Individual $30; Family $40; Business, Patron & Patron Affiliate with Smithsonian Institution $75; Life $350; Heritage Keeper $500 & up.

Bowie

FORT BOWIE NATIONAL HISTORIC SITE, 13 miles south of Bowie on Apache Pass Rd., Bowie, AZ 85605. Mailing Address: P.O. Box 158, Bowie, AZ 85605-0158. Tel.: 520-847-2500. Fax: 520-847-2349.
E-mail: larry_ludwig@nps.gov
Web Site: www.nps.gov/fobo
Founded: 1964.
Congressional District: 5
Key Personnel: Cur., Larry Ludwig.
Personnel Profile: Full-Time Paid 3; Part-Time Paid 1; Part-Time Volunteers 8.
Governing Authority: federal. Administered by National Park Service, Southern Arizona Group Office, 3115 N. 3rd Ave., Ste. 101, Phoenix, AZ 85013. Parent Institution: Chiricahua National Monument. Tax-exempt.
Historic Site: 1858-1894 ruins of military structures; 1858 Apache Pass Overland Mail Station.
Collections: history & natural science books pertaining to area; plants; artifacts; archeological artifacts; military records; period photographs; local history; manuscripts.
Facilities: 850-vol. library of books on history of the Indian Wars, southwest & southwestern natural histories, the Frontier Movement in American history & reference books on the park service & museums available for research on premises; Fort Bowie post records on microfilm. History books, postcards, slides & park guides for sale.
Activities: self-guided tours; lectures; permanent exhibitions.
Publications: booklet, Fort Bowie Official Map & Guide; booklet, Trail Guide to Fort Bowie.
Hours & Admission Prices: Daily 8-4:30. No charge. Closed Thanksgiving; Christmas. ♿
Attendance: 10,000 (accurate)

Buckeye

BUCKEYE MUSEUM, 10th St. & Monroe, Buckeye, AZ 85326. Mailing Address: P.O. Box 292, Buckeye, AZ 85326-0024. Tel.: 623-349-6315. Fax: 623-349-6310.
E-mail: jbrunson@buckeyeaz.gov
Web Site: buckeyeaz.gov
Formerly: Buckeye Valley Museum
Founded: 1954.
Congressional District: 2
Personnel Profile: Full-Time Paid 1; Part-Time Paid 1.
Governing Authority: Parent Institution: Town of Buckeye. Subsidiary Institution: Buckeye Historical Society.
History Museum.
Collections: Buckeye history.
Hours & Admission Prices: Sept.-June Wed.-Thurs. 12-4, Fri.-Sat. 10-4. No charge; donations accepted. Closed holidays.
Attendance: 993 (accurate)
Membership: Individual $5; Family $20; Patron $100. Commercial: Regular $50; Sponsor $100.

Bullhead City

COLORADO RIVER MUSEUM, 2201 Hwy. 68, Bullhead City, AZ 86430. Mailing Address: P.O. Box 1599, Bullhead City, AZ 86430-1599. Tel.: 928-754-3399.
Governing Authority: nonprofit organization.
History Museum.
Collections: area history & culture; photographs; mining; ranching; Native American artifacts; mining equipment; Katherine gold mine replica.
Hours & Admission Prices: Call for hours & admission prices.

Camp Verde

FORT VERDE STATE HISTORIC PARK, 125 E. Holloman, Camp Verde, AZ 86322. Mailing Address: P.O. Box 397, Camp Verde, AZ 86322-0397. Tel.: 928-567-3275. Fax: 928-567-4036.
E-mail: sstubler@azstateparks.gov
Web Site: www.azstateparks.gov
Founded: 1956.

Congressional District: 3
Key Personnel: Park Mgr., Sheila Stubler; Asst. Mgr., Dennis Lockhart.
Personnel Profile: Full-Time Paid 4; Part-Time Paid 1; Part-Time Volunteers 10.
Governing Authority: state. Parent Institution: Arizona State Parks. Tax-exempt.
State Park General Museum: located on site of Fort Verde, Arizona Territory.
Collections: military artifacts; furniture; textiles; weapons; photographs; manuscripts; four historic buildings 1870-1891.
Research Fields: local military history pertaining to military activities in Arizona from 1860-1899; Indian Wars 1865-1895.
Facilities: 700-vol. library of books on history of military in Arizona available on premises.
Activities: living history presentations; permanent & temporary exhibitions. Annual Events: Reenactments in April & October.
Hours & Admission Prices: Daily 8-5. Adults 14 & over $2; discount to groups; children under 13 no charge. Closed Christmas. ♿
Attendance: 30,000 (estimated)

MONTEZUMA CASTLE NATIONAL MONUMENT, 2800 Montezuma Castle Rd., Camp Verde, AZ 86322. Mailing Address: Box 219, Camp Verde, AZ 86322-0219. Tel.: 928-567-3322 & 5276. Fax: 928-567-3597.
E-mail: moca_administration@nps.gov
Web Site: www.nps.gov/moca
Founded: 1906.
Congressional District: 3
Key Personnel: Supt., Kathy M. Davis; Chief Ranger, Ed Cummins; Supvr. Park Ranger, Karen Hughes.
Governing Authority: federal.
Pre-historic Museum.
Collections: archaeology; natural history; Indian artifacts; ethnology.
Facilities: library. Publications for sale.
Activities: lectures; self-guided trail.
Hours & Admission Prices: June-Aug. daily 8-6; Sept.-May daily 8-5. Adults $5; children 15 & under no charge.
Membership: Golden Age Passport (age 62 & over) $10.

Casa Grande

CASA GRANDE VALLEY HISTORICAL SOCIETY & MUSEUM, (M), 110 W. Florence Blvd., Casa Grande, AZ 85222-4033. Tel.: 520-836-2223. Fax: 520-836-5065.
E-mail: info@cgvhs.org
Web Site: www.cgvhs.org
Formerly: Casa Grande History Museum
Founded: 1964.
Congressional District: 5
Key Personnel: Pres., Patty Norris; Archivist, Kay Benedict.
Personnel Profile: Full-Time Paid 1; Part-Time Volunteers 35.
Governing Authority: society. Affiliated with the Arizona Historical Society, 949 E. 2nd St., Tucson. Tax-exempt: 501(c)(3).
History Museum.
Collections: local history; period artifacts; manuscripts; photographs. Historic Building: schoolhouse.
Research Fields: local history.
Facilities: library of books on Arizona history & old newspaper files available on premises; auditorium.
Activities: education program; site preservation projects; guided tours; lectures; permanent & temporary exhibitions.
Publications: newsletter to members & others interested; monographs of local history; newspaper articles on local history; annual journal.
Hours & Admission Prices: Sept. 15-May 15 Mon.-Sat. 1-5; special tours by appointment. Adults $3; members no charge. Closed major holidays. ♿
Attendance: 5,300 (estimated)
Membership: Student $5; Active Single $15; Active Family $25; Associate $35; Sustaining $50; Patron $100; Benefactor $500; Life $1,000.

Cave Creek

CAVE CREEK MUSEUM, (M), 6140 E. Skyline Dr., Cave Creek, AZ 85327. Mailing Address: P.O. Box 1, Cave Creek, AZ 85327-0001. Tel.: 480-488-2764. Fax: 480-595-0838.
E-mail: info@cavecreekmuseum.com
Web Site: cavecreekmuseum.com
Founded: 1968.
Key Personnel: Dir., Evelyn Johnson; Chm. & Pres. (V), Barbara Chatzkel; Administrative Asst., Jean Marsh; Museum Shop Mgr., Faith Pipp; Tech Asst., Karen Friend
History Museum.
Collections: desert foothills history; pioneer living, ranching & mining; Hohokam, Yavapai, & Apache artifacts. Historic Buildings: restored 1920s tuberculosis cabin; 1940s church.
Facilities: Museum-related items for sale.
Hours & Admission Prices: Oct.-May Wed.-Thurs. & Sat.-Sun. 1-4:30, Fri. 10-4:30. Adults $3, seniors 60 & over and students $2; discounts to groups & AAM members. Closed New Year's Day; Easter; Christmas. ♿
Attendance: 5,000 (estimated)

Chandler

ARIZONA RAILWAY MUSEUM, (M), 330 E. Ryan Rd., Chandler, AZ 85224. Mailing Address: P.O. Box 842, Chandler, AZ 85244-0842. Tel.: 480-821-1108.
E-mail: azrymuseum@cox.net
Web Site: www.azrymuseum.org
Founded: 1983.
Congressional District: 6
Key Personnel: Pres. (V), Thomas Klobas; Museum Shop Mgr., Karen Chmiel.
Personnel Profile: Full-Time Volunteers 6; Part-Time Volunteers 25.
Governing Authority: nonprofit organization. Tax-exempt.
Railway Museum.
Collections: railway history of Arizona & the Southwest; railway equipment & artifacts.
Activities: special events.
Hours & Admission Prices: Labor Day to Memorial Day Sat.-Sun. 12-4; other times by appointment. Work Sessions: Sat. 8am to 12pm. No charge; donations accepted.
Attendance: 8,000 (estimated)
Membership: Senior Citizen 62 & over $20; Regular $25; Family $30; Sustaining $50-$499; Life $300; Corporate $500 & up.

CHANDLER MUSEUM, (M), 178 E. Commonwealth Ave., Chandler, AZ 85225-5877. Mailing Address: MS 501, P.O. Box 4008, Chandler, AZ 85244-4008. Tel.: 480-782-2717. Fax: 480-782-2765.
E-mail: chandlermuseum@aol.com
Web Site: www.chandlermuseum.com
Founded: 1969.
Congressional District: 6
Key Personnel: Dir., Jody A. Crago; Coord. Public History, Jean Reynolds; Cur. Education, Mari Dresner; Cur. Collections, Nate Meyers; Visitor Experience & Special Event Coord., Janice Dell.
Personnel Profile: Full-Time Paid 6; Part-Time Paid 1.
Governing Authority: city. Subsidiary Institutions: McCullough Price House, 300 S. Chandler Village Dr., Chandler, AZ; Tumbleweed Ranch, 2250 S. McQueen Rd., Chandler, AZ.
History Museum.
Collections: Chandler area history, art, & cultural artifacts; period records & photographs; Indian artifacts; local artifacts; manuscripts.
Major Exhibits: San Marcos Hotel, 2/10-12/10.
Research Fields: oral history; photographs.
Activities: permanent & temporary exhibitions; school & group tours; lectures; archival reference service.
Publications: newsletter.
Hours & Admission Prices: Tues.-Wed. & Fri.-Sat. 10-4, Thurs. 10-7. No charge; donations accepted. Closed New Year's Day; Martin Luther King Jr. Day; Memorial Day; Independence Day; Labor Day; Veterans Day; Thanksgiving; Christmas. ♿
Attendance: 12,000 (estimated)
Membership: Individual $25; Senior $20; Family $45; Supporting $75; Sponsor $125; Business $250.

HUHUGAM HERITAGE CENTER, 4759 N. Maricopa Rd., Chandler, AZ 85226-5202. Mailing Address: P.O. Box 5041, Chandler, AZ 85226. Tel.: 520-796-3500.
Web Site: www.huhugam.com
Native American Museum.
Collections: Native American culture & history; baskets; paintings.
Hours & Admission Prices: Wed.-Fri. 10-4. Adults $5, seniors & students $3, children 6-12 $2.

Chinle

CANYON DE CHELLY NATIONAL MONUMENT, 3 mi. east of Chinle, Rte. 7, Chinle, AZ 86503. Mailing Address: P.O. Box 588, Chinle, AZ 86503-0588. Tel.: 928-674-5500. Fax: 928-674-5507.
Web Site: www.nps.gov/cach
Founded: 1931.
Congressional District: 4
Key Personnel: WNPA Bookstore, Keith Lyons; WNPA Bookstore, Jennifer Lavris.

Personnel Profile: Full-Time Paid 1; Part-Time Paid 2.
Governing Authority: federal. Parent Institution: Dept. of the Interior; National Park Service. Tax-exempt.
Park Museum.
Collections: archaeology; anthropology; prehistoric Anasazi & Navajo cultures.
Activities: ranger hikes; campfire programs; off-site interpretive programs upon request.
Publications: orientation brochure; park newspaper, Canyon Overlook.
Hours & Admission Prices: Visitor Center: daily 8-5. No charge; donations accepted. Closed Christmas. ♿
Attendance: 1,000,000 (accurate)

Clarkdale

TUZIGOOT NATIONAL MONUMENT, 25 W. Tuzigoot Rd., Clarkdale, AZ 86324. Mailing Address: P.O. Box 219, Camp Vere, AZ 86322-0219. Tel.: 928-634-5564 & 567-5276. Fax: 928-567-3597.
E-mail: MOCA_administration@nps.gov
Web Site: www.nps.gov/tuzi
Founded: 1939.
Congressional District: 3
Key Personnel: Supt., Kathy Davis; Supvr., Karen Hughes.
Governing Authority: federal. Parent Institution: National Park Service, Dept. of Interior, Washington, DC. Tax-exempt.
Park Museum & Visitor Center: located on the Sinagua Indian ruins.
Collections: artifacts found during excavation of Tuzigoot & nearby ruins. Historic Building: 1125-1300 Tuzigoot National Monument.
Research Fields: archeology; anthropology; natural sciences.
Facilities: 300-vol. library of material on archeology, anthropology, botany & zoology available for inter-library loan. Books, slides & postcards for sale.
Activities: guided tours; lectures; films; formally organized education programs for children; permanent exhibitions.
Publications: brochures, published through National Park Service.
Hours & Admission Prices: Winter: daily 8-5; Summer: daily 8-6. Adults $5; children 15 & under and senior citizens with Golden Age Passport no charge.

Coolidge

CASA GRANDE RUINS NATIONAL MONUMENT, 1100 W. Ruins Dr., Coolidge, AZ 85228-3200. Tel.: 520-723-3172. Fax: 520-723-7209.
Web Site: www.nps.gov/cagr
Founded: 1892.
Congressional District: 5
Key Personnel: Administrative Officer, Diana Mills; Administrative Support Asst., Peggy Carter.
Personnel Profile: Full-Time Paid 8; Part-Time Paid 6.
Governing Authority: federal. Affiliated with the National Park Service, Interior Bldg., Washington, DC. Tax-exempt.
Archaeology & Park Museum: located on Hohokam village site dating to approx. A.D. 500-1450.
Collections: Hohokam archaeology; local ethnology; pre-Columbian Hohokam Indian artifacts. Prehistoric Sites: The Casa Grande: c.1300-1350; Hohokam village c.1200-1400.
Research Fields: Hohokam culture archaeology.
Facilities: 1,928-vol. library of archaeology books available on premises by arrangement. Archaeology, ethnology & natural history books of Arizona for sale.
Activities: permanent & temporary exhibitions; ranger talks.
Publications: Archaeology Reports; Technical Series.
Hours & Admission Prices: Daily 9-5. Adults $5; children 15 & under and educational groups no charge. Golden Eagle, Golden Age, Golden Access Passports honored. Closed Thanksgiving; Christmas. ♿
Attendance: 85,000 (accurate)

Cottonwood

VERDE HISTORICAL SOCIETY, CLEMENCEAU HERITAGE MUSEUM, 1 N. Willard, Cottonwood, AZ 86326-3651. Mailing Address: P.O. Box 511, Cottonwood, AZ 86326-0511. Tel.: 928-634-2868.
E-mail: clemenceauheritagem@qwestoffice.net
Web Site: www.clemenceaumuseum.org
Founded: 1989.
Congressional District: 1
Key Personnel: C.E.O., Pres. (V), & Archivist, Betty Gaudy; Dir. & Chm. (V), Helen Killebrew; Museum Shop Mgr., Barbara Evans; Treas., Elnora Jordan.
Personnel Profile: Part-Time Volunteers 50.
Governing Authority: private; nonprofit organization. Tax-exempt: 501(c)(3).
Historical Society Museum: housed in 1923-1924 school building.
Collections: history of the Verde Valley; local artifacts.
Facilities: 600-vol. library; classroom. Museum-related items for sale.
Activities: guided tours. Museum Sponsors: Bar-B-Que; American Arts/Crafts Show; Early Settler Day.
Publications: quarterly newsletter, The Voice.
Hours & Admission Prices: Wed. 9-12, Fri.-Sun. 11-3. No charge; donations accepted. Closed New Year's Day; Easter; Independence Day; Thanksgiving; Christmas. ♿
Attendance: 3,595 (accurate)
Membership: Individual $10; Family $15; Business $50.

Douglas

SLAUGHTER RANCH MUSEUM, 6153 Geronimo Trail, 16 miles East of Douglas, Douglas, AZ 85608. Mailing Address: P.O. Box 438, Douglas, AZ 85608-0438. Tel.: 520-558-2474. Fax: 602-933-3777.
E-mail: sranch@vtc.net
Web Site: slaughterranch.com
Founded: 1982.
Key Personnel: C.E.O. (V), Harvey Finks; Pres. (V), Alan D. Finks; Education & Historian, Dr. Reba Grandrud.
Personnel Profile: Full-Time Paid 4; Part-Time Paid 2; Part-Time Volunteers 2.
Governing Authority: nonprofit. Parent Institution: Johnson Historical Museum of the Southwest. Tax-exempt: 501(c)(3).
Historic Site: located on c.1893 John Slaughter Ranch.
Collections: costumes; furniture; c.1890 ranch & farm implements; 1,000 photos. Historic Buildings: ranch buildings; 1913 U.S. Army 10th Cavalry outpost from Pancho Villa era.
Facilities: 30-vol. library relating to John Slaughter & San Bernardino Valley; 20-seat theater.
Activities: guided tours; films.
Hours & Admission Prices: Wed.-Sun. 10-3. Adults $8; children no charge. Closed New Year's Day; Christmas. ♿
Attendance: 4,000 (estimated)

Dragoon

THE AMERIND FOUNDATION, INC., (M), 2100 N. Amerind Rd., Dragoon, AZ 85609. Mailing Address: P.O. Box 400, Dragoon, AZ 85609-0400. Tel.: 520-586-3666. Fax: 520-586-4679.
E-mail: amerind@amerind.org
Web Site: www.amerind.org
Founded: 1937.
Congressional District: 8
Key Personnel: Chm. (V), William Duncan Fulton; Pres. (V), Michael W. Hard; Dir., Dr. John A. Ware; Cur., Dr. Eric Kaldahl; Public Rels., Karen Peitsmeyer; Museum Shop Mgr., Tammy Stansberry.
Personnel Profile: Full-Time Paid 6; Part-Time Paid 5; Part-Time Volunteers 50.
Governing Authority: nonprofit organization. Tax-exempt: 501(c)(3).
Archaeology & Ethnology Museum and Art Gallery.
Collections: archaeological collections from North America, Mesoamerica & South America; ethnological material from the Southwest, Mexico, Great Plains, Eastern Woodlands, California & the Arctic; oil paintings; sculpture; santos; ivory & scrimshaw; period furniture.
Major Exhibits: And Then, There Were Horses!, 11/09-6/10.
Research Fields: anthropology; archaeology; ethnohistory of the Americas.
Facilities: 25,000-vol. library of research and technical reports, journals, periodicals, manuscripts & books on anthropology, archaeology & natural history available for use by appointment; reading room; separate laboratory operation.
Activities: guided tours; lectures; seminars; artist shows; Visiting Scholar Program.
Publications: Amerind Foundation Archeology Series; Amerind New World Studies Series.
Hours & Admission Prices: Business Office: Mon.-Fri. 8-5. Museum: Tues.-Sun. 10-4. Adults $5, senior citizens $4, children 12-18 $3; discounts to AAM members; members & children under 12 no charge. Closed New Year's Day; Easter; Memorial Day; Independence Day; Labor Day; Thanksgiving; Christmas.
Attendance: 13,000 (accurate)
Membership: Individual $30; Family $40; Cochise Club $100-$499; San Pedro Club $500-$999; Casas Grandes Club $1,000 & up.

Flagstaff

THE ARBORETUM AT FLAGSTAFF, 4001 S. Woody Mountain Rd., Flagstaff, AZ 86001-8776. Tel.: 928-774-1442. Fax: 928-774-1441.
E-mail: steve.yoder@nau.edu
Web Site: www.thearb.org
Founded: 1981.

Congressional District: 6
Key Personnel: Dir., Steve Yoder; Pres. (V), Mike Loven; Dir. Gardens & Facilities, Brian Keeley; Research Scientist, Dr. Kristin Haskins; Mgr. Public Programs, Rachel Edelstein; Visitor Svcs. Mgr., Leslie Fauset.
Personnel Profile: Full-Time Paid 8; Part-Time Paid 10; Part-Time Volunteers 60; Interns 1.
Governing Authority: nonprofit organization. Parent Institution: Transition Zone Horticultural Institute (TZHI). Tax-exempt: 501(c)(3).
Arboretum.
Collections: native plants of the Colorado Plateau including rare & endangered species.
Research Fields: botanical; forestry.
Facilities: 1,500-vol. library pertaining to botany, horticulture & forestry; horticulture center; solar greenhouse; meeting rooms; classrooms; 200 acres of natural & cultivated landscapes; outdoor concert area; 1.6 mile nature trail; constructed wetlands; visitor center. Museum-related items for sale.
Activities: docent program; adult horticultural classes; guided tours; live raptor programs. Annual Events: Plant Sale in June; Penstemon Festival in July; wildflower walks; summer concert series; Arbor Day celebration; children's summer adventure program; science in the park; bird walks; Fall Open House in October.
Publications: quarterly newsletter; annual report; general brochure; membership brochure.
Hours & Admission Prices: April to Oct. daily 9-5. Guided Tours: daily 11 & 1. Adults $6, children 6-17 $1; discounts to AAM members; children under 6 & members no charge. ♿
Attendance: 18,709 (accurate)
Membership: Student $10; Individual $35; Family $50; Cliffrose $100; Ponderosa $250; Columbine Club $500; Penstemon Society $1,000.

ARIZONA HISTORICAL SOCIETY PIONEER MUSEUM, 2340 N. Fort Valley Rd., Flagstaff, AZ 86001-1200. Tel.: 928-774-6272. Fax: 928-774-1596.
E-mail: ahsflagstaff@azhs.gov
Web Site: www.arizonahistoricalsociety.org
Founded: 1864.
Congressional District: 1
Key Personnel: Exec. Dir., Anne I. Woosley, Ph.D.; Northern Arizona Division Dir., Leslie Roe.
Personnel Profile: Full-Time Paid 2; Part-Time Paid 1; Part-Time Volunteers 31; Interns 1.
Governing Authority: bd. of directors. Parent Institution: Arizona Historical Society, 949 E. 2nd St., Tucson, AZ 85719. Tel.: 520-628-5774. Tax-exempt: 501(c)(3).
History Museum.
Collections: industrial, social, institutional & transportation history of Flagstaff & northern Arizona including logging, railroad, livestock, farming and domestic items; 1929 Baldwin logging locomotive #12; Santa Fe Railroad caboose; archives housed at Northern Arizona University. Historic Buildings: 1908 Coconino County Hospital; 1908 Ben Doney homestead cabin.
Research Fields: general history of northern Arizona; lumber industry; community development; architecture; hispanic population.
Facilities: archives of 1,300 linear feet & approximately 30,000 photographs. Museum-related items for sale.
Activities: changing exhibits; school tours. Annual Events: Independence Day Festival; Wool Festival; Heritage Festival.
Publications: quarterly, The Journal of Arizona History; books; monographs; annual report.
Hours & Admission Prices: Mon.-Sat. 9-5. Adults $5, seniors 60 & over and youth 12-18 $4; children 11 & under and members no charge. Closed New Year's Day; Martin Luther King Jr. Day; Presidents' Day; Columbus Day; Veterans Day; Thanksgiving; Christmas.
Attendance: 12,000 (estimated)
Membership: Student $25; Individual $50; Household $65; Sustaining $100; Patron $250; Sponsor $500; Director's Circle $1,000.

COLORADO PLATEAU BIODIVERSITY CENTER, Northern Arizona University, Flagstaff, AZ 86011-0001. Mailing Address: Northern Arizona University, Campus Box 6077, Flagstaff, AZ 86011-0001. Tel.: 928-523-4463. Fax: 928-523-7500.
E-mail: stefan.sommer@nau.edu
Founded: 2004.
Key Personnel: Dir. & Assoc. Cur. Arthropods, Dr. Stefan Sommer; Cur. Arthropods, Dr. Neil Cobb; Cur. Botany, Dr. Randall Scott; Cur. Botany, Dr. Tina Ayers; Cur. Botany, Dr. David Hammond; Cur. Mammals, Dr. Tad Theimer; Cur. Ichthyology, Dr. Linn Montgomery; Cur. Mycology, Dr. Kitty Gehring; Cur. Genetics, Dr. Gery Allan; Cur. Palynology, Dr. Scott Anderson; Cur. Fossil Middens, Dr. Kenneth Cole; Cur. Crustaceans & Non-Arthropods, Dr. Stephen Shuster; Mgr. Paleontology Collections, Sandra Swift; Mgr. Palynology Collections, Susan Smith; Mgr. Arthropod Collections, Robert Delph.
Personnel Profile: Full-Time Paid 10; Full-Time Volunteers 4; Part-Time Paid 17; Part-Time Volunteers 25; Interns 15.
Governing Authority: public university. Parent Institution: Northern Arizona University. Subsidiary Institutions: Colorado Plateau Museum of Arthropod Biodiversity; Deaver Herbarium; NAU Quaternary Sciences Program; NAU Laboratory of Paleoecology. Tax-exempt: 501(c)(3).
Natural History Museum.
Collections: entomology; botany; ichthyology; mammalogy; ornithology; mycology; DNA & tissue collections; palynology; paleontology; herpetology.
Research Fields: entomology; botany; paleontology; genetics; palynology; mycology; mammalogy; ornithology; ichthyology; herpetology.
Facilities: library; 3 auditoriums; educational facilities; 2,000 exhibit space; field research station.
Activities: films; formal education programs for adults & college students; education programs for adults & children; lectures; school loan service; temporary exhibitions; training programs for professional museum workers; broadcast programs; public programs. Annual Event: scientific conferences on the Colorado Plateau.
Hours & Admission Prices: No charge; donations accepted.
Attendance: 15,000 (estimated)

LOWELL OBSERVATORY, 1400 W. Mars Hill Rd., Flagstaff, AZ 86001-4499. Tel.: 928-774-3358. Fax: 928-774-6296.
E-mail: jch@lowell.edu
Web Site: www.lowell.edu
Founded: 1894.
Congressional District: 3
Key Personnel: Dir., Robert L. Millis; Trustee, William Lowell Putnam; Assoc. Dir. Education & Devel., Jeffrey C. Hall; Museum Shop Mgr., Tim Rodriquez.
Personnel Profile: Full-Time Paid 50; Part-Time Paid 17; Part-Time Volunteers 10; Interns 2.
Governing Authority: private. Tax-exempt.
Astronomy Museum & Observatory.
Collections: astronomical photographs; historic & current research instruments; astronomy exhibits; 11 astronomical telescopes.
Research Fields: astronomy; planetary science.
Facilities: 10,000-vol. library of astronomy & mathematic books available for use by special permission; visitor center.
Activities: research; guided tours; school programs; family workshops; youth science programs & nighttime telescope viewings.
Publications: Lowell Observatory Bulletin; quarterly newsletter: The Lowell Observer.
Hours & Admission Prices: Call for hours. Adults $6, children 5-17 $3; discounts to AAA members; members no charge. Closed New Year's Eve & Day; Easter; Independence Day; Thanksgiving; Christmas Eve & Day. ♿
Attendance: 75,716 (accurate)
Membership: Individual $35; Family $50; Friend $100; Contributor $250; Pluto Society $500; Lowell Associate $1,000; Trustee Circle $2,500.

* **MUSEUM OF NORTHERN ARIZONA, (M),** 3101 N. Fort Valley Rd., Flagstaff, AZ 86001-8348. Tel.: 928-774-5213. Fax: 928-779-1527.
E-mail: info@mna.mus.az.us
Web Site: www.musnaz.org
Founded: 1928.
Congressional District: 1
Key Personnel: Dir., Robert G. Breunig, Ph.D.; Chm., Susan G. Garretson; Colbert Cur. Vertebrate Paleontology, David D. Gillette, Ph.D.; Sr. Cur. Anthropology, Dr. David R. Wilcox; Cur. Ecology & Conservation, Dr. Lawrence E. Stevens; Danson Chm. Anthropology, Dr. Kelley Hays-Gilpin; Cur. Museum, Dr. Jennifer McLerran; Collections Mgr., Elaine Hughes; Dir. Devel., Stacy Murison; Mktg. Mgr., Michele Mountain; Membership Mgr., Cheryl Blume; Museum Shop Mgr., Fiona Nagel.
Personnel Profile: Full-Time Paid 29; Part-Time Paid 14; Part-Time Volunteers 300; Interns 12.
Governing Authority: private; nonprofit organization. Bd. of Trustees of Museum of Northern Arizona Inc. Tax-exempt: 501(c)(3).
History Museum.
Collections: prehistoric & ethnographic Southwest Indian artifacts; ceramic repository; geological & paleontological material; herbarium; zoological specimens; Southwestern Anglo & Indian art; archives. Historic Houses: c.1886 The Homestead; Colton House complex, c.1906.
Major Exhibits: Therizinosaur - Mystery of the Sickle Claw Dinosaur (T), 11/09-1/10; Gunnar Widforss, 12/09-5/10; Wings of Time - Dragonfly, 1/10-6/11.
Research Fields: archaeology; ethnology; geology; paleontology; biology; American Indian art.

Facilities: 99,000-vol. reference library; auditorium; nature trail.
Activities: expeditions into backcountry of Colorado Plateau; tours; workshops; inter-museum loan, permanent, temporary & traveling exhibitions; children's programs; lectures; special arts & craft exhibits and demonstrations; lecture series; rental facilities available.
Publications: triannual members newsletter, Museum Notes; biannual magazine, Plateau; occasional research publications.
Hours & Admission Prices: Daily 9-5. Adults $7, senior citizens 65 & over $6, students w/ID $5, children 7-17 & Native People $4; children under 7 & members no charge. ♿
Attendance: 77,500 (accurate)
Membership: Painted Desert Affiliate $60; Sunset Crater Colleague $100; Canyonlands Contributor $150; Chaco Sponsor $275; Black Mesa Assoc. $500; Kaibab Fellow $1,000; Mesa Verde Circle $2,500; Grand Canyon Associate $5,000 & up.

NAU ART MUSEUM, (M), Knoles & McMullen Circle, Bldg. #10, N. NAU Campus, Flagstaff, AZ 86011-0001. Mailing Address: P.O. Box 6021, Flagstaff, AZ 86011-0001. Tel.: 928-523-3471. Fax: 928-523-1424.
E-mail: art.museum@nau.edu
Web Site: www4.nau.edu/art_museum
Formerly: Northern Arizona University Art Museum and Galleries
Founded: 1961.
Congressional District: 3
Key Personnel: Dir., Jennifer McLerran; Cur. & Museum Shop Mgr., Kathleen Battali.
Personnel Profile: Full-Time Paid 1; Part-Time Paid 6.
Governing Authority: state. Affiliated with Northern Arizona University. Tax-exempt.
Art Museum.
Collections: local, state, national & international historic paintings; turn of the century furniture; graphics; paintings; ceramics; sculpture.
Facilities: Artists artwork, baskets, glass & jewelry for sale.
Activities: guided tours; lectures; gallery talks; artists workshops; temporary, traveling & original exhibitions.
Hours & Admission Prices: Museum: Tues.-Sat. 12-5. Beasley Gallery: Mon.-Fri. 11-4. No charge; donations accepted. Closed legal & university holidays. ♿
Attendance: 40,000 (estimated)

RIORDAN MANSION STATE HISTORIC PARK, 409 W. Riordan Rd., Flagstaff, AZ 86001-6440. Tel.: 928-779-4395. Fax: 928-556-0253.
E-mail: mdavis@azstateparks.gov
Web Site: www.pr.state.az.us
Founded: 1983.
Congressional District: 6
Personnel Profile: Full-Time Paid 4; Part-Time Paid 3; Part-Time Volunteers 15; Interns 1.
Governing Authority: state; nonprofit. Parent Institution: State of Arizona. Subsidiary Institution: Arizona State Parks, 1300 W. Washington, Phoenix, AZ 85007.
Historic Mansion: c.1904 site containing a collection of original Craftsman furnishings.
Collections: original furnishings, c.1904; fixtures; furniture; clothing; textiles; decorations; correspondence; photographs; utensils; family mementos.
Facilities: over 13,000 sq. ft. mansion; visitor center; picnic areas.
Activities: guided tours of mansion; self-guided tours of estate surrounding mansion; slide program; children's touch table.
Publications: The Riordan Family of Flagstaff; Riordan Family Recipes.
Hours & Admission Prices: May-Oct. daily 8:30-5; Nov.-April daily 10:30-5; guided tours on the hour. Adults & senior citizens $6, youth (7-13) $2.50; children under 6 no charge. Closed Christmas. ♿
Attendance: 25,000 (accurate)

SUNSET CRATER VOLCANO NATIONAL MONUMENT, 6400 N. U.S. Hwy. 89, Flagstaff, AZ 86004-2759. Tel.: 928-527-0322. Fax: 928-526-4259.
Web Site: www.nps.gov
Founded: 1930.
Congressional District: 6
Key Personnel: Supt., Diane Chung; Cur., Gwenn Gallenstein.
Governing Authority: federal. Parent Institution: Dept. of the Interior, National Park System. Tax-exempt.
Park Museum & Visitor Center.
Collections: geologic specimens of the area, the primary theme being the story of volcanic action which took place in the San Francisco Peaks Volcanic Field; pottery used by people of the period 1064-1250 A.D.
Research Fields: vulcanism; Sinaqua archaeology.
Facilities: visitor center. Postcards, slides, film & publications for sale.
Activities: guided tours; films.
Publications: guide leaflet; orientation brochure.
Hours & Admission Prices: Summer: daily 8-6; Winter: daily 8-5. Admission: $5 per person; discounts to Museum Association of Arizona & AAM members; American disabled citizen and children 16 & under no charge. Golden Age passport available. Closed Christmas. ♿
Attendance: 195,198 (estimated)

WALNUT CANYON NATIONAL MONUMENT, 6400 N. Hwy. 89, Flagstaff, AZ 86004-2759. Tel.: 928-527-0322. Fax: 928-526-4259.
Web Site: www.nps.gov
Founded: 1915.
Congressional District: 3
Key Personnel: Supt., Diane Chung; Cur., Gwenn Gallenstein.
Governing Authority: federal. Parent Institution: Dept. of the Interior, National Park Service. Tax-exempt.
Park Museum: located on the site of prehistoric Indian ruins of the Sinagua Indian culture.
Collections: local history & culture; photographs; period artifacts.
Facilities: library of Sinagua cultural material available under direct supervision of park personnel for on-premise use only. Traveling information, postcards, slides & film for sale.
Activities: self-guided trails.
Publications: brochure; Walnut Canyon Guide.
Hours & Admission Prices: Summer: daily 8-6; Winter: daily 8-5. Admission: $5 per person; discounts to AAM & Museum Association of Arizona members. Closed Christmas. ♿
Attendance: 122,544

WUPATKI NATIONAL MONUMENT, 6400 N. Hwy. 89, Flagstaff, AZ 86004-2759. Tel.: 928-527-0322. Fax: 928-526-4259.
Web Site: www.nps.gov
Founded: 1924.
Congressional District: 6
Key Personnel: Supt., Diane Chung; Cur., Gwenn Gallenstein.
Governing Authority: federal. Parent Institution: National Park Service, Dept. of the Interior, Washington, DC 20240. Tax-exempt.
Historic Site: over 2,600 archaeological sites dating from approximately 1100 A.D.; Hopi ancestral homeland.
Collections: series of displays with artifacts from the sites pertaining to the Sinagua/Anasazi cultural pattern as well as historic Navajo.
Research Fields: archaeology of Sinaqua, Anasazi & historic Navajo cultures.
Facilities: 500-vol. library of material on archaeology, geology & ethnology available for use by special permission. Postcards, slides & publications on the area for sale.
Activities: self-guiding trail of Wupatki Ruin; permanent & temporary exhibits; guided tours of Wupatki Ruins.
Publications: orientation brochure; trail guide leaflets, Volcanoes.
Hours & Admission Prices: Summer: daily 8-6; Winter: daily 8-5. Admission: $5 per person; discounts to AAM & MAA members. Closed Christmas. ♿
Attendance: 251,756

Florence

MCFARLAND STATE HISTORIC PARK, 24 W. Ruggles Ave., Florence, AZ 85232. Mailing Address: P.O. Box 109, Florence, AZ 85232-0109. Tel.: 520-868-5216. Fax: 520-868-9056.
E-mail: cdemille@azstateparks.gov
Web Site: www.co.pinal.az.us/mcfarland
Formerly: McFarland Historical State Park
Founded: 1979.
Congressional District: 6
Key Personnel: Park Mgr., Christopher DeMille.
Personnel Profile: Full-Time Paid 3; Part-Time Paid 1; Part-Time Volunteers 6.
Governing Authority: state government. Subsidiary Institution: Arizona State Parks, 1300 W. Washington, Phoenix, AZ 85007.
Park Museum: housed in 1878 Pinal County Courthouse.
Collections: local historical artifacts; archives of late U.S. Senator E.W. McFarland from private & political careers; Arizona territorial law enforcement history (1863-1912). Historic Building: 1878 county courthouse.
Hours & Admission Prices: Daily 8-5. Adults $3, students 7-13 $1; discounts to groups of 8 or more; children under 14 no charge. Closed Christmas Day. ♿
Attendance: 7,500 (estimated)

PINAL COUNTY HISTORICAL SOCIETY AND MUSEUM, 715 S. Main St., Florence, AZ 85132. Mailing Address: P.O. Box 851, Florence, AZ 85232-0851. Tel.: 520-868-4382.
Founded: 1958.
Congressional District: 3

Key Personnel: Pres., Rowe Gilbert; Vice Pres., Larry Pfeiffer; Recording Sec., Bita Arriola; Treas., Betty Rieffer.
Personnel Profile: Part-Time Paid 1; Part-Time Volunteers 15.
Governing Authority: nonprofit organization. Affiliated with Arizona Historical Society, Tucson, AZ. Tax-exempt: 501(c)(3).
General Museum.
Collections: agriculture; ranching; mining; Indian, Spanish, Mexican & Anglo contributions from residents of Pinal County; Arizona State Prison archives & artifacts; rodeo.
Facilities: 1,000-vol. library; Arizona State Prison Archives. Museum-related items for sale.
Activities: guided tours; lectures; speakers.
Publications: monthly newsletter with page of local history; Florence Tour Guide; A History of Florence; Es Verdad/It Is True; Good Men Bad Men, Lawmen; Florence Images of America.
Hours & Admission Prices: Sept.-July 14 Tues.-Sat. 11-4, Sun. 12-4. No charge; donations accepted. Closed New Year's Day; Easter; Independence Day; Thanksgiving; Christmas. ♿
Attendance: 6,085 (accurate)
Membership: Active $15; Family $25; Single Life $125; Husband & Wife (Life) $150; Corporate $200; Corporate Life $1,000.

Fort Apache

NOHWIKE BAGOWA, THE WHITE MOUNTAIN APACHE CULTURAL CENTER AND MUSEUM, Indian Rte. 46, Fort Apache, AZ 85926. Mailing Address: P.O. Box 507, Fort Apache, AZ 85926-0507. Tel.: 928-338-4625. Fax: 928-338-1716.
Web Site: www.wmat.nsn.us
Founded: 1969.
Key Personnel: Dir., Dr. Karl Hoerig; Tribal Chm., Ronnie Lupe; Museum Shop Mgr., Ann Skidmore.
Personnel Profile: Full-Time Paid 5; Part-Time Paid 2; Part-Time Volunteers 3.
Governing Authority: nonprofit. Parent Institution: White Mountain Apache Tribe. Tax-exempt: 501(c)(3).
Historical Museum.
Collections: Apache culture; Fort Apache artifacts.
Research Fields: Apache culture & Fort Apache history.
Activities: Annual Event: Great Fort Apache Heritage Reunion in May.
Hours & Admission Prices: Winter: Mon.-Fri. 8-5; Summer: Mon.-Sat. 8-5. Adults $5, students $3; children under 7 & tribal members no charge. Closed major holidays. ♿
Attendance: 15,203 (accurate)

Fort Huachuca

FORT HUACHUCA MUSEUM, Boyd & Grierson Sts., Fort Huachuca, AZ 85613. Mailing Address: IMSW-HUA-PLT, Fort Huachuca, AZ 85613-6000. Tel.: 520-533-5736.
Web Site: www.huachuca.army.mil/site/visitor/index.asp
Founded: 1960.
Congressional District: 9
Key Personnel: Dir., Tim Phillips; Cur., Paula Ussery; Exhibits, Marty Matin; Cur. Military Intelligence, Ralph Jackson; Museum Specialist, Steve Gregory; Museum Shop Mgr., Bess Banister.
Personnel Profile: Full-Time Paid 6; Part-Time Volunteers 20; Interns 1.
Governing Authority: federal. Tax-exempt.
History Museum: housed on 1877 Fort, National Historic Landmark.
Collections: military history of the Indian Wars; military & western artifacts.
Research Fields: military history.
Facilities: 2,000-vol. library of books on military & western history available for use on premises. Museum-related items for sale.
Activities: self-guided tour.
Publications: book, Fort Huachuca History; brochures.
Hours & Admission Prices: Mon.-Fri. 9-4, Sat.-Sun. 1-4. No charge; donations accepted. Closed Federal holidays. ♿
Attendance: 70,000 (accurate)
Membership: Individual $10; Annual $15.

Fountain Hills

RIVER OF TIME MUSEUM, 12901 N. La Montana Dr., Fountain Hills, AZ 85268-4742. Tel.: 480-837-2612.
History Museum.
Collections: Verde River Valley & Fountain Hills history & culture; photographs; personal artifacts.
Activities: cultural programs & activities.
Hours & Admission Prices: June-Aug. Fri.-Sat. 1-4; Winter: Tues.-Sat. 1-4; groups by appointment. Adults $3, seniors $2, children 5-12 $1.

Fredonia

PIPE SPRING NATIONAL MONUMENT VISITOR CENTER AND CULTURAL MUSEUM, 406 N. Pipe Spring Rd., Fredonia, AZ 86022. Tel.: 928-643-7245.
History Museum.
Collections: Kaibab Paiutes Indian history; local history & culture; personal artifacts. Historic Building: Winsor Castle built in 1870s.
Facilities: nature trails; picnic area.
Activities: talks; demonstrations; tours; hiking; bird watching; special events.
Hours & Admission Prices: Grounds & Museum: June-Aug. daily 7-5; Sept.-May daily 8-5. Castle: June-Aug. daily 8-4:30; Sept.-May daily 9-4. Closed New Year's Day; Thanksgiving; Christmas.

Ganado

HUBBELL TRADING POST NATIONAL HISTORIC SITE, Hwy. 264, Ganado, AZ 86505. Mailing Address: P.O. Box 150, Ganado, AZ 86505-0150. Tel.: 928-755-3475. Fax: 928-755-3405.
E-mail: E_chamberlin@nps.gov
Web Site: www.nps.gov/hutr/
Founded: 1967.
Congressional District: 1
Key Personnel: Supt., Anne Worthington; Museum Cur., Edward M. Chamberlin; Museum Technician, Kathleen Tabaha; Chief Visitor Svcs., Ailena Benally; Museum Shop Mgr., Steve Pickle.
Personnel Profile: Full-Time Paid 11; Part-Time Paid 2; Part-Time Volunteers 5.
Governing Authority: federal. Parent Institution: National Park Service, Washington, DC. Subsidiary Institution: Western National Parks Association, Friends of Hubbell Trading Post NHS, Inc. Tax-exempt.
Historic Site.
Collections: Native American arts & crafts; art; furnishings for home & trading post; ethnology; graphics; agriculture; archives; sculpture; textiles. Historic Buildings: 1880s Hubbell Trading Post; 1897 Hubbell barn; 1900-1915 Hubbell home; 1930-1943 Hubbell guest hogan.
Research Fields: ethnohistory; history; architecture & furnishings; art.
Facilities: 1,500-vol. library of general & southwestern history available for use on premises. Native American, primarily Navajo, arts & crafts for sale.
Activities: guided tours; permanent exhibitions; demonstration of Navajo weaving & silversmithing. Annual Events: Native American Art Auction in May & fall; Luminaria Night in December.
Publications: orientation brochure; trail guide booklet.
Hours & Admission Prices: May-Sept. daily 8-6 (mountain daylight savings time); Oct.-April daily 8-5. Adults $2; donations accepted. Closed New Year's Day; Thanksgiving; Christmas. ♿
Attendance: 235,000 (accurate)

Gilbert

GILBERT HISTORICAL MUSEUM, (M), 10 S. Gilbert Rd., Gilbert, AZ 85296-1047. Mailing Address: P.O. Box 1484, Gilbert, AZ 85299-1484. Tel.: 480-926-1577.
Web Site: www.gilbertmuseum.com
Founded: 1982.
Key Personnel: Dir., Kayla Kolar; Pres. (V), Dale Hallock.
Personnel Profile: Full-Time Paid 1; Part-Time Volunteers 35.
Governing Authority: Tax-exempt.
History Museum.
Collections: area history & culture.
Hours & Admission Prices: Tues.-Sat. 9-4. Adults $5, seniors $4, children 5-12 $3; children under 5 no charge. Closed holidays. ♿
Attendance: 5,000 (accurate)
Membership: Student $10; Individual $20; Family $40; Sustaining $100; Pioneer Patron & Corporate Bronze $250; Premier & Corporate Silver $500; Corporate Gold $1,000.

Glendale

THE BEAD MUSEUM, (M), 5754 W. Glenn Dr., Glendale, AZ 85301-2559. Tel.: 623-931-2737. Fax: 623-930-8561.
E-mail: info@beadmuseumaz.org
Web Site: www.beadmuseumaz.org
Founded: 1985.
Key Personnel: Chm. (V), Joan Howell; Exec. Dir., Kelly Norton; Collections Mgr., Karen Karn; Museum Shop Mgr., Carol Schluer.
Personnel Profile: Full-Time Paid 2; Part-Time Paid 6; Part-Time Volunteers 30.
Governing Authority: nonprofit. Tax-exempt: 501(c)(3).
Art Museum.
Collections: ancient beads; jewelry; ethnic, tribal, Native American, European

19th century, Asian, S. E. Asian, pre-Columbian, Middle Eastern, Oceanic; trade beads of North & South America; African beads; ancient & modern beads & objects of personal adornment; ethnic, tribal beaded art & artifacts; historical & contemporary artists.
Research Fields: history & identification of beads from archaeological sources; beads; cultural studies; beaded art.
Facilities: library of material relating to the history of beads available to the public by appointment; 6,500 sq. ft. exhibit space. Beads, gift items and beading supplies for sale.
Activities: guided tours; lectures; organized education & outreach programs; classes; loan, traveling, & temporary exhibitions; intern program.
Publications: Connections: The Bead Museum Review; booklet, A Bead Primer; exhibit catalogs.
Hours & Admission Prices: Mon.-Wed. & Fri.-Sat. 10-5, Thurs. 10-8, Sun. 11-4. Adults $5, children 4-12 $2.50; discounts to AAM & ICOM members; Thurs. 4-8 & members no charge. Closed major holidays. ♿
Attendance: 30,000 (estimated)
Membership: Individual $40; Family $55; Supporting $100; Donor $250; Patron $500; Corporate $1,500-$5,000.

GLENDALE COMMUNITY COLLEGE ART COLLECTION, 6000 W. Olive, Glendale, AZ 85302-3090. Tel.: 623-845-3755.
Art Museum.
Collections: paintings; sculptures; drawings; photographs; ceramic works.
Hours & Admission Prices: Fall & Spring Semesters: Mon.-Thurs. 7am-10pm, Fri.-Sat. 7-5; Summer: Mon.-Thurs. 7am-9pm, Sun. 12-5. No charge.

SAHUARO RANCH PARK HISTORIC AREA, 9802 N. 59th Ave., Glendale, AZ 85302-1203. Mailing Address: 5850 W. Glendale Ave., Glendale, AZ 85301-2563. Tel.: 623-930-4200. Fax: 623-915-7587.
Web Site: www.glendaleaz.com/srpha
Founded: 1977.
Congressional District: 2
Key Personnel: Recreation Mgr., Paul Bernardo; Coord. Facilities & Events, Paul King; Coord. Historic Education & Outreach, John Akers.
Personnel Profile: Full-Time Paid 3; Part-Time Paid 2; Part-Time Volunteers 50.
Governing Authority: city government. Parent Institution: City of Glendale Parks & Recreation Dept.
Historic House Museum.
Collections: agricultural history of Sahuaro Ranch & the western Maricopa County.
Research Fields: history of the William Henry Bartlett family; water use in the Salt River Valley; history of Sahuaro ranch owners, operations & laborers.
Facilities: 2,500 sq. ft. exhibit space; educational facilities.
Activities: guided tours; temporary exhibits; school programs; themed events; summer camp. Museum Sponsors: Tractor Shows.
Hours & Admission Prices: Sept.-May Wed.-Fri. 10-2, Sat. 10-4, Sun. 12-4. No charge. Closed Federal holidays; Easter. ♿
Attendance: 50,000 (accurate)

SOUTHWEST MUSEUM OF ENGINEERING, COMMUNICATIONS AND COMPUTATION, 5802 W. Palmaire Ave., Glendale, AZ 85301-2442. Tel.: 623-435-1522.
E-mail: info@smecc.org
Web Site: www.smecc.org
Key Personnel: Archivist, Ed Sharpe
Technology Museum.
Collections: early engineering; communications equipment & memorabilia.
Hours & Admission Prices: Tues.-Sat. 12-3; other times by appointment. Call to confirm. No charge.

Globe

BESH-BA-GOWAH ARCHAEOLOGICAL PARK, 1100 Jesse Hayes Rd., Globe, AZ 85501. Mailing Address: 150 N. Pine St., Globe, AZ 85501-2514. Tel.: 928-425-0320. Fax: 928-402-1071.
Founded: 1987.
Key Personnel: Acting Dir., Lynnette Brandon.
Personnel Profile: Full-Time Paid 3; Part-Time Paid 1; Part-Time Volunteers 3.
Governing Authority: municipal government; nonprofit. Parent Institution: City of Globe. Tax-exempt.
Archaeology Museum & Archaeological Site.
Collections: artifacts from local excavations of Hohokam & Salado prehistoric sites; 1930s & 1980s excavations at Besh-Ba-Gowah.
Activities: Annual Events: Archaeology Month Open House in March; Festival of Lights in December.
Hours & Admission Prices: Daily 9-5. Adults 12-65 $3, senior citizens $2; discounts to AAA members; children under 12 no charge. Closed New Year's Day; Thanksgiving; Christmas. ♿
Attendance: 35,000 (estimated)

GILA COUNTY HISTORICAL MUSEUM, 1330 N. Broad St., Globe, AZ 85501-2712. Mailing Address: P.O. Box 2891, Globe, AZ 85502-2891. Tel.: 928-425-7385.
Founded: 1955.
Congressional District: 4
Key Personnel: C.E.O., Kenneth Hein; Museum Mgr., Dr. Bill Haak.
Personnel Profile: Part-Time Paid 1; Part-Time Volunteers 16.
Governing Authority: nonprofit organization. Parent Institution: Gila County Historical Society. Tax-exempt: 501(c)(3).
History Museum: housed in 1920 mine rescue facility.
Collections: Indian pottery; furniture; glass collections; kitchenware.
Research Fields: archeological; historical.
Facilities: reading room.
Activities: guided tours; lectures.
Publications: books, Copper Bottom Tales; Globe Arizona; Globe's Historic Buildings.
Hours & Admission Prices: Mon.-Fri. 10-4, Sat. 11-3. No charge; donations accepted. Closed major holidays. ♿
Attendance: 4,000 (estimated)
Membership: Individual $15; Family $25.

Goodyear

BIBLE MUSEUM, Hampton Inn & Suites, 2000 N. Litchfield, Goodyear, AZ 85395-1280. Tel.: 623-536-8614. Fax: 623-536-1414.
E-mail: BibleMuseum@hotmail.com
Religious Museum.
Collections: Bible history; Bibles; theological books.
Hours & Admission Prices: Daily.

Grand Canyon National Park

GRAND CANYON NATIONAL PARK MUSEUM COLLECTION, 2C Albright Ave., Grand Canyon Village, South Rim, Grand Canyon National Park, AZ 86023. Mailing Address: P.O. Box 129, Grand Canyon, AZ 86023-0129. Tel.: 928-638-7769 (Museum) & 7888 (National Park). Fax: 928-638-7769.
E-mail: GRCA_Museum_Collection@nps.gov
Web Site: www.nps.gov/grca/photos/museum.htm
Founded: 1919.
Congressional District: 3
Key Personnel: Supt., Steve Martin; Museum Technician, Colleen Hyde; Museum Technician, Kim Besom.
Personnel Profile: Full-Time Paid 3.
Governing Authority: federal. Parent Institution: Grand Canyon National Park. Exhibit Visitor Centers: Tusayan Museum; Yavapai Museum; Canyon View Information Plaza. Tax-exempt.
National Park: the Grand Canyon, a deep gorge of the Colorado River measuring 277 mi. long, 1-18 mi. wide & one mile deep.
Collections: geology; history; natural history; archaeology; prehistoric Indian materials; insects; herbarium; oral history, photography; archives; manuscripts; paleontology.
Research Fields: geology; flora; fauna; history; oral history prehistory; paleontology.
Facilities: 10,000-vol. library available for research on premises only; Exhibit-Visitor Centers located in park: Tusayan Museum; Yavapai Museum; South Rim Visitor Center. Books, children's books & maps for sale.
Activities: guided tours; lectures; films; permanent & temporary exhibitions at Kolb Studio.
Publications: scientific monographs on natural & cultural history; guides to various areas & trails.
Hours & Admission Prices: Park: daily 24 hours. Library & Museum: Mon.-Fri. 8-5. Park: $12 per person; $25 per vehicle. Annual Pass: $50. ♿
Attendance: 5,000,000

Green Valley

TITAN MISSILE MUSEUM, 1580 W. Duval Mine Rd., Green Valley, AZ 85614-4907. Tel.: 520-625-7736 & 4598. Fax: 520-625-9845.
E-mail: ymorris@titanmissilemuseum.org
Web Site: www.titanmissilemuseum.org
Founded: 1986.
Congressional District: 5
Key Personnel: Acting Exec. Dir., Yvonne C. Morris; Chm. (V), Count Ferdinand von Galen.
Personnel Profile: Full-Time Paid 7; Part-Time Paid 4; Part-Time Volunteers 120.
Governing Authority: nonprofit organization. Parent Institution: Arizona Aerospace Foundation. Tax-exempt: 501(c)(3).

Missile Museum: housed in a former operational Titan II ICBM complex.
Collections: 1963 Titan II intercontinental ballistic missile complex & missile related equipment.
Research Fields: Cold War & military technology.
Facilities: classroom. Gift items for sale.
Activities: guided tours.
Hours & Admission Prices: Daily 9-5. Adults $9.50, senior citizens, military & group rate of 20 or more $8.50, students 7-12 $6; discounts to AAA members; members, school groups & children under 6 no charge. Closed Thanksgiving; Christmas. ♿
Attendance: 50,000 (estimated)
Membership: See listing for Pima Air & Space Museum, Tucson, AZ.

Greer

BUTTERFLY LODGE MUSEUM, 4 County Rd. 1126, Greer, AZ 85927. Mailing Address: P.O. Box 76, Greer, AZ 85927-0076. Tel.: 928-735-7514.
E-mail: bflylodge@aol.com
Governing Authority: nonprofit organization.
History Museum: housed in the home of Western writer, James Willard Schultz and his artist son, Hart Merriam Schultz, also known as Lone Wolf. Listed on the National Register of Historic Places.
Collections: original furnishings; personal artifacts; paintings; sculptures.
Activities: special events; education classes.
Hours & Admission Prices: Memorial Day to Labor Day Thurs.-Sun. & holidays 10-5. Adults $2, youth 12-17 $1; children no charge.

Hereford

CORONADO NATIONAL MEMORIAL, 4101 E. Montezuma Canyon Rd., Hereford, AZ 85615-9376. Tel.: 520-366-5515, ext. 22. Fax: 520-366-5705.
Web Site: www.nps.gov/coro
Founded: 1952.
Congressional District: 5
Key Personnel: Supt., Kym A. Hall; Museum Shop Mgr., Linda Connell.
Personnel Profile: Full-Time Paid 2; Part-Time Volunteers 10.
Governing Authority: federal. Parent Institution: National Park Service, Washington, DC. Tax-exempt.
Park Museum & Visitor Center.
Collections: historical books; mid-16th century Spanish costumes documents & weapons; European exploration of the American Southwest 1540-1542.
Research Fields: early Spanish-Mexican history; natural history; Hispanic-Mexican culture.
Facilities: nature trails; picnic area. Historical & natural history books for sale.
Activities: self-guided tours; talks; permanent exhibits.
Publications: brochure, Coronado National Memorial.
Hours & Admission Prices: Daily 9-5. No charge; donations accepted. Closed Thanksgiving; Christmas. ♿
Attendance: 26,000 (accurate)

Holbrook

NAVAJO COUNTY MUSEUM, 100 E. Arizona St., Holbrook, AZ 86025-2698. Tel.: 928-524-2459. Fax: 928-524-1719.
History Museum.
Collections: local history & culture; Native American artifacts; personal artifacts; photographs; period furnishings.
Activities: Indian dance performances in summer.
Hours & Admission Prices: Winter: daily 8-5; Summer: daily extended hours. No charge; donations accepted.

Jerome

GOLD KING MINING MUSEUM AND GHOST TOWN, Perkinsville Rd., Jerome, AZ 86331. Mailing Address: P.O. Box 156, Jerome, AZ 86331-0156. Tel.: 928-634-0053.
Mining Museum.
Collections: local history; mining & mining equipment; period buildings & saw mill; mine shaft.
Facilities: Museum-related items for sale.
Hours & Admission Prices: Call for hours.

JEROME HISTORICAL SOCIETY MINE MUSEUM, 200 Main St., Jerome, AZ 86331. Mailing Address: P.O. Box 156, Jerome, AZ 86331-0156. Tel.: 928-634-5477.
Historical Society Museum.
Collections: mining equipment; ore carts; photographs; personal artifacts; maps; documents.
Facilities: Museum-related items for sale.
Hours & Admission Prices: Daily 9-5. Adults $2, seniors $1; children no charge.

JEROME STATE HISTORIC PARK, 100 Douglas Rd., Jerome, AZ 86331. Mailing Address: P.O. Box D, Jerome, AZ 86331-0097. Tel.: 928-634-5381. Fax: 928-639-3132.
Web Site: www.azstateparks.com
Founded: 1962.
Congressional District: 3
Key Personnel: Supvr., Mike Rollins.
Personnel Profile: Full-Time Paid 4; Part-Time Paid 1; Part-Time Volunteers 4.
Governing Authority: state. Parent Institution: Arizona State Parks Board, Phoenix, AZ. Tax-exempt.
History & Mining Museum.
Collections: mining industry; mineralogy.
Facilities: picnic area. Museum-related items for sale.
Activities: self-guided tours; video program on Jerome history.
Hours & Admission Prices: Daily 8-5. Annual permit $50, adults 14 & over $3; children 13 & under no charge. Closed Christmas. ♿
Attendance: 70,584 (accurate)

Kayenta

KAYENTA VISITOR'S CENTER, Hwy. 160, Kayenta, AZ 86033. Mailing Address: P.O. Box 544, Kayenta, AZ 86033-0544. Tel.: 928-697-3572.
Visitor Center.
Collections: Navajo history & culture; personal artifacts; period furnishings.
Facilities: outdoor amphitheatre. Museum-related items for sale.
Activities: demonstrations; performances; special events.
Hours & Admission Prices: Call for hours.

Kingman

MOHAVE MUSEUM OF HISTORY AND ARTS, 400 W. Beale, Kingman, AZ 86401-5797. Tel.: 928-753-3195. Fax: 928-718-1562.
E-mail: mocohist@citlink.net
Web Site: www.mohavemuseum.org
Founded: 1961.
Congressional District: 1 & 2
Key Personnel: Dir. & C.E.O., Shannon Rossiter; Pres. (V), Jerry Wienke.
Personnel Profile: Full-Time Paid 4; Part-Time Paid 1; Part-Time Volunteers 88.
Governing Authority: Parent Institution: Mohave County Historical Society. Tax-exempt: 501(c)(3).
History Museum: housing Mohave County history.
Collections: Indian artifacts; archaeology; military; mining items; Andy Devine memorabilia; portraits of presidents & their wives; turquoise figurines; maps of area; c.1890 wooden caboose; ranching; wildlife replicas of western animals; 34 ft. mine tunnel replica with gem stones; mine artifacts & wildlife sanctuary murals of western wildlife; manuscripts.
Research Fields: Indian artifacts; archaeology; mining; northwestern Arizona history.
Facilities: library of books and manuscripts of local history photos available for use on premises; microfilms of newspapers & genealogy records; photograph archives relating to area; auditorium. Indian crafts, books & museum-related items for sale.
Activities: lectures; gallery talks; school tours; permanent & temporary exhibitions; monthly Mohave County Genealogical Society meetings. Museum Sponsors: Organ Concerts.
Publications: newsletter, museum exhibits guidebook; walking tour map; local history brochures.
Hours & Admission Prices: Mon.-Fri. 9-5, Sat. 1-5. Adults $4, seniors $3; discounts to AAM members; members no charge. Closed New Year's Day; Easter; Memorial Day; Labor Day; Thanksgiving; Christmas. ♿
Attendance: 30,000
Membership: Individual $25; Family $30; Sustaining $40; Contributing $80; Supporting $130; Business $200; Corporate $500.

ROUTE 66 MUSEUM, 120 W. Andy Devine Ave., Kingman, AZ 86401-5870. Tel.: 928-753-9889.
Founded: 2001.
History Museum: housed in the historical Powerhouse building.
Collections: highway travel history; murals; photographs; dioramas; U.S. Army & Native American artifacts.
Facilities: theater.
Activities: guided tours; school group tours. Museum Sponsors: Fun Hunt.
Hours & Admission Prices: Daily 9-5. Adults $4, seniors 60 & over $3; discounts to groups; children under 12 no charge. ♿

Lake Havasu City

LAKE HAVASU MUSEUM OF HISTORY, 320 London Bridge Rd., Lake Havasu City, AZ 86403-4645. Tel.: 928-854-4938.
Personnel Profile: Part-Time Paid 2; Part-Time Volunteers 30.

Governing Authority: Parent Institution: Lake Havasu City Historical Society. Tax-exempt.
History Museum.
Collections: local history; Chemehuevi Tribe history & culture; mining; steamboats; maps & documents of the lower Colorado river; Parker Dam; London Bridge.
Research Fields: lower Colorado river disputes.
Activities: lectures.
Hours & Admission Prices: Tues.-Sat. 1-4. Adults $4; members and children 12 & under no charge. Closed New Year's Day; Independence Day; Thanksgiving; Christmas. ♿
Attendance: 3,500 (accurate)
Membership: Single $20; Family $30; Sustaining $50; Business $60; Patron $100.

Litchfield Park

WILDLIFE WORLD ZOO & AQUARIUM, 16501 W. Northern, Litchfield Park, AZ 85340-9466. Tel.: 623-935-9453. Fax: 623-935-9499.
Web Site: www.wildlifeworld.com
Founded: 1984.
Key Personnel: Dir., Mickey Ollson; Deputy Dir., Jack Ewert; Education, Antoinette Cancellaro; Museum Shop Mgr., Anna Milts.
Personnel Profile: Full-Time Paid 32; Part-Time Paid 4; Part-Time Volunteers 10; Interns 2.
Governing Authority: private; profit.
Zoo & Aquarium.
Collections: 320 species of exotic animals.
Facilities: 580-vol. library of zoological books; aquarium; 400-seat outdoor theater; zoological park. Zoo-related items for sale.
Activities: formal education programs for children; guided tours; lectures; mobile vans; broadcast programs.
Publications: quarterly newsletter.
Hours & Admission Prices: Daily 9-5. Adults $26.95, senior citizens $25.95, children $13.95. ♿
Attendance: 450,000 (estimated)
Membership: Children $60; Adult $100.

Maricopa

AK-CHIN HIM-DAK ECO-MUSEUM, 47685 N. Eco-Museum Rd., Maricopa, AZ 85239-2850. Tel.: 520-568-9480. Fax: 520-568-9557.
E-mail: epeters@ak-chin.nsn.us
Key Personnel: C.E.O. & Dir., Elaine Peters
Cultural History Museum.
Collections: cultural history; personal artifacts.
Hours & Admission Prices: Mon.-Fri. 9-5, Sat. 8-4 by appointment. No charge; donations accepted.

Mesa

ARIZONA MUSEUM FOR YOUTH, (M), 35 N. Robson, Mesa, AZ 85201-7326. Tel.: 480-644-2467 & 2468. Fax: 480-644-2466.
E-mail: azmus4youth@cityofmesa.org
Web Site: arizonamuseumforyouth.com
Founded: 1980.
Congressional District: 1
Key Personnel: Chm., Deb Dahl; Membership Information, Darlene Zajda; Exec. Dir., Sunnee D. Spencer; Cur., Jeffory Morris; Teacher & Mgr. School Programs, Dena Cruz; Exhibitions Coord., Rex Witte; Exhibits Fabricator, Mark Fromeyer; Business Mgr., Beth Bartholow; Community Arts Coord., Michelle Belani.
Personnel Profile: Full-Time Paid 11; Full-Time Volunteers 10; Part-Time Paid 15; Part-Time Volunteers 10.
Governing Authority: partnership. Parent Institution: City of Mesa, AZ. Tax-exempt: 501(c)(3).
Children's Fine Arts Center.
Collections:
Facilities: classrooms.
Activities: guided tours; formally organized education programs for children.
Publications: triannual newsletters; pre-visit & follow-up brochures for teachers.
Hours & Admission Prices: Tues.-Sat. 10-4, Sun. 12-4. Admission $6.50; discounts to AAM & Association of Children's Museums members; children 1 & under and members no charge. Fee for special exhibits. ♿
Attendance: 70,546 (accurate)
Membership: Family of 2 $50; Family of 4 $70; Family of 6 $120; Family of 8 $175.

ARIZONA MUSEUM OF NATURAL HISTORY, (M), 53 N. MacDonald St., Mesa, AZ 85201-7325. Tel.: 480-644-2230. Fax: 480-644-3424.
E-mail: azmnh.info@mesaaz.gov
Web Site: www.azmnh.org
Formerly: Mesa Southwest Museum
Founded: 1977.
Congressional District: 1
Key Personnel: Dir., Dr. Thomas H. Wilson; Cur. Natural History, Dr. Robert McCord; Cur. Anthropology, Dr. Jerry Howard; Lead Collections Specialist, Margaret MacMimm-Barton; Coord. Exhibits, Tim Walters; Exhibits Preparator, Mike Keller; Collections Specialist, Gavin McCullough; Museum Education Asst., Alice Jung; Cur. Education, Kathy Eastman; Budget Specialist, Sandra Williamson; Administrative Asst., Barbara Dixon; Exhibits Technician, Michael Ramos; Museum Shop Mgr., Terri Karl; Volunteer Coord., Yvonne Petersen; Membership Coord., Nikki Bunnel.
Personnel Profile: Full-Time Paid 15; Part-Time Paid 3; Part-Time Volunteers 300.
Governing Authority: municipal. Parent Institution: City of Mesa. Tax-exempt: 501(c)(3); 170(B)(1)(A).
Natural History Museum.
Collections: natural & cultural history of the American Southwest; over 47,000 objects including: 14,000 photographs; paleontology & mineralogy; archaeology of the Hohokam & other prehistoric cultures of the Southwest & Mesoamerica; ethnology; ethnographic dolls; Spanish mission period; pioneer, Frontier & 1950 domestic life; farming; ranching; transportation; Arizona movie memorabilia; historic photographs; comparative collections: osteology; Arizona geology; prehistoric ceramics. Historic House: Sirrine House.
Research Fields: Southwestern archaeology & ethnology; western paleontology; regional & local history.
Facilities: 7,000-vol. reference library; over 80,000 sq. ft. exhibit space; 150-seat auditorium/theater; Mesa Grande archaeological site. Museum-related items for sale.
Activities: formal docent program; traveling & temporary exhibits; gallery tours; school loan services; children's workshops; lectures; teen volunteer program; symposia; theater; educational outreach & inhouse programs.
Publications: gallery guides; festival programs; docent training manuals; educational school packets; archaeological & paleontological newsletters; scientific publications; archaeological site reports; monograph series; historic surveys; postcards; brochures; volunteer newsletter; symposia proceedings.
Hours & Admission Prices: Tues.-Fri. 10-5, Sat. 12-5, Sun. 1-5. Adults $10, senior citizens 65 & over $9, students $8; children 3-12 $6; discounts to AAA, AAM & ICOM members; children under 3 & members no charge. ♿
Attendance: 135,643 (accurate)
Membership: General $70; Friend $125; Contributor $250; Patron $500; Curator's Circle $1,000; Director's Circle $1,500. Corporate: Friend $1,000; Contributor $2,500; Patron $5,000.

MESA CONTEMPORARY ARTS, One E. Main St., Mesa, AZ 85211. Mailing Address: P.O. Box 1466, Mesa, AZ 85211-1466. Tel.: 480-644-6560.
Web Site: www.mesaartscenter.org
Founded: 1976.
Key Personnel: Exec. Dir., Johann Zietsman; Cur., Patty Haberman
Contemporary Art Museum.
Collections: paintings; sculpture; photography; decorative arts.
Hours & Admission Prices: Tues.-Wed. & Fri.-Sat. 10-5, Thurs. 10-8, Sun. 12-5. Admission $3.50; children 7 & under and Thurs. no charge. ♿

MESA HISTORICAL MUSEUM, (M), 2345 N. Horne, Mesa, AZ 85203-1823. Mailing Address: P.O. Box 582, Mesa, AZ 85211-0582. Tel.: 480-835-7358.
E-mail: info@mesahistoricalmuseum.org
Web Site: www.mesaaz.org
Founded: 1966.
Key Personnel: Pres. & C.E.O., Lisa Anderson; Chm. Bd. (V), Victor Linoff.
Personnel Profile: Full-Time Paid 3; Part-Time Paid 4; Part-Time Volunteers 120.
Governing Authority: private; nonprofit organization. Tax-exempt: 501(c)(3).
History Museum
Collections: history of Mesa, Arizona & the surrounding area.
Facilities: library; 400-seat auditorium; classrooms. Museum-related items for sale.
Activities: docent program; guided tours; lectures; temporary exhibitions.
Publications: monthly members newsletter; books.
Hours & Admission Prices: Tues.-Sat. 9-1. Adults $5, seniors over 65 $4, youth 3-12 $3; discounts to groups; children under 3 & members no charge. Closed major holidays. ♿
Attendance: 28,000 (estimated)

Membership: Individual $35; Family $50; Business $500; Friend $1,000.

Nogales

PIMERIA ALTA HISTORICAL SOCIETY, 136 N. Grand Ave., Nogales, AZ 85621-3211. Mailing Address: P.O. Box 2281, Nogales, AZ 85628-2281. Tel.: 520-287-4621. Fax: 520-287-5201.
Founded: 1948.
Congressional District: 2
Key Personnel: Pres., Kathleen Escalada; Project Dir., Sigrid Maitrejean.
Personnel Profile: Full-Time Paid 1; Full-Time Volunteers 7; Part-Time Paid 2; Part-Time Volunteers 5.
Governing Authority: nonprofit organization. Tax-exempt: 501(c)(3).
Historical Society Museum.
Collections: artifacts of prehistoric & historic Indians of Pimeria Alta; Mexican & American artifacts from period of settlement including items from mining, ranching, local & household industries; 19th- & 20th-century settlement of south Arizona & north Sonora, Mexico; 10,000 regional historic photographs.
Research Fields: history of northwest Sonora, Mexico & southern Arizona.
Facilities: 1,000-vol. library of history & geography books & newspapers dating from 1893, available for use only on premises; archives of Nogales.
Activities: guided tours; lectures; films; permanent exhibitions; trips into Mexico; self guided walking tour; educational & public programming.
Publications: newsletter; annual historic calendar; archaeology reports; local history books; Pimeria Post.
Hours & Admission Prices: Thurs.-Sat. 10-4. No charge; donations accepted. Closed New Year's Day; Thanksgiving; Christmas. ♿
Attendance: 3,359 (accurate)
Membership: Student $1; Individual $20; Family $30; Patron $75; Centennial $100; Silver $250; Gold $500; Medallion $1,000.

Page

JOHN WESLEY POWELL MEMORIAL MUSEUM, 6 N. Lake Powell Blvd., Page, AZ 86040. Mailing Address: Box 547, Page, AZ 86040-0547. Tel.: 928-645-9496. Fax: 928-645-3412.
E-mail: director@powellmuseum.org
Web Site: www.powellmuseum.org
Founded: 1969.
Congressional District: 1
Key Personnel: Dir., Roy Boughton; Pres. (V), Pat Talbott; Museum Shop Mgr., Erin Manzutto.
Personnel Profile: Full-Time Paid 3; Part-Time Paid 1; Part-Time Volunteers 2.
Governing Authority: nonprofit organization. Tax-exempt.
History Museum.
Collections: archives; anthropology; archaeology; ethnology; geology; Indian artifacts; mineralogy; paleontology; philatelic; John Wesley Powell memorial items; films & written records of river runners on the Colorado River & its tributaries; manuscripts.
Major Exhibits: U.S. Dept. of Education Office of Indian Education Student Artist Competition (T), 2/19/10-3/19/10.
Research Fields: historical films & data of area prior to Glen Canyon Dam & city of Page's development.
Facilities: library of books on Colorado River, reclamation, Glen Canyon Dam, Lake Powell, city of Page, John Wesley Powell's life & works, guidebooks of the West & special collections library; reading room. Books & other museum related items for sale.
Activities: guided tours; permanent & temporary exhibitions.
Publications: booklet.
Hours & Admission Prices: Feb. to mid-Dec. Mon.-Sat. 9-5. Adults $5, senior citizens 61 & over $3, children 5-13 $1; members no charge. Closed Thanksgiving; Christmas. ♿
Attendance: 16,594 (accurate)
Membership: Child, Student & Visitor $10; Individual $35; Family $50; Business $150.

Parker

BILL WILLIAMS RIVER NATIONAL WILDLIFE REFUGE, 60911 Hwy. 95, Parker, AZ 85344-9528. Tel.: 928-667-4144.
Key Personnel: Mgr., Richard Gilbert
Wildlife Refuge.
Collections: wildlife & their habitat; natural history; trees; plants; flowers.
Facilities: nature trails.
Activities: hiking.
Hours & Admission Prices: Call for hours.

COLORADO RIVER INDIAN TRIBES MUSEUM, (M), Rte. 1, Parker, AZ 85344. Mailing Address: Rte. 1, Box 23-B, Parker, AZ 85344-7737. Tel.: 928-669-9211, ext. 1335. Fax: 928-669-8262.
Founded: 1970.
Congressional District: 3
Key Personnel: Dir., Michael Tsosie; Librarian & Archivist, Amelia Flores.
Personnel Profile: Full-Time Paid 4; Part-Time Paid 2; Part-Time Volunteers 1.
Governing Authority: Colorado River Indian Tribes. Tax-exempt.
American Indian Museum.
Collections: anthropology; archaeology; Mohave; Chemehuevi; Navajo & Hopi; Anasazi; Hohokam & Patayan tribes; Colorado River area history & ethnology; Japanese Memorial, World War II, Poston, AZ. Historic Buildings: 1917 Old Presbyterian Indian Church; 1860 La Paz, Arizona territorial mining town.
Research Fields: archaeology; linguistics; history; oral history.
Facilities: 2,000-vol. library of books pertaining to the American Indians, Mohave & Chemehuevi archives, microfilm & photograph collection of the reservation available for inter-library loan. Indian-made arts & crafts for sale.
Activities: permanent exhibitions; oral history; crafts workshops; linguistics workshops; La Paz archaeological excavation & reconstruction.
Hours & Admission Prices: Mon.-Fri. 8-5, Sat. 10-3; call for holiday hours. No charge; donations accepted.
Attendance: 4,000 (estimated)

Payson

NORTHERN GILA COUNTY HISTORICAL SOCIETY, INC. - RIM COUNTRY MUSEUM, 700 Green Valley Pkwy., Payson, AZ 85547. Mailing Address: P.O. Box 2532, Payson, AZ 85547-2532. Tel.: 928-474-3483 & 8392. Fax: 928-474-3483.
E-mail: ngchs1@gmail.com
Web Site: www.rimcountrymuseums.com
Founded: 1986.
Congressional District: 4
Key Personnel: Pres., Judy Buettner; Financial Dir., Nancy Purkey; Archivist, Sandy Carson; Security, Jim Buettner; Museum Shop Mgr., Betty Berryman.
Personnel Profile: Part-Time Volunteers 45.
Governing Authority: private; nonprofit organization. Parent Institution: Northern Gila County Historical Society, Inc., Payson, AZ. Tax-exempt: 501(c)(3).
Cultural History Museum.
Collections: archaeological exhibit of Risser Ruin Site; Tonto Apache-Yavapai Indian; Indian/Anglo interaction (advent of cavalry); early pioneer artifacts; local industry.
Research Fields: local histories; landmarks; Tonto Apaches & Yavapai.
Facilities: 300-vol. library of oral histories; 3,200 sq. ft. exhibit space. Gift items for sale.
Activities: art festival; docent program; guided tours; lectures; loan & participatory exhibitions.
Publications: bimonthly newsletter, Northern Gila County Historical Society; books, Rim Country Press.
Hours & Admission Prices: Wed.-Mon. 10-4. Requested Donation: adults $5, seniors 55 & over $4, students 12-18 $3; discounts to seniors & AAM members; members & children under 12 no charge. Closed Easter; Thanksgiving; Christmas. ♿
Attendance: 4,400 (estimated)
Membership: Individual $25; Family $35; Miners Club $50; Settlers Club $100; Loggers Club & Business Booster $250; Ranchers Club $500; Directors Camp & Corporate Sponsor $1,000.

Peoria

CHALLENGER SPACE CENTER OF ARIZONA, 21170 N. 83rd Ave., Peoria, AZ 85382-2458. Tel.: 623-322-2001.
Web Site: www.azchallenger.org
Key Personnel: Exec. Dir., Mary Lynn Kelly; Museum Shop Mgr., Carole LaConte.
Governing Authority: non-profit. 501 (c)(3).
Space Museum.
Collections: interactive exhibits relating to math, science & technology; meteorite collection.
Facilities: planetarium; theater. Museum-related items for sale.
Activities: education programs; simulated space flight missions; youth summer camps; preschool program; scout & youth group activities.
Hours & Admission Prices: Mon.-Fri. 9-4, Sat. 10-4. Adults $6, students 6-18 and seniors 55 & over $4; children 5 & under and members no charge. Closed New Year's Day; Memorial Day; Independence Day; Labor Day; Thanksgiving & day after; Christmas Eve & Day. ♿

Peridot

SAN CARLOS APACHE CULTURAL CENTER, Hwy. 70 at Milepost 272, Peridot, AZ 85542. Mailing Address: P.O. Box 760, Peridot, AZ 85542-0760. Tel.: 928-475-2894.
Cultural Center.
Collections: San Carlos Apaches Indian history & culture; personal artifacts; baskets; paintings; sculptures & carvings.
Activities: educational programs; demonstrations.
Hours & Admission Prices: Mon.-Fri. 9-5. Adults $3, seniors $1.50, students $1; children under 12 no charge.

Petrified Forest National Park

PETRIFIED FOREST NATIONAL PARK, One Park Rd., Petrified Forest National Park, AZ 86028-9997. Mailing Address: P.O. Box 2217, Petrified Forest National Park, AZ 86028-2217. Tel.: 928-524-6228, ext. 267. Fax: 928-524-3567.
E-mail: patricia_thompson@nps.gov
Web Site: www.nps.gov
Founded: 1906.
Congressional District: 1
Key Personnel: C.E.O. & Supt., Cliff Spencer; Chief Resource Mgmt., Pat Thompson; Museum Shop Mgr., Paul DoBell.
Personnel Profile: Full-Time Paid 1.
Governing Authority: federal. Parent Institution: U.S. Dept. of the Interior. Subsidiary Institution: National Park Service, U.S. Dept. of the Interior. Tax-exempt.
National Park.
Collections: vertebrate & invertebrate paleontology specimens; paleobotanical; zoological; geology & archaeology of Petrified Forest National Park. Historic Building: 1924 Painted Desert Inn.
Research Fields: geology, paleontology, archaeology of Petrified Forest National Park.
Facilities: library of material relating to the collections; 40-seat auditorium; 93,533 acres.
Activities: self-guided tours; park orientation film.
Publications: book, Petrified Forest National Park: The Story Behind The Scenery; book, This is Painted Desert; Dawn of the Dinosaur; book, The Painted Desert Land of Light & Shadow; book, The Petrified Forest Thru the Ages; Tapamveni: The Rock Art Galleries of Petrified Forest & Beyond.
Hours & Admission Prices: Summer & Winter: daily 8-5; Spring & Fall call for hours. Car: $10, Bus $5; Golden Eagle, Golden Age & Golden Access passes honored. Closed Christmas. ♿
Attendance: 580,000 (estimated)

Phoenix

ADOBE MOUNTAIN RAILROAD MUSEUM & DESERT RAILROAD, 23280 N. 43rd Ave., Phoenix, AZ 85310. Tel.: 623-670-1904.
Railroad Museum.
Collections: model railroad layouts; small, narrow-gauge 1884 locomotive.
Activities: train rides.
Hours & Admission Prices: Sept.-May Sun. 12-4; other times by appointment.

ARIZONA CAPITOL MUSEUM, (M), 1700 W. Washington St., Phoenix, AZ 85007-2812. Tel.: 602-926-3620. Fax: 602-256-7985.
E-mail: capmus@lib.az.us
Web Site: www.lib.az.us/museum
Founded: 1974.
Congressional District: 1
Key Personnel: Dir., David H. Hoober; C.E.O., GladysAnn Wells; Cur., Brenda McLain; Admin. Asst., Taylor Arrazola; Museum Shop Mgr., Micki Henningsen.
Personnel Profile: Full-Time Paid 9; Part-Time Volunteers 40; Interns 1.
Governing Authority: state. Parent Institution: Arizona State Library, Archives & Public Records. Tax-exempt: 170(b).
History Museum: housed in restored Capitol Building.
Collections: Arizona government history.
Research Fields: Arizona government history.
Facilities: 54,000 sq. ft. of exhibits. Museum-related items for sale.
Activities: guided tours; permanent & temporary exhibits; seminars; lectures.
Hours & Admission Prices: Mon.-Fri. 8-5. No charge. ♿
Attendance: 60,000 (accurate)
Membership: Active & Associate $20; Patron $40.

ARIZONA DOLL AND TOY MUSEUM, 602 E. Adams St. at Heritage Sq., Phoenix, AZ 85004-2351. Tel.: 602-253-9337.
Founded: 1988.
Key Personnel: Pres. (V), Kathleen Lanford; Museum Shop Mgr., Dale Cantrell.
Personnel Profile: Full-Time Paid 1; Part-Time Volunteers 15.
Governing Authority: nonprofit. Tax-exempt.
Doll and Toy Museum.
Collections: period dolls & toys; modern playthings; 1912 schoolroom.
Facilities: Museum-related items for sale.
Activities: tours.
Hours & Admission Prices: Sept.-July Tues.-Sat. 10-4, Sun. 12-4. Call for admission prices; discounts to seniors & handicapped. ♿
Attendance: 7,500 (estimated)

ARIZONA JEWISH HISTORICAL SOCIETY, 4710 N. 16th St., Ste. 201, Phoenix, AZ 85016-4650. Tel.: 602-241-7870. Fax: 602-264-9773.
E-mail: azjhs@aol.com
Web Site: www.azjhs.org
Founded: 1981.
Congressional District: 4
Key Personnel: Exec. Dir., Lawrence Bell, Ph.D.; Pres. (V), Louise Leverant.
Personnel Profile: Full-Time Paid 1; Part-Time Paid 1; Part-Time Volunteers 10.
Governing Authority: private; nonprofit organization. Tax-exempt: 501(c)(3).
Jewish Historical Society.
Collections: photos; documents; maps; artifacts; oral histories.
Research Fields: biography project creating a database of Jewish population of Greater Phoenix from 1860 to the present; oral histories.
Facilities: 300-vol. library of Jewish & Arizona history available for loan; conference room.
Activities: lectures; loan, temporary & traveling exhibitions. Historical Society Sponsors: Fundraising Dinner; Legacy Programs.
Publications: bimonthly newsletter, Heritage.
Hours & Admission Prices: Aug.-June Mon.-Fri. 9:30-3:30. No charge; donations accepted. Closed Memorial Day; Independence Day; Labor Day; Jewish Holidays; Thanksgiving; Christmas.
Membership: Family $50; Oral History $100; Permanent Home $250; Archival Preservation $500; Exhibits $1,000.

ARIZONA MILITARY MUSEUM, Papago Park Military Reservation, 5636 E. McDowell Rd., Phoenix, AZ 85003-2668. Tel.: 602-267-2676 & 253-2378.
Founded: 1981.
Governing Authority: Tax-exempt.
Military Museum.
Collections: uniforms; vehicles; artillery; military artifacts from the Civil War to the Indian and Spanish-American Wars, WWI, WWII, Korea, Vietnam & Desert Storm; POWs & MIAs; military history; Spanish Colonial; conquistadors; pre-Civil War; Desert Storm; War on Terror; Operation Iraqi Freedom.
Facilities: library.
Hours & Admission Prices: Sept.-June Sat.-Sun. 1-4. No charge; donations accepted. ♿
Attendance: 700 (estimated)
Membership: Annual $25; Life $250.

ARIZONA MINING AND MINERAL MUSEUM, 1502 W. Washington, Phoenix, AZ 85007-3210. Tel.: 602-771-1611. Fax: 602-771-1616.
E-mail: curatorazmmm@gmail.com
Web Site: www.mines.az.gov
Founded: 1953.
Congressional District: 1
Key Personnel: Dir., Dr. Madan Singh; Chm. (V), Charlie Connell; Cur., Jan Rasmussen; Museum Shop Mgr., Ann Baker.
Personnel Profile: Full-Time Paid 2; Part-Time Paid 6; Part-Time Volunteers 100.
Governing Authority: state; nonprofit organization. Parent Institution: Dept. of Mines & Mineral Resources. Tax-exempt.
Mineral Museum.
Collections: lapidary; geology; mining artifacts; mining equipment; minerals of Arizona & the world; fossils.
Activities: group programs; lectures; films; formally organized education programs for children & teachers; permanent, temporary & loan exhibits.
Publications: Directory of Earth Science Clubs in Arizona; Directory of Gem & Mineral Shows in Arizona; TeacherKit; Teacher Pac; Mineral Identification Kit; Rocks of Arizona; Minerals of Arizona.
Hours & Admission Prices: Mon.-Fri. 8-5, Sat. 11-4. Adults $2; members & children 17 and under no charge. Closed state holidays. ♿
Attendance: 50,000 (accurate)
Membership: Individual $20; Family $30; Life $200; Patron $250; Small Business $500; Curator $1,000; Corporate $5,000.

ARIZONA SCIENCE CENTER, 600 E. Washington, Phoenix, AZ 85004-2394. Tel.: 602-716-2007. Fax: 602-716-2099.
Web Site: www.azscience.org
Founded: 1984.
Congressional District: 2
Key Personnel: C.E.O. & Pres., Chevy Humphrey; Sr. Dir. Guest Experience, Patrick Weeks; Sr. Dir. Finance, Dwight Middendorf.
Personnel Profile: Full-Time Paid 51; Part-Time Paid 25; Part-Time Volunteers 400; Interns 8.
Governing Authority: nonprofit organization. Tax-exempt: 501(c)(3).
Science Center.
Collections: interactive exhibits: human body, psychology, networks, weather, aerospace, geology & physics.
Facilities: 40,000 sq. ft. exhibit space; 285-seat giant screen IMAX theater; 200-seat Digistar; Nano Seam Dome planetarium; classroom.
Activities: live science demonstrations; education programs; museum excursions.
Publications: quarterly newsletter, Elements; triannual newsletter, Educators Planner.
Hours & Admission Prices: Daily 10-5. Exhibits: adults $12, senior citizens 62 & over & children 3-17 $10. IMAX & Planetarium: additional fee; discounts to members. Closed Thanksgiving; Christmas. ♿
Attendance: 300,000 (accurate)
Membership: Basic $70; Basic Plus $85; Explorer $130; Voyager $250; Adventurer $500; Director's Circle $1,000 & up.

ARIZONA STATE PARKS BOARD, 1300 W. Washington, Phoenix, AZ 85007-2929. Tel.: 602-542-4174. Fax: 602-542-4188.
Web Site: azstateparks.com
Founded: 1957.
Key Personnel: Exec. Dir., Kenneth E. Travous; Chm., William C. Scalzo; Public Information Officer, Ellen Bilbrey; Asst. Dir., Jay Ream; Museum Cur., Michael A. Freisinger; Park Mgr. Fort Verde State Historic Park, Sheila Stubler; Park Mgr. Homolovi Ruins State Park, Karen Berggren; Park Mgr. Jerome State Historic Park, Michael Rollins; Park Mgr. Riordan Mansion State Historic Park, John Schreiber; Park Mgr. Tonto Natural Bridge State Park, John Boeck; Park Mgr. Yuma Crossing State Historic Park, Jerry Emert; Park Mgr. Yuma Territorial Prison State Historic Park, Jesse Torres; Park Mgr. McFarland State Historic Park, Christopher DeMille; Park Mgr. Tombstone Courthouse State Historic Park, Art Austin; Park Mgr. Tubac Presidio State Historic Park, Joe Martinez; Park Mgr. Kartchner Caverns State Park, Richard Ferdon; Park Mgr. Boyce Thompson Arboretum State Park, Tracey Hanley.
Governing Authority: state. Branch Museums: Fort Verde State Historic Park, Camp Verde, AZ; Jerome State Historic Park, Jerome, AZ; McFarland State Historic Park, Florence, AZ; Riordan Mansion State Historic Park, Flagstaff, AZ; Tombstone Courthouse State Historic Park, Tombstone, AZ; Tubac Presidio State Historic Park, Tubac, AZ; Yuma Territorial Prison State Historic Park, Yuma, AZ; Yuma Crossing State Historic Park, Yuma, AZ.
Historical Parks, Museums & Arboretum.
Collections: 28 parks.
Research Fields: history; nature.
Facilities: 50-vol. library of books pertaining to Southwestern history & specific sites available on premises; visitor center; archives; research facility. Books & other museum related items for sale.
Activities: guided tours; lectures; audiovisuals; permanent, temporary & traveling exhibitions.
Publications: printed handouts on historic sites; trails; natural areas.
Hours & Admission Prices: Office: daily 8-5. Parks: adults $4-$10; children under 6 no charge. Phoenix Office closed Christmas. ♿
Attendance: 350,000 (estimated)
Membership: 5 Visits $15; Limited $35; Unlimited $65

ARIZONA ZOOLOGICAL SOCIETY, DBA THE PHOENIX ZOO, (M), 455 N. Galvin Pkwy., Phoenix, AZ 85008-3431. Tel.: 602-273-1341. Fax: 602-273-7078.
E-mail: zooqna@thephxzoo.com
Web Site: www.phoenixzoo.org
Founded: 1961.
Key Personnel: Chm. Bd., Christopher Hogan; C.E.O. & Pres., Norberto J. (Bert) Castro; Volunteer Coord., Gabriele Hebert; C.F.O., Bonnie Mendoza; Exec. Vice Pres. Conservation & Education, Ruth Allard; Dir. Strategic Partnership, Patricia Bump; Registrar, Gretchen Bickert; Security, Steve Roberson; Retail Mgr., Jennifer Hall.
Personnel Profile: Full-Time Paid 197; Part-Time Paid 96; Part-Time Volunteers 400.
Governing Authority: society; nonprofit organization. Parent Institution: Arizona Zoological Society. Tax-exempt: 501(c)(3).
Zoo.
Collections: over 1,300 mammals; birds; reptiles; amphibians; invertebrates.
Facilities: 1,440-vol. library pertaining to zoology, science, husbandry & nutrition; zoological park.
Activities: guided tours; lectures; docent program; formal education programs for children; mobile vans; participatory exhibits.
Publications: bimonthly, Wild Times.
Hours & Admission Prices: Jan. 11-May & Oct.-Nov. 3 daily 9-5; June-Sept. Mon.-Fri. 7-2, Sat.-Sun. 7-4; Nov 4-Jan.10 daily 9-4. Adults $16, senior citizens $11, children $7; discounts to groups; children 2 & under and members no charge. Closed Christmas. ♿
Attendance: 1,484,724 (accurate)
Membership: Individual $50; Couple $70; Family $10 each child; Caretaker Club $120; Keeper's Club $185; Curator's Club $375; Director's Circle $1,000; President's Club $2,500; Chairman's Club $5,000; Robert Maytag Circle $10,000.

BARBARA ANDERSON GIRL SCOUT MUSEUM, Girl Scouts - Arizona Cactus-Pine Council, Inc., 3806 N. 3rd St., Ste. 200, Phoenix, AZ 85012. Mailing Address: P.O. Box 21776, Phoenix, AZ 85036-1776. Tel.: 602-452-7000; 800-352-6133. Fax: 602-452-7100.
E-mail: council@girlscoutsaz.org
Web Site: www.girlscoutsaz.org
Governing Authority: nonprofit organization.
Girl Scout Museum.
Collections: Girl Scout uniforms; handbooks; memorabilia from 1912 to present; Arizona Girl Scouting.
Hours & Admission Prices: By appointment. No charge.

DEER VALLEY ROCK ART CENTER, 3711 W. Deer Valley Rd., Phoenix, AZ 85308-2038. Tel.: 623-582-8007. Fax: 623-582-8831.
E-mail: dvrac@asu.edu
Web Site: dvrac.asu.edu
Founded: 1994.
Congressional District: 3
Key Personnel: Exec. Dir., Kim Arth; Mgr. Education & Programs, Casandra Hernandez; Mgr. Collections, Hannah Kusinitz; Front Desk, Mustafa Karamujic; Front Desk, Katherine Yang; Maintenance Supvr., Edwardo De Luna.
Personnel Profile: Full-Time Paid 3; Part-Time Paid 4; Part-Time Volunteers 75; Interns 2.
Governing Authority: public university; nonprofit. Parent Institution: Arizona State University, School of Human Evolution and Social Change, Tempe, AZ 85281. Tax-exempt: 501(c)(3).
General Museum.
Collections: early rock art site of more than 1,500 boulders with petroglyphs; period archives; photographs.
Major Exhibits: Javelinas: Knowing Our Neighbors, 11/09-9/10.
Research Fields: rock art recording & interpretation; archaeology; native gardening.
Facilities: 1,070-vol. library; art activity/classroom; nature center; nature/petroglyph outdoor trail; outdoor amphitheater; heritage garden. Gifts for sale.
Activities: docent program; films; formal education programs for undergraduate or graduate college students affiliated with university; guided tours; lectures; participatory & temporary exhibitions; children's & family programs.
Publications: quarterly newsletter, Glyph Gazette.
Hours & Admission Prices: May-Sept. Tues.-Sun. 8-2; Oct.-April Tues.-Sat. 9-5, Sun. 12-5. Adults $7, seniors & students $4, children 6-12 $3; discounts to volunteers, AAA & DVRAC members; children 5 & under no charge. ♿
Attendance: 16,000 (accurate)
Membership: Individual $25; Family $40; Friend $100; Director's Circle $500.

* **DESERT BOTANICAL GARDEN, (M),** 1201 N. Galvin Pkwy., Papago Park, Phoenix, AZ 85008-3437. Tel.: 480-941-1225. Fax: 480-481-8124. TDD: 480-481-8143.
E-mail: media@dbg.org
Web Site: www.dbg.org
Founded: 1937.
Congressional District: 1
Key Personnel: Exec. Dir., Ken Schutz; Pres., Lee Bauman Cohn; Pres. Volunteers, Dawn Goldman; Cur. Living Collection, Raul Puente; Dir. Research, Dr. Joe McAuliffe; Dir. Devel., Beverly Duzik; Deputy Dir., MaryLynn Mack; Dir. Retail, Janis Munsil; Dir. Education, Tina Wilson; Asst. Dir. Education, Nancy White; Dir. Human Resources, Mary Catellier; Dir. Exhibits, Elaine McGinn; Dir. Visitor Svcs., Marcia Flynn; Dir. Facilities, Chris McCabe; Controller, Susan Shipka; Librarian, Beth Brand; Dir. Security, Jim Carlson; Mgr. Mktg., John Sallot.

Personnel Profile: Full-Time Paid 94; Part-Time Paid 33; Part-Time Volunteers 1,166.
Governing Authority: incorporated nonprofit educational institution. Tax-exempt: 501(c)(3).
Botanical Garden.
Collections: arid land plants of the world; cactus & leaf succulents; 50,000-sheet herbarium covering Southwest United States & Mexico.
Major Exhibits: Allan Houser Sculpture Exhibit, 1/1/10-5/31/10; Spring Butterfly Exhibit, 3/6/10-5/9/10; Mariposa Monarca, 9/25/10-11/14/10.
Research Fields: basic & applied research into arid land plants; economic botany & plant conservation.
Facilities: library of botanical & arid land related books; 145 acres; 3-acre ethnobotanical area; study areas of natural desert; herbarium; auditorium; educational facility; indoor & outdoor classrooms; rental facility. Museum-related items & botanical prints for sale.
Activities: guided tours; audio tours; lectures; classes; workshops; field trips; permanent displays; special exhibitions; concerts; cultural programs.
Publications: quarterly, The Sonoran Quarterly; plant information leaflets; guide booklet; calendar; event promotional pieces.
Hours & Admission Prices: May-Sept. daily 7-8; Oct.-April daily 8-8. Adults $15, senior citizens over 60 $13.50, students $7.50, children 3-12 $5; discounts to AAA & AAM members; members no charge. Closed Independence Day; Thanksgiving; Christmas. ♿
Attendance: 369,016 (accurate)
Membership: Senita Club $75; Cholla Club $100; Agave Century Club $150; Boojum Tree Club $500; Golden Barrel Club $700; Saguaro $1,250; Curator's Circle $2,500; Director's Circle $5,000; President's Club $10,000; Founder's $25,000.

GEORGE WASHINGTON CARVER MUSEUM AND CULTURAL CENTER, 415 E. Grant St., Phoenix, AZ 85004-2659. Mailing Address: P.O. Box 20491, Phoenix, AZ 85036-0491. Tel.: 602-254-7516. Fax: 602-258-7050.
E-mail: gwcmccphax@qwestoffice.net
Web Site: www.gwcmuseumculturalcenter.org
Key Personnel: Exec. Dir., Princess Crump
History Museum: housed in Arizona's first Black high school, Phoenix Union Colored High, built in 1926.
Collections: local Black history; cultural heritage; works by local & regional visual and performing artists.
Facilities: auditorium; cafe.
Activities: monthly concerts; lectures; workshops; temporary exhibitions; rental facilities.
Hours & Admission Prices: Mon.-Fri. 10-3 by appointment. Adults $3, seniors 60 & over $2.50, youth 6-12 $2, children 3-5 $1.

HALL OF FLAME MUSEUM OF FIREFIGHTING, 6101 E. Van Buren, Phoenix, AZ 85008-3421. Tel.: 602-275-3473. Fax: 602-275-0896.
E-mail: petermolloy@hallofflame.org
Web Site: www.hallofflame.org
Founded: 1961.
Congressional District: 1
Key Personnel: Exec. Dir., Dr. Peter M. Molloy; Pres. (V), George F. Getz; Vice Pres., Bert A. Getz; Vice Pres., Lynn Getz; Sec. & Treas., Michael Olsen; Cur. Public Programs & Education, Mark Moorhead; Restorator, Donald G. Hale; Docent, Michael Lyman; Volunteer Pres., Ron Deutsch.
Personnel Profile: Full-Time Paid 5; Part-Time Paid 4; Part-Time Volunteers 24.
Governing Authority: nonprofit organization. Parent Institution: National Historical Fire Foundation, 6730 N. Scottsdale Rd., Suite 250, Scottsdale, AZ 85253. Tax-exempt: 501(c)(3).
History & Fire Fighting Museum.
Collections: over 130 major pieces of firefighting equipment dating from 1700-1970; over 10,000 objects & graphic materials relating to the history of firefighting; over 40,000 photographs plus 6,000 books, serials & trade catalogs; National Firefighting Hall of Heroes.
Research Fields: history of fire fighting technology; social history of fire fighting in U.S.; structural & wildland firefighting.
Facilities: library; visitor center. Museum-related items for sale.
Activities: guided tours; permanent & temporary exhibitions; workshops & fire safety exhibits for children.
Publications: exhibit catalogue; quarterly newsletter; informational brochure; book, Van Der Heyden's Treatise on Firefighting in Amsterdam.
Hours & Admission Prices: Mon.-Sat. 9-5, Sun. 12-4. Adults $6, senior citizens $5, students 6-17 $4, children 3-5 $1.50; discount to groups & AAA members; members & children under 3 no charge. Closed New Year's Day; Thanksgiving; Christmas. ♿
Attendance: 35,000 (accurate)
Membership: Individual $25; Family $35; Black Helmet Brigade & Fire Professional $60; Red Helmet Brigade $100; White Helmet $250.

* **HEARD MUSEUM, (M),** 2301 N. Central Ave., Phoenix, AZ 85004-1323. Tel.: 602-252-8848. Fax: 602-252-9757.
E-mail: contact@heard.org
Web Site: www.heard.org
Founded: 1929.
Congressional District: 4
Key Personnel: Dir. Collections & Education, Ann E. Marshall, Ph.D.; Dir., Letitia Chambers; Dir. Devel., Geri Wright; Bd. Trustees Pres., John Stiteler; Guild Pres., Ann Gorton; Dir. Finance, Doug Thomey; Dir. American Indian Rels., Wendy Weston; Dir. Mktg. Communications, Juliet Martin; Mktg. Communications Mgr., Nicole Haas; Dir. Educational Svcs., Gina Laczko; Cur. Collections, Diana Pardue; Registrar, Sharon Moore; Assoc. Registrar, Marcus Monenerkit; Dir. Library & Archives, Mario Nick Klimiades; Creative Dir., Lisa MacCollum; Museum Shop Dir., Bruce McGee; Cur. Fine Art, Joe Baker; Assoc. Cur. Heard Museum North, Tricia Loscher; Assoc. Cur. Heard Museum West, Janet Cantley.
Personnel Profile: Full-Time Paid 80; Part-Time Paid 20; Part-Time Volunteers 700; Interns 4.
Governing Authority: nonprofit. Subsidiary Institution: Heard Museum North, 32633 N. Scottsdale Rd., Scottsdale, AZ 85262. Tel.: 480-488-9817. Heard Museum West, 16126 N. Civic Center Plaza, Surprise, AZ 85374. Tel.: 623-344-2200. Tax-exempt: 501(c)(3).
Native Cultures & Art Museum.
Collections: works by American Indians; native arts from the cultures of Africa, Asia, Oceania & upper Amazon; archaeology; ethnology; paintings; sculpture; anthropology.
Research Fields: anthropology; American Indian art; cross-cultural education.
Facilities: 45,000-vol. library of reference material available to the public for reference only. Southwestern Indian crafts, fine art, books & other museum-related items for sale.
Activities: guided tours; lectures; films; gallery talks; arts festivals; regular weekend programs; workshops; permanent, temporary, changing & traveling exhibitions. Annual Events: 19th World Championship Hoop Dance Contest in February; Heard Museum Guild Indian Fair & Market in March; A Gathering of Carvers: Katsina Doll Marketplace in April; Heard Museum Spanish Market; Holidays at the Heard in December.
Publications: newsletter; occasional catalogs & books on Indian arts and crafts, biannual magazine.
Hours & Admission Prices: Mon.-Sat. 9:30-5, Sun. 11-5. Adults $12, senior citizens 65 & over $11, students w/ID $5, children 6-12 $3; discounts to AAM members; children under 6, Native Americans with a tribal enrollment card & members no charge. Closed New Year's Day; Easter; Memorial Day; Independence Day; Labor Day; Thanksgiving; Christmas. ♿
Attendance: 200,000 (estimated)
Membership: Friend $60; Supporter $90; Patron $150; Sustaining Patron $250; Curator's Society $500; Director's Circle $1,250.

MUSICAL INSTRUMENT MUSEUM, (M), (I), Mayo & Tatum Blvd., Phoenix, AZ 85284. Mailing Address: Temporary Headquarters, 8550 S. Priest Dr., Phoenix, AZ 85284. Tel.: 480-481-2460. Fax: 480-481-2459.
Web Site: www.themim.org
Key Personnel: Dir., Dr. Billie DeWalt; Treas., Pat Maney; Registrar, Sharon Aponte Misdea; Cur., Jennifer Post; Cur., Sunni Fass; Cur., Christopher Miller.
Personnel Profile: Full-Time Paid 15.
Governing Authority: private; nonprofit organization.
Musical Instrument Museum.
Collections: instruments from around the world; history & diversity of instruments; music & world cultures; audio & video.
Research Fields: use, conservation, preservation, performance, history, significance and cultural context of musical instruments.
Facilities: library; 75,000 sq. ft. exhibit space; restaurant; classrooms. Museum-related items for sale.
Activities: educational programs; special events.
Hours & Admission Prices: Opening Spring 2010. Call for information. ♿

MYSTERY CASTLE, 800 E. Mineral Rd., Phoenix, AZ 85042-8341. Tel.: 602-268-1581.
Historic Building: built in the 1930s by Boyce Luther Gulley.
Collections: family history; personal artifacts; period furnishings; photographs.
Hours & Admission Prices: Oct. to mid-June Thurs.-Sun. 11-4.

PHOENIX AIRPORT MUSEUM, (M), 3400 Sky Harbor Blvd., Terminal 3, Level 3 W., Phoenix, AZ 85034-4403. Tel.: 602-683-3647.
Personnel Profile: Full-Time Paid 4; Part-Time Paid 2.
Governing Authority: city.
History Museum.

Collections: Arizona's history & cultural heritage.
Activities: permanent & temporary exhibits.
Hours & Admission Prices: Daily 24 hours. No charge. ♿

* **PHOENIX ART MUSEUM,** 1625 N. Central Ave., Phoenix, AZ 85004-1685. Tel.: 602-257-1880. Fax: 602-253-8662.
E-mail: info@phxart.org
Web Site: www.phxart.org
Founded: 1959.
Congressional District: 1
Key Personnel: Pres. Bd. Trustees (V), Ellen Katz; Dir., Cur. American & Western American Art, James K. Ballinger; Asst. to Dir., Samantha Klick; Deputy Dir. Administration, Gary Egan; Deputy Dir. External Affairs, Robert Chamberlain; Public Information Officer, Mindi Carr; Cur. Modern & Contemporary Art, Sara Cochran; Cur. Asian Art, Dr. Janet Baker; Cur. Fashion Design, Dennita Sewell; Research Cur. of Asian Art, Dr. Claudia Brown; Cur. American Art, Jerry Smith; Registrar, Leesha Alston; Librarian, Sandra Wiles; Museum Store Mgr., Lee Werhan.
Personnel Profile: Full-Time Paid 103; Part-Time Paid 41; Part-Time Volunteers 2,442; Interns 15.
Governing Authority: nonprofit. Tax-exempt: 501(c)(3).
Art Museum.
Collections: American, European & Asian paintings and ceramics; sculpture; graphics; decorative arts; 18th, 19th & 20th-century fashion design; Latin & Western American art; Thorne miniatures; modern & contemporary art.
Research Fields: American, European & Oriental paintings & ceramics; sculpture; graphics; decorative arts; fashion design.
Facilities: 50,000-vol. library of art reference books available for use on premises; 55,000 slide collection; 300-seat auditorium; cafe; classrooms; banquet facilities. Museum-related items for sale.
Activities: guided tours; lectures; films; gallery talks; concerts; arts festivals; formally organized education programs; docent program; inter-museum loan, permanent, participatory, temporary & traveling exhibitions; films; rental facilities.
Publications: membership magazine & brochures; exhibition schedule & catalogues; brochures, exhibition highlights; education.
Hours & Admission Prices: Wed. 10-9, Thurs.-Sat 10-5, Sun. 12-5, 1st Fri. of month 10-10. Adults $10, senior citizens & full time students with ID $8, children 6-17 $4; members & children under 6 no charge. ♿
Attendance: 210,000 (accurate)
Membership: General $75; Contributor $100; Supporter $200; Sponsor $400; Patron $750; Director's Circle $1,250; Connoisseurs' Circle $2,500; Trustees' Circle $5,000; President's Circle $10,000; Founders' Circle $25,000.

PHOENIX POLICE MUSEUM, 101 S. Central Ave., Ste. 100, Phoenix, AZ 85004-2410. Tel.: 602-534-7278.
E-mail: mike.nikolin@phoenix.gov
Web Site: phoenixpolicemuseum.com
Founded: 1994.
Key Personnel: Cur., Michael Nikolin.
Governing Authority: Tax-exempt.
Police Museum.
Collections: history & heritage of the police department; hands-on exhibits; memorial room.
Facilities: Museum-related items for sale.
Publications: newsletter.
Hours & Admission Prices: Mon., Wed. & Fri. 9-3. No charge; donations accepted. Closed city holidays. ♿
Attendance: 8,700
Membership: Annual $48.

PHOENIX TROLLEY MUSEUM/ARIZONA STREET RAILWAY MUSEUM, 1218 N. Central Ave., Phoenix, AZ 85004. Mailing Address: P.O. Box 13521, Phoenix, AZ 85002. Tel.: 602-254-0307.
Web Site: www.phoenixtrolley.com
Key Personnel: Pres., Ernest Workman; Sec., Tom Amrheim
Railway Museum.
Collections: restored 1928 Phoenix Street Railway System trolley car; Phoenix trolley system history.
Hours & Admission Prices: Oct.-May Sat. 9-4. Suggested Donation: $1 plus donation; discounts to CAMA members; members no charge. Closed New Year's Day; Thanksgiving; Christmas; holiday weekends.
Attendance: 300 (estimated)
Membership: Students $15; Individual $20; Family $35; Sustaining $100; Corporate $500.

PIONEER ARIZONA LIVING HISTORY VILLAGE & MUSEUM, 3901 W. Pioneer Rd., Exit 225, Interstate 17, Phoenix, AZ 85086. Mailing Address: 3901 W. Pioneer Rd., Phoenix, AZ 85086-7020. Tel.: 623-465-1052. Fax: 623-465-0683.
E-mail: pioneerarizona@earthlink.net
Web Site: www.pioneer-arizona.com
Founded: 1956.
Congressional District: 3
Key Personnel: Pres. (V), C.J. Smith.
Personnel Profile: Full-Time Paid 7; Part-Time Paid 2; Part-Time Volunteers 12.
Governing Authority: nonprofit organization. Parent Institution: Pioneer Foundation, Inc. Tax-exempt: 501(c)(3).
Living History Museum Complex.
Collections: over 20 late 19th-century homes & shops; 19th-century pioneer life artifacts; agricultural items & machinery; Arizona history memorabilia.
Research Fields: social & technological history of 19th-century Arizona; territorial education in rural Arizona.
Facilities: 20+ original & reconstructed buildings arranged in a rural townlike setting; day theatre; restaurant. Crafts & other museum-related items for sale.
Activities: self-guided tours; living history interpretation; special events; children's activities.
Publications: members newsletter; museum guide.
Hours & Admission Prices: June-Sept. Wed.-Sun. 8-2; Oct.-May Wed.-Sun. 9-5. Adults $7, seniors $6, students $5; children under 5 no charge. Guided Tour: $1 extra. Closed Easter; Memorial Day; Independence Day; Labor Day; Thanksgiving; Christmas. ♿
Attendance: 65,000 (estimated)
Membership: Child $20; Individual $30; Family $75; Contributing $250; Pioneer 2000 $2,000.

* **PUEBLO GRANDE MUSEUM AND ARCHAEOLOGICAL PARK, (M),** 4619 E. Washington, Phoenix, AZ 85034-1909. Tel.: 602-495-0901; 877-706-4408 (toll free). Fax: 602-495-5645.
E-mail: pueblo.grande.museum.pks@phoenix.gov
Web Site: www.pueblogrande.com
Founded: 1929.
Congressional District: 1
Key Personnel: C.E.O. & Dir., Roger Lidman; Chm. (V), Thomas Jackson; City Archaeologist, Todd Bostwick; Visitor Svcs., Stacey Mays; Cur. Collections, Holly Young; Museum Shop Mgr., Francine Kavanaugh.
Personnel Profile: Full-Time Paid 15; Part-Time Paid 6; Part-Time Volunteers 40; Interns 3.
Governing Authority: municipal. Parent Institution: City of Phoenix, Parks & Recreation Dept. Tax-exempt.
Archaeological Site Museum.
Collections: greater Southwest archaeological digs artifacts; greater Southwest Native American artifacts; territorial Phoenix archaeological artifacts.
Research Fields: pertaining to collections, the Hohokam of the Salt River Valley & southern Arizona; territorial Phoenix artifacts.
Facilities: 1,500-vol. library of Southwestern archaeology books; ethnology; community room; outdoor trail to Prehistoric Ruin.
Activities: lectures; permanent & changing exhibits; workshops; guided tours for groups by appointment; outreach exhibits & programs. Annual Event: Indian market in December.
Publications: brochures, Pueblo Grande Museum; Hohokam; Anthropological Papers No. 1, 2 & 4.
Hours & Admission Prices: May-Sept. Tues.-Sat. 9-4:45; Oct.-April Mon.-Sat. 9-4:45, Sun. 1-4:45. Adults $6, senior citizens $5, children $3; discounts to Western Museums Assoc., Central Arizona Museum Assoc. & AAM members; members & children under 6 no charge. Closed Memorial Day; Independence Day; Labor Day; Thanksgiving; Christmas. ♿
Attendance: 49,448 (accurate)
Membership: Student $5; Individual $15; Family $20; Contributing $50; Patron $100; Corporate $250.

ROSSON HOUSE MUSEUM, 7th St. & Monroe, Phoenix, AZ 85004. Mailing Address: 113 N. 6th St., Phoenix, AZ 85004-2328. Tel.: 602-262-8070.
Founded: 1982.
Key Personnel: Dir., Darla Harmon; Pres. (V), Liz Zveglich; Museum Shop Mgr., Linda Rork.
Personnel Profile: Part-Time Paid 2; Part-Time Volunteers 65; Interns 4.
Governing Authority: Tax-exempt.
Historic House Museum: built in 1895.
Collections: personal artifacts; period furnishings.
Activities: school tours.
Publications: Heritage Headlines.
Hours & Admission Prices: Wed.-Sat. 10-4, Sun. 12-4. Adults $5, seniors &

students $4, children 6-12 $2; discounts to AAA members, veterans, & active military; children 5 & under no charge. Closed Easter; Independence Day; Thanksgiving; Christmas. ♿
Membership: Student & Active Volunteer $20; General $25; Supporter $50; Sponsor $100.

SHEMER ART CENTER & MUSEUM, 5005 E. Camelback Rd., Phoenix, AZ 85018-3015. Tel.: 602-262-4727. Fax: 602-262-1605.
E-mail: shemer@phoenix.gov
Web Site: phoenix.gov/shemer
Founded: 1984.
Congressional District: 6
Key Personnel: Dir., Brian Flanigan; Cur., Lindsay Palmer; Graphic & Office, Kay Gordon.
Personnel Profile: Full-Time Paid 1; Part-Time Paid 4; Part-Time Volunteers 60; Interns 1.
Governing Authority: municipal. Tax-exempt: 501(c)(3).
Art Museum.
Collections: paintings; photographs; sculpture.
Facilities: classrooms.
Activities: Annual Events: Sunday at Shemer; family arts festival in November.
Publications: quarterly newsletter; class schedules; annual exhibit schedule; exhibition invitations.
Hours & Admission Prices: Tues. 10-9, Wed.-Fri. 10-5, Sat. 10-1. No charge; donations accepted. Closed New Year's Day; Martin Luther King Jr. Day; Presidents' Day; Cesar Chavez's Birthday; Memorial Day; Independence Day; Labor Day; Veterans Day; Thanksgiving & day after; Christmas. ♿
Attendance: 25,000 (estimated)
Membership: Individual $25; Nonprofit Group $50; Patron $100; Business $250; Corporate $500.

SUNNYSLOPE HISTORICAL SOCIETY MUSEUM, 737 E. Hatcher Rd., Phoenix, AZ 85020-2506. Tel.: 602-331-3150.
Web Site: www.sunnyslopehistoricalsociety.org
Founded: 1989.
Key Personnel: Chm. (V), Connie Kreamer.
Personnel Profile: Part-Time Volunteers 30.
Governing Authority: Tax-exempt.
History Museum.
Collections: Sunnyslope history.
Research Fields: community artifacts.
Activities: quarterly educational programs.
Publications: quarterly, The Sunnyslope Heritage.
Hours & Admission Prices: Sept.-May Wed.-Fri. & Sun. 12-4. No charge; donations accepted. ♿
Attendance: 1,000 (estimated)
Membership: $5-$250.

TELEPHONE PIONEER MUSEUM, 20 E. Thomas Rd., Phoenix, AZ 85012-3114. Tel.: 602-630-2060.
Communications Museum.
Collections: history of telecommunications from the 1870s to present day; telephone equipment & memorabilia; early coin phones; phone booths; photographs.
Hours & Admission Prices: Temporarily closed for relocation.

WELLS FARGO HISTORY MUSEUM, (M), 100 W. Washington, Phoenix, AZ 85003-1805. Mailing Address: Wells Fargo Historical Services, 420 Montgomery St., MAC-A0101-106, San Francisco, CA 94163-0001. Tel.: 602-378-1578.
Founded: 2003.
Key Personnel: Cur., Connie Whalen.
Governing Authority: profit-making organization. Affiliated with Wells Fargo Bank.
Company History Museum.
Collections: Concord Stagecoach; Wells Fargo banking & express history; fine art, including paintings by N.C. Wyeth; mining; staging; early Phoenix history.
Activities: guided group tours; audiovisual programs; imaginary rides on replica stagecoach.
Publications: scholarly pamphlets.
Hours & Admission Prices: Mon.-Fri. 9-5. No charge. Closed bank holidays.

Pima

EASTERN ARIZONA MUSEUM AND HISTORICAL SOCIETY OF GRAHAM COUNTY INC., 2 N. Main St., Pima, AZ 85543. Mailing Address: P.O. Box 274, Pima, AZ 85543-0274. Tel.: 928-485-3032.
E-mail: edresbarney@yahoo.com
Founded: 1963.
Congressional District: 1
Key Personnel: Pres., Shawn Wright; Vice Pres., Steve Mattice; Sec., Anna Jane Jarvis; Dir., Edres Barney; Treas., Lesley Talley.
Personnel Profile: Part-Time Paid 2; Part-Time Volunteers 12.
Governing Authority: society; nonprofit organization. Parent Institution: Arizona Historical Society, Tucson. Tax-exempt.
History Museum.
Collections: pioneer & Indian artifacts; photographs; personal & community histories; reproduction of a pioneer home; original notes & copies of trial transcript. of the Wham robbery. Historic House: c.1882 Old Cluff Hall.
Facilities: reading & research room.
Activities: guided tours; permanent & temporary exhibitions.
Publications: booklet, Wham Paymaster Robbery; book, Centennial; Graham County Profiles, Vol. II; Garden of Eden & How It Grew, Mt. Graham.
Hours & Admission Prices: Thurs.-Sat. 10-3; other times by appointment. No charge; donations accepted. ♿
Attendance: 1,824 (accurate)
Membership: Student $3; Family $15; Business $40; Lifetime $100.

Pine

PINE-STRAWBERRY MUSEUM, 3886 Hwy. 87, Pine, AZ 85544. Mailing Address: P.O. Box 564, Pine, AZ 85544-0564. Tel.: 928-476-3547.
History Museum.
Collections: local history & culture; Native American artifacts; Mormon Church; farming implements; period clothing & furniture.
Facilities: Museum-related items for sale.
Hours & Admission Prices: Call for hours. No charge; donations accepted. ♿
Attendance: 2,000 (estimated)

Prescott

HIGHLANDS CENTER FOR NATURAL HISTORY, 1375 S. Walker Rd., Prescott, AZ 86303-6893. Tel.: 928-776-9550. Fax: 928-776-9530.
E-mail: highlands@cableone.net
Web Site: highlandscenter.org
Formerly: Community Nature Center
Founded: 1975.
Congressional District: 3
Key Personnel: Exec. Dir., Dave Irvine; Chm. & Pres. (V), Chris Coleman; Treas., Don Schiller.
Personnel Profile: Part-Time Paid 5; Part-Time Volunteers 150.
Governing Authority: private; nonprofit organization. Branch Museum: Walker Rd. 2 Miles South of Hwy. 69, Prescott, AZ; Lynx Creek Site, 1375 S. Walker Rd., Prescott AZ 86303. Tax-exempt: 501(c)(3).
Nature Center.
Collections: natural history of the Arizona Highlands area.
Research Fields: grasslands project.
Facilities: library; educational facilities; nature/conservation center; amphitheater; riparian (wetland) area; classroom; guided nature trail. Museum-related items for sale.
Activities: docent program; formal education programs; outdoor science fair; docent training; student class. Museum Sponsors: Tracking the Past Workshop; Natural History Workshop; Grow Native! plant sale & educational fair.
Publications: newsletter published three times annually, Highlands Vision; native plants book; book, Wildscaping; curriculum guide, Tracking the Past.
Hours & Admission Prices: April-Sept. 7-7; Oct.-March 8-6. Charge for classes & special events only; donations accepted. Trails open to the public. ♿
Attendance: 5,000 (estimated)
Membership: Student $15; Individual $35; Family $45; Donor $100.

PHIPPEN MUSEUM, (M), 4701 Hwy. 89 N., Prescott, AZ 86301-8303. Tel.: 928-778-1385. Fax: 928-778-4524.
E-mail: phippen@phippenartmuseum.org
Web Site: www.phippenartmuseum.org
Founded: 1974.
Congressional District: 3
Key Personnel: Dir., Kim Villalpando; Chm. (V), Dick Cornwell; Administrative Asst., Edd Kellerman; Bookkeeper, Al Chandler; Events Coord., James Ward; Cur. & Mgr. Collections, Deb Bentlage; Mgr. Information, Tom McCain; Museum Shop Mgr., Deborah Thurston.
Personnel Profile: Full-Time Paid 2; Part-Time Paid 4; Part-Time Volunteers 75.
Governing Authority: nonprofit organization. Parent Institution: George Phippen Memorial Foundation. Tax-exempt: 501(c)(3).
Art of the American West Museum.
Collections: paintings; sculpture; artifacts.
Facilities: art research library; lecture hall; activity hall. Museum-related items for sale.

Activities: guided tours; lectures; organized education programs; temporary & traveling exhibitions; docent led tours. Annual Events: Western Fine Art Show & Sale in May; Fall Gathering BBQ & Branding; Designer Home Showcase; Arizona Holiday Shopping.
Publications: quarterly newsletter; exhibit brochures.
Hours & Admission Prices: Tues.-Sat. 10-4, Sun. 1-4. Adults $5, senior citizens & students $4; discounts to AAM, AAA & ICOM members; museum professionals, children under 12 & members no charge. Closed New Year's Day; Easter; Thanksgiving; Christmas. ♿
Attendance: 8,900 (estimated)
Membership: Individual $35; Family $60; Supporting $120; Business $150; Sustaining $250; Patron $500; Benefactor $1,000.

* **SHARLOT HALL MUSEUM, (M),** 415 W. Gurley St., Prescott, AZ 86301-3691. Tel.: 928-445-3122. Fax: 928-776-9053.
E-mail: gails@sharlot.org
Web Site: www.sharlot.org
Founded: 1928.
Congressional District: 1
Key Personnel: Dir., John Langellier, Ph.D.; Chief Cur., Mick Woodcock; Pres. (V), Chick Hastings; Museum Shop Mgr., Gayle Schambach.
Personnel Profile: Full-Time Paid 15; Part-Time Paid 9; Part-Time Volunteers 350.
Governing Authority: state. Subsidiary Institutions: Sharlot Hall Historical Society & the Prescott Historical Society. Tax-exempt: 170(b)(1)(A).
Regional History Museum.
Collections: regional archives; costumes; vehicles; photographs; Indian archaeological & ethnographic materials; medical; military; decorative arts; transportation. Historic Buildings: 1864 Governor's mansion; 1864 Fort Misery; 1875 John C. Fremont house; 1877 William C. Bashford house.
Major Exhibits: Paint! Breaking the Buckskin Ceiling, 11/09-11/10.
Research Fields: Arizona particularly the Central Mountain Region.
Facilities: library of diaries, books, manuscripts, scrapbooks, files & newspapers available for research on premises; memorial rose garden; herb garden.
Activities: guided tours by prior arrangement; permanent & temporary exhibitions; folk arts demonstrations. Museum Sponsors: annual Folk Arts Fair; Folk Music Festival; Arizona History Adventure; lecture series; Prescott Indian Art Market; Blue Rose Theater Historical Plays.
Publications: bimonthly newsletter; annual history journal. Booklets-Orejana Bull; The Arizona Rough Rider Monument & Captain W. O. O'Neill. Books: Cactus & Pine; Poems of a Ranch Woman; Arizona's First Capitol; Meeting The Four O'Clock Train; The Ernest W. McFarland Papers; Sharlot Herself; Sharlot Hall on the Arizona Strip; The Arizona Rough Riders; Rough Writings; Co-Existing with Urban Wildlife; Historic Photographs of Central Arizona Grasslands and Associated Habitats. Cassette: Grand Canyon Cowboy Band. VHS video tape: Ranch Albu; The Wilderness Around Us.
Hours & Admission Prices: June-Sept. Mon.-Sat. 10-5, Sun. 12-4; Oct.-May Mon.-Sat. 10-4, Sun. 12-4. Adults $5; discounts to AAM members; members and children 18 & under no charge. Closed New Year's Day; Thanksgiving; Christmas. ♿
Attendance: 24,516 (accurate)
Membership: Individual $25; Family $35; Family Circle $75; Heritage Circle $125; Corporate $125-$249; Curator's Circle $250; Director's Circle $500; Sharlot's Circle $1,000; Legacy Circle $5,000.

SMOKI MUSEUM - AMERICAN INDIAN ART & CULTURE, 147 N. Arizona, Prescott, AZ 86301-3184. Mailing Address: P.O. Box 10224, Prescott, AZ 86304-0224. Tel.: 928-445-1230.
E-mail: director@smokimuseum.org
Web Site: www.smokimuseum.org
Founded: 1935.
Congressional District: 3
Key Personnel: Dir., Cynthia Gresser; Pres. (V), Linda Young; Vice Pres., Goodie Berquist; Treas., Kent Robinson; Museum Shop Mgr., Janet Shaw.
Personnel Profile: Full-Time Paid 1; Part-Time Paid 1; Part-Time Volunteers 80.
Governing Authority: private; not-for-profit organization. Tax-exempt: 501(c)(3).
Anthropology Museum.
Collections: prehistoric Southwest Native American artifacts; contemporary basketry & ceramics.
Major Exhibits: Contemporary Native Art, 3/10-5/10; The Spirit of Smoki, 6/10-8/10; Native Jewelry of the Southwest, 9/10-12/10.
Facilities: 600-vol. archaeological & ethnological library on Southwestern Native Americans; 6,000 sq. ft. exhibit space.
Activities: guided tours; lectures; docent program; research facilities. Museum Sponsors: Southwest Indian Arts Festival; Navajo Rug & Indian art auctions.
Publications: quarterly newsletter, "Talking Sun".
Hours & Admission Prices: Tues.-Sat. 10-4, Sun. 1-4. Adults $5, seniors $4, students $3; discounts to AAM members; children 12 & under and Native Americans no charge. Closed Easter; Thanksgiving; Christmas. ♿
Attendance: 4,500 (estimated)
Membership: Student $10; Individual $20; Family $25; Supporting $50; Contributing $75; Sustaining $125; Business $200; Corporate $500.

Quartzsite

TYSON'S WELL STAGE STATION MUSEUM, 161 W. Main St., Quartzsite, AZ 85346. Mailing Address: Quartzsite Historical Society, P.O. Box 331, Quartzsite, AZ 85346-0331. Tel.: 928-927-5229.
Governing Authority: nonprofit organization. Parent Institution: Quartzsite Historical Society.
History Museum: housed in a restored adobe stage station built in 1866.
Collections: local history & culture; photographs; period mining equipment.
Facilities: Museum-related items for sale.
Activities: special events; musical concerts; fundraising events. Museum Sponsors: Quilt Show.
Publications: Quartzsite Arizona, No Ordinary Place; Quartzsite Pioneer Bill Keiser's Lost Mines and Prospector's Lore.
Hours & Admission Prices: April-Oct. Thurs. 9-12; Nov.-March Wed.-Sun. 10-4; other times by appointment. No charge; donations accepted.

Roosevelt

TONTO NATIONAL MONUMENT, Hwy. 188, Roosevelt, AZ 85545. Mailing Address: HC02, Box 4602, Roosevelt, AZ 85545. Tel.: 928-467-2241. Fax: 928-467-2225.
E-mail: TONT_superintendent@nps.gov
Web Site: www.nps.gov/tont
Founded: 1907.
Congressional District: 1
Key Personnel: Supt., Terry Saunders; Park Ranger, Susan Hughes.
Personnel Profile: Full-Time Paid 12; Part-Time Volunteers 4.
Governing Authority: federal. Tax-exempt.
Archaeology Museum.
Collections: clothing, tools, weapons & pottery of the Salado, the prehistoric Indians of the region.
Facilities: picnic area; nature trails.
Activities: guided tours; self-guided trail & tours; audiovisual program.
Publications: Tonto National Monument.
Hours & Admission Prices: Visitor Center & Museum: daily 8-5. Self-Guided Trail: daily 8-4. $3 per person; holders of National Park Pass, Golden Age or Golden Access passes & children under 16 no charge. ♿
Attendance: 80,021 (accurate)

Safford

DISCOVERY PARK CAMPUS, 1651 W. Discovery Park Blvd., Safford, AZ 85546-3909. Tel.: 928-428-6260. Fax: 928-428-8081.
E-mail: harry.swanson@eac.edu
Web Site: www.eac.edu/discoverypark/
Founded: 1995.
Congressional District: 5
Key Personnel: Dean, Harry Swanson, Ph.D.
Personnel Profile: Full-Time Paid 2; Part-Time Paid 2; Part-Time Volunteers 12; Interns 3.
Governing Authority: college. Parent Institution: Eastern Arizona College. Tax-exempt.
Science Center.
Collections: historic, scientific, agricultural & mining exhibits; simulated mine tour; wildlife habitat; research-grade 20" telescope.
Facilities: hiking trails; visitors center; theater; rental facilities.
Activities: guided tours through the Mount Graham International Observatories; formal education programs K-20; hiking trails; films; poetry & prose readings in partnership with Univ. of Arizona Steward Observatory.
Hours & Admission Prices: Mon.-Fri. 8-4, Sat. 4pm-9:30pm. No charge; donations accepted. ♿
Attendance: 7,000 (accurate)

Sahuarita

ASARCO MINERAL DISCOVERY CENTER, 1421 W. Pima Mine Rd., Sahuarita, AZ Tel.: 520-625-7513 & 8233. Fax: 520-625-4756.
E-mail: amdcinfo@asarco.com
Founded: 1997.
Mineral Museum.
Collections: mining history, equipment & process; ball mill model; photographs; haul trucks.
Facilities: theater. Museum-related items for sale.

Activities: demonstrations; guided tours; videos.
Hours & Admission Prices: June-Sept. Tues.-Sat. 9-3.

Saint Michaels

ST. MICHAELS HISTORICAL MUSEUM, 24 Mission Rd., Saint Michaels, AZ 86511. Mailing Address: P.O. Box 680, Saint Michaels, AZ 86511-0680. Tel.: 928-871-4171.
History Museum.
Collections: Navajo culture & history; personal artifacts; photographs; period furnishings.
Activities: educational programs.
Hours & Admission Prices: Memorial Day to Labor Day Mon.-Fri. 9-5.

San Manuel

SAN MANUEL HISTORICAL SOCIETY, 130 N. Redington Rd., San Manuel, AZ 85631-0742. Mailing Address: P.O. Box 742, San Manuel, AZ 85631-0742.
Web Site: www.sanmanuelhistoricalsociety.com
Historical Society Museum.
Collections: local history & culture; photographs; maps; gems; minerals; mining.
Hours & Admission Prices: Sat. 10-1.

Scottsdale

AFRICAN AMERICAN MULTICULTURAL MUSEUM, 617 N. Scottsdale Rd., Scottsdale, AZ 85257-4234. Tel.: 480-314-4400.
E-mail: museum@prodigy.net
Multicultural Museum.
Collections: art; history; culture.
Activities: lectures.
Hours & Admission Prices: Thurs.-Sat. 1-5; other times by appointment. No charge.

CONGREGATION BETH ISRAEL'S SYLVIA PLOTKIN JUDAICA MUSEUM, 10460 N. 56th St., Scottsdale, AZ 85253-1133. Tel.: 480-951-0323. Fax: 480-951-7150.
Web Site: cbiaz.org
Founded: 1966.
Congressional District: 3
Key Personnel: Dir., Rabbi Albert Plotkin; Chm. (V) & Librarian, Carol Reynolds.
Personnel Profile: Part-Time Volunteers 2.
Governing Authority: religious. Parent Institution: Temple Beth Israel. Tax-exempt: 501(c)(3).
Religious Antiques Museum: housed in Temple belonging to oldest Jewish Congregation in the Phoenix area.
Collections: Jewish arts & ceremonials from 1600 to the present; archaeology of Israel; Israeli philatelic collection; Tunisian period gallery of synagogue, original artifacts; pioneer Jews of Arizona 1850-1920; Biblical garden.
Research Fields: Judaica.
Facilities: 12,000-vol. library of books on Judaic studies, art, history, housed in adjoining Temple library; reading room.
Activities: guided tours; lectures; films; gallery talks; concerts; study clubs; TV programs; formally organized education programs; docent program; inter-museum loan exhibitions; permanent & traveling exhibitions.
Publications: annual, HA-OR.
Hours & Admission Prices: By appointment. Donation: adults $3.50. Closed national & Jewish holidays. ♿
Attendance: 500 (estimated)

HOO-HOOGAM KI MUSEUM, 10005 E. Osborn Rd., Scottsdale, AZ 85256-4019. Tel.: 480-850-8190.
E-mail: huhugamki.museaum@srpmic-nsn.gov
Web Site: www.srpmic-nsn.gov/history-culture/museum.asp
Cultural Heritage Museum.
Collections: Salt River Pima-Maricopa cultural heritage & history; Pima basketry; Maricopa pottery; native dress; period furnishings; personal artifacts; sculpture; artwork.
Facilities: Museum-related items for sale.
Hours & Admission Prices: Mon.-Fri. 9:30-4:30. No charge. Closed federal holidays.

HOUSE OF BROADCASTING RADIO & TELEVISION MUSEUM, 7150 E. 5th Ave., Scottsdale, AZ 85251-3238. Mailing Address: 7534 N. 7th St., Phoenix, AZ 85020-4129. Tel.: 602-944-1997. Fax: 602-997-8707.
E-mail: bmaack@cox.net
Web Site: www.houseofbroadcasting.com
Founded: 1996.
Key Personnel: Chm. & Pres. (V), Mary Morrison.
Governing Authority: nonprofit. Tax-exempt: 501(c)(3).
Radio & Television History Museum.
Collections: Arizona's radio & television broadcasting history & personalities; broadcasting artifacts; personal artifacts; photographs; costumes; autographed books.
Activities: book signings by media authors. Annual Events: Golf Tournaments; Celebrity Toast.
Hours & Admission Prices: Daily 10-6. No charge; donations accepted. Closed Thanksgiving; Christmas.
Attendance: 1,500 (estimated)

SCOTTSDALE HISTORICAL MUSEUM, 7333 Scottsdale Mall, Scottsdale, AZ 85251-4414. Mailing Address: P.O. Box 143, Scottsdale, AZ 85252-0143. Tel.: 480-945-4499.
E-mail: info@scottsdalemuseum.com
Web Site: www.scottsdalemuseum.com
Founded: 1991.
Personnel Profile: Part-Time Volunteers 75.
Governing Authority: Parent Institution: Scottsdale Historical Society. Tax-exempt.
History Museum.
Collections: local history; personal artifacts; photographs; newspapers.
Hours & Admission Prices: June & Sept. Wed.-Sun. 10-2; Oct.-May Wed.-Sun. 10-5. No charge. Closed holidays.
Attendance: 25,000 (estimated)
Membership: Senior $10; Individual $25; Family $40; Patron $100; Benefactor $200. Business: Bronze $100-$249; Silver $250-$499; Gold $500 & up.

* **SCOTTSDALE MUSEUM OF CONTEMPORARY ART, (M),** 7374 E. Second St., Scottsdale, AZ 85251-5604. Mailing Address: 7380 E. Second St., Scottsdale, AZ 85251-5604. Tel.: 480-874-4666. Fax: 480-874-4655. TDD: 480-994-2787.
E-mail: smoca@sccarts.org
Web Site: www.smoca.org
Founded: 1999.
Congressional District: 1
Key Personnel: Bd. Chm., Paul Giancola; Sr. Cur., Claire Schneider; Assoc. Cur., Cassandra Coblentz; Mktg. & Public Rels. Mgr., Lesley Oliver; Cur. Education, Carolyn Robbins; Assoc. Cur. Education, Laura Hales; Exhibit Designer, Laura Spalding; Registrar, Pat Evans; Museum Shop Mgr., Janice Bartczak.
Personnel Profile: Full-Time Paid 17; Part-Time Paid 3; Part-Time Volunteers 180; Interns 5.
Governing Authority: nonprofit organization. Parent Institution: Scottsdale Cultural Council. Tax-exempt: 501(c)(3).
Modern & contemporary art, architecture & design.
Collections: modern & contemporary paintings; sculpture; installations; prints; drawings; photographs; architecture and design; James Turrell Skyspace.
Major Exhibits: Rewind, Remix, Replay, 12/19/09-5/23/10; Chuck Close Prints: Process & Collaboration (T), 2/13/10-5/9/10; Soleri Bridges, 5/10-9/10; ArchitectureNET, 5/10-9/10.
Research Fields: modern & contemporary art; architecture; design.
Facilities: 11,000 sq. ft. of galleries; outdoor sculpture garden. Museum-related items for sale.
Activities: guided tours; lectures; arts festivals; organized education programs; docent program; gallery talks; workshops; artists' residencies
Publications: calendar; education program brochures; exhibition catalogues.
Hours & Admission Prices: Winter: Tues.-Wed. & Fri.-Sat. 10-5, Thurs. 10-8, Sun. 12-5; Summer: Wed. & Sun. 12-5, Thurs. 10-8, Fri.-Sat. 10-5. Adults $7, students $5; discounts for AAM & ICOM members; Thurs., members & children under 15 no charge. Closed national holidays. ♿
Attendance: 46,000 (accurate)
Membership: Solo $50; Duet $90; Contributing $150; Sustaining $250; Supporting $500; President's Club $1,250; Circles of Giving $2,500 & up.

Second Mesa

HOPI CULTURAL CENTER, Rte. 264, Second Mesa, AZ 86043. Mailing Address: P.O. Box 67, Second Mesa, AZ 86043-0067. Tel.: 928-734-2401.
History Museum.
Collections: Hope history & culture; Hopi arts & crafts, pottery, weavings, woodcarvings, & silver.
Facilities: restaurant.
Hours & Admission Prices: Call for hours.

Sedona

SEDONA ARTS CENTER, INC., 15 Art Barn Rd., Sedona, AZ 86336-4249. Mailing Address: P.O. Box 569, Sedona, AZ 86339-0569. Tel.: 928-282-3809; 888-954-4442.
E-mail: sac@sedonaartscenter.com
Web Site: www.sedonaartscenter.com
Founded: 1961.
Congressional District: 3
Key Personnel: Exec. Dir., Robert J. Myers; Gallery Dir., Shirley Eichten Albrecht.
Governing Authority: nonprofit organization. Tax-exempt: 501(c)(3).
Art Center.
Collections: various forms of art media.
Facilities: 150-vol. library of general art books & magazines; 2,000 sq. ft. exhibit space; 160-seat theater; drawing & painting, glass & jewelry, ceramics & sculpture classroom studios. Works by local & member artists in crafts & fine art for sale.
Activities: guided tours; lectures; films; concerts; arts festivals; theater; organized educational programs; docent program; traveling exhibitions. Museum Sponsors: Arts & Crafts Show.
Publications: bimonthly newsletter, Previews; occasional exhibition catalogues.
Hours & Admission Prices: Daily 10-5. No charge; donations accepted. Closed major holidays. ♿
Attendance: 58,000 (accurate)
Membership: Individual $50; Family $75; Business $150; Silver $250; Gold $500; Other $1,000 & up.

SEDONA HERITAGE MUSEUM, (M), 735 Jordan Rd., Jordan Historical Park, Sedona, AZ 86336. Mailing Address: Sedona Historical Society, P.O. Box 10216, Sedona, AZ 86339-8216. Tel.: 928-282-7038. Fax: 928-282-7038.
E-mail: sedonamuseum@esedona.net
Founded: 1998.
Congressional District: 1
Personnel Profile: Part-Time Paid 3; Part-Time Volunteers 60.
Governing Authority: Parent Institution: Sedona Historical Society. Tax-exempt.
History Museum: housed in the former farm home of Walter & Ruth Jordan, built in 1930. Listed on the National Register of Historic Places.
Collections: local history & culture; period furnishings; personal artifacts.
Research Fields: local history.
Facilities: Museum-related items for sale.
Activities: special events.
Publications: newsletter; book, Those Early Days; Traveling By Tin Lizzie; Filmography of Sedona.
Hours & Admission Prices: Daily 11-3; tours by appointment. Adults $3; members & children under 12 no charge. ♿
Attendance: 12,000 (accurate)
Membership: Basic $40; Supporting $90; Business Associate $100; Business Colleague & Sustaining $200; Business Partner $500.

Sierra Vista

HENRY F. HAUSER MUSEUM, Ethel Berger Center, 2950 E. Tacoma St., Sierra Vista, AZ 85635-1352. Tel.: 520-417-6980, ext. 560.
History Museum.
Collections: local history & culture; photographs; books.
Facilities: theater. Museum-related items for sale.
Activities: permanent & traveling exhibitions.
Hours & Admission Prices: Mon.-Fri. 9-5.

Somerton

COCOPAH MUSEUM, County 15 and Avenue G, Somerton, AZ 85350. Tel.: 928-627-1992.
Native American History Museum.
Collections: Cocopah Indian artifacts, culture & history; clothing; musical instruments; personal artifacts.
Facilities: Museum-related items for sale.
Hours & Admission Prices: Mon.-Thurs. 8-5, Fri. 9-12. No charge; donations accepted.

Springerville

CASA MALPAIS VISITOR CENTER AND MUSEUM, 418 E. Main St., Springerville, AZ 85938-5220. Tel.: 928-333-5375.
E-mail: malpais@cybertrails.com
History Museum.
Collections: local history & culture; 13th century Mogollon ruins; photographs; period artifacts.
Facilities: visitor center.
Activities: hiking; educational programs.
Hours & Admission Prices: Daily 8-4. Guided Tours: 9am, 11am, & 2pm.

LITTLE HOUSE MUSEUM, S. Fork Rd., Springerville, AZ 85938. Mailing Address: P.O. Box 791, Springerville, AZ 85938-0791. Tel.: 928-333-2286.
History Museum.
Collections: ranching; pioneer life; local history; photographs. Historic Buildings: restored cabins.
Hours & Admission Prices: By appointment. ♿

Superior

* **BOYCE THOMPSON ARBORETUM,** 37615 US Hwy. 60, Superior, AZ 85273-5100. Tel.: 520-689-2723. Fax: 520-689-5858.
E-mail: msiegwar@cals.arizona.edu
Web Site: arboretum.ag.arizona.edu
Formerly: Boyce Thompson Southwestern Arboretum
Founded: 1924.
Congressional District: 4
Key Personnel: Dir., Mark Siegwarth; Chm. (V) & Pres. (V), Mary Irish; Museum Shop Mgr., Lynnea Spencer.
Personnel Profile: Full-Time Paid 23; Part-Time Paid 13; Part-Time Volunteers 120.
Governing Authority: cooperative, nonprofit organization. Parent Institution: Boyce Thompson Southwestern Arboretum Inc. Subsidiary Institution: University of Arizona and Arizona State Parks. Tax-exempt: 501(c)(3).
Arboretum.
Collections: xerophytes; botany; geology; zoology; manuscripts. Historic House: c.1915 Clevenger Homestead; c.1928 Picket Post House.
Research Fields: botany; zoology; floristics; taxonomy; systematics; horticulture.
Facilities: library of biological material; botanical garden; field research station. Color slides, books, mineral specimens & cactus plants for sale.
Activities: guided tours; lectures; permanent & temporary exhibitions; workshops; monthly special events.
Publications: semi-annual journal, Desert Plants.
Hours & Admission Prices: Daily 8-5. Adults $7.50, children 5-12 $3; discounts to AABGA members; members no charge. Closed Christmas. ♿
Attendance: 85,000 (estimated)
Membership: Dual $45; Family $60; Patron $100; Boojum $250; Picketpost Society $500; Director's Circle $1,000.

SUPERIOR HISTORICAL SOCIETY - THE BOB JONES MUSEUM, (M), 300 Main St., Superior, AZ 85173. Mailing Address: P.O. Box 613, Superior, AZ 85173.
History Museum.
Collections: local history; photographs; mining equipment; geology.
Publications: monthly newsletter.
Hours & Admission Prices: Fri. 1-4, Sat.-Sun. 10-4. No charge.
Membership: Individual $8; Family $15; Business $25.

WORLD'S SMALLEST MUSEUM, 1111 W. U.S. Hwy. 60, Superior, AZ 85173-3429. Tel.: 520-689-5857 & 208-0634.
E-mail: sales@smallestmuseum.com
Web Site: www.worldssmallestmuseum.com
General Museum.
Collections: Indian pottery; 1800s wood stove; 1850s frying pan; 1930s 16mm projector; newspaper clippings; 8mm movie camera; photographs; iron kettle.
Facilities: 134 sq. ft. exhibit space. Museum-related items for sale.
Hours & Admission Prices: Wed.-Sun. 8-1:30. No charge; donations accepted. Closed major holidays.

Surprise

WEST VALLEY ART MUSEUM, 17420 N. Avenue of the Arts, Surprise, AZ 85374-2577. Tel.: 623-972-0635. Fax: 602-972-0456.
E-mail: gpalovich@wvam.org
Web Site: www.wvam.org
Formerly: West Valley Art Museum-Sun Cities Museum of Art
Founded: 1980.
Congressional District: 3
Key Personnel: Interim Dir. & Business Mgr., Kendra Amburgey; Pres. Bd., Mrs. Bee Gatliff; Treas., Austin Tingley; Cur., George Palovich; Cur., Lori Toczek; Museum Shop Mgr., Jackie Juergens.
Personnel Profile: Full-Time Paid 7; Part-Time Paid 2; Part-Time Volunteers 300.
Governing Authority: nonprofit. Tax-exempt: 501(c)(3).
Art Museum.

Collections: ethnic dress; international fine prints; Arizona artists.
Major Exhibits: Life Drawing Student Exhibit, 12/4/09-1/10/10; The Art of Barry Goldstein, 12/4/09-2/21/10; Arizona Artists Guild Exhibition, 12/11/09-1/24/10; Red Rohall-Roadside Paintings, 12/11/09-2/14/10; Melissa and Ernie Button, 1/15/10-4/11/10; African Aspects: Adornment and Aquisition, 1/29/10-4/11/10; Paintings of Turner Davis, 1/29/10-4/18/10; John Dawson: Paintings and Sculpture, 2/26/10-5/9/10; James Swinnerton: Visions of the Southwest, 8/10/10-10/24/10; The Woodwork of Tom Deady, 8/20/10-10/10/10.
Facilities: 2,050-vol. library of art history & biography, available to the public; 7,916 sq. ft. exhibit space; tea room; cultural center. Books & museum-related items for sale.
Activities: concerts; formal education programs; guided tours; lectures; temporary & traveling exhibitions; training programs for professional museum workers; home tours; educational outreach to area schools. Annual Events: juried art show; high school & elementary juried art shows; Affair with the Arts.
Publications: quarterly newsletter.
Hours & Admission Prices: Tues.-Sun. 10-4. Adult $7; discounts to AAM members; members no charge. Closed New Year's Day; Easter; Memorial Day; Independence Day; Labor Day; Thanksgiving; Christmas. ♿
Attendance: 35,000 (estimated)
Membership: Art Lovers $50; Family $60; Extended Family $75; Curator $150; President $400; Hoover $1,000; Museum Builder $2,500.

Tempe

AMERICAN HEART ASSOCIATION - HALLE HEART CENTER, 2929 S. 48th St., Tempe, AZ 85282-3145. Tel.: 602-414-2800. Fax: 602-414-5355.
E-mail: halleheartcenter@heart.org
Web Site: www.americanheart.org/halleheartcenter
Founded: 1996.
Key Personnel: Mgr., Jena Long; Chm. (V), Dr. Moschonas.
Personnel Profile: Full-Time Paid 2; Part-Time Paid 16; Part-Time Volunteers 25.
Governing Authority: private; nonprofit organization. Tax-exempt: 501(c)(3).
Science Museum.
Collections: medical equipment; hands-on exhibits.
Facilities: library; 16,000 sq. ft. exhibit space; education facilities; 50-seat large screen & interactive stage; TV theater; activity center; APS electric industrial demonstration kitchen.
Activities: guided & self-guided tours; docent program; lectures; films; formal education for adults, college students & children.
Hours & Admission Prices: Sept.-July Mon.-Fri. 1-4 by appointment. No charge; donations accepted. Closed national holidays. ♿
Attendance: 28,000 (estimated)
Membership: Tree of Life $50-$100; Bronze Hearts $1,000-$4,999; Silver Hearts $5,000-$9,999; Gold Hearts $10,000-$24,999; Presidential Patrons $25,000-$49,000; Presidential Partners $50,000-$99,000; Presidential Pace-Setters $100,000-$249,999; Benefactors $250,000-$350,000.

AMERICAN MUSEUM OF NURSING, ASU Community Svcs. Bldg., 200 E. Curry Rd., 2nd. Fl., Tempe, AZ 85287-0001. Mailing Address: ASU College of Nursing, Extended Campus, P.O. Box 873008, Tempe, AZ 85287-0001. Tel.: 480-965-2195. Fax: 480-965-0619.
Web Site: nursing.asu.edu
Founded: 2002.
Key Personnel: Interim Dir. & Cur., Geri Rosato, MS, R.N.
Personnel Profile: Full-Time Volunteers 1; Part-Time Volunteers 3.
Governing Authority: board of directors. Parent Institution: Arizona State University College of Nursing. Tax-exempt: 501(c)(3).
History & Science Museum of Nursing.
Collections: military, hospital, missionary, and all other types of nursing memorabilia & history: artifacts, photographs, documents, equipment & uniforms.
Research Fields: history of nursing.
Facilities: reference library.
Activities: traveling & loan exhibitions; community programs; book signings.
Hours & Admission Prices: Tues. & Thurs. 10-2; tours & other times by appointment. Admission $2; children 16 & under must be accompanied by an adult.
Attendance: 2,000 (estimated)

ARIZONA HISTORICAL SOCIETY MUSEUM AT PAPAGO PARK, 1300 N. College Ave., Tempe, AZ 85281-1211. Tel.: 480-929-0292. Fax: 480-967-5450.
E-mail: ahstempe@azhs.gov
Web Site: www.arizonahistoricalsociety.org
Founded: 1864.
Congressional District: 5
Key Personnel: Exec. Dir., Anne I. Woosley, Ph.D.; Central Arizona Div. Dir., Peter H. Welsh, Ph.D.; Education & Outreach Div. Dir., Kyle McKoy.
Personnel Profile: Full-Time Paid 10; Part-Time Volunteers 175; Interns 6.
Governing Authority: bd. of directors. Parent Institution: Arizona Historical Society, 949 E. 2nd St., Tucson, AZ 85719. Tel.: 520-628-5774. Tax-exempt: 501(c)(3).
History Museum.
Collections: 20th & 21st century artifacts; news film & visual media; decorative arts; popular culture; textiles; clothing; tools; photographs; books; documents; archives; maps; works by Arizona artists; china; silver; coins; tokens; sports; politics; food preparation; advertising; ephemera; toys; oral histories; architectural drawings. Historic House: Sandra Day O'Connor House.
Major Exhibits: Sandra Day O'Connor, A Citizen for All Seasons, 11/09-12/10.
Research Fields: people & events shaping Arizona since 1900; history of Phoenix & Central Arizona.
Facilities: 2,500-vol. library pertaining to 20th-century Arizona & Western history available for research on premises by appointment; 23,000 sq. ft. exhibition space; 272-seat auditorium; 50-seat theater; catering kitchen; reading room; nature trails.
Activities: lectures; films; formally organized education programs; loan & traveling exhibitions; school loan service; living history outreach program; special events; tours; facility rental.
Publications: quarterly, Journal of Arizona History; books; monographs; annual report.
Hours & Admission Prices: Tues.-Sat. 10-4, Sun. 12-4. Library Archives: call for hours or appointment. Adults $5, seniors 60 & over and youth 12-18 $4; children 11 & under and members no charge. Closed New Year's Day; Independence Day; Veterans Day; Thanksgiving; Christmas. ♿
Attendance: 22,500 (estimated)
Membership: Student $25; Individual $50; Household $65; Sustaining $100; Patron $250; Sponsor $500; Director's Circle $1,000.

ARIZONA STATE UNIVERSITY ART MUSEUM, (M), 10th St. & Mill Ave., Nelson Fine Arts Center, Tempe, AZ 85287-0001. Mailing Address: Box 872911, Tempe, AZ 85287-2911. Tel.: 480-965-2787. Fax: 480-965-5254.
E-mail: asuartmuseum@asu.edu
Web Site: asuartmuseum.asu.edu
Founded: 1950.
Congressional District: 1
Key Personnel: Dir. & Sr. Cur., Heather Lineberry; Sr. Cur., Peter Held; Registrar, Anne Sullivan; Print Collection Mgr., Jean Makin; Curatorial & Museum Specialist Sr., John Spiak; Chief Installationist, Stephen Johnson; Business Mgr., Kathleen Wacker; Museum Shop Mgr., Lareal Eyring.
Personnel Profile: Full-Time Paid 18; Full-Time Volunteers 1; Part-Time Paid 3; Part-Time Volunteers 30; Interns 4.
Governing Authority: university. Parent Institution: Herberger College of Fine Arts, Arizona State University. Tax-exempt: 501(c)(3).
Art Museum & Gallery.
Collections: contemporary art, including new media; Oliver B. James collection of American Art 18th to 20th century; American & European print collection 15th-century to present; crafts; Joseph & Astrid Thomas collection of 19th-century American crockery; contemporary ceramics; Latin American art.
Research Fields: American paintings; American & European prints; American ceramics.
Facilities: 500-vol. library of assorted research materials to American collection available on premises; reading room; seminar rooms; print study room. Museum-related items for sale.
Activities: guided tours; lectures; videos; gallery talks; concerts; arts festivals; curriculum-related education programs; school outreach programs; workshops; demonstrations; docent program; inter-museum loan, temporary & traveling exhibitions; school loan service; student docent program.
Publications: catalogs of selected exhibitions; quarterly newsletter.
Hours & Admission Prices: Fall: Tues. 11-8; Summer: Tues.-Sat. 11-5, Sun. 1-5. No charge. Closed federal & state holidays. ♿
Attendance: 51,000 (accurate)
Membership: Active $50; Supporting $100; Sustaining $500; Patron $1,000.

ARIZONA STATE UNIVERSITY MUSEUM OF ANTHROPOLOGY, (M), Arizona State University, SHESC Bldg., Tempe, AZ 85287-2402. Mailing Address: P.O. Box 872402, Tempe, AZ 85287-2402. Tel.: 480-965-6224. Fax: 480-965-7671.
E-mail: anthro.museum@asu.edu
Web Site: asuma.asu.edu
Founded: 1961.
Key Personnel: Dir. & Interim Dir. Museum Studies, Gwyneira Isaac; Asst.

Cur., Catherine Nichols; Archaeology & Ethography Collections, Arleyn Simon; Cur. Physical Anthropology, Diane Hawkey; Exhibit Developer, Judy Newland.
Personnel Profile: Full-Time Paid 2; Part-Time Paid 3; Part-Time Volunteers 20; Interns 1.
Governing Authority: public university. Parent Institution: Arizona State University. Tax-exempt.
Anthropology Museum.
Collections: archaeology; ethnology; physical anthropology.
Major Exhibits: Que Vivan Los Muertos! 10th Annual Dia de Los Muertos Festival Exhibit, 11/09-1/10; Trade Textiles from the Thomas Hudak Collection, 3/10-8/10.
Research Fields: archaeology; human origins; culture & society.
Facilities: classrooms; laboratories; 2,000 sq. ft. exhibit space.
Activities: changing exhibitions; museum anthropology graduate training program.
Publications: annual, Museum Anthropology Newsletter.
Hours & Admission Prices: Fall & Spring Semesters: Mon.-Fri. 11-3; Winter & Summer: by appointment. No charge. Closed New Year's Eve & Day; Martin Luther King Jr. Day; Memorial Day; Independence Day; Labor Day; Veterans Day; Thanksgiving; Christmas Day & week. ♿
Attendance: 3,500 (accurate)

CENTER FOR METEORITE STUDIES, Arizona State University, Tempe, AZ 85287-0001. Mailing Address: P.O. Box 872504, Tempe, AZ 85287-2504. Tel.: 480-965-6511. Fax: 480-965-4907.
E-mail: meteorites@asu.edu
Web Site: meteorites.asu.edu
Founded: 1961.
Congressional District: 1
Key Personnel: Dir., Meenakshi Wadhwa.
Personnel Profile: Part-Time Paid 1.
Governing Authority: university. Parent Institution: Arizona State University. Tax-exempt.
Meteorite Museum.
Collections: representatives of individual meteorite falls & finds.
Research Fields: meteorite chemistry, identification, history; mineralogy.
Facilities: 14,000-vol. library of books; reprints; microfilmed references available for inter-library loan & upon request; laboratory.
Activities: guided tours; lectures; formally organized education programs for undergraduate & graduate college students; inter-museum loan & permanent exhibitions; scientific & scholarly research.
Hours & Admission Prices: Mon.-Fri. 9-5. No charge; donations accepted. Closed holidays. ♿
Attendance: 3,600 (estimated)

SALT RIVER PROJECT HISTORY MUSEUM, 1521 N. Project Dr., Tempe, AZ 85281-1206. Tel.: 602-236-5900.
History Museum.
Collections: state cultural heritage; photographs; documents; ceramics; stone tools; shell jewelry; grinding wheel; period equipment; films.
Activities: research.
Hours & Admission Prices: Call for hours.

TEMPE HISTORICAL MUSEUM, (M), 809 E. Southern Ave., Tempe, AZ 85282-5205. Tel.: 480-350-5100. Fax: 480-350-5150. TDD: 480-350-5050.
Web Site: www.tempe.gov/museum
Founded: 1972.
Congressional District: 1
Key Personnel: Museum Admin., Amy A. Douglass; Cur. History, W. James Burns; Cur. Collections, Ann Poulos; Cur. Photos & Archives, Richard Bauer; Sec., Jerri Copenhaver; Registrar, Joshua Roffler; Exhibits Coord., Dan Miller.
Personnel Profile: Full-Time Paid 7; Part-Time Paid 5; Part-Time Volunteers 120; Interns 2.
Governing Authority: municipal. Parent Institution: City of Tempe, AZ. Tax-exempt.
History Museum.
Collections: late 19th-20th century domestic artifacts; farm ranch equipment; municipal archives; 20th-century business equipment; historic photographs & archives. Historic House: 1892 Niels Petersen house.
Research Fields: community history; historic preservation; museum studies.
Facilities: research library; photo reproduction & other archives. Gift items for sale.
Activities: guided tours; lecture series; fund-raising events; docent program; school programs; adult classes; internships for university students; multicultural events.
Publications: quarterly newsletter, Time Lines.
Hours & Admission Prices: Museum: closed until March 2010. Niels Petersen House: Tues.-Thurs. & Sat. 10-2. No charge; donations accepted. Closed major holidays. ♿
Attendance: 19,954 (accurate)

Thatcher

GRAHAM COUNTY HISTORICAL SOCIETY, 3430 W. Hwy. 70, Thatcher, AZ 85552. Mailing Address: P.O. Box 290, Thatcher, AZ 85552-0290. Tel.: 928-348-0470.
E-mail: staff@grahammuseum.org
Web Site: www.grahammuseum.org
Founded: 1962.
Congressional District: 4
Key Personnel: Pres., Ralph Smith; Museum Dir., Mel Jones.
Personnel Profile: Part-Time Volunteers 14.
Governing Authority: society. Parent Institution: Arizona Historical Society, 949 E. 2nd St., Tucson, AZ 85719. Tax-exempt: 170(b)(1)(A).
Historical Society Museum.
Collections: Western memorabilia; pioneer & Indian artifacts; archaeology; manuscript collections.
Research Fields: archaeology; historic sites.
Facilities: 500-vol. library of books on Western history available for research on premises & for loan to members.
Activities: guided tours; lectures.
Publications: book, Mount Graham Profiles; annual symposium papers.
Hours & Admission Prices: Jan.-July & mid-Aug. to mid-Dec. Mon.-Tues. & Sat. 10-4; other times by appointment. No charge; donations accepted. Closed holidays. ♿
Attendance: 3,500 (accurate)
Membership: General $15.

Tombstone

BIRD CAGE THEATER MUSEUM, Allen and 6th St., Tombstone, AZ 85638. Tel.: 520-457-3421; 800-457-3423 (Toll Free).
History Museum: built in the 1880s.
Collections: area history; photographs; period furnishings & clothing; theater.
Hours & Admission Prices: Call for hours.

O.K. CORRAL, 326 E. Allen St., Tombstone, AZ 85638. Mailing Address: P.O. Box 367, Tombstone, AZ 85638-0367. Tel.: 520-457-3456. Fax: 520-457-3456.
E-mail: info@ok-corral.com
Web Site: www.okcorral.com
Formerly: Historama
Founded: 1879.
Key Personnel: Dir., Robert Love
History Museum.
Collections: Tombstone history; early Western life & culture; films.
Facilities: theater.
Activities: films; live gunfight reenactments.
Publications: newspaper, Tombstone Epitaph.
Hours & Admission Prices: Daily 9-5. Adults $9. Closed Thanksgiving; Christmas. ♿
Attendance: 100,000 (accurate)

TOMBSTONE COURTHOUSE STATE HISTORIC PARK, 223 E. Toughnut St., Tombstone, AZ 85638. Mailing Address: P.O. Box 216, Tombstone, AZ 85638-0216. Tel.: 520-457-3311. Fax: 520-457-2565.
E-mail: aaustin@pr.state.az.us
Web Site: www.azstateparks.com
Founded: 1959.
Congressional District: 5
Personnel Profile: Full-Time Paid 2; Part-Time Volunteers 2.
Governing Authority: state. Parent Institution: Arizona State Parks Board, 1300 W. Washington St., Phoenix, AZ. Tax-exempt.
Local History Museum: housed in an 1882 Cochise County Courthouse.
Collections: artifacts associated with Tombstone history; glass; china; silver; anthropology; archaeology; mineralogy; medical; natural history; guns; furniture; dolls; wood carving; frontier, pioneer, Old West artifacts until 1929; western cattlemen ranches; domestic, industrial, business & government material.
Major Exhibits: Karl May, 1/10-3/10.
Research Fields: Tombstone history, 1877-1929.
Facilities: Books & museum-related items for sale.
Activities: guided tour of courthouse with advanced reservation; inter-museum loan & temporary exhibitions.
Publications: Nellie Cashman.
Hours & Admission Prices: Thurs.-Mon. 9-5 Adults 14 & over $4, youth 7-13 $1; children 6 & under no charge. Closed Christmas. ♿

Attendance: 59,889 (accurate)

Tonalea

NAVAJO NATIONAL MONUMENT, End of 564 N. Rte., Tonalea, AZ 86044. Mailing Address: HC 71 Box 3, Tonalea, AZ 86044-9708. Tel.: 928-672-2700. Fax: 928-672-2703.
Web Site: www.nps.gov/nava
Founded: 1909.
Congressional District: 4
Key Personnel: Park Archaeologist, Ellen Brennan; Admin., Rose James; WNPA Mgr., Althea James; Supt., Nancy Skinner.
Personnel Profile: Full-Time Paid 9; Part-Time Volunteers 6.
Governing Authority: federal. Parent Institution: U.S. Dept. of Interior. National Park Service, Washington, DC. Tax-exempt.
Archaeological Museum.
Collections: archeological materials of the Kayenta Anasazi & Navajo cultures. Archaeological Sites: 3 prehistoric cliff villages.
Facilities: 2,000-vol. library of history & archaeological books available on premises. Navajo rugs, silver work, paintings, pottery & crafts for sale.
Activities: guided tours; lectures; back country hiking permits to Keet Seel ruin; Navajo artists demonstrations including pottery, rug weaving & basket making.
Publications: orientation brochure, Voices in the Canyon.
Hours & Admission Prices: Visitor Center: May 24-Sept. 13 daily 8-6; Sept. 14-May 22 daily 9-5. No charge. Closed New Year's Day; Christmas. ♿
Attendance: 89,000 (estimated)

Topawa

TOHONO O'ODHAM NATION CULTURAL CENTER & MUSEUM, Fresnal Canyon Rd., Topawa, AZ 85639. Mailing Address: P.O. Box 837, Sells, AZ 85634-0837. Tel.: 520-383-0211.
Native American History Museum.
Collections: Native American culture & history; personal artifacts; photographs; tribal arts & crafts; oral histories; paintings; sculpture.
Activities: educational programs.
Hours & Admission Prices: Mon.-Sat. 10-4. No charge; donations accepted.

Tubac

TUBAC CENTER OF THE ARTS, 9 Plaza Rd., Tubac, AZ 85646-1911. Mailing Address: P.O. Box 1911, Tubac, AZ 85646-1911. Tel.: 520-398-2371. Fax: 520-398-9511.
E-mail: contactus@tubacarts.org
Web Site: tubacarts.org
Founded: 1964.
Congressional District: 5
Key Personnel: Exec. Dir., Annette Brink; Volunteer & Membership Coord., Karin Topping; Exhibit Registrar, Alyson Morvay; Museum Shop Mgr., Lisa Taiz.
Personnel Profile: Full-Time Paid 1; Part-Time Paid 4; Part-Time Volunteers 200.
Governing Authority: board of directors; nonprofit. Parent Institution: Santa Cruz Valley Art Association. Tax-exempt.
Art Center.
Collections: works by regional & national artists.
Facilities: stage. Museum-related items for sale.
Activities: temporary & permanent exhibitions; lectures; performing arts; workshops; children's summer art program; docent program; Juried art Competitions. Museum Sponsors: Christmas Holiday Art Market.
Publications: newsletter; biennial, Arizona Aqueous; national exhibition catalog.
Hours & Admission Prices: Sept.-May Mon.-Sat. 10-4:30, Sun. 1-4:30. Offices: daily. No charge; donations accepted. Closed national holidays. ♿
Attendance: 37,000 (estimated)
Membership: Student $15; Individual $45; Family $60; Business $85; Sustaining $110.

TUBAC PRESIDIO STATE HISTORIC PARK, 1 Burruel St., Tubac, AZ 85646. Mailing Address: P.O. Box 1296, Tubac, AZ 85646-1296. Tel.: 520-398-2252. Fax: 520-398-2685.
E-mail: pmoreno@azstateparks.gov
Web Site: www.azstateparks.com/parks/tupr/index.html
Founded: 1959.
Congressional District: 9
Key Personnel: Park Mgr., Joe Martinez; Park Ranger 2, Patricia Moreno.
Personnel Profile: Full-Time Paid 4; Part-Time Volunteers 35.
Governing Authority: state. Parent Institution: Arizona State Parks Board. Tax-exempt: 501(c)(3).
Park Museum and Visitor Center.
Collections: Indian, Spanish, Mexican & American material culture to demonstrate the interrelationship of these ethnic groups as related to the Presidio & history of Tubac; costumes; archaeology; mining; Washington hand press print shop exhibit; reproduction of Arizona's first newspaper. Historic Buildings: 1885 Old Tubac School House; 1752 Commandant's House (ruin); c.1914 Otero Hall.
Research Fields: Spanish Colonial, Mexican Republic, Arizona territorial periods.
Facilities: picnic area.
Activities: guided tours; lectures; film presentation; demonstration of Washington hand press. Museum Sponsors: Living History program, Spanish Colonial Life at Tubac Presidio c.1752.
Publications: reproduction, The Weekly Arizonian; brochures.
Hours & Admission Prices: Daily 8-5. Adults 14 & over $3; children 13 & under & handicapped no charge. Closed Christmas.
Attendance: 30,000 (estimated)

Tucson

ARIZONA HISTORICAL SOCIETY/ARIZONA HISTORY MUSEUM, (M), 949 E. 2nd St., Tucson, AZ 85719-4898. Tel.: 520-628-5774. Fax: 520-628-5695.
E-mail: ahstucson@azhs.gov
Web Site: www.arizonahistoricalsociety.org
Founded: 1864.
Congressional District: 7
Key Personnel: Exec. Dir., Anne I. Woosley, Ph.D.; Southern Arizona Division Dir., Deborah Shelton; Education & Outreach Division Dir., Kyle McKoy; Publications Division Dir., Bruce Dinges, Ph.D.
Personnel Profile: Full-Time Paid 9; Part-Time Paid 6; Part-Time Volunteers 167; Interns 2.
Governing Authority: bd. of directors. Parent Institution: Arizona Historical Society, 949 E. 2nd St. Tucson AZ 85719. Tel.: 520-628-5774 Tax-exempt: 501(c)(3).
History Museum.
Collections: Spanish colonial; Mexican culture; American military weapons; transportation; ranching equipment; mining equipment; household effects; clothing.
Research Fields: American Southwest, Spanish Colonial, Mexican Republic, northern Mexico & American military history.
Facilities: library & archives including 70,000 books, 1,000,000 photographs, periodicals, newspapers, maps, microfilm, oral history recordings & transcriptions, 2,700 linear feet of vertical files & manuscripts; meeting rooms; auditorium. Museum-related items for sale.
Activities: guided tours; school tours; behind-the-scene tours; seminars; workshops; docent program; lecture series; adult & children's programming; annual events; rental facilities.
Publications: quarterly, Journal of Arizona history; books; monographs; annual report.
Hours & Admission Prices: Museum: Mon.-Sat. 10-4. Adults $5, senior citizens 60 & over and youth 12-18 $4; children 11 & under and members no charge. Library: call for hours. Closed New Year's Day; Martin Luther King Jr. Day; Presidents' Day; Memorial Day; Independence Day; Labor Day; Columbus Day; Veterans Day; Thanksgiving; Christmas. ♿
Attendance: 20,000 (estimated)
Membership: Student $25; Individual $50; Household $65; Sustaining $100; Patron $250; Sponsor $500; Director's Circle $1,000.

* **ARIZONA HISTORICAL SOCIETY DOWNTOWN HISTORY MUSEUM,** 140 N. Stone Ave., Tucson, AZ 85701. Mailing Address: 949 E. 2nd St., Tucson, AZ 85719-4898. Tel.: 520-770-1473.
E-mail: austucson@azhs.gov
Web Site: www.arizonahistoricalsociety.org
Founded: 1864.
Congressional District: 7
Key Personnel: Southern Arizona Division Dir., Deborah Shelton.
Personnel Profile: Part-Time Paid 2.
Governing Authority: bd. of directors. Parent Institution: Arizona Historical Society, 949 E. 2nd St., Tucson, AZ 85719. Tel.: 520-628-5774. Tax-exempt: 501(c)(3).
History Museum.
Collections: history of downtown Tucson; barber shop, drug store, department store, school, hotel, fire & police dept., saloon, cigar store, movie theater, aviation artifacts; 18th century Spanish military; 19th century American military.
Research Fields: history of downtown Tucson.
Activities: guided tours; permanent exhibitions; annual events; special programming.
Publications: quarterly, The Journal of Arizona History; books; monographs; annual report.
Hours & Admission Prices: Tues.-Fri. 10-4. Adults $3, seniors 60 & over and

youth 12-18 $2; children 11 & under and members no charge. Closed New Year's Day; Independence Day; Veterans Day; Thanksgiving; Christmas. ♿
Attendance: 1,600 (estimated)
Membership: Student $25; Individual $50; Household $65; Sustaining $100; Patron $250; Sponsor $500; Director's Circle $1,000.

ARIZONA HISTORICAL SOCIETY FORT LOWELL MUSEUM, 2900 N. Craycroft Rd., Tucson, AZ 85712. Mailing Address: 949 E. 2nd St., Tucson, AZ 85719-4898. Tel.: 520-885-3832.
E-mail: ahstucson@azhs.gov
Web Site: www.arizonahistoricalsociety.org
Founded: 1864.
Congressional District: 8
Key Personnel: Southern Arizona Division Dir., Deborah Shelton.
Personnel Profile: Part-Time Paid 1.
Governing Authority: bd. of directors. Parent Institution: Arizona Historical Society, 949 E. 2nd St., Tucson, AZ 85719. Tel. 520-628-5774. Tax-exempt: 501(c)(3).
Military Museum: housed in a reconstructed officer's quarters from a military post active from 1873 to 1891.
Collections: fort history; period furnishings; costumes of frontier army life; uniforms; military artifacts.
Research Fields: 1873-91 Ft. Lowell; Apache wars in Arizona; frontier army; local history.
Activities: guided tours; permanent exhibits; programs for adults & children; special events. Annual Event: La Reunion de El Fuerte.
Publications: quarterly, The Journal of Arizona History; books; monographs; annual report.
Hours & Admission Prices: Fri.-Sat. 10-4. Adults $3, senior citizens 60 & over and youth 12-18 $2; children 11 & under and members no charge. Closed New Year's Day; Independence Day; Veterans Day; Thanksgiving; Christmas. ♿
Attendance: 1,750 (estimated)
Membership: Student $25; Individual $50; Household $65; Sustaining $100; Patron $250; Sponsor $500; Director's Circle $1,000.

ARIZONA HISTORICAL SOCIETY SOSA-CARRILLO-FRÉMONT HOUSE MUSEUM, 151 S. Granada Ave., Tucson, AZ 85701. Mailing Address: 949 E. 2nd St., Tucson, AZ 85719-4898. Tel.: 520-622-0956.
E-mail: ahstucson@azhs.gov
Web Site: www.arizonahistoricalsociety.org
Founded: 1864.
Congressional District: 7
Key Personnel: Southern Arizona Division Dir., Deborah Shelton.
Personnel Profile: Full-Time Paid 1; Part-Time Paid 2.
Governing Authority: bd. of directors. Parent Institution: Arizona Historical Society, 949 E. 2nd St., Tucson, AZ 85719. Tel.: 520-628-5774. Tax-exempt: 501(c)(3).
Historic House: housed in the former residence of pioneer families Soza & Carrillo; also 1881 residence of John C. Fremont, Governor of Arizona Territory.
Collections: historic house.
Publications: quarterly, The Journal of Arizona History; books; monographs; annual report.
Hours & Admission Prices: Call for hours. Adults $3, senior citizens 60 & over and youth 12-18 $2; children 11 & under and members no charge. Closed New Year's Day; Independence Day; Veterans Day; Thanksgiving; Christmas. ♿
Membership: Student $25; Individual $50; Household $65; Sustaining $100; Patron $250; Sponsor $500; Director's Circle $1,000.

ARIZONA-SONORA DESERT MUSEUM, (M), 2021 N. Kinney Rd., Tucson, AZ 85743-9719. Tel.: 520-883-1380. Fax: 520-883-2500.
E-mail: redison@desertmuseum.org
Web Site: www.desertmuseum.org
Founded: 1952.
Congressional District: 2
Key Personnel: Exec. Dir., Robert J. Edison; Exec. Program Dir., Richard C. Brusca, Ph.D.; Dir. Mktg., Tim Vimmerstedt; Chm. Bd. Trustees, Sophia Kaluzniacki, D.V.M.; Dir. Natural History, Mark A. Dimmitt, Ph.D.; C.F.O., Kathryn Riser; Dir. Facilities, Curt Campbell; Dir. Center for Sonoran Desert Studies, Christine Conte; Assoc. Exec. Dir. Living Collections & Exhibits, Craig Ivanyi; Museum Shop Mgr., Jim Hills.
Personnel Profile: Full-Time Paid 85; Part-Time Paid 14; Part-Time Volunteers 300.
Governing Authority: nonprofit organization. Tax-exempt: 501(c)(3).
Nature Center & Natural History Museum.
Collections: invertebrates; herpetology; ichthyology; ornithology; mammalogy; botany; geology; paleontology; mineralogy: all related to the Sonoran Desert region.
Research Fields: regional natural history research; paleoecology.
Facilities: 6,000-vol. library of books on natural history of the Sonoran Desert, reprints, films & slides; botanical garden; zoological park; aquarium; classrooms; restaurant. Gift items for sale.
Activities: lectures; TV program; formally organized education programs for children; volunteer program; permanent exhibitions; environmental and outreach programs; on-site interpretation activities & demonstrations; special off-site activities & tours for members; interpretive displays & activities conducted daily; special events; Desert Museum Art Institute.
Publications: newsletter; Secret Life of Hummingbirds; Wild Foods of the Sonoran Desert: Discovering the Desert Museum; Tucson Mountains Trail Guide; Mount Lemmon Road Guide; Desert Dogs-Coyotes, Foxes & Wolves; Strangers in Our Midst-the Startling World of Sonoran Desert Arthropods; Sonorasaurus-Dinosaur of the Desert; ASDM Book of Answers; Gardening for Pollinators; (pocket series) Desert Life/Vida Desertica; Natural History of the Sonoran Desert; All About the Arizona-Sonora Desert Museum; My Nana's Remedies; Hummingbirds of the West; Venomous Critters of the Southwest; Outdoor Gizmos; Guide to Birds of the Salton Sea; The Sonoran Desert Tortoise: Natural History, Biology and Conservation; Family Go Guide; Guide to Southern Arizona Bird Nests and Eggs; Desert Museum Scrapbook; Cactaceas de Sonora, Mexico: Su Diversidad, Uso y; Invasive Species in the Sonoran Region.
Hours & Admission Prices: March-Sept. daily 7:30-5; Oct.-Feb. daily 8:30-5. May-Oct. adults $9, children 6-12 $2; Nov.-April adults $12, children 6-12 $4; discounts to groups of 20 or more; children under 6 & members no charge. ♿
Attendance: 462,317 (accurate)
Membership: Los Coatis Kids' Club $25; Individual $40; General $50; Turquoise $150; Copper $300; Silver $600; Gold $1,200.

* **ARIZONA STATE MUSEUM, (M),** University of Arizona, 1013 E. University Blvd., Tucson, AZ 85721-0001. Mailing Address: P.O. Box 210026, Tucson, AZ 85721-0026. Tel.: 520-621-6302 & 6281. Fax: 520-621-2976.
Web Site: www.statemuseum.arizona.edu
Founded: 1893.
Congressional District: 7
Key Personnel: Dir., Beth Grindell, Ph.D.; Administrative Assoc., Elizabeth Cordova; Head Operations, Mackenzie Massman; Co Chm. (V) ASM Advisory Bd., Don Luria; Co Chm. (V) ASM Advisory Bd., Frederick T. Lau; Co Chm. (V) ASM Advisory Bd., Dennis H. Lyon; Co Chm. (V) ASM Advisory Bd., Rick Barrett; Chm. Southwest Native Nations Advisory Bd., Lee Wayne Lomayestewa; Vice Chm. Southwest Native Nations Advisory Bd., Wechoni Shurz; Mktg. Coord., Darlene Lizarraga; Assoc. Cur. & Head of Public Programs, Michael J. Riley, Ph.D.; Asst. Cur. American Indian Rels., Alyce Sadongei; Head Librarian, Mary E. Graham; Head Research & Cur. Archaeology, Michael Brescia; Conservator, Nancy N. Odegaard, Ph.D.; Dir. Ethnohistorical Research, Diana Hadley; Museum Registrar, Mark Cattanach; Museum Shop Mgr., Martin Kim; Dir. Gloria F. Ross Center for Tapestry Studies, Ann Hedlund, Ph.D.; Dir. Education, Lisa Falk; Head Collections, Patrick Lyons, Ph.D.; Antiquity Act & Repatriation Coord., John Madsen.
Personnel Profile: Full-Time Paid 57; Part-Time Paid 27; Part-Time Volunteers 180; Interns 8.
Governing Authority: state. Parent Institution: University of Arizona. Tax-exempt: 701(c)(1).
Anthropology Museum.
Collections: modern & archaeological Indian cultures of the Greater Southwest & Northern Mexico including 26,000 ethnographic items; 150,000 archaeological items; 350,000 photographs; 6,000 osteological remains; 3,300 vertebrate zoo archaeological collections; Japanese & Chinese costumes; West African sculpture & masks; Philippine pottery, basketry & weapons; oil lamps & cuneiform tablets from Middle Eastern archaeological sites; & prehistoric Andean textiles & Old World stone tools.
Research Fields: southwestern archaeology; ethnohistory; ethnology; physical anthropology.
Facilities: 60,000-vol. research library of books pertaining to anthropology, history, technology & museology available for inter-library loan & on premises; reading room; labs; classroom. Publications, contemporary Indian crafts & other museum-related items for sale.
Activities: guided tours; docent program; inter-museum loan, permanent & temporary exhibitions; library archives; administer Arizona antiquities act & issue archaeological permits for research on state lands.
Publications: occasional booklets; exhibit catalogs; brochures; Arizona State Museum Archaeological Series; KIVA: The Journal of SW Anthropology & History.
Hours & Admission Prices: Mon.-Sat. 10-5, Sun. 12-5. Suggested Donation:

adult $3; discounts to AAM & American Anthropological Assoc. Closed state & national holidays. ♿
Attendance: 45,000 (estimated)
Membership: UA/AAHS $20; Individual $30; Family $50; Patron $100; Thompson Circle $250; Haury Circle $500; Cummings Circle $1,000; George W.P. Hunt Heritage Circle $2,500.

CENTER FOR CREATIVE PHOTOGRAPHY, University of Arizona, 1030 N. Olive, Tucson, AZ 85721-0103. Mailing Address: University of Arizona, P.O. Box 210103, Tucson, AZ 85721-0103. Tel.: 520-621-7968. Fax: 520-621-9444.
E-mail: oncenter@ccp.library.arizona.edu
Web Site: www.creativephotography.org
Founded: 1975.
Congressional District: 5
Key Personnel: Dean, Carla Stoffle; Administrative Asst., Joan Klose; Archivist, Leslie Calmes; Registrar, Trinity Parker; Asst. Registrar, Betsi Meissner; Dir. Devel., Linda Truesdale; Asst. Cur., Rebecca Senf; Cur. Education, Cass Fey; Publications, Kari Dahlgren; Head Rights, Reproductions & Imaging, Denise Gose; Information Svcs., Jovan Erfan; Online Store Mgr., Tammy Carter; Design & Prep., Tim Mosman.
Personnel Profile: Full-Time Paid 16; Part-Time Paid 25; Part-Time Volunteers 3; Interns 5.
Governing Authority: university. Parent Institution: University of Arizona. Tax-exempt.
Art Museum.
Collections: major 20th-century photographers; 19th & 20th-century photographs including 80,000 photographs by 2,200 photographers; still photography; manuscripts; archives; personal papers; negatives; ephemera.
Major Exhibits: New Topographics (T), 2/19/10-5/16/10; Joe Deal: West & West, 6/5/10-8/1/10.
Research Fields: photographic history.
Facilities: 20,000-vol. library of photography & photographic history; research center. Center publications for sale.
Activities: lectures; gallery talks; temporary & traveling exhibitions; loans; print viewing by appointment.
Publications: The Archive; exhibition catalogs & books.
Hours & Admission Prices: Mon.-Fri. 9-5, Sat.-Sun. 1-4; guided group tours by appointment. No charge; donations suggested. Closed major holidays. ♿
Attendance: 50,000 (estimated)
Membership: Friends of the Center $500 & up.

DEGRAZIA GALLERY IN THE SUN, 6300 N. Swan Rd., Tucson, AZ 85718-3697. Tel.: 520-299-9191; 800-545-2185. Fax: 520-299-1381.
E-mail: admin@degrazia.org
Web Site: www.degrazia.org
Founded: 1977.
Congressional District: 5
Key Personnel: Exec. Dir., Lance Laber; Dir. Collections & Exhibitions, Kristine Peashock; Mktg. Dir., Susan Vance; Museum Shop Mgr., Lisa Wilkenson.
Personnel Profile: Full-Time Paid 9; Part-Time Paid 2.
Governing Authority: nonprofit organization. Parent Institution: DeGrazia Foundation. Tax-exempt: 501(c)(3).
Art Gallery.
Collections: Southwestern art by Ted DeGrazia includes oils, watercolors, pastels, lithographs, sculpture, textiles, adobe architecture. Historic Buildings: chapel; homes.
Facilities: 500-vol. library of art books; 10-acre adobe campus. Prints, note cards & books for sale.
Activities: guided tours; films; organized education programs for children; participatory, loan, temporary & traveling exhibitions.
Publications: exhibit catalogs & books.
Hours & Admission Prices: Daily 10-4. No charge; donations accepted. Closed New Year's Day; Easter; Thanksgiving; Christmas. ♿
Attendance: 50,000 (estimated)

DINNERWARE CONTEMPORARY ARTS, 264 E. Congress St., Tucson, AZ 85701-1829. Tel.: 520-792-4503. Fax: 520-792-1282.
E-mail: dinnerware@dinnerwarearts.com
Web Site: www.dinnerwareArts.com
Founded: 1979.
Congressional District: 2
Key Personnel: Dir., David Aguirre; Treas., Michael Contreras; Communications Coord., Lucinda Young.
Personnel Profile: Full-Time Paid 1; Interns 3.
Governing Authority: nonprofit. Tax-exempt: 501(c)(3).
Contemporary Art Space: located in historic downtown Tucson arts district.
Collections: works by contemporary artists.
Facilities: 2,400 sq. ft. exhibit space. Exhibit catalogues & other museum-related items for sale.
Activities: guided tours; lectures; traveling exhibitions; concerts; formally organized education programs for undergraduates & graduates. Museum Sponsors: WESTAF Invitational Exhibition; Biennial 7-state Juried Exhibit; Auction Exhibit; Solo/Group shows; travelling shows.
Publications: Retrospective catalog, The First Decade of an Alternative Art Space (1979-1989).
Hours & Admission Prices: Tues.-Sat. 12-5; other times by appointment. No charge. ♿
Attendance: 16,000 (accurate)
Membership: Artist $50; Supporting $35; Lifetime $350; Patron $350-$999; Benefactor $1,000.

FLANDRAU SCIENCE CENTER AND PLANETARIUM, (M), The University of Arizona, 1601 E. University Blvd., Tucson, AZ 85719. Mailing Address: P.O. Box 210091, Tucson, AZ 85721-0091. Tel.: 520-621-STAR. Fax: 520-621-8451.
E-mail: fsc@email.arizona.edu
Web Site: www.flandrau.org
Founded: 1975.
Congressional District: 5
Key Personnel: Exec. Dir., Alexis Faust; Assoc. Dir., William Plant; Technical Svcs. Mgr., Neil McSweeney; Planetarium Mgr., Michael Magee; Asst. Dir. Finance, W. Anthony Major, Jr.; Dir. Mktg. & Outreach, Rob Vugteveen.
Personnel Profile: Full-Time Paid 15; Full-Time Volunteers 1; Part-Time Paid 25; Part-Time Volunteers 6.
Governing Authority: university; nonprofit organization. Parent Institution: The University of Arizona. Tax-exempt.
Science Center, Planetarium & Observatory.
Collections: science exhibits; period & contemporary astronomy instruments; astronomical art; memorabilia from noted astronomers; meteorites; gems & minerals; 16 in. telescope; hands-on exhibits.
Facilities: 125-seat planetarium. Science education materials for sale.
Activities: star shows; lectures; films; formally organized education programs for children & undergraduate college students; volunteer program; permanent & temporary exhibitions; summer science workshops; science demonstrations.
Publications: newsletter.
Hours & Admission Prices: Science Center & Planetarium: Thurs. 9-3, Fri. 9-3 & 6-9, Sat. 12-9, Sun. 12-5. Admission 10 & over $7.50, children 4-9 $5. ♿
Attendance: 50,000 (estimated)
Membership: Individual $25; Family $50; Patron $100; Sponsor $500; Benefactor $1,000.

HISTORY OF PHARMACY MUSEUM, University of Arizona College of Pharmacy, 1703 E. Mabel, Tucson, AZ 85721-0001. Mailing Address: University of Arizona College of Pharmacy, P.O. Box 210202, Tucson, AZ 85721-0202. Tel.: 520-626-1427. Fax: 520-626-4063.
Web Site: www.pharmacy.arizona.edu
Founded: 1966.
Congressional District: 7
Key Personnel: Asst. Dean, Richard Wiedhopf
Pharmacy Museum.
Collections: Arizona pharmacy artifacts c.1880-1950; history of pharmacy; over 60,000 bottles; drug containers; books; store fixtures.
Facilities: Museum-related items for sale.
Activities: tours.
Hours & Admission Prices: Mon.-Fri. 8-5. No charge.

INTERNATIONAL WILDLIFE MUSEUM, 4800 W. Gates Pass Rd., Tucson, AZ 85745-9600. Tel.: 520-629-0100. Fax: 520-618-3561.
Web Site: www.thewildlifemuseum.org
Founded: 1988.
Key Personnel: Dir., Richard S. White; Cur. Education, Kristine Massey.
Personnel Profile: Full-Time Paid 7; Part-Time Paid 5; Part-Time Volunteers 10.
Governing Authority: not-for-profit organization. Parent Institution: Safari Club International Foundation. Tax-exempt: 501(c)(3).
Natural History Museum.
Collections: 62 major natural history dioramas & exhibits; International Collection of the National Heads & Horns collection; Burnham-Eagle-Macomber collection; Wayde bird collection; insects from around the world; wildlife art.
Major Exhibits: Stealing Wildlife, 11/09-5/10; Sharks, 11/09-8/10.
Research Fields: vertebrate paleontology.
Facilities: 100-seat theatre. Gift items for sale.
Activities: educational & interactive computer exhibits; interpretive tours;

school environmental education programs & tours; teacher training & assistance; natural history movies; school outreaches; children's & family programs; classes teaching kits; docent & intern programs.
Publications: Animal Skulls: A Guide for Teachers, Naturalists and Interpreters; Wildlife Classroom Activities; members' newsletter, Tracks; previsitation guides, Discovery Safari.
Hours & Admission Prices: Mon.-Fri. 9-5, Sat.-Sun. 9-6. Adults $7, senior citizens $5.50, children 4-12 $2.50; discounts to AAM & ICOM members & military; children 3 & under and members no charge. Closed Thanksgiving; Christmas. ♿
Attendance: 66,173 (accurate)
Membership: Student $20; Individual $25; Senior $23; Senior Couple $40; Family $45; Friend $125; Life $500.

KITT PEAK NATIONAL OBSERVATORY, State Rte. 86 & Rte. 386, Tucson, AZ 85726-6732. Mailing Address: 950 N. Cherry Ave., Tucson, AZ 85719-4933. Tel.: 520-318-8726. Fax: 520-318-8451.
E-mail: rfedele@noao.edu
Web Site: www.noao.edu
Founded: 1958.
Key Personnel: Mgr. Public Information, Richard Fedele; Museum Shop Mgr., Nick Petrosino.
Personnel Profile: Full-Time Paid 8; Part-Time Paid 9; Part-Time Volunteers 35.
Governing Authority: nonprofit. Parent Institution: National Optical Astronomy Observatory & Aura Inc./NSF. Tax-exempt.
Observatory.
Collections: telescopes; astronomy.
Research Fields: astronomy.
Facilities: 4m, 2.1m & solar telescope.
Activities: night viewing; education programs; classes.
Hours & Admission Prices: Daily 9-3:45; guided tours 10, 11:30 & 1:30. Museum: no charge. Guided Tours: adults $4, children 6-12 $2.50. Closed New Year's Day; Thanksgiving; Christmas. ♿
Attendance: 60,000 (estimated)
Membership: Individual $35; Dual $45; Family $55.

LA PILITA MUSEUM, (M), 420 S. Main Ave., Tucson, AZ 85701-2228. Tel.: 520-882-7454.
History Museum.
Collections: local history & culture; photographs; period artifacts.
Facilities: Museum-related items for sale.
Activities: educational programs; special events; lectures; workshops; concerts.
Publications: A Walk Through Time, Place and Stay; self-guided tour book of Barrio Viejo.
Hours & Admission Prices: Jan. 5-May 14 & Sept. 2-Dec. 20 Mon.-Fri. 11-2; other times by appointment. Suggested Donation: adults $2.
Membership: Amistad de Cobre $25; Amistad de Turquesa $50; Amistad de Oro $100; Amistad de Plata $500.

OLD PUEBLO ARCHAEOLOGY CENTER, 2201 W. 44th St., Tucson, AZ 85713-4575. Mailing Address: P.O. Box 40577, Tucson, AZ 85717-0577. Tel.: 520-798-1201. Fax: 520-798-1966.
E-mail: info@oldpueblo.org
Founded: 1993.
Key Personnel: Exec. Dir., Allen Dart.
Governing Authority: nonprofit organization. Tax-exempt: 501(c)(3).
Archaeology Center.
Collections: archaeology; area history & culture.
Activities: archaeological & historical research programs; educational programs.
Hours & Admission Prices: Call for hours.

OLD WEST MOVIE POSTER MUSEUM, 1300 N. Stone Ave., Tucson, AZ 85705-7338. Tel.: 520-770-1910.
E-mail: info@flamingohoteltucson.com
Web Site: www.flaminghoteltucson.com
Western Movie Poster Museum.
Collections: over 1,000 western movie posters; lobby cards; photographs; autographed star photos; movie memorabilia.
Hours & Admission Prices: Daily 9-5. Hotel guests no charge.

OTIS CHIDESTER SCOUT MUSEUM OF SOUTHERN ARIZONA, 1937 E. Blacklidge Dr., Tucson, AZ 85719-2847. Tel.: 520-326-7669.
Web Site: www.azscoutmuseum.com
Founded: 1986.
Congressional District: 7
Key Personnel: Chm. (V), William White; Pres. (V), James Klein.
Personnel Profile: Part-Time Volunteers 15.
Governing Authority: Tax-exempt.
Scout Museum.
Collections: southern Arizona & Southwest Boy Scouts of America; photographs; audio; personal artifacts.
Activities: tours.
Publications: quarterly newsletter, Museum Dispatch.
Hours & Admission Prices: Thurs. 9am to noon; other times by appointment. No charge.
Attendance: 500 (estimated)
Membership: Individual $20; Family $30.

PIMA AIR & SPACE MUSEUM, 6000 E. Valencia Rd., Tucson, AZ 85756-9403. Tel.: 520-574-0462. Fax: 520-574-9238.
Web Site: www.pimaair.org
Founded: 1966.
Congressional District: 5
Key Personnel: Exec. Dir. & Dir. Titan Missile Museum, Yvonne C. Morris; Chm., Count Ferdinand von Galen; Dir. Collections & Aircraft Restoration, Scott Marchand; Asst. Cur., James Stemm; Museum Shop Mgr., Beth Barksdale.
Personnel Profile: Full-Time Paid 47; Part-Time Paid 17; Part-Time Volunteers 300.
Governing Authority: nonprofit organization. Parent Institution: Arizona Aerospace Foundation. Subsidiary Institution: Arizona Aviation Hall of Fame. Tax-exempt: 501(c)(3).
Aeronautics & Space Museum & Arizona Aviation Hall of Fame.
Collections: aviation memorabilia & 60,000 artifacts; 285 aircraft; static displays of aircraft; photographs; space gallery. Historic Structure: World War II barracks.
Facilities: library of technical repair & operations manuals available for use on premises by appointment; theater; Challenger learning center. Reproductions, museum & aviation-related items for sale.
Activities: guided tours; lectures; temporary exhibitions.
Publications: quarterly newsletter, Skywriting; books, Wonders of the Pima Air & Space Museum; Titan Missile Museum; Contrails.
Hours & Admission Prices: Pima Air & Space Museum: daily 9-5. June-Oct.: adults $13.75, seniors 62 & over and military $9.75, children 7-12 $8; discounts to AAM members; children 6 & under & members no charge. Nov.-May: adults $15.50, seniors 62 & over and military $12.75, children 7-12 $9; discounts to AAM members; children 6 & under and members no charge. ♿
Attendance: 154,099 (accurate)
Membership: Solo $40; Dual $50; Crew $60.

REID PARK ZOO, 1100 S. Randolph Way, Tucson, AZ 85716-5835. Tel.: 520-791-3204. Fax: 520-791-5378.
E-mail: reidzoo@tucsonaz.gov
Web Site: www.tucsonzoo.org
Founded: 1967.
Key Personnel: Dir., Susan Basford; Education & Public Rels., Vivian W. VanPeenen.
Personnel Profile: Full-Time Paid 24; Part-Time Paid 13; Part-Time Volunteers 92; Interns 5.
Governing Authority: municipal; nonprofit. Tax-exempt: 501 (c)(3). Parent Institution: Tucson Parks & Recreation Dept.
Zoo.
Collections: exotic animals from around the world.
Research Fields: animal nutrition.
Facilities: library material available for use on premises; 100-seat cafeteria; zoological park. Zoo-related items for sale.
Activities: docent program; formally organized education programs.
Publications: newsletter, Tucson Zoological Society Quarterly.
Hours & Admission Prices: Gate: daily 9-4. Adults $6, senior citizens $4, children 2-14 $2; discounts to AZA members; members & children under 2 no charge. Closed Christmas. ♿
Attendance: 525,000 (estimated)
Membership: Senior Citizen $20; Single $30; Family $50.

SAGUARO NATIONAL PARK - EASTERN DISTRICT VISITOR CENTER, 3693 S. Old Spanish Trail, Tucson, AZ 85730-5601. Tel.: 520-733-5153.
Natural History Museum.
Collections: local history & culture; Sonoran Desert plants; Native American artifacts; photographs; period furnishings; personal artifacts.
Facilities: Books for sale.
Activities: video; educational programs.
Hours & Admission Prices: Daily 9-5. Closed Christmas.

SAGUARO NATIONAL PARK - WESTERN DISTRICT VISITOR CENTER, 2700 N. Kinney Rd., Tucson, AZ 85743-9719. Tel.: 520-733-5158.
Natural History Museum.

Collections: local natural & cultural history; Native American artifacts; period furnishings; personal artifacts; photographs.
Facilities: Books for sale.
Activities: educational programs; video.
Hours & Admission Prices: Daily 9-5. Closed Christmas.

SAN XAVIER DEL BAC MISSION, 1950 W. San Xavier Rd., Tucson, AZ 85746-7409. Tel.: 520-294-2624. Fax: 520-294-3438.
Church & Religious Museum: built in the late 1700s.
Collections: church history; religious artifacts; wall paintings.
Facilities: Museum-related items for sale.
Activities: video; tours.
Hours & Admission Prices: Self-Guided Tour: 8:30-4:30. Services: call for hours. No charge; donations accepted. ♿

T REX MUSEUM, 3861 N. Oracle Rd., Tucson, AZ 85705-3253. Mailing Address: P.O. Box 91706, Tucson, AZ 85752-1706. Tel.: 520-888-0746 & 907-9107.
E-mail: admin@biopark.org
Web Site: www.trexmuseum.org
Founded: 2003.
Key Personnel: Exec. Dir., Samuel Breidenbach; Creative Dir., Fravarti Breidenbach.
Personnel Profile: Full-Time Volunteers 6; Part-Time Paid 6; Part-Time Volunteers 10.
Governing Authority: private; nonprofit organization. Parent Institution: International Bio Park Foundation. Tax-exempt: 501(c)(3).
Children's Dinosaur Museum.
Collections: history of prehistoric life; dinosaurs; hands-on exhibits; natural history art; reptiles of the past, present & future; fossils; photographs; live zoo animals.
Facilities: 500-vol. library; 75-seat auditorium; snack bar; educational facilities; conservation center; 50-seat theater; zoo. Museum-related items for sale.
Activities: arts festival; docent program; films; formal education programs for children. Annual Events: Dino Fiesta in February; Dino Daze in October.
Hours & Admission Prices: Fri.-Sun. 10-4; other times by appointment. Admission $5. Closed New Year's Day; Independence Day; Thanksgiving; Christmas. ♿
Attendance: 75,000 (estimated)
Membership: Single $40; Family $50; Donor $100; Supporter $500; Lifetime $1,000.

390TH MEMORIAL MUSEUM, (M), 6000 E. Valencia Rd., Tucson, AZ 85756-9403. Tel.: 520-574-0287. Fax: 520-574-3030.
Personnel Profile: Full-Time Paid 2; Full-Time Volunteers 30; Part-Time Paid 1.
Military History Museum.
Collections: 390th unit history & heritage; military aircraft & memorabilia; General James H. Doolittle; paintings; Honor Wall; aircraft models; photographs; B-17G.
Facilities: library; archives.
Activities: research.
Publications: quarterly, Square J Bulletin.
Hours & Admission Prices: Located on the grounds of the Pima Air and Space Museum. Daily 10-4:30. Grounds: fee charged. Memorial Museum: no charge. Closed Thanksgiving; Christmas.
Attendance: 100,000
Membership: 390th B.G. Veterans $20; Non-Veterans $25; Life $500.

TOHONO CHUL PARK INC., (M), 7366 N. Paseo del Norte, Tucson, AZ 85704-4415. Tel.: 520-742-6455, ext. 210. Fax: 520-797-1213.
E-mail: joandonnelly@tohonochulpark.org
Web Site: www.tohonochulpark.org
Founded: 1985.
Congressional District: 5
Key Personnel: C.E.O., Exec. Dir. & Financial Dir., Joan E. Donnelly; Bd. Pres., Donald F. Romano; Cur. Plants, Russ Buhrow; Cur. Exhibits, Vicki Donkersley; Dir. Public Programs, Jo Falls; Dir. Visitor Svcs., Monica Sufaro Spigelman; Dir. Gen. Svcs., Lee Mason; General Mgr. Retail, Linda Wolfe.
Personnel Profile: Full-Time Paid 15; Part-Time Paid 15; Part-Time Volunteers 400; Interns 1.
Governing Authority: nonprofit organization. Tax-exempt: 501(c)(3).
Nature Center.
Collections: Native and adapted plants of desert southwest; limited collection of Native American arts and crafts (contemporary and traditional).
Facilities: 800-vol. library of Southwestern ecology, culture, environment, history & botany; 100-seat auditorium; ethnobotanical garden; performance garden; demonstration garden; children's garden; classroom; nature trails. Items relating to Southwestern culture & environment for sale.
Activities: birding tours, landscape & water conservation tours; art exhibit tours; concerts; docent program; films; educational programs; guided tours; lectures; loaned & temporary exhibitions; demonstrations. Annual Event: Wildflower Festival.
Publications: quarterly newsletter, Desert Corner Journal; The Official Guide to Tohono Chul Park; annual report.
Hours & Admission Prices: Grounds & Tea Room daily 8-5. Exhibits, Museum Shops & Greenhouse: daily 9-5; guided tours by appointment. Adults $7, seniors 62 & over & active military $5, students with valid ID $3, children 5-12 $2; discounts to AAM & AABGA members; members, children under 5 & 1st Tues. of month no charge. Closed New Year's Day; Independence Day; Thanksgiving; Christmas. ♿
Attendance: 170,000 (estimated)
Membership: Senior Single 65 & over $20; Senior Couple 65 & over and Individual $30; Family & Dual $40; Gambel's Quail $75; Desert Tortoise $100; Red-tailed Hawk $250; Bobcat $500; Paloverde $1,000; Saguaro $5,000.

TUCSON BOTANICAL GARDENS, 2150 N. Alvernon Way, Tucson, AZ 85712-3199. Tel.: 520-326-9686, ext. 10. Fax: 520-324-0166.
E-mail: info@tucsonbotanical.org
Web Site: www.tucsonbotanical.org
Founded: 1968.
Congressional District: 5
Key Personnel: Exec. Dir., Michelle Conklin; Bd. Pres. (V), Karen McCloskey; Dir. Horticulture & Facilities, Ken Byrd; Dir. Mktg., Jocelyn Robertson; Dir. Retail & Visitor Svcs., Renee Donaldson.
Personnel Profile: Full-Time Paid 28; Part-Time Paid 5; Part-Time Volunteers 200.
Governing Authority: nonprofit organization. Tax-exempt: 501(c)(3).
Arboretum & Botanical Garden.
Collections: plants adaptable to southern Arizona environments; xeriscape demonstration garden; iris, herb, cactus, succulent, sensory, bird attracting, vegetable & Indian crops gardens; historic Tucson garden; wildflower (gardens); tropical economic greenhouse.
Major Exhibits: Butterfly Magic-Tropical Butterflies, 11/09-4/10; DIG: Prehistoric Gardens, 6/10-9/10.
Research Fields: horticulturally adapted arid land plants.
Facilities: library pertaining to horticulture available for research on premises during open hours; meeting room; education building; nursery; facility rentals available. Plants & plant-related items for sale.
Activities: guided tours; classes & workshops for adults and children horticultural therapy; school gardening programs; after school intersession programs; triannual plant sale. Gardens Sponsors: Home & Garden Tour; Luminaria Nights; Twilight Thursdays Summer Concert Series; Tropical Butterfly exhibit October to April.
Publications: quarterly newsletter, Tucson Botanical Gardens News; bilingual Children's Discovery Guide; self-guided tour brochure; Attracting Birds to Your Garden; A Tucson Herb Garden - Growing Tips from the Tucson Botanical Gardens.
Hours & Admission Prices: Daily 8:30-4:30. Adults $7, children 4-12 $3; members & children under 4 no charge. Closed New Year's Day; Independence Day; Thanksgiving; Christmas Eve & Day. ♿
Attendance: 100,000 (estimated)
Membership: Individual $35, Family $45; Yucca $50; Cholla $100; Agave $250; Ocotillo $500; Saguaro $1,000.

TUCSON CHILDREN'S MUSEUM, (M), 200 S. Sixth Ave., Tucson, AZ 85701-2109. Mailing Address: P.O. Box 2609, Tucson, AZ 85702-2609. Tel.: 520-792-9985. Fax: 520-792-0639.
E-mail: tcm@tucsonchildrensmuseum.org
Web Site: www.tucsonchildrensmuseum.org
Founded: 1986.
Congressional District: 2
Key Personnel: Exec. Dir., Michael Luria; Pres., Dev Sethi; Museum Shop Mgr., Kendra Decker.
Personnel Profile: Full-Time Paid 8; Part-Time Paid 18; Part-Time Volunteers 12; Interns 2.
Governing Authority: nonprofit organization. Tax-exempt: 501(c)(3).
Children's Museum.
Collections: 11,000 sq. ft. of interactive hands on educational exhibits.
Facilities: meeting room.
Activities: guided tours; organized education programs for children; participatory exhibits.
Publications: quarterly newsletter.
Hours & Admission Prices: Winter: Tues.-Sat. 10-5, Sun. 12-5; Summer: Mon.-Sat. 10-5, Sun. 12-5; open Mon. during school holidays. Adults $7, seniors & children $5; members no charge. ♿

Attendance: 95,000 (accurate)
Membership: Parent, Child or Grandparents $40; Family of 4 $75.

* **TUCSON MUSEUM OF ART & HISTORIC BLOCK,** 140 N. Main Ave., Tucson, AZ 85701-8290. Tel.: 520-624-2333. Fax: 520-624-7202.
E-mail: info@tucsonmuseumofart.org
Web Site: www.tucsonmuseumofart.org
Founded: 1924.
Congressional District: 2
Key Personnel: Dir., Robert E. Knight; Deputy Dir. & C.F.O., Carol Bleck; Chief Accountant, Ruth Sons; Collections Mgr. & Registrar, Susan Dolan; Asst. Registrar, Kristen Schmidt; Visitor & Member Svcs., Katherine Wesolowski; Dir. Education, Stephanie Coakley; Dir. Public Rels. & Mktg., Meredith Hayes; Dir. Devel., Leslie Schelle; Cur. Latin American Art, Fatima Bercht; Chief Cur. & Cur. Modern & Contemporary Art, Julie Sasse; Cur. Art of the American West, Thomas Smith; Preparator, David Longwell; Librarian, Jill Provan; Museum Shop Mgr., John McNulty.
Personnel Profile: Full-Time Paid 20; Part-Time Paid 13; Part-Time Volunteers 483; Interns 22.
Governing Authority: nonprofit organization. Tax-exempt: 501(c)(3).
Art Museum.
Collections: pre-Columbian, Spanish colonial, 19th- & 20th-century Latin American & Mexican folk art; contemporary art; 19th- & 20th-century art of America & the American West; World Folk Art; American arts & crafts; 20th-century art of North & South America; Asian, African & European influences on the art of the Americas.
Research Fields: American art; pre-Columbian art; art of the American West; New World art; contemporary art.
Facilities: 6,000-vol. library; 24,000 slide library on primitive & general art available for use on a research basis. Arizona crafts & other museum-related items for sale.
Activities: art classes; docent training; lectures; concerts; gallery talks; tours; competitions; extension department serving Tucson school districts; traveling & changing exhibitions; travel program.
Publications: Museum School brochure; exhibition catalogues; quarterly newsletter; annual report.
Hours & Admission Prices: Tues.-Sat. 10-4, Sun. 12-4. Adults $8, senior citizens 60 & over $6, students 13 & over $3; discounts to AAM & ICOM members; Western Museum Assoc. members, first Sun. of month, children under 12 and members no charge. Closed national holidays. ♿
Attendance: 192,795 (estimated)
Membership: Student $20; Individual $40; Family $50; Sponsor $75; Sustaining $100; Patron $250; President's Circle $500; Director's Circle $1,000; Fellow $5,000; Benefactor $10,000.

TUCSON RODEO PARADE MUSEUM, 4823 S. Sixth Ave., Tucson, AZ 85714-3004. Mailing Address: P.O. Box 1788, Tucson, AZ 85702-1788. Tel.: 520-294-1280.
E-mail: leathercleaner@prodigy.net
Web Site: www.tucsonrodeoparade.org
Founded: 1963.
Key Personnel: Chm. (V), Stan Grimes.
Governing Authority: Parent Institution: Tucson Rodeo Parade Committee, Inc. Tax-exempt.
Western Cultural Museum.
Collections: local history; over 150 horse drawn vehicles; Native American & mining artifacts.
Activities: tours; special events. Museum Sponsors: Tucson Rodeo Parade in February.
Hours & Admission Prices: Jan.-April Mon.-Sat. 9:30-3:30; Dec.-March Mon.-Sat. 9:30-3:30. No charge; donations accepted. Closed New Year's Day.
Attendance: 5,000 (estimated)

UNIVERSITY OF ARIZONA MINERAL MUSEUM, Univ. of Arizona, Flandrau Science Center, Cherry & University, Tucson, AZ 85721-0001. Tel.: 520-621-4227. Fax: 520-621-8451.
E-mail: bailey2@email.arizona.edu
Web Site: www.uamineralmuseum.org
Founded: 1891.
Key Personnel: Cur., Dr. Robert T. Downs; Curatorial Specialist, Sven Bailey.
Personnel Profile: Part-Time Paid 1; Part-Time Volunteers 1.
Governing Authority: university. Tax-exempt.
Mineral Museum.
Collections: over 19,000 mineral specimens representing Arizona & worldwide localities; 7,000 micromounts which may be viewed upon request; excellent meteorite collection.
Research Fields: mineralogical & crystallographic studies in conjunction with Dept. of Geosciences, University of Arizona.
Activities: guided tours; permanent exhibitions.
Hours & Admission Prices: Fri.-Sat. 9-5. School Groups: Tues.-Fri. 9-1. Adults $4; children 4 & under no charge. Closed holidays. ♿

* **THE UNIVERSITY OF ARIZONA MUSEUM OF ART AND ARCHIVE OF VISUAL ARTS, (M),** Park and Speedway, Tucson, AZ 85721-0001. Mailing Address: University of Arizona, P.O. Box 210002, Tucson, AZ 85721-0002. Tel.: 520-621-7567 (Main) & 7568 (Mktg./Public Rels.). Fax: 520-621-8770.
E-mail: dhartman@email.arizona.edu
Web Site: www.artmuseum.arizona.edu
Founded: 1955.
Congressional District: 7
Key Personnel: Exec. Dir., Charles A. Guerin; Deputy Dir. & Museum Shop Mgr., Diane A. Hartman; Asst. Cur., Susannah Maurer; Cur. Education, Carol Petrozzello; Registrar, Kristen Schmidt; Systems Analyst, Robert Hershoff; Business Mgr., Kathleen Kearney; Sr. Exhibits Preparator, John Kelly; Administrative Sec., Christine Aguilar; Ld. Security Officer, Kris Wagman; Security, Andy Leahy; Coord. Public Art, Beth Hancock.
Personnel Profile: Full-Time Paid 11; Part-Time Paid 2; Part-Time Volunteers 56; Interns 6.
Governing Authority: Bd. of Regents. Parent Institution: University of Arizona. Tax-exempt.
Art Museum.
Collections: Samuel H. Kress collection of 14th- to 19th-century European Art including the 15th century altarpiece of Ciudad Rodrigo; 26 paintings by Fernando Gallego and assistants; Edward J. Gallagher Memorial collection of 20th-century & contemporary American & European painting, sculpture & works on paper; old master & contemporary prints; C. Leonard Pfeiffer collection of American painting; Jacques Lipchitz sketches & models.
Research Fields: prints; contemporary art; 15th-century Hispano-Flemish art, education.
Facilities: 14,000 sq. ft. exhibit space. Museum-related items for sale.
Activities: intern programs; tours; research; lectures; family days; permanent, temporary & traveling exhibitions.
Publications: catalogs, Jacques Lipchitz, Sketches and Models; permanent collection print handbook.
Hours & Admission Prices: Tues.-Fri. 9-5, Sat.-Sun. 12-4. Adults $5; UA faculty & staff, students with ID, children & members no charge. Closed major holidays. ♿
Attendance: 33,614 (accurate)
Membership: Basic: Student & Senior $30; Faculty & Staff $40; Senior Couple $50. Associate: Individual $45; Family $75. Partner: Individual $125; Family $175; Sponsor $250; Donor $500; Fellow $1,000; Benefactor $2,500.

UNIVERSITY OF ARIZONA STUDENT UNION GALLERIES, Dept. of Student Programs, Student Union, Rm. 106B, Tucson, AZ 85721-0001. Tel.: 520-621-6142. Fax: 520-621-6930.
E-mail: jsasse@u.arizona.edu
Web Site: www.union.arizona.edu/csil/gallery
Founded: 1971.
Key Personnel: Gallery Cur., Christina Lieberman.
Personnel Profile: Part-Time Paid 5; Interns 1.
Governing Authority: public university; nonprofit.
Art Gallery.
Collections: items purchased or donated from nationally & internationally known artists & supporting University of Arizona student artists.
Facilities: cafeteria.
Activities: guided tours; loan & participatory exhibits; internships in curating & graphic design. Annual Events: alumni exhibit in the fall; student art show in the spring.
Hours & Admission Prices: Mon.-Fri. 10-5, Sat. 12-3. No charge. Closed major holidays & installation day. ♿
Attendance: 11,500 (accurate)

WESTERN ARCHEOLOGICAL & CONSERVATION CENTER, 255 N. Commerce Park Loop, Tucson, AZ 85745-2796. Tel.: 520-791-6400. Fax: 520-791-6465.
Founded: 1952.
Congressional District: 2
Key Personnel: Archivist, Lynn Marie Mitchell; Repository Chief, Stephanie H. Rodeffer; Asst. Conservator, Brynn Bender; Registrar, Kim E. Beckwith; Archivist, Khaleel Saba.
Personnel Profile: Full-Time Paid 5; Part-Time Paid 2; Part-Time Volunteers 12; Interns 1.
Governing Authority: federal. Parent Institution: U.S. Dept. of the Interior, National Park Service. Tax-exempt.
History Museum.

Collections: Southwestern prehistoric, ethnographic artifacts & historic household items; comparative shared library; research archives pertaining to southwest archaeology, ethnography & history; 160,000 image photographic collection; more than 100 current serials/periodicals; natural science.
Research Fields: cultural resources management; archaeology; collections management.
Facilities: 17,000-vol. library on Southwest archaeology, history & ethnography for use on premises; field research station; artifact conservation laboratories; research laboratory.
Activities: work program for graduate students in museology, artifact conservation & cultural resource management; internship program for graduate students in library science and archival management; guided tours for high school, university & community groups by appointment.
Publications: anthropology series.
Hours & Admission Prices: Mon.-Fri. 9-3; library & other times by appointment. No charge. Closed federal holidays. ♿

Tumacacori

TUMACACORI NATIONAL HISTORICAL PARK, 1891 E. Frontage Rd., Tumacacori, AZ 85640. Mailing Address: P.O. Box 8067, Tumacacori, AZ 85640-8067. Tel.: 520-398-2341, ext. 0. Fax: 520-398-9271.
E-mail: roy_simpson@nps.gov
Web Site: www.nps.gov/tuma
Founded: 1908.
Congressional District: 5
Key Personnel: Cur., Roy Simpson; Supt., Ann Razor.
Personnel Profile: Part-Time Paid 1; Part-Time Volunteers 2.
Governing Authority: federal. Parent Institution: U.S. National Park Service. Tax-exempt.
National Park, Historic Site and Museum: site 1795 San Jose de Tumacacori Spanish Mission Church, abandoned in 1848; Los Santos Angeles de Guevavi Mission; San Cayetano de Calabazas Mission.
Collections: Indian & Spanish Colonial artifacts.
Research Fields: Spanish colonial history.
Facilities: 700-vol. library of material on Spanish Colonial exploration, Arizona & Mexico history, church history & related topics available on premises only. Publications for sale.
Activities: guided tours; lectures; films. Museum Sponsors: craft demonstrations.
Publications: brochures; booklet.
Hours & Admission Prices: Daily 9-5. Adults $3; children under 17, Golden Age, Golden Eagle & annual park pass holders no charge. Closed Thanksgiving; Christmas. ♿
Attendance: 60,000 (accurate)

Vail

LA POSTA QUEMADA RANCH MUSEUM, 16721 E. Old Spanish Trail Rd., Vail, AZ 85641. Tel.: 520-647-7275.
History Museum.
Collections: natural & cultural history; Native American artifacts; photographs; personal artifacts; period furnishings; cave history.
Hours & Admission Prices: March 16-Sept. 15 daily 8-5; Sept. 16-March 15 daily 9-5.

Whiteriver

FORT APACHE HISTORIC PARK AND MUSEUM - KINISHBA RUINS, Fort Apache Indian Reservation, Whiteriver, AZ 85941. Mailing Address: P.O. Box 507, Fort Apache, AZ 85926-0507. Tel.: 928-338-4625.
Native American Museum: listed on the National Register of Historic Places.
Collections: Native American culture & history; personal artifacts; photographs; period buildings; prehistoric ruins; military cemetery.
Facilities: Museum-related items for sale.
Activities: tours; art demonstrations; special events.
Hours & Admission Prices: June-Aug. Mon.-Sat. 8-5; Winter: Mon.-Fri. 8-5. Closed major holidays.

Wickenburg

* **DESERT CABALLEROS WESTERN MUSEUM, (M),** 21 N. Frontier St., Wickenburg, AZ 85390-3431. Tel.: 928-684-2272, ext. 100. Fax: 928-684-5794.
E-mail: info@westernmuseum.org
Web Site: westernmuseum.org
Founded: 1960.
Congressional District: 3
Key Personnel: Interim Dir., Mary Ann Igna; Chm. (V), Dallas Gant; Museum Shop Mgr., Marilu Rix; Museum Technician, Paul Hughes.
Personnel Profile: Full-Time Paid 5; Part-Time Paid 3; Part-Time Volunteers 175.
Governing Authority: nonprofit organization. Tax-exempt: 501(c)(3).
General Museum.
Collections: western art; period rooms & dioramas; Native American collection; minerals; cowboy and ranch history; mining history.
Major Exhibits: Photographic Postcards of Arizona, 11/09-9/5/10; Cowgirl Up! Art From the Other Half of the West, 3/26/10-5/2/10; Best of the West, 5/22/10-1/2/11.
Research Fields: history of Arizona.
Facilities: 2,000-vol. library of books on western history & art available on premises; reading room. Museum-related items & publications for sale.
Activities: permanent & temporary exhibitions; lectures; workshops; seminars; classes; trips.
Publications: books, The Town on the Hassayampa a History of Wickenburg, Arizona; The Cowboy's Dream: The Mythic Life and Art of Lon Megargee; annual exhibition catalogue, Cowgirl Up!
Hours & Admission Prices: June-Aug. Tues.-Sat. 10-5, Sun. 12-4; Sept.-May Mon.-Sat. 10-5, Sun. 12-4. Adults $7.50, senior citizens over 55 $6; discounts to AAM members; members & children 16 and under no charge. Closed major holidays. ♿
Attendance: 55,000 (estimated)
Membership: Individual $45; Family $75; Contributor $150; Supporter $250; Sponsor $500; Patron $1,000; Founder $2,500; Board of Governors $5,000.

NATURE CONSERVANCY HASSAYAMPA RIVER PRESERVE VISITOR CENTER, 49614 N. U.S. Hwy. 60, Wickenburg, AZ 85390. Tel.: 928-684-2772.
E-mail: bmccollum@tnc.org
Nature Preserve.
Collections: natural history; wildlife including over 280 species of birds.
Facilities: nature trails.
Activities: hiking; guided tours; special events; educational programs.
Hours & Admission Prices: mid-May to mid-Sept. Fri.-Sun. 7am-11am; mid-Sept. to mid-May Wed.-Sun. 8-5. Adults $5, members $3; children under 12 no charge. Closed New Year's Eve & Day; Thanksgiving; Christmas Eve & Day.

Willcox

CHIRICAHUA NATIONAL MONUMENT, 12856 E. Rhyolite Creek Rd., Willcox, AZ 85643-4722. Tel.: 520-824-3560. Fax: 520-824-3421.
Web Site: www.nps.gov/chir
Founded: 1924.
Congressional District: 5
Key Personnel: Cur., Kathrine Neilsen; Park Ranger, Suzanne Moody.
Governing Authority: federal. National Park Service. Tax-exempt.
Natural History Museum: located in the visitor center. Faraway Ranch & Stafford Cabin offer historical artifacts.
Collections: herbarium; entomology; geology; herpetology; historic furnishings & structures 1880s-1970s.
Facilities: 2,600-vol. library of natural & cultural history available for use on premises.
Activities: conducted programs; guided walks; hiking; camping.
Hours & Admission Prices: Daily 8-4:30. Adults 17 & over $5; children 15 & under no charge. Closed Thanksgiving; Christmas. ♿
Attendance: 128,000

REX ALLEN MUSEUM, 150 N. Railroad Ave., Willcox, AZ 85643-2132. Tel.: 520-384-4583; 877-234-4111.
E-mail: info@rexallenmuseum
Web Site: www.rexallenmuseum.org
Founded: 1989.
Key Personnel: Mgr., Delcie Schultz
Western Movie & Cowboy Museum.
Collections: western movie memorabilia; cowboy artifacts; personal artifacts; local history.
Facilities: theater. Museum-related items for sale.
Hours & Admission Prices: Daily 10-4. Adults $2. Closed New Year's Day; Thanksgiving; Christmas.

Window Rock

NAVAJO NATION MUSEUM, Hwy. 264 & Post Office Loop Rd., Window Rock, AZ 86515. Mailing Address: P.O. Box 1840, Window Rock, AZ 86515-1840. Tel.: 928-871-7941. Fax: 928-871-7942.
E-mail: mwheeler@cia-g.com
Founded: 1961.
Congressional District: 4

Key Personnel: Dir., Manuelito Wheeler; Cur. Collections, Clarenda Begay; Bus. Mgr., Audrey Roberts; Archivist, Eunice Kahn; Cultural Specialist, Robert Johnson.
Personnel Profile: Full-Time Paid 13.
Governing Authority: Navajo Nation. Parent Institution: Navajo Nation Historic Preservation Dept. Tax-exempt: 170(b)(1).
Native American Museum.
Collections: Navajo history; ethnology; fine arts; Southwest archaeology; geology & paleontology; photo archive with more than 40,000 images.
Research Fields: Navajo history & culture.
Facilities: library; rental facilities. Museum-related items for sale.
Activities: permanent & temporary exhibits; group tours; rental facilities.
Publications: book, Navajo-A Century of Progress, 1868-1968; occasional exhibit catalogs.
Hours & Admission Prices: Mon. 8-5, Tues.-Fri. 8-7, Sat. 9-5. No charge; donations accepted. Closed national & tribal holidays. ♿
Attendance: 45,446 (estimated)

NAVAJO NATION ZOO & BOTANICAL PARK, Hwy. 264, Bldg. 36A, Window Rock, AZ 86515. Mailing Address: P.O. Box 1480, Window Rock, AZ 86515-1480. Tel.: 928-871-6574.
Zoo & Botanical Park.
Collections: over 30 species of wild animals; trees; plants; flowers.
Activities: special events.
Hours & Admission Prices: Mon.-Sat. 10-5. No charge. Closed New Year's Day; Christmas.

Winslow

HOMOLOVI RUINS STATE PARK, 87 North, Winslow, AZ 86047. Mailing Address: HCR 63 Box 5, Winslow, AZ 86047-9402. Tel.: 928-289-4106. Fax: 928-289-2021.
E-mail: homolovi@pr.state.az.us
Web Site: www.azstateparks.com
Founded: 1986.
Congressional District: 4
Key Personnel: Park Mgr., Karen Berggren.
Personnel Profile: Full-Time Paid 4; Part-Time Paid 2; Part-Time Volunteers 20.
Governing Authority: state government. Parent Institution: Arizona State Parks. Tax-exempt: 501(c)(3).
State Park.
Collections: prehistoric artifacts from Homolovi sites & associated areas; natural history collections documenting natural resources of Homolovi Ruins State Park; Hopi art.
Facilities: visitor center & bookstore; campground; trails; retail & wholesale Hopi art.
Activities: self-guiding trails; programs & workshops: Native American culture & concerns.
Publications: Homolovi: A Cultural Crossroads; personal notes on Hopi gardening.
Hours & Admission Prices: Park: daily sunrise-sunset; Visitor Center: daily 8-5. Admission $5 per vehicle, 4 people per vehicle $1 for each additional person; Campground: $12 without hookups, $19 with electric hookups (per 6 people). Closed Christmas Day. ♿
Attendance: 26,238 (accurate)

MUSEUM OF ASTROGEOLOGY, METEOR CRATER, Interstate 40, Exit 233, Meteor Crater Rd. 5.5 miles S., Winslow, AZ 86047. Mailing Address: P.O. Box 30940, Flagstaff, AZ 86003-0940. Tel.: 928-289-5898. Fax: 928-289-2598.
E-mail: info@meteorcrater.com
Web Site: www.meteorcrater.com
Founded: 1955.
Key Personnel: Pres., Brad Andes.
Personnel Profile: Full-Time Paid 34; Part-Time Paid 14.
Governing Authority: profit-making organization. Affiliated with Meteor Crater Enterprises.
Astrogeology Museum.
Collections: space capsule: Astronaut Wall of Fame, commemorating all U.S. Astronauts & all U.S. manned space flights. Interactive exhibits: Create a Crater, Shoemaker/Levy 9 Comet Impacts on Jupiter, Earth at Risk, Impact Earth, Ground Zero. Other exhibits: Meteorites, rocks, gems, impact craters throughout our solar system, planetary & astrogeology impact crater mechanics.
Facilities: library of books on meteors & astrogeology. Books for sale.
Activities: lectures; films; audio-visual presentations; formally organized education programs for children, adults & undergraduate college students; permanent exhibitions; weather permitting, daily guided rim tours; interactive computer.
Publications: Meteor Crater Story.
Hours & Admission Prices: Winter: daily 8-5; Summer: daily 7-7. Adults $15, senior citizens 60 & over $14, juniors 6-17 $8; discounts to military & groups; children 5 & under no charge. Closed Christmas. ♿
Attendance: 213,600 (accurate)
Membership: Juniors $9; Seniors $20; Adults $23 (annual pass).

Yuma

ARIZONA HISTORICAL SOCIETY SANGUINETTI HOUSE MUSEUM AND GARDEN, 240 S. Madison Ave., Yuma, AZ 85364-1421. Tel.: 928-782-1841. Fax: 928-783-0680.
E-mail: ahsyuma@azhs.gov
Web Site: www.arizonahistoricalsociety.org
Founded: 1864.
Congressional District: 7
Key Personnel: Exec. Dir., Anne I. Woosley, Ph.D.; Cur., Carol Brooks.
Personnel Profile: Full-Time Paid 2; Part-Time Paid 1; Part-Time Volunteers 51.
Governing Authority: bd. of directors. Parent Institution: Arizona Historical Society, 949 E. 2nd St., Tucson, AZ 85719. Tel.: 520-628-5774. Tax-exempt: 501(c)(3).
History Museum: housed in 1870s residences-Sanguinetti House Museum & Adobe Annex.
Collections: Colorado River area history including photographs, maps, documents, & artifacts; period furnishings; aviaries; historical gardens.
Major Exhibits: Aerial Photos of Yuma, 11/09-11/10.
Research Fields: steamboats; railroad; biographical data; Southwestern Arizona business, domestic, & social history.
Facilities: photographic & manuscript archives. Museum-related gifts for sale.
Activities: extension programs include desert tours, slide programs, history talks, & docent program; facility rental.
Publications: quarterly, The Journal of Arizona History; books; monographs; annual report.
Hours & Admission Prices: Tues.-Sat. 10-4. Adults $3, senior citizens 60 & over and youth 12-18 $2; children 11 & under and members no charge. Closed New Year's Day; Independence Day; Veterans Day; Thanksgiving; Christmas.
Attendance: 5,000 (estimated)
Membership: Student $25; Individual $50; Household $65; Sustaining $100; Patron $250; Sponsor $500; Director's Circle $1,000.

KOFA NATIONAL WILDLIFE REFUGE, 356 W. First St., Yuma, AZ 85364-1410. Tel.: 928-783-7861.
Wildlife Refuge.
Collections: wildlife including white-winged dove, desert tortoise, & desert kit fox; sheep; birds; plants.
Facilities: nature trails.
Activities: hiking.
Hours & Admission Prices: Call for hours.

YUMA ART CENTER MUSEUM - YUMA FINE ARTS, 254 S. Main, Yuma, AZ 85364-1425. Mailing Address: P.O. Box 10295, Yuma, AZ 85366-8295. Tel.: 928-329-6607. Fax: 928-329-6616.
E-mail: yumafinearts@yahoo.com
Web Site: www.yumafinearts.org
Formerly: Yuma Fine Arts Association
Founded: 1962.
Congressional District: 3
Key Personnel: C.E.O., Elza Metzelaar; Pres. (V), Rita Migui; Dir., Louis LeRoy.
Personnel Profile: Full-Time Paid 2; Part-Time Volunteers 6; Interns 1.
Governing Authority: nonprofit organization. Subsidiary Institution: Yuma Art Center. Tax-exempt: 501(c)(3) & 170(b)(1)(A).
Visual Arts Center & Museum.
Collections: contemporary & historic Southwest paintings; ceramics; sculpture; photographs; graphics; fiber; crafts.
Research Fields: contemporary art; contemporary & historical Southwest art.
Facilities: performance space. Museum-related items for sale.
Activities: gallery tours; guest lecturers; art festivals; concerts; temporary & traveling exhibitions.
Publications: quarterly members publications, Art Notes Southwest.
Hours & Admission Prices: Please call for hours. Adults $3; members no charge. ♿
Attendance: 15,000 (estimated)
Membership: Senior Citizen & Student $40; Supporting $50; Individual $60; Family & Donor $100; Sponsor & Business Sponsor $250; Patron & Business Patron $500; Director's Circle & Business Director's Circle $1,000; Silver Circle & Business Silver Circle $2,500; Golden Circle & Business Golden Circle $5,000.

YUMA QUARTERMASTER DEPOT STATE HISTORIC PARK, 201 N. 4th Ave., Yuma, AZ 85364-2336. Tel.: 928-329-0471. Fax: 928-782-7124.
Web Site: www.azstateparks.com
Founded: 1864.
Congressional District: 3
Key Personnel: Park Mgr. & Museum Shop Mgr., Jerry Emert; Asst. Mgr., Gene Laufer.
Personnel Profile: Full-Time Paid 3; Part-Time Paid 6; Part-Time Volunteers 12.
Governing Authority: state. Parent Institution: Arizona State Parks Board, 1300 W. Washington, Phoenix, AZ 85007
History Museum: housed in five original buildings of the Yuma Quartermaster Depot, 1864-1883; two were later used by the Bureau of Reclamation as their Yuma Project Headquarters.
Collections: period furniture; Native American artifacts; military uniforms; maps; wagons; reconstructed steamboat pilothouse; Model T car; Plant Rood exhibit; early western development of the southwest; early military presence in the southwest; early irrigation history of Yuma; photographs chronicling the construction of irrigation works.
Research Fields: history of Fort Yuma Quartermaster Depot.
Facilities: interpretive center.
Activities: guided tours; permanent exhibits; outreach slide programs & video.
Hours & Admission Prices: Daily 8-5. Adult 14 & over $3; children 13 & under no charge. Closed Christmas. ♿
Attendance: 20,000

YUMA TERRITORIAL PRISON STATE HISTORIC PARK, One Prison Hill Rd., Yuma, AZ 85364-8792. Tel.: 928-783-4771. Fax: 928-783-7442.
E-mail: jtorres@pr.state.az.us
Web Site: www.azstateparks.com
Founded: 1940.
Congressional District: 3
Key Personnel: Park Mgr. & Museum Shop Mgr., Jesse Torres.
Personnel Profile: Full-Time Paid 5; Part-Time Paid 1; Part-Time Volunteers 2.
Governing Authority: state. Parent Institution: Arizona State Parks Board, 1300 W. Washington, Phoenix, AZ 85007.
General Museum.
Collections: general history; photographic; domestic artifacts; geological; numismatic; photos & artifacts related to Arizona Territorial Prison (1876-1909).
Research Fields: history of Arizona Territorial Prison.
Facilities: interpretive center; picnic area; hiking trails; cemetery; old prison cells.
Activities: guided tours; permanent exhibits; outreach slide programs & video.
Publications: The Prison Chronicle.
Hours & Admission Prices: Daily 8-5; other times by appointment. Adults 14 & over $5; discounts to AAM & ICOM members; children 13 & under no charge. Closed Thanksgiving; Christmas Eve & Day. ♿
Attendance: 80,000 (accurate)

ARKANSAS

(154 listings)

Arkadelphia

CLARK COUNTY HISTORICAL MUSEUM, 750 S. 5th St., Arkadelphia, AR 71923-6237. Tel.: 870-230-1360.
History Museum.
Collections: local history & culture; photographs; period furnishings.
Hours & Admission Prices: Call for hours.

OUACHITA BAPTIST UNIVERSITY HAMMONS GALLERY, Ouachita St., Arkadelphia, AR 71998-0001. Tel.: 870-245-5129.
Art Gallery.
Collections: works by university students including paintings & sculptures.
Activities: temporary exhibits.
Hours & Admission Prices: Mon.-Fri. 8-5.

REYNOLDS SCIENCE CENTER PLANETARIUM, 514 N. 12th St., Arkadelphia, AR 71998-0001. Tel.: 870-230-5006.
Planetarium.
Collections: astronomy-related exhibits.
Activities: classes; children's programs; tours.
Hours & Admission Prices: Call for hours. Adults $3.

Ashdown

GN & A DEPOT, 180 E. Whitaker, Ashdown, AR 71822-2724. Mailing Address: Chamber of Commerce, P.O. Box 160, Ashdown, AR 71822. Tel.: 870-898-2758. Fax: 870-898-6699.
Governing Authority: Parent Institution: Little River County Chamber of Commerce.
Historic Building: listed on the National Register of Historic Places.
Collections: local history & culture; railroad artifacts; photographs; period furnishings.
Hours & Admission Prices: Call for hours.

HUNTER-COULTER MUSEUM, 310 N. 2nd St., Ashdown, AR 71822-2704. Tel.: 870-898-5200.
Governing Authority: Parent Institution: Little River County Historical Society.
Historic House Museum: built in 1918 by Henry Westbrook. Listed on the National Register of Historic Places.
Collections: local history & culture; period furnishings; early farm tools; education memorabilia; photographs.
Activities: special events. Museum Sponsors: Candlelight Dinner in December.
Hours & Admission Prices: Mon. 12-3.

LITTLE RIVER COUNTY COURTHOUSE, Ashdown, AR 71822. Mailing Address: P.O. Box 160, Ashdown, AR 71822-0160. Tel.: 870-898-5528.
Historic Building: built in 1907. Listed on the National Register of Historic Places.
Collections: local history & culture; photographs; period furnishings.
Hours & Admission Prices: Call for hours.

TWO RIVERS MUSEUM, 15 E. Main St., Ashdown, AR 71822-2825. Mailing Address: 310 N. 2nd St., Ashdown, AR 71822-2704. Tel.: 870-898-3147.
Governing Authority: Parent Institution: Little River County Historical Society.
History Museum.
Collections: local history & culture; photographs; period furnishings; personal artifacts.
Activities: Museum Sponsors: Two Rivers Gala.
Hours & Admission Prices: By appointment.

Batesville

LYON COLLEGE KRESGE GALLERY, Highland & 22nd Sts., Batesville, AR 72503. Tel.: 870-307-7242.
Art Gallery.
Collections: painting; photographs; sculpture.
Hours & Admission Prices: Call for hours.

MARK MARTIN MUSEUM, 1601 Batesville Blvd., Batesville, AR 72501-8372. Mailing Address: P.O. Box 2677, Batesville, AR 72503. Tel.: 870-793-4461.
Founded: 2004.
Racing Museum.
Collections: Mark Martin's cars & trophies; photographs; helmets; firesuits; personal artifacts.
Hours & Admission Prices: Call for hours. No charge.

OLD INDEPENDENCE REGIONAL MUSEUM, 380 S. Ninth St., Batesville, AR 72501-5703. Mailing Address: P.O. Box 4506, Batesville, AR 72503-4506. Tel.: 870-793-2121. Fax: 870-793-2101.
E-mail: oirm@oirm.org
Web Site: www.oirm.org
Founded: 1998.
Congressional District: 1
Key Personnel: Pres. Bd., Jen Smith; Cur., Twyla Wright; Museum Shop Mgr., Frances Mathis.
Personnel Profile: Full-Time Paid 1; Full-Time Volunteers 1; Part-Time Paid 1; Part-Time Volunteers 50; Interns 1.
Governing Authority: private; nonprofit organization. Tax-exempt: 501(c)(3).
History Museum: housed in former National Guard Armory built as a WPA project in 1936 of local sandstone.
Collections: 200 years of North Central Arkansas artifacts; furnishings; photographs; structures.
Major Exhibits: Living Off The Land - Season by Season, 11/09-12/10.
Research Fields: regional history of North Central Arkansas.
Facilities: library; 70-seat auditorium; 10,000 sq. ft. exhibit space. Gift items for sale.
Activities: homeschool days; scouting programs; family day program; day

camp program; guided tours; specialized tours & workshops; monthly educational programs & speakers; docent program.
Publications: semi-annual newsletter, Old Independence Regional Museum; annual report.
Hours & Admission Prices: Tues.-Sat. 9-4:30, Sun. 1:30-4. Adults $3, senior citizens $2, students 6-12 $1; discounts for groups of 10 or more; members & children under 6 no charge. Closed New Year's Day; Easter; Independence Day; Thanksgiving; Christmas. ♿
Attendance: 5,500 (estimated)
Membership: Student & Senior Citizen $20; Individual $30; Family $50; Friend $100; Patron & Day Sponsor $250; Sustainer $500; Benefactor $1,000; Society $1,750.

Bauxite

BAUXITE MUSEUM, 6706 Benton Rd., Bauxite, AR 72011-9124. Mailing Address: P.O. Box 245, Bauxite, AR 72011-0245. Tel.: 501-557-9858.
Governing Authority: Parent Institution: Bauxite Historical Association and Museum. Tax-exempt: 501(c)(3).
History Museum.
Collections: local history & culture; period furnishings; photographs; personal artifacts.
Hours & Admission Prices: Wed. 10-2, Sun. 1:30-4; other times by appointment. No charge.

Bella Vista

BELLA VISTA HISTORICAL MUSEUM, 1885 Bella Vista Way, Bella Vista, AR 72714-3810. Tel.: 479-855-2335.
Founded: 1976.
Congressional District: 3
Key Personnel: Pres. (V), Carole Westby.
Personnel Profile: Part-Time Volunteers 30.
Governing Authority: nonprofit. Parent Institution: Bella Vista Historical Society. Tax-exempt.
History Museum.
Collections: materials & artifacts pertaining to the village of Bella Vista.
Facilities: library of history books & genealogy of Bella Vista; meeting room. Museum-related books for sale.
Activities: guided tours.
Publications: newsletter.
Hours & Admission Prices: March-Nov. Thurs.-Sun. 1-4; other times by appointment. No charge; donations accepted. ♿
Attendance: 600 (estimated)
Membership: Regular $5; Family $10; Contributing $25; Sustaining $50; Sponsor $100; Benefactor $250; Life $500; Founding $1,000.

Benton

GANN MUSEUM OF SALINE COUNTY, 218 S. Market St., Benton, AR 72015-4304. Tel.: 501-778-5513.
E-mail: gannmuseum@up-link.net
Historic House: housed in the former medical office of Dr. Dewel Gann, Sr., built in 1896 using bauxite aluminum ore.
Collections: memorabilia; photographs; period furniture & artifacts.
Hours & Admission Prices: Tues.-Thurs. 10-4; other times by appointment.

Bentonville

COMPTON GARDENS INTERPRETIVE CENTER, 312 N. Main St., Bentonville, AR 72712. Tel.: 479-254-3870. Fax: 479-254-3871.
Key Personnel: Exec. Dir., Leah Whitehead
History Museum.
Collections: Dr. Compton's life, family, books & personal artifacts; photographs; gardens.
Facilities: nature trails; gardens. Museum-related items for sale.
Activities: walking trails.
Hours & Admission Prices: Center: Mon.-Fri. 9:30-3:30. Gardens: dawn to dusk.

MUSEUM OF NATIVE AMERICAN ARTIFACTS, (M), 202 S.W. O St., Bentonville, AR 72712-3641. Tel.: 479-273-2456.
Native American Museum.
Collections: Native American history & culture; personal artifacts; sculpture; paintings; tools; weapons; pottery.
Facilities: Museum-related items for sale.
Hours & Admission Prices: Mon.-Sat. 9-5.

PEEL MANSION MUSEUM & HISTORIC GARDENS, 400 S. Walton Blvd., Bentonville, AR 72712-5705. Tel.: 479-273-9664. Fax: 479-273-9688.
Web Site: www.peelmansion.org
Founded: 1992.
Key Personnel: C.E.O. & Dir., Leah Whitehead; Chm. (V), Joe Thompson.
Personnel Profile: Full-Time Paid 4; Part-Time Paid 3; Part-Time Volunteers 50; Interns 1.
Governing Authority: private; nonprofit organization. Tax-exempt: 501(c)(3).
Historic House Museum: housed in 1875 Italianate villa & 1850 log cabin.
Collections: 19th-century furnishings; photographic collection of historic buildings in the county.
Facilities: 1,000-vol. library of genealogy & Benton County history; botanical garden; 4,000 sq. ft. exhibit space. Museum-related items for sale.
Activities: docent program; guided tours; lectures; rental gallery; temporary exhibitions; living history events; children's educational history programs. Museum Sponsors: Annual Historic Home & Garden Tour; Civil War reenactment.
Publications: quarterly newsletter.
Hours & Admission Prices: Tues.-Sat. 10-4. Adults $3, children $1. Closed Memorial Day; Independence Day; Labor Day; the week between Christmas & New Year's. ♿
Attendance: 2,000 (estimated)
Membership: Friend $35; Pioneer $100; Colonel $500; Presidential $1,000.

WAL-MART VISITOR'S CENTER, 105 N. Main St., Bentonville, AR 72712-5341. Tel.: 479-273-1329.
Web Site: walmartstores.com/AboutUs/287.aspx
History Museum: birthplace of Wal-Mart.
Collections: history of Wal-Mart; period store artifacts; employee manuals; Sam's general headquarters office; Sam's 1979 red Ford F150; personal artifacts.
Facilities: Museum-related items for sale.
Hours & Admission Prices: Tues.-Sat. 9-5. No charge. ♿
Attendance: 50,000

Berryville

HERITAGE CENTER MUSEUM, Public Square, Berryville, AR 72616. Mailing Address: P.O. Box 249, Berryville, AR 72616-0249. Tel.: 870-423-6312.
E-mail: history1880@windstream.net
Web Site: www.rootsweb.com/~arcchs
Founded: 1960.
Congressional District: 3
Key Personnel: Pres., Gordon Hale.
Personnel Profile: Part-Time Paid 2; Part-Time Volunteers 7.
Governing Authority: county; society. Parent Institution: Carroll County Historical Society. Tax-exempt.
Local History Museum: housed in 1880 Carroll County Court House.
Collections: furniture; Connor post office; funeral parlor; school room; photographs; fainting couch; Civil War artifacts; local history memorabilia; miniature railroad; clock collection; pioneer printing office; orphan train display; moonshine still; Mountain Meadows Massacre display. Historic Structures: c.1800 Newberry log cabin; c.1905 log jail cell.
Research Fields: county history; genealogy of county families; Mountain Meadows Massacre exhibit.
Facilities: 1,000-vol. library of books, records & microfilm pertaining to local history available for research on premises.
Activities: guided tours; lectures; loan & permanent exhibitions.
Publications: Carroll County Historical Society Quarterly.
Hours & Admission Prices: Mon.-Fri. 9-4. Family $5, adults $2, children $1; children under 6 no charge. Closed national holidays.
Attendance: 3,000 (estimated)
Membership: Individual $20.

SAUNDERS MEMORIAL MUSEUM, 113-15 E. Madison St., Berryville, AR 72616-3954. Tel.: 870-423-2563.
Founded: 1955.
Congressional District: 3
Key Personnel: Mgr., Rose M. Garrett; Chm. (V), Don Rustuhaltz.
Personnel Profile: Full-Time Paid 1; Part-Time Paid 2.
Governing Authority: municipal. Parent Institution: City of Berryville. Tax-exempt.
Gun & Period Furnishings Museum.
Collections: Colonel C. Burton Saunders' gun collection; silver; china; arts & crafts; Indian artifacts; teakwood furniture; oriental rugs.
Research Fields: guns; teakwood; oriental rugs; paintings; china; silver; American Indian artifacts.
Facilities: Gift items for sale.

Publications: brochures.
Hours & Admission Prices: April 15-first weekend of Nov. Mon.-Sat. 10:30-5. Adults $5, children under 13 $2.50; discount to groups of 10 & over; children under 6 no charge. ♿
Attendance: 3,000 (estimated)

Blytheville

BLYTHEVILLE HERITAGE MUSEUM, 107C Main St., Blytheville, AR 72315-3431. Mailing Address: P.O. Box 234, Blytheville, AR 72316-0234. Tel.: 870-763-2525.
History Museum.
Collections: Blytheville's cotton & logging industries; local history & culture; photographs; pioneer artifacts.
Hours & Admission Prices: Call for hours.

Brinkley

CENTRAL DELTA DEPOT MUSEUM, 100 W. Cypress, Brinkley, AR 72021-2809. Tel.: 870-589-2124.
E-mail: billsayger@yahoo.com
Web Site: www.cddm.org
Founded: 2003.
Key Personnel: Dir., Bill Sayger; Chm. (V), Laura Bussell; Pres. (V), Catherine Jacques.
Personnel Profile: Full-Time Volunteers 1; Part-Time Paid 3; Part-Time Volunteers 1.
Governing Authority: Tax-exempt.
History Museum.
Collections: Central Delta history & culture; Louisiana Purchase; railroad history; photographs; Louis Jordan memorabilia; Southern Pacific caboose. Historic Buildings: train depot; sharecropper's house.
Activities: Annual Event: Choo Choo Ch'Boogie Delta Music Festival.
Publications: quarterly members' newsletter & journal, The Doodlebug.
Hours & Admission Prices: Mon.-Sat. 9-5, Sun. 1-4. Adults $2, children $1; members no charge. ♿
Attendance: 1,230 (accurate)
Membership: Individual $15; Married Couples $25.

Camden

MCCOLLUM-CHIDESTER HOUSE, 926 W. Washington St., Camden, AR 71701-3382. Tel.: 870-836-9243.
E-mail: ochs2003@sbcglobal.net
Web Site: ouachitacountyhistoricalsociety.org
Founded: 1963.
Key Personnel: Pres. (V), Clara Freeland; Docent, Hubert Boddie.
Personnel Profile: Part-Time Paid 1; Part-Time Volunteers 20.
Governing Authority: Parent Institution: Ouachita County Historical Society.
Historic House Museum: built in 1847.
Collections: family history; period furnishings; personal artifacts; Civil War; photographs.
Publications: magazine, Ouachita County Historical Quarterly.
Hours & Admission Prices: Wed.-Sat. 9-4. Adults $5. Closed major holidays. ♿
Attendance: 1,200 (estimated)
Membership: Annual $25.

OUACHITA COUNTY HISTORICAL SOCIETY, 926 Washington St., N.W., Camden, AR 71701-3382. Tel.: 870-836-9243, 3610, 0023 & 0245.
E-mail: ochs2003@sbcglobal.net
Founded: 1963.
Congressional District: 4
Key Personnel: Pres. Ouachita County Historical Society, Clara Freeland; Museum Docent, Hubert Boddie.
Personnel Profile: Part-Time Paid 1; Part-Time Volunteers 20.
Historical Society Museum.
Collections: Victorian furniture, 1863 rare china; glassware, silver; clothing; jewelry; lamps; pictures & frames; law office; Freedmen's Bureau. Historic Buildings: 1847 historic home; 1850 Leake-Ingham library.
Activities: costume guided tours. Museum Sponsors: Daffodil Festival in March; All Hallows Eve Cemetery Walk in October.
Publications: historical quarterly, Quachita County.
Hours & Admission Prices: Wed.-Sat. 9-4. Adults $5, students $2. Closed major holidays. ♿
Attendance: 1,200 (estimated)
Membership: Individual $25.

Charleston

BELLE MUSEUM & PRESBYTERIAN CHAPEL, 322 E. Main, Charleston, AR 72933. Mailing Address: P.O. Box 261, Charleston, AR 72933-0261.
Founded: 1996.
Key Personnel: Dir., Delbert Ervin; Dir., Mary B. Ervin
History & Church Museum.
Collections: local, state & family histories; personal artifacts.
Activities: special events.
Hours & Admission Prices: May-June call for hours. No charge; donations accepted. ♿

Clinton

VAN BUREN COUNTY HISTORICAL MUSEUM, 211 3rd St., Clinton, AR 72031. Mailing Address: P.O. Box 1023, Clinton, AR 72031-1023. Tel.: 501-745-4066.
Key Personnel: Chm. (V), Sharon Baker; Chm. (V), Charlotte West; Pres. (V), Dortha Borecky.
Personnel Profile: Part-Time Volunteers 9.
Governing Authority: Tax-exempt.
Historical Museum.
Collections: family histories; photographs; personal artifacts.
Facilities: library.
Publications: quarterly newsletter; historical calendars.
Hours & Admission Prices: Mon.-Fri. 10-4. No charge; donations accepted. Closed holidays. ♿
Attendance: 500 (estimated)
Membership: Individual $15.

Conway

BAUM GALLERY OF FINE ART, UNIVERSITY OF CENTRAL ARKANSAS, 201 Donaghey Ave., Conway, AR 72035-5001. Mailing Address: McAlister 101, Dept. of Art, UCA, 201 Donaghey Ave., Conway, AR 72035-0001. Tel.: 501-450-5793 & 5000. Fax: 501-450-3670.
E-mail: barbaras@uca.edu
Web Site: www.uca.edu/art/baum
Founded: 1994.
Congressional District: 2
Key Personnel: Dir. & Cur., Barbara Satterfield.
Personnel Profile: Full-Time Paid 1; Part-Time Paid 6; Part-Time Volunteers 20; Interns 2.
Governing Authority: public university; nonprofit. Parent Institution: University of Central Arkansas.
Art Museum.
Collections: contemporary American & European, all media, artists represented include Marshall Arisman, Warren Criswell, Don Netzer, Barry Moser, Raphael Soyer, Larry Zox, Julian Stanczak & Mel Ramos.
Facilities: 3,000 sq. ft. exhibit space.
Activities: docent program; formal education programs for undergraduate students; lecture series; monthly gallery talks; guided tours; labs in standard museum practices; participatory, temporary & traveling exhibits.
Publications: exhibition catalogs.
Hours & Admission Prices: July-May Mon.-Wed. & Fri. 10-5, Thurs. 10-7, Sun. for receptions only. No charge; donations accepted. Closed spring break; summer sessions; Christmas break. ♿
Attendance: 7,300 (accurate)
Membership: Individual $35; Couple Subscriber $50; Associate Members $100; Patrons $500; Sustainers $1,000.

FAULKNER COUNTY MUSEUM, Courthouse Square, 805 Locust St., Conway, AR 72034. Mailing Address: P.O. Box 2442, Conway, AR 72033-2442. Tel.: 501-329-5918.
E-mail: fcm@conwaycorp.net
Web Site: www.faulknerhistory.com/museum
Founded: 1992.
Congressional District: 2
Key Personnel: Dir., Lynita Langley-Ware; Chm. (V), Dr. Sondra Gordy.
Personnel Profile: Full-Time Volunteers 2; Part-Time Paid 2; Part-Time Volunteers 16.
Governing Authority: society; nonprofit organization. Parent Institution: Faulkner County. Subsidiary Institution: Faulkner County Historical Society. Tax-exempt.
History Museum.
Collections: Indian artifacts & campsite; cadron settlement; agricultural tools; medical instruments; general store; political development; cotton culture; genealogy files; Arkansas River history; 1920s kitchen & bedroom; log cabin; 1896 jail building.
Activities: guided tours.

Publications: quarterly magazine, Faulkner Facts & Fiddlings; books, Faulkner County: Its Land & People; Faulkner County, Arkansas: Census of Cemeteries as of December 31, 1987; pamphlet, The Guiding Star: A Guide Book for Catholic Emigrants to the Arkansas River Valley; Pine Mountain Americans; bimonthly newsletter, The Key.
Hours & Admission Prices: Mon.-Thurs. 9-4; groups by appointment. No charge; donations accepted. ♿
Attendance: 1,600 (accurate)
Membership: Individual $35; Family $50.

De Queen

THE SEVIER COUNTY HISTORICAL MUSEUM, 717 N. Maple Ave., De Queen, AR 71832-2506. Tel.: 870-642-6642. Fax: 870-642-6642.
E-mail: seviercountymuseum@windstream.net
Web Site: www.dequeenchamberofcommerce.com/sevier_county_museum.htm
Key Personnel: Dir., Karen Mills; Bd. Pres., Marsha Buford.
Personnel Profile: Full-Time Paid 1; Part-Time Volunteers 6.
Governing Authority: Parent Institution: Sevier County Museum Board. Tax-exempt.
History Museum.
Collections: history of De Queen & Sevier County; United States wars; personal artifacts.
Activities: historical teas; classes; festivals; flower shows. Museum Sponsors: Hoo-Rah Days Festival in October.
Publications: books, Family History; DeQueen Centennial History; Art Cookbook.
Hours & Admission Prices: Tues.-Sat. 12-5. No charge; donations accepted. ♿
Attendance: 3,750

Des Arc

LOWER WHITE RIVER MUSEUM, 2009 Main St., Des Arc, AR 72040-3135. Tel.: 870-256-3711. Fax: 870-256-9202.
E-mail: lowerwhiterivermuseum@arkansas.com
Web Site: www.arkansasstateparks.com
Formerly: Prairie County Museum
Founded: 1971.
Congressional District: 2
Key Personnel: Dir., Neva Boatright; Museum Program Asst. & Sec., Michael Yarberry.
Personnel Profile: Full-Time Paid 2; Part-Time Paid 1; Part-Time Volunteers 1.
Governing Authority: state; nonprofit. Parent Institution: Arkansas Dept. of Parks & Tourism. Branch: Arkansas State Parks Division, Dept. of Parks & Tourism, One Capitol Mall, Little Rock, AR 72201. Tax-exempt: 170(b)(1)(A).
History Museum.
Collections: exhibits emphasizing the history of Lower White River & surrounding environs from settlement-present; clothes; household items; photographs; farm implements.
Research Fields: history of the Lower White River with emphasis on early settlements & commerce from 1831-1931.
Activities: guided tours.
Publications: brochure.
Hours & Admission Prices: Mon.-Sat. 8-5, Sun. 1-5. Adults $3.25, children 6-12 $2. Closed New Year's Day; Thanksgiving; Christmas Eve & Day. ♿
Attendance: 3,969 (accurate)

Dover

MERIKS HISTORICAL SOCIETY, 4504 SR 27, Dover, AR 72837-8114. Mailing Address: P.O. Box 5407, Eugene, OR 97405-0407.
Key Personnel: Pres. (V), Rey Spina; Chmn. (V), Christine Mercorella; Vice Pres. (V), Dana Cullen; Collections Mgmt., Thomas Jurcsek.
Personnel Profile: Full-Time Volunteers 1.
Historical Society.
Research Fields: Genealogical studies.

Dumas

DESHA COUNTY MUSEUM, Hwy. 54 E., Dumas, AR 71639. Mailing Address: P.O. Box 141, Dumas, AR 71639-0141. Tel.: 870-382-4222.
Founded: 1979.
Congressional District: 4
Key Personnel: Bd. Dir., Charlotte Schexnayder; Pres. (V), Martha Clark.
Personnel Profile: Part-Time Paid 1; Part-Time Volunteers 15.
Governing Authority: nonprofit organization. Tax-exempt: 501(c)(3).
Historical & Preservation Society.
Collections: American Indian artifacts; Period farm tools; items from the early years of Desha County; log house farmstead; log house blacksmith shop; potato house & plantation commissary.
Research Fields: history of Desha County.
Facilities: 200-vol. library; reading room.
Activities: guided tours; lectures. Museum Sponsors: concerts by the Arkansas State Symphony.
Hours & Admission Prices: Tues.-Fri. 10-3:30, Sun. 2-4. No charge; donations accepted. ♿
Attendance: 5,500 (estimated)
Membership: Single $10; Family $25.

El Dorado

SOUTH ARKANSAS ARTS CENTER, 110 E. Fifth St., El Dorado, AR 71730-3822. Tel.: 870-862-5474. Fax: 870-862-4921.
E-mail: info@saac-arts.org
Web Site: saac-arts.org
Founded: 1962.
Congressional District: 4
Key Personnel: Exec. Dir., Beth James.
Personnel Profile: Full-Time Paid 4; Part-Time Paid 1.
Governing Authority: nonprofit organization. Tax-exempt.
Art Gallery.
Collections: paintings; Oriental wood block prints; children's Oriental Collection.
Facilities: library; reading room; 250-seat auditorium; community theatre; conference rooms; classrooms.
Activities: lectures; concerts; dance performances; arts festivals; art classes; theatre classes; community theatre productions; art shows & contests; art & drama programs for schools; hobby workshops; formally organized education programs; permanent, temporary & traveling exhibitions.
Publications: bimonthly newsletter.
Hours & Admission Prices: Mon.-Fri. 9-5, Sat. 10-3. No charge; donations accepted. Closed holidays. ♿
Attendance: 30,000 (estimated)
Membership: Senior $15; Student $20; Individual $25; Family $60; Sponsor $100; Donor $200; Patron $750; Benefactor $1,500; Friends of Arts & Education $3,000.

Eureka Springs

AVIATION CADET MUSEUM, 542 CR 2073, Eureka Springs, AR 72632-9630. Tel.: 479-253-5008.
E-mail: av1cadet@arkansas.net
Web Site: www.aviationcadet.com
Founded: 1994.
Key Personnel: Museum Shop Mgr., E.D. Severe.
Personnel Profile: Full-Time Paid 2; Part-Time Volunteers 2.
Governing Authority: Subsidiary Institution: Cadet World. Tax-exempt.
Aviation Museum.
Collections: military aircraft & artifacts; personal artifacts.
Facilities: Museum-related items for sale.
Publications: The Last of a Breed; I Wanna Fly.
Hours & Admission Prices: Wed.-Sat. 10-5; other times by appointment. Adults $10.
Attendance: 400 (estimated)
Membership: $25-$100,000.

BLUE SPRING HERITAGE CENTER, 1537 CR 210, Eureka Springs, AR 72632. Tel.: 479-253-9244. Fax: 479-253-9256.
Heritage Center.
Collections: local history & culture; Native American artifacts; photographs; personal artifacts; gardens.
Activities: classes; educational programs; rental facilities.
Hours & Admission Prices: mid-March to late Nov. daily 9-6. Adults $7.25, students 10-17 $4; children 9 & under no charge.

CASTLE ROGUE'S MANOR, 124 Spring St., Eureka Springs, AR 72632. Tel.: 800-250-5827.
Historic House Museum.
Collections: local history; period furnishings; personal artifacts.
Activities: special events.
Hours & Admission Prices: By appointment. Adults $20; children $10.

CRAZY BONE GALLERY, 37 Spring St., Eureka Springs, AR 72632-3147. Tel.: 479-253-6600; 888-418-8506.
Art Gallery.
Collections: works of local & regional artists.
Hours & Admission Prices: Call for hours.

EUREKA FINE ART GALLERY, 78 Spring St., Eureka Springs, AR 72632-3105. Tel.: 479-253-6595.
Art Gallery.
Collections: paintings; photographs; sculptures.
Hours & Admission Prices: Call for hours.

EUREKA SPRINGS HISTORICAL MUSEUM, 95 S. Main, Eureka Springs, AR 72632-3600. Tel.: 479-253-9417.
E-mail: eshm999@sbcglobal.net
Web Site: www.eshm.org
Founded: 1971.
Key Personnel: Dir., Ginni Miller.
Personnel Profile: Full-Time Paid 1; Part-Time Paid 1; Part-Time Volunteers 3.
Historic House Museum: housed in the Calif House, 1889.
Collections: area history; art; personal artifacts; period furnishings.
Activities: school tours; Victorian tea.
Hours & Admission Prices: March-Nov. Mon.-Sat. 9:30-4, Sun. 11-4. Self-Guided Tours: adults $5, students $2.50; members & children under 10 no charge. Guided Tours: adults $7; discounts to groups of 10 or more. Closed Thanksgiving; Christmas.
Membership: Single $20; Family $30; Business $50.

FAMILY HERITAGE MUSEUM, 2966 CR 207, Eureka Springs, AR 72632-9469. Tel.: 479-253-5444 & 5875. Fax: 479-253-7497.
E-mail: muriels@familyheritagemuseum.com
Web Site: www.familyheritagemuseum.com
Formerly: Gay 90's Button & Doll Museum
Founded: 1971.
Congressional District: 3
Key Personnel: Owner & Cur., Muriel H. Schmidt.
Governing Authority: nonprofit organization. Parent Institution: Destiny of America Foundation, Inc. Tax-exempt: 501(c)(3).
Family Heritage Museum.
Collections: dolls; lamps; dishes; glassware; lace; household accessories; wedding dresses; fabrics; 29 albums combining family history with U.S. history.
Major Exhibits: "Tatting", Summer 2010-Fall 2010; Pearl Button Construction, Summer 2010-Fall 2010; Family Daguerrotypes, Summer 2010-Fall 2010; Homespun & Linsey Woolsey, Summer 2010-Fall 2010; How to Develop Family Journalism, Summer 2010-Fall 2010.
Research Fields: vintage clothing 1800-1950; genealogy of local families; family careers.
Facilities: Museum-related items for sale.
Activities: self-guided tours; lectures; permanent exhibitions.
Publications: My Gi-Gi Has a Museum.
Hours & Admission Prices: By appointment. No charge; donations accepted. ♿
Attendance: 500 (estimated)

THE GREAT PASSION PLAY BIBLE MUSEUM, The Great Passion Play, 935 Passion Play Rd., Eureka Springs, AR 72632-9496. Mailing Address: P.O. Box 471, Eureka Springs, AR 72632. Tel.: 479-253-8559. Fax: 479-253-2302.
E-mail: akovalcik@greatpassionplay.com
Founded: 1968.
Key Personnel: Dir., Anne Kovalcik
Religious Museum.
Collections: Bible history; over 6,000 Bibles, manuscripts; period artifacts; sacred art from the 1500s to present.
Hours & Admission Prices: May-Oct. Mon.-Sat. 10-8. Adults $5, children $2.50. ♿

MUSEUM OF EARTH HISTORY, The Great Passion Play, 935 Passion Play Rd., Eureka Springs, AR 72632-9496. Mailing Address: The Great Passion Play, P.O. Box 471, Eureka Springs, AR 72632. Tel.: 866-566-3565. Fax: 405-872-7500.
E-mail: info@moeh.org
Key Personnel: Pres. & Founder, G. Thomas Sharp
History Museum.
Collections: earth history, science, & faith; dinosaurs; skeletons; Garden of Eden representation; the Ice Age; the Great Flood; fish; fossils.
Facilities: 2,000 sq. ft. exhibit space; aquarium; theater. Museum-related items for sale.
Activities: hands-on exhibits; rental facilities; special events; The Great Passion Play theater performances.
Hours & Admission Prices: May-Oct. call for hours.

ONYX CAVE & MUSEUM, 338 Onyx Cave Lane, Eureka Springs, AR 72632-9631. Tel.: 479-253-9321.
Geology Museum.
Collections: local history; geology; period artifacts & dolls.
Facilities: Museum-related items for sale.
Hours & Admission Prices: April & Oct.-Nov. daily 9-4; May-Sept. daily 8:30-6:30. Adults $4.25, children 13 & under $2.

QUIGLEY'S CASTLE, 274 Quigley Castle Rd., Eureka Springs, AR 72632-9144. Tel.: 479-253-8311.
E-mail: quigleyc@arkansas.net
Web Site: quigleyscastle.com
Historic House Museum: housed in the former home of Elise & Albert Quigley; built in 1943. Listed on the National Register of Historic Places.
Collections: family history; personal artifacts; sculpture; period furnishings.
Activities: guided tours.
Hours & Admission Prices: April-Oct. Mon.-Wed. & Fri.-Sat. 8:30-5. Adults $6.50; children 14 & under no charge.

THE ROSALIE, 282 Spring St., Eureka Springs, AR 72632-3152. Tel.: 479-253-7377.
E-mail: info@therosalie.com
Web Site: www.therosalie.com
Formerly: Rosalie House
Founded: 1889.
Congressional District: 3
Key Personnel: Owner, Charles Ragsdell; Owner, Lori Ragsdell.
Personnel Profile: Full-Time Paid 1; Full-Time Volunteers 2; Part-Time Paid 3; Part-Time Volunteers 2.
Governing Authority: individual operation.
Historic House: built in 1889 by J. W. Hill owner of local livery & stables, and builder of Eureka Springs phone system.
Collections: period furnishings; musical instruments; Hersey memorabilia.
Facilities: banquet facilities.
Activities: tours by appointment; rental facilities.
Hours & Admission Prices: Tours: by appointment. Adults $7.50; children under 6 no charge.
Attendance: 1,000 (estimated)

TURPENTINE CREEK WILDLIFE REFUGE, 239 Turpentine Creek Lane, Eureka Springs, AR 72632-9185. Tel.: 479-253-5841.
Wildlife Refuge.
Collections: big cats & their habitats including lions & tigers.
Activities: educational programs; guided tours.
Hours & Admission Prices: Summer: daily 9-6; Winter: daily 9-5. Adults 13 & over $15, youth 3-12, seniors & veterans $10; children under 3 no charge. Closed Christmas.

Fairfield Bay

LOG CABIN MUSEUM, 335 Snead Dr., Fairfield Bay, AR 72088. Tel.: 501-884-4899.
Historic Building: built in 1850.
Collections: local history & culture; period furnishings; personal artifacts.
Hours & Admission Prices: Call for hours. No charge.

NORTH CENTRAL ARKANSAS ART GALLERY, 337 Snead Dr., Fairfield Bay, AR 72088. Tel.: 501-884-6100.
Art Gallery.
Collections: works by local & national artists including paintings.
Hours & Admission Prices: Call for hours. No charge.

Fayetteville

ARKANSAS AIR MUSEUM, (M), 4290 S. School Ave., Fayetteville, AR 72701-8008. Tel.: 479-521-4947. Fax: 4791-521-4947.
E-mail: arkairmus@aol.com
Web Site: www.arkairmuseum.org
Founded: 1986.
Congressional District: 3
Key Personnel: Pres., Hugh Brewer; Vice Pres., Ray Boudreaux; Treas., Richard Greene; Sec., Jake Lamkins; Museum Shop Mgr., Sally Ebbrecht.
Personnel Profile: Full-Time Paid 1; Part-Time Paid 2; Part-Time Volunteers 4.
Governing Authority: private; nonprofit organization. Tax-exempt.
Air Museum: housed in WWII era wooden truss hangar.
Collections: classic aircraft & artifacts from early flight to present, with emphasis on Arkansas aviators, military & civilian; state historic site; aircraft engine collections piston, jet & rocket; approximately 18 aircrafts, some WWII trainers modern military A-4 Jet Huey & Cobra helicopters.

Research Fields: photographs of general aviation; WWII naval aviation; classic aircraft data.
Facilities: 1,000-vol. of books & aviation magazines; 80-vol. of aviation videos; educational facilities; 30,000 sq. ft. exhibit space; 35-seat theatre. Museum-related items for sale.
Activities: films; guided tours; lectures. Annual Events: Airfest in June; visiting aircraft.
Publications: quarterly newsletter.
Hours & Admission Prices: Sun.-Fri. 11-4:30, Sat. 10-4:30. Family $20, adults $8, children 6-12 $4; discounts to groups, AAC & ICOM members; members no charge. Closed New Year's Day; Thanksgiving; Christmas. ♿
Attendance: 15,000 (estimated)
Membership: Student $10; Individual $25; Family $40; Supporting $75; Patron $100; Life $1,000.

BOTANICAL GARDEN OF THE OZARKS, 4703 N. Crossover Rd., Fayetteville, AR 72764. Mailing Address: P.O. Box 10407, Fayetteville, AR 72703-0042. Tel.: 479-750-2620.
Botanical Garden.
Collections: plants; trees; flowers.
Facilities: nature trails.
Hours & Admission Prices: Feb.-Dec. daily 9-5. Adults 13 & over $5, children 5-12 $2.50; members, children under 5, & Sat. 9-12 no charge. ♿
Attendance: 35,000
Membership: Family $50.

CLINTON HOUSE MUSEUM, 930 California Dr., Fayetteville, AR 72701-4912. Tel.: 479-444-0066; 877-245-6445.
Historic House: housed in the former home of Bill & Hillary Clinton while he was a professor at the University of Arkansas.
Collections: family life & history; personal artifacts; photographs; campaign materials.
Facilities: Museum-related items for sale.
Hours & Admission Prices: Call for hours.

HEADQUARTERS HOUSE MUSEUM, 118 E. Dickson St., Fayetteville, AR 72701-4207. Tel.: 479-521-2970.
E-mail: info@washcohistoricalsociety.org
Web Site: www.washcohistoricalsociety.org/hispro
Key Personnel: Pres., Vince Chadick
History Museum: built in 1853 by Judge Jonas M. Tebbetts, this home served as headquarters for the Federal and Confederate armies during the Civil War.
Collections: personal artifacts; Masonic furniture. Historic Building: Archibald Yell's law office, 1835.
Facilities: period gardens. Museum-related items for sale.
Activities: living history presentations; tours.
Hours & Admission Prices: Tours by appointment. Adults $8, children $1; discounts to members. ♿
Attendance: 4,000 (estimated)
Membership: Senior $15; Family $25.

OZARK MILITARY MUSEUM, 4360 S. School Ave., Fayetteville, AR 72701. Tel.: 479-587-1941. Fax: 479-587-0848.
Key Personnel: Dir., Leonard McCandless
Military Museum.
Collections: military history; WWII, Korean War, & Vietnam artifacts; photographs; personal artifacts; military aircraft & vehicles.
Activities: special events.
Hours & Admission Prices: Sun.-Fri. 11-4:30, Sat. 10-4:30.

THE UNIVERSITY MUSEUM COLLECTIONS, University of Arkansas, Biomass Bldg. Rm. 125, Fayetteville, AR 72701-1201. Tel.: 479-575-3456. Fax: 479-575-7464.
Web Site: www.uark.edu/~museinfo/
Founded: 1873.
Congressional District: 3
Key Personnel: Interim Dir., Dr. Jeannine Durdik; Cur. Collections, Mary Suter; Cur. Zoology, Dr. Nancy G. McCartney.
Personnel Profile: Full-Time Paid 2; Part-Time Volunteers 2.
Governing Authority: university. Parent Institution: Univ. of Arkansas. Tax-exempt: 170(b)(1)(A).
General Museum.
Collections: prehistoric Arkansas Indian artifacts; quartz crystals; bird eggs & nests; malacology; herpetology; ichthyology; geology; herbarium; mineralogy; paleontology; early American pressed glass; early textile equipment & other Americana; ethnological collections from Oceania, Africa & Amerindians.
Research Fields: archaeology; physical anthropology; zoology; geology; paleontology; botany.
Activities: inter-museum loan; collections research; temporary exhibitions.
Hours & Admission Prices: Mon.-Fri. by appointment only. No charge. Closed university holidays. ♿
Attendance: 200 (estimated)

Fordyce

DALLAS COUNTY MUSEUM, 221 S. Main St., Fordyce, AR 71742. Mailing Address: P.O. Box 703, Fordyce, AR 71742-0703. Tel.: 870-352-7202.
History Museum.
Collections: county history & culture; photographs; timber industry; portraits; military artifacts; Paul "Bear" Bryant memorabilia; geology; early agriculture.
Facilities: 12,000 sq. ft. exhibit space.
Activities: group tours.
Hours & Admission Prices: Tues.-Fri. 11-4, Sat. 11-3. No charge. ♿

Foreman

NEW ROCKY COMFORT MUSEUM, 3rd & Schuman, Foreman, AR 71836. Mailing Address: P.O. Box 268, Foreman, AR 71836-0268. Tel.: 870-542-7887. Fax: 870-542-6347.
Historic Building: housed in a restored jail; built in 1902.
Collections: local history & culture; period documents.
Hours & Admission Prices: Call for hours.

Forrest City

ST. FRANCIS COUNTY MUSEUM, (M), 603 Front St., Forrest City, AR 72335-3808. Mailing Address: P.O. Box 1332, Forrest City, AR 72336-1332. Tel.: 870-261-1744. Fax: 870-630-1210.
Web Site: www.sfcmuseum.org
Founded: 1995.
Congressional District: 1
Key Personnel: Dir., H. Wayne Parker; Chm. (V), Rush Beavers; Cur., Shelley Gervasi.
Personnel Profile: Full-Time Paid 1; Part-Time Paid 1; Part-Time Volunteers 6.
Governing Authority: Parent Institution: St. Francis County. Tax-exempt.
Historical & Culturally Specific Museum.
Collections: military history; Native American; Afro-American; medical history; documentations.
Hours & Admission Prices: Mon.-Fri. 10-5. No charge; donations accepted. ♿
Attendance: 4,205 (accurate)

Fort Smith

FORT SMITH AIR MUSEUM, Fort Smith Regional Airport, 6700 McKennon Blvd., Fort Smith, AR 72903. Mailing Address: 3 Glen Haven Dr., Fort Smith, AR 72901-6837. Tel.: 479-785-1839.
Founded: 1999.
Key Personnel: Pres., Wayne Haver; Vice Pres., Carl Riggens; Treas., Ralph Freeman.
Governing Authority: Tax-exempt.
Air Museum.
Collections: aviation history; military aviators; aviation pioneers; aircraft; photographs; personal artifacts.
Hours & Admission Prices: Daily 5:30am-11pm. No charge. ♿
Attendance: 50,000 (estimated)

FORT SMITH ART CENTER, (M), 423 N. Sixth St., Fort Smith, AR 72901-2003. Tel.: 479-784-ARTS (2787). Fax: 479-784-9071.
E-mail: info@fortsmithartcenter.org
Web Site: www.fortsmithartcenter.org
Founded: 1948.
Congressional District: 3
Key Personnel: Dir., Teresa Carver; Pres., Peter Lippencott; Programs Dir., Jason Sacran.
Personnel Profile: Full-Time Paid 3; Part-Time Volunteers 2.
Governing Authority: nonprofit. Tax-exempt: 501(c)(3).
Arts Center: housed in 1870s building.
Collections: contemporary American paintings; graphics; sculpture; decorative arts.
Facilities: Art education building; classrooms.
Activities: guided tours; lectures; gallery talks; arts festivals; rental gazebo; formally organized education programs; permanent & temporary exhibitions. Annual Events: Annual Art Competition in Spring.
Publications: bimonthly bulletin; brochures.

Hours & Admission Prices: Tues.-Sat. 9:30-4:30. No charge; donations accepted. Closed New Year's Day; Memorial Day; Independence Day; Labor Day; Thanksgiving & day after; Christmas Eve & Day. ♿
Attendance: 14,000 (estimated)
Membership: Individual $35; Family $45; Silver $100; Gold $250; Platinum $500; Lifetime $2,500 & up.

FORT SMITH MUSEUM OF HISTORY, 320 Rogers Ave., Fort Smith, AR 72901-1937. Tel.: 479-783-7841. Fax: 479-783-3244.
E-mail: leisa.gramlich@fortsmithmuseum.com
Web Site: www.fortsmithmuseum.com
Founded: 1910.
Congressional District: 3
Key Personnel: C.E.O., Leisa Gramlich; Pres. (V), Greg Smith; Museum Shop Mgr., Joy Sternberg.
Personnel Profile: Full-Time Paid 1; Part-Time Paid 4; Part-Time Volunteers 15; Interns 1.
Governing Authority: nonprofit. Parent Institution: Fort Smith Museum of History Association. Tax-exempt: 501(c)(3).
History Museum: housed in 1906 Atkinson-Williams Building.
Collections: period furniture; textiles; period toys; documents; military items; c.1920 drugstore with operating soda fountain; period vehicles.
Research Fields: furniture industry in Fort Smith Area; Fort Chaffee (US Army Post 1941-present); commercial history (advertising); pharmacy.
Facilities: auditorium; rental facilities.
Activities: workshops; temporary & permanent exhibitions; interpretive programs; school group tours; holiday special events.
Publications: newsletter; Fort Smith: An Illustrated History.
Hours & Admission Prices: June-Aug. Tues.-Sat. 10-5, Sun. 1-5; Sept.-May Tues.-Sat. 10-5. Adults $5, children 6-15 $2; discounts to groups; Fort Smith public schools, children under 6 & members no charge. Closed holidays. ♿
Attendance: 15,000 (estimated)
Membership: Individual $25; Senior Couple $30; Family $50; Investor $100; Silver Benefactor $500-$999; Gold $1,000-$4,999; Diamond $5,000 & up.

FORT SMITH NATIONAL HISTORIC SITE, 301 Parker Ave., Fort Smith, AR 72901-1938. Mailing Address: P.O. Box 1406, Fort Smith, AR 72902-1406. Tel.: 479-783-3961. Fax: 479-783-5307. TDD: 479-783-3961.
E-mail: fosm_interpretation@nps.gov
Web Site: www.nps.gov/fosm/
Founded: 1961.
Congressional District: 3
Key Personnel: Supt., William Black; Museum Technician, Emily Lovick; Chief Interpretation & Resource Mgmt., Nancy Stimson; Administrative Officer, Chuck Shoemaker; Facility Mgr., Gary Smith; Administrative Asst., Quoya Waters.
Personnel Profile: Full-Time Paid 11; Part-Time Paid 2; Part-Time Volunteers 15.
Governing Authority: federal. Parent Institution: Dept. of Interior. Subsidiary Institution: National Park Service. Tax-exempt.
Historic Site: 1817-24 Fort Smith, 1838 regarrisoned at new location, completed larger fort 1849, became the Federal Courthouse and Jail, 1871-1896.
Collections: furnishings; art; photographs; archeological material. Outdoor exhibits include 1817 fort foundations; 1846 Commissary building & reconstructed gallows used by Federal Court.
Research Fields: frontier military history; federal Indian policy; Federal Court for the Western District of Arkansas, deputy marshalls & outlaws.
Facilities: 750-vol. library of history books for use by special request; visitor center in barracks/courthouse building. Books for sale.
Activities: operational film, deputy marshall film, interactive videos on Indian removal & Indian territory; self-guided tour of historic barracks/court house/jail; self-guided walking tour along Arkansas River & Trail of Tears overlook; school tours; children's programs; living history; interpretive talks.
Publications: orientation brochure; quarterly newsletter.
Hours & Admission Prices: Daily 9-5. Seven Day Pass: adults 17 & over $4; National Parks Pass, Golden Age & Gold Access Cardholders and children 16 & under no charge. Closed New Year's Day; Christmas. ♿
Attendance: 100,000 (estimated)

FORT SMITH TROLLEY MUSEUM, 100 S. 4th St., Fort Smith, AR 72901-1947. Tel.: 479-783-0205.
E-mail: info@fstm.org
Web Site: www.fstm.org
Founded: 1979.
Key Personnel: C.E.O. & Pres. (V), Art B. Martin, M.D.; Museum Shop Mgr., Bradley Martin
History Museum.
Collections: Fort Smith's trolley transportation history; 4 original 58 Fort Smith streetcars; Frisco steam engine and tender; cabooses; a former military power car; dining car; boxcars; former Fort Smith buses; 1954 Fort Smith bus used in the filming of Biloxi Blues & Tuskegee Airmen.
Facilities: Museum-related items for sale.
Activities: trolley rides; tours; special events; birthday parties. Museum Sponsors: Open House in May.
Publications: newsletter, Trolley Report.
Hours & Admission Prices: May-Oct. Mon.-Sat. 10-5, Sun. 1-5; Nov.-April Sat. 10-5, Sun. 1-5; other times by appointment. No charge; donations accepted. Trolley Rides: adult $2, children $1. ♿
Attendance: 10,000 (estimated)
Membership: Individual $10; Annual $15; Annual Sponsor $25; Conductor $50; Sustaining $100; 205 Club $205; 224 Club $224; Benefactor $500; Life $1,000.

Garfield

PEA RIDGE NATIONAL MILITARY PARK, 15930 Hwy. 62, Garfield, AR 72732-9532. Tel.: 479-451-8122. Fax: 479-451-0219.
Web Site: www.nps.gov/peri/
Founded: 1956.
Congressional District: 3
Key Personnel: Park Ranger, Troy Banzhaf; Museum Shop Mgr., Lana Samuel; Supt., John Scott.
Personnel Profile: Full-Time Paid 13; Part-Time Volunteers 10.
Governing Authority: federal. National Park Service.
Historical Building: reconstructed Elkhorn Tavern.
Collections: Civil War; military.
Research Fields: Civil War.
Facilities: 300-vol. library of Civil War books.
Activities: guided tours; lectures; films; permanent & temporary exhibits.
Publications: assorted information site bulletins.
Hours & Admission Prices: Daily 8-5. 7 Day Permit: adults 16-61 $5; children under 16 no charge. Closed New Year's Day; Thanksgiving; Christmas. ♿
Attendance: 69,000 (estimated)

Gillett

ARKANSAS POST MUSEUM, 5530 Hwy. 165 S., Gillett, AR 72055-9730. Tel.: 870-548-2634. Fax: 870-548-3003.
E-mail: arkansaspostmuseum@arkansas.gov
Web Site: www.arkansasstateparks.com
Founded: 1960.
Congressional District: 1
Key Personnel: Dir., Christy Murphy.
Personnel Profile: Full-Time Paid 3; Part-Time Paid 2; Part-Time Volunteers 12.
Governing Authority: state. Parent Institution: Arkansas Dept. of Parks & Tourism. Subsidiary Institution: Arkansas State Parks Division. Tax-exempt.
Local History Museum.
Collections: archives; agriculture; archaeology; costumes; history; textiles; transportation; music; glass; schools; child's playhouse; Quapaw Indians; pioneer life; Civil War. Historic House: 1877 Refeld-Hinman Home.
Research Fields: Arkansas Post area history, Grand Prairie Region.
Facilities: Gifts for sale.
Activities: guided tours; programs; lectures; special events.
Hours & Admission Prices: Tues.-Sat. & Mon. holidays 8-5, Sun. 1-5. Family $10, adults $3, children 6-12 $2; children under 6 & school groups no charge. Closed New Year's Day; Thanksgiving; Christmas Eve & Day. ♿
Attendance: 6,000 (accurate)

ARKANSAS POST NATIONAL MEMORIAL, 1741 Old Post Rd., Gillett, AR 72055-9733. Tel.: 870-548-2207. Fax: 870-548-2431.
E-mail: arpo_superintendent@nps.gov
Web Site: www.nps.gov/arpo
Founded: 1964.
Congressional District: 1
Key Personnel: Supt., Edward Wood.
Personnel Profile: Full-Time Paid 10; Part-Time Paid 1; Part-Time Volunteers 8.
Governing Authority: federal. Parent Institution: National Park Service. Tax-exempt: 501(c)(3).
History Museum.
Collections: prehistoric artifacts; early American (pre-Revolutionary War); Colonial (French & Spanish); Revolutionary War; artifacts of Arkansas territorial & early statehood period; Civil War.
Research Fields: Indian, French, Spanish, early American, Civil War & westward expansion.

Facilities: historical trail; picnic area; visitor center.
Activities: films; permanent exhibitions; interpretive programs.
Publications: orientation brochure; quarterly newsletter.
Hours & Admission Prices: Park daily 8-dusk. Visitor Center daily 8-5. No charge; donations accepted. Closed New Year's Day; Thanksgiving; Christmas. ♿
Attendance: 38,180 (accurate)

Gravette

GRAVETTE HISTORICAL MUSEUM, 503 Charlotte, Gravette, AR 72736. Mailing Address: P.O. Box 1371, Gravette, AR 72736-1371. Tel.: 479-787-7334. Fax: 479-787-9910.
Web Site: www.gravette.com
Founded: 1995.
Key Personnel: Chm. (V), John Mitchael; Financial Dir., Michael Von Ree; Museum Shop Mgr., Shiela Martin.
Personnel Profile: Part-Time Paid 1.
Governing Authority: municipal. Parent Institution: City of Gravette. Tax-exempt.
Historical Museum.
Collections: to promote, share & preserve the history of the city of Gravette & its surrounding area; artifacts that depict the life styles of area Native Americans, settlers & residents.
Research Fields: cabin restoration; local site excavations.
Facilities: 1,800 sq. ft. exhibit space.
Activities: temporary exhibitions. Annual Events: Annual Founders Day, State Museum Day.
Hours & Admission Prices: Tues., Thurs. & Sat. 12-4; other times by appointment. No charge; donations accepted. Closed New Year's Day; Christmas. ♿
Attendance: 600 (estimated)

Gurdon

HOO-HOO INTERNATIONAL FORESTRY MUSEUM, 207 Main St., Gurdon, AR 71743-1237. Mailing Address: P.O. Box 118, Gurdon, AR 71743-0118. Tel.: 870-353-4997; 800-979-9950. Fax: 870-353-4151.
E-mail: info@hoo-hoo.org
Web Site: www.hoo-hoo.org
Founded: 1981.
Congressional District: 4
Key Personnel: Exec. Sec., Beth A. Thomas; Chm. Museum Committee, Teeny Johnston.
Personnel Profile: Part-Time Paid 1.
Governing Authority: organization. Parent Institution: The Fraternal Order of Forest Products Industry. Tax-exempt.
Logging & Lumber Museum.
Collections: woodcarvings; tools; artifacts pertaining to forestry; items pertaining to logging & lumber; manuscript collections.
Facilities: 75-seat auditorium.
Activities: permanent exhibitions; school loan service.
Publications: Log & Tally magazine.
Hours & Admission Prices: Mon.-Fri. 9-4. No charge.

Hardy

GOOD OLD DAYS VINTAGE MOTORCAR MUSEUM, INC., 301 W. Main St., Hardy, AR 72542. Mailing Address: P.O. Box 311, Hardy, AR 72542-0311. Tel.: 870-856-4884. Fax: 870-856-4884.
Founded: 1996.
Key Personnel: Dir., Ernest E. Sutherland; Museum Shop Mgr., Mike Reed.
Personnel Profile: Full-Time Paid 1; Part-Time Volunteers 1.
Automobile Museum.
Collections: period automobiles; tools; gas pumps; guns; books.
Facilities: Museum-related items for sale.
Activities: antique auto sales.
Hours & Admission Prices: Mon.-Fri. 9:30-4, Sat. 9-4:30, Sun. 12-5. Adults $8.50, children 12 & under $5; discounts to groups and AAM & ICOM members. Closed Thanksgiving; Christmas. ♿
Attendance: 4,500 (estimated)

Harrison

BOONE COUNTY HERITAGE MUSEUM, 124 S. Cherry St., Harrison, AR 72601-5024. Mailing Address: P.O. Box 1094, Harrison, AR 72602-1094. Tel.: 870-741-3312.
E-mail: bchm@windstream.net
Web Site: www.bchrs.org
Founded: 1987.
Key Personnel: Pres. (V), John Berry; Dir., Roz Slavik
History Museum.
Collections: local history; period artifacts; Civil War; the Missouri & North Arkansas Railroad Co.; Native American artifacts; period clocks; medical & domestic tools.
Research Fields: genealogy.
Facilities: library.
Publications: quarterly, Boone County Historian, Oak Leaves; Boone County History Pictoral.
Hours & Admission Prices: March-Nov. Mon.-Fri. 10-4, Dec.-Feb. Thurs. 10-4. Adults $2. Closed holidays.
Membership: Individual and Husband & Wife $20; Organization & Business $25; Lifetime $250.

BUFFALO NATIONAL RIVER, U.S. Federal Bldg., 402 N. Walnut St. Ste. #136, Harrison, AR 72601-3622. Tel.: 870-741-5443 (park headquarters); 439-2502 (visitor information). Fax: 870-741-7286.
E-mail: caven_clark@nps.gov
Web Site: www.nps.gov/buff/index.htm
Founded: 1972.
Congressional District: 3
Key Personnel: Supt., Kevin G. Cheri; Archaeologist Cur., Caven Clark.
Personnel Profile: Full-Time Paid 1; Part-Time Paid 1.
Governing Authority: federal. Dept. of the Interior, National Park Service. Tax-exempt.
National Park.
Collections: herbarium & other natural history collections; archaeological & historical artifacts; Ozark Mountain settlements dating back 9,000 years. Historic Buildings: c.1860 Beaver Jim Villines Farm; c.1836 Parker-Hickman cabin.
Research Fields: local history & culture; natural history.
Facilities: 700-vol. library on Ozark folklife, park recreation, resource management, available for use on premises; reading room. Books on natural history, Ozark history & folklife for sale.
Activities: guided tours; lectures; films.
Publications: orientation brochure.
Hours & Admission Prices: Ranger Station: daily 8:30-4:30. Tyler Bend Visitor Center: Memorial Day-Labor Day daily 8-5; Sept. to mid-May daily 8:30-4:30. No charge. Closed major holidays. ♿
Attendance: 1,000,000 (accurate)

MARINE CORPS LEGACY MUSEUM, 127 Rush St., Harrison, AR 72601. Mailing Address: P.O. Box 2654, Harrison, AR 72602-2654. Tel.: 870-743-1680.
Military History Museum.
Collections: Marine Corps history from 1775 to present; photographs; uniforms; vehicles; awards.
Activities: educational programs.
Hours & Admission Prices: Tues.-Sat. 10-5.

Heber Springs

OLMSTEAD FUNERAL & HISTORICAL MUSEUM, 108 S. 4th St., Heber Springs, AR 72543-3810. Tel.: 501-362-2422.
E-mail: mail@olmstead.cc
Web Site: www.olmstead.cc/museum.htm
History Museum.
Collections: history of undertaking & funereal directing dating back to 1896; horse drawn hearse.
Activities: tours.
Hours & Admission Prices: Call for appointment.

Helena

DELTA CULTURAL CENTER, 141 Cherry St., Helena, AR 72342-3501. Tel.: 870-338-4350; 800-358-0972. Fax: 870-338-4358.
E-mail: info@deltaculturalcenter.com
Web Site: www.deltaculturalcenter.com
Founded: 1990.
Congressional District: 1
Key Personnel: Dir., Katie Harrington; Chm. Policy Advisory Bd., Emma Petty; Museum Shop Mgr., Kathleen Randall.
Personnel Profile: Full-Time Paid 10; Part-Time Paid 4.
Governing Authority: state government; nonprofit. Parent Institution: Dept. of Arkansas Heritage. Tax-exempt.
Cultural Center: housed in the former St. Louis & Iron Mountain Railroad Depot; c.1912.
Collections: Arkansas Delta history & culture; personal artifacts; photographs.
Hours & Admission Prices: Tues.-Sat. 9-5. No charge; donations accepted. Closed New Year's Day; Thanksgiving; Christmas Eve & Day. ♿
Attendance: 26,988 (accurate)

PHILLIPS COUNTY MUSEUM, 623 Pecan St., Helena, AR 72342-3298. Mailing Address: P.O. Box 38, Helena, AR 72342-0038. Tel.: 870-338-7790. Fax: 870-338-7732.
E-mail: helenamuseum@hnb.com
Founded: 1929.
Congressional District: 1
Key Personnel: Pres. (V), Otis Howe, Jr.; Cur., Anne Pope; Sec., Rose Seaton; Treas., James Billingsley.
Governing Authority: nonprofit organization. Parent Institution: Helena Library & Museum Assoc. Tax-exempt.
History Museum.
Collections: memorabilia of the Civil War, Spanish-American War & World Wars I & II; glassware; china; apparel & accessories covering several generations; early settlement of Phillips County; portraits; furniture; permanent loan from Edison Foundation; early American Indian & area artifacts; contemporary & historical Black art.
Activities: permanent & temporary exhibitions.
Hours & Admission Prices: Tues.-Sat. 10-4. No charge. Closed New Year's Day; Memorial Day; Independence Day; Labor Day; Thanksgiving; Christmas Day & two days after.
Attendance: 3,463 (accurate)
Membership: Membership $5; Sustaining $10.

PILLOW-THOMPSON HOUSE, 718 Perry St., Helena, AR 72342-3134. Mailing Address: P.O. Box 785, Helena, AR 72342-0785. Tel.: 870-338-8535.
E-mail: dussery@pccua.edu
Governing Authority: Parent Institution: Phillips Community College of the University of Arkansas.
Historic House: built in 1896.
Collections: period furnishings; personal artifacts.
Activities: rental facilities.
Hours & Admission Prices: Wed.-Sat. 10-4; groups by appointment. No charge. Closed New Year's Day; Easter; Thanksgiving; Christmas.

Hope

CLINTON BIRTHPLACE HOME, 117 S. Hervey St., Hope, AR 71801-4208. Mailing Address: P.O. Box 1925, Hope, AR 71802-1925. Tel.: 870-777-4455. Fax: 870-722-6929.
E-mail: clinton@arkansas.net
Web Site: www.clintonbirthplace.com
Key Personnel: Dir., Martha Berryman
Historic House: housed in the boyhood home of President William Jefferson Clinton. Listed on the National Register of Historic Places.
Collections: family history; period furnishings; personal artifacts; photographs; replica of the Oval Office rug; memorial garden.
Facilities: garden. Museum-related items for sale.
Activities: special events; permanent & temporary exhibitions.
Hours & Admission Prices: Mon.-Sat. 10-5. Adults $5, senior citizens $4, children 7-18 $3; children 6 & under no charge.

HOPE VISITOR CENTER AND MUSEUM, 100 E. Division St., Hope, AR 71801. Tel.: 870-722-2580.
History Museum: housed in the former Iron Mountain/Missouri Pacific Railroad Depot; built in 1912.
Collections: Bill Clinton memorabilia; railroad history; period furnishings; personal artifacts; photographs.
Hours & Admission Prices: Call for hours.

Hot Springs

GARVAN WOODLAND GARDENS, 550 Arkridge Rd., Hot Springs, AR 71913-8729. Mailing Address: P.O. Box 22240, Hot Springs, AR 71903-2240. Tel.: 501-262-9300; 800-366-4664.
E-mail: gardeninfo@garvangardens.org
Web Site: www.garvangardens.org
Gardens.
Collections: over 160 types of azaleas; roses; shrubs; trees.
Facilities: 210 acre gardens including an Asian garden, bonsai garden, & children's garden.
Hours & Admission Prices: Feb.-March & Oct-Nov. 21. daily 10-5; Nov. 22-Dec. 12-9, April-Sept. daily 9-8. Adults $8, seniors 55 & over $7, children 6-12 $4; discounts to groups of 20 or more. Closed New Year's Day; Thanksgiving; Christmas.

HOT SPRINGS NATIONAL PARK VISITOR CENTER, 369 Central Ave., Bathhouse Row, Hot Springs, AR 71901-3525. Mailing Address: 101 Reserve St., Hot Springs, AR 71901. Tel.: 501-620-6701. Fax: 501-624-3458. TDD: 501-623-2308.
E-mail: hosp_interpretation@nps.gov
Web Site: www.nps.gov/hosp
Founded: 1832.
Congressional District: 4
Key Personnel: Supt., Josie Fernandez; Chief Interpreter, Lisa Garvin; Sec., Gail Sears; Museum Specialist, Sharon Shugart; Interpreter & Museum Shop Coord., Toni P. Cooper; Interpreter & V.I.P. Coord., Jeff Heitzman; Interpreter & Paraprofessional Archeologist, Mark Blaeuer; Museum Shop Mgr., Terri Reedy.
Personnel Profile: Full-Time Paid 6; Part-Time Paid 7.
Governing Authority: federal. Parent Institution: Hot Springs National Park. A branch of National Park Service, U.S. Dept. of Interior, Washington, DC. Tax-exempt: 101(6).
History Building.
Collections: herbarium; geology items; historical memorabilia; Native American artifacts; archives; archaeology artifacts; natural science; insects; Zander electro therapy machines; art nouveau stained glass; 1912 mission style furnishings; photographs; stereographs; blueprints; maps from 1875 to present; period rooms.
Research Fields: hydrology of thermal springs; history of bathing in Hot Springs; bathhouse architecture; spas; medical hydrology & recreation; early history of the city of Hot Springs.
Facilities: 1,500-vol. library of books on human & natural history available on premises; microfilm & Microfiche library; 52-seat auditorium; visitor center. Publications & novaculite whetstones for sale.
Activities: Fordyce Bathhouse self-guided tours; ranger-led outdoor tours for thermal feature tours; summer programs; touch screen exhibit including oral history excerpts.
Publications: orientation brochures, Fire In Folded Rocks; Valley of The Vapors; The Fordyce Bath House; Buckstaff Baths; Historical Reproductions; Hot Springs National Park In Pictures, Ye Hot Springs Picture Book; The Hot Springs of Arkansas Through the Years; American Spa; Didn't All The Indians Come Here?; Geoscenic Tour Guide; Trails of Hot Springs National Park.
Hours & Admission Prices: Daily 9-5. No charge; donations accepted. Closed New Year's Day; Thanksgiving; Christmas. ♿
Attendance: 189,200 (accurate)

MID-AMERICA SCIENCE MUSEUM, 500 Mid America Blvd., Hot Springs, AR 71913-8412. Tel.: 501-767-3461; 800-632-0583 (Arkansas). Fax: 501-767-1170.
E-mail: jmangi1@cablelynx.com
Web Site: www.midamericamuseum.org
Founded: 1979.
Congressional District: 4
Key Personnel: C.O.O., JoAnn Mangione; Chm., Anthony Taylor; Pres. (V), Wayne Roberts; Pres. MASM Foundation, Courtney Crouch, Jr.; Exec. Dir., Andy Marquart; Dir. Devel., Christy Beckwith; Dir. Education, LaJean Burnett; Museum Shop Mgr., Shari Kolar.
Personnel Profile: Full-Time Paid 11; Part-Time Paid 7; Part-Time Volunteers 88.
Governing Authority: Affiliated with Smithsonian Institute. Tax-exempt: 501(c)(3).
General Museum.
Collections: visitor participation exhibits focusing on broad topics of energy, life, matter & human perception.
Facilities: aquarium; theatre; snack bar; nature trail. Museum-related items for sale.
Activities: education programs, school outreach programs & loan materials; virtual reality simulator; camp-ins; field trips; elder hostel programs; Kids' Quest Program.
Publications: quarterly bulletin, The Mid American.
Hours & Admission Prices: Winter: Tues.-Sun. 10-5; Summer: daily 9:30-6. Adults $8, senior citizens 62 & over and children 2-12 $7; discount to AAM & ASTC members; members & children under one no charge. Closed New Year's Day; Thanksgiving; Christmas Eve & Day. ♿
Attendance: 89,151 (accurate)
Membership: Individual $40; Family $65; Grandparent, Aunt, Uncle & Foster $75; Smithsonian $100; Friends Society $250; Dr. Martin Eisele Society $500; Cecil W. Cupp, Jr. Society $1,000.

TOLTEC MOUNDS ARCHEOLOGICAL STATE PARK, 9 Silleda Lane, Hot Springs, AR 71909-3331. Tel.: 501-961-9442. Fax: 501-961-9221.
E-mail: toltecmounds@arkansas.com
Web Site: www.arkansasstateparks.com
Founded: 1975.

Congressional District: 2
Key Personnel: Dir. Toltec Research Station, Dr. Julie Markin; Supt., James Wilborn; Park Interpreter, Robin Gabe; Park Interpreter, Amy Griffin; Museum Shop Mgr., Keryn Cantrell.
Personnel Profile: Full-Time Paid 7; Part-Time Paid 2.
Governing Authority: state. Parent Institution: Dept. of Parks & Tourism, No. 1 Capitol Mall, Little Rock, AR 72201. Tel.: 501-682-1191 & Arkansas Archeological Survey, P.O. Box 1249, Fayetteville, AR 72702. Tel.: 479-375-3556. Tax-exempt.
Archaeological Site.
Collections: archeological research collection.
Research Fields: local environment 1,000 years ago; human use of environment; regional resources; lifeways; social & political systems; Mississippi Valley contacts.
Facilities: field research station; audiovisual room; visitor center; archaeological laboratory; canteen. Maps, books & publications on archaeology & history of the area & gift items for sale.
Activities: tours; films & slide presentations; formally organized education programs for children & adults by group reservation; occasional excavations; rental facility; workshops.
Publications: Emerging Patterns of Plum Bayou Culture; Arkansas Archaeological Survey of 1982; Surveyors of the Ancient Mississippi Valley: Modules & Alignments in Prehistoric Mound Sites; Arkansas Archeological Survey Research Report No. 28; Crossroads of the Past; Arkansas Archeological Survey Popular Series No. 2; Paths of our Children: Historic Indians of Arkansas; Arkansas Archeological Survey Popular Series No. 3; Arkansas Before the Americas Series No. 40.
Hours & Admission Prices: Mon. holidays & Tues.-Sat. 8-5, Sun. 12-5. Adults $3, children 6-12 $2; discounts to groups of 15 or more & schools with reservations; children under 6 no charge. Closed New Year's Day; Thanksgiving; Christmas Eve & Day. ♿
Attendance: 30,000 (accurate)

Jacksonport

JACKSONPORT STATE PARK, 205 Avenue St., Jacksonport, AR 72075. Mailing Address: 205 Avenue St., Newport, AR 72112-8771. Tel.: 870-523-2143. Fax: 870-523-4620.
E-mail: jacksonport@arkansas.com
Web Site: www.arkansasstateparks.com
Formerly: Jacksonport State Park Courthouse Museum
Founded: 1965.
Congressional District: 1
Key Personnel: Supt., Mark Ballard.
Personnel Profile: Full-Time Paid 7; Part-Time Paid 5.
Governing Authority: state. Arkansas Dept. of Parks & Tourism.
Historic Museum: 1872 Courthouse.
Collections: period furnishings; archives; agriculture; courtroom; household items; textiles; transportation; tools; restored sternwheel paddleboat, Mary Woods No. 2; 1872 Courthouse & Clerk's Office.
Major Exhibits: Mirror, Mirror: 19th & 20th Century Women's Fashion, 1/10-2/10; World War II Exhibit, 3/10-2/11.
Facilities: picnic area; rental pavilions; wildflower walk (trail). Museum-related items for sale.
Activities: self-guided & guided tours; hiking; swimming; boating on White River; camping; interpretation programs.
Publications: annual, Stream of History.
Hours & Admission Prices: Please call for hours. Adults $3.25, children $1.75. Closed New Year's Day; Thanksgiving; Christmas Eve & Day. ♿
Attendance: 2,100 (accurate)

Jacksonville

JACKSONVILLE MUSEUM OF MILITARY HISTORY, 100 Veterans' Circle, Jacksonville, AR 72076-4344. Tel.: 501-241-1943.
Web Site: www.jaxmilitarymuseum.org
Founded: 1972.
Congressional District: 2
Key Personnel: Pres. (V), Joan Zumwalt; Dir., Danna Kay Duggar.
Personnel Profile: Full-Time Paid 1; Part-Time Volunteers 30.
Governing Authority: Parent Institution: Little Rock Air Force Base Historical Foundation. Tax-exempt.
Military History Museum.
Collections: military history; personal artifacts; photographs; military equipment & uniforms.
Facilities: library.
Activities: research.
Publications: newsletter.
Hours & Admission Prices: Mon.-Sat. 9-5. Adults $3, seniors & military $2, students $1; members no charge. Closed holidays. ♿
Membership: Basic $100.

Jasper

BRADLEY HOUSE MUSEUM, 403 Clark St., Jasper, AR 72641. Mailing Address: P.O. Box 360, Jasper, AR 72641-0360. Tel.: 870-446-6247.
Personnel Profile: Part-Time Paid 1; Part-Time Volunteers 1.
Governing Authority: Parent Institution: Newton County Historical Society. Tax-exempt.
Historic House Museum: housed in the c.1900 home of Dr. W.A. Bradley.
Collections: personal artifacts; furnishings; farm implements; woodworking tools; Native American artifacts; fossils; photographs; genealogy.
Research Fields: genealogy.
Publications: annual, Newton County Homestead.
Hours & Admission Prices: April-Dec. Tues. 11-4. Adults $1. Closed Independence Day.
Attendance: 500 (estimated)
Membership: Annual $15; Lifetime $150.

HILARY JONES WILDLIFE MUSEUM, 4208 Hwy. 7 N., Jasper, AR 72641. Mailing Address: P.O. Box 277, Jasper, AR 72641-0277. Tel.: 870-446-6180.
Wildlife Museum.
Collections: area wildlife history; elk mounts; fish aquariums; paintings; photographs; videos.
Facilities: Museum-related items for sale.
Activities: video presentations.
Hours & Admission Prices: Call for hours.

Jonesboro

ARKANSAS STATE UNIVERSITY ART GALLERY, 114 S. Caraway Rd., Jonesboro, AR 72467. Mailing Address: P.O. Box 1920, State University, AR 72467-1920. Tel.: 870-972-3050. Fax: 870-972-3932.
E-mail: csteele@astate.edu
Web Site: www.finearts.astate.edu/
Founded: 1967.
Congressional District: 1
Key Personnel: Chm. Gallery Committee, Tom Chaffee; Gallery Committee, Gayle Pendergrass.
Governing Authority: university. Parent Institution: Arkansas State University Dept. of Art, Jonesboro, AR 72467. Tax-exempt.
University Art Gallery.
Collections: contemporary & historical prints; drawings; paintings; sculpture.
Facilities: auditorium; classrooms.
Activities: lectures; gallery talks; formally organized education programs for graduate & undergraduate students; permanent, temporary, traveling & loan exhibitions.
Publications: calendar.
Hours & Admission Prices: Fine Arts Gallery: Mon.-Fri. 10-5. Bradbury Gallery: Tues.-Sat. 12-5, Sun. 2-5. No charge. Closed holidays. ♿
Attendance: 3,600 (estimated)

* **ARKANSAS STATE UNIVERSITY MUSEUM, (M),** Museum Bldg., 110 Cooley Dr., Jonesboro, AR 72401. Mailing Address: P.O. Box 490, State University, AR 72467-0490. Tel.: 870-972-2074. Fax: 870-972-2793.
E-mail: mallen@astate.edu
Web Site: www.museum.astate.edu
Founded: 1933.
Congressional District: 1
Key Personnel: Exec. Dir., Dr. Marti L. Allen; Asst. Dir., Lenore Shoults, M.A.; Cur., Julie MacDonald, M.A.; Office Mgr., Margaret Collier, M.B.A., MSISeC
Personnel Profile: Full-Time Paid 4; Part-Time Paid 2; Interns 4.
Governing Authority: university. Parent Institution: Arkansas State University. Tax-exempt: 501(c)(3).
History & Culture Museum.
Collections: history of Arkansas; archaeology; ethnology; costumes; military; natural history; paleontology; Commemorative China & glass; research collection: fossils, minerals, prehistoric Indian artifacts, clothing, antiques.
Major Exhibits: Portals of the Soul: Ancient Peoples of Northeast Arkansas, 11/09-4/11.
Research Fields: paleobotany; history of northeast Arkansas.
Facilities: library; reading room.
Activities: guided tours; reference service for general public; summer camps for youth; cultural diversity events; iPod tours of Old Town Arkansas; museum studies classes at M.A. & Ph.D. levels.
Publications: brochures.
Hours & Admission Prices: Tues.-Fri. 9-4, Sat.-Sun. 1-5. No charge; donations accepted. Closed national holidays. ♿
Attendance: 48,000 (estimated)

Membership: General $50; Anniversary Donor $100; Heritage Patron $500; Museum Benefactor $1,000; Corporate $5,000; Lifetime Benefactor $10,000.

Lake Village

MUSEUM OF CHICOT COUNTY ARKANSAS, 614 Cokley St., Lake Village, AR 71653. Mailing Address: P.O. Box 762, Lake Village, AR 71653-0762. Tel.: 870-265-2868 & 2358.
E-mail: jpburge@cei.net
Web Site: homeearthlink.net/~diod
Founded: 1994.
Key Personnel: C.E.O., Judge Fred Zieman; Pres., Ellen DiMaggio; Treas., Vera Pesaresi.
Personnel Profile: Part-Time Volunteers 3.
Governing Authority: county; nonprofit. Tax-exempt: 501(c)(3).
Historic Site.
Collections: medical instruments; nursery equipment; surgical table; delivery table; medical supplies. Historic Buildings: c.1910 Victorian house; 1843 log cabin; Italian immigration to Chicot county to near slavery conditions shown through photographs, letters & records.
Research Fields: data on founder, building and doctors who have practiced here; experience of former patients.
Facilities: 14,775 sq. ft. exhibit space.
Activities: guided tours.
Hours & Admission Prices: Mon., Wed. & Fri. 1-4. No charge; donations accepted.
Attendance: 2,500 (estimated)

Lepanto

MUSEUM LEPANTO USA, Main St., Lepanto, AR 72354. Mailing Address: P.O. Box 670, Lepanto, AR 72354-0670. Tel.: 870-475-2222. Fax: 870-475-2384.
Historic Building: housed in a 1915 bank building.
Collections: local history & culture; period artifacts; Native American; replicas of a general store, blacksmith shop, doctor's office; war memorabilia.
Hours & Admission Prices: Wed. & Fri. 1-4; other times by appointment.

Leslie

OZARK HERITAGE ARTS CENTER & MUSEUM, 410 Oak St., Leslie, AR 72645. Mailing Address: P.O. Box 217, Leslie, AR 72645-0217. Tel.: 870-447-2500. Fax: 870-447-2528.
E-mail: ohac@windstream.net
Key Personnel: Exec. Dir., Gary Hall
History Museum.
Collections: regional history from 1820-1960; clothing; documents; mementos; photographs; furniture.
Activities: concerts; theatrical events; permanent & temporary exhibits.
Hours & Admission Prices: April-Dec. Tues.-Sat. 10-4. No charge.

Lincoln

ARKANSAS COUNTRY DOCTOR MUSEUM, (M), 107 N. Starr Ave., Lincoln, AR 72744. Mailing Address: P.O. Box 1004, Lincoln, AR 72744-1004. Tel.: 479-824-4307. Fax: 479-824-4307.
E-mail: countrydoc@pgte.com
Web Site: www.drmuseum.net
Founded: 1994.
Congressional District: 3
Key Personnel: C.E.O. & Pres., David Therneau; Chm. (V) & Education, Dr. Joe B. Hall; Vice Pres., Devel. & Public Rels., Andy Newbill; Treas. & Security, Jerry Leach; Museum Shop Mgr., Diana Hale; Sec., Sue Heisler.
Personnel Profile: Part-Time Paid 2; Part-Time Volunteers 26.
Governing Authority: private; nonprofit organization. Tax-exempt: 501(c)(3).
Country Doctor Museum.
Collections: medical instruments & furnishings; 20th-century medical equipment; iron lung with portable respirators in polio exhibit; 1924 Model T Roadster; 1886 Studebaker Doctors Buggy; carriage house; herb garden.
Research Fields: country doctors & nurses in Arkansas up to 1950.
Facilities: 400-vol. library of medical reference books; botanical garden; 3,650 sq. ft. exhibit space. Museum-related items for sale.
Activities: docent program; films; formal education for area students; guided tours; lectures; loan exhibitions. Annual Events: ice cream social; cookout; yard sale fundraiser.
Publications: newsletter 3 times per year, Arkansas Country Doctor Museum; book, My Spirit is Free - Reflections from an Iron Lung.
Hours & Admission Prices: Feb. 20-Dec. 11 Wed.-Sat. 1-4; other times by appointment. No charge; donations accepted. Closed Independence Day. ♿
Attendance: 800 (estimated)

Membership: Individual $10; Family $15; Patron $50; Sponsor $100; Benefactor $250; Guardian $500; Major Endowment $1,000.

Little Rock

AEROSPACE EDUCATION CENTER, 3301 E. Roosevelt Rd., Little Rock, AR 72206-6709. Tel.: 501-376-IMAX.
Web Site: www.aerospaced.org
Space Museum.
Collections: aviation artifacts; replicas of airplanes & spacecraft; evolution of flight.
Facilities: IMAX theater. Museum-related items for sale.
Activities: special events; educational programs; films; rental facilities; birthday parties; workshops.
Hours & Admission Prices: Museum: Tues.-Thurs. 9:30-2, Fri. 9:30-2 & 6pm-9pm, Sat. 11:30-9, Sun. 11:30-4. IMAX: adults $7.50, seniors 60 & over $6.50, children 12 & under $5.50.

* **THE ARKANSAS ARTS CENTER, (M),** MacArthur Park, 9th & Commerce, Little Rock, AR 72202. Mailing Address: P.O. Box 2137, Little Rock, AR 72203-2137. Tel.: 501-372-4000. Fax: 501-375-8053.
E-mail: nplummer@arkarts.com
Web Site: www.arkarts.com
Founded: 1937.
Congressional District: 2
Key Personnel: Exec. Dir., Dr. Ellen Plummer; Chm. (V), Robert W. Tucker; Pres. (V), Belinda Shults; Deputy Dir. Mktg., Heather Haywood; Deputy Dir. Operations, Rocky Nickles; Registrar, Thom Hall; Deputy Dir. Devel., Clay Mercer; Deputy Dir. Programs, Joseph Lampo; Membership Mgr., Matthew Cleveland; Dir. Children's Theatre, Bradley Anderson; State Svcs., Ned Metcalf; Museum Shop Mgr., Kim White; Volunteer Mgr., Gaynis Boyland.
Personnel Profile: Full-Time Paid 39; Part-Time Paid 34; Part-Time Volunteers 491; Interns 4.
Governing Authority: city; nonprofit organization. Subsidiary Institution: Arkansas Arts Center Foundation. Tax-exempt: 501(c)(3).
Art Museum.
Collections: 19th-20th century American drawings & 15th to 20th-century European drawings; American & European paintings, sculpture, prints & photographs; American, European & Asian decorative arts & contemporary American crafts.
Major Exhibits: World of the Pharaohs: Treasures of Egypt Revealed, 11/09-7/5/10; 52nd Annual Delta Exhibition, 1/29/10-3/14/10; Capturing the Orient, 4/2/10-5/16/10; Young Arkansas Artists 49th Annual Exhibition, 4/9/10-5/23/10.
Research Fields: American & European drawings.
Facilities: 5,000-vol. library on art & drama available for inter-library loan; reading room; museum school; 381-seat theater; 8 galleries; restaurant; 140-seat lecture hall. Museum-related items for sale.
Activities: permanent, temporary & circulating exhibitions; formal organized education program; guided tours; lectures; gallery talks; studio classes for adults & children in visual arts.
Publications: quarterly newsletter, Works; annual report; exhibition & permanent collection catalogues.
Hours & Admission Prices: Mon.-Sat. 10-5, Sun. 11-5. Suggested Donation $5; discount to AAM members; members no charge. Closed major holidays. ♿
Attendance: 298,982 (accurate)
Membership: Individual $55; Family $65; Participating $80; Contributing $150; Associate $300; Supporting $600. Corporate Memberships: Corporate Affiliate $300; Corporate Citizen $600.

ARKANSAS GAME AND FISH COMMISSION, 2 Natural Resources Dr., Little Rock, AR 72205-1572. Tel.: 501-223-6300; 800-364-4263. Fax: 501-223-6465.
Web Site: www.agfc.com
Founded: 1945.
Congressional District: 2
Key Personnel: Dir., Scott Henderson.
Governing Authority: state.
Zoology Museum.
Collections: Arkansas wildlife exhibits; zoology.
Activities: tours.
Publications: magazine, Arkansas Wildlife.
Hours & Admission Prices: Mon.-Fri. 8-4:30. No charge. ♿

CENTRAL HIGH SCHOOL NATIONAL HISTORIC SITE, 2120 Daisy L. Gaston Bates Dr., Little Rock, AR 72202. Tel.: 501-374-1957. Fax: 501-396-3001.
E-mail: CHSC_visitor_center@nps.gov

Web Site: www.nps.gov/chsc/
Formerly: Central High Museum & Visitor Center
Founded: 1995.
Congressional District: 2
Key Personnel: Supt., Robin White.
Personnel Profile: Full-Time Paid 12; Part-Time Paid 3; Part-Time Volunteers 25.
Governing Authority: Parent Institution: National Park Service.
History Museum.
Collections: Central High photographs & artifacts from 1957 crisis.
Research Fields: School Desegregation - Civil Rights.
Facilities: visitor center.
Activities: ranger-led programs; distance learning programs; curriculum-based education programs.
Publications: Lesson Plans; interpretive site bulletins.
Hours & Admission Prices: Daily 9-4:30. No charge; donations accepted. Closed New Year's Day; Thanksgiving; Christmas. ♿
Attendance: 43,277 (accurate)

EMOBA - MUSEUM OF BLACK ARKANSAS, 12th & Louisiana, Little Rock, AR 72214. Mailing Address: P.O. Box 46754, Little Rock, AR 72214-6754. Tel.: 501-661-9903.
Web Site: www.onlinelittlerock.com/emoba.htm
Key Personnel: Founder & Dir., Ernie Dodson.
Governing Authority: Tax-exempt: 501(c)(3).
Black History Museum.
Collections: history & culture of Black Arkansans & their contributions to the state; photographs; personal artifacts.
Activities: special events.
Hours & Admission Prices: Call for hours.

* **HISTORIC ARKANSAS MUSEUM, (M),** 200 E. Third St., Little Rock, AR 72201-1608. Tel.: 501-324-9351. Fax: 501-324-9345. TDD: 501-324-9811.
E-mail: info@historicarkansas.org
Web Site: www.historicarkansas.org
Formerly: Arkansas Territorial Restoration
Founded: 1941.
Congressional District: 2
Key Personnel: Dir. & C.E.O., William B. Worthen, Jr.; Chm. (V), Frances Ross; Pres. (V), Tim Martin, M.D.; Dir. Education, Starr Mitchell; Historic Site Specialist, David Etchieson; Dir. Communications, Ellen Korenblat; Conservator, Andrew Zawacki; Cur. Research, Swannee Bennett; Dir. Devel., Louise Terzia; Registrar, Westley Ashley; Fiscal Mgr., Rebecca Hochradel; Dir. Volunteers & Membership, Tricia Spione; Security Supvr., Gunter Lindermeier; Museum Shop Mgr., Paige James.
Personnel Profile: Full-Time Paid 21; Part-Time Paid 20; Part-Time Volunteers 27; Interns 2.
Governing Authority: state. Parent Institution: Dept. of Arkansas Heritage. Tax-exempt.
History Museum.
Collections: period furnishings; decorative, mechanical & fine arts produced in Arkansas from 1819 to 1890; Arkansas-made art & artifacts from 1700's to present. Historic Buildings: c.1830 Hinderliter House; c.1845 Brownlee House; c.1848 McVicar House.
Research Fields: pre-Civil War Arkansas, Arkansas made Pre-history to The Present.
Facilities: 1,000-vol. library on early Arkansas; 51,000 sq. ft. museum center; gardens; furnished museum houses; art gallery; conservation lab; educational center for school children; exhibition hall in reception center. Museum-related items for sale.
Activities: guided tours; special tours for groups & school children. Annual Events: Christmas Open House; Independence Day open house; Candlelight Gala; Territorial Fair (Mother's Day weekend).
Publications: exhibit catalogues; brochure; newsletter, Collections; A Garden Heritage; Arkansas Made: The Decorative, Mechanical & Fine Arts Produced in Arkansas, 1819-1870, Volumes I & II; The Likeness Trade: Portrait Painting in Arkansas, 1790-1900. (1996)
Hours & Admission Prices: Mon.-Sat. 9-5, Sun. 1-5. Galleries: no charge. Tour: Adults $2.50, senior citizens $1.50, children $1; discount to AAM members; members no charge. Closed New Year's Day; Easter; Thanksgiving; Christmas Eve & Day. ♿
Attendance: 50,000 (estimated)
Membership: Individual $35; Family $50; Supporting $100; Sustaining $250; Founder $500; Cornerstone $1,000 & up.

HISTORICAL RESOURCES AND MUSEUM SERVICES, Arkansas State Parks, One Capitol Mall, Little Rock, AR 72201-1013. Tel.: 501-682-3603. Fax: 501-682-0081.
E-mail: patricia.murphy@arkansas.gov
Web Site: arkansasstateparks.com
Founded: 1979.
Congressional District: 2
Key Personnel: Dir., Patricia Maguire Murphy; Museums Coord., William Long.
Personnel Profile: Full-Time Paid 3.
Governing Authority: state. Parent Institution: Arkansas Dept. of Parks & Tourism. Branch Museums: Prairie County Museum, DesArc, AR; Arkansas Museum of Natural Resources, Smackover, AR; Plantation Agriculture Museum, Scott, AR; AR Post Museum, Gillett, AR. Tax-exempt.
State Agency for Museum Services.
Collections: local history.
Activities: professional & technical advice to state museums; resource library; workshops; administrative services & master planning for affiliated museums.
Publications: occasional publications on museology & museography; workshop papers.
Hours & Admission Prices: Business Office: Mon.-Fri. 8-5. ♿

LITTLE ROCK ZOOLOGICAL GARDENS, One Jonesboro Dr., Little Rock, AR 72205-5401. Tel.: 501-666-2406. Fax: 501-666-7040. TDD: 501-399-3451.
E-mail: mblakely@littlerock.org
Web Site: www.littlerockzoo.com
Founded: 1926.
Congressional District: 2
Key Personnel: C.E.O., Michael E. Blakely; Chm. Bd. Governors, George Mallory; Vice Chm., Blair Allen; Chm. Docent Council (V), Lisa Buehler; Museum Shop Mgr., Barbara Brown.
Personnel Profile: Full-Time Paid 37; Part-Time Paid 11; Part-Time Volunteers 12; Interns 2.
Governing Authority: municipal. Parent Institution: City of Little Rock, AR. Subsidiary Institution: Little Rock Zoo Department.
Zoo.
Collections: 210 species mammals, birds, reptiles, amphibians, invertebrates; 757 specimen.
Research Fields: behavior; blood chemistry; reproductive cycle monitoring through urinalysis.
Facilities: library of science & natural history books; lecture hall.
Activities: guided tours; lectures; Zoo Explorer Post; docent council; miniature train ride; camel rides in summer.
Publications: map; bimonthly newsletter; teachers' guide; education brochures biannual magazine.
Hours & Admission Prices: Summer: daily 9-5; Winter: daily 9-4:30. Adults $8, seniors 60 & over and children 1-12 $6; discounts to AZA institutions; group rates with reservation; zoo members no charge. Closed New Year's Day; Thanksgiving; Christmas. ♿
Attendance: 283,768 (accurate)
Membership: Individual $40; Individual Plus & Dual $50; Family & Grandparents $60; Grandparents Plus $70.

MACARTHUR MUSEUM OF ARKANSAS MILITARY HISTORY, Tower Building of the Little Rock Arsenal, 503 E. Ninth St., Little Rock, AR 72202-3997. Tel.: 501-376-4602.
Web Site: www.arkmilitaryheritage.com
Founded: 2001.
Congressional District: 4
Key Personnel: Exec. Dir., Stephan McAteer
Military History Museum: birthplace of General Douglas MacArthur.
Collections: state's military heritage; artifacts; photographs; weapons; documents; uniforms; military artifacts.
Activities: tours.
Hours & Admission Prices: Tues.-Sat. 10-4, Sun. 1-4. No charge. Closed New Year's Day; Thanksgiving; Christmas Eve & Day. ♿
Attendance: 28,000 (estimated)

MOSAIC TEMPLARS CULTURAL CENTER, (M), 501 W. 9th St., Little Rock, AR 72201-4111. Mailing Address: 1500 Tower Bldg., 323 Center St., Little Rock, AR 72201-2603. Tel.: 501-683-3593.
E-mail: info@mosaictemplarscenter.com
Web Site: www.mosaictemplarscenter.com
African American History Museum.
Collections: African American life, history & culture; photographs; personal artifacts.
Activities: performing arts; conferences; special events; educational programs.

Hours & Admission Prices: Call for hours.

* **MUSEUM OF DISCOVERY: ARKANSAS MUSEUM OF SCIENCE AND HISTORY, (M),** 500 President Clinton Ave., Ste. 150, Little Rock, AR 72201-1757. Tel.: 501-396-7050, ext. 200. Fax: 501-396-7054.
Web Site: www.amod.org
Founded: 1927.
Congressional District: 2
Key Personnel: Exec. Dir., Nan Selz; Chm. (V), Robert Childress; Educator, Animal Caretakers, Nichole Ashley; Educator, Kate Maze; Reservationist, Beth Nelsen; Dir. Collections & Research and Grantwriter, Marci Bynum Robertson; Dir. Mktg., Katie McManners; Educator, David Westbrook; Dir. Finance, Ken Harrison; Dir. Exhibits & Facilities, Joel Gordon; Dir. Programs, Carol Couser; Dir. Devel., Melody Myers; Network Coord., Diane LaFollette; Museum Shop Mgr., Angela Burgess.
Personnel Profile: Full-Time Paid 14; Part-Time Paid 20; Part-Time Volunteers 2,637; Interns 2.
Governing Authority: bd. trustees; nonprofit. Tax-exempt: 501(c)(3).
History & Science Museum.
Collections: birds; mammals; reptiles; invertebrates; Indian artifacts; pottery; pioneer items; South American & African anthropology; interactive exhibits; furniture; appliances; postal jeep; kid's gallery; Kewpie dolls; multicultural masks; Kachina dolls; microscope station.
Major Exhibits: Backyard Science (T), 11/09-3/10; Artifacts Showcase, 11/09-4/10.
Research Fields: traveling exhibits created in-house; early childhood education; immigration into Arkansas; science & technology; biology of live animals; ethnographic studies.
Facilities: 300-vol. library of science & history books; classrooms; theater. Books, crafts, rocks, science materials & historic reproductions for sale.
Activities: gallery talks; TV programs; formally organized education programs for children; docent program; permanent & temporary exhibitions; demonstrations; school extension services.
Publications: seasonal class schedule; Resource Manual; Museum Newsletter; Museum Guide.
Hours & Admission Prices: Closing for renovations in 2010. Call for information. Adults $8; discounts to AAM members; members no charge. ♿
Attendance: 95,773 (accurate)
Membership: Basic $45; Family $75; Contributing: $110.

* **OLD STATE HOUSE MUSEUM, (M),** 300 W. Markham St., Little Rock, AR 72201-1423. Tel.: 501-324-9685. Fax: 501-324-9688. TDD: 501-324-9811.
E-mail: info@oldstatehouse.com
Web Site: www.oldstatehouse.com
Formerly: The Old State House
Founded: 1951.
Congressional District: 2
Key Personnel: Dir., Bill Gatewood; Historic Sites Mgr., Ed Garretson; Devel. Dir., Larry Ahart; Deputy Dir., Duncan Jones; Dir. Public Rels., Amy Peck; Dir. Education, Georganne Sisco; Dir. Exhibits, Gail Moore; Cur., JoEllen Maack; Museum Shop Mgr., David Kennedy.
Personnel Profile: Full-Time Paid 22; Part-Time Paid 18; Part-Time Volunteers 15; Interns 1.
Governing Authority: state. Parent Institution: Dept. of Arkansas Heritage.
History Museum: built 1833-1842, first state capitol (1836-1911).
Collections: history collection; Civil War artifacts; Confederate flags; 19th-century costumes; textiles & decorative arts; Arkansas architectural drawings; wallpaper; 19th- & early 20th-century quilts by Black Arkansans; Arkansas art pottery; Arkansas political history; Arkansas music; first families of Arkansas.
Research Fields: Arkansas political & cultural history.
Facilities: 1,000-vol. library; meeting & classrooms. Museum-related items for sale.
Activities: workshops; scholarly seminars; living history interpretation; historic tours; inter-museum loan; permanent collection & traveling exhibits; formally organized activities for school groups; summer classes for children; special events for members.
Publications: brochures; newsletter, Columns; student newspaper, The Arkansas News; exhibit catalogs; exhibit books.
Hours & Admission Prices: Mon.-Sat. 9-5, Sun. 1-5. No charge; donations accepted. Closed New Year's Day; Thanksgiving; Christmas Eve & Day. ♿
Attendance: 52,866 (accurate)
Membership: Old State House Museum Associates: Basic $30; Supporting $60; Contributing $100; Sustaining $250.

PINNACLE MOUNTAIN STATE PARK, 11901 Pinnacle Valley Rd., Little Rock, AR 72223-5173. Tel.: 501-868-5806. Fax: 501-868-5018.
E-mail: pinnaclemountain@arkansas.com
Web Site: www.arkansasstateparks.com
Founded: 1977.
Congressional District: 2
Key Personnel: Supt., Ron Salley; Asst. Supt., Josh Jeffers; Ranger, Brent Launius; PASC, Alicia Brown; Park Interpreter, Susan Staffeld; Park Interpreter, James Mullins; Park Interpreter, Kristina Root; Museum Shop Mgr., Julie Leggett.
Governing Authority: state. Arkansas Dept. of Parks & Tourism, One Capitol Mall, Little Rock, AR 72201. Tax-exempt.
Environmental Education Center.
Collections: plants; vertebrates; invertebrates; geology; meteorology.
Facilities: 1,200-vol. library of textbooks and Natural Science Guides available for use on premises; classrooms; visitor center; environmental education & conservation center; picnic area; nature trails. Nature-related books, gifts & postcards for sale.
Activities: guided tours; lectures; demonstrations; films; concerts; drama; formally organized education programs; interpretative exhibits; festivals.
Publications: interpretative brochures.
Hours & Admission Prices: April-Sept. Mon.-Fri. 8-5, Sat.-Sun. 8-6; Oct.-March daily 8-5. No charge. Visitor Center closed New Year's Day; Thanksgiving; Christmas. ♿
Attendance: 515,666 (accurate)

UNIVERSITY OF ARKANSAS AT LITTLE ROCK ART DEPARTMENT GALLERY I & II & III, 2801 S. University Ave., Little Rock, AR 72204-1000. Tel.: 501-569-3182. Fax: 501-569-8775.
E-mail: becushman@ualr.edu
Web Site: ualr.edu/art/index.php/home/gallery/
Founded: 1972.
Congressional District: 2
Key Personnel: Dir., Brad Cushman; Chm. Dept. of Art, Win Bruhl; Gallery Asst., Nathan Larson.
Personnel Profile: Full-Time Paid 1; Part-Time Paid 1; Interns 2.
Governing Authority: state university; not for profit organization. Parent Institution: University of Arkansas. Tax-exempt.
University Art Gallery.
Collections: 20th-Century American photography; paintings; prints; drawings; sculpture.
Research Fields: Arkansas artists.
Facilities: 4,300 sq. ft. exhibit space; educational facilities.
Activities: lectures; loan, temporary & traveling exhibitions; gallery talks; docent tours; formally organized educational programs for UALR undergraduate & graduate students.
Publications: biannual, Calendar of Events; exhibition catalogs; postcards.
Hours & Admission Prices: May-Aug. Mon.-Fri. 9-5; other times by arrangement; Sept. to mid-May Mon.-Fri. 9-5, Sat. 10-1, Sun. 2-5. No charge. Closed spring break week; Christmas week; University holidays. ♿
Attendance: 6,000 (estimated)

WILLIAM J. CLINTON PRESIDENTIAL LIBRARY & MUSEUM, 1200 President Clinton Ave., Little Rock, AR 72201-1749. Tel.: 501-372-4242. Fax: 501-244-2883.
E-mail: clinton.library@nara.gov
Web Site: www.clintonlibrary.gov
Founded: 2001.
Key Personnel: Dir., Terri Garner; Education, Kathleen Pate; Registrar, Audra Oliver; Cur., Christine Mouw; Deputy Dir., Emily Robison; Museum Shop Mgr., Connie Fails; Security, Steve Samford.
Personnel Profile: Full-Time Paid 25; Interns 4.
Governing Authority: federal government. Parent Institution: National Archives & Records Administration, Washington, DC.
Presidential History Museum.
Collections: life & career of Bill Clinton; Presidential papers, documents & gifts; personal artifacts; photographs; replicas of the Oval Office & the Cabinet Room.
Facilities: library; restaurant; educational facilities. Museum-related items for sale.
Activities: research; special events; formal educational programs; docent program; guided tours; temporary & traveling exhibitions; acoustiguide.
Hours & Admission Prices: Mon.-Sat. 9-5, Sun. 1-5. Adults 18-61 $7, college students, retired military and senior citizens 62 & over $5, children 6-17 $3; children under 6, school groups w/reservation, active duty, military reservists, National Guard, UACS faculty & staff no charge. Closed New Year's Day; Thanksgiving; Christmas.
Attendance: 300,000 (accurate)
Membership: Individual $35; Family $50.

Malvern

HOT SPRING COUNTY MUSEUM - THE BOYLE HOUSE/1876 LOG CABIN/1868 LOG CABIN, 302 E. Third St., Malvern, AR 72104-3912. Mailing Address; 12697 Hwy. 9, Malvern, AR 72104-6323. Tel.: 501-337-4775.
E-mail: gwjwwest@hughes.net
Founded: 1981.
Congressional District: 4
Key Personnel: C.E.O., Dir. & Chm. (V), Janis West; Cur. & Business Officer, Mary Waniewski.
Personnel Profile: Part-Time Paid 4; Part-Time Volunteers 30.
Governing Authority: county. Subsidiary Institution: Magnet Cove Igneous Complex. Tax-exempt: 501(c)(3).
History Museum.
Collections: artifacts & local history items pertaining to Hot Spring County; first lady doll collection. Historic Buildings: 1892 Boyle House; 1876 log cabin; 1868 log cabin.
Research Fields: local, state & national history.
Activities: guided tours; permanent & temporary exhibitions; school tours.
Publications: brochure.
Hours & Admission Prices: Wed.-Fri. 12:30-4:30; group & school tours by appointment. No charge; donations accepted. Closed holidays. ♿
Attendance: 2,000 (estimated)
Membership: Individual $10; Family $20; Sponsor II $50; Sponsor I $100; Patron III $200; Patron II $300; Patron I $500.

Mammoth Spring

MAMMOTH SPRING STATE PARK, DEPOT MUSEUM, U.S. 63, Mammoth Spring, AR 72554-0036. Mailing Address: P.O. Box 36, Mammoth Spring, AR 72554-0036. Tel.: 870-625-7364. Fax: 870-625-3255.
E-mail: mammothspring@arkansas.com
Web Site: www.arkansasstateparks.com
Founded: 1971.
Congressional District: 1
Key Personnel: Park Supt., Dave Jackson.
Personnel Profile: Part-Time Paid 2.
Governing Authority: state. Parent Institution: Arkansas Dept. of Parks & Tourism, One Capitol Mall, Little Rock, AR 72201.
History Museum: housed in 1886 Frisco Railroad depot.
Collections: railroad memorabilia; early history of Mammoth Spring.
Facilities: picnic area; playground; nature trail.
Activities: guided tours; lectures; permanent exhibitions.
Hours & Admission Prices: Tues.-Sat. 8-5, Sun. 1-5. Adults $2.75, children 6-12 $1.50; discounts to groups of 15 or more; teachers & bus drivers no charge.
Attendance: 7,000 (estimated)

Marianna

MARIANNA-LEE COUNTY MUSEUM ASSOC. INC., 67 W. Main St., Marianna, AR 72360-2243. Mailing Address: 60 McCulloch, Marianna, AR 72360-2030. Tel.: 870-295-2439.
Founded: 1981.
Congressional District: 30
Key Personnel: Cur., Suzy Keasler.
Governing Authority: nonprofit organization. Tax-exempt: 501(c)(3).
Museum Association: housed in 1910 Marianna Elks Club.
Collections: 1835-present, implements & tools used by or made by the first settlers; 1800-1940, kitchen utensils, stoves & cabinets; musical instruments; music box; 1933 Philco radio; early Edisons; zithers, dulcimers, mandolins, horns; costumes, wedding gowns, bustle dresses; needlework; flapper dresses; shoes; Indian artifacts. Historic Building: 1880 one-room schoolhouse.
Activities: lectures; films; permanent & temporary exhibitions.
Publications: quarterly newsletter, Museings.
Hours & Admission Prices: Mon.-Sat. by appointment. No charge; donations accepted. Closed major holidays.
Membership: Student $2.50; Individual $5; Family $7.50; Sustaining $10; Donor $25; Patron, Institutional or Corporate $50 & up; Life $250.

Marked Tree

MARKED TREE DELTA AREA MUSEUM, 308 Frisco St., Marked Tree, AR 72365. Mailing Address: P.O. Box 72, Marked Tree, AR 72365-0072. Tel.: 870-358-4998.
History Museum.
Collections: local history & culture; American Indian pottery; early 1900s telephones; hospital replica; general store.
Hours & Admission Prices: Wed.-Fri. 1-4:30, Sat. 9:30-12:30, Sun. 1-4.

Maynard

MAYNARD PIONEER MUSEUM & PARK, Hwy. 328 W., Maynard, AR 72444. Mailing Address: P.O. Box 486, Maynard, AR 72444-0486. Tel.: 870-647-2701.
Key Personnel: Chm., Bill Eagle
History Museum.
Collections: Randolph County history; period furnishings; photographs; documents; newspaper clippings; personal artifacts.
Facilities: Museum-related items for sale.
Activities: festivals. Annual Event: Pioneer Days in September.
Hours & Admission Prices: May-Oct. 1 Tues.-Sat. 10-3. No charge; donations accepted. Closed Memorial Day.

McNeil

LOGOLY STATE PARK, County Rd. 47 (Logoly Rd.), McNeil, AR 71752. Mailing Address: P.O. Box 245, McNeil, AR 71752-0245. Tel.: 870-695-3561. Fax: 870-695-3729.
E-mail: logoly@arkansas.com
Web Site: www.arkansasstateparks.com
Founded: 1978.
Congressional District: 4
Key Personnel: Supt., Jim Gann; Interpretive Naturalist, Barley Park; Museum Shop Mgr., Pat Swearingen.
Personnel Profile: Full-Time Paid 5; Part-Time Paid 2.
Governing Authority: state; nonprofit. Affiliated with Arkansas Dept. of Parks & Tourism. Tax-exempt.
Park Museum & Nature Center.
Collections: specimens of native wildlife.
Research Fields: environmental education; history of park area.
Facilities: nature center; theater; classrooms; picnic area; nature trails; amphitheater. Gift items for sale.
Activities: guided tours; special events; films; formally organized education programs; camping.
Publications: newsletter, Friends of Logoly; self-guided trail brochure.
Hours & Admission Prices: Park: daily 8am to one hour after sunset. Visitors Center: May-Oct. daily 8-5; Nov.-April Mon.-Fri. 8-5, Sat.-Sun. 1-5. No charge. ♿
Attendance: 25,000 (accurate)

Monticello

DREW COUNTY HISTORICAL MUSEUM, 404 S. Main, Monticello, AR 71655-4818. Tel.: 870-367-7446.
Web Site: www.arkansasroots.com
Founded: 1970.
Congressional District: 4
Key Personnel: Dir., Sheilla Lampkin.
Personnel Profile: Part-Time Paid 4; Part-Time Volunteers 1; Interns 1.
Governing Authority: society. Parent Institution: Drew County Historical Society. Tax-exempt.
History Museum.
Collections: local historical objects; textiles; furniture; Indian artifacts; clothing; war memorabilia; quilts & spinning artifacts.
Research Fields: early Drew County history; Civil War; Indian archaeology.
Facilities: archives.
Activities: classes; special visitor tours.
Publications: monthly, Society and Museum Notes; annual journal.
Hours & Admission Prices: Fri. 1-5, Sat.-Sun. 2-5. No charge; donations accepted. Closed New Year's Day; Thanksgiving; Christmas. ♿
Attendance: 2,500 (estimated)
Membership: Individual (with yearly Journal) $25; Couple $40; Friends $100-$299.99; Associate $300-$499.99; Patron $500-$999.99; Benefactor $1,000 & up.

Morrilton

THE MUSEUM OF AUTOMOBILES, Petit Jean Mountain, 8 Jones Lane, Morrilton, AR 72110-9353. Tel.: 501-727-5427. Fax: 501-727-6482.
E-mail: info@museumofautos.com
Web Site: www.museumofautos.com
Founded: 1964.
Congressional District: 2
Key Personnel: Dir., Buddy Hoelzeman; Pres. (V), Raymond Harrill.
Personnel Profile: Full-Time Paid 3; Part-Time Paid 9.
Governing Authority: nonprofit organization. Tax-exempt: 501(c)(3).
Antique Automobile Museum.
Collections: antique & classic automobiles on loan from collectors.
Facilities: Auto-related items for sale.
Activities: Museum Sponsors: Antique Auto Shows & Swap Meets in June and September.

Hours & Admission Prices: Daily 10-5. Adults $7, seniors 65 & over $6.50, children 6-17 $3.50; discounts for groups of 15 & over; members & children under 6 with parents no charge. Closed Christmas Day. ♿
Attendance: 16,000 (accurate)
Membership: Member $25; Participating $35; Friend $50; Associate $100; Sustaining $250; Contributing $500; Patron $1,000.

Mount Ida

HERITAGE HOUSE MUSEUM OF MONTGOMERY COUNTY, 819 Luzerne St., Mount Ida, AR 71957. Mailing Address: P.O. Box 1362, Mount Ida, AR 71957-1362. Tel.: 870-867-4422.
E-mail: museum@hhmmc.org
Web Site: hhmmc.org
Founded: 1999.
Congressional District: 4
Key Personnel: Dir., Emilie Kinney; Pres. (V) & Museum Shop Mgr., Betty Prince; Treas., Richard Ray.
Personnel Profile: Full-Time Paid 1; Part-Time Volunteers 35.
Governing Authority: private; nonprofit organization. Tax-exempt: 501(c)(3).
History Museum.
Collections: minerals: crystals, mining minerals; papers; photos; Montgomery County artifacts; family history; the building & impact of Lake Quachita; Montgomery County churches.
Research Fields: genealogy of Montgomery County families; county businesses; mining & timber industry; building of Lake Ouachita; Ouachita National Forest.
Facilities: 50-vol. library; 2,500 sq. ft. exhibit space; meeting room. Museum-related items for sale.
Activities: formal education programs for children; guided tours; lectures; temporary exhibitions. Annual Events: Veterans Day Celebration; Arkansas Heritage Month Activity.
Publications: quarterly newsletter; weekly newspaper column, Museum Corner.
Hours & Admission Prices: Mon.-Wed. & Fri. 9-4, Sat.-Sun. 1-4. No charge; donations accepted. Closed New Years Eve & Day; Thanksgiving Eve & Day; Christmas Eve & Day. ♿
Attendance: 1,550 (estimated)
Membership: Member $25; Patron $100; Benefactor & Corporate $200.

Mountain View

THE OZARK FOLK CENTER, 1032 Park Ave., Mountain View, AR 72560-6008. Tel.: 870-269-3851. Fax: 870-269-2909.
E-mail: ozarkfolkcenter@arkansas.com
Founded: 1973.
Congressional District: 1
Key Personnel: Lodge Mgr., Iona Barham; Accountant, Mary A. Smith; Public Information Officer, Jimmy Edwards; Museum Shop Mgr., Wanda Baird.
Personnel Profile: Full-Time Paid 23; Part-Time Paid 275; Part-Time Volunteers 200.
Governing Authority: state. Parent Institution: Arkansas Dept. of Parks and Tourism.
Folk Arts Center.
Collections: traditional crafts of the Ozark Mountain region; artifacts; manuscripts; pre-1920 sheet music; early Ozark life; recordings; field recordings of Ozark folklore; interview transcripts.
Research Fields: Ozark crafts and music.
Facilities: 20,000-vol. library of books, recordings, vertical files related to Ozark Mountain Heritage emphasizing homecrafts & music; reading room; conference center; 1,000-seat auditorium with recording studio; restaurant. Books on crafts & music, records & craft items made in Ozarks for sale.
Activities: concerts; craft & music workshops; live performance of traditional crafts & music, 1840-1940; permanent & temporary exhibitions.
Publications: brochures; workshop newsletter; special event calendar.
Hours & Admission Prices: Craft Village: mid-April to Sept. Wed.-Sat. 10-5; Oct. Tues.-Sun. 10-5. Music Theater: mid-April to Sept. Wed.-Sat. 7:30 pm; Oct.- Tues.-Sat. 7:30 pm. Music or Craft Forum: adults $10, children $6; discount to groups. Daily Combo, 3-Day, Season Tickets, & Family Passes available. ♿
Attendance: 160,000 (estimated)

Murfreesboro

CRATER OF DIAMONDS STATE PARK MUSEUM, 209 State Park Road, Murfreesboro, AR 71958-8947. Tel.: 870-285-3113. Fax: 870-285-4169.
E-mail: crater@arkansas.com
Web Site: www.craterofdiamondsstatepark.com
Founded: 1972.
Congressional District: 4
Key Personnel: Asst. Supt., Bill Henderson; Park Ranger, Matt Briley; Gift Shop Mgr., Patricia Thomas; Park Interpreter, Waymon Cox; Park Interpreter, Margaret Jenks.
Personnel Profile: Full-Time Paid 15; Part-Time Paid 33.
Governing Authority: state. Parent Institution: Department of Parks & Tourism, One Capitol Mall, Little Rock, AR 72201. Tel.: 501-682-7777. Tax-exempt.
Park Interpretative Museum.
Collections: diamonds; semi-precious rocks & minerals; old photos; old records of past diamond mining; modern geology displays; picture displays of past mining of diamonds.
Research Fields: geology & history of Crater of Diamonds State Park area.
Facilities: indoor theater; picnic area; campground; seasonal restaurant; visitors center; amphitheater; Diamond Discovery Center; water park. Gift items for sale.
Activities: guided tours available on advance notice & reservation; interpretative programs.
Hours & Admission Prices: Memorial Day-Labor Day daily 8-8; Sept.-May daily 8-5. Park: no charge. Diamond Mine: adults $7, children 6-12 $4; discounts to groups of 15 or more; children under 6 no charge. Closed New Year's Day; Thanksgiving; Christmas. ♿
Attendance: 154,609 (accurate)

KA-DO-HA INDIAN VILLAGE MUSEUM, 1010 Caddo Dr., Murfreesboro, AR 71958. Mailing Address: P.O. Box 669, Murfreesboro, AR 71958-0669. Tel.: 870-285-3736. Fax: 870-285-4118.
E-mail: caddotc@alltel.net
Web Site: www.caddotc.com
Founded: 1964.
Key Personnel: Owner & Public Rels. Dir., Sam Johnson; Business Officer, Cur. & Gift Shop Mgr., Karen Bush.
Governing Authority: individual operation.
Archaeology Museum: housed on 1,000 A.D. Moundbuilder Village & ceremonial center.
Collections: Indian artifacts from the site as well as other areas.
Research Fields: archaeology.
Facilities: Archaeological books relating to the Moundbuilders & museum-related items for sale.
Activities: guided tours; gallery talks; permanent exhibitions.
Hours & Admission Prices: Summer: daily 9-6; Winter: daily 9-5. Adults $4, children 6-13 $2. Closed Thanksgiving; Christmas Day.

Newport

ARNETT'S DOLL MUSEUM, 2001-B Eastern Ave., Newport, AR 72112-4702. Tel.: 870-523-2194.
Doll Museum.
Collections: over 5,000 dolls.
Hours & Admission Prices: Call for hours.

North Little Rock

ARKANSAS NATIONAL GUARD MUSEUM, Lloyd England Hall, Camp Robinson, North Little Rock, AR 72199-0001. Tel.: 501-212-5215. Fax: 501-212-5228.
E-mail: steve.rucker@ar.ngb.army.mil
Web Site: www.arngmuseum.com
Military Museum.
Collections: history of Arkansas National Guard, Camp Pike & Camp Robinson.
Hours & Admission Prices: Mon.-Fri. 8-3, 1st Sat.-Sun. of month 8-3; call to confirm.

Paris

ARKANSAS HISTORIC WINE MUSEUM, 101 N. Carbon City Rd., Paris, AR 72855-4630. Tel.: 479-963-3990.
E-mail: cowie@cswnet.com
Web Site: www.cowiewinecellars.com
Founded: 1967.
Congressional District: 3
Key Personnel: Dir. (V), Robert G. Cowie.
Personnel Profile: Part-Time Volunteers 3.
Governing Authority: private; nonprofit organization. Tax-exempt: 501(c)(3).
Historic Wine Museum: housed at Cowie Wine Cellars three miles west of Paris.
Collections: concentration on history of bonded wineries in Arkansas; the life & work of Professor Joseph Bachman; the history of home wine making; wine making equipment; small tools; photographs; papers; educational displays.
Research Fields: the history of wine making in Arkansas.
Facilities: 1,750 sq. ft. exhibit space.

Activities: guided tours; lectures. Annual Events: Wine fest in mid-September; Heritage Day on first Saturday in May.
Hours & Admission Prices: Mon.-Sat. 10-6, Sun. 12-6. Adults $1. ♿
Attendance: 3,200 (estimated)
Membership: Individual $20; Family $30; Contributor $50; Patron $75; Sponsor $100; Sustainer $250; Benefactor $500.

LOGAN COUNTY MUSEUM, 202 N. Vine St., Paris, AR 72855-3222. Tel.: 479-963-3936. Fax: 479-963-3936.
Founded: 1972.
Congressional District: 3
Key Personnel: Admin., Jeanne S. Reynolds; Pres. (V), Dan Gray.
Personnel Profile: Part-Time Paid 1; Part-Time Volunteers 20.
Governing Authority: Logan County Museum Association. Tax-exempt.
History Museum: housed in 1886 former Logan County Jail.
Collections: local history.
Activities: guided tours; arts festivals; group tours & activities; living history; educational programs. Museum Sponsors: Independence Day Program; Christmas Tour of Homes.
Publications: newsletter.
Hours & Admission Prices: Tues.-Sat. 12-4. No charge; donations accepted. Closed most federal holidays. ♿
Attendance: 3,000
Membership: Single $15; Couple $25.

Piggott

HEMINGWAY-PFEIFFER MUSEUM AND EDUCATIONAL CENTER, (M), 1021 W. Cherry St., Piggott, AR 72454-1419. Tel.: 870-598-3487. Fax: 870-598-1037.
Founded: 1999.
Congressional District: 1
Key Personnel: Asst. Dir. & Facilities Mgr., Dr. Ruth Hawkins; Asst. Dir. & Facilities Mgr., Diana Sanders; Education Coord., Deanna Dismukes; Administrative Asst., Johnna Redman; Tour Guide & Housekeeper, Karen Trout.
Governing Authority: Parent Institution: Arkansas State University.
Historic House & Barn: listed on the National Historic Register.
Collections: family history; period literature; 1930s world events; agriculture; Northeast Arkansas history; furnishings; Ernest Hemingway timeline.
Facilities: Museum-related items for sale.
Activities: group tours.
Publications: Friends of the Pfeiffer's News.
Hours & Admission Prices: Mon.-Fri. 9-4, Sat. 1-3. Suggested donation: adults $5, seniors $3. Closed New Year's Eve & Day; Memorial Day; Labor Day; Thanksgiving; Christmas Eve & Day. ♿
Attendance: 3,170
Membership: Student $10-$24; Individual $25-$49; Family $50-$99; Century Club $100-$249; Heritage Club $500-$999; Presidents' Council $1,000-$4,999; Corporate Partner $5,000-$9,999; Museum Benefactor $10,000 & up.

Pine Bluff

ARKANSAS ENTERTAINERS HALL OF FAME, One Convention Center Plaza, Pine Bluff, AR 71601-5067. Tel.: 870-536-7660. Fax: 870-850-2105.
E-mail: pbinfo@pinebluff.com
Web Site: www.arkansasentertainershalloffame.com
Founded: 1996.
Congressional District: 4
Hall of Fame.
Collections: Hall of Fame inductees; personal artifacts; photographs.
Hours & Admission Prices: Mon.-Fri. 9-5, Sat.-Sun. call for hours. No charge; donations accepted. ♿
Attendance: 25,000 (estimated)

ARKANSAS RAILROAD MUSEUM, 1700 Port Rd., Pine Bluff, AR 71601-4663. Mailing Address: P.O. Box 2044, Pine Bluff, AR 71613-2044.
Founded: 1983.
Personnel Profile: Part-Time Volunteers 20.
Governing Authority: Parent Institution: Cotton Belt Rail Historical Society, Inc.
Railroad Museum.
Collections: Engine #336, Baldwin 2-6-0; Engine 819; railroad memorabilia; period artifacts.
Publications: quarterly newsletter, Cotton Belt Star.
Hours & Admission Prices: Mon.-Sat. 9-3. No charge; donations accepted. ♿
Attendance: 12,000 (estimated)
Membership: Annual $25.

* **THE ARTS & SCIENCE CENTER FOR SOUTHEAST ARKANSAS, (M),** 701 Main St., Pine Bluff, AR 71601-4903. Tel.: 870-536-3375. Fax: 870-536-3380.
E-mail: info@artssciencecenter.org
Web Site: www.artssciencecenter.org
Founded: 1968.
Congressional District: 4
Key Personnel: Exec. Dir., Janelle Powell; Chm., Patrick Anderson; Chm. (V), Sammye Owen; Chm. (V), Mary Shannon Fikes; Cur. Education, Elise Askew; Mgr. Operations, Rebekah Ray; Facilities Mgr., Charles Isgrig; Receptionist, Kathy Brabsten.
Personnel Profile: Full-Time Paid 4; Part-Time Paid 4; Part-Time Volunteers 125.
Governing Authority: municipal. Tax-exempt: 170(b)(1)(A).
Arts Cultural Center.
Collections: 19th-century European paintings; 20th-century American paintings & prints; John Howard Memorial collection of African-American artists; Arkansas artists; Elsie Mistie Sterling collection of botanical paintings; Delta region paintings & photos.
Major Exhibits: Works of Robyn Horn, 11/09-1/10; The Science of Illusion (T), 11/09-3/10; Africa Unmasked, 12/09-2/10; Work of Jim Hill, 3/10-4/10; Irene Rosenzweig Biennial, 4/10-6/10; Small Works on Paper (T), 7/10-8/10; Pine Bluff Art League, 8/10-10/10; Science & Art (T), 8/10-11/10.
Research Fields: 19th- & 20th-century art.
Facilities: 100-vol. library of reference books available by special request letter; theater; classrooms.
Activities: guided tours; films; gallery talks; concerts; dance recitals; arts festivals; drama; workshops; rental gallery; formally organized education programs; docent program or council; inter-museum loan & traveling exhibitions.
Publications: subscription brochures; quarterly newsletters; invitations; monthly calendar of events; catalogs for exhibitions; annual report; traveling exhibition service.
Hours & Admission Prices: Mon.-Fri. 10-5, Sat. 1-4. No charge; donations accepted. Closed New Year's Day; Easter; Independence Day; Thanksgiving; Christmas Eve & Day. ♿
Attendance: 37,595 (estimated)
Membership: Individual $35; Family $50; Supporter $75; Contributing $125; Patrons $250; Fellow $500; Sponsor $750; Benefactor $1,000; Philanthropist $2,000.

THE BAND MUSEUM, 423 Main St., Pine Bluff, AR 71601-4325. Tel.: 870-534-4676. Fax: 870-541-0350.
E-mail: bandmuseum@hotmail.com
Web Site: bandmuseum.org
Founded: 1994.
Key Personnel: C.E.O., Jerry G. Horne.
Personnel Profile: Full-Time Paid 1; Full-Time Volunteers 1; Part-Time Paid 1; Part-Time Volunteers 1.
Governing Authority: private; nonprofit organization. Tax-exempt: 501(c)(3).
Musical Instruments Museum.
Collections: band instruments from antiquity to 1950.
Facilities: library; 200-seat auditorium; soda fountain. Museum-related items for sale.
Hours & Admission Prices: Mon.-Fri. 10-4, Sat-Sun. by appointment only. No charge; donations accepted. ♿
Attendance: 7,500 (accurate)
Membership: Member $25; 1st Chair $50; Section Leader $100; Soloist $500.

LEEDEL MOOREHEAD-GRAHAM FINE ARTS GALLERY, 1200 N. University, Pine Bluff, AR 71601-2799. Mailing Address: Mail Slot 4925, Pine Bluff, AR 71601. Tel.: 870-575-8236. Fax: 870-575-4636.
E-mail: gaines_c@uapb.edu
Web Site: www.uapb.edu
Founded: 1967.
Congressional District: 4
Key Personnel: Chm., Henri Linton.
Personnel Profile: Part-Time Paid 2.
Governing Authority: public university. Parent Institution: University of Arkansas at Pine Bluff, Pine Bluff, AR. Tax-exempt: 501(c)(3.
Art Museum.
Collections: African American art; history of African Americans in Arkansas; photographs.
Facilities: 3,360 sq. ft. exhibit space.
Activities: loan, traveling & temporary exhibitions; student & faculty exhibitions.
Hours & Admission Prices: Mon.-Fri. 8:30-4:30. No charge. Closed school holidays.
Attendance: 5,000 (estimated)

PINE BLUFF/JEFFERSON COUNTY HISTORICAL MUSEUM, (M), 201 E. 4th, Pine Bluff, AR 71601-4401. Tel.: 870-541-5402. Fax: 870-541-5405.
Web Site: www.pbjc.org
Founded: 1980.
Congressional District: 4
Key Personnel: Dir., Sue Trulock; Cur., Lola Gordon; Mgr. Collections, Rebecca Phillips.
Personnel Profile: Full-Time Paid 2; Part-Time Paid 1; Part-Time Volunteers 21.
Governing Authority: nonprofit organization. Tax-exempt: 501(c)(3).
History Museum: located in the restored Union Depot, built in 1906. Exhibits in keeping with the history of Pine Bluff & Jefferson County.
Collections: artifacts that help in teaching & illustrating the history, culture & lifestyles of Jefferson County; American Indian pottery & artifacts; farm implements; Civil War artifacts; clothing from the Edwardian period; household items; room setting; historical photographs; documentary items; artifacts are from families in Jefferson county; dolls, 1870-1950.
Major Exhibits: History in Battles, 12/09-12/30/10; History of Black Schools in Pine Bluff, 1/1/10-1/11/11.
Research Fields: local history.
Activities: loan & temporary exhibitions; school loan service.
Publications: quarterly newsletters.
Hours & Admission Prices: Winter: Mon.-Fri. 9-4; Summer: Mon.-Fri. 9-5, Sat. 10-2. No charge. Closed legal holidays. ♿
Attendance: 11,000 (accurate)
Membership: Individual $10; Family $15; Contributing $50; Supporting $100; Benefactor $500.

Pine Ridge

LUM & ABNER MUSEUM & JOT 'EM DOWN STORE, 4562 Hwy. 88 W., General Delivery, Pine Ridge, AR 71961-8056. Tel.: 870-326-4442. Fax: 870-326-4539.
E-mail: nlstucker@earthlink.net
Web Site: lum-abner.com
Founded: 1971.
Congressional District: 50
Key Personnel: Co-Dir. & Owner, Noah Lon Stucker; Co-Dir. & Owner, Kathryn Moore Stucker.
Governing Authority: individual operation.
History Museum: housed in c.1904 general merchandise store, on which the Lum & Abner radio program 1931-55 was based.
Collections: photographs & literature from the careers of Lum & Abner; radio tapes; merchandise & dry goods from that era; tools; appliances; clothing; furnishings; radio history books; letters; awards; scripts; posters & advertisements; newspaper articles.
Research Fields: local history as it relates to Lum & Abner, compares to small communities all over the country (school, customs, farming, economy, stores, etc.).
Facilities: Gift items for sale.
Activities: guided tours; radio programs; permanent exhibitions. Affiliated activity-National Lum & Abner Society Convention in June.
Publications: pamphlets; booklets, Lum & Abner's Almanac; Pine Ridge News; Lum & Abner & Their Friends; Hello, This is Lum & Abner-A History of Pine Ridge and Lum & Abner.
Hours & Admission Prices: March-Oct. Tues.-Sat. 9-5, Sun. 12-5; other times by appointment. No charge; donations accepted.

Pocahontas

RANDOLPH COUNTY HERITAGE MUSEUM, 106 E. Everett St., Pocahontas, AR 72455-3309. Tel.: 970-892-4056.
E-mail: heritagemuseum@centurytel.net
Web Site: www.randolphcomuseum.org
Key Personnel: Pres. (V), Museum Admin., & Museum Shop Mgr., Karen Parish; Chm. (V), Bill Carroll.
Personnel Profile: Part-Time Volunteers 9.
Governing Authority: Parent Institution: Five Rivers Historic Preservation. Tax-exempt.
Historical Museum.
Collections: Randolph County history; personal artifacts; photographs.
Hours & Admission Prices: Mon., Wed. & Fri. 10-4. No charge; donations accepted.

Pottsville

POTTS INN MUSEUM, Town Square, Pottsville, AR 72801. Mailing Address: 6368 SR 247, Pottsville, AR 72858-8952. Tel.: 479-968-8369.
Founded: 1978.
Congressional District: 3
Key Personnel: Chm. Bd., Charles Oates; Bd. Member, Lois Morris; Sec., Mary Baker; Bd. Member, Rebecca Stowers; Treas., Bert Page.
Personnel Profile: Full-Time Volunteers 2; Part-Time Volunteers 16.
Governing Authority: county; nonprofit. Affiliated with the Pope County Historical Foundation. Tax-exempt.
Preservation Project: housed in 1850-1858 nine-room home & stage stop of Kirkbride Potts.
Collections: Potts family period artifacts; 100 years of ladies' hats; period furniture; gifts of first settlers. Historic Buildings: milk house; doctor's office; implement barn; c.1827 one-room log cabin.
Activities: guided tours; TV & radio programs; formally organized education programs for children & undergraduate college students affiliated with Arkansas Technical University; permanent exhibitions.
Hours & Admission Prices: Wed.-Sun. 1-5. Adults $3, children $1; discounts to AAM members.
Attendance: 1,900 (estimated)

Prairie Grove

PRAIRIE GROVE BATTLEFIELD STATE PARK, 506 E. Douglas St., Prairie Grove, AR 72753-2731. Tel.: 479-846-2990. Fax: 479-846-4035.
E-mail: prairiegrove@arkansas.com
Web Site: www.arkansasstateparks.com/prairiegrovebattlefield/
Founded: 1957.
Congressional District: 3
Key Personnel: Supt., Jesse Cox; Registrar, Alan Thompson; Museum Shop Mgr., Holly Cherry.
Personnel Profile: Full-Time Paid 7; Part-Time Paid 4; Part-Time Volunteers 4.
Governing Authority: state. Arkansas Dept. of Parks & Tourism.
Civil War Park Museum: located on site of Dec. 7, 1862, Battle of Prairie Grove.
Collections: Civil War artifacts; period furniture; Civil War documents; Civil War & middle 19th-century Ozark Arkansas cultural exhibits; historic buildings; Pioneer Village.
Facilities: library; information center; picnic grounds. Gifts for sale.
Activities: guided tours; arts festivals; audio-visual programs; living history demonstrations; automobile driving tour; walking trail.
Publications: The Effect of the Civil War on Ozark Culture.
Hours & Admission Prices: Daily 8-5. Adults $3, children $2; discounts to groups of 20 or more with appointment; children under 6 no charge. Closed New Year's Day; Thanksgiving; Christmas Eve & Day. ♿
Attendance: 200,000 (accurate)

Prescott

NEVADA COUNTY DEPOT MUSEUM, 403 W. First St. S., Prescott, AR 71857-2067. Tel.: 870-887-5821.
E-mail: online@depotmuseum.org
Web Site: www.depotmuseum.org
Key Personnel: Cur., David Sesser
History Museum.
Collections: Nevada County history; early settlements & settlers; Indian pottery; Civil War; agriculture; railroads; fire fighting equipment; Louisiana Purchase, April 1803.
Activities: tours.
Hours & Admission Prices: Tues.-Sat. 9-5; groups by appointment.

Rison

PIONEER VILLAGE, Mocking Bird Lane &Yaney Dr., Rison, AR 71665. Mailing Address: P.O. Box 134, Rison, AR 71665-0134. Tel.: 870-325-7289.
E-mail: sblisemby@tds.net
Founded: 1976.
Congressional District: 4
Key Personnel: Pres., Lee Moore; Dir., Betty Lisemby; Asst., Dena James.
Governing Authority: society. Affiliated with the Pioneer Village Inc., Rison, AR 71665. Tax-exempt.
Pioneer History Village Museum.
Collections: artifacts pertaining to the history of the County.
Facilities: 125-seat auditorium. Antique bottles, handmade craft items & reproductions for sale.
Activities: guided tours; craft festivals; hobby workshops. Museum Sponsors: Pioneer Craft Festival.
Hours & Admission Prices: March 4th Sat. Adults $1; children under 10 no charge. ♿
Attendance: 4,000 (estimated)

Roger

HOBBS PARK VISITOR CENTER, 21392 E. Hwy. 12, Roger, AR 72756-8183. Mailing Address: P.O. Box 709, Rogers, AR 72757-0709. Tel.: 479-789-2380.
Park Museum & Visitor Center.
Collections: local history; wildlife; natural science; trees; plants; flowers.
Facilities: nature trails; classrooms. Museum-related items for sale.
Activities: educational programs; hiking.
Hours & Admission Prices: Call for hours.

Rogers

ROGERS DAISY AIRGUN MUSEUM, 202 W. Walnut St., Rogers, AR 72756-6665. Tel.: 479-986-6873. Fax: 479-986-6875.
E-mail: info@daisymuseum.com
Web Site: www.daisymuseum.com
Formerly: Daisy International Air Gun Museum
Founded: 2000.
Congressional District: 3
Governing Authority: nonprofit organization.
Air Gun Museum.
Collections: air guns & toy guns.
Publications: brochure, It's a Daisy.
Hours & Admission Prices: Mon.-Sat. 9-5. Adults $2; children 16 & under no charge. Closed major holidays. ♿
Membership: Life $50.

* **ROGERS HISTORICAL MUSEUM, (M),** 322 S. Second St., Rogers, AR 72756-4512. Tel.: 479-621-1154. Fax: 479-621-1155.
E-mail: museum@rogersarkansas.com
Web Site: www.rogersarkansas.com/museum
Founded: 1975.
Congressional District: 3
Key Personnel: C.E.O. & Dir., Gaye K. Bland; Asst. Dir., John Burroughs; Chm. (V), Mike Whitmore; Collections Asst., Jennifer Sweet; Cur. Collections, Terrilyn Wendling; Office Mgr., Pat Campbell; Cur. Education, Janet Hargus; Education Asst., Jessica Whitehead; Adult Programs Asst., Monte Harris; Guide, Robert Rousey.
Personnel Profile: Full-Time Paid 7; Part-Time Paid 4; Part-Time Volunteers 40.
Governing Authority: municipal; nonprofit. Parent Institution: City of Rogers. Tax-exempt.
Historical Building: c.1895 five-room Hawkins House; local history museum.
Collections: local history; Frisco Railroad; Apple Blossom Festival; Coin Harvey, Betty Blake (Mrs. Will) Rogers; quilts; Victorian Period.
Major Exhibits: Rogers Auto Biography, 1/10-12/11; The Civil War: A Nation Divided (T), 6/10; Buried Dreams: Coin Harvey & Montene, 6/10-12/11.
Research Fields: local history; Benton County history; Victorian Period.
Facilities: 1,000 sq. ft. Hawkins House; 5,600 sq. ft. Key Wing containing exhibit galleries & workroom; 6,600 sq. ft. Education Annex.
Activities: guided tours; lectures; organized education programs for children; loan, permanent & temporary exhibitions. Museum Sponsors: Annual Holiday Open House.
Publications: quarterly newsletter, The Friendly Note.
Hours & Admission Prices: Tues.-Sat. 10-4. No charge; donations accepted. Closed major holidays. ♿
Attendance: 15,836 (accurate)
Membership: Individual $10; Family $15; Sponsor $25; Patron $50; Benefactor $100; Endowment $500.

WAR EAGLE CAVERN, 21494 Cavern Rd., Rogers, AR 72756-7493. Tel.: 479-789-2909.
Geology Museum.
Collections: local history & geology.
Facilities: nature trails. Museum-related items for sale.
Activities: hiking; panning; school groups.
Hours & Admission Prices: Mon.-Sat. 9:30-5, Sun. 12-5. Adults $10.50, children 4-11 $5.75; children 3 & under no charge.

Russellville

ARKANSAS RIVER VALLEY ARTS CENTER, 1001 E. B St., Russellville, AR 72801-4252. Mailing Address: P.O. Box 2112, Russellville, AR 72811-2112. Tel.: 479-968-2452.
Founded: 1981.
Key Personnel: Exec. Dir., Betty LaGrone; Admin. Asst., Erica Smith; Teaching Artist, Winston J. Taylor
Art Gallery.
Collections: photographs; paintings.
Facilities: Museum-related items for sale.
Activities: summer art camp; classes; workshops.
Hours & Admission Prices: Mon.-Thurs. 10-5, Fri. 10-4; other times by appointment. No charge. Closed national holidays. ♿
Membership: Students & Seniors $20; Individual $35; Family $50.

ARKANSAS TECH UNIVERSITY MUSEUM, (M), 1502 N. El Paso Ave./Techionery, Russellville, AR 72801-8816. Tel.: 479-964-0826. Fax: 479-964-0872.
Web Site: www.atu.edu/museum
Formerly: Arkansas Tech University Museum of Prehistory and History
Founded: 1989.
Congressional District: 3
Key Personnel: Museum Dir., Judith C. Stewart-Abernathy; Education Coord., Theresa Jureka Johnson; Collections Mgr., Donna Park.
Personnel Profile: Full-Time Paid 1; Part-Time Paid 8; Part-Time Volunteers 1; Interns 1.
Governing Authority: public university; nonprofit. Parent Institution: Arkansas Tech University.
History Museum.
Collections: archaeological; historical; archival.
Major Exhibits: Art and Architecture: Student Exhibition, 3/10-4/10.
Research Fields: history of ATU; establishment, development & history of agriculture school; university students & staff history; prehistory & history of Native American groups indigenous to our region; treaty relations of Native American peoples through our region; Presbyterian Native American boarding school (Dwight Mission) in our area 1820-1828; local regional history; local regional history.
Facilities: 850-vol. library; 25-seat lecture hall; educational facilities; classroom; 2,000 sq. ft. exhibit space; research room. Museum-related items for sale.
Activities: guided tours; teaching lectures. Museum Sponsors: Open House events; Series of Discovery evening lecture & performance programs; exhibit openings.
Publications: Discovery Handbook, all copies sold.
Hours & Admission Prices: Tues.-Thurs. 9-4; other times by appointment. No charge; donations accepted. Closed during university breaks. ♿
Attendance: 6,000 (estimated)

Scott

PLANTATION AGRICULTURE MUSEUM, 4815 Hwy. 161, Scott, AR 72142. Mailing Address: P.O. Box 87, Scott, AR 72142-0087. Tel.: 501-961-1409. Fax: 501-961-1579.
E-mail: plantationagrimuseum@arkansas.com
Web Site: www.arkansasstateparks.com
Founded: 1989.
Congressional District: 2
Key Personnel: Dir., Ben H. Swadley; Cur., Randy Noah; Museum Interpreter, Linda Goza; Museum Shop Mgr., Beverly Long.
Personnel Profile: Full-Time Paid 5; Part-Time Paid 2; Interns 1.
Governing Authority: state. Parent Institution: Arkansas Dept. of Parks & Tourism, Arkansas State Parks, 1 Capitol Mall, Little Rock, AR 72201. Subsidiary Institution: Historical Resources & Museum Services; Region II. Tax-exempt.
History Museum: housed in c.1912 general store.
Collections: tools; equipment; machinery; photographs related to cotton agriculture & plantation life in Arkansas from 1836 until World War II.
Research Fields: cotton agriculture & plantation life in Arkansas from 1836 until World War II.
Facilities: exhibit wing; educational facilities; outdoor exhibit area. Museum-related items for sale.
Activities: tours; exhibitions; special events; 10,000 sq. ft. non-public collection management facility.
Publications: quarterly, Boll Weevil Newsletter.
Hours & Admission Prices: Mon. holidays & Tues.-Sat. 8-5, Sun. 1-5. Adults $3, adult groups of 15 or more $2.75, children 6-12 & school groups $2; discounts to families. Closed New Year's; Thanksgiving; Christmas Eve & Day. ♿
Attendance: 7,200 (estimated)

Sheridan

GRANT COUNTY MUSEUM, 521 Shackleford Rd., Sheridan, AR 72150-7074. Tel.: 870-942-4496.
E-mail: museum4@windstream.net
Founded: 1970.
Congressional District: 4
Key Personnel: Chm. (V), Mary Beth Glover-Wilson; Dir., D.J. Wallace; Financial Dir., Noka Emerson; Magazine Editor, Pat Lucas.
Personnel Profile: Full-Time Paid 3; Part-Time Paid 1.
Governing Authority: county; nonprofit. Tax-exempt.

History Museum.
Collections: history of Arkansas with emphasis on Grant County, Arkansas from prehistoric to present; Civil War artifacts; World War II artifacts & vehicles; archives; photographs; Indian relics; pioneer life; restored buildings including log cabins, church, cafe, corn crib & Victorian house.
Facilities: library containing genealogical material; family research reports; microfilm records & newspaper articles available to the public.
Activities: guided tours; formally organized education programs. Annual Events: Christmas Tour of Homes & Festive Programs.
Publications: historical journal, Grassroots, published three times annually.
Hours & Admission Prices: Tues.-Sat. 9-12 & 1-4; other times by appointment. No charge; donations accepted. Closed legal holidays. ♿
Attendance: 10,000 (estimated)
Membership: Individual $12; Family $15; Supporting $25; Patron $50; Sponsor $100; Life $500; Bless You $1,000.

Siloam Springs

SILOAM SPRINGS MUSEUM, (M), 112 N. Maxwell, Siloam Springs, AR 72761-3174. Mailing Address: P.O. Box 1164, Siloam Springs, AR 72761-1164. Tel.: 479-524-4011.
E-mail: ssmuseum@centurytel.net
Web Site: www.siloamspringsmuseum.com
Founded: 1969.
Congressional District: 3
Key Personnel: Dir. & C.E.O., Donald Warden; Pres. (V), Bill Osgood.
Personnel Profile: Full-Time Paid 2; Part-Time Volunteers 4.
Governing Authority: private. Parent Institution: The Siloam Springs Museum Society. Tax-exempt.
History Museum: housed in 1950 church.
Collections: furniture; uniforms from World War I & II; textiles; clothing; decorative arts; pressed & cut glass; tools; archives: including books, newspapers, manuscripts, photographs & postcards.
Research Fields: local history of Benton County, Arkansas; Southern decorative arts & crafts.
Facilities: archives of 9,500 pieces. Museum-related gifts for sale.
Activities: permanent & temporary exhibitions. Museum Sponsors: Springs Heritage Festival; Spring Home Tour; Fall Music Fundraiser.
Publications: quarterly newsletter.
Hours & Admission Prices: Tues.-Sat. 10-5; other times by appointment. No charge; donations accepted. Closed major holidays. ♿
Attendance: 2,194 (estimated)
Membership: Single Senior Citizen $8; Dual Senior Citizen & Individual $15; Family $25; Contributing $35; Associate $60; Sponsor $125; Patron $300; Capitol $750; Millennium $1,000.

Smackover

ARKANSAS MUSEUM OF NATURAL RESOURCES, 3853 Smackover Hwy., Smackover, AR 71762-9575. Tel.: 870-725-2877. Fax: 870-725-2161.
E-mail: museum@amnr.org
Web Site: amnr.org
Founded: 1977.
Congressional District: 4
Key Personnel: Chm. (V), Phoebe Sellers; Dir., Pam Beasley; Exhibit Specialist, Rhonda Millican; Dir. Education & Research, Shelly Franques; Registrar, Sheri Neely; Cur., Van Zbinden; Museum Shop Mgr., Beth Hooks.
Personnel Profile: Full-Time Paid 9; Part-Time Paid 4; Part-Time Volunteers 48.
Governing Authority: state. Parent Institution: Arkansas Dept. of Parks & Tourism. Tax-exempt.
History & Technology Museum.
Collections: specimens; photographs; archival materials of petroleum & by-products and their relationship to Arkansas history.
Research Fields: Arkansas oil boom; oil & brine industrial technology; timber; geology; Bromine.
Facilities: outdoor oil field exhibit park; collection management facility; education center; woodland walk interpretive trail.
Activities: formally organized education programs; permanent & temporary exhibits; oral history program; guided tours; school loan service. Museum Sponsors: The National State Chautauqua.
Publications: newsletter, The Pipeline; publication, Boom Towns of South Arkansas; brochure, Brine, Bromine, How They Affect Our Lives, Rhene Miller's Circus Truck; visitor guide book; Teacher's Handbook.
Hours & Admission Prices: Mon.-Sat. 8-5, Sun. 1-5. No charge; donations accepted. Closed New Year's; Thanksgiving; Christmas. ♿
Attendance: 24,326 (accurate)
Membership: Single $15; Pipeline Club $30; Arkansas Club $50; Resources Council $100; Ouachita River Club $150; Cross Cut Society $300; Brine Society $500; Gusher Guild $1,000.

Springdale

SHILOH MUSEUM OF OZARK HISTORY, (M), 118 W. Johnson Ave., Springdale, AR 72764-4313. Tel.: 479-750-8165. Fax: 479-750-8693.
E-mail: shiloh@springdalear.gov
Web Site: www.springdalear.gov/shiloh
Founded: 1965.
Congressional District: 3
Key Personnel: Dir., Allyn Lord; Pres. Bd. Trustees, David Whitmore; Collections Mgr., Carolyn Reno; Outreach Coord., Susan Young; Sec., Betty Bowling; Exhibit Designer, Curtis Morris; Education Coord., Pody Gay; Education Asst., Michelle Hearn; Collections Asst., Heather Marie Wells; Photo Archivist, Marie Demeroukas; Library Asst., Cheri Coley; Library Asst., LuAnn Clarkson; Photographer, Amjad Faur; Maintenance, Marty Powers.
Personnel Profile: Full-Time Paid 8; Part-Time Paid 5; Part-Time Volunteers 30.
Governing Authority: municipal. Parent Institution: City of Springdale. Tax-exempt.
History Museum.
Collections: more than half a million indexed photographs; primitive paintings; items related to poultry, fruit, timber industries, pioneer life, and rural town life; farm equipment; domestic tools; hand tools; clothing and textiles; archival material; Native American artifacts; Vaughan-Applegate collection of cameras. Historic Buildings: c.1854 log cabin; c.1871 residence; 1870s post office/general store; 1880s doctor's office; c.1930 barn & outhouse; 1871 church & Odd Fellows lodge.
Major Exhibits: Whats Its, 11/09-3/10; Disaster!, 11/09-4/10; All Dressed Up, 2/10-1/11; Carl Smith's Fayetteville, 4/10-8/10; Springdale's Fire Department, 4/10-9/10; Down By The Old Mill Stream, 8/10-12/10; The Music of Our Lives, 10/10-3/11; Bumper Crop, 12/10-4/11.
Research Fields: prehistory & history of northwest Arkansas; Arkansas Ozarks.
Facilities: library & photo archives dealing with prehistory & history of the region. Museum-related items for sale.
Activities: guided tours; lectures & demonstrations; video & Power Point programs; discovery boxes. Museum Sponsors: Holiday Open House; Regional History Day; Quilt Fair, Sheep-to-Shawl.
Publications: quarterly newsletter; occasional papers; website with podcast program; iTunes U page; annual report.
Hours & Admission Prices: Mon.-Sat. 10-5. No charge; donations accepted. Closed New Year's Day; Thanksgiving; Christmas Eve & Day. ♿
Attendance: 33,309 (accurate)
Membership: Senior Individual $10; School classes $12.50; Individual & Senior couple $15; Family $20; Patron $50; Sponsor $100; Sustaining $250; Benefactor $500; Founding $1,000.

Stuttgart

MUSEUM OF THE ARKANSAS GRAND PRAIRIE, 921 E. 4th St., Stuttgart, AR 72160-4558. Tel.: 870-673-7001. Fax: 870-673-3959.
E-mail: ontheprairiebayou@yahoo.com
Web Site: www.stuttgartmuseum.org
Formerly: Stuttgart Agricultural Museum
Founded: 1974.
Congressional District: 2
Key Personnel: Dir., Melanie Baden; Chm. Bd. Trustees, Bruce Martin; Chm. (V), Beth Hopson; Vice Chm., Garland Demden; Sec., Jean Pollard; Financial Chm., Richard Bell; Cur. Collections, Gena Seidenschwarz; Cur. Restoration-Furniture, Kenneth Bull; Cur. Farm Equip. & Furniture, Jim Gingerich; Educational Dir., Ann Prislovsky; Gen. Asst. & Museum Shop Mgr., Frances Camp.
Personnel Profile: Full-Time Paid 4; Part-Time Volunteers 86.
Governing Authority: city; nonprofit organization. Parent Institution: City of Stuttgart; Stuttgart Agricultural Museum Association. Tax-exempt: 501(c)(3).
Agriculture Museum.
Collections: hay & rice industry farming equipment; agricultural history mural; period duck & turkey calls; period duck & goose decoys; swamp, prairie & wooded area wildlife; crop dusting history; furnishings; Arkansas fish farming; replicas of 1890 prairie home; fire station; printing press office; 1896 2/3 scale replica Lutheran church; mounted ducks in habitats; mounted Albino Canada Goose; guns; vintage clothing; toys; early prairie life & farming; videos; rice milling; fish farming; waterfowlers; waterfowlers of Mississippi Flyway; Hall of Transportation. Historic Building: 1914 schoolhouse.
Research Fields: Rice Branch experiment station-U.S. Dept. of Agriculture.

Riceland foods & Producers rice mill, marketing rice around the world; Aqua Culture Center for fish farming.
Facilities: 200-vol. research library on agricultural equipment, furniture, antiques, rice farming & the history of agriculture; 55-gal. aquarium; theatre. Museum-related items for sale.
Activities: guided tours; lectures; films; formally organized education programs; docent program; permanent & temporary exhibit.
Publications: newsletter; brochure, History of Duck Hunting in Stuttgart; booklet, Arkansas, Its Land & Its People, Of The Grand Prairie; videotapes, Dept. of Interior Fish Farm Biologists.
Hours & Admission Prices: Tues.-Fri. 8-4, Sat. 10-4. No charge; donations accepted. Closed Easter; legal holidays. ♿
Attendance: 13,146 (accurate)
Membership: Annual Seniors, Singles & Students Club $25; Contributor $50; Donor Club $100 & up; Brass Plate $500.

Texarkana

TEX ARK ANTIQUE AUTO MUSEUM, 217 Laurel St., Texarkana, AR 71854-6051. Tel.: 870-772-2886.
E-mail: antauto@texarkaam.org
Web Site: texarkaam.org
Founded: 2004.
Key Personnel: Dir. & Pres. (V), James Jamison; Treas., Charlotte Lipton.
Personnel Profile: Part-Time Volunteers 10.
Governing Authority: municipal. Tax-exempt: 501(c)(3).
Transportation Museum.
Collections: period automobiles, petroleum signs & gasoline pump; tools; literature.
Facilities: library.
Activities: guided tours.
Publications: quarterly newsletter.
Hours & Admission Prices: Sat. 10-4, Sun. 1-4. No charge; donations accepted.
Attendance: 5,000 (estimated)
Membership: Family $25.

Tontitown

TONTITOWN HISTORICAL MUSEUM, 257 E. Henri de Tonti Blvd., Tontitown, AR 72770. Mailing Address: P.O. Box 144, Tontitown, AR 72770-0144. Tel.: 479-361-2498 & 2700.
E-mail: bcortiana@cox.net
Web Site: www.tontitown.com
Founded: 1986.
Congressional District: 3
Key Personnel: Pres. Bd., Bev Cortiana; Cur., Charlotte Piazza.
Governing Authority: city; bd. of commissioners.
History Museum: housed in the former home of two original settlers, sisters Mary and Zelinda Bastianelli.
Collections: Italian immigration; settler families personal artifacts; photographs; period furnishings; early grape press; wine-bottling machine; early farm tools; Catholic church artifacts.
Activities: tours; presentations; research. Museum Sponsors: Tontitown Grape Festival; Arkansas Heritage Month Event in May; Tontitown Old Fashioned Reunion and Polenta Smear in November.
Publications: biannual newsletter, Tontitown Storia.
Hours & Admission Prices: June-Oct. Sat.-Sun. 1-4; other times by appointment. Extended hours during Tontitown Grape Festival. No charge; donations accepted.

Van Buren

BOB BURNS MUSEUM & RIVER VALLEY MUSEUM OF VAN BUREN, 813 Main St., Old Frisco Depot, Van Buren, AR 72956-4315. Mailing Address: P.O. Box 1518, Van Buren, AR 72957-1518. Tel.: 479-474-6164; 800-332-5889. Fax: 501-474-5084.
E-mail: vanburen@vanburen.org
Web Site: www.vanburen.org
Founded: 1994.
Congressional District: 3
Personnel Profile: Full-Time Paid 2; Part-Time Volunteers 24.
Governing Authority: municipal; nonprofit organization. Parent Institution: Van Buren A&P Commission.
Historical Building: 1901 Frisco Depot.
Collections: items related to entertainment career of Bob Burns, a nationally-known 1930s & 1940s radio humorist; Van Buren history.
Activities: guided tours; permanent exhibitions.
Publications: brochures.
Hours & Admission Prices: April-Nov. Mon.-Fri. 8-5, Sat. 9-5; Dec.-March Mon.-Fri. 8-5. No Charge; donations accepted. ♿

Attendance: 30,000 (estimated)
Membership: Student $5; Single $15; Family $25; Corporate $50; Life $100.

Warren

BRADLEY COUNTY HISTORICAL MUSEUM, 200 W. Ash St., Warren, AR 71671-2602. Mailing Address: P.O. Box 311, Warren, AR 71671-0311. Tel.: 870-226-5457.
History Museum: housed in the John Wilson Martin House, c.1857.
Collections: local history; personal artifacts; period furnishings.
Activities: demonstrations; hands-on activities. Museum Sponsors: Open House in June & December.
Hours & Admission Prices: Call for hours. No charge.

Washington

OLD WASHINGTON HISTORIC STATE PARK, 4954 Hwy. 278, Washington, AR 71862. Mailing Address: P.O. Box 129, Washington, AR 71862-0129. Tel.: 870-983-2684. Fax: 870-983-2736.
E-mail: historicwashington@arkansas.com
Web Site: www.historicwashingtonstatepark.com
Founded: 1973.
Congressional District: 4
Key Personnel: Supt., Grady Spann; Asst. Supt., John Spencer; Museum Shop Mgr., Angela McLaughlin; Cur., Glenda Friend.
Personnel Profile: Full-Time Paid 20; Part-Time Paid 8.
Governing Authority: nonprofit organization. Parent Institution: The Arkansas Dept. of Parks & Tourism, Arkansas State Parks, 1 Capitol Mall, Little Rock, AR 72201. Tax-exempt.
History Museum: located in 1824 town.
Collections: archaeology; manuscripts; weapons; hand tools; 19th-century furnishings; documents. Historic Houses: restored examples of southern Greek revival architecture.
Research Fields: southwest Arkansas history 1824-1889.
Facilities: 2,000-vol. library of law books & newspaper clippings on the history of the people & the town; southwest Arkansas regional archives.
Activities: guided tours; permanent exhibitions. Annual Events: Jonquil Festival in March; Frontier Days in September; Civil War weekend in October; Christmas & Candlelight in December.
Publications: information booklets.
Hours & Admission Prices: Daily 8-5. No charge. Guided walking tour of historic sites: adults $8, children 6-12 $4; discount to groups of 20 or more. Closed New Year's Day; Thanksgiving; Christmas. ♿
Attendance: 150,000 (estimated)

SOUTHWEST ARKANSAS REGIONAL ARCHIVES (SARA), 201 Highway 195, Washington, AR 71862. Mailing Address: P.O. Box 134, Washington, AR 71862-0134. Tel.: 870-983-2633. Fax: 870-983-2636.
E-mail: southwest.archives@arkansas.gov
Web Site: www.southwestarchives.com
Founded: 1978.
Congressional District: 4
Key Personnel: Archival Mgr., Peggy S. Lloyd; Administrative Asst., Gail Martin.
Personnel Profile: Full-Time Paid 2.
Governing Authority: Parent Institution: Arkansas History Commission.
Archives & Research Institute: housed in Washington Elementary School.
Collections: history of southwest Arkansas; letters; diaries; newspapers; pamphlets; maps; books including rare historical books; genealogical materials; cemetery records; family histories; periodicals; manuscripts; period photographs; cassettes of oral-history interviews; family collections; ledgers of businesses; family histories; microfilm; publications by county; historical societies.
Research Fields: history of 12 counties in southwest Arkansas; Gulf Plains region.
Facilities: 2,500-vol. library of historical books pertaining to the history of Arkansas & rare volumes of the Civil War available for research on premises only; reading room.
Activities: formally organized education programs for adults & graduate students; temporary exhibitions.
Publications: brochure; quarterly newsletter.
Hours & Admission Prices: Tues.-Sat. 8-4:30. No charge; donations accepted. Closed state & federal holidays. ♿
Attendance: 3,000
Membership: General $25; Contributing $75; Century $100; Patron $250; Lifetime $500; Permanent & Corporate $1,000.

Wilson

HAMPSON ARCHEOLOGICAL MUSEUM STATE PARK, #2 Lake Dr., Wilson, AR 72395. Mailing Address: P.O. Box 156, Wilson, AR 72395-0156. Tel.: 870-655-8622.
E-mail: hampsonarcheologicalmuseum@arkansas.com
Web Site: www.arkansasstateparks.com/hampsonmuseum
Founded: 1961.
Congressional District: 1
Key Personnel: Park Supt., Corinne Fletcher.
Personnel Profile: Full-Time Paid 2.
Governing Authority: state. Parent Institution: Arkansas Dept. of Parks and Tourism, Little Rock, AR. Tax-exempt.
Archaeology Museum.
Collections: late Mississippian culture; archaeological collections.
Research Fields: human osteology; lithic studies; ceramics.
Facilities: picnic area; playground. Museum-related items for sale.
Activities: guided tours; consultations for other museums; group participation-education activity programs, ages 5 and up.
Publications: brochures, museum guide.
Hours & Admission Prices: Tues.-Sat. 8-5, Sun. 1-5. Family $8, adults $2.50, children 6-12 $1.50; discounts to groups of 15 or more with advance reservation. Closed New Year's Day; Thanksgiving; Christmas Eve & Day. ♿
Attendance: 5,100 (estimated)

Wynne

CROSS COUNTY MUSEUM & ARCHIVES, (M), 711 E. Union, Wynne, AR 72396-3029. Mailing Address: P.O. Box 943, Wynne, AR 72396-0943. Tel.: 870-238-4100.
E-mail: crossmuseum@sbcglobal.net
Web Site: www.cchs1862.org
Formerly: Cross County Historical Society
Founded: 1972.
Key Personnel: Pres., Carol Brown; Bd., Richard Hartness.
Personnel Profile: Part-Time Volunteers 12; Interns 1.
Governing Authority: Parent Institution: Cross County Historical Society. Tax-exempt.
Historical Society Museum.
Collections: county history & culture; military artifacts; genealogy; cemetery records.
Research Fields: local history; genealogy.
Facilities: archives.
Activities: Museum Sponsors: Spring Fundraiser; Fall Family Fun Day.
Publications: quarterly newsletter, The Cross County ERA.
Hours & Admission Prices: Mon.-Fri. 10-4. No charge; donations accepted. ♿
Attendance: 1,000 (estimated)
Membership: Individual $15; Family $25; Institutional $35; Sustaining $50; Patron $100; Benefactor $250; Advocate $500; Life $1,000.

CALIFORNIA

(927 listings)

Acton

SHAMBALA PRESERVE, 6867 Soledad Canyon, Acton, CA 93510-2221. Mailing Address: P.O. Box 189, Acton, CA 93510-0189. Tel.: 661-268-0380. Fax: 661-268-8809.
Governing Authority: nonprofit organization. Tax-exempt: 501(c)(3).
Wildlife Preserve.
Collections: over 70 lions, tigers, black & spotted leopards, mountain lions, servals, bobcats, lynxes, Asian leopard cats, a Florida Panther, & a jungle cat.
Facilities: Museum-related items for sale.
Activities: educational programs; safaris.
Publications: newsletter.
Hours & Admission Prices: Safaris: one Sat.-Sun. a month by appointment. Adults 18 & over $40; children under 18 not admitted.

Alameda

USS HORNET MUSEUM, 707 W. Hornet Ave., Alameda, CA 94501-5006. Mailing Address: P.O. Box 460, Alameda, CA 94501-9560. Tel.: 510-521-8448. Fax: 510-521-8327.
E-mail: info@uss-hornet.org
Founded: 1987.
Key Personnel: Dir., Randall Ramian; Chm. (V), Jon Baker.
Governing Authority: Tax-exempt.
Air, Sea, & Space Museum. A National & State Historic Landmark.
Collections: military & personal artifacts; naval artifacts; aircraft; space artifacts including Apollo.
Facilities: Museum-related items for sale.
Hours & Admission Prices: Daily 10-5; groups by appointment. Adults $14, military, students and seniors 65 & over $12, youth 5-17 $6; members and children 4 & under no charge. Closed New Year's Day; Thanksgiving; Christmas.

Alhambra

ALHAMBRA HISTORICAL SOCIETY MUSEUM, 1550 W. Alhambra Rd., Alhambra, CA 91801-2009. Mailing Address: P.O. Box 6687, Alhambra, CA 91802-6687. Tel.: 626-300-8845.
Historical Society Museum.
Collections: local history & culture; period clothing; furnishings; books; photographs.
Activities: guided tours.
Hours & Admission Prices: Thurs. 2-4, 4th Sun. 2-4; groups by appointment. No charge.

Aliso Viejo

SOKA UNIVERSITY ART GALLERY, 1 University Dr., Aliso Viejo, CA 92656-8081. Tel.: 949-480-4108. Fax: 949-480-4110.
Web Site: www.soka.edu
Art Gallery.
Collections: works by national & international artists; paintings; photographs; sculpture.
Facilities: 8,000 sq. ft. exhibit space.
Hours & Admission Prices: Mon.-Fri. 9-5. No charge.

Alleghany

UNDERGROUND GOLD MINERS MUSEUM, 356 Main St., Alleghany, CA 95910-9998. Mailing Address: P.O. Box 907, Alleghany, CA 95910-0907. Tel.: 530-287-3330 & 3223. Fax: 530-287-3455.
E-mail: info@undergroundgold.com
Web Site: undergroundgold.com
Founded: 1995.
Congressional District: 1
Key Personnel: C.E.O. & Museum Shop Mgr., Rae Bell Arbogast; Pres. (V), David Scinto, C.P.A.; Education, Raymond Wittkopp.
Personnel Profile: Part-Time Paid 1; Part-Time Volunteers 4.
Governing Authority: private; nonprofit organization. Tax-exempt: 501(c)(3).
Mining Museum.
Collections: mining technology; mines of Alleghany area; history of Alleghany; mining tools.
Facilities: 25-vol. library; 20-seat theater. Museum-related items for sale.
Activities: guided tours; theater. Annual Event: membership meeting.
Publications: annual newsletter.
Hours & Admission Prices: Memorial Day to Labor Day Sat.-Sun. 1-5. No charge; donations accepted. ♿
Attendance: 1,000 (estimated)
Membership: Student & Senior $15; Annual $30; Lifetime $300.

Allensworth

COLONEL ALLENSWORTH STATE HISTORIC PARK, 4011Grant Dr., Allensworth, CA 93219. Mailing Address: Star Rte. 1, Box 148, Earlimart, CA 93219-9710. Tel.: 661-849-3433. Fax: 661-849-4013.
Founded: 1908.
Congressional District: 18
Key Personnel: State Park Interpreter III, Steven M. Ptomey.
Personnel Profile: Full-Time Paid 4; Part-Time Paid 2; Part-Time Volunteers 50.
Governing Authority: state. Parent Institution: California Dept. of Parks & Recreation, P.O. Box 2390, Sacramento, CA 95811. Tax-exempt.
Park Museum & Interpretive Center: located on the site of 1908 town of Allensworth, created to be a place where black people could live & work without racial prejudice.
Collections: interpretive material. Historic Buildings: Allensworth School; Singleton General Store; post office; drug store; dairy; livery stable; family homes; bakery; hotel.
Research Fields: pertaining to Allensworth & its pioneers.
Facilities: visitors' center; picnic area; campsites.
Activities: guided tours; lectures; films.
Publications: educational brochures.
Hours & Admission Prices: Park: 8-sunset. Visitor Center: daily 10-4. House Museum: by appointment only. Camping Fee: Night $20, Day $6; discounts to seniors & disabled. Call to see if open on particular holiday. ♿

Alturas

MODOC COUNTY HISTORICAL MUSEUM, 600 S. Main St., Alturas, CA 96101-4117. Tel.: 530-233-3280.
Founded: 1967.
Congressional District: 14
Key Personnel: Dir. & Museum Shop Mgr., Paula Murphy.
Personnel Profile: Full-Time Paid 1.
Governing Authority: county. Tax-exempt: 501(c)(3).
Modoc County History Museum.
Collections: settlement & development of Modoc County; period firearms; early settler, pioneer artifacts & Native American artifacts.
Research Fields: local history.
Facilities: Gift items & books for sale.
Activities: guided tours. Historical Society Sponsors: field trips to local historical sites.
Publications: book, The Journal of the Modoc County Historical Society; journals.
Hours & Admission Prices: May-Oct. Tues.-Sat. 10-4. Adults $2; children 16 & under no charge. ♿
Attendance: 6,000 (estimated)
Membership: Modoc County Historical Society: Student $10; Regular $15; Husband & Wife $20; Patron $30.

Amador City

AMADOR/WHITNEY, 14170 Hwy. 49, Amador City, CA 95601. Mailing Address: P.O. Box 181, Amador City, CA 95601-0181. Tel.: 209-267-9310. Fax: 209-267-9310.
Key Personnel: Dir., Joyce Davidson
History Museum.
Collections: local history & culture; contributions of women.
Hours & Admission Prices: Sat.-Sun. 12-4. No charge; donations accepted.

Anaheim

ELIZABETH J. SCHULTZ/ANAHEIM HISTORY ROOM, Anaheim Public Library, 500 W. Broadway, Anaheim, CA 92805-3601. Tel.: 714-765-1850.
Key Personnel: Cur., Jane K. Newell
History Museum.
Collections: Anaheim history; photographs; books.
Hours & Admission Prices: Mon. 9-9, Tues.-Fri. 9-6.

MOTHER COLONY HOUSE MUSEUM, 414 N. West St., Anaheim, CA 92801-5953. Tel.: 714-765-6453.
Web Site: www.anaheimcolony.com/m_colony.htm
Key Personnel: Museum Mgr., Jane Newell
Historic House Museum: State Historical Landmark.
Collections: personal artifacts; period furnishings.
Hours & Admission Prices: Call for appointment. No charge; donations accepted. Closed major holidays

MUZEO, 241 S. Anaheim Blvd., Anaheim, CA 92805-3821. Tel.: 714-956-8936.
E-mail: info@muzeo.org
Web Site: www.muzeo.org/visitor_info.html
Formerly: Anaheim Museum
Congressional District: 38
History Museum.
Collections: local history, heritage, culture & arts.
Facilities: Museum-related items for sale.
Activities: special events; educational programs.
Hours & Admission Prices: Call for hours. Adults $11, seniors 62 & over and students $10, children 3-12 $9; children under 3 no charge. ♿
Attendance: 3,000 (estimated)

OAK CANYON NATURE CENTER, 6700 E. Walnut Canyon Rd., Anaheim, CA 92807-4948. Mailing Address: 200 S. Anaheim Blvd., #433, Anaheim, CA 92805-3820. Tel.: 714-998-8380.
E-mail: ocnc@anaheim.net
Web Site: www.anaheim.net/ocnc/
Nature Center.
Collections: natural history; mounted wildlife.
Facilities: 58 acre park; nature trails.
Activities: hiking; outreach programs.
Hours & Admission Prices: April-May & Sept.-Oct. daily 9-4; June-Aug. daily 9-5; Nov.-March daily 9-3. Closed New Year's Day; Martin Luther King Jr. Day; Presidents' Day; Thanksgiving; Christmas.

WHITE HOUSE MUSEUM & EVENT CENTER, 1238 S. Beach Blvd., Anaheim, CA 92804-4805. Tel.: 714-827-3836 & 527-2323. Fax: 714-236-9762.
Formerly: Doll & Toy Museum
Key Personnel: Dir., Bea De Armond; Museum Shop Mgr., Allan Ansdell, Sr.
Collectables Museum.
Collections: over 6,000 toys & dolls.
Hours & Admission Prices: Daily 10-6.

Angels Camp

ANGELS CAMP MUSEUM & CARRIAGE HOUSE, 753 S. Main St., Angels Camp, CA 95222. Tel.: 209-736-2963.
E-mail: info@angelscamp.gov
Web Site: www.angelscamp.gov/museum.htm
History Museum.
Collections: household artifacts; Pelton water wheel; mining equipment; period carriages, carts & wagons; rocks & minerals.
Facilities: Museum-related items for sale.
Hours & Admission Prices: Jan.-Feb. Sat.-Sun. 10-3; March-Dec. daily 10-3.

Antioch

ANTIOCH HISTORICAL SOCIETY MUSEUM, 1500 W. Fourth St., Antioch, CA 94509-1046. Tel.: 925-757-1326.
Founded: 1998.
Congressional District: 10
Governing Authority: bd. of directors. Parent Institution: Antioch Historical Society.
Historical Society Museum: housed in the former Riverview Union High School; built in 1911. Listed on the National Register of Historical Places.
Collections: local history & culture; photographs; personal artifacts; Antioch Sports Legends Hall.
Hours & Admission Prices: early Jan. to late Dec. Wed. & Sat. 1-4. No charge; donations accepted. Closed holidays; New Year's Eve & Day; Christmas Eve, Day & week. ♿
Attendance: 4,500 (estimated)
Membership: Individual $15; Couple $30.

Apple Valley

VICTOR VALLEY MUSEUM & ART GALLERY, 11873 Apple Valley Rd., Apple Valley, CA 92308-3670. Tel.: 760-240-2111. Fax: 760-240-5290.
E-mail: vvmuseum@hotmail.com
Web Site: www.vvmuseum.com
Founded: 1976.
Congressional District: 35
Key Personnel: Exec. Dir., Carol Carr; Pres., Doug Shumway; Vice Pres., Mike Davis; School Tours, Sarah Puett.
Personnel Profile: Part-Time Paid 4; Part-Time Volunteers 30; Interns 3.
Governing Authority: nonprofit organization. Tax-exempt: 501(c)(3).
Natural History Museum.
Collections: archaeological & geographical artifacts & tools.
Research Fields: history & natural history of Mojave Desert; Serrano Indians; transportation; desert culture.
Facilities: 200-vol. library on local & natural history of California; botanical garden; 90-seat auditorium; 6,000 sq. ft. exhibit space. Books on local history & nature, educational toys & other museum-related items for sale.
Activities: guided tours; lectures; docent program; films; participatory & temporary exhibits.
Publications: quarterly bulletin, VVM.
Hours & Admission Prices: Wed.-Sat. 10-4, Sun. 1-4. Adults $4, seniors $2; members & students no charge. Imagination Station: $1 per child with paid adult general admission. Closed New Year's Day; Easter; Mother's Day; Memorial Day; Father's Day; Labor Day; Thanksgiving; Christmas. ♿
Attendance: 12,000 (estimated)
Membership: Senior 62 & over $25; Senior Couple 62 & over $35; Individual $40; Family & Grandparents $50. Presidents' Circle: Avant Garde $1,000-$1,999; Presidents' Circle $2,500-$4,999; Patron $5,000-$9,999; Sponsor $10,000-$24,999.

Aptos

CABRILLO GALLERY, 6500 Soquel Dr., Bldg. 1000, Rm. 1002, Aptos, CA 95003-3119. Tel.: 831-479-6308. Fax: 831-479-5045.
E-mail: gallery@cabrillo.edu
Web Site: www.cabrillo.edu/services/artgallery
Key Personnel: Gallery Dir., Susan Hoisington; Asst. Dir., Rose Sellery
Art Museum.
Collections: paintings; photographs; drawings; prints.

Hours & Admission Prices: Spring & Fall Mon.-Tues. 9-4 & 7-9, Wed.-Fri. 9-4. Adults $2, youth 12-17 $1; children no charge. ♿
Attendance: 5,000

Arcadia

THE LOS ANGELES COUNTY ARBORETUM & BOTANIC GARDEN, 301 N. Baldwin Ave., Arcadia, CA 91007-2697. Tel.: 626-821-3222. Fax: 626-445-1217.
Web Site: www.arboretum.org
Formerly: The Arboretum of Los Angeles County
Founded: 1947.
Congressional District: 26
Key Personnel: C.E.O., Mark K. Wourms, Ph.D.; Pres. (V) Los Angeles Arboretum Foundation, G. Arnold Mulder, M.D.; Supt., Timothy Phillips; Cur. Living Plant Collection, Jim Bauml, Ph.D.; Librarian, Susan Eubank; Museum Shop Mgr., Marc Hall; Communications & Mktg. Mgr., Cynthia Vargas.
Personnel Profile: Full-Time Paid 48; Part-Time Paid 13; Part-Time Volunteers 600; Interns 6.
Governing Authority: county; board of supervisors. Jointly Managed by: County of Los Angeles Department of Parks & Recreation and the Los Angeles Arboretum Foundation. Tax-exempt.
Arboretum: located on the site of Santa Anita Rancho.
Collections: plants of Australia, Americas, Asia, & Mediterranean region; specialties in orchids, cycads, eucalyptus; callistemon, melaleuca, acacia, palms, bamboo; herbarium consisting of introduced ornamental woody plants of Southern California; California history; children's gardens. Historic Buildings: 1840 Adobe; 1885 Queen Anne Cottage; 1881 Coach Barn; 1890 Santa Fe-Santa Anita Depot.
Research Fields: local history; testing of plants for introduction to California horticulture.
Facilities: 28,000-vol. & 150 periodical library of plant sciences & related topics available for public use & inter-library loan & reference; reading room; greenhouses; demonstration gardens; water conservation garden; meeting rooms; interpretive centers. Books, plants & crafts for sale.
Activities: guided & self-guided tours; tram tours; lectures; concerts; arts festivals; organized educational programs; docent program; permanent & temporary exhibitions; garden walks. Museum Sponsors: flower shows; Environmental Education Fair.
Publications: quarterly newsletter for Foundation members.
Hours & Admission Prices: Daily 9-4:30. Adults $7, seniors & students $5, tram tour $3, children 5-12 $2.50; reciprocal garden memberships; children under 5 & members no charge. Closed Christmas. ♿
Attendance: 300,000 (accurate)
Membership: Senior 62 & over $35; Individual $40; Family $60; Sustainer $125; Sponsor $300; Affiliate $500; Benefactor $1,000.

RUTH AND CHARLES GILB ARCADIA HISTORICAL MUSEUM, 380 W. Huntington Dr., Arcadia, CA 91007. Mailing Address: P.O. Box 60021, Arcadia, CA 91066-6021. Tel.: 626-574-5440. Fax: 626-821-9057.
Founded: 2001.
Congressional District: 26
Key Personnel: Dir., Carolyn Garner-Reagan; Education, Lindsey Sun; Public Rels., Darlene Bradley; Cur., Dana Dunn; Museum Shop Mgr., Roberta Ramsell.
Personnel Profile: Full-Time Paid 1; Part-Time Paid 1; Part-Time Volunteers 14; Interns 2.
Governing Authority: city. Parent Institution: Arcadia Department of Library and Museum Services.
History Museum.
Collections: Arcadia's local history; paintings; photographs; personal artifacts.
Research Fields: Tongva history; Spanish & Mexican Rancho; The E.J. "Lucky" Baldwin family; city of Arcadia civic history; Arcadia community history.
Facilities: 2,000 sq. ft. exhibit space. Museum-related items for sale.
Activities: changing exhibits; children's days & festivals; school tours; brown bag lunch talks; guided tours; lectures; internship, volunteer & docent programs.
Hours & Admission Prices: Tues.-Sat. 10-4. No charge. Closed national holidays. ♿
Attendance: 7,536 (accurate)
Membership: Arcadia Historical Society: Individual $25; Family $30; Business $35; Life $400.

Arcata

HUMBOLDT STATE UNIVERSITY NATURAL HISTORY MUSEUM, (M), 1315 G. St., Arcata, CA 95521-5820. Tel.: 707-826-4479. Fax: 707-826-4477.
E-mail: mlz1@humboldt.edu
Web Site: www.humboldt.edu/~natmus
Founded: 1989.
Key Personnel: Dir., Melissa L. Zielinski; Pres. (V), Karen Reiss; Education & Volunteer Coord., Spring Garrett; Administrative Asst., Michelle Kovry; Museum Shop Mgr., Theresa McLaren; Coord. Membership, Chris House.
Personnel Profile: Full-Time Paid 1; Full-Time Volunteers 10; Part-Time Paid 5; Part-Time Volunteers 30; Interns 2.
Governing Authority: public university; nonprofit. Parent Institution: Humboldt State University. Tax-exempt.
University Natural History Museum.
Collections: Pacific Northwest natural history including butterflies, crabs, mollusks, sponges & corals; birds; minerals; insects; fossils (1.9 billion years ago to present) from around the world; living native animals including a tidepool tank; live honey bee hive; 33 ft. Quetzalcoatlus replica; hominids; North American prehistoric mammals.
Facilities: 200-vol. library of field guides & educational materials; aquarium; educational facilities. Animal models, natural history books & museum-related items for sale.
Activities: docent program; formal educational programs; lectures; school loan service; participatory & temporary exhibitions; audiovisual biodiversity program.
Publications: quarterly newsletter, Nautilus Notes; quarterly program calendar, Nature Adventures.
Hours & Admission Prices: Tues.-Sat. 10-5. Family $10, adults $3, children under 3 $2; ASTC & museum members no charge. Closed New Year's Day; Memorial Day; Independence Day; Labor Day; Thanksgiving; Christmas. ♿
Attendance: 18,500 (estimated)
Membership: Student & Senior $20; Individual $30; Family $55; Friend $75; Sea Star $100; Sand Dollar $250; Lifetime Nautilus $750.

REESE BULLEN GALLERY, (M), Humboldt State University, 1 Harpst St., Arcata, CA 95521-8222. Tel.: 707-826-5802. Fax: 707-826-3628.
Web Site: www.humboldt.edu
Founded: 1970.
Congressional District: 1
Key Personnel: Chm. & Gallery Dir., Martin Morgan; Dir. Asst., Nancy Clark.
Personnel Profile: Full-Time Paid 1; Part-Time Paid 16; Interns 3.
Governing Authority: public college. Parent Institution: Humboldt State University.
University Art Gallery
Collections: 20th-century American & African art.
Facilities: 3,080 sq. ft. exhibit space.
Activities: guided tours; temporary & loan exhibitions; formal education programs for children; training programs for professional museum workers.
Hours & Admission Prices: Sept.-May Mon.-Fri. 11-4. Closed university holidays & semester breaks. ♿
Attendance: 5,400 (accurate)

Arroyo Grande

SOUTH COUNTY HISTORICAL SOCIETY, 134 Mason St., Arroyo Grande, CA 93420. Mailing Address: P.O. Box 633, Arroyo Grande, CA 93421-0633. Tel.: 805-489-8282.
E-mail: schs@sbcglobal.net
Web Site: southcountyhistory.org
Formerly: Paulding History House
Founded: 1976.
Congressional District: 22
Key Personnel: Chm. (V), Chuck Fellows; Pres. (V), Jane Q. Line.
Personnel Profile: Part-Time Volunteers 150.
Governing Authority: Branch Museums: Historic 100F Hall, 128 Bridge St., Arroyo Grande, CA; Heritage House Museum & Garden, 126 S. Mason St., Arroyo Grande, CA; Patricia Loomis History Library, 134 S. Mason St., Arroyo Grande, CA; Santa Manuela Schoolhouse, 127 Short St., Arroyo Grande, CA; The Barn Museum, 127 1/2 Short St., Arroyo Grande, CA; Paulding History House, 551 Crown Hill, Arroyo Grande, CA 93420. Tax-exempt.
Historical Society Museum.
Collections: Native American artifacts; Mexican Land Grant Era; early California statehood, schools, lifestyle & agriculture from 1800-1960; period furnishings; personal artifacts; carvings; Cumash Indian baskets; barn. Historic Buildings: 1902 Historic Hall; 1889 Heritage House Museum; 1904 Santa Manuela Schoolhouse; 1889 Paulding History House; 1888 Ruby's House Resource Center.
Research Fields: South County of San Luis Obispo California history.
Publications: Heritage Press.
Hours & Admission Prices: Heritage Square Museums: Sat. 12-3, Sun. 1-4. Historic 100F Hall: Fri.-Sat. 1-5. Paulding History House: 1st Sat. 12-3. Patricia Loomis History Library Mon.-Fri. 1-5. No charge; donations accepted. Closed New Year's Day; Christmas. ♿

Attendance: 10,000 (estimated)
Membership: Individual $15; Sustaining $100; Patron $200; Life $500; Corporate $1,000, $2,500, $5,000.

Atascadero

CHARLES PADDOCK ZOO, Morro Rd., Hwy. 41, W., Atascadero, CA 93422. Mailing Address: 9305 Pismo Ave., Atascadero, CA 93422-4939. Tel.: 805-461-5080. Fax: 805-461-7625.
E-mail: zoo@atascadero.org
Web Site: charlespaddockzoo.org
Founded: 1955.
Congressional District: 22
Key Personnel: C.E.O., Alan G. Baker; Zoo Society Pres. (V), Jon Jaeger; Zoo Society, Ken Brokamp; Museum Shop Mgr., Kirby Price.
Personnel Profile: Full-Time Paid 7; Part-Time Paid 2; Part-Time Volunteers 50; Interns 4.
Governing Authority: Parent Institution: City of Atascadero. Subsidiary Institution: Zoological Society of San Luis Obispo County. Tax-exempt.
Zoo.
Collections: live animals; plants.
Research Fields: captive breeding & field work.
Publications: newsletter, Zoologic.
Hours & Admission Prices: Summer: daily 10-5; Winter: daily 10-4. Adults 12 & over $5, senior citizens 65 & over $4.25, youth 3-11 $4; AZA members & children under 3 no charge. Closed Thanksgiving; Christmas. ♿
Attendance: 60,000 (estimated)
Membership: Individual $30; Individual Plus One $35; Family $50; Family Plus One $60; Sponsor $100; Benefactor & Zoo Booster (Business) $250.

Atwater

CASTLE AIR MUSEUM, 5050 Santa Fe Dr., Atwater, CA 95301-5154. Tel.: 209-723-2178 & 2182. Fax: 209-723-0323.
Web Site: www.castleairmuseum.org
Founded: 1981.
Congressional District: 18
Key Personnel: C.E.O., Joe Pruzzo; Chm. Bd., Dave Wood; Financial Dir., Nelson Howlett; Sec., Caroline Venable.
Personnel Profile: Full-Time Paid 9; Full-Time Volunteers 4; Part-Time Paid 6; Part-Time Volunteers 149.
Governing Authority: private; nonprofit. Tax-exempt.
Military & Aviation History Museum.
Collections: aviation history including strategic bombardment from World War II to the present including Merced Army Airfield & Castle Air Force Base.
Facilities: 20 acres; 75-seat banquet room; 1,500 sq. ft. exhibit space; picnic grounds. Aviation-related items for sale.
Activities: docent program; guided tours; guest lectures; membership drive.
Publications: quarterly newsletter.
Hours & Admission Prices: April-Oct. daily 9-5; Nov.-March daily 10-4. Adults $10, seniors 60 & up and youth 6-17 $8; active duty, children under 5, & members no charge. Closed New Year's Day; Easter; Thanksgiving; Christmas Eve & Day. ♿
Attendance: 30,000 (accurate)
Membership: Supporting $30; Sustaining $60; Life $1,000; McCarthy $2,500; Eagle $5,000; LeMay $7,500; Doolittle $10,000; Macready $15,000; General Castle $25,000.

Auburn

BERNHARD MUSEUM COMPLEX, 291 Auburn-Folsom Rd., Auburn, CA 95603-5039. Mailing Address: 101 Maple St., Auburn, CA 95603-5026. Tel.: 530-889-6500. Fax: 530-889-6510.
Web Site: www.placer.ca.gov/museum
Key Personnel: Acting Dir., Melanie Barton
History Museum.
Collections: furnishings; period viticulture equipment; farm wagon; zinfandel grapes; vegetables; herbs; flowers.
Hours & Admission Prices: Tues.-Sun. 11-4. Closed holidays. No charge. ♿

PLACER COUNTY MUSEUMS, 101 Maple St., Auburn, CA 95603-5026. Tel.: 530-889-6500. Fax: 530-889-6510.
Web Site: www.placer.ca.gov/museum
Founded: 1948.
Congressional District: 1
Key Personnel: Museum Admin., Melanie Barton; Program Mgr., Ralph Gibson; Cur. Collections, Kasia Woroniecka; Cur. Education, Karen Mattson; Exhibit Preparator, Jason Adair.
Personnel Profile: Full-Time Paid 6; Part-Time Paid 3; Part-Time Volunteers 150.
Governing Authority: county. Subsidiary Institutions: Gold Country Museum; Bernhard Museum Complex; Griffith Quarry Museum; Forest Hill Divide Museum; Golden Drift Museum; Placer County Museum; Placer County Archives. Tax-exempt.
History Museum.
Collections: mining equipment & related items; 1880-1900 furniture & household accessories; agricultural & blacksmith artifacts; logging artifacts; items of daily life; archival records of Placer County; private archival material. Historic Buildings: c.1851 Bernhard Museum; c.1881 Bernhard Wine Processing Building.
Research Fields: history of Placer County.
Activities: guided tours; living history programs; changing exhibits; outreach programs.
Publications: department brochure; newsletter, The Placer; flyers & brochures on current temporary exhibits.
Hours & Admission Prices: Gold Country & Bernhard: Tues.-Sun. 11-4. Placer County: daily 10-4. Griffith Quarry: Sat.-Sun. 12-4. Forest Hill & Gold Drift: Memorial Day-Labor Day Wed. & Sat.-Sun. 12-4. No charge; donations accepted. ♿
Attendance: 30,000

Avalon

CATALINA ISLAND MUSEUM SOCIETY, INC., (M), Casino Bldg., Avalon, CA 90704. Mailing Address: P.O. Box 366, Avalon, CA 90704-0366. Tel.: 310-510-2414. Fax: 310-510-2780.
E-mail: info@catalinamuseum.org
Web Site: www.catalinamuseum.org
Founded: 1953.
Congressional District: 36
Key Personnel: Exec. Dir., Stacey A. Otte; Pres., Steven C. Schreiner; Cur., Jeannine Pedersen; Museum Shop Mgr., John Boraggina; Office Mgr., Marti Winslow; Coord. Membership, Gail Fornasiere.
Personnel Profile: Full-Time Paid 4; Part-Time Paid 5; Part-Time Volunteers 150; Interns 1.
Governing Authority: private; nonprofit corporation. Tax-exempt: 501(c)(3).
History Museum.
Collections: Indian artifacts; historical photographs; ship models; pottery; historical memorabilia.
Research Fields: archaeology; Catalina history.
Facilities: research library on subjects pertaining to Catalina Island available on premises.
Activities: education programs for children; lectures; field trips.
Publications: books, The Casino; The Legends of Old Ben; Avalon Walkabout; The Art of Catalina Clay Products.
Hours & Admission Prices: Jan.-March Fri.-Wed. 10-4; April-Dec. daily 10-4. Adults $5, seniors $4, children 6-15 $2; discounts to AAM members; children under 6 & members no charge. Closed Christmas Day; Thanksgiving Day. ♿
Attendance: 55,000 (estimated)
Membership: Individual $30; Family & Dual $45; Sponsoring $100; Associate $250; Patron $500; Annual Donor $1,000; Benefactor $10,000; Business Friend $100; Business Sponsor $200; Business Associate $500; Business Donor $1,000.

Bakersfield

* **BAKERSFIELD MUSEUM OF ART, (M),** 1930 R St., Bakersfield, CA 93301-4815. Tel.: 661-323-7219. Fax: 661-323-7266.
Web Site: www.bmoa.org
Founded: 1987.
Congressional District: 20
Key Personnel: Exec. Dir., Bernard J. Herman; Bd. Pres., Joe Audelo; Chief Cur., Emily Falke; Asst. Dir., David Gordon.
Personnel Profile: Full-Time Paid 4; Part-Time Paid 11; Part-Time Volunteers 70.
Governing Authority: nonprofit. Parent Institution: Bakersfield Art Foundation. Tax-exempt: 501(c)(3).
Art Museum.
Collections: paintings; sculpture; graphics; complete works of Marion Osborn Cunningham; Phil Paradise serigraphs; California regional artists; works on paper.
Research Fields: California regionalists.
Facilities: 700-vol. library of books, catalogs & magazines available for use by the public; educational facilities; workshop space; reception facilities. Gift items for sale.
Activities: guided tours; lectures; films; gallery talks; arts festivals; formally organized education programs for children; inter-museum loan; participatory, permanent, temporary & traveling exhibitions; docent programs; workshops.
Publications: quarterly newsletter; exhibit catalogs; gallery posters & prints.
Hours & Admission Prices: Tues.-Fri. 10-4, Sat.-Sun. 12-4. Adults $5, seniors

$4, students $2; discounts to AAM & ICOM members; children 6 & under and members no charge. Closed New Year's Day; Martin Luther King Day; Easter; Memorial Day; Independence Day; Labor Day; Thanksgiving; Christmas. ♿
Attendance: 25,000 (estimated)
Membership: Students & Seniors $20; Individual $30; Family $40; Active $100; Contributing $250; Sustaining $500.

BUENA VISTA MUSEUM OF NATURAL HISTORY, 2018 Chester Ave., Bakersfield, CA 93301-4420. Tel.: 661-324-6350. Fax: 661-324-7522.
E-mail: bvmnh@sharktoothhill.com
Web Site: www.sharktoothhill.com
Natural History Museum.
Collections: earth history; paleontology; anthropology; fossils; natural history.
Facilities: Museum-related items for sale.
Activities: workshops; educational programs; geology fieldtrips.
Publications: newsletter, Sharkbites.
Hours & Admission Prices: Thurs.-Sat. 10-5; other times by appointment. Adults $7, senior citizens, children & students $4; discounts to groups of 20 or more; children 5 & under no charge. Closed major holidays.

CALIFORNIA LIVING MUSEUM CALM, 10500 Alfred Harrell Hwy., Bakersfield, CA 93306-9654. Tel.: 661-872-2256. Fax: 661-872-2205.
Web Site: www.calmzoo.org
Key Personnel: Dir., Tom Anspach; Zoo Mgr. & Cur., Lana Fain; Education & Volunteer Svcs., Debby Kroeger; Asst. Cur. Animals, Lloyd Klingenberg
Zoo.
Collections: native California animals; plants; fossils.
Facilities: Museum-related items for sale.
Activities: rental facilities.
Hours & Admission Prices: Feb.-Oct. daily 9-5; Nov.-Jan. daily 9-4. Adults $7, seniors $5, students & children 3-17 $4; discounts to groups; children under 3 no charge. Closed New Year's Day; Easter; Thanksgiving; Christmas Eve & Day.

* **KERN COUNTY MUSEUM, (M),** 3801 Chester Ave., Bakersfield, CA 93301-1345. Tel.: 661-852-5000. Fax: 661-322-6415.
E-mail: kcmuseum@kern.org
Web Site: kcmuseum.org
Founded: 1945.
Congressional District: 18
Key Personnel: Dir., Carola Rupert Enriquez; Chm., Beth Pandol; Asst. Dir., Jeff Nickell; Cur., Lori Wear; Bldg. & Grounds, Scott Fieber; Education Programs, Jackie Brouillette; Educational Asst., Elizabeth Herrera.
Personnel Profile: Full-Time Paid 16; Part-Time Paid 11; Part-Time Volunteers 48.
Governing Authority: county. Parent Institution: Kern County Museum Authority. Subsidiary Institution: Lori Brock Children's Discovery Center. Tax-exempt.
History Museum.
Collections: 57 structure outdoor exhibit; household artifacts; tools & equipment; firearms; Indian artifacts; photographs; historic vehicles; two acre petroleum exhibit.
Research Fields: local history; culture.
Facilities: 2,000-vol. library of local history, museology, geology, mineralogy, Western Americana, California & fiction pertaining to area available on premises by appointment.
Activities: tours for schools; one-room school programs; docent programs; permanent & temporary exhibitions; summer camp. Museum Sponsors: Safe Halloween; Lamplight Tours; Fun Days; Living History Day; Black Gold: The Oil Experience; Early California History Day; Native American Life.
Publications: A Kern County Diary: The Forgotten Photos of Carleton E. Watkins, 1881-1888; cookbook, Nuggets, Nibbles and Nostalgia; quarterly newsletter, The Courier; Historic Kern County: An Illustrated History of Bakersfield and Kern County; Chronicles of Kern County; Hard Drivin' Country: The Honky Tonks, Musicians, and Legends of the Bakersfield Sound.
Hours & Admission Prices: Mon.-Sat. & holidays 10-5, Sun. 12-5; ticket office closes daily at 3. Adults $10, senior citizens over 60 & teens $9, children 6-12 $8, children 3-5 $7; children under 3 & members no charge. Closed New Year's Eve & Day; Easter; Independence Day; Thanksgiving; Christmas Eve & Day. ♿
Attendance: 75,000 (accurate)
Membership: Family $65; Supporting $125; Sustaining $250; Patron $500; Benefactor $1,000.

LORI BROCK CHILDREN'S DISCOVERY CENTER, 3801 Chester Ave., Bakersfield, CA 93301-1345. Tel.: 661-852-5000. Fax: 661-322-6415.
E-mail: kcmuseum@kern.org
Web Site: www.kcmuseum.org/loribrock
Founded: 1976.
Congressional District: 18
Key Personnel: Dir. Museum Svcs., Carola Enriquez; Asst. Dir., Jeff Nickell; Tour Bookings, Lily Soto; Education Program, Jackie Brouillette.
Governing Authority: Parent Institution: Kern County Museum, which is operated by a joint powers agreement between governmental agencies. Tax-exempt: 501(c)(3).
Children's Museum.
Collections: hands-on exhibits.
Facilities: classrooms.
Activities: gallery talks; arts festivals; drama; day camps; formally organized education programs for children.
Publications: quarterly newsletter; summer camp flyer.
Hours & Admission Prices: Mon.-Sat. & holidays 10-5, Sun. 12-5. Adults $8, senior citizens & students 13-17 $7, youth 6-12 $6, children 3-5 $5; children under 3 & members no charge. Closed New Year's Day; Presidents' Day; Memorial Day; Independence Day; Thanksgiving; Christmas Eve & Day. ♿
Attendance: 95,000 (accurate)
Membership: Family $65; Supporting $125; Sustaining $250; Patron $500; Benefactor $1,000.

Banning

GILMAN HISTORIC RANCH AND WAGON MUSEUM, 1937 W. Gilman St., Banning, CA 92220-1861. Tel.: 951-922-9200.
Web Site: riversidecountyparks.org
History Museum: housed in the homestead ranch of James Marshall Gilman.
Collections: California history from Cahuilla Indians to early settlement of southern California & the San Gorgonio Pass.
Hours & Admission Prices: Call for hours.

MALKI MUSEUM, 11-795 Fields Rd., Morongo Indian Reservation, Banning, CA 92220. Mailing Address: P.O. Box 578, Banning, CA 92220-0017. Tel.: 951-849-7289 & 8304. Fax: 951-849-3549.
E-mail: malkimuseummail@gmail.com
Web Site: www.malkimuseum.org
Founded: 1964.
Congressional District: 37
Key Personnel: Dir., Susan Phillips; Pres., Katherine Siva Saubel; Treas., Elaine Mathews.
Personnel Profile: Part-Time Paid 1.
Governing Authority: nonprofit organization. Tax-exempt: 501(c)(3).
Indian Museum.
Collections: Cahuilla & other Southern California Indian tribe artifacts; anthropology; archaeology; history; ethnology; basketry.
Research Fields: California Indians.
Facilities: library of books, pamphlets & other material on the Southern California Indians; ethno-botanical garden. Museum-related gifts for sale.
Activities: school tours; lectures; fiesta; college scholarship program for Southern California Indian students.
Publications: books, A Dried Coyote's Tail; Aboriginal Society in Southern California; Alaawwich (Our Language); Gigyayk Vo'jka! (Walk Strong!); I' isniyatam (Designs); Lost Copper; Luiseno Language; Malki Museum's Native Food-Tasting Experiences; Mirror and Pattern: Laird's World of Chemehuevi Mythology; Stalking the Wild Agave; Studies in Cahuilla Culture: Ethnography of the Cahuilla Indians; Temalpakh (From the Earth); The Cahuilla Indians; The Cahuilla Indians of Southern California; The Chemehuevi Indians of Southern California; The Chumash Indians of Southern California; The First Angelinos; The Luiseno Indians of Southern California; The Serrano Indians of Southern California; Tovangar (World): A Gabrielino Word Book; Wappo Report; Wayta' Yawa' (Always Believe); When the Animals Were People; Willie Boy: A Desert Manhunt; biannual, The Journal of California and Great Basin Anthropology.
Hours & Admission Prices: Tues.-Fri. 10-4. No charge; donations accepted.
Membership: Student $7.50; Single $15; Family $20; Supporting $35; Organization $50; Benefactor $100; Life $500.

Barstow

BARSTOW ROUTE 66 MOTHER ROAD MUSEUM, Historic Harvey House, 681 N. First Ave., Barstow, CA 92311-2201. Tel.: 760-255-1890; 877-997-8366. Fax: 760-256-6776.
E-mail: barstowmuseum@yahoo.com
Web Site: www.route66museum.com
Key Personnel: Mgr. & Cur., Debra Hodkin; Historian, Bill Tomlinson.
Personnel Profile: Part-Time Volunteers 30.

History Museum.
Collections: history of Rte. 66 & the Mojave Desert communities; photographs; automotive history; personal artifacts.
Facilities: Museum-related items for sale.
Activities: tours.
Publications: quarterly newsletter.
Hours & Admission Prices: Fri.-Sun. 10-4; other times by appointment. No charge; donations accepted. ♿

MOJAVE RIVER VALLEY MUSEUM, 270 Virginia Way, Barstow, CA 92312. Mailing Address: P.O. Box 1282, Barstow, CA 92312-1282. Tel.: 760-256-5452.
E-mail: mrvm@verizon.net
Web Site: www.mojaverivervalleymuseum.org
Key Personnel: Pres., Bob Hilburn; Vice Pres., Dave Romero.
Governing Authority: nonprofit organization.
History Museum.
Collections: local history from 1776 to present; photographs; newspapers.
Facilities: Museum-related items for sale.
Activities: field trips; meetings.
Hours & Admission Prices: Daily 11-4. No charge. Closed Christmas.

WESTERN AMERICA RAILROAD MUSEUM - WARM, 685 N. First St., Barstow, CA 92311. Mailing Address: P.O. Box 703, Barstow, CA 92312-0703. Tel.: 760-256-WARM.
E-mail: warm95@verizon.net
Web Site: www.barstowrailmuseum.org
Governing Authority: nonprofit. Tax-exempt.
Railroad Museum.
Collections: railroading history & development; railroad artifacts; art; uniforms; tools; equipment.
Hours & Admission Prices: Fri.-Sun. 11-4.

Bel Air

SONDRA & MARVIN SMALLEY SCULPTURE GARDEN, American Jewish University, 15600 Mulholland Dr., Bel Air, CA 90077-1519. Tel.: 310-476-9777.
Art Museum.
Collections: sculptures.
Hours & Admission Prices: Daily. No charge.

Belmont

PENINSULA MUSEUM OF ART, (M), 10 Twin Pines Lane, Belmont, CA 94002-3889. Tel.: 650-594-1577.
Web Site: www.peninsulamuseum.org
Founded: 2004.
Congressional District: 12
Key Personnel: Chm. & Pres. (V), Ruth Waters; Devel., Linda Stack; Education & Cur., James Daugherty; Public Rels., Jerry Emanuel; Treas., Arabella Decker.
Personnel Profile: Full-Time Volunteers 1; Part-Time Volunteers 36.
Governing Authority: private; nonprofit organization. Tax-exempt: 501(c)(3).
Art Museum.
Collections: paintings; sculpture; Chinese calligraphy; digital art.
Facilities: 900-vol. library; 800 sq. ft. exhibit space. Museum-related items for sale.
Activities: lectures; training programs for professional museum workers.
Publications: quarterly newsletter, Peninsula Museum of Art; exhibition catalogues.
Hours & Admission Prices: Wed.-Fri. 12-4, Sat.-Sun. 1-4. No charge; donations accepted. Closed New Year's Day; Independence Day; Christmas. ♿
Attendance: 1,750 (estimated)
Membership: Individual $45; Family $65; Supporter $100; Benefactor $500; Patron $1,000.

THE WIEGAND GALLERY, Notre Dame de Namur University, 1500 Ralston Ave., Belmont, CA 94002-1908. Tel.: 650-508-3595. Fax: 650-508-3488.
E-mail: ehoward@ndnu.edu
Web Site: www.wiegandgallery.org
Founded: 1970.
Key Personnel: Dir., Robert Poplack; Gallery Coord., Simone Baer; Gallery Coord., Ellen Howard; Art Chm., Betty Friedman.
Personnel Profile: Part-Time Paid 3.
Governing Authority: college. Parent Institution: Notre Dame de Namur University. Tax-exempt: 501(c)(3).
University Art Gallery.
Collections: paintings; sculpture; photographs.
Research Fields: San Francisco Bay area art history.
Facilities: 40-seat theater.
Activities: traveling exhibitions; lectures; gallery talks.
Publications: exhibition catalogues.
Hours & Admission Prices: Sept.-May Tues.-Sat. 12-4. No charge; donations accepted. Closed Christmas. ♿
Attendance: 3,600
Membership: Individual $25; Patron $50; Contributor $100; Supporter $250; Benefactor $500; Director's Circle $1,000.

Benicia

BENICIA FIRE MUSEUM, 900 E. 2nd St., Benicia, CA 94510-3349. Mailing Address: P.O. Box 1251, Benecia, CA 94510-4251. Tel.: 707-745-1688.
Fire-Fighting Museum.
Collections: 1820 Phoenix; 1855 Solano Engine; 1860 Griffin; over 7,000 fire hats; period water grenades & fire extinguishers.
Hours & Admission Prices: 1st three Sun. of month 1-4; other times by appointment. No charge; donations accepted.

BENICIA HISTORICAL MUSEUM, (M), 2024 Camel Rd., Benicia, CA 94510-2339. Mailing Address: 2060 Camel Rd., Benicia, CA 94510-2339. Tel.: 707-745-5435. Fax: 707-745-5869.
E-mail: info@beniciahistoricalmuseum.org
Web Site: beniciahistoricalmuseum.org
Formerly: Benicia Historical Museum and Cultural Foundation (Camel Barn Museum)
Founded: 1985.
Congressional District: 7
Key Personnel: Exec. Dir., Ann Hansen; Chm. (V), Louise Martin; Bd. Pres. (V), David Galligan; Cur., Beverly Phelan; Coord. Elementary Education, Mary Marino; Museum Shop Mgr., Toni Haughey.
Personnel Profile: Full-Time Paid 1; Full-Time Volunteers 1; Part-Time Paid 2; Part-Time Volunteers 120; Interns 4.
Governing Authority: nonprofit organization. Tax-exempt.
Local History Museum: housed in 1853-1857 U.S. Army Arsenal, first arsenal built on Pacific coast & actively used until 1964. Buildings listed in the National Register of Historic Places.
Collections: photographs; documents; maps; artifacts of early Benicia; artifacts from 1847; first store in Solano County; exhibits emphasizing history of the first Arsenal & Camel Auction of 1864.
Major Exhibits: 100th Anniversary of Boy Scouts of America, 2/10; 25th Anniversary Exhibit, 5/10.
Research Fields: conversion from military to civilian life for arsenal & city.
Facilities: library of documents & other printed materials available to the public on a limited basis; 10,000 sq. ft. exhibit space; gardens. Local history-related items for sale.
Activities: education programs: traveling trunk; public outreach at civic events in Benicia; guided tours; concerts; participatory, loan & temporary exhibitions; early California hands-on activities included in school tours; reception room available; concerts; receptions; meeting areas. Museum Sponsors: Spenger Gardent concert series June-October.
Publications: bimonthly newsletter, Camel Tracks.
Hours & Admission Prices: Wed.-Sun. 1-4. Adults $5, seniors & students and Hands-on Early Calif. $3; discounts to groups of 30 or more, CAM & AASLH members; children under 7, Wed. & members no charge. Closed New Year's Day; Easter; Mother's Day; Father's Day; Thanksgiving; Christmas. ♿
Attendance: 15,500 (estimated)
Membership: Student & Senior $20; Individual $30; Family $50; Friend $75; Supporting $100; Patron $150; Camel Corp $225; Dona Benicia $500; Benefactor $1,000; Sponsor $5,000. Corporate: Barracks $250; Quartermaster $500; Arsenal $1,000; Commandant $1,500.

FISCHER-HANLON HOUSE, 135 West G St., Benicia, CA 94510-3114. Tel.: 707-745-3385.
History Museum.
Collections: personal artifacts; furnishings; Steinway piano; wooden toys; quilts.
Hours & Admission Prices: House: Sat.-Sun. 12-3:30. Garden: Wed.-Sun. 10-5. Adults $2, children $1.

Berkeley

THE BADE MUSEUM OF BIBLICAL ARCHAEOLOGY, 1798 Scenic Ave., Berkeley, CA 94709-1323. Tel.: 510-849-8286. Fax: 510-845-8948.
E-mail: bade@psr.edu
Web Site: bade.psr.edu

Formerly: The Bade Institute of Biblical Archaeology and The Howell Bible Collection
Founded: 1926.
Key Personnel: Museum Dir., Aaron Brody; Assoc. Cur., Catherine P. Foster.
Governing Authority: trustees. Parent Institution: Pacific School of Religion. Tax-exempt.
Archaeological Museum.
Collections: biblical archaeology; major collection from Tell en-Nasbeh, Israel, believed to have been the site of Mizpah; artifacts from Egypt, Syria, Cyprus, Greece & Rome; Reformation printed Bibles; European Bibles; facsimiles of early Greek Biblical codices; fragment of Papyri from Oxyrhynchus, Egypt.
Research Fields: near Eastern, especially Syro-Palestinian archaeology.
Facilities: library; 11,000 slides on near Eastern archaeology & world art.
Activities: guided tours; lectures; formally organized educational programs; permanent & traveling exhibitions.
Publications: newsletter.
Hours & Admission Prices: Tues. & Thurs. 10-3; other times by appointment. No charge; donations accepted. ♿

BERKELEY ART CENTER, 1275 Walnut St., Berkeley, CA 94709-1406. Tel.: 510-644-6893. Fax: 510-540-0343.
E-mail: info@berkeleyartcenter.org
Web Site: www.berkeleyartcenter.org
Founded: 1967.
Congressional District: 8
Key Personnel: Exec. Dir., Jill Berk Jiminez; Pres. (V), Susan Klee; Program Coord., Amber Stucke; Music Coord., Marvin Sanders.
Personnel Profile: Full-Time Paid 1; Part-Time Paid 2; Part-Time Volunteers 20; Interns 1.
Governing Authority: private; nonprofit corporation, Berkeley Art Center Association. Tax-exempt.
Art Gallery.
Collections: contemporary art.
Activities: gallery talks; concerts; slides; films; performances; workshops; poetry readings; special events; temporary exhibitions; selected exhibits of Bay Area artists.
Publications: Bodies & Souls, Science Imagined; 10X10: Ten Women, Ten Prints; Asian Roots Western Soil: Japanese Influences in American Culture; Crossings: The Installation Art of Mildres Howard; Ethnic Notions: Black Images in the White Mind; The Whole World's Watching: Peace & Social Justice Movements of the 1960s & 1970s; Sacred Spaces; From Isolation to Connection: Adults Living with Psychiatric Disabilities.
Hours & Admission Prices: Wed.-Sun. 12-5. No charge; donations accepted. Closed holidays. ♿
Attendance: 12,400 (accurate)
Membership: Student & Senior $40; Regular & Senior Artist $45; Artist $50.

BERKELEY ROSE GARDEN, 1200 Euclid Ave., Berkeley, CA 94708. Mailing Address: 2180 Milvia St., Berkeley, CA 94704-1122. Tel.: 510-981-6700. Fax: 510-981-6710.
E-mail: parks@ci.berkeley.ca.us
Web Site: www.ci.berkeley.ca.us/parks/parkspages/berkeleyrosegarden.html
Rose Garden.
Collections: 3,000 rose bushes representing 250 varieties.
Facilities: trails & footbridges; amphitheater.
Activities: special events; weddings.
Hours & Admission Prices: Dawn to dusk. No charge.

ESSIG MUSEUM OF ENTOMOLOGY, UNIVERSITY OF CALIFORNIA, BERKELEY, University of California, Berkeley, CA 94720-0001. Mailing Address: 201 Wellman Hall, MC3112, Berkeley, CA 94720. Tel.: 510-643-0804. Fax: 510-642-7428.
E-mail: gillespi@nature.berkeley.edu
Web Site: essig.berkeley.edu/
Founded: 1939.
Congressional District: 8
Key Personnel: Dir., Rosemary Gillespie; Head Cur., Cheryl B. Barr; Assoc. Cur. Emeritus, J.A. Chemsak; Assoc. Cur. Emeritus, H.V. Daly; Assoc. Cur. Emeritus, W.W. Middlekauff; Assoc. Cur. Emeritus, E.S. Sylvester; Assoc. Cur., Robert Zuparko.
Personnel Profile: Full-Time Paid 1; Part-Time Paid 6; Part-Time Volunteers 7.
Governing Authority: university. Parent Institution: University of California, Berkeley. Tax-exempt.
Entomology Museum.
Collections: 4.5 million insects & terrestrial arthropods.
Research Fields: systematic entomology; California Insect Survey.
Facilities: research collection of 4.5 million insects & terrestrial arthropods; library of books & reprints on biology & taxonomy/systematics of insects available for use on premises.
Activities: displays for the public on Cal Day (campus-wide open house) in April & for other special events.
Publications: Bulletin of the California Insect Survey.
Hours & Admission Prices: Not a public museum, no public admission. ♿
Attendance: 315 (accurate)

HABITOT CHILDREN'S MUSEUM, 2065 Kittredge St., Berkeley, CA 94704-1404. Mailing Address: PMB 326, 1563 Solano Ave., Berkeley, CA 94707. Tel.: 510-647-1111. Fax: 510-647-1110.
E-mail: habitot@lmi.net
Web Site: www.habitot.org
Founded: 1992.
Congressional District: 9
Key Personnel: Dir., Gina Moreland.
Personnel Profile: Full-Time Paid 6; Part-Time Paid 15; Part-Time Volunteers 10; Interns 2.
Governing Authority: Tax-exempt.
Children's Museum.
Collections: hands-on exhibits.
Activities: drop-in art studio; special seasonal & cultural events; children's, parenting & educator classes and workshops; children's summer & winter camps; group visits; birthday parties; family resources; outreach programs. Annual Event: Early Childhood Safety Campaign.
Hours & Admission Prices: Spring & Fall: Mon.-Thurs. 9:30-12:30; Summer: Fri.-Sat. 9:30-4:30; Winter: Fri.-Sun. 9:30-4:30. Admission $8.50; members & children under one no charge. ACM reciprocal admission. Closed New Year's Day; Easter; Independence Day; Labor Day; Thanksgiving; Christmas. ♿
Attendance: 60,000 (estimated)
Membership: Parent-Child $80; Family $110; Family Circle $140.

* **JUDAH L. MAGNES MUSEUM, (M),** 2911 Russell St., Berkeley, CA 94705-2333. Tel.: 510-549-6950. Fax: 510-849-3673.
E-mail: info@magnes.org
Web Site: www.magnes.org
Founded: 1962.
Congressional District: 8
Key Personnel: Acting Exec. Dir. & Chief Cur., Alla Efimova, Ph.D.; Dir. Finance & Operations, Rhonda Grossman; Pres. (V), Irving Rabin; Dir. Emeritus, Seymour Fromer; Collection Mgr. & Registrar, Linda Waterfield; Archivist, Western Jewish History Center, Lara Michels, Ph.D.; Dir. Devel. & Mktg., James G. Leventhal; Cur. Judaica, Elayne Grossbard; Docent, Outreach & Public Program Coord., Allison Green; Exhibitions Registrar, Julie Franklin; Head Research, Francesco Spagnolo.
Personnel Profile: Full-Time Paid 16; Part-Time Paid 6; Part-Time Volunteers 38.
Governing Authority: nonprofit organization. Tax-exempt: 501(c)(3).
Judaica Museum: housed in historic Berkeley mansion.
Collections: Jewish ceremonial art, fine arts, rare books & manuscripts; ritual objects; textiles; costumes; collections from Jews of India & North Africa; Holocaust collection; Magnes & western states Jewish archives.
Research Fields: Western Jewish History Center documents & studies the influence of the Jewish population on the development, character & culture of the Far West; Jewish ceremonial art, manuscripts & rare books; Jewish fine arts.
Facilities: 10,000-vol. Blumenthal Library of Judaica; Western Jewish History Center archives; garden.
Activities: guided tours; lectures; crafts; permanent & traveling exhibits; outreach programs; homepage; URLs; educational workshops/programs; commission for the preservation of Jewish cemeteries & landmarks.
Hours & Admission Prices: Sun.-Thurs. 11-4. Suggested Donation: adults $4; members no charge. Closed Jewish & legal holidays. ♿
Membership: Senior, Educator, Student & National Associate $40; Dual Senior $50; Individual $75; Family $100; Sponsor $250; Patron $500; Benefactor $1,000; Curator's Circle $2,500; President's Circle $5,000. Art & Culture Council $250 & up.

KALA ART INSTITUTE GALLERY, 1060 Heinz Ave., Berkeley, CA 94710-2719. Tel.: 510-549-2977. Fax: 510-540-6914.
E-mail: kala@kala.org
Web Site: www.kala.org/mission.html
Key Personnel: Exec. Dir. & Co Founder, Archana Horsting; Artistic Dir. & Co Founder, Yuzo Nakano
Art Gallery.
Collections: printmaking.
Activities: lectures; classes; workshops.
Hours & Admission Prices: Tues.-Fri. 12-5, Sat. 12-4:30.

LACIS MUSEUM OF LACE & TEXTILES, (M), 2982 Adeline St., Berkeley, CA 94703-2503. Mailing Address: 3163 Adeline St., Berkeley, CA 94703-2401. Tel.: 510-843-7290. Fax: 510-843-5018.
E-mail: jules@lacis.com
Web Site: lacismuseum.org
Founded: 2004.
Key Personnel: Dir., Jules Kliot; Museum Shop Mgr., Erin Algeo
Lace & Textile Museum.
Collections: laces; textiles; period clothing; costumes; books; patterns; lace-making tools; sewing machines.
Major Exhibits: Bobbin Lace, 11/09-2/1/10; The Roaring Twenties, 4/3/10-7/10.
Facilities: Museum-related items for sale.
Activities: classes.
Publications: exhibit catalogs.
Hours & Admission Prices: Mon.-Sat. 12-6. No charge.
Attendance: 6,000 (estimated)

LAWRENCE HALL OF SCIENCE, University of California, Lawrence Hall of Science #5200, Berkeley, CA 94720-0001. Tel.: 510-642-5132. Fax: 510-642-1055.
E-mail: stage@berkeley.edu
Web Site: www.lawrencehallofscience.org
Founded: 1968.
Congressional District: 9
Key Personnel: Dir., Dr. Elizabeth K. Stage; Deputy Dir., Susan Gregory; Dir. Public Science Center, Barbara Ando; Dir. Center for Leadership in Science Teaching, Craig Strang; Dir. Center for Research Evaluation & Assessment, Rena Dorph; Dir. Resource Management, Flori Ramos; Dir. Center for Curriculum Devel. & Implementation, Jacquey Barber; Dir. Exhibits, Brooke Smith; Dir. Center for Mathematics Excellence & Equity, Harold Asturias; Human Resources Mgr., Sandra Colonna; Museum Shop Mgr., Linda Schneider.
Personnel Profile: Full-Time Paid 200; Part-Time Paid 210; Part-Time Volunteers 30; Interns 75.
Governing Authority: university. Parent Institution: University of California. Tax-exempt: 501(c)(3).
Science & Technology Center.
Collections: science education & curriculum materials; Ernest O. Lawrence memorabilia; science & math exhibits and programs; outdoor earth sciences; special exhibits; family discovery labs; extensive live animal & physical science activities; interactive planetarium; hands-on math challenges; real-time seismic monitor.
Research Fields: science education, intellectual development of children; science & math curricula; teacher training; informal education including exhibit evaluation & visitor behavior; mathematics education; development of educational multimedia.
Facilities: 275-seat auditorium; amphitheater; participatory planetarium; exhibit halls with participatory exhibits; discovery-oriented biology labs; Holt Planetarium; classrooms. Star wheels, sunprint kits, specialized educational materials, science & math materials for sale.
Activities: workshops; formally organized education programs for children & adults; permanent & temporary exhibitions; lectures. Center Sponsors: summer science camp; family workshops; teen internships; school programs; special events.
Publications: Curriculum publications & newsletters, GEMS; EQUALS; Family Math; FOSS; SEPUP; Marine Activities, Resources, and Education (MARE); Seeds of Science & Roots of Reading.
Hours & Admission Prices: Daily 10-5. Adults 19-61 $11, youth 7-18, full-time students, disabled and senior citizens 62 & over $9, children 3-6 $6; discounts to groups, ASTC, ICOM & AAM members; UC students, children under 3 & members no charge. Closed Labor Day; Thanksgiving; Christmas Eve & Day. ♿
Attendance: 200,000 (estimated)
Membership: Senior $45; Individual $50; Family & Grandparents $75; Family Plus $100; Sponsor $250; Associate $500; Partners in Science $1,000 & up.

MUSEUM OF PALEONTOLOGY, 1101 Valley Life Sciences Bldg., University of California, Berkeley, CA 94720-0001. Mailing Address: MC: 4780, 1101 Valley Life Sciences Bldg., University of California, Berkeley, CA 94720-0001. Tel.: 510-642-1821. Fax: 510-642-1822.
Web Site: www.ucmp.berkeley.edu
Founded: 1921.
Congressional District: 9
Key Personnel: Cur., David R. Lindberg; Cur., Jere Lipps; Cur., William B. Berry; Cur., Carole S. Hickman; Cur., Kevin Padian; Cur., Walter Alvarez; Cur., Roger Byrne; Cur., William A. Clemens; Cur., James W. Valentine; Cur., Tim White; Cur., Lynn Ingram; Cur., Roy Caldwell; Principal Museum Scientist, Mark B. Goodwin; Museum Scientist, Pat Holroyd; Museum Scientist, Diane Erwin; Museum Scientist, Kenneth L. Finger; Museum Rels., Judy Scotchmoor; Museum Rels., David K. Smith; Webmaster, Josh Frankel; Museum Preparator, Jane Mason.
Personnel Profile: Full-Time Paid 12; Full-Time Volunteers 7; Part-Time Paid 13; Part-Time Volunteers 1.
Governing Authority: state. Parent Institution: University of California. Tax-exempt.
Paleontology Museum.
Collections: fossil vertebrates; invertebrates; plants; recent molluscan shells; foraminifera; vertebrate skeletal elements; marine sediments; protists; sedimentary rock samples, amber; scanning electronic microscope.
Research Fields: all aspects of paleobiology; cytology; anatomy & physiology of protistids; malacology; paleoceanography; morphometrics; ecology; endangered invertebrate species; evolution; systematics.
Facilities: 2.8 million vol. library; molecular sequencing laboratory; vertebrate & microfossil laboratories.
Activities: formally organized education programs for undergraduate & graduate students; public exhibits; tours available for school & other groups; teacher training. Annual Event: Open House in March.
Publications: bulletin, Paleo Bios; manuscripts, U.C. Press-University Publications in Geological Sciences.
Hours & Admission Prices: Mon.-Thurs. 8am-10pm, Fri. 8-5, Sat. 10-5, Sun. 1-10. No charge; donations accepted. Closed national holidays. Call for holiday & summer hours. ♿
Attendance: 15,000 (estimated)
Membership: Donor $25; Sustaining $50; Patron $100; Sponsor $500; Benefactor $1,000.

MUSEUM OF VERTEBRATE ZOOLOGY, University of California, 3101 Valley Life Sciences Bldg., Berkeley, CA 94720-0001. Tel.: 510-642-3567. Fax: 510-643-8238.
Web Site: mvz.berkeley.edu
Founded: 1908.
Congressional District: 7
Key Personnel: Dir. & Cur., Craig Moritz; Cur. Herpetology, James McGuire; Cur. Mammals, Eileen Lacey; Cur. Assoc., Carla Cicero, Ph.D.; Business Mgr., Joyce Leighton.
Personnel Profile: Full-Time Paid 16; Part-Time Paid 6.
Governing Authority: university. Affiliated with University of California. Tax-exempt: 170(b)(1)(A).
University Zoological Research Museum.
Collections: amphibians; reptiles; birds; mammals; natural history; tissues; sound tapes; field notes; photographs.
Research Fields: birds; mammals; herpetology; anatomy; zoology; natural history; ecology; behavior; physiology; genetics; evolution.
Facilities: 1,000-vol. library of books & reprints on vertebrate zoology available by arrangement with individual curators; field research station.
Activities: formally organized education programs for undergraduate & graduate students affiliated with University of California.
Hours & Admission Prices: Open by permission to research scientists, students & agency personnel only. No charge. ♿

* **PHOEBE APPERSON HEARST MUSEUM OF ANTHROPOLOGY, (M), (I),** 103 Kroeber Hall, University of California, Berkeley, CA 94720-0001. Tel.: 510-642-3682. Fax: 510-642-6271.
E-mail: pahma@berkeley.edu
Web Site: hearstmuseum.berkeley.edu
Founded: 1901.
Congressional District: 8
Key Personnel: Interim Dir., Judson King; Information System, Michael Black; Deputy Dir., Sandra Harris; Administrative Asst., Lisa Hart; Collections Mgr., Leslie Freund; Director's Asst., Patricia Franco; Assoc. Research Anthropologist, Ira Jacknis; NAGPRA Coord., Anthony Garcia; Coord. Collections, Victoria Bradshaw; NAGPRA Scientist, Larri Friedricks; Registrar, Joan Knudsen; Business Mgr., Gail Bergunde; Sr. Artist, Marco Centin; Conservator, Madeleine Fang; Education Specialist, Akiko Minaga; Exhibit Preparator, Ben Peters; Museum Shop Mgr., Oliver Fernandez.
Personnel Profile: Full-Time Paid 22; Full-Time Volunteers 5; Part-Time Paid 6; Part-Time Volunteers 34; Interns 3.
Governing Authority: university. Parent Institution: University of California, Berkeley. Tax-exempt.
Anthropology Museum.
Collections: archaeological & ethnological specimens from the Americas, Oceania, Europe, Asia & Africa; human skeletal material; photographic negatives, slides & prints.
Research Fields: archaeology; ethnography; physical anthropology.
Facilities: Ethnic arts & crafts for sale.
Activities: public programs; informal training programs for professional museum workers; inter-museum loan.

Publications: newsletter, Museum News; Classics in California Anthropology; exhibit catalogues.
Hours & Admission Prices: Wed.-Sat. 10-4:30, Sun. 12-4:30; groups of 20 or more by appointment. No charge; donations accepted. Closed national holidays & university administrative holidays. ♿
Attendance: 45,696 (estimated)
Membership: Student, Senior & Disabled $30; Individual $40; Family $50

TILDEN NATURE AREA ENVIRONMENTAL EDUCATION CENTER, 600 Canon Dr., Berkeley, CA 94708-1162. Tel.: 510-525-2233.
E-mail: tnarea@ebparks.org
Web Site: www.ebparks.org/parks/vc/tna
Nature Center.
Collections: history of Wildcat Creek watershed; ecology; farm animals.
Facilities: theater.
Activities: programs; puppet theater.
Hours & Admission Prices: Nature Area: daily 5am-10pm. Center: Tues.-Sun. 10-5. Little Farm: daily 8:30-4. Closed New Year's Day; Thanksgiving; Christmas. ♿

UNIVERSITY & JEPSON HERBARIA, University of California, 1001 Valley Life Sciences Bldg., #2465, Berkeley, CA 94720-0001. Tel.: 510-642-2465 & 643-7008. Fax: 510-643-5390.
E-mail: bbaldwin@berkeley.edu
Web Site: ucjeps.berkeley.edu/
Founded: 1872.
Congressional District: 8
Key Personnel: Dir., Prof. Brent Mishler; Cur. Seed Pants, Dr. Rudolph Schmid; Research Botanist, Algae, Dr. Paul C. Silva; Research Botanist, Ferns & Grasses, Dr. Alan R. Smith; Research Botanist Compositae, Dr. John L. Strother; Collections Mgr. & Research Botanist, Dr. Barbara Ertter; Cur. Jepson Herbarium, Bruce G. Baldwin.
Personnel Profile: Full-Time Paid 15; Full-Time Volunteers 2; Part-Time Paid 6; Part-Time Volunteers 4; Interns 2.
Governing Authority: state; university. Both herbariums are part of University of California at Berkeley. Tax-exempt: 501(c)(3).
Herbaria.
Collections: worldwide plant kingdom; 1.8 million herbarium specimens in two herbariums.
Research Fields: taxonomy; biosystematics; ecology; floristics; computer methods & floristics.
Facilities: 1,350-vol. library of books & pamphlets pertaining to taxonomy.
Activities: guided tours; formally organized education programs for graduate students affiliated with the University of California.
Publications: Jepson Globe.
Hours & Admission Prices: Mon.-Fri. 8-12 & 1-5. No charge. Closed university holidays.

*** UNIVERSITY OF CALIFORNIA BERKELEY ART MUSEUM AND PACIFIC FILM ARCHIVE, (M),** 2626 Bancroft Way, Berkeley, CA 94704. Mailing Address: 2625 Durant Ave., Berkeley, CA 94720-2251. Tel.: 510-642-0808. Fax: 510-642-4889. TDD: 510-642-8734.
E-mail: bampfa@berkeley.edu
Web Site: www.bampfa.berkeley.edu
Founded: 1965.
Congressional District: 8
Key Personnel: Pres. Bd. Trustees, Noel Nellis; Dir., Lawrence Rinder; Security & Operations Dir., Jesse Fisher; Sr. Film Cur., Susan Oxtoby; Film Cur., Kathy Geritz; Film Collection Mgr., Mona Nagai; Cur. Video, Steve Seid; Dir. Education & Academic Rels., Sherry Goodman; Dir. Registration, Lisa Calden; Museum Shop Mgr., Doug McCallister; Dir. Business Svcs., Rebecca Hoag; Chief Cur. and Dir. Programs & Collections, Lucinda Barnes; Cur. Matrix, Elizabeth Thomas; Dir. Devel., Sara Sackner; Dir. Communications, Ariane Bicho.
Personnel Profile: Full-Time Paid 62; Part-Time Paid 125; Part-Time Volunteers 91; Interns 11.
Governing Authority: Regents of the University of California. Parent Institution: University of California. Subsidiary Institution: Berkeley Campus. Tax-exempt: 501(c)(3) & 101(6).
Art Museum.
Collections: 20th-century American & European paintings, sculpture, drawings, prints & photographs; Hans Hofmann paintings; Asian paintings; pre-20th century art; Pacific Film Archive: international contemporary films, Soviet, Japanese & American avant garde, animation & documentaries; film posters; movie stills; prints; videotapes.
Major Exhibits: What's It All Mean: William T. Wiley in Retrospect (T), 3/17/10-6/20/10; James Castle: A Retrospective (T), 2/3/10-4/25/10.
Research Fields: historical art & film periods.
Facilities: film reference library of books, periodicals & clippings; research screening facilities; 234-seat theater; restaurant; sculpture garden. Artbooks, catalogs & other museum-related items for sale.
Activities: permanent & temporary exhibitions; MATRIX: ongoing exhibitions of contemporary art; Pacific Film Archive film exhibition program; video screenings; lectures; gallery talks; poetry readings; public service media program.
Publications: catalogs; brochures; bimonthly calendar of events; MATRIX artists sheets; exhibition handbills.
Hours & Admission Prices: Wed.-Sun. 11-5. Adults $8, seniors, students 13-17 $5 & non-UC Berkeley students & disabled $5; discounts to groups, AAM & ICOM members; UC Berkeley students, faculty & staff and children 12 & under no charge. Closed university holidays. ♿
Attendance: 200,000 (accurate)
Membership: Senior, Student & Disabled Individual $35; Individual $50; Alumni & Staff Double $65; Double & Family $75; Sponsor $150; Patron & Contemporary Arts Forum $300; Donor $500; Chancellor's Committee $1,000; International Fellows $5,000. Business Circle: Associate $1,000-$4,999; Supporter $5,000-$9,999; Benefactor $10,000 and up.

UNIVERSITY OF CALIFORNIA BOTANICAL GARDEN, 200 Centennial Dr., Berkeley, CA 94720-5045. Tel.: 510-643-2755 & 642-0849. Fax: 510-642-5045.
E-mail: garden@berkeley.edu
Web Site: botanicalgarden.berkeley.edu
Founded: 1890.
Congressional District: 8
Key Personnel: Dir., Paul Licht; Education Coord., Christine Manoux; Assoc. Dir. Collections & Horticulture, A. Christopher Carmichael, Ph.D.; Volunteer Coord., Perry Hall; Devel. & Mktg. Officer, Vanessa Crews; Cur., Holly Forbes.
Personnel Profile: Full-Time Paid 26; Part-Time Paid 6; Part-Time Volunteers 250; Interns 2.
Governing Authority: University of California at Berkeley. Tax-exempt: 501(c)(3).
Botanical Garden.
Collections: 13,000 taxa; 9,700 species of plants; 20,000 accessions from around the world including ferns; gymnosperms; flowering plants; succulents; cacti; Rhododendrons; orchids; economically important species; medicinal plants, California rare species & over 1,000 endangered species.
Research Fields: systematics; ecology; evolutionary biology; conservation biology.
Facilities: 1,000-vol. library of books & periodicals on botany & horticulture available for limited access to visitors; 34-acre botanical garden; amphitheater; classroom; conference center; picnic area.
Activities: guided tours; lectures; formally organized educational programs; permanent & temporary exhibitions.
Publications: periodically updated pamphlets; biannual newsletter; biennial seed list; self guided tour booklet; books, Water-Wise Gardening; Math in the Garden; Botany on Your Plate, Native California Plants & People.
Hours & Admission Prices: Daily 9-5. Adults $7, seniors 65 & over $5, juniors 4-17 $3; UC faculty, students & staff, children under 4 and 1st Thurs. of month no charge. Closed first Tues. of the month; New Year's Eve & Day; Martin Luther King Jr. Day; Thanksgiving; Christmas Eve & Day. ♿
Attendance: 40,000 (accurate)
Membership: Current Cal Student $15; Student $15; UCB Affiliate Individual $30; Individual $45; UCB Affiliate Family $55; Family $65; Supporting $100; Sponsor $250; Patron $500; Benefactor $1,000.

Beverly Hills

CALIFORNIA MUSEUM OF ANCIENT ART, (M), Beverly Hills, CA 90213-3515. Mailing Address: P.O. Box 10515, Beverly Hills, CA 90213-3515. Tel.: 818-762-5500.
E-mail: cmaa@att.net
Web Site: cmaa-museum.org
Founded: 1983.
Key Personnel: Pres., John D. Hofbauer; Dir. & Cur., Jerome Berman; C.F.O., Richard Gerber; Sec., John Matrisciano.
Personnel Profile: Full-Time Paid 1; Part-Time Volunteers 15.
Governing Authority: nonprofit organization. Tax-exempt: 501(c)(3).
Near Eastern Art & Archaeology Museum.
Collections: 3500 B.C.-500 A.D., art & artifacts from Sumer, Babylon, Assyria, Elam, the Hittites, Canaan, Israel, Pharaonic & Coptic Egypt.
Research Fields: ancient Near East; publication of artworks in the collection.
Facilities: 150-vol. library of archaeology, art & history of the ancient Near East.
Activities: lectures; symposia; temporary exhibitions; international archaeological tours.
Publications: biannual newsletter, Ancient News.
Hours & Admission Prices: Closed until 2011. Call for more information.
Membership: Individual $40; Couple & Family $65; Sponsor $150; Patron $300; Pharaoh's Circle $1,000; Corporate & Business $1,500; Lifetime $5,000.

THE PALEY CENTER FOR MEDIA, 465 N. Beverly Dr., Beverly Hills, CA 90210-4601. Tel.: 310-786-1000. Fax: 310-786-1086.
E-mail: tebright@paleycenter.org
Web Site: www.paleycenter.org
Formerly: The Museum of Television & Radio
Founded: 1975.
Key Personnel: Pres. & C.E.O. (NY), Pat Mitchell; Vice Pres. & Exec. Dir. (LA), Craig Hitchcock; Dir. Administration & External Rels., Rebecca Faez; Public Rels. Mgr. (LA), Terry Lynn Ebright.
Governing Authority: Tax-exempt.
Communication Museum.
Collections: 75 years of TV & radio programming & advertisements; documentaries; children's programming; comedy shows, etc.
Major Exhibits: William S. Paley Television Festival, 3/10; Paley Fest Fall TV Preview, 9/10.
Facilities: screening rooms; consoles.
Activities: screening series; seminars; children's workshops.
Hours & Admission Prices: Wed.-Sun. 12-5. No charge; donations accepted. ♿
Membership: Senior Citizen & Student $35; General $50; Dual/Family $70; Contributing $150; Supporting $250; Sustaining $500; Patron's Circle $1,000 & up.

VIRGINIA ROBINSON GARDENS, (M), 1008 Elden Way, Beverly Hills, CA 90210-2805. Tel.: 310-276-5367. Fax: 310-276-5352.
E-mail: friendsvrg@gmail.com
Web Site: www.robinsongardens.org
Founded: 1977.
Key Personnel: Dir., Timothy Lindsay
Historic House & Gardens: 1911 Mediterranean Classic Revival home owned by Mr. and Mrs. Harry Winchester Robinson, heirs to the J.W. Robinson department stores empire.
Collections: Gardens: Italian terrace garden; formal mall garden; rose garden; tropical palm garden; kitchen garden. Historic House: furnishings; personal artifacts.
Activities: guided tours.
Hours & Admission Prices: Guided Tours: Tues.-Fri. 10-1 by appointment. Adults $7, seniors 62 & over and students $4, children 5-12 $2.

Big Bear City

BIG BEAR SOLAR OBSERVATORY, 40386 N. Shore Lane, Big Bear City, CA 92314-9672. Tel.: 909-866-5791. Fax: 909-866-4240.
E-mail: pgoode@bbso.njit.edu
Web Site: www.bbso.njit.edu
Key Personnel: Professor & Dir., Phil Goode
Observatory.
Collections: study of the sun.
Hours & Admission Prices: Closed for renovation.

BIG BEAR VALLEY HISTORICAL MUSEUM, 800 N. Greenway, Big Bear City, CA 92314. Mailing Address: P.O. Box 513, Big Bear City, CA 92314-0513. Tel.: 909-585-8100.
Web Site: www.bigbearhistory.org
History Museum.
Collections: Native American artifacts; cattle ranching & lumbering; gold mining. Historic Building: 1875 log cabin.
Hours & Admission Prices: Wed. & Sat.-Sun. 10-4.

Bishop

LAWS RAILROAD MUSEUM AND HISTORICAL SITE, Silver Canyon Rd., Bishop, CA 93514. Mailing Address: P.O. Box 363, Bishop, CA 93515-0363. Tel.: 760-873-5950.
E-mail: lawsmuseum@aol.com
Web Site: www.lawsmuseum.org
Founded: 1966.
Congressional District: 20 & 35
Key Personnel: C.E.O., Admin. & Museum Shop Mgr., Barbara Moss; Chm. (V), Max Cox.
Personnel Profile: Full-Time Paid 4; Part-Time Paid 6; Part-Time Volunteers 10.
Governing Authority: nonprofit organization. Parent Institution: Bishop Museum & Historical Society. Tax-exempt: 501(c)(3).
Railroad Museum Complex: housed in 1883 Laws Railroad Depot & 28 other buildings.
Collections: railroad engines; passenger & freight cars; railroad artifacts; western items; working model railroad; Indian artifacts; old bottle collections; musical instruments; farm wagons & machinery; paintings; guns; sewing machines; barbed wire; doctor's instruments & equipment; cameras; 1870 print shop; rare books; historical village; Death Valley #5.
Research Fields: railroad; local history & pioneer families.
Facilities: 11 acres of ground; reception center. Museum-related gifts for sale.
Activities: guided tours; permanent exhibitions.
Publications: quarterly bulletin.
Hours & Admission Prices: Daily 10-4. Suggested Donation: adults $5; members no charge. Closed New Year's Day; Easter; Thanksgiving; Christmas. ♿
Attendance: 20,000 (accurate)
Membership: Individual $15; Family $25; Organizational $30; Business $60; Life $300; Patron $500; Benefactor $1,000.

Blairsden

PLUMAS-EUREKA STATE PARK, 310 Johnsville Rd., Blairsden, CA 96103-9744. Tel.: 530-836-2380. Fax: 530-836-0498.
Web Site: www.parks.ca.gov
Founded: 1959.
Congressional District: 14
Key Personnel: Ranger, Scott Elliott.
Governing Authority: state; nonprofit. State of California, Dept. of Parks & Recreation, Plumas-Eureka State Park Assoc. Tax-exempt.
Historic Site: High Sierra Mining Town.
Collections: mining & blacksmithing tools & equipment; domestic furnishings; vehicles; tack; photographs; natural history; recreational skiing; carpentry.
Research Fields: history of recreational skiing; mining; mining camp life; domestic life in a remote high-altitude mining camp; early hydro-electric production.
Facilities: picnic area; camping ground; trails; biking; cross-country skiing; intermittent downhill skiing; off highway vehicle access; swimming; fishing; boating.
Activities: guided & self-guided tours; horse-drawn sleigh rides; blacksmithing instruction & demonstration; annual living history events; interpretive hikes; docent program; intern program.
Publications: park brochures.
Hours & Admission Prices: Summer: daily 8-4:30; Winter: call for hours. Campgrounds: $20 per night. Museum: no charge; donations accepted.
Attendance: 40,000
Membership: Individual $5; Family $10; Life $100.

Bolinas

BOLINAS MUSEUM, (M), 48 Wharf Rd., Bolinas, CA 94924. Mailing Address: P.O. Box 450, Bolinas, CA 94924-0450. Tel.: 415-868-0330. Fax: 415-868-0607.
E-mail: info@bolinasmuseum.org
Web Site: bolinasmuseum.org
Founded: 1982.
Congressional District: 6
Key Personnel: Dir., Lucy Van Sands Seeburg; Pres., Roger Peacock; Treas., Terry Donohue.
Personnel Profile: Full-Time Paid 1; Part-Time Paid 2; Part-Time Volunteers 30.
Governing Authority: nonprofit organization. Tax-exempt: 501(c)(3).
Art & History Museum.
Collections: art & history of west Marin County.
Major Exhibits: Contemporary Native American Artists & Ilka Hartmann, 1/23/10-3/7/10; Gordon Cook & Luis Delgado, 3/13/10-4/25/10; Water as Metaphor & Deborah O'Grady, 5/10-6/13/10; Barry McGee & Clare Rojas, also Jona Frank, 6/19/10-8/1/10; 18th Annual Art Auction Preview Exhibition, 8/7/10-9/1/10; Ken Botto: Botto's World in Photographs, 10/20/10-11/14/10; Annual Holiday Mini Show & Michael Light, 11/20/10-12/10.
Facilities: Museum-related items for sale.
Activities: docent program; guided tours; lectures; participatory, loan & temporary exhibitions; workshops. Museum Sponsors: Art Auction; Garden Tour.
Publications: biannual newsletter, Bolinas Museum News.
Hours & Admission Prices: Fri. 1-5, Sat.-Sun. 12-5. No charge; donations accepted. Closed New Year's Day; Thanksgiving; Christmas. ♿
Attendance: 18,000 (estimated)
Membership: Individual $25; Family & Business $50; Sponsor $100; Friend $250; Patron $500; Benefactor $1,000 & up.

Boonville

ANDERSON VALLEY HISTORICAL SOCIETY MUSEUM, 12340 Hwy. 128, Boonville, CA 95415. Mailing Address: P.O. Box 676, Boonville, CA 95415-0676. Tel.: 707-895-3207.
E-mail: sheri@campracheria.com
Web Site: www.andersonvalleymuseum.org
Historical Society Museum.

Collections: artifacts & memorabilia pertaining to Anderson County.
Hours & Admission Prices: Feb.-Nov. Fri.-Sun. 1-4.

Borrego Springs

ANZA-BORREGO DESERT STATE PARK, 200 Palm Cyn Dr., Borrego Springs, CA 92004-5005. Mailing Address: P.O. Box 2001, Borrego Springs, CA 92004-2001. Tel.: 760-767-4037. Fax: 760-767-3427.
E-mail: info@parks.ca.gov
Web Site: www.parks.ca.gov/default.asp?page_ID=638
Founded: 1967.
Congressional District: 52
Key Personnel: Supt., Gail Sevrens; Exec. Dir. Foundation, Linda Carson; Mgr. ABI, Sally Theriault; Mgr. VC, Michael Rodriques; Museum Shop Mgr., Kelley Jorgensen.
Personnel Profile: Full-Time Paid 1; Full-Time Volunteers 4; Part-Time Paid 4; Part-Time Volunteers 125.
Governing Authority: state. Parent Institution: California Dept. of Parks & Recreation, Sacramento, CA. Cooperating Association: Anza-Barrego Foundation and Institute, 586 Palm Canyon Dr., P.O. Box 2001, Borrego Springs, CA 92004. Tel. 760-767-0446; Fax: 760-767-0465. Tax-exempt.
Archaeology & Paleontology Museum: housed inside a subterranean structure, natural face rock without windows.
Collections: paleontological collection; plio-pleistocene mammals, birds, reptiles, archaeological collection; Cahuilla & Kumeyaay pottery & tools; San Dieguito tools; Peninsular Bighorn Sheep Skull collection.
Research Fields: paleontology; archaeology.
Facilities: 3,000-vol. library of natural history of Colorado Desert of California available for research by appointment; botanical garden; separate laboratory operation; 65-seat auditorium & theater; classrooms; outdoor amphitheater. Natural history books, maps & other museum-related items for sale.
Activities: guided tours; lectures; films; docent program.
Publications: park magazine; Anza-Borrego Desert State Park.
Hours & Admission Prices: Visitor center: June-Sept. Sat.-Sun. & holidays 9-5; Oct.-May daily 9-5 No charge; donations accepted; day use fee $6 per vehicle for campgrounds & hiking. ♿
Attendance: 175,774 (accurate)

Boulder Creek

BIG BASIN REDWOODS STATE PARK, 21600 Big Basin Way, Boulder Creek, CA 95006-9063. Tel.: 831-338-8864. Fax: 831-338-8863.
Web Site: bigbasin.org
Founded: 1902.
Congressional District: 15
Key Personnel: Supervising Ranger, Kevin Williams.
Personnel Profile: Full-Time Paid 5; Part-Time Volunteers 8.
Governing Authority: state. Parent Institution: California State Parks. Tax-exempt.
Natural History Museum & State Park.
Collections: fauna & flora of the area; botany; entomology.
Research Fields: botany; history.
Activities: guided tours; organized education programs for children. Museum Sponsors: Celebrating the 100th Anniversary of Big Basin, the oldest state park.
Hours & Admission Prices: Camp Store & Gift Shop daily 10-4. Visitor Center and Nature Museum daily 8-5, call to confirm. Donations accepted for park & trails; $6 per vehicle, senior citizens 62 & over $5 per vehicle. State annual park passes accepted.
Attendance: 750,000 (estimated)

SAN LORENZO VALLEY MUSEUM, 12547 Hwy. 9, Boulder Creek, CA 95006. Mailing Address: P.O. Box 576, Boulder Creek, CA 95006-0576. Tel.: 831-338-8382. Fax: 831-338-8332.
E-mail: slvhm@cruzio.com
Web Site: www.slvmuseum.com
Key Personnel: Exec. Dir., Lynda Phillips.
Governing Authority: Parent Institution: Boulder Creek Historical Society.
History Museum.
Collections: logging history; Native American artifacts; clothing.
Facilities: Museum-related items for sale.
Hours & Admission Prices: Wed. & Fri.-Sun. 12-4; other times by appointment. No charge.

Brea

BREA MUSEUM AND HERITAGE CENTER, 495 S. Brea Blvd., Brea, CA 92821-5395. Mailing Address: P.O. Box 9764, Brea, CA 92822-9764. Tel.: 714-256-2283.
History Museum.
Collections: local history & heritage; photographs; personal artifacts; period furnishings.
Hours & Admission Prices: Sat. 10-3:30; other times by appointment. No charge.

CITY OF BREA ART GALLERY, (M), Brea Civic & Cultural Center, Plaza Level, 1 Civic Center Cir., Brea, CA 92821-5732. Tel.: 714-990-7730. Fax: 714-990-7736.
E-mail: breagallery@cityofbrea.net
Web Site: www.breagallery.com
Founded: 1980.
Key Personnel: C.E.O. & City Mgr., Tim O'Donnell; Dir. & Museum Shop Mgr., Thomas Ciganko; Cultural Arts Comm. Chm., Rick Clark; Arts & Human Svcs. Mgr., Emily Keller; Art Educator, Christina Hasenberg; Coord. Events, Claudia Sandoval.
Personnel Profile: Part-Time Volunteers 2; Interns 1.
Governing Authority: municipal. Parent Institution: Brea Arts Corporation. Tax-exempt.
Art Exhibit Area.
Collections: outdoor large-scale sculptures; paintings; photographs; prints, drawings & graphic arts.
Research Fields: sculptures; public art.
Facilities: county branch library; 200-seat theater; lecture halls; classrooms; meeting rooms; TV studio.
Activities: guided tours; lectures; performing arts; juried art exhibitions; artist workshops; cultural arts commission; volunteer program; TV programs; public sculpture program; consignment art program; gallery available for rental & private receptions.
Publications: newsletter; brochures; exhibit announcements; self-guided Art in Public Places tour guide & catalog.
Hours & Admission Prices: Wed.-Sun. 12-5. Adults $2; discounts to AAM members; members, children under 12 no charge. Closed holidays. ♿
Attendance: 20,000 (accurate)
Membership: Annual $12.

OLINDA HISTORIC MUSEUM AND PARK, 4025 Santa Fe Rd., Brea, CA 92821. Mailing Address: 1 Civic Center Circle, Brea, CA 92821-5792. Tel.: 714-671-4447.
Historic Site.
Collections: local history; geology; Olinda Oil Well #1 drilled in 1897; a jackline pump; records; field office.
Hours & Admission Prices: Wed. & Sat.-Sun. 9-4. No charge.

Brentwood

EAST CONTRA COSTA MUSEUM, 3890 Sellers Ave., Brentwood, CA 94513. Mailing Address: P.O. Box 202, Brentwood, CA 94513-0202. Tel.: 925-625-3553.
History Museum.
Collections: local history; period artifacts; documents; photographs.
Hours & Admission Prices: April-Oct. Sat. & 3rd Sun. of month 2-4.

Bridgeport

BODIE STATE HISTORIC PARK, Hwy. 395, Bridgeport, CA 93517. Mailing Address: P.O. Box 515, Bridgeport, CA 93517-0515. Tel.: 760-647-6445. Fax: 760-647-6486.
Web Site: www.ceres.ca.gov/sierradsp/index.html
Founded: 1962.
Congressional District: 18
Key Personnel: Acting Unit Supervising Ranger, Mark Langner; Museum Cur. II, Judith K. Polanich.
Personnel Profile: Full-Time Paid 5; Part-Time Paid 8; Part-Time Volunteers 8; Interns 1.
Governing Authority: state; nonprofit. Parent Institution: State of California, Dept. of Parks & Recreation, Sierra State Parks Foundation. Tax-exempt.
Historic Site: 1849-1932 Gold Rush Mining Boom Town.
Collections: furnishings; clothing; household goods; mining & milling tools & equipment; vehicles; newspapers; mines; mortuary; cemetery. Historic Structures: schoolhouse; store; hotels; saloons; jail; firehouse; fraternal order buildings; mill.
Research Fields: history of emigration in the West; history of mining in California & Nevada; mining economics; mining camp life.
Facilities: library; archives.
Activities: self-guided & guided tours; school groups; photo workshops.
Publications: teacher's guide; children's activity guide; historic newspaper re-issues; feature length docu-drama historical video: Bodie, Ghost Town Frozen in Time; Self-guide tour brochure; Books: Aurora; Bodie; Esmeralda.
Hours & Admission Prices: Summer: daily 9:30-6; Winter: daily 9-4 (variable access). Adults $3, children 6-12 $1.

Attendance: 190,000 (estimated)
Membership: Copper $20; Silver $35; Gold $50; W.S. Bodey $100; Life $250.

Buena Park

BUENA PARK HISTORICAL SOCIETY, 6631 Beach Blvd., Buena Park, CA 90621-2904. Tel.: 714-562-3570.
E-mail: info@historicalsociety.org
Web Site: www.historicalsociety.org
Founded: 1968.
Congressional District: 30
Key Personnel: Pres. (V), Art Brown; Cur., Dean O. Dixon.
Personnel Profile: Part-Time Paid 1; Part-Time Volunteers 12.
Governing Authority: nonprofit organization. Tax-exempt.
Historic House Museum.
Collections: period furnishings. Historic Houses: 1887 Whitaker-Jaynes House; 1884 Bacon House.
Research Fields: Buena Park history.
Activities: guided tours; lectures; permanent & temporary exhibitions.
Publications: book, The Picture Story of Buena Park; society newsletter; online, Images of America: Buena Park.
Hours & Admission Prices: Thurs. 10:30-2:30, 2nd Sun. of month 1-4. No charge; donations accepted. ♿
Attendance: 684 (accurate)
Membership: Students $2.50; Active $10 (spouse $2.50); Family $15; Life $100.

Burlingame

BURLINGAME MUSEUM OF PEZ & CLASSIC TOY MUSEUM, 214 California Dr., Burlingame, CA 94010-4113. Tel.: 650-347-2301. Fax: 650-347-3840.
E-mail: gary@spectrumnet.com
Web Site: www.burlingamepezmuseum.com
Founded: 1995.
Key Personnel: C.E.O., Gary R. Doss; Museum Shop Mgr., Nancy Doss
General Museum.
Collections: pez dispensers & memorabilia; classic toys including Tinkertoy, Mr. Potato Head, Colorforms, View-Master, Erector, Lincoln Logs, Whee-Lo, Wooly Willy, Ant Factory; original advertising artwork.
Facilities: Museum-related items for sale.
Activities: tours.
Publications: newsletter.
Hours & Admission Prices: Tues.-Sat. 10-6. Adults $3, senior citizens 65 & over and children 4-12 $1; children 3 & under and 1st Thurs. of month no charge. Closed major holidays.

Burney

MCARTHUR-BURNEY FALLS MEMORIAL STATE PARK, 24898 Hwy. 89, Burney, CA 96013-9626. Mailing Address: Interpretive Association, P.O. Box 777, Burney, CA 96013. Tel.: 530-335-2777.
Web Site: www.burney-falls.com
Park Museum & Visitor Center.
Collections: Park: 129-foot Burney Falls. Log Cabin Visitor Center: hands-on exhibits.
Facilities: nature trails. Museum-related items for sale.
Activities: programs; hiking; camping.
Hours & Admission Prices: Daily sunrise-sunset. $6 per vehicle, seniors 62 & over $5 per vehicle.

Calabasas

LEONIS ADOBE MUSEUM, (M), 23537 Calabasas Rd., Calabasas, CA 91302-1311. Tel.: 818-222-6511.
Key Personnel: Ranch & Facility Mgr., Diane Ramadan
Historic House & Gardens: housed in the former home of Miguel Leonis; c.1880.
Collections: late 1800s California ranch life; period furnishings; photographs; personal artifacts.
Facilities: rental facilities. Museum-related items for sale.
Activities: special events; traveling trunk.
Hours & Admission Prices: Wed.-Fri. & Sun. 1-4, Sat. 10-4. Suggested Donations: adults $4, senior citizens $3, children under 12 $1. Closed New Year's Day; Thanksgiving; Christmas Eve & Day.
Membership: Senior & Student $15; Individual $25; Family $40; Caballero $100.

Calistoga

PETRIFIED FOREST MUSEUM, 4100 Petrified Forest Rd., Calistoga, CA 94515-9527. Tel.: 707-942-6667.
E-mail: manager@petrifiedforest.org
Web Site: www.petrifiedforest.org
Forest Museum.
Collections: petrified redwood trees; fossils; area geology; native wildflowers; live oaks, madrone & manzanita trees; 100 ft.-high Ash Fall.
Facilities: picnic area. Museum-related items for sale.
Activities: guided tours.
Hours & Admission Prices: Summer: daily 9-7; Winter: daily 9-5. Adults $6, seniors over 60 & children 12-17 $5, children 6-11 $3.

SHARPSTEEN MUSEUM, (M), 1311 Washington St., Calistoga, CA 94515-1441. Mailing Address: P.O. Box 573, Calistoga, CA 94515-0573. Tel.: 707-942-5911 & 5916 (Mon.-Fri.). Fax: 707-942-6325.
Web Site: sharpsteen-museum.org
Founded: 1978.
Congressional District: 1
Key Personnel: Pres. (V), Tom Andrews; Chm. (V) (books) & Book Shop Mgr., Virginia Heitz; Gift Shop Mgr., Sonya Spencer.
Personnel Profile: Part-Time Volunteers 200.
Governing Authority: municipal government; nonprofit. Tax-exempt.
Historical Society Museum: adjacent to the museum is one of Sam Brannan's original cottages.
Collections: history of the City of Calistoga & other areas in the upper Napa Valley.
Research Fields: geothermal exhibit.
Facilities: library; 3,500 sq. ft. exhibit space. Museum-related items for sale.
Publications: bimonthly newsletter; biography pamphlet, Ben Sharpsteen; books, Sam Brannan; Early Upper Napa Valley; Calistoga Days; Brannan Saga; They Left Their Mark; Anecdotes of Calistoga.
Hours & Admission Prices: 11-4 year round. No charge; donations accepted. Closed Thanksgiving; Christmas. ♿
Attendance: 14,500 (estimated)
Membership: Senior Citizen $20; Individual $25; Business & Associate $50; Sponsor $100; Benefactor $2,500. Lifetime: Individual $300; Family $500; Business $1,000.

Camp Pendleton

CAMP PENDLETON MUSEUMS, Marine Corps Base, Camp Pendleton, CA 92055. Mailing Address: CPAO H&S Bn, History & Museums Office, Marine Corps Base, Box 555019, Camp Pendleton, CA 92055-5019. Tel.: 760-725-2195. Fax: 760-725-5011.
Web Site: www.pendleton.usmc.mil
Governing Authority: Base Museums: World War II & Korea LVT Museum, Bldg. 21561, Boat Basin. Marine Corps Mechanized Command Museum, Bldg. 2612, Vandegrift Blvd. Ranch House Complex: Ranch House Chapel, Bunkhouse Museum, Ranch House.
Military Museum.
Collections: World War II & Korea LVT Museum: amphibious tracked vehicles. Marine Corps Mechanized Command Museum: Marine Corps transport & battle vehicles; Viet Nam & Desert Storm vehicles. Ranch House Complex: Ranch House Chapel; Bunkhouse Museum: military history; early ranch equipment; photographs; period furnishings.
Hours & Admission Prices: By appointment. Submit your written request to the above address. ID required for admittance.

Campbell

CAMPBELL HISTORICAL MUSEUM & AINSLEY HOUSE, (M), 51 N. Central Ave., Campbell, CA 95008-2015. Tel.: 408-866-2119 & 2757. Fax: 408-866-2795.
E-mail: karenb@ci.campbell.ca.us
Web Site: www.ci.campbell.ca.us/museum/tours/htm
Founded: 1964.
Congressional District: 15
Key Personnel: Dir. & Cur., Karen Lange.
Personnel Profile: Full-Time Paid 2; Part-Time Paid 2; Part-Time Volunteers 135.
Governing Authority: municipal. Parent Institution: City of Campbell, CA. Subsidiary Institution: Campbell Museum Foundation. Branch Location: 51 N. Central Ave., Campbell, CA 95008. Tax-exempt.
History Museum: housed in 1951 Fire station which served as the city's first office; 1925 Tudor revival; Carriage House serves as visitor center & museum store.
Collections: local history from early inhabitants to present; artifacts; photographs; archives; farm & agricultural equipment.
Research Fields: local history; genealogy.

Facilities: library pertaining to preservation, rehabilitation, history & museology; research room. Museum-related gift items for sale.
Activities: guided tours; lectures; docent program; oral history program; historic walking tour; historic resource survey; temporary exhibitions; hands-on history exhibits.
Publications: brochure, Campbell Historical Museum Brochure; newsletter, Campbell Visitor.
Hours & Admission Prices: Historical Museum: Mon.-Fri. 8:30-5. Admission $2. Ainsley House: Jan. 3-Dec. 17. Docent Tour: adults $6, senior citizens $4, children 7-17 $2.50; discounts to AAM members; members no charge. Closed New Year's Day; Easter; Thanksgiving Day; Christmas. ♿
Attendance: 6,700 (accurate)
Membership: Senior & Student $20; Individual $25; Family $35; Sponsor $50; Director's Circle $100; Carriage House Circle $250; Benefactor Ainsley House Circle $1,000; Firehouse Circle $2,000; Museum Circle $5,000.

Canoga Park

CANOGA-OWENSMOUTH HISTORICAL MUSEUM, Canoga Park Community Center, 7248 Owensmouth Ave., Canoga Park, CA 91303-1529. Tel.: 818-340-3696 & 346-5252.
History Museum.
Collections: history of San Fernando Valley; photographs; documents; paintings.
Hours & Admission Prices: 2nd & 4th Sun. of month 2-4; other times by appointment. No charge.

ORCUTT RANCH, 23600 Roscoe Blvd., Canoga Park, CA 91304-3057. Tel.: 818-346-7449.
Web Site: www.laparks.org/dos/horticulture/orcuttranch.htm
Historic House: home of William Warren Orcutt & his wife Mary Logan Orcutt, c.1926. Los Angeles Historic-Cultural Monument.
Collections: period furnishings; personal artifacts; gardens; citrus orchard.
Facilities: 24-acre gardens; citrus orchard.
Hours & Admission Prices: Museum: daily sunrise to sunset. Orchards: July call for hours.

Capitola

CAPITOLA HISTORICAL MUSEUM, 410 Capitola Ave., Capitola, CA 95010-3318. Tel.: 831-464-0322.
E-mail: cswift@ci.capitola.ca.us
Web Site: www.capitolamuseum.org
Founded: 1967.
Congressional District: 16
Key Personnel: Dir., Carolyn Swift.
Personnel Profile: Part-Time Paid 2; Part-Time Volunteers 15.
Governing Authority: municipal. Parent Institution: City of Capitola.
General Museum.
Collections: photographs.
Activities: guided tours.
Hours & Admission Prices: Fri.-Sun. 12-4; other time by appointment. No charge; donations accepted. ♿
Attendance: 3,600

Carlsbad

GEMOLOGICAL INSTITUTE OF AMERICA MUSEUM, (M), 5345 Armada Dr., Carlsbad, CA 92008-4602. Tel.: 760-603-4000. Fax: 760-603-4199.
E-mail: emisioro@gia.edu
Web Site: www.gia.edu
Founded: 2001.
Key Personnel: Dir., Elise B. Misiorowski; Registrar & Data Management Specialist, Peggy Walter; Cur., Terri Ottaway; Asst. Cur., Mark Mauthner.
Personnel Profile: Full-Time Paid 5; Part-Time Volunteers 20.
Governing Authority: private; nonprofit organization. Tax-exempt: 501(c)(3).
General Museum.
Collections: gems; gem minerals; jewelry; art; photographs; paintings; books; scientific literature; gemological slides; pre-Columbian jewelry & artifacts.
Facilities: 44,000-vol. library; 140-seat theater; cafeteria; educational facilities.
Activities: docent program; formal education programs for adults & undergraduate or graduate college students; guided tours; lectures; loan, temporary & traveling exhibitions; jr. gemologist program.
Publications: quarterly journal, Gems & Gemology; quarterly magazine, The Loupe; bi-weekly electronic bulletin, The Insider.
Hours & Admission Prices: Mon.-Fri. 8-5. No charge. Closed New Year's Day; Presidents' Day; Memorial Day; Independence Day; Labor Day; Thanksgiving; Christmas.
Attendance: 5,000 (estimated)

MUSEUM OF MAKING MUSIC, A DIVISION OF THE NAMM FOUNDATION, (M), 5790 Armada Dr., Carlsbad, CA 92008-4608. Tel.: 760-438-5996. Fax: 760-438-8964.
E-mail: museum@museumofmakingmusic.org
Web Site: www.museumofmakingmusic.org
Founded: 1998.
Congressional District: 50
Key Personnel: Exec. Dir., Carolyn Grant; C.E.O. & Pres., Joe Lamond; Cur., Tatiana Sizonenko; Museum Shop Mgr., Crystal Babowal.
Personnel Profile: Full-Time Paid 6; Part-Time Paid 2; Part-Time Volunteers 55; Interns 2.
Governing Authority: private; nonprofit organization. Parent Institution: NAMM Foundation. Tax-exempt: 501(c)(3).
Musical Instruments Museum.
Collections: musical instruments; products.
Major Exhibits: Waves of Inspiration: The Legacy of Moog, 11/09-4/10; Saxophones - A History, 6/10-12/10.
Research Fields: history of the music products industry; music education; popular music; music retail business; instrument manufacturing & distribution; music publishing.
Facilities: library; recital & performance space; classroom.
Activities: exhibition-related programming; hands-on workshops; film series; new music series; music & wellness series; concert & conversation series; Saturday afternoon concerts; family activity days.
Publications: newsletter, In Tune.
Hours & Admission Prices: Tues.-Sun. 10-5. Adults $7, senior citizens, students & military $5; discounts to AAM & ICOM members; members no charge. ♿
Attendance: 30,000 (accurate)
Membership: Individual $25; Family $50; Music Enthusiast $100; Music Advocate $250; Music Activist $500; Visionary $1,000.

Carmel

CENTER FOR PHOTOGRAPHIC ARTS, San Carlos & 9th Sts., Carmel, CA 93921. Mailing Address: P.O. Box 1100, Carmel, CA 93921-1100. Tel.: 831-625-5181. Fax: 831-625-5199.
E-mail: info@photography.org
Web Site: www.photography.org/index.html
Photography Museum.
Collections: photography.
Hours & Admission Prices: Tues.-Sun. 1-5.

MISSION SAN CARLOS BORROMEO DEL RIO CARMELO, 3100 Rio Rd., Carmel, CA 93923-9237. Tel.: 831-624-1271, ext. 210. Fax: 831-624-0658.
Web Site: www.carmelmission.org
Founded: 1770.
Congressional District: 5
Key Personnel: Cur., Richard J. Menn.
Governing Authority: Roman Catholic Church. Tax-exempt.
History Museum.
Collections: sculpture; statues; postcards; textiles; Spanish Colonial art & artifacts.
Facilities: library of books published between 1615-1833. Religious articles, books & postcards for sale.
Activities: Sunday services.
Hours & Admission Prices: Mon.-Sat. 9:30-5, Sun. 10:30-5. Adults $5, seniors $4, children under 17 $1.

Carmel-by-the-Sea

CARMEL HERITAGE SOCIETY'S FIRST MURPHY HOUSE, Lincoln & Sixth, Carmel-by-the-Sea, CA 93921. Mailing Address: Carmel Heritage Society, P.O. Box 701, Carmel-by-the-Sea, CA 93921-0701. Tel.: 831-624-4447. Fax: 831-624-1970.
E-mail: info@carmelheritage.org
Web Site: www.carmelheritage.org
Key Personnel: Pres., Dawn Dull
Historical House Museum.
Collections: Carmel history; cultural heritage; garden.
Facilities: garden.
Hours & Admission Prices: House: Wed.-Sun. 1-4. Society Office: Mon.-Thurs. 10-2. No charge.
Membership: Annual $15; Family $30; Sponsor $50; Patron $100; Lifetime $500.

Carmichael

EFFIE YEAW NATURE CENTER, 2850 San Lorenzo Way, Carmichael, CA 95608. Mailing Address: P.O. Box 579, Carmichael, CA 95609-0579. Tel.: 916-489-4918. Fax: 916-489-4983.
E-mail: eync@saccounty.net
Web Site: www.effieyeaw.org
Founded: 1976.
Congressional District: 3
Key Personnel: Dir., Marilee Flannery; Volunteer Coord., Jamie Washington; Dir. Education, Beth Etgen; Exhibit Dir. & Publicity Coord., Betty Cooper; Maidu Cultural Heritage Program, Lynne Pinkerton.
Personnel Profile: Full-Time Paid 5; Part-Time Paid 20; Part-Time Volunteers 200.
Governing Authority: county; nonprofit. Parent Institution: County of Sacramento, Dept. of Parks & Recreation. Subsidiary Institution: American River Natural History Association.
Nature Center.
Collections: mounts & study skins of wildlife native to central California; historic & recreated artifacts of local Sacramento area Native American culture; maps; photographs; demonstration village.
Research Fields: captive hawk behavior modification.
Facilities: 625-vol. library of natural & cultural history of Sacramento region; park management, available for in-house use; 1,800 sq. ft. exhibit space; nature/conservation center; 77-acre nature area; Maidu Indian cultural demonstration area; 4kw solar panel system. Books, nature-related & historical items for sale.
Activities: docent program; formal education programs for children, on & off-site; guided tours; teacher workshops; weekend family programs; participatory & temporary exhibitions. Center Sponsors: Creek Week in April; Maidu Indian Day & The American River Salmon Festival in October.
Publications: field guides, The Outdoor World of the Sacramento Region; Birds of the American River Parkway; The Lower American: Prehistory to Parkway; Biking and Hiking the American River Parkway; children's storybook, Ooti, Child of the Nisenan; curricula; The American River Parkway, a handbook for outdoor exploration and learning; The Valley Nisenan Educator's Guide.
Hours & Admission Prices: Feb.-Oct. Mon.-Tues. 9-1; Nov.-Jan. 9:30-1. Vehicle park entrance fee $5. Museum: no charge; donations accepted. Closed New Year's Day; Thanksgiving; Christmas Day. ♿
Attendance: 83,800 (accurate)
Membership: American River Natural History Association: Student $15; Senior Citizen $20; Individual $25; Family $35; Contributor $60; Sponsor $100; Sustainer $250; Patron $500.

Carpinteria

CARPINTERIA VALLEY HISTORICAL SOCIETY & MUSEUM OF HISTORY, (M), 956 Maple Ave., Carpinteria, CA 93013-2021. Tel.: 805-684-3112. Fax: 805-684-4721.
E-mail: info@carpinteriahistoricalmuseum.org
Web Site: www.carpinteriahistoricalmuseum.org
Founded: 1959.
Congressional District: 23
Key Personnel: Pres., Mary Alice Coffman; Dir. & Cur., David W. Griggs.
Personnel Profile: Full-Time Paid 1; Part-Time Volunteers 75.
Governing Authority: nonprofit organization. Tax-exempt: 170(b)(1)(A) & 501(c)(3).
Local History Museum.
Collections: artifacts of Chumash Indians & early pioneers of Valley; early pioneer furnishings; 1822-1850 Mexican period artifacts; agricultural tools; oral history tapes; photographs; late 19th & early 20th century school artifacts, cameras, costumes, camping & sporting goods, toys.
Research Fields: Chumash Indians; 1769-1850 Hispanic period; pioneer & family history; agriculture; Santa Barbara Channel oil development, asphalt mines.
Facilities: research library; subject & family archives; cross-referenced, triple-indexed photograph & oral history archives.
Activities: docent program; permanent & temporary exhibits; school programs; tours; research facilities; oral history project. Museum Sponsors: Spring Lecture Series; Monthly Flea Market; Annual Potluck Picnic; Holiday Faire.
Publications: bimonthly newsletter, The Grapevine.
Hours & Admission Prices: Tues.-Sat. 1-4. No charge; donations requested.
Attendance: 10,000 (estimated)
Membership: Student $5; Individual $25; Family $35; Contributing $50; Patron $100; Corporate $150; Benefactor $250; Life $500.

Carson

THE INTERNATIONAL PRINTING MUSEUM, 315 Torrance Blvd., Carson, CA 90745-1130. Tel.: 310-515-7166. Fax: 714-538-2443.
E-mail: mail@printmuseum.org
Web Site: www.printmuseum.org
Formerly: The Printing Museum
Founded: 1988.
Key Personnel: Exec. Dir., Mark Barbour; Chm. (V), John Hedlund; Pres., Paul Doucette Ernest Lindner.
Personnel Profile: Full-Time Paid 3; Part-Time Paid 1; Part-Time Volunteers 2.
Governing Authority: private; nonprofit organization. Tax-exempt: 501(c)(3) & 170(b)(1)(A).
Typography Museum.
Collections: period printing machinery & allied trades covering 500 years with an emphasis on the 19th century; research library with 5,000 volumes detailing the history of printing & communications; traveling exhibits.
Hours & Admission Prices: Sat. 10-4. By appointment Tues.-Fri. Adults $8, students, seniors & members $7; preschool children no charge. ♿
Attendance: 20,000 (estimated)

UNIVERSITY ART GALLERY, CSU DOMINGUEZ HILLS, 1000 E. Victoria St., Carson, CA 90747-0001. Tel.: 310-243-3334 & 3310. Fax: 310-217-6967.
E-mail: kzimmerer@csudh.edu
Web Site: www.cla.csudh.edu/artgallery
Founded: 1978.
Congressional District: 31
Key Personnel: Dir., Kathy Zimmerer.
Personnel Profile: Full-Time Paid 1; Part-Time Paid 2; Interns 2.
Governing Authority: university; nonprofit. Parent Institution: CSU Dominquez Hills. Tax-exempt: 501(c)(3).
University Art Gallery.
Collections: paintings; sculpture; photographs.
Major Exhibits: Figurative Dimensions: Tim Ashcraft and Russell McMillin, 11/09-12/09; The Veil: Visible and Invisible Spaces (T), 2/10-3/10; Art of Ink: Traditional and Contemporary Calligraphy, 3/10-4/10; 10th International Shoebox Sculpture Exhibition (T), 2/10-3/11.
Research Fields: contemporary California art with emphasis on multiculturalism; historic California art.
Facilities: 2,150 sq. ft. exhibit space.
Activities: guided tours; lectures; loan exhibitions; formally organized education programs for undergraduates affiliated with CSU Dominguez Hills & surrounding communities; teacher training conferences; K-12 education programs.
Publications: annual newsletter; biannual exhibit catalogues; New Directions in California Sculpture; Painted Light: California Impressionist Paintings from the Gardena High School/LAUSD Collection; An Architectural Stylist: W. Horace Austin and Eclecticism in California; Annual Student Art Exhibition, B.A. Graduates, 2009.
Hours & Admission Prices: Sept.-May Mon.-Thurs. 10-4. No charge; donations accepted. Closed academic holidays: 2 weeks at Christmas; spring break. ♿
Attendance: 10,000 (estimated)
Membership: Individual $15; Patron $25; Sustaining $50; Benefactor $100; Angel $500.

Chatsworth

HOMESTEAD ACRE AND THE HILL-PALMER HOUSE, 10385 Shadow Oak Dr., Chatsworth, CA 91311-2063. Tel.: 818-882-5614.
E-mail: chatsmimi@aol.com
Web Site: www.laparks.org
Historic House Museum.
Collections: period furnishings; gardens; fruit trees; rose bushes.
Hours & Admission Prices: 1st Sun. of month 1-4.

Cherry Valley

EDWARD-DEAN MUSEUM AND GARDENS, 9401 Oak Glen Rd., Cherry Valley, CA 92223-3799. Tel.: 951-845-2626. Fax: 951-845-2628.
Web Site: www.edward-deanmuseum.org
Formerly: Edward-Dean Museum of Decorative Arts
Founded: 1958.
Congressional District: 37
Key Personnel: Asst. Mgr., Terri Bowen.
Personnel Profile: Part-Time Paid 2; Part-Time Volunteers 55.
Governing Authority: county. Parent Institution: Riverside County Economic Development. Tax-exempt.
Decorative Arts Museum.

Collections: European, Oriental & American decorative arts; painting; sculptures; prints; textiles; ceramics; glass; ivory & jade carvings; Asiatic bronzes; paperweights; fans; timepieces; miniatures; cloisonne; Italian creche figures; 16th to 19th-century furniture.
Facilities: 800-vol. library of art reference material; landscaped gardens; special exhibitions; classrooms. Museum-related items for sale.
Activities: guided tours; lectures; workshops; docent program; permanent & temporary exhibitions; educational programs; seminars.
Publications: museum booklet; museum catalog; Selections from the Edward-Dean Museum of Decorative Arts; Robes of China: From the Permanent Collection; catalog, Wedgewood Masterpieces.
Hours & Admission Prices: Fri.-Sun. 10-5. Adults $3, senior citizens $2; children under 12 & members no charge. Guided Tours: $5. Closed national holidays. ♿

Chico

BIDWELL MANSION STATE HISTORIC PARK, 525 Esplanade, Chico, CA 95926-3996. Tel.: 530-895-6144. Fax: 530-895-6699.
Founded: 1964.
Congressional District: 3
Key Personnel: Unit Supvr., Denise Reichenberg; Chm. (V), Museum Shop Mgr. & Guide, Molly McAllister; Guide, Amber Drake; Guide, Susan Zimmer.
Governing Authority: state. California Dept. Parks & Recreation, P.O. Box 2390, Sacramento, CA 95811. Tel. 916-445-2358.
Historic House: 1868 three-story Victorian Italian villa country estate, home of Gen. & Mrs. John Bidwell.
Collections: Victorian era furnishings; books; manuscripts.
Research Fields: the Bidwell family; general state history.
Facilities: 1,000-vol. library available for research by appointment. Books, prints & other museum-related items for sale.
Activities: guided tours; lectures; films; drama; docent program.
Publications: brochure; quarterly newsletter, Bidwell Mansion News & Notes.
Hours & Admission Prices: Tues.-Fri. 12-5, Sat.-Sun. 10-5. Adults 18 & over $4; children 5-17 $2; members and children 4 & under no charge. Closed New Year's Day; Thanksgiving; Christmas. ♿
Attendance: 35,000
Membership: Student & Senior $5; Individual $10; Family $15; Sustaining $25; Patron $50; Life $150.

CHICO CREEK NATURE CENTER, 1968 E. 8th St., Chico, CA 95928-4110. Tel.: 530-891-4671. Fax: 530-891-0837.
E-mail: info@bidwellpark.org
Web Site: bidwellpark.org
Founded: 1990.
Congressional District: 3
Key Personnel: Dir., Tom Haithcock; Pres. (V), Jeanne Boze; Public Rels. & Museum Shop Mgr., Genevieve Mattice.
Personnel Profile: Full-Time Paid 1; Part-Time Paid 5; Part-Time Volunteers 10; Interns 12.
Governing Authority: private; nonprofit organization. Tax-exempt.
Nature Center.
Collections: taxidermy of animals, primarily of the northern California region; non-releasable (injured) live wild animals of the region.
Facilities: small native plant garden; 2,200 sq. ft. exhibit space; Bidwell Park Information & Interpretive Center. Museum-related items for sale.
Activities: environmental educational summer camp; weekend hikes & activities; birthday parties; K-6 environmental education field trips.
Publications: quarterly newsletter, Creekside Notes; Raptors of Bidwell Park.
Hours & Admission Prices: Tues.-Sun. 11-4. No charge; donations accepted. Closed New Year's Day; Easter; Independence Day; Thanksgiving; Christmas. ♿
Attendance: 40,000 (accurate)
Membership: Student & Senior $15; Individual $25; Family $35; Group $80; Supporting $130; Lifetime $500-$1,000.

CHICO MUSEUM, 141 Salem St., Chico, CA 95926. Mailing Address: 270 Boeing Ave., Ste. 1, Chico, CA 95973. Tel.: 530-891-4336 & 892-1525. Fax: 530-892-1524.
E-mail: anne@farwestheritage.org
Web Site: www.farwestheritage.org
Founded: 1980.
Congressional District: 2
Key Personnel: Pres. (V), Dax Kimmelshue; Exec. Dir., Jim Lynch; Administrative Asst., Arlene Ward; Treas., Margaret Skinner; Cur. & Registrar, Anne Seiler.
Personnel Profile: Full-Time Volunteers 1; Part-Time Paid 3; Part-Time Volunteers 40; Interns 2.
Governing Authority: nonprofit organization. Parent Institution: Far West Heritage Assoc. Tax-exempt: 501(c)(3).
History Museum: housed in 1904 Queen Anne & Romanesque Revival style Carnegie Library.
Collections: Chinese Taoist Temple used in Chico 1890-1939; Chico timeline featuring portraits, artifacts & history from 1840 to present.
Research Fields: Chico & the Chico area, prehistoric to modern times.
Facilities: library of local history books & bound newspapers, available for use by appointment; 3,662 sq. ft. exhibit space; mini-theatre. Museum-related items for sale.
Activities: permanent, temporary & traveling exhibits; guided tours; bus tours; lectures; workshops; films. Museum Sponsors: annual meeting; annual volunteer coffee; Annual Founders Day Dinner.
Publications: quarterly membership newsletter, Museum Notes; books related to exhibits & local history.
Hours & Admission Prices: Thurs.-Sun. 11-4, Sat. 10-5. Suggested Donations: adults $2, children $1. Closed New Year's Day; Easter; Independence Day; Thanksgiving; Christmas Eve & Day. ♿
Attendance: 15,000 (accurate)
Membership: Senior $50; Individual $75; Family $100; Settler Society $120; Pioneer Society $300; Explorer's Society $600; Founder's Society $1,200.

JANET TURNER PRINT MUSEUM, California State University, Chico, 400 W. 1st St., Chico, CA 95929-0001. Tel.: 530-898-4476. Fax: 530-898-5581.
E-mail: csullivan@exchange.csuchico.edu
Web Site: www.csuchico.edu/art/galleries/turnergallery.html
Founded: 1981.
Key Personnel: Chm. (V), Joanne Morgan; Cur., Catherine Sullivan Sturgeon; Asst. Collection Mgr., Celia Melton.
Personnel Profile: Part-Time Paid 5; Part-Time Volunteers 4; Interns 3.
Governing Authority: public university; nonprofit. Parent Institution: CSU-Chico. Subsidiary Institution: CSU Foundation. Tax-exempt: 501(c)(3).
Fine Art Print Gallery & Museum Archive.
Collections: original fine art prints, historical & contemporary, from more than 40 countries; professional & student prints.
Research Fields: printmaking artists' biographies; art historical background relating to thematic exhibitions; historical & technical printmaking books.
Facilities: 150-vol. library on the historical techniques of printmaking; 500 sq. ft. exhibit space; auditorium.
Activities: docent program; lectures; intern program; gallery talks; student research projects. Museum Sponsors: student printmaking invitational & biannual National Juried Printmaking Competition & Exhibition.
Hours & Admission Prices: Sept.-May Mon.-Fri. 11-4 during exhibitions; other times by appointment. No charge; donations accepted. Closed spring break; Thanksgiving break; Christmas break. ♿
Attendance: 5,000 (estimated)
Membership: Student $2; Individual $15; Family $25; Patron $100.

MUSEUM OF ANTHROPOLOGY, (M), California State University, Chico, Chico, CA 95929-0001. Tel.: 530-898-5397. Fax: 530-898-6143.
E-mail: anthromuseum@csuchico.edu
Web Site: www.csuchico.edu/anth/Museum
Founded: 1969.
Congressional District: 2
Key Personnel: Co-Dir., Stacy Schafer; Co-Dir., Georgia Fox; Cur., Adrienne Scott.
Personnel Profile: Full-Time Paid 3; Part-Time Paid 3; Part-Time Volunteers 1.
Governing Authority: state university; nonprofit organization. Tax-exempt.
University Anthropology Museum.
Collections: archaeological & ethnographic materials from around the world; emphasis on California prehistory & history.
Major Exhibits: Arctic Peoples, 1/10-7/10.
Research Fields: archaeological; museological.
Facilities: 1,000 sq. ft. exhibit space; educational facilities. Museum-related items for sale.
Activities: guided tours; education programs for children; formally organized education programs for undergraduate & graduate students; cultural enrichment programs; monthly lecture series. Annual Event: photo contest.
Publications: alliance newsletter; exhibit brochure.
Hours & Admission Prices: Sept.-Oct. & Dec.-July Tues.-Sat. 11-3. Office: Summer Mon.-Thurs. 12-4. No charge; donations accepted. ♿
Attendance: 5,000 (accurate)
Membership: Senior Citizen & Student $10; Individual $20; Family $30; Supporting $50; Sustaining $75; Sponsor $150.

NATIONAL YO-YO MUSEUM, 320 Broadway, Chico, CA 95928-5322. Tel.: 530-893-0545, ext. 4.
Web Site: www.nationalyoyo.org/museum/index.htm

Toy Museum.
Collections: yo-yo artifacts & memorabilia.
Hours & Admission Prices: Mon.-Sat. 10-6, Sun. 12-5.

China Lake

U.S. NAVAL MUSEUM OF ARMAMENT & TECHNOLOGY, 1 Pearl Harbor Way, China Lake, CA 93555-2803. Mailing Address: P.O. Box 217, Ridgecrest, CA 93556-0217. Tel.: 760-939-3105.
E-mail: clmf1@ridgenet.net
Web Site: www.chinalakemuseum.org
Founded: 2000.
Key Personnel: Dir., Debra Rios; Pres., Paul B. Homer, (CLMF); Treas., R. Wayne Doucette, (CLMF); Devel., Pat Doucette, (CLMF); Cur., Leroy Doig, III; Museum Shop Mgr., Burnell Hays, (CLMF)
Personnel Profile: Part-Time Paid 2; Part-Time Volunteers 30.
Governing Authority: federal government. Tax-exempt: 501(c)(3).
Military Museum.
Collections: Navy weapons systems from early WWII rockets to modern day smart weapons.
Facilities: 20,000 sq. ft. exhibit space. Museum-related items for sale.
Activities: guided tours; lectures; films. Annual Events: dinner auction; members meeting.
Publications: quarterly newsletter, The China Laker.
Hours & Admission Prices: Mon.-Sat. 10-4. No charge; donations accepted. Closed federal holidays.
Attendance: 7,000 (accurate)
Membership: Regular $25; Contributing $100; Life & Business $1,000; Platinum $5,000.

Chino

CHINO'S OLD SCHOOLHOUSE MUSEUM, 5493 "B" St., Chino, CA 91710-4241. Mailing Address: P.O. Box 972, Chino, CA 91708-0972. Tel.: 909-627-6464.
History Museum: Chino's first schoolhouse built in 1888.
Collections: early local history; photographs.
Hours & Admission Prices: Closed until spring 2010.

PLANES OF FAME AIR MUSEUM, 7000 Merrill Ave. #17, Chino, CA 91710-9085. Tel.: 909-597-3722.
Founded: 1957.
Governing Authority: nonprofit organization. Tax-exempt: 501(c)(3).
Aircraft Museum.
Collections: history of aviation from 1896 Chanute Hang Glider to modern space flight; test & research flight vehicles.
Publications: TAM News.
Hours & Admission Prices: Daily 9-5. Adults $11, seniors & veterans $10, children 5-12 $4; discounts to AAA & seniors; children under 5 & members no charge. Closed Thanksgiving; Christmas. ♿
Attendance: 50,000 (accurate)
Membership: $35; $60; $150; $250; $500; $2,000.

YANKS AIR MUSEUM, 7000 Merrill Ave., Hangar A270, Chino, CA 91710-9091. Mailing Address: 7000 Merrill Ave., Hangar A270, P.O. Box 35, Chino, CA 91710-9091. Tel.: 909-597-1735.
Founded: 1982.
Key Personnel: Dir., Christen Wright
Aviation Museum.
Collections: over 150 flying & static aircraft from WWI to present; drones; aircraft uniforms; flight suits; ejection seats; patches; wings; civil aviation; airliner memorabilia; instrument panels; headgear; turrets; photo archives.
Facilities: Gift items for sale.
Activities: oral history program.
Publications: newsletter.
Hours & Admission Prices: Tues.-Fri. 8-3:30, Sat. 8-2. Adults $10, seniors 62 & over $9; members no charge. Closed holidays. ♿
Membership: Annual $35; Sustaining $150; Life $1,000.

YORBA AND SLAUGHTER FAMILIES ADOBE, 17127 Pomona Rincon Rd., Chino, CA 91708-9285. Mailing Address: c/o San Bernardino Co. Museums, 2024 Orange Tree Lane, Redlands, CA 92374. Tel.: 909-597-8332 & 307-2669. Fax: 909-307-0539.
E-mail: rmckernan@sbcm.sbcounty.gov
Web Site: www.sbcountymuseum.org
Formerly: Yorba-Slaughter Adobe Museum
Founded: 1976.
Congressional District: 35
Key Personnel: Dir., Robert McKernan; Site Mgr., Karen Buma; Cur., Michele Nielsen.
Personnel Profile: Part-Time Paid 1.
Governing Authority: county. Parent Institution: San Bernardino County Museums. Tax-exempt.
Local History and Historic House Museum: housed in c.1853 Adobe home.
Collections: decorative arts; photographs; farm equipment.
Research Fields: local history.
Activities: guided tours; special events.
Hours & Admission Prices: Tues.-Sat. 10-3. No charge; donations requested. Closed New Year's Day; Thanksgiving; Christmas.
Attendance: 1,000 (estimated)

Chiriaco Summit

GENERAL PATTON MEMORIAL MUSEUM, 62-510 Chiriaco Rd., Chiriaco Summit, CA 92201-8203. Tel.: 760-227-3483. Fax: 760-227-3483.
E-mail: contact@generalpattonmuseum.org
Web Site: www.generalpattonmuseum.com
Founded: 1988.
Congressional District: 37
Key Personnel: Pres. (V), Jan Roberts; Conservator, Jacqueline Schindewolf.
Personnel Profile: Part-Time Paid 8.
Governing Authority: not-for-profit organization. Tax-exempt: 501(c)(3).
Military Museum: located near former headquarters of World War II Desert Training Areas.
Collections: exhibits emphasizing Gen. Patton, Desert Training Center, World War II & other eras of military history.
Facilities: 200-vol. library on Gen. Patton, World War II & the military. Museum-related items for sale.
Activities: Annual Events: Veterans Day; Patton's Birthday Celebration.
Publications: newsletter; brochure.
Hours & Admission Prices: Daily 9:30-4:30. Adults 12 & over $4, seniors, teachers & chaperones $3.50; discounts to groups; members military & school-aged children no charge. Bus tours: $3.50 per person. Closed Thanksgiving; Christmas. ♿
Attendance: 73,500 (accurate)
Membership: Annual Individual $25; Annual Family $35; Business $100; Patron $1,000; Benefactor $2,500.

Chula Vista

* **CHULA VISTA NATURE CENTER,** 1000 Gunpowder Point Dr., Chula Vista, CA 91910-8222. Tel.: 619-409-5900 & 5904. Fax: 619-409-5910.
E-mail: tina@chulavistanaturecenter.org
Web Site: www.chulavistanaturecenter.org
Founded: 1987.
Congressional District: 51
Key Personnel: Chm. (V), F.L. Wergeland, Jr., M.D.; Education, Kerry Laube; Museum Shop Mgr., Ben Vallejos.
Personnel Profile: Full-Time Paid 8; Part-Time Paid 3; Part-Time Volunteers 125; Interns 2.
Governing Authority: nonprofit organization. Tax-exempt: 501(c)(3).
Aquarium & Nature Center: located within Sweetwater Marsh National Wildlife Refuge.
Collections: representing an experiential tour of coastal wetlands; live plant & animal specimens; artifacts.
Research Fields: wetland restoration & enhancement; ecology; ornithology.
Facilities: 200-vol. non-circulating library on wetland ecology; aquarium; 125-seat auditorium; botanical garden; classrooms; labs; 6,000 sq. ft. exhibit space; field research station; nature center; 1.5 miles of nature trails Clapper Rail breeding program. Natural history books & supplies for sale.
Activities: docent program; education programs; guided tours; lectures; participatory exhibits; light-footed Clapper Rail captive breeding program.
Publications: quarterly newsletter, Nature News.
Hours & Admission Prices: Tues.-Sun. 10-5. Adults $11, seniors 65 & over, juniors 12-17, and students 18 & over $8, children 4-11 $6; discounts to AAM members & military; children under 4 & members no charge. Closed New Year's Eve & Day; Martin Luther King Jr. Day; Easter; Memorial Day; Independence Day; Labor Day; Veterans Day; Thanksgiving & day after; Christmas Eve & Day; Cesar Chavez Day. ♿
Attendance: 70,000 (accurate)
Membership: Senior, Student & Volunteer $25; Dual Senior, Student & Volunteer & Adult $35; Family $65; call to confirm.

City of Industry

WORKMAN & TEMPLE FAMILY HOMESTEAD MUSEUM, (M), 15415 E. Don Julian Rd., City of Industry, CA 91745-1029. Tel.: 626-968-8492. Fax: 626-968-2048.
E-mail: info@homesteadmuseum.org
Web Site: www.homesteadmuseum.org
Founded: 1981.

Congressional District: 33
Key Personnel: Dir., Karen Graham Wade; Collections Mgr., Paul Spitzzeri; Public Programs Mgr., Alexandra Rasic; Asst. Public Programs Mgr., Lillian Choy; Facilities Coord., Robert Barron; Volunteer Coord., Steven Dugan.
Personnel Profile: Full-Time Paid 10; Part-Time Volunteers 80.
Governing Authority: municipal. Parent Institution: City of Industry. Tax-exempt: 501(c)(1).
Historic Buildings Museum & Site: located on the site of the Rancho la Puente.
Collections: 1830-1930 decorative arts, furniture, textiles, costumes, & artifacts; interior decorative elements consisting of metalwork, tile, wood carvings & stained glass windows; photographic archives. Historic Buildings & Structures: mid-19th century Workman house; 1919-1925 Spanish colonial revival Temple residence; late 19th century Water Tower; 1919 classical revival mausoleum; c.1850 El Campo Santo cemetery.
Research Fields: southern California; California & the United States from 1830-1930; architecture; decorative arts.
Facilities: 600-vol. library pertaining to architecture, art, costumes, decorative arts & history available for research by appointment on premises; exhibit space apart from principal museum; auditorium. Museum-related items for sale.
Activities: guided tours; lectures; films; concerts; formally organized educational programs; volunteer programs; permanent & temporary exhibitions.
Hours & Admission Prices: Wed.-Sun. 1-4, group tours by reservation. No charge; donations accepted. Closed major holidays. ♿
Attendance: 16,000 (estimated)

Claremont

CLAREMONT MUSEUM OF ART, (M), 536 W. First St., Claremont, CA 91711-4618. Tel.: 909-621-3200. Fax: 909-625-1629.
E-mail: info@claremontmuseum.org
Web Site: www.claremontmuseum.org
Key Personnel: Dir., William Moreno
Art Museum.
Collections: paintings; sculptures.
Facilities: Museum-related items for sale.
Activities: educational programs.
Hours & Admission Prices: Wed.-Mon. 11-5. Adults $3; members and children 18 & under no charge.

CLARK HUMANITIES MUSEUM-STUDY, Humanities Bldg., Scripps College, Claremont, CA 91711-3905. Mailing Address: Scripps College, 1030 Columbia Ave., Claremont, CA 91711-3905. Tel.: 909-607-3606. Fax: 909-607-7143.
E-mail: ehaskell@scrippscollege.edu
Founded: 1970.
Congressional District: 34
Key Personnel: Chm. Museum Committee, Dr. Eric T. Haskell.
Governing Authority: college. Affiliated with Scripps College. Tax-exempt: 501(c)(3).
General Museum.
Collections: Gen. Edward Young collection of American paintings; Johnson collection of Japanese prints; Routh collection of Cloisonne; Nagel collection of art & artifacts; Wagner collection of African sculpture; prints; drawings; photographs.
Facilities: Denison Library; Ruth Chandler Williamson Gallery.
Activities: formally organized education programs for undergraduate college students; temporary exhibitions.
Publications: exhibition catalogues.
Hours & Admission Prices: Mon.-Fri. 9-12:30 & 1:30-5. No charge. ♿

PETTERSON MUSEUM OF INTERCULTURAL ART, 730 Plymouth Rd., Claremont, CA 91711. Mailing Address: 660 Avery Rd., Claremont, CA 91711-4222. Tel.: 909-399-5544 & 621-9581. Fax: 909-399-5508.
E-mail: cgil@pilgrimplace.org
Web Site: www.pilgrimplace.org
Founded: 1968.
Congressional District: 33
Key Personnel: Dir., Bill Cunitz; Pres. (V), Dwight Vogel; Cur., Carol Bowdoin Gil.
Personnel Profile: Part-Time Paid 1; Part-Time Volunteers 42.
Governing Authority: nonprofit organization. Parent Institution: Pilgrim Place. Tax-exempt: 501(c)(3).
International Folk & Fine Art Museum.
Collections: international folk & fine art; Chinese bronzes & imperial court robes; Latin American textiles; African masks & woodcarving; intercultural costumes & puppets; masks; international dolls.
Facilities: 2,000-vol. library of books on intercultural arts.
Activities: guided tours; lectures; films; concerts; arts festivals; docent program.
Hours & Admission Prices: Guided Tours: Fri.-Sun. 2-4 or by appointment. No charge; donations accepted. Closed Easter; Thanksgiving; Christmas. ♿
Attendance: 1,500 (estimated)
Membership: Regular $10; Sustaining $25; Patron $50; Petterson Circle $100 & up.

POMONA COLLEGE MUSEUM OF ART, (M), 330 N. College Ave., Claremont, CA 91711-4401. Mailing Address: 333 N. College Way, Claremont, CA 91711-4429. Tel.: 909-621-8283 & 8000. Fax: 909-621-8989.
Web Site: www.pomona.edu/museum
Founded: 1958.
Congressional District: 34
Key Personnel: Dir., Kathleen Howe; Asst. Dir. & Registrar, Steve Comba; Cur., Rebecca McGrew; Administrative Asst., Debbie Wilson; Preparator, Gary Murphy; Museum Coord., Jessica Wimbley; Security & Information Officer, Anne Merten.
Personnel Profile: Full-Time Paid 6; Part-Time Paid 2; Interns 1.
Governing Authority: college. Parent Institution: Pomona College. Tax-exempt: 501(c)(3).
College Art Museum.
Collections: Kress Renaissance paintings; prints, drawings & photographs; American Indian basketry, ceramics & beadwork.
Major Exhibits: Helen Pashgian: Working In Light, 1/10-4/10; Project Series 40: The Institute for Figuring, 1/10-4/10; Pomona Senior Thesis Exhibition, 4/10-5/10.
Research Fields: drawings; prints; American Indian; Kress panels; photographs.
Facilities: Exhibition catalogues & posters for sale.
Activities: lectures; gallery talks; temporary & traveling exhibitions; inter-museum loans; organized education programs for undergraduate students. Museum Sponsors: annual student exhibitions; biennial faculty & faculty Invitation exhibitions.
Publications: exhibition catalogues.
Hours & Admission Prices: Sept.-May Tues.-Fri. 12-5, Sat.-Sun. 1-5. No charge. Closed school & national holidays. ♿
Attendance: 8,460 (accurate)

* **RANCHO SANTA ANA BOTANIC GARDEN, (M),** 1500 N. College Ave., Claremont, CA 91711-3157. Tel.: 909-625-8767, ext. 0. Fax: 909-626-7670.
E-mail: acharlap@rsabg.org
Web Site: www.rsabg.org
Founded: 1927.
Congressional District: 33
Key Personnel: Chm. Bd. Trustees, Richard A. Grant, Jr.; C.E.O. & Exec. Dir., Patrick S. Larkin; Pres. (V), Fraser Pemberton; Dir. Finance, Kristine Crosby; Cur. Herbarium, Steve Boyd; Dir. Education, Lorrae Fuentes; Dir. Horticulture, Susan Jett; Head Librarian, Harvey Brenneise; Mgr. Volunteers, Brenda Bolinger; Dir. Visitor Svcs. & Community Rels., Ann Joslin; Seed Cur., Michael Wall; Museum Shop Mgr., Pamela Conway; Dir. Research, Lucinda McDade; Mgr. Human Resources, Alex Charlap; Dir. Devel., Kent Schell; Dir. Special Projects, Bart O'Brien; Nursery Mgr., Janet Takara.
Personnel Profile: Full-Time Paid 62; Full-Time Volunteers 200; Part-Time Paid 12; Part-Time Volunteers 22; Interns 6.
Governing Authority: nonprofit corp. Tax-exempt: 509(A)(3).
Botanical Garden.
Collections: living plants; herbarium; pollen slides; wood samples; seeds; 1,000,000 specimens.
Research Fields: plant taxonomy; cyto-taxonomy; chemo-taxonomy; mycology; ecology; molecular systematics; monographic revisions; plant anatomy; palynology.
Facilities: 76,747-vol. library of general botanical & horticultural materials available for formal inter-library loan & personal requests; herbarium; laboratories; 100-seat classroom.
Activities: guided tours; formally organized education programs for children; docent program or council; formally organized education programs for graduate students affiliated with Claremont Graduate University. Annual Events: plant sales; biannual symposia; Wildflower Show; Musical Evenings in the Garden.
Publications: biannual scientific journal, Aliso; quarterly newsletter; RSABG Occasional Publications.
Hours & Admission Prices: Daily 8-5. No charge; donations accepted. Closed New Year's Day; Independence Day; Thanksgiving; Christmas. ♿
Attendance: 153,000 (estimated)
Membership: Individual $45; Family $60 (senior & student discount 10% on

either individual or family); Supporting $100; Sustaining $250; Garden Patron $500; Director's Circle $1,000 & up.

*** THE RAYMOND M. ALF MUSEUM OF PALEONTOLOGY, (M),** 1175 W. Baseline Rd., Claremont, CA 91711-2146. Tel.: 909-624-2798. Fax: 909-624-2798.
E-mail: dlofgren@webb.org
Web Site: www.alfmuseum.org
Founded: 1937.
Congressional District: 35
Key Personnel: Dir., Donald Lofgren, Ph.D.; Dir. Outreach, Kathy Sanders; Outreach Asst., Karen McGuirk; Cur., Andrew Farke.
Personnel Profile: Full-Time Paid 3; Part-Time Paid 2; Part-Time Volunteers 15.
Governing Authority: nonprofit organization. Parent Institution: The Webb Schools. Tax-exempt: 501(c)(3).
Paleontology Museum.
Collections: paleontology; rocks; minerals; archaeology; osteology.
Research Fields: paleontology; geology.
Facilities: 60-seat auditorium; classrooms. Museum-related items for sale.
Activities: guided tours; formally organized education programs; permanent & temporary exhibitions; world-wide natural history tours.
Publications: quarterly newsletter, Quest.
Hours & Admission Prices: June-Aug. Mon.-Fri. 8-12 & 1-4; Sept.-May Mon.-Fri. 8-12 & 1-4, Sat. 1-4; groups by appointment. Admission $3; children 4 & under and Wed. no charge. ♿
Attendance: 17,000 (accurate)

RUTH CHANDLER WILLIAMSON GALLERY, SCRIPPS COLLEGE, (M), 1030 Colombia Ave., Claremont, CA 91711-3905. Tel.: 909-607-3397 & 4690. Fax: 909-607-4691.
E-mail: mary.macnaughton@scrippscollege.edu
Web Site: www.scrippscollege.edu/dept/gallery
Founded: 1993.
Congressional District: 34
Key Personnel: Dir., Mary Davis MacNaughton; Sec., Charissa Okamoto; Registrar & Preparator, Kirk Delman; Asst. Preparator, James Coquia; Data Specialist, Krista Coquia.
Personnel Profile: Full-Time Paid 2; Part-Time Paid 4; Part-Time Volunteers 2; Interns 4.
Governing Authority: colleges. Parent Institution: Scripps College, Claremont, CA. Tax-exempt: 501(c)(3).
College Art Gallery.
Collections: Gen. Edward Young collection of American paintings; Dr. & Mrs. William E. Ballard collection of Japanese prints; Fred and Estelle Marer collection of contemporary American, British, Korean, Mexican & Japanese ceramics; Mrs. James Johnson collection of Japanese prints; Dorothy Adler Routh collection of cloissonne; Wagner collection of African sculpture; prints; drawings; photographs; contemporary ceramics.
Research Fields: American paintings; drawings; prints; ceramics.
Facilities: Exhibition catalogues & posters for sale.
Activities: lectures; films; gallery talks; temporary & traveling exhibitions; inter-museum loans; organized education programs for undergraduate students. Museum Sponsors: annual student exhibitions; annual exhibition of contemporary ceramics.
Publications: exhibition catalogues, Larger Than Life: Robert Rahway Zakavitch's Big Bungalow Suite; Annals of My Glass House: Photographs by Julia Margaret Cameron; Revolution in Clay: Marer Collection of Contemporary Ceramics; Johnson, Kaufmann and Coate: Partners in the California Style; Ceramic Annual 2004, 2005, 2006; Alison and Lezley Saar; In the Mind's Sky: Intersections of Art & Science; Matter and Matrix: Kris Cox, Amy Ellingson, Elizabeth Turk, Jane Park Wells; Reading and Meaning: Word and Symbolism in the Art of Squeak Carnwath, Leslie Dill, Leslie Enders Lee, and Anne Siems.
Hours & Admission Prices: Wed.-Sun. 1-5. No charge. Closed school & national holidays. ♿
Attendance: 5,200 (estimated)

Clovis

CLOVIS BIG DRY CREEK HISTORICAL MUSEUM, 401 Pollasky Ave., (at 4th St.), Clovis, CA 93612-1141. Tel.: 559-297-8033. Fax: 559-297-8034.
Web Site: www.clovis-museum.com
Key Personnel: Cur., Peggy Bos
History Museum: site of the historic 1924 bank robbery.
Collections: history of Clovis; Clovis yearbooks signed by Norma Jean Forest, also known as Marilyn Monroe; saddle & chaps owned by cowboy, Happy Jack Hawn; historical artifacts; photographs; military artifacts.
Hours & Admission Prices: Tues.-Sat. 10-2; other times by appointment. No charge; donations accepted.

Coalinga

R.C. BAKER MEMORIAL MUSEUM, INC., 297 W. Elm St., Coalinga, CA 93210-1923. Tel.: 559-935-1914; 877-416-5849. Fax: 559-935-2339.
E-mail: curator@rcbakermuseum.com
Web Site: www.rcbakermuseum.com
Founded: 1961.
Key Personnel: Chm. (V), JoAnn Clark; Cur., Stephanie McHaney
History Museum.
Collections: artifacts & memorabilia pertaining to Pleasant Valley.
Hours & Admission Prices: Mon.-Fri. 10-12 & 1-5. Sat. 11-5. No charge; donations accepted. Closed legal holidays.
Membership: Associate (non-voting) $15; Individual (voting) $25; Commercial & Business $75; Life (voting) $100.

Coarsegold

COARSEGOLD HISTORIC MUSEUM, 31899 Hwy. 41, Coarsegold, CA 93614. Mailing Address: P.O. Box 117, Coarsegold, CA 93614-0117. Tel.: 559-642-4448. Fax: 559-642-4246.
E-mail: 2good@sti.net
Web Site: coarsegoldhistoricmuseum.com
Formerly: Willow Glen Museum
Founded: 1980.
Congressional District: 19
Key Personnel: Office Mgr., Kay Good; Pres. (V), David Dutton.
Personnel Profile: Part-Time Volunteers 34.
Governing Authority: nonprofit. Subsidiary Institution: Coarsegold Historical Society. Tax-exempt.
History Museum.
Collections: local history; personal artifacts; Chukchansi Indian artifacts.
Research Fields: eastern Madera County, CA.
Publications: book, As We Were Told, Vols. I & II.
Hours & Admission Prices: May-Sept. Sun. 12-4, Mon. 9-11:30, Wed.-Sat. 10-2; Oct.-April Sun. 1-4, Mon. 9-11:30; other times by appointment. No charge; donations accepted. ♿
Attendance: 700 (estimated)
Membership: Individual $20; Family $30; Sustaining $50; Life $300.

Coloma

MARSHALL GOLD DISCOVERY STATE HISTORIC PARK, 310 Back St., Coloma, CA 95613. Mailing Address: P.O. Box 265, Coloma, CA 95613-0265. Tel.: 530-622-3470. Fax: 530-622-3472.
E-mail: marshallgold@parks.ca.gov
Web Site: www.parks.ca.gov
Founded: 1890.
Congressional District: 14
Key Personnel: Park Supt., Mark Gibson.
Personnel Profile: Full-Time Paid 8; Part-Time Paid 4; Part-Time Volunteers 130.
Governing Authority: state. Parent Institution: California Dept. of Parks & Recreation. Tax-exempt.
Gold Rush History Museum: located near the site of the discovery of gold in 1848.
Collections: manuscript collections. Historic Buildings: 1867 Thomas House; 1855 Churches; 1849 pioneer cemetery; 1849 Catholic cemetery; 1866-1889 Chalmers winery ruins; 1889 Marshall Monument; 1857 Chinese stores; 1855 Robert Bell's brick store ruins; 1854 Bekearts gunsmith shop; Coloma 1857 stone jail ruins.
Research Fields: history.
Facilities: 1,000-vol. library of books pertaining to the gold rush & pioneer file available on premises; 80-seat lecture room.
Activities: self-guided tours; lectures; films; formally organized education programs for children, adults, undergraduate & graduate college students; permanent & temporary exhibitions.
Publications: brochures; trail guides; teachers guide; historic account of Gold Rush & Marshall's Role, available in translation.
Hours & Admission Prices: Daily 10-4:30. Park: $5 per car; members no charge. Closed New Year's Day; Thanksgiving; Christmas. ♿
Attendance: 250,000 (estimated)
Membership: Individual $15; Family $25; Lifetime $250.

Colton

AGUA MANSA PIONEER MEMORIAL CEMETERY, 2001 W. Agua Mansa Rd., Colton, CA 92324-3388. Mailing Address: c/o San Bernardino Co. Museums, 2024 Orange Tree Lane, Redlands, CA 92374. Tel.: 909-307-2669. Fax: 909-307-0539.
E-mail: rmckernan@sbcm.sbcounty.gov
Web Site: www.sbcountymuseum.org

Founded: 1977.
Congressional District: 36
Key Personnel: Dir., Robert McKernan; Cur., Michele Nielsen; Docent, Jason Bowe.
Personnel Profile: Part-Time Paid 1.
Governing Authority: county. Parent Institution: San Bernardino County Museum. Tax-exempt.
Historic Site & Museum: historic cemetery; oldest remaining cemetery in San Bernardino County (1854).
Collections: photographs & personal memorabilia of local families. Historic Building: chapel.
Research Fields: local history.
Activities: guided tours.
Hours & Admission Prices: Fri. 12-3, Sat. 11-3, 1st Sun. of month 12-2. No charge; donations requested. Closed New Year's Day; Thanksgiving; Christmas. ♿
Attendance: 2,300 (accurate)

COLTON AREA MUSEUM, 380 N. La Cadena Dr., Colton, CA 92324-2928. Mailing Address: P.O. Box 1648, Colton, CA 92324-0851. Tel.: 909-824-8814 & 783-8817. Fax: 909-783-9241.
E-mail: info@coltonmuseum.net
Web Site: www.coltonmuseum.net
Founded: 1984.
Congressional District: 36
Key Personnel: Pres. (V), Don Earp; Museum Shop Mgr., Pam Gregory.
Personnel Profile: Part-Time Volunteers 25.
Governing Authority: private; nonprofit organization. Tax-exempt.
History Museum & Historic Site: housed in 1908 Andrew Carnegie Library building.
Collections: local Colton history & history of the surrounding areas; The Earps; California Portland Cement; San Salvador & Agua Mansa areas; Southern Pacific Railroad; Colton's Federal theatre posters; citrus industry; Ken Hubbs, Chicago Cubs baseball player; local family histories.
Research Fields: Colton newspapers 1877-1972.
Activities: Museum Sponsors: Discover Colton Night; Colton Unity Day; annual quilt display; Wyatt Earp Festival; Library Week.
Publications: biannual, Crossroads: A Journal of Colton Area History; bi-monthly newsletter.
Hours & Admission Prices: Fri. & last Sun. of each month 1-4; tours by appointment. No charge; donations accepted. Closed major holidays. ♿
Attendance: 1,000 (estimated)
Membership: Individual $15; Patron $45; Commercial $250.

Columbia

COLUMBIA STATE HISTORIC PARK, 11255 Jackson St., Columbia, CA 95310-9425. Tel.: 209-536-2888. Fax: 209-532-5064.
E-mail: calhq@parks.ca.gov
Web Site: www.parks.ca.gov
Founded: 1945.
Congressional District: 18
Key Personnel: Ranger, Jennifer "Mac" MacNaughton; Cur., Thonni C. Morikawa.
Personnel Profile: Full-Time Paid 4; Part-Time Paid 6; Part-Time Volunteers 75.
Governing Authority: state. Parent Institution: California Department of Parks & Recreation, P.O. Box 2390, Sacramento, CA 95811. Subsidiary Institution: Chaw Se (Indian Grinding Rocks) State Park; Calaveras Big Trees State Park.
State Park Museum.
Collections: Columbia State Historic Park: 1854 Leavitt-Walker; 1856 St. Charles Saloon-Alberding; 1858 Wells Fargo building; 1856 Duchow; 1860 schoolhouse; 1854-1855 I.O.O.F. Hall-McChesney; grocery store; candy store; general store; saloon; photographs; archives.
Research Fields: 19th century-gardens; folklore; preservation projects; California Gold Rush; Colombia related genealogy.
Facilities: 19th century-garden; picnic area. Museum-related items for sale.
Activities: walking tours; narrated talks for schools & special groups; formally organized education programs for children; permanent exhibitions; stagecoach ride; special events; living history programs.
Publications: brochure.
Hours & Admission Prices: Daily 8-5. No charge. Closed Thanksgiving; Christmas. ♿
Attendance: 467,000 (estimated)

Corona

FENDER MUSEUM OF MUSIC AND THE ARTS, 365 N. Main St., Corona, CA 92880-2040. Tel.: 951-735-2440. Fax: 951-735-2576.
E-mail: member@fendermuseum.com
Web Site: www.fendercenter.org
Founded: 1997.
Key Personnel: Bd. Pres. (V), Jeff Bennett; Exec Dir., Debbie Shuck.
Personnel Profile: Full-Time Paid 4; Part-Time Paid 2; Part-Time Volunteers 100; Interns 1.
Governing Authority: private; nonprofit organization. Tax-exempt.
Music & Art Museum.
Collections: guitars; amps; factory equipment; music memorabilia.
Facilities: 48-track digital recording studio; outdoor amphitheater; visual art gallery; classrooms.
Activities: formal education programs for children.
Publications: newsletter, Plugged In.
Hours & Admission Prices: Wed.-Sat. 11-4. Adults $10, seniors & students $8; children 12 under no charge. Closed major holidays. ♿
Membership: Family: Gold $35; Double Gold $50; Triple Gold $100; Gold Artist $250; Platinum $500; Double Platinum $750; Triple Platinum $1,000; Platinum Artist $2,500. Corporate: Manager $2,500; Promoter $5,000; Producer $10,000.

Corona del Mar

SHERMAN GARDENS, 2647 E. Coast Hwy., Corona del Mar, CA 92625-2103. Tel.: 949-673-2261. Fax: 949-675-5458.
E-mail: info@slgardens.org
Web Site: www.slgardens.org
Founded: 1951.
Congressional District: 40
Key Personnel: C.E.O., Donald Haskell; Pres. (V), Micky Pearlman; Library Dir., Dr. William O. Hendricks; Garden Dir., Wade Roberts; Business Officer, D.T. Daniels; Sales Shop Mgr., Peggy Schmidt.
Personnel Profile: Full-Time Paid 9; Part-Time Paid 9; Part-Time Volunteers 150.
Governing Authority: public charity. Parent Institution: Sherman Foundation. Tax-exempt: 509(a)(1) & 170(b)(A)vi.
Historic Research Institute & Botanical Garden.
Collections: history of the Pacific Southwest; books; maps; microfilmed materials; personal papers; photographs; cacti & succulents to tropical plants.
Research Fields: history of the Pacific Southwest.
Facilities: 6,000-vol. library of books, pamphlets & other printed materials, numerous maps & photographs, microfilm, papers & documents available for research on premises; botanical garden; reading room; 150-seat auditorium; Cafe Jardin, Lunch & Afternoon Tea. Gift items for sale.
Activities: guided tours; lectures; concerts; hobby workshops; formally organized education programs for adults; docent program or council; temporary exhibitions.
Hours & Admission Prices: Gardens: daily 10:30-4. Library: Tues.-Thurs. 9-4:30. Adults & tours $3, children $1; Mon., children 11 & under and members no charge. Closed New Year's Day; Thanksgiving; Christmas. ♿
Attendance: 64,500 (accurate)
Membership: Student & Senior Citizen $25; General $35; Sustaining $100; Contributing $250; Sponsor $500; Benefactor $1,000; Patron $2,000; Life Patron $5,000.

Costa Mesa

DIEGO SEPULVEDA ADOBE ESTANCIA, 1900 Adams, Costa Mesa, CA 92626-4718. Mailing Address: P.O. Box 1764, Costa Mesa, CA 92628-1764. Tel.: 949-631-5918.
Web Site: www.stockteam.com/costa3.html
Founded: 1966.
Governing Authority: Parent Institution: Costa Mesa Historical Society.
History Museum.
Collections: area history; Native American; mission; Spanish; Victorian; mastodon skeleton.
Activities: docent tours 1st & 3rd Saturday of each month.
Hours & Admission Prices: Tours by appointment. No charge; donations accepted.

Crescent City

DEL NORTE COUNTY HISTORICAL SOCIETY, (M), 577 H St., Crescent City, CA 95531-3743. Tel.: 707-464-3922.
E-mail: manager@delnortehistory.org
Web Site: www.delnortehistory.org
Founded: 1951.
Congressional District: 1
Key Personnel: Chm. (V) & Vice Pres., Sean Smith; Pres. (V), Loren Bommelyn.
Personnel Profile: Part-Time Volunteers 34.
Governing Authority: nonprofit. Branch Museums: Main Museum, 6th & H

Sts., Crescent City, CA. 95531; Battery Point Light House, Battery Point Island, Crescent City, CA. Tax-exempt.
Historical Society & Maritime Museum: housed in 1926 County Hall of Records, Jail & Sheriff's office; Battery Point Lighthouse c.1856.
Collections: archaeology; history; lumber industry; marine; mining; naval; shipping; agriculture; genealogy; preservation projects.
Research Fields: local history.
Facilities: library of local history books, photographs, diaries, manuscripts, microfilms & originals of local newspapers, oral history tapes & research files available for use on premises under supervision; reading room.
Activities: permanent & special exhibits.
Publications: quarterly, Del Norte County Historical Society Bulletin.
Hours & Admission Prices: Main Museum: April-Sept. Mon.-Sat. 10-4. Adults $3, students $1. Lighthouse: April-Sept. daily 10-4 (tide permitting). Adults $3, children 17 & under $1; members no charge. Research: $5 per hour (by volunteer); $2 per hour (own research).
Attendance: 3,900 (accurate)
Membership: Senior Citizen $10; Adult $20; Family $30; Lifetime $150 Corporate $1,000.

REDWOOD NATIONAL AND STATE PARKS, 1111 Second St., Crescent City, CA 95531-4123. Tel.: 707-464-6101. Fax: 707-464-1812.
E-mail: redw_superintendent@nps.gov
Web Site: www.nps.gov/redw
Formerly: Redwood National Park
Founded: 1968.
Congressional District: 1
Key Personnel: Supt., Steve Chaney; Cur., James B. O'Barr.
Personnel Profile: Full-Time Paid 104; Part-Time Paid 63; Part-Time Volunteers 10.
Governing Authority: federal. Dept. of the Interior, National Park Service, Washington, DC. Tax-exempt.
National Park.
Collections: items related to natural history, cultural history & history of northcoast California.
Research Fields: coastal redwood ecosystem; Tolowa, Chilula & Yurok history & prehistory; logged lands & mining history.
Facilities: 1,500-vol. library pertaining to coastal redwood ecosystem, northern California coast, history & prehistory of American population & dairy & mining history available for research on premises only; nature trails.
Activities: guided tours; formally organized educational programs; permanent & changing exhibitions.
Publications: trail guides; books, Monarchs of the Mist: the Story of Redwood National Park; Redwood: A Guide to Redwood National & State Parks.
Hours & Admission Prices: Daily 8-5. No charge; donations accepted. Closed New Year's Day; Thanksgiving; Christmas. ♿
Attendance: 500,000 (estimated)

Culver City

MUSEUM OF JURASSIC TECHNOLOGY, 9341 Venice Blvd., Culver City, CA 90232-2621. Tel.: 310-836-6131. Fax: 310-287-2267.
E-mail: info@mjt.org
Web Site: www.mjt.org
Founded: 1989.
Key Personnel: Bd. Pres., Terry Cannon; Museum Dir., David Wilson.
Personnel Profile: Part-Time Paid 12; Part-Time Volunteers 1; Interns 3.
Natural History Museum.
Collections: relics & artifacts from Lower Jurassic.
Hours & Admission Prices: Thurs. 2-8, Fri.-Sun. 12-6. Suggested Donations: adults $5, students & seniors $3; discounts to groups. Closed New Year's Day; Easter; Thanksgiving; Christmas Eve & Day.
Membership: Student & Senior $35; Active $50; Supporter $100; Contributing $200; Sustaining $300; Donor $500; Benefactor $1,000; Founder's Circle $5,000.

STAR ECO STATION, 10101 Jefferson Blvd., Culver City, CA 90232-3519. Tel.: 310-842-8060. Fax: 310-842-8245.
E-mail: ecostation@starinc.org
Web Site: www.ecostation.org
Founded: 1997.
Congressional District: 32
Key Personnel: C.E.O., Katya Bozzi; Chm. (V), Regino Chavez; Pres, (V), Paul Kestenbaum; Treas., Ramiro Vasquez; Cur., Erick Bozzi, II; Asst. Dir., Chandra Huntress Comstock; Education, Katiana Bozzi; Security, Scott Golden; Museum Shop Mgr., Marla Wolkowitz.
Personnel Profile: Full-Time Paid 6; Full-Time Volunteers 4; Part-Time Paid 3; Part-Time Volunteers 5; Interns 10.
Governing Authority: private; nonprofit organization. Parent Institution: Star Education, Inc., 10117 Jefferson Blvd., Culver City, CA 90232. Tax-exempt 501 (c)(3).
Environmental Science Museum.
Collections: indoor & outdoor living wildlife exhibits including mammals, reptiles, birds, amphibians & marine life.
Major Exhibits: African American Art, 2/10.
Research Fields: endangered species management & behavior of birds, reptiles & mammals.
Facilities: 115-vol. library of books available for inter-library loan; aquarium; nature center; zoological park. Museum-related items for sale.
Activities: arts festival; concerts; dance recitals; docent programs; films; formal education programs; guided tours; lectures; mobile vans; study clubs; temporary exhibitions. Annual Events: Dinofaire; African American Art Festival; Children's Earth Day; Children's Art Festival; Creepy Crawly Creature Feature; Enchanted Green Hallow's Eve; Trash to Treasure Fair.
Publications: quarterly, Star Eco Station Newsletter.
Hours & Admission Prices: Summer: Mon.-Fri. 1-5; Winter: Fri. 1-5, Sat.-Sun. 10-4. Adults $8, senior citizens 65 and over $7, children $6; members no charge. Closed New Year's Day; Easter; Independence Day; Thanksgiving; Christmas. ♿
Attendance: 50,000 (estimated)
Membership: Adventurer $45; Wildlife $55; Forest Floor $100; Understory $250; Ecosystem $500; Canopy $1,000; Emergent Layer $5,000.

WENDE MUSEUM, (M), 5741 Buckingham Pkwy., Ste. E, Culver City, CA 90230-6520. Tel.: 310-216-1600. Fax: 310-216-1609.
E-mail: shilger@wendemuseum.org
Web Site: www.wendemuseum.org
Key Personnel: Museum Coord., Silke Hilger.
Governing Authority: nonprofit organization.
History Museum.
Collections: history of the Soviet Union, East Germany & the Cold War; household artifacts; clothing; folk art; photographs; posters; films.
Activities: Museum Sponsors: Open Houses.
Hours & Admission Prices: Museum: Fri. 10-5. Vault Tour: 3pm. No charge. Closed national holidays.

Cupertino

CALIFORNIA HISTORY CENTER & FOUNDATION, 21250 Stevens Creek Blvd., Cupertino, CA 95014-5702. Tel.: 408-864-8987. Fax: 408-864-5486.
E-mail: info@calhistory.org
Web Site: www.calhistory.org
History Museum.
Collections: California history; photographs.
Facilities: library.
Activities: lectures; workshops.
Publications: magazine, The Californian.
Hours & Admission Prices: Sept.-June Tues.-Thurs. 9:30-12 & 1-4, Fri. by appointment. Center: no charge. Library: $5 daily; students & members no charge.

CUPERTINO HISTORICAL SOCIETY & MUSEUM, (M), Quinlan Community Center, 10185 N. Stelling Rd., Cupertino, CA 95014-5732. Tel.: 408-973-1495.
E-mail: cuphistsociety@sbcglobal.net
Web Site: cupertinohistoricalsocietym.org
Founded: 1990.
Congressional District: 13
Key Personnel: Pres., Darryl Stow; Volunteer Coord., Ray Bortner.
Personnel Profile: Part-Time Paid 1; Part-Time Volunteers 19; Interns 1.
Governing Authority: nonprofit organization; society. Parent Institution: Cupertino Historical Society. Tax-exempt: 501(c)(3).
Historical Society Museum.
Collections: historical artifacts; photographs; 1840-1940, archives; clothing; furniture; toys; farm & blacksmith tools; school objects; 1912 Kelly truck.
Research Fields: local history; agricultural life; preservation/buildings.
Facilities: 1,000 sq. ft. exhibit space.
Activities: guided tours; lectures; organized education programs for children; docent program; temporary exhibitions. Annual Events: fundraising BBQ; visit to an historic site.
Publications: The Cornerstone; quarterly newsletter; exhibition catalogs; The Cupertino Chronicle.
Hours & Admission Prices: Wed.-Sat. 10-4. Requested Donation $3; members no charge. ♿
Attendance: 4,000 (accurate)

Membership: Individual $20; Families $35; Contributing $50; Organizations, Clubs & Businesses $75; Patron $125; Sponsor $250; Sustaining $500; Life $1,000.

EUPHRAT MUSEUM OF ART, De Anza College, 21250 Stevens Creek Blvd., Cupertino, CA 95014-5702. Tel.: 408-864-8836. Fax: 408-864-8738.
E-mail: rindfleischjanet@fhda.edu
Web Site: www.deanza.edu/euphrat
Founded: 1971.
Congressional District: 14
Key Personnel: Exec. Dir., Marie Fox Ellison; Dir., Jan Rindfleisch; Co Pres., Margaret Kung; Co Pres., Helen Lewis; Education, Diana Argabrite.
Personnel Profile: Full-Time Paid 1; Part-Time Paid 8; Part-Time Volunteers 10.
Governing Authority: public college/community partnership; nonprofit. Tax-exempt: 501(c)(3).
Art Museum.
Collections: contemporary paintings, prints & photographs; sculpture; installations.
Research Fields: art by recent immigrants to the United States.
Facilities: 1,470 sq. ft. exhibit space.
Activities: formal education programs for children & undergraduate/graduate students affiliated with De Anza College; guided tours; lectures; participatory, traveling & community exhibitions. Annual Events: Family Day (through Arts & Schools Program).
Publications: select exhibition books.
Hours & Admission Prices: late Sept. to mid-June Mon.-Thurs. 10-4; groups by appointment. No charge; donations accepted. ♿
Attendance: 10,000 (estimated)
Membership: Friends of the Euphrat (no specific levels).

FUJITSU PLANETARIUM AT DE ANZA COLLEGE, De Anza College, 21250 Stevens Creek Blvd., Cupertino, CA 95014-5797. Tel.: 408-864-8814 & 8282.
Web Site: www.planetarium.deanza.edu
Formerly: Minolta Planetarium
Founded: 1970.
Governing Authority: Tax-exempt.
Planetarium.
Collections: space science.
Hours & Admission Prices: Field Trips: Mon.-Thurs. mornings, Fri. mornings & afternoons. Call for Family Evenings & Laser Light Show hours & admission prices. ♿

Dana Point

OCEAN INSTITUTE, 24200 Dana Point Harbor Dr., Dana Point, CA 92629-2723. Tel.: 949-496-2274.
E-mail: oi@ocean-institute.org
Web Site: www.ocean-institute.org
Formerly: Orange County Marine Institute
Marine Science Institute.
Collections: hands-on marine science & environmental exhibits.
Activities: maritime history programs; education programs.
Hours & Admission Prices: Mon.-Fri. 8-5 (summer camps & school programs only), Sat.-Sun. 10-3 (public entry). Adults 13 & over $6.50, youth 3-12 $4.50; members and children 2 & under no charge. Closed major holidays.
Membership: Individual $35; Family $60.

Danville

BLACKHAWK MUSEUM (BEHRING-HOFMANN EDUCATIONAL INSTITUTE, INC.), 3700 Blackhawk Plaza Cir., Danville, CA 94506-4652. Tel.: 925-736-2280 & 2277. Fax: 925-736-4818.
E-mail: museum@blackhawkmuseum.org
Web Site: www.blackhawkmuseum.org
Formerly: Blackhawk Automotive Museum (Behring-Hofmann Educational Institute, Inc.)
Founded: 1988.
Key Personnel: C.E.O. & Pres., Don Williams; Education, Nora Wagner; Public Rels., Lawrence Magnus; Special Events Coord., Jon Snyder; Exec. Dir., Dan Dunn; Museum Shop Mgr., Fred Zimmerman.
Personnel Profile: Full-Time Paid 15; Part-Time Paid 6; Part-Time Volunteers 5.
Governing Authority: private; nonprofit organization. Parent Institution: Behring-Hofmann Educational Institute Inc. Affiliate Program Member of the Smithsonian Institution. Tax-exempt: 501(c)(3).
Automobile & History Museum.
Collections: automotive art.
Major Exhibits: Styling, 2/10-8/10; Trains, 11/10-1/11.
Facilities: library; classrooms; 75,000 sq. ft. exhibit space; 600-seat theater. Museum-related items for sale.
Activities: docent program; films; formal educational programs; guided tours; hobby workshops; lectures; loan, participatory, temporary & traveling exhibitions; school loan service; study clubs; training programs for professional museum workers; outreach programs for area schools.
Publications: quarterly newsletter.
Hours & Admission Prices: Wed.-Sun. 10-5. Adults $10, senior citizens & students $7; discounts to groups; children under 6 no charge. Closed New Year's Day; Thanksgiving; Christmas. ♿
Attendance: 62,000 (estimated)
Membership: Individual & Senior Couple $35; Family $45; Friend $100; Patron $150; Contributor $250; Supporter $500; Patron $1,000; Benefactor $2,500; Visionary $5,000.

EUGENE O'NEILL NATIONAL HISTORIC SITE, Danville, CA 94526-0280. Mailing Address: P.O. Box 280, Danville, CA 94526-0280. Tel.: 925-838-0249 & 943-1531. Fax: 925-838-9471.
E-mail: euon_interpretation@nps.gov
Web Site: www.nps.gov/euon
Founded: 1976.
Congressional District: 8
Key Personnel: Chm. (V), Joanne Jarvis; Museum Shop Mgr., Nancy Pierce.
Personnel Profile: Full-Time Paid 5; Part-Time Volunteers 11.
Governing Authority: federal. Administered by National Park Service, U.S. Department of the Interior. Partnering Organization: Eugene O'Neill Foundation. Tax-exempt.
National Historic Site: Tao House was the home of playwright Eugene O'Neill from 1937 to 1944.
Collections: clothing; jewelry; autographed books, paintings; letters; period photographs; furnishings.
Facilities: garden; orchards; visitors center/book store.
Activities: guided tours; occasional special events & performance programs.
Publications: booklet, Eugene O'Neill at Tao House; Eugene O'Neill - official park guide.
Hours & Admission Prices: Wed.-Sun. 10 & 12:30 by reservation only. No charge; donations accepted. ♿
Attendance: 3,475 (accurate)

Davis

DAVIS ART CENTER, 1919 F St., Davis, CA 95616-1163. Mailing Address: P.O. Box 4340, Davis, CA 95617-4340. Tel.: 530-756-4100. Fax: 530-756-3041.
E-mail: davisart@dcn.org
Web Site: davisartcenter.org
Founded: 1959.
Key Personnel: Dir., Erie Vitiello.
Personnel Profile: Full-Time Paid 3; Part-Time Paid 2; Part-Time Volunteers 3; Interns 1.
Governing Authority: nonprofit organization. Tax-exempt: 501(c)(3).
Art Center.
Collections: contemporary art.
Facilities: library; educational facilities; 10,500 sq. ft. exhibit space.
Activities: lectures; concerts; dance recitals; arts festivals; organized educational programs. Annual Events: art & craft sale.
Hours & Admission Prices: Mon.-Thurs. 9:30-7, Fri. 9:30-5. No charge. Closed New Year's Eve & Day; Memorial Day; Independence Day; Labor Day; Christmas Day & week. ♿
Attendance: 40,000 (estimated)
Membership: Senior & Student $20; Individual $30; Family $50; Patron $250.

EXPLORIT SCIENCE CENTER, 2801 2nd St., Davis, CA 95618-7774. Mailing Address: P.O. Box 1288, Davis, CA 95617-1288. Tel.: 530-756-0191. Fax: 530-756-1227.
E-mail: explorit@explorit.org
Web Site: www.explorit.org
Founded: 1982.
Congressional District: 3
Key Personnel: Exec. Dir., Lou Ziskind; Pres. (V), Dr. Rick Baker; Exhibit Coord., Anna Grace; Program Dir, Megan Chiosso; Museum Shop Mgr., Anne Hance.
Personnel Profile: Full-Time Paid 10; Part-Time Paid 11; Part-Time Volunteers 200; Interns 12.
Governing Authority: not-for-profit organization. Tax-exempt: 501(c)(3).
Hands-On Science Center.
Collections: sand; seashells; rocks; fossil paintings.
Major Exhibits: What's Out There? Exploring Our Universe, 12/09-2/10; Wild Planet, 3/10-5/10; Take Matters Into Your Own Hands, 6/10-8/10.
Facilities: Museum-related items for sale.

Activities: education programs for children; lectures; mobile vans; participatory & traveling exhibits; outreach education and exhibit programs for children & adults; changing topics.
Publications: quarterly newsletter, Science Centered.
Hours & Admission Prices: Tues.-Fri. 2-4:30, Sat.-Sun. 11-4:30. Admission $4; discounts to ASTC travel passport program members/Reciprocal admission program; members, teachers, children under 4 & fourth Fri. of each month no charge. Closed New Year's; Memorial Day; Independence Day; Labor Day; Thanksgiving; Christmas. ♿
Attendance: 80,000 (accurate)
Membership: Student & Senior $20; Individual $25; Family & Grandparents $50; Darwin Circle $75; Curie Circle $125; Galileo Circle $250; Einstein Circle $500.

HATTIE WEBER MUSEUM OF DAVIS, 445 C St., Davis, CA 95616-4102. Tel.: 530-758-5637.
Web Site: www.dcn.davis.ca.us/go/hattie
Key Personnel: Dir., Jim Becket
History Museum.
Collections: area history & heritage; personal artifacts.
Hours & Admission Prices: Fall & Winter: Wed.-Sat. 10-4; Summer: Wed. 1:30-4, Sat. 9-2. No charge; donations accepted.

MEMORIAL UNION ART GALLERY, 2nd Fl., Memorial Union Bldg., University of California, Davis, Davis, CA 95616. Mailing Address: University of California, One Shields Ave., Davis, CA 95616-5270. Tel.: 530-752-2885. Fax: 530-754-4387.
E-mail: hmikolaj@ucdavis.edu
Web Site: muartgallery.ucdavis.edu
Founded: 1967.
Key Personnel: Dir., Heather Mikolaj.
Personnel Profile: Full-Time Paid 1; Full-Time Volunteers 1; Part-Time Paid 4; Interns 1.
Governing Authority: university. Parent Institution: University of California, Davis. Affiliated with Memorial Union.
University Art Gallery.
Collections: paintings; photographs; drawings; sculpture.
Research Fields: contemporary art.
Facilities: catalogue collection for public reference.
Activities: guided tours; lectures; films; gallery talks; concerts; arts festivals; volunteer art committee internships; formally organized education programs for undergraduate & graduate college students; inter-museum, permanent & traveling exhibitions. Museum Sponsors: non-degree training program for University of California students.
Publications: biannual exhibit catalogues.
Hours & Admission Prices: Mon., Wed. & Fri. 9-5, Tues. & Thurs. 11-7; other times by appointment. No charge. Closed school holidays. ♿
Attendance: 5,500 (estimated)

PENCE GALLERY, 212 D St., Davis, CA 95616-4513. Tel.: 530-758-3370. Fax: 530-758-4670.
E-mail: penceassistant@sbcglobal.net
Web Site: www.pencegallery.org
Founded: 1975.
Congressional District: 4
Key Personnel: Dir., Natalie Nelson; Asst. Dir., Eileen Hendren; Pres., Sue Smith; Museum Shop Mgr., Cindy Ruff.
Personnel Profile: Part-Time Paid 4; Part-Time Volunteers 30; Interns 6.
Governing Authority: private; nonprofit institution. Land owned by City of Davis, CA. Tax-exempt: 501(c)(3).
Art Association Gallery.
Collections: changing exhibitions of contemporary art, California art & history culture.
Major Exhibits: Crown Point Press Prints, 1/10-3/10; Avery Palmen, 2/10-3/10; Lourdes Carcedo: Microstories, 3/10-4/10; Frankie Hanseberry/Gerry Wallace, 4/10; Not So Common Clay, 5/10; UC Davis MFA Exhibit, 5/10; City of Davis Small Works, 7/10-8/10; 12 Voices (T), 9/10-11/10; Holiday Market, 11/10-12/10.
Facilities: 5,000 sq. ft. exhibit space.
Activities: guided tours; gallery talks; lectures; concerts; exhibitions of works of art; shows of ethnic & folk art, children's art & competitive shows, old master prints & drawings; contemporary painting, sculpture, graphics & photography; art auctions, art related tours & bus excursions; Art Smart Education Program.
Publications: quarterly publication, Pence Events; art catalogues.
Hours & Admission Prices: Tues.-Sun. 11:30-5, 2nd Fri. 6-9. No charge; donations accepted. Closed New Year's Eve & Day; Veterans Day; Thanksgiving; Christmas Eve & Day. ♿
Attendance: 12,500 (estimated)

Membership: Individual $35; Household $60; Sponsor $100; Patron $250; Benefactor $500; Curator's Circle $1,000; Gallery Circle $2,500.

QUAIL RIDGE WILDERNESS CONSERVANCY, 25344 County Rd. 95, Davis, CA 95616. Tel.: 530-758-1387. Fax: 530-758-1316.
E-mail: quailrid@quailridge.org
Web Site: www.quailridge.org
Key Personnel: Exec. Dir., Frank W. Maurer
Conservancy.
Collections: native plants & animals; oak trees; native California bunchgrasses.
Activities: educational workshops; interpretive walks.
Hours & Admission Prices: Call for hours.

R.M. BOHART MUSEUM OF ENTOMOLOGY, Dept. of Entomology, University of California, One Shields Ave., Davis, CA 95616-8584. Tel.: 530-752-0493. Fax: 530-752-9464.
Web Site: bohart.ucdavis.edu
Founded: 1946.
Congressional District: 3
Key Personnel: Dir., Lynn S. Kimsey; Cur., Phil Ward; Cur., Peter S. Cranston; Cur., Penny J. Gullan; Collection Mgr., Steve Heydon; Museum Shop Mgr., M.F. Keller.
Personnel Profile: Full-Time Paid 5; Part-Time Paid 3; Part-Time Volunteers 2.
Governing Authority: University of California. Tax-exempt.
Entomology Museum.
Collections: seven million arthropod specimens.
Research Fields: systematics & insect ecology & behavior.
Facilities: library of entomology texts & periodicals.
Activities: guided tours; formally organized education programs for grades K-12, undergraduate college & graduate students; temporary exhibitions.
Publications: newsletter, Bohart Museum Society.
Hours & Admission Prices: Mon.-Fri. 8-5. No charge; donations accepted. Closed holidays. ♿
Attendance: 4,000 (accurate)
Membership: Student $15; Regular $25; Donor $40; Organization & Patron $100.

RICHARD L. NELSON GALLERY & THE FINE ARTS COLLECTION, UC DAVIS, One Shields Ave., Davis, CA 95616-5270. Mailing Address: Dept. of Art, UC-Davis, CA 95616. Tel.: 530-752-8500. Fax: 530-754-9122.
E-mail: nelsongallery@ucdavis.edu
Web Site: nelsongallery.ucdavis.edu
Founded: 1976.
Congressional District: 4
Key Personnel: Dir., Renny Pritikin; Registrar & Collections Mgr., Robin Bernhard.
Personnel Profile: Full-Time Paid 2; Part-Time Paid 2; Part-Time Volunteers 15; Interns 5.
Governing Authority: public university; nonprofit. Parent Institution: Univ. of California, Davis. Tax-exempt: 501(c)(3).
Art Gallery & Museum.
Collections: 6,000 artifacts including 16th century-present paper, prints, drawings & paintings; contemporary art, emphasizing northern California artists; Chinese & southeast Asian art; European and American art; ceramics.
Major Exhibits: Wayne Thiebaud Hand-Worked Prints, 1/10-3/10; Owen Smith, 3/10-5/10.
Research Fields: contemporary art, with emphasis on northern California.
Facilities: 1,700 sq. ft. exhibit space. Exhibition catalogs for sale.
Activities: guided tours; lectures; loan, traveling & temporary exhibitions; organized education programs for undergraduate & graduate students affiliated with UC Davis Art Dept.
Publications: exhibition catalogs.
Hours & Admission Prices: Mon.-Fri. 11-5, Sun. 2-5. No charge; donations accepted. Closed Martin Luther King Jr. Day; Presidents' Day; Independence Day; Thanksgiving; Christmas. ♿
Attendance: 7,000
Membership: Nelson Art Friends: Student & Senior (65 & over) $25; Individual $35; Dual & Family $60; Patron $150-$999; Business & Corporate Associate $250-$1,999; Benefactor $1,000 and up; Business & Corporate Benefactor $2,000.

UC DAVIS DESIGN MUSEUM, (M), 145 Walker Hall, One Shields Ave., Davis, CA 95616-5200. Mailing Address: 142 Walker Hall, University of California, Davis, One Shields Ave., Davis, CA 95616-5200. Tel.: 530-752-6150. Fax: 530-752-1392.
E-mail: designmuseum@ucdavis.edu
Web Site: www.designmuseum.ucdavis.edu

Formerly: University of California Design Museum
Founded: 1975.
Personnel Profile: Full-Time Paid 2; Interns 6.
Governing Authority: Parent Institution: University of California, Davis. Tax-exempt.
Design Museum.
Collections: national & international design-related materials; textiles; fashion; basketry; porcelain; architecture; furniture.
Research Fields: sustainable exhibition design.
Hours & Admission Prices: Mon.-Fri. 12-4, Sun. 2-4. No charge; donations accepted. Closed holidays; university breaks.
Attendance: 2,000 (estimated)

U.S. BICYCLING HALL OF FAME, (M), Davis, CA 95617. Mailing Address: P.O. Box 73385, Davis, CA 95617. Tel.: 910-253-9349.
E-mail: usbhof@optonline.net
Web Site: usbhof.com
Founded: 1986.
Key Personnel: Pres. Bd., Dawn Wylong.
Governing Authority: bd. of directors. Tax-exempt.
Hall of Fame & Bicycling History Museum.
Collections: cycling greats; photographs; trophies; medals; newspapers; history of cycling; Frank Kramer, 1920s; Greg Lemons, 1980s; Marshall Major Taylor, 1899s.
Activities: racing events. Annual Events: Hall of Fame Dinner; USBHOF Induction Ceremony in November.
Hours & Admission Prices: Call for information.

UC DAVIS ARBORETUM, Valley Oak Cottage, La Rue Rd., University of California, Davis, CA 95616. Mailing Address: One Shields Ave., Davis, CA 95616-5200. Tel.: 530-752-4880. Fax: 530-752-5796.
E-mail: arboretum@ucdavis.edu
Web Site: arboretum.ucdavis.edu
Founded: 1936.
Congressional District: 4
Key Personnel: Dir., Kathleen Socolofsky; Dir. Planning & Collections, Mary T. Burke; Cur., Mia Ingolia; Supt., Warren G. Roberts; Dir. Communications, Diane Cary; Pres., Friends of the Davis Arboretum, Mary Patterson; Dir. Horticulture, Ellen Zagory; Admin. Mgr., Linda Johnson; Resource Devel. Mgr., Amy McGuire; Nursery Mgr., Beth Gale; Asst. Dir., Carmia Feldman; Asst. Dir. Education, Emily Griswold; Grounds Supvr., Robert Bohn; Education Outreach Mgr., Betsy Faber; GIS Mgr., Brian Morgan; Interpretation Coord., Holly Crosson; Youth & Family Outreach Mgr., Elaine Fingerett; Special Projects Asst., Judy Hayes; Business Asst., Sabrina Morgan.
Personnel Profile: Full-Time Paid 14; Part-Time Paid 3; Part-Time Volunteers 100; Interns 10.
Governing Authority: state. Parent Institution: University of California. Tax-exempt.
Arboretum.
Collections: living native & exotic trees & plants: oaks; conifers; eucalyptus; acacias; redwoods; California native plants; American desert plants; drought-tolerant flowering perennial garden.
Research Fields: taxonomy of flowering plants; horticulture of native California plants; California landscape history.
Facilities: 1,000-vol. library of reference material; 100-acre botanical garden.
Activities: guided tours; lectures; elementary school field trips; university courses; field trips; workshops & courses; permanent exhibitions.
Publications: pamphlets; quarterly bulletin.
Hours & Admission Prices: Gardens: daily 24 hours. No charge. Office: Mon.-Fri. 8-12 & 1-5. No charge. ♿
Attendance: 250,000 (estimated)
Membership: Student $15; Individual $40; Family $60; Manzanita Circle $100; Valley Oak Circle $250; Sequoia Circle $500.

Death Valley

DEATH VALLEY NATIONAL PARK VISITOR CENTER AND MUSEUMS, Death Valley National Park, Hwy. 190, Death Valley, CA 92328. Mailing Address: P.O. Box 579, Death Valley, CA 92328-0579. Tel.: 760-786-3200. Fax: 760-786-3283. TDD: 760-786-2471.
E-mail: blair_davenport@nps.gov
Web Site: www.nps.gov/deva
Formerly: Death Valley Visitor Center and Museums
Founded: 1933.
Congressional District: 35
Key Personnel: Supt., James T. Reynolds.
Governing Authority: federal. Parent Institution: National Park Service. Subsidiary Institution: Death Valley National Park. Tax-exempt.
Park Visitor Center, Museum & Historic House.
Collections: archaeology; history; anthropology; geology; herbarium; natural history. Historic Buildings: 1876 charcoal kilns; 1883 Harmony borax works; 1924-1931 Scotty's Castle.
Research Fields: geology; archaeology; botany; biology; ecology; history.
Facilities: 5,000-vol. library available for research on premises; archives. Books for sale.
Activities: guided tours; lectures; permanent exhibitions.
Publications: books; pamphlet; guides; postcards. Published by Death Valley Natural History Association, a cooperating organization.
Hours & Admission Prices: Furnace Creek Visitor Center: daily 8-5; Scotty's Castle Visitor Center: daily 8-5. Tour bus $25-$200, individual vehicles $20, walk-ins & bike-ins $10. Scotty's Castle: Adults $11, seniors (62 & over) $9, children (6-15) & adults with disabilities $6; discounts to Golden Age, Golden Eagle, & Golden Access card holders; children under 6 no charge. ♿
Attendance: 1,000,000 (estimated)
Membership: Death Valley Natural History Association: Individual $20; Sustaining $50; Sponsor $100; Lifetime $1,000.

Delano

DELANO HERITAGE PARK, 330 Lexington, Delano, CA 93215-3602. Tel.: 661-725-6730 & 978-6118. Fax: 661-725-2344.
E-mail: heritagepark1@aol.com
Founded: 1961.
Congressional District: 18
Key Personnel: Pres. (V), Peter Finocchiaro.
Governing Authority: nonprofit organization. Administered by Parks & Recreation Dept. of the city. Affiliated with Delano Historical Society, 330 Lexington St. Tax-exempt: 501(c)(3).
Park Museum.
Collections: local history; agriculture; arboretum. Historic Houses: 1890 Heritage House, Garces & Lexington; 1916 Jasmine School; 1968 Replica Jasmine School Stable; 1876 Jail; 1912 Orcier Famosa Store; 1888 Weaver House; 1800 farm equipment.
Research Fields: local history; agriculture; arboretum.
Facilities: 100-vol. library of local & California history, historical pictures, slides & old books.
Activities: guided tours; lectures; films; permanent exhibitions.
Publications: book, Delano: A Land of Promise, 1965; quarterly bulletin, The Plow.
Hours & Admission Prices: Temporarily closed. Tours by appointment; guided tours for groups. No charge; donations accepted. ♿
Attendance: 1,750 (estimated)
Membership: Individual $25; Business $50.

Desert Hot Springs

CABOT'S PUEBLO MUSEUM, 67-616 E. Desert View Ave., Desert Hot Springs, CA 92240. Mailing Address: P.O. Box 104, Desert Hot Springs, CA 92240-0104. Tel.: 760-329-7610.
Web Site: www.cabotsmuseum.org
Historic House Museum: housed in the former pueblo-style home of Cabot Yerxa.
Collections: local and state cultural heritage & history; Cabot Yerxa's life & family history; Native American pottery; photographs; personal artifacts; early 1900s tools, machinery, & housewares; paintings; sculpture.
Facilities: Books for sale.
Activities: special events.
Hours & Admission Prices: Daily 10-3. Guided Tours: adults $8, students, military, & local residents $6. Closed major holidays.

Donner Pass

WESTERN SKISPORT MUSEUM, Interstate 80 Boreal Ridge Ski Area, Donner Pass, CA 95728. Mailing Address: P.O. Box 729, Soda Springs, CA 95728-0729. Tel.: 530-426-3313, ext. 113. Fax: 530-426-3501.
E-mail: bcasctc@hotmail.com
Web Site: www.auburnskiclub.org
Founded: 1969.
Key Personnel: Dir., Bill Clark; Sec., Laura Clark.
Personnel Profile: Part-Time Paid 1.
Governing Authority: nonprofit organization. Owned & operated by the Auburn Ski Club, Inc., P.O. Box 729, Soda Springs, CA 95728. Tax-exempt.
Ski History Museum.
Collections: steel monument of Snow-Shoe Thompson; memorabilia from Western North America Skisport Hall of Fame; ski history; manuscripts.
Research Fields: pioneer times during snow bound winter months in western states, western Canada & Alaska.
Facilities: 500-vol. library of books, magazines & manuscripts relative to skisport, ski associations, international skisport & Olympic movement available for research by arrangement with custodians or director; reading room; 30-seat theatre.

Activities: guided tours; lectures; films; permanent exhibitions.
Publications: The Lost Sierra.
Hours & Admission Prices: Winter: Fri.-Sun. 10-4; call for extended hours. No charge; donations accepted. ♿
Attendance: 5,000 (estimated)

Downey

DOWNEY MUSEUM OF ART, 10419 S. Rives Ave., Downey, CA 90241. Mailing Address: P.O. Box 4748, Downey, CA 90241-1748. Tel.: 562-861-0419.
E-mail: dmoa.newmuseum@earthlink.net
Web Site: thedmoa.org
Founded: 1957.
Congressional District: 29
Key Personnel: C.E.O. & Consulting, Kate Davies; Pres. (V), Carmela Spencer.
Governing Authority: nonprofit organization. Tax-exempt: 501(c)(3).
Art Museum.
Collections: paintings; sculpture; graphics; photographs.
Research Fields: 20th & 21st century California art.
Facilities: six galleries; community services room.
Activities: guided tours; lectures; gallery talks; young visitors & artists program; in-class high school talks; discovery & exhibitions of new artists.
Hours & Admission Prices: Thurs.-Fri. 1-5; groups by appointment. No charge; donations accepted. Closed holidays. ♿
Attendance: 21,892 (accurate)
Membership: Contributing $40; Associate $100; Sponsor $250; Sustaining $500; Patron $1,000.

Downieville

DOWNIEVILLE MUSEUM, 330 Main St., Downieville, CA 95936. Mailing Address: P.O. Box 1, Downieville, CA 95936-0001. Tel.: 530-289-3506.
E-mail: hangman@jps.net
Founded: 1932.
Congressional District: 14
Key Personnel: Dir. & Chm. (V), Mary Jungi; Treas., Lee Adams; Paid Staff, A. Monjar; Paid Staff, Donald McIntosh; Volunteer, L. Adams, III; Volunteer, Jane Hallman; Volunteer, David Marshall.
Personnel Profile: Part-Time Paid 2; Part-Time Volunteers 5.
Governing Authority: nonprofit organization. Parent Institution: Native Daughters & Native Sons. Tax-exempt.
General Museum: housed in 1852 store.
Collections: artifacts of Gold Rush era, 1849-1920s; replica of gold stamp mill; horse snowshoes; pictures; paper items; Indian & Chinese artifacts; personal & household items of early-day Downieville & surrounding Sierra County; local history.
Facilities: library of histories of Lassen, Plumas & Sierra Counties, La Porte Scrapbook & other volumes of local history, available on premises only.
Hours & Admission Prices: May to mid-Oct. Mon.-Fri. 11-4, Sat.-Sun. 10-5. Suggested Donation: adults $1.
Attendance: 6,500 (accurate)

Duarte

JUSTICE BROTHERS RACING MUSEUM, 2734 Huntington Dr., Duarte, CA 91010-2301. Tel.: 626-359-9174. Fax: 626-357-2550.
E-mail: museum@justicebrothers.com
Web Site: www.justicebrothers.com
Founded: 1985.
Key Personnel: C.E.O. & Pres., Ed Justice, Jr.; Museum Shop Mgr., Caitlin Justice.
Governing Authority: nonprofit organization.
Racing Museum.
Collections: racing vehicles; motorcycles; passenger cars; racing memorabilia.
Facilities: Museum-related items for sale.
Hours & Admission Prices: Mon.-Fri. 9-5. No charge. Closed business holidays. ♿

Durham

PATRICK RANCH MUSEUM, 10381 Midway, Durham, CA 95938. Mailing Address: 270 Boeing Ave., Chico, CA 95973. Tel.: 530-892-1525. Fax: 530-892-1524.
E-mail: office@farwestheritage.org
Web Site: www.farwestheritage.org
Founded: 2004.
Congressional District: 2
Key Personnel: Pres. (V), Dax Kimmelshue; Exec. Dir., Jim Lynch; Treas., Margaret Skinner; Cur. & Registrar, Anne Seiler; Administrative Asst., Arlene Ward; Visitor Svcs., Melinda Rist.
Personnel Profile: Full-Time Volunteers 1; Part-Time Paid 3; Part-Time Volunteers 40; Interns 2.
Governing Authority: Parent Institution: Far West Heritage Assoc. Tax-exempt.
History Museum.
Collections: Sacramento Valley agricultural history including social, cultural and economic artifacts.
Hours & Admission Prices: Closed for restoration.
Membership: Senior $50; Individual $75; Family $100; Settler Society $120; Pioneer Society $300; Explorer's Society $600; Founder's Society $1,200.

Edwards AFB

AIR FORCE FLIGHT TEST CENTER MUSEUM, 405 S. Rosamond Blvd., Edwards AFB, CA 93524-0001. Mailing Address: P.O. Box 57, Edwards, CA 93523-0057. Tel.: 661-277-8050 & 3510 (Public Relations). Fax: 805-277-8051.
E-mail: museum@edwards.af.mil
Web Site: www.afftcmuseum.com/
Founded: 1986.
Key Personnel: Dir. & Cur., Frederick A. Johnsen.
Personnel Profile: Full-Time Paid 2; Full-Time Volunteers 1; Part-Time Volunteers 24.
Governing Authority: federal government; nonprofit. Tax-exempt: 501(c)(3).
Aeronautics Museum.
Collections: concentration on history of Edwards Air Force Base, its antecedents & the history of flight testing.
Facilities: 500-vol. aeronautics library; 8,500 sq. ft. exhibit space; 30-seat theater; six acres of outside exhibit space. Aviation-related items for sale.
Activities: films.
Hours & Admission Prices: Tues.-Sat. 9-5. No charge; donations accepted. Closed federal holidays. ♿
Attendance: 33,000 (accurate)

El Cajon

GROSSMONT COLLEGE HYDE ART GALLERY, 8800 Grossmont College Dr., El Cajon, CA 92020-1798. Tel.: 619-644-7299. Fax: 619-644-7922.
E-mail: ben.aubert@gcccd.edu
Web Site: www.grossmont.edu/artgallery
Founded: 1961.
Congressional District: 43
Key Personnel: Cur., Ben Aubert; Chm. (V) & Dean, Steve Baker; Gallery Asst., Teresa Markey; Head Art Council & Professor, Suda House; Professor, Jennifer Bennett; Art Dept. Chm., Jim Wilsterman.
Governing Authority: college. Parent Institution: Grossmont Community College District. Tax-exempt.
Art Gallery.
Collections: prints; ceramics; photographs; digital.
Activities: films; gallery talks; concerts; loan, temporary & traveling exhibitions.
Publications: exhibit announcements; catalogues.
Hours & Admission Prices: Mon. & Thurs. 10-6:30, Tues.-Wed. 10-8. No charge. Closed all legal holidays. ♿
Attendance: 12,000 (estimated)
Membership: Student $10; Individual $25; Art Council $35; Patron $50; Donor $75; Benefactor $100; Sponsor $250.

HERITAGE OF THE AMERICAS MUSEUM, (M), 12110 Cuyamaca College Dr., W., El Cajon, CA 92019-4317. Tel.: 619-670-5194. Fax: 619-670-5198.
E-mail: hofam@sbcglobal.net
Web Site: www.cuyamaca.edu/museum
Founded: 1993.
Congressional District: 52
Key Personnel: Founder, Bernard Lueck; Exec. Dir., Kathleen Oatsvall; Chm. (V), Ronald Raymond.
Personnel Profile: Full-Time Paid 1; Part-Time Paid 2; Part-Time Volunteers 30.
Governing Authority: private; nonprofit organization. Tax-exempt.
History Museum.
Collections: natural & human history of the Americas.
Activities: lectures; educational programs.
Publications: bimonthly newsletter.
Hours & Admission Prices: Tues.-Fri. 10-4, Sat. 12-4. Adults $3, senior citizens $2; discount to AAM, ICOM & AAA members; youths under 17 & accompanied by an adult & members no charge. ♿
Attendance: 20,000 (accurate)
Membership: Student & Senior $10; Individual $20; Family $30; Contributor $50; Patron $100; Grantor $200.

KNOX HOUSE MUSEUM, 280 N. Magnolia, El Cajon, CA 92020-3906. Mailing Address: P.O. Box 1973, El Cajon, CA 92022-1973. Tel.: 619-444-3800.
E-mail: info@elcajonhistory.org
Web Site: www.elcajonhistory.org
Founded: 1973.
Historical House Museum: built in 1876.
Collections: El Cajon area history; period furnishings.
Activities: community heritage projects; research; guided tours; outreach; fundraising.
Publications: quarterly newsletter.
Hours & Admission Prices: 2nd & 4th Sat. 12:30-3:30, 3rd Sat. 11-1:15. No charge; donations accepted.
Membership: Individual $10; Family $15; Organization $25; Business $35; Life $200; Enhanced Life $500.

El Monte

EL MONTE HISTORICAL SOCIETY MUSEUM, 3150 Tyler Ave., El Monte, CA 91731-3354. Mailing Address: 3150 N. Tyler, El Monte, CA 91731-3354. Tel.: 626-444-3813 & 580-2232. Fax: 626-444-8142.
Founded: 1958.
Congressional District: 29
Key Personnel: Cur., Donna Crippen.
Governing Authority: municipal; nonprofit organization. Parent Institution: City of El Monte. Tax-exempt: 170(b)(1)(A).
History Museum.
Collections: art; archives; glass; furniture; household furnishings; manuscript collections: clothing; jewelry; guns; musical instruments; pictures & history of early settlers & places; newspapers; school materials; maps; land grants & deeds; journals; diaries; church & cemetery records; farm implements; natural history; Indian & Mexican artifacts; tools; blacksmith items; saloon.
Research Fields: limited local & state history of families; genealogy; archeology.
Facilities: 1,500-vol. library of books on local & state history, original manuscripts, diaries & antique books on many subjects available by appointment only; reading room; theater.
Activities: guided tours; lectures; films; drama; formally organized educational programs; docent program or council; permanent & temporary exhibitions.
Publications: quarterly pamphlet, booklet, End of the Santa Fe Trail; book, The History of El Monte; cookbook, Our Pioneer Heritage.
Hours & Admission Prices: Jan. to mid-Dec. Tues.-Fri. 10-4, Sun. 1-3, tours by appointment. No charge; donations requested. Closed national holidays. ♿
Membership: Active $10; Patron $15; Fellowship $30; Life $100.

El Segundo

AUTOMOBILE DRIVING MUSEUM, 610 Lairport St., El Segundo, CA 90245-5004. Tel.: 310-909-0950. Fax: 310-231-4668.
Web Site: www.automobiledrivingmuseum.org
Founded: 2002.
Congressional District: 30
Key Personnel: Pres. (V) & Cur., Earl Rubenstein; Exec. Dir., Jeff Walker; Treas., David R. Zimmerman; Museum Shop Mgr., Raelyn Morgan.
Personnel Profile: Full-Time Paid 3; Part-Time Volunteers 12.
Governing Authority: nonprofit. Tax-exempt: 501(c)(3).
Transportation Museum.
Collections: vehicles from 1915-1970.
Facilities: library; theater; 25,000 sq. ft. exhibit space.
Activities: vehicle rides; concerts; movies. Annual Event: Auto Show.
Publications: quarterly newsletter.
Hours & Admission Prices: Tues.-Sun. 10-4. No charge; donations accepted. Closed holidays. ♿
Attendance: 6,000 (estimated)
Membership: Subscribers $25, $50, $100, $300, $750. Corporate memberships available.

Encinitas

LUX ART INSTITUTE, (M), 1550 S. El Camino Real, Encinitas, CA 92024-4908. Tel.: 760-436-6611. Fax: 760-436-1400.
E-mail: info@luxartinstitute.org
Web Site: www.luxartinstitute.org
Founded: 1998.
Key Personnel: Dir., Reesey Shaw.
Personnel Profile: Full-Time Paid 7; Part-Time Paid 1; Part-Time Volunteers 35; Interns 2.
Governing Authority: Tax-exempt.
Art Museum.
Collections: works by national & international artists.
Major Exhibits: Susan Hauptman, 11/12/09-1/9/10; Iva Gueorguieva, 1/16/10-3/17/10; Robert Lobe, 3/27/10-5/22/10; Sati Zech, 6/6/10-7/10.
Hours & Admission Prices: Thurs.-Fri. 1-5, Sat. 11-5. Adults $10; members & under 21 no charge.
Attendance: 1,800 (estimated)
Membership: Lux $150; Deluxe $500; Luminary $1,000; Visionary $5,000.

SAN DIEGO BOTANIC GARDEN, (M), 230 Quail Gardens Dr., Encinitas, CA 92024-2707. Mailing Address: P.O. Box 230005, Encinitas, CA 92023-0005. Tel.: 760-436-3036. Fax: 760-632-0917.
E-mail: info@sdbgarden.org
Web Site: www.sdbgarden.org
Formerly: Quail Botanical Gardens
Founded: 1958.
Congressional District: 43
Key Personnel: Pres., Julian Duval; Chm., William Rawlings; 1st Vice Chm., Frank Mannen; Dir. Operations, Patricia Hammer; Museum Shop Mgr., Joyce Sapp.
Personnel Profile: Full-Time Paid 13; Part-Time Paid 13; Part-Time Volunteers 19; Interns 1.
Governing Authority: county. Parent Institution: Quail Botanical Gardens Foundation. Tax-exempt: 501(c)(3).
Botanical Garden.
Collections: tropical & sub-tropical trees, shrubs, herbs; fruits; cacti & other succulents; aloe; proteaceae; bamboo; drought resistant California natives & Austral-Asian plants; hibiscus.
Research Fields: drought resistant ornamentals; sub-tropical fruits & bamboo.
Facilities: 500-vol. library of horticultural & botanical books available for research to foundation members on premises; 96-seat auditorium; botanical garden; foundation center; orientation center; bird sanctuary; concession area; walled garden; demonstration garden.
Activities: guided tours; lectures; films; arts festivals; study clubs; hobby workshops; docent program; permanent & temporary exhibitions; concerts; plant sales; art classes; children's programs.
Publications: quarterly bulletin, Quail Tracks.
Hours & Admission Prices: Daily 9-5. Adults $10, seniors, students & military $7, children 3-12 $5; children under 3 no charge. Parking: $1. ♿
Attendance: 140,000 (estimated)
Membership: Senior 60 & over $40; Individual $50; Senior Dual 60 & over $55; Family & Dual $75.

SAN DIEGUITO HERITAGE MUSEUM, 450 Quail Gardens Dr., Encinitas, CA 92024-2711. Mailing Address: Box 230851, Encinitas, CA 92023-0851. Tel.: 760-632-9711. Fax: 760-632-5695.
E-mail: sdheritage@sbcglobal.net
Web Site: www.sdheritage.org
Founded: 1988.
Congressional District: 51
Key Personnel: C.E.O., Shari Fortmueller; Pres., Sue Steele.
Personnel Profile: Part-Time Paid 3; Part-Time Volunteers 75; Interns 1.
Governing Authority: private; nonprofit. Tax-exempt: 501(c)(3).
History Museum.
Collections: local history & culture including seven communities of north coastal San Diego County; Native American artifacts; the Spaniards; the Homesteaders in late 1800; a reconstructed shanty; the first settlers to the 1950s.
Facilities: Handcrafted & other museum-related items for sale.
Activities: docent program; films; guided tours; loan, participatory, temporary & traveling exhibits; videos. Annual Event: barbecue held at 1894 Olivenhain Town Hall.
Publications: quarterly newsletter; book, San Dieguito Heritage.
Hours & Admission Prices: Wed.-Fri. 12-4, last Sat. of month 12-4. No charge; donations accepted. ♿
Attendance: 9,000 (estimated)
Membership: Individual $25; Family $35; Friend $100; Patron $500; Benefactor $1,000 and up.

Escondido

CALIFORNIA CENTER FOR THE ARTS, ESCONDIDO MUSEUM, 340 N. Escondido Blvd., Escondido, CA 92025-2600. Tel.: 760-839-4120. Fax: 760-739-0205.
Web Site: www.artcenter.org
Founded: 1992.
Congressional District: 51
Key Personnel: C.E.O., Vicky Basehore; Museum Dir. & Cur., Olivia Luther; Dir. Education, Tomoko Kuta; Registrar, Mary Johnson.
Personnel Profile: Full-Time Paid 5; Part-Time Paid 5; Part-Time Volunteers 40; Interns 1.
Governing Authority: nonprofit organization. Tax-exempt: 501(c)(3).
Art Museum.
Collections: California & Latin American contemporary artists.

Research Fields: American & regional art since 1950; Latin American art since 1950.
Facilities: library; art studios in use as educational facilities; 10,000 sq. ft. exhibit space; 2,000 sq. ft. sculpture court; 400-seat theater; 1,532-seat concert hall. Art books & catalogues for sale.
Activities: docent program; guided tours for schools K-12; university classes & adult groups; lectures; gallery talks; demonstrations; family workshops; special events; visual & performing arts classes.
Publications: exhibition catalogues.
Hours & Admission Prices: Tues.-Sat. 10-4, Sun. 1-5. Adults $5, senior citizens & active military $4, students $3; discounts to groups, AAM & ICOM members; children under 12 & members no charge. Closed major holidays. ♿
Attendance: 8,200 (accurate)
Membership: Individual $50; Family $100; Patron $250; Connoisseur $500; Aficionado $1,000; Conductor $2,500; California Center Club $5,000.

DEER PARK ESCONDIDO WINERY & AUTO MUSEUM, 29013 Champagne Blvd., Escondido, CA 92026-6002. Tel.: 760-749-1666; 619-298-1666.
Web Site: www.deerparkwine.com
Founded: 1979.
Key Personnel: Education, Rudy Phillips; Security, Paul Williams.
Personnel Profile: Full-Time Paid 3; Full-Time Volunteers 1; Part-Time Paid 4; Part-Time Volunteers 2.
Governing Authority: private.
Winery & Automobile Museum.
Collections: collections from the American Golden Age with emphasis on the development of the convertible automobile & the growth of the American wine industry; appliances; radios; televisions; American popular trends.
Research Fields: convertible car production.
Facilities: library on automobiles & Americana; 10,000 sq. ft. exhibit space; 100-seat cafeteria; nature/conservation center. Museum-related items for sale.
Activities: art festivals; concerts; guided tours; participatory & temporary exhibitions.
Publications: annual calendar & program booklet; quarterly newsletter, Deer Park Winery & Auto Museum.
Hours & Admission Prices: Fri.-Sun. 10-4. Adults $9; discounts to members. Closed holidays.
Attendance: 75,000 (accurate)
Membership: Individual $25; Family $50; Cadillac $100.

ESCONDIDO CHILDREN'S MUSEUM, 380 N. Escondido Blvd., Escondido, CA 92025-2600. Tel.: 760-233-7755.
E-mail: skildoo@escondidochildrensmuseum.org
Web Site: www.escondidochildrensmuseum.org
Key Personnel: Exec. Dir., Steve Kildoo; Mgr., Kelly O'Neil
Children's Museum.
Collections: hands-on exhibits.
Activities: birthday parties.
Hours & Admission Prices: Tues., Thurs. & Sat. 10-3, Wed. & Fri. 12-4. Admission $5; members & children under one no charge. Closed New Year's Day; Easter; Memorial Day; Independence Day; Labor Day; Thanksgiving; Christmas.

ESCONDIDO HISTORY CENTER, (M), 321 N. Broadway, Escondido, CA 92025-2704. Mailing Address: P.O. Box 263, Escondido, CA 92033-0263. Tel.: 760-743-8207. Fax: 760-743-8267.
E-mail: barker@escondidohistory.org
Web Site: www.escondidohistory.org
Formerly: Heritage Walk Museum
Founded: 1956.
Congressional District: 51
Key Personnel: Pres., Ernie Liebman; Exec. Dir., Wendy Barker; Treas., Sally Costello; Registrar, Marie Tuck.
Personnel Profile: Full-Time Paid 2; Part-Time Paid 1; Part-Time Volunteers 70; Interns 1.
Governing Authority: nonprofit organization. Tax-exempt.
Local History Museum: housed in 1894 library & 1888 Santa Fe Railroad Depot; 1890 Victorian house, barn & working blacksmith shop; railroad car with model train layout.
Collections: 1860-present, Escondido history; manuscripts of local residents; newspaper files; photographs.
Research Fields: oral histories & video taping of Escondido residents.
Facilities: 1,100-vol. library of local, county & American history; preservation reference works, available to the public; 6,500 sq. ft. exhibit space. Books & gift items for sale.
Activities: docent program; guided tours; temporary exhibitions; school loan service; videos; monthly lectures series; city walking tours. Annual Events: Car Show in May; Grape Day Festival in September; living history program in October.
Publications: quarterly newsletter, The Grapevine.
Hours & Admission Prices: Office: Mon.-Fri. 8-4. Museum: Tues.-Sat. 1-4. Suggested Donations: adults $3, children $1; members no charge. Closed holidays. ♿
Attendance: 25,000 (estimated)
Membership: Senior $20; Individual $25; Family $50; Supporting $100; Silver Patron $250; Gold Patron $500.

MINGEI INTERNATIONAL MUSEUM, 155 W. Grand Ave., Escondido, CA 92025-2601. Tel.: 760-735-3355. Fax: 760-735-3306.
E-mail: mingei@mingei.org
Web Site: www.mingei.org
Key Personnel: C.E.O. & Dir., Rob Sidner; Museum Mgr., Karen O'Neill; Collectors' Gallery Asst., Patricia Mues; Collectors' Gallery Asst., Cheryl Cady; Admissions Asst., Hildegard Kleiser; Admissions Asst., Eva Hahscom; Security, Nhan Ha.
Personnel Profile: Part-Time Paid 5.
Governing Authority: nonprofit organization. Tax-exempt: 501(c)(3).
International Folk Art, Craft & Design Museum.
Collections: arts of daily life from all cultures of the world.
Major Exhibits: Rite and Ritual-Ceremonial Art Across Cultures, 11/09-10/16/10.
Facilities: education center. Museum-related items for sale.
Activities: docent guided tours; lectures; demonstrations; permanent & traveling exhibitions.
Hours & Admission Prices: Thurs.-Sat. 11-4, 2nd Sat. of month 11-8. Adults $3, seniors, students, youth & military $2; discount to AAM members; members no charge. ♿
Attendance: 5,817 (estimated)
Membership: Individual $45; Friend & Family $60; Contributor $100; Sustainer $250; Patron $500; Director's Circle $1,250.

SAN DIEGO ARCHAEOLOGICAL CENTER, (M), 16666 San Pasqual Valley Rd., Escondido, CA 92027-7001. Tel.: 760-291-0370. Fax: 760-291-0371.
E-mail: info@sandiegoarchaeology.org
Web Site: www.sandiegoarchaeology.org
Founded: 1993.
Congressional District: 49
Key Personnel: Dir., Cindy Stankowski; Pres. (V), Bruce Gallagher; Devel. & Public Rels., Marie Andersen; Education, Annemarie Cox; Registrar, Chris Mirsky; Cur., Margie Burton, Ph.D.
Personnel Profile: Full-Time Paid 4; Full-Time Volunteers 10; Part-Time Paid 4; Part-Time Volunteers 30; Interns 10.
Governing Authority: private; nonprofit organization. Tax-exempt: 501(c)(3).
Archaeology Museum.
Collections: archaeological artifacts & documents; cultural history.
Research Fields: prehistoric groundstone technology; indigenous ceramic typologies & chronology; prehistoric demography & resource use.
Facilities: library; 2,800 sq. ft. exhibit space. Museum-related items for sale.
Activities: docent program; formal education programs; internships; guided tours; hobby workshops; lectures; loan, traveling, participatory & temporary exhibitions; training programs; school loan service. Annual Events: Cultural Resource Management BBQ.
Publications: quarterly, The San Diego Archaeological Center Newsletter.
Hours & Admission Prices: Mon.-Fri. 9-4, Sat. 10-2. Suggested Donation: family $5, individual $2. Closed New Year's Day; Thanksgiving; Christmas.
Attendance: 5,000 (accurate)
Membership: Senior & Student $25; Individual $35; Family $50; Supporter $75; Sponsor $100; Patron $150; Benefactor & Corporation $250.

SAN DIEGO ZOO'S WILD ANIMAL PARK, 15500 San Pasqual Valley Rd., Escondido, CA 92027-7017. Mailing Address: P.O. Box 120551, San Diego, CA 92112-0551. Tel.: 760-738-5018 & 747-8702. Fax: 760-746-7081.
E-mail: csimmons@sandiegozoo.org
Web Site: www.sandiegozoo.org
Founded: 1972.
Congressional District: 14
Key Personnel: C.E.O., Douglas G. Myers; Pres. (V), Bert Dorler; Dir. Wild Animal Park, Robert McClure; Corporate Dir. Merchandising, Yvonne Miles; Dir. Collections, Bob Wiese, Ph.D.; Dir. Veterinary Svcs., Donald Janssen, DVM; Dir. Mktg., Ted Molter; Assoc. Dir. Public Rels., Christina Simmons; Cur. Birds, Michael Mace; Cur. Mammals, Randy Reiches;

Assoc. Dir. Education, Cindy Wallace; Horticulturist, Cary Sharp; Dir. Food Svcs., Beverly Sylvester.
Personnel Profile: Full-Time Paid 800; Part-Time Paid 300.
Governing Authority: society. Parent Institution: Zoological Society of San Diego. Subsidiary Institution: San Diego Wild Animal Park, Division of Conservation and Research for Endangered Species. Tax-exempt: 501(c)(3).
Wildlife Preserve.
Collections: birds, mammals & reptiles of the world; botanical.
Research Fields: veterinary medicine & pathology; animal reproduction & conservation; ecology & habitat preservation.
Facilities: 3,000-vol. library of zoology & natural history; animal hospital; animal care center; amphitheaters; restaurants; 1 1/4 mile hiking trail for photography; Heart of Africa 30-acre walking safari; African marshland exhibit; aviaries; educational campsite; Beckham Center for Conservation & Research. Gifts for sale.
Activities: guided trips through preserve aboard monorail; overnight camping experience; summer Park after Dark experience; guided walking tours through behind-the-scenes areas of park; animal shows; educational programs for pre-school through adult; photo safaris via truck into large animal enclosures; Journey into Africa; African habitat tram tour.
Publications: guidebook, The San Diego Wild Animal Park; magazine, Zoonooz; children's newsletter, Koala Club News; miscellaneous newsletters.
Hours & Admission Prices: Daily 9-4. Adults $28.50, children 3-11 $18.50; discounts to qualifying groups; members and children 2 & under no charge. ♿
Attendance: 1,500,000 (estimated)
Membership: Koala Club 3-11 $21, 12-17 $25; Senior Passes: Single $35; Dual $50; Regular: Single $66; Dual $84; Diamond Club: New $126; Keeper's Club $150; Curator's Club $250; Director's Club $500; President's Associates $1,000; President's Partners $2,500.

Eureka

CLARKE HISTORICAL MUSEUM, (M), 240 E St., Eureka, CA 95501-0433. Tel.: 707-443-1947. Fax: 707-443-0290.
E-mail: clarkehistorical@att.net
Web Site: www.clarkemuseum.org
Formerly: Clarke Memorial Museum, Inc.
Founded: 1960.
Congressional District: 1
Key Personnel: Dir. & Cur., Pam Service; Pres. (V), Jim Moranda; Treas., Wendy Wahlund; Museum Shop Mgr., Constance Clark.
Personnel Profile: Full-Time Paid 1; Part-Time Paid 5; Part-Time Volunteers 22; Interns 1.
Governing Authority: nonprofit corp. Tax-exempt: 501(c)(3).
Regional History Museum.
Collections: Northwestern California Native American basketry & ceremonial regalia; regional & natural history, firearms, Victoriana; decorative arts, costumes, textiles.
Research Fields: Native American culture of the Yurok, Karuk, Hupa, Wiyot & Tolowa; Humboldt County history; American costume & textile.
Facilities: 800-vol. library of regional history; 20,000 photographic archive of Humboldt County scenes.
Activities: docent guided tours for adults & school groups; lectures; temporary & permanent exhibitions; special events; outreach programs to schools.
Publications: books: The Hover Collection of Karuk Baskets, 1993; Baskets and Weavers, 1996; Eureka and Humboldt County California, 2001.
Hours & Admission Prices: Wed.-Sat. 11-4. No charge; donations accepted. ♿
Attendance: 16,000 (accurate)
Membership: Student & Senior $15; Family $25; Sponsor $50; Patron $100; Benefactor $250; Clarke Circle $500.

COLLEGE OF THE REDWOODS ART GALLERY, 7351 Tompkins Hill Rd., Creative Arts Bldg., Eureka, CA 95501-9300. Tel.: 707-476-4558 & 4320.
E-mail: cindy-hooper@redwoods.edu
Web Site: www.redwoods.edu/departments/art/gallery/index.htm
Key Personnel: Head Art Dept., Cindy Hooper
Art Gallery.
Collections: drawings; paintings; sculpture; photography.
Hours & Admission Prices: Call for hours. No charge. Closed during academic breaks.

THE DISCOVERY MUSEUM, 3rd and F Sts., Eureka, CA 95501. Mailing Address: 517 3rd St., Eureka, CA 95501-5105. Tel.: 707-443-9694. Fax: 707-443-7242.
E-mail: info@discovery-museum.org
Web Site: www.discovery-museum.org
Founded: 1995.
Key Personnel: C.E.O., Trey Scott; Dir., Jennifer Taylor
Children's Museum.
Collections: hands-on exhibits.
Facilities: classrooms.
Activities: interactive exhibits; birthday parties; rental facilities; programs for preschoolers, parents & elementary school children; field trips; planetarium shows.
Hours & Admission Prices: Tues.-Sat. 10-4, Sun. 12-4. Admission 2 & over $4; discounts to members.
Membership: Meteorite $25; Asteroid $65; Polaris $100; Comet $250; Nova $500.

HUMBOLDT ARTS COUNCIL/MORRIS GRAVES MUSEUM OF ART, (M), 636 F St., Eureka, CA 95501-1012. Tel.: 707-442-0278. Fax: 707-442-2040.
Web Site: www.humboldtarts.org
Founded: 1966.
Congressional District: 1
Key Personnel: Pres. (V) & C.E.O., Sally Arnot; Cur., Jemima J. Harr.
Personnel Profile: Full-Time Paid 1; Full-Time Volunteers 1; Part-Time Paid 4; Part-Time Volunteers 45; Interns 3.
Governing Authority: private; nonprofit organization. Tax-exempt: 501(c)(3).
Art Museum.
Collections: paintings; prints; drawings; decorative arts; photographs.
Facilities: 200-seat performance rotunda; classroom; 18,000 sq. ft. exhibit space. Museum-related items for sale.
Activities: concerts; dance recitals; docent program; films; formal education programs for children & undergraduate or graduate college students; guided tours; lectures; mobile vans; school loan service; temporary exhibitions; training programs for professional museum workers; broadcast programs.
Hours & Admission Prices: Wed.-Sun. 12-5. No charge; donations accepted. Closed New Year's Day; Easter; Independence Day; Thanksgiving; Christmas.
Attendance: 26,000 (accurate)
Membership: Artist $30; Family $50; Circle of 100 $100; Patron $500; Sponsor $1,000.

WOODEN SCULPTURE GARDEN OF ROMANO GABRIEL, 315 Second St., Eureka, CA 95502-1354. Mailing Address: Eureka Heritage Society, P.O. Box 1354, Eureka, CA 95502-1354. Tel.: 707-445-8775 & 442-8937.
E-mail: info@eurekaheritage.org
Web Site: eurekaheritage.org
Folk Art Museum.
Collections: wooden sculptures.
Hours & Admission Prices: Call for hours.

Fair Oaks

FAIR OAKS HISTORICAL SOCIETY & HISTORY CENTER, Fair Oaks Community Clubhouse, 7997 California Ave., Fair Oaks, CA 95628. Mailing Address: P.O. Box 2044, Fair Oaks, CA 95628-2044. Tel.: 916-961-6912.
Historical Society Museum.
Collections: local history, heritage & culture; photographs; period artifacts.
Hours & Admission Prices: 2nd Sun. of month 1-4.

Fall River Mills

FORT CROOK HISTORICAL MUSEUM, Fort Crook Ave. & Hwy. 299, Fall River Mills, CA 96028. Mailing Address: Box 397, Fall River Mills, CA 96028-0397. Tel.: 530-336-5110.
E-mail: fortcrook@frontiernet.net
Web Site: www.fortcrook.com
Founded: 1934.
Congressional District: 14
Key Personnel: Pres. (V), Charles Thomason; Cur., Dorothy Mason.
Personnel Profile: Part-Time Paid 1; Part-Time Volunteers 18.
Governing Authority: society; nonprofit organization. Parent Institution: Fort Crook Historical Society. Tax-exempt: 170(b)(1)(A).
General Museum.
Collections: agriculture; Indian artifacts; industry; preservation project; transportation; pioneer homemaking, photos, clippings & family histories.
Research Fields: family histories.
Facilities: collection of scrapbooks available on premises; reading room. Museum-related items for sale.
Activities: permanent exhibitions.
Publications: booklet, Reminiscence of Fort Crook Society.
Hours & Admission Prices: May-Oct. Tues.-Sun. 12-4; other times by appointment. No charge; donations accepted.

Attendance: 3,200 (accurate)
Membership: Single $15; Family $25; Business $40; Life $300.

Felicity

MUSEUM OF HISTORY IN GRANITE, Two Center of the World Plaza, Felicity, CA 92183-7777. Tel.: 760-572-0100. Fax: 760-572-3000.
E-mail: ctrworld@aol.com
Web Site: historyingranite.org
Founded: 1973.
Congressional District: 51
Key Personnel: Chm. (V), Jacques Andre Istel; Treas., Felicia Lee; Museum Shop Mgr., Debra Pavey.
Personnel Profile: Part-Time Paid 4; Part-Time Volunteers 11.
Governing Authority: private; nonprofit organization. Parent Institution: Hall of Fame of Parachuting, Inc. Tax-exempt: 501(c)(3).
History Museum.
Collections: granite monuments.
Research Fields: world research.
Facilities: library; 60 acre site; 72-seat restaurant; classrooms. Museum-related items for sale.
Activities: films; guided tours. Museum Sponsors: Dedications.
Hours & Admission Prices: Outdoor Exhibits: daily. Shop & Restaurant: Thanksgiving to Easter. No charge; donations accepted.
Attendance: 20,000 (estimated)

Ferndale

FERN COTTAGE, 2121 Centerville Rd., Ferndale, CA 95536-9719. Mailing Address: P.O. Box 1286, Ferndale, CA 95536-1286. Tel.: 707-786-4835.
Key Personnel: Chm., Irene Harville Hannaford.
Governing Authority: Parent Institution: Fern Cottage Foundation.
Historic House Museum: Russ family farm house, built in 1866.
Collections: personal artifacts; furnishings.
Hours & Admission Prices: Call for hours.

FERNDALE MUSEUM, 515 Shaw Ave., Ferndale, CA 95536. Mailing Address: P.O. Box 431, Ferndale, CA 95536-0431. Tel.: 707-786-4466.
Founded: 1976.
Congressional District: 1
Governing Authority: Tax-exempt.
History Museum.
Collections: local history & heritage; period artifacts; furniture.
Hours & Admission Prices: Feb.-May & Oct.-Dec. Wed.-Sat. 11-4, Sun. 1-4; June-Sept. Tues.-Sat. 11-4, Sun. 1-4. Adults $1; members no charge. ♿

Fillmore

FILLMORE HISTORICAL MUSEUM, INC., 350 Main St., Fillmore, CA 93015-2040. Mailing Address: P.O. Box 314, Fillmore, CA 93016-0314. Tel.: 805-524-0948. Fax: 805-524-0516.
E-mail: fillmore.museum@sbcglobal.net
Founded: 1971.
Key Personnel: Pres. (V) & Administrative Officer, Martha Gentry; Research Librarian, Ynez Haase.
Personnel Profile: Part-Time Volunteers 8.
Governing Authority: nonprofit corporation. Tax-exempt: 501(c)(3).
General Historical Museum: housed in c.1887 former Southern Pacific Depot; 1905 Hinckley House; 1905 Craftsman House; 1919 Rancho Sespe Bunk House.
Collections: photos; memorabilia.
Research Fields: Fillmore area history.
Activities: guided tours.
Publications: newsletter published three times annually.
Hours & Admission Prices: Tues.-Fri. 10-4, Sat. 10:30-3. Adults $4; members no charge; donations accepted. ♿
Attendance: 1,500
Membership: Individual $30; Family $40; Business $50; Contributing $75; Sustaining $100; Patron $500; Benefactor $1,000.

Folsom

THE FOLSOM CITY ZOO SANCTUARY, 403 Stafford St., Folsom, CA 95630-2643. Tel.: 916-351-3527.
E-mail: kbanyard@folsom.ca.us
Web Site: www.folsom.ca.us/depts/parks_n_recreation/zoo.asp
Key Personnel: Zoo Mgr., Jocelyn Smeltzer; Zoo Education, Vicki Valentine
Zoo.
Collections: wildlife & their habitats including peacocks, black bears, wolves, parrots, red foxes, pigs, horses, raccoons, sheep, snakes, & monkeys.
Hours & Admission Prices: Tues.-Sun. 10-4. Adults 13 & over $4, senior citizens 55 & over and children 2-12 $3; children under 2 no charge.

FOLSOM HISTORY MUSEUM, 823 Sutter St., Folsom, CA 95630-2440. Tel.: 916-985-2707. Fax: 916-985-7288.
E-mail: info@folsomhistorymuseum.org
Web Site: www.folsomhistorymuseum.org
Founded: 1960.
Congressional District: 4
Key Personnel: C.E.O. & Dir., Melissa Pedroza; Chm. (V), Patrick Maxfield; Museum Shop Mgr., Pam Conrad.
Personnel Profile: Full-Time Paid 2; Full-Time Volunteers 5; Part-Time Paid 1; Part-Time Volunteers 50; Interns 1.
Governing Authority: nonprofit organization. Tax-exempt: 501(c)(3).
Historical Society Museum: site of Pony Express terminus from June 1860 to October 1861; Wells Fargo Assay Office, 1860-1871.
Collections: history of Folsom area including Pony Express; Sacramento Valley Railroad (first railroad west of the Mississippi); Folsom Powerhouse, one of first to transmit long distance electricity in the world; Mother Lode gold mining (northern mines).
Research Fields: area history.
Facilities: archives, research by appointment; 2,300 sq. ft. exhibit space. Museum-related items for sale.
Activities: guided tours; lectures; temporary & loan exhibits; docent program. Annual Events: Antique Quilt Show in August and September.
Publications: quarterly newsletter, Tailings.
Hours & Admission Prices: Memorial Day to Labor Day daily 11-4; Sept.-May Tues.-Sun. 11-4. Adults $4, youth $2; members no charge. Closed New Year's Day; Easter; Mother's Day; Thanksgiving; Christmas. ♿
Attendance: 18,500 (estimated)
Membership: Senior $15; Individual & Senior Family $25; Family & Non-profit $35; Supporting, Business & Professional $75; Corporate $200.

Fontana

MARY VAGLE NATURE CENTER, 11501 Cypress Ave., Fontana, CA 92337. Mailing Address: 9460 Sierra Ave., Fontana, CA 92335-2411. Tel.: 909-428-8386.
E-mail: rdean@fontana.org
Web Site: www.fontana.org/main/parks_rec/vagle.htm
Nature Center.
Collections: astronomy; rocks & minerals; Native American.
Facilities: trails.
Hours & Admission Prices: Wed.-Sun. 12-5; other times by appointment. No charge; donations accepted. Closed Federal holidays.

Forbestown

YUBA-FEATHER MUSEUM, 19096 New York Flat Rd., Forbestown, CA 95941. Tel.: 530-675-1025.
History Museum.
Collections: mining & logging tools; photographs; period clothing; toys; home furnishings; Maidu baskets & jewelry.
Hours & Admission Prices: Memorial Day-Labor Day Sat.-Sun. 12-4. No charge; donations accepted.

Foresthill

FORESTHILL DIVIDE MUSEUM, 24601 Harrison St., Foresthill, CA 95631. Mailing Address: The Forest Hill Divide Historical Society, P.O. Box 646, Foresthill, CA 95631-0646. Tel.: 530-367-3988.
Web Site: mmoffet.mystarband.net/museum.htm
Governing Authority: Parent Institution: Placer County Museums. Tax-exempt.
History Museum.
Collections: late 19th & early 20th centuries; Gold Rush artifacts; Native Americans; recreation; transportation.
Hours & Admission Prices: mid-May to mid-Oct. Sat.-Sun. & major holidays 12-4. No charge; donations accepted.
Membership: Individual $8; Family $15; Lifetime $120.

Fort Bragg

FORT BUILDING, 430 N. Franklin St., Fort Bragg, CA 95437-3210. Tel.: 707-961-2840.
Military Museum: last remaining structure of the 1857-1864 military post.
Collections: photographs; post history; model of fort.
Hours & Admission Prices: Mon.-Fri. 9-5. No charge. Closed major holidays.

THE GUEST HOUSE MUSEUM, 343 N. Main St., Fort Bragg, CA 95437. Mailing Address: P.O. Box 71, Fort Bragg, CA 95437-0071. Tel.: 707-964-4251 & 2404.
E-mail: ds1923@hotmail.com
Founded: 1950.
Congressional District: 2
Key Personnel: C.E.O. & Pres. (V), Mark Ruedrich; Museum Shop Mgr., Denise Stenberg.
Personnel Profile: Part-Time Volunteers 24.
Governing Authority: municipal. Parent Institution: Fort Bragg. Subsidiary Institution: Mendocino Coast Historical Society. Tax-exempt.
Logging & Lumber Museum: housed in 1892 C.R. Johnson Home.
Collections: logging & lumber mill artifacts; photos; Fort Bragg historical artifacts.
Activities: permanent & temporary exhibitions.
Publications: quarterly, Voice of the Past.
Hours & Admission Prices: June-Oct. Mon.-Fri. 11-2, Sat.-Sun. 10-4; Nov.-May Thurs.-Sun. 11-2. Families $5, adults $2; members & children under 12 no charge. Closed New Year's Day; Thanksgiving; Christmas.
Attendance: 8,500 (estimated)
Membership: Individual $20; Couple $30.

MENDOCINO COAST BOTANIC GARDEN, 18220 N. Hwy. 1, Fort Bragg, CA 95437-8773. Tel.: 707-964-4354.
E-mail: info@gardenbythesea.org
Web Site: www.gardenbythesea.org/about
Key Personnel: Exec. Dir., Christopher Woods
Botanic Garden.
Collections: coastal pine forest; fern-covered canyons; plants; flowers; birds.
Facilities: cafe. Museum-related items for sale.
Activities: education programs; weddings; docent tours.
Hours & Admission Prices: March-Oct. daily 9-5; Nov.-Feb. daily 9-4. Adults 18 & over $10, seniors 60 & over $7.50, juniors 13-17 $4, children 6-12 $2; children 5 & under and members no charge. Closed Thanksgiving; Christmas.

TRIANGLE TATTOO & MUSEUM, 356 B. N. Main St., Fort Bragg, CA 95437-3406. Tel.: 707-964-8814. Fax: 707-964-1193.
E-mail: info@triangletattoo.com
Web Site: www.triangletattoo.com
Founded: 1992.
Key Personnel: C.E.O. & Museum Shop Mgr., M. Chinchilla; C.E.O. & Museum Shop Mgr., Mr. G.
Governing Authority: private; nonprofit.
Tattoo History Museum.
Collections: tattoo art & artifacts; photographs; tattoo implements; historical items pertaining to the development of the Electric Tattooing era.
Research Fields: documenting old tattoos & tattooed people.
Facilities: working tattoo parlor.
Activities: tours.
Publications: books, Stewed, Screwed & Tattooed (3rd revised printing 2005); Electric Tattooing by Women 1900-2003; Electric Tattooing by Men 1900-2004.
Hours & Admission Prices: Daily 12-6. No charge; donations accepted. Closed Christmas.
Attendance: 5,000 (estimated)

Fort Jones

FORT JONES MUSEUM, 11913 Main St., Fort Jones, CA 96032. Mailing Address: P.O. Box 428, Fort Jones, CA 96032-0428. Tel.: 530-468-5568.
Founded: 1947.
Congressional District: 2
Key Personnel: Dir., Cecelia Reuter Mayor Tom McCulley; City Clerk, Linda Romaine.
Personnel Profile: Full-Time Volunteers 2; Part-Time Volunteers 25.
Governing Authority: municipal. Branch Museum: The Fort Jones Museum Carriage House, Corner of Sterling & East St., Fort Jones, CA 96032. Tel.: 530-468-2281. Tax-exempt: 170(b)(1)(A).
Historical Museum.
Collections: Indian beads, baskets; guns; clothing; tools; military, Civil War, WWI & WWII. Carriage House: 9 horse drawn vehicles.
Hours & Admission Prices: Memorial Day to Labor Day Mon.-Fri. 10-4, Sat. 11-3; other times by appointment. No charge; donations accepted. ♿
Attendance: 3,000 (estimated)

Fortuna

CHAPMAN'S GEM AND MINERAL MUSEUM, Hwy. 101, Fortuna, CA 95540. Mailing Address: P.O. Box 32, Carlotta, CA 95528-0032. Tel.: 707-725-2714.
Founded: 1950.
Key Personnel: Owner, Lyle Brown; Dir., Sharon Brown.
Personnel Profile: Full-Time Paid 2; Part-Time Paid 1.
Governing Authority: private. Tax-exempt.
Gem & Mineral Museum.
Collections: petrified palms; precious stones; Indian & pre-Columbian artifacts; fossils.
Hours & Admission Prices: Daily 10-5. No charge; donations accepted. Closed New Year's Day; Easter; Thanksgiving; Christmas. ♿
Attendance: 8,500 (estimated)

FORTUNA DEPOT MUSEUM, 3 Park St., Fortuna, CA 95540-2461. Tel.: 707-725-7645.
Founded: 1976.
Key Personnel: Cur., Caroline Weed.
Personnel Profile: Part-Time Paid 1; Part-Time Volunteers 4.
Governing Authority: Parent Institution: City of Fortuna.
History Museum.
Collections: Eel River Valley history; railroad, farm & war memorabilia; dolls; fishing gear & lures; Fortuna High School year books; Indian baskets; period household artifacts; hands-on exhibits.
Hours & Admission Prices: June-Aug. daily 12-4:30; Sept.-May Thurs.-Sun. 12-4:30. No charge; donations accepted.
Attendance: 5,000 (estimated)

Fremont

ARDENWOOD HISTORIC FARM, 34600 Ardenwood Blvd., Fremont, CA 94555-3645. Tel.: 510-791-4196.
Web Site: www.ebparks.org/parks/arden.htm
Founded: 1985.
Personnel Profile: Full-Time Paid 14; Part-Time Paid 7; Part-Time Volunteers 400.
Living History Museum.
Collections: 1870s agricultural practices; hands-on exhibits.
Facilities: Organic vegetables for sale.
Activities: educational programs; planting, tending & harvesting; farm chore demonstrations. Museum Sponsors: Christmas program.
Hours & Admission Prices: Tues.-Sun. 10-4. April-Nov. 20 Tues.-Wed. & Sat.: adults $2, children 4-17 $1, Thurs.-Fri. & Sun.: adults $5, seniors 62 & over and children 4-17 $4; Nov. 21-March Tues.-Sun. adults $2, children $1. Closed Thanksgiving; Christmas. ♿

LOUIE-MEAGER ART GALLERY, Ohlone College, 43600 Mission Blvd., Gary Soren Smith Center for the Fine & Performing Arts, Rm SC-143, Fremont, CA 94539-0390. Mailing Address: P.O. Box 3909, Fremont, CA 94539-0390. Tel.: 510-659-6176. Fax: 510-659-6188.
E-mail: kmencher@ohlone.edu
Key Personnel: Dir. & Cur., Kenney Mencher
College Art Gallery.
Collections: works by local & regional artists.
Activities: art workshops; school programs.
Hours & Admission Prices: Mon.-Tues. & Thurs.-Fri. 12-3, Wed. by appointment. No charge. Closed campus holidays & breaks.

MISSION SAN JOSE CHAPEL AND MUSEUM, 43300 Mission Blvd., Fremont, CA 94539-5829. Mailing Address: P.O. Box 3159, Fremont, CA 94539-0315. Tel.: 510-657-1797.
History Museum.
Collections: Ohlone artifacts; period furnishings.
Facilities: Museum-related items for sale.
Hours & Admission Prices: Daily 10-5. Adults $3, student $2. Closed New Year's Day; Easter; Thanksgiving; Christmas.

MUSEUM OF LOCAL HISTORY, 190 Anza St., Fremont, CA 94539-5802. Tel.: 510-623-7907.
E-mail: info@museumoflocalhistory.org
History Museum.
Collections: Fremont's history; historical books & documents.
Facilities: library.
Activities: research.
Hours & Admission Prices: Wed., Fri. & 2nd Sat.-Sun. of month 10-4; groups by appointment.

NILES DEPOT MUSEUM, 36997 Mission Blvd., Fremont, CA 94536. Mailing Address: Niles Depot Historical Foundation, P.O. Box 2716, Fremont, CA 94536-0716. Tel.: 510-797-4449.
E-mail: tcsmendhf@att.net
Web Site: nilesdepot.railfan.net/ndhfhome.html
Founded: 1982.
Key Personnel: Pres. (V), Stanley B. Keeser.
Governing Authority: Tax-exempt.
Railroad Museum.
Collections: railroad & local history museum; HO & N scale model trains; photographs; track equipment; signals; locomotive artifacts & uniforms.
Facilities: library.
Hours & Admission Prices: Temporarily closed. No charge; donations accepted.
Membership: Annual $25.

Fresno

VETERANS MEMORIAL MUSEUM, HOME OF THE LEGION OF VALOR, 2425 Fresno St., Fresno, CA 93721-1841.
Formerly: Legion of Valor Veterans Museum
Founded: 1991.
Key Personnel: C.E.O., Arthur J. Hill; Chm. (V), Judy Jones; Museum Shop Mgr., Raymond Lee
Military Museum.
Collections: citations; photographs; personal artifacts; uniforms; military equipment.
Hours & Admission Prices: Mon.-Sat. 10-3. No charge.

ARTE AMERICAS, 1630 Van Ness Ave., Fresno, CA 93721-1129. Tel.: 559-266-2623. Fax: 559-268-6130.
E-mail: grace@arteamericas.org
Web Site: www.arteamericas.org
Key Personnel: Dir., Grace Solis; Asst. Dir., Mary Ellen G. Clay; Program Dir., Diana Hernandez; Cur., Kristen Sierra
Art Museum.
Collections: arts in Mexico, Latin America, the Southwest & California.
Facilities: library; classrooms. Museum-related items for sale.
Activities: education programs.
Publications: newsletter, Arte Americas.
Hours & Admission Prices: Tues.-Wed. & Fri.-Sat. 11-5, Thurs. 11-8. Admission $3, senior citizens & students $2; members & children under 5 no charge.

COKE HALLOWELL CENTER FOR RIVER STUDIES, 11605 Old Friant Rd., Fresno, CA 93730-9701. Tel.: 559-433-3190. Fax: 559-433-0634.
Web Site: www.riverparkway.org/rivercenter.asp
Key Personnel: Exec. Dir., Dave Koehler
Natural History Museum.
Collections: culture & natural history of the San Joaquin River; 1890s ranch house.
Facilities: rose garden; picnic area; orchard; vineyard. Museum-related items for sale.
Activities: education programs & activities; art workshops; readings; gardening classes; kids' crafts; rental facilities.
Hours & Admission Prices: Ranch House: Fri.-Sun. 11-3; other times by appointment. Grounds: daily 8-5.

THE DISCOVERY CENTER, 1937 N. Winery Ave., Fresno, CA 93703-2828. Mailing Address: 1944 N. Winery, Fresno, CA 93703-2829. Tel.: 559-251-5533. Fax: 559-251-5531.
E-mail: office@thediscoverycenter.net
Web Site: www.thediscoverycenter.net
Founded: 1956.
Congressional District: 17
Key Personnel: C.E.O., Roni Weil; Exec. Dir., Janet Berry; Sec., Karen Perkins.
Personnel Profile: Full-Time Paid 2; Part-Time Paid 6; Part-Time Volunteers 7.
Governing Authority: nonprofit organization. Grounds owned by Fresno City. Tax-exempt: 501(c)(3).
Participatory, Natural History & Natural Science Museum.
Collections: participatory science exhibits; central California natural history; local Native American Indian baskets & artifacts.
Facilities: six-acre science center; freshwater pond; cactus garden; picnic area; urban wildlife center. Museum-related items for sale.
Activities: hands-on exhibits; summer stargazing parties; outdoor equipment & science classes. Center Sponsors: summer science workshops PS-6th grade; Saturday science workshop PS-6th grade; Star Lab inflatable planetarium.
Publications: newsletter.
Hours & Admission Prices: Mon.-Fri. 9-5, Sat. 10-4. No charge; donations accepted. Closed New Year's Day; Easter; Independence Day; Thanksgiving; Christmas. ♿
Attendance: 35,000 (estimated)
Membership: Individual 25; Family $40; Friend $250; Corporate $1,000 & up.

DOWNING PLANETARIUM, 5320 N. Maple Ave. M/S DP132, California State University, Fresno, Fresno, CA 93740-0001. Tel.: 559-278-4121. Fax: 559-278-4070.
E-mail: stevenwh@csufresno.edu
Web Site: www.downing-planetarium.org
Founded: 2000.
Planetarium.
Collections: photographs; solar system scale; elements scale; gravity well; sundial; science toys; meteorites.
Facilities: 74-seat theater. Museum-related items for sale.
Hours & Admission Prices: Call for hours.
Attendance: 24,000

FORESTIERE UNDERGROUND GARDENS, 5021 W. Shaw Ave., Fresno, CA 93722-5026. Tel.: 559-271-0734.
E-mail: tours@undergroundgardens.info
Web Site: www.undergroundgardens.info/
General Museum: Baldasacre Forestiere spent 40 years sculpting this underground complex using only hand tools.
Collections: underground rooms, niches, courts, patios & passageways including a kitchen, living room, 2 bedrooms, library, bath, & chapel; fish pond, aquarium; auto tunnel; trees.
Activities: tours.
Hours & Admission Prices: Tours: April-May & Sept.-Nov. Sat.-Sun. 11am, 12pm, 1pm & 2pm; Memorial Day to Labor Day Thurs.-Fri. & holidays 11am, 12pm, 1pm & 2pm, Sat.-Sun. 10am, 11am, 12pm, 1:30pm & 2:30pm. Adults $12, seniors 60 & over $10, teens 13-17 $8, children 5-12 $7; children 4 & under no charge.

* **FRESNO ART MUSEUM, (M),** 2233 N. First St., Fresno, CA 93703-2364. Tel.: 559-441-4221. Fax: 559-441-4227.
E-mail: info@fresnoartmuseum.org
Web Site: www.fresnoartmuseum.org
Formerly: Fresno Art Center
Founded: 1949.
Congressional District: 17
Key Personnel: C.E.O., Michael Mazur; Pres., Dr. Robin Smit; Dir. Devel. & Communications, Eva Torres; Cur., Jacquelin Pilar; Registrar, Emily Krause; Exhibitions Technician & Community Outreach, Brandon Drake; Preparator, Steve Ruppel; Curatorial Asst., Rebecca Shepard; Dir. Finance, Michael Kerr; Coord. Special Events, Starr Lopez; Mgr. Education Programs, Elizabeth Powell; Art Instructor & Special Projects, Erika Morales; Office Mgr. & Exec. Asst., Debbie Horton; Receptionist, Betty Peralta; Facility Maintenance, Sarkis Kglyan; Membership Asst. & Special Events, Raziel Cortes; Security Guard, Abel Fernandes; Security Guard, Adan Mireles.
Personnel Profile: Full-Time Paid 15; Part-Time Paid 2; Part-Time Volunteers 175; Interns 3.
Governing Authority: nonprofit organization. Tax-exempt: 501(c)(3).
Modern & Contemporary Art Museum.
Collections: pre-Columbian, Mexican, Peruvian & contemporary local & California works of art; American sculpture; graphics; photographs.
Research Fields: pre-Columbian; French late 19th-century printmaking.
Facilities: art reference library; galleries; sculpture garden; classrooms; rental gallery; auditorium. Museum-related items for sale.
Activities: tours; lectures; films; formally organized education programs; docent council; inter-museum loan, temporary & traveling exhibitions; school art class service; concerts; school outreach.
Publications: catalogues of exhibitions; newsletter; quarterly, Preview.
Hours & Admission Prices: Tues.-Wed. & Fri.-Sun. 11-5, Thurs. 11-8. Adults $4, seniors & students $2; discounts to AAM & WMK members; Sun. & members no charge. Closed national holidays. ♿
Attendance: 21,000 (estimated)
Membership: Individual: Student, Educator & Senior $25; Individual & Couple: Student, Educator & Senior $35; Family & Dual $50; Family Plus $85; Contributing $100; Sustaining $250; Benefactor $500; Director's Circle $1,000; Corporate Council $1,500-$5,000.

FRESNO CHAFFEE ZOO, 894 W. Belmont Ave., Fresno, CA 93728-2807. Tel.: 559-498-5910. Fax: 559-264-9226.
E-mail: info@fresnochaffeezoo.com
Web Site: fresnochaffeezoo.com
Formerly: Chaffee Zoological Gardens of Fresno

Founded: 1929.
Congressional District: 18
Key Personnel: C.E.O., Scott Barton; Chm., Colin Doughtery; Interim Dir. Mktg. & Devel., Terri Mejorado; Museum Shop Mgr., Chris Schiefer.
Personnel Profile: Full-Time Paid 50; Full-Time Volunteers 6; Part-Time Paid 35; Part-Time Volunteers 200.
Governing Authority: nonprofit. Parent Institution: Fresno's Chaffee Zoo Corp. Tax-exempt: 501(c)(3).
Zoo.
Collections: 204 species; 629 specimens of mammals, birds, reptiles, amphibians & fish; herpetology building; aviary; quarantine station; Asian elephant exhibit; tropical rainforest; Australian aviary; Sunda forest.
Research Fields: artificially induced reproduction in amphibians & reptiles.
Facilities: 150-vol. library of zoology & veterinary books. Refreshments & novelties for sale.
Activities: guided tours; lectures; films; zoomobile; wildlife workshops.
Publications: Zoo News.
Hours & Admission Prices: Daily 9-4. Adults $7, senior citizens & children 2-11 $3.50; AZA reciprocal zoos & aquariums; members & children under 2 no charge. ♿
Attendance: 429,272 (accurate)
Membership: Senior Citizens & Students $25; Individual $35; Plus-One $45; Family & Grandparent $50; Keeper Club $145; Safari Club $500; Toucan Club $1,000.

FRESNO CITY AND COUNTY HISTORICAL SOCIETY, (M), 7160 W. Kearney Blvd., Fresno, CA 93706-9520. Tel.: 559-441-0862. Fax: 559-441-1372.
E-mail: frhistsoc@aol.com
Web Site: www.valleyhistory.org
Key Personnel: Exec. Dir., Jill Moffat
Historical Society Museum.
Collections: city & county history and culture; pioneer records; documents; photographs; scrapbooks; letters; diaries; early local government records.
Hours & Admission Prices: Call for hours.

* **FRESNO METROPOLITAN MUSEUM OF ART & SCIENCE,** 1555 Van Ness Ave., Fresno, CA 93721-1212. Tel.: 559-441-1444. Fax: 559-441-8607.
E-mail: danat@fresnomet.org
Web Site: www.fresnomet.org
Founded: 1984.
Congressional District: 18
Key Personnel: Bd. Chm. (V), Betsy Reeves; Bd. Pres. (V), Paul Gottlieb; Exec. Dir., Dana L. Thorpe; Dir. Membership & Mktg., Candice Pendergrass; Mgr. Mktg., John English; Devel. Mgr., Hamilton Arnold; Cur. Permanent Collections, Kristina Hornback; Receptionist, Gabriella Tanori; School Tour & Volunteer Mgr., Ann Wanger; Education Mgr., Ariana Addington; Chief Preparator & Art Handler, Mike Weatherson; Coord. Membership & Special Events, Diana Enriquez; Educator, Jamie Meadows; Dir. Finance, Denise Russell; Finance & IT Asst., Nicole Jacomet; Visitor Svcs. & Museum Shop Mgr., Bryan Miller; Mktg. Coord., Amanda Allen; Store Asst. Mgr., Ceilidh Benoit; Devel. Mgr., Ellen Mata; Exec. Asst. & Security, Nina Acosta; Curatorial Asst., Sarah Vargas; Visitor Svcs. Assoc., Victoria Robinson; Education Coord., Tory Johnson; Educator, Jackie Cha; Educator, Lance Truong.
Personnel Profile: Full-Time Paid 20; Part-Time Paid 12; Part-Time Volunteers 120; Interns 2.
Governing Authority: nonprofit organization. Tax-exempt: 501(3)(c).
Art & Science Museum: housed in 1922 Italian Renaissance-style building, formerly the Fresno Bee Newspaper Building.
Collections: 17th- to 20th-century American European still-life & Trompe-l'oeil paintings; Ansel Adams photographs; antique Chinese snuff bottles; writings & memorabilia of William Saroyan; Native American cradleboards; puzzles.
Major Exhibits: A Forest Journey (T), 1/10-8/10; Creatures of the Abyss (T), 2/10-5/10; Mexico: Festival of Toys (T), 2/10-5/10; Andre Kertesz: On Reading (T), 5/10-6/10; Fantasies & Fairytales: Maxfield Parish and the Art of Printmaking (T), 7/10-10/10; Jim Henson's Fantastic World (T), 7/10-10/10; Adventure's With Clifford the Big Red Dog (T), 9/10-1/11; Mystery of the Mayan Medallion (T), 10/10-12/10; Gather Up the Fragments: The Andrews Shaker Collection (T), 10/10-1/11; Holidays at the Met, 11/10-1/11.
Research Fields: Art History.
Facilities: 5,000-vol. library pertaining to art available for research on premises only by appointment. Books, catalogs & other museum-related items for sale.
Activities: guided tours; lectures; films; gallery talks; education programs for children & adults; loan, permanent, temporary & traveling exhibitions.
Publications: quarterly newsletter, Met Report; books, Oscar & Maria Salzer Collection of Still Life & Trompe L'Oeil Painting; Strands of Time, Yokuts, Mono & Miwok Baskets; 4,000 Years of Chinese Jade; Variations on a Theme: American Prints From Pop Art to Minimalism.
Hours & Admission Prices: Wed.-Sun. 11-5. Adults $9, senior citizens & students $7, children 3-12 $5; discounts to AAM, ICOM & ASTC reciprocal members; children under 3 & members no charge. Closed New Year's Day; Easter; Memorial Day; Independence Day; Labor Day; Thanksgiving; Christmas. ♿
Attendance: 101,000 (estimated)
Membership: Junior $15; Student & Senior $30; General $75; Contributing $150; Sustaining $250; Metropolitan $500; Museum Society $1,000; Curator's Council $2,000; Business & Professional Partner $3,000.

KEARNEY MANSION MUSEUM, 7160 W. Kearney Blvd., Fresno, CA 93706-9520. Tel.: 559-441-0862. Fax: 559-441-1372.
E-mail: frhistsoc@aol.com
Web Site: www.valleyhistory.org
Founded: 1919.
Congressional District: 15
Key Personnel: Exec. Dir., Jill Moffat; Pres. (V), John Boogaert; Dir. Public Rels., Christina Perryman; Archivist, Maria Ortiz; Cur. Collections & Education Coord., Sharon Hiigel; Tour Coord. & Museum Shop Mgr., Amy Lawrence; Bookkeeper & Membership, Barbara James Higgins; Oral History Coord., Ruth Lang.
Personnel Profile: Full-Time Paid 6; Part-Time Paid 1; Part-Time Volunteers 225.
Governing Authority: nonprofit organization. FCCHS Board of Trustees, contributions from Fresno County & City. Parent Institution: Fresno Historical Society. Tax-exempt: 501(c)(3).
Historic Site Museum: housed in 1900 original Kearney Mansion.
Collections: costumes & accessories; furniture; textiles; Native American artifacts; household & agricultural implements; musical instruments; archives: 1860s-1960s regional history including photos, negatives, business, individual & family manuscript collections; local government records; maps; biography indexes; ephemera.
Research Fields: local history; agriculture; local families; logging; fire department; regional Indian tribes; hydroelectric development.
Activities: guided tours; bus tours; docent program; temporary exhibitions; field trips; history lectures; outreach programs in schools; historic preservation advocacy. Museum Sponsors: Annual Heritage Home Tour; Traveling History Trunks; Time Travelers Day Camp; Living History at Kearney Park.
Publications: quarterly journal, Fresno Past & Present; quarterly newsletter, Grapevine; books, Evolution of Fruit Vale Estate, reprint of 1904 original; Imperial Fresno, reprint of 1897 original; Evans & Sontag; M. Theo Kearney-Prince of Fresno; California Homes & Industries; Fresno Illustrated.
Hours & Admission Prices: Kearney Mansion Tours: Fri.-Sun. 1, 2 & 3pm. Adults $5, seniors & students $4, children $3; children under 12 & members no charge. Closed New Year's Day; Easter; Independence Day; Thanksgiving; Christmas. ♿
Attendance: 9,023 (accurate)
Membership: Student & Educator $20; Individual $35; Contributing $45; Sustaining $100; Sponsor $250; Patron $500; Benefactor $1,000 and up; Corporate Partners $1,000-$5,000.

MEUX HOME MUSEUM, (M), 1007 R St., Fresno, CA 93721-1312. Mailing Address: P.O. Box 70, Fresno, CA 93707-0070. Tel.: 559-233-8007. Fax: 559-233-2331.
E-mail: judi@meux.mus.ca.us
Web Site: www.meux.mus.ca.us
Founded: 1979.
Key Personnel: Pres., John R. Campbell; Vice Pres., Shirley Emrick; Treas., Evelyn Pipkin.
Personnel Profile: Part-Time Volunteers 25.
Governing Authority: private; nonprofit organization. Parent Institution: Meux Home Corp. Tax-exempt: 501(c)(3).
Historic House: 1888 Victorian house.
Collections: Victorian lifestyle: costumes, textiles, furniture, books, pictures; family artifacts; Dr. Meux' Civil War uniform & medical books; Dr Meux' daughter's 1907 wedding gown.
Research Fields: late 19th-century Fresno; history of Meux family's migration from England to Tennessee to California; Victorian clothing.
Facilities: library on Victorian period; 4,600 sq. ft. exhibit space; educational facilities for pre-school through college tours; rose gardens; facilities available for private special events. Museum-related items for sale.
Activities: guided tours; docent program; weddings; special events; rental facilities. Annual Events: Wedding Re-Enactment; Field Hospital Re-Enactment; Teddy Bear Picnic; Victorian Teas.
Publications: quarterly newsletter, Meux Home Gazette.

Hours & Admission Prices: Feb. to Dec. Fri.-Sun. 12-3:30; private & school tours during week. Adults $5, students $4, children $3; special events rates vary. Closed holidays. ♿
Attendance: 30,000 (estimated)
Membership: Individual $35; Close Friend of the Family $50; Distant Relative $100; Member of the Family $500; Heir $1,000.

SIMONIAN FARMS, 2629 S. Clovis Ave., Fresno, CA 93725-9307. Tel.: 559-237-2294. Fax: 559-441-1198.
E-mail: simonian@lightspeed.net
Web Site: www.simonianfarms.com
Farm Museum.
Collections: period bicycles; peddle cars; porcelain signs; mannequins; vintage gas pumps; model train.
Hours & Admission Prices: No charge.

Friant

MILLERTON COURTHOUSE, Department of Parks & Recreation, 5290 Millerton Rd., Friant, CA 93626. Tel.: 559-822-2225. Fax: 209-822-2319.
Historic Building Museum.
Collections: archaeology; basketry; birds; ethnic & tribal art; history; mammals; mineralogy.
Activities: children's classes; guided tours; school outreach program.
Hours & Admission Prices: June-Sept. Sat. 10-6. Courthouse: no charge. Parking: fee charged.

Fullerton

ANTHROPOLOGY TEACHING MUSEUM, CALIFORNIA STATE UNIVERSITY, FULLERTON, Fullerton, CA 92834-6846. Mailing Address: Dept. of Anthropology, Cal-State Univ., Fullerton, P.O. Box 6846, Fullerton, CA 92834-6846. Tel.: 657-278-3626. Fax: 657-278-5001.
E-mail: anthropology@exchange.fullerton.edu
Web Site: www.anthro.fullerton.edu
Founded: 1970.
Congressional District: 39
Key Personnel: Coord. Administrative Support, Rose Calderon; Dept. Chm., Dr. John Bedell.
Personnel Profile: Full-Time Paid 1; Part-Time Paid 1.
Governing Authority: university; nonprofit. Parent Institution: CSU Fullerton. Tax-exempt: 501(c)(3).
Anthropology Museum.
Collections: southern California, southwest, midwest prehistoric artifacts; ethnographic specimens from South Pacific, Near East, Mexico & South America; faunal, mineral, sherd comparative collections.
Research Fields: southern California; Honduras.
Facilities: 1,640-vol. research library & local faunal, mineral, sherd research collections for use on premises; archaeology laboratory; classrooms; 1,800 sq. ft. exhibit space.
Activities: guided tours; lectures; organized educational programs for undergraduate & graduate student affiliated with CSU Fullerton; temporary exhibitions.
Hours & Admission Prices: School Year: Mon.-Thurs. & by appointment; School Vacation: holidays & weekends by appointment. No charge; donations accepted. ♿

BECKMAN COULTER HERITAGE EXHIBIT, Beckman Coulter, Inc. Corp. Headquarters., 4300 N. Harbor Blvd., Fullerton, CA 92835-1091. Tel.: 714-773-6924. Fax: 714-773-8389.
E-mail: paashton@beckman.com
Web Site: www.beckman.com/hr/ourcompany/oc_heritage_exhibit.asp
Founded: 1980.
Personnel Profile: Full-Time Paid 1; Part-Time Volunteers 20.
Governing Authority: Parent Institution: Beckman Coulter, Inc.
Corporate History Museum.
Collections: Beckman Coulter's contributions to industry, science & medicine.
Hours & Admission Prices: Mon.-Fri. 9-4. No charge. Closed holidays. ♿
Attendance: 3,000 (estimated)

THE FULLERTON ARBORETUM, (M), 1900 Associated Rd., Fullerton, CA 92831-1659. Mailing Address: c/o California State University, Fullerton, P.O. Box 6850, Fullerton, CA 92834-6850. Tel.: 657-278-3579 & 3407. Fax: 657-278-7066.
E-mail: farboretum@fullerton.edu
Web Site: arboretum.fullerton.edu
Founded: 1972.
Congressional District: 39
Key Personnel: Dir., Gregory T. Dyment; Pres. Fullerton Arboretum Commission, Eugene C. Jones; Pres. Friends of the Fullerton Arboretum (V), Mary Dalesci.
Personnel Profile: Full-Time Paid 10; Part-Time Paid 12; Part-Time Volunteers 600.
Governing Authority: municipal & university under joint-powers agreement. Parent Institution: California State University, Fullerton. Tax-exempt: 170(b)(1)(A).
Arboretum & Historic House: 1894 home & office of Dr. George Clark, moved to site of the Gilman Ranch, where first Valencia oranges grown in Orange County were planted.
Collections: plant collection: 3,500 accessions, emphasis on drought tolerant plants suitable to coastal plain of southern California; historical collection: house, outbuildings & artifacts including c.1890 doctor's equipment, office & pharmacy; musical instruments, family memorabilia; Victoriana; furniture & furnishings.
Research Fields: local history; suitability of plants for coastal plain of southern California.
Facilities: library of botanical material available for use on premises; botanical gardens. Plants & plant-oriented gifts for sale.
Activities: guided & self-guided tours; formally organized education programs for children; docent program; temporary exhibitions.
Publications: brochures; newsletter.
Hours & Admission Prices: Arboretum: daily 8-4:45. Heritage House: Sat.-Sun. 2-4; other times by appointment. No charge; donations accepted. Closed New Year's Day; Thanksgiving; Christmas. ♿
Attendance: 120,000 (estimated)
Membership: Individual $40; Family $75; Partner $100; Steward $250; Patron $500.

FULLERTON COLLEGE ART GALLERY, (M), 321 E. Chapman Ave., Bldg. 1000, Fullerton, CA 92832-2011. Tel.: 714-992-7329. Fax: 714-992-7320.
E-mail: kjohnson@fullcoll.edu
Web Site: art.fullcoll.edu
Key Personnel: Dir., Beth Solomon Marino
Art Gallery.
Collections: paintings; photographs; sculpture.
Facilities: 2,000 sq. ft. exhibition space.
Activities: special events; permanent & temporary exhibitions.
Hours & Admission Prices: Mon. & Wed.-Thurs. 10-2, Tues. 10-2 & 5-7.

FULLERTON MUSEUM CENTER, (M), 301 N. Pomona Ave., Fullerton, CA 92832-1927. Tel.: 714-738-6545. Fax: 714-738-3124.
E-mail: danniellem@ci.fullerton.ca.us
Web Site: www.cityoffullerton.com/depts/museum
Founded: 1971.
Congressional District: 39
Key Personnel: C.E.O., Cindy Yount; Dir., Dannielle Mauk; Museum Shop Mgr., Kelly Chidester.
Personnel Profile: Full-Time Paid 6; Part-Time Paid 7; Part-Time Volunteers 12.
Governing Authority: nonprofit organization. Parent Institution: City of Fullerton Cultural Services Div. Tax-exempt.
General Museum.
Collections: Leo Fender related collections of musical instruments & inventions.
Facilities: 4,500 sq. ft. rotating exhibitions; 5,000 sq. ft. outdoor plaza & stage; 75-seat auditorium. Museum-related items for sale.
Activities: changing exhibitions; lectures; workshops; educational programs for region; permanent exhibitions.
Publications: newsletter; exhibition catalogs.
Hours & Admission Prices: Tues.-Wed. & Fri.-Sun. 12-4, Thurs. 12-8. Adults $4, senior citizens & students $3, children 6-12 $1; discounts for AAM & ICOM members; children 5 & under and members no charge. ♿
Attendance: 30,000 (estimated)
Membership: Student & Senior $30; Individual $35; Family $50. Fender Levels: Seafoam Green $100; Fiesta Red $250; Silver Mist Metallic $500; Shoreline Gold $1,000.

MAIN ART GALLERY, CALIFORNIA STATE UNIVERSITY, FULLERTON, 800 N. State College Blvd., Visual Arts Center, Fullerton, CA 92834-6850. Mailing Address: P.O. Box 6850, Visual Arts Dept., Fullerton, CA 92834-6850. Tel.: 657-278-3262 & 7750. Fax: 657-278-2390.
E-mail: mmcgee@fullerton.edu
Web Site: www.fullerton.edu/arts/art
Founded: 1967.
Congressional District: 39
Key Personnel: Gallery Dir., Mike McGee; Asst. to Dir., Marilyn Moore; Technical Asst., Marty Lorigan.
Governing Authority: university; Affiliated with California State University, Fullerton Art Dept.
University Art Gallery.

Collections: outdoor sculpture; contemporary prints.
Facilities: 1,500-vol. library of museum catalogs & publications relating to museums, their operations & studies, available for research by special permission; 150-seat auditorium; theater; classrooms; cafeteria. Exhibition catalogs & prints for sale.
Activities: guided tours; lectures; films; gallery talks; arts festivals; formally organized education programs for children, adults, undergraduate & graduate students; docent program or council; training programs for professional museum personnel; temporary & traveling exhibitions.
Publications: quarterly, exhibition catalogues.
Hours & Admission Prices: Tues.-Fri. 12-4, Sat. 12-2, call to confirm. No charge; donations accepted. Parking Tues-Fri. $5. Closed national holidays. ♿
Membership: Student $10; Member $25; Sponsor $50; Patron $100; Donor $250; Benefactor $500.

MUCKENTHALER CULTURAL CENTER AND MANSION MUSEUM, 1201 W. Malvern Ave., Fullerton, CA 92833-2429. Tel.: 714-738-6595 & 6340. Fax: 714-738-6366.
E-mail: info@themuck.org
Web Site: www.themuck.org
Founded: 1965.
Congressional District: 39
Key Personnel: Exec. Dir., Zoot Velasco; Pres. (V), Jane Parker; Museum Shop Mgr., Peggy Albert.
Personnel Profile: Full-Time Paid 4; Part-Time Paid 8; Part-Time Volunteers 90; Interns 7.
Governing Authority: foundation. Muckenthaler Cultural Center Foundation. Tax-exempt.
Cultural Center: housed in 1923 home of Walter Muckenthaler.
Collections: paintings; photographs; sculpture.
Major Exhibits: Contemporary Decorative Metalworks, 2/10-3/10; Heather Hendrickson & Chris Gallup Design Planters, 2/10-3/11; Fullerton High School Art Exhibit, 4/10; Concept Car Drawings, 5/10; Pine Design: Cub Scout Pinewood Derby Cars, 5/10; Muckenthaler Cultural Center/Student Show, 6/10; Korean Cultural Center of LA Shows, 7/10-9/10; Jose Lozano Solo Drawings, Paintings & Prints, 10/10-1/11.
Facilities: garden; 250-seat amphitheatre; classrooms; 2,300 sq. ft. exhibit space.
Activities: guided tours; lectures; gallery talks; arts festivals; drama; rental gallery; formally organized education programs for children, adults, undergraduate students; docent programs; traveling exhibitions; arts & craft classes; theater presentations. Jazz Institute: jazz concerts & classes. Muckenthaler Repertory: theatre productions; theatre classes. Museum Sponsors: Spoken Word Series, Poetry Open Mic Night; Film Series; Easter & Christmas Holiday Festivals.
Publications: catalogues; quarterly Muckenthaler newsletter.
Hours & Admission Prices: Wed.-Sun. 12-4. No charge; donations accepted. Closed holidays.
Attendance: 45,000 (accurate)
Membership: Student & Senior Citizen $30; Individual $60; Family $100; 500 Club $500; Millennium Club $1,000; President's Circle $5,000; Founder's Circle Mucketymucks $10,000.

Garden Grove

GARDEN GROVE HISTORICAL SOCIETY, 12174 Euclid St., Garden Grove, CA 92840. Mailing Address: P.O. Box 4297, Garden Grove, CA 92842-4297. Tel.: 714-530-8871. Fax: 714-534-2611.
E-mail: gardengrovehistsoc@att.net
Founded: 1966.
Congressional District: 38
Key Personnel: Pres. (V), Tim Dull; Vice Pres., Stanley Beitler; Treas., Beulah Miller.
Personnel Profile: Part-Time Volunteers 40.
Governing Authority: society. Tax-exempt: 501(c)(3) & 170(b)(1)(A).
Historic House Museum: building completed 1892 by E.G. Ware, one of the first pioneers of Garden Grove.
Collections: agriculture; antiques; medical & dental items; restored barbershop; general store; fire station; history; 1926 American La France fire truck. Historic Buildings: c.1878 Original Garden Grove Post Office; 1880's homes; 1916 craftsman style home.
Research Fields: Life in Garden Grove, Orange County & Southern California during the late 1800s and early 1900s.
Facilities: library; archive; research room. Handmade crafts & museum-related books for sale.
Activities: guided tours; monthly meetings; volunteer days Mon.-Fri.
Publications: pamphlets; brochures; monthly newsletter.
Hours & Admission Prices: 1st & 3rd Sun. of month 1:30; other times by appointment. Suggested Donation: adults $5, students under 18 $1.
Attendance: 800 (accurate)
Membership: Student $5; Individual $15; Family $25; Business & Organization $30; Sustaining $50; Patron $100; Business Patron $200; Life $500; Centennial $1,874.

Gilroy

CITY OF GILROY MUSEUM, 195 Fifth St., Gilroy, CA 95020-5703. Tel.: 408-846-0446. Fax: 408-847-5604.
Web Site: www.ci.gilroy.ca.us
Formerly: Gilroy Historical Museum
Founded: 1958.
Congressional District: 12
Key Personnel: Supvr., Cathy Mirelez.
Personnel Profile: Part-Time Paid 2; Part-Time Volunteers 35.
Governing Authority: municipal government. Tax-exempt: 501(c)(3).
Local History Museum: housed in 1910 Carnegie Library.
Collections: local history & culture from the Ohlone Indians to present; clothing; accessories; furniture; household items; Ohlone artifacts; tools; toys; archives.
Research Fields: Henry Miller, local cattle king; early California history; family histories & genealogies; local history.
Facilities: 150-vol. library of local, regional & state history; 275-vols. local newspapers; 100-vols. local municipal archives available to the public; 2,500 sq. ft. exhibit space. Museum-related printed material for sale.
Activities: guided tours; lectures; temporary exhibitions; Traveling Trunk Program (two themes: filled with reproductions, photos, reference material; available for check-out to schools and community groups. No charge); two theme trunks: Kids 1890's Trunk and Ohlone Indians Trunk. Annual Events: Young Artists Show; Art & Culture Exhibition; summer concert series; Victorian Christmas.
Publications: quarterly newsletter, The Society Page.
Hours & Admission Prices: Tues. & Thurs. 10-5, Wed. by appointment, 1st Sat. of month 10-2. Call for admission information. Closed New Year's Day; Presidents' Day; Memorial Day; Independence Day; Labor Day; Veterans Day; Thanksgiving; Christmas.
Attendance: 2,415 (accurate)

Glen Ellen

JACK LONDON STATE HISTORIC PARK, 2400 London Ranch Rd., Glen Ellen, CA 95442-9749. Tel.: 707-938-5216. Fax: 707-938-5216.
E-mail: jacklondonshp@gmail.com
Web Site: www.jacklondonpark.com
Founded: 1959.
Congressional District: 2
Key Personnel: Unit Ranger, Sheryl Lawton.
Personnel Profile: Full-Time Paid 2; Part-Time Paid 10; Part-Time Volunteers 50.
Governing Authority: state. Parent Institution: the State of California Department Parks & Recreation, Box 942896, Sacramento, CA 94296. Tax-exempt.
State Park Museum.
Collections: history; paintings; sculpture. Historic Houses: 1913 ruins of Jack London's Wolf House mansion; 1919 House of Happy Walls; Jack London's ranch cottage & barns.
Major Exhibits: Cruise of the Snark, 11/09-12/10.
Facilities: Books for sale.
Activities: guided tours.
Publications: brochures.
Hours & Admission Prices: Museum: daily 10-5. Park: daily 9:30-5. Admission per car $8, senior citizens 62 & over $7. Museum: closed New Year's Day; Thanksgiving; Christmas. ♿
Attendance: 90,000 (estimated)

Glendale

BRAND LIBRARY & ART CENTER, 1601 W. Mountain St., Glendale, CA 91201-1200. Tel.: 818-548-2051. Fax: 818-548-5079.
E-mail: info@brandlibrary.org
Web Site: www.brandlibrary.org
Founded: 1956.
Key Personnel: Sr. Library Supvr., Alyssa Resnick; Librarian, Cathy Billings.
Personnel Profile: Full-Time Paid 5; Part-Time Paid 15; Part-Time Volunteers 4.
Governing Authority: municipal. Parent Institution: City of Glendale. Subsidiary Institution: Glendale Public Library. Tax-exempt.
Library & Art Center.
Collections: art & music books; videos; DVDs; slides; records; CDs; framed prints.
Facilities: library; art gallery; recital hall.
Activities: professional concerts; art exhibits; dance programs; art tours; lecture series.

Publications: catalogs; Annual Art Exhibition catalog.
Hours & Admission Prices: Tues. & Thurs. 1-9, Wed. 1-6, Fri.-Sat. 1-5. No charge; donations accepted. ♿
Attendance: 130,000
Membership: Regular $20; Supporting $55; Patron $100; Benefactor $500 & up.

CASA ADOBE DE SAN RAFAEL, 1330 Dorothy Dr., Glendale, CA 91202-1610. Tel.: 818-548-2000. Fax: 818-548-3789.
Founded: 1867.
Congressional District: 22
Key Personnel: C.E.O. & Chm. (V), Merry Franzen; Pres. (V), Doyle Kutch; Dir. Parks, Recreation & Community Svcs., Nello Iacono.
Personnel Profile: Part-Time Volunteers 2.
Governing Authority: municipal. Affiliated with Parks, Recreation & Community Services Division, City of Glendale. Parent Institution: Glendale Beautiful. Tax-exempt.
Historic Building Museum: Early Mexican-American heritage.
Collections: early California furniture; artifacts.
Facilities: library of historical material pertaining to the era of the Casa Adobe de San Rafael not available for public use.
Activities: guided tours.
Publications: pamphlet, History of Casa Adobe De San Rafael.
Hours & Admission Prices: morning to dusk; group tours by reservation. No charge. ♿
Attendance: 1,400 (estimated)
Membership: Annual $7.

DOCTORS' HOUSE MUSEUM, Brand Park, 1601 W. Mountain Ave., Glendale, CA 91201-1200. Tel.: 818-548-2147.
E-mail: tghs@glendalehistorical.org
Web Site: www.glendalehistorical.org
History Museum.
Collections: period furnishings, medical implements & supplies.
Hours & Admission Prices: Jan.-July & Sept.-Nov. Sun. 2-4, last tour at 3:40; Dec. call for hours. Adults $1; children 15 & under and members no charge. Closed major holidays.

FOREST LAWN MUSEUM, 1712 S. Glendale Ave., Glendale, CA 91205-3320. Tel.: 800-204-3131. Fax: 323-551-5329.
E-mail: museum@forestlawn.com
Web Site: forestlawn.com
Founded: 1951.
Key Personnel: Chm. (V), John Llewellyn; Supvr. Operations & Museum Shop Mgr., Elizabeth Bloess; Exhibit Designer & Cur., Joan Adan.
Personnel Profile: Full-Time Paid 4; Part-Time Paid 2.
Governing Authority: nonprofit organization. Parent Institution: Forest Lawn Cemetery Assoc. Branch Museum: Hall of Liberty, 6300 Forest Lawn Dr., Los Angeles, CA 90068. Tax-exempt: 501(c)(3).
General History Museum.
Collections: American history from 1770 to present; pre-Colombian Mexican history; American bronze & marble statuary; over 2,000 stained glass windows; paintings; pre-Christian & Christian era coins; gems; autographs; manuscripts.
Major Exhibits: Paintings by Chris Hopkins of Northwest Native Americans, 1/29/10-4/25/10; Light & Passion, 2/13/10-6/10; Francisco Goya: The Caprichos Etchings (T), 5/14/10-8/1/10; Light & Color, 6/10-11/10; Animals in Art, 8/20/10-1/2/11; Light & Hope, 11/26/10-2/7/11.
Research Fields: American history from 1770; Renaissance art with special reference to Leonardo da Vinci & Michelangelo; pre-Colombian Mexican history.
Facilities: theater. Mementos of museum & park for sale.
Activities: films; concerts; public school field trips; permanent exhibitions.
Hours & Admission Prices: Tues.-Sun. 10-5. No charge. ♿
Attendance: 50,000 (accurate)

Goleta

RANCHO LA PATERA - THE STOW HOUSE G.V.H.S., 304 N. Los Carneros Rd., Goleta, CA 93117-1502. Tel.: 805-964-4407 & 681-7216. Fax: 805-681-7217.
E-mail: info@goletahistory.com
Web Site: goletahistory.org
Formerly: Stow House/Museum of Goleta Valley History
Founded: 1967.
Congressional District: 19
Key Personnel: Pres. (V), Robin H. Cederlof; Treas., Dan Marchiando; Coord. Events, Dacia Harwood; Caretaker, Linda Foster; Caretaker, Ron Foster.
Personnel Profile: Part-Time Paid 3; Part-Time Volunteers 100; Interns 2.
Governing Authority: nonprofit organization. Tax-exempt: 501(c)(3).
Historical Society Museum: housed in c.1872 Stow House ranch.
Collections: wedding gowns c.1860-1960; farm machinery; five Goleta cannons from 18th & 19th centuries; furnishings.
Facilities: library material available for use on premises; small acreage & lake. Grounds available for weddings & receptions. Books of local history & other museum-related items for sale.
Activities: docent program; guided tours; temporary exhibits; concerts. Annual Events: Old-Fashioned 4th of July; Fiddler's Convention in October; Holiday at the Ranch.
Publications: quarterly newsletter, GVHS Newsletter; biannual publication of Goleta Valley History.
Hours & Admission Prices: Sat.-Sun. 2-4; hours vary for special events. Museum no charge. House Tour: $5. Closed New Year's Day; Easter; Thanksgiving; Christmas.
Attendance: 10,000 (estimated)
Membership: Individual $30; Family $50; Friend $100; Pioneer $250; Goodlander $500; Preservationist $1,000.

SOUTH COAST RAILROAD MUSEUM AT GOLETA DEPOT, 300 N. Los Carneros Rd., Goleta, CA 93117-1502. Tel.: 805-964-3540. Fax: 805-964-3549.
E-mail: director@goletadepot.org
Web Site: www.goletadepot.org
Founded: 1983.
Congressional District: 19
Key Personnel: Exec. Dir., Gary B. Coombs; Asst. Dir., Phyllis J. Olsen; Pres. (V), Noel Langle.
Personnel Profile: Full-Time Paid 1; Part-Time Paid 2; Part-Time Volunteers 50; Interns 1.
Governing Authority: nonprofit organization. Parent Institution: Institute for American Research. Tax-exempt: 501(c)(3).
Railroad Museum: housed in 1901 Southern Pacific railroad depot.
Collections: railroad items; Southern Pacific railroad; local history.
Research Fields: local history; railroad history.
Facilities: 250-vol. library of railroading & area history material; 14-seat theater. Railroad items & local history books for sale.
Activities: guided tours; films; organized education programs for children; docent program; temporary exhibitions; annual events.
Publications: quarterly newsletter, Depot Dispatch; annual booklet, Publications in Local History Series.
Hours & Admission Prices: Wed.-Sun. 1-4. Donation Requested: adults $1. Closed New Year's Day; Easter; Thanksgiving; Christmas. ♿
Attendance: 22,000 (estimated)
Membership: Volunteer $7; Junior Engineer & Active $15; Sustaining $25; Contributing & Corporate $50; Life $200.

Grass Valley

GRASS VALLEY MUSEUM, 410 S. Church St., Grass Valley, CA 95945-6722. Tel.: 530-273-5509.
History Museum: housed in the former orphanage used during Gold Rush times; established by Father William Dalton in 1865 for children orphaned by mining accidents.
Collections: local history from Gold Rush to 1930s; period clothing & furnishings; paintings; early doctor's office; Gold Rush classroom; 130 year old rose garden.
Hours & Admission Prices: Tues.-Fri. 12:30-3:30; other times by appointment. No charge.

LOLA MONTEZ HOME, 248 Mill St., Grass Valley, CA 95945-6712. Tel.: 530-273-4667.
History Museum.
Collections: period furnishings.
Hours & Admission Prices: Mon.-Fri. 9-5. No charge; donations accepted.

Gridley

HISTORICAL AND WILDLIFE MUSEUM, Kentucky & Hazel Sts., Gridley, CA 95948. Tel.: 530-846-4482.
Founded: 1996.
History Museum.
Collections: Gridley history; photographs; military uniforms; period school artifacts.
Hours & Admission Prices: Wed. & Fri. 10-2, 2nd & 4th Sat. 12-3.

Groveland

GROVELAND YOSEMITE GATEWAY MUSEUM, 18990 Main St., Groveland, CA 95321-9442. Tel.: 209-962-0300.
E-mail: grovelandmuseum@mlode.com

Web Site: www.grovelandmuseum.org
Founded: 2000.
Congressional District: 19
Key Personnel: Pres., Marc Fossum; Cur., Gordon R. Norris; Museum Shop Mgr., Cheryl Hernandez.
Personnel Profile: Part-Time Volunteers 25.
Governing Authority: private; nonprofit organization. Parent Institution: Southern Tuolumne County Historical Society, Groveland, CA. Tax-exempt: 501(c)(3).
History Museum.
Collections: history of southern Tuolumne County, CA; newspapers; paintings; photographs; films; furnishings; personal artifacts.
Facilities: 40-vol. library; 12-seat theater. Museum-related items for sale.
Activities: concerts; docent program; temporary exhibitions; theater. Annual Event: fundraising picnic.
Hours & Admission Prices: Daily 1-4:30. No charge; donations accepted. ♿
Attendance: 2,500 (estimated)
Membership: Family & Individual $20; Business $100; Life $250.

Gustine

GUSTINE MUSEUM, 397 Fourth St., Hwy. 33, Gustine, CA 95322-1131. Mailing Address: 803 Laurel Ave., Gustine, CA 95322. Tel.: 209-854-2344.
Founded: 1990.
Congressional District: 18
Key Personnel: Museum Shop Mgr., Patricia S. Snoke.
Personnel Profile: Part-Time Paid 1; Part-Time Volunteers 50.
Governing Authority: Parent Institution: Gustine Historical Society. Tax-exempt.
History Museum.
Collections: Gustine history; photographs; memorial plaques; cowboy tack & gear; early dairy industry artifacts; Yokuts Indians.
Facilities: history center.
Publications: newsletter, The Magpie.
Hours & Admission Prices: Thurs. & Sun. 1-4. No charge; donations accepted. Closed all holidays. ♿
Attendance: 1,000 (estimated)

Hacienda Heights

YOUTH SCIENCE CENTER, Wedgeworth Elementary School, 16949 Wedgeworth Dr., Hacienda Heights, CA 91745. Mailing Address: P.O. Box 5723, Hacienda Heights, CA 91745-0723. Tel.: 626-854-9825. Fax: 626-855-3790.
E-mail: ysc@youthsciencecenter.org
Web Site: www.youthsciencecenter.org
Founded: 1962.
Congressional District: 38
Key Personnel: C.E.O., Ling-Ling Chang; Chm. (V), Ron Chong.
Personnel Profile: Full-Time Paid 1; Full-Time Volunteers 1; Part-Time Paid 6; Part-Time Volunteers 25.
Governing Authority: Tax-exempt.
Science Center.
Collections: hands-on science exhibits.
Facilities: video and book library. Science-related items for sale.
Activities: family activities; educational programs.
Publications: e-newsletter.
Hours & Admission Prices: Sept.-July Tues. & Thurs. 12-3:45, Sat. 11-3. No charge.
Attendance: 2,000 (estimated)
Membership: Sustaining $50; Business $100; Life $250.

Half Moon Bay

COASTAL ARTS LEAGUE MUSEUM, 300 Main St., Half Moon Bay, CA 94019-1784. Tel.: 650-726-6335.
Web Site: www.coastalartsleague.com
Governing Authority: nonprofit organization.
Art Museum.
Collections: paintings; photographs; sculpture; ceramics.
Facilities: Museum-related items for sale.
Activities: facility rental; educational programs; classes.
Publications: newsletter.
Hours & Admission Prices: Thurs.-Mon. 11-5. No charge.

Hanford

CLARK CENTER FOR JAPANESE ART AND CULTURE, 15770 Tenth Ave., Hanford, CA 93230-9533. Tel.: 559-582-4915. Fax: 559-582-9546.
E-mail: info@ccjac.org
Web Site: www.ccjac.org
Formerly: The Ruth & Sherman Lee Institute for Japanese Art
Founded: 1995.
Congressional District: 5
Key Personnel: Dir., Andreas Marks; Chm. (V), Richard L. Schafer.
Personnel Profile: Full-Time Paid 4; Part-Time Paid 1; Part-Time Volunteers 50; Interns 2.
Governing Authority: bd. of directors. Tax-exempt.
Art Museum.
Collections: Japanese paintings, sculpture & decorative arts; Buddhist paintings & sculpture; bonsai trees.
Major Exhibits: Lethal Beauty: Samurai Weapons & Armor, 11/09-1/10; The Splendor of the Japanese Screen, 2/10-4/10; They Swim, Fly, Wiggle, Walk, or Slither: The Hidden Code of Animals & Japanese Art (T), 3/10-5/10; Modern Japanese Baskets from the Clark Center for Japanese Art & Culture and the Art of Motoko Maio (T), 5/10-9/5/10; Delightful Pursuits: Highlights from the Clark Center (T), 8/10-12/10.
Facilities: library.
Publications: newsletter, Tokonoma.
Hours & Admission Prices: Sept.-July Tues.-Sat. 12:30-5. Adults $5, children & students $3; members no charge. Closed major holidays. ♿
Attendance: 3,500 (estimated)

HANFORD CARNEGIE MUSEUM, 109 E. 8th St., Hanford, CA 93230-3933. Tel.: 559-584-1367.
Web Site: www.irwinstreetinn.com/carnegie-museum.html
Founded: 1975.
Key Personnel: Dir., JoAnn Gibbons; Pres. Bd., Carolyn Limjoco.
Personnel Profile: Part-Time Paid 1.
History Museum.
Collections: Hanford's history; personal artifacts; photographs; furnishings; clothing; toys; Yokuts Indians.
Hours & Admission Prices: Wed.-Sat. 10-2. Adults $2, children, students & seniors $1.
Attendance: 2,750 (estimated)
Membership: Carnegie Individual $15; Carnegie Family $25; Historian $50; Cornerstone $100; Preservationist $250; Landmark $500.

TAOIST TEMPLE AND MUSEUM, 12 China Alley, Hanford, CA 93230. Mailing Address: P.O. Box 728, Hanford, CA 93232-0728. Tel.: 559-582-4508.
Web Site: www.visithanford.com/hfdvis23e.html
Key Personnel: Pres. (V), Arianne Wing; Museum Shop Mgr., Camille Wing.
Personnel Profile: Part-Time Volunteers 10.
Governing Authority: Tax-exempt.
History Museum.
Collections: furnishings; Hanford's Chinese residents; photographs; Chinese herb store artifacts; gambling houses; kitchen artifacts from homes & restaurants; Chinese temple including altar & furnishings.
Facilities: Museum-related items for sale.
Hours & Admission Prices: Call for hours. No charge; donations accepted.
Attendance: 1,271 (estimated)
Membership: Student $5; Individual $15; Family $25; Patron $50; Sustaining $100.

Hayward

C.E. SMITH MUSEUM OF ANTHROPOLOGY, CSU East Bay, Hayward, CA 94542-3039. Tel.: 510-885-3168 & 3104. Fax: 510-885-3353.
E-mail: george.miller@csueastbay.edu
Web Site: class.csueastbay.edu/anthropologymuseum/
Founded: 1975.
Key Personnel: Dir. & Cur., Prof. George Miller.
Personnel Profile: Part-Time Paid 5.
Governing Authority: university. Parent Institution: Cal State University East Bay. Subsidiary Institution: College of Letters, Arts & Social Sciences.
Anthropology Museum.
Collections: Jack Lee Kachina collection; American Southwest artifacts; Native American baskets; African art; Philippine artifacts; California Bay Area & Gold Rush artifacts; Andean textiles.
Research Fields: Hopi kachinas; Bay Area archaeology.
Facilities: library, available to the public.
Activities: docent program; temporary exhibitions; museum coursework.
Hours & Admission Prices: Mon.-Fri. 10-4 during exhibits. No charge; donations accepted. Closed federal holidays; university holidays. ♿
Attendance: 2,000 (estimated)
Membership: Student $5; Individual $20; Supporting $35; Sustaining $50; Sponsor $200; Patron $500.

HAYWARD AREA HISTORICAL SOCIETY, (M), 22701 Main St., Hayward, CA 94541-5113. Tel.: 510-581-0223. Fax: 510-581-0217.
Web Site: www.haywardareahistory.org
Founded: 1956.
Congressional District: 13
Key Personnel: C.E.O., Myron Freedman; Pres. (V), Jackie Grissom; Collections Mgr., Heather Farquhar; Dir. Devel., Alison Wenz; Museum Shop Mgr., Carrie Santell; Curator, Diane Curry; Educational Asst., Adriana Abrams; Museum Asst., Mae Vecchio.
Personnel Profile: Full-Time Paid 6; Part-Time Paid 4; Part-Time Volunteers 50; Interns 8.
Governing Authority: private; nonprofit organization. Subsidiary Institution: McConaghy House, Hayward, CA. Tax-exempt: 501(c)(3).
Historical Society.
Collections: focus on the history of Eden Township; furnishings; personal artifacts; recreational artifacts.
Research Fields: local history.
Facilities: 500-vol. library of local history books; 1,800 sq. ft. exhibit space. Victoriana, local history books & other museum-related items for sale.
Activities: docent program; formal education programs for children; lectures; participatory & temporary exhibits; walking tours. Annual Event: Preservation Gala & Awards.
Publications: quarterly newsletter, Adobe Trails.
Hours & Admission Prices: Tues.-Sat. 11-4. No charge; donations accepted. Closed New Year's; Independence Day; Thanksgiving; Christmas. ♿
Attendance: 4,371 (accurate)
Membership: Senior $20; Student & Teacher $25; Individual $30; Senior Family $35; Family $40; Nonprofit $50; Silver $75; Business & Club $100; Gold $125; Diamond $200; Historian $1,000.

MCCONAGHY HOUSE, 18701 Hesperian Blvd., Hayward, CA 94541-2247. Mailing Address: 22701 Main St., Hayward, CA 94541-5113. Tel.: 510-581-0223. Fax: 510-581-0217.
Web Site: www.haywardareahistory.org
Founded: 1976.
Congressional District: 13
Key Personnel: C.E.O., Myron Freedman; Chm. (V), Esther Jorgensen; Pres. (V), Jackie Grissom; Cur., Diane Curry; Collections Mgr., Heather Farguhar; Dir. Devel., Alison Wenz; Education Asst., Adriana Abrams; Admin. Asst., Carrie Santell; Museum Shop Mgr., Lucille Lorge.
Personnel Profile: Full-Time Paid 5; Part-Time Paid 3; Part-Time Volunteers 25.
Governing Authority: private; nonprofit. Parent Institution: Hayward Area Historical Society, Hayward CA. Tax-exempt: 501(c)(3).
Historic Home: 1886 Victorian farmhouse depicting the lifestyle of one of the area's first pioneer families.
Collections: Victorian furnishings & decorative arts; carriage house; tank house.
Research Fields: family history.
Facilities: 6,000 sq. ft. exhibit space. Victoriana for sale.
Activities: docent program; formal education programs for children; guided tours.
Publications: quarterly newsletter, HAHS Adobe Trails.
Hours & Admission Prices: Fri.-Sun. 1-4. Adults $3, senior citizens $2, children $.50; discounts AAM members; members no charge. Closed New Year's; Thanksgiving; Christmas.
Attendance: 4,583 (accurate)
Membership: Individual $15; Family $20; Supporting $40; Company $55; Sustaining $100; Patron $200; Individual Life $500.

SULPHUR CREEK NATURE CENTER, 1801 D St., Hayward, CA 94541-4434. Tel.: 510-881-6747. Fax: 510-888-0129.
E-mail: sulphurcreek@haywardrec.org
Web Site: www.hard.dst.ca.us
Founded: 1961.
Congressional District: 14
Key Personnel: Coord., Wendy Winsted.
Personnel Profile: Full-Time Paid 1; Part-Time Paid 12; Part-Time Volunteers 150; Interns 1.
Governing Authority: municipal. Parent Institution: Hayward Area Recreation & Park District, 1099 E St., Hayward, CA 94541. Tax-exempt.
Nature Center.
Collections: native wildlife including live mammals, birds, reptiles, amphibians & various invertebrates.
Facilities: nature center; hiking trail; picnic area.
Activities: wildlife education programs for school groups & the general public; tours; on-site field explorations; special topic programs; outreach programs; wildlife rehabilitation; animal rental library; nature study classes; summer camps; special events; volunteer programs; docent program; live animal presentations.
Publications: bimonthly newsletter; quarterly schedule of programs & activities.
Hours & Admission Prices: Tues.-Sun. 10-5. No charge; donations accepted. Closed New Year's Day; Martin Luther King Jr. Day; Presidents' Day; Easter; Veterans Day; Thanksgiving & day after; Christmas Eve & Day.
Attendance: 40,000 (accurate)

SUN GALLERY, 1015 E St., Hayward, CA 94541-5210. Tel.: 510-581-4050. Fax: 510-581-3384.
E-mail: sungallery@comcast.net
Web Site: sungallery.org
Founded: 1975.
Congressional District: 10
Key Personnel: Chm. (V) & Pres. (V), Valerie Caveglia; Asst. to Bd. of Dir., Christine Bender; Museum Shop Mgr., Audrey LePell.
Personnel Profile: Part-Time Paid 1; Part-Time Volunteers 10; Interns 3.
Governing Authority: nonprofit. Parent Institution: Hayward Area Forum of the Arts, Inc. Tax-exempt: 501(c)(3).
Visual Arts Center.
Collections: contemporary art by northern California artists; works by artists of 1960s & 1970s.
Major Exhibits: 21st Annual Children's Book Illustrator Exhibit, 1/10-4/10; The Wild, Wild West II, 4/10-5/10; Hottest Show in Town III, 8/10-9/10.
Facilities: art classroom. Ceramics, glass, wood items & jewelry for sale.
Activities: guided tours; lectures; gallery talks; arts festivals; docent program or council; school field trips; hands-on art activities; summer art classes for children; training programs; permanent & temporary exhibitions.
Publications: newsletter, Sun Gallery
Hours & Admission Prices: Wed.-Sat. 11-5. No charge; donations accepted. Closed major holidays. ♿
Attendance: 5,000 (estimated)
Membership: Student $10; Senior Citizen $25; Individual $35; Family $50; Sponsor $100; Silver $250; Gold $500; Platinum $1,000.

Healdsburg

HEALDSBURG MUSEUM, 221 Matheson St., Healdsburg, CA 95448. Mailing Address: P.O. Box 952, Healdsburg, CA 95448-0952. Tel.: 707-431-3325. Fax: 707-473-4471.
E-mail: healdsburg@sbcglobal.net
Web Site: www.healdsburgmuseum.org
Key Personnel: Cur., Daniel Murley
History Museum.
Collections: local history; photographs.
Facilities: library.
Activities: educational programs; special events.
Publications: newsletter.
Hours & Admission Prices: Museum: Tues.-Sun. 11-4. Research Archives: Thurs.-Sat. by appointment. No charge.

TILE HERITAGE FOUNDATION, (M), Healdsburg, CA 95448. Mailing Address: Box 1850, Healdsburg, CA 95448-1850. Tel.: 707-431-8453. Fax: 707-431-8455.
E-mail: foundation@tileheritage.org
Web Site: www.tileheritage.org
Founded: 1987.
Congressional District: 1
Key Personnel: Pres., Joseph A. Taylor; Financial Dir., Sheila A. Menzies.
Personnel Profile: Full-Time Paid 2; Part-Time Paid 2; Part-Time Volunteers 3.
Governing Authority: public charity; nonprofit organization. Tax-exempt: 501(c)(3).
Art Foundation: for the research & preservation of ceramic surfaces.
Collections: archival library of historic & contemporary information on ceramic surfaces in the U.S.; designers; manufacturers; showroom sites; photographs; slides; books; catalogs; collection of historic & contemporary tiles (not on display).
Research Fields: to promote ceramic surfaces as an integral part of America's cultural heritage; to encourage the growth of organized information regarding the history & preservation of ceramic surfaces; to demonstrate that through continued research, the information gathered can be effectively added to the growing store of knowledge & provide a workable resource to enhance educational programs throughout the nation; to strengthen the network of people willing to share information for the common goal of promoting & preserving ceramic surfaces; to enhance the visibility of the Tile Heritage Foundation nationally as an organization dedicated to the research & preservation of this important artistic medium.
Facilities: 300-vol. library; 28,000 document archives; field research station. Museum-related items for sale.
Activities: guided tours of tile sites; workshops; lectures; school loan services; loan & temporary exhibits.

Publications: journal, Tile Heritage: A Review of American Tile History; newsletter, E-News.
Hours & Admission Prices: Mon.-Sat. 10-4 by appointment only. No charge; donations accepted. Closed Easter; Independence Day; Thanksgiving; Christmas week. ♿
Membership: Individuals & Families: Regular $45; Supporting $60; Sustaining $75; Friend $150; Guardian $300; Patron $500. Businesses & Corporations: Centurian $100; Sponsor $250; Donor $500; Benefactor $1,000.

Hemet

FINGER PRINTS YOUTH MUSEUM, 123 S. Carmalita St., Hemet, CA 92543-4210. Mailing Address: 418 E. Florida Ave., Hemet, CA 92543-4210. Tel.: 951-765-1223. Fax: 951-652-0064.
E-mail: director@fingerprintsyouthmuseum.com
Web Site: www.fingerprintsmuseum.com
Formerly: The KidZone Riverside County Youth Museum
Governing Authority: Tax-exempt: 501(c)(3).
Children's Museum.
Collections: hands-on exhibits.
Hours & Admission Prices: Tues.-Sun. 9-5. Admission $5, seniors 55 & over $4; children under 2 no charge.
Membership: Family of 4 $50; Family of 8 $80.

HEMET MUSEUM, Santa Fe Depot/State & Florida, Hemet, CA 92543. Mailing Address: P.O. Box 2521, Hemet, CA 92546-2521. Tel.: 951-929-4409 & 5885.
Web Site: www.hemetmuseum.org
Founded: 1973.
Congressional District: 65
Key Personnel: Cur.8, Anne B. Jennings; Museum Shop Mgr., Virginia Sisk.
Personnel Profile: Part-Time Volunteers 40.
Governing Authority: private; nonprofit organization. Parent Institution: Hemet Area Museum Assoc. Tax-exempt.
History Museum: housed in 1898 freight house of the historic Santa Fe Depot.
Collections: concentration on Hemet area history from prehistoric to modern era; photographs; documents; artifacts; memorabilia; clothes; household wares; business equipment; fossils dating to the Pleistocene era.
Research Fields: local history.
Facilities: 100-vol. library of California & local history; garden. Museum-related items for sale.
Activities: guided tours; special tours for school children. Museum Sponsors: Open House; Old Timer Gatherings; Pioneer Picnic; outreach program in elementary schools.
Publications: book, Valley, River, Mountain - Fortune Favors the Brave Revisited: A History of the Lake Hemet Water Co; San Jacinto Valley Railway; Whittier, Fuller & Co; Vignettes of the Valley.
Hours & Admission Prices: Sept.-July Tues.-Sun. 11-3. No charge; donations accepted. Closed New Year's Day; Independence Day; Labor Day; Thanksgiving; Christmas. ♿
Attendance: 4,510 (accurate)
Membership: Individual $10; Family $15; Organization, Business & Contributing $25; Lifetime Individual $150; Lifetime Couple $250.

WESTERN CENTER FOR ARCHAEOLOGY AND PALEONTOLOGY, (M), 2345 Searl Pkwy., Hemet, CA 92543-9706. Tel.: 951-791-0033. Fax: 951-791-0032.
Web Site: westerncentermuseum.org
Founded: 1999.
Congressional District: 45
Key Personnel: Interim Dir., Tracy J. Frick; Chm. (V), Bruce Wallis; Museum Shop Mgr., Joyce Simanek.
Personnel Profile: Full-Time Paid 8; Part-Time Paid 9; Part-Time Volunteers 45; Interns 6.
Governing Authority: Tax-exempt.
Archaeology & Paleontology Museum.
Collections: archaeology; paleontology; fossils; Diamond Valley Lake artifacts.
Facilities: classrooms; banquet facilities.
Activities: educational programs; teaching laboratory; field trips; science Saturdays.
Hours & Admission Prices: Tues.-Sun. 10-5. Adults $8, seniors 62 & over and students 13-22 $6.50, youth 5-12 $6; members, military and children 4 & under no charge. ♿
Attendance: 45,000 (accurate)
Membership: Student $30; Senior $40; Individual $50; Family $75.

Hermosa Beach

HERMOSA BEACH HISTORICAL MUSEUM, 710 Pier Ave., Hermosa Beach, CA 90254-3940. Tel.: 310-318-9421.
E-mail: hbhs@hermosabeachhistoricalsociety.org
Web Site: www.hermosabeachhistoricalsociety.org
Founded: 1987.
Personnel Profile: Part-Time Paid 1.
Governing Authority: Parent Institution: Hermosa Beach Historical Society. Tax-exempt.
Historical Society Museum.
Collections: local history; photographs; personal artifacts.
Major Exhibits: Lifeguards and Paddleboards, 11/09-2/10.
Hours & Admission Prices: Wed. 10-12, Sat.-Sun. 2-4. No charge; donations accepted. Closed holidays.

Hollister

SAN BENITO COUNTY HISTORICAL SOCIETY MUSEUM, 498 5th St., Hollister, CA 95023-3841. Tel.: 831-635-0335.
E-mail: info@sbchistoricalsociety.org
Web Site: sbchistoricalsociety.org
Founded: 1956.
Key Personnel: Pres. & Dir., Peter Sonne.
Governing Authority: nonprofit organization.
History Museum.
Collections: photographs; artifacts; clothing; farm and farm-life related tools & equipment. Historic Buildings: c.1860 home with outhouse; c.1890 one-room schoolhouse; early 1900s public bar; large dance hall; several open-faced barns; blacksmith & carpenter shops; print shop; gas engine shop; 1890s drug store.
Hours & Admission Prices: Historical Society Museum: Sat.-Sun. 1-3; groups by appointments. No charge; donations accepted. Historical Village: daily dawn to dusk. Parking fee: $3.
Membership: Junior (under 18) $3; Individual $20; Family $30; Premier $50.

Hollywood

HOLLYWOOD GUINNESS WORLD OF RECORDS MUSEUM, 6764 Hollywood Blvd., Hollywood, CA 90028-4622. Mailing Address: 6767 Hollywood Blvd., Hollywood, CA 90028-4623. Tel.: 323-463-6433. Fax: 323-462-3953.
Web Site: www.hollywoodwax.com
Founded: 1991.
Key Personnel: Pres., Tej Sundher; Dir., Chanchil Sundher; Dir., Raubi Sundhon.
Personnel Profile: Full-Time Paid 20.
Governing Authority: company organized for profit. Parent Institution: World of Records Exhibition, LTD (Licensor) Beaulieu Hampshire England.
Guinness Book of World Records Museum: housed c.1913 Hollywood's first movie theatre.
Collections: world record facts, feats & record holders; photographs; personal artifacts; movie memorabilia.
Facilities: 15,000 sq. ft. exhibit space.
Hours & Admission Prices: Sun.-Thurs. 10-12, Fri.-Sat. 10-1. Adults $15.95, senior citizens $13.95, children 6-12 $6.95. ♿
Attendance: 125,000 (estimated)

HOLLYWOOD HERITAGE MUSEUM, 2100 Highland Ave., Hollywood, CA 90068-3241. Mailing Address: P.O. Box 2586, Hollywood, CA 90078-2586. Tel.: 323-874-2276 & 4005; 323-467-0287. Fax: 323-465-5993.
E-mail: kxiaojie@aol.com
Web Site: www.hollywoodheritage.org
Formerly: Hollywood Studio Museum
Founded: 1982.
Congressional District: 13
Key Personnel: Dir., Cur. & Museum Shop Mgr., Marc Wanamaker.
Personnel Profile: Part-Time Volunteers 15.
Governing Authority: nonprofit. Parent Institution: Hollywood Heritage, Inc., P.O. Box 2586, Hollywood. Subsidiary Institution: Hollywood Heritage Museum in the Lasky-DeMille Barn. Tax-exempt: 501(c)(3).
Early Hollywood History & Heritage Museum: housed in restored 1895 barn which was adapted for use as a film studio in Hollywood in 1912; became Paramount Studios in 1916; state historic landmark in 1955.
Collections: the development & history of the film industry in Southern California, predominantly Hollywood & Los Angeles; the early years of filmmaking & silent films from 1906-1931; history of the principals of the Jesse L. Laskey Feature Play Co., Famous Players Co., and Paramount Pictures Co.
Research Fields: history of film industry in Southern California; silent film

industry; musical scores of silent films; excavation of film set of The Ten Commandments; architecture of historically significant Hollywood buildings.
Facilities: 600-vol. library; 3,000 sq. ft. exhibit space. Film-related items for sale.
Activities: guided tours; lectures; docent program; films; temporary exhibits; film screenings. Museum Sponsors: quarterly Paper Collectible Show & Sale.
Publications: quarterly newsletter, Hollywood Heritage Inc.
Hours & Admission Prices: Thurs.-Sun. 12-4. Adults $5, seniors $3, children under 12 $1; members no charge. Closed New Year's Day; Thanksgiving; Christmas. ♿
Membership: Senior/Student $20; Individual $35; Household $50; Triangle $100; Kalem $250; Bison $500; Keystone $1,000; Majestic $2,500.

HOLLYWOOD HISTORY MUSEUM, 1660 N. Highland Ave., Hollywood, CA 90028-6121. Tel.: 323-464-7776.
E-mail: info@thehollywoodmuseum
Web Site: www.thehollywoodmuseum.com
Movie History Museum: housed in the landmark Max Factor building.
Collections: movie memorabilia; personal artifacts; photographs; clothing.
Hours & Admission Prices: Wed.-Sun. 10-5. Adults $15, seniors & students under 21 $12, children under 5 $5.

HOLLYWOOD WAX MUSEUM, INC., 6767 Hollywood Blvd., Hollywood, CA 90028-4623. Tel.: 323-462-8860. Fax: 323-462-3953.
E-mail: contact@hollywoodwax.com
Web Site: www.hollywoodwax.com
Founded: 1965.
Key Personnel: Financial Dir., Chanchil Sundher; Cur., Ken Horn; Public Rels., Raubi Sundher.
Personnel Profile: Full-Time Paid 30; Part-Time Paid 3.
Governing Authority: company organized for profit.
Wax Museum: housed in c.1929 former Embassy Club.
Collections: sculptures.
Facilities: Tourist novelties for sale.
Hours & Admission Prices: Call for hours. Adults $15.95, senior citizens $13.95, children 6-12 $6.95; children under 5 no charge.
Attendance: 130,000 (estimated)

Homewood

TAHOE MARITIME MUSEUM, (M), 5205 W. Lake Blvd., Homewood, CA 96141. Mailing Address: P.O. Box 627, Homewood, CA 96141-0627. Tel.: 530-525-9253. Fax: 530-525-9283.
Founded: 1988.
Key Personnel: Exec. Dir., William Kraus; Pres. (V), Thomas Bredt.
Personnel Profile: Full-Time Paid 3; Part-Time Paid 1.
Governing Authority: nonprofit organization. Tax-exempt: 501(c)(3).
Maritime Museum.
Collections: local maritime history; boats; photographs; period artifacts.
Activities: special tours; childrens programs; lectures. Museum Sponsors: Living History Day; Marine Swap Meet.
Publications: Tahoe Maritimes.
Hours & Admission Prices: May 24-Sept. Thurs.-Tues. 10-5; Oct.-April Fri.-Sun. 10-5. Adults $5; members & children under 12 no charge. ♿
Membership: $40; $100; $200; $300; $500; $1,000; Friend $1,000; Sustaining Friend $2,500.

Hoopa

HOOPA VALLEY TRIBAL MUSEUM, Hwy. 96, Hoopa, CA 95546. Mailing Address: P.O. Box 1348, Hoopa, CA 95546-1348. Tel.: 530-625-4110.
E-mail: hvtm@pcweb.net
Web Site: bss.sfsu.edu/calstudies/hupa/hoopa.htm
Founded: 1979.
Personnel Profile: Full-Time Paid 2; Part-Time Paid 1; Part-Time Volunteers 1; Interns 1.
Governing Authority: nonprofit. Parent Institution: Hoopa Valley Tribe. Tax-exempt.
Tribal Museum.
Collections: culture & history of native people of northern California; Hupa, Yurok, & Karuk artifacts; basketry; ceremonial regalia; redwood dugout canoes; tools.
Activities: Hupa language classes; basketry classes; village tours; storytelling events; dance demonstrations.
Hours & Admission Prices: Mon.-Fri. 8-12 & 1-5, Sat. 10-12 & 1-4. Village Tours: $10 per person, groups of 6 or more $50.
Attendance: 2,518 (accurate)

Huntington Beach

BOLSA CHICA CONSERVANCY, 3842 Warner Ave., Huntington Beach, CA 92649-4263. Tel.: 714-846-1114. Fax: 714-846-4065.
E-mail: info@bolsachica.org
Web Site: www.bolsachica.org
Key Personnel: Exec. Dir., Grace Adams; Dir. Education & Wetland Research Coord., Laura Bandy.
Governing Authority: nonprofit organization.
Conservatory.
Collections: preservation, restoration, & enhancement of Bolsa Chica Wetlands; native plants.
Facilities: library.
Hours & Admission Prices: Tues.-Fri. 10-4, Sat. 9-12, Sun. 12:30-3:30.

FINE ARTS GALLERY AT GOLDEN WEST COLLEGE, 15744 Goldenwest Street, Huntington Beach, CA 92647-2748. Tel.: 714-892-7711, ext. 51032.
E-mail: dhudson@gwc.cccd.edu
Web Site: www.goldenwestcollege.edu/gallery
Art Museum.
Collections: paintings; photographs.
Activities: special events.
Hours & Admission Prices: Mon. & Thurs. 10-2, Tues.-Wed. 10-2 & 5-8, Fri. by appointment.

HUNTINGTON BEACH INTERNATIONAL SURFING MUSEUM, 411 Olive Ave., Huntington Beach, CA 92648. Mailing Address: P.O. Box 782, Huntington Beach, CA 92648-0782. Tel.: 714-960-3483. Fax: 714-960-1434. TDD: 714-960-3483.
E-mail: info@surfingmuseum.org
Web Site: www.surfingmuseum.org
Founded: 1987.
Congressional District: 42
Key Personnel: Chm., Jodi McKay; Vice Chm., Dave Reynolds; Sec., Linda Miller; Treas. & Museum Shop Mgr., Tom Gibbons; Business Admin., Gary Sahagen.
Personnel Profile: Full-Time Volunteers 2; Part-Time Volunteers 1; Interns 3.
Governing Authority: nonprofit organization. Tax-exempt: 501(c)(3).
Surfing Museum: housed in restored Art Deco building.
Collections: c.1800-present surfboards; photos; art; sculpture; film; books; magazines; posters; clothing; surf guitars; albums; cameras; documents.
Major Exhibits: Surfboard Shapers, 11/09-10/10.
Research Fields: surf lifesaving; surfing history.
Facilities: 2,000 sq. ft. exhibit space. Museum-related items for sale.
Activities: docent program; films; guided tours; loan, temporary, participatory & traveling exhibitions; broadcast programs.
Publications: quarterly newsletter, Shore Break.
Hours & Admission Prices: Mon.-Fri. 12-5, Sat.-Sun. 11-6. No charge; donations accepted. Closed New Year's Day; Christmas. ♿
Attendance: 10,000 (estimated)
Membership: Individual $20; Family $35; Patron $500; Lifetime $250.

Imperial

PIONEERS' MUSEUM, 373 E. Aten Rd., Imperial, CA 92251-9653. Tel.: 760-352-3211. Fax: 760-352-5411.
Governing Authority: nonprofit organization.
History Museum.
Collections: local history & culture; archaeology; period artifacts; baskets; Native American artifacts; furniture.
Activities: lectures; special events; fundraisers.
Hours & Admission Prices: Tues.-Sun. 10-4. Adults $2, children 6-12 $1.50; children under 6 no charge.

Independence

EASTERN CALIFORNIA MUSEUM, 155 N. Grant St., Independence, CA 93526. Mailing Address: P.O. Box 206, Independence, CA 93526-0206. Tel.: 760-878-0364 & 0258. Fax: 760-878-0412.
E-mail: ecmuseum@inycounty.us
Web Site: inyocounty.us/ecmuseum/index.html
Founded: 1928.
Congressional District: 40
Key Personnel: Museum Svcs. Admin., Jon Klusmire; Museum Specialist, Beth Sennett Porter; Museum Asst., Roberta Harlan; Museum Asst., Donna Stanger.
Personnel Profile: Full-Time Paid 2; Part-Time Paid 2.
Governing Authority: county. Parent Institution: Inyo County. Tax-exempt: 501(c)(3); 170(b)(1)(A).
Local & Natural History Museum.

Collections: Paiute & Shoshone Indian basketry & other cultural artifacts; Inyo County Pioneer artifacts & memorabilia relating to mining & farming, exhibits on Manzanar Japanese American War Relocation Center (World War II); narrow gauge steam locomotive. Historic Houses: 1865 Edwards House; 1883 Commander's House.
Research Fields: anthropology, history & oral history.
Facilities: non-circulating reference library; herbarium. Museum-related items for sale.
Activities: scientific, cultural programs, including history lectures; field trips.
Publications: annual newsletter; Music Box Cassette; book, Mountains to Desert.
Hours & Admission Prices: Wed.-Mon. 10-4. No charge; donations accepted. Edward's House & Commander's House temporarily closed. Closed New Year's Day; Easter; Thanksgiving; Christmas. ♿
Attendance: 10,000 (accurate)
Membership: Individual $25; Family $40; Contributing $100; Business & Organization $150; Patron $250; Sustaining $500; Benefactor $1,000 & up.

Indio

COACHELLA VALLEY HISTORICAL SOCIETY MUSEUM AND CULTURAL CENTER, (M), 82-616 Miles Ave., Indio, CA 92201-4228. Mailing Address: P.O. Box 595, Indio, CA 92202-0595. Tel.: 760-342-6651. Fax: 760-863-5232.
E-mail: cvmuscc1@aol.com
Web Site: www.coachellavalleymuseum.org
Founded: 1984.
Congressional District: 44
Key Personnel: Exec. Dir., Jessie Seiss; Pres. Bd., Hugh Mason; Registrar & Cur., Connie Cowan; Administrative Asst., Felma Wilson; Museum Shop Mgr., Doris Wilkie.
Personnel Profile: Part-Time Paid 1; Part-Time Volunteers 35.
Governing Authority: private; nonprofit organization. Parent Institution: Coachella Valley Historical Society, Inc. Tax-exempt: 501(c)(3).
History Museum: 1926 adobe house built by Dr. Harry Smiley, known as Smiley Place.
Collections: farm tools; horse drawn farm machinery; Cahuilla Indian artifacts; railroad; pioneer families; water development; Coachella Valley artifacts; date culture; blacksmith shop. Historic House: 1909 schoolhouse.
Research Fields: Coachella Valley history; women pioneers; date culture history.
Facilities: library & archives; art studio; 4,000 sq. ft. exhibit space; gardens.
Activities: educational tours; docent program; summer art classes for children; permanent & temporary exhibitions; special events. Annual Events: Heritage Day; Aki Matsuri Festival.
Publications: quarterly newsletter, Scratches in the Sand; annual magazine, The Periscope; pictorial history book.
Hours & Admission Prices: Thurs.-Sat. 10-4, Sun. 1-4. Adults $3, senior citizens & students $2, children 6-12 $1; AAM members, children under 5 & members no charge. Closed holidays.
Attendance: 4,000 (accurate)
Membership: Individual $20; Family $45; Contributor $75; Sponsor & Organizations $100; Benefactor & Business $150; Life $500.

S.C.R.A.P. GALLERY, (M), 46-350 Arabia St., Indio, CA 92201-5824. Tel.: 760-863-7777. Fax: 760-863-8973.
E-mail: info@scrapgallery.org
Web Site: scrapgallery.org
Founded: 1996.
Key Personnel: C.E.O., Karen Riley; Pres. (V), Marilyn Glassman; Treas., Donna Pease.
Personnel Profile: Full-Time Paid 1; Part-Time Paid 2; Part-Time Volunteers 20; Interns 2.
Governing Authority: private; nonprofit organization.
Art Museum.
Collections: art objects created with reused or recycled materials.
Facilities: educational facilities; conservation center; 10,000 sq. ft. exhibit space. Museum-related items for sale.
Activities: formal education programs for children; guided tours; mobile vans; participatory exhibits; school loan service.
Publications: Landfill Lunch Box; The Eco Deck; Don't Trash My Planet.
Hours & Admission Prices: Sept.-July Mon.-Fri. 9-5, Sat. special hours monthly. No charge. Closed major holidays. ♿
Attendance: 270,000 (accurate)

Irvine

BEALL CENTER FOR ART AND TECHNOLOGY, 712 Arts Plaza, Claire Trevor School of the Arts, UC Irvine, Irvine, CA 92697-2775. Tel.: 949-824-4339. Fax: 949-824-2450.
Web Site: beallcenter.uci.edu
Formerly: University of California Art Gallery and Beall Center for Art and Technology
Founded: 1965.
Key Personnel: Dir., Eleanore Stewart; Assoc. Dir., David Familian.
Personnel Profile: Full-Time Paid 1; Part-Time Paid 2.
Governing Authority: university. Parent Institution: University of California, Irvine. Tax-exempt.
Art Museum.
Collections: new media art.
Major Exhibits: Emergence, 1/8/10-5/7/10.
Activities: public & private tours. Museum Sponsors: Family Art Days.
Hours & Admission Prices: Tues.-Wed.12-5, Thurs.-Sat. 12-8. No charge. Closed New Year's Day; Easter; Christmas Eve & Day; university breaks. ♿
Attendance: 10,000

IRVINE FINE ARTS CENTER, 14321 Yale Ave., Irvine, CA 92604-1901. Tel.; 949-724-6880. Fax: 949-552-2137.
E-mail: rmcgraw@cityofirvine.org
Web Site: www.cityofirvine.org/depts/cs/finearts
Arts & Crafts Museum.
Collections: painting; ceramics; photography; jewelry; culinary arts.
Facilities: Museum-related items for sale.
Activities: workshops.
Hours & Admission Prices: Mon.-Thurs. 9-9, Fri.-Sat. 9-5. No charge.

THE IRVINE MUSEUM, 18881 Von Karman Ave., Ste. 100, Irvine, CA 92612-6541. Tel.: 949-476-0294. Fax: 949-476-2437.
Web Site: www.irvinemuseum.org
Founded: 1992.
Key Personnel: Exec. Dir., Mr. Jean Stern; Museum Shop Mgr., Don Bridges.
Personnel Profile: Full-Time Paid 5; Part-Time Paid 1; Part-Time Volunteers 15.
Governing Authority: nonprofit. Tax-exempt.
Art Museum.
Collections: early California Impressionist paintings, c.1890-1930.
Publications: A California Womens Story, 2006; California This Golden Land of Promise, 2001; The Life and Art of Paul de Longpre, 2001; All Things Bright and Beautiful, 1998; California Impressionists, 1996; Joseph Kleitsch, A Kaleidoscope of Color, 2007; Native Grandeur, Preserving California's Vanishing Landscapes, 2003; Reflections of California The Athalie Richardson Irvine Clarke Memorial Exhibition, 1994; Romance of the Bells, The California Missions in Art, 1995; Selections from The Irvine Museum, 1992; East Coast West Coast and Beyond; Colin Campbell Cooper American Impressionist, 2006; Guy Rose American Impressionist, 1996; Impressions of California, Early Currents in Art 1850-1930, 1996; Masters of Light, Plein-Air Painting in California, 1890-1930, 2002; In Nature's Temple, The Life and Art of William Wendt, 2008, Palette of Light, 1995.
Hours & Admission Prices: Tues.-Sat. 11-5. No charge. Closed major holidays. ♿
Attendance: 19,442 (accurate)

UNIVERSITY OF CALIFORNIA IRVINE ARBORETUM, University of California, North Campus Dr. & Jamboree Rd., Irvine, CA 92697-0001. Tel.: 949-824-5833. Fax: 949-824-6146.
Web Site: arboretum.bio.uci.edu
Founded: 1965.
Congressional District: 40
Key Personnel: Dir., Dr. Peter Bowler.
Governing Authority: university. Parent Institution: University of California, Irvine. Tax-exempt: 170(b)(1)(A).
Arboretum.
Collections: African xerophytes, Petalloid monocot plants; iridaceae, liliaceae, amaryllidaceae, geraniaceae; California native plants.
Research Fields: general botany; conservation; plant propagation & breeding.
Facilities: botanical garden.
Activities: lectures; formally organized education programs for undergraduate & graduate college students affiliated with the University of California; permanent exhibitions.
Publications: book, Plant Extinctions: A Global Crisis; quarterly newsletter, Index Seminum.
Hours & Admission Prices: Mon.-Sat. 9-3. No charge; donations accepted. Closed holidays.
Attendance: 14,100
Membership: Regular $30; Active $50; Sustaining $100; Builder $250; Patron $500; Benefactor $1,000.

Jackson

AMADOR COUNTY MUSEUM, 225 Church St., Jackson, CA 95642-2303. Mailing Address: 810 Court St., Jackson, CA 95642-2132. Tel.: 209-223-6386. Fax: 209-223-0749.
E-mail: museum@volcano.net
Founded: 1949.
Congressional District: 14
Key Personnel: Cur. & Museum Shop Mgr., Georgia Fox.
Personnel Profile: Full-Time Paid 1; Part-Time Paid 1; Part-Time Volunteers 4.
Governing Authority: county. Tax-exempt.
General Museum: housed in c.1859 house.
Collections: Western history; gold rush history, equipment & memorabilia; gold mining artifacts; furnishings; photos; mine models; Indian & Chinese artifacts; William Lemos (1910) painting of Yosemite, CA; Bordello history; gambling; jazz pianist, Dave Brubeck.
Research Fields: pioneer families; Gold Rush era.
Activities: guided tour of the Head Frame of the Kennedy Mine Model.
Hours & Admission Prices: Museum: Feb.-Nov. Wed.-Sun. 10-4. Kennedy Gold Mine Model Tours: Sat.-Sun. 11-3 on the hour; group tours by reservation. Mime Model Tours: $2. Museum: no charge; donations accepted. ♿
Attendance: 9,000 (estimated)

Jenner

FORT ROSS STATE HISTORIC PARK VISITOR CENTER AND MUSEUM, 19005 Coast Hwy. One, Jenner, CA 95450. Tel.: 707-847-3437. Fax: 707-847-3601.
Congressional District: 6
Key Personnel: Dir., Lyn Kalani; Pres. (V), Sarah Sweedler; Museum Shop Mgr., Lake Perry.
Personnel Profile: Part-Time Paid 4.
Governing Authority: private; nonprofit organization. Tax-exempt.
History Museum.
Collections: local history; archaeology; baskets; Native American artifacts.
Major Exhibits: Rotchen House Museum, Summer 2010.
Research Fields: Russian archives, preservation & restoration of Rotchen House.
Facilities: library; visitor center. Museum-related items for sale.
Activities: presentations; environmental living program; lectures; art shows; conferences; private tours. Museum Sponsors: Cultural Heritage Day; Harvest Festival.
Publications: Fort Ross and Salt Point newsletters, books & brochures; e-newsletter; audio-visual productions.
Hours & Admission Prices: Daily 10-4:30. Park: adults $8 per car, seniors $7 per car. Museum: no charge. Closed Thanksgiving; Christmas.
Attendance: 200,000 (estimated)
Membership: Senior & Student $15; Regular $20; Family $25; Organization $30.

Jolon

MISSION SAN ANTONIO DE PADUA, Mission Creek Rd., Jolon, CA 93928. Mailing Address: P.O. Box 803, Jolon, CA 93928-0803. Tel.: 831-385-4478. Fax: 831-386-9332.
E-mail: sam1771@redshift.com
Web Site: www.missionsanantonio.net
Formerly: San Antonio Mission
Founded: 1771.
Congressional District: 29
Key Personnel: Lay Coord., Teresa Carey.
Governing Authority: church. Parent Institution: Catholic Diocese of Monterey. Tax-exempt: 501(c)(3).
Historic Museum: restored old San Antonio Mission.
Collections: wine press of Spanish colonial period; Indian relics; manuscripts; archives.
Research Fields: soldiers barracks; Indian dwellings; buildings; archaeology.
Facilities: Religious articles & mission-related items for sale.
Activities: special guided tours; occasional inter-museum loan, permanent & temporary exhibitions.
Publications: books, Padres & People of Mission San Antonio; Herbs of Mission (used by Indians); History of Mission of San Antonio.
Hours & Admission Prices: Summer: daily 8-6; Winter: daily 8-5. Donation Accepted: $2. Closed Easter; Thanksgiving; Christmas Eve & Day. ♿
Attendance: 10,000

Julian

JULIAN PIONEER MUSEUM, 2811 Washington St., Julian, CA 92036. Tel.: 760-765-0227.
History Museum.
Collections: personal artifacts; period clothing from 1896-1913; photographs; mining equipment; Victorian era pianos; Native American artifacts.
Hours & Admission Prices: Call for hours.

Kentfield

MARIN COMMUNITY COLLEGE ART GALLERY, Sir Francis Drake Blvd., Kentfield, CA 94904. Tel.: 415-485-9494.
Art Museum.
Collections: paintings; sculpture.
Hours & Admission Prices: Call for hours.

Kernville

KERN RIVER VALLEY HISTORICAL SOCIETY MUSEUM, 49 Big Blue Rd., Kernville, CA 93238. Mailing Address: P.O. Box 651, Kernville, CA 93238-0651. Tel.: 760-376-6683.
E-mail: info@krvhistoricalsociety.org
Web Site: www.krvhistoricalsociety.org/museum.htm
Key Personnel: Pres., Ron Bolyard; Cur., Jon Partin
Historical Society Museum.
Collections: local history & culture; Old West; Native American artifacts; gold mining; farming; ranching; Western movies; works by local artists.
Hours & Admission Prices: Thurs.-Sun. 10-4; other times by appointment. No charge.

Kingsburg

KINGSBURG HISTORICAL PARK, 2321 Sierra St., Kingsburg, CA 93631. Mailing Address: P.O. Box 282, Kingsburg, CA 93631-1457.
History Museum.
Collections: schoolroom; period farm tools; clothing; appliances; photographs; early printing press. Historic Buildings: medical building; grocery store; schoolhouse; service station; windmill; firehouse.
Hours & Admission Prices: Thurs.-Sat. 1-4. Adults $3, children under 12 $.50; discounts to groups; members no charge.

Klamath

END OF THE TRAIL MUSEUM, 15500 Hwy. 101 N., Klamath, CA 95548-9351. Mailing Address: P.O. Box 96, Klamath, CA 95548-0096. Tel.: 707-482-2251.
E-mail: tofm@treesofmystery.net
Web Site: treesofmystery.net
Founded: 1950.
Key Personnel: Museum Shop Mgr., Debbie Thompson
History Museum.
Collections: Native American history & culture; personal artifacts; baby carriers.
Facilities: Museum-related items for sale.
Hours & Admission Prices: No charge. Closed Christmas. ♿
Attendance: 300,000

La Canada Flintridge

* **DESCANSO GARDENS GUILD, INC., (M),** 1418 Descanso Dr., La Canada Flintridge, CA 91011-3102. Tel.: 818-952-4401 & 4408; 949-4200. Fax: 818-790-3291.
E-mail: dbrown@descansogardens.org
Web Site: www.descansogardens.org
Founded: 1957.
Congressional District: 22
Key Personnel: Exec. Dir., David R. Brown; Chm. (V), Simon Harrison; Financial Dir., Juliann Rooke; Dir. Devel., Linda Mitchell; Public Rels., Mary Ellen Walker; Museum Shop Mgr., David Crocker.
Personnel Profile: Full-Time Paid 49; Part-Time Paid 25; Part-Time Volunteers 400; Interns 1.
Governing Authority: nonprofit organization. Tax-exempt: 501(c)(3).
Botanical Garden: housed in the former home of E. Manchester Boddy; c.1930s.
Collections: Camellia collection: 30,000 plants under an oak forest canopy; 9 acres of native plant area; 5-acre rose garden; 1 1/2 Descanso Lake & bird sanctuary with over 150 species of birds.
Facilities: library; botanical garden; rental facilities; 55-seat patio cafe; educational facilities; 2,800 sq. ft. exhibit space; Bird Observation Center. Horticulturally-related items for sale.

Activities: guided tours; lectures; rental facilities; films; dance recitals; arts festivals. Museum Sponsors: Plant sales; Winter Holiday Show; Horticultural events; Spring Festival of Flowers late March thru late April; Pumpkin Festival in October; Japanese Garden Festival in November; Labor Day Picnic.
Publications: quarterly, Descanso News.
Hours & Admission Prices: Daily 9-4:30. Adults $8, senior citizens & students $6, children 5-12 $3; Guild members & children under 5 no charge. Closed Christmas Day. ♿
Attendance: 300,000 (accurate)
Membership: Kid-care pass $25; Senior Individual $55; Individual $60; Senior Couple $65; Couple $70; Family & Grandparents $80; Patron $150, $250, $500 & $1,000.

LANTERMAN HOUSE, 4420 Encinas Dr., La Canada Flintridge, CA 91011-3113. Tel.: 818-790-1421. Fax: 818-952-8450.
E-mail: mpatton@bilrc.caltech.edu
Web Site: lantermanfoundation.org
Founded: 1993.
Key Personnel: Exec. Dir., Melissa Patton; Pres. (V), Joe Thompson.
Personnel Profile: Part-Time Paid 2; Part-Time Volunteers 68; Interns 2.
Governing Authority: Parent Institution: City of La Canada Flintridge. Tax-exempt.
Historic House: c.1915.
Collections: period furnishings; hand-painted wall & ceiling ornamentation; personal artifacts; medical equipment.
Research Fields: local history; CA political history; 20th-century music; arts and crafts architecture & decorative arts.
Facilities: archive.
Activities: lectures; period events; member tours.
Hours & Admission Prices: Sept.-July Tues., Thurs., 1st & 3rd Sun. of month 1-4. Adults $3, students 12-18 $1; discounts to AAM members; children under 12 no charge. Closed holidays. ♿
Attendance: 2,000 (accurate)
Membership: Sponsor $35; Sustainer $60; Associate $100; Benefactor $250; Life $1,000.

La Habra

CHILDREN'S MUSEUM AT LA HABRA, 301 S. Euclid, La Habra, CA 90631-5412. Tel.: 562-905-9693 & 9793. Fax: 562-905-9698.
E-mail: museumstaff@lahabra
Web Site: www.lhcm.org
Founded: 1977.
Congressional District: 39
Key Personnel: Museum Dir., Kimberly Albarian; Administrative Asst., Richard Williams; Outreach Program Coord., Cristy Watkins; Bilingual Programs Mgr., Maria Tinaiero Dowdle; Bilingual Coord., Cynthia Estay; Tour Leader, Dorothy Fite; Exhibits Coord., Lisa Reckon; Tour Guide, Patrice Sorokin; Receptionist, Charlene Underwood; Floor Supvr., Laura Venegas; Education Programs Coord., Jane Ivory; Sec., Yolanda Flores; Cur., April Morales; Museum Shop Mgr., Virginia Wyckoff.
Personnel Profile: Full-Time Paid 6; Full-Time Volunteers 1; Part-Time Paid 9; Part-Time Volunteers 150; Interns 6.
Governing Authority: municipal; nonprofit organization. Parent Institution: City of La Habra, CA. Subsidiary Institution: Friends of the Children's Museum. Tax-exempt: 170(b)(1)(A); 509(A)(1); 501(c)(3).
Children's Museum: housed in a renovated 1923 Mission Style Union Pacific Railroad Depot.
Collections: local historical artifacts; taxidermied local animals; exhibits cover scientific, cultural & historical topics; fullsize railroad cars; live bee observatory; gems; minerals; model train village; railroad cars; children's art; Dentzel carousel; toys; dolls; theatre costumes & props; physical science exhibits; infant & toddler exhibits; transportation; dinosaur fossils; stuffee health program.
Research Fields: local history.
Facilities: permanent & temporary exhibits; multipurpose room; classroom. Gift items for sale.
Activities: arts festivals; craft workshops; art camp; hospital visits; docent program or council; permanent & temporary exhibitions; special exhibit events; outreach programs; birthday parties.
Publications: Kid's Guide to La Habra; La Habra: The Good Old Days and the Way It Was; A Bell in the Barranca; quarterly newsletter.
Hours & Admission Prices: Tues.-Fri. 10-4, Sat. 10-5, Sun. 1-5. Adults $7, La Habra residents $6; discount to ASTC members; children under 2 & members no charge. Closed national holidays. ♿
Attendance: 100,000 (accurate)
Membership: Family $45.

La Jolla

BIRCH AQUARIUM AT SCRIPPS, SCRIPPS INSTITUTION OF OCEANOGRAPHY, UNIVERSITY OF CALIFORNIA, SAN DIEGO, 2300 Expedition Way, La Jolla, CA 92037. Mailing Address: 9500 Gilman Dr., #0207, La Jolla, CA 92093-0207. Tel.: 858-534-5301. Fax: 858-534-7114.
E-mail: heiock@ucsd.edu
Web Site: aquarium.ucsd.edu
Founded: 1905.
Congressional District: 41
Key Personnel: Exec. Dir., Nigella Hillgarth, Ph.D.; Cur. Aquarium, Robert Burhans; Mgr. Mktg., Lydia Cobb; Head Facilities, Mick Curzon; Dir. Operations, Pat Helbling; Dir. Education, Kristin Evans; Dir. Special Events, Barbara Ramsey; Mgr. Membership, Paula Smith; Mgr. Finance, Ken Steitz; Mgr. Museum Shop, Susan Malk; Mgr. Exhibits, Charles Langsett; Program Scientist, Cheryl Peach; Program Scientist, Debbie Zmarzly.
Personnel Profile: Full-Time Paid 54; Part-Time Volunteers 302.
Governing Authority: university. Parent Institutions: Scripps Institution of Oceanography (SIO), University of Calif., San Diego (UCSD). Tax-exempt.
Aquarium-Museum.
Collections: living, pacific marine life; Scripps research.
Research Fields: aquaculture; fish diseases.
Facilities: 11,000 sq. ft. aquarium; education center; seawater system; 6,000 sq. ft. exhibit court; 4,500 sq. ft. Tidepool Plaza; service areas. Museum-related items for sale.
Activities: guided tours; lectures; films; formally organized educational programs; docent programs; permanent & traveling exhibitions; career experience program for high school students; special events.
Publications: quarterly members newsletter, OnBoard; education materials; monthly e-newsletter, Explorations.
Hours & Admission Prices: Daily 9-5. Adults $11, seniors 60 & over $9, college students with ID & youth 3-12 $7.50; children under 2 & members no charge. ♿
Attendance: 400,000 (estimated)
Membership: Scripps Oceanographic Society: Individual $55; Dual $68; Family $75; Adopt-a-Fish $100-$1,000; Supporting $100 & up; Voyager $150 & up; Discovery $300 & up; Expedition $600 & up.

JAMES S. COPLEY LIBRARY, 1134 Kline St., La Jolla, CA 92037-4565. Mailing Address: P.O. Box 1530, La Jolla, CA 92038-1530. Tel.: 858-454-0411. Fax: 858-729-8051.
E-mail: ron.vanderhye@copleypress.com
Founded: 1966.
Congressional District: 41
Key Personnel: Registrar & Mgr., Carol Beales; OCLC, Ronald Vanderhye; Restoration & Conservation, Harold Kopelke; Consultant, Richard Reilly.
Personnel Profile: Full-Time Paid 3.
Governing Authority: company organized for profit. Parent Institution: Copley Newspapers.
Library.
Collections: presidential letters; fine press books; Benito Juarez collection; John Charles Fremont; American Revolutionary War manuscripts and 1st edition books; various books & letters from Samuel Langhorne Clemens and Robinson Jeffers and other American authors & artists.
Research Fields: American Revolutionary War; Samuel Clemens; John Charles Fremont expeditions.
Facilities: 2,000-vol. library of American Revolution material, including 300 books and letters of Samuel Clemens available to the public on premises only; 440 sq. ft. exhibition space; educational facilities.
Activities: guided tours; lectures; participatory & temporary exhibitions.
Hours & Admission Prices: Mon.-Fri. 10-12 & 1-3. No charge. Closed New Year's Day; Memorial Day; Independence Day; Labor Day; Thanksgiving and day after; Christmas Day. ♿
Attendance: 4,000 (estimated)

LA JOLLA HISTORICAL SOCIETY, (M), 7846 Eads Ave., La Jolla, CA 92037-4211. Tel.: 858-459-5335.
Personnel Profile: Full-Time Paid 2; Part-Time Paid 2; Part-Time Volunteers 100; Interns 2.
Governing Authority: Tax-exempt.
Historical Society Museum.
Collections: local history & heritage; photographs; period artifacts. Historic House: Wisteria Cottage.
Activities: educational programs.
Publications: Historic La Jolla Walking Tour.
Hours & Admission Prices: Mon.-Fri. 10-4 by appointment.
Membership: $50; $100; $250; $500; $1,000; $5,000.

* **MUSEUM OF CONTEMPORARY ART SAN DIEGO, (M),** 700 Prospect St., La Jolla, CA 92037-4291. Tel.: 858-454-3541. Fax: 858-454-6985.
E-mail: info@mcasd.org
Web Site: www.mcasd.org
Founded: 1941.
Congressional District: 43
Key Personnel: Dir., Hugh M. Davies; Pres. Bd. Trustees, Dr. Peter C. Farrell; Vice Pres., David C. Copley; Vice Pres., Maryanne Pfister; Vice Pres., Matthew Strauss; Deputy Dir., Charles E. Castle; Dir. External Affairs, Anne Farrell; Chief Advancement Officer, Jeanna Yoo; Dir. Devel., Cynthia Tuomi; Sr. Cur., Stephanie Hanor; Dir. Communications, Denise Montgomery; Registrar, Anne Marie Purkey Levine; Museum Store Mgr., Monique Fuentes.
Personnel Profile: Full-Time Paid 43; Part-Time Paid 40; Part-Time Volunteers 105; Interns 6.
Governing Authority: nonprofit organization. Additional Location: MCASD Downtown, 1001 & 1100 Kettner Blvd., San Diego, CA 92101. Tax-exempt: 501(c)(3).
Art Museum.
Collections: contemporary art including paintings, sculptures, drawings & prints; photography; video art; installation.
Major Exhibits: Automatic Cities: The Architectural Imaginary in Contemporary Art, 11/09-1/10; Museums in Miniature: Works by Marcel Duchamp and Joseph Cornell, 11/09-1/10; Collectors XXV, 2/10-5/10; Here Not There, 5/10-9/10; Kim MacConnell, 10/10-1/11.
Research Fields: contemporary art.
Facilities: 14,300 sq. ft. exhibit space; 500-seat auditorium; 31,000 sq. ft. outdoor sculpture garden; cafe. Museum-related items for sale.
Activities: lectures; films; seminars; gallery talks; educational programs; concerts; inter-museum loans, temporary & traveling exhibitions.
Publications: quarterly newsletter with calendar of events; exhibition catalogs; educational brochures; membership brochure; general information brochure.
Hours & Admission Prices: Thurs.-Tues. 11-5, third Thurs. of month 11-7. Adults $10, senior citizens & military $5; discounts to AAM & ICOM members; 25 & under and members no charge. Admission valid for 7 days at all MCASD locations. Closed New Year's Day; Thanksgiving; Christmas. ♿
Attendance: 168,000 (estimated)
Membership: Artist & Student $35; Active $75; Contributor $150; Patron $300; Donor $600-$1,499; Benefactor $1,500-$2,499; stART Up $2,500; Contemporary Collectors $5,000; International Collectors $10,000. Corporate Members: $1,500 & up.

STUART COLLECTION, University of California, San Diego-0010, 105 Pepper Canyon Hall, La Jolla, CA 92093-0001. Mailing Address: UCSD 0010, 9500 Gilman Dr., La Jolla, CA 92093-0001. Tel.: 858-534-2117. Fax: 858-534-9713.
E-mail: mbeebe@ucsd.edu
Web Site: stuartcollection.ucsd.edu
Founded: 1981.
Congressional District: 49
Key Personnel: Dir., Mary L. Beebe; Projects Mgr., Mathieu Gregoire; Office Mgr., Jane Peterson.
Personnel Profile: Full-Time Paid 2; Part-Time Paid 1; Part-Time Volunteers 3.
Governing Authority: public university. Parent Institution: UCSD. Tax-exempt.
University Art Collection.
Collections: 17 contemporary outdoor commissioned sculpture throughout 1,200-acre campus.
Facilities: 2,000-vol. library of catalogues & books available to public by appointment.
Activities: guided tours; lectures; study clubs; temporary exhibitions.
Publications: brochure; map; book, Landmarks: Sculpture Commissions for the Stuart Collection at the University of California, San Diego, 2001.
Hours & Admission Prices: Daily 24 hours. No charge; donations accepted. ♿
Membership: Friends of the Stuart Collection $1,500.

UNIVERSITY ART GALLERY, UNIVERSITY OF CALIFORNIA, SAN DIEGO, 9500 Gilman Dr., La Jolla, CA 92093-5004. Tel.: 858-534-2107. Fax: 858-822-3548.
E-mail: uag@ucsd.edu
Web Site: uag.ucsd.edu
Founded: 1974.
Congressional District: 41
Key Personnel: Coord. Exhibitions, Isabelle Lutterodt; Cur., Stephen Hepworth.
Personnel Profile: Full-Time Paid 2; Part-Time Paid 2; Part-Time Volunteers 10.
Governing Authority: public university. Parent Institution: University of California, San Diego. Subsidiary Institution: Department of Visual Arts.
University Art Gallery.
Collections: paintings; photographs; sculpture.
Research Fields: contemporary art.
Activities: receptions; members' art tours; graduate student studio tours.
Publications: exhibition catalogs.
Hours & Admission Prices: Tues.-Sat. 11-5. No charge. ♿
Attendance: 15,000 (estimated)

VILLAGE GALLERY, 8100 Pasea Del Ocaso, Ste. B, La Jolla, CA 92037-3115. Tel.: 858-459-1196.
Web Site: www.lajollaart.org
Key Personnel: Gallery Dir., Gwen Nobil; Dir. Exhibitions, Carrie Barton
Art Museum.
Collections: paintings; drawings; sculptures; photography.
Activities: lectures; docent tours; demonstrations.
Hours & Admission Prices: Daily 11-5. No charge.

La Mesa

HORSELESS CARRIAGE FOUNDATION & AUTOMOTIVE RESEARCH LIBRARY, 8186 Center St., Ste. F, La Mesa, CA 91942-2959. Mailing Address: P.O. Box 369, La Mesa, CA 91944-0369. Tel.: 619-464-0301. Fax: 619-464-0301.
E-mail: research@hcfi.org
Web Site: www.hcfi.org
Founded: 1984.
Key Personnel: C.E.O. & Pres. (V), Donald Sable, II; Chm. (V) & Archivist, Jack Garrison; Pres. (V) & Devel., Greg Long; Exec. Dir., Roberta Watkins; Treas., Thomas E. Kettenburg; Public Rels., Reid Carroll.
Personnel Profile: Full-Time Paid 1; Part-Time Paid 4; Part-Time Volunteers 9.
Governing Authority: board of directors; nonprofit. Tax-exempt: 501(c)(3).
Research Library.
Collections: automotive literature from 1895-1943 which includes factory sales catalogs & operation manuals; technical data.
Research Fields: technological research related to specific makes of automobiles for private individuals, museums, historical societies, the media & academic researchers, some of which are foreign clients in 35 countries.
Facilities: 18,400-vol. library; reading room; research facility.
Activities: education programs for children; guided tours; lectures; childrens' car rides; elementary school show. Annual Events: general meeting; Annual Reception in February; Director's Reception; Patron's Reception.
Publications: quarterly, H.C.F. Research Library Newsletter.
Hours & Admission Prices: Jan. to mid-Dec. Tues.-Fri. 10-4. No charge; donations accepted. Closed major holidays. ♿
Attendance: 100 (estimated)
Membership: Patron $35; Century $100; Benefactor $250; Life $5,000.

La Puente

LA PUENTE VALLEY HISTORICAL SOCIETY, INC., 15900 E. Main St., La Puente, CA 91744-4719. Mailing Address: P.O. Box 522, La Puente, CA 91747-0522. Tel.: 626-855-1500. Fax: 626-855-4626.
Founded: 1960.
Congressional District: 34
Key Personnel: Pres., Patricia McIntosh; Vice Pres., C. Wictor; Sec., Heather Barron; Treas., John C. Butler.
Personnel Profile: Part-Time Volunteers 30.
Local History Museum.
Collections: furniture & belongings of the Rowland family & early La Puente Valley families; Indian artifacts & early ranch items; local history.
Research Fields: La Puente Valley history.
Facilities: 200-vol. library of general & California history, available on premises by appointment.
Activities: guided tours; school tours; slide shows; docent program.
Publications: bimonthly newsletter, The Bridge; book, La Puente Kaleidoscope Part I & Part II; Footsteps to the Past; booklet, John Rowland; brochure, La Puente Historic Points of Interest.
Hours & Admission Prices: Rowland & Dibble Museum: by appointment. Heritage Room: Thurs. 1-4. No charge; donations accepted. Closed holidays. ♿
Attendance: 1,900 (estimated)
Membership: General $10; Life $100.

Laguna Beach

LAGUNA ART MUSEUM, (M), 307 Cliff Dr., Laguna Beach, CA 92651-1696. Tel.: 949-494-8971. Fax: 949-494-1530.
E-mail: director@lagunaartmuseum.org
Web Site: www.lagunaartmuseum.org

Founded: 1996.
Key Personnel: Dir., Bolton Colburn; Museum Shop Mgr., Mike Stice.
Governing Authority: private; nonprofit organization. Tax-exempt.
Art Museum.
Collections: sculptures; paintings.
Research Fields: California Art 1900 to present.
Facilities: library; rental facilities. Museum-related items for sale.
Activities: art auctions; lecture panels; film screenings; plein air painting invitational.
Publications: newsletter; exhibition books & catalogs; members' magazine.
Hours & Admission Prices: Daily 11-5. Adults $10, senior citizens & students $8; children under 12 no charge. ♿
Attendance: 50,000 (accurate)
Membership: Student $25; Individual $60; Family $75; Friend $125; Contributor $250; Patron $500.

Lake Arrowhead

MOUNTAIN SKIES ASTRONOMICAL SOCIETY & SCIENCE CENTER, 2001 Observatory Way, Lake Arrowhead, CA 92352. Mailing Address: P.O. Box 1169, Lake Arrowhead, CA 92352-1169. Tel.: 909-336-1699.
E-mail: stargazersmail@mountain-skies.org
Web Site: www.mountain-skies.org
Founded: 1989.
Key Personnel: Pres. & Chm., Dr. Lorann Parker, D.Sc., Ph.D.
Science Center & Observatory.
Collections: hands-on exhibit; Solar System models; tools; photographs and memorabilia (historical).
Facilities: library. Museum-related items for sale.
Activities: public programs; private group programs; special events.
Hours & Admission Prices: Thurs.-Tues. 10-3. Donations accepted. Sat. night programs open to public. At door $9, advance $7. Call for information. ♿
Membership: Classroom $15; Student $20; Senior $25; Single $30; Family $40; Business $80; Life $500.

Lakeport

LAKE COUNTY HISTORIC COURTHOUSE MUSEUM, (M), 255 N. Main St., Lakeport, CA 95453. Mailing Address: 255 N. Forbes St., Lakeport, CA 95453-4790. Tel.: 707-263-4555. Fax: 707-263-7918.
E-mail: museum@co.lake.ca.us
Web Site: www.lakecounty.com/things/museums.html
Formerly: Lake County Museum
Founded: 1936.
Personnel Profile: Part-Time Paid 4; Part-Time Volunteers 1; Interns 1.
Governing Authority: county. Owned & operated by the County of Lake. Tax-exempt.
History Museum: housed in 1871 Lake County Courthouse.
Collections: Pomo baskets; Native American tools; projectile points; groundstone; minerals & gems found in the county; clothing & artifacts from the 1800s & 1900s. Genealogical & research library with reference books; a 10,000 page manuscript by Henry Mauldin on local history; photographs & family histories.
Research Fields: local history.
Facilities: research library of local history books.
Activities: genealogy society; docent program.
Publications: quarterly newsletter, The Muse; Legend of Moon Tear; Pomo Legend Coloring Book.
Hours & Admission Prices: Sun. 12-4, Wed.-Sat. 10-4. No charge; donations accepted. Closed most holidays. ♿
Attendance: 6,000 (accurate)
Membership: Individual $15; Friend $25; Sponsor $50; Steward $100; Patron $250; Benefactor $500.

Lakeside

BARONA CULTURAL CENTER AND MUSEUM, (M), 1095 Barona Rd., Lakeside, CA 92040-1541. Tel.: 619-443-7003, ext. 2. Fax: 619-443-0173.
E-mail: museum@baronmuseum.org
Web Site: www.baronamuseum.org
Key Personnel: Dir. & Cur., Cheryl Hinton; Chm., Phyllis Van WanSeele; Gift Shop Coord., Robin Edmonds
History Museum.
Collections: Native American culture & history; photographs; basketry; pottery making; stone tools.
Hours & Admission Prices: Tues.-Fri. 12-5, Sat. 10-4. No charge.

Lancaster

ANTELOPE VALLEY CALIFORNIA POPPY NATURAL RESERVE, 15101 W. Lancaster Rd., Lancaster, CA 93536-9733. Mailing Address: 43779 15th St., W., Lancaster, CA 93534-4754. Tel.: 661-942-0662 & 724-1180 (reserve). Fax: 661-940-7327.
E-mail: mdic@parks.ca.gov
Web Site: www.parks.ca.gov
Founded: 1982.
Congressional District: 20
Key Personnel: District Supt., Ron Krueper; Pres. (V), Milt Starck; Museum Shop Mgr., Pat Treadwell.
Personnel Profile: Full-Time Paid 1; Part-Time Paid 4; Part-Time Volunteers 30.
Governing Authority: state. Parent Institution: California Dept. of Parks & Recreation, Mojave Sector, Tehachap District, 43779 15th St. W., Lancaster, CA 93534. Subsidiary Institution: Poppy Reserve Interpretive Center. Tax-exempt: 501(c)(3).
Nature Center.
Collections: nature exhibits; 155 Jane S. Pinheiro wildflower watercolor paintings.
Research Fields: wildflowers; poppies.
Facilities: nature & conservation center; 8 mile hiking trails; picnic area. Park-related items for sale.
Activities: guided tours; docent program; permanent exhibitions; school programs.
Publications: pamphlet.
Hours & Admission Prices: Visitor Center: call for hours. mid-March to mid-May $5 per vehicle, senior citizens (62 & above) $4; mid-May to mid-March $2 per car, seniors $1.
Attendance: 70,000 (accurate)
Membership: Poppy Reserve/Mojave Desert Interpretive Association: Full-time Student $5; Regular $10; Sustaining & Family $15; Organization & Patron $30; Lifetime $1,000.

ANTELOPE VALLEY INDIAN MUSEUM, 15701 E. Ave. M, Lancaster, CA 93535-7059. Mailing Address: 43779 15th St. West, Lancaster, CA 93534-4754. Tel.: 661-946-3055 & 6900. Fax: 661-946-6116.
E-mail: pronning@parks.ca.gov
Web Site: www.avim.parks.ca.gov
Founded: 1928.
Congressional District: 20
Key Personnel: Cur., Peggy Ronning; Coop. Assoc. & Museum Shop Mgr., Mary Shoemaker.
Personnel Profile: Full-Time Paid 1; Part-Time Paid 1; Part-Time Volunteers 39.
Governing Authority: state. Parent Institution: California State Dept. of Parks & Recreation, Tehachapi District, Mojave Sector, 43779 15th St. W., Lancaster, CA 93534-4754; Friends of Antelope Valley Indian Museum Cooperative Association. Tax-exempt: 501(c)(3).
American Indian Cultural Museum.
Collections: artifacts from California, the Great Basin & the Southwest; Sea Grass Weavings; Kachina Dolls; regional American Indian items & implements; rugs; blankets; pottery; murals, paintings & portraits by Edwards & other artists; American Indian art.
Research Fields: American Indian culture groups Californian, Western Great Basin, Southwestern region; prehistoric & ethnographic.
Facilities: library; 3,000 sq. ft. exhibit space; nature trail; picnic area. Museum-related items for sale.
Activities: guided & self-guided tours; docent program; permanent & temporary exhibitions; guest artists; touch table. Museum Sponsors: American Indian educational demonstrations; workshops; occasional ceremonial & vendor events.
Publications: brochures, Nature Trail Guide; booklet, American Indian Peoples of the Antelope Valley, Western Mojave Desert, CA: 12,000 Years of Culture & History.
Hours & Admission Prices: Closed until spring 2010. ♿
Attendance: 9,000 (estimated)
Membership: FAVIM: Individual $10; Family $15; Organization $25; Patron $50; Life $200.

LANCASTER MUSEUM/ART GALLERY, (M), 44801 N. Sierra Hwy., Lancaster, CA 93534-3226. Mailing Address: 44933 N. Fern Ave., Lancaster, CA 93534-2461. Tel.: 661-723-6250. Fax: 661-948-1322.
E-mail: njwest@cityoflancasterca.org
Web Site: www.cityoflancasterca.org
Founded: 1984.
Congressional District: 20
Key Personnel: Dir. Parks, Recreation & Arts, Bob Greene; Cur., Nicholas West.

Personnel Profile: Full-Time Paid 2; Part-Time Paid 6.
Governing Authority: municipal government. Parent Institution: City of Lancaster. Tax-exempt.
Art & History Museum.
Collections: Lancaster history; Native American artifacts; photographs; historical documents; paintings; works on paper.
Research Fields: local history; art history.
Facilities: 100-vol. library of local history. Museum-related items for sale.
Activities: guided tours; lectures; organized educational programs.
Publications: Exhibition Catalogues.
Hours & Admission Prices: Tues.-Sat. 11-4. Suggested Donation: $2. Closed New Year's Day; Easter; Memorial Day; Independence Day; Labor Day; Thanksgiving; Christmas. ♿
Attendance: 20,000 (estimated)

WESTERN HOTEL/MUSEUM, 557 W. Lancaster Blvd., Lancaster, CA 93534-2533. Mailing Address: 44933 N. Fern Ave., Lancaster, CA 93534-2461. Tel.: 661-723-6250. Fax: 661-948-1322.
E-mail: lmagreceptionist@cityoflancasterca.org
Web Site: www.cityoflancasterca.org/index.aspx?page=69
Key Personnel: Cur., Nicholas West.
Personnel Profile: Full-Time Paid 2; Part-Time Paid 3.
Governing Authority: municipal. Parent Institution: City of Lancaster. Tax-exempt.
History Museum: c.1880s hotel.
Collections: local Antelope Valley Native American & pioneer history artifacts; clothing; photographs; furniture.
Research Fields: local history; anthropology.
Activities: educational programs; guided tours; outdoor events.
Hours & Admission Prices: 2nd & 4th Fri.-Sat. 11-4. No charge. Closed holidays.

Larkspur

SCHWARTZ COLLECTION OF SKIING HERITAGE, 761 Old Quarry Rd. S., Larkspur, CA 94939-2200. Tel.: 415-435-1076. Fax: 415-435-5027.
E-mail: info@picturesnow.com
Founded: 1986.
Key Personnel: C.E.O., Gary Schwartz; Cur., Rhoda Valowitz; Archivist & Registrar, Dorte Larsen; Public Rels., Gabrielle Disario.
Personnel Profile: Full-Time Volunteers 4; Part-Time Volunteers 1.
Governing Authority: private; nonprofit.
Sports Museum.
Collections: historic snow skiing artwork & communication artifacts; photographs; advertising illustrations; posters.
Research Fields: bibliography of all known English language books about skiing; compilation of all known general release films containing skiing scenes; compilation of historic material from America's first major ski resort, Sun Valley, Idaho.
Facilities: 3,000-vol. library of historic skiing books & periodicals covering the 16th century to the present; field research station.
Activities: loan exhibition.
Hours & Admission Prices: By appointment only. No charge. ♿
Attendance: 100 (estimated)

Lebec

FORT TEJON STATE HISTORIC PARK, 4201 Fort Tejon Rd., Lebec, CA 93243. Mailing Address: P.O. Box 895, Lebec, CA 93243-0895. Tel.: 661-248-6692. Fax: 661-248-8373.
Web Site: www.parks.ca.gov
Founded: 1939.
Congressional District: 18
Key Personnel: Park Supt., Stephen Bylin; Interpreter, Sean T. Malis.
Personnel Profile: Full-Time Paid 2; Part-Time Paid 3; Part-Time Volunteers 600.
Governing Authority: state. Parent Institution: California Dept. of Parks & Recreation, P.O. Box 942896 Sacramento, CA 94296-0001.
State Historic Park: site of 1854-64 U.S. Army fort.
Collections: interpretive collections.
Facilities: visitor center; picnic area; group camp.
Activities: permanent exhibitions; guided tours. Museum Sponsors: Civil War reenactments; Dragoon Era Living History Program; California Volunteer Living History Program.
Publications: brochure.
Hours & Admission Prices: Call for hours. Park: adults $2; children 16 & under no charge. Special Events: adults $5, children $3. Closed New Year's Day; Thanksgiving; Christmas. ♿
Attendance: 85,000 (estimated)
Membership: Fort Tejon Historical Association: Individual $20; Family $30.

Lemoore

SARAH A. MOONEY MEMORIAL MUSEUM, 542 W. 'D' St., Lemoore, CA 93245. Mailing Address: P.O. Box 413, Lemoore, CA 93245-0413. Tel.: 559-925-0321.
Web Site: www.lemoore.com/sammm.htm
Personnel Profile: Part-Time Volunteers 20.
Governing Authority: bd. of directors.
Historic House Museum: built in 1893.
Collections: period furnishings; clothing; personal artifacts; office equipment.
Hours & Admission Prices: No charge; donations accepted.

Lodi

MICKE GROVE ZOO, 11793 N. Micke Grove Rd., Lodi, CA 95240-9426. Tel.: 209-331-7270. Fax: 209-331-7271.
E-mail: parks@sjgov.org
Web Site: www.mgzoo.com
Founded: 1957.
Congressional District: 14
Key Personnel: C.E.O. & Zoo Mgr., Kenneth C. Nieland; Chm. (V), Claude Brown; Gen. Cur., Matt McKim; Purchasing. Supt., Arthur Head; Museum Shop Mgr., Judy Kaszer.
Personnel Profile: Full-Time Paid 10; Part-Time Paid 8; Part-Time Volunteers 65.
Governing Authority: county. Parent Institution: San Joaquin County. Tax-exempt.
Zoo.
Collections: birds, primates & carnivores representing 80 species & 160 individuals.
Research Fields: behavioral animal research.
Facilities: 150-vol. library of zoology reference materials available for staff use & to public on special request; zoological park; auditorium.
Activities: guided tours; lectures; formally organized education programs for children; docent program or council; permanent exhibitions.
Publications: bimonthly newsletter, Paw Prints; Micke Grove Zoo News.
Hours & Admission Prices: May-Sept. Mon.-Fri. 10-5, Sat.-Sun. 10-6; Oct.-April Mon daily 10-5. Adults & senior citizens $2, children $1; children under 2 no charge. Parking fee; weekdays $2 per car, weekends $4 per car. Closed Christmas. ♿
Attendance: 200,000 (estimated)
Membership: Individual $15; Senior & Student $20; Dual $35; Family $45; Life $200.

* **SAN JOAQUIN COUNTY HISTORICAL SOCIETY & MUSEUM, (M),** 11793 N. Micke Grove Rd., Lodi, CA 95240-9426. Mailing Address: P.O. Box 30, Lodi, CA 95241-0030. Tel.: 209-331-2055. Fax: 209-331-2057.
E-mail: info@sanjoaquinhistory.org
Web Site: www.sanjoaquinhistory.org
Founded: 1966.
Congressional District: 14
Key Personnel: Exec. Dir., David R. Stuart; Pres. (V), Dee Anne Gillick; Collections & Exhibits Mgr., Julie Blood; Mgr. Education & Visitors Svcs. and Museum Shop Mgr., Robin Wood; Archivist, Leigh Johnsen; Administrative Mgr., Ute Gampp; Bookkeeper, Judy Rodman; Maintenance Supvr., Mike Mason.
Personnel Profile: Full-Time Paid 4; Part-Time Paid 7; Part-Time Volunteers 130.
Governing Authority: society; county; nonprofit organization. Parent Institution: San Joaquin County Historical Society Affiliated with San Joaquin County Historical Museum. Tax-exempt: 501(c)(3).
Regional History Museum.
Collections: Floyd J. Locher tool collection; anthropology; agricultural tools & implements; transportation; textiles & costumes; Crawler & wheeled tractors; trucks; Joseph Tope & C. Gregory Crampton, California & Southern mines collections; local history; county historical documents; Charles M. Weber collection; grape, wine, fruit & nut industries; vineyard.
Major Exhibits: Past Tents: The Way We Camped (T), 8/15/10-12/17/10.
Research Fields: agricultural development; early American hand tools; cultural & ethnic groups in county.
Facilities: over 5,000-vol. library of history & maps; botanical garden of native California flora; county archives.
Activities: guided tours; craft demonstrations; summer museum youth camp; agriculture demonstrations; student environmental living program.
Publications: The Harness Maker & His Tools; William George Micke; Man of the Soil; Chinese Clothing & Theatrical Costumes; The Heritage of Claude H. Erickson; Charles M. Weber, Founder of Stockton, San Joaquin Historian, News & Notes; Land of Bright Promise; On The Road Again: Final Journey of Julia Weber Home; Visiting Our County Museum.
Hours & Admission Prices: Summer: Wed.-Sun. 10-5; Winter: Wed.-Sun. 11-4;

guided tours by appointment. Adults $5, senior citizens & teens $4, children 6-12 $2; San Joaquin County Historical Society members no charge. Closed New Year's Day; Independence Day; Thanksgiving & day after; Christmas Eve & Day. ♿
Attendance: 50,000 (estimated)
Membership: Individual & Family $35; Business $50; Sponsor $100; Patron $250; Sustainer $500; Benefactor $1,000.

Loleta

WIYOT HERITAGE CENTER, 1000 Wiyot Dr., Loleta, CA 95551. Tel.: 707-733-5055; 800-388-7633. Fax: 707-733-5601.
Key Personnel: Cultural Dir., Helene Rouvier
Heritage Center.
Collections: Wiyot culture & history; photographs; personal artifacts.
Activities: special events; educational programs.
Hours & Admission Prices: Mon.-Fri. 8-5. Closed holidays.

Lomita

LOMITA RAILROAD MUSEUM, 2137 W. 250th St., Lomita, CA 90717-2217. Mailing Address: P.O. Box 339, Lomita, CA 90717-0339. Tel.: 310-326-6255.
E-mail: m.martinez@lomita.com
Web Site: www.lomita-rr.org
Key Personnel: Mgr., Faith Bilyeu; Cur., Alice Abbott
Railroad Museum.
Collections: railroad artifacts; Southern Pacific Railroad steam locomotive; Union Pacific caboose.
Hours & Admission Prices: Thurs.-Sun. 10-5. Adults $4, children under 12 $2. Closed Thanksgiving; Christmas.

Lompoc

LA PURISIMA MISSION STATE HISTORIC PARK, 2295 Purisima Rd., Lompoc, CA 93436-9647. Tel.: 805-733-3713. Fax: 805-733-2497.
E-mail: lpminfo@parks.ca.gov
Web Site: www.lapurisimamission.org
Founded: 1935.
Congressional District: 19
Key Personnel: Chm. (V), Robert Wilson; Museum Shop Mgr., Audrey Bowman.
Personnel Profile: Full-Time Paid 8; Part-Time Paid 7; Part-Time Volunteers 95.
Governing Authority: state. California Dept. of Parks & Recreation.
History Museum: housed in 1813-1821 restored adobe buildings.
Collections: 1787-1834 Mission period artifacts from local sites; documentary records; translations; data on architectural studies during restoration of 1934-41. Historic Building: 1934-41 Civilian Conservation Corps.
Research Fields: mission history; contemporary restoration c.1935-1941.
Facilities: 200-vol. library of books on history of California Missions, 1787-1834 natural history & interpretive materials, available for use by reservation; mission livestock display; botanical garden.
Activities: guided tours; mission craft demonstrations; self guided tours; living history events.
Publications: booklet, J.H. Engbeck La Purisima Mission State Historic Park.
Hours & Admission Prices: Daily 9-5. $4 per vehicle. Closed New Year's Day; Thanksgiving; Christmas. ♿
Attendance: 200,000 (accurate)
Membership: Active Docent $3; Associate $10; Supporting $25; Business $100.

LOMPOC MUSEUM, (M), 200 S. H St., Lompoc, CA 93436-7297. Tel.: 805-736-3888. Fax: 805-736-2840.
E-mail: lompocmuseum@verizon.net
Web Site: www.lompocmuseum.org
Founded: 1969.
Congressional District: 19
Key Personnel: Dir. & Cur. Anthropology, Dr. Lisa Renken; Pres., Theodore Suchecki; Administrative Asst., Angie Pasquini.
Personnel Profile: Part-Time Paid 2; Part-Time Volunteers 22.
Governing Authority: society; board of trustees; nonprofit organization. Lompoc Museum Associates, Inc. Tax-exempt: 501(c)(3).
Anthropology Museum: housed in 1910 Carnegie Library Building.
Collections: Chumash Indian artifacts; natural history & wildlife exhibits; mining & uses of Diatomaceous Earth; historical articles relating to the human development & customs of the area.
Research Fields: local archaeology; local history.
Activities: guided tours; films; lectures; gallery talks; permanent & temporary exhibitions; demonstrations.
Publications: newsletter 3 times a year, Galleries.
Hours & Admission Prices: Tues.-Fri. 1-5, Sat.-Sun. 1-4. Donation Requested: adults $1; children no charge. Closed New Year's Day; Easter; Thanksgiving; Christmas.
Attendance: 3,645 (accurate)
Membership: Single $20; Family $25; Sustaining $50; Business & Group $150; Life $500.

LOMPOC VALLEY HISTORICAL SOCIETY, INC., 207 N. L St., Lompoc, CA 93436-5901. Mailing Address: P.O. Box 88, Lompoc, CA 93438-0088. Tel.: 805-735-4626.
E-mail: myra@best1.net
Web Site: lompochistory.org
Founded: 1964.
Congressional District: 19
Key Personnel: Pres., Dennis Headrick; 1st Vice Pres., Oscar Cook; Corresponding Sec., Beverly Preece; Recording Sec., Debbie Manfrina; Treas., Jeannette Miller Wynne.
Personnel Profile: Part-Time Volunteers 26.
Governing Authority: nonprofit organization. Tax-exempt.
Historical Society Museum: housed in 1875 Fabing-McKay-Spanne House.
Collections: clothing; house furnishings; farm implements; vehicles; photographs; Lompoc artifacts; blacksmith shop; carriage house.
Research Fields: genealogy; Lompoc history.
Facilities: reference & research historical library.
Activities: permanent & temporary exhibitions.
Publications: quarterly newsletter, Hodge Podge; quarterly bulletin, Lompoc Legacy.
Hours & Admission Prices: Mon. & Thurs. 8:30-11, 4th Sat. of month 10-2; special tours by appointment. No charge; donations accepted. Closed major holidays. ♿
Attendance: 500 (estimated)
Membership: Junior (under 18) $5; Single $25; Family $35; Patron $250; Life $250; Family Lifetime $350; Organization $500.

Lone Pine

THE BEVERLY & JIM ROGERS MUSEUM OF LONE PINE FILM HISTORY, U.S. 395, Lone Pine, CA 93543. Mailing Address: P.O. Box 111, Lone Pine, CA 93545-0111. Tel.: 760-876-9909.
E-mail: lonepinemovies@aol.com
Web Site: www.lonepinefilmhistorymuseum.org
History Museum.
Collections: props; costumes; still & moving images; movie memorabilia; period artifacts.
Activities: special events.
Hours & Admission Prices: Mon. & Wed.-Sun 10-4

Long Beach

AMERICAN MUSEUM OF STRAW ART, 2324 Snowden Ave., Long Beach, CA 90815-2234. Tel.: 562-431-3540. Fax: 562-598-0457.
E-mail: curator@strawartmuseum.org
Web Site: www.strawartmuseum.org
Founded: 1984.
Congressional District: 39
Key Personnel: Dir. & Cur., Morgyn Owens-Celli; Archivist, Carol Thompson; Devel., Bob McCashey.
Personnel Profile: Part-Time Paid 7; Interns 4.
Governing Authority: private; nonprofit organization. Parent Institution: American Foundation for the Straw Arts. Tax-exempt: 501(c)(3).
Decorative & Folk Art Museum.
Collections: concentration on decorative & folk arts in straw; 12 distinct categories including straw applique, coiled straw, straw hats & bonnets, straw plait and Swiss straw work.
Facilities: library; 1,400 sq. ft. exhibit space; educational facilities. Museum-related items for sale.
Activities: guided tours; workshops; lectures; loan & traveling exhibits; docent program; educational programs; broadcast programs. Annual Event: Festival Days.
Publications: quarterly magazine, The Straw Chronicles.
Hours & Admission Prices: Temporarily closed.
Membership: Annual $15; Friend of Museum $50; Contributing $60; Patron $250; Benefactor $1,000.

AQUARIUM OF THE PACIFIC, 100 Aquarium Way, Long Beach, CA 90802-8126. Tel.: 562-590-3100. Fax: 562-951-1629.
E-mail: aquariumofpacific@lbaop.org
Web Site: www.aquariumofpacific.org
Formerly: Long Beach Aquarium of the Pacific
Founded: 1998.

Key Personnel: Pres. & C.E.O., Jerry Schubel; Chm. (V), Mario Molina; Vice Pres. Finance & C.F.O., Vanessa Lewis; Vice Pres. Govt. Rels. & Special Projects and Corporate Sec., Barbara Long; Vice Pres. Devel., Jeanne Brodeur; Dir. Mktg., Cecile Fisher; Education, Amy Rosenberg; Vice Pres. Human Resources, Kathie Nirschl; Vice Pres. Devel., Rick Larkin; Facilities, Tom Vantress; Retail Operations Mgr., Jeff Spofford; Dir. Husbandry, Perry Hampton; Dir. Operations, John Rouse.
Personnel Profile: Full-Time Paid 200; Part-Time Volunteers 500.
Governing Authority: nonprofit organization. Tax-exempt.
Aquarium.
Collections: 12,500 marine animals representing 550 species.
Facilities: teacher resource center; restaurant; 170-seat auditorium. Gift items for sale.
Activities: shows; lectures; educational programs.
Publications: membership newsletter, Pacific Currents.
Hours & Admission Prices: Daily 9-6. Adults $22.95, seniors 62 & over $20.95, children 3-11 $11.95. ♿
Attendance: 1,400,000 (accurate)
Membership: Senior $45; Individual $55; Senior Couple $75; Dual $95; Family $125.

*** CALIFORNIA STATE UNIVERSITY, LONG BEACH, UNIVERSITY ART MUSEUM, (M),** 1250 Bellflower Blvd., Long Beach, CA 90840-0004. Tel.: 562-985-5761. Fax: 562-985-7602.
E-mail: kaplan@csulb.edu
Web Site: www.csulb.edu/uam
Founded: 1949.
Congressional District: 32
Key Personnel: Dir., Chris Scoates; Pres. (V), Michael Patrick Porter; Assoc. Dir., Ilee Kaplan; Cur. Education, Brian Trimble; Registrar & Cur. Collections, Angela Barker; Dir. Publications & Public Rels., Sarah G. Vinci.
Personnel Profile: Full-Time Paid 7; Part-Time Paid 18; Part-Time Volunteers 50.
Governing Authority: university; nonprofit. Parent Institution: California State University, Long Beach. Tax-exempt: 501(c)(3).
University Art Museum.
Collections: modern & contemporary works of art on paper; site-specific sculpture; the Gordon F. Hampton collection.
Research Fields: art history; museology & museography.
Facilities: library; reading room; auditorium; theatre; classrooms; restaurants on campus.
Activities: guided tours; lectures; films; gallery talks; formally organized education programs for adults, undergraduate & graduate students; training programs for museum professionals; inter-museum loan, temporary & traveling exhibitions; Certificate in Museum Studies given by the university recognizing the four semester training program in museology at the graduate level.
Publications: catalogues; brochures; newsletter.
Hours & Admission Prices: Sept.-May Tues.-Wed. & Fri. 12-5, Thurs. 12-8; Summer: Tues.-Sat. 12-5. Adults $4; discounts to AAM members; students & staff of CSULB and members no charge. Closed university holidays. ♿
Attendance: 60,000 (estimated)
Membership: CSULB Student $15; Faculty & Staff $25; Friend $35; Fellow $100; Partner $300; Contemporary Council $500; Benefactor $1,000.

EARL BURNS MILLER JAPANESE GARDEN, California State University Long Beach, Earl Warren Dr., Long Beach, CA 90840-0001. Mailing Address: California State University Long Beach, 1250 Bellflower Blvd., Long Beach, CA 90840-0001. Tel.: 562-985-5930 & 8889.
E-mail: jgcoordinators@csulb.edu
Web Site: www.csulb.edu/~jgarden
Founded: 1981.
Governing Authority: Parent Institution: California State University, Long Beach. Tax-exempt.
Japanese-style Garden.
Collections: bamboo; Japanese black pine; sculptures.
Publications: newsletter, The Lantern.
Hours & Admission Prices: Jan. 25-Dec. 16 Tues.-Fri. 8-3:30, Sun. 12-4; call to confirm; groups of 10 or more by appointment. Tours: no charge. Closed spring break; Independence Day; Thanksgiving & weekend after. ♿
Attendance: 60,000 (estimated)

EL DORADO NATURE CENTER, 7550 E. Spring St., Long Beach, CA 90815-1698. Tel.: 562-570-1745 & 1748. Fax: 562-570-8530.
Web Site: www.lbparks.org
Founded: 1969.
Congressional District: 38
Key Personnel: Co Dir. & Park Naturalist, Donnie Haigh; Co Dir. & Park Naturalist, Meaghan O'Neill.
Personnel Profile: Full-Time Paid 2; Part-Time Paid 20; Part-Time Volunteers 80; Interns 1.
Governing Authority: municipal. Parent Institution: City of Long Beach, Parks Recreation & Marine Dept. Tax-exempt.
Nature Center.
Collections: natural history of region.
Facilities: gallery; 102.5 acres with trails; one-quarter mile paved access trail. Museum-related items for sale.
Activities: guided tours; self-conducted tours; classes of various natural history & outdoor topics; school outreach - environmental & cultural; stewardship, service learning opportunity; focus on sustainability & interdependence.
Publications: volunteer newsletter, On the Trail.
Hours & Admission Prices: Trail: Tues.-Sun. 8-5. Museum: Tues.-Fri. 10-4, Sat.-Sun. 8:30-4. Parking: Mon.-Fri. $5 per car; Sat.-Sun. $7 per car, holidays $8 per car, school buses $27, commercial buses $32. Closed Christmas. ♿
Attendance: 150,000 (estimated)
Membership: Friends of EDNC $35; $50; $100; $250; $500; $1,000.

LONG BEACH FIRE MUSEUM, Old Station 10, 1445 Peterson Ave., Long Beach, CA 90813-2325.
E-mail: lbfdmuseum@verizon.net
Web Site: www.lbfdm.org
Key Personnel: Cur., Herb Bramley
Fire-Fighting Museum.
Collections: fire equipment; badges; photographs; clothing.
Hours & Admission Prices: Wed. 7:30am-11:45am, 2nd Sat. of month 10-3; other times by appointment. No charge.

*** LONG BEACH MUSEUM OF ART, (M),** 2300 E. Ocean Blvd., Long Beach, CA 90803-2442. Tel.: 562-439-2119. Fax: 562-439-3587.
Web Site: www.lbma.org
Founded: 1950.
Congressional District: 34
Key Personnel: Dir., Ronald C. Nelson; Dir. Collections, Sue Ann Robinson; Dir. Finance, Suzanne Rivera.
Personnel Profile: Full-Time Paid 28; Full-Time Volunteers 250; Part-Time Paid 25.
Governing Authority: private. Long Beach Museum of Art Foundation. Tax-exempt.
Art Museum.
Collections: Milton Wichner Collection; Jawlensky, Kandinsky, Feininger; Art of Southern California & European 1850-present; contemporary sculpture; American decorative arts; contemporary ceramics & turned wood; English & French ceramics.
Research Fields: Blue Four; modern German art; arts of Southern California; 20th-century American art; American decorative arts; French & English ceramics.
Facilities: 1,200-vol. library of art history books & catalogs of exhibitions; gallery; sculpture garden. Bookstore & art-related items for sale.
Activities: lectures; performance; docent tours; art festivals; art making workshops for children.
Publications: exhibition catalogues: Milton Wichner Collection, Abraham Walkowitz; Drawings by Painters; Video, A Retrospective Long Beach Museum of Art 1974-1984; Media Arts; Southland Video Anthology; California Video; Art of Music Video; New California Video; Video Poetics; Alexej Jawlensky; Gary Hill; Selina Trieff; Bettina Brendel; Matthew Thomas; New Visions: Video 1998; Bountiful Harvest: American Decorative Arts from the Gail-Oxford Collection; For A New Nation: American Decorative Arts from the Gail Oxford Collection; Imps On A Bridge: Wedwood Fairyland & Other Lustres; Evocations: Sharon Ellis, 1991-2001; The Modernist Jewelry of Clair Falkenstein; Enigma Variations: The Sculpture of John Frame, 1980-2005; Mineo Mizuno; Painting with Fire: Masters of Enameling in America, 1930-1980.
Hours & Admission Prices: Tues.-Sun. 11-5. Adults $7, students & seniors over 62 $6; discounts to AAM & ICOM members; members, children under 12 & Fri. no charge. Closed New Year's Day; Independence Day; Thanksgiving; Christmas. ♿
Membership: Student, Senior & Educator $40; Individual $50; Family & Dual $75; Patron $150; Sponsor $500; Director's Circle $1,000; Collector's Circle $1,500; President's Circle $2,500; Milbank Philanthropic Circle $5,000.

MUSEUM OF LATIN AMERICAN ART, (M), 628 Alamitos Ave., Long Beach, CA 90802-1513. Tel.: 562-437-1689. Fax: 562-437-7043.
E-mail: info@molaa.org
Web Site: www.molaa.org
Founded: 1996.
Key Personnel: Chm. (V), Robert Gumbiner; Vice Pres. Operations, Lee

Gumbiner; Vice Pres. Exhibits & Special Projects, Alex Slato; Assoc. Vice Pres. Exhibits, Cynthia MacMullin; Vice Pres. Public Rels. & Mktg., Susan Golden; Museum Shop Mgr., Vanessa Castillo.
Personnel Profile: Full-Time Paid 30; Part-Time Paid 5; Part-Time Volunteers 15; Interns 3.
Governing Authority: private; nonprofit organization. Tax-exempt: 501(c)(3).
Art Museum.
Collections: contemporary fine art of Mexico, Central & South America and the Spanish-speaking Caribbean.
Research Fields: contemporary art of Latin America.
Facilities: 600-vol. library; 12,000 sq. ft. exhibit space; cafe; education/entertainment center. Museum-related items for sale.
Activities: art festivals; concerts; dance recitals; docent program; films; formal education programs for children; guided tours; lectures; temporary & traveling exhibitions; theater. Annual Events: Day of the Dead; Cinco de Mayo.
Publications: quarterly newsletter; monthly calendar of events.
Hours & Admission Prices: Tues.-Fri. 11:30-7, Sat. 11-7, Sun. 11-6. Adults $7.50, seniors & students $5; discounts for tours & groups; children under 12 & members no charge. Closed New Year's Day; Thanksgiving; Christmas. ♿
Attendance: 75,000 (estimated)
Membership: Student (with ID) $20; Basic $40; Family $60; Friend $100; Colleagues $250; Associate $500; Directors Circle $1,000.

QUEEN MARY, 1126 Queens Hwy., Long Beach, CA 90802-6390. Tel.: 562-435-3511. Fax: 562-437-4531.
E-mail: marketing@queenmary.com
Web Site: www.queenmary.com
Founded: 1971.
Congressional District: 38
Key Personnel: C.E.O. & Pres., Joseph F. Prevratil; Museum Dir., Lovetta Kramer; Gen. Mgr., Jay Primaveria.
Personnel Profile: Full-Time Paid 500; Part-Time Paid 100; Part-Time Volunteers 17.
Governing Authority: municipal. Operated by Hostmark Hospitality Group, City of Long Beach.
Maritime Museum: located aboard the Queen Mary, retired British ocean liner.
Collections: Art Deco architecture; 56 varieties of wood; acid etched glass; memorabilia from the 30s & 40s; two 40,000 HP steam turbine engines & power train.
Facilities: retired British ocean liner: 307 hotel staterooms; 3 restaurants; 3 lounges & bars; 17 salons & ballrooms; shops; wedding chapel; convention accommodations; meeting facilities; marketplace.
Activities: self-guided & guided tour of Queen Mary including bridge, captain's quarters, engine room; historical displays.
Publications: Mailcall!
Hours & Admission Prices: Daily 10-5:30. Adults $24.95, senior citizens & military $21.95, children 5-11 $12.95.
Attendance: 1,300,000 (accurate)
Membership: Quartermaster $30; Purser $60; First Officer $100; Captain $500; Commodore $1,000.

RANCHO LOS ALAMITOS, 6400 Bixby Hill Rd., Long Beach, CA 90815-4706. Tel.: 562-431-3541. Fax: 562-430-9694.
E-mail: info@rancholosalamitos.com
Web Site: www.rancholosalamitos.com
Founded: 1970.
Congressional District: 32
Key Personnel: Exec. Dir., Pamela Seager; Educational Programs, Ms. Michael Powers; Cur., Pamela Young Lee; Museum Shop Mgr., Teresa Barbee.
Personnel Profile: Full-Time Paid 8; Part-Time Paid 8; Part-Time Volunteers 167.
Governing Authority: municipal government. Owned by City of Long Beach; operated by Rancho Los Alamitos Foundation. Tax-exempt.
Historic Site Museum: Native American site, c.1800 adobe is part of the 1790 300,000-acre Manuel Nieto land grant.
Collections: local history from 500 A.D.; furniture & decorative arts; tools; farm implements and equipment; Indian artifacts; 4-acre historic garden; livestock. Historic Buildings: ranch house; stallion barn; dairy barn; blacksmith's shop; feed shed.
Research Fields: local & California history; California ranching; landscape & garden history.
Activities: adult, school & special tours; docent program; permanent exhibitions; public events; heritage programs; lectures; Native American cultural workshops for children. Museum Sponsors: California Ranch Day; Fall Festival; Japanese & Hispanic Heritage Celebrations; Cultural Arts Showcase; Dramatic Period Presentation at Christmas.
Hours & Admission Prices: Wed.-Sun. 1-5. No charge; donations accepted. Closed national holidays. ♿
Attendance: 25,000
Membership: Rancho Los Alamitos Foundation: Friend $30; Supporter $75; Partner $200; Patron $500; Benefactor $1,000.

RANCHO LOS CERRITOS HISTORIC SITE, 4600 Virginia Rd., Long Beach, CA 90807-1916. Tel.: 562-570-1755. Fax: 562-570-1893.
E-mail: ellen.calomiris@longbeach.gov
Web Site: www.rancholoscerritos.org
Founded: 1955.
Congressional District: 32
Key Personnel: Historic Sites Officer, Ellen Calomiris; Pres. (V), Thomasina Parker; Historical Cur., Stephen C. Iverson; Horticulturist, Marie Barnidge-McIntyre; Museum Shop Mgr., Cheryl Bryan; Pres. Foundation (V), Lovetta Kramer.
Personnel Profile: Full-Time Paid 3; Part-Time Paid 5; Part-Time Volunteers 100; Interns 1.
Governing Authority: municipal. Parent Institution: Dept. of Parks, Recreation & Marine, City of Long Beach, CA 90815. Tax-exempt: 501(c)(3)
Historic Site Museum: located on 1790 Spanish land grant to Manuel Nieto; 2-story adobe constructed 1844.
Collections: furniture; tools; costumes; quilts; coverlets; photographs; gardens of original & native plants; archaeology. Historic Building: 1844, 2-story Monterey style adobe built by John Temple & remodeled in 1930 in the mission colonial revival style; c.1850-1940 historic gardens.
Research Fields: local & California history; California ranching; John Temple, Jotham Bixby & Sarah Bixby Smith families; adobe architecture; Ralph Cornell, landscape architect for Rancho.
Facilities: 5,500-vol. research library & archives, books, maps, manuscripts.
Activities: guided tours; school tours; slide programs; formally organized education programs for children; docent program or council; permanent & changing exhibitions; nonprofit fundraising foundation; annual family events, workshops & lectures; teen docent program.
Publications: membership newsletter, Friends Footnotes; Rancho Review.
Hours & Admission Prices: Wed.-Sun. 1-5, hourly tours Sat.-Sun. No charge; donations accepted. Closed holidays. ♿
Attendance: 19,000
Membership: Student $10; Senior $35; Individual $40; Family $50; Patron $100; Cog Stone Society $250.

Los Altos

LOS ALTOS HISTORY MUSEUM AKA ASSOCIATION OF THE LOS ALTOS HISTORICAL MUSEUM, 51 S. San Antonio Rd., Los Altos, CA 94022-3056. Tel.: 650-948-9427. Fax: 650-559-0268.
E-mail: info@losaltoshistory.org
Web Site: www.losaltoshistory.org
Founded: 1977.
Congressional District: 14
Key Personnel: Exec. Dir., Laura Bajuk, E.D.; Pres. (V), Jim Thurber; Treas. (V), Ann Foxen; Collections Mgr., Lisa Robinson; Museum Shop Mgr., Jean Kenny; Museum Shop Mgr., Diane Simmons.
Personnel Profile: Full-Time Paid 1; Part-Time Paid 4; Part-Time Volunteers 300; Interns 2.
Governing Authority: private; nonprofit organization. Tax-exempt: 501(c)(3).
Historic House Museum: 1905 farmhouse built by J. Gilbert Smith, a local farmer.
Collections: newspapers, photos & documents of Los Altos & Los Altos Hills.
Major Exhibits: It's A Small World, 11/09-1/17/10; Through Thick & Thin: The Complicated But Enduring Bond Between the Larger-Than-Life Sisters Sarah Winchester & Isabelle Merriman, 1/28/10-6/6/10; No Life Without Water, 8/26/10-1/2/11.
Research Fields: local history.
Facilities: classroom with AV equipment; 1,500 sq. ft. exhibit space. Museum-related items for sale.
Activities: docent programs; formal third and fourth grade education programs; lectures; temporary & traveling exhibitions; cable TV programs; rental facilties. Annual Events: Antique Shows; Historical Essay Contest for 3rd - 6th grade students.
Publications: quarterly newsletter, Under the Oaks.
Hours & Admission Prices: Thurs.-Sun. 12-4. No charge; donations accepted. Closed New Year's Day; Easter; Independence Day; Thanksgiving; Christmas. ♿
Attendance: 16,000 (accurate)
Membership: Student & Senior $25; Individual $35; Household $50; Business $75; Sponsor $100; Supporter $250; Patron $500; Benefactor $1,000.

Los Angeles

A + D ARCHITECTURE AND DESIGN MUSEUM, (M), 6032 Wilshire Blvd., Los Angeles, CA 90036. Tel.: 323-932-9393.
Founded: 2001.
Architecture & Design Museum.
Collections: architecture; interior, landscape, fashion, & product design; regional, national & international designers; photographs.
Activities: educational programs.
Hours & Admission Prices: Tues.-Fri. 10-6, Sat.-Sun. 11-5. Adults $5, students & seniors $2.50; members no charge.

THE AMERICAN FILM INSTITUTE, 2021 N. Western Ave., Los Angeles, CA 90027-1625. Mailing Address: 1180 Avenue of the Americas, 10th Fl., New York, NY 10036-8402. Tel.: 323-856-7600. Fax: 323-467-4578.
Web Site: www.afi.com
Founded: 1967.
Key Personnel: Chm. Bd. Directors, John Avnet; Chm. Bd. Trustees, Howard Stringer; Dir. & Exec. Vice Pres., Jonathan Estrin.
Personnel Profile: Full-Time Paid 135; Part-Time Volunteers 19.
Governing Authority: nonprofit organization. Branch Institution: The AFI National Film Theater, The John F. Kennedy Center for the Performing Arts, Washington, DC 20566; 1180 Ave. of the Americas, 10th Fl., New York, NY 10032. Tax-exempt: 501(c)(3).
National Arts Organization: a national trust dedicated to preserving the heritage of film & television & presenting the moving image as an art form.
Collections: film & TV script collection; seminar & oral history transcriptions; personal papers & manuscripts of leading film figures.
Research Fields: motion pictures; television; video; education for moving image community.
Facilities: 10,000-vol. Louis B. Mayer Library containing books; periodicals; clipping files; 3,000 motion pictures, television series & long films; oral history transcripts & tapes.
Activities: arts festivals; advanced technology courses; film festivals.
Publications: monthly theater program guide, Preview; annual report; Life Achievement Award Tribute books; board newsletter, Dialogue; AFI catalog of feature films.
Hours & Admission Prices: Call for hours and prices. Library: Mon.-Fri. 9-6 no charge to use library. ♿
Membership: Individual $20; National $35; TDC $250; Film Club $350; SDC $1,500.

* **AUTRY NATIONAL CENTER OF THE AMERICAN WEST, (M),** 4700 Western Heritage Way, Los Angeles, CA 90027-1462. Tel.: 323-667-2000. Fax: 323-660-5721.
Web Site: www.autrynationalcenter.org
Formerly: Autry Museum of Western Heritage
Founded: 1984.
Congressional District: 29
Key Personnel: Pres. & C.E.O., John L. Gray; Founding Chm., Jackie Autry; Founding Pres., Joanne D. Hale; Chm. Bd. Trustees, Tom Lee; Vice Pres. Exhibitions & Exec. Dir. of the Museum of the American West, Jonathan Spaulding; Asst. Cur. Arms & Armor, Julia Bourbois; Cur. Visual Arts, Amy Scott; Assoc. Cur. Social & Cultural History, Jeffrey Richardson; Dept. Dir. Inst. & Asst. Cur. Western Women's History, Carolyn Brucken; Sr. Media Producer & Mgr. Exhibits, Paula Kessler; Sr. Dir. Collections, Linda A. Strauss; Registrar, Acquisitions, Steven Walsh; Registrar, Loans & Exhibits, Andi Alameda; Registrar, Permanent Collections, Lalena Lewark; Exec. Dir. Institute for the Study of the American West, Stephen Aron; Editor & Assoc. Dir. Publications, Marlene Head; Dir. Publications & Assoc. Dir. Institute, Marva Felchlin; Dir. Education, Erik Greenberg; Dir. Programs, Robyn Hetrick; Dir. Major Gifts, Anna Norville; Assoc. Dir. Corp. Giving, Brooke Glazer; Dir. Foundation Rels., Jan Frazier; Dir. Government Affairs & Special Projects, David Burton; Dir. Membership & Visitor Svcs., Chrystina Geagan; Sr. Dir. Mktg. & Communications, Joan Cumming; Production & Traffic Mgr., Denise Arguijo; Controller, Angelica Castro; Vice Pres. Advancement, Elizabeth Kennedy; Conservator, Richard Moll; Vice Pres. & C.O.O., Luke Swetland; Dir. Human Resources, Valerie Nelson; Human Resources Coord., Amanda Trease; Dir. Facilities, Mike Garcia; Dir. Security, Everett Drayton; Dir. Retail Operations, Jo Valiulis; Museum Shop Mgr., Jasmine Aslanyan; Dir. Special Events & Donor Rels., Cathy Crowser; Assoc. Dir. Event Sales & Services, Wendy Esensten; Mgr. Visitor Svcs., Sara Bornstein.
Personnel Profile: Full-Time Paid 129; Part-Time Paid 27; Part-Time Volunteers 296; Interns 4.
Governing Authority: nonprofit organization. Parent Institution: Autry National Center. Tax-exempt.
Western History & Culture Museum.
Collections: 300,000 objects; art & artifacts of Native American cultures; the multicultural American West; popular culture & fine arts.
Research Fields: history, material culture & iconography of the American West.
Facilities: 40,000-vol. library; archives.
Activities: docent tour; seminars; permanent & temporary loan exhibitions of Western & Native American art & artifacts; fund raising; outreach; special events.
Publications: biannual scholarly publication, Convergence; quarterly calendar; brochures; books; gallery guides; exhibition catalogs; quarterly membership magazine, The Autry.
Hours & Admission Prices: Southwest Museum of the American Indian: temporarily closed. Museum of the American West: July-Aug. Tues.-Wed. & Fri. 10-4, Thurs. 10-8, Sat.-Sun. 11-5; Sept.-June Tues.-Fri. 10-4, Sat.-Sun. 11-5. Adults $9, senior citizens & students $5, children 3-12 $3; discounts to groups, AAM, ICOM & Southern CA Auto Club members; museum members, 2nd Tues. of month & Thurs. after 4 no charge. Closed New Year's Day; Independence Day; Labor Day; Thanksgiving; Christmas. ♿
Attendance: 162,000 (accurate)
Membership: Individual $45; Dual $55; Family $65; Turquoise $160; Copper $250; Shell $500; Silver $1,250; Gold $2,500.

AVILA ADOBE, 10 E. Olvera St., Los Angeles, CA 90012-2921. Mailing Address: 845 N. Almeda St., Los Angeles, CA 90012-2901. Tel.: 213-628-1274.
Web Site: www.cityofla.org/elp
Key Personnel: Cur., Suellen Chang
Historic House Museum: housed in c.1818 home of Don Francisco Avila; also served as headquarters for Commodore Robert Stockton during the Mexican American War.
Collections: 1840s Los Angeles lifestyle.
Hours & Admission Prices: Daily 9-4.

BEN MALTZ GALLERY AT OTIS COLLEGE OF ART AND DESIGN, (M), 9045 Lincoln Blvd., Los Angeles, CA 90045-3505. Tel.: 310-665-6905 & 6800. Fax: 310-665-6908.
E-mail: galleryinfo@otis.edu
Web Site: www.otis.edu/benmaltzgallery
Formerly: OTIS Gallery, OTIS College of Art and Design
Founded: 1940.
Key Personnel: Dir., Meg Linton; Exhibitions Coord. & Registrar, Jinger Heffner; Mgr. & Outreach Coord., Kathy MacPherson; Public Programs Coord., Trinidad Ruiz.
Personnel Profile: Full-Time Paid 4; Part-Time Paid 1; Part-Time Volunteers 1; Interns 5.
Governing Authority: private; nonprofit college. Parent Institution: Otis College of Art and Design. Tax-exempt: 501(c)(3).
Art Gallery.
Collections: Emerson Woelffer paintings and drawings.
Research Fields: contemporary art and design.
Facilities: 3,500 sq. ft. gallery.
Activities: traveling exhibitions; curated shows of local, national & international emerging artists; group shows; installations; one-person retrospectives; international artist-in-residence program.
Publications: exhibition catalogs; limited edition artworks.
Hours & Admission Prices: Tues.-Wed. & Fri.-Sat. 10-5, Thurs. 10-7. No charge. Closed mid-Dec.-New Year's Day; Martin Luther King weekend; President's Day weekend; Memorial Day weekend; Labor Day weekend; Thanksgiving weekend. ♿
Attendance: 16,000 (estimated)

CALIFORNIA AFRICAN-AMERICAN MUSEUM, (M), 600 State Dr., Exposition Park, Los Angeles, CA 90037-1267. Tel.: 213-744-7432. Fax: 213-744-2050.
Web Site: www.caam.ca.gov
Founded: 1981.
Congressional District: 48
Key Personnel: Exec. Dir., Charmaine Jefferson; Chm. Bd., Eric Lawrence Frazier; History Program Mgr., Christopher Jimenez Y West; Cur. History, Tiffini Bowers; Exhibit Design Supvr., Edward Garcia; Visual Arts Program Mgr., Mar Hollingsworth; Librarian, Ann Shea; Mgr. Visual Arts Program, Michelle Elizabeth Lee.
Personnel Profile: Full-Time Paid 19; Part-Time Paid 7.
Governing Authority: state; nonprofit. Tax-exempt.
African-American Culture Museum.
Collections: African-American culture: fine art; sculpture; prints; photographs; costumes; decorative arts; documents; books; manuscripts; audiovisual materials; Pan-African art works; implements; instruments & artifacts of the people of African descent in California and west of the Mississippi.
Major Exhibits: America I Am, 11/09-3/10.

Research Fields: African Americans in theater & film; contemporary art, music, sports & popular culture.
Facilities: 8,950-vol. library of books, periodicals, audio & video tapes, records & boxes of archival material available for inter-library loan by special request & available to the public for use in-house by appointment; theatre; 40 sq. ft. exhibit space; educational facilities. Catalogues, books, jewelry, African clothing, decorative items, posters, cards, audio visual recordings for sale.
Activities: guided tours; lectures; school loan service; loan, temporary & traveling exhibitions; films; concerts; formally organized education programs for undergraduate & graduate students.
Publications: published biannually to bimonthly: calendar of events, Museum Notes.
Hours & Admission Prices: Tues.-Sat. 10-5, Sun. 11-5. No charge; donations accepted. Parking $8. Closed New Year's Day; Thanksgiving; Christmas. ♿
Attendance: 45,000 (estimated)
Membership: Individual $35; Family $50; Patron $100; Sponsor $250; Supporting $500; Benefactor & Corporate $1,000; Corporate & Program Support $5,000.

* **CALIFORNIA SCIENCE CENTER, (M),** 700 Exposition Park Dr., Los Angeles, CA 90037. Tel.: 213-744-7400 & 2019. Fax: 213-744-2034.
Web Site: www.californiasciencecenter.org
Founded: 1880.
Congressional District: 33
Key Personnel: Pres., Jeffrey Rudolph; Deputy Dir. Administration, Cheryl Tateishi; Deputy Dir. Education, Dr. Ron Rohovit; Vice Pres. Retail Operations, Kent Jones; Deputy Dir. Exhibits, Dr. Diane Perlov; Sr. Vice Pres. & Chief Financial Officer, Cynthia Pygin; Deputy Dir. Operations, Tony Budrovich; Sr. Vice Pres. Devel. & Mktg., William T. Harris; Cur. World Ecology, Dr. Chuck Kopczak; Cur. Technology, Dr. David Bibas; Cur Aerospace, Dr. Kenneth E. Phillips.
Personnel Profile: Full-Time Paid 202; Part-Time Paid 169; Part-Time Volunteers 126.
Governing Authority: state. Parent Institution: State of California. Tax-exempt.
Science and Technology Museum.
Collections: biology; geology; high wire bicycle; air & space.
Facilities: 3-D IMAX theater; cafe.
Activities: lectures; films; formally organized education programs for children; permanent & traveling exhibitions; workshops & demonstrations; live programs; teacher professional development.
Publications: quarterly newsletter; brochures; Discovery Guide; World of Life book; educational programming.
Hours & Admission Prices: Daily 10-5. No charge; donations accepted. Closed New Year's Day; Thanksgiving; Christmas. ♿
Attendance: 1,300,000 (estimated)
Membership: Explorer Family $50; Discover Family $100; Adventure Family $300; Pioneer Family $500.

CENTER FOR THE STUDY OF POLITICAL GRAPHICS (CSPG), 8124 W. Third St., Ste. 211, Los Angeles, CA 90048-4340. Tel.: 323-653-4662. Fax: 323-653-6991.
E-mail: cspg@politicalgraphics.org
Web Site: www.politicalgraphics.org
Founded: 1988.
Key Personnel: C.E.O., Dir. & Cur., Carol A. Wells; Program Dir., Mary Sutton; Archivist, Joy Novak.
Personnel Profile: Full-Time Paid 4; Part-Time Paid 2; Part-Time Volunteers 5; Interns 2.
Governing Authority: private; nonprofit organization. Tax-exempt: 501(c)(3).
History Museum.
Collections: over 60,000 domestic & international political and protest posters from early 20th century to present including Viet Nam War Era, Civil Rights Movement, African American, Asian, Latino & Native American Rights, Women's Rights, Human Rights, Los Angeles, Black Panther Party, Che Guevara & Latin America, racism, sexism & homophobia.
Facilities: research facility. Museum-related items for sale.
Activities: guided tours; lectures; loan, participatory & traveling exhibitions. Annual Event: Party and Art Auction.
Publications: biannual newsletter, Poligrafiks.
Hours & Admission Prices: Mon.-Fri. 9-6 by appointment. No charge; donations accepted.
Attendance: 1,500 (estimated)

CHINESE AMERICAN MUSEUM, 425 N. Los Angeles St., Los Angeles, CA 90012-2939. Mailing Address: El Pueblo de Los Angeles, 125 Paseo de la Plaza, Ste. 400, Los Angeles, CA 90012. Tel.: 213-485-8567. Fax: 213-485-8238.
Web Site: www.camla.org
Founded: 1984.
Chinese American Museum.
Collections: local Chinese American history.
Facilities: Museum-related items for sale.
Hours & Admission Prices: Tues.-Sun. 10-2. Suggested Donation: adults $3; members no charge. Closed major holidays. ♿
Membership: Student & Senior 60 & over $25; Individual $50; Corporate $500.

CORITA ART CENTER, (M), 5515 Franklin Ave., Los Angeles, CA 90028-5901. Tel.: 323-450-4650. Fax: 323-466-2150.
E-mail: sasha@corita.org
Web Site: www.corita.org
Founded: 1995.
Congressional District: 30
Key Personnel: Dir., Alexandra Carrera; Asst. to Dir., Corrie Siegel; Web Designer, Jorge Lopez.
Personnel Profile: Full-Time Paid 1; Part-Time Paid 2; Part-Time Volunteers 4; Interns 1.
Governing Authority: private; nonprofit organization. Parent Institution: Immaculate Heart Community, Los Angeles, CA. Tax-exempt: 501(c)(3).
Art Museum.
Collections: serigraphs & watercolors of Corita Kent; archives.
Research Fields: life & artistic works of Corita Kent.
Facilities: 600 sq. ft. exhibit space. Prints & reproductions for sale.
Activities: tours by appointment; art education programs; permanent & traveling exhibition.
Publications: quarterly newsletter, Corita Art Center News.
Hours & Admission Prices: Mon.-Fri. 10-4, one Sat. a month by appointment; original artwork sales by appointment only. No charge; donations accepted. Closed New Year's week; Christmas week; national holidays. ♿
Attendance: 200 (estimated)
Membership: Primary Colors $35; Everyday Miracles $75; Different Drummers $150; Moon Flowers $500; Dancing Stars $1,000; Visionaries $5,000; Joyous Revolutionaries $10,000.

COUNTY OF LOS ANGELES FIRE MUSEUM, 1320 N. Eastern Ave., Los Angeles, CA 90063-3244. Mailing Address: P.O. Box 3325, Alhambra, CA 91803-0325. Tel.: 323-881-2411 & 357-0311. Fax: 323-267-0668.
Web Site: www.clafma.org
Founded: 1974.
Key Personnel: Dir., Paul Schneider.
Governing Authority: nonprofit organization.
Fire-Fighting Museum.
Collections: historic fire equipment & memorabilia; 1852 button hand pumper; 1903 steam engine; c.1970 Squad 51; hand-drawn ladder truck; photographs; books; helmets; badges.
Facilities: 520 sq. ft. exhibit space.
Activities: Museum Sponsors: Fire Service Day; Fire Musters; Open House in April.
Publications: quarterly newsletter, The Fire Warden.
Hours & Admission Prices: By appointment. No charge; donations accepted. ♿
Attendance: 1,400 (estimated)
Membership: Retired $12; Regular $24.

CRAFT AND FOLK ART MUSEUM - CAFAM, 5814 Wilshire Blvd., Los Angeles, CA 90036-4501. Tel.: 323-937-4230.
Web Site: www.cafam.org
Founded: 1973.
Key Personnel: C.E.O. & Dir., Maryna Hrushetska; Museum Shop Mgr., Yuko Makuuchi.
Personnel Profile: Full-Time Paid 6; Part-Time Paid 1; Part-Time Volunteers 4; Interns 4.
Governing Authority: Tax-exempt.
Art Museum.
Collections: folk art; contemporary craft; world cultures.
Major Exhibits: Nomadic Legacy: Textiles from Central Asia and Iran (T), 1/10-5/10; The Art and History of Tarot, 1/10-5/10; Some Assembly Required: Race, Gender and Culture (T), 5/10-9/10; Aaron Kramer Solo Exhibit, 5/10-9/10; De La Torre Brothers Exhibit, 9/10-1/11.
Facilities: Museum-related items for sale.
Activities: K-12 school tours; internships; family art workshops; adult workshops; curator's lectures; concerts; film screenings; studio tours; dance performances; artist demonstrations.
Publications: quarterly newsletter.
Hours & Admission Prices: Tues.-Wed. & Fri. 11-5, Thurs. 11-7, Sat.-Sun. 12-6. Adults $5, students & senior citizens $3; discounts to AAM & ICOM

members; members, children 12 & under and first Wed. of month no charge. Closed New Year's Day; Easter; Independence Day; Thanksgiving; Christmas. ♿
Attendance: 15,000 (estimated)
Membership: Individual $45; Family $60; Believer $100; Enthusiast $250; Worldly Traveler $500; Visionary $1,000; Cultural Ambassador $2,500 & up.

EL PUEBLO HISTORICAL MONUMENT, 125 Paseo de la Plaza, Ste. 400, Los Angeles, CA 90012-2959. Tel.: 213-628-1274 & 680-2525. Fax: 213-485-8238.
Web Site: cityofla.org/elp/
Founded: 1953.
Congressional District: 25
Key Personnel: Gen. Mgr., Robert Andrade; Museum Shop Mgr., Gloria Giangiuli.
Personnel Profile: Full-Time Paid 27; Part-Time Paid 25; Part-Time Volunteers 30; Interns 4.
Governing Authority: city. Owned by City of Los Angeles, CA. Tax-exempt.
Historic District & Museum Complex.
Collections: manuscript collections; architectural drawings; slides; archival collections; photographs; artifact & archaeological collections. Historic Buildings: 1890 Garnier Block; c.1900 Hellman-Quon Building; 1884 Firehouse Museum; 1870 Pico House; 1870 Merced Theatre; 1858 Masonic Hall Museum; 1894 Jones-Simpson Building; c.1888 Jones Building; 1910 10 W. Olvera St.; 1887 Sepulveda House Museum; c.1855 Pelanconi House; 1908 Italian Hall; 1909 Hammel Building; 1926 Plaza United Methodist Church; 1926 Biscailuz Building; 1904 Plaza Substation; c.1818 Avila Adobe Museum; 1870-1914 Winery; 1888 Vickrey/Brunswig Building; 1883 Plaza House; 1818-1822 Plaza Catholic Church; c.1912 Brunswig Warehouse; 1897 Brunswig Annex; 1924 Old Brunswig Co. Laboratory.
Research Fields: Los Angeles history; Chinese American history; development of El Pueblo Park.
Facilities: library of books, periodicals & photographs pertaining to the history of Los Angeles available for research on premises by appointment; visitors center; restaurants. Gift items for sale.
Activities: guided tours; bus tours; slide lectures; school programs; docent program; film on early history of Los Angeles; changing exhibits. Olvera St. Merchants Sponsor: Mardi Gras; Blessing of the Animals in April; Flower & Camera Day in June; Rose Queen Tour in early December; Las Posadas week before Christmas. Park Sponsors: City Birthday Celebration in September; Cinco de Mayo; Mexican Independence Weekend event.
Publications: brochures, general & on specific buildings.
Hours & Admission Prices: Visitors Center, Sepulveda House & Avila Adobe: daily 9-4. Firehouse: Tues.-Sun. 10-3. Masonic Hall: Tues.-Fri. 10-3. Tours: Tues.-Sat. 10-1; discounts to AAM members; special group tours by reservations only, call for hours of the various museums. No charge; donations accepted. For further information call the History Division 213-680-2525 or tour reservations office 213-628-1274. ♿
Attendance: 260,000 (accurate)
Membership: Individual $25; Donor $50; Contributing $100; Patron $250; Sustaining $500; Supporting $1,000; Corporate or Benefactor $5,000.

FERNDELL NATURE MUSEUM, 5375 Red Oak Dr., Los Angeles, CA 90068-2531. Tel.: 323-666-5046.
Nature Museum.
Collections: California sycamores; over 50 fern species; tropical plants & flowers.
Hours & Admission Prices: Daily 6am-10pm.

FIDM MUSEUM & GALLERIES, (M), 919 S. Grand Ave., Los Angeles, CA 90015-1421. Tel.: 213-623-5821. Fax: 213-624-7617.
Web Site: www.fidmmuseum.org
Founded: 1977.
Congressional District: 35
Key Personnel: Acting Dir., Barbara Bundy; Pres., Tonian Hohberg; Treas., Annie Johnson; Cur., Kevin L. Jones; Collections Mgr., Christina Johnson; Public Rels., Shirley Wilson; Registrar, Meghan Grossman; Security, Ivan Chapel; Museum Shop Mgr., Judy Yaras.
Personnel Profile: Full-Time Paid 10; Part-Time Paid 4; Part-Time Volunteers 1; Interns 3.
Governing Authority: private; nonprofit organization. Parent Institution: Fashion Institute of Design & Merchandising. Subsidiary Institute: FIDM Museum & Library, Inc. Tax-exempt: 501(c)(3).
Costume Museum.
Collections: 10,000 costumes from 18th century to present; 20th century couture and ready-to-wear.
Facilities: 12,000-vol. library; 12,500 sq. ft. exhibit space. Museum-related items for sale.
Activities: guided tours; loan & temporary exhibitions; receptions; lectures.
Publications: annual exhibition brochures.
Hours & Admission Prices: Feb. to mid-Dec. daily call for hours. No charge. Closed major holidays. ♿
Attendance: 40,000 (estimated)

FOWLER MUSEUM AT UCLA, (M), W. Sunset Blvd. & Westwood Plaza, 1586 Fowler Bldg., Los Angeles, CA 90095-1549. Mailing Address: Box 951549, Los Angeles, CA 90095-1549. Tel.: 310-825-4361 & 206-7004. Fax: 310-206-7007.
E-mail: fowlerws@arts.ucla.edu
Web Site: www.fowler.ucla.edu
Formerly: UCLA Fowler Museum of Cultural History
Founded: 1963.
Congressional District: 23
Key Personnel: Dir., Marla C. Berns; Dir. Center for Study Rgnl. Dress, Patricia Anawalt; Asst. Dir., David Blair; Exec. Asst., Betsy Escandor; Dir. Communications, Stacey Ravel Abarbanel; Exhibit Designer, Sebastian Clough; Cur. Southeast Asia & Oceania, Roy Hamilton; Dir. Devel., Nicole Dunn; Dir. Education, Betsy D. Quick; Cur. Archaeology, Wendy Teeter; Collections Mgr., Rachel Raynor; Traveling Exhibits Coord., Karyn Zarubica; Registrar, Charles Carroll; Dir. Publications, Daniel Brauer; Dir. Photography, Don Cole; Museum Shop Mgr., Stella Krieger.
Personnel Profile: Full-Time Paid 42; Part-Time Paid 32; Part-Time Volunteers 31; Interns 3.
Governing Authority: university; state. Parent Institution: University of California, 405 Hilgard Ave., Los Angeles, CA 90024. Tax-exempt: 501(c)(3).
Cultural History Museum.
Collections: African, Oceanic, S.E. Asian, North, Middle & South American art, archaeology & material culture.
Major Exhibits: Nick Cave: Meet Me at the Center of the Earth (T), 1/10-5/10.
Research Fields: ancient & non-Western art, archaeology; ethnology.
Facilities: 10,000-vol. library of books & periodicals relating to the collections available by request; 320-seat auditorium; 20,000 sq. ft. exhibit space. Museum publications for sale.
Activities: arts festivals; guided tours; hobby workshops; lectures; gallery talks; formally organized education programs for college students, children & adults; inter-museum, participatory, traveling & temporary exhibitions. Museum Sponsors: Satellite & Peripatetic Museum programs; instruction in museology.
Publications: exhibition catalogs; occasional papers; Museum Monogram Series.
Hours & Admission Prices: Office: Mon.-Fri. 8:30-5. Gallery: Wed.-Sun. 12-5, Thurs. 12-8. No charge. Closed university holidays. ♿
Attendance: 60,000 (estimated)
Membership: Student $20; UCLA Faculty & Staff $25; Senior & UCLA Alumni $35; Individual $50; Family & Dual $75; Contributing $150; Supporting $275; Patron $500; MANUS $1,500; Curator's Circle $2,500; Director's Circle $5,000. Fowler Textile Council: Individual $50; Couple $75; Student $25.

GEORGE J. DOIZAKI GALLERY, Japanese American Cultural & Community Center, 244 S. San Pedro St., Los Angeles, CA 90012-3856. Tel.: 213-628-2725. Fax: 213-617-8576.
E-mail: info@jaccc.org
Web Site: www.jaccc.org
Key Personnel: Dir., Chris Alhara
Art Gallery.
Collections: paintings; ceramics; sculptures.
Hours & Admission Prices: Tues.-Fri. 12-5, Sat.-Sun. 11-4. No charge.

GRAMMY MUSEUM, Figueroa St., Los Angeles, CA 90015. Mailing Address: 800 W. Olympic Blvd., Ste. A245, Los Angeles, CA 90015-1366. Tel.: 213-765-6800.
Key Personnel: Exec. Dir., Bob Santelli
Music History Museum.
Collections: music history; recordings & recording artists; photographs; Hall of Fame.
Facilities: Museum-related items for sale.
Activities: mix & produce music; videos; hands-on exhibits; educational programs.
Hours & Admission Prices: Sun.-Fri. 11:30-7:30, Sat. 10-7:30. Adults $14.95, students and seniors 65 & over $11.95, youth 6-17 $10.95; members and children 5 & under no charge. ♿

GRIER MUSSER MUSEUM, 403 S. Bonnie Brae St., Los Angeles, CA 90057-3009. Tel.: 213-413-1814.
E-mail: griermusser@hotmail.com
Web Site: griermussermuseum.com

Founded: 1984.
Congressional District: 43
Key Personnel: Dir., Susan Tejada.
Governing Authority: individual operation; organized for profit.
Antiques Museum: housed in c.1898 Queen Ann Victorian house.
Collections: monthly holiday exhibits; postcards of old Los Angeles.
Activities: guided tours; lectures; theatre; traveling exhibitions; weekly postcard show of old Los Angeles.
Publications: newsletter, Parlour Talk.
Hours & Admission Prices: Wed.-Sat. 12-4, call for reservations. Adults $10, senior citizens & students $7, children $5; tours & family group rates available. Closed most holidays.
Attendance: 500 (accurate)

GRIFFITH OBSERVATORY, 2800 E. Observatory Rd., Los Angeles, CA 90027-1299. Tel.: 213-473-0800. Fax: 213-473-0816.
Web Site: www.griffithobservatory.org
Founded: 1935.
Congressional District: 24
Key Personnel: Dir., Dr. Edwin C. Krupp; Pres. Friends Of The Observatory, David Primes.
Personnel Profile: Full-Time Paid 31; Part-Time Paid 200.
Governing Authority: municipal. City of Los Angeles. Tax-exempt: 170(b)(1)(A).
Public Observatory, Planetarium & Astronomy Museum.
Collections: astronomy & related sciences; artwork & illustration; photographs; astronomical instruments & artifacts.
Research Fields: astronomy.
Facilities: 6,650-vol. library of books on astronomy available by special arrangements; telescope observatory housing a 12 in. Zeiss refracting telescope.
Activities: live planetarium performances; guided tours; special lectures; films; gallery talks; observatory telescopes open to public on clear evenings.
Publications: monthly magazine, Griffith Observer.
Hours & Admission Prices: Tues.-Fri. 12-10, Sat.-Sun. 10-10; hours are subject to change. Oschin Planetarium: adults $7, seniors & students $5, children 5-12 $3; discounts to members. Closed Thanksgiving; Christmas. ♿
Attendance: 1,000,000 (accurate)
Membership: Friends Of The Observatory: Planet $45; Star $100; Supernova $250; Galaxy $500; Celestial Circle $1,000; Copernicus Society $2,500; Galileo Society $5,000; Newton Society $10,000.

GRUNWALD CENTER FOR THE GRAPHIC ARTS, HAMMER MUSEUM, (M), 10899 Wilshire Blvd., Los Angeles, CA 90024-4343. Tel.: 310-443-7076. Fax: 310-443-7099. TDD: 310-443-7094.
E-mail: cdixon@hammer.ucla.edu
Web Site: www.hammer.ucla.edu
Formerly: Grunwald Center for the Graphic Arts, UCLA Hammer Museum of Art and Cultural Center
Founded: 1956.
Congressional District: 30
Key Personnel: Dir. & Chief Cur., Cynthia Burlingham; Curatorial Assoc., Claudine Dixon; Conservation Technician, Maureen McGee; Preparator, Lynne Blaikie; Assoc. Cur., Allegra Pesenti; Asst. Registrar, Kate Bergeron.
Personnel Profile: Full-Time Paid 5; Part-Time Paid 1.
Governing Authority: university. Parent Institution: University of California at Los Angeles.
Art Museum & Study Center.
Collections: 45,000 prints, drawings, photographs & artists' books.
Research Fields: history of graphic arts.
Facilities: print study room.
Activities: guided tours; lectures; gallery talks; temporary & traveling exhibitions.
Publications: selected areas of graphic arts collection; temporary & traveling exhibitions.
Hours & Admission Prices: Grunwald Center Study Room: Mon.-Fri. 10-4, by appointment only. No charge. ♿
Membership: Friends of the Graphic Arts: Advocate $150; Associate $1,000.

HAMMER MUSEUM, 10899 Wilshire Blvd., Los Angeles, CA 90024. Tel.: 310-443-7020 & 7000. Fax: 310-443-7099.
E-mail: info@hammer.ucla.edu
Web Site: www.hammer.ucla.edu
Founded: 1990.
Congressional District: 30
Key Personnel: Dir., Ann Philbin; Chm. & Pres., John V. Tunney; Dept. Dir. Finance & Admin., Deborah Snyder; Dir. Admin., Jenni Kim; Museum Shop Mgr., Maggie Sarkissian.
Personnel Profile: Full-Time Paid 83; Part-Time Paid 6; Part-Time Volunteers 20; Interns 34.
Governing Authority: university. Parent Institution: University of California at Los Angeles. Subsidiary Institution: UCLA Grunwald Center for the Graphic Arts, 10899 Wilshire Blvd., 2nd Fl., Los Angeles, CA. Tax-exempt.
Art Museum.
Collections: French 19th-century works; European paintings; American artists from 18th to 20th centuries; sculpture garden; Hammer Daumier collection; Hammer contemporary collection.
Major Exhibits: Heat Waves in a Swamp: The Paintings of Charles Burchfield (T), 11/09-1/10; Chen Quilin, 11/09-1/10; Hammer Permanent Collection, 11/09-1/10; The Bible Illuminated: R. Crumb's Book of Genesis, 11/09-2/10; Rob Fischer, 11/09-4/10; Rembrandt Prints, 1/10-4/10; Rachel Whiteread: Drawings (T), 1/10-5/10; Desiree Holman, 2/10-5/10.
Research Fields: history of graphic arts; modern sculpture; American & contemporary art.
Facilities: video library & viewing room; public program space; theater; cafe. Bookstore.
Activities: concerts; readings; lectures; screenings; discussions; guided tours; gallery talks; temporary & traveling exhibitions.
Publications: newsletter; temporary exhibitions catalogues.
Hours & Admission Prices: Tues.-Wed. & Fri.-Sat. 11-7, Thurs. 11-9, Sun. 11-5. Adults $7, senior citizens & alumni members $5; members, students, staff, children, AAM & ICOM members, and Thurs. no charge. Closed New Year's Day; Independence Day; Thanksgiving; Christmas. ♿
Attendance: 150,000 (estimated)
Membership: Full Time Student & Artist $40; Individual $50; Friend $75; Contributor $125; Supporter $350; Hammer Fellow $1,000; Hammer Patron $2,500.

HANCOCK MEMORIAL MUSEUM, University Avenue at Childs Way, Los Angeles, CA 90089-0189. Mailing Address: USC Libraries, Special Collections, 3550 Trousdale Pkwy., Los Angeles, CA 90089-0189. Tel.: 213-740-5141. Fax: 213-740-2343.
E-mail: melindah@usc.edu
Web Site: www.usc.edu
Key Personnel: Cur., Melinda Hayes
History Museum: housed in four rooms dismantled from the original Hancock mansion.
Collections: period furnishings; personal artifacts; paintings; Steinway piano c.1910; family heirlooms.
Hours & Admission Prices: By appointment.

HERITAGE SQUARE MUSEUM, (M), 3800 Homer St., Los Angeles, CA 90031-1530. Tel.: 323-225-2700. Fax: 323-225-2725.
E-mail: admin@heritagesquare.org
Web Site: www.heritagesquare.org
Founded: 1969.
Congressional District: 27
Key Personnel: C.E.O., Saline Davies; Treas., Charles Horton; Dir. Devel., Brian Sheridan; Dir. Museum Administration & Operations, Jessica Maria Alicea; Cur. Grounds & Gardens, Steven Ormenyi; Cur. Architecture, Justin Gershuny; Education Mgr., Jessica Rivas; Museum Shop Mgr., Leticia Munoz.
Personnel Profile: Full-Time Paid 3; Part-Time Paid 3; Part-Time Volunteers 70.
Governing Authority: private; nonprofit organization. Parent Institution: Cultural Heritage Foundation of Southern California, Inc., Los Angeles, CA 90031. Tax-exempt: 501(c)(3).
History Museum.
Collections: 8 Victorian structures from Los Angeles & Pasadena; related furniture & personal artifacts; textiles; medical, communication, transportation & business equipment and artifacts.
Research Fields: life of John Ford, master woodcarver & former owner of one of the homes; Southern California rural and urban development, history, agriculture, horticulture and gardening after 1865; structures & families that occupied them.
Facilities: 1,200 sq. ft. exhibit space. Museum-related items for sale.
Activities: living history programs; guided tours; docent program; lectures; temporary exhibitions. Museum Sponsors: MOTA Day, Annual Open House; Silent & Classic Movie Nights in July; Halloween Mourning Tours in October; Holiday Lamplight-Christmas tours; Victorian Fashion Show.
Publications: quarterly member newsletter, On the Square; quarterly volunteer newsletter, The Chronicle.
Hours & Admission Prices: April-Sept. Fri.-Sun. & holiday Mon. 12-5; Oct.-March Fri.-Sun. & holiday Mon. 11:30-4:30. Adults $10, senior citizens $8, children 6-12 $5; discounts to AAM, AAA & Time Travelers member institutions; members no charge. Closed New Year's Day; Thanksgiving; Christmas Day.
Attendance: 8,797 (accurate)

Membership: Friends of Heritage Square: Volunteer $25; Individual $35; Family $50; Sustaining $75; Contributing $100. Heritage Square Society: Member $250; Donor $500; Sponsor $1,000; Patron $2,500.

HOLLYHOCK HOUSE, Barnsdall Park, 4800 Hollywood Blvd., Los Angeles, CA 90027-5302. Tel.: 323-664-6269.
E-mail: met_scannon@sbcglobal.net
Web Site: www.hollyhockhouse.net
Founded: 1971.
Key Personnel: Dir. Education, Sara L. Cannon; Cur. Historic Site, Virginia Kazor; Cur. Historic Site, Jeffrey Herr.
Personnel Profile: Full-Time Paid 3; Part-Time Volunteers 35.
Governing Authority: Parent Institution: Dept. of Recreation & Parks, Los Angeles. Subsidiary Institution: Dept. of Cultural Affairs, Los Angeles. Tax-exempt.
History Museum: home of oil heiress Aline Barnsdall designed by architect Frank Lloyd Wright, c.1919.
Collections: furnishings.
Research Fields: architecture of Frank Lloyd Wright and Rudolf Schindler.
Hours & Admission Prices: Wed.-Sun. 12:30, 1:30, 2:30 & 3:30. Groups of 10 & up call for reservation. Adults $7, students & seniors $3; children under 12 no charge. ♿
Attendance: 10,000

HOLLYWOOD BOWL MUSEUM, (M), 2301 N. Highland Ave., Los Angeles, CA 90068-2742. Tel.: 323-850-2058.
E-mail: museum@laphil.org
Web Site: www.hollywoodbowl.com
Founded: 1984.
Key Personnel: Dir. & Cur., Dr. Carol Merrill-Mirsky.
Personnel Profile: Full-Time Paid 1; Part-Time Paid 4; Part-Time Volunteers 60; Interns 1.
Governing Authority: Parent Institution: Los Angeles Philharmonic Association. Tax-exempt.
Music & Performing Arts Museum.
Collections: photographs; films; audio; documents; ephemera; 20th-century musical artists of the Hollywood Bowl.
Research Fields: music & performing arts.
Facilities: resource center; permanent & temporary exhibition galleries; performance space; education area.
Activities: changing exhibits on musical topics; educational, volunteer & docent programs; concert & lecture series.
Publications: Exiles in Paradise l991.
Hours & Admission Prices: July-Sept. 18 Tues.-Sat. 10-8; Sept.19-June Tues.-Fri. 10-5, Sat. by appointment. No charge. Closed New Year's Day; Thanksgiving; Christmas. ♿
Attendance: 27,000 (accurate)

HOLYLAND EXHIBITION, 2215 Lake View Ave., (cor. Allesandro Way & Lake View Ave.), Los Angeles, CA 90039-3635. Tel.: 323-664-3162.
Founded: 1924.
Key Personnel: C.E.O. & Pres. (V), Christine Kirkegaard; Dir. & Cur., Betty J. Shepard.
Personnel Profile: Full-Time Volunteers 2.
Governing Authority: nonprofit organization. Parent Institution: Holyland Exhibit.
Religious Museum.
Collections: collections from Egypt; Persia; Palestine; Syria; Rome; Greece; pottery; mummy case; coins; oil lamps; furniture; paintings; tapestries; artifacts.
Research Fields: the Holy Lands of the Bible; artifacts.
Facilities: auditorium. Museum-related items for sale.
Activities: guided tours; photographic presentations; refreshments.
Publications: Futterer's Eye-Ographic Bible System.
Hours & Admission Prices: 2 hour guided tour by appointment only. Donations Requested: adults $2.50, students & children under 16 $2.

* **THE J. PAUL GETTY MUSEUM, (M), (I),** 1200 Getty Center Dr., Ste. 1000, Los Angeles, CA 90049-1687. Tel.: 310-440-7330. Fax: 310-440-7751. TDD: 310-440-7305.
E-mail: administration-museum@getty.edu
Web Site: www.getty.edu
Founded: 1953.
Congressional District: 27
Key Personnel: Dir., Michael Brand; Pres. & C.E.O. Getty Trust, James Wood; Assoc. Dir. Administration, Thomas Rhoads; Assoc. Dir. Collections, David Bomford; Assoc. Dir. Exhibitions, Quincy Houghton; Asst. Dir. Education, Toby Tannenbaum; Asst. Dir. Public Affairs, John Giurini; Sr. Cur. Antiquities, Karol Wight; Sr. Cur. Sculpture & Decorative Arts, Antonia Bostrom; Mgr. Exhibition Design, Merritt Price; Sr. Cur. Paintings, Scott Schaefer; Sr. Cur. Manuscripts, Thomas Kren; Acting Sr. Cur. Photographs, Judith Keller; Head & Retail Merchandise, Susan DeLand; Museum Shop Mgr., Chloe Simon; Sr. Cur. Drawings, Lee Hendrix; Sr. Conservator, Decorative Arts & Sculpture, Brian Considine; Sr. Conservator, Paintings, Mark Leonard; Sr. Conservator, Antiquities, Jerry Podany; Sr. Conservator, Paper Conservation, Marc Harnly; Head Preparator, Bruce Metro; Mgr. Visitor Svcs., Thomas Hook; Chief Registrar, Sally Hibbard; Head Collection Information & Access, Erin Coburn; Mgr. Museum Events, Ivy Okamura; Mgr. Imaging Svcs., Stanley Smith; Publisher, Gregory Britton; Dir. Security, Bob Combs.
Personnel Profile: Full-Time Paid 350; Part-Time Paid 29; Part-Time Volunteers 980; Interns 6.
Governing Authority: nonprofit organization. Parent Institution: The J. Paul Getty Trust. Tax-exempt: 501(c)(3).
Art Museum.
Collections: Greek & Roman antiquities; pre-20th century Western European paintings, drawings; manuscripts; sculpture; decorative arts; 19th to 20th-century American & European photographs.
Research Fields: fields pertaining to collections & conservation.
Facilities: 450-seat auditorium; cafe; restaurant. Museum publications for sale.
Activities: lectures; gallery talks; permanent exhibitions; concert series; special exhibits; seminars; general education programs for schools & adults; theatrical performances; family programs; interactive touchscreen access system.
Publications: exhibitions catalogues; Getty Villa & Museum guides; books, art history, antiquities, conservation, photography, European paintings, drawings, manuscripts, sculpture, & decorative arts.
Hours & Admission Prices: Museum: Tues.-Fri. & Sun. 10-5:30, Sat. 10-9. Villa: Thurs.-Mon. 10-5. Museum: no charge. Villa: call for admission prices. Parking $10. Closed New Year's Day; Independence Day; Thanksgiving; Christmas. ♿
Attendance: 1,600,000 (estimated)

* **JAPANESE AMERICAN NATIONAL MUSEUM, (M),** 369 E. First St., Los Angeles, CA 90012-3901. Mailing Address: 111 N. Central Ave., Los Angeles, CA 90012-3910. Tel.: 213-625-0414. Fax: 213-625-1770.
Web Site: www.janm.org
Founded: 1985.
Congressional District: 35
Key Personnel: Pres. & C.E.O., Irene Hirano; Chm., Margaret Oda; Pres. (V), Carole Yamakoshi; Sr. Vice Pres. Programs, Akemi Kikumura-Yano; Vice Pres. Devel., Lawrence Wilson; Vice Pres. External Rels., Carol Komatsuka; Controller & Dir. Administration, Kyla Lee; Dir. Collections Management & Access, Cristine Paschild; Dir. Community Affairs, Nancy Araki; Dir. Curatorial & Exhibitions, Karin Higa; Dir. Program Initiatives, Kristine Kim; Dir. Public Programs, Sabrina Motley; Dir. Retail & Visitor Svcs., Maria Kwong; Dir. Special Events, Cayleen Nakamura; Mgr. Human Resources & Volunteer Svcs., Myrna Mariona; Vice Pres. Natl. Center for Preservation of Democracy, Eileen Kurahashi.
Personnel Profile: Full-Time Paid 90; Full-Time Volunteers 200; Part-Time Volunteers 100.
Governing Authority: organization; nonprofit. Subsidiary Institution: National Center for the Preservation & Democracy. Tax-exempt: 501(c)(3).
History Museum.
Collections: Japanese American historical artifacts; three-dimensional objects; documents; printings; photographs; moving images; oral histories; 85,000 sq. ft. Pavilion designed by Gyo Obata.
Research Fields: early immigration & settlement; World War II incarceration & military service; post WWII resettlement; Japanese American communities; Japanese American art.
Facilities: 500-vol. library of books & newspapers; classrooms; 18,000 sq. ft. exhibit space; media arts center. Crafts, books of literature & scholarship for sale.
Activities: guided tours; lectures; films; formal educational programs; docent program; temporary exhibitions of your own collections; participatory, loan & traveling exhibitions; family programs; rental facility available.
Publications: annual report; quarterly, calendar of events; museum member magazine; Donor Recognition publication.
Hours & Admission Prices: Tues.-Wed. & Fri.-Sun. 11-5, Thurs. 11-8. Adults $8, seniors (62 & over) $5, students with ID & youth 6-17 $4; discounts to groups & AAM members; Thurs. 5-8 & every 3rd Thurs. of month, members, children 5 & under no charge. Closed New Year's Day; Thanksgiving; Christmas. ♿
Attendance: 120,000 (estimated)
Membership: Individual $35; Family $50; Contributing $125; Supporting $250; Sustaining $500; Director's $1,000-$2,499; President's $2,500-$9,999; Chairman's $10,000 & up.

KOREAN AMERICAN MUSEUM, 3727 W. Sixth St., Ste. 400, Los Angeles, CA 90020-5112. Tel.: 213-388-4229. Fax: 213-381-1288.
E-mail: info@kamuseum.org
Web Site: www.kamuseum.org
Key Personnel: Program Coord., Irene Hong
Korean American Museum.
Collections: Korean-American history & culture.
Hours & Admission Prices: Call for hours.

LABAND ART GALLERY, LOYOLA MARYMOUNT UNIVERSITY, One LMU Dr., Los Angeles, CA 90045-2650. Tel.: 310-338-2880. Fax: 310-338-6024.
E-mail: labandin@lmu.edu
Web Site: cfa.lmu.edu/laband
Founded: 1984.
Congressional District: 36
Key Personnel: Dir. & Cur., Carolyn Peter.
Personnel Profile: Full-Time Paid 1; Part-Time Paid 5; Part-Time Volunteers 1.
Governing Authority: university. Parent Institution: Loyola Marymount University. Tax-exempt: 170(b)(1)(A).
University Art Gallery.
Collections: Warschaw Collection of Flemish & Italian Baroque art; Max Thalmann drawings & prints.
Facilities: 212-seat auditorium; 2,300 sq. ft. exhibit space; classrooms; gallery.
Activities: guided tours; lectures; films; gallery talks; concerts; dance recitals; arts festivals; formally organized education programs for undergraduate college students.
Publications: catalogs & brochures in conjunction with exhibition programs.
Hours & Admission Prices: mid-Sept. to May Wed.-Fri. 12-4. No charge; donations accepted. ♿
Attendance: 3,850 (accurate)

LACE (LOS ANGELES CONTEMPORARY EXHIBITIONS), 6522 Hollywood Blvd., Los Angeles, CA 90028-6210. Tel.: 323-957-1777. Fax: 323-957-9025.
E-mail: info@welcometolace.org
Web Site: www.welcometolace.org
Founded: 1977.
Key Personnel: Pres., David Richards; Exec. Dir., Carol Stakenas; Vice Pres., Deborah Hong; Sec., Vincent Ruiz-Abogado; Treas., Chad Clark; Bd. Member, Adam Comeau; Bd. Member, Glen R. Phillips; Bd. Member, Blake Koh; Bd. Member, Grace Kim; Bd. Member, Synderela Peng; Bd. Member, Sean McDonald.
Personnel Profile: Full-Time Paid 3; Part-Time Volunteers 20; Interns 10.
Governing Authority: not-for-profit organization. Tax-exempt: 501(c)(3).
Visual Arts Center
Collections: present works of art in all media including performance art & video.
Research Fields: panels & forums in areas related to contemporary art criticism.
Facilities: 3,472 sq. ft. gallery.
Activities: exhibitions of contemporary art; performances; dialogs; film & video screenings; panels; lectures & readings.
Publications: catalog, Major Shows; brochures.
Hours & Admission Prices: Wed.-Thurs. & Sat.-Sun. 12-6, Fri. 12-9. Suggested Donation: $3; members no charge. ♿
Attendance: 15,000 (accurate)
Membership: Artist $25; Friend $50; Advocate $100; Silver Circle (Solo) $250; Silver Circle (Duo) $500; Presenter's Circle $1,000 & up; Vanguard $5,000 & over.

THE LOS ANGELES ART ASSOCIATION/GALLERY 825, 825 N. La Cienega Blvd., Los Angeles, CA 90069-4707. Tel.: 310-652-8272. Fax: 310-652-9251.
E-mail: gallery825@laaa.org
Web Site: www.laaa.org
Founded: 1925.
Congressional District: 5
Key Personnel: Exec. Dir., Peter Mays.
Personnel Profile: Full-Time Paid 2; Part-Time Paid 1; Part-Time Volunteers 53; Interns 1.
Governing Authority: nonprofit organization. Tax-exempt: 501(c)(3).
Southern California Art Gallery/Association.
Collections: paintings; photographs; sculpture; drawings.
Activities: changing exhibits; lectures; round tables; annual film & video event.
Publications: biannual newsletter, Artline.
Hours & Admission Prices: Tues.-Sat. 10-5. No charge. Closed New Year's Day; Easter; Independence Day; Thanksgiving; Christmas. ♿
Attendance: 5,000 (estimated)
Membership: Friends $50; Artists & Active $250; Corporate $500; Patron $1,000; Benefactor $2,500.

LOS ANGELES (CENTRAL) PUBLIC LIBRARY, 630 W. Fifth St., Los Angeles, CA 90071-2002. Tel.: 213-228-7000 & 7470. Fax: 213-228-7429. TDD: 800-735-2922.
E-mail: aconnor@lapl.org
Web Site: www.lapl.org
Founded: 1872.
Congressional District: 25
Key Personnel: Dir. Central Library, Anne Connor; Head Literature Dept., David Kelly; Head Art, Rec., & Music, Sheila Nash; Head History Dept., Cindy McNaughton; Head Adult Outreach, Daniel Dupill; Coord. Exhibits, Toria Aiken; Coord. Exhibits, Gloria Gerace; Cur. Photographs, Carolyn Cole.
Personnel Profile: Full-Time Paid 165; Part-Time Volunteers 80; Interns 2.
Governing Authority: municipal. Tax-exempt.
Library with Collections.
Collections: California prints; Japanese prints; Leo Politi Bunker Hill paintings; 240,000 images, historic photographs; Gladys English original children's book illustrations; 3 million photographs & 2.6 million Herald Examiner newspaper clippings.
Facilities: 2,600,000-vol. library of books & periodicals of general & special interest available for inter-library loan & on premises; reading room.
Activities: guided tours; permanent, temporary & traveling exhibits; reference services.
Publications: book lists.
Hours & Admission Prices: Mon.-Thurs. 10-8, Fri.-Sat. 10-6, Sun. 1-5. No charge. Closed national & state holidays. ♿
Attendance: 2,140,620 (accurate)

*** LOS ANGELES COUNTY MUSEUM OF ART, (M), (I),** 5905 Wilshire Blvd., Los Angeles, CA 90036-4598. Tel.: 323-857-6000. Fax: 323-857-6214. TDD: 323-857-0098.
E-mail: publicinfo@lacma.org
Web Site: www.lacma.org
Founded: 1910.
Congressional District: 24
Key Personnel: Dir., Michael Govan; Pres. & C.O.O., Melody Kanschat; Chm. Bd., Andrew Gordon; C.F.O., Ann Rowland; Mgr. Mktg., Rachel Mullennix; Mgr. Special Events, Terri Bradshaw; Gen. Counsel, Fred Goldstein; Asst. Dir. Exhibition Program, Irene Martin; Dir. Conservation, Mark Gilberg; Sr. Cur. Modern Art, Stephanie Barron; Cur. South & Southeast Asian Art, Stephen A. Markel; Cur. Japanese Art, Robert Singer; Dept. Head and Sr. Cur. Costumes & Textiles, Sharon Takeda; Chief Cur. European Art, J. Patrice Marandel; Dir. Membership, Alvaro Vasquez; Deputy Dir. Art Administration & Collections, Nancy K. Thomas; Dept. Head & Cur. Decorative Arts, Wendy Kaplan; Head Music Programs, Mitch Glickman; Head Film Programs, Ian Birnie; Asst. Vice Pres. Museum Education, Jane E. Burrell; Cur. Photography, Charlotte Cotton; Chief Information Officer, Peter Bodell; Asst. Dir. Collections Mgmt., Renee Montgomery; Head Registrar, Nancy Russell; Asst. Vice Pres. Merchandising, Cim B. Castellon.
Personnel Profile: Full-Time Paid 240; Part-Time Paid 30; Part-Time Volunteers 3,300; Interns 53.
Governing Authority: county; nonprofit organization. Tax-exempt: 501(c)(3).
Art Museum.
Collections: American furniture; Chinese, Korean & Japanese paintings, sculptures, ceramics & works on paper; Egyptian & Greco-Roman sculptures & antiquities; European & American art & decorative arts; Islamic art; South, Southeast & later West Asian paintings, sculpture, textiles, jades & metal works; European, Asian, North & South American art textiles and costumes; 20th-century painting, sculpture, prints & drawings.
Major Exhibits: Luis Melendez, 11/09-1/3/10; New Topographics, 11/09-1/3/10; Indian Comic Books, 11/09-2/7/10; Renoir, After Impressionism (1890-1919), 2/14/10-5/9/10; Telling Tales: American Genre Painting (1700-1920), 2/28/10-5/23/10; Robin Rhode, 3/11/10-6/6/10.
Research Fields: all curatorial departments.
Facilities: 117,000-vol. library available for use by appointment; 10,000 sq. ft. children's gallery; conservation center; 600-seat theatre; restaurant & cafe. Art books, catalogs, post cards, posters & other museum-related items for sale.
Activities: guided tours; lectures; films; gallery talks; concerts; art rental gallery; formally organized educational programs; docent program; 116-seat lecture hall; 10-volunteer councils; inter-museum loan, permanent, temporary & traveling exhibitions; tours for the hearing & visually impaired.
Publications: descriptive bulletins; monthly magazine, At LACMA; Inside LACMA; exhibition & permanent collection catalogs; members magazines, Connect; Insider.

Hours & Admission Prices: Mon.-Tues. & Thurs. 12-8, Fri. 12-9, Sat.-Sun. 11-8. Adults $12, senior citizens 62 & over and students 18 & over with I.D. $8; discounts to AAM & ICOM members; members, children under 17 & 2nd Tues. of month no charge. Closed Thanksgiving; Christmas. After 5 pay what you wish. ♿
Attendance: 825,000 (accurate)
Membership: Student $25; Active $90; Patron $200; Supporting $600; Community Partner $1,200; President's Circle Avant-Garde $1,000; President's Circle $2,500; President's Circle Patron $5,000; President's Circle Sponsor $10,000; Director's Circle $25,000; Director's Circle Scholar $50,000. Add MUSE to any level $50.

LOS ANGELES MUNICIPAL ART GALLERY - BARNSDALL ART PARK, 4800 Hollywood Blvd., Los Angeles, CA 90027-5302. Tel.: 323-644-6269. Fax: 323-644-6271. TDD: 213-660-4254.
E-mail: cadmag@sbcglobal.net
Founded: 1952.
Congressional District: 24
Key Personnel: Pres., Michael Fuller; Exec. Dir, Mark Steven Greenfield; Cur., Scott Canty; Dir. Museum Education & Tours, Sara L. Cannon; Preparator, Michael Miller; Registrar, Sidney Taylor.
Personnel Profile: Full-Time Paid 6; Part-Time Paid 24; Part-Time Volunteers 50; Interns 4.
Governing Authority: municipal. Parent Institution: Dept. of Cultural Affairs, Los Angeles, 201 N. Figueroa Street, Los Angeles, CA 90012. Tax-exempt: 501(c)(3).
Contemporary Art Gallery.
Collections: contemporary southern California art; original furniture; Wright Drawings. Historic House: 1921 Frank Lloyd Wright Hollyhock House.
Major Exhibits: 20th Anniversary - Los Angeles Printmaking Society National Exhibition, 11/09-1/10; Ideational Architectures, 1/10-4/10; COLA, 5/10-7/10; Juried Exhibition, 8/10-10/10.
Research Fields: contemporary southern California art history; Frank Lloyd Wright.
Facilities: library; 300-seat theater; art studio & classrooms; 10,000 sq. ft. exhibit space; slide registry of contemporary artists. Museum-related items for sale.
Activities: guided tours; changing exhibitions of predominantly contemporary southern California artists; improvisational tours; outreach programs to hospitals, schools & senior citizen center facilities; internship program; teacher workshops; conversations with exhibiting artists; spoken work reading program in the gallery; performances emphasizing interrelationships of the arts; formal educational programs; lectures. Museum Sponsors: Barnsdall Art Park Open House; F.L. Wright Birthday Party.
Publications: exhibition catalogs; COLA Individual Artist Fellowship.
Hours & Admission Prices: No charge; donations accepted. ♿
Attendance: 50,000 (accurate)
Membership: Student & Senior $20; Active $35; Patron $100.

LOS ANGELES MUSEUM OF THE HOLOCAUST, 6435 Wilshire Blvd., Los Angeles, CA 90048-4907. Tel.: 323-651-3704. Fax: 323-651-3706.
Web Site: www.lamoth.org
Founded: 1961.
Congressional District: 23
Key Personnel: Dir., Mark Rothman; Chm., E. Randol Schoenberg; Exec. Sec., Jodi Shapiro; Chief Docent, Ilaria Benzoni-Clark.
Personnel Profile: Full-Time Paid 4; Part-Time Paid 2; Part-Time Volunteers 20; Interns 5.
Governing Authority: religious institution. Parent Institution: Jewish Federation Council. Tax-exempt: 170(b)(1)(A).
Holocaust History Museum.
Collections: photo-narrative exhibits; artifacts; artworks; documents; oral histories; scale model of Sobibor Death Camp; videodisc presentation of archival material & oral histories.
Facilities: 2,500-vol. library of reference materials on the Holocaust period, art, insurance, claims, art of survivors & art of the holocaust and pre-war Jewish life in Europe & North Africa.
Activities: guided tours; lectures; films; organized educational programs; docent program; participatory, loan, traveling & temporary exhibitions; school loan service; annual conference; meetings; social programs; outreach programs; curriculum writing; educators credit programs. Museum Sponsors: Annual Yom Hashoah observance.
Publications: quarterly newsletter, PAGES; exhibit catalogues, Polluting the Pure, Odyssey, Kaleidoscopes, Guide to Righteous Gentiles, Anne Frank, Schindler's List, Denying History (University of California Press).
Hours & Admission Prices: Mon.-Thurs. 10-4, Fri. 10-2, Sun. 12-4. No charge; donations accepted. Closed national & Jewish holidays. ♿
Attendance: 15,000 (estimated)
Membership: Basic $75; Supporting $100; Patron $150; Sustaining $250.

LOS ANGELES POLICE HISTORICAL SOCIETY & MUSEUM, 6045 York Blvd., Los Angeles, CA 90042-3503. Tel.: 323-344-9445. Fax: 323-344-9516.
E-mail: info@laphs.com
Web Site: www.laphs.com
Founded: 1989.
Key Personnel: Chm. (V), Greg Meyer.
Governing Authority: private; nonprofit organization. Tax-exempt.
Historical Society Museum.
Collections: memorabilia; history of Los Angeles Police Dept.
Hours & Admission Prices: Adults $5; senior citizens $4; children under 12 no charge. ♿
Membership: Auxiliary Booster $25; Regular $48; Supporting $100; Family $250; Sustaining $500; Chief's Circle $1,000.

*** THE LOS ANGELES ZOO AND BOTANICAL GARDENS,** 5333 Zoo Dr., Los Angeles, CA 90027-1451. Tel.: 323-644-4200. Fax: 323-662-9786.
Web Site: www.lazoo.org
Founded: 1912.
Congressional District: 24
Key Personnel: Pres. Greater LA Zoo Assoc., Connie Morgan; Zoo Dir., John R. Lewis; Asst. Gen. Mgr., Denise Verret; Mktg. & Public Rels. Dir., Jason Jacobs; Visitor Svcs. & Gen. Mgr., Greg Edgar; Dir. Research, Dr. Cathleen Cox; Museum Shop Mgr., Denise Demont.
Personnel Profile: Full-Time Paid 271; Part-Time Paid 89; Part-Time Volunteers 800.
Governing Authority: municipal. Subsidiary Institution: Greater Los Angeles Zoo Assoc. (GLAZA). Tax-exempt.
Zoo.
Collections: mammals; birds; reptiles; amphibians; botanical gardens.
Research Fields: mammals; reptiles; birds.
Facilities: library of zoological books available for use on grounds. Zoo-related items for sale.
Activities: guided tours; lectures; films; formally organized education programs for children; permanent exhibitions.
Publications: quarterly magazine, Zooview; monthly newsletter, Zooscape.
Hours & Admission Prices: Daily 10-5. Adults 13 & over $13 and seniors 62 & over $10, children 2-12 $8; discounts to groups; members & children under 2 no charge. Closed Christmas. ♿
Attendance: 1,600,000 (accurate)
Membership: Regular $45; Couple $60; Family $75; Family Deluxe $125; Contributor $250; Wildlife Assoc. $500; Conservation Circle $1,000.

LUMMIS HOME: EL ALISAL, 200 E. Ave. 43, Los Angeles, CA 90031. Mailing Address: P.O. Box 93487, Pasadena, CA 91109-3487. Tel.: 323-222-0546 & 460-5632. Fax: 323-798-4170.
E-mail: hssc@socalhistory.org
Web Site: www.socalhistory.org
Founded: 1883.
Congressional District: 25
Key Personnel: Asst. Dir., Robert D. Montoya; Pres. (V), John O. Pohlmann.
Personnel Profile: Full-Time Paid 2; Part-Time Paid 3; Part-Time Volunteers 10.
Governing Authority: municipal; nonprofit organization. Headquarters of Historical Society of Southern California Museum, Los Angeles, CA 90031. Tax-exempt: 501(c)(3).
Historic House: 1897-1912 home of Charles F. Lummis.
Collections: archaeology; ethnology; history; Indian artifacts; photography; books by builder.
Facilities: water-conserving garden. Books on local & Southern California history & gardening for sale.
Activities: guided tours; lectures; permanent exhibitions; water conservation garden.
Publications: Southern California Quarterly; Letters from the Orange Empire; California Bibliographies; Land of Fiction; Centennial History of HSSC; Manana Land; A Guide to Historical Outing in Southern California; Land of Fact; An End and a Beginning: The South Coast and Los Angeles 1850-1887; Those Powerful Years: The South Coast and Los Angeles 1887-1917; Southern California's Spanish Heritage: An Anthology; At the Arroyo's Edge: A History of Linda Vista; A Companion and Guide to the Waterwise Garden; Southern California Local History: A Gathering of the Writings of W.W. Robinson; Month by Month in a Waterwise Garden; El Alisal: Where History Lingers; The St. Francis Dam Disaster Revisited; Women in the Life of Southern California: An Historical Anthology; Angels Flight; Griffith Park; Painting with Light; Mission San Fernando Rey de Espana; John Rowland & William Workman: 1841 So. CA Pioneers; Golden Odyssey; video, Museums Along the Arroyo; Pasadena Sketchbook, Man-made Disaster; Duncan Gleason: Artist, Athlete, and Author; Founding Documents of Los Angeles: A Bilingual Edition.

Hours & Admission Prices: Fri.-Sun. 12-4. No charge; donations accepted. Closed major holidays. ♿
Attendance: 10,000 (estimated)
Membership: Student $25; Individual & Institutional $75; Contributing $125; Patron $300; Benefactor $600; President's Circle $1,250.

MILDRED E. MATHIAS BOTANICAL GARDEN, University of California, 777 S. Tiverton Ave., Los Angeles, CA 90095-0001. Mailing Address: UCLA, Box 951606, Los Angeles, CA 90095-0001. Tel.: 310-825-3620 & 1260 (office). Fax: 310-206-3987.
E-mail: agibson@biology.ucla.edu
Web Site: www.botgard.ucla.edu.
Founded: 1929.
Congressional District: 23
Key Personnel: Dir., Dr. Arthur C. Gibson; Staff Research Assoc., Dr. Barry Prigge.
Personnel Profile: Full-Time Paid 5; Part-Time Volunteers 20.
Governing Authority: university. Parent Institution: Univ. of California at Los Angeles. Tax-exempt: 501(c)(3).
Arboretum; Botanical Garden-Herbarium.
Collections: subtropical ornamentals.
Research Fields: landscape potentialities of plants, species & hybrids.
Facilities: library of reference material on botany available for use by approval of director.
Activities: university-related research & instruction.
Publications: newsletter, MEMBG.
Hours & Admission Prices: Mon.-Fri. 8-5, Sat. 8-4. No charge; donations accepted. Closed university holidays. ♿
Attendance: 36,000
Membership: Student $15; Individual $25; Family & Couple $40; Sustaining $100; Sponsor $250; Patron $1,000.

THE MUSEUM OF AFRICAN AMERICAN ART, 4005 Crenshaw Blvd., 3rd Fl., Los Angeles, CA 90008-2534. Mailing Address: P.O. Box 8418, Los Angeles, CA 90008-0418. Tel.: 323-294-7071. Fax: 323-294-7084.
E-mail: info@maaa-la.org
Web Site: www.maaa-la.org
Founded: 1976.
Congressional District: 27
Key Personnel: Pres. (V), Belinda Fontenot-Jamerson; Mgr., Harvey Lehman.
Governing Authority: nonprofit. Tax-exempt: 501(c)(3).
African American Art Museum.
Collections: arts of African & African-descendant peoples; soapstone sculpture of the Shona people of S.E. Africa; Makonde sculpture of E. Africa; traditional sculpture of W. African peoples; sculpture, paintings, prints, ceramics, of Caribbean & South American peoples paintings, prints & sculptures of leading contemporary American artists; Harlem Renaissance Art.
Research Fields: African & African-American art.
Facilities: 300-vol. library of African, African-American art, literature & history available for research on premises; reading room. Periodicals on African-American art & other museum-related gifts for sale.
Activities: lectures; films; gallery talks; study clubs; docent program or council; training programs for professional museum workers; loan, permanent, temporary & traveling exhibitions.
Publications: book, Art: African American; International Review of African American Art; The Art of Elizabeth Catlett.
Hours & Admission Prices: Thurs.-Sat. 11-6, Sun. 12-5. No charge; donations accepted. ♿
Attendance: 1,500 (estimated)
Membership: Individual $35; Family $50; Active $100; Sponsor $250; Patron $500; Trustees Circle $1,250.

* **THE MUSEUM OF CONTEMPORARY ART, LOS ANGELES, (M),** 250 S. Grand Ave., Los Angeles, CA 90012-3021. Tel.: 213-626-6222. Fax: 213-620-8674. TDD: 213-626-6222.
Web Site: www.moca.org
Founded: 1979.
Congressional District: 25
Key Personnel: Chm. Bd. Trustees (V), Clifford J. Einstein; Pres. (V), Willem Mesdag; Dir., Jeremy Strick; C.F.O., Jack Wiant; Chief Cur., Paul Schimmel.
Personnel Profile: Full-Time Paid 95; Part-Time Paid 15; Part-Time Volunteers 105; Interns 33.
Governing Authority: board of trustees; nonprofit organization. Tax-exempt: 501(c)(3).
Art Museum.
Collections: contemporary works after 1940.
Research Fields: contemporary art in all media, including painting, sculpture, prints, photography, architecture, film, video & performance.
Facilities: 75,000 sq. ft. exhibit space.
Activities: educational programs; performances; special events.
Publications: quarterly newsletter, The Contemporary; museum catalogues.
Hours & Admission Prices: Mon. & Fri. 11-5, Thurs. 11-8, Sat.-Sun. 11-6. Adults $10, students & seniors $5; discounts to AAM & ICOM members; children under 12, Thurs. 5-8 & members no charge. ♿
Attendance: 325,000 (accurate)
Membership: Student $30; Artist $40; Member $65; Household $85; Contributing Member $155; Moca Associate $325; Art Advocate $625; Curator's Circle $1,200; Executive Forum & Director's Forum $3,000; MOCA Partners $10,000.

MUSEUM OF NEON ART, (M), 136 W. 4th St., Los Angeles, CA 90013. Mailing Address: P.O. Box 862307, Los Angeles, CA 90086-2307. Tel.: 213-489-9918. Fax: 213-489-9932.
E-mail: info@neonmona.org
Web Site: www.neonmona.org
Founded: 1981.
Congressional District: 25
Key Personnel: Exec. Dir., Kim Koga.
Personnel Profile: Full-Time Paid 1; Part-Time Paid 1; Part-Time Volunteers 24.
Governing Authority: nonprofit. Tax-exempt: 501(c)(3).
Neon, Electric & Kinetic Art Museum.
Collections: contemporary fine art in electric media; historic neon signs.
Research Fields: history of neon, electric & kinetic art; outdoor advertising art; legal & cultural ramifications of neon art.
Facilities: 500-vol. library of books, slides & videotapes pertaining to art & neon art available for research on premises only by written request; classrooms. Books, electronic jewelry & other museum related items for sale.
Activities: guided tours; lectures; films; gallery talks; concerts; workshops; rental gallery; formally organized education programs.
Publications: quarterly newsletter.
Hours & Admission Prices: Thurs.-Sat. 12-7, Sun. 12-5. Adults $7, seniors 65 & over and students 13-22 $5, children 5-12 $3; children under 5 no charge. ♿
Attendance: 6,000 (accurate)
Membership: Student $25; Neon $35; Argon $50; Helium $100; Krypton $250; Plasma $500; Xenon $1,000.

MUSEUM OF TOLERANCE, 9786 W. Pico Blvd., Los Angeles, CA 90035-4720. Tel.: 310-553-8403 & 9036. Fax: 310-553-4521.
Web Site: www.museumoftolerance.com
Founded: 1993.
Congressional District: 23
Key Personnel: Founder & Dean, Rabbi Marvin Hier; Assoc. Dir., Rabbi Abraham Cooper; Exec. Dir., Rabbi Meyer H. May; Museum Dir., Liebe Geft; C.F.O. & C.A.O., Susan Burden; Dir. Membership Devel., Marlene F. Hier; Dir. Public Rels, Avra Shapiro; Dir. Communications, Michele E. Alkin; Dir. Media Projects, Richard Trank; Dir. Major Gifts, Janice Prager; Dir. Library & Archive Svcs., Adaire Klein.
Governing Authority: nonprofit organization. Parent Institution: Simon Wiesenthal Center, Inc., 1300 S. Roxbury Dr., Los Angeles, CA. Tax-exempt: 501(c)(3).
Holocaust & Human Rights Museum.
Collections: Nazi Holocaust; World War II; 20th-century genocide; racism; concentration camps; Holocaust artifacts; human rights; tolerance; Civil Rights; antisemitism; art; photographs.
Major Exhibits: The Power to Play: Toys That Reflect A Child's Imagination (Co-sponsored with Christian Children's Fund) (T), 11/09-1/10.
Research Fields: war crimes & criminals; history of the Holocaust; historical & contemporary antisemitism; contemporary human rights issues; prejudice; aggression; tolerance; ethnic relations in the U.S.; multiculturalism.
Facilities: library; archives; 3,500 sq. ft. exhibit space.
Activities: guided tours; lectures; broadcast programs; docent programs; loan, traveling & temporary exhibitions; research; reference assistance; oral history program; Moriah Films. Annual Event: Yom Hashoah Commemoration.
Publications: Occupation: Nazi Hunter: The Continuing Search for the Perpetrators of the Holocaust; Genocide: Critical Issues of the Holocaust: A Companion to the Film, Genocide; Confronting Omnicide: Jewish Reflections on Weapons of Mass Destruction; Simon Wiesenthal Center Annual; Codename: The Long Sobbing; Dignity & Defiance: The Confrontation of Life & Death in the Warsaw Ghetto; Beit Hashoah: Museum of Tolerance; Ministry of Lies: The Truth Behind the Nation of Islam, The Secret Relationship Between Blacks & Jews; Mirror of Conflict: The Black Press & Major Issues of Jewish Concern; The Water Crisis; The Next Middle East Conflict; The Neo-Nazi Movement in Germany: An Eyewitness Documentary; The BNL Blunder: How U.S. Policy Allowed a Bank in Atlanta to

Help Finance Saddam Hussein's War Machine; The Poison Gas Connection: Western Suppliers of Unconventional Weapons & Technologies to Iraq & Libya; Weapons of Mass Destruction: The Cases of Iran, Libya & Syria; In Their Own Words: Interviews with Leaders of Hamas, Islamic & the Muslim Brotherhood: Damascus, Amman, Gaza; Holocaust Denial: Bigotry in the Guise of Scholarship; Genocide; Echoes That Remain; Liberation; Liberation & the companion book Codename: The Long Sobbing: Genocide & Echoes That Remain; Genocide, Echoes That Remain & Liberation; Genocide, Echoes That Remain, Liberation & the companion book to Liberation; Courage to Remember.
Hours & Admission Prices: April-Oct. Mon.-Fri. 10-5, Sun. 11-5; Nov.-March Mon.-Thurs. 10-5, Fri. 10-3, Sun. 11-5. Adults $15, senior citizens 62 & over $12, students w/ID & youth 5-18 $11; members no charge. Closed New Year's Day; Independence Day; Labor Day; Thanksgiving; Christmas; Jewish holidays. ♿
Attendance: 250,000 (estimated)
Membership: Students & Seniors $30; Individual $45; Dual & Family $65; Sustainer $100; Associate $250; Colleague $500; Director's Circle $1,000.

* **NATURAL HISTORY MUSEUM OF LOS ANGELES COUNTY, (M),** 900 Exposition Blvd., Los Angeles, CA 90007-4057. Tel.: 213-763-DINO. Fax: 213-743-4843.
E-mail: info@nhm.org
Web Site: www.nhm.org
Founded: 1910.
Congressional District: 28
Key Personnel: Pres. & Dir., Dr. Jane G. Pisano; Chief Deputy Dir., Jural J. Garrett; Sr. Vice Pres. Advancement, Tom Jacobson; Legal Counsel & Vice Pres. Government Affairs, James R. Gilson; Div. Chief Research & Collections, Margaret Hardin; Deputy Dir. Administration & Operations, Leonard Navarro; Dir. Budgeting & Financial Reporting, Linda Ross; Vice Pres. Mktg. & Communications, Cynthia Wornham; Dir. Human Resources, Micah Mullens; Vice Pres. Education, Karen Wise; Volunteer Coord., Julie McAdam; Museum Shop Mgr., Trino Marquez.
Personnel Profile: Full-Time Paid 300; Part-Time Paid 5; Part-Time Volunteers 520.
Governing Authority: county. Parent Institution: Los Angeles County Museum of Natural History Foundation. Branch Museums: Page Museum at the La Brea Tar Pits, Hancock Park, 5801 Wilshire Blvd., Los Angeles; William S. Hart Park and Museum, 24151 Newhall Ave., Newhall, CA 91321. Tax-exempt: 501(c)(3) & 170(b)(1)(A).
Natural History Museum.
Collections: ethnology; ichthyology; archaeology; anthropology; archives; botany; entomology; herpetology; California & general American history; mineralogy; paleontology; ornithology; mammalogy; invertebrate zoology: crustacea, echinoderms, mollusks & polychaets.
Research Fields: anthropology; archaeology; botany; entomology; ethnology; geology; herpetology; California & general American history; American Indians; mineralogy; vertebrate & invertebrate paleontology; ichthyology; ornithology; mammalogy; invertebrate zoology.
Facilities: 150,000-vol. library of books & periodicals on zoology; botany; mineralogy; paleontology; archaeology; ethnology & California & general American history available for reference use only; 350-seat auditorium; classrooms. Books, prints & ethnic art objects reproductions for sale.
Activities: guided tours; lectures; films; gallery talks; classes, workshops & field trips for children & adults; outreach programs to elementary schools, special education facilities, senior citizen centers & rest homes; Discovery Center; insect zoo; teacher workshops; docent program; inter-museum, permanent & temporary exhibitions; school loan service; Earthmobile & Seamobile, mobile science museum for schools; high school research program.
Publications: Baja California Travels Series: Contributions in Science; Science Series; Technical Reports; books & catalogues in history, natural sciences, anthropology & archaeology; member magazine, Naturalist.
Hours & Admission Prices: Daily 9:30-5. Adults $9, students & seniors $6.50, children 5-12 $2; children under 5, visitors on first Tues. of month & members no charge. Closed New Year's Day; Independence Day; Thanksgiving; Christmas. ♿
Attendance: 650,000 (estimated)
Membership: Family $70; Patron $185; Naturalist $325; Explorer $600; Fellows $1,500.

ORAN Z'S PAN AFRICAN BLACK FACTS & WAX MUSEUM, 3742 W. Martin Luther King Blvd., Los Angeles, CA 90008-1751. Tel.: 323-299-8829.
Black History Museum.
Collections: black history & culture; period clothing; uniforms; personal artifacts; black wax figures; autographs; photographs; postcards; sculptures.
Hours & Admission Prices: Call for hours.

PAGE MUSEUM AT THE LA BREA TAR PITS, 5801 Wilshire Blvd., Los Angeles, CA 90036-4596. Tel.: 323-934-7243.
Web Site: www.tarpits.org
Archaeology Museum.
Collections: fossils; Ice Age plants & animals; Los Angeles history.
Facilities: Museum-related items for sale.
Hours & Admission Prices: Mon.-Fri. 9:30-5, Sat.-Sun. & holidays 10-5. Adults $7, seniors 62 & over, students $4.50, children 5-12 $2; 1st Tues. of month, members & children under 5 no charge. Closed New Year's Day; Independence Day; Thanksgiving; Christmas.

PETERSEN AUTOMOTIVE MUSEUM, 6060 Wilshire Blvd., Los Angeles, CA 90036-3605. Tel.: 323-964-6356 & 6357. Fax: 323-930-6642.
E-mail: info@petersen.org
Web Site: www.petersen.org
Founded: 1994.
Congressional District: 4
Key Personnel: Dir., Richard Messer; Chm. (V), Steven E. Young; Cur., Leslie Kendall; Membership, Teresa Markowitz; Special Events, Kari Lusti; Museum Shop Mgr., J.C. Lepe.
Personnel Profile: Full-Time Paid 30; Part-Time Paid 4; Part-Time Volunteers 70; Interns 2.
Governing Authority: Parent Institution: Petersen Automotive Museum Foundation. Tax-exempt: 501(c)(3).
Automotive Museum.
Collections: works on paper; automobiles & related objects in the permanent collection reflect the history of the automobile & its impact on American life & culture using Los Angeles as the prime example.
Research Fields: automobiles built in Los Angeles & southern California.
Facilities: education facilities; banquet facilities; 100,000 sq. ft. exhibit space; children's discovery center. Museum-related items for sale.
Activities: docent program; guided tours; lectures; rental gallery; traveling exhibitions; hands-on children's exhibits.
Publications: quarterly newsletter; Petersen Quarterly.
Hours & Admission Prices: Tues.-Sun. 10-6. Adults $10, senior citizens & students $5, children 5-12 $3; discounts to AAA members; members no charge. ♿
Attendance: 150,000 (estimated)
Membership: Station Wagon $55; Convertible $65; Vintage $150; Classic $250; Concourse $500; Checkered Flag $1,200.

PLAZA DE LA RAZA, INC. & BOATHOUSE GALLERY, 3540 N. Mission Rd., Los Angeles, CA 90031-3195. Tel.: 323-223-2475. Fax: 323-223-1804.
Web Site: www.plazadelaraza.org
Founded: 1969.
Congressional District: 30
Key Personnel: Exec. Dir., Rose Marie Cano; Chm. (V), Armando G. Ramirez; Dir. Education, Maria Jimenez-Torres; Museum Shop Mgr., Rosalie Portillo; Coord., Kay Rosser; Dir. Devel., Tomas J. Benitez; Dir. Mktg., Melissa Richardson Banks.
Personnel Profile: Full-Time Paid 9; Part-Time Paid 27; Part-Time Volunteers 220; Interns 2.
Governing Authority: nonprofit organization. Tax-exempt: 501(c)(3), 170(b)(1)(A).
Art Museum: housed in historic boathouse gallery.
Collections: Mexican-American folk arts of southern California; artwork by Latino artists; photos by Jose Galvez.
Research Fields: Mexican-American folk life of southern California.
Activities: films; concerts; dance recitals; art festivals; organized educational programs; loan & traveling exhibitions; hispanic arts.
Publications: annual catalogues, Celebration; plaza newsletter; brochures.
Hours & Admission Prices: Mon.-Fri. 10-5, Sat. 10-2. Suggested Donations: adults $3, children $1. Closed Columbus Day; Veterans Day; Thanksgiving. ♿
Membership: Amigo $35; Familia $50; Maestro $100; Padrino $250; Amigo Distinguido $500.

PSYCHIATRY: AN INDUSTRY OF DEATH MUSEUM, 6616 Sunset Blvd., Los Angeles, CA 90028-7104. Tel.: 323-467-4242; 800-869-2247.
E-mail: humanrights@cchr.org
Web Site: www.cchr.org
Psychiatry Museum.
Collections: psychiatric history, drugs & medical practices; documentaries.
Facilities: Museum-related items for sale.
Activities: films.
Hours & Admission Prices: Mon.-Fri. 10-10, Sat.-Sun. 10-6. No charge.

SEPULVEDA HOUSE, 622 N. Main St., Los Angeles, CA 90012-1822. Tel.: 213-628-1274.
Key Personnel: Cur., Suellen Chang
Historic House Museum: housed in former boardinghouse, built in 1887.
Collections: period artifacts & furnishings.
Activities: film.
Hours & Admission Prices: Mon.-Fri. 9-4, Sat.-Sun. 10-3. No charge.

SKIRBALL CULTURAL CENTER, (M), 2701 N. Sepulveda Blvd., Los Angeles, CA 90049-6833. Tel.: 310-440-4500 & 4642. Fax: 310-440-4728.
E-mail: mrasmussen@skirball.org
Web Site: www.skirball.org
Founded: 1996.
Congressional District: 29
Key Personnel: Chief of Staff, Kathryn Girard; C.E.O., Uri D. Herscher; Museum Dir., Robert Kirschner; Cur., Grace Cohen Grossman; Assoc. Cur. Archaeology, Erin Clancey; Dir. Programs, Jordan Peimer; Controller, Rob Harrison; Dir. Education, Sheri Bernstein; Mgr. Membership, Sabrina Wurf; Vice Pres. Advancement, Jocelyn Tetel; Assoc. Cur., Tal Gozani; Museum Shop Mgr., Pam Balton.
Personnel Profile: Full-Time Paid 167; Part-Time Paid 13; Part-Time Volunteers 309; Interns 6.
Governing Authority: board of trustees. Tax-exempt: 501(c)(3).
Art & History Museum.
Collections: Kirschstein Collection of Jewish ceremonial art; Dr. Nelson Glueck Memorial Collection of archaeological artifacts; Joseph Hamburger numismatic collection; I. Solomon & L. Grossman collections of engravings & photo prints; manuscripts, paintings, sculpture, prints & drawings by artists of Jewish origins & on Jewish themes; textiles; decorative arts; Israel archaeology; graphics; American Jewish ethnography.
Research Fields: Jewish culture & ceremonial art; contemporary Jewish artists; Jewish history artifacts.
Facilities: conference center; resource center; classrooms; restaurant; amphitheater; children's museum. Museum-related items for sale.
Activities: guided tours; lectures; films; concerts; children's workshops; docent program; classes.
Publications: catalogs; exhibition brochures; museum calendar.
Hours & Admission Prices: Tues.-Wed. & Fri. 12-5, Thurs. 12-9, Sat.-Sun. 10-5. Adults $10, students w/ID & seniors $8, children 2-12 $5; discounts to AAM members & museum professionals w/ID; children under 2 & members no charge. Closed national & Jewish holidays. ♿
Attendance: 500,000 (accurate)
Membership: Student & Senior $50; Individual $55; Senior Dual $65; Dual $70; Family $95; Family Plus $195; Supporting $300; Corporate $650; Curator's Circle $1,500, $2,500, $5,000.

TRAVEL TOWN TRANSPORTATION MUSEUM, 5200 Zoo Dr., Los Angeles, CA 90027-1472. Mailing Address: Travel Town Planning and Development, Department of Recreation and Parks, 3900 W. Chevy Chase Dr. (MS 656/3), Los Angeles, CA 90039. Tel.: 323-662-5874. Fax: 818-243-0041.
Web Site: www.laparks/grifmet/tt/index.htm
Founded: 1952.
Congressional District: 29
Key Personnel: Dir., Linda J. Barth; Asst. Dir., Thomas W. Breckner; Museum Shop Mgr., Nancy Gneier.
Personnel Profile: Full-Time Paid 5; Part-Time Paid 15; Part-Time Volunteers 150.
Governing Authority: municipal government; nonprofit. Parent Institution; Recreation & Parks, City of Los Angeles. Tax-exempt.
Transportation Museum: located on the site of the Civilian Conservation Corp. camp, which was used as a P.O.W. camp during World War II. One building on site is a c.1900 relocated freight depot.
Collections: railroad equipment with emphasis on steam locomotives used in the American West & Southwest chiefly in the period 1880-1940; wagons used locally 1860s-1910s; local & California general & transportation history; model train display.
Research Fields: development of Los Angeles & southern California as it relates to railroading; role & impact of railroads in culture; history of interurbans in Los Angeles County.
Facilities: library of railroad ephemera; 10,000 sq. ft. exhibit space; 7 acre exhibit space apart from buildings. Museum-related items for sale.
Activities: docent program; formal education & exhibit programs for children; temporary exhibitions; miniature train ride. Museum Sponsors: full-size railroad equipment operations; teacher's guide on railroad history.
Publications: quarterly newsletter, Green Eye.
Hours & Admission Prices: Mon.-Fri. 10-4, Sat.-Sun. & holidays 10-5. No charge; donations accepted. Closed Christmas. ♿
Attendance: 350,000 (estimated)

* **USC FISHER MUSEUM OF ART, (M),** 823 Exposition Blvd., Los Angeles, CA 90089-0172. Mailing Address: USC Fisher Museum of Art, University Park, Harris Hall Rm. 126, Los Angeles, CA 90089-0001. Tel.: 213-740-4561. Fax: 213-740-7676.
E-mail: fmoa@usc.edu
Web Site: fisher.usc.edu
Founded: 1939.
Congressional District: 28
Key Personnel: Dir., Dr. Selma Holo; Assoc. Dir., Kay Allen; Administrative Asst., Raphael Gatchalian; Cur., Ariadni Liokatis; Education & Programs Coord., Katherine Goar; Collections Mgr. & Registrar, Courtney Lynch; Chief Preparator, Richard Ruhe.
Personnel Profile: Full-Time Paid 7; Part-Time Volunteers 1; Interns 6.
Governing Authority: university. Parent Institution: University of Southern California. Tax-exempt: 103(6).
University Art Museum.
Collections: paintings; sculpture; graphics; European & American paintings, prints & drawings; Armand Hammer & Elizabeth Holmes Fisher Collection of 15th- to 20th-century paintings.
Research Fields: ancient through 20th-century art.
Facilities: fine arts library; School of Fine Arts.
Activities: guided tours; lectures; films; family festivals; gallery talks; inter-museum loan, permanent, traveling & temporary exhibitions.
Publications: exhibition catalogs including most recently: The Art of Exaggeration & Piranesi's Perspectives on Rome (spring '95); LAX: The Los Angeles Exhibition, 1992; Body to Earth: 3 Artists from Brazil, 1993; Richard Diebenkorn: Works on Paper from the Harry W. & Mary Margaret Anderson Collection, 1993; Locus, Contemporary Israeli Art Exhibition, 1993; Light in Darkness: Women in Japanese Prints of Early Showa (1926-1945), 1996; Ut Poesis Pictura: J.M.W. Turner's Illustrations to the British Poets, 1997; L.A. Obscura: The Architectural Photography of Julius Shulman, 1998; Open House West: Museum Architecture and Changing Civic Identity, 1999; Lost and Found: Rediscovering Early Photographic Processes, 2001; Willie Robert Middlebrook, 2001; Global Address, 2002; Mixed Feelings, 2002; Fashion and Transgression, 2003; Human Conditions, 2003; UnNaturally, 2003; Transfictions, 2004; Peter Plagens, An Introspective, 2004; Albert Contreras, Luminous Scapes and Environments, Fall 2005; Contemporary Soliloquies on the Natural World, Winter 2005-2006; Michael Mazur and Dante: A Different Paradise, Fall 2006; The Bone-and-Bird Art of Joyce Cutler-Shaw and Sarah Perry, Spring 2007; Material Affinities: To Clay and Back, Fall 2007; Robert Graham: Body of Work, Spring 2009; Donald Bandler: A Roving Eye on Cyprus, Spring 2009; Victor Raphael: Travels and Wanderings, 1979-2009.
Hours & Admission Prices: Tues.-Sat. 12-5, during exhibitions. No charge. ♿
Attendance: 20,000 (estimated)

WATTS TOWERS ARTS CENTER & CHARLES MINGUS YOUTH ARTS CENTER, 1727 E. 107th St., Los Angeles, CA 90002-3621. Tel.: 213-847-4646 & 485-1795. Fax: 323-564-7030.
E-mail: cadwattsctr@earthlink.net
Web Site: culturela.org
Founded: 1975.
Congressional District: 37
Key Personnel: Dir., Rosie Lee Hooks.
Personnel Profile: Full-Time Paid 4; Part-Time Paid 15; Interns 1.
Governing Authority: municipal; nonprofit organization. Parent Institution: City of Los Angeles Dept. of Cultural Affairs, 201 N. Figueroa St., Ste. 1400, Los Angeles, CA 90012. Tax-exempt: 501(c)(3).
Arts Center & Gallery.
Collections: The Watts Towers, Simon Rodia built using from seashells, tiles, bottles & various broken pieces of ceramics; art gallery exhibitions of local & world renowned contemporary artists.
Facilities: classrooms.
Activities: lectures; films; concerts; arts festivals drama; organized education programs for children; loan & temporary exhibitions; art instruction classes. Museum Sponsors: annual Simon Rodia; Watts Towers Jazz Festival; Day of the Drum Festival in September.
Hours & Admission Prices: Watts Towers Arts Center: Tues.-Sat. 10-4, Sun. 12-4. Tours: adults $7, seniors $3; military and children under 12 no charge. Simon Rodia's Watts Towers: Sat. 10-4, Sun. 12-4. Tours: Thurs.-Fri. 11-3, Sat. 10:30-3, Sun. 12:30-3; please call for information. Closed New Year's Day; Christmas. ♿
Attendance: 25,000 (estimated)
Membership: Associate $15; Individual $30; Family $40; Sponsor $100; Patron $500.

WELLS FARGO HISTORY MUSEUM, 333 S. Grand Ave., Los Angeles, CA 90071-1504. Mailing Address: Wells Fargo Historical Services, 420 Montgomery St., MAC A0101-106, San Francisco, CA 94163-0001. Tel.: 213-253-7166.
Founded: 1982.
Congressional District: 25
Key Personnel: Cur., Juan Colato; Asst. Cur., Ileana Bonilla.
Governing Authority: profit-making organization. Affiliated with Wells Fargo Bank.
Company History Museum.
Collections: Concord Stagecoach; Wells Fargo banking & express history; gold scales; mining; Southern California.
Activities: guided tours; audiovisual programs; permanent & temporary exhibitions; replica stagecoach on which visitors may take imaginary ride.
Publications: scholarly pamphlets.
Hours & Admission Prices: Mon.-Fri. 9-5. No charge. Closed bank holidays. ♿
Attendance: 100,000 (estimated)

ZIMMER CHILDREN'S MUSEUM, 6505 Wilshire Blvd., Ste. 100, Los Angeles, CA 90048-4908. Tel.: 323-761-8989 & 8992. Fax: 323-761-8990.
E-mail: info@zimmermuseum.org
Web Site: www.zimmermuseum.org
Formerly: Zimmer Children's Museum of Jewish Community Centers of Greater Los Angeles
Founded: 1991.
Key Personnel: C.E.O., Esther Netter; Dir., Esther Shapiro; Pres. (V), Wendy Moss Klein.
Personnel Profile: Full-Time Paid 5; Part-Time Paid 5; Part-Time Volunteers 50; Interns 1.
Governing Authority: private; nonprofit organization. Tax-exempt: 501(c)(3).
Children's Museum.
Collections: hands-on focus on Jewish culture, traditions & history.
Hours & Admission Prices: Tues., Thurs. & Sun. 12:30-5, Wed.10-5, Fri. 10-12:30. Adults $8, children 3-12 $5; discounts to AAM members & groups; grandparents, members & children under 3 no charge. Closed all national & Jewish holidays; holiday Sundays. ♿
Attendance: 25,000 (accurate)
Membership: Family $75; Family Plus $185; Silver Patron $250; Gold Patron $500; Diamond Patron $1,000 and up; President's Circle $2,500 & up; Museum Founder $5,000 & up.

Los Banos

RALPH MILLIKEN MUSEUM, 905 Pacheco Blvd., Los Banos, CA 93635. Mailing Address: P.O. Box 2294, Los Banos, CA 93635-2294. Tel.: 209-826-5505.
Founded: 1954.
Key Personnel: Sec., June Erreca.
Governing Authority: county. Support Institution: Milliken Museum Society. Tel: 209-826-5747.
Cultural Museum.
Collections: agriculture; archaeology; military uniforms; Indian artifacts; paleontology; photographs.
Research Fields: genealogy; history; biography; photography.
Facilities: library of old historic value newspapers; account books; maps; minutes; documents available for use on premises.
Activities: permanent & rotating displays; museum society monthly meetings.
Publications: pamphlets; brochures.
Hours & Admission Prices: Tues.-Sun. 1-4, special tours by arrangement. No charge; donations accepted.
Attendance: 1,000

Los Gatos

MUSEUMS OF LOS GATOS, 75 Church St. & 4 Tait Ave., Los Gatos, CA 95030. Mailing Address: P.O. Box 1904, Los Gatos, CA 95031-1904. Tel.: 408-395-7375 & 354-2646. Fax: 408-395-7386.
E-mail: ed@museumsoflosgatos.org
Web Site: www.museumsoflosgatos.org
Formerly: Los Gatos Museum Association
Founded: 1965.
Congressional District: 13
Key Personnel: Exec. Dir., Elke Groves; Pres., Sandy Decker; Cur. Art, Catherine Politopoulos.
Personnel Profile: Full-Time Paid 1; Part-Time Paid 5; Part-Time Volunteers 950.
Governing Authority: nonprofit organization. Parent Institution: Los Gatos Museum Association. Branch Museum: History Museum of Los Gatos, Forbes Mill, 75 Church St., Los Gatos, CA 95030. Tel: 408-395-7375; Art & Nature Museums of Los Gatos, 4 Tait Ave., Los Gatos, CA 95030. Tel: 408-354-2646. Tax-exempt.
Art & History Museum.
Collections: local history; art displays; cultural displays; two historic buildings.
Research Fields: local mortuary records.
Activities: guided tours; educational programs.
Publications: book, Walking Tour of Los Gatos.
Hours & Admission Prices: Wed.-Sun. 12-4. No charge; donations accepted. Closed holidays. ♿
Attendance: 10,000 (accurate)
Membership: Student & Senior $25; Individual $35; Household $50; Supporting & Business $100; Sponsor $250; Benefactor $500.

YOUTH SCIENCE INSTITUTE AT VASONA PARK, 296 Garden Hill Dr., Los Gatos, CA 95032-7669. Tel.: 408-356-4945.
E-mail: info@ysi-ca.org
Web Site: www.ysi-ca.org/vasona/vshome.html
Science Center.
Collections: local animals; native plants; dinosaurs.
Activities: science classes; science day camp in summer.
Hours & Admission Prices: Mon.-Fri. 9-4:30, Sat.-Sun. by appointment.

Los Olivos

WILDLING ART MUSEUM, (M), 2928 San Marcos Ave., Los Olivos, CA 93441. Mailing Address: P.O. Box 907, Los Olivos, CA 93441-0907. Tel.: 805-688-1082. Fax: 805-686-8339.
E-mail: info@wildlingmuseum.org
Web Site: www.wildlingmuseum.org
Founded: 1997.
Congressional District: 24
Key Personnel: Exec. Dir., Elizabeth P. Knowles; Pres. (V), Patti Jacquemain; Treas., Dave Gledhill; Dir. Communications & Membership, Holly Cline; Mgr. Visitor Svcs., Amy Mutza.
Personnel Profile: Full-Time Paid 2; Part-Time Paid 1; Part-Time Volunteers 30.
Governing Authority: private; nonprofit organization. Tax-exempt.
Art Museum.
Collections: paintings, prints, drawings, photographs & sculpture depicting America's wilderness and wildlife including flora & fauna.
Facilities: library; 900 sq. ft. exhibit space; education center. Museum-related items for sale.
Activities: formal education programs for adults; guided tours; lectures; artists workshops; art classes for children; field trips. Annual Events: Wilderness Spirit Award Dinner; Vivan Los Californios BBQ; Santa Ynez Valley Artists' Studio Tour.
Publications: quarterly newsletter, The Fox Tale; brochures; exhibition monographs; catalogue, Endangered Species: Flora & Fauna in Peril.
Hours & Admission Prices: Wed.-Sun. 11-5. Donation Requested: adults $3; museum, AAM & ICOM members no charge. Closed New Year's Day; Easter; Independence Day; Thanksgiving; Christmas. ♿
Attendance: 8,000 (estimated)
Membership: Individual $45; Family $60; Wilderness Circle $150; Meadow Guild $250; Foothills Council $500; Pinnacle Group $1,000; Summit Stars $5,000.

Madera

MADERA COUNTY MUSEUM, 210 W. Yosemite Ave., Madera, CA 93637. Mailing Address: Madera County Historical Society, P.O. Box 150, Madera, CA 93639-0150. Tel.: 559-673-0291.
Web Site: www.maderahistory.org
Founded: 1955.
Congressional District: 18
Key Personnel: Pres. (V), Sheryl Berry; Cur., Dorothy Foust; Museum Shop Mgr., Lou Emmertt.
Personnel Profile: Part-Time Volunteers 15.
Governing Authority: county. Affiliated with Madera County Historical Society. Tax-exempt.
General Museum: housed in the 1900, first Madera County Court House.
Collections: photographs; mining; local Indian artifacts; home furnishings; lumber; agriculture; period artifacts; law enforcement.
Research Fields: family histories; industry; county history.
Facilities: 400-vol. library of material of historical information, education, health, law, & literature available on premises.
Activities: guided tours.
Publications: semiannual bulletin, Madera County Historian; quarterly newsletter.
Hours & Admission Prices: Sat.-Sun. 1-4. No charge; donations accepted. Closed New Year's Day; Easter; Mother's Day; Christmas.

Attendance: 1,141 (accurate)
Membership: Student $2; Individual $15; Family & Sustaining $25; Life $150.

Malibu

FREDERICK R. WEISMAN MUSEUM OF ART, Pepperdine University, 24255 Pacific Coast Hwy., Malibu, CA 90263-3999. Tel.: 310-506-7257. Fax: 310-506-4556.
E-mail: michael.zakian@pepperdine.edu
Web Site: arts.pepperdine.edu/museum/
Founded: 1992.
Congressional District: 24
Key Personnel: Dir., Michael Zakian.
Personnel Profile: Full-Time Paid 1; Part-Time Paid 1.
Governing Authority: private university; not-for-profit. Tax-exempt: 501(c)(3).
University Art Museum.
Collections: 20th-century American art; contemporary California art.
Research Fields: contemporary California art.
Facilities: 3,000 sq. ft. exhibit space.
Activities: temporary exhibits.
Hours & Admission Prices: Tues.-Sun. 11-5. No charge. Closed New Year's Eve, Day & week; Memorial Day; Independence Day; Labor Day; Thanksgiving; Christmas Day & week. ♿
Attendance: 20,000 (estimated)
Membership: Bronze $50; Silver $100; Sterling $150; Gold $300; Platinum $500; Diamond $1,000.

MALIBU LAGOON MUSEUM, 23200 Pacific Coast Hwy., Malibu, CA 90265-4937. Mailing Address: P.O. Box 291, Malibu, CA 90265-0291. Tel.: 310-456-8432 & 1770.
Web Site: www.adamsonhouse.org
Founded: 1982.
Key Personnel: Chm. (V), Katherine Mesi; Pres. (V), Devel. & Membership, Deborah Miller; Public Rels., Beverly Gosnell; Gift Shop Mgr., Joan Page.
Personnel Profile: Part-Time Volunteers 90.
Governing Authority: state; nonprofit organization. California Dept. of Parks & Recreation; Malibu State Beach Interpretive Assoc. Tax-exempt: 501(c)(3).
Historic House & Museum; botanical gardens.
Collections: Malibu history from Chumash Indians to present day; Chumash Indian artifacts; ceramics; photographs; coins; early ranching items; documents. Historic House: 1929 Adamson House.
Research Fields: Chumash Indians; chain of title of Malibu Land Grant; tile & ceramic products from Malibu Potteries; Rindge family history; Malibu Railroad; 1920s & 1930s California & Mediterranean architects & architecture.
Facilities: library; meeting space; botanical garden. Museum-related items & books for sale.
Activities: guided tours; lectures; organized education programs for children; docent program.
Publications: monthly newsletter, Information for Volunteers; quarterly newsletter, Information for Membership.
Hours & Admission Prices: Wed.-Sat. 11-3, last house tour 2; groups of 10 & over by appointment only. Adults $5. Closed holidays. ♿
Attendance: 19,709 (estimated)
Membership: Individual $25; Family $50; Sponsor $100; Associate $250; Patron $500.

Mammoth Lakes

DEVILS POSTPILE NATIONAL MONUMENT, Mammoth Lakes, CA 93546. Mailing Address: P.O. Box 3999, Mammoth Lakes, CA 93546-3999. Tel.: 760-934-2289. Fax: 760-934-4780.
Web Site: nps.gov/depo
Founded: 1911.
Congressional District: 15
Key Personnel: Park Mgr., Deanna Dulen.
Governing Authority: federal. Parent Institution: National Park Service, U.S. Dept. of Interior, Washington, DC. Tax-exempt: 501(c)(3).
Park Museum.
Collections: rocks; pressed flowers; herbarium; volcanic rock; colored slide collection.
Research Fields: geology of volcanic rocks.
Facilities: Selected books & slides for sale.
Activities: conducted walks; campfire programs.
Hours & Admission Prices: May 26-Oct. daily 9-5 weather permitting. Adult $7, child 3-15 $4; not to exceed $20 per carload. Park Camping: daily.

MAMMOTH SKI MUSEUM, (M), 100 College Pkwy., Mammoth Lakes, CA 93546. Tel.: 760-934-6592.
E-mail: info@mammothskimuseum.org
Web Site: www.mammothskimuseum.org
Key Personnel: Dir. & Cur., Kendra Knight
Ski Museum.
Collections: ski history; sport & culture of skiing; fine art; literature.
Major Exhibits: Peak Advantage: The 10th Mountain Dive, 11/09-12/10; Children & Skiing, 11/09-12/10; Andrea Mead Lawrence, 11/09-12/10; The New Yorker, 11/09-12/10; Skiing & Photography, 11/09-12/10; Canada & The Olympics, 1/10-12/10.
Facilities: library. Museum-related items for sale.
Hours & Admission Prices: Wed.-Sat. 10-5. Adults $5; discounts to AAM members; members no charge. ♿
Attendance: 1,000
Membership: Rope Tow $50; Flying Skis $150; Black Diamond $500.

Manhattan Beach

OCEANOGRAPHIC TEACHING STATION INC. - ROUNDHOUSE MARINE STUDIES LAB & AQUARIUM, Manhattan Beach Pier, Manhattan Beach, CA 90266. Mailing Address: P.O. Box 1, Manhattan Beach, CA 90267-0001. Tel.: 310-379-8117. Fax: 310-937-9366.
E-mail: roundhouse.aquarium@verizon.net
Web Site: www.roundhouseaquarium.org
Founded: 1979.
Congressional District: 36
Key Personnel: Pres. OTS Bd. (V), Matt Friedman; Chm. (V), Dave Weldon; Treas., Chuck Milam; Dir. Aquarium, Christine Buckius; Dir. Aquarium, Eric Martin; Dir. Aquarium, Valerie Hill.
Personnel Profile: Full-Time Paid 3; Part-Time Paid 3; Part-Time Volunteers 30; Interns 2.
Governing Authority: private; nonprofit organization. Tax-exempt 501 (c)(3).
Aquarium.
Collections: Santa Monica Bay marine life & artifacts.
Facilities: aquarium; educational facilities; field research station.
Activities: summer camp; school programs & field trips; docent program; formal education programs; guided tours. Annual Events: Halloween Event; Earth Day; Coastal Clean Up Day.
Publications: monthly newsletter, Roundhouse Newsletter.
Hours & Admission Prices: Mon.-Fri. 3pm to sunset, Sat.-Sun. 10am to sunset. No charge; donations accepted. Closed New Year's Day; Thanksgiving; Christmas. ♿
Attendance: 49,900 (estimated)

Manteca

MANTECA HISTORICAL SOCIETY AND MUSEUM, 600 W. Yosemite Ave., Manteca, CA 95337-5402. Mailing Address: P.O. Box 907, Manteca, CA 95336-1137. Tel.: 209-825-3021.
Founded: 1989.
Key Personnel: Dir., Evelyn Prouty; Chm. (V), Phyllis Abram; Pres. (V), Leon Sucht; Museum Shop Mgr., Pat Metzler.
Personnel Profile: Part-Time Paid 1.
Governing Authority: Tax-exempt.
Historical Society Museum.
Collections: local history & culture; photographs; personal artifacts; documents.
Activities: special events. Museum Sponsors: Gourmet Sampler; Summer Barbecue.
Publications: monthly newsletter.
Hours & Admission Prices: Tues.-Wed. 1-3, Thurs. & Sun. 1-4; groups by appointment. No charge; donations accepted. ♿
Attendance: 7,000 (estimated)
Membership: Individual $15; Couple $25; Family $50; Business Sustaining $100; Business $250; Supporter $500; Benefactor $1,000; Life $5,000.

Mariposa

CALIFORNIA STATE MINING & MINERAL MUSEUM, 5005 Fairgrounds Dr., Mariposa, CA 95338. Mailing Address: P.O. Box 1192, Mariposa, CA 95338-1192. Tel.: 209-742-7625. Fax: 209-966-3597.
E-mail: mineralmuseum@sierratel.com
Web Site: www.parks.ca.gov
Founded: 1880.
Congressional District: 19
Key Personnel: Acting Dir., Peggy Ronning.
Personnel Profile: Full-Time Paid 2; Part-Time Paid 5; Part-Time Volunteers 15.
Governing Authority: state government; nonprofit. Parent Institution: California State Department of Parks and Recreation, P.O. Box 942896, Sacramento, CA 94296. Tax-exempt: 501(c)(3).
Mineralogy Museum.
Collections: California minerals; replica mine tunnel & model stamp mill.

Facilities: 4,000 sq. ft. exhibit space. Museum-related items for sale.
Activities: docent program; formal educational programs; guided tours; hobby workshops; lectures; temporary exhibitions; junior ranger programs; special events; living history.
Hours & Admission Prices: May-Sept. daily 10-6; Oct.-April Wed.-Mon. 10-4. Adults $3; members & children under 16 no charge. Closed New Year's Day; Thanksgiving; Christmas. ♿
Attendance: 15,229 (accurate)
Membership: General $10; Business $25; Sustaining $100; Patron $500.

MARIPOSA MUSEUM AND HISTORY CENTER INC., (M), 5119 Jessie St., Mariposa, CA 95338. Mailing Address: P.O. Box 606, Mariposa, CA 95338-0606. Tel.: 209-966-2924. Fax: 209-966-2924.
E-mail: mmhc@sti.net
Web Site: www.mariposamuseum.com
Founded: 1957.
Congressional District: 19
Key Personnel: Pres. (V), Ron Loya; Museum Shop Mgr., Sandi Rohrig.
Personnel Profile: Part-Time Paid 2; Part-Time Volunteers 82.
Governing Authority: society. Tax-exempt: 501(c)(3).
Historical Society Museum.
Collections: Indian artifacts; mining; Gold Rush period material; local history; manuscripts.
Research Fields: family & local history.
Facilities: 150-vol. library of books on Mariposiana, California & Yosemite available on premises by request; reading room. Books & postcards for sale.
Activities: guided school tours; lectures; docent program or council.
Publications: quarterly, The Sentinel.
Hours & Admission Prices: Daily 10-4. Adults $3; children under 16 & members no charge. Closed New Year's Eve & Day; Thanksgiving; Christmas Eve & Day. ♿
Attendance: 10,719 (accurate)
Membership: Senior $20; Single $25; Grubsteak (Family) $40; Patron $50; Business $100; Life $250.

Markleeville

ALPINE COUNTY MUSEUM, School St., Markleeville, CA 96120. Mailing Address: P.O. Box 517, Markleeville, CA 96120-0517. Tel.: 530-694-2317. Fax: 530-694-1087.
E-mail: acm@gbis.com
Web Site: www.co.alpine.ca.us/dept/museum/museum.htm
Founded: 1963.
Congressional District: 3
Key Personnel: Cur., Wanda Coyan; Pres. (V), Rick Dustman.
Personnel Profile: Full-Time Paid 1; Part-Time Paid 1; Part-Time Volunteers 15.
Governing Authority: Parent Institution: Historical Society of Alpine County. Tax-exempt.
History Museum.
Collections: Alpine County history; old country store; blacksmith shop; Washoe Indian basketry; watch maker's desk; doctor's black bag with tools; toys & dolls; mining; pioneer family; clothing; photographs; paintings. Historic Buildings: ore stamp mill; 1882 Old Webster School; Old Log Jail.
Major Exhibits: Blacksmith's Exhibit, 11/09-12/10.
Research Fields: local genealogy; mining history.
Facilities: Museum-related items for sale.
Activities: Annual Events: Pioneer Day; Silver Mountain Tour.
Publications: Alpine Heritage; Images of Alpine County; various oral histories; Summit City History.
Hours & Admission Prices: Memorial Day to Oct. Thurs.-Mon. 11-4. No charge; donations accepted. ♿
Attendance: 5,000 (accurate)
Membership: Individual $15; Family $20; Business & Prof. $50; Benefactor $100; Life $250.

Martinez

JOHN MUIR NATIONAL HISTORIC SITE, 4202 Alhambra Ave., Martinez, CA 94553-3826. Tel.: 925-228-8860. Fax: 925-228-8192.
E-mail: JOMU_interpretation@nps.gov
Web Site: www.nps.gov/jomu
Founded: 1964.
Congressional District: 7
Key Personnel: C.E.O., Martha Lee.
Personnel Profile: Full-Time Paid 8; Part-Time Paid 4; Part-Time Volunteers 35.
Governing Authority: federal. Affiliated with National Park Service, Dept. of Interior, Washington, DC. Tax-exempt: 501(c)(3).
Historic Site.
Collections: period artifacts; ranching & family life of John Muir; Victorian furnishings. Historic Buildings: 1882-83 John Muir house; 1849 Martinez adobe; 1885 John Muir carriage house.
Research Fields: history.
Facilities: visitor center; auditorium. Postcards, posters, slides & books for sale.
Activities: guided & self-guided tours; lectures; films; special events.
Publications: pamphlets.
Hours & Admission Prices: Wed.-Sun. 10-5. Adults $3; Golden Age, National Park Pass, Golden Eagle Pass holders & children 15 & under no charge. Closed New Year's Day; Thanksgiving; Christmas. ♿
Attendance: 31,000 (accurate)

MARTINEZ MUSEUM, (M), 1005 Escobar, Martinez, CA 94553. Mailing Address: P.O. Box 14, Martinez, CA 94553-0001. Tel.: 510-228-8160.
Web Site: martinezhistory.org
Founded: 1974.
Congressional District: 7
Key Personnel: Dir., Andrea Blachman; Pres., John Curtis.
Governing Authority: Parent Institution: Martinez Historical Society.
History Museum.
Collections: local history; period artifacts; scrapbooks of civic groups; microfilm; photographs.
Research Fields: microfilm; accessor's books; scrapbooks; ledgers; paper files; maps; family history.
Activities: tours. Museum Sponsors: dedications; open house; parades; teas; treasure hunts.
Publications: bimonthly newsletter, Martinez Historical Society; Martinez A California Town.
Hours & Admission Prices: Tues. & Thurs. 11:30-3, Sun. 1-4. No charge; donations accepted.
Attendance: 1,700 (accurate)
Membership: Student $5; Individual $10; Family $15; Contributing $25; Supporting $50; Patron $75; Life $500.

Marysville

CHINESE-AMERICAN MUSEUM OF NORTHERN CALIFORNIA, 232 1st St., Marysville, CA 95901-6002. Tel.: 510-710-2342.
History Museum.
Collections: artifacts & memorabilia pertaining to Chinese history; replicas of a Chinese general store & Sanfow Bean Sprout Plant.
Hours & Admission Prices: 1st Sat. of the month 12-4. No charge.

HONDA FOOD CULTURE MUSEUM AND COMMUNICATION EDUCATION CENTER, 1744 Feather River Blvd., Marysville, CA 95901. Tel.: 530-749-0568.
General Museum.
Collections: food & agricultural products.
Hours & Admission Prices: Tues.-Fri. 10-5, Sat.-Sun. 10-4.

MARY AARON MEMORIAL MUSEUM, 704 D St., Marysville, CA 95901-5319. Tel.: 530-743-1004.
Key Personnel: Pres., Peppie Schrader
Historic House Museum: built in 1855.
Collections: photographs; costumes; furnishings.
Hours & Admission Prices: Thurs.-Sat. 1-4; other times by appointment. No charge.

MUSEUM OF THE FORGOTTEN WARRIORS, 5865 A Rd., Marysville, CA 95901-8017. Tel.: 530-742-3090.
E-mail: cws21779@aol.com
Web Site: museumoftheforgottenwarriors.org
Military Museum.
Collections: over 50,000 military artifacts.
Hours & Admission Prices: Thurs. 7pm-9pm, Sat. 10-3. No charge.

McClellan

AEROSPACE MUSEUM OF CALIFORNIA, (M), 3200 Freedom Park Dr., McClellan, CA 95652-2432. Tel.: 916-643-3192. Fax: 916-643-0389.
Web Site: www.aerospacemuseumofcalifornia.org
Founded: 1986.
Congressional District: 5
Key Personnel: Exec. Dir., Roxanne Yonn; Pres. (V), James W. Hopp, Maj. Gen. USAF (Ret.); Cur., Barry Bauer; Museum Shop Mgr., Marianne Laws.
Personnel Profile: Full-Time Volunteers 4; Part-Time Paid 8; Part-Time Volunteers 197.
Governing Authority: Tax-exempt.
Aviation & Aerospace Museum.
Collections: aviation & aerospace industries.

Hours & Admission Prices: Mon.-Sat. 9-5, Sun. 10-5. Adults $8, seniors 65 & over and youth 13-18 $6, children 6-12 $5; active military and children 5 & under no charge. ♿
Attendance: 75,000 (estimated)
Membership: Senior 65 & over, Teacher, & Student $45; Individual $75; Family $100; Business Bronze $250; Business Silver $500; Business Gold $1,000; Life 65 & over $1,200; Life under 65 $2,000.

Mendocino

FORD HOUSE VISITOR CENTER AND MUSEUM, 735 Main St., Mendocino, CA 95460. Mailing Address: P.O. Box 1387, Mendocino, CA 95460-1387. Tel.: 707-937-5397.
E-mail: fordhouse@mcn.org
Key Personnel: Mgr., Jenny Heckeroth
History Museum.
Collections: miniature model of the Village of Mendocino; Pomo Indian artifacts; natural history.
Hours & Admission Prices: Daily 11-4. Suggested Donation: $2.

KELLEY HOUSE MUSEUM, 45007 Albion St., Mendocino, CA 95460. Mailing Address: P.O. Box 922, Mendocino, CA 95460-0922. Tel.: 707-937-5791. Fax: 707-937-2156.
E-mail: info@kelleyhousemuseum.org
Web Site: www.kelleyhousemuseum.org
Founded: 1973.
Congressional District: 1
Key Personnel: Exec. Dir., Nancy Freeze.
Personnel Profile: Part-Time Paid 2; Part-Time Volunteers 25.
Governing Authority: nonprofit organization. Parent Institution: Kelley House Museum, Inc. Tax-exempt: 501(c)(3).
Historical Society Museum: 1861 Kelley House.
Collections: photographs & documents relating to Mendocino history; logging items; North Coast genealogical references.
Research Fields: California History
Facilities: library; botanic garden. Museum-related items for sale.
Activities: guided tours; study clubs; docent program; temporary exhibitions. Annual Events: House & Historic Building Tour in May; BBQ & jazz on the lawn in July; Silent Auction in October; lighting of the town Christmas tree in December.
Publications: annual, MHR Review; quarterly, members newsletter.
Hours & Admission Prices: Museum: June-Aug. Thurs.-Tues. 11-4; Sept.-May Fri.-Mon. 11-4; walking tours by appointment. Office: Tues.-Fri. 9-4. Research by appointment. $2 per person. Tours: $10 per person; discounts on purchases of MHR, Inc. publications for members; members no charge. Closed New Year's Day; Thanksgiving; Christmas. ♿
Attendance: 3,500 (estimated)
Membership: Associate $25; Subscribing $40; Nonprofit & Family $50; Business $70; Sustaining $100; Lifetime $1,000.

Merced

AGRICULTURE MUSEUM, 4498 E. Hwy. 140, Merced, CA 95340-9388. Tel.: 209-383-1912.
Web Site: www.agmuseum.us/webpage_001.htm
Founded: 1993.
Agriculture Museum.
Collections: dairy equipment; household artifacts; toys; blacksmith shop; dental equipment; washing machines; beauty shop.
Facilities: Museum-related items for sale.
Activities: special events.
Hours & Admission Prices: Tues.-Sun. 8-5. No charge; donations accepted. ♿

APPLEGATE PARK ZOO, 1045 W. 25th St., Merced, CA 95340-3500. Mailing Address: 690 W. 16th St., Merced, CA 95340-4721. Tel.: 209-385-6840. Fax: 209-384-5805.
E-mail: borban@cityofmerced.org
Founded: 1962.
Congressional District: 18
Key Personnel: Dir. Parks & Community Svcs., Alexander Hall; Pres. (V), Marlene Murphy; Recreation Supvr., Norene Borba; Lead Zookeeper, Donna McDowell; Zookeeper, Alisha Costa.
Personnel Profile: Full-Time Paid 2; Part-Time Paid 2; Part-Time Volunteers 10.
Governing Authority: municipal. Parent Institution: City of Merced. Subsidiary Institution: The Merced Zoological Society, P.O. Box 408, Merced, CA 95341. Tax-exempt: 501(c)(3).
Zoo.
Collections: animals; plants.
Facilities: 2-acre zoological park; picnic facilities. Wildlife-related items for sale.
Activities: summer educational zoo camp programs; zoo tours with a zookeeper by appointment; workshops; wildlife programs; presentations; special events.
Publications: book, Take A Walk on the Wild Side.
Hours & Admission Prices: March-Oct. daily 10-5; Nov.-Dec. daily 10-4. Admission 11-59 $1.50, children 3-10 $1, senior citizens 60 & over $.75; discounts to AZA, AAZK & reciprocal institution members; museum members, Merced Zoological Society members, children under 3 and 2nd Tues. afternoon of the month no charge. Closed New Year's Day; Thanksgiving; Christmas. ♿
Attendance: 52,000 (estimated)
Membership: Student & Senior Citizen $7; Individual $10; Family & Grandparents Plus $20; Organization $50; Lifetime $150; Lifetime Family $250.

MERCED COUNTY COURTHOUSE MUSEUM, (M), 21st and N Sts., Merced, CA 95340-3790. Tel.: 209-723-2401. Fax: 209-723-8029.
E-mail: info@mercedmuseum.org
Web Site: www.mercedmuseum.org
Founded: 1975.
Congressional District: 15
Key Personnel: C.E.O. & Dir., Sarah Lim; Pres., Bob Souza; Pres.-Elect, Patti Kishi; Financial Dir., Grey Roberts; Sec., John Hofmann; Museum Shop Mgr., Ann Carson.
Personnel Profile: Full-Time Paid 1; Part-Time Paid 4; Part-Time Volunteers 114; Interns 2.
Governing Authority: nonprofit. Parent Institution: Merced County Historical Society. Tax-exempt.
Local History Museum: 1875 Italianate style Courthouse.
Collections: local period photographs; clothing; 1870-1930s county assessor records; Chinese temple; blacksmith shop; cultural artifacts from prehistory to 1920s.
Research Fields: Merced County & surrounding areas.
Facilities: 8,499 sq. ft. exhibit space. Museum-related items for sale.
Activities: guided tours; lectures; organized education programs for children; history trunks used in elementary classrooms; docent program; participatory, loan, traveling & temporary exhibitions. Museum Sponsors: Christmas Open House.
Publications: quarterly newsletter, For The Record; occasional local histories.
Hours & Admission Prices: Wed.-Sun. 1-4. No charge; donations accepted. Closed New Year's Day; Easter; Independence Day; Thanksgiving; Christmas Eve & Day. ♿
Attendance: 8,000 (estimated)
Membership: Junior $2; Senior $15; Individual $20; Family $35; Sustaining Individual $50; Sustaining Business $100; Benefactor $250; Patron $500; Founders Circle $1,000.

Mill Valley

MUIR WOODS NATIONAL MONUMENT, Muir Woods National Monument, Mill Valley, CA 94941-2696. Mailing Address: Golden Gate National Recreation Area, Bldg. 201, Fort Mason, San Francisco, CA 94123. Tel.: 415-388-2595 & 2596. Fax: 415-389-6957.
Web Site: www.nps.gov/muwo
Founded: 1908.
Congressional District: 6
Key Personnel: Supt., Brian O'Neill.
Governing Authority: federal. Parent Institution: National Park Svc. Subsidiary Institution: Golden Gate National Recreational Area. Tax-exempt.
National Park.
Collections: herbarium; history.
Facilities: visitors center; nature trails. Books, maps & posters for sale.
Activities: daily walks; children's program.
Publications: Muir Woods: Trail Guides; Muir Woods: Redwood Refuge.
Hours & Admission Prices: Daily 8 to sunset. Adults 18 & over $5; children 15 & under, Golden Eagle and Access Passes no charge. ♿
Attendance: 1,446,256 (estimated)
Membership: Golden Gate National Park Association: $25-$1,000.

Milpitas

SAN FRANCISCO BAY BIRD OBSERVATORY, 524 Valley Way, Milpitas, CA 95035-4106. Tel.: 408-946-6548. Fax: 408-946-9279.
Web Site: www.sfbbo.org
Key Personnel: Exec. Dir., Scott Smithson
Bird Conservatory.
Collections: birds & their habitats.
Activities: guided walks.
Hours & Admission Prices: Call for hours.

Mission Hills

HISTORICAL MUSEUM-ARCHIVAL CENTER, 15151 San Fernando Mission Blvd., Mission Hills, CA 91345-1109. Tel.: 818-365-1501. Fax: 818-361-3276.
Founded: 1962.
Key Personnel: Dir. & Archivist, Msgr. Francis J. Weber, A.C.A.; Adjunct Archivist, Kevin Feeney, A.C.A.
Governing Authority: church. Parent Institution: Roman Catholic Archdiocese of Los Angeles, 1531 W. Ninth St., Los Angeles, CA 90015. Tax-exempt.
Museum & Archival Center: located on the grounds of the San Fernando Mission.
Collections: documents; letters; historical memorabilia associated with the Catholic Church in Southern California; manuscripts.
Research Fields: ecclesial history; western Americana.
Facilities: 8,000-vol. library of material pertaining to ecclesial & western Americana.
Activities: guided tours; hobby workshops; reading room; docent program; Las Damas Archivistas; permanent exhibitions.
Publications: quarterly newsletter, Friends of Archival Center.
Hours & Admission Prices: Mon. & Thurs. 1-3; other times by appointment. No charge. Closed national holidays. ♿
Membership: Friends of Archival Center: Student & Senior Citizen $10; Supporting $25; Sustaining $100; Benefactor $500; Life $1,000.

SAN FERNANDO MISSION, 15151 San Fernando Mission Blvd., Mission Hills, CA 91345-1109. Tel.: 818-361-0186. Fax: 818-361-3276.
Founded: 1797.
Key Personnel: Dir. & Admin., Msgr. Francis J. Weber; Chm., Archbishop Roger Mahony; Business Officer, Kevin Feeney; Sales Shop Mgr., Monica Mejorado.
Governing Authority: church; nonprofit organization. Parent Institution: Roman Catholic Archdiocese of Los Angeles, 3424 Wilshire Blvd., Los Angeles, CA 90010-2241. Tel: 213-637-7000. Tax-exempt.
Museums & Mission Complex: founded in 1797 by Fray Fermin Lasuen and later restored.
Collections: Museum: mission baskets; pictorial history; pottery; santos; trade & commerce items. Mayordomo's House: 1806 home belonging to the foreman of mission ranch. Convento: 1822 adobe building with 21 Roman arches; iron grilles; painting; pipe organ; vestments; Hispanic furniture. West Garden: rare trees; wine vats; adobe displays; 1686 & 1720 bells from the Escaray collection. Fourth Mission Church: c.1804 replica of earlier edifice. East Garden; replica of Cordova fountain; rare trees; cacti; seasonal flowers; cemetery. Workshops: recreating carpentry; pottery; saddle; blacksmiths shop; weaving room; furnishings from the provincial era; manuscripts. Piczek Tableaus. Archival Center (see separate listing).
Research Fields: mission registers.
Facilities: 1,760-vol. Biblioteca Montereyensis-Angelorum Diocese library pertaining to apologetics, scripture, theology & history available for research on premises. Religious & museum-related items for sale.
Activities: self-guided tours; lectures; concerts; reading room; permanent exhibitions.
Publications: brochures; pamphlet.
Hours & Admission Prices: Daily 9-4:30. Adults $4, children 7-15 $3; discounts to AAA members; children under 7 no charge. Closed Thanksgiving; Christmas. ♿

SAN FERNANDO VALLEY HISTORICAL SOCIETY, INC., 10940 Sepulveda Blvd., Mission Hills, CA 91346. Mailing Address: P.O. Box 7039, Mission Hills, CA 91346-7039. Tel.: 818-365-7810. Fax: 818-365-7810.
E-mail: sfvhs@verizon.net
Web Site: sfvhs.com
Founded: 1943.
Congressional District: 21
Key Personnel: Corresponding Sec., Tesa Becica; Recording Sec. & Cur., Dr. Richard Doyle.
Personnel Profile: Full-Time Volunteers 2; Part-Time Volunteers 8.
Governing Authority: municipal; society. Parent Institution: Los Angeles Dept. of Recreation & Parks.Tax-exempt: 501(c)(3).
History Museum.
Collections: archives; paintings; decorative arts; costumes; history; Indian artifacts; manuscripts. Historic House: 1834 Andres Pico Adobe.
Research Fields: San Fernando Valley & California history.
Facilities: 5,000-vol. library of books & pamphlets on San Fernando Valley & California history available for use on premises by public for research; reading room.
Activities: guided tours; lectures; films; inter-museum loan, permanent & temporary exhibitions.
Publications: monthly newsletter, The Valley; guide.
Hours & Admission Prices: Mon. 10-3; 3rd Sun. of month 1-4; tours by appointment. No charge; donations accepted. Closed New Year's Day; Easter; Thanksgiving; Christmas.
Attendance: 300 (estimated)
Membership: Student $10; Individual $18; Couple & Organization $28; Sustaining $50; Business, Professional & Corporate $100; Life $250.

Modesto

GREAT VALLEY MUSEUM OF NATURAL HISTORY, 1100 Stoddard Ave., Modesto, CA 95350-5818. Tel.: 209-575-6196. Fax: 209-575-6466.
E-mail: crawfordl@mjc.edu
Web Site: yosemite.cc.ca.us/community/great-valley
Founded: 1973.
Congressional District: 12
Key Personnel: Pres. (V), Roger Gohring; Dir., Louise J. Crawford; Gift Shop Mgr., Tana Dennen.
Personnel Profile: Full-Time Paid 1; Part-Time Paid 12; Part-Time Volunteers 16.
Governing Authority: nonprofit organization. Parent Institution: Yosemite Community College District. Subsidiary Institution: Modesto Junior College. Tax-exempt: 501(c)(3) & 170(b)(1)(A).
Natural History Museum.
Collections: mammals; invertebrates; birds; fish; shells; geological specimens.
Facilities: educational facilities. Science-related books & materials for sale.
Activities: guided tours; lectures; participatory exhibits; docent program; field trips; school loan service; annual events.
Publications: quarterly, newsletter.
Hours & Admission Prices: July daily 10-4; Sept.-June Tues.-Fri. 9-4:30, Sat. 10-4. Families $3, adults $2.50, senior citizens 65 & over and children 5-17 $1.50; members and children 6 & under no charge. Closed major holidays. ♿
Attendance: 3,314 (estimated)
Membership: Student $15; Senior Citizen $20; Individual $25; Family $35; Supporting $50; Contributor $100; Institution (schools) $200; Donor $250; Sponsor $500; Sustaining Friend $1,000.

MCHENRY MUSEUM, (M), 1402 I St., Modesto, CA 95354-1032. Tel.: 209-577-5366. Fax: 209-491-4407.
Web Site: www.mchenrymuseum.org
Founded: 1965.
Congressional District: 15
Key Personnel: Cultural Svcs. Mgr., Wayne A. Mathes; Exhibit Designer, Laura Mesa; Museum Shop Mgr., Anne Hatheway; Sec., Ellen LaCoste.
Personnel Profile: Full-Time Paid 2; Part-Time Paid 4; Part-Time Volunteers 80.
Governing Authority: municipal government; nonprofit organization. Parent Institution: City of Modesto. Tax-exempt: 170(b)(1).
History Museum: housed in 1911 library building.
Collections: over 5,000 photographs & documents on local history; 1880-1910 room exhibits; blacksmith shop; doctor & dentist office; gold mining; barber shop; school-room; fire display; costumes; accessories & linens.
Research Fields: local history.
Facilities: library; 90-seat auditorium. Museum-related items for sale.
Activities: guided tours; lectures; concerts; docent program; temporary exhibitions.
Publications: quarterly newsletter; brochure.
Hours & Admission Prices: Tues.-Sun. 12-4. No charge; donations accepted. Closed New Year's Day; Easter; Thanksgiving; Christmas. ♿
Attendance: 25,000 (estimated)
Membership: Individual $25; Family & Couple $45; Benefactor $100-$299; Patron $300-$499; Corporate $500-$999; Life $1,000.

Modjeska Canyon

ARDEN - THE HELENA MODJESKA HISTORIC HOUSE & GARDENS, 29042 Modjeska Canyon Rd., Modjeska Canyon, CA 92676-9793. Mailing Address: c/o Heritage Hill Historical Park, 25151 Serrano Rd., Lake Forest, CA 92630-2534. Tel.: 949-923-2230. Fax: 949-855-6321.
E-mail: ardenmodjeska@ocparks.com
Web Site: www.ocparks.com/modjeskahouse/
Founded: 1990.
Congressional District: 47
Personnel Profile: Full-Time Paid 7; Full-Time Volunteers 30; Part-Time Paid 1; Part-Time Volunteers 30.
Governing Authority: county. Tax-exempt.
Historic House Museum: housed in the home of Polish American Shakespearean actress, Madame Helena Modjeska.
Collections: period furniture; personal artifacts.
Facilities: gardens; ponds.

Activities: docent program; formal education programs for children; guided tours.
Publications: biannual newsletter, The Helena Modjeska Foundation.
Hours & Admission Prices: Jan.-Nov. 1st & 3rd Tues. and 2nd & 4th Sat. by appointment only. Admission $5. ♿
Attendance: 3,600 (accurate)
Membership: Foundation $25.

Montebello

JUAN MATIAS SANCHEZ ADOBE, 946 Adobe Ave., Montebello, CA 90640. Tel.: 323-887-4592.
E-mail: gbrougher@sbcglobal.net
Key Personnel: Cur., Bud Sanchez.
Governing Authority: Parent Institution: Montebello Historical Society.
Historic House Museum: built in 1844 by Dona Maria Casilda de Lobo.
Collections: period artifacts & furnishings.
Publications: The Adobe Dust; newsletter, Montebello Historical Society and Museum.
Hours & Admission Prices: Sat. 1-4. No charge. ♿
Attendance: 200 (estimated)
Membership: Student $10; Individual $15; Family $25; Historical Society $45; Business & Civic $100.

Monterey

CASA AMESTI, 516 Polk St., Monterey, CA 93940-2884. Tel.: 831-372-8173. Fax: 831-372-2808.
Founded: 1954.
Key Personnel: Pres., Pam McCollough.
Governing Authority: nonprofit organization. Parent Institution: Property of the National Trust for Historic Preservation, 1785 Massachusetts Ave., N.W., Washington, DC 20036. Operated with the cooperation of the Monterey History and Art Association. Tax-exempt: 501(c)(3).
Historic House: c.1834-1846 now used by the Old Capital Club as a private men's luncheon club.
Collections: sculpture; personal artifacts.
Activities: guided tours.
Hours & Admission Prices: Sat.-Sun. 2-4; other times by appointment. Adults over 12 $1; children & members no charge. Closed holidays.

COLTON HALL MUSEUM, (M), City Hall, Pacific St., Monterey, CA 93940-2806. Tel.: 831-646-5640. Fax: 831-646-3422.
E-mail: museumpt@ci.monterey.ca.us
Web Site: www.monterey.org/museum/
Founded: 1949.
Congressional District: 16
Key Personnel: Chm. (V), Elizabeth Schneider; Museum & Cultural Arts Mgr., Jim Conway; Cultural Arts Asst., Chalet Catlin.
Personnel Profile: Full-Time Paid 1; Part-Time Paid 5; Part-Time Volunteers 10.
Governing Authority: municipal. Parent Institution: City of Monterey. Subsidiary Museum: Old Monterey Jail.
Regional History Museum: housed in Colton Hall, 1849 town hall & public school, site of 1849 California Constitutional Convention.
Collections: documents, library material & furnishings relating to the Constitutional Convention; local history artifacts, photos & documents.
Research Fields: research files on California's Constitutional Convention & delegates; local history information files.
Facilities: 200-vol. library of historical material available for research on premises.
Activities: guided tours; special exhibits; educational programs.
Publications: leaflet, Path of History Guide; booklet, Historic Monterey.
Hours & Admission Prices: Daily 10-4. No charge; donations accepted. Closed New Year's Day; Thanksgiving; Christmas.
Attendance: 20,000 (estimated)

MARITIME MUSEUM OF MONTEREY, (M), 5 Custom House Plaza, Monterey, CA 93940-2430. Tel.: 831-372-2608. Fax: 831-655-3054.
E-mail: info@montereyhistory.org
Web Site: www.montereyhistory.org
Founded: 1970.
Congressional District: 16
Key Personnel: Exec. Dir., John N. Bailey; Pres. (V), William D. Curtis; Registrar, Deborah Silguero; Museum Shop Mgr., Anne LaVigne.
Personnel Profile: Full-Time Paid 8; Part-Time Paid 4; Part-Time Volunteers 100; Interns 15.
Governing Authority: nonprofit association. Parent Institution: Monterey History and Art Association. Tax-exempt: 501(c)(3).
Maritime Museum.
Collections: marine artifacts; ship models; paintings; photographs; manuscripts.
Research Fields: fishing; whaling; naval history; sailing-ship era; lighthouses.
Facilities: library of maritime-related books; theater; community room. Museum-related items for sale.
Activities: guided tours; lectures; permanent & temporary exhibitions.
Publications: flyer descriptive of museum with map of local historical places; seasonal announcements; quarterly newsletter, Noticias.
Hours & Admission Prices: Tues.-Sun. 10-5. No charge. Closed Thanksgiving; Christmas. ♿
Attendance: 73,500 (accurate)
Membership: Nonprofit $15; Single $35; Dual $45; Family $60.

MONTEREY BAY AQUARIUM, 886 Cannery Row, Monterey, CA 93940-1085. Tel.: 831-648-4800. Fax: 831-648-4810.
Web Site: www.montereybayaquarium.org
Founded: 1984.
Congressional District: 17
Key Personnel: Exec. Dir., Julie Packard; Chm. (V), Dr. Peter Bing; Mng. Dir., Jim Hekkers; Vice Pres. & C.F.O., Ed Prohaska; Vice Pres. Exhibitions, Don Hughes; Vice Pres. Communications, Hank Armstrong; Vice Pres. Human Resources, Teresa Merry; Vice Pres. & Dir. The Center for the Future of The Oceans, Mike Sutton; Dir. Mktg., Mimi Hahn; Dir. Conservation Research, Dr. Christopher Harrold; Chief Devel. Officer, Cristina Fekeci; Vice Pres. Conservation, Education & Research, Cynthia Vernon; Vice Pres. Husbandry, Randy Hamilton; Vice Pres. Facilities, Charles Aslanian; Museum Shop Mgr., Andrew Fischer.
Personnel Profile: Full-Time Paid 328; Part-Time Paid 51; Part-Time Volunteers 1,028; Interns 26.
Governing Authority: nonprofit organization. Parent Institution: Monterey Bay Aquarium Foundation. Tax-exempt: 501(c)(3).
Aquarium: on former site of Hovden Cannery.
Collections: live aquatic displays representing 550 species; canning industry history; California sea otters; kelp forest exhibit; live video feed of deep-sea research; periodic displays of great white sharks; jellies; giant octopus; penguins.
Major Exhibits: The Secret Lives of Sea Horses, 11/09-9/5/12; Hot Pink Flamingos, 3/27/10-9/2/13.
Research Fields: tuna research & conservation; research & conservation of sea otters; health & maintenance of marine organisms; basic biology & physiology of deep-sea & open-ocean marine organisms; vessel bay sails.
Facilities: 4,200-vol. library available to public by appointment; aquarium; 273-seat auditorium; cafeteria; restaurant; classrooms; field research station. Books & gift items for sale.
Activities: guided tours; field trips; lectures; teacher training; organized educational programs; docent program; participatory exhibits; day sails; diving experiences for children 8-13; live animal feedings & shows; educational programs & presentations.
Publications: quarterly newsletter, Shorelines; monthly e-newsletter, Sea Notes; annual review; conservation research report; natural history books; blog, Sea Notes.
Hours & Admission Prices: Summer: Mon.-Fri. 9:30-6, Sat.-Sun. 9:30-8, holidays 9:30-6:30; Winter: daily 10-6. Adults $29.95, seniors 65 & over and students 13-17 $27.95, children 3-12 & disabled $20.95; discounts to military & groups; members & children under 3 no charge. Closed Christmas. ♿
Attendance: 1,902,806 (accurate)
Membership: Senior & Student $75; Member $149; Member Plus $250; Supporter $300; Sustainer $500; Associate $1,000; Packard's Circle $2,500.

MONTEREY COUNTY YOUTH MUSEUM (MY MUSEUM), 425 Washington St., Monterey, CA 93940-3023. Tel.: 831-649-1304.
E-mail: info@mymuseum.org
Web Site: www.mymuseum.org
Key Personnel: Exec. Dir., Lauren Cohen; Devel. Dir., Ann Packer; Assoc. Dir., Kelly Lepai.
Personnel Profile: Full-Time Paid 3; Part-Time Paid 8.
Children's Museum.
Collections: hands-on exhibits.
Facilities: 2,700 sq. ft. exhibit space.
Activities: birthday parties; field trips.
Hours & Admission Prices: Mon.-Tues. & Thurs.-Sat. 10-5, Sun. 12-5. Multivisit card $40 for 10 visits, adults & children $7; children under 2 no charge.

MONTEREY HISTORY AND ART ASSOCIATION, 5 Custom House Plaza, Monterey, CA 93940-2430. Tel.: 831-372-2608. Fax: 831-655-3054.
E-mail: info@montereyhistory.org
Web Site: www.montereyhistory.org

Founded: 1931.
Congressional District: 16
Key Personnel: Exec. Dir., John N. Bailey; Pres. (V), William D. Curtis; Museum Shop Mgr., Christy O'Neil.
Personnel Profile: Full-Time Paid 8; Part-Time Paid 4; Part-Time Volunteers 100; Interns 15.
Governing Authority: nonprofit organization. Subsidiary Institution: Monterey Maritime & History Museum. Tax-exempt: 501(c)(3).
Maritime Museum & History Center.
Collections: paintings; costumes; manuscripts; maritime artifacts; artwork; books; Casa Serrano Adobe period paintings & furnishings; Jo Mora sculptures. Historic Buildings: c.1845 Serrano Adobe; c.1845 Fremont House; 1876 Mayo Hayes O'Donnell Library; 1865 Francis Doud house; Perry Downer House: costumes.
Research Fields: Monterey & California history.
Facilities: 1,500-vol. library of California history books available for use on premises. Gift items for sale.
Activities: guided tours; permanent & temporary exhibitions. Association Sponsors: LaMirenda celebration of Monterey's birthday; re-enactment of historic landing by Commodore John Drake Sloat on July 7, 1846.
Publications: quarterly bulletin, Noticias del Puerto de Monterey; quarterly newsletter.
Hours & Admission Prices: Mayo Hayes O'Donnell Library: Wed. & Fri.-Sun. 1-4. No charge. Maritime Museum of Monterey: Thurs.-Tues. 10-5. No charge. Closed New Year's Day; Thanksgiving Day; Christmas. ♿
Attendance: 60,000 (estimated)
Membership: Educational & Nonprofit $15; Active (Single) $35; Active (Couple & Dual) $45; Active Family $60; Sustaining (Single) $85; Sustaining (Dual) $110; Sustaining Family $125; Life (Individual) $750; Life (Couple & Dual) $1,000.

* **MONTEREY MUSEUM OF ART, (M),** 559 Pacific St., Monterey, CA 93940-2805. Tel.: 831-372-5477. Fax: 831-372-5680.
Web Site: www.montereyart.org
Founded: 1959.
Congressional District: 17
Key Personnel: Pres., Craig L. Johnson; Exec. Dir., E. Michael Whittington; Dir. Devel., Robin Venuti; Dir. Communications, Sara Beth Newell; Chief Cur., Marcelle Polednik; Museum Shop Mgr., Nanci Markey; Curatorial Asst., Helaine Glick.
Personnel Profile: Full-Time Paid 14; Part-Time Paid 6; Interns 1.
Governing Authority: nonprofit organization. Branch Museum: La Mirada, 720 Via Mirada, Monterey, CA 93940. Tel: 831-372-3689. Tax-exempt: 501(c)(3).
Art Museum.
Collections: California art from the 19th century to the present within a national & international context.
Major Exhibits: In Process: Mark Licari, 11/09-2/14/10; Made In Monterey, 1/24/10-10/24/10.
Research Fields: relating to collections & exhibits.
Facilities: library of art books, catalogues & magazines available for use on premises. Museum-related items for sale.
Activities: changing exhibitions; lectures; art workshops; bus tours; docent programs; youth activities; exhibition openings.
Publications: e-newsletter; catalogues, Henrietta Shore: A Retrospective 1900-1963; Yesterday's Artists on the Monterey Peninsula; The Monterey Photographic Tradition: The Weston Years; The Artist & the Myth; Armin Hansen: A Centennial Salute; From Old Timer to New Timer: The Life & Work of Mark M. Walker; Colors & Impressions: The Early Work of E. Charlton Fortune; Armin Hansen: The Jane & Justin Dart Collection; Dody Weston Thompson: Photographs; Henry Gilpin: Photographs.
Hours & Admission Prices: Wed.-Sat. 11-5, Sun. 1-4. Adults $5, students & military w/ID $2.50; discounts to NARM members; members & children under 12 no charge. Closed New Year's Day; Thanksgiving; Christmas. ♿
Attendance: 31,387 (accurate)
Membership: Student, Teacher, & Military $20; Individual $40; Dual Out of Town $50; Dual & Family $60; Contributor $100; Supporter $250; Enthusiast $500; Curator's $1,000; Director's Circle $2,500; President's Circle $5,000; Benefactor's Circle $10,000; Connoisseurs' Circle $15,000; Patron's Circle $20,000.

MONTEREY STATE HISTORIC PARK, 20 Custom House Plaza, Monterey, CA 93940-2430. Tel.: 831-649-7118. Fax: 831-647-6236.
Web Site: www.parks.ca.gov
Founded: 1938.
Congressional District: 16
Key Personnel: Cur., Kris N. Quist; Guide Supvr., Stephanie Price.
Personnel Profile: Full-Time Paid 12; Part-Time Paid 12.
Governing Authority: state. Parent Institution: California State Department of Parks & Recreation, P.O. Box 942896, Sacramento, CA 94296. Tax-exempt.
State Historic Park Museum: consisting of 12 buildings, gardens & sites in Monterey.
Collections: history; preservation projects; anthropology; archaeology; manuscripts; Native American; costumes; historic theater. Historic Houses: 1827 Custom House; 1832 Cooper-Holera Adobe; 1835 Robert Louis Stevenson House (see separate listing); 1835 Larkin House; 1844 Casa Soberanes; 1847 Pacific House; 1847 First Brick House. Concession-Operated Bldgs.: 1841 Casa Guitierrez; 1845 Casa Del Oro (Boston Store); 1847 First Theatre; 1847 Whaling Station.
Activities: guided tours; slide presentations; drama; permanent exhibitions.
Hours & Admission Prices: Daily 7-5:30. No charge. Closed New Year's Day; Thanksgiving; Christmas. ♿
Attendance: 180,000

MONTEREY STATE HISTORIC PARK/ROBERT LOUIS STEVENSON HOUSE, 530 Houston St., Monterey, CA 93940-3226. Mailing Address: 20 Custom House Plaza, Monterey, CA 93940. Tel.: 831-649-7118. Fax: 831-647-6236.
Web Site: www.historicmonterey.org
Founded: 1941.
Congressional District: 16
Key Personnel: Cur., Kris N. Quist; Guide Supvr., Stephanie Price; District Supt., Dennis Hanson.
Personnel Profile: Full-Time Paid 12; Part-Time Paid 12.
Governing Authority: state. Parent Institution: California Department of Parks & Recreation, P.O. Box 942896, Sacramento, CA 95811.
Historic House: hotel in which Robert Louis Stevenson stayed in 1879, located in Monterey State Historic Park.
Collections: costumes; period furnishings; largest collection of Stevenson's personal materials in U.S.; manuscripts; fine arts.
Facilities: 500-vol. library of Stevenson works.
Activities: guided tours; permanent exhibitions.
Hours & Admission Prices: Daily 8-4. No charge. Closed New Year's Day; Thanksgiving; Christmas. ♿
Attendance: 25,000

MY MUSEUM, 425 Washington St., Monterey, CA 93940-3023. Tel.: 831-649-6444. Fax: 831-649-1304.
E-mail: info@mymuseum.org
Web Site: www.mymuseum.org
Key Personnel: Exec. Dir., Lauren Cohen; Pres., Kandis Malfyt; Vice Pres., Debra Panelli
Children's Museum.
Collections: hands-on exhibits.
Hours & Admission Prices: Mon.-Tues. & Thurs.-Sat. 10-5, Sun. 12-5. Admission $5.50; children under 2 no charge.

OLD MONTEREY JAIL, City Hall, 580 Pacific St., Monterey, CA 93940-2806. Tel.: 831-646-5640. Fax: 831-646-3917.
Web Site: www.monterey.org/museum/
Founded: 1949.
Congressional District: 16
Key Personnel: Museum Mgr., Jim Conway.
Personnel Profile: Full-Time Paid 1; Part-Time Paid 5; Part-Time Volunteers 15.
Governing Authority: municipal. Parent Institution: City of Monterey. Tax-exempt.
Historic Building: 1854 Old Monterey jail.
Collections: jail artifacts, records & cells.
Research Fields: Monterey jails.
Activities: self-guided tours.
Publications: brochure.
Hours & Admission Prices: Daily 10-4. No charge; donations accepted. Closed New Year's Day; Thanksgiving; Christmas.
Attendance: 20,000 (estimated)

THOMAS KINKADE GALLERY, 361 Lighthouse Ave., Monterey, CA 93940-1418. Tel.: 831-655-3349. Fax: 831-655-5525.
Web Site: www.thomaskinkade.com
Founded: 2001.
Congressional District: 17
Key Personnel: Owner, Rick Barnett.
Personnel Profile: Full-Time Paid 2; Part-Time Paid 1.
Governing Authority: private; nonprofit organization. Tax-exempt: 501(c)(3).
Art Museum: housed at the Casa Gutierrez Adobe.
Collections: Kinkade originals including oils & sketches.
Research Fields: Casa Gutierrez; Thomas Kinkade.
Facilities: 785 sq. ft. exhibit space; garden.
Activities: loan, temporary & traveling exhibitions.

Publications: biannual newsletter, Thomas Kinkade Museum Patron Newsletter.
Hours & Admission Prices: Daily 10-5. No charge. Closed New Year's Day; Easter; Thanksgiving; Christmas. ♿
Attendance: 3,000 (estimated)

Moraga

* **HEARST ART GALLERY, ST. MARY'S COLLEGE, (M),** 1928 St. Mary's Rd., Moraga, CA 94556-2744. Mailing Address: P.O. Box 5110, Moraga, CA 94575-5110. Tel.: 925-631-4379. Fax: 925-376-5128.
E-mail: cbrewste@stmarys-ca.edu
Web Site: heartstartgallery.org
Founded: 1977.
Congressional District: 10
Key Personnel: Chm. (V), Clark Vilas; Dir., Carrie Brewster; Registrar & Collections Mgr., Julie Armistead; Public Programming & Information Mgr., Heidi Donner; Gallery Mgr., Thea Grigsby; Preparator, Jim Whiteaker.
Personnel Profile: Full-Time Paid 5; Part-Time Volunteers 15; Interns 2.
Governing Authority: college bd. of trustees. Parent Institution: St. Mary's College of California. Tax-exempt: 501(c)(3).
College Art Gallery.
Collections: William Keith paintings & other California landscapes; Eastern European icons; medieval sculpture; ancient ceramics; Morris Graves works; Don Quixote collection.
Research Fields: William Keith; American art.
Facilities: picnic area; meeting room; food service available. Museum publications & gift items for sale.
Activities: lectures; tours; inter-museum loan & temporary exhibitions. Annual Events: Family Festival; biennial Master Art Tribute.
Publications: exhibition catalogues; leaflets; William Keith: The Saint Mary's College Collection; Modern British Art: Vorticism & the Grosvenor School; African Alchemy; Manuel Neri: A Sculptor's Drawings.
Hours & Admission Prices: Wed.-Sun. 11-4:30. Suggested Donation $3; members no charge. Closed major holidays & between exhibitions. ♿
Attendance: 10,498 (accurate)
Membership: Senior $40; Individual $50; Family $75; Friend & Patron $100; Connoisseur $250; Director's Circle $1,000; President's Circle $1,500.

Morro Bay

MORRO BAY AQUARIUM, 595 Embarcadero, Morro Bay, CA 93442-2217. Tel.: 805-772-7647.
Web Site: www.morrobay.com/morrobayaquarium
Governing Authority: nonprofit organization.
Aquarium.
Collections: harbor seal; sea lions; fish; sharks; octopus; eels; abalone sea anemones; horseshoe crabs.
Facilities: Museum-related items for sale.
Hours & Admission Prices: Daily 9:30-5. Admission 12 & over $2, children 5-11 $1; children 4 & under no charge.

MORRO BAY STATE PARK MUSEUM OF NATURAL HISTORY, 20 State Park Rd., Morro Bay, CA 93442-2430. Tel.: 805-772-2694, ext. 105. Fax: 805-772-7129.
E-mail: rouvaishyana@hearstcastle.com
Web Site: ccnha.org
Founded: 1962.
Congressional District: 16
Key Personnel: Chm. (V), Louise Abbott; CCNHA Exec. Dir., Mary Golden; Nature Store Mgr., Dorian Farrow.
Personnel Profile: Full-Time Paid 1; Part-Time Paid 2; Part-Time Volunteers 5.
Governing Authority: state. Parent Institution: California State Dept. of Parks & Recreation, P.O. Box 942896, Sacramento, CA 94296. Tax-exempt.
Natural History Museum.
Collections: Chumash Indians; birds & mammals study skins; live mounts; reptiles; insects & other invertebrates; plants including marine algae; rocks; minerals; fossils; shells; estuary below museum.
Facilities: 400-vol. library of reference books on natural & local history available on premises by appointment; 76-seat auditorium.
Activities: guided tours & walks; lectures; films; docent program; school groups.
Publications: monthly newsletter; activities schedule; booklets, Wanderer; The Monarch Butterfly; Estuary; newsletter, Nature Notes Public; monthly e-newsletter, The Bear's Den.
Hours & Admission Prices: Daily 10-5. Adults $2; discounts for State Park Pass holders; members, children 16 & under and school groups with reservation no charge. Closed New Year's Day; Thanksgiving; Christmas. ♿
Attendance: 60,000 (accurate)

Membership: Individual $25; Family $50; Advocate $100; Conservator $500; Guardian $1,000.

Mount Shasta

SISSON MUSEUM, #1 N. Old Stage Rd., Mount Shasta, CA 96067-9701. Tel.: 530-926-5508. Fax: 530-926-5508 (call first).
E-mail: sissonmuseum@sbcglobal.net
Web Site: www.mountshastasissonmuseum.org
Formerly: Sisson Hatchery Museum
Founded: 1983.
Congressional District: 2
Key Personnel: Pres., H. "Bud" Hamilton; Treas., Marcia Smith; Museum Shop Mgr., Gene Greenland.
Personnel Profile: Part-Time Volunteers 30.
Governing Authority: private; nonprofit organization. Tax-exempt: 501(c)(3).
History Museum.
Collections: Mt. Shasta historical artifacts; furnishings; recreational artifacts; paintings; photographs; geological.
Facilities: 80-seat auditorium; 4,000 sq. ft. exhibit space. Museum-related items for sale.
Activities: concerts; temporary exhibitions. Annual Events: Mt. Shasta Dance Theater H2O Manifesto; History Night; Quilt Show; Art Show; Yard Sale.
Publications: quarterly newsletter, Sisson Mirror.
Hours & Admission Prices: April-May & Oct.-Dec. daily 1-4, call to confirm; June-Sept. Mon.-Sat. 10-4, Sun. 1-4. Suggested Donations: adults 16 & over $1. Closed New Year's Day; Easter; Thanksgiving; Christmas Eve & Day. ♿
Attendance: 8,743 (accurate)
Membership: Senior 62 & over $5; Adult $10; Family $20; Commercial $30; Senior Life $60.

Mountain View

COMPUTER HISTORY MUSEUM, (M), 1401 N. Shoreline Blvd., Mountain View, CA 94043-1311. Tel.: 650-810-1010. Fax: 650-810-1055.
Web Site: www.computerhistory.org
Key Personnel: Chm. Bd., Len Shustek; Pres. & C.E.O., John Hollar
History Museum.
Collections: history of computers; hardware; software; documentation; film; video; audio; ephemera.
Activities: tours.
Hours & Admission Prices: Wed.-Fri. & Sun. 12-4, Sat. 11-5. No charge; donations accepted.

Murphys

OLD TIMERS MUSEUM, 470 Main St., Murphys, CA 95247. Mailing Address: P.O. Box 94, Murphys, CA 95247-0094. Tel.: 209-728-1160.
Key Personnel: Dir., Robert Frew; Public Rels., Bob Buchanan; Treas., Michael F. Davis; Archivist, Chris Sellman.
Personnel Profile: Part-Time Volunteers 10.
Governing Authority: private; nonprofit organization. Tax-exempt: 501(c)(3).
Historic Building Museum.
Collections: local history & culture; photographs; period artifacts; documents; family artifacts.
Facilities: library; 1,200 sq. ft. exhibit space. Museum-related items for sale.
Activities: guided tours.
Hours & Admission Prices: Winter: Sat.-Mon. 12-4; Summer: Fri.-Mon. 12-4. No charge; donations accepted. Closed holidays.
Attendance: 11,008

Napa

COPIA: THE AMERICAN CENTER FOR WINE, FOOD & THE ARTS, 500 First St., Napa, CA 94559-2629. Tel.: 707-259-1600; 888-512-6742. Fax: 707-257-8601.
E-mail: info@copia.org
Web Site: www.copia.org
Founded: 1990.
Congressional District: 1
Key Personnel: Pres. & C.E.O., Garry McGuire; Exec. Asst., Christi Skibbins; Chm. (V), Lauren Ackerman; C.O.O., Kurt Nystrom; Dir. Exhibitions, Neil Harvey; Chief Mktg. Officer, Larry Tsai; Dir. Human Resources, Marina Kreager; Museum Retail Mgr., Christina Taylor-Godwin; Dir. Visitor Svcs., Betty Teller; Dir. Visitor Rels., Lynn Norris; Mgr. Public Rels., Kathleen Iudice.
Personnel Profile: Full-Time Paid 77; Part-Time Paid 20; Part-Time Volunteers 204; Interns 2.
Governing Authority: private; nonprofit organization. Tax-exempt: 501(c)(3).
Wine, Food and Art Museum.

Collections: contemporary art, photographs, design & artifacts related to food & wine; Julia Child's copper cookware.
Facilities: 13,000 sq. ft. exhibition galleries; 3.5 acre garden; 500-seat outdoor river concert terrace; 260-seat theater; 75-seat tiered lecture & demonstration room; 3 40-seat classrooms; 75-seat dining room; children's garden; wedding pavilion; cafe. Museum-related items for sale.
Activities: formal & informal education programs for adults, children, professionals & the general public; concerts; lectures; films; garden classes; wine & food tastings; participatory & temporary exhibitions; festivals; special events; rental facilities.
Publications: quarterly calendar & catalogues.
Hours & Admission Prices: Summer: daily 10-6; Winter: Fri.-Sun. 10-6. Adults $12.50, students & seniors $10, youth $7.50; discounts to AAM & ICOM members; members no charge. ♿
Attendance: 180,000 (estimated)
Membership: Individual $60; Dual $75; Family $100; Reciprocal $125; Community Partner $250; Trustee Circle $500-$25,000.

NAPA COUNTY HISTORICAL SOCIETY, 1219 First St., Napa, CA 94559-2929. Tel.: 707-224-5933.
E-mail: director@napahistory.org
Web Site: www.napahistory.org
Founded: 1948.
Personnel Profile: Full-Time Paid 1; Part-Time Paid 1; Part-Time Volunteers 25; Interns 4.
Governing Authority: Tax-exempt.
Historical Society Museum.
Collections: Napa County history & culture; photographs; books; period directories & maps; manuscripts; videos.
Facilities: library.
Activities: research.
Publications: Gleanings.
Hours & Admission Prices: Tues.-Sat. 12-4. No charge; donations accepted. ♿
Attendance: 3,000
Membership: Senior & Student $25; Individual $30; Dual $40; Patron $75; Business $100; Life $500; Business Life $1,000.

NAPA FIREFIGHTERS MUSEUM, INC., 1201 Main St., Napa, CA 94559-2636. Tel.: 707-259-0609.
E-mail: info@napafirefightersmuseum.org
Web Site: www.napafirefightersmuseum.org
Founded: 1997.
Congressional District: 1
Fire-Fighting Museum.
Collections: firefighting equipment; personal artifacts; photographs.
Hours & Admission Prices: Wed.-Sat. 11-4; other times by appointment. No charge.

Needles

HAVASU NATIONAL WILDLIFE REFUGE, 317 Mesquite Ave., Needles, CA 92363. Mailing Address: P.O. Box 3009, Needles, CA 92363-2045. Tel.: 760-326-3853.
Wildlife Refuge.
Collections: natural history; wildlife & their habitats; plants; trees; flowers.
Facilities: nature trails.
Activities: hiking.
Hours & Admission Prices: Call for hours.

Nevada City

MINERS FOUNDRY CULTURAL CENTER, 325 Spring St., Nevada City, CA 95959-2420. Mailing Address: P.O. Box 1991, Nevada City, CA 95959-1940. Tel.: 530-265-5040. Fax: 530-265-5462.
E-mail: info@minersfoundry.org
Web Site: www.minersfoundry.org
Founded: 1989.
Congressional District: 2
Key Personnel: Dir., Gretchen Bond; Pres. (V), Ardyce Minch.
Personnel Profile: Full-Time Paid 1; Part-Time Paid 3; Part-Time Volunteers 50.
Governing Authority: Parent Institution: Nevada County Cultural Preservation Trust. Tax-exempt.
Mining Museum: site of the Pelton wheel.
Collections: use of original building as a foundry; Victorian artifacts.
Activities: lectures; theatre; concerts.
Hours & Admission Prices: Mon.-Fri. 10-4; docent tours available by appointment. No charge; donations accepted. ♿
Attendance: 50,000 (estimated)
Membership: Associate & Volunteer $25; Hearthstone $50; Cornerstone $150; Patron $300; Founders Circle $500; Lester Pelton Society $1,000.

NEVADA COUNTY HISTORICAL SOCIETY, INC., 214 Church St., Nevada City, CA 95959-1300. Mailing Address: P.O. Box 1300, Nevada City, CA 95959-1300. Tel.: 530-265-5910.
E-mail: info@nevadacountyhistory.org
Web Site: www.nevadacountyhistory.org
Founded: 1945.
Congressional District: 14
Key Personnel: Pres. (V), Alan de Negris; Cur. Mining Museum, Glenn Jones; Librarian, Searls Historic Library, Ed Tyson; Cur. Transportation Museum, Brian Blair; Cur. Firehouse Museum, Wally Hagaman.
Personnel Profile: Full-Time Volunteers 3; Part-Time Paid 1; Part-Time Volunteers 35.
Governing Authority: society; nonprofit corporation. Branch Museums: Firehouse No. 1 Museums, 214 Main St., Nevada City 95959. Tel. 530-265-5468; Mining Museum & Pelton Wheel Exhibit, Mill St., Grass Valley, CA 95945. Tel. 530-273-4255; Searls Historical Library, 214 Church St., Nevada City 95959. Tel. 530-265-5910; Transportation Museum, 5 Kidder Court, Nevada City 95959. Tax-exempt.
Historical Society Museums.
Collections: cultural; Native American; Chinese; railroad; communications; transportation; mining; agriculture; period furnishings; genealogies; county records; photography; videos; gold rush era history; Cornish miners history; emigrant trail history.
Research Fields: genealogy; Gold Rush history.
Facilities: library of genealogical records, archives, county records & photographs.
Activities: lectures; guided tours of the area; demonstrations.
Publications: quarterly newsletter; quarterly bulletin; pamphlets; brochures; maps; books.
Hours & Admission Prices: Firehouse No. 1 Museums, Mining Museum & Pelton Wheel Exhibit: May to Oct. 15 10-5. Searls Memorial Library: Mon.-Sat. 1-4. Research: $20 hour. Transportation Museum: May-Oct. Fri.-Tues. 10-4; Nov.-April Sat.-Sun. 10-4. No charge; donations accepted. Closed New Year's Day; Thanksgiving; Christmas. ♿
Attendance: 2,000 (estimated)
Membership: Individual $25; Business $50.

Newbury Park

STAGECOACH INN MUSEUM COMPLEX, (M), 51 S. Ventu Park Rd., Newbury Park, CA 91320-3943. Tel.: 805-498-9441. Fax: 805-498-6375.
E-mail: stagecoach@stagecoachmuseum.org
Web Site: www.stagecoachmuseum.org
Founded: 1967.
Congressional District: 24
Key Personnel: Pres., Elaine Williams; Dir., Sandra Hildebrandt; Cur. Education, Jackie Pizitz; Cur. History, Miriam Sprankling; Cur. Anthropology & Archaeology, Dr. Thomas Maxwell; Museum Shop Mgr., Constance Clarke; Museum Shop Mgr., Carol Salyer.
Personnel Profile: Part-Time Paid 2; Part-Time Volunteers 186.
Governing Authority: society. Parent Institution: Conejo Valley Historical Society. Subsidiary Institution: Conejo Recreation & Park. Tax-exempt: 501(c)(3).
History Museum: housed in 1876 Grand Union Hotel.
Collections: local history & culture; Chumash native people, Spanish-Mexican & Anglo-American, from 1846-1930; shells; fossils; minerals. Tri-Village Complex: Chumash hut, Spanish adobe, pioneer house, Conejo Valley history & culture; Carriage House; replica of 1889 Timber School.
Research Fields: anthropology; local history; botany; prehistoric Indian culture; costumes; decorative arts & textiles.
Facilities: approx. 1,500-vol. library of pioneer & natural history including flora, fauna, geology & paleontology; Indian & decorative arts; nature trails. Handcrafted items for sale.
Activities: docent guided tours for visitors, elementary school classes & special groups; living history program; weddings.
Publications: Chumash Indian pamphlet; Newbury Park; Mad Agnes & Pierre: A Spirited History of the Stagecoach Inn Museum.
Hours & Admission Prices: Wed.-Sun. 1-4. Adults $4, senior citizens & youth 13-21 $3, children 5-12 $1; members & children under 5 no charge. Closed New Year's Day; Easter; Thanksgiving; Christmas. ♿
Attendance: 10,902 (accurate)
Membership: Children under 18 & Senior Citizens $15; Individual $20; Family $30; Organization (nonprofit) $40; Business & Supporter $50; Backer $75; Friend $100; Patron $150; Sponsor $250; Sustaining $500; Benefactor $1,000.

Newhall

WILLIAM S. HART COUNTY PARK & MUSEUM, 24151 Newhall Ave., Newhall, CA 91321-2908. Tel.: 661-254-4584. Fax: 661-254-6499.
E-mail: information@hartmuseum.org

Web Site: www.hartmuseum.org
Founded: 1958.
Congressional District: 22
Key Personnel: Dir. Natural History Museum, Dr. Jane Pisano; Park Supt., Norman Phillips; Volunteer Coord., Kristyn Van Wy; Gift Store Mgr., Becki Basham.
Personnel Profile: Full-Time Paid 2; Part-Time Paid 2; Part-Time Volunteers 50.
Governing Authority: county. Parent Institution: L.A. County Dept. of Parks & Recreation. Subsidiary Institution: L.A. County Natural History Museum. Tax-exempt.
Historic Building & Site: 1927 home of silent film star William S. Hart.
Collections: paintings including Russell, De Yong, J.M. Flagg, Remington; sculpture; woodcarvings; Navajo blankets & rugs; Native American artifacts; 1920s-1930s furniture, clothing & housewares; barnyard animals; bison herd.
Research Fields: William S. Hart; early filmmaking; Western film; period architecture & furnishings.
Activities: guided tours; permanent exhibitions.
Publications: brochures.
Hours & Admission Prices: Museum: Wed.-Sun. 11-3:30. Park: mid-June to Labor Day daily 8-6; Sept. to mid-June daily 8-5. No charge; donations accepted. Closed New Year's Day; Thanksgiving; Christmas. ♿
Attendance: 35,000 (accurate)
Membership: Senior Citizens $15; Volunteer $25; Individual & Family $40; Sponsor $75; Patron $125; Silver Benefactor $250; Gold Benefactor $500; Diamond Benefactor $1,000; Corporate Benefactor $2,500.

Newport Beach

ORANGE COUNTY MUSEUM OF ART, 850 San Clemente Dr., Newport Beach, CA 92660-6399. Tel.: 949-759-1122. Fax: 949-759-5623.
Web Site: www.ocma.net
Founded: 1918.
Congressional District: 34
Key Personnel: Dir., Dennis Szakacs; Chm. & Pres., David Emmes, II; Dir. Museum Shop, Hayley Miller; Deputy Dir. Programs & Chief Cur., Elizabeth Armstrong; Cur. Collections and Dir. Public Programs & Education, Karen Moss; Dir. Devel., Kellie Webb.
Personnel Profile: Full-Time Paid 40; Part-Time Paid 10; Part-Time Volunteers 150; Interns 10.
Governing Authority: private; nonprofit corp. Branch Museum: South Coast Plaza Crate and Barrel Wing, 3333 Bear Street, Costa Mesa, CA 92626. Tax-exempt: 501(c)(3).
Visual Art Museum.
Collections: art from 19th century to present.
Research Fields: modern & contemporary art.
Facilities: library of art books & catalogues available for use by request; auditorium; classrooms. Cards, magazines, jewelry, art books & posters for sale.
Activities: guided tours; lectures; educational programs.
Publications: quarterly newsletter; catalogs of current exhibits.
Hours & Admission Prices: Wed. & Fri.-Sun. 11-5, Thurs. 11-8. Adults $10, students $8; discounts to AAA, AAM & ICOM members; members, children under 12 & 3rd Thurs. of month no charge. Closed Easter; Independence Day; Thanksgiving; Christmas. ♿
Attendance: 80,000 (accurate)
Membership: Member $60; Family Donor $100; Friend $250; Supporter $500; Advocate $1,500; Patron $2,500; Contributing Patron $5,000; Distinguished Patron $10,000.

Nipomo

DANA ADOBE, 671 S. Oak Glen Ave., Nipomo, CA 93444-9009. Tel.: 805-929-5679.
E-mail: dana@danaadobe.org
Web Site: danaadobe.org
Founded: 1997.
Key Personnel: Exec. Dir., Kathy Kubiak; Pres. (V), Herb Kandel; Museum Shop Mgr., Helen Daurio.
Personnel Profile: Full-Time Paid 1; Part-Time Paid 1; Part-Time Volunteers 30.
Governing Authority: tax-exempt.
Historic Home & Rancho; History Museum.
Collections: period artifacts.
Publications: newsletter.
Hours & Admission Prices: May-Oct. Sat.-Sun. 12-4; Winter: Sun. 12-4. No charge; donations accepted. ♿
Attendance: 2,000 (estimated)
Membership: Single $25; Family $40.

North Fork

SIERRA MONO INDIAN MUSEUM, 33103 Rd. 228, North Fork, CA 93643-9442. Tel.: 559-877-2115.
Web Site: www.sierramonomuseum.org
Founded: 1969.
Congressional District: 6
Key Personnel: Dir., Barbara Ezell; Dir., Jordan Clark; Chm. (V), Sharon Carter; Pres. (V), Kelly Marshall; Museum Shop Mgr., Jordan Clark.
Personnel Profile: Full-Time Paid 1; Part-Time Paid 1; Part-Time Volunteers 15; Interns 1.
Governing Authority: Tax-exempt.
Native American Museum.
Collections: North Fork Mono Tribe; fishing; hunting; cooking; healing; basketmaking; games; ceremonies; Tettleton wildlife collection; California Native American baskets; Crane Valley artifacts; animal dioramas; California Native Mono Tribe beadwork; Indian village.
Research Fields: anthropology; California Native Mono Tribe.
Facilities: nature trail. Museum-related items for sale.
Activities: guided tours by appointment. Museum Sponsors: Pow Wow in August.
Publications: newsletter, Nuck-a-Hee.
Hours & Admission Prices: Tues.-Fri. 10-3:30. Suggested Donation: $5; discounts to AAM members. ♿
Attendance: 5,000 (estimated)
Membership: Annual $25.

North Hollywood

CAMPO DE CAHUENGA, 3919 Lankershim Blvd., North Hollywood, CA 91604-3419. Mailing Address: P.O. Box 956, North Hollywood, CA 91603-0956. Tel.: 818-762-3998, ext. 2. Fax: 818-762-2734.
E-mail: campodecahuenga1847@hotmail.com
Web Site: www.campodecahuenga.com
Key Personnel: Dir., Deuk Perrin.
Governing Authority: Tax-exempt: 501(c)(3).
History Museum: site of the signing of the Treaty of Cahuenga in 1847.
Collections: plaques; monuments; documents.
Activities: special programs; meetings.
Hours & Admission Prices: Sat. 11-3; call to confirm. Closed holidays.

THE PORTAL OF THE FOLDED WINGS SHRINE TO AVIATION AND MUSEUM, 10621 Victory Blvd., North Hollywood, CA 91606-3918. Tel.: 818-763-9121. Fax: 818-763-3801.
Web Site: www.portalofthefoldedwings.com
Founded: 1996.
Congressional District: 24
Key Personnel: Dir., John Torres; Gen. Mgr. Cemetery, Oliver Yeo.
Personnel Profile: Part-Time Paid 1; Part-Time Volunteers 6.
Governing Authority: nonprofit.
Memorial Park.
Collections: burial place for 13 of America's most noted aviation pioneers from the Wright brothers to Lockheed Aircraft; photographs.
Research Fields: biographies of aviators buried at Portal.
Facilities: 36 sq. ft. exhibit space.
Activities: guided tours; lectures. Annual Event: Memorial Day Celebrations.
Hours & Admission Prices: Tours 1st Sun. of each month 1-3; other times by appointment. No charge. ♿
Attendance: 2,000 (estimated)

Northridge

ART GALLERIES, CALIFORNIA STATE UNIVERSITY, NORTHRIDGE, 18111 Nordhoff St., Northridge, CA 91330-8299. Tel.: 818-677-2226 (gallery) & 2156 (office). Fax: 818-677-5910.
Web Site: www.csun.edu/artgalleries/
Founded: 1972.
Congressional District: 21, 23 & 26
Key Personnel: Interim Dir., Jim Sweeters; Exhibitions Coord., Michelle Giacopuzzi; Museum Shop Mgr., Dorothy Goggin.
Personnel Profile: Full-Time Paid 2; Part-Time Volunteers 80; Interns 10.
Governing Authority: university; nonprofit organization. Parent Institution: California State University, Northridge. Volunteer Institution: Arts Council for California State University, Northridge. Tax-exempt.
University Art Gallery.
Collections: paintings; photographs; sculpture.
Research Fields: contemporary art; international art.
Facilities: classrooms; 3,200 sq. ft. exhibit space. Gallery-related items for sale.
Activities: guided tours; lectures; gallery talks; formally organized education programs for children & graduate students; docent program or council; training programs for professional museum workers.

Publications: exhibition catalogues; brochures.
Hours & Admission Prices: June-Aug. Mon.-Fri. 12-4; Sept.-May Mon.-Wed. & Fri.-Sat. 12-4; Thurs. 12-8. No charge; donations accepted. Closed holidays. ♿
Attendance: 32,000 (estimated)
Membership: Annual $30.

CAL STATE NORTHRIDGE BOTANIC GARDEN, Biology Dept., 18111 Nordhoff St. - MC 8303, Northridge, CA 91330-0001. Tel.: 818-677-3496. Fax: 818-677-2034.
E-mail: botanicgarden@csun.edu
Web Site: www.csun.edu/botanicgarden
Founded: 1958.
Key Personnel: Chm. (V), Brenda Kanno.
Personnel Profile: Part-Time Volunteers 12.
Governing Authority: Parent Institution: California State University, Northridge Biology Department.
Botanical Garden.
Collections: 3,000 plant species, CA Natives; cacti; tropical plants; native grasses; New Zealand plants; palms; herbs; redwood trees; orchids; bromeliads; ferns; pond; waterfall.
Facilities: 1.5-acre garden.
Activities: tours.
Hours & Admission Prices: Mon.-Fri. 8-4:45. No charge. Closed holidays. ♿
Attendance: 10,000 (estimated)
Membership: Individual $30; Family $40

Norwalk

HARGITT HOUSE, 12426 Mapledale, Norwalk, CA 90650-6026. Tel.: 562-864-9663.
Historic House Museum: housed in the home of Charles & Ida Hargitt, built in 1891 by the D.D. Johnston family.
Collections: period furnishings.
Hours & Admission Prices: 1st & 3rd Sun. of month 1-4.

Novato

MARIN MUSEUM OF THE AMERICAN INDIAN, 2200 Novato Blvd., (in Miwok Park), Novato, CA 94947-2079. Tel.: 415-897-4064. Fax: 415-892-7804.
E-mail: office@marinindian.com
Web Site: marinindian.com
Formerly: Marin Museum Society
Founded: 1967.
Congressional District: 6
Key Personnel: C.E.O., Colleen Hicks; Pres. (V), Robert Baguio; Dir. Education, Kristi Lauchstedt.
Personnel Profile: Full-Time Paid 2; Part-Time Paid 2; Part-Time Volunteers 20; Interns 2.
Governing Authority: private; board of directors; nonprofit organization. Parent Institution: Marin Museum Society, Inc. Tax-exempt.
Archaeological & Anthropological Museum: located on prehistoric site once occupied by Coast Miwok Indians.
Collections: archaeological, ethnographic & archival materials ranging from Alaska to Peru, pertaining to Native Americans of Marin County, California & the Western Americas; photographic materials pertaining to California Indians; original Edward S. Curtis photogravures.
Major Exhibits: Living Tradition, 11/09-1/15/10.
Research Fields: California Indian culture.
Facilities: non-circulating reference library; classroom; outdoor classroom; native plant garden; 35-acre park with nature trail. Books, & other museum-related gifts for sale.
Activities: tours; lectures; hands on education programs for pre-kindergarten thru adult ages; formally organized classes for children; family field trips; docent training program; intermuseum loans; permanent, temporary & traveling exhibitions; interpretative kit loans for schools & organizations.
Publications: bibliographies; curriculum materials; native plant garden guide; teachers Resource Pack.
Hours & Admission Prices: Tues.-Fri. 12-5, Sat.-Sun. 12-4. Adults $5; members no charge.
Attendance: 25,000 (estimated)
Membership: Individual $25; Family $35; Patron $100; Sponsor $250; Benefactor $1,000.

NOVATO HISTORY MUSEUM, 815 De Long Ave., Novato, CA 94945-7005. Mailing Address: City of Novato, 75 Rowland Way, Ste. 200, Novato, CA 94945. Tel.: 415-897-4320.
E-mail: skimpel@ci.novato.ca.us
Web Site: www.cityofnovato.org/museum
Founded: 1976.
Congressional District: 6
Key Personnel: Pres. (V), Ron Vela; Dir., Samantha Kimpel; Museum Shop Mgr., Pat Johnstone.
Personnel Profile: Full-Time Paid 1; Part-Time Volunteers 50.
Governing Authority: municipal; nonprofit. Parent Institution: City of Novato. Subsidiary Institution: Novato Historical Guild. Tax-exempt.
History Museum: located in 1850 Postmaster's House, a Greek Revival two-story farmhouse typical of the era.
Collections: concentration on northern Marin County, California, particularly the Novato area.
Research Fields: oral history; video projects; historic architecture of downtown Novato; agriculture & ranching life in Novato; history & impact of Hamilton airfield.
Facilities: 240-vol. library of local newspapers & regional history; 1,200 sq. ft. exhibit space. Gift items for sale.
Activities: docent program; adult programming; formal education programs for children; guided tours; lectures; four general meetings with lecturers.
Publications: quarterly newsletter & historic journal, The Novato Historian; book, Novato Township.
Hours & Admission Prices: Wed.-Thurs. & Sat. 12-4; other times by appointment. No charge; donations accepted. Closed major holidays. ♿
Attendance: 2,500 (estimated)
Membership: Historical Guild: Student $5; Individual $15; Family $25; Business $50; Patron $100; Life $500.

Oakdale

OAKDALE COWBOY MUSEUM, 355 E. F St., Oakdale, CA 95361-4084. Mailing Address: P.O. Box 1155, Oakdale, CA 95361-1155. Tel.: 209-847-5163. Fax: 209-847-4183.
E-mail: christie@oakdalecowboymuseum.org
Web Site: www.oakdalecowboymuseum.org
Founded: 1995.
Key Personnel: Exec. Dir., Christie Camarillo
Cowboy History Museum.
Collections: history of local rodeo cowboys & ranchers; cowboy memorabilia; World Champion Rodeo.
Hours & Admission Prices: Mon.-Sat. 10-2. Adults $1; members no charge. Closed holidays. ♿
Attendance: 5,000 (accurate)
Membership: Individual $25; Family $50; Business $100.

OAKDALE MUSEUM & HISTORY CENTER, 277 N. 2nd Ave., Oakdale, CA 95361-3042. Mailing Address: P.O. Box 2212, Oakdale, CA 95361-5212. Tel.: 209-845-3591. Fax: 209-845-3592.
E-mail: history@lanset.com
Web Site: www.oakdalehistory.com
Founded: 1985.
Congressional District: 18
Key Personnel: Dir., Cheryl Bolin; Chm. (V), William Wood; Pres., Don Riise; Vice Pres., Barbara Torres.
Personnel Profile: Part-Time Paid 1; Part-Time Volunteers 7.
Governing Authority: municipal government. Parent Institution: City of Oakdale. Tax-exempt: 501(c)(3).
Local History Museum: housed in 1869 residence.
Collections: Haidlen historical photographs, interviews & mementos; Sandl art; microfilm collection of Oakdale newspapers, 1881-present; obituaries 1884-present; tax records 1907-1951.
Research Fields: history of Oakdale & area; people; businesses; structures; events.
Facilities: 25-vol. library of local history books, available to the public; microfilm library: Oakdale, Stockton & Modesto newspapers, Stanislaus Co. census.
Activities: arts festivals; docent program; formal education programs for children; guided tours; temporary & traveling exhibitions. Annual Events: Benefit Dinner in June; 1890s Day in September; Christmas Boutique.
Publications: quarterly newsletter, The Live Oak.
Hours & Admission Prices: Mon.-Fri. 12-4. No charge; donations accepted. Closed major holidays. ♿
Attendance: 2,500 (estimated)
Membership: Adult $10; Family $15.

Oakhurst

CHILDREN'S MUSEUM OF THE SIERRA, 49269 Golden Oak Dr., Oakhurst, CA 93644-8536. Mailing Address: P.O. Box 1200, Oakhurst, CA 93644-1200. Tel.: 559-658-5656. Fax: 559-658-5656.
Web Site: www.childrensmuseumofthesierra.org
Founded: 1997.
Key Personnel: Dir. & Chm. (V), Jean Hand; Devel., Linda Priest; Education,

Donna Marks; Public Rels., Ronda Clarke; Treas. & Cur., Jim Elliott; Registrar, Angelo Pizelo; Museum Shop Mgr., Lian Rausch.
Personnel Profile: Full-Time Volunteers 1; Part-Time Paid 2; Part-Time Volunteers 3.
Governing Authority: private; nonprofit organization. Tax-exempt: 501(c)(3).
Children's Museum.
Collections: hands-on exhibits.
Facilities: 150-vol. library; 3,500 sq. ft. exhibit space; party room; theater. Museum-related items for sale.
Activities: arts festivals; hobby workshops; school loan service; rodeos; local events; travel trunk. Annual Events: Breakfast with Santa; Parking Lot Sale.
Publications: quarterly newsletter, The Museum Messenger.
Hours & Admission Prices: July-Aug. Tues.-Sat. 10-5; Sept.-June Tues.-Sat. 10-4, Sun. 1-4. Admission $3; discounts to groups. Closed Mother's Day; major holidays.
Attendance: 12,518 (accurate)
Membership: Family $45; Contributor $50-$99; Patron $100-$199; Sponsor $200-$499.

FRESNO FLATS HISTORICAL PARK, 49777 Rd. 427, Oakhurst, CA 93644. Mailing Address: P.O. Box 451, Oakhurst, CA 93644-0451. Tel.: 559-683-6570. Fax: 559-658-2161.
E-mail: fresnoflatsmuseum@sti.net
Web Site: fresnoflatsmuseum.org
Founded: 1968.
Congressional District: 19
Key Personnel: Pres., Don Ashton; 1st Vice Pres., Pat Pinckney; 2nd Vice Pres., Ray Edmondson; Treas., Barbara Skowrenski; Sec., Shirley Halderman; Ways & Means, Roger Shickler.
Personnel Profile: Full-Time Volunteers 40; Part-Time Paid 2; Part-Time Volunteers 15.
Governing Authority: private; nonprofit organization. Parent Institution: Sierra Historic Site Association, P.O. Box 451, Oakhurst, CA 93644. Tax-exempt: 501(c)(3).
History Museum.
Collections: the period from the California Gold Rush to 1930 with emphasis on late 19th & early 20th-century in the foothills & mountains of central California; log house; two schoolhouses; blacksmith shop; two jailhouses.
Research Fields: life in the foothills & mountains of central California 1850-1930.
Facilities: 1,500-vol. library of local history, California history, national history & museum manuals; 134,000 sq. ft. exhibit space. Museum-related items for sale.
Activities: docent programs; guided tours; rental facilities. Museum Sponsors: Film Festival in April; Heritage Days in September.
Publications: quarterly newsletter, Fresno Flats Gazette.
Hours & Admission Prices: Museum: Mon.-Fri. 10-3, Sat.-Sun. 12-4. Library: Mon.-Fri. 10-3. Grounds: daily dawn to dusk. Museum & Tours: adults $4, children $2; members no charge. ♿
Attendance: 7,000 (estimated)
Membership: General $25; Bronze $50; Silver $300; Gold $500; Platinum $1,000.

KING VINTAGE CLOTHING MUSEUM, 40680 Hwy. 41, Oakhurst, CA 93644. Mailing Address: P.O. Box 303, Oakhurst, CA 93644-0303. Tel.: 559-658-6999. Fax: 559-683-3094.
E-mail: kingvintagemuseum@sti.net
Web Site: www.kingvintagemuseum.org
Founded: 2002.
Key Personnel: Chm. (V), Toni Lagunoff; Museum Shop Mgr., Mary Ann Hutcherson.
Personnel Profile: Part-Time Paid 1; Part-Time Volunteers 10.
Governing Authority: Tax-exempt.
History Museum.
Collections: period clothing from the 1790 to 1990s including war memorabilia.
Major Exhibits: Abraham Lincoln Self-Made in America (T), 3/5/10-4/2/10.
Hours & Admission Prices: Wed.-Sat. 11-5, Sun. 1-4. Adults $3. ♿
Attendance: 925 (estimated)
Membership: Individual $25; Family $50; Business $100; Life $500.

Oakland

AFRICAN-AMERICAN MUSEUM AND LIBRARY AT OAKLAND, 659 14th St., Oakland, CA 94612-1242. Tel.: 510-637-0200. Fax: 510-637-0204. TDD: 510-652-8634.
Web Site: www.oaklandlibrary.org
Founded: 1965.
Congressional District: 7
Key Personnel: C.E.O. & Pres. Trustees (V), Melvin Terry; Cur. & Museum Mgr., Rick Moss; Museum Cur. Asst., Erica L. Watkins; Librarian, Veronica L. Lee; Librarian, Linda Jolivet.
Personnel Profile: Full-Time Paid 7; Part-Time Paid 2.
Governing Authority: nonprofit organization. Parent Institution: Oakland Public Library. Tax-exempt: 501(c)(3).
African-American History Museum.
Collections: California's African-American history; books; photographs; documents; artifacts; videotapes & audiotapes.
Research Fields: California history of African Americans; Western, California & Northern California Black History.
Facilities: 1,000-vol. library & archives of general Black history, available for research on premises during office hours; reading room.
Activities: guided tours; lectures; films; permanent & temporary exhibitions.
Hours & Admission Prices: Tues.-Sat. 12-5:30. ♿

THE CAMRON-STANFORD HOUSE PRESERVATION ASSOCIATION, 1418 Lakeside Dr., Oakland, CA 94612-4307. Tel.: 510-444-1876 & 874-7802 (office). Fax: 510-874-7803.
E-mail: pelican@cshouse.org
Web Site: www.cshouse.org
Founded: 1971.
Congressional District: 8
Key Personnel: Vice Pres. Collections & House Committee, Frankie Rhodes; Vice Pres. House Administrative, Elaine Oldham; Consulting Cur., Wayne Mathes.
Personnel Profile: Part-Time Volunteers 20.
Governing Authority: nonprofit organization. Parent Institution: Camron-Stanford House Preservation Assoc. Tax-exempt: 501(c)(3).
Historic House & Preservation Project: 1876 four-story Victorian House, former Oakland Museum.
Collections: period rooms; paintings; sculpture; 1875-85 decorative arts & furnishings; 19th-century women's needle & craft work; 19th-century artifacts, history & household items; photographs.
Research Fields: 1875-1885 decorative arts; 19th-century gardens, construction, craft techniques, customs, living styles, parties & Christmas practices.
Facilities: 200-vol. library of books, magazines, slides & slide tapes pertaining to all aspects of the Victorian era available for research by special request; reading room; 40-seat auditorium; meeting rooms; reception facilities. Museum-related items for sale.
Activities: guided tours; lectures; films; docent program & council; formally organized education programs for children; permanent & temporary exhibitions; rental facilities.
Publications: newsletter, Camron-Stanford House Newsletter; brochure.
Hours & Admission Prices: 3rd Wed. of month 1-5. Adults $5, senior citizens $4, juniors 12-18 $3; children under 12, school tours and 1st Sun. no charge.
Attendance: 400 (estimated)
Membership: Student $10; Individual $35; Family $50; Preservationist $100; Victorian $150; Italianate $250.

CHABOT SPACE & SCIENCE CENTER, 10000 Skyline Blvd., Oakland, CA 94619-2450. Tel.: 510-336-7373. Fax: 510-336-7491.
Web Site: www.chabotspace.org
Formerly: Chabot Observatory & Science Center
Founded: 1883.
Congressional District: 9
Key Personnel: C.E.O. & Dir., Alexander Zwissler; Chm., Jean Quan; Museum Shop Mgr., Lara Miranda.
Personnel Profile: Full-Time Paid 60; Part-Time Volunteers 180; Interns 6.
Governing Authority: Tax-exempt.
Science Center.
Collections: astronomy; space sciences; global climate change; environment.
Facilities: classrooms; theater; digital planetarium; three observatories. Museum-related items for sale.
Activities: simulated space mission; hands-on exhibits & activities; telescope viewing.
Publications: e-Voyager; Astronotes; podcasts.
Hours & Admission Prices: Summer: Tues.-Thurs. 10-5, Fri.-Sat. 10-10, Sun. 11-5. Telescope Viewing: dusk to 10:30. Adults $14.95, youth 3-12 $10.95; discounts to military; children under 3 & members no charge. Closed Independence Day; Thanksgiving; Christmas. ♿
Attendance: 150,000 (estimated)
Membership: Earth Adult $60; Earth Active & Earth Parent $75; Earth Family $99; Earth Family Plus $125; Neptune $250; Saturn $500; Jupiter $750.

COHEN-BRAY HOUSE, 1440 29th Ave., Oakland, CA 94601-2309. Tel.: 510-536-1703.
Historic House Museum.
Collections: personal artifacts; period furnishings.
Activities: special events.
Hours & Admission Prices: 4th Sun. of month 2pm.

DUNSMUIR HELLMAN HISTORIC ESTATE, 2960 Peralta Oaks Ct., Oakland, CA 94605-5320. Tel.: 510-619-5994. Fax: 510-562-8294.
E-mail: jimd@dunsmuir.org
Web Site: www.dunsmuir.org
Founded: 1971.
Congressional District: 9
Key Personnel: Chm. (V), Dinah Benson; Dir., Jim DeMersman; Museum Shop Mgr., Debra Bresso.
Personnel Profile: Full-Time Paid 5; Part-Time Paid 10; Part-Time Volunteers 65; Interns 2.
Governing Authority: Tax-exempt.
Historic Estate: a 37-room Neoclassical Revival mansion built in 1899.
Collections: furnishings; personal artifacts. Historic Buildings: milk barn; carriage house; 1928 residence; chauffeur cottage.
Research Fields: Edwardian life in America; Jewish American experience in the West.
Facilities: 50 acres. Museum-related items for sale.
Activities: Museum Sponsors: Family First Sundays; Scottish Highland Games; Oktoberfest & Pumpkin Patch; Summer Movie Under the Stars; Holidays at Dunsmuir in December.
Publications: quarterly newsletter.
Hours & Admission Prices: Grounds: Mon.-Fri. 10-4. Mansion Tours: April 5-Sept. 27 Wed. 11am. Adults $5, seniors $4; discounts to AAM members; children 13 & under no charge.
Attendance: 65,125 (accurate)
Membership: Individual $40; Family $60; Century Club $100; Peralta Club $250; Dunsmuir Club $500; Hellman Club $1,000.

JUNIOR CENTER OF ART AND SCIENCE, Lakeside Park, 558 Bellevue Ave., Oakland, CA 94610-5026. Tel.: 510-839-5777. Fax: 510-839-8102.
E-mail: jrcenter@sbcglobal.net
Web Site: www.juniorcenter.org
Founded: 1954.
Congressional District: 9
Key Personnel: Exec. Dir., Tammara Katsikas; Cur., Daniel McClain
Children's Museum.
Collections: hands-on exhibits; California Native American tools, games, baskets, & artifacts.
Activities: workshops; demonstrations.
Hours & Admission Prices: June-Aug. Mon.-Thurs. 8:30-5:30; Sept.-May Tues.-Fri. 10-6, Sat. 10-3. No charge.

KENNEDY ART CENTER GALLERY AT HOLY NAMES UNIVERSITY, 3500 Mountain Blvd., Oakland, CA 94619-1627. Tel.: 510-436-1457.
Art Gallery.
Collections: paintings; music recordings; art history slides.
Facilities: classrooms; theater.
Activities: performances.
Hours & Admission Prices: Sat.-Sun. 12-5; other times by appointment.

MERRITT MUSEUM OF ANTHROPOLOGY, 12500 Campus Dr., Library Bldg., Oakland, CA 94619-3107. Tel.: 510-436-2607. Fax: 415-922-0905.
Founded: 1973.
Congressional District: 7
Key Personnel: Dir., Dr. Barbara Joans; Cur. Conservation, Leslie Fleming; Cur. & Museum Assoc., Lisa Valcenier.
Governing Authority: college. Parent Institution: Peralta Community College District. Tax-exempt.
Anthropology Museum.
Collections: ethnological material from North & South America, Africa, the Pacific & Asia; prehistoric collection; European collection.
Research Fields: contemporary United States, South Africa & Mexico.
Facilities: classrooms.
Activities: guided tours; lectures; films; formally organized education programs for undergraduate college students; training programs for paraprofessional museum workers; loan, temporary & permanent exhibits. Museum Sponsors: satellite exhibits at various locations in surrounding communities.
Hours & Admission Prices: Mon.-Thurs. 7:45-7, Fri. 7:45-3. No charge. Closed academic holidays. ♿
Attendance: 300 (estimated)
Membership: Individual $5.

MILLS COLLEGE ART MUSEUM, (M), 5000 MacArthur Blvd., Oakland, CA 94613-1302. Tel.: 510-430-2164. Fax: 510-430-3168.
E-mail: museum@mills.edu
Web Site: www.mills.edu/campus_life/art_museum
Founded: 1925.
Congressional District: 8
Key Personnel: Dir., Jessica Hough; Asst. Dir., Stacie Daniels.
Personnel Profile: Full-Time Paid 2; Full-Time Volunteers 8; Interns 20.
Governing Authority: college. Parent Institution: Mills College. Tax-exempt: 501(c)(3).
College Art Gallery.
Collections: international prints & drawings; Asian & Latin American textiles; 20th-century American ceramics; Japanese ceramics; California regionalist paintings; contemporary photography & new media.
Research Fields: art of the San Francisco Bay Area.
Activities: lectures.
Publications: Mills College Art Museum Bulletin; posters; exhibition brochures; catalogues.
Hours & Admission Prices: Tues. & Thurs.-Sun. 11-4, Wed. 11-7:30. No charge; donations accepted. ♿
Attendance: 10,100 (accurate)
Membership: Friends of Mills College Art Museum $100.

OAKLAND AVIATION MUSEUM, 8252 Earhart Rd., Oakland, CA 94621. Mailing Address: P.O. Box 2248, Oakland, CA 94621-0148. Tel.: 510-638-7100. Fax: 510-638-6530.
Web Site: www.oaklandaviationmuseum.org
Formerly: Western Aerospace Museum
Founded: 1981.
Key Personnel: Dir. & Museum Shop Mgr., Pamela Kruse-Buckingham; Pres. (V), Carol Hill.
Personnel Profile: Full-Time Paid 1; Part-Time Volunteers 54; Interns 2.
Governing Authority: private; not-for-profit. Tax-exempt: 501(c)(3).
Aviation History Museum: housed in 1940 Army Air Corps hangar on historic Oakland Airport, North Field.
Collections: aircraft; furnishings & personal artifacts of aviation; photographs; prints & films; history of Oakland Airport 1922-1965.
Research Fields: history of aviation in San Francisco Bay area & northern California.
Facilities: 3,000-vol. library on aviation; 30,500 sq. ft. exhibit space; classroom. Books, t-shirts, postcards, model aircraft, toys & other museum-related items for sale.
Activities: guided tours; lectures; loan exhibitions; films; docent programs. Annual Events: Members' Meeting; Aviation Authors Book Signing.
Publications: quarterly newsletter, Chatter from the Flight Line.
Hours & Admission Prices: Wed.-Sun. 10-4. Adults $9, senior citizens 55 & over $8, child 6-12 $5; discounts to groups, CSAA Airline Crew, military, ICOM & AAM members; children 5 & under and members no charge. Closed New Year's Eve & Day; Thanksgiving; Christmas. ♿
Attendance: 5,168 (accurate)
Membership: Individual $35; Family $60; Golden Gater $100; Life $600.

*** OAKLAND MUSEUM OF CALIFORNIA, (M),** 1000 Oak St., Oakland, CA 94607-4892. Tel.: 510-238-2200 & 3404 (director's office). Fax: 510-238-2258. TDD: 510-451-3322.
E-mail: equist@museumca.org
Web Site: www.museumca.org
Founded: 1969.
Congressional District: 8 & 9
Key Personnel: Chm., Christopher M. McLain; Exec. Dir., Lori Fogarty; Chief Cur. Art, Philip Linhares; Chief Cur. Education, Barbara Henry; Sr. Cur. Art, Karen Tsujimoto; Cur. Art Photography, Drew Johnson; Registrar Art, Arthur Monroe; Cur. History, Costumes & Textiles, Inez Brooks-Myers; Docent Coord., Joan Collignon; Registrar, History & Natural Science, Carolyn Rissanen.
Personnel Profile: Full-Time Paid 76; Part-Time Paid 37; Part-Time Volunteers 887; Interns 10.
Governing Authority: partnership. Parent Institution: City of Oakland. Subsidiary Institution: Oakland Museum of California Foundation. Tax-exempt: 170(b)(1)(A); 501(c)(3).
Regional Multidisciplinary Museum.
Collections: California environment, history & art; archives, fine art & historical photography; paintings, sculpture; fine crafts; decorative arts; aquatic biology; regional ecology; California Library of Natural Sounds; California Indian artifacts; California history & cultures from prehistory to present.
Research Fields: California landscape & contemporary art, history, historic costume & textiles, nature sounds, biotic zones & ecology; the arts & crafts movement; Dorothea Lange photo collection.
Facilities: gardens; theater; lecture hall; classroom; restaurant. Museum-related items for sale.
Activities: guided tours; lectures; gallery talks; concerts; plays, films; ethnic festivals; formally organized education programs for children; docent program; museum-school partnerships; youth interpreter & junior docent

programs; inter-museum loan; permanent, temporary & traveling exhibitions; school loan service; teacher training; travel program. Museum Sponsors: Earth Day Fest; Annual Wildflower Show.
Publications: 4-5 annual catalogs; quarterly magazine, The Museum of California; brochures.
Hours & Admission Prices: Wed.-Sat. 10-5, Sun. 12-5. Adults $8, seniors & students $5; discounts to non-Oakland school groups, AAM members; children under 6, Oakland school groups, members & Fri. 5-9 no charge. Closed New Year's Day; Independence Day; Thanksgiving; Christmas. ♿
Attendance: 130,000 (accurate)
Membership: Senior Citizens $43; Active $54; Contributor $80; Supporter $125; Sponsor $250; Patron $500; Colleague $1,000.

OAKLAND MUSEUM OF CALIFORNIA-SCULPTURE COURT AT CITY CENTER, 1111 Broadway, Oakland, CA 94607-4139. Mailing Address: 1000 Oak St., Oakland, CA 94607-4892. Tel.: 510-238-2200 & 6836. Fax: 510-238-6838.
Web Site: www.museumca.org
Key Personnel: Exec. Dir., Lori Fogarty; Chief Cur. Art, Philip Linhares; Chief Cur. Natural Sciences, Tom Steller; Sr. Cur. History, P. Christian Klieger; Cur. Education, Barbara Henry; Museum Shop Mgr., Katherine Rolph
Sculpture Court.
Collections: contemporary California sculptures.
Hours & Admission Prices: Mon.-Fri. 7-7, third Thurs. each month 7am-8pm. No charge. Closed holidays.

OAKLAND ZOO, 9777 Golf Links Rd., Oakland, CA 94605-4925. Mailing Address: P.O. Box 5238, Oakland, CA 94605-0238. Tel.: 510-632-9525, ext. 132. Fax: 510-635-5719.
E-mail: nancy@oaklandzoo.org
Web Site: www.oaklandzoo.org/
Founded: 1922.
Congressional District: 9
Key Personnel: Exec. Dir., Dr. Joel J. Parrott, D.V.M.; C.F.O. & C.A.O., Vince Forte; Animal Cur., Colleen Kinzley; Dir. Mktg., Nancy Filippi; Grounds, Jorge Urbina; Dir. Operations, Tim Love; Dir. Park Svcs., Bob Westfall; Dir. Education & Conservation, Randi Meyer; Museum Shop Mgr., Lynn Greer-Thompson.
Personnel Profile: Full-Time Paid 109; Part-Time Paid 17; Part-Time Volunteers 375.
Governing Authority: municipal; nonprofit organization. Operated by East Bay Zoological Society; development through the East Bay Zoological Society. Tax-exempt: 501(c)(3).
Adult & Children's Zoo.
Collections: over 660 native & exotic animals.
Research Fields: ChimpanZoo project.
Facilities: 150-vol. library; educational facilities; amphitheater; botanical garden; 60 acres exhibit space; snack shop. Zoo-related items for sale.
Activities: guided tours; lectures; formal educational programs; docent program; Zoomobile programs; members nights. Annual Events: Walk in the Wild; Fundraiser; Earth Day; Celebrating Elephants; Discovering Primates; Boo at the Zoo; Feasts for the Beasts; Paws & Claus; Zoolights.
Publications: quarterly newsletter, Roar; annual report.
Hours & Admission Prices: Daily 10-4. Adults 15-55 $10.50, children 2-14 $7; discounts to groups; members no charge. Parking: bus $10, car $6. Closed Thanksgiving; Christmas. ♿
Attendance: 550,000 (estimated)
Membership: Student & Senior $40; Individual $50; Dual Senior $65; Individual Plus & Single Parent $70; Grandparents $75; Family $80; Family Plus $99; Sustaining $150; Contributing $250; Sponsor $500.

THE PARDEE HOME MUSEUM, 672 11th St., Oakland, CA 94607-3651. Tel.: 510-444-2187. Fax: 510-444-7120.
E-mail: info@pardeehome.org
Web Site: www.pardeehome.org
Founded: 1982.
Key Personnel: Dir., David Nicolai; Chm. (V), Stan Stidham; Registrar, Vicki Wiese.
Personnel Profile: Full-Time Paid 1; Part-Time Paid 2; Part-Time Volunteers 2.
Governing Authority: nonprofit organization. Tax-exempt: 501(c)(3).
Historic House: c.1868 former residence of Gov. George Pardee.
Collections: 1850-1980 Pardee family furniture; ethnography; archives; photographs.
Facilities: 165-vol. library of collections management; historic preservation; collections research & identification available for use by the public; archival research room; 5,000 sq. ft. exhibit space.
Activities: docent program; guided tours. Museum-related items for sale.
Publications: newsletter, Pardee Home Museum.
Hours & Admission Prices: Tours: Wed. & Fri.-Sat. 12-3; groups by appointment. Adults $5; children under 12 & members no charge.
Attendance: 875 (accurate)
Membership: Students & Seniors $10; Individual $20; Family $30.

PEERLESS COFFEE & TEA COMPANY MUSEUM, 260 Oak St., Oakland, CA 94607-4587. Tel.: 800-310-KONA; 410-763-1763. Fax: 510-763-5026.
Founded: 2001.
Key Personnel: Pres. & Cur., Sonja Vukasin
Company Museum.
Collections: coffee memorabilia; period coffee grinders; tins & tea bins; jewelry; Vukasin family history; 1922 Model T Ford Depot Hack; Peerless Coffee Company & Tea heritage.
Facilities: Museum-related items for sale.
Hours & Admission Prices: Mon.-Fri. 10-4; groups by appointment. No charge. ♿

ROTARY NATURE CENTER, 600 Bellevue Ave., Oakland, CA 94610-5000. Tel.: 510-238-3739. Fax: 510-238-7962.
E-mail: sbenavidez@oaklandnet.com
Web Site: www.lakemerritt.org
Founded: 1953.
Congressional District: 8
Key Personnel: Supervising Naturalist, Stephanie Benavidez.
Personnel Profile: Full-Time Paid 2; Part-Time Paid 13; Part-Time Volunteers 10.
Governing Authority: municipal. Parent Institution: Oakland Office of Parks & Recreation. Tax-exempt.
Natural History Museum.
Collections: mounted birds; live specimens; mammals; reptiles; study skins.
Research Fields: water birds.
Facilities: approx. 600-vol. library of books on Western U.S. natural sciences available for use on premises; reading room; nature center; wildlife refuge; 75-seat auditorium.
Activities: guided tours; classes in nature & ecology; films; walks; nature art & day camps; school loan service. Center Sponsors: wildlife & animal demonstrations.
Publications: bimonthly program of activities; brochures.
Hours & Admission Prices: Daily & holidays 10-5. Feedings 3:30pm. No charge; donations accepted. ♿
Attendance: 35,000 (estimated)

Oceanside

CALIFORNIA SURF MUSEUM, 312 Pier View Way, Oceanside, CA 92054. Tel.: 760-721-6876.
E-mail: csm@surfmuseum.org
Web Site: www.surfmuseum.org
Founded: 1986.
Key Personnel: Pres. (V), Jim Kempton; Operations Mgr., Julie Cox; Museum Shop Mgr., Todd Quinn.
Personnel Profile: Full-Time Paid 1; Part-Time Paid 3; Part-Time Volunteers 30; Interns 4.
Governing Authority: nonprofit organization. Tax-exempt: 501(c)(3).
Surf Museum.
Collections: surfboards & surf-related equipment; photographs; clothing; art; posters; vintage film; surf-related board games; magazines; trophies; skateboards.
Major Exhibits: History of Women's Surfing, 3/10.
Research Fields: surfing; California beach culture.
Facilities: Museum-related items for sale.
Activities: surf film festival; exhibit opening parties; VIP events; concerts; book signings; lectures. Annual Events: an exhibit highlighting one pioneering legend of surfing; Gala Fundraiser; Legends Day.
Publications: quarterly newsletter, Outside.
Hours & Admission Prices: Mon.-Wed. & Fri.-Sun. 10-4, Thurs. 10-8. Adults $3, seniors 62 & over, military with ID and students with ID $1; members & Thurs. no charge.
Attendance: 25,000 (accurate)
Membership: Gremmie & Legend $25; Surfer $50; Otlana $75; Malibu Chip $100, $250, $500.

MISSION SAN LUIS REY MUSEUM, 4050 Mission Ave., Oceanside, CA 92057-6402. Tel.: 760-757-3651. Fax: 760-757-4613.
E-mail: museumdesk@sanluisrey.org
Web Site: www.sanluisrey.org
Founded: 1798.
Congressional District: 40
Key Personnel: Admin., Edward Gabarra; Exec. Dir., Bro. James Lockman, O.F.M.; Dir. & Cur., Bradford Claybourn; Museum Assoc. & Tour Coord., Beverly Perna.

Personnel Profile: Full-Time Paid 2; Part-Time Paid 1; Part-Time Volunteers 21.
Governing Authority: Parent Institution: Franciscan Friars of the Santa Barbara Province. Subsidiary Institution: Old Mission San Luis Rey, Inc. Tax-exempt: 501(c)(3).
Historic Building & Site: 1798 San Luis Rey Mission.
Collections: Native American baskets; decorative & fine arts from Spanish occupation; Spanish, Mexican American & Native American ecclesiastical furnishings; church vestments; polychrome statues; books from mission period; religious vessels.
Research Fields: Spanish colonial mission period in Alta California.
Facilities: picnic grounds; meeting rooms available. Native American, mission history & religious articles for sale.
Activities: guided tours to groups with reservations.
Publications: Mission News.
Hours & Admission Prices: Daily 10-4. Adult $6, seniors & active military $5, youth $4; discounts to families; children 5 & under no charge. Behind the Scenes Guided Tours: adults $10. Closed New Year's Day; Easter; Thanksgiving; Christmas. ♿
Attendance: 55,000 (accurate)
Membership: Individual $35; Dual $50; Family $75; Franciscan Circle $250; Patron $500; Serra Circle $1,500; Sponsor $2,500 & up.

OCEANSIDE MUSEUM OF ART, (M), 704 Pier View Way, Oceanside, CA 92054-2802. Tel.: 760-435-3720. Fax: 760-966-5819.
E-mail: skip@oma-online.org
Web Site: oma-online.org
Founded: 1995.
Congressional District: 48
Key Personnel: Exec. Dir., James R. Pahl; Dir. Devel., Beth Smith; Asst. Dir., Danielle Susalla; Dir. Exhibitions & Collections, Teri Sowell, Ph.D.; Mgr. Facilities, Erika Koga; Membership Mgr., Teresa Ellis.
Personnel Profile: Full-Time Paid 6; Part-Time Paid 2; Part-Time Volunteers 50; Interns 1.
Governing Authority: private; nonprofit organization. Tax-exempt: 501(c)(3).
Art Museum.
Collections: regional art from 1900 to present.
Major Exhibits: Allison Renshaw, 1/31/10-6/20/10; The Art of WWII, 4/18/10-9/5/10; Contemporary Native American Art, 7/11/10-11/14/10; Quilt Visions, 9/26/10-2/20/11.
Facilities: 9,000 sq. ft. exhibit space. Gift items for sale.
Activities: docent program; tours to other museums & cultural destinations; lectures; school of art; temporary & permanent exhibitions. Annual Events: Dinner Dance/Formal; receptions; Culinary Cinema Series; Vigilucci's Jazz at the Museum; Mardi Gras; Museum Ball; Art After Dark; Free Family Art Days.
Publications: newsletter; catalog, James Hubbell Retrospective; Chouinard: A Living Legacy; Masterpieces of San Diego Painting: Fifty Works from Fifty Years; Damngorgeous: A Daughters Memoir of Millard Owen Sheets; Art of the WPA Era; Worn With Pride: Celebrating Samoan Artistic Heritage; Deloss McGraw: The Circus Loosely; Ethel Green: Surrealist Painter; Convergence: The Studio Furniture of Tasmania and America; James Hubbell: Meditations on Nature and Life.
Hours & Admission Prices: Tues.-Sat. 10-4, Sun. 1-4. Adults $8; discounts to AAM & ICOM members; members, students, and active military & their dependents no charge. Closed major holidays. ♿
Attendance: 53,000 (accurate)
Membership: Student & Military $30; Individual $45; Artist Alliance $55; Dual & Family $60; Artist Alliance Dual $65; Patron $150; President's Circle $500; Millennium Club $2,500.

Ojai

OJAI VALLEY HISTORICAL SOCIETY AND MUSEUM, (M), 130 W. Ojai Ave., Ojai, CA 93023-3212. Mailing Address: P.O. Box 204, Ojai, CA 93024-0204. Tel.: 805-640-1390. Fax: 805-640-1342.
E-mail: ojaivalleymuseum@ojai.net
Web Site: ojaivalleymuseum.org
Founded: 1966.
Key Personnel: Pres. (V), Ann Scanlin; Chm. (V), Fran Love; Museum Shop. Mgr., Bobbie Boschan.
Personnel Profile: Part-Time Paid 2; Part-Time Volunteers 80.
Governing Authority: Tax-exempt.
Historical Society Museum.
Collections: concentration on Ojai Valley & the early Chumash Indians to pioneer settlers; natural history collection featuring animals indigenous to the area.
Activities: lectures & family programs; Chumash day camp.
Publications: Rack card; quarterly newsletter.
Hours & Admission Prices: Thurs.-Fri. 1-4, Sat. 10-4, Sun. 12-4, Wed. tours by appointment. Adults $3, children 6-18 $1; members & children under 6 no charge. Closed New Year's Day; Independence Day; Thanksgiving; Christmas. ♿
Attendance: 5,952 (accurate)
Membership: Individual $30; Family $45; Business $75; Patron $100; Sustaining $250.

Old Sacramento

OLD SACRAMENTO STATE HISTORIC PARK, 111 I St., Old Sacramento, CA 95814-2204. Tel.: 916-445-7387. Fax: 916-327-5655. TDD: 916-324-2667.
E-mail: csrmlibrary@csrmf.org
Web Site: www.csrmf.org
Founded: 1976.
Congressional District: 3
Key Personnel: Dir., Paul J. Hammond; Chief Cur., Stephen E. Drew; Dir. Collections, Ellen L. Halteman; Maintenance Chief, Dennis Pruitt.
Personnel Profile: Full-Time Paid 40; Part-Time Paid 15; Part-Time Volunteers 900.
Governing Authority: state. Affiliated with California State Parks, P.O. Box 942896 Sacramento, CA 94296. Parent Institution: California State Railroad Museum. Tax-exempt.
State Park Museum: located in Old Sacramento State Historic Park.
Collections: original State Supreme Court Chambers & Wells Fargo Bank; artifacts of 1st transcontinental telegraph & western terminus of the Pony Express.
Facilities: Eagle Theatre; B.F. Hastings Building; McDowell Building; Tehama Block Building; Pony Express Monument.
Activities: guided tours; talks to groups; permanent exhibits; docent program.
Hours & Admission Prices: Daily 10-5. Call for schedule of activities. No charge. Closed New Year's Day; Thanksgiving; Christmas. ♿
Attendance: 60,000 (estimated)

Ontario

GRABER OLIVE HOUSE MUSEUM, 315 E. 4th St., Ontario, CA 91764-2709. Mailing Address: P.O. Box 511, Ontario, CA 91762-8511. Tel.: 909-983-1761; 800-996-5483. Fax: 909-984-2180.
Web Site: www.graberolives.com
Founded: 1894.
Key Personnel: C.E.O. & Dir., Clifford C. Graber, II
Historic House Museum: housed in the home of the Graber Family, growers & producers of Graber Olives since 1894.
Collections: grading, curing & canning Graber Olives.
Activities: tours.
Hours & Admission Prices: Daily 9-5:30; group tours by appointment. No charge. Closed major holidays. ♿

MUSEUM OF HISTORY & ART, ONTARIO, (M), 225 S. Euclid Ave., Ontario, CA 91762-3812. Tel.: 909-395-2510. Fax: 909-983-8978.
Web Site: www.ci.ontario.ca.us/index.cfm/1605
Founded: 1979.
Congressional District: 34
Key Personnel: Pres. Bd., Chris Kueng; Dir., Theresa Hanley; Pres. (V) Museum Assoc., Virginia Eaton; Cur., Steve Thomas; Cur. & Education Coord., Marcilyn Callejo; Gallery Attendant, Irene Gapido; Office Asst., Tammi Rendon; Museum Asst., Leslie Matamora; Museum Asst., Jacqueline Aguilar-Sathi; Museum Asst., Stephen Clugston.
Personnel Profile: Full-Time Paid 3; Part-Time Paid 5; Part-Time Volunteers 30.
Governing Authority: municipal; nonprofit. Parent Institution: City of Ontario. Tax-exempt: 501(c)(3).
Local History & Art Museum.
Collections: history of Ontario, inland Southern California, citrus, social and home life, local businesses, viticulture, mining & assaying history; 20th-century California paintings.
Research Fields: history of agricultural & industrial development of Ontario & region; major collections include Hotpoint/General Electric appliance collection; Biane Family Winery collection; Barnes family mining, agricultural & home life collection; citrus industry; Latimer family; local citrus & pioneer family; regional & California artists collection.
Facilities: 75-seat auditorium & meeting space. Museum-related items for sale.
Activities: guided tours; lectures; temporary exhibitions school & community workshops & activities; film presentations; reading & discussion groups; lectures; docent programs.
Publications: museum newsletter; local history & California history publications.
Hours & Admission Prices: Wed.-Sun. 12-4. No charge; donations accepted. Closed New Year's Eve & Day; Easter; Memorial Day; Christmas. ♿

Attendance: 20,000 (estimated)
Membership: Student & Senior Citizen $15; Individual $25; Family $35; Contributing $100; Sponsor $250; Benefactors $1,000; $2,500; $5,000.

Orange

CHAPMAN UNIVERSITY GUGGENHEIM GALLERY, (M), One University Dr., Moulton Center, Orange, CA 92866-1005. Tel.: 714-997-6815.
Art Gallery.
Collections: paintings; sculpture; photographs.
Activities: special events; receptions.
Hours & Admission Prices: Call for hours.

Oroville

BOLT'S ANTIQUE TOOL MUSEUM, 1650 Broderick St., Oroville, CA 95965-4809. Mailing Address: 1735 Montgomery St., Oroville, CA 95965-4820. Tel.: 530-538-2415. Fax: 530-538-2417.
E-mail: boltmuseum@cityoforoville.org
Founded: 1999.
Congressional District: 2
Key Personnel: Chm. (V), Bud Bolt; Cur., David Dewey; Museum Shop Mgr., Liala Bolt.
Personnel Profile: Part-Time Paid 2; Part-Time Volunteers 20.
Governing Authority: municipal.
Tool Museum.
Collections: over 5,000 hand tools; power tools; manufacturing documents.
Research Fields: tool history.
Facilities: library; 3,000 sq. ft. exhibit space. Museum-related items for sale.
Activities: docent program; guided tours; lectures.
Hours & Admission Prices: Tues.-Sun. 11:45-3:45. Adults $3, AAA members & groups of 15 or more $2.50; children under 12 no charge. Closed national holidays. ♿
Attendance: 1,902 (accurate)

BUTTE COUNTY PIONEER MEMORIAL MUSEUM, 2332 Montgomery St., Oroville, CA 95965-4924. Mailing Address: 1735 Montgomery St., Oroville, CA 95965-4820. Tel.: 530-538-2497. Fax: 530-538-2417.
Web Site: www.cityoforoville.org/pioneermuseum.html
Founded: 1932.
Congressional District: 2
Key Personnel: Cur., David Dewey.
Personnel Profile: Part-Time Paid 2; Part-Time Volunteers 30.
Governing Authority: municipal government. Tax-exempt.
History Museum.
Collections: early pioneering; Gold Rush Era of California; early area artifacts.
Facilities: 3,600 sq. ft. exhibit space. Museum-related items & books for sale.
Activities: docent program; formal education programs for children; guided tours. Annual Event: Open House in February.
Hours & Admission Prices: Feb. 2-Dec. 14 Fri.-Sun. 12-4. Adults $3, AAA members & groups of 15 or more $2.50; children under 12 no charge.
Attendance: 1,000 (estimated)

C.F. LOTT HISTORIC HOME, 1067 Montgomery St., Oroville, CA 95965. Mailing Address: 1735 Montgomery St., Oroville, CA 95965-4820. Tel.: 530-538-2497. Fax: 530-538-2417.
Web Site: www.cityoforoville.org/cflotthome.html
Founded: 1963.
Congressional District: 2
Key Personnel: Cur., David Dewey.
Personnel Profile: Part-Time Paid 2; Part-Time Volunteers 30.
Governing Authority: municipal government. Tax-exempt.
History Museum.
Collections: furniture; paintings; rugs; textiles; clothes; 1849-1915 silver & glassware.
Facilities: Museum-related items for sale.
Activities: docent program; formal education programs for children; guided tours; temporary exhibitions. Annual Event: Mistletoe Party - Open House.
Hours & Admission Prices: Feb.-Dec. 14 Sun.-Mon. & Fri. 11:30-3:30. Adults $3; discounts to AAA members & groups of 15 or more.
Attendance: 891 (accurate)

MILITARY MUSEUM OF BUTTE COUNTY, (M), 4514 Pacific Heights Rd., Oroville, CA 95965-9266. Tel.: 530-534-9956. Fax: 530-534-1170.
Military History Museum.
Collections: military history; personal artifacts; photographs; memorabilia; military uniforms, vehicles & weapons.
Hours & Admission Prices: Mon.-Sat. 8-6. No charge.

OROVILLE CHINESE TEMPLE, 1500 Broderick St., Oroville, CA 95965-4871. Mailing Address: 1735 Montgomery St., Oroville, CA 95965-4820. Tel.: 530-538-2497 & 888-OROVILLE. Fax: 530-538-2417.
Web Site: www.cityoforoville.org/chinesetemple.html
Founded: 1949.
Congressional District: 2
Key Personnel: C.E.O. & Dir. Parks, Charles Miller; Cur., David Dewey.
Personnel Profile: Part-Time Paid 2; Part-Time Volunteers 30.
Governing Authority: municipal. City of Oroville, 1735 Montgomery St., Oroville, CA. Tax-exempt.
Religious Museum: 1863 Chinese Temple.
Collections: restored Chinese Temple; religious figures; tapestries; writings; screens; altars; Chinese immigrants during California gold rush.
Facilities: library. Postcards & gifts for sale.
Activities: guided tours; permanent exhibitions; school group tours.
Hours & Admission Prices: Feb.-Dec. 15 daily 12-4; groups by appointment. Adults $3, AAA members & groups of 15 or more $2.50; children under 12 no charge.
Attendance: 4,886 (accurate)

Oxnard

CARNEGIE ART MUSEUM, (M), 424 S. C St., Oxnard, CA 93030-5944. Tel.: 805-385-8157 & 8179. Fax: 805-483-3654.
Web Site: www.vcnet.com/carnart
Founded: 1980.
Congressional District: 19
Key Personnel: Dir., Suzanne Bellah; Cur. Education, Jeanette LaVere; Pres. (V), Stacy Roscoe.
Personnel Profile: Full-Time Paid 3; Part-Time Paid 4; Part-Time Volunteers 20; Interns 1.
Governing Authority: municipal; nonprofit. Parent Institution: City of Oxnard. Subsidiary Institution: Carnegie Art Museum Cornerstones. Tax-exempt: 501(c)(3).
Art Museum: housed in 1906 former library & city hall.
Collections: over 1,500 works of California art; Eastwood Collection: archaeological & anthropological artifacts; Hollywood portrait photography.
Research Fields: art history.
Facilities: classroom.
Activities: guided tours; lectures; performances; concerts; permanent, temporary & traveling exhibitions; school tour program; adult & children's art classes; workshops.
Publications: brochure, Municipal Art Collection of Oxnard; book, Sacha Moldovan, Expressionist 1901-1982; catalog, The Pastel Landscapes of Theodore Lukits; museum newsletter; exhibit gallery guides.
Hours & Admission Prices: Thurs.-Sat. 10-5, Sun. 1-5. Adults $3, senior citizens & students $2, children 6-16 $1; discounts to AAM & WMG members; Fri. 3-5, members & children under 6 no charge. Closed Easter; Memorial Day; Independence Day; Labor Day; Thanksgiving; Christmas.
Attendance: 20,000 (estimated)
Membership: Student & Senior $25; Individual $35; Family $45; Sustaining $60; Patron $100; Angel $250; Golden Circle $1,000.

GULL WINGS CHILDREN'S MUSEUM, 418 W. Fourth St., Oxnard, CA 93030-5995. Tel.: 805-483-3005. Fax: 805-483-3226.
E-mail: gullwings1@netzero.com
Web Site: www.gullwings.org
Founded: 1989.
Key Personnel: Dir., Melissa Baffa.
Personnel Profile: Full-Time Paid 3; Part-Time Paid 3; Part-Time Volunteers 6.
Governing Authority: Tax-exempt.
Children's Museum.
Collections: hands-on exhibits.
Facilities: Museum-related items for sale.
Activities: school programs; birthday parties; special events.
Publications: newsletter.
Hours & Admission Prices: Tues.-Sat. 10-5. Admission $4; children under 2 no charge.
Attendance: 15,000 (estimated)
Membership: Grandparent $30; Family $50; Daycare Punchcard $55; Extended Family $60.

VENTURA COUNTY MARITIME MUSEUM, INC., (M), 2731 S. Victoria Ave., Oxnard, CA 93035-2947. Tel.: 805-984-6260.
E-mail: vcmm@aol.com
Web Site: www.vcmm.org
Founded: 1991.
Congressional District: 23
Key Personnel: Exec. Dir., Bill Conroy; Trustee Chm., Joyce Nelson; Trustee Pres., William Buenger; Chm. (V), Pat Hart; Cur. Art, Jackie Cavish.

Personnel Profile: Full-Time Paid 1; Part-Time Paid 4; Part-Time Volunteers 100.
Governing Authority: not-for-profit organization. Tax-exempt: 501(c)(3).
Maritime Museum.
Collections: sailing ship models; 17th- to 20th-century maritime art; shipboard items; Ventura County maritime history; 18th century POW bone models.
Major Exhibits: ASMA Aqueous III, 12/09-1/10; Nautica 2010, 2/10-3/10; Oxnard Union High School District Art, 4/10; Model Ship Expo, 5/10; Plein-Air 2010, 6/10-7/10; ISMP, 8/10-12/10.
Research Fields: California & European maritime history; American maritime history, 17th to 19th-century.
Facilities: 2,000-vol. library of maritime history & art.
Activities: docent program; formal education programs for children; guided tours; school outreach programs; tall ship visits; educational field trips; ship model guild.
Publications: quarterly newsletter; books, Port Hueneme: A History; Ventura County's Maritime Legacy.
Hours & Admission Prices: Daily 11-5. No charge; donations accepted. Closed New Year's Eve & Day; Thanksgiving; Christmas. ♿
Attendance: 20,000 (accurate)
Membership: Individual $35; Family $50; Lieutenant $100; Commander $250; Captain & Business $500; Commodore $1,000.

Pacific Grove

PACIFIC GROVE ART CENTER ASSOCIATES, INC., 568 Lighthouse Ave., Pacific Grove, CA 93950-2624. Mailing Address: P.O. Box 633, Pacific Grove, CA 93950-0633. Tel.: 831-375-2208. Fax: 831-375-2208.
E-mail: pgart@mbay.net
Web Site: www.pgartcenter.org
Founded: 1969.
Congressional District: 16
Key Personnel: Pres. (V), Babs Dupont Hanneman; Dir., Joan Jeffers Mc-Cleary; Preparator, Julie Brown Smith.
Personnel Profile: Part-Time Paid 2; Part-Time Volunteers 20.
Governing Authority: bd. of directors; nonprofit organization. Tax-exempt: 501(c)(3).
Art Center.
Collections: paintings; graphics; photographs; sculpture.
Major Exhibits: Image Makers Photography, 2/26/10-4/9/10; Gaby Hahn Paintings, 4/16/10-5/27/10; Artists Equity of Monterey County, 9/10/10-10/21/10; Patrons' Show Annual Fundraiser, 10/29/10-12/16/10; Monterey Bay Metal Arts Guild, 10/29/10-12/16/10.
Facilities: artists' studios; classroom.
Activities: rotating exhibits; art & rental of studios; art & dance classes; concerts.
Publications: PGAC newsletter.
Hours & Admission Prices: Wed.-Sat. 12-5, Sun. 1-4. No charge; donations accepted. Closed legal holidays.
Attendance: 16,000 (accurate)
Membership: Student $20; Single $25; Family $30; Business $100; Sponsor $150; Patron $500; Lifetime $1,000; Corporate Sponsor $1,200.

* **PACIFIC GROVE MUSEUM OF NATURAL HISTORY, (M),** 165 Forest Ave., Pacific Grove, CA 93950-2698. Tel.: 831-648-5716. Fax: 831-372-3256.
Web Site: www.pgmuseum.org
Founded: 1881.
Congressional District: 16
Key Personnel: Chm. (V), John Courtney; Pres. (V), Robert Frischmuth; Dir., Paul M. Finnegan; Asst. Cur., Ron L. Kettlewell; Museum Shop Mgr., N.J. Taylor.
Personnel Profile: Full-Time Paid 2; Part-Time Paid 2; Part-Time Volunteers 80.
Governing Authority: municipal. Parent Institution: City of Pacific Grove, CA. Subsidiary Institution: Pt. Pinos Lighthouse. Tax-exempt: 170(b)(1)(A).
Natural History Museum.
Collections: birds; mammals; reptiles; amphibians; marine life; plants; insects of Monterey County; zoology; botany; geology; herbarium; ethnology. Historic House: 1853 Point Pinos Lighthouse.
Research Fields: natural history of Monterey County.
Facilities: 2,000-vol. library of reference material available on premises; botanical garden. Books, educational toys & games, minerals and fossils for sale.
Activities: guided tours; lectures; inter-museum loan; permanent, temporary & traveling exhibitions. Museum Sponsors: annual wildflower show.
Publications: Supplement to the Vascular Plants of Monterey County, California; quarterly newsletter, Horizons; Wildflowers of Monterey County: A Field Companion.
Hours & Admission Prices: Tues.-Sat. 10-5. No charge; donations accepted. Closed major holidays. ♿

Attendance: 115,400 (accurate)
Membership: Student $5; Active $10; Family $20; Contributing $50; Sustaining $100; Supporting $250; Corporate $500 & up.

THE STOWITTS MUSEUM & LIBRARY, 591 Lighthouse Ave., Pacific Grove, CA 93950-2662. Tel.: 831-655-4488. Fax: 831-655-4489.
E-mail: info@stowitts.org
Web Site: www.stowitts.org
Founded: 1995.
Congressional District: 17
Key Personnel: C.E.O., Robert W. Packard; Chm. (V), Sally Higgins; Pres. (V), Ford Minton; Financial Dir., Patricia Hamilton; Chief Cur., Anne Holliday; Archivist & Education, Elizabeth Hunter; Devel., Angus Whyte; Dir., Public Rels., Christine Gary; Security, Bud Giles; Museum Shop Mgr., Judie Najariar.
Personnel Profile: Full-Time Paid 3; Full-Time Volunteers 2; Part-Time Paid 4; Part-Time Volunteers 20; Interns 10.
Governing Authority: private; nonprofit organization. Tax-exempt: 501(c)(3).
Art Museum.
Collections: 20th century arts archives 1900-1950; paintings, prints, photographs, sculpture, theatrical costumes, performing arts books, films, and archives for early ballet & dance films; Russian history artifacts; letters & book manuscripts.
Research Fields: 20th-century dance history; early 20th-century Asian history; performing arts; film studies.
Facilities: 1,900-vol. library; 2,700 sq. ft. exhibit space; theater; educational facility. Museum-related items for sale.
Activities: films; formal education programs; guided tours; lectures; participatory, loan, temporary & traveling exhibitions. Museum Sponsors: Stowitts Spirit Awards Dinner in June.
Publications: bimonthly newsletter, Phoenix Rising; monographs on dance history; exhibition catalogues.
Hours & Admission Prices: Library: by appointment only. Museum: Wed.-Sat. 1-5; members visit anytime. No charge; donations accepted. Closed New Year's Day; Passover; Easter; Independence Day; Labor Day; Christmas.
Attendance: 4,500 (estimated)
Membership: Senior & Student $10; Individual $25; Family $50; Donor $100; Corporate $500.

Pacific Palisades

WILL ROGERS STATE HISTORIC PARK, 1501 Will Rogers State Park Rd., Pacific Palisades, CA 90272-3941. Tel.: 310-454-8212, ext. 104. Fax: 310-459-2031.
E-mail: rnicholas@parks.ca.gov
Web Site: www.ugf.edu/aboutugf/galerietrinitas
Founded: 1944.
Key Personnel: District Supt., Ron Schafer; Topanga Supt., Lynette Hernandez; Museum Cur., Rochelle Nicholas-Booth.
Personnel Profile: Full-Time Paid 11; Part-Time Paid 10; Part-Time Volunteers 45; Interns 2.
Governing Authority: state. Parent Institution: California Dept. of Parks & Recreation, Sacramento, CA.
Historic Building & Site Museum: housed in 1924-1935 original home of Will Rogers.
Collections: personal belongings of Will Rogers; cowboy souvenirs; American Indian artifacts; books; Western art, principally Charles M. Russell & Edward Borein.
Facilities: visitor center; picnic grounds. Books & museum-related items for sale.
Activities: house tours; paths & hiking trails; polo games; orientation film.
Publications: brochure, Will Rogers.
Hours & Admission Prices: Park: 8-sunset. Visitors Center & House: call for hours. Ranch Tour: Tues.-Sat. 11, 1 & 2. $7 per vehicle. Polo Games: April-Sept. Sat. 2-5, Sun. 10-1. Ranch Tours: closed New Year's Day; Thanksgiving; Christmas. ♿
Attendance: 230,000 (estimated)

Pacifica

SANCHEZ ADOBE HISTORIC SITE, 1000 Linda Mar Blvd., Pacifica, CA 94044-3545. Tel.: 650-359-1462. Fax: 650-359-1462.
E-mail: sanchezadobe@historysmc.org
Web Site: www.historysmc.org/sanchez.html
Founded: 1947.
Congressional District: 1
Key Personnel: Exec. Dir., Mitch Postel; Site Mgr., Linda Corwin; Chm. (V), Charline Smith; Education Coord., Carmen Blair.
Personnel Profile: Part-Time Paid 3; Part-Time Volunteers 20.
Governing Authority: county. Parent Institution: San Mateo County Historical Museum Assoc. Tax-exempt.

Historic House Site: historic rancho built 1842-46 site of Mission Dolores farming outpost (1783-1828); Pruristac village site for Ohlone Indians.
Collections: period furnishings; interpretive exhibits; artifacts from archaeological digs.
Facilities: library.
Activities: guided tours; lectures; living history programs.
Publications: descriptive brochures, The Sanchez Adobe; historic booklet, Journal of the San Mateo County Historical Association.
Hours & Admission Prices: Tues.-Thurs. 10-4, Sat.-Sun. 1-5. No charge; donations accepted. Closed legal holidays.
Attendance: 6,103

Paicines

PINNACLES NATIONAL MONUMENT, 5000 Hwy. 146, Paicines, CA 95043-9770. Tel.: 831-389-4486, ext. 233. Fax: 831-389-4489.
Web Site: www.nps.gov
Founded: 1908.
Congressional District: 17
Key Personnel: Supt., Eric Brunnemann; Pres. (V), Veronica Johnson; Museum Shop Mgr., Linda Regan.
Governing Authority: federal. Parent Institution: National Park Service. Subsidiary Institution: Pinnacles Partnership. Tax-exempt: 501(c)(3).
Natural History Museum.
Collections: herbarium; herpetology; entomology; geology; zoology.
Facilities: 300-vol. library of natural history books available for use by special request; visitor center.
Activities: on-site natural history study collections.
Publications: booklets, Natural History of Pinnacles National Monument.
Hours & Admission Prices: Winter: daily 7:30-6; Summer: daily 7:30-8. Vehicle $5 for 7 days; Walk-in $3 for 7 days; children under 16 & educational groups with advanced waiver no charge. Bear Gulch Visitor Center: daily 9-5. ♿
Attendance: 171,000 (estimated)

Pala

SAN ANTONIO DE PALA ASISTENCIA, 3015 Mission Rd., Pala, CA 92059. Mailing Address: P.O. Box 70, Pala, CA 92059-0070. Tel.: 760-742-1600. Fax: 760-742-3040.
Web Site: missionsanantonio.org
Founded: 1816.
Key Personnel: Museum Shop Mgr., Sr. Barbara Jackson.
Personnel Profile: Full-Time Paid 1.
History Museum: housed in a sub-mission of Mission San Luis Rey de Francia.
Collections: Indian art; period artifacts.
Activities: religious services.
Hours & Admission Prices: Office & Store: Tues.-Fri. 9:30-4:30, Sat. 9:30-3, Sun. 9:30-1. Mass: Mon.-Fri. 8am, Sat. 5pm, Sun. 8:30am & 11:30 (English), 10:30am (Spanish). Closed Thanksgiving; Christmas.

Palm Desert

THE LIVING DESERT, 47900 Portola Ave., Palm Desert, CA 92260-6156. Tel.: 760-346-5694, ext. 2102. Fax: 760-568-9685.
E-mail: sjohnson@livingdesert.org
Web Site: livingdesert.org
Founded: 1970.
Key Personnel: C.E.O. & Pres., Mr. Stacey Johnson; Pres. (V), Nick Steffanoff; Chm. Bd., Mrs. Peggy Bernthal; Dir. Public Rels. & Mktg., Kimberly Bowers; Dir. Conservation & Education, Peter Siminski; Dir. Accounting, Steve Lake; Cur. Garden Dept., Kirk Anderson; Cur. Education Dept., Mike Chedester; Cur. Animals, Liz Hile; Dir. Devel., Jane Twedt; Museum Shop Mgr., Brooke Ancheta.
Personnel Profile: Full-Time Paid 95; Part-Time Paid 28; Part-Time Volunteers 500.
Governing Authority: nonprofit organization. Tax-exempt.
Zoo & Gardens.
Collections: 6,000 slide photographic library; desert fauna & flora; Colorado desert herbarium; inanimate zoological & botanical materials; Cahuilla Indian art & artifacts; North American & African aviaries; live animals including birds of prey; coyotes, mountain lions, Mexican wolves, bighorn sheep, giraffe, cheetahs, leopards, zebra, & nocturnal species; art.
Major Exhibits: Fanciful Flyers: Butterfly & Hummingbird Exhibit, 11/09-4/10.
Research Fields: zoology; botany; geology.
Facilities: 9,000-vol. reference library of natural history books available for use by written request; botanical garden; walk-through aviaries; 300-seat auditorium; 600-seat outdoor amphitheater; visitors center; picnic & party facilities. Museum-related items for sale.
Activities: guided tours; lectures; docent program; permanent & temporary exhibitions; nature & hiking trails; art craft & natural history classes; field trips; concert series; wildflower program; volunteer program; volunteer trainging; summer nature school. Museum Sponsors: annual desert plant sale; Earth Day Celebration.
Publications: newsletter, L.D. Newsletter; annual report; Living Desert coloring book; book, Desert Wildflower.
Hours & Admission Prices: June 16 to Aug. daily 8-1:30; Sept. to mid-June daily 9-5 (last admission 4). Summer: adults $9.50, children 3-12 $5.25; Winter: adults $12.50, children 3-12 $7.50 accompanied by an adult; discounts to AZA & AAA members, senior citizens, groups & schools; members no charge. ♿
Attendance: 305,102 (accurate)
Membership: Individual $45; Family $65; General $75; Contributing $100; Supporting $135; Donor $250; Sustaining $500; Curator $1,000; Director $2,500; Life $5,000. Corporate: $350; $500; $1,000; $2,500; $5,000.

Palm Springs

AGUA CALIENTE CULTURAL MUSEUM, 219 S. Palm Canyon Dr., Palm Springs, CA 92262-6310. Mailing Address: 471 E. Tahquitz Canyon Way, Palm Springs, CA 92262-6620. Tel.: 760-778-1079. Fax: 760-322-7724.
Web Site: www.accmuseum.org
Founded: 1993.
Congressional District: 37
Key Personnel: Pres. & Chm. (V), Mildred Browne; Exec. Dir., Dr. Michael Hammond; Dir. Devel., Steve Sharp; Assoc. Dir. Devel., Mary Perry; Asst. Dir. Devel., Sydne Heidrich; Cur. & Dir. Programs, Ginger Ridgway; Archivist, Jon Flectcher; Asst. Cur., Dawn Wellman; Dir. Education, O'Jay T. Vanegas; Staff Accountant, Larry Soriano; Exec. Asst., Sharon May; Registrar, Laurie Egan; Education Specialist, Luis Rodriguez; Curatorial Asst., Cierra Teel; Museum Interpreter, Rita Dickey; Museum Interpreter, Ursula Cripps; Museum Interpreter, Susan Myers; Museum Interpreter, Don Karvelis; Administrative Asst., Claire Victor.
Personnel Profile: Full-Time Paid 12; Part-Time Paid 6; Part-Time Volunteers 3.
Governing Authority: private; nonprofit organization. Tax-exempt: 501(c)(3).
History Museum.
Collections: cultural & heritage artifacts from the Agua Caliente Band of Cahuilla Indians; baskets; pottery.
Research Fields: rock art; native & nonnative interactions from 1780 to present.
Facilities: 2,000-vol. library; educational facilities; 800 sq. ft. exhibit space. Museum-related items for sale.
Activities: formal education programs; lectures. Annual Events: Dinner in the Canyons (fundraiser); Native American Cultural Weekend.
Publications: quarterly, The Spirit.
Hours & Admission Prices: Memorial Day to Labor Day Fri.-Sat. 10-5, Sun. 12-5; Sept.-May Wed.-Sat. 10-5, Sun. 12-5. No charge; donations accepted. Closed New Year's Day; Thanksgiving; Christmas.
Attendance: 14,000 (estimated)
Membership: Senior $30; Individual $40; Family $50; Paloverde $100; Mesquite $250; Palm $500; Eagle $1,000; Eagle Bronze $2,500; Eagle Silver $5,000; Eagle Gold $10,000.

MOORTEN BOTANIC GARDEN AND CACTARIUM, 1701 S. Palm Canyon Dr., Palm Springs, CA 92264-8936. Tel.: 760-327-6555.
E-mail: clarkmoorten@yahoo.com
Founded: 1938.
Congressional District: 37
Key Personnel: Exec. Dir. & C.E.O., Patricia Moorten; Cur., Clark Moorten.
Governing Authority: profit-making organization; individual operation.
Botanical Garden.
Collections: botany; geology; natural history; over 3,000 varieties of worldwide desert plants, including rare & endangered species. Historic House: 1915 pioneer home, Cactus Castle.
Research Fields: botany; geology; natural history.
Facilities: 300-vol. library of botanical books of desert plants available for use on premises & by appointment; desert plant nursery.
Activities: guided tours; lectures; films; formally organized education programs for children, adults, undergraduate & graduate college students; inter-museum loan, permanent, temporary & traveling exhibitions; Desert Lore classes for children; conservation education.
Publications: book, Desert Plants for Desert Gardens.
Hours & Admission Prices: Mon.-Sat. 9-4:30, Sun. 10-4. Adults $3, children age 5-15 $1.50; children under 5 no charge.

PALM SPRINGS AIR MUSEUM, (M), 745 N. Gene Autry Trail, Palm Springs, CA 92262-5464. Tel.: 760-778-6262, ext. 222.
E-mail: sharon@palmspringsairmuseum.org

Web Site: www.palmspringsairmuseum.org
Key Personnel: Dir., Sharon Maguire; Museum Shop Mgr., Judy Hauseur.
Governing Authority: nonprofit organization. Tax-exempt: 501(c)(3).
Air Museum.
Collections: WWII military aircraft; period automobiles; aviation art; photographs; aircraft & ship models.
Activities: educational programs; seminars; flight demonstrations; temporary exhibitions.
Hours & Admission Prices: Daily 10-5. Adults $12, seniors 65 & over, military and youth 13-17 $10, children 6-12 $5; children under 6 and active military no charge. Closed Thanksgiving; Christmas.

* **PALM SPRINGS ART MUSEUM, (M),** 101 Museum Dr., Palm Springs, CA 92262-5659. Mailing Address: P.O. Box 2310, Palm Springs, CA 92263-2310. Tel.: 760-322-4800. Fax: 760-327-5069.
E-mail: info@psmuseum.org
Web Site: www.psmuseum.org
Formerly: Palm Springs Desert Museum, Inc.
Founded: 1938.
Congressional District: 37
Key Personnel: Chm., Harold J. Meyerman; Exec. Dir., Steven A. Nash, Ph.D.; Chief Cur., Katherine Hough; Sr. Cur. & Deputy Dir. Art, Daniell Cornell; Deputy Dir. Education & Public Programs, Robert Brasier; Dir. Devel. & Membership, Scott Schroeder; Dir. Finance, Fred Clewell; Registration & Collections Mgmt., Kathy Clewell; Deputy Dir. Facilities, Steve Hubbard; Deputy Dir. External Affairs, Lisa Vossler; Museum Shop Mgr., Betty Rinnig.
Personnel Profile: Full-Time Paid 68; Part-Time Paid 5; Interns 2.
Governing Authority: nonprofit organization. Subsidiary Institution: 8 support councils. Tax-exempt: 501(c)(3).
Art Museum.
Collections: 19th- & 20th-century art with emphasis on contemporary international art, classic Western American & Native American art, Mesoamerican art, Mexican art, European modern sculpture, American mid-20th century architecture, and American photography; glass studio art.
Major Exhibits: Linda Connor Photographs (T), 12/09-4/10; Architecture of John Lautner (T), 2/10-5/10; Color of the West: Birger Sandzen (T), 4/10-6/10; Richard Avedon Photography (T), 10/10-12/10; Retablos from the Thiebaud Collection (T), 10/10-12/10.
Research Fields: photography by Bill Anderson and Stephen Willard; Albert Frey, E. Stewart Williams architects; George Montgomery Collection.
Facilities: 12,000-vol. library of art books available for use on premises; 53,000 sq. ft. exhibition space; 90-seat lecture hall; three sculpture gardens; nature trail; 435-seat theater; 2 classrooms; cafe; educational center. Museum-related items for sale.
Activities: guided tours; lectures; films; gallery talks; concerts; dramatic productions; dance recitals; formally organized educational programs; inter-museum loan, permanent, temporary & traveling exhibitions; docent program or council.
Publications: Duane Hanson: Virtual Reality; NW x SW: Painted Fictions; Michael Todd: 25-Year Survey; California Grandeur and Genre; Transforming the Western Image; Namingha: Timeless Land and Enduring Images; American Arts & Crafts from the Collection of Alexandra and Sidney Sheldon; Agnes Pelton: Poet of Nature; Collaborations: William Allan, Robert Hudson, William Wiley; Icons and Legends: The Photography of Michael Childers; Stephen H. Willard: Photography and Archive; Contemporary Desert Photography: The Other Side of Paradise; Lights! Camera! Glamour! George Hurrell at 100; quarterly member magazine; D.J. Hall Thirty-Five Year Retrospective; Picasso to Moore: Modern Sculpture from the Weiner Collection; Portrait: Robert Mapplethorpe; 70 Years of Painting: Wayne Thiebaud.
Hours & Admission Prices: Tues.-Wed. & Fri.-Sun. 10-5, Thurs. 12-8. Adults $12.50, seniors 62 & over $10.50, students & military personnel with I.D. $5; discounts to CAM, WMA, AAM, ICOM & AAMD members; NARM, members & Thurs. 4-8 no charge. Closed major holidays. ♿
Attendance: 130,000 (accurate)
Membership: Individual $50; Family & Dual $85; Supporting $125; Contributing $350; Patron $750; President's Circle $1,500.

RUDDY'S 1930S GENERAL STORE MUSEUM, 221 S. Palm Canyon Dr., Palm Springs, CA 92262-6310. Tel.: 760-327-2156.
History Museum.
Collections: re-created 1930s general store; period artifacts.
Hours & Admission Prices: July-Sept. Sat.-Sun. 10-4; Oct.-June Thurs.-Sun. 10-4. Adults $.95; children under 12 no charge.

VILLAGE GREEN HERITAGE CENTER, 221 S. Palm Canyon Dr., Palm Springs, CA 92262-6310. Mailing Address: P.O. Box 1498, Palm Springs, CA 92263-1498. Tel.: 760-323-8297. Fax: 760-320-2561.
Governing Authority: nonprofit organization. Parent Institution: Palm Springs Historical Society.
Historical Society Museum.
Collections: local history & culture; personal artifacts; photographs; Native American artifacts. Historic Buildings: two 19th century pioneer homes.
Hours & Admission Prices: mid-Oct. to May Wed. & Sun. 12-3, Thurs.-Sat. 10-4. Adults $2; children no charge.

Palo Alto

MUSEUM OF AMERICAN HERITAGE, 351 Homer Ave., Palo Alto, CA 94301-2727. Mailing Address: P.O. Box 1731, Palo Alto, CA 94302-1731. Tel.: 650-321-1004. Fax: 650-473-6950.
Key Personnel: Exec. Dir., Gwenyth Claughton
Technology Museum.
Collections: early 20th century life & technology; electrical & mechanical devices; inventions.
Activities: hands-on experiments; educational programs.
Hours & Admission Prices: Fri.-Sun. 11-4. No charge.

PALO ALTO ART CENTER, 1313 Newell Rd., Palo Alto, CA 94303-2909. Tel.: 650-329-2366. Fax: 650-326-6165.
E-mail: artcenter@cityofpaloalto.org
Web Site: www.cityofpaloalto.org/artcenter
Founded: 1971.
Congressional District: 12
Key Personnel: Dir., Karen Kienjle; Cur., Signe Mayfield; Studio Supvr., Gary Clarien; Operations & Sales Mgr., Rebecca Barbee; Volunteer Coord., Janette Herceg; Dir. Children's Classes, Larnie Fox; Dir. Project Look!, Ariel Feinberg; Museum Shop Mgr., Diane Master; Publications, Sharon Fox.
Personnel Profile: Full-Time Paid 9; Part-Time Paid 21; Part-Time Volunteers 150.
Governing Authority: municipal. Parent Institution: City of Palo Alto. Affiliated with the Division of Arts & Culture, City of Palo Alto. Tax-exempt: 501(c)(1).
Visual Art Center.
Collections: contemporary & historical fine art; Palo Alto Art in public places; fine craft & design.
Research Fields: contemporary art & design; fine crafts.
Facilities: sculpture gardens; auditorium; art education laboratory; meeting rooms. Museum-related items for sale.
Activities: permanent & temporary exhibitions; guided tours; lectures; films; workshops; classes; gallery talks; concerts; dance recitals; formally organized educational programs; docent program.
Publications: exhibition catalogues & brochures; quarterly calendar & newsletter.
Hours & Admission Prices: Tues.-Thurs. 10-5 & 7pm-10pm, Fri.-Sat. 10-5, Sun. 1-5. No charge; donations accepted. ♿
Attendance: 79,000 (accurate)
Membership: Individual $50; Family & Dual $75; Enthusiast $150; Advocate $250; Benefactor $500; Visionary $1,000; Director $2,500.

PALO ALTO JUNIOR MUSEUM AND ZOO, 1451 Middlefield Rd., Palo Alto, CA 94301-3351. Tel.: 650-329-2111. Fax: 650-473-1965.
Web Site: www.cityofpaloalto.org
Founded: 1934.
Congressional District: 12
Key Personnel: Zoo Cur., Robert Steele; Dir. Education, Karen Miel; Exhibits Cur., Darin Wacs; Receptionist, Ines Thiessen.
Personnel Profile: Full-Time Paid 5; Part-Time Paid 13; Part-Time Volunteers 30.
Governing Authority: municipal. Parent Institution: City of Palo Alto. Affiliated with Division of Recreation Open Spaces & Sciences of Palo Alto, CA.
Children's Museum & Zoo.
Collections: natural history; anthropological; historical; living; ethnographic.
Research Fields: informal education.
Facilities: classrooms.
Activities: lectures; art & science classes; field trips; school loan service; changing participatory science exhibition; hands-on science outreach program; animal demonstrations.
Publications: monthly, activities bulletin; quarterly, activities bulletin; current exhibition guide; brochure; quarterly membership newsletter.
Hours & Admission Prices: Tues.-Sat. 10-5, Sun. 1-4. No charge; donations accepted. Closed state & federal holidays; day after Thanksgiving. ♿
Attendance: 165,000 (estimated)

Membership: $45; $100; $250; $500; $1,000.

Palomar Mountain

PALOMAR OBSERVATORY, 35899 Canfield Rd., Palomar Mountain, CA 92060-0200. Tel.: 760-742-2119.
E-mail: palomar-info@astro.caltech.edu
Web Site: www.astro.caltech.edu/palomarnew
Governing Authority: nonprofit organization. Tax-exempt: 501(c)(3).
Observatory.
Collections: astronomical photographs; discoveries at Palomar Observatory; Hale Telescope.
Facilities: Museum-related items for sale.
Hours & Admission Prices: Daily 9-4. Closed Christmas Eve & Day.

Paradise

GOLD NUGGET MUSEUM, 502 Pearson Rd., Paradise, CA 95969-5114. Mailing Address: P.O. Box 949, Paradise, CA 95967-0949. Tel.: 530-872-8722. Fax: 530-872-1050.
E-mail: goldnuggetmuseum@aol.com
Web Site: goldnuggetmuseum.com
History Museum.
Collections: old country store; one-room schoolhouse; walk-through mine; farm & mining equipment; old West mining town replica; working blacksmith shop; gold panning sluices; in-ground Maidu grinding rock.
Facilities: picnic area.
Hours & Admission Prices: Wed.-Sun. 12-4.

Pasadena

GAMBLE HOUSE, 4 Westmoreland Pl., Pasadena, CA 91103-3593. Tel.: 626-793-3334.
E-mail: gamblehs@usc.edu
Web Site: www.gamblehouse.org
Key Personnel: Dir., Edward R. Bosky; Museum Shop Mgr., Sarah Smith Stehly.
Personnel Profile: Full-Time Paid 5; Part-Time Paid 4; Part-Time Volunteers 180.
Governing Authority: Parent Institution: bd. of overseers. Tax-exempt.
Historic House Museum: home of David & Mary Gamble of the Procter and Gamble Company, c.1908.
Collections: furnishings; personal artifacts; period fixtures.
Facilities: archives. Books for sale.
Activities: craftsman tours; lectures.
Publications: The Gamble House.
Hours & Admission Prices: Guided Tours: Thurs.-Sun. 12-4; last tour begins at 3. Adults $10, seniors 65 & over and students $7; discounts to National Historic Trust members; members & children under 12 no charge. Closed national holidays.
Attendance: 25,000 (estimated)
Membership: Individual $40; Active $125; Supporting $250; Patron $500; Director's Circle $1,000; Life $2,500.

KIDSPACE CHILDREN'S MUSEUM, 480 N. Arroyo Blvd., Pasadena, CA 91103-3269. Tel.: 626-449-9144, ext. 5215. Fax: 626-449-9985.
E-mail: maearp@kidspacemuseum.org
Web Site: www.kidspacemuseum.org
Founded: 1979.
Congressional District: 23
Key Personnel: Exec. Dir., Tracy Bechtold; Pres. Bd., Greg Johnson; Dir. Education, Valerie R. Oguss; Vice Pres. Devel., Craig Prizant; Dir. Business Operations, Mary Ann Earp; Museum Shop Mgr., Susan Cardosi-Albert.
Personnel Profile: Full-Time Paid 25; Part-Time Paid 30.
Governing Authority: nonprofit. Tax-exempt: 501(c)(3).
Children's Participatory Museum.
Collections: interactive exhibits; raindrop climber; wisteria climber; wildlife pond.
Facilities: cafe. Museum-related items for sale.
Activities: interactive & exploratory programs in the arts, sciences, & humanities.
Publications: newsletter; calendar of events; guest guide; early childhood programs brochure; education program guide; membership brochure.
Hours & Admission Prices: June-Aug. Mon.-Fri. 9:30-5, Sat.-Sun. 10-5; Sept.-May Tues.-Fri. 9:30-5, Sat.-Sun. 10-5. Admission $10; children under one no charge. Closed New Year's Day; Thanksgiving; Christmas. ♿
Attendance: 225,000 (estimated)
Membership: 6 Month Permit to Play $89; 6 Month License to Play $135; 12 Month Permit to Play $160; 12 Month License to Play $250.

NORTON SIMON MUSEUM, 411 W. Colorado Blvd., Pasadena, CA 91105-1825. Tel.: 626-449-6840. Fax: 626-796-4978.
E-mail: info@nortonsimon.org
Web Site: www.nortonsimon.org
Formerly: Pasadena Art Museum
Founded: 1924.
Key Personnel: Pres., Walter W. Timoshuk; Senior Cur., Sara Campbell; Chief Cur., Carol Togneri; Cur., Gloria Williams; Cur., Christine Knoke; Asst. Cur., Leah Lehmbeck; Registrar, Lisa Escovedo; Rights & Reproductions, Giselle Arteaga-Johnson; Public Rels., Leslie Denk; Exec. Admin., Sally Swaney; Security, Wayne Horton; Museum Shop Mgr., Andrew Uchin.
Personnel Profile: Full-Time Paid 46; Part-Time Paid 108; Interns 1.
Governing Authority: nonprofit organization. Tax-exempt: 501(c)(3).
Art Museum.
Collections: European paintings, drawings & sculpture from the early Renaissance through the 20th century; stone & bronze sculpture from India, Nepal & southeast Asia; tapestries; Galka Scheyer Blue Four Collection; 20th century American Art; Picasso, Rembrandt & Goya graphics; Degas sculpture.
Facilities: theater; Garden Cafe. Museum-related items for sale.
Activities: guided tours; family programs; lectures; musical performances; dance performances; adult education.
Publications: Selected Paintings at the Norton Simon Museum; Masterpieces from the Norton Simon Museum; book, The Blue Four Collection at the Norton Simon Museum; Vincent van Gogh: Painter, Printmaker, Collector; Rembrandt Etchings; Picasso: Graphic Magician; Radical P.A.S.T.: Contemporary Art & Music in Pasadena, 1960-1974; Painted Poems: Rajput Paintings from the Ramesh and Urmil Kapoor Collection; Asian Art at the Norton Simon Museum Vol. I-III; The Collectible Moment: Photographs in the Norton Simon Museum; Handbook of the Norton Simon Museum; Nineteenth-Century Art in the Norton Simon Museum, Volume 1.
Hours & Admission Prices: Wed.-Thurs. & Sat.-Mon. 12-6, Fri. 12-9. Call for tours. Adults $8, seniors $4; members & students no charge. Closed New Year's Day; Thanksgiving; Christmas. ♿
Attendance: 200,000 (estimated)
Membership: Active $65; Participating $100; Contributing $150; Sponsoring $275; Patron $550; Benefactor $1,000.

PACIFIC ASIA MUSEUM, 46 N. Los Robles Ave., Pasadena, CA 91101-2071. Tel.: 626-449-2742, ext. 0. Fax: 626-449-2754.
E-mail: info@pacificasiamuseum.org
Web Site: www.pacificasiamuseum.org
Founded: 1971.
Congressional District: 22
Key Personnel: Exec. Dir., Joan Marshall; Chm. (V), Bruce Blumstrom; Cur., Dr. Kendall Brown; Mgr. Membership, Chelsea Mason; Controller, Yoon Lee; Cur. Education, Amelia Chapman; Visitor Svcs. & Facility Rental, Gabriella Karsch; Mgr. Collections, Bridget Bray; Exhibition Coord., John Cline; Library Mgr., Sally McKay; Volunteer Coord., Sunny Stevenson; Museum Shop Mgr., Tai-Ling Wong.
Personnel Profile: Full-Time Paid 13; Part-Time Paid 15; Part-Time Volunteers 400; Interns 4.
Governing Authority: nonprofit organization. Tax-exempt: 501(c)(3).
Museum of Asian and Pacific Island Art: housed in a Chinese Imperial Palace style building; built in 1924.
Collections: Asian artifacts in all media including Chinese ceramics & textiles; Japanese paintings & prints; Himalayan sculpture; Pacific Island cultural artifacts.
Research Fields: arts relating to Chinese ceramics, Pacific Island tapas, Chinese textiles, Japanese Art.
Facilities: 7,500-vol. library of material relating to Asian & Pacific Island Arts, available for research to members & scholars by appointment only; 100-seat auditorium; classrooms. Books, gift items & art objects for sale.
Activities: permanent, temporary & traveling exhibitions; guided tours; lectures; films; concerts; dance programs; gallery talks; formally organized educational programs; docent training program; travel programs; 8 Asian Arts Councils; Docent Council; Service Council; Family Festival Days.
Publications: quarterly museum newsletter; catalogues pertaining to the exhibitions; posters.
Hours & Admission Prices: Wed.-Sun. 10-6. Adults $9, seniors & students $7; discounts to AAM members; children under 12 & members no charge. Closed New Year's Eve & Day; Independence Day; Thanksgiving; Christmas. ♿
Attendance: 53,275 (accurate)
Membership: Active $55; Donor $100; Friend $250; Patron $500; Benefactor $1,000; Associate $1,500-$5,000; Collector's Circle $3,000.

PASADENA MUSEUM OF CALIFORNIA ART, 490 E. Union St., Pasadena, CA 91101-1790. Mailing Address: 495 E. Colorado Blvd., Pasadena, CA 91101-2024. Tel.: 626-568-3665. Fax: 626-568-3674.
E-mail: info@pmcaonline.org
Web Site: www.pmcaonline.org
Founded: 2002.
Key Personnel: Exec. Dir., Jenkins Shannon; Chm., Reed Halladay; Gallery Mgr., Emmett Clements; Dir. Public Rels., Emma Jacobson-Sive; Bookstore & Membership Mgr., Matthew Howard; Vice Chm., David Partridge; Exhibition Designer, Sergio Gomez; Mgr. Special Events, Ceres Botros; Exhibition Mgr. & Registrar, Shirlae Cheng; Mgr. Mktg. & Devel., Christine Goo.
Personnel Profile: Full-Time Paid 5; Part-Time Paid 6; Part-Time Volunteers 10; Interns 8.
Governing Authority: private; nonprofit organization. Tax-exempt: 501(c)(3).
Art Museum.
Collections: California art, design & architecture from 1850 to present.
Research Fields: contemporary & historic California art.
Facilities: 500-vol. library; 16,000 sq. ft. exhibit space. Museum-related items for sale.
Activities: concerts; docent program; guided tours; lectures; loan & traveling exhibitions. Museum Sponsors: California Design Biennial. Annual Event: California Art Club Gold Medal Exhibition.
Publications: quarterly newsletter.
Hours & Admission Prices: Wed.-Sun. 12-5. Adults $7, senior citizens & students $5; 1st Fri. of month, children under 12 & members no charge. Closed New Year's Day; Independence Day; Thanksgiving; Christmas. ♿
Attendance: 55,000
Membership: Senior & Student $25; Studio $50; Guild $200; Director $500.

PASADENA MUSEUM OF HISTORY, (M), 470 W. Walnut St., Pasadena, CA 91103-3562. Tel.: 626-577-1660. Fax: 626-577-1662.
E-mail: info@pasadenahistory.org
Web Site: www.pasadenahistory.org
Formerly: Pasadena Historical Museum
Founded: 1924.
Congressional District: 44
Key Personnel: Exec. Dir., Jeannette O'Malley; Pres., Karen Craig; Dir. Exhibitions & Public Programming, Ardis Willwerth; Archivist, Laura Verlaque; Mgr. Special Events, Linda Sturgeon; Coord. Membership, Michelle Turner; Coord. Visitor Svcs., Katie Volz; Coord. Exhibitions & Volunteers, Diane Siegel.
Personnel Profile: Full-Time Paid 6; Part-Time Paid 10; Part-Time Volunteers 200.
Governing Authority: private; nonprofit organization. Tax-exempt: 501(c)(3).
Historic House Museum: 1906 Pasadena home belonging to the Fenyes Family & descendents; mansion served as Finnish consulate.
Collections: manuscripts; photographs; architectural records; books; pamphlets; 19-century Finnish folk art; costumes; 17th- & 18th-century period furnishings & furniture; early California paintings.
Research Fields: history.
Facilities: 10,000-vol. library for Pasadena & surrounding area; 2 acre garden; 10,000 sq. ft. exhibit space. Museum-related items for sale.
Activities: guided tours; lectures; historical exhibits; concerts.
Publications: quarterly newsletter; pamphlets.
Hours & Admission Prices: History Center & Store: Wed.-Sun. 12-5. Library & Archives: Wed.-Sun. 1-4. Fenyes Mansion Tours: Fri.-Sun. 1:30 & 3. General $5, Mansion Tours $4; discounts to seniors, students & AAM members; children under 12 no charge. ♿
Attendance: 16,000 (accurate)
Membership: Active $50; Friend $75; Sponsor $125; Donor $250; Business Sponsors $300; Patron $500; Founders Circle $1,000 & up.

TOURNAMENT HOUSE AND WRIGLEY GARDENS, 391 S. Orange Grove Blvd., Pasadena, CA 91184-0002. Tel.: 626-449-4100. Fax: 626-449-9066.
E-mail: rosepr@rosemail.org
Web Site: www.tournamentofroses.com/aboutus/house.asp
Historic House Museum: housed in former home of chewing gum manufacturer William Wrigley, Jr.
Collections: personal artifacts; portraits.
Hours & Admission Prices: Feb.-Aug. House: Thurs. 2-4. Gardens: daily.

Paso Robles

PASO ROBLES ART ASSOCIATION, 2208 Golden Hill Rd., Paso Robles, CA 93446-6379. Mailing Address: P.O. Box 2219, Paso Robles, CA 93447-2219. Tel.: 805-238-5473.
Web Site: www.pasoroblesartassociation.org
Formerly: Call-Booth House Gallery
Key Personnel: Dir., Jerry Boxen
History & Art Museum.
Collections: paintings.
Hours & Admission Prices: Wed.-Sun. 11-3.

Penn Valley

MUSEUM OF ANCIENT & MODERN ART, (M), 11392 Pleasant Valley Rd., Penn Valley, CA 95946-0975. Mailing Address: P.O. Box 975, Penn Valley, CA 95946-0975. Tel.: 530-432-3080. Fax: 530-272-0184.
Web Site: www.mama.org
Founded: 1981.
Congressional District: 14
Key Personnel: Chm. Bd. (V), Dr. Ann-Victoria Hopcroft; Pres. (V), Cur. Science & Technology, Dr. Claude Needham; Vice Pres. & Dir. Children's Art Academy, Zoe Alowan; C.F.O., David Franco; Dir. Public Rels., Morgan Fox; Public Rels. Coord. & Museum Shop Mgr., Jewel McInroy; Program Devel. & Cur. 19th- & 20th-Century Works on Paper, Linda Corriveau; Cur. Antiquities, Jeff Spencer; Assoc. Cur. Stellar Astronomy, Dr. James D. Wrey; Cur. Mathematics & Science, David Christie; Cur. Interactive Multimedia, Tim Elston; Conservator (Ancient), Nancy Christie; Conservator (Modern), Robbert Trice; Librarian, Nancy Burns; Computer Archivist, Wayne Hoyle.
Personnel Profile: Part-Time Volunteers 30.
Governing Authority: nonprofit organization. Tax-exempt: 501(c)(3).
Art Museum.
Collections: dioramas of ancient history from prehistoric times; 18th-century Dynasty Amarna artifacts from 1926-27 Pendlebury digs; Theodora Van Runkel collection of ancient gold; objects of daily use; jewelry; African masks; dinosaur fossils; meteorites; early books; works on paper from the 16th century; modern & contemporary art.
Research Fields: ancient technologies; comparative lifestyles; ancient rituals; cultural influences; ancient dance; slime molds.
Facilities: 1,500-vol. library for research & reference upon special request; Children's Art Academy. Museum-related items for sale.
Activities: guided tours; Children's Art Academy; field trips; workshops; seminars; lectures; docent program; SHARE & TAP tour, Traveling Art Program offering exhibits on ancient Egypt & Dinosaurs (Mummies, Myth & More & Dinosaurs in my Garden) which travel to school; Art Appreciation program; temporary & traveling exhibitions; concerts; gallery talks. Museum Sponsors: From a Kid's Point of View Annual Children's Art Festival; special preview events.
Publications: exhibition catalogs; quarterly literary journal for children, SeeSaw; quarterly newsletter of Children's Art Academy, Art is Fun!; bimonthly newsletter, DIMENSIONS.
Hours & Admission Prices: Call for hours. No charge; donations accepted. ♿
Attendance: 18,000 (estimated)
Membership: Individual $25; Family $35; Supporting $100; Sustaining $1,000.

Perris

LAKE PERRIS REGIONAL INDIAN MUSEUM (HOME OF THE WIND), 17801 Lake Perris Dr., Perris, CA 92571-8400. Tel.: 951-657-0676. Fax: 951-657-5659.
Founded: 1985.
Congressional District: 44
Key Personnel: Acting Park Supt., Norbert Ruhmke.
Personnel Profile: Full-Time Paid 1; Part-Time Paid 1; Part-Time Volunteers 3.
Governing Authority: Parent Institution: California State Parks. Tax-exempt.
Park & Museum.
Collections: Southern California Native Americans.
Facilities: nature trails.
Activities: school group tours; animal tracking; basket weaving; story tellers; cultural & nature walks; special events; camping; water sports; equestrian trails. CA Dept. Parks & Recreation: boating, fishing, camping, hiking, bicycling.
Publications: maps; bird guides.
Hours & Admission Prices: Museum: Wed. 10-2, Sat.-Sun. 10-4; groups by appointment. No charge with park entrance fee; donations accepted. ♿
Attendance: 12,000 (accurate)

ORANGE EMPIRE RAILWAY MUSEUM, 2201 S. A St., Perris, CA 92570-9318. Mailing Address: P.O. Box 548, Perris, CA 92572-0548. Tel.: 951-943-3020. Fax: 951-943-2676.
E-mail: info@oerm.org
Web Site: www.oerm.org
Founded: 1956.
Congressional District: 42
Key Personnel: C.E.O. & Pres. (V), Thomas N. Jacobson; Chm. (V), Fred Nicas.

Personnel Profile: Full-Time Paid 3; Full-Time Volunteers 3; Part-Time Paid 1; Part-Time Volunteers 250.
Governing Authority: nonprofit organization. Tax-exempt: 501(c)(3).
Railway Museum: on the historical Santa Fe line from Riverside to San Diego.
Collections: steam, diesel & electric locomotives; electric streetcars & interurbans; passenger cars; freight cars, including maintenance-of-way cars and cabooses. Historical House: 1882 dugout-type pioneer house; 1892 Santa Fe depot.
Research Fields: railway technology; railway history.
Facilities: picnic area; rental facilities. Gift items for sale.
Activities: special events. Museum Sponsors: Rail Festival in April.; Swap Meets in spring & fall; A Day Out With Thomas in November.
Publications: monthly newsletter; web-based publications.
Hours & Admission Prices: Daily 9-5. Museum: no charge except for gated events. Weekend Rides: adults $12, children 5-11 $8; discounts to Assoc. of Railway Museums members; children under 5 no charge. Closed Thanksgiving; Christmas. ♿
Attendance: 40,000 (estimated)
Membership: Junior Affiliate $15; Associate $30; Individual $40; Family $60; Sustaining $100; Benefactor $250; Corporate $500; Life $800.

Pescadero

ANO NUEVO STATE RESERVE, 1 New Years Creek Rd., Pescadero, CA 94060. Mailing Address: P.O. Box 942896, Sacramento, CA 94296. Tel.: 650-879-2025. Fax: 650-879-2031.
Web Site: www.parks.ca.gov
Founded: 1980.
Key Personnel: Supervising Ranger, Gary Strachan.
Governing Authority: state. Parent Institution: California State Parks. Tax-exempt.
Historic Building & Park Museum: housed in c.1880 Dickerman Dairy Barn.
Collections: shipwreck artifacts; early farm equipment & tools; elephant seal pictures; photographs; archaeology; Indian boats & tools; flora & fauna exhibits.
Research Fields: early Indian; whaling; farming; natural history; elephant seals; marine mammals.
Facilities: nature/conservation center. Books, photos & other museum-related items for sale.
Activities: guided tours; lectures; formally organized education programs for children, undergraduate & graduate college students; guided disabled tours; docent program; permanent & temporary exhibitions.
Publications: brochure, Ano Nuevo State Reserve.
Hours & Admission Prices: Self-Guided Walks: April-Oct. daily 8:30-3:30; Nov. daily 8:30-3. Guided Walks: Dec. 15 to March daily 8:45-2:45. Vehicle: $7. Guided Walks: $7 per person; discounts to groups, disabled, and seniors 62 & over. ♿
Attendance: 105,000
Membership: Individual $15; Family $25; Supporting $50; Sponsor $100.

Petaluma

PETALUMA ADOBE STATE HISTORIC PARK, 3325 Adobe Rd., Petaluma, CA 94954. Tel.: 707-762-4871. Fax: 707-762-4871.
E-mail: petadobe@parks.ca.gov
Web Site: www.petalumaadobe.com
Founded: 1951.
Key Personnel: Ranger, Crystal Shoaf.
Personnel Profile: Full-Time Paid 1; Part-Time Paid 3; Part-Time Volunteers 15.
Governing Authority: state. Parent Institution: State of California, Dept. of Parks & Recreation.
Historic Building: 1836 Vallejo's adobe ranch headquarters.
Collections: furnishings; tools pertaining to 1840 ranch life.
Facilities: picnic area.
Activities: self-guided tours; special events.
Publications: brochures.
Hours & Admission Prices: Daily 10-5. Adults $2; children 16 & under and members no charge. Closed New Year's Day; Thanksgiving; Christmas. ♿
Attendance: 71,000
Membership: Annual: Sonoma State Historic Park Association $20.

PETALUMA HISTORICAL LIBRARY AND MUSEUM, (M), 20 Fourth St., Petaluma, CA 94952-3004. Tel.: 707-778-4398. Fax: 707-762-3923.
E-mail: info@petalumamuseum.com
Web Site: petalumamuseum.com
Founded: 1978.
Key Personnel: Pres., Joe Noriel.
Personnel Profile: Part-Time Paid 2; Part-Time Volunteers 60; Interns 1.
Governing Authority: Parent Institution: City of Petaluma. Tax-exempt.
History Museum.
Collections: local history; Miwok Indian artifacts; poultry & agricultural industries; period furnishings.
Activities: guided tours; outreach programs; research; internships; special events. Annual Event: Victorian Tea.
Hours & Admission Prices: Thurs.-Sat. 10-4, Sun. 12-3; other times by appointment. No charge; donations accepted. Closed holidays. ♿
Attendance: 8,234 (accurate)

WILDLIFE MUSEUM AT PETALUMA HIGH SCHOOL, 201 Fair St., Petaluma, CA 94952-2594. Tel.: 707-778-4787. Fax: 707-778-4603.
Web Site: www.petalumawildlifemuseum.org/default.htm
Formerly: Petaluma Wildlife and Natural Science Museum
Founded: 1990.
Key Personnel: Dir., Cur. & Instructor, Marsi H. Wier; Pres., George Grossi.
Personnel Profile: Full-Time Paid 1; Part-Time Paid 1; Part-Time Volunteers 12.
Governing Authority: private; nonprofit. Tax-exempt: 501(c)(3).
Natural Science Museum.
Collections: North American, African & Asian taxidermy specimens; minerals; fossils; live & stuffed marine animals; forestry & logging; live mammals & reptiles; African artifacts; dinosaurs.
Facilities: research & reference library; aquarium; classroom; 8,000 sq. ft. exhibit space; nature/conservation center; zoological park.
Activities: docent program; formal education program for children; guided tours; school loan service; broadcast programs; blind & handicapped program. Annual Events: Pasta Feed-local dinner & tours for public; dinner, raffle & auction.
Publications: annual newsletter, Museum News & Update; quarterly letter to donors regarding animal adoption.
Hours & Admission Prices: 1st Sat. of month 11-3; other times by appointment. Admission $2; discounts to groups; children 4 & under no charge. Closed major holidays; Easter & Christmas vacations. ♿
Attendance: 2,000 (estimated)
Membership: Family $25; Silver Ram Foundation $250 & up.

Piercy

CONFUSION HILL GRAVITY HOUSE, 75001 N. Hwy. 101, Piercy, CA 95587-8805. Tel.: 707-925-6456. Fax: 707-925-6477.
E-mail: confusion@asis.com
Web Site: www.confusionhill.com
Founded: 1949.
Key Personnel: Owner & Operator, Doug Campbell; Owner & Operator, Carol Campbell
Logging Museum.
Collections: hands-on exhibits; period logging equipment.
Facilities: Museum-related items for sale.
Activities: train ride; self-guided tour.
Hours & Admission Prices: May-Sept. 9-6; Oct.-April 9-5. Train Ride: adults $7, children 4-12 $5; children 3 & under no charge.

Piru

RANCHO CAMULOS MUSEUM, Rte. 126, Piru, CA 93040. Mailing Address: P.O. Box 308, Piru, CA 93040-0308. Tel.: 805-521-1501.
Historic Site: listed on the National Register of Historic Places; a National Historic Landmark.
Collections: California history & culture; photographs; 1853 adobe.
Facilities: 1,800 acre ranch.
Activities: living history presentations; special events; docent tours.
Hours & Admission Prices: Feb.-Nov. Wed. & Sat.-Sun. 1-4; other times by appointment.

Pittsburg

LOS MEDANOS COLLEGE ART GALLERY, 2700 E. Leland Rd., Pittsburg, CA 94565-5197. Tel.: 925-439-2181, ext. 3493.
Web Site: www.losmedanos.net/groups/art/default.htm
Key Personnel: Cur., Dawn Black
Art Gallery.
Collections: paintings; sculpture.
Hours & Admission Prices: Tues.-Thurs. 12:30-2:30 & 6:30-8:30.

Placentia

GEORGE KEY RANCH, 625 W. Bastanchury Rd., Placentia, CA 92870-2230. Tel.: 714-973-3190 & 3191.
E-mail: keyranch@ocparks.com
Web Site: www.ocparks.com/keyranch
Historic House Museum.

Collections: farm equipment; hand tools; orange grove; garden.
Facilities: 2.2 acres; garden; orange grove; botanical preserve; picnic area.
Activities: interpretive programs.
Hours & Admission Prices: Tues.-Fri. & 1st Sat. of month 12:15-5.

Placerville

EL DORADO COUNTY HISTORICAL MUSEUM, 104 Placerville Dr. Fairgrounds, Placerville, CA 95667-3910. Tel.: 530-621-5865. Fax: 530-621-6644.
E-mail: museum@co.el-dorado.ca.us
Web Site: www.co.el-dorado.ca.us/museum
Founded: 1974.
Congressional District: 14
Key Personnel: Museum Admin., Mary Cory.
Personnel Profile: Full-Time Paid 1; Part-Time Volunteers 70.
Governing Authority: county; nonprofit. Parent Institution: El Dorado County. Subsidiary Institution: Museums Foundation. Tax-exempt: 501(c)(3).
History Museum.
Collections: archives; history; Indian artifacts; mine equipment; historical artifacts from El Dorado County; country store; Victorian room display; early transportation display.
Research Fields: El Dorado County history.
Facilities: collection of material pertaining to historical places and people of El Dorado County available for use on premises.
Activities: permanent & temporary exhibitions.
Publications: pamphlets; books.
Hours & Admission Prices: Wed.-Sat. 10-4, Sun. 12-4. No charge; donations accepted. Closed holidays. ♿
Attendance: 20,000 (accurate)

Pleasanton

MUSEUM ON MAIN, 603 Main St., Pleasanton, CA 94566-6603. Tel.: 925-462-2766. Fax: 925-462-2779.
E-mail: info@museumonmain.org
Web Site: www.museumonmain.org
Formerly: Amador-Livermore Valley Historical Society
Founded: 1963.
Congressional District: 9
Key Personnel: Exec. Dir., Jim DeMersman; Pres., Roz Wright; Dir. Education, Jennifer Amiel; Cur., Ken MacLennan; Office Mgr., Kris Jarvis.
Personnel Profile: Full-Time Paid 2; Part-Time Paid 2; Part-Time Volunteers 35; Interns 2.
Governing Authority: society. Parent Institution: Amador-Livermore Valley Historical Society. Tax-exempt: 501(c)(3).
General Museum: housed in c.1914 Town Hall.
Collections: tools; household items; local artifacts; photographs; textiles; manuscripts; newspapers; film.
Research Fields: local history.
Facilities: library & archives of local history available for research. Books & museum-related items for sale.
Activities: guided tours; lectures; volunteer program; permanent & traveling exhibits; rotating cultural exhibits.
Publications: books; pamphlets; prints
Hours & Admission Prices: Wed.-Sat. 11-4, Sun. 1-4. Donation: family $5, individual $2. ♿
Attendance: 19,000 (estimated)
Membership: Family $25; Sustaining $50; Supporting $100; Donor $250; Sponsor $500.

Point Arena

POINT ARENA LIGHTHOUSE AND MUSEUM, 45500 Lighthouse Rd., Point Arena, CA 95468. Mailing Address: P.O. Box 11, Point Arena, CA 95468-0011. Tel.: 877-725-4448; 707-882-2777. Fax: 707-882-2111.
E-mail: palight@mcn.org
Web Site: www.pointarenalighthouse.com
Founded: 1870.
Key Personnel: Exec. Dir., Rae Radtkey
Lighthouse & History Museum.
Collections: structure; period artifacts.
Facilities: Museum-related items for sale.
Hours & Admission Prices: Winter: daily 10-3:30. Adults $7, children $1
Membership: Individual $40; Life Individual $400; Life Family $550.

Point Reyes

POINT REYES NATIONAL SEASHORE, 1 Bear Valley Rd., Point Reyes, CA 94956-9703. Tel.: 415-464-5100 & 5125 (Curator). Fax: 415-663-8132.
Web Site: www.nps.gov/pore
Founded: 1962.
Congressional District: 6
Key Personnel: Park Supt., Don L. Neubacher; Chief Interpretation, John Dell'Osso; Archivist, Carola DeRooy.
Governing Authority: federal. Parent Institution: National Park Service, U.S. Dept. of the Interior. Tax-exempt.
Natural & Cultural Museum.
Collections: natural history; archaeology; history; 16th Century porcelain shards; Maritime radio. Historic Building: 1870 Point Reyes Lighthouse.
Research Fields: Applied Natural Resources Studies.
Facilities: library of natural history, local history, collections, archives & research available for use on premises. Interpretive museums & visitors centers. Books on park-related subjects for sale.
Activities: lectures; demonstration.
Publications: pamphlets; books; posters.
Hours & Admission Prices: Bear Valley Visitor Center: Mon.-Fri. 9-5, Sat.-Sun. & holidays 8-5. Ken Patrick Visitor Center: Sat.-Sun. & holidays 10-5. Lighthouse & Lighthouse Visitor Center: Thurs.-Mon. 10-4:30. Library & Study collection: Mon.-Fri. 8-4:30, by appointment only. No charge; donations accepted. ♿
Attendance: 500,000 (accurate)
Membership: Point Reyes National Seashore Association.

Point Richmond

GOLDEN STATE MODEL RAILROAD MUSEUM, 900-A Dornan Dr., Point Richmond, CA 94801-4126. Mailing Address: P.O. Box 71244, Point Richmond, CA 94807-1244. Tel.: 510-234-4884.
E-mail: info@gsmrm.org
Web Site: www.gsmrm.org
Founded: 1985.
Congressional District: 7
Key Personnel: C.E.O., John Morrison; Financial Dir. & Museum Shop Mgr., Martin Jahner; Dir. Public Rels., Sean Dexter.
Personnel Profile: Part-Time Volunteers 50.
Governing Authority: private; nonprofit organization. Tax-exempt: 501(c)(3).
Model Railroad Museum.
Collections: historic scale model railroad equipment & steam locomotives; modern diesel & intermodal trains; PFM - Bill Ryan brass locomotives.
Facilities: library; 10,000 sq. ft. exhibit space.
Activities: hobby workshop.
Publications: quarterly newsletter, Zephyr.
Hours & Admission Prices: April-Dec. Sat.-Sun. 12-5. Train operations only on Sun. Family $9, adults $4; members & Sat. no charge.
Attendance: 7,672 (accurate)
Membership: Individual $24; Family $45; Assessed $120.

Pomona

ADOBE DE PALOMARES, 491 E. Arrow Hwy., Pomona, CA 91767-2264. Mailing Address: Historical Society of Pomona Valley, 585 E. Holt Ave., Pomona, CA 91767. Tel.: 909-620-0264; 909-623-2198.
Web Site: www.pomonahistorical.org/palomares
Historic House Museum.
Collections: period furniture; personal artifacts; herb garden; blacksmith shop.
Facilities: garden.
Hours & Admission Prices: Sun. 2-5. No charge. Closed Easter; Memorial Day; Labor Day; Thanksgiving.

AMERICAN MUSEUM OF CERAMIC ART, (M), 340 S. Garey Ave., Pomona, CA 91766-1722. Tel.: 909-865-3146. Fax: 909-629-1067.
E-mail: frontdesk@ceramicmuseum.org
Web Site: www.ceramicmuseum.org
Founded: 2004.
Key Personnel: Dir. & Cur., Christy Johnson; Devel. & Museum Shop Mgr., Edward Escarsega; Pres., David Armstrong; Registrar Asst., Nicole Frazer; Asst. Cur., Ansley Davies.
Personnel Profile: Full-Time Paid 4; Part-Time Volunteers 2; Interns 1.
Governing Authority: private; nonprofit organization. Tax-exempt: 501(c)(3).
Art Museum.
Collections: works of ceramics artists from around the world.
Facilities: 2,200 sq. ft. exhibit space. Museum-related items for sale.
Activities: arts festivals; concerts; films; guided tours; hobby workshops; lectures; loan exhibition; theater; temporary & traveling exhibitions. Museum Sponsors: Pottery Market in summer & winter; member only events.
Publications: quarterly newsletter; exhibition catalogues.
Hours & Admission Prices: Wed.-Sat. 12-5, 2nd Sat. of month 12-9. Adults $3, senior citizens & students $2; members no charge. Closed New Year's Day; Thanksgiving; Christmas Eve & Day. ♿
Attendance: 7,635 (estimated)

Membership: Student $25; Active $40; Sustaining $75; Cobalt $100; Celadon $250; Silver Luster $500; Gold Luster $1,000; Armstrong Society $5,000 & up.

LA CASA PRIMERA DE RANCHO SAN JOSE, 1569 N. Park Ave., Pomona, CA 91768-1835. Mailing Address: Historical Society of Pomona Valley, 585 E. Holt Ave., Pomona, CA 91767. Tel.: 909-623-2198.
Web Site: www.laokay.com/lacasaprimera.htm
History Museum.
Collections: 19-century furnishings; period artifacts.
Hours & Admission Prices: Sun. 2-5.

LATINO ART MUSEUM, (M), 281 S. Thomas St., Ste. 105, Pomona, CA 91766-1750. Tel.: 909-620-6009.
E-mail: latinoartmuseum@msn.com
Web Site: www.lamoa.net
Founded: 2001.
Key Personnel: Dir., Graciela H. Nardi.
Governing Authority: Branch Museum: Latino Art Museum, Ontario Emporia District, 119 W. Transit St. #D, Ontario, CA 91762.
Art Museum.
Collections: paintings; photographs; Latin American art; international art.
Facilities: rental facilities. Museum-related items for sale.
Activities: special events; lectures; poetry. Museum Sponsors: Art Walk & Opening Reception; Pot-Luck.
Publications: Yearbook, 2008; Yearbook 2009; Biennale 2006; Biennale 2004.
Hours & Admission Prices: Wed.-Sat. 3:30-6:30, 2nd & last Sat. of month 3:30-9:30. No charge; donations accepted.
Attendance: 500
Membership: Senior & Student $15; Individual $25; Family $40; Sponsor $100; Benefactor $1,000; Corporate Benefactor $2,500.

SOUTHERN CALIFORNIA CHAPTER RAILWAY & LOCOMOTIVE HISTORICAL SOCIETY, Los Angeles County Fairgrounds, 1100 McKinley, Pomona, CA Mailing Address: P.O. Box 2250, Pomona, CA 91769-2250. Tel.: 909-623-0190.
E-mail: rlhs-pomona@rrmail.com
Web Site: www.trainweb.org/rlhs
Founded: 1954.
Key Personnel: Chm. (V), Loren R. Martens; Membership, Edward Cheetham.
Personnel Profile: Full-Time Volunteers 200.
Governing Authority: private; not-for-profit organization. Parent Institution: Railway & Locomotive Historical Society. Tax-exempt: 501(c)(3).
Railroad Historical Society Museum.
Collections: railroad steam & diesel motive power including largest remaining locomotives in the world; rail signal systems; tools; telegraph systems; related hardware; reference books; photographs; original documents; employee timetables; historical steam engine display: Union Pacific Engine 4014, Santa Fe Engine 3450, Southern Pacific Engine 5021, Union Pacific Engine 9000, Outer Harbor Engine 2, Fruit Growers Engine 3, Union Pacific Engine 6915, U.S. Potash Engine 3; Santa Fe Horse Express 1993; Pullman 8 Dining-Lounge Car; Santa Fe Caboose 1314; General American Reefer 67806; Arcadia Santa Fe Depot.
Facilities: Santa Fe arcadia depot & static display.
Activities: Museum Sponsors: Open House second weekend each month except Mothers' Day; LA County Fair in September.
Publications: monthly newsletter; biannual books, railroad history.
Hours & Admission Prices: 2nd Sat.-Sun. each month 10-4; other times by appointment. No charge; donations accepted.
Attendance: 5,000 (estimated)
Membership: Annual $52.

WALLY PARKS NHRA MOTORSPORTS MUSEUM, Fairplex Gate 1, 1101 W. McKinley Ave., Bldg. 3A, Pomona, CA 91768-1639. Tel.: 909-622-2133. Fax: 909-622-1206.
E-mail: tthacker@nhra.com
Web Site: www.museum.nhra.com
Founded: 1998.
Key Personnel: Exec. Dir., Tony Thacker; Cur., Greg Sharp; Mgr. Mktg. & Advertising, Rose Dickinson; Coord. Museum Svcs., Sheri Watson
Motorsports and Transportation Museum.
Collections: vintage & historical racing vehicles; photographs; trophies; helmets; driving uniforms; paintings; motorsports memorabilia.
Major Exhibits: 50th Anniversary of National Dragster, 11/09-8/10.
Facilities: Museum-related items for sale.
Hours & Admission Prices: Wed.-Sun. 10-5. Adults $7, seniors 60 & over and children 6-15 $5; discount to Automotive Club of Southern California members; children under 5 & NHRA members no charge. Closed Easter; Thanksgiving; Christmas. ♿
Attendance: 100,000

Port Hueneme

U.S. NAVY SEABEE MUSEUM, 99 23rd Ave., Port Hueneme, CA 93043-0001. Mailing Address: 99 23rd Ave., Bldg. 99, Port Hueneme, CA 93043-0001. Tel.: 805-982-5165. Fax: 805-982-5595.
E-mail: lara.godbille@navy.mil
Web Site: www.history.navy.mil
Formerly: U.S. Navy Civil Engineer Corps/Seabee Museum
Founded: 1947.
Congressional District: 21
Key Personnel: Dir., Lara Glodbille; Cur., Kimberlyn Crowell; Archivist, Gina Nichols.
Personnel Profile: Full-Time Paid 5; Part-Time Volunteers 12; Interns 2.
Governing Authority: federal. Parent Institution: Naval Historical Center, Washington, DC. Tax-exempt.
Military History Museum.
Collections: military weapons; uniforms; models of military equipment; cultural & art displays; wearing apparel & native artifacts from many countries of the world; personal papers & books of high ranking officers; unit plaques & flags; dioramas; nuclear power plant model & displays from Antarctic & Alaska.
Research Fields: history of the Civil Engineer Corps/Seabees; projects; equipment.
Facilities: archives including records for CEC & Seabees; 20,000 sq. ft. exhibit space. Museum-related items for sale.
Activities: films; tours.
Publications: brochure.
Hours & Admission Prices: Tues.-Fri. 8-4, Sat. 10-3. No charge. Closed federal holidays; Christmas week. ♿
Attendance: 15,000 (estimated)

Porterville

PORTERVILLE HISTORICAL MUSEUM, 257 N. D St., Porterville, CA 93257-3622. Tel.: 559-784-2053. Fax: 559-784-4009.
Founded: 1965.
Congressional District: 21
Key Personnel: Chm., Jerry Lynch; Co-Chm., Wayne Foltz; Assoc. Dir., Bill Scruggs; Treas., Sharon Noble; Sec., Beverly Faul; Cur., Sherry Perry.
Personnel Profile: Full-Time Paid 1; Full-Time Volunteers 4; Part-Time Volunteers 8.
Governing Authority: board of directors. Tax-exempt.
History Museum: housed in c.1913 Southern Pacific Railroad passenger depot.
Collections: Indian artifacts; farm implements; china; glass; vignettes.
Research Fields: heritage & anthropology; history of the Yokuts Indians.
Activities: guided tours; lectures; blacksmith shop; permanent & temporary exhibitions. Museum Sponsors: local model train society exhibit in December.
Publications: quarterly newsletter.
Hours & Admission Prices: Summer: Thurs.-Sat. 9-3; Winter: Thurs.-Sat. 10-4. Adults $4, students 6-12 $1; discounts to Friends of the Museum; members & children under 6 no charge. Closed New Year's Day; Fair Week (second week in May); Thanksgiving; Christmas. ♿
Attendance: 7,000 (estimated)
Membership: Individual $20; Family $35; Sponsor $250, $500 & $1,000.

ZALUD HOUSE, 393 N. Hockett St., Porterville, CA 93257-3639. Mailing Address: 291 N. Main, Porterville, CA 93257-3737. Tel.: 559-782-7548. Fax: 559-791-7854.
E-mail: jperrine@ci.porterville.ca.us
Founded: 1976.
Congressional District: 21
Key Personnel: C.E.O., Jim Perrine; Cur., Lynn Shell.
Personnel Profile: Full-Time Paid 1; Part-Time Paid 2; Part-Time Volunteers 1.
Governing Authority: municipal; nonprofit organization.
Historic House: built in 1892.
Collections: late 1800-1950 Zalud house; personal items including furniture, hats & clothing; Victorian garden; history of the City of Porterville & Tulare County.
Research Fields: preservation & conservation of items; paranormal.
Facilities: 600-vol. library of books & magazines; botanical garden.
Activities: docent program; guided tours; temporary exhibitions; weddings & events in garden; paranormal nighttime investigations. Annual Events: June Weddings; Old Fashioned Christmas.
Hours & Admission Prices: Feb.-Dec. Wed.-Sat. 10-4, Sun. 2-4. Adults & senior citizens $2, students $.25-$.50, children $.50. Closed Easter; Independence Day; Thanksgiving; Christmas. ♿
Attendance: 2,888 (accurate)

Portola

WESTERN PACIFIC RAILROAD MUSEUM, 700 Western Pacific Way, Portola, CA 96122-8636. Mailing Address: P.O. Box 608, Portola, CA 96122-0608. Tel.: 530-832-4131. Fax: 530-832-1854.
E-mail: david-epling@wplives.org
Web Site: www.wplives.org
Formerly: Portola Railroad Museum
Founded: 1984.
Congressional District: 2
Key Personnel: Dir., Rod McClure; Treas., Mike Coen; Membership, Eugene Vicknair; Museum Mgr., David W. Epling.
Personnel Profile: Full-Time Paid 1; Full-Time Volunteers 6; Part-Time Paid 1; Part-Time Volunteers 40.
Governing Authority: private; nonprofit organization. Parent Institution: Feather River Rail Society. Tax-exempt.
Railroad Museum: former Western Pacific shop & service facility.
Collections: Western railroad history & equipment; including the Western Pacific Railroad & diesel-electric locomotive development; 38 diesel locomotives from 1929-1971; 99 freight, passenger cars, & cabooses; maintenance of way equipment.
Facilities: archives; 65,250 sq. ft. exhibit space; 60-seat cafeteria. Museum-related items for sale.
Activities: Annual Events: Railroad Days; Rail Fan Day; Run-A-Locomotive Program March to November.
Publications: bimonthly newsletter, Train Sheet; semiannual bulletin, The Headlight.
Hours & Admission Prices: March & Nov. daily 11-4; April-Oct. daily 10-5. Train Rides: Memorial Day to Labor Day. Adults $5, children $2. Closed Easter; Thanksgiving; Christmas.
Attendance: 10,000 (accurate)
Membership: Associate $20; Active $40; Family $60; Sustaining $100; Life $300-$1,200.

Presidio of San Francisco

PRESIDIO HISTORICAL ASSOCIATION, Funston Ave. & Lincoln Blvd., Bldg. T-3, Presidio of San Francisco, CA 94129. Mailing Address: P.O. Box 29163, San Francisco, CA 94129-0163. Tel.: 415-561-2278. Fax: 415-561-2279.
E-mail: fppha@aol.com
Web Site: www.presidioassociation.org
Founded: 1959.
Congressional District: 5
Key Personnel: Pres. (V), Gary Widman; Vice Pres., Redmond F. Kernan; Treas., Roy Borgonovo.
Personnel Profile: Part-Time Paid 1; Part-Time Volunteers 15.
Governing Authority: nonprofit. Tax-exempt: 501(c)(3).
Historical Society.
Research Fields: history of the west; military history; Presidio of San Francisco history.
Activities: guided tours; lectures; temporary exhibitions.
Publications: newsletter, Communique.
Hours & Admission Prices: By appointment only.
Membership: Participating $30; Associate $50; Contributing $100; Sustaining $250; Donor $500; Corporate $1,000.

Quincy

PLUMAS COUNTY MUSEUM, 500 Jackson St., Quincy, CA 95971-9412. Tel.: 530-283-6320. Fax: 530-283-6081.
E-mail: pcmuseum@digitalpath.net
Web Site: wwwplumasmuseum.org
Founded: 1964.
Congressional District: 4
Key Personnel: Dir., Scott J. Lawson; Asst. Dir., Paul Russell; Bd. Dir. Chm. (V), Mr. John Weddle; Bd. Trustees Pres. (V), Mr. Pat Cook; Chm. (V), Mr. Jerry Holland.
Personnel Profile: Full-Time Paid 2; Full-Time Volunteers 6; Part-Time Volunteers 30.
Governing Authority: county. Subsidiary Institution: Plumas County Museum Association, Inc. Tax-exempt.
Historical Museum.
Collections: Indian artifacts; geology; costumes; Maidu basketry; wildlife specimens; local historic artifacts; bottles; tools; mining & logging; ranching; railroad artifacts; photographs; negatives; documents; oral history tapes; historical books & maps; restored 1878 historic house.
Research Fields: local history; mining; lumbering; railroad; water rights; transportation.
Facilities: library & archives. Local photographs & cookbooks for sale.
Activities: guided tours; lectures; permanent & temporary exhibitions.
Publications: Plumas County Historical Cookbook; History of Plumas County 1882; Wildflower Coloring Book; Historical Diaries of Plumas County Pioneers; History of Rich Bar; quarterly newsletter; Growing Up In Plumas County 1850-1920; The Diary of Sarah M. Dean, 1864-1865; books, Plumas County-History of the Feather River Region; "Recollections of a 49er".
Hours & Admission Prices: Tues.-Sat. 9-4:30. Adults $2, children 12-17 $1; children under 12 & members no charge. Closed major holidays Oct.-April. ♿
Attendance: 11,532 (accurate)
Membership: Individual $25; Family $35; Patron $100; Business $150; Sustaining $1,000.

Ramona

CLASSIC ROTORS, Ramona Airport, 2898 Montecito Rd., Hangar G, Ramona, CA 92065-1638. Tel.: 760-803-0244.
E-mail: communications@rotors.org
Web Site: www.classicrotors.org
Founded: 1992.
Helicopter Museum.
Collections: period helicopters.
Activities: Museum Sponsors: Air Shows.
Hours & Admission Prices: Fri.-Mon. 10-4, Tues.-Thurs. by appointment.

GUY B. WOODWARD MUSEUM, 645 Main St., Ramona, CA 92065-2043. Mailing Address: Ramona Pioneer Historical Society, P.O. Box 625, Ramona, CA 92065. Tel.: 760-789-7644.
E-mail: info@woodwardmuseum.org
Web Site: www.woodwardmuseum.org/index.shtml
Governing Authority: nonprofit organization. Tax-exempt: 501(c)(3).
History Museum.
Collections: photographs; Ramona Sentinel newspapers from 1894; period tools & equipment; period clothing; furniture; toys; historic records.
Hours & Admission Prices: Thurs.-Sun. 1-4; other times by appointment.

Rancho Cucamonga

CASA DE RANCHO CUCAMONGA, 8810 Hemlock St., Rancho Cucamonga, CA 91730-2319. Tel.: 909-989-4970.
Web Site: www.co.san-bernardino.ca.us/museum/branches/rains.htm
Historic House Museum.
Collections: personal artifacts; furnishings; photographs.
Hours & Admission Prices: Tues.-Sat. 10-3. No charge; donations requested.

CHAFFEY COMMUNITY ART ASSOCIATION MUSEUM OF ART, 12467 Base Line Rd., North Wing of the J. Filippi Winery, Rancho Cucamonga, CA 91739-9522. Mailing Address: P.O. Box 3902, Rancho Cucamonga, CA 91729-3902. Tel.: 909-463-3733.
E-mail: info@ccaamuseum.org
Web Site: www.ccaamuseum.org
Founded: 1941.
Congressional District: 26
Key Personnel: Pres. (V), George Morris.
Personnel Profile: Part-Time Paid 1.
Art Museum.
Collections: paintings.
Major Exhibits: Milford Zornes, 1/3/10-2/14/10; Annual Juried Show, 2/26/10-4/11/10; Permanent Collection, 6/18/10-8/29/10; Inland Empire Gold, 9/10/10-10/17/10; Annual Miniature Exhibit, 10/29/10-12/12/10.
Publications: newsletter.
Hours & Admission Prices: Fri.-Sun. 12-5. No charge; donations accepted. ♿
Attendance: 2,800 (accurate)
Membership: Senior $30; Individual $35; Family $60; Patron $125; Sponsor $250; Benefactor $500; Corporate $1,000; Life $2,500.

JOHN RAINS HOUSE, 8810 Hemlock Ave., Rancho Cucamonga, CA 91730-2319. Mailing Address: c/o San Bernardino Co. Museums, 2024 Orange Tree Lane, Redlands, CA 92374. Tel.: 909-989-4970 & 307-2669. Fax: 909-307-0539.
E-mail: rmckernan@sbcm.sbcounty.gov
Web Site: www.sbcountymuseum.org
Formerly: Casa de Rancho Cucamonga
Founded: 1972.
Congressional District: 35
Key Personnel: Dir., Robert McKernan; Site Mgr., Pam Strunk; Cur., Michele Nielsen.
Personnel Profile: Part-Time Paid 1; Part-Time Volunteers 25.
Governing Authority: county. Parent Institution: San Bernardino County Museums, 2024 Orange Tree Lane, Redlands, CA. Tax-exempt.

Historic House Museum: housed in c.1860 John & Merced Rains home; house of original rancho, oldest fired brick house in San Bernardino County.
Collections: period furniture; local historical items; decorative arts.
Research Fields: local history.
Activities: guided tours. Special Events: Holidays, Rancho Days.
Hours & Admission Prices: Tues.-Sat. 10-3. No charge; donations accepted. Closed New Year's Day; Thanksgiving; Christmas. ♿
Attendance: 3,500 (accurate)

WIGNALL MUSEUM OF CONTEMPORARY ART, (M), Chaffey College, 5885 Haven Ave., Rancho Cucamonga, CA 91737-3002. Tel.: 909-652-6492. Fax: 909-652-6491.
E-mail: wignall.staff@chaffey.edu
Web Site: www.chaffey.edu/wignall
Founded: 1972.
Congressional District: 35
Key Personnel: Dir. & Cur., Rebecca Trawick; Asst. Cur., Roman Stollenwerk.
Personnel Profile: Full-Time Paid 2; Part-Time Paid 8.
Governing Authority: Parent Institution: Chaffey Community College. Tax-exempt: 501(c)(3).
Contemporary art.
Collections: works by contemporary artists.
Major Exhibits: Haute, 1/25/10-3/6/10; Suzanne Erickson, 1/25/10-3/6/10; Student International 2010, 4/19/10-5/22/10.
Facilities: 2,100 sq. ft. exhibit space.
Activities: lectures; arts festivals; concerts; organized education programs for children & undergraduate college students.
Publications: exhibition catalogs.
Hours & Admission Prices: Aug.-May Mon.-Thurs. 10-4, Sat. 12-4. No charge; donations accepted. Closed college holidays. ♿
Attendance: 5,000 (accurate)

Rancho Mirage

CHILDREN'S DISCOVERY MUSEUM OF THE DESERT, 71-701 Gerald Ford Dr., Rancho Mirage, CA 92270-1934. Tel.: 760-321-0602. Fax: 760-321-1605.
E-mail: lvanderbeck@cdmod.org
Web Site: www.cdmod.org
Founded: 1987.
Congressional District: 37
Key Personnel: C.E.O. & Exec. Dir., LeeAnne Vanderbeck; Pres., Scott Wilson; C.F.O., Bill Hartung; Assoc. Exec. Dir., Judi Miller; Sec., Walter Russo; Mgr. Gallery Experience, Kim Hatten; Administrative Mgr., Carey Morales; Special Events Coord., Kathy Ashkins; Museum Shop Mgr. & Visitors Svcs., Debi Jensen.
Personnel Profile: Full-Time Paid 6; Full-Time Volunteers 50; Part-Time Paid 8; Part-Time Volunteers 250; Interns 6.
Governing Authority: nonprofit organization. Tax-exempt: 501(c)(3).
Children's Museum.
Collections: hands-on exhibits: strobe light & fan; rope maze; climbing wall; archaeological dig; paint the car; supermarket; pizza parlor; attic; animation station.
Facilities: 8,000 sq. ft. exhibit space; facility rental; gardens; groves; multipurpose & performing arts facility. Educational toys & gifts for sale.
Activities: arts festivals; adult & youth docent programs; school tours; participatory exhibits; school outreach, community service & special holiday, vacation & summer programs.
Publications: newsletter, Discovery-Gram.
Hours & Admission Prices: Jan.-April daily 10-5; May-Dec. Tues.-Sun. 10-5. Admission 2 & over $8; members, ACM reciprocal members & children under 2 no charge. Closed New Year's Day; Easter; Memorial Day; Independence Day; Labor Day; Thanksgiving; Christmas. ♿
Attendance: 65,000 (accurate)
Membership: Individual $25.

HEARTLAND, THE CALIFORNIA MUSEUM OF THE HEART, 39600 Bob Hope Dr., Rancho Mirage, CA 92270-3265. Mailing Address: 644 Indian Trail, Palm Springs, CA 92264-7625. Tel.: 760-324-3278.
Founded: 1988.
Congressional District: 37
Key Personnel: Dir., Cur. & Exhibit Construction, Adam Rubinstein; Chm. (V), Jack J. Sternleib, M.D.; Pres. (V) & Museum Shop Mgr., Rebbecca Rogeway; Vice Pres., Dennis Modrich; Sec., Jeffrey Fromberg; Treas., Michael Brabo; Devel. & Membership, Nancy A. Yablon.
Personnel Profile: Full-Time Paid 3; Part-Time Paid 1; Part-Time Volunteers 149.
Governing Authority: nonprofit organization. Parent Institution: Heart Institute of the Desert Foundation. Tax-exempt: 501(c)(3).
Heart Health Museum.
Collections: interactive heart health educational exhibits.
Research Fields: heart valves; artificial hearts; public health.
Facilities: 150 video tape library of heart surgeries available to the public; 108-seat auditorium & theater; 1,000 sq. ft. exhibit space; laboratory; video suites; 45-seat restaurant. Heart-related gift items for sale.
Activities: guided tours; lectures; films; theater; organized education programs for children; docent program; participatory exhibits.
Publications: semiannual newsletter, Heart Health Today TV Program.
Hours & Admission Prices: Mon.-Sat. 7:30am-7pm; other times by appointment. Donation: adults $2, children & students $1. ♿
Attendance: 90,000 (accurate)
Membership: Associates Club $25; Associates Active $50; Annual Founder $1,000; Lifetime Founder $10,000.

Rancho Palos Verdes

PALOS VERDES ART CENTER, 5504 W. Crestridge Rd., Rancho Palos Verdes, CA 90275-4998. Tel.: 310-541-2479. Fax: 310-541-9520.
E-mail: info@pvartcenter.org
Web Site: www.pvartcenter.org
Founded: 1931.
Congressional District: 30
Key Personnel: C.E.O., Robert A. Yassin; Chm. (V), Donald Crocker; Pres. (V), Allen Lay; Dir. Exhibits, Scott Canty; Administrative Dir., Ann Willens; Dir. Publicity, Kathy Shinkle; Dir. Education, Angela Hoffman; Dir. Programs, Gail Phinney.
Personnel Profile: Full-Time Paid 11; Part-Time Paid 60; Part-Time Volunteers 600.
Governing Authority: nonprofit organization. Tax-exempt: 501(c)(3).
Art Gallery.
Collections: historical & contemporary California cultural exhibits.
Major Exhibits: Surf and Turf, 11/09-1/10; Kites, 1/29/10-3/27/10; About Van Gogh, 4/9/10-6/20/10; Children's Art, 5/10; Juried All Media, 7/10-8/10.
Research Fields: art of southern California.
Facilities: 50,000 PCS, book & slide library; banquet facility; ceramic, photography, print making & fine art studios; studio classrooms; professional kitchen (not a restaurant).
Activities: changing exhibitions; programs related to exhibitions; workshop classes.
Publications: quarterly members newsletter & class brochure; gallery exhibit announcements; special programs; exhibition catalogues.
Hours & Admission Prices: Galleries: Mon.-Sat. 10-4, Sun. 1-4. No charge; donations accepted. Closed New Year's Day; President's Day; Memorial Day; Independence Day; Labor Day; Thanksgiving; Christmas. ♿
Attendance: 80,000 (estimated)
Membership: Individual $50; Family $60; Supporting $100; Contributing $150; Sustaining $250; Art Patron $500; Art Patron Silver $1,000; Gold Art Patron $2,500; Platinum Art Patron $5,000.

Rancho Santa Fe

RANCHO SANTA FE ART GUILD, 6004 Paseo Delicias, Rancho Santa Fe, CA 92067. Mailing Address: P.O. Box 773, Rancho Santa Fe, CA 92067-0773. Tel.: 858-759-3545.
Art Gallery.
Collections: paintings; photographs; sculpture.
Activities: special events.
Hours & Admission Prices: Tues.-Sat. 11-4:30.

Randsburg

RANDSBURG DESERT MUSEUM, 161 Butte Ave., Randsburg, CA 93554. Mailing Address: P.O. Box 307, Randsburg, CA 93554-0307. Tel.: 760-374-2359.
E-mail: jdietrichson@yahoo.com
Key Personnel: Dir., Judith Dietrichson
General Museum.
Collections: history of Randsburg; gold, silver & tungsten rush history; gems; minerals; photographs; maps.
Facilities: library.
Hours & Admission Prices: Sat.-Sun. 10-5; other times by appointment. No charge; donations accepted.

Red Bluff

KELLY-GRIGGS HOUSE MUSEUM, 311 Washington St., Red Bluff, CA 96080-3430. Mailing Address: P.O. Box 9082, Red Bluff, CA 96080-6068. Tel.: 530-527-1129.
Founded: 1965.
Congressional District: 2
Key Personnel: C.E.O. & Pres. (V), Sharon Wilson.

Personnel Profile: Part-Time Volunteers 40.
Governing Authority: nonprofit. Tax-exempt: 501(c)(3).
Local History Museum: housed in 1880 Victorian home.
Collections: period furniture & furnishings; art collection spanning over a century; Indian artifacts including original arrowheads & possessions of Ishi; pioneer artifacts; period photographs; Victorian costumes.
Research Fields: local history.
Facilities: 1880s Victorian home.
Activities: guided tours; permanent, temporary & traveling exhibitions; bi-monthly activity: coffee hours with museum-related programs. Museum Sponsors: Victorian Christmas champagne party (members only); old-fashioned ice cream social; band concert; outdoor art show.
Publications: pamphlet, Map Tour of Victorian Red Bluff, California; bi-monthly newsletter & guide schedule, Kelly-Gram; publication, A Sketch-book From Indian Ways To Victorian Days.
Hours & Admission Prices: Thurs.-Sun. 1-4; groups by appointment. No charge; donations accepted. Closed New Year's Day; Easter; Independence Day; Thanksgiving; Christmas.
Attendance: 3,500 (estimated)
Membership: Associate (Individual) $10; Sustaining $50; Charter $100 plus $10 annual; Memoriam $100; Life $200; Patron $500; Benefactor $1,000.

WILLIAM B. IDE ADOBE STATE HISTORIC PARK, 21659 Adobe Rd., Red Bluff, CA 96080-9392. Tel.: 530-529-8599. Fax: 530-529-8598.
E-mail: dchakarun@parks.ca.gov
Founded: 1951.
Congressional District: 2
Key Personnel: Interpreter, Debbie Chakarun.
Personnel Profile: Full-Time Paid 1; Part-Time Paid 2; Part-Time Volunteers 100.
Governing Authority: state. Parent Institution: CA Dept. of Parks & Recreation. Tax-exempt.
Park & Historic House: 1850 adobe cabin, memorial to William B. Ide, president of the California Republic.
Collections: artifacts & reproductions relating to the site & its interpretive period, 1845-1854; adobe smokehouse; carriage shed; small cattle corral; woodworker's shop.
Research Fields: local history.
Facilities: 50-vol. library relating to the history of the area. Gift items for sale.
Activities: guided tours; lectures; formally organized education programs for children; docent program; living history events.
Publications: brochure; quarterly newsletter, The Adobe Ferry Ledger.
Hours & Admission Prices: Sunrise to sunset daily. $5 per vehicle. ♿
Attendance: 30,000 (estimated)
Membership: Ide Adobe Interpretive Association: Individual $8; Family $10; Institutional $20; Life $100.

Redding

SHASTA COLLEGE MUSEUM & RESEARCH CENTER, 11555 Old Oregon Trail, Redding, CA 96003-7692. Mailing Address: P.O. Box 496006, Redding, CA 96049-6006. Tel.: 530-242-7520. Fax: 530-225-3946.
E-mail: dsmith@shastacollege.edu
Founded: 1970.
Congressional District: 1
Key Personnel: Vice Pres. Academic Affairs, Bill Cochran; Dean, Dr. Ralph Perrin.
Personnel Profile: Part-Time Paid 1.
Governing Authority: public school district. Affiliated with Shasta-Tehama-Trinity Joint Community College District. Tax-exempt: 501(c)(3).
History Museum.
Collections: artifacts, papers, & photographs of local history; Shasta County coroners' reports, 1851-1939; farming equipment; 1872 Buffalo Pitts Separator-Thresher; logging tools; early logging drag saws; mining tools; commercial records of a grocery store; clothing & accessories; 6-ton petroglyph; Northern Sacramento Valley prehistory; 1920s John Deer Tractor; narrow garage railroad car; 1920s Harvester; c. 1900 buggy & wagon.
Research Fields: local history & prehistory.
Facilities: workshop.
Activities: temporary exhibitions; loan services; research facilities; weekend classes.
Publications: annual, Museum Report.
Hours & Admission Prices: Temporarily closed. ♿
Attendance: 1,000

TURTLE BAY EXPLORATION PARK, 840 Sundial Bridge Dr., Redding, CA 96001. Mailing Address: 1335 Arboretum Dr., Ste. A, Redding, CA 96003-3628. Tel.: 530-243-8850; 800-887-8532. Fax: 530-243-8898.
E-mail: info@turtlebay.org
Web Site: www.turtlebay.org
Formerly: Turtle Bay Museums & Arboretum on the River
Founded: 1990.
Congressional District: 2
Key Personnel: C.E.O., Mike Warren; Chm. (V), Steve Gaston; C.O.O., Maggie Redmon; Exhibits Mgr., Julia Cronin; Public Rels. Mgr., Mktg. & Sales Officer, Toby Osborn; Dir. Human Resources, Jacque Holden; Visitor Svcs. Mgr., Carrian Harwig.
Personnel Profile: Full-Time Paid 44; Part-Time Paid 13; Part-Time Volunteers 350.
Governing Authority: private; nonprofit. Tax-exempt: 501(c)(3).
History, Art & Nature Museum.
Collections: regional history; California art; regional Native American artifacts; archeological; photography; natural science; forestry; ecology & water resources.
Major Exhibits: The Art of Mt. Shasta, 1/15/10-5/2/10; Turtle Travels (T), 1/23/10-4/18/10; Native Images, 1/23/10-4/18/10; GPS Adventures (T), 5/10-9/6/10; Thoreaus Walden: A Journey in Photographs By Scot Miller (T), 5/15/10-9/12/10; Out of this World (T), 10/9/10-1/9/11.
Research Fields: Northern California history, art & natural science.
Facilities: 220-acre arboretum; gardens; amphitheatre; classrooms. Museum-related items for sale.
Activities: temporary exhibitions; arts festivals; docent program; formal educational programs; guided tours; hobby workshops; lectures; school loan service; teacher training.
Publications: trimonthly member's calendar; exhibition catalogs.
Hours & Admission Prices: March 15-Sept. daily 9-5; Oct.-March 14 Wed.-Sat. 9-4, Sun. 10-4. Adults $13, children 4-15 $9; discounts to ASTC, AAM & ICOM members; members no charge. ♿
Attendance: 145,000 (estimated)
Membership: College Student $30; Individual $55; Family $80; Contributor $160; Patron $310; Benefactor $510; Leader $1,010.

Redlands

ASISTENCIA: SAN GABRIEL MISSION OUTPOST, 26930 Barton Rd., Redlands, CA 92373-4312. Mailing Address: c/o San Bernardino Co. Museums, 2024 Orange Tree Lane, Redlands, CA 92374. Tel.: 909-793-5402 & 307-2669. Fax: 909-307-0539.
E-mail: rmckernan@sbcm.sbcounty.gov
Web Site: sbcountymuseum.org
Founded: 1937.
Congressional District: 35
Key Personnel: Dir., Robert McKernan; Site Mgr., Mark Turpin; Cur., Michele Nielsen.
Personnel Profile: Part-Time Paid 1; Part-Time Volunteers 3.
Governing Authority: county. Parent Institution: San Bernardino County Museums, 2024 Orange Tree Lane, Redlands, CA 92374. Tax-exempt.
History Museum: 1930s early California mission style ranch buildings.
Collections: history of local California Mission & Rancho era.
Research Fields: California mission era.
Facilities: 100-seat auditorium.
Activities: concerts; guided tours; lectures; temporary exhibitions; rental space for private weddings & receptions. Annual Events: History Day; Astronomy Evening.
Hours & Admission Prices: Tues.-Sat. 10-3. No charge; donations accepted. Closed New Year's Day; Thanksgiving; Christmas.
Attendance: 8,500 (accurate)

HISTORICAL GLASS MUSEUM, 1157 N. Orange St., Redlands, CA 92374-3218. Mailing Address: P.O. Box 921, Redlands, CA 92373-0281. Tel.: 909-798-0868.
E-mail: glassmuseums@aol.com
Web Site: www.glassmuseums.com
Founded: 1976.
Key Personnel: C.E.O. & Dir., Frank Herendeen.
Personnel Profile: Part-Time Paid 1; Part-Time Volunteers 12.
Governing Authority: bd. dirs. Tax-exempt.
Historical American Glass Museum.
Collections: 6000 artifacts of American glassware including glass beaded purses; art glass; milk glass; cruets; perfume bottles.
Facilities: Museum-related items for sale.
Hours & Admission Prices: Sat.-Sun. 12-4. Suggested donation: adults $3; members no charge. Closed major holidays.
Membership: $25.

KIMBERLY CREST HOUSE & GARDENS, 1325 Prospect Dr., Redlands, CA 92373-7049. Mailing Address: P.O. Box 206, Redlands, CA 92373-0061. Tel.: 909-792-2111. Fax: 909-798-1716.
E-mail: info@kimberlycrest.org

Web Site: www.kimberlycrest.org
Founded: 1981.
Congressional District: 35
Key Personnel: Exec. Dir., Terry deVries.
Personnel Profile: Full-Time Paid 3; Full-Time Volunteers 1; Part-Time Paid 2; Part-Time Volunteers 80.
Governing Authority: private; nonprofit organization. Parent Institution: Kimberly-Shirk Association. Tax-exempt: 501(c)(3).
Historic Site: housed in an 1897 French chateau-style house & carriage house, formal 1909 Italian gardens and citrus grove.
Collections: decorative arts (original furnishings of Kimberly family); fine arts; archives; architecture; gardens; photography; family history.
Research Fields: architecture; decorative arts; landscape design.
Facilities: 6-acre site; garden structure & pathways.
Publications: newsletter, View from Kimberly Crest.
Hours & Admission Prices: Thurs.-Sun. 1-4. Suggested Donation: adults $7, seniors & students $6, children 6-12 $3; discounts AAM & ICOM members; children 5 & under no charge. Closed Easter; Thanksgiving; Christmas . ♿
Attendance: 13,000 (estimated)
Membership: Friend $35; Partner $50; Contributing $100; Supporter $250; Patron $500; Benefactor $1,000; Mary Kimberly Shik Circle $5,000.

LINCOLN MEMORIAL SHRINE, 125 W. Vine St., Redlands, CA 92373-4761. Tel.: 909-798-7632 (administrative) & 7636. Fax: 909-798-7566.
E-mail: archives@akspl.org
Web Site: www.lincolnshrine.org
Founded: 1932.
Congressional District: 37
Key Personnel: Pres. (V), James Hofer; Cur. & Archivist, Donald McCue; Assoc. Archivist, Nathan Gonzales; Assoc. Archivist, Jeff Smith.
Personnel Profile: Full-Time Paid 4; Part-Time Paid 2; Part-Time Volunteers 30; Interns 2.
Governing Authority: municipal. Parent Institution: A. K. Smiley Public Library, 125 W. Vine St. Tax-exempt: 501(c)(3).
History Museum.
Collections: rare manuscripts & documents of Lincoln & leading Civil War generals, soldiers & civilians; artifacts of Lincoln & the Civil War period; sculpture; murals; paintings; manuscript collections.
Research Fields: Lincoln and Civil War.
Facilities: 5,000-vol. library of manuscripts, pamphlets newsletters, rare & new books on the Civil War period available for use on premises. Museum-related items for sale.
Activities: guided tours; lectures; docent program or council; permanent & temporary exhibitions.
Publications: quarterly newsletter; annual keepsakes dealing with the collections & Lincoln/Civil War history.
Hours & Admission Prices: Feb. 12 & Tues.-Sun. 1-5, special hours by appointment. No charge; donations accepted. Closed holidays. ♿
Attendance: 14,000 (estimated)
Membership: Individual $15; Family $25; Corporate $35.

* **SAN BERNARDINO COUNTY MUSEUM, (M),** 2024 Orange Tree Lane, Redlands, CA 92374-4560. Tel.: 909-307-2669 & 798-5719. Fax: 909-307-0539.
E-mail: rmckernan@sbcm.sbcounty.gov
Web Site: www.sbcountymuseum.org
Founded: 1957.
Congressional District: 37
Key Personnel: Dir., Robert L. McKernan; Cur. History, Michele Nielsen; Senior Cur. Geological Sciences, Kathleen Springer; Research Biologist, Gerald Braden; Cur. Exhibitions, Carey Smith; Cur. Anthropology, Dr. Adella Schroth; Cur. Education, Jolene Redvale; Registrar, Andrea Morics.
Personnel Profile: Full-Time Paid 57; Full-Time Volunteers 5; Part-Time Paid 55; Part-Time Volunteers 75; Interns 1.
Governing Authority: county. Subsidiary Institution: San Bernardino County Museum Association. Branch Museums: John Rains' House, 8810 Hemlock, Rancho Cucamonga, CA; Mousley Museum of Natural History, 35350 Panorama Dr., Yucaipa, CA; Asistencia: San Gabriel Mission Outpost, 26930 Barton Rd., Redlands, CA; Agua Mansa Pioneer Memorial & Cemetery, 270 E. Agua Mansa Rd., Colton, CA; Yorba and Slaughter Families Adobe, 17127 Pomona Rincon Rd., Chino, CA; Yucaipa Adobe, 32183 Kentucky St., Yucaipa, CA 92399. Tax-exempt.
General Museum.
Collections: archaeology; anthropology; art; history; natural history; geology; ornithology; paleontology; photographs; hands-on exhibits.
Research Fields: archaeology; history; natural history; paleontology; mineralogy.
Facilities: 6,000-vol. library on ornithology, anthropology & history available on premises only; botanical garden; field research station; classrooms. Museum-related items for sale.
Activities: guided tours; field trips; lectures; hobby workshops; docent program; permanent exhibitions; school loan service.
Publications: monthly newsletter, San Bernardino County Museum Assn; quarterly, & occasional papers.
Hours & Admission Prices: Tues.-Sun. 9-5. Adults $6, seniors & students $5, children $4; discounts to AAM & AAA members; members no charge. Closed New Year's Day; Thanksgiving; Christmas. ♿
Attendance: 100,000 (accurate)
Membership: Individual $30; Family $40; Family Plus $50; Subscriber $60; Sustaining $75; Contributing $100; Corporate-Patron $500-$999; Benefactor $1,000-$5,000.

Redwood City

LATHROP HOUSE, 627 Hamilton St., Redwood City, CA 94063. Mailing Address: P.O. Box 1273, Redwood City, CA 94064-1273. Tel.: 650-365-5564.
Historic House: built in 1863.
Collections: period furnishings.
Facilities: Museum-related items for sale.
Hours & Admission Prices: Sept.-July Wed. & 3rd Sat. 11-3. No charge; donations accepted.

MARINE SCIENCE INSTITUTE, 500 Discovery Pkwy., Redwood City, CA 94063-4746. Tel.: 650-364-2760. Fax: 650-364-0416.
E-mail: gail@sfbaymsi.org
Web Site: www.sfbaymsi.org
Key Personnel: Exec. Dir., Marilou S. Seiff
Marine Science Museum.
Collections: hands-on science & environmental exhibits.
Activities: education programs.
Hours & Admission Prices: Call for hours.

* **SAN MATEO COUNTY HISTORICAL ASSOCIATION AND MUSEUM, (M),** 2200 Broadway, Redwood City, CA 94063-1639. Tel.: 650-299-0104. Fax: 650-299-0141.
E-mail: info@historysmc.org
Web Site: www.historysmc.org
Founded: 1935.
Congressional District: 11
Key Personnel: Pres., Mitchell Postel; Chm. Bd. Dirs., Keith Bautista; Archivist, Carol Peterson; Mktg. Coord., Diane C. Rummel; Business Mgr., Misa Sakaguchi; Deputy Dir., Carmen Blair; Assoc. Dir. Education, Dawn Distasio; Site Mgr., Becky Christ; Site Mgr., Marilyn Murphy.
Personnel Profile: Full-Time Paid 12; Part-Time Paid 7; Part-Time Volunteers 150; Interns 1.
Governing Authority: bd. directors. Branch Museums: 1846, Sanchez Adobe, Pacifica; 1854; Woodside Store, Woodside. Tax-exempt: 501(c)(3).
San Mateo County History Museum.
Collections: archives of local history; horse drawn vehicles; 19th-century tools; photographs; assessment records; costumes; local material culture.
Major Exhibits: 75 Years of Capturing History, 1/10-6/10; Centennial Boy Scouts, 2/10-12/10; 100 Year Dome, 6/10-12/10.
Research Fields: local government, society, industry; Native American, Spanish & Mexican heritage.
Facilities: library of pamphlets, photographs, manuscripts, monographs & documents of the history of San Mateo County available on premises.
Activities: guided tours; lectures; films; gallery talks; docent programs; educational activities for children; outreach programs for schools; inter-museum loan, permanent & temporary exhibitions designed for self-touring of the visually impaired.
Publications: semiannual journal, La Peninsula; monthly newsletter, Historical Happenings; books, Sawmills in the Redwoods (republished); Carolands Hillsboro; San Mateo County: A Sesquicentennial History; exhibit catalogue, Land of Opportunity: The Immigrant Experience in San Mateo County.
Hours & Admission Prices: Tues.-Sun. 10-4. Adults $4, seniors 65 and over & students $2; children under 5 no charge. ♿
Attendance: 52,000 (accurate)
Membership: Student & Senior $40; Individual $50; Family Time Traveler $100; Archivist $250; Historian $500; Curator $1,000.

Reedley

MENNONITE QUILTING CENTER, 1012 G St., Reedley, CA 93654-2936. Tel.: 559-638-3560.
Governing Authority: Tax-exempt: 501(c)(3).
Quilt Museum.

Collections: quilts; wall hangings.
Facilities: Museum-related items for sale.
Activities: quilting & handmade rug making; workshops; quilting classes.
Hours & Admission Prices: Mon.-Fri. 10-5, Sat. 10-4; groups of 10 or more by appointment. No charge; donations accepted. Closed holidays.

REEDLEY MUSEUM, 1752 10th St., Reedley, CA 93654-2933. Tel.: 559-638-1913.
History Museum.
Collections: Reedley history & culture.
Hours & Admission Prices: Tues. 10-12, Sat. 9:30-12. Adults $1; students & children under 18 no charge

Represa

RETIRED CORRECTIONAL PEACE OFFICERS MUSEUM AT FOLSOM PRISON, 312 3rd St., Represa, CA 95671-0001. Tel.: 916-985-2561, ext. 4589.
Founded: 1994.
Key Personnel: Operations Mgr., Jim Brown.
Personnel Profile: Part-Time Volunteers 7.
History Museum: housed in an old prison house, c.1898.
Collections: documents; personal artifacts; handcuffs; license plates; newspaper clippings; hanging rope; weapons; artwork; crafts.
Research Fields: historical research of family trees.
Hours & Admission Prices: Daily 10-4. Adults $2; school groups, law enforcement & military no charge. Closed New Year's Day; Thanksgiving; Christmas.
Attendance: 10,000 (accurate)

Rialto

RIALTO HISTORICAL SOCIETY, 201-205 N. Riverside Ave., Rialto, CA 92376. Mailing Address: P.O. Box 413, Rialto, CA 92377-0413. Tel.: 909-875-1750 & 1175.
Founded: 1971.
Congressional District: 36
Key Personnel: Pres., Jean Randall; Vice Pres., Jo Elliott; Sec. & Treas., Judy Roberts; Historian, John Adams; Corresponding Sec., Shirley Knowles; Computer Technician, Richard McInnis.
Personnel Profile: Part-Time Volunteers 12.
Governing Authority: society; nonprofit. Tax-exempt: 501(c)(3).
Historical Society Museum: adjacent to historic church building.
Collections: carpenters tools; medical equipment; clothing; orange crate labels; orange industry equipment; Rialto Record newspapers; photographs; local citrus labels; Victorian memorabilia & furniture; library; maps; water history; military artifacts; cameras; local artists' works; Native American. Historic Building: c.1848 Old Adobe in Bender Park.
Research Fields: Rialto area history.
Facilities: Kristina Dana Hendrickson Cultural Center: reading room, meeting room; weddings.
Activities: school tours; arts festivals; lectures; music recitals; travelogues; reading room; permanent & temporary exhibitions. Museum Sponsors: monthly luncheon & speakers October to June.
Publications: newsletter, Rialto Landmarks & Homes Prior to 1900; books, History of Rialto; Then and Now; Rialto-Images of America; The Little Girl in the Window.
Hours & Admission Prices: Wed. 2-4, Sat. 10-2; other times by appointment. No charge; donations accepted. Closed holidays.
Attendance: 400 (estimated)
Membership: Annual $5; Contributing $10; Sustaining $25; Organizational & Benefactor $100; Life $500; Perpetual $1,000.

Richmond

RICHMOND ART CENTER, 2540 Barrett Ave., Richmond, CA 94804-1600. Tel.: 510-620-6772. Fax: 510-620-6771.
E-mail: admin@therichmondartcenter.org
Web Site: www.therichmondartcenter.org
Founded: 1936.
Congressional District: 11
Key Personnel: C.E.O., Suzanne Tan; Pres. (V), Hershell West; Exec. Dir., Nancy M. Servis; Dir. On-site Education, Kato Jaworski.
Personnel Profile: Full-Time Paid 2; Full-Time Volunteers 5; Part-Time Paid 4; Part-Time Volunteers 50; Interns 2.
Governing Authority: nonprofit organization, board of directors. Tax-exempt: 501(c)(3) & 170(b)(1)(A).
Art Center.
Collections: rotating exhibits.
Facilities: sculpture court; classrooms; six studios; four galleries; resource room.
Activities: extension exhibition program; class program; tours; lectures; temporary exhibitions. Center Sponsors: scholarship programs; outreach instruction programs.
Publications: catalogues; calendar of exhibition & events; newsletter; class schedule.
Hours & Admission Prices: Tues.-Sat. 11-5. No charge; donations accepted. ♿
Attendance: 50,000 (estimated)
Membership: Senior Citizen $35; Individual $45; Family $60; Patron $100 & up; Sponsor $250 & up; Benefactor $500 & up; Major Benefactor $1,000 & up.

RICHMOND MUSEUM OF HISTORY, 400 Nevin Ave., Richmond, CA 94801-3017. Mailing Address: P.O. Box 1267, Richmond, CA 94802-0267. Tel.: 510-235-7387.
E-mail: donaldbastin@comcast.net
Web Site: richmondmuseumofhistory.org
Founded: 1954.
Congressional District: 11
Key Personnel: Pres., C.E.O. (V) & Programs, Lois H. Boyle; Exec. Dir., Donald Bastin.
Personnel Profile: Part-Time Paid 4; Part-Time Volunteers 110.
Governing Authority: nonprofit organization. Parent Institution: Richmond Museum Association. Tax-exempt: 501(c)(3)
History Museum.
Collections: World War II Richmond shipyard years; photographs; archives; decorative arts; costumes; 1931 Model A automobile.
Research Fields: Richmond & the surrounding areas.
Facilities: 640-vol. library.
Activities: permanent & temporary exhibitions; lectures; films; organized educational programs for youth; docent program; guided tours.
Publications: quarterly, The Mirror.
Hours & Admission Prices: Wed.-Sun. 1-4. Adults $2, seniors & students $1; children & members no charge. Closed legal holidays. ♿
Attendance: 2,900 (accurate)
Membership: Student $15; Seniors $20; Individual $25; Family & Organization $35; Contributing $50; Sustaining $100; Patron $500; Benefactor $1,000.

Ridgecrest

MATURANGO MUSEUM OF THE INDIAN WELLS VALLEY, (M), 100 E. Las Flores, Ridgecrest, CA 93555-3654. Tel.: 760-375-6900. Fax: 760-375-0479.
E-mail: matmus6@maturango.org
Web Site: www.maturango.org
Founded: 1962.
Congressional District: 22
Key Personnel: Dir., Harris Brokke; Bd. Pres., Carolyn Shepherd; Cur. Archaeology, Alexander K. Rogers; Cur. Natural History, Camille Anderson; Cur. History, Elizabeth Babcock; Gallery Coord., Sylvia Winslow Art Gallery, Rosemary Lackaye; Bookkeeper, Mary Adler; Petroglyph Tour Coord., Fran Van Valkenburgh; Education Coord., Nora Nuckles.
Personnel Profile: Full-Time Paid 1; Part-Time Paid 11; Part-Time Volunteers 150.
Governing Authority: nonprofit organization. Tax-exempt: 501(c)(3).
Cultural and Natural History.
Collections: minerals; mining tools & equipment; history; flora & fauna of the upper Mojave desert; archaeology, paleontology; geology; entomology; mammals; reptiles; prehistoric rock art; Emma Lou Davis library & archives; artwork of local & regional artists.
Research Fields: Native American archaeology prehistoric rock art of the Coso Range & adjacent Indian Wells Valley; regional botanical & zoological species.
Facilities: 2,000-vol. library of archaeology & local history & desert natural history; local tourist information; video library of lectures & programs; Xeriscape garden; labyrinth; observatory; Death Valley Tourist Center; Northern Mojave Visitor Center. Museum-related items for sale.
Activities: guided tours; lectures; formally organized education programs for children; docent program; inter-museum, permanent & temporary exhibitions; foreign study tours; observatory star parties. Museum Sponsors: guided tours of Coso petroglyphs in Little Petroglyph Canyon; wildflower show in spring.
Publications: monthly newsletter; annual report; books, Rock Drawings of the Coso Range; Art & Poetry of Gladys Merrick; Before the Navy; Epsom Salts Monorail; Ayers Rock; Millennium Conference Proceedings; Following the Shaman's Path: A Walking Guide to Little Petroglyph Canyon, Coso Range, CA; A Festschrift Honoring the Contributions of California Archaeologist Jay Von Werlhof; DVD, Somewhere on the Edge of Nowhere; booklet, Common Sense in Desert Travel; Fossil Mammals of the Indian Wells Valley, history of the Indian Wells Valley; Adventures with a Desert

Bush Pilot; Coso Rock Art: A New Prospective; Maturango Country-Discover It; recipe book, Maturango Museum Luncheons; videos on various lectures & programs available for loan to members; tourist brochures.
Hours & Admission Prices: Daily 10-5. Adults $5, Seniors & children $3; discounts to AAM members with ID; children under 6 & members no charge. Closed New Year's Day, Memorial Day; Independence Day, Labor Day, Thanksgiving, Christmas. ♿
Attendance: 24,119 (accurate)
Membership: Senior Citizen 55 & over $35; Individual $40; Senior Family $45; Family $50.

Rio Vista

RIO VISTA MUSEUM, 16 N. Front St., Rio Vista, CA 94571-1837. Tel.: 707-374-5169.
History Museum.
Collections: history of Rio Vista; photographs; newspapers; clothing; farm equipment; wedding gowns from 1876-1920.
Hours & Admission Prices: Sat.-Sun. 1:30-4:30.

Riverside

JURUPA MOUNTAINS CULTURAL CENTER, 7621 Granite Hill Dr., Riverside, CA 92509-1299. Tel.: 951-685-5818. Fax: 951-685-1240.
E-mail: jmccmail@hotmail.com
Web Site: www.jmcc.us
Founded: 1964.
Congressional District: 43
Key Personnel: Exec. Dir., Mary Burns; Pres., Dan Rodriguez; Cur., Jack Neiburger; Office Mgr., Victoria Blevins.
Personnel Profile: Full-Time Paid 6; Full-Time Volunteers 1; Part-Time Paid 3; Part-Time Volunteers 30; Interns 1.
Governing Authority: private; nonprofit organization. Tax-exempt: 501(c)(3).
Earth Science Museum.
Collections: rocks; minerals; fossils; fluorescent minerals; Native American artifacts; gems; dinosaur eggs from China.
Facilities: library; 86 acre site; educational facilities. Museum-related items for sale.
Activities: guided tours; formal education programs; hobby workshops; lectures; participatory, loan & temporary exhibitions; school loan service. Annual Events: Greenfaire; Olive Curing.
Publications: monthly newsletter, Smoke Signals.
Hours & Admission Prices: Center & Earth Science Museum: Tues.-Sat. 8-4. Adults $3, teens $2, children 6-12 $1. Public Tours: Sat. 9 & 12. Pre-arranged Group Tours: Tues.-Fri. for groups of 25 or more. Groups: $8-$12 per person; discounts to members & AAA members. Closed New Year's Day; Easter; Independence Day; Thanksgiving; Christmas. ♿
Attendance: 27,500 (estimated)
Membership: Individual $20; Family $35.

MARCH FIELD AIR MUSEUM, 22550 Van Buren Blvd., Riverside, CA 92518-2400. Mailing Address: P.O. Box 6463, March ARB, CA 92518-0394. Tel.: 909-697-6600 & 6602. Fax: 909-697-6605.
E-mail: info@marchfield.org
Web Site: www.marchfield.org
Founded: 1979.
Congressional District: 43
Key Personnel: C.E.O., Patricia Korzec; Pres. (V), Jamil DaDa; Collections Mgr., Michelle Sifuentes; Events, Paula Ramos; Museum Shop Mgr., Katheryn Dodd.
Personnel Profile: Full-Time Paid 7; Part-Time Paid 3; Part-Time Volunteers 121.
Governing Authority: nonprofit. Parent Institution: March Field Museum Foundation. Tax-exempt: 501(c)(3).
Aviation History.
Collections: 72 aircraft; over 20,000 military & aviation artifacts; uniforms; aircraft engine displays; Korea, Vietnam & Desert Storm artifacts; photographs; weapons; World War I, World War II & 15th Air Force artifacts; memorabilia of famous flyers; aviation films.
Research Fields: oral history program; intern program for local college students.
Facilities: aviation library; theater; reading & lounge area. Museum-related items for sale.
Activities: walking tours to aircraft display area daily; tour groups welcome; reunions & conferences welcome; special commemorative weeks for groups such as the Tuskegee Airmen.
Publications: foundation newsletter, Flightline.
Hours & Admission Prices: Daily 9-4. Adults $8; discounts to AAM members; members no charge. Closed major holidays. ♿
Attendance: 90,000 (accurate)
Membership: Individual $41; Family $65; Sustaining $125; Corporate $250.

MISSION INN FOUNDATION/MUSEUM, (M), 3696 Main St., Riverside, CA 92501-2839. Tel.: 951-781-8241. Fax: 951-341-6574.
E-mail: info@missioninnmuseum.com
Web Site: www.missioninnmuseum.com
Founded: 1976.
Key Personnel: Chm. (V), John Brown; Exec. Dir., John Worden; Museum Shop Mgr., Sharla Wright; Collection Mgr., Steve Spiller; Office Administration, Randi Brewer; Dir. Mktg., Virginia Fesunoff.
Personnel Profile: Full-Time Paid 5; Part-Time Paid 5; Part-Time Volunteers 125.
Governing Authority: private; nonprofit. Tax-exempt: 501(c)(3).
Historic House & Site: restored turn-of-the-century resort hotel now a national historic landmark.
Collections: arts & crafts furniture; paintings; sculpture; Oriental art; dolls; bells; crosses; Mission memorabilia. Inn features arcades, gardens, turrets, domes, flying buttresses, circular staircases, stained glass, wrought iron & tile.
Facilities: 2,400 sq. ft. exhibit space. Museum publications, posters, T-shirts, postcards & other museum-related items for sale.
Activities: guided tours; lectures; docent program; temporary exhibits. Annual Event: 5/10K Run in November.
Hours & Admission Prices: Daily 9:30-4. Museum: $2. Tours $12. Closed Easter; Mother's Day; Thanksgiving; Christmas.
Attendance: 45,000 (accurate)
Membership: Student $10; Individual $25; Family $35; Contributor $100; Corporate $250; Curator's Circle $1,000; Director's Circle $2,500; President's Circle $5,000.

RIVERSIDE ART MUSEUM, (M), 3425 Mission Inn Ave., Riverside, CA 92501-3368. Tel.: 951-684-7111. Fax: 951-684-7332.
Web Site: www.riversideartmuseum.org
Founded: 1931.
Congressional District: 36
Key Personnel: Exec. Dir., Daniel Foster; Sr. Cur., Peter Frank; Museum Shop Mgr., Debbie Martin.
Personnel Profile: Full-Time Paid 5; Part-Time Paid 6; Part-Time Volunteers 45; Interns 8.
Governing Authority: nonprofit; board of trustees. Subsidiary Institution: Art Alliance of Riverside Art Museum. Tax-exempt: 501(c)(3).
Art Museum: housed in 1929 building, designed by Julia Morgan, architect for Hearst Castle.
Collections: paintings; sculpture; decorative arts; graphics.
Research Fields: contemporary, American art.
Facilities: rental gallery; courtyard restaurant. Gift items for sale.
Activities: guided tours; lectures; films; gallery talks; arts festivals; formally organized education programs for children & adults; permanent, temporary & traveling exhibitions.
Publications: quarterly newsletter; exhibition catalogues.
Hours & Admission Prices: Mon.-Sat. 10-4. Adults $5, students and seniors 65 & over $2; members & children 12 and under no charge. Closed holidays. ♿
Attendance: 70,000 (estimated)
Membership: General $40; Enhanced $100; Julia Morgan Society $500; Julie Morgan Society Patron $1,000; Julia Morgan Society Benefactor $2,500; Julia Morgan Society Medici $5,000; Life $20,000.

RIVERSIDE COMMUNITY COLLEGE ART GALLERY, 4800 Magnolia Ave., Riverside, CA 92506-1201. Tel.: 951-222-8358. Fax: 909-222-8740.
E-mail: julia.buckley@rcc.edu
Web Site: academic.rcc.edu/art/exhibitions.jsp
Key Personnel: Coord. Art Gallery, Leslie A. Brown
Art Gallery.
Collections: paintings.
Activities: film series; lectures; research; outreach to schools.
Hours & Admission Prices: Mon.-Wed. & Fri. 10-3, Thurs. 10-3 & 5:30-8.

RIVERSIDE HERITAGE HOUSE, 8193 Magnolia Ave., Riverside, CA 92504-3409. Mailing Address: 3580 Mission Inn Ave., Riverside, CA 92501-3321. Tel.: 951-826-5273.
Web Site: www.riversideca.gov/museum/heritage.asp
Historic House Museum.
Collections: period furnishings; personal artifacts.
Activities: docent tours; special events.
Hours & Admission Prices: Sept.-June Fri. 12-3, Sat.-Sun. 12-3:30. Suggested Donations: adults $3, children $1. Closed federal holidays.

* **RIVERSIDE METROPOLITAN MUSEUM, (M),** 3580 Mission Inn Ave., Riverside, CA 92501-3321. Tel.: 951-826-5273. Fax: 951-369-4970.
E-mail: enusbaum@riversideca.gov
Web Site: www.riversideca.gov/museum
Formerly: Riverside Municipal Museum
Founded: 1925.
Congressional District: 36
Key Personnel: Museum Dir., Ennette Nusbaum; Chm. Bd. (V), Norton Younglove; RMA Pres. (V), Skipper Wood; Cur. Natural History, James Bryant; Cur. Collections, Brenda Buller-Focht, Ph.D.; Cur. Historic Structures & Collections, Lynn Voorheis; Cur. Educator, Allison Campbell; Restoration Specialist, Gary Ecker; Admin. Analyst, Jolene Church; Cur. Anthropology, Maggie Wetherbee; Archivist, Kevin Hallaran; Assoc. Cur. Collections, Teresa Woodard; Maintenance, German Ponce; Maintenance, Mario Zuniga; Clerical Asst., Lucy Morin; Office Specialist, Toni Kinsman; Cur. History, Dean Ayer.
Personnel Profile: Full-Time Paid 14; Part-Time Paid 3; Part-Time Volunteers 130; Interns 6.
Governing Authority: municipal. Parent Institution: City of Riverside, 3900 Main St., Riverside, 92522. Subsidiary Institution: Riverside Museum Associates. Tax-exempt: 170(b)(1)(A).
Natural History Museum.
Collections: ethnology; archaeology; history; photo & document archives; decorative arts; rocks; minerals; fossils; mammals; birds; reptiles; insects; herbarium; Citrus label art; quilts; costumes. Historic House: 1891 Queen Anne Victorian House.
Research Fields: history; anthropology; archaeology; zoology; geology; paleontology; botany; art & decorative arts.
Facilities: 2,000-vol. library pertaining to museum collections available for use on premises by appointment; gardens. Books, pamphlets of local importance & other museum-related items for sale.
Activities: hands on programs; lectures; education programs for children; docent program or council; inter-museum loan, permanent & temporary exhibitions; school loan service; family programs. Annex: local history research available by appointment. Historic House Sponsors: community outreach ice cream social; Christmas Open House.
Publications: books; exhibit & collection pamphlets; brochure; newsletters, Native American Basketry of Central California, American Indian Basketry of Northern California, Native American Basketry of Southern California, A History of Citrus in the Riverside Area, Fading Images: Indian Pictographs of Western Riverside County.
Hours & Admission Prices: Museum: Tues.-Wed. & Fri. 9-5, Thurs. 9-9, Sat. 10-5, Sun. 11-5. Heritage House: Sept.-June Thurs.-Fri. 12-3, Sun. 12-3:30; groups by appointment. No charge; donations requested. Closed major holidays. ♿
Attendance: 75,000 (estimated)
Membership: Junior $1; Active $15; Individual $20; Family $30; Associate $50; Sustaining $75; Contributing $100; Life $1,000; Patron $2,500; Benefactor $5,000 & up.

SHERMAN INDIAN MUSEUM, 9010 Magnolia Ave., Riverside, CA 92503-4431. Tel.: 951-276-6719.
E-mail: lsisquoc@charter.net
Web Site: www.shermanindianmuseum.org
Key Personnel: Cur., Lorene Sisquoc
Native American Museum.
Collections: Native American history & culture; photographs; basketry; Navajo rugs; paintings.
Facilities: library.
Hours & Admission Prices: By appointment.

SWEENEY ART GALLERY, UNIVERSITY OF CALIFORNIA, 3800 Main St, Riverside, CA 92501-3624. Tel.: 951-827-3755. Fax: 951-827-3798.
E-mail: krapp@pop.ucr.edu
Web Site: sweeney.ucr.edu
Founded: 1963.
Congressional District: 36
Key Personnel: Dir., Karen Rapp; Gallery Mgr., Jennifer Frins.
Personnel Profile: Full-Time Paid 2; Part-Time Volunteers 2; Interns 4.
Governing Authority: state university; nonprofit organization. Tax-exempt: 501(c)(3).
University Art Gallery.
Collections: various portfolios on paper; Jules Cheret vintage prints; Vigango sculpture of East Africa; basic study collection; contemporary California.
Facilities: 500-vol. non-circulating library of exhibition catalogues; 2,000 sq. ft. exhibit space.
Activities: lectures; loan & traveling exhibitions.
Publications: quarterly newsletter for members; catalogues for some exhibitions.
Hours & Admission Prices: Tues.-Sat. & 1st Sun. of month 12-5. No charge; donations accepted. Closed major holidays. ♿
Attendance: 7,500 (estimated)
Membership: Subscriber $50; Friend $120; Fellow $500; Patron $1,000; Benefactor $2,500; Corporate $5,000.

UCR/CALIFORNIA MUSEUM OF PHOTOGRAPHY, 3824 Main St., Riverside, CA 92501-3624. Mailing Address: UCR/California Museum of Photography, Riverside, CA 92521-0001. Tel.: 951-827-4787. Fax: 951-827-4797.
E-mail: colin.westerbeck@ucr.edu
Web Site: www.cmp.ucr.edu/
Founded: 1973.
Congressional District: 43
Key Personnel: Dir. & Prof. Art & Art History, Colin Westerbeck; Asst. Cur., Kristine Thompson; Store Contact, Emily Papavero; Preparator, Jason Chakravarby; Cur. Collections, Leigh Gleason; Cur. Digital Media, Georg Burwick; Administrative Mgr., Zelda Glenn.
Personnel Profile: Full-Time Paid 9; Full-Time Volunteers 2; Part-Time Paid 10; Part-Time Volunteers 25; Interns 10.
Governing Authority: university; nonprofit organization. Parent Institution: University of California at Riverside, Riverside, CA. Tax-exempt.
Photography Museum.
Collections: 19th- & 20th-century photographs; Keystone-Mast Stereoview collection; stereoview negatives & prints; 19th- & 20th-century Bingham cameras & photographic apparatus; 20th century master prints & contemporary works.
Research Fields: history of photography; media; culture & optically generated images.
Facilities: library of photographically related monographs & serials available for research on premises only; digital studio; 12,000 sq. ft. exhibit space; separate laboratory operation. Museum-related items for sale.
Activities: temporary exhibitions exploring photography & video's relationship to art, society & politics; new music & performance art events; lectures & symposia; cooperative photography & video exhibitions with K-12 schools; hands-on optics & photographic technology for children; guided tours; formally organized education programs for undergraduate & graduate college students affiliated with UCR & other area universities; loan, permanent, temporary & traveling exhibitions; internet gallery.
Publications: occasional catalogues & artists' books; quarterly newsletter, FOTOTEXT.
Hours & Admission Prices: Tues.-Sat. 12-5. Adults $3; members, students & seniors no charge. Closed New Year's Day; Thanksgiving; Christmas. ♿
Attendance: 35,000 (estimated)
Membership: Student & Senior $25; Participating $35; Supporting $65; Contributing $125; Sustaining $500; Museum Fellow $1,000.

WORLD MUSEUM OF NATURAL HISTORY, (M), La Sierra Univ., 4500 Riverwalk Pkwy., Riverside, CA 92505-3344. Tel.: 951-785-2500 (Mon.-Thurs.); 2209 (Sat.). Fax: 951-785-2478.
E-mail: ajordane@lasierra.edu
Web Site: www.lasierra.edu/wmnh
Founded: 1971.
Congressional District: 43
Key Personnel: C.E.O. & Pres. La Sierra Univ., Randal Wisbey; Cur., Dr. Billy Hankins; Cur., Dr. Virchel Wood.
Personnel Profile: Part-Time Volunteers 5.
Governing Authority: La Sierra University. Tax-exempt: 501(c)(3).
Natural History Museum.
Collections: reptiles; birds of southeast Asia; mammals; minerals; fluorescent; meteorites; tektites; petrified woods.
Facilities: 200-seat auditorium; arboretum; 2,000 sq. ft. exhibit space; educational facilities.
Activities: videos; formal education programs for children & undergraduate or graduate college students affiliated with La Sierra University; guided tours.
Publications: occasional newsletter.
Hours & Admission Prices: Sat. 2-5; other times by appointment. No charge; donations accepted. ♿
Attendance: 8,000 (estimated)

Rohnert Park

UNIVERSITY ART GALLERY, SONOMA STATE UNIVERSITY, 1801 E. Cotati Ave., Rohnert Park, CA 94928-3609. Tel.: 707-664-2295. Fax: 707-664-2054.
E-mail: carla.stone@sonoma.edu
Web Site: www.sonoma.edu/artgallery/
Founded: 1977.
Key Personnel: Dir., Michael Schwager; Exhibition Coord., Carla Stone.
Personnel Profile: Full-Time Paid 1; Part-Time Paid 1; Interns 10.

Governing Authority: university; nonprofit organization. Parent Institution: Sonoma State University. Tax-exempt: 501(c)(3).
Art Gallery.
Collections: 20th-century American art works on paper; Asian art works; Garfield collection.
Major Exhibits: SSU Art Faculty Exhibit, 2/10; Juried Student Exhibition, 4/10; BFA Exhibition, 5/10.
Research Fields: 20th-century American art.
Activities: lectures; organized educational programs; training programs for professional museum workers; loan exhibitions; organized education programs for undergraduate or graduate students affiliated with Sonoma State University.
Publications: exhibition catalogues; posters.
Hours & Admission Prices: Sept.-May Tues.-Fri. 11-4, Sat.-Sun. 12-4. No charge. Closed holidays. ♿
Attendance: 2,000 (estimated)
Membership: Special $15; Active $35; Contributing $50; Patron $100; Benefactor $1,000.

Roseville

MAIDU MUSEUM AND HISTORIC SITE, (M), 1970 Johnson Ranch Dr., Roseville, CA 95661-3749. Tel.: 916-774-5934. Fax: 916-772-6161. TDD: 916-774-5220.
E-mail: kstevens@roseville.ca.us
Web Site: www.roseville.ca.us/indianmuseum
Formerly: Maidu Interpretive Center
Founded: 2001.
Congressional District: 4
Key Personnel: Dir. & Devel., Kris Stevens; Education, Heidi Franz; Education, Rick Adams; Public Rels., Theresa Williams; Registrar, April Farnham; Coord. Events, Linda Grindstaff; Museum Shop Mgr., Rick Doyle; Customer Service, Sara Ebi; Historic Site Restoration Coord., Robin Rietz; Security, Rich Douglas.
Personnel Profile: Full-Time Paid 2; Part-Time Paid 11; Part-Time Volunteers 42; Interns 1.
Governing Authority: municipal; nonprofit. Parent Institution: City of Roseville, CA.
Historic Site: listed on the National Register of Historic Places.
Collections: Nisenan Maidu & other Maiduan history & culture from 5000 BC to present.
Facilities: 3,000 sq. ft. exhibit space. Museum-related items for sale.
Activities: docent program; formal education programs; guided tours; lectures; participatory, temporary & traveling exhibitions. Annual Events: Leafing Out of Spring Cultural Celebration.
Publications: newsletter, Ah Kapa (Bear Rock) News.
Hours & Admission Prices: Mon.-Fri. 9-4 & 2nd Sat. of month. Adults $4, children & seniors $3.75; discounts to groups. Closed major holidays. ♿
Attendance: 34,500 (accurate)

ROSEVILLE UTILITY EXPLORATION CENTER, 2090 Hilltop Cir., Roseville, CA 95747-9704. Tel.: 919-746-1550.
E-mail: ruec@roseville.ca.us
Web Site: www.roseville.ca.us/explore
Key Personnel: Dir., Bob Garrison
Environmental Preservation Museum.
Collections: environmental preservation & conservation; energy technology; recycling.
Activities: educational programs.
Hours & Admission Prices: Tues.-Thurs. 10-7, Fri.-Sat. 10-5. No charge.

Sacramento

CALIFORNIA AUTOMOBILE MUSEUM, 2200 Front St., Sacramento, CA 95818-1107. Tel.: 916-442-6802. Fax: 916-442-2646.
E-mail: director@calautomuseum.org
Web Site: www.calautomuseum.org
Formerly: Towe Auto Museum
Founded: 1982.
Key Personnel: Pres., Joe Hensler; Vice Pres., Al Buescher; Dir., Karen McClaflin; Museum Shop Mgr., Derek Fleming.
Personnel Profile: Full-Time Paid 5; Part-Time Paid 5; Part-Time Volunteers 300.
Governing Authority: nonprofit membership organization. Parent Institution: California Vehicle Foundation. Tax-exempt: 501(c)(3).
Transportation Museum.
Collections: period American automobiles 1900 to present day; automobile artifacts & memorabilia; period costumes from 1900-1959; vehicle parts including heaters, chassis & tires.
Research Fields: Henry Ford; Ford Motor Company; historic automobiles; general automotive history; evolution of American automobile through 100 years; role of the automobile in changing American society.
Facilities: automotive research library; banquet facilities. Museum-related items for sale.
Activities: guided tours; lectures; films; organized education programs; docent program; participatory & temporary exhibitions; annual events; educational classes; educational tours; rental facilities.
Publications: newsletter; annual report.
Hours & Admission Prices: Daily 10-6; last admission at 5pm. Adults $8, senior citizens $7, students $4; discounts to AAA members & groups; children under 5 & members no charge. Closed New Year's Day; Thanksgiving; Christmas. ♿
Attendance: 40,000 (estimated)
Membership: Student $25; General $50; Dual & Family $75; Car Club $100-$150; Executive $150; Corporate $300.

THE CALIFORNIA MUSEUM FOR HISTORY, WOMEN AND THE ARTS, (M), 1020 O St., Sacramento, CA 95814-5704. Tel.: 916-653-7524. Fax: 916-653-0314.
E-mail: kbitz@sos.ca.gov
Web Site: www.californiamuseum.org
Formerly: California State History Museum
Founded: 1998.
Congressional District: 5
Key Personnel: Exec. Dir., Claudia French; Chm., Dina Eastwood; Business Mgr., Diane Masters; Dir. Exhibitions & Programs, Amanda Meeker; Dir. Mktg., Sandra Kopp; Deputy Dir., John O'Connor; Museum Shop Mgr., Mika Visante.
Personnel Profile: Full-Time Paid 16; Part-Time Paid 3; Part-Time Volunteers 20; Interns 2.
Governing Authority: private; nonprofit organization. Tax-exempt: 501(c)(3).
General Museum.
Collections: archives; artifacts; manuscripts; ephemera related to California; multimedia exhibit technology; state-of-the-art technology; documents & artifacts.
Facilities: 260-seat auditorium; classrooms; 30,000 sq. ft. exhibit space.
Activities: Annual Events: family oriented events with California themes; California Hall of Fame Induction Ceremony in December.
Hours & Admission Prices: Tues.-Sat. 10-5, Sun. 12-5. Adults $7.50, senior citizens & students $6, children 6 -13 $5; discounts to AAM members & groups; members and children 5 & under no charge. Closed New Year's Day; Thanksgiving; Christmas. ♿
Attendance: 62,000 (accurate)
Membership: Student, Senior & Teacher $40; Individual $50; Family & Dual $85; Friend $250.

CALIFORNIA STATE CAPITOL MUSEUM, 10th St., Rm. B-27, Sacramento, CA 95814. Tel.: 916-324-0333. Fax: 916-445-3628. TDD: 916-324-2092.
E-mail: capitol@parks.ca.gov
Web Site: www.statecapitolmuseum.ca.gov
Founded: 1981.
Congressional District: 3
Key Personnel: Museum Dir., Mr. Todd Thames; Pres. (V), Loraine Donnelly; Cur. Collections, V. Joseph Sgromo; Museum Shop Mgr., Sandra May.
Personnel Profile: Full-Time Paid 23; Part-Time Paid 19; Part-Time Volunteers 121.
Governing Authority: state. Parent Institution: California Dept. of Parks & Recreation. Subsidiary Institution: Gold Rush District. Tax-exempt.
Historic Building Museum: c.1860-1874 restored California State Capitol.
Collections: architectural features from the State Capitol; late 19th-century office furnishings; tools & materials from the restoration of the State Capitol; documents & other items related to the state; 1900-1906 executive officers; interior & exterior images of the Capitol.
Research Fields: history of California government; State Capitol building; legislature, executive & judicial offices; general office practices of 1900-1910.
Facilities: theater; 200-seat cafeteria. Items made from original capitol architectural fragments, books & other museum-related items for sale.
Activities: guided tours; films; formally organized education programs; docent program; loan, permanent & temporary exhibitions.
Publications: California State Capitol Restoration: A Pictorial History, 1983; California's Historic Capitol, 1983; The Governors of California and Their Portraits.
Hours & Admission Prices: Tours: daily 9-4. No charge. Closed New Year's Day; Thanksgiving; Christmas. ♿
Attendance: 513,000 (estimated)
Membership: Volunteer Association: Active $10; Sustaining $18; Supporting $25.

CALIFORNIA STATE INDIAN MUSEUM, 2618 K St., Sacramento, CA 95816-5104. Tel.: 916-324-0971. Fax: 916-322-5231.
Web Site: www.parks.ca.gov/indianmuseum
Founded: 1940.
Congressional District: 3
Key Personnel: Interpretive Svcs., Connie McGough; Cur., Ileana Maestas; Dir., Rob Wood; Museum Shop Mgr., Helen Kawello.
Personnel Profile: Full-Time Paid 3; Part-Time Paid 4; Part-Time Volunteers 30.
Governing Authority: state. Affiliated with California State Dept. of Parks & Recreation, P.O. Box 2390, Sacramento, CA 95811.
California Native American Cultural & Historical Museum.
Collections: California Indian artifacts; contemporary California Native American art work.
Facilities: hands-on area. Native-made items for sale.
Activities: gallery talks upon request; groups by reservation. Museum Sponsors: Annual Honored Elders Day; Acorn Day; Indian Arts & Crafts Marketplace in spring; Holiday Arts & Crafts Fair in fall.
Publications: brochures.
Hours & Admission Prices: Daily 10-5. Adults 17 & up $2; youth 6-17 $1; children 5 & under no charge. Closed New Year's Day; Thanksgiving; Christmas. ♿
Attendance: 40,000 (estimated)

THE CALIFORNIA STATE MILITARY MUSEUM, 1119 Second St., Sacramento, CA 95814-3203. Tel.: 916-442-2883. Fax: 916-442-7532.
E-mail: daniel.sebby@us.army.mil
Web Site: www.militarymuseum.org
Founded: 1991.
Congressional District: 1
Key Personnel: Dir., Dan Sebby; Deputy Dir. Library, Bill Davies; Deputy Dir. Special Projects, Ernie McPherson; Deputy Dir. Grants, Marilyn Starbuck; Administration, Butch Dixon; Museum Shop Mgr., Lynden Larsen; Security, Neil Strasbauch; Exhibit Specialist, Ricardo Davis.
Personnel Profile: Full-Time Paid 4; Part-Time Paid 4; Part-Time Volunteers 60.
Governing Authority: nonprofit. Parent Institution: California State Military Dept. Branch Museums: Camp Roberts, southern Monterey County; Camp San Luis Obispo; Fresno Air National Guard Base; Los Alamitos Joint Forces Training Base, Orange County. Tax-exempt: 501(c)(3).
Military Museum.
Collections: military artifacts; photographs; personal artifacts.
Research Fields: California military history.
Facilities: library.
Activities: tours.
Hours & Admission Prices: Tues.-Sun. 10-4. Adults $5, children 6-17 $3; members and children 5 & under no charge. Closed New Year's Day; Easter; Thanksgiving; Christmas. ♿
Attendance: 70,000 (estimated)

CALIFORNIA STATE RAILROAD MUSEUM, 125 I St., Sacramento, CA 95814-2265. Mailing Address: 111 I St., Sacramento, CA 95814-2265. Tel.: 916-445-6645 & 7387. Fax: 916-327-5655.
E-mail: rrmuseuminfo@parks.ca.gov
Web Site: www.csrmf.org
Founded: 1976.
Congressional District: 3
Key Personnel: Dir., Paul J. Hammond; Chief Cur., Stephen E. Drew; Cur. History & Technology, Kyle K. Wyatt; Dir. Collections, Ellen L. Halteman; Archivist, Kathryn Santos; Dir. Foundation, Pamela Horan; Chm. Foundation (V), Robert Slobe; Exhibits, Paul Brown; Librarian, Cara Randall; Maintenance Chief, Dennis Pruitt; Museum Shop Mgr., Tom Grenache.
Personnel Profile: Full-Time Paid 45; Full-Time Volunteers 6; Part-Time Paid 15; Part-Time Volunteers 1,000; Interns 3.
Governing Authority: state. Parent Institution: California State Parks. Related Organization: California State Railroad Museum Foundation. Tax-exempt.
Railroad Museum: in Old Sacramento State Historic Park.
Collections: railroads and railroading in California, Nevada & the West; 200 historic steam locomotives, diesels & cars; artifacts; archival materials; manuscripts; Railtown 1897 State Historic Park. Historic Buildings: Big Four Building; Dingley Spice Mill; Central Pacific Railroad Passenger Station; Central Pacific Railroad Freight Depot.
Research Fields: railroads & railroading in the United States, emphasizing California, Nevada & the West.
Facilities: library of books, photographs, manuscripts, archival materials regarding railroading in California & the United States, available for research use; reading room; two 135-seat theaters; classrooms; restaurant. Books & other memorabilia for sale.
Activities: guided tours; lectures; films; gallery talks; live steam train rides; formally organized educational programs; docent programs; permanent & temporary exhibitions; biannual living history. Museum Sponsors: National Handcar Races.
Publications: museum brochure; guidebook; On Track!
Hours & Admission Prices: Daily 10-5. Adults $8, children 6-17 $3; children under 6 & members no charge. Closed New Year's Day; Thanksgiving; Christmas. ♿
Attendance: 525,000 (estimated)
Membership: Children's Caboose Club $15; Student & Senior Citizen $25; Fireman $35; Conductor $50; Engineer $100; Trainmaster $250. Corporate: Copper Spike $250; Bronze Spike $500; Silver Spike $750; Gold Spike $1,000; Platinum Spike $5,000.

CENTER FOR SACRAMENTO HISTORY, 551 Sequoia Pacific Blvd., Sacramento, CA 95811-0229. Tel.: 916-264-7072. Fax: 916-264-7582.
E-mail: meymann@cityofsacramento.org
Web Site: www.sacramenities.com/history/
Formerly: Sacramento Archives and Museum Collection Center
Founded: 1953.
Congressional District: 3
Key Personnel: Mgr., Marcia Eymann; Senior Archivist, Patricia Johnson; Archivist, Dylan McDonald; Cur. History, Lisa Prince.
Personnel Profile: Full-Time Paid 5; Part-Time Paid 3; Part-Time Volunteers 25; Interns 3.
Governing Authority: municipal. Parent Institution: City of Sacramento. Subsidiary Institutions: Sacramento History Museum; Sacramento Science Center; Sacramento City Cemetery. Tax-exempt: 170(b)(1)(A).
Historic Agency.
Collections: transportation; history; city and county records; archives; photographs; printing; California newspapers; manuscripts; business records.
Research Fields: local history; ethnic studies; textiles; theater; transportation; printing; California journalism; television news.
Facilities: 15,000-vol. library, including news collection, documentary photographs, architectural drawings, American west maps; local government archive; local television film library available for use on premises.
Activities: lectures; graduate & undergraduate student intern program; community outreach.
Publications: reports, Old Sacramento Historic Illustrations Guide; Telling the Sacramento Story; booklets, Old Sacramento, A Reference Point in Time; Sidewalk History: Pioneer Sites in Old Sacramento; book, The City of the Plain, Sacramento in the 19th Century; The Sacramento Museum; Recommendations for Planning and Development in the Old Sacramento State Historic Park; catalogue, For the Record; quarterly journal, Interchange; History of the Lower American River.
Hours & Admission Prices: Tues. 1-4:30, Wed. 4-7:45, Thurs.-Fri. 8:15-12, Sat. 8:15-12 and 1:15-4:30 & by appointment only. No charge; donations accepted. Closed city holidays. ♿
Attendance: 5,000 (estimated)

* **CROCKER ART MUSEUM, (M),** 216 O St., Sacramento, CA 95814-5399. Tel.: 916-808-7000. Fax: 916-808-7372. TTY CA Relay: 1-888-877-5379.
E-mail: cam@cityofsacramento.org
Web Site: www.crockerartmuseum.org
Founded: 1885.
Congressional District: 3
Key Personnel: Dir., Lial A. Jones; Acting Dir. Devel., Linda Farley; Dir. Admin., Cheri Johnson; Cur., Scott Shields; Finance, David Separovich; Dir. Mktg., LeAnne Ruzzamenti; Deputy Dir., Randy Roberts; Museum Store Mgr., Michelle Mckenzie.
Personnel Profile: Full-Time Paid 34; Part-Time Paid 15; Part-Time Volunteers 200; Interns 10.
Governing Authority: partnership. Parent Institution: Crocker Art Museum Association. Subsidiary Institution: City of Sacramento. Tax-exempt.
Art Museum: housed in 1872 E.B. Crocker Art Gallery; Crocker Mansion Wing; R.A. Herold Wing.
Collections: master drawings; California art; European paintings; photography; international ceramics; Asian art.
Research Fields: master drawings; California painting & sculpture.
Facilities: 20,000-vol. library of books on art available for use on premises by appointment only.
Activities: guided tours; lectures; films; concerts; arts festivals; formally organized educational programs; docent program; formal inter-museum loan, temporary & traveling exhibitions.
Publications: exhibition catalogs; ArtLetter.
Hours & Admission Prices: Tues.-Sun. 10-5, 1st & 3rd Thurs. 10-9. Adults $6, senior citizens $4, students with ID $3; discounts to AAM members; members & children 6 and under no charge. Closed New Year's Day; Thanksgiving; Christmas. ♿
Attendance: 160,000 (accurate)

Membership: Individual $45; Family $55; Supporter $85; Associate $150; Contributor $250; Benefactor $500; Director's Circle Patron $1,250; Director's Circle Trustee $2,500; Director's Circle President $5,000; Crocker Council Founder $10,000.

DISCOVERY MUSEUM, SACRAMENTO MUSEUM OF HISTORY, SCIENCE AND TECHNOLOGY, (M), Discovery Museum, 3615 Auburn Blvd., Sacramento, CA 95821-2097. Tel.: 916-575-3942. Fax: 916-575-3925.
E-mail: marlenec@thediscovery.org
Web Site: www.thediscovery.org
Founded: 1994.
Congressional District: 4
Key Personnel: Interim Exec. Dir., Michele Wong; Dir. Science Public Programs, Susan Douglas; Challenger Flight Dir., Catherine Gray; Museum Shop Mgr., Janice Wagaman.
Personnel Profile: Full-Time Paid 14; Full-Time Volunteers 4; Part-Time Paid 2; Part-Time Volunteers 250; Interns 2.
Governing Authority: nonprofit organization. Branch Location: Science & Space Center, 3615 Auburn Blvd., Sacramento, CA 95821. Tel.: 916-575-3941. Fax: 916-575-3925. Tax-exempt: 501(c)(3).
History, Science & Space Museum.
Collections: local historical objects & artifacts; insects; fossils; rocks & minerals; shells; live animals; native & drought tolerant plants.
Facilities: Museum-related items for sale. Science & Space Center: planetarium; classroom; amphitheatre; 14 acres of nature trail; wildlife pond.
Activities: guided tours; docent program; planetarium shows; hands-on temporary exhibits; traveling science programs to schools & other locations; youth classes; teacher training; rental facility.
Publications: newsletter; brochures; educational program booklet.
Hours & Admission Prices: Daily 10-5. Adults $5, children 13-17 & seniors $4, children 4-12 $3; discounts to AAM & ASTC members; members & children under 3 no charge. Closed New Year's Day; Thanksgiving; Christmas. ♿
Attendance: 120,000 (accurate)
Membership: Student & Senior $35; Individual $40; Family & Grandparents $50; Donor $75; Sustainer $150; Patron $250; Benefactor $500.

GOVERNOR'S MANSION STATE HISTORIC PARK, 1526 H St., Sacramento, CA 95814-2005. Tel.: 916-323-3047. Fax: 916-322-4775.
Web Site: www.parks.ca.gov/governorsmansion
Founded: 1967.
Congressional District: 3
Key Personnel: Supervising Lead Guide, Eva Ross-Forney; Cur. & Mgr., Kendra Dillard.
Personnel Profile: Full-Time Paid 3; Part-Time Paid 6; Part-Time Volunteers 75.
Governing Authority: state. California State Dept. of Parks and Recreation, P.O. Box 2390, Sacramento, CA 95811. Subsidiary Institution: California Historic Governor's Mansion Foundation. Tax-exempt.
Historic House Museum: housed in Victorian mansion, built in 1877.
Collections: furnishings collected by 13 California governors from 1903-1967; Albert & Clemenza Gallatin's hardware c.1877.
Research Fields: printed & oral history of residents.
Activities: guided tours; special events; rental facilities. Museum Sponsors: Living History Days; Halloween after dark tours; Gala Christmas Celebration.
Publications: Golden Notes #1; Golden Notes #2; The Historic Governor's Mansion; Governor's Mansion Cookbook; Governor's Mansion Coloring Book; Earthquake Days (1906); California Gold; Sacramento and The California Delta; Governor's Mansion Traditional Family Recipes; History books; Day Hikers Guide to California State Parks.
Hours & Admission Prices: Tours: 10-4; groups by appointment. Park: 10-5. Adults $4, children 6-16 $2; children under 6 no charge. Closed New Year's Day; Thanksgiving; Christmas. ♿
Attendance: 39,078 (estimated)

GREGORY KONDOS GALLERY, Sacramento City College - FA9, 3835 Freeport Blvd., Sacramento, CA 95822-1318. Tel.: 916-558-2210.
E-mail: dauberc@scc.losrios.edu
Web Site: web.scc.losrios.edu/art/gallery
Key Personnel: Dir., Chris Daubert
Art Gallery.
Collections: works by regional artists; Gregory Kondos paintings & prints.
Hours & Admission Prices: Mon. & Thurs.-Fri. 10-4, Tues.-Wed. 10-4 & 6-8.

LA RAZA/GALERIA POSADA, 1022 22nd St., #1024, Sacramento, CA 95816-4908. Tel.: 916-446-5133. Fax: 916-446-1324.
E-mail: larazagaleria@sbcglobal.net
Web Site: www.larazagaleriaposada.org
Congressional District: 5
Key Personnel: Dir., Marie Acosta; Chm. (V), Mario Gutierrez; Gallery Coord., Juanishi V. Orosco.
Personnel Profile: Full-Time Paid 1; Part-Time Paid 1; Part-Time Volunteers 100.
Governing Authority: nonprofit organization. Tax-exempt: 501(c)(3).
Art Center & Museum: housed in the Heilbron Mansion, a Victorian landmark.
Collections: poster art by national Chicano artists; traditional folk & fine art by Native American, Latino & Chicano.
Research Fields: Mexican, Chicano & Latino art movement.
Facilities: workshops. Books, folk art & museum-related items for sale.
Activities: guided tours; temporary & traveling exhibitions of museum collections; story-telling for children; mask-making workshops. Annual Events: Canto Poetry & Music Series; Christmas Folk Art Sale.
Publications: annual catalogue of books, La Raza Galeria Posada.
Hours & Admission Prices: Wed.-Sat. 12-6, 2nd Sat. of month 12-9. Suggested Donation: $5. Closed Easter; Thanksgiving; Christmas. ♿
Attendance: 25,000 (estimated)
Membership: Student & Senior Citizen $15; Individual $30; Family $40; Contributor $50; Sponsor $100; Benefactor $500; Patron, Business & Group Sponsor $1,000.

OLD SACRAMENTO SCHOOLHOUSE MUSEUM, 1200 Front St., Sacramento, CA 95814-3247. Mailing Address: 5325 Ridgefield Ave., Carmichael, CA 95608-2109. Tel.: 916-483-8818. Fax: 916-972-7041.
E-mail: info@oldsacschoolhouse.org
Web Site: www.scoe.net/oldsacschoolhouse
Founded: 1977.
History Museum.
Collections: 19th century school life in California; pot-bellied stove; period furnishings; student desks.
Activities: one hour lesson from the 1800s for school children. Museum Sponsors: Gingerbread Holiday House Contest in December.
Hours & Admission Prices: Mon.-Sat. 10-4, Sun. 12-4. No charge. ♿

ROBERT ELSE GALLERY, California State University Sacramento, 6000 'J' St., Kadema Hall, First Fl., Sacramento, CA 95819-2605. Tel.: 916-278-6166.
Web Site: www.csus.edu/galleries/else.html
Art Gallery.
Collections: works by student artists.
Activities: special events.
Hours & Admission Prices: Academic Year: Mon.-Fri. 12-4:30. No charge.

SACRAMENTO ZOO, 3930 W. Land Park, Sacramento, CA 95822-1123. Tel.: 916-808-5166. Fax: 916-264-5887.
E-mail: saczooinfo@cityofsacramento.org
Web Site: www.saczoo.com
Founded: 1927.
Congressional District: 5
Key Personnel: Exec. Dir. & C.E.O., Mary Healy; Pres. (V), Terry Kastanis; Cur., Jim Schnormeier; Museum Shop Mgr., Fred Klinker.
Personnel Profile: Full-Time Paid 58; Part-Time Paid 26; Part-Time Volunteers 1,400.
Governing Authority: society. Parent Institution: Sacramento Zoological Society. Tax-exempt.
Zoo.
Collections: 413 specimens of exotic animals; 131 species.
Research Fields: behavioral research through University of California at Davis; Chimpanzoo (Jane Goodall Institute).
Facilities: 300-vol. library of zoology material not available for inter-library loan; botanical garden; zoological park; banquet facilities. Gift items for sale.
Activities: guided tours; lectures; fund raising events; outreach programs; formally organized education programs for children, adults, undergraduate & graduate students; docent program or council; permanent exhibitions.
Publications: quarterly newsletter, Maagizo.
Hours & Admission Prices: Feb.-Oct. daily 9-4; Nov.-Jan. daily 10-4. Mon.-Fri. adults $9, seniors $8.25, children 3-12 $6.50; discounts to groups of 25 or more; AZA, children 2 & under and members no charge. Sat.-Sun. adults $9.50, seniors $8.75, children 3-12 $7; discounts to groups of 25 or more; AZA, children 2 & under and members no charge. Closed Thanksgiving; Christmas. ♿
Attendance: 500,000 (estimated)
Membership: Individual $35; Member plus Guest $50; Family $75; Family Plus $115; Zoo Builder $250; Zoo Patron $500.

SIERRA SACRAMENTO VALLEY MEDICAL SOCIETY MUSEUM OF MEDICAL HISTORY, 5380 Elvas Ave., Sacramento, CA 95819-2300. Tel.: 916-456-3152. Fax: 916-452-2690.
E-mail: ssvmsmus@winfirst.com
Web Site: www.ssvms.org
Founded: 2001.
Key Personnel: Chm. (V) & Cur., Dr. Bob LaPerriere.
Personnel Profile: Part-Time Volunteers 8.
Governing Authority: Parent Institution: Sierra Sacramento Valley Medical Society. Tax-exempt.
Medical History Museum.
Collections: history of medicine including surgery, clinical diagnosis, infectious disease, pharmacy, radiology, Chinese medicine, obstetrics & gynecology, and medical quackery; books; journals; medical artifacts.
Facilities: 1,200 sq. ft. exhibit space.
Activities: guided tours.
Hours & Admission Prices: Mon.-Fri. 9-4. No charge; donations accepted. Closed holidays. ♿
Attendance: 1,000 (estimated)

SUTTER'S FORT STATE HISTORIC PARK, 2701 L St., Sacramento, CA 95816-5613. Tel.: 916-445-4422. Fax: 916-442-8613.
E-mail: info@parks.ca.gov
Web Site: www.parks.ca.gov/suttersfort
Founded: 1839.
Congressional District: 3
Key Personnel: Interpreter II, Bob Russo; Museum Tech, Judy Russo; Unit Ranger, Karen Meltzer; Museum Shop Mgr., Sparky Anderson.
Personnel Profile: Full-Time Paid 2; Part-Time Paid 2; Part-Time Volunteers 125.
Governing Authority: state. Parent Institution: California State Dept. of Parks & Recreation, P.O. Box 2390, Sacramento 95811. Tax-exempt.
State Park Museum.
Collections: 1839-1850 period artifacts; pre-California gold rush story.
Facilities: Museum-related items for sale.
Activities: talks; electronic self-guided tour in English, German, Spanish & Japanese; environmental living program with school groups; docent training program. Museum Sponsors: living history days & demonstrations; authentic 1840s Trade Faire in April; costumed interpreters & demonstrations in summer.
Publications: costume manual; brochures, Teacher Guide; California Historical Landmarks; Gold Rush Era.
Hours & Admission Prices: Daily 10-5. Call for admission prices. Closed New Year's Day; Thanksgiving; Christmas. ♿
Attendance: 200,000 (estimated)

WELLS FARGO HISTORY MUSEUM, 400 Capitol Mall, Sacramento, CA 95814-4407. Mailing Address: Wells Fargo Historical Services, 420 Montgomery St., MAC-A0101-106, San Francisco, CA 94163-0001. Tel.: 916-440-4161.
Founded: 1992.
Key Personnel: Cur., Indulis Kalnins.
Governing Authority: profit-making organization. Affiliated with Wells Fargo Bank.
Company History Museum.
Collections: Concord stagecoach; Wells Fargo banking & express history; gold mining; gold specimens; original gold scales; Livingston collection of Sacramento Postal; Wells Fargo express covers.
Activities: guided tours.
Publications: scholarly pamphlets.
Hours & Admission Prices: Mon.-Fri. 9-5. No charge. Closed bank holidays. ♿

WELLS FARGO HISTORY MUSEUM, 1000 Second St., Sacramento, CA 95814-3202. Mailing Address: Wells Fargo Historical Services, 420 Montgomery St., MAC-A0101-106, San Francisco, CA 94163-0001. Tel.: 916-440-4263.
Founded: 1984.
Key Personnel: Cur., Denise M. Pranza.
Governing Authority: profit-making organization. Affiliated with Wells Fargo Bank.
Company History Museum.
Collections: original gold scales; model Concord Stagecoach; Wells Fargo banking & express history; staging; Pony Express; mining; local items.
Activities: guided group tours; permanent & temporary exhibitions.
Publications: scholarly pamphlets.
Hours & Admission Prices: Daily 10-5. No charge. Closed New Year's Day; Easter; Thanksgiving; Christmas. ♿

Saint Helena

BALE GRIST MILL STATE HISTORIC PARK, 3369 St. Helena Hwy. N., Saint Helena, CA 94515. Mailing Address: 3801 St. Helena Hwy. N., Calistoga, CA 94515-9617. Tel.: 707-942-4575. Fax: 707-942-9560.
Web Site: www.parks.ca.gov/
Founded: 1975.
Congressional District: 7
Key Personnel: Supvr., Eileen Bielecki.
Personnel Profile: Part-Time Paid 2; Part-Time Volunteers 12.
Governing Authority: nonprofit co-op assoc. state. Tax-exempt: 501(c)(3).
History Museum: housed in a grist mill built in 1844-47.
Collections: tools specific to milling grain; photographs.
Facilities: 11,000 sq. ft. exhibit space. Gift items for sale.
Activities: guided tours; informal education programs for children; school groups. Annual Events: Old Mill Days in October; Pioneer Christmas in December.
Publications: newsletter, Napa Valley State Parks Association.
Hours & Admission Prices: Park: daily. Buildings: Summer daily; Sept.-June Sat.-Sun. Adults $2; children under 16 no charge. Closed major holidays. ♿
Attendance: 14,000 (accurate)
Membership: Senior & Student $15; Individual $20; Family $30; Business & Sponsor $50 & up.

ST. HELENA HISTORICAL SOCIETY, (M), St. Helena Public Library, Saint Helena, CA 94574. Mailing Address: P.O. Box 87, Saint Helena, CA 94574-0087. Tel.: 707-967-5502.
Key Personnel: Pres., Skip Lane
Historical Society Museum.
Collections: local history & culture; books; photographs.
Activities: research.
Hours & Admission Prices: By appointment.

SILVERADO MUSEUM - ROBERT LOUIS STEVENSON COLLECTION, (M), 1490 Library Lane, Saint Helena, CA 94574-1143. Mailing Address: P.O. Box 409, Saint Helena, CA 94574-0409. Tel.: 707-963-3757. Fax: 707-963-0917.
Founded: 1969.
Congressional District: 2
Key Personnel: Chm. (V), William von Metz; Dir. & Cur., Dorothy Mackay-Collins; Asst. Dir., Dianne Fraser.
Personnel Profile: Full-Time Paid 2; Part-Time Paid 2; Part-Time Volunteers 7.
Governing Authority: nonprofit. Parent Institution: The Vailima Foundation, P.O. Box 409. Tax-exempt.
History & Literary Museum.
Collections: first editions, manuscripts, letters, memorabilia of Robert Louis Stevenson; books, periodicals, paintings, photographs & sculptures relating to Stevenson.
Research Fields: life and works of Robert Louis Stevenson, his immediate family & associates.
Facilities: library of books related to Robert Louis Stevenson & his family; original letters & manuscripts; photographs; periodicals; paintings; prints; sculptures; memorabilia. Publications written & related to Stevenson for sale.
Activities: guided tours; lectures; docent program; permanent & temporary exhibitions.
Publications: The Silverado Squatters; Prayers Written at Vailima; The New Lighthouse on the Dhu Heartache Rock; Play-If I'm Spared; Treasured Recipes; books, Robert Louis Stevenson biographies.
Hours & Admission Prices: Wed.-Sun. 12-4; other times by appointment. No charge; donations accepted. Closed New Year's Day; Easter; Independence Day; Memorial Day; Thanksgiving; Christmas. ♿
Attendance: 4,000 (accurate)

Salinas

HARVEY-BAKER HOUSE, Salinas Transportation Center, Salinas, CA 93901. Mailing Address: Monterey County Historical Society, P.O. Box 3576, Salinas, CA 93912-3576. Tel.: 831-424-7155.
Historic House Museum: housed in the home of Isaac Harvey, the first mayor of Salinas, built in 1868.
Collections: period furnishings.
Hours & Admission Prices: 1st Sun. of month 1-4; other times by appointment. No charge.

JOSE EUSEBIO BORONDA ADOBE, 333 Boronda Rd., Salinas, CA 93907-1808. Mailing Address: P.O. Box 3576, Salinas, CA 93912-3576. Tel.: 831-757-8085.
Historic House Museum: built in the 1840s.
Collections: local & family history; period furnishings; personal artifacts; photographs.

Hours & Admission Prices: Mon.-Fri. 10-3.

NATIONAL STEINBECK CENTER, 1 Main St., Salinas, CA 93901-3436. Tel.: 831-796-3833. Fax: 831-796-3828.
E-mail: info@steinbeck.org
Web Site: www.steinbeck.org
Founded: 1983.
Congressional District: 17
Key Personnel: Dir., Steven A. Hoffman; Museum Shop Mgr., Jesse Garcia.
Personnel Profile: Full-Time Paid 12; Part-Time Paid 3; Part-Time Volunteers 100; Interns 3.
Governing Authority: private; nonprofit. Tax-exempt: 501(c)(3).
Literary, Agriculture & Art Museum.
Collections: 30,000 objects, manuscripts, letters, photographs, oral history tape, truck, screen plays & reviews related to the life & art of John Steinbeck.
Research Fields: the life, legacy & art of John Steinbeck.
Facilities: archives; 215-seat meeting area; 12,000 sq. ft. exhibit space. Museum-related items for sale.
Activities: volunteer program; lectures; book group; temporary exhibitions; educational programs; festivals; literary programs; art activities.
Publications: quarterly newsletter.
Hours & Admission Prices: Daily 10-5. Adults $10.95, seniors $8.95, youth 13-17 $7.95, children $5.95; members and children 5 & under no charge. Closed New Year's Day; Thanksgiving; Christmas. ♿
Attendance: 70,000 (estimated)
Membership: Individual $45; Dual & Family $65; Literary Guild $125; Pulitzer Prize Circle $250; Author's Circle $500.

Samoa

HUMBOLDT BAY MARITIME MUSEUM, Hwy. 255, Samoa, CA 95564. Mailing Address: P.O. Box 282, Samoa, CA 95564-0282. Tel.: 707-444-9440.
E-mail: joshhbmm@suddenlinkmail.com
Web Site: www.humboldtbaymaritimemuseum.com
Key Personnel: Chm., Joshua Smith; Operations, Dalene Zerlang.
Governing Authority: nonprofit. Tax-exempt: 501(c)(3).
Maritime Museum.
Collections: regional maritime history; photographs; local culture.
Activities: educational programs; group tours.
Hours & Admission Prices: Tues.-Wed. & Fri.-Sat. 11-4.

SAMOA COOKHOUSE & LOGGING MUSEUM, 908 Vance Ave., Samoa, CA 95564. Mailing Address: 2841 E St., Eureka, CA 95501-4331. Tel.: 707-442-1659. Fax: 707-442-1699.
Web Site: www.samoacookhouse.net/samoa-cookhouse-museum.html
Key Personnel: Mgr., Jeff Brustman; Asst. Mgr., Sharon Nichols
Lumber & Logging Industry Museum.
Collections: Cookhouse & logging history; period artifacts; photographs.
Facilities: cookhouse.
Hours & Admission Prices: Daily 7am-8pm. No charge.

San Andreas

CALAVERAS COUNTY ARCHIVES, 891 Mountain Ranch Rd., San Andreas, CA 95249-9713.
E-mail: archives@goldrush.com
Key Personnel: Archivist, Shannon Van Zant.
Personnel Profile: Part-Time Paid 1.
Governing Authority: Parent Institution: Calaveras County.
County History Museum.
Collections: Indian artifacts & baskets; Chinese artifacts from the California Gold Rush era; county documents, 1851-1960.
Research Fields: genealogy; Calaveras County history; Mother Lode history; mining; farming; state parks.
Activities: special historic & cultural programs; research.
Hours & Admission Prices: Mon. & Wed. 8-4. No charge. Research $10 per hour. ♿

CALAVERAS COUNTY HISTORICAL SOCIETY MUSEUM, 30 N. Main St., San Andreas, CA 95249. Mailing Address: P.O. Box 721, San Andreas, CA 95249-0721. Tel.: 209-754-4658 & 1058. Fax: 209-754-1086.
E-mail: cchs@goldrush.com
Web Site: www.calaverascohistorical.com
Founded: 1936.
Congressional District: 18
Key Personnel: Pres. Calaveras Historical Society, Donna Shannon; Cur., Karen Nicholson.
Personnel Profile: Full-Time Paid 1; Part-Time Paid 2; Part-Time Volunteers 5.
Governing Authority: county. Subsidiary Institution: Red Barn Museum, 891 Mountain Ranch Rd., San Andreas, CA 95249. Tel.: 209-754-0800. Tax-exempt.
County History Museum.
Collections: Indian artifacts & baskets; 1849 gold rush mining & pioneer artifacts. Historic Buildings: 1867 courthouse & jail; 1893 Hall of Records.
Research Fields: Calaveras County & Mother Lode history; Calaveras County mining; genealogical research.
Facilities: library.
Activities: special historic & cultural programs.
Publications: quarterly published by C.C. Historical Society, Las Calaveras.
Hours & Admission Prices: Daily 10-4. Adults $3, senior citizens $2, children under 12 $1; discounts to student groups; members no charge. Closed New Year's Day; Easter; Christmas Day. ♿
Attendance: 3,000 (estimated)
Membership: County Historical Society: Individual $22; Life $440.

RED BARN MUSEUM, Government Center, 891 Mountain Ranch Rd., San Andreas, CA 95249-9713. Tel.: 209-754-0800. Fax: 209-754-1086.
E-mail: cchs@goldrush.com
Web Site: www.calaverascohistorical.com
Key Personnel: Cur., Rosemary Faulkner
Historic Building: housed in the former dairy barn of the old County Hospital.
Collections: county history; agriculture; mining; logging; ranching; mining carts; farm wagons; paintings; tools; farming; pioneer artifacts.
Activities: hands-on exhibits.
Hours & Admission Prices: Thurs.-Sun. 10-4. Adults $3, senior citizens 60 & over $2, children under 12 $1. Closed New Year's Day; Easter; Christmas.

San Bernardino

* **ROBERT V. FULLERTON ART MUSEUM, CALIFORNIA STATE UNIVERSITY, SAN BERNARDINO, (M),** 5500 University Pkwy., San Bernardino, CA 92407-2318. Tel.: 909-537-3373. Fax: 909-537-7068.
E-mail: artmuseum@csusb.edu
Web Site: museum.csusb.edu
Founded: 1965.
Congressional District: 36
Key Personnel: Pres. University, Dr. Albert Karnig; Dir. & Cur., Eva Kirsch; Pres. Advisory Bd., Art Butler.
Personnel Profile: Full-Time Paid 5; Part-Time Paid 1; Part-Time Volunteers 8; Interns 4.
Governing Authority: public university. Parent Institution: California State University System. Subsidiary Institution: San Bernardino Campus. Tax-exempt: 501(c)(3).
University Art Museum.
Collections: Asian & Etruscan ceramics; African sculpture; Egyptian antiquities; contemporary prints; drawings; paintings; sculptures.
Major Exhibits: PAN: A Graphic Art Time Capsule of Avant-garde Europe 1895-1900, 11/09-1/23/10; Tomoko Suzuki: Rain, 11/09-2/20/10; Contemporary Works on Paper from the Permanent Collection, 11/09-2/20/10; Coming Home, 1/13/10-2/10; David Olivant, 2/21/10-5/15/10; Dylan Palmer & Colby Bird, 2/21/10-5/15/10; Timeless Enchantment: Richard Wagner's Ring of the Nibelung in Visual Arts, 4/8/10-7/10; 40th Annual Student Art Exhibition, 6/17/10-7/10.
Research Fields: Egyptian art; African sculpture.
Facilities: educational facilities; 6,500 sq. ft. exhibit space.
Activities: formal education programs for undergraduate students; art history lectures; gallery talks. Annual Events: Summer Egyptian Art Workshop for kids; Friends Holiday Event.
Publications: annual exhibition catalogs.
Hours & Admission Prices: Sept.-July Tues.-Wed. & Fri.-Sat. 10-5, Thurs. 10-7. Special Exhibits: admission fee charged; discounts to AAM, NARM & WMG members. Parking: $5. Closed major holidays. ♿
Attendance: 10,000 (estimated)
Membership: Student, Faculty, Staff & Senior $35; Individual $50; Family $75; Associate $100; Contributor $500; Benefactor $1,000.

San Carlos

HILLER AVIATION INSTITUTE, 601 Skyway Rd., San Carlos, CA 94070-2702. Tel.: 650-654-0200. Fax: 650-654-0220.
E-mail: museum@hiller.org
Web Site: www.hiller.org
Founded: 1995.
Congressional District: 12
Key Personnel: C.E.O. & Pres., Jeffrey Bass; Chm. (V), Steve Hiller; Vice Pres. Devel., Bernadette Mellott, MPA; Vice Pres. Mktg., Willie Turner; Archivist & Historian, Gordon Werne; Dir. Volunteers and Exhibits, North E. West; Education Programs Mgr., Jon Welte; Private Events Mgr., Lanie

Agulay; Registrar, Nicole DeGuzman; Dir. Merchandising & Retail, Duncan Chadwick; Restoration Shop Mgr., Newton Craven.
Personnel Profile: Full-Time Paid 8; Part-Time Paid 5; Part-Time Volunteers 140.
Governing Authority: private; nonprofit organization. Tax-exempt: 501(c)(3).
Aviation Museum & Research Center: housed at the historic San Carlos Airport.
Collections: aviation artifacts; past, present & future aviation technology.
Research Fields: progress of air transportation.
Facilities: classrooms; 35,000 sq. ft. exhibit space; 50-seat theater; aircraft restoration shop. Museum-related items for sale.
Activities: docent program; films; formal education programs for adults, children & college students; guided tours; lectures; rental gallery; temporary & traveling exhibitions; theater; conferences & seminars for scholars and corporate leaders to exchange ideas; special events; guest speakers. Museum Sponsors: Teacher Curriculum Guides; Flight Night (paper airplane contest for ages 8-17); Explorer Scout Post; Members Previews & Receptions.
Publications: quarterly, Briefings.
Hours & Admission Prices: Daily 10-5. Adults $10, senior citizens 65 & over and youth 5-17 $6; discounts to groups of 15 or more; members & children under 5 no charge. Closed New Year's Day; Easter; Thanksgiving; Christmas; occasional special event. ♿
Attendance: 75,000 (accurate)
Membership: Senior $35; Individual $50; Family $75; Sustaining $100; Supporting $250; Director's Circle $500; Patron $1,000; Benefactor $2,500; Trustee's Circle $5,000; Founder's Circle $10,000 & up.

San Diego

ANTHROPOLOGY MUSEUM, UNIVERSITY OF SAN DIEGO, (M), 5998 Alcala Park, San Diego, CA 92110-2476. Tel.: 619-260-4238. Fax: 619-260-2245.
E-mail: joycea@sandiego.edu
Web Site: www.sandiego.edu/anthropology/maycollection.php
Key Personnel: Dir., Dr. Alana Cordy-Collins; Mgr. Collections, Joyce Antorietto.
Personnel Profile: Part-Time Paid 1; Interns 1.
Governing Authority: private university.
Anthropology Museum.
Collections: Native American art & artifacts of southwestern U.S. and California from prehistoric to modern times; Alaskan & Northwest coast cultures; Baja California; Mexico Indians; Indians of Middle & South America.
Activities: lectures; loan, temporary & traveling exhibitions; artist-in-residence.
Hours & Admission Prices: Tues. & Thurs.-Fri. 1-3; other times by appointment. No charge. Closed university holidays. ♿
Attendance: 200 (estimated)

CABRILLO NATIONAL MONUMENT, 1800 Cabrillo Memorial Dr., San Diego, CA 92106-3601. Tel.: 619-557-5450. Fax: 619-226-6311. TTY: 619-222-8211.
Web Site: www.nps.gov/cabr/
Founded: 1913.
Congressional District: 49
Key Personnel: Acting Supt., Wendy Janssen; Chief of Interpretation, Karl Pierce; Historian, Robert Munson; Museum Technician, Tracie Cobb; Museum Shop Mgr., Karen Eccles.
Personnel Profile: Full-Time Paid 15; Part-Time Paid 10; Part-Time Volunteers 300; Interns 1.
Governing Authority: federal. Parent Institution: National Park Service. Tax-exempt.
Historic Site: commemorating the exploration of California coast & San Diego Bay by Juan Rodriguez Cabrillo in 1542.
Collections: commemorates the role that the historic Old Point Loma Lighthouse played in the development of maritime economy in San Diego & California; the WWI & WWII coastal defenses protecting San Diego Harbor; the ecologically sensitive coastal sage scrub and rocky intertidal communities & the ecology & annual migration of the Pacific gray whale. Historic Buildings: 1854 Old Point Loma Lighthouse furnished with artifacts of the period; coastal defense structures from WWI and WWII; exhibit in former army radio building.
Facilities: 1,500-vol. library of history & natural history books available for use on premises; 100-seat auditorium; reading room. Books & other museum-related items for sale.
Activities: informal introduction of film; formally organized educational programs; permanent & temporary exhibitions; environmental education films & discussions.
Publications: books, Cabrillo National Monument; Whale Primer; The Old Point Loma Lighthouse; Cabrillo's Log; The Cabrillo Era; Account of the Voyage of Juan Rodriguez Cabrillo; quarterly newsletter, Explorer; biannual park visitors guide, Cabrillo Journal; Junior Ranger Program; booklet, Just for Kids, Understanding the Life of Point Loma.
Hours & Admission Prices: Daily 9-5. $5 per vehicle, $3 per person; children under 16, seniors over 61, disabled U.S. citizens, members with annual Cabrillo, Golden Age, Golden Access, America the Beautiful Interagency, Senior or Access Pass no charge. ♿
Attendance: 886,620 (accurate)
Membership: Individual $35; Duo (2 people in same household) $60; Family (2 adults & 2 children) $75; Supporting $100; Sustaining $500; Benefactor $1,000.

COMMAND MUSEUM, MARINE CORPS RECRUIT DEPOT, SAN DIEGO, (M), off Old Town Exit by Freeway, Gate 4-Bldg. 26, 1600 Henderson Ave., San Diego, CA 92140-0001. Mailing Address: Bldg. 26 1600 Henderson Ave., Suite 212, San Diego, CA 92140-0001. Tel.: 619-524-6719, 6720 & 6038. Fax: 619-524-0076.
E-mail: barbara.mccurtis@usmc.mil
Web Site: www.usmchistory.com
Founded: 1987.
Congressional District: 41
Key Personnel: Dir., Barbara S. McCurtis; Business Mgr., Patricia Hawkins; Museum Shop Mgr., Bunny Hand.
Personnel Profile: Full-Time Paid 8; Full-Time Volunteers 25; Part-Time Paid 4; Part-Time Volunteers 30; Interns 1.
Governing Authority: federal; nonprofit. Parent Institution: Headquarters Marine Corps, Historical Center, Bldg. 58, Washington Navy Yard, Washington, DC 20374-0580 & G-3 Command Museum Sponsor. Subsidiary Institution: Commanding General, MCRD; Museum Historical Society. Tax-exempt: 501(c)(3).
Military Museum.
Collections: USMC military equipment, battlefield souvenirs; reference material; personal papers; accoutrements & historic costumes, 1846-present; photos; artwork; film; archives; U.S. Marine Corps & the Recruit Depot and the city of San Diego.
Research Fields: role of U.S. Marine Corps in southern California & the Pacific, 1846-present.
Facilities: 5,000-vol. library of military history, tactics, & technology material; 50-seat theater; 25,000 sq. ft. exhibit space; educational facilities. Gift items for sale.
Activities: guided tours; films; undergraduate & graduate internship programs with San Diego State University & the University of San Diego; docent program; temporary exhibitions.
Publications: quarterly newsletter.
Hours & Admission Prices: Mon.-Wed. & Fri.-Sat. 8-4, Thurs. 8-4:30. Photo ID required for admittance. No charge; donations accepted. Closed federal holidays. ♿
Attendance: 175,000 (accurate)
Membership: Historical Society: Regular $25; Family $35; Contributing $100.

FIREHOUSE MUSEUM, 1572 Columbia St., San Diego, CA 92101-2913. Tel.: 619-232-FIRE.
E-mail: info@thesdfirehousemuseum.org
Web Site: www.thesdfirehousemuseum.org
Key Personnel: C.E.O., Mike Colafrancesco
Fire-Fighting Museum.
Collections: fire-fighting equipment & memorabilia; photographs.
Hours & Admission Prices: Thurs.-Fri. 10-2, Sat.-Sun. 10-4. Adults $3, seniors & children $2.

FLYING LEATHERNECK AVIATION MUSEUM, (M), T-4203 Anderson Ave., San Diego, CA 92145-0001. Mailing Address: P.O. Box 452008, San Diego, CA 92145-2008. Tel.: 877-359-8762.
Web Site: www.flyingleathernecks.org
Personnel Profile: Full-Time Paid 7; Full-Time Volunteers 2; Part-Time Volunteers 60.
Governing Authority: Parent Institution: MCAS Miramar. Tax-exempt.
U.S. Marine Corps Aviation Museum.
Collections: Marine Corps aviation & aviators; period aircraft; portraits; military clothing & weapons; Marine women; trophies; Marine Corps Aviation Assoc. awards & trophies.
Hours & Admission Prices: Tues.-Sun. 9-3:30. No charge; donations accepted. ♿
Attendance: 30,000 (accurate)
Membership: Individual $35.

HISTORICAL SHRINE FOUNDATION OF SAN DIEGO COUNTY, 2482 San Diego Ave., San Diego, CA 92110-2838. Tel.: 619-297-9327.
Web Site: www.sandiegohistory.org
Founded: 1956.

Congressional District: 41
Key Personnel: Dir., Gary Beck; Vice Pres., David Todd.
Governing Authority: nonprofit organization; county. Tax-exempt.
Historic House Museum.
Collections: Historic Houses: 1856 Whaley House Museum; 1868 theater; 1869-1871 courthouse; 1851 Derby-Pendleton House, shipped from Maine; 1852 old town drugstore.
Research Fields: Whaley Papers - Old Town.
Facilities: Paperback books & pamphlets for sale.
Activities: research; lectures; rose garden; scent & savory garden; old town history program for 4th graders. Annual Event: Halloween Celebration.
Publications: Consignments to El Dorado; Thomas Whaley 1849 Journal; Thomas Whaley House, California's Oldest Town.
Hours & Admission Prices: Sun.-Tues. & Thurs. 10-9, Fri.-Sat. 10am-11pm. Daytime (before 7pm) adults $5, seniors 55 & over $4, children 3-12 $3; children under 2 no charge. Nighttime (after 7pm) adults $10, children $5. Halloween Oct. 28-31 10am-midnight. ♿
Attendance: 24,000 (accurate)
Membership: Individual $15; Family (3+) $35; Individual Patron $75; Sponsor $150.

JAPANESE FRIENDSHIP GARDEN SOCIETY OF SAN DIEGO, (M), 2215 Pan American Rd. E., San Diego, CA 92101-1656. Mailing Address: Balboa Park Administration Bldg., 2125 Park Blvd., San Diego, CA 92101-4792. Tel.: 619-232-2721. Fax: 619-232-0917.
E-mail: jfgsd@niwa.org
Web Site: www.niwa.org
Founded: 1979.
Key Personnel: Exec. Dir., Luanne Lao-Kanzawa; Pres., Dennis Otsuji; Chm. (V), Tom Yanagihara.
Personnel Profile: Full-Time Paid 6; Part-Time Paid 9; Part-Time Volunteers 5.
Governing Authority: Tax-exempt.
Japanese Gardens.
Collections: Japanese heritage & culture; plants; trees; sculptures; personal artifacts.
Major Exhibits: Shibori & Bingata Art, 1/10-2/10; Book Art, 3/10; Ceramic & Japanese Calligraphy, 4/10; Children's Day (T), 5/10; Japanese Paintings, 6/10-8/10; Miya Hannan Solo Exhibit, 9/10-11/10.
Activities: workshops; educational programs; classes.
Publications: newsletter.
Hours & Admission Prices: Memorial Day to Labor Day Mon.-Fri. 10-5, Sat.-Sun. 10-4; Sept.-May Tues.-Sun. 10-4. Adults $4, seniors, students & military $2.50; children 6 & under no charge.

MARITIME MUSEUM OF SAN DIEGO, 1492 N. Harbor Dr., San Diego, CA 92101-3309. Tel.: 619-234-9153. Fax: 619-234-8345.
E-mail: info@sdmaritime.org
Web Site: www.sdmaritime.org
Founded: 1948.
Congressional District: 44
Key Personnel: Pres. & C.E.O., Raymond E. Ashley; Dir. Devel., Karen Sowell Dyer; Event Coord., James Davis; Dir. Mktg., Robyn Gallant; Controller, Grace Rodriquez; Cur. Models & Collections Mgr., Kevin Sheehan; (V) Coord., Jeff Loman; Curriculum Coord., Susan Sirota; Editor, Mains'l Haul, Neva Sullaway; Cur. Exhibits, Mark Montijo; Office Mgr., Erminia Taranto; Dir. Group Sales, Gregg Doherty; Museum Store Mgr., Carolyn Goben.
Personnel Profile: Full-Time Paid 37; Full-Time Volunteers 15; Part-Time Paid 50; Part-Time Volunteers 400.
Governing Authority: nonprofit organization. Tax-exempt: 501(c)(3).
Maritime Museum: housed aboard four ships.
Collections: small crafts; ship models; navigation instruments; luxury liner memorabilia; tools; photographs; U.S. Navy artifacts; marine engineering; pleasure boating; maritime research library; submarines: USS Dolphin & Soviet b-39; replica ships Californian & Surprise. Historic Ships: 1863 Star of India; 1898 ferryboat Berkeley; 1904 steam yacht Medea, 1914 Pilot.
Major Exhibits: Masterpieces in Miniature, 11/09-5/10; Treasures from the Lost Galleon, 11/09-8/16/10; Mapping the Pacific Coast (T), 6/10/10-3/30/11.
Research Fields: San Diego, California & Pacific Ocean maritime history.
Facilities: library pertaining to maritime history and research available to accredited students & members on premises. Maritime & museum-related items for sale.
Activities: guided tours; speakers bureau; lectures; films; loan, permanent & temporary exhibits; demonstrations; membership program; historic boat rides; day sailing adventures. Educational programs available: docent guided tours (K-12 and beyond), Science of Seafaring workshops (grades K-8), Living history on the Star of India (grades 4-8), Science environmental studies and technology, field trips (Day on the Bay, Transportation Adventures) and Sea Chest Loan Program.
Publications: quarterly, Mains'l Haul: A Journal of Pacific Maritime History; newsletter, Full'n By.
Hours & Admission Prices: Daily 9-8. Adults $14, senior citizens & military $11, children 5-17 $8; discounts to groups, AAM & ICOM members; children under 5 & members no charge. ♿
Attendance: 225,504 (accurate)
Membership: Navigator (Senior 62 & over) & Apprentice (Student) $35; Mariner (Individual) $40; Crew (Family) $65; Boatswain $150; First Mate $500; Captain's Table $1,000; Captain's Cabin $5,000.

*** THE MARSTON HOUSE/SAN DIEGO HISTORICAL SOCIETY,** 3525 7th Ave., San Diego, CA 92103-5008. Mailing Address: 1649 El Prado, Ste. 3, San Diego, CA 92101-1664. Tel.: 619-298-3142. Fax: 619-232-6297.
Web Site: www.sandiegohistory.org
Formerly: George White and Anna Gunn Marston House/San Diego Historical Society
Founded: 1928.
Key Personnel: Dir., David Kahn; Pres. (V), Robert F. Adelizzi; Archivist, Jane Kenealy; Dir. Retail Operations, Ginger Raaka; Museum Shop Mgr., Trina Brewer.
Personnel Profile: Full-Time Paid 22; Part-Time Paid 14; Part-Time Volunteers 100; Interns 5.
Governing Authority: private; nonprofit organization. Parent Institution: San Diego Historical Society, P.O. Box 81825, San Diego 92138. Branch Museums: Villa Montezuma, 1925 K St., Serra Museum, 2727 Presidio Dr., Museum of San Diego History, 1649 El Prado, Ste. 3, San Diego, CA 92101. Tel.: 619-232-6203. Tax-exempt: 501(c)(3).
Historic House: built in 1905 for George Marston, a prominent San Diego merchant & civic leader, this structure is an early example of the work of San Diego architects William Hubbard & Irving Gill.
Collections: furnishings & decorative arts from the c.1900 arts & crafts movements.
Facilities: Gift items & books relating to the craftsman era for sale.
Activities: docent program; guided tours; special events; festivals & fairs.
Publications: quarterly newsletter, The San Diego Historical Society Times; quarterly, The Journal of San Diego History.
Hours & Admission Prices: Fri.-Sun. call for hours. Adults $5, students, seniors, military and groups $4, children 6-17 $2; discounts to National Trust, Time Travelers, KPBS, AAM & AAA members; members no charge. Closed New Year's Day; Thanksgiving; Christmas Eve & Day.
Attendance: 3,862 (accurate)
Membership: Student, Senior & Military $35; Individual $40; Family $60; Associate $100; Scholar's $250; Curator's Circle $500; Director's Circle $1,000; Chairman's Circle $2,500.

*** MINGEI INTERNATIONAL MUSEUM, (M),** 1439 El Prado, San Diego, CA 92101-1617. Tel.: 619-239-0003. Fax: 619-239-0605.
E-mail: mingei@mingei.org
Web Site: www.mingei.org
Founded: 1974.
Congressional District: 43
Key Personnel: C.E.O. & Dir., Rob Sidner; C.F.O., Alan Strang; Chair, Bd. Trustees (V), Frances Hamilton-White; Dir. Mktg., Charlotte Cagan; Dir. Devel., Cathy Sang; Registrar, Terri Bryson; Dir. Public Rels., Martha Ehringer; Mgr. Membership, Lotus Fragola; Coord. Devel., Heather Barnes; Administrative Asst., Karine Muschinske; Asian Art Cur., Lennox Tierney; Installation Coord. & Exhibit Designer, Jeremiah Maloney; Exhibition Preparator, Michael Grant; Collectors' Gallery Coord. & Museum Shop Mgr., Amy Schindler; Exhibition Preparator, Jenny Merullo; Exhibition Preparator, Jim Woodard; Exhibition Preparator, Dandridge Mitchell; Collectors' Gallery Asst., Marielle Mudgett-Olson; Collectors' Gallery Asst., Jessica Walker; Collectors' Gallery Asst., Schorsch Kaffenberger; Docent Coord., Linda Hirshberg; Dir. Education, Alison Rossi; Photographer, Anthony Scoggins; Coord. Library Svcs. & Volunteer Coord., Kristi Ehrig-Burges; Reception & Coord. Visitor Rels., Gloria Cooper; Admissions Asst., Mary Ann Balestrieri; Admission Asst., Dina Keppler; Registration Asst., Anne Dugger; Registration Asst., Sarah Winston; Dir. Security, Simon Leader; Security, Luis Flores; Security, Nhan Ha; Security, Dandridge Mitchell.
Personnel Profile: Full-Time Paid 23; Part-Time Paid 9; Part-Time Volunteers 150; Interns 7.
Governing Authority: nonprofit organization. Branch Museum: Mingei International Museum Escondido, 155 W. Grand Ave., Escondido, CA 92025. Tel: 760-735-3355, Fax: 760-735-3306. Tax-exempt: 501(c)(3).
International Folk Art, Craft & Design Museum.
Collections: arts of daily life from all cultures of the world.
Major Exhibits: Masters of Mid-Century California Modernism-Evelyn and

Jerome Aecerman, 11/09-1/10/10; Sonabai-Another Way of Seeing, 11/09-9/5/10; June Schwarcz-Enamel Vessels, 11/09-7/4/10; Fisch Out of Water, 11/09-12/10.
Research Fields: international exhibition materials; folk art; craft; design.
Facilities: 7,500-vol. library of audiovisual art reference library; theater; multimedia education center. Exhibition-related items for sale.
Activities: docent guided tours; illustrated lectures; artist craftsmen demonstrations; volunteer council; permanent collection loans; traveling exhibitions; outreach programs for San Diego Community.
Publications: 39 documentary publications; 21 DVDs & videotapes.
Hours & Admission Prices: Tues.-Sun. 10-4. Adults $7, seniors $5, youth 6-17, students, & military with ID $4; AAM members & members no charge. Closed national holidays. ♿
Attendance: 97,500 (estimated)
Membership: Individual $45; Friends & Family $60; Contributor $100; Sustainer $250; Patron $500; Director's Circle $1,250.

MISSION SAN DIEGO DE ALCALA, 10818 San Diego Mission Rd., San Diego, CA 92108-2498. Tel.: 619-283-7319. Fax: 619-283-7762.
E-mail: info@missionsandiego.com
Web Site: www.missionsandiego.com
Founded: 1769.
Key Personnel: Pastor, Rev. Msgr. Richard F. Duncanson; Assoc. Pastor, Rev. Bill Springer; Historian, Janet Bartel; Mgr., Rosie Cisneros; Museum Shop Mgr., Rhonda Sosa.
Personnel Profile: Part-Time Paid 1; Part-Time Volunteers 50.
Governing Authority: church. Affiliated with Roman Catholic Diocese of San Diego, 3888 Paducah Dr., San Diego 92117. Tax-exempt: 501(c)(3).
Historic Site Museum.
Collections: Native American baskets; American & Spanish colonial period artifacts; ecclesiastical artifacts; archaeological findings; archives.
Research Fields: archaeology.
Facilities: Gift items, reproductions & postcards for sale.
Activities: tote-a-tape tour; formally organized education programs for undergraduate & graduate students; permanent exhibitions.
Publications: booklet, Mission San Diego de Alcala; annual brochure, Mission San Diego de Alcala; book, San Diego de Alcala.
Hours & Admission Prices: Daily 9-4:45. Suggested Donation: adults $3, seniors $2, children $1. Closed Thanksgiving; Christmas. ♿
Attendance: 75,000 (estimated)

MUSEUM OF CONTEMPORARY ART SAN DIEGO - DOWNTOWN, 1001 & 1100 Kettner Blvd., San Diego, CA 92101. Mailing Address: 700 Prospect St., La Jolla, CA 92037-4291. Tel.: 858-454-3541. Fax: 619-814-4670.
Web Site: www.mcasd.org
Founded: 1941.
Key Personnel: Dir., Hugh M Davies; Pres. Bd. Trustees, Dr. Peter C. Farrell; Vice Pres., David C. Copley; Vice Pres., Maryanne Pfister; Vice Pres., Matthew Strauss; Deputy Dir., Charles E. Castle; Dir. External Affairs, Anne Farrell; Chief Advancement Officer, Jeanna Yoo; Sr. Cur., Stephanie Hanor; Dir. Communications, Denise Montgomery; Dir. Devel., Cynthia Tuomi; Registrar, Anne Marie Purkey Levine; Museum Shop Mgr., Monique Fuentes.
Personnel Profile: Full-Time Paid 43; Part-Time Paid 40; Part-Time Volunteers 105; Interns 6.
Governing Authority: nonprofit organization. Additional Location: MCASD, 700 Prospect St., La Jolla, CA 92037. Tax-exempt: 501(c)(3).
Art Museum.
Collections: contemporary art including paintings, sculpture, drawings & prints; photography; video art; installation.
Major Exhibits: Tara Donovan (T), 11/09-2/10; Laerke Lavta, 3/10-6/10; Cerca Series: Lael Corbin, 3/10-6/10; Ruben Ochoa, 3/10-6/10; Cerca Series: Mara De Luca, 3/10-6/10; Viva La Revolucion: A Dialogue With The Urban Landscape, 7/10-11/10.
Research Fields: contemporary art.
Facilities: 17,000 sq. ft. exhibit space; 120-seat auditorium. Museum-related items for sale.
Activities: lectures; films; seminars; gallery talks; educational programs; concerts; inter-museum loans, temporary & traveling exhibitions.
Publications: quarterly newsletter with calendar of events; exhibition catalogs; educational brochures; membership brochure; general information brochure.
Hours & Admission Prices: Thurs.-Tues. 11-5, third Thurs. 11-7. Adults $10, senior citizens & military $5; discounts to AAM & ICOM members; 25 & under and members no charge. Closed New Year's Day; Thanksgiving; Christmas. Admission valid for 7 days at all MCASD locations. ♿
Attendance: 168,000 (estimated)
Membership: Artist & Student $35; Active $75; Contributor $150; Patron $300; Donor $600-$1,499; Benefactor $1,500-$2,499; stART Up $2,500; Contemporary Collectors $5,000; International Collectors $10,000. Corporate Members: $1,500 & up.

* **MUSEUM OF PHOTOGRAPHIC ARTS, (M),** 1649 El Prado, Balboa Park, San Diego, CA 92101. Tel.: 619-238-7559. Fax: 619-238-8777.
E-mail: info@mopa.org
Web Site: www.mopa.org
Founded: 1983.
Congressional District: 49
Key Personnel: Dir., Deborah Klochko; Pres. Bd., Gail Bryan; Deputy Dir., Vivian Kung Haga; Operations Asst., John Hogan; Accounting Mgr., Catherine Anderson; Registrar, Barbara Pope; Dir. Exhibitions & Design, Scott Davis; Cur. Photography, Carol McCusker; Sales & Events Coord., Melissa Pfeiffa; Mgr. Membership, Susan George; Mktg. & Communications Coord., Aki Martin; Dir. Education & Public Programs, Amber Lucero-Criswell; Docent & Youth Programs Coord., Lori Sokolonski; Film & Public Programs Mgr., Priscilla Parra; Outreach & Educator Programs Mgr., Shana Cinquemani; Education Asst., Farzad Nikbakht; Mgr. Library, Holland Kessinger; Store & Visitor Svcs. Mgr., Kristen Hurst; Tour & Visitor Svcs. Coord., Kristie Muller; Guest Svcs. Coord., Sam Renauldo; Library Asst., Ingrid Martis; Volunteer Coord., Heather Thomas; Care Mgr., Julie Lawrence.
Personnel Profile: Full-Time Paid 17; Part-Time Paid 13; Part-Time Volunteers 25; Interns 10.
Governing Authority: nonprofit organization. Tax-exempt: 501(c)(3).
Photographic Arts.
Collections: photography.
Major Exhibits: Picturing the Process: Beauty & Body Image, 1/30/10-7/25/10; State of Minds: The 2010 California Invitational, 2/6/10-5/16/10.
Facilities: 27,000-vol. library pertaining to photography; 5,500 sq. ft. exhibit space; 228 seat theater; classrooms. Museum-related items for sale.
Activities: lectures; docent program; film programs; traveling exhibitions; workshops; school tours; educator packets for selected exhibitions; children summer camps; special events; photographic workshops for adults.
Publications: periodic exhibition catalogues; bi-weekly e-newsletter.
Hours & Admission Prices: Tues.-Sun. 10-5; docent tours by appointment. Gallery: adults $6, students, seniors & active military $4; children under 12, members, & San Diego residents on 2nd Tues. of the month no charge. Closed New Year's Day; Thanksgiving; Christmas Day . ♿
Attendance: 101,019 (accurate)
Membership: Student $25; Senior & Educator $40; Individual $50; Duo Senior $70; Duo & Family $75; Photographer's Circle $150; Silver Circle $250; Platinum Circle $500; Curator's Circle $1,000; Director's Circle $2,500.

MUSEUM OF SAN DIEGO HISTORY AND RESEARCH LIBRARY, 1649 El Prado, Ste. 3, San Diego, CA 92101-1664. Tel.: 619-232-6203, ext. 109. Fax: 619-232-6297.
E-mail: angela.sieckman@sandiegohistory.org
Web Site: www.sandiegohistory.org
Formerly: San Diego Historical Society Museum and Research Archives
Founded: 1928.
Congressional District: 4
Key Personnel: Dir., David Kahn; Bd. Pres. (V), Robert Adelizzi; Museum Shop Mgr., Trina Brewer.
Personnel Profile: Full-Time Paid 22; Full-Time Volunteers 14; Part-Time Paid 14; Part-Time Volunteers 107.
Governing Authority: private; nonprofit organization. Tax-exempt: 501(c)(3).
History Museum & Research Archives.
Collections: concentration on San Diego's history & growth since the 1840s; photographic negatives; historical & art-related materials.
Facilities: library; 100-seat theater; research archives with reading room. Books & gift items for sale.
Activities: school programs; public programs; tours; lectures; temporary & permanent exhibitions.
Publications: quarterly newsletter, The San Diego Historical Society Times; quarterly, The Journal of San Diego History; newsletter, The Times.
Hours & Admission Prices: Museum: daily 10-5. Adults $5, seniors, students & military with ID $4, children 6-17 $2; discounts to groups & AAM members; members and children 5 & under no charge. Research Library: Thurs.-Sat. 9:30-1. Adults $6, students with ID $2. Closed New Year's Day; Thanksgiving; Christmas Eve & Day. ♿
Attendance: 25,200 (accurate)
Membership: Family & Household Circle $60; Century Circle $100; Scholar's Circle $250; Curator's Circle $500; Director's Circle $1,000.

NEW AMERICANS MUSEUM, (M), 2825 Dewey Rd., Ste. 102, San Diego, CA 92106-6147. Tel.: 619-255-8908. Fax: 619-269-3499.
E-mail: contactus@namuseum.org
Web Site: www.newamericansmuseum.org
Formerly: New Americans Immigration Museum & Learning Center

Founded: 2001.
Key Personnel: Exec. Dir., Gayle Hom; Founder, Deborah Szekely; Chm. (V), Stacey Goto; Program Dir., Miguel-Angel Soria.
Personnel Profile: Full-Time Paid 4; Part-Time Volunteers 28; Interns 2.
Governing Authority: private; nonprofit organization. Tax-exempt: 501(c)(3).
Cultural Center.
Collections: American immigrants.
Hours & Admission Prices: Wed.-Sun. 11-5. No charge; donations accepted. Closed major holidays. ♿
Membership: Student, Senior & Military $25; Individual $50.

THE NEW CHILDREN'S MUSEUM, 200 W. Island Ave., San Diego, CA 92101-6850. Tel.: 619-233-8792. Fax: 619-233-8796.
Web Site: www.thinkplaycreate.org
Formerly: Children's Museum/Museo de Los Ninos San Diego
Founded: 1981.
Congressional District: 41
Key Personnel: Bd. Pres., Patsy Marino; Exec. Dir., Rachel Teagle; C.O.O., Donna Gough; Dir. External Affairs & Mktg., Jessica Hanson York.
Personnel Profile: Full-Time Paid 22; Part-Time Paid 30; Part-Time Volunteers 40; Interns 8.
Governing Authority: nonprofit organization. Tax-exempt: 501(c)(3).
Children's Museum.
Collections: learning through the arts, providing hands-on, minds-on experiences for all ages.
Facilities: performance studio; cafe; classrooms. Museum-related items for sale.
Activities: organized educational programs for children; volunteer program; student internships offered to college students; rental facilities; birthday parties; participatory exhibitions; Teen Advisory Council; school visits; workshops; summer camps.
Hours & Admission Prices: Call for hours. Adults $10; discounts to AAM members. ♿
Attendance: 190,000 (accurate)
Membership: Family $85; Friend $150; Neighbor $500.

OLD TOWN SAN DIEGO STATE HISTORIC PARK, 4002 Wallace St., San Diego, CA 92110-2743. Mailing Address: 4477 Pacific Hwy., San Diego, CA 92110-3136. Tel.: 619-220-5422. Fax: 619-220-7387.
Web Site: www.parks.ca.gov
Founded: 1968.
Congressional District: 41
Key Personnel: District Supt., Ronilee Clark.
Personnel Profile: Full-Time Paid 10; Part-Time Paid 12; Part-Time Volunteers 75.
Governing Authority: state. Parent Institution: California Department of Parks & Recreation, P.O. Box 2390, Sacramento, CA 95814. Tax-exempt.
State Park Museum.
Collections: preservation project. Historic Houses: 1827 Casa de Estudillo; 1835 Casa de Machado y Stewart; 1865 Mason Street school; 1868 San Diego Union building; c.1830 Casa de Machado y Silvas; 1829 Casa de Bandini; c.1869 Seeley Stables; Casa de Rodriguez; Pedrorena Adobe; c.1850 U.S. House; c.1847 Light & Freeman Adobe; c.1851 Wrightington Adobe; c.1862 McCoy House; c.1853 Robinson Rose.
Research Fields: preservation project; archaeology; history of California.
Activities: guided tours; lectures; formally organized education programs for children; permanent exhibitions; craft demonstrations; living history programs.
Publications: tour guide, Old Town San Diego State Historic Park; map, California State Park.
Hours & Admission Prices: Daily 10-5. No charge; donations accepted. Closed New Year's Day; Thanksgiving; Christmas. ♿
Attendance: 7,000,000 (estimated)
Membership: Individual $7-$10.

REUBEN H. FLEET SCIENCE CENTER, 1875 El Prado, Balboa Park, San Diego, CA 92101-1625. Mailing Address: P.O. Box 33303, San Diego, CA 92163-3303. Tel.: 619-238-1233. Fax: 619-685-5771.
E-mail: jkirsch@rhfleet.org
Web Site: www.rhfleet.org
Founded: 1973.
Congressional District: 42
Key Personnel: Exec. Dir., Dr. Jeffrey W. Kirsch; Bd. Pres., Dr. Chuck Wheatley, III; C.O.O., Craig Blower; Consulting Astronomer, Grant Miller; Dir. Devel., Dan Vecchitto; Deputy Exec. Dir. Education & Exhibition Programs, Lynne Kennedy; Dir. Mktg. & Communications, Jennifer Lee; Sr. Dir. Engineering & Facilities, Dave McGrew; Museum Shop Mgr., David Miller.
Personnel Profile: Full-Time Paid 45; Part-Time Paid 64; Part-Time Volunteers 150; Interns 30.
Governing Authority: board of trustees. Parent Institution: San Diego Space & Science Foundation. Tax-exempt: 501(c)(3).
Science Center & IMAX Dome Theater.
Collections: interactive science exhibits; IMAX films & planetarium presentations, simulator rides, virtual reality exhibit.
Research Fields: cognitive issues relating to scientific concepts.
Facilities: hemisphere screen; 340-seat planetarium theatre with Omnimax Film Projection System; 4 wheelchair spaces & 122-seat lecture hall; 23-seat motion base simulator; 180-seat community forum; Challenger Learning Center. Scientific books, kits & other educational items for sale.
Activities: lectures; films; science workshops; audience participation; simulator rides; Nierman Challenger Learning Center missions; traveling & permanent exhibitions; corporate special events; teachers inquiry institute; senior programs; Kid City.
Publications: annual report; quarterly/monthly newsletter members only newsletter; monthly e-newsletter.
Hours & Admission Prices: Daily 9:30 (closing times varies). Galleries: adults $10, seniors 65 & over and juniors 3-12 $8.75; members no charge. Gallery & IMAX: adults $14.50, seniors 65 & over and juniors 3-12 $11.75, members $9.75. ♿
Attendance: 477,557 (accurate)
Membership: Individual & Senior $52; Exhibit Experience $53; Family $79. Discovery Society: Adventurer $150; Voyager $300; Explorer $500; Pioneer $1,000; Innovator $2,500. Corporate Partnerships: Friend $250; Associate $500; Sponsor $1,000; Patron $2,500; Benefactor $5,000; Leader $10,000 & up.

ROBINSON-ROSE HOUSE, 4002 Wallace St., San Diego, CA 92110-2743. Tel.: 619-220-5422.
Web Site: www.parks.ca.gov
Key Personnel: Supervising Ranger, Gary Olson
Historic House Museum: housed in the original commercial center of old San Diego.
Collections: local history; model of Old Town in 1872.
Hours & Admission Prices: Daily 10-5. No charge. Closed New Year's Day; Thanksgiving; Christmas.

* **SAN DIEGO AIR & SPACE MUSEUM,** 2001 Pan American Plaza, San Diego, CA 92101-1636. Tel.: 619-234-8291, ext. 10. Fax: 619-233-4526.
Web Site: www.sandiegoairandspace.org
Formerly: San Diego Aerospace Museum
Founded: 1961.
Congressional District: 41
Key Personnel: Pres., James Kidrick; Chm., Lynda Moerschvalcher; Exec. Asst., Jessica Packard.
Personnel Profile: Full-Time Paid 31; Full-Time Volunteers 5; Part-Time Paid 14; Part-Time Volunteers 241.
Governing Authority: nonprofit organization. Subsidiary Institutions: San Diego Air & Space Technology Center; San Diego Aerospace Foundation. Tax-exempt: 501(c)(3) & 170(b)(1)(A).
History Museum.
Collections: aviation; space; technology; historical aircraft & engines; N. Paul Whittier Historical Aviation Library; aeronautical books, magazines, manuals, documents & photographs.
Research Fields: aviation; science; history.
Facilities: 18,000-vol. library of historical, books pertaining to aviation available on premises by special arrangements.
Activities: films; inter-museum loan & permanent exhibitions; temporary aviation art shows.
Publications: magazine; bimonthly newsletter; Air Capital of the West; quarterly newsletter, Flight Lines.
Hours & Admission Prices: Winter: daily 10-4:30; Summer: extended hours. Adults 12 & over $15, seniors, students & retired military $12, youth 3-11 $6; discounts to groups, AAM & Smithsonian Institution Museum of Flight members; children under 3, active military, & members no charge. Closed New Year's Day; Thanksgiving; Christmas. ♿
Attendance: 175,000 (accurate)
Membership: Senior $30; Individual $40; Family $55; Wings Club $150; Mercury $500; Apollo $1,000.

SAN DIEGO AUTOMOTIVE MUSEUM, 2080 Pan American Plaza, Balboa Park, San Diego, CA 92101-1636. Tel.: 619-231-2886. Fax: 619-231-9869.
E-mail: info@sdautomuseum.org
Web Site: www.sdautomuseum.org
Founded: 1988.
Congressional District: 49

Key Personnel: Exec. Dir., Paula Brandes; Mgr. Exhibits, David Woodin; Dir. Education, Kenn Colclasure; Accounting, Faye Levy; Retail Mgr., Bruce Bassham; Librarian, Guy Preuss; Cur., Rebecca Morales, Ph.D.; Asst. Cur., David Woodin.
Personnel Profile: Full-Time Paid 5; Part-Time Paid 8; Part-Time Volunteers 48.
Governing Authority: private; nonprofit organization. Tax-exempt: 501(c)(3).
Transportation Museum: housed in a structure built in 1935 for the Pan American Exposition as the California State Building.
Collections: international automobiles & automotive memorabilia, motorcycles, engines and related archival & attendant accoutrements.
Major Exhibits: Cars & Society, 1/10-12/10.
Research Fields: automotive history 1890s-present.
Facilities: library; 40,000 sq. ft. exhibit space. Gift items for sale.
Activities: docent program; guided tours; hobby workshops; lectures; loan, participatory & temporary exhibitions; clubs; show roll-outs.
Publications: quarterly newsletter, Auto Museum News.
Hours & Admission Prices: Daily 10-5. Adults $8, senior citizens 65 & over and active military w/ID $6, students $5, children 6-15 $4; children under 6 & members no charge. Closed New Year's Day; Thanksgiving; Christmas. ♿
Attendance: 100,000 (estimated)
Membership: Individual $45; Car Club $55; Family $65; Friend of the Museum $200; Patron $1,000; Wheels 100 $10,000.

SAN DIEGO CHINESE HISTORICAL MUSEUM, 404 Third Ave., San Diego, CA 92101-6803. Tel.: 619-338-9888. Fax: 619-338-9889.
E-mail: info@sdchm.org
Web Site: www.sdchm.org
Key Personnel: Pres., Michael Lee; Cur., Murray K. Lee.
Governing Authority: nonprofit organization. Admission $2; members & children under 12 no charge.
Culturally Specific.
Collections: Chinese culture; maps; books; period art; personal artifacts; embroidered shoes; teapots.
Facilities: library; garden.
Activities: research.
Hours & Admission Prices: Tues.-Sat. 10:30-4, Sun. 12-4. No charge; donations accepted.

SAN DIEGO HALL OF CHAMPIONS SPORTS MUSEUM, 2131 Pan American Plaza, Balboa Park, San Diego, CA 92101-1683. Tel.: 619-234-2544. Fax: 619-234-4543.
E-mail: info@sdhoc.com
Web Site: www.sdhoc.com
Founded: 1961.
Congressional District: 44
Key Personnel: C.E.O., Pres. & Exec. Dir., Alan Kidd; Chm. (V), Ron Fowler; Cur., Todd Tobias; Museum Shop Mgr., Gil Johnson.
Personnel Profile: Full-Time Paid 14; Part-Time Paid 6; Part-Time Volunteers 60; Interns 4.
Governing Authority: nonprofit organization. Tax-exempt: 501(c)(3).
Sports Museum & Breitbard Hall of Fame: housed in the Federal Building in Balboa Park.
Collections: sports memorabilia & artifacts.
Research Fields: sport.
Facilities: resource center including library containing volumes, periodicals, films & tapes pertaining to sports.
Activities: guided tours; films; permanent exhibitions; seminars; clinics & counseling.
Publications: quarterly newsletter.
Hours & Admission Prices: Daily 10-4:30. Adults $8, senior citizens, military & students with ID $6, children 7-17 $4; discounts to AAM & ICOM members; members & children under 7 no charge. Closed New Years Day; Thanksgiving; Christmas. ♿
Attendance: 94,000 (accurate)
Membership: Friends of Bob $100; Patron $500; Bronze $1,000; Silver $2,500; Gold $5,000; Platinum $10,000.

* **SAN DIEGO MODEL RAILROAD MUSEUM, INC., (M),** 1649 El Prado, San Diego, CA 92101-1662. Tel.: 619-696-0199. Fax: 619-696-0239.
Web Site: www.sdmrm.org
Founded: 1980.
Congressional District: 41
Key Personnel: C.E.O. & Pres., Jay Styron; Exec. Dir., John A. Rotsart; C.F.O. Treas., Robert McBane; Gift Shop Mgr., Veronique Rotsart.
Personnel Profile: Full-Time Paid 1; Part-Time Paid 25; Part-Time Volunteers 300; Interns 1.
Governing Authority: nonprofit organization. Tax-exempt: 501(c)(3).
Model Railroad Museum: housed on site of 1915 Panama-California Exposition in the Casa de Balboa building.
Collections: 24,000 sq. ft. of working model railroads depicting railroads in southern California, San Diego County & Western roads; toy trains which include interactive throttles; history & significance of railroads & the development of model railroading; full-size railroad artifacts including a working semaphore signal; model railroad magazines.
Research Fields: southern California railroads, including San Diego & Arizona Eastern, Santa Fe & Southern Pacific; history of model railroading.
Facilities: 5,000-vol. library pertaining to railroads. Railroad-related items for sale.
Activities: operating model trains; guided tours; films & videos on actual railroads; arts festivals; hobby workshops; traveling & participatory exhibits; field trips; study clubs; traveling slide show & lecture on the museum exhibits.
Publications: quarterly newsletter, San Diego Telegraph; self-guided tour brochure.
Hours & Admission Prices: Museum: Tues.-Fri. 11-4, Sat.-Sun. 11-5; guided tours by appointment. Library: see website for hours. Adults $7, senior citizens 65 & over $6, students $3, military & dependents $2.50; discounts to CAM, Assoc. of RR Museums, SD Inter-Museum Promotion Council members, AAM & ICOM members; members, San Diego county residents 1st Tues. of month & children 15 and under no charge. Closed Thanksgiving; Christmas. ♿
Attendance: 133,000 (accurate)
Membership: Annual $20; Family $30; Contributing $50; Life $500; Benefactor $1,000; Patron $2,500; Founder $7,500.

* **SAN DIEGO MUSEUM OF ART, (M),** Balboa Park, 1450 El Prado, San Diego, CA 92101. Mailing Address: P.O. Box 122107, San Diego, CA 92112-2107. Tel.: 619-232-7931. Fax: 619-232-9367.
E-mail: library@sdma.org
Web Site: www.sdmart.org
Founded: 1925.
Congressional District: 42
Key Personnel: Pres. (V), Dr. Kenneth J. Widder, Ph.D.; Cur. Asian Art, Sonya Quintanilla, Ph.D.; Deputy Dir. Curatorial Affairs, Julia Marciari-Alexander; Cur. European Art, John Marciari; Deputy Dir. Education & Interpretation, Vas Prabhu; Deputy Dir. Operations & Finance, Julianne Markow; Deputy Dir. External Affairs, Katy McDonald; Human Resources Mgr., Laura Boyd; Library Mgr., James Grebl; Museum Store Mgr., Warren Herman.
Personnel Profile: Full-Time Paid 54; Part-Time Paid 10; Part-Time Volunteers 259; Interns 5.
Governing Authority: nonprofit organization. Tax-exempt: 501(c)(3).
Art Museum: housed in a Spanish plateresque-style building located on the site of the Panama/California International Exposition.
Collections: 14th- to 20th-century European paintings, sculpture & decorative arts including Italian Renaissance & Spanish Baroque painting; Asian arts, including Chinese, Japanese, Korean, Thai, & Indian painting, sculpture, ceramics, stone & metal work; contemporary painting & sculpture; Edward Binney 3rd Collection of Indian paintings.
Research Fields: pertaining to works in the museum collections.
Facilities: non-circulating library with 30,000 art books & catalogs; slides; subject & artists files available on premises; 400-seat auditorium; cafe. Books & museum-related items for sale.
Activities: guided tours; lectures; gallery talks; concerts; formally organized education programs for children, adults & undergraduate college students; inter-museum loan; permanent, temporary & traveling exhibitions; art school for children, teens, & adults; K-12 art exhibition.
Publications: quarterly magazine; electronic newsletter, Muse News; exhibition catalogs.
Hours & Admission Prices: Summer: Tues.-Wed. & Fri.-Sun. 10-6, Thurs. 10-9; Winter: Tues.-Sun. 10-6. Adults $10, seniors & military $8, students $7, children 6-17 $4; AAM members, members and children 5 & under no charge. Closed New Year's Day; Thanksgiving; Christmas. ♿
Attendance: 350,000 (accurate)
Membership: Student & Educator $35; Individual $45; Dual & Household $75; Friend $175; Sponsor $500; President's Circle $1,500; Patron's Circle $3,000; Director's Circle $5,000; Benefactor's Circle $10,000. Seniors & Active Military discounts available.

* **SAN DIEGO MUSEUM OF MAN, (M),** 1350 El Prado, Balboa Park, San Diego, CA 92101-1681. Tel.: 619-239-2001. Fax: 619-239-2749.
E-mail: mbrooksgonyer@museumofman.org
Web Site: www.museumofman.org
Founded: 1915.
Congressional District: 49

Key Personnel: Chm. & Pres. (V), Karen Berger; C.O.O., MaryAnn Brooks-Gonyer; Registrar, Linda Fisk; Librarian, M. Jane Bentley; Cur. Physical Anthropology, Tori Randall; Dir. Devel., Gail Alsobrook; Museum Shop Mgr., Dennis Fox.
Personnel Profile: Full-Time Paid 27; Part-Time Paid 11; Part-Time Volunteers 40; Interns 10.
Governing Authority: society. Tax-exempt: 501(c)(3).
Anthropology Museum.
Collections: over 140,000 artifacts, photographs & cultural objects relating to ethnological & archaeological collections pertaining to peoples of the Western Americas; physical anthropology primarily from California, the Southwest & Peru; Egyptian antiquities from Tell el-Amarna, Abydos & other sites. Historical Building: 1915 California Building.
Major Exhibits: Costume: Identity & Power in the Americas, 2/10; Games, 6/10.
Research Fields: field work in California archaeology; The Kuna of Panama; physical anthropology; Western Hemisphere aborigines.
Facilities: 13,510-vol. library of books and 72 archival manuscripts & periodicals on anthropology, archaeology, ethnology available for inter-library loan & for scholars, teachers & graduate students. Arts & craft items from the Southwest & around the world for sale.
Activities: guided tours; formally organized education programs for children; curatorial seminar series; docent program or council; permanent & temporary exhibitions.
Publications: San Diego Museum Papers; Ethnic Technology Notes; leaflets; Journey to the Copper Age: Archeology in the Holy Land, 2007.
Hours & Admission Prices: Daily 10-4:30. Adults $10, seniors, students, military & youth 13-17 $7.50, children 3-12 $5; discounts to AAM & ICOM members; members & children under 3 no charge. Closed Thanksgiving; Christmas. ♿
Attendance: 189,364 (accurate)
Membership: Student $20; Individual $45; Family & Grandparent $60; Friend $125; Sponsor $250; President's Associate $500; Patron $1,000; Los Compadres $5,000.

* **SAN DIEGO NATURAL HISTORY MUSEUM, (M),** 1788 El Prado, Balboa Pk., San Diego, CA 92101. Mailing Address: P.O. Box 121390, San Diego, CA 92112-1390. Tel.: 619-232-3821. Fax: 619-232-0248.
E-mail: mhager@sdnhm.org
Web Site: www.sdnhm.org
Founded: 1874.
Congressional District: 49
Key Personnel: Pres. & C.E.O., Dr. Michael W. Hager; Bd. Chm., Stephen Cohen; Bd. Pres., Eleanor Navarra; Vice Pres. Institutional Advancement, Ann Ladden; C.O.O., George Brooks-Gonyer; Vice Pres., Public Programs, James Stone; Dir. Devel. & Membership, Eowyn Bates; Dir. Biodiversity Research Center of the Californias, Michael Wall; Dir. Mktg. & Public Rels., Delle Willett; Dir. Binational Education, Doretta Winkelman; Dir. Exhibits, Tim Murray; Dir. Research Library, Margaret Dykens; Dir. Volunteer Svcs., Janet Morris; Dir. Visual Media, Cary Canning; Dir. Foundation Rels., Elizabeth Castillo; Cur. Botany, Dr. Jon Rebman; Cur. Paleontology, Dr. Thomas Demere; Cur. Herpetology, Dr. Brad Hollingsworth; Mgr. Ornithology & Mammalogy Collections, Phil Unitt; Museum Shop Mgr., Nancy Stevens; Mgr. AV Svcs., Alexis McKee; Mgr. Public Programs, Lindy Villa; Mgr. School Programs, Sara Aglietti.
Personnel Profile: Full-Time Paid 105; Part-Time Paid 63; Part-Time Volunteers 645; Interns 20.
Governing Authority: society. Parent Institution: San Diego Society of Natural History. Tax-exempt: 501(c)(3).
Natural History Museum
Collections: botany; entomology; geology; herpetology; mammalogy; marine invertebrates; mineralogy; ornithology; regional ecology & paleontology
Major Exhibits: Darwin (T), 11/09-2/10; Dinosaurs (T), 3/27/10-9/6/10; Gems and Minerals, 5/10-5/12; Lizards and Snakes Alive (T), 10/10-3/11.
Research Fields: botany; entomology; herpetology; mammalogy; mineralogy; ornithology; paleontology; marine invertebrates.
Facilities: 90,000-vol. research library; research center; science center; 300-seat large-format theatre; 4 classrooms; 8,500 sq. ft. exhibit space; catering facilities. Museum-related items for sale.
Activities: traveling exhibitions; large-format films; natural history classes, field trips, & lecture series for all ages; scout badge overnights; summer camps; school tours & lab programs; specimen loan library; school outreach programs; binational teacher education; free public nature hikes; guided hikes for the visually impaired; long-range expedition travel; activities for members & volunteers.
Publications: member newsletter, Field Notes; education programs catalog; proceedings; occasional papers.
Hours & Admission Prices: Daily 10-5. Adults $13, seniors, military, student & youth 13-17 $11, children 3-12 $7; discounts to college, KPBS, & AAA members; children 2 & under and members no charge. Closed Thanksgiving; Christmas. ♿
Attendance: 743,446 (accurate)
Membership: Student $25; Senior $35; Dual Senior & Individual $55; Grandparents & Family $70; Kate Sessions Circle $175-$274; Daniel Cleveland Circle $275-$524; A.R. Valentein Circle $525-$1,199; John Audubon $1,200-$2,499; John Muir $2,500-$4,999; Carl Linnaeus $5,000-$9,999; Charles Darwin $10,000 & up.

* **SAN DIEGO ZOO, (M),** 2920 Zoo Dr., San Diego, CA 92101-1693. Mailing Address: P.O. Box 120551, San Diego, CA 92112-0551. Tel.: 619-231-1515 & 685-3291. Fax: 619-557-3970.
E-mail: publicrelations@sandiegozoo.org
Web Site: www.sandiegozoo.org
Founded: 1916.
Congressional District: 41
Key Personnel: C.E.O., Douglas G. Myers; Zoo Dir., Richard Farrar; Collections Dir., Bob Wiese, Ph.D.; Chm. & Pres. (V), Berit Durler; Deputy Dir., Matthew Musella; Dir. Conservation & Science, Allison Alberts, Ph.D.; Deputy Dir. Conservation & Science, Alan Lieberman; Cur. Mammals, Carmi Penny; Cur. Birds, David Rimlinger; Gen. Cur. Reptiles, Donal Boyer; Devel. Dir., Mark Stuart; Mktg. Dir., Ted Molter; Registrar, Toni Giezendanner; Veterinary Svcs., Patrick Morris, D.V.M.; Nutritionist, Michael Schlegel, Ph.D.; Pathologist, Bruce Rideout, D.V.M., Ph.D.; Geneticist, Oliver Ryder, Ph.D.; Assoc. Education Dir., Victoria Garrison; Architecture & Planning Dir., David E. Rice, FAIA; Library Mgr., Linda Coates; Food Svcs. Dir., John Kling; Reproductive Physiologist, Barbara Durrant, Ph.D.; Dir. Corporate Merchandising & Museum Shop Mgr., Yvonne Miles.
Personnel Profile: Full-Time Paid 2,000.
Governing Authority: society. Parent Institution: Zoological Society of San Diego. Subsidiary Institution: San Diego Wild Animal Park, CRES. Tax-exempt: 501(c)(3).
Zoo & Botanical Garden.
Collections: birds, mammals, reptiles & amphibians of the world; botany; scientific & photo library collections; cytogenetic collections (cell strings, semen & eggs).
Research Fields: veterinary medicine & pathology; zoology; animal reproduction & conservation; in situ conservation.
Facilities: 400,000 image photographic library supporting museum & collections; botanical gardens; nature center; 200-seat auditorium; 1,500-seat & 3,000-seat amphitheaters; restaurant; classrooms. Books, artifacts, jewelry & other museum-related items for sale.
Activities: guided tours; TV & radio programs; formally organized educational programs; animal shows; lecture & special events for members; ecotourism; nighttime zoo experience; worldwide tours; interactive website.
Publications: monthly magazine, Zoonooz; guidebook, The San Diego Zoo; quarterly children's newsletter, Koala Club News; miscellaneous publications; books, A World of Animals, The San Diego Zoo; Mr. Zoo-The Life & Legacy of Dr. Charles Schroeder.
Hours & Admission Prices: June 21-Labor Day daily 9-10; Sept.-June 20 daily 9-4. Adults 12 & over $34, children 3-11 $24; discounts to groups; Koala Club members, children under 3 & members no charge. ♿
Attendance: 3,200,000 (accurate)
Membership: Koala Club 3-11 $21, 12-17 $25; Senior Passes: Single $35; Dual $50; Regular: Single $66; Dual $84; Diamond Club New: $126; Keeper's Club $150; Curator's Club $250; Director's Club $500; President's Associates $1,000; President's Partners $2,500.

SEAWORLD SAN DIEGO, 500 Sea World Dr., San Diego, CA 92109-7995. Tel.: 800-257-4268. Fax: 619-226-3996. TDD: 619-226-3907.
Web Site: www.seaworldsandiego.com
Founded: 1964.
Congressional District: 41
Key Personnel: Exec. Vice Pres. & Gen. Mgr., Andy Fichthorn; Vice Pres. Zoological Operations, Michael Scarpuzzi; Vice Pres. Mktg., Marilyn Hannes; Vice Pres. Entertainment, Adrian Fischer; Vice Pres. Operations, David Cromwell.
Personnel Profile: Full-Time Paid 500; Part-Time Paid 2,500.
Governing Authority: corporation. Owned by Anheuser-Busch Companies. Managed by Busch Entertainment Corp.
Aquarium, Marine Museum and Oceanarium.
Collections: marine life.
Research Fields: marine science.
Facilities: 500-vol. library of books on marine sciences available for research on premises by appointment; botanical garden; zoological park; aquarium; underwater theater; restaurants; snack bars. Gift items for sale.
Activities: guided tours; TV & radio programs; formally organized education

programs for children, adults, undergraduate & graduate students; field projects; shows; rides; play area; outreach education programs.
Hours & Admission Prices: Visit website for information. ♿
Attendance: 4,000,000
Membership: Visit website for information.

SERRA MUSEUM/SAN DIEGO HISTORICAL SOCIETY, 2727 Presidio Dr., Presidio Park, San Diego, CA 92103. Mailing Address: 1649 El Prado, Ste. 3, San Diego, CA 92101-1664. Tel.: 619-297-3258. Fax: 619-232-6297.
Web Site: www.sandiegohistory.org
Formerly: Junipero Serra Museum/San Diego Historical Society
Founded: 1928.
Congressional District: 49
Key Personnel: Dir., David Kahn; Pres. (V), Robert F. Adelizzi; Archivist, Jane Kenealy; Museum Shop Mgr., Trina Brewer.
Personnel Profile: Full-Time Paid 22; Part-Time Paid 14; Part-Time Volunteers 100; Interns 5.
Governing Authority: private; nonprofit organization. Parent Institution: San Diego Historical Society. Branch Museums: The Villa Montezuma Museum, 1925 K St., San Diego, CA 92110; Museum of San Diego History, 1649 El Prado, San Diego, CA 92101, Tel.: 619-232-6203; Marston House, 3525 Seventh Ave., San Diego, CA. Tel.: 619-298-3142. Tax-exempt: 501(c)(3).
History Museum: housed in a mission-style 1929 structure constructed to commemorate the site where Father Junipero Serra & Captain Gaspar de Portola established the first mission and military outpost on the west coast of the U.S. & Canada.
Collections: concentration on artifacts including housewares, period clothing, furniture & tools from the Native American, Spanish and Mexican periods through 1835.
Facilities: archaeological excavations of original presidio. Museum-related items for sale.
Activities: lectures; guided tours; films; docent program; formal education programs for children; temporary exhibitions.
Publications: quarterly newsletter, The San Diego Historical Society Times; quarterly magazine, The Journal of San Diego History.
Hours & Admission Prices: June-Sept. 3 daily 10-4:30; Sept.4-May call for hours. Adults $5, senior citizens, students with ID & military $4, children 6-17 $2; discounts to AAA, KPBS, National Trust members; members & children under 5 no charge. Closed New Year's Day; Thanksgiving & day after; Christmas Eve & Day.
Attendance: 14,625 (accurate)
Membership: Student, Senior & Military $35; Individual $40; Family $60; Associate $100; Scholar Circle $250; Curator's Circle $500; Director's Circle $1,000; Chairman's Circle $2,500.

SUSHI PERFORMANCE AND VISUAL ART, 964 5th Ave., Ste. 228, San Diego, CA 92101. Mailing Address: 390 11th Ave., San Diego, CA 92101-7413. Tel.: 619-235-8466. Fax: 619-235-8552.
E-mail: info@sushiart.org
Web Site: www.sushiart.org
Founded: 1980.
Congressional District: 49
Key Personnel: Exec. Dir. & Artistic Dir., Lynn Schuette; Business Mgr., Frances V. Carrillo.
Personnel Profile: Full-Time Paid 1; Part-Time Paid 1; Part-Time Volunteers 10; Interns 1.
Governing Authority: nonprofit. Tax-exempt: 501(c)(3).
Art Museum
Collections: innovative projects by contemporary visual, performance & movement artists.
Facilities: 1,500 sq. ft. exhibit space; 100-seat theater.
Activities: art festivals; guided tours; lectures; participatory exhibits; theater; art auction; performance festivals & dance.
Publications: monthly post-card exhibition announcements; monthly performance brochures.
Hours & Admission Prices: Call for appointment.
Attendance: 40,000
Membership: Artist, Student & Senior $20; Individual $30; Household $50; Opening night pass $100; Any Nite Pass $150.

THOMAS WHALEY HOUSE MUSEUM, 2476 San Diego Ave., San Diego, CA 92110-2730. Tel.: 619-297-7511. Fax: 619-291-3576.
E-mail: soho-1@sohosandiego.org
Web Site: www.whaleyhouse.org
Founded: 1969.
Key Personnel: Exec. Dir., Bruce Coons; Pres., Curtis Drake; Museum Shop Mgr., Alana Coons.
Personnel Profile: Full-Time Paid 4; Full-Time Volunteers 1; Part-Time Paid 18; Part-Time Volunteers 11.
Governing Authority: private; nonprofit organization. Parent Institution: SOHO. Tax-exempt.
House Museum.
Collections: 1850-1880 furnishings.
Activities: guided tours; docent program.
Publications: quarterly magazine, Our Heritage.
Hours & Admission Prices: Memorial Day to Labor Day daily 10-10; Sept.-May Sun.-Tues. 10-5, Thurs.-Sat. 10-10. Daily 10-7: adults $6, senior citizens $5, students & children $4; members no charge. Thurs.-Sun. 5pm-10pm: adults $10, children $5; children 2 & under no charge. Closed Thanksgiving; Christmas. ♿
Attendance: 120,000 (estimated)
Membership: Adult $35.

TIMKEN MUSEUM OF ART, (M), 1500 El Prado, Balboa Park, San Diego, CA 92101-1620. Tel.: 619-239-5548. Fax: 619-531-9640.
E-mail: info@timkenmuseum.org
Web Site: www.timkenmuseum.org
Founded: 1965.
Congressional District: 4
Key Personnel: Exec. Dir., John Wilson, Ph.D.; Pres. (V), Gary Meads; Deputy Dir., Carrie Cottriall; Dir. Operations, James Petersen; Dir. Education, Kristina Rosenberg; Controller, Denise Lamas.
Personnel Profile: Full-Time Paid 5; Part-Time Paid 12; Part-Time Volunteers 20.
Governing Authority: nonprofit organization. Parent Institution: The Putnam Foundation. Tax-exempt: 501(c)(3).
Art Museum.
Collections: 14th to 19th-century Old Masters European paintings; 19th-century American paintings; Gobelin Tapestries; 15th to 19th-century Russian Icons.
Facilities: 200-vol. director's library of art books.
Activities: docent tours.
Publications: Timken Museum of Art, European Works of Art, American Paintings and Russian Icons in the Putnam Foundation Collection, 1996; Timken Museum Acquisitions 1995-2005, 2006; Guercino: Stylistic Evolution in Focus, 2006; Rembrandt's Apostles, 2005; Benjamin West: Allegory and Allegiance, 2004; Portraiture in Paris Around 1800: Cooper Penrose by Jacques-Louis David, 2003; The Portraits of Bartolomeo Veneto, 2002; Luca Carlevarijs: Views of Venice, 2001; John Singleton Copley and Margaret Kemble Gage: Turkish Fashion in 18th Century America, 1998; Art & Devotion in Siena after 1350: Luca de Tomme & Niccolo di Buonaccorso, 1997; Eastman Johnson: The Cranberry Harvest, Island of Nantucket, 1990.
Hours & Admission Prices: Tues.-Sat. 10-4:30, Sun. 1:30-4:30. No charge; donations accepted. Guided Tours: Tues. & Thurs. 10-12. Closed legal holidays. ♿
Attendance: 140,811 (accurate)
Membership: Friends: $100 & up; $250 & up; $500 & up. Patrons Society: $1,000 & up; Ames Circle $2,500 & up; Putnam Circle $5,000 & up; Timken Circle $10,000 & up; Founder's Society $25,000 & up.

UNIVERSITY ART GALLERY SAN DIEGO STATE UNIVERSITY, (M), 5500 Campanile Dr., San Diego, CA 92182-0003. Mailing Address: School of Art, Design & Art History, San Diego, CA 92182-0001. Tel.: 619-594-5171. Fax: 619-594-1217.
E-mail: artgallery@sdsu.edu
Web Site: artgallery.sdsu.edu
Key Personnel: Dir., Tina Yapelli.
Governing Authority: university. Tax-exempt: 501(c)(3).
University Art Gallery.
Collections: contemporary art; study collection of Asian sculpture; African & Mexican art.
Research Fields: contemporary art in all media.
Facilities: 2,500 sq. ft. gallery space.
Activities: lectures; organized educational programs for adults & undergraduate or graduate college students affiliated with SDSU; traveling exhibitions; artists' lectures.
Publications: exhibition catalogues & brochures.
Hours & Admission Prices: Sept.-May Mon.-Thurs. & Sat. 12-4. No charge; donations accepted. Closed holidays. ♿
Attendance: 5,000 (estimated)
Membership: Annual $50.

USS MIDWAY MUSEUM, (M), 910 N. Harbor Dr., San Diego, CA 92101-5811. Tel.: 619-544-9600. Fax: 619-544-9188.
E-mail: mmclaughlin@midway.org
Web Site: www.midway.org

Formerly: San Diego Aircraft Carrier Museum
Key Personnel: Pres., Mac McLaughlin; C.F.O., Rich Benard
Military Museum.
Collections: over 19 restored aircraft; flight simulators; military history; personal artifacts.
Facilities: cafe. Museum-related items for sale.
Activities: self-guided audio tour; flight simulators.
Hours & Admission Prices: Daily 10-5; groups of 15 or more by appointment. Adults $17, seniors 62 & over and students $13, retired military $10, youth 6-17 $9; children 5 & under no charge. Closed Thanksgiving; Christmas.

VILLA MONTEZUMA MUSEUM, 1925 K St., San Diego, CA 92102-3828. Mailing Address: 657 20th St., San Diego, CA 92102. Tel.: 619-255-9367.
Web Site: www.villamontezuma.org
Founded: 1928.
Governing Authority: Tax-exempt: 501(c)(3).
Historic House Museum: housed in the former home of musician Jesse Shepard; built in 1887. Listed on the National Register of Historic Places.
Collections: late 19th-century furnishings & decorative arts; stained glass windows; personal artifacts; photographs.
Facilities: 4,000 sq. ft. exhibit space. Museum-related items for sale.
Activities: special events.
Hours & Admission Prices: Closed for renovations.
Membership: Individual $25; Professional $50; Supporting $100; Patron $250; Benefactor $500.

WELLS FARGO HISTORY MUSEUM, 2733 San Diego Ave., San Diego, CA 92110-2731. Mailing Address: Wells Fargo Historical Services, 420 Montgomery St., MAC-A0101-106, San Francisco, CA 94163-0001. Tel.: 619-238-3929.
Founded: 1990.
Key Personnel: Cur., Allan E. Peterson; Asst. Cur., Casey (William) Gill.
Governing Authority: profit-making organization. Affiliated with Wells Fargo Bank.
Company History Museum.
Collections: Concord Stagecoach; Wells Fargo banking & express history; mining; staging; local items.
Activities: guided group tours; permanent & temporary exhibitions; audiovisual programs.
Publications: scholarly pamphlets.
Hours & Admission Prices: Daily 10-5. No charge. Closed bank holidays. ♿

WILLIAM HEATH DAVIS HOUSE MUSEUM ADMINISTERED BY GASLAMP QUARTER HISTORICAL FOUNDATION, 410 Island Ave., San Diego, CA 92101-6925. Tel.: 619-233-4692. Fax: 619-233-4148.
E-mail: info@gaslampquarter.org
Web Site: www.gaslampquarter.org
Founded: 1984.
Key Personnel: Exec. Dir., Melissa Trew; Cur., Mary Joralmon; Museum Shop Mgr., Keiliki Rodriguez.
Personnel Profile: Full-Time Paid 2; Part-Time Paid 2; Part-Time Volunteers 100.
Governing Authority: private; nonprofit organization. Tax-exempt: 501(c)(3).
Historic House & Museum.
Collections: William Heath Davis House, the oldest wooden structure in San Diego; each room has been decorated to represent a different period of time in the life of the house from 1850-1940.
Research Fields: genealogical study of William Heath Davis.
Facilities: urban park available for rental. Museum-related items for sale.
Activities: guided tours of Gaslamp Quarter; children's tours. Annual Event: Fall Back Festival Children's Historic Street Faire.
Hours & Admission Prices: Tues.-Sat. 10-6, Sun. 9-3. Adults 12 & over $5, seniors 55 & over $4. Guided walking tour of Gaslamp district: Sat. 11. Adults $10, seniors & students $8 (includes admission to museum); group tours available with two weeks notice; children 11 & under no charge. Closed New Year's Day; Easter; Memorial Day; Independence Day; Thanksgiving; Christmas. ♿
Attendance: 30,000 (accurate)
Membership: Individual $25; Family $50, $100; Corporate $250, $500; Benefactor $1,000.

San Fernando

LOPEZ ADOBE, 1100 Pico St., San Fernando, CA 91340-3514. Mailing Address: 117 Macheil St., San Fernando, CA 91340-2911.
History Museum: listed as a National Historical Site.
Collections: period furnishings.
Hours & Admission Prices: 4th Sun. of month 1-4.

San Francisco

ALCATRAZ ISLAND, Pier 33, San Francisco, CA 94123. Mailing Address: Natl. Park Svc., Golden Gate Natl. Rec. Area, Bldg. 201, Fort Mason, San Francisco, CA 94123-1307. Tel.: 415-981-7625.
Web Site: www.nps.gov/alcatraz
Key Personnel: Gen. Supt., Brian O'Neill
Historic Site: federal prison 1934-1963.
Collections: island history; prison remnants; American Indian history; military history 1850-1933.
Facilities: theater; gardens.
Activities: video presentation; Alcatraz inmates & correctional officers audio tour.
Hours & Admission Prices: Ferry: departs every 30 minutes beginning at 9am. Island Tours: Summer: 10-6:30; Winter: 10-4:30. Closed New Year's Day; Christmas; extreme weather.

ALEXANDER F. MORRISON PLANETARIUM, Calif. Academy of Sciences, 55 Music Concourse Dr., San Francisco, CA 94118-4503. Tel.: 415-750-7127 & 7138.
E-mail: planet@calacademy.org
Web Site: www.calacademy.org/planetarium
Founded: 1952.
Key Personnel: Dir., Ryan Watt; Asst. Dir., Bing Quock; Production Coord., Molly Michelson.
Personnel Profile: Full-Time Paid 3; Part-Time Volunteers 1.
Governing Authority: nonprofit organization. Parent Institution: California Academy of Sciences. Tax-exempt: 501(c)(3).
Planetarium: housed in Natural History Museum.
Collections: astronomy; space science.
Facilities: planetarium.
Activities: lectures; formally organized educational programs; permanent exhibitions.
Hours & Admission Prices: Mon.-Sat. 9:30-5, Sun. 11-5. Adults $24.95, seniors 65 & over and youth 12-17 $19.95, children 7-11 $14.95; children 6 & under no charge. Closed Thanksgiving; Christmas. ♿
Attendance: 140,000 (estimated)
Membership: Family $60.

* **ASIAN ART MUSEUM OF SAN FRANCISCO, CHONG-MOON LEE CENTER FOR ASIAN ART AND CULTURE, (M),** 200 Larkin St., San Francisco, CA 94102-4734. Tel.: 415-581-3500. Fax: 415-581-4700. TDD: 415-861-2035.
Web Site: www.asianart.org
Formerly: Asian Art Museum of San Francisco, The Avery Brundage Collection
Founded: 1966.
Congressional District: 8
Key Personnel: C.O.O., Mark McLoughlin; Dir., Jay Xu; Chm. (V) Asian Art Commission, Doris Lee; Pres. (V), Sarah Hambrecht; Dir. Human Resources, Valerie Pechenik; Chief Cur. & Wattis Cur. of South & Southeast Asian Art, Forrest McGill; Cur. Japanese Art, Yoko Woodson; Cur. Korean Art, Cheeyun Kwon; Senior Cur. Chinese Art, Michael Knight; Dir. Education, Deborah Clearwaters; Dir. Devel., Amory Sharpe; Dir. Mktg. & Communications, Tim Hallman; Librarian, John Stucky; Museum Shop Mgr., Peri Danton.
Personnel Profile: Full-Time Paid 134; Part-Time Paid 11; Part-Time Volunteers 655; Interns 1.
Governing Authority: Asian Art Commission of San Francisco, an agency of the City & County of San Francisco. Tax-exempt: 501(c)(3).
Art Museum.
Collections: over 15,000 art objects spanning 6,000 years of history & representing countries and cultures throughout Asia which includes ceramics; bronze; jade; lacquer; sculpture; architectural elements; metalwork; glass; ivory; textiles; applied art; painting & screens.
Research Fields: Asian art, with emphasis on China, Korea, Japan, India, Nepal, Bhutan, Tibet, Southeast Asia & Iran.
Facilities: 34,000-vol. library on Asian art & culture available for use on premises; conservation & photography laboratories; resource room; 3 multi-purpose classrooms; cafe. Museum slides for sale.
Activities: guided tours; courses & lectures; films; performances; family festivals; intern program for graduate students; docent council; speakers bureau programs available to public; inter-museum loan; permanent, temporary & traveling exhibitions; docent tours for the deaf; live demonstrations; hands-on activities.
Publications: handbooks; catalogues on museum collections & traveling shows; slides; photographs; Members' Magazine.
Hours & Admission Prices: Tues.-Wed. & Fri.-Sun. 10-5, Thurs. 10-9. Adults $12, seniors $8, youth & college students $7; discounts Thurs. after 5pm;

AAM & ICOM members, children 12 & under, SFUSD students, 1st Sun. of month and members no charge. Closed New Year's Day; Thanksgiving; Christmas. ♿
Attendance: 262,482 (accurate)
Membership: Student & Teacher & Out of Region $40; Senior Active $55; Active $65; Senior Family & Friends $75; Friends & Family $85; Senior Contributor $115; Contributor $125; Donor $300; Sponsor $600; Patron $1,000.

*** CALIFORNIA ACADEMY OF SCIENCES, (M),** 55 Music Concourse Dr., San Francisco, CA 94118-4503. Tel.: 415-379-8000.
E-mail: info@calacademy.org
Web Site: www.calacademy.org
Founded: 1853.
Congressional District: 9
Key Personnel: Exec. Dir., Gregory Farrington; Chm. Bd. (V), William Paterson; Pres. (V), Dr. John Hefernik; Dir. Steinhart Aquarium, Chris Andrews; Chm. Anthropology, Dr. Zeray Alemseged; Chm. Aquatic Biology, Dr. John McCosker; Chm. Botany, Dr. Frank Almeda; Chm. Entomology, Dr. Wojciech Pulawski; Chm. Ichthyology, Dr. Tomio Iwamoto; Chm. Herpetology, Dr. Alan Leviton; Chm. Ornithology & Mammalogy, Dr. John Dumbacher; Chm. Invertebrate Zoology & Geology, Dr. Gary Williams; Public Information Officer, Stephanie Stone.
Personnel Profile: Full-Time Paid 320; Part-Time Paid 250; Part-Time Volunteers 1,100; Interns 35.
Governing Authority: nonprofit organization. Tax-exempt: 501(c)(3) & 170(b)(1)(A).
Natural History Museum, Aquarium & Planetarium.
Collections: ichthyology; invertebrate zoology; ornithology; mammalogy; natural history; botany; entomology; herpetology; anthropology; paleontology; geology; minerals; artifacts; diatoms.
Major Exhibits: Extreme Mammals (T), 4/10-10/10.
Research Fields: anthropology; botany; entomology; geology; herpetology; ichthyology; invertebrate zoology; ornithology; mammalogy; aquatic biology.
Facilities: 210,000-vol. library of science books on botany, zoology, geology & related topics available for inter-library loan & on premises; aquarium. Books, museum reproductions & other related items for sale.
Activities: guided tours; lectures; formally organized education programs for children & adults; docent program or council; inter-museum loan, permanent & temporary exhibitions.
Publications: newsletters; scientific papers; memoirs; proceedings; occasional papers.
Hours & Admission Prices: Mon.-Sat. 9:30-5, Sun. 11-5. Adults $24.95, youth 12-17, senior citizens 65 & over and students $19.95, children 7-11 $14.95; children 6 & under no charge. Closed Thanksgiving; Christmas. ♿
Attendance: 1,500,000 (accurate)
Membership: Senior $59; Individual $99; Family $159; Family Plus $250; Associate $500; Guild $750.

CALIFORNIA HISTORICAL SOCIETY, 678 Mission St., San Francisco, CA 94105-4014. Tel.: 415-357-1848. Fax: 415-357-1850.
E-mail: info@calhist.org
Web Site: www.calhist.org
Founded: 1871.
Congressional District: 8
Key Personnel: Exec. Dir., David Crosson; Dir. Education & Public Programs, Lisa Eriksen; Pres. (V), Jan Berckefeldt; Dir. Library & Archives, Mary Morganti; Dir. Devel., Derlene Plumtree; Dir. Operations, Liliana Vasquez; Editor California History, Janet Fireman; Dir. Finance, Pamela Garcia; Museum Shop Mgr., Sy Russell.
Personnel Profile: Full-Time Paid 10; Part-Time Paid 7; Part-Time Volunteers 12; Interns 4.
Governing Authority: private; nonprofit organization. Partnerships with Bancroft Library & Autry National Center, USC. Tax-exempt: 501(c)(3).
Historical Society Museum.
Collections: California history from the pre-Gold Rush days to the present; photography; fine art; books; manuscripts; artifacts; costumes.
Major Exhibits: Think California, 11/09-9/10.
Research Fields: exhibition-specific research on art, photography, and library collections.
Facilities: 506,500-vol. library of books, pamphlets, photographs, periodicals, archival collections & manuscripts; 3,300 sq. ft. exhibit space. Museum-related items for sale.
Activities: lectures; loan, participatory, temporary & traveling exhibitions; training programs for professional museum workers; family days; walking tours. Museum Sponsors: Holiday Party; Hats-Off Benefit.
Publications: quarterly peer-reviewed scholarly journal, California History; quarterly newsletter, California Chronicle.
Hours & Admission Prices: Wed.-Sat. 12-4:30. Suggested Donations: adults $3, senior citizens & students $1; discounts to AAM & ICOM members; members & children no charge. Closed New Year's Day; Martin Luther King Jr. Day; Presidents' Day; Memorial Day; Independence Day; Labor Day; Thanksgiving & day after; Christmas. ♿
Attendance: 12,000 (estimated)
Membership: Student, Teachers $40; Senior $45; Libraries & Nonprofit $50; Regular $55; Plus $75; Friend $125; Contributor $250; Benefactor $500; Silver Circle $1,000.

CARTOON ART MUSEUM, 655 Mission St., San Francisco, CA 94105-4126. Tel.: 415-227-8666, ext. 300. Fax: 415-243-8666.
E-mail: office@cartoonart.org
Web Site: www.cartoonart.org
Founded: 1984.
Key Personnel: Acting Dir., Summerlea Kashar; Chm., Ron Evans; Cur., Andrew Farago; Bookstore Mgr., Heather Plankett.
Personnel Profile: Full-Time Paid 4; Part-Time Paid 1; Part-Time Volunteers 25; Interns 6.
Governing Authority: nonprofit organization. Tax-exempt: 501(c)(3).
Cartoon Art Museum.
Collections: original cartoon art, flat graphics-animation cels; videos & film; toys; figurines; ephemera.
Research Fields: cartoon art; cartooning.
Facilities: library available to the public for research only; 3,400 sq. ft. exhibit space. Museum-related items for sale.
Activities: guided tours; lectures; artist appearances; loan, traveling & temporary exhibitions. Museum Sponsors: Saturday cartooning classes, one Saturday a month during school year, two Saturdays a month during summer.
Publications: newsletter, Cartoon Times; exhibition catalogs.
Hours & Admission Prices: Tues.-Sun. 11-5. Adults $6, students & seniors $4, children 6-12 $2; discounts to AAM & ICOM members; CAM members & children 5 and under no charge. Closed New Year's Day; Easter; Independence Day; Thanksgiving; Christmas Eve & Day. ♿
Attendance: 35,000 (estimated)
Membership: Student & Senior $25; Individual $35; Family $50; Friend $100; Patron $250; Sponsor $500; Benefactor $1,000-$4,999; Business Friend $5,000-$9,999.

CCA WATTIS INSTITUTE FOR CONTEMPORARY ARTS, 1111 Eighth St., San Francisco, CA 94107-2247. Tel.: 415-551-9210. Fax: 415-551-9209.
E-mail: wattis@cca.edu
Web Site: www.wattis.org
Founded: 1998.
Congressional District: 9
Personnel Profile: Full-Time Paid 4; Part-Time Paid 1; Interns 2.
Governing Authority: college. Parent Institution: California College of The Arts. Branch Museums: 1111 8th St., San Francisco, CA 94107. Tax-exempt.
Art Gallery.
Collections: contemporary culture.
Activities: lectures; gallery talks; contemporary exhibitions of fine art, fine craft, architecture & design; education programs.
Publications: books, Searchlight: Consciousness at the Millennium; Rock My World - Recent Art and the Memory of Rock 'n Roll; After the Gold Rush; The Artist's World; Utopia Now; How Extraordinary That the World Exists!; Sudden Glory; Extra Art: A Survey of Artist's Ephemera; Reality Check: Painting in the Exploded Field; Baja to Vancouver: The West Coast and Contemporary Art; Likeness: Portraits of Artists by Other Artists; Monuments for the USA; What We Want is Free; A Brief History of Invisible Art; Spaced Out: Late 1990's Works from the Vicki and Kent Logan Collection; Prophets of Deceit; Pioneers, Apocalypse Now: The Theater of War, Amateurs; Capp Street Project: Mario Ybarra, Jr.; Capp Street Project: Tim Lee: Capp Street Project: Abraham Cruzvillegas; Capp Street: Beatriz Santiago Munoz; The Wizard of Oz; Paul McCarthy's Low Life Slow Life; Moby Dick.
Hours & Admission Prices: Logan Center Galleries: Tues. & Thurs. 11-7, Wed., Fri. & Sat. 11-6. No charge; donations accepted. Closed major holidays; during installation. ♿
Attendance: 28,000 (estimated)

CHINESE CULTURE CENTER OF SAN FRANCISCO, 750 Kearny St., 3rd. Fl., San Francisco, CA 94108-1887. Tel.: 415-986-1822. Fax: 415-986-2825.
E-mail: info@c-c-c.org
Web Site: www.c-c-c.org
Founded: 1965.
Congressional District: 5

Key Personnel: Co Chm., Richard Lee, M.D.; Co Chm., Colin C. Wong, D.D.S.; Pres., Russell E. Leong, M.D.; Exec. Dir., Albert Cheng; Program Dir., Abby Chen.
Personnel Profile: Full-Time Paid 2; Part-Time Paid 5; Part-Time Volunteers 20.
Governing Authority: nonprofit organization. Parent Institution: Chinese Culture Foundation. Tax-exempt: 501(c)(3).
Art Gallery.
Collections: historical photographs on Chinese-Americans; Chinese art; Chinese folk arts; crafts.
Research Fields: pertaining to exhibits; special research.
Facilities: 400-seat auditorium; classrooms; north gallery; collector's corner; community gallery. Museum-related items for sale.
Activities: youth genealogy research programs; guided tours; lectures; gallery talks; TV & radio programs; docent program; classes & workshops; visual arts exhibitions; performing arts & festivals.
Publications: exhibition catalogues; educational brochures; newsletters.
Hours & Admission Prices: Tues.-Sat. 10-4. No charge; donations accepted. Closed major holidays. ♿
Attendance: 65,000 (estimated)
Membership: Senior Citizens 65 & over & Full-Time Students $25; Individual $35; Family $50; Contributing $200; Benefactor $500; Business & Corporate $1,000; Life $10,000.

CHINESE HISTORICAL SOCIETY OF AMERICA, 965 Clay St., San Francisco, CA 94108-1527. Tel.: 415-391-1188. Fax: 415-391-1150.
E-mail: info@chsa.org
Web Site: www.chsa.org
Founded: 1962.
Key Personnel: Dir., Sue Lee; Pres., Paul Fong
Chinese Historical Society.
Collections: Chinese history & culture; photographs; chalkware; trade cards; sheet music; toys.
Hours & Admission Prices: Tues.-Fri. 12-5, Sat. 11-4. Adults $3, college students & seniors $2, children 6-17 $1; members & children 5 & under no charge. Closed New Year's Day; Veterans Day; Independence Day; Christmas.

CONTEMPORARY JEWISH MUSEUM, (M), 736 Mission St., San Francisco, CA 94103-3113. Tel.: 415-655-7800. Fax: 415-655-7815.
E-mail: info@thecjm.org
Web Site: www.thecjm.org
Founded: 1984.
Congressional District: 8
Key Personnel: Dir. & C.E.O., Connie Wolf; Chm. (V), Roselyne Swig; Museum Shop Mgr., Kevin Grenon.
Personnel Profile: Full-Time Paid 29; Part-Time Paid 31; Part-Time Volunteers 146; Interns 15.
Governing Authority: nonprofit organization. Tax-exempt: 501(c)(3).
Art Museum & Center.
Collections: Jewish art & culture.
Major Exhibits: There's A Mystery There: Sendak on Sendak, 11/09-1/19/10; The Scribe Project, 11/09-12/10; Notre Combat, 2/10-6/10; Reinventing Ritual, 4/10-9/10; Maira Kalman, 7/10-10/10; Reclaimed: Paintings from the Collection of Jacques Goudstrikker, 10/10-3/11; Charlotte Salomon: Life? or Theater?, 11/10-3/11.
Research Fields: Jewish art, culture & traditions; Jewish education; museum education.
Facilities: 11,700 sq. ft. exhibit space.
Activities: traveling exhibition; artists' invitational exhibits; community-based exhibitions; guided tours; lecture series; educational programs for children, adults & elders; intergenerational program; college guides; films; contemporaries. Museum Sponsors: family holiday celebrations; fund-raising auction.
Publications: exhibition catalogues.
Hours & Admission Prices: Thurs. 1-8, Fri.-Tues. 11-5. Adults $10; youth 18 & under and members no charge. Closed New Year's Day; Passover; Independence Day; Rosh Hashanah; Yom Kippur; Thanksgiving. ♿
Attendance: 150,000 (estimated)
Membership: Senior $40; Dual Senior $55; Individual $60; Household $75; Supporter $150; Sponsor $250; Patron $500; Circle of Friends $1,000 & up.

THE EXPLORATORIUM, 3601 Lyon St., San Francisco, CA 94123-1099. Tel.: 415-563-7337. Fax: 415-561-0307. TDD: 415-567-0709.
E-mail: pubinfo@exploratorium.edu
Web Site: www.exploratorium.edu
Founded: 1969.
Congressional District: 5
Key Personnel: Exec. Dir., Dennis M. Bartels; Chm. Bd. Trustee (V), George W. Cogan; Exec. Assoc. Dir., Robert J. Semper; C.F.O., Laura Zander; Dir. Exhibitions & Public Programs, Thomas Rockwell; Dir. Mktg., Joyce Gardella; Museum Shop Mgr., Mark Giberson.
Personnel Profile: Full-Time Paid 209; Part-Time Paid 115; Part-Time Volunteers 220; Interns 4.
Governing Authority: nonprofit organization. Tax-exempt.
Science Museum & Center.
Collections: participatory exhibits & art works explore & illustrate the physical nature of world & sensory mechanisms through which we perceive; commissioned art works dealing with natural phenomena.
Major Exhibits: Geometry Playground, 6/10-9/10.
Research Fields: exhibit-based education; exhibit & curriculum development; research & development of multi-media learning tools; visitor learning research.
Facilities: classrooms; cafe; theater.
Activities: lectures; films; concerts; field trips; festivals; special theme exhibitions; demonstrations; performances; teachers workshops.
Publications: monthly newsletter; Exploratorium Cookbooks (exhibit construction manuals); supplemental curriculum materials & exhibit plans for teachers, including Science Snackbook series, Scale & Structure, Human Body Explorations & Math/Science Across Cultures; reference charts, Electromagnetic Spectrum, Sound Spectrum, History of the Alphabet Cycles & Language Families of the World; trade books for children, families & curious readers, Explorabook, The Science Explorer series, Math Explorer and Exploratopia.
Hours & Admission Prices: Tues.-Sun. 10-5. Adults $14, senior citizens & youth 13-17 $11, children 4-12 $9; discounts to AAM & ICOM members; children under 4, 1st Wed. of month & members no charge. Closed Thanksgiving; Christmas. ♿
Attendance: 600,000 (estimated)
Membership: Senior & Disabled $50; Active $60; International $75; Family $85; Family Plus $140; Supporting $250; Sustaining $500; Associate $1,000.

THE FINE ARTS MUSEUMS OF SAN FRANCISCO, DE YOUNG MUSEUM, 50 Hagiwara Tea Garden Dr., San Francisco, CA 94118-4502. Tel.: 415-750-3600. Fax: 415-750-7692.
E-mail: guestbook@famsf.org
Web Site: www.deyoungmuseum.org
Founded: 1894.
Congressional District: 8
Key Personnel: Dir., John E. Buchanan, Jr.; Pres. Bd. Trustees (V), Dede Wilsey; Assoc. Dir., Robert Futernick; Administrative Asst. to Dir., Lauren Ito; C.F.O., Nicholas Elsishans; Deputy Dir. Devel., Martha Brigham; Dir. Mktg. & Communications, Susannah Stringam; Cur. Prints & Drawings, Achenbach Foundation for Graphic Arts, Karin Breuer; Ednah Root Cur. American Arts, Timothy Anglin Burgard; Cur. Africa, Oceania & Americas, Kathleen Berrin; Cur. European Paintings, Dr. Lynn Federle Orr; Cur. Ancient Art & Interpretation, Renee Dreyfus; Advertising & Promotion, Gina Yrrizarry; Dir. Education, Sheila Pressley; Museum Shop Mgr., Stuart Hata; Media Rels., Jill Lynch; Publications, Ann Heath Karlstrom.
Personnel Profile: Full-Time Paid 420; Part-Time Volunteers 600.
Governing Authority: municipal; county. Tax-exempt.
Fine Arts Museums.
Collections: paintings, prints & drawings; sculpture & decorative arts from America; traditional arts of Africa, Oceania & the Americas; rugs; textiles; photographs.
Research Fields: European & American painting; decorative arts; conservation; African art; art of Oceania.
Facilities: auditorium; theatre; cafe; conservation laboratories. Museum-related items for sale.
Activities: temporary exhibitions; lectures; docent tours; films; concerts; community outreach programs; musical programs; school programs.
Publications: quarterly members magazine, Fine Arts; collection & exhibition catalogues.
Hours & Admission Prices: Tues.-Thurs. & Sat.-Sun. 9:30-5:15, Fri. 9:30-8:45. Adults $10; 1st Tues. of month & members no charge. Closed New Year's Day; Independence Day; Thanksgiving; Christmas. ♿
Attendance: 750,000
Membership: Student $45; Senior $50; Teacher $55; Out of State $60; Individual $80; Family/Dual $95; Contributing $175; Supporting $300; Sustaining $500; Friend $1,000.

* **THE FINE ARTS MUSEUMS OF SAN FRANCISCO, LEGION OF HONOR, (M),** 100 34th Ave., San Francisco, CA 94121-1677. Mailing Address: c/o deYoung, 50 Hagiwara Tea Garden Dr., San Francisco, CA 94118. Tel.: 415-750-3600. Fax: 415-750-3656.
E-mail: guestbook@famsf.org
Web Site: www.legionofhonor.org
Formerly: California Palace of the Legion of Honor
Founded: 1924.

Congressional District: 8
Key Personnel: Dir., John E. Buchanan, Jr.; Pres. Bd. Trustees (V), Dede Wilsey; Assoc. Dir., Robert Futernick; Administrative Asst. to Dir., Lauren Ito; C.F.O., Nicholas Elsishans; Dir. Mktg. & Communications, Susannah Stringam; Deputy Dir. Devel., Martha Brigham; Cur. Prints & Drawings, Achenbach Foundation for Graphic Arts, Karin Breuer; Ednah Root Cur. American Arts, Timothy Anglin Burgard; Cur. Africa, Oceania & American, Kathleen Berrin; Cur. European Art, Dr. Lynn Federle Orr; Cur. Ancient Art & Interpretation, Renee Dreyfus; Advertising & Promotion, Gina Yrrizarry; Dir. Education, Shelia Pressley; Museum Shop Mgr., Stuart Hata; Media Rels., Jill Lynch; Webmaster, Andrew Fox; Publications, Ann Heath Karlstrom; European Decorative Arts & Sculpture, Martin Chapman.
Personnel Profile: Part-Time Volunteers 600.
Governing Authority: county. Tax-exempt.
Fine Arts Museum.
Collections: paintings, sculpture & decorative arts from Europe and England; tapestries; prints; drawings; arts of ancient Egypt, Greece & Rome.
Research Fields: European & American painting; decorative arts; conservation.
Facilities: auditorium; theatre; cafe; conservation laboratories. Museum-related items for sale.
Activities: temporary exhibitions; lectures; docent tours; films; concerts; community outreach programs; musical programs; school programs.
Publications: quarterly members magazine, Fine Arts; collection & exhibition catalogues.
Hours & Admission Prices: Tues.-Sun. 9:30-5:15. Adults $10, seniors over 65 $7, children 12-17 $6; discounts to AAM members; members, children 12 & under, San Francisco public and private school students K-12 with ID & 1st Tues. of month no charge. Closed New Year's Day; Independence Day; Thanksgiving; Christmas. ♿
Attendance: 500,000
Membership: Student $45; Senior $50; Teacher $55; Out of State $60; Individual $80; Family/Dual $95; Contributing $175; Supporting $300; Sustaining $500; Friend $1,000.

FORT POINT NATIONAL HISTORIC SITE, Presidio of San Francisco, Bldg. 989, San Francisco, CA 94129. Mailing Address: Fort Mason, Bldg. 201, San Francisco, CA 94123-1307. Tel.: 415-556-1693. Fax: 415-561-4390. TDD: 415-556-0505.
Web Site: www.nps.gov/fopo
Founded: 1970.
Congressional District: 5
Key Personnel: Supt., Brian O'Neill.
Personnel Profile: Full-Time Paid 2; Full-Time Volunteers 8; Part-Time Paid 1; Interns 1.
Governing Authority: federal government. Parent Institution: Dept. of the Interior, National Park Service.
Historic Site: c.1853-1861 Fort Point which is the only third system fort on the west coast.
Collections: items related to the history of Fort Point & the garrisons who served there.
Research Fields: military history of Fort Point.
Facilities: 200-vol. library relating to military history & Fort Point, available for use on premises. Publications, posters & postcards for sale.
Activities: guided tours; formally organized education programs for children; permanent exhibitions; video; audiotour.
Publications: book, Fort Point; color photo book; video, Fort Point: Guardian of the Golden Gate; audiotour, A Day in the Life of a Fort Point Soldier.
Hours & Admission Prices: Fri.-Sun. 10-5. No charge; donations accepted. Closed New Year's Day; Thanksgiving; Christmas. ♿
Attendance: 300,000
Membership: Golden Gate National Park Conservancy or Fort Point & Presidio Historical Association. $35-$100.

GOLDEN GATE NATIONAL RECREATION AREA, Fort Mason, Bldg. 201, San Francisco, CA 94123-0022. Tel.: 415-561-2831. Fax: 415-441-8272. TDD: 415-556-2766.
E-mail: jonathan_bayless@nps.gov
Web Site: www.nps.gov/goga/
Founded: 1972.
Congressional District: 6, 8 & 12
Key Personnel: Supt., Brian O'Neill; Cur., Jonathan Bayless; Museum Specialist, Lulu Chye; Archivist, Susan Ewing Haley; Chief Interpretation, Howard Levitt; Registrar, John Weingardt; Security, Yvette Ruan.
Personnel Profile: Full-Time Paid 370; Part-Time Volunteers 5,000.
Governing Authority: federal government; nonprofit. Parent Institution: Dept. of the Interior. Subsidiary Institution: National Park Service. Tax-exempt.
Park Museum: the Golden Gate National Recreation Area, including Muir Woods National Monument & Fort Point National Historic Site, sits at the juncture & overlapping of two ecological provinces & its innate diversity is increased, which has resulted in unique biological communities & species found together.
Collections: concentration on interpretive themes & periods, which represent approximately 10,000 years of human history & prehistory; natural resources of the north & south Pacific border regions of the California coast; 180,000 historic documents; 6,000 plants, including 12 distinct communities; 20,000 photographic images; 700 historic structures; historical & military architecture; coastal defense systems.
Research Fields: cultural landscape of history army airfields; small mammal predators; historic furnishings & structures of World War II & Cold War era; historic furnishings of Civil War fortification; historic resources of Presidio of San Francisco & coastal fortifications.
Facilities: library related to park resources for use on premises; 4,000 sq. ft. exhibit space. Gift items for sale.
Activities: concerts; docent program; formal education programs for children; guided tours.
Publications: quarterly newsletter, The Park; quarterly event calendar, Park Events.
Hours & Admission Prices: Daily 10-5. No charge; donations accepted. Closed New Year's Day; Thanksgiving; Christmas. ♿
Attendance: 13,803,382 (estimated)
Membership: Golden Gate National Park Association: Student & Senior $15; Senior Dual $20; Individual $25; Associate $50; Participant $100.

HAAS-LILIENTHAL HOUSE, 2007 Franklin St., San Francisco, CA 94109-2909. Tel.: 415-441-3000. Fax: 415-441-3015.
E-mail: info@sfheritage.org
Web Site: www.sfheritage.org
Founded: 1973.
Congressional District: 5
Key Personnel: Pres., Charles Olsen; Exec. Dir., Jack Gold; Operations Mgr., Barbara Roldan.
Personnel Profile: Full-Time Paid 4; Part-Time Paid 2; Part-Time Volunteers 100; Interns 1.
Governing Authority: nonprofit. Parent Institution: San Francisco Architectural Heritage, 2007 Franklin St., San Francisco, CA. Tax-exempt: 501(c)(3).
Historic House: c.1886 Queen Anne style Victorian.
Collections: late 1800s & turn-of-the-century furniture, accessories & paintings.
Research Fields: architectural history of San Francisco; feasibility studies for renovation; adaptive reuse of significant buildings in San Francisco; preservation & conservation of city structures.
Facilities: room & house rentals.
Activities: docent-guided tours; special programs; lectures; architectural walking tours; preservation & conservation of old city buildings; heritage architectural walks; slide-lectures; school program.
Publications: bimonthly newsletter; Splendid Survivors - San Francisco's Downtown Architectural Heritage; Jessie Street Substation: Adaptive Reuse Feasibility Study & Proposal; Directory 77: Rehabilitation Advice & Useful Sources For Owners of Vintage Buildings; Victorian Sampler: A Walk in Pacific Heights & the Haas Lilienthal House.
Hours & Admission Prices: Wed. & Sat. 12-3, Sun. 11-4. Adults $8, children under 12 & senior citizens $5; discount to AAA & Travel with Visa members; members no charge.
Attendance: 6,000 (estimated)
Membership: Student & Senior Citizen $35; Individual $50; Family $75; Supporting $125; Contributing $250; Sustaining $500.

HENRY WILSON COIL MASONIC LIBRARY & MUSEUM, (M), 1111 California St., San Francisco, CA 94108-2252. Tel.: 415-776-7000, ext. 143.
History Museum.
Collections: Freemasonry history; photographs.
Facilities: library.
Activities: lectures.
Hours & Admission Prices: Call for hours.

INTERNATIONAL MUSEUM OF WOMEN, (M), 101 Howard St., Ste. 480, San Francisco, CA 94105-6123. Mailing Address: P.O. Box 190038, San Francisco, CA 94119-0038. Tel.: 415-543-4669. Fax: 415-543-4668.
E-mail: info@imow.org
Web Site: www.imow.org
Founded: 1985.
Key Personnel: Pres., Chris Yelton; Chm. (V), Elizabeth Colton; C.F.O., Nancy Daum; Vice Pres. Exhibitions & Programs, Catherine King; Mgr. Education & Public Programs, Dr. Constanza Svidler; Mgr. Mktg. & Communications, Jo Beaton.
Personnel Profile: Full-Time Paid 12; Part-Time Paid 3; Interns 2.

Governing Authority: nonprofit organization. Tax-exempt: 501(c)(3).
History Museum.
Collections: artifacts & archives relating to women's history.
Research Fields: women's history.
Facilities: development office.
Activities: Speaker series; art & education program for K-12.
Publications: quarterly newsletter.
Hours & Admission Prices: Please call for further information.
Membership: Student & Senior $35; Individual $50; Family $75; Auxiliary $100-$499; Initiator $500-$4,999; Ambassador $1,000-$4,900; Emissary $5,000-$9,999.

THE MEXICAN MUSEUM, Fort Mason Center, Bldg. D., San Francisco, CA 94123.
Web Site: www.mexicanmuseum.org
Founded: 1975.
Congressional District: 5
Key Personnel: Chm. (V), Victor Marquez; Exec. Dir., William Moreno; Cur. Collections, Tere Romo; Coord. Education, Rachel Cox; Museum Shop Mgr., Teo Dane; Devel. Assoc., Michael Gary; Registrar, Maren Jones; Asst. to Exec. Dir., Eva Jimenez.
Personnel Profile: Full-Time Paid 2; Part-Time Paid 6; Part-Time Volunteers 30; Interns 2.
Governing Authority: nonprofit organization. Tax-exempt: 501(c)3.
Fine Arts Museum.
Collections: pre-conquest art; Colonial & Popular art; modern & contemporary Mexican and Latino art; Chicano art.
Research Fields: Mexican & Chicano-Mexican American fine arts; pre-conquest art; colonial art; popular art; Mexican & Latino art; Mexican American & Chicano contemporary art.
Facilities: 300-vol. library of Mexican art & culture. Books, Mexican folk art & other museum-related items for sale.
Activities: guided tours; lectures; temporary exhibitions; family day workshops & presentations.
Publications: catalogues, The Nelson A. Rockefeller Collection of Mexican Folk Art, Witness to the Self; Rodolfo Morales; Colonial Mexican & Popular Religious Art; Leonora Carrington; Patssi Valdez: A Precarious Comfort.
Hours & Admission Prices: Wed.-Sat. 11-5. No charge; donations accepted. Closed holidays. ♿
Attendance: 5,000 (estimated)
Membership: Student & Senior Citizen $25; Teacher $30; Individual $35; Family $55; Supporting $100; Patron $250; Sponsor $500 & up.

MISSION CULTURAL CENTER FOR LATINO ARTS, 2868 Mission St., San Francisco, CA 94110-3908. Tel.: 415-821-1155. Fax: 415-648-0933.
E-mail: info@missionculturalcenter.org
Web Site: www.missionculturalcenter.org
Founded: 1977.
Congressional District: 6
Key Personnel: Exec. Dir., Jennie Rodriguez; Video Dept. Coord., Adrian Arias; Graphic Design Coord., Ruben Antonio; Mission Grafica Coord., Juan Fuentes; Facilities Coord., J. Angel Varela; Youth Program Coord, Jose Leon; Gallery Asst. Cur., Carolina Lucero; Gallery Coord., Patricia Rodriguez.
Personnel Profile: Full-Time Paid 2; Part-Time Paid 5; Part-Time Volunteers 7.
Governing Authority: municipal; nonprofit. Parent Institution: Neighborhood Arts Program, 45 Hyde St., #319, San Francisco, CA 94102. Tel.: 415-558-3463. Tax-exempt: 170(b)(1)(A).
Civic Art, Cultural Center.
Collections: private collection of artists work; posters of events housed at the Mission Cultural Center & from gallery shows.
Research Fields: local, Mexican, Central & South American Culture.
Facilities: 200-seat theatre; stage; graphic services; T-shirt Press; dance/music studios; 6,000 sq. ft. gallery.
Activities: performing events; lectures, films; on-going classes & workshops; receptions; site-visits, tours.
Publications: quarterly cultural arts magazine, Humanizarte.
Hours & Admission Prices: Tues. & Sat. 10-5. Adults $2. Closed holidays. ♿
Attendance: 20,000 (estimated)

MISSION SAN FRANCISCO DE ASIS (MISSION DOLORES), 3321 Sixteenth St., San Francisco, CA 94114-1712. Tel.: 415-621-8203.
Historic Building: c.1791.
Collections: archives; ethnic & tribal art; furniture; paintings.
Activities: children's classes; guided tours.
Hours & Admission Prices: Daily 9-4. Adults $5, children $3; children under 6 no charge. Closed Thanksgiving; Christmas Day.

THE MUSEE MECANIQUE, Pier 45, Shed A, San Francisco, CA 94133. Tel.: 415-346-2000.
E-mail: coad01@yahoo.com
Web Site: www.museemecaniquesf.com
Key Personnel: Owner, Daniel Galand Zelinsky
General Museum.
Collections: over 300 coin-operated mechanical art machines.
Hours & Admission Prices: Mon.-Fri. 10-7, Sat.-Sun. & holidays 10-8. No charge. ♿

MUSEO ITALOAMERICANO, Ft. Mason Center, Bldg. C, San Francisco, CA 94123-1301. Tel.: 415-673-2200. Fax: 415-673-2292.
E-mail: sfmuseo@sbcglobal.net
Web Site: www.museoitaloamericano.org
Founded: 1978.
Congressional District: 5
Key Personnel: Dir., Paola Bagnatori; Pres. (V), Clemente Deamicis; Museum Shop Mgr., Susan Filippo.
Personnel Profile: Full-Time Paid 1; Full-Time Volunteers 1; Part-Time Paid 4; Part-Time Volunteers 45.
Governing Authority: nonprofit. Tax-exempt.
Contemporary Italian, Italian-American Art Museum & Italian Cultural Center.
Collections: 20th-century paintings, sculpture & photographs by Italian & Italian-American artists; changing exhibits.
Facilities: library. Museum-related items for sale.
Activities: Italian language & conversation classes; art & culture lectures; Culinary Arts Series; concerts; CIAO (Children's Italian Art Outreach Program); Italian film program.
Publications: newsletter; Italian American Studies Curriculum Unit; exhibition catalogs.
Hours & Admission Prices: Tues.-Sun. 12-4. No charge; donations accepted. Closed holidays. ♿
Attendance: 8,450 (accurate)
Membership: Senior Citizens $35; Next Generation $50; Dual Senior $60; Dual Family $75; Special Friend $100; Sponsor $150; Supporter $250; Benefactor $500; Silver Circle $1,000 & up; Gold Circle $5,000 & up; Platinum Circle $10,000 & up.

MUSEUM OF CRAFT AND FOLK ART, (M), 51 Yerba Buena Ln., San Francisco, CA 94103-3183. Tel.: 415-227-4888. Fax: 415-227-4351.
E-mail: officemgr@mocfa.org
Web Site: www.mocfa.org
Formerly: San Francisco Craft and Folk Art Museum
Founded: 1983.
Congressional District: 6
Key Personnel: Dir., Jennifer McCabe; Bd. Pres., Zachary Walton; Honorary Chm. (V), Gertrud Parker; Dir. School Program, Linda Janklow; Dir. Devel., Juanita Carroll Young; Administrative Dir., Betsy Herczeg-Konecny; Museum Store Mgr., Kpoene' Kofi-Bruce.
Personnel Profile: Full-Time Paid 5; Part-Time Paid 5; Part-Time Volunteers 10; Interns 3.
Governing Authority: nonprofit organization. Tax-exempt: 501(c)(3).
Craft & Folk Art Museum.
Collections: contemporary craft; folk art.
Research Fields: Crafts and Folk Art world-wide.
Activities: lectures; films; organized education programs; traveling exhibitions.
Publications: catalogs: Native Arts of Luzon; Textiles of Old Japan: Color & Dye; Sun & Moon: Traditional Arts of Yi Dynasty Korea; The Quiet Eye: Pottery of Shoji Hamada & Bernard Leach; Classical Chinese Wood Furniture; quarterly publication: A Report; Riches from Rags; Land of the Morning; Treasures of the Philippines; June Schwarcz/Forty Years: Forty Pieces; Intimate Views: The Books of Kay Sekimachi; Beyond the Obvious: Rethinking Jewelry; Enamelist (video); Explorations in Cloth. Bob Stocksdale: 88 Turnings; Fusing Traditions: Transformation in Glass by Native American artists.
Hours & Admission Prices: Mon.-Tues. & Fri. 11-6, Sat.-Sun. 11-5. Adults $5, senior citizens 62 & over $4; discounts to AAM members & groups; members & children under 18 no charge. Closed major holidays. ♿
Attendance: 20,000 (estimated)
Membership: Out of Town, Artist, Teacher, Senior & Student $36; Individual $45; Dual & Family $65; Young Collectors $90; Enthusiasts $200; Patron $500; Director's Circle $1,000; President's Circle $2,500.

MUSEUM OF RUSSIAN CULTURE, (M), 2450 Sutter St., San Francisco, CA 94115-3016. Tel.: 415-921-4082. Fax: 415-921-4082.
Founded: 1948.
Key Personnel: Pres., Nicholas Koretsky; Vice Pres., Yuri Tarala; Cur., Nicholas Diachkoff.
Governing Authority: nonprofit. Tax-exempt: 501(c)(3).

Ethnic History Museum.
Collections: archives; history; military; ethnology; numismatic; manuscripts.
Research Fields: Russian history & immigration.
Activities: lectures; inter-museum loan & permanent exhibitions;.
Publications: biennial, Sbornik Museia Russkoy Kultury.
Hours & Admission Prices: Wed. & Sat. 10:30-2:30. No charge. Closed holidays.
Membership: Annual $6.

MUSEUM OF THE AFRICAN DIASPORA, 685 Mission St., San Francisco, CA 94105-4126. Tel.: 415-358-7200. Fax: 415-358-7252.
E-mail: kbrown@moadsf.org
Web Site: www.moadsf.org
Founded: 2003.
Key Personnel: Chm. (V), Ernest Urquhart; Devel., Kathleen Brown; Education, Demetrie Broxton; Financial Dir., Yen Nguyenle; Cur. Public Programs, Shiree Dyson.
Personnel Profile: Full-Time Paid 7; Part-Time Paid 2; Part-Time Volunteers 50; Interns 5.
Governing Authority: nonprofit organization. Tax-exempt: 501(c)(3).
Art Museum.
Collections: art, history & culture of African Diaspora.
Major Exhibits: African Continuum (T), 1/10.
Facilities: 10,000 sq. ft. exhibit space; 85-seat auditorium; educational facilities. Museum-related items for sale.
Activities: docent program; films; formal education programs for adults; guided tours; lectures.
Hours & Admission Prices: Wed.-Sat. 11-6, Sun. 12-5. Adults $10, senior citizens 65 & over and students $5; children 12 & under and members no charge. Closed New Year's Day; Labor Day; Thanksgiving; Christmas.
Attendance: 70,000 (accurate)
Membership: Senior, Teacher & Student $45; Individual $65; Dual & Family $85; Supporter $150; Contributor $250; Donor $500; Sustaining $1,000; Patron $1,500; Sponsor $2,500; Benefactor $5,000.

MUSEUM OF VISION, 655 Beach St., San Francisco, CA 94109-1342. Tel.: 415-561-8500. Fax: 415-561-8533.
E-mail: museum@aao.org
Web Site: www.museumofvision.org
Formerly: Museum of Vision Foundation of the American Academy of Ophthalmology
Founded: 1980.
Key Personnel: Dir. Museum of Vision, Jenny Benjamin.
Personnel Profile: Full-Time Paid 1.
Governing Authority: nonprofit organization. Parent Institution: The Foundation of the American Academy of Ophthalmology. Tax-exempt.
Medical History Museum.
Collections: history of ophthalmology from the 14th century-present; spectacles; diagnostic & surgical instruments; pharmaceuticals; stamps & coins; photography; memorabilia; literature & oral histories; archives.
Research Fields: 1600-present history of ophthalmology.
Facilities: 500-vol. library & archive pertaining to ophthalmology; 600 sq. ft. exhibit space.
Activities: history resource services; educational resources & collections; traveling exhibitions.
Publications: brochure; oral histories; Eye Openers; Art and Vision: Seeing in 3-D; Discover Your Eye Q!; Eye Qs: Activities with Vision.
Hours & Admission Prices: Mon.-Fri. 9-5. Tours by appointment only. No charge; donations accepted. Closed national holidays. ♿
Attendance: 300

NATIONAL JAPANESE AMERICAN HISTORICAL SOCIETY PEACE GALLERY, 1684 Post St., San Francisco, CA 94115-3604. Tel.: 415-921-5007. Fax: 415-921-5087.
Historical Society Museum.
Collections: Japanese American culture & history; paintings; personal artifacts; photographs.
Facilities: Museum-related items for sale.
Activities: educational programs; special events; workshops.
Publications: journal; newsletters.
Hours & Admission Prices: Mon.-Fri. & 1st Sat. of month 12-5.

NATIONAL LIBERTY SHIP MEMORIAL/S.S. JEREMIAH O'BRIEN, 1275 Columbus Ave., Ste. 300, San Francisco, CA 94133. Tel.: 415-544-0100. Fax: 415-544-9890.
E-mail: liberty@ssjeremiahobrien.org
Web Site: www.ssjeremiahobrien.org
Founded: 1978.
Key Personnel: Chm., Carl Nolte
Merchant Marine Ship Museum and U.S. Naval Armed Guard: built in 1943.
Collections: WWII artifacts.
Facilities: Museum-related items for sale.
Activities: tours; cruises.
Publications: quarterly, Steady As She Goes.
Hours & Admission Prices: Daily 9-4. Adults $8, seniors $5, juniors 6-14 $4; active military & children under 6 no charge. Closed New Year's Day; Thanksgiving; Christmas Day.
Membership: Student $20; Individual $50; Family $100; Sponsor $250; Life $800; Corporate $1,500.

OCTAGON HOUSE, 2645 Gough St., San Francisco, CA 94123-4402. Tel.: 415-441-7512.
Historic House: octagonal in shape, used as a family residence until the late 1920s. Listed on the National Register of Historic Places.
Collections: period furnishings; portraits; silver; pewter; ceramics; documents bearing signatures of 54 of the 56 Signers of the Declaration of Independence.
Hours & Admission Prices: Feb.-Dec. 2nd Sun. & 2nd and 4th Thurs. 12-3. No charge; donations accepted. Closed legal holidays.
Attendance: 1,249

RANDALL MUSEUM, 199 Museum Way, San Francisco, CA 94114-1429. Tel.: 415-554-9600. Fax: 415-554-9609.
E-mail: info@randallmuseum.org
Web Site: www.randallmuseum.org
Founded: 1937.
Congressional District: 6
Key Personnel: Exec. Dir., Chris Boettcher; Cur. Science, John Dillon; Dir. Devel., Traci McCollister; Ceramics Instructor, Dennis Treanor; Animal Exhibit Asst., Molly Bradley; Science Instructor, Margaret Goodale; Cur. Science, Susan Way; Arts Coord., Julie Dodd Tetzlaff; Animal Exhibit Mgr., Nancy Ellis; Receptionist, Della Young; Gardener, Hugh McDermott.
Personnel Profile: Full-Time Paid 11; Part-Time Paid 1; Part-Time Volunteers 25; Interns 3.
Governing Authority: municipal; county. Parent Institution: San Francisco Recreation & Park Dept. Subsidiary Institution: Randall Museum Friends. Tax-exempt.
Community Museum.
Collections: rocks & minerals; fossils; shells; butterflies; live animals.
Facilities: 180-seat Children's Theater; woodworking shop; art studio; ceramics studio; lapidary shop; photography darkroom; live animal room; model railroad; seismograph; classroom; greenhouse; gardens; park.
Activities: guided tours; lectures; films; workshops for children & adults; permanent & temporary exhibits.
Publications: quarterly newsletter; class flyer published five times annually.
Hours & Admission Prices: Tues.-Sat. 10-5. No charge; donations accepted. Closed New Year's Day; Independence Day; Veterans Day; Thanksgiving; Christmas; state & federal holidays. ♿
Attendance: 85,000 (estimated)
Membership: Individual $30; Family $40; Associate $50; Sponsor $100; Patron $250 & up.

SAN FRANCISCO AFRICAN AMERICAN HISTORICAL AND CULTURAL SOCIETY, INC., 762 Fulton St., 2nd Fl., San Francisco, CA 94102-4119. Tel.: 415-292-6172.
E-mail: info@sfblackhistory.org
Founded: 1955.
Congressional District: 5
Key Personnel: Admin., Vandean Philpott.
Governing Authority: nonprofit organization. Affiliated with the Association for Study of Afro-American Life & History, 1528 9th St., N.W., Washington DC 20001. Subsidiary Institution: Center for African & African American Art. Tax-exempt: 501(c)(3).
African American Cultural Center.
Collections: Sargent Johnson, Mary Ellen Pleasant, R. Alan Williams & Dorothy Haywood collections; Haitian art.
Research Fields: African American Western history; African American national history of Africa and South America; Caribbean Islands; African American curriculum development.
Facilities: 3,000-vol. library of books, pamphlets, photographs, periodicals, magazines & encyclopedia available for use on premises & for inter-library loan; reading room; 100-seat auditorium; classroom.
Activities: guided tours; lectures; films; gallery talks; concerts; arts festivals; drama; study clubs; permanent & temporary exhibitions. Museum Sponsors: youth programs; African American history classes; senior history & crafts.
Publications: quarterly newsletter.
Hours & Admission Prices: Wed.-Sun. 12-5. Suggested Donations: adults $2, children $1. Closed New Year's Eve & Day; Memorial Day; Independence Day; Labor Day; Thanksgiving; Christmas. ♿

Attendance: 55,000
Membership: Senior & Youth $10; Individual $25; Family $40; Sustaining $100 or more; Life $500; Organization-small $1,000; Organization-large $2,500.

SAN FRANCISCO ART INSTITUTE - WALTER & MCBEAN GALLERIES, 800 Chestnut St., San Francisco, CA 94133-2299. Tel.: 415-749-4563. Fax: 415-351-3516.
E-mail: exhibitions@artists.sfai.edu
Web Site: www.sfai.edu
Founded: 1871.
Congressional District: 6
Key Personnel: Pres., Chris Bratton; Dir. Exhibitions & Public Programs, Hou Hanru; Dean, Okwui Enwezor; Asst. Cur., Mary Ellyn Johnson.
Personnel Profile: Full-Time Paid 2; Part-Time Paid 8.
Governing Authority: nonprofit organization. Parent Institution: San Francisco Art Institute. Tax-exempt: 501(c)(3).
Art Museum.
Collections: works by contemporary artists.
Major Exhibits: Everyday Miracles (T), 10/09-2/10.
Research Fields: contemporary art.
Facilities: 27,000-vol. library; slide library of works by contemporary artists; 250-seat auditorium; 3,000 sq. ft. galleries.
Activities: contemporary exhibitions program; performance; video & film series; active visiting artists program.
Publications: exhibition catalogs/artists' books, Sue Williams; Joyce J. Scott; Lee Bul Live Forever; Sarkis, Wherever We Go; Allora & Calzadilla; Jen Haaning, 5/09; Teddy Cruz; Pedro Reyes; Yan Pei Ming; Aleksander Komarov; Atelier Bow-Wow; Cyprien Gaillard; Jimmie Durham; Knut Asdam; Mark Lewis; Sam Samore; Hamra Abbas; Jewyo Rhii; Kan Xuan; Ringo Bunoan; Cao Fei.
Hours & Admission Prices: Tues.-Sat. 11-6. No charge. Closed holidays. ♿
Attendance: 18,000

SAN FRANCISCO BOTANICAL GARDEN AT STRYBING ARBORETUM, 1199 9th Ave., (at Lincoln Way), San Francisco, CA 94122-2370. Tel.: 415-661-1316. Fax: 415-661-3539.
E-mail: info@sfbotanicalgarden.org
Web Site: www.sfbotanicalgarden.org
Founded: 1937.
Congressional District: 5
Key Personnel: Dir., Brent Dennis; Pres., Ann Cameron; Supt., Susan Nervo; Exec. Dir., Michael McKechnie; Plant Collections Mgr., Mona Bourell; Volunteer Coord., Tom Laursen; Head Librarian, Barbara Pitschel; Asst. Librarian, Brandy Kuhl; Children's Education, Annette Huddle; Shop Mgr., Dennis Guttman; Membership, Stephanie Perez; Adult Education, Fred Bove.
Personnel Profile: Full-Time Paid 27; Part-Time Paid 7; Part-Time Volunteers 300; Interns 16.
Governing Authority: municipal. A branch of the Recreation & Park Dept. of the City & County of San Francisco, McLaren Lodge, Golden Gate Park, CA 94117. Subsidiary Institution: San Francisco Botanical Garden Society. Tax-exempt.
Arboretum & Botanical Gardens.
Collections: plants from Mediterranean climates; Asiatic magnolias, Vireya rhododendrons; conifers; California natives; primitive plants; fragrance garden for blind; demonstration garden; Mexican cloud forest; periodicals.
Facilities: 25,000-vol. Helen Crocker Russell Library; The County Fair Building with 2 lecture rooms; auditorium; 55-acres of gardens.
Activities: guided tours; lecture series; outdoor education school program, elementary through college; work study program; docent training program; training programs for professional museum workers; horticultural therapy workshops to train activity directors & volunteers.
Publications: garden guide; plant guide list; newsletter; self-guiding pamphlets.
Hours & Admission Prices: Mon.-Fri. 8-4:30, Sat.-Sun. & holidays 10-5. No charge; donations requested. ♿
Attendance: 500,000 (estimated)
Membership: Avid Gardener $60; Garden Friend $75; Garden Lover $125; Garden Steward $250; Garden Patron $500; Strybing Circle $1,000.

SAN FRANCISCO CAMERAWORK, 657 Mission St., San Francisco, CA 94105-4104. Tel.: 415-512-2020. Fax: 415-512-7109.
E-mail: info@sfcamerawork.org
Web Site: www.sfcamerawork.org
Founded: 1974.
Congressional District: 6
Key Personnel: Exec. Dir., Sharon Tanenbaum; Pres. (V), Kristen Wolfe; Dir. Devel., Melissa Fever; Cur, Chuck Mobley; Gallery Mgr., Dina Howard; Education Coord., Erik Auerbach; Operations Coord., Andrew Goodrich.
Personnel Profile: Full-Time Paid 5; Part-Time Paid 1; Part-Time Volunteers 20; Interns 10.
Governing Authority: nonprofit organization. Tax-exempt: 501(c)(3).
Photography Museum.
Collections: photographic reference library.
Facilities: reference library of photography books and catalogs available for research on premises. Museum-related items for sale.
Activities: On-going exhibitions program; temporary & traveling exhibitions; lectures and workshops; critique sessions; video and film screenings; book signing events.
Publications: biannual, Camerawork: A Journal of Photographic Arts; exhibition catalogs.
Hours & Admission Prices: Tues.-Sat. 12-5. Adults $5, students & seniors $2. Closed national holidays. ♿
Attendance: 30,000 (estimated)
Membership: Senior & Student $30; Subscribing Member $50; Household $85; Sponsor $200; Collector $350 & up.

SAN FRANCISCO FIRE DEPARTMENT MUSEUM, 655 Presidio Ave., San Francisco, CA 94115-2424. Tel.: 415-558-3546 & 563-4630.
E-mail: sffdhs@sffiremuseum.org
Web Site: www.sffiremuseum.org
Founded: 1964.
Congressional District: 5
Key Personnel: Dir., Paul L. Barry; Chief Dept., Joanne Hayes-White.
Governing Authority: municipal. Sponsored by: San Francisco Fire Dept. Historical Society. Tax-exempt: 501(c)(3).
Fire Museum.
Collections: artifacts, memorabilia & apparatus relating to the firefighting history of San Francisco.
Research Fields: San Francisco Fire Dept. history.
Activities: firemen's musters throughout the west; special demonstrations.
Publications: newsletter, St. Francis Hook & Ladder Society.
Hours & Admission Prices: Thurs.-Sun. 1-4 by appointment. No charge; donations accepted. ♿
Membership: Student & Senior Citizen $15; General $25; Business & Professional $50; Life $1,000 & up.

* **SAN FRANCISCO INTERNATIONAL AIRPORT; SAN FRANCISCO AIRPORT MUSEUMS, (M),** San Francisco International Airport, San Francisco, CA 94128. Mailing Address: P.O. Box 8097, San Francisco, CA 94128-8097. Tel.: 650-821-6700. Fax: 650-821-6777.
E-mail: Comments@sfoArts.org
Web Site: www.sfoarts.org
Founded: 1980.
Congressional District: 12
Key Personnel: Pres. Airport Commission, Larry Mazzola; Dir. Airport, John L. Martin; Dir. & Chief Cur., Blake Summers; Exec. Administrative Asst., Kathleen Smookler; Asst. Dir., Abe Garfield; Cur. Aviation, John Hill; Cur. Administration & Special Projects, Sonya Knudsen; Cur. Registration, Barbara Geib.
Personnel Profile: Full-Time Paid 27; Part-Time Paid 10; Part-Time Volunteers 60; Interns 2.
Governing Authority: municipal. Parent Institution: City & County of San Francisco. Subsidiary Institution: Airport Commission. Tax-exempt.
General Museum.
Collections: commercial aviation in the Pacific region.
Major Exhibits: Ancient Mediterranean Black and Red Figure Pottery, 11/09-3/10; Flippers, Bumpers, and Silver Balls A Brief History of Pinball, 11/09-4/10; For Amusement Only-Slot Machines, Trade Simulators, and other Gambling Devices of the Mechanical Age, 11/09-5/10; Chinese Jade from the Asian Art Museum, 12/09-5/10; Japan Airlines: Sixty Years of Service, 2/10-8/10; Meissenware: Early European Porcelain from Germany, 3/10-9/10; Better City, Better Life-High-Rise Architecture and the Remaking of China's Gateway to the World, 4/10-10/10; West African Helmet Masks from the Phoebe A. Hearst Museum of Anthropology, 6/10-11/10; Pacific Mail Call: The Jon E. Krupnick Aerophilatelic Collection, 8/10-2/11; China Clipper, 8/10-4/11.
Research Fields: commercial aviation.
Facilities: 84,835 sq. ft. exhibit space.
Activities: temporary exhibitions in Airport terminals.
Publications: exhibition brochures.
Hours & Admission Prices: Airport Terminals: daily twenty-four hours a day. No charge. Aviation Library & Museum: Sun.-Fri. 10-4:30. No charge. ♿
Attendance: 4,517,339 (estimated)

* **SAN FRANCISCO MARITIME NATIONAL HISTORICAL PARK,** Fort Mason Ctr., Bldg. E, San Francisco, CA 94123. Tel.: 415-561-7000. Fax: 415-556-1624.
E-mail: lynn_cullivan@nps.gov

Web Site: www.nps.gov/safr
Founded: 1951.
Congressional District: 8
Key Personnel: Supt. & Dir., Kate Richardson; Chief Cultural Resources, Robbyn Jackson; Chief Facilities & Maintenance, Al Mayton; Chief Interpretation, Marc Hayman; Chief Administration, Shelley Neidernhofer; Cur. Maritime History, Steve Canright; Cur. Small Craft, Bill Doll; Prin. Librarian, David Hull; Cur. Exhibits, Richard Everett; Mgr. Collections, Keri Koehler; Public Affairs Officer, Lynn Cullivan; Coord. (V), Terry Dorman.
Personnel Profile: Full-Time Paid 103; Part-Time Volunteers 500; Interns 2.
Governing Authority: federal. Parent Institution: National Park Service, Dept. of the Interior. Tax-exempt.
Maritime Museum Complex.
Collections: 250,000 photographs & negatives of ships & shipping ports, primarily West Coast; 120,000 sheets of ship plans; 4,000 log books & charts; manuscripts; scrimshaw; paintings & other fine arts & decorative arts; ship models; 16,000 books & periodicals, tape recordings of interviews with seafaring men & shipowners; artifacts from historic vessels; steam machinery; small craft. Historic Ships: Balclutha, square-rigged ship; C.A. Thayer, schooner; Eureka, walking-beam ferry; Hercules, steam tug; Alma, scow schooner; Eppleton Hall, paddle-wheel tug, located at Hyde Street Pier; Clipper-Bowed Monterey, fishing boat; Wapama, steam schooner.
Research Fields: maritime history with emphasis on West Coast & Pacific Area; maritime culture, its lifestyles & folkways which are unique and set its men & women apart from the majority of society.
Facilities: bayfront recreation area. Museum-related items for sale.
Activities: permanent exhibits; special exhibits; lectures; living history program; special tours; environmental living program for school children; volunteer program; small boat restoration program; films.
Publications: monthly newsletter; brochure, quarterly park newsletter.
Hours & Admission Prices: Museum: daily. No charge. Visitor Center & Hyde Street Pier: daily 9:30-5. No charge. Historic Ships: daily 9:30-5. Adults 17 & over $5, children & federal pass holders no charge. ♿
Attendance: 4,042,022 (accurate)

SAN FRANCISCO MUSEUM OF CRAFT+DESIGN, 550 Sutter St., San Francisco, CA 94102. Tel.: 415-773-0303; 877-487-3623. Fax: 415-773-0306.
E-mail: info@sfmcd.org
Web Site: www.sfmcd.org
Founded: 2004.
Key Personnel: Exec. Dir., JoAnn Edwards; Pres. (V), Steven B. Kaplan; Museum Shop Mgr., Raymond McKenzie.
Personnel Profile: Full-Time Paid 1; Part-Time Paid 1.
Craft & Design Museum.
Collections: works of contemporary craft & design.
Major Exhibits: Designers on Jewelry: 12 Years of Jewelry Production by Chi ha paura...? (T), 1/10-5/10; Designocracy: Karim Rashid's Designs for Living (T), 6/10-10/10; Fashioning Felt (T), 11/10-1/11.
Activities: group tours by appointment; art education for children; speaker series.
Hours & Admission Prices: Tues.-Wed. & Fri.-Sat. 10-5, Thurs. 10-7, Sun. 12-5. Suggested Donations: adults $3, seniors 62 & over and students $2; children under 18 no charge. Closed holidays.

* **SAN FRANCISCO MUSEUM OF MODERN ART, (M),** 151 Third St., San Francisco, CA 94103-3159. Tel.: 415-357-4000. Fax: 415-357-4037. TDD: 415-357-4154.
Web Site: www.sfmoma.org
Founded: 1935.
Congressional District: 8
Key Personnel: Chm., Charles Schwab; Dir., Neal Benezra; Deputy Dir. Collection & Exhibitions, Ruth Berson; Deputy Dir. & Admin. Finance, Ikuko Satoda; Dir. ISS, Leo Ballate; Head Registrar, Tina Garfinkel; Sr. Cur. Painting & Sculpture, Gary Garrels; Cur. Painting & Sculpture, Janet C. Bishop; Cur. Media Arts, Rudolf Frieling; Sr. Cur. Photography, Sandra S. Phillips; Cur. Architecture & Design, Henry Urbach; Dir. Collections & Conservation, Jill Sterrett; Dir. Retail & Wholesale Operations, Jana Machin; Dir. Human Resources, Sanchie Fernandez.
Personnel Profile: Full-Time Paid 189; Part-Time Paid 49; Part-Time Volunteers 143; Interns 17.
Governing Authority: nonprofit organization. Tax-exempt: 501(c)(3).
Art Museum.
Collections: early 20th-century to present international paintings, sculpture, graphics, photography, architecture, design, digital projects & media arts.
Major Exhibits: The View From Here, 1/10-6/10; Christian Marclay, 1/10-6/10; 75 Years of Looking Forward, 1/10-7/10; Luc Tuymans (T), 2/10-5/10; How Wine Became Modern, 6/10-1/11.
Research Fields: modern & contemporary paintings, sculpture, graphics, photography, architecture, design & media arts.
Facilities: 80,000-vol. library of modern art books, periodicals & exhibit catalogues available for use on premises by appointment; painting & works on paper conservation laboratory; classrooms; 299-seat theater; art rental & sale gallery; cafe. Art books, gifts & other museum-related items for sale.
Activities: guided docent tours; lectures; concerts; formally organized educational programs; inter-museum loan, permanent, temporary & traveling exhibitions; random-access (CD-ROM based) audio tours of permanent collection.
Publications: bimonthly exhibition & program guide; annual report; exhibition catalogs; Web based member newsletters; web site.
Hours & Admission Prices: Memorial Day-Labor Day Thurs. 10-9, Fri.-Tues. 10-6; Sept.-May Thurs. 11-9, Fri.-Tues. 11-6. Adults $15, senior citizens 62 & over and students with ID $9; discounts to AAM & ICOM members and on Thurs. 6-9; first Tues. of every month, AFMOMA & museum members, and children 12 & under accompanied by an adult no charge. Closed New Year's Day; Independence Day; Thanksgiving; Christmas. ♿
Attendance: 550,000 (estimated)
Membership: Senior $45; Dual Senior $65; Individual $80; Dual Family $105; Supporting $250; Contributing $500; Benefactor $1,000.

SAN FRANCISCO ZOOLOGICAL GARDENS, 1 Zoo Rd., San Francisco, CA 94132-1098. Mailing Address: 731 Sansome St., Fl. 4, San Francisco, CA 94111-1723. Tel.: 415-753-7080. Fax: 415-681-2039.
E-mail: webmaster@sfzoo.org
Web Site: www.sfzoo.org
Founded: 1929.
Congressional District: 6
Key Personnel: Dir. Finance, Wayne Reading; Chm. (V), Gordon Dean; Pres. (V), Fred Carroll; Veterinarian, Freeland Dunker, D.V.M.; Cur. Collections, Myron I. Sulak; Dir. Public Rels., Nancy Chan; Dir. Public Rels. & Mktg., Lora LaMarca; Dir. Membership, Eric Maul; Dir. Animal Care & Conservation, Bob Jenkins; Human Resources, Arturo Aleman; Assoc. Cur., David Bocian; Assoc. Cur., Michele Rudovsky; Dir. Special Collections, Roger Hoppes; Museum Shop Mgr., Stacey Adams.
Personnel Profile: Full-Time Paid 220; Part-Time Volunteers 350; Interns 15.
Governing Authority: Parent Institution: San Francisco Zoological Society. Tax-exempt.
Zoo.
Collections: 210 wild species & 900 wild specimens of mammals, birds, amphibians & reptiles; 64 species & 6,500 specimens of invertebrates.
Research Fields: zoology; animal sciences.
Facilities: 600-vol. library of materials on zoology available on request; children's zoo; botanical garden; insect zoo. Gift items for sale.
Activities: guided tours; lectures; films; formally organized education programs for children, adults & undergraduate students; permanent & temporary exhibitions; zoomobile program; avian conservation program.
Publications: quarterly, ZOO VIEWS.
Hours & Admission Prices: Daily & holidays 10-5. Adults 15-64 $15, senior citizens 65 & over $12, youth 4-14 $9; discounts to residents; AZA reciprocating zoos, children 3 & under, members & children's zoo no charge. ♿
Attendance: 1,000,000 (estimated)
Membership: Student & Senior Citizen $45; Individual $60; Family & Dual $75; Friend $85; Patron $150; Supporting $250; Sustaining $500; Guardian $1,000.

THE SOCIETY OF CALIFORNIA PIONEERS, 300 Fourth St., San Francisco, CA 94107-1207. Tel.: 415-957-1849. Fax: 415-957-9858.
Web Site: californiapioneers.org
Founded: 1850.
Key Personnel: C.E.O., Peter J. Flagg; Pres., Erin D. Ebeling; Education, Tim Evans; Bookkeeper, Mercedes Devine; Librarian, Patricia Keats.
Personnel Profile: Full-Time Paid 7; Part-Time Paid 2; Interns 4.
Governing Authority: private; nonprofit organization. Tax-exempt: 501(c)(3.
Art Museum.
Collections: California paintings, prints, drawings, artifacts, books, manuscripts, journals, newspapers, photographs & decorative arts.
Research Fields: California art, history & culture.
Facilities: 10,000-vol. library; educational facilities; 3,000 sq. ft. exhibit space; 25-seat theater. Museum-related items for sale.
Activities: concerts; films; formal education programs; guided tours; lectures; loan, temporary & traveling exhibitions. Annual Events: Discovery of Gold Party; President's Picnic; Shumate lecture; Holiday Party.
Publications: annual journal, The Pioneer; biannual exhibition catalogues.
Hours & Admission Prices: Wed.-Fri. & 1st Sat. of month 10-4. Adults $5, senior citizens & students $2.50; discounts to Friends, AAM & ICOM members; members & children no charge. Closed Martin Luther King Jr.

Day; Presidents' Day; Memorial Day; Independence Day; Labor Day; Veterans Day; Thanksgiving & day after; Christmas Eve to New Year's Day. ♿
Attendance: 4,500 (estimated)

THE WALT DISNEY FAMILY MUSEUM, LLC, (M), 104 Montgomery St., The Presidio of San Francisco, San Francisco, CA 94129-1718. Tel.: 415-345-6821. Fax: 415-345-6896.
E-mail: info@wdfmuseum.org
Web Site: www.waltdisney.org
Founded: 2009.
Congressional District: 8
Key Personnel: Exec. Dir., Richard Benefield; Treas., Kathy Trudeau; Education, Donna Tuggle; Dir. Visitor Svcs., Michael Re; Public Rels., Elaine Mellis; Dir. Human Resources, Rosalind Cohen-Baruch; Dir. Collections, Michael Labrie; Facilities & Operations, Nancy Wolf; Museum Shop Mgr., Katy Dashiell.
Personnel Profile: Full-Time Paid 30; Part-Time Volunteers 37.
Governing Authority: private; nonprofit organization. Parent Institution: Walt Disney Family Foundation. Tax-exempt: 501(c)(3).
Disney Family History Museum.
Collections: Walt Disney's life, work & family history; animation development & art; 20th century theme parks; personal artifacts; period furnishings; family photographs & home movies; films; Oscar statuettes; drawings; animation cells; personal papers & belongings of Walt Disney; early movie posters.
Research Fields: 1930s art; Snow White and the Seven Dwarfs art; original plans & opening of Disneyland.
Facilities: 114-seat large screen theater; 114-seat auditorium; two studios; restaurant. Museum-related items for sale.
Activities: animation classes; listening stations; videos; concerts; films; formal education programs for adults & children; guided tours; lectures; participatory, temporary, & traveling exhibits; theater.
Publications: quarterly member newsletter.
Hours & Admission Prices: Wed.-Mon. 10-6. Adults $20, seniors & students $15, children 6-17 $12.50; children under 6 & members no charge. ♿
Membership: Senior $55; Individual $75; Senior Dual $95; Dual $125; Family $175; Founding $500.

WAX MUSEUM AT FISHERMAN'S WHARF, 145 Jefferson St., Ste. 500, San Francisco, CA 94133-1295. Tel.: 800-439-4305.
E-mail: sales@waxmuseum.com
Web Site: www.waxmuseum.com
Founded: 1963.
Wax Museum
Collections: over 250 wax figures.
Facilities: Museum-related items for sale.
Hours & Admission Prices: Daily 10-9. Adults $12.95, senior 55 & over and junior 12-17 $9.95, child 6-11 $6.95. ♿
Attendance: 436,000 (accurate)

WELLS FARGO HISTORY MUSEUM, Wells Fargo Bank, Historical Services, 420 Montgomery St., MAC-A010-106, San Francisco, CA 94163-0001. Tel.: 415-396-2619 & 4157. Fax: 415-975-7430.
Founded: 1929.
Key Personnel: Mgr., Glen T. Myers; Cur., Joycee Wong.
Governing Authority: profit-making organization. Affiliated with Wells Fargo Bank.
Company History Museum: located in Wells Fargo Bank's corporate headquarters.
Collections: Concord Stagecoach; Wells Fargo banking & transportation history; San Francisco & Gold Rush California exhibits; mining tools; gold specimens & coins; Wiltsee Collection of western stamps & postal history.
Activities: guided group tours; permanent & temporary exhibitions; imaginary rides on replica stagecoach; audiovisual programs.
Publications: scholarly pamphlets. History of Wells Fargo.
Hours & Admission Prices: Mon.-Fri. 9-5. No charge. Closed bank holidays. ♿

YERBA BUENA CENTER FOR THE ARTS, 701 Mission St., San Francisco, CA 94103-3138. Tel.: 415-978-2700 & ARTS (2787). Fax: 415-978-9635.
E-mail: kbudas@ybca.org
Web Site: www.ybca.org
Founded: 1986.
Key Personnel: Exec. Dir., Kenneth Foster; Pres. Bd., Janis M. Zivic; Asst. Cur. Performing Arts, Angela Mattox; Visual Arts Cur., Bethi-Sue Hertz; Dir. Mktg., Kathy Budas; Film Video Cur., Joel Shepard.
Personnel Profile: Full-Time Paid 50; Part-Time Paid 15; Part-Time Volunteers 50; Interns 5.
Governing Authority: private; nonprofit organization. Tax-exempt: 501(c)(3).
Arts Center.
Collections: visual art; performing arts; film.
Facilities: 10,000 sq. ft. exhibit space; 750, 600 & 100-seat theaters. Gift items for sale.
Activities: concerts; dance recitals; docent program; films; lectures; theater; exhibitions; music; dance; film/video; new media (hi-tech installations); educational programs.
Publications: calendar magazine, Life Amplified; season performance brochure.
Hours & Admission Prices: Tues.-Wed. & Fri.-Sun. 12-5, Thurs. 12-8. Adults $7, senior citizens, students, teachers & children $5; members no charge. ♿
Attendance: 200,000 (accurate)
Membership: Senior $45; Basic $65; Household $85; Discoverer $165; Groundbreaker $300; Curator's Circle $500; Director's Forum $1,000.

ZEUM, 221 Fourth St., San Francisco, CA 94103-3116. Tel.: 415-820-3320. Fax: 415-820-3330.
E-mail: info@zeum.org
Web Site: www.zeum.org
Founded: 1998.
Key Personnel: C.E.O., Audrey Yamamoto; Dir. Devel. & Mktg., Joy Wong Daniels; Dir. Finance & Operations, Anne Amis.
Personnel Profile: Full-Time Paid 20; Part-Time Paid 31; Part-Time Volunteers 25.
Governing Authority: Tax-exempt.
Children's Museum.
Collections: interactive visual arts; performing & media arts technology; community & youth artwork; 1906 Charles Looff carousel.
Facilities: technology studios; 200-seat theater. Museum-related items for sale.
Activities: digital art, animation, sound & video production; live performance; traveling international & community art exhibits; art workshops; preschool workshops; youth docent internships; professional (teacher) development programs; school field trips; carousel rides.
Hours & Admission Prices: Summer: Tues.-Sun. 11-5; Sept.-June Wed.-Fri. 1-5, Sat.-Sun. 11-5. Adults $10, children $8; discounts to ASTC members; members no charge. ♿
Membership: Individual $55; Family $70; Family & Caregiver $85; Organization $200.

San Gabriel

SAN GABRIEL MISSION MUSEUM, 428 S. Mission Dr., San Gabriel, CA 91776-1252. Tel.: 626-457-3035. Fax: 626-282-5308.
E-mail: alsgm1@aol.com
Web Site: www.sangabrielmission.net
Founded: 1771.
Congressional District: 29
Key Personnel: Dir., Rev. Steve Niskanen, C.M.F.; Business Mgr., Alfred Sanchez; Museum Shop Mgr., C. Lyons.
Personnel Profile: Part-Time Volunteers 14.
Governing Authority: church. Parent Institution: San Gabriel Mission Catholic Church. Tax-exempt.
Religious Museum: fourth in a chain of 21 California Missions founded Sept. 8, 1771, site of San Gabriel Mission.
Collections: Old Mission church; books; artifacts; furnishings of old mission; manuscripts; paintings; statues; photographs; plants.
Facilities: Museum-related items for sale.
Activities: self-guided tours; formally organized education programs for groups by appointment; permanent exhibitions.
Hours & Admission Prices: Daily 9-4:30. Adults $5, seniors 62 & over $4, youth 6-17 $2. ♿
Attendance: 50,000 (estimated)

San Jacinto

SAN JACINTO MUSEUM, 695 Ash St., San Jacinto, CA 92583. Mailing Address: P.O. Box 922, San Jacinto, CA 92581-0922. Tel.: 951-654-4952. Fax: 909-654-9270.
Web Site: www.ci.san-jacinto.ca.us
Founded: 1939.
Congressional District: 37
Key Personnel: Asst., Betty Jo Dunham.
Personnel Profile: Part-Time Paid 1; Part-Time Volunteers 6.
Governing Authority: municipal. Parent Institution: City of San Jacinto. Tax-exempt.
History Museum.
Collections: Indian archaeology; geology; mineralogy; paleontology; period artifacts; San Jacinto & Hemet area history.

Research Fields: local history.
Activities: permanent & temporary historical exhibitions.
Hours & Admission Prices: Fri.-Sun. 11-4. No charge; donations accepted. Closed New Year's Day; Thanksgiving; Christmas. ♿
Attendance: 3,000 (accurate)
Membership: Single $10; Couples & Family $15; Organization $25.

San Jose

CHILDREN'S DISCOVERY MUSEUM OF SAN JOSE, 180 Woz Way, San Jose, CA 95110-2780. Tel.: 408-298-5437, ext. 0. Fax: 408-298-6826.
E-mail: contactus@cdm.org
Web Site: www.cdm.org
Founded: 1982.
Congressional District: 16
Key Personnel: Exec. Dir. & Devel. Dir., Marilee Jennings Gandelman; Exec. Dir., Connie Martinez; Pres. Bd. of Dir. (V), Bruce Chizen; Vice Pres. Bd. of Dir., Randy Pond; Dir. Exhibits, Tom Lindsay; Financial Dir., Susan Clark; Dir. Education & Programs, Jenni Martin; Assoc. Dir. Education, Amity Sandage; Mktg. & Community Rels. Mgr., Cathy Fisher; Devel. & Membership Mgr., Debbie McKenzie; Human Resource Mgr., Patience Davidson; Retail & Visitor Svcs. Mgr. & Museum Shop Mgr., Carolyn Nelson.
Personnel Profile: Full-Time Paid 36; Part-Time Paid 57; Part-Time Volunteers 100.
Governing Authority: nonprofit organization. Legal Name: San Jose Children's Discovery Museum. Tax-exempt.
Children's Museum: housed in Ricardo Legorreta-designed structure.
Collections: San Jose regional history; health & physiognomy; energy; environmental sciences; cultural arts; early childhood education; communications; banking; postal service; media studio; digital communications; city & historical vehicles.
Research Fields: related to collections.
Facilities: 33,500 sq. ft. exhibit space; 120-seat black box theatre; 48-seat cafe; outdoor garden & amphitheatre.
Activities: films; concerts; theatre; school visitation program; outreach programs to schools; participatory exhibits; parent & child workshops; creative arts; environmental & science programs.
Publications: bimonthly calendar, Discovery Dates; annual report.
Hours & Admission Prices: Summer: Mon.-Sat. 10-5, Sun. 12-5; Sept. to mid-June Tues.-Sat. 10-5, Sun. 12-5; call for holiday hours. Admission $8, senior citizens over 60 $7; members and children one & under no charge. ♿
Attendance: 295,062 (accurate)
Membership: Grandparent & Family $75; Family Plus $105; Family Childcare Provider & Explorer's Circle $150; Developer's Circle $250; Partner's Circle $500; Leader's Circle $1,000 & up.

CHINESE CULTURAL GARDEN/OVERFELT GARDENS, 368 Educational Park Dr., San Jose, CA 95133-1711. Tel.: 408-251-3323. Fax: 408-251-2865.
Web Site: chineseculturalgarden.org
Key Personnel: Park Ranger, Will Bick; Gardener, Sheila Strand
General Museum.
Collections: sculptures; Chinese culture & history; gardens.
Facilities: 6 acres.
Hours & Admission Prices: Daily 10 to sunset. No charge. Closed major holidays.

HAPPY HOLLOW PARK & ZOO, 1300 Senter Rd., San Jose, CA 95112-2520. Tel.: 408-277-4193 & 3999. Fax: 408-975-9369.
Web Site: www.happyhollowparkandzoo.org
Founded: 1967.
Congressional District: 16
Key Personnel: C.E.O. & Zoo Dir., Gregg Owens.
Personnel Profile: Full-Time Paid 12; Part-Time Paid 5; Part-Time Volunteers 45.
Governing Authority: Parent Institution: City of San Jose. Subsidiary Institution: Happy Hollow Corporation.
Zoo.
Collections: live animals; birds.
Facilities: snack bar; education classroom.
Activities: rides. Museum Sponsors: feasts with the beasts; exhibit grand opening; annual membership party; Earth Day; Halloween event.
Publications: quarterly newsletter.
Hours & Admission Prices: Closed for renovations until March 2010. ♿
Attendance: 337,123 (accurate)
Membership: Sr. Student $20; Individual $30; Family $60; Donor $100; Patron $250; Sustaining $500.

* **HISTORY SAN JOSE,** 1650 Senter Rd., San Jose, CA 95112-2599. Tel.: 408-287-2290. Fax: 408-287-2291.
E-mail: abray@historysanjose.org
Web Site: www.historysanjose.org
Formerly: History Museums of San Jose
Founded: 1971.
Congressional District: 13
Key Personnel: Pres. & C.E.O., Alida Bray; Chm. Bd., Jim Towery; Dir. Operations, Barbara Johnson; Pres. (V), Joan Shepley; Dir. Resource Management, Linda Spencer; Cur. Interactive Media, Melissa Johnson; Archivist, James Reed; Cur. Art & Photography, Sarah Puckitt; Dir. Events & Museum Shop Mgr., Pam Watson; Devel. Assoc., Monica Tucker-Harley; Finance Mgr., Maggie Williams; Preparator, Joseph Cowart; Sr. Accountant, Sarita Rosario; Education Asst., Barbara Johnston; Admin. Asst., Tracy Saravanan; Facilities Mgr., Todd Shaffer.
Personnel Profile: Full-Time Paid 15; Full-Time Volunteers 20; Part-Time Paid 15; Part-Time Volunteers 200.
Governing Authority: nonprofit organization. Tax-exempt: 501(c)(3).
History Museum.
Collections: local historic furniture; household accessories; textiles; archaeology; vehicles; business equipment; archives of city records, maps, local history documents & photographs; medical instruments; California art; 16 historic structures; 10 recreated structures; Chinese temple; Portuguese Imperio; operating trolley restoration barn. Historic Houses: 1797 Peralta Adobe; 1855 Fallon House.
Research Fields: local & regional history.
Facilities: cafe. Gift items for sale.
Activities: guided tours; lectures; formally organized educational programs; docent program; research activities; history makers; summer camp; adult literacy program; rental facilities. Annual Events: Chinese Summer Festival; Heritage Days; Portuguese Festival.
Publications: quarterly membership newsletter, The Exchange; monthly volunteer newsletter, Volunteer Voices.
Hours & Admission Prices: History Park in Kelley Park: Tues.-Sun. 12-5. Peralta Adobe & Fallon House: by appointment. No charge; donations accepted. Closed New Year's Day; Independence Day; Thanksgiving; Christmas. ♿
Attendance: 100,000 (accurate)
Membership: Senior $35; Family $50; Associate $100; Partner $250; Advocate $500; Patron $1,000. Corporate: Concierge $500; Associate $1,000; Partner $2,500; Advocate $5,000; Patron $10,000 & up.

NATALIE & JAMES THOMPSON ART GALLERY, School of Art and Design SJSU, San Jose, CA 95192-0089. Tel.: 408-924-4320 & 4327. Fax: 408-924-4326.
E-mail: thompsongallery@cadre.sjsu.edu
Web Site: www.sjsu.edu
Formerly: San Jose State University Art Galleries
Founded: 1959.
Key Personnel: Gallery Dir., Jo Farb Hernandez; Asst. Dir., Theta Belcher.
Personnel Profile: Full-Time Paid 2; Part-Time Paid 6; Part-Time Volunteers 2; Interns 2.
Governing Authority: university. Affiliated with the State of California. Parent Institution: San Jose State University. Tax-exempt.
University Art Gallery.
Collections: paintings; photographs; sculpture.
Major Exhibits: Pictorial Art Faculty, 1/10-2/10; Richard Barnes: Animal Logic, 3/10-4/10; Nathan Oliveira: Fetish Series, 4/10-5/10; Miguel Palma, 8/10-9/10.
Research Fields: exhibitions & projects; fine arts; traditional arts; design.
Facilities: lecture hall.
Activities: gallery talks; formally organized education programs for undergraduate & graduate college students; temporary exhibitions; visiting artists program; weekly lecture series; class presentations; workshops.
Publications: catalogues; brochures; monthly announcements & newsletters.
Hours & Admission Prices: Sept.-May Mon. & Wed.-Fri. 11-4, Tues. 11-4 & 6-7:30. No charge. Closed semester breaks; national holidays. ♿
Attendance: 15,000 (accurate)

NEW ALMADEN QUICKSILVER MINING MUSEUM, 21350 Almaden Rd., San Jose, CA 95120-4306. Tel.: 408-323-1107. Fax: 408-323-0943.
Founded: 1998.
Key Personnel: Museum Mgr. & Museum Shop Mgr., Robin Schaut; Docent Coord., Kitty Monahan.
Personnel Profile: Full-Time Paid 2; Part-Time Volunteers 15.
Governing Authority: Parent Institution: Santa Clara County Parks.
Mining Museum.
Collections: history of mercury mining; area mining communities; mine shaft replica; Cornish, Mexican & Chinese mining families.
Hours & Admission Prices: July-Aug. Fri.-Sun. 10-4; Sept.-June Fri. 12-4,

Sat.-Sun. 10-4; other times by appointment. No charge; donations accepted. Closed New Year's Day; Thanksgiving; Christmas. ♿
Attendance: 7,500 (estimated)

PERALTA ADOBE, 175 W. Saint John St., San Jose, CA 95110-2434. Mailing Address: 1650 Senator Rd., San Jose, CA 95112. Tel.: 408-993-8300. Fax: 408-993-8008.
E-mail: kmccaman@historysanjose.org
Web Site: www.historysanjose.org/visiting_hsj/peralta_fallon
Historic Building: built in 1797.
Collections: structure; furnishings; outside working oven; daily life during the Spanish & Mexican periods.
Hours & Admission Prices: Thurs.-Sun. 11-4. Adults $6, seniors $5, youth $3.

PORTUGUESE HISTORICAL MUSEUM, 1650 Senter Rd., San Jose, CA 95112-2599. Mailing Address: Portuguese Heritage Society of California, P.O. Box 18277, San Jose, CA 95158. Tel.: 650-964-0406.
E-mail: aldutra@aol.com
Web Site: www.portuguesemuseum.org
Key Personnel: Bd. Pres., Al Dutra
Cultural History Museum.
Collections: Portuguese heritage & culture.
Hours & Admission Prices: Sat.-Sun. 1-5; other times by appointment.

ROSICRUCIAN EGYPTIAN MUSEUM, 1660 Park Ave., San Jose, CA 95191-0001. Mailing Address: 1342 Naglee Ave., San Jose, CA 95191-0001. Tel.: 408-947-3600 & 3636. Fax: 408-947-3638.
E-mail: curator@egyptianmuseum.org
Web Site: www.egyptianmuseum.org
Founded: 1929.
Congressional District: 13
Key Personnel: Dir., Julie Scott; Mgr., Nancy Leonard; Cur., Steven Armstrong.
Personnel Profile: Full-Time Paid 11; Part-Time Volunteers 16.
Governing Authority: society. Parent Institution: Rosicrucian Order AMORC. Tax-exempt: 501(c)(3).
Egyptian History Museum.
Collections: Assyrian, Babylonian & Egyptian antiquities; astronomy; paintings; sculpture; graphics; archaeology; Coptic textiles; utensils; scarabs; jewelry; statuary; amulets; human & animal mummies; replica of an Egyptian rock tomb; 18th Dynasty Egyptian garden.
Major Exhibits: Alchemical Inspirations, 6/10-5/11.
Research Fields: Egyptology.
Facilities: art gallery; temporary & permanent exhibits. Egyptian arts, crafts, statuary & books for sale.
Activities: guided tours; lectures; films; gallery talks; special tours for the blind & school groups; workshops.
Publications: catalogue, Treasures of the Rosicrucian Egyptian Museum; Hieroglyphic Coloring Book; catalogue, Women of the Nile; teacher's guide; postcard book of collection; blog, The Scribe.
Hours & Admission Prices: Mon.-Fri. 9-5, Sat.-Sun. 11-6. Adults $9, students with ID & senior citizens $7, children 5-10 $5; discounts to military, KQED, AAM & AAA members; children 4 & under & members no charge. Planetarium Showtimes: Mon.-Fri. 2, Sat.-Sun. 2 & 3:30. Closed major holidays.
Attendance: 100,000 (accurate)
Membership: Senior, Student & Teacher $20; Individual $35; Family $50; Friends of Anubis $75; Friends of NUT $125; Friends of Sekhmet $250; Friends of Isis $500; Friends of Osiris $1,000; Friends of RA $2,500.

* **SAN JOSE MUSEUM OF ART, (M),** 110 S. Market St., San Jose, CA 95113-2383. Tel.: 408-271-6840 & 6880. Fax: 408-294-2977.
E-mail: info@sjmusart.org
Web Site: www.sanjosemuseumofart.org
Founded: 1969.
Congressional District: 16
Key Personnel: Exec. Dir., Susan Krane; Pres. (V), Deborah Rappaport; Deputy Dir. Operations, Deborah Norberg; Deputy Dir. External Affairs, Patricia McLeod; Financial Officer, Lynn Schuyler-King; Dir. Mktg. & Communications, Nicole McBeth; Sr. Cur., JoAnne Northrup; Sr. Scholar, Susan Landauer; Cur. Education, Lucy Larson; Asst. Cur., Kristen Evangelista; Curatorial Asst., Jodi Throckmorton; Chief Design & Installation, Richard Karson; Facilities Mgr., John Renzel; Museum Store Mgr., Pat Downward; Events Mgr., Julia Wagner.
Personnel Profile: Full-Time Paid 24; Part-Time Paid 35; Part-Time Volunteers 300; Interns 3.
Governing Authority: nonprofit organization. Parent Institution: San Jose Museum of Art Association. Tax-exempt: 501(c)(3).
Contemporary Art Museum.
Collections: 20th and 21st-century art.
Major Exhibits: Juicy Paint, 12/09-6/10; Wayne Thiebaud: 70 Years of Painting (T), 2/10-7/10; Leo Villareal, 8/10-1/11.
Research Fields: 20th & 21st-century art with special emphasis on contemporary art.
Facilities: reference library; 78,000 sq. ft. exhibit space; two sculpture courts; cafe. Museum-related items for sale.
Activities: docent tours; lectures; gallery talks; local school art program; art classes for children & adults; poetry readings; concerts; art demonstrations; rental facilities. Annual Events: quarterly signed exhibition tours; quarterly Kids Art Sunday: free hands-on workshops & performing arts; opera at the museum.
Publications: exhibition brochures; annual donor acknowledgement; quarterly newsletter; Art Works! education brochure.
Hours & Admission Prices: Tues.-Sun.11-5. Adults $8; discounts to AAM members; members no charge. Closed New Year's Day; Thanksgiving; Christmas. ♿
Attendance: 105,000 (estimated)
Membership: Individual $50; Young Professional $65; Dual & Family $75; Art Advocate $150; Contributor $300; Benefactor $600; Collector $1,000; Curator $2,500.

SAN JOSE MUSEUM OF QUILTS & TEXTILES, (M), 520 S. First St., San Jose, CA 95113-2806. Tel.: 408-971-0323, ext. 16. Fax: 408-971-7226.
E-mail: jane@sjquiltmuseum.org
Web Site: www.sjquiltmuseum.org
Founded: 1977.
Congressional District: 10
Key Personnel: Bd. Pres., Connie Tiegel; Dir., Jane Przybysz; Museum Shop Mgr., Jeanne Holmes; Educational Outreach, Sylvia Carroll; Business Mgr., Drew Goings; Deputy Dir., Connie DeWitt.
Personnel Profile: Full-Time Paid 3; Full-Time Volunteers 1; Part-Time Paid 4; Part-Time Volunteers 100; Interns 1.
Governing Authority: board of directors. Tax-exempt: 501(c)(3).
Quilt & Textile Museum
Collections: over 500 quilts & textiles from 1850 to present.
Major Exhibits: Still Crazy, 11/17/09-2/7/10; Poetic License: The Art of Joan Schultze, 2/16/10-5/9/10; Navajo Weaving in the Present Tense: The Art of Lucy and Ellen Begay, 2/16/10-5/9/10; Hawaii's Alfred Shaheen: Fabric and Fashion, 5/18/10-8/8/10.
Research Fields: contemporary fiber art & quilt history.
Facilities: Museum-related items for sale.
Activities: guided tours; lectures; organized education programs for children; docent program; participatory, loan, temporary & traveling exhibitions; education outreach to local 2nd & 5th grade students, call museum for schedule.
Publications: quarterly newsletter, Connections.
Hours & Admission Prices: Tues.-Wed. & Fri.-Sun. 10-5, Thurs. 10-8. Adults $6.50; discounts to AAM members; children 12 & under and 1st Fri. of month no charge. Closed major holidays. ♿
Attendance: 20,000 (estimated)
Membership: Individual $40; Family $55; Patron $100; Sponsor $250; Benefactor $500.

THE TECH MUSEUM, 201 S. Market St., San Jose, CA 95113-2008. Tel.: 408-294-TECH. Fax: 408-279-7167.
E-mail: info@thetech.org
Web Site: www.thetech.org
Formerly: The Tech Museum of Innovation
Founded: 1990.
Key Personnel: C.E.O. & Pres., Peter Friess; Chm., Ann Bowers; Mktg. & Public Rels., Elizabeth Williams; Mktg. & Public Rels., Roqua Montez; Operations, Bill Bailor.
Personnel Profile: Full-Time Paid 90; Part-Time Paid 44; Part-Time Volunteers 440.
Governing Authority: Tax-exempt.
Science & Technology Museum.
Collections: technology & how it affects our lives; innovation; the internet; the human body; exploration; hands-on exhibits.
Major Exhibits: Star Trek (T), 11/09-4/10.
Facilities: 295-seat IMAX Dome Theater; Robert N. Noyce Center for Learning; 4,000 sq. ft. used for educational media & science/technology labs; 80-seat cafe. Museum-related items for sale.
Activities: hands-on learning workshops.
Publications: Innovation calendar for members only.
Hours & Admission Prices: Daily 10-5. Admission $10; members no charge. Closed Christmas. ♿
Attendance: 500,000 (accurate)
Membership: Individual $25; Family $80; Sustaining $250; Explorer $500; Leadership Circle $1,000 & up.

YOUTH SCIENCE INSTITUTE, Penitencio Creek Rd., San Jose, CA 95127. Mailing Address: 296 Garden Hill Dr., Los Gatos, CA 95032-7669. Tel.: 408-258-4322. Fax: 408-358-3683.
E-mail: info@ysi-ca.org
Web Site: www.ysi-ca.org
Founded: 1953.
Congressional District: 10, 12, 13
Key Personnel: Exec. Dir., Susane Mulcahy; Pres. (V), Mark Lohbeck; Administrative Asst., Marion Blair; YSI Center Mgr. Sanborn & Animal Cur. Sanborn, Laura Weiss; Animal Cur. Alum Rock, Dorothy Johnson; Dir. Education, Bonnie Lemat.
Personnel Profile: Full-Time Paid 7; Part-Time Paid 30; Part-Time Volunteers 25.
Governing Authority: nonprofit organization. Branch Museums: Alum Rock Nature Center, 16260 Alum Rock Ave., San Jose, CA 95127. Tel.: 408-258-4322; Vasona Park Nature Center, 296 Garden Hill Dr., Los Gatos, CA 95032. Tel.: 408-356-4945; Sanborn Park Nature Center, 16055 Sanborn Rd., Saratoga, CA 95070. Tel.: 408-867-6940. Tax-exempt: 501(c)(3).
Children's Natural History Museum & Nature Center.
Collections: Alum Rock Center: houses a live animal collection of vertebrate species. Holmes bird collection: 300 species & hands-on exhibitry. Vasona Discovery Center: physics, watershed, live animals; hands-on exhibits. Sanborn Discovery Center: insect zoo, live amphibian & reptile collection, rock & mineral collection; hands-on natural history displays.
Facilities: 200-vol. library of science material available for inter-library loan & to the public; aquarium; nature & conservation center; educational facilities; 1,000 sq. ft. exhibit space at each center. Science games & toys for sale.
Activities: lectures; organized educational programs; training programs for animal caretakers; docent program; participatory exhibits. Museum Sponsors: Wildlife Festival & Insect Fair.
Publications: quarterly newsletter; summer programs & general brochures; curriculum guide to the Viola Anderson Native Plant Trail; checklist of birds of Alum Rock Park.
Hours & Admission Prices: Summer: Tues.-Sun. 12-4:30; School Groups: Mon.-Fri. 9-5. Alum Rock: adults $1, children $.50. Sanborn & Vasona locations donations accepted. ♿
Attendance: 70,000 (estimated)

San Juan Bautista

MUSEUM, MISSION SAN JUAN BAUTISTA, 406 Second St., San Juan Bautista, CA 95045. Mailing Address: P.O. Box 400, San Juan Bautista, CA 95045-0400. Tel.: 831-623-2127. Fax: 831-623-2433.
E-mail: ann@oldmissionsjb.org
Web Site: www.oldmissionsjb.org/history.html
Founded: 1797.
Congressional District: 25
Key Personnel: Pastor, Rev. Edward Fitz-Henry; Museum Shop Mgr., Jackie Ferreira.
Governing Authority: church.
Historic Site: one of the original California missions founded by Franciscan Fathers.
Collections: adobe walls with original Indian decorations; local Indian, Spanish, Mexican & religious artifacts; archives; convent wing containing Spanish colonial period artifacts; chairs; candelabra; figures of saints; baptismal fonts.
Research Fields: mission & local history.
Facilities: Museum-related items for sale.
Activities: self-guided tour.
Publications: Guide to Old Mission SJB.
Hours & Admission Prices: Office: Mon.-Fri. 9-12 & 1-4. Museum: daily 9:30-4:30. Suggested Donations: adults $2, students & seniors $1. Closed New Year's Day; Good Friday; Thanksgiving; Christmas. ♿
Membership: Individual $5; Family $10.

SAN JUAN BAUTISTA STATE HISTORIC PARK, 2nd St., Washington & Mariposa Sts., San Juan Bautista, CA 95045-0787. Mailing Address: P.O. Box 787, San Juan Bautista, CA 95045-0787. Tel.: 831-623-4881 & 4526. Fax: 831-623-4612.
Web Site: www.parks.ca.gov
Founded: 1933.
Congressional District: 16
Key Personnel: Supt., Eddie Guaracha; Pres. (V), Bob Cable; Chm. (V), Nikki Combs; Cur., Kris N. Quist; Chief Interpreter, Pat Clark-Gray; Museum Shop Mgr., Joanna McMahon.
Personnel Profile: Full-Time Paid 8; Part-Time Paid 8; Part-Time Volunteers 36.
Governing Authority: state. Parent Institution: California Dept. of Parks & Recreation, P.O. Box 942896, Sacramento, CA 95811. Tax-exempt.
State Historic Park: located next to a Franciscan mission.
Collections: furniture; house furnishings; wagons & buggies; blacksmith tools & equipment; period clothing; 1880 fire wagon. Historic Buildings: Castro/Breen Adobe; Plaza Hotel; Plaza Stable; Plaza Hall (Zanetta home); jail; settler's cabin.
Research Fields: Spanish, Mexican & early American California.
Facilities: gardens available for small parties; Plaza Hotel Barroom available for smaller parties, call for reservations.
Activities: self-guided & guided tours by reservation; hornito & tortilla demonstrations and living history demonstrations on selected weekends; video. Museum Sponsors: 1st Sat. of every month, Living History Day; entertainment in Plaza Hotel Barroom in cooperation with the Plaza History Assoc.
Publications: general information brochure; video on the town of San Juan Bautista's History; video on the Castro and Breen families.
Hours & Admission Prices: Daily 10-4:30. Adults $2; children 16 & under no charge. Closed New Year's Day; Thanksgiving; Christmas. ♿
Attendance: 99,600 (accurate)
Membership: Individual $10; Family $15; Historical Association $25; Sustaining $50; Corporate $100.

San Juan Capistrano

MISSION SAN JUAN CAPISTRANO MUSEUM, 26801 Ortega Hwy., San Juan Capistrano, CA 92675-2601. Tel.: 949-234-1300. Fax: 949-493-8747.
Web Site: www.missionsjc.com
Founded: 1980.
Congressional District: 48
Key Personnel: Exec. Dir., Mechelle Lawrence-Adams; Devel. & Mktg., Barb Beier; Museum Conservator, Catherine Hayes.
Personnel Profile: Full-Time Paid 20; Part-Time Paid 10; Part-Time Volunteers 100.
Governing Authority: Diocese of Orange County California; nonprofit. Tax-exempt.
Historic & Archaeological Site.
Collections: four historic murals; photographs; artifacts of the Spanish rancho era c.1800; local American Indian collections; 13 acres of botanical gardens with flowers from 60 different countries; Spanish-Moorish adobe ruins 225 years old; ruins of Great Stone Church which fell in earthquake of 1812.
Facilities: lecture & media room; educational gardens; 10.5 acres of grounds.
Activities: audio tours; special events; community activities; hands-on exhibits; children's education programs; docent programs; living history programs; summer camp programs; summer concert series.
Publications: quarterly newsletter, The Jewel.
Hours & Admission Prices: Daily 8:30-5. Adults $9, seniors 60 & over and children 4-11 $5; children 3 & under no charge. Closed Thanksgiving; Christmas. ♿
Attendance: 500,000 (estimated)
Membership: Individual $30; Family $50; Supporting $100; Patron $500.

San Luis Obispo

APPLE FARM MILL HOUSE, 2015 Monterey St., San Luis Obispo, CA 93401-2695. Tel.: 805-544-2040.
E-mail: info@applefarm.com
Web Site: www.applefarm.com
Key Personnel: Dir. Mktg., Kim Wykoff
Technology Museum.
Collections: working grist mill; gardens; waterfalls.
Facilities: gardens.
Activities: system of pulleys, shafts, gears & water produces stone-ground wheat, fresh apple cider & ice cream.
Hours & Admission Prices: Call for hours.

DALLIDET ADOBE AND GARDENS, 1185 Pacific St., San Luis Obispo, CA 93401-3301. Tel.: 805-543-6762. Fax: 805-783-2919.
Web Site: www.slochs.org/dalliet.asp
Key Personnel: Exec. Dir., Kimberly Alfaro
History Museum.
Collections: furniture; paintings; personal artifacts.
Activities: rental facilities.
Hours & Admission Prices: Fri. 10-1, 2nd Sun. of month 1-4.

MISSION SAN LUIS OBISPO DE TOLOSA, 751 Palm St., San Luis Obispo, CA 93401-3521. Tel.: 805-543-6850 (gift shop) & 781-8220. Fax: 805-781-8214.
Web Site: www.sanluisobispo.org
Founded: 1772.
Key Personnel: Pastor, Rev. Russell Brown; Mgr. Gift Shop & Museum, Minerva Soto.
Governing Authority: church; nonprofit. Parent Institution: Diocese of Monterey. Tax-exempt: 170(b)(1)(a).

Religious & History Museum: 1772 Mission San Luis Obispo de Tolosa.
Collections: area artifacts; Chumash Indian collection; original stations of the cross; robes; original altar pieces.
Facilities: Religious goods, books on the history of the Mission & religious themes & other museum-related items for sale.
Activities: docent guided tour by appointment.
Publications: tapes & books by Fr. Nisbet.
Hours & Admission Prices: Memorial Day to Labor Day daily 9-5; Sept.-May daily 9-4. Suggested Donation: $2. Closed New Year's Day; Easter; Thanksgiving; Christmas. ♿
Attendance: 2,000,000 (estimated)

SAN LUIS OBISPO ART CENTER, 1010 Broad St., San Luis Obispo, CA 93401-3505. Tel.: 805-543-8562.
Web Site: www.sloartcenter.org
Founded: 1967.
Key Personnel: Dir., Karen M. Kile.
Governing Authority: Tax-exempt.
Art Museum.
Collections: paintings; sculpture.
Hours & Admission Prices: July 4 to Labor Day daily 11-5; Sept.-July 3 Wed.-Mon. 11-5. No charge; donations accepted. Closed New Year's Day; Easter; Independence Day; Christmas.
Attendance: 42,000 (estimated)
Membership: Student $20; Senior $25; Individual $30; Family $45; Business $125.

SAN LUIS OBISPO COUNTY HISTORICAL SOCIETY & MUSEUM, 696 Monterey St., San Luis Obispo, CA 93401-3515. Tel.: 805-543-0638. Fax: 805-783-2919.
E-mail: kalfaro@slochs.org
Web Site: www.slochs.org/
Founded: 1956.
Congressional District: 20
Key Personnel: Pres. (V), Elise Wheeler; Exec. Dir., Kimberly Alfaro; Assoc. Dir., Dan Carpenter.
Personnel Profile: Full-Time Paid 2; Full-Time Volunteers 1; Part-Time Paid 1; Part-Time Volunteers 100; Interns 1.
Governing Authority: Parent Institution: San Luis Obispo County Historical Society. Tax-exempt: 501(c)(3).
History Museum.
Collections: 40,000 miscellaneous historic artifacts; archives; textiles; decorative arts; folklore; history items; photographs; newspapers; ledgers; maps; Historic Houses: 1838 Dana Adobe; 1853 Dallidet Adobe.
Research Fields: local & California history.
Facilities: 1,000-vol. library of history books relating to city, county & state of California available for use on the premises; reading room.
Activities: temporary exhibitions.
Publications: monthly newsletter; local history books.
Hours & Admission Prices: Wed.-Sun. 10-4; other times by appointment. No charge; donations accepted. Closed New Year's Day; Easter; Memorial Day; Labor Day; Thanksgiving; Christmas. ♿
Attendance: 16,000 (accurate)
Membership: Historical Society: Individual $25; Dual & Family $40; Sustaining $100; Business Membership $125; Institutional $250; Life $1,000.

San Marcos

BOEHM GALLERY, 1140 W. Mission Rd., San Marcos, CA 92069-1415. Tel.: 760-744-1150, ext. 2304. Fax: 760-744-8123.
E-mail: jbigfeather@palomar.edu
Web Site: www.palomar.edu/art/BoehmGallery.html
Founded: 1964.
Congressional District: 43
Key Personnel: Dir., Joanna Bigfeather; Pres. Palomar College, Robert Deegan; Librarian, Daniel Arnsan; Dir. Public Rels., Mike Norton.
Personnel Profile: Full-Time Paid 1; Part-Time Paid 3; Part-Time Volunteers 2; Interns 2.
Governing Authority: college. Parent Institution: Palomar College. Tax-exempt.
Art Gallery.
Collections: over 200 pieces by major & local artists dating from the 16th century to present.
Research Fields: contemporary San Diego artists.
Activities: lectures; gallery talks; temporary exhibitions.
Publications: catalogues.
Hours & Admission Prices: Tues. 10-4, Wed.-Thurs. 10-7, Fri.-Sat. 10-2. No charge; donations accepted. Closed school holidays. ♿
Attendance: 6,500 (accurate)

San Marino

HUNTINGTON LIBRARY, ART COLLECTIONS, AND BOTANICAL GARDENS, 1151 Oxford Rd., San Marino, CA 91108-1218. Tel.: 626-405-2140 & 2100. Fax: 626-405-0225.
E-mail: publicinformation@huntington.org
Web Site: www.huntington.org
Founded: 1919.
Congressional District: 22
Key Personnel: Chm. Bd. Trustees, Stewart R. Smith; Chm. Bd. Overseers, Ken McCormick; Pres., Dr. Steven S. Koblik; Dir. Art Collections, John Murdoch; Cur. Manuscripts, Mary Robertson; Cur. Rare Books, Alan Jutzi; Dir. Botanical Gardens, James P. Folsom; Dir. Library, David Zeidberg; Dir. Research, Robert C. Ritchie; Vice Pres. Financial Affairs, Alison Sowden; Readers' Svcs. Librarian, Laura Stalker; Head Technical Svcs., Lorraine Perrotta; Vice Pres. Communications, Susan Turner-Lowe; Vice Pres. Advancement, George Abdo; Museum Shop Mgr., Janet Crockett.
Personnel Profile: Full-Time Paid 225; Part-Time Paid 70; Part-Time Volunteers 1,000; Interns 20.
Governing Authority: nonprofit organization. Tax-exempt: 501(c)(3).
Library, Art Gallery & Botanical Gardens.
Collections: 18th-century British & European art; paintings; drawings; watercolors; manuscripts; books; sculpture; silver; miniatures; furniture; porcelain; French 18th-century paintings, decorative arts; Renaissance paintings & bronzes; c.1730-1930 American paintings; botanical collections of camellias, roses, trees and rare & endangered succulents.
Research Fields: British & American history & literature; art history, history of science.
Facilities: 600,000-vol. library; 150-acre botanical garden; 500-seat auditorium; classrooms; 175-seat restaurant. Books & gift items for sale.
Activities: guided tours; gallery talks; formally organized education programs for children; permanent & temporary exhibitions; public programs; invitational programs; a teaching greenhouse.
Publications: reprints; pamphlets; scholarly research books; calendar of events; magazine, Frontiers; annual report; exhibition catalogues.
Hours & Admission Prices: Wed.-Mon. 12-4:30. Call for admission prices. Closed New Year's Day; Independence Day; Thanksgiving; Christmas Eve & Day. ♿
Attendance: 500,000 (accurate)

OLD MILL MUSEUM, EL MOLINO VIEJO - OLD MILL FOUNDATION, 1120 Old Mill Rd., San Marino, CA 91108-1840. Tel.: 626-449-5458. Fax: 626-449-1057.
E-mail: oldmill@sbcglobal.net
Web Site: old-mill.org
Founded: 1816.
Congressional District: 22
Key Personnel: Pres. (V), Warren Weber; Vice Pres., Jack McQueen.
Governing Authority: nonprofit institution. Parent Institution: Old Mill Foundation.
History Museum.
Collections: history of California; art; period paintings & furnishings; photographs; operating model of the mill.
Facilities: library; garden.
Activities: historic tours; lectures; films.
Publications: quarterly journal, California History; books; pamphlets; bulletins; catalogs.
Hours & Admission Prices: Tues.-Sun. 1-4. No charge. Closed holidays.
Membership: Senior Citizen & Student $35; Contributor $50; Benefactor & Guardian $100; Sponsor $250; Ambassador $500.

San Martin

WINGS OF HISTORY AIR MUSEUM, 12777 Murphy Ave., San Martin, CA 95046-9527. Mailing Address: P.O. Box 495, San Martin, CA 95046-0495. Tel.: 408-683-2290. Fax: 408-683-2291.
E-mail: wohoffice@sbcglobal.net
Web Site: wingsofhistory.org
Founded: 1983.
Congressional District: 12
Key Personnel: C.E.O. & Pres. (V), Thomas Sharpee; Education, Peter Talbot; Prop Maker, Guy Watson; Restoration, Dave Thompson; Office Mgr., Susan Talbot; Museum Shop Mgr., Claire Kushner; Librarian, Norm Zimmerman; Cur., Frank Nichols.
Personnel Profile: Part-Time Volunteers 40.
Governing Authority: private; nonprofit organization. Tax-exempt.
Aeronautics Museum.
Collections: homebuilt & pre-war aircraft; propellers; engines; models; aviation artifacts.
Facilities: 2,000-vol. library on aviation. Gift items for sale.
Activities: docent program; films; formal educational programs; guided tours; temporary exhibitions. Annual Event: Open House and Fly-In.

Publications: monthly newsletter, The Vintage Flyer.
Hours & Admission Prices: Tues. & Thurs. 10-3, Sat.-Sun. 11-4; other times by appointment. Recommended Donation: adults $5; members no charge. Closed New Year's Day; Easter; Thanksgiving; Christmas. ♿
Attendance: 5,000 (estimated)
Membership: Student $10; Member $40; Sustaining $100.

San Mateo

COYOTE POINT MUSEUM FOR ENVIRONMENTAL EDUCATION, 1651 Coyote Point Dr., San Mateo, CA 94401-1097. Tel.: 650-342-7755. Fax: 650-342-7853.
E-mail: info@coyoteptmuseum.org
Web Site: www.coyoteptmuseum.org
Founded: 1953.
Congressional District: 12
Key Personnel: Pres. Volunteer Council, Frank Babbitt; Pres. Bd. Trustees, Linda Lanier; Dir., Rachel Meyer; Dir. Wildlife, Nikii Finch-Morales; Exec. Asst., Myra Sinkamo.
Personnel Profile: Full-Time Paid 24; Part-Time Paid 17; Part-Time Volunteers 116; Interns 1.
Governing Authority: Coyote Point Museum Association. Tax-exempt: 501(c)(3).
Natural Science Environmental Education Museum.
Collections: living & nonliving collections: birds; mammals; insects; plants; shells; reptiles; amphibians, from the San Francisco Bay Area.
Facilities: 500-vol. library of natural science books available on premises; zoological park; nature & conservation center; classrooms; wildlife center. Science books, field supplies & natural science notions for sale.
Activities: guided tours; lectures; films; formally organized educational programs; docent program and council; summer camp; youth training programs. Museum Sponsors: conservation-oriented field trips.
Publications: quarterly newsletter, Naturally; visitors guides; volunteer newsletter, Coyote Trails.
Hours & Admission Prices: Tues.-Sat. 10-5, Sun. 12-5. Adults $7, seniors over 61 & students 13-18 $5, children 3-12 $3; discounts to AAM, AZA, KQED, AAA & ASTC members; museum members & 1st Sun. each month no charge. Closed New Year's Day; Thanksgiving; Christmas. ♿
Attendance: 74,556 (accurate)
Membership: Senior Citizen & Student $35; Individual $45; Family $65; Premium $100-$499; Contributing $500-$999.

SAN MATEO ARBORETUM SOCIETY, INC., 101 9th Ave., San Mateo, CA 94401-4202. Tel.: 650-579-0536. Fax: 650-343-8416.
Web Site: www.sanmateoarboretum.org
Founded: 1975.
Congressional District: 11
Key Personnel: Pres. (V), Brian Silk; Treas., Jack Bennett.
Personnel Profile: Part-Time Volunteers 12.
Governing Authority: municipal; nonprofit organization. Affiliated with the San Mateo Arboretum Society. Tax-exempt: 170(b)(1)(A).
Arboretum: housed in 1874 Kohl Pump House.
Collections: approx. 300 specimen trees; flowering plants; Native American plants.
Facilities: turn-of-century lawns & flower beds; Japanese Garden; display garden; botanical garden.
Activities: guided tours; lectures, seasonal workshops & classes; demonstrations; gardening information.
Publications: quarterly newsletter, San Mateo Arboretum Society Newsletter.
Hours & Admission Prices: Green House: Tues., Thurs. & Sun. 10-3. Japanese Garden: daily 9-4. No charge; donations accepted. ♿
Attendance: 200 (estimated)
Membership: Senior Citizen $15; Individual or Senior Citizen Couple $20; Couple $25; Garden Clubs $30; Commercial or Sponsor $50; Patron $100; Life $1,000.

San Miguel

MISSION SAN MIGUEL, 775 Mission St., San Miguel, CA 93451. Mailing Address: P.O. Box 69, San Miguel, CA 93451-0069. Tel.: 805-467-3256. Fax: 805-467-2448.
Web Site: www.missionsanmiguel.org
Founded: 1797.
Congressional District: 16
Key Personnel: C.E.O., Bill Short, O.F.M.
Personnel Profile: Full-Time Paid 1; Part-Time Paid 4.
Governing Authority: church. Parent Institution: Franciscan Friars, Santa Barbara Province. Tax-exempt.
Religious Museum: housed in 1797 Mission.
Collections: artifacts of old mission days; original rooms; murals; paintings.
Facilities: religious articles for sale.
Activities: self-guided tours; permanent exhibitions.
Hours & Admission Prices: Mission: daily 9.30-4.30. Donation Suggested. Mass: Sun. 7 & 11. Closed New Year's; Easter; Thanksgiving; Christmas. ♿
Attendance: 30,000 (estimated)

RIOS-CALEDONIA ADOBE, 700 S. Mission St., San Miguel, CA 93451. Mailing Address: P.O. Box 326, San Miguel, CA 93451-0326. Tel.: 805-467-3357.
Founded: 1968.
Historic House Museum: built in 1835.
Collections: local history; personal artifacts.
Facilities: Museum-related items for sale.
Hours & Admission Prices: Fri.-Sun. 11-4. No charge.

San Pablo

ALVARADO ADOBE & THE BLUME HOUSE, 13831 San Pablo Ave., San Pablo, CA 94806-3703. Tel.: 510-215-3092.
Web Site: www.ci.san-pablo.ca.us/main/museums.htm
Governing Authority: Parent Institution: San Pablo Historical Society.
Alvarado Adobe: reconstructed home of California Governor Juan Bautiste Alvarado, 1848-1882. Blume House: 1905 farm house.
Collections: Adobe Museum: furnishings; personal artifacts. Blume House: period artifacts & furnishing.
Hours & Admission Prices: Alvarado Adobe: 1st Sun. of month 12-4. Blume House: 2nd Sun. of month 12-4; other times by appointment.

San Pedro

ANGELS GATE CULTURAL CENTER, 3601 S. Gaffey St., San Pedro, CA 90731-6969. Tel.: 310-519-0936. Fax: 310-519-8698.
E-mail: info@angelsgateart.org
Web Site: www.angelsgateart.org
Key Personnel: Exec. Dir., Nathan Birnbaum
Art Museum.
Collections: works by local & international artists.
Facilities: Museum-related items for sale.
Activities: classes; workshops; rental facilities.
Hours & Admission Prices: Gallery: Tues.-Sun. 10-5. Office: Tues.-Fri. 10-5.

CABRILLO MARINE AQUARIUM, 3720 Stephen M. White Dr., San Pedro, CA 90731-7012. Tel.: 310-548-7562. Fax: 310-548-2649.
E-mail: mike.schaadt@lacity.org
Web Site: www.cabrillomarineaquarium.org
Formerly: Cabrillo Marine Museum
Founded: 1935.
Congressional District: 32
Key Personnel: Dir. CMA, Mike Schaadt; Exec. Dir., Friends of CMA, Paula Moore; Membership Coord., Friends of CMA, Jan Hirata.
Personnel Profile: Full-Time Paid 34; Part-Time Paid 52; Part-Time Volunteers 500; Interns 6.
Governing Authority: city. Affiliated with the city of Los Angeles, Dept. of Recreation & Parks. Tax-exempt.
Aquarium & Marine Museum.
Collections: southern California marine plants & animals; marine invertebrates; shore birds; marine fossils; sea shells; fish; whales.
Research Fields: population studies of intertidal invertebrates & gray whales; water quality monitoring; invertebrate & fish propagation; grunion monitoring.
Facilities: 16,500 sq. ft. exhibit space; classroom; research laboratories; 300-seat auditorium.
Activities: guided tours; lectures; gallery talks; formally organized education programs for children, adults, undergraduate & graduate college students; teacher workshops; outreach program for schools; docent program; research internship for students. Special Events: Whale Fiesta in January; Earth Day in April; Annual Autumn Sea Fair in October.
Publications: quarterly, Tidelines; education brochures; visitors guides (English & Spanish); Whales of Baja boat trip brochure; Meet the Grunion Flyers & CMA Sealife Rack cards; membership applications.
Hours & Admission Prices: Tues.-Fri. 12-5, Sat.-Sun. 10-5. Suggested Donations: adults $5, senior citizens & children $1; beach parking fee $7 per car. Closed Thanksgiving; Christmas. ♿
Attendance: 301,633 (accurate)
Membership: Senior $30; Individual $40; Family $50; Sponsor $125; Benefactor $ 250; Patron $500; Partner $1,000.

FORT MACARTHUR MUSEUM, 3601 S. Gaffey St. at Battery Osgood-Farley, San Pedro, CA 90731-6969. Mailing Address: P.O. Box 268, San Pedro, CA 90733-0268. Tel.: 310-548-2631. Fax: 310-241-0847.
E-mail: director@ftmac.org
Web Site: www.ftmac.org
Founded: 1985.
Key Personnel: Dir. & Cur., Stephen R. Nelson.
Personnel Profile: Full-Time Paid 1; Part-Time Paid 4; Part-Time Volunteers 10.
Governing Authority: municipal; nonprofit. Parent Institution: City of Los Angeles Dept. of Recreation and Parks. Subsidiary Institution: Fort MacArthur Museum Association. Tax-exempt.
Military History Museum.
Collections: 1916-1945 Coast Artillery; The Cold War; 1945-1975 NIKE Missile; operational military vehicles, radios & equipment.
Research Fields: coast artillery; local military history; local photo collection; World Wars I & II; Nike missile sites; coast artillery weapons; 1920s & 1930s Cold War.
Facilities: 12-seat theater.
Activities: docent program; films; guided tours; lectures. Museum Sponsors: Old Ft. MacArthur Days; Artillery Show; monthly living history program.
Publications: quarterly newsletter, Alert; brochures; pamphlets.
Hours & Admission Prices: Tues., Thurs. & Sat.-Sun. 12-5. Requested Donation $3; 10% gift shop discount for AAM members. ♿
Attendance: 35,000 (estimated)
Membership: Individual $25; Sustaining $35; Supporting $100.

LOS ANGELES MARITIME MUSEUM, (M), Berth 84, (foot of 6th St.), San Pedro, CA 90731. Tel.: 310-548-7618. Fax: 310-832-6537.
Web Site: www.lamaritimemuseum.org
Founded: 1980.
Congressional District: 32
Key Personnel: Dir., Marifrances Trivelli; Admin. Sec., Franceen McClung; Registrar, Lucy Ruggirello; Museum Shop Mgr., Jean Olson.
Personnel Profile: Full-Time Paid 8; Part-Time Paid 6; Part-Time Volunteers 100.
Governing Authority: municipal; nonprofit. Parent Institution: City of Los Angeles. Tax-exempt: 501(c)(3).
Maritime Museum: housed in 1941 former Los Angeles Municipal Ferry Building, built in Art Deco style.
Collections: California maritime history; shipbuilding; transportation technology; longshoring; naval history; fishing industry history; history of maritime trades, port of Los Angeles; historic harbor tug.
Research Fields: California maritime history; shipbuilding; Pacific fleet.
Facilities: 5,000-vol. library, maritime records and archives available to the public by appointment; 45-seat auditorium. Maritime history books, nautical objects & gifts for sale.
Activities: guided tours; lectures; films; docent program; participatory & permanent exhibits.
Publications: quarterly members' newsletter, Channel Crossings.
Hours & Admission Prices: Tues.-Sat. 10-5, Sun. 12-5; last admission at 4:30. Adults $3; members, children & school groups no charge. Closed holidays. ♿
Attendance: 75,000 (estimated)
Membership: Individual $25; Family $40; Sponsor $100; Benefactor $500; Patron $1,000.

MULLER HOUSE MUSEUM, 1542 S. Beacon St., San Pedro, CA 90731-4849. Tel.: 310-831-1788.
Web Site: www.sanpedrochamber.com/champint/mulrhsmu.htm
Historic House Museum: built in 1899.
Collections: period furnishings.
Facilities: library.
Hours & Admission Prices: first 3 Sun. of month 1-4; other times by appointment. Suggested Donation: $3.

POINT FERMIN LIGHTHOUSE, 807 W. Paseo del Mar, San Pedro, CA 90731-7131. Tel.: 310-241-0684. Fax: 310-241-0732.
Web Site: www.pointferminlighthouse.org
Founded: 2003.
Key Personnel: Cur., Kristen Heather.
Personnel Profile: Full-Time Paid 1; Part-Time Paid 2; Part-Time Volunteers 30.
Governing Authority: municipal.
Lighthouse & Museum.
Collections: lighthouse history.
Research Fields: lighthouse history; architecture; family history.
Facilities: botanical garden; 1,000 sq. ft. exhibit space. Museum-related items for sale.
Activities: docent program; guided tours; temporary exhibitions. Annual Event: Lighthouse Birthday.
Hours & Admission Prices: Tues.-Sun. 1-4. No charge; donations accepted. Closed holidays; special events.
Attendance: 15,000 (accurate)

San Quentin

SAN QUENTIN PRISON MUSEUM, Dolores Way, Bldg. #106, San Quentin, CA 94964. Mailing Address: Bldg. #106, Dolores Way, P.O. Box 205, San Quentin, CA 94964-0205. Tel.: 415-454-8808.
Founded: 1985.
Key Personnel: Pres., R.A. Nelson
Prison Museum.
Collections: prison history; prison cell model; miniature gas chamber; artifacts from original gallows & the Dungeon.
Facilities: library. Museum-related items for sale.
Hours & Admission Prices: Mon.-Fri. 10-4, Sat. 11:45-3:15; call to confirm hours; no cameras allowed inside the gate. Admission 12-55 $2, seniors, students & State employees $1. ♿

San Rafael

FALKIRK CULTURAL CENTER, 1408 Mission Ave., San Rafael, CA 94901-1971. Mailing Address: P.O. Box 151560, San Rafael, CA 94915-1560. Tel.: 415-485-3328. Fax: 415-485-3404.
E-mail: jane.lange@ci.san-rafael.ca.us
Web Site: www.falkirkculturalcenter.org
Founded: 1974.
Congressional District: 5
Key Personnel: Dir., Jane Lange; Cur., Beth Goldberg; Pres. (V), Margaret Farley; Public Programs & Public Rels., Cory Bytof.
Personnel Profile: Full-Time Paid 1; Part-Time Paid 4; Part-Time Volunteers 30.
Governing Authority: municipal. Parent Institution: City of San Rafael. Tax-exempt.
Contemporary Arts Center: housed in 1888 National Historic Place, previous home of Robert Dollar.
Collections: furnishings of mansion; Dollar family archives.
Research Fields: contemporary arts; history preservation; Bay Area poetry.
Facilities: classroom; poetry reading room; gardens; lecture rooms; private rental facilities; 1927 vintage greenhouse; reflecting pool; gardener's cottage; outdoor kitchen; reception facilities; 11 acres of wooded land. Located on premises: Marin Poetry Center.
Activities: artist lectures; concerts; education programs; writers' workshops; poetry readings; symposia; art classes, docent lead tours. Annual Events: juried exhibition; summer camp; Alice in Wonderland Egghunt; Showcase in December.
Publications: quarterly newsletter; exhibition catalogues; special event announcements.
Hours & Admission Prices: Mon.-Fri. 1-5, Sat. 10-1. No charge; donations requested. Closed legal holidays. ♿
Attendance: 35,000 (estimated)
Membership: Student & Artist $20; Individual $30; Family $50; Copper $100; Silver $250; Gold $5,000; Platinum $5,000 and up.

MARIN HISTORY MUSEUM, (M), 1125 B St., San Rafael, CA 94901-2907. Tel.: 415-454-8538. Fax: 415-454-6137.
E-mail: info@marinhistory.org
Web Site: www.marinhistory.org
Formerly: Marin County Historical Society
Founded: 1935.
Congressional District: 6
Key Personnel: Pres. (V), Carleton Prince; Exec. Dir., Merry Alberigi; Devel. Assoc., Amy Foster; Collections Mgr., Michelle Kaufman; Chief Cur., Dawn Laurant; Public Programs, Monica Burrowes; Librarian, Jocelyn Moss; Office Mgr., Shelley Hamner.
Personnel Profile: Full-Time Paid 5; Part-Time Paid 4; Part-Time Volunteers 30; Interns 2.
Governing Authority: board of directors. Tax-exempt.
Historical Museum.
Collections: memorabilia; artifacts; newspapers; photographs; books; newspaper clippings; pamphlets; brochures; maps; clothing; San Quentin Prison photos, books, papers of Clinton Duffy (warden); explorer Louise A. Boyd's photos, papers, artifacts from her 1920 to 1940 expeditions to the Arctic & Greenland.
Major Exhibits: Marin Rocks-The History of Rock & Roll in Marin County, 1/10-12/10.
Research Fields: Marin County history; genealogy; architecture.
Facilities: library of books & newspapers on history of Marin; historic photo archives; collections facility.

Activities: guided tours; lectures; trips to historic sites; dinners with guest speakers on local history; family programs; films, author series; oral histories; internships.
Publications: newsletter; historic photo calendars; special publications.
Hours & Admission Prices: Tues.-2nd & 3rd. Sat. of month 11-4. No charge; donations accepted. Closed legal holidays. ♿
Attendance: 1,200 (estimated)
Membership: Friend $30; Contributor $50; Supporter $100; Sponsor $250; Patron $500; Benefactor $1,000.

MISSION SAN RAFAEL ARCANGEL, 1104 Fifth Ave., San Rafael, CA 94901-2916. Tel.: 415-454-8141, ext. 12. Fax: 415-454-8193.
Founded: 1817.
Key Personnel: Cur., Theresa Brunner; Museum Shop Mgr., Helen Bernardoni
History Museum.
Collections: religious artifacts; Native American artifacts.
Publications: newsletter, The Mission News.
Hours & Admission Prices: Mon.-Sat. 11-4, Sun. 10-4. No charge.

WILDCARE, 76 Albert Park Lane, San Rafael, CA 94901-3929. Tel.: 415-453-1000.
E-mail: info@wildcarebayarea.org
Web Site: www.wildcarebayarea.org
Key Personnel: Exec. Dir., Karen Wilson
Natural History Museum.
Collections: hands-on exhibits.
Hours & Admission Prices: Daily 9-5. No charge; donations accepted.

San Simeon

* **HEARST CASTLE, (M),** 750 Hearst Castle Rd., San Simeon, CA 93452-9740. Tel.: 805-927-2020. Fax: 805-927-2031. TDD: 800-274-7275.
E-mail: curator@hearstcastle.com
Web Site: www.hearstcastle.com
Formerly: Hearst Castle-Hearst San Simeon State Historical Monument
Founded: 1957.
Congressional District: 22
Key Personnel: District Supt., Nicholas Franco; Museum Dir., Hoyt Fields; Supt. Coastal Sector, Juventino Ortiz; Chief Guide, Diane McGrath.
Personnel Profile: Full-Time Paid 250; Part-Time Paid 150; Part-Time Volunteers 275.
Governing Authority: state. Parent Institution: California State Parks, P.O. Box 942896, Sacramento, CA 94296. Tel. 916-653-8380. Tax-exempt.
Historic House.
Collections: Hearst family life & history; decorative & fine arts of Gothic & Renaissance Spain & Italy; architectural elements; silver; paintings; sculpture; antiquities; tapestries; textiles; Oriental rugs; 127 acres including gardens, pools & guest houses.
Research Fields: William Randolph Hearst; Julia Morgan; construction of Hearst castle; the art collection.
Facilities: visitor center. Museum-related items for sale.
Activities: guided tours; films; permanent exhibitions.
Hours & Admission Prices: Tours: daily 8:20-3:20; times may vary; reservations recommended, call 800-444-4445. Discounts to groups of 12 or more; children under 6 no charge. Closed New Year's Day; Thanksgiving; Christmas. ♿
Attendance: 860,000 (accurate)
Membership: Friends of Hearst Castle $45-$5,000.

Sanger

SANGER DEPOT MUSEUM, 1700 7th St., Sanger, CA 93657-2804. Mailing Address: P.O. Box 44, Sanger, CA 93657-0044. Tel.: 559-875-2848.
Web Site: www.webcitypress.com/sanger
History Museum.
Collections: artifacts & memorabilia pertaining to the city of Sanger.
Hours & Admission Prices: Fri. 9:30-12:30, Sun. 1-4. Adults $1, children $.25.

Santa Ana

* **BOWERS MUSEUM, (M),** 2002 N. Main St., Santa Ana, CA 92706-2776. Tel.: 714-567-3601. Fax: 714-567-3603.
E-mail: pkeller@bowers.org
Web Site: www.bowers.org
Founded: 1936.
Congressional District: 40
Key Personnel: Pres., Peter C. Keller, Ph.D.; Chm. Bd., Frank O'Bryan; C.F.O., Thuy Nguyen; Vice Pres. Education, Nancy Warzer Brady; Dir. Mktg. & Public Rels., Heidi Simonian; Dir. Collections & Registrar, Jennifer Ring; Exhibit Design & Fabrication, Paul Johnson; Dir. Retail Sales, Pauline Rusterholtz.
Personnel Profile: Full-Time Paid 36; Part-Time Paid 39; Part-Time Volunteers 300.
Governing Authority: nonprofit organization. Tax-exempt: 501(c)(3).
Art & Cultural Arts Museum.
Collections: South Pacific; Native North and South America; Pre-Columbian; African; Asian; 19th & 20th-century American paintings; Orange County historic photography; Southern California history.
Research Fields: cultures of the Americas, Pacific Rim, Oceania & Africa.
Facilities: education center; 800-seat auditorium; restaurant. Museum-related items for sale.
Activities: guided tours; lectures; films; studio workshops; community festivals; African Cultural Arts Council; California Art Council; Docent Guild; Indian Cultural Arts Council; Persian Arts Council; Hispanic Arts Council; Chinese Cultural Art Council; Collector's Council; Orange County American Italian Renaissance Foundation; Bead Society of Orange County; Plein Air Art Council; Bells; education programs for children & adults; permanent, temporary & traveling exhibitions; mobile museum exhibits; intermuseum loan; speakers bureau; mini-museum classroom kits.
Publications: monthly calendar of events; exhibit catalogs; gallery guides.
Hours & Admission Prices: Tues.-Sun. 10-4. Adults $17-$19, seniors & students $12-$14; discounts to AAM, ICOM & WMA members; children under 5 & members no charge. ♿
Attendance: 132,300 (accurate)
Membership: Senior & Student $45; Active $65; Contributor $175; Patron $500; Fellow $1,000; Corporate Fellow $2,000.

DISCOVERY SCIENCE CENTER, 2500 N. Main St., Santa Ana, CA 92705-6600. Tel.: 714-542-CUBE. Fax: 714-542-2828.
Science Center.
Collections: hands-on science exhibits; environment; physics; earth; dinosaurs; air & space; hockey; perception.
Major Exhibits: Science of Circles (T), 1/10-5/10; Bubblefest, 3/10-4/10; Tinkertoys (T), 5/10-9/10; Grossology (T), 5/10-9/10; Dragons & Fairies (T), 10/10-12/10; Science of Gingerbread, 11/10-12/10.
Facilities: restaurant; rental facilities.
Activities: teacher programs; summer camp; camp-ins; rental facilities.
Hours & Admission Prices: Daily 10-5. Adults $12.95, children 3-17 $9.95; members and children 2 & under no charge. Closed Thanksgiving; Christmas. ♿
Attendance: 440,000 (accurate)
Membership: Individual $60; Family $99; Family Plus $149; Family & Friends $179.

DR. HOWE-WAFFLE HOUSE AND MEDICAL MUSEUM, 120 Civic Center Dr., Santa Ana, CA 92701-7505. Tel.: 714-547-9645.
Web Site: www.santaanahistory.com/house.html
Founded: 1974.
Key Personnel: Chm. & Pres. (V), Alison Young; Special Project Leader, Guy Ball.
Personnel Profile: Part-Time Volunteers 20.
Governing Authority: Parent Institution: Santa Ana Historical Preservation Society. Tax-exempt.
Historic House & Medical Museum: built in 1889 by Orange County physicians, Alvin & Willella Howe.
Collections: period furnishings; personal artifacts; medical equipment & supplies.
Facilities: digital photographic archives.
Activities: living history tours & events.
Publications: quarterly newsletter; books, Logan Barrio; O.C. Fruit Crate Labels.
Hours & Admission Prices: Feb., April, June, Aug., Oct. & Dec. 1st Sat. each month 12-4. Adults $5; discounts to members.
Attendance: 3,000 (estimated)
Membership: $20 to $1,000.

OLD COURTHOUSE MUSEUM, (M), 211 W. Santa Ana Blvd., Santa Ana, CA 92701-7554. Tel.: 714-834-6605 & 973-6607. Fax: 714-834-2280.
Web Site: www.ocparks.com
Founded: 1987.
Congressional District: 47
Key Personnel: Cur., Marshall Duell; Education Coord., Carey Baughman.
Personnel Profile: Full-Time Paid 2; Part-Time Volunteers 15; Interns 1.
Governing Authority: county government. Tax-exempt.
County History Museum: housed in 1901 Richardsonian Romanesque style county courthouse.
Collections: law & government artifacts; court documents; photographs.

Major Exhibits: Abraham Lincoln: Self-Made in America (T), 1/29/10-2/26/10; Bear in Mind (T), 6/6/10-10/10/10; Class Action, 10/10-2/11.
Research Fields: local & regional history.
Facilities: 70-seat auditorium. Gift items for sale.
Activities: docent program; guided tours; lectures; loan, temporary & traveling exhibitions.
Publications: The Court Reporter.
Hours & Admission Prices: Mon.-Fri. 9-5. No charge. Closed state holidays. ♿
Attendance: 18,000 (estimated)
Membership: Individual $10; Family $15; Sustaining & Organization $25: Business $35.

ORANGE COUNTY NATURAL HISTORY MUSEUM, Interstate 5, Santa Ana, CA 92701. Mailing Address: P.O. Box 716, Santa Ana, CA 92702-0716.
Web Site: www.ocnhm.org
History Museum.
Collections: community heritage.
Activities: lectures; special programs; nature walks; youth & school programs.
Hours & Admission Prices: Temporarily closed for relocation.

SANTA ANA COLLEGE ART GALLERY, 1530 W. 17th St., Santa Ana, CA 92706-3398. Tel.: 714-564-5615. Fax: 714-564-5629.
Web Site: www.sac.edu/art
Founded: 1970.
Key Personnel: Dir., Phillip Marquez.
Personnel Profile: Full-Time Paid 2; Part-Time Paid 4; Part-Time Volunteers 10.
Governing Authority: public university. Rancho Santiago Community College District. Branch Location: SAC Arts at the Santora, Santora Arts Complex, 207 N. Broadway, Suite Q, Santa Ana, CA 92701. Tax-exempt.
College Art Gallery.
Collections: works by student artists.
Facilities: library of exhibit catalogs; 1,120 sq. ft. exhibit space.
Activities: guided tours; lectures; organized education programs for adults. Museum Sponsors: monthly Artwalk in Artists Village.
Publications: exhibition brochures.
Hours & Admission Prices: Santa Ana College Main Art Gallery: School Year: Mon. & Thurs. 10-2, Tues.-Wed. 10-2 & 6:30pm-8:30pm. No charge; donations accepted. Closed holidays; spring, summer & winter breaks. SAC Arts at the Santora: Thurs.-Sat. 12-4. No charge; donations accepted. Closed holidays; spring & winter break. ♿
Attendance: 15,000 (estimated)

SANTA ANA ZOO, 1801 E. Chestnut Ave., Santa Ana, CA 92701-5001. Tel.: 714-647-6575. Fax: 714-953-7401.
E-mail: kyamaguchi@santa-ana.org
Web Site: santaanazoo.org
Founded: 1952.
Key Personnel: Dir., Kent Yamaguchi; Devel., Cathi Decker; Zoo Cur., Suzanne Werner.
Personnel Profile: Full-Time Paid 20; Part-Time Paid 14; Part-Time Volunteers 65.
Governing Authority: municipal; nonprofit. Parent Institution: City of Santa Ana. Subsidiary Institution: Recreation & Community Services.
Zoo.
Collections: mammals; birds; reptiles; amphibians; fish.
Facilities: library; educational facility; zoological park. Educational supplies, animal & conservation-related items for sale.
Activities: guided tours; formal educational programs; docent program; mobile vans.
Publications: bimonthly newsletter, Animal Tales.
Hours & Admission Prices: Memorial Day-Labor Day Mon.-Fri. 10-5, Sat.-Sun.10-6; Sept.-May daily 10-5; last ticket sold 1 hour before closing. Adults $8, senior citizens 60 & over and children 3-12 $5; children 2 & under, handicapped, reciprocal zoos, AZA & members no charge. ♿
Attendance: 268,878 (accurate)
Membership: Individual $35; Couple $45; Family $55.

Santa Barbara

CARRIAGE AND WESTERN ART MUSEUM, 129 Castillo St., Santa Barbara, CA 93101-5725. Mailing Address: P.O. Box 1587, Santa Barbara, CA 93102-1587. Tel.: 805-962-2353.
Web Site: www.carriagemuseum.org/
Founded: 1972.
Personnel Profile: Full-Time Paid 2; Part-Time Paid 16.
History Museum.
Collections: history of the west; 50 saddles once belonging to famous people including Cisco Kid, Will Rogers, & Clark Gable; mud wagons; army wagons; circus wagons; photographs.
Activities: special events.
Publications: quarterly newsletter.
Hours & Admission Prices: Mon.-Fri. 9-3; groups by appointment. No charge; donations accepted. ♿
Membership: Family $25.

THE CASA DEL HERRERO FOUNDATION, 1387 E. Valley Rd., Santa Barbara, CA 93108-1202. Tel.: 805-565-5653. Fax: 805-969-2371.
E-mail: casatour@silcom.com
Web Site: www.casadelherrero.com
Founded: 1995.
Key Personnel: Dir., Molly Barker; Devel., Olga Rogers; Volunteer Dir., Susannah Gordon.
Personnel Profile: Full-Time Paid 4; Part-Time Paid 1; Part-Time Volunteers 40.
Governing Authority: private; nonprofit organization. Tax-exempt: 501(c)(3).
Historic House Museum: former home of George Fox Steedman designed by architect George Washington Smith, built in 1925. National Historic Landmark.
Collections: 14th-18th century Spanish furnishings; period artifacts; handmade silver; paintings.
Facilities: library; botanical garden; 4,000 sq. ft. exhibit space. Museum-related items for sale.
Activities: docent program; members luncheons & dinner parties; guided tours; lectures. Annual Events: Architecture Tours Fundraiser; Volunteer Recognition Events; Art in the Garden Fundraiser; Holiday Tours & Auction.
Publications: quarterly membership newsletter, Newsletter of the Casa del Herrero.
Hours & Admission Prices: Public Tours: Feb. to mid-Nov. Wed. & Sat. 10 & 2. Group Tours: Tues.-Sat. 10 & 2 by appointment. Adults $20; discounts to National Trust for Historic Preservation; children under 10 not admitted. Closed New Year's Day; national holidays.
Attendance: 3,225 (estimated)
Membership: Friend $40; Household $100; Partner $250; Patron $500; Supporter $1,000; Benefactor $2,500; Director's Club $5,000.

HISTORIC SANTA BARBARA COURTHOUSE, 1100 Anacapa St., Santa Barbara, CA 93101-2099. Tel.: 805-962-6464.
Web Site: www.santabarbaracourthouse.org/sbch/
Key Personnel: Pres., Pam Stoney
History Museum.
Collections: functional courthouse; clock tower; gardens.
Facilities: gardens.
Activities: special events.
Hours & Admission Prices: Museum: Mon.-Fri. 8-5, Sat.-Sun. 10-4. Tours: Mon.-Tues. & Fri. 10:30 & 2, Wed.-Thurs. & Sat. 2. No charge; donations accepted. Closed Christmas.

REYNOLDS GALLERY AT WESTMONT COLLEGE, 955 La Paz Rd., Santa Barbara, CA 93108-1099. Tel.: 805-565-6162.
Web Site: www.reynoldsgallery.org
Key Personnel: Dir., Judy L. Larson.
Personnel Profile: Full-Time Paid 2.
Governing Authority: Parent Institution: Westmont College. Tax-exempt.
Art Museum.
Collections: works on paper; sculpture.
Activities: special events; receptions.
Hours & Admission Prices: Mon.-Sat. 11-5. No charge. Closed college holidays.
Membership: Chagall Circle $45; Cassatt Circle $100; Rodin Circle $200; Monet Circle $500; Rembrandt Circle $1,500; Medici Circle $3,500.

* **SANTA BARBARA BOTANIC GARDEN, (M),** 1212 Mission Canyon Rd., Santa Barbara, CA 93105-2199. Tel.: 805-682-4726, ext. 101. Fax: 805-563-0352.
E-mail: info@sbbg.org
Web Site: www.santabarbarabotanicgarden.org
Formerly: The Botanic Garden at Santa Barbara and Ojai
Founded: 1926.
Congressional District: 19
Key Personnel: Chm. Bd. Trustees, The Honorable Fife Symington, III; Pres. & C.E.O., Edward L. Schneider, Ph.D.; Vice Pres. Finance & Administration, Robert Sherwood; Vice Pres. Programs & Collections, Dieter Wilken, Ph.D.; Vice Pres. Mktg. & Government Rels., Nancy Johnson; Vice Pres. Devel., Gina Benesh; Dir. Horticulture, Andrew Wyatt; Dir. Nursery, Bruce Reed; Dir. Education, Sally Isaacson; Cur. Herbarium, Steve Junak;

Librarian, Joan Ariel; Museum Shop Mgr., Gail Meadows Milliken; Human Resources & Volunteer Mgr., Cherie Welsh.
Personnel Profile: Full-Time Paid 25; Part-Time Paid 18; Part-Time Volunteers 308; Interns 1.
Governing Authority: nonprofit organization. Tax-exempt: 501(c)(3).
Arboretum/Botanical Garden: located at site of Old Mission Dam & Aqueduct.
Collections: native California plants; plants from California offshore islands including rare & endangered California plants as part of Garden's program in rare plant conservation; over 1,000 living California plants; 15,000 books & journals; 140,000 preserved plant specimens.
Research Fields: plant systematics, evolution & ecology; structural botany; conservation biology.
Facilities: 15,000-vol. library; regional maps; series of oral history tapes; herbarium of over 140,000 specimens; 78 acre gardens. California native & Mediterranean plants, prints, stationery, books & handcrafted gifts for sale.
Activities: guided tours; lectures; symposia; workshops; formally organized programs for children, including pre-school; Master Gardening Certificate & Certificate in So. Calif. Gardening, Garden Grower Certificate (retail nursery management) programs; cooperative graduate program with the Univ. of California, Santa Barbara for M.A., M.S. & Ph.D. degrees in botanical science; docent programs; field trips; camping trips; environmental education programs.
Publications: Flora of the Santa Barbara Region; Flora of Santa Cruz Island; Trees of Santa Barbara; quarterly newsletter, Ironwood; occasional books; Alice's Garden.
Hours & Admission Prices: March-Oct. daily 9-6; Nov.-Feb. daily 9-5. Adults $8, seniors 60 & over $6, teens 13-17, full-time students & active military $6, children 2-12 $4; discounts to AAM members; members & children under 2 no charge. Closed New Year's Day; Thanksgiving; Christmas Eve & Day; occasional special events. ♿
Attendance: 96,000 (accurate)
Membership: Individual $50; Family & Dual $75; Wildflower Guild $150; Seasons Guild $300; Ironwood Circle $600; Director's Circle $1,000; President's Circle $2,500; Corporate President's Circle $5,000.

SANTA BARBARA CONTEMPORARY ARTS FORUM, 653 Paseo Nuevo, Santa Barbara, CA 93101-3392. Tel.: 805-966-5373. Fax: 805-962-1421.
E-mail: lmermel@sbcaf.org
Web Site: www.sbcaf.org
Key Personnel: Exec. Dir., Mike Garcia; Communications Coord., Lauren Mermel; Dir. Operations, Margie Yahyavi
Contemporary Arts Center.
Collections: works by local, regional, national & international artists; contemporary art.
Activities: performances.
Hours & Admission Prices: Tues.-Sat. 11-5, Sun. 12-5.

THE SANTA BARBARA HISTORICAL MUSEUM, (M), 136 E. De la Guerra St., Santa Barbara, CA 93101-2205. Tel.: 805-966-1601. Fax: 805-966-1603.
E-mail: dbisol@sbhistorical.org
Web Site: www.santabarbaramuseum.com
Founded: 1932.
Congressional District: 19
Key Personnel: Exec. Dir., David S. Bisol; Cur. Collections, Gabriel Ramirez-Ortiz; Dir. Research, Michael Redmon; Mktg. Coord., Eleanor Van Cott; Membership Coord., Fran Wisielewski.
Personnel Profile: Full-Time Paid 7; Part-Time Paid 11; Part-Time Volunteers 50.
Governing Authority: society. Tax-exempt: 501(c)(3).
Local History Museum.
Collections: history; clipping books; genealogical material; artifacts covering Spanish, Mexican & American Periods; local newspapers; old photographs; manuscript collections. Historic Houses: 1825 Historic Adobe; 1817 Covarrubias Adobe; 1854 Trusell-Winchester Adobe; 1861 Fernald Mansion.
Research Fields: Santa Barbara & California history & genealogy.
Facilities: 6,000-vol. library of California history books available for use on premises. Local history books & postcards of museum artifacts for sale.
Activities: pre-arranged tours; lectures; reading room; formally organized education programs for children; docent program or council; inter-museum loan, permanent & temporary exhibitions.
Publications: quarterly, Noticias.
Hours & Admission Prices: Tues.-Sat. 10-5, Sun. 12-5. Suggested Donation: general $5, children 12 & under $2. Closed New Year's Day; Easter; Memorial Day; Independence Day; Thanksgiving; Christmas. ♿
Attendance: 15,400 (accurate)
Membership: Individual $45; Family $50; Supporter $75; Sustainer $125; Sponsor $250; Benefactor $500; Patron $1,000; Mayor Benefactor $5,000; President's Circle $10,000.

SANTA BARBARA MARITIME MUSEUM, 113 Harbor Way, Ste. 190, Santa Barbara, CA 93109-2344. Tel.: 805-962-8404. Fax: 805-962-7634.
E-mail: museum@sbmm.org
Web Site: www.sbmm.org
Founded: 1994.
Congressional District: 22
Key Personnel: Pres., Trevor Large; Exec. Dir., Greg Gorga; Vice Pres., Cindy Makela; Treas., Gail Anikouchine; Controller, Pauline Keeble; Cur. & Dir. Education, Abby Chamberlain; Education & Volunteer Coord., Alyssa Morris; Facilities Mgr., Shawn Balla.
Personnel Profile: Full-Time Paid 6; Part-Time Paid 3; Part-Time Volunteers 180; Interns 1.
Governing Authority: private; nonprofit organization. Tax-exempt: 501(c)(3).
Maritime Museum.
Collections: nautical instruments & objects related to maritime endeavors; maritime history & archaeology; photographs; documents.
Research Fields: Santa Barbara & central coast maritime history; archaeological remains of local shipwrecks.
Facilities: library; 88-seat theater & auditorium; 8,500 sq. ft exhibit space. Museum-related items for sale.
Activities: docent program; films; formal education programs for adults; guided tours; lectures; floating & participatory exhibits; rental facilities.
Publications: quarterly newsletter, Maritime Currents; Seafarers; Santa Barbara Fisheries.
Hours & Admission Prices: Memorial Day-Labor Day Thurs.-Tues. 10-6; Sept.-May Thurs.-Tues. 10-5. Adults $7, seniors, students, youth 6-17 $4, children 1-5 $2; members, CAMM & AASLH members no charge. Closed Thanksgiving; Christmas. ♿
Attendance: 25,909 (accurate)
Membership: Students (with ID) & Senior Citizens 65 & up $25; Individual $40; Crew (family) $55; Mariner $125; Navigator $500; Explorer $1,000; Astronavigator $2,500; Circumnavigator $5,000.

SANTA BARBARA MISSION MUSEUM, 2201 Laguna St., Santa Barbara, CA 93105-3611. Tel.: 805-682-4713, ext. 166. Fax: 805-687-7841 & 6067.
E-mail: museumtours@sboldmission.org
Web Site: www.santabarbaramission.org
Mission Museum.
Collections: religious artifacts; period furnishings.
Facilities: Museum-related items for sale.
Hours & Admission Prices: Museum: daily 9-4:30. Tours: adults $5, seniors $4, youth 6-16 $1; children under 6 no charge. Closed Easter; Thanksgiving; Christmas. Church: Sat. 4pm, Sun. 7:30am, 9am, 10:30am, 12pm.

* **SANTA BARBARA MUSEUM OF ART, (M),** 1130 State St., Santa Barbara, CA 93101-2746. Tel.: 805-963-4364. Fax: 805-966-6840.
E-mail: info@sbma.net
Web Site: www.sbma.net
Founded: 1941.
Congressional District: 5
Key Personnel: Chm. Bd. Trustees (V), Marshall C. Milligan; Dir., Larry J. Feinberg; C.F.O., Diane Wondolowski; Dir. Education, Patsy Hicks; Cur. Asian Art, Susan Shin-tsu Tai; Cur. Contemporary Art, Julie Joyce; Cur. Photography, Karen Sinsheimer; Registrar, Cherie Summers; Museum Store Mgr. & Visitor Svcs. Mgr., Georgia McDermott; Dir. Devel., Kristi Wallace.
Personnel Profile: Full-Time Paid 59; Part-Time Paid 42; Part-Time Volunteers 215; Interns 15.
Governing Authority: nonprofit organization. Tax-exempt: 501(c)(3).
Art Museum.
Collections: Greek, Roman, Egyptian antiquities; Asian sculpture, woodblock prints; painting, ceramic & decorative arts; American paintings from colonial period to present; works on paper from Renaissance to present; European paintings & sculpture; photographs; modern & contemporary art.
Research Fields: 19th-century French lithographs, American Modernism, Japanese Meiji woodblock prints.
Facilities: art library & education center for art classes; 153-seat auditorium. Books & cards for sale.
Activities: docent guided tours; lectures; films; gallery talks; formally organized education programs for children; docent program; permanent & temporary exhibitions; national & international museum sponsored trips.
Publications: catalogs; calendars; announcements; reports.
Hours & Admission Prices: Tues.-Sun. 11-5. Adults $9, seniors $7, students with ID & children 6-17 $6; discounts to AAM & ICOM members; members, children under 6 & Sun. no charge. Closed some holidays. ♿
Attendance: 130,000 (estimated)
Membership: General $60; Associate Patron $125; Gallery Patron $250; Collector's Patron $500; Curator's Patron $750; Director's Patron $1,500; Benefactor's Circle $3,000.

* **SANTA BARBARA MUSEUM OF NATURAL HISTORY, (M),** 2559 Puesta del Sol Rd., Santa Barbara, CA 93105-2998. Tel.: 805-682-4711, ext. 117. Fax: 805-569-3170.
E-mail: info@sbnature2.org
Web Site: www.sbnature.org
Founded: 1916.
Congressional District: 19
Key Personnel: Exec. Dir., Dr. Karl L. Hutterer; Dir. Finance & Admin., Diane E. Wondolowski; Pres. (V), Stephen M. Hicks; Cur. Vertebrate Zoology, Paul W. Collins; Librarian, Terri Sheridan; Cur. Anthropology, Dr. John R. Johnson; Cur. Invertebrate Zoology, Dr. F. G. Hochberg; Dir. Collections & Research, Dr. Henry Chaney; Dir. Education & Exhibits, Heather Mossat; Dir. Facilities, Gary Robinson; Mgr. Exhibits, Simon Allen; Dir. Retail & Visitor Svcs., Amy Carpenter; Mktg. & Public Rels Mgr., Easter Moorman; Dir. Devel., Caroline Grange.
Personnel Profile: Full-Time Paid 50; Full-Time Volunteers 1; Part-Time Paid 45; Part-Time Volunteers 200; Interns 3.
Governing Authority: nonprofit organization. Subsidiary Institution: Sea Center. Tax-exempt: 501(c)(3).
Natural History Museum.
Collections: natural history & prehistoric life of Pacific Coast; anthropology; invertebrate zoology; vertebrate zoology; paleontology; mineralogy; historical archive; antique & natural history art.
Research Fields: anthropology; invertebrate zoology; vertebrate zoology.
Facilities: 40,000-vol. library of science & natural history available for inter-library loan & for use on premises by special permission from librarian; separate laboratory operation; planetarium; 350-seat & 100-seat auditoriums; classrooms; historical archives & nature art; marine aquariums. Books, laboratory supplies, specimens & limited specialty items for sale.
Activities: guided tours; field trips; lectures; films; study clubs; formally organized educational programs; formally organized education programs for undergraduate & graduate students affiliated with University of California, Santa Barbara campus; inter-museum loan, permanent, temporary & traveling exhibitions.
Publications: monthly public program calendars; books; teacher guides & papers.
Hours & Admission Prices: Daily 10-5. Adults $10, youths 13-17 & senior citizens $7, children 2-12 $6; discounts to ASTC & AAM members; last Sun. of month, children under 2 & members no charge. Closed New Year's Day; Thanksgiving; Christmas. ♿
Attendance: 110,000 (accurate)
Membership: Individual $50; Family Plus $75; Naturalist $90; Contributor $150; Explorer $275; Benefactor $500; Patron $1,000; Director's Circle $2,500; President's Circle $5,000.

SANTA BARBARA ORCHID ESTATE, 1250 Orchid Dr., Santa Barbara, CA 93111-2914. Tel.: 805-967-1284; 800-553-3387. Fax: 805-683-3405.
E-mail: sboe@sborchid.com
Web Site: www.sborchid.com
Orchid Estate.
Collections: thousands of orchid species & hybrids.
Facilities: 5 acres.
Activities: special events.
Hours & Admission Prices: Mon.-Sat. 8-4:30, Sun. 11-4. Closed New Year's Day; Presidents' Day; Easter; Memorial Day; Independence Day; Labor Day; Thanksgiving; Christmas.

SANTA BARBARA TRUST FOR HISTORIC PRESERVATION, (M), 123 E. Canon Perdido, Santa Barbara, CA 93101-2215. Tel.: 805-965-0093. Fax: 805-568-1999.
Web Site: www.sbthp.org
Founded: 1961.
Key Personnel: Dir., Dr. Jarrell Jackman; Chm. (V), Craig Makela; Treas., Sally Fouhse; Devel., Kendra Rhodes; Education, Karen Anderson; Public Rels., Jared Brach; Cur., Anne Peterson; Archivist, Laurie Hannah; Museum Shop Mgr., Joan Stewart.
Personnel Profile: Full-Time Paid 8; Part-Time Paid 14; Part-Time Volunteers 100.
Governing Authority: private; nonprofit organization. Casa de la Guerra, 15 E. de la Guerra St., Santa Barbara, CA. Tax-exempt.
Historic Buildings: El Presidio de Santa Barbara State Historic Park - adobe fort built by the Spanish as they colonized California in the late 18th century. Casa de la Guerra - adobe house, home of early 19th century commandant of El Presidio.
Collections: archives pertaining to Spanish colonization of California; archaeological.
Research Fields: Spanish borderlands & colonization.
Facilities: library. Museum-related items for sale.
Activities: arts festivals; concerts; dance recitals; docent programs; films; education programs; guided tours; lectures; loan & temporary exhibitions; rental gallery; training programs for professional museum workers; fundraising events; archaeological dig. Annual Event: Living History.
Publications: quarterly newsletter, La Campana.
Hours & Admission Prices: El Presidio: daily 10:30-4:30. Casa de la Guerra: Thurs.-Sun. 12-4. Adults $5; discounts to seniors, AAA & AAM members; members no charge. Closed Thanksgiving; Christmas. ♿
Attendance: 20,000 (accurate)
Membership: Student $15; Individual $40; Dual $50; Preservationist $100; Steward $250.

SANTA BARBARA ZOOLOGICAL GARDENS, 500 Ninos Dr., Santa Barbara, CA 93103-3798. Tel.: 805-962-5339. Fax: 805-962-1673.
E-mail: zooinfo@sbzoo.org
Web Site: www.sbzoo.org
Founded: 1963.
Congressional District: 19
Key Personnel: Dir. & C.E.O., Richard Block; Pres. (V), Thomas Luria; C.O.O., Nancy Hollenbeck McToldridge; C.F.O., Carol Bedford; Dir. Animal Programs & Conservation, Alan Varsik; Asst. Dir. Animal Programs, Sheri Horiszny; Dir. Animal Medicine, Karl Hill, D.V.M.; Dir. Education, Heather Johnson; Asst. Dir. Education, Christopher Horrigan; Dir. Devel., Jill Rode, CFRE; Asst. Dir. Devel., Pieter van Meeuwen; Asst. Dir. Devel., Membership, Kimberly Roberson; Dir. Food Service, Chris Gambler; Asst. Dir. Food Svcs., Cameron Parton; Dir. Human Resources, Corinne Santini; Dir. Guest Svcs., David Velazquez; Asst. Dir. Guest Svcs., Jess Frasier; Dir. Facilities & Horticulture, Abelardo Landeros; Dir. Mktg., Dean Noble; Asst. Dir. Mktg., Events, Katharine Buford; Dir. Retail Operations, Ross Beardsley; Dir. Safety & Security, Chris Briggs.
Personnel Profile: Full-Time Paid 68; Full-Time Volunteers 180; Part-Time Paid 51; Part-Time Volunteers 400; Interns 5.
Governing Authority: nonprofit organization. Parent Institution: Santa Barbara Zoological Foundation. Tax-exempt: 501(c)(3).
Zoo.
Collections: live zoological collection; 600 specimens including 175 species of invertebrates, amphibians, reptiles, birds & mammals.
Research Fields: reproductive physiology; behavioral.
Facilities: classrooms; picnic facilities. Animal-oriented gift items, books, art, games & film for sale; restaurant; catering.
Activities: guided tours; formally organized educational programs; docent program; permanent exhibitions; workshops; Zoo Camp.
Publications: quarterly newsletter, Zoo News; annual report.
Hours & Admission Prices: Daily 10-5. Adults $10, children & senior citizens $8. School Tours: students over 12 $9, students 2-12 $7; discounts to AZA members; members no charge. Closed Thanksgiving; Christmas. ♿
Attendance: 431,753 (accurate)
Membership: Individual $40; Individual plus one (Santa Barbara Zoo Admission Only) $50; Family $65; Supporting $125; Society Couple $250; Donor $500 & up.

* **UNIVERSITY ART MUSEUM, SANTA BARBARA, (M),** 552 University Rd. - UCSB, Santa Barbara, CA 93106-7130. Tel.: 805-893-2951 & 2724 (Architecture & Design). Fax: 805-893-3013.
E-mail: uam@uam.ucsb.edu
Web Site: www.uam.ucsb.edu
Founded: 1959.
Congressional District: 22
Key Personnel: Dir., Kathryn Kanjo; Asst. to Dir. & Museum Shop Mgr., Marie Vierra; Cur. Fine Arts, Elyse Gonzales; Designer, Rollin Fortier; Preparator, Todd Anderson; Registrar, Susan Lucke; Business Mgr., Victoria Stuber; Security Officer, Bill Durham.
Personnel Profile: Full-Time Paid 6; Part-Time Paid 2; Interns 6.
Governing Authority: university. Parent Institution: University of California. Tax-exempt: 501(c)(3).
Art Museum.
Collections: Morgenroth Collection of Renaissance medals & plaquettes; Sedgwick Collection of Old Master paintings; Feitelson Collection of Old Master Drawings; Dreyfus Collection of Luristan Bronzes, Near Eastern ceramics & pre-Columbian art; Ala Story Graphic Arts Collection (15th-18th centuries); Ruth S. Shaffner Collection of Contemporary Art; Ken Trevey Collection of American Realist Prints; Fernand Lungren paintings & drawings; various paintings, sculpture, drawings, prints, photography & ceramics with emphasis on contemporary; separately housed collection of over 750,000 architectural drawings & related materials, largely the work of California architects.
Research Fields: contemporary art; modern architecture; Renaissance medals & plaquettes; California artists; Old Master drawings; ethnographic art; works on paper.
Facilities: Books for sale.

Activities: docent guided tours; lectures; gallery talks; permanent, temporary & traveling exhibitions; education programs for children, adults & university students.
Publications: exhibition catalogs; Lasting Impressions: MFA08.
Hours & Admission Prices: Wed.-Sun. 12-5. No charge; donations accepted. Closed major holidays. ♿
Attendance: 30,000 (estimated)
Membership: Gaucho $20; Household $50-$99; Contributor $100-$499; Patron $500-$999; Director's Circle $1,000-$2,500.

Santa Clara

* **DE SAISSET MUSEUM, (M),** Santa Clara University, 500 El Camino Real, Santa Clara, CA 95053-0001. Tel.: 408-554-4528. Fax: 408-554-7840.
E-mail: rnadel@scu.edu
Web Site: www.scu.edu/desaisset
Founded: 1955.
Congressional District: 13
Key Personnel: Dir., Rebecca M. Schapp; Asst. Dir. Exhibitions, Education & Community Outreach, Karen Kienzle; Collections Mgr., Jean MacDougall; Administrative Asst. to Dir., Ramona Nadel; Preparator, Ernest Jolly.
Personnel Profile: Full-Time Paid 3; Part-Time Paid 2; Part-Time Volunteers 60.
Governing Authority: university. Parent Institution: Santa Clara University. Tax-exempt: 501(c)(3).
Art & History Museum.
Collections: 19th-century to present American art including graphics, painting, sculpture, photography & video; 15th-century to contemporary European painting, sculpture & graphic arts; American, European & Oriental decorative art; Native American (Costanoan); California Mission & University of Santa Clara History collection.
Research Fields: California art & history; modern American & European art; ecclesiastical textiles of the California missions.
Facilities: 1,200-vol. library of books, catalogs & periodicals; video archive, video art & video tapes; interviews with New Deal artists; 200-seat auditorium. Museum catalogs for sale.
Activities: guided tours; inter-museum loan program; permanent, temporary & traveling exhibitions.
Publications: exhibition catalogs; member newsletter.
Hours & Admission Prices: Tues.-Sun. 11-4. No charge; donations accepted. Closed national holidays; Martin Luther King Jr. Day; Good Friday; Thanksgiving weekend; short periods between exhibitions. ♿
Attendance: 10,713 (accurate)
Membership: Santa Clara Community $25; Seniors, Educators, & Artists $35; Individual & Senior Dual $50; Family $70; Sponsor $100; Friend $250; Benefactor $500; President's Circle $1,000.

INTEL MUSEUM, 2200 Mission College Blvd., Robert Noyce Bldg., Santa Clara, CA 95054-1537. Tel.: 408-765-0503.
E-mail: tracey.mazur@intel.com
Web Site: www.intel.com/museum
Founded: 1992.
Key Personnel: Cur., Tracey Mazur; Archivist, Rachel Stewart; Education, Elizabeth Jones; Technical Network Systems Engineer, Elyse Polhaupessy; Museum Shop Mgr., Richard Smith.
Personnel Profile: Full-Time Paid 3; Part-Time Volunteers 10.
Governing Authority: corporate; nonprofit. Parent Institution: Intel Corp.
Corporate History, Science & Technology Museum.
Collections: hands-on exhibits; corporate history; industry records, artifacts, products, documents & images; 80,000 records in database.
Research Fields: early & current intel product & corporate development.
Facilities: learning lab; 10,000 sq. ft. exhibit space. Museum-related items for sale.
Activities: formal education programs; hands-on exhibits; guided tours.
Publications: monthly newsletter; brochure; anniversary publications; product timeline charts.
Hours & Admission Prices: Mon.-Fri. 9-6, Sat. 10-5. No charge. Parking no charge. Closed New Year's Day; Washington's Birthday; Memorial Day; Independence Day; Labor Day; Thanksgiving; Christmas. ♿
Attendance: 116,847 (accurate)

TRITON MUSEUM OF ART, 1505 Warburton Ave., Santa Clara, CA 95050-3791. Tel.: 408-247-3754. Fax: 408-247-3796.
E-mail: info@tritonmuseum.org
Web Site: www.tritonmuseum.org
Founded: 1965.
Congressional District: 12
Key Personnel: Exec. Dir. & Senior Cur., George Rivera; Pres., Rosalie Wilson; Registrar & Assoc. Cur., Stephanie Learmonth; Assoc. Cur., Preston Metcalf; Asst. Dir., Jill Meyers; Preparator, Ron Garcia.
Personnel Profile: Full-Time Paid 3; Part-Time Paid 9; Part-Time Volunteers 40.
Governing Authority: private; nonprofit corporation. Tax-exempt: 170(b)(1)(A) & 501(c)(3).
Art Museum & Center.
Collections: c.1859-1939 paintings by California artist Theodore Wores; American artists; Vivan Woodward Elmer Majolica collection; contemporary American drawings & prints; 19th to 21st-century artists; Native American art & artifacts; 20th to 21st-century Bay Area art. Historic House: 1866 Jamison-Brown house.
Research Fields: pertaining to permanent collection & temporary exhibitions.
Facilities: 1,000-vol. library of books & journals available for staff, docents & members; sculpture garden. Gift items for sale.
Activities: guided tours; slide lectures; gallery talks; workshops; auctions; luncheons; studio art classes for children; docent tours of exhibitions; outreach program, ARTREACH; docent out-reach program to schools & senior centers; rental space.
Publications: catalogues; A Catalog of the Paintings by Theodore Wores in the Permanent Collection of the Triton Museum of Art; Austen D. Warburton Collection of American Indians Art & Artifacts; Expressions from the Soul: Bay Area Korean - American Women; Iku K. Nagai; Los Tres: Jose Clemente Orozco, Diego Rivera & David Alfaro Siqueiros; A Visual Heritage: Bay Area African-American Artists; A Bay Area Connection: Works from the Anderson Collection 1954-1984; brochures related to exhibitions; quarterly calendar & newsletter.
Hours & Admission Prices: Thurs. 11-9, Fri.-Wed. 11-5. No charge; donations accepted. Closed national holidays. ♿
Attendance: 40,000 (estimated)
Membership: Student & Senior $15; Individual $35; Family $50; Curator's Circle $100; Director's Circle $250; Patron $500; Benefactor $1,000.

Santa Cruz

ARBORETUM AT UC SANTA CRUZ, University of California, 1156 High St., Santa Cruz, CA 95064-1077. Tel.: 831-427-2998. Fax: 831-427-1524.
E-mail: arboretum@ucsc.edu
Web Site: ucsc.edu/arboretum/
Founded: 1964.
Congressional District: 16
Key Personnel: Exec. Dir., Daniel Harder, Ph.D.; Pres. (V), Peggy Williams; Dir. of Horticulture, Brett Hall; Dir. Education, Stephen McCabe; Harry O. Warren Cur. of New Zealand Collection, Thomas Sauceda; Admin., Susie Bower; Cur. Australian Collection, Melinda Johnson; Cur. Native Collection, Rick Flores; Cur. African Collection, Ron Arruda; Nursery Asst. Mgr., Stephanie Hudson; Facilities Mgr. & Horticulturist, Francis Campbell.
Personnel Profile: Full-Time Paid 11; Full-Time Volunteers 25; Part-Time Volunteers 200; Interns 6.
Governing Authority: Parent Institution: University of California Santa Cruz. Tax-exempt: 501(c)(3).
Arboretum & Botanical Gardens.
Collections: living plants of scientific, educational or ornamental value.
Research Fields: horticulture; evolution of plants; conifers; bulbs; natives; land management; rare fruit collections; primitive angiosperms; Australian; South African; New Zealand; California natives.
Facilities: botanical garden. Plants & gift items for sale.
Activities: guided tours; lectures; docent program or council; formally organized education programs for undergraduate college students affiliated with UCSC; permanent exhibitions; teaching; public outreach; conservation.
Publications: quarterly bulletin, Arboretum Associates.
Hours & Admission Prices: Daily 9-5. Adults $5; members no charge.
Attendance: 55,000 (estimated)
Membership: Individual $50; Dual & Family $65; Kauri $100-$249; Erica $250-$499; Banksia $500-$999; Protea $1000 & up; Life $2500.

ELOISE PICKARD SMITH GALLERY, Cowell College, University of California, Santa Cruz, CA 95064. Tel.: 831-459-2953.
E-mail: lapope@ucsc.edu
Web Site: cowell.ucsc.edu/smith.gallery/main.php
Key Personnel: Dir. & Gallery Cur., Linda Pope
Art Gallery.
Collections: Monterey Bay region contemporary art & photographs. ♿
Attendance: 3,200

MARY PORTER SESNON ART GALLERY, (M), UC Santa Cruz, Porter College, Santa Cruz, CA 95064. Mailing Address: Porter Faculty Svcs., Porter College, UC Santa Cruz, Santa Cruz, CA 95064. Tel.: 831-459-3606. Fax: 831-459-3535.
E-mail: sgraham@ucsc.edu

Web Site: arts.ucsc.edu/sesnon
Founded: 1971.
Key Personnel: Dir. & Cur., Shelby Graham; Gallery Mgr., Leslie Fellows.
Personnel Profile: Full-Time Paid 1; Part-Time Paid 4; Part-Time Volunteers 1; Interns 1.
Governing Authority: tax-exempt. Parent Institution: University of California.
Art Gallery.
Collections: archives; drawings; video; paintings.
Publications: exhibition catalogues.
Hours & Admission Prices: Sept.-June 15 Tues.-Sat. 12-5. No charge. ♿
Attendance: 3,500 (estimated)

MISSION SANTA CRUZ, 130 Emmet St., Santa Cruz, CA 95060. Mailing Address: 126 High St., Santa Cruz, CA 95060-3711. Tel.: 831-426-5686.
Web Site: missiontour.org/santacruz/index.htm
Founded: 1791.
Religious Museum.
Collections: replica of the original mission church.
Hours & Admission Prices: Tues.-Sat. 10-4, Sun. 10-2. Closed holidays.

MUSEUM OF ART AND HISTORY AT THE MCPHERSON CENTER, 705 Front St., Santa Cruz, CA 95060-4508. Tel.: 831-429-1964. Fax: 831-429-1954.
E-mail: director@santacruzmah.org
Web Site: www.santacruzmah.org
Founded: 1996.
Congressional District: 16
Key Personnel: Exec. Dir., Paul Figueroa; Pres. (V), Peter Orr; Chm. (V), Glenn Peters; Dir. Exhibitions, Susan Hillhouse; Cur. Education, Ashley Adams; Administrative Dir., Kala Haines; Volunteer Coord. & Special Events, Allie Wilson; Museum Shop Mgr., Katie Horner.
Personnel Profile: Full-Time Paid 12; Part-Time Paid 5; Part-Time Volunteers 120; Interns 2.
Governing Authority: nonprofit organization. Tax-exempt.
Museum of Art & History, Archives Library on Site.
Collections: art & historical artifacts.
Research Fields: Santa Cruz County, CA history.
Facilities: auditorium. Museum-related items for sale.
Activities: guided tours; lectures; films; organized education programs for adults; docent program; children's workshops; family fun days.
Publications: quarterly newsletter; yearly history journal; exhibition catalogs; Lime Kiln Legacies; Sidewalk Companion to Santa Cruz Architecture; Legal History Santa Cruz County; Surf, Sand and Streetcars; A Gathering of Voices - The Native Peoples of the Central California Coast.
Hours & Admission Prices: Tues.-Sun. 11-5. Adults $5, students 18 and over & senior citizens $4; discounts to AAM members; members, students under 18 & children under 12 no charge. Closed legal holidays. ♿
Attendance: 36,000 (estimated)
Membership: Educator & Student $20; Individual $40; Dual & Family $60; Director's Circle $125; Artist's Circle $250; Collector's Circle $500; Trustee's Circle $1,000; President's Circle $2,500; Patron's Circle $5,000.

THE PAPERWEIGHT MUSEUM, 123 Locust St., Santa Cruz, CA 95060-3907. Tel.: 831-427-1177. Fax: 831-427-0111.
E-mail: lselman@paperweight.com
Web Site: www.theglassgallery.com
Paperweight Museum.
Collections: paperweights.
Hours & Admission Prices: Mon.-Fri. 9-5, Sat. 10-4, Sun. by appointment.

SANTA CRUZ ART LEAGUE, INC., 526 Broadway, Santa Cruz, CA 95060-4622. Tel.: 831-426-5787. Fax: 831-426-5789.
E-mail: cindy@scal.org
Web Site: www.scal.org
Founded: 1919.
Congressional District: 16
Key Personnel: Pres. (V), Stephanie Schriver; Dir. Operations, Kim Scheiblauer; Gift Shop Mgr., Nancy Howe; Administrative Asst., Margot Kuhre; Theater Mgr., Barry Brown; Weekend Receptionist & Docent, Inglis Carre.
Personnel Profile: Part-Time Paid 4; Part-Time Volunteers 50; Interns 5.
Governing Authority: nonprofit organization. Tax-exempt: 501(c)(3).
Art Gallery.
Collections: pioneer paintings of local area artists; sculpture from the 1915 Panama Pacific Expo (San Francisco).
Research Fields: local art and artists.
Facilities: 1,800 sq. ft. main gallery; 62-seat performance space; 700 sq. ft. classroom; kitchen.
Activities: gallery talks; art classes; art demonstrations & workshops; theater performances; outdoor art fairs.
Publications: monthly members' bulletin.
Hours & Admission Prices: Wed.-Sat. 12-5, Sun. 12-4. No charge; donations accepted. ♿
Attendance: 20,000
Membership: Students & Seniors $35; Individual $55; Family $70.

SANTA CRUZ MUSEUM OF NATURAL HISTORY, (M), 1305 E. Cliff Dr., Santa Cruz, CA 95062-3722. Tel.: 831-420-6115 & 6119. Fax: 831-420-6451.
E-mail: staff@santacruzmuseums.org
Web Site: www.santacruzmuseums.org
Founded: 1904.
Congressional District: 16
Key Personnel: Pres. Bd. (V), Patty Quillin; Dir., Jenifer Lienau-Thompson; Administrative Asst., Sally Heine.
Personnel Profile: Full-Time Paid 2; Part-Time Paid 4; Part-Time Volunteers 40.
Governing Authority: municipal. Branch Museum: Santa Cruz Surfing Museum at Lighthouse Point; Tel. 831-420-6289. Subsidiary Institution: Santa Cruz Surfing Museum. Tax-exempt.
Regional Natural History Museum: centered on the Northern Monterey Bay Region of California.
Collections: regional surfing & natural history; California & Native American ethnological artifacts; historical artifacts; regional art collection; surfing artifacts.
Research Fields: local natural history; paleontology; archaeology; regional history & art.
Facilities: 1,200-vol. library of natural history reference materials available on request; 2,500 sq. ft. permanent exhibit space; meeting room; educational facilities. Books relating to permanent & special exhibits for sale.
Activities: guided tours; activities; lectures; formally organized education programs for children; permanent & temporary exhibitions.
Publications: bimonthly newsletter; Fossil Invertebrates & Geology of the Marine Cliffs at Capitola; Tide Drift Shells of the Monterey Bay Region; Fossil Sharks & Rays of the Southern Santa Cruz Mountains.
Hours & Admission Prices: Tues.-Sun. 10-5. Surfing Museum: Wed.-Mon. 12-4. Adults $2.50, seniors 60 & over $1.50; youth under 18 & members no charge. Closed New Year's Day; Martin Luther King Day; Easter; Memorial Day; Independence Day; Labor Day; Thanksgiving & day after; Christmas. ♿
Attendance: 100,000 (estimated)
Membership: Student & Senior $15; Individual $25; Family $35; Donor $50-$249; Sponsor $250-$499; Patron $500 & up. Business Membership: Bobcat $100-$249; Friend $250-$499; Patron $500-$999.

Santa Fe Springs

HATHAWAY RANCH MUSEUM, 11901 E. Florence Ave., Santa Fe Springs, CA 90670-4494. Tel.: 562-777-3444. Fax: 562-945-1892.
Founded: 1986.
Key Personnel: C.E.O. & Exec. Dir., Francine Rippy; Pres. (V), Chad Hathaway.
Personnel Profile: Full-Time Paid 1; Part-Time Paid 2; Part-Time Volunteers 15.
Governing Authority: HRM bd. dirs. Tax-exempt.
History Museum.
Collections: 19th- & 20th-century American furnishings; farm buildings & equipment; 3,000 local history photographs; oil field & feed lot artifacts; household articles; clothing.
Research Fields: Southern California oil industry; Santa Fe Springs; early ranching.
Facilities: archives; visitors center; picnic area; 30-seat meeting room; banquet facilities.
Activities: historical lectures; farm equipment demonstrations; hay wagon rides; tours.
Publications: pamphlets: From Fulton Wells to Santa Fe Springs; Los Nietos-at the Crossroads of History; Lovingly Yours - the Letters of Lola McCarric to Jesse Hathaway; Pre-tour educational materials: Discovery Packet; self guided tour information; booklets: Settlers of Southern California, Vols. 1-9; quarterly, HRM Newsletter.
Hours & Admission Prices: Mon.-Tues. & Thurs. 11-4, Fri.-Sun. & group tours by appointment. Suggested Donation: adults $4. Closed major holidays. ♿
Attendance: 800 (estimated)
Membership: Individual $5; Family $10.

Santa Maria

THE NATURAL HISTORY MUSEUM OF SANTA MARIA, 412 S. McClelland, Santa Maria, CA 93454-5117. Mailing Address: P.O. Box 5254, Santa Maria, CA 93456-5254. Tel.: 805-614-0806. Fax: 805-614-0806.
Web Site: www.naturalhistorysantamaria.com
Formerly: Samuel J. Perry Natural History Museum
Founded: 1996.
Congressional District: 33
Key Personnel: Pres., Laura Mohajer; Treas., Bailey Hudson.
Personnel Profile: Part-Time Paid 1; Part-Time Volunteers 20; Interns 1.
Governing Authority: private; nonprofit organization. Tax-exempt: 501(c)(3).
Natural History Museum: housed in the historic Hart Home.
Collections: natural history; wildlife dioramas & their habitats.
Activities: bird kit & curriculum; bug kit & curriculum; rock and fossil kits. Special Events: Live! At the Museum each month.
Publications: The Meadowlark quarterly members newsletter.
Hours & Admission Prices: Wed.-Sat. 11-4, Sun. 1-4. No charge; donations accepted. Closed holidays. ♿
Attendance: 4,850 (accurate)
Membership: Individual $25; California Quail $50; Meadowlark $100; Great Horned Owl $250; Golden Eagle $500; Red Tailed Hawk $1,000; California Condor $2,000.

SANTA MARIA MUSEUM OF FLIGHT, INC., (M), 3015 Airpark Dr., Santa Maria, CA 93455-1821. Tel.: 805-922-8758. Fax: 805-922-8958.
E-mail: info@smmof.org
Web Site: www.smmof.org
Founded: 1984.
Congressional District: 19
Key Personnel: Pres., Michael Geddry, Sr.; Registrar, Jerry Nicholson; Museum Shop Mgr., Tom Reedy.
Personnel Profile: Full-Time Volunteers 12; Part-Time Volunteers 20.
Governing Authority: public benefit nonprofit corporation. Tax-exempt: 501(c)(3).
Aeronautics Museum.
Collections: aircraft & aviation artifacts from early flight to current space activities with special emphasis on the aviation & space history of the central coast of California; Stinson Reliant, Fleet Model 2, Rand KR2, Sonerii Fly Baby, 1931 Great Lakes, rocket engines, satellite simulator; rotating display of aircraft; the Topping collection of miniature aircrafts; dioramas; F-4 Phantom; full scale Wright 1902 glider & F-86 sabre; H1 (Howard Hughes) full scale replica; A-4; Flight of the Phoenix scale movie prop; Folland Gnat.
Research Fields: national flying schools of the late 20s & early 30s; Flight of the Southern Cross; early aviation of central coast of California; pilot training & the original 9 primary flight training schools (1939-1945); history of North American Aviation Company.
Facilities: 2,100-vol. library & 1,600 VCR tapes on aviation; 11,000 sq. ft. exhibit space. Museum-related items for sale.
Activities: guided tours; docent training. Annual Event: Warbirds Aircraft Fly In; Ford Car Show.
Publications: quarterly newsletter, The Flight Plan.
Hours & Admission Prices: Fri.-Sun. 10-4; groups & other times by appointment. Suggested Donation: adults $5, seniors $4, students $3, children 6 & under $1; members, military & their dependents no charge. Closed New Year's Day; Christmas. ♿
Attendance: 10,000 (estimated)
Membership: Student & Senior $20; Individual $35; Family $50; Business $100; Life 55 & over $250; Life under 55 $350.

SANTA MARIA VALLEY HISTORICAL MUSEUM, 616 S. Broadway, Santa Maria, CA 93454-5111. Mailing Address: P.O. Box 264, Santa Maria, CA 93456-0264. Tel.: 805-922-3130.
Web Site: www.smvrhm.org
Formerly: Santa Maria Valley Historical Society, Inc.
Founded: 1955.
Key Personnel: Pres., Dave Carey; Museum Dir., Richard Chenoweth; Sec., Jim O'Neill.
Personnel Profile: Full-Time Paid 1; Part-Time Paid 2; Part-Time Volunteers 30.
Governing Authority: nonprofit organization. Tax-exempt: 501(c)(3).
General Museum: housed in building constructed on site of c.1900 1st municipal water works.
Collections: Indian artifacts; Rancho period memorabilia; pioneer profile room displays; models; Santa Maria Valley history.
Research Fields: local & valley history.
Facilities: library; reading room. Books & museum-related items for sale.
Activities: guided tours; lectures; films; education programs; temporary exhibits.
Publications: quarterly newsletter; book, This Is Our Valley - Santa Maria Historical Photo Album; Santa Maria Style Barbecue.
Hours & Admission Prices: Closed for relocation. ♿
Attendance: 4,320 (estimated)
Membership: Active $20; Family $30; Patron $50; Vaquero & Townbuilder $100; Pioneer Patriot $250; Founder's Circle $500; Lifetime $1,000.

Santa Monica

ANGELS ATTIC MUSEUM, Heritage Square, Santa Monica, CA 90401. Mailing Address: Volunteers of America Los Angeles, Ste. 1500, 3600 Wilshire Blvd., Los Angeles, CA 90010-2603. Tel.: 310-394-8331. Fax: 310-656-6865.
E-mail: angelsattic516@yahoo.com
Web Site: www.angelsattic.com
Founded: 1984.
Key Personnel: Museum Dir., Nicole Dickerson; Dir., Eleanor La Vove; Museum Shop Mgr., Susan Baker.
Personnel Profile: Full-Time Paid 1; Full-Time Volunteers 2; Part-Time Paid 3; Part-Time Volunteers 20.
Governing Authority: private; nonprofit. Tax-exempt: 501(c)(3).
Toy & Doll Museum: housed in a c.1895 Queen Anne Victorian House.
Collections: dollhouses; miniatures; toys; dolls.
Facilities: Gift items for sale.
Hours & Admission Prices: Thurs.-Sun. 12:30-4:30. Adults $6.50; discounts to seniors & children under 12. ♿
Attendance: 5,000 (estimated)
Membership: Individual $35; Angel $100.

CALIFORNIA HERITAGE MUSEUM, 2612 Main St., Santa Monica, CA 90405-4002. Tel.: 310-392-8537. Fax: 310-396-0547.
E-mail: calmuseum@earthlink.net
Web Site: californiaheritagemuseum.org
Founded: 1977.
Key Personnel: Dir., Tobi Smith; Chm. (V), Mary Ann Hays; Museum Shop Mgr., Arlene Encell.
Personnel Profile: Full-Time Paid 3; Part-Time Paid 4; Part-Time Volunteers 35; Interns 2.
Governing Authority: Tax-exempt.
Historic House.
Collections: California decorative arts, fine art, folk art, pottery & tile 1900-1930; photo archive; photography; culture & heritage of the state.
Research Fields: California history & decorative arts; photography archive.
Publications: Hawaiian Style; Arts & Crafts Movement; International Masks, Masks of the World; Monterey Furniture - California Spanish Revival; California Tile, The Golden Era 1910-1940; Saints & Sinners - Mexican Devotional Art; Everyday Life in California - Regional Watercolors.
Hours & Admission Prices: Wed.-Sun. 11-4. Adults $5, senior citizens & students $3; discount to AAA members; children under 12 & members no charge. Closed major holidays ♿
Attendance: 17,500 (estimated)
Membership: Student & Senior $25; General $35; Patron $100; Collector's Club $250; Roy Jones Society $1,000 & up.

SANTA MONICA HISTORY MUSEUM, (M), 1350 7th St., Santa Monica, CA 90401. Mailing Address: P.O. Box 3059, Santa Monica, CA 90408-3059. Tel.: 310-395-2290. Fax: 310-395-2290 (call first).
Web Site: www.santamonicahistory.org
Founded: 1975.
Key Personnel: Pres. & C.E.O., Louise Gabriel; Chm. (V), Jean McNeil Wyner; Museum Shop Mgr., Jean Ann Holbrook.
Personnel Profile: Full-Time Paid 1; Part-Time Paid 1.
Governing Authority: Tax-exempt.
History Museum.
Collections: local history & culture; photographs; artwork; architectural drawings; newspapers; books; period artifacts.
Major Exhibits: Cirque du Soleil Early Costumes, 2/10; Senator John P. Jones, Santa Monica Co-Founder, 7/10.
Publications: quarterly newsletter; monthly e-zine.
Hours & Admission Prices: Tues. & Thurs. 12-8, Wed. 10-4, Fri-Sat. 11-5. Adults $5, seniors & students $2; children 12 & under and members no charge. ♿
Attendance: 2,000 (accurate)
Membership: Individual $40; Family/Organization $50; Sustaining $60; Patron $100; Business $200; Life $500.

SANTA MONICA MUSEUM OF ART, (M), Bergamot Station, 2525 Michigan Ave., Bldg. G1, Santa Monica, CA 90404-4042. Tel.: 310-586-6488. Fax: 310-586-6487.
E-mail: info@smmoa.org
Web Site: www.smmoa.org
Founded: 1988.
Congressional District: 27
Key Personnel: Exec. Dir., Elsa Longhauser; Deputy Dir. Exhibitions & Programs, Lisa Melandri; Dir. Education, Asuka Hisa; Dir. Communications, Miranda Carroll; Dir. Admin. & Finance, Patricia Scharf; Dir. Devel., Tracy Mizkaui; Registrar, Royce Kunze; Membership, Anna Nickila; Gracie Cur., Amy Coane.
Personnel Profile: Full-Time Paid 11; Part-Time Paid 2; Part-Time Volunteers 50; Interns 5.
Governing Authority: nonprofit organization; board of trustees. Tax-exempt: 501(c)(3).
Contemporary Art Museum.
Collections: works by contemporary artists.
Major Exhibits: Diane Thater, 1/16/10-4/17/10; Project Rm 1: Jeffrey Wells, 1/16/10-4/17/10; Project Rm 2: Nira Pereg: Shabat, 1/16/10-4/17/10; Andrew Lord, 5/15/10-8/21/10; Alberto Burri, 9/11/10-12/18/10.
Facilities: 6,000 sq. ft. exhibit space plus education and orientation rooms.
Activities: educational & outreach programs; lectures; temporary exhibitions; intern program.
Publications: exhibition catalogs.
Hours & Admission Prices: Tues.-Sat. 11-6. Suggested Donations: adults $5, artists, senior citizens & students $3; members no charge. Closed legal holidays. ♿
Attendance: 35,000
Membership: Artist, Student & Senior $40; Individual $55; Partner $100; Family $300; SMMOA Fellows $500; Curatorial Corps $1,000; Director's Salon $3,000 & up.

Santa Paula

CALIFORNIA OIL MUSEUM, 1001 E. Main St., Santa Paula, CA 93060-2809. Mailing Address: P.O. Box 48, Santa Paula, CA 93061-0048. Tel.: 805-933-0076. Fax: 805-933-0096.
E-mail: info@oilmuseum.net
Web Site: www.oilmuseum.net
Formerly: Santa Paula Union Oil Museum
Founded: 1950.
Congressional District: 23
Key Personnel: Dir., Jeanne Orcutt; Chm., Mary Alice Henderson.
Personnel Profile: Full-Time Paid 1; Part-Time Paid 1; Part-Time Volunteers 15; Interns 2.
Governing Authority: city. Tax-exempt.
Museum of the Oil Industry.
Collections: oil industry artifacts; photographs; paintings; publications.
Research Fields: oil history in California.
Facilities: facility available for receptions & special events.
Publications: Pipelines museum newsletter.
Hours & Admission Prices: Museum: Wed.-Sun. 10-4. Guided Tours: Wed.-Sun. 11-2:30, other times & groups of 10 or more by appointment. Adults $4, senior citizens $3, children $1; discounts to AAM & ICOM members; members no charge. Closed major holidays. ♿
Attendance: 12,000 (accurate)
Membership: Single & Dual $35; Family $50; Business $100; Premier $500; Corporate $1,000.

Santa Rosa

CALIFORNIA INDIAN MUSEUM & CULTURAL CENTER, 5250 Aero Dr., Santa Rosa, CA 95403-8069. Tel.: 707-579-3004. Fax: 707-579-9019.
E-mail: CIMandCC@aol.com
Web Site: www.cimcc.org
Key Personnel: Pres. (Pomo), Andrew Maisel; Vice Pres., Jerry Burroni; Exec. Dir., Nicole Myers-Lim; Project Mgr., David Lim; Devel. Specialist, Carol Oliva; Administrative Asst., Ramona Cruz
Indian Museum.
Collections: art; traveling exhibits; photo displays.
Activities: lectures; walking tours; community events.
Publications: book, The California Indian.
Hours & Admission Prices: Mon.-Fri. 9-5. No charge; donations accepted.
Membership: Members $25; Sponsor $50; Patron $100; Benefactor $1,000; President's Circle $1,000 & up.

CHARLES M. SCHULZ MUSEUM AND RESEARCH CENTER, (M), 2301 Hardies Lane, Santa Rosa, CA 95403-2668. Tel.: 707-579-4452, ext. 260. Fax: 707-579-4436.
E-mail: inquiries@schulzmuseum.org
Web Site: www.schulzmuseum.org
Founded: 2002.
Congressional District: 1
Key Personnel: Dir., Karen Johnson; Pres. (V), Jean F. Schulz.
Personnel Profile: Full-Time Paid 11; Part-Time Paid 9; Part-Time Volunteers 120.
Governing Authority: Tax-exempt.
Art Museum.
Collections: morphing Snoopy wood sculpture; tile mural featuring the images of Charlie Brown & Lucy composed of 3,588 Peanuts comic strips; 96 sq. ft. wall from early Schulz home containing characters painted by Charles Schulz; original Peanuts comic strip drawings; photographs & memorabilia related to life of Charles Schulz.
Major Exhibits: The Facts Behind the Funnies, 11/09-1/10; Peanuts Cooks, 11/09-2/10; Sunday at the Funnies, 12/09-4/10; May I Have This Dance?, 1/10-4/10; Peanuts...Naturally, 2/10-6/10; Language of Lines: How Cartoonists Create Imaginary Lines, 4/10-8/10; Youth Culture, 5/10-9/10; From Highland Park Caddy, 6/10-10/10; The Legacy of Peanuts, 8/10-1/11; Failed Experiments in Peanuts, 9/10-2/11.
Research Fields: cartoon art history, life & art of Charles Schulz.
Facilities: 27,384 sq. ft. exhibit space; 100 seat auditorium; classroom; outdoor gardens.
Activities: permanent & temporary exhibits.
Publications: exhibitions catalogs; quarterly newsletter, Musings.
Hours & Admission Prices: Memorial Day to Labor Day Mon.-Fri. 11-5, Sat.-Sun. 10-5; Sept.-May Mon. & Wed.-Fri. 11-5, Sat.-Sun. 10-5. Adults $8, seniors & youth $5; discounts to AAM, CAM, AAA & WMA members; members no charge. Closed New Year's Day; Easter; Independence Day; Thanksgiving; Christmas Eve & Day. ♿
Attendance: 60,000 (estimated)
Membership: Individual $40; Family $70; Fan $100; Super Fan $250; Legacy $500; Golden Legacy $1,000; Patron $2,500; Sponsor $5,000; Corporate Levels: Contributing $500; Supporting $1,000; Associate $2,500; Benefactor $5,000.

JESSE PETER MUSEUM, Santa Rosa Junior College, 1501 Mendocino Ave., Santa Rosa, CA 95401-4332. Tel.: 707-527-4479. Fax: 707-524-1861.
E-mail: bbenson@santarosa.edu
Web Site: www.santarosa.edu/museum
Formerly: Jesse Peter Native American Art Museum
Founded: 1932.
Congressional District: 2
Key Personnel: C.E.O., Margaret Bond; Dir., Sandra Holliman; Exhibit Coord., Christine Vasquez.
Personnel Profile: Full-Time Paid 1; Part-Time Paid 4; Interns 3.
Governing Authority: college. Affiliated with Santa Rosa Junior College. Tax-exempt.
Multicultural Museum.
Collections: Native American cultural art; Latino, African & Asian material culture.
Research Fields: material culture of North American Indians with emphasis on California & the Southwest.
Facilities: research center.
Activities: rotating exhibits; guided tours; lectures; demonstrations. Annual Event: A Day Under the Oaks, California Native American Cultural Festival in May.
Publications: occasional monographs & teacher's guides.
Hours & Admission Prices: mid-Aug. to mid-May Mon.-Fri. 9-5; Summer: call for hours. No charge; donations accepted. Closed holidays & vacations. ♿
Attendance: 17,000 (accurate)

LUTHER BURBANK HOME & GARDENS, (M), Santa Rosa Ave. at Sonoma Ave., Santa Rosa, CA 95402. Mailing Address: 100 Santa Rosa Ave., Rm. 10, Santa Rosa, CA 95404-4957. Tel.: 707-524-5445. Fax: 707-524-5827.
E-mail: burbankhome@lutherburbank.org
Web Site: www.lutherburbank.org
Founded: 1979.
Congressional District: 2
Key Personnel: Bd. Chm. (V), Frank Haeg; Chm. (V), Richard Russ; Treas., Toni Hower; Archivist, Rebecca Baker; Museum Shop Mgr., Sharlene McCaw.
Personnel Profile: Full-Time Paid 2; Part-Time Volunteers 150.
Governing Authority: municipal. Parent Institution: City of Santa Rosa. Tax-exempt.
Historic House & Garden: 1884 Luther Burbank Home; 1889 greenhouse.
Collections: furnishings; tools; photographs; plants; documents.
Research Fields: Burbank life & work.
Facilities: 450-vol. library of catalogs, photographs & publications available

for research by application on premises only; demonstration gardens. Museum-related items for sale.
Activities: guided tours; plant sales. Annual Events: mid-summer Garden Tea in July; holiday open house in December.
Publications: Luther Burbank: Gardener to the World; Fifty Famous Favorites, Plant Introductions by Luther Burbank; A Gardener Touched with Genius: The Life of Luther Burbank; Here a Plant, There a Plant, Children's Biography on Luther Burbank.
Hours & Admission Prices: April-Oct. Tues.-Sun. 10-3:30; groups by appointment. Guided & cell phone audio tours $7; tours $5; Friends of Luther Burbank no charge. Gardens: daily 8 to dusk. No charge. ♿
Attendance: 75,000 (accurate)
Membership: Individual $30; Family $45; Senior Citizens & Students $20; Benefactor $125 & up.

PACIFIC COAST AIR MUSEUM, N. Laughlin at Becker, Santa Rosa, CA 95403. Mailing Address: 2230 Becker Blvd., Santa Rosa, CA 95403-8275. Tel.: 707-575-7900. Fax: 707-545-2813.
E-mail: director@pacificcoastairmuseum.org
Web Site: www.pacificcoastairmuseum.org
Founded: 1990.
Key Personnel: Pres. (V), Mike Voorhees; Exec. Dir., Dave Pinsky; Public Rels., Doug Clay; Museum Shop Mgr., Bob Conz.
Personnel Profile: Full-Time Paid 1; Part-Time Volunteers 150.
Governing Authority: private; nonprofit organization. Tax-exempt.
Aircraft Museum.
Collections: aircraft including BAC 167 Strikemaster, IL-14, F-8, A-4, F-14, F-4, A-6, C-118, F-16, A-26, T-38, T-37, T-33, F-84, F-86, F-105, F-106, H-34 helicopter, RF86, HU-16E & a UH-1 on display; indoor exhibits of WWII material; civil artifacts.
Facilities: Museum-related items for sale.
Activities: docent program; guided tours. Annual Event: Air Show.
Publications: monthly newsletter, Straight Scoop.
Hours & Admission Prices: Tues., Thurs. & Sat.-Sun. 10-4. Suggested Donation: adults $5; discount to California Assoc. of Museums; children 12 & under no charge. Closed New Year's Day; Thanksgiving; Christmas. ♿
Attendance: 23,569 (accurate)
Membership: Individual $30; Family $45.

SANTA ROSA JR. COLLEGE ART GALLERY, Frank P. Doyle Library, 1501 Mendocino Ave., Santa Rosa, CA 95401-4395. Tel.: 707-527-4298.
Web Site: www.santarosa.edu/artgallery/
Key Personnel: Dir., Stephanie Sanchez; Exhibition Specialist, Michael McGinnis
College Art Gallery.
Collections: works by student & faculty artists.
Activities: programs; temporary exhibitions. Museum Sponsors: Annual Student Art Show; Art Faculty Exhibits.
Hours & Admission Prices: Winter: Tues.-Fri. 10-4, Sat. 12-4 during shows. No charge; donations accepted. Closed all school holidays.

SONOMA COUNTY MUSEUM, (M), 425 Seventh St., Santa Rosa, CA 95401-5233. Tel.: 707-579-1500. Fax: 707-579-4849.
E-mail: info@sonomacountymuseum.org
Web Site: www.sonomacountymuseum.org
Founded: 1976.
Congressional District: 2
Key Personnel: Exec. Dir., Diane Evans; Cur. Exhibitions, Eric Stanley; Cur. Education, Laurie Cox; Education, Visitor Svcs. Coord. & Museum Shop Mgr., Michelle Novosel; Museum Coord., Sarah-Jane Andrew; Bookkeeping Mgr., Kirsten Olney.
Personnel Profile: Full-Time Paid 6; Part-Time Paid 1; Part-Time Volunteers 125; Interns 5.
Governing Authority: nonprofit organization. Parent Institution: Sonoma County Museum Foundation. Tax-exempt: 501(c)(3).
Contemporary Art & History Museum.
Collections: fine art from 19th century to present with emphasis on San Francisco Bay area & northern California; Christo & Jeanne Claude 19th-20th century Sonoma County history.
Major Exhibits: Richard Shaw: Five Decades of Ceramics, 1/29/10-5/10; Polaridad Complimentaria: Recent Works from Cuba (T), 6/16/10-9/5/10.
Research Fields: art history; Christo & Jeanne Claude.
Facilities: Books, crafts & museum-related items for sale.
Activities: guided tours; lectures; films; arts festivals; docent program; temporary & traveling exhibitions; public programs; family days; school loan service; education materials; educational releases; history & exhibitions outreach; teacher open house; school tours; fundraisers; social activities; bus tours.
Publications: newsletter, The Muse; exhibit catalogues.
Hours & Admission Prices: Tues.-Sun. 11-5. Adults $5, seniors, disabled & students $2; discounts to AAM members; children under 12, museum members & school groups no charge. Closed New Year's Day & day after; Martin Luther King Jr. Day; Easter; Memorial Day; Independence Day; Labor Day; Thanksgiving & day after; Christmas Eve, Day & day after. ♿
Attendance: 30,000 (estimated)
Membership: Discount & Individual $35; Partner $50; Supporting $125; Sustaining $250; Friend $500; Curator's Circle $1,000; Patrons Circle $2,500; Director's Circle $5,000.

Santa Ynez

SANTA YNEZ VALLEY HISTORICAL SOCIETY, (M), 3596 Sagunto St., Santa Ynez, CA 93460-9110. Mailing Address: P.O. Box 181, Santa Ynez, CA 93460-0181. Tel.: 805-688-7889. Fax: 805-688-1109.
E-mail: syvm@verizon.net
Web Site: www.santaynezmuseum.org
Founded: 1961.
Key Personnel: Exec. Dir., Chris Bashforth; Pres. (V), Bill Reynolds; Cur. & Archivist, John Crockett.
Personnel Profile: Full-Time Paid 2; Part-Time Paid 2; Part-Time Volunteers 30.
Governing Authority: private; nonprofit organization. Tax-exempt: 501(c)(3).
History Museum.
Collections: local historical artifacts. Carriage House: carriages & stage coaches
Facilities: 500-vol. library of local & state history books. Museum-related items for sale.
Activities: docent program; guided tours; lectures; temporary exhibitions. Annual Events: Vaquero Show; Jamboree Auction, Dinner, Dance.
Publications: quarterly newsletter, Valley Heritage.
Hours & Admission Prices: Wed.-Sun. 12-4. Adults $4; members and children 16 & under no charge. Closed major holidays. ♿
Attendance: 9,000 (estimated)
Membership: Individual $35; Family $50; Sponsor $150; Patron $300; Lifetime $2,500.

Santa Ysabel

SANTA YSABEL ASISTENCIA, 23013 Hwy. 79, Santa Ysabel, CA 92070. Mailing Address: P.O. Box 129, Santa Ysabel, CA 92070-0129. Tel.: 760-765-0810.
Founded: 1818.
Personnel Profile: Full-Time Paid 1; Part-Time Paid 1.
Indian Museum.
Collections: Indian artifacts; period furnishings.
Facilities: Museum-related items for sale.
Hours & Admission Prices: Daily 8-3. No charge; donations accepted.

Santee

CREATION AND EARTH HISTORY MUSEUM, 10946 Woodside Ave., N., Santee, CA 92071-3272. Mailing Address: Life and Light Foundation, 9336 Abraham Way, Santee, CA 92071. Tel.: 619-596-1104.
Web Site: www.lifeandlightfoundation.org
Formerly: ICR Museum of Creation & Earth History
Founded: 1976.
Key Personnel: Museum Shop Mgr., Sue Sisco.
Governing Authority: Parent Institution: Life and Light Foundation. Tax-exempt.
Earth History & Science Museum.
Collections: earth history & science; butterfly collection; live animals; fossils; archaeology; Middle East.
Hours & Admission Prices: Mon.-Sat. 9-4. No charge; donations accepted. Closed New Year's Day; Presidents' Day; Memorial Day; Independence Day; Labor Day; Thanksgiving & two days after; Christmas Eve, Day & day after. ♿
Attendance: 16,000 (estimated)

Saratoga

HAKONE ESTATE AND GARDENS, 21000 Big Basin Way, Saratoga, CA 95070-5755. Mailing Address: Hakone Foundation, P.O. Box 2324, Saratoga, CA 95070. Tel.: 408-741-4994. Fax: 408-741-4993.
E-mail: hakone@hakone.com
Web Site: www.hakone.us
Key Personnel: Exec. Dir., Lon Saavedra; Japanese Garden Specialist, Jack Tomlinson; Asst. Gardener, Raul Alvarez
Japanese-style Gardens.
Collections: bamboo garden; tea garden; zen garden; statues.
Facilities: Museum-related items for sale.

Hours & Admission Prices: Mon.-Fri. 10-5, Sat.-Sun. 11-5. Adults $5, seniors & students $3.50; members no charge. Closed New Year's Day; Christmas.

MONTALVO ARTS CENTER, 15400 Montalvo Rd., Saratoga, CA 95070-6327. Mailing Address: P.O. Box 158, Saratoga, CA 95071-0158. Tel.: 408-961-5800. Fax: 408-961-5850.
Web Site: www.montalvoarts.org
Founded: 1930.
Congressional District: 12
Key Personnel: Exec. Dir., Bill Melis; Pres. (V), Charmaine Warmenhoven; Dir. Mktg. & Communications, Ariane Bicho.
Personnel Profile: Full-Time Paid 27; Part-Time Paid 10; Part-Time Volunteers 400; Interns 5.
Governing Authority: nonprofit. Parent Institution: Montalvo Association. Tax-exempt: 501(c)(3).
Art Museum, Arboretum & Historic House/Site.
Collections: decorative arts. Historic Houses: 1912 Villa Montalvo; 1912 carriage house.
Facilities: 175-acre park & nature preserve; 275-seat Carriage House theatre; 1,250-seat Garden theatre.
Activities: guided tours; lectures; gallery talks; concerts; artist in residence program; arts festivals; drama; permanent exhibitions; education programs.
Publications: monthly calendar; monthly e-newsletter.
Hours & Admission Prices: Park & Gallery during exhibits: 9-5. No charge, fee for concert goers. Closed New Year's Day; Thanksgiving; Christmas. ♿
Attendance: 250,000 (estimated)
Membership: Student $30; Educator $45; Individual $60; Family $100; Senator's Circle $250; Griffin Circle $500; Phelan Circle $1,000; Villa Circle $2,500; Artist Circle $5,000; Creative Circle $10,000.

YOUTH SCIENCE INSTITUTE, SANBORN NATURE CENTER, 16055 Sanborn Rd., Sanborn-Skyline Park, Saratoga, CA 95070-9746. Mailing Address: Va Sona Nature Center, 296 Garden Hill Dr., Los Gatos, CA 95032-7669. Tel.: 408-867-6940. Fax: 408-867-0196.
E-mail: info@ysi-ca.org
Web Site: www.ysi-ca.org
Founded: 1953.
Key Personnel: Exec. Dir., Suzanne Mulchay; YSI Center Mgr., Bonnie Lemat; Project Dir., Daniel Margulies.
Governing Authority: nonprofit. Parent Institution: Youth Science Institute, Vasona Park, CA. Tax-exempt: 501(c)(3).
Youth & Science Museum.
Collections: geology items; taxidermied items & invertebrate zoo; living & nonliving insects; California Indian artifacts; redwood ecology.
Research Fields: community garden program.
Facilities: botanical garden; educational facilities; 1,000 sq. ft. exhibit space; nature center.
Activities: lectures; organized educational programs; docent program; temporary exhibitions. Museum Sponsors: Insect Fair.
Publications: quarterly newsletter Explore.
Hours & Admission Prices: Mon.-Sat. 8-4:30 No charge; donations accepted. Education program fee. Closed New Year's Day; Thanksgiving; Christmas. ♿
Attendance: 16,500 (estimated)
Membership: Individual $20; Family $35; Supporting $50; Patron $100; Donor $250; Gavilan $500; Sponsor $750; Benefactor & Corporate $1,000.

Sausalito

BAY AREA DISCOVERY MUSEUM, Fort Baker, 557 McReynolds Rd., Sausalito, CA 94965-2601. Tel.: 415-339-3900. Fax: 415-339-3901.
Web Site: www.baykidsmuseum.org
Founded: 1984.
Key Personnel: Pres. (V), Eve Niquette; Dir., Richard Winefield; Treas., John Park; Museum Shop Mgr., Ted Payton.
Personnel Profile: Full-Time Paid 40; Part-Time Paid 20; Part-Time Volunteers 100; Interns 2.
Governing Authority: nonprofit organization. Tax-exempt: 501(c)(3).
Children's Museum.
Collections: art; nature; science; culture of the Bay Area; photography.
Research Fields: early childhood education; outdoor education; children's creativity.
Activities: weekend programs & workshops.
Publications: Discoveries.
Hours & Admission Prices: Tues.-Fri. 9-4, Sat.-Sun. 10-5. Adults $10, children 1-17 & seniors 62 & over $8; discounts to AAM & ICOM members; family level membership & children under one no charge. ♿
Attendance: 300,000 (accurate)
Membership: Time for Two: $85; Fun for Four $105; Family Passport $120; Anchor $150; Adventurer $250; Explorer $1,500.

SAN FRANCISCO BAY MODEL VISITOR CENTER, 2100 Bridgeway, Sausalito, CA 94965-1764. Tel.: 415-332-3871. Fax: 415-332-0761.
Web Site: www.spn.usace.army.mil/bmvc/
Founded: 1956.
Congressional District: 6
Key Personnel: Chm. (V), Paul Anderson; Park Mgr., Chris Gallagher.
Personnel Profile: Full-Time Paid 7; Full-Time Volunteers 20; Part-Time Volunteers 30.
Governing Authority: federal; U.S. Army Corps. of Engineers. Tax-exempt.
Park Museum: located within the Bay Model Regional Visitor Center, an hydraulic testing facility.
Collections: biota of San Francisco Bay & how hydraulic modeling is used to study the bay; interactive video program; Corps of Engineers.
Research Fields: study hydraulic problems that affect the San Francisco Bay & the Sacramento/San Joaquin Delta.
Facilities: archival library pertaining to tests that have been conducted on the Bay Model; 125-seat auditorium; 6,000 sq. ft. gallery area. Books on local environment & maritime history for sale.
Activities: guided tours; lectures; films; volunteer program; audio tours available in 6 languages: German, French, Spanish, Japanese, Russian, English; orientation program also available in 5 languages.
Publications: brochure, Bay Model User's Guide; self-guiding brochure.
Hours & Admission Prices: Winter: Tues.-Sat. 9-4; Summer: Tues.-Fri. 9-4, Sat.-Sun. & holidays 10-5. No charge, donations accepted. ♿
Attendance: 108,257 (accurate)
Membership: Seastar $35; Pelican $50; Harbor Seal $100; Shark $250; Gray Whale $500.

Scotia

PALCO, 125 Main. St., Scotia, CA 95565. Mailing Address: P.O. Box 37, Scotia, CA 95565-0037. Tel.: 707-764-4472. Fax: 707-764-4171.
Web Site: www.palco.com
Formerly: The Pacific Lumber Company
Founded: 1869.
Congressional District: 1
Key Personnel: C.E.O., George O'Brien; Chm. (V), Mary Bullwinkel.
Personnel Profile: Part-Time Paid 3; Part-Time Volunteers 1.
Logging & Lumber Museum: housed in 1920 First National Bank of Scotia, all redwood building.
Collections: period logging equipment; pictorial history of The Pacific Lumber Co. Historic Building: 1920 Winema Theatre located nearby.
Hours & Admission Prices: June-Sept. Mon.-Fri. 8-4:30; other times by request. No charge. Closed holidays.
Attendance: 15,000 (estimated)

Seal Beach

SEAL BEACH HISTORICAL & CULTURAL SOCIETY/RED CAR MUSEUM, Electric Ave. & Main, Seal Beach, CA 90470. Mailing Address: P.O. Box 152, Seal Beach, CA 90740-0152. Tel.: 562-430-1450.
Founded: 1971.
Congressional District: 46
Key Personnel: Pres. (V), Marie Antos
Historic Train Car: a roving machine shop used to troubleshoot problems along the Pacific Electric LA-Newport Line; built in 1925.
Collections: local history; railroad artifacts; signs; tickets; pins; photographs; video.
Publications: quarterly newsletter.
Hours & Admission Prices: 2nd & 4th Sat. 12-3. No charge.
Attendance: 1,000
Membership: Student $7; Single $15; Family $25; Life $200.

Shafter

MINTER FIELD AIR MUSEUM, 401 Vultee St., Shafter, CA 93263. Mailing Address: P.O. Box 445, Shafter, CA 93263-0445. Tel.: 661-393-0291. Fax: 661-393-3296.
E-mail: mfam@minterfieldairmuseum.com
Web Site: www.minterfieldairmuseum.com
Founded: 1981.
Congressional District: 20
Key Personnel: Chm. Bd., Maj. Gen. James T. Whitehead, Jr. USAF Ret.; Vice Chm., Dean Craun; Cur., Dr. David Day.
Personnel Profile: Part-Time Paid 1; Part-Time Volunteers 30.
Governing Authority: private; nonprofit organization. Tax-exempt: 501(c)(3).
Military Aeronautics Museum.
Collections: World War II aircraft & vehicles; historical artifacts.
Facilities: 200-vol. World War II aircraft; 5,000 sq. ft. exhibit space. Museum-related items for sale.
Activities: guided tours; airworthy restoration of L-3 & BT-13L Link trainer &

military vehicle restorations; parades; fly-ins; helicopter H-34 Vietnam era; Aermachi jet trainer. Open Houses: tour includes P-51, AT-6, PT-17, PT-26, L-5, 2 Reno Air Racers, AT-6 Miss T-N-T & P-51 Strega; UC-78 Bamboo Bomber - restoration project. Museum Sponsors: Annual Auction and Awards Dinner; Airshow.
Publications: monthly newsletter, Snap Roll II.
Hours & Admission Prices: Sat. 9-2; other times by appointment. No charge; donations accepted. Closed most holidays. ♿
Attendance: 12,000 (estimated)
Membership: Family $50; Senior Pilot $100; Command Pilot $250; Squadron Commander (Life) $500; Wing Commander (Life) $1,000; Division Commander (Life) $2,000; A.F. Commander (Life) $5,000; Supreme Commander (Life) $10,000.

SHAFTER DEPOT MUSEUM, 150 Central Valley Hwy., Shafter, CA 93263-2002. Mailing Address: Shafter Historical Society, P.O. Box 1088, Shafter, CA 93263-1088. Tel.: 661-746-4423.
Web Site: www.shafter.com/index.asp?NID=14
Key Personnel: Cur., Stan Wilson
History Museum
Collections: railroad artifacts; agriculture; local history.
Publications: quarterly newsletter.
Hours & Admission Prices: Sat. 10-2; other times by appointment. ♿
Membership: Student $10; Individual $15; Family $25.

Shasta

SHASTA STATE HISTORIC PARK, 15312 Hwy. 299 W., Shasta, CA 96087. Mailing Address: P.O. Box 2430, Shasta, CA 96087-2430. Tel.: 530-225-2065 & 243-8194. Fax: 530-225-2038.
E-mail: lcooper@parks.ca.gov
Founded: 1937.
Key Personnel: Cur., Linda L. Cooper.
Personnel Profile: Full-Time Paid 2; Part-Time Paid 2; Part-Time Volunteers 20.
Governing Authority: state.
State Park Museum.
Collections: early California paintings; gold rush & mining materials; extensive archives pertaining to Shasta County; Native American basketry; artifacts.
Facilities: visitor center; picnic area.
Activities: permanent exhibitions.
Hours & Admission Prices: Wed.-Sun. 10-5. Adults $2; children 17 & under no charge. Closed New Year's Day; Thanksgiving; Christmas.
Attendance: 36,000 (accurate)

Shoshone

SHOSHONE MUSEUM, 118 Hwy. 127, Shoshone, CA 92384. Mailing Address: P.O. Box 38, Shoshone, CA 92384-0038. Tel.: 760-852-4524.
E-mail: shoshonemus@veawb.coop
Web Site: deathvalleychamber.org
Founded: 1986.
Key Personnel: Dir., Jennifer Viereck; Pres. (V), Susan Sorrells.
Personnel Profile: Part-Time Paid 4; Part-Time Volunteers 3.
Governing Authority: Tax-exempt.
Historic Building: built in Greenwater in 1906, moved to Zabriskie & later to its present location where it served as a store & gas station.
Collections: area history; mining & farming equipment; mammoth skeleton; natural history; Native American artifacts; minerals; mining; pioneers; T&T Railroad.
Publications: triannual newsletter, The Shoshone Museum Reader.
Hours & Admission Prices: Summer: Wed.-Mon. 10-4; Winter: daily 10-4. No charge; donations accepted. Closed Federal holidays. ♿
Attendance: 55,000 (accurate)
Membership: Individual $15; Family $35; Business & Nonprofit $50.

Sierra City

SIERRA COUNTY HISTORICAL SOCIETY (KENTUCKY MINE MUSEUM), 100 Kentucky Mine Rd., Sierra City, CA 96125. Mailing Address: P.O. Box 260, Sierra City, CA 96125-0260. Tel.: 530-862-1310.
Key Personnel: Dir., Cur. & Museum Shop Mgr., Virginia Lutes; Pres., Bud Buczkowske; Vice Pres., Joleen Torris; Chm. Membership, Suzi Schoensee; Sec., Patrick Manning; Treas., William Copren; Caretaker, Toni Strine.
Personnel Profile: Part-Time Paid 2; Part-Time Volunteers 2.
Governing Authority: private; nonprofit organization. Tax-exempt: 501(c)(3).
History Museum.
Collections: mine history; mining tools & equipment.
Research Fields: archaeology; Native American history; bat biology.
Facilities: 100-vol. library. Museum-related items for sale.
Activities: concerts; docent program; guided mine & stamp mill tours; temporary exhibitions.
Publications: quarterly membership newsletter, The Sierran.
Hours & Admission Prices: Memorial Day to Labor Day Wed.-Sun. 10-4. Adults $1. Guided Tours: adults $7, children 17 & under $3.50; children under 6 no charge.
Attendance: 1,000 (estimated)
Membership: Adults $20; Family & Institutions $25; Business & Supporting $35; Sustaining $50; Life $300.

Silverado

TUCKER WILDLIFE SANCTUARY, 29322 Modjeska Canyon Rd., Silverado, CA 92676-9784. Tel.: 714-649-2760. Fax: 714-649-2760.
E-mail: kcornell@exchange.fullerton.edu
Web Site: www.tuckerwildlife.org
Founded: 1938.
Key Personnel: Dir., Karon Cornell; Site Mgr., Marcella Gilchrist.
Governing Authority: university. Parent Institution: California State University, Fullerton, CA. Tax-exempt.
Wildlife Sanctuary.
Collections: botany; entomology; geology; herpetology; ornithology.
Research Fields: flora & fauna of the Santa Ana Mountains; entomology; ornathology; native wildlife.
Facilities: visitor center; picnic area; amphitheater; gardens. Museum-related items for sale.
Activities: K-12 school tours; public groups tours; bird observation area; workshops; special events.
Publications: quarterly newsletter; bird list; plant guide.
Hours & Admission Prices: Tues.-Sun. 9-4. Suggested Donation: $3 per person. Naturalist Guided Group Tours: $6 per person. Closed major holidays. ♿
Attendance: 30,000
Membership: Senior Quail $20; Hummingbird $25; Red Tailed Hawk $50; Eagle $100.

Simi Valley

R.P. STRATHEARN HISTORICAL PARK AND MUSEUM, 137 Strathearn Place, Simi Valley, CA 93065-1605. Mailing Address: P.O. Box 940461, Simi Valley, CA 93094-0461. Tel.: 805-526-6453. Fax: 805-526-6462.
E-mail: simihistorian@sbcglobal.net
Web Site: www.simihistory.com
Founded: 1970.
Congressional District: 20
Key Personnel: Dir., Patricia Havens; Pres. (V), Georgia Trumble.
Personnel Profile: Part-Time Paid 3; Part-Time Volunteers 100; Interns 1.
Governing Authority: society; nonprofit organization. Parent Institution: Rancho Simi Recreation & Parks District & Simi Valley Historical Society, 1692 Sycamore Dr. Tax-exempt: 170(b)(1)(A).
Historic Buildings.
Collections: period artifacts; letters; documents; books; farm implements; furniture; papers; household items; ranch tools; school & business records; financial records; clothing. Historic Buildings: c.1800 Simi Adobe; 1890s Victorian house; 1890s Strathearn home; 1889 The Colony House; St. Rosa Lima Church.
Research Fields: history of Simi Valley, Southern California & Ventura County.
Facilities: library of books & letters; reading room.
Activities: guided tours; lectures; demonstrations; field trips for school children & other groups.
Publications: books, Straw Roads-A Story of Simi Valley from 1908-1960; Simi Grows Up; Moorpark, Star of the Valley; Simi Valley - A Journey through Time (Earliest days through 1997); Strathearn Letters - Windows on the Past, 2009.
Hours & Admission Prices: Tours: Wed.-Fri. 1 pm, Sat.-Sun. 1-4. Park: Mon.-Fri. 9-3. Requested Donation: adults $3; members and children 17 & under no charge. Closed Easter; Christmas.
Attendance: 6,000 (estimated)
Membership: Single $15; Family $25; Sustaining $50-$100; Patron $500; Benefactor $1,000.

RONALD REAGAN PRESIDENTIAL LIBRARY AND MUSEUM, (M), 40 Presidential Dr., Simi Valley, CA 93065-0699. Tel.: 800-410-8354. Fax: 805-577-4074.
Web Site: www.reagan.utexas.edu
Founded: 1991.
Congressional District: 23
Key Personnel: Dir., R. Duke Blackwood; Deputy Dir., Tony Chauveaux; Registrar, Jennifer Torres; Gift Shop Mgr., Carolyn Mente.

Personnel Profile: Full-Time Paid 30; Part-Time Paid 10; Part-Time Volunteers 182; Interns 2.
Governing Authority: federal. A unit of the National Archives and Records Administration, Washington, D.C. 20408. Tax-exempt: 170(b)(1)(A).
Presidential Library.
Collections: personal papers; government records; still photographs; motion pictures; audio & video tapes; head of state gifts; gifts from private citizens; political campaign items; personal & family memorabilia.
Research Fields: the Reagan presidency; the 1980s; life, times, and career of Ronald Reagan and his family.
Facilities: archival reading room; 400-seat auditorium; classroom; conference spaces.
Activities: guided tours; lectures; conferences; changing exhibits; organized educational programs for children & adults; docent program.
Publications: exhibit-related brochures & catalogs; curriculum guides; volunteer newsletter; membership newsletter.
Hours & Admission Prices: Daily 10-5. Adults $12, seniors 62 & over $9, children 11-17 $3; children 10 & under no charge. Closed New Year's Day; Thanksgiving; Christmas. ♿
Attendance: 300,000 (accurate)
Membership: Friends of the Reagan Library & Museum: Individual $35; Family $50; Diplomat $100; Cabinet $250; Chairman's Club $1,000.

Smith River

SHIP ASHORE RESORT MUSEUM, 12370 Hwy. 101 N., Smith River, CA 95567-9448. Tel.: 800-487-3141; 707-487-3141. Fax: 707-487-7070.
E-mail: shipashore@charterinternet.com
Web Site: www.ship-ashore.com
Maritime Museum.
Collections: local historic artifacts; seashells; rocks & minerals; natural history.
Facilities: Museum-related items for sale.
Hours & Admission Prices: Call for hours. No charge.

Soledad

MISSION NUESTRA SENORA DE LA SOLEDAD, 36641 Fort Romie Rd., Soledad, CA 93960. Mailing Address: P.O. Box 515, Soledad, CA 93960-0515. Tel.: 831-678-2586.
Web Site: missiontour.org/soledad/index.htm
Founded: 1791.
Congressional District: 17
Key Personnel: Chm. (V) & Museum Shop Mgr., Nancy Morrison; Pres. (V), Carlene Bell.
Governing Authority: Tax-exempt.
Religious Museum.
Collections: religious artifacts.
Activities: special services; weddings.
Hours & Admission Prices: Daily 10-4. Mass: 1st Sun. of month. No charge; donations requested. Closed New Year's Day; Easter; Independence Day; Thanksgiving; Christmas. ♿
Attendance: 16,000 (estimated)

Solvang

ELVERHOJ MUSEUM OF HISTORY AND ART, 1624 Elverhoy Way, Solvang, CA 93463-2704. Mailing Address: P.O. Box 769, Solvang, CA 93464-0769. Tel.: 805-686-1211. Fax: 805-686-1822.
E-mail: info@elverhoj.org
Web Site: www.elverhoj.org
Founded: 1988.
Key Personnel: C.E.O., Esther Jacobsen Bates.
Personnel Profile: Full-Time Paid 1; Part-Time Paid 1; Part-Time Volunteers 50.
Governing Authority: nonprofit. Tax-exempt.
History and Art Museum.
Collections: local history; Danish culture; photographs; porcelain; silverware.
Facilities: garden; picnic gazebo.
Activities: special events; tours.
Publications: newsletter.
Hours & Admission Prices: Wed.-Thurs. 1-4, Fri.-Sun. 12-4. No charge; donations accepted. Closed New Year's Day; Easter; Thanksgiving; Christmas Eve & Day. ♿
Attendance: 11,200 (accurate)
Membership: Individual $35; Couple & Family $50; Business $100; Benefactor $250; Patron $500.

HANS CHRISTIAN ANDERSEN MUSEUM, 1680 Mission Dr., Solvang, CA 93463-3602. Tel.: 805-688-2052.
Founded: 1989.
Personnel Profile: Part-Time Volunteers 2.
Governing Authority: nonprofit organization. Parent Institution: Ugly Duckling Foundation.
General Museum.
Collections: Andersen's life & work; period tools; Andersen's first & early edition tales; travel journals; letters; photographs; Andersen's artwork.
Activities: tours; lectures. Annual Event: Andersen's Birthday Celebration in April.
Hours & Admission Prices: Daily 10-5; groups by appointment.

OLD MISSION SANTA INES, 1760 Mission Dr., Solvang, CA 93463-2625. Mailing Address: P.O. Box 408, Solvang, CA 93464-0408. Tel.: 805-688-4815. Fax: 805-686-4468.
E-mail: Office@missionsantaines.org
Web Site: www.missionsantaines.org
Founded: 1804.
Key Personnel: Archives, Sheila Benedict; Gift Shop Mgr., Vonnie Abbott.
Governing Authority: church. Roman Catholic Archdiocese of Los Angeles.
Historic Site & Historic Building: 1804 Old Mission Santa Ines.
Collections: religious vestments; Mexican & Spanish Colonial art; tools.
Activities: recorded tours.
Publications: brochures; book, Mission Santa Ines, The Hidden Gem.
Hours & Admission Prices: Winter & Summer: daily 9-5:30. Adults $3; discounts for groups; children under 16 no charge. Closed New Year's Day; Easter; Thanksgiving; Christmas. ♿
Attendance: 50,000 (estimated)

Sonoma

DEPOT PARK MUSEUM, (M), 270 First St., W., Sonoma, CA 95476. Mailing Address: P.O. Box 861, Sonoma, CA 95476-0861. Tel.: 707-938-1762. Fax: 707-938-1762.
E-mail: depot@vom.com
Web Site: www.vom.com/depot
Founded: 1979.
Congressional District: 6
Key Personnel: Pres., John Ambrose; Mgr., Dir. & Cur., Diane Smith.
Personnel Profile: Part-Time Paid 1; Part-Time Volunteers 50.
Governing Authority: council. Parent Institution: Sonoma Valley Historical Society. Tax-exempt.
Art & History Museum.
Collections: exhibits & artifacts relating to pioneers & settlers of Sonoma Valley; native American collection; Victorian & early Sonoma period furniture & artifacts; railroad equipment.
Research Fields: genealogy of local early Sonoma families; buildings, history.
Facilities: research library.
Activities: lectures; films; permanent & temporary exhibitions; tours.
Publications: books, Saga of Sonoma; Sonoma Mission; Sonoma Valley Legacy; monthly, historical society newsletter; Sonoma Valley Notes; Pioneer Sonoma; Schools & Scows in Early Sonoma; The Men of The California Bear Flag Revolt and Their Heritage; Images of America Sonoma Valley.
Hours & Admission Prices: Wed.-Sun. 1-4:30. No charge; donations accepted. ♿
Attendance: 5,000 (estimated)
Membership: Student under 18 $10; Individual $25; Family $35; Business & Supporter $50; Friend $100; Patron $200; Life $300.

SONOMA STATE HISTORIC PARK, 363 3rd St., W., Sonoma, CA 95476-5632. Tel.: 707-938-1519. Fax: 707-938-1406.
Web Site: www.parks.ca.gov
Founded: 1906.
Congressional District: 6
Key Personnel: Mission Guide, Jim Danaher; State Historian II, Marianne Hurley; Vallejo Home Guide, Michele Kazeminejad; State Park Ranger, Chrystal Shoaf; Museum Cur., Carol A. Dodge; Museum Shop Mgr., Sue Vargas; Maintenance Supvr., Tom Jager.
Personnel Profile: Full-Time Paid 1; Part-Time Paid 3; Part-Time Volunteers 10.
Governing Authority: state. Dept. of Parks & Recreation, P.O. Box 2390, Sacramento, CA 95811. Tax-exempt.
State Historic Park Museum Complex.
Collections: furnishings; Jorgonsen paintings of California Missions. Historic Houses: c.1870 Toscano Hotel; 1852 Vallejo Home; 1852 Swiss Chalet; 1823 San Francisco Solano Mission; 1836 Sonoma Barracks.
Research Fields: Mission San Francisco Solano de Sonoma; California history 1823-1846; General Vallejo 1807-1890.
Facilities: visitor centers at Mission San Francisco, Swiss Chalet & Sonoma Barracks.

Activities: formally organized environmental education programs for children; permanent exhibitions; guided tours for school groups with advanced reservations.
Publications: descriptive brochure.
Hours & Admission Prices: Daily 10-5. Adults $2; children 16 & under no charge. Closed New Year's Eve & Day; Thanksgiving; Christmas.
Attendance: 602,398

SONOMA VALLEY MUSEUM OF ART, (M), 551 Broadway, Sonoma, CA 95476-6601. Mailing Address: P.O. Box 322, Sonoma, CA 95476-0322. Tel.: 707-939-7862. Fax: 707-939-1080.
Web Site: www.svma.org
Founded: 1998.
Congressional District: 1
Key Personnel: Exec. Dir., Kate Eilertsen; Bd. Pres., Jane Milotich; Registrar, Lesley Hunter.
Personnel Profile: Full-Time Paid 3; Part-Time Paid 2; Part-Time Volunteers 100; Interns 4.
Governing Authority: private; nonprofit organization. Tax-exempt: 501(c)(3).
Art Museum.
Collections: fine arts from around the world.
Facilities: 5,000 sq. ft. exhibit space. Museum-related items for sale.
Activities: concerts; docent program; films; formal education programs for adults & children; guided tours; lectures; loan & traveling exhibitions. Annual Event: Wet Paint Gala Auction Fundraiser.
Publications: quarterly museletter.
Hours & Admission Prices: Wed.-Sun. 11-5 during exhibitions. Adults $5; discounts to groups of 15 or more; members, students K-12 & Sun. no charge. Closed New Year's Day; Presidents' Day; Memorial Day; Independence Day; Labor Day; Thanksgiving; Christmas. ♿
Attendance: 15,000 (accurate)

Sonora

TUOLUMNE COUNTY MUSEUM & HISTORY CENTER, 158 W. Bradford Ave., Sonora, CA 95370-4920. Mailing Address: P.O. Box 299, Sonora, CA 95370-0299. Tel.: 209-532-1317.
Historic Building: housed in a former jail built in 1857 and rebuilt in 1865 after being destroyed by a fire that killed the inmate who allegedly started it. Listed on the National Register of Historic Places.
Collections: local history & culture; genealogy; photographs; personal artifacts; firearms.
Facilities: gardens; rental facilities.
Activities: rental facilities.
Hours & Admission Prices: Call for hours.

South Lake Tahoe

LAKE TAHOE HISTORICAL SOCIETY & MUSEUM, 3058 Lake Tahoe Blvd., South Lake Tahoe, CA 96150-7810. Mailing Address: P.O. Box 404, South Lake Tahoe, CA 96156-0404. Tel.: 530-541-5458.
Founded: 1968.
Congressional District: 14
Key Personnel: Chm., Diane Johnson; Pres. (V), Lynne Bajuk; Museum Shop Mgr., Peggy Bourland.
Personnel Profile: Full-Time Paid 1; Part-Time Volunteers 12.
Governing Authority: society; nonprofit. Parent Institution: Lake Tahoe Historical Society. Tax-exempt: 501(c)(3).
Historical Society Museum.
Collections: Washo Indian: photographs; artifacts related to South Lake Tahoe historical significance, industry, commerce & gaming; R/R display in the Bijou Community Park.
Research Fields: historic slides; photographs; oral histories.
Facilities: library & archives available by special arrangement. Books & notepaper for sale.
Activities: guided tours; lectures; films; slide presentation; library; permanent & temporary exhibitions; school loan service.
Publications: books, Lake Valley's Past; Legends of Lake Tahoe; Railroads & Steamers of Lake Tahoe; The Steamer Tahoe; A Short History of the Lake Tahoe Basin; Sierra Trailblazers; Hank Monk, He'll Get You There on Time; member newsletter.
Hours & Admission Prices: Memorial Day to Labor Day Wed.-Mon. 11-3. No charge; donations accepted. ♿
Attendance: 1,750 (estimated)
Membership: Individual $25; Family $40; Business $65; Lifetime $300.

Stanford

IRIS & B. GERALD CANTOR CENTER FOR VISUAL ARTS AT STANFORD UNIVERSITY, (M), 328 Lomita Drive, Stanford, CA 94305-5060. Tel.: 650-723-4177. Fax: 650-725-0464.
Web Site: museum.stanford.edu
Founded: 1891.
Congressional District: 12
Key Personnel: Dir., Thomas K. Seligman; Cur. European Art & Mgr. Publication, Bernard Barryte; Cur. Modern & Contemporary Art, Hilarie Faberman; Registrar, Susan Roberts-Manganelli; Cur. Education, Patience Young; Cur. Arts of Africa & the Americas, Barbara Thompson; Cur. Asian Art, Xiaoneng Yang; Museum Shop Mgr., Arlene Gutowski.
Personnel Profile: Full-Time Paid 35; Part-Time Paid 20; Part-Time Volunteers 75.
Governing Authority: university. Affiliated with Stanford University. Tax-exempt: 501(c)(3).
Art Museum.
Collections: photographs; paintings; sculpture; Rodin collection; decorative arts; archaeology; prints & drawings; Oriental; ancient; pre-Columbian; African; coins & medals; textiles; Stanford family memorabilia.
Major Exhibits: From Their Studios, 11/09-1/3/10; Frank Lobdell Figure Drawings, 11/11/09-2/14/10; Tracing the Past, Drawing the Future: Master Ink Painters in 20th-Century China (T), 2/17/10-7/4/10; William Trost Richards-True to Nature: Drawings, Watercolors and Oil Sketches at Stanford University, 6/23/10-9/26/10; Mami Wata: Arts for Water Spirits in Africa and Its Diasporas, 8/4/10-1/2/11; Vodoun/Vodounon: Portraits of Initiates, 10/13/10-2/13/11.
Research Fields: American, Ancient, Oriental & European art from 1500.
Facilities: auditorium; cafe. Museum-related items for sale.
Activities: guided tours; lectures; gallery talks; concerts; inter-museum loan, permanent, temporary & traveling exhibitions.
Publications: exhibition catalogs; The Cantor Arts Center Journal.
Hours & Admission Prices: Wed. & Fri.-Sun. 11-5, Thurs. 11-8. No charge; donations accepted. Closed Thanksgiving; Christmas. ♿
Attendance: 250,950 (accurate)
Membership: Individual $50; Family & Couple $75; Sponsor $150; Patron $250; Benefactor $500; Artists' Circle $1,000; Connoisseurs' Circle $2,500; New Founders' Circle $5,000; Director's Circle $10,000.

Stinson Beach

AUDUBON CANYON RANCH, 4900 Hwy. 1, Stinson Beach, CA 94970. Tel.: 415-868-9244. Fax: 415-868-1699.
E-mail: acr@egret.org
Web Site: www.egret.org
Founded: 1962.
Key Personnel: Exec. Dir., Maurice A. Schwartz; Pres. Bd., Bryant Hichwa; Treas., Bill Richardson; Education, Diane Jacobson; Museum Shop Mgr., Yvonne Pierce.
Personnel Profile: Full-Time Paid 20; Part-Time Volunteers 450.
Governing Authority: nonprofit organization. Subsidiary Institutions: Cypress Grove Research Center, Marshall, CA; Bouverie Preserve, Glen Ellen, CA. Tax-exempt: 501(c)(3).
Nature Center.
Collections: local natural & environmental history; Coast Miwok Indian history.
Research Fields: monitoring grasses; shore birds, egrets, great blue herons; native plants & animals.
Facilities: 800-vol. library of natural history material; educational facilities; field research station. Natural history items for sale.
Activities: guided tours; lectures; organized educational programs; workshops; docent program.
Publications: semiannual seminar schedule, ACR Bulletin; monthly newsletters, The Heron & The Nutshell.
Hours & Admission Prices: mid-March to mid-July Sat.-Sun. & holidays 10-4, Tues.-Fri. by appointment. No charge; donations accepted. ♿
Attendance: 20,000 (estimated)

Stockton

ALAN SHORT GALLERY, 928 E. Rose St., Stockton, CA 95202-1849. Tel.: 209-462-8208 & 948-5759. Fax: 209-948-9042.
E-mail: asc@ddso.org
Web Site: www.ddso.org
Art Museum.
Collections: photographs.
Hours & Admission Prices: Daily 8-4. No charge; donations accepted. Closed national holidays

CHILDREN'S MUSEUM OF STOCKTON, 402 W. Weber Ave., Stockton, CA 95203-3108. Tel.: 209-465-4386. Fax: 209-465-4394.
E-mail: gina.delucchi@ci.stockton.ca.us
Web Site: stocktongov.com
Founded: 1991.
Congressional District: 11
Key Personnel: Pres. (V), Gary S. Giovanetti; Dir., Gina Delucchi; Asst. Dir., Nancy Collum.
Personnel Profile: Full-Time Paid 3; Part-Time Paid 10; Part-Time Volunteers 20.
Governing Authority: private; nonprofit organization. Tax-exempt: 501(c)(3).
Children's Museum.
Collections: hands-on exhibits.
Publications: monthly calendar; bimonthly newsletter; summer camp brochure.
Hours & Admission Prices: June-Aug. Mon.-Fri. 9-4, Sat. 10-5; Sept.-May Tues.-Fri. 9-4, Sat. 10-5, Sun. 12-5. Admission $4.50; discounts to school groups; children under 2 & members no charge. Closed Easter; Thanksgiving; Christmas. ♿
Attendance: 60,000 (estimated)
Membership: Individual $35; Grandparent $40; Family $45; Friendship $100; Bronze $250; Gold $500; Platinum $1,000.

THE HAGGIN MUSEUM, (M), 1201 N. Pershing Ave., Stockton, CA 95203-1604. Tel.: 209-940-6311. Fax: 209-462-1404.
E-mail: info@hagginmuseum.org
Web Site: www.hagginmuseum.org
Founded: 1928.
Congressional District: 14
Key Personnel: Pres. (V), Thomas Bowe III; Exec. Dir. & Cur. History, Tod Ruhstaller; Dir. Devel., Susan Obert; C.F.O., Karen Richards; Cur. Archival Collections, Kimberly Bowden; Cur. Collections, Kylee Denning; Cur. Education, Lisa Cooperman; Registrar, Erin Hicks; Webmaster, Eddie Hargreaves; Museum Store Mgr., Patty Huntley; Facilities Supt., Ray Shermantine; Membership & Mktg., Kristen Anema.
Personnel Profile: Full-Time Paid 13; Part-Time Paid 5; Part-Time Volunteers 300; Interns 6.
Governing Authority: nonprofit organization. Affiliated with the San Joaquin Pioneer & Historical Society. Tax-exempt: 509(a)(1).
Art & History Museum.
Collections: 19th century French & American paintings; American, European & Oriental decorative arts; glass; folk art; California Central Valley history artifacts including agricultural technology, furnishing, personal effects, replicas of local historic interiors & Indian artifacts, primarily California basketry.
Research Fields: late 19th & early 20th-century agricultural technology; Stockton manufacturing history; general Stockton history.
Facilities: library of books, photographs & ephemera on California & local history & art available on the premises by appointment; Holt Archives of Industrial & Agricultural Technology; Stephens Brothers Shipbuilding Archives.
Activities: guided tours; lectures; gallery talks; concerts; art workshops for children; docent council; inter-museum loan, permanent, temporary & traveling exhibitions.
Publications: quarterly activities calendar; history publications; catalogue, Haggin Art Collection.
Hours & Admission Prices: Wed.-Sun. 1:30-5, 1st & 3rd Thurs. of month 1:30-9. Adults $5; discounts to AAM & ICOM members; members no charge. Closed New Year's Day & day after; Easter; Independence Day; Thanksgiving & day after; Christmas Eve & Day. ♿
Attendance: 45,000 (estimated)
Membership: Student $15; Individual $25; Couple $35; Family $45; Sustaining $60; Supporting $100; Cornerstone $300-$2,500; Business $500-$1,500; Life $1,000; Life Founder $5,000.

THE HERBARIUM OF THE UNIVERSITY OF THE PACIFIC, Classroom Bldg., Stockton, CA 95211-0001. Mailing Address: Dept. Biological Sciences, Univ. of the Pacific, Stockton, CA 95211-0001. Tel.: 209-946-2181. Fax: 209-946-3022.
E-mail: mbrunell@pacific.edu
Founded: 1851.
Congressional District: 14
Key Personnel: Pres. Univ., Donald DeRosa; Cur., Mark Brunell.
Personnel Profile: Full-Time Paid 1; Part-Time Paid 1.
Governing Authority: university. Parent Institution: University of the Pacific.
Herbarium.
Collections: botany.
Research Fields: herbarium; botany.
Activities: loans for research to accredited herbaria.
Hours & Admission Prices: Mon.-Fri. 8-5. No charge; donations accepted. Closed university holidays. ♿

HOLT-ATHERTON SPECIAL COLLECTIONS, University of the Pacific Library, 3601 Pacific Ave., Stockton, CA 95211-0001. Tel.: 209-946-2431 & 2404. Fax: 209-946-2942.
E-mail: trichards@pacific.edu
Web Site: library.pacific.edu/ha
Key Personnel: Head Special Collections, Shan Sutton; Archivist, Michael Wurtz; Special Collections Asst., Trish Richards
History Museum.
Collections: research materials including manuscripts, photographs & specialized books; Dave Brubeck; John Muir papers; Locke-Hammond Family papers; Jedediah Strong Smith papers; pamphlets; maps; history of Stockton.
Hours & Admission Prices: Mon.-Fri. 10-5.

Suisun City

THE WESTERN RAILWAY MUSEUM, (M), 5848 State Hwy. 12, Suisun City, CA 94585-9641. Tel.: 707-374-2978. Fax: 707-374-6742.
Web Site: www.wrm.org
Founded: 1946.
Congressional District: 4
Key Personnel: C.E.O. & Chm. (V), Bill Kluver; Treas., Alan Stangenberger; Gen. Mgr., Mike Drieling; Exec. Dir., Phil Kohlmetz; Sec., John Krauskopf.
Personnel Profile: Full-Time Paid 1; Part-Time Paid 3; Part-Time Volunteers 100.
Governing Authority: company. Parent Institution: Bay Area Electric Railroad Association, Inc. Tax-exempt: 501(c)(3).
Transportation Museum.
Collections: trolley cars; electric interurbans; freight and work cars; Pullman cars; electric, diesel & steam locomotives.
Research Fields: vintage construction techniques for restoration.
Facilities: 4,000-vol. library on railways available by written request to curator; display and restoration buildings for large artifacts; photographic and corporate records files. Railway books for sale.
Activities: guided tours; films; permanent & temporary exhibitions; demonstration railway for living history experience.
Publications: monthly newsletter, The Review.
Hours & Admission Prices: Memorial Day-Labor Day Wed.-Sun. 10:30-5; Sept.-May Sat.-Sun. 10:30-5. Adults $10, seniors $9, children 2-14 $7; discounts to Association of Railway Museums & AAM members; members no charge. ♿
Attendance: 25,000 (accurate)
Membership: Individual $45; Family $65; Sustaining $100; Patron $500; Benefactor $1,000.

Sunnyvale

THE LACE MUSEUM, 552 S. Murphy Ave., Sunnyvale, CA 94086-6116. Tel.: 408-730-4695.
E-mail: jamele1@earthlink.net
Web Site: www.thelacemuseum.org
Founded: 1980.
Congressional District: 12
Key Personnel: Co Chm., Cherie Helm; C.E.O. & Co-Chm., Eleanore Schwartz; Volunteer Dir., Suzanne Meyer.
Personnel Profile: Part-Time Volunteers 25.
Governing Authority: nonprofit organization. Tax-exempt: 501(c)(3).
Lace Museum.
Collections: lace-trimmed clothing; books; old & recent laces; decorative items; lace-making tools; family heirlooms; original patterns dated from the late 1800s; costumes.
Research Fields: identification & verification of laces & lace artifacts.
Facilities: 300-vol. library pertaining to the research of lace. Threads, needles, books & patterns for sale.
Activities: guided tours; lectures; classes; films; study clubs; video programs; docent programs; participatory & loan exhibits; demonstrations & classes of several lace-making techniques.
Publications: quarterly newsletter.
Hours & Admission Prices: Tues.-Sat. 11-4. Private Tours: 10-11. Private Tour Fee: $3 per person. Closed first week in July; Thanksgiving; Christmas; week between Christmas & New Year's Day. ♿
Attendance: 3,500 (estimated)
Membership: Lace Museum Guild: Senior Citizen & Student $6; General $12; Patron $25 & up.

SUNNYVALE HISTORICAL SOCIETY AND MUSEUM ASSOCIATION, 570 E. Remington Dr., Sunnyvale, CA 94087-2652. Mailing Address: P.O. Box 61301, Sunnyvale, CA 94088-1301. Tel.: 408-749-0220. Fax: 408-732-4726.
E-mail: info@heritageparkmuseum.org
Web Site: www.heritageparkmuseum.org
Founded: 1973.
Congressional District: 12
Key Personnel: Pres., Michael Coggiola; Vice Pres., Floyd Frederickson.
Personnel Profile: Part-Time Volunteers 120.
Governing Authority: nonprofit organization. Parent Institution: Sunnyvale Historical Society & Museum Association. Branch Museum: Orchard Heritage Park, 550 Remington, Sunnyvale, CA 94087. Tax-exempt.
History Museum: located on site of Martin Murphy, Jr. home.
Collections: personal items of Ida Trubschenck, first city clerk; photographs; old newspapers, oral history tapes; furnishings from Martin Murphy, Jr. home; artifacts from Hendy Iron Works, Delmonte Seed Dept.; some early electronics games from Atari; early farm tools & equipment; early office equipment; model of U.S.S. Macon (dirigible) stationed at Sunnyvale Naval Air Station; model of Sparrowhawk, fighter plane of U.S.S. Macon.
Research Fields: local history; Martin Murphy, Jr. family.
Facilities: 300-vol. library of books available for use on site by prior arrangement.
Activities: lectures; gallery talks; docent program or council; permanent, temporary & traveling exhibitions; school loan service; walking tour of Murphy Ave. (100 S. Murphy); school docent program.
Publications: monthly newsletter.
Hours & Admission Prices: Tues., Thurs. & Sun. 12-4; other times by appointment. No charge. Closed national holidays. ♿
Attendance: 2,500
Membership: Senior $20; Individual $25; Senior Family $35; Contributing $50; Business & Organization $100; Lifetime $400; Business Lifetime $1,000.

Sunol

GOLDEN GATE RAILROAD MUSEUM, Niles Canyon Railway, Brightside Yard, 5550 Niles Canyon Rd., Sunol, CA 94586. Mailing Address: 1755 E. Bayshore Rd., Ste. 19A, Redwood City, CA 94063-4153. Tel.: 650-365-2472. Fax: 650-385-2473.
E-mail: 2472info@ggrm.org
Web Site: www.ggrm.org
Founded: 1985.
Key Personnel: Pres. (V), Dave Hensarling; Mgr. Operations, Dave Roth; Treas., Ronald Vane.
Personnel Profile: Full-Time Paid 1; Part-Time Volunteers 100.
Governing Authority: private; nonprofit organization. Tax-exempt: 501(c)(3).
Railroad Museum: housed within the former U.S. Navy Hunters Point Shipyard.
Collections: railroad equipment & artifacts pertaining to the San Francisco Bay area's regional rail transportation history; 60 locomotives & railcars; technical drawings & blueprints from Southern Pacific Company.
Publications: monthly newsletter, Stack Talk.
Hours & Admission Prices: Temporarily closed.
Membership: Special Participating $25 plus 30 hrs. work; Regular $35; Participating $75.

Susanville

LASSEN HISTORICAL MUSEUM, (M), N. Weatherlow St., Susanville, CA 96130. Mailing Address: P.O. Box 321, Susanville, CA 96130-0321. Tel.: 530-257-3292 & 1031.
Founded: 1958.
Congressional District: 14
Key Personnel: Pres., Tony Jones.
Personnel Profile: Part-Time Volunteers 14.
Governing Authority: municipal. Lassen County Historical Society. Tax-exempt: 501(c)(3).
Regional History Museum.
Collections: historical items related to Lassen County history.
Research Fields: genealogy & County history.
Facilities: Historic information for sale.
Activities: permanent & special exhibitions; monthly meetings with presentations of local history; field trips.
Publications: pamphlets; books; monthly newsletter.
Hours & Admission Prices: May-Oct. Mon.-Fri. 10-4, Sat. call for hours; other times by appointment. No charge; donations accepted. ♿
Membership: Individual $10; Family $15.

Sylmar

NETHERCUTT COLLECTION, 15200 Bledsoe St., Sylmar, CA 91342-2711. Tel.: 818-364-6464. Fax: 818-364-6466.
E-mail: info@nethercuttcollection.org
Web Site: www.nethercuttcollection.org
Founded: 1971.
Automobile & Musical Instrument Museum.
Collections: period automobiles; mechanical musical instruments; period furniture.
Hours & Admission Prices: Thurs.-Sat. 10-1:30 by appointment. No charge. Closed New Year's Eve & Day; Memorial Day weekend; Independence Day; Labor Day weekend; Thanksgiving weekend; Christmas Eve, Day & week. ♿

Taft

WEST KERN OIL MUSEUM, 1168 Wood St., Taft, CA 93268-4336. Mailing Address: P.O. Box 491, Taft, CA 93268-0491. Tel.: 661-765-6664. Fax: 661-765-9175.
Oil History Museum.
Collections: California's oil industry; local history; photographs; equipment; books.
Major Exhibits: Taft Oildorado Exhibit, 10/10.
Publications: quarterly newsletter, The Pumper.
Hours & Admission Prices: Thurs.-Sat. 10-4, Sun. 1-4. No charge; donations accepted. Closed New Year's Day; Independence Day; Thanksgiving; Christmas.
Attendance: 1,057 (estimated)
Membership: Single $12.50; Family $15; Supporting $35; Patron $75; Memorial & Life $250; Benefactor $500.

Tahoe City

GATEKEEPER'S MUSEUM & MARION STEINBACH INDIAN BASKET MUSEUM, (M), 130 W. Lake Blvd., Tahoe City, CA 96145. Mailing Address: P.O. Box 6141, Tahoe City, CA 96145-6141. Tel.: 530-583-1762. Fax: 530-583-8992.
E-mail: info@northtahoemuseums.org
Web Site: www.northtahoemuseums.org
Founded: 1969.
Congressional District: 4
Key Personnel: Exec. Dir., Stefanie Givens; Pres. (V), Dick Morton; Treas., Jim Arthur.
Personnel Profile: Full-Time Paid 3; Part-Time Paid 1; Part-Time Volunteers 10.
Governing Authority: private; nonprofit organization. Parent Institution: North Lake Tahoe Historical Society. Branch Museums: Watson Cabin Museum; Marion Steinbach Indian Basket Museum; Gatekeeper's Museum. Tax-exempt: 501(c)(3).
Historical Society Museum: site of prehistoric summer camping site & Washoe camp site.
Collections: archaeological artifacts; research library. Marion Steinbach Indian Basket Museum: over 1,000 American Indian baskets, research library, dolls & artifacts.
Research Fields: Lake Tahoe history; Native American basketry.
Facilities: 600-vol. library; 5,000 sq. ft. exhibit space. Museum-related items for sale. Gatekeeper's Museum/Marion Steinbach Indian Basket Museum/Watson Cabin Museum/William B. Layton Park.
Activities: guided tours; hobby workshops; temporary exhibitions. Museum Sponsors: basket weaving classes; weavers market.
Hours & Admission Prices: May-June 15 & Sept. Wed.-Sun. 11-5; June 16-Aug. daily 11-5; Oct.-April Sat.-Sun. 11-3 weather permitting. Adults 13-54 $3, seniors citizens 55 & over $2, children 6-12 $1; children under 6 & members no charge. ♿
Attendance: 30,000 (estimated)
Membership: Individual $30; Family $40; Business $50; Sponsor $100; Patron $150; Benefactor $250.

Tahoma

PINE LODGE (EHRMAN MANSION), Ed Z'berg Sugar Pine Point State Park, Tahoma, CA 96142. Mailing Address: Sugarpine Point State Park, Hwy. 89, P.O. Box 266, Tahoma, CA 96142-0266. Tel.: 530-525-7232. Fax: 530-525-3380.
Web Site: www.parks.ca.gov
Founded: 1965.
Congressional District: 14
Key Personnel: Lake Sector Supt., Susan Grove; Unit Supervising Ranger, Don Schmidt; Museum Cur. II, Judith K. Polanich.
Governing Authority: state; nonprofit. Parent Institution: State of California, Dept. of Parks & Recreation, Sierra State Parks Foundation. Tax-exempt.

Nature & Visitor Center: housed in c.1901 historic shingle style resort home complex.
Collections: period non-primary domestic furnishings; natural history specimens.
Research Fields: Lake Tahoe resort living 1900-1940s.
Facilities: trails; picnic areas; grounds available for weddings; campground.
Activities: guided tours; interpretive hikes & campfire programs; annual living history event; cross country skiing; swimming.
Publications: The Ehrman Mansion.
Hours & Admission Prices: Mansion: mid-June to Labor Day daily 11-4, tours on the hour. Adults $5, children 6-12 $3; children under 6 no charge. Parking $5.
Attendance: 20,000 (estimated)

VIKINGSHOLM, Emerald Bay State Park, Hwy. 89, Tahoma, CA 96142. Mailing Address: Emerald Bay State Park, P.O. Box 266, Hwy. 89, Tahoma, CA 96142-0266. Tel.: 530-525-7232. Fax: 530-525-3380.
Web Site: www.parks.ca.gov
Founded: 1953.
Congressional District: 14
Key Personnel: Supervising Ranger, Brian Barton; Museum Cur. II, Judith K. Polanich; Lake Sector Supt., Susan Grove.
Personnel Profile: Full-Time Paid 5; Part-Time Paid 5; Interns 4.
Governing Authority: state; nonprofit. Parent Institution: California Dept. of Parks & Recreation. Subsidiary Institution: Friends of Vikingsholm. Tax-exempt.
Visitor Center: housed in c.1929 historic Scandinavian styled resort home.
Collections: primary historic domestic furnishings; 16th-century European gate locks; Scandinavian furniture; architectural details; historic buildings.
Research Fields: domestic resort life at Lake Tahoe in 1930s & 1940s.
Facilities: visitor center; trails; picnic area.
Activities: guided tours.
Publications: Vikingsholm; Tahoe's Hidden Castle.
Hours & Admission Prices: mid-June to Labor Day daily 10-4, tours on the half hour. Adults $5, children 6-12 $3.
Attendance: 40,000 (estimated)

Taylorsville

INDIAN VALLEY MUSEUM, 4288 Cemetery St., Taylorsville, CA 95983. Mailing Address: P.O. Box 194, Taylorsville, CA 95983-0194. Tel.: 530-284-7785.
E-mail: IVM@frontiernet.net
Web Site: www.indianvalley.net/iv-museum
Founded: 1963.
History Museum.
Collections: local history & culture; Native American artifacts from 1860-1940.
Hours & Admission Prices: Memorial Day to Oct. Sat.-Sun. 1-4; other times by appointment. No charge.

Tehachapi

MOURNING CLOAK RANCH AND BOTANICAL GARDENS, 22101 Old Town Rd., Tehachapi, CA 93561-8886. Tel.: 661-822-1661. Fax: 661-822-5062.
Botanical Garden.
Collections: 2,200 plants.
Hours & Admission Prices: May-Oct. Mon.-Sat. 10-3.

Tehama

TEHAMA COUNTY MUSEUM, 275 C St., Tehama, CA 96090-0275. Mailing Address: P.O. Box 275, Tehama, CA 96090-0275. Tel.: 530-384-2595.
Web Site: tehamamuseum.110mb.com
History Museum.
Collections: local history & culture; photographs; personal artifacts.
Hours & Admission Prices: Fri.-Sun. 1-4. No charge.

Temecula

PENNYPICKLE'S WORKSHOP, 42081 Main St., Temecula, CA 92590-2769. Tel.: 951-308-6370. Fax: 951-695-0636.
E-mail: phineas@pennypickles.org
Web Site: www.pennypickles.org
Formerly: Imagination Workshop - Temecula Children's Museum
Founded: 2004.
Key Personnel: Museum Mgr., Robin Gilliland.
Personnel Profile: Full-Time Paid 1; Part-Time Paid 10; Part-Time Volunteers 2.
Children's Museum.
Collections: hands-on exhibits.
Facilities: Museum-related items for sale.
Hours & Admission Prices: Tues.-Thurs. & Sat. Session 1: 10-12, Session 2: 12:30-2:30, Session 3: 3-5, Fri. Session 1: 10-12, Session 2: 12:30-2:30, Session 3: 3-5, Session 4: 5:30-7:30, Sun. Session 1: 12:30-2:30, Session 2: 3-5. Admission 3 & over $4.50; discounts to groups & ACM Reciprocal members; children 2 & under no charge. ♿
Attendance: 50,000 (estimated)
Membership: $100.

TEMECULA VALLEY MUSEUM, 28314 Mercedes St., Temecula, CA 92590-1837. Tel.: 951-694-6452. Fax: 951-506-6871.
E-mail: wendell.ott@cityoftemecula.org
Web Site: www.ci.temecula.ca.us/cityhall/commserv/museum/index.htm
Founded: 1985.
Congressional District: 48
Key Personnel: Museum Svcs. Mgr., Wendell Ott; Pres., Pam Grender; Sec., Agnes Gaertner; Treas., Margaret Cushing; Museum Shop Mgr., Jo Ann Lamb.
Personnel Profile: Full-Time Paid 1; Part-Time Paid 5; Part-Time Volunteers 57.
Governing Authority: Parent Institution: City of Temecula. Tax-exempt.
History Museum.
Collections: focus on photographs, documents, tools & household goods from local ranches & frontier towns; artifacts & photographs relating to local Native American cultures. Special collections relate to the Roripaugh & Vail ranching families, & to Erle Stanley Gardner, author of the Perry Mason stories.
Research Fields: Luiseno history & culture; Vail Ranch history.
Facilities: 7,200 sq. ft. exhibit. Museum-related items for sale.
Activities: guided tours; lectures; docent program.
Publications: Temecula Valley Museum Docent Handbook; Temecula Valley Museum Newsletter; High Country Magazine.
Hours & Admission Prices: Tues.-Sat. 10-4, Sun. 1-4. Suggested Donation: $2; discount to AAM & ICOM members. ♿
Attendance: 19,008 (accurate)

Thousand Oaks

CONEJO VALLEY ART MUSEUM, 3143 Potter Ave., Thousand Oaks, CA 91358-0616. Mailing Address: P.O. Box 1616, Thousand Oaks, CA 91358-0616. Tel.: 805-373-0054 & 492-2147. Fax: 805-492-7677. TDD: 805-492-7677.
E-mail: dessornes@earthlink.net
Web Site: www.cvam.us
Founded: 1977.
Congressional District: 21
Key Personnel: C.E.O. & Pres. (V), Maria E. Dessornes.
Personnel Profile: Full-Time Volunteers 1; Part-Time Volunteers 50; Interns 2.
Governing Authority: not-for-profit organization. Tax-exempt: 501(c)(3).
Art Museum.
Collections: various medias of art.
Facilities: 2,500 sq. ft. exhibit space. Books, tapes, folk art, fiber arts & pottery cards for sale.
Activities: concerts; lectures; loan exhibitions; rental gallery; traveling exhibitions; formal education programs for adults. Museum Sponsors: ArtWalk (a fine art & designer craft fair) in June.
Publications: monthly newsletter; calendar of events.
Hours & Admission Prices: Temporarily closed for relocation. ♿
Attendance: 12,000 (estimated)
Membership: Students & Seniors $10; General & Family $25; Sponsor $50; Patron $100-$249; Silver Patron $250-$499; Gold Patron $500-$999; Benefactor $1,000-$1,499; Corporate Donor $2,500 & up.

SANTA MONICA MOUNTAINS NATIONAL RECREATION AREA, 401 W. Hillcrest Dr., Thousand Oaks, CA 91360-4223. Tel.: 805-370-2300.
E-mail: philip_holmes@nps.gov
Web Site: www.nps.gov/samo/
Founded: 1978.
Congressional District: 21, 23, 24, 26, 27
Key Personnel: Supt., Woody Smeck; Cultural Anthropologist, Phil Holmes; Deputy Supt., Lorenza Fong.
Personnel Profile: Full-Time Paid 1.
Governing Authority: federal. Parent institution: National Park Service, U.S. Dept. of the Interior. Tax-exempt.
National Park: Collections consist of natural history specimens, local archaeological & historical artifacts and park archives. Satwiwa Native American Indian Culture Center.
Collections: natural & cultural history items.
Research Fields: Santa Monica Mountains history & natural history.

Facilities: Satwiwa Native American Culture Center; visitor center. Books & museum-related items for sale.
Activities: seminars; concerts; theme events; naturalist programs; self-guided tours; education programs for children.
Publications: quarterly calendar, Outdoors.
Hours & Admission Prices: Visitor Center: Mon.-Sat. 8-5. Park Site: daily. No charge. Closed major holidays. ♿
Attendance: 500,000 (estimated)
Membership: Friends of Satwiwa: Student & Elder $10; Individual $25; Family $35; Associate $100; Life $500; Patron $1,000; Corporate $5,000.

SATWIWA NATIVE AMERICAN INDIAN CULTURE CENTER, 4126 Potrero Rd., Thousand Oaks, CA 91320-5239. Mailing Address: 401 W. Hillcrest Dr., Thousand Oaks, CA 91360-4223. Tel.: 805-499-2837.
Web Site: www.nps.gov/samo
Native American Museum.
Collections: Chumash & Gabrielino/Tongva cultures.
Activities: workshops; programs.
Hours & Admission Prices: Sat.-Sun. 9-5.

Three Rivers

SEQUOIA AND KINGS CANYON NATIONAL PARKS, 47050 Generals Hwy., Three Rivers, CA 93271-9599. Tel.: 559-565-3133. Fax: 209-565-3730.
Web Site: www.sequoia.national-park.com/info.htm
Founded: 1933.
Congressional District: 17
Key Personnel: Chief Park Interpreter, Colleen Bathe; Archaeologist, Thomas L. Burge; Museum Technician, Ward Eldredge.
Personnel Profile: Full-Time Paid 2; Part-Time Paid 1.
Governing Authority: federal. Parent Institution: National Park Service, U.S. Dept. of the Interior, Washington, DC. Tax-exempt: 501(c)(3).
Park Museum & Visitor Centers: located at Ash Mountain, Lodgepole & Grant Grove.
Collections: archives; biological & geological specimens, prehistoric & historic artifacts & an extensive historic photographic file of black & white images.
Facilities: 1,500-vol. reference library of natural history books available at park headquarters. Publications for sale.
Activities: visitor centers.
Hours & Admission Prices: Lodgepole Visitor Center: June-Sept. daily 8-5; Oct.-May Sat.-Sun. 9-5. Grant Grove Visitor Center: daily 8-5. Foothills Visitor Center: daily 8-4:30. Visitor Centers: no charge; donations accepted. Parks: fee charged. ♿

Tiburon

ANGEL ISLAND STATE PARK, Tiburon, CA 94920. Mailing Address: P.O. Box 318, Tiburon, CA 94920-0318. Tel.: 415-435-5390. Fax: 415-435-0850.
E-mail: aivc@parks.ca.gov
Web Site: www.angelisland.org
Formerly: U.S. Immigration Station
Founded: 1954.
Historic Buildings & Sites.
Collections: immigration & quarantine history; Civil War through Cold War; military site.
Activities: Museum Sponsors: Civil War Days in June; Victorian House Tours in August; Victorian Christmas in November.
Hours & Admission Prices: 8am to sunset, call to confirm. Park entrance fee included in price of ferry ticket; discounts to school groups K-12. ♿

BELVEDERE-TIBURON LANDMARKS SOCIETY, 1550 Tiburon Blvd., Tiburon, CA 94920. Mailing Address: 1550 Tiburon Blvd., Ste. M, Tiburon, CA 94920-2529. Tel.: 415-435-1853.
Web Site: landmarks-society.org
Founded: 1959.
Congressional District: 6
Key Personnel: Pres. (V), David Gotz.
Personnel Profile: Part-Time Paid 4; Part-Time Volunteers 60.
Governing Authority: society; nonprofit organization. Branch Museums: Old St. Hilary's Landmark, Esperanza St., Tiburon CA, 94920; China Cabin, Beach Rd. Belvedere, CA 94920. Tiburon Railroad-Ferry Museum, 1920 Paradise Dr. Tiburon, CA 94920; Landmarks Art & Garden Centor, site of 1870 brick kiln & bunkhouse, 841 Tiburon Blvd. Tiburon, CA 94920. Tax-exempt: 501(c)(3).
Old St. Hilary's: Preservation Project & Museum: housed in 1888 Carpenter Gothic style church with wildflower preserve. China Cabin: restored social hall of the SS China, 1866-1886.
Collections: society archives: photographs; art collection; social and architectural history; artifacts of early California domestic life; railroad-ferry system. Historic Buildings: Tiburon Railroad-ferry Museum Depot 1884; Brickkiln Bunkhouse Landmark.
Research Fields: local history; architecture; native flora.
Activities: botanic & historic tours; art exhibits; concerts; historic lectures; railroad-ferry museum exhibits.
Publications: books, A Garland for John Thomas Howell; Both Sides of the Track; Excerpts of Marin History; Glimpses II; Old St. Hilary's; Pictorial History of Tiburon; Shark Point, High Point Index; A Pictorial History of Belvedere; 1890-1990.
Hours & Admission Prices: April-Oct. Wed. & Sun. 1-4; other times by appointment. No charge; donations accepted; charge for group tours, off hours. ♿
Attendance: 3,500 (estimated)
Membership: Friends $50; Preservationists $100; Patron $250; Historian $500; Steward $1,000; Guardian $2,500.

OLD ST. HILARY'S LANDMARK & WILDFLOWER PRESERVE, 249 Esperanza, Tiburon, CA 94920. Mailing Address: 1550 Tiburon Blvd., Ste. M, Tiburon, CA 94920-2529. Tel.: 415-435-1853.
Formerly: Old St. Hilary's Church Museum & St. Hilary's Preserve
Founded: 1959.
Key Personnel: Pres., Dave Gotz.
Governing Authority: Parent Institution: Belvedere Tiburon Landmarks Society.
Historical Museum: housed in a 19th-century Carpenter Gothic-style church, built in 1886.
Collections: religious artifacts. Preserve: wildflower garden containing 217 species of plants.
Publications: newsletter, The Landmark.
Hours & Admission Prices: April-Oct. Wed. & Sun. 1-4.

Tomales

TOMALES REGIONAL HISTORY CENTER, (M), 26701 State Hwy. #1, Tomales, CA 94971. Mailing Address: P.O. Box 262, Tomales, CA 94971-0262. Tel.: 707-878-9443.
E-mail: info@tomaleshistory.com
Web Site: tomaleshistory.com
Founded: 1978.
Key Personnel: Bd. Pres., Liz Mitchell; Cur., Ginny Mackenzie Magan; Museum Shop Mgr., Nancy Conzett.
Governing Authority: nonprofit organization. Tax-exempt.
History Center.
Collections: period artifacts; photographs; costumes; painting; prints & drawings.
Activities: childrens classes; lectures; performances; living history program; research; fundraising events; yearly week-long study unit of interactive California & local history for two fourth grade classes; periodic lecture series.
Publications: quarterly history journal, TRHC Bulletin; book, Tomales Township: A History.
Hours & Admission Prices: Fri.-Sun. 1-4; other times by appointment. No charge; donations accepted. Closed major holidays. ♿
Membership: Individual $15; Family $20; Life $250.

Torrance

TORRANCE ART MUSEUM, (M), 3320 Civic Center Dr. N., Torrance, CA 90503-5016. Tel.: 310-618-6340. Fax: 310-618-2399.
E-mail: torranceartmuseum@tornet.com
Web Site: www.torranceartmuseum.com
Founded: 1985.
Congressional District: 36
Key Personnel: Dir. & Head Cur., Max Presneill; Asst. Cur., Ryan Callis; Asst. Cur., Colton Stenke; Volunteer Coord., Regina Taylor.
Personnel Profile: Full-Time Paid 3; Part-Time Paid 3; Part-Time Volunteers 40.
Governing Authority: municipal.
Art Museum.
Collections: contemporary art.
Major Exhibits: The Reflected Glaze, 1/14/10-2/20/10; Fax (T), 1/14/10-2/20/10; Sunrise-Ryan Taber, 3/4/10-4/17/10; Set Theory-Roland Reiss, 4/29/10-6/12/10; Baker's Dozen, 6/24/10-7/10/10; Susan Collis, 4/29/10-6/12/10; The Rise of Rad, 7/22/10-9/4/10; Zoom 2, 9/16/10-11/6/10; South Bay Focus, 11/18/10-12/4/10.
Research Fields: contemporary art.
Facilities: 500-vol. library; educational facilities; 4,000 sq. ft. exhibit space.
Activities: concerts; dance recitals; docent program; lectures; temporary & participatory exhibits.

Publications: exhibition catalogs.
Hours & Admission Prices: Tues.-Sat. 11-5. No charge; donations accepted. Closed New Year's Day; Memorial Day; Armed Forces Day; Independence Day; Labor Day; Thanksgiving & day after; Christmas week. ♿
Attendance: 6,821 (accurate)

WESTERN MUSEUM OF FLIGHT, 3315 Airport Dr., Red Baron #3, Torrance, CA 90505-6152. Tel.: 310-326-9544. Fax: 310-326-9556.
E-mail: wmofschaf@um.att.com
Web Site: www.wmof.com
Key Personnel: Pres., Cindy Macha Skjonsby.
Governing Authority: nonprofit organization. Parent Institution: Southern California Historical Aviation Foundation.
Aviation History Museum.
Collections: Southern California's aviation history; airplanes; target drones; piston & jet aircraft engines; World War II instruments; aircrew accessories; model aircrafts.
Facilities: Museum-related items for sale.
Activities: educational programs for children.
Hours & Admission Prices: Wed. & Fri.-Sun. 10-3. Adults $3; members & children under 12 no charge.

Tracy

TRACY HISTORICAL MUSEUM, 1141 Adam St., Tracy, CA 95376-3506. Tel.: 209-832-7278.
E-mail: tracymuseum@sbcglobal.net
Web Site: www.tracymuseum.org
Governing Authority: city. Operated by the West Side Pioneer Association.
History Museum: housed in the former Tracy Post Office building; built in 1937.
Collections: local history & culture; photographs; period artifacts.
Hours & Admission Prices: June-Sept. Sun., Wed. & Fri. 1-4. No charge; donations accepted.

Travis AFB

TRAVIS AIR MUSEUM, 461 Burgan Blvd., Bldg. 80, Travis AFB, CA 94535. Tel.: 707-424-5605.
E-mail: curator@travisairmuseum.org
Web Site: www.travisairmuseum.org
Military Museum.
Collections: aircraft artifacts & memorabilia.
Hours & Admission Prices: Tues.-Sat. 9-4. No Charge. Closed federal holidays.

Trinidad

STONE LAGOON RED SCHOOLHOUSE MUSEUM AT REDWOOD TRAILS, 265 Idlewood Lane, Trinidad, CA 95570-9641. Mailing Address: 265 Redwood Trails Cir., P.O. Box 1240, Trinidad, CA 95570. Tel.: 707-488-2061.
E-mail: info@rv4fun.com
Historic Building: housed in former one-room schoolhouse, c.1894.
Collections: period furnishings; structure.
Hours & Admission Prices: Memorial Day to Labor Day. No charge.

Truckee

DONNER MEMORIAL STATE PARK AND EMIGRANT TRAIL MUSEUM, 12593 Donner Pass Rd., Truckee, CA 96161-3858. Tel.: 530-582-7892. Fax: 530-550-2347.
Web Site: www.parks.ca.gov
Founded: 1962.
Congressional District: 14
Key Personnel: Unit Supervising Ranger, Don Schmidt; Ranger, Mike Rominger; Cur., Judith K. Polanich.
Personnel Profile: Full-Time Paid 6; Part-Time Paid 3; Part-Time Volunteers 5; Interns 1.
Governing Authority: state; nonprofit. Parent Institution: Dept. of Parks & Recreation. Subsidiary Institution: Sierra State Parks Foundation. Tax-exempt.
Historic Site & Museum.
Collections: California Emigrant Trail-Truckee routes; Donner Emigrant Party; Central Pacific Railroad; weapons; photographs.
Research Fields: Westward Emigration; Native American culture; Chinese American culture; winter survival.
Facilities: operational; outdoor text & photo panel interpretive exhibit; self-guided nature trails; camping grounds; biking; swimming; boating (no launch); cross country skiing; fishing.
Activities: interpretive hikes & campfire programs.
Publications: trail guides; park brochure; coloring book.
Hours & Admission Prices: Daily 9-4. Museum: no charge; donations accepted. Closed New Year's Day; Thanksgiving; Christmas. No winter camping. ♿
Attendance: 75,000 (accurate)

KIDZONE MUSEUM, 11711 Donner Pass Rd., Truckee, CA 96161-4954. Tel.: 530-587-KIDS. Fax: 530-587-0200.
E-mail: info@kidzonemuseum.org
Key Personnel: Dir., Carol Meagher; Exhibits Mgr., Liz Bordner; Facilities Mgr., Lea Anne Weiss
Children's Museum.
Collections: hands-on exhibits.
Hours & Admission Prices: June-July Tues.-Sat. 9-1; Winter: Tues.-Sat. 10-5, Sun. 10-3. Children: Non-Resident $7, Placer & Nevada County resident $5, adults $3, seniors $2; children under one no charge.

TRUCKEE'S OLD JAIL MUSEUM, Near the Corner of Jibbom and Spring Sts., Truckee, CA 96160. Mailing Address: P.O. Box 893, Truckee, CA 96160-0893. Tel.: 530-582-0893.
E-mail: info@truckeehistory.org
Web Site: www.truckeehistory.org
Formerly: Truckee-Donner Historical Society Jail Museum
Key Personnel: Cur., Chelsea Walterscheid; Coord. Special Group Tours, Don Colclough.
Governing Authority: Operated by the Truckee-Donner Historical Society.
Historic Building: served as jailhouse from 1875 to 1968.
Collections: local historical artifacts; photographs; lumbering; box manufacturing; ice harvesting; film industry; Truckee's early winter sports.
Facilities: garden.
Hours & Admission Prices: Memorial Day-Sept. Sat.-Sun. 11-4; group tours by appointment. Requested Donation: $2.

Tujunga

BOLTON HALL HISTORICAL MUSEUM, 10110 Commerce Ave., Tujunga, CA 91042-2313. Mailing Address: P.O. Box 203, Tujunga, CA 91043-0203. Tel.: 818-352-3420.
Founded: 1957.
Key Personnel: Pres. (V) & Museum Shop Mgr., Lloyd Hitt.
Personnel Profile: Part-Time Volunteers 25; Interns 2.
Governing Authority: Tax-exempt.
Community Historic Museum.
Collections: photographs; newspapers; cemetery records; directories; Rancho Tujunga artifacts.
Facilities: library; photoarchives.
Activities: tours. Museum Sponsors: programs September to June.
Publications: newsletter.
Hours & Admission Prices: Sun. & Tues. 1-4. No charge; donations accepted. ♿
Attendance: 1,500 (estimated)
Membership: Individual $15; Family $25; Patron & Business $50; Lifetime $350.

Tulare

HERITAGE COMPLEX ANTIQUE FARM EQUIPMENT MUSEUM AND AGVENTURES LEARNING CENTER, 4500 S. Laspina St., Tulare, CA 93274-9165. Tel.: 559-688-1030. Fax: 559-686-5527.
E-mail: katy@farmshow.org
Web Site: www.heritagecomplex.org
Founded: 2000.
Congressional District: 31
Key Personnel: Chm. (V), Bernie Cargyl; Pres. (V), David Eddy.
Personnel Profile: Full-Time Paid 24; Part-Time Volunteers 1,300.
Governing Authority: Parent Institution: International Agri-Center. Tax-exempt.
Agriculture Museum.
Collections: period tractors; farming equipment; steam engine equipment; hands-on exhibits.
Hours & Admission Prices: Daily. No charge; donations accepted. ♿
Attendance: 10,000

TULARE HISTORICAL MUSEUM, 444 W. Tulare Ave., Tulare, CA 93274-3831. Mailing Address: P.O. Box 248, Tulare, CA 93275-0248. Tel.: 559-686-2074. Fax: 559-686-9295.
Web Site: www.tularehistoricalmuseum.org
Founded: 1985.
Congressional District: 21

Key Personnel: Exec. Dir., Terry Brazil; Financial Dir., Archivist & Historian, Bob Bandy; Devel., Cathy Mederos; Coord. Docent, Derryl Dumermuth; Cur., Kary Mancebo-Ingram; Public Rels., Linda Ruminer; Museum Shop Mgr., Helen McCourt.
Personnel Profile: Part-Time Paid 3; Part-Time Volunteers 75.
Governing Authority: private; nonprofit organization. Parent Institution: Tulare City Historical Society. Tax-exempt: 501(c)(3).
History Museum.
Collections: Tulare history & heroes memorabilia; period furniture; art glass; photographs; books; military uniforms & artifacts.
Facilities: library; 117-seat auditorium; 6,356 sq. ft. exhibit space. Museum-related items for sale.
Activities: concerts; docent program; lectures; loan & traveling exhibitions; training programs for professional museum workers. Annual Events: holiday luncheon; Lovely Way to Spend an Evening; Taste Treats in Tulare; Reverse Drawing.
Publications: quarterly newsletter, Then & Now.
Hours & Admission Prices: June-Aug. Thurs.-Sat. 10-4; Sept.-May Thurs.-Sat. 10-4, 3rd Sun. of month 12:30-4. Adults $5, senior citizens $3, students $2; members, children under 5 & 3rd Sun. of month no charge. Closed New Year's Day; Easter; Mother's Day; Father's Day; Independence Day; Thanksgiving & day after; Christmas. ♿
Attendance: 7,000 (estimated)
Membership: Student $10; Individual $25; Contributing $35; Family $40; Supporting $50; Patron $100; Business & Corporate $250.

Tulelake

LAVA BEDS NATIONAL MONUMENT, 1 Indian Wells Headquarters, Tulelake, CA 96134. Tel.: 530-667-1800. Fax: 530-667-2737.
Web Site: www.nps.gov/labe/
Founded: 1925.
Congressional District: 1
Key Personnel: Supt., Dave Kruse.
Governing Authority: federal.
History/Natural History Museum.
Collections: geology of shield volcanoes & lava tubes; desert ecology; history; archaeology; Modoc Indian artifacts.
Publications: publications pertaining to natural history; human history; Modoc Indian War 1872-73.
Hours & Admission Prices: Memorial Day weekend-Labor Day weekend daily 8-6; Sept.-May daily 8:30-5. Monument: $10 per car; annual pass $20; federal lands pass holders no charge. ♿
Attendance: 100,000 (estimated)

Tustin

MARCONI AUTOMOTIVE MUSEUM, 1302 Industrial Dr., Tustin, CA 92780-6416. Tel.: 714-258-3001. Fax: 714-258-9117.
E-mail: mdanielson@marconimuseum.org
Web Site: www.marconimuseum.org
Founded: 1994.
Key Personnel: C.E.O., Priscilla "Bo" Marconi; Exec. Dir., Marianne Danielson; Dir. Operations, Miguel De la Cerda.
Governing Authority: nonprofit.
Automobile Museum.
Collections: historical, exotic, & classic cars.
Activities: facility rental.
Hours & Admission Prices: Mon.-Fri. 9-4:30 by appointments. Adults $5; children no charge. Closed major holidays. ♿

Twentynine Palms

JOSHUA TREE NATIONAL PARK, OASIS VISITOR CENTER, 74485 National Park Dr., Twentynine Palms, CA 92277-3597. Tel.: 760-367-5522 & 5500, ext. 0. Fax: 619-367-6392.
Web Site: www.nps.gov/jotr
Formerly: Twentynine Palms Oasis Visitor Center, Joshua Tree National Park
Founded: 1936.
Congressional District: 40 & 44
Key Personnel: Supvr., Cynthia Von Halle.
Governing Authority: federal. Parent Institution: National Park Service. Tax-exempt: 501(c)(3).
Park Museum.
Collections: archaeology; geology; zoology; botany; desert flora & fauna; palm trees; rabbits; birds; reptiles.
Research Fields: natural history, cultural history.
Facilities: 750-vol. library of books on history & natural history of the area; 9 camp grounds. Educational literature of the area for sale.
Activities: orientation talks; programs on the park and its history; guided walks on nearby nature trail & historic site.
Publications: Guide to Joshua Tree National Park.
Hours & Admission Prices: Museum: daily 8-5. No charge. Park: One Week Pass: $15 per vehicle ♿
Attendance: 1,256,928 (accurate)
Membership: Annual Passes: Joshua Tree NP $25; National Parks Golden Eagle Pass $50.

Ukiah

GRACE HUDSON MUSEUM & SUN HOUSE, (M), 431 S. Main St., Ukiah, CA 95482-4923. Tel.: 707-467-2836. Fax: 707-467-2835.
E-mail: gracehudson@pacific.net
Web Site: www.gracehudsonmuseum.org
Founded: 1975.
Congressional District: 2
Key Personnel: Chm. (V), Mary Louise Chase; Dir., Sherrie Smith-Ferri; Cur., Marvin Schenck; Museum Shop Mgr., Sandy Dockins; Registrar, Karen Holmes.
Personnel Profile: Full-Time Paid 2; Part-Time Paid 4; Part-Time Volunteers 60.
Governing Authority: municipal. Parent Institution: City of Ukiah. Subsidiary Institution: Sun House Guild, Grace Hudson Museum Endowment Fund, Inc. Tax-exempt.
Historic House: 1911 home of Dr. John W. Hudson & Artist Grace Carpenter Hudson; specialized, family collection; interdisciplinary (art, history & anthropology).
Collections: Artwork of Grace Carpenter Hudson; Hudson-Carpenter manuscript & photographic collections; ethnographic materials of Pomo culture; 19th & 20th-century decorative art & furnishings.
Research Fields: Mendocino County history; California regional art; Pomo culture; Grace Hudson's art & life; Hudson-Carpenter family; John Hudson's research & ethnographic collection.
Facilities: Sun House, historical craftsman home; 11,000 sq. ft. museum; public meeting room. Museum-related items for sale.
Activities: guided tours; docent program or council; permanent & temporary exhibitions; lectures; symposia related to purposes.
Hours & Admission Prices: Wed.-Sat. 10-4:30, Sun. 12-4:30. Admission fee: $10 per family, $4 per person, $3 students & seniors; discount to AAM & ICOM members. Closed holidays. ♿
Attendance: 11,000
Membership: Annual $15-$150; Life $1,500; Endowment Society $5,000.

HELD-POAGE MEMORIAL HOME AND RESEARCH LIBRARY, 603 W. Perkins St., Ukiah, CA 95482-4726. Tel.: 707-462-6969.
E-mail: mchs@pacific.net
Founded: 1970.
Congressional District: 1
Personnel Profile: Full-Time Volunteers 1; Part-Time Volunteers 10.
Governing Authority: society. Parent Institution: Mendocino County Historical Society Inc. Tax-exempt: 501(c)(3).
Historical Society Museum: housed in 1903 Queen Ann Victorian home of William D. L. Held.
Collections: Native American artifacts & research material; local historical artifacts; kitchen furniture; library displays; children's toys; manuscript collections.
Research Fields: county, state & U.S. history.
Facilities: 5,000-vol. library of books; 13,000 historical photographic negatives, microfilms, documents, maps, scrapbooks, Great Registers, genealogies relating to history of northern California; county records; newspapers & magazines available for use on premises; reading room. Publications for sale.
Activities: guided tours.
Publications: quarterly newsletter, from Mendocino County Historical Society, Inc.
Hours & Admission Prices: Mon.-Fri. 1-4; other times by appointment. No charge; donations accepted. ♿
Attendance: 600 (estimated)
Membership: Regular $20; Couple $25; Contributing $50; Life $300.

Upland

COOPER REGIONAL HISTORY MUSEUM, 217 A St., Upland, CA 91786-6024. Mailing Address: P.O. Box 772, Upland, CA 91785-0772. Tel.: 909-982-8010.
E-mail: lola@coopermuseum.org
Web Site: www.coopermuseum.org
Founded: 1965.
Congressional District: 35
Key Personnel: Exec. Dir., Marilyn Anderson; Pres., David W. Stevens.
Personnel Profile: Full-Time Volunteers 13; Part-Time Volunteers 5.

Governing Authority: nonprofit organization. Parent Institution: Chaffey Communities Cultural Center. Tax-exempt: 501(c)(3).
History Museum.
Collections: domestic life; citrus industry; local history; hunting; Native American; seasonal exhibits.
Research Fields: history & culture of Upland, Ontario, Montclair, Mt. Baldy, and Rancho Cucamonga, California from 1800-present.
Facilities: 100-seat meeting room.
Activities: lectures; films; oral history program with local residents.
Publications: bulletin published three times annually; book, Oranges for Health-California for Wealth.
Hours & Admission Prices: Fri. 1-4, Sat.-Sun. 11-5. No charge; donations accepted. Closed national holidays. ♿
Attendance: 5,000 (accurate)
Membership: Individual $15; Family $25.

Vacaville

VACAVILLE MUSEUM, 213 Buck Ave., Vacaville, CA 95688-3835. Tel.: 707-447-4513. Fax: 707-447-2661.
E-mail: vacamuseum@sbcglobal.net
Web Site: vacavillemuseum.org
Founded: 1981.
Congressional District: 1
Key Personnel: Dir., Shawn Lum; Cur. Collections, Annie Farley; Cur. Exhibits, Philip Nollar; Registrar, Heidi Casebolt; Office Mgr., Sheri Ware.
Personnel Profile: Full-Time Paid 3; Part-Time Paid 6; Part-Time Volunteers 100.
Governing Authority: nonprofit organization. Tax-exempt: 501(c)(3).
History Museum.
Collections: pre-history through present local history items.
Research Fields: agricultural history; Japanese-American history; Spanish-American history; women's history; water history in Solano County.
Facilities: 1,600 sq. ft. gallery; conference room; native plant garden area. Museum-related items for sale.
Activities: guided tours; lectures; workshops; TV & radio programs; organized educational programs; docent program; traveling, permanent, temporary & changing exhibitions.
Publications: quarterly newsletter, Vacaville Museum News & Notes; exhibit catalogue, Berryessa Valley: The Last Year; book, Solano's Gold - The People and Their Orchards; memories & reminiscences of Vacaville's Japanese community, Omo i de; cookbook.
Hours & Admission Prices: Wed.-Sun. 1-4:30. Adults $3, children & students $2; discounts to AAM & ICOM members; CAM & WMA members no charge. Closed holidays. ♿
Attendance: 10,000 (estimated)
Membership: Participating $50; Supporting & Family $75; Sponsor $145; Principal $250; Patron $500; Benefactor $1,200; Life $5,000.

Vallejo

SIX FLAGS DISCOVERY KINGDOM, 2001 Marine World Pkwy., Vallejo, CA 94589-4001. Tel.: 707-644-4000. Fax: 707-644-0241. TDD: 707-643-6769.
Web Site: www.sixflags.com
Formerly: Six Flags Marine World
Founded: 1968.
Key Personnel: Gen. Mgr., Rick Mcurley; Dir. Mktg., Dwayne McNeil; Mgr. Merchandise & Museum Shop Mgr., Mike Southern; Supvr. Education, Terran Rosenberg; Mgr. Oceanarium, Kathy France; Dir. Opers., Tim Ready; Show Productions, David Miller; Mgr. Public Rels., Jeff Jouett; Dir. Animal Operations, David Blasko.
Personnel Profile: Full-Time Paid 175; Part-Time Paid 1,500.
Governing Authority: City of Vallejo.
Wildlife Theme Park.
Collections: live marine & land mammals, birds, reptiles, fish & invertebrates on exhibit & performing in educational shows.
Research Fields: dolphin communication; sea lions; otter conservation; killer whale vocalizations and behavior; communication & cognition; artificial insemination; reproductive cycles in killer whales & elephants.
Facilities: 1,200-vol. library of materials for staff use only; restaurants; classrooms; discovery center; show stadiums; animal displays. Gift items for sale.
Activities: guided tours; lectures; TV & radio programs; formally organized education programs; rides; mobile vans.
Publications: A Closer Look; Teacher Guides on Marine Mammals, Tropical Rain Forests, Vanishing Animals & Habitats available on request; teacher's guide on Sharks.
Hours & Admission Prices: Memorial Day to Labor Day Mon.-Thurs. 10-8, Fri.-Sun. 10-9. Adults $44.99, senior citizens $26.99, children 4-12 $29.99; discounts to groups; children 2 & under no charge. ♿
Attendance: 1,950,000 (accurate)

VALLEJO NAVAL & HISTORICAL MUSEUM, (M), 734 Marin St., Vallejo, CA 94590-5992. Tel.: 707-643-0077. Fax: 707-643-2443.
E-mail: valmuse@pacbell.net
Web Site: www.vallejomuseum.org
Founded: 1974.
Congressional District: 7
Key Personnel: Dir., James E. Kern; Pres. (V), Mike Browne; Museum Shop Mgr., Mimi Farone.
Personnel Profile: Full-Time Paid 1; Part-Time Paid 2; Part-Time Volunteers 50.
Governing Authority: nonprofit organization. Tax-exempt: 501(c)(3).
Historical Museum: located in Vallejo's Old City Hall.
Collections: history of Vallejo & the nearby Mare Island Naval Shipyard from 1850-present.
Research Fields: local history.
Facilities: 6,000-vol. library pertaining to local & maritime history; 125-seat auditorium; classroom. Books & museum-related items for sale.
Activities: guided tours; lectures; concerts; organized education programs for children; docent program; temporary exhibitions.
Publications: bimonthly newsletter, Valmuse.
Hours & Admission Prices: Wed.-Sat. 12-4. Adults $5, seniors & students 12-17 $3; discounts to AAM & ICOM members; members & children under 12 no charge. Closed holidays. ♿
Attendance: 9,000 (estimated)
Membership: Individual $30; Family $45; Sustaining $100; Supporting $150; Patron $275; Sponsor $650; Benefactor $1,000; Director's Circle $5,000.

Valley Glen

LOS ANGELES VALLEY COLLEGE ART GALLERY, 5800 Fulton Ave., Valley Glen, CA 91401-4062. Tel.: 818-778-5536.
Web Site: www.lavc.edu/arts/artgallery.html
Founded: 1960.
Art Gallery.
Collections: works by student & faculty artists; contemporary & ethnic art.
Hours & Admission Prices: Call for hours.

Van Nuys

THE JAPANESE GARDEN, 6100 Woodley Ave., Van Nuys, CA 91406-6450. Tel.: 818-756-8166. Fax: 818-756-9648.
E-mail: betty.ethridge@lacity.org
Web Site: www.thejapanesegarden.com
Founded: 1984.
Congressional District: 27
Key Personnel: Dir., Gene Green; Chm. (V), Barbara Shellow; Landscape Architect, Patrick Rigney; Technician, Julius Luna; Office Mgr., Betty Ethridge; Tour Desk Staff, Lori Stewart; Tour Desk Staff, Melanie Schuyler; Museum Shop Mgr., Jan E. Abrams.
Personnel Profile: Full-Time Paid 4; Part-Time Paid 2; Part-Time Volunteers 70.
Governing Authority: Parent Institution: city of Los Angeles. Subsidiary Institution: Bureau of Sanitation. Tax-exempt.
Cultural Garden.
Collections: plants; flowers; trees; local wildlife; culturally significant structures & decorative elements.
Research Fields: Japanese culture; water reclamation process.
Facilities: selected areas for weddings, luncheons, meetings, filming & photography available for rent. Museum-related items for sale.
Activities: Museum Sponsors: Taiko Drumming; Origami; Ikebana; Kimono exhibition & demonstration.
Hours & Admission Prices: Mon.-Thurs. 12-4, Sun. 10-4. Tours: Mon.-Thurs. 9:30, 10 & 10:30. Adults $3, children under 10 and seniors 62 & over $2; members no charge. Closed holidays.
Attendance: 12,629 (accurate)
Membership: Senior $35; Individual $40; Family $60; Patron $100.

Ventura

ALBINGER ARCHEOLOGICAL MUSEUM, 113 E. Main St., Ventura, CA 93001-2606. Tel.: 805-648-5823.
E-mail: jscott@ci.ventura.ca.us
Web Site: www.albingermuseum.org
Key Personnel: Mgr., Jeanne Scott.
Personnel Profile: Part-Time Paid 1.
Archaeology Museum.
Collections: Chumash, Spanish, Chinese, American & Mexican cultures.
Hours & Admission Prices: Winter: Wed.-Fri. 10-2, Sat.-Sun. 10-4; Summer: Wed.-Sun. 10-4. No charge. ♿

Attendance: 12,000

CHANNEL ISLANDS NATIONAL PARK, ROBERT J. LAGOMARSINO VISITOR CENTER, 1901 Spinnaker Dr., Ventura, CA 93001-4354. Tel.: 805-658-5730. Fax: 805-658-5799.
Web Site: www.nps.gov/chis
Founded: 1980.
Congressional District: 23
Key Personnel: Supt., Russell E. Galipeau, Jr.; Chief Interpretation, Yvonne Menard; Western National Parks Association, Carolyn Westberg; Supervisory Park Ranger, John Curwen.
Governing Authority: federal. U.S. Dept. of the Interior, National Park Service, Washington, DC. Subsidiary Institution: S.W. Parks & Monuments. Tax-exempt.
National Park & Museum; Natural History Museum.
Collections: cultural, historical & archaeological objects; photographs; documents; natural preserved animals; plant collection; native plant garden; radio carbon dating 11,500 years.
Research Fields: natural & cultural resources of the California Channel Islands.
Facilities: 2,000-vol. library pertaining to diverse Channel Islands & National Park Service subjects; reading room; archival material; film & video tape library; visitor center; tide pool; native plant garden. Publications & museum-related items for sale.
Activities: guided tours; organized educational programs for children; permanent & temporary exhibits; slide program; off-site program; evening programs in the summer.
Publications: trail guides, Anacapa: An Island, a State of Mind; Canyon View Nature Trail, Santa Barbara Island; monthly schedule of events; all island site bulletins; Park newspaper.
Hours & Admission Prices: Daily 8:30-5. Park: no charge; donations accepted. Closed Thanksgiving; Christmas. ♿
Attendance: 321,492 (accurate)

MUSEUM OF VENTURA COUNTY, (M), 89 S. California St., Ventura, CA 93001-2828. Tel.: 805-641-1876, ext. 308. Fax: 805-653-5900.
E-mail: director@venturamuseum.org
Web Site: www.venturamuseum.org
Formerly: Ventura County Museum of History & Art
Founded: 1913.
Congressional District: 19
Key Personnel: Pres. Bd. Dir. (V), John Orr; Pres. Docent Council (V), Pat Masterson; C.E.O., Tim Schiffer; Librarian, Charles Johnson; Dir. Education, Wendy VanHorn; Operations Mgr., Jeanne Scott; Cur. Collections, Anna Rios Bermudez; Dir. Devel., Robin C. Woodworth; Dir. Mktg., Susan Gerrard; Museum Shop Mgr., Linden Royce.
Personnel Profile: Full-Time Paid 11; Part-Time Paid 10; Part-Time Volunteers 165; Interns 1.
Governing Authority: nonprofit organization. Subsidiary Institution: Ventura County Historical Society. Tax-exempt: 501(c)(3).
History & Art Museum.
Collections: art & artifacts from the region before European contact to the present; George Stuart historical figures; 5,000 maps, newspapers, books & periodicals relating to regional history; 25,000 photographs; 40,000 negatives; early & contemporary California art; farm machinery; implements & tools; oil industry artifacts.
Major Exhibits: The Art of Master Painter Omar DiLeon, 12/10/09-2/10; Becoming Art At the Seams, 3/13/10-5/30/10; George Stuart: American History, 6/4/10-9/6/10.
Research Fields: Ventura County, California.
Facilities: Museum-related items for sale.
Activities: special lectures & programs; monthly family arts & crafts; gallery openings; speakers bureau; school outreach; docent networking program; member travel program.
Publications: quarterly journal, Journal of Ventura County; newsletter; exhibit catalogs; books on county history; collection catalog.
Hours & Admission Prices: Tues.-Sun. 11-6. Museum: no charge; donations accepted. Fee charged for some events. Closed New Year's Day; Thanksgiving; Christmas. ♿
Attendance: 65,000 (accurate)
Membership: Individual $45; Dual $60; Family $70; Associate $100; Business & Professional $150; Supporter $250; Donor & Business Member Plus $500; Friend $1,000; Patron $2,500; Benefactor $5,000.

ORTEGA ADOBE, 215 W. Main St., Ventura, CA 93001. Mailing Address: P.O. Box 99, Ventura, CA 93002. Tel.: 805-644-4346.
Web Site: www.ventura.com/points_of_interest/ortegaadobe
History Museum: built in 1857 by Miguel Emigdio Ortega.
Collections: period artifacts; structure.
Hours & Admission Prices: Daily 9-4 by appointment. No charge.

SAN BUENAVENTURA MISSION MUSEUM, 225 E. Main St., Ventura, CA 93001-2622. Mailing Address: 211 E. Main St., Ventura, CA 93001-2691. Tel.: 805-643-4318. Fax: 805-643-7831.
E-mail: mission@sanbuenaventuramission.org
Web Site: www.sanbuenaventuramission.org
Founded: 1782.
Congressional District: 38
Key Personnel: Pastor, Rev. Michael Carcerano; Gift Shop Mgr., Kyra Samaniego.
Personnel Profile: Full-Time Paid 1; Part-Time Paid 3.
Governing Authority: church. Roman Catholic Archbishop of Los Angeles. Tax-exempt.
Historical Museum: housed in 1782 San Buenaventura Mission, founded by Fray Junipero Serra.
Collections: paintings; statues; Indian artifacts; military; wooden bells; Chumash baskets; Juan Camarillo II artifacts; 23 sets of vestments from the mission; books comprising the Bibliotheca Sancti Bonaventurae; historical mementos; religious artifacts. Historic Structures: 1829 Adobe Settling Tank; 1809 San Buenaventura Church.
Facilities: Literature on the history of the mission for sale.
Activities: guided tours; formally organized education programs for children in conjunction with the Ventura County Historical Museum; permanent exhibitions; Latin Mass on Sundays.
Hours & Admission Prices: Mon.-Sat. 10-5, Sun. 10-4. Adults $2. Mass schedule: daily 7:30 am, Sat. 5:30 pm, 7:30 pm (Spanish), Sun. 7:30, 9, 10:30 (Spanish), 12 & 1:30 (Latin). No charge; donations accepted. Closed New Year's; Easter; Thanksgiving; Christmas. ♿
Attendance: 66,000 (estimated)

Victorville

CALIFORNIA ROUTE 66 MUSEUM, 16825 (Ste. 1 & 2) Route 66 D St., Victorville, CA 92395. Mailing Address: P.O. Box 2151, Victorville, CA 92393-2151. Tel.: 760-951-0436. Fax: 760-951-0509.
E-mail: cart66musm@mscomm.com
Web Site: califrt66museum.org
Formerly: Old Town Victorville Heritage Preservation, Inc. dba California Route 66 Museum
Founded: 1995.
Congressional District: 40
Key Personnel: Chm. (V) & Pres. (V), Eldon Kingston; Public Rels., Registrar & Museum Shop Mgr., Betty A. Halbe.
Personnel Profile: Full-Time Volunteers 2; Part-Time Volunteers 4.
Governing Authority: nonprofit corporation. Tax-exempt: 501(c)(3).
History Museum.
Collections: Hula Ville folk art & panorama from early 20th century to present; Victorville community from 1800s to present.
Research Fields: Route 66 & the eight states that the highway goes through.
Facilities: library available for research on the premises; educational facilities. Museum-related items for sale.
Activities: films, formal education programs; guided tours; lectures; loan & temporary exhibitions.
Hours & Admission Prices: Thurs.-Mon. 10-4, Sun. 11-3; other times by appointment. No charge; donations accepted. Closed Memorial Day; Independence Day; Labor Day; Thanksgiving; Christmas. ♿
Attendance: 4,876 (accurate)

Visalia

IMAGINEU CHILDREN'S MUSEUM, 700 E. Main St., Visalia, CA 93292-6447. Mailing Address: P.O. Box 688, Visalia, CA 93279-0688. Tel.: 559-733-5975 & 0735. Fax: 559-733-0871.
E-mail: imagineumuseum@sbcglobal.net
Web Site: www.imagineumuseum.org
Key Personnel: Exec. Dir., Angela Huerta-Reyna.
Governing Authority: nonprofit organization. Tax-exempt: 501(c)(3).
Children's Museum.
Collections: hands-on exhibits.
Activities: birthday parties; classes.
Hours & Admission Prices: Tues.-Sat. 10-5. Admission $3; members no charge.

TULARE COUNTY MUSEUM AT MOONEY GROVE PARK, 27000 S. Mooney Blvd., Visalia, CA 93277-9341. Tel.: 559-733-6616 & 6291 (Parks Division). Fax: 559-730-2653.
Founded: 1948.
Congressional District: 17
Key Personnel: Dir & Cur., Kathy McGowan.
Personnel Profile: Full-Time Paid 1; Part-Time Paid 1; Part-Time Volunteers 25.

Governing Authority: county. Parent Institution: Resource Management Agency-County of Tulare. Tax-exempt.
History Museum.
Collections: sculpture of James Earle Frasher, End of the Trail; Indian relics; agricultural implements; wagons; buggies; clothing. Historical Buildings: 1854 log cabin; 1872 jail; c.1890 home, library, blacksmith; 1863 home; 1888 & 1890 schools.
Activities: guided tours by appointment.
Publications: quarterly bulletin, Los Tulares.
Hours & Admission Prices: Summer: Mon. & Wed.-Fri. 10-4, Sat.-Sun. 10-5; Spring & Fall: Thurs.-Mon. 10-4; Winter: Thurs.-Mon. 10-4, Sat.-Sun. 1-4. Car admission fee for Mooney Grove Park $6, admission to museum included in park entrance fee. Closed New Year's Eve & Day; Thanksgiving; Christmas Eve & Day. ♿
Attendance: 125,000 (accurate)

Vista

ANTIQUE GAS & STEAM ENGINE MUSEUM, INC., 2040 N. Santa Fe Ave., Vista, CA 92083-1534. Tel.: 760-941-1791. Fax: 760-941-0690.
E-mail: rod_agsem@yahoo.com
Web Site: www.agsem.com
Founded: 1976.
Congressional District: 43
Key Personnel: C.E.O., Jeanette Stevens; Dir., Rod Groenewold; Museum Shop Mgr., Glenda Garrison.
Personnel Profile: Full-Time Paid 2; Full-Time Volunteers 3; Part-Time Volunteers 500; Interns 2.
Governing Authority: nonprofit organization. Tax-exempt: 501(c)(3).
Agriculture & Industrial Museum Complex: located on 40 acres of farm land.
Collections: archival materials; steam & gas powered engines; horse drawn equipment used in farming, industrial & construction industries.
Facilities: wheat crop grown for demonstration of antique farm equipment; exhibitions of large & small stationary steam & gas powered engines; blacksmith & wheelwright shops; sawmill; farmhouse with parlor; 1/3 scale train operational during special shows.
Activities: guided tours; organized education programs for children; participatory exhibits. Museum Sponsors: Threshing Bees & Antique Engine Shows in June & October.
Publications: newsletter, Ignitor.
Hours & Admission Prices: Daily 10-4. Adults $3. Closed Christmas. ♿
Attendance: 55,000 (estimated)
Membership: Student & Associate $15; Member $30; Family $50; Lifetime $600.

VISTA HISTORICAL MUSEUM, 2317 Old Foothill Dr., Vista, CA 92084. Mailing Address: P.O. Box 1032, Vista, CA 92085-1032. Tel.: 760-630-0444. Fax: 760-295-9993.
E-mail: vhm67@1882.sdcoxmail.com
Web Site: www.vhsm.org
Founded: 1994.
Congressional District: 5
Key Personnel: Pres. (V), Diane Echert; Financial Dir., Richard Sepulveda; Devel., Sandi Graham; Museum Shop Mgr., Rosemary Conway.
Personnel Profile: Part-Time Paid 1; Part-Time Volunteers 20.
Governing Authority: private; nonprofit organization. Parent Institution: Vista Historical Society, Vista, CA. Tax-exempt: 501(c)(3).
Historical Museum.
Collections: artifacts from indigenous people of North County; relating to the discovery, diversity & destiny of Vista, San Diego & California.
Facilities: 2,400 sq. ft. exhibit space; theater.
Activities: docent program; films; guided tours; lectures; temporary exhibitions; tours for school groups & other societies; bimonthly programs.
Publications: monthly newsletter, Vista Historical Society.
Hours & Admission Prices: Temporarily closed for relocation. ♿
Attendance: 3,500 (estimated)
Membership: Individual $25; Family $45; Business $100.

Walnut Creek

BEDFORD GALLERY AT THE DEAN LESHER REGIONAL CENTER FOR THE ARTS, 1601 Civic Dr., Walnut Creek, CA 94596-4299. Tel.: 925-295-1417. Fax: 925-295-1486.
E-mail: lederer@bedfordgallery.org
Web Site: www.bedfordgallery.org
Founded: 1963.
Congressional District: 7
Key Personnel: Dir. Cultural & Community Svcs., Gary Pokorny; Cur., Carrie Lederer; Preparator, Erik Mortensen.
Personnel Profile: Full-Time Paid 2; Part-Time Paid 4; Part-Time Volunteers 100.
Governing Authority: municipal. Tax-exempt.
Municipal Art Gallery.
Collections: paintings; photographs; sculpture.
Facilities: slide & art library; 3,500 sq. ft. gallery; learning center; 800-seat theatre; 300-seat theatre.
Activities: guided tours; docent program or council; gallery talks; 5-6 annual exhibitions in all media; formally organized education programs for children, adults, undergraduate & graduate college students; in-school program; lecture series; changing exhibitions of contemporary art; school programs.
Publications: calendar of exhibitions; exhibit announcements; magazine, Diablo Arts.
Hours & Admission Prices: Tues.-Wed. & Sun. 12-5, Thurs.-Sat. 12-5 & 6-8. Adults $5, students 17 & under $3; children under 12 no charge. Closed national holidays. ♿
Attendance: 45,000

* **LINDSAY WILDLIFE MUSEUM,** 1931 First Ave., Walnut Creek, CA 94597-2540. Tel.: 925-935-1978. Fax: 925-935-8015.
Web Site: www.wildlife-museum.org
Founded: 1955.
Congressional District: 7
Key Personnel: Pres., John Kikuchi; Exec. Dir., Loren Behr; Cur. Live Collections, Michele Setter; Financial Dir., Suzie Mahaffay; Dir. Wildlife Rehabilitation, Susan Heckly; Deputy Dir. & Dir. Wildlife Svcs., Nancy Anderson, DVM, Ph.D., A.V.B.P.; Dir. Operations, Chris Bernard; Dir. Education, Patti Harris; Cur. Natural History & Dir. Operations, Marty Buxton; Museum Shop Mgr., Christine Garcia.
Personnel Profile: Full-Time Paid 25; Part-Time Paid 19; Part-Time Volunteers 600; Interns 5.
Governing Authority: bd. of directors; nonprofit. Tax-exempt: 501(c)(3).
Natural History Museum.
Collections: live wild animals; taxidermied specimens; Indian artifacts; entomology; botany; marine.
Research Fields: wildlife release & rehabilitation; natural history of California.
Facilities: classrooms; discovery room. Books & other museum-related items for sale.
Activities: guided tours; trips; lectures; formally organized educational programs; docent program & council; permanent, temporary & traveling exhibitions; mobile vans; school loan service; volunteer training to work with animals; petting area.
Publications: quarterly newsletter, Volunteer News; Public Program brochure.
Hours & Admission Prices: Jan.-June 15 Thurs.-Fri. 12-5, Sat.-Sun. 10-5; June 16-Aug. Wed.-Sun. 10-5; Sept.-Dec. Wed.-Fri. 12-5, Sat.-Sun. 10-5. Adults $7, senior citizens 65 & over $6, children 2-17 $5; discount to ASTC reciprocal members & groups of 15-35; members & children under 2 no charge. Closed Independence Day; Thanksgiving; Christmas. ♿
Attendance: 114,911 (accurate)
Membership: Individual $35; Family & Grandparents $65; Member Plus $100; Friends $250 & up.

Wasco

WASCO HISTORICAL SOCIETY MUSEUM, 918 6th St., Wasco, CA 93280-1902. Mailing Address: P.O. Box 186, Wasco, CA 93280-0186. Tel.: 661-758-8948.
Historical Society Museum.
Collections: local history & culture; photographs; personal artifacts.
Hours & Admission Prices: Call for hours.

Watsonville

ELKHORN SLOUGH NATIONAL ESTUARINE RESEARCH, 1700 Elkhorn Rd., Watsonville, CA 95076-9218. Tel.: 831-728-2822. Fax: 831-728-1056.
E-mail: info@elkhornslough.org
Web Site: www.elkhornslough.org
Key Personnel: Reserve Mgr., Becky Suarez
Natural History Museum.
Collections: tidal salt march; live plants; animals; birds; fish nursery.
Facilities: Museum-related items for sale.
Hours & Admission Prices: Wed.-Sun. 9-5. No charge.

PAJARO VALLEY HISTORICAL ASSOCIATION, 332 E. Beach St., Watsonville, CA 95076. Mailing Address: P.O. Box 623, Watsonville, CA 95077-0623. Tel.: 831-722-0305. Fax: 831-722-5501.
E-mail: pvhahistory@cruzio.com
Web Site: www.pajarovalleyhistory.org
Founded: 1940.
Congressional District: 16

Key Personnel: Pres., Judy Campbell; Sec., Cathy Moresco-Schimpeler; Treas., Eileen Sambrailo; Online Store Mgr., Alice Leyland; Administrative Sec., Gerianne Simmons.
Personnel Profile: Part-Time Paid 3; Part-Time Volunteers 50.
Governing Authority: nonprofit organization. Tax-exempt: 501(c)(3).
History Museum: housed in the Bockius-Orr House.
Collections: Pajaro Valley; photographs; vignettes; clothing & costumes; textiles; post cards of Pajaro Valley; slides of buildings & houses in Watsonville; archives. Historic Buildings: Volck Home & Carriage House.
Research Fields: oral histories; old homes, schools, businesses, genealogy, maps, local history & anything on Pajaro Valley history.
Facilities: over 500-vol. library of books & mansucripts available for use on premises by appointment only.
Activities: monthly board meetings; special events & fundraising activities; group tours; school group programs. Museum Sponsors: annual meeting in February; Fourth of July Barbecue; Christmas Tea; Membership Party.
Publications: quarterly newsletter.
Hours & Admission Prices: Tues.-Thurs. 11-3. No charge; donations accepted. ♿
Attendance: 750 (estimated)
Membership: Donor $35; Sponsor $50; Supporter $100; Benefactor $250; Patron $500 & up.

Weaverville

J.J. JACKSON MEMORIAL MUSEUM, 780 Main St., Weaverville, CA 96093. Mailing Address: Box 333, Weaverville, CA 96093-0333. Tel.: 530-623-5211. Fax: 530-623-5053.
E-mail: jake@trinitymuseum.org
Web Site: www.trinitymuseum.org
Founded: 1968.
Congressional District: 1
Key Personnel: Dir., Bridget Carson; Pres., Rich Lorenz; Museum Shop Mgr., Pat Williams.
Personnel Profile: Part-Time Paid 6; Part-Time Volunteers 25.
Governing Authority: county; society. Parent Institution: Trinity County Historical Society. Tax-exempt.
History Museum & Research Center.
Collections: Gold Rush artifacts; Chinese & Native American culture & history; pioneer artifacts; textiles; photographs & documents of Trinity history; blacksmith shop; tin shop; paymaster mine stampmill; ditch tender's cabin; stagecoach & buggy barn.
Research Fields: county records; geneaological research; Trinity County history.
Facilities: history center; park & picnic area. Gift items, booklets & stationery for sale.
Activities: permanent exhibitions; blacksmith shop demonstrations. Museum Sponsors: stampmill demonstrations on 3-day weekends & Independence Day.
Publications: books, Trinity County Historic Sites, Tales of the Trinity; yearbook, Trinity, From the Known to the Unknown, Flowers and Trees of the Trinity Alps.
Hours & Admission Prices: Jan.-March Tues.-Sat. 12-4; April & Nov.-Dec. daily 12-4; May-Oct. daily 10-5. No charge; donations accepted. ♿
Attendance: 11,750 (accurate)
Membership: Individual $15; Family $25; Supporter $50; Friend $100; Patron $200; Benefactor $500.

WEAVERVILLE JOSS HOUSE, State Historic Park, 630 Main St., Weaverville, CA 96093. Mailing Address: P.O. Box 1217, Weaverville, CA 96093-1217. Tel.: 530-623-5284.
Web Site: www.parks.ca.gov
Founded: 1956.
Key Personnel: Historic Monument Guide, Jack Frost.
Personnel Profile: Full-Time Paid 1; Part-Time Paid 2.
Governing Authority: state. Affiliated with State of California Department of Parks & Recreation, P.O. Box 942896, Sacramento, CA 94296-0001.
Historic Building: housed in a Chinese temple; built in 1874.
Collections: history of the Taoist temple of worship; temple equipment; Chinese art objects; photographs; mining tools; wrought iron weapons used in the 1854 Tong War.
Activities: guided tours; permanent exhibitions; guided tours for educational groups of high school level or below upon written request.
Hours & Admission Prices: Wed.-Sun. 10-5. Adults $3, children 6-17 $2.
Attendance: 20,000

Weed

LIVING MEMORIAL SCULPTURE GARDEN, Hwy. 97, Weed, CA 96094. Mailing Address: P.O. Box 301, Weed, CA 96094-0301. Tel.: 530-842-2477.
Web Site: livingmemorialsculpturegarden.org
Founded: 1987.
Key Personnel: Pres. (V), Susan Breceda.
Personnel Profile: Part-Time Volunteers 7.
Governing Authority: Parent Institution: Kiwanis Club of Weed/Lake Shastina.
War Memorial Sculpture Garden.
Collections: war memorial sculptures.
Activities: Annual Events: Memorial Services in May & November.
Publications: brochures; newsletter, 3 times annually.
Hours & Admission Prices: Daily sunrise-sunset. No charge.
Attendance: 6,000 (estimated)
Membership: Annual $25; Contributor $50; Lifetime Individual $400; Sponsor $1,000.

Weott

HUMBOLDT REDWOODS STATE PARK VISITOR CENTER, 17119 State Rte. 254, Weott, CA 95571. Mailing Address: P.O. Box 276, Weott, CA 95571-0276. Tel.: 707-946-2263. Fax: 707-946-2618.
E-mail: hrsp@humboldtredwoods.org
Web Site: www.humboldtredwoods.org
Founded: 1979.
Congressional District: 1
Key Personnel: State Park Liaison, John O'Rourke; Chm., Susan O'Hara; Dist. Supt., Steve Horvitz; Museum Shop Mgr., Dave Stockton.
Personnel Profile: Full-Time Paid 1; Full-Time Volunteers 30; Part-Time Paid 1; Part-Time Volunteers 25.
Governing Authority: nonprofit organization. Parent Institution: Humboldt Redwoods State Park. Tax-exempt.
Park Museum & Visitor Center.
Collections: plant & animal specimens native to north coast Redwood habitat.
Facilities: nature & conservation center. Museum-related items for sale.
Activities: lectures; films; docent program.
Publications: Humboldt Redwoods Trail Guide; Avenue of the Giants Auto Tour Guide; The Killen Eel.
Hours & Admission Prices: March-Oct. daily 9-5; Nov.-Feb. daily 10-4. No charge; donations accepted. ♿
Attendance: 79,160 (accurate)
Membership: Student & Senior $10; Individual $25; Supporting $50; Life $250; Patron $500; Endowment $1,000; Redwood Crown $2,500.

West Covina

HURST RANCH HISTORICAL FOUNDATION, 1227 S. Orange Ave., West Covina, CA 91790-3320. Tel.: 626-813-0116. Fax: 626-919-1133.
E-mail: info@hurstranch.com
Web Site: www.hurstranch.com
Founded: 1996.
Congressional District: 28
Key Personnel: C.E.O. & Pres. (V), Bill Berger; Treas., Stan Daubenbis.
Personnel Profile: Part-Time Volunteers 28.
Governing Authority: Tax-exempt.
History Museum.
Collections: 19th-century furniture; tools; farm implements; kitchen utensils; Coca-Cola memorabilia; books; early automobiles; fully maintained agricultural garden.
Hours & Admission Prices: Call for hours & admission prices. ♿
Attendance: 1,600 (estimated)
Membership: Friend $25; Family $50; Patron $100; Bronze $250; Silver $500; Gold $1,000; Platinum $2,500.

West Hollywood

MAK CENTER FOR ART AND ARCHITECTURE AT THE SCHINDLER HOUSE, 835 N. Kings Rd., West Hollywood, CA 90069-5409. Tel.: 323-651-1510, ext. 5 & ext. 10. Fax: 323-651-2340.
E-mail: office@makcenter.org
Web Site: www.makcenter.org
Founded: 1994.
Key Personnel: C.E.O., Peter Noever; Pres., Robert Sweeney, FOSH; Dir., Kimberli Meyer; Asst. Programs Coord., Janet Owen; Museum Shop Mgr., Angelica Fuentes; Security, Omar Velazquez.
Personnel Profile: Full-Time Paid 4; Part-Time Paid 1; Part-Time Volunteers 25; Interns 2.

Governing Authority: private; nonprofit organization. Parent Institution: Museum for Angewandte Kunst, Stubenring 5, Vienna, Austria A1010. Subsidiary Institution: MAK, Vienna, Austria. Tax-exempt: 501(c)(3).
Center for Art & Architecture: R.M. Schindler's landmark Kings Road House/Studio (1921-22)
Collections: paintings; photographs; historic building.
Research Fields: history of R.M. Schindler's work for exhibition.
Facilities: library; 1,500 sq. ft. exhibit space; outdoor courtyard. Books for sale.
Activities: docent program; films; guided tours; lectures; loan & traveling exhibitions. Museum Sponsor: annual architectural tour of Schindler homes.
Publications: catalogues for exhibitions.
Hours & Admission Prices: Wed.-Sun. 11-6. Adults $7, seniors & students $6; members no charge. Closed New Year's Day; Independence Day; Labor Day; Christmas. ♿
Attendance: 9,400 (accurate)
Membership: Student $25; General $45; Active $100; Charitable $250; Sustaining $500; Contributor $1,500; Supporter $5,000; Donor $10,000.

Whiskeytown

WHISKEYTOWN UNIT, WHISKEYTOWN-SHASTA-TRINITY NATIONAL RECREATION AREA, Hwy. 299 W., Whiskeytown, CA 96095-0188. Mailing Address: P.O. Box 188, Whiskeytown, CA 96095-0188. Tel.: 530-242-3451 & 246-1225. Fax: 530-246-5154.
Web Site: www.nps.gov/whis
Founded: 1965.
Congressional District: 2
Key Personnel: Supt., Jim F. Milestone.
Personnel Profile: Part-Time Paid 1.
Governing Authority: federal. Administered by National Park Service, U.S. Department of the Interior. Tax-exempt.
Anthropology, History Museum: located in former gold rush area. Tower House Historic District is on the National Register of Historic Places.
Collections: mining tools & memorabilia; Indian artifacts; natural history; archaeological sites relating to the occupation of the California Northern Wintu; historic structures dating back to the California gold rush era.
Facilities: visitor center. Postcards, slides & books for sale.
Activities: tours; gold panning; educational programs.
Hours & Admission Prices: Recreation Area: daily 10-4. Visitor Center: daily 9-6. Park Headquarter Mon.-Fri. 8-4:30. Vehicle Pass: annual $25, weekly $10, daily $5; Golden Age, Golden Access & Golden Eagle Passport members no charge. Closed New Year's Day; Thanksgiving; Christmas. ♿
Attendance: 715,000 (estimated)

Whittier

JONATHAN BAILEY HOME, 13421 E. Camilla St., Whittier, CA 90601-4608. Mailing Address: Whittier Historical Society, 6755 Newlin Ave., Whittier, CA 90601. Tel.: 562-945-3871.
Web Site: www.whittiermuseum.org/5.htm
Founded: 1975.
Congressional District: 38
Key Personnel: C.E.O. & Exec. Dir., Myra Hilliard.
Personnel Profile: Part-Time Volunteers 25.
History Museum.
Collections: period furnishings; personal artifacts; tools.
Hours & Admission Prices: Guided Tours: Sun. 1-4. No charge; donations accepted.

WHITTIER MUSEUM, 6755 Newlin Ave., Whittier, CA 90601. Tel.: 562-945-3871. Fax: 562-945-9106.
E-mail: info@whittiermuseum.org
Web Site: www.whittiermuseum.org
Founded: 1981.
Congressional District: 38
Key Personnel: C.E.O. & Exec. Dir., Myra Hilliard; Chm. (V), Janna Roznos; Pres. (V), Audrey Gee.
Personnel Profile: Full-Time Paid 3; Part-Time Volunteers 50; Interns 4.
Governing Authority: Tax-exempt.
History Museum.
Collections: archives; textiles; period artifacts.
Major Exhibits: Fly Your Colors - Patriotism in Whittier, 11/09-1/10; Show Me The Money - Banking In Whittier, 3/10-7/10; Death & Taxes, 9/10-1/11.
Facilities: archives by appointment.
Activities: Museum Sponsors: Chili Cookoff; Victorian Feast; Wine Tasting; Tea & Fashion Show.
Publications: members' monthly newsletter, Gazette.
Hours & Admission Prices: Call for hours. No charge; donations accepted. ♿
Attendance: 4,000 (estimated)
Membership: Individual $25; Family $40.

Williams

SACRAMENTO VALLEY MUSEUM, 1491 E St., Williams, CA 95987. Mailing Address: P.O. Box 1437, Williams, CA 95987-1437. Tel.: 530-473-2978. Fax: 530-473-2978.
E-mail: sacvalleymuseum@frontiernet.net
Web Site: www.sacvalleymuseum.com
Founded: 1963.
Key Personnel: Dir., Kathy Manor; Archive Mgr., Emily Conrado
History Museum: former building of Williams High School, built in 1911.
Collections: party line phone switchboard; sheriff's desk; landscape paintings & portraits; horse buggies; early fire equipment; California Native Tribal artifacts; pioneer quilts; toys; dolls; apothecary shop; Asian heritage; period clothing; military memorabilia; saddler & blacksmith shops; bedroom & parlor furnishings.
Publications: members quarterly newsletter.
Hours & Admission Prices: mid-March to mid-Nov. Thurs.-Sat. 10-4; other times by appointment. Adults $3, children 4-17 $2; members no charge.
Attendance: 651 (accurate)
Membership: Individual $15; Family $20; Business $30; Sponsor $100; Patron $250; Benefactor $500.

Willits

MENDOCINO COUNTY MUSEUM, (M), 400 E. Commercial St., Willits, CA 95490-3204. Tel.: 707-459-2736. Fax: 707-459-7836.
E-mail: museum@co.mendocino.ca.us
Web Site: www.co.mendocino.ca.us/museum/
Founded: 1972.
Congressional District: 1
Key Personnel: C.E.O. & Dir., Herbert E. Pruett; Cur., Elaine Hamby; Guest Cur. Archaeology, Dr. Thomas N. Layton; Guest Cur. Textiles, Mrs. Dian Crayne; Archivist, Dr. Russell Bartley; Archivist, Mrs. Sylvia Bartley; Administration & Museum Shop Mgr., Nikki Burgess; Reception, Eileen Pinsky.
Personnel Profile: Full-Time Paid 4; Part-Time Paid 2; Part-Time Volunteers 30; Interns 1.
Governing Authority: county. Parent Institution: County of Mendocino (CA) board of supervisors. Subsidiary Institution: Grassroots History Publications. Tax-exempt.
History & Railroad Museum.
Collections: artifacts representing all aspects of Mendocino County life including furniture, clothing, tools, vehicles, art, machinery & household utensils; archives; steam powered logging & railroad equipment; 1850 Frolic shipwreck; Seabiscuit exhibition; Carlos Hittel 1902 oil paintings; L.P. Latimer 1915 oil paintings.
Research Fields: Native American & American ethnic cultural history; Pomo basketry; historic textiles; archaeology; historic preservation; rural environmental adaptation; family & community history; railroad logging history.
Facilities: research library. Books & museum-related items for sale.
Activities: volunteer projects; rotating exhibits; grassroots history publication series; workshops; artifact conservation; photograph darkroom. Annual Events: Steam-Ups with free train rides.
Publications: Grassroots History Publications.
Hours & Admission Prices: Wed.-Sun. 10-4:30. No charge; donations accepted. Closed most holidays. ♿
Attendance: 20,000 (estimated)

Willow Creek

WILLOW CREEK - CHINA FLAT MUSEUM, 38949 Hwy. 299, Willow Creek, CA 95573. Mailing Address: P.O. Box 102, Willow Creek, CA 95573-0102. Tel.: 530-629-2653.
Web Site: bigfootcountry.net
Personnel Profile: Part-Time Volunteers 20.
History Museum.
Collections: area historical artifacts; bigfoot/sasquatch research material.
Hours & Admission Prices: May-Sept. Wed.-Sun. 10-4; Oct. Fri.-Sun. 10-4. No charge; donations accepted. ♿
Membership: Individual $10; Family $25.

Willows

WILLOWS MUSEUM, 336 W. Walnut St., Willows, CA 95988-2819. Mailing Address: P.O. Box 1242, Willows, CA 95988-1242. Tel.: 530-934-5644.
History Museum.
Collections: historical artifacts.
Hours & Admission Prices: Thurs. & Sat.-Sun. 1-4; other times by appointment. No charge; donations accepted.

Wilmington

BANNING MUSEUM, (M), 401 E. M St., Wilmington, CA 90744-2610. Mailing Address: P.O. Box 397, Wilmington, CA 90748-0397. Tel.: 310-548-7777. Fax: 310-548-2644.
Web Site: www.thebanningmuseum.org
Founded: 1974.
Congressional District: 32
Key Personnel: C.E.O., Ed Beall; Pres. (V), Bonnie Winters; Dir., Michael Sanborn; Devel. & Membership, Dina Dini; Cur., Tara Fansler; Public Rels., Marty Washington.
Personnel Profile: Full-Time Paid 5; Part-Time Paid 5; Part-Time Volunteers 107; Interns 2.
Governing Authority: municipal. Parent Institution: Getty Grant Program. Subsidiary Institution: Banning Residence Museum & Friends of Banning Museum. Tax-exempt: 501(c)(3).
History Museum: 1864 Greek Revival home of Phineas Banning.
Collections: 19th-century decorative arts; textiles & costumes; furniture; glass & ceramics; silver; books; photographs; Los Angeles harbor development & transportation 1851-1975.
Research Fields: 19th & early 20th-century history of Southern California.
Facilities: library available to public for research; 10,000 sq. ft. exhibit space. Books, paper goods & gift items for sale.
Activities: guided tours; lectures; organized educational programs; docent programs; participatory & temporary exhibitions. Museum Sponsors: Victorian Christmas.
Publications: biannual newsletter, Banning and Company.
Hours & Admission Prices: Tours: Tues.-Thurs. 12:30, 1:30 & 2:30, Sat.-Sun. 12:30, 1:30, 2:30 & 3:30; groups of 10 or more by appointment. Requested Donation: adults $5, children under 12 $1. Closed legal holidays.
Attendance: 22,000 (accurate)
Membership: Friends of Banning Museum: Individual $55; Family $100; Sponsoring $250; Patron $500; President's Circle $1,000; Preservation Circle $2,500; Vanguard Circle $5,500.

DRUM BARRACKS CIVIL WAR MUSEUM, 1052 Banning Blvd., Wilmington, CA 90744-4604. Tel.: 310-548-7509. Fax: 310-548-2946.
E-mail: susan.ogle@lacity.org
Web Site: www.drumbarracks.org
Founded: 1987.
Congressional District: 32
Key Personnel: Dir., Susan Ogle; Museum Shop Mgr., Kathy Ralston.
Personnel Profile: Full-Time Paid 1; Part-Time Paid 4; Part-Time Volunteers 18; Interns 1.
Governing Authority: state; nonprofit. Parent Institution: Recreation & Parks Dept. City of Los Angeles. Support Group: Drum Barracks Garrison & Society. Tax-exempt.
History Museum.
Collections: Civil War library; Civil War weaponry, firearms & uniforms; officers' sitting room & family bedroom; small scale 1863 site model; 34 star battle flag from Vicksburg; autograph book of 50 Union general's signatures.
Research Fields: California participation in Civil War period & 1861-1871, American Indian Wars; officers stationed at Wilmington/San Pedro camp; American Civil War.
Facilities: library of national & local military Civil War material, including historical magazines available to the public by appointment.
Activities: guided tours; organized education programs for children, adults, undergraduate & graduate college students; docent program; temporary exhibitions; annual events; internships.
Publications: monthly newsletter, Reveille.
Hours & Admission Prices: Tours: Tues.-Thurs. 10, 11, 12 & 1, Sat.-Sun. 11:30, 12:30, 1:30 & 2:30. Requested Donation: Adults $5. Closed New Year's Day; Good Friday; Easter; Memorial Day; Independence Day; Labor Day; Thanksgiving; Christmas.
Attendance: 9,097 (accurate)
Membership: Individual $20; Family $30; Sustaining $50; Sponsor $100; Patron $250; Founder $500; Corporate $1,000.

Woodland

GIBSON HOUSE, 512 Gibson Rd., Woodland, CA 95695-4843. Tel.: 530-666-1045. Fax: 530-666-3690.
E-mail: ychmoffice@sbcglobal.net
Web Site: www.yolo.net/vme/ychm
Formerly: Yolo County Historical Museum
Founded: 1979.
Congressional District: 4
Key Personnel: Sec., Marilyn Wirth; Treas., Barbara Shreve.
Personnel Profile: Part-Time Paid 1; Part-Time Volunteers 50; Interns 2.
Governing Authority: nonprofit organization. Tax-exempt: 501(c)(3).
Historic House Museum: c.1857 Greek Revival mansion.
Collections: regional history; paintings; photographs; Native American artifacts; clothing; furniture; furnishings; agriculture.
Research Fields: Yolo County history.
Facilities: library; 2.5-acre parkland. Gift items for sale.
Activities: concerts; docent program; guided tours; lectures; temporary exhibitions; weddings; receptions; special events; rental facilities; festivals; family programs; school tours & activities.
Publications: exhibit catalogs; quarterly newsletter; annual report.
Hours & Admission Prices: Thurs.-Sun. 12-4. Adults $5, children 5-17 $2; members & children under 4 no charge. Closed major holidays. ♿
Attendance: 6,000 (accurate)
Membership: Youth $15; Senior Citizen $20; Individual $25; Family $35; Sustaining $50; Donor $100; Patron $250; Life $1,000.

HAYS ANTIQUE TRUCK MUSEUM, 1962 Hays Lane, Woodland, CA 95776-6216. Mailing Address: P.O. Box 2347, Woodland, CA 95776-2347. Tel.: 530-666-1044. Fax: 530-666-5777.
Web Site: truckmuseum.org
Founded: 1982.
Key Personnel: Exec. Dir., Ed Rocha
Transportation Museum.
Collections: period trucks; history of trucking.
Hours & Admission Prices: Mon.-Fri. 10-5, Sat. 10-6, Sun. 10-4. Adults $7, seniors 62 & over $6, children 6-14 $4; children under 6 no charge.

Woodside

FILOLI CENTER, 86 Canada Rd., Woodside, CA 94062-4144. Tel.: 650-364-8300. Fax: 650-367-0724.
E-mail: friends@filoli.org
Web Site: www.filoli.org
Founded: 1976.
Congressional District: 12
Key Personnel: Exec. Dir., Jane A. Risser; Pres. (V), Antoinette Barrack; Dir. Interpretation, Lynn Norns; Gift Shop Mgr., Cat Bishop.
Personnel Profile: Full-Time Paid 32; Part-Time Paid 20; Part-Time Volunteers 1,100; Interns 3.
Governing Authority: nonprofit. Property of the National Trust for Historic Preservation; operated by the Filoli Center Inc. Affiliated with The Friends of Filoli. Tax-exempt: 501(c)(3).
Formal Garden, Historic House & Nature Preserve: 1915-1917 residence designed by Willis J. Polk for William B. Bourn, II; gardens designed by Bruce Porter.
Collections: botanical; library; furnishings.
Research Fields: landscape architecture; S.F. Bay Historic Estates & Gardens.
Facilities: 16 acres of gardens; nature education center.
Activities: guided & self-guided tours; docent-led nature hikes.
Publications: self-guided brochure.
Hours & Admission Prices: mid-Feb. to late Oct. Tues.-Sat. 10-3:30, Sun. 11-3:30; call for tour schedule & reservations Tel.: 650-364-8300, ext. 507. Adults $12, students 5-17 $5; discounts to National Trust for Historic Preservation; children under 5 & members no charge. Closed Federal holidays. ♿
Attendance: 110,000 (accurate)
Membership: Individual Senior $35; Individual $50; Dual Senior $60; Dual $75; Family $85; Friend $150; Filoli $250; President $500; Bourn $1,000; Roth $2,500.

WOODSIDE STORE HISTORIC SITE, 3300 Tripp Rd., Woodside, CA 94062-3632. Tel.: 650-851-7615.
E-mail: woodsidestore@historysmc.org
Founded: 1954.
Congressional District: 12
Key Personnel: Pres., Mitchell P. Postel; Chm., Umang Gupta; Dir. Education, Carmen Blair; Coord. Educational Programs, Marilyn Murphy.
Personnel Profile: Part-Time Paid 2; Part-Time Volunteers 20; Interns 1.
Governing Authority: county. Parent Institution: San Mateo County Historical Association. Tax-exempt.
Historic Building: c.1854 general store.
Collections: hands-on museum of 1880s general store.
Research Fields: Local history.
Activities: guided tours for groups; educational programs.
Hours & Admission Prices: Tues. & Thurs. 10-4, Sat.-Sun. 12-4. No charge; donations accepted. Closed national holidays. ♿

Yermo

CALICO GHOST TOWN AND THE LANE HOUSE & MUSEUM, 36600 Ghost Town Rd., Yermo, CA 92398. Mailing Address: P.O. Box 638, Yermo, CA 92398-0638. Tel.: 760-254-3679. Fax: 760-254-2047.
Web Site: www.calicotown.com
Governing Authority: Parent Institution: County of San Bernardino.
History Museum.
Collections: Town: life of miners & townspeople. House & Museum: local history; natural history; furnishings; mining equipment & artifacts; photographs.
Hours & Admission Prices: Town: daily 9-5. House & Museum: daily 10-4; other times by appointment. Adults $6, youth 6-15 $3; children 5 & under no charge.

Yorba Linda

RICHARD NIXON LIBRARY & BIRTHPLACE, 18001 Yorba Linda Blvd., Yorba Linda, CA 92886-3949. Tel.: 714-993-5075. Fax: 714-528-0544.
E-mail: rexjht@msn.com
Web Site: www.nixonlibraryfoundation.org
History Museum.
Collections: personal artifacts; presidential papers; furnishings; photographs.
Hours & Admission Prices: Mon.-Sat. 10-5, Sun. 11-5. Adult 12 & over $9.95, seniors 62 & over and military $6.95, student $5.95, children 7-11 $3.75; children 6 & under no charge. Closed Thanksgiving; Christmas.

Yosemite

THE ANSEL ADAMS GALLERY, 9031 Village Dr., Yosemite, CA 95389. Tel.: 209-372-4413. Fax: 209-372-4714.
E-mail: yosemite@anseladams.com
Web Site: www.anseladams.com
Key Personnel: Pres., Matthew Adams; Cur., Glenn Crosby; Workshops, Sara Bateman
Art Gallery.
Collections: photographs.
Facilities: Museum-related items for sale.
Hours & Admission Prices: Call for hours.

Yosemite National Park

THE YOSEMITE MUSEUM, NATIONAL PARK SERVICE, (M), Museum Bldg., Yosemite National Park, CA 95389. Mailing Address: P.O. Box 577, Yosemite Nation, CA 95389-0577. Tel.: 209-372-0297 & 0281. Fax: 209-372-0255.
E-mail: yose_museum@nps.gov
Founded: 1915.
Congressional District: 19
Key Personnel: Cur., Jonathan Bayless; Cur. Collections, Barbara L. Beroza; Archivist, Paul Rogers; Asst. Archivist, Brenna Lissoway; Librarian, Linda Eade; Registrar, Miriam Luchans.
Personnel Profile: Full-Time Paid 6; Part-Time Paid 2; Part-Time Volunteers 15.
Governing Authority: federal. Parent Institution: National Park Service. Tax-exempt: 101(6).
History, Ethnography & Natural Science Museum.
Collections: anthropology; archaeology; archives; entomology; ethnology; geology; herbarium; history; Indian culture; natural history; photography; zoology. Historic Houses: 1880-1915 Pioneer Yosemite History Center; 1880-1900 park trail cabins.
Research Fields: natural history; history; ethnography; photography.
Facilities: 20,000-vol. library; visitor centers; history center. Museum-related items for sale.
Activities: guided tours; talks; films; self-guiding displays; formally organized education programs for children; inter-museum loan, permanent & temporary exhibitions; field seminars; living history demonstrations.
Publications: books; pamphlets; periodicals.
Hours & Admission Prices: Yosemite Valley Visitor Center: Memorial Day-Labor Day daily 8-6; Sept.-May daily 9-5. Call for hours for Pioneer Yosemite History Center; Hill's Studio; Indian Village. No charge. ♿
Attendance: 485,000 (estimated)
Membership: Yosemite Association: Individual $30; Joint & Family $35; Supporting $50; Contributing $100; Sustaining $250; Patron $500; Benefactor $1,000.

Yountville

NAPA VALLEY MUSEUM, 55 Presidents Circle, Yountville, CA 94599. Mailing Address: P.O. Box 3567, Yountville, CA 94599-3567. Tel.: 707-944-0500. Fax: 707-945-0500.
E-mail: rick@napavalleymuseum.org
Web Site: www.napavalleymuseum.org
Founded: 1973.
Congressional District: 1
Key Personnel: Exec. Dir., Rick Deragon; Pres., Shirley Robinson Von Karl.
Personnel Profile: Full-Time Paid 3; Part-Time Paid 3; Part-Time Volunteers 100; Interns 1.
Governing Authority: private; nonprofit organization. Tax-exempt: 501(c)(3).
Local History, Art & Natural Science Museum.
Collections: area history, art & environment heritage including the Wappo Indians, Chinese, Mexicans, pioneers, ranchos, viticulture, Napa River; 19th century painter Sophie Alstrom Mitchell art; Henry Evans botanical prints.
Research Fields: Wappo Indians; Chinese history; history & culture in Napa Valley; cultural heritage of the Napa Valley.
Facilities: education center; collections & resource center. Museum-related items for sale.
Activities: arts festivals; concerts; dance recitals; lectures; rental gallery; organized educational programs; guided tours; workshops; school loan service; docent program; loan & temporary exhibitions; internships. Annual Events: Angel Gala Fundraiser.
Publications: Napa Valley Museum; monthly mailer, Napa Valley Museum Events & Programs; exhibit catalogue.
Hours & Admission Prices: Wed.-Mon. 10-5. Adults $4.50, senior citizens & students $3.50, youth $2.50; discounts to AAM members; members & children under 7 no charge. Closed New Year's Day; Easter; Christmas. ♿
Attendance: 20,000 (estimated)
Membership: Individual $35; Family $60; Donor $125; Supporter $300; Sponsor $500; Patron $1,000; Benefactor $2,500; Leader $5,000.

Yreka

SISKIYOU COUNTY MUSEUM, 910 S. Main St., Yreka, CA 96097-3373. Tel.: 530-842-3836. Fax: 530-842-3166.
E-mail: hismus@inreach.com
Web Site: www.co.siskiyou.ca.us/museum/
Founded: 1950.
Congressional District: 1
Key Personnel: Dir., Michael Hendryx; Museum Asst., Richard Terwilliger.
Personnel Profile: Full-Time Paid 1; Part-Time Paid 2; Part-Time Volunteers 50.
Governing Authority: county. Tax-exempt: 501(c)(3).
Local History Museum.
Collections: prehistoric marine, plant & animal fossils; ethnographic Indian & Chinese artifacts; trapping paraphernalia; gold mining, agricultural & transportation artifacts; lumbering, settlement, turn-of-the-century, Depression & other 20th-century objects. Outdoor Museum: 1856 log cabin; 1870 miner's cabin; church; schoolhouse; Blacksmith shop; 1912 logging skid shack; operating general merchandise store.
Facilities: 17,000-vol. research library including 18,000 catalogued photographs, 1864-1983 county newspapers & pamphlet files on local history, complete set Bancroft History volumes & pioneer biographies; voter registers; scrapbooks from early 1900s to present.
Activities: special interpretive exhibits; lectures; films; monthly meetings county historical society; field trips; school programs. Annual Events: Christmas Candlelight event; Living History Celebration in summer.
Publications: annual, The Siskiyou Pioneer; Occasional Paper, No. 1, Siskiyou County: A Time of Change; Occasional Paper, No. 2, Gold Mining in Siskiyou County 1850-1900, technical leaflet, Siskiyou Horizontal Log Construction; Plants & the People, the Ethnobotany of the Karuk Tribe; State of Jefferson; Walking the Medicine Path; Poor, But Not So Poor-Depression Mining in Siskiyow County.
Hours & Admission Prices: Tues.-Fri. 9-5, Sat. 9-4. Adults $2, children 7-12 $.75; children under 7 no charge. Closed national holidays. ♿
Attendance: 21,000 (estimated)
Membership: Individual $20; Institution $50; Sponsor $60; Life $2,000.

Yuba City

COMMUNITY MEMORIAL MUSEUM OF SUTTER COUNTY, (M), 1333 Butte House Rd., Yuba City, CA 95993-2301. Mailing Address: P.O. Box 1555, Yuba City, CA 95992-1555. Tel.: 530-822-7141. Fax: 530-822-7291.
E-mail: museum@syix.com
Web Site: www.co.sutter.ca.us/
Founded: 1975.

Congressional District: 4
Key Personnel: Dir., Julie Stark; Chm. (V), Rebecca Flower; Asst. Cur., Sharyl Simmons.
Personnel Profile: Full-Time Paid 2; Part-Time Paid 3; Part-Time Volunteers 30.
Governing Authority: county. Parent Institution: County of Sutter. Tax-exempt.
History Museum.
Collections: Maidu Indian artifacts; Sutter County related artifacts including furniture, clothing & agricultural items; documents; photo collection.
Major Exhibits: Past Tents (T), 1/10-3/10; Multiply by Six Million (T), 6/10-7/10.
Research Fields: Sutter County.
Facilities: 200-vol. library of local history books, tax lists, California history, documents, & photos available for research on premises only. Books & other museum-related items for sale.
Activities: guided tours; lectures; workshops; permanent, temporary & historical exhibition; volunteer auxiliary.
Publications: membership newsletter.
Hours & Admission Prices: Tues.-Fri. 9-5, Sat.-Sun. 12-4. No charge; donations accepted. Closed New Year's Day; Memorial Day; Labor Day; Thanksgiving; Christmas. ♿
Attendance: 8,000 (estimated)
Membership: Student & Senior Citizen $20; Individual $25; Organizations & Clubs $35; Family $40; Business & Sponsor $100; Corporate & Benefactor $1,000.

Yucaipa

OAK GLEN SCHOOL HOUSE MUSEUM, 11911 S. Oak Glen Rd., Yucaipa, CA 92399-9488. Tel.: 909-797-1691.
E-mail: oakglenshmuseum@yahoo.com
Founded: 1981.
Governing Authority: San Bernardino City Special District # 63. Tax-exempt.
History Museum.
Collections: local history; works on paper; school books from 1880s to 1965.
Facilities: nature walks.
Activities: concerts; educational events.
Publications: biannual newsletter.
Hours & Admission Prices: Oct. Wed.-Sun. 12-4; Nov.-Sept. Sat. 12-4, Sun. 1-5; other times by appointment. No charge; donations accepted.
Attendance: 3,000
Membership: Seniors & Students $10; Individual $15; Family $30; Supporting $50.

YUCAIPA ADOBE, 32183 Kentucky St., Yucaipa, CA 92399-1768. Mailing Address: c/o San Bernardino Co. Museums, 2024 Orange Tree Lane, Redlands, CA 92374. Tel.: 909-795-3485 & 307-2669. Fax: 909-307-0539.
E-mail: rmckernan@sbcm.sbcounty.gov
Web Site: www.sbcountymuseum.org
Founded: 1958.
Congressional District: 35
Key Personnel: Dir., Robert McKernan; Site Mgr., Tony Webb; Cur., Michele Nielsen.
Personnel Profile: Part-Time Paid 1.
Governing Authority: county. Parent Institution: San Bernardino County Museums. Tax-exempt.
Local History and Historic House Museum: housed in late 1850s adobe house.
Collections: local history; farm equipment; decorative arts; blacksmith shop; historic houses.
Research Fields: Local History.
Activities: guided tours; holiday open house; grounds available for weddings.
Hours & Admission Prices: Tues.-Sat. 10-3. No charge; donations suggested. Closed New Year's Day; Thanksgiving Day; Christmas.
Attendance: 500 (accurate)

YUCAIPA VALLEY HISTORICAL SOCIETY MUSEUM, 35308 Panorama Dr., Yucaipa, CA 92399-3532. Mailing Address: P.O. Box 297, Yucaipa, CA 92399-0297. Tel.: 909-790-4685. Fax: 909-790-4685.
E-mail: yucaipahistory@cybertime.net
Formerly: Mousley Museum of Natural History
Founded: 1970.
Congressional District: 37
Key Personnel: Pres., Claire Teeters; Pres., Harry Birkbeck; Vice Pres., David Stirdivant; Vice Pres., Jan Lemon.
Personnel Profile: Part-Time Paid 1; Part-Time Volunteers 26.
Governing Authority: county. Parent Institution: Yucaipa Valley Historical Society. Tax-exempt.
Natural History Museum.
Collections: Yucaipa Valley period artifacts; minerals; nature; primitive artifacts.
Facilities: 100-seat presentation hall. Museum-related items for sale.
Activities: temporary & permanent exhibitions; meetings; research. Museum Sponsors: Touch & Feel Exhibit.
Publications: brochures; books on local history.
Hours & Admission Prices: Wed. 5-9, Sat. 10-3. No charge; donations accepted. ♿
Attendance: 40 (accurate)
Membership: Individual $15; Corporate Sponsor $30; Cornerstone $100; Landmark & Scholarship Endowment $250; Heritage $500; Founder $1,000.

Yucca Valley

HI-DESERT NATURE MUSEUM, (M), 57116 29 Palms Hwy., Yucca Valley, CA 92284-2930. Tel.: 760-369-7212. Fax: 760-369-1605.
E-mail: museum@yucca-valley.org
Web Site: www.hidesertnaturemuseum.org
Founded: 1964.
Congressional District: 67
Key Personnel: Supvr., Lynne Richardson; Cur., Stefanie Ritter; Registrar, Peggy Pourtemour; Museum Asst., Janine Cleveland.
Personnel Profile: Full-Time Paid 3; Part-Time Paid 1; Part-Time Volunteers 1.
Governing Authority: Parent Institution: Town of Yucca Valley. Subsidiary Institution: Hi-Desert Nature Museum Assocation. Tax-exempt.
Natural History Museum.
Collections: butterflies from local & foreign countries; fossils from paleozoic times; rocks; gems; minerals; pine cones; copper ore; pressed desert wild flowers; Indian artifacts; rare & unusual implements; points; pottery; manos; pestels; bird eggs & nest; petrified wood; live reptiles; sea shells; mini-zoo of small desert animals & reptiles; pictures; mounted golden eagle, deer, badger, bobcat & reptiles, various birds.
Major Exhibits: 45 Years of the Hi-Desert Nature Museum, 1/10-3/10; Reduce, Reuse, Recycle, 3/10-4/10; Yucca Valley High School Art Show, 5/10-6/10; Firemaking Tools (T), 6/10-8/10; Missions of California, 9/10-11/10; Season of Light, 11/10-12/10.
Research Fields: plants; insects; geology; reptiles; birds; local history; earthquakes.
Facilities: mini zoo.
Activities: tours; education program for children; lecture series; junior naturalist program; temporary exhibits; wildflower festival. Museum Sponsors: Starry Nights Festival; Earth Day Fair.
Publications: e-newsletter, Tortoise Tales.
Hours & Admission Prices: Tues.-Sun. 10-5. No charge; donations accepted. Closed holidays. ♿
Attendance: 33,236 (accurate)
Membership: Youth $2; Annual $6; Two Adults Same Household $15; Business $25; Organizational $25; Life $150.

COLORADO

(259 listings)

Alamosa

ADAMS STATE COLLEGE LUTHER BEAN MUSEUM, (M), Richardson Hall, #256, Alamosa, CO 81102-0001. Mailing Address: 208 Edgemont Blvd., Alamosa, CO 81102-0001. Tel.: 719-587-7151; 800-824-6494. Fax: 719-587-7547.
E-mail: asclutherbean@adams.edu
Web Site: adams.edu/lutherbean
Founded: 1921.
Congressional District: 3
Key Personnel: Pres., Dr. David Svaldi; Treas., Bill Mansheim; Museum Dir., Kat Olance; Security, Joel Schultz.
Personnel Profile: Full-Time Paid 1; Part-Time Paid 1.
Governing Authority: college. Tax-exempt: 501(c)(3).
Anthropology, Ethnology Indian & History Museum.
Collections: Paleo-Indian folsom points; Pueblo Indian cultural artifacts, primarily pottery; Navajo weaving; Spanish culture; Santos; Spanish history primarily San Luis Valley & Southwest; Woodard period artifacts; works by Stephen Quiller; Bill Moyers bronzes; Native American pottery, paintings & artifacts.
Research Fields: archaeology & local history; pioneer history of the San Luis Valley.
Facilities: 100-vol. library of museology books available for use on premises; planetarium; 500-seat auditorium; classrooms; 40 sq. ft. exhibit space.
Activities: permanent & temporary exhibitions; guided tours.
Publications: quarterly alumni magazine, A-Stater.
Hours & Admission Prices: Tues.-Fri. 8-5; other times by appointment only. No charge; donations accepted. Closed New Year's Eve & Day; Labor Day; Memorial Day; Thanksgiving; Christmas Eve, Day & week; national holidays. ♿

Attendance: 3,000 (estimated)

SAN LUIS VALLEY MUSEUM, 401 Hunt Ave., Alamosa, CO 81101. Mailing Address: P.O. Box 1593, Alamosa, CO 81101-1593. Tel.: 719-587-0667.
Formerly: San Luis History Center
Founded: 1992.
Key Personnel: Chm. (V), Dorothy M. Brandt; Mgr. & Museum Shop Mgr., Joyce Gunn.
Personnel Profile: Full-Time Paid 1; Part-Time Volunteers 15; Interns 2.
Governing Authority: Tax-exempt.
History Museum.
Collections: local history; multicultural heritage; photographs; period artifacts; ranch & farm life; Native American; military; early railroading.
Activities: lectures; art shows.
Publications: annual report; semiannual newsletter; operational plan; museum brochure.
Hours & Admission Prices: Tues.-Sat. 10-4; other times by appointment. Adults $2, students $1; members no charge. ♿
Attendance: 1,400 (estimated)
Membership: Single $15; Couples $25.

Arvada

ARVADA CENTER FOR THE ARTS AND HUMANITIES, (M), 6901 Wadsworth Blvd., Arvada, CO 80003-3499. Tel.: 720-898-7200. Fax: 720-898-7217. TDD: 720-898-7203.
Web Site: www.arvadacenter.org
Founded: 1976.
Congressional District: 2
Key Personnel: Exec. Dir., Gene Sobczak; Chm. (V), Kimberly Wagner; History Museum Cur., William Henning; Museum Shop Coord., Debra Sanders; Administrative Clerk, Bernita Christenson; Dir. Performing Arts, Rod Lansberry; Dir. Education, Mickey McVey; Dir. Mktg., Cynthia DeLarber; Exhibit Designer, Collin Parson.
Governing Authority: municipal. Parent Institution: City of Arvada. Tax-exempt.
Art and History Museum.
Collections: 19th century photography; contemporary art & crafts; outdoor sculpture.
Research Fields: humanities programming in museums; Arvada area history.
Facilities: 500-seat auditorium; classrooms.
Activities: guided tours; lectures; films; concerts; dance recitals; arts festivals; theater; study clubs; organized education programs; docent program; participatory, loan & temporary exhibitions.
Publications: quarterly magazine, Center.
Hours & Admission Prices: Mon.-Fri. 9-6, Sat. 9-5, Sun. 1-5. No charge; donations accepted. Closed New Year's Day; Memorial Day; Independence Day; Labor Day; Thanksgiving; Christmas. ♿
Attendance: 360,000 (estimated)
Membership: General $40.

ARVADA FLOUR MILL, 5580 Old Wadsworth Blvd., Arvada, CO 80002-3104. Tel.: 303-431-1261.
Governing Authority: Parent Institution: Arvada Historical Society.
Historic Building: restored flour mill; built in 1926. Listed on the National Register of Historic Places.
Collections: mill history; late 1800s equipment.
Activities: guided tours.
Hours & Admission Prices: By appointment. Adults $1.50, children 12 & under $.50.

ARVADA HISTORICAL SOCIETY, 7307 Grandview Ave., Arvada, CO 80002-2507. Tel.: 303-431-1261.
Historical Society Museum.
Collections: area history & culture; photographs; personal artifacts; books; documents.
Hours & Admission Prices: Tues.-Sat. 11-3.

Aspen

* **ASPEN ART MUSEUM, (M),** 590 N. Mill St., Aspen, CO 81611-1510. Tel.: 970-925-8050. Fax: 970-925-8054.
E-mail: info@aspenartmuseum.org
Web Site: www.aspenartmuseum.org
Founded: 1979.
Key Personnel: Dir. & Chief Cur., Heidi Zuckerman Jacobson; Asst. Dir. Devel., Christy Sauer; Campaign Coord., Grace Brooks; Asst. Dir. Finance, Dara Coder; Curatorial Assoc. & Museum Shop Mgr., Nicole Kinsler; Coord. Special Events, Wendy Wilhelm; Public Rels. & Mktg. Mgr., Jeffrey Murcko; Phtographer, Karl Wolfgang; Graphic Designer, Jared Rippy; Asst. Dir. External Affairs, John-Paul Schaefer; Visitor Svcs. Asst., Dasa Bausova; Visitor Svcs. Asst., Karyn Andrade; Chief Preparator & Facilities Mgr., Dale Benson; Registrar, Pam Taylor; Assoc. Cur., Matthew Thompson; Coord. Visitor Svcs., Dorie Shellenergar; Membership Asst., Elizabeth Closuit; Web & Design Assoc., Rachel Rippy.
Personnel Profile: Full-Time Paid 18; Part-Time Paid 2; Part-Time Volunteers 45.
Governing Authority: nonprofit. Tax-exempt: 501(c)(3).
Art Museum.
Collections: outdoor sculpture.
Major Exhibits: Kris Martin, 12/10/09-1/24/10; Claire Fontaine, 12/10/09-1/10; Disembodied, 2/11/10-4/11/10; Mark Bradford, 2/11/10-4/14/10; Restless Empathy, 5/20/10-7/18/10; Sergej Jenson, 8/10-9/11/10; Mark Manders, 11/10-12/10.
Research Fields: contemporary art.
Facilities: library of slides & periodicals available for research.
Activities: guided tours; lectures; educational programs; docent program; loan & traveling exhibitions; art workshops for children & adults.
Publications: books, One Hour Ahead: The Avant Garde in Aspen, 1945-2004; Simon Evans: How to Get About, 2006; Doug Aitken 99 cent Dreams; Yutaka Sone (co-published with The Renaissance Society at the University of Chicago, and Kunsthalle Bern); exhibition catalogues, Amy Adler; Like Color in Pictures; Sculptors' Drawings; Belief and Doubt; Jeremy Deller; Aida Ruilova: The Singles 1999-Now; Friedrich Kunath; Phil Collins; Now You See It; Fred Tomaselli.
Hours & Admission Prices: Tues.-Wed. & Fri.-Sat. 10-6, Thurs. 10-7, Sun 12-6. No charge; donations accepted. Art After Hours: Thurs: 5-7. Closed New Year's Day; Thanksgiving; Christmas. ♿
Attendance: 24,500 (accurate)
Membership: Individual $35; Family $50; Art Addict $150; Sustainer $250; Donor $500; Patron $1,000; Benefactor's Circle $3,000; Director's Circle $5,000; President's Circle $10,000; Founder's Circle $25,000; Visionaries Circle $50,000.

ASPEN HISTORICAL SOCIETY, (M), 620 W. Bleeker St., Aspen, CO 81611-1230. Tel.: 970-925-3721. Fax: 970-925-5347.
Web Site: www.aspenhistory.org
Formerly: Heritage Aspen
Founded: 1963.
Congressional District: 3
Key Personnel: Pres. (V), Jenna Weatherred; Dir., Georgia Hanson; Cur., Lisa Hancock.
Personnel Profile: Full-Time Paid 8; Part-Time Paid 3; Part-Time Volunteers 40; Interns 3.
Governing Authority: society; nonprofit. Branch Museum: Holden-Marolt Ranching & Mining Museum, Aspen; Wheeler-Stallard Museum; Independence & Ashcroft Ghost Towns. Tax-exempt: 501(c)(3).
Housed in 1888 Wheeler-Stallard House.
Collections: Aspen and Roaring Fork Valley history & lifestyles; domestic life; mining; ranching; skiing & culture; textiles; manuscripts; newspapers; photographs.
Research Fields: Aspen & Roaring Fork Valley history.
Facilities: 1,000-vol. library of books on Aspen and Roaring Fork Valley history; 200 Aspen Times Newspapers; written materials including brochures, stocks, bonds & other forms of original documentation; 6,000 sq. ft. exhibit space.
Activities: docent program; adult & children's educational programs; films; guided tours; walking tours of historic West End & downtown Aspen; temporary exhibitions.
Publications: quarterly newsletter.
Hours & Admission Prices: Summer: Tues.-Sat. 1-5. Winter: Tues.-Fri. 1-5. Adults $6, seniors $5, children $3; children under 5 & members no charge. Closed Christmas. ♿
Attendance: 25,000 (estimated)
Membership: Student & Limited Income $18.79; Individual $35; Family $60; Business $125; Contributing $300; Collaborator $700; Sustaining $1,000.

Aurora

AURORA HISTORY MUSEUM, (M), 15051 E. Alameda Pkwy., Aurora, CO 80012-1554. Tel.: 303-739-6660. Fax: 303-739-6657.
Web Site: www.auroramuseum.org
Founded: 1979.
Congressional District: 2, 6
Key Personnel: Exec. Dir., Dr. Gordon Davis; Acting Co-Dir. & Cur. Education, Jennifer Kuehner; Cur. Exhibits, MaryJane Valade; Acting Co-Dir. & Cur. Collections, Michael Thompson; Facility Mgr., Ken Clinton; Historic Preservation Asst., Jeanne Ramsay.
Personnel Profile: Full-Time Paid 7; Full-Time Volunteers 3; Part-Time Paid 10; Part-Time Volunteers 125.

Governing Authority: municipal. Parent Institution: City of Aurora. Tax-exempt.
History Museum.
Collections: local history collections reflecting rural Great Plains agricultural and 19th- & 20th-century suburban development; Indian culture of the Aurora area encompassing Adams & Arapahoe Counties; manuscripts. Historic Buildings: Gully Homestead; DeLaney Farm and Round Barn; Coal Creek School; Centennial House.
Research Fields: Great Plains agricultural, late Victorian suburban & 20th-century urban history; historic preservation.
Facilities: archive & library of periodicals & manuscripts on Aurora, Colorado, Western history, museology & historic preservation available for research on premises; meeting rooms.
Activities: guided tours; lectures; films; gallery talks; formally organized educational programs; permanent & temporary exhibitions.
Publications: Aurora: Gateway to the Rockies; First Sun. of Colorado, Aurora
Hours & Admission Prices: Tues.-Fri. 9-4, Sat.-Sun. 11-4; call for Gully Homestead and Centennial House hours. No Charge. Closed holidays. ♿
Attendance: 15,164 (accurate)
Membership: Student 18 & under $5; Senior Citizens 60 & over $10; Senior Couple & Individual $15; Family & General $25; Sustaining $50; Century Club $100; Benefactor $250.

PATROL SQUADRON COLORADO, 3657 S. Uravan St., Aurora, CO 80013-3459. Mailing Address: 13207 W. Luke Ave., Litchfield Park, AZ 85340-8380. Tel.: 303-699-8611. Fax: 303-699-8611.
Founded: 1982.
Congressional District: 5
Key Personnel: Commander, Arnold Zaharia.
Governing Authority: nonprofit organization. Tax-exempt: 501(c)(3).
Military History Museum.
Collections: military equipment; static displays.
Activities: guided tours; air-ground combat reenactments; parades; fly-bys; air shows; dances.
Publications: monthly newsletter.
Hours & Admission Prices: Special events, call for information. ♿
Membership: Cadet & Auxiliary $15; Regular Member $25; Corporation & Business Member $500 & up.

PLAINS CONSERVATION CENTER, 21901 E. Hampden Ave., Aurora, CO 80013-5000. Tel.: 303-693-3621. Fax: 303-693-3379.
E-mail: info@plainscenter.org
Web Site: www.plainscenter.org
Founded: 1949.
Key Personnel: C.E.O. & Dir., Tudi Arneill; Pres. (V), Gordon C. Tucker.
Personnel Profile: Full-Time Paid 6; Part-Time Paid 8; Part-Time Volunteers 100; Interns 1.
Governing Authority: Parent Institution: West Arapahoe Conservation District. Tax-exempt.
General Museum.
Collections: natural & cultural heritage; replica sod village, schoolhouse, blacksmith shop, & barn; live animals; period furnishings.
Research Fields: paleontology; zoology; prairie ecology.
Facilities: library; 6,800 acres of short grass prairie; visitor center; hiking trails.
Activities: nature walks & programs; historical interpretation programs of Plains Indians & 1880s.
Publications: quarterly newsletter.
Hours & Admission Prices: Sat. 9-5. No charge. ♿
Attendance: 20,000 (accurate)
Membership: Individual $20; Family $30; Business & Supporting $60.

Beaver Creek

THE MAY GALLERY, PATRON'S LOUNGE, Vilar Center for the Arts, 68 Avondale Lane, Beaver Creek Resort, Beaver Creek, CO 81620. Mailing Address: P.O. Box 3822, Avon, CO 81620-3822. Tel.: 970-845-8497; 888-920-2787. Fax: 970-748-1396.
E-mail: ksabel@vvf.org
Web Site: vilarcenter.org
Formerly: The May Gallery, A Program of the Vail Valley Arts Council
Founded: 1972.
Congressional District: 56
Key Personnel: Vice Pres. Cultural Programming, Kris Sabel; Pres. (V), Bob Jamar; Dir. Mktg., Shelley Woodworth.
Personnel Profile: Full-Time Paid 3; Part-Time Paid 3; Part-Time Volunteers 150.
Governing Authority: Vail Valley Foundation; private; nonprofit organization. Tax-exempt: 501(c)(3).
Art Museum & Center.
Collections: paintings.
Facilities: 100-vol. library of periodicals; 2,247 sq. ft. exhibit space. Museum-related items for sale.
Activities: arts festivals; docent program; formal education programs; guided tours; hobby workshops; lectures; loan & traveling exhibitions.
Publications: quarterly newsletter; exhibition brochures & catalogues.
Hours & Admission Prices: By appointment only. No charge. ♿
Attendance: 20,000 (estimated)
Membership: Artist, Student & Educator $25; Friend $50; Supporting $100; Sustaining $250; Benefactor $500; Inner Circle: $1,000-$2,500 (per Year for 5 years); Collector's Group: $2,500, $3,000 & $5,000; Donor $5,000; Major Donor $10,000.

Berthoud

LITTLE THOMPSON VALLEY PIONEER MUSEUM, 224 Mountain Ave., Berthoud, CO 80513. Tel.: 970-532-2147.
History Museum.
Collections: local history & culture; photographs; personal artifacts.
Facilities: Museum-related items for sale.
Hours & Admission Prices: Wed.-Sun. 1-5; other times by appointment.

Boulder

BOULDER HISTORY MUSEUM, (M), 1206 Euclid Ave., Boulder, CO 80302-7224. Tel.: 303-449-3464. Fax: 303-938-8322.
E-mail: info@boulderhistory.org
Web Site: www.boulderhistorymuseum.org
Formerly: Boulder Museum of History
Founded: 1944.
Congressional District: 2
Key Personnel: C.E.O., Nancy Geyer; Dir. Devel., Stephany Precourt; Cur. Exhibits & Facilities, Julie Schumaker; Cur. Education, Laura Stroud; Mktg. & Public Rels., Susan Linde.
Personnel Profile: Full-Time Paid 5; Part-Time Paid 3; Part-Time Volunteers 30; Interns 2.
Governing Authority: society. Affiliated with Boulder Historical Society. Tax-exempt: 501(c)(3).
History Museum: housed in the Harbeck-Bergheim house built in 1899.
Collections: 35,000 material objects; 2,500 early clothing items; 200,000 period photographs.
Research Fields: local history.
Activities: guided tours; in-house programs; lectures; permanent & rotating interpretive exhibits; outreach programs; festivals; workshops.
Publications: informational brochures; newsletter.
Hours & Admission Prices: Tues.-Fri. 10-5, Sat.-Sun. 12-4. Adults $6, seniors $4, children & students $2; discounts to AAM & ICOM members; members & children under 5 no charge. Closed major holidays. ♿
Attendance: 8,000 (accurate)
Membership: Senior $25; Individual $35; Senior Couple $40; Family $55; Supporting $100; Sustaining $250; Patron $500; Leadership Circle $1,000.

BOULDER MUSEUM OF CONTEMPORARY ART, 1750 13th St., Boulder, CO 80302-6226. Tel.: 303-443-2122. Fax: 303-447-1633.
E-mail: info@bmoca.org
Web Site: www.bmoca.org
Founded: 1972.
Congressional District: 2
Key Personnel: Co Exec. Dir. & Sr. Cur., Joan Markowitz; Co Exec. Dir., Sr. Admin., Finance, Penny Barnow; Assoc. Cur., Kirsten Gerdes Stoltz.
Personnel Profile: Full-Time Paid 1; Part-Time Paid 7; Part-Time Volunteers 100; Interns 4.
Governing Authority: bd. directors. Tax-exempt.
Contemporary Art Museum.
Collections: contemporary art.
Facilities: 10,000 sq. ft. exhibit space.
Activities: visual art exhibitions; performance; education; outreach.
Publications: newsletter, BMOCA; catalogs.
Hours & Admission Prices: Tues.-Fri. 11-5, Sat. 9-4, Sun. 12-3. Adults $5, senior citizens, educators & students $4; discounts to school groups, NARP & AAM members; Modern & Contemporary and North American members reciprocal program; members & children 11 and under no charge. ♿
Attendance: 35,000 (accurate)
Membership: Senior Citizen & Student $25; Individual $35; Family $55; Contributor $100; Supporter $150; Benefactor $250; Sustainer $500.

CU ART GALLERIES, (M), 318 UCB, Sibell Wolle Fine Arts Bldg., University of Colorado/Boulder, Boulder, CO 80309-0001. Tel.: 303-492-8300. Fax: 303-735-4197.
Web Site: www.colorado.edu/cuartmuseum

Founded: 1939.
Key Personnel: Dir., Lisa Tamiris; Collections Mgr., Bridget Carlin; Exhibitions Mgr., Stephen Martonis; Outreach Coord., Carrie Olson; Galleries & Administrative Coord., Evan Cantor.
Personnel Profile: Full-Time Paid 4; Part-Time Paid 11; Part-Time Volunteers 8; Interns 7.
Governing Authority: university. Parent Institution: University of Colorado at Boulder. Tax-exempt.
Art Gallery.
Collections: 19th & 20th-century paintings & prints; 15th to 20th-century drawings, watercolors, sculptures & ceramics; 20th-century photographs.
Research Fields: contemporary art.
Facilities: 5,000 sq. ft. exhibit space.
Activities: lectures; participatory, loan, temporary & traveling exhibitions.
Publications: catalogs.
Hours & Admission Prices: Call for information. ♿
Attendance: 20,000 (accurate)

CU HERITAGE CENTER, (M), University of Colorado, Boulder Campus, 3rd Fl. Old Main, Boulder, CO 80302. Mailing Address: Campus Box 459, Boulder, CO 80309-0001. Tel.: 303-492-6329. Fax: 303-492-1244.
E-mail: kay.oltmans@cufund.org
Web Site: cuheritage.org
Founded: 1985.
Congressional District: 2
Key Personnel: Dir., Kay Oltmans; Asst. Dir., Allyson Smith.
Personnel Profile: Part-Time Paid 2; Part-Time Volunteers 10; Interns 1.
Governing Authority: university; nonprofit. Parent Institution: University of Colorado Foundation. Tax-exempt: 501(c)(3).
History Museum: first campus building opened in 1876, housed the president & his family, classrooms, library & chapel.
Collections: photographs, trophies, books, furniture, clothing & uniforms; artifacts from the university's 13 astronauts, distinguished alumni & presidents; buffalo collection, space exploration & sports-related artifacts; campus architecture exhibits; Glenn Miller's gold records.
Research Fields: university history.
Facilities: conference room.
Activities: guided tours; docent program; lectures; reunions; receptions; events.
Hours & Admission Prices: Mon.-Fri. 10-4. No charge. Closed New Year's Day; Memorial Day; Thanksgiving; Christmas; university holidays. ♿
Attendance: 21,600 (estimated)

LEANIN' TREE MUSEUM OF WESTERN ART, (M), 6055 Longbow Dr., Boulder, CO 80301-3296. Mailing Address: Box 9500, Boulder, CO 80301-9500. Tel.: 303-530-1442; 800-777-8716.
E-mail: artmuseum@leanintree.com
Web Site: www.leanintreemuseum.com
Founded: 1974.
Congressional District: 2
Key Personnel: C.E.O. & Pres., Thomas E. Trumble; Dir. & Chm., Edward P. Trumble.
Personnel Profile: Full-Time Paid 3; Part-Time Paid 6.
Governing Authority: company organized for profit. Parent Institution: Leanin' Tree, Inc., 6055 Longbow Dr., Boulder, CO 80301.
Art Museum of the American West.
Collections: contemporary & deceased masters, Western cowboy & Indian art; 85 Western bronze sculptures; 300 paintings.
Facilities: Gift items & paper products for sale.
Activities: guided & self-guided tours; permanent & temporary exhibits.
Publications: souvenir book, Leanin' Tree Museum of Western Art.
Hours & Admission Prices: Mon.-Fri. 8-5, Sat.-Sun. 10-5. No charge. Closed national holidays. ♿
Attendance: 50,000 (accurate)

SHELBY AMERICAN COLLECTION, 5020 Chaparral Ct., Boulder, CO 80301-3351. Mailing Address: P.O. Box 19228, Boulder, CO 80308-2228. Tel.: 303-516-9565. Fax: 303-447-1380.
Web Site: www.carollshelby.com
Founded: 1996.
Key Personnel: C.E.O., Steven B. Volk; Archivist, Dave Murray.
Governing Authority: private; nonprofit organization.
Automotive Museum.
Collections: race cars manufactured by Carroll Shelby from 1962-1967; Shelby Cobras; Ford GT 40s; Shelby Mustang GT 350s.
Facilities: 2,000-vol. library of automotive books; 10,000 sq. ft. exhibit space; 25-seat large screen theater. Museum-related items for sale.
Activities: guided tours. Museum Sponsors: annual fundraiser with Carroll Shelby in December.
Hours & Admission Prices: Sat. 10-4; groups & clubs by appointment. Adults $5; children 12 & under no charge. ♿
Attendance: 3,000 (estimated)

*** UNIVERSITY OF COLORADO MUSEUM OF NATURAL HISTORY, (M),** Broadway, between 15th & 16th St., Boulder, CO 80309-0001. Mailing Address: 218 UCB, Boulder, CO 80309-5002. Tel.: 303-492-6892 & 6297. Fax: 303-492-4195.
E-mail: cumuseum@colorado.edu
Web Site: cumuseum.colorado.edu
Founded: 1902.
Congressional District: 2
Key Personnel: Dir. & Prof. Biology, Pat Kociolek; Prof. Emeritus Anthropology, Linda S. Cordell; Cur. Museography & Prof. Emeritus, John R. Rohner; Collections Mgr. Botany, Tim Hogan; Collections Mgr. Botany, Nan Lederer; Cur. & Prof. Anthropology, Stephen Lekson; Cur. Botany Emeritus, William A. Weber; Cur. Entomology & Prof. Biology, M. Deane Bowers; Collections Mgr. Entomology, Virginia Scott; Cur. Invertebrate Paleontology & Assoc. Prof. Geological Sciences, Dena Smith; Assoc. Prof. Emeritus, Natural History, Judith A. Harris; Cur. Paleontology & Assoc. Prof. Geological Sciences, Karen Chin; Cur. Paleontology & Asst. Prof., Jaelyn Eberle; Cur. Zoology Emeritus, Shi-Kuei Wu; Collections Mgr. Zoology, Mariko Kageyama; Cur. Invertebrate Zoology & Assoc. Prof Biology, Robert Guralnick; Cur. Vvertebrate Zoology & Asst. Prof. Biology, Christy McCain; Coord. Exhibits, Charles Counter; Exhibits Technician, William Moats; Asst. Dir., Jim S. H. Hakala; Coord. Public Programs, Dulce Aldama; Museum & Field Studies Graduate Program Coord., Kathy Freeman; Bldg. Coord., Kory Katsimpalis; Admin. & Museum Store Mgr., Susan S. Reinke; Asst. to Dir., Susanna Drogsvold; Information Coord., Tara Hess; Collection Mgr. Anthropolgy, Christina Cain; Collection Mgr. Invertebrate Paleontology, Kathy Hollis; Collection Mgr. Vertebrate Paleontology, Toni Culver.
Personnel Profile: Full-Time Paid 12; Part-Time Paid 12; Part-Time Volunteers 80.
Governing Authority: state; university. Parent Institution: University of Colorado. Tax-exempt: 170(b)(1)(A).
Natural History & Anthropology Museum.
Collections: Native American textiles; U.S. Southwestern archeology; Colorado insects, especially butterflies & bees; Colorado mammals, birds; vertebrate and invertebrate fossils. Artic, Alpine, Colorado & Western U.S. plants.
Research Fields: anthropology; archaeology; ethnology; botany; lichenology; malacology; bryology; floristics; geology; vertebrate & invertebrate paleoecology; zoology; mammalogy; herpetology; paleontology; entomology.
Facilities: research labs.
Activities: lectures; formally organized education programs for undergraduate & graduate students affiliated with University of Colorado; Master's program in museum & field studies; education outreach kits; pamphlets; field trips; inter-museum loan; continuing, temporary & traveling exhibitions; K-12 guided tours; teacher & adult workshops; family programs.
Publications: episodic, Natural History Guides; Natural History Inventories of Colorado; leaflets; newsletter.
Hours & Admission Prices: Mon.-Fri. 9-5, Sat. 9-4, Sun. 10-4. No charge; donations accepted. Closed university holidays; New Year's Day; Easter; Independence Day; Thanksgiving; Christmas. ♿
Attendance: 25,600 (estimated)
Membership: Student $10; Educator $20; Individual $25; Family $45; Sponsoring $100; Sustaining $250; Curator's Circle $500; Director's Circle $1,000.

Breckenridge

BARNEY FORD HOUSE MUSEUM, 111 E. Washington Ave., Breckenridge, CO 80424. Mailing Address: P.O. Box 2460, Breckenridge, CO 80424-2460. Tel.: 800-980-1859.
Historic House: former home of Barney L. Ford, an escaped slave who became a prominent entrepreneur and Black civil rights pioneer in Colorado; built in 1882.
Collections: family history; period furnishings.
Hours & Admission Prices: Daily 11-4.

EDWIN CARTER MUSEUM, 111 N. Ridge St., Breckenridge, CO 80424-8830. Mailing Address: P.O. Box 2460, Breckenridge, CO 80424. Tel.: 800-980-1859.
Historic House Museum: housed in the former home of Edwin Carter.
Collections: local history & culture; personal artifacts.
Hours & Admission Prices: Call for hours.

MOUNTAIN TOP CHILDREN'S MUSEUM, 605 S. Park Ave., Breckenridge, CO 80424. Mailing Address: P.O. Box 4359, Breckenridge, CO 80424-4359. Tel.: 970-453-7878.
E-mail: mtntopmuseum@aol.com
Web Site: www.mtntopmuseum.org
Founded: 2002.
Key Personnel: Exec. Dir., Laura Horvath.
Governing Authority: nonprofit organization. Tax-exempt: 501(c)(3).
Children's Museum.
Collections: hands-on exhibits.
Facilities: Museum-related items for sale.
Activities: rental facilities; day camp; outreach programs; birthday parties.
Hours & Admission Prices: April 20-May 18 & Sept. 4-Dec. 12 Fri.-Mon. 10-4:30; Dec. 12-April 20 daily 10-4:30. Children $7, adults $5; children under one & seniors no charge. Closed New Year's Eve & Day; Christmas Eve, Day & week. ♿
Attendance: 10,000 (accurate)

SUMMIT HISTORICAL SOCIETY, 111 N. Ridge St., Breckenridge, CO 80424. Mailing Address: P.O. Box 745, Breckenridge, CO 80424-0745. Tel.: 970-453-9022.
E-mail: mail@summithistorical.org
Web Site: www.summithistorical.org
Founded: 1966.
Congressional District: 13
Key Personnel: Pres. (V), Pete Peterson; Vice Pres., Terry Merrick; Treas., Charles Bond; Sec., Jane Young.
Personnel Profile: Part-Time Paid 3; Part-Time Volunteers 40.
Governing Authority: society; nonprofit. Branch Office: Edwin Carter Museum, 111 N. Ridge St., Breckenridge, CO 80424; Dillon Schoolhouse Museum, 403 LaBonte, Dillon, CO 80435. Tel.: 303-453-9022; Main St. Museum, 111 S. Main St., Breckenridge, CO 80424. Tax-exempt.
Historical Society Museums: 1870 Cabin - Edwin Carter Museum, 1883 Dillon School House & 1885 Lula Myers Cabin & 1936 honeymoon cabin.
Collections: furnishings from old Dillon, Breckenridge, Frisco, Montezuma & Kokomo schools; old domestic furnishings; Victorian parlor; 19th-century general store; blacksmith shop with original tools; taxidermy; photographs; W.W. Boyd artistic & corrective horseshoes. Historic Structures: 1883 Dillon Schoolhouse, Dillon; 1936 Slate Creek Hall, Slate Creek; 1896 William Harrison Briggle House Museum, Breckenridge; 1880 Alice G. Milne House, Breckenridge; 1880 Washington mine, Breckenridge; 1900 Gold Dredge Boat, Breckenridge; 1884 Montezuma Schoolhouse, Montezuma; 1885 Lula Myers Cabin, Dillon; 1930s Honeymoon Cabin, Dillon; Rice Born, Dillon Co., Barney Ford House Museum; Breckenridge, Silverthorne Museum, Silverhorne.
Research Fields: local history.
Facilities: 200-vol. library of books & manuscripts relating to local history available for use on the premises only. Books & other museum-related items for sale.
Activities: guided tours; library; temporary exhibitions.
Publications: annual, Newsletter; books, A History of Montezuma, Sts. John & Argentine; The Blue River Valley Wonderland; Southern Summit; Roadside Summit; Summit County's High Altitude Cookbook; Memoirs of Montezuma; Friends in Feathers and Fur; Roadside Summit II; A Strew of Wonder; Dillon, Denver & The Dam; Small Spectaculars; Men, Mining & Machines; Stalking the Wild Flower.
Hours & Admission Prices: Guided Tours: June-Sept. daily 10-7; Oct.-May call for hours. Tours: $3 per person. ♿
Attendance: 33,000 (accurate)
Membership: Individual $25; Family $45, Sponsor $100, Patron $250, Historian $500.

Brighton

ADAMS COUNTY HISTORICAL SOCIETY MUSEUM, 9601 Henderson Rd., Brighton, CO 80601-8127. Tel.: 303-659-7103. Fax: 303-659-7988.
Founded: 1987.
Congressional District: 4
Key Personnel: Pres., Mel Bacon; Admin., Dixie Pierce; Sec., Casey Hayes; Treas., Richard Hoffman.
Personnel Profile: Part-Time Paid 3; Part-Time Volunteers 150; Interns 3.
Governing Authority: society; nonprofit. Parent Institution: Adams County Historical Society. Tax-exempt: 501(c)(3).
Historical Society Museum.
Collections: prehistoric life & geology; Native American periods up to 1850; mountain men & explorers, 1820-1840; early western settlement, 1840-1902; Adams County; World War I; earth science; blacksmith shop; newspapers 1892-1936; Japanese inspired garden; period equipment. Historic Structures: 1930s era Conoco gas station; 1920s one room schoolhouse; 1887 Victorian House; 1930 red caboose.
Facilities: 50-vol. library of art & art related books; 8,000 sq. ft. exhibit space. Books, note cards, earth science & other museum-related items for sale.
Activities: guided tours by appointment; temporary & traveling exhibitions; school tour service; craft shows. Museum Sponsors: book sale in February; Mother's Day Tea in May; Family Hertiage Day in September; Plowboy Poetry Gathering; Moonlight Gala in October; Christmas Tea in December.
Publications: quarterly newsletter, Hi-Story News; craft show flyers; brochures.
Hours & Admission Prices: Jan. 3-Dec. 21 Tues.-Sat. 10-4. No charge; donations accepted. Closed Independence Day; Thanksgiving. ♿
Attendance: 9,000 (accurate)
Membership: Individual $15; Family $25; Supporting $35; Supporting Business $100; Corporation $150; Life & Life Plus $500.

Broomfield

BROOMFIELD DEPOT MUSEUM, 2201 W. 10th Ave., Broomfield, CO 80020-6713. Mailing Address: 212 Agate Way, Broomfield, CO 80020-2312. Tel.: 303-466-3663.
History Museum.
Collections: Broomfield's history; photographs; personal artifacts; railroad artifacts & history.
Activities: school tours.
Hours & Admission Prices: Sun. 2-4. Closed holidays.

BROOMFIELD VETERANS MEMORIAL MUSEUM, 12 Garden Center, Ste. 230, Broomfield, CO 80020-7036. Tel.: 303-460-6801.
Founded: 2003.
Military Museum.
Collections: military history; war memorabilia; photographs; uniforms; personal artifacts.
Hours & Admission Prices: Tues. 7pm-9pm, Sat. 1-4; other times by appointment.

Brush

BRUSH AREA MUSEUM AND CULTURAL CENTER, 314 S. Clayton, Brush, CO 80723. Mailing Address: P.O. Box 341, Brush, CO 80723-0341. Tel.: 970-842-9879.
E-mail: engineer@kci.net
History Museum: housed in the former Knearl School building; built in 1910.
Collections: local history & culture; photographs; period furnishings; personal artifacts.
Activities: hands-on exhibits; educational programs; permanent & temporary exhibits.
Hours & Admission Prices: Fri.-Sat. 10-4, Sun. 1-4; other times by appointment.
Membership: Single $10; Family $25; Small Business $50; Corporate $100.

Buena Vista

BUENA VISTA HERITAGE MUSEUM, 506 E. Main St., Buena Vista, CO 81211. Mailing Address: P.O. Box 1414, Buena Vista, CO 81211-1414. Tel.: 719-395-8458.
E-mail: buenavistaheritage@msn.com
Web Site: www.buenavistaheritage.org
Founded: 1974.
Personnel Profile: Full-Time Paid 1; Part-Time Paid 2.
History Museum.
Collections: personal artifacts; clothing; furniture; rocks & minerals; schoolroom; period artifacts.
Hours & Admission Prices: Memorial Day to Sept. 10-5. Adults $5; members no charge. ♿
Attendance: 3,500 (accurate)
Membership: Individual $20; Family $30; Business $100; Corporate $250.

Burlington

OLD TOWN MUSEUM, 420 S. 14th St., Burlington, CO 80807-2300. Tel.: 719-346-7382; 800-288-1334.
E-mail: oldtown@plains.net
History Museum.
Collections: period furnishings & equipment; books; photographs; dolls; saddles; tools; printing press; Native American artifacts. Old Town Buildings: barn; depot, c.1889; law office; bank; barber shop; cream station; general store; blacksmith shop, built late 1800s; caretakers house; sod house; school house, c.1911; church, c.1921; doll house; manor house, built early 1900s; drug store; leather shop; wood shop; jail house; The Longhorn Saloon; The Burlington Blade; Heritage Hall.
Activities: special events.

Hours & Admission Prices: Mon.-Sat. 9-5, Sun. 12-5.

Canon City

DINOSAUR DEPOT MUSEUM, (M), 330 Royal Gorge Blvd., Canon City, CO 81212-6739. Mailing Address: 330 Royal Gorge Blvd. #A, Canon City, CO 81212-6740. Tel.: 719-269-7150. Fax: 719-269-7227.
E-mail: office@dinosaurdepot.com
Web Site: www.dinosaurdepot.com
Founded: 1995.
Congressional District: 5
Key Personnel: Exec. Dir., Jon P. Stone.
Personnel Profile: Full-Time Paid 3; Full-Time Volunteers 1; Part-Time Volunteers 55.
Governing Authority: private; nonprofit organization. Parent Institution: Garden Park Paleontology Society. Tax-exempt: 501(c)(3).
Paleontology Museum.
Collections: Garden Park Fossil Area discoveries; fossils; rocks; minerals; tools & equipment.
Research Fields: Garden Park Fossil area; historical quarry mapping.
Facilities: 700-vol. library of geology & paleontology books; 4,000 sq. ft. exhibit space; classrooms. Museum-related items for sale.
Activities: docent program; formal education programs; guided tours; school loan service; temporary & traveling exhibitions; paleontology field training program.
Publications: bimonthly newsletter, Tracks in Time.
Hours & Admission Prices: Memorial Day to Labor Day daily 9-5; Winter: Wed.-Sun. 10-4. Adults $4, children $2; members no charge. Closed New Year's Day; Thanksgiving; Christmas. ♿
Attendance: 20,000 (accurate)
Membership: Student $5; Senior Citizens $7.50; Individual $15; Family $25; Supporting $100; Patron $250; Benefactor $500.

MUSEUM OF COLORADO PRISONS, 201 N. 1st St., Canon City, CO 81212-3219. Tel.: 719-269-3015. Fax: 719-269-9148.
E-mail: museumprisons@aol.com
Web Site: www.prisonmuseum.org
Founded: 1987.
Congressional District: 5
Key Personnel: Dir., M. Kay Ellison; Cur., Pat Kant
Prison Museum.
Collections: Colorado Corrections history; hangman's noose used for last execution; confiscated inmate weapons & contraband; gas chamber; photographs.
Facilities: Museum-related items for sale.
Activities: Annual Event: Ghost Walk in May to September.
Publications: quarterly newsletter.
Hours & Admission Prices: May & Sept. to mid-Oct. daily 10-5; Memorial Day to Labor Day daily 8:30-6; mid-Oct. to April Wed.-Sun. 10-5; other times by appointment. Adults $7, seniors 65 & over $6, youth 6-12 $5; discounts to AAA members, Dept. of Corrections & active military. Closed New Year's Day; Easter; Thanksgiving; Christmas. ♿
Attendance: 15,000 (accurate)
Membership: Individual $30; Family $50; Sustaining $100; Benefactor $250; Corporate $500.

ROYAL GORGE REGIONAL MUSEUM & HISTORY CENTER, 612 Royal Gorge Blvd., Canon City, CO 81212-3751. Mailing Address: P.O. Box 1460, Canon City, CO 81215-1460. Tel.: 719-269-9036.
E-mail: historycenter@canoncity.org
Web Site: www.royalgorgehistory.org
Formerly: Canon City Municipal Museum
Founded: 1928.
Congressional District: 3
Key Personnel: Dir., Susan Ooton; Archivist & Cur., Cliff Hight.
Personnel Profile: Full-Time Paid 4; Part-Time Paid 1; Part-Time Volunteers 15.
Governing Authority: municipal. Parent Institution: City of Canon City. Tax-exempt.
History Museum.
Collections: material & natural history of the Fremont County region; textiles; decorative arts, guns, fossils; minerals. Historic Buildings: 1927 building; 1880s house; 1860s cabin.
Research Fields: local history; genealogy; labor history; environmental history.
Activities: permanent & loan exhibitions.
Publications: brochure; newsletter.
Hours & Admission Prices: Wed.-Sat. 10-4. No charge; donations accepted. Closed major holidays. ♿

Carbondale

MT. SOPRIS HISTORICAL MUSEUM, 499 Weant Blvd., Carbondale, CO 81623. Mailing Address: P.O. Box 2, Carbondale, CO 81623-0002. Tel.: 970-963-7041.
History Museum: housed in a cabin built by homesteaders in the late 1800s.
Collections: local history & culture; Native American artifacts; photographs; personal artifacts.
Facilities: library.
Activities: research; special events.
Hours & Admission Prices: Call for hours.

Centennial

B'S BALLPARK MUSEUM, (M), 8611 E. Otero Place, Centennial, CO 80112-3317. Mailing Address: 3600 S. Yosemite St., Ste. 600, Denver, CO 80237. Tel.: 720-351-0665. Fax: 303-694-1462.
Founded: 1999.
Key Personnel: Dir. & Pres., Bruce S. Hellerstein.
Governing Authority: private; nonprofit organization. Tax-exempt: 501(c)(3).
Baseball Ballpark Museum.
Collections: stadium seats; signs; postcards; stadium artifacts; bricks; lithographs.
Facilities: 100-vol. library; 600 sq. ft. exhibit space.
Activities: films; guided tours; lectures.
Hours & Admission Prices: Sat. 9-5, Sun. 9-1. Adults $5, senior citizens & children under 11 $2.
Attendance: 400 (estimated)

Central City

CENTRAL CITY OPERA HOUSE ASSOCIATION, 124 Eureka St., Central City, CO 80427. Mailing Address: 400 S. Colorado Blvd., Ste. 530, Denver, CO 80246-1253. Tel.: 303-292-6500. Fax: 303-292-4958.
E-mail: marketing@centralcityopera.org
Web Site: www.centralcityopera.org
Founded: 1932.
Congressional District: 4
Key Personnel: Chm. Bd., Jeannie Fuller; Pres. Bd., J. Landis Martin; Gen. Dir., Pelham G. Pearce; Artistic Dir. Emeritus, John Moriarty.
Personnel Profile: Full-Time Paid 18.
Governing Authority: nonprofit organization. Tax-exempt.
Historic Opera House & Teller House Hotel Museum; built in 1878. A National Historic Landmark.
Collections: over 30 Victorian era properties; restored parlours & rooms, Victorian era Hotel. Historical Buildings: 1878 Opera House; 1872 Teller House; 1876 Williams Stable; 1863 Medical Building; 1869 Weckbaugh House; 1884 McFarlane House.
Research Fields: early theater & western Americana.
Facilities: theatre. Museum-related gifts for sale.
Activities: summer opera festival; guided tours; lectures; arts festivals; permanent exhibitions. Annual Event: Summer Festival June to August.
Publications: Central City Opera High Notes; Central City Opera Season Program.
Hours & Admission Prices: Opera Tickets $45-$99. Closed major holidays. ♿
Attendance: 28,000
Membership: Associates $100; Patron's Circle $500; Artist's Circle $1,000; Conductor's Circle $2,500; Director's Circle $5,000; President's Circle $10,000; Chairman's Circle $25,000; Eureka Circle $50,000; Guarantor $75,000; Grand Guarantor $100,000 & up.

GILPIN HISTORY MUSEUM, 228 E. High St., Central City, CO 80427. Mailing Address: P.O. Box 247, Central City, CO 80427-0247. Tel.: 303-582-5283.
Web Site: www.gilpinhistory.org
Founded: 1971.
Congressional District: 4
Key Personnel: Exec. Dir., James Prochaska.
Personnel Profile: Part-Time Paid 1; Part-Time Volunteers 5.
Governing Authority: society; nonprofit. Affiliated with Gilpin County Historical Society. Branch Museum: The Thomas House. Tax-exempt: 501(c)(3).
Historical Society Museum: housed in c.1870 Gilpin County Public School.
Collections: personal items, furniture and tools of pioneers and early residents of Gilpin county; living room; parlor; kitchen; school room; clothing fashions; general store; carriage collection; dolls; doctors office; pharmacy; law office; bank display; assay office; barber shop; sheriffs office; saloon; tools; mineral exhibits; fire fighting equipment; maps and photos of the railroad and tram; fraternal organizations badges and paraphernalia; opera house. Historic Buildings: 1870 2-story stone school; 1874 Greek Revival house; mine shaft building.
Research Fields: Gilpin county cemeteries; genealogy; mining.

Activities: guided tours; permanent exhibitions.
Publications: brochure, History of Building and Society; Mining Gold to Mining Wallets: Central City 1854-1999; Little Kingdom of Gilpin.
Hours & Admission Prices: Memorial Day to Labor Day daily 11-4. Adults $5; discounts to AAM members; senior citizens, children under 12 & members no charge.
Attendance: 1,200 (accurate)
Membership: Individual $20; Family $35; Patron $50; Business Associate $100.

Clark

HAHNS PEAK AREA HISTORICAL SOCIETY AND SCHOOL HOUSE, General Delivery, Hahns Peak Village, Clark, CO 80428-9999. Mailing Address: P.O. Box 803, Clark, CO 80428-0803. Tel.: 970-879-7291.
Founded: 1972.
Congressional District: 4
Key Personnel: Pres. (V) & Cur., Marge Eardley; Vice Pres., Tim Wright; Vice Pres., Dean Moss; Treas., LeeLee Wright.
Governing Authority: nonprofit organization. Parent Institution: Hahns Peak Area Historical Society. Tax-exempt: 501(c)(3).
History Museum: located on the site of the first permanent settlement in Routt County & N.W. Colorado.
Collections: school furnishing including desks; piano; books; mining artifacts; furniture. Historic Buildings: schoolhouse; Wither cabin.
Research Fields: local history; mining methods; wildlife & native plants.
Facilities: 100-vol. library of original school texts & local history books & papers to be used on premises.
Activities: lectures; films.
Publications: book, Historic Hahns Peak.
Hours & Admission Prices: June-Sept. daily 12-4. No charge; donations accepted.
Attendance: 1,000
Membership: Annual $5; Life $100.

Colorado Springs

AIR FORCE ACADEMY CHAPEL AND VISITORS CENTER, 2346 Academy Dr., Colorado Springs, CO 80840-9401. Tel.: 719-333-2025.
Chapel & Visitors Center.
Collections: religious artifacts; paintings; 4,334 pipe organ.
Facilities: visitor center; chapel.
Activities: worship services for the needs of all faiths; self-guided tours.
Hours & Admission Prices: Tours: Mon.-Sat. 9-5. Call for religious worship services. ♿

AMERICAN NUMISMATIC ASSOCIATION MONEY MUSEUM, 818 N. Cascade Ave., Colorado Springs, CO 80903-3279. Tel.: 719-632-2646. Fax: 719-634-4085.
E-mail: museum@money.org
Web Site: www.money.org
Formerly: Museum of the American Numismatic Association
Founded: 1967.
Congressional District: 5
Key Personnel: Exec. Dir., Larry Shepherd; Pres., Barry Stuppler; Sr. Administrative Mgr. & Membership Operations, Kim Kiick; Museum Dir., Tiffanie Bueschel; Controller, Carol Shuman; Treas., Austin M. Sheheen, Jr.; Cur., Douglas Mudd; Dir. Mktg. & Public Rels., Jay Beeton; Mgr. Library, RyAnn Scott.
Personnel Profile: Full-Time Paid 34; Part-Time Paid 1; Part-Time Volunteers 9; Interns 1.
Governing Authority: private; nonprofit organization. Parent Institution: American Numismatic Association. Tax-exempt: 501(c)(3).
Numismatic Museum.
Collections: coins, medals, tokens, paper money and related materials from c.700 B.C.
Research Fields: numismatics.
Facilities: 50,000-vol. library of numismatic books & tapes; 5,000 sq. ft. exhibit space. Museum-related items for sale.
Activities: hobby workshops; lectures; participatory, loan, temporary & traveling exhibitions; training programs for professional museum workers. Annual Events: summer & early spring conventions; summer seminars.
Publications: monthly magazine, The Numismatist; ANA journal.
Hours & Admission Prices: Tues.-Fri. 9-5, Sat. 10-5, Sun. 12-5; groups by appointment. Adults $5, seniors, active military & students $4; discounts to groups; members no charge. Closed federal holidays. ♿
Attendance: 23,000 (accurate)
Membership: Junior $26; Senior $41; Regular $46.

CHEYENNE MOUNTAIN ZOOLOGICAL PARK, 4250 Cheyenne Mountain Zoo Rd., Colorado Springs, CO 80906-5755. Tel.: 719-633-9925. Fax: 719-633-2254.
E-mail: info@cmzoo.org
Web Site: www.cmzoo.org
Founded: 1926.
Congressional District: 5
Key Personnel: Chm., Kevin Kratt; Pres. & C.E.O., Bob Chastain; Exec. Asst., Holly Ray; General Cur., Tracy Leeds; Registrar, Randy Barker; Cur. Education, Nicole Mantz; Cur. Horticulture, Frank Haas; Dir. Conservation, Animal Health & Staff Veterinarian, Dr. Della Garelle; Vice Pres. Devel. & Financial Growth, Tracey Gazibara; Public Rels. & Special Events Mgr., Sean Anglum; Mgr. Operations, Ed Bedford; Dir. Mktg., Diane Loschen; Guest Svcs. Mgr., Jane Majeske; Museum Shop Mgr., Todd Langfield.
Personnel Profile: Full-Time Paid 69; Part-Time Paid 34; Part-Time Volunteers 200; Interns 5.
Governing Authority: society. Parent Institution: Cheyenne Mountain Zoological Society. Tax-exempt: 501(c)(3).
Zoo.
Collections: mammals; birds; reptiles; amphibians; breeding herd of reticulated giraffe; breeding colony of orangutan; felines & hoofed mammals; tram; period carousel.
Research Fields: animal reproduction.
Facilities: 150-seat education center. Gift items for sale.
Activities: guided tours; films; formally organized education programs for children; docent program or council; permanent exhibitions; sky ride.
Publications: Cheyenne Mountain Zoological Park Annual Report; quarterly newsletter.
Hours & Admission Prices: Memorial Day to Labor Day: daily 9-6; Sept.-May daily 9-5. Adults 12-64 $14.25, seniors 65 & over $12.25, children 3-11 $7.25; discounts to AZA & AAA members & military; members & children 2 & under no charge. ♿
Attendance: 468,039 (accurate)
Membership: Individual Plus $58.25; Family & Grandparent $82.50; Family Plus $102.50; Contributing $152.50; Conservator $252.50; Patron $502.50; Patron Gold $1,002.50.

* **COLORADO SPRINGS FINE ARTS CENTER (TAYLOR MUSEUM), (M),** 30 W. Dale St., Colorado Springs, CO 80903-3210. Tel.: 719-634-5581. Fax: 719-634-0570.
E-mail: info@csfineartscenter.org
Web Site: www.csfineartscenter.org
Founded: 1936.
Congressional District: 5
Key Personnel: Interim Pres. & C.E.O., Shawn Raintree; Exec. Asst., Kendall Kullman; Dir. Facilities, Charlie Hagen; Information Technology Specialist, John Trujillo; Dir. Devel., Susan Weisgerber; Exhibition Preparator, Laurel Swab; Dir. Bemis School of Art, Tara Thomas; Dir. Membership, Angie Weddle; Museum Shop Mgr., Naoma Ingo; Dir. Mktg. & Public Rels., Charlie Snyder; Chief of Security, Dan Puhtila; Graphic Designer, Serena Wolford; Accountant, Nikki Simmons.
Personnel Profile: Full-Time Paid 46; Part-Time Paid 85; Part-Time Volunteers 225.
Governing Authority: nonprofit organization. Parent Institution: Colorado Springs Fine Arts Center. Subsidiary Institution: Taylor Museum; FAC Modern, 121 S. Tejon St., Ste. 100, Colorado Springs, CO. Tax-exempt: 501(c)(3).
Art Museum.
Collections: historic & contemporary art & material culture of the Southwest United States including major Hispanic & Native American collections; 20th-century American & contemporary art.
Research Fields: art & culture of the Southwest United States; 20th century American & contemporary art.
Facilities: 450-seat theater; 48,000 sq. ft. exhibit space; classrooms; sculpture courtyard; art school; 140-seat recital room; conference facilities; restaurant. Museum-related items for sale.
Activities: docent tours; lectures; films; gallery talks; art classes; performing arts programming; inter-museum loan; permanent, temporary & traveling exhibitions; repertory theatre company.
Publications: Artsfocus; exhibition catalogs; scholarly publications on Southwest studies; annual report.
Hours & Admission Prices: Tues.-Fri. & Sun. 10-5, Sat. 10-8. Adults $12; discounts to members. Closed federal holidays. ♿
Attendance: 200,000 (estimated)
Membership: Individual $45; Dual $55; Family $60; Contributing $110.

COLORADO SPRINGS MUSEUM, 215 S. Tejon St., Colorado Springs, CO 80903-2206. Tel.: 719-385-5990. Fax: 719-385-5645.
E-mail: cosmuseum@springsgov.com
Web Site: www.cspm.org

Founded: 1937.
Congressional District: 5
Key Personnel: Dir., Matt Mayberry; Chm. (V), Kathie Walker; Archivist, Leah Davis Witherow; Cur. & Registrar, David Ryan; Museum Shop Mgr., Carol Denning.
Personnel Profile: Full-Time Paid 6; Part-Time Paid 2; Part-Time Volunteers 190; Interns 3.
Governing Authority: city. Tax-exempt.
History Museum: housed in the former El Paso County Courthouse, 1903.
Collections: history & culture of the Pikes Peak region; period artifacts; Van Briggle art pottery; regional art; Native American artifacts; mining & agricultural history.
Research Fields: regional history & art.
Facilities: 200-seat auditorium; meeting rooms.
Activities: guided & self-guided tours; permanent & temporary exhibits; lecture series; special events.
Publications: quarterly newsletter; gallery guides; educational materials; pamphlets; monographs.
Hours & Admission Prices: Tues.-Sat. 10-4. No charge; donations accepted. Closed holidays; Thanksgiving week. ♿
Attendance: 55,818 (accurate)
Membership: Senior $15; Individual $25; Family $30; Sustaining $50; Business $250; Life $1,000.

DR. LESTER L. WILLIAMS FIRE MUSEUM, 375 Printers Pkwy., Colorado Springs, CO 80901. Mailing Address: P.O. Box 119, Colorado Springs, CO 80901-0119. Tel.: 719-385-5950.
History Museum.
Collections: fire memorabilia; firefighting history; personal artifacts; photographs.
Publications: newsletter.
Hours & Admission Prices: Mon.-Fri. 8-5.

EL POMAR FOUNDATION CARRIAGE MUSEUM, 10 Lake Cir., Colorado Springs, CO 80906-4201.
Web Site: elpomar.org
Founded: 1941.
Key Personnel: C.E.O., Robert J. Hilbert; Cur., Jason J. Campbell.
Personnel Profile: Full-Time Paid 1; Part-Time Paid 2.
Governing Authority: nonprofit. Parent Institution: El Pomar Foundation. Tax-exempt.
Transportation Museum.
Collections: period carriages; covered wagons; stage coaches.
Hours & Admission Prices: Mon.-Sat. 9-5, Sun. 1-5. No charge. Closed New Year's Day; Easter; Thanksgiving; Christmas. ♿
Attendance: 6,800 (estimated)

GALLERY OF CONTEMPORARY ART, UNIVERSITY OF COLORADO, COLORADO SPRINGS, 1420 Austin Bluffs Pkwy., Colorado Springs, CO 80918-3733. Mailing Address: P.O. Box 7150, Colorado Springs, CO 80933-7150. Tel.: 719-255-3567. Fax: 719-262-3183. TDD: 262-3621.
E-mail: gallery@uccs.edu
Web Site: www.galleryuccs.org
Founded: 1981.
Congressional District: 5
Key Personnel: Interim Dir., Caitlin Green.
Personnel Profile: Full-Time Paid 1; Part-Time Paid 3; Part-Time Volunteers 2; Interns 2.
Governing Authority: university. Parent Institution: University of Colorado. Tax-exempt: 501(c)(3); 170(b)(A).
Art Museum & Center.
Collections: works by contemporary artists.
Research Fields: contemporary art; art history.
Facilities: classrooms.
Activities: guided tours; lectures; concerts; educational programs; docent program; education programs for undergraduate college students affiliated with University of Colorado; training programs for professional museum workers; museum studies; group exhibitions with a specific theme or medium; loan & traveling exhibitions.
Hours & Admission Prices: Tues.-Fri. 12-6; other times by appointment. No charge; donations accepted. Closed major holidays. ♿
Attendance: 28,000 (estimated)
Membership: Student & Senior $10; Individual $20; Friend $35-$99; Patron $100-$499; Donor $500-$999; Founder $1,000-$2,499; Benefactor $2,500.

GARDEN OF THE GODS VISITOR & NATURE CENTER, 1805 N. 30th St., Colorado Springs, CO 80904-1247. Tel.: 719-634-6666. Fax: 719-634-0094.
Nature Center.
Collections: hands-on exhibits; local history; geology; plants; wildlife.
Facilities: visitor center; cafe. Museum-related items for sale.
Activities: lectures; special events; scout & school programs; guided tours; picnic area; hiking.
Hours & Admission Prices: Park: May-Oct. daily 5am-11pm; Nov.-April daily 5am-9pm. Visitor Center: Memorial Day to Labor Day daily 8-8; Winter: daily 9-5. No charge.

GHOST TOWN MUSEUM, 400 S. 21st St., Colorado Springs, CO 80904-3755. Tel.: 719-634-0696.
E-mail: history@ghosttownmuseum.com
History Museum.
Collections: old west town history; Colorado heritage; period furnishings; hands-on exhibits; structures.
Facilities: Museum-related items for sale.
Activities: hands-on activities; film.
Hours & Admission Prices: June-Aug. Mon.-Sat. 9-6, Sun. 11-6; Sept.-May Mon.-Sat. 10-5, Sun. 11-5. ♿

MAY NATURAL HISTORY MUSEUM AND MUSEUM OF SPACE EXPLORATION, John May Museum Center, 710 Rock Creek Canyon Rd., Colorado Springs, CO 80926-9799. Tel.: 719-576-0450; 800-666-3841. Fax: 719-576-3644.
E-mail: maymuseum2001@yahoo.com
Web Site: www.maymuseum-camp-rvpark.com
Founded: 1941.
Congressional District: 5
Key Personnel: C.E.O. & Pres. (V), John M. May; Museum Shop Mgr., Louise N. Steer.
Personnel Profile: Full-Time Paid 1; Full-Time Volunteers 1; Part-Time Paid 5; Part-Time Volunteers 2.
Governing Authority: individual operation. Parent Institution: John May Museum Center. Tax-exempt: 501(c)(3) & 509(a)(2).
Natural History, Entomology & Space Exploration Museum.
Collections: entomological specimens; primitive artifacts; geological; space photography; models; NASA films; New Guinea artifacts.
Research Fields: entomology.
Facilities: 250-vol. library of entomology and astronomy; nature center; nature trails. Curios, Indian artifacts & clothing for sale.
Activities: guided tours; permanent exhibitions; hiking; public & private school programs.
Publications: annual brochures.
Hours & Admission Prices: May-Sept. daily 9-6; Oct.-April by appointment. Adults $6, seniors 60 & over $5, children 6-12 $3; discounts to schools, senior citizens & AAA members; children under 6 with family no charge. ♿
Attendance: 30,000 (estimated)

MCALLISTER HOUSE MUSEUM, (M), 423 N. Cascade Ave., Colorado Springs, CO 80903-3391. Tel.: 719-635-7925.
E-mail: curator@mcallisterhouse.org
Web Site: www.mcallisterhouse.org
Founded: 1961.
Congressional District: 5
Key Personnel: Chm., Mary Anne Sehorn; Treas., Barbara Rasmussen; Cur., Karen Lakes.
Personnel Profile: Part-Time Paid 1; Part-Time Volunteers 30.
Governing Authority: society. Parent Institution: The National Society of The Colonial Dames in the State of Colorado. Tax-exempt.
Historic House: c.1873 Major Henry McAllister Home.
Collections: late Victorian era furnishings; Downing Gothic Style Cottage.
Facilities: banquet facilities; limited meeting space.
Activities: guided tours; lecture series. Museum Sponsors: Victorian Ice Cream Social; Victorian Christmas.
Publications: book, Henry McAllister: Colorado Pioneer.
Hours & Admission Prices: Feb.-April & Sept.-Dec. Thurs.-Sat. 10-4; May-Aug. Wed.-Sat. 10-4, Sun. 12-4. Adults $5, seniors, students & members $4, children 6-12 $3; discount to AAM members; children under 6 no charge. Closed major holidays.
Attendance: 3,000 (estimated)
Membership: Individual $15; Family $25; Sponsor $50; Patron $100; Life $500.

OLD COLORADO CITY HISTORICAL SOCIETY, One South 24th St., Colorado Springs, CO 80904-3319. Tel.: 719-636-1225.
E-mail: history@oldcolo.com
Web Site: www.history.oldcolo.com
Congressional District: 5
Key Personnel: Pres., Suzanne Schorsch.
Governing Authority: bd. of directors. Tax-exempt.

Historical Society Museum.
Collections: area history & culture; photographs; personal artifacts.
Research Fields: early El Paso county history & culture.
Facilities: research library. Museum-related items for sale.
Activities: research library; rental facilities; monthly educational programs; tours.
Publications: newsletter, West Word.
Hours & Admission Prices: Tues.-Sat. 11-4. No charge; donations accepted. Closed holidays. ♿
Membership: Single & Student $20; Family $25; Business $50; Life $150.

PRO RODEO HALL OF FAME & MUSEUM OF THE AMERICAN COWBOY, 101 Pro Rodeo Dr., Colorado Springs, CO 80919-2396. Tel.: 719-528-4761. Fax: 719-548-4874.
E-mail: prorodeo@prorodeo.com
Web Site: www.prorodeo.com
Founded: 1979.
Congressional District: 5
Key Personnel: Exec. Dir., Larry McCormack; Museum Shop Mgr., Sammi Snow.
Personnel Profile: Full-Time Paid 8; Part-Time Paid 2.
Governing Authority: nonprofit organization. Tax-exempt: 501(c)(3).
Rodeo & Cowboy History Museum.
Collections: sculptures; paintings; saddles; chaps; ropes; boots; clothing & artifacts tracing history of rodeo 1865-present; memorabilia, trophies & artifacts of champions & notables; buckles; books; periodicals; Wild West show memorabilia; rodeo programs; photographs.
Research Fields: rodeo history; ranching & livestock history.
Facilities: 1,500-vol. library of rodeo records & history available for research on premises; two electronic multi-media theaters; 40,000 sq. ft. exhibit space; garden. Prints & other museum-related items for sale.
Activities: guided tours; lectures; films; loan & permanent exhibitions; demonstrations. Museum Sponsors: Pro Rodeo Week.
Publications: brochures; pamphlets; newsletter.
Hours & Admission Prices: Summer: daily 9-5; Winter: Wed.-Sun. 9-5. Adults $6, seniors $5, children 6-12 $3; discount to groups; members & children 5 & under no charge. Closed New Year's Day; Easter; Thanksgiving; Christmas. ♿
Attendance: 50,000 (estimated)
Membership: Hall of Fame Society: Wrangler $20; Pewter $30; Bronze $50; Silver $100; Gold $500; Platinum $1,000.

ROCK LEDGE RANCH HISTORIC SITE, 30th St. & Gateway Rd., Colorado Springs, CO 80904. Mailing Address: 1401 Recreation Way, Colorado Springs, CO 80905-1024. Tel.: 719-578-6777. Fax: 719-578-6965.
Personnel Profile: Full-Time Paid 2; Part-Time Paid 2; Part-Time Volunteers 50.
Governing Authority: city. Tax-exempt.
Historic Site: listed on the National Register of Historic Places.
Collections: American Indian history; late 1860s homesteading. Historic Houses: 1880 farm house; 1907 estate house.
Facilities: Museum-related items for sale.
Activities: special events; horse drawn equipment demonstrations; musical performances; lectures. Annual Events: Fall Harvest Festival; Holiday Evenings Celebration.
Hours & Admission Prices: June to Labor Day Wed.-Sun. 10-5; Winter: call for special events. Adults $6, seniors 55 & over and students 13-18 $4, youth 6-12 $2; discounts to groups; children under 6 no charge. ♿
Attendance: 65,000 (accurate)
Membership: Senior $10; Senior Couple $15; Individual $20; Family $30; Contributing $50; Supporting $100.

SEVEN FALLS, 2850 S. Cheyenne Canyon Rd., Colorado Springs, CO 80906-2919. Tel.: 719-632-0765. Fax: 719-632-0781.
Natural History Museum.
Collections: local history; wildlife; ecology.
Facilities: nature trails.
Activities: hiking.
Hours & Admission Prices: Day: adults $9, seniors $8, children 6-15 $5.50; children 5 & under no charge. Night: adults $10.50, seniors $9.50, children 6-15 $6.50; children 5 & under no charge.

U.S. OLYMPIC VISITOR CENTER, 1 Olympic Plaza, Colorado Springs, CO 80909. Tel.: 719-632-5551.
Web Site: www.olympic-usa.org
Sports Museum.
Collections: Olympic history; hands-on exhibits; Hall of Fame; photographs.
Facilities: Museum-related items for sale.
Activities: guided tours.
Hours & Admission Prices: Mon.-Sat. 9-6, Sun. 10-5. No change.

* **WESTERN MUSEUM OF MINING & INDUSTRY, (M),** 225 N. Gate Blvd., Colorado Springs, CO 80921-3002. Tel.: 719-488-0880; 800-752-6558. Fax: 719-488-9261.
E-mail: info@wmmi.org
Web Site: www.wmmi.org
Founded: 1970.
Congressional District: 5
Key Personnel: Exec. Dir., David Carroll; Chm. (V), Marriott W. Smart; Museum Shop Mgr., Steve Stanton.
Personnel Profile: Full-Time Paid 5; Part-Time Paid 6; Part-Time Volunteers 82; Interns 1.
Governing Authority: nonprofit. Tax-exempt: 501(c)(3).
Mining & Technology History Museum.
Collections: metal mining & milling machinery; steam, water & electrically powered prime movers; electrical equipment; machine tools; exhibit dealing with western hard rock mining; placer mining & milling; social history of miners, mining districts & art; mine reclamation & environmental science; operating reconstructed stamp mill; locomotives; steeple-compound steam stamp & walking beam engine on outdoor display. Historic House: 19th-century farmhouse & barn; blacksmith shop & hoist house.
Research Fields: metallurgy; industrial archaeology of the American West; mining engineering.
Facilities: 13,000-vol. library of texts, original histories, trade catalogs & serials relating to electrical, mechanical, hydraulic, civil & mine engineering; 15,000 sq. ft. exhibit space; picnic area.
Activities: guided tours; classes; lectures; permanent & temporary exhibitions.
Publications: quarterly newsletter; annual report; catalogue; Mining History & Technology Series Vol. I: A Concise History of Mine Hoisting.
Hours & Admission Prices: Mon.-Sat. 9-4. Adults $8, military $7, seniors 60 & over, children 13-18 $4; discounts to AAM members; children under 3 & members no charge. ♿
Attendance: 54,403 (accurate)
Membership: Individual $30; Dual $40; Family $50; Centennial $100; Silver Medallion $250; Gold Medallion $500; Heritage $1,000.

WORLD FIGURE SKATING MUSEUM & HALL OF FAME, (M), 20 First St., Colorado Springs, CO 80906-3624. Tel.: 719-635-5200. Fax: 719-635-9548.
Web Site: www.worldskatingmuseum.org
Founded: 1965.
Key Personnel: Assoc. Exec. Dir., Kim Fox; Mktg. & Public Rels. Mgr., Linda Famula; Museum Admin. Coord. & Museum Shop Mgr., Karen Cover; Administrative Asst., Angela Terrazas.
Personnel Profile: Full-Time Paid 1; Part-Time Paid 3; Part-Time Volunteers 5.
Governing Authority: nonprofit organization. Parent Institution: U.S. Figure Skating. Tax-exempt: 501(c)(3).
Sports Museum.
Collections: figure skating history from 800 AD to present; skating in art, 16th- to 20th century; prints; films; photographs; video archive; official repository for world amateur figure skating records & memorabilia; costumes; trophies; US & World Hall of Fame.
Major Exhibits: 2009 U.S. Champions, 11/09-1/10.
Research Fields: skating in art as part of European & American cultures; history of the development of the skate blade over 1,200 years; study of U.S., World & Olympic champions & medalists since 1908.
Facilities: library.
Activities: films; guided tours; loan, temporary & traveling exhibitions; special event fundraising. Annual Event: U.S. & World Halls of Fame induction.
Publications: Figure Skating: A History.
Hours & Admission Prices: May-Oct. Mon.-Sat. 10-4; Nov.-April Mon.-Fri. 10-4. Adults $3, children 6-12 & seniors over 60 $2; discounts to military & AAA members; children 5 & under and USFSA members no charge. Closed New Year's Eve & Day; Memorial Day; Independence Day; Labor Day; Thanksgiving; Christmas. ♿
Attendance: 15,000 (estimated)

Cortez

CORTEZ CULTURAL CENTER, 25 N. Market St., Cortez, CO 81321-3212. Tel.: 970-565-1151.
Key Personnel: Exec. Dir., Deb Avery
Native American Museum.
Collections: Native American history, culture & life; personal artifacts; photographs; paintings; mural.
Activities: storytellers; lectures; special events; music & cultural programs. Museum Sponsors: Native American Dances in summer.
Hours & Admission Prices: May & Sept.-Oct. daily 10-6; June-Aug. daily 10-10; Nov.-April daily 10-5. No charge; donations accepted.

CROW CANYON ARCHAEOLOGICAL CENTER, 23390 County Rd. K, Cortez, CO 81321-9408. Tel.: 970-565-8975. Fax: 970-565-4859.
E-mail: gprior@crowcanyon.org
Web Site: www.crowcanyon.org
Founded: 1983.
Key Personnel: C.E.O., Ricky Lightfoot, Ph.D.; Chm. (V), Sue Anschutz-Rodgers.
Personnel Profile: Full-Time Paid 43; Part-Time Paid 5; Part-Time Volunteers 3; Interns 10.
Governing Authority: private; nonprofit organization. Tax-exempt: 501(c)(3).
Archaeological Center.
Collections: archaeological artifacts.
Hours & Admission Prices: March-Oct. Mon.-Fri. 8:30-5. No charge. Day program: June-Aug. adults $50, children $25. ♿
Attendance: 3,000 (estimated)
Membership: Youth under 18 $30; Adult $50; Family $75; Research Assistant $100; Research Fellow $250; Research Benefactor $500. Chairman's Council $1,000; Director's Circle $2,500; President's Circle $5,000.

NOTAH DINEH MUSEUM, 345 W. Main, Cortez, CO 81321-3132. Tel.: 800-444-2024.
E-mail: notah@fone.net
Key Personnel: Owner, Greg Leighton
Native American Museum.
Collections: Navajo rugs; Native American weavings; Native American art including hand carved wooden Kachinas; sculpture; sandpaintings; beaded baskets; cradle boards; moccasins; beadwork; 14k & sterling silver jewelry.
Facilities: Museum-related items for sale.
Hours & Admission Prices: Mon.-Sat. 9-6:30.

Craig

MUSEUM OF NORTHWEST COLORADO, 590 Yampa Ave., Craig, CO 81625-2612. Tel.: 970-824-6360. Fax: 970-824-1098.
Web Site: www.museumnwco.org
Founded: 1964.
Congressional District: 3
Key Personnel: Dir., Dan Davidson; Pres. (V), Delaine Voloshin; Asst. Dir., Jan Gerber.
Personnel Profile: Full-Time Paid 2; Part-Time Paid 4; Part-Time Volunteers 24.
Governing Authority: county. Parent Institution: Moffat County. Tax-exempt.
Local History Museum.
Collections: Indian artifacts; local history; home of the Cowboy & Gunfighter Museum; wildlife photography; largest stretched canvas oil painting on the western slope of Colorado, depicting Craig 1895.
Research Fields: local buildings; local genealogy.
Publications: museum brochure.
Hours & Admission Prices: Mon.-Sat. 9-5. No charge; donations accepted. ♿
Attendance: 16,500 (accurate)

WYMAN MUSEUM, 94350 E. Hwy. 40, Craig, CO 81625. Mailing Address: P.O. Box 339, Craig, CO 81626-0339. Tel.: 970-824-6346. Fax: 970-824-5890.
E-mail: wymanmuseum@earthlink.net
Web Site: wymanmuseum.com
Founded: 2006.
Key Personnel: Co Dir., Lou Wyman; Co Dir., Paula Wyman; Chm. (V), Al Shepherd; Museum Shop Mgr., Nicky Boulger.
Personnel Profile: Full-Time Paid 1; Part-Time Paid 2.
Living History Museum.
Collections: chain saws; personal artifacts; trophies; farm equipment; live animals.
Facilities: picnic area. Museum-related items for sale.
Activities: hay rides. Museum Sponsors: Wymans Wacky Winter Festival in February; Grand Olde West Days in May; Sheep Wagon Days in September.
Hours & Admission Prices: Mon.-Fri. 9-5, Sat.-Sun. 11-4. No charge; donations accepted. Closed major holidays. ♿
Attendance: 10,395 (accurate)

Creede

CREEDE UNDERGROUND MINING MUSEUM, 503 Forest Service Rd. #9, Creede, CO 81130. Mailing Address: P.O. Box 422, Creede, CO 81130-0422. Tel.: 719-658-0811.
E-mail: creedeminingmuseum@hotmail.com
Key Personnel: Museum Shop Mgr., Ricky Brown; Museum Shop Mgr., Dianna Brown.
Personnel Profile: Full-Time Paid 1; Part-Time Paid 3.
Mining Museum.
Collections: mining history; mining equipment.
Facilities: Museum-related items for sale.
Hours & Admission Prices: Memorial Day to Labor Day daily 10-4; Fall & Spring Mon.-Fri. 10-3. Tour: $15 per person.

Crested Butte

CENTER FOR THE ARTS PIPER GALLERY, 606 6th St., Crested Butte, CO 81224-1819. Mailing Address: P.O. Box 1819, Crested Butte, CO 81224-1819. Tel.: 970-349-7487. Fax: 970-349-5626.
Key Personnel: Exec. Dir., Jenny Birnie
Art Gallery.
Collections: works by local & regional artists; photographs; pottery; oil pastels.
Facilities: auditorium.
Activities: special events.
Hours & Admission Prices: Call for hours.

CRESTED BUTTE MOUNTAIN HERITAGE MUSEUM, (M), 331 Elk Ave., Crested Butte, CO 81224. Mailing Address: P.O. Box 2480, Crested Butte, CO 81224-2480. Tel.: 970-349-1880.
Founded: 1991.
Key Personnel: C.E.O., Gio Cunningham.
Personnel Profile: Part-Time Paid 3; Part-Time Volunteers 25.
History Museum.
Collections: history of Crested Butte; Ute Indians; immigrant miners; ranchers; skiers; mountain bikers; personal artifacts; coal stove; period furniture & artifacts; photographs; model railroad; mining diorama; textiles; history of skiing; Mountain Bike Hall of Fame.
Activities: programs; special events. Museum Sponsors: Annual Black & White Ball in July.
Hours & Admission Prices: Summer: daily 10-8; Winter: daily 12-6; Spring & Fall: call for hours. Adults $3; discounts to AAM & ICOM members; AASLH members no charge. ♿
Attendance: 27,000 (accurate)
Membership: Individual $15; Family $30; Business $50; Supporter $100; Guarantor $200; Sponsor $500; Benefactor $1,000.

Cripple Creek

CRIPPLE CREEK DISTRICT MUSEUM, INC., (M), 500 E. Bennett Ave., Cripple Creek, CO 80813. Mailing Address: P.O. Box 1210, Cripple Creek, CO 80813-1210. Tel.: 719-689-9540 & 2634. Fax: 719-689-9540.
Web Site: www.cripple-creek.co.us
Founded: 1953.
Congressional District: 6
Key Personnel: Pres., Steve Mackin; Dir., Jan MacKell; Vice Pres., John Bowman; Bd. Member, Milford Ashworth; Bd. Member, Ike Hern; Bd. Member, Bonnie Mackin; Bd. Member, John Sharpe; Bd. Member, Georganna Peiffer; Bd. Member, Art Tremayne; Museum Shop Mgr., Johnna Luck.
Personnel Profile: Full-Time Paid 2; Part-Time Paid 4; Part-Time Volunteers 1.
Governing Authority: nonprofit organization. Tax-exempt: 990-A.
Historic Buildings.
Collections: pioneer artifacts; mining & geological displays; Victorian furniture; assay office; paintings & art objects; photographic history gallery; photographs; local newspapers 1896-present; gold ore. Historic Buildings: 1895 Midland Jerminal Railroad Depot; 1893 Colorado Trading & Transfer Co.; 1890s Assay Office.
Research Fields: mining & local history.
Facilities: 50-vol. collection of old books available for use by appointment. Historical books & other museum-related items for sale.
Activities: guided tours; demonstrations; permanent exhibitions.
Hours & Admission Prices: May-Oct. 15 daily 10-5; Oct. 16-April Fri.-Sun. 10-4. Adults $5, locals $4, military, senior citizens & children 7-12 $3; discounts to groups; members and children 6 & under no charge. Closed New Year's Day; Thanksgiving; Christmas. ♿
Attendance: 15,000
Membership: Friends of the Museum: Seniors 10% discount on all levels; Single Jack $50; Double Jack $75; Nugget $150; Sylvanite $250; High Grade $500.

MOLLIE KATHLEEN GOLD MINE, U.S. Hwy. 67, Cripple Creek, CO 80813. Mailing Address: P.O. Box 339, Cripple Creek, CO 80813-0339. Tel.: 719-689-2466.
Mining Museum.
Collections: area history; coal mining industry; photographs.
Facilities: Museum-related items for sale.
Activities: mine tours.
Hours & Admission Prices: April 2-May 14 & Oct. daily 10-4; May 15-Sept.

15 daily 9-5; Sept. 16-Sept. 30 daily 10-5. Adults $15, children 3-12 $10; children 2 & under no charge.

Del Norte

RIO GRANDE COUNTY MUSEUM AND CULTURAL CENTER, 580 Oak St., Del Norte, CO 81132-2210. Tel.: 719-657-2847; 800-233-4403. Fax: 719-657-2627.
E-mail: ajtaylor@rgcm.org
Key Personnel: Dir., A. J. Taylor
History Museum.
Collections: cultural & natural history of the area; early settlers; Indian rock art; Western art; period furnishings; personal artifacts; Old Spanish Trail.
Facilities: library. Museum-related items for sale.
Activities: seminars; workshops; lectures; special events.
Hours & Admission Prices: Tues.-Sat. 10-5; other times by appointment. Families $2.50, children $1.50, adults $1; donations accepted. Closed New Year's Day; Thanksgiving; Christmas.

Delta

DELTA COUNTY MUSEUM, 251 Meeker St., Delta, CO 81416-1914. Tel.: 970-874-8721.
E-mail: deltamuseum@aol.com
Founded: 1964.
Congressional District: 3
Key Personnel: Chm. (V), Bernice Musser; Pres. (V), David Mangum; Cur., James K. Wetzel.
Personnel Profile: Part-Time Paid 1; Part-Time Volunteers 40.
Governing Authority: nonprofit organization. Parent Institution: Delta County Historical Society. Tax-exempt: 170(b)(1)(A).
History Museum.
Collections: Vivian Jones dinosaur collection; butterflies; county newspapers; manuscripts; barbed wire; cameras; photographs; agriculture; Indian artifacts; transportation; industrial; c.1883 to present.
Research Fields: local history.
Facilities: 200-vol. library of Delta County books & newspapers on microfilm, directories, town records & magazines, available for research on premises.
Activities: permanent exhibitions.
Publications: quarterly newsletter.
Hours & Admission Prices: May-Sept. Tues.-Sat. 10-4; Oct.-April Wed. & Sat. 10-4. Adults $2, seniors $1; children under 12 with adult & members no charge. Closed legal holidays. ♿
Attendance: 3,500 (estimated)
Membership: Senior $7.50; Individual $10; Family $20; Business $30; Sponsor $50; Lifetime $150.

FORT UNCOMPAHGRE HISTORY MUSEUM, 205 Gunnison River Dr., Delta, CO 81416-1847. Mailing Address: 360 Main St., Delta, CO 81416-1837. Tel.: 970-874-1718. Fax: 970-874-1353.
E-mail: wilma.erven@delta-co.gov
Web Site: www.deltafort.org
Founded: 1990.
Congressional District: 3
Key Personnel: C.E.O., Wilma Erven; Cur., Ken Reyher.
Personnel Profile: Full-Time Paid 1; Part-Time Paid 2; Part-Time Volunteers 15.
Governing Authority: municipal. Parent Institution: City of Delta.
General Museum.
Collections: fur trade period items ranging from firearms & traps to tools & livestock.
Research Fields: Antoine Robidoux & the southwest fur trade.
Facilities: Museum-related items for sale.
Activities: self guided tours; hobby workshops; lectures; training programs for professional museum workers. Annual Events: Christmas Open House; Seasonal Special Occasions.
Hours & Admission Prices: Daily 10-3. Admission $3.50. Closed major holidays. ♿
Attendance: 3,000 (estimated)

Denver

BLACK AMERICAN WEST MUSEUM & HERITAGE CENTER, 3091 California St., Denver, CO 80205-3044. Tel.: 303-482-2242. Fax: 303-382-1981.
E-mail: executivedirector@blackamericanwestmuseum.com
Web Site: www.blackamericanwestmuseum.com
Founded: 1971.
Congressional District: 1
Key Personnel: C.E.O., LaWanna Larson; Co Chm., Terry Gentry; Co Chm., Thelma Craig.
Personnel Profile: Full-Time Paid 2; Part-Time Paid 1; Part-Time Volunteers 15.
Governing Authority: state & federal; nonprofit. Tax-exempt: 501(c)(3).
History Museum: located in the home of Dr. Justina L. Ford, the first Black female physician in Colorado.
Collections: concentration on the history, achievements & contributions of Black Americans in the building of the American West.
Facilities: Books, T-shirts, Western-oriented items & jewelry of African heritage for sale.
Activities: concerts; formal educations programs for adults; guided tours; lectures; loan, temporary & traveling exhibitions. Annual Events: Western Dance; Jamboree; Awards Ceremony.
Publications: book; Crossing over Jordon: A History of the Black Church in Colorado.
Hours & Admission Prices: June-Aug. Tues.-Sat. 10-5; Sept.-May Tues.-Sat. 10-2. Adults $8, senior citizens over 65 $7, children 12 & under $6; members no charge. Closed New Year's Day; Easter; Memorial Day; Independence Day; Labor Day; Thanksgiving; Christmas. ♿
Attendance: 12,500 (estimated)
Membership: Student & Senior $20; Individual $25; Family $35; Pioneer $50; Heritage $100; Organization $250; Life $1,000; Corporate $2,500.

BYERS-EVANS HOUSE MUSEUM, 1310 Bannock St., Denver, CO 80204-2719. Tel.: 303-620-4933. Fax: 303-620-4795.
E-mail: kevin.gramer@chs.state.co.us
Web Site: www.coloradohistory.org/be
Founded: 1990.
Congressional District: 1
Key Personnel: Admin., Kevin Gramer; Museum Asst., Shawn Snow.
Personnel Profile: Full-Time Paid 1; Part-Time Paid 2; Part-Time Volunteers 35; Interns 1.
Governing Authority: state government. Parent Institution: Colorado Historical Society, 1300 Broadway, Denver, CO 80203. Tax-exempt.
Historic House: 1883 Italianate style home.
Collections: 1912-1924 Restoration period, Evans family furnishings.
Facilities: Books on Denver history for sale.
Activities: docent program; guided tours; educational programs for children.
Hours & Admission Prices: Tues.-Sun. 11-3. Adults $5, senior citizens & students $4, children 6-12 $3; discounts to AAM & ICOM members; members & children under 6 no charge. Closed state holidays. ♿
Attendance: 10,038 (accurate)

CHILDREN'S MUSEUM OF DENVER, (M), 2121 Children's Museum Dr., Denver, CO 80211-5200. Tel.: 303-433-7444. Fax: 303-433-9520.
E-mail: information@cmdenver.org
Web Site: www.mychildsmuseum.org
Founded: 1973.
Congressional District: 1
Key Personnel: Pres., Tom Downey; Chm. (V), Deborah Wapensky-Nugent; Vice Pres. Guest Experience, Mike Yankovich; Vice Pres. Devel., Gretchen Kerr; Dir. Exhibits, Dennis Meyer; C.F.O., Cyndi Kerins.
Personnel Profile: Full-Time Paid 31; Part-Time Paid 10; Part-Time Volunteers 828; Interns 2.
Governing Authority: nonprofit organization. Tax-exempt: 501(c)(3).
Children's Museum.
Collections: hands-on exhibits.
Major Exhibits: Junior Jobsite, 6/10-9/10; Storybook Farm, 8/10-9/10.
Facilities: resource center.
Activities: interactive exhibits for children, newborn through 8 yrs. old & their caregivers; theater performances; educational programs; special events; community outreach; school groups.
Publications: newsletter, Brain Bubbles; Teachable Moment articles; Grand Play articles; Recipes for Play; Playtime Pointers.
Hours & Admission Prices: Mon.-Tues. & Thurs.-Fri. 9-4, Wed. 9-7:30, Sat.-Sun. 10-5. Admission 2-59 $7.50, senior citizens 60 & over and children one year old $5.50; discounts to AAM members; children under 1 & members no charge. Closed New Year's Day; Easter; Thanksgiving; Christmas Eve & Day. ♿
Attendance: 288,407 (accurate)
Membership: Just for Two $70; Grandparent $75; Family & Childcare Provider $90; ACM $140.

CLYFFORD STILL MUSEUM, 13th & Bannock Sts., Denver, CO 80202. Mailing Address: 201 W. Colfax Ave., Dept. 1007, Denver, CO 80202-5329. Tel.: 720-865-4317. Fax: 720-865-4315.
Web Site: clyffordstillmuseum.org
Founded: 2005.
Congressional District: 1
Key Personnel: Dir., Dean Sobel; Chm. (V), Christopher Hunt.

Personnel Profile: Full-Time Paid 1; Part-Time Paid 2; Interns 1.
Governing Authority: private; nonprofit organization. Tax-exempt: 501(c)(3).
Art Gallery.
Collections: over 2,000 works of art by Clyfford Still.
Activities: temporary exhibit; lectures.
Hours & Admission Prices: Opening 2010. Call for information.

COLORADO SPORTS HALL OF FAME, INVESCO Field at Mile High, 1701 Bryant St., Ste. 500, Denver, CO 80204. Tel.: 720-258-3888. Fax: 303-244-1003.
Sports Museum.
Collections: Colorado's athletes, coaches & sports industry leaders; photographs; personal artifacts; sports memorabilia, equipment & uniforms.
Hours & Admission Prices: June-Aug. Tues.-Sat. 10-3; Sept.-May Thurs.-Sat. 10-3.

COLORADO STATE CAPITOL, 200 E. Colfax Ave., Denver, CO 80203-1776. Tel.: 303-866-2604.
E-mail: simon.maghakyan@state.co.us
Web Site: www.colorado.gov
Key Personnel: Asst. Visitor Svcs. Mgr., Simon Maghakyan
Historic Building: built in the 1890s.
Collections: Colorado history; photographs; period furnishings; war artifacts; portraits; murals.
Hours & Admission Prices: June-Aug. Mon.-Fri. 9-3:30; Sept.-May Mon.-Fri. 9:15-2:30; reservations for groups & those with special needs. No charge. Closed most legal holidays. ♿

* **DENVER ART MUSEUM, (M),** 100 W. 14th Ave. Pkwy., Denver, CO 80204-2788. Tel.: 720-865-5000. Fax: 720-913-0001.
E-mail: info@denverartmuseum.org
Web Site: www.denverartmuseum.org
Founded: 1893.
Congressional District: 1
Key Personnel: Chm., Frederic C. Hamilton; Dir., Lewis I. Sharp; Interim Pres., Cathey Finlan; Pres. (V), Roberta Bhasin; Dir. Conservation, Sarah Melching; Chief Cur. & Cur. New World Pre-Columbian, Margaret Young-Sanchez; Dir. Communications, Andrea Fulton; Dir. Petrie Institute of Western American Art, Thomas Smith; Registrar, Lori Iliff; Dir. Exhibitions & Collections, Michele Assaf; Dir. Education, Melora McDermott-Lewis; Gates Cur. Paintings & Sculpture, Timothy J. Standring; Cur. Asian, Ronald Otsuka; Cur. Native Arts, Nancy Blomberg; Deputy Dir. and Polly & Mark Addison Cur. Modern & Contemporary Art, Christoph Heinrich; Cur. New World Spanish Colonial, Donna Pierce; Cur. Photography, Eric Paddock; Cur. Textile Art, Alice Zrebiec; AIGA Asst. Cur. & Graphics, Darrin Alfred; Sr. Scholar, Institute of Western American Art, Joan C. Troccoli; Museum Shop Mgr., Greg McKay.
Personnel Profile: Full-Time Paid 136; Part-Time Paid 160; Part-Time Volunteers 475; Interns 42.
Governing Authority: municipal. Subsidiary Institution: Denver Art Museum Foundation. Tax-exempt: 501(c)(3).
Art Museum.
Collections: Native arts, including works of North America, Africa & Oceania; Asian art; architecture, design & graphics; modern & contemporary art; photography; paintings & sculpture, featuring works by Monet, Renoir, Matisse & Degas; pre-Columbian & Spanish colonial art; textile art; Western American art.
Major Exhibits: The Masterworks of Charles M. Russel A Retrospective of Paintings & Sculpture (T), 11/09-1/10/10; Allen True's West (T), 11/09-3/10; Fritz Schdder: A New Indian Image, 11/09-5/10; A Visual Alphabet: Herbert Bayer's Anthology Paintings, 11/09-12/10; Embrace!, 11/14/09-4/4/10; Charles Deas & 1840s America, 8/21/10-11/28/10.
Research Fields: art history & education.
Facilities: over 40,000-vol. library in administrative annex, call 720-913-0100. Museum-related items for sale.
Activities: guided tours; docent tours by appointment; lectures; slide talks; seminars; symposia; youth & adult art appreciation classes; performing arts events; permanent, temporary & traveling exhibitions.
Publications: annual report; exhibition catalogs; permanent collection catalogs; books, Herbert Bayer Collection & Archive at the Denver Art Museum; The Denver Art Museum: The First 100 Years; annual publication, Western Passages.
Hours & Admission Prices: Museum: Tues.-Thurs. & Sat. 10-5, Fri. 10-10, Sun. 12-5. Library: by appointment; located in the administrative annex. Adults in-state $10, out-of-state $13, senior citizens & students in-state $8, out-of-state $10, youth 6-18 in-state $3, out-of-state $5; discounts to AAM & ICOM members; children 5 & under and members no charge. Closed New Year's Day; Thanksgiving; Christmas Eve & Day. ♿
Attendance: 500,000 (accurate)
Membership: Senior, Student, Teacher $45; Individual $50; Dual & Family $70; Sustaining $125; Supporting $500; Benefactor $1,000; Associate $2,500.

* **DENVER BOTANIC GARDENS, INC., (M),** 1005 York St., Denver, CO 80206-3014. Mailing Address: 909 York St., Denver, CO 80206-3751. Tel.: 720-865-3502 & 3585. Fax: 720-865-3713. TDD: 720-865-3745.
Web Site: botanicgardens.org
Founded: 1951.
Congressional District: 1
Key Personnel: C.E.O., Brian Vogt; Chm. (V), Jerry D. Ladd; Dir. Education, Matthew Cole; Dir. Horticulture, Sarada Krishnan; C.F.O., Florence Welch; Dir. Garden Operations, Tom Aljinovich; Dir. Mktg., Robin Doerr.
Personnel Profile: Full-Time Paid 93; Part-Time Paid 10; Part-Time Volunteers 1,147; Interns 30.
Governing Authority: city & county of Denver; private, nonprofit corporation. Parent Institution: Dept. of Parks & Recreation, 1805 Bryant St., Denver 80204. Branch Facility: Denver Botanic Gardens at Chatfield, 8500 Deer Creek Canyon., Littleton, CO 80123. Tax-exempt: 501(c)(3).
Botanical Gardens & Arboretum.
Collections: herb garden; Japanese garden, rock-alpine garden; high plains garden; scripture garden; western perennial border fragrance garden; xeriscape garden; aquatic garden; rose garden; lilac garden; Montane garden; low-maintenance garden; vegetable garden; Water-Smart garden; xeriscape collection; tropical conservatory; herbarium with 29,000 sheets; water lily gardens; endangered plants garden; research collections of endangered species; original watercolors of Colorado wildflowers; Mt. Goliath; Chatfield, 84 woody windbreak species & Western dryland perennial collections; Sacred Earth Garden (tribes of Four Corners Region); birds & bees garden; children's secret path; PlantAsia garden; Sensory garden; Cloud Forest Tree with orchids & bromeliads; cutting garden.
Research Fields: 59,000 specimen vascular plant & mycological herbarium with accompanying extensive mycological laboratory & library; 29 endangered species as a Center for Plant Conservation participant; vascular plants; alpine plant identification/conservation; grassland restoration; floristic inventories.
Facilities: 28,000-vol. library with 1,000 periodicals, 7,200 current pamphlets, 8,500 current seed & nursery catalogs, rare book room including a bromeliad-literature collection; herbarium; conservatory & greenhouses; Orchid-Bromeliad House; Cactus & Succulent House; 350-seat auditorium & show facility; accessible classrooms; mycological research lab; Mt. Goliath alpine nature trail & Dos Chapelle Nature Center at Mt. Evans; 700-acre Denver Botanic Gardens at Chatfield in Littleton; Cloud Forest Tree. Books, gardening accessories & other museum-related items for sale.
Activities: 2 certification programs, Botanical Art, Illustration & Rocky Mountain Gardening; certificate training: applied plant conservation; community garden program; Ask The Expert plant information service; educational programs for adults & children; flower shows; guided tours of Chatfield, conservatory, outside gardens & sensory garden; classes, lectures & field trips. Botanic Gardens Sponsors: annual plant & book sale, 2-day holiday sale; summer concerts in outdoor amphitheater; pumpkin festival; corn maze; Earth Day event; winter evening light show; summer college intern program.
Publications: book, Rocky Mountain Alpines; bimonthly membership magazine; education programs; summer brochure, Summertime Kids Program; Denver Botanic Gardens at Chatfield brochure; Visitors Guide; interpretive brochures.
Hours & Admission Prices: Sept. 14-May 9 daily 9-5; May 10-Sept. 12 Wed.-Fri. 9-5, Sat.-Tues. 9-8. Call for admission prices. Closed New Year's Day; Thanksgiving; Christmas. ♿
Attendance: 503,000 (accurate)
Membership: Individual $40; Individual Plus One $50; General $70; General Plus $160; Supporter $325; Patron $625.

THE DENVER CENTER FOR THE PERFORMING ARTS, 1101 13th St., Denver, CO 80204-5319. Tel.: 303-893-4100. Fax: 303-595-9634.
History Museum.
Collections: theater history; paintings; cast autographs; props; costumes; stages.
Facilities: theater.
Activities: guided tours; performances.
Hours & Admission Prices: Tours: Mon. & Sat. 10 am by appointment. Adults $8.

DENVER FIREFIGHTERS MUSEUM, 1326 Tremont Pl., Denver, CO 80204-2120. Tel.: 303-892-1436. Fax: 303-893-4835.
E-mail: info@denverfirefightersmuseum.org
Web Site: www.denverfirefightersmuseum.org
Founded: 1978.

Congressional District: 1
Key Personnel: Exec. Dir. & Museum Shop Mgr., Angela Rayne; Pres. (V), Robert Vallero; Treas., Mike Berlin; Sec., Diane Ensminger.
Personnel Profile: Full-Time Paid 2; Part-Time Paid 1; Part-Time Volunteers 120.
Governing Authority: private; nonprofit organization. Tax-exempt: 501(c)(3).
History Museum.
Collections: historic photographs; firefighting artifacts; hand-drawn to motorized fire fighting vehicles; books; archives.
Research Fields: history of Denver Fire Department.
Facilities: 400-vol. library; 12,000 sq. ft. exhibit space. Museum-related items for sale.
Activities: hands-on children's museum; fire safety programs; guided tours; available to rent for parties & meetings.
Publications: newsletter, Four Rings.
Hours & Admission Prices: Mon.-Sat. 10-4. Adults $6, senior citizens & students $5, children 1-12 $4; discounts to groups; children under one & members no charge.
Attendance: 20,000 (accurate)
Membership: Hook & Ladder $36-$49; Hose Reel $50-$149; Steamer $150-$499; Engine $500-$999; Truck $1,000-$4,999; Tower $5,000 & up.

DENVER MUSEUM OF MINIATURES, DOLLS AND TOYS, (M), 1880 Gaylord St., Denver, CO 80206-1211. Tel.: 303-322-1053. Fax: 303-322-3704.
E-mail: director@dmmdt.org
Web Site: www.dmmdt.org
Founded: 1981.
Congressional District: 1
Key Personnel: Dir., Wendy Littlepage; Pres. Bd., Margery Smith; 1st Vice Pres., Pat Vick; Treas., Carol Kluver; Volunteer Coord., Stasia Steele; Museum Shop Mgr., Deanna Thomas.
Personnel Profile: Full-Time Paid 1; Part-Time Paid 1; Part-Time Volunteers 125; Interns 2.
Governing Authority: nonprofit organization. Tax-exempt: 501(c)(3).
Miniatures, Dolls & Toys Museum.
Collections: miniatures; dolls & toys from prehistoric to modern times; doll houses; board games; paper dolls; tin toys; trains; international dolls; crafts; archives; mechanical toys; doll furniture.
Research Fields: miniatures; dolls; toys.
Facilities: 100-vol. library; classroom; 6,000 sq. ft. exhibit space. Miniatures, toys & dolls for sale.
Activities: lectures; hobby workshops; temporary exhibitions; children's art programs. Annual Events: spring & fall.
Publications: quarterly newsletter.
Hours & Admission Prices: Wed.-Sat. 10-4, Sun. 1-4. Adults $6, senior citizens $5, children $4; discounts to groups, AAA, CAA, & CHS members; members no charge. Closed major holidays. ♿
Attendance: 7,809 (accurate)
Membership: Senior Individual $25; Individual $30; Family $45; Sponsor $100; Benefactor $125; Patron $150; Contributing $250; Fellow $500; President's Circle $1,000.

∗ **DENVER MUSEUM OF NATURE & SCIENCE, (M),** 2001 Colorado Blvd., Denver, CO 80205-5798. Tel.: 303-322-7009. Fax: 303-331-6492. TDD: 303-370-8257.
E-mail: feedback@dmns.org
Web Site: www.dmns.org
Formerly: Denver Museum of Natural History
Founded: 1900.
Congressional District: 1
Key Personnel: Pres. & C.E.O., George Sparks; Vice Pres. Research & Collections, Dr. Kirk Johnson; Cur. Anthropology & Dept. Chair Archaeology, Dr. Stephen Nash; Cur. Vertebrate Zoology, Dr. John Dembroski; Cur. Archaeology, Dr. Steve Holen; Cur. of Planetary Sciences & Dept. Chair, Dr. Steve Lee; Cur. Human Health & Vice Pres. Strategic Partnerships & Programs, Dr. Bridget Conghlin; Cur. Space Science, Dr. Ka Chun Yu; Cur. Lower Vertebrate Paleontology & Chief Preparator, Dr. Ken Carpenter; Cur. Astrobiology, Dr. David Grinspoon; Vice Pres. Visitor Experience, Mary Hacking; Archivist & Dept. Chair, Kris Haglund; Cur. Invertebrate Zoology & Dept. Chair, Dr. Paula Cushing; Librarian, Katherine B. Gully; Image Archivist, Rene Payne; C.F.O., Juliet Gustafson; Vice Pres. Devel., Sandi Garcia; Vice Pres. Information Technology, Dave Noel; Conservator & Dept. Conservation Chair, Jude Southward.
Personnel Profile: Full-Time Paid 203; Part-Time Paid 212; Part-Time Volunteers 1,467.
Governing Authority: private; nonprofit organization. Tax-exempt: 501(c)(3).
Natural History Museum.
Collections: archaeology; ethnography; ornithology; mammalogy; herpetology; entomology; conchology; geology; mineralogy; vertebrate paleontology; paleobotany; space science; natural history art.
Research Fields: North American archaeology and ethnography with emphasis on Southwest & Plains; Colorado mineralogy & Western interior paleontology; ornithology, mammalogy & entomology; space sciences; planetary sciences; astrobiology.
Facilities: 25,000-vol. library of natural history & anthropology books and journals; archives & 300,000 photographic images; IMAX theater; planetarium; health education center; cafe. Museum-related items for sale.
Activities: guided tours; adults lectures & courses; children's workshops; permanent & temporary exhibitions; gallery demonstrations; teen program; IMAX & Planetarium shows; outreach programs; internships; classroom programs; learning lab.
Publications: newsletter, Museum magazine; exhibit catalogs; symposia proceedings; annual report; scientific books & papers; teacher's guides.
Hours & Admission Prices: Museum: daily 9-5. Adults $11, juniors 3-18, students, and senior citizens 65 & over $6; members no charge. IMAX: adults $8, juniors 3-18, students, and seniors 65 & over $6; discounts to members. Museum & IMAX Combination: adults $16, juniors 3-18, seniors 65 & over, and youth 3-18 $10; discounts to members. Closed Christmas. ♿
Attendance: 1,252,300 (accurate)
Membership: Senior Individual $35; Individual $40; Senior Dual $50; Dual $55; Family $75; Family Plus $100; Curator's Club $200-$499; Benefactor $500-$999; Patron $1,000-$1,499; Naturalist's Club $1,500; Collector's Circle $3,000; Director's Circle $6,000; Campion Circle $10,000.

DENVER ZOOLOGICAL GARDENS, 2300 Steele St., Denver, CO 80205-4899. Tel.: 303-376-4800. Fax: 303-376-4801.
E-mail: zooinfo@denverzoo.org
Web Site: www.denverzoo.org
Founded: 1896.
Congressional District: 1
Key Personnel: C.E.O. & Pres., Craig Piper; Chm. Bd., Patrick E. Green; C.O.O., Kyle D. Burks; Treas., Donna Mei Lin Driscoll; Vice Pres. Mktg., Ana Bowie; Vice Pres. Devel., Ben Duke; Vice Pres. Operations, Dennis Smith; Vice Pres. Education, Jacque Taylor; Vice Pres. Planning, George Pond; Veterinarian, Felicia Knightley, V.M.D.
Personnel Profile: Full-Time Paid 228; Part-Time Paid 54; Part-Time Volunteers 569; Interns 44.
Governing Authority: municipal; nonprofit organization. Parent Institution: City & County of Denver. Subsidiary Institution: Denver Zoological Foundation, Inc. Tax-exempt.
Zoo.
Collections: 3,667 specimens; 682 species; 1,850 specimens biofact collection.
Research Fields: ethology; nutrition; conservation policy; field conservation.
Facilities: 500-vol. research library of zoology books; 80-acre campus with 90 buildings and exhibits; cafe. Museum-related items for sale.
Activities: field trips; tours; lectures; summertime daily wildlife theatre shows.
Publications: annual report; quarterly, Zoo Review; monthly, On the Wildside.
Hours & Admission Prices: Summer: daily 9-6. Adults $12, children $7. Winter: daily 10-5. Adults $9, children $5; discount to seniors; AZA Professional members & members no charge. ♿
Attendance: 1,711,593 (accurate)
Membership: Individual $40; Individual & Guest $55; Family $75; Family Plus $100; Curator's Club $250; Director's Circle $500; President's Circle $1,000; Conservation Society $2,500.

DOWNTOWN AQUARIUM, 700 Water St., Denver, CO 80211-5210. Tel.: 303-561-4450. Fax: 303-561-4465.
Aquarium.
Collections: freshwater fish; Sumatran tigers.
Facilities: restaurant.
Hours & Admission Prices: Sun.-Thurs. 10-9, Fri.-Sat. 10-9:30. Adults 12-64 $13.75, seniors 65 & over $12.95, children 3-11 $8.25; children under 2 no charge.

FORNEY MUSEUM OF TRANSPORTATION, 4303 Brighton Blvd., Denver, CO 80216-3702. Tel.: 303-297-1113. Fax: 303-297-3113.
E-mail: museum@forneymuseum.org
Web Site: www.forneymuseum.org
Founded: 1955.
Key Personnel: Pres. Bd., Jack D. Forney; Dir. Museum, Amy Newman; Mgr. Visitor Svcs., Beverly Little.
Personnel Profile: Full-Time Paid 2; Part-Time Paid 3; Part-Time Volunteers 4; Interns 1.
Governing Authority: nonprofit organization. Tax-exempt: 501(c)(3).
Transportation Museum.
Collections: period automobiles, trains, carts, carriages, wagons, aircraft, fire

engines, Denver cable car, bicycles, motorcycles, trolleys, sleighs, steam tractor, & clothing.
Research Fields: transportation.
Facilities: library. Gift items for sale.
Activities: tours; lectures; rental facilities; birthday parties. Museum Sponsors: Kid's Club; Senior Day in February; Transportation Safety Expo in April; Big Boy Day in June; Forney Fall Fest in October; Denver Art Week; Museum Day.
Publications: The Transportation Times; Forney Kid's Club News; Forney Museum of Transportation Coloring Book.
Hours & Admission Prices: Mon.-Sat. 10-4. Adults $7, seniors 62 & over $6, youth 11-15 $4.50, child 5-10 $3.50; discounts to disabled, military, AAA, AAM & ICOM members; children under 5 no charge. Closed New Year's Day; Thanksgiving; Christmas. ♿
Attendance: 15,000 (estimated)
Membership: Unicycle (Individual) $30; Tandem (Dual) $40; Minivan (Family of 4) $50; Big Rig (Extended Family of 8) $75; Trolley (Group of 10) $100; Club Coach (Group of 30) $300. Sustaining: Locomotive $500; Concorde $1,000; Booster Rocket $5,000 & up.

FOUR MILE HISTORIC PARK, (M), 715 S. Forest St., Denver, CO 80246-2324. Tel.: 720-865-0800. Fax: 720-865-0801.
E-mail: info@fourmilepark.org.
Web Site: www.fourmilepark.org
Founded: 1977.
Congressional District: 1
Key Personnel: C.E.O. & Dir., Barbara Gibson; Chm. (V), Larry Harte; Artifact Mgr., Bonnie Bowman; Dir. Educational Programs, Karla Zelvis; Rental & Special Events Dir., Aimee Pellet; Bookkeeper, Connie Wyatt; Asst. Site Mgr., Jeff Suhr; Coord. (V), Mary Jane Bradbury; Museum Shop Mgr., Scotty Wilkins.
Personnel Profile: Full-Time Paid 6; Part-Time Paid 6; Part-Time Volunteers 150.
Governing Authority: nonprofit. Parent Institution: Four Mile Historic Park, Inc. Tax-exempt: 501(c)(3).
Historic Site: 1859 & 1883 Four Mile House, log house, which served as stage stop, wayside inn, tavern & farmhouse.
Collections: reconstructed middle 19th-century farm/ranch, log barn, stallion barn, carriage barn; furniture & furnishings of the period 1859-1883; collection of early photographic material; objects recovered from archaeological studies & excavations.
Research Fields: archaeology; history & rural life; 1859-1883 agricultural history transportation history.
Facilities: Museum-related items for sale.
Activities: guided tours; workshops; living history demonstrations; formally organized educational programs; docent program; permanent exhibits. Museum Sponsors: special events.
Publications: Denver's Four Mile House.
Hours & Admission Prices: April-Sept. Wed.-Fri. 12-4, Sat.-Sun. 10-4; Oct.-March Sat.-Sun. 12-4. Suggested Donations: adults $3.50, students & senior citizens $2; discount to AAA & National Trust members; children 5 & under no charge. ♿
Attendance: 43,500 (accurate)
Membership: Pioneer $35; Settler $50; Homesteader $100; 59'er $250; Wagon Master $500; Trail Blazer $1,000; Corporate memberships available.

GRANT-HUMPHREYS MANSION, 770 Pennsylvania St., Denver, CO 80203-3619. Tel.: 303-894-2505. Fax: 303-894-2508.
E-mail: rentalsghm@chs.state.co.us
Web Site: coloradohistory.org/ghm
Founded: 1976.
Congressional District: 1
Key Personnel: Admin., Kevin Gramer; Events Coord., Debbie Golden.
Personnel Profile: Full-Time Paid 2; Part-Time Paid 2; Part-Time Volunteers 5.
Governing Authority: state. Parent Institution: Colorado Historical Society, 1300 Broadway, Denver, CO 80203. Tax-exempt.
Historic House Museum: 1902 Beaux-Arts style home.
Collections: early 20th-century decorative & fine arts belonging to the Humphreys family.
Facilities: banquet facilities. Books on Denver history for sale.
Activities: special programs.
Hours & Admission Prices: Mon.-Fri. 9-5. No charge; donations accepted. ♿
Attendance: 20,294 (accurate)
Membership: See State Historical Society of Colorado for membership information.

* **HISTORY COLORADO, THE COLORADO HISTORICAL SOCIETY, (M),** 1300 Broadway, Denver, CO 80203-5600. Tel.: 303-866-3682. Fax: 303-866-5739.
E-mail: information@chs.state.co.us
Web Site: www.coloradohistory.org
Founded: 1879.
Congressional District: 1
Key Personnel: Pres. & C.E.O., Edward C. Nichols; C.F.O., Susan Riehl; Chm. (V), W. Bart Berger; C.O.O., Kathryn Hill; Dir. Devel., Jill Cowperthwaite; State Archaeologist & Deputy SHPO, Susan M. Collins; Historic Preservation & Deputy SHPO, Steve Turner; Mng. Editor, Steve Grinstead; State Historian, William J. Convery; Dir. Library, Rebecca Lintz; Dir. Education, J.J. Rutherford; Dir. Facilities Svcs., Joseph Bell; Cur. Decorative & Fine Arts, Moya Hansen; Cur. Books & Manuscripts, Keith Schrum; Dir. Collections, Elisa Phelps.
Personnel Profile: Full-Time Paid 122; Part-Time Paid 9; Part-Time Volunteers 547; Interns 7.
Governing Authority: state. Parent Institution: State of Colorado. Colorado Commission on Higher Education. The State Historical Society of Colorado. Regional Museums: Grant-Humphreys Mansion (303-894-2505), Byers-Evans House (303-620-4933), Pearce-McAllister Cottage (303-322-1053), Denver; Fort Garland & Pikes Stockade (719-379-3512), Fort Garland; Georgetown Loop Historic Mining & Railroad Park (303-569-2788), Georgetown; Healy House & Dexter Cabin (719-486-0487), Leadville; Ute Indian Museum (970-249-3098), Montrose; Fort Vasquez (970-785-2832), Platteville; El Pueblo History Museum (719-583-0453), Pueblo; Trinidad History Museum comprising Santa Fe Trail Museum, Baca House, Bloom Mansion & Historic Gardens (719-846-7217), Trinidad. Tax-exempt: 501(c)(3).
Historical Society Museum.
Collections: history & prehistory of Colorado and the American West to present; over 140,000 artifacts including American Indian, archaeological, Hispanic, domestic life, industrial, military, transportation, crafts & industries, graphic arts & advertising, fine arts, political & community life, religious, costume & textiles, sports, firearms, furniture; over 750,000 historic photographs, moving images and negatives; Approximately 14 million documents, microfilm, books, serials and ephemera collections.
Major Exhibits: Allen True's West (T), 11/09-3/10.
Research Fields: history of Colorado & the American West; archaeology; American Indian studies; ethnic communities.
Facilities: 14,000,000-item library including books, maps, newspapers, photographs, microfilm, manuscripts, tapes & film; reading room; classrooms; 36,000 sq. ft. exhibit space; 400-seat auditorium. Museum-related items for sale.
Activities: special, permanent exhibitions; guided tours; lectures; films; gallery talks; formally organized education programs; training programs for professional museum workers & classroom teachers; school loan service; inter-museum loan service; inventory, nomination & restoration of historic & archaeological sites under National Register Program; State Historical Fund preservation grant program; review of environmental impact statements; historic markers program; publications program; friends groups & volunteer organizations.
Publications: bimonthly magazine, Colorado Heritage; monthly e-newspaper, Colorado History Now; books.
Hours & Admission Prices: Colorado History Museum: Mon.-Sat. 10-5, Sun. 12-5. Library Tues.-Sat. 10-4:30. Adults $7, students with I.D. & senior citizens 65 & over $6, children 6-12 $5; discounts to AAM & AAA members; members no charge. Closed major holidays; some state holidays. ♿
Attendance: 229,509 (accurate)
Membership: Individual $50; Family & Group $65; Associate $75; Explorer $125; Centennial $250; Historian $500; Heritage Club $1,000.

KIRKLAND MUSEUM OF FINE & DECORATIVE ART, (M), 1311 Pearl St., Denver, CO 80203-2518. Tel.: 303-832-8576. Fax: 303-832-8404.
E-mail: info@kirklandmuseum.org
Web Site: www.kirklandmuseum.org
Formerly: Vance Kirkland Museum
Founded: 1996.
Congressional District: 1
Key Personnel: Dir., Hugh Grant; Deputy Dir., Gerald Horner; Registrar, Christopher Herron; Mktg. Dir., Holly Victor; Visitor Svcs. Coord. & Museum Shop Mgr., Katrina Boldry; Volunteer & Public Program Coord., Mary Beth Orr; Mktg. & Membership Coord., Maya Wright; Collections Asst., Alisha Stovall.
Personnel Profile: Full-Time Paid 7; Part-Time Paid 3; Part-Time Volunteers 28.
Governing Authority: private; nonprofit. Tax-exempt.
Art Museum: housed in a 1910-1911 commercial art building, which was inaugurated as The Student's School of Art by artist Henry Read; the building was later acquired by Colorado painter Vance Kirkland, who used the structure as the Kirkland School of Art from 1932-1946 & continued to paint at this location until his death in 1981. National Trust Associate Site.
Collections: decorative art from 1880-1980 including Arts & Crafts, Art

Nouveau, Glasgow Style, Wiener Werkstatte, De Stijl, Bauhaus, Art Deco, Modern and Pop Art; regional modernist art; painter, Vance Kirkland.
Facilities: 1,580-vol. library on American & European artists and American dinnerware & ceramics available to public by special arrangement; 2,100 sq. ft. exhibit space. Posters, postcards & Vance Kirkland exhibition catalogs for sale.
Activities: lectures; loan, temporary & traveling exhibitions; broadcast programs.
Hours & Admission Prices: Tues.-Sat. 11-5, Sun. 1-5. Adults $7, seniors, teachers & students $6; discounts to groups, museum employees, AAA & AAM members; members no charge. Children under 13 not admitted. Closed major holidays. ♿
Attendance: 14,426 (accurate)
Membership: Senior, Student & Teacher $30; Individual $35; Dual $45; Individual & Guest $50; Sustaining $100.

METROPOLITAN STATE COLLEGE OF DENVER/CENTER FOR VISUAL ART, (M), 1734 Wazee St., Denver, CO 80202-1232. Tel.: 303-294-5207. Fax: 303-294-5210.
E-mail: mscd-cva@mscd.edu
Web Site: www.metrostatecva.org
Founded: 1991.
Congressional District: 1
Key Personnel: Dir. & Cur., Jennifer Garner; Asst. Dir. & Cur., Cecily Cullen.
Personnel Profile: Full-Time Paid 4; Part-Time Paid 6; Part-Time Volunteers 2; Interns 1.
Governing Authority: university; nonprofit. Parent Institution: Metropolitan State College of Denver. Tax-exempt: 501(c)(3).
Art Gallery.
Collections: works of contemporary art.
Research Fields: contemporary art.
Facilities: 3,500 sq. ft. exhibit space.
Activities: adult & children's programs; temporary exhibits.
Publications: quarterly newsletter.
Hours & Admission Prices: Tues.-Fri. 11-6, Sat. 12-5. No charge; donations accepted. Closed all major holidays. ♿
Attendance: 15,000 (accurate)
Membership: Student & Senior Citizen $25; Individual $40; Family & Dual $65; Other $100 & up.

MIZEL MUSEUM, (M), 400 S. Kearney St., Denver, CO 80224-1238. Tel.: 303-394-9993. Fax: 303-394-1119.
E-mail: ellen@mizelmuseum.org
Web Site: www.mizelmuseum.org
Founded: 1982.
Congressional District: 1
Key Personnel: Chm. Bd., Larry A. Mizel; Exec. Dir., Ellen Premack; Dir. Education, Jan Cooper Nadav; Special Projects, Deanne Kapnik; Database & Office Mgr., Maggi Junor; Cur., Georgina Kolber.
Personnel Profile: Full-Time Paid 5; Full-Time Volunteers 30; Part-Time Paid 30; Part-Time Volunteers 45.
Governing Authority: nonprofit organization. Subsidiary Institution: The C.E.L.L. Tax-exempt: 501(c)(3).
Cultural Museum.
Collections: ritual & religious objects of the synagogue; historical artifacts; contemporary Judaica.
Research Fields: Jewish history & culture; multicultural education.
Facilities: 400-vol. library pertaining to Jewish art & ceremony.
Activities: guided tours; lectures; films; workshops; art classes; organized educational programs & exhibitions; docent program; participatory, traveling & temporary exhibitions.
Publications: quarterly newspaper, Mizel Tov; biannual education brochure.
Hours & Admission Prices: Mon.-Thurs. 8:30-5, Fri. 8:30-3. No charge; donations accepted. Closed Jewish holidays.
Attendance: 120,000 (accurate)
Membership: Seniors & Students $15; Individual $35; Family & Duo $50; Pissaro Society $150; Chagall Society $250; Agam Society $500.

MOLLY BROWN HOUSE MUSEUM, 1340 Pennsylvania St., Denver, CO 80203-2417. Tel.: 303-832-4092, ext. 16. Fax: 303-832-2340.
E-mail: admin@mollybrown.org
Web Site: www.mollybrown.org
Founded: 1970.
Congressional District: 1
Key Personnel: Exec. Dir. Historic Denver, Annie Levinsky; Chm., Karen Jonas; Cur. Collections, Kelly Rasmussen; Dir. Operations, Andrea Malcomb.
Personnel Profile: Full-Time Paid 6; Part-Time Paid 6; Part-Time Volunteers 90; Interns 2.
Governing Authority: nonprofit organization. Historic House Museum & Preservation Society. Parent Institution: Historic Denver, Inc. Tax-exempt: 501(c)(3).
Historical & Preservation Society.
Collections: furnishings; fashions. Historic House: 1889 Molly Brown House.
Research Fields: architectural; Victoriana; community revitalization; urban preservation; women's history.
Facilities: 200-vol. library of materials dealing with turn-of-the-century life in Denver.
Activities: guided tours; lectures; Victorian eating experiences; educational outreach programs.
Publications: monthly newsletters, Historic Denver News; Life of Margaret (Molly) Brown.
Hours & Admission Prices: Winter: Tues.-Sat. 10-4, Sun. 12-4; Summer: Mon.-Sat. 10-4, Sun. 12-4. Adults $8, senior citizens 65 & over $6, children 6-12 $4; discounts to Historic Denver members; members no charge. Closed major holidays. ♿
Attendance: 47,980 (accurate)
Membership: Annual $40; Friend $100.

MUSEO DE LAS AMERICAS, 861 Santa Fe Dr., Denver, CO 80204-4344. Tel.: 303-571-4401. Fax: 303-607-9761.
E-mail: patty@museo.org
Web Site: www.museo.org
Founded: 1991.
Congressional District: 1
Key Personnel: Exec. Dir., Patty Ortiz; Operations Mgr., David Dadone; Bd. Pres., George Martinez; Dir. Education, Judy Kelly; Collections Mgr., Kristi Martens; Public Rels. & Mktg., Nicole Reusch; Membership, Ricardo Farias; Museum Shop Mgr., Claudia Moran.
Personnel Profile: Full-Time Paid 5; Part-Time Volunteers 24; Interns 2.
Governing Authority: private; nonprofit organization. Tax-exempt: 501(c)(3).
Art & History Museum.
Collections: focus on the art & culture of Latin America from ancient times to contemporary.
Research Fields: Latin American arts ancient, folk art, and contemporary.
Activities: tours; youth education programs; lectures; film; symposia; Spanish Happy Hour; bilingual programs.
Publications: newsletter, Notitas.
Hours & Admission Prices: Tues.-Fri. 10-5, Sat.-Sun. 12-5. Adults $4, students and seniors 65 & over $3; discounts to AAM members; members & children under 13 no charge. Closed New Year's Day; Independence Day; Thanksgiving; Christmas. ♿
Attendance: 30,000 (accurate)
Membership: Onyx (Student, Teacher & Senior) $25; Coral (Individual) $30; Amber (Family) $45; Opal $75; Turquoise $125; Obsidian $250; Jade $500; Sapphire $1,000; Corporate & Major Donors $3,000.

MUSEUM OF ANTHROPOLOGY, UNIVERSITY OF DENVER, (M), (I), 2000 Asbury Ave. #146, Denver, CO 80208. Tel.: 303-871-2688. Fax: 303-871-2437.
E-mail: ckreps@du.edu
Web Site: www.du.edu/duma/duma.html
Founded: 1932.
Congressional District: 1
Key Personnel: Dir., Dr. Christina Kreps; Cur. Collections, Ms. Brook Rohde; Dept. of Anthropology Faculty Member, Dr. Dean Saitta; Dept. of Anthropology Faculty Member, Dr. Bonnie Clark.
Personnel Profile: Full-Time Paid 1; Part-Time Paid 1; Interns 15.
Governing Authority: university; nonprofit. Parent Institution: University of Denver. Tax-exempt: 501(c)(3).
Anthropology Museum.
Collections: textiles; period artifacts.
Research Fields: ethnology, archaeology of the Southwest US.
Facilities: archaeology lab.
Activities: educational outreach; lecture series.
Hours & Admission Prices: Sept.-June Mon.-Fri. 9-4. No charge. Closed university holidays. ♿
Attendance: 1,000 (estimated)
Membership: Student $5; Non-Student $10; Patron $25; Donor $50.

MUSEUM OF CONTEMPORARY ART, (M), 1485 Delgany, Denver, CO 80202-1100. Tel.: 303-298-7554.
Key Personnel: Exec. Dir. & Chief Cur., Cydney Payton
Art Museum.
Collections: paintings; sculpture; photography.
Activities: special events; education programs.
Hours & Admission Prices: Tues.-Thurs. & Sat.-Sun. 10-6, Fri. 10-10. Adults $10, students, teachers and seniors 62 & over $5; children under 6 & members no charge.

RED ROCKS AMPHITHEATRE & VISITOR CENTER, 18300 W. Alameda Pkwy., Denver, CO 80465. Tel.: 720-865-2475.
History Museum.
Collections: Red Rocks geologic & music history; Hall of Fame; wildlife.
Facilities: amphitheatre; visitor center; nature trail. Museum-related items for sale.
Activities: guided tours; hiking; hands-on exhibits; videos.
Hours & Admission Prices: May-Sept. daily 8-7; Oct.-April daily 9-4. Adults $6, seniors & children $3.

STILES AFRICAN AMERICAN HERITAGE CENTER, INC., 2607 Glenarm Place, Denver, CO 80205-3151. Tel.: 303-294-0597.
Founded: 1998.
Heritage Center.
Collections: African American history & culture; photographs; memorabilia; personal artifacts.
Facilities: classrooms.
Activities: guided tours; research; workshops.
Hours & Admission Prices: Mon., Wed. & Fri. 11-3, Sat. 2-4; other times by appointment.

UNIVERSITY OF DENVER, SCHOOL OF ART & ART HISTORY, VICTORIA H. MYHREN GALLERY, 2121 E. Asbury Ave., Denver, CO 80208-0001. Tel.: 303-871-3716. Fax: 303-871-4112.
E-mail: galleryinfo@du.edu
Web Site: www.du.edu/art
Founded: 1940.
Key Personnel: Dir., Dan Jacobs; Chm. (V), Victoria H. Myhren.
Personnel Profile: Full-Time Paid 1; Part-Time Paid 2; Interns 2.
Governing Authority: private university; not-for-profit. Parent Institution: University of Denver School of Art & Art History. Tax-exempt: 501(c)(3).
University Art Gallery.
Collections: late 19th- & early 20th-century European & regional masters; digital art; performance art; photographs.
Facilities: 2,564 sq. ft. exhibit space; educational facilities.
Activities: guided tours; lectures; loan & participatory exhibits; educational programs for undergraduate & graduate students affiliated with the Univ. of Denver; concerts.
Publications: newsletter; exhibition catalogs.
Hours & Admission Prices: Exhibitions: daily 12-4. Office: Mon.-Fri. 9-4. No charge. ♿

WINGS OVER THE ROCKIES AIR & SPACE MUSEUM, 7711 E. Academy Blvd., Denver, CO 80230-6929. Tel.: 303-360-5360, ext. 110. Fax: 303-360-5328.
E-mail: ceo@wingsmuseum.org
Web Site: wingsmuseum.org
Founded: 1994.
Key Personnel: C.E.O. & Pres., Greg Anderson; Cur., Matthew Burchette.
Personnel Profile: Full-Time Paid 8; Part-Time Paid 3; Part-Time Volunteers 160; Interns 1.
Governing Authority: Tax-exempt.
Air & Space Museum: housed in World War II vintage hangar.
Collections: over 36 air & spacecraft spanning 8 decades including a full-size Star Wars X-Wing Fighter; aircraft armament; full-size mockup of a manned space station crew module; Colorado astronaut tribute.
Facilities: library; photo archive; photo reproduction laboratory. Museum-related items for sale.
Publications: newsletter, Wingspan.
Hours & Admission Prices: Mon.-Sat. 10-5, Sun. 12-5. Adults $9, seniors 65 & over $8, children 4-12 $6; discounts to groups; members & children under 4 no charge. Closed major holidays. ♿
Attendance: 150,000 (accurate)
Membership: Individual $30; Family $40; Patron $300; Lifetime $1,000.

Dillon

DILLON SCHOOLHOUSE MUSEUM, 403 La Bonte, Dillon, CO 80435. Mailing Address: P.O. Box 745, Breckenridge, CO 80424-0745. Tel.: 970-468-2207.
Governing Authority: Tax-exempt.
Historic Building: originally used as a schoolhouse until 1910 when it became a church; built in 1883.
Collections: local history; period artifacts; desks; slates; individual learning stations; Centennial flag; chemistry set; kerosene slide projector; phonograph; piano; organ; clothing; jewelry.
Hours & Admission Prices: Call for hours.

Dolores

BUREAU OF LAND MANAGEMENT - ANASAZI HERITAGE CENTER - CANYONS OF THE ANCIENTS NATIONAL MONUMENT, 27501 Hwy. 184, Dolores, CO 81323-9217. Tel.: 970-882-5600. Fax: 970-882-7035.
E-mail: rene_farias@blm.gov
Web Site: www.co.blm.gov/ahc
Founded: 1988.
Congressional District: 3
Key Personnel: Mgr., LouAnn Jacobson; Museum Shop Mgr., Robert DeNyke; Museum Shop Mgr., Diana Donohue.
Personnel Profile: Full-Time Paid 12; Part-Time Paid 2; Part-Time Volunteers 72; Interns 3.
Governing Authority: federal government; not-for-profit. Parent Institution: Bureau of Land Management. Tax-exempt.
Archaeology Museum.
Collections: focus on the northern San Juan Ancestral Puebloan people from Basketmaker to Pueblo III periods; over 3 million artifacts from federal lands in SW Colorado; Native American cultures of the Four Corners region.
Research Fields: Southwest archaeology.
Facilities: research lab.
Activities: interpretation & visitor services.
Hours & Admission Prices: March-Oct. daily 9-5; Nov.-Feb. daily 10-4. March-Oct. adults $3; Nov.-Feb. no charge. America the Beautiful passes accepted. Closed New Year's Day; Thanksgiving; Christmas. ♿
Attendance: 22,066 (accurate)
Membership: Annual Pass $6.

Durango

ANIMAS MUSEUM, 3065 W. 2nd Ave., Durango, CO 81301-4209. Mailing Address: P.O. Box 3384, Durango, CO 81302-3384. Tel.: 970-259-2402. Fax: 970-259-4749.
E-mail: animasmuseum@frontier.net
Web Site: www.animasmuseum.org
Founded: 1978.
Congressional District: 3
Key Personnel: Dir. & Museum Shop Mgr., Robert McDaniel; Pres. (V), Mary Jane Hood; Treas., Emily Ter Maat; Registrar, Janet Postler.
Personnel Profile: Full-Time Paid 1; Part-Time Paid 2; Part-Time Volunteers 25.
Governing Authority: private; nonprofit. Parent Institution: LaPlata Co. Historical Society. Tax-exempt: 501(c)(3).
Historical Society Museum: housed in the former 1904 Animas City School building, a 3-story sandstone structure; a c.1870s hand hewn log cabin is also located on the grounds.
Collections: concentration on San Juan Basin history with a focus on La Plata County.
Major Exhibits: Land of Opportunity - Settling & Developing La Plata County, 11/09-12/10.
Facilities: 225-vol. library of books relating to local & regional history/culture, southwest archaeology, genealogy and historical preservation; restored classroom; 3,000 sq. ft. exhibit space. Southwest Indian arts & crafts, books, cards and museum-related items for sale.
Activities: formal education programs for children; guided tours; lectures; school loan service; temporary exhibitions. Annual Events: May Fair; Community Heritage Award; Christmas Bazaar; Durango Heritage Celebration.
Publications: newsletter published five times annually, Artifacts; Historic Durango.
Hours & Admission Prices: May-Oct. Mon.-Sat. 10-6; Nov.-April Tues.-Sat. 10-4. Adults $3, children 7-12 $1; discounts to groups & tours; children 6 and under & members no charge. ♿
Attendance: 5,010 (accurate)
Membership: Pioneer (over 65) & Student $25; Single $40; Family $50; Centennial $125; Small Commercial $150; Corporate $300; Chief Ouray (Single Life) $1,200; Otto Mears (Family Life) $1,800.

CENTER OF SOUTHWEST STUDIES/FORT LEWIS COLLEGE, 1000 Rim Dr., Durango, CO 81301-3911. Tel.: 970-247-7456. Fax: 970-247-7422.
E-mail: britz_k@fortlewis.edu
Web Site: swcenter.fortlewis.edu
Founded: 1964.
Congressional District: 3
Key Personnel: Dir., Kevin Britz; FLC Pres., Dr. Brad Bartel; Cur., Jeanne Brako; Archivist, Nik Kendziorski; Librarian, Elayne Silversmith; Coord. Special Events, Julie Tapley Booth; Asst. Librarian & Archivist, Jen Pack.

Personnel Profile: Full-Time Paid 6; Full-Time Volunteers 10; Part-Time Paid 10; Part-Time Volunteers 20; Interns 10.
Governing Authority: college; nonprofit organization. Fort Lewis College. Tax-exempt: 501(c)(3).
Art Museum.
Collections: American Southwest with emphasis on Four Corners area; ranching heritage; ancestral Puebloan history; books; archives; art; anthropology; ethnology; archaeology; college memorabilia.
Research Fields: training Native Americans in cultural heritage management & museum studies.
Facilities: 15,000-vol. library; 105-seat auditorium; restaurant; classrooms; labs; 4,400 sq. ft. exhibit space; field research station.
Activities: arts festival; concerts; dance recitals; docent program; films; formal education programs; guided tours; hobby workshops; lectures; loan, participatory, temporary & traveling exhibitions; rental gallery; study clubs; training programs. Annual Events: Hozhoni Days in March; Hispanic Heritage Days in May.
Publications: occasional papers series; magazine, Timelines.
Hours & Admission Prices: Galleries: Mon.-Wed. & Fri.-Sat. 1-4, Thurs. 1-7. No charge; donations accepted. Closed state & federal holidays. ♿
Attendance: 35,000 (estimated)

CHILDREN'S MUSEUM OF DURANGO, 802 E. 2nd Ave., 2nd Fl., Durango, CO 81301-5426. Tel.: 970-259-9234. Fax: 970-259-6320.
E-mail: info@childsmuseum.org
Web Site: www.childsmuseum.org
Key Personnel: Dir., Amy De Prospo
Children's Museum.
Collections: hands-on exhibits.
Facilities: 1,100 sq. ft. exhibit space.
Activities: special events; educational programs; rental facilities.
Hours & Admission Prices: Wed.-Sat. 9:30-4:30, Sun. 1-5. Adults $5.50, children 3 & over $4; children under 3 & grandparents no charge.

THE STRATER HOTEL, 699 Main Ave., Durango, CO 81301-5423. Tel.: 970-247-4431. Fax: 970-259-2208.
E-mail: mthom@strater.com
Web Site: www.strater.com
Founded: 1887.
Congressional District: 3
Key Personnel: C.E.O., Rod Barker.
Governing Authority: corp.
Historic Building: c.1887 operative Victorian hotel & saloon.
Collections: 93 rooms of early American Victorian walnut furnishings 1860-1910 period; carved walnut beds, wash stands & armoires.
Research Fields: Victorian era.
Facilities: restaurant; theatre.
Activities: guided tours. Museum Sponsors: plays June to Sept.
Publications: book, Strater Hotel Story.
Hours & Admission Prices: Daily 24 hours. Regularly scheduled tours. No charge; donations accepted.
Attendance: 36,000 (estimated)

Eaton

A.J. EATON HOUSE MUSEUM, 207 Elm Ave., Eaton, CO 80615-3428. Tel.: 970-454-2236.
Key Personnel: Pres., Nancy Donahoo
Historic House Museum: housed in the former home of A.J. Eaton.
Collections: US military, wars & flag history; uniforms; photographs; personal memorabilia; newspapers; magazines; scrapbooks.
Hours & Admission Prices: Tues., Thurs. & Sat. 2-4. No charge; donations accepted.

ANTIQUE WASHING MACHINE MUSEUM, 35901 WCR 31, Eaton, CO 80615. Tel.: 970-454-1856.
E-mail: lee@oldewash.com
Web Site: www.oldewash.com
Washing Machine Museum.
Collections: over 1,000 period washing machines.
Publications: book, Save Womens Lives.
Hours & Admission Prices: By appointment only.

Englewood

THE MUSEUM OF OUTDOOR ARTS, 1000 Englewood Pkwy., Ste. #2-230, Englewood, CO 80110-2373. Tel.: 303-806-0444, ext. 410. Fax: 303-806-0504.
Web Site: www.moaonline.org
Founded: 1982.
Congressional District: 6
Key Personnel: Pres. & Exec. Dir., Cynthia Madden Leitner; C.O.O., Rodney Lontine; Administrative Dir., Tatum Hayes; Project Mgr., Timothy Vacca; Technical Dir., Kelley Bergmann; Research Coord. & Archivist, Paul Leitner; Creative Dir., Lonnie Hanzon.
Personnel Profile: Full-Time Paid 8; Part-Time Paid 1; Part-Time Volunteers 6; Interns 20.
Governing Authority: nonprofit organization. Tax-exempt: 501(c)(3).
Art Museum.
Collections: fine arts.
Research Fields: public art; outdoor performing arts.
Facilities: 18,000-seat amphitheatre.
Activities: concerts; arts festivals; arts education classes; outdoor public art; exhibitions; college student internships; collaborative performances.
Publications: collections & information brochure; walking tour guides.
Hours & Admission Prices: Gallery: Mon.-Thurs. 9-5, Fri. 9-4; guided tours by arrangement. No charge; donations accepted. Closed federal holidays. ♿
Attendance: 250,000 (estimated)

Estes Park

ENOS MILLS CABIN MUSEUM & GALLERY, 6760 Hwy. 7, Estes Park, CO 80517-6404. Tel.: 970-586-4706.
E-mail: enosmillscbn@earthlink.net
Governing Authority: private.
Historic House Museum: built in 1885 by 15 year old Kansan Enos A. Mills. Listed on the National Register of Historic Places.
Collections: personal artifacts; photographs; letters; books.
Hours & Admission Prices: Summer: Thurs.-Sat. 11-4. Winter: Sat. 11-4; other times by appointment. Adults $5, children 6-12 $2.50.

ESTES PARK MUSEUM, (M), 200 4th St., Estes Park, CO 80517-6339. Tel.: 970-586-6256. Fax: 970-577-3768.
E-mail: bkilsdonk@estes.org
Web Site: www.estesnet.com/museum
Formerly: Estes Park Area Historical Museum
Founded: 1962.
Congressional District: 4
Key Personnel: Dir., Betty Kilsdonk; Pres. Friends Bd., John Roehl; Cur. Education, Kate Miller; Cur. Collections & Exhibits, Derek Fortini; Museum Shop Mgr., Elaine Hunt-Downey.
Personnel Profile: Full-Time Paid 3; Part-Time Paid 1; Part-Time Volunteers 50.
Governing Authority: municipal. Parent Institution: Town of Estes Park. Tax-exempt.
History Museum.
Collections: local history; photographs; textiles; archives; paintings; furnishings; Stanley Steamer automobile. Historic Buildings: early 20th century cabin; Rocky Mountain National Park administration building; 1909 Hydroplant Interpretive Center.
Research Fields: Estes Park history.
Activities: guided tours; permanent & temporary exhibits; lectures.
Publications: books: Weaving Mountain Memories; This Was Estes Park; The Ways of the Mountains; In the Vale of Elkanah; Early Narratives of Estes Park Vols. I-IV; Rocky Mountain Celts: The Scottish & Irish in Early Estes Park.
Hours & Admission Prices: May-Oct. Mon.-Sat. 10-5, Sun. 1-5; Nov.-April Sat. 10-5, Sun. 1-5. No charge; donations accepted. Closed major holidays. ♿
Attendance: 20,000 (estimated)
Membership: Individual $30; Family $50; Business & Organization $100; Contributor $150; Sustaining $300; Patron $500; Donor $1,000.

MACGREGOR RANCH, 180 MacGregor Lane, Estes Park, CO 80517. Mailing Address: P.O. Box 4675, Estes Park, CO 80517-4675. Tel.: 970-586-3749. Fax: 970-586-1092.
Historic House Museum: housed in the MacGregor family home, c.1896.
Collections: period furnishings & agricultural equipment; personal artifacts; oil paintings; photographs. Historic Buildings: milkhouse; blacksmith shop; root cellar; smokehouse.
Facilities: nature trails; nature center.
Activities: hiking; camping; wagon rides; tours. Annual Event: Children's History Camp in summer.
Hours & Admission Prices: June-Aug. Tues.-Fri. 10-4; other times by appointment.

ROCKY MOUNTAIN NATIONAL PARK, 1000 Highway 36, Estes Park, CO 80517-8311. Tel.: 970-586-1340. Fax: 970-586-1387. TTY: 970-586-1319.
E-mail: tim_burchett@nps.gov

Web Site: www.nps.gov/romo
Founded: 1915.
Congressional District: 2, 3 & 4
Key Personnel: Supt., Vaughn Baker; Cur., Tim Burchett; Archeologist, Bill Butler; Chief Interpretation & Education, Larry Frederick.
Personnel Profile: Full-Time Paid 1; Part-Time Volunteers 3.
Governing Authority: federal. Parent Institution: Department of the Interior. Subsidiary Institution: National Park Service.
Cultural & Natural History Museum.
Collections: herbarium; zoological; geology; botany; archaeological; historical; art.
Research Fields: Alpine ecology; archaeology history; glaciology; air quality; wildlife; natural history.
Facilities: Literature pertaining to surrounding national park for sale.
Activities: guided tours; talks; films; permanent exhibitions.
Hours & Admission Prices: Open to researchers only; call for appointment. No charge. ♿
Attendance: 3,000,000 (estimated)

STANLEY MUSEUM, 517 Big Thompson Ave., Estes Park, CO 80517-9661. Mailing Address: P.O. Box 788, Estes Park, CO 80517-0788. Tel.: 970-577-1903. Fax: 970-577-1924.
Founded: 1985.
Key Personnel: Dir., Donald Hoke
Transportation Museum.
Collections: automotive & transportation history; 1909 Model R Stanley Roadster; personal artifacts.
Hours & Admission Prices: June-Oct. daily 10-5; Nov.-May Wed.-Mon. 10-5; by appointment. No charge; donations accepted.

Evergreen

HIWAN HOMESTEAD MUSEUM, 4208 S. Timbervale Dr., Evergreen, CO 80439-8456. Mailing Address: 700 Jefferson County Pkwy., Golden, CO 80401-6025. Tel.: 720-497-7650. Fax: 303-670-7746.
Web Site: hiwan.jeffco.us
Founded: 1974.
Congressional District: 25
Key Personnel: Dir., Ralph Schell; Admin., John Steinle.
Personnel Profile: Full-Time Paid 4; Part-Time Paid 14; Part-Time Volunteers 150.
Governing Authority: county. Parent Institution: Jefferson County Open Space. Tax-exempt: 501(c)(3).
History Museum & Heritage Center: housed in 1880s 17-room log mansion, Camp Neosho, later renamed Hiwan Ranch.
Collections: Native American artifacts from the Douglas collection; Julia Douglas dolls; 6,000 catalogued historical photos; catalogued oral histories; manuscripts; Jefferson County historical items; religious objects; period furnishings.
Research Fields: Jefferson County history.
Facilities: 250-vol. library of local history & period books available for use on premises; nature trail; classrooms; Victorian gardens.
Activities: guided tours; lectures; docent program; formally organized education programs for children; special tours for blind, physically handicapped & nursing home seniors; after school specials; pioneer shop for printing & carpentry.
Publications: Indian Hills: The Place, The Times, The People; Mountain Memories; From Camp Neosho to the Hiwan Homestead; Evergreen; Upper Side of the Pie Crust.
Hours & Admission Prices: Jan. 8-May & Sept.-Dec. Tues.-Sun. 12-5; June-Aug. Tues.-Sun. 11-5. No charge; donations accepted. ♿
Attendance: 11,986 (accurate)
Membership: Student $2; Regular Individual $10; Family $15; Sustaining $25; Patron $100; Life $250.

HUMPHREY MEMORIAL PARK & MUSEUM, 620 S. Soda Creek Rd., Evergreen, CO 80439-9263. Mailing Address: P.O. Box 2122, 620 S. Soda Creek Rd., Evergreen, CO 80437-2122. Tel.: 303-674-5429. Fax: 303-674-5807.
E-mail: humphreymuseum@wispertel.net
Key Personnel: Dir., Peggy Shaw.
Governing Authority: nonprofit organization. Tax-exempt: 501(c)(3).
History Museum.
Collections: Humphrey family's personal artifacts; period furnishings; wall hangings; photographs; letters; scrapbooks.
Activities: Summer Events: plays; concerts; dance recitals; poetry readings; Writer's Festival.
Hours & Admission Prices: By appointment.

Fairplay

SOUTH PARK CITY MUSEUM, (M), 100 4th, Fairplay, CO 80440-0634. Mailing Address: P.O. Box 634, Fairplay, CO 80440-0634. Tel.: 719-836-2387. Fax: 719-836-9855.
E-mail: southparkhistorical@wildblue.net
Web Site: www.southparkcity.org
Founded: 1957.
Congressional District: 3
Key Personnel: Dir., Linda Bjurklund; Pres. (V), Harley Hamilton; Cur., Carol Davis.
Personnel Profile: Full-Time Paid 2; Part-Time Paid 10; Part-Time Volunteers 15.
Governing Authority: nonprofit organization. Parent Institution: South Park Historical Foundation, Inc. Tax-exempt: 501(c)(3).
Historic Village Museum: located on the site of a Colorado mining town.
Collections: furnishings; 34 representative pieces of architecture (1860-1900). Historic Buildings: c.1876 South Park Lager Beer Brewery; 1879 Summer Saloon. (Listed on the National Register of Historic Places).
Research Fields: culture & history of the South Park area 1860-1920.
Facilities: visitors center. Fine art reproductions & museum-related items for sale.
Activities: self-guided tours; permanent exhibitions; video.
Publications: video tour, A Town is Born; books, A Town is Born; South Park City.
Hours & Admission Prices: mid-May to late May daily 9-5; Memorial Day-Labor Day daily 9-7; Sept. to mid-Oct. daily 10-6. Adults $7.50, senior citizens 62 & over $6, children 6-12 $4; discounts to members of Time Travelers affiliated institutions AAM, ICOM, AAA members & groups; members & children under 6 no charge. ♿
Attendance: 14,682 (accurate)
Membership: Individual $15; Family $45.

Fleming

FLEMING HISTORICAL SOCIETY, Heritage Museum Park, Fleming, CO 80728. Mailing Address: P.O. Box 351, Fleming, CO 80728-0351. Tel.: 970-265-2591 & 3611.
Founded: 1965.
Congressional District: 4
Key Personnel: C.E.O., Donald D. Langdon.
Governing Authority: society; nonprofit. Tax-exempt: 501(c)(3).
Historical Society Museum: housed in 1905 Philarado, a one-room schoolhouse & Burlington Depot.
Collections: local history; Indian artifacts.
Research Fields: history of the early settlers in this area.
Facilities: Philarado school; Burlington Depot.
Activities: permanent exhibitions. Museum Sponsors: Pioneer Day Activities in September.
Publications: books, Memories of Our Pioneers, Our Pioneer Heritage.
Hours & Admission Prices: June-Aug. Sun. 1-4 or by appointment. No charge; donations accepted. ♿
Attendance: 200 (estimated)

Florence

PRICE PIONEER MUSEUM, 100 E. Front St., Florence, CO 81226. Tel.: 719-784-1904.
Founded: 1964.
Congressional District: 3
Key Personnel: Pres., Olive Tripp; Vice Pres., Don Vitullo; Treas., Jean Pittman; Sec., Goldie Vitullo; Museum Cur., Roberta Miller.
Personnel Profile: Part-Time Paid 1; Part-Time Volunteers 14.
Governing Authority: municipal. Parent Institution: Pioneer Day Board Assoc. Tax-exempt.
Pioneer Museum: housed in 1894 building.
Collections: industrial; general; folklore; Indian artifacts; mineralogy; manuscripts. Historic House: 1875 first city jail.
Facilities: 300-vol. library of newspaper files, historic documents; scrapbooks; general reference files available for research on premises; reading room.
Activities: guided tours; permanent exhibitions.
Hours & Admission Prices: mid-May to Sept. Tues.-Sun. 1-4; other times by appointment. No charge; donations accepted.
Attendance: 1,500 (estimated)
Membership: Annual $25.

Florissant

FLORISSANT FOSSIL BEDS NATIONAL MONUMENT, 15807 Teller County Rd. #1, Florissant, CO 80816. Mailing Address: P.O. Box 185, Florissant, CO 80816-0185. Tel.: 719-748-3253. Fax: 719-748-3164.
Web Site: www.nps.gov/flfo
Founded: 1969.
Congressional District: 5
Key Personnel: Chief Interpretation & Resources Mgmt. & Visitor Protection, Rick Wilson; Supt., Keith Payne; Paleontologist, Dr. Herbert W. Meyer; Volunteer Coord., Jeff Wolin.
Personnel Profile: Full-Time Paid 8; Part-Time Paid 2; Part-Time Volunteers 20; Interns 6.
Governing Authority: federal. Parent Institution: Department of the Interior, National Park Service, Washington, DC 20240. Tax-exempt.
Historic House Museum.
Collections: fossil insects, leaves, fish, & several other categories of fossils of the Eocene period, approximately 34 to 35 million years ago; archaeological specimens 5,000 to 8,000 years old.
Research Fields: paleontology especially paleoentomology and paleobotany; modern flora & fauna; history.
Facilities: 900-vol. library of scientific books, available for use by prior notice on premises only; hiking trails. Interpretive books & postcards for sale.
Activities: self-guided hiking trails year-round; ranger-guided tours during summer; off-site lectures; school programs on & off-site year-round; junior ranger.
Publications: biannual newspaper.
Hours & Admission Prices: Daily 9-5. Adults $3; senior citizens & children under 16 no charge. Federal Lands Passes accepted. Closed New Year's Day; Thanksgiving; Christmas. ♿
Attendance: 62,000 (accurate)

Fort Collins

AVENIR MUSEUM OF DESIGN AND MERCHANDISING, (M), Colorado State University, 1574 Campus Delivery, Fort Collins, CO 80523-1574. Tel.: 970-491-1983. Fax: 970-491-4376.
E-mail: carlson@cahs.colostate.edu
Web Site: www.colostate.edu/depts/dm
Formerly: Gustafson Gallery/Design & Merchandising
Founded: 1986.
Congressional District: 4
Key Personnel: Cur., Linda Carlson.
Personnel Profile: Full-Time Paid 1; Part-Time Paid 1; Part-Time Volunteers 15; Interns 2.
Governing Authority: Colorado State University. Tax-exempt: 501(c)(3).
Costume, Textiles & Interior Furnishings Museum.
Collections: 19th-20th century western dress; Asian costume & textiles; period chairs.
Major Exhibits: Artisans of the Silk Road, 2/10-5/10; Blackwell Retrospective, 9/10-12/10.
Research Fields: influence of films on fashion styles & trends; middle 19th-century men's dress in the American west; quilting traditions.
Facilities: 200-vol. library of costume history books & magazines; classrooms; labs.
Activities: exhibit openings with curator talks; formal education programs for undergraduate or graduate students affiliated with Colorado State University; guided tours; lectures; temporary exhibitions; traveling trunk program.
Publications: exhibit catalogs, Kimono; Women's Suits: Transformations in Form & Fabric, 1890-1990; quarterly newsletter, Friends of Gustafson Gallery Update; Window to the World, 2009.
Hours & Admission Prices: Mon.-Wed. & Fri. 11-6, Thurs. 11-8. No charge; donations accepted. Closed Thanksgiving; Christmas. ♿
Attendance: 500 (estimated)
Membership: Associate $20; General $40; Groups & Organizations $50; Sponsor $100; Benefactor $250.

AVERY HOUSE, 328 W. Mountain Ave., Fort Collins, CO 80521-2702. Tel.: 970-221-0533.
Historic House: former home of Franklin Avery, founder of the First National Bank; built in 1879. Listed on the National Register of Historic Places.
Collections: family history; period furnishings.
Activities: special events.
Hours & Admission Prices: Sun. & Wed. 1-3.

BEE FAMILY CENTENNIAL FARM MUSEUM, 4320 E. County Rd., 58, Fort Collins, CO 80524-9326. Tel.: 970-482-9168.
E-mail: info@beefamilyfarm.com
Web Site: www.beefamilyfarm.org
Founded: 2004.
Key Personnel: Chm. (V), Liz Harrison; Pres. (V), Adam Thomas; Museum Shop Mgr., Eva Wallace.
Personnel Profile: Part-Time Volunteers 8.
Governing Authority: nonprofit organization. Tax-exempt.
Farm Museum.
Collections: family history; period farm equipment; early irrigation methods; personal artifacts; pioneer farming.
Activities: demonstrations.
Publications: brochure; interpretive guide; introduction DVD.
Hours & Admission Prices: May-Oct. Fri.-Sat. 9-4; other times by appointment. Adults $5, children $2. ♿
Attendance: 600 (estimated)

COLORADO STATE UNIVERSITY ART MUSEUM, (M), Univ. Center for the Arts Campus 1778, Fort Collins, CO 80523-0001. Tel.: 970-491-1989.
E-mail: linda.frickman@colostate.edu
Web Site: www.artmuseum.colostate.edu
Formerly: Hatton Gallery, Colorado State University
Founded: 2008.
Congressional District: 4
Key Personnel: Dir., Linda Frickman; Program Coord., Keith Jentzsch; Collections Mgr., Suzanne Hale.
Personnel Profile: Full-Time Paid 2; Part-Time Paid 1; Part-Time Volunteers 10; Interns 8.
Governing Authority: public university. Parent Institution: Colorado State University. Tax-exempt: 501(c)(3).
University Art Museum.
Collections: Japanese prints; African art; South Seas art; modern & contemporary works on paper.
Research Fields: contemporary poster design; African art.
Activities: contemporary artists & art historical exhibitions; formal education programs for adults & undergraduate or graduate students affiliated with Colorado State University; K-12 partnerships; lectures; loan, temporary & traveling exhibitions.
Publications: Colorado International Invitational poster exhibition catalogs; critic & artist residency series catalogs; annual calendar.
Hours & Admission Prices: Tues.-Sat. 11-7. No charge; donations accepted. Closed university & major holidays. ♿
Attendance: 10,000 (estimated)

CURFMAN GALLERY, Colorado State University, Fort Collins, CO 80523-0001. Mailing Address: 8033 Campus Delivery, Lory Student Center, Colorado State University, Fort Collins, CO 80523-0001. Tel.: 970-491-2810. Fax: 970-491-3746.
E-mail: lsc_artsmanager@mail.colostate.edu
Web Site: www.curfman.colostate.edu
Founded: 1969.
Congressional District: 4
Key Personnel: Graduate Asst. & Dir., Nick Croghan; Designer, Jack Curfman.
Personnel Profile: Full-Time Paid 1; Part-Time Paid 7.
Governing Authority: public university. Parent Institution: Colorado State University. Tax-exempt.
Exhibit Area & Gallery.
Collections: posters; Native American artifacts; African tribal artifacts.
Facilities: 1,700 sq. ft. exhibit area.
Activities: Annual Events: juried student exhibit; Biennial Event: Colorado International Invitational Poster Exhibition.
Publications: schedule of exhibits.
Hours & Admission Prices: mid-Jan. to May & Sept. to mid-Dec. Mon.-Thurs. 9-9, Fri. 9-9:30, Sat. 12-4. No charge; donations accepted. Closed university holidays. ♿
Attendance: 35,000 (estimated)

DISCOVERY SCIENCE CENTER, 703 E. Prospect Rd., Fort Collins, CO 80525-1108. Mailing Address: 200 Mathews St., Fort Collins, CO 80524-2817. Tel.: 970-472-3990. Fax: 970-472-3997.
E-mail: dcsm@dcsm.org
Web Site: www.dcsm.org
Founded: 1989.
Key Personnel: Exec. Dir., Annette Geiselman; Dir. Devel., Annette Pontillo; Assoc. Dir., Jason Wolvington; Volunteer Coord., Kate Kosakowski.
Personnel Profile: Full-Time Paid 4; Part-Time Paid 5; Part-Time Volunteers 130.
Governing Authority: private; not-for-profit organization. Tax-exempt: 501(c)(3).
Science Museum.
Collections: large-scale hands-on science & technology exhibits which include

electricity, biology, communication, light & optics, energy & motion, simple machines & the human body.
Facilities: Museum-related items for sale.
Activities: classes; field trips; special events & programs.
Hours & Admission Prices: Tues.-Sat. 10-5. Adults 13-59 $7, senior citizens 60 & over $5.50, children 3-12 $5; ASTC Travel Passport Program; children under 3, ASTC Reciprocal members & members no charge. Closed New Year's Day; Independence Day; Thanksgiving; Christmas. ♿
Attendance: 32,000 (accurate)
Membership: Individual $20; Grandparent $50; Family $60; Deluxe $75.

FORT COLLINS MUSEUM, (M), 200 Mathews, Fort Collins, CO 80524-2817. Tel.: 970-221-6738. Fax: 970-416-2236.
E-mail: bhiggins@fcgov.com
Web Site: fcgov.com/museum/
Founded: 1940.
Congressional District: 4
Key Personnel: City Mgr., Darin Atteberry; Mayor, Doug Hutchinson; Dir., Cheryl Donaldson; Asst. Dir., Brent Carmack; Public Rels. & Devel. Coord., Beth Higgins; Education Cur., Kerry Doyle; NAGPRA Coord., Brenda Martin; Collections Mgr., Linda Moore; Exhibitions Technician, Cory Gundlach; Education Coord., Toby Swaford; Museum Shop Mgr., Brad Thrush.
Personnel Profile: Full-Time Paid 4; Part-Time Paid 5; Part-Time Volunteers 60; Interns 3.
Governing Authority: municipal. Parent Institution: City of Fort Collins. Subsidiary Institution: Cultural, Library & Recreational Services. Tax-exempt.
History Museum: housed in historic Carnegie library.
Collections: human interaction with nature through the history of the Cache La Poudre River Valley; Paleolithic material; American Indian artifacts; early military & pioneer materials of Larimer Co.: furniture, clothing, personal artifacts, tools & equipment. Historic Structures: Boxelder Schoolhouse (1905); Franz-Smith Cabin (1882); the Elizabeth Auntie Stone Cabin (1864); the Antoine Janis Cabin (1854).
Research Fields: history; Folsom archaeology; material culture; Western history.
Facilities: Museum-related items for sale.
Activities: special exhibits; guided group tours with reservation; outreach trunk program; workshops & classes; hands-on programs for families; special events. Museum Sponsors: Rendezvous in July; Carol Fest in December.
Publications: postcard notebook, Fort Collins Memories; book, Diary of Ann Sloan Sargisson.
Hours & Admission Prices: Tues.-Sat. 10-5, Sun. 12-5. No charge; donations accepted. Closed national holidays. ♿
Attendance: 25,000 (accurate)

FORT COLLINS MUSEUM OF CONTEMPORARY ART, (M), 201 S. College Ave., Fort Collins, CO 80524-3182. Tel.: 970-482-2787. Fax: 970-482-0804.
Web Site: www.fcmoca.org
Founded: 1990.
Congressional District: 4
Key Personnel: Chm. (V), Gretchen Gaede; Exec. Dir., Marianne Lorenz.
Personnel Profile: Full-Time Paid 3; Part-Time Paid 1; Part-Time Volunteers 75; Interns 4.
Governing Authority: private; nonprofit. Tax-exempt: 501(c)(3).
Contemporary Art Museum.
Collections: works by contemporary artists.
Major Exhibits: Todd Siler Art Science, 1/10-2/10; Myth, Object & the Animal William Morris Glass, 8/10-10/10.
Facilities: art library; art school.
Activities: gallery education programs; tours (including studio); lectures.
Publications: quarterly newsletter.
Hours & Admission Prices: Tues.-Fri. 10-5, Sat. 12-5. Suggested Donation: adults $2; discount to AAM & ICOM members; students, senior citizens & members no charge. Closed holidays. ♿
Attendance: 15,000 (estimated)
Membership: Student & Senior $25; Individual $40; Family $75; Contributor $150; Patron $500; Benefactor $1,000; Masterpiece $2,500.

Fort Garland

FORT GARLAND MUSEUM, 29477 Hwy. 159, Fort Garland, CO 81133. Mailing Address: P.O. Box 368, Fort Garland, CO 81133-0368. Tel.: 719-379-3512. Fax: 719-379-3479.
E-mail: rick.manzanares@chs.state.co.us
Web Site: www.fortgarlandmuseumfriends.org
Formerly: Old Fort Garland
Founded: 1945.
Congressional District: 3
Key Personnel: Dir., Rick Manzanares.
Personnel Profile: Full-Time Paid 2; Part-Time Volunteers 30.
Governing Authority: state. State Historical Society of Colorado, 1300 Broadway, Denver, CO 80203. Tax-exempt.
Military & Pioneer Museum: housed in c.1858-1883 Old Fort Garland.
Collections: military; pioneer and Indian; dioramas pertaining to period of Fort operation, from Spanish exploration-1880.
Facilities: Historical publications & post cards for sale.
Activities: self-guided tours. Special Events: military reenactments.
Publications: monthly magazine, Colorado Heritage.
Hours & Admission Prices: April-Oct. daily 9-5; Nov.-March Thurs.-Mon. 10-4. Adults $4, senior citizens $3.50, children $2.50; children under 6 & C.H.S. members no charge. Closed New Year's Day; Thanksgiving; Christmas. ♿
Attendance: 15,000 (accurate)
Membership: Senior $40; Seniors Family, Groups & Individual $50; Family & Group $60; Associate $65; Explorer $100; Centennial $250; Historian $500; Heritage Club $1,000; Millenium $2,100.

Fort Morgan

* **FORT MORGAN MUSEUM, (M),** 414 Main St., City Park, Fort Morgan, CO 80701. Mailing Address: P.O. Box 184, Fort Morgan, CO 80701-0184. Tel.: 970-542-4009 & 4010. Fax: 970-542-4012.
E-mail: fortmorganmuseum@ftmorganmus.org
Web Site: www.ftmorganmus.org/
Founded: 1969.
Congressional District: 4
Key Personnel: Pres., Don Ostwald; Dir., Marne Jurgemeyer; Registrar, Nikkie Cooper; Educator, Andrew Dunehoo.
Personnel Profile: Full-Time Paid 3; Part-Time Paid 1; Part-Time Volunteers 20; Interns 1.
Governing Authority: private foundation. Parent Institution: Fort Morgan Heritage Foundation. Tax-exempt: 501(c)(3).
General Museum.
Collections: prehistoric & historic Indian relics; agricultural implements; ranching equipment; quilts; china; photographs; textiles; clothing; Fort Morgan Times on microfilm from 1884 to present; small Glenn Miller archive; small Great Western (beet) sugar archive; documents.
Research Fields: history of Morgan County & northeastern Colorado.
Facilities: research center; meeting room. Museum-related items for sale.
Activities: guided tours on request; lectures; docent program; inter-museum loan, permanent, temporary & traveling exhibitions; school loan service; school outreach program; research.
Publications: books, 111 Trees; Best of Friends Cookbook; Instructor's Delights: Cooking Schools I-IV; Early Fort Morgan; Fort Morgan; A Step Back in Time; Patchwork Chatelaine; Windows To The Past; From The Steppes To The Prairies; Memories of Morgan County; Platte Reflections; Baker... More Than A School.
Hours & Admission Prices: Mon. & Fri. 10-5, Tues.-Thurs. 10-8, Sat. 11-5. Research Room: Wed. & Fri. mornings, Tues.-Thurs. afternoons. No charge; donations accepted. Closed national holidays. ♿
Attendance: 12,605 (accurate)
Membership: Individual $20; Family $30; Sustaining $50; Patron $100; Benefactor $300; Philanthropist $500.

Fraser

COZENS RANCH MUSEUM, 77849 U.S. Hwy. 40, Fraser, CO 80442. Mailing Address: P.O. Box 165, Hot Sulphur Springs, CO 80451-0165. Tel.: 970-726-5488. Fax: 970-725-0129.
E-mail: crm@rkymtnhi.com
Web Site: www.grandcountymuseum.com
Founded: 1990.
Congressional District: 4
Key Personnel: Pres., Yvonne Knox; Treas. & Sec., Barbara Mitchell; Dir., Don Woster.
Personnel Profile: Full-Time Paid 3; Part-Time Paid 1; Part-Time Volunteers 25.
Governing Authority: nonprofit organization. Parent Institution: Grand County Historical Association. Tax-exempt: 501(c)(3).
Historic House: 1874 ranch built by William & Mary Cozens, among the first homesteaders to ranch in the Fraser Valley.
Collections: c.1900 furnishings.
Research Fields: county settlement; transportation; county ranches; post offices.
Facilities: County history books & Cozens special interest items for sale.
Activities: lectures; docent program.
Publications: quarterly newsletter, The Spoke; annual journal.
Hours & Admission Prices: Memorial Day to Labor Day Tues.-Sat. 10-5;

Sept.-May Wed.-Sat. 10-4. Families $10, adults $4, senior citizens $3, students $2; discounts to tour groups, seniors & locals; children under 6 & members no charge. ♿
Attendance: 1,836 (accurate)
Membership: Individual $25; Couple $40; Explorer $80; Historian $125; Pioneer $250; Heritage $500.

Frisco

FRISCO HISTORIC PARK & MUSEUM, (M), 120 Main St., Frisco, CO 80443. Mailing Address: P.O. Box 4100, Frisco, CO 80443-4100. Tel.: 970-668-3428. Fax: 970-668-0694.
Web Site: www.townoffrisco.com
Formerly: Frisco Historical Society
Founded: 1983.
Key Personnel: Mgr., Simone Belz; Museum Asst., Melissa Stabile; Museum Asst., Angela McCarthy.
Personnel Profile: Full-Time Paid 1; Part-Time Paid 2; Part-Time Volunteers 30.
Governing Authority: Parent Institution: Town of Frisco. Tax-exempt.
History Museum: located in c.1900 Frisco Schoolhouse Museum.
Collections: local history, 1880s to 1960s; town of Frisco & Summit County, CO.
Research Fields: local history.
Facilities: 50-seat Gazebo. Museum-related items for sale.
Activities: arts festivals; concerts; formal educational programs; guided tours; lectures; rental facilities. Annual Events: children's halloween program; Founder's Day celebration; Night at The Museum Series.
Hours & Admission Prices: May-Sept. Tues.-Sat. 9-5, Sun. 9-3; Oct.-April Tues.-Sat. 10-4, Sun. 10-2. No charge. Closed Thanksgiving; Christmas. ♿
Attendance: 26,000 (estimated)

Fruita

COLORADO NATIONAL MONUMENT, Monument Rd., Fruita, CO 81521-0001. Tel.: 970-858-3617. Fax: 970-858-0372.
Web Site: www.nps.gov
Founded: 1911.
Congressional District: 4
Key Personnel: Resource Management Chief, David Price; Park Ranger, Lisa Klaussen.
Personnel Profile: Part-Time Paid 1; Part-Time Volunteers 1.
Governing Authority: federal. Parent Institution: National Park Service. Tax-exempt.
Park Museum.
Collections: geology; cultural & natural history.
Facilities: 500-vol. library of natural history and geology books available for on-site use; study collection of plant & animal specimens.
Activities: research; interpretive programs.
Publications: NPS-CRM publication.
Hours & Admission Prices: Visitor Center: Memorial Day-Labor Day daily 8-6; Sept.-May daily 9-5. Visitor Center no charge; Park: $5. Closed Christmas. ♿
Attendance: 385,000 (estimated)

DINOSAUR JOURNEY, 550 Jurassic Court, Fruita, CO 81521-7707. Mailing Address: P.O. Box 2000, Grand Junction, CO 81502-5020. Tel.: 970-858-7282.
Web Site: www.dinosaurjourney.org
Dinosaur Museum.
Collections: dinosaurs; dinosaur skeletons; hands-on exhibits; dinosaur history; fossils.
Hours & Admission Prices: Mon.-Sat. 10-4, Sun. 12-4. Adults $7, seniors $6, children $4; members no charge.

Gateway

GATEWAY COLORADO AUTOMOBILE MUSEUM, 43224 Hwy. 141, Gateway, CO 81522. Mailing Address: P.O. Box 339, Gateway, CO 81522-0339. Tel.: 970-931-2895.
Founded: 2006.
Key Personnel: Exec. Dir., Preston Patterson
Automobile Museum.
Collections: over 40 cars depicting America's automobile history, science, design and social impact; hands-on exhibits.
Facilities: 30,000 sq. ft. exhibit space. Museum-related items for sale.
Activities: hands-on exhibits.
Publications: book, The Performing Art of The American Automobile.
Hours & Admission Prices: Sun.-Mon. 10-5, Tues.-Sat. 10-7. Adults $9, seniors 65 & over $7, youth 6-12 $5; discounts to groups; children 5 & under and members no charge. Closed Thanksgiving; Christmas.

Georgetown

GEORGETOWN ENERGY MUSEUM, 600 Griffith St., Georgetown, CO 80444. Mailing Address: 600 Griffith St., P.O. Box 398, Georgetown, CO 80444-0398. Tel.: 303-569-3557.
E-mail: gtnem@juno.com
Web Site: georgetownenergymuseum.org
Founded: 1900.
Governing Authority: nonprofit organization. Tax-exempt: 501(c)(3).
History Museum: housed in fully functioning and operational hydroelectric generating plant.
Collections: hydroelectric power history; photographs; early electrical household appliances.
Activities: tours.
Hours & Admission Prices: June to early Oct. Mon.-Sat. 10-4, Sun. 12-4; mid-Oct. to May Mon.-Fri. by appointment; groups by appointment. No charge; donations accepted.

HAMILL HOUSE MUSEUM, 305 Argentine, Georgetown, CO 80444. Mailing Address: P.O. Box 667, Georgetown, CO 80444-0667. Tel.: 303-569-2840. Fax: 303-569-2111.
E-mail: preservation@historicgeorgetown.org
Web Site: www.historicgeorgetown.org
Formerly: Historic Georgetown Inc.
Founded: 1970.
Congressional District: 4
Key Personnel: Exec. Dir., Sharon Rossino; Chm. (V), Matt Schmalz; Museum Shop Mgr., Tristen Greenleaf.
Personnel Profile: Full-Time Paid 2; Part-Time Paid 5; Part-Time Volunteers 50.
Governing Authority: society. Tax-exempt: 501(c)(3).
Historic Houses Museum: located in the Georgetown-Silver Plume Historic District.
Collections: original furnishings & woodwork. Historic Buildings: c.1867-1881 William A. Hamill House & 1880-1881 Hamill office building, stable & carriage house; 1892 Bowman-White House; Tucker-Rutherford House; 1875-1880 Miner's cottage; 1870 log cabin.
Research Fields: general Georgetown history & architecture; biography of William A. Hamill; biographies of John H. Bowman & J. J. White; Christmas at Hamill House.
Facilities: Books & memorabilia of Colorado history & the Victorian period for sale.
Activities: tours; lectures; auctions; Biennial house tour; facility rental. Museum Sponsors: Christmas market; biennial Gala Auction Benefit.
Publications: quarterly newsletter; journal; Guide to the Georgetown-Silver Plume Historic District; William A. Hamill, The Gentleman from Clear Creek; annual report.
Hours & Admission Prices: Hamill House: June-Sept. daily 10-4; Winter: call for hours. Adults $6, seniors & students $4; discounts for AAA, Colorado Historical Society members & groups of 10 or more; member no charge. Closed New Year's Day; Thanksgiving; Christmas. Bowman-White House: closed for restoration. ♿
Attendance: 18,000 (estimated)
Membership: Annual Memberships, Domestic/Foreign: Regular $30-$35; Associate $50-$55; Sustaining $100-$105; Supporting $500-$505. Lifetime Memberships: Johnson Log Cabin $1,500; Tucker/Rutherford $2,500; Kneisel House & Bowman-White House $10,000; Hamill House $25, 000.

HOTEL DE PARIS MUSEUM, 409 6th Ave., Georgetown, CO 80444. Mailing Address: 1510 E. 10th Ave., #3F, Denver, CO 80218-3139. Tel.: 303-569-2311. Fax: 303-756-8768.
Web Site: www.hoteldeparismuseum.org
Founded: 1954.
Congressional District: 2
Key Personnel: Chm. (V), Mrs. Polly S. Flobeck; Pres. (V), Mrs. Jean Gray McGinnis; Dir., James H. Bert.
Personnel Profile: Full-Time Paid 1; Part-Time Paid 4; Part-Time Volunteers 20.
Governing Authority: nonprofit organization. Parent Institution: The National Society of The Colonial Dames of America in Colorado. Subsidiary Institution: The National Society of Colonial Dames in America in the State of Colorado (NASCDA in CO). Tax-exempt.
Historic Building Museum: built in 1875.
Collections: original furniture, dishes & kitchen utensils pertaining to a 19th-century hotel with a strong French influence; academic library.
Activities: guided tours; permanent exhibitions.
Publications: booklets; tour booklets; pamphlet, The Hotel de Paris Museum; DVD.
Hours & Admission Prices: Memorial Day-Labor Day daily 10-4:30. Adults $5, senior citizens $4, children 6-12 $2, group tours over 10 people $3 per

person; discounts to AAA members; children under 6 no charge. Les Amis de L'Hotel de Paris Museum: donations accepted. ♿
Attendance: 6,500 (accurate)

Glenwood Springs

FRONTIER HISTORICAL SOCIETY AND MUSEUM, 1001 Colorado, Glenwood Springs, CO 81601-3319. Tel.: 970-945-4448. Fax: 970-384-2477.
E-mail: history@rof.net
Web Site: www.glenwoodhistory.com
Founded: 1963.
Key Personnel: Exec. Dir., Cindy Hines; Pres., Ann Gremel; Vice Pres., Mark Howard; Sec. & Treas., Scott Werking; Archivist & Registrar, Patsy Stark; Education, Sue Plush.
Personnel Profile: Full-Time Paid 1; Part-Time Paid 2; Part-Time Volunteers 75.
Governing Authority: private; nonprofit organization. Tax-exempt: 501(c)(3).
General Museum.
Collections: Glenwood Springs history particularly around 1900.
Facilities: 200-vol. library; 1,000 sq. ft. exhibit space. Museum-related items for sale.
Activities: formal education programs for children; guided tours; lectures; temporary exhibitions. Annual Event: Cemetery Ghost Walk.
Publications: quarterly newsletter, Frontier Times; monthly newspaper article, Frontier Diary.
Hours & Admission Prices: May-Oct. 1 Mon.-Sat. 11-4; Oct. 2-April Mon. & Thurs.-Sat. 1-4. Adults $3, senior citizens $2, children 12 & under $1; discounts to groups; members no charge. Closed New Year's Day; Memorial Day; Independence Day; Labor Day; Thanksgiving; Christmas.
Attendance: 3,513 (accurate)
Membership: Old Timer $15; Old Timer Couple $20; Frontier $30; Vintage Family $50; Pioneer $100; Antique $250; Historian $500; Nostalgia Sponsor $1,000.

GLENWOOD RAILROAD MUSEUM, 413 7th St., Glenwood Springs, CO 81601-3442. Tel.: 970-945-7044.
Founded: 2003.
Key Personnel: Gen. Mgr., Jan Girardot; Cur., Dick Helmke.
Governing Authority: Tax-exempt: 501(c)(3).
Railroad Museum: housed in the historic Glenwood Springs Railroad Station; built in 1904.
Collections: railroad history, memorabilia & artifacts; photographs; large scale model railroad; telegraphs; railroad semaphore signals.
Facilities: Museum-related items for sale.
Activities: school tours.
Hours & Admission Prices: Fri.-Mon. 12-4.

Golden

ASTOR HOUSE MUSEUM, (M), 822 12th St., Golden, CO 80401-1112. Mailing Address: 923 10th St., Golden, CO 80401. Tel.: 303-278-3557. Fax: 303-278-8916.
E-mail: shannon@astorhousemuseum.org
Web Site: www.astorhousemuseum.org
Founded: 1972.
Key Personnel: Exec. Dir., Shannon Voirol.
Personnel Profile: Full-Time Paid 2; Part-Time Paid 4; Part-Time Volunteers 225; Interns 1.
Governing Authority: nonprofit organization. Parent Institution: City of Golden. Subsidiary Institution: Friends of the Astor House Museum & Clear Creek History Park. Tax-exempt: 501(c)(3).
Historic House Museum: housed in c.1867 Astor House hotel.
Collections: decorative art of the frontier period; furniture; clothing; historical objects from collections predate 1908.
Research Fields: local history; architectural survey of city; late 19th-century decorative arts & architecture.
Activities: guided tours; lectures; formally organized education programs for children; docent program or council; training programs; loan, permanent & temporary exhibitions; call for information on living history demonstrations & living history day camp for children. Museum Sponsors: Tea Time at the Astor House.
Publications: quarterly newsletter, Dear Friends; volunteer monthly newsletter, Friendly Reminder.
Hours & Admission Prices: Tues-Sat. 10-4:30. Adults $4, senior citizens 65 & over $3, children 6-16 $2; members no charge. Closed major holidays. ♿
Attendance: 12,705 (accurate)
Membership: Volunteer $12-$23; Prospector $24-$49; Bridge Builder $50-$149; Merchant $150-$499; Hotelier $500-$999; City Founder $1,000-$4,999; Territorial Legislator $5,000 & up.

BUFFALO BILL MUSEUM & GRAVE, (M), 987 1/2 Lookout Mountain Rd., Golden, CO 80401-9646. Tel.: 303-526-0747 & 0744. Fax: 303-526-0197.
E-mail: buffalobill.museum@ci.denver.co.us
Web Site: www.buffalobill.org
Formerly: Buffalo Bill Memorial Museum
Founded: 1921.
Key Personnel: Dir., Steve Friesen; Educational Programs Coord., Betsy Martinson; Collections Mgr., Shelley Howe; Exhibits Designer, Melanie Irvine.
Personnel Profile: Full-Time Paid 5; Part-Time Paid 1; Part-Time Volunteers 60.
Governing Authority: municipal. Affiliated with City & County of Denver, Dept. of Parks & Recreation, 1805 Bryant St., Denver, CO 80202. Tax-exempt: 170(b)(1)(A).
History Museum: Founded by Johnny Baker, a close friend of Buffalo Bill & an important member of Buffalo Bill's Wild West Show.
Collections: items connected with the life & associations of William F. Cody, Buffalo Bill; Indian artifacts; paintings; photographs; manuscripts.
Research Fields: William F. Cody; Buffalo Bill's Wild West.
Facilities: 400-vol. library of Wild West Show programs, couriers, rosters & books available for use under supervision of museum personnel.
Activities: permanent & temporary exhibitions; special events; orientation video. Annual Event: Buffalo Bill's Birthday in February.
Publications: quarterly newsletter, Scout's Dispatch.
Hours & Admission Prices: May-Oct. daily 9-5; Nov.-April Tues.-Sun. 9-4. Adults $4, children 6-15 $1; children under 6 no charge. ♿
Attendance: 64,000 (accurate)
Membership: Individual $10; Family $15.

CLEAR CREEK HISTORY PARK, 1020 11th St., Golden, CO 80401. Mailing Address: 822 12th St., Golden, CO 80401-1112. Tel.: 303-278-3557. Fax: 303-278-8916.
Web Site: www.clearcreekhistorypark.org
Founded: 1999.
Key Personnel: Exec. Dir., Shannon Voirol
Living History Park.
Collections: Homestead Structures: 2 cabins, barn, chicken coop, one-room schoolhouse.
Activities: guided tours; concerts; formally organized educational programs; docent programs; training program; children's living history day program.
Publications: quarterly newsletter, Dear Friends; monthly volunteer newsletter, The Friendly Reminder.
Hours & Admission Prices: May & Sept. Sat. 10-4:30; June-Aug. Tues.-Sat. 10-4:30, Sun. 11-3; Oct.-April groups by appointment. Adults $3, seniors $2.50, youth $2; discounts to AASLH & AAM members; children 5 & under and members no charge. Closed major holidays. ♿
Attendance: 9,610

COLORADO RAILROAD MUSEUM, (M), 17155 W. 44th Ave., Golden, CO 80403-1621. Mailing Address: P.O. Box 10, Golden, CO 80402-0010. Tel.: 303-279-4591; 800-365-6263. Fax: 303-279-4229.
Web Site: www.coloradorailroadmuseum.org
Founded: 1958.
Congressional District: 2
Key Personnel: Exec. Dir., Donald Tallman; Business Mgr., Bonnie Prater.
Personnel Profile: Full-Time Paid 12; Part-Time Paid 5; Part-Time Volunteers 120; Interns 1.
Governing Authority: nonprofit organization. Parent Institution: The Colorado Railroad Historical Foundation, Inc. Tax-exempt: 501(c)(3).
Railroad Museum.
Collections: rolling stock of Colorado railroads; interior exhibits of Colorado railroad items, documents; photos; memorabilia; manuscripts.
Research Fields: railroads of Colorado & adjoining states.
Facilities: 10,000-vol. library of railroad related materials available by request; research facilities. Railroad books & museum-related items for sale.
Activities: lectures; films; slide & history shows; school talks; permanent & temporary exhibitions.
Publications: Iron Horse News & Colorado Rail Annual.
Hours & Admission Prices: Daily 9-5. Family (2 adults & children) $16, adults $8, senior citizens $7, children under 16 $5; members no charge. Closed New Year's Day; Thanksgiving; Christmas.
Attendance: 60,453 (accurate)
Membership: Individual $30; Family $50; Family Premium $80; Patron $250; Life $1,000.

COLORADO SCHOOL OF MINES GEOLOGY MUSEUM, 1301 Maple St., Golden, CO 80401-1887. Tel.: 303-273-3823 & 3815. Fax: 303-273-3244.
E-mail: geomuseum@mines.edu
Web Site: www.mines.edu/academic/geology/museum
Founded: 1874.
Congressional District: 2
Key Personnel: Dir., Bruce Geller; Cur., Diana Bartos.
Personnel Profile: Full-Time Paid 1; Part-Time Paid 12; Part-Time Volunteers 1.
Governing Authority: state. Parent Institution: Colorado School of Mines. Tax-exempt.
Geology & Mineralogy Museum.
Collections: mineralogy; paleontology; mining.
Research Fields: mineralogy; paleontology.
Activities: guided tours; permanent & temporary exhibitions; teaching kits for loan.
Hours & Admission Prices: July-Aug. Mon.-Sat. 9-4; Sept.-June Sun. 1-4, Mon.-Sat. 9-4. No charge. Closed New Year's Day; Easter; Memorial Day; Independence Day; Thanksgiving; Christmas; CSM school holidays. ♿
Attendance: 30,000 (estimated)

FOOTHILLS ART CENTER, 809 15th St., Golden, CO 80401-1813. Tel.: 303-279-3922.
Web Site: www.foothillsartcenter.org
Key Personnel: Exec. Dir., Reilly Sanborn; Cur., Michael Chavez
Art Museum.
Collections: works by local, regional & national artists.
Facilities: Museum-related items for sale.
Hours & Admission Prices: Mon.-Sat. 10-5, Sun. 1-5; call to confirm. Adults $5, seniors $3; members, children & students no charge. ♿
Membership: Senior $25; Individual $30; Senior Dual $35; Dual Family $40; Patron $100; Sustaining $250; Benefactor $500 & up.

GOLDEN OLDY CYCLERY, 17224 W. 17th Place, Golden, CO 80401-2509. Tel.: 303-271-1998.
Web Site: www.goldenoldy.org
Bicycle Museum.
Collections: late 1800s bicycles; 1889 bicycle repair shop; early bicycle headlamps; period clothing & accessories; over 500 poems; history & people of cycling; photographs.
Facilities: library.
Activities: research.
Hours & Admission Prices: Call for hours.

GOLDEN PIONEER MUSEUM, 1620 Washington Ave., Golden, CO 80401-1927. Tel.: 303-278-7151. Fax: 303-278-2755.
E-mail: info@goldenpioneermuseum.com
Web Site: www.goldenpioneermuseum.com
Founded: 1939.
Congressional District: 6
Key Personnel: Pres., Robert Harmsen; Business Mgr., Barbara B. Mills; Treas., Robert Sorgenfrei; Coord. Education, Karen Kuchta.
Personnel Profile: Full-Time Volunteers 4; Part-Time Volunteers 72; Interns 2.
Governing Authority: municipal; private; nonprofit organization. Parent Institution: City of Golden, CO. Tax-exempt: 501(c)(3)
History Museum.
Collections: Golden, Colorado history from prehistoric to 1930s with an emphasis on when Golden was the Territorial Capitol of Colorado.
Facilities: 270-vol. library of genealogy research, Golden & Jefferson County history. Gift items for sale.
Activities: docent programs; guided tours; lectures; participatory & temporary exhibits; training programs for professional museum workers; lecture series; educational activities. Museum Sponsors: Christmas tour of historic homes & buildings; Benefit Tea & Book Dramatization.
Publications: quarterly newsletter, Artifacts. The History of Golden Schools; Changing Face of Golden; History of Golden; Golden Then & Now.
Hours & Admission Prices: June-Aug. Mon.-Sat. 10-4:30, Sun. 11-3; Sept.-May Mon.-Sat. 10-4:30. Adults $3; discounts to AAM members; members no charge. Closed Memorial Day; Independence Day; Labor Day; Thanksgiving; Christmas. ♿
Attendance: 14,500 (estimated)
Membership: Senior $15; Senior Dual $25; Family & Individual $30; Contributing $50; Patron $100; Sustaining $250; Benefactor $500. Business: $30; $50; $100; $250; $500; $1,000.

ROCKY MOUNTAIN QUILT MUSEUM, (M), 1213 Washington Ave., Golden, CO 80401. Mailing Address: Sandra Dallas Library, 910 13th St., Ste. 300, Golden, CO 80401-0732. Tel.: 303-277-0377. Fax: 303-215-1636.
Web Site: www.rmqm.org
Founded: 1982.
Congressional District: 6
Key Personnel: Exec. Dir., Brenda Ohlschwager; Pres. (V), Carol Born; Mgr. Collections & Exhibits, Karen Roxburgh; Finance Mgr., Rhonda Schneider; Volunteer Mgr., Kathy Williams.
Personnel Profile: Full-Time Paid 1; Part-Time Paid 9; Part-Time Volunteers 111.
Governing Authority: nonprofit organization. Tax-exempt: 501(c)(3).
Quilt Museum.
Collections: quilts from 1800s to contemporary times.
Research Fields: quilts; textiles.
Facilities: 1,000-vol. research library; 2,000 sq. ft. exhibit space. Museum related items for sale.
Activities: guided tours; temporary exhibitions. Annual Events: membership reception; anniversary reception; trunk shows.
Publications: quarterly membership newsletter.
Hours & Admission Prices: Mon.-Sat. 10-4. Adults $6, seniors $4, children 6-12 $3; discounts to groups over 15; children 5 & under, 1st Sat. of quarter and members no charge. Closed New Year's Day; Thanksgiving; Christmas. ♿
Attendance: 12,000 (accurate)
Membership: Senior $25; Individual $30; Family $45; Patron $70; Donor $125; Associate $250; Benefactor $500; Founder $1,000.

Grand Junction

THE ART CENTER, 1803 N. 7th, Grand Junction, CO 81501-3009. Tel.: 970-243-7337, ext. 4. Fax: 970-243-2482.
Web Site: www.gjartcenter.org
Formerly: Western Colorado Center for the Arts
Founded: 1953.
Congressional District: 4
Key Personnel: C.E.O., Cheryl McNab; Pres. (V), Robbie Breaux; Exhibition & Education Cur., Camille Silverman; Events & Communications Mgr., Lee Borden; Resident Artist - Ceramics, Terry Shepherd; Museum Shop Mgr., Carolyn Gillette.
Personnel Profile: Full-Time Paid 4; Part-Time Paid 3; Part-Time Volunteers 125; Interns 6.
Governing Authority: nonprofit. Tax-exempt: 501(c)(3).
Arts & Crafts Museum.
Collections: works by Western artists; Navajo blankets & rugs; Anasazi pottery; Paul Pletka, Harold Bryant & Alfred Nestler works; contemporary Colorado paintings & ceramics.
Facilities: 250-vol. library of art history available for use on premises; sculpture court; Japanese garden; auditorium; classrooms. Gift items for sale.
Activities: lectures; gallery talks; studio instruction for adults & children; formally organized education programs; loan exhibitions.
Publications: bimonthly newsletter; catalogue, WCAA - The Permanent Collection (2001).
Hours & Admission Prices: Tues.-Sat. 9-4. Adults & children $3; discounts to AAM & ICOM members; Tues. & members no charge. Closed national holidays. ♿
Attendance: 31,000 (estimated)
Membership: Senior Citizen & Student $25; Senior Couple & Individual $35; Family $50; Supporter $100; Patron $500; Benefactor $1,000.

CROSS ORCHARDS HISTORIC FARM, 3073 F Rd., Grand Junction, CO 81504. Tel.: 970-434-9814. Fax: 970-242-3960.
Historic Site: housed on an early 1900s apple orchard. National Register of Historic Sites & Places.
Collections: early 1900s furnishings & farm equipment; train cars; Grand Valley pioneers; bunkhouse; barn; Uintah narrow gauge railway cars.
Hours & Admission Prices: April 10 to mid-Oct. Tues.-Sat. 9-4. Adults $4, seniors $3, children $2.50.

* **MUSEUM OF WESTERN COLORADO, (M),** 462 Ute Ave., Grand Junction, CO 81501-2516. Mailing Address: P.O. Box 20000, Grand Junction, CO 81502-5001. Tel.: 970-242-0971. Fax: 970-242-3960.
Web Site: www.museumofwesternco.org
Founded: 1965.
Congressional District: 4
Key Personnel: Exec. Dir., Michael L. Perry; Chm. Bd. & Pres., Dale Tooker; Cur. Paleontology, Dr. John R. Foster; Cur. History & Dir. Western Investigations Team, David Bailey; Cur. Collections & Registrar, Zebulon Miracle; Asst. Dir. Operations, Kay Fiegel; Cur. Archives & Registrar,

Michael Menard; Business Mgr., Erik Vliek; Asst. Business Mgr., Joan Cron; Facilities Mgr., Don Kerven; Dir. Devel., Miffie Blozvich; Cultural Heritage Specialist, Ronna Lee Sharpe.
Personnel Profile: Full-Time Paid 12; Part-Time Paid 12; Part-Time Volunteers 312; Interns 2.
Governing Authority: private; nonprofit. Branch Sites: Cross Orchards Living History Site, 3073 F Rd., Grand Junction. Tel.: 970-434-9814; Museum of the West, 462 Ute Ave. Grand Junction, CO 81501; Whitman Education Bldg., 248 S. Fourth St.; Dinosaur Journey, 550 Jurassic Ct., Fruita, CO 81521, Tel: 970-858-7282. Tax-exempt: 501(c)(3).
Cultural & Natural History Museum.
Collections: small arms; costumes; archaeology; paleontology; geology; mineralogy; archives; ethnology; botany; zoology; Western Colorado history.
Research Fields: western Colorado history; paleontology; anthropology; genealogy.
Facilities: auditorium; classrooms. Outdoor Sites: Rabbit Valley research natural area. Gifts & museum-related items for sale.
Activities: guided tours; lectures; inter-museum loan; permanent, temporary & traveling exhibitions; school loan service; educational programs; archival research; children's & adult programs; living history farm; animated dinosaur exhibit; dinosaur digs; interpretive walks.
Publications: books, Familiar Insects of Mesa County; Biography of Cinosauria 1667-1986; Mesa County Colorado: A 100 Year History; Grand Heritage: A Photographic History of Grand Junction; Cross Times Cookin 1896-1996; 125 Years 125 People-A History of Grand Junction; tri-annual museum journal, Pathways; quarterly newsletter, Museum Times; monthly activity calendars.
Hours & Admission Prices: History Museum: Winter: 10-3; Summer: Mon.-Sat. 9-5, Sun. 1-4. Family $16, adults $5.50, seniors $4.50, children $3. Cross Orchards Living History Site: May-Sept. Tues. & Fri.-Sat. 10-3. May to mid-Oct. family $10, adults $4, seniors $3, children $2.50. Dinosaur Journey: daily 9-5. Family $20, adults $7, seniors $6, children $4; discounts to AAA, CCA & Time Traveler members. ♿
Attendance: 112,000 (estimated)
Membership: Student & Senior $15; Senior Couple $20; Individual $25; Family $40; Supporting $100; Sponsor $250; Patron $500; Benefactor $1,000.

WESTERN COLORADO CENTER FOR THE ARTS, 1803 N. 7th St., Grand Junction, CO 81501-3009. Tel.: 970-243-7337.
E-mail: info@gjartcenter.org
Art Gallery.
Collections: paintings; photographs; sculpture.
Facilities: Museum-related items for sale.
Activities: art classes; workshops.
Hours & Admission Prices: Tues.-Sat. 9-4. Adults $3; members, children under 12 & Tues. no charge.

Grand Lake

GRAND LAKE AREA HISTORICAL SOCIETY, Lake Ave. at Pitkin St., Grand Lake, CO 80447. Mailing Address: Box 656, Grand Lake, CO 80447-0656. Tel.: 970-627-9644. Fax: 970-627-3693.
E-mail: glhistory@rkymtnhi.com
Founded: 1973.
Key Personnel: Pres., Jim Cervenka; Treas., Patti Stahl; Sec., Elin Capps.
Governing Authority: nonprofit organization; society. A member of the State Historical Society of Colorado, Colorado State Museum, 200 Fourteenth Ave., Denver, CO 80203. Tax-exempt: 170(b)(1)(A).
Historical Society Museum: housed in 1892 Ezra Kauffman Tourist Hotel/Residence.
Collections: furniture, furnishings & artifacts of the period; manuscripts.
Research Fields: Grand Lake from the time of the Ute Indians-present.
Activities: guided tours; self-guided walking tours; lectures; films; gallery talks; formally organized education programs; docent program; permanent exhibitions.
Publications: Stagecoach Stops; Where the Colorado River Began; The Kauffman House; Grand Lakes 100th Year 1881-1981; A Walking Tour of Historic Grand Lake.
Hours & Admission Prices: Memorial Day to Labor Day daily 11-5; Sept. Sat.-Sun. 11-5; tours & other times by appointment. No charge; donations accepted. ♿
Attendance: 5,500 (accurate)
Membership: Individual $15; Family $25; Business $50; Sustaining $100.

Greeley

CENTENNIAL VILLAGE MUSEUM, 1475 A St., Greeley, CO 80631-2185. Mailing Address: 714 8th St, Greeley, CO 80631-3910. Tel.: 970-350-9220. Fax: 970-350-9700.
E-mail: museums@greeleygov.com
Web Site: www.greeleymuseums.com
Founded: 1976.
Congressional District: 4
Key Personnel: Museum Mgr., Erin Quinn; Pres. (V), Don Wiegel; Research Coord., Peggy A. Ford; Education Coord., Sheryl Kippen; Leisure Svcs., Ken d'Amato; Special Events Coord., Ann Schmidt; Registrar, JoAnna Stull; Historic Sites Coord., Bruce Murdoch; Exhibits Cur., Nancy Lynch; Museum Shop Mgr., Jody Lopez.
Personnel Profile: Full-Time Paid 10; Part-Time Paid 10; Part-Time Volunteers 350; Interns 6.
Governing Authority: municipal. Parent Institution: City of Greeley, Department of Leisure Services, Division of Museums. Tax-exempt.
Historic Houses.
Collections: 30 historic structures; personal artifacts; 1860-1940 furnishings.
Research Fields: local, county & regional history.
Facilities: meeting rooms; special events area. Handcrafted items, books, notecards & other museum-related items for sale.
Activities: festivals; guided tours; organized educational programs for children; permanent, temporary exhibitions; lectures; slide presentations; seasonal activities; concerts. Museum Sponsors: History Fest; Potato Day; Trick or Treat at the Village; Homesteaders' Holiday.
Publications: newsletter.
Hours & Admission Prices: May-Sept. Tues.-Sat. 10-4. Adult $7, senior citizens $5, children 6-12 $3; discounts to Time Travelers, AAM, ICOM, active military, & AAA members; children under 6 & members no charge. Closed Independence Day. ♿
Attendance: 19,000 (accurate)
Membership: Individual $15; Family $25; Contributor $50; Special Donor $100 & up.

GREELEY HISTORY MUSEUM, (M), 714 8th Street, Greeley, CO 80631-3910. Tel.: 970-350-9220. Fax: 970-350-9570.
E-mail: museums@greeleygov.com
Web Site: www.greeleymuseums.com
Formerly: Municipal Archives
Founded: 2005.
Congressional District: 4
Key Personnel: Education Coord., Sheryl Kippen; Research Cur., Peggy A. Ford; Exhibits Cur., Nancy Lynch; Registrar, JoAnna Stull; Cur. Collections, Erin Quinn; Special Events Coord., Ann Schmidt; Historic Sites Coord., Bruce Murdoch; Museum Shop Mgr., Jody Lopez.
Personnel Profile: Full-Time Paid 8; Part-Time Paid 8; Part-Time Volunteers 400; Interns 3.
Governing Authority: municipal. Parent Institution: City of Greeley, Department of Leisure Services, Division of Museums. Tax-exempt.
History Museum.
Collections: city records; photographs; archival documents; scrapbooks; maps; books.
Major Exhibits: Ghost Towns and Boom Towns, 11/09-8/10; .
Research Fields: local, county & regional history.
Facilities: 2,000-vol. library of historical books, ledgers, diaries & local history scrap books available on premises only.
Activities: guided tours; organized education programs; seasonal activities; special events; historic neighborhood tours.
Publications: e-newsletter.
Hours & Admission Prices: Tues.-Fri. 8:30-4:30, Sat. 10-4. No charge; donations accepted. Closed major holidays. ♿
Attendance: 12,851 (accurate)
Membership: Individual $15; Family $25; Contributor $50; Special Donor $100 & up.

MARIANI GALLERY, UNIVERSITY OF NORTHERN COLORADO, 8th Ave. & 18th St., Greeley, CO 80639-0001. Mailing Address: School of Visual Arts Galleries, Campus Box 30, Guggenheim Hall University of Northern CO, Greeley, CO 80639-0001. Tel.: 970-351-2184. Fax: 970-351-2299.
Web Site: www.arts.unco.edu/visarts/visarts_galleries.html
Founded: 1972.
Key Personnel: Dir., Joan Shannon-Miller.
Personnel Profile: Part-Time Paid 7.
Governing Authority: public university; not-for-profit organization. Parent Institution: University of Northern Colorado. Subsidiary Institution: Oak Room Gallery. Tax-exempt.
University Art Gallery.
Collections: works by contemporary artists.
Hours & Admission Prices: Sept.-May Mon.-Tues. & Thurs.-Fri. 10-3, Wed. 1-6. No charge. ♿
Attendance: 10,680 (accurate)

MEEKER HOME MUSEUM, 1324 9th Ave., Greeley, CO 80631-4608. Mailing Address: 714 8th St., Greeley, CO 80631-3910. Tel.: 970-350-9220. Fax: 970-350-9570.
E-mail: museums@greeleygov.com
Web Site: www.greeleymuseums.com
Founded: 1929.
Key Personnel: Dir., Ken d'Amato; Research Cur., Peggy A. Ford; Mktg. & Special Events Coord., Ann Schmidt; Cur. Collections, Erin Quinn; Coord. Historic Sites, Bruce Murdoch; Cur. Exhibits, Nancy Lynch; Coord. Education, Sheryl Kippen; Museum Shop Mgr., Jody Lopez; Registrar, Joanna Stull.
Personnel Profile: Full-Time Paid 8; Part-Time Paid 8; Part-Time Volunteers 400; Interns 6.
Governing Authority: municipal; nonprofit organization. Parent Institution: City of Greeley, Leisure Services Dept., Division of Museums. Tax-exempt: 501(c)(3).
Historic House: 1870 home of Nathan C. Meeker, founder of Greeley.
Collections: personal artifacts; material culture of local area, 1870-1882.
Research Fields: local, county & regional history.
Activities: guided tours; organized educational programs for children; seasonal activities. Museum Sponsors: Mr. Meeker's Neighborhood Walking Tours; Nathan Meeker's Birthday Party.
Publications: newsletter.
Hours & Admission Prices: May-Oct. 1st Sat. of month 10-4. No charge; donations accepted. ♿
Attendance: 600 (accurate)
Membership: Individual $15; Family $25; Contributor $50; Special Donor $100 and up.

PLUMB FARM LEARNING CENTER, 955 39th Ave., Greeley, CO 80634-1549. Mailing Address: 714 8th St., Greeley, CO 80631-3910. Tel.: 970-350-9220. Fax: 970-350-9570.
E-mail: museums@greeleygov.com
Web Site: www.greeleymuseums.com
Formerly: Plumb Farm Museum
Founded: 1997.
Key Personnel: Dir. Leisure Svcs., Ken d'Amato; Supt., Chris Dill; Coord. Research, Peggy A. Ford; Coord. Education, Sheryl Kippen; Coord. Collections, Erin Quinn; Coord. Historic Sites, Bruce Murdoch; Coord. Mktg., Ann Schmidt; Registrar, JoAnna Stull; Cur. Exhibits, Nancy Lynch.
Personnel Profile: Full-Time Paid 10; Part-Time Paid 8; Part-Time Volunteers 400.
Governing Authority: municipal. Parent Institution: City of Greeley, Department of Leisure Services, Division of Museums.
Historic Farm Museum.
Collections: farm house; potato cellar; several out buildings; gardens; 1870 flood irrigation system; farm tools & equipment.
Research Fields: local, county & regional agricultural history.
Facilities: gardens.
Activities: guided tours; museum classes for children; seasonal activities. Museum Sponsors: Baby Animal Days in April & May.
Publications: newsletter.
Hours & Admission Prices: April-Oct. tours by appointment. Special Event Days: call for information. No charge; donations accepted. ♿
Attendance: 8,000 (estimated)
Membership: Individual $15; Family $25; Contributor $50; Special Donor $100 and up.

Gunnison

GUNNISON ARTS CENTER, 102 S. Main St., Gunnison, CO 81230. Tel.: 970-641-4029.
Art Center.
Collections: works by local artists.
Facilities: Museum-related items for sale.
Activities: visual art classes; workshops.
Hours & Admission Prices: Tues.-Fri. 10-6, Sat. 10-4. No charge.

GUNNISON COUNTY PIONEER AND HISTORICAL SOCIETY, S. Adams St. & Hwy. 50, Gunnison, CO 81230. Mailing Address: P.O. Box 824, Gunnison, CO 81230-0824. Tel.: 970-641-4530.
Founded: 1930.
Key Personnel: C.E.O. & Pres., C.J. Miller.
Personnel Profile: Full-Time Volunteers 12; Part-Time Volunteers 40.
Governing Authority: nonprofit. Tax-exempt: 501(c)(3).
Historical Society Museum.
Collections: geology; costumes; mineralogy; transportation; railroad artifacts; agriculture; period cars; 50 vintage cars; telephones & telephone equipment. Historic Buildings: 1890 Log Barn; 1904 Paragon School House; 1890 Train Depot; c.1880 Log Post Office; 1881 narrow-gauge railroad train.
Research Fields: historic buildings.
Facilities: 500-vol. library of old textbooks from Paragon School & bound volumes of Gunnison newspapers, 1880-1950.
Activities: guided tours; permanent exhibitions.
Publications: annual news sheet, Gunnison Museum.
Hours & Admission Prices: Memorial Day to Sept. Mon.-Sat. 9-5, Sun. 11-5. Adults $7, children 6-12 $3; discounts to groups of 10 or more.
Attendance: 5,000 (accurate)
Membership: Individual $20.

Holyoke

PHILLIPS COUNTY MUSEUM, 109 S. Campbell Ave., Holyoke, CO 80734-1501. Tel.: 970-854-2129.
E-mail: pcmuseum@pctelcom.coop
Web Site: www.rootsweb.ancestry.com/~copchs/
Founded: 1967.
Congressional District: 4
Key Personnel: Pres., Mike Coyne; Vice Pres., Jean Clayton; Sec., Diane Rahe; Treas., Sharrie Ellis.
Governing Authority: nonprofit society. Parent Institution: Phillips County Historical Society. Tax-exempt: 501(c)(3).
Historical Society Museum.
Collections: agricultural tools; pioneer household items; dolls; photographs; Native American artifacts; weapons; furnishings from the 1920s; vintage filling station; one-room schoolhouse.
Research Fields: local history.
Facilities: 400-vol. library of books & microfilm of old newspapers, available for use on the premises; reading room.
Activities: lectures; special guest exhibitions.
Publications: book, Those Were The Days, vols. I & II.
Hours & Admission Prices: Memorial Day to Labor Day Sun. 2-5, Wed. 2-4; other times by appointment. No charge. ♿
Attendance: 850 (estimated)
Membership: Individual $5; Family $15; Business $25.

Hot Sulphur Springs

GRAND COUNTY MUSEUM, 110 E. Byers, Hot Sulphur Springs, CO 80451. Mailing Address: P.O. Box 165, Hot Sulphur Springs, CO 80451-0165. Tel.: 970-725-3939. Fax: 970-725-0129.
E-mail: gcha@grandcountymuseum.com
Web Site: www.grandcountymusuem.com
Founded: 1974.
Congressional District: 4
Key Personnel: C.E.O. & Dir., Don Woster; Pres. (V), Yvonne Knox; Treas. & Sec., Barbara Mitchell.
Personnel Profile: Full-Time Paid 2; Part-Time Paid 1; Part-Time Volunteers 50.
Governing Authority: nonprofit organization. Parent Institution: Grand County Historical Association. Tax-exempt.
History Museum: housed in c.1924 school house.
Collections: pertaining to the settlement of Grand County. Historical Buildings; 1870 Grand County Pioneer Museum; 1924 Grand County Museum; 1915 ranch house; blacksmith shop; Grand County court house; Grand County jail; Eight Mile school.
Research Fields: Windy Gap Indian digs; county history.
Facilities: 7,000 photographs on file & manuscripts; library of records available for use under supervision only.
Activities: guided tours; oral history; site designations; school programs; permanent exhibitions; special displays; historic treks; lectures; receptions; programs. Museum Sponsors: two annual meetings.
Publications: pamphlets; journals; newsletter.
Hours & Admission Prices: Memorial Day-Labor Day Tues.-Sat. 10-5, Sun. 1-5; Sept.-May Wed.-Sat. 10-4. Adults $4, senior citizens 62 & over $3, children 6-18 $2; discounts for tours, locals & AAM members; members & children under 6 no charge. ♿
Attendance: 2,350 (accurate)
Membership: Individual $25; Couple $40; Explorer $80; Historian $125; Pioneer $250; Heritage $500; Centennial $1,000.

Hugo

LINCOLN COUNTY MUSEUM, 617 Third Ave., Hugo, CO 80821. Mailing Address: P.O. Box 115, Hugo, CO 80821-0115. Tel.: 719-740-0107. Fax: 719-743-2447.
E-mail: twbndee@yahoo.com
Formerly: Headlund House Museum

Founded: 1972.
Congressional District: 4
Key Personnel: Pres., Dee Ann Blevins; Treas., Garald Ensign; Representative, Gary Ensign; Contact, Terry Blevins.
Governing Authority: municipal. Parent Institution: Lincoln County Historical Society. Tax-exempt.
History Museum: located on c.1880 site of the homestead of Hugo's founder.
Collections: period furniture & furnishings; utensils; glass; photos; postcards; period clothing; guns.
Research Fields: Lincoln County History.
Activities: guided tours.
Hours & Admission Prices: Memorial Day to Labor Day Fri. 4-7, Sat. 1-7, Sun. 1-4; other times by appointment. No charge; donations accepted.
Attendance: 400 (accurate)
Membership: Lincoln County Historical Society: Annual $3; Lifetime $50.

Idaho Springs

ARGO GOLD MINE & MILL MUSEUM, 2350 Riverside Dr., Idaho Springs, CO 80452. Mailing Address: P.O. Box 1990, Idaho Springs, CO 80452-1990. Tel.: 303-567-2421. Fax: 303-567-9304.
E-mail: argo2350@aol.com
Web Site: www.historicargotours.com
Founded: 1977.
Key Personnel: C.E.O., James N. Maxwell; Dir., Robert N. Maxwell.
Personnel Profile: Full-Time Paid 2; Part-Time Paid 3.
Governing Authority: nonprofit organization. Tax-exempt.
Mining & Milling Museum: housed in 1913 six-story Argo Gold Mill.
Collections: original mill equipment; historic milling & mining items; photographic displays; journals, ledgers & other written material of relevance to the history of Clear Creek County.
Facilities: Museum-related items for sale.
Activities: self-guided tours; educational & guided tours by appointment; permanent exhibitions; gold panning; demonstrations.
Publications: Argo Tailing Guide.
Hours & Admission Prices: mid-April to mid-Oct. daily 9-6; Winter: by appointment. Adults $15, children 7-12 $7.50; discounts to AAA, AAM, ICOM members & groups of 25 or more with reservation; children 6 & under no charge.
Attendance: 15,000 (estimated)

THE HERITAGE MUSEUM, 2060 Miner St., Idaho Springs, CO 80452-1318. Mailing Address: P.O. Box 1318, Idaho Springs, CO 80452-1318. Tel.: 303-567-4382.
E-mail: njohnson@historicidahosprings.com
Web Site: www.historicidahosprings.com
Founded: 1964.
Congressional District: 4
Key Personnel: Pres. (V), Robert Bowland; Museum Shop Mgr., Carliss Allan; Exec. Asst., Nancy Johnson.
Personnel Profile: Part-Time Paid 5; Part-Time Volunteers 25.
Governing Authority: nonprofit organization. Operated by the Historical Society of Idaho Springs. Tax-exempt: 170(b)(1)(A).
History Museum.
Collections: local history & culture from 1860-1940s; mining & mining tools; Indian artifacts; fire department equipment; geological specimens; hand crafts; photographs; paintings; costumes; furnishings from 1800s to early 1900s; George Jackson's discovery of gold.
Research Fields: genealogy; photos.
Facilities: Gift items for sale.
Activities: permanent exhibitions; walking tour of homes & cemetery. Museum Sponsors: 150th Anniversary of the Colorado Gold Rush; Tommyknocker Mining Competition.
Publications: quarterly, The Idahoe; books, Tailing, Track & Tommyknockers: History of Clear Creek County; Historical Highlights of Idaho Springs; Historical Walking Tour of Idaho Springs; The Waterwheel; Motherlode of Metal Miners' Mealtime Munchies.
Hours & Admission Prices: Daily 9-5. No charge; donations accepted. Closed New Year's Day; Easter; Thanksgiving; Christmas. ♿
Attendance: 25,000 (estimated)
Membership: Senior Citizen $25; Single $35; Senior Family $40; Family $50; Business $100; Sustaining $500; Patron $1,000; Life Patron $5,000.

UNDERHILL MUSEUM, 1418 Miner St., Idaho Springs, CO 80452-1318. Mailing Address: P.O. Box 1318, Idaho Springs, CO 80452-1318. Tel.: 303-567-4382.
Web Site: www.historicidahosprings.com
Key Personnel: Pres. (V), Robert Bowland; Exec. Asst., Nancy Johnson.
Personnel Profile: Part-Time Paid 4; Part-Time Volunteers 3.
Governing Authority: nonprofit organization. Operated by the Historical Society of Idaho Springs. Tax-exempt: 170(b)(1)(A).
Historic House & Mining Engineer Office: housed in the former home & office of college professor & U.S. Mineral Surveyor, James Underhill; built in 1912.
Collections: mining equipment; early photographs; furnishings; garden.
Facilities: garden.
Hours & Admission Prices: Memorial Day to Sept. 10:30-4. No charge; donations accepted.
Attendance: 3,700 (accurate)
Membership: Senior Citizen $25; Single $35; Senior Family $40; Family $50; Business $100; Sustaining $500; Patron $1,000; Life Patron $5,000.

Ignacio

SOUTHERN UTE CULTURAL CENTER AND MUSEUM, (M), 14826 State Hwy. 172, Ignacio, CO 81137. Mailing Address: Box 737, Ignacio, CO 81137-0737. Tel.: 970-563-9583. Fax: 970-563-4641.
E-mail: sum@frontier.net
Web Site: www.southernutemuseum.org
Founded: 1972.
Congressional District: 3
Key Personnel: Chm., Robert Burch; Museum Technician, Timothy Ryder; Museum Shop Mgr., Raquel Taylor; Administrative Asst., Marian Gilmore.
Personnel Profile: Full-Time Paid 6; Part-Time Paid 1; Part-Time Volunteers 10; Interns 1.
Governing Authority: Parent Institution: Southern Ute Indian tribe. Subsidiary Institution: Southern Ute Cultural Center. Tax-exempt: 501(c)(3).
Native American History & Ethnology Museum: located on Southern Ute Indian reservation.
Collections: photographss & artifacts pertaining to Ute Indians & other Native American tribes.
Research Fields: Southern Ute oral history.
Facilities: 50-vol. library of Native American history, arts & crafts available for use by the public & inter-library loan; restaurant; archives. Native American items for sale.
Activities: arts festivals; Native American dance recitals; docent program; films; guided tours; hobby workshops; lectures; school loan service; participatory, temporary & traveling exhibitions; broadcast programs.
Publications: Southern Ute Tribal History; Ute Dictionary, Grammar & Narrative; educational packet, The Ute Legacy: video tape, history books, study guides & poster; video tape, The Colorado Ute Legacy.
Hours & Admission Prices: May 15-Oct. 15 Mon.-Fri. 10-6, Sat.-Sun. 10-3; Oct. 16-May 14 Mon.-Fri. 10-5:30. Adults $1, children 12 & under $.50; discounts for guided tour with videotape for groups of 4 or more; Southern Ute Tribal Members no charge. ♿
Attendance: 15,000 (estimated)
Membership: Senior Citizen & Student $5; Individual $10; Family $20; Institution $25; Sponsor $50; Life $200.

Julesburg

DEPOT MUSEUM, 201 W. 1st St., Julesburg, CO 80737. Mailing Address: Fort Sedgwick Historical Society, 114 E. 1st St., Julesburg, CO 80737-1501. Tel.: 970-474-2264. Fax: 970-474-2061.
E-mail: history@kci.net
Web Site: www.kci.net/~history
Formerly: Pioneer Museum
Founded: 1940.
Congressional District: 4
Key Personnel: Pres. (V), Doris Heath; Vice Pres., Dallas Williams.
Personnel Profile: Full-Time Volunteers 1; Part-Time Paid 1; Part-Time Volunteers 15.
Governing Authority: society. Affiliated with Fort Sedgwick Historical Society, Julesburg, CO 80737. Branch Museum: Fort Sedgwick Museum, 114 E. 1st St., Julesburg, CO 80737. Tax-exempt.
History Museum: housed in the Union Pacific Railroad Depot; built in 1930.
Collections: agriculture; archaeology; archives; folklore; glass; history; Indian artifacts; mineralogy; military; music; natural history; transportation; manuscripts; railroad; Pony Express home station.
Research Fields: natural history; local architecture; genealogy.
Facilities: archives; research room.
Activities: permanent & temporary exhibitions; guest programs; tours; research.
Publications: History of Sedgwick County Vol. I & II; booklets; brochures; biannual newsletter.
Hours & Admission Prices: Tues.-Sat. 10-4, Sun. 1-4 & by appointment. Adults $1, children under 12 $.50; school groups & members no charge. ♿
Attendance: 801 (accurate)
Membership: Individual $10; Family $25; Business $50; Lifetime $200.

FORT SEDGWICK MUSEUM & ARCHIVES, 114 E. 1st St., Julesburg, CO 80737-1501. Mailing Address: Fort Sedgwick Historical Society, 114 E. 1st St., Julesburg, CO 80737. Tel.: 970-474-2061.
Key Personnel: Pres. (V), Doris Heath; Vice Pres., Dallas Williams.
Personnel Profile: Full-Time Volunteers 1; Part-Time Paid 1; Part-Time Volunteers 5.
Governing Authority: society. Affiliated with Fort Sedgwick Historical Society, Julesburg, CO 80737. Branch Museum: Depot Museum, 201 W. 1st, Julesburg, CO 80737. Tax-exempt.
History Museum.
Collections: cannons; military artifacts.
Facilities: research room.
Activities: research; special events.
Publications: biannual newsletter.
Hours & Admission Prices: Memorial Day to Labor Day Tues.-Sat. 10-4, Sun. 1-4; Sept.-May Tues.-Fri. 9-1. Adults $1, children $.50; members no charge. Closed national holidays. ♿
Attendance: 900
Membership: Individual $10; Family $25; Business $50; Lifetime $200.

HIPPODROME THEATRE, 215 Cedar St., Julesburg, CO 80737-1521. Tel.: 970-474-9977.
Web Site: www.rivertrailonline.org/users/hippodrome
Governing Authority: nonprofit organization.
Historic Building: housed in a functioning movie theater; built in 1919.
Collections: historic building; movies.
Hours & Admission Prices: Shows: Fri.-Sat. 7:30pm, Sun. 2pm & 6pm. Admission $4; children 3 & under no charge. ♿

Keenesburg

THE WILD ANIMAL SANCTUARY, 1946 WCR 53, Keenesburg, CO 80643. Tel.: 303-536-0118.
E-mail: information@wildlife-sanctuary.org
Governing Authority: nonprofit organization.
Wildlife Sanctuary.
Collections: lions; tigers; bears; jaguars; leopards; mountain lions; lynx; bobcats; wolves.
Activities: observation decks.
Hours & Admission Prices: Daily 9-4. Adults $10, children $5.

Kiowa

ELBERT COUNTY HISTORICAL SOCIETY AND MUSEUM, 515 Comanche St., Hwy. 86, Kiowa, CO 80117. Mailing Address: P.O. Box 43, Kiowa, CO 80117-0043.
History Museum.
Collections: county history & culture; photographs; personal artifacts; manuscripts; documents.
Hours & Admission Prices: Memorial Day to Labor Day.

Kit Carson

KIT CARSON HISTORICAL SOCIETY, 202 W. Hwy. 287, Kit Carson, CO 80825. Mailing Address: P.O. Box 67, Kit Carson, CO 80825-0067. Tel.: 719-962-3306.
Web Site: www.kcdr1.org
Founded: 1968.
Congressional District: 5
Key Personnel: C.E.O., Carl Randel; Pres. (V), Penny McPherson; Vice Pres. & Dir., Victor Gibbs; Dir. & Treas., Ronald White; Dir., Polly Johnson; Dir., Deb Dwyer; Dir. & Sec., Charles Oswald; Dir., Marilyn Bullock.
Personnel Profile: Full-Time Volunteers 7; Part-Time Volunteers 45.
Governing Authority: nonprofit organization. Tax-exempt: 501(c)(3).
History Museum.
Collections: Indian artifacts; natural history; manuscripts; railraod caboose. Historic Building: 1904 Union Pacific Depot; 1928 Signal Maintainers House; steam era stone pump house.
Activities: guided tours; permanent & temporary exhibitions. Annual Events: pancake supper; Memorial Day Picnic.
Publications: books: Homesteaders & Other Early Settlers (1900-1930); Kit Carson Colorado, Home of the Famous Scout; Friendly People & Prime Beef Cattle.
Hours & Admission Prices: May & Sept. Sat.-Sun. 9-5; Memorial Day-Labor Day daily 9-5. No charge; donations accepted. ♿
Attendance: 877 (accurate)
Membership: Active $5; Supporting $25; Life $100.

La Junta

BENT'S OLD FORT NATIONAL HISTORIC SITE, 35110 Hwy. 194 E., La Junta, CO 81050-9523. Tel.: 719-383-5010. Fax: 719-383-2129.
E-mail: beol_cultural_resources@nps.gov
Web Site: www.nps.gov/beol
Founded: 1963.
Congressional District: 4
Key Personnel: Cur., Kate Hogue; Supt., Alexa Roberts; Museum Shop Mgr., Elaine Leadabrand.
Personnel Profile: Full-Time Paid 11; Part-Time Paid 11; Part-Time Volunteers 120; Interns 1.
Governing Authority: federal. Parent Institution: National Park Service. Tax-exempt.
Living History Museum.
Collections: archaeological artifacts from excavation of original 1830-1849 trading post; reconstructed adobe fort with period reproductions & furnishings c.1833-1849; archival documents & photographs; herbarium of native plants.
Research Fields: American Southwest fur trade; Santa Fe Trail; Bent St. Vrain Company; Bent family; St. Vrain family; the War with Mexico.
Facilities: 1,000-vol. reference library relating to the American Southwest & early 19th-century history; picnic area. Books, reproduction trade goods & other museum-related items for sale.
Activities: guided tours; living history training program; craft demonstrations; special events.
Publications: brochures; worldwide web home page.
Hours & Admission Prices: June-Aug. daily 8-5:30; Sept.-May daily 9-4. Adults $3, children 6-12 $2; children 5 & under no charge; America the Beautiful passes honored. Closed New Year's Day; Thanksgiving; Christmas.
Attendance: 35,000 (estimated)

KOSHARE INDIAN MUSEUM, INC., 115 W. 18th, La Junta, CO 81050-3302. Mailing Address: P.O. Box 580, La Junta, CO 81050-0580. Tel.: 719-384-4411. Fax: 719-384-8836.
E-mail: jeremy.manyik@ojc.edu
Web Site: koshare.org
Founded: 1949.
Key Personnel: Program Dir. & Cur., Jeremy Manyik.
Personnel Profile: Full-Time Paid 4; Part-Time Paid 5; Part-Time Volunteers 65.
Governing Authority: college. Affiliated with Otero Junior College. Tax-exempt.
Indian Art & Artifacts Museum.
Collections: paintings; archaeology; anthropology; plains & pueblo Indian art & artifacts; two-dimensional artwork with emphasis on southwest.
Research Fields: anthropology.
Facilities: 2,000-vol. library of Indian lore, archaeology & anthropology books available by request. Indian arts, crafts & other museum-related items for sale in Kiva Trading Post.
Activities: guided tours; gallery talks; hobby workshops; permanent & temporary exhibitions. Museum Sponsors: interpretive Indian dances. Annual Events: Kiva presents artist series featuring a different artist 1st. Sun. each month, no charge.
Publications: book, Koshare; brochure; biannual newsletter, Koshare News; artist calendar, Kiva Presents.
Hours & Admission Prices: June-Aug. daily 10-5; Sept.-May call for hours. Adults $5, students $3; members no charge. Interpretive Indian Dances: mid-June to Aug. Sat. 7:30pm; Dec. 27-Jan. 4 call for hours. Show: adults $8, children 3-18 $5. Closed major holidays. ♿
Attendance: 24,000 (estimated)
Membership: Jr. Feather Clan: Student (18 & under) $10; Adult (19-24) $25. Adult Feather Clan: Individual (25 & up) $50; Family $75. Kokopelli $100-$249; Chippewa $200 & up; Warriors $250-$499; Dreamcatchers $500-$999; Kira Society $1,000-$2,999; Burshears Circle $3,000 & up.

OTERO MUSEUM ASSOCIATION, (M), 218 Anderson St., La Junta, CO 81050-0223. Mailing Address: P.O. Box 223, 218 Anderson St., La Junta, CO 81050-0223. Tel.: 719-384-7500. Fax: 719-384-7500.
E-mail: oteromuseum@centurytel.net
Web Site: www.coloradoplains.com/otero/museum
Founded: 1984.
Congressional District: 4
Key Personnel: Pres. (V), Cur. & Public Rels., Don Lowman; Treas. & Devel., Donna Aldea; Recording Sec., Marilyn Mast.
Personnel Profile: Full-Time Volunteers 2; Part-Time Volunteers 21.
Governing Authority: private; nonprofit organization. Tax-exempt: 501(c)(3).
General Museum.
Collections: 1876-1950 local history; displays of life in early La Junta & Otero

County; ranching & farming displays; transportation; railroad memorabilia; Santa Fe Railroad memorabilia; doctor's office; post office; volunteer fire dept. display building; clocks; agricultural implements; war artifacts from civil war to Vietnam era; chinaware; 137 mustache cups; guns. Historic Houses: Daniel Sciombato Home/Grocery Store; Nancy Wickham Home; 1873 railroad workers boarding house; 1876 log cabin school; Coach House: 1867 Concord stage coach, chuck wagon, 1905 Reo.
Research Fields: irrigation in the Arkansas River Valley; early fire fighting.
Facilities: 160-vol. library; 29,000 sq. ft. exhibit space. Museum-related items for sale.
Activities: guided tours; arts festivals. Annual Events: video programs April to October; Art Shows in May & November; Bean Supper (Fundraiser) in June; antique appraisal program June to October; school tours in spring.
Hours & Admission Prices: June-Sept. Mon.-Sat. 1-5; Oct.-May & groups by appointment only. No charge; donations accepted.
Attendance: 2,750 (estimated)
Membership: Family $25; Contributing $50; Sustaining $100.

La Veta

FRANCISCO FORT MUSEUM, 306 S. Main St., La Veta, CO 81055. Mailing Address: P.O. Box 263, LaVeta, CO 81055-0263. Tel.: 719-742-5501.
Founded: 1965.
Congressional District: 3
Key Personnel: Dir., Judy Heble; Treas., Shirley Jameson; Chm. (V), Gary Bailey; Museum Shop Mgr., Yvonne Hedrick.
Personnel Profile: Part-Time Paid 2; Part-Time Volunteers 18; Interns 3.
Governing Authority: nonprofit organization. Parent Institution: Huerfano County Historical Society. Tax-exempt.
Historical Society Museum: housed on 1862 adobe fort and other historic buildings.
Collections: American Indian artifacts of area; 1800s furniture of area settlers; old post office; general store; switchboard; doctors office; blacksmith shop & tools; farm & ranch implements; 1860-1940 clothes; Civil War to WWII weaponry; steam engines; spinning wheels; Lincoln letter of 1850; chuck-wagon; taxidermy collection; musical instruments; one-room school; coal mining artifacts; Edison sound & light inventions; mammoth tooth, fossilized coral, dinosaur fossilized footprint; Hispanic artifacts; Hispanic exhibits & penitente; religious articles.
Major Exhibits: Villains of Southern Colorado (T), 4/10-8/10; Postal Service 1865-1945, 4/10-9/10; Archuleta Penitente Collection (T), 5/10-10/10; 1890-1910 Women's Clothing, 5/10-10/10; Western Frontier Justice (T), 6/10-9/10; Gov. Charles Bent's 1770s Tapalo, 6/10-10/10; Georgia Colony, 7/10-9/10.
Research Fields: local history; projectile points; genealogy.
Facilities: library of taped oral histories, maps, photos, general & local history, old local newspapers available for research by permission from board of directors; reading room. Museum-related items for sale.
Activities: guided tours; gallery talks; permanent & temporary exhibitions; oral history project with LaVeta Public Library; children's treasure hunt; special events. Museum Sponsors: Saloon Nite in June; Francisco Fort Days in July.
Publications: annual newsletter; brochures, HCHS Museums; quarterly newsletter.
Hours & Admission Prices: Memorial Day to early Oct. Tues.-Sat. 10-4, Sun. 12-4; other times by appointment. Adults $6, senior citizens & children 10-17 $3; discounts to groups of 8 or more & railroad riders; members & children under 10 no charge. ♿
Attendance: 6,044 (estimated)
Membership: Individual $15; Family $25; Business $50; Corporate $250; Life $1,000.

Lafayette

LAFAYETTE MINERS MUSEUM, (M), 108 E. Simpson St., Lafayette, CO 80026-2322. Tel.: 303-665-7030.
E-mail: minersmuseum@cityoflafayette.com
Founded: 1976.
Congressional District: 2
Key Personnel: Vice Pres. & Acting Dir., Dick Schillawski; Cur., Claudia Lund.
Personnel Profile: Part-Time Paid 1; Part-Time Volunteers 25.
Governing Authority: nonprofit society. Parent Institution: Lafayette Historical Society. Tax-exempt.
Coal Mining Museum: housed in c.1892 Lewis House. Listed on the National Register of Historic Places.
Collections: coal mining artifacts; period furniture & furnishings; photographs; newspapers; rocks & minerals; local obituary file; mine union records; mine company time books; war memorabilia from the Spanish-American War to the Gulf War; local high school memorabilia; personal artifacts.
Research Fields: coal mining; local history.
Facilities: archives; picnic area.
Activities: guided & self-guided tours; lectures; formally organized education programs for children; slide presentations; demonstrations; bimonthly community program at Lafayette Public Library. Museum Sponsors: Peach Festival; Lafayette Days; Oatmeal Festival.
Publications: book: Lafayette Centennial History, Lafayette, Colorado Volunteer Fire Department 1893 to 2001 Squirt to Telesquirt; Slaughter in Serene: The Columbine Coal Strike Reader; A Wide-Awake Woman-Josephine Roche in the Era of Reform; History of Waneka Lake; The Price of Colorado Coal; The Cherokee Trail; area coal mining maps; Cherry Blossom Comrades; Lincoln Highway in Colorado; Remember Ludlow.
Hours & Admission Prices: Thurs. & Sat. 2-4; tours by appointment. No charge; donations accepted. Closed holidays. ♿
Attendance: 1,500 (accurate)
Membership: Individual $10; Family $15; Business $30; Life $100.

WOW! CHILDREN'S MUSEUM (WORLD OF WONDER), 110 N. Harrison Ave., Lafayette, CO 80026-2336. Tel.: 303-604-2424.
Web Site: www.wowmuseum.com
Key Personnel: Co-Founder & Exec. Dir., Lisa Atallah; Mgr., Susan Rasmussen; Mgr. Mktg., Katie MacDonald
Children's Museum.
Collections: hands-on exhibits.
Facilities: Museum-related items for sale.
Activities: special events; parties; workshops; theater & dance performances.
Hours & Admission Prices: June-Aug. 18 Mon.-Wed. 9-5, Thurs.-Sat. 10-6; mid-Aug. to May Tues.-Wed. 9-5, Thurs.-Sat. 10-6, Sun. 12-4; other times by appointment. Children $7; discounts to groups; adults and children 14 months & under no charge. Closed New Year's Day; Memorial Day; Father's Day; Labor Day; Thanksgiving; Christmas.

Lakewood

LAKEWOOD'S HERITAGE CENTER, (M), 801 S. Yarrow St., Lakewood, CO 80226-4372. Tel.: 303-987-7850. Fax: 303-987-7851. TDD: 303-987-4862.
E-mail: andmil@lakewood.org
Web Site: www.lakewood.org
Founded: 1976.
Congressional District: 6
Key Personnel: HCA Mgr., Michelle Nierling; Admin., Andrea Miller; Office Mgr., Julie Elan; Volunteer Coord., Mark Smith; Mktg. Coord., Rhetta Shead.
Personnel Profile: Full-Time Paid 7; Part-Time Paid 2; Part-Time Volunteers 100.
Governing Authority: municipal. Parent Institution: City of Lakewood. Tax-exempt: 170(b)(1)(A).
History Museum.
Collections: culture, pertaining to the Foothills area of the Eastern Slope of Colorado; restored vintage farm machinery; local history; archival, local art; 18 historic structures.
Research Fields: agricultural history; 20th-Century Lakewood area history; farming; ranching; homesteading; transportation; local history; natural history.
Facilities: library of Lakewood Colorado history, Jefferson County history & early farm methodology, available for use on premises; classrooms; meeting rooms; kitchen areas; picnic areas; nature trail; outdoor amphitheater; festival area; cultural center with 300-seat indoor theater.
Activities: lectures; films; gallery talks; discovery trunks; summer camps; art classes; exhibits; tours; performances; community events.
Publications: brochures; quarterly, Bravo Lakewood; membership quarterly, The Review.
Hours & Admission Prices: Tues.-Sat. 10-4. Adults $5, seniors citizens $4, youth $3; discounts to AAM members; children 3 & under members no charge. Closed holidays. ♿
Attendance: 45,238 (accurate)
Membership: Young Professional: Individual $50, Dual $70; Supporter $150; Benefactor 250; Patron $500.

ROBERT H. JOHNSON PLANETARIUM, 200 Kipling St., Lakewood, CO 80226-1046. Tel.: 303-982-7278. Fax: 303-982-7277.
Formerly: Jefferson County Schools Planetarium
Founded: 1963.
Key Personnel: Dir., Kathy Miller; Coord. Scheduling, Lisa Delameter.
Governing Authority: public school district. Parent Institution: Jefferson County Public Schools, 809 Quail. Branch Observatories: Jefferson County Lab School, Upper Bear Creek; Windy Peak, Bailey, CO. Tax-exempt.
Planetarium & Observatories.
Collections: astronomy; space science.

Facilities: approx. 500-vol. library of astronomy & related subjects; 120-seat planetarium.
Activities: lectures; films; education programs for students K-6.
Publications: curriculum guides.
Hours & Admission Prices: Sept.-June Mon.-Fri. 9-3. Admission $3. Closed holidays. ♿
Attendance: 32,000

ROCKY MOUNTAIN COLLEGE OF ART + DESIGN GALLERIES, 1600 Pierce Ave., Lakewood, CO 80214-1897. Tel.: 800-888-ARTS. Fax: 303-759-4970.
E-mail: cstell@rmead.edu
Web Site: www.rmcad.edu/exhibitions
Founded: 1963.
Congressional District: 4
Key Personnel: C.E.O., Steven Steele; Treas., Susan Pivoda; Cur., Cortney Stell; Recruitment, Angela Carlson; Registrar, Eleni Stoycos; Alumni, V.A. Hayman.
Personnel Profile: Full-Time Paid 40; Part-Time Paid 50.
Governing Authority: private college; profit. The Philip J. Steele Gallery.
College Art Gallery.
Collections: paintings; sculptors; graffiti.
Facilities: library; educational facilities; 450 sq. ft. exhibit space. Art supplies for sale.
Activities: formal education programs offering Bachelor of Fine Art degrees; affiliated with Rocky Mountain College of Art & Design; lectures; gallery forums for the public.
Hours & Admission Prices: Mon.-Sat. 12-5. No charge. Closed New Year's Day; Independence Day; Labor Day; Thanksgiving; Christmas.

Lamar

BIG TIMBERS MUSEUM, 7515 US Hwy. 50, Lamar, CO 81052. Mailing Address: P.O. Box 362, Lamar, CO 81052-0362. Tel.: 719-336-2472. Fax: 719-336-2472.
E-mail: bigtimbers@prowerscounty.net
Web Site: www.bigtimbersmuseum.org
Founded: 1966.
Congressional District: 3
Key Personnel: Cur., Kathleen Scranton.
Personnel Profile: Full-Time Paid 1; Part-Time Paid 3; Part-Time Volunteers 5.
Governing Authority: nonprofit organization. Sponsored by Prowers County Historical Society. Tax-exempt: 501(c)(3).
History Museum: housed in the original AT&T Co. repeater station.
Collections: history; WWI poster collection; Charles Frederick Worth gown exhibit; Indian arrowhead collection; furniture.
Facilities: 100-vol. library of newspaper files.
Activities: permanent & temporary exhibitions.
Publications: A Prowers Country History.
Hours & Admission Prices: June-Aug. Mon.-Sat. 10-5, Sun. 1-5; Sept.-May daily 1-4; tours by appointment. Family $5, adults $3. Closed New Year's Day; Good Friday; Thanksgiving; Christmas.
Attendance: 1,300 (accurate)
Membership: Individual $7; Family $10; Patron $25; Life $100.

Las Animas

KIT CARSON MUSEUM, (M), 9th St. & Bent Ave., Las Animas, CO 81054. Mailing Address: P.O. Box 68, Las Animas, CO 81054-0068. Tel.: 719-456-2507.
Web Site: bentcounty.org
Founded: 1959.
Key Personnel: Cur., Andy Thomas.
Personnel Profile: Part-Time Volunteers 3.
Governing Authority: society. Affiliated with Pioneer Historical Society. Tax-exempt: 501(c)(3).
General Museum.
Collections: Native American artifacts; cattle industry items; carriages; railroad room; agricultural room; Fort Lyon room; Santa Fe room; Llewellyn Thompson memorial room; history. Historic Buildings: 1876 county jail; 1891 schoolhouse; 1860 stage coach station; blacksmith shop.
Research Fields: local history.
Facilities: Books & cards for sale.
Activities: guided tours; lectures; permanent & temporary exhibitions.
Publications: yearly newsletter; pamphlet, Kit Carson Museum.
Hours & Admission Prices: Memorial Day-Labor Day daily 12-4 by appointment. No charge; donations accepted. ♿
Attendance: 900
Membership: Regular $5; Sustaining $10; Life $100.

Leadville

HEALY HOUSE-DEXTER CABIN, 912 Harrison Ave., Leadville, CO 80461-3321. Tel.: 719-486-0487. Fax: 719-486-2557.
E-mail: maureen.scanlon@chs.state.co.us
Web Site: www.coloradohistory.org
Founded: 1947.
Congressional District: 5
Key Personnel: Dir., Ed Nichols.
Personnel Profile: Part-Time Paid 5.
Governing Authority: state. Parent Institution: Colorado Historical Society, 1300 Broadway, Denver, CO 80203. Tax-exempt.
Historic Buildings.
Collections: Victorian household items. Historic Buildings: 1878 Healy House; 1879 Dexter Cabin.
Research Fields: Leadville history.
Activities: tours of house & cabin; Leadville Mining District 4 wheel drive tours.
Hours & Admission Prices: mid-May to Sept. daily 10-4:30; other times tours by appointment. Adults $5, senior citizens $4.50, children 6-16 $3.50; discounts to AAM members, school & group tours; children under 6 & members no charge.
Attendance: 8,000

HERITAGE MUSEUM & GALLERY, 102 E. Ninth St., Leadville, CO 80461-3302. Mailing Address: P.O. Box 962, Leadville, CO 80461-0962. Tel.: 719-486-1878.
Founded: 1971.
Congressional District: 5
Key Personnel: Pres. (V), Carl Schaefer; C.E.O., Ray Stamps; Museum Shop Mgr., Nancy Manly; Museum Shop Mgr., Barbara Beck.
Personnel Profile: Full-Time Paid 1; Part-Time Paid 1; Part-Time Volunteers 20.
Governing Authority: nonprofit organization. Parent Institution: Lake County Civic Center Association. Tax-exempt: 501(c)(3).
History Museums: located in Historic Leadville District.
Collections: mining artifacts; ore samples; diorama display-Leadville mining history; Oak Room furnishings; clothing; personal articles & household artifacts; 1/4-inch scale replica of Leadville's 1896 Ice Palace. Historic Buildings: 1880s The Old Church; 1902 Heritage Museum; 1870 Prospector's cabin.
Research Fields: Leadville/Lake county history.
Facilities: 250-vol. books; manuscripts, newspaper & census microfilm; 2,500 photographs on Lake County history available for research within the Lake County Public Library; Prospector Park. Leadville history booklets, crafts, newspaper reproductions & other museum-related items for sale.
Activities: self-guided tours; art exhibits; school & educational tours.
Publications: quarterly newsletter, The Tallyboard.
Hours & Admission Prices: May-Oct. daily 10-6. Adults $6, seniors $5, children 6-16 $3; children under 6 & members no charge. ♿
Attendance: 9,000 (accurate)
Membership: Annual $20; Patron $30; Contributing $50; Donor $100.

THE HISTORICAL TABOR OPERA HOUSE, 308 Harrison Ave., Leadville, CO 80461-3612. Tel.: 719-486-8409.
E-mail: info@taboroperahouse.net
Web Site: www.taboroperahouse.net
Founded: 1955.
Key Personnel: C.E.O., Dir. & Cur., Sharon Bland; Chm. (V), Marylee Mosqovoy.
Personnel Profile: Full-Time Volunteers 1; Part-Time Volunteers 12.
Governing Authority: individual operation.
Historic Theater Museum: listed on the National Register of Historic Places.
Collections: paintings; theater; history; original scenery; Leadville & Tabor.
Research Fields: paintings; theater; history; original scenery.
Facilities: Books, pictures & museum-related items for sale.
Activities: guided tours; lectures; films; drama; permanent exhibitions.
Publications: books, The Tabor Opera House; Silver Dollar Tabor; Leadville Crystal Carnival 1896; My Search for Augusta Pierce Tabor; Leadville's First Lady.
Hours & Admission Prices: House: Memorial Day to Labor Day Mon.-Sat. 10-5. Adults $5; discounts to seniors, AAA & military. Tabor's Second Story: by appointment. Adults $5. House & Second Story: $7. ♿

HOUSE WITH THE EYE MUSEUM, 127 W. Fourth St., Leadville, CO 80461-3629. Mailing Address: P.O. Box 911, Leadville, CO 80461-0911. Tel.: 719-486-0860.
Founded: 1964.
Congressional District: 3
Key Personnel: Cur., Barbara M. Bost.

Governing Authority: individual operation.
Historic House Museum: 1879 House with the Eye, built by noted French architect Robitaille for his bride; features a gingerbread front & hand-crafted wainscoting.
Collections: carriages; mining tools; pianos; jewelry; guns; old bottles; picture albums; clocks; boomtown memorabilia.
Research Fields: Leadville history.
Activities: guided tours.
Publications: descriptive brochure.
Hours & Admission Prices: June-Labor Day daily 10-4. Adults $2.50, children $.75; discounts to senior citizens.

LEADVILLE NATIONAL MINING HALL OF FAME & MUSEUM, 120 W. 9th St., Leadville, CO 80461-3403. Mailing Address: P.O. Box 981, Leadville, CO 80461-0981. Tel.: 719-486-1229. Fax: 719-486-3927.
Web Site: www.mininghalloffame.org
Founded: 1987.
Key Personnel: Dir. & Pres., Robert Hartzell; Chm. (V), Dick Moolick.
Personnel Profile: Full-Time Paid 2; Part-Time Paid 10; Part-Time Volunteers 10; Interns 1.
Mining Museum.
Collections: mining history; mining pioneers.
Facilities: Museum-related items for sale.
Publications: High Grad Newsletter.
Hours & Admission Prices: Daily 11-4. Adults 12 & over $7, seniors 62 & over $6, children 6-12 $4; discounts to AAM members; children under 6 no charge. Closed New Year's Day; Thanksgiving; Christmas. ♿
Attendance: 25,000 (estimated)
Membership: Individual $35; Family $50; Contributing $150; Benefactor $1,000; Life $2,500.

MATCHLESS MINE MUSEUM, 120 W. 9th St., Leadville, CO 80461-3403. Mailing Address: P.O. Box 981, Leadville, CO 80461-0981. Tel.: 719-486-1229. Fax: 719-486-3927.
E-mail: director@mininghalloffame.org
Web Site: www.mininghalloffame.org
Founded: 1953.
Congressional District: 6
Key Personnel: Dir. & Chm. (V), Robert Hartzell; Museum Shop Mgr., Lynn Webster.
Personnel Profile: Full-Time Paid 2; Part-Time Paid 3.
Governing Authority: nonprofit organization. Tax-exempt.
Mining Museum.
Collections: period mine artifacts.
Activities: guided tours.
Hours & Admission Prices: May 6 to Oct. 1 daily 9-5. Adults $7, seniors $6, children 6-12 $3; discounts to groups & AAM members; members no charge. ♿
Attendance: 10,000 (estimated)

Limon

LIMON HERITAGE MUSEUM, 899 First St., Limon, CO 80828. Mailing Address: P.O. Box 341, Limon, CO 80828-0341. Tel.: 719-775-8605. Fax: 719-775-8808.
E-mail: limonmuseum@hotmail.com
Web Site: townoflimon.com.tourism
Founded: 1990.
Congressional District: 4
Key Personnel: C.E.O., Tony Wernsman; Pres. (V), Vivian Lowe; Chm. (V), Education & Devel., Lucille Reimer; Treas. & Registrar, Barbara Berry.
Personnel Profile: Full-Time Volunteers 30; Part-Time Paid 2; Part-Time Volunteers 35; Interns 1.
Governing Authority: private; nonprofit organization. Parent Institution: Limon Heritage Society. Tax-exempt: 501(c)(3).
History Museum: housed in a restored Union Depot.
Collections: local history of the Colorado high plains, the Union Pacific & Rock Island Railroads, ranching & farming; sheepherder's wagons; period farm machinery; one-room schoolhouse; Houtz Native American artifacts.
Research Fields: homesteaders prior to 1910; ancient plains, geology of area.
Facilities: 5,200 sq. ft. exhibit space.
Activities: concerts; docent program; guided tours; temporary exhibitions. Annual Events: Western Festival & Parade; Heritage Celebration & Lost Arts Demonstrations.
Publications: annual newsletter, Windbreak.
Hours & Admission Prices: Memorial Day-Labor Day Mon.-Sat. 1-8. No charge; donations accepted. ♿
Attendance: 5,000 (estimated)
Membership: Student $5; Adult $15; Family $25; Donor $100; Business $150.

Littleton

COLORADO GALLERY OF THE ARTS/ARAPAHOE COMMUNITY COLLEGE, 5900 S. Santa Fe Dr., 1st Fl. Annex Bldg., Littleton, CO 80120-1801. Tel.: 303-797-5649.
Founded: 1979.
Congressional District: 6
Key Personnel: Gallery Coord., Trish Sangelo.
Governing Authority: university. Parent Institution: Arapahoe Community College. Tax-exempt.
Art Gallery.
Collections: exhibitions of loaned & leased art objects.
Facilities: 2,128 sq. ft. exhibition area.
Activities: guided tours; lectures; films; concerts; rental gallery; organized educational programs; docent program; loan & traveling exhibitions.
Publications: quarterly newsletter.
Hours & Admission Prices: Mon. & Wed.-Fri. 12-5, Tues. 12-7; other times by appointment. No charge. Closed holidays. ♿
Attendance: 14,000
Membership: Student & Senior Citizen $10; Individual $15; Family & Dual $20; Associate $35; Patron $100 & up; Donor $500 & up.

*** LITTLETON MUSEUM, (M),** 6028 S. Gallup St., Littleton, CO 80120-2703. Tel.: 303-795-3950. Fax: 303-730-9818.
E-mail: tnimz@littletongov.org
Web Site: www.littletongov.org/museum/default.asp
Formerly: Littleton Historical Museum
Founded: 1969.
Congressional District: 6
Key Personnel: Dir., Tim Nimz; Cur. Exhibits, Bill Hastings; Deputy Dir. & Cur. Collections, Lorena Donohue; Administrative Coord., Margene Hamilton; Cur. Education & Interpretation, Suellen Winstead.
Personnel Profile: Full-Time Paid 13; Part-Time Paid 7; Part-Time Volunteers 150; Interns 2.
Governing Authority: municipal. Parent Institution: City of Littleton. Tax-exempt.
General Museum: history museum & living history farms.
Collections: agriculture; archives; manuscripts; costumes; decorative arts; industry; medicine; transportation. Historic Buildings: 1863 log schoolhouse; 1890 blacksmith shop; ice house; two living history farms: 1860s & 1895-1905.
Research Fields: general; agriculture; archives; costumes; decorative arts; industry; medicine; transportation.
Facilities: 600-vol. library of public & private records, papers on local history, newspapers & photographs available for research under supervision by staff.
Activities: guided tours; lectures; arts festivals; formally organized education programs for children; permanent & temporary exhibitions.
Publications: pamphlets; brochures; museum news.
Hours & Admission Prices: Tues.-Fri. 8-5, Sat. 10-5, Sun. 1-5. No charge; donations accepted. Closed holidays. ♿
Attendance: 128,686 (accurate)

Longmont

AGRICULTURAL HERITAGE CENTER AT THE LOHR-MCINTOSH FARM, (M), 8348 Ute Hwy. 66, Longmont, CO 80503-9232. Tel.: 303-776-8848.
Heritage Center.
Collections: local history & heritage; photographs; period furnishings; farm equipment.
Hours & Admission Prices: April-Oct. Fri.-Sun. 10-5; Winter: 1st Sat. of month 10-5.

LONGMONT MUSEUM, (M), 400 Quail Rd., Longmont, CO 80501-8989. Tel.: 303-651-8374. Fax: 303-651-0483. TDD: 303-651-8799.
Web Site: www.ci.longmont.co.us/museum
Founded: 1940.
Congressional District: 4
Key Personnel: Dir., Martha Clevenger; Bd. Chm., Glendora Shaffer; Bd. Vice Chm., Richard Luke; Pres. Friends, Chris Caron; Cur. Exhibits, Jared Thompson; Cur. Education, Jill Overlie; Cur. Collections, Cathey Dunn; Cur. Research & Information, Erik Mason; Discovery Days Coord., Stephanie Ohlsen; Art in Public Places Admin., Lauren Greenfield; Museum Asst., Joann McCoy; Museum Shop Mgr., Christina Mehler.
Personnel Profile: Full-Time Paid 7; Part-Time Paid 6; Part-Time Volunteers 65; Interns 2.
Governing Authority: municipal. Parent Institution: City of Longmont, Dept. of Community Services. Tax-exempt: 170(b)(1)(A).
Regional History Museum.

Collections: history & culture of the region; development of the Longmont area.
Research Fields: Longmont & the St. Vrain Valley cultural history prehistoric to present.
Facilities: photograph & document archives available for research on premises only. Museum-related items for sale.
Activities: guided & self-guided tours; inter-museum loan, permanent & traveling exhibitions; programs for children, adults & families; special events; volunteer program; internship program; panoramic view of the mountains & plains.
Publications: quarterly newsletter of events & exhibits.
Hours & Admission Prices: Tues. & Thurs.-Sat. 9-5, Wed. 9-8, Sun. 1-5. No charge; donations accepted. Closed holidays. ♿
Attendance: 71,831 (accurate)
Membership: Senior $20; Individual $25; Family $35; Supporting $125; Business $275.

Louisville

LOUISVILLE HISTORICAL MUSEUM, (M), 1001 Main St., Louisville, CO 80027-1725. Mailing Address: City Hall, 749 Main St., Louisville, CO 80027. Tel.: 303-665-9048.
Key Personnel: Museum Coord., Bridget Bacon
History Museum.
Collections: Louisville history; coal mining. Historic Buildings: Jacoe Store: period artifacts; photographs; coal mining; industrial equipment. Tomeo House: period furnishings.
Hours & Admission Prices: Tues.-Thurs. & 1st Sat. of month 10-3.

Loveland

* **LOVELAND MUSEUM GALLERY, (M),** 503 N. Lincoln Ave., Loveland, CO 80537-5619. Tel.: 970-962-2410. Fax: 970-962-2910.
Web Site: ci.loveland.co.us
Founded: 1956.
Key Personnel: C.E.O. & Dir. Curatorial Svcs., Susan P. Ison; Pres. Historical Society (V), Ed Fisher; Cur. Interpretation, Tom Katsimpalis; Cur. Collections, Jennifer Slichter; Cur. Exhibits, Janice Currier; Business Svcs. Coord., Suzanne Jassen; Exhibits Preparator, David L. Phelps; Administrative Specialist, Claudette Phelps; Cultural Events Coord., Kim Akeley-Charron; Youth Activities Coord., Jenni Dobson.
Personnel Profile: Full-Time Paid 9; Part-Time Volunteers 10; Interns 6.
Governing Authority: municipal; nonprofit. Tax-exempt: 170(b)(1)(A).
Art and History Museum.
Collections: social, natural, cultural & art history of Loveland.
Research Fields: history of the Larimer County Fairground; Great Western Sugar Co.; Germans from Russia; history of community business, architecture & social development.
Facilities: library; auditorium. Museum-related items for sale.
Activities: concerts; docent program; films; teen coffeehouses; Lone Tree School schoolhouse program; after school art programs; guided tours; hobby workshops; lectures; loan, participatory & traveling exhibitions; school loan service; art exhibits. Annual Events: Cherry Pie Festival; Halloween Fun Festival.
Publications: Fifth & Lincoln News; books, Loveland's Historic Downtown; Stone Quarrying in Loveland's Foothills; Historic Loveland Churches; A Guide to Historic Loveland; Exploring Loveland's Hidden Past: People and Places of Early Loveland, Colorado; Germans from Russia in the Loveland Area.
Hours & Admission Prices: Tues.-Wed. & Fri. 10-5, Thurs. 10-9, Sat. 10-4, Sun. 12-4. No charge; donations accepted. Closed New Year's Day; Easter; Independence Day; Thanksgiving & day after; Christmas. ♿
Attendance: 49,088
Membership: Individual $15; Family $25; Contributing $100; Patron $250; Corporate $1,000.

TIMBERLANE FARM MUSEUM, 2306 E. First St., Loveland, CO 80537-5906. Tel.: 970-663-7348. Fax: 970-663-7364.
Web Site: www.timberlanefarmmuseum.org
Farm Museum.
Collections: local history & farm life from 1860 to 1940; farm equipment; restored home; farm buildings.
Activities: working farm.
Hours & Admission Prices: Call for hours. ♿

Lyons

THE LYONS REDSTONE MUSEUM, 340 High St., Lyons, CO 80540. Mailing Address: P.O. Box 9, Lyons, CO 80540-0009. Tel.: 303-823-6692 & 5271. Fax: 303-823-8257.
E-mail: lavern921@aol.com
Founded: 1973.
Congressional District: 2
Key Personnel: C.E.O., Chm. (V) & Pres. (V), LaVern M. Johnson; Vice Pres., Jerry L. Johnson; Historic Asst., Calvin Schilling; Deputy Dir., Maxine Harkalis; Museum Shop Mgr., Terri Weir.
Personnel Profile: Full-Time Volunteers 2; Part-Time Paid 3; Part-Time Volunteers 5; Interns 2.
Governing Authority: nonprofit organization. Parent Institution: Lyons Historical Society. Subsidiary Institution: Town of Lyons. Tax-exempt: 501(c)(3).
History Museum: housed in c.1881 school building.
Collections: local artifacts; E.S. Lyon & family artifacts; sandstone tools; old books; household items; photographs; period artifacts; Lyon Post office boxes c.1890; early Arapaho Indian artifacts; square grand piano; player organ of the Loukonen family; power pole; 577 telephone insulators; horse drawn mail cart; Lyons State Bank; teller cage (1907-1983); c.1880 Friden Family, pump organ; Lyons Drug Store artifacts (1924-1970); Lyons Historic District, 15 sandstone buildings in the Lyons area from 1880-1917; Lyons area people and business files.
Research Fields: local history.
Facilities: 50-vol. library of books printed in the 1880s & old school books available for research on premises or by special permission. Books, crafts & other gift items for sale.
Activities: guided tours; historic walking tours; history programs; formally organized education programs; loan, permanent & temporary exhibitions.
Publications: special reports & events; small oral history books of area pioneers and their families on ES Lyon family founder of town of Lyons; video, history of sandstone quarries & geology; book, The Sandstone - 1800s; 2006 Lyons Timeline; Billie Welch Resort; History of Sandstone Quarries; History of Old Stone Church; History of Pella, (Refuge in the Valley) Altoona District; Big Elk Meadows; Homestead Acres; Lyons - The Gateway to the Rockies - 1900s; Lyons - The Quarry Town - 1800s; tour maps.
Hours & Admission Prices: June-Sept. Sat. 9:30-4:30, Sun. 12:30-4:30. No charge, donations accepted.
Attendance: 1,000 (estimated)
Membership: Senior & Student & Family $5; Friend $10; Business Contributor $25; Sustaining $50; Supporting $100; Life $500.

Manassa

JACK DEMPSEY MUSEUM AND PARK, 412 Main St., Manassa, CO 81141. Mailing Address: P.O. Box 130, Manassa, CO 81141-0130. Tel.: 719-843-5207.
Founded: 1966.
Governing Authority: city.
History Museum: housed in the cabin where heavyweight boxing champion, Jack Dempsey was born.
Collections: Dempsey's career; boxing gloves from his NY fight; personal artifacts; photographs.
Hours & Admission Prices: Memorial Day to Labor Day Tues.-Sat. 10-5. No charge; donations accepted. ♿

Manitou Springs

CAVE OF THE WINDS, 100 Cave of the Winds Rd., Manitou Springs, CO 80829. Mailing Address: P.O. Box 826, Manitou Springs, CO 80829-0826. Tel.: 719-685-5444. Fax: 719-685-1712.
Natural History Museum.
Collections: natural history.
Activities: guided tours; rental facilities.
Hours & Admission Prices: Summer daily 9-9; Winter: daily 10-5. Adults $18, children 6-11 $9; children 5 & under no charge.

CLIFF DWELLINGS MUSEUM, U.S. Hwy. 24, Manitou Springs, CO 80829. Mailing Address: P.O. Box 272, Manitou Springs, CO 80829-0272. Tel.: 719-685-5242; 800-354-9971.
E-mail: info@cliffdwellingsmuseum.com
Web Site: www.cliffdwellingsmuseum.com
Natural History Museum.
Collections: Anasazi cliff dwellings; American Indian culture; archaeology; natural history preserve; stone mesa-top building; Anasazi baking oven; native flowers, herbs, trees & plants.
Facilities: picnic area; nature trail. Museum-related items for sale.
Activities: tours. Museum Sponsors: daily Indian dances June to mid-Aug.
Hours & Admission Prices: March-April & Oct.-Nov. daily 9-5; May-Sept. daily 9-6; Dec.-Feb. daily 10-4. Adults 12 & over $9.50, seniors 60 & over $8.50, children 7-11 $7.50; discounts to groups; handicapped and children 6 & under no charge. Closed Thanksgiving; Christmas.

GARDEN OF THE GODS TRADING POST, 324 Beckers Lane, Manitou Springs, CO 80829. Tel.: 800-874-4515; 719-685-9045.
Art Gallery.
Collections: works by Colorado fine artists; traditional & contemporary jewelry; Native American jewelry; Navajo rugs; sand paintings; Pueblo pottery.
Facilities: cafe. Museum-related items for sale.
Hours & Admission Prices: Summer: daily 8-8; Winter: daily 9-5. Closed Thanksgiving; Christmas.

MIRAMONT CASTLE MUSEUM, 9 Capitol Hill Ave., Manitou Springs, CO 80829-1618. Tel.: 719-685-1011; 888-685-1011.
Founded: 1976.
Congressional District: 5
Key Personnel: Pres. Bd., Lance Michels; Exec. Dir., Kelly Hunter; Treas. & Museum Shop Mgr., Peggie Yager.
Personnel Profile: Full-Time Paid 3; Full-Time Volunteers 12; Part-Time Paid 3; Part-Time Volunteers 12.
Governing Authority: nonprofit organization. Parent Institution: Manitou Springs Historical Society. Tax-exempt: 501(c)(3).
Historic Building Museum: built in 1895.
Collections: Victorian period furniture & furnishings; period artifacts, books, maps, papers & records of the Manitou Springs area; paintings; worldwide dolls; miniatures from around the world.
Research Fields: local history.
Facilities: library; banquet facilities; tea room. Museum-related items for sale.
Activities: self-guided tours; lectures; meetings; concerts; arts festivals; seminars; guided group tours; community events.
Hours & Admission Prices: Memorial Day-Labor Day daily 9-5; Sept.-May Tues.-Sun. 10-4; groups by appointment. Adults $6, seniors over 59 $5.50, children 6-12 $2; children under 6 & members no charge. ♿
Attendance: 34,943 (accurate)
Membership: Golden Age $5; Individual $10; Family $15; Life $100; Sustaining $250; Benefactor $500; Patron $1,000.

Meeker

THE WHITE RIVER MUSEUM, 565 Park St., Meeker, CO 81641. Mailing Address: P.O. Box 413, Meeker, CO 81641-0413. Tel.: 970-878-9982.
E-mail: wrmuseum@nctelecom.net
Web Site: www.meekercolorado.com/whiterivermuseum.htm
Founded: 1956.
Key Personnel: Cur., Ardith Douglass.
Governing Authority: society; nonprofit organization. Affiliated with Rio Blanco County Historical Society.
History Museum: housed in 1880 Officer's Quarters.
Collections: rocks; furniture; Indian artifacts; clothing; musical instruments; stoves; wooden tools; school furnishings; early photographs including Theodore Roosevelt hunting in 1901; period money; period furnishings.
Research Fields: local history.
Activities: tours.
Hours & Admission Prices: May-Oct. Mon.-Fri. 9-5, Sat.-Sun. 10-5; mid-Nov. to mid-April call for hours. No charge; donations accepted. Closed New Year's Day; Easter; Mother's Day; Father's Day; Thanksgiving; Christmas. ♿
Membership: Annual $10.

Mesa Verde National Park

MESA VERDE NATIONAL PARK MUSEUM, Mesa Verde National Park, CO 81330. Mailing Address: P.O. Box 8, Mesa Verde National Park, CO 81330-0008. Tel.: 970-529-5074 & 5073. Fax: 970-529-1117.
Web Site: www.nps.gov/meve
Founded: 1917.
Congressional District: 3
Key Personnel: Supt., Larry Wiese; Museum Cur., Carolyn Landes; Chief Research & Resource Mgmt., Scott Travis; Chief, Interpretation, Tessy Shirakawa; Park Archivist, Greg Cox.
Personnel Profile: Full-Time Paid 1; Part-Time Paid 1; Interns 1.
Governing Authority: federal. Parent Institution: National Park Service. Tax-exempt.
Park Museum: archaeological & ethnographic exhibits; ancestral Puebloan archaeological sites dating from AD 550-1300.
Collections: ancestral Puebloan archaeology; Southwest ethnology; archives, archaeology & park history; photographs, excavation, stabilization & park history; historical, park, Civilian Conservation Corps.
Research Fields: archaeology; geology; biology.
Facilities: 7,200-vol. library of archaeological & ethnographic books available for research on premises & through inter-library loan; campground; cafeteria; picnic area. Slides, postcards, books, pamphlets, trail guides & museum-related items for sale.
Activities: permanent exhibitions; guided & self-guided tours; inter-museum loan.
Publications: The Story of Mesa Verde National Park; The Towers of Hovenweep; The Coming of Gray Owl; Cliff Dwellings of the Mesa Verde; Indians of the Mesa Verde; Archeological Techniques used at Mesa Verde National Park.
Hours & Admission Prices: mid-April to mid-Oct. daily 8-6:30; mid-Oct. to mid-April daily 8-5. Park entrance fee $10 per car. Tickets available at Far View Visitor Center for guided tours to 3 major sites during summer season, $1.75 per person. ♿
Attendance: 623,000 (estimated)
Membership: Individual $30; Family $45; Heritage $1,000.

Monte Vista

MONTE VISTA HISTORICAL SOCIETY HISTORY CENTER, 110 Jefferson St., Monte Vista, CO 81144-1700. Mailing Address: P.O. Box 323, Monte Vista, CO 81144-0323. Tel.: 719-852-4396 & 2518.
E-mail: mvhs123@msn.com
History Museum.
Collections: period documents; photographs; area history.
Hours & Admission Prices: May-Sept. Mon.-Fri. 2-5; Winter: by appointment. No charge; donations accepted.

TRANSPORTATION OF THE WEST MUSEUM, 916 First Ave., Monte Vista, CO 81144-1445. Mailing Address: P.O. Box 323, Monte Vista, CO 81144-0323. Tel.: 719-852-8864.
E-mail: mvhs123@msn.com
Transportation Museum.
Collections: early modes of transportation; 1880s-1900s railroad; farming; sports; photographs.
Hours & Admission Prices: May-Sept. Mon.-Sat. call for hours. No charge; donations accepted.

Montrose

MONTROSE COUNTY HISTORICAL MUSEUM, 21 N. Rio Grande, Montrose, CO 81401-3467. Mailing Address: P.O. Box 1882, Montrose, CO 81402-1882. Tel.: 970-901-9270 (winter); 249-2085 (summer).
E-mail: debbarr@rmi.net
Founded: 1974.
Key Personnel: Pres. (V), Zilla May Brown; Vice Pres., Marge Morgenstern; Sec., Ruth Heath; Treas., Steve Gray; Cur., Deb Barr.
Personnel Profile: Part-Time Paid 1; Part-Time Volunteers 35.
Governing Authority: society. Parent Institution: Montrose County Historical Society. Tax-exempt.
Historical Society Museum: housed in c.1912 Denver & Rio Grande Western Depot.
Collections: farm machinery; mining & railroad memorabilia; Indian artifacts; tools; country store; children's room; homesteader's cabin; scrapbooks; tapes; old newspapers; dolls; Union Pacific railroad caboose; cowboy cabin.
Research Fields: pioneers; old time buildings; pictures; newspapers, 1896-1940.
Activities: children's workshops; monthly programs. Museum Sponsors: Open House; Historic Treks; History & Culture Fair.
Publications: book, Experience in Lieu of Education; Montrose-100 Years; quarterly newsletter.
Hours & Admission Prices: May-Oct. Mon.-Sat. 10-4. Adults $4, seniors $3, students $1, children $.50; discounts to AAA members; members no charge. Closed holidays.
Attendance: 3,500 (accurate)
Membership: Individual $25; Family $40; Business $50; Life $175; Family Lifetime $300; Business Lifetime $500.

UTE INDIAN MUSEUM/MONTROSE VISITOR CENTER, 17253 Chipeta Dr., Montrose, CO 81403-4748. Tel.: 970-249-3098. Fax: 970-252-8741.
E-mail: cj.brafford@state.co.us
Founded: 1956.
Congressional District: 3
Key Personnel: C.E.O. & Museum Shop Mgr., C.J. Brafford.
Personnel Profile: Full-Time Paid 1; Part-Time Paid 5; Part-Time Volunteers 20; Interns 1.
Governing Authority: state. Parent Institution: Colorado Historical Society, 1300 Broadway, Denver, CO 80203. Tax-exempt.
Indian History Museum: located on the site of Chief Ouray, leader of the Uncompahgve Utes.
Collections: ethnology of the Ute Indians; Indian artifacts; history; archaeology; paintings; anthropology; clothing; Ute Indian baskets, dioramas & wickiup.

Facilities: picnic area; visitor center; 8 1/2-acre farm. Books & other museum-related items for sale.
Activities: self-guided tours.
Publications: Colorado History News.
Hours & Admission Prices: May 31-Oct. Mon.-Sat. 9-4:30, Sun. 11-4:30; Nov.-May Mon.-Sat. 9-4:30. Adults $3.50, seniors $3, students 6-16 $1.50, school groups $1.25 per child & $1 per adult; co-historical society members & children under 6 no charge. ♿
Attendance: 17,000 (accurate)
Membership: Students $15; Senior Citizens $20; Individual $25; Senior Couple $30; Family $35; Centennial $100; Patron $300; Annual Corp. $1,000.

Morrison

MORRISON NATURAL HISTORY MUSEUM, 501 Colorado Hwy. 8, Morrison, CO 80465. Mailing Address: P.O. Box 564, Morrison, CO 80465-0564. Tel.: 303-697-1873. Fax: 303-697-8752.
E-mail: info@mnhm.org
Key Personnel: Dir., Matthew T. Mossbrucker
Natural History Museum.
Collections: hands-on exhibits; local history; rocks & fossils; life-size sculpture of a baby stegosaurus.
Facilities: Museum-related items for sale.
Activities: tours; special events; birthday parties; volunteer programs.
Hours & Admission Prices: March-Oct. daily 10-6; Nov.-Feb. daily 10-4. Closed New Year's Day; Easter; Thanksgiving; Christmas Eve & Day.

Mosca

GREAT SAND DUNES NATIONAL MONUMENT AND PRESERVE, 11500 Hwy. 150, Mosca, CO 81146-9502. Tel.: 719-378-6363. Fax: 719-378-6360.
E-mail: phyllis_bovin@nps.gov
Founded: 1932.
Congressional District: 3
Key Personnel: Supt., Steve Chaney; Resource Mgmt., Fred Bruch; Cur., Phyllis Pineda Bovin.
Personnel Profile: Full-Time Paid 1; Part-Time Paid 1.
Governing Authority: federal. Parent Institution: National Park Service. Tax-exempt.
Park Museum.
Collections: geology; general; natural history; anthropology; archaeology; Indian artifacts; herbarium; insects.
Research Fields: geology; zoology; botany.
Facilities: 1,500-vol. library of natural science & resource books available for inter-library loan & for use to public upon written request to superintendent; reading room. Slides, postcards, books, pamphlets & trail guides for sale.
Activities: guided tours; lectures; gallery talks; permanent exhibits.
Publications: information handouts.
Hours & Admission Prices: Visitor Center: Summer: daily 9-6; Spring & Fall daily 9-5; Winter: daily 9-4:30. Adults 17 & over $3.

Naturita

RIMROCKER HISTORICAL MUSEUM OF WEST MONTROSE COUNTY, 411 W. 2nd Avenue, Naturita, CO 81422. Mailing Address: P.O. Box 913, Nucla, CO 81424-0913. Tel.: 970-865-2100.
E-mail: rimrocker@fone.net
Founded: 1980.
Congressional District: 3
Key Personnel: Chm. (V), Marie Templeton; Pres. (V), Mary Helen de Koevend; Hostess, Carol Legge.
Personnel Profile: Part-Time Paid 1; Part-Time Volunteers 8.
Governing Authority: society. Tax-exempt.
Historical Society Museum: housed in Old Naturita Elementary School House.
Collections: Uranium mining; Indian artifacts; outside exhibit-mining & farming; blacksmith shop displaying tools of the trade; ranch artifacts; household items; dolls; costumes; tools; collection depicting history of the Pinon colony, the Colorado Cooperative Co., which built irrigation ditch to irrigate Tabequacke Park c.1894-1904; Umetco's video collection of mining & milling operations; pioneer kitchen, bedroom & business safe; hanging flume model; obituaries; file of articles of local people, schools, businesses, sports events, organizations & churches.
Research Fields: local history.
Facilities: Museum-related items for sale.
Activities: guided tours; temporary & permanent exhibitions. Museum Sponsors: Annual Mine Tour; Labor Day Picnic.
Publications: books, Spell of the Tabeguache; The Visionaries; pamphlets; newsletter; Naturita, Where the Past Meets the Present.
Hours & Admission Prices: June-Labor Day Tues.-Sat. 2-4; Winter: Wed. 2-4. No charge; donations accepted. ♿

Attendance: 450 (estimated)
Membership: Individual $10; Family $20.

Nunn

DRYLANDERS MUSEUM, 755 3rd St., Nunn, CO 80648. Tel.: 970-897-3125 (summer) 2671 (winter).
History Museum.
Collections: area history & culture; period artifacts; pioneer life.
Activities: tours; lectures.
Hours & Admission Prices: Summer: Sun. 1-4; other times by appointment.

Ouray

OURAY COUNTY HISTORICAL SOCIETY MUSEUM, 420 6th Ave., Ouray, CO 81427. Mailing Address: P.O. Box 151, Ouray, CO 81427-0151. Tel.: 970-325-4576.
E-mail: ochs@ouraynet.com
Historical Society Museum: housed in the former St. Joseph's Miners' Hospital; built in 1886.
Collections: local history & culture; mining; ranching; railroading; minerals; Native American artifacts; photographs; personal artifacts.
Facilities: library.
Hours & Admission Prices: April 15-May 14 Thurs.-Sat. 1-4:30; May 15-Sept. Mon.-Sat. 10-4:30, Sun. 12-4:30; Oct.-Nov. Thurs.-Sat. 10-4:30. Adults $5, seniors 60 & over $3, children 12 & under $1; discounts to groups; members no charge.

Pagosa Springs

FRED HARMAN ART MUSEUM, 85 Harman Park Dr., Pagosa Springs, CO 81147. Mailing Address: P.O. Box 192, Pagosa Springs, CO 81147-0192. Tel.: 970-731-5785. Fax: 970-731-4832.
E-mail: info@harmanartmuseum.com
Web Site: www.harmanartmuseum.com
Founded: 1979.
Congressional District: 3
Key Personnel: C.E.O., Cur. & Chm. (V), Fred C. Harman, III; Financial Dir. & Treas., Alan Kuyendall; Devel., Membership & Museum Shop Mgr., Norma Harman; Dir. Public Rels., Michael McLachlan; Security, Pat Curtis.
Personnel Profile: Full-Time Volunteers 2; Part-Time Volunteers 2.
Governing Authority: nonprofit organization. Tax-exempt: 501(c)(3).
Art Museum: home of Fred Harman, artist & cartoonist, creator of the Red Ryder & Little Beaver comics; one of the founders of the Cowboy Artists of America.
Collections: Harman oil paintings; pen & inks; books; original studio intact; saddles; firearms; photographs of rodeo & movie stars; awards; western memorabilia.
Research Fields: history of Fred Harman.
Facilities: 2,000 sq. ft. exhibit space. Museum-related items for sale.
Activities: guided tours; lectures.
Hours & Admission Prices: Feb.-March by appointment only; April-May & Sept.-Jan. Mon.-Fri. 10:30-5; Memorial Day-Labor Day Mon.-Sat. 10:30-5, Sun. 12:30-4. Adults $4, students & children $.50; discounts to CWYN, AAM & ICOM members; members no charge. ♿
Attendance: 4,950 (estimated)
Membership: Individual $25; Family $50; Friend $100; Supporting $250; Patron $500; Sustaining $1,000; Life $10,000.

Palmer Lake

LUCRETIA VAILE MUSEUM, 66 Lower Glenway St., Palmer Lake, CO 80133. Mailing Address: Palmer Lake Historical Society, P.O. Box 662, Palmer Lake, CO 80133-0662. Tel.: 719-559-0837.
Web Site: www.ci.palmer-lake.co.us/plhs/museum.shtml
Founded: 1956.
Congressional District: 20
Key Personnel: Dir., Roger Davis.
Personnel Profile: Part-Time Volunteers 6.
Governing Authority: society. Parent Institution: Palmer Lake Historical Society. Tax-exempt: 501(c)(3).
Historical Society Museum.
Collections: local relics & photographs; manuscripts; Timeline 1873 to present.
Research Fields: local history.
Facilities: 10-vol. collection of old books available for use under supervision on premises.
Activities: lectures; films.
Publications: Palmer Lake Narrative; Palmer Lake Historic Landmarks; Estemere Estate of Palmer Lake; Monument-Faded Neighbor Towns; Through the Years at Monument.

Hours & Admission Prices: June-Aug. Wed. 1-4, Sat. 10-2; Sept.-May Sat. 10-2. No charge; donations accepted. Closed national holidays. ♿
Attendance: 750 (estimated)

Parker

WILDLIFE EXPERIENCE MUSEUM, (M), 10035 S. Peoria St., Parker, CO 80134-9600. Tel.: 720-488-3300.
E-mail: info@twexp.org
Web Site: www.thewildlifeexperience.org
Natural History Museum.
Collections: natural history; fine art; film; paintings; sculpture; photography.
Facilities: theater; conference rooms; restaurant. Museum-related items for sale.
Activities: educational programs; conservation classes; films; school tours; Meet the Artist programs; special events.
Hours & Admission Prices: Tues.-Sun. 9-5. Adults 13-64 $7.95, seniors 65 & over $6.95, children 2-12 $4.95; discounts to groups; children under 2 no charge. Additional fee for theater & shows. Closed Thanksgiving; Christmas.
Membership: Individual $35; Dual $50; Family & Grandparent $75; Patron $125; Supporting $200; Benefactor $500; Life $900-$1,800.

Peterson Air Force Base

PETERSON AIR & SPACE MUSEUM, 21st Space Wing/MU, 150 E. Ent Ave., Peterson Air Force Base, CO 80914-1255. Tel.: 719-556-4915. Fax: 719-556-8509.
E-mail: 21sw.mu@peterson.af.mil
Web Site: www.petemuseum.org
Founded: 1981.
Personnel Profile: Full-Time Paid 2; Part-Time Volunteers 40.
Governing Authority: Parent Institution: National Museum of the U.S. Air Force. Tax-exempt.
Military Museum.
Collections: aviation & space history of Colorado Springs and Peterson Air Force Base; 16 aircraft; 4 missiles; models; uniforms; WWII.
Facilities: theater. Museum-related items for sale.
Hours & Admission Prices: Tues.-Sat. 9-4 by appointment. No charge; donations accepted. Closed federal holidays. ♿
Attendance: 14,000 (estimated)
Membership: Annual $25; Family $50; Life $325; Sponsor $500. Eagle Wings: Kitty Hawk $1,000-$4,999; Lightning $5,000-$9,999; Spirit of St. Louis $10,000-$24,999; Thunderbolt $25,000-$49,999; Super Connie $50,000-$74,999; Eagle Wings $75,000 & up.

Platteville

FORT VASQUEZ MUSEUM, 13412 U.S. Hwy. 85, Platteville, CO 80651-8017. Tel.: 970-785-2832.
Web Site: www.coloradohistory.org
Founded: 1958.
Congressional District: 4
Key Personnel: Dir., Susan Hoskinson.
Personnel Profile: Full-Time Paid 1; Part-Time Paid 1; Interns 1.
Governing Authority: state; society. Parent Institution: Colorado Historical Society, 1300 Broadway, Denver, CO 80203-2137. Tax-exempt: 501(c)(3).
Fur Trade and Native American Museum: reconstructed adobe fort on site of original 1835 trading post. Fort Vasquez trading post archaeological site and the Works Progress Administration adobe fort are listed in the National Register of Historic Places.
Collections: items related to Rocky Mountain fur trade era, 1830-1840s; items created by Arapahoe, Cheyenne, Sioux, & Ute during late 19th century, interpretation of archaeological investigation at Fort Vasquez trading post sites in the late 1960s. Historic Structure: 1935-1936 Works Progress Administration reconstructed Fort Vasquez fur trading post.
Research Fields: Plains Indians; historic archaeology; history of Rocky Mountain fur trade.
Facilities: Museum-related items for sale.
Activities: guided tours; lectures; living history demonstrations of Plains Indians and fur trade life.
Publications: Colorado History Now.
Hours & Admission Prices: Memorial Day-Labor Day daily 9-4:30, call to confirm. Adults $1; children 4 & under no charge. Closed New Year's Day; Thanksgiving; Christmas. ♿
Attendance: 9,565 (accurate)
Membership: Contact Colorado Historical Society membership office.

Pueblo

COLORADO MENTAL HEALTH INSTITUTE AT PUEBLO MUSEUM, 13th & Francisco Sts., Pueblo, CO 81003. Mailing Address: 1600 W. 24th St., Pueblo, CO 81003-1411. Tel.: 719-543-2012.
E-mail: info@cmhipmuseum.org
Web Site: www.cmhipmuseum.org
Key Personnel: Dir., Bob Mitchell; Asst. Dir., Nell Mitchell; Dir. Volunteer Svcs., Eunice Wolther.
Governing Authority: nonprofit organization.
Psychiatry Museum: listed on the National Register of Historic Places.
Collections: institute history; treatment of mentally ill; personal artifacts; historical documents; photographs; medical equipment; awards.
Activities: research.
Hours & Admission Prices: Tues. 10-4; other times by appointment. No charge.

EL PUEBLO HISTORY MUSEUM, 301 N. Union, Pueblo, CO 81003-4266. Tel.: 719-583-0453. Fax: 719-583-8214.
E-mail: deborah.espinosa@chs.state.co.us
Web Site: www.coloradohistory.org
Founded: 1959.
Congressional District: 3
Key Personnel: Dir., Deborah Espinosa; Administrative Asst., Kathleen Byers; Education Coord., Kathleen Eriksen; Trades, Truman Pooler.
Personnel Profile: Full-Time Paid 1; Part-Time Paid 3; Part-Time Volunteers 65.
Governing Authority: state; Parent Institution: Colorado Historical Society. Tax-exempt: 501(c)(3).
Historical Society Museum.
Collections: Spanish period of occupation; prehistoric & historic Indian artifacts; artifacts related to cattle industry; early man; Plains Indians; Spanish/Mexican Period; Pueblo's industrialization & European immigration to the city until 1900; historic site, El Pueblo Trading Post; archaeological dig; 1921 flood; 20th-century Pueblo.
Research Fields: Spanish/Mexican settlement in southern Colorado; archaeology of El Pueblo Trading Post; history of Pueblo, Colorado, 19th & 20th centuries.
Activities: formally organized education programs for children. Annual Event: Mercado (Frontier Market, Living History) and Chile Festival. Museum Sponsors: Children's Day; Women's History Week; Family Saturdays.
Publications: quarterly, Colorado Heritage; monthly, Colorado History NOW.
Hours & Admission Prices: Tues.-Sat. 10-4. Adults $4; discounts to AAM members & military; children 12 & under no charge. Closed major holidays. ♿
Attendance: 23,000 (accurate)
Membership: Student $18; Seniors over 65 $25; Individual $30; Institution $35; Family $40; Centennial $100; Patron $300; Heritage Club $1,000.

INFOZONE NEWS MUSEUM, (M), 100 E. Abriendo Ave., Pueblo, CO 81004-4232. Tel.: 719-553-0205.
Key Personnel: Dir., Maria Sanchez-Kennedy.
Personnel Profile: Full-Time Paid 2; Part-Time Volunteers 10.
Governing Authority: city. Parent Institution: County Library District. Tax-exempt.
History Museum.
Collections: Pueblo history & culture; hands-on exhibits.
Facilities: 100-seat theater.
Activities: hands-on exhibits; educational programs; films.
Hours & Admission Prices: Mon.-Thurs. 9-9, Fri.-Sat. 9-6, Sun. 1-5. No charge. ♿
Attendance: 25,000 (accurate)

PUEBLO ART GUILD AND GALLERY, 1500 N. Santa Fe, Pueblo, CO 81003-3700. Tel.: 719-543-2455.
Web Site: www.puebloartguild.com
Key Personnel: Pres., Freda Moore
Art Gallery: housed in the historic boathouse in Mineral Palace Park.
Collections: works by local artists.
Hours & Admission Prices: Spring, Summer & Fall Wed.-Sun. 12-4. Winter: call for hours. No charge; donations accepted. Closed most holidays.

PUEBLO COUNTY HISTORICAL SOCIETY MUSEUM AND EDWARD H. BROADHEAD LIBRARY, 201 W. "B" St., Pueblo, CO 81003-3403. Tel.: 719-543-6772.
E-mail: info@pueblohistory.org
Web Site: www.pueblohistory.org
Founded: 1976.
Congressional District: 3
Key Personnel: Pres., Dwight Hunter.

Personnel Profile: Part-Time Volunteers 13.
Governing Authority: Parent Institution: Pueblo County Historical Society. Tax-exempt.
Historical Society Museum & Library.
Collections: railroad furniture; memorabilia; Native American; Pueblo saddlery; baseball; prehistoric artifacts.
Research Fields: meta physical.
Activities: monthly membership meetings.
Publications: monthly, The Pueblo Lore; books related to the history & heritage of Pueblo & southern Colorado.
Hours & Admission Prices: Tues.-Sat. 10-4. No charge; donations accepted. Closed holidays. ♿
Attendance: 6,000 (estimated)
Membership: Student $12; Single $20; Family $28; Supporting $50; Sponsor $1,000.

PUEBLO WEISBROD AIRCRAFT MUSEUM, 31001 Magnuson Ave., Pueblo, CO 81001-4822. Tel.: 719-948-9219. Fax: 719-948-2437.
E-mail: phas@pwam.org
Web Site: www.pwam.org
Formerly: International B-24 Museum
Key Personnel: Pres. (V), R.J. Black Schultz; Vice Pres., D.R. Fry.
Personnel Profile: Part-Time Volunteers 25.
Governing Authority: bd. of directors.
Aircraft & Military History Museum.
Collections: US military aviation; military aircraft.
Activities: special events.
Publications: newsletter.
Hours & Admission Prices: Mon.-Sat. 10-4, Sun. 1-4. Adults $7; military with proper ID no charge. ♿
Membership: Annual $25; Life Time 60 & over $125; 40-59 $150; Under 40 $175.

PUEBLO ZOO, 3455 Nuckolls Ave., Pueblo, CO 81005-1234. Tel.: 719-561-1452, ext. 100. Fax: 719-561-8686.
E-mail: director@pueblozoo.org
Web Site: www.pueblozoo.org
Founded: 1903.
Congressional District: 4
Key Personnel: Exec. Dir., Jonnene McFarland; Pres., John Ercul; Cur., Marilyn McBirney; Mktg., Linda Frakes; Education, Marti Osborn; Museum Shop Mgr., Betty Wilkinson.
Personnel Profile: Full-Time Paid 19; Part-Time Paid 10; Part-Time Volunteers 75; Interns 2.
Governing Authority: private; nonprofit. Tax-exempt: 501(c)(3).
Zoo.
Collections: over 425 exotic & domestic animals of 135 species.
Facilities: 400-vol. library covering zoological-related topics; classroom. Zoo-related items for sale.
Activities: docent program; formal education programs for children; guided tours; lectures; participatory exhibits. Annual Events: Zoofari; Senior Safari; ElectriCritters.
Publications: newsletter, Pueblo Zoo News; annual report.
Hours & Admission Prices: May Mon.-Fri. 9-4, Sat.-Sun. 9-5; June-Aug. daily 9-5; Sept.-April Mon.-Sat. 9-4, Sun. 12-4. Adults $8, children 3-16 $5; discounts to groups & AZA members; members no charge. Closed New Year's Day; Thanksgiving; Christmas. ♿
Attendance: 70,795 (accurate)
Membership: Senior & Student $25; Individual $35; Senior Couple $40; Family & Grandparents $50.

ROSEMOUNT MUSEUM, (M), 419 W. 14th St., Pueblo, CO 81003-2707. Tel.: 719-545-5290. Fax: 719-545-5291.
Web Site: www.rosemount.org
Founded: 1967.
Congressional District: 3
Key Personnel: C.E.O. & Exec. Dir., Deb Darrow; Pres., Kathlyn Thatcher Vail; Office & Volunteer Coord., Carolyn Wainwright; Collections Mgr. & Housekeeping, Susan Kittinger; Maintenance & Groundskeeper, Roger Cain; Museum Shop Mgr., Patricia Bedard.
Personnel Profile: Full-Time Paid 4; Part-Time Paid 1; Part-Time Volunteers 80.
Governing Authority: nonprofit organization. Tax-exempt: 501(c)(3).
Historic House Museum: housed in an 1893 Victorian mansion, the John A. Thatcher residence; Henry Hudson Holly, architect.
Collections: late Victorian decorative arts; personal artifacts; period furnishings; photographs; 1904 McClelland Collection of World Curiosities.
Research Fields: late Victorian period.
Facilities: research library; restaurant. General gift items for sale.
Activities: guided tours; lectures; concerts; educational programs; community events.
Publications: brochure; quarterly newsletter; school workbooks; Victorian cookbook.
Hours & Admission Prices: Feb.-Dec. Tues.-Sat. 10-3:30. Adults $6, senior citizens $5, children 6-18 $4; members & children under 6 no charge. Closed holidays.
Attendance: 7,000 (accurate)
Membership: Seniors $15; Individual $25; Family $40; Contributor $75; Patron & Corporate $150; Benefactor $250; Collectors Council $500 & up.

*** SANGRE DE CRISTO ARTS CENTER & CONFERENCE CENTER, (M),** 210 N. Santa Fe Ave., Pueblo, CO 81003-4133. Tel.: 719-295-7200. Fax: 719-295-7230.
E-mail: mail@sdc-arts.org
Web Site: www.sdc-arts.org
Formerly: Sangre de Cristo Arts Center & Buell Children's Museum
Founded: 1972.
Congressional District: 3
Key Personnel: Exec. Dir. & C.E.O., Maggie Divelbiss; Chm. (V), Sally Berryman; Vice Chm., Cathy Valenzuela; Assoc. Dir., Judy Voss; Cur. Visual Arts, Karin Larkin; Cur. Children's Museum, Donna Stinchcomb; Asst. Cur. Children's Museum, Joleen Ryan; Dir. Dance, Karen Schaffenburg; Cur. Education, Gary Holder; Asst. Education Cur. & Cur. Asst., Diane Pirraglia; Accountant & Controller, Rochelle Spoone; Box Office Coord., Cheryl Califano; Facilities & Beverage Mgr., Lorrie Marquez; Office Asst. & Museum Shop Mgr., Julie Gallegos; Receptionist, Dan Masterson.
Personnel Profile: Full-Time Paid 17; Part-Time Paid 41; Part-Time Volunteers 97; Interns 1.
Governing Authority: nonprofit organization. Tax-exempt: 501(c)(3).
Arts Center & Children's Museum.
Collections: historic & contemporary art of the American West.
Research Fields: Western American paintings; Gene Kloss intaglio prints.
Facilities: library; theater; conference & banquet facilities; children's museum. Gift items for sale.
Activities: guided tours; lectures; films; concerts; theater; workshops; dance school; permanent, temporary, traveling & loan exhibitions; docent program; conferences; outdoor summer concerts; performing arts.
Publications: quarterly newsletter, Town & Center Mosaic; education brochure; exhibit catalogs; books, Gene Kloss: Impressions of the Land & People; Joseph Hitchins: The Passionate Landscape; The Art of C.M. Russell & Northern Plains Indians; Colorado on Canvas: A Pictorial Survey of Early Colorado; Francis King Collection; South by Southwest: 25th Anniversary Catalog.
Hours & Admission Prices: Children's Museum: Tues.-Thurs. & Sat. 11-4, Fri. 9-4. Adults $4, children $3; discounts to military; members no charge. Office: Mon.-Fri. 9-5. Closed legal holidays. ♿
Attendance: 222,000 (accurate)
Membership: Student $20-$74; Senior $25-$74; One-Person $30-$74; Two-Person $35-$74; Grandparents $40-$74; Family $45-$74; Contributor $75-$149; Patron $150-$274; Sponsor $275-$549; Benefactor $550-$1,449; Premiere Club $1,500 & up.

SOUTHEASTERN COLORADO HERITAGE CENTER, 201 W. B St., Pueblo, CO 81003-3403. Tel.: 719-295-1517. Fax: 719-295-0040.
Founded: 1997.
Key Personnel: Museum Coord., Fran Reed.
Personnel Profile: Full-Time Paid 1; Part-Time Volunteers 24.
Governing Authority: bd. of directors. Tax-exempt: 501(c)(3).
History Museum: listed on the National Register of Historic Buildings.
Collections: southern Colorado history & culture; saddles; period telephones; railroad artifacts.
Facilities: library.
Activities: school tours; Legacy trunk education outreach; cultural organizations workshops. Museum Sponsors: Heritage Days Festival.
Hours & Admission Prices: Tues.-Sat. 10-4. No charge; donations accepted. Closed New Year's Day; Independence Day; Thanksgiving & day after; Christmas. ♿
Attendance: 9,000 (accurate)

Rangely

RANGELY OUTDOOR MUSEUM, 150 Kennedy Dr., Rangely, CO 81648-3503. Mailing Address: Rangely Museum Society, P.O. Box 131, Rangely, CO 81648. Tel.: 970-675-2612.
History Museum.
Collections: local history; Native American; pioneers; ranching from 1883 to 1946; energy development from 1946 to present.
Hours & Admission Prices: April-May & Sept.-Oct. Fri.-Sat. 10-4; June-Aug. Mon.-Sat. 10-4; other times by appointment.

Ridgway

RIDGWAY RAILROAD MUSEUM, US Hwy. 550 & Colorado State Hwy. 62, Ridgway, CO 81432. Mailing Address: P.O. Box 588, Ridgway, CO 81432-0588. Tel.: 970-252-1110.
Governing Authority: nonprofit organization. Tax-exempt: 501(c)(3).
Railroad Museum.
Collections: railroading history & equipment; photographs; personal artifacts.
Facilities: library.
Activities: educational programs; special events.
Publications: book, Narrow Gauge Railroading in the San Juan Triangle.
Hours & Admission Prices: June-Sept. daily 9-4; Oct.-May Mon.-Fri. 10-3. No charge; donations accepted.

Rifle

RIFLE CREEK MUSEUM, 337 East Ave., Rifle, CO 81650-2333. Tel.: 970-625-4862.
Founded: 1967.
Congressional District: 3
Key Personnel: Pres. (V), Crystal Anderson; Vice Pres., Millie Sawyer; Dir., Kim Fazzi; Sec., Vivian Langstaff; Treas., Irma Meisner.
Personnel Profile: Part-Time Paid 1; Part-Time Volunteers 10.
Governing Authority: nonprofit. Tax-exempt.
General Museum.
Collections: natural history; history; Indian artifacts; Garrison photos; textiles.
Research Fields: local history.
Activities: guided tours; slide shows.
Hours & Admission Prices: May-Oct. Mon.-Fri. 10-4; other times by appointment. Adults $2.50, senior citizens $2, students $1.50; under 5 & members no charge. ♿
Attendance: 2,500 (estimated)
Membership: Individual $10; Family $15; Business $25; Sustaining (3 years) $100; Lifetime $1,000.

Rocky Ford

ROCKY FORD HISTORICAL MUSEUM, 1005 Sycamore Ave., Rocky Ford, CO 81067-1760. Mailing Address: P.O. Box 835, Rocky Ford, CO 81067-0835. Tel.: 719-254-6737.
Founded: 1940.
Congressional District: 3
Key Personnel: Bd. Pres., Brian Liekam; Bd. Sec., Nancy Martin; Cur., William B. Hodges, Jr.
Personnel Profile: Part-Time Paid 1; Part-Time Volunteers 4.
Governing Authority: board of trustees. Parent Institution: City of Rocky Ford.
General Museum.
Collections: Swink family; American Crystal Sugar Co.; produce farming; furnishings; first fire engine; military; photography; oral history tapes; archieves; ethnography; rocks & minerals; fossils; Indian artifacts.
Research Fields: local history.
Facilities: 1909 Carnegie Library building; school yearbooks, photographs & newspapers available for research.
Activities: guided tours.
Hours & Admission Prices: Memorial Day to Labor Day Tues.-Fri. 1-5, Sat. 10-2; Sept.-May Wed. 1-5; other times by appointment. No charge; donations accepted.
Attendance: 700 (estimated)

Saguache

HAZARD HOUSE MUSEUM, 807 Pitkin Ave., Saguache, CO 81149. Mailing Address: P.O. Box 589, Saguache, CO 81149. Tel.: 719-655-2805.
Founded: 1998.
Personnel Profile: Part-Time Volunteers 10.
Governing Authority: Parent Institution: Saguache County Museum. Tax-exempt.
History Museum: housed in a 1908 home.
Collections: Hazard family artifacts; period furnishings; Steinway piano; oriental rugs; silver flatware; tea sets; personal artifacts.
Hours & Admission Prices: Memorial Day to 3rd week of Sept. daily 9-4. Adults $2, children under 12 $.50.

SAGUACHE COUNTY MUSEUM, Hwy. 285, Saguache, CO 81149. Mailing Address: P.O. Box 569, Saguache, CO 81149-0558. Tel.: 719-256-4272 & 655-2557.
E-mail: ginny@amigo.net
Web Site: slumuseumtrail.com
Founded: 1958.
Congressional District: 3
Key Personnel: Chm. (V), Virginia Sutherland; C.E.O., Margaret B. Finnerty; Co-Chm. (V), Thad Englert.
Personnel Profile: Part-Time Paid 6; Part-Time Volunteers 6.
Governing Authority: county. Parent Institution: Saguache County Museum Board. Tax-exempt: 501(c)(3).
Pioneer Museum & National Historic Site.
Collections: history artifacts; mineralogy; geology; glass; early pioneer memorial; archaeology; Indian artifacts; zoology; family histories. Historic Houses: 1870 school & jailer's residence; 1908 Saguache County jail; c.1880 blacksmith shop.
Facilities: library of early school, law & medical books, documents, letters, pictures & papers, historical books & works by local authors, available for research by people or organizations upon permission of the board. Books on local history for sale.
Activities: inter-museum loan, permanent & temporary exhibitions; special tours for groups of children. Museum Sponsors: Memorial weekend parade; Annual Fall Festival in Saguache Co. in September; crafts sales by local artisans.
Publications: pamphlets on local history; Frontier Eyewitness - Diary of John Lawrence; Images of The Past, Vol. I, II & III - Saguache County History People, Places & Events Vol. IV; Images of Past Vol. V; Sunny San Luis Valley. 1875 Episcopal Minister; Bonanza G. Kerber Creek; Images VI, 2007.
Hours & Admission Prices: Memorial Day-Labor Day daily 9-4; 3rd week in Sept. to Oct. by appointment. Adults $5, children under 12 $1; discounts to groups of 50 or more; members no charge. ♿
Attendance: 1,315 (accurate)
Membership: Sustaining $15-$100.

Salida

SALIDA MUSEUM, 406 1/2 W. Rainbow Blvd., Salida, CO 81201-2236. Tel.: 719-539-4602 & 7483.
Founded: 1954.
Congressional District: 3
Key Personnel: Pres., Judy Micklich.
Personnel Profile: Full-Time Volunteers 6; Part-Time Volunteers 2.
Governing Authority: municipal. Tax-exempt.
General Museum.
Collections: local historic artifacts; Indian artifacts; mineralogy; mining; homesteading; textiles.
Research Fields: newspapers; recorded stories; pictures.
Hours & Admission Prices: Memorial Day to Labor Day daily 11-5; tours by appointment. Adults $3, children 12-18 $1.50, youth 7-11 $1; children 6 & under and members no charge. ♿
Attendance: 2,000 (estimated)
Membership: Annual $10; Lifetime $100 & up.

San Luis

SAN LUIS MUSEUM AND CULTURAL CENTER, 401 Church Place, San Luis, CO 81152. Tel.: 719-672-3611.
E-mail: morada@amigo.net
History Museum.
Collections: murals; paintings.
Facilities: theater. Museum-related items for sale.
Activities: special events.
Hours & Admission Prices: Summer: daily 10-4; Winter: Mon.-Fri. 9-4. Adults $2, seniors & students $1.

Silt

SILT HISTORICAL SOCIETY, 707 Orchid, Silt, CO 81652. Mailing Address: P.O. Box 401, Silt, CO 81652-0401. Tel.: 970-876-5801.
E-mail: silthist@rof.net
Founded: 1982.
Congressional District: 3
Key Personnel: C.E.O. & Pres. (V), Randell Gorsett; Cur. & Museum Shop Mgr., Alice Jones; Cur., Lois Ferbrache; Public Rels., Joan Nestor.
Personnel Profile: Full-Time Volunteers 12; Part-Time Volunteers 12.
Governing Authority: private; nonprofit organization. Tax-exempt: 501(c)(3).
Living History Museum.
Collections: Native American artifacts; horse drawn machinery. 10 Historic Buildings 1880s-1930s: school, house, store, office, saloon, shop, blacksmith shop, cow camp, & machine sheds.
Research Fields: family histories & history of towns in the area.
Facilities: 662-vol. library of National Geographic books, school books, booklets, pamphlets & scrapbooks. Museum-related items for sale.
Activities: guided tours; lectures; temporary exhibitions; artisan demonstrations. Museum Sponsors: early 1900 Hey Day in May; Family Fair Day in August.
Publications: Garfield County, First 100 Years; Reflections, Rifle Early and

Late; Reflections, Dry Hollow Ranch Memories; Reflections, Yes I Remember; Reflections, The Family History of Mary Wright; Reflections, The Century of My Life; Silt, Colorado Homesteads, 1880-1940.
Hours & Admission Prices: May-Oct. Tues.-Sat. 10-3. No charge; donations accepted. ♿
Attendance: 3,000 (estimated)
Membership: Family $10; Business $50; Patron $100.

Silver Cliff

SILVER CLIFF MUSEUM, 606 Main St., Silver Cliff, CO 81252. Mailing Address: P.O. Box 154, Silver Cliff, CO 81252-0154. Tel.: 719-783-2615. Fax: 719-783-4480.
E-mail: silverclifftown@centurytel.net
Founded: 1959.
Congressional District: 3
Key Personnel: C.E.O., Susan Hutton; Chm. (V), Carol Franta; Chm. (V), Alan Urban.
Personnel Profile: Part-Time Paid 2; Part-Time Volunteers 6.
Governing Authority: municipal. Tax-exempt.
General Museum.
Collections: clothes; silver pieces; photographs; c.1800 fire cart; period furnishings; paintings.
Research Fields: local history.
Facilities: 100-vol. library.
Activities: guided tours.
Publications: brochure.
Hours & Admission Prices: Memorial Day to Labor Day. Fri.-Sun. 1-5; other times by appointment. No charge; donations accepted.
Attendance: 310 (accurate)

Silver Plume

GEORGE ROWE MUSEUM, 315 Main St., Silver Plume, CO 80476. Mailing Address: P.O. Box 935, Silver Plume, CO 80476-0935. Tel.: 303-569-2562.
Founded: 1960.
Key Personnel: Chm. (V), Judith Caldwell.
Personnel Profile: Part-Time Paid 3.
Governing Authority: Parent Institution: People for Silver Plume, Inc. Tax-exempt.
History Museum.
Collections: area history; 19th century school room; period furnishings; mining.
Publications: Recipes-Remedies from the Kitchens of Silver Plume.
Hours & Admission Prices: Memorial Day to Labor Day daily 10-4; Sept. Sat.-Sun. 10-4. Adults $2.50; members and Sliver Plume residents No charge.
Attendance: 1,409 (accurate)
Membership: Senior Individual $10; Individual & Senior Family $15; Family $25; Sponsor $25; Sponsor $50; Sustaining $100; Life $500.

Silverton

SAN JUAN COUNTY HISTORICAL SOCIETY MUSEUM, 1557 Greene, Silverton, CO 81433. Mailing Address: P.O. Box 154, Silverton, CO 81433-0154. Tel.: 970-387-5838 & 5609. Fax: 970-387-5144.
E-mail: silvertonarchive@aol.com
Web Site: silvertonhistoricalsociety.org
Founded: 1964.
Congressional District: 3
Key Personnel: Chm. (V), Beverly Rich; Treas. & Sec., Scott Fetchenhier; Museum Shop Mgr., Duane Murphy.
Personnel Profile: Part-Time Paid 2; Part-Time Volunteers 7; Interns 1.
Governing Authority: society. Tax-exempt: 170(b)(1)(A).
Local History Museum.
Collections: mining equipment; office & home furniture; china, glass & paper work from businesses; railroad cars; hardware; archives of photographs, mine records & oral history; records; home furnishings; clothing. Historic Buildings: 1904 San Juan County Jail; 1882 Denver & Rio Grande Western Railroad Depot; 1900 Silverton Northern Railroad Depot; 1912 Silverton Northern Railroad Engine House, Power House & Mule barn; 1929 Mayflower Gold Processing Mill.
Research Fields: history of San Juan County.
Facilities: 200-vol. library of microfilm copies of Silverton newspapers, business records & bound books.
Activities: permanent exhibitions; programs of local, regional & oral history.
Publications: yearly, San Juan Courier.
Hours & Admission Prices: Memorial Day-Sept. daily 9-5; Oct. daily 10-3. Adults $3.50. Mayflower Gold Mill: Memorial Day-Sept. 30 daily 10-4:30. Tours on half hour: adults $8.50, children 5-12 $4.50; discounts to groups; members & children under 5 no charge.
Attendance: 14,000 (estimated)
Membership: Member $10; Family $15; Supporting $25; Lifetime $350.

Snowmass Village

ANDERSON RANCH ARTS CENTER & MUSEUM, 5263 Owl Creek Rd., Snowmass Village, CO 81615. Mailing Address: P.O. Box 5598, Snowmass Village, CO 81615-5598. Tel.: 970-923-3181. Fax: 970-923-3871.
E-mail: info@andersonranch.org
Web Site: www.andersonranch.org
Founded: 1966.
Key Personnel: Pres., Hunter O'Hanian; Chm. (V), Mary Scanlan; Museum Shop Mgr., Shannon Bolona.
Personnel Profile: Full-Time Paid 25; Part-Time Paid 2; Part-Time Volunteers 20; Interns 17.
Art School & Gallery.
Collections: works by Ranch artists.
Facilities: cafe. Museum-related items for sale.
Activities: workshop program; residency program.
Hours & Admission Prices: Oct.-May Mon.-Fri. 9-5. No charge. ♿
Attendance: 5,000

Steamboat Springs

STEAMBOAT ART MUSEUM, (M), 801 Lincoln Ave., Steamboat Springs, CO 80488. Mailing Address: P.O. Box 883434, Steamboat Springs, CO 80488-3434. Tel.: 970-870-1755.
Art Museum.
Collections: western art; paintings; sculpture.
Activities: workshops.
Hours & Admission Prices: Tues.-Sat. 11-7.

TREAD OF PIONEERS MUSEUM, (M), 800 Oak St., Steamboat Springs, CO 80477. Mailing Address: P.O. Box 772372, Steamboat Springs, CO 80477-2372. Tel.: 970-879-2214. Fax: 970-879-6109.
E-mail: topmuseum@springsips.com
Web Site: www.treadofpioneers.org
Founded: 1959.
Congressional District: 6
Key Personnel: Dir., Candice Lombardo; Cur., Katie Peck.
Personnel Profile: Full-Time Paid 2; Part-Time Paid 1; Part-Time Volunteers 56.
Governing Authority: bd. of directors.
Local History Museum.
Collections: skiing history; ranching; Routt County historical documents; southwestern Native American artifacts; pioneer & turn-of-the-century home furnishings; mining & agricultural history.
Major Exhibits: When the School Bell Rings: A Story of Education in Routt Co., 11/09-5/10.
Activities: guided tours; temporary & permanent exhibitions & programs.
Publications: biannual newsletter; annual report.
Hours & Admission Prices: Tues.-Sat. 11-5; call for seasonal extended hours. Adults $5, senior citizens $4, children 6-12 $1; discounts to AAA members; members & Routt County residents no charge. ♿
Attendance: 9,111 (accurate)
Membership: Chairlift $25; Chuck Wagon $50; Stagecoach $100; Haystack $250; Homestead $500; Pioneer Circle $1000.

Sterling

OVERLAND TRAIL MUSEUM, Junction I-76 & Hwy. 6E., Sterling, CO 80751. Mailing Address: Box 4000, Sterling, CO 80751-0400. Tel.: 970-522-3895. Fax: 970-521-0632.
E-mail: krich@sterlingcolo.com
Web Site: www.sterlingcolo.com
Founded: 1936.
Congressional District: 4
Key Personnel: C.E.O., Larry Huggins; Pres. (V), Norma Nab; Cur., Kay L. Brigham Rich; Asst., Marilyn Hutt; Asst., Lana Tramp; Asst., Perry Johnson; Asst., Emily Singer.
Personnel Profile: Full-Time Paid 1; Part-Time Paid 4; Part-Time Volunteers 8.
Governing Authority: municipal. Parent Institution: City of Sterling. Subsidiary Institution: Logan County Historical Society. Tax-exempt.
General Museum: located on the site of the Overland Trail, near the Valley Station of Ben Holladay Stage line.
Collections: Indian artifacts; rock & lapidary; local natural history; mammal & marine fossils; frontier rifles; shot guns; relics of Civil, Spanish-American & later wars; cattle branding irons; frontier saddles; ranch & farm equipment; hand tools; hand-weaving, spinning wheel & loom; furniture; household items; one room schoolhouse; county church; blacksmith shop;

19th-century baby clothes; men & women's garments & accessories; musical instruments; dolls; country store; barn.
Research Fields: local history; Western history.
Facilities: nature & conservation center. Postcards & books for sale.
Activities: guided tours; lectures; permanent exhibits.
Hours & Admission Prices: April-Oct. Mon.-Sat. 9-5, Sun. 1-5, Holidays 10-5; Nov.-March Tues.-Sat. 10-4. Adults $2-$4. ♿
Attendance: 14,000 (estimated)
Membership: Individual $6; Family $10.

Strasburg

COMANCHE CROSSING HISTORICAL SOCIETY & MUSEUM, 56060 E. Colfax Ave., Strasburg, CO 80136. Mailing Address: P.O. Box 647, Strasburg, CO 80136-0647. Tel.: 303-622-4322.
E-mail: csmith80136@tds.net
Founded: 1969.
Congressional District: 6
Key Personnel: C.E.O., Vencil Welp; Treas., Kathleen Burnet; Cur., Clifford Smith; Museum Shop Mgr., Beth Smialek.
Personnel Profile: Part-Time Volunteers 40.
Governing Authority: nonprofit organization. Parent Institution: Comanche Crossing Historical Society. Tax-exempt: 501(c)(3).
Historical Society Museum: Comanche Crossing is the location where the first continuous chain of rails was completed by the Kansas Pacific Railroad, Aug. 15, 1870.
Collections: reconstructed first bank, post office, drug store; Union Pacific caboose; printing press; Hickok paper ruler; linotype; tools; fossils; Indian artifacts; fencing tools; impact wrenches; cameras; watches; books; maps; quilts; minerals; polished rocks; buggies; clothing; antique cars; military memorabilia; dolls; Halladay's Mill windmill; early 20th century room areas. Historical Buildings: 1891 Living Springs schoolhouse; 1910 Leslie Dyer Homestead; 1904 frame schoolhouse; 1917 Railroad Depot.
Research Fields: stage stations; trails; family history.
Facilities: library of old books, encyclopedias & maps available for loan by signing a legal request & posting an amount of funds to cover their value; classrooms. Centennial celebration & other museum-related items for sale.
Activities: special tours; lectures; guided tours; wheat thrashing; horse pull; tractor pull. Museum Sponsors: Pioneer School in July.
Publications: Comanche Crossing Centennial; History of Depot & Caboose.
Hours & Admission Prices: June-Aug. daily 1-4; other times by appointment. No charge; donations accepted. ♿
Attendance: 800 (estimated)
Membership: Annual $10; Lifetime $100.

Telluride

TELLURIDE HISTORICAL MUSEUM, (M), 201 W. Gregory Ave., Telluride, CO 81435. Mailing Address: P.O. Box 1597, Telluride, CO 81435-1597. Tel.: 970-728-3344. Fax: 970-728-6757.
E-mail: museum@telluridecolorado.net
Web Site: www.telluridemuseum.org
Founded: 1964.
Congressional District: 3
Key Personnel: Exec. Dir., Lauren Bloemsma; Asst. Dir., Kathy Rohrer; Pres., Carol Kammer.
Personnel Profile: Full-Time Paid 2; Part-Time Paid 1; Part-Time Volunteers 40.
Governing Authority: bd. of directors. Tax-exempt.
General Museum: housed in 1896 community hospital building.
Collections: anthropology; costumes; glass; history; Indian artifacts; mineralogy; mining; photographs of San Miguel County dating from 1875 to the present; early local fraternal lodge memorabilia; the Rio Grande Southern Railroad; manuscripts; toys; 1890s bedroom & kitchen; medical equipment; L.L. Nunn & Tesla alternating current artifacts.
Research Fields: genealogy; mining; photographs; AC current electricity; Native American-early Pueblo history.
Facilities: 1,300-vol. library of books on the San Miguel area, available for research. Books of local interest for sale.
Activities: lectures; films; permanent exhibitions; school programs.
Publications: brochures; newsletter; Telluride Tales of Two Early Pioneers; Tellurides Victorian Vernacular.
Hours & Admission Prices: Summer: Tues.-Sat. 11-5, Sun. 1-5; Winter: Tues.-Sat. 11-5. Adults $5, seniors & students $3; discounts to AAM members; children 5 & under & members no charge. Closed major holidays. ♿
Attendance: 6,000 (estimated)
Membership: Quartz $35; Galena $60; Nickel $100; Business $125; Zinc $150; Copper $300; Silver $500; Gold $1,000; Prospector $1,500; Historian $2,500.

Trinidad

ARTHUR ROY MITCHELL MEMORIAL MUSEUM, 150 E. Main St., Trinidad, CO 81082-2709. Mailing Address: P.O. Box 95, Trinidad, CO 81082-0095. Tel.: 719-846-4224. Fax: 719-846-2004.
Founded: 1979.
Congressional District: 4
Key Personnel: Dir. & Museum Shop Mgr., Debra Krumm; Pres., Cosette Henritz; Vice Pres., Barbara Snow; Treas., John N. Beardan.
Personnel Profile: Full-Time Paid 1; Part-Time Volunteers 19.
Governing Authority: nonprofit organization. Parent Institution: A. R. Mitchell Memorial, Inc. Tax-exempt: 501(c)(3) & 170(b)(1)(A).
Art Museum: housed in c.1906 building.
Collections: paintings by Arthur Roy Mitchell, Harvey Dunn, Harold von Schmidt, Nick Eggenhofer, Frank Street, Ned Jacob, Frank Hoffman, Grant Reynard, Paul Milosevich, Dave Powell & Otto Kuhler; drawings; sketches; Indian artifacts; Western memorabilia; Hispanic religious folk art; Arthur Roy Mitchell's personal papers; Aultman photography, representing 106 years of continuous photography work within a family-owned studio, begun by Oliver E. Aultman in 1889.
Facilities: Books, magazines, Indian jewelry & weavings for sale.
Activities: guided tours; docent program; loan & temporary exhibitions.
Hours & Admission Prices: May-Sept. Tues.-Sat. 10-4; other times by appointment. Adult $3; members & children under 12 no charge. ♿
Attendance: 2,500 (accurate)
Membership: Individual $25; Family $50; Sponsor $100; Sustaining $500; Benefactor $1,000.

LOUDEN-HENRITZE ARCHAEOLOGY MUSEUM, Trinidad State Junior College, 600 Prospect St., Trinidad, CO 81082-2356. Tel.: 719-846-5508. Fax: 719-846-5050.
E-mail: loretta.martin@trinidadstate.edu
Web Site: www.trinidadstate.edu/museum
Founded: 1955.
Congressional District: 4
Key Personnel: Dir., Loretta Martin.
Personnel Profile: Part-Time Paid 1; Part-Time Volunteers 2.
Governing Authority: Trinidad State Junior College. Tax-exempt.
Natural History Museum.
Collections: archaeology; geology; paleontology; paleogeology; ethnobotany; history.
Activities: guided tours by appointment; formally organized education programs for undergraduate college students; permanent & temporary exhibitions.
Hours & Admission Prices: Jan.-Nov. Mon.-Thurs. 10-3; groups by appointment. No charge. Closed national & state holidays. ♿
Attendance: 2,322 (accurate)

TRINIDAD HISTORY MUSEUM - COLORADO HISTORICAL SOCIETY, 312 E. Main St., Trinidad, CO 81082-2713. Mailing Address: P.O. Box 377, Trinidad, CO 81082-0377. Tel.: 719-846-7217. Fax: 719-845-0117.
Web Site: www.trinidadco.com/thm; www.coloradohistory.org
Founded: 1955.
Key Personnel: Pres., Ed Nichols; Dir., Paula Manini.
Personnel Profile: Full-Time Paid 2; Part-Time Paid 7; Part-Time Volunteers 20; Interns 1.
Governing Authority: state. Parent Institution: Colorado Historical Society, 1300 Broadway, Denver, CO 80203. Tax-exempt.
Historic Site.
Collections: Hispanic; Victorian; Santa Fe Trail; ranching. Historic Buildings: 1870 adobe Baca House; 1882 Bloom Mansion.
Research Fields: local history.
Activities: children, adult, & family programs; research.
Publications: monthly, Colorado History News; quarterly, Colorado Heritage Magazine.
Hours & Admission Prices: Museum: May-Sept. Mon.-Sat. 10-4. Adults $6; discounts to AAM & ICOM members; members no charge. Research: by appointment. Closed holidays.
Attendance: 9,000 (accurate)

USAF Academy

U.S. AIR FORCE ACADEMY VISITOR CENTER, (M), 2346 Academy Dr., USAF Academy, CO 80840-9401. Tel.: 719-333-2025. Fax: 719-333-4402.
E-mail: pa.comrel@usafa.af.mil
Web Site: usafa.af.mil
Founded: 1955.
Congressional District: 5

Key Personnel: Chief Visitor Svcs. Branch, Melissa Porter; Bldg. Mgr., Larry Wells.
Governing Authority: Parent Institution: United States Air Force Academy. Tax-exempt: 170(b)(1)(A).
Military Museum.
Collections: pictorial & audiovisual exhibits explaining the history & current programs of the U.S. Air Force Academy.
Research Fields: aviation & aerospace history.
Facilities: theater; snack bar. Air Force Academy-related items for sale.
Activities: guided & self-guided tours; film; permanent exhibits.
Publications: self-guided tour map.
Hours & Admission Prices: Daily 9-5. No charge. ♿
Attendance: 370,658 (accurate)

Vail

COLORADO SKI & SNOWBOARD MUSEUM, (M), 231 S. Frontage Rd., Level 3-Vail Village Transportation Center, Vail, CO 81657. Mailing Address: P.O. Box 1976, Vail, CO 81658-1976. Tel.: 970-476-1876. Fax: 970-476-1879.
E-mail: info@skimuseum.net
Web Site: www.skimuseum.net
Founded: 1976.
Congressional District: 3
Key Personnel: Exec. Dir., Susie Tjossem; Chm., David Scott; Cur., Justin Henderson; Museum Shop Mgr., Cathy Whiston.
Personnel Profile: Full-Time Paid 1; Part-Time Paid 3; Part-Time Volunteers 40.
Governing Authority: nonprofit. Tax-exempt: 501(c)(3).
Ski and Snowboard History Museum.
Collections: history of skiing & snowboarding in Colorado; artifacts; photographs; books; ski, boot & pole exhibit; ski clothing; cross-country skiing; military skiing & safety equipment; military skiing, 10th mountain division; Hall of Fame; chronology of skiing exhibit; United States Forest Services; World Ski Championship exhibit; snowboarding; pamphlets; videos; films; magazines.
Research Fields: Colorado skiing history.
Facilities: 100-vol. library of books on the history & techniques of skiing; theater; banquet facilities. Museum-related items for sale.
Activities: guided tours; lectures; films; docent program; permanent, temporary & loan exhibitions; videos.
Publications: quarterly newsletter.
Hours & Admission Prices: June-Sept. & Nov.-April Tues.-Sun. 10-5; guided tours by appointment. Suggested Donation $1. Closed New Year's Day; Easter; Thanksgiving; Christmas. ♿
Attendance: 50,000 (estimated)
Membership: Individual $50; Family $100; Supporting $150; Sustaining $250; Corporate $500; Patron $1,000 & up.

Victor

VICTOR LOWELL THOMAS MUSEUM, 3rd St. & Victor Ave., Victor, CO 80860. Mailing Address: P.O. Box 238, Victor, CO 80860-0238. Tel.: 719-689-5509.
Governing Authority: nonprofit organization. Parent Institution: Victor Improvement Association. Tax-exempt: 501(c)(3).
History Museum: built in 1899.
Collections: local history & culture; photographs; personal artifacts.
Facilities: Museum-related items for sale.
Activities: gold panning; special events.
Hours & Admission Prices: Memorial Day to Labor Day Wed.-Sun. 9:30-5:30; Sept. to Columbus Day Sat.-Sun. 9:30-5:30. Adults $4, seniors 60 & over $3; discounts to groups; children 12 & under no charge.

Walsenburg

HUERFANO COUNTY HISTORICAL SOCIETY, INCLUDING THE WALSENBURG MINING MUSEUM & FT. FRANCISCO MUSEUM OF LA VETA, 112 W. 5th St., Walsenburg, CO 81089-1941. Mailing Address: P.O. Box 134, Walsenburg, CO 81089-0134. Tel.: 719-738-1992. Fax: 719-738-6218.
Founded: 1987.
Congressional District: 3
Key Personnel: Dir. Walsenberg, Margaret Gleisberg; Museum Shop Mgr., Marge Figal.
Personnel Profile: Part-Time Volunteers 10.
Governing Authority: society; nonprofit. Parent Institution: Huerfano County Historical Society. Subsidiary Institutions: Francisco Ft. Museum of La Veta, Francisco Plaza, La Veta, CO. Tax-exempt: 501(c)(3).
Mining Museum: housed in c.1896 jail building.
Collections: Southern Colorado coal mining industry artifacts; mining equipment; miner's personal equipment; mine records & maps; photographs; letters; UMWA, IWW items; coalfield wars & strikes items.
Research Fields: mining industry.
Facilities: 56-vol. library of mining material available for viewing on premises. Museum-related books & other gift items for sale.
Publications: books, Hiram Vasquez, All Our Yesterdays, Romance of the Spanish Peaks, In the Shadow of the Peaks.
Hours & Admission Prices: Walsenburg Mining Museum: May-Oct. Mon.-Fri. 10-4. Adults $2, teens $1; children under 12 no charge. Ft. Francisco Museum: Mon.-Sat. 10-4, Sun. 1-4. Adults $6, children & seniors $3.
Attendance: 1,500 (estimated)
Membership: Huerfano County Historical Society: Senior & Student $10; Sustaining Individual $20; Sustaining Family $30; Sponsor Patron $50; Associate Patron $100; Corporate $500; Executive Patron $1,000.

Westminster

BUTTERFLY PAVILION, 6252 W. 104th Ave., Westminster, CO 80020-4107. Tel.: 303-469-5441. Fax: 303-657-5944.
E-mail: marketing@butterflies.org
Web Site: www.butterflies.org
Founded: 1995.
Key Personnel: Dir., Robert Bonacci; Museum Shop Mgr., Cynthia Killingbeck.
Personnel Profile: Full-Time Paid 25; Part-Time Paid 25; Part-Time Volunteers 125; Interns 4.
Governing Authority: Tax-exempt.
Tropical Conservatory.
Collections: over 1,200 butterflies; invertebrate; aquatic animals.
Major Exhibits: Dr. Entomo's Palace of Exotic Wonders (T), 3/10-7/10; Eight-Legged Beasts (T), 8/10-12/10.
Facilities: nature trails; conservatory. Museum-related items for sale.
Activities: special events; school groups; workshops; scholarships; classes; camps; storytime.
Publications: newsletter, Flutterings.
Hours & Admission Prices: Daily 9-5. Closed New Year's Day; Christmas Eve & Day. Adults $7.95, seniors 65 & over $5.95, children 2-12 $4.95; members & children under 2 no charge. Closed Thanksgiving; Christmas. ♿
Attendance: 250,000 (accurate)
Membership: Individual $25; Family $65; Lace Wing $115.

Wheat Ridge

WHEAT RIDGE HISTORIC PARK, 4610 Robb St., Wheat Ridge, CO 80033-2537. Mailing Address: P.O. Box 1833, Wheat Ridge, CO 80034-1833. Tel.: 303-421-9111. Fax: 303-467-0023.
Formerly: Wheat Ridge Soddy
Founded: 1970.
Congressional District: 6
Key Personnel: Pres. (V), Charlotte Whetsel; Vice Pres. & Museum Shop Mgr., Claudia Worth.
Personnel Profile: Part-Time Volunteers 3.
Governing Authority: municipal; nonprofit organization. Parks Dept., City of Wheat Ridge; Wheat Ridge Historical Society. Tax-exempt.
History Museum.
Collections: local history & culture; period furnishings; local industry. Historic Buildings: 1859, homestead cabin; 1913 post office; 1910 farmhouse; c.1860s sod house.
Major Exhibits: A Woman's Work is Never Done, 1/10-3/10.
Research Fields: local history; homestead families & identification of original homesteads; schools.
Facilities: library of local history available for research by request.
Activities: guided tours; lectures; craft workshops; permanent & temporary exhibitions; special events. Museum Sponsors: May Festival-Antique Road Show; Cider Day in October.
Publications: brochure; books, History of Pioneer Wheat Ridge; Activities 1976-Centennial-Bicentennial Year; Biographical Sketches-Early Settlers of Wheat Ridge; Guide to the Collection of the Wheat Ridge Historical Society Museum & Library.
Hours & Admission Prices: Fri. 10-3; other times by appointment. Adults $2. Closed national holidays. ♿
Attendance: 3,100 (estimated)
Membership: Individual $10; Family $15; Sustaining $25; Individual Life $50. Family Life $100.

Windsor

WINDSOR MUSEUM, 301 Walnut St., Windsor, CO 80550-5141. Tel.: 970-674-2443. Fax: 970-674-2456.
E-mail: cknight@windsorgov.com

Web Site: www.windsorgov.com
Founded: 2003.
Congressional District: 4
Key Personnel: Mgr. Arts & Heritage, Carrie Knight; Cur., Elizabeth Handwerk Kurt.
Personnel Profile: Full-Time Paid 3.
Governing Authority: municipal.
History Museum.
Collections: Windsor's residents, cultural history, businesses, & events. Historic Buildings: railroad depot; 1890s rural schoolhouse; pioneer church.
Research Fields: Western rural schoolhouses & education; immigration of Germans to Russia.
Activities: formal education programs; guided tours; temporary exhibitions. Annual Events: Octoberfest; Creepy Crawl.
Hours & Admission Prices: June 12-Sept. 1 Tues.-Sat. 10-4. No charge; donations accepted.
Attendance: 5,000 (estimated)

Woodland Park

ROCKY MOUNTAIN DINOSAUR RESOURCE CENTER, 201 S. Fairview St., Woodland Park, CO 80863-1154. Tel.: 719-686-1820.
E-mail: info@rmdrc.com
Web Site: www.rmdrc.com
Founded: 2004.
Key Personnel: Pres., J.J. Triebold.
Personnel Profile: Full-Time Paid 25.
Paleontology Museum.
Collections: prehistoric life including dinosaurs; marine reptiles; flying reptiles; fish.
Facilities: Museum-related items for sale.
Activities: educational workshops.
Hours & Admission Prices: Mon.-Sat. 9-6, Sun. 10-5. Call for admission prices. Closed New Year's Day; Easter; Thanksgiving; Christmas. ♿

Wray

WRAY MUSEUM, 205 E. Third St., Wray, CO 80758-1106. Mailing Address: P.O. Box 161, Wray, CO 80758-0161. Tel.: 970-332-5063.
Web Site: www.wrayco.net
Founded: 1969.
Congressional District: 4
Key Personnel: Dir., Ardith Hendrix; EYCHS Pres. (V), Lou Ann Deterding.
Personnel Profile: Full-Time Paid 1; Part-Time Paid 2.
Governing Authority: society. Parent Institution: City of Wray and the East Yuma County Historical Society. Tax-exempt.
History Museum.
Collections: permanent Smithsonian archaeological exhibit on Paleo Indians; bison; arrowheads; diorama of Beecher Island Battle of 1868; paintings; textiles; photographs; big game animal trophies; general store display.
Research Fields: archaeology; local family history; history of trails; post offices; towns; old ranches.
Activities: tours; educational programs; permanent, traveling & temporary exhibits. Museum Sponsors: The Greater Prairie Chickens - Sandhills dancers in March & April.
Hours & Admission Prices: Tues.-Sat. 12-4. Adults $1, children $.50; members no charge. ♿
Attendance: 2,000 (accurate)
Membership: Individual $10; Civic Clubs & Organization $15; Commercial Business $20; Family $35; Patron & Business $50; Life Individual $100; Lifetime $125; Corporate $1,000.

CONNECTICUT

(247 listings)

Ansonia

ANSONIA NATURE & RECREATION CENTER, 10 Deerfield Rd., Ansonia, CT 06401. Tel.: 203-736-1053.
Key Personnel: Dir., Donna Lindgren
Nature Center.
Collections: natural history; plants; trees; butterfly & hummingbird garden; wildflowers.
Activities: educational programs; special events; classes.
Hours & Admission Prices: Park: sunup to sundown. Center: daily 9-5. Closed major holidays.

GENERAL DAVID HUMPHREY'S HOUSE, 37 Elm St., Ansonia, CT 06401-3312. Mailing Address: P.O. Box 331, Derby, CT 06418-0331. Tel.: 203-735-1908.
E-mail: derbyhistorical@att.net
Web Site: www.derbyhistorical.org/humphrey.htm
Key Personnel: Dir., Robert J. Novak, Jr.
Governing Authority: Parent Institution: Derby Historical Society.
Historic House: built in 1698.
Collections: family history; period furnishings.
Activities: school group programs; special events.
Hours & Admission Prices: Mon.-Fri. 1-4.

Avon

THE AVON HISTORICAL SOCIETY, INC., 8 E. Main St., Avon, CT 06001. Mailing Address: P.O. Box 448, Avon, CT 06001-0448. Tel.: 860-678-7621.
E-mail: ahs.mail.1830@sbcglobal.net
Web Site: www.ahsct.org
Founded: 1974.
Congressional District: 5
Key Personnel: Pres., Terri Wilson.
Personnel Profile: Part-Time Volunteers 12.
Governing Authority: nonprofit organization. Branch Museums: Pine Grove School House & The Derrin House, W. Avon Rd., Avon, CT. Tax-exempt: 501(c)(3).
Historical Society Museum; housed in two 19th century schoolhouses & farmhouse.
Collections: concentration on local Avon history; archives.
Publications: Avon, Connecticut...An Historical Story; Avon, Connecticut - Photographs 1880-1940.
Hours & Admission Prices: Living Museum & Pine Grove Schoolhouse: June-Oct. Sun. 2-4. Derrin House: call for hours. Library: 2-4; other times by appointment. No charge; donations accepted.
Attendance: 600 (estimated)
Membership: Senior Citizen & Student $20; Individual $25; Family $35; Business $100; Life $500.

FARMINGTON VALLEY ARTS CENTER (FVAC), 25 Arts Center Lane, Avon, CT 06001-3746. Tel.: 860-678-1867. Fax: 860-674-1877.
Founded: 1974.
Key Personnel: Exec. Dir., Marty Rotblatt.
Personnel Profile: Full-Time Paid 2; Part-Time Paid 3; Part-Time Volunteers 60.
Governing Authority: Tax-exempt.
Arts Center.
Collections: paintings; sculpture.
Facilities: Museum-related items for sale.
Activities: educational programs; classes; workshops; summer camp; birthday parties.
Publications: catalogue 3 times per year, Connections.
Hours & Admission Prices: Call for hours. No charge.
Attendance: 6,000 (estimated)
Membership: Individual $30; Household $60.

THE LIVING MUSEUM OF AVON, 8 E. Main St., Avon, CT 06001. Tel.: 860-678-7621.
History Museum: housed in a 19th-century schoolhouse.
Collections: photographs; farm implements; household artifacts; period clothing.
Hours & Admission Prices: June-Sept. by appointment. No charge; donations accepted.

Bethlehem

BELLAMY-FERRIDAY HOUSE & GARDEN, 9 Main St. N., Bethlehem, CT 06751. Mailing Address: P.O. Box 181, Bethlehem, CT 06751. Tel.: 203-266-7596.
Historic House: built in 1754.
Collections: family history & culture; personal artifacts; period furnishings; photographs.
Facilities: garden.
Hours & Admission Prices: May-Aug. Wed. & Fri.-Sun. 11-4; Sept.-Oct. Sat.-Sun. 11-4; groups by appointment. Adults $7, students and seniors 65 & over $6, children 6-18 $4; children under 6 no charge.

OLD BETHLEHEM HISTORICAL SOCIETY, 4 Main St. N., Bethlehem, CT 06751. Mailing Address: P.O. Box 132, Bethlehem, CT 06751-0132. Tel.: 203-266-5196.
Founded: 1968.

Key Personnel: Pres. (V), Carol Ann Brown
Historical Society Museum.
Collections: Bethlehem history & culture; photographs; personal artifacts.
Hours & Admission Prices: June-Aug. Sun. 1-4; other times by appointment. No charge; donations accepted. Closed holidays. ♿

Bloomfield

OLD FARM SCHOOL, 151 School St., Bloomfield, CT 06002-2718. Mailing Address: Wintonbury Historical Society, P.O. Box 7454, Bloomfield, CT 06002. Tel.: 860-243-1531.
E-mail: oldfarmschool@bloomfieldcthistory.org
Web Site: www.bloomfieldcthistory.org
Key Personnel: Pres., Fannie Gabriel.
Governing Authority: Parent Institution: Wintonbury Historical Society. Subsidiary Institutions: Southwest District School, Simsbury Rd., Bloomfield, CT; Captain Oliver Filley House, 130 Mountain Ave., Bloomfield, CT.
Historic Building: built c.1840. Listed on the National Register of Historic Places.
Collections: local history; period furnishings; paintings.
Hours & Admission Prices: May 15-Oct. 15 Sun. 1-4.

Branford

HARRISON HOUSE, 124 Main St., Branford, CT 06405-3523. Mailing Address: P.O. Box 504, Branford, CT 06405-0504. Tel.: 203-488-4828.
Web Site: branfordhistory.org
Founded: 1960.
Congressional District: 3
Key Personnel: Pres. (V), Peter Black.
Personnel Profile: Part-Time Volunteers 40.
Governing Authority: society; nonprofit organization. Parent Institution: Society for the Preservation of New England Antiquities, 141 Cambridge St. Boston, MA 02114. Tel. 617-227-3956. Operated by the Branford Historical Society. Tax-exempt: 501(c)(3).
Historic House: c.1724 restored by architect J. Frederick Kelly.
Collections: furnishings; town memorabilia; farm tools.
Facilities: reference library.
Activities: guided tours; programs.
Publications: newsletter; local histories.
Hours & Admission Prices: June-Sept. Sat. 2-5; other times by appointment. No charge; donations accepted.
Attendance: 125 (estimated)
Membership: Student $5; Individual $10; Family $15; Sustaining $25; Contributing $50.

Bridgeport

THE BARNUM MUSEUM, 820 Main St., Bridgeport, CT 06604-4912. Tel.: 203-331-1104. Fax: 203-331-0079.
Web Site: www.barnum-museum.org
Founded: 1893.
Congressional District: 4
Key Personnel: Exec. Dir. & Cur., Kathleen Maher; Dir. Education, Jaime Knoedler; Administrative Asst., Debbie Saviello.
Personnel Profile: Full-Time Paid 3; Part-Time Paid 3; Part-Time Volunteers 29; Interns 3.
Governing Authority: Parent Institution: The Barnum Museum Foundation, Inc. Subsidiary Institution: City of Bridgeport, CT. Tax-exempt: 501(c)(3).
History Museum: housed in original 1893 structure.
Collections: 19th-century historical & scientific society; biological specimens; period relics; colonial artifacts; 19th century industrial & decorative arts including paintings, furniture, and costumes; P.T. Barnum documents & personal items; 1920 miniature circus model.
Research Fields: P.T. Barnum & his genre in 19th century American history; social & material culture; American decorative arts; industrial & entertainment histories.
Facilities: archive library available by appointment; 15,000 sq. ft. exhibit space. Museum-related items for sale.
Activities: school & family programs; lectures; films; gallery talks; TV & radio programs; weekend guided tours by reservation.
Publications: newsletter, The Barnum Herald; calendar of events.
Hours & Admission Prices: Tues.-Sat. 10-4:30, Sun. 12-4:30. Adults $7, students & senior citizens $5, children $4; discounts to AAA & AAM members; children under 4 & members no charge. Closed most national holidays. ♿
Attendance: 25,000 (estimated)
Membership: Single $25; Family $45; Family Plus $60; Sustaining $150; Patron Circle $500; Director's Circle $1,000.

BLACK ROCK ART CENTER, 2838 Fairfield Ave., Bridgeport, CT 06605-3210. Mailing Address: P.O. Box 1919, Bridgeport, CT 06604. Tel.: 203-367-7917. Fax: 203-333-0603.
Art Gallery.
Collections: paintings; photographs; sculpture; films.
Facilities: theater; cafe.
Activities: temporary exhibits; educational programs.
Hours & Admission Prices: Call for hours.
Attendance: 25,000 (estimated)
Membership: $35-$500.

CITY LIGHTS GALLERY, 37 Markle Ct., Bridgeport, CT 06604-4816. Tel.: 203-334-7748.
Art Gallery.
Collections: paintings; photographs; sculpture.
Activities: art programs; receptions; workshops; demonstrations; rental facilities; classes.
Hours & Admission Prices: Mon.-Fri. 9:30-5:30, Sat. 11-4. No charge.

CONNECTICUT'S BEARDSLEY ZOO, 1875 Noble Ave., Bridgeport, CT 06610-1646. Tel.: 203-394-6569. Fax: 203-394-6566.
E-mail: gdancho@beardsleyzoo.org
Web Site: www.beardsleyzoo.org
Founded: 1922.
Congressional District: 7
Key Personnel: Chm., Richard Perusi; Zoo Dir., Gregg Dancho; Cur. Education, Tedor Whitman; Dir. Animal Care & Operations, Don Goff; Chm. (V), Tracy Benham; Museum Shop Mgr., Rose Ryan.
Personnel Profile: Full-Time Paid 42; Part-Time Paid 25; Part-Time Volunteers 125; Interns 30.
Governing Authority: state; nonprofit organization. Parent Institution: Connecticut Zoological Society. Tax-exempt: 501(c)(3).
Zoo.
Collections: endangered animals of North & South America; New England farmyard contains minor breeds of domestic animals.
Facilities: 300-vol. library of zoology references; classrooms; botanical garden; 400-seat Gazebo; zoological park. Gifts, jewelry & other items for sale.
Activities: guided tours; lectures; school loan service; mobile vans; formally organized education programs; docent program.
Publications: quarterly newsletter, The Zootimes.
Hours & Admission Prices: Daily 9-4. Adults $11, senior citizens & children $9; discount to groups; AZA members & members no charge. Closed New Year's Day; Thanksgiving; Christmas. ♿
Attendance: 262,000 (estimated)
Membership: Individual $50; Family $80; Director's Circle $150; President's Circle $250; Benefactor $500.

THE DISCOVERY MUSEUM, INC., 4450 Park Ave., Bridgeport, CT 06604-1098. Tel.: 203-372-3521. Fax: 203-374-1929.
E-mail: malkin@discoverymuseum.org
Web Site: www.discoverymuseum.org
Founded: 1958.
Congressional District: 4
Key Personnel: Chm. (V), Phil Rubin; Exec. Dir., Linda Malkin; Dir. Devel., Donna Curran; Dir. Finance & Admin., Lynn Kiernan; Dir. Mktg. & Communications, Jane Hollis; Dir. Exhibits & Public Programming, John Labate; Dir. Facilities, Jerry McKoy; Dir. Education, Alan Winick.
Personnel Profile: Full-Time Paid 12; Part-Time Paid 6; Part-Time Volunteers 35.
Governing Authority: nonprofit corporation. Subsidiary Institution: Soundview Community Media public access television station. Tax-exempt: 501(c)(3).
Science Museum & Planetarium.
Collections: over 100 interactive physical science exhibits; planetarium.
Research Fields: interrelationship of art & science.
Facilities: planetarium; 125-seat auditorium; classrooms; childrens learning area; learning center. Gift items for sale.
Activities: guided tours; lectures; large format film center; gallery talks; formally organized education programs for children; permanent & temporary exhibitions; weekend science & art workshops; special programs for the handicapped; volunteer training programs; summer programs for children; planetarium shows; science shows; educational programs; learning center.
Publications: bimonthly newsletter; catalogues.
Hours & Admission Prices: Summer: Mon.-Sat. 10-5, Sun. 12-5; Sept.-June Tues.-Sat. 10-5, Sun. 12-5. Planetarium Shows: Tues.-Fri. 1 & 3:30. Adults $8.50, children 5-17, senior citizens & college students with ID $7; discounts to Auto Club of America members; members & children under 5

no charge. Closed New Year's Day; Easter; Memorial Day; Independence Day; Labor Day; Thanksgiving; Christmas. ♿
Attendance: 103,274 (accurate)
Membership: Individual $25; Senior Couple $30; Grandparent $45; Family $50; Friend $150; Supporting $300; Council $1,000.

HOUSATONIC MUSEUM OF ART, (M), 900 Lafayette Blvd., Bridgeport, CT 06604-4704. Tel.: 203-332-5052. Fax: 203-332-5123.
E-mail: rzella@hcc.commnet.edu
Web Site: www.hctc.commnet.edu/artmuseum/index.html
Founded: 1967.
Congressional District: 4
Key Personnel: Dir. & Cur., Robbin Zella.
Personnel Profile: Full-Time Paid 1; Part-Time Paid 1; Part-Time Volunteers 3; Interns 4.
Governing Authority: state. Parent Institution: Housatonic Community College. Tax-exempt.
College Museum.
Collections: 19th- & 20th-century European & American art; contemporary Latin American & Connecticut artists; ethnographic collections in African, Asian & South Seas artifacts.
Facilities: 2,000-vol. art library; classrooms; slides; cafeteria.
Activities: guided tours; lectures, films; gallery talks; inter-museum loan, permanent & temporary exhibitions.
Publications: exhibition catalogs, Housatonic Museum of Art.
Hours & Admission Prices: June-Aug. Mon.-Wed. & Fri. 8:30-5:30, Thurs. 8:30-7; Sept.-May Mon.-Wed. & Fri. 8:30-5:30, Thurs. 8:30-7, Sat. 9-3, Sun. 12-4. No charge; donations accepted. ♿
Attendance: 7,500 (estimated)

Bristol

AMERICAN CLOCK AND WATCH MUSEUM, INC., 100 Maple St., Bristol, CT 06010-5092. Tel.: 860-583-6070. Fax: 860-583-1862.
E-mail: info@clockmuseum.org
Web Site: www.clockandwatchmuseum.org
Founded: 1952.
Congressional District: 1
Key Personnel: Exec. Dir., Donald Muller; Pres. (V), Gary Plonski; Office Coord., Jill Godbout; Cur., Chris H. Bailey; Asst. Cur., Mary Jane Dapkus; Dir. Interpretation, Colleen Nicastro; Museum Shop Mgr., Jean Haines.
Personnel Profile: Full-Time Paid 2; Part-Time Paid 6; Part-Time Volunteers 40.
Governing Authority: nonprofit organization. Tax-exempt: 501(c)(3).
Horological Museum: housed in 1801 Miles Lewis House & 1956 Ebenezer Barnes Wing & 1987 Edward Ingraham Wing.
Collections: manuscripts; clocks, watches & other horological items.
Research Fields: horology; historical; technical.
Facilities: 2,000-vol. library of horological books & journals; local & state history books available by special appointment with curator; 1801 garden.
Activities: lectures; permanent exhibitions; video presentations; special exhibits.
Publications: quarterly newsletter; semi-annual journal, The Timepiece Journal; booklets, reproductions of scarce horological trade catalogs.
Hours & Admission Prices: April-Nov. daily 10-5; Dec.-March by appointment only. Families $9, adults $5, senior citizens $4, children 8-15 $2; discounts to AAM & AAA members; members no charge. Closed Thanksgiving. ♿
Attendance: 4,261 (accurate)
Membership: Annual $30; Family $45; Contributing $100; Life $1,500.

IMAGINE NATION MUSEUM, One Pleasant St., Bristol, CT 06010-6254. Tel.: 860-314-1400.
E-mail: info@imaginenation.org
Web Site: www.imaginenation.org
Founded: 2004.
Key Personnel: Dir., Doreen Stickney; C.E.O., Michael Suchopar; Dir. Devel., Ellen Zoppo-Sassu; Dir. Education, Deron Ash; Volunteer Coord., Grace Vogel.
Personnel Profile: Full-Time Paid 4; Part-Time Paid 13; Part-Time Volunteers 100.
Governing Authority: nonprofit organization. Parent Institution: The Bristol Boys & Girls Club and Family Center of Bristol. Tax-exempt.
Children's Museum.
Collections: hands-on exhibits.
Activities: educational field trips; scout badge programs; state licensed camp programs; birthday parties. Museum Sponsors: Family Festivals.
Hours & Admission Prices: Winter: Wed.-Fri. 9:30-5, 1st Fri. of month 9:30-8, Sat. 11-5, Sun. 12-5; Summer: call for extended hours. Admission $5; children under one no charge. Special Events: admission prices vary. Closed New Year's Day; Thanksgiving; Christmas. ♿
Attendance: 40,000
Membership: Family $100.

THE NEW ENGLAND CAROUSEL MUSEUM, 95 Riverside Ave., Bristol, CT 06010-6390. Tel.: 860-585-5411. Fax: 860-314-0483.
E-mail: info@thecarouselmuseum.org
Web Site: thecarouselmuseum.org
Founded: 1989.
Congressional District: 6
Key Personnel: Exec. Dir., Louise L. DeMars; Pres. (V), John S. Driscoll; Education, Eileen Norkun; Museum Mgr., Mary Moret; Head of Restoration, Judith Baker; Visitor Svcs., Elaine Lipton; Museum Shop Mgr., Linda Kozikowski.
Personnel Profile: Full-Time Paid 4; Part-Time Paid 16; Part-Time Volunteers 10.
Governing Authority: private; nonprofit organization.Tax-exempt: 501(c)(3).
Carousel Museum: housed in a restored hosiery factory.
Collections: turn-of-the-century wooden carousel pieces including horses, menagerie animals, chariots, rounding boards, shields & band organs; fine arts; firefighting history.
Research Fields: history, art & science of the carousel; history of Lake Compunce & its carousel.
Facilities: reference library available to public; art room; 7,000 sq. ft. exhibit space. Museum-related items for sale.
Activities: docent program; formal education programs for children; guided tours; lectures; loan, participatory & temporary exhibitions. Museum Sponsors: art classes for children.
Publications: biannual newsletter, The Carousel.
Hours & Admission Prices: April-Nov. Mon.-Sat. 10-5, Sun. 12-5; Dec.-March Thurs.-Sat. 10-5, Sun. 12-5. Adults $5, senior citizens $4.50, children 4-14 $2.50; discounts to groups, AAM, AAA, Lets Go Arts & Chamber of Commerce members; members no charge. Closed New Year's Day; Easter; Independence Day; Labor Day; Thanksgiving; Christmas. ♿
Attendance: 10,745 (accurate)
Membership: Cherub $10 (under 16); Individual $30; Family & Dual $50.

Brookfield

BROOKFIELD CRAFT CENTER, 286 Whisconier Rd., Brookfield, CT 06804. Mailing Address: P.O. Box 122, Brookfield, CT 06804-0122. Tel.: 203-775-4526. Fax: 203-740-7815.
E-mail: info@brookfieldcraftcenter.org
Web Site: www.brookfieldcraftcenter.org
Founded: 1954.
Congressional District: 8
Key Personnel: Interim Exec. Dir., Richard Herrmann; Registrar, Alice Smith; Sales Shop Mgr., Betsy Halliday.
Personnel Profile: Full-Time Paid 2; Part-Time Paid 3; Part-Time Volunteers 100; Interns 3.
Governing Authority: nonprofit. Tax-exempt: 501(c)(3).
Craft Gallery: housed in 1780 old grist mill.
Collections: contemporary national profile artists.
Research Fields: crafts.
Facilities: Museum-related items for sale.
Activities: classes; workshops; temporary & traveling exhibitions; lectures; seminars.
Publications: 4 catalogs of courses each year.
Hours & Admission Prices: Mon.-Sat. 9-5, Sun. 12-5. No charge. Closed major holidays.
Attendance: 10,000
Membership: Senior 65 & over $40; Individual $50; Family $100; Sponsor $250; Lifetime $2,500.

BROOKFIELD MUSEUM AND HISTORICAL SOCIETY, 165 Whisconier Rd., Brookfield, CT 06804. Mailing Address: P.O. Box 5231, Brookfield, CT 06804-5231. Tel.: 203-740-8140.
E-mail: brookfieldhistsoc@snet.net
Web Site: www.brookfieldcthistory.org
Founded: 1968.
Congressional District: 5
Key Personnel: Pres. (V), John D. Furlong; Vice Pres., Robert Brown; Museum Shop Mgr., Jan Furlong.
Personnel Profile: Part-Time Volunteers 15.
Governing Authority: Tax-exempt.
Historical Society Museum.
Collections: Brookfield history & culture; photographs.
Publications: newsletter.
Hours & Admission Prices: Sat. & 1st Sun. of month 12-4; other times by appointment. No charge. ♿
Attendance: 1,500 (estimated)

Membership: Family $15.

MOTHER EARTH GALLERY & MINING COMPANY, 806 Federal Rd., Brookfield, CT 06804. Tel.: 203-775-6272. Fax: 203-775-5620.
Web Site: www.motherearthcrystals.com
Founded: 1987.
Personnel Profile: Full-Time Paid 1; Part-Time Paid 2.
Mining Museum.
Collections: mining history; natural & cultural artifacts; geology.
Facilities: Museum-related items for sale.
Activities: hands-on activities; children dig for gemstones in re-created mine.
Hours & Admission Prices: Mon. & Wed.-Sat. 10-6, Sun. 12-5.
Attendance: 6,000

Burlington

SESSIONS WOODS WILDLIFE MANAGEMENT AREA & CONSERVATION EDUCATION CENTER, 341 Milford St., Burlington, CT 06013-1550. Mailing Address: P.O. Box 1550, Burlington, CT 06013-1550. Tel.: 860-675-8130.
Nature Center.
Collections: wildlife & their habitats; natural history.
Activities: demonstrations; hiking; educational programs.
Hours & Admission Prices: Call for hours.

Canterbury

PRUDENCE CRANDALL MUSEUM, 1 S. Canterbury Rd., Canterbury, CT 06331-1536. Mailing Address: P.O. Box 58, Canterbury, CT 06331-0058. Tel.: 860-546-7800. Fax: 860-546-7803.
E-mail: crandall.museum@ct.gov
Web Site: www.cultureandtourism.org
Founded: 1984.
Congressional District: 2
Key Personnel: Dir., Karen Senich; Cur. II, Kazimiera Kozlowski.
Personnel Profile: Full-Time Paid 1; Part-Time Volunteers 6.
Governing Authority: state. Parent Institution: Commission on Culture & Tourism, State of Connecticut, 1 Constitution Plaza, Hartford, CT 06103. Tax-exempt.
Historic House & Site: housed in 1805 Prudence Crandall House.
Collections: life & work of Prudence Crandall; black history; books; manuscripts, newspapers.
Research Fields: Afro-American history; Canterbury history; education; women's history; local history materials; Afro-American history.
Facilities: 1,000-vol. library of books & pamphlets.
Activities: lectures; changing exhibitions.
Hours & Admission Prices: Check website for current hours. Adults $3, senior citizens & youth $2; children under 5 no charge. Closed major holidays. ♿
Attendance: 1,500 (accurate)

Canton

GALLERY ON THE GREEN, 5 Canton Green Rd., Canton, CT 06019. Mailing Address: P.O. Box 281, Canton, CT 06019. Tel.: 860-693-4102.
Art Gallery: housed in a c.1790 schoolhouse.
Collections: paintings; photographs; sculpture.
Facilities: Museum-related items for sale.
Hours & Admission Prices: Fri.-Sun. 1-5.

ROARING BROOK NATURE CENTER, 70 Gracey Rd., Canton, CT 06019-2113. Tel.: 860-693-0263.
Nature Center.
Collections: wildlife & their habitat; Native American artifacts; farming; period artifacts.
Facilities: nature trails. Museum-related items for sale.
Activities: educational programs; hiking.
Hours & Admission Prices: July-Aug. Mon.-Sat. 10-5, Sun. 1-5; Sept.-June Tues.-Sat. 10-5, Sun. 1-5. Adults $5, seniors $4, children $3; members no charge.

Chaplin

CHAPLIN MUSEUM, 1 Chaplin St., Chaplin, CT 06235. Tel.: 860-455-9209.
History Museum.
Collections: local history & culture; period furnishings; personal artifacts; photographs.
Hours & Admission Prices: Temporarily closed.

Cheshire

THE BARKER CHARACTER, COMIC AND CARTOON MUSEUM, 1188 Highland Ave. (Rte. 10), Cheshire, CT 06410-1624. Tel.: 203-699-3822.
E-mail: museum@barkeranimation.com
Web Site: www.barkermuseum.com
Founded: 1997.
Key Personnel: Owners, Herbert Barker; Owners, Gloria Barker; Dir. & Cur., Judy Fuerst.
Personnel Profile: Full-Time Paid 1; Part-Time Paid 2.
General Museum.
Collections: over 80,000 items including toys & character collectibles from 1873 to present; TV & advertising collection; cartoon memorabilia; Celebriducks; the California Raisins & Gumby.
Activities: tours.
Hours & Admission Prices: Wed.-Sat. 12-4; group tours for ages 8 & over by appointment. Adults $5, children 12 & under $3. Closed holidays. ♿
Attendance: 20,000 (estimated)

Clinton

STANTON HOUSE, 63 E. Main St., Clinton, CT 06413-2036. Tel.: 860-669-2132.
E-mail: curator@stantonhousect.com
Web Site: www.stantonhousect.com/
Founded: 1916.
Congressional District: 33
Key Personnel: Cur., Edward P. Lang.
Personnel Profile: Full-Time Volunteers 1.
Governing Authority: Parent Institution: Fleet Bank, Trustee. Tax-exempt: 501(c)(3).
Historic House: 1789 Stanton House.
Collections: period furniture; china; glass; 18th Century store.
Activities: guided tours.
Hours & Admission Prices: By appointment. No charge; donations requested.
Attendance: 1,200 (estimated)

Collinsville

CANTON HISTORICAL MUSEUM, 11 Front St., Collinsville, CT 06019-3118. Tel.: 860-693-2793.
E-mail: cantonhistoric@sbcglobal.net
Web Site: www.cantonmuseum.org
Founded: 1969.
Congressional District: 1
Key Personnel: Pres. (V), Paul J. Therrien; Museum Shop Mgr., Curt Edgar.
Personnel Profile: Part-Time Paid 2; Part-Time Volunteers 27.
Governing Authority: Tax-exempt.
History Museum: housed in c.1865 building used for finishing agricultural plows.
Collections: 19th century artifacts; period fire equipment & medical instruments; Almond D. Fisk burial case; reconstructed 19th century general store, post office, barber shop & blacksmith shop.
Research Fields: genealogy; historic sites.
Activities: tours; winter lectures. Museum Sponsors: Open House; Christmas Boutique; fundraisers.
Publications: newsletter.
Hours & Admission Prices: Wed. & Fri.-Sun. 1-4, Thurs. 1-8. Adults $3. Closed Easter; Christmas.
Attendance: 2,000 (accurate)
Membership: Single $15; Family $25; Sustaining $50; Life $200.

Cos Cob

* **HISTORICAL SOCIETY OF THE TOWN OF GREENWICH A/K/A BUSH-HOLLEY HISTORIC SITE, (M),** 39 Strickland Rd., Cos Cob, CT 06807-2727. Tel.: 203-869-6899, ext. 10. Fax: 203-861-9720.
E-mail: mcouture@hstg.org
Web Site: www.hstg.org
Founded: 1931.
Congressional District: 4
Key Personnel: C.E.O., Debra Mecky; Chm., Susan Larkin; Museum Shop Mgr., Michele Couture.
Personnel Profile: Full-Time Paid 9; Part-Time Paid 6; Part-Time Volunteers 200; Interns 2.
Governing Authority: nonprofit corporation. Parent Institution: The Historical Society of the Town of Greenwich Inc. Tax-exempt: 501(c)(3).
History Museum: housed in Bush-Holley House; site of Connecticut's first art colony. A National Historic Landmark.
Collections: 18th, 19th & 20th-century Connecticut & American decorative

arts; paintings by American Impressionists; period furnishings; regional history artifacts; manuscripts. Historic Buildings: c.1730 Bush-Holley House; c.1805 Justus Luke Bush storehouse; c.1850 Brush House.
Research Fields: local history & genealogy; Cos Cob art colony & architecture.
Facilities: library; archives; visitors & education center.
Activities: guided tours; lecture series; family programs; school programs; summer camp; historic markers program.
Publications: Childe Hassam in Connecticut; Chains Unbound; Slave Emancipations in the Town of Greenwich, Connecticut; Greenwich Grows Up; On Home Ground: Elmer Livingston MacRae at The Holley House. Greenwich Before 2000; Building Greenwich: Architecture and Design, 1640 to the Present (2006); Bush-Holley Historic Site Guide; Carved with Rasps and Chisels: The Sculpture of Margaret Brassler Kane.
Hours & Admission Prices: Library & Archives: Wed.-Thurs. 10-4; other times by appointment. Bush Holley House & Museum: Jan.-Feb. Fri.-Sun. 12-4; March-Dec. Wed.-Sun. 12-4. House Tours: 1, 2 & 3. Adults $10, senior citizens & students $8; discounts to AAM & ICOM members; children under 6 & museum members no charge. Closed New Year's Day; Easter; Independence Day; Thanksgiving; Christmas. ♿
Attendance: 16,000 (accurate)
Membership: Seniors & Teachers $ 30; Individual $40; Family $65; Sponsor $100; Donor $250; Patron $500; Benefactor $1,000.

Coventry

NATHAN HALE HOMESTEAD MUSEUM, 2299 South St., Coventry, CT 06238. Mailing Address: P.O. Box 760, Coventry, CT 06238-0760. Tel.: 860-742-6917.
Founded: 1948.
Key Personnel: Dir., Sheryl Hack.
Personnel Profile: Part-Time Paid 18; Part-Time Volunteers 10; Interns 1.
Governing Authority: Parent Institution: Connecticut Landmarks. Tax-exempt.
History Museum: site of Capt. Nathan Hale's birth in 1755; Hale family built present structure in 1776 & moved in a month after Nathan's death.
Collections: Hale family artifacts; period furniture.
Facilities: nature trails. Museum-related items for sale.
Activities: tours; living history & hearth cooking programs; birthday parties; summer camp; educational programs for school & scout groups; 18th-century demonstration garden; hands-on activities; horseback riding; nature walks.
Publications: newsletter.
Hours & Admission Prices: May & Sept.-Oct. Sat.-Sun. 11-4; June-Aug. Wed. & Fri.-Sun. 11-4. Family $15, adults $7, seniors $6, students $4; discounts to AAM & ICOM members; members & children under 6 no charge. ♿
Attendance: 8,000 (estimated)
Membership: Individual $35; Family $50; Preservation Circle $100-$249; Collector's Circle $250-$499.

Danbury

THE DANBURY MUSEUM & HISTORICAL SOCIETY, (M), 43 Main St., Danbury, CT 06810-8011. Tel.: 203-743-5200. Fax: 203-743-1131.
E-mail: info@danburymuseum.org
Web Site: www.danburymuseum.org
Founded: 1942.
Congressional District: 5
Key Personnel: Exec. Dir. & Museum Shop Mgr., Brigid Guertin; Pres., Robert Young.
Personnel Profile: Full-Time Paid 1; Part-Time Paid 2; Part-Time Volunteers 10; Interns 3.
Governing Authority: society. Tax-exempt: 501(c)(3).
History Museum.
Collections: 18th-, 19th- & early 20th-century furnishings; textiles & costumes; hatting & woodworking tools; Charles Ives memorabilia; DAR & the Revolutionary War. Historic Buildings: 1785 John & Mary Rider House; c.1790 John Dodd Shop; c.1829 Charles Ives Birthplace; Marian Anderson Studio.
Research Fields: local history; hatting; Charles Ives; genealogy.
Facilities: library & archives; Huntington Hall; Marian Anderson Studio. Museum-related items for sale.
Activities: guided tours; lectures; films; workshops; permanent & temporary exhibits.
Publications: newsletter.
Hours & Admission Prices: Tues.-Thurs. by appointment, Sat. 10-4. No charge; donations accepted. ♿
Attendance: 4,000 (estimated)
Membership: Student 21 & under and Senior Citizens 65 & over $20; Individual $25; Family $50; Fellowship $100; Special Friend $200; Patron $500; Corporate $1,000.

DANBURY RAILWAY MUSEUM, 120 White St., Danbury, CT 06810-6642. Mailing Address: P.O. Box 90, Danbury, CT 06813-0090. Tel.: 203-778-8337. Fax: 203-778-1836.
E-mail: info@danburyrail.org
Web Site: www.danburyrail.org
Founded: 1994.
Congressional District: 5
Key Personnel: Pres., Ira Pollack; Museum Shop Mgr., Patty Osmer.
Governing Authority: nonprofit organization.
Railway Museum.
Collections: railroad history; rolling stock; railroad artifacts.
Facilities: Museum-related items for sale.
Activities: rail excursions; hands-on railroad work at 12 inches to the foot scale; birthday parties; special events.
Publications: monthly newsletter, Railyard Local.
Hours & Admission Prices: Memorial Day to Labor Day Mon.-Sat. 10-5, Sun. 12-5; Sept.-May Wed.-Sat. 10-4, Sun. 12-4. Adults $6, seniors 60 & over $5, children 3-12 $4; children under 3 & members no charge. Closed New Year's Day; Thanksgiving; Christmas.
Attendance: 20,000 (estimated)
Membership: Retired Railroader $20; Individual $40; Family $50; Patron $200; Lifetime $400; Corporate $500.

MILITARY MUSEUM OF SOUTHERN NEW ENGLAND, 125 Park Ave., Danbury, CT 06810-7504. Tel.: 203-790-9277. Fax: 203-790-0420.
E-mail: usmilitarymuseum@yahoo.com
Web Site: www.usmilitarymuseum.org
Founded: 1985.
Congressional District: 5
Key Personnel: Pres., John V. Valluzzo; Vice Pres., Joseph Di Candido; Exec. Dir. & Sec., Samuel Johnson; Treas., John Purtill.
Personnel Profile: Full-Time Paid 1; Part-Time Volunteers 65.
Governing Authority: nonprofit organization. Tax-exempt: 501(c)(3).
Military Museum.
Collections: World War I-present armored vehicles & weapons; special collection of World War II tank destroyer vehicles & weapons; heavy weapons, books, technical manuals, uniforms, insignia.
Research Fields: restoration of military vehicles & weapons; tank destroyer history; weapons research.
Activities: guided tours; lectures; temporary & traveling exhibitions.
Publications: quarterly newsletter.
Hours & Admission Prices: April-Nov. Tues.-Sat. 10-5, Sun. 12-5; Dec.-March Fri.-Sat. 10-5, Sun. 1-5. Adults $6, senior citizens, children 6-18 & active duty military $4; children under 5 & members no charge. ♿
Attendance: 7,000 (estimated)
Membership: Junior $10; Individual $20; Family $40; Sustaining $100; TD Vets Honor Roll $500; Regular Life $1,000.

Danielson

KILLINGLY HISTORICAL AND GENEALOGICAL SOCIETY, INC., 196 Main St., Danielson, CT 06239-2823. Mailing Address: P.O. Box 6000, Danielson, CT 06239. Tel.: 860-779-7250.
Web Site: www.killinglyhistory.org
Formerly: Killingly Historical Center
Founded: 1972.
Congressional District: 2
Key Personnel: Dir., Marilyn Labbe; Pres. (V), Lynn LaBerge
History Museum.
Collections: local history & culture; genealogy; photographs.
Activities: lectures; programs.
Publications: newsletter.
Hours & Admission Prices: Wed.-Sat. 10-4. No charge; donations accepted. Closed New Year's Eve & Day; Christmas Eve, Day & week.
Attendance: 200 (estimated)
Membership: Individual $20; Family $20 (1st person) $10 (each additional person); Nonprofit & Libraries $25; Business $100; Life $200.

Darien

BATES-SCOFIELD HOMESTEAD, THE DARIEN HISTORICAL SOCIETY, (M), 45 Old King's Hwy., N., Darien, CT 06820-4607. Tel.: 203-655-9233. Fax: 203-656-3892.
E-mail: info@darienhistorical.org
Web Site: historical.darien.org
Founded: 1954.
Congressional District: 5
Key Personnel: Pres., Enid Oresman; Exec. Dir., Judith Groppa; Cur. Costume, Babs White; Cur. Quilt, Catherine Malloch.
Personnel Profile: Part-Time Paid 3; Part-Time Volunteers 25.
Governing Authority: society. Parent Institution: The Darien Historical Society. Tax-exempt: 501(c)(3).

Historic House: housed in c.1736 structure.
Collections: costumes; archives; quilts; manuscripts.
Research Fields: Darien history; Fairfield county history; decorative arts.
Facilities: 900-vol. library of New England historical & genealogical books available for use on premises; reading room.
Activities: guided tours; lectures; slide shows; antiques show; trips; eight formally organized education programs; temporary exhibitions.
Publications: book, Darien-Historical Sketches; quarterly newsletter.
Hours & Admission Prices: Library: Tues. & Fri. 9-2, Wed.-Thurs. 9-4. Museum: Wed.-Thurs. 2-4. Adults $3; members no charge. Closed major holidays.
Attendance: 2,000 (estimated)
Membership: Friend $25; Contributing $50; Family $100; Patron $250; Sustaining $500; Benefactor $1,000.

Deep River

STONE HOUSE, 245 Main St., Deep River, CT 06417-2055. Tel.: 860-526-5811.
Governing Authority: Parent Institution: Deep River Historical Society.
Historic House: built in 1840.
Collections: period furnishings; personal artifacts; portraits; musical instruments.
Hours & Admission Prices: Call for hours.

Derby

KELLOGG ENVIRONMENTAL CENTER, 500 Hawthorne Ave., Derby, CT 06418. Tel.: 203-734-2513.
Science Center.
Collections: natural history; environment; geology.
Facilities: nature trails.
Activities: workshops; educational programs; lectures; hiking.
Hours & Admission Prices: Tues.-Sat. 9-4:30. No charge; donations accepted.

OSBORNE HOMESTEAD MUSEUM, 500 Hawthorne Ave., Derby, CT 06418-1020. Tel.: 203-734-2513. Fax: 203-922-7833.
E-mail: christiana.jones@po.state.ct.us
Web Site: www.ct.gov/dep
Key Personnel: Cur., Christiana Jones
History Museum: housed in the former estate of Frances Osborne Kellogg, an accomplished businesswomen & conservationist who was dedicated to preserving land for future generations.
Collections: history of the Osborne family; period furniture; fine art.
Facilities: gardens.
Activities: guided tours; school programs; special programs; hands-on activities.
Hours & Admission Prices: May-Oct. Thurs.-Fri. 10-3, Sat. 10-4, Sun. 12-4; Nov. 27-Dec. 20 Thurs.-Sun. 10-4.

East Granby

OLD NEW-GATE PRISON AND COPPER MINE, 115 Newgate Rd., East Granby, CT 06026-9545. Mailing Address: P.O. Box 254, East Granby, CT 06026-0254. Tel.: 860-653-3563 & 566-3005. Fax: 860-844-2142.
Founded: 1969.
Congressional District: 6
Key Personnel: Dir., Karin Peterson; Museum Asst., Lance Kozikowski.
Personnel Profile: Full-Time Paid 1; Part-Time Paid 5.
Governing Authority: state. Parent Institution: Connecticut Commission on Culture & Tourism, 1 Constitution Plaza., Hartford. Tax-exempt.
History Museum: abandoned underground copper mine used as first state prison from 1773 to 1827.
Collections: photos; mining & prison memorabilia.
Research Fields: American Revolution; mining & copper mining; prisons.
Facilities: hiking trails; picnic area. Museum-related items for sale.
Activities: guided tours; lectures; permanent exhibitions; living history programs.
Hours & Admission Prices: May-Oct. Fri.-Sun. 10-4. Adults $10, senior citizens 60 & over and college students $8, children 6-17 $6; discounts to groups; children under 6 no charge. Closed Memorial Day; Independence Day; Labor Day; Columbus Day. ♿
Attendance: 18,114 (accurate)

East Haddam

ALLEGRA FARM & HORSE-DRAWN CARRIAGE AND SLEIGH MUSEUM, 69 Town Rd., East Haddam, CT 06415. Mailing Address: P.O. Box 455, East Haddam, CT 06423-0455. Tel.: 860-537-8861.
Transportation Museum.
Collections: horse-drawn carriages, wagons & equipment.
Activities: hay & sleigh rides; educational programs.
Hours & Admission Prices: By appointment.

GILLETTE CASTLE STATE PARK, 67 River Rd., East Haddam, CT 06423-1462. Tel.: 860-526-2336. Fax: 860-4244070.
E-mail: dep.stateparks@ct.gov
Web Site: www.ct.gov/dep
Key Personnel: Park Supvr., Bill Mattioli.
Governing Authority: state. Subsidiary Institution: Department of Environmental Protection.
Historic Building: housed in a twenty four room mansion built for actor, director, & playwright, William Hooker Gillette, c.1914.
Collections: period furnishings; personal artifacts.
Facilities: nature trails.
Activities: hiking; picnicking; camping.
Hours & Admission Prices: Park: daily 8am to sunset. No charge. Castle: Memorial Day to Columbus Day daily 10-4:30. Adults $5, children 6-17 $3; children 5 & under no charge.

GOODSPEED OPERA HOUSE, 6 Main St., East Haddam, CT 06423-1302. Tel.: 860-873-8668 & 8664.
Historic Building: housed in a Victorian theater built in 1876 by shipping magnate William Goodspeed. Listed on the National Register of Historic Places.
Collections: opera house history; period furnishings; photographs.
Activities: guided tours; performances.
Hours & Admission Prices: June-Oct. Sat. 10:30-1. Adults $5, children under 12 $1.

East Hartford

EDWARD E. KING MUSEUM, Raymond Library, 840 Main St., 2nd Fl., East Hartford, CT 06108-3128. Tel.: 860-289-6429.
History Museum.
Collections: tobacco & aviation history.
Hours & Admission Prices: Jan.-Sept. Mon.-Thurs. 9-9, Fri.-Sat. 9-5; Oct.-April Mon.-Thurs. 9-9, Fri.-Sat. 9-5, Sun. 1-4.

East Haven

SHORE LINE TROLLEY MUSEUM, 17 River St., East Haven, CT 06512-2519. Tel.: 203-467-6927. Fax: 203-467-7635.
E-mail: berasltm18@sbcglobal.net
Web Site: www.bera.org
Founded: 1945.
Congressional District: 3
Key Personnel: Dir. & Sec., George Boucher; Chm. (V), Louis Levinson; Pres., William J. Wall; Treas., Ronald Kupin; Dir. Vehicle Collection Management, Theodore Eickmann; Dir. Library, Michael Schreiber; Dir. Exhibits, Frederick Sherwood; Dir. Mktg., Katherine Slinsky; Museum Shop Mgr., David A. Cohen.
Personnel Profile: Full-Time Paid 2; Part-Time Paid 1; Part-Time Volunteers 50.
Governing Authority: nonprofit corporation. Operated by Branford Electric Railway Association, Inc. Tax-exempt: 501(c)(3).
Transportation: Technology & Operating Railway Museum.
Collections: urban, suburban & interurban electric railway cars & equipment; buses; trolley bus.
Research Fields: history of electric railway operations; evolution of mass transit; urban rail transit & its role in urban life.
Facilities: reception center; picnic area.
Activities: guided tours; permanent & temporary exhibitions; rides on operating electric cars. Members: Car operation; car restoration; maintenance & operation of the museum railway & associated facilities as volunteers using authentic tools, vehicles, & procedures.
Publications: monthly newsletter; guidebook; semi-annual journal.
Hours & Admission Prices: April & Nov. Sun. 10:30-4:30; May & Sept.-Oct. Sat.-Sun. 10:30-4:30; Memorial Day to Labor Day, daily 10:30-4:30. Adults $8, senior citizens $6, children 2-15 $4; discounts to groups, AAM, AAA & ARM members; children under 2 & members no charge. ♿
Attendance: 16,293 (accurate)
Membership: Associate $20; Regular $40; Family $65; Supporting $75; Sustaining $150; Benefactor $500.

East Windsor

CONNECTICUT FIRE MUSEUM, 58 North Rd. (Rte. 140), East Windsor, CT 06088. Mailing Address: P.O. Box 297, East Windsor, CT 06088-0297. Tel.: 860-627-6540. Fax: 860-627-6510.
E-mail: ctfiremuseum@hotmail.com
Web Site: ct-trolley.org/firemuseum
Founded: 1968.
Congressional District: 1
Key Personnel: Pres. (V), Bert Johanson; Treas., Anna Tefft; Devel. & Museum Shop Mgr., Alan Walker.
Personnel Profile: Part-Time Volunteers 11.
Governing Authority: private; nonprofit organization. Tax-exempt: 501(c)(3).
Fire-Fighting Museum.
Collections: early fire apparatus & equipment; fire sleigh c.1894; 1967 Walter airport crash truck.
Facilities: library; 6,900 sq. ft. exhibit space.
Activities: guided tours. Annual Events: Parades.
Hours & Admission Prices: Memorial Day-Labor Day Mon. & Wed.-Sat. 10-4, Sun. 12-4; Sept. to Thanksgiving Sat. 10-4, Sun. 12-4. Adults $8, senior citizens $7, children $5.
Attendance: 16,250 (estimated)
Membership: Associate $10; Active $15; Family $25.

CONNECTICUT TROLLEY MUSEUM, 58 North Rd., East Windsor, CT 06088-9606. Mailing Address: P.O. Box 360, East Windsor, CT 06088-0360. Tel.: 860-627-6540. Fax: 860-627-6510.
E-mail: office@ceraweb.org
Web Site: www.ct-trolley.org
Founded: 1940.
Congressional District: 6
Key Personnel: Pres. (V), Galen Semprehon; Chm., Brian O'Leary; Business Mgr., Carol Zenczak.
Personnel Profile: Full-Time Paid 1; Full-Time Volunteers 1; Part-Time Paid 2; Part-Time Volunteers 65.
Governing Authority: nonprofit organization. Parent Institution: Connecticut Electric Railway Association, Inc. Tax-exempt: 501(c)(3).
Trolley Museum.
Collections: electric transportation equipment from 1880-1947; 1894 Steeple-Cab electric locomotive; streetcars; 4-wheeled ex-horse cars; interurban & suburban passenger cars; railway cars.
Research Fields: histories of street railways.
Facilities: collection of documents & historic papers of Southern New England railways & street railway companies available for use by written application. Museum-related items for sale.
Activities: guided tours (3-mile round trip); lectures; films; formally organized education programs for children; permanent exhibitions. Annual Events: Halloween & December programs.
Publications: quarterly newsletter, Connecticut Electric News; books, The Cleveland Railway; New York, New Haven & Hartford Railroad Electrification; Heisler; Metropolitan Subway & Elevated Systems.
Hours & Admission Prices: March to mid-June Sat. 10-5, Sun. 12-5; mid-June to Labor Day Mon. & Wed.-Sat. 10-5, Sun. 12-5; groups of 10 or more by appointment. See website for additional hours. Unlimited rides: adults $8, senior citizens 62 & up $7, children 2-12 $5; discounts to seniors, AAA, MTA, ALA & ARM members & trolley museum members with ID; children under 2 no charge. Closed Thanksgiving; Christmas.
Attendance: 36,000 (estimated)
Membership: Senior $20; Individual $30; Family $50; Contributing $100; Supporting $250; Sustaining $500; Patron $1,000.

SCANTIC ACADEMY MUSEUM, EAST WINDSOR HISTORICAL SOCIETY, INC., 115 Scantic Rd., Rte. 191, East Windsor, CT 06088-9737. Tel.: 860-623-5327.
E-mail: eastwindsorhistory@att.net
Web Site: eastwindsorhistory.home.att.net
Founded: 1965.
Congressional District: 1
Key Personnel: Pres. (V), Michael Hunt; Treas., Jean Lamenzo; Sec., Robert Goff.
Personnel Profile: Part-Time Volunteers 10.
Governing Authority: private. Tax-exempt.
General Museum: housed in 1817 Scantic Academy Building.
Collections: industry; agriculture; paintings; transportation.
Research Fields: local history; genealogy.
Facilities: 130-vol. library of books on local history.
Activities: annual meetings & dinners; town community day program.
Publications: book: History of East Windsor Through the Years; newsletter, New HS.
Hours & Admission Prices: Sat. 9-12; other times by appointment. No charge; donations accepted. ♿
Attendance: 150 (estimated)
Membership: Individual $10; Family $15; Corporate $50.

Enfield

MARTHA A. PARSONS HOUSE MUSEUM, 1387 Enfield St., Enfield, CT 06082-5524. Mailing Address: Enfield Historical Society, P.O. Box 586, Enfield, CT 06083-0586. Tel.: 860-745-6064.
Founded: 1950.
Historic House Museum: built in 1782 by John Meacham.
Collections: period furnishings; personal artifacts.
Hours & Admission Prices: May-Oct. Sun. 2-4:30; other times by appointment. No charge.

OLD TOWN HALL MUSEUM, 1294 Enfield St., Enfield, CT 06082-4928. Mailing Address: Enfield Historical Society, P.O. Box 586, Enfield, CT 06083. Tel.: 860-745-1729.
Founded: 1960.
Personnel Profile: Part-Time Volunteers 40.
Governing Authority: Tax-exempt.
Historic Building: housed in the former meeting house of the First Ecclesiastical Society; c.1774. Listed on the National Register of Historic Places.
Collections: Enfield's history & culture; photographs; period furnishings; personal artifacts; farming implements; industrial machinery; Shaker artifacts.
Hours & Admission Prices: May-Oct. Sun. 2-4:30; other times by appointment. No charge. Closed major holidays.
Membership: Individual $10; Family $15; Contributing $20; Sustaining $40; Supporting $100; Corporate $200; Life $250; Benefactor $500.

Essex

* **CONNECTICUT RIVER MUSEUM, (M),** 67 Main St., Essex, CT 06426-1150. Tel.: 860-767-8269. Fax: 860-767-7028.
Web Site: www.ctrivermuseum.org
Founded: 1974.
Congressional District: 2
Key Personnel: Exec. Dir., Jerry Roberts; Cur., Amy Trout; Chm. Bd. Trustees, Tim Boyd; Front Desk & Shop Mgr., Helen Davis; Business Mgr., Joan Meek; Dir. Education, Jennifer White-Dobbs.
Personnel Profile: Full-Time Paid 4; Part-Time Paid 5; Part-Time Volunteers 125.
Governing Authority: nonprofit organization. Parent Institution: The Connecticut River Foundation at Steamboat Dock, Inc. Tax-exempt: 501(c)(3).
Maritime & River Museum: housed in 1878 wooden warehouse.
Collections: objects related to Connecticut River Valley agriculture; industry; small craft collection; archaeology; model of American Turtle, first submarine. Historical Building: 1813 Chandlery of Capt. Richard Hayden.
Research Fields: Connecticut River maritime & River Valley history; cultural landscape of the Connecticut River; river ecology.
Facilities: library of unpublished documents on Connecticut & U.S. maritime subjects available for research by appointment.
Activities: guided tours; lectures; formally organized education programs for children; permanent & temporary exhibitions.
Publications: quarterly newsletter, Steamboat Log; walking map, A Walking Tour of Essex; books, Connecticut River Master Mariners; Potapaug Quarter, The First Settlers of Essex, Connecticut; Life in the Connecticut River Valley; booklet, Life In the Connecticut River Valley 1800-1840; prints of river scenes.
Hours & Admission Prices: Tues.-Sun. 10-5. Adults $8, senior citizens, students, & AAA members $7, children $5; discounts to AAM members; children under 6 & members no charge. ♿
Attendance: 16,000 (accurate)
Membership: Individual $35; Two People $50; Family $60; Supporting $100; Sustaining $250; Benefactor $500; Life $1,500.

ESSEX HISTORICAL SOCIETY, INC., 22 Prospect St., Essex, CT 06426-1021. Mailing Address: P.O. Box 123, Essex, CT 06426-0123. Tel.: 860-767-0681 & 0375.
Web Site: essexhistory.org
Founded: 1955.
Congressional District: 2
Key Personnel: Pres. (V), Mary Ann Pleva; Cur., Celia Francis.
Personnel Profile: Part-Time Volunteers 100.
Governing Authority: society. Tax-exempt.
History Museum.
Collections: late 1700s furnishings displayed in a home setting; 18th-19th century records & items relating to industrial & domestic history of Essex & vicinity. Historic Houses: c.1732 Pratt House; 1832 Hills Academy.
Research Fields: local history; early New England style of living.

Facilities: 50-vol. library of local history available by arrangement.
Activities: lectures; films; individual & group tours.
Publications: The British Raid on Essex: April 8, 1814; The Oliver Cromwell; The Golden Rule Days of Essex; From Bicycles to Buicks, The Story of Behrems and Bushnell.
Hours & Admission Prices: Pratt House: June-Aug. Sat.-Sun. 1-4; Sept.-May by appointment. No charge; donations accepted.
Attendance: 400 (estimated)
Membership: Student $10; Individual $20; Family, Business & Professional $30; Sustaining $50; Patron $100; Sponsor & Life $500.

Fairfield

BELLARMINE MUSEUM, FAIRFIELD UNIVERSITY, 1073 N. Benson Rd., Fairfield, CT 06824. Tel.: 203-254-4000, ext. 2215. Fax: 203-249-5513.
E-mail: jdeupi@fairfield.edu
Web Site: www.fairfield.edu/museum
Founded: 2009.
Congressional District: 4
Key Personnel: Dir., Jill Deupi, J.D., Ph.D.; Registrar, Carey Weber.
Personnel Profile: Full-Time Paid 1; Part-Time Paid 1; Interns 2.
Governing Authority: private university. Parent Institution: Fairfield University, Fairfield, CT. Tax-exempt: 501(c)(3).
Art Musuem.
Collections: Kress study collection of Italian paintings, 1200-1800; cast collection of Greco Roman antiquities; non-western art.
Research Fields: Kress collection of paintings; 18th century Italian art & culture.
Facilities: 250 sq. ft. exhibit space; educational facilities.
Activities: guided tours; lectures; formal education programs for undergraduate or graduate college students; loan, permanent & temporary exhibitions.
Hours & Admission Prices: Mon.-Fri. 10-4. No charge; donations accepted. Closed national holidays.

CONNECTICUT AUDUBON BIRDCRAFT MUSEUM, 314 Unquowa Rd., Fairfield, CT 06824-5018. Tel.: 203-259-0416. Fax: 203-259-1344.
E-mail: birdcraft@ctaudubon.org
Web Site: www.ctaudubon.org
Founded: 1914.
Congressional District: 4
Key Personnel: Pres., Robert Martinez; Chm. (V), Stephen B. Oresman; Dir., Nelson North; Site Mgr., Deborah T. Callan.
Personnel Profile: Full-Time Paid 2; Part-Time Paid 2; Part-Time Volunteers 10.
Governing Authority: private; nonprofit. Parent Institution: Connecticut Audubon Society, Fairfield, CT. Tax-exempt: 501(c)(3).
Natural Science & Ornithology Museum: founded in 1914 by Mabel Osgood Wright, who played a major role in establishing the American conservation movement.
Collections: biological collections focusing on the zoology of Connecticut, particularly the coastal area; bird mounts & artifacts from around the world; African animal mounts; fossils; minerals; insects; botanical; nature & avian decorative arts & artifacts; specimens & artifacts collected by Wright & naturalist, G.B. Grinnell.
Research Fields: migratory birds of Connecticut; Mabel Osgood Wright, conservationist & author; monk parakeet distribution in Greater Bridgeport, Connecticut; bird banding station.
Facilities: library; 1,550 sq. ft. exhibit space; field research station; nature & conservation center; 6-acre sanctuary. Museum-related items for sale.
Activities: docent program; films; formal education programs; guided tours; hobby workshops; lectures; loan, participatory & temporary exhibitions. Annual Event: International Migratory Bird Day in May.
Hours & Admission Prices: Tues.-Fri. 9-5, Sat. 12-5; other times by appointment. Adults $2, children $1; discounts to AAM, ICOM & Connecticut Ornithological Assoc. members; members no charge. Closed major holidays. ♿
Attendance: 15,000 (accurate)
Membership: Individual $35; Family $50; Sustaining, Associated Organization & Supporting $75; Contributing $100; Donor $200; Patron $500; Benefactor $1,000.

CONNECTICUT AUDUBON CENTER AT FAIRFIELD, (M), 2325 Burr St., Fairfield, CT 06824-1806. Tel.: 203-259-0416, ext. 109. Fax: 203-254-7673.
E-mail: bmucci@ctaudubon.org
Web Site: www.ctaudubon.org
Founded: 1898.
Key Personnel: Sr. Dir. Southwest CT Operations, Nelson North; Dir. Education, Carol Kratzman; Museum Shop Mgr., Deborah Callan.
Personnel Profile: Full-Time Paid 4; Part-Time Paid 3; Part-Time Volunteers 150; Interns 2.
Governing Authority: private; nonprofit environmental education organization. Parent Institution: Connecticut Audubon Society, 2325 Barr St., Fairfield, CT 06824. Tax-exempt: 501(c)(3).
Nature Center.
Collections: living & mounted animal specimens; 160-acre wildlife sanctuary.
Research Fields: colonial waterbird survey.
Facilities: nature center; aquarium; classrooms; 1,000 sq. ft. exhibit space; 160-acre wildlife sanctuary. Birdseed, nature books, field guides & museum-related items for sale.
Activities: guided tours; lectures; temporary & participatory exhibits; school loan service; docent program; formal education programs for children; internships. Annual Events: Friends Event; Halloween Event; Volunteers Dinner.
Publications: quarterly membership newsletter; CT Audubon Society News.
Hours & Admission Prices: Tues.-Sat. 10-3. Adults $2, children $1; members no charge. Closed major holidays. ♿
Attendance: 12,000 (estimated)
Membership: Individual $40; Supporting $75; Contributing $100; Donor $200; Patron $500; Benefactor $1,000.

CONNECTICUT AUDUBON SOCIETY, 2325 Burr St., Fairfield, CT 06824-1806. Tel.: 203-259-6305, ext. 101. Fax: 203-254-7673.
E-mail: rmartinez@ctaudubon.org
Web Site: www.ctaudubon.org
Founded: 1898.
Congressional District: 4
Key Personnel: Pres., Robert Martinez; Chm. (V), Stephen B. Oresman; Dir. Finance & Human Resources, Frank Thiel; Dir. Connecticut Audubon Fairfield, Rgnl. Programs, Nelson North; Dir. Connecticut Audubon Center at Glastonbury, Sally Carbone; Dir. Devel., Ann O'Leary; Dir. Mktg. & Communications, Mara Neville; Emeritus, Barbara Strickland.
Personnel Profile: Full-Time Paid 30; Part-Time Paid 4; Part-Time Volunteers 100.
Governing Authority: nonprofit organization; society. Branch Museums: Connecticut Audubon Center at Fairfield, 2325 Burr St., Fairfield, CT 06430; Connecticut Audubon Center at Glastonbury, 1361 Main St., Glastonbury, CT 06033; Connecticut Audubon Coastal Center at Milford Point, 1Milford Point Rd., Milford; Connecticut Audubon Birdcraft Museum, 314 Unquowa Rd., Fairfield; Connecticut Audubon Environmental Center, 118 Oak St., Hartford; Connecticut Audubon Center at Pomfret, 189 Pomfret St. (Rte. 169), Pomfret Center, CT 06259; 19 statewide sanctuaries. Tax-exempt: 401(c)(3).
Natural History Museum.
Collections: 4,000 mounted birds of Connecticut; study skins.
Research Fields: ornithology; wildlife ecology & environmental issues; bird banding program.
Facilities: 3,000-vol. library; teacher resource center; field research station; 200-seat auditorium; classrooms; animal care facility; 16 wildlife sanctuaries. Nature-related items for sale.
Activities: guided tours; lectures; films; summer classes; educational programs; permanent & temporary exhibitions; school loan service; local, regional, international field trips.
Publications: quarterly, Connecticut Audubon News Bulletin; Capitol Alert.
Hours & Admission Prices: July-Aug. Tues.-Sat. 9-4:30; Sept.-June Tues.-Sat. 9-4:30, Sun. 12-4. Adults $2, children $1. Closed major holidays. ♿
Attendance: 50,000 (accurate)
Membership: Individual $40; Family $55; Contributing $100; Donor $200; Patron $500; Benefactor $1,000.

FAIRFIELD MUSEUM AND HISTORY CENTER, (M), 370 Beach Rd., Fairfield, CT 06824-6639. Tel.: 203-259-1598, ext. 101. Fax: 203-255-2716.
E-mail: info@fairfieldhs.org
Web Site: www.fairfieldhs.org
Formerly: Fairfield Historical Society
Founded: 1902.
Congressional District: 4
Key Personnel: C.E.O., Michael A. Jehle; Pres., Barbara Geddis Wooten; Cur., Adrienne Saint-Pierre; Dir. Education, Christine Jewell; Librarian, Bonnie Collier; Prog. & Volunteer Coord., Walter Matis.
Personnel Profile: Full-Time Paid 7; Part-Time Paid 4; Part-Time Volunteers 90; Interns 5.
Governing Authority: society. Parent Institution: Fairfield Historical Society. Branch Museum: Ogden House, 1520 Bronson Rd., Fairfield. Tax-exempt: 101(6).
History Museum & Library.
Collections: personal artifacts; furnishings; paintings; photographs; maps; manuscripts.

Research Fields: local genealogy & history; decorative arts.
Facilities: 8,000-vol. library of genealogical & historical interest for use on premises.
Activities: guided tours; seminars, workshop & lecture series; changing exhibits. Annual Event: Fall Festival.
Publications: quarterly newsletter; books, Fairfield, The Biography of a Community, 1639-2000; History of Fairfield County Men In The Revolution; Walking Through History-The Seaports of Black Rock & Southport; Cooking with Fire: Open Hearth Cooking & Recipes; Clocks & Clockmakers of Fairfield 1736-1813; Fairfield Bicycle Tour: Travel Back in Time; Fairfield Printmaker: John Taylor Arms; Visions of Home and Abroad; Images of America: Fairfield, Connecticut.
Hours & Admission Prices: Mon.-Fri. 10-4, Sat.-Sun. 12-4. Adults $5; discounts to AAM members; members no charge. ♿
Attendance: 30,000 (estimated)
Membership: Individual $30 Family $50; Contributing & Business $100; Sustaining $250; Patron $500; Benefactor $1,000.

THE GALLERY OF CONTEMPORARY ART - SACRED HEART UNIVERSITY, 5151 Park Ave., Fairfield, CT 06825-1000. Tel.: 203-365-7650. Fax: 203-396-8361.
E-mail: gevass@sacredheart.edu
Founded: 1989.
Key Personnel: Dir., Sophia Gevas
Art Gallery.
Collections: works by contemporary artists.
Activities: special events; educational programs.
Hours & Admission Prices: mid-Sept. to May Mon.-Thurs. 12-5, Sun. 12-4.

THOMAS J. WALSH ART GALLERY, QUICK CENTER FOR THE ARTS AT FAIRFIELD UNIVERSITY, (M), 1073 N. Benson Rd., Fairfield, CT 06824-5171. Tel.: 203-254-4000, ext. 2969. Fax: 203-254-4113.
E-mail: info@quickcenter.com
Web Site: www.quickcenter.com
Founded: 1990.
Congressional District: 4
Key Personnel: Exec. Dir., Thomas V. Zingarelli; Gallery Dir., Dr. Diana Dimodica Mille.
Personnel Profile: Full-Time Paid 1; Part-Time Volunteers 7; Interns 4.
Governing Authority: nonprofit. Parent Institution: Fairfield University. Tax-exempt: 501(c)(3).
University Art Gallery.
Collections: pre-Columbian, African, Oceanic, Eastern and Indian sculpture; contemporary art-20th century; Renaissance paintings.
Research Fields: art history.
Facilities: 2,200 sq. ft. exhibit space; theater.
Activities: lectures; films; concerts; arts festivals; theater; organized education programs for children, adults, undergraduate & graduate college students affiliated with Fairfield Univ.; training programs for professional museum workers; participatory, loan & traveling exhibitions.
Publications: catalogue, Images of the Divine.
Hours & Admission Prices: Tues.-Sat. 11-5, Sun. 12-4. No charge; donations accepted. Closed Memorial Day; Labor Day; Thanksgiving; Christmas. ♿
Attendance: 10,000 (estimated)
Membership: Friend $50; Member $100; Sustainer $250; Patron $500; Benefactor $1,000.

Falls Village

FALLS VILLAGE-CANAAN HISTORICAL SOCIETY, 44 Railroad St., Falls Village, CT 06031. Mailing Address: P.O. Box 206, Falls Village, CT 06031-0206. Tel.: 860-824-8226. Fax: 860-824-4506.
Web Site: www.betweenthelakes.com/canaan/hist_society.htm
Founded: 1952.
Congressional District: 6
Key Personnel: Pres. (V), Judy Jacobs; Cur. South Canaan Meeting House, Mrs. H. DeVries; Cur. Falls Village Depot, Cheryl Aeschliman; Cur. Beebe Hill Schoolhouse, Mary Lu Sinclair.
Governing Authority: nonprofit organization. Tax-exempt.
Historical Society Museum.
Collections: costumes; local history items; railroad artifacts.
Facilities: 200-vol. library of genealogy, ledgers & day books, local history, & children's books available for use on premises.
Activities: school groups; temporary exhibitions; concerts. Special Events: semiannual Peddler's Markets; Antique Tool Show in June; Living History Demonstrations in October; Lecture Series June to August.
Publications: quarterly newsletter; pamphlet, South Canaan Congregational Church; The Two Canaans-Division of the Town of Canaan; 1853 map of the Town of Canaan; Lemuel Haynes; Chronicles of Old Canaan; book, Canaan: A Small New England Town During the Revolutionary War; book, Country Depots in the Connecticut Hills; book, Exploring the Berkshire Hills; book, Iron Country Revisited; Mumbet.
Hours & Admission Prices: Falls Village: Sat. 10-1; other times by appointment. No charge; donations accepted. ♿
Attendance: 175 (estimated)
Membership: Single $15; Family $25; Business $50; Friends of the Society $100.

Farmington

* **HILL-STEAD MUSEUM, (M),** 35 Mountain Rd., Farmington, CT 06032-2304. Tel.: 860-677-4787. Fax: 860-677-0174.
E-mail: cagenelloc@hillstead.org
Web Site: www.hillstead.org
Founded: 1946.
Congressional District: 6
Key Personnel: Dir. & C.E.O., Sue Sturtevant; Dir. Education & Curatorial Svcs., Cynthia Cormier; Dir. Devel. & Communications, Marie Dalton-Meyer; Pres. (V), Margaret C. Darby; Museum Shop Mgr., Denise Bowen; Mgr. Communications, Cynthia Cagenello; Dir. Operations, David Perbeck; Office Mgr., Cindy Stanley; Assoc. Cur., Melanie A. Bourbeau.
Personnel Profile: Full-Time Paid 15; Part-Time Paid 30; Part-Time Volunteers 200; Interns 10.
Governing Authority: nonprofit organization. Tax-exempt: 501(3)(c).
Art Museum: housed in c.1901 building designed by Theodate Pope Riddle in collaboration with McKim, Mead & White. Period garden based on plan by Beatrix Farrand.
Collections: French Impressionist paintings; prints; sculpture; furniture; porcelain.
Research Fields: art; architecture.
Facilities: research library available to scholars by appointment; gardens. Museum-related books for sale.
Activities: guided tours; permanent exhibitions; nature & educational programs; poetry; music.
Publications: quarterly newsletters; booklets, House Guide; Theodate Pope Riddle: Her Life & Her Work; brochures, Garden & Grounds; Flip card; Sunken Garden guide; Theodate Pope Riddle: A Pioneer Woman Architect; Oriental Carpets in the Collections of H-S Museum; Hill-Stead, An Illustrated Museum Guide; Dearest of Geniuses, A Life of Theodate Pope Riddle; annual reports; Hill-Stead Plant Book; poetry chapbooks.
Hours & Admission Prices: Call for hours. Adults $9; discounts for AAA & AAM members; members no charge. Closed major holidays. ♿
Attendance: 33,563 (accurate)
Membership: Student & Individual $50; Family & Household $75; Contributor $150; Sponsor $300; Theodate Pope Riddle Society $500 & up.

STANLEY-WHITMAN HOUSE, FARMINGTON, 37 High St., Farmington, CT 06032-2314. Tel.: 860-677-9222. Fax: 860-677-7758.
E-mail: lisa@stanleywhitman.org
Web Site: www.stanleywhitman.org
Founded: 1935.
Congressional District: 6
Key Personnel: C.E.O., Lisa Johnson; Chm. (V), Jane Dalal.
Personnel Profile: Full-Time Paid 2; Part-Time Paid 5; Part-Time Volunteers 70; Interns 4.
Governing Authority: nonprofit organization. Parent Institution: Farmington Village Green & Library Association, Main St., Farmington, CT. Tax-exempt: 501(c)(3).
Historic House Museum: c.1719-1772 Stanley-Whitman House; interpretation of 18th-century Farmington.
Collections: 1642-1880 Farmington history; 18th-century furniture & decorative arts; local artifacts; herb garden.
Research Fields: Colonial Farmington life; furniture; decorative arts; 17th- & 18th-century furniture & decorative arts; historic house investigation; 18th-century dooryards & gardens; agriculture; Judah Woodruff, constructor of houses, barns, mid-late 18th-century; 17th century New England culture & witchcraft trials.
Facilities: education building annex. Museum-related gifts for sale.
Activities: house tours; school programs; member events; exhibition previews.
Publications: newsletter; A Short History of Farmington, Connecticut; A Guide to Historic Farmington, Connecticut; The Preservation of the Stanley-Whitman House; The Stanley-Whitman House: A Dwelling House and Homestead.
Hours & Admission Prices: Wed.-Fri. 9-4, Sat.-Sun. 12-4. House Tours: Wed.-Sun. 12-4. Adults $5, senior citizens & group rate per person $4; discounts to New England Museum Assoc. members; Greater Hartford Assoc. of Historic Houses & museum members no charge. Closed national holidays. ♿
Attendance: 12,000 (estimated)
Membership: Full Time Student $18; Individual $20; Family $30; Friend (2

guest passes) $45; Donor (4 guest passes) $65; Sponsor (6 guest passes) $100; Patron (8 guest passes) $150; Benefactor (10 guest passes) $500.

Franklin

BLUE SLOPE COUNTRY MUSEUM, 138 Blue Hill Rd., Franklin, CT 06254-1601. Tel.: 860-642-6413.
E-mail: museum@blueslope.com
Web Site: www.blueslope.com/museum.html
Key Personnel: Dir., Sandy Staebner
History Museum.
Collections: early farming; period farm equipment & furnishings; personal artifacts.
Facilities: Museum-related items for sale.
Activities: special events; educational programs.
Hours & Admission Prices: Call for hours.

Gales Ferry

NATHAN LESTER HOUSE, Long Cove & Vinegar Hill Rds., Gales Ferry, CT 06335. Tel.: 860-464-8540.
Historic House: housed in an 18th century farmhouse.
Collections: period furnishings; personal artifacts; photographs; outbuildings.
Facilities: nature trails.
Activities: hiking.
Hours & Admission Prices: House: Memorial Day to Labor Day Tues. & Thurs. 2-4, Sat.-Sun. 1-4:30; other times by appointment. Grounds: daily. No charge; donations accepted.

Glastonbury

HISTORICAL SOCIETY OF GLASTONBURY, 1944 Main St., Glastonbury, CT 06033-2901. Mailing Address: P.O. Box 46, Glastonbury, CT 06033-0046. Tel.: 860-633-6890. Fax: 860-633-6890.
E-mail: hsglastonbury@sbcglobal.net
Web Site: www.hsgct.org
Founded: 1936.
Congressional District: 1
Key Personnel: Exec. Dir., James Bennett; Pres., Donna Henrikson; Treas., David Motycka; Cur., Linda Scarduzio; Librarian, Phylis Reed.
Personnel Profile: Full-Time Paid 2; Part-Time Paid 1; Part-Time Volunteers 40.
Governing Authority: nonprofit organization. Branch Museum: Welles-Shipman-Ward House, 972 Main St., S., Glastonbury, CT 06073. Tax-exempt: 501(c)(3).
Historical Society Museum: housed in c.1840 Old Town Hall.
Collections: local history; Indian artifacts; historical documents; textiles; folk art; Colonial artifacts; Civil War; WW I & WW II artifacts; early industries; maps.
Research Fields: Indians; historic site surveys; local businesses.
Facilities: 200-vol. library pertaining to local history; genealogy, Native Americans & New England folkways; herb garden. Books, pewter spoons & other related items for sale.
Activities: guided tours; lectures; organized educational programs; docent program; loan & temporary exhibitions.
Publications: quarterly newsletter; annual journal, The Publick Post; books, The Glastonbury Express; Glastonbury: From Settlement to Suburb; The Letter Kills But the Spirit Gives Life; Moments in History.
Hours & Admission Prices: Welles-Shipman-Ward: April-Nov. 3rd Sun. of month and 2nd & 4th Tues. of month 1-4. Museum on the Green: Mon.-Tues. & Thurs. 9-4, 3rd Sun. of month 1-4; other times by appointment. No charge; donations accepted. Closed national holidays.
Attendance: 3,800 (estimated)
Membership: Senior 62 & over $12; Individual $25; Family $35; Contributing $75; Sustaining $100; Patron $200; Life $500; Life Couple $750.

Goshen

ACTION WILDLIFE FOUNDATION, 337 Torrington Rd., Rte. 4, Goshen, CT 06756-2031. Tel.: 860-482-4465; 491-9191. Fax: 860-482-8337.
E-mail: info@actionwildlife.org
Web Site: www.actionwildlife.org
Key Personnel: Museum Dir., Jim Mazzarelli; Animal Mgr., Sue Tracy; Sec., Julie Mazzarelli
Foundation.
Collections: mounted wildlife scenes; live exotic animals.
Hours & Admission Prices: Daily 10-5. Adults $10, children under 12 $8. ♿

GOSHEN HISTORICAL SOCIETY, 21 Old Middle St., Goshen, CT 06756. Mailing Address: P.O. Box 457, Goshen, CT 06756-0457. Tel.: 860-491-9610 & 3129.
E-mail: jvnkuq@juno.com
Web Site: goshenhistoricalct.org
Founded: 1955.
Congressional District: 5
Key Personnel: Pres. (V), Henrietta C. Horvay.
Personnel Profile: Full-Time Volunteers 5; Part-Time Volunteers 4.
Governing Authority: private. Tax-exempt.
History Museum.
Collections: pewter; rocks & shells; history; Indian artifacts; medical; natural history; textiles; dolls; farm tools; historic flags.
Facilities: 300-vol. library of historical subjects available for research use by appointment.
Activities: lectures; formally organized education programs for children; permanent exhibitions.
Publications: annual letter.
Hours & Admission Prices: April-Nov. Tues. 9-12; other times by appointment only. No charge. ♿
Attendance: 300 (estimated)
Membership: Sustaining $15; Life $500.

Granby

SALMON BROOK HISTORICAL SOCIETY, INC., 208 Salmon Brook St., Granby, CT 06035. Mailing Address: P.O. Box 840, Granby, CT 06035-0840. Tel.: 860-653-9713.
Web Site: www.salmonbrookhistorical.org
Founded: 1959.
Congressional District: 6
Key Personnel: Pres. (V), Charles Dickson; Archivist & Genealogist, Carol Laun.
Personnel Profile: Part-Time Volunteers 20.
Governing Authority: society. Tax-exempt: 501(c)(3).
History Museum: housed in c.1732 Abijah Rowe House.
Collections: household & farm furniture; history; local genealogy; manuscript collections; personal & farming artifacts; documents. Historic Buildings: 1790 Weed-Enders House; 1870 Cooley Rd. School; 1900 Tobacco Barn.
Research Fields: local, area & state history.
Facilities: 1,000-vol. library of books & documents pertaining to history & genealogy of local interest available for research on premises; collection of newspapers dating back to pre-Civil War period; Reference & Educational Center open to public.
Activities: permanent & special exhibits; tours of house; lectures & classes.
Publications: books, The Heritage of Granby, 1786-1967; Collections of the Salmon Brook Historical Society Vol. I, II, III, IV & V; Granby, Connecticut: A Brief History 1786-1986, 1986; Selectmen's Records 1786-1850, 1986; Bicentennial Quilt Booklet, 1986; Tempest in a Small Town, 1996; The Holcomb Collection, 1998; Burials in the Granby Center Cemetery, 1998. Beneath These Stones, 2003; Burials in the Granby Center Cemetery, Revised 2004; Wintonbury Church Records, 2004.
Hours & Admission Prices: June-Sept. Sun. 2-4; other times by appointment. Adults $4; members no charge.
Attendance: 600 (estimated)
Membership: Student $3; Single $15; Family $20; Sustaining $30; Life $300.

Greenwich

AUDUBON GREENWICH, 613 Riversville Rd., Greenwich, CT 06831-2624. Tel.: 203-869-5272. Fax: 203-869-4437.
E-mail: greenwich_center@audubon.org
Web Site: greenwich.audubon.org
Founded: 1942.
Key Personnel: Exec. Dir., Tom Baptist; Center Dir., Karen A. Dixon; Environmental Education Specialist, Edward S. Gilman; Environmental Education Specialist, Lindsay DeVito; Environmental Education Specialist, James Flynn; Education Mgr., Jeff Cordulack; Nature Shop Mgr., Brian O'Toole; Office Mgr., Gigi Lombardi.
Personnel Profile: Full-Time Paid 9; Part-Time Volunteers 30; Interns 1.
Governing Authority: society; nonprofit. Affiliated with National Audubon Society, 225 Varick St., New York, NY 10014. Tel.: 212-979-3000. Tax-exempt: 501(c)(3).
Nature Center.
Collections: natural history; wildlife & their habitats; hands-on exhibits.
Research Fields: bird banding.
Facilities: 686 acres; nature trails. Museum-related items for sale.
Activities: guided tours; lectures; films; formally organized education programs for children & adults; permanent exhibitions; children's learning center; bird observation; summer & winter camp programs for K-10.
Publications: Audubon Greenwich in Flight.

Hours & Admission Prices: Daily 9-5. Adults $3, children & senior citizens over 62 $1.50; discount to AAM members; members no charge. ♿
Attendance: 30,000 (estimated)
Membership: National Audubon Society $35.

* **BRUCE MUSEUM, (M),** One Museum Dr., Greenwich, CT 06830-7157. Tel.: 203-869-0376. Fax: 203-869-0963.
Web Site: www.brucemuseum.org
Formerly: Bruce Museum of Arts and Science
Founded: 1912.
Congressional District: 4
Key Personnel: C.E.O. & Exec. Dir., Peter C. Sutton; Co Chm. (V), Nathaniel Day; Co Chm. (V), Tamara Holliday; Dir. Public Rels., Michael Horyczun; Dir. Education, Robin Garr; Cur. Science, Carolyn Rebbert; Assoc. Dir. Devel., Whitney Rosenberg; Dir. Exhibits, Anne von Stuelpnagel; Dir. Finance & C.F.O., Gregory Hollop; Registrar, Jack Coyle; Dir. Devel., Liz Hopper; Museum Shop Mgr., Justine Matteis.
Personnel Profile: Full-Time Paid 35; Part-Time Paid 12; Part-Time Volunteers 475; Interns 6.
Governing Authority: private. Parent Institution: Bruce Museum, Inc. Subsidiary Institution: Seaside Center. Tax-exempt: 501(c)(3).
Arts, Science & History.
Collections: American painting; sculpture & decorative art; Native American art & artifacts; photography; costumes & textiles; North American mounted mammals & birds; fossils; minerals; shells.
Major Exhibits: Highlights from the Bruce Museum Collection, 1/23/10-4/25/10; World Maps, 1/30/10-4/4/10; Costumes from the Bruce Museum Collection, 5/15/10-9/5/10; Circus! Art & Science Under the Big Top, 9/24/10-1/9/11.
Research Fields: art history; geology.
Facilities: 150-seat lecture gallery; educational workshop; Seaside Museum annex. Museum-related gifts for sale.
Activities: lectures; films; docent program; permanent, temporary & traveling exhibitions; college student interns; school & adult tours; family events & activities; afterschool programs.
Publications: bimonthly calendar of events; exhibition catalogs; e-newsletter; online teacher resources.
Hours & Admission Prices: Tues.-Sat. 10-5, Sun.1-5. Adults $7, students & senior citizens $6; discounts to AAM & ASTC members; Tues., children under 5 & members no charge. Closed New Year's Day; Easter; Memorial Day; Independence Day; Thanksgiving; Christmas. ♿
Attendance: 71,282 (accurate)
Membership: Student & Educator $35; Senior $40; Individual $60; Senior Couple $60; Young Friend $150; Patron $250; Benefactor $750. Robert Bruce Circle: Bronze $2,000; Silver $3,000; Gold $6,000; Platinum $10,000; Director's Diamond $25,000.

PUTNAM COTTAGE, 243 E. Putnam Ave., Greenwich, CT 06830-4808. Tel.: 203-869-9697.
E-mail: info@putnamcottage.org
Web Site: www.putnamcottage.org
Founded: 1900.
Key Personnel: Pres. (V), Mrs. Wedgbury Jayes; Museum Shop Mgr., Mrs. Sally Bretschger.
Personnel Profile: Full-Time Volunteers 20; Part-Time Volunteers 30.
Governing Authority: organization. Parent Institution: Israel Putnam House Association. Tax-exempt.
History Museum: housed in c.1700 Knapps Tavern.
Collections: early Americana; period Greenwich artifacts; archives; 18th century furnishings; General Putnam memorabilia; c.1690 gunstock posts; fieldstone fireplaces.
Facilities: genealogical library; herb garden.
Activities: guided tours. Museum Sponsors: American History essay contests; Historical Battle Reenactment in February.
Hours & Admission Prices: April-Dec. Sun. 1-4; other times by appointment. Adults $6; children under 12 no charge. Closed holidays.
Attendance: 300 (estimated)

Groton

SUBMARINE FORCE MUSEUM AND HISTORIC SHIP NAUTILUS, (M), 1 Crystal Lake Rd., Groton, CT 06340-2464. Mailing Address: P.O. Box 571 NAVSUBASE, New London, Groton, CT 06349-5571. Tel.: 860-694-3174; 800-343-0079. Fax: 860-694-4150.
Web Site: www.ussnautilus.org
Founded: 1954.
Key Personnel: Dir., Commander Gregory Caskey; Supervisory Cur., Stephen Finnigan; Archives Technician, Wendy Gulley; Museum Aide, Martha Barber; Museum Specialist, Thaddeus Wakefield; Tour Coord. & Sec., Linda Williams.
Personnel Profile: Full-Time Paid 5; Part-Time Volunteers 1.
Governing Authority: federal. Parent Institution: Dept. of the Navy. Tax-exempt.
Naval Museum: housed on USS Nautilus submarine & adjacent museum.
Collections: historic submarine: USS Nautilus, first nuclear-powered submarine; objects, documents & photographs related to the history of the U.S. Submarine Force; working periscopes; mini-theaters; ship models; torpedoes.
Research Fields: U.S. submarines.
Facilities: 5,000-vol. submarine research library.
Activities: self-guided tours of museum and submarine Nautilus.
Hours & Admission Prices: Museum: May-Oct. Tues. 1-5, Wed.-Mon. 9-5; Nov.-April Wed.-Mon. 9-4. Library: Mon.-Fri. by appointment only. No charge; donations accepted. Closed New Year's Day; Thanksgiving; Christmas. ♿
Attendance: 141,800 (accurate)

Guilford

HENRY WHITFIELD STATE HISTORICAL MUSEUM, 248 Old Whitfield St., Guilford, CT 06437-3459. Tel.: 203-453-2457. Fax: 203-453-7544.
E-mail: whitfieldmuseum@ct.gov
Web Site: cultureandtourism.org
Founded: 1899.
Congressional District: 3
Key Personnel: Dir., Karin Senich; Cur., Michael A. McBride; Asst. Cur., Michelle E. Parrish; Guide, Chris Collins.
Personnel Profile: Full-Time Paid 2; Part-Time Paid 1; Part-Time Volunteers 10.
Governing Authority: state. Parent Institution: Connecticut Commission on Culture & Tourism, One Constitution Plaza, 2nd Fl., Hartford, CT 06103. Tax-exempt: 170(b)(1)(a).
National Historic Landmark: 1639 oldest building in Connecticut, oldest stone house in New England; first state-owned museum in Connecticut (1899), colonial revival restorations by Norman Isham in 1902-1904 & J. Frederick Kelly in the 1930s.
Collections: 17th-19th century European & American furniture; textiles & household furnishings; herb garden; firearms; manuscripts.
Research Fields: all aspects of the 17th century & the Whitfield family; Guilford & Connecticut history.
Facilities: 600-vol. library of local historical materials available on application; herb garden; local & state historical materials; landscaped grounds; visitor & tourist info center. Museum-related items for sale.
Activities: self-guided tours; programs; group tours by appointment; changing exhibits.
Publications: book, Henry Whitfield House.
Hours & Admission Prices: See website for current hours. Adults $4, seniors $3, youth $2.50; children 5 & under no charge. Closed major holidays. ♿
Attendance: 4,000 (accurate)

THE HYLAND HOUSE, 84 Boston St., Guilford, CT 06437-2874. Mailing Address: P.O. Box 229, Guilford, CT 06437-0229. Tel.: 203-453-9477 & 3850.
E-mail: jack@carles.us
Web Site: www.hylandhouse.com
Founded: 1918.
Key Personnel: Pres. (V) Bd. Dir. Dorothy Whitfield Historic Society, John Carles; Treas., Paul Shuell; Cur., Pamela Besse; Membership, Sally Leighton; Education, Teresa Buchannon.
Personnel Profile: Part-Time Paid 4; Part-Time Volunteers 18.
Governing Authority: private; nonprofit organization. Tax-exempt.
General Museum.
Collections: 17th to early 18th century furniture; decorative arts; early colonial life & architecture; hearth tools; cooking implements.
Research Fields: historic structures; Dorothy Whitfield Historic Society & the colonial revival; Ebenezer Parmelee & Connecticut clockmaking.
Activities: concerts; formal education programs; guided tours; lectures; temporary exhibitions; hands-on workshops for Guilford 4th graders. Museum Sponsors: Annual Antiques Show in March.
Publications: newsletter, Hyland House Times.
Hours & Admission Prices: April 15 to May by appointment only; June-Columbus Day Tues.-Sat. 10-4:30, Sun. 12-4:30. No charge; donations accepted.
Attendance: 1,835 (accurate)
Membership: Dorothy Whitfield Historic Society: Single $15; Family $20; Contributing $30; Sustaining $100.

THE THOMAS GRISWOLD HOUSE AND MUSEUM, 171 Boston St., Guilford, CT 06437. Mailing Address: P.O. Box 363, Guilford, CT 06437-0363. Tel.: 203-453-3176.
E-mail: info@guilfordkeepingsociety.com
Web Site: guilfordkeepingsociety.com
Founded: 1947.
Congressional District: 3
Key Personnel: Pres., Thomas Black; Dir., Patricia Lovelace; Vice Pres., Winnie Seibert; Treas., Thomas Williams; Public Rels., Stuart Wilkie; Programs, Robert Donahue.
Personnel Profile: Part-Time Paid 6; Part-Time Volunteers 200.
Governing Authority: private; nonprofit organization. Parent Institution: Historical & Preservations Societies. Branch Museum: The Medad Stone Tavern and Museum, 197 Three Mile Course, Guilford, CT 06437. Tel.: 203-453-2263. Tax-exempt: 501(c)(3).
Historic House: built in 1774.
Collections: 19th & 20th century glass plates & photographs; documents; deeds; genealogical data from 1639; furniture & household items from the 18th & 19th century.
Research Fields: genealogical research on Guilford ancestors.
Facilities: library of books on Guilford historical data on families, deeds; early photos & town documents available to the public. Museum-related items for sale.
Activities: concerts; formal education for children; guided tours; temporary exhibitions. Annual Events: Antiques Festival; Memorial Day Picnic; Wine Tasting & Silent Auction.
Publications: quarterly newsletter, Society News.
Hours & Admission Prices: June-Sept. Tues.-Sun. 11-4; other times for pre-arranged groups. Adults & students $2; discounts to NEMA members & groups; children & members no charge.
Attendance: 1,500 (estimated)
Membership: Individual $20; Family $40; Contributing $75; Sustaining $150; Life $500.

Hamden

ELI WHITNEY MUSEUM, INC., 915 Whitney Ave., Hamden, CT 06517-4036. Tel.: 203-777-1833. Fax: 203-777-1229.
E-mail: kl@eliwhitney.org
Web Site: www.eliwhitney.org
Founded: 1976.
Congressional District: 3
Key Personnel: Pres., Jon Alander; Dir., William Brown; Treas., Ray Fair; Dir. Design, Sally Hill; Mgr., Karen Lenahan.
Personnel Profile: Full-Time Paid 8; Part-Time Paid 45; Interns 2.
Governing Authority: nonprofit organization. Tax-exempt: 501(c)(3).
Experimental Learning Workshop & Museum.
Collections: period arms; photographs; maps; history of manufacturing & the effect of technology on American society; Whitney armory firearms; A.C. Gilbert toys & artifacts. Historic Building: 1816 barn.
Research Fields: history of education in non scholastic subjects.
Activities: tours; lectures; workshops; organized education programs for children; experimental learning; wood working; temporary & permanent exhibitions.
Publications: brochure; catalog, Windows on the Works: Industry on the Whitney site: 1798-1976.
Hours & Admission Prices: Memorial Day to Labor Day daily 11-4; Sept.-May Wed.-Fri. & Sun. 12-5, Sat. 10-3. No charge; donations accepted. Closed Easter; Christmas. ♿
Attendance: 48,000 (estimated)
Membership: Family $45.

HAMDEN HISTORICAL SOCIETY, INC., 105 Mt. Carmel Ave., Hamden, CT 06518. Mailing Address: P.O. Box 5512, Hamden, CT 06518-0512. Tel.: 203-288-0017.
Founded: 1928.
Congressional District: 3
Key Personnel: Museum Shop Mgr., Lois Casey.
Governing Authority: society. Tax-exempt: 501(c)(3).
History Museum: housed in 1792 Jonathan Dickerman House.
Collections: herbarium; late 18th century period furnishings & artifacts; 1800 Dickerman Talmade Cider Mill/Barn.
Research Fields: local history, structure & homes in Hamden.
Facilities: collection of history books; land deeds; photographs available for use by the public.
Activities: guided tours; lectures; films; permanent & temporary exhibitions.
Publications: Hamden: Our Architectural Heritage; Images of America: Hamden.
Hours & Admission Prices: July-Aug. Sat.-Sun. 1-4. No charge; donations accepted.
Attendance: 400 (estimated)
Membership: Individual $15; Family $25; Life $250.

Hartford

CRRA TRASH MUSEUM, 211 Murphy Rd., Hartford, CT 06114-2100. Tel.: 860-757-7765. Fax: 860-278-8471.
Web Site: www.crra.org/pages/Trash_Museum.htm
Trash Museum.
Collections: waste management solutions; recycling; early disposal methods; mural.
Facilities: 6,500 sq. ft. exhibit space. Museum-related items for sale.
Activities: view the Container Processing Facility.
Hours & Admission Prices: July-Aug. Tues. 10-2, Wed.-Fri. 10-4; Sept.-June Wed.-Fri. 12-4. No charge. Closed New Year's Day; Good Friday; Independence Day; Thanksgiving & day after; Christmas Day & day after. ♿

CONNECTICUT HISTORICAL SOCIETY, 1 Elizabeth St., Hartford, CT 06105-2292. Tel.: 860-236-5621. Fax: 860-236-2664.
E-mail: ask_us@chs.org
Web Site: www.chs.org
Founded: 1825.
Congressional District: 1
Key Personnel: Exec. Dir., Kate Steinway; Pres., James C. Williams; Florence S. Marcy Crofut Dir. Collections, Dr. Susan P. Schoelwer; Dir. Public Programs, Andrea Rapacz; Dir. Collections Access, Richard Malley; Dir. Admin., Kevin Hughes; Dir. Education, Rebecca Furer.
Personnel Profile: Full-Time Paid 28; Part-Time Paid 8; Part-Time Volunteers 300; Interns 10.
Governing Authority: Tax-exempt: 501(c)(3).
Historical Society Museum & Library.
Collections: 33,000 artifacts including: 17th-18th century Connecticut furniture & decorative arts; painting & miniatures; 18th to early 19th-century American tavern signs; sculpture; clocks & clock tools; silver, gold & jewelry; glass & ceramics; metalware including 20th-century chromium household artifacts; industrial artifacts; costumes; textiles; 230,000 graphics including drawings, watercolors & pastels; lithographs by the Kelloggs of Hartford; 20th-century prints; 1,200 maps; 4,000 broadsides; 17th-20th century manuscripts.
Research Fields: Connecticut & New England history; genealogy; material culture; decorative arts; graphic arts; industry & technology; women's history; domestic life; Civil War.
Facilities: research library focusing on Connecticut & New England history & genealogy; print & photograph study room; hands-on activity room; meeting rooms; auditorium.
Activities: interactive exhibitions; educational outreach programs & curriculum materials; family programs; lectures & workshops; guided tours; gallery talks.
Publications: quarterly newsletter; exhibition catalogs.
Hours & Admission Prices: Exhibition Galleries: Tues.-Sat. 12-5; groups by appointment. Library Reading Room: Tues.-Sat. 10-5. Photograph Study Room: Mon.-Fri. 1-5 by appointment. Adults $6, senior citizens & students $3; discount to AAM members; children 6 & under, members & first Sat. of each month 9-1 no charge. Closed New Year's Day; Easter; Independence Day; Thanksgiving Day; Christmas. ♿
Attendance: 60,000 (estimated)
Membership: Individual $30; Family & Household $45; Sustaining $150; Benefactor $300; Sponsor $500; Presidents' Circle $1,000.

CONNECTICUT LANDMARKS, 255 Main St., 4th Fl., Hartford, CT 06106-1821. Tel.: 860-247-8996. Fax: 860-249-4907.
E-mail: info@ctlandmarks.org
Web Site: www.ctlandmarks.org
Formerly: The Antiquarian and Landmarks Society, Inc.
Founded: 1936.
Congressional District: 1
Key Personnel: Exec. Dir., Sheryl N. Hack; Exec. Sec. & Office Mgr., Tina Daly; Mktg. & Devel. Administrative Asst., Jamie-Lynn Fontaine; Cur., Beverly Lucas; Property Mgr., Joseph Pukas; Education Asst., Cynthia Riccio; Dir. Communications & Mktg., Rochelle Simon.
Personnel Profile: Full-Time Paid 6; Part-Time Paid 2; Part-Time Volunteers 10.
Governing Authority: society. Parent Institution: The Antiquarian & Landmarks Society, Inc. Branch Museums: 1678 Joshua Hempsted House, New London, CT; 1854 Isham-Terry House, Hartford, CT; 1720 Buttolph-Williams House, Wethersfield, CT; 1761 & 1794 Phelps-Hatheway House, Suffield, CT; 1776 Nathan Hale Homestead, Coventry, CT; 1816 Amasa Day House, Moodus, CT; 1759 Nathaniel Hempsted House, New London, CT; 1782 Butler-McCook House & Garden, Hartford, CT; Bellamy-Ferriday House & Garden, Bethlehem, CT. Tax-exempt: 501(c)(3).
Historic Houses & Historic Site concerned with Connecticut's Social History.

Collections: decorative arts.
Research Fields: architecture & furnishings; state history.
Activities: guided tours; lectures; workshops; living history programs; bus tours; formally organized education programs for students; docent program; permanent exhibitions.
Publications: quarterly newsletter.
Hours & Admission Prices: Call or see website for hours. Adults $7, students, teachers & seniors $6, children 6-18 $4; discounts to groups of 10 or more, New England Museum Assoc. & AAM members; members & children under 6 no charge.
Attendance: 20,000 (estimated)
Membership: Individual $40; Family $55; Contributing $125; Preservation $250; Landmark $500; George Dudley Seymour Circle $1,000.

* **HARRIET BEECHER STOWE CENTER, (M),** 77 Forest St., Hartford, CT 06105-3296. Tel.: 860-522-9258. Fax: 860-522-9259.
E-mail: info@stowecenter.org
Web Site: www.harrietbeecherstowecenter.org
Founded: 1941.
Congressional District: 1
Key Personnel: Exec. Dir. & C.E.O., Katherine Kane; Chm., Christiana N. Gianopulos; Collections Mgr., Elizabeth Giard; Mgr. Education & Visitor Svcs., Shannon Burke; Visitor Center Coord., Kathleen Rounds; Dir. Devel., Andrea Spak; Dir. Mktg., Mary Ellen White; Office Mgr., Carol Ann Stephenson.
Personnel Profile: Full-Time Paid 8; Part-Time Paid 20.
Governing Authority: nonprofit foundation. Tax-exempt: 501(c)(3).
Historic Buildings: housed in the home of activist author Harriet Beecher Stowe; located on Nook Farm, the 19th-century neighborhood where Mark Twain, Isabella Beecher Hooker & William H. Gillette also resided.
Collections: 180,000 manuscripts; 5,000 photographs; 7,000 broadsides, posters, prints & drawings; 12,000 books; 4,000 pamphlets; 100 scrapbooks related to decorative art, memorabilia and art work of & by Stowe & extended Beecher family; artifacts relating to abolition, suffrage, architecture, African-Americans & women; gardens. Historic Houses: 1871 Stowe House; 1884 Katharine Seymour Day House; 1873 Carriage House.
Major Exhibits: Uncle Tom's Cabin: A Moral Battle Cry for Freedom, 11/09-12/10; Reforming the Season, 12/09-1/10.
Research Fields: abolition; slavery; African American history; suffrage movement; 19th-century domestic life; architecture; decorative arts; Nook Farm residents; 19th & early 20th-century theater; genealogy.
Facilities: 12,000-vol. library; 4,000 pamphlets & 180,000 manuscript items with emphasis on 19th-century architecture, decorative arts, history & literature; Victorian gardens; visitor center. Museum-related items for sale.
Activities: Programs using Harriet Beecher Stowe's life and impact to inspire people to work for positive change. Guided tours, lectures, community activities, programs to preserve & interpret Harriet Beecher Stowe's home & the Stowe Center's collections.
Publications: members monthly e-newsletter; Victorian Blossoms; Harriet Beecher Stowe Hartford Home; Unfolding History; Harriet Beecher Stowe in Europe; Nook Farm; Portraits of a Nineteenth Century Family; Harriet Beecher Stowe Reader; The Minister's Wooing; Poganuc People; American Woman's Home.
Hours & Admission Prices: June-Sept. Tues.-Sat. 9:30-4:30, Sun. 12-4:30; Oct.-May Wed.-Sat. 9:30-4:30, Sun. 12-4:30. Adult 17-64 $9, seniors 65 & over $8, children 5-16 & students $6; discounts to groups & AAM members; members no charge. Closed New Year's Day; Easter; Independence Day; Thanksgiving; Christmas Eve & Day.
Attendance: 22,785 (accurate)
Membership: Student $15; Individual $25; Household $45; International $50; Sustaining $100; Library $175; Associate $250; Benefactor $500 & up; HBS Society $1,000 & up.

* **THE MARK TWAIN HOUSE & MUSEUM,** 351 Farmington Ave., Hartford, CT 06105-4401. Tel.: 860-247-0998. Fax: 860-278-8148.
E-mail: info@marktwainhouse.org
Web Site: www.marktwainhouse.org
Founded: 1929.
Congressional District: 1
Key Personnel: Exec. Dir., Jeffrey Nichols; Pres. (V), Dede D. DeRosa; Supvr. Buildings & Grounds, William Perez; Beatrice Fox Averbach Chief Cur., Patti Philippon.
Personnel Profile: Full-Time Paid 17; Part-Time Paid 39; Part-Time Volunteers 8; Interns 1.
Governing Authority: nonprofit. Tax-exempt: 501(c)(3).
Historic Building: Mark Twain House, author's home 1874-1891 designed by Edward Tuckerman Potter; Alfred M. Thorp & decorated by Louis C. Tiffany and Associated Artists in 1881.
Collections: memorabilia, photographs, furniture of Mark Twain; period house furnishings; 19th-century American paintings, prints & drawings; decorative arts; Louis C. Tiffany collection of furniture & art glass; Candace Wheeler collection of fabrics & memorabilia; study samples of 19th-century wallpaper & textiles; rare books & manuscripts.
Research Fields: Mark Twain; Louis C. Tiffany; architecture; decorative arts, history and literature from 1850-1900.
Facilities: library of 4,000 books & 3,000 manuscript items; autographed copies of first editions; inscribed copies; foreign translations; documents & photographic file on Mark Twain, his family & 19th century. Museum-related items for sale.
Activities: guided tours; lectures; symposia; family programs; musical performances; dramatic readings.
Publications: quarterly newsletter; exhibition catalogues.
Hours & Admission Prices: Jan.-March Wed.-Mon. 9:30-5:30; April-Dec. Mon.-Sat. 9:30-5:30, Sun. 12-5:30; group tours by appointment. Adults $14, seniors $12, children 6-16 $8; discounts to AAM members & groups of 10 or more; children under 6 & members no charge. Closed New Year's Day; Easter; Independence Day; Thanksgiving; Christmas Eve & Day. ♿
Attendance: 67,855 (accurate)
Membership: National $40; Individual $50; Household $75; Sustaining $150.

MUSEUM OF CONNECTICUT HISTORY, Connecticut State Library, 231 Capitol Ave., Hartford, CT 06106-1569. Tel.: 860-757-6535. Fax: 860-757-6533.
Web Site: www.museumofcthistory.org/
Founded: 1910.
Congressional District: 1
Key Personnel: Admin., Dean E. Nelson; Cur. Education, Patrick Smith; Cur. Collections, David J. Corrigan.
Personnel Profile: Full-Time Paid 3.
Governing Authority: state. Parent Institution: Connecticut State Library. Tax-exempt: 170(c).
History Museum.
Collections: Connecticut history; governors' portraits; industrial; military; political; numismatic; general history.
Research Fields: Connecticut & American history.
Facilities: 500,000-vol. library containing 2,000,000 manuscripts on history, law & genealogy; archives dating from 1636; books available for inter-library loan; manuscripts available on premises; reading room.
Activities: permanent & temporary exhibitions.
Hours & Admission Prices: Mon.-Fri. 9-4, Sat. 9-3. No charge. Closed state holidays. ♿
Attendance: 25,000 (accurate)

OLD STATE HOUSE, 800 Main St., Hartford, CT 06103-2301. Tel.: 860-522-6766. Fax: 860-522-2812.
E-mail: ctoldstatehouse@cga.ct.gov
Web Site: www.ctosh.org
Founded: 1975.
Congressional District: 1
Key Personnel: Dir. Educational & Programming, Sally Whipple; Mgr. Programming & Curriculum, Rebecca Taber-Conover.
Personnel Profile: Full-Time Paid 10; Part-Time Paid 10.
Governing Authority: state legislature. Parent Institution: Connecticut General Assembly, Joint Committee on Legislative Management. Tax-exempt.
Historic Federal Building: built in 1796, designed by Charles Bulfinch; site of first meeting house, George Washington's meeting with Comte de Rochambeau and the French troops; first Amistad Trial.
Collections: Connecticut history from 1636 to present; portrait of George Washington by Gilbert Stuart; 18th-20th century furnishings & paintings; Joseph Steward's Museum of Curiosities; American Puppet Theater.
Research Fields: Old State House history; Hartford history; Connecticut state government history; civics.
Facilities: 6,000 sq. ft. exhibit space; educational center; rental facilities; theater. Museum-related items for sale.
Activities: guided tours; formally organized educational programs; historical reenactments; permanent & temporary exhibitions; audio tours; hands-on activities; media experiences.
Publications: newsletters.
Hours & Admission Prices: Tues.-Sat. 10-5. Guided Tours: adults $6, senior citizens, students & children 6-17 $3; children 5 & under no charge. Closed major holidays. ♿
Attendance: 32,368 (accurate)

STATE CAPITOL, HARTFORD, CONN., 210 Capitol Ave., Hartford, CT 06106-1535. Tel.: 860-240-0222. Fax: 860-240-8627.
E-mail: capitol.tours@cga.ct.gov
Web Site: www.cga.ct.gov/capitoltours
Founded: 1878.
Congressional District: 1

Key Personnel: Dir., Kimberly Fabrizio; Asst. Dir., Susan Lakin.
Personnel Profile: Full-Time Paid 2; Part-Time Paid 2; Part-Time Volunteers 21; Interns 1.
Governing Authority: Parent Institution: League of Women Voters of Connecticut Education Fund. Tax-exempt.
Historic Building.
Collections: Hall of Flags; Charter Oak Chair; figureheads; models; Israel Putnam's tombstone; furniture.
Activities: guided tours; educational tours.
Publications: leaflet, This Is Your General Assembly; How a Bill Becomes A Law; Directory of Connecticut's Federal & State Elected Officials; Connecticut: A Guide to State Government; self-guided tour pamphlets.
Hours & Admission Prices: One-hour Tours: April-June & Sept.-Oct. Mon.-Fri. 9:15, 10:15, 11:15, 12:15 & 1:15, Sat. 10:15, 11:15, 12:15, 1:15 & 2:15; July-Aug. Mon.-Fri. 9:15, 10:15, 11:15, 12:15, 1:15 & 2:15; Sat. 10:15, 11:15, 12:15, 1:15 & 2:15. Nov.-March Mon.-Fri. 9:15, 10:15, 11:15, 12:15 & 1:15. No charge; donations accepted. Closed state & national holidays and holiday weekends. ♿
Attendance: 30,228 (accurate)

* **WADSWORTH ATHENEUM MUSEUM OF ART, (M),** 600 Main St., Hartford, CT 06103-2990. Tel.: 860-278-2670. Fax: 860-527-0803.
E-mail: info@wadsworthatheneum.org
Web Site: www.wadsworthatheneum.org
Formerly: Wadsworth Atheneum
Founded: 1842.
Congressional District: 1
Key Personnel: Dir., Susan Lubowsky Talbott; Dir. Institutional Advancement, Jeffrey Wolfman; Dir. Finance, Judy Mihalko; Georgette Averbach Koopman Dir. Education, Johanna Plummer; Dir. Facility, Alan Barton; Chief Cur. & Cur. Krieble American Painting & Sculpture, Elizabeth Mankin Kornhauser; Cur. Susan H. Hilles European Art, Eric M. Zafran; Senior Cur. and Charles C. & Eleanor Lamont Cunningham Cur. European Decorative Arts, Linda H. Roth; Coord. Exhibitions, Adria Patterson; Head Museum Design, Cecil Adams; Collection Imaging Mgr., Allen Phillips; Visitors Svcs. Mgr., Susan Carey; Registrar, Mary Schroeder; Sr. Assoc. Registrar, Edd Russo; Assoc. Registrar, Mary Busick; Chief Paintings Conservator, Stephen Kornhauser; William G. DeLana Archivist & Cur., Austin House, Eugene R. Gaddis; Assoc. Conservator, Zen Gansziniec; Librarian & Cur. Special Book Collection, John Teahan; Senior Conservator, Ulrich Birkmaier; Cur. Film & Theater, Deborah Gaudet; Dir. Public Rels. & Mktg., Kimberly Reynolds; Museum Shop Mgr., Stacey Stachow; Museum Shop Asst. Mgr., Jane Gallagher; Membership & Special Events Mgr., Vivian Nabeta; Exec. Dir., The Amistad Center for Art & Culture, Olivia White; Dir. Human Resources, Shawn Lewinson.
Personnel Profile: Full-Time Paid 87; Part-Time Paid 33; Part-Time Volunteers 353; Interns 20.
Governing Authority: nonprofit organization. Branch Museum: Austin House, 130 Scarborough St., Hartford, CT. Tax-exempt: 170(b)(1)(A).
Art Museum.
Collections: classical bronzes; Renaissance & Baroque art; Spanish, Italian & 17th-century Dutch & northern European art; Wallace Nutting collection of American furniture; two fully restored American period rooms removed from their original homes; 18th-century French & German porcelains; 19th century American & European art; 20th-century art; American paintings, sculpture, drawings & decorative arts; French & American Impressionist paintings; African-American art; European & American costumes & textiles; English & American silver; contemporary paintings, sculpture; Sol LeWitt wall drawings; Matrix series.
Research Fields: paintings; sculpture; decorative arts; costumes; textiles; African-American & contemporary art.
Facilities: Auerbach Library: 32,000-vols. on art history, museology & art education; archives; 287-seat theater; cafe. Museum publications for sale.
Activities: lectures; films; gallery talks; guided group tours for students & adults; teachers workshops; children's studio programs & summer art camp; docent program; college internship program; costume & textile society; decorative arts council; permanent, temporary & traveling exhibitions. Women's Committee Organizes: Festival of Trees & Traditions; Fine Art & Flowers.
Publications: members quarterly; artist sheets, MATRIX; collection catalogs; exhibition catalogs; annual report; gallery & special exhibition guides.
Hours & Admission Prices: Museum: Tues.-Fri. 11-5, Sat.-Sun. 10-5, first Thurs. of month 11-8. Adults $10, senior citizens $8, students 13 to college $5; discounts first Thurs. of month & AAM members; children 12 & under and members no charge. Library: Wed.-Thurs. 11-5. Closed New Year's Day; Independence Day; Thanksgiving; Christmas. ♿
Attendance: 117,500 (accurate)
Membership: Individual $45; Amistad & Atheneum Individual $55; Household $60; Amistad & Atheneum Household $70; Supporting $120; Reciprocal $170; Patron $370; Premier Levels $1,000-$25,000 & up.

WIDENER GALLERY, AUSTIN ARTS CENTER, TRINITY COLLEGE, 300 Summit St., Hartford, CT 06106-3100. Tel.: 860-297-5232 & 2199. Fax: 860-297-5349.
E-mail: felice.caivano@mail.trincoll.edu
Web Site: www.trincoll.edu/artsattrinity
Founded: 1964.
Congressional District: 1
Key Personnel: Dir. Studio Arts & Chm. Fine Arts Dept., Patricia Tillman; Cur., Felice Caivano.
Governing Authority: college. Tax-exempt: 170(b)(1)(A).
College Gallery.
Collections: teaching collections; The Samuel H. Kress Collection.
Facilities: theatre.
Activities: education programs for college students affiliated with Trinity college & the public.
Hours & Admission Prices: Sun.-Fri. 1-6. No charge. Closed academic holidays & recesses.

Ivoryton

MUSEUM OF FIFE AND DRUM, 63 N. Main St., Ivoryton, CT 06442-0277. Mailing Address: P.O. Box 277, Ivoryton, CT 06442-0277. Tel.: 860-767-2237. Fax: 860-767-9765.
E-mail: companyhq@companyoffifeanddrum.org
Web Site: www.companyoffifeanddrum.org
Founded: 1965.
Congressional District: 2
Key Personnel: Pres. (V), Sylvia Hooghkirk; Treas., Jack Doyle; Cur. & Archivist, Ed Olsen; Devel. Public Rels., Randy Stack; Education, George Carteris; Security, Joseph Franklin.
Personnel Profile: Full-Time Volunteers 10; Part-Time Volunteers 15.
Governing Authority: private; nonprofit organization. Parent Institution: The Company of Fifers & Drummers. Tax-exempt: 501(c)(3).
Musical Instruments Museum.
Collections: instruments; photographs; uniforms; documents; drums dating back to American Revolution; archives.
Research Fields: history & development of fifing & drumming.
Facilities: library available only to scholars & historians; 250-seat auditorium. Museum-related items for sale.
Activities: guided tours; formal education programs for undergraduate or graduate college students as requested; company & committee meetings; lectures as requested. Annual Events: summer concerts; Jaybird (Old-Timers) Day.
Publications: quarterly magazine, The Ancient Times.
Hours & Admission Prices: June 30-Labor Day Sat.-Sun. 1-5 by appointment only. Adults $3, youth 13-17 & seniors 60 and over $2; children 12 & under no charge.
Attendance: 1,150 (estimated)
Membership: Individual $15; Drum Corps. $60; Individual Life & Patron Drum Corps. $1,000.

Kensington

NEW BRITAIN YOUTH MUSEUM AT HUNGERFORD PARK, 191 Farmington Ave., Kensington, CT 06037-1220. Tel.: 860-827-9064. Fax: 860-827-1266.
E-mail: marketing@newbritainyouthmuseum.org
Web Site: newbritainyouthmuseum.org
Founded: 1984.
Congressional District: 6
Key Personnel: Dir., Ann F. Peabody; Chm. (V), Robert Ramsey.
Personnel Profile: Full-Time Paid 6; Part-Time Paid 5; Part-Time Volunteers 20; Interns 4.
Governing Authority: nonprofit organization. Parent Organization: New Britain Institute. Branch Museum: New Britain Youth Museum. Tax-exempt: 501(c)(3).
Children's Museum & Nature Center.
Collections: mounted specimens; geological & agricultural tools; farm & exotic animals; pets; local history; natural history & environmental issues.
Facilities: nature & conservation center; classroom; kitchen workshop; nature trails. Items related to natural science for sale.
Activities: guided tours; lectures; films; study clubs; organized education programs for children; docent program; participatory & temporary exhibitions.
Publications: brochures, Visitors Guide; Trail Guide; quarterly newsletter, Ramblings.
Hours & Admission Prices: Tues.-Sat. 10-4:30. Adults $4, senior $3, children $2; discounts to AAM members; members & children under 2 no charge. Closed major holidays. ♿
Attendance: 23,732 (accurate)

Membership: Individual $25; Family $40; Supporting $50; Sustaining $100; Patron $250.

Kent

CONNECTICUT ANTIQUE MACHINERY ASSOCIATION MUSEUM, 31 Kent-Cornwall Rd., Kent, CT 06757. Tel.: 860-927-0050.
History Museum.
Collections: industrial & agricultural heritage & history; machinery.
Activities: special events.
Hours & Admission Prices: May-Oct. Wed.-Sun. 10-4; other times by appointment. Adults $3; children under 12 no charge.

CONNECTICUT COMMISSION ON CULTURE & TOURISM - SLOANE-STANLEY MUSEUM, 31 Kent Cornwall Rd., Rte. 7, Kent, CT 06757. Mailing Address: P.O. Box 917, Kent, CT 06757-0917. Tel.: 860-927-3849 (Museum) & 256-2760 (Hartford Office). Fax: 860-256-2811 (Hartford) & 927-2152 (Museum).
E-mail: sloanestanley.museum@ct.gov
Web Site: www.cultureandtourism.org
Formerly: Sloane-Stanley Museum and Kent Furnace
Founded: 1969.
Congressional District: 6
Key Personnel: Museum Dir., Karin Peterson.
Personnel Profile: Part-Time Paid 2.
Governing Authority: state. Parent Institution: Connecticut Commission on Culture & Tourism, Historic Preservation & Museum Division, One Constitution Plaza, 2nd Fl., Hartford, CT 06103. Tax-exempt: 170(c)(1).
Early American Tools & Implements Museum: located on the site of the ruins of Kent Iron Furnace.
Collections: early American tools; diorama of early iron industry at Kent Furnace; paintings by Eric Sloane; recreation of Sloane's art studio from his Connecticut home.
Research Fields: early American tools & implements; early iron industry.
Activities: lectures; permanent exhibitions.
Publications: books by Eric Sloane relating to tools, implements & carpentry, and signed & numbered prints for sale.
Hours & Admission Prices: May -Oct. Sun. 10-4. Adults $8, senior citizens 60 & over $6, students 6-17 $5; special rates for school groups; children 5 & under no charge.
Attendance: 5,000 (accurate)

THE KENT ART ASSOCIATION, 21 S. Main St., Kent, CT 06757. Mailing Address: P.O. Box 202, Kent, CT 06757-0202. Tel.: 860-927-3989. Fax: 860-927-4218.
E-mail: info@kentart.org
Web Site: www.kentart.org
Founded: 1923.
Key Personnel: Pres. (V), Carolyn Fisher; Exec. Dir., Davia Kennedy Fink.
Governing Authority: private; nonprofit organization.
Art Museum.
Collections: paintings; drawings; sculpture.
Activities: rental gallery. Annual Events: spring show; member's show; President's show; fall show; student art show; charity events; Elected artist exhibition; Catalogs with each show .
Publications: quarterly newsletter; quarterly catalogs; show catalogs.
Hours & Admission Prices: During Shows & Holidays: Thurs.-Sun. 1-5. No charge; donations accepted.
Attendance: 5,000 (estimated)
Membership: Associate $30; Sustaining $40; Patron $65; Family $80; Life $300.

Lakeville

SALISBURY CANNON MUSEUM, 15 Millerton Rd., Lakeville, CT 06039-1401. Mailing Address: P.O. Box 553, Salisbury, CT 06068-0553. Tel.: 860-435-0566.
E-mail: lbucceri@yahoo.com
Web Site: www.salisburycannonmuseum.org
Key Personnel: Cur., Lou Bucceri.
Governing Authority: nonprofit organization. Parent Institution: Salisbury Association, Inc.
History Museum.
Collections: cannon-making; musket; powder horn; Revolutionary War uniforms; cannonballs; military weapons.
Activities: educational programs.
Hours & Admission Prices: Temporarily closed.

Lebanon

LEBANON HISTORICAL SOCIETY, 856 Trumbull Hwy., Lebanon, CT 06249-1546. Mailing Address: P.O. Box 151, Lebanon, CT 06249. Tel.: 860-642-6579.
Key Personnel: Dir., Donna K. Baron.
Personnel Profile: Part-Time Paid 3.
Governing Authority: Tax-exempt.
Historical Society Museum.
Collections: local history & culture; photographs; period furnishings.
Research Fields: history of Lebanon, CT; eastern CT; CT & American Revolution; genealogy.
Facilities: Museum-related items for sale.
Activities: educational programs.
Hours & Admission Prices: Wed.-Sat. 12-4. No charge; donations accepted. ♿

Litchfield

* **LITCHFIELD HISTORICAL SOCIETY AND MUSEUM, (M),** 7 South St., On-the-Green, Litchfield, CT 06759. Mailing Address: P.O. Box 385, Litchfield, CT 06759-0385. Tel.: 860-567-4501. Fax: 860-567-3565.
E-mail: cfields@litchfieldhistoricalsociety.org
Web Site: www.litchfieldhistoricalsociety.org
Founded: 1856.
Congressional District: 6
Key Personnel: Dir., Catherine Keene Fields; Cur., Julie Frey; Librarian & Archivist, Linda Hocking; Museum Shop Mgr., Kate Zullo; Cur. Education, Linda Loveday.
Personnel Profile: Full-Time Paid 5; Part-Time Paid 6; Part-Time Volunteers 60; Interns 2.
Governing Authority: society. Tax-exempt: 501(c)(3).
Historical Society Museum & Historic House: Tapping Reeve House & Law School, America's first law school.
Collections: documents & manuscripts; furniture; textiles; decorative arts; paintings; artifacts of daily life. Historic Buildings: 1774 Tapping Reeve House; 1784 Litchfield Law School.
Research Fields: local history; genealogy.
Facilities: 10,000-vol. library of books, 40,000 manuscripts available for researchers & students; four galleries of changing exhibits. Museum-related items for sale.
Activities: educational program; guided tours; walking tours; lecture series; curriculum projects; outreach programs; workshops; changing exhibitions.
Publications: quarterly newsletter, Discover Litchfield; children's workbook; catalogs, Tho Inanimate They Speak: Ralph Earl Paintings in the Collection of the LHS; To Ornament Their Minds: Sarah Pierce's Litchfield Female Academy, 1792-1833.
Hours & Admission Prices: Museum & Tapping Reeve House: mid-April to Nov. Tues.-Sat. 11-5, Sun. 1-5. Adults $5, senior citizens & students $3 (combined admission to Reeve House, Law School & Museum); AAM & museum members no charge. ♿
Attendance: 13,000 (estimated)
Membership: Individual $25; Family $40; Contributing $100; Donor $250; Benefactor $500; Tapping Reeve Society $1,000.

WHITE MEMORIAL CONSERVATION CENTER, INC., 80 Whitehall Rd., Litchfield, CT 06759-3914. Mailing Address: P.O. Box 368, Litchfield, CT 06759-0368. Tel.: 860-567-0857. Fax: 860-567-2611.
E-mail: info@whitememorialcc.org
Web Site: whitememorialcc.org
Founded: 1964.
Congressional District: 6
Key Personnel: Exec. Dir., Keith R. Cudworth; Dir. Administration & Devel., Gerri Griswold; Pres., Arthur Hill Diedrick; Dir. Education, Jeffrey Greenwood; Dir. Research, James Fischer; Museum Shop Mgr., Lois Melaragno.
Personnel Profile: Full-Time Paid 5; Part-Time Paid 2; Part-Time Volunteers 75.
Governing Authority: nonprofit organization. Affiliated with White Memorial Foundation. Tax-exempt: 501(c)(3).
Natural History Museum: located on 4,000-acre preserve of the White Memorial Foundation.
Collections: live animals; native fauna & flora; rocks & minerals; natural history interpretive exhibits; dioramas & life-like exhibits.
Research Fields: wildlife censusing & banding of birds; forestry.
Facilities: nature & conservation center; classroom; 200-seat auditorium; nature trails; food service facility. Books & educational aids related to natural history for sale.
Activities: guided tours; lectures; films; formally organized educational programs; permanent & changing exhibitions; self-guiding trails.
Publications: quarterly newsletter.
Hours & Admission Prices: Museum: Tues.-Sat. 9-5, Sun. 12-5. Suggested

Donations: adults $5, children $2.50. Guided Tours up to 25 people $75. Closed major holidays. ♿
Attendance: 20,100 (accurate)
Membership: Individual $30; Family $45.

Madison

MADISON HISTORICAL SOCIETY, Lee Academy, 14 Meeting House Lane, Madison, CT 06443. Mailing Address: P.O. Box 17, Madison, CT 06443-0017. Tel.: 203-245-4567.
E-mail: contact@madisoncthistorical.org
Web Site: www.madisonhistorical.org
Founded: 1917.
Congressional District: 3
Key Personnel: Pres. (V), Lynn Friedman.
Personnel Profile: Part-Time Paid 3; Part-Time Volunteers 25.
Governing Authority: society. Branch Museum: The Lee Academy, 14 Meeting House Ln., Madison, CT 06443. Tax-exempt: 501(c)(3).
History Museum: housed in c.1785 Allis-Bushnell House.
Collections: costumes; dolls; furniture; toys; farming, carpentry, housekeeping, spinning & weaving tools & equipment; manuscripts; ship construction half models; shipbuilding; shoemaking; textiles.
Research Fields: Madison history.
Facilities: 650-vol. library of books on history, genealogy, theology; pamphlets; maps available during regular hours; reading room.
Activities: guided tours; lectures; films; education programs for children; permanent & temporary exhibits.
Publications: books, Madison's Heritage; Daniel Hand of Madison, Connecticut, 1801-1891; Madison: Three Hundred Years by the Sea; pamphlet, Madison's Unique Contribution to Summer Theatre in America.
Hours & Admission Prices: June-Aug. Sat. 11-4; Winter by appointment. No charge; donations accepted.
Attendance: 500 (estimated)
Membership: Junior (under 18) $3; Individual $25; Couple $35; Contributing $40-$99; Business $75; Sustaining $100 & up; Life $300.

Manchester

CHENEY HOMESTEAD, 106 Hartford Rd., Manchester, CT 06040-5921. Tel.: 860-643-5588; 674-9983.
E-mail: ManchesterHistory@Juno.com
Web Site: www.manchesterhistory.org
Founded: 1969.
Congressional District: 1
Key Personnel: C.E.O., David Smith; Pres. (V), John Dormer.
Personnel Profile: Full-Time Paid 1; Part-Time Volunteers 6.
Governing Authority: nonprofit. Parent Institution: Manchester Historical Society, Inc. Tel: 860-647-9983. Tax-exempt.
Historic House Museum.
Collections: Manchester history. Historic House: 1785 Cheney homestead; replica 1751 Keeney Schoolhouse.
Research Fields: Manchester history.
Activities: guided tours; permanent & temporary exhibitions.
Hours & Admission Prices: By appointment. Adults $2; children 12 & under accompanied by adult and members no charge. Closed legal holidays.
Attendance: 1,200 (accurate)

LUTZ CHILDREN'S MUSEUM, 247 S. Main St., Manchester, CT 06040-6561. Tel.: 860-643-0949.
E-mail: reckert@lutzmuseum.org
Web Site: www.lutzmuseum.org
Founded: 1953.
Congressional District: 1
Key Personnel: Dir. & C.E.O., Bob Eckert; Pres. (V), Kristen Addabbo; Operations Dir., Stephanie Radowitz; Arts Cur., Laura Diller; Volunteer Coord., Joanna Snyder; Visitor Svcs., Greta Vrissis.
Personnel Profile: Full-Time Paid 8; Full-Time Volunteers 2; Part-Time Paid 4; Part-Time Volunteers 65; Interns 4.
Governing Authority: nonprofit organization. Tax-exempt: 501(c)(3).
Children's Museum.
Collections: live animals; history; natural history; ethnology; art.
Research Fields: child participation; educational teaching aids & kits.
Facilities: 53-acre nature center; classrooms; outdoor playscape. Museum-related gifts for sale.
Activities: guided tours; lectures; formally organized education programs for children; field trips; participatory exhibits; craft demonstrations; school loan service; family programs; parent-child workshops, classes, resource lessons; live animals.
Publications: membership newsletter; quarterly teacher newsletter; educational services catalogue.
Hours & Admission Prices: Tues.-Fri. 9-5, Sat.-Sun. 12-5; Nature Trails dawn-dusk. Admission $5; members no charge. Closed some holidays. ♿
Attendance: 30,000 (estimated)
Membership: Child & Senior $10; Adult $15; Family $40.

OLD MANCHESTER MUSEUM, (M), 126 Cedar St., Manchester, CT 06040-5839. Mailing Address: Manchester Historical Society, 175 Pine St., Manchester, CT 06040. Tel.: 860-647-9983.
E-mail: manchesterhistory@juno.com
Web Site: www.manchesterhistory.org
Founded: 1965.
Key Personnel: Pres., John A. Dormer.
Personnel Profile: Full-Time Volunteers 2; Part-Time Paid 1; Part-Time Volunteers 20; Interns 1.
Governing Authority: Parent Institution: Manchester Historical Society. Tax-exempt.
History Museum: housed in c.1859 school house.
Collections: Manchester history.
Research Fields: Manchester history; genealogy; local history.
Facilities: Museum-related items for sale.
Activities: guided tours; permanent & temporary exhibitions.
Publications: quarterly newsletter, The Courier.
Hours & Admission Prices: Sat. 10-4, Sun. 1-4; other times by appointment. Adults $2; discounts to AAM members; members no charge. Closed holidays. ♿
Attendance: 1,500 (accurate)
Membership: Student $5; Individual $15; Family $25; Contributing Individual $45; Contributing Family $75; Corporate $200; Life Individual $250; Life Couple $400.

Mashantucket

MASHANTUCKET PEQUOT MUSEUM AND RESEARCH CENTER, (M), 110 Pequot Trail, Mashantucket, CT 06338-3180. Mailing Address: P.O. Box 3180, Mashantucket, CT 06338-3180. Tel.: 800-411-9671; 860-396-6945. Fax: 860-396-7013.
E-mail: bkingsland@mptn-nsn.gov
Web Site: www.pequotmuseum.org
Founded: 1998.
Congressional District: 2
Key Personnel: Exec. Dir., Kimberly Hatcher-White; Dir. Finance, Selma Ward; Cur., Steve Cook; Education, Trudie Richmond; Registrar, Meredith Vasta; Security, George Eleazor, Sr.; Museum Shop Mgr., Donna Johnson.
Personnel Profile: Full-Time Paid 32; Part-Time Paid 18; Part-Time Volunteers 15; Interns 12.
Governing Authority: nonprofit. Parent Institution: Mashantucket Pequot Tribal Nation (Tribal Council). Tax-exempt: 170(b)(1)(A).
Native American Museum.
Collections: personal artifacts; tribal history; area land history; archaeology; ethnographic. Historic House: c.1780 farmstead.
Major Exhibits: Through the Eyes of the Eagle: Illustrating Healthy Living for Children (T), 2/10-5/10; North by Northeast: Akwasasne, Mohawk, Tuscarora and Wabanak, Traditional Arts (T), 6/10-9/10; Native Works, Native Warriors (T), 10/10-12/10.
Research Fields: ethnohistory; material culture studies; archaeology; ethnobotany.
Facilities: 45,000-vol. library; 328-seat auditorium; 268-seat restaurant; archaeology & conservation labs; classrooms; 80,000 sq. ft. exhibit space; 7 theaters; observation tower. Museum-related items for sale.
Activities: interactive computer programs; concerts; dance recitals; films; formal education programs for children, University of Connecticut & Connecticut College students; guided tours; hobby workshops; lectures; theater; teacher seminars. Annual Events: Strawberry Festival; Gifts of the Land and Waters.
Publications: quarterly calendar of events, Native Visions.
Hours & Admission Prices: Wed.-Sat. 10-4; last admission 3pm. Adults $15, senior citizens $13, children 6-15 $10; discounts to AAM members & groups; members & children 5 and under no charge. Closed New Year's Eve & Day; Thanksgiving Eve & Day; Christmas Eve & Day. ♿
Attendance: 100,000 (estimated)
Membership: Individual & Educator $40; Military $48; Family & Dual $60; Contributing & Library $250; Supporting $500; Patron $1,000; Corporate $2,500-$25,000.

Meriden

MERIDEN HISTORICAL SOCIETY, INC., 1090 Hanover St., Morehouse Research Center, Meriden, CT 06451-6207. Mailing Address: P.O. Box 3005, Meriden, CT 06450-9305. Tel.: 203-639-1913.
E-mail: meridenhistoricalsociety@gmail.com
Web Site: www.meridenhistoricalsociety.org

Founded: 1893.
Congressional District: 5
Key Personnel: C.E.O. & Pres. (V), Lesley Solkoske; Treas., Kathy McMahon; Cur., Allen Weathers; Sec., Dorothy Heffernan.
Governing Authority: society. Tax-exempt: 990A(SF).
Local History Museum & Research Library: museum housed in 1760 Andrews Homestead; Research Library: 1090 Hanover Rd., South Meriden, CT 06451.
Collections: glass & china; history; industry; dolls; furniture; manuscripts; maps; books; items manufactured locally; schools; churches; wars; art; design; photographs; period silver; International Silver Co. historic silver collection & library.
Research Fields: Victorian silverplate, early local silver manufacturers.
Facilities: history library, with catalogs, maps, patents & original photographs.
Activities: special exhibits.
Publications: annual reports; quarterly newsletter.
Hours & Admission Prices: Research Center: Wed. 2-4; tours by appointment. No charge; donations accepted. Closed holidays.
Membership: Senior $10; Regular $15; Corporate $50; Life Senior $125; Life $250.

Middlebury

THE GOLDEN AGE OF TRUCKING MUSEUM, (M), 1101 Southford Rd., Middlebury, CT 06762-3212. Mailing Address: P.O. Box 1314, Middlebury, CT 06762-7314. Tel.: 203-577-2181. Fax: 203-577-2404.
Web Site: www.goldenagetruckmuseum.com
Founded: 1998.
Key Personnel: Dir. & Pres. (V), Kathleen Jones; Asst. Dir., Pamela Palmer; Chm. (V), John Dwyer; Treas., Robert Dionne.
Personnel Profile: Full-Time Paid 2; Part-Time Volunteers 25.
Governing Authority: private; nonprofit organization. Tax-exempt: 501(c)(3).
Trucking Museum.
Collections: restored trucks; period trucks.
Facilities: library; educational facilities; 32,000 sq. ft. exhibit space; 80-seat theater. Museum-related items for sale.
Activities: guided tours; lectures; loan exhibitions; arts festivals. Annual Events: Antique & Classic Truck Fest; fundraiser in February; Saturday Seminars: Jan., March, and April; Earth Day Celebration in April; Tuesday evening, cruise nights June-Aug; Truck Fest in September; Harvest Fest in October; Art Opening in November; Santa & Mrs. Claus in December.
Hours & Admission Prices: Tues.-Sat. 10-4, Sun. 12-4. Adults $8, senior citizens $7, students & children $5; discounts to groups; members no charge. Closed New Year's Eve & Day; Easter; Independence Day; Thanksgiving; Christmas Eve & Day. ♿
Attendance: 20,000 (estimated)
Membership: Senior $35; Individual $50; Senior Couple $75; Family $100; Corporate $500; Golden $5,000.

Middletown

DAVISON ART CENTER, WESLEYAN UNIVERSITY, 301 High St., Middletown, CT 06459-3232. Tel.: 860-685-2500. Fax: 860-685-2501.
Web Site: www.wesleyan.edu/dac
Founded: 1952.
Congressional District: 2
Key Personnel: Cur., Clare Rogan; Registrar Collections & Mgr. Museum Information Svcs., Robert Lancefield; Gallery Supvr., Lee Berman.
Personnel Profile: Full-Time Paid 2; Part-Time Paid 1.
Governing Authority: university. Parent Institution: Wesleyan University. Tax-exempt.
Art Museum: housed in c.1838-40 Alsop House, a pre-Civil War mansion.
Collections: prints from the mid-15th century to the present; photographs from the 1840s to the present; period wall decorations in Alsop House.
Research Fields: prints & photographs.
Facilities: 3,000-vol. library of art history & print reference available for use under university regulations; reading room; classrooms.
Activities: lectures; gallery talks.
Publications: exhibition catalogs; exhibition announcements.
Hours & Admission Prices: Sept.-May Tues.-Sun. 12-4. No charge; donations accepted. Closed holidays; academic vacations. ♿
Attendance: 3,000 (accurate)
Membership: Individual $30; Family $50; Sustaining $100; Donor $250; Patron $500; Life $1,000.

EZRA AND CECILE ZILKHA GALLERY, Center for the Arts, Wesleyan University, Middletown, CT 06459-0001. Mailing Address: Wesleyan University, 283 Washington Terr., Middletown, CT 06459-0001. Tel.: 860-685-2695. Fax: 860-685-2061.
E-mail: cparente@wesleyan.edu
Web Site: wesleyan.edu/cfa
Founded: 1973.
Congressional District: 2
Key Personnel: Dir., Pamela Tatge; Cur. Exhibitions, Nina Felshin.
Personnel Profile: Part-Time Paid 2.
Governing Authority: affiliated with Wesleyan University. Tax-exempt.
Art Gallery.
Collections: contemporary art.
Activities: lectures; gallery talks; video.
Publications: exhibition brochures & catalogs.
Hours & Admission Prices: Tues.-Sun. 12-4. No charge; donations accepted. Closed holidays; during academic recess. ♿
Attendance: 9,500 (accurate)

KIDCITY CHILDREN'S MUSEUM, 119 Washington St., Middletown, CT 06457-2817. Tel.: 860-347-0495.
E-mail: info@kidcitymuseum.com
Web Site: www.kidcitymuseum.com
Key Personnel: Exec. Dir., Jennifer Alexander
Children's Museum.
Collections: hands-on exhibits.
Activities: birthday parties.
Hours & Admission Prices: Sun.-Tues. 11-5, Wed.-Sat. 9-5. Admission $7; children under one no charge. ♿

MIDDLESEX COUNTY HISTORICAL SOCIETY, 151 Main St., Middletown, CT 06457-3423. Tel.: 860-346-0746. Fax: 860-346-0746.
E-mail: middlesexhistory@wesleyan.edu
Web Site: www.middlesexhistory.org
Founded: 1901.
Congressional District: 2
Key Personnel: Dir., Deborah D. Shapiro; Pres., William Ryczek.
Personnel Profile: Full-Time Paid 1; Part-Time Volunteers 4; Interns 2.
Governing Authority: nonprofit organization. Tax-exempt: 170(c).
Historical Society Museum: housed in 1810 General Mansfield house.
Collections: decorative arts; archives; manuscripts; Civil War uniforms & artifacts.
Research Fields: Civil War; genealogy; 18th-century shipping; history of Middlesex County.
Facilities: library of Frank Farnsworth Starr genealogy materials; 18th-century manuscripts & account books available for use by appointment.
Activities: guided tours; lectures; permanent & temporary exhibitions, Middletown Heritage Trail (self guided walking tour with 23 historical markers throughout downtown area).
Publications: Historical Observer.
Hours & Admission Prices: Museum: Winter: Tues.-Thurs. 10-3, Fri. 10-12; Summer: call for hours. Research: Mon.-Thurs. 10-3 by appointment. Adults $5; discount to AAM members; members no charge. Closed holidays & holiday weekends. ♿
Membership: Student $10; Individual $25; Family $35; Business & Contributing $50; Patron $100; Life $500.

Milford

MILFORD HISTORICAL SOCIETY, 34 High St., Milford, CT 06460-4732. Mailing Address: P.O. Box 337, Milford, CT 06460-0337. Tel.: 203-874-2664.
E-mail: mhsoc@hotmail.com
Formerly: Eells-Stow House, Milford Historical Society
Founded: 1930.
Congressional District: 3
Key Personnel: Co Pres. (V), Ardienne Damicis; Co Pres. (V), Michael Elgee; Museum Shop Mgr., Barbara Arnt.
Personnel Profile: Full-Time Volunteers 4; Part-Time Volunteers 50.
Governing Authority: society. Parent Institution: Milford Historical Society, Inc., P.O. Box 337, Milford, CT. Tax-exempt: 501(c)(3).
General Museum: housed in c.1700 Eells-Stow House.
Collections: period artifacts; Claude C. Coffin Indian collection; furniture. Historic Buildings: 1780 Clark Stockade House; Wharf Lane complex.
Major Exhibits: Local Milford History Exhibit, 6/10-10/15/10.
Facilities: 200-vol. library of historical books available for use on premises for reference use only; gardens. Museum-related items for sale.
Activities: guided tours; temporary & permanent exhibitions; walking tours; bimonthly lectures; summer programs; school group tours.
Publications: newsletter, Wharf Lane Newsletter.
Hours & Admission Prices: June to mid-Oct. Sat.-Sun. 1-4; other times by appointment. Adults $3, children $1; members no charge.
Attendance: 2,000
Membership: Student $5; Individual $15; Family $30; Life $400.

Monroe

MONROE HISTORICAL SOCIETY, 31 Great Ring Rd., Monroe, CT 06468-1328. Mailing Address: P.O. Box 212, Monroe, CT 06468-0212. Tel.: 203-261-8554.
Web Site: www.monroehistoricsociety.org
Founded: 1959.
Congressional District: 5
Key Personnel: Pres. (V), Nancy Zorena; Historian, Edward Coffey; Vice Pres., Judy Standerford.
Personnel Profile: Part-Time Volunteers 12.
Governing Authority: society. Tax-exempt.
General Museum.
Collections: costumes; folklore; agriculture; archives; history; mineralogy. Historic Buildings: 1790 East Village Schoolhouse; 1770 Beardsley House; 1811 East Village Meeting House.
Research Fields: genealogy; title research for old homes in Monroe.
Facilities: 100-vol. library of history & genealogy books housed in the Monroe Public Library.
Activities: guided tours; slide lectures of Old Monroe; formally organized education programs for children; traveling exhibitions; 19th-century school day programs upon request; Hands on History summer program.
Publications: quarterly newsletter.
Hours & Admission Prices: By appointment. No charge; donations accepted.
Attendance: 500 (estimated)
Membership: Senior $10; Individual $20; Family $25; Friend $50; Business Associate $200; Life $350.

Moodus

AMASA DAY HOUSE MUSEUM, 33 Plains Rd., Moodus, CT 06469. Mailing Address: 255 Main St., 4th Fl., Hartford, CT 06106-1821. Tel.: 860-247-8996, ext. 12.
Historic House: built in 1816.
Collections: Day family furnishings; photographs; period artifacts.
Hours & Admission Prices: By appointment. Adults $7, students, teachers & seniors $6, children 6-18 $4; discounts to groups; children under 6 & members no charge.

Mystic

DENISON PEQUOTSEPOS NATURE CENTER, 109 Pequotsepos Rd., Mystic, CT 06355-3045. Mailing Address: P.O. Box 122, Mystic, CT 06355-0122. Tel.: 860-536-1216. Fax: 860-536-2983.
E-mail: info@dpnc.org
Web Site: www.dpnc.org
Founded: 1946.
Congressional District: 18
Key Personnel: C.E.O. & Exec. Dir., Margarett L. Jones; Pres. (V), Dorrit Castle; Treas., Theodore Liston; Treas., Daniel Brannegan; Dir. Finance, Mayada Wadsworth; Education, Kim Macklin; Public Rels., Jennifer Johnson; Museum Shop Mgr., Christine Anderson.
Personnel Profile: Full-Time Paid 5; Full-Time Volunteers 3; Part-Time Paid 6; Part-Time Volunteers 60; Interns 2.
Governing Authority: private; nonprofit. Tax-exempt: 501(c)(3).
Natural Science & Environmental Education.
Collections: natural history of southeastern Connecticut; forest, wetland & meadow habitats, including live birds of prey, frogs, snakes & turtles; mounted birds, mammals & insects.
Research Fields: resident breeding bird populations; distribution of Pink Lady slippers in a small nature preserve; horseshoe crabs; amphibian monitoring.
Facilities: wildflower garden; 80-seat classroom; 2,000 sq. ft. exhibit space; small theater; 300-acre sanctuary with over eight miles of trails. Educational toys, games, jewelry & locally produced items for sale.
Activities: formal & early childhood education programs; lectures; participatory exhibits; ecological area field trips; workshops; seasonal farmer's market featuring organically grown produce from June-October; field guides, bird feeders & seed; state licensed nature-based preschool for ages 3-5. Annual Events: Lady's Slipper Festival in May; Earth Day Celebration; Summer Nature Camp; Summer Eco-luncheon or Eco-evening; Wild Mushroom Festival in September; Halloween Spooky Nature Trail.
Publications: quarterly newsletter, The Chickadee.
Hours & Admission Prices: Mon.-Sat. 9-5, Sun. 10-4. Adults $8, seniors & children under 12 $5; discounts to military, ANCA & AAA members. Closed New Year's Day; Easter; Thanksgiving; Christmas.
Attendance: 50,000 (estimated)
Membership: Senior 65 & over $20; Individual $25; Senior Couple $35; Single Parent Family & Couple $40; Family $50; Library & Nonprofit $100.

MYSTIC AQUARIUM & INSTITUTE FOR EXPLORATION, 55 Coogan Blvd., Mystic, CT 06355-1997. Tel.: 860-572-5955. Fax: 860-572-5969.
E-mail: info@mysticaquarium.org
Web Site: www.mysticaquarium.org
Founded: 1973.
Congressional District: 2
Key Personnel: Pres. & C.E.O., Dr. Stephen Coan; Chm. Bd. (V), George M. Milne, Jr., Ph.D.; C.F.O., Denise H. Armstrong; Sr. Vice Pres. Mktg. & Public Affairs, Peter P. Glankoff; Vice Pres. Facilities, Keith P. Sorensen; Dir. Mktg., Jacinta Simoncini; Vice Pres. Devel., Diane Generous; Dir. Education & Public Conservation Programs, Kelly E. Matis; Dir. Guest & Member Svcs., Celinda A. Beaudreau; Sr. Vice Pres. Research & Zoological Operations, Dr. Tracy A. Romano.
Personnel Profile: Full-Time Paid 115; Part-Time Paid 130; Part-Time Volunteers 550; Interns 6.
Governing Authority: nonprofit organization. Parent Institution: Sea Research Foundation, Inc., 55 Coogan Blvd., Mystic, CT 06355. Tax-exempt: 501(c)(3).
Aquarium & Marine Museum.
Collections: marine mammals; invertebrates; fishes; plants; penguins; water fowl; marine archaeological artifacts.
Research Fields: marine mammal behavior, biology & medicine; fish reproductive biology & medicine; invertebrate biology; water chemistry; deep sea archaeology & exploration.
Facilities: 1,000-vol. library of books, journals & magazines pertaining to natural history & husbandry of marine animals available for research on premises by appointment; theater; classrooms. Books, sculpture, shells & other museum-related items for sale.
Activities: public programs; formally organized education programs for children, adults, undergraduate & graduate students; training programs for museum workers; permanent exhibitions; marine mammal demonstrations.
Publications: quarterly newsletters.
Hours & Admission Prices: Daily 9-6. Adults $26; members no charge. Closed Thanksgiving; Christmas. ♿
Attendance: 714,425 (accurate)
Membership: Individual $60; Couple $119; Single Parent Family & Single Grandparent $139; Family $169; Grandparent $169; Member Plus $249.

MYSTIC ARTS CENTER, 9 Water St., Mystic, CT 06355-2592. Tel.: 860-536-7601. Fax: 860-536-0610.
Web Site: www.mysticarts.org
Founded: 1914.
Congressional District: 2
Key Personnel: Exec. Dir., Karen Barthelson; Pres., Christine Brady; Treas., Fred Conti.
Personnel Profile: Full-Time Paid 4; Part-Time Paid 12; Part-Time Volunteers 150.
Governing Authority: nonprofit organization. Tax-exempt: 501(c)(3).
Art Museum Center.
Collections: works by founding & early artists.
Activities: concerts; films; formal educational programs; lectures; temporary exhibitions; studio classes; outreach program; cultural programs. Annual Events: Mystic Photo Show; Regional Show; Members Show.
Publications: Gallery Newsletter.
Hours & Admission Prices: Daily 11-5. Suggested Donation: adults $3. Closed New Year's Day; Easter; Thanksgiving; Christmas Eve & Day. ♿
Attendance: 10,000 (estimated)
Membership: Junior $15; Individual $35; Elected Artist $40; Family $45; Donor $100; Patron $500; Benefactor $1,000.

*** MYSTIC SEAPORT - THE MUSEUM OF AMERICA AND THE SEA, (M),** 75 Greenmanville Ave., Mystic, CT 06355-0990. Mailing Address: 75 Greenmanville Ave., P.O. Box 6000, Mystic, CT 06355-0990. Tel.: 860-572-0711. Fax: 860-572-5326. TDD: 860-572-5319.
E-mail: info@mysticseaport.org
Web Site: www.mysticseaport.org
Founded: 1929.
Congressional District: 2
Key Personnel: Pres., Stephen C. White; Chm. Bd., Dick Victor; Vice Pres. Finance & Administration, Marcy Withington; Vice Pres. Education & Public Programs, Susan Funk; Vice Pres. Watercraft Preservation & Programs, Dana Hewson; Dir. Facilities Management, William Parent; Dir. Information Technology, Michael Lehnertz; Dir. Exhibitions, Jonathan Shay; Dir. Visitor Svcs., Sally Ackley; Dir. Shipyard, Quentin Snediker; Senior Cur., William Peterson; Dir. Maritime Studies, James Carlton; Dir. Finance, Caroleen Frey; Vice Pres. Advancement, J. Nathaniel Arata; Cur. Photography & Dir. Intellectual Property, Mary Anne Stets; Dir. Administrative Svcs., Mark Dulin; Dir. Devel. & Membership, Cheryl Mattson; Dir. Food Svcs., Gary Holland; Dir. Publications, Andy German; Librarian, Paul J. O'Pecko.

Personnel Profile: Full-Time Paid 216; Part-Time Paid 98; Part-Time Volunteers 872.
Governing Authority: bd. of trustees. Tax-exempt: 501(c)(3) & 170(b)(1)(A).
Maritime History.
Collections: America's historic & contemporary relationship with the sea; maritime art & artifacts; historic film footage & photographs; manuscripts; ships' plans; maps & charts; books & periodicals; small craft collection; historic buildings in a New England maritime village setting. Historic Ships: Charles W. Morgan; Joseph Conrad; L. A. Dunton; Emma C. Berry; Sabino; Brilliant; Roann.
Research Fields: American social & cultural history with emphasis on the relationship of America & the sea; 19th century maritime communities; vessel documentation; shoreside industries; ethnomusicology; literature; women's studies; marine biology & oceanography; coastal life; ethnic studies in maritime America.
Facilities: 70,000-vol. research library; 2,000 roles of microfilm; 1,000 ship registers; 1,000,000 manuscript pieces; 1,200 log books; 600 audiotaped interviews; 200 videotaped interviews; 9,000 charts & maps; planetarium; film & video archives; classrooms; children's museum; food service available. Museum-related items for sale.
Activities: internet home page; guided tours; films; gallery talks; concerts; education programs for special needs visitors, children, adults, undergraduate & graduate college students; inter-museum loan, permanent & temporary exhibitions; sail education programs; live interpretations; crafts demonstrations; video production; river cruises; scholarly research & symposia; planetarium classes & programs; workshops; lectures; boat livery; weekend events; music festival; daytime & overnight camps; historic holiday re-enactments; family activities & programs; music; elderhostel programs; curriculum units for school children; teacher institutes; first & third person interpretation; maritime skills demonstrations; sign language interpreter; signature exhibition, Voyages: Stories of America and the Sea; Inspiration Station for hands on visual and performing arts activities.
Publications: triannual magazine, Mystic Seaport; book series, American Maritime Library; quarterly newsletter, Wind Rose; America and the Sea: A Maritime History; exhibition catalog, Voyages: Stories of America and the Sea.
Hours & Admission Prices: Ships & Exhibits: April-Oct. daily 9-5; Nov.-March daily 10-4. Adults $24, seniors, military & students $22, youth 6-17 $15; members and children 5 & under no charge. Closed Christmas Eve & Day. ♿
Attendance: 300,000 (accurate)
Membership: Individual $45; Dual $65; Family & Grandparent $90; Mariner $104; Sustaining $199; Associate $300; Benefactor $500; Champion $750.

Naugatuck

NAUGATUCK HISTORICAL SOCIETY, 195 Water St., Naugatuck, CT 06770-2826. Mailing Address: P.O. Box 317, Naugatuck, CT 06770-0317. Tel.: 203-729-9039.
E-mail: naugatuckhistory@sbcglobal.net
Web Site: www.naugatuckhistory.com
Founded: 1959.
Congressional District: 5
Key Personnel: Pres. (V), Charles Marino; Museum Shop Mgr., Mary Doback.
Personnel Profile: Part-Time Paid 1; Part-Time Volunteers 15.
Governing Authority: bd. of directors. Tax-exempt.
Historical Society Museum: housed in former railroad station.
Collections: Naugatuck town history; rare books; photographs; photographs; manuscripts; city directories (census) dating back to 1877; rubber industry items; local manufacturing.
Research Fields: rubber industry.
Activities: tours; outreach; research.
Publications: newsletter.
Hours & Admission Prices: Wed.-Fri. 12-4, Sat. 10-2; other times by appointment. Adults $2, senior citizens 55 & up $1.50, children 18 & under $1; discounts to AAM & ICOM members; members no charge. ♿
Attendance: 1,500 (estimated)
Membership: Children 18 & under and Seniors 55 & up $12; Individual $15; Family $35; Life Individual $150; Life Couple $250.

New Britain

CENTRAL CONNECTICUT STATE UNIVERSITY ART GALLERIES, University Galleries, Maloney Hall, S.T. Chen Fine Arts Center, 1615 Stanley St., New Britain, CT 06050-2439. Tel.: 860-832-2620 & 2633. Fax: 860-832-2634.
E-mail: rodiamond2@yahoo.com
Web Site: www.art.ccsu.edu/gallery.html
Formerly: Museum of Central Connecticut State University
Founded: 1965.
Key Personnel: Co Dir., Sean Gallagher; Co Dir., Mark Strathy.
Personnel Profile: Part-Time Paid 1; Interns 1.
Governing Authority: state. Parent Institution: Connecticut State University, 1615 Stanley St., New Britain, CT. Tax-exempt.
Art Museum.
Collections: anthropology; paintings; sculpture; graphics; decorative arts; archaeology; folklore; industry; textiles; architectural drawings & models.
Facilities: library of books and other materials related to the history of art & art education available on premises.
Activities: formally organized education programs for undergraduate and graduate college students.
Hours & Admission Prices: Mon.-Fri. 1-4. No charge; donations accepted. ♿
Attendance: 3,000 (estimated)

NEW BRITAIN INDUSTRIAL MUSEUM, 185 Main St., I.I.E.T. Bldg., Fl. 2, New Britain, CT 06051-2296. Tel.: 860-832-8654.
E-mail: mailnbim@sbcglobal.net
Web Site: www.nbim.org
Founded: 1995.
Key Personnel: Pres. (V), Warren E. Kingsbury; Chm. (V), Nancy Schatz; Museum Shop Mgr., Newspaper Editor & Membership Chm., Lois L. Blomstrann.
Governing Authority: Parent Institution: New Britain Institute. Tax-exempt.
Industrial Museum.
Collections: manufactured products from invention to production developed in New Britain, CT including The Stanley Works; Fafnir Bearing; Landers; American Hardware; and North & Judd.
Research Fields: industrial history.
Publications: quarterly newsletter featuring articles on history of New Britain Industry.
Hours & Admission Prices: Mon.-Tues. & Thurs.-Fri. 2-5, Wed. 12-5. No charge. ♿
Attendance: 5,000
Membership: Senior & Student $15; Individual $20; Contributing $25; Sponsor $100; Patron $500; Benefactor $1,000.

* **NEW BRITAIN MUSEUM OF AMERICAN ART, INC., (M),** 56 Lexington St., New Britain, CT 06052-1412. Tel.: 860-229-0257. Fax: 860-229-3445.
E-mail: nbmaa@nbmaa.org
Web Site: www.nbmaa.org
Founded: 1903.
Congressional District: 5
Key Personnel: Chm. (V), Kathryn Cox; Dir., Douglas Hyland; Dir. Devel., Claudia Thesing; Dir. Finance, Patricia Levandoski; Deputy Dir. & Cur. Education, Maura O'Shea; Collections Mgr., John Urgo; Museum Shop Mgr., Donna Downes; Museum Shop Mgr., Judith Gaffney.
Personnel Profile: Full-Time Paid 18; Part-Time Paid 9; Part-Time Volunteers 420; Interns 52.
Governing Authority: nonprofit corporation. Tax-exempt: 170(b)(1)(A) & 501(c)(3).
Art Museum.
Collections: American art from colonial times to contemporary; paintings; sculpture; graphics; Sanford Low Memorial collection of illustration.
Major Exhibits: NEW/NOW: Sandra Allen, 11/09-1/10; Hudson River School Paintings from the Metropolitan Museum of Art, 11/09-9/10; John Haberle: Master of Illusion (T), 12/09-3/10; NEW/NOW: Kwabena Slaughter, 1/10-4/10; The Great American Watercolor, 4/10-7/10; NEW/NOW: Elana Herzog, 4/10-7/10; Daniel Truth, 6/10-9/10; NEW/NOW: Jon Rappleye, 7/10-10/10; NEW/NOW: Christopher Pugliese, 10/10-1/11.
Research Fields: American art.
Facilities: 200-vol. library; auditorium; cafe; study room; art studio; outdoor sculpture garden. Museum-related items for sale.
Activities: docent-led tours by appointment; free I-hour Sunday Masterpiece tours; Take 20 at 12 Friday gallery talks; art activities & teacher services; workshops & packets for pre- and post-visit classroom activities; age-appropriate classes offered weekly; lectures; gallery talks; monthly art programs; monthly films & concerts; quarterly art & literature series. Museum Sponsors: monthly First Friday jazz evenings; quarterly Museum After Dark social events for young professionals; Annual Juneteenth Celebration; Annual Gala/Art Auction; The Art of Wine & Food Benefit.
Publications: quarterly newsletter, Art & Insight; quarterly calendar of events; catalogues, New Britain Museum of American Art: Highlights of the Collection: Volumes I & II; Charles Ethan Porter: African-American Master of Still-Life; Double Lives: American Painters as Illustrators 1850-1950; John Haberle: Master of Illusion; 15-page illustrated brochure: The Christopher Hyland Collection of Photography, By Way of These Eyes: The Sublime, Exotic and Familiar; Electronic: www.nbmaa.org.
Hours & Admission Prices: Tues.-Wed. & Fri. 11-5, Thurs. 11-8, Sat. 10-5, Sun. 12-5. Adults $9, seniors $8, students & educators $7; discounts to AAM & ICOM members; members, children under 12, & Sat. 10-12 no

charge. Closed New Year's Day; Easter; Memorial Day; Independence Day; Thanksgiving; Christmas. ♿
Attendance: 75,459 (accurate)
Membership: Basic: Educator & Student $35; Senior $40; Individual $45; Senior Household $70; Household $75. Contributing: Friend's Circle $100; Artist's Circle $250; Collector's Circle $500. Premier: American Art Circle $1,000; John Butler Talcott Society $2,500-$10,000

NEW BRITAIN YOUTH MUSEUM, (M), 30 High St., New Britain, CT 06051-4227. Tel.: 860-225-3020. Fax: 860-229-4982.
E-mail: nbymdwtn@yahoo.com
Web Site: www.newbritainyouthmuseum.org
Founded: 1956.
Congressional District: 6
Key Personnel: Acting Dir., Ann F. Peabody; Chm. Bd., Robert Ramsey; Programs & Education, Christine J. Lawton; Mktg. & Special Events, Donna M. Veach.
Personnel Profile: Part-Time Paid 3; Part-Time Volunteers 1.
Governing Authority: nonprofit organization Parent Institution: New Britain Institute. Subsidiary Institution: New Britain Youth Museum at Hungerford Park. Tax-exempt: 501(c)(3).
Children's Museum & Nature Center.
Collections: circus miniatures; children's clothing & toys; period dolls; Native American & international artifacts; live animals; farming tools; natural history specimens.
Research Fields: natural history; period dolls & doll houses; ethnology; natural sciences; arts & cultures; Indian artifacts; illustration; cartoons; American circus.
Facilities: 300-vol. library on circus history & fiction; available for use on premises and for inter-library loan; classrooms; Hungerford park site.
Activities: guided tours by appointment; education programs for children; temporary & participatory exhibits; school loan service; docent program.
Publications: brochures; quarterly newsletter, Ramblings.
Hours & Admission Prices: Museum: Tues.-Fri. 1-5, Sat. 10-4. No charge; donations accepted. New Britain Youth Museum, Hungerford Park: Tues.-Fri. 1-5, Sat. 10-5. Adults $4; discounts to AAM members; members no charge. Closed federal & state holidays. ♿
Attendance: 31,505 (accurate)
Membership: Individual $25; Patron $250.

New Canaan

NEW CANAAN HISTORICAL SOCIETY, (M), 13 Oenoke Ridge, New Canaan, CT 06840-4195. Tel.: 203-966-1776. Fax: 203-972-5917.
E-mail: newcanaan.historical@snet.net
Web Site: www.nchistory.org
Founded: 1889.
Congressional District: 4
Key Personnel: Exec. Dir., Mrs. Janet Lindstrom; Pres. (V), Susan Bishop; Librarian, Sharon Turo; Historian, Joseph C. Sweet; Cur. Cody Drug Store, George Cody.
Personnel Profile: Full-Time Paid 2; Part-Time Paid 2; Part-Time Volunteers 102.
Governing Authority: nonprofit organization. Tax-exempt.
History Museum.
Collections: history; costumes; sculpture; medical; archives; manuscripts; antique tool museum; old printing press; dolls; pewter; furniture. Historic Buildings: 1764 Hanford-Silliman House; 1825 Town House; 1878 John Rogers Studio; 1845 Cody Drug Store; 1799 Rock Schoolhouse; 1960 Irwin Pavilion.
Research Fields: local history; genealogical.
Facilities: 3,000-vol. library of history & genealogical books and bound newspapers. Books, pamphlets, postcards for sale.
Activities: lectures; permanent & temporary exhibitions; school tours.
Publications: annual magazine; books, Readings in New Canaan History; Landmarks of New Canaan; Portrait of New Canaan, the History of a Connecticut Town; A New Canaan Private in the Civil War: Letters of Justus M. Silliman; Records of World War II, Vols. I, II & III; Philip Johnson in New Canaan; John Rogers & the Rogers Groups; The Merritt Parkway; Wampum to Wall Street; various pamphlets; books, Impressions of the Hour, The Diary of an Early New Canaan Teacher; New Canaan, Texture of a Community; quarterly newsletter, Tydings.
Hours & Admission Prices: Library: Tues.-Sat. 9:30-4:30. Museums: call for hours. No charge; donations accepted. Closed Memorial Day; Easter; Independence Day; Thanksgiving; Christmas. ♿
Attendance: 5,000 (estimated)
Membership: Individual $35; Family $50; Supporting $100; Sustaining $250; Patron $500; Benefactor $1,000.

NEW CANAAN NATURE CENTER, 144 Oenoke Ridge, New Canaan, CT 06840-4198. Tel.: 203-966-9577. Fax: 203-966-6536.
Web Site: www.newcanaannature.org
Founded: 1960.
Congressional District: 5
Key Personnel: Pres. (V), Mary Otocka; Exec. Dir., Laura Heckman.
Personnel Profile: Full-Time Paid 15; Part-Time Paid 15; Part-Time Volunteers 500; Interns 2.
Governing Authority: nonprofit organization. Tax-exempt: 501(c)(3).
Nature Center.
Collections: live birds of prey, native vertebrates & invertebrates; mounts of birds, mammals & insects; rock & mineral specimens; shells; 40 acres of diverse habitats; arboretum; sugar house; cider house; bird & butterfly garden; wildflower & herb gardens; naturalist's garden.
Research Fields: bird migration.
Facilities: 8 classrooms; gardens; arboretum; sanctuary; nature trails. Gift items for sale.
Activities: lectures; field trips; seminars; workshops; courses & programs; 725 programs for school classes each year; licensed nursery school; apple cider & maple syrup making demonstrations; licensed summer camp for ages 3-17. Center Sponsors: Spring Horticulture Symposium; Spring Garden Market; Fall Fair; Secret Gardens Tour; Holiday Market.
Publications: New Canaan Nature Center newsletter; annual report; programs brochures.
Hours & Admission Prices: Mon.-Sat. 10-4. No charge; donation accepted. Closed major holidays. ♿
Attendance: 70,000 (estimated)
Membership: Individual $35; Family $55; Supporter $100; Sustainer $250; Benefactor $500.

PHILIP JOHNSON GLASS HOUSE, Visitor Center, 199 Elm St., New Canaan, CT 06840. Tel.: 203-594-9884.
Key Personnel: Cur. & Collections Mgr., Irene Shum Allen
Architecture Museum.
Collections: house history; contemporary art; sculptures.
Facilities: 47-acre site; visitor center. Museum-related items for sale.
Activities: guided tours; educational programs.
Hours & Admission Prices: Tours: April-Oct. 10:30 & 2:30 by appointment. Admission 10 & over $30-$45; not recommended for children under 10.

SILVERMINE GUILD ARTS CENTER, 1037 Silvermine Rd., New Canaan, CT 06840-4398. Tel.: 203-966-9700, ext. 14. Fax: 203-966-2763.
E-mail: sgac@silvermineart.org
Web Site: www.silvermineart.org
Founded: 1922.
Congressional District: 4
Key Personnel: Exec. Dir., Pamela Davis; Gallery Dir., Jeffrey Mueller; Dir. Silvermine School of Art, Anne Connell; Chm. (V), Fran Henry-Meehan; Museum Shop Mgr., Nancy Woodward.
Personnel Profile: Full-Time Paid 9; Part-Time Paid 6; Part-Time Volunteers 300; Interns 2.
Governing Authority: nonprofit organization. Tax-exempt: 501(c)(3).
Art Gallery: housed in c.1890 barn & galleries located in the Silvermine area, a small, pre-revolutionary community, one of the first art colonies in the United States, founded by sculptor Solon Borglum in the early 1900s.
Collections: graphics; award winners of the National Print Biennial Exhibition; 160 works in all print media from 1960-present.
Facilities: auditorium; classrooms. Pottery, jewelry, prints, paintings & sculpture for sale.
Activities: guided tours; lectures; gallery talks; concerts; arts festivals; formally organized education programs; temporary exhibitions.
Publications: quarterly newsletter; exhibition catalogs.
Hours & Admission Prices: Tues.-Sat. 11-5, Sun. 1-5. No charge; donations accepted. Closed New Year's Day; Easter; Independence Day; Thanksgiving; Christmas. ♿
Attendance: 12,000 (estimated)
Membership: Individual $55; Family $75; Supporting $125; Patron $250; Conservator $1,000 & up.

New Haven

CONNECTICUT CHILDREN'S MUSEUM, 22 Wall St., New Haven, CT 06511-6528. Tel.: 203-562-5437. Fax: 203-787-9414.
E-mail: info@childrensbuilding.org
Web Site: childrensbuilding.org
Key Personnel: Dir., Sandra Malmquist
Children's Museum.
Collections: hands-on exhibits.
Activities: educational field trips; programs.

Hours & Admission Prices: Educational Field Trips: Tues.-Thurs. by appointment. General Public: Fri.-Sat. 12-5. Admission $5. ♿

HARVEY CUSHING/JOHN HAY WHITNEY MEDICAL LIBRARY, HISTORICAL LIBRARY, 333 Cedar St., New Haven, CT 06510-3206. Mailing Address: P.O. Box 208014, New Haven, CT 06520-8014. Tel.: 203-785-4354. Fax: 203-785-5636.
E-mail: toby.appel@yale.edu
Web Site: www.med.yale.edu/library/historical/
Founded: 1941.
Congressional District: 3
Key Personnel: Dir. Medical Library, Regina Kenny Marone; Librarian Medical History, Toby Appel; Preservation Librarian, Sarah Burge; Library Asst., Historical, Florence Gillich; Research Specialist, Historical, Thomas Falco; Cur. Prints & Drawings, Susan Wheeler.
Personnel Profile: Full-Time Paid 3; Part-Time Paid 2; Part-Time Volunteers 1.
Governing Authority: university. Parent Institution: Yale University. Tax-exempt: 501(a).
Medical Library.
Collections: graphics; paintings; weights & measures; medical instruments.
Facilities: 400,000-vol. library of books & periodicals available to health practitioners & historians; reading room.
Activities: permanent & temporary exhibitions.
Publications: catalog of print collection.
Hours & Admission Prices: Library: Mon.-Fri. 9-4:30. No charge. Closed New Year's Day; Independence Day; Thanksgiving; Christmas. ♿
Membership: Associates of Cushing/Whitney Medical Library: Contributing $35; Sustaining $100; Life $1,000.

JOHN SLADE ELY HOUSE, 51 Trumbull St., New Haven, CT 06510-1004. Tel.: 203-624-8055. Fax: 203-624-2306.
E-mail: info@elyhouse.org
Web Site: www.elyhouse.org
Founded: 1960.
Congressional District: 3
Key Personnel: Cur., Paul Clabby.
Personnel Profile: Part-Time Paid 1; Interns 2.
Governing Authority: nonprofit organization. Parent Institution: John Slade Ely Trust. Tax-exempt.
Art Gallery.
Collections: permanent collection of paintings & sculpture of the New Haven Paint & Clay Club.
Facilities: meeting rooms.
Activities: temporary exhibitions by groups or individuals; changing exhibits featuring contemporary work by Connecticut & Greater New Haven artists; internships; concerts; lectures. Gallery Sponsors: annual juried exhibitions; Connecticut Women Artists; New Haven Paint & Clay Club; Connecticut Water Color Society; Calligraphers Guild of New Haven.
Publications: annual calendar; brochures; catalog, 15 painters & Sculptors: An Invitational Exhibition of Connecticut Commission on the Arts Grant Recipients, 1972-1985; poster, Chinese Protest Calligraphy, 1989; exhibition catalog, Artists from People's Republic of China: Min Wang, Tong Wang, Yue-Mei Zhang & Liang Wei; also poster for the 1991 exhibition; exhibition catalog: Architecture & Process 1992; John McCrillis: 50 Years in Design 1994.
Hours & Admission Prices: Wed.-Fri. 11-4, Sat.-Sun. 2-5. No charge; donations accepted. ♿
Attendance: 5,000 (estimated)

KNIGHTS OF COLUMBUS MUSEUM, One State St., New Haven, CT 06511-6702. Tel.: 203-865-0400 & 0320. Fax: 203-865-0351.
Web Site: www.kofcmuseum.org
Formerly: Knights of Columbus Headquarters Museum
Founded: 1982.
Congressional District: 3
Key Personnel: Supreme Knight & C.E.O., Carl A. Anderson; Dir., Lawrence D. Sowinski; Cur. Museum, Mary Lou Cummings; Archivist, Susan Brosnan; Asst. to Dir., Kathy Cogan; Museum Shop Mgr., Olga Lapaeva; Administrative Asst., Erica Ruzbarsky.
Personnel Profile: Full-Time Paid 9; Full-Time Volunteers 1; Part-Time Paid 3.
Governing Authority: nonprofit organization. Parent Institution: Knights of Columbus Museum, Inc. Tax-exempt: 501(c)(3).
History Museum; Catholic Fraternal Society.
Collections: fine & decorative art; paintings; prints; sculpture; costumes; rare book collection on Christopher Columbus; memorabilia & manuscripts relating to the history, formation & activities of the K of C from 1882 to present day.
Major Exhibits: Mother Teresa, 3/10-7/10.
Research Fields: history of K of C, Catholic Church & Christopher Columbus.
Facilities: archives & library with manuscripts & other archival material pertaining to the history of K of C, Catholic Church & secular history in America available for research by appointment; reading room.
Activities: guided tours; permanent & temporary exhibitions. Annual Event: Christmas Tree Festival.
Publications: brochure; post cards; posters; fact sheet; exhibit catalogues; note cards.
Hours & Admission Prices: May to Labor Day daily 10-5; Tues. after Labor Day to April Wed.-Sat. 10-5, Sun. 11-5; groups by appointment. No charge, donations accepted. Closed Good Friday; Thanksgiving; Christmas. ♿
Attendance: 20,120 (accurate)

NEW HAVEN MUSEUM, 114 Whitney Ave., New Haven, CT 06510-1238. Tel.: 203-562-4183. Fax: 203-562-2002.
Web Site: www.newhavenmuseum.org
Formerly: New Haven Museum & Historical Society
Founded: 1862.
Congressional District: 3
Key Personnel: Chief Administrative Officer & Pres. (V), Walter R. Miller; Librarian, James W. Campbell.
Personnel Profile: Full-Time Paid 2; Part-Time Paid 5; Part-Time Volunteers 14; Interns 2.
Governing Authority: bd. of directors. Tax-exempt: 501(c)(3).
History Museum.
Collections: fine, decorative & inventive arts of New Haven; photographs of New Haven, The New Haven Colony & Connecticut.
Research Fields: social, cultural, economic, technological, political & ethnic-racial history of New Haven; fine, decorative & inventive arts.
Facilities: 30,000-vol. library of archival, photographic & oral history material on New Haven & Connecticut for use on premises; 100-seat auditorium; 35-seat education center. Gift items for sale.
Activities: lectures; films; gallery talks; history workshops; education programs; docent program; inter-museum loan, permanent, temporary & traveling exhibitions.
Publications: newsletter; exhibition catalogs.
Hours & Admission Prices: Tues.-Fri. 10-5, Sat. 12-5. Adults $4, senior citizens $3, students 6-17 $2; discounts to AAM, AAA AASLH & NEMA; children under 6 & members no charge. Closed New Year's Day; Martin Luther King Day; President's Day; Memorial Day; Independence Day; Labor Day; Columbus Day; Thanksgiving; Christmas. ♿
Attendance: 10,000 (estimated)
Membership: Student $20; Senior $35; Individual $40; Household $65; Contributing $100; Supporting $250; Director's Circle $500; President's Cabinet $1,000.

* **PEABODY MUSEUM OF NATURAL HISTORY, (M),** Yale University, 170 Whitney Ave., New Haven, CT 06511-8118. Mailing Address: P.O. Box 208118, New Haven, CT 06520-8118. Tel.: 203-432-5050. Fax: 203-432-9816.
E-mail: peabody.webmaster@yale.edu
Web Site: www.peabody.yale.edu
Founded: 1866.
Congressional District: 3
Key Personnel: Dir., Cur. Invertebrate Paleontology, Derek E. G. Briggs; Asst. Dir. Public Programs & Deputy Dir., Jane Pickering; Asst. Dir. Collections & Operations, Tim White; Cur. Anthropology, Michael Dove; Cur. Anthropology, Roderick McIntosh; Cur. Anthropology, Eric Sargis; Cur. Paleobotany, Leo J. Hickey; Cur. Vertebrate Paleontology & Vertebrate Zoology, Elisabeth Vrba; Cur. Vertebrate Zoology, Thomas Near; Cur. Vertebrate Zoology, David Skelly; Cur. Vertebrate Paleontology & Vertebrate Zoology, Jacques A. Gauthier; Cur. Invertebrate Paleontology, Adolf Seilacher; Cur. Entomology, Antonia Monteiro; Assoc. Cur. Entomology, Leonard E. Munstermann; Cur. Invertebrates, Leo W. Buss; Cur. Botany, Michael J. Donoghue; Cur. Mineralogy, Jay Ague; Cur. Meteorites & Planetary Science, Karl K. Turekian; Cur. Historical Scientific Instruments, David F. Musto; Cur. Vertebrate Zoology, Richard O. Prum; Public Rels. & Mktg. Mgr., Melanie Brigockas; Business Mgr., Susan L. Voigt; Sr. Conservator, Catherine Sease; Dir. Devel., Eliza Cleveland; Head, Peabody Fellows Program, Laura Fawcett; Head, Education & Outreach, David Heiser; Museum Shop Mgr., Kathleen Sullivan.
Personnel Profile: Full-Time Paid 66; Part-Time Paid 19; Part-Time Volunteers 217; Interns 3.
Governing Authority: university. Parent Institution: Yale University. Tax-exempt: 501(c)(3).
University Natural History Museum.
Collections: anthropology; botany; paleobotany; invertebrate paleontology; vertebrate paleontology; invertebrate zoology; entomology; ichthyology; herpetology; ornithology; mammalogy; mineralogy; meteorites; historic scientific instruments; The Age of Reptiles & The Age of Mammals, murals by Rudolph F. Zallinger.

Major Exhibits: Disease Detectives (T), 11/09-1/10; Coffee: The World in Your Cup, Summer 2010 (T).
Research Fields: anthropology; botany; paleobotany; invertebrate paleontology; vertebrate paleontology; invertebrate zoology; entomology; ichthyology; herpetology; ornithology; mammalogy; mineralogy; meteorites; historic scientific instruments.
Facilities: 12,000-vol. library; biological field station on Long Island Sound; 175-seat auditorium. Museum-related items for sale.
Activities: formally organized education programs for schools, events for children & adults in the museum; guided tours by docents; lectures; field trips; diversified volunteer program; permanent & temporary exhibitions.
Publications: monograph series, Bulletin of the Peabody Museum of Natural History, Yale University Publications in Anthropology; shorter papers, Postilla; irregular serial; quarterly newsletter, Explorer; proceedings from scientific meetings.
Hours & Admission Prices: Mon.-Sat. 10-5, Sun. 12-5. Adults $7, senior citizens 65 & over $6, children 3-18 $5; discounts to AAM, ASTC & ICOM w/ID & Friends of Museum Associates; members, children under 3, Yale Univ. faculty & students w/ID no charge. Closed New Year's Day; Easter; Independence Day; Thanksgiving; Christmas Eve & Day. ♿
Attendance: 140,000 (estimated)
Membership: Full-time Student $15; Discounted Individual $30; Individual $40; Discounted Household $45; Dual $50; Household $60; Sustaining $125; Rudy Zallinger Club $250; Deinonychus Circle $500; Torosaurus Society $2,500; Lifetime $7,500.

WEST ROCK NATURE CENTER, 1080 Wintergreen Ave., New Haven, CT 06515. Mailing Address: P.O. Box 2969, New Haven, CT 06515-0069. Tel.: 203-946-8016. Fax: 203-946-8024.
E-mail: wwilliam@newhavenct.net
Web Site: www.cityofnewhaven.com/parks/ranger/westrock.asp
Founded: 1946.
Congressional District: 3
Key Personnel: Park Ranger, Wray Williams; Park Ranger, Joe Milone; Park Ranger, Chris Guerette.
Personnel Profile: Full-Time Paid 3; Part-Time Volunteers 40.
Governing Authority: municipal government. Parent Institution: New Haven Dept. of Parks, Rec. & Trees Affiliated with Connecticut Assoc. of Environmental Educators, Southern Connecticut State University & New Haven Public School System. Tax-exempt.
Nature Center.
Collections: indoor snake collection; native snakes; turtles; insects; reptiles.
Research Fields: Connecticut wildlife.
Facilities: library of books & magazines; nature trails; sledding slope; interpretive building; sundial; organic garden; native reptile display.
Activities: nature study; educational programs; school visitation; New Haven ranger program; volunteer programs; youth volunteer programs; interactive activities.
Hours & Admission Prices: Mon.-Fri. 10-4. No charge; donations accepted. Closed city holidays.
Attendance: 20,000 (estimated)

YALE CENTER FOR BRITISH ART, (M), 1080 Chapel St., New Haven, CT 06510-2302. Mailing Address: P.O. Box 208280, New Haven, CT 06520-8280. Tel.: 203-432-2800; 877-BRIT-ART. Fax: 203-432-4538.
E-mail: ycba.info@yale.edu
Web Site: ycba.yale.edu
Founded: 1977.
Congressional District: 3
Key Personnel: Dir., Amy Meyers; Deputy Dir., Constance Clement; Assoc. Dir. Finance & Administration, David Mills; Assoc. Dir. Devel. & External Affairs, Beth Miller; Cur. Paintings & Sculpture and Operations Mgr., Angus Trumble; Asst. Cur. Paintings & Sculpture and Security Supvr., Cassandra Albinson; Cur. Prints & Drawings and Special Events Coord., Scott Wilcox; Assoc. Cur. Prints & Drawings, Gillian Forrester; Cur. Rare Books & Manuscripts, Elisabeth Fairman; Cur. Education, Linda Friedlaender; Chief Conservator, Theresa Fairbanks; Registrar, Timothy Goodhue; Museum Shop Mgr., Lizbeth O'Connor; Public Rels. & Mktg. Mgr., Amy McDonald; Head Librarian, Kraig Binkowski; Membership Mgr., Linda Jerolmon; Paintings Conservator, Mark Aronson; Volunteer Coord., Aviva Luria; Operations Mgr., George Conte; Security Supvr., Len Costenza; Special Events Coord., Julienne Richardson.
Personnel Profile: Full-Time Paid 77; Part-Time Paid 30; Part-Time Volunteers 46; Interns 6.
Governing Authority: university. Parent Institution: Yale University. Tax-exempt: 501(c)(3).
Art Museum.
Collections: British art from 16th-century to present including 1,900 paintings, 20,000 drawings, 30,000 prints & 30,000 books & manuscripts; 100 sculptures.
Research Fields: British art & related British cultural studies.
Facilities: 25,000-vol. non-circulating art reference library specializing in British art from 1550-present; conservation laboratory; 200,000 photo archive of British art worldwide; 200-seat auditorium; classrooms. Museum-related items for sale.
Activities: guided tours; permanent & temporary exhibitions; lectures; films; gallery talks; concerts; symposia; special programs for children; docent program; visiting fellowship program.
Publications: exhibition catalogs; postcards; notecards; slides.
Hours & Admission Prices: Tues.-Sat. 10-5, Sun. 12-5. No charge; donations accepted. Closed New Year's Eve & Day; Memorial Day; Independence Day; Thanksgiving; Christmas Eve & Day. ♿
Attendance: 100,000 (estimated)
Membership: Joint Membership with Yale University Art Gallery: Student $15; Individual $50; Dual Family $75; Contributor $125; Sponsor $250; Benefactor $500; Kahn Fellow $1,000. Friends of British Art: $1,100, $2,500, $5,000.

* **YALE UNIVERSITY ART GALLERY,** 1111 Chapel St., New Haven, CT 06510-2300. Mailing Address: P.O. Box 208271, New Haven, CT 06520-8271. Tel.: 203-432-0600. Fax: 203-432-9523.
E-mail: artgalleryinfo@yale.edu
Web Site: artgallery.yale.edu
Founded: 1832.
Congressional District: 3
Key Personnel: Dir., Jock Reynolds; Chm. (V), Robert W. Doran; Deputy Dir. Finance & Internal Operations, Louisa Cunningham; Deputy Dir. Collections & Education, Pam Franks; Deputy Dir. Museum Resources & Stewardship, Jill Westgard; Assoc. Dir. Public Information, Ana Davis; Chief Conservator, Ian McClure; Cur. American Decorative Arts, Patricia Kane; Cur. Education & Academic Affairs, Kate Ezra; Cur. Asian Art, David Sensabaugh; Cur. African Art, Frederick Lamp; Cur. Coins & Medals, William E. Metcalf; Cur. Prints, Drawings & Photographs, Suzanne Boorsch; Assoc. Cur. Public Education, Jessica Sack; Assoc. Dir. Exhibitions, Jeffrey Yashimine; Cur. American Paintings & Sculpture, Helen Cooper; Cur. Early European, Laurence Kanter; Cur. Ancient Art, Susan B. Matheson; Cur. Modern & Contemporary Art, Jennifer Gross; Dir. Collection & Technology Initiatives, Carol DeNatale; Coord. Visitor Svcs., Annabel Rhodeen.
Personnel Profile: Full-Time Paid 124; Part-Time Paid 9; Part-Time Volunteers 25; Interns 96.
Governing Authority: university. Parent Institution: Yale University. Tax-exempt: 501(c)(3).
Art Museum.
Collections: American painting & decorative arts; Greek & Roman art including artifacts from the ancient Roman City of Dura-Europos; Jarves, Griggs, & Rabinowitz collections of early Italian paintings; European, Asian, & African art including the Charles B. Benenson collection of African art; art of the ancient Americas; Societe Anonyme collection of early 20th century European & American art; Impressionist, modern, & contemporary works.
Major Exhibits: Eero Saarinen: Shaping the Future, 2/16/10-5/2/10; Italian Paintings from the Richard L. Feigen Collection, 5/28/10-9/12/10; John La Farge's Second Paradise: Voyages in the South Seas, 1890-1891, 10/19/10-1/2/11.
Research Fields: all fields pertaining to collections.
Facilities: Books relating to collections & other museum-related items for sale.
Activities: guided tours; lectures; gallery talks; concerts; permanent & loan exhibitions; family programs; school group tours.
Publications: Yale University Art Gallery Bulletin; interpretive guides to the collection; exhibition catalogues & catalogue raisonnes; membership magazine; calendar of events.
Hours & Admission Prices: July-Aug. Tues.-Sat.-10-5, Sun. 1-6; Sept.-June Tues.-Wed. & Fri.-Sat. 10-5, Thurs. 10-8, Sun. 1-6. Tours: no charge. Group Tours: call for fees & information. Closed major holidays. ♿
Attendance: 132,000 (estimated)
Membership: Student $15; Individual $50; Dual & Family $75; Contributor $125; Sponsor $250; Benefactor $500; Fellow $1,000; Patron $2,500, $5,000, & $10,000.

YALE UNIVERSITY COLLECTION OF MUSICAL INSTRUMENTS, 15 Hillhouse Ave., New Haven, CT 06511-6823. Mailing Address: P.O. Box 208278, New Haven, CT 06520-8278. Tel.: 203-432-0822. Fax: 203-432-8342.
E-mail: musinst@pantheon.yale.edu
Web Site: www.yale.edu/musicalinstruments
Founded: 1900.
Congressional District: 3
Key Personnel: Interim Dir., William Purvis; Assoc. Cur., Nicholas Renouf; Cur., Susan E. Thompson.

Governing Authority: university. Tax-exempt: 501(c)(3).
Musical Instruments Museum.
Collections: 16th-18th centuries keyboard instruments; 17th-20th centuries stringed instruments; 15th-20th centuries American & European instruments; bells; mechanical instruments.
Research Fields: musical instruments; organology.
Facilities: 400-vol. library of catalogs, books, brochures, treatises & facsimiles pertaining to the history & identification of musical instruments available for use by approval of university librarian. Publications, recordings, photographs & postcards for sale.
Activities: guided tours; lectures; gallery talks; concerts; formally organized education programs for undergraduate & graduate college students; permanent & temporary exhibitions.
Publications: various catalogs & checklists.
Hours & Admission Prices: Sept.-June Tues.-Fri. 1-4, Sun. 1-5. Adults $2. Closed university recesses, summer & national holidays.
Membership: Student & Senior Citizens over 65 $5; Single $10; Family $20; Regular Associate $25; Family Associate $45; Sustaining $50; Patron $100; Life $500.

New London

CONNECTICUT COLLEGE ARBORETUM, 270 Mohegan Ave., New London, CT 06320-4150. Mailing Address: Campus Box 5201, 270 Mohegan Ave., New London, CT 06320. Tel.: 860-439-5020 & 5060. Fax: 860-439-5482.
E-mail: arbor@conncoll.edu
Web Site: arboretum.conncoll.edu
Founded: 1931.
Congressional District: 2
Key Personnel: Dir., Glenn D. Dreyer; Asst. Dir., Kathy Dame; Arboretum Horticulturist, Leigh S. Knuttel; Groundsperson, Bryan Goulet; Senior Groundsperson, Charles A. McIlwain, III; Staff Asst., Elene Anthopolos; Cur. & Information Resource Mgr., Mary Villa.
Personnel Profile: Full-Time Paid 6; Part-Time Paid 2; Part-Time Volunteers 50.
Governing Authority: college. Parent Institution: Connecticut College. Tax-exempt: 501(c)(3).
Arboretum.
Collections: woody plants native to N.E.U.S.; ornamental trees & shrubs; natural areas.
Research Fields: naturalistic landscaping; terrestrial & wetland ecology; vegetation management with fire and herbicides.
Facilities: nature trails.
Activities: guided tours; lectures; formally organized education programs for adults & undergraduate students; children's activities; demonstrations.
Publications: Arboretum Bulletins & research papers.
Hours & Admission Prices: Daily sunrise-sunset. No charge.
Attendance: 12,000 (estimated)
Membership: Student $10; Individual $30; Organization $40; Sustaining $50; Supporting $100.

* **LYMAN ALLYN ART MUSEUM, (M),** 625 Williams St., New London, CT 06320-4199. Tel.: 860-443-2545. Fax: 860-443-2060.
E-mail: stula@lymanallyn.org
Web Site: www.lymanallyn.org
Formerly: Lyman Allyn Museum of Art at Connecticut College
Founded: 1932.
Congressional District: 2
Key Personnel: Exec. Dir. & Cur., Nancy Stula; Pres., William A. Lieber; Dir. Devel., Nancy Hileman; Asst. to Dir., Ann Wicks.
Personnel Profile: Full-Time Paid 9; Part-Time Paid 6; Part-Time Volunteers 40; Interns 1.
Governing Authority: nonprofit corp. Tax-exempt: 501(c)(3).
Art Museum.
Collections: 10,000 objects of art: contemporary, modern & early American fine arts; American Impressionist paintings; Connecticut decorative arts; 17th-19th century European works on paper. Historic House: The Deshon-Allyn Mansion.
Major Exhibits: Play Things: Toys and the Invention of Modern Childhood, 3/27/10-9/5/10.
Facilities: 10,000-vol. library of art reference books available by appointment on premises; 78-seat auditorium.
Activities: guided tours; lectures; gallery talks; travel program; docent program; inter-museum loan, permanent & temporary exhibitions; children's art workshops; adult & kids education programs; corporate partnership programs. Museum Sponsors: Monthly Free First Sundays.
Publications: catalogues: The American Collection; Beatrice Cumming 1903-1974; John Day; The Devotion Family; Dolls and Doll Houses and Toys; Charles Ebert; Elizabeth Enders; Lyman Allyn Art Museum Handbook; Mirror of Fashion; Rollie McKenna; New Artist Drawings; New London Silver; A New London Whaler on the California Gold Rush; Painters of Light and Color; The Shakers of Sabbathday Lake; Through the Eyes of Charles Chu; The Barkley L. Hendricks Experience; American Artists Abroad and Their Inspiration; The Vision and Influence of Winslow Ames; James Britton; At Home and Abroad: The Transcendental Landscapes of Christopher Cranch.
Hours & Admission Prices: Tues.-Sat. 10-5, Sun. 1-5. Adults $8, students & seniors $7; AAM, museum members, New London residents, children under 12, Connecticut College faculty, staff & students no charge. Closed major holidays. ♿
Attendance: 25,000 (accurate)
Membership: Student $25; Individual $40; Family $60; Sustaining $250; Patron $500; Harriet Allyn Society $1,000.

NEW LONDON COUNTY HISTORICAL SOCIETY, (M), 11 Blinman St., New London, CT 06320-5677. Tel.: 860-443-1209. Fax: 860-443-1209.
E-mail: info@newlondonhistory.org
Web Site: newlondonhistory.org/
Founded: 1870.
Congressional District: 2
Key Personnel: Exec. Dir., Edward D. Baker; Pres., Deborah J. Donovan; Librarian, Tricia Royston.
Personnel Profile: Full-Time Paid 1; Part-Time Paid 2; Part-Time Volunteers 28; Interns 3.
Governing Authority: private; nonprofit organization. Subsidiary Institution: Shaw Mansion. Tax-exempt: 501(c)(3).
Historic House Museum: housed in the 1756 Shaw Mansion, used as Connecticut's Naval Office during the Revolution.
Collections: Shaw family portraits, furniture; 1,300 manuscripts including early history of New London & inhabitants; decorative arts; textiles; tools; paintings; naval activities during the Revolutionary War; newspapers; whaling; Amistad exhibit documents; Frances M. Caulkins collection.
Major Exhibits: New London and the Resolute, 11/09-9/10; Scrimshaw: The Folk Art of Whalemen, 11/09-11/10.
Research Fields: local history; genealogy; history of the African American community in Southeastern Connecticut; maritime history; whaling & sealing.
Facilities: 5,000-vol. library of books on genealogy & history; reading room; botanical gardens. Museum-related items for sale.
Activities: guided tours; permanent & temporary exhibitions; lecture series; historic bus tours; History Club for middle school students; special events.
Publications: bimonthly newsletter, The NLCHS Newsletter; Diary of Joshua Hempstead, c.1711-1758; Life on a Whaler; Tapestry, A History of Blacks in South East Connecticut; Greetings from New London, A Collection of Early 20th-Century Postcards; Black Roots in Southeastern CT 1650-1900; The Amistad Incident as Reported in the New London Gazette; History of the Amistad Captives; A View from the Sixties: The Black Experience in Southeastern CT; The History of New London, Frances M. Caulkins, 1860; The History of Norwich, Frances M. Caulkins, 1866.
Hours & Admission Prices: Winter: Wed.-Fri. 1-4; Summer: Wed.-Fri. 1-4, Sat. 10-4. Library: by appointment only. Adults $5, senior citizens $4, children under 12 $2; discounts to AAM & NEMA members and groups of 10 or more; members no charge. Closed national holidays; Thanksgiving; Christmas. ♿
Attendance: 3,100 (estimated)
Membership: Senior $15; Individual & Senior Couples $25; Family $35; Contributing $50; Sustaining $100; Patron $250; Life $1,000.

U.S. COAST GUARD MUSEUM, U.S. Coast Guard Academy, 15 Mohegan Ave., New London, CT 06320-4195. Tel.: 860-444-8511. Fax: 860-701-6700.
E-mail: arlyn.s.danielson@uscg.mil
Web Site: www.uscg.mil/hq/cg092/museum
Founded: 1967.
Congressional District: 2
Key Personnel: Cur., Arlyn Danielson.
Personnel Profile: Full-Time Paid 1.
Governing Authority: federal. Parent Institution: U.S. Coast Guard. Subsidiary Institution: U.S. Coast Guard Academy. Tax-exempt.
Maritime Museum.
Collections: lighthouse lenses; rescue equipment; ship & airplane models; paintings & artifacts relating to the U.S. Coast Guard & its predecessors, the Revenue-Cutter service, Lighthouse service & Life-Saving service.
Research Fields: Coast Guard history.
Facilities: 160,000-vol. college undergraduate library, available for use by appointment; military academy.
Activities: small changing exhibits.
Hours & Admission Prices: Mon.-Fri. 9-4:30. No charge; donations accepted. Closed federal holidays. ♿
Attendance: 25,000 (accurate)

New Milford

THE NEW MILFORD HISTORICAL SOCIETY, 6 Aspetuck Ave., New Milford, CT 06776. Mailing Address: P.O. Box 359, New Milford, CT 06776-0359. Tel.: 860-354-3069. Fax: 860-210-0263.
Web Site: www.nmhistorical.org
Founded: 1915.
Congressional District: 5
Key Personnel: Pres. Bd. Trustees (V), Joanne Lillis; Dir., Paula Walton; Corresponding Sec., Susan Metcalf.
Personnel Profile: Part-Time Paid 3; Part-Time Volunteers 10.
Governing Authority: board of trustees. Tax-exempt.
Historical Society Museum.
Collections: glass; china; silver; pewter; Wannopee pottery; miniatures; portraits including those by Ralph Earl & Richard Jennys; costumes, samplers, quilts & other textiles; toys, including dolls; furniture; historical & genealogical records; New Milford memorabilia; photographs. Historic Buildings: early 19th-century Knapp House; c.1796 Boardman Store; c.1820 Bank of Litchfield County; c.1843 Hill & Plain Schoolhouse #1.
Research Fields: genealogy; New Milford history.
Activities: tours; lectures; classes; special events.
Publications: books, Edith Newton's New Milford; Howard Peck's New Milford; Voices From The Past; The Courage of Sarah Noble; pamphlet, Two Tales of New Milford; maps; prints of New Milford scenes.
Hours & Admission Prices: May-Oct. Thurs.-Fri. & Sun. 1-4; other times by appointment. Adults $5; discounts to students; members no charge. Closed legal holidays. ♿
Membership: Individual $25; Family $50; Sustaining $75; Corporate $95; Life $300.

Newington

ENOCH KELSEY HOUSE, 1702 Main St., Newington, CT 06111-3938. Mailing Address: 679 Willard Ave., Newington, CT 06111-2615. Tel.: 860-666-7118.
E-mail: NGTNheritage@aol.com
Web Site: www.newingtonhistoricalsociety.org/index.htm
Governing Authority: Parent Institution: Newington Historical Society & Trust, Inc.
Historic House Museum: home built by Enoch Kelsey & his son David, c.1799.
Collections: period furnishings; personal artifacts.
Hours & Admission Prices: April-Nov. 1st & 3rd Sun. of month 1-3. Closed holidays.

KELLOGG-EDDY HOUSE AND MUSEUM, 679 Willard Ave., Newington, CT 06111-2615. Tel.: 860-666-7118.
E-mail: NGTNheritage@aol.com
Web Site: www.newingtonhistoricalsociety.org/index.htm
Key Personnel: Dir., Dorothy Abbott.
Governing Authority: Parent Institution: Newington Historical Society & Trust, Inc.
Historic House Museum: housed in the former home of General Martin Kellogg, built in 1808.
Collections: period furnishings; personal artifacts.
Hours & Admission Prices: April-Nov. 1st Sun. of month 1-3. Closed holidays.

Niantic

CHILDREN'S MUSEUM OF SOUTHEASTERN CONNECTICUT, (M), 409 Main St., Niantic, CT 06357-3103. Tel.: 860-691-1111. Fax: 860-691-1194.
E-mail: pr.relations@childrensmuseumsect.org
Web Site: childrensmuseumsect.org
Founded: 1992.
Congressional District: 2
Key Personnel: Exec. Dir., Christy Hammond; Pres. (V), Ivan Sadler; Dir. Guest Svcs., Melissa Gula; Education Coord., Diane Dusza; Graphic Design Coord., Julie Clements-Reagan.
Personnel Profile: Full-Time Paid 3; Part-Time Paid 9; Part-Time Volunteers 125; Interns 3.
Governing Authority: private; nonprofit organization. Tax-exempt: 501(c)(3).
Children's Museum.
Collections: educational items pertinent to the culture & history of Connecticut; permanent & teaching collections.
Facilities: 5,000 sq. ft. exhibit space; classroom; planetarium. Museum-related items for sale.
Activities: concerts; films; formal education programs for adults, children & undergraduate or graduate college students affiliated with internships; school loan service; traveling exhibitions. Annual Events: Fairy Tale Ball; fashion show.
Publications: quarterly newsletter, Building Blocks; annual report.
Hours & Admission Prices: Tues.-Sat. 9:30-5, Sun. 12-5. Adults $6, tour groups $4.75; discounts to AAM, ACM & NEMA members; members & children under one no charge. Closed Easter; Memorial Day; Independence Day; Labor Day; Thanksgiving; Christmas. ♿
Attendance: 56,451 (accurate)
Membership: Grandparent $35; Basic $45; Library & Supporting $100; Contributing $250; Corporate $1,000.

EAST LYME HISTORICAL SOCIETY/THOMAS LEE HOUSE, W. Main St., Niantic, CT 06357. Mailing Address: P.O. Box 112, East Lyme, CT 06333-0112. Tel.: 860-739-9660. Fax: 860-444-6661.
E-mail: info@eastlymehistoricalsociety.org
Web Site: www.eastlymehistoricalsociety.org
Founded: 1894.
Congressional District: 2
Key Personnel: Pres., Norman B. Peck, III; Treas., Ruth Ames; Museum Shop Mgr., Russell DeGrafft.
Personnel Profile: Part-Time Volunteers 40.
Governing Authority: society. Tax-exempt: 501(c)(3).
Historical Society Museum.
Collections: furnishings; personal artifacts. Historic Buildings: c.1660 Thomas Lee House; Little Boston Schoolhouse c.1734.
Activities: guided tours; lectures; temporary exhibitions; elementary education programs.
Publications: quarterly newsletter.
Hours & Admission Prices: mid-June to Labor Day Tues.-Sun. 1-4; other times by appointment. No charge; donations accepted.
Attendance: 500 (estimated)
Membership: Individual $5; Family $10; Sustaining $25; Life $150.

Noank

NOANK HISTORICAL SOCIETY, INC., 17 Sylvan St., Noank, CT 06340-5742. Mailing Address: P.O. Box 9454, Noank, CT 06340-9454. Tel.: 860-536-3021 & 3029.
E-mail: noankhist@sbcglobal.net
Web Site: www.noankhistoricalsociety.org
Founded: 1966.
Congressional District: 2
Key Personnel: Pres., Deborah Bates; Vice Pres., Justin Carmarata; Cur., Mary Anderson; Historian, Arnold Crossman; Treas., Steven Anderson.
Governing Authority: society; nonprofit organization. Subsidiary Institution: Latham/Chester Store Museum, 108 Main St., Noank, CT 06340. Tax-exempt: 501(c)(3).
History Museum: housed in c.1847 mercantile building.
Collections: marine; naval; local history; medical & domestic paraphernalia; art; historical photographs; shipbuilder's tools; exhibition of local fisheries.
Research Fields: Indian; marine; shipbuilding; fishing; histories of old houses; local history; genealogy.
Facilities: Books, early maps, photos & other museum-related items for sale.
Activities: quarterly meetings; group tours; local history program; lectures. Annual Events: Independence Day Art Show & Celebration.
Publications: quarterly newsletter; book, Noank: From the Papers of Claude Chester. Noank: The Ethereal Years; The Log of Downit; Captains B. F. Rathbun of Noank; Noank Celebrating A Maritime Heritage.
Hours & Admission Prices: July-Columbus Day Wed. & Sat.-Sun. 2-5; other times by appointment. No charge; donations accepted.
Attendance: 1,000 (estimated)
Membership: Individual $10; Family $15; Contributing $25 & over.

Norfolk

NORFOLK HISTORICAL MUSEUM, 13 Village Green, Norfolk, CT 06058. Mailing Address: P.O. Box 288, Norfolk, CT 06058-0288. Tel.: 860-542-5761.
E-mail: norfolkhistorical@sbcglobal.net
Web Site: www.norfolkhistoricalsociety.org
Founded: 1960.
Congressional District: 6
Key Personnel: Pres. (V), Barry Webber; 1st Vice Pres., Richard Byrne; 2nd Vice Pres., Eric Anderson; Treas., Susan Dyer; Sec., Sally Vaun.
Personnel Profile: Part-Time Paid 1; Part-Time Volunteers 15.
Governing Authority: nonprofit corporation. Norfolk Historical Society, Inc. Tax-exempt: 501(c)(3).
Historical Society Museum.
Collections: decorative arts; costumes; folklore; maps; manuscripts; artifacts; farm tools; photographs; genealogical material; local history archive including Norfolk area.
Research Fields: early Norfolk history & residents.

Facilities: 200-vol. library of books on local history & genealogy available on premises.
Activities: lectures; permanent & temporary exhibitions.
Publications: pamphlets; annual society newsletter, The Muse.
Hours & Admission Prices: June-Oct. 10 Sat.-Sun. 12-4; Nov.-April 1st Thurs. of month 1-5; other times by appointment. No charge; donations accepted. ♿
Membership: Family & Friends $10-$25; Supporting $50-$75; Donor $100-$300; Patron $500.

North Haven

NORTH HAVEN HISTORICAL SOCIETY, 27 Broadway, North Haven, CT 06473-2302. Tel.: 203-239-7722.
Web Site: www.northhavenhistoricalsociety.org
Founded: 1957.
Key Personnel: Pres., Bruce Dumelin; Vice Pres., Steve Nugent; Treas., Walter Brockett; Cur., Gloria Furnival; Sec., Arline Tolette.
Personnel Profile: Part-Time Paid 1; Part-Time Volunteers 15.
Governing Authority: nonprofit organization. Tax-exempt: 501(c)(3).
History Museum.
Collections: local history & culture; documents, deeds, manuscripts, diaries, journals & account books pertaining to North Haven; genealogical material; Indian artifacts; projectile points; textiles; looms; agricultural items; historic buildings.
Research Fields: local history.
Facilities: library pertaining to basic research & rare books available for research on premises by special arrangement with librarian.
Activities: guided tours; lectures; films; formally organized education programs for children; temporary exhibitions; scholarship fund for North Haven High School senior. Annual Event: Trolly Tour of Town.
Publications: booklets, North Haven in the Revolution; The Quinnipiac; Two to Eight - A Country Childhood When the Century was New; Amidst Cultivated & Pleasant Fields, A Bicentennial History of North Haven, CT; On the Green, The Old Center Cemetery in North Haven, Connecticut 1723-1882.
Hours & Admission Prices: Winter & Spring: Tues. & Thurs. 1-4:30; Summer: Thurs. 1-4:30; Fall: Wed. 7pm-9pm, Tues. & Thurs. 1-4:30. No charge; donations accepted. Closed New Year's Eve & Day; Christmas Eve, Day & week.
Membership: Individual $15; Family $25; Supporting $75; Life Individual $125; Life Family $200.

Norwalk

ART GALLERY AT NORWALK COMMUNITY COLLEGE, 188 Richards Ave., Norwalk, CT 06854. Tel.: 203-857-7000.
Art Gallery.
Collections: paintings; prints; photography; sculpture.
Hours & Admission Prices: Mon.-Thurs. 9-9, Fri. 9-4, Sat. 9-12. No charge. Closed holidays.

CENTER FOR CONTEMPORARY PRINTMAKING, Mathews Park, 299 West Ave., Norwalk, CT 06850-4002. Tel.: 203-899-7999. Fax: 203-899-7997.
E-mail: info@contemprints.org
Web Site: www.contemprints.org
Founded: 1995.
Key Personnel: Exec. Dir., Leslie Nolan; Chair, Diana Wedge
Printmaking Museum.
Collections: prints; printmaking.
Hours & Admission Prices: Mon.-Sat. 9-5. No charge. ♿

LOCKWOOD-MATHEWS MANSION MUSEUM, 295 West Ave., Norwalk, CT 06850-4002. Tel.: 203-838-9799. Fax: 203-838-1434.
E-mail: info@lockwoodmathewsmansion.com
Web Site: www.lockwoodmathewsmansion.com
Founded: 1966.
Congressional District: 4
Key Personnel: Pres. & Exec. Dir., Sheldon Gerarden; Chm. (V), Chris Cooke.
Personnel Profile: Full-Time Paid 1; Part-Time Paid 2; Part-Time Volunteers 50.
Governing Authority: nonprofit organization. Tax-exempt.
Historic House Museum: c.1868 Elm Park Home.
Collections: Victorian furniture; decorative wall paintings; inlaid & carved woodwork; historic costume collection; 19th-century decorative arts, paintings & archival collections.
Research Fields: Victorian arts & architecture.
Facilities: Victorian gifts for sale.
Activities: guided tours; lectures; arts festivals; formally organized education programs for children; docent program; traveling exhibitions.
Publications: quarterly newsletter; books, LeGrand Lockwood; The Lockwood Mathews Mansion; Nineteenth Century Architects: Building a Profession; Nineteenth Century Women Photographers: A New Dimension in Leisure; The Tiffanys.
Hours & Admission Prices: Tours: Jan to mid-March by appointment only; mid-March to Dec. Wed.-Sun. 12-3. Adults $10, senior citizens $8, youth 8-18 $6; children under 8 & members no charge. Closed major holidays. ♿
Attendance: 23,000 (estimated)
Membership: Individual $35; Family $55; Circle Donor $100; Circle Sponsor $250; Circle Patron $500; Circle Benefactor $1,000; Circle Angel $2,500.

THE MARITIME AQUARIUM AT NORWALK, 10 N. Water St., Norwalk, CT 06854-2228. Tel.: 203-852-0700, ext. 2232. Fax: 203-838-5416.
Web Site: www.maritimeaquarium.org
Founded: 1988.
Congressional District: 4
Key Personnel: C.E.O. & Pres., Jennifer Herring; Education, Jack Schneider; Mktg., Chris Loynd; Dir. Exhibits, Judith Bacal; Museum Shop Mgr., Angela Catigano.
Personnel Profile: Full-Time Paid 50; Part-Time Paid 50; Part-Time Volunteers 175; Interns 20.
Governing Authority: nonprofit organization. Tax-exempt: 501(c)(3).
Aquarium: housed in 19th-century iron works foundry.
Collections: aquarium of marine life indigenous to Long Island Sound, including harbor seals & sharks; sea turtles; jelly fish; River otters; artifacts of the oystering industry in Norwalk; marine science & culture; Ray touch tank; intertidal animals touch tank.
Major Exhibits: African Penguins, 11/09-12/10.
Research Fields: monitoring physical & chemical water quality parameters, including dissolved oxygen; marine population studies in Long Island Sound; harbor seal census.
Facilities: aquarium; 200-seat restaurant; classrooms; laboratories; 75,000 sq. ft. exhibit space; 337-seat IMAX theatre; 1 research vessel. Environmental education center: classrooms, laboratory, 180-seat school cafeteria. Museum-related items for sale.
Activities: docent program; IMAX films; formal educational programs; guided tours; ecology cruises; lectures; loan, temporary & traveling exhibitions; mobile vans; interactive exhibits; gallery rental; theatre; conferences; festivals. Annual Events: Holiday Programs; Members Reception; Harbor Seal Symposium.
Publications: quarterly newsletter, The Maritimes; school programs brochure.
Hours & Admission Prices: Aquarium: adults $11.75, seniors 62 & over $10.75, children 2-12 $9.75; members no charge. Closed Thanksgiving; Christmas. ♿
Attendance: 500,000
Membership: Individual Plus One $69; Family $90; Family & AuPair $110; Family Plus $130; Family Deluxe $250; Friends Society $1,000 & up.

SHEFFIELD ISLAND LIGHTHOUSE, Hope Dock (Ferry Svc.), Washington St. & N. Water St., Norwalk, CT 06854. Mailing Address: Norwalk Seaport Association, 132 Water St., 06854, CT 06854. Tel.: 203-838-9444.
Historic Lighthouse: housed on Sheffield Island; built in 1868.
Collections: lighthouse; period artifacts.
Hours & Admission Prices: Ferry Service: May-Sept. call for schedule. Adults $20, seniors $18, children 4-12 $12, children 3 & under $5.

SONO SWITCH TOWER MUSEUM, 77 Washington St., Norwalk, CT 06854-3086. Tel.: 203-246-6958.
Historic Building: built in 1896.
Collections: railroad & switch tower history; railroad memorabilia; period artifacts; photographs.
Hours & Admission Prices: May-Oct. Sat.-Sun. 12-5. No charge; donations accepted.

STEPPING STONES MUSEUM FOR CHILDREN, (M), 303 West Ave., Mathews Park, Norwalk, CT 06850-4002. Tel.: 203-899-0606. Fax: 203-899-0530.
E-mail: information@steppingstonesmuseum.org
Web Site: www.steppingstonesmuseum.org
Founded: 1998.
Key Personnel: Exec. Dir., Rhonda Kiest; Devel., Michelle Jordan; Chm. Bd., John Foster; Dir. Education, Hyla Crane; Mgr. Mktg. & Communications, Robin Wexler; C.F.O. & Dir. Business Devel., David Sklar; Museum Shop Mgr., Dina Berger.
Personnel Profile: Full-Time Paid 25; Part-Time Paid 25; Part-Time Volunteers 230; Interns 3.
Governing Authority: private; nonprofit organization. Tax-exempt: 501(c)(3).
Children's Museum.
Collections: hands-on science, the arts, culture & heritage.

Research Fields: early childhood development; K-5 learning standards; environmental design; community collaboration.
Facilities: 1,000-vol. library; 80-seat auditorium; 20-seat cafeteria; 10,000 sq. ft. exhibit space; learning labs; resource center; outdoor courtyard. Museum-related items for sale.
Activities: formal education programs; guided tours; hobby workshops; lectures; participatory exhibits; rental gallery; study clubs; summer drop-off program; parent education; scout workshops & badge-earning activities.
Publications: quarterly newsletter, Stepping Stones Museum for Children - Get Into It!; monthly e-newsletter; annual report.
Hours & Admission Prices: Memorial Day to Labor Day daily 10-5; Sept.-May Tues. 1-5, Wed.-Sun. 10-5. Adults $9, seniors $7; discounts to groups of 15 or more & ACM members; children under 1 & members no charge. Closed New Year's Day; Easter; Thanksgiving; Christmas. ♿
Attendance: 200,000 (accurate)
Membership: Family $125; Family Plus $175; Friend $300.

Norwich

FAITH TRUMBULL CHAPTER, DAUGHTERS OF THE AMERICAN REVOLUTION, INC., MUSEUM AND CHAPTER HOUSE, 42 Rockwell St., Norwich, CT 06360-3537. Tel.: 860-887-8737.
Founded: 1893.
Congressional District: 2
Key Personnel: Regent, Polly Gunther; Cur., Marianne Vanden Bout.
Personnel Profile: Full-Time Paid 1; Part-Time Volunteers 10.
Governing Authority: nonprofit organization. Parent Institution: The National Society Daughters of the American Revolution. Tax-exempt.
Historical Society Museum.
Collections: furniture; clothing; local portraits; local history; genealogy books. Historic Houses: 1750 Nathaniel Backus House; 1818 Rockwell House.
Research Fields: genealogical tracing; Faith Trumbull DAR Chapter.
Facilities: library of local history books available for use by appointment only.
Activities: guided tours; permanent exhibitions. Museum Sponsors: six area high school scholarships.
Hours & Admission Prices: 2nd & 4th Sun. of month 1-3:30; other times by appointment. No charge; donations accepted. Closed holidays.

THE LEFFINGWELL HOUSE MUSEUM, 348 Washington St., Norwich, CT 06360-2444. Mailing Address: P.O. Box 13, Norwich, CT 06360-0013. Tel.: 860-889-9440. Fax: 860-887-4551.
Founded: 1901.
Congressional District: 2
Key Personnel: Pres., Ann-etta Cannon; Museum Shop Mgr., Pauline Sullivan.
Personnel Profile: Part-Time Volunteers 20.
Governing Authority: nonprofit. Parent Institution: Society of the Founders of Norwich, CT, Inc. Branch Museums: 1772, Joseph Carpenter Silversmith Shop, 73 E. Town St., Norwich; 1789 E. District School Children's Historical Museum, Norwich. Tax-exempt: 501(c)(3).
Historic House Museum: 1675-1715-1760 The Leffingwell Inn.
Collections: period dolls; Norwich silver; Indian artifacts; genealogical & historical local material; early Norwich colonial silver & pewter; antiques of local origin.
Facilities: 150-vol. library of books pertaining to Norwich historical background; genealogical material pertaining to Norwich families; old deeds; newspapers & documents available for research by properly accredited persons. Books on Norwich history & museum-related items for sale.
Activities: guided tours.
Publications: annual report; books, Samuel Huntington & His Family; Craftsmen & Artists of Norwich; The History of Norwich; A Definitive Index of Caulkins' History; The Autobiography of James L. Smith; Norwich-Century of Growth.
Hours & Admission Prices: May-Oct. Sat.-Sun. 12-4 & also by appointment. Adults $5, students & senior citizens $3, children under 12 $2; discounts to groups of 10 or more; members no charge.
Attendance: 1,500 (estimated)
Membership: Student $10; Senior Citizens (over 65) $15; Single $20; Family $30; Sustaining $60; Patron $150; Life $500.

THE SLATER MEMORIAL MUSEUM - NORWICH FREE ACADEMY, (M), 108 Crescent St., Norwich, CT 06360-3556. Tel.: 860-887-2506 & 425-5560. Fax: 860-885-0379.
E-mail: zoev@norwichfreeacademy.com
Web Site: www.norwichfreeacademy.com
Founded: 1886.
Congressional District: 2
Key Personnel: Chm. (V), Richard DesRoches; Dir., Vivian F. Zoe; Museum Educator, Mary Anne Hall; Asst. Dir., Leigh Smead.
Personnel Profile: Full-Time Paid 3; Part-Time Paid 5; Part-Time Volunteers 30.
Governing Authority: nonprofit organization. Parent Institution: Norwich Free Academy Corp. Tax-exempt: 501(c)(3).
Art Museum: housed in an historic building designed by Worcester architect, Stephen Earle c.1886; located on the campus of the Norwich Free Academy.
Collections: casts of early Greek, Roman & Renaissance statues; American paintings, sculpture, graphics & furnishings; Oriental art; African & South Sea Islands art; costumes; Native American & marine items; guns; decorative arts; textiles.
Research Fields: John Denison Crocker; Alexander Hamilton Emmons.
Facilities: Converse Art Gallery.
Activities: guided tours; lectures; gallery talks; permanent & rotating exhibitions.
Publications: pamphlet, The Slater Memorial Museum; The Slater Museum Cast catalogue; Greek Myths for Young People; quarterly newsletter, The Muse.
Hours & Admission Prices: Tues.-Fri. 9-4, Sat.-Sun. 1-4. Adults $3, seniors & students $2; discounts to NEMA, AAM & ICOM members; museum members no charge. Closed holidays.
Attendance: 12,000 (estimated)
Membership: Friends of Slater Museum: Student $10; Senior Citizen $15; Individual $25; Family $35; Contributing $50; Patron $100; Sustaining $200; Benefactor $500.

Oakdale

THE DINOSAUR PLACE AT NATURE'S ART, 1650 Hartford New London Turnpike, Oakdale, CT 06370. Tel.: 860-443-4367. Fax: 860-443-0253.
Mineralogy Museum.
Collections: local history; minerals; fossils.
Facilities: Museum-related items for sale.
Activities: hands-on exhibits; special events; birthday parties.
Hours & Admission Prices: Call for hours.

Old Lyme

* **FLORENCE GRISWOLD MUSEUM, (M),** 96 Lyme St., Old Lyme, CT 06371-1426. Tel.: 860-434-5542. Fax: 860-434-9778 (administrative offices).
E-mail: jeff@flogris.org
Web Site: www.florencegriswoldmuseum.org
Founded: 1936.
Congressional District: 2
Key Personnel: C.E.O. & Dir., Jeffrey W. Andersen; Pres., Mary Ann Besier; Facilities Mgr., Ted Gaffney; Dir. Devel., Janie Stanley; Dir. Education & Outreach, David Rau; Museum Educator, Mollie Clarke; Business Mgr., Therese Kus; Membership Coord., Shawn Savage; Registrar, Nicole Wholean; Asst. to Dir., Donna Carlson; Cur., Amy Kurtz Lansing; Dir. Mktg., Tammi Amaya Flynn; Dir. Finance, Laura Alden; Fundraising Office, Sarah Carpenter; Visitor Svcs. Coord. & Museum Shop Mgr., Matt Greene; Mktg. Assoc., Elizabeth Reid.
Personnel Profile: Full-Time Paid 14; Part-Time Paid 4; Part-Time Volunteers 375; Interns 2.
Governing Authority: nonprofit. Parent Institution: Lyme Historical Society, Inc. Tax-exempt: 501(c)(3).
Art Museum.
Collections: American paintings; Lyme Art Colony paintings; decorative arts; archives. Historic Houses: c.1794, Huntley-Brown House; William Chadwick Studio; 1817 Florence Griswold House.
Research Fields: regional history; paintings of the Old Lyme Art Colony; art of Connecticut.
Facilities: library & archives on regional history & American art available for use on premises; Hartman Education Center. Books & museum-related items for sale.
Activities: guided tours; lectures; films; classes.
Publications: catalogues; books, Miss Florence & the Artists of Old Lyme; Hamburg Cove Past and Present; The Lieutenant River; The Lymes' Heritage Cookbook; catalogs, Edward F. Rook American Impressionist; Connecticut and American Impressionism; Clark Voorhees, 1871-1933; Old Lyme: The American Barbizon; Bruce Crane: American Tonalist; The Whites of Waterford; Harry L. Hoffman: A World of Color; En Plein Air: The Art Colonies of East Hampton & Old Lyme, 1880-1930; Thomas W. Nason: New England Virtues; Carved in Wood; portfolio, The Connecticut Impressionists at Old Lyme; Childe Hassam in Connecticut; The Harmony of Nature; The Art and Life of Frank Vincent DuMond; A World Observed: The Art of Everett Longley Warner; Faces of Change: The Art of Ivan Olinsky; A Noble Tradition: American Paintings from the National Arts Club; Lines of Thought: American Works on Paper from a Private Collection; Wilson Henry Irvine and The Poetry of Light; Henry Ward Ranger and The Humanized Landscape; The American Artist in Connecticut, 2002; May Night, Willard Metcalf in Old Lyme, 2005; Visions of

Mood: Henry C. White Pastels, 2009; Lyme in Mind: The Clement C. Moore Collection, 2009.
Hours & Admission Prices: Tues.-Sat. 10-5, Sun. 1-5. Adults $9, senior & students with ID $8; discounts to AAA & AAM members; children under 12 & members no charge. ♿
Attendance: 57,708 (accurate)
Membership: Individual $50; Family $75; Business Sponsor & Supporting $125 & up; Sustaining $250 & up; Patron $500 & up; Leader $1,000 & up; Life $2,500; Benefactor $5,000 & up.

Pine Meadow

NEW HARTFORD HISTORICAL SOCIETY, 367 Main St., Pine Meadow, CT 06061. Mailing Address: P.O. Box 41, New Hartford, CT 06057-0041. Tel.: 860-379-6894.
Historical Society Museum.
Collections: New Hartford history; photographs; personal artifacts.
Activities: lectures; meetings; school programs; research.
Hours & Admission Prices: Wed. 2-4, Sat. 10-12; other times by appointment.

Pleasant Valley

STONE MUSEUM, Greenwoods Rd., Pleasant Valley, CT 06063. Mailing Address: P.O. Box 1, Pleasant Valley, CT 06063. Tel.: 860-379-2469.
Historic Building: built in 1934.
Collections: local history & culture; mounted wildlife; natural history; photographs; Native American artifacts.
Facilities: nature trails.
Activities: hiking; special events.
Hours & Admission Prices: Memorial Day to June & Sept to Columbus Day Sun.; July-Aug. Sat.-Sun.

Plymouth

ARTWORKS ART STUDIO & GALLERY, 109 Wilton Rd., Plymouth, CT 06782. Tel.: 860-283-6272.
Art Gallery.
Collections: works by local artists; sculpture; pottery; paintings; pastels.
Activities: classes; birthday parties; summer camps; temporary exhibitions.
Hours & Admission Prices: Mon.-Fri. 9-6, Sat.-Sun. 10-4. No charge.

Ridgefield

THE ALDRICH CONTEMPORARY ART MUSEUM, (M), 258 Main St., Ridgefield, CT 06877-4935. Tel.: 203-438-4519. Fax: 203-438-0198.
E-mail: general@aldrichart.org
Web Site: www.aldrichart.org
Founded: 1964.
Congressional District: 5
Key Personnel: Chm., Mark Goldstein; Dir., Harry Philbrick.
Personnel Profile: Full-Time Paid 18; Part-Time Paid 30; Part-Time Volunteers 35; Interns 3.
Governing Authority: nonprofit organization. Tax-exempt: 170(b)(1)(A).
Contemporary Art Museum.
Collections: works by contemporary artists.
Research Fields: Contemporary Art.
Facilities: sculpture garden.
Activities: exhibition related events, tours, lectures, film; nationally recognized education programs; changing exhibitions focusing on contemporary art with an emphasis on emerging & mid-career artists.
Publications: catalog of changing exhibitions; newsletter; exhibition posters.
Hours & Admission Prices: Tues.-Sun. 12-5. Adults $7, senior citizens & college students $4; discount to AAM members; children 18 & under, members and Tues. no charge. Closed New Year's Day; Thanksgiving; Christmas. ♿
Attendance: 25,000 (estimated)
Membership: Friend $100; Family $125; Partner $500; Donor $1,000; Sponsor $2,500.

KEELER TAVERN MUSEUM, 132 Main St., Ridgefield, CT 06877-4931. Mailing Address: P.O. Box 204, Ridgefield, CT 06877-0204. Tel.: 203-438-5485 & 431-0815. Fax: 203-438-9953.
E-mail: keelertavernmuseum@earthlink.net
Web Site: keelertavernmuseum.org
Founded: 1966.
Congressional District: 5
Key Personnel: Pres., Cheryl Crowl; 1st Vice Pres., Ken Friedman; Treas., George Stuek; Co.-Dir., Mary Ann Connors; Co.-Dir., Brenda DeVos; Museum Shop Mgr., Margo McEachern.
Personnel Profile: Full-Time Paid 1; Full-Time Volunteers 75; Part-Time Paid 2; Part-Time Volunteers 100.
Governing Authority: society. Parent Institution: Keeler Tavern Preservation Society, Inc. Tax-exempt: 501(c)(3).
Historic Building Museum.
Collections: period tavern furnishings; cannon ball shot by cannon into corner post during battle of Ridgefield still in sight; 18th to 19th-century furnishings, including original family pieces, pewter, woodenware, china, milkglass & costumes; 1890-1930 Joseph Hartmann photographic collection from glass plate negative. Historic Buildings: 1907 summer home of architect Cass Gilbert; 1915 garden house; barn; 1713 tavern & stagecoach inn.
Research Fields: local history.
Facilities: garden; banquet facilities. Gifts & museum-related items for sale.
Activities: guided tours; lectures; temporary exhibitions. Museum Sponsors: Colonial Day; Traditional Christmas Luncheon in Cass Gilbert Garden House in December.
Publications: books, the Diary of Anna M. Resseguie (1851-67); A View From the Inn; The Keeler Family Book.
Hours & Admission Prices: Feb.-Dec. Wed. & Sat.-Sun. 1-4, last tour 3:30 p.m.; special tours by appointment. Adults $5, senior citizens $3, children under 12 $2; members no charge. Closed Easter; Christmas.
Attendance: 4,600 (estimated)
Membership: Individual $25; Family $50; Contributing $100; Patron & Business $250; Life $1,000.

RIDGEFIELD HISTORICAL SOCIETY, 4 Sunset Lane, Ridgefield, CT 06877-4643. Tel.: 203-438-5821.
E-mail: ridgefieldhistory@sbcglobal.net
Web Site: www.ridgefieldhistoricalsociety.org
Key Personnel: Pres., Gary Singer
Historical Society Museum.
Collections: Ridgefield history & culture; photographs.
Hours & Admission Prices: Tues.-Thurs. 1-5.

Riverton

GREENWOOD GLASS BLOWING STUDIO GALLERY, 3 Robertsville Rd., Riverton, CT 06065. Tel.: 860-738-9464.
Art Gallery: housed in historic Union Church; built in 1829.
Collections: contemporary hand-blown art glass chandeliers; wall sculptures; glass furniture; lighting; goblets; paintings.
Activities: demonstrations; glass-blowing classes; guided tours; workshops.
Hours & Admission Prices: Tues.-Sat. 9-5 by appointment. No charge.

Rocky Hill

ACADEMY HALL MUSEUM OF THE ROCKY HILL HISTORICAL SOCIETY, INC., 785 Old Main St., Rocky Hill, CT 06067-1519. Mailing Address: P.O. Box 185, Rocky Hill, CT 06067-0185. Tel.: 860-563-6704.
E-mail: info@rockyhillhistory
Web Site: www.rockyhillhistory.org
Founded: 1962.
Congressional District: 1
Key Personnel: Pres. (V), Mike Martino.
Personnel Profile: Part-Time Volunteers 10.
Governing Authority: society. Tax-exempt: 501(c)(3).
History Museum: housed in 1803 schoolhouse.
Collections: Indian artifacts; domestic implements; 19th-century clothing & accessories; hats; fans; farming equipment; tools; furniture; 500 salts; handmade quilts; early lamps.
Research Fields: local history.
Facilities: 600-vol. library of local & general historical material available in the society's library. Booklets for sale.
Activities: permanent & special exhibitions.
Publications: quarterly newsletter, Rocky Hill Historical Society.
Hours & Admission Prices: June-Sept. Tues. 10-12, 4th Thurs. 7-9, Sat. 12:30-3; Oct.-May Tues. 10-12, Sat. 12:30-3; other times by appointment. No charge.
Attendance: 340 (accurate)
Membership: Individual $15; Family $25; Business & Groups $35; Contributing $100; Life $250.

DINOSAUR STATE PARK, 400 West St., Rocky Hill, CT 06067-3506. Tel.: 860-529-8423. Fax: 860-257-1405.
E-mail: info@dinosaurstatepark.org
Web Site: www.dinosaurstatepark.org
Founded: 1968.
Congressional District: 1
Key Personnel: Pres. (V), Kathy Kennedy; Vice Pres., Susan Lionberger; Dir., Meg Enkler; Maintainer III, Lawrence Butts; Maintainer III, Alan Bielawski; Park Naturalist, Christine Witkowski; Treas., Jan Locke; Sec., Maryanne Marchinski; Museum Shop Mgr., Joseph Panitch.

Personnel Profile: Full-Time Paid 5; Part-Time Paid 5; Part-Time Volunteers 40.
Governing Authority: state. Parent Institution: CT Dept. of Environmental Protection. Subsidiary Institution: Bureau of Outdoor Recreation, State Parks Div. Tax-exempt.
State Park.
Collections: sandstone trackway with 2,000 dinosaur tracks; slabs with tracks; living woody plants of families from Mesozoic Era; geological specimens; herbarium; dioramas; early plants.
Research Fields: dinosaur tracks; local flora & fauna.
Facilities: 1,000-vol. library of geology texts, reprints, bulletins & nature study handbooks available for use on premises by permission of staff; nature trail; picnic area; 100-seat auditorium; classroom; arboretum; butterfly garden; native plant garden. Museum-related items for sale.
Activities: guided tours; temporary & permanent exhibitions; lectures; films; special programs; track casting area.
Publications: bimonthly newsletter; Tracks and Trails.
Hours & Admission Prices: Exhibit Center: Tues.-Sun. 9-4:30. Park: daily 9-4:30. Trails: daily 9-4. Exhibit Center: adults 13 & over $10, youth 6-12 $4; children 5 & under no charge. Closed New Year's Day; Thanksgiving; Christmas. ♿
Attendance: 53,000 (estimated)
Membership: Friends of Dinosaur Park Assoc. Inc.: Individual $15; Family $20; Supporting $40; Coelophysis Club $75; Dilophosaurus Club $150; Corporate $250; Life $400.

Rowayton

ROWAYTON ARTS CENTER, 145 Rowayton Ave., Rowayton, CT 06853-1444. Tel.: 203-866-2744.
Founded: 1960.
Key Personnel: Dir., Debra Randall; Pres., Hu Lindsay; Vice Pres., Jessica Huse.
Governing Authority: Tax-exempt.
Art Center.
Collections: paintings; sculpture.
Major Exhibits: Students and Teachers, 1/10-10-1/24/10; Walter Brooks Memorial Watercolor, 1/31/10-2/21/10; All Media/Juried Show, 2/28/10-3/21/10; Photography & Sculpture, 3/28/10-4/18/10; Community Sponsored All Media, 4/25/10-5/16/10; Drawings, Prints, Pastels, Mixed, Computer, 5/23/10-6/13/10; My Kind of Town, Our Town, 6/20/10-7/11/10; Alternative Visions/Abstract, 7/18/10-8/8/10; Wet Paint/Oil and Acrylic, 8/15/10-9/6/10; Mavis Fenner Memorial, 10/10/10-11/7/10.
Facilities: Museum-related items for sale.
Activities: adult & children's classes; fundraising events; workshops; demonstrations; receptions. Museum Sponsors: Art in the Park in May; Plein Air Art Walk & Show in June; Holiday Gift Sale in November & December.
Publications: quarterly newsletter.
Hours & Admission Prices: Tues.-Sat. 12-5, Sun. 1-4. No charge. Closed Thanksgiving; Christmas.
Membership: Supporting: Individual $30; Family $55; Art Angel $200. Exhibiting: Individual $45; Family $60; Art Angel $200.

Scotland

D'ELIA ANTIQUE TOOL MUSEUM, 21 Brook Rd., Scotland, CT 06264. Mailing Address: P.O. Box 164, Scotland, CT 06264-0164. Tel.: 860-456-1516.
E-mail: info@deliatoolmuseum.com
Web Site: www.deliatoolmuseum.com
Tool Museum.
Collections: over 1,000 woodworking hand planes; patents; early planemakers.
Hours & Admission Prices: Sat.-Sun. 10-4; other times by appointment.

HUNTINGTON HOMESTEAD, 36 Huntington Rd., Scotland, CT 06264-2209. Mailing Address: P.O. Box 231, Scotland, CT 06264-0231. Tel.: 860-456-8381.
E-mail: info@huntingtonhomestead.org
Web Site: huntingtonhomestead.org
Founded: 1994.
Governing Authority: Parent Institution: Governor Samuel Huntington Trust, Inc., P.O. Box 231, Scotland, CT 06264. Tax-exempt.
Historic House: the birthplace of Samuel Huntington, a signer of the Declaration of Independence.
Collections: period artifacts; photographs; Samuel Huntington signed documents.
Facilities: Museum-related items for sale.
Publications: annual newsletter, The Signature.
Hours & Admission Prices: May-Oct. 1st & 3rd Sat. of month 10:30-3:30. No charge; donations accepted.
Membership: Individual $15; Family $20; Citizen $50; Parishioner $100; Lawyer $250; Justice $500; Councilor $1,000; Congressman $5,000; Governor $10,000; President $10,000 & up.

Sharon

SHARON AUDUBON CENTER, 325 Cornwall Bridge Rd., Sharon, CT 06069-2512. Tel.: 860-364-0520. Fax: 860-364-5792.
Web Site: www.audubon.org/local/sanctuary/sharon
Founded: 1961.
Congressional District: 6
Key Personnel: Dir., Scott Heth; Land Mgr., Mike Dudek; Museum Shop Mgr. & Office Mgr., Dawn Osborne; Environmental Education Specialist, Wendy Miller; Animal Rehabilitation & Outreach Coord., Erin O'Connell; Caretaker, Dave Paton.
Personnel Profile: Full-Time Paid 6; Part-Time Paid 1; Part-Time Volunteers 10; Interns 2.
Governing Authority: nonprofit. Parent Institution: National Audubon Society, 700 Broadway, New York, NY 10003. Tax-exempt: 501(c)(3).
Nature Center.
Collections: 1,147 acre area with fields, forest, pond, stream, marsh, trees & plants; wildlife refuge; bird sanctuary; raptor aviaries including 10 species of live birds of prey.
Research Fields: education, woodlot & wildlife management.
Facilities: 900-vol. library of natural history & conservation books available for use on premises; nature center; nine nature trails; trail for handicapped. Books, stationery & museum-related items for sale.
Activities: guided tours; films; hobby workshops for adults; formally organized educational programs; permanent & temporary exhibitions; outreach to local camps; summer day camp for children. Center Sponsors: Maple Sugaring Festival in March; Sharon Audubon Festival in August.
Publications: newsletter, The Otter and the Hawk.
Hours & Admission Prices: Trails: dawn-dusk. Tues.-Sat. 9-5, Sun. 1-5. Adults $3, children under 18 & seniors $1.50; discounts to National Audubon Society members; members no charge. Closed holidays. ♿
Attendance: 10,000 (estimated)
Membership: Annual $20; National Audubon Society $35.

SHARON HISTORICAL SOCIETY, (M), 18 Main St., Sharon, CT 06069-2052. Mailing Address: P.O. Box 511, Sharon, CT 06069-0511. Tel.: 860-364-5688.
Web Site: www.sharonhist.org
Founded: 1911.
Key Personnel: Exec. Dir., Elizabeth G. Shapiro; Chm. (V), Edward Kirby; Education, Janet Nickson; Treas., Allen Reiser; Cur., Margaret McAvoy.
Personnel Profile: Part-Time Paid 3; Part-Time Volunteers 80.
Governing Authority: private; nonprofit organization. Tax-exempt: 501(c)(3).
Historical Society Museum.
Collections: local, regional & state history and culture; decorative arts; period artifacts.
Facilities: library; 750 sq. ft. exhibit space. Museum-related items for sale.
Activities: films; formal education programs; guided tours; hobby workshops; lectures; participatory & temporary exhibitions; training programs for professional museum workers. Annual Events: Independence Day Special Event; Tree Lighting Open House.
Publications: quarterly newsletter, Sharon Archives.
Hours & Admission Prices: Jan. 4-Dec. 27 Tues.-Fri. 10-4; other times by appointment. No charge; donations accepted. Closed New Year's Day; Thanksgiving; Christmas Day & week. ♿
Attendance: 1,200 (estimated)
Membership: Annual $25; Sustaining $150; Benefactor $300; Sponsor $500; Trustee's Circle $1,000.

Shelton

SHELTON HISTORICAL SOCIETY, 70 Ripton Rd., Shelton, CT 06484. Tel.: 203-929-7963.
Historical Society Museum: housed in a one-room school house; built in 1871.
Collections: local history & culture; period furnishings; photographs.
Hours & Admission Prices: Call for hours.

Sherman

NORTHROP HOUSE MUSEUM, 10 Rte. 37 Center, Sherman, CT 06784-1503. Tel.: 860-350-3475 & 354-3083.
Governing Authority: Parent Institution: Sherman Historical Society.
Historic House Museum: built in 1829.
Collections: Northrop family history; personal artifacts; period furnishings; photographs.
Hours & Admission Prices: By appointment.

Simsbury

SIMSBURY HISTORICAL SOCIETY, PHELPS TAVERN, MUSEUM, (M), 800 Hopmeadow St., Simsbury, CT 06070-1825. Mailing Address: P.O. Box 2, Simsbury, CT 06070-0002. Tel.: 860-658-2500. Fax: 860-651-4354.
E-mail: info@simsburyhistory.org
Web Site: www.simsburyhistory.org
Founded: 1911.
Congressional District: 6
Personnel Profile: Full-Time Paid 2; Full-Time Volunteers 4; Part-Time Paid 2; Part-Time Volunteers 120; Interns 4.
Governing Authority: Parent Institution: Simsbury Historical Society Inc. Tax-exempt: 501(c)(3).
History Museum.
Collections: Higley coppers; fuse machinery; sleighs; carriages; artifacts; memorabilia; manuscripts. Historic Houses: 1795 Hendrick Cottage; 1740 First Simsbury School House; replica of 1683 First Meeting House; 1771 Captain Elisha Phelps House, Barn & Outbuildings; mid-19th century Victorian Carriage House; 1876 Simsbury Probate court building.
Research Fields: local & family history; transportation; early manufacturing.
Facilities: 5,000-vol. library and extensive manuscript collection. Commemorative items & publications for sale.
Activities: guided tours; lecture series; historic portrayals; local history programs for children; organized education programs for children; permanent & temporary exhibitions. Annual Event: antique show.
Publications: books, A Spy at Ticonderoga, Newgate From Copper Mine to State Prison; annual calendar; quarterly, Archival; newsletter, The Sign Post.
Hours & Admission Prices: Tours: Tues.-Sat. 12-4. Adults $6, senior citizens over 65 $5, children 6-17 $4; discount to groups & AAA members; members and children 5 & under no charge. Library & Archives: Thurs.-Sat. 12-4. Closed federal holidays.
Attendance: 3,800 (accurate)
Membership: Individual $15; Family $25; Sustaining $40; Corporate $75.

South Norwalk

NORWALK MUSEUM, (M), 41 N. Main St., South Norwalk, CT 06854-2702. Tel.: 203-866-0202. Fax: 203-866-0675.
E-mail: sgunnbromley@norwalkct.org
Web Site: www.norwalkct.org/norwalkmuseum
Key Personnel: Dir., Susan Gunn Bromley
History Museum.
Collections: local history & culture; Norwalk's industry; photographs; oystering; railroads; historic buildings; pottery; quilts.
Facilities: library.
Hours & Admission Prices: Museum: Wed.-Sun. 1-5. Archives: by appointment.

South Windsor

SOUTH WINDSOR HISTORICAL SOCIETY, 771 Ellington Rd., Rte. 74, South Windsor, CT 06074. Mailing Address: P.O. Box 216, South Windsor, CT 06074-0216.
Historical Society Museum.
Collections: local history; period artifacts; books; manuscripts; photographs. Historic Building: 19th-century one-room schoolhouse.
Hours & Admission Prices: April-June & Sept.-Nov. 1st Sun. of month 1-4; July-Aug. Tues. & Thurs. 12-4, 1st Sun. of month 1-4. No charge; donations accepted.

Southbury

AUDUBON CENTER AT BENT OF THE RIVER, 185 E. Flat Hill Rd., Southbury, CT 06488-1151. Tel.: 203-264-5098. Fax: 203-264-6332.
Wildlife Sanctuary.
Collections: wildlife & their habitats.
Facilities: nature trails.
Activities: educational programs; hiking.
Hours & Admission Prices: Center: Mon.-Fri. 9-5. Trails: daily dawn to dusk. No charge; donations accepted.

Southington

BARNES MUSEUM, 85 N. Main St., Southington, CT 06489-2518. Tel.: 860-628-5426. Fax: 860-628-0488.
E-mail: secondom@southington.org
Web Site: barnesmuseum.wordpress.com
Founded: 1973.
Key Personnel: Dir., Marie Secondo.
Personnel Profile: Full-Time Paid 1; Part-Time Paid 1; Part-Time Volunteers 4.
Governing Authority: Tax-exempt.
History Museum.
Collections: period furniture; personal artifacts; diaries; photographs; newspapers; magazines; family Bibles.
Activities: tours.
Hours & Admission Prices: July-Aug. Mon.-Wed. & Fri. 1-5, Thurs. 1-7; Sept.-June Mon.-Wed., Fri., 1st & last Sat. of month 1-5, Thurs. 1-7.
Attendance: 5,500 (estimated)

Stamford

BARTLETT ARBORETUM & GARDENS, 151 Brookdale Rd., Stamford, CT 06903-4199. Tel.: 203-322-6971, ext. 10. Fax: 203-595-9168.
E-mail: admin@bartlettarboretum.org
Web Site: bartlettarboretum.org
Formerly: Bartlett Arboretum, University of Connecticut
Founded: 1965.
Congressional District: 5
Key Personnel: Pres. (V), Kenneth A. Della Rocco.
Personnel Profile: Full-Time Paid 8; Part-Time Paid 2; Part-Time Volunteers 100.
Governing Authority: state & university. Tax-exempt: 501(c)(3).
Arboretum, Herbarium & Library.
Collections: plant collections; woody trees; shrubs; vines; dwarf & unusual conifers; ericaceous plants; herbarium including plant specimens from 1887 to present; over 3,000 sheets of preserved plants from around the world.
Research Fields: botany; herbarium.
Activities: guided tours; lectures; formally organized education programs.
Publications: brochures; seasonal, Bartlett Arboretum Newsletter.
Hours & Admission Prices: Grounds: daily 8:30-sunset. Office: Mon.-Fri. 8:30-4. Adults $6; members no charge. Closed Christmas.
Attendance: 20,000 (estimated)
Membership: Senior $50; Individual $60; Family $75.

RICHARD AND HINDA ROSENTHAL GALLERY, Rich Forum, 307 Atlantic St., Stamford, CT 06901-3506. Mailing Address: 61 Atlantic St., Stamford, CT 06901-3506. Tel.: 203-358-2305.
Art Gallery.
Collections: paintings; photographs; sculpture.
Hours & Admission Prices: Call for hours.

SACKLER ART GALLERY, Palace Theatre, 61 Atlantic St., Stamford, CT 06901-2403. Tel.: 203-358-2305.
Art Gallery: housed in a former vaudeville theatre; built in 1927.
Collections: paintings; sculpture; photographs.
Hours & Admission Prices: Call for hours.

SOUNDWATERS COASTAL EDUCATION CENTER, Cove Island Park, 1281 Cove Rd., Stamford, CT 06902-5457. Tel.: 203-323-1978.
Education Center.
Collections: local history; environment; paintings; photographs; freshwater & saltwater fish.
Facilities: aquarium.
Activities: hands-on exhibits; workshops; lectures; educational programs.
Hours & Admission Prices: Memorial Day to Labor Day Tues.-Sat. 10-5.

STAMFORD HISTORICAL SOCIETY, INC., 1508 High Ridge Rd., Stamford, CT 06903-4107. Tel.: 203-322-1565 & 329-1183. Fax: 203-322-1607.
E-mail: administrator@stamfordhistory.org
Web Site: www.stamfordhistory.org
Founded: 1901.
Congressional District: 4
Key Personnel: C.E.O. & Pres., Thomas Zoubek; Chm. (V), Pam Coleman; Administrative Asst., Haideh Molavi; Senior Librarian, Ron Marcus; Museum Shop Mgr., Rosemary Vacca.
Personnel Profile: Part-Time Paid 2; Part-Time Volunteers 40; Interns 1.
Governing Authority: nonprofit organization. Subsidiary Institution: Hoyt Barnum House. Tax-exempt: 170(b)(1)(A).
History & Decorative Arts Museum.
Collections: 17th- to 19th-century Americana; manuscripts; farm implements; needlework; quilts; dolls; household equipment; early pottery & craft tools; archives; costumes; Stamford business & city agency records, 1960-present. Historic House: Hoyt-Barnum House, 18th-century farmhouse begun in 1699.
Research Fields: local industrial history; decorative arts; genealogy.
Facilities: 2,500-vol. non-circulating library of books & pamphlets relating to history of Stamford available for use by public.

Activities: guided tours; lectures; permanent & temporary exhibitions; formally organized educational programs.
Publications: books, Stamford Revolutionary War Damage Claims; Springdale Remembered; Stamford - Pictures From The Past; Stamford In The Gilded Age; Fort Stamford - A Concise Study; Elizabeth Clawson: Thou Deserveth To Dye; Stamford Past And Present; Stamford Post Offices And Post Master; History of the Cove in Stamford; Poems on Stone in Stamford, Connecticut; Bibliography of Stamford References. The Civil War Diaries of Noah Webster Hoyt.
Hours & Admission Prices: Museum: Tues.-Sat. 12-4; Hoyt-Barnum House seasonal & by appointment only. Adults $5, members $2, children $1; discounts to AAM, ICOM & NEMA members. Closed New Year's Day; Thanksgiving; Christmas. ♿
Attendance: 10,000 (estimated)
Membership: Student & Senior Citizen $25; Individual $35; Family $50; Contributing $100; Supporting $250; Patron $500; Corporate $1,000.

STAMFORD MUSEUM & NATURE CENTER, 39 Scofieldtown Rd., Stamford, CT 06903-4096. Tel.: 203-322-1646. Fax: 203-322-0408.
E-mail: info@stamfordmuseum.org
Web Site: www.stamfordmuseum.org
Founded: 1936.
Congressional District: 4
Key Personnel: Exec. Dir., Melissa H. Mulrooney; Pres., Juanita James; Dir. Finance, William King; Farm Dir., Lauren Satterfield; Cur. Collections, Rosa Portell.
Personnel Profile: Full-Time Paid 20; Part-Time Paid 30; Part-Time Volunteers 35.
Governing Authority: nonprofit organization. Tax-exempt: 501(c)(3).
General Museum.
Collections: agriculture; paintings; sculpture; graphics; astronomy; botany; entomology; geology; herpetology; Native American artifacts, clothing & furnishings; mineralogy; natural history; live domestic & native animals; native wildfowl; cultural artifacts; photography; working farm.
Research Fields: astronomy; variable stars.
Facilities: classrooms; planetarium; observatory; hiking trails.
Activities: formally organized educational programs; permanent & temporary exhibitions; special events. Museum Sponsors: Maple Sugar Sunday; Spring on the Farm; Harvest Spooktacular.
Publications: bimonthly newsletter; quarterly magazine.
Hours & Admission Prices: Mon.-Sat. & holidays 9-5, Sun. 11-5. Adults $8, senior citizens $6, children $4; Stamford residents on Wed., children under 3, members, AAM & ICOM members no charge. Closed New Year's Day; Independence Day; Thanksgiving; Christmas. ♿
Attendance: 110,000 (accurate)
Membership: Seniors 65 & over $30; Individual $35; Senior Couple $50; Family $80; Family Plus & Contributing $150; Supporting $250; Benefactor $500; Patron $1,000 & up.

UKRAINIAN MUSEUM & LIBRARY, (M), 161 Glenbrook Rd., Stamford, CT 06902-3002. Tel.: 203-323-8866 & 327-7899. Fax: 203-357-7681.
E-mail: ukrmulrec@optonline.net
Web Site: ukrainianmuseumlibrary.org
Founded: 1935.
Key Personnel: Dir., John M. Terlecky; Cur., Lubow Wolynetz.
Personnel Profile: Full-Time Paid 2; Full-Time Volunteers 1; Part-Time Paid 2; Part-Time Volunteers 2.
Governing Authority: Library: 39 Clovelly Place, Stamford, CT. Tax-exempt.
Culturally Specific.
Collections: Ukrainian culture & heritage; fine arts; folk arts; religious art; books; periodicals; recordings; photographs; archives; numismatics.
Major Exhibits: Ukrainian Woodcarvings, 11/09-9/10; Ukrainian Folk Costumes, 1/10-12/10; Byzantine Ukrainian Icons, 1/10-12/10; Cossacks in Art-Painting Exhibit, 1/10-12/10; Pysanky Ukrainian Easter Eggs, 3/10-12/10.
Activities: workshops for children & adults in embroidery; Christmas tree decorating.
Publications: brochure.
Hours & Admission Prices: Wed.-Fri. 1-5, Sat.-Tues. by appointment. No charge; donations accepted. Closed major holidays. ♿
Attendance: 4,000
Membership: Senior & Student $25; Individual $50; Family & Institution $100; Supporter $500; Patron $1,000; Sponsor $2,500; Benefactor $5,000.

WHITNEY MUSEUM AT CHAMPION, One Champion Plaza, Stamford, CT 06921-0001. Tel.: 203-358-7652.
Art Museum.
Collections: works of contemporary American art.
Activities: educational programs; lectures; tours; film & video presentations; workshops.
Hours & Admission Prices: Tues.-Sat. 11-5. No charge. ♿

Stonington

CAPTAIN NATHANIEL B. PALMER HOUSE - HOME OF THE DISCOVERER OF ANTARCTICA, 40 Palmer St., Stonington, CT 06378-1014. Mailing Address: The Stonington Historical Society, Inc., P.O. Box 103, Stonington, CT 06378. Tel.: 860-535-8445.
E-mail: director@stoningtonhistory.org
Web Site: www.stoningtonhistory.org/palmer
Founded: 1996.
Congressional District: 2
Key Personnel: Pres. Stonington Historical Society (V), Meredith Brown; Dir., Mary E. Baker; Treas., Bryan Bentz.
Personnel Profile: Full-Time Paid 1; Part-Time Paid 3; Part-Time Volunteers 50; Interns 3.
Governing Authority: Parent Institution: Stonington Historical Society, Inc. Subsidiary Institutions: The Richard Woolworth Library & Research Center; The Old Lighthouse Museum. Tax-exempt.
History Museum.
Collections: memorabilia of Nathaniel's Antarctica discovery; Palmer brothers' personal artifacts; Stonington family portraits, furnishings & artifacts; historic house.
Research Fields: local history; genealogy; maritime.
Facilities: library.
Activities: lectures; programs; special events.
Publications: quarterly newsletter, Footnotes; monographs; biography; history.
Hours & Admission Prices: May-Oct. Wed.-Sun. 1-5. Palmer House & Old Lighthouse Museum: adults $8; members no charge.
Attendance: 2,500 (estimated)
Membership: Individual $30; Family $50; Contributing $100; Sustaining $200; Life $1,000; Life Couple $1,500.

OLD LIGHTHOUSE MUSEUM - STONINGTON HISTORICAL SOCIETY, 7 Water St., Stonington, CT 06378-1422. Tel.: 860-535-1440.
E-mail: pittaway@snet.net
Web Site: www.stoningtonhistory.net
Founded: 1925.
Congressional District: 2
Key Personnel: Exec. Dir. Stonington Historical Society, Mary Beth Baker; Cur. & Museum Shop Mgr., Louise D. Pittaway.
Personnel Profile: Full-Time Paid 1; Part-Time Paid 3; Part-Time Volunteers 5.
Governing Authority: society. Parent Institution: Stonington Historical Society. Tax-exempt.
Historic Site Museum.
Collections: history; paintings; archives; furniture; 17th-19th century historical artifacts of the town including whaling & War of 1812 relics; Fresnel lighthouse lens; photographs of Long Island Lights; maritime artifacts; children's toys; doll house.
Research Fields: genealogy.
Facilities: 500-vol. library of history & genealogy available by appointment, Call: 860-535-1131; reading room.
Activities: guided tours; lectures; formally organized education programs for children; permanent & temporary exhibitions; climb tower for view of 3 states.
Publications: quarterly magazine, Historical Footnotes; books, Stonington Graveyards; map of Stonington graveyards; An Hour Walk Through the Borough of Stonington; The Davis Homestead; The Battle of Stonington, War of 1812; Stonington Ice 1874-1947; The Stonington Tragedy.
Hours & Admission Prices: May-Nov. daily 10-5; other times by appointment. Call for admission prices.
Attendance: 7,500 (accurate)
Membership: Individual $30; Family $50; Contributing $100; Sustaining $200; Benefactor $500; Life $1,000; Dual Life $1,500.

Storrs

THE BALLARD INSTITUTE & MUSEUM OF PUPPETRY, School of Fine Arts, Depot Campus, 6 Bourn Pl., U-5212, Storrs, CT 06269-0001. Tel.: 860-486-0339.
E-mail: bimp@uconn.edu
Web Site: www.bimp.uconn.edu
Key Personnel: Dir., Dr. John Bell.
Governing Authority: university.
Puppetry Museum.
Collections: student built puppets; puppets of all types that are hundreds of years old & from around the world.
Activities: theater performances.
Hours & Admission Prices: Fri.-Sun. 12-5. Suggested Donations: Adult $5, seniors, students & children $4.

CONNECTICUT STATE MUSEUM OF NATURAL HISTORY AND CONNECTICUT ARCHAEOLOGY CENTER, University of Connecticut, Unit 1023, 2019 Hillside Rd., Storrs, CT 06269-0001. Tel.: 860-486-4460. Fax: 860-486-0827.
E-mail: csmnhinfo@uconn.edu
Web Site: www.cac.uconn.edu
Founded: 1982.
Congressional District: 2
Key Personnel: Dir., Leanne Kennedy Harty; Coord. Membership, Emily R.M. Lanz; Coord. Public Information, David C. Colberg; Exhibits Planner, Collin Harty; State Archaeologist, Dr. Nicholas F. Bellantoni; Coord. Programs, Cheri Collins.
Personnel Profile: Full-Time Paid 5; Part-Time Paid 3; Part-Time Volunteers 150.
Governing Authority: college; nonprofit. Parent Institution: University of Connecticut. Subsidiary Institution: University of Connecticut Foundation. Tax-exempt: 501(c)(3).
Natural History Museum.
Collections: Native American artifacts; mammals; birds; reptiles & amphibians; insects; mollusks; minerals; photographs.
Research Fields: biology; anthropology; Connecticut archaeology; ecology.
Facilities: 2 classrooms.
Activities: major events: special events; family programs; guided tours; lectures; education programs for children; workshops; field trips.
Publications: newsletter; activities program; membership brochure; annual report.
Hours & Admission Prices: Wed.-Fri. 10-4. No charge; donations accepted. Closed holidays. ♿
Attendance: 90,000 (accurate)
Membership: Student & Senior Citizen $25; Individual & Senior Couple $35; Couple $40; Family $45. Donor: Saw-Whet Owl $75; Snow Owl $150; Screech Owl $300; Barn Owl $600.

J. ROBERT DONNELLY HUSKY HERITAGE SPORTS MUSEUM, UConn Alumni Center, 2384 Alumni Dr., Unit-3053, Storrs, CT 06269-0001. Tel.: 888-822-5861.
E-mail: ucaa@uconn.edu
Web Site: www.uconnhuskies.com/trads/museum.html
Formerly: Alumni Center - Husky Heritage Sports Museum
Key Personnel: Exec. Dir., Lisa Lewis; Center Mgr., Julie Sweeney.
Governing Authority: university.
Sports Museum.
Collections: sports memorabilia which reflects more than 100 years of UConn athletic competition; personal artifacts; photographs.
Activities: special events.
Hours & Admission Prices: Mon.-Fri. 8-5. No charge.

MANSFIELD HISTORICAL SOCIETY MUSEUM, 954 Storrs Rd., Storrs, CT 06268-2611. Mailing Address: P.O. Box 145, Storrs, CT 06268-0145. Tel.: 860-429-6575.
E-mail: mansfieldhistorical@snet.net
Web Site: mansfieldct-history.org
Founded: 1957.
Congressional District: 2
Key Personnel: Pres., John Meyers; Dir., Ann Galonska; Treas., Howard Raphaelson.
Personnel Profile: Part-Time Paid 1.
Governing Authority: nonprofit; society. Parent Institution: Mansfield Historical Society. Tax-exempt: 501(c)(3).
History Museum: housed in former Mansfield Town Office building & adjacent Town Hall c.1843.
Collections: furniture; household equipment; tools; farm equipment; industry; textiles; archives; photographs of local houses and people; 18th-19th century costumes of Connecticut town.
Research Fields: early houses in town.
Facilities: 500-vol. library on history, manuscripts & old account books; local genealogy.
Activities: guided tours; permanent & temporary exhibitions.
Publications: Chronology of Mansfield, Connecticut 1702-2002; That Sacred Plant of Paradise; Farming In Mansfield 1690-1955; George Freeman, Miniaturist, 1789-1868. On The Trail of a Legend, Separatist Movement in Mansfield, Ct., 1745-1769; Listen to the Echoes: Early History of Spring Hill; The Mansfield Poor House 1861-1922; World War II on the Home-front: Mansfield (excerpts from the diaries of Edwina Maud Whitney); The Constant Years; Historic Mansfield Center.
Hours & Admission Prices: June-Sept. Thurs. & Sun. 1:30-4:30; tours by appointment. Adults $2; members no charge.
Attendance: 1,000 (estimated)
Membership: Student $10; Individual $20; Family $30; Contributing $50; Small Business $75; Sustaining $100; Patron $150; Corporate $250.

THE WILLIAM BENTON MUSEUM OF ART, (M), Univ. of Conn., 245 Glenbrook Rd. U-2140, Storrs, CT 06269-0001. Tel.: 860-486-4520. Fax: 860-486-0234.
E-mail: thomas.bruhn@uconn.edu
Web Site: www.thebenton.org
Founded: 1966.
Congressional District: 2
Key Personnel: Acting Dir. & Cur. Collections, Thomas P. Bruhn; Business Mgr., Karen Sommer; Registrar, Toni Hulse; Coord. Membership, Lynn Eriksson; Educational Coord., Tracy Lawlor; Public Rels. & Mktg. Coord., Diane Lewis; Preparator, Philip Hollister; Museum Shop Mgr., Jeanne Ahern Mogayzel; Museum Store Assoc., Samantha Smith.
Personnel Profile: Full-Time Paid 5; Part-Time Paid 5; Part-Time Volunteers 25; Interns 2.
Governing Authority: university. Parent Institution: University of Connecticut. Tax-exempt: 501(c)(1).
Art Museum.
Collections: over 5,000 European, American & Asian works in various media from 15th century to present; Kathe Kollwitz and Reginald Marsh prints & drawings.
Research Fields: 19th-21st century paintings, graphics & photography.
Facilities: cafe. Museum-related items for sale in shop.
Activities: temporary exhibitions; lectures; gallery talks; symposia; interdisciplinary programs; concerts; exhibition-related films; digital media; on-line exhibitions.
Publications: triennial calendar; exhibition catalogs.
Hours & Admission Prices: Thurs.-Fri. 10-4:30, Sat.-Sun. 1-4:30. No charge; donations accepted. Closed between some exhibitions; national holidays. ♿
Attendance: 42,000 (estimated)
Membership: Student $10; Single $30; Family $40; Supporting $75; Contributing $125; Sustaining $250; Donor $500; Patron $1,000 & up.

Stratford

BOOTHE MEMORIAL PARK AND MUSEUM, 5744 Main St. Putney, Stratford, CT 06614. Mailing Address: P.O. Box 902, Stratford, CT 06615-0902. Tel.: 203-381-2046.
Founded: 1984.
Key Personnel: Dir. Friends of Boothe Park, Bessie Burton; Pres. (V), Ken Burton.
Personnel Profile: Part-Time Volunteers 40; Interns 4.
Governing Authority: Tax-exempt.
Americana.
Collections: Boothe family artifacts; baskets; period artifacts. Historic Buildings: homestead building; blacksmith shop; lighthouse; windmill; carriage building shop.
Facilities: 32 acre park; rose garden.
Activities: picnic grounds.
Publications: newsletter.
Hours & Admission Prices: Museum: call for hours. No charge; donations accepted. ♿
Attendance: 10,000 (estimated)
Membership: Single $10; Family $25.

GARBAGE MUSEUM, 1410 Honeyspot Rd. Extension, Stratford, CT 06615-7142. Tel.: 203-381-9571. Fax: 203-377-1930.
Web Site: www.crra.org/pages/contact_garbage_museum.htm
Environmental Education Center.
Collections: solutions & practices for solid waste disposal & recycling.
Hours & Admission Prices: July-Aug. Tues.-Fri. 10-4; Sept.-June Wed.-Fri. 12-4; groups by appointment. Closed New Year's Day; Good Friday; Independence Day; Thanksgiving Day & after; Christmas Eve & Day.

NATIONAL HELICOPTER MUSEUM, INC., 2480 Main St., Stratford, CT 06615-5940. Mailing Address: P.O. Box 775, Stratford, CT 06615-0775. Tel.: 203-375-8857.
Web Site: www.nationalhelicoptermuseum.org
Founded: 1983.
Congressional District: 3
Key Personnel: Pres. (V), Ken Pike; Cur., Raymond E. Jankowich, M.D.; Museum Shop Mgr., Gail Whittemore.
Governing Authority: Tax-exempt.
Helicopter Museum.
Collections: helicopter history; photographs; documents; models; videos; Cabin Sikorsky S76; gas turbine T S3 engine; cabin cockpit S76; Sikorsky Helicopter.
Hours & Admission Prices: Memorial Day to mid-Oct. Wed.-Sun. 1-4. No charge; donations accepted. ♿
Attendance: 1,400 (accurate)
Membership: Annual $10; 3-Year $25; Lifetime $100.

PERRY HOUSE VISITORS CENTER, 1128 W. Broad St., Stratford, CT 06615. Tel.: 203-377-3779.
Historic House: built c.1690.
Collections: local history & culture; period furnishings; personal artifacts.
Activities: educational programs; special events.
Hours & Admission Prices: Daily 12-4. No charge.

THE STRATFORD HISTORICAL SOCIETY & CATHERINE B. MITCHELL MUSEUM, 967 Academy Hill, Stratford, CT 06615-0382. Mailing Address: P.O. Box 382, Stratford, CT 06615-0382. Tel.: 203-378-0630. Fax: 203-378-2562.
E-mail: judsonhousestfd@aol.com
Web Site: www.stratfordhistoricalsociety.com
Founded: 1925.
Congressional District: 3
Key Personnel: Pres. (V), Rudolph Mastroianni; Cur., Carol Lovell; Archivist, Gloria Duggan.
Personnel Profile: Part-Time Paid 4; Part-Time Volunteers 10.
Governing Authority: society; nonprofit. Parent Institution: Stratford Historical Society. Tax-exempt: 501(c)(3).
Historical Society Museum: housed in 1750 Capt. David Judson Home, located on the original common of 1639.
Collections: archives; decorative arts; baskets; costumes; clothing; glass; china; silver; period Stratford items; toys; dolls; textiles; tools, Revolutionary & Civil Wars; early kitchen items; paintings; photographs; quilts; local artifacts; Native American artifacts; furniture.
Research Fields: local genealogy.
Facilities: 1,300-vol. library; 10,000 sq. ft. exhibit space. Museum-related items for sale.
Activities: guided tours; lectures; films; formally organized education programs; permanent & temporary exhibitions.
Publications: bimonthly newsletter.
Hours & Admission Prices: June-Oct. Wed. & Sun. 12-4. Family $5, adults $3, students $1; museum members no charge. ♿
Attendance: 1,000 (estimated)
Membership: Senior Citizen $15; Adult $20; Corporate $50; Life $200.

Suffield

THE KING HOUSE MUSEUM, 232 S. Main St., Suffield, CT 06078. Mailing Address: P.O. Box 893, Suffield, CT 06078-0893. Tel.: 860-668-5256.
Web Site: www.suffieldhistoricalsociety.org/kinghouse.htm
Key Personnel: Pres. (V), Edward Chase, III; Cur., Lester Smith.
Governing Authority: Parent Institution: Suffield Historical Society.
Historic House Museum: built in 1764.
Collections: family & local history; early Connecticut Valley furniture; tobacco industry; early flasks & bottles; Bennington pottery.
Activities: special events.
Publications: newsletter.
Hours & Admission Prices: May-Sept. Wed. & Sat. 1-4; other times by appointment. Adults $1; students no charge.

Terryville

LOCK MUSEUM OF AMERICA, INC., 230 Main St., Rte. 6, Terryville, CT 06786-5900. Mailing Address: P.O. Box 104, Terryville, CT 06786-0104. Tel.: 860-589-6359. Fax: 860-589-6359 (call first).
E-mail: thomasnsc@aol.com
Web Site: www.lockmuseum.com/
Founded: 1972.
Congressional District: 6
Key Personnel: Pres. & Asst. Cur., Thomas Hennessy, Jr.; Vice Pres., Gilbert Wade; Cur., Thomas F. Hennessy; Sec. & Librarian, Reggie Murawski; Membership Sec., Theresa Kovaleski.
Governing Authority: nonprofit organization. Tax-exempt.
Lock Museum: located on the site of the original offices of the Eagle Lock Co., built in 1859.
Collections: American locks, keys & ornate hardware.
Facilities: 1,000-item library of catalogs, books, financial & sales records of Sargent & Greenleaf Co. & the Eagle Lock Co. from c.1900-1930 available for research on premises; meeting room.
Publications: newsletter.
Hours & Admission Prices: May-Oct. Tues.-Sun. 1:30-4:30. Adults $3, senior citizens $2.50; members no charge. ♿
Attendance: 1,000 (estimated)
Membership: Single $20; Family $25; Company & Organization $100; Individual Life $200; Company Life $1,000.

Thomaston

RAILROAD MUSEUM OF NEW ENGLAND, 242 E. Main St., Thomaston, CT 06787-0400. Mailing Address: P.O. Box 400, Thomaston, CT 06787-0400. Tel.: 860-283-7245. Fax: 860-283-7245.
E-mail: info@rmne.org
Web Site: www.rmne.org
Key Personnel: Pres., Ralph Harris
History Museum: housed in the New England Thomaston Station; built in 1881.
Collections: railroad heritage, history, & artifacts; New England rolling stock including locomotives, passenger cars, freight cars, & cabooses.
Facilities: Museum-related items for sale.
Activities: train rides; special events.
Hours & Admission Prices: Train Rides: May-Aug. Sun. 12 & 2, Tues. 10am; Sept.-Oct. Tues. 10am, Sat.-Sun. 12 & 2. Adults $12, seniors 62 & over $10, children 3-12 $8; discounts to groups; children 2 & under no charge.

Tolland

DANIEL BENTON HOMESTEAD, Metcalf Rd., Tolland, CT 06084. Mailing Address: P.O. Box 107, Tolland, CT 06084-0107. Tel.: 860-974-1875.
E-mail: tolland.historical@snet.net
Web Site: www.tollandhistorical.org/danielbentonhomestead
Founded: 1969.
Key Personnel: Pres. (V), Stewart R. Joslin; Museum Dir., Gail W. White.
Personnel Profile: Part-Time Volunteers 25.
Governing Authority: society. Tolland Historical Society, Inc., P.O. Box 107, Tolland, CT 06084. Tax-exempt: 501(c)(3).
Historic Building: 1720 house.
Collections: local history; period furnishings.
Facilities: nature trails.
Activities: guided tours; lectures; workshops; formally organized education programs for children; French & Indian War weekend; Revolutionary War Encampment; 18th-century Artisans & Sutlers Market.
Publications: semi-annual newsletter; books, Tolland, An Old Post Road Town; Tolland on the Green.
Hours & Admission Prices: May-Oct. Sun. 1-4; other times by appointment. Donation $2. ♿
Membership: Single $5; Family $10; Associate $25; Corporate $100.

HICKS-STEARNS FAMILY MUSEUM, 42 Tolland Green, Tolland, CT 06084-3042. Tel.: 860-875-7552.
Key Personnel: Dir., Beatrice White-Ramirez
Historic House Museum.
Collections: family artifacts; period furnishings.
Facilities: Museum-related items for sale.
Activities: summer concerts. Museum Sponsors: Christmas Open House in December.
Hours & Admission Prices: mid-May to mid-Oct. Sun. & Wed. 1-4; other times by appointment. No charge; donations accepted.

TOLLAND HISTORICAL SOCIETY - TOLLAND COUNTY JAIL & MUSEUM, 52 Tolland Green, Tolland, CT 06084. Mailing Address: P.O. Box 107, Tolland, CT 06084-0107. Tel.: 860-870-9599.
E-mail: tolland.historical@snet.net
Web Site: www.tollandhistorical.org
Founded: 1856.
Congressional District: 2
Key Personnel: Dir., Kathy Bach; Pres., Stewart Joslin; Museum Shop Mgr., Sue Errickson.
Personnel Profile: Part-Time Volunteers 25.
Governing Authority: society. Parent Institution: Tolland Historical Society. Tax-exempt: 501(c)(3).
Historic Society Museum: housed in old jail cell block & jailer's home.
Collections: Native American artifacts; farm implements; 18th & 19th-century clothing; furniture; early schools & industries.
Activities: guided tours; demonstrations; reenactments. Annual Event: Tolland Antiques Show.
Publications: book; quarterly newsletter, Tolland Monthly.
Hours & Admission Prices: mid-May to mid-Oct. Sun. 1-4; other times by appointment. No charge; donations accepted. ♿
Attendance: 3,030 (accurate)

Torrington

ARTWELL GALLERY, 19 Water St., Torrington, CT 06790-5319. Tel.: 860-482-5122. Fax: 860-492-5122.
Art Gallery.
Collections: paintings; photographs; sculpture.

Activities: educational programs; classes; performances; special events.
Hours & Admission Prices: Tues.-Fri. 10-5, Sat.-Sun. 12-5.

TORRINGTON HISTORICAL SOCIETY, INC., (M), 192 Main St., Torrington, CT 06790-5201. Tel.: 860-482-8260.
E-mail: torringtonhistorical@snet.net
Web Site: www.torringtonhistoricalsociety.org
Founded: 1944.
Congressional District: 1
Key Personnel: Exec. Dir., Mark McEachern; Pres. (V), David R. Bennett; Cur., Gail Kruppa; Librarian, Carol Clapp.
Personnel Profile: Full-Time Paid 2; Part-Time Paid 3; Part-Time Volunteers 35; Interns 1.
Governing Authority: society. Tax-exempt: 501(c)(3).
Local History Museum.
Collections: history of Torrington; artifacts & archives; Hendey machine shop artifacts; historic buildings; John Brown birthplace memorial. Historic Building: Hotchkiss-Fyler House, 1900.
Research Fields: historical; genealogical; industrial.
Facilities: 2,000-vol. library of local history & genealogy available for use on premises.
Activities: guided tours; lectures; outreach programs; concerts; children's programs.
Publications: booklets, First Church of Torrington 1741-1841; First Church of Torrington 1841-1942; Torrington Town Meeting 1740-1765; Gleanings from Early Torrington History; The Formative Years, 1740-1852; The Growth Years, 1852-1923; The Annealing Years, 1923-1976; History of Torrington, Conn. (1878) reprint; Erastus Hodges 1781-1847; The John Brown Birthplace; Gertrude Fyler Hotchkiss.
Hours & Admission Prices: House Museum: April 15-Oct. Tues.-Sat. 12-4. History Museum: April 15-Oct. Tues.-Fri. 10-4, Sat.-Sun. 12-4. Library: Tues.-Fri. 1-4. House Museum: adults $5. History Museum: adults $2; discounts to AAM members; members no charge. Closed legal holidays. ♿
Attendance: 6,000 (estimated)
Membership: Senior Citizens $15; Individual $20; Family $30; Contributing $50; Sustaining $100; Patron $250.

Uncasville

TANTAQUIDGEON INDIAN MUSEUM, Rte. 32, 1819 Norwich-New London Rd., Uncasville, CT 06382-1320. Tel.: 860-848-0594. Fax: 860-862-6025.
E-mail: museum@moheganmail.com
Founded: 1931.
Key Personnel: Exec. Dir., Melissa Tantaquidgeon Zobel; Cur., Stacy Dufresne.
Governing Authority: individual operation.
Indian Museum.
Collections: crafts made by Mohegan & other New England craftsmen of past & present; objects of stone, wood & bone; baskets; bowls; ladles; archaeology; artifacts from Southwestern & Northern Plains Tribes. Historic Church: c.1831 Mohegan Congregational Church.
Hours & Admission Prices: May-Nov. Wed.-Sat. 10-4. No charge. Closed holidays. ♿

Unionville

UNIONVILLE MUSEUM, 15 School St., Unionville, CT 06085-1029. Tel.: 860-673-2231.
Key Personnel: Pres., Frank Corbeil
History Museum: housed in the restored Andrew Carnegie free public library building, c.1917.
Collections: photographs; letters; advertising items; period clothing; blacksmith tools; paintings.
Activities: Museum Sponsors: annual vintage car parades; suppers.
Publications: historic calendar.
Hours & Admission Prices: Wed. & Sat.-Sun. 2-4. No charge; donations accepted.

Vernon

NEW ENGLAND CIVIL WAR MUSEUM, 14 Park Pl., Vernon Memorial Hall, 2nd Fl, Vernon, CT 06066-3291. Mailing Address: P.O. Box 153, Vernon, CT 06066. Tel.: 860-870-3563.
E-mail: necwm@hotmail.com
Web Site: pages.cthome.net/ne.civilwar.mus
Founded: 1995.
Key Personnel: Exec. Dir., Matt Reardon; Librarian & Cur., Jerry Caroon; Librarian & Cur., Alex Oliphant.
Personnel Profile: Full-Time Volunteers 1; Part-Time Volunteers 2.
Governing Authority: Parent Institution: Alden Skinner Camp #45, Sons of Union Veterans of the Civil War. Tax-exempt.
Civil War Museum.
Collections: Civil War artifacts; personal artifacts of Thomas F. Burpee, Hirst Brothers, & Weston including a sword, belts, cap boxes, holster, photographs & a trumpet; memorial hall.
Hours & Admission Prices: 1st Thurs. of month 3-7, 2nd & 4th Sun. of month 12-3; other times by appointment. No charge; donations accepted. ♿
Attendance: 1,200 (accurate)

VERNON HISTORICAL SOCIETY MUSEUM, 734 Hartford Turnpike, Vernon, CT 06066-5127. Mailing Address: P.O. Box 2055, Vernon, CT 06066-1455. Tel.: 860-875-4326.
E-mail: vernonhs@sbcglobal.net
Web Site: vhsvernonct.tripod.com
Historical Society Museum.
Collections: local history & culture; paintings; etchings; books; photographs; period artifacts.
Activities: special events.
Hours & Admission Prices: Thurs. & 2nd Sun. of month 2-4. No charge; donations accepted.

Wallingford

WALLINGFORD HISTORICAL SOCIETY, INC., 180 S. Main St., Wallingford, CT 06492-4217. Mailing Address: P.O. Box 73, Wallingford, CT 06492-0073. Tel.: 203-294-1996.
Founded: 1916.
Congressional District: 3
Key Personnel: Pres. (V), Raymond A. Chappell; 1st Vice Pres., Robert Beaumont.
Personnel Profile: Part-Time Volunteers 8.
Governing Authority: society. Tax-exempt: 501(c)(3).
General Museum: housed in 1759 Parsons House.
Collections: costumes; Bibles; scrapbooks; diaries; school books & notebooks.
Research Fields: local history.
Facilities: 200-vol. library of genealogies & newspapers available on premises by permission.
Activities: guided tours; lectures; permanent & temporary exhibitions.
Publications: Wallingford, in the Images of America Series.
Hours & Admission Prices: Memorial Day-Labor Day Sun. 2-4:30; other times by appointment. No charge; donations accepted.
Attendance: 900 (estimated)
Membership: Individual $5; Couple $8; Life $50.

Washington

GUNN MEMORIAL LIBRARY AND MUSEUM, (M), 5 Wykeham Rd., Washington, CT 06793. Mailing Address: P.O. Box 1273, 5 Wykeham Rd., Washington, CT 06793-0273. Tel.: 860-868-7756. Fax: 860-868-7247.
E-mail: gunnmuseum@sbcglobal.net
Web Site: www.gunnlibrary.org
Founded: 1899.
Congressional District: 6
Key Personnel: Exec. Dir., Jean Chapin; Pres., Steven Haas; Pres. (V), Rod Pleasants; Cur., Stephen Bartkus; Asst. Cur., Margaret Freeland.
Personnel Profile: Full-Time Paid 1; Part-Time Paid 1; Part-Time Volunteers 8.
Governing Authority: private; bd. of trustees. Parent Institution: Gunn Memorial Library. Tax-exempt.
General Museum: housed in 1781 building.
Collections: letter; archives; manuscripts; 17th- to 19th-century furnishings; Revolutionary, Civil War, & World War I items; letters of George Washington & Thomas Jefferson; manuscript collections; textiles; china & glass; pewter & silver; spinning wheels; dolls & doll houses; 19th- & early 20th-century costumes & portraits; 19th-century farm & carpentry tools.
Research Fields: archives; textiles; glass; doll house & dolls; portraits; photographs.
Facilities: 180-vol. library of history books available for use on premises; Connecticut Room: genealogical, state & local history reference.
Activities: lectures; gallery talks; loan, permanent & temporary exhibitions.
Publications: Return to Arcadia - The Architecture of Ehrick Rossiter; Rossiter: Country Houses of Washington, Connecticut.
Hours & Admission Prices: Jan.-April Thurs.-Sat. 10-4; May-Dec. Thurs.-Sat. 10-4, Sun. 12-4. No charge; donations accepted. Closed holidays.
Attendance: 1,500 (accurate)

THE INSTITUTE FOR AMERICAN INDIAN STUDIES (IAIS), 38 Curtis Rd., Washington, CT 06793-0260. Mailing Address: P.O. Box 1260, Washington, CT 06793-0260. Tel.: 860-868-0518. Fax: 860-868-1649.
E-mail: iais@charter.net

Web Site: www.birdstone.org
Founded: 1975.
Congressional District: 6
Key Personnel: Dir., Elizabeth McCormick; Archaeologist, Dir. Research & Collections, Dr. Lucianne Lavin; Asst. Cur. Collections, Lisa Piastuch-Temmen; Education Coord., Ruth Barr; Museum Shop Mgr., Christine Peschel; Dir. Camp, Matt Barr.
Personnel Profile: Full-Time Paid 4; Full-Time Volunteers 2; Part-Time Paid 7; Part-Time Volunteers 10; Interns 3.
Governing Authority: nonprofit. Tax-exempt: 501(c)(3).
American Indian Culture & Archaeology Museum.
Collections: prehistoric & historic artifacts primarily from Connecticut & Northeastern United States; ethnographic items from most North American culture areas; contemporary Native art; reconstructed American Indian village; plants the American Indians used in the region over the last 10,000 years.
Research Fields: Southern New England historic & prehistoric American Indian cultural & post white contact culture.
Facilities: 2,000-vol. library available for research for IAIS members, scholars & students with letter from Professor for use on premises only; nature trail; classrooms; arboretum. Books & other gifts for sale.
Activities: guided tours; lectures; films; gallery talks; formally organized education programs for children, adults, college students affiliated with colleges of Hartford, Fairfield, Wesleyan & others; loan, permanent, temporary & traveling exhibitions; school loan service; craft programs; Native American studies program. Museum Sponsors: summer field schools training sessions in archaeology; summer camps & year-round workshops.
Publications: 4 membership newsletters; Occasional Papers; teacher materials; educational pamphlets; books; videos.
Hours & Admission Prices: Mon.-Sat. 10-5, Sun. 12-5. Adults $5, seniors $4.50, children $3; discounts to AAM & ICOM members; members no charge. Closed New Year's Day; Easter; Memorial Day; Independence Day; Thanksgiving; Christmas. ♿
Attendance: 60,000
Membership: Senior Citizen $30; Individual $40; Family $55; Contributor $100; Benefactor $250; Sponsor $500; Patron $1,000.

Waterbury

* **THE MATTATUCK MUSEUM ARTS AND HISTORY CENTER, (M),** 144 W. Main St., Waterbury, CT 06702-1298. Tel.: 203-753-0381, ext. 10. Fax: 203-756-6283.
E-mail: info@mattatuckmuseum.org
Web Site: www.mattatuckmuseum.org
Formerly: The Mattatuck Museum of the Mattatuck Historical Society
Founded: 1877.
Congressional District: 5
Key Personnel: C.E.O. & Exec. Dir., Marie Galbraith; Pres. (V), M. Catherine Smith; Cur., Cynthia Roznoy, Ph.D.; Dir. Bldg. Svcs., Darryl Dilday; Education, Laurie Pasteryak; Business Mgr., Jan Doughty.
Personnel Profile: Full-Time Paid 10; Part-Time Paid 12; Part-Time Volunteers 200.
Governing Authority: society. Parent Institution: The Mattatuck Historical Society, Inc. Tax-exempt: 501(c)(3).
History & Art Museum: housed in renovated Masonic Temple.
Collections: Connecticut artists collection; 17th-20th century decorative arts; 18th century regional furniture; brass industry; historical material relating to state & local history; colonial; industrial; manuscripts.
Research Fields: Connecticut artists; brass worker's history.
Facilities: library pertaining to local history & Connecticut artists available for use on premises by request; auditorium; cafe. Books, crafts & gift items for sale.
Activities: guided tours; lectures; gallery talks; formally organized educational programs; docent program; permanent, temporary & traveling exhibitions; art classes for children & adults; field trips; performing arts; teacher training.
Publications: annual report; books, Waterbury Pictorial History; Metal, Minds & Machines: Waterbury at Work; Fiddlebacks & Crooked Backs: Elijah Booth & Other Joiners in Newton and Woodbury 1750-1820; Images of Contentment: John Frederick Kensett & the Connecticut Shore; Artist of the Litchfield Hills.
Hours & Admission Prices: Tues.-Sat. 10-5, Sun. 12-5. Suggested Donation: adults $5, seniors $4; members no charge. Closed major holidays. ♿
Attendance: 45,000 (accurate)
Membership: Student $10; Seniors $25; Individual $40; Family $60; Sustaining $100; Supporting $200; Patron $500; Fellow $1,000; Benefactor $2,500; Sponsor $5,000; Life $10,000.

TIMEXPO MUSEUM, 175 Union St., Brass Mill Commons, Waterbury, CT 06706-1236. Tel.: 203-755-8463; 800-225-7742. Fax: 203-755-8531.
E-mail: cconti@timexpo.com
Web Site: www.timexpo.com
Founded: 2001.
Congressional District: 5
Key Personnel: Pres., Michael Friend; Dir., Cathy Conti.
Personnel Profile: Full-Time Paid 2; Part-Time Paid 1; Part-Time Volunteers 10.
Governing Authority: Parent Institution: Timexpo Corporation.
History Museum.
Collections: watches & clocks from Waterbury Clock Co. & Waterbury Watch Co., Ingersoll, U.S., Time Corp. & Timex; related letters, photographs & ads; Reed boat from Bolivia; replicas of artifacts from Easter Island, Peru, Egypt, Middle East; videos; interactive exhibits; theories & discoveries of Dr. Thor Heyerdahl, the Norwegian explorer and scientist, with emphasis on ocean navigation by ancient civilizations.
Facilities: 60-seat multi-purpose room; 8,000 sq. ft. exhibit space. Museum-related items for sale.
Hours & Admission Prices: Tues.-Sat. 10-5. Adults $6, seniors $5, children 5-12 $4; discounts to groups with reservation; children under 5 no charge. Closed major holidays. ♿
Membership: Senior & Teacher $20; Individual $25; Family $60; Patron $150.

Waterford

HARKNESS MEMORIAL STATE PARK, 275 Great Neck Rd., Waterford, CT 06385-3895. Tel.: 860-443-5725. Fax: 860-441-6151.
E-mail: dep.stateparks@ct.gov
Web Site: www.ct.gov/dep
Founded: 1953.
Key Personnel: Park & Recreations Supvr., Mark Darin.
Personnel Profile: Full-Time Paid 4; Part-Time Paid 1.
Governing Authority: state. Connecticut Dept. of Environmental Protection, Division of Parks & Recreation, Hartford, CT 06106.
Park Museum: 1906 Eolia, summer residence of the Edward S. Harkness family. The estate & mansion are located near the confluence of the Thames River & Long Island Sound on the promontory, Goshen Point.
Collections: cutting garden; Italian Garden; Oriental Garden; 42-room mansion; greenhouses; stable; water tower.
Research Fields: virgin shoreline on Long Island Sound; open meadow lands.
Facilities: picnic area.
Activities: picnicking; fishing. Park Sponsors: recreation site for the handicapped.
Publications: brochures.
Hours & Admission Prices: Grounds: daily 8-sunset. In-State cars Mon.-Fri. $5, Sat.-Sun. & holidays $7; out-of-state cars Mon.-Fri. $7, Sat.-Sun. & holidays $10. Season Pass: CT residents $50; Out of State residents $75. Mansion Tours: Memorial to Labor Day Sat.-Sun. & holidays 10-2. No charge; donations accepted. ♿
Membership: Individual $15; Family $25; Patron $50; Supporter $100; Benefactor $250; Corporate $500; Eolian $1,000.

Watertown

WATERTOWN HISTORICAL SOCIETY, INC., 22 DeForest St., Watertown, CT 06795-2116. Tel.: 860-274-1050.
E-mail: watertownctmuseum@sbcglobal.net
Web Site: www.watertownhistoricalsociety.org
Founded: 1947.
Congressional District: 6
Key Personnel: C.E.O. & Pres., Jeffrey S. Grenier; Vice Pres., Jan J. Guidess; Treas., JoAnn Zanavich; Archivist, John F. Pillis.
Personnel Profile: Part-Time Volunteers 10.
Governing Authority: society. Tax-exempt: 501(c)(3).
Local History Museum: housed in 1846 building.
Collections: articles, utensils, tools & furniture manufactured in Watertown; manuscripts.
Research Fields: town history; genealogies.
Facilities: library of books & files.
Activities: guided tours; lectures; formally organized education programs for children; permanent & temporary exhibitions.
Publications: semiannual newsletter.
Hours & Admission Prices: Wed. 2-4; groups by appointment. No charge; donations accepted. Closed major holidays.
Attendance: 300 (estimated)
Membership: Senior $12; Individual $30; Couple $45; Museum Sponsor $100; Heminway Circle $250; Lifetime $500.

West Hartford

THE CHILDREN'S MUSEUM, (M), 950 Trout Brook Dr., West Hartford, CT 06119-1492. Tel.: 860-231-2824. Fax: 860-232-0705.
E-mail: info@thechildrensmuseumct.org

Web Site: www.thechildrensmuseumct.org
Formerly: Science Center of Connecticut
Founded: 1927.
Congressional District: 1
Key Personnel: Pres. & C.E.O., Kevin Sullivan; Chm. (V), Elaine McDonald; Dir. Guest Rels. & Museum Shop Mgr., Beth Weller; Dir. Education, Sue Carroll; Dir. Travelers Science Dome & Gengras Planetarium, Kristie Mazzoni.
Personnel Profile: Full-Time Paid 21; Part-Time Paid 49; Part-Time Volunteers 80.
Governing Authority: nonprofit corporation. Tax-exempt: 501(c)(3).
Children's Museum.
Collections: fossils; math exhibit; natural history; technology; physical science; hands-on exhibits.
Facilities: planetarium; nature center; wildlife sanctuary.
Activities: birthday parties; rental facilities; summer & vacation science camps; youth group programs; field trips; outreach; nature walks; teacher training; after school programs; evening astronomy programs; science preschool.
Publications: teacher resource guide; annual fund brochure; newsletters; program brochure.
Hours & Admission Prices: Summer: Mon.-Sat. 10-5, Sun. 11-4; Winter: Tues.-Sat. 9-4, Sun. 11-4. Admission 2-62 $11, senior citizens 63 & over $10; children under 2 no charge. Closed Easter; Memorial Day; Independence Day; Labor Day; Thanksgiving; Christmas Eve & Day.
Attendance: 210,000 (accurate)
Membership: One Plus One $60; Family & Grandparent $85; Family Plus & Grandparent Plus $125.

JOSELOFF GALLERY, HARTFORD ART SCHOOL, UNIVERSITY OF HARTFORD, Harry Jack Gray Center, 200 Bloomfield Ave., West Hartford, CT 06117-1545. Tel.: 860-768-4090. Fax: 860-768-5159.
E-mail: joseloff@hartford.edu
Web Site: www.joseloffgallery.org
Founded: 1970.
Congressional District: 1
Key Personnel: Dir., Zina Davis; Gallery Mgr., Lisa Gaumond.
Personnel Profile: Full-Time Paid 2; Part-Time Paid 5.
Governing Authority: university; nonprofit. Parent Institution: University of Hartford/Hartford Art School. Tax-exempt: 501(c)(3).
Art Gallery.
Collections: paintings; photographs; sculpture.
Major Exhibits: 6th Annual Distinguished Artists Symposium & Exhibition, 11/6/09-1/17/10; Alexander A. Goldfarb Student Exhibition, 2/17/10-3/21/10; Chuck Close: A Couple of Ways of Doin Something from the Aperture Foundation (T), 4/14/10-6/27/10.
Facilities: 200-seat auditorium; 3,500 sq. ft. exhibit space.
Publications: annual calendar of events; catalogues & brochures.
Hours & Admission Prices: Tues.-Fri. 11-4, Sat.-Sun. 12-4. No charge; donations accepted. Closed major university & national holidays. ♿
Attendance: 10,000 (estimated)

NEIL'S AMERICAN DREAM MUSEUM, 124-126 Raymond Rd., West Hartford, CT 06107-2542. Tel.: 860-561-5311.
Key Personnel: Owner & Cur., Neil Sakow
Collectibles Museum.
Collections: toys; sports & cowboy memorabilia; early television collectibles; Americana advertising.
Hours & Admission Prices: By appointment.

* **NOAH WEBSTER HOUSE/WEST HARTFORD HISTORICAL SOCIETY, (M),** 227 S. Main St., West Hartford, CT 06107-3430. Tel.: 860-521-5362. Fax: 860-521-4036.
E-mail: comments@noahwebsterhouse.org
Web Site: www.noahwebsterhouse.org
Formerly: Noah Webster House Museum of West Hartford History
Founded: 1965.
Congressional District: 1
Key Personnel: Exec. Dir., Chris Dobbs; Pres. (V), Connie B. Robinson; Dir. Education, Jennifer Matos; Museum Shop Mgr., Pattie McCleary.
Personnel Profile: Full-Time Paid 4; Part-Time Paid 19; Part-Time Volunteers 80; Interns 2.
Governing Authority: nonprofit organization. Tax-exempt: 501(c)(3).
History Museum: housed in 18th-century Noah Webster House.
Collections: period furnishings & decorative arts of 18th century; 18th to 20th-century period clothing; local & regional manuscripts; Webster publications; paintings & photographs.
Research Fields: West Hartford history; Noah Webster's life & works; Webster family.
Facilities: 800-vol. library of regional & topical history & the life of Noah Webster, available for research by special appointment; 50-seat auditorium; schoolhouse theater. Museum-related items for sale.
Activities: guided tours; special events; lectures; films; gallery talks; outreach educational programs; walking tours; formally organized education programs for children, undergraduate & graduate college students affiliated with museum internships; permanent & temporary exhibitions; cable access monthly TV show; summer camp.
Publications: occasional books & booklets, Noah Webster; From Colonial Parish; filmstrip, A Brief Appreciation of West Hartford; The Blue-backed Speller; filmstrip, Noah Webster: Schoolmaster of America; quarterly newsletter, Spectator.
Hours & Admission Prices: Thurs.-Mon. 1-4. Adults $7, senior citizens $5, children 6-18 $4; discounts for groups, AAM, NEMA, & GHAHHM members. Closed national holidays. ♿
Attendance: 17,500 (accurate)
Membership: Library $10; Student $20; Single $25; Family $40; Sustaining $75.

SAINT JOSEPH COLLEGE ART GALLERY, (M), 1678 Asylum Ave., West Hartford, CT 06117-2791. Tel.: 860-231-5399. Fax: 860-231-5754.
E-mail: artgallery@sjc.edu
Web Site: www.sjc.edu/artgallery
Founded: 1937.
Congressional District: 1
Key Personnel: Dir. & Cur., Ann H. Sievers; Collection Mgr. & Registrar, Rochelle L. R. Oakley.
Personnel Profile: Full-Time Paid 2; Part-Time Paid 3; Part-Time Volunteers 4; Interns 3.
Governing Authority: private college; nonprofit. Tax-exempt: 501(c)(3).
Art Museum.
Collections: early 20th-century American paintings; original prints by European & American artists dating from the 15th-century to the present; Japanese woodblock prints; Thomas Nast wood engravings.
Facilities: print study room; 2,150 sq. ft. gallery space.
Activities: formal education programs for undergraduate & graduate college students; temporary exhibitions.
Publications: exhibition checklists.
Hours & Admission Prices: Tues.-Wed. & Fri.-Sat. 11-4, Thurs. 11-7, Sun. 1-4. No charge. Closed national holidays. ♿
Attendance: 5,000 (estimated)
Membership: Student & Recent Alumni $10; Senior $20; Educator K-12 $25; Individual $35; Family & Household $50; Patron $100; Sponsor $250; Benefactor $500; Director's Circle $1,000; Kelly Associate $10,000.

West Haven

SAVIN ROCK MUSEUM, 6 Rock St., West Haven, CT 06516-5846. Tel.: 203-937-3666.
Web Site: www.savinrockmuseum.com
Key Personnel: Cur., Harold Hartmann
History Museum.
Collections: local history & culture; photographs; period furnishings; personal artifacts.
Hours & Admission Prices: April 5-Sept. 14 Tues. 9am-12pm, Wed. & Fri. 1-4, Sat.-Sun. 4-7; Sept. 17-Dec. 21 Wed. & Fri.-Sun. 1-4. Adults $4, seniors & children under 12 $2.

Westbrook

MILITARY HISTORIANS, HEADQUARTERS & MUSEUM, N. Main St., Westbrook, CT 06498-1944. Tel.: 860-399-9460.
E-mail: military.historians@snet.net
Formerly: The Company of Military Historians Headquarters and Museum
Founded: 2000.
Key Personnel: Admin., Maj. William R. Reid; Cur. Uniforms, Insignia & Photos, Earl Vincent; Librarian, Kenneth Reid.
Personnel Profile: Full-Time Volunteers 2; Part-Time Volunteers 3.
Governing Authority: nonprofit organization. Tax-exempt: 501(c)(3).
Military Uniform Museum.
Collections: military uniforms from 1775 to date; military music & art; military vehicles from World War II to present.
Research Fields: military units of North America.
Facilities: library of books, films, DVDs & photos dealing with the military available for research by special request; reading room.
Activities: guided tours; lectures; films, concerts; permanent exhibitions.
Hours & Admission Prices: Tues.-Fri. 8-2:30; other times by appointment. No charge, donations accepted.

STEWART B. MCKINNEY NATIONAL WILDLIFE REFUGE, 733 Old Clinton Rd., Westbrook, CT 06498-1760. Tel.: 860-399-2513. Fax: 860-399-2515.
Key Personnel: Mgr., Barry Parrish

Wildlife Refuge.
Collections: wildlife & their habitats; ecology; natural history; geology.
Activities: educational programs.
Hours & Admission Prices: Call for hours.

Weston

THE COLEY HOMESTEAD & BARN MUSEUM, 104 Weston Rd., Weston, CT 06883. Mailing Address: P.O. Box 1092, Weston, CT 06883-0092. Tel.: 203-226-1804.
Founded: 1961.
Congressional District: 5
Key Personnel: Pres. (V), Reg Bowden.
Personnel Profile: Part-Time Volunteers 15.
Governing Authority: society. Parent Institution: The Weston Historical Society. Tax-exempt.
Agriculture Museum: housed in 1835 Old Barn & Victorian house.
Collections: early handicrafts; furnishings; old farm tools; herb garden.
Research Fields: old houses; Weston genealogy.
Facilities: 100-vol. library of old history books.
Activities: guided tours; lectures; formally organized education programs for children; permanent exhibits.
Publications: Weston, the Forging of a Connecticut Town; quarterly newsletter, The Chronicle.
Hours & Admission Prices: Call for hours. No charge; donations accepted.
Attendance: 5,000 (estimated)
Membership: Sustaining $25-$99; Renovator $100-$249; Restorer $250-$399; Preserver $400 & up.

WESTON WOODS INSTITUTE, (M), 389 Newtown Tpke., Weston, CT 06883-1116. Tel.: 203-222-8000 & 454-4005. Fax: 203-222-2263.
E-mail: uryy@sbcglobal.net
Web Site: www.infowestonwoodsinstitute.org
Founded: 1983.
Congressional District: 4
Key Personnel: C.E.O. & Chm. (V), Morton Schindel.
Personnel Profile: Part-Time Paid 1; Part-Time Volunteers 1; Interns 2.
Governing Authority: private; nonprofit organization. Tax-exempt: 501(c)(3).
Children's Museum.
Collections: original animation cels; early mechanical music devices; stereoptical & projection devices.
Research Fields: communication techniques for children.
Facilities: 1,000-vol. library of children's books; 2,500 sq. ft. exhibit space.
Activities: films; formal education programs for children; guided tours; mobile vans; participatory, temporary & traveling exhibitions.
Hours & Admission Prices: By appointment or invitation. No charge.
Attendance: 750 (estimated)

Westport

* **EARTHPLACE - THE NATURE DISCOVERY CENTER, (M),** 10 Woodside Lane, Westport, CT 06880-2322. Mailing Address: P.O. Box 165, Westport, CT 06881-0165. Tel.: 203-227-7253. Fax: 203-227-8909.
E-mail: info@earthplace.org
Web Site: www.earthplace.org
Formerly: Nature Center for Environmental Activities, Inc.
Founded: 1958.
Congressional District: 4
Key Personnel: Exec. Dir., John D. Horkel, Ph.D.; Chm., Rob Chasin; Pres., Cardyn Trabuco.
Personnel Profile: Full-Time Paid 12; Part-Time Paid 21; Part-Time Volunteers 100; Interns 5.
Governing Authority: nonprofit organization. Tax-exempt: 501(c)(3) & 170(b)(1)(A).
Natural History Museum & Environmental Studies Center.
Collections: geology; entomology; ornithology; mineralogy; mammalogy; ichthyology; malacology.
Research Fields: environmental studies; botany; ornithology.
Facilities: nature center; water quality research laboratory; 100-seat auditorium; classrooms; wild animal shelter.
Activities: bird & butterfly demonstration garden; native plant court; guided tours; lectures; films; formally organized educational programs; family local & regional excursions; inter-museum loan; permanent, temporary & traveling exhibitions; water-quality monitoring and research program; nature trails including universal access trail.
Publications: newsletter.
Hours & Admission Prices: Mon.-Sat. 9-5, Sun. 1-4. Suggested Donations: adults $7, seniors 62 & over and children 1-12 $5; members no charge. Closed New Year's Day; Easter; Memorial Day; Independence Day; Labor Day; Thanksgiving; Christmas. ♿
Attendance: 70,000 (estimated)
Membership: Seniors 62 & over $25; Single $35; Family $75; Sponsor $125; Friend $250; Patron $500; Benefactor $1,000.

ROLNICK OBSERVATORY, 182 Bayberry Lane, Westport, CT 06880. Tel.: 203-227-0925.
Observatory.
Collections: 25 inch Newtonian telescope; astronomy.
Activities: classes.
Hours & Admission Prices: Wed.-Thurs. 8pm-10pm. No charge.

WESTPORT ARTS CENTER, 51 Riverside Ave., Westport, CT 06880. Tel.: 203-222-7070.
Art Gallery.
Collections: contemporary art; paintings; sculpture.
Activities: educational programs; hands-on activities.
Hours & Admission Prices: Mon.-Fri. 10-4, Sat.-Sun. 12-4. No charge. ♿

WESTPORT HISTORICAL SOCIETY, 25 Avery Place, Westport, CT 06880-3215. Tel.: 203-222-1424. Fax: 203-221-0981.
E-mail: info@westporthistory.org
Web Site: westporthistory.org
Founded: 1899.
Congressional District: 4
Key Personnel: Exec. Dir., Susan Gold; Pres. Westport Historical Society, Dorothy Curran; Vice Pres. Finance, Elliott Netherton; Museum Shop Mgr., Olivia Yule.
Personnel Profile: Full-Time Paid 1; Part-Time Paid 3; Part-Time Volunteers 30.
Governing Authority: society; not-for-profit. Tax-exempt: 501(c)(3).
History Museum.
Collections: genealogy; house history; photographs; costumes & textiles; period rooms: parlor, bedroom, kitchen in the Victorian style; Westport history; diorama of historic downtown.
Research Fields: house history; genealogy; costumes; textiles.
Facilities: archives. Gift items for sale.
Activities: formal education programs for children; adult workshops; lectures; temporary exhibitions. Annual Events: Holiday House Tour; Garden Tour.
Publications: bimonthly newsletter; annual report.
Hours & Admission Prices: Mon.-Fri. 10-4, Sat. 12-4. No charge; donations accepted. ♿
Attendance: 5,000 (estimated)
Membership: Student & Senior Citizen $30; Individual $35; Senior Family $50; Family $60; Patron $100; Minuteman $250; Patron $500; Benefactor $1,000.

Wethersfield

BUTTOLPH-WILLIAMS HOUSE, 249 Broad St., Wethersfield, CT 06109. Mailing Address: 211 Main St., Wethersfield, CT 06109-2339. Tel.: 860-247-8996. Fax: 860-529-0460.
Governing Authority: Parent Institution: The Antiquarian & Landmarks Society.
Historic House: built c.1711.
Collections: period furnishings; personal artifacts.
Hours & Admission Prices: Wed.-Mon. 10-4. Adults $4, children $2; members no charge.

* **THE WEBB-DEANE-STEVENS MUSEUM, (M),** 211 Main St., Wethersfield, CT 06109-2339. Tel.: 860-529-0612. Fax: 860-571-8636.
E-mail: info@webb-deane-stevens.org
Web Site: www.webb-deane-stevens.org
Founded: 1919.
Congressional District: 1
Key Personnel: Pres. (V), Torrey Cooke; Dir., Charles T. Lyle; Education Coord., Tari-Lynn Joyce; Curatorial Asst., Ellen Goldberg; Curatorial Asst., Sal Cormosino; Rentals, Katie Sullivan.
Personnel Profile: Full-Time Paid 3; Part-Time Paid 22; Part-Time Volunteers 40; Interns 1.
Governing Authority: society. Parent Institution: The National Society of The Colonial Dames of America in the State of Connecticut. Tax-exempt: 501(c)(3).
Historic Houses: restored 18th-century houses.
Collections: American furniture; decorative arts; ceramics; silver; American needlework; gardens; research library; archives; toys; games; children's items; early 20th-century murals & tea room.
Research Fields: local history; Connecticut Valley furniture & architecture; 18th-century social history; multi-culturalism in 18th century; slavery; colonial revival; women's organizations; American Revolution child life in the early 14th century; Wallace Nutting and the Colonial Revival Movement.

Facilities: 5,000-vol. library of history & decorative arts materials. Museum-related items for sale.
Activities: guided tours; school tours; museum school programs; family programs; academic programs for undergraduate college students affiliated with the greater Hartford Consortium of Colleges; summer internship program; seminars on decorative arts; special events; special interpretive tours. Museum Sponsors: 1772 Thanksgiving Holiday Tour, 1840 & 1925 Christmas Holiday Tours.
Publications: newsletter.
Hours & Admission Prices: Jan-March by appointment; April & Nov. Sat. 10-4, Sun. 1-4; May-Oct. Wed.-Mon. 10-4, Sun. 1-4; last tour at 3:30; Nov.-April Sat. 10-4, Sun. 1-4; last tour at 3:30. House: adults $8, seniors $7, students $4; discounts to AAA & AAM members; members no charge. ♿
Attendance: 10,000 (estimated)
Membership: Family $15.

THE WETHERSFIELD HISTORICAL SOCIETY, (M), 150 Main St., Wethersfield, CT 06109-3126. Tel.: 860-529-7656. Fax: 860-563-2609.
E-mail: society@wethhist.org
Web Site: www.wethhist.org
Founded: 1932.
Congressional District: 1
Key Personnel: Interim Dir., Amy Northrop; Pres., Dorene Ciarcia; Vice Pres., Robert L. Fisher; Dir. Mktg. & Events, Margaret Longey.
Personnel Profile: Full-Time Paid 2; Part-Time Paid 6; Part-Time Volunteers 100.
Governing Authority: historical society. Branch Museums: 1804 Old Academy & Library; 1690 The Cove Warehouse; 1793 Capt. James Francis House; 1804 Hurlbut-Dunham House; 1787 Standish House; 1893 Robert Allan Keeney Memorial. Tax-exempt: 501(c)(3).
History Museum.
Collections: local history; historic properties & buildings; tools & crafts; regional furniture; decorative arts; costumes; paintings; wallpaper; marine artifacts. Historic Buildings: 18th century brick Georgian house; 18th century Cove Warehouse.
Research Fields: local history; genealogy.
Facilities: research library; reading room; meeting rooms; lecture halls; visitors center. Museum-related items for sale.
Activities: guided tours; lectures; seminars; docent program; temporary exhibitions; formally organized education programs; daily life programs.
Publications: quarterly newsletter; periodic booklets & books.
Hours & Admission Prices: Old Academy & Research Library: Tues.-Fri. 10-4 & by appointment. No charge. Wethersfield Museum at Keeney Memorial: Mon.-Sat. 10-4, Sun. 1-4. Adults $3; discounts to AAM members; members, children 16 and under & town residents no charge. Hurlbut-Dunham House: mid-May to mid-Oct., Sat. 10-4, Sun. 1-4. Adults $3. Cove Warehouse: mid-May to mid-Oct. Sat. 10-4, Sun. 1-4. Donation: adults $1; children no charge. ♿
Attendance: 10,000 (estimated)
Membership: Student $10; Senior $20; Individual $30; Senior Citizen Couple 62 & over $35; Family $40; Friend $75; Sponsor $100; Patron $250; Benefactor $500.

Willimantic

CONNECTICUT EASTERN RAILROAD MUSEUM, off Bridge St., Willimantic, CT 06226. Mailing Address: P.O. Box 665, Willimantic, CT 06226-0665. Tel.: 860-456-9999.
E-mail: info@cteastrrmuseum.org
Founded: 1992.
Key Personnel: Pres. (V), Mark F. Granville; Museum Shop Mgr., M. Jean Lambert.
Governing Authority: nonprofit organization. Parent Institution: Connecticut Eastern Chapter, NRHS, Inc. Tax-exempt: 501(c)(3).
Railroad Museum.
Collections: locomotives; rolling stock; railroad buildings; replica 1850s style pump car.
Publications: newsletter, Ghost Train Journal; annual calendar.
Hours & Admission Prices: May-Oct. Sat.-Sun. 10-4; other times by appointment. Adults $5, seniors 62 & over $4, children 8-12 $1; children under 8 no charge.
Membership: Friend $25; Sponsor $50.

WINDHAM TEXTILE AND HISTORY MUSEUM (THE MILL MUSEUM), 411 Main St., Willimantic, CT 06226-3173. Tel.: 860-456-2178.
E-mail: millmuseum@sbcglobal.net
Web Site: www.millmuseum.org
Founded: 1985.
Congressional District: 2
Key Personnel: Exec. Dir., Brooke Shannon; Pres., Steve Kenton; Educator, Beverly York.
Personnel Profile: Part-Time Paid 2; Part-Time Volunteers 73; Interns 1.
Governing Authority: private; nonprofit organization. Tax-exempt: 501(c)(3).
Textile & History Museum: located in 1877 buildings built as a company store & library for the Willimantic Linen Company.
Collections: material culture of the working families & owners - factory, home life & community life; manuscript collection includes more than 20,000 architectural & engineering drawings, photos and business records.
Research Fields: American, Connecticut & Windham textile industry history; oral history; water power; immigration & migration; mill architecture.
Facilities: 1,850-vol. library; 6,770 sq. ft. exhibit space; field research station. Museum-related items for sale.
Activities: arts festivals; concerts; dance recitals; docent program; films; formal education programs for adults, graduate & undergraduate students affiliated with the University of Connecticut and Eastern Connecticut State University; guided tours; hobby workshops; lectures; loan & temporary exhibitions; rental gallery; school loan service; Girl Scout & Boy Scout badge activities. Annual Events: Meet the Artist; architectural tours; spinning bee; Victorian crafts.
Publications: quarterly newsletter, The Gazette; school curriculum guides; three publications, Willimantic Women: Their Lives and Labors; Willimantic Industry and Community: The Rise & Decline of a Connecticut Textile City; A Tour of The Oaks (Worker Housing); Mills and Meadows, A Pictorial of Windham & Tolland Counties.
Hours & Admission Prices: May-Oct. Tues. & Fri.-Sun. 10-4; Nov.-April Fri.-Sun. 10-4. Adults $5, senior citizens & students $3.50; discounts to groups, AAM & ICOM members; children under 5 & members no charge. Closed New Year's Day; Easter; Thanksgiving; Christmas. ♿
Attendance: 7,000 (estimated)
Membership: Seniors & Students $10; Individual $15; Family $25; Sustaining $30; Patron $50; Benefactor $1,000; Business $150.

Wilton

WEIR FARM NATIONAL HISTORIC SITE, 735 Nod Hill Rd., Wilton, CT 06897-1309. Tel.: 203-834-1896. Fax: 203-834-2421.
Web Site: www.nps.gov/wefa/
Founded: 1990.
Congressional District: 5
Key Personnel: Supt., Linda Cook.
Personnel Profile: Full-Time Paid 8; Part-Time Paid 3; Part-Time Volunteers 40; Interns 1.
Governing Authority: federal government; nonprofit. Parent Institution: U.S. Dept. of Interior, National Park Service, Northeast Region. Private Partner: Weir Farm Trust. Tax-exempt: 501(c)(3).
Historic Site: comprised of 60 acres of J. Alden Weir's farm (1852-1919) in Branchville, CT. Listed on the National Register of Historic Places.
Collections: focus on J. Alden Weir, American Impressionist painter & owner of the farm from 1882-1919; Weir's art & person artifacts; other artists associated with Weir Farm; furnishings; personal items; archives & manuscript materials relating to Weir's private & professional life. Historic Structures: 3 historic farm houses, two barns, two artists' studios.
Research Fields: historic structures report on all historic buildings; cultural landscape study focusing on the landscape since 1882; historic furnishings report for Weir's house & painting studio & Mahonri Young's sculpture studio; historic painting sites study to locate sites where paintings, drawings & etchings were executed on site.
Facilities: visitor center. Publications about Weir & postcards for sale.
Activities: guided tours; lectures; docent program; formal educational programs; orientation video; computer station of site-related artwork; children's art classes; Resident Artist Programs; art demonstrations; meetings. Annual Event: Jazz in the Garden.
Publications: site bulletin; brochures; exhibit activity guides; quarterly newsletter Weir Farm News; volunteer newsletter.
Hours & Admission Prices: Visitor Center: Wed.-Sun. 9-5; Grounds: daily dawn to dusk. Tours of historic art studios & grounds available, call for schedule. No charge; donations accepted. Closed New Year's Day; Thanksgiving; Christmas.
Attendance: 17,000 (accurate)
Membership: Weir Farm Art Center: Seniors $25; Associate $35; Family $50; Contributor $100; Sponsor $250; Patron $500; Benefactor $1,000.

WILTON HISTORICAL MUSEUMS, (M), 224 Danbury Rd., Wilton, CT 06897-6000. Tel.: 203-762-7257. Fax: 203-762-3297.
E-mail: info@wiltonhistorical.org
Web Site: www.wiltonhistorical.org
Formerly: Wilton Heritage Museum
Founded: 1938.
Congressional District: 4

Key Personnel: Pres., Greg Chann; Vice Pres. Mktg. & Communications, William Mathews; Cur., Andrea Wulffleff.
Personnel Profile: Full-Time Paid 3; Part-Time Paid 3; Part-Time Volunteers 40.
Governing Authority: Wilton Historical Society, Inc. Tax-exempt.
Historical Society Museum.
Collections: 18th to early 20th-century furnishings & accessories; 1740-1910 period rooms; costumes; textile collection; toys; dolls & dollhouses; Norwalk Redware; ceramics; 18th-20th century kitchen equipment; tools. Historic Buildings: c.1739 Betts-Sturges Blackmar House; c.1770 Raymond-Fitch House; 19th century barn; mid 19th century Abbott Barn; working blacksmith shop.
Research Fields: genealogy; local history; survey of 18th & 19th-century houses.
Facilities: research library of history, genealogy & manuscripts pertaining to Wilton history & families. Museum-related items for sale.
Activities: guided house tours; tours to historic sites; lectures; blacksmith shop; educational programs; traveling exhibitions. Museum Sponsors: antiques show; crafts show.
Publications: semiannual newsletter, Eighteenth Century Dwellings In Wilton; Annals of Wilton, Vol. I, II & III; Cannondale: A Connecticut Neighborhood; A Difinitive History of Wilton; Wilton Connecticut - Three Centuries of People, Places & Progress.
Hours & Admission Prices: Mon.-Thurs. 10-4:30, Sun. 1-4 for special exhibits & programs. Adults $4; discounts to AAM members; members no charge. ♿
Attendance: 5,500 (estimated)
Membership: Individual & Family $35; Sustaining $50; Patron $100.

WOODCOCK NATURE CENTER, 56 Deer Run Rd., Wilton, CT 06897. Tel.: 203-762-7280.
Nature Center.
Collections: natural history; wildlife & their habitats; plants; flowers; trees.
Facilities: Museum-related items for sale.
Hours & Admission Prices: Center: Summer: Mon.-Fri. 9:30-4; Winter: Mon.-Fri. 9:30-4, Sat. call for hours. Trails: daily dawn to dusk. No charge; donations accepted.

Windsor

OLIVER ELLSWORTH HOMESTEAD AND MUSEUM, 778 Palisado Ave., Windsor, CT 06095-2097. Mailing Address: P.O. Box 791, Windsor, CT 06095-0791. Tel.: 860-688-8717.
Web Site: www.ctdar.org/oeh/index.html
Founded: 1903.
Key Personnel: Chm. (V), Jean E. Kelsey; Pres. (V), Jennie May Rehnberg.
Personnel Profile: Part-Time Volunteers 30.
Governing Authority: Parent Institution: Ellsworth Memorial Association, Inc. Tax-exempt.
Historic House Museum: built in 1781.
Collections: family history; personal artifacts; photographs; portraits; period furnishings.
Activities: special events.
Hours & Admission Prices: May 15-Oct. 15 Wed.-Thurs. & Sat. 12-4, last Sun. of month 1-4. Requested Donation: adults $4; children 12 & under and CT DAR members no charge.
Attendance: 1,000 (estimated)

Windsor Locks

NEW ENGLAND AIR MUSEUM, Bradley International Airport, 36 Perimeter Rd., Windsor Locks, CT 06096-1069. Tel.: 860-623-3305. Fax: 860-627-2820.
E-mail: staff@neam.org
Web Site: www.neam.org
Founded: 1959.
Congressional District: 1
Key Personnel: Exec. Dir., Michael P. Speciale; Chm. (V), Cornelius P. O'Leary; Visitor Svcs. Mgr., Gina Maria Alimberti.
Personnel Profile: Full-Time Paid 4; Part-Time Paid 14; Part-Time Volunteers 165.
Governing Authority: nonprofit organization. Owned by Connecticut Aeronautical Historical Association, Inc. Tax-exempt: 501(c)(3).
Aeronautics Museum.
Collections: aircraft; propulsion systems and associated material in aeronautics; manuscripts.
Research Fields: New England aeronautics.
Facilities: 1,000-vol. library of aeronautical, scientific, & transportation books available for use by approval and appointment; indoor & outdoor exhibits featuring aircraft. Aeronautical pamphlets, postcards, photographs, models & museum-related items for sale.
Activities: lectures; inter-museum loan, permanent & temporary exhibitions.
Publications: brochure; pamphlets; Tour Guide; quarterly newsletter.
Hours & Admission Prices: Daily 10-5. Adults $10, senior citizens 65 & over $9, children 4-11 $6; discounts to groups; CAHA members & children 3 and under no charge. Closed New Year's Day; Thanksgiving; Christmas. ♿
Attendance: 61,000 (accurate)
Membership: CAHA: Individual $60; Family $70; Benefactor $100; Regular Life $1,000.

NODEN-REED FARM MUSEUM, 58 West St., Windsor Locks, CT 06096-1808. Mailing Address: P.O. Box 733, Windsor Locks, CT 06096-0733. Tel.: 860-627-9212.
E-mail: winlocks@aol.com
Key Personnel: Dir., Ruth Bonito; Cur., James Anderson
History Museum: housed in Victorian farmhouse. Listed on National Register of Historical Places.
Collections: period furnishings; farm tools.
Facilities: nature trails.
Hours & Admission Prices: May-Oct. Sun. 1-5. No charge.

Woodbridge

AMITY AND WOODBRIDGE HISTORICAL SOCIETY, 1907 Litchfield Turnpike, Woodbridge, CT 06525-1264. Tel.: 203-387-2823.
E-mail: donaldmenzies@sbcglobal.net
Web Site: www.woodbridgehistory.org
Founded: 1936.
Congressional District: 3
Key Personnel: C.E.O. & Pres., Donald Menzies.
Governing Authority: nonprofit organization. Tax-exempt.
Local History & Historical Society Museum: housed in Thomas Darling House.
Collections: local history; period artifacts.
Activities: guided tours; lectures.
Publications: Amity & Woodbridge Historical Society Journal.
Hours & Admission Prices: By appointment. No charge; donations accepted.
Attendance: 200 (estimated)
Membership: Individual $10; Family $20; Sustaining $50; Life $100.

Woodbury

FLANDERS NATURE CENTER, 5 Church Hill Rd., Woodbury, CT 06798-1718. Tel.: 203-263-3711.
Key Personnel: Exec. Dir., Arthur S. Milnor
Nature Center.
Collections: wildlife & their habitats.
Facilities: nature trails.
Activities: hiking; educational programs; special events.
Hours & Admission Prices: Daily dawn to dusk. No charge.

THE GLEBE HOUSE MUSEUM AND GERTRUDE JEKYLL GARDEN, 49 Hollow Rd., Woodbury, CT 06798. Mailing Address: Box 245, Woodbury, CT 06798-0245. Tel.: 203-263-2855. Fax: 203-263-6726.
E-mail: ghmgjg@snet.net
Web Site: www.theglebehouse.org
Founded: 1923.
Congressional District: 6
Key Personnel: Dir., Judith Kelz; Pres., Carter Booth; Museum Shop Mgr., Rebecca Otten.
Personnel Profile: Full-Time Paid 1; Full-Time Volunteers 1; Part-Time Volunteers 101.
Governing Authority: society. Governed by the Seabury Society for the Preservation of the Glebe House. Tax-exempt: 501(c)(3).
Historic Building: c.1750 The Glebe House, birthplace of American Episcopacy.
Collections: original paneling; period furnishings; historical documents relating to Samuel Seabury; birthplace of American Episcopacy; 18th-century prints & painting; books & documents; 18th century furniture.
Research Fields: Episcopal Church history; state & local history; 18th-century culture; Gertrude Jekyll Gardens & Horticulture.
Facilities: garden. Photographs, brochures & gift-related items for sale.
Activities: guided tours; formally organized educational programs; lectures, demonstrations, concerts & Symposia; cemetery tours. Museum Sponsors: Fall Colonial Fair; Fall All Hollow's Eve; Holiday Festival.
Publications: brochures & pamphlets; postcards; writing paper; newsletter.
Hours & Admission Prices: May-Oct. Wed.-Sun. 1-4; Nov. Sat.-Sun. 1-4; other times by appointment only. Adults $5, children $2; members no charge.
Attendance: 5,000 (estimated)
Membership: Individual $35; Dual $60; Sponsor $100; Patron $500; Benefactor $1,000.

Woodstock

ROSELAND COTTAGE, 556 Rte. 169, Woodstock, CT 06281-2344. Mailing Address: 141 Cambridge St., Boston, MA 02114-2702. Tel.: 860-928-4074. Fax: 860-963-2208.
E-mail: roselandcottage@historicnewengland.org
Web Site: www.historicnewengland.org
Founded: 1970.
Congressional District: 2
Key Personnel: Site Mgr., Lisa Centola.
Personnel Profile: Full-Time Paid 1; Part-Time Paid 4; Part-Time Volunteers 40.
Governing Authority: society; nonprofit organization. Parent Institution: Historic New England, 141 Cambridge St., Boston, MA 02114. Tel.: 617-227-3956. Tax-exempt: 501(c)(3).
Historic House: 1846 Gothic Revival cottage.
Collections: Gothic Revival furniture; Bowen family possessions; carriage house; outbuildings.
Facilities: garden.
Activities: guided tours; lectures; special events; school & youth programs; functions.
Publications: Guide to Historic New England; magazine, Historic New England.
Hours & Admission Prices: June-Oct. 15 Wed.-Sun. 11-5. Adults $8; discounts to AAM members; members & Historic New England members no charge. ♿
Attendance: 13,272 (accurate)
Membership: National $35; Individual $45; Household $55; Garden & Landscape $75; Institutional $85; Contributing $100; Historic Homeowner $200; Supporting $250.

WOODSTOCK HISTORICAL SOCIETY, INC., 523 Rte. 169, Woodstock, CT 06281. Mailing Address: P.O. Box 65, Woodstock, CT 06281-0065. Tel.: 860-928-1035.
Web Site: www.woodstockhistoricalsociety.org
Founded: 1967.
Congressional District: 3
Key Personnel: Pres. (V), Gail White; Treas., Earl Brazeal; Museum Shop Mgr., Judy Gilliland.
Personnel Profile: Part-Time Volunteers 20.
Governing Authority: society. Tax-exempt: 170(b)(1)(A).
Historical Society Museum.
Collections: agricultural artifacts; personal artifacts; books & documents; photographs. Historic Buildings: Red-White School; Palmer Hall.
Research Fields: agriculture; architecture; history; genealogy
Facilities: seminar space.
Activities: lectures; field trips; research.
Publications: book, Samuel Sewall & the Town He Named Woodstock; booklet; sketches; Mrs. Dr. Bowen's Bustle & Apple Molasses.
Hours & Admission Prices: April-Oct. Sun. 12-4. No charge; donations accepted. Closed major holidays. ♿
Attendance: 200 (estimated)
Membership: Individual $20; Life $500.

DELAWARE

(78 listings)

Bear

WHALE WALLOW NATURE CENTER - LUMS POND STATE PARK, 1068 Howell School Rd., Bear, DE 19701. Tel.: 302-368-6989.
Nature Center.
Collections: local natural history & wildlife; plants; photographs.
Facilities: nature trails.
Activities: educational programs.
Hours & Admission Prices: Park: daily 8am to sunset. Center: Memorial Day to Labor Day daily 12-6.

Bridgeville

BRIDGEVILLE HISTORICAL SOCIETY, 102 S. Williams St., Bridgeville, DE 19933. Mailing Address: P.O. Box 306, Bridgeville, DE 19933-0336. Tel.: 302-337-8595.
Key Personnel: Dir., Mike Collison; Pres., Howard E. Hardesty
Historical Society.
Collections: local history; over 450 dolls.
Hours & Admission Prices: By appointment.

Christiana

CHRISTIANA HISTORICAL SOCIETY, 49 N. Old Baltimore Pike, Christiana, DE 19702-1637. Mailing Address: P.O. Box 6031, Stanton, DE 19804-6031. Tel.: 302-286-6223.
E-mail: kendigger@aol.com
Web Site: www.xtinahs.org/xtinahistoricalsociety.html
Key Personnel: Pres., Ken Baumgardt
Historical Society Museum.
Collections: local history & culture; photographs; personal artifacts.
Hours & Admission Prices: Call for hours.

Claymont

ROBINSON HOUSE, 1 Naamans Rd., Claymont, DE 19703-2701. Tel.: 302-792-0285.
Web Site: www.robinsonhousede.org
Governing Authority: Parent Institution: Claymont Historical Society.
Historic House Museum.
Collections: period furniture.
Facilities: Museum-related items for sale.
Activities: tours. Annual Event: Christmas House Tour in December.
Hours & Admission Prices: By appointment.

Delaware City

FORT DELAWARE SOCIETY, 33 Staff Lane, Ft. Dupont State Park, Delaware City, DE 19706. Mailing Address: P.O. Box 553, Delaware City, DE 19706-0553. Tel.: 302-834-1630. Fax: 302-834-1630.
E-mail: society@fortdelaware.org
Web Site: www.fortdelaware.org
Founded: 1950.
Key Personnel: Pres. (V), William G. Robelen, IV; Chm. (V), William E. Craven, Jr.
Personnel Profile: Part-Time Paid 1.
Governing Authority: state. Division of Parks, affiliated with Fort Delaware Society Bd. of Directors in association with state. Tax-exempt: 170(b)(1)(A).
Military & Park Museum Complex: located in c.1859 former barracks of Civil War Fort Delaware on Pea Patch Island, accessible by boat only.
Collections: materials & artifacts relating to Delaware's role in the Civil War & to the fort on Pea Patch Island; military artifacts; acoutrements; marine items; archaeology finds; gun emplacements; 32 lb. sea coast artillery cannon.
Research Fields: military.
Facilities: picnic area. Books and pamphlets for sale.
Activities: guided tours; films; formally organized education programs for children; permanent & temporary exhibitions; historical interpretations.
Publications: Fort Delaware Notes; quarterly, Fort Delaware Newsletter; books & pamphlets, A Fort Delaware Journal; Confederate Prisoners of War at Fort Delaware; Fort Delaware in the Civil War; Fort Delaware; They died at Fort Delaware; General M. Jeff Thompson in Fort Delaware; The Story of Fort Delaware; The Chains of Glory; Prison Times; Fire in the Hole.
Hours & Admission Prices: mid-June to Sept. Wed.-Sun. & holidays 10-6. Boat Fee: Adults $11, children $6; discounts to groups, senior citizens & active military. ♿
Attendance: 25,000 (accurate)
Membership: Active $25; Couple or Family $35; Supporting $60; Life $500.

Delmar

DELMAR RAILROAD MUSEUM, Delmar Public Library, 101 N. Bi-State Blvd., Delmar, DE 19940. Tel.: 302-846-9894.
Railroad Museum.
Collections: railroad artifacts; period artifacts; photographs.
Hours & Admission Prices: Call for hours.

Dover

BIGGS MUSEUM OF AMERICAN ART, (M), 406 Federal St., Dover, DE 19901-3615. Mailing Address: P.O. Box 711, Dover, DE 19903-0711. Tel.: 302-674-2111. Fax: 302-674-5133.
E-mail: ldanko@biggsmuseum.org
Web Site: www.biggsmuseum.org
Formerly: Sewell C. Biggs Museum of American Art
Founded: 1989.
Congressional District: 1
Key Personnel: Dir., Linda A.K. Danko; Chm. (V), Charles Terry Jackson, II; Membership & Communications Coord., Sarah DiMondi; Cur., Ryan Grover; Education & Events Coord., Rebecca Cooper; Museum Mgr., Ellen Arthur.

Personnel Profile: Full-Time Paid 5; Part-Time Paid 4; Part-Time Volunteers 12; Interns 2.
Governing Authority: private; nonprofit association. Tax-exempt.
American Art Museum: housed in 1858 County Office Building.
Collections: American fine & decorative arts from 1700-present with emphasis on Delaware & the Delaware Valley including J. Hesselius, the Peale Family, G. Stuart, A. Bierstadt, T. Cole & the Hudson River School, W.M. Chase, F. Schoonover & other Brandywine School Illustrators; Delaware & Philadelphia-region furniture & silver; modern & contemporary Delaware painters.
Major Exhibits: Arts Connected, 11/09-2/21/10; Ships & Seas, 3/5/10-6/20/10; Award Winners, 7/2/10-10/21/10.
Research Fields: American fine & decorative arts.
Facilities: 3,000-vol. art library; family archives.
Activities: guided tours; adults & children's activities; lectures; art workshops; crafts; special exhibitions; public celebrations; fundraisers; gala.
Publications: bimonthly, Museletter & calendar; 2-vol. catalogue, The Sewell C. Biggs Collection of American Art; Almost Forgotten: Delaware Women Artists; Delaware Clocks; Greetings from Delaware and Other Artist Communities; Delaware Silver.
Hours & Admission Prices: Tues.-Sat. 9-4:30, Sun. 1:30-4:30. No charge; donations accepted. Closed New Year's Day; Easter; Thanksgiving; Christmas. ♿
Attendance: 15,000 (estimated)
Membership: Student, Instructor, Military, & Senior $30; Individual $40; Household $50; Family $60.

DELAWARE AGRICULTURAL MUSEUM AND VILLAGE, 866 N. Dupont Hwy., Dover, DE 19901-2012. Tel.: 302-734-1618. Fax: 302-734-0457.
E-mail: damv@verizon.net
Web Site: www.agriculturalmuseum.org
Founded: 1974.
Congressional District: 1
Key Personnel: Pres. (V), Ed Kee; Museum Coord., Di Rafter; Mgr. Maintenance, Michael Grimes.
Personnel Profile: Full-Time Paid 1; Part-Time Paid 3; Part-Time Volunteers 100.
Governing Authority: nonprofit; bd. of trustees. Tax-exempt: 501(c)(3).
Museum of Rural Life and Agricultural History and Technology.
Collections: artifacts dating from early settlement; manuscript collections; farm equipment; folk art collection; tractors; interpretive poultry & dairy exhibits; horse drawn & transportation equipment; tools; housewares; store furnishings; replica of a 19th century water-powered mill. Historic Structures: c.1890 furnished two-story farm house with summer kitchen; c.1900 barn; c.1880 wagon shed, grainery; c.1860 blacksmith shop; c.1850 one-room schoolhouse; c.1825 cornhouse; c.1820 meathouse; c.1870 country store; c.1860 train station; c.1900 barbershop; c.1858 church.
Research Fields: Delaware farming; general farm life; agricultural technology.
Facilities: 2,000-vol. library pertaining to farming & agriculture available for research; reading room; re-created 1890's village & farmstead, 40,000 sq. ft. exhibit building; 80-seat auditorium. Books, reproductions, craft & other museum-related items for sale.
Activities: guided tours; lectures; youth summer camps; formally organized education programs; intern program; docent program; permanent & temporary exhibits. Special Events: town ball, Springtime on the Farm, Fall Harvest Festival; 1890 Great Country fair; Ghost walk in October; Farmer's Christmas in December featuring lamplight tour.
Publications: newsletter, Museum Gazette; brochures; annual report.
Hours & Admission Prices: Tues.-Sat. 10-3. Adults $5, senior citizens & youths 4-17 $3; discounts for groups, AAA members & Time Travelers; members & children under 3 no charge. Closed New Year's Day; Easter; Thanksgiving; Christmas. ♿
Attendance: 22,000 (accurate)
Membership: Student & Senior Citizen $15; Senior Couple & Individual $25; Family $40; Patron $75; Sponsor $150; Business $500; Corporate $1,000; Endowment $5,000.

DELAWARE ARCHAEOLOGY MUSEUM, 316 S. Governors Ave., Dover, DE 19904-6706. Mailing Address: 406 Federal St., Dover, DE 19901-3615. Tel.: 302-739-4266 & 3260. Fax: 302-739-3943.
E-mail: bev.laing@state.de.us
Web Site: history.delaware.gov
Key Personnel: Dir., Tim Slavin; Museum Shop Mgr., Bridget Warner.
Governing Authority: Parent Institution: Division of Historical & Cultural Affairs.
Archaeology Museum: housed in the former Presbyterian Church, built in 1790.
Collections: Delaware's Native Americans; archaeology; arrowheads; ceramics; stone & bone tools; personal artifacts.
Research Fields: Middle Atlantic archaeology including pre-contact & contact periods.
Activities: tours; special events; monthly family focus programs. Museum Sponsors: Old Dover Days in May; Delaware's Archaeology Month in May.
Hours & Admission Prices: Tues.-Sat. & state holidays 9-4:30, Sun. 1:30-4:30; groups by appointment. No charge; donations accepted. Closed New Year's Day; Easter; Christmas. ♿

DELAWARE DIVISION OF HISTORICAL & CULTURAL AFFAIRS, 21 The Green, Dover, DE 19901-3611. Tel.: 302-736-7400. Fax: 302-739-6712.
Web Site: history.delaware.gov
Formerly: Delaware State Museums
Founded: 1931.
Key Personnel: Dir., Timothy Slavin; Deputy Dir., Steve Marz; Cur. Archaeology, Charles H. Fithian; Cur. Collections, Ann M. Baker Horsey; Cur. Education, Madeline Dunn; Cur. Collections Management, Claudia F. Leister; Landscape Supt., Diane D. Crom; Site Supvr. New Castle, Cynthia Snyder; Site Mgr., Beverly Laing; Site Supvr. Dover, Stacey Johnson; Site Supvr. John Dickinson Plantation, Gloria Henry; Site Supvr. Zwaanendael Museum, Andrea Anderson; Museum Shop Mgr., Bridget Warner.
Personnel Profile: Full-Time Paid 30; Part-Time Paid 45.
Governing Authority: state. Parent Institution: Department of State, Division of Historical & Cultural Affairs. Branch Museums: Archaeology Museum, Museum of Small Town Life, 316 S. Governors Ave., Dover; Old State House, The Green, Dover; State Visitor Center, Federal St., Dover; Johnson Victrola Museum, Corner of Bank Ln. & New St., Dover; Buena Vista State Conference Center, 661 S. DuPont Hwy., New Castle; Old New Castle Courthouse, The Green, New Castle; John Dickinson Plantation, Kitts Hummock Rd., Dover; Octagonal Schoolhouse, Cowgills Corner, Route 9, Dover; Belmont Hall Conference Center, Smyrna; Zwaanendael Museum, Lewes. Monuments: Cooch's Bridge Monument, Old Baltimore Pike, Newark; DeVries Monument, Pilotown Rd., Lewes.
State Historical Agency & Museums: Meeting House Galleries: housed in c.1790 Presbyterian Church now the State Archaeology gallery & 1880 Sunday School Building; Old State House: c.1792; Johnson Victrola Museum; Buena Vista: 1845-47, home of John M. Clayton now used as a conference center; Old New Castle Courthouse: located on the Green laid out by Peter Stuyvesant in 1655; in 1776 the Declaration of Independence & the first Constitution of Delaware were approved; State Visitor Center & Gallery; John Dickinson Plantation, c.1740, historic house, with reconstructed Afro-American tenant house & farm buildings, boyhood home of John Dickinson who wrote, Letters from a Farmer in Pennsylvania, & signed Articles of Confederation & U.S. Constitution; Octagonal Schoolhouse, 1831, one of Delaware's oldest remaining school buildings; Zwaanendael Museum, housed in a 1931 adaptation of the Old Town Hall in Hoorn, Holland. Monuments: Cooch's Bridge Monument commemorating September 3, 1777 skirmish with British; DeVries Monument commemorating landing of the Dutch in 1631, the first settlement in Delaware; c.1770, Belmont Hall Conference Center, home of last President of Delaware.
Collections: lifestyles, government, politics, & decorative arts of Delaware citizens; state archaeological collection; official state portraits. Meeting House Galleries: state archaeology; Main Street Delaware on small towns. Johnson Victrola Museum: phonographs; advertising; records; ephemera; papers of Eldridge Reeves Johnson, founder of the Victor Talking Machine Company. Zwaanendael Museum: early history of Lewes & Sussex County; maritime archaeology of the HMS DeBraak which sank in 1798.
Research Fields: Delaware prehistory, history & culture; legislative, judicial & executive history & material culture; Victor Talking Machine Co. sound archives.
Facilities: 1,000-vol. library on eastern North American prehistory; reading rooms; archaeological laboratory & field research station; visitor center. Museum-related items for sale.
Activities: guided tours; gallery talks; lectures; permanent & temporary exhibitions; inter-museum loan program; formally organized programs for children; museum internship opportunities for undergraduates; archaeological excavation & survey; internship program; in-service training programs for teachers; special educational programs.
Publications: brochures.
Hours & Admission Prices: Buena Vista Conference Center: by appointment. Old New Castle Courthouse: Tues.-Sat. 10-3:30, Sun. 1:30-4:30. Delaware Visitor's Center and Galleries, Delaware Archaeology Museum, Museum of Small Town Life, Johnson Victrola Museum & Historic Old State House: Mon.-Sat. 9-4:30, Sun. 1:30-4:30. John Dickinson Plantation: Jan.-Feb. Tues.-Sat. 10-3:30; March-Dec. Tues.-Sat. 10-3:30, Sun. 1:30-4:30. Zwaanendael: Tues.-Sat. 10-4:30, Sun. 1:30-4:30. No charge; donations accepted. Closed state holidays. For specific information on tour arrangements, call State Visitor Center, Dover, 302-645-1148, or write to State Visitor Center, Federal St., 406 Federal St., Dover, DE 19901. ♿
Attendance: 100,000 (estimated)

DELAWARE PUBLIC ARCHIVES, 121 Duke of York St., Dover, DE 19901-3638. Tel.: 302-744-5000. Fax: 302-739-2578.
E-mail: aarchives@state.de.us
Web Site: www.archives.delaware.gov
Founded: 1905.
Key Personnel: Dir., James R. Frazier
Archives.
Collections: history; culture; genealogy; probates; tax assessments; family histories.
Activities: research; tours; genealogy; presentations; workshops.
Hours & Admission Prices: Mon.-Fri. 8-4:15, 1st Sat. of month 9-4:45. No charge. Closed state holidays.

DELAWARE STATE POLICE MUSEUM, 1425 N. DuPont Hwy., Dover, DE 19903. Mailing Address: P.O. Box 430, Dover, DE 19903-0430. Tel.: 302-739-7700. Fax: 302-739-7707.
E-mail: dspmuseum@aol.com
Web Site: www.delawaretrooper.com/museum
Key Personnel: Pres., Maj. Raymond Deputy; Vice Pres., Capt. Peter Steil; Treas., Maj. Robert Gouge; Cur., Sgt. John Alstadt
Police Museum.
Collections: criminal investigation methods; highway safety; major crime scenes; police vehicles & equipment; uniforms; weapons.
Activities: tours.
Hours & Admission Prices: Mon.-Fri. 9-3, 3rd Sat. of month 11-3; other times by appointment. No charge.

DELAWARE VISITOR'S CENTER AND GALLERIES, 406 Federal St., Dover, DE 19901-3615. Tel.: 302-739-4266. Fax: 302-739-3943.
Web Site: history.delaware.gov/
Founded: 1950.
Key Personnel: Dir., Tim Slavin.
Governing Authority: state. Parent Institution: Division of Historical & Cultural Affairs, 21 The Green, Dover, DE 19901.
History Museum & Visitor's Center.
Collections: Delaware history.
Facilities: 500 sq. ft. exhibit space. Museum-related items for sale.
Activities: guided tours; lectures; temporary exhibitions; monthly special programs. Annual Event: Old Dover Days.
Publications: local & state information.
Hours & Admission Prices: Tues.-Sat. & state holidays 9-4:30, Sun. 1:30-4:30; groups by appointment. No charge; donations accepted. Closed New Year's Day; Easter; Christmas. ♿

JOHN DICKINSON PLANTATION, 340 Kitts Hummock Rd., Dover, DE 19901-7016. Tel.: 302-739-3277. Fax: 302-739-3173.
Web Site: www.history.delaware.gov
Founded: 1956.
Key Personnel: Supvr., Gloria Henry.
Governing Authority: Parent Institution: State of Delaware. Subsidiary Institution: Division of Historical and Cultural Affairs.
History Museum.
Collections: period history; plantation life; decorative arts; archaeology; architecture; slavery. Historic Buildings: 18th century plantation home; farm buildings.
Activities: demonstrations; tours.
Hours & Admission Prices: Wed.-Sat. 10-3:30, Sun. 1:30-4:30. No charge; donations accepted. Closed state holidays. ♿

JOHNSON VICTROLA MUSEUM, 375 S. New St., Dover, DE 19901. Mailing Address: 406 Federal St., Dover, DE 19901-3615. Tel.: 302-739-4266. Fax: 302-739-3943.
E-mail: stacey.johnson@state.de.us
Web Site: history.delaware.gov/museums/jvm/jvm_main.shtml
Founded: 1960.
Key Personnel: Dir., Tim Slavin; Site Supvr., Stacey Johnson.
Governing Authority: state. Parent Institution: Division of Historical & Cultural Affairs, 21 The Green, Dover, DE 19901.
Technology Museum: Eldridge Reeves Johnson, founder of the Victor Talking Machine Company in 1901, later known as RCA.
Collections: life & work of Eldridge Reeves Johnson; Victor talking machines; phonographs; memorabilia; personal artifacts; paintings; Victor records.
Facilities: 2,000 sq. ft. exhibit space.
Activities: guided tours; monthly family focus programs. Annual Event: Old Dover Day.
Hours & Admission Prices: 1st Sat. of month 9-4:30; groups by appointment. No charge; donations accepted. Closed New Year's Day; Easter; Christmas.

MUSEUM OF SMALL TOWN LIFE, 316 S. Governors Ave., Dover, DE 19901. Mailing Address: 406 Federal St., Dover, DE 19901-3615. Tel.: 302-739-4266. Fax: 302-739-3943.
Web Site: history.delaware.gov/
Founded: 1950.
Key Personnel: Dir., Tim Slavin.
Governing Authority: state. Parent Institution: Division of Historical & Cultural Affairs, 21 The Green, Dover, DE 19901.
Historic Site: housed in the former Presbyterian Church Sunday School; build in 1880.
Collections: household artifacts; industrial equipment from 1880-1900s; print shops; pharmacy; general store; wood working shop; post office.
Research Fields: printing methods; 19th century household products; 19th century pharmacy methods.
Facilities: 2,000 sq. ft. exhibit space.
Activities: guided tours; monthly family focus programs. Annual Event: Old Dover Days.
Hours & Admission Prices: Temporarily closed. ♿

THE OLD STATE HOUSE, 25 The Green, Dover, DE 19901. Mailing Address: 406 Federal St., Dover, DE 19901-3615. Tel.: 302-739-4266. Fax: 302-739-3943.
E-mail: stacey.johnson@state.de.us
Web Site: history.delaware.gov/museums/sh/sh_main.shtml
Founded: 1976.
Key Personnel: Dir., Tim Slavin; Site Supvr., Stacey Johnson.
Governing Authority: state. Parent Institution: Division of Historical & Cultural Affairs, 21 The Green, Dover, DE 19901.
Historic Site: housed in the restored capitol building; built in 1792.
Collections: architecture; period furnishings; archival documents.
Research Fields: political records, laws & government.
Facilities: 3,500 sq. ft. exhibit space.
Activities: concerts; guided tours; lectures; monthly family focus programs. Annual Event: Old Dover Days.
Hours & Admission Prices: Tues.-Sat. & state holidays 9-4:30, Sun. 1:30-4:30; groups by appointment. No charge; donations accepted. Closed New Year's Day; Easter; Christmas. ♿

Dover AFB

AIR MOBILITY COMMAND MUSEUM, (M), 1301 Heritage Rd., Dover AFB, DE 19902-5301. Tel.: 302-677-5938 & 5939. Fax: 302-677-5940.
E-mail: museum@dover.af.mil
Web Site: www.amcmuseum.org
Founded: 1986.
Key Personnel: C.E.O., Michael D. Leister; Pres., Donald Sloan; Cur., James R. Leech; Operations Mgr., John Taylor; Restoration Chief, Rick Veller; Archivist, Harry Heist; Education, Dick Caldwell; Registrar & Collections Mgr., Deborah Sellars; Museum Shop Mgr., Jim Stewart.
Personnel Profile: Full-Time Paid 4; Full-Time Volunteers 2; Part-Time Paid 3; Part-Time Volunteers 100.
Governing Authority: federal; nonprofit. Parent Institution: USAF Museum. Tax-exempt: 501(c)(3).
Military Museum: housed in a WWII hanger.
Collections: 27 aircraft.
Research Fields: airlift history.
Facilities: 750-vol. library of military aviation; 20,000 sq. ft. exhibit space; 70-seat theater; outdoor air park; commemoration park. Museum-related items for sale.
Activities: films; formal education programs for adults; guided tours; lectures; loan, temporary & traveling exhibitions; training programs for professional museum workers; broadcast/cable programs. Museum Sponsors: Community Appreciation Day.
Publications: quarterly foundation newsletter, Hangar Digest.
Hours & Admission Prices: Tues.-Sun. 9-4. No charge; donations accepted. Closed federal holidays. ♿
Attendance: 48,000 (accurate)
Membership: Individual $20; Family $30; Patron $100; Aircraft Sponsor & Corporate $200.

Fenwick Island

DISCOVERSEA SHIPWRECK MUSEUM, 708 Coastal Hwy., Fenwick Island, DE 19944. Tel.: 302-539-9366; 888-743-5524. Fax: 302-539-1285.
E-mail: dsmuseum@aol.com
Web Site: www.discoversea.com
Key Personnel: Dir., Dale W. Clifton, Jr.
Maritime History Museum.
Collections: maritime history; shipwreck artifacts.
Activities: lecture; educational programs.

Hours & Admission Prices: June-Aug. daily 11-8; Sept.-May Sat.-Sun. 11-4; groups by appointment. No charge; donations accepted.

FENWICK ISLAND LIGHTHOUSE & MUSEUM, Rt. 54, Fenwick Island, DE 19944. Mailing Address: New Friends of the Fenwick Island Lighthouse, P.O. Box 1001, Selbyville, DE 19975. Tel.: 302-436-8100.
Web Site: www.fenwickislandlighthouse.org
Governing Authority: state.
Historic Lighthouse: built in 1858.
Collections: local & lighthouse history; period artifacts; photographs.
Facilities: Museum-related items for sale.
Hours & Admission Prices: May to Columbus Day: Thurs.-Tues. No charge; donations accepted.

Frederica

BARRATT'S CHAPEL AND MUSEUM, 6362 Bay Rd., Frederica, DE 19946-1505. Tel.: 302-335-5544. Fax: 302-335-5750.
E-mail: barratts@aol.com
Web Site: barrattschapel.org
Founded: 1964.
Congressional District: 33
Key Personnel: Dir., Kenyon Camper; Site Administrator, Barb Duffin; Conference Historian, Rev. Philip Lawtor.
Personnel Profile: Part-Time Paid 2; Part-Time Volunteers 5.
Governing Authority: church denominational group. Parent Institution: Peninsula-Delaware Conference of The United Methodist Church. Tax-exempt.
Religious Museum.
Collections: conference journals; Methodist magazines & artifacts; printed biographies & autobiographies of 18th to 20th-century preachers; reconstructed 18th-century vestry.
Research Fields: Methodist history on Delmarva peninsula.
Facilities: 2,500-vol. library of religious books, conference journals & church records.
Activities: guided tours; lectures; permanent exhibitions.
Publications: New Light on Old Barratts; Cultivating the Methodist Garden.
Hours & Admission Prices: Sat.-Sun. 1:30-4:30; other times by appointment. No charge; donations accepted. ♿
Attendance: 4,007 (accurate)
Membership: Friends $20.

Georgetown

DELAWARE AVIATION MUSEUM, 21513 Rudder Lane, Georgetown, DE 19947-2016. Tel.: 302-854-0244.
Aviation Museum.
Collections: military aviation history; photographs; WWII & Cold War era artifacts.
Facilities: over 3,000-vol. library.
Hours & Admission Prices: Sat.-Sun. 10-4.

ELSIE WILLIAMS DOLL COLLECTION, Seashore Hwy., Rte. 18 & Rte. 404, Georgetown, DE 19947. Mailing Address: Delaware Technical and Community College, Owens Campus, P.O. Box 610, Georgetown, DE 19947. Tel.: 302-856-9033. Fax: 302-858-5462.
E-mail: treasures@dtcc.edu
Web Site: www.treasuresofthesea.org/other.html#doll
Founded: 1988.
Key Personnel: Dir., Dr. James Soles.
Personnel Profile: Full-Time Paid 1.
Governing Authority: Parent Institution: Delaware Technical & Community College Educational Foundation. Tax-exempt.
Doll Museum.
Collections: over 700 dolls including some donated by Elsie Steele Williams, the wife of U.S. Senator John Williams.
Hours & Admission Prices: Mon.-Thurs. 9am-10pm, Fri. 8-4:30, Sat. 9-1. No charge. Closed major holidays; Christmas break. ♿

MARVEL CARRIAGE MUSEUM, 510 S. Bedford St., Georgetown, DE 19947-1852. Tel.: 302-855-9660.
E-mail: marvelmuseum@juno.com
Web Site: www.marvelmuseum.com
Formerly: Nutter D. Marvel Museum
Key Personnel: Pres., Jim Bowden.
Governing Authority: Parent Institution: Georgetown Historical Society.
Historic Buildings.
Collections: personal artifacts; horse drawn carriages; photographs; newspaper clippings; books; Georgetown history. Historic Buildings: two barrel roof barns; 100 year old church; one room school house; blacksmith shop; two period railroad freight buildings.
Hours & Admission Prices: By appointment.

OLD SUSSEX COUNTY COURTHOUSE, 10 S. Bedford St., Georgetown, DE 19947-1852. Tel.: 302-855-9660.
Governing Authority: Parent Institution: Georgetown Historical Society.
Historic Building: built in 1791.
Collections: period furnishings; law & government artifacts.
Hours & Admission Prices: 1st Wed. of month; other times by appointment.

TREASURES OF THE SEA EXHIBIT, Delaware Technical & Community College, Seashore Hwy., Rte. 18/404, Georgetown, DE 19947-0610. Mailing Address: P.O. Box 610, Georgetown, DE 19947-0610. Tel.: 302-856-5700 & 5482. Fax: 302-858-5462.
E-mail: treasures@dtcc.edu
Web Site: www.treasuresofthesea.org
Founded: 1988.
Congressional District: Delaware
Key Personnel: Chm. (V), James R. Soles; Pres., Dr. Orlando George; Dir., Robert Hearn; Education, Registrar & Museum Shop Mgr., Gayle L. Chandler; Public Rels., Leanne Phillips-Lowe; Security, William Wood.
Personnel Profile: Full-Time Paid 1; Part-Time Paid 3; Interns 2.
Governing Authority: college; nonprofit. Parent Institution: Delaware Technical & Community College. Tax-exempt: 501(c)(3).
Maritime Museum.
Collections: shipwreck artifacts: coins, firearms, jewelry, gold & silver bars, cannons; dolls; arboretum of trees of the 50 states.
Facilities: 75-vol. library of books & video cassettes on shipwreck archaeology available to the public; 10-gallon aquarium; 200-seat auditorium; 40-seat & 200-seat cafeteria; 30-seat theatre; nature trail; picnic area; meeting rooms. Souvenirs & other museum-related items for sale.
Activities: guided tours.
Hours & Admission Prices: Jan. by appointment; Feb. to mid-Dec. Mon.-Tues. 10-4, Fri. 12-4, Sat. 9-1. Adults $3, senior citizens $2.50, students $1; discounts to AAM, WHYY & AAA members; children 4 & under no charge. Closed major holidays. ♿
Attendance: 2,294 (accurate)

Harrington

HARRINGTON HISTORICAL SOCIETY, 108-110 Fleming St., Harrington, DE 19952-1145. Tel.: 302-398-3698.
Formerly: Harrington Railroad Museum
Founded: 1978.
Key Personnel: Cur., Jean Miller; Pres. (V), Herman Zeitler
Railroad History Museum.
Collections: railroad & city history; photographs.
Activities: tours. Annual Event: Heritage Day.
Hours & Admission Prices: By appointment. No charge; donations accepted.
Membership: Members $5.

MESSICK AGRICULTURE MUSEUM, 325 Walt Messick Rd., Taylor and Messick, Inc., Harrington, DE 19952-3300. Tel.: 302-398-3729.
Agriculture Museum.
Collections: agriculture history; period John Deere tractors & bicycles.
Hours & Admission Prices: Mon.-Fri. 7:30-4:30. No charge; donations accepted.

Hockessin

DELAWARE NATURE SOCIETY, 3511 Barley Mill Rd., Hockessin, DE 19707-9393. Mailing Address: P.O. Box 700, Hockessin, DE 19707-0700. Tel.: 302-239-2334. Fax: 302-239-2473.
E-mail: dnsinfo@delawarenaturesociety.org
Web Site: www.delawarenaturesociety.org
Founded: 1964.
Key Personnel: Exec. Dir., Michael E. Riska; Pres., Thomas C. Shea, Jr.; Vice Pres., Sharon Struthers; Sec., Richmond Williams; Treas., Clifford H. Hunter.
Personnel Profile: Full-Time Paid 21; Part-Time Paid 58; Part-Time Volunteers 1,000; Interns 6.
Governing Authority: nonprofit organization. Branch Museums: Abbott's Mill Nature Center, 15411 Abbott's Pond Rd., Milford, DE; Ashland Nature Center, Barley Mill & Brackenville Rd., Hockessin, DE; Coverdale Farm, 543 Way Rd., Greenville, DE; DuPont Environmental Education Center, 1400 Delmarva Lane, Wilmington, DE. Tax-exempt: 501(c)(3).
Nature Center.
Collections: books; taxidermy specimens; butterfly house.
Research Fields: environmental.

Facilities: library; nature trails; auditorium.
Activities: teacher workshops; education programs for children, adults, families, schools & special interest groups; internships; Environmental Institution Management Course; environmental issue conferences; environmental advocacy; natural area preservation; native plant demonstration garden. Museum Sponsors: Harvest Moon Festival; Autumn at Abbott's; Native Plant Sale.
Publications: quarterly newsletter; program brochures; Delmarva butterflies field guide; reference book, Birds of Delaware; Amphibians & Reptiles of Delaware.
Hours & Admission Prices: Mon.-Fri. 8:30-4:30, Sat. 9-3. Trail: $2; ANCA & society members no charge. Closed holidays. ♿
Attendance: 80,000 (estimated)
Membership: College Student & Senior Citizen $30; Individual $40; Household $55; Household Plus $85; Sustaining $125; Supporting $250; Sponsor $500; Director's Circle $1,000.

MT. CUBA CENTER, 3120 Barley Mill Rd., Hockessin, DE 19707. Mailing Address: P.O. Box 3570, Greenville, DE 19807-0570. Tel.: 302-239-4244. Fax: 302-239-5366.
E-mail: info@mtcubacenter.org
Horticultural Center.
Collections: wildflower gardens; native plants.
Facilities: 650 acre site.
Activities: educational programs; research; conservation; classes; docent tours.
Hours & Admission Prices: By appointment.

Laurel

BALD CYPRESS NATURE CENTER, Trap Pond State Park, 33587 Baldcypress Lane, Laurel, DE 19956-2988. Tel.: 302-875-5163. Fax: 302-875-2697.
Nature Center.
Collections: local history; wildlife; plants; bald cypress trees.
Facilities: nature trails. Gift items for sale.
Activities: hiking; camping; fishing; boating; educational programs.
Hours & Admission Prices: Daily 8 to sunset.

BALDCYPRESS NATURE CENTER - TRAP POND STATE PARK, 33587 Baldcypress Lane, Laurel, DE 19956-2988. Tel.: 302-875-2392.
Web Site: www.destateparks.com
Nature Center.
Collections: local natural history & wildlife; geology; plants; flowers.
Facilities: nature trails.
Activities: educational programs; hiking.
Hours & Admission Prices: Daily 8am to sunset.

Lewes

LEWES HISTORICAL SOCIETY, (M), 110 Shipcarpenter St., Lewes, DE 19958-1210. Tel.: 302-645-7670. Fax: 302-645-2375.
E-mail: info@historiclewes.org
Web Site: www.historiclewes.org
Founded: 1961.
Congressional District: 37
Key Personnel: Pres. (V), F. Rogers Jones; Dir., E. Michael DiPaolo; Museum Shop Mgr., Ann Hilaman.
Personnel Profile: Full-Time Paid 1; Full-Time Volunteers 6; Part-Time Paid 4; Part-Time Volunteers 300; Interns 1.
Governing Authority: society. Tax-exempt.
History & Marine Museum.
Collections: early American furniture; Swedish log cabin furnished as an early settlers cabin; early physician's office; 1800 country store in operation during summer; two colonial houses; 1884 lifesaving station.
Research Fields: Lewes history, genealogy.
Facilities: Period furnishings & other museum-related items for sale.
Activities: lectures; films; annual craft fair; seminars; guided & self-guided tours. Annual Events: antiques show; art show; Christmas tour of Lewes.
Publications: quarterly newsletter; Pictorial History of Lewes; Victorian Lewes & Her Architecture; Journal of the Lewes Historical Society; Swanendael in New Netherland.
Hours & Admission Prices: Memorial Day to Labor Day Mon.-Sat. 10-4. Guided Tours: June & mid-Sept. to mid-Oct. by appointment. Adults $5; AASLH members & members no charge.
Attendance: 33,000 (estimated)
Membership: Individual $25; Joint $35; Contributing $50; Century $100; Supporting $250; Life $1,000.

PACKARD REATH GALLERY, 109 W. Market St., Lewes, DE 19958. Mailing Address: 142 Second St., Ste. 2A, Lewes, DE 19958-1396. Tel.: 302-644-7513.
Web Site: www.packardreathgallery.com
Art Gallery.
Collections: works by contemporary & upcoming photographic artists.
Hours & Admission Prices: Daily 11-5.

SEASIDE NATURE CENTER - CAPE HENLOPEN STATE PARK, 15099 Cape Henlopen Dr., Lewes, DE 19958-3153. Tel.: 302-645-8983.
Web Site: www.destateparks.com
Nature Center.
Collections: ocean life; ecology; natural history; photographs.
Facilities: nature trails.
Activities: educational programs; hiking; guided tours.
Hours & Admission Prices: Center: Mon.-Sat. 9-4, Sun. 12-4. Park: daily 8am to sunset.

ZWAANENDAEL MUSEUM, Savannah Rd. & Kings Hwy., Lewes, DE 19958. Mailing Address: 21 The Green, Dover, DE 19901-3611. Tel.: 302-645-1148.
Key Personnel: Site Supvr., Bridget Warner
Historic Building: built in 1931.
Collections: county history; War of 1812; Cape Henlopen Lighthouse artifacts; H.M.S. DeBraak & H.M.S. Severn shipwreck artifacts; political & military history including uniforms & weapons.
Activities: Annual Events: Zwaanendael Heritage Garden Tour in June; Christmas House Tour in December.
Hours & Admission Prices: Tues.-Sat. 10-4:30, Sun. 1:30-4:30. No charge; donations accepted. Closed state holidays.

Milford

ABBOTT'S MILL NATURE CENTER, 15411 Abbott's Pond Rd., Milford, DE 19963-3549. Tel.: 302-422-0847. Fax: 302-422-1849.
E-mail: dnsinfo@delawarenaturesociety.org
Web Site: www.delawarenaturesociety.org/abbotts.html
Key Personnel: Exec. Dir., Michael E. Riska.
Governing Authority: Parent Institution: Delaware Nature Society.
Nature Center.
Collections: wildlife & their habitats; plants; ecology; pine woods. Historic Building: grist mill.
Facilities: nature trails.
Activities: educational programs; classes. Museum Sponsors: Autumn at Abbott's Mill Festival in October.
Hours & Admission Prices: Mon.-Fri. 9-4; other times by appointment.

DUPONT NATURE CENTER, 2992 Lighthouse Rd., Milford, DE 19963. Tel.: 302-422-1329.
Web Site: www.dupontnaturecenter.org
Nature Center.
Collections: wildlife & their habitats.
Activities: educational programs; special events.
Hours & Admission Prices: April-Sept. Tues.-Sun. 10-4; Oct.-March Mon.-Fri. 10-4. No charge; donations accepted. ♿

MILFORD HISTORICAL SOCIETY, 501 N.W. Front St., Milford, DE 19963-1015. Mailing Address: P.O. Box 352, Milford, DE 19963-0352. Tel.: 302-422-3115.
Formerly: Parson Thorne Mansion
Founded: 1961.
Personnel Profile: Part-Time Volunteers 7.
Governing Authority: Parent Institution: Milford Historical Society.
Historic House Museum: housed in the former home of Milford's founder, Parson Sydenham Thorne; built c.1735. Listed on the National Register of Historic Places.
Collections: family history; period furnishings.
Activities: special events.
Hours & Admission Prices: June 1st Sat. of month; Sept. last Sat. of month; other times by appointment. Admission $2.
Attendance: 1,000
Membership: Individual $10; Joint $15.

MILFORD MUSEUM, 121 S. Walnut St., Milford, DE 19963-1955. Tel.: 302-424-1080 & 422-2187.
E-mail: dkenton@cbmove.com
Founded: 1983.
Congressional District: 1
Key Personnel: Chm., Dave Kenton; Dir. Public Rels., Al Lauckner; Sec., Barbara Jones.

Personnel Profile: Full-Time Volunteers 25; Part-Time Paid 1; Part-Time Volunteers 10.
Governing Authority: municipal; nonprofit. Parent Institution: City of Milford. Tax-exempt: 501(c)(3).
Local History Museum: housed in c.1910 Federal style brick building.
Collections: local history from 1680-present; marble trim; store items; costumes; photographs; documents; decorative arts; awards to citizens; shipbuilding items; Indian artifacts.
Major Exhibits: Rock & Roll History - Milford, 3/10-12/10; Milford Shipbuilding, 3/10-12/11; Civil War History, 3/10-12/11.
Research Fields: local history.
Facilities: 116-vol. library pertaining to local history.
Activities: films; temporary exhibitions; programs pertaining to current exhibits.
Publications: semiannual newsletter, Museum Musings.
Hours & Admission Prices: Tues.-Thurs. 10-2, Sat.-Sun. 2-4; groups by appointment. No charge; donations accepted. Closed New Year's Day; Easter; Independence Day; Christmas. ♿
Attendance: 1,500 (estimated)
Membership: Student $5; Individual $10; Family $20; Patron $50; Corporate $100.

Millsboro

MILLSBORO ART LEAGUE, 203 Main St., Millsboro, DE 19966. Tel.: 302-934-6440.
Web Site: www.millsboroartleague.com
Art Gallery.
Collections: works by local & national artists.
Activities: classes; workshops; educational programs.
Hours & Admission Prices: Fri.-Sat. 11-3, Sun. 12-3.

NANTICOKE INDIAN MUSEUM, 27073 John J. Williams Hwy., Millsboro, DE 19966-4642. Tel.: 302-945-7022.
E-mail: nanticok@verizon.net
Personnel Profile: Part-Time Paid 4; Part-Time Volunteers 1.
History Museum.
Collections: history of the Nanticoke Indians; stone artifacts; carvings; pottery; clothing; photographs.
Facilities: library. Museum-related items for sale.
Activities: video presentations. Annual Event: Nanticoke Indian Powwow in Sept.
Hours & Admission Prices: Tues.-Sat. 10-4. Adults $2, children $1.

Milton

MILTON HISTORICAL SOCIETY AND THE LYDIA BLACK CANNON MUSEUM, 210 Union St., Milton, DE 19968-1620. Mailing Address: P.O. Box 112, Milton, DE 19968-0112. Tel.: 302-684-1010.
E-mail: info@historicmilton.org
Web Site: www.historicmilton.org
Founded: 1970.
Key Personnel: Dir., Melinda Linderer Huff; Pres. (V), Dennis Hughes.
Personnel Profile: Full-Time Paid 1; Part-Time Paid 1; Part-Time Volunteers 60; Interns 3.
Governing Authority: Tax-exempt.
History Museum: housed in the newly restored 1857 Methodist Church.
Collections: area history & culture; photographs; personal artifacts; shipbuilding tools & records; area agriculture; button press.
Hours & Admission Prices: Wed.-Sat. 11-4; other times by appointment. No charge; donations accepted. Closed federal holidays.
Attendance: 7,000 (estimated)
Membership: Individual $25; Family $35; Supporting $250; Sustaining $500; Partnering $1,000.

PRIME HOOK NATIONAL WILDLIFE REFUGE, 11978 Turkle Pond Rd., Milton, DE 19968-3759. Tel.: 302-684-8419. Fax: 302-684-8504.
E-mail: fw5rw_phnwr@fws.gov
Web Site: www.fws.gov/northeast/primehook
Governing Authority: Parent Institution: U.S. Fish & Wildlife Service.
Wildlife Refuge.
Collections: wildlife & their habitat including birds, mammals, reptiles, amphibian; fish; plants.
Hours & Admission Prices: Refuge: daily sunrise to sunset. Visitor Contact Station & Store: Mon.-Fri. 7:30-4. Visitor Center: April-Nov. Sat.-Sun. 9-4.

New Castle

NEW CASTLE COURT HOUSE MUSEUM, 211 Delaware St., New Castle, DE 19720-4815. Tel.: 302-323-4453. Fax: 302-323-5319.
E-mail: cynthia.snyder@state.de.us
Web Site: history.delaware.gov
Governing Authority: Parent Institution: Delaware Department of State Division of Historical & Cultural Affairs. Tax-exempt.
Historic Site.
Collections: Delaware history & government; legal history; underground railroad history.
Activities: special events. Museum Sponsors: Day In Old New Castle in May; Separation Day in June; New Castle Christmas in December.
Hours & Admission Prices: Tues.-Sat. 10-3:30, Sun. 1:30-4:30. No charge; donations accepted. Closed state holidays. ♿
Attendance: 14,000 (accurate)

NEW CASTLE HISTORICAL SOCIETY, 2 E. Fourth St., New Castle, DE 19720-5014. Tel.: 302-322-2794. Fax: 302-322-8923.
E-mail: nchistorical@aol.com
Web Site: www.newcastlehistory.org
Founded: 1934.
Key Personnel: Dir., Michael Connolly; Pres. (V), Richard R. Cooch; Coord. Education, Bruce Dalleo.
Personnel Profile: Part-Time Paid 18; Part-Time Volunteers 120; Interns 1.
Governing Authority: society. Tax-exempt: 501(c)(3).
Historical Society Museum.
Collections: early Dutch furnishings; 18th-century furnishings. Historic Houses: c.1700 Dutch House; 1730 Amstel House.
Major Exhibits: New Castle Nuptials, 5/10-9/10; Symbolizing Civic Power, 5/10-12/10.
Research Fields: local history; early Dutch settlement; colonial America.
Activities: traveling exhibit. Museum Sponsors: annual exhibit at Old Library Museum. Annual Event: Historic Preservation Award.
Publications: book, New Castle on the Delaware; Buildings, Books & Blackboards: Education in New Castle 1657 to 1930; Dr. Constance Cooper, 350 Years of New Castle Delaware: Chapter's in a Town's History.
Hours & Admission Prices: April-Dec. Tues.-Sat. 11-4, Sun. 1-4. Amstel House or Dutch House: adults $4, children under 12 $1.50; Combination Tickets: adults $7, children 2-12 $2.50; children under 6, members no charge. Old Library Museum Sat.-Sun. 1-4. no charge. Closed national holidays.
Attendance: 10,500 (accurate)
Membership: Individual $30; Family $50; Business $65; Patron $100; Benefactor $250.

OLD LIBRARY MUSEUM, 40 E. 3rd St., New Castle, DE 19720. Mailing Address: 2 E. 4th St., New Castle, DE 19720-5014. Tel.: 302-322-2794. Fax: 302-322-8923.
E-mail: nchistorical@aol.com
Web Site: www.newcastlehistory.org
Historic Building: housed in a hexagonal brick structure; built in 1892.
Collections: local history & culture; period furnishings; personal artifacts; photographs.
Hours & Admission Prices: April-Dec. Sat.-Sun. 1-4.

READ HOUSE & GARDENS, 42 The Strand, New Castle, DE 19720-4826. Tel.: 302-322-8411. Fax: 302-322-8557.
Web Site: www.dehistory.org
Personnel Profile: Full-Time Paid 2; Part-Time Paid 25; Part-Time Volunteers 10.
Governing Authority: Parent Institution: Delaware Historical Society. Tax-exempt.
Historic House: built in 1801 by George Read Jr., the son of one of Delaware's signers of the Declaration of Independence.
Collections: period furnishings; personal artifacts; photographs; gardens.
Activities: demonstrations; tours; school programs.
Hours & Admission Prices: Jan.-Feb. Sat. 10-4, Sun. 11-4; other times by appointment; March-Dec. Wed.-Fri. & Sun. 11-4, Sat. 10-4. Adults $5, senior citizens over 65, military, & students 13-21 $4, children 6-12 $2; discounts to groups; children under 6 no charge. Closed major holidays.
Attendance: 18,000 (estimated)

Newark

CHAMBERS HOUSE NATURE CENTER AT WHITE CLAY CREEK STATE PARK, 1475 Creek Rd., Newark, DE 19711. Mailing Address: 425 Wedgewood Rd., Newark, DE 19711-2123. Tel.: 302-368-6560 & 6900.
Nature Center.
Collections: natural history; photographs; geology.

Facilities: library.
Activities: educational programs; special events; guided tours.
Hours & Admission Prices: May-Oct. Sat.-Sun. 11-4. ♿

HALE BYRNES HOUSE, 606 Stanton Christiana Rd., Newark, DE 19713-2109. Tel.: 302-737-5792.
Web Site: www.halebyrnes.org
Key Personnel: Resident Property Mgr. & Cur., Ralph Burdick; Resident Property Mgr. & Cur., Kim Burdick.
Governing Authority: Parent Institution: Delaware Division of Historical and Cultural Affairs.
Historic House: housed in the building used as a meeting place for General George Washington & his staff between the Battle of Cooch's Bridge in Delaware and the Battle of Brandywine in Pennsylvania in 1777; built in 1750. Listed on the National Register of Historic Places.
Collections: local history; period furnishings.
Hours & Admission Prices: 1st Wed. of month 12-3; other times by appointment.

IRON HILL MUSEUM, (M), 1355 Old Baltimore Pike, Newark, DE 19702-1110. Tel.: 302-368-5703. Fax: 302-369-4287.
E-mail: ironhillmuseum@verizon.net
Web Site: www.ironhill-museum.org
Founded: 1965.
Key Personnel: Exec. Dir., Katherine Larrivee; Pres. (V), James P. Neal; Chm. (V), Brian Shertz.
Personnel Profile: Full-Time Paid 1; Part-Time Paid 6; Part-Time Volunteers 11.
Governing Authority: Parent Institution: Delaware Academy of Sciences. Tax-exempt.
Natural History Museum.
Collections: human & natural history of Iron Hill region; rocks & minerals; Delaware animals; natural history; earth science; Lenni Lenape Indians; archaeology.
Facilities: nature trail.
Activities: outreach programs; educational programs; teacher workshops; summer camps; public programs; guided tours; Native American program.
Publications: newsletter, News and Views.
Hours & Admission Prices: Tues.-Fri. 9-2; other times by appointment. Adults $4; discounts to ASTC & AASLH members; members no charge. ♿
Attendance: 6,000 (estimated)
Membership: Individual $20; Grandfamily $30; Family $40; Patron $100; Lifetime $500.

UNIVERSITY MUSEUMS, UNIVERSITY OF DELAWARE, 209 Mechanical Hall, Newark, DE 19716. Mailing Address: 208 Mechanical Hall, University of Delaware, Newark, DE 19176. Tel.: 302-831-8037. Fax: 302-831-8057. TDD: 302-831-4563.
E-mail: jat@udel.edu
Web Site: www.udel.edu/museums
Founded: 1978.
Congressional District: 1
Key Personnel: Dir., Janis A. Tomlinson, Ph.D.; Cur. African American Art, Julie L. McGee; Cur. Collections, Janet Gardner Broske; Cur. Mineralogical Collection, Sharon L. Fitzgerald; Preparator, Brian Kamen.
Personnel Profile: Full-Time Paid 7; Part-Time Volunteers 2; Interns 4.
Governing Authority: university. Parent Institution: University of Delaware. Branch Museums: University Gallery, Study Room, Old College; Mechanical Hall Gallery; Mineralogical Museum, Penny Hall. Tax-exempt: 501(c)(3).
University Gallery: housed in 1832 first major Greek Revival structure in the state. Mechanical Hall: renovated 1898 building.
Collections: Brandywine School; Gertrude Kasebier; African American art; minerals; 20th century American works on paper; Inuit art; pre-Columbian ceramics; survey study collection.
Major Exhibits: Abstract Relations, 2/10-5/10; Warhol: Behind the Camera, Spring 2010.
Research Fields: multi-disciplinary.
Activities: loan, traveling, permanent & temporary exhibitions.
Publications: exhibit catalogues & brochures.
Hours & Admission Prices: Sept. to May Wed. & Fri.-Sat. 12-5, Thurs. 12-8; Summer: see website for hours. No charge. Closed during installation; university holidays. ♿
Attendance: 6,000 (accurate)

Odessa

HISTORIC HOUSES OF ODESSA, 109 Main St., Odessa, DE 19730. Mailing Address: P.O. Box 697, Odessa, DE 19730-0697. Tel.: 302-378-4119. Fax: 302-378-4050.
E-mail: info@historicodessa.org
Web Site: www.historicodessa.org
Governing Authority: Parent Institution: Historic Odessa Foundation.
Historic Houses.
Collections: local history; period furnishings; photographs. Historic Buildings: Corbit-Sharp House c.1774; Wilson-Warner House c.1769; Collins-Sharp House c.1700; Brick Hotel c.1822; Odessa Bank c.1853.
Hours & Admission Prices: March-Dec. Thurs.-Sun. 10-4:30. Adults $10, students $8; discounts to members; children under 5 no charge. Closed Easter; Independence Day; Thanksgiving; Christmas Eve & Day.

Port Penn

PORT PENN INTERPRETIVE CENTER, Rte. 9 & Rd. 2, Port Penn, DE 19731. Mailing Address: P.O. Box 170, Delaware City, DE 19706. Tel.: 302-836-2533.
History Museum: housed in a former schoolhouse; built in 1886.
Collections: local history & culture; period hunting decoys; fishing & fur trapping equipment; paintings.
Hours & Admission Prices: Memorial Day to Labor Day Fri.-Sun. 9-5; groups by appointment.

Rehoboth Beach

INDIAN RIVER LIFE-SAVING STATION, 25039 Coastal Hwy., Rehoboth Beach, DE 19971. Tel.: 302-227-6991. Fax: 302-227-6438.
Historic Building: built in 1876. Listed on the National Register of Historic Places.
Collections: U.S. Life Saving Service history; photographs.
Facilities: Museum-related items for sale.
Hours & Admission Prices: Daily 8am to sunset.

REHOBOTH ART LEAGUE, INC., 12 Dodds Lane, Rehoboth Beach, DE 19971-1668. Tel.: 302-227-8408. Fax: 302-227-4121.
Web Site: www.rehobothartleague.org
Founded: 1938.
Congressional District: 7
Personnel Profile: Full-Time Paid 3; Part-Time Paid 5; Part-Time Volunteers 150; Interns 1.
Governing Authority: R.A.L. Board of Trustees. Tax-exempt.
Historic Buildings & Art League: one gallery & studio in c.1740s homestead, two galleries & a studio located on 3 1/2 acres of formal & informal gardens.
Collections: sculpture; paintings; decorative arts; art books. Historic Building: Homestead Museum.
Major Exhibits: Regional Juried Show, 7/23/10-8/23/10.
Facilities: classrooms.
Activities: art classes; concerts; music programs; art shows for members; shows of work for visiting artists; craft exhibitions; Cottage Tour of Art; outdoor Art & Craft exhibit; bus trips to art museums & theaters; workshops by visiting artists; lectures on art & art history.
Publications: annual brochure; pamphlets, Sand in Your Brush; Story of the Homestead.
Hours & Admission Prices: April-Oct. Mon.-Sat. 10-4, Sun 12-4. No charge; donations accepted; Closed New Year's Day; Thanksgiving; Christmas. ♿
Membership: Individual $50; Joint $75; Family $100; Sponsor $125; Patron $250; Benefactor $500.

Seaford

GOVERNOR ROSS PLANTATION, 1101 N. Pine St. Ext., Seaford, DE 19973-5754. Mailing Address: 203 High St., Seaford, DE 19973-3909. Tel.: 302-628-9500. Fax: 302-628-2984.
E-mail: seafordsociety@verizon.net
Web Site: www.seafordhistoricalsociety.com
Founded: 1976.
Key Personnel: Pres., Rudy Wilson; Treas., John Watson; Public Rels., Ann Nesbitt; Tour Dir. & Museum Shop Mgr., Margaret Alexander.
Personnel Profile: Part-Time Paid 1; Part-Time Volunteers 80.
Governing Authority: private; nonprofit organization. Parent Institution: Seaford Historical Society. Branch Museum: Seaford Museum, 203 High St. Seaford. Tax-exempt: 501(c)(3).
Historic House & Historical Society Museum: c.1860 Italian Villa style home built by Delaware Governor William Ross.

Collections: decorative arts objects appropriate for furnishing a 13-room home; Ross family's personal artifacts; original granary; carriage house; log slave quarters; corn cribs; smokehouse.
Research Fields: slavery & Civil War era in Delaware.
Facilities: library.
Activities: guided tours. Annual Events: Town & Country Fair; Heritage Days during Memorial Day weekend; Victorian Christmas.
Publications: quarterly newsletter, Seaford Historical Society.
Hours & Admission Prices: Sat.-Sun. 1-4; other times by appointment. Adults $3; discount to groups of 10 or more; members & children under 12 no charge. Closed state holidays. ♿
Attendance: 6,000 (accurate)
Membership: Individual $20; Family $35; Individual Life $300; Family Life $600

SEAFORD MUSEUM, 203 High St., Seaford, DE 19973-3909. Tel.: 302-628-9828. Fax: 302-628-2984.
E-mail: seafordsociety@verizon.net
Web Site: www.seafordhistoricalsociety.com
Founded: 1997.
Congressional District: 39
Key Personnel: Museum Shop Mgr., Shirley Skinner.
Personnel Profile: Part-Time Paid 3; Part-Time Volunteers 90.
Governing Authority: Parent Institution: Seaford Historical Society. Tax-exempt.
History Museum: housed in the former post office; built in 1930s.
Collections: local history & culture; period furnishings; Native American artifacts; photographs.
Facilities: Museum-related items for sale.
Publications: quarterly newsletter.
Hours & Admission Prices: Thurs.-Sun. 1-4. Adults $3. Closed holidays. ♿
Attendance: 2,000 (accurate)
Membership: Individual $20; Family $35; Life $300; Family $600.

Smyrna

BOMBAY HOOK NATIONAL WILDLIFE REFUGE, 2591 Whitehall Neck Rd., Smyrna, DE 19977-2912. Tel.: 302-653-9345. Fax: 302-653-0684.
E-mail: fw5rw_bhnwr@fws.gov
Web Site: www.fws.gov/northeast/bombayhook
Key Personnel: Mgr., Michael Stroeh
Wildlife Refuge.
Collections: migrating & wintering ducks & geese; mammals.
Facilities: nature trails; picnic area.
Activities: bird watching; hiking; educational programs; workshops.
Hours & Admission Prices: March-May & Sept. to mid-Dec. Mon.-Fri. 8-4, Sat.-Sun. 9-5; mid-Dec. to Feb. Mon.-Fri. 8-4.

SMYRNA MUSEUM, 11 S. Main St., Smyrna, DE 19977-1430. Mailing Address: P.O. Box 335, Smyrna, DE 19977-0335. Tel.: 302-653-1320. Fax: 302-653-8844.
Key Personnel: Pres., Brooks Keen.
Governing Authority: Parent Organization: Duck Creek Historical Society.
History Museum.
Collections: local artifacts; toys & dolls; Native American artifacts; paintings; over 400 pitchers; mid-1700s plank house.
Hours & Admission Prices: Tues., Thurs. & Sat. 10-1; other times by appointment. No charge; donations accepted.

Wilmington

ARDEN CRAFT SHOP MUSEUM, 1807 Millers Rd., Wilmington, DE 19810-4052. Tel.: 302-529-1510.
Art Museum.
Collections: paintings; sculpture; prints; woodcarvings.
Hours & Admission Prices: Sun. 1-3, Wed. 7:30pm-9pm. No charge.

BELLEVUE HALL MANSION - BELLEVUE STATE PARK, 800 Carr Rd., Wilmington, DE 19809-2163. Tel.: 302-761-6963.
Web Site: www.destateparks.com
Historic House.
Collections: local history & culture; photographs; period furnishings; personal artifacts.
Facilities: nature trails.
Activities: hiking.
Hours & Admission Prices: Park: daily 8am to sunset. Mansion: by appointment.

BRANDYWINE CREEK NATURE CENTER, 41 Adams Dam Rd., Wilmington, DE 19807. Mailing Address: P.O. Box 3782, Greenville, DE 19807-0782. Tel.: 302-655-5740.
Nature Center.
Collections: natural history; photographs.
Facilities: nature trails. Museum-related items for sale.
Activities: educational programs.
Hours & Admission Prices: Daily 8am to sunset.

BRANDYWINE ZOO, 1001 N. Park Dr., Wilmington, DE 19802-3801. Tel.: 302-571-7747. Fax: 302-571-7787.
Web Site: www.brandywinezoo.org
Founded: 1905.
Key Personnel: C.E.O. & Zoo Dir., Nancy M. Falasco; Pres. (V), Greg Ellis; Cur. Education, Jill Karlson; Asst. Cur. Education, Melody Hendricks; Museum Shop Mgr., Patty Tiano.
Personnel Profile: Full-Time Paid 8; Part-Time Paid 20; Part-Time Volunteers 40; Interns 38.
Governing Authority: state. Subsidiary Institution: Delaware Zoological Society. Tax-exempt.
Zoo.
Collections: North & South America; Temperate Asia.
Facilities: zoological park; classroom. Gift items for sale.
Activities: education programs for school groups; guided tours; outreach programs; teacher workshops; volunteer & docent program; public programs for toddlers & seniors; special events; informal education programs; loan kits; summer camp for children.
Publications: quarterly newsletter, Zoo News; education program guides.
Hours & Admission Prices: Daily 10-4. June-Sept. adults $5, senior citizens $4, children 3-11 $3. Oct.-May adults $4, senior citizens & children 3-11 $2; discount to groups; members & children under 3 no charge. ♿
Attendance: 90,000 (estimated)
Membership: Individual $25; Senior $35; Household $45; Donor $75; Naturalist $100; Zoo Gooder $250; Animal Enthusiast $500; Rare Bird $1,000.

* **DELAWARE ART MUSEUM, (M),** 2301 Kentmere Pkwy., Wilmington, DE 19806-2096. Tel.: 302-571-9590. Fax: 302-571-0220.
Web Site: www.delart.org
Founded: 1912.
Congressional District: 6
Key Personnel: Exec. Dir., Danielle Rice, Ph.D.
Personnel Profile: Full-Time Paid 35; Part-Time Paid 14; Part-Time Volunteers 132.
Governing Authority: nonprofit organization. Tax-exempt: 501(c)(3).
Art Museum.
Collections: The Samuel and Mary R. Bancroft Memorial Collection of British Pre-Raphaelite Art (1848-1915); collection of work by American illustrator Howard Pyle (1853-1911) and other American illustrators from the period 1876-1940; collection of work by American artist John Sloan (1871-1951) and related artists; survey of American art in various media from the early 19th century to the present.
Major Exhibits: Dinotopia: The Fantastical Art of James Gurney (T), 2/10-5/10; Fifty Works for the First State: The Dorothy and Herbert Vogel Collection, 6/10-8/10; Images of the Jewish Experience: Art from the Collection of Sigmund R. Balka, 9/10-1/11.
Research Fields: American art & illustration; British Pre-Raphaelite art.
Facilities: library; archives; educational facilities; interactive children's learning area; outdoor sculpture garden; cafe. Museum-related items for sale.
Activities: guided tours; lectures; gallery talks; studio art classes; education programs; permanent, temporary & traveling exhibitions.
Publications: bimonthly newsletter; studio art classes booklet; summer art camp brochure; school & teacher programs booklet; annual report; E-Bulletin; exhibition catalogs.
Hours & Admission Prices: Wed.-Sat. 10-4, Sun. 12-4. Adults $12, seniors $10, students & youth $6; discounts to AAM & ICOM members; members & children 6 and under no charge. ♿
Attendance: 70,000 (accurate)
Membership: Individual $50; Household $70; Friend $100; Associate $250; Patron $500; Benefactor $1,000. Director's Circle: John Sloan Society $1,500; Bancroft Society $2,500; Howard Pyle Society $5,000; Rossetti Circle $10,000.

DELAWARE CENTER FOR THE CONTEMPORARY ARTS, (M), 200 S. Madison St., Wilmington, DE 19801-5100. Tel.: 302-656-6466, ext. 7102. Fax: 302-656-6944.
E-mail: info@thedcca.org
Web Site: www.thedcca.org
Founded: 1979.
Congressional District: 1

Key Personnel: Exec. Dir, Maxine Gaiber; Pres. (V), James Headley; Treas., Jeff Mitchell; Education Cur., Victoria Eastburn; Cur., Carina Evangelista; Dir. Mktg. & Public Rels., John Van Heest; Dir. Special Events, Ashlee Lukoff; Museum Shop Mgr., Whitney Marsden.
Personnel Profile: Full-Time Paid 12; Part-Time Paid 8; Part-Time Volunteers 28; Interns 2.
Governing Authority: private; nonprofit organization. Tax-exempt: 501(c)(3).
Art Museum.
Collections: workd by national & regional contemporary artists in all media & crafts.
Major Exhibits: Jamey Grimes, 11/09-1/10; Amy Orr, 11/09-2/10; Neon!, 11/19/09-4/4/10; Talia Greene, 11/27/09-1/10/10; Andrew Wapinski, 1/19/10-4/18/10; Lee Arnold, 2/12/10-5/2/10; Gabriela Bulisova, 3/9/10-5/30/10; Lawrence Cromwell, 4/27/10-7/25/10; Tannaz Farsi, 5/14/10-8/8/10; Joseph Barbaccia, 6/8/10-8/29/10.
Facilities: 100-seat auditorium; educational facilities; 6,000 sq. ft. exhibit space. Museum-related items for sale.
Activities: concerts; films & video; formal education programs; internships for college students; guided tours; lectures; temporary, participatory & traveling exhibitions. Annual Event: Fundraiser & Art Auction in Fall.
Publications: bimonthly e-newsletter, DCCA News; annual report, DCCA Annual Report; exhibition catalogues.
Hours & Admission Prices: Tues. & Thurs.-Fri. 10-5, Wed. & Sun. 12-5. No charge. Closed major holidays. ♿
Attendance: 16,000 (estimated)
Membership: Art Student & Senior $40; Individual $45; Household $65; Supporting $125; Sponsor $250; Patron $500; Visionary $1,000.

DELAWARE CHILDREN'S MUSEUM, 550 Justison St., Wilmington, DE 19801. Mailing Address: 110 S. Poplar St., Ste. 103, Wilmington, DE 19801-5034. Tel.: 302-654-2340.
Children's Museum.
Collections: hands-on exhibits.
Hours & Admission Prices: Call for hours & admission prices.

DELAWARE HISTORICAL SOCIETY, (M), 505 Market St., Wilmington, DE 19801-3091. Tel.: 302-655-7161. Fax: 302-655-7844.
E-mail: deinfo@dehistory.org
Web Site: www.dehistory.org
Founded: 1864.
Congressional District: 1
Key Personnel: Exec. Dir., Joan R. Hoge; Pres., Anne Canby; Dir. Museum Programs, Stephanie Przybylek; Dir. Library, Constance Cooper; Read House Site Admin., Michele Anstine; Education & Programs Coord., Andrea Gomez.
Personnel Profile: Full-Time Paid 15; Part-Time Paid 36; Part-Time Volunteers 25; Interns 4.
Governing Authority: society. Tax-exempt: 501(c)(3).
History Museum.
Collections: documents & artifacts related to Delaware history; Delaware silver; furniture; decorative arts; costumes; paintings; restored jail cells; newspapers; maps; photographs; manuscripts. Historic Houses: 1798 Old Town Hall; c.1748-1801 Willingtown Square; 1801 Read House & Gardens.
Major Exhibits: Dutch E. Swedes (T), 12/09-3/10; Railroad Industry in Delaware (T), 3/10-12/10.
Research Fields: Delaware history; material culture; architecture; decorative arts.
Facilities: 85,000-vol. library of Delaware history books; 11,000 sq. ft. exhibit space; meeting facilities. Museum-related items for sale.
Activities: guided tours; walking tours of New Castle; lectures; changing exhibitions; formally organized education programs; family discovery room.
Publications: biannual magazine, Delaware history; biannual newsletter; catalogue, Delaware Collections: The Historical Society of Delaware; exhibition catalogues.
Hours & Admission Prices: Library: Mon. 1-9, Tues.-Fri. 9-5. Delaware History Museum: Wed.-Fri. 11-4, Sat. 10-4. Read House: Wed.-Fri. 11-4, Sat. 10-4, Sun. 12-4. Adults $4, senior citizens & children 12-21 $3.50, children 6-12 $2; discounts to groups & AAM members; library & members no charge. Closed Federal holidays. ♿
Attendance: 60,000 (accurate)
Membership: Student & Institutional $15; Individual $40; Family $55; Contributing $75; Sustaining $100; Sponsor $250; Patron $500; Benefactor $1,000.

DELAWARE MUSEUM OF NATURAL HISTORY, 4840 Kennett Pike, Wilmington, DE 19807-1827. Mailing Address: P.O. Box 3937, Wilmington, DE 19807-0937. Tel.: 302-658-9111. Fax: 302-658-2610.
E-mail: hspruance@delmnh.org
Web Site: www.delmnh.org
Founded: 1957.
Congressional District: 1
Key Personnel: Dir., Halsey Spruance; Pres. Bd., William Spence; Dir. Collections & Cur. Ornithology, Dr. Jean Woods; Cur. Mollusks, Dr. Liz Shea; Dir. Exhibits & Graphic Arts, Gary Bloomer; Dir. Communications, Teresa Messmore; Controller, Judy Julis; Dir. Devel., Dawn Swartout; Dir. Visitor Svcs., Terri Reed.
Personnel Profile: Full-Time Paid 26; Part-Time Paid 18; Part-Time Volunteers 70.
Governing Authority: nonprofit organization. Tax-exempt: 501(c)(3).
Natural History Museum.
Collections: birds; bird eggs; mollusks; mammals; dinosaurs.
Major Exhibits: Supercroc, 11/09-1/10; Attack of the Bloodsuckers, 2/2/10-5/16/10; Tree Houses, 5/29/10-9/6/10; Be The Dinosaur, 10/2/10-1/9/11.
Research Fields: taxonomic ornithology; malacology; mammalogy.
Facilities: 10,000-vol. library of mollusk, bird & other biology manuscripts & archives; discovery room. Molluscan & ornithological research books for sale.
Activities: lectures; films; formally organized educational programs; inter-museum loan; permanent, temporary & school loan exhibits.
Publications: journal, Nemouria & Indo-Pacific Mollusca; books, Exotic Conchology; Living Volutes; Philippine Birds; South Pacific Birds; Woodpeckers of the World; Index Nudibranchia; Ranellidae; Marine Mollusks of Bermuda.
Hours & Admission Prices: Mon.-Sat. 9:30-4:30, Sun. 12-4:30. Adults $7, seniors $6, children 3-17 $5; discounts to groups & AAM members; children under 3 & members no charge. Closed New Year's Day; Independence Day; Thanksgiving; Christmas. ♿
Attendance: 82,591 (accurate)
Membership: Individual $30; Grandparent $45; Household $55; Sustaining $70; Patron $125; Gold Patron $500; Explorer Society $1,000.

DELAWARE SPORTS MUSEUM AND HALL OF FAME, Frawley Stadium, 801 Shipyard Dr., Wilmington, DE 19801. Tel.: 302-425-3263. Fax: 302-425-3713.
E-mail: desports@cavtel.net
Web Site: www.desports.org
Founded: 1976.
Key Personnel: Dir., Jon Rafal.
Personnel Profile: Full-Time Paid 1.
Governing Authority: Tax-exempt: 501(c)(3).
Sports Museum.
Collections: sports memorabilia & artifacts; uniforms; photographs; 272 inductees; books; videos; Hall of Fame.
Activities: special events; induction ceremony.
Hours & Admission Prices: April-Oct. Tues.-Sat. 12-5; Nov.-March by appointment. Adults $4, seniors over 50 $3, youth 13-19 $2; children 12 & under and Hall of Fame inductees & members no charge. ♿
Membership: Individual $40.

*** HAGLEY MUSEUM AND LIBRARY, (M),** 298 Buck Rd. E., Wilmington, DE 19807-2106. Mailing Address: P.O. Box 3630, Wilmington, DE 19807-0630. Tel.: 302-658-2400. Fax: 302-658-0568.
E-mail: ghalfpenny@hagley.org
Web Site: www.hagley.org
Founded: 1952.
Congressional District: 1
Key Personnel: Exec. Dir., Geoff Halfpenny; Head External Affairs & Devel., Jill A. MacKenzie; Andrew W. Mellon Cur. Prints & Photographs, Jon Williams; Cur. Collections & Exhibits, Debra Hughes; Deputy Dir. Library Administration, Terry Snyder; Finance Dir., Jeanne Belk; Head Manuscripts, Lynn Catanese; Objects Conservator, Ebenezer Kotei; Mgr. Visitor Svcs., Candace Dunson; Registrar, Amy Martina; Museum Shop Mgr., Carole Katchur; Industrial Exhibits Specialist, John McCoy; Supt. Svcs., Michael Downs.
Personnel Profile: Full-Time Paid 85; Part-Time Paid 90; Part-Time Volunteers 475.
Governing Authority: nonprofit organization. A division of the Eleutherian Mills-Hagley Foundation, Inc. Tax-exempt: 501(c)(3).
History & Technology Museum: located on the original site of Du Pont powder yards c.1802-1921.
Collections: archaeology; technology; patent models; industry; textiles; ceramics; manuscripts, imprints & photographs of the history of business and technology. Historic Buildings: 1803 Eleutherian Mills; 1813 Henry Clay

Factory, textile mill; 1817 Brandywine Manufacturer's Sunday School; 1840 Gibbons House; 1858 Millwright/Machine Shop; several 19th-century powder mills.
Research Fields: industrial, economic, social & technological history.
Facilities: research library of manuscript & pictorial collections; indoor exhibits in numerous buildings; narrated bus ride through grounds along Brandywine River. Museum-related items for sale.
Activities: guided tours; lectures; education programs for children; formally organized Fellowship education programs for graduate students affiliated with University of Delaware; research grants for visiting scholars; docent program; permanent, temporary & traveling exhibitions; school loan service.
Publications: guidebooks, Impressions of Hagley; Eleutherian Mills; booklet series, Hagley Museum's Industry In America; catalogues of collections & exhibits; quarterly newsletter; annual report; collections guides.
Hours & Admission Prices: Jan. to mid-March Sat.-Sun. 9:30-4:30, Mon.-Fri. Tour 1:30; mid-March to Dec. daily 9:30-4:30. Adults $11, seniors & students $9, children 6-14 $4; discounts to AAM, ICOM, AASLH & ASTC members; children under 6 & members no charge. Tours: bus $7.50, children tours $3.50, full-day tour $12; group tours by advance reservation. Closed Thanksgiving; Christmas. ♿
Attendance: 63,657 (accurate)
Membership: Individual $30; Scholar $35; Staff & Volunteers $50; Household $60; Patron $150-$499; Sponsor $500-$999; Benefactor $1,000 & up.

HOLY TRINITY (OLD SWEDES) CHURCH & HENDRICKSON HOUSE MUSEUM, 606 Church St., Wilmington, DE 19801-4421. Tel.: 302-652-5629. Fax: 302-652-8615.
E-mail: oldswedes@aol.com
Web Site: www.oldswedes.org
Founded: 1947.
Congressional District: 1
Key Personnel: Pres. (V), Max Dooley; Dir., Carol E. Mason; Museum Shop Mgr. & C.E.O., Jo Thompson.
Personnel Profile: Full-Time Paid 1; Full-Time Volunteers 16; Part-Time Paid 1; Part-Time Volunteers 1.
Governing Authority: nonprofit organization. Tax-exempt: 501(c)(3).
Historic Church & House: 1698 Holy Trinity (Old Swedes) Church.
Collections: early colonial life, Swedish culture; genealogical. Historic House: 1690 Andrew Hendrickson House.
Research Fields: Wilmington colonial history; genealogy; birth, baptism, marriage & burial records of Old Swede Church.
Facilities: 150-vol. library pertaining to Wilmington history. Gift items for sale.
Activities: guided tours; permanent exhibitions; historical & genealogical research DE and neighboring states; church services.
Publications: annual newsletter, Foundation News.
Hours & Admission Prices: Wed.-Sat. 10-4. Adults $2; discounts to members; children no charge. ♿
Attendance: 2,500 (estimated)
Membership: Student & Senior Citizen $15; Individual $25; Family $45; Patron $100; Life $500.

MERIKS AQUARIUM, 6 S Union St. #871, Wilmington, DE 19805-3828.
Key Personnel: Pres. (V), Voleen Paul; COO, Margaret Deeds; Assoc. Dir., Antoinette Harvey; Volunteer Coord., Danielle Marcus.
Personnel Profile: Full-Time Paid 1; Full-Time Volunteers 3; Part-Time Volunteers 3.
Aquarium.
Research Fields: aquaculture; fish diseases.
Publications: newsletter, Fish Tales.

MUSEUM OF BUSINESS HISTORY AND TECHNOLOGY, 1200 Philadelphia Pike, Wilmington, DE 19809-2040. Tel.: 302-798-2100.
Web Site: www.mbht.org
History Museum.
Collections: business technology; inventions; business machines from 1873-1940; 1795 copier; 1820 calculator; early typewriters; books; patents; manuals.
Hours & Admission Prices: By appointment.

NEMOURS MANSION AND GARDENS, 1600 Rockland Rd., Wilmington, DE 19803-3607. Tel.: 800-651-6912. Fax: 302-651-6933.
E-mail: tours@nemours.org
Web Site: www.nemoursmansion.org
Founded: 1977.
Key Personnel: Registrar, Francesca Biella Bonny; Exec. Dir., Grace Gary; Estate Supt., James Solge.
Personnel Profile: Full-Time Paid 21; Part-Time Paid 38.
Governing Authority: nonprofit organization. Parent Institution: The Nemours Foundation. Tax-exempt.
Historic House & Gardens: housed in 1910 Louis XVI-style chateau.
Collections: 14th to 20th-century American, European & Oriental fine & decorative arts; porcelain; paintings; prints; drawings; photographs; sculpture; silver; textiles; tapestries; oriental rugs; furniture; innovative technical equipment.
Research Fields: European fine & decorative arts.
Facilities: formal French gardens.
Activities: guided tours.
Publications: booklet, Nemours Mansion and Gardens.
Hours & Admission Prices: May-Dec. Adults $12; visitors must be at least 12 years old; reservations recommended. Closed Thanksgiving; Christmas. ♿
Attendance: 12,000 (estimated)

ROCKWOOD PARK, (M), 610 Shipley Rd., Wilmington, DE 19809-3609. Tel.: 302-761-4340. Fax: 302-761-4345.
E-mail: pnord@nccde.org
Web Site: www.rockwood.org
Founded: 1976.
Congressional District: 6
Key Personnel: Dir., Philip Nord; Cur., Carey Lockman Corbin; Horticulturist, Dena Kirk.
Personnel Profile: Full-Time Paid 3; Part-Time Paid 4; Part-Time Volunteers 25.
Governing Authority: county. Parent Institution: New Castle County.
Historic House & Museum Gallery: English Victorian Mansion & grounds.
Collections: American & European turn of the century furnishings; architecture; horticulture; specimen trees; family documents & photographs.
Research Fields: Victorian life.
Facilities: 72 acres of park grounds; self-service cafe; picnic area.
Activities: guided tours of mansion & grounds; special events. Annual Events: Partner with Delaware Shakespeare Festival; Holiday Open House.
Publications: Romantic Rockwood.
Hours & Admission Prices: Museum: Tues.-Sun. 10-3. Grounds: daily 7-10. Adults $5, children 2-12 $2; children under 2 no charge. Closed major holidays.
Attendance: 20,000 (estimated)

Winterthur

* **WINTERTHUR MUSEUM & COUNTRY ESTATE, (M),** Rte. 52, (5105 Kennett Pike), Winterthur, DE 19735. Tel.: 302-888-4600; 800-448-3883. Fax: 302-888-4820. TDD: 302-888-4907.
E-mail: tourinfo@winterthur.org
Web Site: www.winterthur.org
Formerly: Winterthur, An American Country Estate
Founded: 1951.
Congressional District: 1
Key Personnel: Dir. & C.E.O., Leslie Greene Bownan; Chm. (V), John L. McGraw; C.F.O., Robert Necarsulmer; Dir. Museum Affairs, J. Thomas Savage; Dir. Human Resources, Lisbeth Selsor; Dir. Exhibitions, Felice Jo Lamden; Museum Shop Mgr., Ellen Taviano; Dir. Garden & Estate, Christopher Strand.
Personnel Profile: Full-Time Paid 225; Part-Time Paid 208; Part-Time Volunteers 1,883; Interns 6.
Governing Authority: nonprofit organization. Tax-exempt: 501(c)(3).
Decorative Arts & Cultural History Museum: housed in 1839 building with additions in the 1920s, 1930s, 1950s & 1990s.
Collections: American decorative arts, 17th century to 1860: interior architecture, furniture, metalwork, ceramics, glass, textiles, paintings, prints, & sculpture; English & continental 17th- to 19th-century fabrics, glass, lighting fixtures, pottery & porcelain; Chinese export porcelain; English & Oriental carpets; manuscript collections.
Research Fields: decorative arts; American material culture; horticulture; conservation of historic & artistic objects.
Facilities: 70,000-vol. library of books, manuscripts, microfilm, periodicals & photographs relating to the American arts & their European, English, & Oriental antecedents available for research; botanical gardens; 350-seat auditorium; classrooms; restaurant. Museum-related items for sale.
Activities: guided tours; lectures; school tours; outreach educational programs; formally organized education programs; formally organized education programs for graduate students affiliated with the University of Delaware; training programs for professional museum workers; permanent & temporary exhibitions. Museum Sponsors: Point-to-Point Races; annual Delaware Antiques Show; Garden Fair.
Publications: member magazine; Winterthur Portfolio; books, catalogs & monographs on decorative arts; school newsletter; donor newsletter.
Hours & Admission Prices: Tues.-Sun. & holiday Mon. & the Yuletide tour 10-5. Adults $18, students & seniors $16, children 2-11 $10; discounts to

groups by advance arrangement, AAM, ICOM, MAAM & AAMD members; members & children under 2 no charge. Closed New Year's Day; Thanksgiving; Christmas. ♿
Attendance: 156,215 (accurate)
Membership: Individual $50; Dual $65; Family $70; Contributor $125; Patron $250; Benefactor $500; Associate $1,000; Director $2,500.

Yorklyn

AUBURN HEIGHTS PRESERVE, 3000 Creek Rd., Yorklyn, DE 19736. Mailing Address: Friends of Auburn Heights Inc., P.O. Box 61, Yorklyn, DE 19736-0061. Tel.: 800-349-2134; 302-239-2385.
Web Site: www.auburnheights.org
Governing Authority: nonprofit organization. Tax-exempt: 501(c)(3).
Historic House: housed in the Marshall family home & carriage house. Listed on the National Register of Historic Places.
Collections: family & automobile history; personal artifacts; period furnishings; early automobiles including Stanley Steamers, Packards, & electric cars; steam train; photographs.
Activities: outreach programs; guided tours; rental facilities.
Hours & Admission Prices: Call for hours. Museum: adults $10, children 2-12 $7.

DISTRICT OF COLUMBIA

(104 listings)

Fort McNair

U.S. ARMY CENTER OF MILITARY HISTORY, MUSEUM DIVISION, 103 Third Ave., Fort McNair, DC 20319-5058. Tel.: 202-685-2452. Fax: 202-685-2113.
E-mail: julia.simon@us.army.mil
Web Site: www.history.army.mil
Founded: 1946.
Key Personnel: Chief Military History, Dr. Jeffrey J. Clarke; Acting Dir. Army Museums & Chief Museum Programs, J. Terry Dougherty; Chief Collections, Dennis P. Mroczkowski.
Personnel Profile: Full-Time Paid 26.
Governing Authority: federal. Parent Institution: Dept. of the Army. Subsidiary Institution: Center of Military History. Tax-exempt.
History Museum and Military Museums.
Collections: Active Army Museums and Museum Activities. Please call for a complete list of museums and other activities.
Research Fields: military history.
Facilities: 1,000-vol. library.
Activities: training & educational programs; programs for soldier/ leaders & professional museum staff; temporary & permanent exhibitions.
Publications: bimonthly, Army Museum Memo; books, The Guide to U.S. Army Museums; Guide for Coordinator of Volunteers in U.S. Army Museums; Certification Inspection Handbook; Professional Assistance Directory; Handbook for Supervisors of Museums; Museum Standing Operating Procedures; Army Museum Information System (AMIS); Army Regulation 870-20; Army Museums, Historical Artifacts, and Art.
Hours & Admission Prices: Library: Mon.-Fri. 9-4. No charge. ♿
Attendance: 1,200,000

Washington

AFRICAN AMERICAN CIVIL WAR MEMORIAL FREEDOM FOUNDATION AND MUSEUM, 1200 U St., N.W., Washington, DC 20009-4443. Tel.: 202-667-2667. Fax: 202-667-6771.
E-mail: info@afroamcivilwar.org
Web Site: afroamcivilwar.org
Key Personnel: Exec. Dir., Dr. Frank Smith, Jr.; Cur., Harold Jones
History Museum.
Collections: African Americans in the Civil War; period history; photographs; documents; newspaper articles; clothing; uniforms; weapons.
Facilities: Museum-related items for sale.
Activities: special events; educational programs.
Hours & Admission Prices: Mon.-Fri. 10-5, Sat. 10-2.

THE AMERICAN CENTER OF POLISH CULTURE, 2025 "O" St., N.W., Washington, DC 20036-5913. Tel.: 202-785-2320. Fax: 202-785-2159.
E-mail: assistant@polishcenterdc.org
Web Site: www.polishcenterdc.org
Founded: 1997.
Key Personnel: Chm. (V), Patricia Koproski; Dir., Patricia Whitelaw-Hill.
Personnel Profile: Full-Time Paid 1; Part-Time Paid 3; Part-Time Volunteers 1.
Governing Authority: Tax-exempt.
Cultural History Museum.
Collections: Polish history & cultural heritage; Polish, Jewish & American relations; photographs; paintings; sculpture; decorative arts; textiles; costumes; graphic arts; documentary film.
Research Fields: Polish history & culture.
Facilities: library.
Activities: youth programs; speeches; book presentations; discussions; concerts.
Publications: The Center Line.
Hours & Admission Prices: Mon.-Fri. 10-4. No charge; donations accepted.
Membership: Senior $50; Individual $75; Couple & Family $100.

AMERICAN UNIVERSITY MUSEUM AT THE KATZEN ARTS CENTER, (M), 4400 Massachusetts Ave., N.W., Washington, DC 20016-8003. Tel.: 202-885-1300. Fax: 202-885-1140.
E-mail: rasmusse@american.edu
Web Site: www.american.edu/museum
Formerly: Watkins Gallery, American University
Founded: 2005.
Key Personnel: Dir. & Cur., Jack Rasmussen; Asst. Dir., Stefanie Fedor; Chief Preparator & Registrar, Bruce Wick.
Personnel Profile: Full-Time Paid 3; Part-Time Paid 5; Part-Time Volunteers 55.
Governing Authority: university. Parent Institution: American University. Tax-exempt.
Art Museum.
Collections: 1900-present American & European paintings, prints & drawings.
Facilities: 30,000 sq. ft. exhibit space.
Hours & Admission Prices: Tues.-Sun. 11-4. No charge. ♿

ANACOSTIA COMMUNITY MUSEUM, (M), 1901 Fort Pl., Washington, DC 20560-0001. Tel.: 202-633-4820. Fax: 202-287-3183. TDD: 202-357-1729.
E-mail: ACMinfo@si.edu
Web Site: anacostia.si.edu
Formerly: Anacostia Museum and Center for African American History & Culture
Founded: 1967.
Key Personnel: Dir., Camille Akeju; Deputy Dir., Sharon Reinckens; Asst. Dir. Education, Robert Hall; Sr. Cur., Portia James; Historian, Gail Lowe; Devel. Officer, Joanne Leese.
Personnel Profile: Full-Time Paid 19; Part-Time Volunteers 40; Interns 20.
Governing Authority: Parent Institution: Smithsonian Institution, Washington, DC, which is a nonprofit federally-chartered corporation. Branch Museum: 1901 Fort Pl., S.E., Washington, DC 20560-0004. Tax-exempt: 501(c)(3) & 170(b)(1)(A).
Family & Community History Museum.
Collections: African American social & cultural history; family & community history.
Major Exhibits: Lorenzo Dow Turner, 8/9/10-10/27/11.
Research Fields: 19th & 20th-century African American history & culture; contemporary African American culture & community life; urban issues.
Facilities: library; laboratory.
Activities: guided tours; workshops; teacher workshops; performances; educational programs; films. Annual Observances: Martin Luther King Jr. Program.
Publications: exhibit catalogues; newsletter; resource guides; educational materials.
Hours & Admission Prices: Daily 10-5. No charge. Closed Christmas. ♿

ARCHIVES OF AMERICAN ART, SMITHSONIAN INSTITUTION, 750 9th Street, N.W., Ste. 2200, Washington, DC 20001. Mailing Address: P.O. Box 37012, Victor Bldg., Ste. 2200, MRC 937, Washington, DC 20013-7012. Tel.: 202-633-7940. Fax: 202-633-7994.
E-mail: aaaemref@si.edu
Web Site: www.aaa.si.edu
Founded: 1954.
Key Personnel: Dir., John W. Smith; Asst. Dir. Operations, Jody Pettibone; Senior Cur., Elizabeth S. Kirwin; Chief Reference, Marisa Bourgoin; Chief Collections Processing, Barbara J. Aikens; Archives Catalog Database Mgr., Karen B. Weiss; Registrar, Susan Cary.
Personnel Profile: Full-Time Paid 38; Part-Time Paid 9; Part-Time Volunteers 4; Interns 3.
Governing Authority: bureau of the Smithsonian Institution, Washington, DC, which is a nonprofit federally chartered corporation & the board of trustees, Archives of American Art. Regional Centers: New York Center, 1285 Avenue of the Americas, New York, NY 10019; Washington Center, 750 9th St., N.W., Washington, DC 20560; Lawrence A. Fleischman Gallery at the Reynolds Centers, 8th & F Sts., N.W., Washington, DC 20013-7012. Parent Institution: Smithsonian Institution. Tax-exempt: 501(c)(3) & 170(b)(1)(A).

Research Institution.
Collections: the personal & professional records of American artists, dealers, critics, curators & collectors; records of galleries, museums & art societies; oral history material; manuscripts.
Research Fields: American art history.
Facilities: microfilmed archives collection available in research & reading areas of branch offices in: Boston Public Library; New York; San Francisco M.H. deYoung Museum; Washington, DC; Los Angeles, Amon Carter Museum & through inter-library loan.
Activities: inter-museum loans; temporary exhibitions; occasional documentary exhibitions.
Publications: 10-vol. card catalogue of the manuscript collection; 1-vol. card catalogue of the Oral History Collection; quarterly journal, Archives of American Art Journal; books, Collection of Exhibition Catalogues; Directory of Resources; Checklist of the Collection; Arts in America: A Bibliography. guides: Art-related Archival Materials in the Philadelphia Region, 1984-1989 Survey; Inventory of the Records of the National Arts Club, 1898-1960; Art-related Archival Materials in the Chicago Area; Paris: A Guide to Archival Sources for American Art History; A Finding Aid to the Walter Pach Papers; A Finding Aid to the Rockwell Kent papers.
Hours & Admission Prices: Mon.-Fri. 9-5. No charge. Closed Federal holidays. ♿
Attendance: 555 (estimated)
Membership: Sustaining $65; Associate $125; Sponsor $250; Patron $500; Fellow $1,000; Benefactor $2,500; Chairman's Circle $5,000.

ART MUSEUM OF THE AMERICAS, OAS, 201 18th St., N.W., Washington, DC 20006-5606. Mailing Address: 1889 F St., N.W., Washington, DC 20006-4401. Tel.: 202-458-6016 & 6019. Fax: 202-458-6021.
E-mail: artmus@oas.org
Web Site: www.museum.oas.org
Founded: 1976.
Key Personnel: Coord. Education, Adriana Opsina; Cur. Permanent Collection, Maria Leyva; Cur. Temporary Exhibits, Fabian Goncalves Borrega; Public & Media Rels., Gregory Svitil; Administrative, Charo Marroquin.
Governing Authority: nonprofit. Parent organization: Organization of American States. Tax-exempt.
Latin American Contemporary Art Collection.
Collections: Latin American 20th-century art; paintings; sculpture; graphics; drawings; works by Latin American & Caribbean artists.
Research Fields: Latin American Art.
Facilities: library & archives available for research only on premises.
Activities: guided tours; lectures & seminars; films; inter-museum loan, permanent, temporary & traveling exhibitions; color slides & films on Latin American art & archaeology; documentaries on the lives of the artists of the Americas.
Publications: Audio-visual catalog; exhibition catalogs.
Hours & Admission Prices: Tues.-Sun. 10-5. No charge; donations accepted. Closed major holidays; Good Friday.
Membership: Individual $100; Couple $150.

ARTS CLUB OF WASHINGTON, 2017 I St., N.W., Washington, DC 20006-1804. Tel.: 202-331-7282. Fax: 202-857-3678.
E-mail: membership@artsclubofwashington.org
Web Site: www.artsclubofwashington.org
Founded: 1916.
Key Personnel: Pres. (V), June Hajjar; Vice Pres., Walter Burns; Gen. Mgr., Brennan Hurley; Gallery Mgr., William Owens; Business Mgr., Shelly Gardiner.
Personnel Profile: Full-Time Paid 2; Part-Time Paid 2.
Governing Authority: nonprofit corporation.
Art Gallery: housed in 1802 home of President James Monroe.
Collections: Washington art.
Research Fields: local history.
Activities: promotion of cooperation among artists in all fields; student aid in the creative and performing arts.
Hours & Admission Prices: Sept.-July Tues.-Fri. 10-5, Sat. 10-2. No charge; donations accepted.

B'NAI B'RITH KLUTZNICK NATIONAL JEWISH MUSEUM, (M), 2020 K St., N.W., 7th Fl., Washington, DC 20006-1806. Tel.: 202-857-6647. Fax: 202-857-6601.
E-mail: museum@bnaibrith.org
Web Site: www.bnaibrith.org
Founded: 1957.
Key Personnel: Cheryl Kempler.
Personnel Profile: Full-Time Paid 1.
Governing Authority: denominational group. Parent Institution: B'nai B'rith Henry Monsky Foundation. Tax-exempt: 501(c)(3).
Jewish Heritage & Culture Museum.
Collections: pre-20th century Jewish ceremonial & folk art; Israeli archaeology; Jewish historical documents; contemporary Jewish art.
Research Fields: Jewish ceremonial folk art; Jewish history; history of B'nai B'rith.
Activities: guided tours; permanent exhibitions; classes for adults & children; films; lectures; concerts; organized trips to places of Jewish interest.
Publications: permanent collection, In the Spirit of Tradition; changing exhibit catalogues
Hours & Admission Prices: Mon.-Thurs. 12-3 by appointment. No charge; donations accepted. Closed legal & major Jewish holidays. ♿
Membership: Seniors & Students $45; Families $65.

BUREAU OF ENGRAVING & PRINTING, (M), 14th and C Sts., S.W., Washington, DC 20228-0001. Tel.: 202-874-2330; 866-874-2330 (Toll Free).
Key Personnel: Dir., Larry R. Felix
History Museum.
Collections: security documents including U.S. paper currency, U.S. passports, Homeland Security, military ID cards, Immigration & Naturalization certificates.
Activities: view paper currency production.
Hours & Admission Prices: Call for hours.

* **THE CORCORAN GALLERY OF ART, (M),** 17th St. & New York Ave., N.W., Washington, DC 20006. Mailing Address: 500 17th St., N.W., Washington, DC 20006-4899. Tel.: 202-639-1700. Fax: 202-639-1779.
Web Site: www.corcoran.org
Founded: 1869.
Key Personnel: Dir. & Pres., Paul Greenhalgh; Chm. Bd., Harry F. Hopper; C.O.O., Sam Sweet; Head Public Rels., Kristing Guiter; Mgr. Mktg., Jessica Semler; Mgr. Special Events, Allie Gallo; Visitor & Membership Svcs., Kathleen Kane; Registrar, Nancy Swallow.
Personnel Profile: Full-Time Paid 184; Part-Time Paid 39; Part-Time Volunteers 250; Interns 25.
Governing Authority: nonprofit organization. Tax-exempt: 501(c)(3).
Art Museum.
Collections: American paintings & sculptures from 18th-20th century; European paintings, sculptures & decorative arts; American and European drawings, prints & photographs; contemporary art.
Research Fields: William A. Clark collection.
Facilities: 35,000-vol. library of art & art history books available by appointment; archival repository: gallery records including exhibition records & correspondence with American artists available for research by appointment; restaurant. Museum-related items for sale.
Activities: guided tours; lectures; films; gallery talks; docent program; concerts; arts festivals; drama; formally organized education programs; permanent, temporary & traveling exhibitions.
Publications: exhibition catalogs.
Hours & Admission Prices: Wed. & Fri.-Sun. 10-5, Thurs. 10-9. Adults $10, senior citizens 62 & over and students with ID $8; children under 12 & members no charge. Closed New Year's Day; Christmas. ♿
Attendance: 350,000 (estimated)
Membership: Senior 65 & over $45; Individual $55; Senior Dual & Senior Family $75; Dual & Family $85; 1869 Society $105; Friend of the Corcoran $110; Supporting $205; Sponsoring $330; Contributing $555; Fellow of the Gallery $1,000; Chairman's Guild Sustainer $1,500; Chairman's Guild Patron $2,500; Chairman's Guild Inner Circle $5,000; Chairman's Guild President's Council $10,000.

* **DAUGHTERS OF THE AMERICAN REVOLUTION MUSEUM, (M),** 1776 D St., N.W., Washington, DC 20006-5392. Tel.: 202-879-3241. Fax: 202-628-0820.
E-mail: museum@dar.org
Web Site: www.dar.org/museum
Founded: 1890.
Key Personnel: Museum Dir. & Chief Cur., Diane L. Dunkley; Chm. (V), Michelle Mott Juehring; Cur. Education, Raina Boyd; Asst. Cur. Education, Kendall Edwards; Cur. Collections, Olive Graffam; Cur. Furnishings, Patrick Sheary; Cur. Textiles & Costumes, Alden O'Brien; Collections Mgr., Anne Ruta; Assoc. Registrar, Stephanie Randall; Museum Shop Mgr., Cynthia Carson.
Personnel Profile: Full-Time Paid 12; Part-Time Paid 2; Part-Time Volunteers 100; Interns 7.
Governing Authority: society. Parent Institution: National Society, Daughters of the American Revolution. Tax-exempt: 501(c)(3).
Decorative Arts & History Museum: housed in 1904 Memorial Continental Hall.
Collections: decorative arts made or used in America in the pre-industrial period; quilts; coverlets; needlework; costumes; ceramics; glass; silver;

pewter; furniture; paintings; miniatures; musical instruments; toys; dolls; Revolutionary War artifacts; 31 American period rooms.
Research Fields: quilts, coverlets & needlework; American material culture, 1700-1840.
Facilities: 2,000-vol. library on decorative arts available for use on premises. Slides, postcards, notecards & handicrafts for sale.
Activities: guided tours; textile identification clinics; lectures; quilt workshops; docent program; inter-museum loan, permanent & temporary exhibitions; organized education programs for children, adults & undergraduate or graduate college students; internship program; costume workshop; summer camps.
Publications: First Flowerings: Early Virginia Quilts; Magnificent Intentions: Decorative Arts of the District of Columbia, 1791-1861; Souvenirs from the Voyage of Life; American Case Furniture 1680-1840: Selections from the DAR Museum Collection; Youth is the Time for Progress: The Importance of American Schoolgirl Art; Preserving the American Spirit at the DAR Museum.
Hours & Admission Prices: Museum: Mon.-Fri. 9:30-4, Sat. 9-5. Period Room Tours: Mon.-Fri. 10-3, Sat. 9-4:30. Call to confirm hours. No charge; donations accepted. Closed major holidays. ♿
Attendance: 23,000 (estimated)
Membership: Regular $10; Sustaining $25; Sponsor $50; Life & Memorial Tribute $200; Patron $500; Benefactor $5,000.

DECATUR HOUSE MUSEUM, 748 Jackson Pl., N.W., Washington, DC 20006-4912. Mailing Address: 1610 H St., N.W., Washington, DC 20006-4907. Tel.: 202-842-0920. Fax: 202-842-0030.
E-mail: decatur_house@nthp.org
Web Site: www.decaturhouse.org
Founded: 1956.
Key Personnel: Exec. Dir., Cynthia B. Malinick; Chm. (V), Thomas R. Pickering; Dir. Special Events, Arioth Harrison; Dir. Public Rels. & Mktg., Mame Croze; Museum Shop Mgr., Rosemary Rudd Cohen.
Personnel Profile: Full-Time Paid 6; Part-Time Paid 21; Part-Time Volunteers 3; Interns 4.
Governing Authority: nonprofit organization. Parent Institution: National Trust for Historic Preservation, 1785 Massachusetts Ave., N.W., Washington, DC 20036. Tax-exempt: 501(c)(3).
Historic House Museum: 1819 Commodore Stephen Decatur House, designed by B. Latrobe.
Collections: 18th-, 19th- & 20th-century decorative arts.
Research Fields: residents of house; political & social history of Washington, D.C.; Early 19th Century decorative Arts.
Facilities: rental facilities available. Books & gift items for sale.
Activities: guided tours; lectures; temporary exhibitions; school programs; special events; walking tours.
Publications: Jackson Place Journal.
Hours & Admission Prices: Tues.-Sat. 10-5, Sun. 12-4. Suggested Donation: adult $5. Closed New Year's Day; Thanksgiving; Christmas. ♿
Attendance: 25,000 (estimated)
Membership: Decatur House Friends: Palladian Society $50; Jackson Place Society $100; Beale Society $250; Decatur Society $500; Lafayette Square Associates $1,000; Latrobe Society $5,000 & up.

DEPARTMENT OF THE TREASURY, Office of the Curator, Rm. 1225, 15th & Pennsylvania N.W., Dept. of the Treasury, Washington, DC 20220-0001. Mailing Address: 1500 Pennsylvania Ave., N.W., Washington, DC 20220-0002. Tel.: 202-622-1250. Fax: 202-622-2294.
E-mail: richard.cote@do.treas.gov
Web Site: www.ustreas.gov/curator
Key Personnel: Cur., Richard Cote; Tour Coord., Mary Edwards; Preservation Specialist, Guy Munsch.
Personnel Profile: Full-Time Paid 4; Part-Time Volunteers 25; Interns 2.
Governing Authority: federal government.
Architecture Museum: 1836-1869 U.S. Treasury Building.
Collections: 19th & 20th-century office furniture; original artwork; portraits of former Secretaries of the Treasury; architectural fragments.
Hours & Admission Prices: Tours: Sat. 9, 9:45, 10:30 & 11:15 by appointment only through your congressional office. ♿

DIPLOMATIC RECEPTION ROOMS, DEPARTMENT OF STATE, (M), MIFA, Rm. 8213, 2201-C St., N.W., Washington, DC 20520-0001. Tel.: 202-647-1990. Fax: 202-647-3428.
Web Site: www.state.gov/m/drr
Founded: 1961.
Key Personnel: Dir. & Cur., Marcee F. Craighill; Registrar, Lynn M. Turner; Museum Specialist, Virginia K. Burden; Project Coord., Hope E. Kosier.
Governing Authority: federal, Dept. of State. Tax-exempt.
National Agency.
Collections: American period furnishings; paintings; decorative period arts.
Research Fields: American furniture; paintings of 18th & 19th century; Chinese Export porcelain; American silver; oriental rugs.
Activities: guided tours.
Publications: Becoming A Nation.
Hours & Admission Prices: By appointment: Mon.-Fri. 9:30, 10:30, 2:45. Fine Arts Tour: recommended age is 12 & up; photo ID required for adults. No charge; donations accepted. For reservations call or fax 90 days in advance: Department of State, Washington, DC 20520. Tel.: 202-647-3241. Web: https://receptiontours.state.gov. TDD: 202-736-4474; Fax: 202-736-4232. ♿
Membership: Contributing $500 & up; Sustaining $1,000 & up; Patron $5,000 & up; Sponsors $10,000 & up; Major Sponsors $25,000 & up; Benefactor $50,000 & up; Major Benefactors $100,000 & up; Philanthropists $250,000 & up; Major Philanthropists $500,000 & up; Grand Patrons $1,000,000.

DISTRICT OF COLUMBIA ARTS CENTER, 2438 18th St., N.W., Washington, DC 20009-2004. Tel.: 202-462-7833. Fax: 202-328-7099.
E-mail: info@dcartcenter.org
Web Site: www.dcartscenter.org
Founded: 1989.
Key Personnel: Dir., B. Stanley; Chm. (V), Bruce Kogod; Pres. (V), Jay Bothwell.
Personnel Profile: Full-Time Paid 1; Part-Time Paid 4; Part-Time Volunteers 4; Interns 2.
Governing Authority: Tax-exempt.
Visual & Performing Arts Center.
Collections: works by local artists.
Activities: theater performances; special events.
Hours & Admission Prices: Wed.-Sun. 2-7 & during theater performances. No charge.
Attendance: 4,000 (estimated)

* **DUMBARTON HOUSE, (M),** 2715 Que St., N.W., Washington, DC 20007-3071. Tel.: 202-337-2288. Fax: 202-337-0348.
E-mail: info@dumbartonhouse.org
Web Site: www.dumbartonhouse.org
Founded: 1932.
Congressional District: 1
Key Personnel: Chm. (V), Mrs. Philip Heeth Grantham; Pres. (V), Hilary Gripekoven; Exec. Dir., Karen L. Daly; Museum Cur., Scott S. Scholz; Dir. Education, Jennifer Michaelree; Mgr. Mktg. & Events, Melissa Hoggan Groppel.
Personnel Profile: Full-Time Paid 8; Part-Time Paid 30; Part-Time Volunteers 46; Interns 6.
Governing Authority: society. Parent Institution: The National Society of The Colonial Dames of America (NSCDA). Tax-exempt.
Historic House: c.1800 Dumbarton House.
Collections: federal period furnishings & decorative arts; Nourse family papers; Morris family papers.
Major Exhibits: Fran, Have You Supplied the Table? Foods, Service and Etiquette in the Federal Era, 11/09-6/10.
Research Fields: Federal period decorative arts; Georgetown, DC history; Washington, DC history; Nourse family; Anthony Morris family; United States Treasury.
Facilities: 120-seat assembly hall.
Activities: tours; lectures; special events; concerts; school programs; scout programs; public programs; private events; rental facilities.
Publications: newsletters; calendar; exhibition catalogues.
Hours & Admission Prices: Tours: Tues.-Sat. 10:15, 11:15, 12:15 & 1:15. Adults $5; discounts to AAA, AAM & ICOM members; school groups & students w/ID no charge. Closed Christmas Eve; most national holidays. ♿
Attendance: 15,000 (estimated)

DUMBARTON OAKS RESEARCH LIBRARY & COLLECTIONS, (M), (I), 1703 32nd St., N.W., Washington, DC 20007-2961. Tel.: 202-339-6414. Fax: 202-339-6419.
E-mail: dumbartonoaks@doaks.org
Web Site: www.doaks.org
Founded: 1940.
Key Personnel: Dir., Prof. Jan Ziolkowski; Dir. Pre-Columbian Studies, Joanne Pillsbury; Dir. Studies in Landscape Architecture, John Beardsley; Dir. Byzantine Studies, Margaret Mullet; Dir. Museum, Gudrun Buehl; Cur. Image Collections & Fieldwork Archives, Gerrianne Schaad; Mgr. House Collection & Archivist, James Carder; Supt. Gardens & Grounds, Gail Griffin.
Personnel Profile: Full-Time Paid 74; Part-Time Paid 22; Part-Time Volunteers 16.
Governing Authority: trustees for Harvard University. Parent Institution: Harvard University. Tax-exempt.
Library & Art Museum.

Collections: Byzantine; Pre-Columbian artifacts; some European & American paintings, sculpture & decorative arts; rare books & manuscripts in garden history & history of landscape architecture.
Research Fields: Byzantine; Pre-Columbian; studies in landscape architecture & garden history.
Facilities: 125,150-vol. library on Byzantine research, pre-Columbian studies, & gardens available to accredited scholars by special permission; gardens. Handbooks of the collections & other museum-related items for sale.
Activities: public lectures; permanent exhibitions; conferences; fellowships; concerts.
Publications: handbook, The Byzantine Collection; handbook, The Robert Woods Bliss Collection of Pre-Columbian Art; monographs; conference proceedings; catalogues; guidebook, Dumbarton Oaks: The Collections.
Hours & Admission Prices: Museum: Tues.-Sun. 2-5. No charge. Gardens: April-Oct. Tues.-Sun. 2-6; Nov.-March Tues.-Sun. 2-5. Adults $7, children & senior citizens $5. Closed national holidays. ♿
Attendance: 38,000 (estimated)

FEDERAL RESERVE BOARD, (M), 20th & C Sts., N.W., Washington, DC 20551-0001. Tel.: 202-452-3302. Fax: 202-736-5680.
Web Site: www.federalreserve.gov/generalinfo/virtualtour
Founded: 1975.
Key Personnel: Dir., Stephen Bennett Phillips; Chm. (V), Richard J. Kelly; Vice Chm., Leatrice Eagle; Fine Arts Program Asst., Joan B. Mulcahy; Collections Asst., Rhonda Gray-Young.
Governing Authority: federal government. Tax-exempt: 170(b)(1)(A).
Art Gallery: housed in a 1935-37 building by Paul Philippe Cret.
Collections: 19th- & 20th-century American and European paintings, prints & works on paper.
Activities: loan exhibitions.
Publications: exhibition brochures.
Hours & Admission Prices: Mon.-Fri. 10-3:30 by appointment. Please call 202-452-3778 or Fax: 202-736-5680. No charge. Closed federal holidays. ♿

FOLGER SHAKESPEARE LIBRARY, 201 E. Capitol St., S.E., Washington, DC 20003-1094. Tel.: 202-544-4600. Fax: 202-544-4623.
E-mail: webmaster@folger.edu
Web Site: www.folger.edu
Founded: 1932.
Congressional District: 1
Key Personnel: C.E.O. & Dir., Gail Kern Paster; Chm. (V), Paul T. Ruxin; Dir. Research, Dr. David Schalkwyk; Librarian, Dr. Stephen Enniss; Reference Librarian, Dr. Georgianna Ziegler; Dir. Public Programs, Janet Griffin; Dir. Devel., Beverly C. With; Museum Shop Mgr., Barbara Jacoby; Controller, Howard Parks; Head External Rels., Garland Scott.
Personnel Profile: Full-Time Paid 100; Part-Time Volunteers 45.
Governing Authority: Trustees of Amherst College. Tax-exempt: 501(c)(3).
Private Independent Research Library.
Collections: rare books & manuscripts of 15th-18th century on continental & English Renaissance; Shakespeare; theater history from Middle Ages to 20th century; theater memorabilia.
Research Fields: Renaissance; Shakespeare; history of drama.
Facilities: 310,000-vol. library of printed books & 55,000 manuscripts on Renaissance civilization of England & the continent available for use on premises by scholars & graduate students completing doctoral dissertations; reading room; 250-seat Elizabethan theatre. Books, maps, postcards, CDs & DVDs for sale.
Activities: guided tours; public readings & lectures; gallery talks; concerts; seminars; poetry readings; docent program; theatrical performances; drama; education programs; exhibitions.
Publications: magazine, Folger; Shakespeare Quarterly; Folger Library Shakespeare Editions; exhibition catalogs.
Hours & Admission Prices: Library: Mon.-Fri. 8:45-4:45, Sat. 9-12 & 1-4:30. Exhibits Gallery: Mon.-Sat. 10-5. No charge; donations accepted. Closed federal holidays. ♿
Attendance: 200,000 (estimated)
Membership: Friends of the Folger: For information call 202-675-0359.

FONDO DEL SOL VISUAL ARTS & MEDIA CENTER/EL MUSEO DE CULTURAS Y HERENCIAS AMERICANAS/MOCHA, (M), 2112 R St., N.W., Washington, DC 20008-1932. Tel.: 202-265-9235. Fax: 202-265-1045.
E-mail: fondodelsol@earthlink.net
Web Site: www.fondodelsol.org
Founded: 1973.
Key Personnel: Dir. & Chief Cur., W. Marc Zuver; Co Chm. (Jamaica), A. Michael Auld; Co Chm. (Cuba), Osvaldo Mesa; Co Chm., Dr. Floyd Coleman; Deputy Dir., Education & Website, Alan Urtecho; Dir. Communications & Publications, Sanne Tikjoeb; Asst. Dir. (Peru), Manuel Pereira.
Personnel Profile: Full-Time Paid 1; Part-Time Paid 6; Part-Time Volunteers 2; Interns 2.
Governing Authority: nonprofit. Tax-exempt: 501(c)(3) & 509.
Art Museum & Media Center.
Collections: pre-Columbian & Hispanic Santero collection; contemporary Latino, Chicano & Puerto Rican art.
Research Fields: contemporary Hispanic, Chicano, Puerto Rican, & Latin American art; Native American, Caribbean & Afro American art.
Facilities: film & video library pertaining to Hispanic artists in the U.S.
Activities: guided tours; lectures; films & videos; concerts; arts festivals; TV & radio programs; organized programs for children; internship program; loan, temporary & traveling exhibitions; mobile vans; film & video services for museums & private groups.
Publications: monthly brochures & catalogues for exhibits; monthly program notes for video & media programs.
Hours & Admission Prices: Wed.-Sat. 1-5. Suggested Donation: $3; members & children no charge. Closed major holidays. ♿
Attendance: 50,000
Membership: Mailing $30; Assistant Sponsor $50; Sponsor $100; Patron $500; Benefactor & Corporate $1,000-$5,000.

FORD'S THEATRE NATIONAL HISTORIC SITE (LINCOLN MUSEUM), 511 10th St., N.W., Washington, DC 20004. Tel.: 202-426-6924. Fax: 202-426-1845. TDD: 202-426-1749.
Web Site: www.nps.gov/foth/
Founded: 1933.
Key Personnel: Site Mgr., Rae Emerson; Asst . Site Mgr., Claudia Anderson; Supt., Kay Fielder.
Personnel Profile: Full-Time Paid 20; Part-Time Volunteers 15.
Governing Authority: federal. Parent Institution: National Park Service. Subsidiary Institution: National Capital Parks-Central, 900 Ohio Dr., S.W., Washington, DC 20242. Tax-exempt.
Historic Site & History Museum.
Collections: Lincoln memorabilia; period furnishings; Oldroyd collection of Lincoln artifacts; John Wilkes Booth gun. Historic Buildings: 1849 Petersen House, where Lincoln died; 1863 Ford's Theatre.
Research Fields: Lincoln's life; his assassination; Civil War period.
Facilities: Books, pamphlets, maps & posters for sale.
Activities: lectures; self-guided tours; permanent exhibitions.
Hours & Admission Prices: Daily 9-5. No charge. Closed Christmas.
Attendance: 1,029,000 (accurate)

* **FREDERICK DOUGLASS NATIONAL HISTORIC SITE,** 1411 W Street, S.E., Washington, DC 20020-4813. Mailing Address: c/o National Parks-East, 1411 W. St., S.E., Washington, DC 20020. Tel.: 202-426-5961. Fax: 202-426-0880. TDD: 202-426-1452.
E-mail: cathy_ingram@nps.gov
Web Site: www.cr.nps.gov/csd/exhibits/douglass
Founded: 1916.
Key Personnel: Rgnl. Dir., Peggy O'Dell; Park Supt., Gayle Hazelwood; Cur., Cathy Ingram.
Personnel Profile: Full-Time Paid 6; Part-Time Volunteers 3.
Governing Authority: federal. Parent Institution: National Capital Parks-East, National Park Services, U.S. Dept. of the Interior, 1900 Anacostia Dr., S.E., Washington DC. Tax-exempt.
Historic Site.
Collections: films; furnishings, documents & personal artifacts of Frederick Douglass.
Research Fields: writings, letters, documents related to the activities of Douglass.
Facilities: library of historic records available by appointment; visitor center. Museum-related items for sale.
Activities: guided tours; films; special interpretive programs.
Publications: interpretive pamphlets.
Hours & Admission Prices: April-Oct. daily 9-5; Nov.-March daily 9-4. Adults $3, senior citizens $1.50; children under 6 & school groups with approved waiver no charge. ♿
Attendance: 33,000 (accurate)

FREER AND SACKLER GALLERIES OF ART, 1050 Independence Ave., S.W., Washington, DC 20013-7012. Mailing Address: MRC 707, P.O. Box 37012, Washington, DC 20013-7012. Tel.: 202-633-4880. Fax: 202-357-4911. TDD: 202-786-2374.
E-mail: publicaffairsasia@si.edu
Web Site: www.asia.si.edu
Founded: 1906.
Key Personnel: Dir., Dr. Julian Raby; Exhibitions Coord., Cheryl Sobas; Deputy Dir., Dr. James Ulak; Assoc. Dir. & Cur. Ancient China, Keith Wilson; Assoc. Cur. Chinese Art, Joseph Chang; Cur. Ceramics, Louise Cort; Chief Cur. & Cur. Islamic Art, Dr. Massumeh Farhad; Sr. Assoc. Cur.,

Ann Yonemura; Assoc. Cur., Lee Glazer; Research Spec. Chinese Literature & History, Stephen Allee; Head Librarian, Reiko Yoshimura; Head Collection Management, Elizabeth Duley; Research Assoc. (Nepalese/Tibetan Art), Dr. Mary Slusser; Mgr. Shops, Peter Musolino; Head, Imaging & Photographic Svcs., John Tsantes; Head Digital Publications, Web & Digital Media, Karen Sasaki; Head Finance & Administration, Pat Kennedy Graham; Dir. External Affairs, Katie Ziglar.
Personnel Profile: Full-Time Paid 141; Part-Time Volunteers 20; Interns 25.
Governing Authority: federal; nonprofit corporation. Parent Institution: Smithsonian Institution, Washington, DC. Tax-exempt: 501(c)(3) & 170(b)(1)(A).
Asian Art Gallery.
Collections: Chinese, Japanese, Korean, Islamic, Ancient Near Eastern art; South & Southeast Asian bronze; jade; sculpture; painting; lacquer; pottery; porcelain; manuscripts; metalwork & glass; works by 19th & early 20th century American artists including James McNeill Whistler; slides; photographs; archives includes Charles Lang Freer papers, Bishop papers, Pope papers, Empress Dowager Cizi photographs, Ernst Herzfeld papers, Myron Bement Smith collection, Dwight William try on papers, Freer-Whistler correspondence.
Research Fields: Asian art history; 19th & early 20th century American art.
Facilities: 80,000-vol. library of books, pamphlets & periodicals half of which are in Chinese & Japanese pertaining to collections available for research in reading room; archives; 300-seat auditorium. Museum-related items for sale.
Activities: guided tours; lectures; gallery talks; permanent & temporary exhibitions; films; concerts; educational programs; after hours events.
Publications: Ars Orientalis; 2 series of monographs, Freer Gallery of Art Oriental Studies; Freer Gallery of Art Occasional Papers; exhibition catalogs; various booklets & pamphlets.
Hours & Admission Prices: Daily 10-5:30. No charge. Closed Christmas. ♿
Attendance: 723,868 (accurate)
Membership: Friends of the Freer & Sackler Galleries: Patrons' Circle $1,200; Directors' Circle $3,000; Founders' Circle $5,000; Sponsors' Circle $10,000.

GEORGETOWN UNIVERSITY ART COLLECTION, Georgetown University, Healy Hall, Room #107, 3700 O St., N.W., Washington, DC 20057-1174. Mailing Address: Georgetown Univ., Lauinger Library, Special Collections, 5th Fl., 3700 O St., N.W., Washington, DC 20057-1174. Tel.: 202-687-1469. Fax: 202-687-7501.
E-mail: artcollection@georgetown.edu
Web Site: www.library.georgetown.edu/dept/speccoll/guac/
Founded: 1789.
Key Personnel: Cur. Art, LuLen Walker; Asst. Cur., Christen Runge; Head Special Collections, John Buchtel.
Personnel Profile: Full-Time Paid 2; Part-Time Paid 2.
Governing Authority: university. Parent Institution: Georgetown University. Tax-exempt: 501(c)(3).
Art and History Museum: housed in 1879 Healy Hall on the Georgetown University campus.
Collections: historical objects; works by Van Dyck & Gilbert Stuart; paintings; sculpture; graphics; American portraits; religious objects; decorative arts; period rooms.
Research Fields: historical objects; paintings; sculpture.
Activities: gallery talks; formally organized education programs for undergraduate college students; permanent & temporary exhibitions.
Publications: catalog of the collection.
Hours & Admission Prices: Call for hours. No charge. ♿

HERITAGE PRESERVATION, (M), 1012 14th St., N.W., Ste. 1200, Washington, DC 20005-3408. Tel.: 202-233-0800. Fax: 202-233-0807.
E-mail: lreger@heritagepreservation.org
Web Site: www.heritagepreservation.org
Founded: 1972.
Key Personnel: C.E.O. & Pres., Lawrence Reger; Exec. Vice Pres., Moira Egan; Chm. (V), Merv Richard; Treas., Tom Clareson; Vice Pres. Emergency Programs, Jane Long; Vice Pres. Collections Care Programs, Kristen Laise; Dir. Conservation Assessment Program, Sara Gonzales.
Personnel Profile: Full-Time Paid 10; Part-Time Paid 3.
Governing Authority: private; nonprofit organization. Tax-exempt: 501(c)(3).
Heritage Preservation.
Publications: Caring For Your Collections; Caring For Your Historic House; Caring For Your Family Treasures; Heritage Preservation Update; SOS! Update; Capabilities; Field Guide to Emergency Response; The Emergency Response and Salvage Wheel; A Public Trust At Risk: The Heritage Health Index Report on the State of America's Collections.
Hours & Admission Prices: Mon.-Fri. 9-5:30. Closed New Year's Day; Martin Luther King Jr. Day; Presidents' Day; Memorial Day; Independence Day; Labor Day; Columbus Day; Veterans Day; Thanksgiving; Christmas. ♿

Membership: Member $150; Supporting $500; Sustaining $1,000; Benefactor $1,001 & up.

* **HILLWOOD ESTATE, MUSEUM & GARDENS, (M), (I),** 4155 Linnean Ave., N.W., Washington, DC 20008-3806. Tel.: 202-686-8500. Fax: 202-966-7846.
E-mail: info@hillwoodmuseum.org
Web Site: www.hillwoodmuseum.org
Founded: 1976.
Key Personnel: Bd. Pres. (V), Ellen MacNeille Charles; C.E.O. & Exec. Dir., Frederick J. Fisher; Assoc. Dir. & Dir. Interpretation & Visitor Svcs., Angie Dodson; Acting Dir. Collections, Chief Cur. & Sr. Cur. Western European Art, Liana Paredes; Asst. Dir. Collections & Collections Mgr., Ruthann Uithol; Assoc. Cur. Russian & Eastern European Art, Scott Ruby; Cur. American Material Culture & Historian, Estella Chung; Asst. Cur. Costumes & Textiles, Howard Kurtz; Archives & Visual Resources Mgr., Heather Corey; Asst. Registrar, Stephanie Thornton; Chief Art Librarian, Kristen Regina; Head Preservation & Exhibitions, Scott Brouard; Head Interpretation, Audra Kelly; Mgr. Youth Audiences, Rebecca Singer; Mgr. Adult Audiences, Erin McCormally; Interpretation Volunteer Coord., Lisa Leyh; Horticulture Volunteer Coord., Bill Johnson; Head Communications & Mktg., Marie Marcogliese; Head Communications & Media Rels., Lynn Rossotti; Head Visitor Svcs., Michael Kruelle; Tourism & Visitor Rels. Coord., Laura Andersen; Group Tours & Special Events Coord., Stephen Stuart; Head Merchandising, Lauren Chapin Salazar; Dir. Human Resources, Cathy Grantham; Dir. Devel., Joan Wetmore; Dir. Finance & Admin. and C.F.O., Madge Minor; Controller, Charles Parnell; Dir. Facilities, Don Rogers; Dir. Horticulture, Brian Barr; Dir. Security, Wickie Lyons.
Personnel Profile: Full-Time Paid 72; Part-Time Paid 16; Part-Time Volunteers 252; Interns 2.
Governing Authority: nonprofit organization. Administered by Hillwood Museum & Gardens Foundation. Tax-exempt: 501(c)(3).
Decorative Art Museum: housed in Washington residence of Marjorie Merriweather Post, founder of Hillwood Museum & Gardens Foundation.
Collections: Russian decorative arts; Russian & French books, paintings, sculptures & prints; Russian icons; 18th-century French furniture & porcelain; East Asian works of art; memorabilia & furnishings assembled by Mrs. Post; European paintings & prints; American decorative & fine arts; American material culture; botanical collections; gardens; orchids.
Major Exhibits: Sevres Then and Now: Tradition and Innovation in Porcelain, 1750-2000 (T), 11/09-5/10.
Research Fields: Russian decorative arts; European, fine & decorative arts; East Asian works of art; American decorative arts, paintings, & material culture; 20th-century interior design; 20th-century American history; historic landscape preservation; horticultural sciences.
Facilities: 32,000-vol. library relating to Russian & French decorative arts including rare books, sales catalogues, periodicals & horticultural publications; archives; visitor center; cafe; 13 acres of formal gardens; theater. Museum-related items for sale.
Activities: guided, special interest & audio tours; public programs for adults & children.
Publications: visitor's companion book, Hillwood Museum & Gardens: Majorie Merriweather Post's Art Collector's Personal Museum; The Hillwood Post newsletter; A Taste for Splendor: Russian Imperial & European Treasures from the Hillwood Museum (catalogue of collection); Hillwood Collection Series: Faberge at Hillwood; Russian Icons at Hillwood; Sevres Porcelain at Hillwood; Russian Imperial Porcelain at Hillwood; Russian Glass at Hillwood; French Furniture in the Hillwood Museum Collection; Tradition in Transition: Russian Icons in the Age of the Romanovs; Hillwood: Thirty Years of Collecting 1977-2007; Treasures into Tractors: The Selling of Russia's Cultural Heritage, 1918-1938; Sevres Then and Now: Tradition and Innovation in Porcelain, 1750-2000.
Hours & Admission Prices: Museum: Feb.-Dec. Tues.-Sat. 10-5. Office: Mon.-Fri. 9-5. Estate Donation: adults $12, seniors $10, students $7, children 6-18 $5; discounts to AAM & ICOM members. Closed national holidays. ♿
Attendance: 49,384 (accurate)
Membership: Friend $50 ($40 beyond DC/MD/VA); Dual & Family Friend $75; Contributing Friend $100; Contributing Dual & Family $150; Patrons $250; Donors $500; Sponsors $1,000; Corporate Neighbor $2,500; Corporate Supporter $5,000; Corporate Sponsor $10,000; Corporate Partner $25,000.

HIRSHHORN MUSEUM AND SCULPTURE GARDEN, SMITHSONIAN INSTITUTION, (I), Seventh St. & Independence Ave., S.W., Washington, DC 20560-0001. Mailing Address: P.O. Box 37012/HMSG MRC 350, Washington, DC 20013-7012. Tel.: 202-633-4674. Fax: 202-786-2682. TDD: 202-357-1729.
E-mail: sawyerd@si.edu
Web Site: hirshhorn.si.edu

Founded: 1966.
Key Personnel: Exec. Dir., Richard Koshalek; Dir. Art & Public Programs, Kerry Brougher; Dir. External Affairs, Gabriel Riera; Program Dir., Milena Kalinovska; Registrar, Barbara Freund; Librarian, Anna Brooke; Chief Conservator, Susan Lake; Chief Exhibits & Design, Al Masino; Security Chief, Adolf Smith; Building Mgr., Fletcher Johnston; Communications & Mktg. Specialist, Erin Baysden; Publications Mgr., Vanessa Mallory; Museum Shop Mgr., Tina Mallett; Dir. Devel., Kevin Chrysler.
Personnel Profile: Full-Time Paid 61; Part-Time Volunteers 100; Interns 33.
Governing Authority: nonprofit organization. Parent Institution: Smithsonian Institution. Tax-exempt.
Art Museum.
Collections: international modern & contemporary art; 19th- & 20th-century sculpture.
Research Fields: 19th- & 20th-century international paintings, sculpture & graphic art; contemporary art.
Facilities: 43,000-vol. library of art books & catalogs available to scholars by appointment on museum premises; 280-seat auditorium.
Activities: guided tours; lectures; films; gallery talks; concerts; education programs for children, adults, undergraduate & graduate college students; docent program; inter-museum loan, permanent, temporary & traveling exhibitions.
Publications: exhibition catalogues & brochures; gallery handouts; seasonal calendars of events.
Hours & Admission Prices: Daily 10-5:30. No charge; donations accepted. Closed Christmas. ♿
Attendance: 690,544 (accurate)
Membership: Associates' Circle $100-$249; Contributor's Circle $250-$499; Inner Circle $500-$999; Friend's Circle $1,000-$2,499; Curator's Circle $2,500-$4,999; Donor's Circle $5,000-$9,999; Benefactor's Circle $10,000-$24,999; Director's Circle $25,000 & up.

HISTORICAL SOCIETY OF WASHINGTON, DC, 801 K St., N.W., (@ Mt. Vernon Sq.), Washington, DC 20001-3746. Tel.: 202-383-1850.
E-mail: info@historydc.org
Web Site: www.historydc.org
Key Personnel: Exec. Dir., Sandy Bellamy
Historical Society Museum.
Collections: history; culture; government documents; photographs; books; videos; personal artifacts.
Facilities: library.
Activities: permanent & temporary exhibitions.
Hours & Admission Prices: Library: Tues.-Sat. 10-5. No charge. Closed New Year's Day; Thanksgiving; Christmas.

HOUSE OF THE TEMPLE, 1733 16th St., N.W., Washington, DC 20009-3103. Tel.: 202-232-3579. Fax: 202-464-0487.
E-mail: hcalloway@scottishrite.org
Web Site: www.scottishrite.org
Formerly: The Supreme Council
Founded: 1807.
Key Personnel: C.E.O., Ronald A. Seale; Librarian & Cur., Joan Sansbury; Archivist, Art de Hoyos; Asst. Librarian, Larissa Watkins; Dir. Special Programs, Heather Calloway.
Personnel Profile: Full-Time Paid 3; Part-Time Paid 1.
Governing Authority: private; nonprofit organization. Parent Institution: Scottish Rite of Freemasonry. Tax-exempt: 501(c)(3).
Masonic/Fraternal Museum.
Collections: Masonic history with concentration on the Scottish Rite; Burl Ives collection.
Research Fields: Freemasonry; fraternal history.
Facilities: 267,000-vol. library.
Activities: guided tours.
Publications: The Scottish Rite Journal; books.
Hours & Admission Prices: Mon.-Thurs. 10-4. No charge; donations accepted. Closed Federal holidays.
Attendance: 10,450 (estimated)

HOWARD UNIVERSITY GALLERY OF ART, 2455 6th St., N.W., Fine Arts Bldg., Rm. 1025, Washington, DC 20059-0001. Tel.: 202-806-7070. Fax: 202-806-6503.
Web Site: www.howard.edu/library/art@howard/goa/default.htm
Founded: 1928.
Key Personnel: Dir., Dr. Tritobia H. Benjamin; Asst. Dir., Scott Baker; Registrar, Eileen Johnston.
Governing Authority: federal. Parent Institution: Howard University. Tax-exempt.
Art Gallery.
Collections: African-American & American painting, sculpture, graphic art; Alain LeRoy Locke African collection; European graphic art; Samuel H. Kress study collection of Italian paintings and sculpture; Irving Gumbel prints.
Research Fields: African-American art.
Activities: inter-museum loan; temporary, permanent & traveling exhibitions.
Publications: catalogs.
Hours & Admission Prices: Winter: Mon.-Fri. 9:30-5, Sun. 12-4. Summer: Mon.-Fri. 9:30-4:30, Sun. call for hours. No charge; donations accepted. Closed national holidays. ♿

HOWARD UNIVERSITY MUSEUM, MOORLAND SPINGARN RESEARCH CENTER, 500 Howard Pl., N.W., Washington, DC 20059-0001. Tel.: 202-806-7239. Fax: 202-806-6405.
Web Site: www.founders.howard.edu/moorland-spingarn
Founded: 1914.
Key Personnel: Dir., Dr. Thomas C. Battle; Adminstrative Officer, Rosa Anthony.
Personnel Profile: Full-Time Paid 35; Part-Time Paid 1.
Governing Authority: Parent Institution: Howard Univ., 2400 6th St. N.W., Washington DC 20059. Tax-exempt.
Black History Museum.
Collections: African artifacts; historic materials relative to the Black experience.
Research Fields: all areas related to Black history.
Facilities: library & research center containing manuscripts, photographs, tapes, microforms, periodicals & other documents relating to the Black experience, available for use on premises. Museum-related items for sale.
Activities: guided tours; lectures; temporary & permanent exhibitions.
Publications: exhibition catalogs
Hours & Admission Prices: Mon.-Fri. 9-4:30. No charge. ♿

INDIAN ARTS AND CRAFTS BOARD, 1849 C St., N.W., Rm. 2528, MIB, U.S. Dept. Interior, Washington, DC 20240-0001. Tel.: 202-208-3773. Fax: 202-208-5196.
E-mail: iacb@ios.doi.gov
Founded: 1935.
Key Personnel: Dir., Meridith Stanton.
Governing Authority: federal. Affiliated with the U.S. Department of the Interior. Branch Museums: Museum of the Plains Indian, Browning, MT; Southern Plains Indian Museum, Anadarko, Okla.; Sioux Indian Museum, Rapid City, SD. Tax-exempt.
American Indian & Alaska Native Arts Museum.
Collections: contemporary American Indian & Alaska Native arts of the U.S.
Research Fields: pertaining to collection.
Publications: Source Directory of Native American owned & operated arts & crafts businesses; brochures, Know The Law Brochure; The Indian Arts and Crafts Act.
Hours & Admission Prices: Mon.-Fri. 7:45-4:15. No charge. Closed national holidays. ♿

INTERNATIONAL SPY MUSEUM, (M), 800 F St., N.W., Washington, DC 20004-1505. Tel.: 202-393-7798. Fax: 202-393-7797.
E-mail: aabrell@spymuseum.org
Web Site: www.spymuseum.org
Founded: 2002.
Key Personnel: Exec. Dir., E. Peter Earnest; Media Rels., Amanda Abrell.
Governing Authority: private.
Spy Museum.
Collections: over 600 artifacts; tradecraft, history & contemporary role of espionage; international espionage artifacts; espionage tools & techniques; lipstick pistol; Enigma cipher machine; counterfeit currency; disguised weapons; miniature cameras; concealment devices for weapons; radio transmitters & receivers; dead drops; objects related to specific espionage cases & historic figures such as John Walker, Mata Hari & George Washington; KGB & historic photographs; espionage stories.
Facilities: theater; rental space. Museum-related items for sale.
Activities: audio-visual programs; computer interactives; hands-on components; lectures; tours; book signings; temporary exhibits; special events.
Hours & Admission Prices: Daily 10am. Adults $18, seniors 65 & over $17, children 5-11 $15. Operation Spy: adults 12 & over $14. Operation Spy & Main Exhibit: adults 12 & over $25. Closed New Year's Day; Thanksgiving; Christmas. ♿
Membership: Spy $65; Spy Partners $95; Spy Family $175; Spy Master $275.

KENILWORTH PARK AND AQUATIC GARDENS, 1550 Anacostia Ave., N.E., Washington, DC 20019-2028. Mailing Address: 1900 Anacostia Dr., S.E., Washington, DC 20020-6722. Tel.: 202-426-6905. Fax: 202-426-5991.
Web Site: www.nps.gov/keaq/index.htm
Founded: 1882.

Key Personnel: Park Supt., Gayle Hazelwood; Park Ranger, Kate Bucco; Gardener Foreman, Doug Rowley.
Personnel Profile: Full-Time Paid 10; Part-Time Volunteers 32.
Governing Authority: federal. Parent Institution: National Capital Parks-East, National Park Service, U.S. Dept. of Interior. Tax-exempt.
Aquatic Garden.
Collections: water plants; tropical & hardy water lilies & lotus.
Research Fields: aquatic ecosystems; tidal marshes; urban river water quality.
Facilities: visitor center.
Activities: guided tours; self-guided walks; birding.
Publications: brochure.
Hours & Admission Prices: Grounds: daily 8-dusk. Aquatic Garden: daily 7-4. Closed New Year's Day; Thanksgiving; Christmas. ♿
Attendance: 75,000 (estimated)

THE KREEGER MUSEUM, (M), 2401 Foxhall Rd., N.W., Washington, DC 20007-1149. Tel.: 202-337-3050. Fax: 202-337-3051.
E-mail: publicrelations@kreegermuseum.org
Web Site: www.kreegermuseum.org
Founded: 1994.
Key Personnel: Dir., Judy A. Greenberg; Financial Officer, Basil Arendse; Head Mktg., Molly McMullen; Head Education, Erich Keel; Visitor Svcs. Mgr., Antonia Valdes Dapena.
Personnel Profile: Full-Time Paid 7; Full-Time Volunteers 1; Part-Time Paid 2; Part-Time Volunteers 80; Interns 2.
Governing Authority: private; nonprofit foundation. Parent Institution: The David Lloyd Kreeger Foundation. Tax-exempt: 501(c)(3).
Art Museum: housed in the former residence of Carmen & David Lloyd Kreeger; designed by Philip Johnson.
Collections: museum designed by the renowned architect Philip Johnson, showcases the Kreeger's personal art collection of 19th- & 20th-century painting and sculpture, as well as traditional African art. Artists featured: Monet, Picasso, Braque, Miro, Kandinsky, Dubuffet, Moore.
Research Fields: 19th- & 20th-century European, American, African & Indian art.
Facilities: library.
Activities: docent tours; artists talks; concerts; intern program; master class programs; lecture series; guest speakers; community educational projects; story time for preschool aged children; children's workshops; panel discussions; temporary exhibitions.
Publications: Gilliam in 3D; Remembering the Present; William Christenberry: Changing Landscape - The Source Revisited; The True Artist is an Amazing Luminous Fountain; The Kreeger Museum Catalogue; Kendell Buster: Inventory of Imagined Places; Tim Rollins & KOS, The Creation; Gene Davis: Interval; The Houses of Philip Johnson; Philip Johnson: Architecture As Art.
Hours & Admission Prices: Sept.-July Sat. 10-4. Tours: Tues.-Fri. 10:30 & 1:30 by appointment. Adults $10, seniors 65 & over and student $7; discounts to museum professionals, ICOM & AAM members; members no charge. Closed New Year's Day; Martin Luther King Jr. Day; Presidents' Day; Memorial Day; Independence Day; Labor Day; Columbus Day; Thanksgiving & day after; Christmas Eve & Day.
Attendance: 10,000 (estimated)
Membership: Friend $100; Sustainer $250; Foxhall Circle $500; Patron's Circle $1,000; Director's Circle $5,000; Founder's Circle $10,000; Kreeger Circle $25,000.

LIBRARY OF CONGRESS, 101 Independence Ave., S.E., Washington, DC 20540-0002. Mailing Address: Library of Congress, Washington, DC 20540-0001. Tel.: 202-707-5000 (general) & 8000 (visitor information). Fax: 202-707-1714.
E-mail: libofc@loc.gov
Web Site: www.loc.gov
Founded: 1800.
Key Personnel: Librarian of Congress, James H. Billington; C.O.O., Jo Ann Jenkins; Assoc. Librarian Strategic Initiatives, Laura Campbell; Assoc. Librarian, Library Svcs., Deanna Marcum; Dir. Congressional Research Svcs., Daniel P. Mulhollan; Dir. American Folklife Center, Peggy Bulger; Acting Law Librarian, Donna Scheeder; Register of Copyrights, Copyright Office, Marybeth Peters; Interpretive Programs Officer, William Jacobs; Dir. Publishing Office, W. Ralph Eubanks; Dir. Preservation, Dianne Van Der Reyden; Chief Prints & Photographs Div., Helen Zinkham; Chief, Packard Campus of the Natl. Audiovisual Conservation Center, Patrick Loughney; Head Retail Mktg. Unit, Anna S. Lee.
Governing Authority: federal. Parent Institution: United States Congress.Tax-exempt: 501(c)(3) Title 26, U.S. Code.
National library with collections housed in the Thomas Jefferson Building, constructed between 1889-1897; the James Madison Memorial Building, constructed between 1970-1981; & the 1939 John Adams Building.
Collections: over 138,000,000 item library of books & pamphlets including Americana, written in 470 languages; bound worldwide newspapers; manuscripts relating to American history & civilization; maps & views; classical to modern music recordings; photographic negatives, prints & slides, including those made by Mathew Brady; prints & drawings, including the Joseph Pennell collection of Whistleriana; motion-picture reels, including Fred Ott's Sneeze, the first to be copyrighted; microfilm; braille volumes; talking books on records & magnetic tape; caricatures & cartoons; early American history; creating the United States.
Research Fields: research in fields pertaining to legislation for members & committees of Congress; legal research in domestic & international copyright; research for other government agencies & preparation of resulting analyses bibliographies, etc.; technology to improve reading materials for blind & handicapped persons; technology in the preservation of all types of library materials; application of automation to library operations; cataloging, classification & standards for all types of library materials; digitization of library materials.
Facilities: library; Jefferson building: 20,000 sq. ft. exhibit space; reading rooms; auditorium; James Madison Memorial Building: 64-seat projection room. Selected LC publications, facsimiles, music & spoken recordings & other library-related items for sale.
Activities: guided tours; audio tours for major exhibitions; video orientation; national preservation program; lectures & symposia; concerts; dramatic & poetry readings; broadcasts by educational stations in U.S.; inter-library loan; exhibitions, many available for travel to other institutions; permanent exhibitions; coordination of folklife activities for a national constituency; a national program through a network of cooperating libraries to provide reading materials to blind & physically handicapped readers; the digitization of the library's collections of unique American materials.
Publications: biweekly, Library of Congress Information Bulletin; monthly, Calendar of Events in the Library of Congress to addresses within 100 miles of Washington; quarterly, Folklife Center News.
Hours & Admission Prices: Exhibition Halls: Mon.-Fri. 8:30am-9:30pm, Sat. 8:30am-6:30pm. General Reading Rooms: call 201-707-6400 for various hours. No charge. Closed all federal government holidays. ♿
Attendance: 1,600,000 (estimated)

LIBRARY OF THE SUPREME COUNCIL, 33 DEGREES, 1733 16th St., N.W., Washington, DC 20009-3199. Tel.: 202-232-3579. Fax: 202-464-0487.
E-mail: jsansbury@srmason-sj.org
Web Site: www.srmason-sj.org
Founded: 1888.
Key Personnel: Sovereign Grand Commander, Ronald A. Seale; Cur. & Librarian, Joan Sansbury; Archivist & Historian, Art de Hoyos; Asst. Librarian, Larissa Watkins; Dir. Special Programs, Heather Calloway.
Personnel Profile: Full-Time Paid 3; Part-Time Paid 1.
Governing Authority: Ancient & Accepted Scottish Rite of Freemasonry, Supreme Council.
Masonic & Americanism Museum.
Collections: medals; jewels; patents; art objects; manuscripts; flag carried to the moon by Buzz Aldrin; masonic book collection; J. Edgar Hoover Collection; Lincoln Collection; Robert Burns Collection; Burl Ives Collection, 1997.
Research Fields: freemasonry; general collection of old non-fiction.
Facilities: 200,000-vol. library of books relating to Masons; religion; history; biography available for research by request, accompanied by Masonic or educational institution reference.
Activities: guided tours.
Publications: magazine, The Scottish Rite Journal.
Hours & Admission Prices: Mon.-Thurs. 8-5. No charge; donations accepted. Closed federal holidays. ♿
Attendance: 3,600 (estimated)

LILLIAN AND ALBERT SMALL JEWISH MUSEUM, (M), 701 3rd St., N.W., Washington, DC 20001-2624. Mailing Address: 701 4th St., N.W., Washington, DC 20001-2607. Tel.: 202-789-0900. Fax: 202-789-0485.
E-mail: info@jhsgw.org
Web Site: www.jhsgw.org
Founded: 1975.
Key Personnel: Exec. Dir., Laura C. Apelbaum; Pres. (V), Stuart Zuckerman.
Personnel Profile: Full-Time Paid 7; Part-Time Paid 1; Part-Time Volunteers 5; Interns 3.
Governing Authority: private; nonprofit organization. Parent Institution: Jewish Historical Society of Greater Washington. Tax-exempt.
Historical Society Museum: housed in the 1876 Old Adas Israel Synagogue, the first structure built in Washington, DC as a Jewish house of worship.
Collections: letters, photographs, documents, records, scrapbooks, diaries, objects & related artifacts which document the Jewish people & the Jewish communities of greater Washington, DC; artifacts related to the origins or

historical development of customs, beliefs, activities or material culture as practiced by Jews of the greater Washington, DC area.
Research Fields: communal & social life of Jews in Washington area.
Facilities: 50-vol. library on American Jewish history & Jewish art; 500 sq. ft. exhibit space.
Activities: docent program; guided tours; lectures; temporary & traveling exhibitions; video programs of exhibits; internships. Annual Event: meeting of the Jewish Historical Society of Greater Washington.
Publications: newsletter, Third Street Echoes; annual journal, The Record.
Hours & Admission Prices: Sun.-Thurs. by appointment. No charge; donations accepted. Closed major Jewish holidays.
Attendance: 3,000 (estimated)
Membership: Individual $36; Family $54; Donor $100; Patron $150; Sponsor $300; Guardian $1,000; Historian $1,800; Heritage $2,500; Legacy $5,000; Benefactor $10,000; President's Club $25,000.

LINCOLN MEMORIAL, W. Potomac Park @ 23rd St., N.W., Washington, DC 20024. Mailing Address: National Mall & Memorial Parks, 900 Ohio Dr., S.W., Washington, DC 20242-0002. Tel.: 202-426-6841.
Web Site: www.nps.org/linc
Key Personnel: Supervisory Park Ranger, Toni Braxton
Historic Building: built in 1917 to honor the 16th president of the United States, Abraham Lincoln.
Collections: 19 ft. marble statue of President Abraham Lincoln; 2 murals; inscriptions of his 2nd inaugural address & the Gettysburg Address.
Facilities: Books & gift items for sale.
Hours & Admission Prices: Park Rangers on duty: daily 9:30am-11:30pm. No charge.

LINDA K. JORDAN GALLERY, GALLAUDET UNIVERSITY, Washburn Arts Bldg. #127, 800 Florida Ave., N.E., Washington, DC 20002-3600. Tel.: 202-651-5480. Fax: 202-651-5618.
Founded: 2006.
Key Personnel: Chm., Dr. Marguerite Glass
Art Gallery.
Collections: photographs; paintings; drawings; ceramics.
Hours & Admission Prices: Call for hours.

THE LUTHER W. BRADY ART GALLERY, 805 21st St., N.W., Washington, DC 20052-0029. Tel.: 202-994-1525. Fax: 202-994-1632.
E-mail: bradyart@gwu.edu
Web Site: www.gwu.edu/~bradyart
Formerly: The George Washington University Art Gallery
Founded: 1966.
Key Personnel: Dir. University Art Galleries, Lenore D. Miller; Asst. Cur., Olivia Kohler.
Personnel Profile: Full-Time Paid 2; Part-Time Paid 5; Interns 1.
Governing Authority: university. Parent Institution: George Washington University. Tax-exempt: 101(6).
Art Gallery.
Collections: paintings; sculpture; graphic arts & photographs from 18th, 19th & 20th centuries, with special emphasis on American art; W. Lloyd Wright Collection of Washingtoniana; works pertaining to George Washington; U. S. Grant Collection of photographs, documents, prints & newspaper clippings; collection of prints by Joseph Pennell; pre-Columbian artifacts.
Research Fields: art history; documentation of permanent collections.
Facilities: study room.
Activities: graduate & undergraduate programs in museum problems; intermuseum loan & temporary exhibitions; lectures; visual literacy programs for children.
Publications: exhibition catalogs.
Hours & Admission Prices: Tues.-Fri. 10-5. No charge. Closed during school breaks, summer & national holidays. ♿
Attendance: 3,500 (estimated)

MADAME TUSSAUDS WASHINGTON D.C., 1001 F St., Washington, DC 20004. Tel.: 888-923-0334.
E-mail: info@madametussaudsdc.com
Wax Museum.
Collections: wax figures including historical & political figures, musicians, sports stars, world leaders, & Hollywood stars.
Activities: special events.
Hours & Admission Prices: mid-April to early Sept. Sun.-Fri. 10-6, Sat. 10-8; early Sept. to mid-April Sun.-Thurs. 10-6, Fri.-Sat. 10-8. Adults $20, seniors 60 & over $18, children 3-12 $15; discounts to groups; children 2 & under no charge.

MARIAN KOSHLAND SCIENCE MUSEUM, 6th & E Sts., N.W., Washington, DC 20001. Mailing Address: The National Academies, 500 5th St., N.W., Washington, DC 20001-2736. Tel.: 202-334-1201. Fax: 202-334-1548.
E-mail: ksm@nas.edu
Web Site: www.koshlandsciencemuseum.org
Founded: 2004.
Key Personnel: Dir., Patrice Legro; Chm., Donald Kennedy; Operations & Museum Shop Mgr., Johann Yurgen; Financial & Administrative Officer, Lisa Alston; Deputy Dir., Erika Shugart; Exhibits & Programs, Sapna Batish; Communications Officer, Annie Drinkard.
Personnel Profile: Full-Time Paid 8; Part-Time Paid 1; Part-Time Volunteers 22.
Governing Authority: private; nonprofit organization. Parent Institution: National Academy of Sciences. Subsidiary Institution: National Academies, Washington, DC. Tax-exempt: 501(c)(3).
Science Museum.
Collections: science; engineering; medicine.
Research Fields: by requests from Congress or private organizations: agriculture; behavioral & social science; chemistry; earth science; education; health & medicine; physics; technology.
Facilities: 5,000 sq. ft. exhibit space.
Activities: docent program; films; guided tours; lectures; participatory & traveling exhibitions; public programs; field trip program.
Hours & Admission Prices: Wed.-Mon. 10-6. Adults $5, senior citizens, military & students $3. Closed New Year's Day; Thanksgiving; Christmas. ♿
Attendance: 30,000 (accurate)

MARY MCLEOD BETHUNE COUNCIL HOUSE NATIONAL HISTORIC SITE, 1318 Vermont Ave., N.W., Washington, DC 20005-3607. Tel.: 202-673-2402. Fax: 202-673-2414.
Web Site: www.nps.gov/mamc
Founded: 1979.
Key Personnel: Supt., Gayle Hazelwood; Deputy Supt., Alex Romero; Park Mgr., Robert Parker; Archivist, Kenneth Chandler; Park Ranger, Joy Kinard; Park Guide, Kenvi Phillips; Park Guide, Toi Barnes; Museum Shop Mgr., Margaret Coleman.
Personnel Profile: Full-Time Paid 5; Part-Time Volunteers 1; Interns 26.
Governing Authority: nonprofit. Parent Institution: National Park Service. Tax-exempt.
Historic House.
Collections: photographs; communication artifacts; archives.
Research Fields: Mary McLeod Bethune; African American Women's History.
Facilities: archives.
Activities: programs.
Hours & Admission Prices: Mon.-Sat. 9-5. No charge, donations accepted. Closed New Year's Day; Thanksgiving; Christmas.
Attendance: 8,631 (accurate)

MERIDIAN INTERNATIONAL CENTER, (M), 1624 Crescent Pl., N.W., Washington, DC 20009-4004. Mailing Address: 1630 Crescent Pl., N.W., Washington, DC 20009-4004. Tel.: 202-667-6800. Fax: 202-939-5512.
E-mail: tkharvey@meridian.org
Web Site: www.meridian.org
Formerly: Meridian International Center-Cafritz Galleries
Founded: 2009.
Key Personnel: Pres. & C.E.O., Ambassador Stuart W. Holliday; Chm. (V), Jim Blanchard; Vice Pres. for the Arts, Dr. Curtis Sandberg; Dir. Exhibitions, Terry Harvey.
Personnel Profile: Full-Time Paid 100; Part-Time Volunteers 25; Interns 2.
Governing Authority: nonprofit organization. Tax-exempt: 501(c)(3).
International Arts & Cultural Center.
Collections: French furnishings; over-door paintings; Mortlake tapestry; portraits. Historic Buildings: 1911, White-Meyer House; 1921, Meridian House, both designed by John Russell Pope.
Research Fields: intercultural exchange programs.
Facilities: library; reception & conference facilities; formal gardens; 5,000 sq. ft. exhibit space.
Activities: organizes, presents & circulates international art & historical exhibitions; lectures; films; concerts; center provides programs, orientation & services to international visitors & diplomats.
Publications: newsletter; exhibition catalogues.
Hours & Admission Prices: Wed.-Sun. 2-5. No charge; donations accepted. Closed major holidays. ♿
Attendance: 25,000 (estimated)
Membership: Individual $100; Family $175.

MID-ATLANTIC ASSOCIATION OF MUSEUMS, (M), 2300 N St., N.W. Ste. 710, Washington, DC 20037-1263. Tel.: 202-452-8040. Fax: 202-833-3636.
E-mail: director@midatlanticmuseums.org
Web Site: www.midatlanticmuseums.org
Founded: 1947.
Key Personnel: Exec. Dir., Graham Hauck; Pres. (V), Kim Fortney; Treas., Carole Wharton.
Personnel Profile: Full-Time Paid 1; Full-Time Volunteers 2; Part-Time Paid 2; Part-Time Volunteers 1; Interns 1.
Governing Authority: nonprofit organization. Tax-exempt.
Museum Service Organization.
Activities: training programs for professional museum workers; workshops. Organization Sponsors: Annual three-day conference.
Publications: quarterly newsletter, Courier; professional publication, Forum; occasional paper series.
Hours & Admission Prices: Mon.-Fri. 9-5. Closed national holidays.
Attendance: 400
Membership: Retired & Student $25; Individual & Individual Affiliate $40; Supporting $60; Contributing $100; Institutional Affiliate $250. Institutional Membership: under 50,000 $50; 50,000-100,000 $75; 100,000-250,000 $100; 250,000-500,000 $150; 500,000-1,000,000 $200; 1,000,000-2,500,000 $250; over 2,500,000 $300.

MILLENNIUM ARTS CENTER, 65 "I" St., S.W., Washington, DC 20024. Mailing Address: 1330 Mass Ave., N.W., Washington, DC 20005-4155. Tel.: 202-479-2572. Fax: 202-479-0946.
E-mail: info@millenniumartscenter.org
Web Site: milleniumartscenter.org
Key Personnel: Dir., William Wooby
Art Center.
Collections: works by national & international artists.
Activities: performances; educational programs; special events.
Hours & Admission Prices: Wed.-Sat. 11-5; other times by appointment.

NATIONAL ACADEMY OF SCIENCES, (M), 2101 Constitution Ave., N.W., Washington, DC 20418-0006. Mailing Address: 500 Fifth St., N.W., NAS 269, Washington, DC 20001-2736. Tel.: 202-334-2436. Fax: 202-334-1690.
E-mail: cpnas@nas.edu
Web Site: www.nationalacademies.org/arts
Founded: 1980.
Key Personnel: Dir., Mr. J.D. Talasek; Sr. Program Assoc., Ms. Alana Quinn.
Personnel Profile: Full-Time Paid 2.
Governing Authority: private; nonprofit organization. Tax-exempt: 501(c)(3).
Art & Science Museum.
Collections: art & science; engineering & medicine; paintings; photographs; decorative arts.
Facilities: 650-seat auditorium.
Activities: concerts; guided tours; lectures; temporary & traveling exhibitions. Annual Events: Artist Receptions and Lectures; Classical and Jazz Concerts.
Publications: biannual calendar of events, Exhibitions and Cultural Programs Calendar.
Hours & Admission Prices: Mon.-Fri. 9-5. No charge. Closed New Year's Day; Martin Luther King Jr. Day; Presidents' Day; Memorial Day; Independence Day; Labor Day; Thanksgiving & day after; Christmas Eve & Day.
Attendance: 5,000 (estimated)

*** NATIONAL AIR AND SPACE MUSEUM, (M),** Sixth St. & Independence Ave., S.W., Washington, DC 20560-0001. Mailing Address: Office Communications, MRC 321, P.O. Box 37012, Washington, DC 20013-7012. Tel.: 202-633-2370 & 1000. Fax: 202-633-8174. TDD: 202-357-1505.
Web Site: www.nasm.si.edu
Founded: 1946.
Key Personnel: Dir., John R. Dailey; Chm. Center for Earth & Planetary Studies, John Grant; Chm. Space History Dept., Michael Neufeld; Chm. Aeronautics Dept., F. Robert van der Linden; Assoc. Dir. Collections & Research, Peter Jakab; Assoc. Dir. Planning Programs, John Benton; Asst. Dir. Communications, Claire Brown; Dir. Devel., Monecia Taylor; Asst. Dir. Special Events, Linda Hicks; Museum Shop Mgr., Frank Byrne.
Personnel Profile: Full-Time Paid 235; Part-Time Paid 28; Part-Time Volunteers 131; Interns 19.
Governing Authority: federal; nonprofit corporation. Parent Institution: Smithsonian Institution. Subsidiary Institutions: Steven F. Udvar-Hazy Center. Tax-exempt: 501(c)(3) & 170(b)(1)(A).
Aeronautics & Space Museum.
Collections: aeronautical & astronautical items; air & space craft; instruments; equipment; art; uniforms; personal memorabilia; manuscripts.
Research Fields: aviation & aerospace history; flight science technology; earth & planetary studies; contributions of flight to the economy; pioneering efforts of early aviators & astronauts.
Facilities: 40,000-vol. library of material on history of flight & aerospace development; aircraft & space vehicle photographic collection available for inter-library loan, for use on premises & by request; planetarium; theater; reading room; education resource center; cafeteria. Model airplane & space kits, books & other museum-related items for sale.
Activities: guided tours; lectures; films; gallery talks; daily science demonstrations; formally organized education programs for children; docent program or council; inter-museum loan, permanent, temporary & traveling exhibitions.
Publications: periodic series, Studies in Air & Space; Famous Aircraft of the National Air & Space Museum; exhibition booklets; quarterly calendars; monographs; commemorative books published on special anniversaries; leaflets; catalogs; e-newsletters; official guide to the National Air and Space Museum.
Hours & Admission Prices: Daily 10-5:30. No charge; donations accepted. Closed Christmas. ♿
Attendance: 8,179,218 (accurate)
Membership: Wright Flyer $35; Spirit of St. Louis $50; Glamorous Glennis $100; Friendship $250; Eagle $500; Enterprise $1,000; Voyager Solar System Spacecraft $2,500; North American X-15 $5,000.

THE NATIONAL AQUARIUM IN WASHINGTON DC, Department of Commerce Bldg., Rm. B-077, 14th St. & Constitution Ave., Washington, DC 20230-0001. Tel.: 202-482-2826 & 2825. Fax: 202-482-4946.
E-mail: info@nationalaquarium.com
Web Site: www.nationalaquarium.org
Founded: 1873.
Key Personnel: C.E.O., Robert A. Ramin; Chm. (V), Peter Welles; Mgr. Mktg., Celia Lourens; Museum Shop Mgr., Tammy Ward.
Personnel Profile: Full-Time Paid 9; Part-Time Paid 5.
Governing Authority: society; nonprofit. Subsidiary Institution: National Aquarium in Baltimore. Tax-exempt.
Aquarium & Fishery Museum.
Collections: approx. 260 species of freshwater & marine animals; 1,700 specimens.
Facilities: Museum-related items for sale.
Activities: educational programs for local school groups.
Publications: quarterly newsletter.
Hours & Admission Prices: Daily 9-5. Adults $7, seniors & military $6, children 2-10 $3.50; discounts to groups; members no charge. Closed Thanksgiving; Christmas. ♿
Attendance: 200,000 (estimated)
Membership: Individual $25; Couple $40; Family $55; Family Plus $75; Lionfish $150.

NATIONAL ARCHIVES EXPERIENCE, 700 Pennsylvania Ave., N.W., Washington, DC 20408-0002. Mailing Address: Museum Programs, National Archives Bldg., 700 Pennsylvania Ave., Washington, DC 20408-0001. Tel.: 202-357-5000. Fax: 202-357-5926.
E-mail: museumprograms@nara.gov
Web Site: www.archives.gov/nae
Formerly: National Archives and Records Administration
Founded: 1934.
Key Personnel: Acting Archivist, Adrienn Thomas; Exec. Dir. Foundation, Thora Colot; Exec. Dir. Museum Programs, Marvin Pinkert; Dir. Mktg. & Admin., Frank Cordes; Dir. Retail Operations, Chris Derderian.
Governing Authority: federal. Maintains National Archives Exhibition Hall, Washington, DC; National Archives at College Park, MD; Franklin D. Roosevelt Library, Hyde Park, NY; Harry S. Truman Library, Independence, MO; Herbert Hoover Library; West Branch, IA; Dwight D. Eisenhower Library, Abilene, KS; John F. Kennedy Library, Boston, MA; Lyndon B. Johnson Library, Austin, TX; Gerald Ford Library, Ann Arbor, MI; Gerald Ford Museum, Grand Rapids, MI; Jimmy Carter Library, Atlanta, GA; Ronald Reagan Library, Simi Valley, CA; Bush Library, College Station, TX; William J. Clinton Presidential Materials Project, Little Rock, AR; 13 Regional Centers. Tax-exempt.
History Museum: housed in the National Archives building; built 1931-1935.
Collections: federal government archives of the United States from 1774 to present including the original Declaration of Independence, the Constitution & the Bill of Rights; photographic records, sound recordings; motion pictures; maps; charts; aerial photographs; textual records; electronic records; the 1297 Magna Carta.
Research Fields: U.S. history & foreign relations.
Facilities: reference library, research rooms; 294-seat theatre; classrooms; snack bar; learning center. Gift items for sale.

Activities: guided tours; conferences; lectures; films; formally organized education programs for children, adults, undergraduate & graduate students; inter-museum loans; permanent, temporary & traveling exhibitions.
Publications: leaflets; facsimiles of documents; exhibit catalogs; quarterly journal, Prologue; annual reports; finding aids; curriculum materials, documentary publications; archives administration publications; presidential library publications; records management handbooks; publications of the Federal Register; monthly calendar of events.
Hours & Admission Prices: Winter: daily 10-5:30; Spring & Summer: daily 10-7. No charge. Research Rooms: Mon. & Wed. 8:45-5, Tues. & Thurs.-Fri. 8:45-9, Sat. 8:45-4:45. Closed Thanksgiving; Christmas. ♿
Attendance: 1,000,000 (estimated)

NATIONAL BUILDING MUSEUM, 401 F St., N.W., Washington, DC 20001-2637. Tel.: 202-272-2448, ext. 3458. Fax: 202-272-2564.
E-mail: jweber@nbm.org
Web Site: www.nbm.org
Founded: 1980.
Key Personnel: Exec. Dir., Chase Rynd; Vice Pres. Finance & Admin., Betsy May-Salazar; Sr. Vice Pres. Special Projects, G. Martin Moeller, Jr.; Vice Pres. Devel., Shar Taylor; Vice Pres. Education, Scott Kratz; Dir. Exhibitions & Collections, Cathy Crane Frankel; Vice Pres. Mktg. & Communication and Govt. Affairs, Bryna Lipper; Dir. Visitor Svcs., Kristi Cotner; Dir. Special Events, Chris Frame; Museum Shop Mgr., Michael Higdon; Exec. Asst., Emily Daniels; Controller, Diane Beckham.
Personnel Profile: Full-Time Paid 30; Part-Time Paid 54; Part-Time Volunteers 120; Interns 6.
Governing Authority: nonprofit organization. Tax-exempt: 501(c)(3).
Architecture Museum.
Collections: local history & culture; manuscripts; drawings; blueprints; models; photographs; books; artifacts.
Major Exhibits: House of Cars, 11/09-7/11/10.
Research Fields: architectural history; architectural projects & trends; design field; urban planning; engineering; construction technology; material technology.
Facilities: bakery. Museum-related items for sale.
Activities: guided tours; lectures; films; docent program; intern programs for undergraduate & graduate students; day trips/tours; traveling exhibitions; family & outreach programs; rental facilities; youth education.
Publications: monthly calendar of programs; exhibition catalogs; books; annual report.
Hours & Admission Prices: Mon.-Sat. 10-5, Sun. 11-5. Suggested Donation: $5. Closed New Year's Day; Thanksgiving; Christmas. ♿
Attendance: 398,550 (accurate)
Membership: Student w/ID $30; Senior $40; Individual $50; Dual $70; Family $80; Builder Friend $125; Builder Fellow $250; Builder Contributor $500; Corinthian Friend $1,000-$2,500; Corinthian Fellow $2,500-$5,000; Corinthian Contributor $5,000-$10,000; Corinthian Patron $10,000 & up.

NATIONAL CHILDREN'S MUSEUM, (M), (I), 955 L'Enfant Plaza North, S.W., Ste. 5100, Washington, DC 20024-2103. Tel.: 202-675-4120. Fax: 202-675-4140.
E-mail: info@ncm.museum
Web Site: www.ncm.museum
Formerly: Capital Children's Museum
Founded: 1974.
Key Personnel: Pres., Kathy Dwyer Southern; Chm. (V), S. Ross Hechinger.
Personnel Profile: Full-Time Paid 26.
Governing Authority: nonprofit organization. Tax-exempt: 501(c)(3).
Children's Museum.
Collections: hands-on exhibits.
Publications: quarterly newsletter.
Hours & Admission Prices: Closed until 2013. ♿

* **NATIONAL GALLERY OF ART, (M), (I),** 4th St. & Constitution Ave., N.W., Washington, DC 20565-0001. Mailing Address: 2000B S. Club Dr., Landover, MD 20785. Tel.: 202-737-4215. TDD: 202-842-6176.
Web Site: www.nga.gov
Founded: 1937.
Key Personnel: Dir., Earl A. Powell, III; Pres. (V), Victoria P. Sant; Chm. (V), John Wilmerding; Deputy Dir. & Chief Cur., Franklin W. Kelly; Admin., Darrell R. Willson; Treas., James E. Duff; Sec. Gen. Counsel, Elizabeth A. Croog; Exec. Officer, Devel. & External Affairs, Joseph J. Krakora; Dean, Center for Advanced Study in Visual Arts, Elizabeth Cropper; Cur. Northern Baroque Paintings, Arthur K. Wheelock, Jr.; Cur. Italian Paintings, David Alan Brown; Cur. Northern Renaissance Paintings, John Hand; Cur. Early European Sculpture, Alison Luchs; Cur. Modern & Head, Contemporary Art, Harry Cooper; Sr. Cur. & Head Dept. Photographs, Sarah Greenough; Cur. Special Projects in Modern Art, Ruth Fine; A.W. Mellon Sr. Cur. Prints & Drawings, Andrew C. Robison; Cur. & Head Old Master Prints, Peter Parshall; Cur. & Head Old Master Drawings, Margaret Morgan Grasselli; Cur. & Head Modern Prints & Drawings, Judith Brodie; Cur. & Head Dept., Sculpture & Decorative Arts, Mary Levkoff; Cur. & Head Dept., American & British Paintings, Nancy Anderson; Chief of Conservation, Mervin Richard; Sr. Conservator & Head Painting Conservation, Sarah Fisher; Head Paper Conservation, Kimberly Schenck; Sr. Conservator & Head Object Conservation, Shelley Sturman; Sr. Conservator & Head Textile Conservation, Julia Burke; Head Scientific Research Dept., E. Rene de la Rie; Exec. Librarian, Neal T. Turtell; Chief Library Image Collections, Gregory P.J. Most; Chief Exhibitions, D. Dodge Thompson; Sr. Cur. & Chief Design, Mark Leithauser; Head Education, Lynn Russell; Head Film Programs, Margaret Parsons; Editor in Chief, Publishing Office, Judy Metro; Chief Registrar, Sally Freitag; Chief Imaging & Visual Svcs., Alan Newman; Head Loans & Natl. Lending Svcs., Stephanie T. Belt; Head Digital Imaging Svcs., Robert Grove; Head Visual Svcs., Barbara Bernard; Chief Protocol & Special Events, Carol W. Kelley; Chief Devel. & Corporate Rels. Officer, Christine M. Myers; Chief Press & Public Information Officer, Deborah Ziska; Personnel Officer, Michael Bloom; Chief Horticulture Svcs., Cynthia Kaufmann; Deputy Chief Admin. Visitor Svcs., Elizabeth Thomas; Chief Gallery Archives, Maygene Daniels; Chief Gallery Shop Div., Ysabel L. Lightner; Special Projects Officer, Pamela Jenkinson.
Personnel Profile: Full-Time Paid 1,055; Part-Time Paid 10; Part-Time Volunteers 513; Interns 20.
Governing Authority: independent establishment of the U.S.; nonprofit organization. Tax-exempt: 170(b)(1)(A); 501(c)(3).
Art Museum.
Collections: European & American painting, sculpture, decorative arts & graphic arts from 13th-21st century; European Old Master paintings; French, Spanish, Italian, American & British 18th- & 19th-century paintings; sculpture from late Middle Ages to present; Renaissance bronzes; Chinese porcelains; medals & plaquettes; modern & contemporary art.
Research Fields: art history; conservation; Center for Advanced Studies in the Visual Arts.
Facilities: library; photographic archives; four restaurants; sculpture garden; education studio. Museum-related items for sale.
Activities: guided tours; illustrated lectures; films; gallery talks; concerts; family activities; docent program; inter-museum loan, permanent & temporary exhibitions; loan teaching services.
Publications: exhibition catalogs; illustrated collection catalogs; catalogue raisones on specific artists; Studies in the History of Art, which includes Conservation Research, symposium papers, and anniversary volumes; the CASVA (Center for Advanced Study in the Visual Arts) annual report; Kress Foundation Studies in the History of European Art; Andrew W. Mellon Lectures in the Fine Arts; National Gallery of Art Bulletin; National Gallery of Art; annual report; bimonthly calendar of events; quarterly film calendar; quarterly, NGA Kids.
Hours & Admission Prices: Mon.-Sat. 10-5, Sun. 11-6. No charge. ♿
Attendance: 4,500,000 (estimated)
Membership: Circle: Contributing $1,000; Supporting $2,500; Sustaining $5,000; Patron $10,000.

NATIONAL GEOGRAPHIC MUSEUM, (M), National Geographic Society, 1145 17th St., N.W., Washington, DC 20036-4707. Tel.: 202-857-7455, 7588 & 7000. Fax: 202-857-5864. TDD: 202-857-7198.
Web Site: www.ngmuseum.org
Founded: 1930.
Key Personnel: C.E.O. & Pres., John M. Fahey, Jr.; Chm., Gilbert M. Grosvenor; Exec. Vice Pres., Terry Garcia; Vice Pres. & C.O.O. Mission Programs, Sarah Laskin; Vice Pres. NG Live, Explorers Hall Museum & Dir. Museum, Gregory McGruder; Dir. Museum & Special Events, Susan E.S. Norton; Mgr. Administration, Nancy Beers Parsons; Mgr. Special Events, Rita Dooley; Dir. Exhibits, Richard McWalters; Dir. Libraries, Susan Fifer Canby.
Personnel Profile: Full-Time Paid 11; Part-Time Paid 1; Interns 1.
Governing Authority: nonprofit organization. Parent Institution: National Geographic Society. Tax-exempt: 501(c)(3).
Science Museum & Geography Center.
Collections: paleontology; aeronautics; natural history; anthropology; meteorology; archaeology; marine, land & space explorations; astronomy; Indian artifacts; archives; photographs; geography; maps.
Major Exhibits: Terra Cotta Warriors, 11/19/09-3/10; Art of National Geographic, 4/10-8/10; Design for the Other 90% (T), 4/28/10-9/6/10; Geckos-Tails to Toepads, 9/24/10-1/9/11; Wild Music (T), 10/10-1/2/11.
Research Fields: scientific disciplines.
Facilities: 65,000-vol. library of geography oriented books available for research on premises; reading room; auditorium. All National Geographic Society publications & maps for sale.

Activities: films; TV programs; permanent & temporary exhibitions; lectures; geography education program; cultural programs.
Publications: National Geographic Society publications; videos; filmstrips; maps.
Hours & Admission Prices: Mon.-Sat. & holidays 9-5, Sun. 10-5. No charge; donations accepted. Closed Christmas. ♿
Attendance: 244,227 (accurate)

*** NATIONAL MUSEUM OF AFRICAN ART, SMITHSONIAN INSTITUTION, (M),** 950 Independence Ave., S.W., Washington, DC 20560-0006. Mailing Address: P.O. Box 37012, NMAfA MRC 708, Washington, DC 20013-7012. Tel.: 202-633-4600. Fax: 202-357-4879. TDD: 202-357-4814.
E-mail: nmafaweb@si.edu
Web Site: www.si.edu/nmafa
Founded: 1964.
Key Personnel: Assoc. Dir. Administrative Operations & Facility, Alan Knezevich; Interim Asst. Dir. External Affairs, Dale Mott; Assoc. Dir. Devel., Anita Henri; Cur., Bryna Freyer; Cur., Christine Mullen Kreamer; Asst. Cur., Andrea Nicolls; Cur. Photographic Archives, Amy Staples; Chief Conservator, Stephen Mellor; Registrar, Julie Haifley; Librarian, Janet Stanley.
Personnel Profile: Full-Time Paid 45.
Governing Authority: nonprofit. Bureau of the Smithsonian Institution, Washington, DC. Tax-exempt: 501(c)(3).
Art Museum.
Collections: 7,000 objects of African art, wood, metal, ceramic, ivory & fiber; Eliot Elisofon Photographic Archives of 200,000 color slides, 78,000 black & white negatives & 140,000 ft. of motion picture film & videotape on African art & culture.
Research Fields: African art & culture.
Facilities: 20,000-vol. library of books and periodicals on African arts & culture, providing reference & information service by appointment to the public, by telephone, or by mail; a branch of the Smithsonian Institution Libraries. Books, exhibition catalogues & museum-related items for sale.
Activities: guided tours; lectures; credit courses in African art for area universities; varied public program department: residency fellowship program administered by the Smithsonian Institution makes research facilities available for advanced scholarly research; outreach programs; demonstrations; performances; films permanent exhibits.
Publications: exhibition catalogs; pamphlets; audiovisual material; instructional material for use by elementary & secondary school teachers.
Hours & Admission Prices: Daily 10-5:30. No charge. Closed Christmas. ♿
Attendance: 300,000 (estimated)
Membership: Patron $500; Advocate $1,000; Benefactor $2,500; Collector's Society $5,000; Director's Circle $10,000.

*** NATIONAL MUSEUM OF AMERICAN HISTORY, (M),** 1400 Constitution Ave., N.W., Washington, DC 20560-0001. Mailing Address: P.O. Box 37012, Washington, DC 20013-7012. Tel.: 202-633-1000. Fax: 202-633-8053. TTY: 202-633-5285.
Web Site: americanhistory.si.edu
Founded: 1964.
Key Personnel: Dir., Brent D. Glass; Chm. (V), John Rogers; Assoc. Dir. Curatorial, David K. Allison; Assoc. Dir. Management & Administration, Janice G. Lilja; Assoc. Dir. Capital Campaign & External Affairs, Maggie Webster; Assoc. Dir., Judith Gradwohl; Dir. Public Affairs, Melinda Machado; Museum Shop Mgr., Kathy Sklar.
Personnel Profile: Full-Time Paid 200; Part-Time Volunteers 545; Interns 150.
Governing Authority: bureau of the Smithsonian Institution, Washington, DC, a nonprofit federally chartered corporation. Tax-exempt: 501(c)(3) & 170(b)(1)(A).
American History & Technology Museum.
Collections: agriculture & natural resources; armed forces history; ceramics & glass items; community life items; costumes & dress; computers; domestic life; electricity & modern physics; engineering & industry; graphic arts; medical sciences; musical instruments; numismatics; photographic history; physical sciences & mathematics; political history; textiles; transportation; popular culture.
Research Fields: agriculture; architecture; archives; astronomy; business history; ceramics; furnishings; costumes; folk; general; glass; graphic arts; industrial; marine; medical; military; music; manufacturing; mining; photography; political; presidential; preservation methods; naval; numismatic; philatelic; science; technology; textile; transportation.
Facilities: 165,000-vol. library of books & periodicals on American history, technology, science, culture & the military, available for inter-library loan & use on premises; separate laboratory operation; 271-seat auditorium; restaurant. Museum-related items for sale.
Activities: guided tours; lectures; films; gallery talks; concerts; docent program; formally organized education programs for undergraduate & graduate college students; permanent, temporary & traveling exhibitions; hands-on exhibits.
Publications: catalogs; guidebooks; scholarly publications; monographs; pamphlets.
Hours & Admission Prices: Daily 10-5:30. No charge; donations accepted. Closed Christmas. ♿
Attendance: 3,000,000 (estimated)

NATIONAL MUSEUM OF AMERICAN JEWISH MILITARY HISTORY, 1811 R St., N.W., Washington, DC 20009-1603. Tel.: 202-265-6280. Fax: 202-462-3192.
E-mail: nmajmh@nmajmh.org
Web Site: www.nmajmh.org
Founded: 1958.
Key Personnel: Natl. Exec. Dir., Col. Herb Rosenbleeth; Pres. (V), David L. Magidson; Dir. Operations, Larry Richardson.
Personnel Profile: Full-Time Paid 35; Full-Time Volunteers 1; Part-Time Paid 1; Part-Time Volunteers 15; Interns 10.
Governing Authority: nonprofit. Parent Institution: Jewish War Veterans of the U.S.A. Tax-exempt: 501(c)(3).
National Museum of American Jewish Military History.
Collections: photos; uniforms; firearms; medals; personal papers; documents; history of JWV organization.
Research Fields: Jewish individuals who participated in the U.S. military.
Facilities: 2,550-vol. library; classrooms; 25,000 sq. ft. exhibit space; rental facilities.
Activities: guided tours; lectures; films; temporary & traveling exhibitions.
Publications: quarterly newsletter; calendar; catalogues, GIs Remember: Liberating the Concentration Camps, Centennial - 100 Years of the JWV; An American, A Sailor and A Jew: The Life and Career of Uriah Phillips Levy USN (1792-1862); Women in the Military: A Jewish Perspective.
Hours & Admission Prices: Mon.-Fri. 9-5, Sun. by appointment only;. No charge; donations accepted. Closed federal & Jewish holidays. ♿
Attendance: 3,000 (estimated)
Membership: Individual $25; Family $36; Patron $50; Sustaining $75; Guardian $100; Life $1,000.

NATIONAL MUSEUM OF CRIME & PUNISHMENT, 575 7th St., N.W., Washington, DC 20004-1607. Tel.: 202-393-1099.
E-mail: media@crimemuseum.org
Web Site: www.crimemuseum.org/
Founded: 2008.
Key Personnel: Dir., Janine Vaccarello.
Personnel Profile: Full-Time Paid 29; Part-Time Paid 7.
Governing Authority: Parent Institution: Attraction Concepts.
History Museum.
Collections: history of crime & punishment; photographs; crime solving & fighting.
Facilities: Museum-related items for sale.
Activities: high-speed police chase simulators; simulated FBI shooting range; police lineup; child fingerprinting; autopsy table.
Publications: newsletter, American Police Beat.
Hours & Admission Prices: March 20-Aug. daily 9-9; Sept.-March 19 daily 10-8. Adults 12-59 $19.95, seniors 60 & over, military, law enforcement $16.95, children 5-11 $14.95; members & children under 5 no charge. Closed New Year's Day; Thanksgiving; Christmas. ♿
Membership: Individual $75; Couple $115; Family $190.

NATIONAL MUSEUM OF HEALTH AND MEDICINE, 6900 Georgia Ave. & Elder St., N.W., Washington, DC 20307-0001. Mailing Address: 6825 16th St., N.W., Washington, DC 20306-0003. Tel.: 202-782-2200. Fax: 202-782-3573.
E-mail: nmhminfo@afip.osd.mil
Web Site: www.nmhm.washingtondc.museum
Formerly: Army Medical Museum
Founded: 1862.
Key Personnel: Dir., Adrianne Noe, Ph.D.; Admin. & Museum Shop Mgr., Donna White; Collections Mgr. Historical Collections, Alan Hawk; Archivist, Michael Rhode; Asst. Archivist, Kathleen Stocker; Collection Mgr., Neuroanatomical, Archie Fobbs; Public Programs Mgr., Andrea Schierkolk; Public Affairs Officer, Tim Clarke, Jr.; Exhibits Mgr., Steve Hill; Tour Program Mgr., Gwen Nelmes; Registrar, Beth Eubanks.
Personnel Profile: Full-Time Paid 30; Part-Time Volunteers 16; Interns 4.
Governing Authority: federal. Dept. of Defense. Parent Institution: Armed Forces Institute of Pathology. Tax-exempt.
Medical History Museum.
Collections: anatomy; anthropology; forensic sciences; history & sociology of medical science & technology; materia medica; medical research; military medicine; parasitology; pathology; paleopathology; public health.

Research Fields: anatomy; anthropology; ethnomedicine & ethnopharmacology; forensic sciences; history & sociology of medical science & technology; medical research; military medicine; parasitology; pathology; paleopathology; public health & health education.
Facilities: research library of books & periodicals on medicine, medical research & public health; archives; facilities for visiting scholars; 110-seat auditorium.
Activities: permanent & special exhibits; education programs for children, students, adults; volunteer docent program; guided tours.
Publications: quarterly newsletter; pamphlet on exhibits; catalogues; Billings Microscope Collection, 2nd Ed.; Computer print-out lists of collections; monthly electronic newsletter.
Hours & Admission Prices: Daily 10-5:30. No charge; donations accepted. Closed Christmas. ♿

* **NATIONAL MUSEUM OF NATURAL HISTORY, (M),** 10th St. & Constitution Ave., N.W., Washington, DC 20560-0001. Mailing Address: P.O. Box 37012, Washington, DC 20013-7012. Tel.: 202-357-1300. Fax: 202-357-4779. TTY: 202-357-1729.
E-mail: info@si.edu
Web Site: www.mnh.si.edu
Founded: 1846.
Key Personnel: Acting Dir., Dr. Cristian Samper; Chm. (V), Roger W. Sant; Staff Asst. & Bd. Liaison, Donna Attaway-Dancy; Assoc. Dir. Public Programs, Elizabeth Duggal; Assoc. Dir. Research & Collections, Hans-Dieter Sues; Assoc. Dir. Operations, Susan Fruchter; Sr. Biological Diversity Advisor, Dr. Scott Miller; Chm. Dept. Paleobiology, Dr. Conrad Labandeira; Chm. Dept. Anthropology, Dr. Daniel Rogers; Chm. Dept. Entomology, Dr. Terry Erwin; Chm. Dept. Botany, Dr. Warren Wagner; Chm. Dept. Invertebrate Zoology, Stephen D. Cairns; Deputy Assoc. Dir & Special Projects, Jerry Conlon; Public Affairs Mgr., Randall Kremer; Museum Shop Mgr., Betty Stolarun.
Personnel Profile: Full-Time Paid 470; Part-Time Paid 85; Part-Time Volunteers 902; Interns 200.
Governing Authority: nonprofit corporation. Parent Institution: Smithsonian Institution, Washington, DC. Tax-exempt: 501(c)(3) & 170(b)(1)(A).
Natural History Museum.
Collections: anthropology; invertebrate & vertebrate zoology; entomology; botany; fossils; minerals, rocks, gems & meteorites.
Research Fields: anthropology; botany; paleobiology, vertebrate & invertebrate zoology; entomology; mineral sciences including volcanology, meteorites; biodiversity.
Facilities: 250,000-vol. library of books on natural history; restaurant; theater. Books & other museum-related items for sale.
Activities: education programs for children, students & adults; docent program; lectures; films; tours; hands-on exhibits; electronic classroom.
Publications: irregular series, Contributions to: Anthropology, Botany, Earth Sciences, Marine Sciences, Paleobiology, Zoology, Handbook of North American Indians; Quest; calendar of events; annual report; AnthroNotes.
Hours & Admission Prices: Winter: daily 10-5:30; Spring & Summer: call for hours. No charge. Closed Christmas. ♿
Attendance: 5,542,000 (accurate)

NATIONAL MUSEUM OF THE AMERICAN INDIAN, 4th St. and Independence Ave., S.W., National Mall, Washington, DC 20024. Tel.: 202-633-1000.
Web Site: www.americanindian.si.edu
Key Personnel: Dir., Kevin Grover; Dir. Pub. Affairs, Eileen Maxwell.
Governing Authority: Parent Institution: Smithsonian Institution.
Native American Museum.
Collections: Native American history & culture; wood & stone carvings; masks; painted & quilled hides; clothing & feathered bonnets; pottery & basketry; 18th-century materials from Great Lakes region; C.B. Moore collection; Navajo weavings; works on paper & canvas; Caribbean archaeological objects; ceramics from Costa Rica, Central Mexico & Peru; carved jade from the Olmec & Maya peoples; textiles & gold from Andean cultures; funerary, religious & ceremonial objects; films.
Facilities: theater; cafe; resource center. Museum-related items for sale.
Activities: films; theater; special events.
Publications: magazine, American Indian.
Hours & Admission Prices: Daily 10-5:30; groups of 10 or more by appointment. No charge. Closed Christmas. ♿
Membership: Golden Prairie Circle $25; Riverbed Circle $35; Everglades Circle $50; Sky Meadows Circle $100; Boundary Waters $250; Desert Sands Circle $500; Director's Council of Friends $1,000, $2,500, $5,000.

* **NATIONAL MUSEUM OF THE UNITED STATES NAVY, (M),** 805 Kidder Breese St., S.E., Washington, DC 20374-5060. Tel.: 202-433-4882. Fax: 202-433-8200. TDD: 202-433-4882.
E-mail: karin.hill@navy.mil
Web Site: www.history.navy.mil
Founded: 1961.
Key Personnel: Dir., Kim Nielsen; Cur., Dr. Edward M. Furgol; Dir. Public Programs, Karin Hill; Museum Shop Mgr., Andre Dyson; Security, James Creasman.
Personnel Profile: Full-Time Paid 11; Part-Time Paid 5; Part-Time Volunteers 18; Interns 10.
Governing Authority: federal. Parent Institution: Dept. of the Navy. Subsidiary Institution: Naval Historical Center. Tax-exempt.
Naval History Museum: housed in the former Breech Mechanism Shop of the old Naval Gun Factory.
Collections: documents; paintings; weapons; photographs; medals; decorations; memorabilia relating to naval personalities; awards; ship models; swords; ordnance; maps; prints; uniforms; flags; scientific instruments; Destroyer Barry (DD-933); 19th & 20th-century guns, cannons submarines, naval artifacts.
Research Fields: U.S. Naval history.
Activities: guided tours; permanent & temporary exhibits pertaining to naval history; educational program; lecture series; musical programs. Museum Sponsors: US Navy in the Korean War exhibit.
Publications: quarterly newsletter, Naval Historical Foundation, Pull Together.
Hours & Admission Prices: April to Labor Day Mon.-Fri. 9-5, Sat.-Sun. 10-5; Sept.-May Mon.-Fri. 9-4, Sat.-Sun. 10-5. No charge; donations accepted. Closed New Year's Day; Thanksgiving; Christmas Eve & Day. ♿
Attendance: 215,000 (accurate)
Membership: Active $25; Sustaining $50; Associate $75; Fellowship $100; Life $500.

NATIONAL MUSEUM OF WOMEN IN THE ARTS, 1250 New York Ave., N.W., Washington, DC 20005-3970. Tel.: 202-783-5000. Fax: 202-393-3235.
Web Site: www.nmwa.org
Founded: 1981.
Key Personnel: C.E.O. & Dir., Dr. Susan Fisher Sterling; Chm. (V), Wilhelmina Cole Holladay; Pres. (V), Mary V. Mochary; Cur. Education, Deborah Gaston; Sr. Cur., Jordana Pomeroy; Registrar, Alan Francisco; Dir. Library & Research Center, Jason Stieber; Dir. Membership, Ruth White; Dir. Communications & Mktg., Michelle Cragle; Dir. National Programs, Ilene Gutman; Dir. Retail & Wholesale Operations, Lynda Marks.
Personnel Profile: Full-Time Paid 50; Full-Time Volunteers 129; Part-Time Paid 54; Part-Time Volunteers 175; Interns 20.
Governing Authority: nonprofit organization. Tax-exempt: 501(c)(3).
Art Museum: housed in 1908 second Renaissance revival style structure.
Collections: works by over 800 women artists including paintings, sculptures, pottery, prints, drawings, books, silver, special collections including over 18,500 files on women artists, Irene Rice Pereira's library, 19th & 20th century bookplates & 650 artists' books & photography. Art from the Renaissance to the present.
Research Fields: women artists' history & contributions.
Facilities: 18,500-vol. library & research center of books, monographs, exhibition catalogs, & periodicals pertaining to women artists; 200-seat auditorium; 500-seat banquet hall with kitchen; cafe; classrooms. Bookstore with museum-related items for sale.
Activities: guided tours; lectures; films; concerts; symposia; member previews; organized education programs; docent program; loan, temporary, & traveling exhibitions.
Publications: quarterly news magazine; catalogs & brochures.
Hours & Admission Prices: Museum: Mon.-Sat. 10-5, Sun. 12-5. Adults $10, seniors & students w/ID $8; discounts to AAM members; children under 18 & members no charge. Library: by appointment. Closed New Year's Day; Thanksgiving; Christmas. ♿
Attendance: 126,637 (accurate)
Membership: Individual $40; Supporter $50; Dual $70; Family $75; Friend $100; Business & Professional Women's Council & Sustainer $250; Benefactor $500; President's Club $1,000; Library Fellows $1,200; Museum Council $2,000. Corporate Memberships: Supporter $5,000; Patron $10,000; Fellow $15,000; Leader $25,000; Benefactor $50,000.

NATIONAL PARK SERVICE, 1201 Eye St., N.W. 2265, Washington, DC 20005-5905. Mailing Address: 1849 C St., N.W., (2202), Washington, DC 20240-0001. Tel.: 202-354-2000. Fax: 202-371-6757.
E-mail: ronald_wilson@nps.gov
Web Site: www.nps.gov/history/museum/
Founded: 1916.
Key Personnel: Chief Cur., Ronald C. Wilson; Museum Registrar, Kathleen

Byrne; Museum Cur., Joan Bacharach; Sr. Cur. Natural History, Greg McDonald; Archivist, John W. Roberts; Information Management Specialist, Lynn Black.
Governing Authority: federal. Parent Institution: National Park Service, U.S. Dept. of the Interior, 18th & C Sts., N.W., Washington, DC 20240. Tax-exempt.
National Park Service.
Collections: archeology; ethnology; history; archives; biology; geology; paleontology; 124 million objects, specimens & archival documents in 365 park units.
Research Fields: all areas of collections.
Facilities: library of reference works in museology, history, technology & decorative arts available for use on premises.
Activities: collections management policy & training for National Park System.
Publications: NPS Museum Handbook; Conserve-O-Grams; ANCS & User Manual.
Hours & Admission Prices: Offices: Mon.-Fri. 7:45-4:15. Closed national holidays. ♿

NATIONAL PARK SERVICE - PEIRCE BARN, 5200 Glover Rd., N.W., Washington, DC 20015. Tel.: 202-895-6222. Fax: 202-895-6230.
E-mail: ricardo_perez@nps.gov
Web Site: www.nps.gov/rocr
Formerly: Peirce Mill and Peirce Barn
Founded: 1936.
Key Personnel: Park Supt., Adrienne Coleman; Park Ranger, Ricardo Perez.
Personnel Profile: Full-Time Paid 1.
Governing Authority: federal. Administered by U.S. Dept. of the Interior, National Park Service, Rock Creek Park.
Historic Building: c.1820 Grist Mill & Peirce Mill located in Rock Creek Park.
Collections: water paddle wheel; Peirce Mill machinery; furniture; records; library. Peirce Barn: The Mills of Rock Creek Valley & The Peirce Estate.
Research Fields: local history.
Facilities: 250-vol. library of books on mill operation, construction & history, and Northwest Washington, D.C. history.
Activities: guided tours; demonstrations; curriculum-based education programs for adults & children.
Publications: brochure, Peirce Mill.
Hours & Admission Prices: Mill: temporarily closed for renovation. Barn: Sat. 12-4. Research Facility: by appointment only. Closed federal holidays.

* **NATIONAL PORTRAIT GALLERY, (M),** Eighth & F Sts., N.W., Donald W. Reynolds Center for American Art & Portraiture, Washington, DC 20001. Mailing Address: P.O. Box 37012, Victor Bldg., Ste. 410, MRC-973, Washington, DC 20013-7012. Tel.: 202-633-8300. Fax: 202-633-8243. TDD: 202-633-8229.
E-mail: npgweb@si.edu
Web Site: www.npg.si.edu
Founded: 1962.
Key Personnel: Dir., Martin Sullivan; Deputy Dir., Carolyn Carr; Assoc. Dir. Operations, Nik Apostolides; Administrative Officer, Annetta McRae; Chm., Mallory Walker; Librarian, Cecilia Chin; Conservator, Cindy Lou Molnar; Historian, Sidney Hart; Facilities Mgr., Andrew Smith; Dir. Education Program, Rebecca Kasemeyer; Dir. Devel., Sherri Weil; Cur. of Painting & Sculpture, Ellen Miles; Exhibitions & Collections Management Dir., Beverly Cox; Cur. Prints & Drawings, Wendy Wick Reaves; Cur. Photographs, Ann Shumard; Photographer, Mark Gulezian; Chief, Design & Production, Nello Marconi; Keeper, Center for Electronic & Outreach Svcs., Linda Thrift; Assoc. Registrar Collections, John McMahon; Assoc. Registrar Exhibitions, Molly Grimsley; Publications Officer, Dru Dowdy; Museum Shop Mgr., Myra Cones.
Personnel Profile: Full-Time Paid 61; Part-Time Paid 3; Interns 55.
Governing Authority: nonprofit organization. Parent Institution: Smithsonian Institution. Tax-exempt: 501 (c)(3) & 170(b)(1)(A).
Art & History Museum: housed in c.1840, former U.S. Patent Office building.
Collections: portraits of men & women who have made notable contributions to the history & development of the United States.
Major Exhibits: Outwin Boochever Portrait Competition 2009, 11/09-8/22/10; Portraiture Now: Communities, 11/6/09-7/5/10; One Life: Echoes of Elvis, 1/8/10-8/29/10; From FDR to Obama: Presidents on TIME, 2/12/10-9/6/10; One Life: Katharine Graham, 10/10-5/20/11; Hide/Seek: Difference and Desire in American Portraiture, 10/22/10-2/6/11; Elvis at 21, 10/30/10-1/23/11.
Research Fields: American portraiture; biography; history.
Facilities: 60,000-vol. library of American art, history & biography available for inter-library loan & to qualified persons; field research station; reading room; 346-seat auditorium; classrooms; restaurant. Books, catalogs, reproductions & other museum related items for sale.
Activities: guided tours; lectures; films; gallery talks; formally organized educational programs; docent program; inter-museum loan, permanent & temporary exhibitions.
Publications: catalogs of special exhibitions & various segments of the permanent collection.
Hours & Admission Prices: Daily 11:30-7. No charge. Closed Christmas. ♿
Attendance: 100,000
Membership: National Portrait Gallery & Smithsonian American Art Museum: Associate $50; Sponsor $150; Sustainer $250; Patron $500.

NATIONAL POSTAL MUSEUM, SMITHSONIAN INSTITUTION, 2 Massachusetts Ave., N.E., Washington, DC 20002. Tel.: 202-633-5555. Fax: 202-633-9393. TTY: 202-633-9849.
E-mail: npm@npm.si.edu
Web Site: www.postalmuseum.si.edu.
Founded: 1993.
Key Personnel: Dir., Allen Kane.
Personnel Profile: Full-Time Paid 39; Part-Time Paid 1; Part-Time Volunteers 50; Interns 2.
Governing Authority: federal. Parent Institution: Smithsonian Institution, 900 Jefferson Dr., S.W., Washington, D.C. 20560. Tax-exempt: 501(c)(3).
Postal History Museum: housed in 1914 Old City Post Office Building.
Collections: stamp collection; postal history material pre-dating stamps; postal vehicles; mailboxes; meters; greeting cards; letters & stationery; barcode readings.
Research Fields: postal history; Philately.
Facilities: Museum shop & stamp store.
Activities: hands-on activities; lectures; films.
Publications: books, Reaching Rural America; Great American Post Offices; Mail on the Move; Motorized Mail; Horse-Drawn Mail; Illustrated Guide to the National Postal Museum; Owney: The Mascot of the Railway Service; quarterly member newsletter, En Route.
Hours & Admission Prices: Daily 10-5:30. No charge; donations accepted. Closed Christmas. ♿
Attendance: 500,000 (accurate)
Membership: Annual $25.

NATIONAL SOCIETY OF THE CHILDREN OF THE AMERICAN REVOLUTION MUSEUM, 1776 D St., N.W., Rm. 224, Washington, DC 20006-5303. Tel.: 202-638-3153. Fax: 202-737-3162.
E-mail: hq@nscar.org
Web Site: www.nscar.org
Founded: 1895.
Key Personnel: Sr. National Pres., Lois Schmidt.
Governing Authority: society. Affiliated with the National Society, Daughters of the American Revolution. Tax-exempt: 501(c)(3).
History Museum.
Collections: decorative & applied arts.
Activities: guided tours; inter-museum loan, permanent & temporary exhibitions.
Hours & Admission Prices: Mon.-Fri. 8:30-4, Sat. 9-5. No charge; donations accepted.

NATIONAL TRUST FOR HISTORIC PRESERVATION, (M), 1785 Massachusetts Ave., N.W., Washington, DC 20036-2117. Tel.: 202-588-6000. Fax: 202-588-6038.
E-mail: feedback@nthp.org
Web Site: www.preservationnation.org
Founded: 1949.
Key Personnel: Vice Pres. Stewardship of Historic Sites, Jim Vaughan; Administrative Dir., Stewardship of Historic Sites, Lyn Moriarity; Dir. Museum Collections, Terri Anderson; Dir. Interpretation & Education, Max Van Balgooy; Graham Gund Architect of the Natl. Trust, Barbara Campagna, FAIA, LEED AP; Assoc. Architect, Elizabeth Milnarik; Sr. Archaeologist, Lynne Lewis.
Governing Authority: nonprofit organization. National Trust collection includes 29 historic sites: African Meeting House & Abiel Smith School, Boston, MA; African Meeting House, Nantucket, MA; Belle Grove, Middletown, VA; Brucemore, Cedar Rapids, IA; Chesterwood, Stockbridge, MA; Cliveden, Philadelphia, PA; Cooper-Molera Adobe, Monterey, CA; Decatur House, Washington, DC; Drayton Hall, Charleston, SC; Farnsworth House, Plano, IL; Filoli, Woodside, CA; Frank Lloyd Wright Home & Studio, Oak Park, IL; Frank Lloyd Wright's Pope-Leighey House, Mount Vernon, VA; Frederick C. Robie House, Chicago, IL; Gaylord Building, Lockport, IL; James Madison's Montpelier, Montpelier Station, VA; Kykuit, Tarrytown, NY; Lower East Side Tenement Museum, New York, NY; Lyndhurst, Tarrytown, NY; Oatlands, Leesburg, VA; Shadows-on-the-Teche, New Iberia, LA; Touro Synagogue, Newport, RI; Woodlawn, Mount Vernon, VA; Woodrow Wilson House, Washington, DC; President Lincoln & Soldiers' Home National Monument, Washington, DC; Philip Johnson's Glass House, New Canaan, CT; Villa Finale, San Antonio, TX;

Acoma Sky City, Acoma, NM; Hotel de Paris, Georgetown, CO. Tax-exempt: 501(c)(3).
Historical Society.
Collections: decorative & fine arts; local historic artifacts; documents; archaeological artifacts.
Research Fields: American history & culture.
Activities: tours; educational programs; special events.
Publications: bimonthly magazine, Preservation; bimonthly professional journal, Forum, Preservation Information Series, brochures & pamphlets.
Hours & Admission Prices: See individual listings for their hours & admission fees. ♿
Attendance: 809,204 (accurate)
Membership: Individual $20; Family $24; Contributing $50; Sustaining $100; Participating $250; Donor & Corporate $1,000.

NATIONAL WWII MEMORIAL, 17th St., (between Constitution & Independence Aves.), Washington, DC 20006. Mailing Address: National Park Service, 900 Ohio Dr., S.W., Washington, DC 20242-0002. Tel.: 202-619-7222; 800-639-4992.
E-mail: wwiicustserv@americancustomercare.com
Web Site: www.wwiimemorial.com
Military Memorial.
Collections: World War II history.
Activities: special events.
Hours & Admission Prices: Daily 24 hrs. Rangers on duty to answer questions daily 9:30-11:30.

NATIONAL ZOOLOGICAL PARK, SMITHSONIAN INSTITUTION, 3001 Connecticut Ave., N.W., Washington, DC 20008-2598. Tel.: 202-633-4800. Fax: 202-673-4607.
Web Site: www.si.edu/natzoo
Founded: 1889.
Key Personnel: Acting Dir. & Assoc. Dir. Conservation and Science, Dr. Steven Montfort; Chm. (V), Clark Bunting; Assoc. Dir. Communications, Pamela Baker-Masson; Assoc. Dir. Animal Care, Dr. Don Moore; Assoc. Dir. Education, Joseph Sacco; Chief Management Svcs. Office, Alexander Beim; Project Exec., Debra Nauta-Rodriguez; Sr. Nutritionist, Mike Maslanka; Assoc. Dir. Exhibits & Park Management, Charles Fillah; Head Veterinarian, Dr. Suzan Murray; Head Pathologist, Dr. Timothy Walsh; Chief of Police, Russell Walkowich; Safety Mgr., Donald Williams; Exec. Dir. Friends of the National Zoo (FONZ), Robert Lamb.
Personnel Profile: Full-Time Paid 247; Part-Time Volunteers 1,086.
Governing Authority: federal, nonprofit. Parent Institution: Smithsonian Institution. Tax-exempt: 501(c)(3) & 170(b)(1)(A).
Zoological Park.
Collections: mammals: 131 species, 1,337 individuals; birds: 152 species, 971 individuals; reptiles: 72 species, 482 individuals; amphibians: 19 species, 285 individuals; invertebrates: 110 species; 3,945 individuals.
Research Fields: wildlife ecology & management; animal behavior, breeding, husbandry & conservation; exotic animal medicine & pathology; zoo education; comparative zoology, nutrition, reproductive physiology.
Facilities: 7,000-vol. library of zoological material available for inter-library loan & on premises to qualified scholars; 300-seat auditorium; classrooms; resource room; 163-acre zoological park.
Activities: curriculum guides & teacher resources; cooperative teaching programs with local medical & veterinary school; study grants for students & internships for veterinarians; zoo society, Friends of the National Zoo; series of symposia, seminars & lectures; research fellowships, wildlife management training for officials of developing countries.
Publications: Zoogoer Magazine; Smithsonian New Zoo; Self-Guides for Teachers; How to Zoo: An Educator's Guide to the Smithsonian National Zoo.
Hours & Admission Prices: Grounds: April-Oct. daily 6-8; Nov.-March daily 6-6. Buildings: April-Oct. daily 10-6; Nov.-April daily 10-4:30. No charge; donations accepted. Parking fee $20 maximum. Closed Christmas. ♿
Attendance: 2,600,000 (estimated)
Membership: Senior Citizen $35; Individual $40; Household $55.

NAVAL HISTORY AND HERITAGE COMMAND, Washington Navy Yard, Navy Art Collection, Bldg. 67, 805 Kidder Breese, S.E., Washington, DC 20374-5060. Tel.: 202-433-3815.
Formerly: Naval Historical Center
History Museum.
Collections: U.S. naval history; over 15,000 paintings, prints, drawings, & sculpture.
Hours & Admission Prices: Mon.-Fri. 9-3:30. Closed Federal holidays.

NEWSEUM, 555 Pennsylvania Ave., N.W., Washington, DC 20001-2114. Tel.: 888-639-7386.
E-mail: info@newseum.org
Web Site: www.newseum.org
Founded: 1997.
Key Personnel: C.E.O., Charles Overby; Exec. Dir., Joe Urschel; Pres., Ken Paulson; Vice Pres. Broadcasting & Programs, Paul Sparrow; Sr. Vice Pres. Devel., Mary Kay Blake; Vice Pres. Mktg., Collections & Exhibits, Susan Bennett; Vice Pres. Operations, Security & Visitor Svcs., James Thompson.
Personnel Profile: Full-Time Paid 218; Part-Time Volunteers 103.
Governing Authority: private foundation; nonprofit. Parent Institution: Freedom Forum. Tax-exempt: 501(c)(3).
Interactive Museum.
Collections: newspapers; photographs; media technology artifacts & personal artifacts related to major news figures; history of news development & technology.
Major Exhibits: Manhunt: Chasing Lincoln's Killer, 11/09-2/10; G-Men and Journalists: Top News Stories of the FBI's First Century, 11/09-12/10.
Research Fields: news history; people; technology; techniques.
Hours & Admission Prices: Daily 9-5. Adults $20, seniors $18, youth $13; discounts to AAM members & groups. Closed New Year's Day; Thanksgiving; Christmas. ♿
Membership: Individual $75; Dual $125; Family $175.

* **THE OCTAGON MUSEUM,** 1799 New York Ave., N.W., Washington, DC 20006-5207. Tel.: 202-638-3221. Fax: 202-626-7420.
E-mail: info@theoctagon.org
Web Site: www.archfoundation.org/octagon/
Founded: 1942.
Key Personnel: Dir. Museum & Collections, Sherry C. Birk; Asst. to Dir., Edward Bates.
Personnel Profile: Full-Time Paid 2; Part-Time Paid 5; Part-Time Volunteers 40.
Governing Authority: nonprofit organization. Parent Institution: The American Architectural Foundation. Tax-exempt.
Architecture Museum & Historic House: 1799-1801 Federal townhouse built for Colonel John Tayloe III, based on designs by Dr. William Thornton, served as first temporary White House during the winter of 1814-1815 for President James & Dolley Madison; the Treaty of Ghent was signed there, ending the War of 1812.
Collections: original architectural drawings & photographs; changing exhibits of architecture & allied arts; archaeological artifacts; decorative arts of the period 1800-1828.
Research Fields: architecture; decorative & design arts; Washington history.
Facilities: Gift shop with exhibition catalogs & books for sale.
Activities: guided tours; lectures; inter-museum loan; temporary exhibitions.
Publications: exhibit catalogues; books; research series focusing on the Federal Period through catalogues & exhibitions.
Hours & Admission Prices: Closed for renovation. Call for information.
Attendance: 36,000 (estimated)
Membership: Individual Friend $35; Family & Dual Friend $65; Director's Circle $100; President's Circle $365; Octagon Society $1,000; 1799 Society $5,000.

THE OLD STONE HOUSE, 3051 M St., N.W. (Georgetown), Washington, DC 20007-3702. Mailing Address: 3545 Williamsburg Lane, Washington, DC 20008-1207. Tel.: 202-426-6851. Fax: 202-895-6230. TDD: 202-426-0125.
Web Site: www.nps.gov/olst
Founded: 1950.
Key Personnel: Asst. Park Supt., Cynthia Cox; Park Ranger, Ron Harvey.
Personnel Profile: Full-Time Paid 3; Part-Time Paid 1; Part-Time Volunteers 3.
Governing Authority: federal. Administered by U.S. Dept. of the Interior, National Park Service. Tax-exempt.
Historic Building: 1765 pre-Revolutionary building located in the Georgetown area of the District of Columbia.
Collections: 18th-century furniture; glassware; cooking ware; kitchen; gardens.
Research Fields: local history.
Facilities: 250-vol. library of books on crafts & history.
Activities: guided tours; formally organized education programs for children, adults & undergraduate college students; permanent & temporary exhibitions.
Publications: brochure, The Old Stone House.
Hours & Admission Prices: Daily 12-5; groups by appointment. No charge; donations accepted. Closed federal holidays. ♿
Attendance: 70,000 (accurate)

* **THE PHILLIPS COLLECTION, (M),** 1600 21st St., N.W., Washington, DC 20009-1090. Tel.: 202-387-2151, ext. 200. Fax: 202-387-2436.
E-mail: webmaster@phillipscollection.org
Web Site: www.phillipscollection.org

Founded: 1921.
Key Personnel: Dir., Dorothy Kosinski; Chm. Bd. Trustees (V), George Vradenburg; Vice Chm., Linda Lichtenberg Kaplan; Vice Chm., Leo E. Zickler; Chief Cur., Eliza Rathbone; Chief Administrative & Financial Officer, Susan J. Nichols; Assoc. Cur., Elsa Smithgall; Asst. Cur., Sue Behrends Frank; Dir. Budgeting & Reporting, Cheryl Nichols; Assoc. Dir. Center for the Study of Modern Art, Ruth Perlin; Installations Mgr., William Koberg; Dir. Music, Caroline Mousset; Chief Registrar, Joseph Holbach; Librarian, Karen Schneider; Dir. Devel., Barbara Hall; Assoc. Registrar, Sarah Anderson; Mgr. Membership, Jeffrey Petrie; Chief Information Officer, Darci Vanderhoff; Dir. of Education, Suzanne Wright; Dir. Mktg. & Communications, Ann Greer; Dir. Human Resources, Angela Gillespie; Dir. Security & Facilities, Dan Datlow; Museum Shop Mgr., Cathy Wetmiller.
Personnel Profile: Full-Time Paid 75; Part-Time Paid 91; Part-Time Volunteers 70; Interns 8.
Governing Authority: nonprofit organization. Tax-exempt: 501(c)(3).
Art Museum: housed in the former residence of Duncan Phillips family, 1897 Georgian Revival home.
Collections: 19th & 20th-century European & American paintings & sculpture; 2,500 works of art; historic house.
Major Exhibits: Man Ray, African Art and the Modernist Lens, 10/10/09-1/10/10; Georgia O'Keeffe: Abstraction, 2/6/10-5/9/10; Susan Rothenberg, 6/10-9/10.
Research Fields: 19th- & 20th-century European & American art.
Facilities: 9,000-vol. library of books, periodicals & catalogues, available for museum members, scholars & researchers by appointment only; auditorium; classroom; meeting facilities; seminar room. Books, catalogues, reproductions & other museum-related items for sale.
Activities: permanent & temporary exhibitions; guided tours; lectures; parent/child workshops; training programs for Art Educators; school tours; gallery talks. Dupont-Kalorama Museums Consortium: Museum Walk Weekend in June; introductory tours; Artful Evenings; Sunday Concerts.
Publications: books, brochures; catalogs of special exhibitions & loan exhibitions; member magazine.
Hours & Admission Prices: Tues.-Wed. & Fri.-Sat. 10-5, Thurs. 10-8:30, Sun. 11-6. Concerts: Oct.-May Sun. 4pm. Admission prices vary. Closed Federal holidays except Veterans Day. ♿
Attendance: 150,000 (estimated)
Membership: Individual $60; Dual & Family $100; Contemporary $125 (for younger members); Associate $175; Friend $300; Contributing Friend $600; Supporting Friend $1,000; Patron $2,000; Galley Patron $3,500; Collection Patron $5,000; Chairman's Circle $10,000; Leadership Circle $25,000; Executive Circle $50,000.

POPE JOHN PAUL II CULTURAL CENTER, 3900 Harewood Rd., N.E., Washington, DC 20017-1505. Tel.: 202-635-5400. Fax: 202-635-5411.
E-mail: info@jp2cc.org
Web Site: www.jp2cc.org
Founded: 2001.
Key Personnel: Dir., Rev. Steven Boguslowski, O.P.; Chm. (V), Archbishop Donald Wuerl; Pres. (V), Cardinal Adam Maida; Museum Shop Mgr., Veronica Osborne.
Personnel Profile: Full-Time Paid 23; Part-Time Paid 30; Part-Time Volunteers 3; Interns 2.
Governing Authority: Tax-exempt.
Cultural Center.
Collections: Catholic Church history; Papal & Polish heritage; photographs; paintings; statues; interactive exhibits.
Major Exhibits: Joy to the World - Creches, 11/09-2/10; Love, Hope & Art, 2/10-5/10; Africa Through the Eyes of Pope John Paul II, 5/10-9/10; Hispanic Heritage, 9/10-11/10.
Facilities: chapel; cafe. Museum-related items for sale.
Activities: children's activities; lectures; movies.
Hours & Admission Prices: Tues. & Thurs.-Sat. 10-5, Sun. 12-5. Suggested Donations: families $15, individuals $5, seniors & students $4; discounts to members. Closed Federal holidays. ♿
Attendance: 29,000 (estimated)
Membership: Individual $35.

PRESIDENT LINCOLN'S COTTAGE, Rock Creek Church Rd., N.W., (at Upshur St. N.W.), Washington, DC 20011. Mailing Address: AFRH-W 1315, 3700 N. Capitol St., N.W., Washington, DC 20011-8400. Tel.: 202-829-0436, ext. 31231. Fax: 202-829-0437.
Web Site: www.lincolncottage.org
Founded: 2008.
Key Personnel: Dir., Dr. Frank D. Milligan; Devel., George Rogers; Education, Callie Hawkins; Coord. Devel., Alison Mitchell; Registrar, Katie Derr; Cur., Erin Carlson Mast; Museum Shop Mgr., Jamie Cooper.
Personnel Profile: Full-Time Paid 6; Part-Time Paid 8; Part-Time Volunteers 2; Interns 2.
Governing Authority: private; nonprofit organization. Parent Institution: National Trust for Historic Preservation, Washington, DC. Tax-exempt: 501(c)(3).
Historic House: housed in the summer home of Lincoln and his family during his presidency.
Collections: Lincoln history; sculpture; prints; period furnishings.
Research Fields: house; diaries; personal artifacts.
Facilities: library; educational facilities; 25-seat theater. Museum-related items for sale.
Activities: formal education programs; guided tours; lectures; permanent, loan & temporary exhibitions; public programs.
Publications: quarterly newsletter, President Lincoln's Cottage News.
Hours & Admission Prices: Mon.-Sat. 9:30-4:30, Sun. 11:30-5:30. Adults $12, students 6-12 $5; discounts to members, military & groups; children under 6 no charge. Closed New Year's Day; Thanksgiving; Christmas.
Membership: Individual $25; Dual $50; Family $100; Sponsor $250; Presidential Guard $500; Lincoln Cabinet $1,000.

PROVISIONS LIBRARY, 1875 Connecticut Ave., N.W., Ste. 1100, Washington, DC 20009-5758. Tel.: 202-299-0460. Fax: 202-232-1651.
E-mail: pl@provisionslibrary.org
Web Site: www.provisionslibrary.org
Founded: 2004.
Key Personnel: Exec. Dir. & Cur., Donald Russell; Chm. (V), Ethelbert Miller.
Personnel Profile: Full-Time Paid 2; Full-Time Volunteers 1; Part-Time Paid 1; Part-Time Volunteers 5; Interns 2.
Governing Authority: private; nonprofit organization. Tax-exempt: 501(c)(3).
Library & Art Museum.
Collections: books & periodicals on global social issues.
Research Fields: global social change.
Facilities: library; educational facilities.
Activities: arts festivals; films; formal education programs for adults & college students; guided tours; workshops; lectures; participatory & traveling exhibits; study clubs; training programs for professional museum workers.
Hours & Admission Prices: Tues.-Fri. 12-5. No charge; donations accepted. ♿
Attendance: 25,000 (estimated)
Membership: Basic $95; Family $150; Sponsor $250 & up.

RAILS-TO-TRAILS CONSERVANCY, The Duke Ellington Building, 2121 Ward Ct., NW, 5th Fl., Washington, DC 20037-1247. Tel.: 202-331-9696. Fax: 202-331-9680.
Web Site: www.railtrails.org
Founded: 1985.
Key Personnel: Pres., Keith Laughlin; Chm. (V), Joe Louis Barrow, Jr.
Personnel Profile: Full-Time Paid 26; Interns 2.
Governing Authority: nonprofit organization. State Chapters: RTC-Michigan, Lansing, MI; RTC-Florida, Tallahassee, FL; RTC-Pennsylvania, Harrisburg, PA; RTC-Ohio, Columbus, OH. Tax-exempt: 501(c)(3).
National Agency.
Collections: files documenting the nation's 1,000 rail-trails open to the public & the 400 in development.
Research Fields: economic benefits to local communities; corridor acquisition & trail development; impacts on adjacent property; technological & legal matters.
Facilities: Publications & trail-related products for sale.
Activities: Annual Events: Regional Seminars; Biennial National Conference.
Publications: quarterly magazine, Rails-To-Trails: A Celebration of Trails and Greenways; annual directory of rail-trails, America's Rail-Trails.
Hours & Admission Prices: Mon.-Fri. 9-5. No charge. Closed federal holidays. ♿
Membership: Individual $18; Family $25; Sustaining $35; Patron $50; Benefactor $100.

RENWICK GALLERY OF THE SMITHSONIAN AMERICAN ART MUSEUM, 1661 Pennsylvania Ave., N.W., (at 17th St.), Washington, DC 20006. Mailing Address: P.O. Box 37012, MRC 510, Washington, DC 20013-7012. Tel.: 202-633-7970. Fax: 202-786-2810.
E-mail: info@saam.si.edu
Web Site: www.americanart.si.edu
Formerly: Renwick Gallery of the National Museum of American Art, Smithsonian Institution
Founded: 1972.
Key Personnel: Dir., Elizabeth Broun; Chief, Renwick Gallery, Robyn Kennedy; Cur., Jane Milosch.
Governing Authority: Dept. of the Smithsonian American Art Museum, a unit of the Smithsonian Institution, Washington, DC, a nonprofit federally chartered corporation. Tax-exempt: 501(c)(3) & 170(b)(1)(A).
American Crafts Museum.
Collections: contemporary American crafts.

Research Fields: contemporary & historical American crafts; fellowship program.
Activities: videos; lectures; concerts; craft demonstrations; temporary exhibitions.
Publications: exhibition catalogues & checklists; pamphlets; triannual calendar of events.
Hours & Admission Prices: Daily 10-5:30. No charge. Closed Christmas. ♿
Attendance: 134,650 (accurate)

ROCK CREEK NATURE CENTER, 5200 Glover Rd., N.W., Washington, DC 20015-1095. Mailing Address: 3545 Williamsburg Lane, N.W., Washington, DC 20008-1207. Tel.: 202-895-6070. Fax: 202-895-6230. TDD: 202-426-6829.
Web Site: www.nps.gov/rocr
Founded: 1960.
Congressional District: 5
Key Personnel: Asst. Park Supt., Cynthia Cox.
Governing Authority: federal. Parent Institution: National Park Service. Subsidiary Institution: Dept. of Interior. Tax-exempt.
Nature Center.
Collections: botany; entomology; geology; zoology; observation bee hive.
Facilities: reference library of books on natural history in all basic categories: Native Americans, astronomy, conservation and the National Parks available for research on premises by request; auditorium; planetarium. Guides, postcards, charts, books & teaching materials for sale.
Activities: guided nature walks; planetarium shows; animal demonstrations; films; educational programs for school, community & special population groups are regularly scheduled & by reservation; touch tables.
Publications: brochure, Rock Creek Park; Rock Creek Park monthly calendar of events.
Hours & Admission Prices: Wed.-Sun. 9-5. No charge; donations accepted. Closed federal holidays. ♿
Attendance: 35,000 (accurate)

SECURITIES AND EXCHANGE COMMISSION HISTORICAL SOCIETY, Washington, DC 20004-2514. Mailing Address: 1101 Pennsylvania Ave., N.W., Ste. 600, Washington, DC 20004-2514. Tel.: 202-756-5015. Fax: 202-756-5014.
E-mail: c.rosati@sechistorical.org
Web Site: www.sechistorical.org
Founded: 2002.
Key Personnel: Exec. Dir., Carla L. Rosati, CFRE
Governing Authority: society; nonprofit organization.
Virtual Museum.
Collections: history of the U.S. Securities and Exchange Commission from 1930s to present; securities industry; photographs; oral histories.
Activities: educational programs.
Hours & Admission Prices: Online access only.

SEWALL-BELMONT HOUSE AND MUSEUM, (M), 144 Constitution Ave., N.E., Washington, DC 20002-5608. Tel.: 202-546-1210. Fax: 202-546-3997.
E-mail: info@sewallbelmont.org
Web Site: www.sewallbelmont.org
Founded: 1929.
Congressional District: 2
Key Personnel: Exec. Dir., Page Harrington; Pres., Dianne Chasen Lipsey; Mktg. Mgr. & Museum Shop Mgr., Becky Gilmore; Collection Mgr., Jennifer Krafchik; Admin. & Devel. Coord., Rachel Sloan; Interpretation & Education Mgr., Abigail Newkirk.
Personnel Profile: Full-Time Paid 5; Part-Time Paid 10; Part-Time Volunteers 20; Interns 3.
Governing Authority: nonprofit organization. Parent Institutions: National Woman's Party; National Capital Park-East, National Park Service, Dept. of Interior. Tax-exempt: 501(c)(3).
Women's History Museum: housed in c.1800 structure later added on, 1800 residence of Albert Gallatin 1801-1813 and 1929-1972 office & home of Alice Paul, founder of the National Woman's Party & author of the ERA.
Collections: fine arts; photographs; banners; scrapbooks; memorabilia of suffrage & equal rights campaign.
Research Fields: Equal Rights & Women's Suffrage Movement.
Facilities: research library; classroom; tented garden.
Activities: guided tours; lectures; films; gallery talks; docent program; permanent exhibitions; volunteer program.
Publications: e-news, Sewall Belmont; Kids Guide to Sewall-Belmont.
Hours & Admission Prices: Wed.-Sun. 12-4. Suggested Donation: $5. Closed holidays.
Attendance: 15,000 (estimated)
Membership: Annual $35.

* **SMITHSONIAN AMERICAN ART MUSEUM, (M),** 8th & F Streets N.W., Washington, DC 20006. Mailing Address: MRC 970, P.O. Box 37012, Washington, DC 20013-7012. Tel.: 202-633-7970. Fax: 202-633-8535.
E-mail: saaminfo@si.edu
Web Site: www.americanart.si.edu
Formerly: National Museum of American Art
Founded: 1829.
Key Personnel: Dir. The Margaret and Terry Stent, Elizabeth Broun; Deputy Dir., Rachel M. Allen; Chief Cur., Eleanor Jones Harvey; Deputy Chief Cur., George Gurney; Consulting Sr. Cur. Film & Media Arts, John G. Hanhardt; Cur. Photography, Toby Jurovics; The James Dicke Cur. Contemporary Art, Joanna Marsh; Sr. Cur., Virginia M. Mecklenburg; Sr. Cur. Graphic Arts, Joann G. Moser; Sr. Cur., William H. Truettner; Special Projects Dir. & Acting Chief Exhibitions, Claire F. Larkin; Devel. Officer, Elaine Webster; Chief External Affairs, Jo Ann Sims; Registrar, Melissa Kroning; Chm. Lunder Educational, Susan Nichols; Chief Publications Office, Theresa J. Slowik; Chief Research & Scholars, Christine Hennessey; Acting Chief Information Technology, Mitzi Harp; Chief Renwick Gallery, Robyn L. Kennedy; Administrative Officer, Doug Wild; Public Affairs Officer, Laura Baptiste; Office of Public Affairs, Amy Hutchins; Mgr. Visitor Svcs., Janet Walker; Exhibition Coord., Marie Elena Amatangelo; Head New Media, Nancy Proctor.
Personnel Profile: Full-Time Paid 113; Part-Time Paid 14; Part-Time Volunteers 96; Interns 36.
Governing Authority: nonprofit federally chartered corporation. Parent Institution: Smithsonian Institution, Washington, DC. Subsidiary Museum: Renwick Gallery, 17th & Pennsylvania Ave. N.W., Washington, DC 20560. Tax-exempt: 501(c)(3) & 170(b)(1)(A).
Art Museum: housed in 1836 Old Patent Office Building.
Collections: American art from the colonial period to the present, including paintings, sculpture, graphics, photography, folk art, and contemporary crafts at the Museum's Renwick Gallery; 19th century landscape painting; 19th & 20th century sculpture; art of the 1930-1940s; African-American art; Latino art; manuscript & clipping files.
Research Fields: all aspects of the collections; American art; active fellowship program.
Facilities: 80,000-vol. library; archives of slides & photographs; restaurant. Museum-related items for sale.
Activities: symposia; lectures; films; concerts; organized education programs; museum intern training; inter-museum loans; permanent, temporary & traveling exhibitions; self-guided & docent-guided tours; family programs; conservation clinics & tours; music performances. Museum Sponsors: monthly jazz performances.
Publications: scholarly journal, American Art; exhibition catalogs; books on American art & artists; pamphlets and booklets on the museum, its collections & programs; quarterly members newsletter & calendar of events.
Hours & Admission Prices: Daily 11:30-7. No charge. Closed Christmas. ♿
Membership: Member $50; Sponsor Member $150; Patron Member $500; Director's Circle $1,500.

SMITHSONIAN INSTITUTION, 1000 Jefferson Dr., S.W., Washington, DC 20560-0009. Mailing Address: 1000 Jefferson Dr., S.W., Rm. 369, MRC033, Washington, DC 20560-0009. Tel.: 202-633-1000. Fax: 202-786-2377. TTY: 202-633-5285.
E-mail: porterj@si.edu
Web Site: www.smithsonian.org
Founded: 1846.
Key Personnel: Acting Under Sec. Science, Scott Miller; Pres., Tom Ott; Dir. Communications & Public Affairs, Evelyn Lieberman.
Personnel Profile: Full-Time Paid 6,250; Part-Time Volunteers 5,500; Interns 900.
Governing Authority: nonprofit independent trust instrumentality of the United States. Museums & Galleries: Anacostia Museum; Cooper-Hewitt, National Design Museum, New York, NY; Freer Gallery of Art; Hirshhorn Museum & Sculpture Garden; National Air & Space Museum; National Museum of African Art; Smithsonian American Art Museum; National Museum of American History; National Museum of the American Indian; National Museum of Natural History; National Portrait Gallery; National Postal Museum; National Zoological Park; Renwick Gallery; Arthur M. Sackler Gallery; Smithsonian Institution Building (the Castle); National Museum of African American History & Culture. Tax-exempt: 501(c)(3) & 170(b)(1)(A).
National Museum.
Collections: natural history specimens; rare books; artworks; science & technology artifacts; rare U.S. & international stamps & coins; U.S. history collections; the national collections (U.S.A.); exotic living animals.
Research Fields: anthropology; biology; ecology; astrophysics; geodesy;

meteoritics; space sciences; botany; oceanography; mineral sciences; conservation of natural resources, wildlife, museum object & library materials; the arts; history; museology; exhibit techniques; international, governmental & social history; molecular systematics entomology; vertebrate & invertebrate zoology; paleobiology; artists' papers; Latino Center; American Indian Cultural Resources Center; African American Center; folk life & cultural studies; conservation; tropical rain forests; marine environments; armed forces history; musical instruments; Native American history; archaeology; design; advances in technology; Asian art; African art; American arts & crafts; transportation history; philately; numismatics; political history; Asian Studies Center.

Facilities: 1.5 million-vol. library system including 40,000 rare books, specializing in natural history; horticulture; conservation science; American ethnology; zoology; anthropology; history of astronautics & aeronautics; astrophysics; American history & culture; history of science & technology; philately; American painting, sculpture, portraiture & biography; decorative arts & design; early works of travel & scientific exploration; volcanism; marine systems; tropical biology; Chesapeake Bay area ecology; museology; available for inter-library loan & for use by qualified scholars. Other research facilities include: Astrophysical Observatory; Environmental Research Center; Tropical Research Institute; the Archives of American Art.

Activities: guided tours; lectures; films; gallery talks; concerts; dance performances; arts festivals; workshops; educational activities; special workshops for teachers; Campus on the Mall courses; docent program; training programs for professional museum workers; inter-museum loans; permanent, temporary & traveling exhibitions; biodiversity & other scientific research; study tours; international exchange of scientific publications; scholarly study; virtual tours on the Web; heritage month celebrations. Museum Sponsors: Spring Kite Festival; Summer Smithsonian Folklife Festival; Smithsonian Craft Show.

Publications: monthly magazine, Smithsonian; bimonthly magazine, Air & Space/Smithsonian; books; serials; exhibition catalogs; guides; pamphlets; quarterly research newsletter; bimonthly newsletter about Native American related activities; and multi-volume works on selected subjects, as well as CD-ROMs, music recordings of remastered originals and web pages on the internet; learned journals.

Hours & Admission Prices: Daily 10-5:30. Visitor Center: daily 8:30-5:30. No charge (except Cooper-Hewitt). Closed Christmas. ♿

Attendance: 20,100,000 (estimated)

Membership: Young Benefactors & Individual $35; Double & Family $50.

THE SOCIETY OF THE CINCINNATI AT ANDERSON HOUSE, (M), 2118 Massachusetts Ave., N.W., Washington, DC 20008-3640. Tel.: 202-785-2040. Fax: 202-785-0729.

E-mail: admin@societyofthecincinnati.org

Web Site: www.societyofthecincinnati.org

Founded: 1938.

Key Personnel: Exec. Dir., Jack D. Warren, Jr.; Deputy Dir. & Cur., Emily L. Schulz; Dir. Library, Ellen McCallister Clark; Coord. Museum Visitor Svcs., Caren A. Pauley; Museum Collections Mgr., Lindsay Borst.

Personnel Profile: Full-Time Paid 12; Part-Time Paid 6; Part-Time Volunteers 26; Interns 3.

Governing Authority: nonprofit organization. Parent Institution: The Society of the Cincinnati. Tax-exempt: 501(c)(3).

Historic House Museum: housed in 1902-1905 Anderson House, a beaux arts mansion designed by Little & Browne of Boston.

Collections: Anderson house original furnishings; sculpture; paintings; textiles; ceramics; Asian & European decorative arts; artifacts; manuscripts & books related to the history of the Society of the Cincinnati; armaments, silver, maps, manuscripts, and rare books of the period of the American Revolution; manuscripts, books, and photographs relating to Larz & Isabel Anderson III.

Major Exhibits: Virginia in the American Revolution, 11/09-3/10; New Hampshire in the American Revolution, Fall 2010-Spring 2011.

Research Fields: American Revolution; Society of the Cincinnati history; art of war in the 18th century; the lives and collection's of Larz & Isabel Anderson III; Washington history.

Facilities: 45,000-vol. research & reference library on history of the American Revolution, Society of the Cincinnati, Washington DC, and collections; reading room; garden.

Activities: guided tours; lectures; concerts; docent program; volunteer positions available; internships possible; inter-museum loan, permanent & temporary exhibitions.

Publications: biannual journal, Cincinnati Fourteen; Why America is Free; The Insignia of the Society of the Cincinnati; George Rogers Clark lectures; exhibition catalogues.

Hours & Admission Prices: Museum: Tues.-Sat. 1-4. Library: Mon.-Fri. 10-4 by appointment only. No charge; donations accepted. Closed legal holidays & during society meetings. ♿

Attendance: 8,708 (accurate)

THE SUPREME COURT OF THE UNITED STATES, Office of the Curator, One First St., N.E., Washington, DC 20543-0001. Tel.: 202-479-3298 & 3000 (tours); 888-539-4438 (gift shop). Fax: 202-479-2926.

E-mail: curator@supremecourt.gov

Web Site: www.supremecourtus.gov

Founded: 1973.

Key Personnel: Cur., Catherine E. Fitts; Assoc. Cur., Matthew Hofstedt; Collections Mgr., Franz Jantzen; Collections Mgr., Devon Burge; Programs Asst., Gwen Fernandez; Photographer, Steve Petteway; Curatorial Asst., Emily Rosolowski.

Personnel Profile: Full-Time Paid 7; Part-Time Paid 2; Part-Time Volunteers 20; Interns 5.

Governing Authority: federal agency. Tax-exempt.

Historic Agency & Building.

Collections: portraits of all former Justices; marble busts of the Chief Justices & certain Associate Justices; historic photos, etchings & drawings of the Justices & the architecture of the building; memorabilia; archival & manuscript materials on Supreme Court history; 18th & 19th-century American & English furniture & decorative arts; architectural drawings & plans of Supreme Court Building.

Research Fields: lives of the Supreme Court Justices, the traditions of the Court; architecture & furnishings of Supreme Court Building; administrative history of Supreme Court.

Facilities: library of reference books related to the Supreme Court history available for use in the Curator's Office; cafeteria. Gifts items for sale.

Activities: courtroom lectures; film; permanent & temporary exhibitions.

Publications: booklet, The Supreme Court of the United States; pamphlets, Visitor's Guide to the Supreme Court; Visitor's Guide to Oral Argument; exhibit catalogues, John Jay, The First Chief Justice; Charles Evans Hughes, The Eleventh Chief Justice; William Howard Taft, President and Chief Justice; Documenting the Constitution: A Manuscript History.

Hours & Admission Prices: Mon.-Fri. 9-4:30. Courtroom lectures every hour on the half-hour 9:30-3:30 when court is not sitting. No charge. Closed federal holidays. ♿

Attendance: 300,000 (estimated)

* **THE TEXTILE MUSEUM, (M),** 2320 S St., N.W., Washington, DC 20008-4088. Tel.: 202-667-0441. Fax: 202-483-0994.

E-mail: info@textilemuseum.org

Web Site: www.textilemuseum.org

Founded: 1925.

Key Personnel: C.E.O., Maryclaire Ramsey; Pres. Bd. (V), Bruce P. Baganz; C.F.A.O., Doug Maas; Mgr. Devel., Liz Kelly; Exec. Asst. Devel., Ingrid Faulkerson; Communications & Mktg. Asst., Kathryn Clune; Research Assoc. Western Hemisphere, Ann Rowe; Cur. Eastern Hemisphere, Sumru Krody; Dir. Conservation, Esther Methe; Registrar, Rachel Shabica; Research Assoc. Southeast Asian Textiles, Mattiebelle Gittinger; Assoc. Cur. Eastern Hemisphere, Lee Talbot; Collections Conservator, Anne Ennes; Cur. Education, Tom Groehner; Research Assoc. Contemporary Textiles, Rebecca Stevens; Asst. Registrar, Latasha Richards; Devel. Asst., Sheila Freeman; Librarian, Gina Schoen; Dir. Mktg. & Communications, Cyndi Bohlin; Dir. Facilities & Exhibitions Production, Richard Timpson; Dir. Retail Operations, Chabrina Williams.

Personnel Profile: Full-Time Paid 25; Part-Time Paid 5; Part-Time Volunteers 75; Interns 5.

Governing Authority: nonprofit organization. Tax-exempt: 501(c)(3).

Textile Museum.

Collections: over 18,000 historic & ethnographic handmade textiles; Oriental carpets; pre-Columbian, Peruvian, Islamic, Coptic, Caucasian, southeast & central Asian, indigenous Latin American & North American textiles. Changing exhibitions highlight areas of the permanent collection as well as contemporary fiber art, American quilts & other areas of the textile arts which lie outside the realm of the museum's collection.

Major Exhibits: Recent Acquisitions, 11/09-1/3/10; Contemporary Japanese Fashion: The May Baskett Collection (T), 11/09-4/11/10; The Art of Living: Textile Furnishings from the Permanent Collection, 2/12/10-7/10; Art By The Yard: Woven Design Mid-Century Britain, 5/15/10-9/12/10; Colors of the Oasis: Central Asian Ikats, 10/16/10-4/11.

Research Fields: preservation; exhibition; study of permanent collections.

Facilities: 20,000-vol. research & reference library of books; periodicals; pamphlets on technical, historical & artistic aspects of rugs & textiles; conservation laboratory. Museum-related items for sale.

Activities: guided tours; lectures; films; gallery talks; docent program; inter-museum loan, temporary & traveling exhibitions; classes in textile techniques; workshops; looking exercises; cultural stories; video; weekly rug & textile appreciation sessions; school & family programs.

Publications: biannual journal; quarterly, Bulletin; exhibition catalogues; books relating to Museum's collection & activities.

Hours & Admission Prices: Tues.-Sat. 10-5, Sun. 1-5. Suggested Donation $5. Closed Federal holidays. ♿

Attendance: 28,000 (estimated)
Membership: Student $25; Mid-Atlantic $50; National $45; Foreign $50; Myers Fellow $100; Supporters $250; Sponsors $500; Patron $1,000; Connoisseurs Circle $5,000; Benefactor $10,000.

TUDOR PLACE HISTORIC HOUSE & GARDEN, 1644 31st St., N.W., Washington, DC 20007-2924. Tel.: 202-965-0400, ext. 100. Fax: 202-965-0164.
E-mail: info@tudorplace.org
Web Site: tudorplace.org
Formerly: Tudor Place Foundation, Inc.
Founded: 1966.
Congressional District: 1
Key Personnel: Pres., S. Allen Chambers, Jr.; Exec. Dir., Leslie Buhler; Mgr. Collections, Fay Winkle.
Personnel Profile: Full-Time Paid 10; Part-Time Paid 5; Part-Time Volunteers 5; Interns 10.
Governing Authority: public; nonprofit organization. Tax-exempt: 501(c)(3).
Historic House & Garden: house designed by Dr. William Thornton, first architect of the U.S. Capitol, completed 1816.
Collections: Washington-Custis-Peter memorabilia; furniture; silver; porcelain; sculpture; paintings; textiles; photographs; manuscripts; household items; historic trees, shrubs & flowers.
Research Fields: Custis-Peter Family; Georgetown and Washington history; Federal period architecture & gardens; Sculpture of Paul Wayland Bartlett, 1865-1925.
Facilities: 5 1/2 acre garden.
Activities: guided tours. Annual Events: Holiday Evenings; Fall Garden Day; Kids Summer History Weeks.
Publications: annual report; quarterly newsletter.
Hours & Admission Prices: Tues.-Sat. 10, 11, 12, 1, 2, 3, Sun. 12, 1, 2, 3. Adults $8; discounts to AAA, NTHP, & AAM members, senior citizens & students; members no charge. Closed New Year's Day; Independence Day; Thanksgiving; Christmas.
Attendance: 17,500 (estimated)
Membership: Individual $40; Family & Dual $75.

U.S NATIONAL ARBORETUM, 3501 New York Ave., N.E., Washington, DC 20002-1958. Tel.: 202-245-4523 & 2726. Fax: 202-245-4575.
E-mail: nancy.luria@ars.usda.gov
Web Site: www.usna.usda.gov
Founded: 1927.
Key Personnel: Dir., Dr. Thomas Elias; Unit Leader, Education, Nancy Luria; Unit Leader, Gardens, Scott Aker; Unit Leader, Research, Dr. Margaret Pooler; Administrative Officer, Deborah Cicala; Administrative & Mktg. Mgr., Allison Opicka.
Personnel Profile: Full-Time Paid 100; Part-Time Paid 10; Part-Time Volunteers 150; Interns 10.
Governing Authority: federal. Parent Institution: U.S. Dept. of Agriculture. Subsidiary Institution: Agricultural Research Service. Tax-exempt 170(c)(1).
Arboretum.
Collections: horticulture; azaleas; rhododendrons; camellias; native plants; ferns; magnolias; holly; perennials; ornamental cherries; crabapples; annuals; Asian plants; ornamental trees & shrubs; herbarium; outdoor museum; national bonsai collection; national herb garden.
Research Fields: test plantings; taxonomy; plant breeding.
Facilities: 10,000-vol. library of books & periodicals on botany & ornamental horticulture available on premises.
Activities: guided tours; lectures; classes; symposia; temporary exhibitions. Annual Events: flower shows.
Publications: U.S. National Arboretum News and Notes (electronic); National Arboretum Contributions.
Hours & Admission Prices: Daily & holidays 8-5. Bonsai Pavilions daily 10-4. No charge; donations accepted. Closed Christmas. ♿
Attendance: 450,000 (estimated)
Membership: Individual $35; Family & Joint $50.

*** UNITED STATES BOTANIC GARDEN, (M),** 245 First St., S.W., Washington, DC 20024-3201. Tel.: 202-226-8333. Fax: 202-225-1561.
E-mail: usbg@aoc.gov
Web Site: www.usbg.gov
Founded: 1820.
Key Personnel: Acting Dir., Stephen Ayers; Exec. Dir., Holly H. Shimizu; Admin. Officer, Elizabeth Spar; Safety Officer, Courtney Nichols; Facility Mgr., John Gallagher; Public Programs Mgr., Christine A. Flanagan; Acting Horticulture Mgr., Frank Brooks.
Personnel Profile: Full-Time Paid 66; Part-Time Paid 2; Part-Time Volunteers 173; Interns 4.
Governing Authority: federal. Parent Institution: U.S. Government (Legislative Branch): Architect of the Capitol. Tax-exempt.
Botanical Garden.
Collections: tropical, sub-tropical & temperate plants: orchids, cacti & succulents; medicinal & other economic plants; ferns; cycads; bromeliads; epiphytes; carnivorous (insectivorous) plants; rare endangered, threatened plants; native plants (mid-Atlantic U.S.).
Major Exhibits: Holiday Exhibit, 11/10-1/11.
Research Fields: plant & culture evaluation.
Facilities: conservatory.
Activities: guided tours by advance appointment; permanent & temporary exhibitions; public classes in botany, horticulture, botanical art & the environment; school programs; teacher workshops; special events; professional conferences.
Publications: assorted horticultural, botanical & environmental information sheets; quarterly, Calendar of Events; book, A Botanic Garden for the Nation; workbook, Junior Botanist.
Hours & Admission Prices: Conservatory: daily 10-5. No charge. ♿
Attendance: 850,000 (estimated)

UNITED STATES CAPITOL, (M), U.S. Capitol, Architect of the Capitol, Washington, DC 20515-0001. Tel.: 202-228-1222. Fax: 202-228-4602.
E-mail: bwolanin@aoc.gov
Web Site: www.aoc.gov
Founded: 1793.
Key Personnel: Acting Architect of the Capitol, Steven T. Ayers, AIA; Cur., Dr. Barbara A. Wolanin; Photo Branch, Michael Dunn; Registrar, Pamela Violante McConnell.
Governing Authority: federal. Under the direction of the Joint Committee on the Library, U.S. Congress. Branch Facility: U.S. Botanic Garden. Tax-exempt: 501(c)(1).
National Agency & Art Museum.
Collections: 19th & 20th-century paintings, sculpture & decorative arts, including works by Franzoni, Crawford, Rogers, Powers, Roberts, French, Peale, Trumbull, Vanderlyn, Weir, Leutze & Brumidi; restored historic chambers; 100,000 architectural drawings; 70,000 photographs; archives pertaining to the U.S. Capitol art & architecture.
Research Fields: architecture; art; decorative arts; history of the U.S. Capitol complex; history of Washington, D.C.
Facilities: 1,500-vol. specialized reference library & archives pertaining to architecture, art & history of the Capitol, available for consultation on premises; cafeteria & restaurant.
Activities: guided tours; inter-museum loan & permanent exhibitions.
Publications: book, Art in the United States Capitol: A Brief Architecture History; occasional publications.
Hours & Admission Prices: Mon.-Sat. 8:30-4:30. No charge. Closed federal holidays. ♿

UNITED STATES DEPARTMENT OF THE INTERIOR MUSEUM, (M), 1849 C Street, N.W. Mail Stop 2266, Washington, DC 20240-0001. Tel.: 202-208-4743. Fax: 202-208-1535.
E-mail: diana_l_ziegler@nbc.gov
Web Site: www.doi.gov/interiormuseum
Founded: 1938.
Key Personnel: C.E.O., Dr. David McKinney; Program & Outreach Coord., Diana Ziegler; Registrar, Erin McKeen; Museum Technician, Kirk Dietz.
Personnel Profile: Full-Time Paid 5; Interns 2.
Governing Authority: federal. Parent Institution: U.S. Dept. of the Interior, Office of the Secretary Museum Services Branch, Washington, DC 20240. Tax-exempt.
General Museum.
Collections: American Indian, Eskimo, Micronesia, Virgin Island and Guam handicraft & artifacts; rocks; fossils; paintings; sculptures; maps; charts; mapping & surveying equipment; mining equipment; models & dioramas.
Research Fields: land management; North American Indians material culture; federal history.
Activities: lunch time lectures on topics related to the Dept.
Publications: brochure.
Hours & Admission Prices: Mon.-Fri. 8:30-4:30, 3rd Sat. of every month 1-4. No charge. Photo I.D. required for adults at entrance. Closed national holidays. ♿
Attendance: 30,000 (estimated)

*** UNITED STATES HOLOCAUST MEMORIAL MUSEUM, (M), (I),** 100 Raoul Wallenberg Place, S.W., Washington, DC 20024-2126. Tel.: 202-488-0400. Fax: 202-488-2690. TDD: 202-488-0406.
E-mail: visitorsmail@ushmm.org
Web Site: www.ushmm.org
Founded: 1993.
Key Personnel: Dir. United States Holocaust Memorial Museum, Sara J.

Bloomfield; Chm. United States Holocaust Memorial Council, Fred S. Zeidman; Dir. Exhibitions, Steve Goodell; Deputy Dir. Exhibitions, Edward Phillips; Chief of Staff, William Parsons; Cur. Permanent Exhibition, Steven Luckert; Dir. External Affairs, Dara Goldberg; Dir. Center for Advanced Holocaust Studies, Paul Shapiro; Dir. Institutional Stewardship, Diane Saltzman; Sr. Advisor, Arthur S. Berger; Dir. Media Rels., Andrew Hollinger; Dir. Human Resources, Antonio Guzman; Dir. Collections, Michael Grunberger; Dir. Collections Management, Travis Roxlau; Dir. Film & Video, Raye Farr; Chief Conservator, Jane Klinger; Assoc. Cur. Art & Artifacts, Suzy Snyder; Dir. Oral History, Joan Ringelheim; Dir. Photographic Reference Collection, Judith Cohern; Dir. NIHE, Sarah Ogilvie; Dir. Education, Daniel Napolitano; Dir. Survivor Affairs, Ellen Blalock; Sr. Project Mgr. NIHE, Kristine Donly; Chief Archivist, Henry Mayer; Museum Shop Mgr., Marylou Withem; Dir. Museum Svcs., Paul Garver; Dir. Library, Ronald Coleman; Chief Information Officer Information & Technology, Lawrence Swiader; C.F.O., John Fawsett; Dir. Devel., Jordan Tannenbaum; Dir. Membership, Dana Weinstein.

Personnel Profile: Full-Time Paid 400; Part-Time Paid 10; Part-Time Volunteers 320; Interns 22.

Governing Authority: federal. Tax-exempt: 170(b)(1)(A).

History Museum.

Collections: reflecting the events of the Holocaust of 1933-1945, including artifacts, photographs, films, video, oral histories, books, archives.

Research Fields: Holocaust Studies

Facilities: 55,000-vol. library of Holocaust-related material in 18 languages available for use by the public on the premises only; auditorium; restaurant; resource center; classrooms; 50,000 sq. ft. exhibit space; theatre. Museum-related items for sale.

Activities: research; public programs.

Publications: quarterly, The United States Holocaust Memorial Museum; Journal of Holocaust & Genocide Studies & select papers issued by the Museum's Center for Advanced Holocaust Studies; exhibition catalogues.

Hours & Admission Prices: Daily 10-5:30. No charge; donations accepted. Closed Christmas; Yom Kippur. ♿

Attendance: 1,373,589 (accurate)

Membership: Associate $25; Member $36; Supporting $100; Sustaining $500; Circle of Remembrance $1,000.

UNITED STATES SENATE COMMISSION ON ART, Rm. S-411, U.S. Capitol Bldg., Washington, DC 20510-0001. Tel.: 202-224-2955. Fax: 202-224-8799.

E-mail: curator@sec.senate.gov

Web Site: www.senate.gov

Founded: 1968.

Key Personnel: Cur., Diane K. Skvarla; Assoc. Cur., Melinda K. Smith; Admin., Scott M. Strong; Museum Specialist, Richard L. Doerner; Registrar, Courtney D. Morfeld; Collections Specialist, Theresa Malanum; Historic Preservation Officer, Kelly Steele; Curatorial Asst., Amy Elizabeth Burton; Staff Asst., Amy Camilleri; Collections Mgr., Deborah Wood.

Personnel Profile: Full-Time Paid 10; Interns 4.

Governing Authority: federal. Parent Institution: U.S. Senate. A commission of the U.S. Senate, Washington, DC 20510. Tax-exempt.

Preservation Projects: c.1850 Old Senate & Old Supreme Court Chambers & other historic areas of the U.S. Capitol Building & exhibits.

Collections: paintings; sculpture; prints; furnishings; documents.

Research Fields: American fine arts & decorative arts; cultural & political history; heritage of U.S. Senate.

Facilities: 250,000-vol. library; food services available.

Activities: guided tours; lectures; internships for undergraduate college students; permanent & temporary exhibitions.

Publications: catalog of collections; guide to exhibits; guides to restored chambers; exhibition posters & catalogs.

Hours & Admission Prices: Daily 9-4:30. No charge. Closed New Year's Day; Thanksgiving; Christmas. ♿

Attendance: 1,500,000 (estimated)

U.S. CAPITOL HISTORICAL SOCIETY, 200 Maryland Ave., N.E., Washington, DC 20002-5724. Tel.: 202-543-8919; 800-887-9318. Fax: 202-544-8244.

E-mail: uschs@uschs.org

Web Site: www.uschs.org

Founded: 1963.

Key Personnel: Pres., Ronald A. Sarasin, CAE; Vice Pres. Merchandising, Diana Wailes; Dir. Mktg., Mary Hughes; Museum Shop Mgr., Sharron Randolph.

Personnel Profile: Full-Time Paid 35; Full-Time Volunteers 4; Part-Time Volunteers 20; Interns 4.

Governing Authority: Parent Institution: United States Congress. Tax-exempt.

Historical Society Museum.

Collections: history of capitol building & congress; documents; videos.

Research Fields: history of the Capitol & Congress.

Activities: seminars; educational outreach programs.

Publications: We, The People, Washington: Past & Present; Young Person Guide to the Capitol; Understanding Congress; Exploring Capitol Hill; Where the People Speak; A Vision of Freedom; Outstanding Members of Congress Series; The Capitol: Designing and Decorating a National Icon.

Hours & Admission Prices: Daily 9-4:30. No charge; donations accepted. Closed holidays. ♿

Attendance: 8,000,000 (estimated)

Membership: Charter $35; Freedom $50; Cornerstone $100; Rotunda $250; Architect of History $500; Capitol Circle $1,000; Benefactor $2,500; Founder $5,000; Brumidi $10,000.

U.S. NAVY MEMORIAL FOUNDATION AND NAVAL HERITAGE CENTER, 701 Pennsylvania Ave., N.W., Suite 123, Washington, DC 20004-2688. Tel.: 202-737-2300, ext. 710 & 725. Fax: 202-737-2308.

E-mail: library@lonesailor.org

Web Site: www.navymemorial.org

Founded: 1991.

Key Personnel: C.E.O. & Pres., RADM Edward K. Walker, SC, USN (Ret.); Chm. (V), Richard C. Vie; Treas., Edward Walker, USN, (Ret.); Vice Pres. Operations, Cindy Collins; Cur. & Educator, Mark T. Weber; Devel., M. C. Dunn; Vice Pres. Mktg. & Communications, Taylor Kiland; Registrar, Don Dupuis; Museum Shop Mgr., B'journ Liverpool.

Personnel Profile: Full-Time Paid 13; Full-Time Volunteers 1; Part-Time Paid 6; Part-Time Volunteers 25; Interns 3.

Governing Authority: private; nonprofit organization. Tax-exempt: 501(c)(3).

Naval Museum.

Collections: information on 610,000 sea service veterans; naval art; naval history books; personal accounts; 30,000 photographs.

Major Exhibits: Navy Explosive Ordnance Disposal (T), 11/09-11/10; USS Liberty, 1/10-12/10; Year of Navy Supply, 4/10-3/11.

Research Fields: sea service veterans.

Facilities: 1,500-vol. library; 250-seat auditorium; 250-seat large screen theater; 2,500 sq. ft. exhibit space. Museum-related items for sale.

Activities: arts festival; concerts; docent program; films; guided tours; lectures; rental gallery; loan, traveling & temporary exhibitions; theater. Museum Sponsors: Blessing of the Fleet; Historical Wreath-laying; official Navy events including retirements, re-enlistments & change of command.

Publications: quarterly newsletter, The Lone Sailor.

Hours & Admission Prices: Daily 9:30-5. No charge; donations accepted. Closed New Year's Day; Thanksgiving; Christmas. ♿

Attendance: 70,000 (estimated)

Membership: $25 & up.

WASHINGTON NATIONAL CATHEDRAL, (M), 3101 Wisconsin Ave., N.W., Washington, DC 20016-5000. Tel.: 202-537-6200. Fax: 202-364-6611.

E-mail: tours@cathedral.org

Web Site: www.nationalcathedral.org

Founded: 1893.

Key Personnel: Bishop, Rt. Rev. John Bryson Chane; Dean, The Very Rev. Samuel Lloyd, III; Dir., Kathleen Cox; Dir. Visitor Programs, Julie Cooke; Vicar, Rev. Steve Huber.

Personnel Profile: Full-Time Paid 90; Part-Time Volunteers 1,200.

Governing Authority: Parent Institution: Protestant Episcopal Cathedral Foundation. Tax-exempt: 509(a)(1).

Religious Institution: housed in a Gothic cathedral.

Collections: religious art & architecture, including stained glass windows, wrought iron, wood & stone carvings, gargoyles & grotesques, needlepoint & tapestries; a stained glass window with embedded moon rock; an altar painting by N.C. Wyeth; garden sculpture of Prodigal Son by Heinz Warneke; bronze sculpture of Abraham Lincoln by Walker Hancock; exterior sculpture by Frederick Hart; exterior fountain & artwork. Nine chapels. Bishop's Garden and Olmsted Woods. 10,650-pipe organ, 10-bell peal, carillon and choirs. Interred remains of Helen Keller, Woodrow Wilson, Adm. George Dewey, Cordell Hull, and others.

Facilities: Bishop's Garden and Olmsted Woods. Gift-related items for sale.

Activities: audio & guided tours; daily worship services; specialty tours; temporary exhibitions; workshops; spirituality speakers; special events. Annual Events: Evensong seasonally; Tour and Tea; Behind the Scenes Tours; Flower Mart in May; Shrove Tuesday Pancake Race; Blessing of the Animals in October.

Publications: brochures; self-guided tours; fact sheets; quarterly magazine, Cathedral Age; Cathedral Voice; books.

Hours & Admission Prices: Winter: Sun.-Fri. 10-5:30, Sat. 10-4; Summer: call for extended hours; groups by appointment. Requested Donation: family $15, adults $5, seniors $3. ♿

Attendance: 775,000 (accurate)

* **THE WHITE HOUSE,** 1600 Pennsylvania Ave., N.W., Washington, DC 20502-0001. Tel.: 202-456-2550. Fax: 202-456-6820.
Web Site: www.whitehouse.gov
Founded: 1792.
Key Personnel: Cur., William G. Allman; Asst. Cur., Lydia S. Tederick; Asst. Cur., Melissa C. Naulin; Collections Mgr., Donna A. Hayashi Smith.
Governing Authority: federal. Tax-exempt.
Historic House Museum: 1792-1800, The White House.
Collections: American & European furniture, decorative & fine arts from the late 18th, 19th and 20th centuries; collections of Presidential porcelain, silver & glassware; portraits of the Presidents, First Ladies and other national notables; late 18th, 19th and 20th-century paintings and prints; archival & manuscript materials on White House history.
Research Fields: relating to the history of the White House, its furnishings and collections.
Facilities: library of books & other materials relating to all aspects of White House history, the Presidency & White House families.
Activities: tours; permanent & temporary exhibits.
Publications: books, The White House: An Historic Guide; The Presidents of the United States; The First Ladies; The Living White House; The President's House: A History; Art in the White House: A Nation's Pride; The White House: It's Historic Furnishings and First Families; White House Glassware: Two Centuries of Presidential Entertaining; journal, White House History.
Hours & Admission Prices: Please call 202-456-7041 for information. Tours: Tues.-Thurs. 7:30-11, Fri. 7:30-12, Sat. 7:30-1. No charge. ♿

* **WOODROW WILSON HOUSE, (M),** 2340 S St., N.W., Washington, DC 20008-4016. Tel.: 202-387-4062. Fax: 202-483-1466.
E-mail: faucella@woodrowwilsonhouse.org
Web Site: www.woodrowwilsonhouse.org
Founded: 1963.
Key Personnel: Museum Dir., Frank J. Aucella; Chm. (V), Stuart J. Brahs; Cur., John Powell; Dir. Devel., Claudia Bismark; Museum Shop Mgr., Sarah Andrews.
Personnel Profile: Full-Time Paid 4; Part-Time Paid 24; Part-Time Volunteers 1; Interns 2.
Governing Authority: nonprofit. Parent Institution: National Trust for Historic Preservation, 1785 Massachusetts Ave., N.W., Washington, DC 20036. Tax-exempt: 501(c)(3).
Historic House Museum: housed in the former home of President Wilson.
Collections: original furnishings; memorabilia of World War I; early 20th-century decorative arts & political memorabilia; World War I photos & posters; textiles; gifts from various heads of state.
Research Fields: political & social history; interior design.
Facilities: meeting & banquet space; gardens.
Activities: guided tours; school programs; lectures; special events; walking tours. Museum Sponsors: Wilson Symposium.
Publications: newsletter; exhibit catalogues.
Hours & Admission Prices: Tues.-Sun. 10-4. Adults $7.50, children & senior citizens $6.50; discounts to AAM, ICOM & National Trust members; members no charge. Closed major holidays. ♿
Attendance: 15,025 (accurate)
Membership: Basic $50; Family $100; Patron $250; Heritage $1,000.

ZENITH GALLERY, 1429 Iris St., N.W., Washington, DC 20012. Mailing Address: P.O. Box 55295, Washington, DC 20040-5295. Tel.: 202-783-2963.
E-mail: art@zenithgallery.com
Web Site: www.zenithgallery.com
Key Personnel: Dir., Margery Goldberg
Art Gallery.
Collections: works by local & regional artists.
Hours & Admission Prices: By appointment.

FLORIDA

(406 listings)

Anna Maria Island

ANNA MARIA ISLAND HISTORICAL MUSEUM, 402 Pine Ave., Anna Maria Island, FL 34216. Mailing Address: P.O. Box 4315, Anna Maria, FL 34216-4315. Tel.: 941-778-0492.
Web Site: www.amihs.org
Founded: 1992.
Key Personnel: Chm., Nelson L. Roberts; Pres. (V), Thea Kelley.
Governing Authority: private; nonprofit organization. Parent Institution: Anna Maria Island Historical Society.
History Museum.
Collections: island history & culture; personal artifacts; photographs; videos; shells; fossils; period office equipment; tools.
Activities: educational programs; scholarships.
Hours & Admission Prices: Memorial Day to Labor Day Tues.-Thurs. & Sat. 10-12; Sept.-May Tues.-Thurs. & Sat. 10-3. No charge.

Apalachicola

JOHN GORRIE MUSEUM STATE PARK, 46 6th St. & Avenue D, Apalachicola, FL 32329. Mailing Address: P.O. Box 267, Apalachicola, FL 32329-0267. Tel.: 850-653-9347.
Web Site: baynavigator.com
Founded: 1955.
Congressional District: 2
Key Personnel: Dir. Florida Park Service, Mike Bullock; Park Mgr., Mark Knapke; Ranger, Willie McNair.
Personnel Profile: Full-Time Paid 1.
Governing Authority: state. Parent Institution: St. George Island State Park. Dept. of Environmental Protection, Div. of Recreation and Parks, 3900 Commonwealth Blvd., Tallahassee, FL 32303. Tax-exempt.
History Museum.
Collections: replica of the first ice-making machine invented by Dr. John Gorrie; first refrigeration & air conditioning; history of Apalachicola River & Town.
Activities: tours.
Hours & Admission Prices: Thurs.-Mon. 9-5. Admission $2; children 5 & under no charge. Closed New Year's Day; Thanksgiving; Christmas. ♿

Apopka

MUSEUM OF APOPKANS, (M), 122 E. 5th St., Apopka, FL 32703-5314. Tel.: 407-703-1707. Fax: 407-703-1773.
E-mail: director@apopkamuseum.org
Web Site: www.apopkamuseum.org
Founded: 1968.
Key Personnel: Mgr., Reba Wilson.
Personnel Profile: Full-Time Paid 1; Part-Time Volunteers 20.
Governing Authority: Parent Institution: Apopka Historical Society. Tax-exempt.
History Museum.
Collections: history of Apopkans; photographs; personal artifacts; Native American artifacts.
Research Fields: NW Orange County history.
Facilities: library; meeting room; rental facilities.
Activities: permanent & temporary exhibitions; film; guest speakers; educational tours; traveling plays for schools; Power Point presentations for schools; membership meetings. Annual Events: Mother's Day Tea; Festival of Trees; Fireball Roberts Memorial Celebration.
Publications: quarterly newsletter, News and Views.
Hours & Admission Prices: Wed.-Thurs. 10-4, Sat. 10-2; other times by appointment. No charge; donations accepted. ♿
Attendance: 3,000 (estimated)
Membership: Junior $10; Individual $15; Couple $25; Family $35; Business $75; Lifetime Single $200; Lifetime Couple $300.

Avon Park

AVON PARK DEPOT MUSEUM, 3 N. Museum Ave., Avon Park, FL 33825-3153. Tel.: 863-453-3525.
E-mail: museum@strato.net
Web Site: www.hsaponline.org
Governing Authority: Tax-exempt: 501(c)(3).
History Museum.
Collections: Avon Park history & culture; photographs; personal artifacts.
Facilities: library.
Activities: research.
Hours & Admission Prices: Tues.-Fri. 10-3. No charge; donations accepted.

SOUTH FLORIDA COMMUNITY COLLEGE MUSEUM OF FLORIDA ART AND CULTURE, 600 W. College Dr., Avon Park, FL 33825-9356. Tel.: 863-784-7240.
E-mail: mofac@southflorida.edu
Web Site: www.mofac.org
Key Personnel: Cur., Mollie Doctrow
Art Museum.
Collections: works by Florida artists.
Hours & Admission Prices: Sept.-May Wed.-Fri. 12:30-4:30. ♿

Barberville

PIONEER SETTLEMENT FOR THE CREATIVE ARTS, 1776 Lightfoot Lane, Barberville, FL 32105. Mailing Address: P.O. Box 6, Barberville, FL 32105-0006. Tel.: 386-749-2959. Fax: 386-749-2087.
E-mail: info@pioneersettlement.org
Web Site: www.pioneersettlement.org
Founded: 1976.
Key Personnel: Pres. (V), Carl McClancy; Dir. Education, Jewel Tompkins; Coord. Special Events, Dale Barnhart.
Personnel Profile: Full-Time Paid 5; Part-Time Paid 9; Part-Time Volunteers 400.
Cultural Heritage Museum.
Collections: state and regional cultural heritage.
Research Fields: Florida settlement; family histories; early architecture.
Facilities: Museum-related items for sale.
Activities: special events. Annual Events: Folk Art Days in February; Spring Fest & Frolic in April; Summer Folk School in June & July; Harvest Celebration in September; Fall County Jamboree in November; Florida Christmas Remembered in December.
Publications: quarterly newsletter, Pioneer Press.
Hours & Admission Prices: Mon.-Sat. 9-4. Adults $6, children 6-12 $4; members & children under 5 no charge. Closed major holidays. ♿
Attendance: 65,000
Membership: Student $20; Teacher & Senior Individual $25; Individual $30; Senior Couple $35; Couple $40; Family $50; Patron $100; Small Business $300; Advocate $500; Booster $1,000.

Bartow

POLK COUNTY HISTORICAL MUSEUM, (M), 100 E. Main St., Bartow, FL 33830-4629. Tel.: 863-534-4386. Fax: 863-534-4387.
E-mail: museum@polk-county.net
Web Site: www.polkcountymuseum.org
Founded: 1998.
Congressional District: 12
Key Personnel: Dir., Tom Muir; Museum Asst., Maria Trippe.
Personnel Profile: Full-Time Paid 2; Part-Time Volunteers 12.
Governing Authority: county government; nonprofit. Parent Institution: Polk County Board of County Commissioners. Tax-exempt.
History Museum.
Collections: history of Polk County, Florida from prehistoric to modern times; pioneer life; political history; agriculture; industry; contemporary life of Polk County; general store; hands-on children's exhibits; military artifacts; c.1908 & c.1926 courtrooms.
Facilities: 10,000 sq. ft. exhibit space.
Activities: self-guided tours; participatory exhibits.
Publications: The Historical Marker.
Hours & Admission Prices: Tues.-Fri. 9-5, Sat. 9-3. No charge; donations accepted. Closed New Year's Day; Martin Luther King Jr. Day; Memorial Day; Independence Day; Labor Day; Veterans Day; Thanksgiving weekend; Christmas. ♿
Attendance: 20,000 (estimated)

Bay Lake

DISNEY'S ANIMAL KINGDOM THEME PARK, 1200 N. Savannah Circle E., Bay Lake, FL 32830. Mailing Address: P.O. Box 10000, Lake Buena Vista, FL 32830-1000. Tel.: 407-939-6382. Fax: 407-939-6240.
Web Site: www.disneyworld.com
Founded: 1998.
Congressional District: 9
Key Personnel: Vice Pres., Jacqueline J. Ogden, Ph.D.; Vice Pres., Val Bunting; Administrative Asst., Leah Logan; Administrative Asst., Jill Martin; Animal & Environmental Initiative Policies & Standards Technical Dir., John Lehnhardt; Dir. Dept. of Animal Health, Mark Stetter, D.V.M., Dipl. A.C.Z.M.; Dir. Education & Science, Jill Mellen, Ph.D.; Sr. Research Biologist, Tamara Bettinger, Ph.D.; Sr. Conservation Biologist, Anne Savage, Ph.D.; Cur. Education, Kathy Lehnhardt; Cur. Education, Allyson Atkins; Dir. Operations Learning & Devel., Amy Groff; Asst. Cur. Records, Lynn S. McDuffie; Veterinary Svcs. Operations Mgr., Elizabeth C. Nolan, D.V.M., Dipl. A.C.Z.M.; Veterinary Svcs. Operations Mgr., Don Neiffer, V.M.D., Dipl. A.C.Z.M.; Veterinarian, Greg Fleming, D.V.M., Dipl. A.C.Z.M.; Veterinarian, Deidre Fontenot, D.V.M.; Cur. Birds, Chelle Plasse; Animal Operations Mgr., Mammals, Joe Christman; Dir. Animal Operations, Matt Hohne; Asst. Cur. Ectotherms, Andre J. Daneault; Animal Operations Mgr., Rafiki's Planet Watch, Jerry Brown; Cur. Disney's Animal Kingdom Lodge, Greg Peccie; Veterinary Svcs. Operations Mgr. & Pathologist, Scott P. Terrell, D.V.M., Dipl. A.C.V.P.; Nutritionist, Eduardo V. Valdes, Ph.D.; Gen. Mgr. Park Operations, Dale A. Stafford; Gen. Mgr. Food & Beverage, Jeannie Colaizzi; Dir. Engineering Svcs., Rachel Hutter; Mgr. Horticulture Svcs., Wendy Andrew; Cur. Mammals, Jeff Bolling; Mgr. Human Resources, Scott Gobetz; Gen. Mgr. Merchandise, Kent L. Mitchell.
Governing Authority: Parent Institution: Walt Disney World Resort, a division of Walt Disney Parks and Resorts U.S., Inc., Lake Buena Vista, FL.
Zoological Park.
Collections: 350 species (more than 6,000 specimens) of mammals, birds, reptiles, amphibians, invertebrates & fish; 4 million trees, plants, shrubs, vines, grasses & ferns representing more than 3,000 species.
Research Fields: botany; animal health; applied research related to animal management; reproductive physiology/endocrinology & behavior.
Facilities: library; aquarium; botanical garden; restaurants; classrooms; 500 acre exhibit space; nature center; zoological park. Museum-related items for sale.
Activities: formal education programs; guided tours; lectures; training programs for professional museum workers; children's fossil play maze; wooly mammoth bone dig; guest educational research. Annual Events: Earth Day; Plant Conservation Day; International Migratory Bird Day; Party for the Planet.
Publications: weekly brochures.
Hours & Admission Prices: Summer: 9-8; Winter 9-5. Adults $79.88, children 3-9 $67.10. ♿

Big Cypress Seminole Indian Reservation

* **AH-TAH-THI-KI MUSEUM, (M),** County Rd. 833 & W. Boundary Rd., Big Cypress Seminole Indian Reservation, FL 33440. Mailing Address: HC-61, Box 21-A, Clewiston, FL 33440. Tel.: 863-902-1113. Fax: 863-902-1117.
Web Site: www.seminoletribe.com/museum
Founded: 1989.
Key Personnel: Exec. Dir., Tina M. Osceola; Museum Dir., David Blackard; Education, Dr. Cynthia Kasee; Coord. Community Outreach, Brian Zepeda; Museum Shop Mgr., Louise Osceola; Operations Mgr., Gene Davis; Security, Vicky Knouse.
Personnel Profile: Full-Time Paid 35; Part-Time Paid 1; Part-Time Volunteers 1; Interns 1.
Governing Authority: nonprofit. Parent Institution: Seminole Tribe of Florida, Hollywood, FL.
Tribal Museum.
Collections: Seminole & Southeastern Indian materials with historically related items; Seminole genre paintings by Seminole and non-Indian artists; Seminole war period militaria; botanical park with resident fauna.
Research Fields: Seminole culture & history.
Facilities: 255-vol. library; 8,530 sq. ft. exhibit space; botanical garden; 45-seat large screen theater. Museum-related items for sale.
Activities: guided tours; temporary exhibitions.
Publications: newsletter, Ah-Tah-Thi-Ki Museum News.
Hours & Admission Prices: Daily 9-5. Adults $9, senior citizens & students $6; discounts to AAM members & groups; children under 6 & members no charge. Closed New Year's Day; Easter; Independence Day; Veterans Day; Thanksgiving Day; Christmas; Native American Day. ♿
Attendance: 26,793 (accurate)
Membership: Individual $30; Family Clan $60; Osceola Circle $250; Bandolier Bag $500, Chairman's Circle $1,000.

Boca Grande

BOCA GRAND LIGHTHOUSE MUSEUM AND VISITOR'S CENTER, Gasparilla Island State Park, Boca Grande, FL 33921. Mailing Address: P.O. Box 637, Boca Grande, FL 33921-0637. Tel.: 941-964-0060. Fax: 941-964-0054.
Web Site: www.barrierislandparkssociety.org
Key Personnel: Dir., Sharon McKenzie
History Museum.
Collections: displays on Native Americas & Spanish, local fishing industry, history of the lighthouse, railroad development, Port Boca Grande, the town of Boca Grande & tarpon fishing.
Hours & Admission Prices: June-July & Sept.-Oct. Wed.-Sat. 10-4, Sun. 12-4; Nov.-May Mon.-Sat. 10-4, Sun. 12-4. Closed New Year's Day; Martin Luther King Jr. Day; Easter; Memorial Day; Independence Day; Labor Day; Thanksgiving; Christmas.

Boca Raton

BOCA RATON HISTORICAL SOCIETY, 71 N. Federal Hwy., Boca Raton, FL 33432-3919. Tel.: 561-395-6766, ext. 106. Fax: 561-395-4049.
E-mail: info@bocahistory.org
Web Site: www.bocahistory.org
Founded: 1972.
Congressional District: 23

Key Personnel: Dir., Mary Csar; Cur., Susan Gillis; Educator, Laurie Lynn Jones; Administrative Asst., Jean Scanlen; Museum Shop Mgr., Sandy McCoy.
Personnel Profile: Full-Time Paid 4; Full-Time Volunteers 1; Part-Time Paid 1; Part-Time Volunteers 150; Interns 2.
Governing Authority: private; nonprofit organization. Tax-exempt: 501(c)(3).
Historical Society Museum.
Collections: Boca Raton history from the late 1890s to modern times; timeline; biographies; map; history of Palm Beach County cities, people & events; restored streamline railcars at F.E.C. Depot.
Research Fields: Boca Raton history; historic architecture.
Facilities: research library; 2,000 sq. ft. exhibit space. Museum-related items for sale.
Activities: lectures; loan, temporary & traveling exhibitions; weekly historic tours of city and Boca Raton Resort & Club. Annual Events: Benefit; House Tour; Holiday Gift Show; Wine Festival.
Publications: annual, Spanish River Papers; academic publication on local history.
Hours & Admission Prices: Mon.-Fri. 10-4. No charge; donations accepted. Closed state holidays. ♿
Attendance: 25,000 (estimated)
Membership: Junior $20; Individual $30; Family $50; Patron $100; Benefactor & Corporate $500.

* **BOCA RATON MUSEUM OF ART, (M),** Mizner Park, 501 Plaza Real, Boca Raton, FL 33432-3982. Tel.: 561-392-2500, ext. 200. Fax: 561-391-6410.
E-mail: info@bocamuseum.org
Web Site: www.bocamuseum.org
Founded: 1950.
Congressional District: 22
Key Personnel: Pres., Paul W. Carman; Exec. Dir., George S. Bolge; Dir. Devel., Louise C. Adler; Dir. Administration, Roberta Stewart; Dir. Education, Claire Clum; Sr. Cur., Wendy M. Blazier; Asst. to Exec. Dir., Valerie Johnson; Dir. Mktg. & Public Rels., Bruce Herman; Dir. Art School, Rebecca Sanders; Registrar, Martin Hanahan; Mgr. Special Events, Aloysius Gigl; Dir. Finance, Linda Ursillo; Museum Shop Mgr., Laura Toia.
Personnel Profile: Full-Time Paid 27; Part-Time Paid 5; Part-Time Volunteers 500; Interns 8.
Governing Authority: nonprofit organization. Tax-exempt: 501(c)(3).
Art Museum.
Collections: 19th-20th century and contemporary European & American painting, drawing, sculpture & graphics; photography from 1840 to present; The Dr. & Mrs. John J. Mayers Collection of Modern Masters (including Braque, Degas, Demuth, Matisse, Modigliani, Picasso, Prendergast, Seurat and others); The Jean & David Colker Collection of Pre-Columbian Art; West African tribal art of artifacts; Oceanic sculpture, textiles and basketry; Asian sculpture & ceramics; 19th-century English Victorian Doulton-Lambeth stoneware.
Major Exhibits: An Unfinished Conversation: Collecting Enrique Martinez Celaya, 11/17/09-1/10/10; Why Tribal? African, Oceanic and Meso-American, 11/17/09-6/13/10; The Magical World of M.C. Escher, 1/19/10-4/11/10; Mary Cassatt: Works on Paper, 1/19/10-4/11/10; Remembering Stanley Boxer (T), 4/20/10-6/13/10; Elvis at 21: New York to Memphis (T), 4/20/10-6/13/10; 59th All Florida Juried Competition and Exhibition, 6/22/10-8/29/10; Armando Morales, 9/7/10-11/7/10; Fernando Botero: Bronzes and Works on Paper, 9/7/10-11/7/10; Valerio Adami, 11/16/10-1/9/11.
Research Fields: 20th century European & American modernism, African, Oceanic, Pre-Columbian; photography.
Facilities: 4,000-library of art history; sculpture gardens. Museum-related items for sale.
Activities: guided tours; lectures; films; gallery talks; concerts; study clubs; docent program; traveling exhibitions. Annual Event: Boca Museum Juried Art Festival.
Publications: quarterly newsletter; catalogs for changing exhibitions.
Hours & Admission Prices: Tues. & Thurs.-Fri. 10-5, Wed. 10-9, Sat.-Sun. 12-5. Adults $8, senior citizens $6, students with ID $4; discounts to groups & AAM members; members, children 12 & under, & Wed. 5-9 no charge. Admission may change for special exhibits. Closed major holidays. ♿
Attendance: 150,000 (estimated)
Membership: Individual $80; Dual $100; Contributing $150; Supporting $300; Sustaining $600; Patrons $1,250; Director $2,500; Trustee $5,000; President $10,000; Benefactor $25,000.

CHILDREN'S MUSEUM, INC., 498 Crawford Blvd., Boca Raton, FL 33432-3752. Tel.: 561-368-6875. Fax: 561-395-7764.
Founded: 1979.
Congressional District: 14
Key Personnel: Exec. Dir., Poppi Mercier; Pres. (V), Penny Morey.
Personnel Profile: Full-Time Paid 1; Part-Time Paid 6; Part-Time Volunteers 60.
Governing Authority: nonprofit. Tax-exempt: 501(c)(3).
Children's Museum: housed in c.1912 unaltered wooden structure.
Collections: Sophia S. Kuzmick dolls; Korvetz Shell collection; Florida Pioneer Kitchen artifacts; Charles Weiner carousel animals; World of Play toys.
Facilities: 600-vol. library; 1,400 sq. ft. exhibit space; nature & conservation center. Museum-related items for sale.
Activities: docent program; guided tours; temporary, traveling & loan exhibitions; formally organized education programs for children.
Publications: quarterly newsletter, Connections.
Hours & Admission Prices: Tues.-Sat. 9:30-11:45 (reserved for groups), 12-4 (public hours). $3 per person; infants & members no charge. Closed New Year's Day; Memorial Day; Independence Day; Labor Day; Thanksgiving; Christmas. ♿
Attendance: 50,000 (estimated)
Membership: Individual/Teacher $25; Florida Plus $50; Friend $100; Supporter $250; Patron $500.

CHILDREN'S SCIENCE EXPLORIUM AT SUGAR SAND PARK, 300 S. Military Trail, Boca Raton, FL 33486-4302. Tel.: 561-347-3913. Fax: 561-347-3910.
E-mail: explorium@myboca.us
Web Site: www.scienceexplorium.org
Founded: 1998.
Key Personnel: Science Center Coord., Jennifer Yates; Coord. Exhibits, Harry Robelen; Science Center Educator, Heather Peete.
Personnel Profile: Full-Time Paid 4; Part-Time Paid 6; Part-Time Volunteers 22.
Governing Authority: nonprofit; municipal government. Tax-exempt.
Children's Science Museum.
Collections: interactive physical science exhibits.
Facilities: 155-seat auditorium; demo classroom; 4,000 sq. ft. exhibit space; outdoor science playground.
Activities: traveling exhibitions; formal education programs for children; science camps; guided tours; public programs.
Hours & Admission Prices: Mon.-Fri. 9-6, Sat.-Sun. & holidays 10-5. Suggested Donation $2. Closed Thanksgiving; Christmas. ♿
Attendance: 86,000 (estimated)

UNIVERSITY GALLERIES, FLORIDA ATLANTIC UNIVERSITY, 777 Glades Rd., Boca Raton, FL 33431-6496. Tel.: 561-297-2966 & 2661. Fax: 561-297-2166.
E-mail: wfaulds@fau.edu
Web Site: www.fau.edu/galleries
Founded: 1970.
Key Personnel: Dir., W. Rod Faulds.
Personnel Profile: Full-Time Paid 2; Part-Time Paid 6; Part-Time Volunteers 20; Interns 4.
Governing Authority: Parent Institution: Florida Atlantic University. Tax-exempt.
Contemporary Art Museums & Galleries.
Collections: Artinian collection of self-portraits by Florida artists; Albert Binny Backus paintings.
Major Exhibits: Biennial Faculty Exhibition, 11/14/09-1/23/10; Thirst Design-Rick Valicenti, 2/13/10-4/3/10.
Research Fields: contemporary art; art, humanities & popular culture.
Facilities: 5,000 sq. ft. exhibit space.
Activities: docent training for undergraduate students; traveling exhibitions; exhibition-related programs; artists lectures, presentations & residencies to create on-site exhibition projects.
Publications: exhibit catalogues; exhibition announcements; brochures.
Hours & Admission Prices: Ritter Art Gallery & Schmidt Center Gallery: Tues.-Fri. 1-4, Sat. 1-5. No charge; donations accepted. ♿
Attendance: 15,000 (accurate)
Membership: Individual $30; Family $50.

Bokeelia

KOUCKY GALLERY, 5971 Bay Point Rd, Bokeelia, FL 33922-2860. Tel.: 239-283-4414. Fax: 231-547-2455; 239-283-4495.
E-mail: kouckygallery@gmail.com
Web Site: www.kouckygallery.com
Art Museum.
Collections: fine arts; paintings; sculptures; jewelry.
Hours & Admission Prices: Winter: Mon.-Sat. 9-5; Summer: call for hours.

Bonita Springs

ART LEAGUE OF BONITA SPRINGS, (M), 26100 Old 41 Rd., Bonita Springs, FL 34135-8613. Tel.: 239-495-8989. Fax: 239-495-3999.
E-mail: albs@artinusa.com
Web Site: www.artcenterbonita.org
Founded: 1959.
Key Personnel: Exec. Dir., Susan Bridges.
Personnel Profile: Full-Time Paid 11; Part-Time Paid 2; Part-Time Volunteers 1,102; Interns 25.
Governing Authority: Tax-exempt.
Art Museum.
Collections: paintings; photographs; sculpture.
Activities: educational programs; classes; special events & activities; lectures; festivals; luncheons. Museum Sponsors: Beaux Arts Ball and Auction.
Hours & Admission Prices: Mon.-Fri. 10-4, Sat. 1-5. No charge; donations accepted. Closed New Year's Day; Christmas. ♿
Attendance: 85,000 (estimated)
Membership: Student $25; Individual $70; Family $95; Business Patron $300; Business Patron Circle $600; Corporate $1,000.

Bowling Green

PAYNES CREEK HISTORIC STATE PARK, 888 Lake Branch Rd., Bowling Green, FL 33834-4078. Tel.: 863-375-4717. Fax: 863-375-4510.
E-mail: jackson.mosley@dep.state.fl.us
Web Site: www.floridastateparks.org
Formerly: Paynes Creek State Historic Site
Founded: 1981.
Congressional District: 10
Key Personnel: Park Mgr., Jacks Mosley; Park Ranger, Ray N. Gilmore; Pres. (V) & Park Ranger, Sam Hale.
Personnel Profile: Full-Time Paid 3; Full-Time Volunteers 6; Part-Time Paid 2; Part-Time Volunteers 10.
Governing Authority: state. Parent Institution: Dept. of Environmental Protection. Tax-exempt.
Historic Site: located near c.1850 Ft. Chokonikla, Seminole Indian War Fort Visitor Center.
Collections: trading post items; Seminole costumes; military uniforms; historic paintings; c.1850 cannon; artifacts from Ft. Chokonikla: bullets, bottles, buttons, utensils & pipes.
Facilities: 65-seat theatre.
Activities: guided tours; organized education programs for children.
Hours & Admission Prices: Daily 8am to sundown. $3 per vehicle. ♿
Attendance: 31,000 (estimated)

Boynton Beach

THE SCHOOLHOUSE CHILDREN'S MUSEUM, 129 E. Ocean Ave., Boynton Beach, FL 33435-4536. Tel.: 561-742-6780. Fax: 561-742-6781.
E-mail: susanne@schoolhousemuseum.org
Web Site: www.schoolhousemuseum.org
Key Personnel: Interim Dir., Susanne Berman; Pres. (V), Stacey Accardi.
Personnel Profile: Full-Time Paid 5; Part-Time Paid 5; Part-Time Volunteers 25.
Governing Authority: Parent Institution: City of Boynton Beach. Subsidiary Institution: Boynton Cultural Centre. Tax-exempt.
Children's Museum.
Collections: hands-on exhibits.
Facilities: Museum-related items for sale.
Activities: birthday parties; special events; holiday workshops; educational programs.
Hours & Admission Prices: Tues.-Sat. 10-5. Adults $5, grandparents $4, children 2-17 $3; discounts to groups of 10 or more. ♿
Membership: Individual $25; Grandparents $35; Basic $50; National Reciprocal $100; Supporting $250.

Bradenton

ARTCENTER MANATEE, 209 9th St., W., Bradenton, FL 34205-8627. Tel.: 941-746-2862. Fax: 941-746-2319.
E-mail: acm@artcentermanatee.org
Web Site: www.artcentermanatee.org
Formerly: Art League of Manatee County
Founded: 1937.
Congressional District: 10
Key Personnel: Dir., Diane Shelly.
Personnel Profile: Full-Time Paid 4; Part-Time Paid 2; Part-Time Volunteers 200.
Governing Authority: board of directors; nonprofit organization. Tax-exempt.
Arts Center.
Collections: works by local, regional & national artists.
Major Exhibits: American Watercolor Society (T), 1/15/10-2/28/10; Delicious - A Culinary Open Show, 3/2/10-3/26/10; A Perfect 10 - ACM Member Show, 3/30/10-4/23/10; Flashback: A 60s Retrospective, 5/25/10-6/18/10.
Facilities: 3,000-vol. library on art, artists, artist's material & techniques available on premises or by special permission; reading room. Handcrafts, art works & gifts for sale.
Activities: lectures; films; gallery talks; arts festivals; workshops; formally organized education programs; instruction in painting, pottery, drawing, sumie & fine crafts; children's programs; temporary exhibits.
Publications: exhibition & class schedules; e-newsletters.
Hours & Admission Prices: Mon. & Fri.-Sat. 9-5, Tues.-Thurs. 9-6. No charge; donations accepted. Closed New Year's Eve & Day; Memorial Day; Independence Day; Labor Day; Thanksgiving; Christmas Eve & Day. ♿
Attendance: 30,000 (estimated)
Membership: Student $20; Adult $50; Family $70.

DESOTO NATIONAL MEMORIAL, 75th St., N.W., Bradenton, FL 34209. Mailing Address: P.O. Box 15390, Bradenton, FL 34280-5390. Tel.: 941-792-0458, ext. 105. Fax: 941-792-5094.
E-mail: deso_ranger_activities@nps.gov
Web Site: www.nps.gov/deso/
Founded: 1948.
Congressional District: 13
Key Personnel: Supt., Scott Pardue; Park Ranger, Ben Sims.
Personnel Profile: Full-Time Paid 6; Part-Time Paid 5; Part-Time Volunteers 20.
Governing Authority: federal. Parent Institution: Dept. of the Interior. Affiliated with the National Park Service. Tax-exempt.
Park Museum.
Collections: 16th-century European military artifacts; pre-historic Native American artifacts.
Research Fields: Spanish period of 16th century & related fields.
Facilities: 1,000-vol. library of 16th-century history of the Spanish, Native Americans, Europeans & National Park material available for use on premises; auditorium; 16th-century living history camp; visitor center; nature trails.
Activities: narrative film; permanent exhibits; self-guiding nature trail. Museum Sponsors: living history camp with demonstrations mid-Dec. to mid-April.
Publications: informational brochure.
Hours & Admission Prices: Visitor Center: daily 9-5. History Camp: mid-Dec. to mid-April daily 10-4, call to confirm. No charge; donations accepted. Closed New Year's Day; Thanksgiving; Christmas. ♿
Attendance: 275,505 (accurate)

MANATEE VILLAGE HISTORICAL PARK, 1404 Manatee Ave. E., Bradenton, FL 34208-1360. Tel.: 941-741-4075. Fax: 941-708-5924.
E-mail: dean.dixon@manateeave.e
Web Site: www.manateeclerk.com
Founded: 1974.
Congressional District: 10
Key Personnel: Supvr., Dean Dixon; Chm. (V), Mark Barneby.
Personnel Profile: Full-Time Paid 4; Part-Time Volunteers 50.
Governing Authority: county government. Parent Institution: Manatee County Clerk of Circuit Courts. Tax-exempt: 501(c)(3).
Local History Museum.
Collections: Manatee County history, 1841-1914; period furniture & furnishings; children's hands-on exhibits; Florida barn; smokehouse; sugar kettle & mill; boat works. Historic Buildings: 1866 courthouse; 1887 church; 1912 farm house; 1903 general store; 1908 one-room schoolhouse; 1920s cowhunter bunkhouse; Turpentine Still; blacksmith shop.
Research Fields: Manatee County history.
Facilities: 50-vol. library of Manatee County history books, available for use by public; educational facilities; children's hands-on room.
Activities: guided tours; lectures; organized education programs for children; docent program; participatory, loan, temporary & traveling exhibitions; school loan service. Museum Sponsors: Heritage Days in March; Manatee County History Fair in November.
Publications: monthly newsletter, The Cabbage Head Gazette.
Hours & Admission Prices: July-Aug. Mon.-Fri. 9-4:30; Sept.-June Mon.-Fri. & 2nd & 4th Sat. of month 9-4:30. No charge; donations accepted. Closed holidays. ♿
Attendance: 40,000 (estimated)

SOUTH FLORIDA MUSEUM, BISHOP PLANETARIUM & PARKER MANATEE AQUARIUM, (M), 201 10th St., W., Bradenton, FL 34205-8635. Mailing Address: P.O. Box 9265, Bradenton, FL 34206-9265. Tel.: 941-746-4131, ext. 18. Fax: 941-747-2556.
Web Site: www.southfloridamuseum.org

Founded: 1946.
Congressional District: 10
Key Personnel: Dir., Brynne Anne Besio; Chm. & Pres. (V), William Blalock; Office Mgr. & Sec., Debi Applebee; Museum Shop Mgr., Ellen Ferraro.
Personnel Profile: Full-Time Paid 10; Part-Time Paid 16; Part-Time Volunteers 120; Interns 2.
Governing Authority: bd. of directors; nonprofit organization. Tax-exempt: 501(c)(3).
General Museum & Planetarium.
Collections: archaeology; astronomy; live manatee exhibit; geology; history; Indian artifacts; science & natural history; paleontology; medical; ethnology; costumes; manuscripts; transportation; maritime history; decorative arts.
Research Fields: ongoing projects with manatee.
Facilities: educational facilities; hands-on environmental classroom. Educational books & gifts for sale.
Activities: docent program or council; permanent & temporary exhibitions; film series. Museum Sponsors: school programs.
Publications: brochures; leaflets; museum notes; quarterly newsletter.
Hours & Admission Prices: Museum: Jan.-April & July Mon.-Sat. 10-5, Sun. noon-5; May-June & Aug.-Dec. Tues.-Sat. 10-5, Sun. noon-5. Museum, Aquarium & Planetarium: adult $15.95, senior 60 & over $13.95, children 4-12 $11.95; discounts to groups & ASTC members; members & children under 4 no charge. Closed New Year's Day; Thanksgiving; Christmas. ♿
Attendance: 85,000 (estimated)
Membership: Individual $50; Family $125; Sponsor $250; Patron $500; Benefactor $750.

Bristol

TORREYA STATE PARK, 2576 N.W. Torreya Park Rd., Bristol, FL 32321-2203. Tel.: 850-643-2674. Fax: 850-643-2987.
E-mail: steven.cutshaw@dep.state.fl.us
Web Site: www.floridastateparks.org/torreya
Key Personnel: Park Mgr., Steve Cutshaw.
Personnel Profile: Full-Time Paid 2; Part-Time Paid 1; Part-Time Volunteers 1.
Governing Authority: state. Tax-exempt.
Park & Historic House Museum.
Collections: Historic House: Gregory House built in 1849.
Activities: guided tours.
Hours & Admission Prices: Park: 8-sunset. Tours: Mon.-Fri. 10am, Sat.-Sun. & state holidays 10am, 2pm & 4pm. Adults $3, children 12 & under $2; children under 6 no charge.

Brooksville

HERNANDO HERITAGE MUSEUM, 601 Museum Ct., Brooksville, FL 34601-2631. Tel.: 352-799-0129. Fax: 352-799-4766.
E-mail: info@hernandohistoricalmuseumassoc.com
Web Site: hernandohistoricalmuseumassoc.com/index.htm
Founded: 1980.
Key Personnel: C.E.O., Virginia Jackson; Chm. (V), Virginia Rusk.
Personnel Profile: Part-Time Volunteers 25.
Governing Authority: Parent Institution: Hernando Historical Museum Assoc. Inc.
Historic House Museum: built c.1856. Listed on the National Register of Historic Places.
Collections: personal artifacts; summer kitchen; photographs; school room; war room; doctors room; 1885 train depot; Cracker Country display.
Activities: Living history; annual events: Museum Sponsors: Brooksville Raid Festival in January.
Publications: quarterly newsletters; histories.
Hours & Admission Prices: Tues.-Sat. 12-3. Suggested Donation: adults $5, children $2; students & scouts no charge. ♿
Attendance: 35,000 (estimated)

Bunnell

BULOW PLANTATION RUINS HISTORIC STATE PARK, 3501 S. Old Kings Rd., 9 mi. S.E. of Bunnell State Rd. 5, Bunnell, FL 32110. Mailing Address: P.O. Box 655, Bunnell, FL 32110-0655. Tel.: 386-517-2084.
Web Site: www.floridastateparks.org/bulowplantation/default.cfm
Founded: 1945.
Congressional District: 4
Key Personnel: Head Ranger, Nicky Makouski; Park Mgr., Benny Woodham.
Personnel Profile: Full-Time Paid 1; Part-Time Paid 2.
Governing Authority: state. Dept. of Environmental Protection, Div. of Recreation & Parks, Commonwealth Bldg., 3900 Commonwealth Blvd., Tallahassee, FL 32303, Tel: 850-488-9872.
History Museum: interpretive center.
Collections: sugar kettle and mill ruins; artifacts & small tools used on plantation; springhouse ruins.
Research Fields: plantation life of early 1800s.
Facilities: nature trail; picnic area with pavilion building; boat ramp; fishing dock.
Activities: permanent exhibitions; occasional tours.
Publications: park brochure.
Hours & Admission Prices: Thurs.-Mon. 9-5. $3 per vehicle, $1 bicycles & walk-ins. Canoe Rentals: $10 hr., $40 day. Pavilion Rental: $30 plus tax. ♿

Bushnell

DADE BATTLEFIELD HISTORIC STATE PARK, 7200 County Rd. 603, S. Battlefield Dr., Bushnell, FL 33513-3538. Tel.: 352-793-4781. Fax: 352-793-4230.
Web Site: www.floridastateparks.org
Formerly: Dade Battlefield State Historic Site
Founded: 1921.
Congressional District: 6
Key Personnel: Park Mgr., Tracey Stardridge; Pres. (V), Jean Mcnary; Park Ranger, Chuck Wicks; Park Ranger, George Webb.
Personnel Profile: Full-Time Paid 3; Part-Time Paid 1; Part-Time Volunteers 6.
Governing Authority: state. Parent Institution: Dept. of Environmental Protection, Div. of Recreation and Parks, Commonwealth Bldg., 3900 Commonwealth Blvd., Tallahassee, FL 32303. Tax-exempt.
Historic Site and Park Museum: site of a battle between Seminole & US soldiers on Dec. 28, 1835.
Collections: interpretive exhibits; artifacts of the battle; video.
Facilities: picnic area; nature trail; rental hall.
Activities: guided tours, permanent exhibitions, interpretive programs for organized groups can be arranged by contacting site six weeks in advance. Annual Events: WWII Commemorative Day in August; Battle Reenactments in late Dec. & early Jan.
Hours & Admission Prices: Museum: daily 9-5. Grounds: daily 8am to sunset. $3 per vehicle, $1 bicycles & walk-ins. Bus fee $40 or $1 per person. ♿
Attendance: 30,000 (estimated)
Membership: Dade Battlefield Society: Individual Adult $10. Florida Park Service Annual Permit: Individual $30; Family $60.

Cape Coral

CAPE CORAL HISTORICAL MUSEUM, 544 Cultural Park Blvd., Cape Coral, FL 33990-1212. Mailing Address: P.O. Box 150637, Cape Coral, FL 33915-0637. Tel.: 239-772-7037. Fax: 239-573-7518.
E-mail: ccoralmuseum@embarqmail.com
Web Site: www.capecoralhistoricalmuseum.org
Founded: 1986.
Key Personnel: Cur., Anne C. Cull.
Personnel Profile: Part-Time Paid 1; Part-Time Volunteers 40.
Governing Authority: private; nonprofit organization. Tax-exempt.
History Museum.
Collections: local history & culture; photographs; personal artifacts.
Activities: monthly speakers.
Publications: members monthly newsletter.
Hours & Admission Prices: Sept.-June Wed.-Thurs. & Sun. 1-4. Suggested Donation: $2. Closed holidays. ♿
Attendance: 1,500 (estimated)
Membership: Single $15; Family $20; Corporate $500.

Carrabelle

CAMP GORDON JOHNSTON MUSEUM, City Complex, Gray Ave., 302 Marine St., Carrabelle, FL 32322. Tel.: 850-697-8575.
E-mail: campgordon@fairpoint.net
Web Site: campgordonjohnston.com
Key Personnel: Dir., Linda Manachelli
World War II Museum.
Collections: camp history; WWII soldier's heritage; photographs; uniforms; military artifacts.
Facilities: theater. Museum-related items for sale.
Hours & Admission Prices: Mon.-Thurs. 1-4, Fri. 12-4, Sat. 10-2. No charge; donations accepted.

Cedar Key

CEDAR KEY HISTORICAL SOCIETY MUSEUM, 2nd St. at State Rd. 24, Cedar Key, FL 32625. Mailing Address: P.O. Box 222, Cedar Key, FL 32625-0222. Tel.: 352-543-5549.
E-mail: cedarcedar@bellsouth.net
Web Site: www.cedarkeymuseum.org
Founded: 1979.
Congressional District: 2
Key Personnel: Pres. (V), George Sresovich; Dir., Galina Binkley; Vice Pres., John Andrews.

Personnel Profile: Part-Time Paid 1; Part-Time Volunteers 20.
Governing Authority: society; nonprofit. Tax-exempt.
Historical Society Museum: housed in c.1871 former private residence.
Collections: from prehistoric to modern times: fossils; shells; pencil & lumber industry; railroad history; maps & charts of early Florida; photographic collection; Indian artifacts & history; commercial fishing industry in Cedar Key.
Facilities: more than 60-vol. library of material on Florida & Cedar Key history; 2,500 sq. ft. exhibit space. Museum-related items for sale.
Publications: semiannual newsletter, The Beacon.
Hours & Admission Prices: Sun.-Fri. 1-4, Sat. 11-5. Adults $1, children over 12 $.50; members no charge. Closed Christmas & part of Christmas week. ♿
Attendance: 9,000
Membership: Student $10; Individual & Family $20; Small Business $25; Supporting $50; Contributing & Corporate Contributing $100; Sustaining $250; Corporate Sustaining & Patron $500; Benefactor & Corporate Benefactor $1,000.

CEDAR KEY MUSEUM STATE PARK, 12231 S.W. 166 Court, Cedar Key, FL 32625-6200. Tel.: 352-543-5350 & 5567. Fax: 352-543-0187.
E-mail: Charles.Neese@dep.state.fl.us
Web Site: www.floridastateparks.org
Founded: 1962.
Congressional District: 4
Key Personnel: C.E.O. & Exec. Dir., Michael W. Sole; Park Ranger, Charles Neese; Park Mgr., Kristin Ebersol.
Personnel Profile: Full-Time Paid 1; Part-Time Volunteers 5.
Governing Authority: state. Dept. of Environmental Protection, Div. of Recreation & Parks, Commonwealth Bldg., 3900 Commonwealth Blvd., Tallahassee, FL 32303. Tax-exempt.
State Museum.
Collections: Cedar Key history; shell collection; natural history.
Activities: permanent exhibitions.
Hours & Admission Prices: Thurs.-Mon. 10-5. Admission $2. Closed Christmas. ♿
Attendance: 20,408

Charlotte Harbor

CHARLOTTE COUNTY HISTORICAL CENTER, (M), 22959 Bayshore Rd., Charlotte Harbor, FL 33980-2000. Tel.: 941-629-7278. Fax: 941-743-3917.
E-mail: historicalcenter@charlottefl.com
Web Site: charlottecountyfl.com/historical
Formerly: Florida Adventure Museum of Charlotte County
Founded: 1969.
Congressional District: 72
Key Personnel: Historical Supvr., Linda Coleman.
Personnel Profile: Full-Time Paid 2; Part-Time Paid 1; Part-Time Volunteers 369.
Governing Authority: Parent Institution: Charlotte County Parks, Recreation & Cultural Resources Dept. Tax-exempt.
General Museum.
Collections: personal artifacts; archives; local & state history.
Major Exhibits: Florida Girls & Boys and Their Toys (T), 1/10-5/10.
Facilities: Books & museum-related items for sale.
Activities: self-guided tours; organized education programs; docent program; participatory, temporary & traveling exhibitions; school loan service; annual festival.
Publications: newsletter, The Charlotte Historian.
Hours & Admission Prices: Tues.-Fri. 10-5, Sat. 10-3. Adults $2, children $1; discounts to ASTC members; members no charge. Closed holidays. ♿
Attendance: 8,000 (accurate)
Membership: Individual $20; Family & Grandparent $35; Friend $50; Donor $100; Benefactor $500; Angel $1,000.

Chokoloskee

TED SMALLWOOD'S STORE, INC., 360 Mamie St., Chokoloskee, FL 34138. Mailing Address: P.O. Box 367, Chokoloskee, FL 34138-0367. Tel.: 239-695-2989. Fax: 239-695-4454.
E-mail: ishtoholo@ataol.com
Web Site: www.florida-everglades.com/chokol/smallw.tm
Founded: 1989.
Key Personnel: Exec. Dir., Ms. Lynn Smallwood McMillin.
Governing Authority: private; nonprofit organization.
History Museum: housed in 1906 Indian Trading Post.
Collections: Florida history from prehistoric to modern times with emphasis on Chokoloskee.
Activities: killing Mr. Watson reenactment. Museum Sponsors: Seminole Day, 100 Year Celebration.
Hours & Admission Prices: May 2-Nov. Fri.-Tues. 10-4; Dec.-May 1 daily 10-5. Adults $3, senior citizens $2.50; discounts to groups of 10 or more; children under 12 no charge. Closed Thanksgiving; Christmas Eve & Day.
Attendance: 32,000 (estimated)
Membership: Student $5; Senior Citizen $15; Adult $25; Family $40.

Christmas

FORT CHRISTMAS HISTORICAL PARK, 1300 Fort Christmas Rd., Christmas, FL 32709-9427. Tel.: 407-568-4149. Fax: 407-568-9790.
E-mail: cheryl.wasserman@ocfl.net
Web Site: parks.onetgov.net
Founded: 1977.
Key Personnel: Historic Site Supvr., Trudy Trask; Recreation Specialist, Vickie Prewett; Recreation Specialist, Joseph Adams; Recreation Leader, Shirley Truex; Recreation Leader, Cheryl Wasserman; Museum Shop Mgr., Mary Clark; Senior Parks Specialist, Mike Heller; Park Specialist, Jeff Hamilton.
Personnel Profile: Full-Time Paid 7; Full-Time Volunteers 2; Part-Time Paid 2; Part-Time Volunteers 10.
Governing Authority: county. Tax-exempt.
History Museum.
Collections: military artifacts; period furnishings.
Research Fields: family history; architectural history of structures; interviews & oral histories.
Facilities: library; pavilions for outdoor classrooms. Museum-related items for sale.
Activities: formal education programs for children; lectures. Museum Sponsors: Cracker Christmas; Historic Military Encampments; Bluegrass Festival; Pioneer Homecoming.
Hours & Admission Prices: Park: Summer: daily 8-8; Winter: daily 8-6. Museum: Tues.-Sat. 10-5, Sun. 1-5. Pioneer Homes: Tues.-Sat. 10-12 & 1-3:30, Sun. 1-3:30. No charge; donations accepted. Closed holidays. ♿
Attendance: 123,775 (estimated)
Membership: Individual $10; Family $15; Patron $50; Life $350.

Clearwater

CLEARWATER MARINE AQUARIUM, 249 Windward Passage, Clearwater, FL 33767-2244. Tel.: 727-441-1790, ext. 240. Fax: 727-445-1139.
E-mail: fdame@cmaquarium.org
Web Site: www.seewinter.com
Founded: 1972.
Congressional District: 9
Key Personnel: Chm., Tom Orr; Vice Chm., John Draheim; Dir., David Yates; Sec., Ellen Bilgore; Treas., Bruce Veghte; Exec. Vice Pres., Frank Dame; Dir. Merchandising, Patty Belcher.
Personnel Profile: Full-Time Paid 30; Part-Time Paid 15; Part-Time Volunteers 500; Interns 25.
Governing Authority: nonprofit organization. Tax-exempt: 501(c)(3).
Aquarium & Marine Museum.
Collections: specializing in education, marine research & the rescue, rehabilitation & release of injured or sick whales, dolphins, otters & sea turtles.
Research Fields: marine mammal & sea turtle rescue & rehabilitation.
Facilities: library pertaining to sea life; aquarium; educational facilities. Museum-related items for sale.
Activities: films; formal educational programs; guided tours; lectures; temporary exhibitions of your own collections; traveling exhibitions; broadcast programs. Museum Sponsors: Annual Coastal Clean-up.
Publications: quarterly newsletter, Lifelines.
Hours & Admission Prices: Sun. 10-5, Mon.-Thurs. 9-5, Fri.-Sat. 9-9. Adults $11, children $6.50; discounts to FAA & AAA members & groups; children under 3 & members no charge. Closed New Year's Day; Easter; Thanksgiving; Christmas Eve & Day. ♿
Attendance: 100,000 (estimated)
Membership: Senior Citizen $25; Individual $40; Couple $55; Party of Four $75; Six Pack $99; Eight Pack $250; Sponsor $1,000.

MOCCASIN LAKE NATURE PARK, AN ENVIRONMENTAL & ENERGY EDUCATION CENTER, 2750 Park Trail Lane, Clearwater, FL 33759-2602. Tel.: 727-793-2976. Fax: 727-793-2978. TDD: 727-562-4833.
E-mail: cliff.norris@myclearwater.com
Web Site: www.myclearwater.com
Founded: 1982.
Key Personnel: Nature Park Supvr., Cliff Norris; Nature Park Programmer, Lloyd Simmons; Nature Park Support Technician, Dave Weitzel.
Personnel Profile: Full-Time Paid 4; Part-Time Volunteers 135; Interns 1.
Governing Authority: municipal government. Parent Institution: City of Clearwater. Subsidiary Institution: Parks & Recreation Dept. Tax-exempt: 501(c)(3).

Nature Center & Conservation Area; Alternative Energy Demonstration Center.
Collections: plants native to Florida; natural history; alternative/renewable energy systems; permanently injured birds of prey native to Florida; arboretum; live reptiles & amphibian displays; fish tanks; exotic nuisance plants & animals of Florida.
Facilities: library of natural history & energy books; herbarium; 100-seat classroom; educational facilities; nature trail; wildlife preserve. Gift items for sale.
Activities: alternative/renewable energy demonstrations; Families Exploring Nature Club; guided tours; lectures; organized educational programs; docent program; temporary & interactive exhibitions; local chapter meetings of Sierra Club, Audubon & Suncoast Herpetological Society; Science Safari Educational Company nature camps; Native Plant Society.
Publications: quarterly magazine, Clearwater.
Hours & Admission Prices: June-Aug. Mon.-Fri. 9-5; Sept.-May Tues.-Fri. 9-5, Sat. 10-5. Additional hours for special programming. Nonresidents adults $3, Clearwater Residents adults $2; children under 3 no charge. Closed city holidays. ♿
Attendance: 51,000 (accurate)

NAPOLEONIC SOCIETY OF AMERICA, INC., (M), 1115 Ponce de Leon Blvd., Clearwater, FL 33756-1040. Mailing Address: 6000A W. Irving Park Rd., Chicago, IL 60634-2520. Tel.: 773-794-1804. Fax: 773-794-1769.
E-mail: staff@napoleonic-society.com
Web Site: www.napoleonic-society.com
Founded: 1983.
Congressional District: 8
Key Personnel: Exec. Dir. & Contact, Todd Fisher.
Personnel Profile: Part-Time Paid 2.
Governing Authority: nonprofit organization. Parent Institution: Napoleonic Society of America. Tax-exempt: 501(c)(3).
History Museum.
Collections: books & prints of the life & times of Napoleon Bonaparte; artifacts, weapons.
Facilities: 800-vol. library of Napoleonic material available to the public; 800 sq. ft. exhibit space. Prints, certificates & plates for sale.
Activities: guided tours to Europe; annual conferences.
Publications: quarterly, Member's Bulletin.
Hours & Admission Prices: Mon.-Fri. 10-5. No charge; donations accepted.
Attendance: 1,000 (estimated)
Membership: Students $24; Regular Member $48. Foreign: Canada $52; all other $60.

Clewiston

CLEWISTON MUSEUM, INC., 109 Central Ave., Clewiston, FL 33440-3701. Tel.: 863-983-2870.
E-mail: clewistonmuseum@embarqmail.com
Web Site: www.clewistonmuseum.org
Founded: 1984.
Congressional District: 12
Key Personnel: Chm. (V), Miller Couse.
Personnel Profile: Full-Time Volunteers 1; Part-Time Volunteers 2.
Governing Authority: nonprofit organization. Parent Institution: Friends of the Museum. Tax-exempt: 501(c)(3).
Heritage & History Museum: housed in c.1928 Clewiston News Building.
Collections: agriculture; Seminole Indians; World War II; community history.
Facilities: 60-seat theater. Books & crafts for sale.
Activities: traveling exhibitions; films & lectures on the sugar cane & citrus industry of the south Lake Okeechobee area.
Publications: Pioneering in the Everglades by Beardsley.
Hours & Admission Prices: Mon.-Fri. 9-4; other times by appointment. Adults $4, seniors $3. Closed major holidays. ♿
Attendance: 1,000 (estimated)
Membership: Individual $15; Family $30; Sponsor $50; Patron $100; Corporate $250; Corporate Silver $500; Corporate Gold $1,000.

Cocoa

ASTRONAUT MEMORIAL PLANETARIUM AND OBSERVATORY, Brevard Community College, 1519 Clearlake Rd., Cocoa, FL 32922-6598. Tel.: 321-433-7373. Fax: 321-433-7646.
E-mail: leslies@brevardcc.edu
Web Site: www.brevardcc.edu/planet
Founded: 1976.
Congressional District: 11
Key Personnel: Dir., Mark Howard; Assoc. Dir., Suzanne Leslie.
Personnel Profile: Full-Time Paid 3; Part-Time Paid 3; Part-Time Volunteers 20.
Governing Authority: community college; nonprofit. Parent Institution: Brevard Community College.
Astronomy Museum.
Collections: telescope; Minolta Infinium Star Projector.
Research Fields: laser graphics; astrophotography & imagining; U.S., Soviet/Russian/CIS, & all other international astronauts, cosmonauts, and spationautes; advanced exhibit development.
Facilities: planetarium; observatory; IWERKS theater; classroom.
Activities: films; formal education programs for children and undergraduate & graduate college students; guided tours; participatory & temporary exhibits; portable planetarium; special programs.
Publications: quarterly newsletter, Focal Point.
Hours & Admission Prices: Exhibit Halls: Wed. 1:30-4:30, Fri.-Sat. 6:30pm-10:30pm. Public Shows: Wed. 2 & 3, Fri.-Sat. 7pm, 8pm & 9pm. Observatory: Fri. -Sat. dusk-10pm. Single Show: adults $7, seniors, students, & military $6, children 12 & under $4. Planetarium & Movie: adults $11, seniors, students, & military $9, children 12 & under $7. Planetarium, Movie, & Laser: admission $16. ♿
Attendance: 40,000 (estimated)
Membership: Single $35; Family $70; Sponsor $120; Corporate $500 & up.

BREVARD MUSEUM OF HISTORY & SCIENCE, 2201 Michigan Ave., Cocoa, FL 32926-5618. Tel.: 321-632-1830 & 1920. Fax: 321-631-7551.
E-mail: bmhs@brevardmuseum.org
Web Site: www.brevardmuseum.org
Founded: 1969.
Congressional District: 29
Key Personnel: C.E.O. & Dir., JaNeen Kniprath Smith; Pres. (V), Carol Ellis; Museum Shop Mgr. & Receptionist, Brandon L. Brown.
Personnel Profile: Full-Time Paid 1; Part-Time Paid 3; Part-Time Volunteers 32; Interns 1.
Governing Authority: nonprofit organization. Tax-exempt: 501(c)(3).
History & Natural Science Museum.
Collections: natural science; archaeology; local history; children's discovery room; Windover, 8,000 year old dig exhibit.
Research Fields: anthropology, archaeology, local history, malacology, ornithology, botany, ecology, entomology.
Facilities: 60-seat classroom; laboratory; discovery room; picnic pavilion & nature center with trails.
Activities: school & adult group programming.
Publications: brochures; History of the Cape Canaveral Lighthouse; printed material on special exhibits; cookbook; calendar; bimonthly newsletter, The Dillo's Tale.
Hours & Admission Prices: June-Aug. Thurs.-Sat. 10-4; Sept.-May Tues.-Sat. 10-4. Adults $6, seniors $5.50, college students $5, children 5-16 $4.50; members no charge. Closed New Year's Day; Easter; Thanksgiving; Christmas Eve & Day. ♿
Attendance: 25,000 (accurate)
Membership: Student $20; Teacher $25; Individual $30; Couple $40; Family $50; Corporate $2,500.

FLORIDA HISTORICAL SOCIETY, 435 Brevard Ave., Cocoa, FL 32922-7901. Tel.: 321-690-1971. Fax: 321-690-4388.
Founded: 1856.
Key Personnel: Dir., Benjamin Brotemarkle; Museum Shop Mgr., Debra Wynne.
Personnel Profile: Full-Time Paid 4; Part-Time Paid 2; Part-Time Volunteers 20.
Governing Authority: Tax-exempt.
Historical Society Museum.
Collections: local history & culture; photographs; manuscripts.
Facilities: research library.
Publications: Florida historical quarterly.
Hours & Admission Prices: Tues.-Sat. 10-4:30. No charge; donations accepted. ♿

Coconut Grove

THE BARNACLE HISTORIC STATE PARK, 3485 Main Hwy., Coconut Grove, FL 33133-5915. Tel.: 305-442-6866. Fax: 305-442-6872.
E-mail: katrina.boler@dep.state.fl.us
Web Site: www.floridastateparks.org/TheBarnacle
Founded: 1973.
Key Personnel: Pres., Jonathan Hill; Park Mgr., Katrina A. Boler; Park Svcs. Specialist, Kim Good.
Personnel Profile: Full-Time Paid 2; Part-Time Paid 3; Part-Time Volunteers 20; Interns 2.
Governing Authority: state; nonprofit. Tax-exempt: 501(c)(3).
Historic House.
Collections: memorabilia of pioneer and yacht designer Commodore Ralph

Middleton Munore & his family; marine artifacts; photographs; cameras; furniture; household items; handmade family quilts; boathouse; tools.
Facilities: Museum-related items for sale.
Activities: arts festivals; concerts; docent program; guided tours; hobby workshops; grounds rental. Museum Sponsors: Regatta (traditional Sailboats); Old-fashioned Independence Day Picnic; Commodore's Birthday Party (volunteer recruit); Firefly Lawn Party (fundraiser); monthly Moonlight Concerts; Old Time Dances; Yoga by the Sea; Washington's Birthday Regatta; Earth Day Celebration.
Publications: quarterly newsletter, The News Packet.
Hours & Admission Prices: Fri.-Mon. 9-5. Tours: 10, 11:30, 1 & 2:30. Group Tours: Wed-Thurs. with advanced reservations. Admission $1. Closed New Year's Day; Thanksgiving; Christmas. ♿
Attendance: 32,000 (estimated)
Membership: Senior Citizen $15; Individual $25; Family $30; Sustaining $50; Contributing $100; Patron $250; Corporate $500; Life $1,000.

Coral Gables

CORAL GABLES MUSEUM, (M), 285 Aragon Ave., Coral Gables, FL 33134. Mailing Address: P.O. Box 141687, Coral Gables, FL 33114-1687. Tel.: 305-910-3996.
E-mail: info@coralgablesmuseum.org
Web Site: www.coralgablesmuseum.org
Founded: 2003.
Congressional District: 18
Key Personnel: Chm. (V), George Kakouris.
Governing Authority: Tax-exempt.
History Museum: housed in the Phineas Paist Police and Fire Station built in 1936.
Collections: local history & culture; paintings; photographs; documents.
Activities: educational programs; special events.
Hours & Admission Prices: Closed until late 2010.

* **FAIRCHILD TROPICAL BOTANIC GARDEN, (M),** 10901 Old Cutler Rd., Coral Gables, FL 33156-4296. Tel.: 305-667-1651. Fax: 305-661-8953.
E-mail: clewis@fairchildgarden.org
Web Site: www.fairchildgarden.org
Founded: 1938.
Congressional District: 19
Key Personnel: Pres. (V), Bruce W. Greer; Dir., Carl E. Lewis, Ph.D.; Dir. Museum Shop, Erin Fitts.
Personnel Profile: Full-Time Paid 100; Part-Time Paid 19; Part-Time Volunteers 440; Interns 2.
Governing Authority: nonprofit organization. Tax-exempt: 501(c)(3).
Botanical Garden.
Collections: living tropical & sub-tropical plants.
Research Fields: tropical botany & horticulture.
Facilities: 15,000-vol. library of books on tropical botany & horticulture available on premises by appointment. Books for sale.
Activities: guided tours; lectures; classes; plant shows & sales. Museum Sponsors: International Mango Festival; International Orchid Festival; ramble; International Chocolate Festival; Family Harvest Day.
Publications: quarterly magazine, The Tropical Garden.
Hours & Admission Prices: Daily 9:30-4:30. Adults $20, seniors $15, children 6-17 $10; children 5 & under no charge. Closed Christmas. ♿
Attendance: 146,388 (accurate)
Membership: Student $25; Associate $40; Associate Plus $60; Family & Friends $80; Sustaining $125; Supporting $250; Signature $500; Fellow $1,000-$2,499; Silver Fellow $2,500-$4,999; Gold Fellow $5,000-$9,999; Platinum Fellow $10,000 & up.

* **LOWE ART MUSEUM, UNIVERSITY OF MIAMI, (M),** 1301 Stanford Dr., Coral Gables, FL 33146-2099. Tel.: 305-284-3535. Fax: 305-284-2024.
Web Site: www.lowemuseum.org
Founded: 1950.
Congressional District: 18
Key Personnel: Dir. & Chief Cur., Brian A. Dursum; Assoc. Dir., Denise M. Gerson; Adjunct Cur. African Art., Marcilene Wittmer; Adjunct Cur. Renaissance, Perri L. Roberts; Dir. Membership, Yina Balarezo-Badenjki; Asst. Dir., Kara Schneiderman; Assoc. Preparator, Martin Casuso; Cur. Education, Jodi Sypher; Fiscal Officer, Jason Janik; Special Events Coord., Irene Bergmann; Receptionist, Janie Graulich; Head Security, Maria Milhomme; Curatorial Asst., Gita Shonek; Museum Shop Mgr., Lorraine Stassun.
Personnel Profile: Full-Time Paid 14; Part-Time Paid 2; Part-Time Volunteers 200; Interns 2.
Governing Authority: Parent Institution: University of Miami. Tax-exempt: 501(c)(3).
Art Museum.
Collections: Samuel H. Kress collection of Renaissance & Baroque Art; Alfred I. Barton collection of North American Indian Art; Samuel K. Lothrop collection of Guatemalan Textiles; pre-Columbian Art; Asian sculpture, bronzes, ceramics & painting; African Art; Art of the Pacific; European & American painting, sculpture & works on paper; Greco-Roman antiquities.
Research Fields: all fields pertaining to collections.
Facilities: classroom; studio. Paintings, sculptures, books, cards & jewelry for sale.
Activities: guided tours; lectures; films; gallery talks; concerts; arts festivals; family days; formally organized educational programs; educational outreach program; docent program; inter-museum loan; intra-campus lending program; permanent, temporary & traveling exhibitions.
Publications: quarterly newsletter, The Lowe; catalogs; brochures.
Hours & Admission Prices: Tues.-Sat. 10-4, Sun. 12-4. Adults $10, senior citizens & students $5; discounts to AAM members; children under 12 & members no charge. Closed major holidays. ♿
Attendance: 49,710 (accurate)
Membership: Academic $30; Cintas Individual $50; Kress Family $65; Barton $100; Contemporary $150; Friends of Art $350; Director's Circle $1,200.

Coral Springs

CORAL SPRINGS MUSEUM OF ART, (M), 2855 Coral Springs Dr., Coral Springs, FL 33065-3825. Tel.: 954-340-5000. Fax: 954-346-4424.
E-mail: ctbok@coralsprings.org
Web Site: www.csmart.org
Founded: 1997.
Congressional District: 19
Key Personnel: Exec. Dir., Barbara O'Keefe; Pres. (V), Dr. Kerry Kuhn.
Personnel Profile: Full-Time Paid 4; Part-Time Paid 3; Part-Time Volunteers 67.
Governing Authority: private; nonprofit organization. Tax-exempt: 501(c)(3).
Art Museum.
Collections: visual art; contemporary.
Facilities: 10,000 sq. ft. exhibit space; classrooms. Museum-related items for sale.
Activities: formal education programs; guided tours; lectures; temporary exhibitions; artist in residence program.
Hours & Admission Prices: Summer: Mon.-Sat. 10-5; Winter: Mon.-Wed. & Fri.-Sat. 10-5, Thurs. 10-8. Adults $5, seniors $4, students $3; discounts to AAM & ICOM members; Wed., children 12 & under and members no charge. Closed major holidays. ♿
Attendance: 31,000 (estimated)
Membership: Mondrian $50; Calder $75; Monet $100; Pollock $250; Cezanne $500; Picasso $1,000; Michelangelo $5,000.

Cross Creek

MARJORIE KINNAN RAWLINGS HISTORIC STATE PARK, 18700 S. County Rd. 325, Cross Creek, FL 32640-8403. Tel.: 352-466-3672 & 9273. Fax: 352-466-4743.
E-mail: valerie.rivers@dep.state.fl.us
Web Site: www.floridastateparks.org
Formerly: Marjorie Kinnan Rawlings State Historic Site
Founded: 1970.
Key Personnel: Park Mgr., Valerie Rivers.
Personnel Profile: Full-Time Paid 3; Part-Time Paid 5; Part-Time Volunteers 12; Interns 1.
Governing Authority: state. Dept. of Environmental Protection, Division of Recreation & Parks, 3900 Commonwealth Blvd., Commonwealth Bldg., Tallahassee, FL 32303. Tax-exempt.
Historic House Museum: c.1930's citrus farm & home of Marjorie Kinnan Rawlings, a rambling Cracker farmhouse. A National Historic Landmark.
Collections: furnishings of Marjorie Kinnan Rawlings author of The Yearling, Cross Creek, and other books.
Activities: guided tours.
Hours & Admission Prices: Daily 9-5. $3 per car. House Tours: Oct.-July Thurs.-Sun. 10-4. Adults $3, children 6-12 $2; children under 6 no charge. Closed Thanksgiving; Christmas. ♿
Attendance: 25,000
Membership: CSO - Friends of the Marjorie Kinnan Rawlings Farm $20.

Crystal River

COASTAL HERITAGE MUSEUM, 532 Citrus Ave., Crystal River, FL 34428-4017. Tel.: 352-795-1755 & 563-0097. Fax: 352-341-6445.
E-mail: crcoastalmuseum@aol.com
Web Site: citrushistorical.org

Formerly: The Museum of Citrus County History-Coastal Heritage
Founded: 1986.
Congressional District: 6
Key Personnel: Chm. (V), Sharon Padgett.
Personnel Profile: Part-Time Volunteers 20.
Governing Authority: county. Parent Institution: Citrus County Historical Society. Tax-exempt: 501(c)(3).
Local History Museum: housed in 1939 old City Hall.
Collections: west Citrus County history; archaeological artifacts; furniture; photographs.
Research Fields: Citrus County history & pre-history.
Facilities: archival repository. Museum-related items for sale.
Activities: guided tours; docent program. Annual Event: Tour of Historic Homes in March.
Publications: bimonthly newsletter, At Home; brochures; calendar; book, A History of Crystal River, Florida; brochure, Historic Tour Guide of Crystal River, Florida.
Hours & Admission Prices: Aug.-June Tues.-Sat. 10-2. No charge, donations accepted. Closed holidays. ♿
Attendance: 2,100 (accurate)
Membership: Student $5; Individual $15; Family $22; Business $30; Supporting $100; Life $250; Corporate $500.

CRYSTAL RIVER ARCHAEOLOGICAL STATE PARK, 3400 N. Museum Pt., Crystal River, FL 34428-6207. Tel.: 352-795-3817. Fax: 352-795-6061.
Web Site: floridastateparks.org
Founded: 1965.
Congressional District: 6
Key Personnel: Park Mgr., Nicholas D. Robbins; Park Ranger & Chm. (V), Henry L. Smith; Park Ranger & Museum Shop Mgr., Michael Petellat.
Personnel Profile: Full-Time Paid 3.
Governing Authority: state. Parent Institution: Florida Dept. of Environmental Protection. Tax-exempt.
State Park Museum.
Collections: archaeology; ancient Florida Indian artifacts.
Research Fields: pre-Columbian Indians.
Facilities: visitor center.
Activities: guided tours for groups.
Publications: brochure.
Hours & Admission Prices: Museum: Thurs.-Mon. 9-5. Park: daily 8am to sundown. Park Entrance: car: $3; motorcycle & pedestrian $2. ♿
Attendance: 21,000 (estimated)

Dade City

PIONEER FLORIDA MUSEUM ASSOCIATION, INC., 15602 Pioneer Museum Rd., Dade City, FL 33523. Mailing Address: P.O. Box 335, Dade City, FL 33526-0335. Tel.: 352-567-0262. Fax: 352-567-1262.
E-mail: curator@pioneerfloridamuseum.org
Web Site: www.pioneerfloridamuseum.org
Founded: 1961.
Congressional District: 12
Key Personnel: C.E.O. & Pres. (V), Robert Sumner; Dir., Christine Smith; Museum Shop Mgr., Susan Bayes.
Personnel Profile: Full-Time Paid 1; Part-Time Paid 3; Part-Time Volunteers 150.
Governing Authority: bd. of trustees; nonprofit organization, Pioneer Florida Museum Association, Inc. Tax-exempt: 501(c)(3).
Pioneer Museum.
Collections: local pioneer family life & culture including records & personal information; sugar cane patch & grinding exhibit; moon shine still; natural stream; citrus packing house. Historic Buildings: restored school-house, church, depot, C.C. Smith General Store & 1860's home; restored shoe repair shop & two Cypress buildings from Cumner Sons Cypress Saw Mill Company.
Research Fields: pioneer Florida living.
Activities: guided tours; permanent exhibitions; research. Special Events: Christmas at the Museum; Labor Day, Pioneer Florida Day Celebration; Quilt & Antiques Show & Sale.
Hours & Admission Prices: Tues.-Sat. 10-5; group tours by appointment. Adults $6, seniors 55 & over $5, students 6-18 $2; members and children 5 & under no charge. Closed major holidays. ♿
Attendance: 20,000 (estimated)
Membership: Individual $25; Family $35; Individual Life $150; Life Couple $250. Mabel Jordan Barn Fund Donation: Pathfinder $100; Settler $250; Pioneer $500; Trailblazer $1,000.

Dania Beach

INTERNATIONAL GAME FISH ASSOCIATION - FISHING HALL OF FAME AND MUSEUM, 300 Gulf Stream Way, Dania Beach, FL 33004-2118. Tel.: 954-922-4212. Fax: 954-924-4220.
E-mail: hq@igfa.org
Web Site: www.igfa.org
Key Personnel: Dir., Ryan Dick; Pres., Rob Kramer.
Governing Authority: Parent Institution: International Game Fish Association. Tax-exempt.
History Museum.
Collections: Hall of Fame inductees; fishing history; angling literature.
Facilities: library. Museum-related items for sale.
Activities: birthday parties; rental facilities; educational programs.
Publications: The International Angler; The International Junior Angler; The World Records Book.
Hours & Admission Prices: Mon.-Sat. 10-6, Sun. 12-6. Adults $8, children $5. Closed Thanksgiving; Christmas. ♿
Attendance: 70,000
Membership: Junior $20; Regular $40; Family $55.

Davie

BUEHLER PLANETARIUM AND OBSERVATORY, Broward College, 3501 Davie Rd., Davie, FL 33314-1604. Tel.: 954-201-6681. Fax: 954-201-6316.
Web Site: www.iloveplanets.com
Planetarium & Observatory.
Collections: Zeiss M1015 star projector; astronomy.
Activities: star shows; astronomical programs; children's programs. Museum Sponsors: Stories for A Starry Night.
Hours & Admission Prices: Observatory: Wed. & Fri.-Sat. 8pm-10pm. No charge.

FINE ARTS GALLERY AT BROWARD COLLEGE, A. HUGH ADAMS CAMPUS, 3501 S.W. Davie Rd., Bldg. 3, Davie, FL 33314-1604. Tel.: 954-201-6984. Fax: 954-201-6518.
E-mail: cgallery@broward.edu
Web Site: www.geocities.com/bccfineartsgallery
Founded: 1965.
Key Personnel: Dir., Harumi Abe.
Governing Authority: Tax-exempt.
Art Gallery.
Collections: paintings; sculpture; drawings; photographs.
Major Exhibits: Sara Stites, 1/14/10-2/3/10; Annual Adjunct Exhibition, 2/11/10-3/3/10; Group Show, 3/11/10-3/31/10; 31st Annual Student Show, 4/8/10-5/5/10; BC Potters Guild, 5/13/10-6/17/10.
Activities: permanent & temporary exhibitions; receptions.
Hours & Admission Prices: Mon., Wed. & Fri. 9-2, Thurs. 10-6. No charge; donations accepted.

FLAMINGO GARDENS, EVERGLADES WILDLIFE SANCTUARY, 3750 Flamingo Rd., Davie, FL 33330-1698. Tel.: 954-473-2955. Fax: 954-473-1738.
Web Site: www.flamingogardens.org
Founded: 1969.
Key Personnel: Exec. Dir., Stan W. Wood.
Governing Authority: Tax-exempt.
Wildlife Sanctuary & Historic Home: housed in the former residence of founders Floyd L. & Jane Wray, built in 1933.
Collections: area natural & cultural heritage; plants; birds; personal artifacts; early South Florida settlers.
Facilities: cafe. Museum-related items for sale.
Activities: tram rides.
Hours & Admission Prices: June-Nov. Tues.-Sun. 9:30-5; Dec.-May daily 9:30-5. Adults $17, children 4-11 $8.50; discounts to seniors, students, military, & groups. Closed Thanksgiving; Christmas. ♿
Attendance: 125,000 (accurate)
Membership: Individual $40; Single Parent $55; Dual $75; Family $90; Sustaining $195.

OLD DAVIE SCHOOL HISTORICAL MUSEUM, 6650 Griffin Rd., Davie, FL 33314-4331. Tel.: 954-797-1044. Fax: 954-797-1047.
E-mail: director@olddavieschool.org
Web Site: www.olddavieschool.org
Founded: 1984.
Key Personnel: Dir., Patti Koch; Pres., Kathy Cox; Education, Judy Maxwell.
Personnel Profile: Full-Time Paid 2; Part-Time Paid 1; Part-Time Volunteers 40.
Governing Authority: private; nonprofit organization. Tax-exempt: 501(c)(3).

History Museum: housed in a 1918 two-story masonry school building designed by August Geiger. Listed on the National Register of Historic Places.
Collections: Western Broward County & Everglades history from prehistoric to modern times; town of Davie history. Historic Buildings: 1912 Viele House; c.1912 Walsh-Osterhoudt home; early pioneer homes.
Facilities: 200-seat auditorium; 2,400 sq. ft. exhibit space. Museum-related items for sale.
Activities: school tours; educational programs; special events; temporary exhibits; docent program; guided tours; theater. Annual Events: Back to School Dinner; Generations of Taste Pioneer Dinner; Old Davie Christmas.
Publications: quarterly newsletter, The Report Card.
Hours & Admission Prices: Tues.-Sat. 10-2. Adults $10, seniors & children $7; discounts to AAM & ICOM members; members no charge. Closed New Year's Day; Memorial Day; Independence Day; Labor Day; Thanksgiving; Christmas. ♿
Attendance: 14,000 (estimated)
Membership: Individual $25; Family $50; Business $100; Dean's List $250; Principal's List $500; Honor Roll $1,000.

YOUNG AT ART CHILDREN'S MUSEUM, 11584 W. State Rd. 84, Davie, FL 33325-4022. Tel.: 954-424-0085, ext. 23. Fax: 954-370-5057.
E-mail: visitorservices@youngatartmuseum.org
Web Site: www.youngatartmuseum.org
Founded: 1987.
Congressional District: 15
Key Personnel: Exec. Dir., Mindy Shrago; Assoc. Dir., Esther Shrago; Chm. Bd., John Voigt; Vice Chm., David Esack; Dir. Operations & Visitor Svcs., Kathy Bradley Dean.
Personnel Profile: Full-Time Paid 10; Part-Time Paid 14; Part-Time Volunteers 60.
Governing Authority: nonprofit organization. Tax-exempt: 501(c)(3).
Children's Museum.
Collections: teaching collections; art; paintings; sculpture; hands-on exhibits.
Facilities: 9,500 sq. ft. exhibit space; Art Institute including a photo lab, ceramic studio, painting and drawing studio. Museum-related items for sale.
Activities: formal education programs for children; guided tours; loan, traveling & participatory exhibitions.
Publications: quarterly newsletter, The Drawing Board.
Hours & Admission Prices: Mon.-Sat. 10-5, Sun. 12-5. Adults $8, seniors $7.50; discounts to groups; members & children under 2 no charge. Closed New Year's Day; Easter; Thanksgiving; Christmas. ♿
Attendance: 92,000 (accurate)
Membership: Family $65; Grandparents $100; Sponsor $150; Donor $500; Family Plus $10 each additional.

Daytona Beach

DAYTONA 500 EXPERIENCE, 1801 W. International Speedway Blvd., Daytona Beach, FL 32114-1215. Tel.: 386-681-6800. TTY: 386-681-6530.
E-mail: srobinson@daytona500experience.com
Web Site: www.daytonausa.com
Formerly: Daytona USA
Racing History Museum.
Collections: Daytona history; stock car champions & their cars; racing history & memorabilia; photographs.
Facilities: IMAX theater. Museum-related items for sale.
Activities: hands-on activities; motion simulator rides; video arcade; tram tour.
Hours & Admission Prices: Daily 10-6; call for extended hours. Adults $24, seniors & children 6-12 $19; children under 5 no charge. Closed Thanksgiving; Christmas.

HALIFAX HISTORICAL MUSEUM, 252 S. Beach St., Daytona Beach, FL 32114-4407. Tel.: 386-255-6976. Fax: 386-255-7605.
E-mail: mail@halifaxhistorical.org
Web Site: www.halifaxhistorical.org
Founded: 1949.
Congressional District: 4
Key Personnel: Dir., Fayn LeVeille.
Personnel Profile: Full-Time Paid 2; Full-Time Volunteers 6; Part-Time Volunteers 25.
Governing Authority: society. Parent Institution: Halifax Historical Society. Tax-exempt: 501(c)(3).
Local History Museum.
Collections: Native American artifacts of the area & artifacts from early local plantations; Civil War through WWII military memorabilia; mementos from Pioneer & Victorian families; auto racing history; postcards; period clothing; vintage housewares; Grandma's Attic; maps.
Research Fields: early local history; automobile racing; genealogy.
Facilities: 1,500-vol. library of Florida history books; newspaper files from 1883-present & extensive photographic & vertical files available for research on premises by appointment; 50-seat theatre with films on local history & Florida; research room houses over 10,000 photographs, 5,000 antique post cards, 60 drawers of vertical files, library with over 1,500 rare and out of print books; research facility used by genealogists, authors, home researchers. Fee $10/day; volunteer researcher on staff 3 days/week (fee $10/hr).
Activities: permanent & temporary exhibitions; educational programs & tours.
Publications: semiannual The Halifax Herald; quarterly newsletter to members; books, Daytona Beach and the Halifax River Area; A Brief History of the Halifax Historical Society.
Hours & Admission Prices: Tues.-Sat. 10-4. Adults $5, children 12 & under $1; members no charge. Closed major holidays. ♿
Attendance: 10,000 (estimated)
Membership: Individual $30; Family $40, $50, $75, $100, $500, $1,000. Seniors 10% discount 65 & over.

* **THE MUSEUM OF ARTS AND SCIENCES, INC. AND CENTER FOR FLORIDA HISTORY, (M),** 352 South Nova Rd., Daytona Beach, FL 32114-4597. Tel.: 386-255-0285. Fax: 386-255-5040.
E-mail: info@moas.org
Web Site: www.moas.org
Founded: 1971.
Congressional District: 7
Key Personnel: Exec. Dir., Wayne D. Atherholt; Pres. (V), Debbie Allen; Asst. to Exec. Dir., Pattie Pardee; Dir. Membership, Bonnie Tremblay; Public Rels. & Mktg. Dir., Christina Lane; Cur. Gary R. Libby Art & Chief Cur., Cynthia Duval; Operations Mgr., Eric Goire; Finance & Human Resources Dir., Linda Ippolito; Sr. Cur. Education & History, Zach Zacharias; Admin. Old St. Augustine Village, Lenore Welty; Physical Plant Asst., Israel Taylor; Visitor Svcs., Patti Cournoyer.
Personnel Profile: Full-Time Paid 18; Full-Time Volunteers 2; Part-Time Paid 14; Part-Time Volunteers 100; Interns 2.
Governing Authority: nonprofit. Parent Institution: The Museum of Arts & Sciences. Subsidiary Institutions: Old St. Augustine Village. Tax-exempt: 501(c)(3).
General Museum.
Collections: contemporary Florida paintings, prints & photos by major Florida artists; Pleistocene fossils; regional natural history; Timucuan Indian material from Tick and Stone Island, Florida; Frischer sculpture garden; Cuban paintings of the 18th-20th centuries; African, pre-Columbian, 19th-century European, Central American and Cuban fine & folk art; American fine & decorative arts 1640-1900; European & American works on paper, Oriental fine & decorative arts; Persian miniatures; art; European decorative arts; Indian miniature painting; Olga Hirshhorn collection of Ashante gold objects; sloth skeleton; children's hands on exhibits.
Major Exhibits: Reflections: Paintings of Florida 1865-1965 From the Collection of Cici and Hyatt Brown, 11/21/09-5/17/10; The Paintings of Tom Reis, 5/10-8/10; Stories of Community: Self-taught Art From the Hill Collection, 9/10-11/10.
Research Fields: Florida contemporary arts & fine arts; Florida history & archaeology; Pleistocene material; Cuban fine arts; American fine and decorative art including jewelry 1785-1885; international decorative art.
Facilities: 9,000-vol. library of general reference works available to members on premises; nature trails; planetarium; 268-seat multidisciplinary hall.
Activities: guided tours; lectures; films; marine biology programs; foreign & domestic travel; county-wide outreach programs; changing art exhibits; summer art history & science programs; formally organized education programs; planetarium workshops; daily planetarium shows; educational star shows; Florida history programs & activities; changing science exhibitions.
Publications: Arts and Sciences Magazine; yearly monograph; exhibit catalogs; triannual members' bulletin; Cuba: A History in Art in full color; Coast to Coast: The Contemporary Landscape in Florida in full color; A Treasury of American Art: Selections from the American Collection; Great Masters of Cuban Art - Ramos Collection.
Hours & Admission Prices: Tues.-Sat. & Mon. holidays 9-5, Sun. 11-5. Adults $12.95, seniors $10.95, children 6-17 $6.95; discounts to groups, AAM, ICOM, HIA & SEMC members; children 5 & under and members no charge. Closed Thanksgiving; Christmas. ♿
Attendance: 154,000 (accurate)
Membership: Student $20; Senior Citizen $25; Single $30; Senior Citizen Couple $35; Family $60; Friends of the Museum $125; Renaissance $200-$10,000.

SOUTHEAST MUSEUM OF PHOTOGRAPHY, (M), Daytona State College, 1200 W. International Speedway Blvd., Daytona Beach, FL 32114. Mailing Address: P.O. Box 2811, Daytona Beach, FL 32120-2811. Tel.: 386-506-3350. Fax: 386-506-4487. TDD: 386-506-3023.
E-mail: romnesj@daytonastate.edu

Web Site: www.SMPonline.org
Founded: 1979.
Congressional District: 4
Key Personnel: Dir., Kevin R. Miller; Asst. Dir. Exhibitions & Collections, Juliana Romnes; Cur. Education, Christina Katsolis.
Personnel Profile: Full-Time Paid 5; Part-Time Paid 15; Part-Time Volunteers 12; Interns 4.
Governing Authority: public college. Parent Institution: Daytona State College. Tax-exempt.
Photography Museum.
Collections: contemporary & historical photography.
Major Exhibits: Journal - Annabel Clarke (T), 11/09-12/09; Double Exposure, 1/10-5/10; The Bikeriders (T), 2/10-5/10; Stella Johnson, 2/10-5/10; I Still Do - Judith Fox, 9/10-11/10; Intended Consequences (Rwanda) (T), 9/10-11/10; Still Life - Home, 9/10-12/10; Elaine Ling, 9/10-12/10; Linda Conner, 11/10-2/11.
Research Fields: contemporary & historical photography.
Facilities: 1,000-vol. library on museology & photography; 500-seat auditorium; 8,000 sq. ft. exhibit space.
Activities: films; formal education programs for undergraduate college students affiliated with Daytona State College; guided tours; lectures; summer camp; after school program for ages 10 & 11.
Publications: annual report; occasional catalogs & monographs.
Hours & Admission Prices: Jan.-May & Aug.-Nov. Tues. & Thurs.-Fri. 11-4, Wed. 11-7, Sat.-Sun. 1-5; June-July & Dec. Tues.-Sun. 12-4. Adults $3; discounts to AAM & ICOM members; members no charge. Closed New Year's Eve & Day; Independence Day; Thanksgiving & weekend after; Christmas Eve, Day & week. ♿
Attendance: 60,000 (accurate)
Membership: Student $20; Individual $30; Family $40; Supporting $100; Patron $250; Benefactor $500; Endowment $1,000.

De Land

AFRICAN AMERICAN MUSEUM OF THE ARTS, 325 S. Clara Ave., De Land, FL 32720-5884. Tel.: 386-736-4004. Fax: 386-736-4088.
E-mail: art@africanmuseumdeland.org
Web Site: www.africanmuseumdeland.org
Key Personnel: Exec. Dir., Mary Allen.
Personnel Profile: Part-Time Paid 1.
Governing Authority: nonprofit organization. Tax-exempt: 501(c)(3).
Art Museum.
Collections: African American & Caribbean American cultures & art; photographs; paintings; sculptures; masks.
Activities: lectures; drama; dance; meetings; reading & creative writing programs.
Hours & Admission Prices: Thurs.-Sat. 10-4. No charge; donations accepted. ♿
Membership: Student 6-18 $10; Individual $20; Family $50; Supporter $100; Corporate $250; Organization $200.

THE DUNCAN GALLERY OF ART, Sampson Hall, Stetson University, De Land, FL 32723-0001. Mailing Address: Campus Box 8252, Stetson University, 421 N. Woodland Blvd., De Land, FL 32723-0001. Tel.: 386-822-7266.
E-mail: cnelson@stetson.edu
Web Site: www.stetson.edu/departments/art
Founded: 1965.
Key Personnel: Gallery Dir., Dan Gunderson; Asst. to Gallery Dir. & Admin. Specialist, Christine Nelson.
Personnel Profile: Full-Time Paid 2; Part-Time Paid 5.
Governing Authority: university. Parent Institution: Stetson University. Tax-exempt.
Art Gallery.
Collections: contemporary drawings, prints, watercolors, oils, ceramics & sculpture; photographs; collection of American Modernist Artist Oscar Bluemner.
Research Fields: contemporary art of the Southeast.
Facilities: 2,385 sq. ft. gallery.
Activities: gallery talks; workshops; demonstrations; formally organized education programs for undergraduate college students; traveling exhibitions.
Publications: exhibition catalogs.
Hours & Admission Prices: Sept.-April Mon.-Fri. 10-4, Sun. call for hours. No charge. Closed university & national holidays. ♿
Attendance: 8,400 (estimated)
Membership: Friends of Art: Student $5-$34; Individual $35-$59; Family $60-$99; Associate $100-$249; Benefactor $250-$499; Investor $500-$999; President's Circle $1,000 & up.

THE GILLESPIE MUSEUM - STETSON UNIVERSITY, 234 E. Michigan Ave., De Land, FL 32724-3539. Mailing Address: Stetson University, 421 N. Woodland Blvd., Unit 8403, De Land, FL 32723-0001. Tel.: 386-822-7330. Fax: 386-822-7328.
E-mail: gillespie@stetson.edu
Web Site: www.gillespiemuseum.stetson.edu
Formerly: Gillespie Museum of Minerals, Stetson University
Founded: 1958.
Congressional District: 4
Key Personnel: Exec. Dir., Dr. Robert S. Chauvin; Cur., Dr. Bruce C. Bradford; Assoc. Dir., Holli M. Vanater.
Personnel Profile: Full-Time Paid 1; Part-Time Paid 1; Part-Time Volunteers 10; Interns 10.
Governing Authority: university. Parent Institution: Stetson University. Tax-exempt: 501(c)(3).
Earth & Environmental Science Museum.
Collections: minerals; teaching collection of major rock groups; thematic minerals; environmental science.
Activities: self-guided tours; lectures; formally organized education programs for primary, secondary & college students; permanent exhibitions.
Hours & Admission Prices: Academic Year: call for hours. Adults $2, seniors & students $1; discounts to groups & ASTC members; members no charge. Closed national & university holidays. ♿
Attendance: 5,000 (estimated)
Membership: Students $10; Seniors 55 & over $15; Individuals $20; Senior Couples 55 & over $25; Family $35; Corporate $175; Bronze $1,000; Silver $2,500; Gold $5,000; Honorary Curator $10,000.

DeLand

DELAND NAVAL AIR STATION MUSEUM, 910 Biscayne Blvd., DeLand, FL 32724-2009. Tel.: 386-738-4149. Fax: 386-738-5405.
E-mail: contact@delandnavalairstation.org
Web Site: www.delandnavalairstation.org
Key Personnel: Exec. Dir., Chris Stubbs.
Governing Authority: private; nonprofit organization.
Military Museum.
Collections: U.S. Naval history; military artifacts; documents; F-14 fighter jet; WWII TBF Avenger torpedo bomber.
Hours & Admission Prices: Tues.-Sat. 12-4. No charge; donations accepted.

HENRY A. DELAND HOUSE MUSEUM, 137 W. Michigan Ave., DeLand, FL 32720-3418. Tel.: 386-740-6813. Fax: 386-740-6813.
E-mail: delandhouse@msn.com
Web Site: www.delandhouse.com
Governing Authority: Parent Institution: West Volusia Historical Society.
Historic House: housed in the former home of DeLand's first attorney, Arthur George Hamlin; built in 1886.
Collections: period furnishings; personal artifacts; photographs.
Facilities: Museum-related items for sale.
Hours & Admission Prices: Tues.-Sat. 12-4; other times by appointment.

MEMORIAL HOSPITAL MUSEUMS, 230 N. Stone St., DeLand, FL 32720-4010. Tel.: 386-740-5800.
Governing Authority: Parent Institution: West Volusia Historical Society.
Hospital Museum: listed on the National Register of Historic Buildings.
Collections: medical equipment & history; pharmacy; period electrical systems; personal artifacts; veterans memorabilia.
Hours & Admission Prices: Wed.-Sat. 10-3. No charge. ♿

MUSEUM OF FLORIDA ART, (M), 600 N. Woodland Blvd., DeLand, FL 32720-3447. Tel.: 386-734-4371. Fax: 386-734-7697.
E-mail: peterson@museumoffloridaart.org
Web Site: www.museumoffloridaart.org
Formerly: The DeLand Museum of Art
Founded: 1951.
Congressional District: 7
Key Personnel: Exec. Dir., Jennifer Coolidge; Pres. (V), Parke Teal; Admin. & Mktg. Dir., Kathryn Peterson; Coord. Exhibitions, David Fithian.
Personnel Profile: Full-Time Paid 5; Part-Time Paid 2; Part-Time Volunteers 100; Interns 20.
Governing Authority: nonprofit corporation. Tax-exempt: 501(c)(3).
Art Museum: located in DeLand Cultural Arts Center.
Collections: art of Florida; Florida artists.
Major Exhibits: Tony Eitharong, 12/11/09-2/28/10; Volusia Students Create, 3/12/10-3/28/10; Dowis Sculpture, 3/12/10-5/30/10; Biennial V, 4/9/10-5/30/10; Mollie Doctrow, 6/11/10-8/22/10; Permanent Collection, 6/11/10-8/22/10; Roig-Messersmith-Burggraf, 6/11/10-8/22/10; Trent Tomengo, 9/3/10-11/28/10; Jeff Whipple, 9/3/10-11/28/10; Barbara Sorensen (T), 12/10/10-2/13/11.

Research Fields: Florida art.
Facilities: meeting rooms; classrooms. Museum-related gifts for sale.
Activities: guided tours; lectures; gallery talks; workshops; formally organized education programs; docent program or council; outreach exhibitions & activities; inter-museum loan; permanent, temporary & traveling exhibitions; travel program.
Publications: monthly newsletter; catalogues; exhibition brochures & programs.
Hours & Admission Prices: Tues.-Sat. 10-4, Sun. 1-4. Adults $3, students & children 3-12 $1; discounts to AAA, AAM & ICOM members; Southeastern & North American reciprocal membership members, children under 3, members & staff no charge. Closed national holidays. ♿
Attendance: 30,000 (estimated)
Membership: Student $15; Teacher $20; Senior Individual $25; Individual $35; Senior Couple $45; Family $55. Renaissance: Contributor $100-$249; Advocate $250-$499; Patron $500-$999; Investor $1,000-$2,499; Sustainer $2,500-$4,999; Benefactor $5,000 & up.

ROBERT M. CONRAD RESEARCH AND EDUCATIONAL CENTER, 137 W. Michigan Ave., DeLand, FL 32720-3418. Tel.: 386-740-6813.
Web Site: www.delandhouse.com/conrad.htm
Governing Authority: Parent Institution: West Volusia Historical Society.
History Museum.
Collections: local history; personal artifacts; photographs; newspaper clippings; videos.
Facilities: library.
Activities: research; educational programs.
Hours & Admission Prices: Tues.-Sat. 12-4; other times by appointment.

Deerfield Beach

DEERFIELD BEACH HISTORICAL SOCIETY, (M), 380 E. Hillsboro Blvd., Deerfield Beach, FL 33441-3540. Mailing Address: P.O. Box 755, Deerfield Beach, FL 33443-0755. Tel.: 954-429-0378. Fax: 954-429-0378.
E-mail: carolyn.morris@deerfield-history.org
Web Site: www.deerfield-history.org
Founded: 1973.
Key Personnel: Pres., Henry Gould; Vice Pres., Ronald LaVergne; Sec., Catherine Coney; Treas., Dave Noderer; Dir., Carolyn Morris.
Personnel Profile: Part-Time Volunteers 12.
Governing Authority: private; nonprofit organization. Subsidiary Institutions: Butler House Museum; 1920 Deerfield School; 1940 Kester Cottage; 1926 Deerfield Beach Elementary School; 1926 Seaboard Airline Railway Station. Tax-exempt: 501(c)(3).
History Museum.
Collections: archives; photographs; oral histories; costumes; period furnishings; artifacts.
Facilities: library. Museum-related items for sale.
Activities: docent training program; internship program; lectures; workshops; guided tours; traveling & permanent exhibits; school programs; historic trail. Annual Events: Pioneer Days; cemetery walk; Breakfast with Santa; History at High Noon; 1/2 day in 1920s classroom; Ice Cream Social; Fall Ball Costume Gala.
Publications: quarterly newsletter; annual lecture series; oral history transcripts; photo essay.
Hours & Admission Prices: Mon.-Fri. 9-4, Sat. by appointment. Suggested Donation: $2; discounts to AAM members. ♿
Attendance: 8,000 (estimated)
Membership: Individual $40; Family $50; Professional $100; Sponsor $175; Corporate $200.

SOUTH FLORIDA RAILWAY MUSEUM, 1300 W. Hillsboro Blvd., Deerfield Beach, FL 33442-1716. Tel.: 954-698-6620. Fax: 561-790-4191.
Web Site: www.sfrm.org/
Key Personnel: Pres., Vic Zarzycki; Dir., Richard Bretone
Transportation Museum.
Collections: railroad history; model railroad; historic artifacts.
Hours & Admission Prices: Closed for renovation until 2010.

Delray Beach

AMERICAN ORCHID SOCIETY, 16700 AOS Lane, Delray Beach, FL 33446-4351. Tel.: 561-404-2000. Fax: 561-404-2034 & 2100.
E-mail: TheAOS@aos.org
Web Site: www.aos.org
Botanical Garden.
Collections: orchids.
Hours & Admission Prices: Daily 10-4:30. Adults $10; children 12 & under no charge.

CASON COTTAGE HOUSE MUSEUM, 5 N.E. 1st St., Delray Beach, FL 33444-3707. Tel.: 561-243-0223 & 243-2577.
E-mail: info@db-hs.org
Governing Authority: Parent Institution: Delray Beach Historical Society.
Historic House Museum: housed in the home of Rev. John R. Cason, a community leader & Methodist minister; built in 1915.
Collections: Florida lifestyle c.1915-1935; personal artifacts; furnishings.
Hours & Admission Prices: Tues.-Fri. 10-4. Adults $4. ♿

CORNELL MUSEUM OF ART & AMERICAN CULTURE, 51 N. Swinton Ave., Delray Beach, FL 33444-2631. Tel.: 561-243-7922. Fax: 561-243-7018.
E-mail: museum@oldschool.org
Web Site: www.oldschool.org/oldschool
Founded: 1990.
Congressional District: 14
Key Personnel: Dir. Museum (V), Gloria Rejune Adams; Pres. (V), Brian Cheslack; Museum Asst., Pam Mendelsohn.
Personnel Profile: Full-Time Paid 2; Part-Time Volunteers 60.
Governing Authority: nonprofit. Parent Institution: Old School Square. Tax-exempt: 501(c)(3).
Art History Museum: housed in 1913 building.
Collections: Black women's achievements against the odds; early 1900s classroom memorabilia. Historic Buildings: 1925 Crest Theatre; 1926 gymnasium.
Major Exhibits: Pinball Palooza, 12/09-3/28/10; Stuff II: The Joy of Collecting, 4/12/10-9/25/10; Cats: Not The Musical, 10/10-4/11.
Facilities: educational facilities.
Activities: arts festivals; concerts; docent program; films; guided tours; lectures; loan, temporary & traveling exhibitions; school loan service.
Publications: e-newsletter.
Hours & Admission Prices: June-Oct. Tues.-Sat. 10:30-4:30; Nov.-May Tues.-Sat. 10:30-4:30, Sun. 1-4:30. Adults $6, seniors & students 6-21 w/ID $4, children 5-12 $2; discounts to Florida Trust members; children under 5 & members no charge. Closed New Year's Day; Good Friday; Easter; Memorial Day; Independence Day; Labor Day; Thanksgiving & day after; Christmas Eve & Day. ♿
Attendance: 50,000 (accurate)

*** THE MORIKAMI MUSEUM AND JAPANESE GARDENS, (M),** 4000 Morikami Park Rd., Delray Beach, FL 33446-2305. Tel.: 561-495-0233. Fax: 561-499-2557.
E-mail: morikami@pbcgov.com
Web Site: www.morikami.org
Founded: 1977.
Congressional District: 14
Key Personnel: Dir. & Sr. Cur., Thomas Gregersen; Trustee Pres., David Schmidt; Park Admin., Bonnie White Lemay; Dir. Advancement, Amy Hever; Dir. Education, Reiko Nishioka; Membership Mgr., Della Henderson; Volunteer Coord., Elizabeth Kelley; Events Mgr., Kizzy Sanchez; Operations Supvr., Debbie Towers; School Programs Specialist, Beth Kawazura; Cur. Japanese Art, Susanna Brooks Lavallee; Cur. Collections, Veljko Dujin; Facility Rental Coord., Alanna Rainey; Exhibit Preparator, Stacey Garcia; Museum Shop Mgr., Sallie Chisholm.
Personnel Profile: Full-Time Paid 42; Part-Time Paid 7; Part-Time Volunteers 265.
Governing Authority: county. Parent Institution: Palm Beach County Parks & Recreation Dept., 2700 Sixth Ave. S., Lake Worth, FL 33461. Tax-exempt.
Ethnology Museum specializing in Japanese culture.
Collections: Yamato Colony of Japanese settlers; Japanese fine art, folk art, & ethnological materials; Gulf Stream Bonsai.
Research Fields: history of the Yamato Colony of Japanese farmers.
Facilities: 4,000-vol. library of materials related to Japan, including some in Japanese, available for use on premises by request; 200-acre park with Japanese Gardens; 225-seat theater; picnic facilities.
Activities: guided tours; docent program; permanent, temporary & loan exhibitions; seasonal celebrations; special events. Annual Events: Oshogatsu Japanese New Year; Hatsume Fair; Gala Dinner-Dance; Children's Day; Bon Festival.
Publications: quarterly newsletter & calendar; exhibition catalog.
Hours & Admission Prices: Museum: Tues.-Sun. 10-5. Adults $12, seniors $11, children 6-17 & college students $7; discounts to groups of 15 or more; members & children under 6 no charge. Park: daily sunrise to sundown. No charge. Closed New Year's Day; Easter; Independence Day; Thanksgiving; Christmas. ♿
Attendance: 230,432 (accurate)
Membership: Student $30; Origami (Individual Adult) $55; Daruma (Two Adults) & Sakura (Individual & One Guest) $80; Netsuke $135; Taiko $275; Samurai $550; Wisdom Ring $1,500.

MUSEUM OF LIFESTYLE & FASHION HISTORY, 322 N.E. 2nd Ave., Delray Beach, FL 33482. Mailing Address: P.O. Box 6127, Delray Beach, FL 33482-6127. Tel.: 561-243-2662. Fax: 561-495-8785.
E-mail: info@mlfhmuseum.org
Web Site: mlfhmuseum.org
Governing Authority: nonprofit organization. Tax-exempt: 501(c)(3).
General Museum.
Collections: hosts exhibits including period fashion designs, popular culture art, decorative arts, interior designs, architecture history; ethnic cultures.
Activities: community outreach programs; special events.
Hours & Admission Prices: Temporarily closed.

SPADY CULTURAL HERITAGE MUSEUM, 170 N.W. 5th Ave., Delray Beach, FL 33444-2653. Tel.: 561-279-8883.
E-mail: cfjones@spadymuseum.org
Web Site: www.spadymuseum.com/
Key Personnel: Exec. Dir., Daisy Fulton; Dir. Programs, Charlene Jones; Educator, Brandy Brownlee.
Governing Authority: nonprofit organization.
Cultural Heritage Museum: housed in the former home of Solomon D. Spady, a prominent African American educator & community leader in Delray Beach from 1922-1957.
Collections: black history & culture.
Hours & Admission Prices: Mon.-Fri. 11-4, Sat. 10-2. Adults $5, seniors $3; students & members no charge.

Doral

MUSEUM OF THE AMERICAS, (M), 2500 N.W. 79th Ave., Ste. 104, Doral, FL 33122-1071. Tel.: 305-599-8088 & 8089.
E-mail: americasmuseum@aol.com
Web Site: www.museumamericas.org
Founded: 1991.
Key Personnel: Dir., Raul M. Oyuela
Art Museum.
Collections: 20th-century Latin American & Caribbean art.
Activities: educational programs.
Hours & Admission Prices: Tues.-Fri. 11-5, Sat. by appointment. No charge.

Dunedin

DUNEDIN FINE ART CENTER, 1143 Michigan Blvd., Dunedin, FL 34698-2799. Tel.: 727-298-3322.
Founded: 1974.
Key Personnel: Exec. Dir., George Ann Bissett, C.F.R.E.
Personnel Profile: Full-Time Paid 9; Full-Time Volunteers 2; Part-Time Paid 4; Part-Time Volunteers 75; Interns 1.
Governing Authority: bd. of directors. Tax-exempt: 501(c)(3).
Art Center.
Collections: paintings; sculpture; photographs; children's hands-on art exhibits.
Activities: lectures; studio classes; workshops; educational & cultural programming.
Hours & Admission Prices: Mon.-Fri. 10-5, Sat. 10-2, Sun. 1-4. Adults $4, senior citizens $3; children 2 & under and members no charge.

DUNEDIN HISTORICAL SOCIETY & MUSEUM, (M), 349 Main St., Dunedin, FL 34698-5700. Mailing Address: P.O. Box 2393, Dunedin, FL 34697-2393. Tel.: 727-736-1176. Fax: 727-736-4756.
E-mail: dunedinhistory@yahoo.com
Web Site: www.dunedinmuseum.org
Founded: 1970.
Congressional District: 5
Key Personnel: Pres., Susan Littlejohn; Admin. Asst., Sandy Kinzer; Dir., Vincent Luisi; Museum Shop Mgr., Carol Venherm.
Personnel Profile: Full-Time Paid 1; Part-Time Paid 2; Part-Time Volunteers 100; Interns 2.
Governing Authority: society. Subsidiary Institution: Andrews Memorial Chapel, 1899 San Mateo, Dunedin, FL 34698. Tax-exempt: 501(c)(3).
Local History Museum: housed in 1923 Atlantic Coastline Passenger Station; The Old Freight Warehouse, adjacent to Passenger Station.
Collections: Dunedin and Pinellas photographs & artifacts.
Research Fields: history of Dunedin area, county & state; documentation for historic preservation; transportation.
Facilities: library of books on history of area, related collections & newspaper articles available for use by appointment only on premises; meeting room. History books & reproductions of documents for sale.
Activities: guided tours; lectures; loan exhibitions; docent program.
Publications: bimonthly newsletter, Dunedin Days; booklet, Historical Highlights-First 100 Years of Settlement; book, Dunedin Thru The Years, 1st & 2nd editions; Arcadia Press - Images of Dunedin; Arcadia Press - Images of Pinellas County.
Hours & Admission Prices: Tues.-Sat. 10-4. Suggested Donation: adults $2; discounts to AAM members; members & children under 12 no charge. Closed legal holidays. ♿
Attendance: 14,500 (accurate)
Membership: Individual $25; Family $35.

Eatonville

ZORA NEALE HURSTON NATIONAL MUSEUM OF FINE ARTS, 227 E. Kennedy Blvd., Eatonville, FL 32751-5303. Tel.: 407-647-3307. Fax: 407-539-2192.
E-mail: info@zorafestival.com
Web Site: zoranealehurstonmuseum.com
Art Museum.
Collections: works by African American artists.
Activities: Annual Event: festival.
Hours & Admission Prices: Mon.-Fri. 9-4; groups by appointment. No charge; donations accepted.

Eglin Air Force Base

AIR FORCE ARMAMENT MUSEUM, 100 Museum St., Eglin Air Force Base, FL 32542-1497. Tel.: 850-651-1808 & 882-4062. Fax: 850-882-3990.
E-mail: info@afarmamentmuseum.com
Web Site: www.afarmamentmuseum.com
Founded: 1985.
Key Personnel: Interim Dir., George Jones; Chm. (V), Cleta Halvorson; Museum Specialist, Timothy Savoir; AFAM Foundation Mgr., Doug Ferris.
Personnel Profile: Full-Time Paid 1; Part-Time Paid 1; Part-Time Volunteers 25.
Governing Authority: federal; nonprofit. Parent Institution: Air Force Museum AFB Wright-Patterson, OH. Subsidiary Institution: Eglin AFB, FL. Tax-exempt.
Military Museum.
Collections: armament; gun vault collection; missiles; rockets; aircraft: SR-71, B-17, B-25, F100, P47, P51, F4, F-105, C-47, B-57, F-86, F-89, F101, B-52, F-15, F-104, RB-47, MIG 21, F-111, F-16, A-10, C-130, F-80, T-33, MIG-21, UH-1H, C-131, 02.
Facilities: 25,000 sq. ft. exhibit space; 60-seat theater. Military & local souvenir items for sale.
Activities: films; docent program; participatory & traveling exhibitions.
Publications: quarterly historical record.
Hours & Admission Prices: Mon.-Sat. 9:30-4:30. No charge; donations accepted. Closed federal holidays. ♿
Attendance: 94,000 (estimated)
Membership: Individual $15.

Ellenton

THE JUDAH P. BENJAMIN CONFEDERATE MEMORIAL AT GAMBLE PLANTATION HISTORIC STATE PARK, 3708 Patten Ave., Ellenton, FL 34222-2152. Tel.: 941-723-4536. Fax: 941-723-4538.
Web Site: dep.state.f1.us/parks
Founded: 1926.
Congressional District: 13
Key Personnel: Park Mgr., Kevin Kiser.
Personnel Profile: Full-Time Paid 4; Part-Time Volunteers 18.
Governing Authority: state. Parent Institution: State of Florida, Division of Recreation & Parks, 3900 Commonwealth Blvd., Commonwealth Bldg., Tallahassee, FL 32303. Tax-exempt.
Historic House: 1840-60 plantation home of Robert Gamble. 1844-1865, Gamble Mansion, the main house of the Gamble sugar plantation; Greek revival vernacular construction.
Collections: antebellum furnishings.
Facilities: picnic shelter; visitor center.
Activities: guided tours.
Publications: brochures.
Hours & Admission Prices: Visitor Center: Thurs.-Mon. 8-5. Park Grounds: daily 8am-sunset. Tours: Thurs.-Mon. 9:30, 10:30 & 1, 2, 3, & 4. Adults $6, children 6-12 $4; under 6 no charge. ♿
Attendance: 33,500 (estimated)

Estero

KORESHAN STATE HISTORIC SITE, 3800 Corkscrew Rd., Estero, FL 33928-1919. Tel.: 239-992-0311. Fax: 239-992-1607.
E-mail: kate.anthony@dep.state.fl.us
Web Site: koreshan.mwweb.org
Founded: 1961.

Congressional District: 13
Key Personnel: Park Mgr., Robert Brooks; Asst. Park Mgr., Karen LaCivita; Pres. (V), Bill Grace.
Personnel Profile: Full-Time Paid 11; Part-Time Paid 2; Part-Time Volunteers 60; Interns 1.
Governing Authority: state; nonprofit. Parent Institution: Florida Park Service. Subsidiary Institution: Koreshan Unity Alliance. Tax-exempt.
Historic Building Complex: 1894-1982 utopian settlement.
Collections: ephemera related to Koreshan members; historic buildings.
Research Fields: communal studies; women's issues; cultural landscape; architecture; music; drama; archaeology.
Facilities: botanical garden; historic buildings.
Activities: docents; special events; weekend guided tours; ghost walks; theatre festival; antique engine show; campfire programs; rental facility; canoe tours.
Publications: brochures; self-guided tour booklet.
Hours & Admission Prices: Daily 8 to sundown. Adults $5 per vehicle; members no charge. ♿
Attendance: 50,000 (estimated)
Membership: Koreshan Unity Alliance, Citizen Support Organization: Student $5; Individual $10; Family $20; Sustaining $25; Sponsor $100; Contributor $500; Patron & Corporate $1,000.

Eustis

EUSTIS HISTORICAL MUSEUM & PRESERVATION SOCIETY, INC., 536 N. Bay St., Eustis, FL 32726-3439. Tel.: 352-483-0046.
E-mail: eustishist@embarqmail.com
Web Site: www.eustishistoricalmuseum.com
Founded: 1983.
Congressional District: 6
Key Personnel: Pres., Betty McClellan; Treas., John Blankenship; Cur., Tammy Treadwell-Morris; Historian, Louise Carter; Education, Elizabeth Le Fevre; Public Rels., Ethel I. Ryan.
Personnel Profile: Part-Time Paid 1; Part-Time Volunteers 18.
Governing Authority: municipal. Branch Museums: Citrus Museum & Tool Museum. Tax-exempt.
Historic House Museum: housed in the residence of G.D. Clifford, an early settler.
Collections: Florida historical & cultural artifacts; preservation of Florida landmarks; furniture; memorabilia.
Research Fields: history of the area; the citrus industry in central Florida.
Facilities: library; Unity-Bell-Clifford Pavilion available to rent for parties & weddings.
Activities: guided tours; special temporary exhibits; educational programs; meetings. Annual Events: antique appraisal clinic; Christmas in Eustis; Eustis fourth grade history essay contest.
Publications: monthly newsletter; Days of Yesteryear 1875-1911; Eustis, Our Town 1912-1945.
Hours & Admission Prices: Mon.-Fri. & 1st Sat. of month 1-5. No charge; donations accepted. Closed Easter; Memorial Day; Independence Day; Labor Day; Thanksgiving; Christmas. ♿
Attendance: 25,000 (estimated)
Membership: Student $10; Individual $20; Family $25; Business $55; Life $500.

LAKE EUSTIS MUSEUM OF ART, (M), 200 E. Orange Ave., Eustis, FL 32726-4139. Tel.: 352-483-2900.
E-mail: lodensusan@gmail.com
Web Site: lakeeustismuseumofart.org
Founded: 1994.
Congressional District: 8
Key Personnel: Dir., Susan Loden; Pres. (V), Mary Ziegengeist.
Personnel Profile: Full-Time Paid 1; Part-Time Volunteers 30; Interns 4.
Governing Authority: Tax-exempt.
Fine Art Museum.
Collections: fine art.
Major Exhibits: Vivid Reality, Tropical Intensity: Victor Bokas, 1/10-2/21/10; Evolution & Emotion vs Color & Steel: Pollpeter & Cruz, 2/26/10-3/28/10; Hypnotic Eccentricities from a Whimsical Universe: Lynn & John Whipple, 2/2/10-5/11/10; So Much to Say: Fletcher Crossman, 6/11/10-7/18/10; Industrial Strength: Jason Barrell, 9/24/10-10/24/10; Ahun: A Painted Life, 10/29/10-12/5/10.
Facilities: gallery; classroom.
Activities: special events; art exhibits; classes; workshops; gallery talks; docent project. Museum Sponsors: Art Escapade in February.
Publications: newsletter, Artcentric; annual brochure; posters; postcards.
Hours & Admission Prices: Mon.-Fri. 10-4, Sat.-Sun. 12-4. Adults $5; discount to AAM & NARM members; members no charge. Closed major holidays. ♿
Attendance: 6,000 (accurate)
Membership: Senior/Student $25; Individual $40; Family $60; Individual NARM $100; Contributor $150; Sustaining $250; Patron $1,000.

Fernandina Beach

AMELIA ISLAND MUSEUM OF HISTORY, (M), 233 S. Third St., Fernandina Beach, FL 32034-4210. Tel.: 904-261-7378. Fax: 904-261-9701.
E-mail: info@ameliamuseum.org
Web Site: www.ameliamuseum.org
Founded: 1986.
Congressional District: 4
Key Personnel: Dir., Phyllis Davis; Bd. Pres., Pat Panella; Asst. Dir. Programs, Alex Buell; Volunteer Coord., Thea Seagraves; Elderhost Coord., Brenda Brubeck; Assoc. Dir. Creative Devel. & Operations, Liz Norris; References & Archives, Teen Peterson; Museum Shop Mgr., Janet Kohler.
Personnel Profile: Full-Time Paid 4; Part-Time Paid 4; Part-Time Volunteers 180.
Governing Authority: nonprofit organization. Tax-exempt: 501(c)(3).
History Museum: housed in c.1937 Nassau County Jail building.
Collections: Nassau County history; over 3000 photos; glassplate negatives; Spanish land grants; 18th-20th century newspapers; textiles; Native American artifacts; 19th century weapons, photography equipment, maps & charts; Victoria era relics; cemetery surveys; city directories; architectural files.
Research Fields: Amelia Island & Nassau County c.2500 B.C.-present.; Civil War; local historic district; Spanish colonial history.
Facilities: library; research facility; archives; 7,000 sq. ft. exhibit space; 100-seat auditorium. Museum & local history-related publications for sale.
Activities: guided tours; Speakers Bureau; student & senior programs; Elderhostel; holiday tours; veterans oral history project; facility rental; lectures.
Publications: monthly & quarterly newsletter; five monographs on local history, Timucuan Indian through early 19th century.
Hours & Admission Prices: Mon.-Sat. 10-4, Sun. 1-4. Museum & Spoken History Tour: 11am & 2pm. Adults $7, students & military $4. Centre Street Historic District Tours: Sept.-June Fri.-Sat.; Summer: call for hours. Admission $10. Ghost Tours: Fri. 6pm. Admission $10. Closed all major holidays. ♿
Attendance: 35,000 (accurate)
Membership: Individual $50; Family $75; Patron $100; Business Partnership $300.

FORT CLINCH STATE PARK, 2601 Atlantic Ave., Fernandina Beach, FL 32034-2203. Tel.: 904-277-7274. Fax: 904-277-7225.
Web Site: www.floridastateparks.org
Founded: 1935.
Key Personnel: C.E.O., Michael Bullock; Park Mgr., Peter Scalco; Sec. Florida DEP, Michael W. Sole.
Personnel Profile: Full-Time Paid 13; Part-Time Paid 4; Part-Time Volunteers 150.
Governing Authority: state. Parent Institution: Dept. of Environmental Protection, Division of Recreation & Parks, Commonwealth Bldg., 3900 Commonwealth Blvd., Tallahassee, FL 32399. Tax-exempt.
Historic Building: 1864 restored Fort Clinch.
Collections: local history & culture; Civil War era armament.
Facilities: visitor center; nature trails.
Activities: Museum Sponsors: living history demonstrations, life of the 1864 Union soldier at Fort Clinch; Union Garrison Weekend monthly; Confederate Garrison in October.
Publications: quarterly newsletter.
Hours & Admission Prices: Park: daily 8-sundown. $6 per vehicle up to 8 persons. Fort: daily 9-5. $2 per person over 6. Fort: evening programs $3 per person over 6. ♿
Attendance: 214,630 (estimated)
Membership: Citizen support organization formed Friends of Fort Clinch.

Fort Lauderdale

* **BONNET HOUSE MUSEUM & GARDENS, (M),** 900 N. Birch Rd., Fort Lauderdale, FL 33304-3326. Tel.: 954-563-5393. Fax: 954-561-4174. TDD: 954-563-5393.
Web Site: www.bonnethouse.org
Founded: 1987.
Congressional District: 22
Key Personnel: C.E.O., Karen L. Beard; Bd. Chm. (V), William L. Stanton; Treas., Brad H. Clifton; Dir. Education & Tour Coord., Linda Schaller; Asst. Dir., Susan M. Parker; Museum Shop Mgr., Bobbie Burke.
Personnel Profile: Full-Time Paid 7; Part-Time Paid 7; Part-Time Volunteers 200.
Governing Authority: nonprofit. Parent Institution: Florida Trust for Historic

Preservation, Tallahassee, FL. Subsidiary Institution: Bonnet House, Inc. Tax-exempt: 501(c)(3).
Historic House: house built in 1920; property consists of 35 acres from the Atlantic Ocean to the Intracoastal Waterway. Listed on the National Register of Historic Places.
Collections: personal furnishings & collections of Frederic C. & Evelyn F. Bartlett; artwork; wood carvings; carousel animals; rare china; orchids.
Facilities: rental facilities; 2 film schools. Museum-related items for sale.
Activities: guided tours; lecture series; traveling exhibitions; music series; family days.
Publications: newsletter, Bonnet House Newsletter.
Hours & Admission Prices: Tours: Tues.-Sat. 10-4, Sun. 12-4. Adults $20, senior citizens $18, children 6-12 $ 16, groups over 15 people $11, grounds only $10; discounts to AAM & AAA members; members & children under 6 no charge. Closed New Year's Day; Thanksgiving; Christmas. ♿
Attendance: 60,000 (estimated)
Membership: Individual $55; Couples $95; Parrot & Family $125; Monkey $250; Swan $500; Golden Shell $1,000.

BROWARD COUNTY HISTORICAL COMMISSION, 301 S.W. 13th Ave., Fort Lauderdale, FL 33312. Tel.: 954-765-4670. Fax: 954-765-4437.
Web Site: www.broward.org/history
Founded: 1972.
Congressional District: 14, 15 & 16
Key Personnel: Chm. (V), Phyllis Loconto; Admin. & County Historic Preservation Officer, Dave Baber; Cur., Denyse Cunningham; County Archaeologist, Mathew DeFelice; County Historian, Helen Landers; Administrative Coord., Marlia Selding.
Personnel Profile: Full-Time Paid 4; Part-Time Paid 2; Part-Time Volunteers 10.
Governing Authority: county. Parent Institution: Broward County Board of County Commissioners. Tax-exempt.
Historic Commission.
Collections: books, maps, microfilm, prints, artifacts, documents & photographs related to the exploration, settlement & urbanization of South Florida, particularly Broward County; oral history tapes; manuscripts.
Research Fields: early Broward & courthouse history; biographies of pioneers.
Facilities: 1,500-vol. library of historical books available for research on premises or for limited loan; reading room; archives; microfilms.
Activities: temporary exhibitions; oral history interviews. Commission Sponsors: seminars; county historical festival; identification of historical sites.
Publications: annual magazine, Broward Legacy.
Hours & Admission Prices: Mon.-Thurs. 8-4:30. No charge; donations accepted. Closed county, state & federal holidays. ♿
Attendance: 5,000

FORT LAUDERDALE HISTORICAL SOCIETY, 219 S.W. 2nd Ave., Fort Lauderdale, FL 33301-1825. Tel.: 954-463-4431, ext. 15. Fax: 954-523-6228.
E-mail: villageinfo@oldfortlauderdale.org
Web Site: oldfortlauderdale.org
Formerly: Old Fort Lauderdale Museum of History
Founded: 1962.
Congressional District: 12
Key Personnel: Interim Exec. Dir., Wil Trower; Pres. (V), Paul McCawley; Museum Shop Mgr., Linda Rosen.
Personnel Profile: Full-Time Paid 7; Part-Time Paid 5; Part-Time Volunteers 15; Interns 1.
Governing Authority: society; nonprofit. Parent Institution: Fort Lauderdale Historical Society. Tax-exempt: 501(c)(3).
Historical Society Museum.
Collections: 8,000 three-dimensional artifacts; 250,000 photographic images; 5,000 architectural drawings; 2,000 maps and books; 250 community scrapbooks; manuscript and photographic collections.
Research Fields: local history; historic preservation.
Facilities: 3,000-vol. library of local & Florida history, available by request for use on premises; reading room; archives; photographic archives. Books for sale.
Activities: temporary & permanent exhibitions; historic preservation; educational programs & workshops; lecture series; walking tours.
Publications: membership newsletter, Inn Sider.
Hours & Admission Prices: Museum: Tues.-Sat. 10-5, Sun. 12-5. Archives: Wed. & Fri. 10-4, Sat. 12-4. Adults $10; discounts to AAM members; members no charge. Closed major holidays. ♿
Attendance: 40,000 (estimated)
Membership: Student & Teacher $35; Individual $50; Family $75; Sustainer $100; Benefactor $250; Steward $500; King's Creek Villager $2,500; Heritage Villager $5,000.

INTERNATIONAL SWIMMING HALL OF FAME, INC., One Hall of Fame Dr., Fort Lauderdale, FL 33316-1694. Tel.: 954-462-6536. Fax: 954-525-4031.
Web Site: www.ishof.org
Founded: 1965.
Congressional District: 15
Key Personnel: C.E.O., Bruce Wigo, Ed.D.; Pres., Richard Korhammer; Chm. (V), Mark Spitz; Cur., Bob Duenkel; Museum Shop Mgr. & Displays Mgr., Laurie Marchwinski.
Personnel Profile: Full-Time Paid 6; Part-Time Paid 4.
Governing Authority: nonprofit organization. Tax-exempt: 501(c)(3).
Aquatic Sports Museum.
Collections: murals, photos, films, books, sculpture & other works of art, devoted primarily to aquatic lore & memorabilia; Olympic medals; swimming; diving; water polo; synchronized swimming; lifesaving masters & open water swimming; Olympic and historic swimming & bathing attire; 2 Olympic size pools; diving platforms & springboards.
Research Fields: Aquatic field.
Facilities: 200-seat auditorium; 24-seat theater; meeting room. Museum-related items for sale.
Activities: guided tours for groups; films; Hall of Fame Sponsors: International Diving Meet; Annual College Swim Coaches Forum; National and Regional swimming, diving, water polo and synchronized swimming meets.
Publications: quarterly newsletter; induction ceremony books.
Hours & Admission Prices: Daily 9-5. Adults $8, seniors $6, children $4; discounts to groups of 10 or more; children under 12 & members no charge. ♿
Attendance: 50,000 (estimated)
Membership: Basic Member (U.S.) $35; International Member $50; Contributor/Family Member $100; Competitor Member $250; Champion Member $500. Patrons of Swimming: Century Club Member $1,000; Chairman's Club $5,000; Benefactor's Club $10,000 & up.

* **MUSEUM OF ART/FORT LAUDERDALE, (M),** One E. Las Olas Blvd., Fort Lauderdale, FL 33301-1807. Tel.: 954-525-5500. Fax: 954-524-6011.
Web Site: www.moafl.org
Formerly: Museum of Art, Inc.
Founded: 1958.
Congressional District: 12
Key Personnel: Exec. Dir., Irvin Lippman; Pres., Mike Jackson; Dir. Devel. & Community Affairs, Lynn Mandeville; Dir. Education, Anthony Lauro; Mgr. Special Events, Gail Vilone; Communications Mgr., Nicole Gargotta; Controller, Robert Schwartz; Cur. Collection, Jorge Santis; Registrar, Rachel Talent-Ivers; Coord. Maintenance, Rick Powers; Museum Shop Mgr., Douglas Ratcliff; Head Exhibition Design, Annegreth Nill.
Personnel Profile: Full-Time Paid 26; Part-Time Paid 11; Part-Time Volunteers 628; Interns 2.
Governing Authority: nonprofit organization. Tax-exempt: 501(3)(c).
Art Museum.
Collections: 20th-century European & American art including: Picasso, Dali, Warhol, Mapplethorpe & Stella; William Glackens collection; post-World War II Northern European Expressionist CoBrA art; African, South Pacific, Pre-Columbian, contemporary Cuban & Native American art.
Facilities: 1,000-vol. non-circulating library of art reference books; 256-seat auditorium for meetings & lectures; Miriam & Bernard Peck Sculpture Terrace for weddings & special events; Satellite Learning Center, classrooms for 4th & 5th grades. Museum-related items for sale.
Activities: inter- & intra-museum loan exhibitions; guided gallery tours; lectures; seminars; arts festivals; school coordinated educational programs; acoustiguide; docent training program.
Publications: catalogs for changing exhibitions; gallery guides; newsletters.
Hours & Admission Prices: June-Sept. call for hours; Oct.-May Thurs. 11-8, Fri.-Wed. 11-5. Adults $10, senior citizens 65 & over, students 6-17, & military $7; members & children 5 & under no charge. Special exhibit hours & prices may vary. Closed national holidays. ♿
Attendance: 100,000 (estimated)
Membership: Family & Dual $75; Reciprocal $150; Supporter $250; Patron $500; Benefactor $1,000; Director's Circle $2,500.

* **MUSEUM OF DISCOVERY AND SCIENCE,** 401 S.W. Second St., Fort Lauderdale, FL 33312-1707. Tel.: 954-467-6637, ext. 311. Fax: 954-467-0046.
E-mail: kcavendish@mods.net
Web Site: www.mods.org
Founded: 1976.
Congressional District: 15
Key Personnel: C.E.O. & Pres., Kim L. Cavendish; Chm. (V), Jon Ferrando; Dir. Devel., Tracy Roloff; Vice Pres. Finance & C.F.O., Patty Ackerman; Vice Pres. Devel., Patrick Flynn; Bldg. Supt., Jaime Menendez; Vice Pres.

Mktg. & Communications, Marlene Janetos; Dir. Programs & Exhibits, Joe Cytacki; Museum Shop Mgr., Kevin Stradtner.
Personnel Profile: Full-Time Paid 45; Part-Time Paid 60; Part-Time Volunteers 150; Interns 6.
Governing Authority: nonprofit organization. Tax-exempt: 501(c)(3).
Science Center.
Collections: live specimens related to Florida ecology; health, physical sciences & space artifacts; fossils; Great Gravity Clock.
Major Exhibits: Grossology (T), 1/10-5/10; Water Works (T), 5/10-9/10.
Research Fields: education techniques; ecology; aquariology; corals.
Facilities: educational facilities; IMAX theater; lecture hall; cafe; video/demonstration theater. Museum-related items for sale.
Activities: films; traveling exhibitions; summer camps; snake shows; outreach programs; IMAX films; demonstrations; table talks; school tours; science labs; mall camps; scout programs; camp-ins; sea turtle walks; flight simulators; ride simulator; Youth Advisory Council; Teen Science Track; nanotechnology lectures.
Publications: visitors guide; school services brochure; membership brochure; annual report; quarterly magazine, Explorations.
Hours & Admission Prices: Mon.-Sat. 10-5, Sun. 12-6. Exhibits: adults $10; ASTC & members no charge. IMAX: adults $9; discounts to members & ASTC members. Exhibits & IMAX: adults $15, seniors $14, children $12. ♿
Attendance: 449,142 (accurate)
Membership: Dual & Grandparent $65; Family $95; Contributing $150; Sponsoring $275.

MY JEWISH DISCOVERY PLACE CHILDREN'S MUSEUM, 6501 W. Sunrise Blvd., Fort Lauderdale, FL 33313-6036. Tel.: 954-792-6700. Fax: 954-792-4839.
E-mail: dhochman@sorefjcc.org
Web Site: sorefjcc.org
Key Personnel: Dir., Debbie Hochman; Asst. Dir., Donald Graw
Children's Museum.
Collections: hands-on exhibits; Jewish culture & history.
Hours & Admission Prices: Tues.-Thurs. 12-4. Admission 2 & over $5; adult accompanied by child no charge.
Membership: Family with one child $36; Family with 2 children $54; Family with 3 or more children $72.

OLD DILLARD MUSEUM, 1009 N.W. 4th St., Fort Lauderdale, FL 33311-8935. Tel.: 754-322-8828. Fax: 754-322-8824.
Key Personnel: Dir., Ernestine Ray
History Museum.
Collections: African American history, culture, & art; personal artifacts; photographs.
Activities: educational programs.
Hours & Admission Prices: Mon.-Fri. 11-4; groups by appointment. No charge; donations accepted.

STRANAHAN HOUSE, INC., (M), 335 S.E. 6th Ave., Fort Lauderdale, FL 33301-2256. Tel.: 954-524-4736. Fax: 954-525-2838.
E-mail: stranahanl@aol.com
Web Site: www.stranahanhouse.org
Founded: 1981.
Congressional District: 22
Key Personnel: Exec. Dir., Barbara W. Keith; Pres., Joseph Smith; Vice Pres., Sandra Casteel; Sec., Eric Von Salzen; Treas., John Abel; Asst. Dir. & Special Events Coord., Ellen Murton; Security, John Della Cerra; Gift Shop Mgr., Linda Fox; Education Specialist, Marlene Schotanus.
Personnel Profile: Full-Time Paid 3; Part-Time Paid 3; Part-Time Volunteers 35.
Governing Authority: nonprofit organization. Tax-exempt: 501(c)(3).
Historic Building & Site.
Collections: period furnishings; photographs; personal artifacts.
Facilities: Museum-related items for sale.
Activities: guided tours; education programs for children; docent program. Annual Events: fundraisers; Ghost Tours in October; Christmas Party; socials.
Publications: quarterly newsletter, The Trading Post.
Hours & Admission Prices: Guided Tours: daily 1, 2, & 3. Adults $12, seniors $11, students $7; discounts for AAM members; special rates available for large groups (reservations required). Closed most holidays.
Attendance: 30,000 (estimated)
Membership: Individual $35; Family $50; Pioneer $100; Trading Partners $250; Settler $500; Golden Trader $1,000. Corporate Memberships: Corporate $250; Silver Trader $500; Golden Trader $1,000; Platinum Trader $2,500; Emerald Trader $5,000-$10,000.

TERRAMAR VISITORS CENTER - HUGH TAYLOR BIRCH STATE PARK, 3109 E. Sunrise Blvd., Fort Lauderdale, FL 33304-3313. Tel.: 954-564-4521. Fax: 954-762-3737.
History Museum: housed in the former home of Chicago attorney, Hugh Taylor Birch; built in 1940.
Collections: natural & cultural history; personal artifacts; photographs; period furnishings.
Facilities: 180-acre park; nature trails.
Activities: hiking. canoeing; camping; fishing.
Hours & Admission Prices: Call for hours.

Fort Myers

BOB RAUSCHENBERG GALLERY AT EDISON STATE COLLEGE, (M), Lee County Campus, Humanities Hall Bldg. L, 8099 College Pkwy., S.W., Fort Myers, FL 33919-5598. Tel.: 239-489-9313. Fax: 239-489-9482.
E-mail: rbishop@edison.edu
Web Site: bobrauschenberggallery.com
Founded: 1979.
Congressional District: 13
Key Personnel: Dir., Ron Bishop.
Personnel Profile: Full-Time Paid 2; Part-Time Paid 2; Part-Time Volunteers 26; Interns 2.
Governing Authority: state; college. Parent Institution: Edison College. Tax-exempt.
Art Center.
Collections: works of modern & contemporary artists.
Facilities: library; 194-seat auditorium; classrooms; cafeteria.
Activities: guided tours; films; docent program.
Publications: catalogs from past exhibitions available; Marc Chagall: Works on Paper; Don Saff, Sculpture; Contemporary Woodblock Prints; Edward Potthast, American Impressionist; Kings, Queens & Souptureens (Campbell Collections); The Art of Architecture; Pritzker Prize Laureates.
Hours & Admission Prices: Mon.-Fri. 10-4, Sat. 11-3. No charge; donations accepted. Closed holidays. ♿
Attendance: 10,000 (accurate)

CALUSA NATURE CENTER AND PLANETARIUM, 3450 Ortiz Ave., Fort Myers, FL 33905-7811. Tel.: 239-275-3435. Fax: 239-275-9016.
E-mail: info@calusanature.org
Web Site: www.calusanature.org
Founded: 1970.
Congressional District: 13
Key Personnel: Dir., Sanders E. Lewallen; Pres., Chuck Reynolds; Museum Shop Mgr., Grayce Smith.
Personnel Profile: Full-Time Paid 8; Part-Time Paid 4; Part-Time Volunteers 150; Interns 2.
Governing Authority: private; nonprofit organization. Tax-exempt: 501(c)(3).
Nature Center.
Collections: natural history; wildlife; native plants; astronomy.
Facilities: 10,000-vol. library of books, periodicals, vertical files & videos; 2,023 sq. ft. educational facilities; 13,700 sq. ft. exhibit space; nature & conservation center; planetarium; 90-seat theater; nature trails; intern apartment; aviary. Gift items for sale.
Activities: films; formal educational programs; guided tours; hobby workshops; lectures; participatory exhibits. Museum Sponsors: laser light shows; astronomy shows; telescope viewing; off-site outreach; field trips. Annual Events: Reptile Day; Bug Day; Creepy Crawlie Fair.
Publications: monthly newsletter, Naturally Speaking; volunteer quarterly newsletter, Voluncheer.
Hours & Admission Prices: Mon.-Sat. 9-5, Sun. 11-5. Adults $9, children 3-12 $6; discount to groups; members & children under 3 no charge. ♿
Attendance: 60,000 (estimated)
Membership: Individual Senior & Student $25; Individual Adult $30; Family $45; Organization $100; N.E.S.T. $100-$200; Business $500-$1,000; Life $2,000-$5,000.

EDISON & FORD WINTER ESTATES, 2350 McGregor Blvd., Fort Myers, FL 33901-3315. Mailing Address: P.O. Box 2368, Fort Myers, FL 33902-2368. Tel.: 239-334-7419. Fax: 239-461-2688.
E-mail: info@efwefla.org
Web Site: www.efwefla.org
Founded: 1947.
Congressional District: 14
Key Personnel: C.E.O. & Pres., Chris Pendleton; Chm., Suzanne Edwards; Exec. Asst., Sarah Reding; Public Rels. & Mktg. Mgr., Lisa Sbuttoni; Museum Store Mgr., Patti Wensel.
Personnel Profile: Full-Time Paid 27; Part-Time Paid 42; Part-Time Volunteers 150; Interns 10.
Governing Authority: nonprofit organization. Operated by Thomas Edison and Henry Ford Winter Estate, Inc. Tax-exempt: 501(c)(3).

History & Science Museum.
Collections: historical & scientific artifacts; Edison's & Ford's inventions; manuscripts; banyan tree extending 400 ft. around the trunk; cycads; prototype Model T; 200 Edison phonographs; memorabilia related to Edison's life; historical plants; period cars; Florida history; 9 historic buildings.
Research Fields: history of technology; social & botanical history; Henry Ford & Edison in Fort Myers, their inventions & business.
Facilities: 500-vol. library; botanical garden. Museum-related items for sale.
Activities: guided & self-guided tours; temporary & permanent exhibitions; education programs; living history programs; elder hostel programs.
Publications: Estates Guide Book; newsletters; recipe book; English & German audio tour devices; French, Spanish, & German print tour material.
Hours & Admission Prices: Daily 9-5:30. Adults $20, children 7-12 $11; discounts to AAM & ICOM members, groups, FL Trust, FL Historic Passport & American Horticulture Society; children under 6 no charge. Closed Thanksgiving; Christmas. ♿
Attendance: 225,000 (accurate)
Membership: $50-$5,000.

FLORIDA GULF COAST UNIVERSITY ART GALLERY, 10501 FGCU Blvd. S., FGCU Library, Fort Myers, FL 32965-6565. Tel.: 239-590-7199. Fax: 239-590-7270.
E-mail: asturdiv@fgcu.edu
Key Personnel: Interim Gallery Dir., Anica Sturdivant; Preparator & Studio Mgr., Andy Morris
Art Museum.
Collections: contemporary art; paintings; sculpture.
Activities: special events; receptions; rental facilities.
Hours & Admission Prices: Mon.-Fri. 10-4, Sat. 11-2; other times by appointment.

IMAGINARIUM HANDS-ON MUSEUM, 2000 Cranford Ave., Fort Myers, FL 33916-4006. Tel.: 239-321-7420. Fax: 239-344-5915.
E-mail: imag@cityftmyers.com
Web Site: www.imaginariumfortmyers.com
Founded: 1989.
Congressional District: 14
Key Personnel: Gen. Mgr., Matt Johnson; Business Mgr., Shelby Baucom.
Personnel Profile: Full-Time Paid 9; Part-Time Paid 5; Part-Time Volunteers 18.
Governing Authority: Parent Institution: City of Fort Myers. Subsidiary Institution: Imaginarium Group, Inc. Tax-exempt: 501(c)(3).
Science & Technology Center/Museum: housed in 1938 historic building.
Collections: hands-on exhibits.
Facilities: 100-seat theater; conference center; outdoor pavilion.
Publications: newsletter.
Hours & Admission Prices: Mon.-Sat. 10-5, Sun. 12-5. Adults $12, seniors $10, children 3-12 $8; discounts for ASTC members; museum members & children under 3 no charge. Closed Thanksgiving; Christmas. ♿
Attendance: 75,000 (accurate)
Membership: Individual $55; Family $75; Extended Family $100; Helping Hand $250.

SOUTHWEST FLORIDA MUSEUM OF HISTORY, (M), 2031 Jackson St., Fort Myers, FL 33901. Tel.: 239-321-7430. Fax: 239-344-5914.
E-mail: museuminfo@cityftmyers.com
Web Site: www.swflmuseumofhistory.com
Formerly: Fort Myers Historical Museum
Founded: 1982.
Congressional District: 14
Key Personnel: Gen. Mgr., Matthew H. Johnson; Business Mgr., Shelby Baucom; Public Rels. & Mktg. Mgr., Helena Finnegan; Education Asst., Victor Zarick; Visitors Svc., Monica Norton; Museum Clerk, Harriett Winn-Smith.
Personnel Profile: Full-Time Paid 4; Part-Time Paid 2; Part-Time Volunteers 10.
Governing Authority: municipal government. Parent Institution: City of Ft. Myers. Tax-exempt: 170(b)(1)(A).
Regional History Museum: housed in 1924 ACL Railroad Depot.
Collections: Calusa & Seminole Indian artifacts; Florida fossils; drawings & photographs of Fort Myers area from 1200B.C.-present; 20-ft. dugout canoe; Ethel Cooper Glass Collection; working switchboard; 10,000 photographs; regional history archives; Paleo Indian plants, animals & typography; Land of Giants: Paleo Florida exhibit; scale models of Historic Buildings: 1874 Jacob Summerlin House; 1856 Fort in Fort Myers; 84 ft. long, 101 ton Pullman private rail car Esperanza built in 1929; Cracker House dwelling built in the late 1800s to early 1900s.
Research Fields: Southwest Florida History.
Facilities: 200-vol. library of Southwest Florida history; educational center; Esperanza railcar & Cracker House. Historical books & related items for sale.
Activities: guided group tours; organized education programs for children; docent program; school loan service; participatory, temporary & traveling exhibitions; audio tour. Museum Sponsors: Escorted Day Trips January to April; Downtown Walking Tours January to April; monthly Authors Evenings September to April.
Publications: brochures; newsletters.
Hours & Admission Prices: Tues.-Sat. 10-4. Adults $9.50, seniors $8.50, students $5, children 3-12 $4; discounts to AAA, AAM & ICOM members; children under 3 & members no charge. Closed all major holidays. ♿
Attendance: 11,000 (accurate)
Membership: Student $15; Individual $25; Family $45; Donor $75; Benefactor $100; Supporting Donor $500; Sustaining Donor $1,000; Patron Donor $5,000; Founder $10,000.

Fort Pierce

A.E. BACKUS MUSEUM, 500 N. Indian River Dr., Fort Pierce, FL 34950-3080. Tel.: 772-465-0630.
E-mail: info@backusmuseum.com
Web Site: www.backusmuseum.com
Founded: 1960.
Key Personnel: Dir., Kathleen P. Fredrick
Art Museum.
Collections: works by A.E. Backus, Florida Highwaymen, & Indian River School artists.
Hours & Admission Prices: June-Aug. by appointment; Sept.-May Wed.-Sun. 11-4. No charge.
Attendance: 28,000 (estimated)
Membership: Individual $50.

HEATHCOTE BOTANICAL GARDENS, INC., 210 Savannah Rd., Fort Pierce, FL 34982-3447. Tel.: 772-464-4672. Fax: 772-489-2748.
E-mail: info@heathcotebotanicalgardens.org
Web Site: www.heathcotebotanicalgardens.org
Founded: 1985.
Congressional District: 16
Key Personnel: Dir., Amy Dahan; Pres. & Chm. (V), Cris Adams; Vice Pres. (V), Pat Linley; Treas., Gloria Moore.
Personnel Profile: Full-Time Paid 3; Part-Time Paid 3; Part-Time Volunteers 350.
Governing Authority: nonprofit organization. Tax-exempt: 501(c)(3).
Botanical Garden.
Collections: Japanese garden; subtropical palm walk; native plants; herb garden; trees; shrubs; flowers. Historic Buildings: pioneer house; 1922 home office.
Facilities: botanical garden. Museum-related items for sale.
Activities: guided tours; educational classes; rental facility; concert series. Annual Events: Fall Garden Festival; Holiday Nonprofit Market; Artist Days; Hidden Gardens Tour; Bloomin' Art & Plant Sale.
Publications: quarterly newsletter; brochures.
Hours & Admission Prices: May-Oct. Tues.-Sat. 9-5; Nov.-April Tues.-Sat. 9-5, Sun. 1-5. Adults $6, seniors $5, children 6-12 $2; discounts to groups; children under 6, members & AHS reciprocal members no charge. Closed major holidays. ♿
Attendance: 18,000 (estimated)
Membership: Student $10; Individual $35; Family $45; Contributing $100; Small Business & Sustaining $250; Sponsor $500; Benefactor $1,000.

NATIONAL NAVY UDT-SEAL MUSEUM, (M), 3300 N. Hwy. A1A, North Hutchinson Island, Fort Pierce, FL 34949-8520. Tel.: 772-595-5845. Fax: 772-595-5847.
E-mail: udtsealm@bellsouth.net
Web Site: www.navysealmuseum.com
Founded: 1985.
Congressional District: 16
Key Personnel: Exec. Dir., Michael R. Howard; Pres. (V), Willard Snyder; Cur., Ruth McSween; Dir. Mktg. & Media, Rolf Snyder; Education Coord., Suzi Howard; Funds Mgr., Marisa Moffett.
Personnel Profile: Full-Time Paid 4; Full-Time Volunteers 2; Part-Time Paid 2; Part-Time Volunteers 24.
Governing Authority: county; nonprofit. UDT/SEAL Museum Association Inc. Tax-exempt.
Military Museum: located on the 1943-1946, site where the Navy first trained Frog Men (Underwater Demolition Teams).
Collections: 1943-present, equipment used by the Underwater Demolition Teams & SEAL Teams; scuba equipment; weapons; boats; uniforms;

photos; explosive devices; dioramas of operations from World War II to Desert Storm; present day Navy SEALs.
Research Fields: various operations performed by UDT/SEALs; other countries with similar programs.
Facilities: library of histories & roster of the teams available to the public; 20-seat theater; 4,000 sq. ft. exhibit space; field research station. Gift items for sale.
Activities: guided tours; lectures; films; theater; organized education programs; temporary & traveling exhibitions. Museum Sponsors: UDT/SEAL reunion; Annual "Muster"-Veterans Day Celebration in November.
Publications: quarterly, Fire in the Hole.
Hours & Admission Prices: Jan.-April Mon.-Sat. 10-4; May-Dec. Tues.-Sat. 10-4, Sun. 12-4. Adults $6, children 6-12 $3; discounts to groups; members & children under 5 no charge. Closed New Year's Eve & Day; Martin Luther King Jr. Day; Presidents' Day; Easter; Memorial Day; Independence Day; Labor Day; Thanksgiving & day after; Christmas Eve & Day. ♿
Attendance: 30,000 (estimated)
Membership: Annual $50; Sponsor $100; Lifetime $800.

ST. LUCIE COUNTY HISTORICAL MUSEUM, 414 Seaway Dr., Fort Pierce, FL 34949-3138. Tel.: 772-462-1795.
Web Site: www.st-lucie.lib.fl.us/museum
Founded: 1965.
Congressional District: 10
Key Personnel: Supt., John Donlon.
Personnel Profile: Full-Time Paid 2; Part-Time Paid 3; Part-Time Volunteers 65.
Governing Authority: county. St. Lucie County Commission. Tax-exempt.
History Museum.
Collections: Seminole Indian artifacts; Spanish treasure fleet, early settler living; archives; manuscripts; maps; photographs; cattle brands, farm tools & equipment; paintings; firefighting equipment; 1907 Florida cracker house.
Research Fields: local historical sites & history.
Facilities: 1,000-vol. research library of history & genealogy books available for use on premises; Memorial Garden; reading room.
Activities: guided tours; permanent, temporary & traveling exhibits; special exhibits & events.
Publications: book, Pictorial History of St. Lucie County, 1565-1910.
Hours & Admission Prices: Tues.-Sat. 10-4; guided tours by appointment. Adults $4, seniors $3.50, children 6-17 $1.50; children under 6 no charge. Closed county holidays. ♿
Attendance: 15,000

Fort Walton Beach

CITY OF FORT WALTON BEACH HERITAGE PARK & CULTURAL CENTER, 139 Miracle Strip Pkwy., S.E., Fort Walton Beach, FL 32548-5817. Mailing Address: P.O. Box 4009, Fort Walton Beach, FL 32549-4009. Tel.: 850-833-9595. Fax: 850-833-9675.
Web Site: www.fwb.org/museum
Formerly: Indian Temple Mound Museum
Founded: 1962.
Congressional District: 1
Key Personnel: Dir., Ellen Middlebrook Herron; Coord. Education, Gail Lynn Meyer; Volunteer Coord., Ernie Masters; Coord. Programming, Mike Thomin; Museum Shop Mgr. & Museum Educator, Alicia Gardner; Facilities, Joe Carson.
Personnel Profile: Full-Time Paid 4; Part-Time Paid 2; Part-Time Volunteers 12.
Governing Authority: municipal. Parent Institution: City of Fort Walton Beach, P.O. Box 4009. Tax-exempt.
Heritage Park & Cultural Center: Fort Walton Temple Mound National Historic Landmark.
Collections: lithic & ceramic artifacts of local aboriginal origin; ethnologic & replica items; Indian artifacts; Walton Guard during the Civil War; NW Florida one-room schoolhouse artifacts; postal memorabilia. Historic Buildings: Camp Walton Schoolhouse, c.1912; Garnier Post Office, c.1918.
Major Exhibits: Pirates: Curse of the Caribbean, 6/10-8/10.
Research Fields: archaeology & related field notes; anthropology; museology; history.
Facilities: 1,200-vol. library of books, pamphlets & quarterlies on archaeology, museology & history available on premises; reading room. Indian handcrafts, replicas, books, pamphlets & postcards for sale.
Activities: guided tours; lectures; films; gallery talks; formally organized education programs for children; Friends of the Museum; special program by arrangement; inter-museum loan; permanent & temporary exhibitions; school loan service.
Publications: booklets, Excavations at the Fort Walton Temple Mound; The Buck Burial Mound; reprint papers, Florida Anthropologist extracts; Pottery of the Fort Walton Period; Fort Walton Beach Heritage Walk.
Hours & Admission Prices: Mon.-Sat. 10-4; call for holiday hours. Adults 18 & over $5, Seniors 55 & over & military with ID $4.50, children 4-17 $3; discounts to groups of 12 or more; children under 3 no charge. ♿
Attendance: 20,000 (estimated)
Membership: Friends of the Museums: Individual $25; Family $35; Patron $100; Life $1,000.

EMERALD COAST SCIENCE CENTER, 139 Brooks St., Fort Walton Beach, FL 32548-5826. Tel.: 850-664-1261. Fax: 850-664-6862.
E-mail: bobg@ecscience.org
Web Site: www.ecscience.org
Founded: 1989.
Key Personnel: Exec. Dir., James "Jamie" LaFollette.
Personnel Profile: Full-Time Paid 2; Part-Time Paid 3; Part-Time Volunteers 1.
Science Center.
Collections: hands-on exhibits.
Activities: picnics; parties.
Hours & Admission Prices: June-Aug. Mon.-Fri. 9-4, Sat.-Sun. 11-4; Sept.-May Mon.-Fri. 9-2, Sat.-Sun. 11-4. Adults $5, seniors 55 & over and youth 13-17 $4, children 3-12 $3.50; discounts to groups of 15 or more; children 2 & under no charge. Closed New Year's Day; Independence Day; Thanksgiving; Christmas.
Attendance: 50,000

FLORIDA'S GULFARIUM, 1010 Miracle Strip Pkwy., S.E., Fort Walton Beach, FL 32548. Tel.: 850-243-9046; 800-247-8575.
E-mail: info@gulfarium.com
Aquarium.
Collections: over 200 marine mammals including dolphins, sea lions, penguins, otters, & fish; birds, reptiles.
Activities: marine shows; educational programs; camps; rental facilities; feed demonstrations; special events.
Hours & Admission Prices: Daily 9-6. Adults 11 & over $18.75, seniors 62 & over $16.75, children 3-10 $11; children 2 & under no charge. Closed Thanksgiving; Christmas Eve & Day.

Gainesville

ALACHUA COUNTY HISTORIC TRUST: MATHESON MUSEUM, INC., 513 E. University Ave., Gainesville, FL 32601-5451. Tel.: 352-378-2280. Fax: 352-378-1246.
E-mail: info@mathesonmuseum.org
Web Site: www.mathesonmuseum.org
Founded: 1994.
Congressional District: 3
Key Personnel: Dir., Jessica Aiken; Pres. (V), Patricia Hilliard-Nunn, Ph.D
Personnel Profile: Part-Time Paid 3; Part-Time Volunteers 20; Interns 1.
Governing Authority: private; nonprofit organization. Tax-exempt: 501(c)(3).
History Museum.
Collections: culture & history of Gainesville, Alachua County & North Central Florida region. Historic House: 1867 historic home.
Facilities: 2,300-vol. library of Florida history books; archives; 1,600 sq. ft. exhibit space. Museum-related items for sale.
Activities: lectures; rental gallery; temporary & traveling exhibitions; tours of historic towns & neighborhoods; educational & public programs; docent led tours.
Publications: semi-annual newsletter, The Album.
Hours & Admission Prices: By appointment. Suggested Donation: $5 per person. Closed New Year's Day; Martin Luther King Jr. Day; Easter; Memorial Day; Independence Day; Labor Day; Veterans Day; Thanksgiving & day after; Christmas Day & day after. ♿
Attendance: 7,000 (estimated)
Membership: Student $15; Senior Individual $25; Individual $30; Family $40; Contributor & Corporate $100; Benefactor $250; Sponsor $500; Patron $1,000; Investor $2,500.

* **FLORIDA MUSEUM OF NATURAL HISTORY, (M),** S.W. 34th St. & Hull Rd., Gainesville, FL 32611-0001. Mailing Address: P.O. Box 117800, Gainesville, FL 32611-7800. Tel.: 352-846-2000 & 392-1721. Fax: 352-392-8783 & 846-0253.
E-mail: sfaze@flmnh.ufl.edu
Web Site: flmnh.ufl.edu
Formerly: Florida State Museum
Founded: 1917.
Congressional District: 4
Key Personnel: Dir. & Cur. Invertebrate Paleontology, Dr. Douglas S. Jones; Asst. Dir., Beverly Sensbach; Asst. Dir. Exhibits, Public Programs & Butterfly Rainforest Shop, Dr. Douglas R. Noble; Asst. Dir. Budget & Human Resources, Darlene Novak; Assoc. Dir. Collections & Research and Cur. Ornithology, Dr. David W. Steadman; Dir. Devel., Josh McCoy; Dir.

Mktg. & Public Rels., Paul Ramey; Assoc. Cur. Informatics, Dr. Reed S. Beaman; Assoc. Cur. Vertebrate Paleontology, Dr. Jonathan I. Bloch; Asst. Cur. Herbarium, Dr. Nico Cellinese; Distinguished Research Cur., Spanish Colonial Archaeology, Dr. Kathleen A. Deagan; Graduate Research Professor Paleobotany, Dr. David L. Dilcher; Assoc. Scientist & Program Dir. Center for Informal Science Education, Dr. Betty A. Dunckel; Assoc. Cur. Environmental Archaeology, Dr. Katherine F. Emery; Dir. McGuire Center for Lepidoptera & Biodiversity, Dr. Thomas C. Emmel; Cur. Caribbean Archaeology, Dr. William F. Keegan; Cur. Vertebrate Paleontology, Dr. Bruce J. MacFadden; Cur. Paleobotony, Dr. Steven R. Manchester; Cur. FL Archaeology, Dr. William H. Marquardt; Cur. Latin American Art & Archaeology, Dr. Susan Milbrath; Cur. Lepidoptera, Dr. Jacqueline Y. Miller; Cur. Herpetology, Dr. Max A. Nickerson; Interim Cur. Ichthyology, Dr. Lawrence Page; Cur. Marine Malacology, Dr. Gustav Paulay; Cur. History of Science, Dr. Charlotte M. Porter; Assoc. Cur. Mammals, Dr. David L. Reed; Ordway Professor, Dr. Scott K. Robinson; Distinguished Professor, Molecular Systematics & Evolutionary Genetics, Dr. Pamela S. Soltis; Cur. Malacology, Dr. Fred G. Thompson; Asst. Scientist FL Archaeology, Dr. Karen J. Walker; Cur. Botany & Keeper of the Herbarium, Dr. Norris H. Williams; Asst. Cur. Lepidoptera, Dr. Keith R. Willmott.

Personnel Profile: Full-Time Paid 125; Part-Time Paid 200; Part-Time Volunteers 624.

Governing Authority: university bd. of trustees. Parent Institution: University of Florida. Branch Museums: Randell Research Center, Pineland, FL; McGuire Center for Lepidoptera and Biodiversity. Tax-exempt.

Natural History Museum.

Collections: Southeastern U.S. & Caribbean area mammals; birds; bird eggs; fish; bioacoustics; lepidoptera; herbarium; reptiles; amphibians; invertebrate fossils; vertebrate fossils; marine & freshwater mollusks; environmental archaeology; archaeology; ethnology; fossil plants; pollen; physical anthropology.

Research Fields: paleoecology; ecology; anthropology; archaeology; vertebrate paleontology; lepidoptera; conservation; ethnology; environmental archaeology; herpetology; ornithology; systematics and natural history; zoology; ichthyology; mammalogy; invertebrate paleontology; malacology; botany; zoology; paleobotany; marine malacology; molecular systematics.

Facilities: natural history exhibits; butterfly rainforest; classrooms; research laboratories; collectors shop. Educational materials relating to museum programs for sale.

Activities: guided tours, lectures; films; formally organized education programs; docent program or council; inter-museum loan, permanent, temporary & traveling exhibitions; school loan service. Museum Sponsors: summer program for superior students; travel programs.

Publications: Bullen Monographs; Contributions in Anthropology & History; Natural Science Bulletin; Bulletin of the Allyn Museum of Entomology.

Hours & Admission Prices: Mon.-Sat. 10-5, Sun. 1-5. No charge. Butterfly Rainforest & Special Exhibits: call for admission prices. Closed Thanksgiving; Christmas. ♿

Attendance: 175,939 (accurate)

Membership: Out-of-Town & Student $25; Individual $50; Dual $75; Family & Group $100; Supporting $150; Explorer $250; Benefactor $500; Fellow $1,000; Patron $2,500; Director's Circle $5,000.

KANAPAHA BOTANICAL GARDENS, 4700 S.W. 58th Dr., Gainesville, FL 32608-0808. Tel.: 352-372-4981. Fax: 352-372-5892.

E-mail: kanapgard@aol.com

Web Site: www.kanapaha.org

Governing Authority: Operated By: North Florida Botanical Society.

Botanical Gardens.

Collections: bamboos; herbs; plants.

Facilities: 62-acrea site. Museum-related items for sale.

Activities: weddings; receptions; conferences; special events.

Hours & Admission Prices: Mon.-Wed. & Fri. 9-5, Sat.-Sun. 9 to dusk. Adults $6, children 6-13 $3; discounts to groups; children under 6 no charge.

MORNINGSIDE NATURE CENTER, 3540 E. University Ave., Gainesville, FL 32641-6057. Tel.: 352-334-2170. Fax: 352-334-2248.

Founded: 1972.

Congressional District: 3

Key Personnel: C.E.O., Gary A. Paul; Pres. (V), Penny Weber; Nature Operations Mgr., Steve Phillips; Nature Program Coord., George Chappell.

Personnel Profile: Full-Time Paid 10; Part-Time Paid 10; Part-Time Volunteers 5.

Governing Authority: municipal; nonprofit organization. Parent Institution: City of Gainesville. Subsidiary Institution: Dept. of Recreation & Parks. Tax-exempt.

Nature Center: includes working turn-of-the-century farm & five relocated buildings of historic significance for architecture & time period.

Collections: live representatives of Florida native animal species; taxidermied specimens; animal artifacts; period furnishings & reproductions of turn-of-the-century time period; Timucua Indian family compound.

Facilities: 400-vol. library; educational facilities; nature & conservation center.

Activities: arts festivals; docent program; formal educational programs; guided tours; lectures.

Publications: bimonthly newsletter, The Longleaf Pine.

Hours & Admission Prices: Center: daily 9-5. Living History Farm: Sat. only. Adults $2, children $1. Closed New Year's Day; Easter; Memorial Day; Labor Day; Thanksgiving; Christmas. ♿

Attendance: 30,000 (estimated)

Membership: Friends of Morningside: Adult $10; Family $20; Contributing $50.

* **SAMUEL P. HARN MUSEUM OF ART, (M), (I),** University of Florida, S.W. 34th St. & Hull Rd., Gainesville, FL 32611-0001. Mailing Address: P.O. Box 112700, Gainesville, FL 32611-0001. Tel.: 352-392-9826. Fax: 352-392-3892.

E-mail: coral@harn.ufl.edu

Web Site: www.harn.ufl.edu

Founded: 1990.

Congressional District: 6

Key Personnel: Dir. & Lecturer, Rebecca Martin Nagy; Sr. Dir. Devel., Phyllis Delaney; Chief Cur. & Cur. Asian Art, Charles Q. Mason; Cur. Modern Art, Dulce Roman; Cur. Contemporary Art, Kerry Oliver-Smith; Cur. Photography, Thomas Southall; Dir. Finance & Operations, Mary B. Yawn; Cur. African Art, Susan Cooksey; Registrar, Laura Nemmers; Dir. Mktg. & Public Rels., Tami Wroath; Coord. Membership, Tracy Pfaff; Coord. School & Family Programs, Eva Rosin; Chief Preparator, Michael Peyton; Dir. Education, Bonnie Bernau; Coord. Adult & Docent Programs, Rebecca Fitzsimmons.

Personnel Profile: Full-Time Paid 33; Full-Time Volunteers 167; Part-Time Paid 13; Part-Time Volunteers 150; Interns 18.

Governing Authority: nonprofit; University of Florida. Tax-exempt: 501(c)(3).

Art Museum.

Collections: American, pre-Columbian, African & Asian art.

Research Fields: 20th-century American art; African art.

Facilities: library; 86,800 sq. ft. facility; 250-seat auditorium; 32,773 sq. ft. exhibit space; 820 sq. ft. museum study center; object study room; classroom. Cafe; art books & other gift items for sale.

Activities: guided tours; lectures; gallery talks; films & videos; concerts; performances; organized education programs for children, adults, undergraduate & graduate students; docent program; school programs; teacher training; training programs for professional museum workers; internships; traveling & temporary exhibitions.

Publications: members' bimonthly newsletter; annual report; exhibition brochures & catalogues.

Hours & Admission Prices: Tues.-Fri. 11-5, Sat. 10-5, Sun. 1-5. No charge; donations accepted. Closed New Year's Day; Martin Luther King Jr. Day; Memorial Day; Independence Day; Labor Day; Veterans Day; Thanksgiving & day after; Christmas. ♿

Attendance: 78,807 (accurate)

Membership: Student $30; Individual $50; Dual $75; Associate $125; Fellow $250; Patron $500. Director's Circle: Sustainer $1,000; Benefactor $2,500. Business & Professional Friends: Contributor $250; Donor $500; Leader $1,000; Corporate Club $2,500.

SANTA FE COMMUNITY COLLEGE TEACHING ZOO, 3000 N.W. 83rd St., Gainesville, FL 32606-6200. Tel.: 352-395-5601. Fax: 352-395-7365.

E-mail: anita.courtot@sfcollege.edu

Web Site: www.sfcollege.edu/zoo

Founded: 1971.

Congressional District: 6

Key Personnel: Zoo Dir., Jack Brown; Zoo Cur., Kathleen Coyne-Russell; Asst. Dir., Jonathan Miot; Asst. Cur. & Exhibit Mgr., Shawn Jacobs; Asst. Cur., Shawntal Abram.

Governing Authority: college. Parent Institution: The Santa Fe Community College. Tax-exempt.

Zoo.

Collections: representative animal collection used in zoo animal technology.

Research Fields: captive reproductive biology.

Facilities: 100-vol. library of zoological material available for research on premises.

Activities: guided tours; formally organized education programs for undergraduate college students affiliated with Santa Fe Community College; permanent exhibits.

Hours & Admission Prices: Mon.-Fri. 9-2 by appointment, Sat.-Sun. 9-2. Adults $4, seniors 60 & over and children 4-12 $3; SFCC students & staff no charge. Closed holidays & university holidays. ♿

Attendance: 33,000 (estimated)

SANTA FE GALLERY, 3000 N.W. 83rd St., Bldg. M, Rm. 147, Gainesville, FL 32606-6210. Tel.: 352-395-5621. Fax: 352-395-4432.
E-mail: jayne.grant@sfcollege.edu
Web Site: dept.sfcollege.edu/vpa/gallery/schedule.html
Founded: 1978.
Congressional District: 6
Key Personnel: Gallery Mgr., Jayne Grant; Gallery Asst., Daniel Barker.
Personnel Profile: Part-Time Paid 1.
Governing Authority: nonprofit. Parent Institution: Santa Fe Community College. Tax-exempt: 501(c)(3).
Art Gallery.
Collections: paintings; sculpture; photographs.
Facilities: 1,800 sq. ft. exhibit space.
Hours & Admission Prices: Mon.-Fri. 12-4. No charge; donations accepted. Closed all college holidays & breaks. ♿
Attendance: 10,000

THOMAS CENTER GALLERIES, 302 N.E. 6th Ave., Gainesville, FL 32601-5476. Tel.: 352-334-5064. Fax: 352-334-2314.
E-mail: friedbereh@cityofgainsville.org
Web Site: www.gvlculturalaffairs.org/website/programs_events/programs.html#galleries
Founded: 1929.
Key Personnel: Dir., Erin H. Friedberg.
Personnel Profile: Full-Time Paid 1; Part-Time Volunteers 10.
Governing Authority: municipal government.
Art Gallery.
Collections: paintings; sculpture; drawings.
Activities: rental space available for workshops; lectures; musical performances; receptions; artist lectures.
Publications: brochures; postcards.
Hours & Admission Prices: Mon.-Fri. 8-5, Sat.-Sun. 1-4. No charge. Closed city holidays; New Year's Day; Independence Day; Thanksgiving; Christmas. ♿
Attendance: 10,000 (estimated)

UNIVERSITY GALLERY, (M), University of Florida, 400 S.W. 13th St., Fine Arts Bldg. B, Gainesville, FL 32611-0001. Mailing Address: P.O. Box 115803, University of Florida, Gainesville, FL 32611-5803. Tel.: 352-273-3041. Fax: 352-846-0266.
E-mail: amyv@ufl.edu
Web Site: www.arts.ufl.edu/galleries
Founded: 1965.
Congressional District: 5
Key Personnel: C.E.O. & Dir., Amy Vigilante.
Personnel Profile: Full-Time Paid 2; Part-Time Paid 7; Interns 2.
Governing Authority: university. Parent Institution: University of Florida, College of Fine Arts, School of Art & Art History. Tax-exempt: 501(c)(3).
Art Gallery.
Collections: master of fine arts student collection; contemporary art.
Research Fields: contemporary art.
Facilities: 30,000-vol. library of books & periodicals on general art & architecture available for inter-library loan.
Activities: lectures; gallery talks; inter-museum loan; temporary & traveling exhibitions.
Publications: exhibitions catalogues.
Hours & Admission Prices: Sept.-April 23 Tues.-Wed. & Fri. 10-5, Thurs. 10-7, Sat. 12-4. No charge. Closed academic & national holidays. ♿
Attendance: 8,000 (estimated)
Membership: Individual $25; Family $50; Patron $100 & up; Supporter $250; Donor $500; Title Sponsor $1,000 & up.

Geneva

MUSEUM OF GENEVA HISTORY, 165 First St., Geneva, FL 32732. Mailing Address: Geneva Historical & Genealogical Society, Inc., P.O. Box 91, Geneva, FL 32732-0091.
E-mail: genevahgs@aol.com
Key Personnel: Chm. (V), Mary Jo Martin; Pres. (V), Cindy Simonton.
Governing Authority: Parent Institution: Geneva Historical and Genealogical Society, Inc. Tax-exempt.
History Museum.
Collections: Geneva history; period furnishings; personal artifacts; military uniforms.
Publications: newsletter, Village Crier.
Hours & Admission Prices: Oct.-May 2nd & 4th Sun. of month 2-4; other times by appointment. No charge; donations accepted.
Attendance: 750 (accurate)

Green Cove Springs

MILITARY MUSEUM OF NORTH FLORIDA, One Bunker Ave., Green Cove Springs, FL 32043. Tel.: 904-284-8053.
E-mail: information@militarymuseumofnf.com
Web Site: www.militarymuseumofnorthflorida.com
Key Personnel: Pres. & Treas., Bud Nelson; Exec. Dir. & Cur., Herb Steigelman
Military Museum.
Collections: military artifacts; photographs; uniforms; weapons; equipment.
Facilities: library.
Hours & Admission Prices: Call for hours.

Gulf Breeze

GULF ISLANDS NATIONAL SEASHORE, 1801 Gulf Breeze Pkwy., Gulf Breeze, FL 32563-5000. Tel.: 850-934-2600. Fax: 850-932-9654.
E-mail: guis_fl_interpretation@nps.gov
Web Site: www.nps.gov/guis/
Founded: 1971.
Congressional District: 1
Key Personnel: Supt., Jerry A. Eubanks; Deputy Supt., Nina Kelson; Chief of Interpretation, Gail Bishop; Florida Dist. Interpreter, Stanley Lawhead; Chief Science & Resources Management, Rick Clark; Admin. Officer, Cathy Losher; Contract Specialist, Evans Ward; Exhibit Specialist, Jeff Halstead.
Governing Authority: federal. National Park Services, Dept. of the Interior, Washington, DC (See the listings for Fort Pickens Area-Gulf Islands National Seashore, Santa Rosa Island, FL & William M. Colmer Visitor Center, Ocean Springs, MS for additional information.)
National Park & Historic District: barrier islands stretch from Cat Island in Mississippi, 240 kilometers (160 miles) eastward to the far end of Santa Rosa Island in Florida.
Collections: A portion of the Gulf Islands National Seashore collection was lost due to Hurricane Ivan in 2004 & Hurricane Katrina in 2005. The surviving collection was temporarily transferred to Timucuan Ecological and Historic Preserve in Jacksonville, FL. William M. Colmer Visitor Center with natural history exhibits at Ocean Springs, MS. Historic Military Posts: 1834 Ft. Pickens, FL.; 1844 Ft. Barrancas, FL. (located at Pensacola Naval Air Station); 1859 Advanced Redoubt, FL. (located on board NAS Pensacola;) 1866 Ft. Massachusetts, Ship Island, MS.
Major Exhibits: Horn Island by Walter Anderson, 11/09-6/11.
Research Fields: history; natural history; archeology.
Facilities: campsites; visitor centers; picnic areas; nature trails; 40-seat auditorium. Books & publications for sale.
Activities: guided tours; films; self guided trails; boat tours; concession boat trip to West Ship Island from Gulfport, MS (April-Oct.) swimming & scuba diving; fishing; formally organized education program for children; volunteer program; permanent exhibitions; talks.
Publications: newsletter, The Gulf Islands Guide; history & natural history pamphlets; folder, Gulf Islands.
Hours & Admission Prices: Ft. Pickens closed due to Hurricane Ivan. Entrance fee collected at Perdido Key area of seashore. All centers & facilities no charge. ♿

THE ZOO, 5701 Gulf Breeze Pkwy., Gulf Breeze, FL 32563-9553. Tel.: 850-932-2229. Fax: 850-932-8575.
E-mail: annzoonwf@bellsouth.net
Web Site: www.thezoonorthwestflorida.org
Founded: 1984.
Key Personnel: Exec. Dir., Danyelle Lantz; Gen. Cur., Diane Norris; Dir. Operations, Terry Whitman; Dir. Visitor Svcs., Christi Maeda; Dir. Education, Susan Leveille.
Personnel Profile: Full-Time Paid 30; Part-Time Paid 30; Part-Time Volunteers 25.
Governing Authority: nonprofit. Tax-exempt: 501(c)(3).
Zoo & Botanical Garden.
Collections: over 700 animals; hundreds of birds; flowers; exotic plants; children's zoo.
Facilities: 300-vol. library of zoo & zoo-related books & magazines; 200-seat outdoor amphitheatre; 50-acre zoo; snack bar. Stuffed animals, zoological souvenirs, books, gifts & tee shirts for sale.
Activities: films; docent program; formal educational programs; mobile vans; loan, participatory & traveling exhibitions; broadcast programs; adopt-an-animal program; African photo safaris; zoo camp for kids. Zoo Sponsors: Zoo Lights in December.
Publications: biannual newsletter, The ZOOsletter
Hours & Admission Prices: Summer: daily 9-5; Winter: daily 9-4. Adults $11.50, senior citizens $10.50, children 3-11 $8.25; discounts to groups; children under 3 no charge. Closed Thanksgiving; Christmas. ♿
Attendance: 175,000

Membership: Individual $40; Grandparent & Family $75.

Hollywood

AH-TAH-THI-KI MUSEUM AT OKALEE, 5710 Seminole Way, Ste. S-2, Hollywood Seminole Indian Reservation, Hollywood, FL 33314-6405. Tel.: 954-797-5570.
Web Site: www.ahtahthiki.com
Founded: 1997.
Key Personnel: Museum Mgr., Barbara Butera; Exec. Dir., Tina M. Osceola; Museum Dir., Anne McCudden; Education, Dr. Cynthia Kasee; Museum Shop Mgr., Louise Osceola; Coord. Community Outreach, Brian Zepeda; Mgr. Physical Plant, Gene Davis; Security, Vicky Knouse
Native American.
Collections: Seminole Tribe of Florida: history & culture.
Facilities: 4,000 sq. ft. exhibit space; 1.5 mile nature walk; plants are marked by name & how they were used by the tribe for medicine and food. Museum-related items for sale.
Publications: membership newsletter.
Hours & Admission Prices: Daily 9-5. Adults $9, children 5-18, military and seniors 55 & over $6; discounts to groups of 10 or more; children 4 & under no charge. Closed major holidays.
Membership: Individual $30; Family Clan $60; Osceola Circle $250; Bandolier Bag $500; Chairman's Circle $1,000; Tribal Elder Corporate Sponsorship $5,000.

ART AND CULTURE CENTER OF HOLLYWOOD, 1650 Harrison St., Hollywood, FL 33020-6806. Tel.: 954-921-3274. Fax: 954-921-3273.
E-mail: info@artandculturecenter.org
Web Site: www.artandculturecenter.org
Founded: 1978.
Congressional District: 16
Key Personnel: C.E.O. & Exec. Dir., Joy Satterlee; Chm. (V), Alan Koslow, Esq.; Bookkeeper, Elizabeth Veszi; Asst. Dir. & Dir. Education, Susan Rakes; Mktg. & Design Mgr., Alesh Houdek; Technical Dir., Joseph Popejoy; Theater Mgr., Gustavo Ortiz; Dir. Devel., Jeff Rusnak; Front Desk Asst., Elise Viola; Public Rels. & Membership Mgr., Charmain Yobbi; Asst. to Dir., Jeff Lynn; Cur. Exhibitions, Jane Hart.
Personnel Profile: Full-Time Paid 9; Part-Time Paid 9; Part-Time Volunteers 350; Interns 2.
Governing Authority: private; nonprofit organization. Tax-exempt: 501(c)(3).
Multi-disciplinary Arts Center
Collections: contemporary paintings & sculpture; ethnographic arts.
Major Exhibits: Time & Temp: Surveying the Shifting Climate of Painting in South Florida, 11/14/09-1/10/10; Abracadabra: 3rd Annual Fundraising Art Exhibition and Raffle, 1/23/10-2/19/10; Balbone Martinez Site Specific Installation, 1/23/10-2/19/10; Adler Guerrier, 2/27/10-5/23/10; Nathan Sawaya: Replay, 6/5/10-8/15/10; Adaptation, 6/5/10-8/15/10.
Research Fields: pertaining to the permanent collection & exhibitions.
Facilities: library of art history available for use by special permission; reading room; 500-seat auditorium.
Activities: guided tours; lectures; films; gallery talks; formally organized education programs for children & adults; docent program; permanent exhibitions; master dance classes.
Publications: catalog.
Hours & Admission Prices: Mon.-Sat. 10-5, Sun. 1-4. Adults $7, seniors & students $4; discounts to AAA members & groups of 10 or more; Miami-Dade & Broward teachers, firefighters, police, members and children 13 & under no charge. Closed New Year's Day; Easter; Independence Day; Thanksgiving; Christmas. ♿
Attendance: 52,000 (estimated)
Membership: Student $25; Individual $40; Family $60; Friend $100.

HOLOCAUST DOCUMENTATION & EDUCATION CENTER, INC., 2031 Harrison St., Hollywood, FL 33020-5019. Tel.: 954-929-5690. Fax: 954-929-5635.
E-mail: info@hdec.org
Web Site: www.hdec.org
Founded: 1979.
Congressional District: 17
Key Personnel: Exec. Vice Pres., Rositta E. Kenigsberg; Pres. (V), Harry A. (Hap) Levy; Dir. Educational Outreach, Merle Saferstein; Documentation Dept. Coord., Rita Hofrichter.
Personnel Profile: Full-Time Paid 5; Full-Time Volunteers 2; Part-Time Paid 2; Part-Time Volunteers 350.
Governing Authority: nonprofit organization. Tax-exempt: 501(c)(3).
Holocaust Educational Resource Center.
Collections: video & audio tapes of survivors, liberators & protectors of the Holocaust; World War II & Holocaust memorabilia; paintings.
Research Fields: oral history; prejudice-reduction.
Activities: films; broadcast programs; organized education programs for children, adults & undergraduate & graduate college students; docent program for community exhibits; participatory exhibits; interviewer training; teachers' seminars; visual arts & writing contest for students. Center Sponsors: Holocaust Remembrance; Student Awareness Days; Teachers' Institute on Holocaust Studies; interviews of survivors & eyewitnesses of the Holocaust.
Publications: State of Florida Task Force on Holocaust Education Resource Manuals for grades 4-6; annual newsletter.
Hours & Admission Prices: Mon.-Fri. 9-5. No charge. Closed national & Jewish holidays. ♿
Membership: Individual $36; Supporting $100; Sustaining $250; Patron $500; Benefactor $1,000; Founder $1,500.

Homeland

HOMELAND HERITAGE PARK, (M), 249 Church Ave., Homeland, FL 33847. Tel.: 863-534-3766.
Historical Park, Sites & Buildings.
Collections: local history & culture; period furnishings; personal artifacts. Historic Buildings: Homeland School, 1878; Old Homeland Methodist Church, 1887; Raulerson House, 1880; English family log cabin & barn, 1888.
Facilities: 5-acre site; rental facilities.
Activities: rental facilities.
Hours & Admission Prices: Mon.-Fri. 8-5, Sat. by appointment.

Homestead

BISCAYNE NATIONAL PARK, 9700 S.W. 328th St., Homestead, FL 33033-5634. Tel.: 305-230-1144. Fax: 305-230-1190.
Web Site: www.nps.gov/bisc
Founded: 1968.
Congressional District: 20
Key Personnel: Supt., Mark Lewis; Park Science Coord., Richard Curry; Admin. Officer, Nancy Sanchez; Agent-Florida National Parks & Monument Association & Visitor Center Coord., Bob Showler; Chief Information Officer, Susan Gonshor.
Governing Authority: federal. Parent Institution: Dept. of the Interior, Washington, DC. Tax-exempt.
National Park & Nature Center.
Collections: natural history objects related to the ecology of the park; lobster sanctuary; crabs; seashells; plants; turtles; birds; sponges.
Research Fields: oceanography; marine biology; terrestrial biology; archaeology.
Facilities: 2,280-vol. library of books, journals, reports & documents all pertaining to the history of the park available for research on premises; on-site use or loan of duplicate copies to recognized research organizations; 180,000 acres of tropical marine & subtropical terrestrial natural area; field research station. Publications on natural history for sale.
Activities: guided tours; lectures; formally organized education programs for children; temporary & traveling exhibitions; glass bottom boat; snorkel & scuba tours.
Publications: Seascape, biannual park newsletter.
Hours & Admission Prices: Convoy Point Visitor Center: daily 7-5:30. Dante Fascell Visitor Center: daily 9-5. No charge. Call 305-230-7275 for information. ♿
Attendance: 500,000 (estimated)

EVERGLADES NATIONAL PARK, 40001 State Rd. 9336, Homestead, FL 33034-6733. Tel.: 305-242-7826 & 7700. Fax: 305-242-7711. TDD: 305-242-7826.
E-mail: nancy_russell@nps.gov
Web Site: www.nps.gov/ever
Founded: 1947.
Congressional District: 20
Key Personnel: Supt., Dan Kimball; Cur., Nancy Russell.
Personnel Profile: Full-Time Paid 2; Part-Time Paid 6; Part-Time Volunteers 1; Interns 3.
Governing Authority: federal. U.S. Dept. of the Interior, National Park Service, Washington, DC 20240. Tax-exempt.
National Park; pre & early settlement, southern Florida.
Collections: herbarium; birds; mammals; herps; fish; insects; corals; tree snails; historical & archaeological artifacts; research archives; 60,000 natural history specimens.
Research Fields: botany; wildlife; ecology; archaeology; history; hydrology.
Facilities: 5,000-vol. library including 4,000 photographs pertaining to natural science available for research on premise; South Florida Research Center Archives; visitor centers: Parachute Key & Flamingo; field research station; 100-seat auditorium. Books on park subjects & other museum related items for sale.

Activities: guided tours; lectures; formally organized education programs for children; permanent & temporary exhibitions.
Publications: biannual park newspaper.
Hours & Admission Prices: Visitor Center's: daily 8-5. Park: $20 per car; senior citizens with Golden Age Passport no charge. ♿
Attendance: 1,000,000 (estimated)
Membership: Annual Pass $50.

Indian Rocks Beach

GULF BEACH ART CENTER, 1515 Bay Palm Blvd., Indian Rocks Beach, FL 33785-2827. Tel.: 727-596-4331. Fax: 727-596-4331.
E-mail: arts1515@aol.com
Web Site: beachartcenter.org
Founded: 1978.
Congressional District: 8
Key Personnel: Exec. Dir., Grace Dimm.
Personnel Profile: Full-Time Paid 1; Part-Time Volunteers 14.
Governing Authority: nonprofit organization. Tax-exempt: 501(c)(3).
Art Gallery & School.
Collections: paintings; sculpture drawings.
Facilities: 300-vol. library of artists & painting material available to members; 1,400 sq. ft. exhibit space; educational facilities.
Activities: arts festivals; hobby workshops; organized education programs for children and adults; temporary exhibitions.
Publications: monthly newsletter.
Hours & Admission Prices: Sept.-June Mon.-Thurs. 8:30-4, Fri. 9-12. No charge; donations accepted. Closed Thanksgiving; Christmas. ♿
Membership: Member $15; Family & Patron $25; Sponsor $50; Lifetime $150; Benefactor $300.

Inverness

THE OLD COURTHOUSE HERITAGE MUSEUM, (M), One Courthouse Square, Inverness, FL 34450-4808. Tel.: 352-341-6428. Fax: 352-341-6445.
Formerly: The Museum of Citrus County History-Old Courthouse
Founded: 1985.
Congressional District: 6
Key Personnel: Pres. Historical Society, John Grannan; Pres. Museum, Linda Bega; Vice Pres., Beverly Drinkhouse; Dir. of Historical Resources, Kathy Turner.
Governing Authority: county. Parent Institution: Citrus County Historical Society, Inc. Tax-exempt: 501(c)(3).
History Museum: housed in 1911 Old Courthouse.
Collections: county archives 1885-current; pioneer settlers; photographs; diaries; manuscripts.
Research Fields: pioneer settlement.
Facilities: archival repository available for use by public. Museum-related items & gifts for sale.
Activities: guided tours; docent program.
Publications: bimonthly newsletter, At Home; brochures; calendars; book, Back Home.
Hours & Admission Prices: Museum: Mon.-Fri. 10-4. Historical Resource: Mon.-Fri. 10-5. No charge; donations accepted. ♿
Attendance: 20,000 (estimated)
Membership: Student (Grades 1-12) $1; Individual $10; Household $15; Organization $20; Life $250; Benefactor $500.

Islamorada

FLORIDA KEYS HISTORY OF DIVING MUSEUM, (M), 82990 Overseas Hwy., Islamorada, FL 33036-3600. Tel.: 305-664-9737.
E-mail: info@divingmuseum.org
Web Site: www.divingmuseum.org
Founded: 2000.
Key Personnel: Pres., Sally E. Bauer; Dir., Debra A. Illes; Museum Shop Mgr., Karenanne Gilbert.
Personnel Profile: Full-Time Paid 2; Full-Time Volunteers 2; Part-Time Paid 2; Part-Time Volunteers 12.
Governing Authority: Tax-exempt: 501(c)(3).
Diving Museum.
Collections: diving history; photographs; period artifacts; diving equipment; research documents; sunken treasure; Florida history.
Hours & Admission Prices: Daily. Adults $12, children 5-12 $6; discount to AAM members; AASLH members, members & children under 5 no charge. Closed New Year's Day; Thanksgiving; Christmas. ♿
Attendance: 7,300 (estimated)
Membership: $25; $50; $100; $150.

Jacksonville

ALEXANDER BREST MUSEUM AND GALLERY, 2800 University Blvd. N., Jacksonville, FL 32211-3321. Tel.: 904-256-7374. Fax: 904-256-7375.
Founded: 1977.
Congressional District: 3
Key Personnel: Dir. & Cur., Prof. Jack Turnock.
Personnel Profile: Full-Time Paid 1; Part-Time Paid 1; Interns 3.
Governing Authority: private university; nonprofit. Parent Institution: Jacksonville University. Tax-exempt.
University Art Museum.
Collections: decorative arts; ivory; Steuben glass; Chinese porcelain & cloisonne; Tiffany glass; Boehm porcelains; Persian carpets; pre-Columbian art & artifacts.
Facilities: 4,250 sq. ft. exhibit space.
Activities: guided tours; lectures; docent program; concerts; temporary exhibits.
Publications: A Guide to the Collection: The Alexander Brest Museum & Gallery.
Hours & Admission Prices: Mon.-Fri. 9-4:30, Sat. 12-5. No charge. Closed Memorial Day; Independence Day; Labor Day; Veterans Day; Thanksgiving; Christmas. ♿
Attendance: 12,000 (estimated)
Membership: Friends of Fine Arts $35 & up.

* **CUMMER MUSEUM OF ART & GARDENS, (M),** 829 Riverside Ave., Jacksonville, FL 32204-3336. Tel.: 904-356-6857. Fax: 904-353-4101.
Web Site: www.cummer.org
Founded: 1958.
Congressional District: 3
Key Personnel: Dir., Hope McMath; Chm., James Van Vleck; Cur., Holly Keris; Dir. Finance, Wendy Steve; Registrar, Kristen Bucher; Dir. Education, Susan Gallo; Dir. Visitor Svcs., Susan Mahla; Museum Shop Mgr., Susan Tudor.
Personnel Profile: Full-Time Paid 26; Part-Time Paid 16; Part-Time Volunteers 1,785; Interns 8.
Governing Authority: nonprofit organization. A branch of The DeEtte Holden Cummer Museum Foundation. Tax-exempt: 509(a); 4942(j)(3).
Art Museum & Gardens.
Collections: European & American paintings, sculpture; works on paper & decorative arts; early Meissen porcelain; Asian art; ancient art.
Major Exhibits: Botanical Watercolors by Jacques le Moyne, 11/09-1/10; Jazz ABZ: An A to Z Collection of Jazz Portraits by Paul Rogers, 1/10-8/10; Collectors Choice: Works from Jacksonville Private Collections, 5/10-9/10.
Research Fields: early Meissen porcelain; American art.
Facilities: 12,000-vol. library of art books; historic gardens. Art books, catalogs, postcards & art objects for sale.
Activities: guided tours; lectures; concerts; permanent, temporary & traveling exhibitions; interactive educational center; art studios.
Publications: The Wark Collection of Early Meissen Porcelain, 1984; collection Catalogue (2000), The Cummer Museum of Art & Gardens; Vision 2002: The Cummer Contemporary; Passion and Clarity: The Art of Joseph Jeffers Dodge; A Legacy in Bloom: Celebrating a Century of Gardens at The Cummer (2008).
Hours & Admission Prices: Wed.-Fri. 10-4, Sat. 10-5, Sun. 12-5. Adults $10, senior citizens, military & students $6; discounts to AAM & ICOM members; children 5 & under, members & Tues. 4-9 no charge. Closed major holidays. ♿
Attendance: 112,815 (accurate)
Membership: Seniors, Military & Educators $5 off any level; Student $30; Individual $50; Family $85; Associate $200; Fellow $300; Sponsor $500; Ponce de Leon $1,000 & up.

FLORIDA COMMUNITY COLLEGE, KENT CAMPUS MUSEUM/GALLERY, 3939 Roosevelt Blvd., Jacksonville, FL 32205-8946. Tel.: 904-381-3674.
E-mail: Kwarren@fccj.org
Web Site: www.fccj.org
Founded: 1971.
Key Personnel: Dir., Kelly Warren; Support Specialist, Angie Fogle.
Personnel Profile: Part-Time Paid 4.
Governing Authority: college. Parent Institution: Florida Community College at Jacksonville, 501 W. State St., Jacksonville, FL 32202. Tax-exempt.
Art Museum.
Collections: paintings; sculpture.
Facilities: 80-seat auditorium.
Activities: guided tours; lectures; gallery talks; arts festivals; TV programs; temporary & traveling exhibitions.
Publications: Kalliope

Hours & Admission Prices: Mon.-Thurs. 10-4, Fri. 10-3. No charge. Closed holidays. ♿
Attendance: 1,200 (estimated)

JACKSONVILLE FIRE MUSEUM, 1406 Gator Bowl Blvd., Jacksonville, FL 32202-1310. Tel.: 904-630-0618. Fax: 904-630-4202.
E-mail: lindat@coj.net
Web Site: www.jacksonvillefiremuseum.com
Founded: 1974.
Congressional District: 3
Key Personnel: C.E.O. & Cur., Linda S. Treadwell; Pres. (V), Wayne Doolittle.
Personnel Profile: Full-Time Paid 1.
Governing Authority: municipal; nonprofit. Tax-exempt: 501(c)(3).
Fire Museum: housed in 1902 single Bay Fire Station. Listed on the National Registered Historical Building.
Collections: antique fire apparatus & artifacts on fire fighting history; history of fire fighting in the city of Jacksonville, Florida.
Facilities: 35-vol. library of fire station log books & accounting records from 1902; 1,200 sq. ft. exhibit space.
Activities: guided tours; fire safety training for school children.
Hours & Admission Prices: Mon.-Fri. 9-4; groups by appointment. No charge; donations accepted.
Attendance: 60,000 (estimated)

JACKSONVILLE MARITIME MUSEUM SOCIETY, 1015 Museum Circle, Unit 2, Jacksonville, FL 32207-9006. Tel.: 904-398-9011. Fax: 904-398-7248.
E-mail: jaxmarmus@bellsouth.net
Web Site: www.jaxmaritimemuseum.org
Founded: 1985.
Key Personnel: Chm. (V), Ray Lake, Jr.; Dir., Catherine M. Krueger.
Personnel Profile: Interns 2.
Maritime Museum.
Collections: Jacksonville maritime history; model ships; paintings; photographs; period artifacts.
Publications: monthly newsletter.
Hours & Admission Prices: Mon.-Fri. 10:30-3; Sat.-Sun. 1-5. No charge; donations accepted.
Attendance: 7,000 (estimated)
Membership: Individual $25; Family $50; Sustaining $100; Patron $500; Golden Patron $1,000; Corporate $1,500-$2,500.

JACKSONVILLE ZOO AND GARDENS, 370 Zoo Pkwy., Jacksonville, FL 32218-5799. Tel.: 904-757-4463, ext. 110. Fax: 904-757-4315.
E-mail: zooadmin@jacksonvillezoo.org
Web Site: www.jacksonvillezoo.org
Founded: 1914.
Congressional District: 3
Key Personnel: Exec. Dir., Tony Vecchio; Chm. (V), Ann Baker; Museum Shop Mgr., Tena Barnidge; Volunteer Coord., Matt Lemonds.
Personnel Profile: Full-Time Paid 161; Part-Time Paid 91; Part-Time Volunteers 340; Interns 1.
Governing Authority: nonprofit society. Jacksonville Zoological Society. Tax-exempt: 501(c)(3).
Zoo and Garden.
Collections: mammals; birds; reptiles; amphibians; invertebrates; fish; plants.
Research Fields: field zoology.
Facilities: auditorium; outdoor picnic area; 2 restaurants; 2 snack shops; gardens; meeting facilities. Gift items for sale.
Activities: organized school programs & tours; teacher & family workshops; speakers bureau; docent program or council; sleepovers; after dark programs; night tours; stroller tours; preschool programs; outreach; behind the scenes tour; day camps; Trout River Lodge meeting facility; after-hours rentals.
Publications: quarterly magazine, Wild; bimonthly, Teacher & Educator Newsletter; members e-newsletter, Animals in Your Box.
Hours & Admission Prices: Daily 9-5. Adults $13, seniors $11, children 3-12 $8; discounts to groups, military, AAA & zoo members; members & children under 3 no charge. Closed Thanksgiving; Christmas. ♿
Attendance: 687,283 (accurate)
Membership: Individual $40; Friend $70; Family $90; Family Plus One $100; Family Plus Two $135; Director's Circle: $200, $300, $500, & $1,000.

KINGSLEY PLANTATION, 11676 Palmetto Ave., Jacksonville, FL 32226-2449. Mailing Address: 13165 Mt. Pleasant Rd., Jacksonville, FL 32225-1227. Tel.: 904-251-3537. Fax: 904-251-3577. TDD: 904-251-3537.
E-mail: timu_interpretation@nps.gov
Web Site: www.nps.gov/timu
Founded: 1991.
Congressional District: 4
Key Personnel: Supt., Barbara Goodman; Museum Cur., Anne Lewellen.
Personnel Profile: Full-Time Paid 25; Part-Time Paid 5; Part-Time Volunteers 15.
Governing Authority: federal. Parent Institution: National Park Service. Subsidiary Institution: Timucuan Ecological & Historic Preserve, 13165 Mt. Pleasant Rd., Jacksonville, FL 32225. Tax-exempt.
Historic Site.
Collections: history; archaeological. Historic Buildings: 19th century Kitchen House; Carriage House & slave cabins; 18th century Plantation House.
Facilities: interpretive garden.
Activities: guided tours; permanent exhibitions.
Publications: book, Junior Ranger Activity Book.
Hours & Admission Prices: Daily 9-5. No charge; donations accepted. Closed New Year's Day; Thanksgiving; Christmas. ♿
Attendance: 60,000 (accurate)

MANDARIN MUSEUM AND HISTORICAL SOCIETY, (M), 11964 Mandarin Rd., Jacksonville, FL 32223-1339. Mailing Address: P.O. Box 23601, Jacksonville, FL 32241-3601. Tel.: 904-268-0784. Fax: 904-268-0752.
E-mail: mandarinmuseum@bellsouth.net
Web Site: mandarinmuseum.net
Founded: 1992.
Congressional District: 4
Key Personnel: Dir., Andrew Morrow; Pres. (V), John Cooksey.
Personnel Profile: Full-Time Paid 1.
Governing Authority: Subsidiary Institution: Walter Jones Historical Park, 11964 Mandarin Rd., Jacksonville, FL; Store & Post Office, 12471 Mandarin Rd., Jacksonville, FL. Tax-exempt.
Historic Buildings & Park.
Collections: Mandarin Store & Post Office: period furnishings; local history; Timacua artifacts; Steamboat Maple Leaf artifacts. Walter Jones Historical Park: 1800s homestead; 1875 farmhouse; 1876 barn & sawmill.
Research Fields: historical Florida.
Activities: lectures; educational programs; family events; school groups.
Publications: newsletter; Adventures in Mandarin 1876-1886.
Hours & Admission Prices: Museum: Tues. & Thurs.-Fri. 1-4, Sat. 9-4. Park: daily 7am-10pm. Store & Post Office: 1st & 3rd Sat. 1-3. No charge; donations accepted. Closed holidays. ♿
Attendance: 600 (accurate)
Membership: Orange Picker $35; May $50; Maple Leaf $100; Walter Jones Society & Stowe Society $500.

MUSEUM OF CONTEMPORARY ART JACKSONVILLE, (MOCA JACKSONVILLE), (M), 333 N. Laura St., Jacksonville, FL 32202-3505. Tel.: 904-366-6911. Fax: 904-366-6901.
E-mail: info@mocajacksonville.org
Web Site: www.mocajacksonville.org
Formerly: Jacksonville Museum of Modern Art
Founded: 1948.
Congressional District: 3
Key Personnel: Dir., Deborah Broder; Chm. (V), Preston Haskell; Assoc. Cur. & Registrar, Ben Thompson; Assoc. Dir. Education, Cathy Fitzpatrick; Museum Shop Mgr., Amie Barr.
Personnel Profile: Full-Time Paid 10; Part-Time Paid 8; Interns 4.
Governing Authority: nonprofit. Parent Institution: University of North Florida.Tax-exempt: 501(c)(3).
Contemporary Art Museum.
Collections: emphasis on works from 1960 to present include paintings, printmaking, sculpture, photography.
Major Exhibits: Life as a Legend: Marilyn Monroe (T), 1/10-4/10.
Research Fields: contemporary art; historical Jacksonville architecture; contemporary & modern art.
Facilities: 625-vol. library of professional & reference books pertaining to art available for research on premises by application; reading room; exhibit space; 125-seat auditorium; children's interactive area; classroom art facilities: darkroom, printing, ceramics, painting studios. Art, handcrafted items, books & cards for sale.
Activities: guided tours; films; gallery talks; arts festivals; professionally conducted workshops; formally organized education programs; docent program; inter-museum loan, permanent, temporary & traveling exhibitions; school art center for loans of art reproductions, slides & prints to teachers; art enrichment (Outreach) program for public schools.
Publications: quarterly newsletter.
Hours & Admission Prices: Tues.-Wed. & Fri.-Sat. 10-4, Thurs. 10-8, Sun. 12-4. Adults $8, senior citizens 65 & over, students & military $4; children under 2, families on Sun., members & 1st Wed. of month 5pm-9pm no charge. Closed New Year's Day; Martin Luther King Day; President's Day;

Easter; Memorial Day; Independence Day; Labor Day; Veterans Day; Thanksgiving; Christmas. ♿
Attendance: 58,000 (accurate)
Membership: Student, Educator & Senior Citizen $30; Individual $50; Dual & Family $75.

*** MUSEUM OF SCIENCE & HISTORY OF JACKSONVILLE, (M),** 1025 Museum Circle, Jacksonville, FL 32207-9053. Tel.: 904-396-6674, ext. 218. Fax: 904-396-7900. TDD: 904-348-3972.
E-mail: admin@themosh.org
Web Site: www.themosh.org
Founded: 1941.
Congressional District: 3 & 4
Key Personnel: Exec. Dir., Maria Hane; Chm., Dori Walton; Dir. Finance, Jacquelyn Blanchard; Dir. Education, Christy Turner; Dir. Visitor Svcs. & Facilities, John Rouge.
Personnel Profile: Full-Time Paid 20; Part-Time Paid 15; Part-Time Volunteers 425; Interns 3.
Governing Authority: board of trustees; nonprofit organization. Tax-exempt: 501(c)(3).
Science & History Museum/Planetarium.
Collections: archaeology; ethnology; geology; natural history; natural science; physical science; health science; history; Floridian material culture; decorative arts; costumes; toys, antique dolls.
Major Exhibits: A-mazing Sea (T), 1/30/10-5/2/10; Florida's Timucua Natives, 2/20/10-10/31/10; Dino Scenes (T), 5/15/10-8/10; Trains!, 11/20/10-1/30/11.
Research Fields: museum collections, exhibitions & educational programs.
Facilities: galleries of permanent regional history & science exhibitions, physical science interactive & changing exhibitions; classrooms & theaters; 60 ft. dome planetarium; live animal exhibitions; outdoor interpretive courtyard; store collection storage; support spaces.
Activities: tours; lectures; formally organized educational programs; crafts classes; exhibit related trips; science demonstrations; astronomy programs; live animal demonstrations; planetarium programs; day camps; camp-ins; teacher training workshops.
Publications: museum brochure; annual report to members; annual teachers guide; bimonthly newsletter; annual summer programs brochure.
Hours & Admission Prices: Oct.-Aug. Mon.-Fri. 10-5, Sat. 10-6, Sun. 1-6; call for Sept. hours. Adults $9, children $7; discounts to active duty military & senior citizens, AAM & ASTC members; members no charge. Closed major holidays. ♿
Attendance: 198,580 (accurate)
Membership: Individual $50; Family $65; Family Plus $75; Patron $150; Benefactor $250; Grand Benefactor $500.

MUSEUM OF SOUTHERN HISTORY, 4304 Herschel St., Jacksonville, FL 32210-2210. Tel.: 904-388-3574.
E-mail: vseagraves@comcast.net
Web Site: www.museumsouthernhistory.com
Founded: 1975.
Key Personnel: Chm. Bd., Richard Henderson; Vice Pres. Bd., Ben Willingham; Treas., Randy Kerlin; Cur., Van Seagraves.
Personnel Profile: Full-Time Paid 1; Part-Time Volunteers 16.
Governing Authority: private; nonprofit organization. Tax-exempt: 501(c)(3).
General Museum.
Collections: local history & culture; photographs; period artifacts; military weapons; flags.
Research Fields: Black soldiers in Confederate service.
Facilities: 3,000-vol. library; 3,500 sq. ft. exhibit space. Museum-related items for sale.
Activities: guided tours; lectures; loan & participatory exhibits. Annual Event: Battle of Olustee in February.
Publications: quarterly newsletter, The Florida Sandspur.
Hours & Admission Prices: Tues.-Sat. 10-4. Adults $3; senior citizens, students, members & children 16 & under no charge. Closed holidays. ♿
Attendance: 7,000 (estimated)
Membership: Individual $25; Family $35; Booster $50; Sponsor $100; Benefactor $300.

RITZ THEATRE AND MUSEUM, 829 N. David St., Jacksonville, FL 32202-4734. Tel.: 904-632-5555. Fax: 904-632-5553.
Web Site: www.ritzjacksonville.com
Formerly: Ritz Theatre & LaVilla Museum
Founded: 1999.
Congressional District: 3
Key Personnel: Dir., Carol J. Alexander; Museum Admin., Lydia P. Stewart.
Personnel Profile: Full-Time Paid 7; Full-Time Volunteers 1; Part-Time Paid 2; Part-Time Volunteers 7.
Governing Authority: city. Tax-exempt.
History Museum.
Collections: Jacksonville's African American community history from 1800s to 1960s; furnishings; personal artifacts; photographs.
Major Exhibits: Through Our Eyes - Each One Teach One: The Artist As Mentor, 11/09-5/10.
Research Fields: development of educational institutions, businesses & roles of women in Jacksonville's African American community in the 1800s & 1900s.
Facilities: 11,000 sq. ft. exhibit space; 400-seat theater.
Activities: concerts; dance recitals; docent program; films; guided tours; lectures; loan, temporary & traveling exhibitions; theater. Annual Event: jazz concerts.
Hours & Admission Prices: Tues.-Fri. 10-6, Sat. 10-2, Sun. 2-5. Adults $6, senior citizens, children & students $3; discounts to groups of 25 or more. Closed New Year's Day; Martin Luther King Jr. Day; Presidents' Day; Memorial Day; Independence Day; Labor Day; Veterans Day; Thanksgiving; Christmas. ♿
Attendance: 5,000 (estimated)

TIMUCUAN ECOLOGICAL AND HISTORIC PRESERVE AND FORT CAROLINE NATIONAL MEMORIAL, 12713 Fort Caroline Rd., Jacksonville, FL 32225-1240. Mailing Address: 13165 Mt. Pleasant Rd., Jacksonville, FL 32225-1227. Tel.: 904-641-7155. Fax: 904-641-3798.
E-mail: timu_interpretation@nps.gov
Web Site: www.nps.gov/timu
Founded: 1953.
Congressional District: 4
Key Personnel: Supt., Barbara Goodman; Chief Interpretation, Brian Loadholtz; Museum Cur., Anne R. Lewellen.
Personnel Profile: Full-Time Paid 25; Part-Time Paid 5; Part-Time Volunteers 15.
Governing Authority: federal; not-for-profit. Parent Institution: National Park Service.
Historic & Natural History Museum.
Collections: furnishings; archaeological remains; Native American culture; colonization of the French colony of La Caroline; plantation period and slavery; Timucuan people exhibits & objects.
Research Fields: plantation operations; slavery; 16th-20th century Native American & European inhabitants; wetland natural history.
Facilities: Books, postcards, field guides & local history publications for sale.
Activities: guided tours; formal education programs for children; natural history walks.
Publications: book, Junior Ranger Activity Book.
Hours & Admission Prices: Daily 9-5. No charge. Closed New Year's Day; Thanksgiving; Christmas. ♿
Attendance: 1,000,000 (estimated)

Jacksonville Beach

BEACHES MUSEUM & HISTORY CENTER, (M), 380 Pablo Ave., Jacksonville Beach, FL 32250-5539. Mailing Address: P.O. Box 50646, Jacksonville Beach, FL 32240-0646. Tel.: 904-241-5657. Fax: 904-241-6243.
Formerly: Beaches Area Historical Society
Key Personnel: Exec. Dir., Deborah B. Guglielmo; Pres. (V), Steve Williams; Museum Shop Mgr., Jane Alexander.
Personnel Profile: Full-Time Paid 4; Part-Time Paid 1; Part-Time Volunteers 48; Interns 2.
Governing Authority: Parent Institution: Beaches Area Historical Society. Tax-exempt.
History Museum.
Collections: local history & culture; photographs.
Major Exhibits: The A, B, & C's of the Beaches, 1/10-2/10.
Research Fields: first coast beaches in Florida.
Facilities: library; archives.
Activities: lectures; summer camp; educational tours.
Publications: bimonthly newsletter, Tidings.
Hours & Admission Prices: Tues.-Sat. 10-4:30. Archives: Tues.-Thurs. 10-4:30. Adults $5; discounts to AAM members, military & seniors; members no charge. ♿
Attendance: 12,000 (accurate)
Membership: Individual $30; Family $50; Sustaining $100; Corporate $250-$500.

Jensen Beach

FPL ENERGY ENCOUNTER, 6501 S. Ocean Dr., Jensen Beach, FL 34957-2041. Tel.: 877-375-4386. Fax: 772-467-7565.
E-mail: energy_encounter@fpl.com
Web Site: www.fpl.com/learning/energy_encounter
Founded: 1990.

Key Personnel: Dir., Vicki Spencer.
Personnel Profile: Full-Time Paid 2; Part-Time Paid 1.
General Museum.
Collections: energy, electricity & nuclear power displays.
Activities: Annual Event: Atomic Energy Merit Badge for Boy Scouts; teacher workshop - nuclear energy in January.
Hours & Admission Prices: Mon.-Fri. 10-4; groups by appointment. No charge.
Attendance: 25,000 (accurate)

MARITIME & CLASSIC BOAT MUSEUM, (M), 1707 N.E. Indian River Dr., Jensen Beach, FL 34957. Tel.: 772-692-1234. Fax: 772-463-3204.
E-mail: mym34994@comcast.net
Web Site: www.mymflorida.com
Formerly: Maritime and Yachting Museum of Florida
Founded: 1993.
Key Personnel: Dir., Sheila Stewart-Leach.
Personnel Profile: Full-Time Paid 2; Part-Time Paid 3; Part-Time Volunteers 25; Interns 2.
Governing Authority: private; nonprofit organization. Tax-exempt.
Maritime Museum.
Collections: maritime & yachting history; period wooden boats; ship models; maritime paintings, prints & photographs; navigator's instruments; marine engines; boatbuilding tools.
Facilities: library.
Activities: educational programs; boat shows; workshops; meetings; boat restoration; tours; seminars; symposia; lectures.
Publications: newsletter.
Hours & Admission Prices: Mon. & Wed.-Sat. 10-5, Tues. 10-7, Sun. 1-4. Adults $5, children 5-12 $4; children under 5 & members no charge. Closed major holidays. ♿
Attendance: 2,500 (estimated)

Juno Beach

LOGGERHEAD MARINELIFE CENTER, 14200 U.S. Hwy. 1, Loggerhead Park, Juno Beach, FL 33408-1406. Tel.: 561-627-8280. Fax: 561-627-8305.
E-mail: info@marinelife.org
Web Site: www.marinelife.org
Formerly: Marinelife Center of Juno Beach
Founded: 1980.
Key Personnel: Chm. (V), Ray Graziotto; Exec. Dir., Nanette Lawrenson; Membership & Adoption Coord., Brandon Gardner; Dir. Education, Jennifer Royce; Biologist, Chris Johnson; Communications & Devel. Mgr., Tom Longo; Museum Shop Mgr., Karen Bell.
Personnel Profile: Full-Time Paid 7; Part-Time Paid 1; Part-Time Volunteers 150; Interns 1.
Governing Authority: nonprofit organization; board of directors. Tax-exempt: 501(c)(3).
Marine Museum: housed in c.1950 ranch house.
Collections: sea turtle specimens; live sea turtles; fish; crab & shell collection; touch tank; shark tank.
Research Fields: leatherback sea turtle (Dermochelys coriacea) clutch survivability; nesting documentation (3 varieties of sea turtle); electronic mapping of nesting activity.
Facilities: library of reference books available for inter-library loan & for use by public; aquarium; educational facilities; 1,500 sq. ft. exhibit space; 2,500 sq. ft. saltwater tank yard; field research station; nature center; zoological park. Educational items & gifts for sale.
Activities: guided tours; lectures; organized educational programs; docent program; participatory, loan, temporary & traveling exhibitions.
Publications: quarterly newsletter, Turtle Times.
Hours & Admission Prices: Mon.-Sat. 10-5, Sun. 12-4. No charge; donations accepted. Closed New Year's Day; Easter; Memorial Day; Independence Day; Labor Day; Thanksgiving; Christmas. ♿
Attendance: 100,000 (accurate)
Membership: Individual $35; Family $65; Sponsor $150; Patron $250.

Jupiter

BURT REYNOLDS & FRIENDS MUSEUM, 100 U.S. Hwy. #1, Jupiter, FL 33468. Mailing Address: P.O. Box 264, Jupiter, FL 33468-0264. Tel.: 561-743-9955. Fax: 561-743-9922.
E-mail: mdaniel@burtreynoldsmuseum.org
Web Site: www.burtreynoldsmuseum.org
Key Personnel: Pres., Kenneth Kay.
Celebrity Museum.
Collections: celebrity artifacts; photographs.
Hours & Admission Prices: Call for hours.

HIBEL MUSEUM OF ART, 5353 Parkside Dr., Jupiter, FL 33458-2906. Tel.: 561-622-5560. Fax: 561-622-4881.
E-mail: info@hibelmuseum.org
Web Site: hibelmuseum.org
Founded: 1977.
Congressional District: 12
Key Personnel: Dir., Nancy Walls; Chief Cur. Artworks & Exhibitions, Edna Hibel.
Personnel Profile: Full-Time Paid 3; Part-Time Paid 6; Part-Time Volunteers 8.
Governing Authority: nonprofit organization. Parent Institution: Edna Hibel Art Foundation. Tax-exempt: 501(c)(3).
Art Museum dedicated to the works of Edna Hibel who specializes in Classical, Impressionist, Figurative & Oriental styles of painting, drawing, original graphics & sculpture.
Collections: preservation of paintings, sculptures, drawings, graphics, porcelain art, crystal art and dolls by Edna Hibel; Oriental & Western antique furniture; period paperweights; Oriental dolls; snuff bottles.
Research Fields: works and life of Edna Hibel; art history of various cultures.
Facilities: 200-vol. library of cultural & art history; gallery space & function space for community groups; piano for chamber concerts. Videotapes & films available & art-related items for sale.
Activities: guided tours; lectures; films; concerts; docent program; temporary, traveling & loan exhibitions; traveling & lending film program.
Publications: educational booklets; catalogs; books; newsletters; brochures; films and video documentaries.
Hours & Admission Prices: April-Oct. Tues.-Fri. 11-4; Nov.-March Tues.-Sat. 11-5, Sun. 1-5. No charge; donations accepted. Closed major holidays. ♿
Attendance: 6,000 (accurate)
Membership: Friends of the Hibel Museum of Art: Annual $50; Gold One-Year Family Membership $100.

LOXAHATCHEE RIVER HISTORICAL SOCIETY - JUPITER INLET LIGHTHOUSE & MUSEUM, (M), 500 Captain Armour's Way, Jupiter, FL 33469-3508. Tel.: 561-747-8380. Fax: 561-575-3292.
E-mail: visit@jupiterlighthouse.org
Web Site: www.jupiterlighthouse.org
Founded: 1971.
Congressional District: 12
Key Personnel: Bd. Pres., James Snyder; Vice Chair, Bill Wood; Pres. & C.E.O., Jamie Stuve; Asst. Dir., Kathleen Glover; Lighthouse Mgr., Chris McKnight; Archivist & Research, Lynn Drake.
Personnel Profile: Full-Time Paid 3; Part-Time Paid 5; Part-Time Volunteers 116; Interns 3.
Governing Authority: nonprofit organization. Subsidiary Institution: DuBois Pioneer Home, Jupiter Inlet Lighthouse & Museum. Tax-exempt: 501(c)(3).
General History Museum: lighthouse & historic homes.
Collections: 1860 lighthouse with fresnel lens & related artifacts; regional history; marine & agricultural development; lifesaving station; Seminole Wars; WW II; railroads. Historic Buildings: c.1898 DuBois Pioneer home; Jupiter Inlet Oil House; 1892 Tindall House; WW II barracks building.
Major Exhibits: Five Thousand Years on the Loxahatchee, 11/09-12/10.
Research Fields: north Palm Beach County; south Martin County; documentation; archaeology.
Facilities: library pertaining to local history for use on premises only by appointment; snack shop. Gifts for sale.
Activities: guided tours; lecture series; summer camps; weddings; special events; indoor & outdoor history exhibits; organized educational programs; speakers; temporary & permanent exhibitions.
Publications: newsletters, Update; quarterly periodical; Loxahatchee Currents; booklet, Jupiter Inlet Lighthouse.
Hours & Admission Prices: Tues.-Sun. 10-5, last tour leaves at 4. Adults $7, children 6-18 $5; discounts to groups; children under 5, active military & members no charge. Closed major holidays. ♿
Attendance: 58,575 (accurate)
Membership: Individual $35; Family $60; Sustaining $100; Patron $250; Benefactor $500. 1860 Society: Bright Lights $250; Lighthouse Keepers $1,000; Captain Yorke Club $2,500; General Meade $5,000.

Key Biscayne

BILL BAGGS CAPE FLORIDA STATE PARK, 1200 S. Crandon Blvd., Key Biscayne, FL 33149-2795. Tel.: 305-361-8779. Fax: 305-365-0003.
Web Site: www.floridastateparks.org
Founded: 1935.
Congressional District: 18
Key Personnel: Park Supt., Robert Yero.
Personnel Profile: Full-Time Paid 19; Part-Time Paid 3; Part-Time Volunteers 25; Interns 2.
Governing Authority: state. Dept. of Environmental Protection Division of Recreation & Parks, Commonwealth Bldg., 3900 Commonwealth Blvd., Tallahassee, FL 32303. Tax-exempt.

Historic Building: c.1825 restored Lighthouse; reconstruction of Keeper's house.
Collections: native plants; endangered species.
Activities: guided tours; interpretation of the early history of South Florida, Second Seminole War.
Hours & Admission Prices: Park: 8am to sunset. Cape Florida Lighthouse Tours: Thurs.-Mon. 10 & 1; children 8 & under not permitted to top of lighthouse. No charge; donations accepted.
Attendance: 700,000 (estimated)
Membership: Florida State Parks Annual Pass (good at all parks): Individual $31.95; Family $63.90.

Key West

AUDUBON HOUSE & TROPICAL GARDENS, 205 Whitehead St., Key West, FL 33040-6522. Tel.: 305-294-2116. Fax: 305-294-4513.
E-mail: audubonhouse@audubonhouse.org
Web Site: www.audubonhouse.org
Founded: 1960.
Congressional District: 19
Key Personnel: Pres. (V), Louis Wolfson, III; Public Rels., Mktg. Dir. & Retail Mgr., Elizabeth Amneus; Cur. & Museum Mgr., Robert Merritt.
Personnel Profile: Full-Time Paid 4; Part-Time Paid 5.
Governing Authority: nonprofit organization. Owned & operated by the Mitchell Wolfson Family Foundation, P.O. Box 012440, Miami, FL 33101. Tax-exempt: 501(c)(3).
Historic House Museum & Tropical Gardens: early 19th-century home of Capt. John H. Geiger which commemorates John James Audubon's visit to Key West in 1832.
Collections: original period furniture; original Audubon engravings; the Geiger Archives.
Research Fields: historic home restoration & preservation.
Facilities: botanical garden.
Activities: guided tours; lectures; gallery talks.
Publications: Tropical Garden Catalogue.
Hours & Admission Prices: Daily 9:30-5. Adults $10, students $6.50, children 6-12 $5; discounts to military, and AAA, ICOM & AARP members; children under 6 & members no charge.
Attendance: 40,000 (accurate)
Membership: Student $10; Individual $15; Family $25; Donor $100; Contributor $250; Patron $500; Affiliate $1,000; Corporate $1,500.

DONKEY MILK HOUSE, HISTORIC HOME, 613 Eaton St., Key West, FL 33040-6802. Tel.: 305-296-1866. Fax: 305-296-0922.
Founded: 1992.
Key Personnel: C.E.O., Denison Tempel.
Personnel Profile: Full-Time Volunteers 2.
Historic House: located in 1866 10-room mansion; tropical version of Classic Revival architecture containing rare 19th-century interior detailing, including 1890 Italian decorated ceilings; home of U.S. Marshall Williams & family for over 120 years.
Collections: period furniture & furnishings (c.1830-1930) representing items owned by Peter Williams when he built the house & acquisitions over the next 100 years by subsequent generations.
Research Fields: 120 year stewardship of Peter A. Williams & descendants; great fire of 1886, home survived fire due to Marshall Williams deflection with blasts of dynamite.
Facilities: tropical garden.
Activities: garden and part of historical home available for special events.
Hours & Admission Prices: Tours by appointment. Adults $5, senior citizens & members $4, students $2.50; discounts to AAM & ICOM members; children under 12 no charge. ♿

DRY TORTUGAS NATIONAL PARK, Key West, FL 33041. Mailing Address: P.O. Box 6208, Key West, FL 33041-6208. Tel.: 305-242-7700. Fax: 305-242-7711.
E-mail: ever_reception@nps.gov
Web Site: www.nps.gov/drto
Founded: 1960.
Congressional District: 19
Key Personnel: Public Affairs Officer, Richard Cook.
Governing Authority: federal. National Park Service, Everglades National Park, P.O. Box 279, Homestead, FL 33030. Tel. 305-242-7700.
National Park & Preservation Project: c.1846 Fort Jefferson, third order coastal defense.
Collections: artillery; weaponry; Sooty Tern Rookery; Brown Noddies & frigate birds in their natural habitat.
Research Fields: cultural & natural history.
Facilities: camping; picnic area; snorkeling; fishing; 12-seat auditorium. Reference & marine books for sale.
Activities: visitor interaction computer programming; self-guided trail; intermittent ranger-guided activities.
Publications: brochure.
Hours & Admission Prices: Daily 8-5. Park Entrance: $5. Access to island available from Key West by chartered boat or commercial seaplane. ♿
Attendance: 95,000

EAST MARTELLO MUSEUM, 3501 S. Roosevelt Blvd., Key West, FL 33040-5209. Mailing Address: 281 Front St., Key West, FL 33040-8313. Tel.: 305-296-3913. Fax: 305-296-6206.
Web Site: www.kwahs.org
Founded: 1951.
Congressional District: 20
Key Personnel: C.E.O. & Exec. Dir., Claudia L. Pennington; Pres., Kerry Shelby; Site Supvr., Jack Holland; Admissions, Annalisa Beck; Admissions, Irene Loeber.
Personnel Profile: Full-Time Paid 5; Part-Time Paid 4; Part-Time Volunteers 3.
Governing Authority: society; nonprofit organization. Parent Institution: Key West Art & Historical Society. Tax-exempt: 501(c)(3).
Historical Museum and Art Gallery: housed in 1861 brick fort.
Collections: local historic & military artifacts; Mario Sanchez folk art collection; Stanley Papio folk art collections; costumes; WPA paintings; local paintings; period furnishings.
Research Fields: Florida Keys history.
Facilities: Museum-related items for sale.
Activities: monthly art exhibitions; permanent & temporary exhibitions; permanent military displays; tours; educational & cultural programs.
Publications: e-newsletter, The Ghosts of East Martello.
Hours & Admission Prices: Daily 9:30-4:30. Adults $6, seniors 62 & over $5, students & children $3; children under 5, school tours & museum members no charge. Closed Christmas. ♿
Attendance: 13,288 (accurate)
Membership: Student $10; Individual $25; Family $45; Contributing $50; Patron $100; Life $250.

ERNEST HEMINGWAY HOUSE MUSEUM, 907 Whitehead, Key West, FL 33040-7473. Tel.: 305-294-1136. Fax: 305-294-2755.
E-mail: hemingwy@bellsouth.net
Web Site: www.hemingwayhome.com
Founded: 1964.
Key Personnel: Gen. Mgr., Jacque Sands; Dir. Events, Dave Gonzales; Museum Shop Mgr., Linda Mendez.
Personnel Profile: Full-Time Paid 22; Part-Time Paid 1.
Governing Authority: individual operation.
Historic House: 1931-1961 Ernest Hemingway Home, built in Spanish Colonial Style of native rock hewn from the grounds.
Collections: furniture; rugs; chandeliers; tile & other mementos from Spain, Africa, France, Cuba and other parts of the world.
Facilities: first swimming pool in Key West; poolhouse; gardens. Ernest Hemingway books for sale.
Activities: museum & garden facilities available for rent; tours.
Publications: books.
Hours & Admission Prices: Daily 9-5. Adults $12, groups of 12 or more $10, children 6-12 $6; discounts to military, groups & AAA members; children under 5 no charge. ♿

FORT ZACHARY TAYLOR HISTORIC STATE PARK, End of Southard St., Truman Annex, Key West, FL 33040. Mailing Address: P.O. Box 6560, Key West, FL 33041-6560. Tel.: 305-292-6713. Fax: 305-292-6881.
E-mail: david.foster@dep.state.fl.us
Web Site: www.floridastateparks.org/forttaylor
Founded: 1985.
Congressional District: 8
Key Personnel: Park Mgr., David Foster.
Governing Authority: state; nonprofit. Parent Institution: Florida Dept. of Environmental Protection. Subsidiary Institution: Division of Recreation & Parks. Tax-exempt.
Military Museum: housed in 1845-1866 fort.
Collections: Civil War items; Spanish-American war items; World War I & II items.
Research Fields: Civil War; Spanish-American War; World War I & II.
Facilities: 50-vol. library of Civil War material available to the public; educational facilities; picnic area.
Activities: guided tours; organized education programs for children.
Hours & Admission Prices: Park: 8-sunset. Museum: temporarily closed. Vehicle (up to 8 passengers): $6 per car, $.50 per person, Walk-ins $2.50 per person; children under 6 no charge. ♿
Attendance: 411,000 (accurate)
Membership: Friends of Fort Taylor $20; Family $30; Business $50.

HARRY S. TRUMAN LITTLE WHITE HOUSE MUSEUM, 111 Front St., Key West, FL 33040-8311. Mailing Address: P.O. Box 6443, Key West, FL 33041-6443. Tel.: 305-294-9911. Fax: 305-294-9988.
E-mail: bwolz@trumanlittlewhitehouse.com
Web Site: www.trumanlittlewhitehouse.com
Founded: 1991.
Congressional District: 20
Key Personnel: Exec. Dir., Robert J. Wolz; Chm., Christopher Belland; Pres., Edwin Swift; Financial Dir., Benjamin McPherson; Cur., Bert Whitt; Public Rels., Piper Smith.
Personnel Profile: Full-Time Paid 12; Part-Time Paid 4.
Governing Authority: state. Parent Institution: Key West Harry S. Truman Foundation, Inc. Tax-exempt: 501(c)(3).
Historic House: built in 1890 as the Navy Base Commander home, and used by Presidents' Taft, Truman, Eisenhower, John F. Kennedy, Carter & Clinton.
Collections: furnishings; video presentations.
Major Exhibits: A Very Merry 1940 Christmas, 12/09-1/10; With Love Harry, 2/10-3/10; Truman's Far East Legacy, 4/10-6/10.
Facilities: 100-vol. library of Truman & US Presidency books; 30-seat theater. Museum-related items for sale.
Activities: docent programs; formal education for adults & children; temporary exhibitions. Annual Event: Educational Conference with Truman Presidential Library.
Publications: newsletter & electronic newsletter.
Hours & Admission Prices: Daily 9-5; last tour begins 4:30 p.m. Adults $15, seniors $13, students $5; discounts to AAM, AASLH & ICOM members; members no charge. ♿
Attendance: 99,000 (accurate)
Membership: Student Aide $15; Diplomat $50; Ambassador $100; Representative $250; Senator $500; Cabinet $1,000. Business & Corporate: Contributor $100; Sponsor $250; Supporter $500; Patron $750; Benefactor $1,000.

HERITAGE HOUSE MUSEUM AND ROBERT FROST COTTAGE, 410 Caroline St., Key West, FL 33040-6502. Tel.: 305-296-3573.
E-mail: heritagehouse@aol.com
Web Site: www.heritagehousemuseum.org
Founded: 1992.
History Museum: housed in a 1830s Caribbean Colonial House owned by the Porters, a notable Key West family; Robert Frost was a family friend who spent many winters in a cottage located in the tropical garden of this home.
Collections: period furnishings; seafaring artifacts; personal artifacts.
Facilities: garden.
Activities: tours; poetry festivals; writers' workshops; lectures; cultural events; weddings; special events.
Hours & Admission Prices: Oct. 2-Aug. 1 Mon.-Sat. 10-4. Adults $9 (guided), $6 (self-guided); discounts to AAM & ICOM members. Closed New Year's Day; Christmas. ♿

KEY WEST LIGHTHOUSE MUSEUM, 938 Whitehead St., Key West, FL 33040-7423. Tel.: 305-295-6616, ext. 16. Fax: 305-296-6206.
Web Site: www.kwahs.org
Founded: 1966.
Congressional District: 19
Key Personnel: C.E.O. & Dir., Claudia L. Pennington; Pres., Kerry Shelby; Museum Shop Mgr., Linda Hardy; Site Operations, Bob Wandres.
Personnel Profile: Full-Time Paid 20.
Governing Authority: county; federal. Parent Institution: Key West Art & Historical Society, 281 Front St., Key West, FL. Tax-exempt: 501(c)(3).
General Museum: housed in 1887 lighthouse keepers home & 1846 lighthouse museum.
Collections: artifacts relating to the history of the Key West Lighthouse & the lighthouses of the Florida Keys; lenses; photographs; household items; archaeological; models.
Research Fields: lighthouses.
Publications: monthly e-newsletter.
Hours & Admission Prices: Daily & holidays 9:30-4:30. Adults $10, seniors 62 & over $9, children 7-12 $5; discounts to groups, AAA members, & local residents; children under 6 & members no charge. Closed Christmas. ♿
Attendance: 92,674 (accurate)
Membership: Individual $55; Dual $100; Family $125.

KEY WEST MUSEUM OF ART AND HISTORY, (M), 281 Front St., Key West, FL 33040-8313. Tel.: 305-295-6616, ext. 16. Fax: 305-295-6649.
Web Site: www.kwahs.org
Founded: 1951.
Congressional District: 20
Key Personnel: Exec. Dir., Claudia L. Pennington; Pres., Kerry Shelby; C.F.O., Kathleen Moody; Programs Coord., Gerri Sidoti; Webmaster, Jane Rohrschneider; Education & Group Tours, Suzanne Periera; Public Rels., Michael Haskins; Site Supvr., Jack Holland; Cur., Norman Aberle; Museum Shop Mgr., Linda Hardy.
Personnel Profile: Full-Time Paid 20; Part-Time Paid 6; Part-Time Volunteers 10; Interns 3.
Governing Authority: private; nonprofit organization. Branch Museums: East Martello Museum, Key West, FL; Key West Lighthouse, Key West, FL. Tax-exempt: 501(c)(3).
Art & History Museum: housed in c.1891 Custom House.
Collections: fine art; folk art; historic artifacts; documents; photographs from 1860s to present.
Research Fields: history of Key West & Florida Keys.
Facilities: 2,000-vol. library; 18,000 sq. ft. exhibit space. Museum-related items for sale.
Activities: arts festivals; concerts; guided tours; lectures; loan, traveling & participatory exhibitions; adult programs; children's classes.
Publications: monthly e-newsletter.
Hours & Admission Prices: Daily 9:30-4:30. Adults $10, seniors $9, children & students $5; discount to AAA members & local residents; members & children under 6 no charge. Closed Christmas. ♿
Attendance: 78,358 (accurate)
Membership: Individual $55; Dual $100; Family $125.

KEY WEST SHIPWRECK HISTOREUM MUSEUM, 1 Whitehead St., Key West, FL 33040-6634. Tel.: 305-292-8990. Fax: 305-292-1617.
E-mail: shipwreck@historictours.com
Web Site: www.shipwreckhistoreum.com
Historic Ship Museum.
Collections: artifacts & memorabilia from the 1985 rediscovery of the wrecked vessel Isaac Allerton.
Hours & Admission Prices: Daily 9:40-5. Adults $10.80, children 4-12 $4.50; children under 4 no charge.

KEY WEST TROPICAL FOREST & BOTANICAL GARDEN, 5210 College Rd., Key West, FL 33040-4302. Tel.: 305-296-1504. Fax: 305-296-2242.
Web Site: www.keywestbotanicalgarden.org
Founded: 1988.
Congressional District: 18
Key Personnel: Dir., Carolann Sharkey; Gen. Mgr., Sharon Agee; Chm. (V), Todd German; Dir. Client Svcs., Misha D. McRae.
Personnel Profile: Full-Time Paid 6; Part-Time Paid 1; Part-Time Volunteers 70; Interns 2.
Governing Authority: private; nonprofit organization. Tax-exempt: 501(c)(3).
Botanical Garden.
Collections: native fragrant plants; tropical fruit trees; native palms; tropical spices; local herbs; flowers.
Facilities: botanical garden; nature center. Museum-related items for sale.
Activities: docent program; lectures; formal education programs. Annual Events: Garden Fest Key West in March; Migration Mania in April.
Hours & Admission Prices: Daily 10-4. Suggested Donations: adults $5, seniors $4; members & children under 12 no charge. Closed New Year's Day; Christmas. ♿
Attendance: 25,000 (accurate)
Membership: Student $10; Individual $35; Household Family $50; Patron $120; Ruby $300; Emerald $600; Diamond $1,100.

* **MEL FISHER MARITIME HERITAGE SOCIETY,** 200 Greene St., Key West, FL 33040-6516. Tel.: 305-294-2633, ext. 15. Fax: 305-294-5671.
E-mail: info@melfisher.org
Web Site: www.melfisher.org
Founded: 1982.
Congressional District: 20
Key Personnel: C.E.O., Melissa Kendrick; Chm. (V), Mr. John Harrison; Vice Pres., Mr. George Robb; Archivist, Monica Brook; Devel., Candy Pierce-Watson; Museum Shop Mgr., Steven LaPoint; Chief Cur. & Traveling Exhibition Coord., Dylan Kibler; Archaeology, Corey Malcom; Membership, Jim Kelly.
Personnel Profile: Full-Time Paid 25; Full-Time Volunteers 3; Part-Time Paid 13; Part-Time Volunteers 15; Interns 3.
Governing Authority: society. Not-for-profit. Tax-exempt: 501(c)(3).
Maritime Museum.
Collections: 17th- & 18th-century coins; decorative arts; ceramics; Slave Trade artifacts; maritime artifacts.
Research Fields: 15th- to 18th-century shipping & shipbuilding.
Facilities: 2,200-vol. library of maritime history & Colonial Spanish history available for use by the public; 50-seat theater. Museum-related items for sale.

Activities: formal education programs for children; guided tours; lectures; permanent & traveling exhibitions; elder hostel; summer camps.
Publications: bimonthly newsletter, Navigator; biannual historical magazine, Astrolabe.
Hours & Admission Prices: Daily 8:30-5. Adults $12, children $6; discounts to groups, Monroe County residents, AAM, ICOM, AARP & Florida Assoc. of Museums members; members no charge. ♿
Attendance: 206,114 (accurate)
Membership: Individual $55; Patron $100; Business $500 & up.

THE OLDEST HOUSE & GARDEN MUSEUM, 322 Duval St., Key West, FL 33040. Mailing Address: P.O. Box 689, Key West, FL 33041-0689. Tel.: 305-294-9501. Fax: 305-294-4509.
E-mail: oldisland@bellsouth.net
Web Site: www.oirf.org
Founded: 1975.
Congressional District: 19
Key Personnel: Exec. Dir., Michael Driscoll; Pres., Anthony S. Minore.
Personnel Profile: Full-Time Paid 1; Full-Time Volunteers 5; Part-Time Paid 4; Part-Time Volunteers 10.
Governing Authority: nonprofit organization. Parent Institution: Old Island Restoration Foundation. Tax-exempt.
Maritime Museum: housed in c.1829 Conch House, home of local sea captain & wrecker.
Collections: 19th-century furniture; Key West history; toys; paintings; documents related to 19th-century wrecking in Key West.
Research Fields: genealogy; local maritime history.
Facilities: gardens.
Activities: guided tours; docent program. Museum Sponsors: garden party.
Publications: brochure, Old Island Days; A Guide to Historic Key West on the Pelican Path.
Hours & Admission Prices: Mon.-Tues. & Thurs.-Sat. 10-4. Adults $5, children $1; discounts to groups; members no charge. ♿
Attendance: 4,288 (accurate)
Membership: Old Island Restoration Foundation: Single $25; Couples $40; Business $75; Patron $100; Benefactor $250; Life $1,000.

PIRATE SOUL MUSEUM, 524 Front St., Key West, FL 33040-6658. Tel.: 305-292-1113. Fax: 305-292-1125.
E-mail: sknott@piratesoul.com
Web Site: www.piratesoul.com
Founded: 2005.
Key Personnel: C.E.O., Kelly Croce Sorg; Dir., Sarah Knott; Museum Shop Mgr., Thomas Lockyear
History Museum.
Collections: pirate artifacts; Captain Kidd; pirate treasure chest.
Hours & Admission Prices: Mon.-Fri. 9-5, Sat.-Sun. 10-5. Adults $13.95, children $7.95. ♿

RIPLEY'S BELIEVE IT OR NOT!, 108 Duval St., Key West, FL 33040-6506. Tel.: 305-293-9939. Fax: 305-293-9709.
E-mail: museum@ripleyskeywest.com
Web Site: www.ripleys.com
Founded: 1927.
Key Personnel: Mgr., Kevin Hays.
Personnel Profile: Full-Time Paid 10.
Governing Authority: private; profit-making organization. Parent Institution: Ripley Corp., 5720 Major Blvd., Ste. 700, Orlando, FL 32819.
General Museum.
Collections: antiquities & oddities; Asian artifacts; primitive tribal artifacts; human oddities; arcane art.
Facilities: 30-vol. library of Hemingway works available to the public; 30-seat large-screen theater; 10,000 sq. ft. exhibit space. Ripley's Believe It or Not! memorabilia for sale.
Activities: guided tours; theater; participatory & traveling exhibitions.
Hours & Admission Prices: Daily 9:30am-11pm. Adults $14.95, children 5-12 $11.95; children 4 & under no charge. ♿
Attendance: 86,000 (accurate)

Kissimmee

OSCEOLA CENTER FOR THE ARTS, 2411 E. Irlo Bronson Memorial Hwy., Kissimmee, FL 34744-5430. Tel.: 407-846-6257. Fax: 407-846-7902.
E-mail: emoore@ocfta.com
Web Site: www.ocfta.com
Founded: 1964.
Key Personnel: Dir., Ed Moore; Chm. (V), Ed Kilroy.
Personnel Profile: Full-Time Paid 6; Part-Time Paid 2; Part-Time Volunteers 20; Interns 1.
Governing Authority: Tax-exempt.
Art Gallery.
Collections: works by local & regional artists.
Facilities: 250-seat theater.
Activities: visual & performing art classes; special events.
Publications: quarterly event guides.
Hours & Admission Prices: Museum: June-July Mon.-Fri. 9-5, Sat. 10-4; Aug.-May Mon.-Fri. 10-6, Sat. 10-4. Roadside Gallery: daily. No charge; donations accepted. Closed New Year's Day; Independence Day; Labor Day; Christmas Day. ♿
Attendance: 6,000 (estimated)
Membership: Single $100; Family $150; Corporate $250 & up.

VETERANS TRIBUTE AND MUSEUM OF OSCEOLA COUNTY, INC., (M), 3831 W. Vine St., #46, Kissimmee, FL 34741-4650. Tel.: 407-931-3133.
E-mail: veteranstribute@embarqmail.com
Web Site: veteranstributemuseum.com
Key Personnel: Chm. (V), Donald Smith.
Personnel Profile: Full-Time Paid 1.
Military Museum.
Collections: artifacts; military relics; photographs; memorabilia.
Hours & Admission Prices: Tues.-Sun. 12-6. No charge; donations accepted.

WHITE 1 FOUNDATION - WWII AIRCRAFT MUSEUM, 233 N. Hoagland Blvd., Kissimmee, FL 34741-4531. Tel.: 727-365-1713; 407-473-3957. Fax: 407-622-9308.
E-mail: white1foundation@yahoo.com
Web Site: www.white1foundation.org
Founded: 1998.
Key Personnel: Dir. & Cur., Dr. M.J. Timken; Devel., Gene Davidson; Public Rels., Melissa Timken; Treas., Peter Lackman; Museum Shop Mgr., G. Murphy, Ph.D.
Personnel Profile: Full-Time Volunteers 4; Part-Time Volunteers 1.
Governing Authority: private; nonprofit organization.
Military History Museum.
Collections: WWII aviation history; aircraft; pilot gear & survival equipment; technical data; Focke Wulf FW 190.
Research Fields: performance of period fighter aircraft to present day; construction techniques.
Facilities: library; educational facilities; 2,000 sq. ft. exhibit space. Museum-related items for sale.
Activities: formal education programs; guided tours; hobby workshops; lectures; participatory, temporary & traveling exhibitions; broadcast programs.
Publications: monthly newsletter email.
Hours & Admission Prices: Mon.-Fri. 9-5, Sat.-Sun. by appointment. No charge; donations accepted. ♿
Attendance: 5,000 (estimated)
Membership: Individual $40.

LaBelle

LABELLE HERITAGE MUSEUM, 150 S. Lee St., LaBelle, FL 33935. Mailing Address: P.O. Box 2846, LaBelle, FL 33975-2846. Tel.: 863-674-0034.
Founded: 1991.
Key Personnel: Pres. (V), Joseph H. Thomas; Museum Shop Mgr., Rhoda Spang.
Personnel Profile: Part-Time Paid 32; Part-Time Volunteers 16.
Governing Authority: Tax-exempt.
Historical Museum.
Collections: local history & artifacts; fossils; clothing; family books; furniture; photographs; personal artifacts.
Activities: group tours; special events; Annual events: Old Timers Dinner; Swamp Cabbage Festival in February.
Publications: newsletter.
Hours & Admission Prices: Summer: Thurs.-Fri. 2-5; Winter: Thurs.-Sat. 2-5; other times by appointment. No charge; donations accepted. ♿
Attendance: 150 (estimated)
Membership: Single $20; Couple $35; Sponsor $50; Patron $100; Corporate $150.

Lake City

LAKE CITY COLUMBIA COUNTY HISTORICAL MUSEUM, INC., 157 S.E. Hernando Ave., Lake City, FL 32025-4428. Mailing Address: P.O. Box 3276, Lake City, FL 32056-3276. Tel.: 386-755-9096. Fax: 904-755-6605.
E-mail: edisto1@alltel.net
Founded: 1984.

Congressional District: 2
Key Personnel: Dir. & Cur., Pat McAlhany; Vice Pres., Paulette Lord; Sec., Sean McMahon, Ph.D.; Education, Margie Stanfield.
Personnel Profile: Full-Time Volunteers 10; Part-Time Volunteers 2.
Governing Authority: private; nonprofit organization. Tax-exempt: 501(c)(3).
History Museum: located in a Historic House.
Collections: display of civil war memorabilia; items relating to history & growth of area; old house furniture.
Research Fields: local family history.
Facilities: 40-vol. library containing civil war references, area history & local family references available to the public; 2,500 sq. ft. exhibit space. Museum-related items for sale.
Activities: guided tours; participatory exhibits.
Hours & Admission Prices: Wed. 10-1. No charge; donations accepted. Closed New Year's Day; Easter; Independence Day; Christmas. ♿
Attendance: 3,000 (estimated)
Membership: Youth & Senior $5; Individual $10; Family $25.

Lake Wales

BOK TOWER GARDENS, 1151 Tower Blvd., Lake Wales, FL 33853-3470. Tel.: 863-676-1408. Fax: 863-676-6770.
E-mail: info@boktower.org
Web Site: www.boktowergardens.org
Formerly: Historic Bok Sanctuary
Founded: 1929.
Congressional District: 12
Key Personnel: Pres., David Price; Financial Dir., Steve Jolley; Public Rels. & Mktg., Cassie Jacoby; Dir. Retail Svcs., Sandra Dent; Dir. Horticulture, Nick Baker.
Personnel Profile: Full-Time Paid 47; Part-Time Paid 21; Part-Time Volunteers 427; Interns 2.
Governing Authority: nonprofit organization. Tax-exempt: 501(c)(3).
Botanical Garden.
Collections: cultivated plants; rare & endangered plants; endemic plants; camellias; decorative arts; local historic objects. Historic Building: 1930s Mediterranean-style Mansion.
Research Fields: rare & endangered plant species of the region.
Facilities: 2,600-vol. library of carillon-related material, including 1,000 carillon tapes; 3,000 botanic & historic slides, available to the public on a limited basis; botanical garden; nature walks & nature preserve trail; 23,000 sq. ft. Education and Visitor Center which includes meeting facilities, orientation theatre and interpretive exhibits & cafe. Museum-related items for sale.
Activities: guided tours; lectures; films; indoor & outdoor concerts; organized education programs for children, adults, undergraduate & graduate students in carillon studies; horticulture internships; docent program; participatory & temporary exhibitions; garden wedding ceremonies; facility rentals.
Publications: quarterly newsletter; annual report.
Hours & Admission Prices: Daily 8-6. Adults $10, children 5-12 $3; discount to groups; children under 5, AABGA members & members no charge; AABGA reciprocal. ♿
Attendance: 130,000 (estimated)
Membership: Individual $35; Duo $45; Family $60; Sustainer $85; Donor $125; Patron $250; Sponsor $500; Bok Tower Club $1,000; President's Council $2,500; Chairman's Council $5,000.

LAKE WALES DEPOT MUSEUM & CULTURAL CENTER, 325 S. Scenic Hwy., Lake Wales, FL 33853-3873. Tel.: 863-678-4209. Fax: 863-678-4299.
E-mail: lwdepot@historiclakewales.org
Web Site: www.cityoflakewales.com
Founded: 1976.
Congressional District: 12
Key Personnel: Dir., Mimi Reid Hardman; Cur. & Administrative Asst., Stephanie Carter; Administrative Asst., Jennifer Nanek.
Personnel Profile: Full-Time Paid 1; Full-Time Volunteers 1; Part-Time Paid 4; Part-Time Volunteers 3.
Governing Authority: municipal government. Parent Institution: City of Lake Wales. Subsidiary Institution: Seaboard Freight Depot. Branch Museum: Historic Lake Wales Society; Stuart-Dunn-Oliver Historic House Museum; Children's Museum, Lake Wales, FL. Tax-exempt.
Local History Museum: housed in 1928 ACL & Seaboard Coastline Railroad Depot.
Collections: local history artifacts including railroad, turpentine, citrus, cattle exhibits; 1916 Pullman car, 1926 Seaboard Air Line caboose, 1944 engine; photographs and documentary archives; quilt, clothing, toys, Native American & patriotic rotating exhibits. Additional facilities located on the CSX Historic Corridor are the 1916 Seaboard Air Line Freight Depot, the 1920 Children's Museum, & the 1920 Stuart-Dunn-Oliver Historic House Museum, originally a founder's home.
Research Fields: historic building preservation; local history; local black history.
Facilities: 100-vol. library pertaining to local history; documentary & photograph archives; biographical files & manuscripts.
Activities: lectures; dance recitals; theater; hobby workshops; organized education programs; temporary & traveling exhibitions. Museum Sponsors: Local Pioneer Day Festival.
Publications: quarterly newsletter.
Hours & Admission Prices: Mon.-Fri. 9-5, Sat. 10-4. No charge; donations accepted. Closed major holidays. ♿
Attendance: 20,000 (estimated)
Membership: Historic Lake Wales Society: Student & Associate $10; Individual $25; Family $50; Life $200; Corporate $300.

Lake Worth

MUSEUM OF THE CITY OF LAKE WORTH, 414 Lake Ave., Lake Worth, FL 33460-3807. Tel.: 561-586-1700. Fax: 561-586-1651.
Founded: 1982.
Congressional District: 14
Key Personnel: C.E.O., Cur. & Treas., Beverly Mustaine.
Personnel Profile: Full-Time Paid 1; Part-Time Volunteers 5.
Governing Authority: municipal; nonprofit. Tax-exempt: 509(a)(1).
History Museum.
Collections: Lake Worth history & the surrounding area; photograph collection; period clothing; dishes; tools; office equipment; cameras; kitchen equipment; ethnic displays.
Research Fields: Major General Worth, The Man; 80th Anniversary of the City of Lake Worth; research materials of the area.
Facilities: 500-vol. research library on Florida history available to the public; 3,000 sq. ft. exhibit space; 65-seat auditorium.
Activities: guided tour of museum & city; formal educational programs.
Publications: brochure, Walk & Ride Historical Brochure; book, On Lake Worth.
Hours & Admission Prices: Mon.-Fri. 9:30-4:30. No charge; donations accepted. Closed New Year's Day; Independence Day; Thanksgiving; Christmas.
Attendance: 2,500 (accurate)

NATIONAL MUSEUM OF POLO AND HALL OF FAME, INC., (M), 9011 Lake Worth Rd., Lake Worth, FL 33467-3617. Tel.: 561-969-3210. Fax: 561-964-8299.
E-mail: polomuseum@att.net
Web Site: www.polomuseum.com
Founded: 1984.
Key Personnel: C.E.O. & Chm. (V), Stephen Orthwein; Exec. Dir. & Vice Pres., George DuPont; Dir. Devel., Brenda Lynn; Pres. (V), Martin S. Cregg.
Personnel Profile: Full-Time Paid 2.
Governing Authority: federal; nonprofit organization. Tax-exempt: 501(c)(3).
Polo Sports History & Hall of Fame.
Collections: books; record books; scrapbooks; polo sporting equipment; trophies; photographs; research material; art work.
Research Fields: polo sports history.
Facilities: 300-vol. library available to the public; 2,000 sports related magazines; 763 sq. ft. exhibit space; field research station. Museum-related items for sale.
Activities: films; docent program; temporary & traveling exhibitions.
Publications: annual newsletter.
Hours & Admission Prices: Jan.-April Mon.-Fri. 10-4, Sat. 10-2; other times by appointment. No charge; donations accepted. ♿

Lakeland

EXPLORATIONS V CHILDREN'S MUSEUM, 109 N. Kentucky Ave., Lakeland, FL 33801-5057. Tel.: 863-687-3869.
E-mail: info@explorationsv.com
Web Site: www.explorationsv.com
Founded: 1991.
Key Personnel: C.E.O., Georgann Carlton
Children's Museum.
Collections: hands-on exhibits.
Facilities: Museum-related items for sale.
Hours & Admission Prices: Mon.-Sat. 9-5:30. Admission $5; children 2 and under & members no charge. Closed major holidays.
Membership: $50; $100.

FLORIDA AIR MUSEUM AT SUN'N FUN, (M), 4175 Medulla Rd., Lakeland, FL 33811-1249. Tel.: 863-644-0741. Fax: 863-648-9264.
Web Site: www.floridaairmuseum.org

Formerly: International Sport Aviation Museum (ISAM)
Founded: 1989.
Key Personnel: Mgr., Ernest Sanborn; Museum Shop Mgr., Susan Highley.
Personnel Profile: Full-Time Paid 3; Part-Time Paid 2; Part-Time Volunteers 25.
Governing Authority: nonprofit organization. Parent Institution: Sun 'n Fun Fly-In, Inc. Tax-exempt: 501(c)(3).
Aviation Museum.
Collections: period aircraft; classic aircraft; experimental aircraft; Howard Hughes aviation archives.
Facilities: 20,000 sq. ft. exhibit space. Gift items for sale.
Activities: seminars & workshops; organized education programs for children; temporary exhibitions.
Publications: bimonthly newsletter, Sun'n Fun News.
Hours & Admission Prices: Mon.-Fri. 9-5, Sat. 10-4, Sun. 12-4. Contribution: adults $8, senior citizens $6, students 8-12 $4; children 7 & under and members no charge. Closed New Year's Day; Christmas. ♿
Attendance: 60,000 (estimated)
Membership: Personal $35; Family $50; Personal & Engraved Brick $99.

* **POLK MUSEUM OF ART, (M),** 800 E. Palmetto St., Lakeland, FL 33801-5529. Tel.: 863-688-7743. Fax: 863-688-2611.
E-mail: destetson@PolkMuseumofArt.org
Web Site: www.PolkMuseumofArt.org
Founded: 1966.
Congressional District: 12
Key Personnel: Exec. Dir., Daniel E. Stetson; Pres., Dr. Anne Kerr; Exec. Asst., Palemeschia "Pal" Rivers Powell; Art Cur., Todd Behrens; Exhibits Specialist, Gregory Mills; Admin., Terri D'Orsaneo; Operations Mgr., Bill O'Connell; Museum Shop Mgr., Terry Aulisio.
Personnel Profile: Full-Time Paid 12; Part-Time Paid 9; Part-Time Volunteers 200; Interns 2.
Governing Authority: board of trustees; nonprofit organization. Tax-exempt: 501(c)(3).
Art Museum.
Collections: pre-Columbian art; 15th to 18th-century European decorative arts; photography; contemporary American & Florida artists; American paintings and works on paper; 20th-century contemporary Japanese ceramics; Asian decorative arts; contemporary art.
Research Fields: contemporary Florida Art; pre-Columbian art; American Contemporary Art.
Facilities: 37,000 sq. ft. building; 3,500-vol. research library with arts - related volumes, periodicals & computer with terminal access & gallery collections; computer graphics teaching laboratory; photography laboratory; ceramics studio; permanent & changing exhibition galleries; student gallery & art discovery room; multi-purpose room; teaching auditorium; sculpture garden; studio classrooms. Museum-related items for sale.
Activities: guided tours; lectures; film series; exhibitions; concerts; workshops; formally organized educational programs; docent program; summer program for children; high school for visual arts; traveling exhibitions; school loan service. Museum Sponsors: Mayfaire By-The-Lake Art Festival; Festival of Arts and Athletes.
Publications: quarterly newsletter; exhibition catalogues; educational services brochure; traveling exhibition service brochure; annual report; self-guided tour brochure; family gallery guides.
Hours & Admission Prices: Tues.-Sat. 10-5, Sun. 1-5. Adults $5, senior citizens $4; discounts to AAM & ICOM members; members no charge. Closed holidays. ♿
Attendance: 125,000 (estimated)
Membership: Individual $40; Family & Household $60; Sponsor $100; Advocate $250; Benefactor $500; Patron $1,000; Gold Patron $2,500; Platinum Patron $5,000.

Largo

THE ARMED FORCES MILITARY MUSEUM, (M), 2050 34th Way N., Largo, FL 33771-3960. Tel.: 727-539-8371.
E-mail: info@armedforcesmuseum.com
Web Site: www.armedforcesmuseum.com
Founded: 1996.
Congressional District: 10
Key Personnel: Dir. & Pres. (V), John J. Piazza, Sr.; Museum Shop Mgr., William Puckett.
Personnel Profile: Full-Time Paid 5; Part-Time Paid 3; Part-Time Volunteers 4.
Governing Authority: Tax-exempt.
Military Museum.
Collections: displays illustrating WWI & II, D-Day landings, the attack on Pearl Harbor, Korea, Vietnam & other conflicts.
Facilities: meeting & conference space.
Activities: tours; military history classes; special events; open houses; civic events; memorial walk; engraved brick program; field trip program for schools.
Publications: bimonthly newsletter.
Hours & Admission Prices: Tues.-Sat. 10-4. Adults $8, children 7-12 $5; discounts to AAM & AAA members and groups of 15 or more; children 6 & under and active & retired military with ID no charge. Closed New Year's Day; Easter; Thanksgiving; Christmas. ♿
Membership: Patriotic $25; Community Partner $100; Founding Silver $1,500-$2,499; Founding Gold $2,500-$4,999; Founding Platinum $5,000 & up.

HERITAGE VILLAGE, (M), 11909-125 St., N., Largo, FL 33774-3611. Tel.: 727-582-2127. Fax: 727-582-2211.
E-mail: ebabb@co.pinellas.fl.us
Web Site: www.pinellascounty.org/heritage
Founded: 1961.
Congressional District: 8
Key Personnel: Operations Mgr., Ellen Babb; Cur. Collections, Alison Giesen; Museum Interpreter, Paige W. Noel.
Personnel Profile: Full-Time Paid 4; Part-Time Paid 11.
Governing Authority: county. Parent Institution: Pinellas County Government. Subsidiary Institution: Gulf Beaches Historical Museum, 115 10th Ave., St. Pete Beach, FL 33706. Tel.: 727-552-1610. Tax-exempt: 170(b)(1)(A).
Living History Museum.
Collections: over 9,000 photographs of early St. Petersburg, Clearwater & surrounding communities in Pinellas County; audiovisuals; postcards; school & college annuals; books & ledgers; maps & atlases; city directories; newspapers; scrapbooks; census records; clip files; genealogical materials; primitives & home furnishings of early Pinellas Pioneers; early textiles. 28 Historic Buildings: 1907 House of Seven Gables; 1879 Moore House; 1896 Plant-Sumner House; Victorian bandstand; c.1900 gazebo; sugar cane mill; 1911 Lowe Barn; c.1852 Coachman-McMullen Log House; 1876 Boyer Cottage; 1924 Sulphur Springs Depot; 1905 Safety Harbor Church; 1888 Greenwood House; 1890 Safford Pavilion; 1915 Walsingham House; 1915 H.C. Smith store, barber shop, garage & filling station; 1888 Lowe House; 1868 Daniel McMullen House; 1915 Union Academy; Harris School & Firehouse with 1919 LaFrance fire engine; c.1930 Tarpon Springs sponge warehouse.
Research Fields: Pinellas County & Florida history.
Facilities: 3,500-vol. library & archives.
Activities: guided walking tours; craft demonstrations; fiber arts demonstrations; historic preservation; Pinellas County Historical Society.
Publications: annual scholarly publication, Punta Pinal; quarterly newsletter, Village Post.
Hours & Admission Prices: Wed.-Sat. 10-4, Sun. 1-4. No charge; donations accepted. ♿
Attendance: 125,000 (estimated)
Membership: Pinellas County Historical Society: College Student $10; Individual $20; Family $35; Contributing $50; Sustaining $100; Patron $500; Benefactor $1,000.

NATIONAL COMEDY HALL OF FAME, (M), 9011 Park Blvd., Ste. 202, Largo, FL 33777-4123. Mailing Address: P.O. Box 20492, St. Petersburg, FL 33742-0492.
E-mail: comedyhall@aol.com
Web Site: comedyhall.com
Key Personnel: Exec. Dir., Tony Belmont
Comedy Museum.
Collections: history of comedy in American theater; comedy legends.
Facilities: library. Museum-related items for sale.
Hours & Admission Prices: Call for hours.

Live Oak

SUWANNEE COUNTY HISTORICAL MUSEUM, 208 N. Ohio Ave., Live Oak, FL 32064-2455. Tel.: 386-362-1776.
E-mail: suwanneemuseum@yahoo.com
Web Site: suwanneemuseum.org
Founded: 1981.
Key Personnel: Dir., Randy S. Torrance.
Personnel Profile: Full-Time Paid 1.
Governing Authority: nonprofit. Tax-exempt.
History Museum.
Collections: Suwannee County history; railroad layout; railroad artifacts; telephones; early American kitchen; Timucuan Indian artifacts; post office & farm equipment; photographs.
Activities: special events; seasonal program events & lectures. Museum

Sponsors: Civil War Living History Event in February; Chili-Challenge Cook-Off in Spring; Railroad Festival in September; Holiday Open House in December.
Publications: quarterly newsletter, The Suwannee Freight Line.
Hours & Admission Prices: Tues.-Sat. 9-3. No charge; donations accepted.
Membership: Household & Family $10; Corporate & Business $50.

Longboat Key

LONGBOAT KEY CENTER FOR THE ARTS, 6860 Longboat Dr. S., Longboat Key, FL 34228-1036. Tel.: 941-383-2345. Fax: 941-383-7915.
Web Site: www.lbkca.org
Founded: 1952.
Key Personnel: Dir., Jane Buckman; Public Rels. & Galleries & Special Events, Marlene Hauck.
Personnel Profile: Full-Time Paid 1; Part-Time Paid 4; Part-Time Volunteers 250.
Arts & Crafts Museum.
Collections: paintings; photographs; sculpture.
Facilities: library pertaining to art history & all phases of art for education; educational facilities. Museum-related items for sale.
Activities: arts festivals; formal educational programs; guided tours; hobby workshops; lectures; participatory exhibits. Annual Events: Fine Arts & Crafts Festival; Jazz Concerts in the Gallery; Gift Gallery.
Publications: yearbook of schedule of events; newsletters.
Hours & Admission Prices: Jan.-March daily 9-4; April & Oct.-Dec. Mon.-Fri. 9-4; May-July & Sept. Mon.-Thurs. 9-4. No charge; donations accepted. Closed Easter; Memorial Day; Independence Day; Thanksgiving; Christmas. ♿
Attendance: 20,000 (estimated)
Membership: Single $60; Family $100; Sustaining $125; Patron $250; Benefactor $500; Palette & Chisel $1,000; Medici Circle $2,500.

Madison

NORTH FLORIDA COMMUNITY COLLEGE ART GALLERY, 325 N.W. Turner Davis Dr., Madison, FL 32340-1611. Tel.: 850-973-1642. Fax: 850-973-9288.
E-mail: bardenl@nfcc.edu
Founded: 1975.
Congressional District: 2
Key Personnel: Pres., Morris Steen; Dir., William F. Gardner, Jr.
Governing Authority: college. Affiliated with North Florida Community College. Tax-exempt.
College Art Gallery.
Collections: permanent collection.
Facilities: theater; classrooms.
Activities: guided tours; lectures; films; gallery talks; arts festivals; formally organized education programs; permanent exhibitions.
Hours & Admission Prices: Mon.-Fri. 10-12 & 1-3; Sun. special openings. No charge. ♿

Maitland

HOLOCAUST MEMORIAL RESOURCE AND EDUCATION CENTER OF FLORIDA, INC., 851 N. Maitland Ave., Maitland, FL 32751-4461. Mailing Address: P.O. Box 941508, Maitland, FL 32794. Tel.: 407-628-0555, ext. 284. Fax: 407-628-1079.
E-mail: info@holocaustedu.org
Web Site: www.holocaustedu.org
Founded: 1983.
Key Personnel: Exec. Dir., Pam Kancher; Chm. (V), Tess Wise; Pres. (V), Randall Ellington; First Vice Pres., Stanley Creel; Second Vice Pres., Jim Shapiro; Sec., Diane Jacobs; Treas., Phillip Senderowitz; Cur., Anita Lam; Archivist, Alice Gamson; Devel., Susan Mitchell; Education, Mitchell Bloomer; Public Rels., Eva Ritt; Admin. Asst., Mary Johnson.
Personnel Profile: Full-Time Paid 4; Part-Time Paid 2; Part-Time Volunteers 13; Interns 1.
Governing Authority: private; nonprofit organization. Tax-exempt: 501(c)(3).
History Museum.
Collections: Holocaust artifacts; original art by professional artists.
Facilities: 5,000-vol. library of books.
Activities: film series; education programs for students; teacher training; courses for adults; traveling & documentary exhibitions. Museum Sponsors: commemorative programs for Kristallnacht & Holocaust; Remembrance Day.
Publications: semiannual newsletter; Holocaust Education Curricula; exhibit & field trip guides.
Hours & Admission Prices: Mon.-Thurs. 9-4, Fri. 9-1, Sun. 1-4. No charge; donations accepted. Closed Jewish holidays; national holidays. ♿
Attendance: 20,000 (estimated)
Membership: Student $18; Friend $36; Family $100; Patron $150; Supporter $250; Sustainer $500; Benefactor $1,000; Builder $1,500; Founder $5,000.

MAITLAND ART CENTER, (M), 231 W. Packwood Ave., Maitland, FL 32751-5596. Tel.: 407-539-2181. Fax: 407-539-1198.
Web Site: www.maitlandartcenter.org
Founded: 1972.
Congressional District: 8
Key Personnel: Admin., Margaret Anglin; Chm. (V), Victor Diaz; 1st Vice Chm., Roger Pickar; 2nd Vice Chm., John Wacker; Treas., Bill Dacko; Security & Maintenance, Jeffrey Hendley; Cur., Richard D. Colvin; Coord. Education, Ann E. Colvin; Coord. Membership, Ana Hidalga-Bartolomei; Administrative Asst., Margaret Pytel; Program Coord., Gloria Capozzi; Receptionist & Museum Shop Mgr., Dierdre Peeler.
Personnel Profile: Full-Time Paid 7; Part-Time Paid 6; Interns 19.
Governing Authority: nonprofit organization; board of trustees. Parent Institution: Maitland Art Association. Tax-exempt: 501(c)(3).
Art Center.
Collections: works of artists who lived on the grounds since 1937; works of founder, Andre Smith.
Research Fields: works of founder, Jules Andre Smith (1880-1959) & those artists who were participants as Bok Fellows at the Center, 1938-1959.
Facilities: outdoor gardens & chapel. Books, catalogs, jewelry, art reproductions & other museum-related items for sale.
Activities: quarterly studio art classes; guided tours of grounds; changing & permanent exhibition; docent program; lecture series; concerts in the gardens. Center Sponsors: Dinner with the Artists; Artist-in-Action Program; Art Auction in April; Annual Children's Art Festival in April; Founders Birthday Celebration in December.
Publications: annual reports; quarterly: newsletter & school schedule; exhibition catalogues.
Hours & Admission Prices: Tues.-Sat. 9-5:30, Sun. 12-5:30. Admission 12 & over $3; members no charge. Closed major holidays. ♿
Attendance: 66,926 (accurate)
Membership: Individual Senior Citizens $20; Dual Senior Citizens, Artists & Students $25; Individual $30; Family & Dual $40; Donor $50; Cheraphin $100; Seraphim $250; Patron $500; Benefactor $1,000. Maitland Resident: Individual Senior Citizen $15; Dual Senior, Artists & Students $20; Individual $25; Family & Dual $35.

MAITLAND HISTORICAL SOCIETY AND MUSEUMS, (M), 840 Lake Lily Dr., Maitland, FL 32751-5613. Mailing Address: P.O. Box 941001, Maitland, FL 32794-1001. Tel.: 407-644-2451. Fax: 888-316-5729.
E-mail: info@maitlandhistory.org
Web Site: www.maitlandhistory.org
Founded: 1970.
Congressional District: 9 & 13
Key Personnel: C.E.O., Andrea Bailey Cox; Pres. Bd. (V), Michael Culbertson.
Personnel Profile: Full-Time Paid 4; Part-Time Paid 5; Part-Time Volunteers 100.
Governing Authority: private; nonprofit organization. Tax-exempt: 501(c)(3).
Historic Museums: four museums including Waterhouse Residence Museum, Carpentry Shop, Maitland Historical Museum, & the Telephone Museum.
Collections: history of Maitland. Telephone Museum: telephone technology from days of early phone service in Maitland. Historic Waterhouse Residence Museum & Carpentry Shop: Maitland and Waterhouse family history, furnishings, tools & textiles.
Activities: educational programs; special events; research.
Publications: book, History of Maitland; quarterly newsletter; membership brochure; events calendar; education brochure; general museum brochure.
Hours & Admission Prices: Thurs.-Sun. 12-4. Adults $3, children $2; discounts to AAM members; members no charge. ♿
Attendance: 20,000 (accurate)
Membership: Pioneer $15; Individual $20; Dual $30; Family $50; Patron $100; Business $200; Heritage $500.

Marathon

CRANE POINT, 5550 Overseas Hwy., Marathon, FL 33050-2713. Mailing Address: P.O. Box 500536, Marathon, FL 33050-0536. Tel.: 305-743-3900 & 9100 (museum). Fax: 305-743-0429.
E-mail: info@cranepoint.net
Web Site: www.cranepoint.net
Founded: 1990.
Congressional District: 20
Key Personnel: Exec. Dir., Audrey Moir; Dir. Outreach, Laura Fowler; Dir. Education, Elizabeth Moore; Outreach Coord., Alisha Adrianse.
Personnel Profile: Full-Time Paid 6; Full-Time Volunteers 0; Part-Time Paid 3; Part-Time Volunteers 40.

Governing Authority: nonprofit organization. Parent Institution: Florida Keys Land & Sea Trust. Tax-exempt: 501(c)(3).
Natural History Museum.
Collections: photos; shipwreck artifacts; dioramas; railroad; nature trail; shells; hardwoods; butterflies; cultural history development of Florida Keys. Historic Adderley Village: restored 1903 Conch home, kitchen house & garden;
Facilities: 64 acre nature trail system. Gift items for sale.
Activities: concerts; docent program; formal education programs for children; guided tours; lectures; participatory exhibits. Museum Sponsors: Trailblazers Summer Day Camp (8-10 yr.); migrating bird festival; Super Science Saturdays (9-11 yr.).
Publications: quarterly newsletter.
Hours & Admission Prices: Mon.-Sat. 9-5, Sun. 12-5. Adults $11, senior citizens 65 & over $9, students 6-12 $7; discounts to groups; children under 6 & members no charge. Closed Christmas. ♿
Attendance: 30,000 (accurate)
Membership: Individual $25; Family $60; Conservator $150; Patron $500; Benefactor & Corporate $1,000 plus $15 per employee.

Marco Island

MARCO ISLAND HISTORICAL SOCIETY, (M), 168 Royal Palm Dr., Marco Island, FL 34145-2010. Mailing Address: P.O. Box 2282, Marco Island, FL 34146-2282. Tel.: 239-394-6917.
Web Site: www.themihs.org
Key Personnel: Pres., Darcie Guerin.
Governing Authority: Branch Museum: Marco Island Area Assoc. of Realtors, 140 Waterway Dr., Marco Island, FL.
Historical Society Museum.
Collections: local history & culture; photographs.
Hours & Admission Prices: Key Marco Museum: daily Mon.-Fri. 9-4. Museum at Old Marco: daily 7-7.

Melbourne

BREVARD ART MUSEUM, (M), 1463 Highland Ave., Melbourne, FL 32935-6562. Tel.: 321-242-0737. Fax: 321-242-0798.
E-mail: info@brevardartmuseum.org
Web Site: www.brevardartmuseum.org
Formerly: Brevard Museum of Art and Science, Inc.
Founded: 1978.
Congressional District: 15
Key Personnel: Pres. & C.E.O., Steven Maklansky; Cur. Art, Jackie Borsanyi; Bd. Pres., Susan Hopkins; Office Mgr., Tina Murray; Dir. Museum School, Bobbie McMillan; Registrar, Jose Marquez; Fiscal Admin., Laura Settembrino.
Personnel Profile: Full-Time Paid 7; Part-Time Paid 4; Part-Time Volunteers 300; Interns 4.
Governing Authority: nonprofit organization. Tax-exempt: 501(c)(3).
Art Museum.
Collections: works by women artists; works on paper; contemporary artists; Chase collection of Industrial Design.
Facilities: 1,000-vol. library of art reference books & magazines; galleries; 100-seat auditorium; ceramics & sculpture studio; print laboratory; photo laboratories; painting & drawing studios. Museum-related items for sale.
Activities: guided tours; lectures; films; gallery talks; concerts; arts festivals; formally organized education programs; docent program and council; loan & traveling exhibitions.
Publications: quarterly, Museletter; gallery guides; class brochures; e-newsletter.
Hours & Admission Prices: Tues.-Sat. 10-5, Thurs. 10-7, Sun. 1-5. Adults $5, seniors $3, children & students $2; members, & ASTC members no charge. Closed major holidays. ♿
Attendance: 70,000 (estimated)
Membership: Senior & Student $25; Family $55; Patron $150; Renaissance $1,000 & up.

FLORIDA INSTITUTE OF TECHNOLOGY BOTANICAL GARDENS, Florida Tech, 150 W. University Blvd., Melbourne, FL 32901-6982. Tel.: 321-674-8962. Fax: 321-674-7257.
Web Site: www.facilities.fit.edu/botanical_gardens.php
Key Personnel: Dir., John Milbourne
Botanical Gardens.
Collections: palm trees; tropical plants.
Facilities: 30-acres.
Hours & Admission Prices: Daily dawn to dusk.

LIBERTY BELL MEMORIAL MUSEUM, 1601 Oak St., Melbourne, FL 32901-4516. Tel.: 321-727-1776.
Web Site: home.att.net/%7EhonorAmerica/libertybell/
History Museum.
Collections: full-size replica of the original Liberty Bell; U.S. flags; documents; local history; American War artifacts; model warships & airplanes; weapons; clothing.
Facilities: Museum-related items for sale.
Hours & Admission Prices: Tues.-Fri. 10-4, Sat. 10-2. No charge; donations accepted. ♿
Attendance: 15,000
Membership: Regular $20; Freedom Fighters $25; Patriots $50; Standard Bearer $100; Arsenal of Democracy $500; Corporate Sponsorships available.

Merritt Island

NASA KENNEDY SPACE CENTER, SR 405, Merritt Island, FL 32899. Kennedy Space Center, FL 32899-. Tel.: 321-867-5000; 866-737-5235.
Space Museum.
Collections: past, present & future space program artifacts; rockets; Space Shuttle Explorer; Astronaut Hall of Fame; NASA's launch headquarters.
Facilities: restaurant; theater. Museum-related items for sale.
Activities: tours; launch programs; NASA programs; interactive space flight simulators.
Hours & Admission Prices: Visitors Center: daily 9-7. Hall of Fame: daily 9-8. Space Center Tour: adults $31, children 3-11 $21. Hall of Fame: adults $17, children 3-11 $13. Closed Christmas; occasional launch days.

Miami

BAY OF PIGS MUSEUM & LIBRARY, (M), 1821 S.W. 9th St., Miami, FL 33135-5101. Tel.: 305-649-4719. Fax: 305-649-8719.
E-mail: bgd2506@bellsouth.net
Web Site: www.brigada2506.com/museum.htm
Founded: 1979.
Key Personnel: C.E.O., Esteban Bovo; Museum Shop Mgr., Jorge Marquet.
Personnel Profile: Part-Time Paid 2; Part-Time Volunteers 2.
Governing Authority: Parent Institution: Bay of Pigs Veterans Association. Tax-exempt.
History Museum.
Collections: history of the Bay of Pigs; maps; uniforms; arms; organization charts; names of Brigade members; photographs; books; film.
Facilities: library.
Publications: magazine, Giron.
Hours & Admission Prices: Mon.-Fri. 10-9, Sat. 10-2; other times by appointment. No charge; donations accepted. ♿
Attendance: 2,000 (estimated)

BLACK HERITAGE MUSEUM, 15801 S.W. 102nd Ave., Miami, FL 33157-1653. Mailing Address: P.O. Box 570327, Miami, FL 33257-0327. Tel.: 786-346-8038. Fax: 305-252-3535.
E-mail: blkhermu@yahoo.com
Web Site: lets.showmywebsite.com
Founded: 1987.
Key Personnel: Pres., Priscilla G. Stephens Kruize; Financial Dir. & Treas., Gary Roberts; Sec., Eva Cofield.
Governing Authority: nonprofit organization. Tax-exempt: 501(c)(3).
Cultural Arts & History Museum.
Collections: art & artifacts of the Black heritage from around the world; tribal artifacts from Africa & New Guinea; Black Americana; Nigeria's terracotta.
Research Fields: Black heritage & culture; cultural exchanges.
Activities: guided tours; lectures; dance recitals; concerts; permanent & temporary exhibits; special exhibitions.
Publications: newsletter.
Hours & Admission Prices: Call for hours; groups by appointment. No charge; donations accepted. Closed New Year's Day; Easter; Christmas. ♿
Attendance: 4,010
Membership: Active $25; Family $35; Associate $50; Patron $100; Corporate $500.

DEERING ESTATE AT CUTLER, 16701 S.W. 72nd Ave., Miami, FL 33157-2500. Tel.: 305-235-1668. Fax: 305-254-5866.
Web Site: www.deeringestate.org
Key Personnel: Exec. Dir., Mary Petit
Historic Estate.
Collections: family history; paintings; sculpture; personal artifacts; period furnishings; archaeology; historic buildings.
Activities: classes; programs.
Hours & Admission Prices: Daily 10-5. Adults $10, youth 4-14 $5; discounts to groups. Closed Thanksgiving; Christmas.

GALLERY NORTH, MIAMI-DADE COMMUNITY COLLEGE, NORTH CAMPUS, 11380 N.W. 27th Ave., Miami, FL 33167-3418. Tel.: 305-237-1532. Fax: 305-237-1850.
Key Personnel: Dir. Communications, Juan Mendieta
Art Museum.
Collections: paintings; sculpture; photographs.
Activities: lectures.
Hours & Admission Prices: Mon.-Thurs. 9-5, Fri. 9-2. No charge.

GOLD COAST RAILROAD MUSEUM, INC., 12450 S.W. 152nd St., Miami, FL 33177-1402. Tel.: 305-253-0063 & 505-5405; 888-608-7246 (Toll Free). Fax: 305-233-4641.
E-mail: gcrm@askchuck.com
Web Site: www.goldcoast-railroad.org
Founded: 1957.
Congressional District: 18
Key Personnel: C.E.O. & Exec. Dir., Michael D. Hall; Pres., Alan Deems; Vice Pres., Connie Greer; Treas., John McLean; Gift Shop Mgr., Patricia Huffman.
Personnel Profile: Full-Time Paid 4; Full-Time Volunteers 20; Part-Time Paid 1; Part-Time Volunteers 20; Interns 1.
Governing Authority: nonprofit organization. Tax-exempt: 501(c)(3).
Railroad Museum: located on historic NAS RICHMOND, second largest Airship Naval Base World War II.
Collections: Presidential Pullman, Ferdinand Magellan; California Zephyr, Silver Crescent & Silver Stag, FEC Steam Locomotives #113 & 153; FEC Coach Belle Glade & #136; model train area; freight equipment; 7 diesel locomotives & passenger sleepers, coaches, diner & lounge cars; helium tank car; 4 cabooses; cranes. Historic Buildings: Princeton Station; buildings remaining from Richmond Naval Air Station.
Facilities: educational facilities; 52 acres exhibition space. Museum-related items for sale.
Activities: guided tours; training programs for professional museum workers; rental facilities; school summer programs. Annual Events: Dade Heritage Days; Railroad Days; Tropical Agricultural Fiesta in July.
Publications: newsletter, Steam & Steel.
Hours & Admission Prices: Grounds: Tues.-Wed. & Fri. 10-4, Thurs. 10-7, Sat.-Sun. 11-4. Train Bldg.: Mon.-Fri. 11-2, Sat.-Sun. 11-4. Coach: 2nd weekend each month. Cab Rides: $12. Children's Railroad: $2.50. Coach Rides: $6; discounts to local community organization, groups & AAM members; members & children 3 & under no charge. ♿
Attendance: 120,000 (estimated)
Membership: General $35; Family $50.

HAITIAN HERITAGE MUSEUM, (M), 4141 N.E. 2nd Ave., Ste. 105C, Miami, FL 33137. Mailing Address: P.O. Box 370809, Miami, FL 33137-0809. Tel.: 305-371-5988. Fax: 305-432-3792.
Key Personnel: Exec. Dir., Eveline Pierre; Dir. Operations, Serge Rodriguez; Mgr. Education, Lawrence Gonzalez
Heritage Museum.
Collections: Haiti's history & culture; personal artifacts; photographs; Haitian art & music.
Facilities: 200-seat theater.
Hours & Admission Prices: Tues.-Fri. 10-5; other times by appointment.

* **HISTORICAL MUSEUM OF SOUTHERN FLORIDA,** 101 W. Flagler St., Miami, FL 33130-1504. Tel.: 305-375-1492. Fax: 305-375-1609.
E-mail: info@hmsf.org
Web Site: www.hmsf.org
Founded: 1940.
Congressional District: 18
Key Personnel: C.E.O. & Pres., Robert McCammon; Chm., Dr. Edmund I. Parnes; Senior Vice Pres., Roxanne Cappello; Cur. Research, Rebecca A. Smith; Chief Cur., Dr. Joanne Hyppolite; Vice Pres. External Rels., Cristina Blanco; Vice Pres. Education, Cecilia Slesnick; Cur. Objects, Jorge Zamanillo; Museum Shop Mgr., Susan Garcia.
Personnel Profile: Full-Time Paid 25; Part-Time Paid 22; Part-Time Volunteers 15; Interns 4.
Governing Authority: society. Parent Institution: Historical Association of Southern Florida. Tax-exempt: 501(c)(3).
History Museum.
Collections: historical artifacts of south Florida; archives & manuscripts; archaeology; maps; photographs; Audubon's Birds of America; recreational powerboats; aviation.
Research Fields: history, folk life & archaeology of southern Florida and Caribbean, West Indies.
Facilities: research center; theater; meeting rooms. Books & gifts for sale.
Activities: lectures; formally organized educational programs; permanent & temporary exhibitions; historic tours; travel programs; eco-history tours. Annual Event: Miami International Map Fair & Fundraiser.
Publications: annual journal, Tequesta; quarterly periodical, South Florida History.
Hours & Admission Prices: Tues.-Fri. 10-5, 3rd Thurs. 10-9, Sat.-Sun. 12-5. Adults $8, seniors & students $7, children 6-12 $5; discounts to seniors, students, and AAM & ICOM members; children under 6 & members no charge. Closed New Year's Day; Martin Luther King Jr. Day; Presidents' Day; Memorial Day; Independence Day; Labor Day; Columbus Day; Veteran's Day; Thanksgiving; Christmas. ♿
Attendance: 94,000 (estimated)
Membership: Student $25; Educator $30; Institution & Senior $35; Senior Family & Individual $45; Tropee $50; Dual $55; Family $65; Tropee Family $75; History Buff $100; Trail Blazer $250; Fellow $500.

JUNGLE ISLAND, 1111 Parrot Jungle Trail, Miami, FL 33132-1611. Tel.: 305-400-7000. Fax: 305-400-7290.
E-mail: education@jungleisland.com
Web Site: www.jungleisland.com
Formerly: Parrot Jungle Island
Founded: 1936.
Congressional District: 19
Key Personnel: Pres., Dr. Bern M. Levine; Education, Krishawana Thornton; Mktg. Dir., Sandra Edwards; Human Resources, Bobbie Ibarra; Animal Science, Dr. Jason Chatfield; Operations, Cesar Navascues; Museum Shop Mgr., Yvette Khayata.
Personnel Profile: Full-Time Paid 180; Part-Time Paid 60; Interns 5.
Governing Authority: individual operation. Parent Institution: PJ Birds, Inc.
Aviary & Botanical Garden.
Collections: botanical gardens; exotic plants; birds; reptiles; primates.
Facilities: auditoriums; botanical garden; 200-seat restaurant; meeting rooms; nature & conservation center; 18-acre walk-through park. Gifts & books for sale.
Activities: guided tours; docent program; formal educational programs; lectures; study clubs. Museum Sponsors: plant sales & holiday events.
Hours & Admission Prices: Daily 10-6. Adults $29.95, seniors $25.95, children 3-10 $23.95; discounts to groups, AAM members & contracted travel agents. Annual Passes available. ♿
Attendance: 500,000 (estimated)
Membership: Adult $39.95; Children 3-10 $30.95.

* **MIAMI ART MUSEUM, (M),** 101 W. Flagler St., Miami, FL 33130-1504. Tel.: 305-375-3000. Fax: 305-375-1725.
E-mail: mamnews@miamiartmuseum.org
Web Site: www.miamiartmuseum.org
Founded: 1978.
Congressional District: 17
Key Personnel: Chm., Aaron Podhurst; Pres. (V), Gail S. Meyers; Dir., Terence Riley; Asst. Dir. Programs & Sr. Cur., Peter Boswell; Cur. Education, Esther "Chipi" Morales; MAM Store Mgr., Cristina Velez.
Personnel Profile: Full-Time Paid 30; Part-Time Paid 29; Part-Time Volunteers 45.
Governing Authority: nonprofit organization. Tax-exempt: 501(c)(3).
Art Museum.
Collections: 20th & 21st centuries international art.
Facilities: auditorium; sculpture court & outdoor plaza; picnic area. Art-related items for sale in MAM store.
Activities: traveling & temporary exhibitions; lectures; films; guided tours available by reservation. Museum Sponsors: Jam at MAM, the museum's happy hour with art, music & entertainment - 3rd Thurs. of each month 5-9; free hands-on activities for children and their families - 2nd Sat. of each month.
Publications: newsletter: MAM Portrait; Triumph of the Spirit: Carlos Alfonzo, A Survey 1975-1991; Modern Photographs: the Machine, The Body & The City; Jan Dibbets: Perspective Collection; Work in Progress: Herzog & de Meuron's Miami Art Museum; Wifredo Lam at Miami Art Museum.
Hours & Admission Prices: Tues.-Fri. 10-5, third Thurs. 10-9, Sat.-Sun. 12-5. Adults $8, seniors $4; discounts to AAM, ICOM & AAA members; students, members, children under 12 no charge. ♿
Attendance: 62,500 (estimated)
Membership: Individual $45; Dual $60; Family $75; Sustaining $125; Contributing $250; Supporting $500; Friends $1,000; Museum Circle $2,500 & up.

MIAMI CHILDREN'S MUSEUM, 980 MacArthur Causeway, Miami, FL 33132-1604. Mailing Address: Finance Dept., 980 MacArthur Causeway, Miami, FL 33132. Tel.: 305-373-5437, ext. 100. Fax: 305-373-5431.
E-mail: info@miamichildrensmuseum.org
Web Site: miamichildrensmuseum.org

Founded: 1984.
Congressional District: 19
Key Personnel: Pres. (V), Jeffrey Berkowitz; C.E.O. & Exec. Dir., Deborah Spiegelman; Dir. Museum Experiences, Amy Padolf; Dir. Exhibits, Mike Neufeld; Dir. External Rels., Hannah Hausman; Museum Shop Mgr., Johanne Bitton.
Personnel Profile: Full-Time Paid 35; Part-Time Paid 90; Part-Time Volunteers 50; Interns 1.
Governing Authority: nonprofit organization. Tax-exempt: 501(c)(3).
Children's Museum.
Collections: hands-on educational exhibits.
Activities: gallery tours; school outreach. resource center; drop-in activities; early childhood series. Museum Sponsors: Children's Film Festival.
Publications: teacher & student educational packets.
Hours & Admission Prices: Daily 10-6. Adults $15; discount to Florida residents; members no charge. Closed Thanksgiving; Christmas. ♿
Attendance: 113,617 (accurate)
Membership: Grandparent $100; Family & Patron $150; Sponsor $500; Benefactor $1,000.

MIAMI-DADE COLLEGE KENDALL CAMPUS ART GALLERY, 11011 S.W. 104th St., Miami, FL 33176-3393. Tel.: 305-237-2322. Fax: 305-237-2901. TDD: 800-955-8771.
E-mail: lfontana@mdc.edu
Web Site: www.mdc.edu/kendall/art/default.asp
Founded: 1970.
Congressional District: 19
Key Personnel: Acting Dir., Lilia Fontana.
Personnel Profile: Full-Time Paid 1; Part-Time Paid 3.
Governing Authority: college. Tax-exempt: 170(b)(1)(A).
Art Gallery.
Collections: contemporary paintings, prints, sculpture, photography, fibre, video & electronic media; 16th to 19th-century engravings, etchings & lithographs; artists' books.
Research Fields: contemporary, African Diaspora, Latin American & Hispanic art; art of the minorities.
Facilities: 300-seat auditorium; 300-seat restaurant; 3,000 sq. ft. exhibit space.
Activities: guided tours; lectures; films; docent program; training programs for professional museum workers; organized education programs for college students affiliated with Miami-Dade Community College; temporary, loan & traveling exhibitions.
Publications: exhibition catalogues.
Hours & Admission Prices: Sept.-July Mon.-Thurs. 8-7:30, Fri. 8-4, Sat. 9:30-4:30. No charge. ♿
Attendance: 9,500 (estimated)

MIAMI METROZOO, 12400 S.W. 152nd St., One Zoo Blvd., Miami, FL 33177-1402. Tel.: 305-251-0400, ext. 84913. Fax: 305-378-6381.
Web Site: www.miamimetrozoo.com
Founded: 1980.
Congressional District: 19
Key Personnel: Dir., Eric Stephens; Asst. Dir., Carol Kruse; Admission & Concessions, Julio Mesa; Museum Shop Mgr., Nicole Anderson.
Personnel Profile: Full-Time Paid 192; Part-Time Paid 110; Part-Time Volunteers 120.
Governing Authority: county. Parent Institution: Dade County Park & Recreation Department. Tax-exempt.
Zoo.
Collections: birds; mammals; ecotherms.
Research Fields: breeding of endangered species, specializing in crocodilians, birds, & ungulates.
Facilities: library; 300-acre exhibit site; amphitheatre; classroom facilities; monorail. Museum-related items for sale.
Activities: wildlife shows; outreach & in-house education programs; field trips; groups events; party packages; special events; safari cycle rental; guided tram tours; giraffe & pelican feedings; camel rides; zookeeper talks.
Publications: book, Toucan Talk.
Hours & Admission Prices: Daily 9:30-5:30 (gates close at 4). Adults $15.95, children 3-12 $11.95; children 2 & under, American Zoo and Aquarium Association members no charge. ♿
Attendance: 650,133 (accurate)
Membership: Zoological Society of Florida: Senior Dual $64; Dual $64; Family $109.

* **MIAMI SCIENCE MUSEUM, (M),** 3280 S. Miami Ave., Miami, FL 33129-2899. Tel.: 305-646-4200. Fax: 305-646-4300.
E-mail: gthomas@miamisci.org
Web Site: www.miamisci.org
Founded: 1949.
Congressional District: 18
Key Personnel: Pres. & C.E.O., Gillian Thomas; Chm. (V), Trish Bell; Chm. (V), Dan Bell; C.F.O., Nancy McKee; Vice Pres. Exhibits, Sean Duran; Dir. Wildlife Center, Greta Meally.
Personnel Profile: Full-Time Paid 60; Part-Time Paid 37; Part-Time Volunteers 600.
Governing Authority: county; nonprofit organization. Tax-exempt: 501(c)(3).
Science Museum.
Collections: anthropology; archaeology; astronomy; entomology; ethnology; geology; Florida Indian artifacts; marine; mineralogy; nature center; South Florida birds; dynamic hands on light; sound; optics; chemistry; biology; physics; energy; science; technology; invention; wildlife center with walk-in aviary, insects & reptiles; gallery, The Body in Action, explores wonders of the human body; natural science specimens.
Research Fields: radio; photography; marine life; archaeology; botany; astronomy; meteorology; mineralogy; herpetology; conchology; malacology; ornithology; tropical ecology.
Facilities: 5,000-vol. library of scientific books & material relating to all scientific fields available for inter-library loan & by application; two computer labs; environmental information center; nature center; planetarium; 240-seat theater; 230-seat planetarium; Macintosh Training Center; theater; classrooms; observatory; dark rooms; mini-science theater. Scientific items, items relating to South Florida & other museum-related gifts for sale.
Activities: guided tours; lectures; films; gallery talks; concerts; radio drama; study clubs; hobby workshops; TV & radio programs; formally organized education programs; docent program or council; permanent, temporary & traveling exhibitions; school loan service. Museum Sponsors: Latin-oriented programs; technology training center; teacher training.
Publications: summer camp guide; newsletter, Miamisci.
Hours & Admission Prices: Daily 10-6. Adults $14.95, students & seniors $16, children 3-12 $10.95; discounts to museum members & ASTC members; children under 3 no charge. Closed Thanksgiving; Christmas. ♿
Attendance: 300,000 (estimated)
Membership: Student & Individual $40; Family $60; Family Plus $80; 21st Century Club $150; Contributor $250; Donor $500; Benefactor $1,000.

MIAMI SEAQUARIUM, 4400 Rickenbacker Causeway, Miami, FL 33149-1095. Tel.: 305-361-5705. Fax: 305-361-6077.
E-mail: cperrina@msq.cc
Web Site: www.miamiseaquarium.com
Founded: 1955.
Congressional District: 15
Key Personnel: Gen. Mgr., Andrew Hertz; Veterinarian, Maya Menchaca, D.V.M.; Financial Dir., Sherryl Moody; Dir. Operations, Charles Gaudio; Museum Shop Mgr., Rosa White.
Governing Authority: business organized for profit. Wometco Enterprises, Inc., 3195 Ponce de Leon, Coral Gables, FL 33134. Tel: 305-529-1400.
Aquarium.
Collections: killer whale; bottlenose dolphins; Pacific white-sided dolphin; Florida manatee; assorted species of shark, sea turtles, tropical & subtropical fishes; sea lions.
Research Fields: study & raising of sea turtle hatchlings; behavioral & nutritional studies concerning Florida manatee husbandry.
Facilities: botanical garden; aquarium; 230-seat cafeteria. Museum-related items for sale.
Activities: occasional lectures; slides; permanent exhibitions; educational activities; swim with the dolphins.
Hours & Admission Prices: Daily 9:30-6. Adults $35.95, children $26.95; discounts to senior citizens, military, AAA & AAM members. Annual Pass: adult $38.90, children $31.90. ♿
Attendance: 650,000

* **THE PATRICIA & PHILLIP FROST ART MUSEUM, (M),** 10975 S.W. 17th St., Miami, FL 33199-0001. Tel.: 305-348-2890 & 6186. Fax: 305-348-2762.
E-mail: artinfo@fiu.edu
Web Site: www.thefrost.fiu.edu
Formerly: The Art Museum at Florida International University
Founded: 1977.
Congressional District: 16
Key Personnel: Dir., Carol Damian, Ph.D.; Budget & Finance Mgr., Mary Alice Manella; Preparator, Andy Vasquez; Registrar, Debbye Taylor; Cur. Education, Linda Powers; Administrative Asst., Elisabeth Gonzalez; Communications, Jessica Delgado; Exhibition Designer, Chip Steeler; Curatorial Coord., Catalina Jarami; Dir. Devel., Etain Connor; Museum Studies Coord., Annette B. Fromm; Asst. Registrar, Sherry Zambrano; Security Mgr., Julio Alvarez; Security Guard, Ragan Williams.
Personnel Profile: Full-Time Paid 14; Part-Time Paid 6; Part-Time Volunteers 2; Interns 15.

Governing Authority: state. Parent Institution: Florida International University. Tax-exempt: 170(b)(1)(A).
Art Museum.
Collections: European, North & South American paintings, drawings, prints & sculpture; African, Oriental & pre-Columbian artifacts; international outdoor sculpture park, ArtPark; Cintas Fellows collection of contemporary Cuban-American artists.
Research Fields: fields pertaining to collections.
Facilities: library of art books, magazines & catalogues available on premises; sculpture park; auditorium; classrooms.
Activities: museum curated & traveling exhibitions; Critics' Lecture Series; formally organized educational programs; bus tours; artist walkthroughs; ArtSmart tours. Museum Sponsors: Target Wednesday After Hours.
Publications: newsletter; exhibition catalogues; pamphlets; calendars.
Hours & Admission Prices: Tues.-Sat. 10-5, Sun. 12-5. No charge; donations accepted. Closed holidays. ♿
Attendance: 112,000 (estimated)
Membership: University Community $35; Family $75; Contributor $125; Sustainer $250; Connoisseur Couple $1,500.

* **VIZCAYA MUSEUM AND GARDENS, (M),** 3251 S. Miami Ave., Miami, FL 33129-2897. Tel.: 305-250-9133, ext. 2252. Fax: 305-285-2004. TDD: 800-955-8771.
E-mail: joel.hoffman@vizcayamuseum.org
Web Site: www.vizcayamuseum.org
Founded: 1952.
Congressional District: 18
Key Personnel: Exec. Dir., Joel M. Hoffman; Chm. (V), Cathy Jones; Deputy Dir. Finance & Administration, Luis Correa; Asst. to Dir., Kyndal Campbell; Deputy Dir. Advancement, Dennis Fruitt; Deputy Dir. Collections & Curatorial Affairs, Flaminia Gennari; Deputy Dir. Learning, Ann Loshaw; Collections & Archives, Remko Jansonius; Dir. Mktg., Holly Blount; Dir. Events, Adrienne Kaiser; Mgr., School, Youth & Family Programs, Wendy Wolf; Collections Care Specialist, Gina Wouters; Grants Mgr., Anne Doten; Security Supvr., Ralph Castillo; Maintenance Supvr., Jim Rustin.
Personnel Profile: Full-Time Paid 41; Part-Time Paid 6; Part-Time Volunteers 200; Interns 2.
Governing Authority: county. Tax-exempt.
Historic House: 1916 European-Inspired Villa, Gardens & 11-building village on 50 acres of grounds, formerly the estate of International Harvester Executive James Deering.
Collections: European interiors of 16th- to 19th-century; mixed with American original paneling; murals; ceilings; doors; mantels; mirrors from palaces in Italy, France, Spain, England; historic period furnishings & art objects of marble, bronze, wood, textile, ceramic & ivory; decorated gardens; extensive photographie; drawing & document archives.
Research Fields: architecture; decorative arts; gardens.
Activities: guided tours; lectures; concerts; performing arts events; permanent exhibitions.
Hours & Admission Prices: Daily 9:30-4:30. Adults $15, seniors & students $10, children 6-12 $6; discounts to county residents; children 5 & under, AAM members & members no charge. ♿
Attendance: 175,000 (accurate)

WINGS OVER MIAMI AIR MUSEUM, INC., 14710 S.W. 128 St., Miami, FL 33196-2002. Tel.: 305-233-5197. Fax: 305-232-4134.
E-mail: wingsovermiami@aol.com
Web Site: www.wingsovermiami.com
Formerly: Weeks Air Museum
Founded: 2001.
Congressional District: 21
Key Personnel: Chm. (V), William H. Walker; Museum Shop Mgr., Konstantine Oulianov.
Personnel Profile: Full-Time Paid 2; Part-Time Volunteers 100.
Governing Authority: nonprofit organization. Tax-exempt: 501(c)(3).
Aeronautics Museum: located inside Kendall-Tamiami Executive Airport.
Collections: aircraft; engines; instruments; propellers; aviation history of south Florida; airline memorabilia.
Research Fields: restoration of aircraft from beginning of flight to end of World War II era.
Facilities: video booths. Model airplanes, books, pins, patches, bomber jackets & shirts for sale.
Activities: guided tours; facility rental. Museum Sponsors: Member's Day & Open Cockpit Day; Air Show.
Publications: quarterly newsletter.
Hours & Admission Prices: Thurs.-Sun. 10-5. Adults $10, senior citizens $7, children 12 & under $6; discounts to groups, AAA, ICOM & AAM members; members no charge. Closed Thanksgiving; Christmas. ♿
Attendance: 3,700 (estimated)
Membership: Student $15; Associated $20; Individual $30; Family $40.

WOLFSON GALLERIES MIAMI-DADE COLLEGE, 300 N.E. 2nd Ave., Ste. 1365, Miami, FL 33132-2204. Tel.: 305-237-3417. Fax: 305-237-7309.
E-mail: mquiroga@mdcc.edu
Key Personnel: Dir., Mercedes A. Quiroga
Art Museum.
Collections: works by national & international artists.
Hours & Admission Prices: Mon.-Wed. & Fri. 10-4, Thurs. 12-6. No charge. ♿

Miami Beach

ARTCENTER/SOUTH FLORIDA, 924 Lincoln Rd., #205, Miami Beach, FL 33139-2602. Tel.: 305-674-8278. Fax: 305-674-8772.
E-mail: email@artcentersf.org
Web Site: www.artcentersf.org
Founded: 1984.
Congressional District: 18
Key Personnel: C.E.O. & Exec. Dir., Jeremy Chestler; Chm., Richard Shack; Dir. Education, Tammy Key Johnston.
Personnel Profile: Full-Time Paid 8; Part-Time Paid 6; Part-Time Volunteers 20; Interns 2.
Governing Authority: Branch Locations: 800 & 810 Lincoln Rd., Miami Beach, FL. Tax-exempt.
Art Museum.
Collections: works by Miami artists.
Facilities: art education classrooms.
Activities: art programs & classes.
Hours & Admission Prices: Mon.-Thurs. 2-10, Fri.-Sun. 11-11. No charge; donations accepted. ♿
Attendance: 132,000 (accurate)
Membership: Individual $45; Dual & Family $75; Friend $250; Art Partner $500; Corporate Art Partner $1,000.

* **BASS MUSEUM OF ART, (M),** 2121 Park Ave., Miami Beach, FL 33139-1756. Tel.: 305-673-7530. Fax: 305-673-7062.
E-mail: info@bassmuseum.org
Web Site: www.bassmuseum.org
Founded: 1963.
Congressional District: 18
Key Personnel: Exec. Dir., Silvia Karman Cubina; Chm. (V) & Pres. (V), George Lindemann; Asst. Dir. Operations, Jean Ortega; Dir. Mktg. & Public Rels., Lee Ortega; Devel. Assoc., Membership & Volunteer Coord., Denise Wolpert; Registrar & Exhibitions Coord., Chelsea Guerdat; Education Program Coord., Anna Barten; Chief Preparator & Exhibition Technician, Jan Galliardt; Administrative Asst. to Dir., Elisa Alonso; Bldg. Supvr., James Lawrence; Admissions Clerk, Gabrielle Peters; Museum Shop Mgr., William Llanes.
Personnel Profile: Full-Time Paid 10; Part-Time Paid 18; Part-Time Volunteers 50; Interns 5.
Governing Authority: board of trustees. Parent Institution: City of Miami Beach. Tax-exempt: 170(b)(1)(A). Friends of the Bass Museum. Tax-exempt: 501(c)(3).
Art Museum.
Collections: Encyclopedic collection ranging from Old Master paintings, sculpture, textiles; ecclesiastic artifacts; Oriental bronzes; ceramics; decorative arts; 20th-century American graphics, paintings & sculpture; architectural drawings & prints; photography; Latin American & Haitian art.
Major Exhibits: DZine, 11/09-1/10/10; Kent Henrickson, 11/09-1/10/10; Selections from the Jumex Collection, 12/3/09-3/14/10; Ritualistic, 4/2/10-7/18/10; Francis Alys "Night Watch" Project, 6/10-7/10; Fabric Workshop: Selections from the Collection, 8/6/10-10/10/10.
Research Fields: European art & other collections.
Facilities: 7,200 sq. ft. exhibition space. Museum-related items for sale.
Activities: permanent & special exhibitions; lectures; gallery talks; concerts; films; docent program; multidisciplinary symposia; new media projects & presentations.
Publications: collections & special exhibitions catalogues; newsletter; brochures.
Hours & Admission Prices: Sun. 11-5, Tues.-Sat. 10-5. General Admission $8, senior citizens & students with valid ID $6; discounts to AAM & ICOM members; Miami Beach residents, members & children under 6 no charge. Call for list of reciprocal memberships. Additional charge for special exhibitions. Closed holidays. ♿
Attendance: 40,000 (estimated)
Membership: Student $25; Individual $50; Family & Dual $75; Sustaining $100; Contributing $250; Donor $500; Silver Director's Circle $1,000; Gold Director's Circle $2,500; Platinum Director's Circle $5,000.

∗ **JEWISH MUSEUM OF FLORIDA, (M),** 301-311 Washington Ave., Miami Beach, FL 33139-6965. Tel.: 305-672-5044, ext. 3163. Fax: 305-672-5933.
E-mail: mzerivitz@jewishmuseum.com
Web Site: www.jewishmuseum.com
Founded: 1995.
Congressional District: 18
Key Personnel: C.E.O., Marcia Jo Zerivitz; Pres., Leonard A. Wien, Jr.; Assoc. Dir., JoAnn Arnowitz; Cur., Maria Ordonel; Designer, Ira Newman; Education, Sid Krupkin; Museum Shop Mgr., Eva Shvedova; Bookkeeper, Irene Warner; Registrar, Mike Knoll; Administrative Asst., Roberta Gordon.
Personnel Profile: Full-Time Paid 11; Part-Time Paid 2; Part-Time Volunteers 115; Interns 2.
Governing Authority: private; nonprofit organization. Tax-exempt: 501(c)(3).
Jewish History of Florida Museum: housed in a 1936 art deco-style building which served as a synagogue with Moorish copper dome & 80 stained-glass windows.
Collections: photographs, artifacts, documents & ephemera relating to Florida Jewish history, documented from 1763 to present; Mosaic-Jewish life in Florida.
Major Exhibits: Judy Chicago: Jewish Identity, 11/09-2/7/10; 48 JEWS: What It Means to be Jewish - Paintings by Abshalom Jac Lahav, 11/09-4/4/10; Jewish Film Posters, in collaboration with Jewish Film Festival, 1/12/10-1/31/10; Seeking Justice: The Leo Frank Case Revisited, 1/18/10-8/14/11; Florida Jews in the Military, 2/23/10-9/12/10; Lox With Black Beans & Rice: Portraits of Cuban Jews in South Florida, 4/13/10-9/5/10; Last Days of the Four Seasons: Holocaust Survivors Live Life to the Fullest, 10/5/10-1/2/11; Auktion 392: Reclaiming the Galerie Stern Dusseldorf, 10/5/10-4/17/11.
Research Fields: Jewish history of Florida; to document Jewish life in America began in Florida in the 1500s, not in New York in 1654.
Facilities: 150-vol. library of Florida history & general Judaic material; 150-seat auditorium; 400-seat auditorium; educational facilities; 4,000 sq. ft. exhibit space; cafe. Museum-related items for sale.
Activities: concerts; docent program; films; formal educational programs; guided tours; lectures; loan, traveling, temporary & participatory exhibitions.
Publications: quarterly newsletter, Tiles; exhibit monographs.
Hours & Admission Prices: Tues.-Sun. 10-5. Adults $6, senior citizens & students $5, children $2.50; discounts to groups, AAA & PBS members; children under 6, members & Sat. no charge. Closed New Year's Day; Memorial Day; Independence Day; Labor Day; Thanksgiving; Jewish holidays. ♿
Attendance: 47,000 (accurate)
Membership: Senior Individual $30; Individual $36; Senior Couple & Single Parent Family $40; Basic Family $50; Donor $125; Patron $250; Sponsor & Corporate Sponsor $500; Benefactor & Corporate Benefactor $1,000.

∗ **THE WOLFSONIAN - FLORIDA INTERNATIONAL UNIVERSITY, (M), (I),** 1001 Washington Ave., Miami Beach, FL 33139-5017. Tel.: 305-531-1001 & 535-2617. Fax: 305-531-2133.
E-mail: leffc@fiu.edu
Web Site: www.wolfsonian.org
Founded: 1986.
Congressional District: 18
Key Personnel: Dir., Cathy Leff; Deputy Dir. Finance Administration & Operations, Jeanne Brace; Assoc. Dir. Curatorial Affairs & Education, Marianne Lamonaca; Chm. (V), Charles Cowles; Pres. (V), Ray E. Marchman; Assoc. Dir. Business & Finance, Daniel Nolan, Jr.; Registrar, Kimberly Bergen; Exhibition Designer, Richard Miltner; Asst. Dir. Mktg., Member Rels. & New Media, Ian Rand; Chief Librarian, Francis X. Luca; Museum Shop Mgr., Paola La Rivera.
Personnel Profile: Full-Time Paid 35; Part-Time Paid 14; Part-Time Volunteers 11; Interns 6.
Governing Authority: university. Parent Institution: Florida International University. Tax-exempt: 501(c)(3).
Art, Design, Decorative Arts & Architecture Museum: housed in restored building in the historic Art Deco District.
Collections: over 120,000 art & design objects from 1885-1945 including decorative, design & architectural arts; sculpture; paintings; graphics; industrial design; transportation objects; rare books.
Major Exhibits: Styled for the Road: The Art of Automobile Design, 11/09-3/14/10; Rhythms of Modern Life: British Prints, 1914-1939, 11/20/09-2/28/10; Speed Limits, 9/17/10-2/20/11.
Research Fields: Fellowship Program based in areas of collecting focus.
Facilities: 40,000-vol. library containing rare books & periodicals pertaining to decorative & propaganda arts; 15,000 sq. ft. exhibit space.
Activities: guided tours; lectures; films; concerts; loan, temporary & traveling exhibitions; formal education programs for adults & families; docent program.
Publications: catalogues; books; journal, The Journal of Decorative and Propaganda Arts.
Hours & Admission Prices: Academic Year: Mon.-Tues. & Sat. 12-6, Thurs.-Fri. 12-9; Summer: call for hours. Adults $7, seniors, students & children 6-12 $5; discounts to ICOM members; AAM, ICOM & Wolfsonian members, 6pm-9pm on Fri., children under 6 and students, faculty & staff of state university system of Florida no charge. ♿
Attendance: 35,000 (estimated)
Membership: Artist, Educator, Senior & Student $30; Popular $50; Dual & Family $75; Propagandist $125 & up; Diplomat $250; Ally $500 & up; Patriot $1,000 & up; Futurist $2,500 & up.

WORLD EROTIC ART MUSEUM, (M), 1205 Washington Ave., Miami Beach, FL 33139-4613. Tel.: 305-532-9336. Fax: 305-695-1209.
E-mail: missnaomi@weam.com
Founded: 2005.
Key Personnel: Dir., Pres. (V) & Cur., Naomi Wilzig; Public Rels., Robert G. Harbour; Gen. Mgr. & Security, J.C. Harris; Asst. Cur. & Archivist, Charles G. Haak.
Personnel Profile: Full-Time Paid 4; Part-Time Paid 4.
Governing Authority: municipal.
Art Museum.
Collections: erotic art from Biblical to contemporary.
Facilities: 250-vol. library; 12,000 sq. ft. exhibit space. Museum-related items for sale.
Activities: guided tours; lectures; rental facilities.
Hours & Admission Prices: Daily 11am to midnight; children not admitted. Adults $15, senior citizens $14, students $13.50. Closed New Year's Day; Christmas. ♿
Attendance: 5,000 (estimated)
Membership: Annual $100.

Miami Gardens

ST. THOMAS UNIVERSITY LIBRARY, 16401 N.W. 37th Ave., Miami Gardens, FL 33054-6313. Tel.: 305-628-6668. Fax: 305-628-6666.
Web Site: www.stu.edu/Library/tabid/395/Default.aspx
Key Personnel: Dir., L. Bryan Cooper, Ph.D.
Library.
Collections: books; manuscripts; photographs; prints; posters; personal papers; corporate records.
Hours & Admission Prices: Mon.-Thurs. 8am-11pm, Fri. 8-5, Sat. 9-5, Sun. 2-10 by appointment. Closed major holidays.

Micanopy

MICANOPY HISTORICAL SOCIETY MUSEUM, 607 N.E. First St., Micanopy, FL 32667-4112. Mailing Address: P.O. Box 462, Micanopy, FL 32667-0462. Tel.: 352-466-3200. Fax: 352-466-1150.
E-mail: micanopymuseum@aol.com
Web Site: www.afn.org/~micanopy
Founded: 1980.
Congressional District: 6
Key Personnel: Dir., Patricia Crass; Publicity, Liselotte Hof.
Personnel Profile: Full-Time Volunteers 1; Part-Time Volunteers 36.
Governing Authority: private; nonprofit organization. Parent Institution: Micanopy Historical Society. Tax-exempt.
History Museum.
Collections: Micanopy history; farm & family life from 1860 to present; Seminole portraits.
Facilities: Museum-related items for sale.
Activities: elderhostels; children's programs for 4th grade & up; history simulation.
Publications: museum brochure; newsletter, Micanopy Historical Society; book, Story of Historic Micanopy; walking tour brochure.
Hours & Admission Prices: Daily 1-4. Suggested Donation: $2. Closed New Year's Day; Thanksgiving; Christmas. ♿
Attendance: 5,629 (accurate)
Membership: Individual $10; Family $20; Supporter $50; Contributor $100; Patron $500.

Milton

ARCADIA MILL ARCHAEOLOGICAL SITE, 5709 Mill Pond Lane, Milton, FL 32583-1788. Tel.: 850-626-3084.
E-mail: troberts@uwf.edu
Web Site: www.historicpensacola.org/arcadia.cfm
Founded: 2004.
Congressional District: 1
Key Personnel: Site Mgr., Tim Roberts.
Personnel Profile: Full-Time Paid 2; Part-Time Paid 3.

Governing Authority: Parent Institution: West Florida Historic Preservation, Inc./University of West Florida. Subsidiary Institution: T.T. Wentworth; Florida State Museum; Historic Pensacola Village. Tax-exempt: 501(c)(3).
Historic Archaeological Site: housed in a mid-19th century industrial complex.
Collections: archaeological; structural remains.
Research Fields: local historical technology and related people & families.
Facilities: visitors center; nature trail.
Activities: guided tours; archaeological excavations in summer.
Hours & Admission Prices: Tues.-Sat. 10-4. No charge; donations accepted. Closed New Year's Day; Independence Day; Veterans Day; Thanksgiving & day after; day after Christmas. ♿
Attendance: 15,000 (estimated)

WEST FLORIDA RAILROAD MUSEUM, 5003 Henry St., Milton, FL 32570-6790. Mailing Address: P.O. Box 770, Milton, FL 32572-0770. Tel.: 850-623-3645.
Founded: 1989.
Key Personnel: Pres. (V), Art Tuttle.
Personnel Profile: Part-Time Volunteers 10.
Governing Authority: Tax-exempt.
Railroad History Museum.
Collections: Northwest Florida & South Alabama railroad history.
Hours & Admission Prices: Fri.-Sat. 10-3; other times by appointment. No charge; donations accepted. ♿
Membership: Annual $30.

Mount Dora

MOUNT DORA CENTER FOR THE ARTS, 138 E. 5th Ave., Mount Dora, FL 32757-5573. Tel.: 352-383-0880. Fax: 352-383-7753.
E-mail: center@mountdoracenterforthearts.org
Web Site: www.mountdoracenterforthearts.org
Founded: 1985.
Congressional District: 5
Key Personnel: Exec. Co.-Chair, Nancy Zinkofsky; Exec. Co.-Chair, Christina Padgett; Admin. Asst., Cliffette Nicholls.
Personnel Profile: Full-Time Paid 1; Part-Time Paid 3; Part-Time Volunteers 10; Interns 2.
Governing Authority: nonprofit organization. Tax-exempt: 501(c)(3).
Art Center.
Collections: Best of Show pieces from Mount Dora Arts Festival.
Facilities: 700 sq. ft. exhibit space. Gift items for sale.
Activities: arts festivals; formal educational programs; lectures; participatory & temporary exhibitions.
Publications: quarterly, MDCA Newsletter.
Hours & Admission Prices: Mon.-Fri. 10-4, Sat. 10-2. No charge; donations accepted. Closed major holidays. ♿
Attendance: 35,000 (accurate)
Membership: Student & Senior $20; Individual $25; Senior Couple $30; Family $35; Sponsor $50; Sustaining & Business $100; Associate $250; Patron $500; Benefactor $1,000.

MOUNT DORA HISTORY MUSEUM, 450 Royellou Lane, Mount Dora, FL 32757-5554. Mailing Address: P.O. Box 1166, Mount Dora, FL 32756-1166. Tel.: 352-383-0006. Fax: 813-769-6117.
E-mail: royellou@yahoo.com
Web Site: www.mountdorahistoricalsociety.com
Formerly: Royellou Museum
Founded: 1978.
Key Personnel: Dir. & Pres. (V), Andrew Mulen; Museum Shop Mgr., Mary Pezzo.
Personnel Profile: Full-Time Volunteers 1; Part-Time Volunteers 4; Interns 1.
Governing Authority: Tax-exempt.
History Museum: housed in the old city jail built in 1923.
Collections: Mount Dora history & photographs; jail cell; moonshine still; personal artifacts; clothing.
Hours & Admission Prices: Thurs. & Sat. 1-4; other times by appointment. Adults $2; discounts to AAM & ICOM members; AAA members & students no charge. ♿
Attendance: 900 (estimated)
Membership: Student $5; Individual $15; Family $25.

Mulberry

MULBERRY PHOSPHATE MUSEUM, (M), 101 S.E. 1st St., Mulberry, FL 33860-3169. Mailing Address: P.O. Box 707, Mulberry, FL 33860-0707. Tel.: 863-425-2823. Fax: 863-425-0188.
Web Site: www.mulberrychamber.org/attractions.htm
Founded: 1985.
Congressional District: 10
Key Personnel: Dir., Lewetta Haag.
Personnel Profile: Full-Time Paid 1; Part-Time Paid 1.
Governing Authority: municipal. Parent Institution: City of Mulberry. Tax-exempt: 501(c)(3).
Natural History Museum: housed in c.1899 Mulberry Train Depot.
Collections: Cenozoic fossils.
Research Fields: Ice Age animals living in Florida during the Cenozoic Era.
Activities: guided tours; lectures; organized educational programs; docent program; loan, temporary & traveling exhibitions; school loan service.
Hours & Admission Prices: Tues.-Sat. 10-4:30. No charge; donations accepted. Closed New Year's Day; Memorial Day; Thanksgiving; Christmas. ♿
Attendance: 35,000

Naples

CHILDREN'S MUSEUM OF NAPLES, (M), 15080 Livingston Rd., Naples, FL 34109. Mailing Address: P.O. Box 2423, Naples, FL 34106-2423. Tel.: 239-784-1879.
Web Site: www.cmon.org
Founded: 2002.
Key Personnel: Dir., Joseph P. Cox; Pres. (V), Julie Koester; Treas., Karysia Demarest.
Personnel Profile: Full-Time Paid 4; Part-Time Paid 1; Part-Time Volunteers 30.
Governing Authority: nonprofit organization. Tax-exempt: 501(c)(3).
Children's Museum.
Collections: hands on participatory exhibits.
Activities: arts festivals; concerts; docent program; guided tours; workshops; lectures; rental gallery; temporary & traveling exhibits.
Publications: quarterly newsletter, C'mon; e-newsletters.
Hours & Admission Prices: Opening Fall 2010.

COLLIER COUNTY MUSEUM, (M), 3301 Tamiami Trail E., Naples, FL 34112-4961. Tel.: 239-252-8476. Fax: 239-252-8580.
E-mail: curator11@att.net
Web Site: www.colliermuseums.com
Founded: 1978.
Key Personnel: C.E.O., Ron D. Jamro; Cur., Jennifer Guida; Education, David Southall; Volunteer Coord. & Museum Shop Mgr., Mary Margaret Gruszka; Mgr., Lee Mitchell; Mgr., Timothy England; Mgr., Gary Vincent; Museum Asst., Martha Schramm; Museum Asst., Jon Nickerson; Museum Asst., Susan Maunz; Administrative Asst., Judy Lusher.
Personnel Profile: Full-Time Paid 13; Part-Time Volunteers 200.
Governing Authority: county. Subsidiary Institutions: Museum of the Everglades, Everglades City, FL; Immokalee Pioneer Museum at Roberts Ranch; Naples Depot Museum, downtown Naples. Tax-exempt: 501(c)(3).
History Museum.
Collections: history & archaeology of Collier County; several restored structures; a steam logging locomotive.
Major Exhibits: For Everglades: Photography by Clyde Butcher & Jeff Ripple (T), 1/10-4/10; At The Crossroads - Documenting Florida's Rural Voices (T), 2/10-3/10.
Research Fields: historic site & structures in Collier County; construction of the Tamiami Trail 1923-1928; Calusa Indians in southwest Florida.
Facilities: 700-vol. non-circulating research library relating to Florida history, Collier County archaeology, Seminole Indians, general American & southern history; botanical garden; educational facilities; 10,000 sq. ft. exhibit space; archaeology laboratory. Museum-related items for sale.
Activities: formal education programs; guided tours; lectures; participatory, temporary & traveling exhibitions. Annual Events: Old Florida Festival; Florida Archaeology Week.
Hours & Admission Prices: Mon.-Fri. 9-5, Sat. 9-4. No charge; donations accepted. Closed national & county holidays. ♿
Attendance: 75,000 (estimated)
Membership: Student & Senior Citizen $15; Individual $25; Family $40; Friend $100; Sponsor $500; Patron $1,000.

CONSERVANCY OF SOUTHWEST FLORIDA NATURE CENTER, 1450 Merrihue Dr., Naples, FL 34102-3449. Tel.: 239-262-0304. Fax: 239-262-0672.
Web Site: www.conservancy.org
Founded: 1964.
Key Personnel: C.E.O., Andrew McElwaine
Nature Center.
Collections: owls; hawks; pelicans; bald eagle; injured birds, mammals & reptiles; freshwater & saltwater fish.
Facilities: 21 acres; nature trails. Museum-related items for sale.
Activities: summer camp; school programs; visitor programs; field excursions; canoe & kayak rentals; electric boat tours.
Publications: Conservancy Update.
Hours & Admission Prices: May-Nov. 4 Mon.-Sat. 9-4:30; Nov. 5-April 29

Mon.-Sat. 9-4:30, Sun. 12-4. Adults $9, children 3-12 $2; children under 3 & members no charge.
Membership: Family $35; Protector $50; Friend $100; Partner $250; Advocate $500; Conservator $1,000; Guardian $2,000; Benefactor $5,000.

HOLOCAUST MUSEUM OF SOUTHWEST FLORIDA, 4760 Tamiami Trail N., Ste. 7, Naples, FL 34103-3065. Tel.: 239-263-9200. Fax: 239-263-9500.
Founded: 2001.
Personnel Profile: Full-Time Paid 4; Part-Time Paid 3; Part-Time Volunteers 150; Interns 1.
Governing Authority: Tax-exempt.
History Museum.
Collections: Holocaust & WWII history & artifacts; survivor documents & stories.
Activities: special events.
Hours & Admission Prices: Tues.-Sun. 1-4. Adults $8; members no charge. Closed public holidays. ♿
Attendance: 8,300 (accurate)
Membership: $18; $36; $54; $200; $300; $1,000; $1,500. Window of Hope: $1,000-$100,000.

NAPLES BOTANICAL GARDEN, 4820 Bayshore Dr., Naples, FL 34112-7336. Tel.: 239-643-7275. Fax: 239-649-7306.
E-mail: jbarry@naplesgarden.org
Web Site: www.naplesgarden.org
Founded: 1993.
Congressional District: 14
Key Personnel: Exec. Dir., Brian Holley; Chm. (V), Juliet C. Sproul; C.O.O., Joyce Zirkle; Dir. External Affairs, Jill Barry; Museum Shop Mgr., Janele Smith.
Personnel Profile: Full-Time Paid 20; Full-Time Volunteers 1; Part-Time Paid 4.
Governing Authority: Tax-exempt.
Botanical Garden.
Collections: natural science; plants; art; history; gardens.
Facilities: 160 acreas; garden; laboratory; nature trail.
Hours & Admission Prices: Daily 9-5. Adults $9.95; members no charge. ♿
Attendance: 30,000 (estimated)
Membership: Individual $50; Family $75; Contributing $125; Sustainer $500; Garden Fellow $1,000; Royal Palm Society $1,500, $3,000, $5,000, $10,000.

PATTY AND JAY BAKER NAPLES MUSEUM OF ART, (M), 5833 Pelican Bay Blvd., Naples, FL 34108-2740. Tel.: 239-597-1111. Fax: 239-596-7526.
E-mail: museum@thephil.org
Web Site: www.thephil.org
Formerly: Naples Museum of Art and the Philharmonic Center for the Arts Galleries
Founded: 1989.
Congressional District: 13
Key Personnel: Founder, Chm. & C.E.O., Myra Janco Daniels; Dir. & Chief Cur., Michael Culver, Ph.D.; Registrar, Jacqueline Zorn; Preparator, Blake Millard; Exhibitions Designer, Chris Erickson; Dir. Finance, Renee Neville; Mgr. Devel., Sally Bettin; Membership, Steve Pederson; Volunteer Coord., Carolyn Williams; Cur. Education, Jessica Wozniak; Art Handler, William Teague; Art Handler, Steven Kravec; Museum Coord., Diane Shaheen; Museum Shop Mgr., Carol Rushing.
Personnel Profile: Full-Time Paid 10; Part-Time Paid 4; Part-Time Volunteers 239; Interns 3.
Governing Authority: nonprofit. Parent Institution: Philharmonic Center for the Arts. Tax-exempt: 501(c)(3).
Art Gallery.
Collections: photography; sculpture garden; painting; American modernism; 20th century Mexican & Latin American art; contemporary art; photography; video; miniatures; glass (chiculy).
Major Exhibits: Esphyr Slobodkina: Rediscovering a Pioneer of Abstraction (T), 11/09-12/27/09; The Art of Janet Fish, 11/09-1/17/10; Latin American Painting Now, 11/09-1/10/10; Woman: The Art of Gaston Lachaise (T), 1/12/10-4/10; Chihuly: Recent Work (T), 1/23/10-4/25/10; People, Places and Things: The Art of Ben Aronson, Joel Babb & Alec Smith, 2/2/10-4/18/10; Associated American Artists, Art by Subscription (T), 5/9/10-6/10.
Research Fields: on permanent collection objects & subjects of temporary & traveling exhibitions.
Facilities: 200 & 1,221-seat theaters; 22,000 sq. ft. exhibit space.
Activities: permanent, loan & traveling exhibitions; guided tours; docent program; lectures; gallery talks; art trips; performances; formally organized education programs; museum family days.
Publications: catalogues of permanent collections & exhibitions; member newsletter, Dome; annual community report; annual brochures, Showtime, Naples Philharmonic Orchestra, Naples Museum of Art; quarterly magazine, The Phil; Family Entertainment Guide: An Adventure in Family Entertainment; This Week at the Museum.
Hours & Admission Prices: May-June & Oct. Tues.-Sat. 10-4, Sun. 12-4; Nov.-April Tues.-Sat. 10-5, Sun. 12-5. Adults $8, students $4; discounts to AAM & ICOM members; members no charge. Additional fee for special exhibitions. Closed New Year's Eve & Day; Easter; Memorial Day; Thanksgiving; Christmas Eve & Day. ♿
Attendance: 100,000 (estimated)
Membership: Individual $50; Household $125; Donor $200-$499; Patron $500-$999; Benefactor $1,000-$4,999; Associate $5,000-$9,999; Circle $10,000 & up.

THE VON LIEBIG ART CENTER - THE NAPLES ART ASSOCIATION, 585 Park St., Naples, FL 34102-6611. Tel.: 239-262-6517. Fax: 239-262-5404.
E-mail: info@naplesart.org
Web Site: www.naplesart.org
Founded: 1954.
Congressional District: 14
Key Personnel: Pres., Frank Nappo; Vice Pres., Bob Saltarelli; Vice Pres., Richard Stevens; Exec. Dir., Joel Kessler; Asst. Dir., Ginamarie Pugliese; Devel. & Finance Support Mgr., Joan Esler; Cur., Jack O'Brien; Public Rels. & Mktg. Mgr., Robin DeMattia; Mgr. Volunteer Svcs., Yvonne Gibb; Registration, Sheri Chase; Librarian, Patricia Treusch; Museum Shop Mgr., Nancy Baxter; Dir. Education, Nicole DuPont Strub; Dir. Festivals, Marianne Megela; Coord. Festivals, Nancy Doyal; Coord. Festivals, Tom Taylor; Preparator & Art Handler, Ken Andexlee; Finance, Aimee Schlehr; Security, Jerry Dylag.
Personnel Profile: Full-Time Paid 10; Part-Time Paid 7; Part-Time Volunteers 380; Interns 60.
Governing Authority: private; nonprofit organization. Parent Institution: Naples Art Association. Tax-exempt: 501(c)(3).
Art Museum.
Collections: paintings; sculpture; photography; works on paper.
Facilities: 2,000-vol. library; six classrooms/studios; 2,500 sq. ft. exhibit space. Museum-related items for sale.
Activities: changing exhibitions; education programs; classes; workshops; lectures; facility rental. Annual Events: From His Collection to Yours in January; Naples National Art Festival in February; Nuts About the von Liebig Family Day in February; Goddess Night in April; Art in the Park Nov.-April.
Publications: semiannual newsletter; monthly e-newsletter.
Hours & Admission Prices: Gallery: Mon.-Sat. 10-4, Sun. 1-4. Administration Office: Mon.-Fri. 9-5. No charge; donations accepted. Closed Easter; Memorial Day; Independence Day; Labor Day; Thanksgiving; Christmas. ♿
Attendance: 40,250 (accurate)
Membership: Individual $65; Family $125; Supporting $250; Patron $650; Corporate $1,000.

New Port Richey

WEST PASCO HISTORICAL SOCIETY MUSEUM AND LIBRARY, 6431 Circle Blvd., New Port Richey, FL 34652-2360. Tel.: 727-847-0680.
E-mail: wb2ium@sanctum.com
Founded: 1983.
Congressional District: 5
Key Personnel: Pres. (V), David Prace; Treas., Steve Brooks; Museum Shop Mgr., Audrey O'Neill.
Personnel Profile: Part-Time Volunteers 20.
Governing Authority: society. Parent Institution: West Pasco Historical Society, Inc. Tax-exempt: 501(c)(3).
Historical Society Museum: housed in 1913 two-room schoolhouse.
Collections: Wedgewood china; local history displays; local artifacts; pre-Columbian artifacts; arrowheads; vintage clothing; quilts; period household furnishings; typewriters; Native American clothing; arrowheads; pottery; jewelry; library.
Research Fields: local history; local photograph collection.
Facilities: 2,000-vol. library of books; newspaper files, available for use by public; classrooms; 2,000 sq. ft. exhibit space. Books & gift items for sale.
Activities: guided tours; lectures; films; arts festivals; docent program; participatory & temporary exhibitions; field trips. Museum Sponsors: fashion show; Christmas Dinner Auction; Rummage Sale.
Publications: quarterly, WPHS Newsletter; books on local history.
Hours & Admission Prices: Tues. 10-1, Fri.-Sat. 1-4. No charge; donations accepted. Closed legal holidays. ♿
Attendance: 3,500 (estimated)
Membership: Student $5; Adult $15; Family $25; Business $50; Life $100.

New Smyrna Beach

ATLANTIC CENTER FOR THE ARTS, INC., 1414 Art Center Ave., New Smyrna Beach, FL 32168-5560. Tel.: 386-427-6975. Fax: 386-427-5669.
E-mail: program@atlanticcenterforthearts.org
Web Site: www.atlanticcenterforthearts.org
Founded: 1977.
Congressional District: 7
Key Personnel: Dir., Ann Brady; Chm. (V), Margery Pabst; Treas., Ed Leerdam; Devel. & Public Rels., Kelle Groom; Security, Tom Kurtzhals; Museum Shop Mgr., Brenda Owens.
Personnel Profile: Full-Time Paid 12; Part-Time Volunteers 130; Interns 1.
Governing Authority: private; nonprofit organization. Tax-exempt: 501(c)(3).
Art Center.
Collections: works by former master artists-in-residence.
Facilities: 500-vol. library; 200-seat auditorium; artist studios; 4,000 sq. ft. exhibit space. Museum-related items for sale.
Activities: arts festivals; formal education programs; guided tours; hobby workshops; lectures; temporary & traveling exhibitions.
Publications: yearly annual report, ACA Annual Report; quarterly newsletter, ACA Newsletter.
Hours & Admission Prices: Tues.-Fri. 10-4, Sat. 10-2. Closed Martin Luther King Jr. Day; Presidents' Day; Memorial Day; Independence Day; Labor Day; Thanksgiving & day after; Christmas week. ♿
Attendance: 5,000 (estimated)
Membership: Artist-in-Residence $25; Individual & Volunteer League $40; Family $70; Art Angel $100; Salon $250; Patron Images & Patron Horsin' Around $1,000; Preservationist $2,500.

Niceville

MATTIE KELLY ARTS CENTER GALLERIES AT NORTHWEST FLORIDA STATE COLLEGE, (M), 100 College Blvd., Niceville, FL 32578-1347. Tel.: 850-729-6044. Fax: 850-729-5286.
E-mail: williamk@nwfsc.edu
Formerly: Mattie Kelly Arts Center at Okaloosa-Walton College
Founded: 1997.
Congressional District: 1
Key Personnel: Division Dir., Fine & Performing Arts, Dr. Cliff Herron; Gallery Dir., K.C. Williams; Assoc. Dir., The Arts Center, Jeanette Shires.
Personnel Profile: Full-Time Paid 1; Part-Time Paid 3; Part-Time Volunteers 32; Interns 2.
Governing Authority: Parent Institution: Northwest Florida State College. Tax-exempt.
College Art Museum.
Collections: works by national & international artists.
Major Exhibits: Florida Visual Arts Fellowship Exhibition (T), 1/10-2/10; Arnie Hart Juried Student Exhibition, 3/10-4/10; 18th Annual Arts & Design Society Southeast Regional Juried Fine Arts Exhibition, 5/10; Flight Path, 6/10-7/10; Pastel Society of North Florida's 11th Biennial National Pastel Exhibition, 11/10.
Facilities: 1,650-seat theater.
Activities: education programs; performances.
Hours & Admission Prices: Mon.-Thurs. 9-4, Sun. 1-4. No charge. Closed holidays.
Attendance: 9,000 (estimated)

North Miami

* **MUSEUM OF CONTEMPORARY ART (MOCA), (M),** 770 N.E. 125th St., North Miami, FL 33161-5654. Mailing Address: Joan Lehman Bldg., 770 N.E. 125th St., North Miami, FL 33161. Tel.: 305-893-6211. Fax: 305-891-1472.
E-mail: info@mocanomi.org
Web Site: www.mocanomi.org
Founded: 1981.
Congressional District: 10
Key Personnel: Exec. Dir. & Chief Cur., Bonnie Clearwater; Chm. Bd. Dir., Michael Collins; Museum Shop Mgr., Alan Waufle.
Personnel Profile: Full-Time Paid 15; Part-Time Paid 9; Part-Time Volunteers 30; Interns 1.
Governing Authority: nonprofit organization. Branch Museum: MOCA at Goldman Warehouse, 404 N.W. 26th St., Wynwood Arts District, Miami, FL 33127. Tax-exempt: 501(c)(3).
Visual Contemporary Art.
Collections: contemporary art.
Major Exhibits: The Reach of Realism, 12/09-2/21/10; Ceal Floye, 3/11/10-5/6/10; Claire Fontaine, 6/2/10-8/22/10.
Facilities: 23,000 sq. ft. exhibit space.
Activities: guided tours; lectures; films; organized education programs for children organized education & enrichment programs for teens; loan exhibitions; tours to artists' studios; temporary exhibitions of contemporary, national & international artists; monthly jazz concerts.
Publications: quarterly newsletter; catalogs; MOCA'zine teen magazine.
Hours & Admission Prices: MOCA North Miami: Tues. & Thurs.-Sat. 11-5, Wed. 1-5, Sun. 12-5. Adults $5, seniors & students $3; North Miami residents, children under 12 & members no charge. Tues. donations accepted. MOCA at Goldman Warehouse: Wed.-Sat. 12-5. No charge; donations accepted. Closed Thanksgiving; Christmas. ♿
Attendance: 65,000 (accurate)
Membership: Artist, Student & Educator $30; Individual $50; Family $70; MOCA Shaker $150; Patron $500; Associate $1,000; Benefactor $2,500; International Collector Circle $5,000.

North Miami Beach

ANCIENT SPANISH MONASTERY OF ST. BERNARD DE CLAIRVAUX CLOISTERS, 16711 W. Dixie Hwy., North Miami Beach, FL 33160-3714. Tel.: 305-945-1462 & 1461. Fax: 305-945-4052.
Web Site: www.spanishmonastery.com
Founded: 1952.
Key Personnel: Exec. Admin. & C.E.O., Rev. Dr. Ronald N. Fox; Museum Shop Mgr., Tania Witten; Parish Sec., Mayten Battalle.
Governing Authority: church. Parent Institution: Episcopal Diocese of S.E. Florida. Tax-exempt.
Art Museum: housed in The Cloister and Refectory, reconstruction of monastery, built in 1141 in Segovia, Spain, with original stones brought to United States by William Randolph Hearst.
Collections: paintings; sculpture; historical artifacts of religious nature; historical architectural artifacts.
Facilities: Religious articles, books & related items for sale.
Activities: guided tours; arts festivals; drama; inter-museum loan & permanent exhibitions.
Hours & Admission Prices: Mon.-Sat. 9-5, Sun. 12-5. Adults 12-55 $5, senior citizens 55 & over $2.50, students 12 & under $1. ♿

North Palm Beach

JOHN D. MACARTHUR BEACH STATE PARK & NATURE CENTER, 10900 Jack Nicklaus Dr., North Palm Beach, FL 33408-3440. Tel.: 561-624-6952 & 6950.
E-mail: friends@macarthurbeach.org
Web Site: www.macarthurbeach.org
Park & Nature Center.
Collections: aquariums; video; natural history.
Facilities: picnic area. Museum-related items for sale.
Activities: recreational activities; video; education programs.
Hours & Admission Prices: Nature Center: daily 9-5. Park: daily 8 to sunset. Entrance Fee: $5 per vehicle.

Ocala

APPLETON MUSEUM OF ART, 4333 E. Silver Springs Blvd., Ocala, FL 34470-5000. Tel.: 352-291-4455. Fax: 352-291-4460.
E-mail: ormej@cf.edu
Web Site: www.appletonmuseum.org
Founded: 1986.
Congressional District: 6
Key Personnel: Dir., Dr. John Lofgren; Staff Asst. III, Joyce Orme; Mgr. Membership & Events, Colleen Harper; Coord. Facilities, Russell Days; Registrar, David Reutter; Devel. Officer, Pamela Mock; Coord. Events & Mktg., Steve Specht; Educator, Korene Wilbanks; Museum Operations Coord., Lisa Moline.
Personnel Profile: Full-Time Paid 13; Part-Time Paid 27; Part-Time Volunteers 100; Interns 2.
Governing Authority: nonprofit organization. Parent Institution: Central Florida Community College. Tax-exempt.
Fine Arts Museum.
Collections: fine arts, including European, Pre-Columbian, African, Asian, Islamic & decorative arts; contemporary art; Florida artists antiquities.
Major Exhibits: New Reality: Frontier of Realism in the 21st Century (T), 1/10-3/10; Southern Journeys (T), 4/10-6/10; Appleton Museum of Art Biennial (T), 6/10-8/10.
Research Fields: all items pertaining to collections.
Facilities: art reference library; 250-seat auditorium; conference rooms; 39,000 sq. ft. exhibit space. Museum-related items for sale.
Activities: guided tours; lectures; films; concerts; organized education programs for children, adults, undergraduate & graduate college students; docent program; loan, temporary & traveling exhibitions; tours in Spanish & French available upon request; workshops.
Publications: calendar of events; quarterly newsletter.
Hours & Admission Prices: Tues.-Sat. 10-5, Sun. 12-5. Call for admission

prices. Reciprocal memberships with other museums. Closed New Year's Day; Thanksgiving; Christmas. ♿
Attendance: 50,000 (accurate)
Membership: Students & Educator $15; Senior $25; Individual $30; Dual Senior $40; Dual Family $50; Director's Circle $100-$499, $500-$999, $1,000-$2,499, $2,500-$4,999, $5,000 & up.

CFCC WEBBER CENTER GALLERY, 3001 S.W. College Rd., Ocala, FL 34474-4415. Mailing Address: P.O. Box 1388, Ocala, FL 34478-1388. Tel.: 352-873-5809. Fax: 352-873-5886.
E-mail: moodym@cf.edu
Web Site: www.cf.edu
Founded: 1995.
Congressional District: 6
Key Personnel: Dir. Visual & Performing, Dr. Jennifer Fryns; Exhibits Coord., Molly Moody.
Personnel Profile: Full-Time Paid 1; Part-Time Paid 3; Part-Time Volunteers 1.
Governing Authority: Parent Institution: Central Florida Community College. Tax-exempt.
Art Museum.
Collections: paintings; photographs; prints; drawings; graphic arts; sculpture.
Major Exhibits: Carnaval! (T), 6/17/10-8/11/10.
Facilities: 2,000 sq. ft. exhibit space; conference room; outside patio.
Activities: videos; films; seminars; lectures; poetry readings; story-tellings; musical offerings; temporary exhibitions.
Hours & Admission Prices: Tues.-Fri. 11-5, Sat. 10-2. No charge; donations accepted. Closed college observed holidays. ♿
Attendance: 9,000 (estimated)

DISCOVERY SCIENCE AND OUTDOOR CENTER, 701 N.E. Sanchez Ave., Ocala, FL 34470. Tel.: 352-401-3900. Fax: 352-401-3939.
E-mail: discover@ocalafl.org
Web Site: www.ocalafl.org
Founded: 1993.
Congressional District: 5
Key Personnel: Asst., Nora Davie.
Personnel Profile: Full-Time Paid 1; Part-Time Paid 6; Part-Time Volunteers 200.
Governing Authority: nonprofit organization. Parent Institution: City of Ocala. Tax-exempt.
Science Center.
Collections: hands-on science & nature exhibits.
Facilities: 23 acre park setting; nature walk. Gift items for sale.
Activities: educational programs; participatory, loan & traveling exhibitions; explainer program.
Publications: Science Matters.
Hours & Admission Prices: Tues.-Fri. 9-4, Sat. 10-2. ♿
Attendance: 25,000 (estimated)
Membership: Adult $30; Single $35; Family $50; Friend $125.

DON GARLITS MUSEUM OF DRAG RACING INC., 13700 S.W. 16th Ave., I-75, Exit 341, Ocala, FL 34473-3918. Tel.: 352-245-8661; 877-271-3278 (toll-free). Fax: 352-245-6895.
E-mail: garlits@mfi.net
Web Site: www.garlits.com
Founded: 1976.
Congressional District: 6
Key Personnel: C.E.O. & Chm., Donald G. Garlits; Vice Chm., Donna Garlits Perry; Treas., Gay Lyn Capitano; Dir. & Sec., Pat Garlits; Dir., Carl Schiefer; Dir., Chris Karamesines; Dir. Legal, George Albright; Museum Shop Mgr., Peggy Hunnewell; Comptroller, Raj Kumar.
Personnel Profile: Full-Time Paid 6; Part-Time Paid 2; Part-Time Volunteers 4.
Governing Authority: board of directors. Tax-exempt: 501(c)(3).
Drag Racing & Antique Cars & Tools Museum.
Collections: drag racing from late 1940s-present; race cars; engine exhibits; early parts; pictures; model exhibits; period cars.
Research Fields: drag racing.
Facilities: 5000-vol. library pertaining to drag racing; video theater. Auto-related items for sale.
Activities: guided tours; films; organized education programs; loan & temporary exhibitions.
Publications: membership newsletter.
Hours & Admission Prices: Daily 9-5. Adults $15, senior citizens & students $13, children $6; discounts to AAA members; children under 5 no charge. Closed Christmas. ♿
Attendance: 75,000 (accurate)
Membership: Annual $25.

SILVER RIVER MUSEUM & ENVIRONMENTAL EDUCATION CENTER, 1445 N.E. 58th Ave., Ocala, FL 34470-1189. Tel.: 352-236-5401. Fax: 352-236-7142.
E-mail: scott.mitchell@marion.k12.fl.us
Web Site: www.silverrivermuseum.com
Founded: 1991.
Congressional District: 6
Key Personnel: Dir., Cur. & Public Rels., Scott Mitchell; Financial Dir., Archivist, Registrar & Museum Shop Mgr., Linda La Mont; Education, Dorothy Lorch.
Personnel Profile: Full-Time Paid 4; Part-Time Paid 6; Part-Time Volunteers 25.
Governing Authority: public school district; nonprofit organization. Parent Institution: Marion County School System. Tax-exempt.
History & Natural History of Florida Museum.
Collections: history; natural history; archaeology; paleontology; geology.
Research Fields: Florida natural & cultural history.
Facilities: research library; educational facilities. Museum-related items for sale.
Activities: educational program; docent program.
Hours & Admission Prices: Student Tours: Mon.-Fri. General Public: June-July Tues.-Fri. 10-4, Sat.-Sun. 9-5; Aug.-May Sat.-Sun. 9-5. Adults $2; children 6 & under no charge. ♿
Attendance: 20,000 (estimated)

Ochopee

BIG CYPRESS NATIONAL PRESERVE, Oasis Visitors Center, 52105 Tamiami Trail E., Ochopee, FL 34141. Mailing Address: HCR 61 Box 11, Ochopee, FL 34141. Tel.: 239-695-1201 & 2000. Fax: 239-695-3901.
Web Site: nps.gov/bicy
Founded: 1974.
Congressional District: 12, 19 & 16
Key Personnel: Supt., Pedro Ramos.
Governing Authority: federal. Parent Institution: National Park Services, Dept. of the Interior, Washington, DC.
National Park & Visitor Center.
Collections: archeological findings stored at the Southeast Archeological Center, Tallahassee, FL; 2,400 sq. miles consisting of sandy islands of slash pine; mixed hardwood hammocks; wet prairies; marshes; estuarine mangrove forests; airplants; bromeliads; orchids; animals in natural habitat.
Research Fields: natural sciences; south Florida environment.
Facilities: small resource library.
Hours & Admission Prices: Oasis Visitor Center: daily 9-4:30. No charge. Closed Christmas. ♿

Oldsmar

THE CENTER FOR CIVIL WAR PHOTOGRAPHY, (M), Oldsmar, FL 34677. Mailing Address: P.O. Box 1740, Oldsmar, FL 34677-1740. Tel.: 813-951-4962.
E-mail: info@civilwarphotography.org
Web Site: www.civilwarphotography.org
Founded: 1999.
Congressional District: 19
Key Personnel: Pres., Bob Zeller; Vice Pres., Garry Adelman; Treas., Sec. & Exec. Dir., Jennifer Kon; Dir., Justin A. Shaw; Dir. Devel., Charles Morrongiello; Dir. Imaging, John Richter.
Personnel Profile: Part-Time Paid 1; Part-Time Volunteers 6.
Governing Authority: private; nonprofit organization. Tax-exempt: 501(c)(3).
History Museum.
Collections: 1,000 negatives of Gettysburg Battlefield, 1930s-1950s; slide-mounted Civil War stereographs; Civil War books, artwork, video & audiotape; photographs.
Research Fields: Civil War photography.
Activities: school outreach program; lectures; temporary exhibitions; video & audiotape presentations. Annual Event: Civil War Photography Seminar in October.
Publications: semiannual newsletter, The Battlefield Photographer; 99 Historic Photographs of Culp's Hill; 99 Historic Images of Fredericksburg and Spotsylvania Civil War Sites; 99 Historic Images of Richmond Civil War Sites; 99 Historic Images of Civil War Washington; 99 Historic Images of Civil War Petersburg; 99 Historic Images of Harpers Ferry; 99 Historic Images of Civil War Charleston.
Membership: Student $25; Individual $35; Family $50; Ambrotype $100; Daguerrotype $250; Folio $500.

Olustee

OLUSTEE BATTLEFIELD HISTORIC STATE PARK, 5815 Battlefield Trail Rd., Olustee, FL 32072. Mailing Address: P.O. Box 40, Olustee, FL 32072-0040. Tel.: 386-758-0400.
E-mail: olusteecso@yahoo.com
Web Site: www.battleofolustee.org
Founded: 1909.
Key Personnel: Park Mgr., Benjamin Faure; Park Ranger, Francis J. Loughran.
Governing Authority: state. Dept. of Natural Resources, Div. of Recreation & Parks, 3900 Commonwealth Blvd., Commonwealth Bldg., Tallahassee, FL 32303.
State Historic Site & Military Museum.
Collections: military artifacts; battlefield monument.
Facilities: nature trails.
Activities: permanent exhibitions; interpretive programs.
Publications: brochures.
Hours & Admission Prices: Park: Daily: 8-5. Visitor Center: daily 9-5. No charge; donations accepted; (except for special events). Closed Thanksgiving; Christmas. ♿

Orange Park

MUSEUM OF GREAT CHRISTIAN PREACHERS & MINISTRIES, (M), 2941 Greenridge Rd., Orange Park, FL 32073-6411. Tel.: 904-375-0047.
Founded: 2000.
Key Personnel: Dir., Minister Donald L. Crutch; Chm. (V), Shaun Harper; Pres. (V), Lisa A. Crutch; Devel. & Cur., Samuel Alston; Education & Public Rels., Joni Meyers; Treas., Patricia A. Strader; Registrar & Museum Shop Mgr., Marcus Debnam.
Personnel Profile: Full-Time Paid 1; Full-Time Volunteers 6; Interns 2.
Governing Authority: private; nonprofit organization. Tax-exempt: 501(c)(3).
Religious Art Museum.
Collections: lives & travel of Christian leaders; wax figures of Christian leaders; photographs.
Research Fields: religions; Bible.
Activities: concerts. Annual Event: Gospel Music Concert.
Hours & Admission Prices: Oct.-Aug. Mon.-Fri. 10-6, Sat. 9-12. Adults $7, senior citizens, students & children $3. Closed New Year's Eve & Day; Martin Luther King Jr. Day; Lincoln's Birthday; Washington's Birthday; Good Friday; Memorial Day; Independence Day; Thanksgiving & day before; Christmas Eve & Day.
Attendance: 400

Orlando

ANITA S. WOOTEN GALLERY AT VALENCIA COMMUNITY COLLEGE EAST CAMPUS, 701 N. Econlockhatchee Trail, Orlando, FL 32825-6404. Mailing Address: P.O. Box 3028, Orlando, FL 32802-3028. Tel.: 407-582-2298. Fax: 407-582-8917.
Web Site: www.valenciacc.edu/gallery
Founded: 1967.
Congressional District: 5
Key Personnel: Dir., Jackie Otto-Miller.
Personnel Profile: Part-Time Paid 2.
Governing Authority: college. Parent Institution: Valencia Community College. Tax-exempt: 501(c)(3).
Art Museum.
Collections: contemporary art; Florida art; small works.
Facilities: 30-vol. library of artists books available for inter-library loan; educational facilities; 1,200 sq. ft. exhibit space.
Activities: guided tours; lectures; films; concerts; dance recitals; theatre; broadcast programs; organized education programs for adults & undergraduate or graduate college students; temporary, loan & traveling exhibitions. Museum Sponsors: Small Works Competition.
Publications: exhibition catalogs.
Hours & Admission Prices: Summer: Mon.-Thurs. 8:30-4:30, Fri. 8:30am-12pm; Winter: Mon.-Fri. 8:30-4:30. No charge. ♿
Attendance: 18,000 (estimated)

HARRY P. LEU GARDENS, 1920 N. Forest Ave., Orlando, FL 32803-1537. Tel.: 407-246-2620. Fax: 407-246-2849.
E-mail: rbowden@cityoforlando.net
Web Site: www.leugardens.org
Founded: 1961.
Key Personnel: Dir., Robert E. Bowden; Membership Coord., Lynn Williams; Mktg., Tracy Micciche; Museum Shop Mgr., Miriam Maldanado.
Personnel Profile: Full-Time Paid 20; Part-Time Paid 15; Part-Time Volunteers 200.
Governing Authority: municipal; board of trustees; nonprofit. Parent Institution: City of Orlando. Tax-exempt: 501(c)(3).
Botanical Garden.
Collections: camellias; roses; citrus; palms; cycads; bromeliads.
Facilities: library of horticulture books available to the public; classroom; lecture hall; meeting rooms; archives; herbarium. Museum-related items for sale.
Activities: concerts; docent program; formal educational programs; guided tours; hobby workshops; lectures. Annual Events: Spring & Fall Moonstrolls; International Christmas, plant sales, fall gardening festival.
Publications: quarterly newsletter, Garden View; quarterly class schedule, Leu Gardens Classes & Workshops.
Hours & Admission Prices: Daily 9-5. Adults $7, children grades K-12 $2; discounts to groups & American Horticultural Society; Mon., museum members & members of AABGA RAP program no charge. ♿
Attendance: 140,000 (accurate)
Membership: Individual $30; Family $35; Contributing $60; Sustaining $125; Orchid $300; Rose $500; Camellia $1,000.

MENNELLO MUSEUM OF AMERICAN ART, (M), 900 E. Princeton St., Orlando, FL 32803-1437. Tel.: 407-246-4278. Fax: 407-246-4329.
E-mail: mennellomuseum@cityoforlando.net
Web Site: www.mennellomuseum.com
Founded: 1998.
Congressional District: 8
Key Personnel: C.E.O., Frank Holt; Chm. (V), Lawrence Hefler; Pres. (V), John Rigsby; Office & Museum Shop Mgr., Kim Robinson.
Personnel Profile: Full-Time Paid 2; Part-Time Paid 3; Part-Time Volunteers 16; Interns 2.
Governing Authority: Parent Institution: City of Orlando. municipal; not-for-profit. Tax-exempt: 501(c)(3).
American Art Museum.
Collections: paintings by Earl Cunningham; American Folk art; early 20th-century paintings.
Major Exhibits: Ulysses Davis (T), 11/09-1/10; Regional Dialect (T), 11/09-2/7/10; Auspicious Vision (T), 2/10-5/10.
Research Fields: identification & research on American Folk artists; Earl Cunningham & early 20th century American modernism.
Facilities: library; 3,511 sq. ft. exhibit space; lakeside grounds. Museum-related items for sale.
Activities: docent program; guided tours; lectures; loan & traveling exhibitions.
Publications: member's newsletter; exhibit catalogs; American Folk Art Masters; Earl Cunningham: Dreams Realized.
Hours & Admission Prices: Tues.-Sat. 10:30-4:30, Sun. 12-4:30. Adults $4, seniors $3, students $1; discounts to AAM members; members & children under 12 no charge. Closed major holidays. ♿
Attendance: 18,000 (accurate)
Membership: Student & Senior $15; Individual $35; Family $50; Sponsor $100; Patron $500; Benefactor $1,000.

* **ORANGE COUNTY REGIONAL HISTORY CENTER, (M),** 65 E. Central Blvd., Orlando, FL 32801-2401. Tel.: 407-836-8500. Fax: 407-836-8550.
E-mail: sara.vanarsdel@ocfl.net
Web Site: www.thehistorycenter.org
Formerly: Orange County Historical Museum
Founded: 1957.
Congressional District: 5 & 9
Key Personnel: Exec. Dir., Sara Van Arsdel; Chm. (V), Alesandra Saunders; Pres. (V), Michael Crosbie; Museum Shop Mgr., Henry Nauman.
Personnel Profile: Full-Time Paid 29; Part-Time Paid 4; Part-Time Volunteers 125; Interns 5.
Governing Authority: county government. Parent Institution: Orange County Historical Society, Inc. Affiliated with the Board of County Commissioners. Subsidiary Institution: Historical Society of Central Florida, Inc. Tax-exempt: 501(c)(3).
Local Central Florida History & American History (12,000 years ago to the present).
Collections: permanent & special exhibits, tracing central Florida history; national & international exhibits on historical subjects; furniture collections; Indian artifacts; Seminoles; Pioneers; early Florida industries including: cattle, citrus, aviation, transportation & tourism; Heritage Square park & plaza; restored 1927 Courtroom B; community exhibits.
Major Exhibits: Out of This World: Extraordinary Costumes from Film & Television (T), 2/6/10-5/16/10; History of Harness Racing, 8/27/10-11/7/10.
Research Fields: Floridiana; oral history; citrus industry; tourism.
Facilities: 5,000-vol. library; theater; photo archives; old city directories; telephone books; maps; ledgers; scrapbooks; yearbooks; postcards; archival material.
Activities: educational programs for children, students & adults; rental facility; social events; seminars; lectures; family fun events; special exhibits; tours; hands-on activities; camps.

Publications: newsletter; brochures, educational pamphlets; quarterly magazine.
Hours & Admission Prices: Mon.-Sat. 10-5, Sun. 12-5. Adults $9, seniors 60 & over $7, children 3-12 $6; discounts to AAM members & Orange County employees; children under 3, members & regional Florida teachers no charge. Closed county holidays. ♿
Attendance: 100,000 (accurate)
Membership: Senior Citizen & Student $40; Individual $50; Senior Family $65; Family $75; Contributing Patron $125; Sustaining Patron $250; Director's Circle Patron $500; Special Patron $1,000; Legacy Patron $1,500; 1892 Cornerstone Patron $1,892; History Maker Patron $2,500.

* **ORLANDO MUSEUM OF ART, (M),** 2416 N. Mills Ave., Orlando, FL 32803-1483. Tel.: 407-896-4231. Fax: 407-896-9920.
E-mail: info@omart.org
Web Site: www.omart.org
Founded: 1924.
Congressional District: 8
Key Personnel: Exec. Dir., Marena Grant Morrisey; Chm. (V), Thomas P. Warlow, III; Pres. (V), Curtis B. McWilliams; C.F.O., Beryl H. Davis; Chief Operations, Alex Garcia; Public Rels. & Mktg. Mgr., Linda Cegelis; Cur. Education, Jane Ferry; Cur., Hansen Mulford; Museum Shop Mgr., Jamieson Thomas.
Personnel Profile: Full-Time Paid 25; Part-Time Paid 5; Part-Time Volunteers 739; Interns 5.
Governing Authority: nonprofit organization. Tax-exempt: 501(c)(3) & 170(b)(1)(A).
Art Museum.
Collections: American art; art of the ancient Americas; African art.
Major Exhibits: Nature and Spirit: American Landscape Painting from Florida Private Collections, 1/9/10-3/21/10; Without A Trace: Artists Imagine A World Without Us, 1/9/10-3/21/10; Transcending Vision: American Impressionism 1870-1940, Spring 2010 (T); Knuffle Funny: The Art and Whimsy of Mo Willems, Summer 2010 (T).
Research Fields: 18th-, 19th- & 20th-century American art; art of the Ancient Americas & African art.
Facilities: 2,500-vol. reference library; 250-seat auditorium; classrooms; meeting rooms.
Activities: guided tours; lectures; films; art classes; concerts; docent program; permanent & temporary exhibitions; school loan service; corporate lease program; facility rental program.
Publications: newsletters; exhibition catalogs; e-calendar.
Hours & Admission Prices: Tues.-Fri. 10-4, Sat.-Sun. 12-4. Adults $8, seniors 65 & over, college students, & military $7, children 4-17 $5; discount to groups of 10 or more; children 3 & under and members no charge. Closed national holidays. ♿
Membership: Student $40; Individual $55; Dual & Family $80; Contributing $125; Supporting $250; Sustaining $500; Ambassador $1,000-$25,000.

* **ORLANDO SCIENCE CENTER, INC.,** 777 E. Princeton St., Orlando, FL 32803-1291. Tel.: 407-514-2000. Fax: 407-514-2277.
E-mail: info@osc.org
Web Site: www.osc.org
Founded: 1959.
Congressional District: 8
Key Personnel: C.E.O. & Pres., Dr. Brian Tonner; Chm. (V), Theodore Bradford; Vice Pres. Finance & C.F.O., John Mallozzi; Vice Pres. & C.O.O., JoAnn Newman; Dir. Public Rels., Jeff Stanford; Vice Pres. Participant Experience, Kim Hunter.
Personnel Profile: Full-Time Paid 70; Part-Time Paid 50; Part-Time Volunteers 200; Interns 10.
Governing Authority: nonprofit organization. Tax-exempt: 501(c)(3) & 509(a).
Science & Technology Center.
Collections: interactive exhibits focusing on physical, natural, space & health sciences; applied technology-aerospace, lasers, simulation & entertainment; career; early childhood; CineDome: 15/70 film, Digistrar II planetarium; Observatory: 10-inch refractor telescope.
Research Fields: educational research; visitor studies.
Facilities: 300-seat combination Iwerks large film format theater & planetarium; astronomical observatory; meeting rooms; 250-seat theater; restaurant. Books, science games, educational & science-related items for sale.
Activities: classes & courses; volunteer training program; formally organized education programs for pre-K through undergraduate college students, teachers & adults; large-scale demonstrations & science theater; permanent & temporary exhibitions; planetarium shows; educational tours; workshop.
Publications: magazine, SCOPE.
Hours & Admission Prices: Thurs.-Tues. 10-5. Adults $17, students & seniors 55 & over $16, children 3-11 $12; discounts to active military, ASTC members, reciprocal participants & corporate sponsor employees; members no charge. Closed Thanksgiving; Christmas. ♿
Attendance: 390,000 (accurate)
Membership: Individual $80; Couple $95; Family $110.

RIPLEY'S BELIEVE IT OR NOT! MUSEUM, 8201 International Dr., Orlando, FL 32819-9326. Tel.: 407-363-4418 & 351-5803.
E-mail: museum@ripleysorlando.com
Web Site: www.ripleysorlando.com
General Museum.
Collections: antiquities & oddities from around the world; personal artifacts.
Facilities: Museum-related items for sale.
Activities: tours.
Hours & Admission Prices: Daily 9:30am to midnight. Adults $18.95, children 4-12 $11.95; discounts to groups of 15 or more.

TERRACE GALLERY-CITY OF ORLANDO, City Hall, 400 S. Orange Ave., Orlando, FL 32801-3360. Mailing Address: City Hall, P.O. Box 4990, Orlando, FL 32802-4990. Tel.: 407-246-4279. Fax: 407-246-3434.
E-mail: paul.wenzel@cityoforlando.net
Web Site: www.cityoforlando.net/arts
Founded: 1992.
Congressional District: 8
Key Personnel: Cur. & Public Art Coord., Paul F. Wenzel.
Personnel Profile: Full-Time Paid 2; Interns 1.
Governing Authority: municipal. Parent Institution: City of Orlando. Branch Gallery: Harry P. Leu Gardens, Garden House Gallery, 1920 N. Forest Ave., Orlando, FL. Tax-exempt: 501(c)(3).
Art Gallery.
Collections: contemporary Florida artists; 850 works in all media.
Research Fields: Florida art.
Facilities: 3,000 sq. ft. exhibit space.
Activities: guided tours; lectures; loan, temporary & traveling exhibitions.
Publications: exhibit catalogs.
Hours & Admission Prices: Terrace Gallery: Mon.-Fri. 8-9, Sat.-Sun. 12-5. No charge. Mayor's Gallery: Mon.-Fri. 8-5. No charge. Garden House Gallery: daily 9-5. Adults $5, children $1. ♿
Attendance: 35,000 (estimated)

UNIVERSITY OF CENTRAL FLORIDA ART GALLERY, Visual Arts Bldg. #51, Orlando, FL 32816-0001. Mailing Address: P.O. Box 161342, Orlando, FL 32816-1342. Tel.: 407-823-3161 & 2975. Fax: 407-823-6470.
E-mail: tlolz@mail.ucf.edu
Web Site: www.art.ucf.edu
Key Personnel: Dir., Theo Lotz; Asst. Dir., Janet Kilbride.
Governing Authority: public university.
Art Museum.
Collections: paintings; sculpture; photography.
Activities: guided tours; special events.
Hours & Admission Prices: Mon.-Fri. 9-5:30. No charge.

WYCLIFFE DISCOVERY CENTER, 11221 John Wycliffe Blvd., Orlando, FL 32832-7013. Mailing Address: P.O. Box 628200, Orlando, FL 32862-8200. Tel.: 407-852-3626. Fax: 407-852-3781.
Web Site: www.wycliffe.org/wordspring
Formerly: WordSpring Discovery Center
Founded: 2002.
Congressional District: 24
Key Personnel: Dir., Patricia Cox; Mgr. Events, Brian Shaffer; Mgr. Education Program, Dorcas Winfrey; Museum Shop Mgr., Tim Holloran.
Personnel Profile: Full-Time Paid 6; Part-Time Volunteers 8.
Governing Authority: private; nonprofit organization. Parent Institution: Wycliffe Bible Translators. Tax-exempt: 501(c)(3).
Religious Museum.
Collections: Bible translations; ethnic costumes from around the world; audio samples of the world's languages.
Research Fields: linguistics; literacy.
Facilities: 500-vol. library of Bibles in different languages; 5,300 sq. ft. exhibit space; auditorium; cafe; 35-seat theater. Museum-related items for sale.
Activities: films; guided tours; lectures; participatory exhibits; theater.
Hours & Admission Prices: Mon.-Fri. 9-4, Sat. & holidays call for hours. Adults $8, seniors $7, children grades 1-12 $6; discounts to groups; children under 5 no charge. ♿
Attendance: 15,000 (accurate)
Membership: Children $12; Senior $14; Adult $16.

Ormond Beach

ORMOND MEMORIAL ART MUSEUM & GARDEN, (M), 78 E. Granada Blvd., Ormond Beach, FL 32176-6534. Tel.: 386-676-3347. Fax: 386-676-3244.
E-mail: omam78e@aol.com

Web Site: www.ormondartmuseum.org
Founded: 1946.
Congressional District: 4
Key Personnel: Dir., Susan Tucker; Chm. (V) & Pres. (V), Theresa Gryer; Pres. (V), Mary Greenlees; Vice Pres., Patti Alexander; Treas., Alexis Lenssen; Cur. Education, Barbara Saunders; Cur. Education, Regina Stengel; Cur. Education, Linda King; Administrative Coord., Vanessa Elliott.
Personnel Profile: Full-Time Paid 3; Part-Time Paid 3; Part-Time Volunteers 110.
Governing Authority: private; nonprofit. Tax-exempt: 501(c)(3).
Art Museum & Botanical Garden: the museum is located in a four-acre botanical garden.
Collections: symbolic paintings by Malcolm Fraser.
Facilities: botanical garden; 4,500 sq. ft. exhibit space.
Activities: arts festivals; docent program; formal education program for children; guided tours; lectures; loan, temporary & traveling exhibitions. Annual Events: Starry Starry Night in January; holiday exhibitions & receptions; Presidents Day School Alternative in February.
Publications: quarterly newsletter.
Hours & Admission Prices: Mon.-Fri. 10-4, Sat.-Sun. 12-4. Donation: adults $2; discounts to AAM members; members, seniors 60 & over and children no charge. Closed New Year's Day; Good Friday; Easter; Memorial Day; Independence Day; Labor Day; Thanksgiving; Christmas. ♿
Attendance: 18,000 (estimated)
Membership: Retiree & Individual $25; Family $35. Heritage Club: Sponsor $85; Benefactor $150; Patron $500.

Osprey

* **HISTORIC SPANISH POINT,** 337 N. Tamiami Trail, Osprey, FL 34229-8911. Mailing Address: P.O. Box 846, Osprey, FL 34229-0846. Tel.: 941-966-5214. Fax: 941-966-1355.
E-mail: laura@historiespanishpoint.org
Web Site: historicspanishpoint.org
Founded: 1980.
Congressional District: 13
Key Personnel: C.E.O. & Exec. Dir., Linda W. Mansperger; Pres., Mary Gonter; Dir. Education, Mike Sprout; Cur., Hope Kocian; Site Horticulturist, Nancy Paul; Museum Shop Mgr., Tess Herschman.
Personnel Profile: Full-Time Paid 8; Part-Time Paid 4; Part-Time Volunteers 200.
Governing Authority: nonprofit organization. Parent Institution: Gulf Coast Heritage Association Inc. Tax-exempt: 501(c)(3).
Historic Site.
Collections: late 19th-century pioneer artifacts; prehistoric Indian artifacts; shell tools; pottery; textiles.
Research Fields: local & regional history; archaeology; environmental studies.
Facilities: visitors center, nature trails; 500 sq. ft. exhibit gallery space; pioneer buildings; archaeological exhibition; picnic area. Museum-related items for sale.
Activities: guided tours; lectures; organized education programs; docent program; temporary exhibitions.
Publications: quarterly newsletter, Vision.
Hours & Admission Prices: Mon.-Sat. 9-5, Sun. 12-5. Adults $9, children 6-12 $3; discounts to senior citizens on Mon., AAA & AAM members; children under 6, NARM & members no charge. Closed New Year's Day; Easter; Thanksgiving; Christmas. ♿
Attendance: 30,000 (estimated)
Membership: Individual $40; Family $65; Donor $125; Settler $250; Heritage Club $500 & up.

Palatka

RAVINE GARDENS STATE PARK, 1600 Twigg St., Palatka, FL 32177-5637. Tel.: 386-329-3721. Fax: 386-329-3718.
E-mail: donna.rhein@dep.state.fl.us
Web Site: www.floridastateparks.org/ravinegardens/default.cfm
Founded: 1933.
Key Personnel: Park Mgr., Nathan Sommons.
Personnel Profile: Full-Time Paid 10; Part-Time Paid 3; Part-Time Volunteers 12.
Governing Authority: state government. Tax-exempt.
Botanical Garden.
Collections: plants; flowers; trees.
Facilities: 240-seat auditorium; 4 meeting rooms.
Activities: guided tours; guided trail walks; garden tours; wagon tours.
Publications: Park & Trail Guides.
Hours & Admission Prices: Daily 8-sunset. Cars with up to 8 people $5, motorcycle & single occupant cars $4, bicycles & walk-ins $2; children under 6 no charge. Annual park passes available. ♿
Attendance: 145,963 (accurate)
Membership: The Friends of Ravine Gardens (CSO) Citizen Support Organization: Student $5; Individual $10; Family $20; Corporation $30.

Palm Beach

* **FLAGLER MUSEUM, (M), (I),** Cocoanut Row & Whitehall Way, Palm Beach, FL 33480. Mailing Address: P.O. Box 969, Palm Beach, FL 33480-0969. Tel.: 561-655-2833. Fax: 561-655-2826.
E-mail: mail@flaglermuseum.us
Web Site: www.flaglermuseum.us
Formerly: Henry Morrison Flagler Museum
Founded: 1959.
Congressional District: 14
Key Personnel: Exec. Dir., John Michael Blades; Business Mgr., Donovan Owen; Chief Cur., Tracy Kamerer; Dir. Visitor & Member Svcs., Sarah Brutschy; Dir. Public Affairs, David Carson; Chief Security, William Fallacaro; Facilities Mgr., John Gordon; Dir. Education, Allison Goff.
Personnel Profile: Full-Time Paid 37; Part-Time Paid 14; Part-Time Volunteers 90.
Governing Authority: nonprofit organization. Tax-exempt: 501(c)(3).
Historic House: Whitehall, 1902 Gilded Age estate of Henry Morrison Flagler.
Collections: furnishings original to Flagler's Gilded Age estate and other period objects.
Research Fields: America's Gilded Age; Henry Flagler's role in the development of Florida; Florida history.
Facilities: library available by application.
Activities: guided tours; lectures; concerts; docent program; permanent & temporary exhibitions; special events.
Publications: video, The Wilderness Shall Bloom; newsletter, Inside Whitehall; exhibit catalogues, Palm Beach Panorama; Henry M. Flagler's Paintings - The Taste of a Gilded Age Collector; Romance of the Season: Five Florida East Coast Hotel Novelettes from 1904 (facsimile reproduction); guidebook, Flagler Museum: An Illustrated Guide; exhibit catalogue, A Society of Painters: Flagler's St. Augustine Art Colony; exhibit catalogue, A Young Man's Legacy: Rare Photographs of the Titanic; video/DVD, Whitehall: A National Historic Landmark; exhibit catalogue, Tiffany at the World's Columbian Exposition.
Hours & Admission Prices: Tues.-Sat. 10-5, Sun. 12-5. Adults $15, youth 13-18 $8, children 6-12 $3; discount to groups & AAM members; members no charge. Closed New Year's Day; Thanksgiving; Christmas. ♿
Attendance: 85,000 (accurate)
Membership: Individual $75; Family $125; Sustaining $225; Sponsor $500; Patron $1,000 Benefactor $2,500; Associate $5,000.

* **THE SOCIETY OF THE FOUR ARTS,** 2 Four Arts Plaza, Palm Beach, FL 33480-4102. Tel.: 561-655-7227. Fax: 561-655-7233.
Web Site: www.fourarts.org
Founded: 1936.
Congressional District: 11
Key Personnel: Pres., Ervin S. Duggan; Chm. Bd., Mrs. F. Eugene Dixon, Jr.
Personnel Profile: Full-Time Paid 22; Part-Time Paid 5.
Governing Authority: corporation. Tax-exempt: 501(c)(3) & 170(b)(1)(A).
General Museum.
Collections: paintings; sculptures; Japanese & Chinese porcelain; Japanese & Chinese textiles; shells.
Major Exhibits: Florida's Wetlands, 12/09-11/10; Fashioning Kimono: Art Deco and Modernism in Japan (T), 12/5/09-1/10/10; The Grandeur of Americas Age of Sail: The Paintings of John Stobart (T), 1/23/10-2/10; Paintings from the Reign of Victoria: The Royal Holloway Collection, London (T), 3/13/10-4/18/10.
Research Fields: paintings; sculpture.
Facilities: 60,000-vol. library of general books available for inter-library loan & on premises; children's library; reading room; sculpture garden; botanical garden; 700-seat auditorium.
Activities: lectures; films; concerts; dance & opera; formally organized education programs for children; inter-museum loan & traveling exhibitions.
Publications: catalogs of exhibitions; triannual calendar; annual schedule of events.
Hours & Admission Prices: Gallery: Dec. to mid-April Mon.-Sat. 10-5, Sun. 2-5. Adults $5. Children's Library: May-Oct. Mon.-Fri. 10-5; Nov.-April Mon.-Fri. 10-5, Sat. 10-1. Adult Library: June-Oct. Mon.-Tues. & Thurs.-Fri. 10-5, Wed. 10-6; Nov.-May Mon.-Tues. & Thurs.-Fri. 10-5, Wed. 10-6, Sat. 10-3. Sculpture & Botanical Gardens: daily 10-5 (weather permitting). Met. Operas $22. Concerts: $35-$40. Films: $3; discounts to AAM members & groups; members no charge. Closed major holidays. ♿
Attendance: 96,572 (estimated)
Membership: Individual $1,000.

Palm Coast

FLORIDA AGRICULTURAL MUSEUM, 7900 Old Kings Rd., Palm Coast, FL 32137-8285. Tel.: 386-446-7630. Fax: 386-446-7631.
E-mail: famuseum@pcfl.net
Web Site: www.myagmuseum.com
Founded: 1983.
Congressional District: 7
Key Personnel: C.E.O., Bruce J. Piatek; Chm. (V), Tom Torrence; Trustee, Doyle Conner; Trustee, Ben Hill Griffin, III; Trustee, Brenda Tucker Boyd; Trustee, Michael Kenney; Trustee, William Livingston; Trustee, Louis Parrish; Trustee, Clark Bailey; Trustee, Frank Ford; Trustee, Rudy Bradley.
Personnel Profile: Full-Time Paid 3; Part-Time Paid 4; Part-Time Volunteers 45; Interns 2.
Governing Authority: public; nonprofit. Tax-exempt: 501(c)(3).
Agriculture Museum.
Collections: period artifacts; specimens; historical documents & heirlooms representing the history of Florida agriculture; heritage livestock breeds including endangered Florida Cracker horses and cattle. Historic Buildings: 1890s farmstead & outbuildings; 1900s dry goods store & commissary.
Research Fields: Florida agricultural history; Florida shortline railroads; rural Florida architecture & lifeways; heritage livestock breeds.
Facilities: 10,000-vol. library of historic & contemporary agriculture; 400 acres of grounds.
Activities: guided tours; lectures; monthly community projects.
Hours & Admission Prices: Wed.-Sun. 9-5. Adults $5, children $3; members no charge. ♿
Attendance: 20,000 (estimated)

THE LILLYWHITE FAMILY MUSEUM, (M), Nibliers Reach, Hammock Dunes, 4 Riviera Pl., Palm Coast, FL 32137-2270. Tel.: 386-446-3679. Fax: 386-446-3679.
E-mail: jwlillywhite@mac.com
Founded: 2007.
Congressional District: 7
Key Personnel: Dir. & Cur., John W. Lillywhite; Chm. (V), Elisabet G. Wauters-Lillywhite.
Personnel Profile: Full-Time Volunteers 2.
Governing Authority: private.
Family Sports History Museum.
Collections: family sports memorabilia; sporting goods; photographs; illustrations; ephemera; books; family business of manufacturing & retailing of sporting goods from 1844 to present.
Research Fields: life & times of the Victorian Lillywhite Family of sportsmen & business entrepreneurs.
Facilities: 300-vol. library; 300 sq. ft. exhibit space.
Activities: traveling exhibitions.
Hours & Admission Prices: Mon.-Fri. 9-1 by appointment only. No charge; donations accepted. Closed holidays.
Attendance: 300 (estimated)

WASHINGTON OAKS GARDENS STATE PARK, 6400 N. Ocean Shore Blvd., Palm Coast, FL 32137-2415. Tel.: 386-446-6780. Fax: 386-446-6781.
E-mail: matgeo@mail.state.fl.us
Web Site: www.floridastateparks.org/washingtonoaks
Founded: 1970.
Key Personnel: Park Mgr., Douglas Carter; Asst. Mgr., Renee Paolinc.
Personnel Profile: Full-Time Paid 10; Part-Time Paid 2; Part-Time Volunteers 10.
Governing Authority: state. Department of Environmental Protection, Commonwealth Bldg., 3900 Commonwealth Blvd., Tallahassee, FL 32303.
State Gardens.
Collections: botanical.
Publications: park brochures.
Hours & Admission Prices: Park: daily 8-sundown. Vehicle (up to 8 people) $5, Single Occupant Vehicle$4, Pedestrians & Bicyclists $1; children 5 & under no charge.

Palm Harbor

NORTH PINELLAS HISTORICAL MUSEUM, 2043 Curlew Rd., Palm Harbor, FL 34683-6820. Tel.: 727-724-3054.
Formerly: Palm Harbor Historical Museum
Founded: 1997.
Congressional District: 10
Key Personnel: Dir., Arlene Brandt.
Personnel Profile: Part-Time Volunteers 12.
Governing Authority: private; nonprofit organization. Parent Institution: Palm Harbor Historical Society, Inc. Tax-exempt: 501(c)(3).
History Museum.
Collections: local & regional history; photographs; audiovisuals; personal artifacts.
Facilities: library. Museum-related items for sale.
Activities: guided tours; temporary exhibitions; broadcast programs; luncheons for groups of 20 or more by appointment. Annual Events: Pioneer Days; English High Tea.
Hours & Admission Prices: Mon. & Sat. 10-4; groups of 10 or more by appointment. No charge; donations accepted. Closed New Year's Day; Thanksgiving; Christmas. ♿
Attendance: 900 (estimated)
Membership: Cracker Club (Grades 6-12) $5; Single $25; Family $40; Business $75.

Panama City

GULF COAST COMMUNITY COLLEGE ART GALLERY, 5230 W. Hwy. 98, Panama City, FL 32401-1058. Tel.: 850-872-3887. Fax: 850-872-3836.
E-mail: tmarinuzzi@gulfcoast.edu
Art Gallery.
Collections: paintings; sculpture; photographs.
Hours & Admission Prices: Mon.-Fri. 8-4. No charge.

THE JUNIOR MUSEUM OF BAY COUNTY, 1731 Jenks Ave., Panama City, FL 32405-4626. Tel.: 850-769-6128. Fax: 850-769-6129.
Web Site: www.jrmuseum.org
Founded: 1969.
Congressional District: 1
Key Personnel: Exec. Dir., Rae Cotton; Dir. Education, Mickey Busby; Admin., Sarah Sapp.
Personnel Profile: Full-Time Paid 4; Part-Time Paid 2; Part-Time Volunteers 120.
Governing Authority: nonprofit organization. Tax-exempt: 501(c)(3).
Children's Museum.
Collections: pioneer Florida log structures; grist mill; Bay County historical material; agriculture implements; nature trail; science & nature hands-on exhibits.
Research Fields: local history; natural sciences.
Facilities: 80-seat auditorium; classrooms; nature trail. Museum-related items for sale.
Activities: self-guided tours; children summer classes; weekend programs; permanent & temporary exhibits.
Publications: brochures; newsletter, The Adventures.
Hours & Admission Prices: Mon.-Fri. 10-5, Sat. 10-4. Adults $5; discounts to groups & military; teachers & members no charge. Closed major holidays. ♿
Attendance: 27,000 (accurate)
Membership: Individual $35; Family & Grandparents $60; Enhanced Family $125; Patron $250; Benefactor $500; Sustaining $1,000.

VISUAL ARTS CENTER OF NORTHWEST FLORIDA, 19 E. 4th St., Panama City, FL 32401-3106. Tel.: 850-769-4451. Fax: 850-785-9248.
E-mail: visualartscenterofnwfla@comcast.net
Web Site: www.vac.org.cn
Founded: 1988.
Key Personnel: Exec. Dir., Ellen Killough; Operations Mgr., Stacey Dyer; Exhibits & Education, Jayson Kretzer; Volunteer Coord., Bonnie Rodenburg.
Personnel Profile: Full-Time Paid 2; Part-Time Paid 2; Part-Time Volunteers 36.
Governing Authority: nonprofit organization. Parent Institution: Panama Art Association. Tax-exempt: 501(c)(3).
Art Gallery; 1925 former city courthouse, jail & fire station.
Collections: permanent collections focus on artists of northwest Florida; paintings in watercolor, oil, acrylics, pen & ink; drawings; photographs; sculpture.
Facilities: large main gallery; smaller Higby gallery; art studios; children's hands-on interactive gallery. Museum-related items for sale.
Activities: lecture series; workshops; tours.
Publications: newsletter, Images.
Hours & Admission Prices: Tues. & Thurs. 10-8, Wed. & Fri.-Sat. 10-6, Sun. 1-5. No charge; donations accepted. Closed New Year's Eve & Day; Christmas. ♿
Attendance: 10,078 (accurate)
Membership: Student, Senior Citizen 55 & over and Educator $15; Senior Couple 55 & over $25; Individual $35; Family $60; Group (10 or more) $75; O'Keefe $100l; Picasso $250; Monet $500; Renoir $1,000; Van Gogh $2,500; Rembrandt $5,000; Michelangelo $10,000.

Panama City Beach

MAN IN THE SEA MUSEUM, 17314 Panama City Beach Pkwy., Panama City Beach, FL 32413-6038. Tel.: 850-235-4101. Fax: 850-235-4101.
E-mail: momits@bellsouth.net
Web Site: www.maninthesea.org
Formerly: The Museum of Man In the Sea, Inc.
Founded: 1980.
Congressional District: 1
Key Personnel: Mgr., Leslie Baker; Pres. (V), Michael A. Zinszer; Education & Museum Shop Mgr., Sarah Hough.
Personnel Profile: Full-Time Paid 2; Part-Time Paid 1; Part-Time Volunteers 36.
Governing Authority: not-for-profit organization. Parent Institution: Institute of Diving, Inc., 17413 Panama City Beach Pkwy., Panama City Beach, FL 32413. Tax-exempt: 501(c)(3).
History & Science Museum.
Collections: how man can live, work & play underwater; SCUBA; commercial & military diving equipment; underwater habitats; diving bells; submersibles; armored diving suits; recreational diving equipment; history of diving.
Research Fields: commercial; military & recreational diving equipment; underwater habitats; artificial reefs; marine pollution; marine archaeology; history of diving.
Facilities: 300-vol. library. Books, jewelry & T-shirts for sale.
Activities: guided tours; lectures; loan & participatory exhibits; school loan service.
Publications: quarterly, Institute of Diving Newsletter.
Hours & Admission Prices: Tues.-Sun. 10-4. Admission $5; members & children under 6 no charge. Closed New Year's Day; Thanksgiving; Christmas. ♿
Attendance: 30,080 (accurate)
Membership: Annual $35; Three-Year Individual $90; Lifetime $1,000.

Parrish

FLORIDA RAILROAD MUSEUM, INC., U.S. 301, 12210 83rd St. E., Parrish, FL 34219. Mailing Address: P.O. Box 355, Parrish, FL 34219-0355. Tel.: 877-869-0800. Fax: 941-917-0081.
Web Site: www.frrm.org
Formerly: Florida Gulf Coast Railroad Museum
Founded: 1983.
Congressional District: 11
Key Personnel: Pres. (V), Steven Wonderly; Sec., Dr. Edward Dunham; Treas., William Maddock.
Personnel Profile: Full-Time Paid 1; Full-Time Volunteers 30; Part-Time Volunteers 30; Interns 5.
Governing Authority: board of directors. Tax-exempt.
Railroad Museum.
Collections: concentration on railroad history from 1890s to present with emphasis on Florida railroad history & the economic history of the railroad industry; steam engine #12; operating railroad.
Research Fields: economic impact of the railroads on Florida history.
Activities: guided tours; docent program; formal education program for adults; operation of a branch line passenger train. Annual Events: WWII & Civil War Reenactments; Halloween specials; Hole in Head Gang Train Robbers; Christmas Train.
Publications: members newsletter, Tracks.
Hours & Admission Prices: Train rides: Sat.-Sun. 11 & 2. Adults $12, children $8, extra charge for special events, please visit website for special event dates; members no charge. Closed New Year's Day; Christmas.
Attendance: 45,000 (estimated)
Membership: Individual $30; Family $100; Sustaining $500; Trainmaster $1,000.

Pembroke Pines

THE ART GALLERY, BROWARD COMMUNITY COLLEGE SOUTH CAMPUS, 7200 Hollywood Blvd., Pembroke Pines, FL 33024-7225. Tel.: 954-210-8895. Fax: 954-201-8934.
E-mail: kbelan@broward.edu
Web Site: www.broward.edu/locations/south/artgallery
Key Personnel: Dir., Dr. Kyra Belan
Art Gallery.
Collections: paintings; photographs; sculpture.
Hours & Admission Prices: Mon.-Fri. 10-2. No charge.

Pensacola

ANNA LAMAR SWITZER CENTER FOR VISUAL ARTS, Pensacola Junior College, 1000 College Blvd., Pensacola, FL 32504-8910. Tel.: 850-484-2554 & 2550. Fax: 850-484-2564.
E-mail: vspencer@pjc.edu
Web Site: www.pjc.edu/visarts
Formerly: Visual Arts Gallery
Founded: 1970.
Congressional District: 3
Key Personnel: Dir., Vivian Spencer.
Personnel Profile: Full-Time Paid 2; Part-Time Paid 6; Interns 7.
Governing Authority: college. Parent Institution: Pensacola Junior College. Tax-exempt.
College Art Museum.
Collections: contemporary drawings; prints; paintings; photography; crafts; sculpture.
Major Exhibits: PJC Art Faculty, 11/09-12/11/09; Jing Zhou, Switzer Distinguished Artist, 1/25/10-3/12/10; Art Student Honors Exhibition, 4/5/10-5/3/10; Best of the Coast - Local Artist Series Pat Regan Retrospective, 5/25/10-7/22/10; Green Light: A Juried Exhibition of Emerging Artists with Disabilities, 5/25/10-7/22/10.
Facilities: studio complex.
Activities: guided tours; formally organized education programs for college students; loan & temporary exhibitions.
Publications: brochures; catalogs; announcements; posters.
Hours & Admission Prices: Sept.-May Mon.-Thurs. 8-9, Fri. 8-3:30, Sat. 9-3. No charge. Closed holidays. ♿
Attendance: 28,000 (accurate)

HISTORIC PENSACOLA VILLAGE, 120 Church St., Pensacola, FL 32502-5941. Mailing Address: P.O. Box 12866, Pensacola, FL 32591-2866. Tel.: 850-595-5985, ext. 100. Fax: 850-595-5989.
E-mail: rbrosnaham@uwf.edu
Web Site: www.historicpensacola.org
Founded: 1967.
Congressional District: 1
Key Personnel: Exec. Dir., Richard Brosnaham; Chm. (V), J. Earle Bowden; Assoc. Dir., Robert Overton; Special Events Coord., Casey Campbell; Chief Cur., B. Lynne Robertson; Registrar, Carolyn Prime; Archivist, Jacquelyn Wilson; Dir. Education, Dena Bush; Educator, Sheyna Priest; Cur. Exhibits, Gale Messerschmidt; Living History Program, Jim McMillen; Museum Shop Mgr., Wendi Davis.
Personnel Profile: Full-Time Paid 16; Part-Time Paid 8; Part-Time Volunteers 60; Interns 2.
Governing Authority: Parent Institution: University of West Florida, West Florida Historic Preservation, Inc. Subsidiary Institution: T.T. Wentworth Jr., FL State Museum. Tax-exempt: 501(c)(3).
Historic Houses & Buildings.
Collections: T.T. Wentworth Jr. collection of 150,000 Southeastern U.S. historical artifacts and archives, primarily 19th & 20th century: paintings, lithographs, photographs, documents, weapons, hardware, household items, furniture, textiles, farming equipment, broadsides and newspapers, transportation vehicles; marine artifacts; archaeology; doll houses; local Civil War artifacts & documents. Historic Houses: 1803 Lavalle House; 1805 Julee Cottage; 1810 Walton House; 1879 Moreno Cottage; 1871 Dorr House; c.1835 Barkley House; 1903 L & N Marine Terminal; 1930 Piney Woods sawmill; 1888 Christ Church parish school; 1888 Lear house; 1832 Old Christ Church; 1876 Pfeiffer house; 1870 & 1890 warehouses (museums of commerce & industry); 1888 Manuel Barrios Cottage; 1880 McMillan House; 1885 Shotgun House.
Research Fields: regional historical, architectural & archaeological research; maritime & industrial history.
Facilities: 1,500-vol. research library; 50,000 sq. ft. exhibit space in eleven museum buildings; archives.
Activities: guided tours; inter-museum loan, permanent & temporary exhibitions; living history program.
Publications: quarterly newsletter; monthly calendar of living history demonstrations & events.
Hours & Admission Prices: Village: Tues.-Sat. 10-4. Adults $6, children $3; discounts to senior citizens, groups over 20 & military personnel; AAM, ICOM & museum members no charge. T.T. Wentworth, Jr. Florida State Museum: Mon.-Sat. 10-4. No charge. Closed New Year's Day; Martin Luther King Jr. Day; Memorial Day; Independence Day; Labor Day; Veterans Day; Thanksgiving & day after; Christmas. ♿
Attendance: 100,000 (estimated)
Membership: Student $20; Individual $35; Couple $45; Family $60; Patron $100; Supporter $250; Grand Benefactor $500.

* **NATIONAL NAVAL AVIATION MUSEUM,** 1750 Radford Blvd., Ste. C, Pensacola, FL 32508-5402. Tel.: 850-452-3604. Fax: 850-452-3296.
E-mail: museuminfo.navalaviation@mchsi.com
Web Site: navalaviationmuseum.org
Founded: 1963.
Congressional District: 1
Key Personnel: Dir., Capt. Robert Rasmussen, USN (Ret); Found. Pres. & C.E.O., VADM (Ret) G.L. Hoewing, USN (Ret); Admin., David Darville; Dir. Mktg., Shelley Ragsdale; Flight Deck Museum Shop Mgr., Pat Hickman; Deputy Dir. & Cur., Robert Macon; Education Coord., Sam Shilling; IMAX Operations, Fred Geiger; C.F.O., Steve Flint; MIS, Gary Petersen.
Personnel Profile: Full-Time Paid 30; Part-Time Volunteers 405.
Governing Authority: federal government. Tax-exempt: 501(c)(3).
Naval Aviation Museum.
Collections: history of naval aviation depicted by photographs, charts, diagrams, artifacts, scale models. More than 150 full size aircraft, models & aviation art trace the history of naval aviation from the dawn of flight to the exploration of space.
Research Fields: aeronautics.
Facilities: Naval aviation research library; cafe. Museum-related items for sale.
Activities: guided tours; historical movies; audiovisual exhibits; permanent & temporary exhibitions; IMAX; flight simulators; flight adventure deck.
Publications: exhibit & program brochures; Foundation magazine; newsletter, Fly By.
Hours & Admission Prices: Daily 9-5. No charge; donations accepted. Closed New Year's Day; Thanksgiving; Christmas. ♿
Attendance: 717,649 (accurate)
Membership: One Year $35; Two Year $65; Three Year $90; Benefactor's Circle (Lifetime) $1,000.

PENSACOLA HISTORICAL SOCIETY, 110 Church St., Pensacola, FL 32502-5962. Mailing Address: P.O. Box 12866, Pensacola, FL 32591. Tel.: 850-595-5840. Fax: 850-595-5842.
E-mail: rbrosnaham@uwf.edu
Web Site: www.pensacolahistory.org
Founded: 1933.
Congressional District: 1
Key Personnel: Exec. Dir., Richard Brosnaham; Chm. (V), J. Earle Bowden; Assoc. Dir., Robert Overton; Facilities Mgr., Pat Paterson; Chief Cur., B. Lynne Robertson; Registrar, Carolyn Prime; Archivist, Jacki Wilson.
Personnel Profile: Full-Time Paid 16; Part-Time Paid 2; Part-Time Volunteers 30; Interns 2.
Governing Authority: Parent Institution: West Florida Historic Preservation, Inc. Tax-exempt: 501(c)(3).
History Museum: housed in historic Arbona Building.
Collections: clothing; local family silver; 19th-century men's & women's accessories; American Indian artifacts; local bottles; 19th-century household items; Viola A. Blount fine art glass; the Carpenter glass negative collection; Escambia County & Pensacola history including archaeological materials; library collection: Indian, maritime, multicultural & military themes; manuscripts.
Research Fields: history of Pensacola, Escambia County & northwest Florida; history & genealogy of inhabitants; history of 19th-century businesses; area brick manufacture 18th-20th centuries.
Facilities: 2,000-vol. library of material relevant to the history of Pensacola, Escambia County & extreme northwest Florida; technical reference section; oral history section; microfilm; microfiche; tape recordings; 1780-1910 censuses; reading area; 60,000 photographs & negatives. Library relocated to 110 E. Church St., Pensacola. Books, publications, postcards, stationery & map reprints for sale.
Activities: guided tours; lectures; films; TV programs; educational programs.
Publications: booklets; magazine, Pensacola History Illustrated; monthly newsletter, Pensacola History Today; educational sheets for elementary & middle school level.
Hours & Admission Prices: Tues.-Thurs. 10-4, Sat. 10-3. Research & Library: $5; members no charge. Closed state & university holidays. ♿
Attendance: 15,000 (estimated)
Membership: Student $10; Individual $40; Family $55; Sustaining $100; Business & Patron $250.

* **PENSACOLA MUSEUM OF ART,** 407 S. Jefferson St., Pensacola, FL 32502-5901. Tel.: 850-432-6247. Fax: 850-469-1532.
E-mail: info@pensacolamuseumofart.org
Web Site: www.pensacolamuseumofart.org
Founded: 1954.
Congressional District: 1
Key Personnel: Exec. Dir., Sonya Davis; Pres. (V), David Bear; Exec. Asst. & Coord. Membership, Kate Moloney; Assoc. Cur., Leah Griffin; Coord. Education, Patrick Jennings; Coord. Devel., Kate Sutley; Registrar & Preparator, Nick Christopher; Media Coord., Stephanie Kress.
Personnel Profile: Full-Time Paid 6; Part-Time Paid 2; Part-Time Volunteers 120.
Governing Authority: Pensacola Museum of Art, Inc. Tax-exempt: 501(c)(3).
Art Museum: housed in 1908 old city jail.
Collections: glass, paintings & graphics with emphasis on American contemporary artists.
Facilities: 1,500-vol. library of art reference material available for inter-library loan or use by responsible persons or any institution; 100-seat auditorium; classrooms. Museum-related items for sale.
Activities: guided tours; lectures; films; formally organized educational programs; loan, permanent & traveling exhibitions.
Publications: newsletter; catalogues for major exhibitions.
Hours & Admission Prices: Tues.-Fri. 10-5, Sat.-Sun. 12-5. Adults $5, students $2; children 5 & under, Tues., and members no charge. Closed national holidays. ♿
Attendance: 75,000 (accurate)
Membership: Student $15; Individual $40; Family $75; Sustaining $250; Patron $500; Benefactor $1,000; Corporate $250-$10,000.

T.T. WENTWORTH, JR. FLORIDA STATE MUSEUM, 330 S. Jefferson St., Pensacola, FL 32502-5943. Mailing Address: P.O. Box 12866, Pensacola, FL 32591-2866. Tel.: 850-595-5985, ext. 100. Fax: 850-595-5989.
E-mail: rbrosnaham@uwf.edu
Web Site: www.historicpensacola.org
Founded: 1988.
Congressional District: 1
Key Personnel: Exec. Dir., Richard Brosnaham; Chm. (V), J. Earle Bowden; Assoc. Dir., Robert Overton; Registrar, Carolyn Prime; Museum Educator, Dena Bush; Chief Cur., B. Lynne Robertson; Cur. Exhibits, Gale Messerschmidt.
Personnel Profile: Full-Time Paid 16; Part-Time Paid 8; Part-Time Volunteers 60; Interns 2.
Governing Authority: Parent Institution: University of West Florida, West Florida Historic Preservation, Inc., Pensacola, Fl. Subsidiary Institution: Historic Pensacola Village, Pensacola, Fl. Tax-exempt: 501(c)(3).
Historic Building: housed in the former Pensacola City Hall building.
Collections: period artifacts; photographs; artifacts from local land & underwater sites.
Research Fields: local & regional history.
Facilities: 1,500-vol. library; 7,000 sq. ft. exhibit space; archives.
Activities: formal education programs for University of West Florida students; guided tours; inter-museum loan, participatory & temporary exhibitions. Annual Event: Open House in June.
Publications: quarterly newsletter; monthly calendar.
Hours & Admission Prices: Mon.-Sat. 10-4. No charge; donations accepted. Closed New Year's Day; Martin Luther King Jr. Day; Memorial Day; Independence Day; Labor Day; Veterans Day; Thanksgiving & day after; Christmas. ♿
Attendance: 100,000 (estimated)
Membership: Student $20; Individual $35; Couple $45; Family $60; Patron $100; Supporter $250; Grand Benefactor $500.

UNIVERSITY OF WEST FLORIDA ART GALLERY, 11000 University Pkwy., Bldg. 82, Pensacola, FL 32514-5750. Tel.: 850-474-2696. Fax: 850-474-2043.
E-mail: artgallery@uwf.edu
Web Site: uwf.edu/art
Founded: 1970.
Congressional District: 1
Key Personnel: Gallery Dir., Holly Collins.
Personnel Profile: Full-Time Paid 1; Part-Time Paid 1; Part-Time Volunteers 6; Interns 5.
Governing Authority: university; state. Parent Institution: University of West Florida. Tax-exempt.
University Art Gallery.
Collections: contemporary paintings; photographs.
Activities: guided tours; visiting artists & scholar's lecture series; films; gallery talks; concerts; loan, curated, temporary & traveling exhibitions.
Publications: catalogues; flyers; posters.
Hours & Admission Prices: Mon.-Fri. 10-5, during school year. No charge. Closed Easter; Memorial Day; Independence Day; Veterans Day; Thanksgiving. ♿
Attendance: 14,000 (accurate)

WEST FLORIDA HISTORIC PRESERVATION, INC., (M), 120 Church St., Pensacola, FL 32502-5941. Mailing Address: P.O. Box 12866, Pensacola, FL 32591-2866. Tel.: 850-595-5985. Fax: 850-595-5989.
E-mail: rbrosnaham@uwf.edu
Web Site: www.historicpensacola.org
Founded: 1967.
Congressional District: 1
Key Personnel: Dir., Richard Brosnaham; Chm. (V), J. Earle Bowden; Museum Shop Mgr., Wendi Davis; Assoc. Dir., Robert Overton; Facilities Mgr., Pat Paterson; Chief Cur., B. Lynne Robertson; Cur. Exhibits, Gale Messerschmidt; Registrar, Carolyn Prime; Dir. Education, Dena Bush; Archivist, Jacquelyn Wilson; Museum Educator, Sheyna Priest; Living History Program, Jim McMillen; Coord. Special Events, Casey Campbell.
Personnel Profile: Full-Time Paid 18; Part-Time Paid 10; Part-Time Volunteers 60; Interns 2.
Governing Authority: Parent Institution: University of West Florida. Subsidiary Institution: Pensacola Historical Society. Branch Museums: Historic Pensacola Village; T.T. Wentworth, Jr. Florida State Museum; Arcadia Mill Archaeological Site, Milton, FL. Tax-exempt: 501(c)(3).
Preservation Society.
Collections: archives; local history; photographs.
Research Fields: local & regional history; genealogy.
Activities: research; permanent & temporary exhibits; formal education programs for Univ. of West FL students; guided tours; rental facilities; lecture series.
Publications: monthly calendar; quarterly newsletter.
Hours & Admission Prices: Offices & Archives: Mon.-Fri. 8-4:30. Research: Tues.-Fri. by appointment. Research: $5 per day; discounts to AAM & ICOM members. Closed New Year's Eve & Day; Martin Luther King Jr. Day; Memorial Day; Independence Day; Labor Day; Veterans Day; Thanksgiving & day after; Christmas Eve, Day & week. ♿
Attendance: 100,000 (estimated)
Membership: Student, Senior, & Out of Town $20; Individual $35; Couple $45; Family $60; Patron $100; Supporter $250; Grand Benefactor $500. Time only members: 80 hrs volunteer time annually.

Perry

FOREST CAPITAL STATE MUSEUM, S. U.S. Hwy. 19, 204 Forest Park Dr, Perry, FL 32348-6320. Tel.: 850-584-3227. Fax: 850-584-3488.
Web Site: www.floridastateparks.org
Founded: 1973.
Key Personnel: Park Ranger, Jim Greist.
Personnel Profile: Full-Time Paid 1; Part-Time Paid 2.
Governing Authority: state. Tax-exempt: 47-04-023952-52C/2.
Logging & Lumber Museum: Timber Industry Museum & Forestry including c.1865 Pioneer-Cracker Homestead.
Collections: exhibits interpreting turpentine production, virgin forest cutting, modern forest practices; indigenous tree species; turn-of-the-century furnishings; turn-of-the-century interpretive homestead area.
Facilities: picnic area.
Activities: guided tours. Museum Sponsors: Florida Forest Festival in October.
Publications: State Parks Guide.
Hours & Admission Prices: Thurs.-Mon. 9-5. Adults $2; children 5 & under & Florida public school groups no charge. Closed New Year's Day; Thanksgiving; Christmas. ♿
Attendance: 7,000 (estimated)

Pine Island Center

MUSEUM OF THE ISLANDS, 5728 Sesame, Pine Island Center, FL 33956. Mailing Address: P.O. Box 305, Saint James City, FL 33956-0305. Tel.: 239-283-1525.
E-mail: info@museumoftheislands.com
Web Site: www.museumoftheislands.com
Founded: 1990.
Congressional District: 14
Key Personnel: Pres. (V), Sharon Traylor; Museum Shop Mgr., Barbara "Bobbie" Mahaffey.
Personnel Profile: Part-Time Volunteers 20.
Governing Authority: Tax-exempt.
General Museum.
Collections: Pine Island history; seashells; photographs; portraits; dolls; period household artifacts; fishing gear.
Hours & Admission Prices: May-Oct. Tues., Thurs. & Sat. 11-3; Nov.-April Tues.-Sat. 11-3, Sun. 1-4; groups by appointment. Adults $2, children $1. Closed Easter; Thanksgiving; Christmas. ♿
Attendance: 8,000 (estimated)
Membership: Individual $10; Family $15; Club $25; Sponsor $50; Life $100.

Plant City

DINOSAUR WORLD, 5145 Harvey Tew Rd., Plant City, FL 33565. Tel.: 813-717-9865. Fax: 813-707-9776.
Natural History Museum.
Collections: over 150 life size dinosaurs; dinosaur eggs; raptor claws.
Facilities: theatre; picnic area. Museum-related items for sale.
Activities: educational programs; classes; fossil dig; outreach programs; scout programs; special events; birthday parties.
Hours & Admission Prices: Feb.-Nov. daily 9-6; Dec.-Jan. daily 9-5. Adults $12.75, seniors over 60 $10.75, children 3-12 $9.75; discounts to groups & military dependents; active military no charge.

EAST HILLSBOROUGH HISTORICAL SOCIETY, INC., 605 N. Collins St., Plant City, FL 33563-3321. Tel.: 813-757-9226.
Formerly: 1914 Plant City High School Community Center
Founded: 1974.
Key Personnel: Pres. (V) & Archivist, Shelby Bender; Vice Pres., Roberta Jordan.
Personnel Profile: Part-Time Paid 2; Part-Time Volunteers 20.
Governing Authority: private; nonprofit organization. Tax-exempt: 501(c)(3).
Pioneer Heritage Museum: housed in c.1914 high school bldg.
Collections: local pioneer family artifacts.
Facilities: 1,000-vol. library; 500-seat auditorium; 8,500 sq. ft. exhibit space.
Activities: formal education programs for adults; guided tours; hobby workshops; genealogical workshops. Annual Events: Pioneer Day; Christmas Candlelight Tour of Homes in Historic District.
Hours & Admission Prices: Pioneer Museum: call for hours. Quintilla Geer Bruton Archives Center: Tues. 10-5, Wed.-Sat. 1-5, evenings by appointment. No charge; donations accepted. ♿
Attendance: 10,000 (estimated)
Membership: Individual $15; Family & Business $25; Lifetime $100; Patron $1,000.

Plantation

PLANTATION HISTORICAL MUSEUM, 511 N. Fig Tree Lane, Plantation, FL 33317-1849. Tel.: 954-797-2722. Fax: 954-797-2717.
E-mail: museum511@aol.com
Web Site: www.plantation.org/Museum/index.html
Founded: 1975.
Congressional District: 20
Key Personnel: Cur., Shirley Schuler; Office Mgr., Rosemary Schafer; Facility Attendant, Sandy Franz.
Personnel Profile: Part-Time Paid 3; Part-Time Volunteers 15.
Governing Authority: municipal; society; nonprofit organization. Parent Institution: City of Plantation, FL. Tax-exempt: 501(c)(3).
Local History Museum.
Collections: 20th century artifacts; fire-fighting equipment; 1956 GMC front-end pumper Fire Engine No. 1; 1957 Fire Engine No. 1.
Facilities: Locally handmade items for sale.
Activities: guided tours; hobby workshops; temporary & traveling exhibitions; oral history program of pioneer residents.
Publications: monthly newsletter; city quarterly; county quarterly.
Hours & Admission Prices: Tues. & Thurs.-Sat. 9-12 & 1-4, Wed. 1-4; groups by appointment. No charge; donations accepted. Closed national holidays. ♿
Attendance: 12,000 (estimated)
Membership: Individual $15; Family $25; Life $150.

SCHACKNOW MUSEUM OF FINE ARTS, (M), 7080 Northwest 4th St., Plantation, FL 33317-2201. Tel.: 954-583-5551. Fax: 954-583-5557.
Web Site: www.smofa.com/
Founded: 2000.
Key Personnel: Founder & Dir., Max Schacknow
Art Museum.
Collections: paintings; photography; sculpture.
Hours & Admission Prices: Tues.-Sat. 10-5. Adults $5, seniors & children over 12 $3; members no charge. ♿
Membership: Individual $75; Couple $95; 4 or More $100.

Point Washington

EDEN STATE GARDENS AND MANSION, County Rd. 395, Point Washington, FL 32459. Mailing Address: 181 Eden Garden Rd., Point Washington, FL 32459-5973. Tel.: 850-231-4214.
Historic House: housed in the former home of William Henry Wesley, founder of a timber company; built in 1890.
Collections: family & local history; period artifacts; Louis XVI furniture; personal artifacts; photographs; gardens.
Facilities: rental facilities; gardens. Museum-related items for sale.

Activities: rental facilities.
Hours & Admission Prices: Tours: Thurs.-Mon.

Polk City

AMERICAN WATER SKI EDUCATIONAL FOUNDATION, 1251 Holy Cow Rd., Polk City, FL 33868-8200. Tel.: 863-324-2472. Fax: 863-324-3996.
E-mail: awsefhalloffame@cs.com
Web Site: waterskihalloffame.com
Founded: 1968.
Key Personnel: Exec. Dir., Carole Lowe; Chm., Jim Grew; Pres., Robert Reich; Treas., Mark Harvat.
Personnel Profile: Full-Time Paid 1.
Governing Authority: nonprofit organization. Subsidiary Museum: Water Ski Museum & Hall of Fame, Polk City, FL. Tax-exempt: 501(c)(3).
Sports Museum.
Collections: first water skis, 1922; show ski costumes; water ski ropes & handles; photographs; archives; memorabilia.
Facilities: library; resource center.
Activities: films; formal education programs; participatory exhibits; annual ceremony.
Publications: newsletter, Water Ski Hall of Fame.
Hours & Admission Prices: Mon.-Fri. 10-5. Adults $5, seniors $4, children 6-12 $3; discounts to AAM members; children 5 & under no charge. Closed New Year's Day; Martin Luther King Jr. Day; Memorial Day; Independence Day; Thanksgiving; Christmas. ♿
Attendance: 10,000 (estimated)
Membership: Regular $25; Supporting $100; Sponsor $250; Patron $500; Benefactor $1,000; Founder $50,000.

FANTASY OF FLIGHT, 1400 Broadway Blvd., S.E., Polk City, FL 33868-9109. Tel.: 863-984-3500.
Web Site: www.fantasyofflight.com
Key Personnel: Owner, Kermit Weeks
Aircraft Museum.
Collections: aircraft from early flight to 1950s.
Facilities: Museum-related items for sale.
Activities: biplane & hot air balloon rides.
Hours & Admission Prices: Daily 10-5. Adults $28.95, children 6-15 $14.95; discounts to groups & military; children 4 & under no charge. Closed Thanksgiving; Christmas.

Ponce Inlet

PONCE DELEON INLET LIGHTHOUSE PRESERVATION ASSOCIATION, INC., (M), 4931 S. Peninsula Dr., Ponce Inlet, FL 32127-7301. Tel.: 386-761-1821. Fax: 386-761-3121.
E-mail: lighthouse@ponceinlet.org
Web Site: www.ponceinlet.org
Founded: 1972.
Congressional District: 4
Key Personnel: Exec. Dir., Ed Gunn; Pres. (V), Robyn Hurd; Dir. Operations, Mike Bennett; Cur., Ellen Henry; Program Mgr., Bob Callister.
Personnel Profile: Full-Time Paid 11; Part-Time Paid 16; Part-Time Volunteers 31.
Governing Authority: nonprofit organization. Tax-exempt: 501(c)(3).
History Museum, Historic Site & National Historic Landmark.
Collections: local history & lighthouse keepers' lives. Historic Structures: c.1887 Lighthouse Tower; 3 Keepers' Houses; 4 out-buildings; Lens exhibit building.
Facilities: 10-acre grounds. Museum-related items for sale.
Activities: guided tours; lectures; video theater.
Publications: quarterly newsletter; brochure.
Hours & Admission Prices: Memorial Day to Labor Day daily 10-9; Sept.-May daily 10-6. Adults $5, children $1.50; members no charge. Closed Christmas Day. ♿
Attendance: 121,004 (accurate)
Membership: General $20; Family $40.

Port St. Joe

CONSTITUTION CONVENTION MUSEUM STATE PARK, 200 Allen Memorial Way, Port St. Joe, FL 32456-2342. Tel.: 850-229-8029.
Web Site: www.floridastateparks.org/constitutionconvention/
Formerly: Constitution Convention State Museum
Founded: 1955.
Congressional District: 2
Key Personnel: Park Mgr., Brian Addison; Asst. Mgr., Danny Kemp; Park Ranger, William Wilkinson.
Personnel Profile: Full-Time Paid 1; Part-Time Paid 1.
Governing Authority: state. Parent Institution: St. Joseph Peninsula State Park. Tax-exempt.
History Museum: site of the Constitution Convention for the Territory of FL.
Collections: Old St. Joseph history.
Activities: guided tours; permanent exhibitions.
Hours & Admission Prices: Visitor Center: Thurs.-Mon. 9-12 & 1-5. Adults $2; children 4 & under no charge. Closed New Year's Day; Thanksgiving; Christmas. ♿
Attendance: 3,500 (estimated)

Punta Gorda

MILITARY HERITAGE MUSEUM, (M), 1200 W. Retta Esplanade, Unit 48, Punta Gorda, FL 33950-5325. Tel.: 941-575-9002.
Founded: 2001.
Congressional District: 16
Key Personnel: Exec. Dir., Kim Lovejoy; Chm. (V), Marilyn Smith-Mooney.
Personnel Profile: Full-Time Paid 2; Part-Time Volunteers 40.
Governing Authority: nonprofit organization. Tax-exempt: 501(c)(3).
Military Heritage Museum.
Collections: military heritage, history, & artifacts; photographs; personal artifacts; war memorabilia.
Hours & Admission Prices: Summer: Mon.-Sat. 10-6, Sun. 12-5; Winter: call for extended hours. No charge; donations accepted. ♿
Attendance: 47,643 (accurate)
Membership: Student $15; Adult $25; Corporate $250; Life $500.

Quincy

GADSDEN ARTS CENTER, 13 N. Madison, Quincy, FL 32351-2409. Tel.: 850-875-4866. Fax: 850-627-8606.
E-mail: grace@gadsdenarts.org
Web Site: www.gadsdenarts.org
Founded: 1994.
Congressional District: 2
Key Personnel: Exec. Dir., Grace Maloy; Pres. (V), Altha Manning; Cur., Angela Barry; Museum Shop Mgr., Becky Reep.
Personnel Profile: Full-Time Paid 2; Part-Time Paid 1; Part-Time Volunteers 100; Interns 12.
Governing Authority: Parent Institution: Gadsden Arts, Inc. Tax-exempt.
Fine Arts Museum.
Collections: paintings; sculpture; American art including southern vernacular & contemporary regional.
Major Exhibits: FAMU Faculty Exhibition, 1/10-2/10; Eric Baret, William McKeown, & Clay Lovel, 3/10-5/10; Trudy Wheeler Photography & Don Taylor Watercolor, 6/10-8/10; Mark Lindquist: 40 Years, 9/10-10/10; 22nd Annual Art in Gadsden, 11/10-12/10.
Facilities: studios.
Activities: guided tours; art classes; workshops; lectures; summer camps.
Publications: monthly e-newsletter, GAC.
Hours & Admission Prices: Tues.-Sat. 10-5, Sun. 1-5. Adults $1; discounts to AAM & ICOM members; members no charge. Closed holidays. ♿
Attendance: 18,000 (estimated)
Membership: Student $10-$25; Individual $25-$50; Family $45-$100; Artists Guild $100; Corporate $250-$10,000.

Safety Harbor

SAFETY HARBOR MUSEUM OF REGIONAL HISTORY, 329 Bayshore Blvd. S., Safety Harbor, FL 34695-4053. Tel.: 727-726-1668. Fax: 727-725-9938.
E-mail: info@safetyharbormuseum.org
Web Site: www.safetyharbormuseum.org
Founded: 1970.
Congressional District: 9
Key Personnel: Pres., Les Griffith; Dir. Operations, Bobbie Davidson; Dir. Exhibits, Ronald Fekete; Dir. Education, Robert S. Anderson.
Personnel Profile: Full-Time Paid 1; Part-Time Paid 2; Part-Time Volunteers 30; Interns 2.
Governing Authority: private; nonprofit organization. Tax-exempt: 501(c)(3).
Florida & Regional History Museum.
Collections: dioramas depicting key events in Florida history; fossils; displays & artifacts pertaining to the pre-history of the Tocobaga Indians, paleo & archaic periods; the recorded history of the Spanish encounter; pioneer era of Odet Philippe; Heritage Gallery collection of Safety Harbor memorabilia.
Major Exhibits: Highwaymen Artists, 1/10-3/10; Cracker Exhibit, 4/10-6/10; Civil War Exhibit, 7/10-9/10.
Research Fields: Florida archaeology; Florida history; history of Safety Harbor area.
Activities: guided tours; lectures; public school tour with lecture.

Publications: newsletters; brochure, Tocobaga Fishing Industry in Tampa Bay; biography, Odet Philippe.
Hours & Admission Prices: Wed. & Fri. 10-4, Thurs. 10-7, Sat. 10-2, Sun. 1-4; other times by appointment. Adults $4, seniors $3; discounts to AAA members; children under 7 & members no charge. Closed major holidays. ♿
Attendance: 8,783 (accurate)
Membership: Individual $25; Family $50; Supporter $100; Sponsor $250; Corporate $500.

Saint Augustine

CASTILLO DE SAN MARCOS NATIONAL MONUMENT, One S. Castillo Dr., Saint Augustine, FL 32084-3252. Tel.: 904-829-6506. Fax: 904-823-9388.
Web Site: www.nps.gov/casa
Founded: 1935.
Congressional District: 4
Key Personnel: Supt., Gordon J. Wilson; Eastern National Bookstore, Bruce Harris.
Governing Authority: federal. Parent Institution: National Park Service, Dept. of the Interior, Washington, DC 20240. Tax-exempt.
Park Museum: housed in 1672-95 restored Spanish Castillo de San Marcos.
Collections: Indian, Spanish & English pottery shards; artillery; manuscripts.
Research Fields: St. Augustine fort.
Activities: guided tours; lectures; films; permanent exhibitions; living history demonstrations.
Publications: folder, Castillo de San Marcos, Florida; handbook, The Building of Castillo de San Marcos.
Hours & Admission Prices: Daily 8:45-4:45. Adults $6; children under 16 no charge. Closed Christmas. ♿

COLONIAL SPANISH QUARTER MUSEUM, 29 St. George St., Saint Augustine, FL 32084-3607. Mailing Address: P.O. Box 210, St. Augustine, FL 32085-0210. Tel.: 904-825-6830. Fax: 904-825-6874.
E-mail: sqmuse@aug.com
Web Site: www.historicstaugustine.com
Formerly: The Spanish Quarter Museum
Founded: 1959.
Congressional District: 4
Key Personnel: Museum Mgr., Susan K. Van Vleet; Museum Clerk, Annmarie Smith.
Personnel Profile: Full-Time Paid 8; Part-Time Paid 5; Part-Time Volunteers 20.
Governing Authority: municipal government, City of St. Augustine.
Living History Museum.
Collections: Spanish & Spanish-Colonial artifacts & reproductions, fine & decorative arts; preservation project; history; historical archeology; 26 restored or reconstructed colonial buildings from the 18th & 19th centuries.
Research Fields: history; historical archaeology; colonial culture; cultural anthropology; ethnohistory; architectural history.
Facilities: 3,000-vol. library related to preservation project, including microfilms of Spanish documents. Craft products & period merchandise for sale.
Activities: living history; craft demonstrations; outdoor museum; permanent & temporary exhibits; special events.
Publications: brochures & occasional booklets; pamphlet; walking tour leaflet; educational materials.
Hours & Admission Prices: Daily 9-5:30. Family $16.95, adults $6.95, senior citizens 62 & over $5.95, children 6-17 $4.25; discounts to AAM members & St. Johns county residents. Closed New Year's Day; Thanksgiving; Christmas Eve & Day. ♿
Attendance: 52,000 (accurate)
Membership: Senior & Student $20; Individual $25; Family & Dual $35; Sustaining $50; Associate $100; Donor $250; Patron $500; Benefactor $1,000.

FORT MATANZAS NATIONAL MONUMENT, 8635 A1A S., Saint Augustine, FL 32080-8411. Tel.: 904-829-6506, ext. 227 (Headquarters). Fax: 904-471-7605.
E-mail: linda_chandler@nps.gov
Web Site: www.nps.gov/foma
Founded: 1935.
Congressional District: 4
Key Personnel: District Ranger, Andrew Rich; Park Ranger, Linda Chandler; Bookstore Mgr., Bruce Harris; Supt., Gordon Wilson.
Personnel Profile: Full-Time Paid 3; Part-Time Paid 3; Part-Time Volunteers 5.
Governing Authority: federal. Parent Institution: National Park Service, Dept. of the Interior, Washington, DC 20240. Museum Shop: Eastern National Parks & Monuments Association. Tax-exempt.
Park Museum: Site of first European battle for control of New World.
Collections: Historic Building: 1742 Fort Matanzas, Spanish fort.
Research Fields: all aspects related to the defense at Matanzas Inlet as accessory to the fort at St. Augustine.
Facilities: nature trail; picnic area. Publications & postcards for sale.
Activities: orientation video; permanent exhibitions; guided tours; free ferry service to Fort & living history demonstrations; school group lectures; nature trails.
Publications: brochure in English & Spanish; self-guiding map to Ft. Manzas N.M.
Hours & Admission Prices: Daily 9-5:30. Ferry: 9:30-4:30. No charge for admission. Cooperative association with National Park Service. Closed Christmas. ♿
Attendance: 700,000 (accurate)

LIGHTNER MUSEUM, (M), City Hall, Museum Complex, 75 King St., Saint Augustine, FL 32084. Mailing Address: P.O. Box 334, Saint Augustine, FL 32085-0334. Tel.: 904-824-2874. Fax: 904-824-2712.
E-mail: info@lightnermuseum.org
Web Site: www.lightnermuseum.org
Founded: 1948.
Congressional District: 4
Key Personnel: C.E.O., Robert W. Harper, III; Chm. (V), David C. Drysdale; Cur., Barry W. Myers, Jr.; Visitor Svcs., Helen Ballard; Registrar, Irene Lawrie; Asst. to Dir., Helen C. Amato; Business Mgr., Angela Blankenship.
Personnel Profile: Full-Time Paid 6; Part-Time Paid 7; Part-Time Volunteers 64.
Governing Authority: municipal; nonprofit organization. Tax-exempt: 501(c)(3).
General Museum: housed in 1887 Alcazar Hotel.
Collections: 19th-century fine & decorative arts & material culture, featuring American & European glass, ceramics, metal work & furniture; natural science, industry & anthropology collection.
Research Fields: 19th-century decorative arts material culture.
Facilities: 6,000-vol. reference library; permanent & changing exhibition galleries; meeting room; restaurant; courtyard garden. Museum-related items for sale.
Activities: demonstrations of 19th century mechanical musical instruments; lectures; concerts; seminars.
Publications: exhibition catalogs; reproduction postcards; guide books; multilingual guides; Lost Colony - The Artists of Saint Augustine, 1930-1950.
Hours & Admission Prices: Daily 9-5. Adults $10, active military with ID $6; college students with ID & youth 12-18 $5 students $5; discount to groups, military & AAM members; children under 12 with adult no charge. Closed Christmas. ♿
Attendance: 106,424 (accurate)

OLD FLORIDA MUSEUM, 259 San Marco Ave., Saint Augustine, FL 32084-1628. Mailing Address: P.O. Box 528, Saint Augustine, FL 32085-0528. Tel.: 800-813-3208; 904-824-8874.
E-mail: info@oldfloridamuseum.com
Web Site: www.oldfloridamuseum.com
Founded: 1996.
Key Personnel: Dir., Charles F. Ponce, Jr.
History Museum.
Collections: hands-on exhibits; Florida history.
Hours & Admission Prices: Daily 10-5. Call for admission prices. ♿

OLDEST HOUSE MUSEUM COMPLEX, 14 St. Francis St., Saint Augustine, FL 32084-5047. Mailing Address: 271 Charlotte St., St. Augustine, FL 32084-5033. Tel.: 904-824-2872. Fax: 904-824-2569.
E-mail: sahsdirector@bellsouth.net
Web Site: www.oldesthouse.org
Founded: 1883.
Congressional District: 7
Key Personnel: C.E.O., Dr. Susan R. Parker; Pres. (V), Dr. Barbara Wingo; Office Mgr., Jill Ruland.
Personnel Profile: Full-Time Paid 6; Part-Time Paid 15; Part-Time Volunteers 27.
Governing Authority: society. Parent Institution: St. Augustine Historical Society, 271 Charlotte St., Saint Augustine, FL. Tax-exempt: 501(c)(3).
Historic Houses, Military Museum & Ornamental Garden.
Collections: Spanish, English & American antiques, 1727-present; St. Augustine history items; interpretive exhibits including tools used by the Spanish & English; manuscripts; maps & photographs.
Research Fields: St. Augustine history: domestic, social & military.
Facilities: library; archives.
Activities: tours; school programs; elder hostels; lecture series.
Publications: annual journal, El Escribano; semiannual newsletter, East Florida Gazette; books, The Oldest City; St. Augustine: A Saga of Survival;

The Houses of St. Augustine; Awakening of St. Augustine; bimonthly members' newsletter, St. Augustine Historical Society News.
Hours & Admission Prices: Daily 9-5. Adults $8, seniors $7, students & adult tours $4; discounts to groups & military; members & children under 6 no charge. Closed Easter; Thanksgiving; Christmas. ♿
Attendance: 37,433 (accurate)
Membership: Student $20; Individual $35; Family $50; Contributor $100; Supporter $250; Benefactor $500; Guardian $1,000. Organizations & Firms: Associate $100; Promoter $250; Sustainer $500; Developer $1,000; Patron $2,500.

OLDEST STORE MUSEUM, 4 Artillery Lane, Saint Augustine, FL 32084-3269. Tel.: 904-829-9729.
Key Personnel: Museum Shop Mgr., John Stabley
History Museum.
Collections: over 100,000 period artifacts.
Facilities: Museum-related items for sale.
Hours & Admission Prices: June-Aug. Mon.-Sat. 9-5, Sun. 10-5; Sept.-May Mon.-Sat. 9-5, Sun. 12-5. Adults $5, children $1.50.

THE PENA-PECK HOUSE MUSEUM, 143 St. George St., Saint Augustine, FL 32084-3642. Tel.: 904-829-5064. Fax: 904-829-3898.
E-mail: lthom2007@aol.com
Founded: 1932.
Congressional District: 4
Key Personnel: Pres. (V), Linda Thompson; Museum Shop Mgr., Sue Dixon.
Personnel Profile: Full-Time Paid 1; Part-Time Paid 2; Part-Time Volunteers 60.
Governing Authority: municipal; private; nonprofit organization. The Woman's Exchange. Tax-exempt.
History Museum: Housed in ante bellum home of Dr. Seth & Sarah Lay Peck. Built in 1870 with original furnishings dating back to 1837.
Collections: home & furnishings of a family who came to St. Augustine from Connecticut in the early 1830s.
Research Fields: Peck-Burt records.
Facilities: Museum-related items for sale.
Activities: guided tours; candlelight evening tours by appointment.
Publications: book, The Treasurer's House.
Hours & Admission Prices: Tours: daily 12:30-4. Shop: Mon.-Sat. 10-5, Sun. 12-5. No charge; donations accepted. Closed most major holidays.
Attendance: 5,000 (estimated)

POTTER'S WAX MUSEUM, 17 King St., Saint Augustine, FL 32084. Tel.: 800-584-4781.
E-mail: info@potterswax.com
Web Site: www.potterswax.com
Founded: 1948.
Congressional District: 7
Key Personnel: C.E.O. & Dir., Chuck Ponce.
Personnel Profile: Full-Time Paid 2; Part-Time Paid 6.
Wax Museum.
Collections: 160 wax figures including presidents, athletes, entertainers, authors, artists, inventors, scientists & explorers.
Facilities: theater. Museum-related items for sale.
Activities: tours.
Hours & Admission Prices: Sun.-Thurs. 10-5, Fri.-Sat. 10-8. Adults $9, seniors 55 & over $8, children 6-12 $6, discount to local, military & AAA members; children 5 & under no charge.
Attendance: 60,000 (estimated)

RIPLEY'S BELIEVE IT OR NOT! MUSEUM, 19 San Marco Ave., Saint Augustine, FL 32084-3278. Tel.: 904-824-1606.
Web Site: staugustine.ripleys.com
Key Personnel: Mgr., Ed Shaffer
General Museum.
Collections: over 800 antiquities & oddities from around the world; personal artifacts.
Hours & Admission Prices: Sun.-Thurs. 9-7, Fri.-Sat. 9-8. Adults 12 & over $14.99, senior citizens 55 & over $12.26, children 5-11 $7.99.

ST. AUGUSTINE ALLIGATOR FARM, 999 Anastasia Blvd., Saint Augustine, FL 32080-4619. Tel.: 904-824-3337, ext. 10. Fax: 904-829-6677.
E-mail: jbrueggen1@aol.com
Web Site: www.alligatorfarm.com
Founded: 1893.
Key Personnel: Dir., John Brueggen; Gift Shop Mgr., Natalie Hurtado.
Personnel Profile: Full-Time Paid 27; Part-Time Paid 3.
Zoological Park.
Collections: 23 species of crocodiles from around the world; tropical birds.
Hours & Admission Prices: June-Aug. daily 9-6; Sept.-May daily 9-5. Adults $21.95, children 3-11 $10.95; discounts to seniors, groups, AAM, ICOM & AAA members; children under 3 & members no charge. ♿
Attendance: 213,000 (estimated)
Membership: Individual $49.95; Photo; $59.95; Grandparent $69.95; Family $79.95.

ST. AUGUSTINE ART ASSOCIATION, (M), 22 Marine St., Saint Augustine, FL 32084-4438. Tel.: 904-824-2310. Fax: 904-824-0716.
E-mail: staart@bellsouth.net
Web Site: www.staaa.org
Founded: 1924.
Art Museum.
Collections: paintings; photographs; period artifacts.
Major Exhibits: Jean Troemel Retrospective, 2/10; Lost Colony Artists, 9/10.
Activities: lectures; classes; children's programs & camps; special events; master artist workshops & demonstrations; walking tours.
Publications: newsletter.
Hours & Admission Prices: Tues.-Sat. 12-4, Sun. 2-5. No charge; donations accepted. Closed holidays. ♿
Membership: Student $25; Individual $50; Family $65; Patron $250; Life $1,000.

ST. AUGUSTINE LIGHTHOUSE & MUSEUM, INC., (M), 81 Lighthouse Ave., Saint Augustine, FL 32080-4650. Tel.: 904-829-0745. Fax: 904-808-1248.
E-mail: info@staugustinelighthouse.com
Web Site: www.staugustinelighthouse.com
Founded: 1988.
Congressional District: 4
Key Personnel: Dir., Kathy Allen Fleming; Deputy Dir., Rick Cain; Dir. Education, Chris Kastle; Dir. Sales, Lee Capitano; Volunteer Coord., Debe Thompson; Dir. Museum Advancement, Mollie Malloy.
Personnel Profile: Full-Time Paid 25; Part-Time Paid 11; Part-Time Volunteers 280.
Governing Authority: nonprofit. Tax-exempt.
Maritime & History Museum: National Register site.
Collections: lightkeepers' implements; historic lens on loan from U.S. Coast Guard.
Research Fields: lighthouse history & preservation; maritime archaeology; shrimping history.
Facilities: rental gallery.
Activities: Museum Sponsors: Lighthouse Festival in March; Luminary Light in December.
Publications: member's newsletter, The Spyglass.
Hours & Admission Prices: Winter: daily 9-6; Summer: call for extended hours. Adults $9, seniors 60 & over $7.50, children 12 & under $7; discounts to AAM members; retired, active military & members no charge. Closed Thanksgiving; Christmas Eve & Day. ♿
Attendance: 198,866 (accurate)
Membership: Keeper $30; Keeper's Family $50; Family Plus $100; Guardians $100 for 5 years; Heritage Club $25 for 5 years; Legacy Circle $500 for 5 years; Founding $1,000 for 5 years.

ST. PHOTIOS GREEK ORTHODOX NATIONAL SHRINE, 41 St. George St., Saint Augustine, FL 32084-3607. Tel.: 904-829-8205; 800-222-6727. Fax: 904-829-8707.
E-mail: info@stphotios.com
Web Site: www.stphotios.com
Founded: 1982.
Congressional District: 4
Key Personnel: Dir., Polexeni M. Hillier; Chm. (V), His Eminence Demetrios; Pres. (V), Metropolitan Alexios of Atlanta; Museum Shop, Fernando Arango; Museum Shop, Nicole Ouimette; Admin., Chia Hsuan Lin.
Personnel Profile: Full-Time Paid 2; Part-Time Paid 2; Part-Time Volunteers 7; Interns 3.
Governing Authority: nonprofit organization. Parent Institution: Greek Orthodox Archdiocese of America. Tax-exempt: 501(c)(3).
History Museum: housed in 1740 Avero House. Listed on the National Register of Historic Places.
Collections: 1768 Greek landing with Minorcans, Italians, Corsicans & Greeks; frescoes; icons; artifacts reflecting the Hellenic Heritage & teachings of the Orthodox Christian Faith; early life of Greeks in America; photographs; historical documents.
Research Fields: Greeks in America.
Facilities: 300-vol. library of Greek-related material available to the public; 25-seat video theater. Greek items & items relating to Greek Orthodoxy for sale.
Activities: lectures; films; loan exhibitions. Museum Sponsors: St. Photios

Feast Day; Annual St. Photios National Shrine Pilgrimage in February; House of Worship Tours in February; Lecture Series in February, June & October; Renewal retreat in June; Greek Landing Day in June.
Publications: annual newsletter, Friends.
Hours & Admission Prices: Mon.-Sat. 9-5, Sun. 12-6. No charge; donations accepted. Closed New Year's Day; Greek Orthodox Good Friday; Independence Day; Thanksgiving; Christmas. ♿
Attendance: 86,400 (estimated)
Membership: Friend $50; Supporter $100; Sustainer $250; Patron $500; Benefactor $1,000; Wall-of-Tribute $2,000.

WORLD GOLF HALL OF FAME, One World Golf Pl., Saint Augustine, FL 32092-2724. Tel.: 904-940-4000. Fax: 904-940-4391.
E-mail: info@wghof.org
Web Site: www.wgv.com
Founded: 1998.
Congressional District: 7
Key Personnel: Sr. Vice Pres. & C.O.O., Jack Peter; Gen. Mgr. Hall of Fame, Bruce Lahti; Sr. Dir. Mktg., Mary Altman; Dir. Communications, Jane Fader.
Personnel Profile: Full-Time Paid 40; Part-Time Paid 25; Part-Time Volunteers 250.
Governing Authority: nonprofit organization. Parent Institution: World Golf Foundation. Tax-exempt: 501(c)(3).
Sports Museum.
Collections: golf clubs & equipment used by famous golfers; paintings; ceramics; trophies; medals; sculpture; photographs; period clubs, balls & other golf memorabilia; clothing; jewelry.
Major Exhibits: Class of 2009, 11/09-11/10; Bob Hope: Shanks for the Memory (T), 11/09-12/10.
Research Fields: database on Hall of Fame members.
Facilities: 300-seat IMAX theater; 18-hole putting course; cafe; walk of champions. Museum-related items for sale.
Activities: interactive exhibits including golf simulator & putting surfaces; audio tour; mini theaters.
Publications: annual, World Golf Hall of Fame.
Hours & Admission Prices: Mon.-Sat. 10-6, Sun. 12-6. Adults $19.50, seniors & students $17.50, children 5-12 $9; members & children under 5 no charge. IMAX: adults $8, seniors & students $7, children 3-12 $5. Closed Thanksgiving; Christmas. ♿
Attendance: 250,000 (estimated)
Membership: see website for updated information on membership.

XIMENEZ-FATIO HOUSE MUSEUM, 20 Aviles St., Saint Augustine, FL 32084-4442. Tel.: 904-829-3575. Fax: 904-829-3445.
Governing Authority: Parent Institution: The National Society of The Colonial Dames of America in the State of Florida.
Historic House Museum.
Collections: local history & culture; period furnishings; personal artifacts.
Hours & Admission Prices: Tues.-Sat. 11-4. Adults $5, students 6-17 $4, seniors $3. ♿

Saint George Island

ST. GEORGE ISLAND VISITOR CENTER AND LIGHTHOUSE MUSEUM, 2 E. Gulf Beach Dr., Saint George Island, FL 32328-2883. Tel.: 888-927-7744.
Web Site: www.seestgeorgeisland.com
Maritime History Museum.
Collections: local history & culture; lighthouse.
Hours & Admission Prices: Visitor Center: Fri.-Wed. 10-5. Lighthouse Tours: Mon.-Wed. 9-12 & 1-3, Sat. 9-1, Sun. 1-3. Adults $5, children 16 & under $3; Lighthouse Assn. members & children 6 and under no charge.

Saint Marks

SAN MARCOS DE APALACHE HISTORIC STATE PARK, 148 Old Fort Rd., Saint Marks, FL 32355-0027. Mailing Address: 3600 Indian Mounds Rd., Tallahassee, FL 32303-2300. Tel.: 850-922-6007. Fax: 850-488-0366.
Web Site: www.floridastateparks.org
Founded: 1964.
Key Personnel: Park Mgr., Barry Burch; Administrative Asst., Shirley Deal.
Personnel Profile: Full-Time Paid 1.
Governing Authority: state. Dept. of Environmental Protection, Div. of Recreation and Parks, 3900 Commonwealth Blvd., Tallahassee, FL 32303. Tax-exempt.
State History Museum: second-oldest fortification in Florida.
Collections: archaeology; military; Indian artifacts; fort ruins.
Facilities: military cemetery.
Activities: interpretive video.

Publications: site specific brochure.
Hours & Admission Prices: Thurs.-Mon. 9-5. Adults $1; children under 6 no charge. Closed New Year's Day; Thanksgiving; Christmas Day. ♿
Attendance: 15,000 (estimated)

Saint Petersburg

* **FLORIDA HOLOCAUST MUSEUM, (M),** 55 5th St., S., Saint Petersburg, FL 33701-4146. Tel.: 727-820-0100; 800-960-7448. Fax: 727-821-8435.
E-mail: eblankenship@flholocaustmuseum.org
Web Site: www.flholocaustmuseum.org
Founded: 1989.
Congressional District: 10
Key Personnel: Exec. Dir., David Schafer; Cur. Exhibitions & Collections, Erin Blankenship.
Personnel Profile: Part-Time Volunteers 270; Interns 1.
Governing Authority: private; nonprofit organization. Subsidiary Institution: Sarasota-Manatee Arch Family Holocaust Education Center. Tax-exempt: 501(c)(3).
History Museum.
Collections: principle concentration on items related to the time of the Holocaust; additional items of Judaica, artwork concerning the Holocaust, genocide & the human condition; mixed media; traveling art & cultural exhibits.
Facilities: 7,000-vol. library on the Holocaust, human rights & other genocides; 12,000 sq. ft. exhibit space; Teaching Trunks for classrooms K-12. Museum-related items for sale.
Activities: docent & teacher training; guided tours; education programs & outreach; traveling art exhibits; Survivor services & video testimony; self-guided audio tours. Annual Events: Kristallnacht Night of Broken Glass Commemoration; ...To Life Award Dinner; Yom HaShoah (Day of Remembrance) Commemoration; Summer Institutes for Teachers K-16; Student Awareness Days; Anne Frank Humanitarian Award.
Publications: Newsletter; exhibit catalogues; curricula.
Hours & Admission Prices: Daily 10-5; last admission at 4. Adults $14, senior citizens 65 & over $12, college students $10, students under 18 $8; discounts to groups and AAM & ICOM members; members no charge. Closed New Year's Day; Rosh Hashanah; Yom Kippur; Thanksgiving; Christmas. ♿
Attendance: 60,000 (accurate)
Membership: Student $10; Educator $18; Senior $20; Young Friend (18-35) $25; Individual $36; Family $65; Circle of Friends $250; Circle of History $500; Circle of Heritage $1,000; Circle of Hope $3,000; Circle of Tolerance $5,000; Circle of Equality $10,000.

THE FLORIDA INTERNATIONAL MUSEUM AT ST. PETERSBURG COLLEGE, 244 2nd Ave. N., Saint Petersburg, FL 33701-3318. Tel.: 727-341-7900. Fax: 727-341-7908.
Web Site: www.spcollege.edu/fimuseum
Founded: 1994.
Congressional District: 10
Key Personnel: Dir., Kathleen C. Oathout; Cur., Christine Renc-Carter; Dir. Volunteers, Windy Crowder.
Personnel Profile: Full-Time Paid 5; Part-Time Volunteers 100.
Governing Authority: private; nonprofit organization. Parent Institution: St. Petersburg College. Tax-exempt: 501(c)(3).
Exhibition Gallery.
Collections: photographs; paintings; sculpture.
Major Exhibits: Rooted In Tradition - Art Quilts from the Rocky Mountain Quilt Museum (T), 11/6/09-1/10/10; Best of Show - Pinellas County Quilters, 11/6/09-1/10/10.
Facilities: 9,000 sq. ft. exhibit space. Museum-related items for sale.
Activities: education programs for children; lectures; loan & traveling exhibitions; special events; celebrations appropriate to the theme of the current exhibition; public programs.
Publications: exhibition catalogs; gallery guides.
Hours & Admission Prices: During exhibitions: Tues.-Sat. 10-5, Sun. 12-5. Adults $8, seniors & military $6, students $5; discounts to groups; children under 6 no charge. Closed New Year's Eve & Day; Memorial Day; Labor Day; Thanksgiving; Christmas Eve & Day. ♿
Attendance: 100,000 (estimated)

GREAT EXPLORATIONS CHILDREN'S MUSEUM, 1925 Fourth St. N., Saint Petersburg, FL 33704-4307. Tel.: 727-821-8992. Fax: 727-823-7287.
E-mail: colleen@greatex.org
Web Site: www.greatexplorations.org
Founded: 1986.
Congressional District: 10
Key Personnel: Exec. Dir., David Penn; Pres. (V), Dr. H. William Heller; Museum Store Mgr., Yusy Hernandez.

Personnel Profile: Full-Time Paid 12; Part-Time Paid 19; Part-Time Volunteers 120.
Governing Authority: private; nonprofit organization. Tax-exempt.
Children's Museum.
Collections: science, art & history interactive exhibits; teaching collection for outreach & demonstrations (snakes, spiders, scorpions, millipedes, beetles); sound; sailboats; racecars; roleplay; baby garden; air pressure; electromagnetism; climbing wall.
Facilities: 1926 Mediterranean Revival building.
Activities: daily preschool; youth leadership program; afterschool program; summer & holiday camps; educational demonstrations & outreach shows; puppet theatre; workshops; special events.
Publications: newsletter, Great News!; education guide.
Hours & Admission Prices: Mon.-Sat. 10-4:30, Sun. 12-4:30. Adults $9, seniors 55 & over $8; discounts for ASTC members & reciprocal members with ACM; children under one no charge. ♿
Attendance: 200,000 (accurate)
Membership: Individual $50; Family $100; Joint $125; Platinum $150.

THE MOREAN ARTS CENTER, (M), 719 Central Ave., Saint Petersburg, FL 33701-3627. Tel.: 727-822-7872. Fax: 727-821-0516.
Web Site: www.theartscenter.org
Key Personnel: Exec. Dir., Katee Tully; Cur., Amanda Cooper
Art Museum.
Collections: contemporary art.
Activities: art shows.
Hours & Admission Prices: June-Aug. Mon.-Sat. 10-5; Sept.-May Mon.-Sat. 10-5, Sun. 12-4. Adults $8, seniors 65 & over $6, students & children $5; children 5 & under no charge.

* **MUSEUM OF FINE ARTS OF ST. PETERSBURG, FLORIDA, (M),** 255 Beach Dr., N.E., Saint Petersburg, FL 33701-3498. Tel.: 727-896-2667. Fax: 727-894-4638.
Web Site: www.fine-arts.org
Founded: 1961.
Congressional District: 10
Key Personnel: Bd. Chm. & Pres., Seymour Gordon; Dir., Dr. John E. Schloder; Asst. Dir., Roger Zeh; Chief Cur., Dr. Jennifer Hardin; Dir. Devel., Judith Whitney; Devel. Asst., Kimberly Francis; Registrar, Louise Reeves; Asst. Cur. Education, Anna Alexander; Curatorial Asst., Robin O'Dell; Coord. Exhibitions, Kelly Reynolds; Financial Officer, Donald G. Bremer; Photography & Installations, Thomas U. Gessler; Installations & Technical Support, Thaddeus Root; Dir. Public Rels., David O. Connelly; Mgr. Events Mktg., Ellen Rivera; Museum Store Mgr., Ellen Holte; Coord. Store Merchandising, Jenny Noyes; Librarian, Jordana Weiss; Membership Coord., Steve Hack; Asst. to Dir., Vicki Sofranko.
Personnel Profile: Full-Time Paid 19; Part-Time Paid 9; Part-Time Volunteers 600.
Governing Authority: board of trustees; nonprofit organization. Tax-exempt: 501(c)(3).
Art Museum.
Collections: American & European paintings, drawings, prints, sculpture & photographs; Ancient Greek & Roman, pre-Columbian, Native American, African & Asian Art; decorative arts; sculpture garden; gallery of Steuben glass.
Major Exhibits: The Baroque World of Fernando Botero (T), 1/9/10-4/4/10; Transcending Vision: American Impressionism 1870-1940 (T), 8/28/10-1/16/11.
Facilities: 27,000-vol. library of art reference books; 225-seat theatre & recital hall; cafe; gardens; glass conservatory. Museum-related items for sale.
Activities: docent tours; lectures; films; gallery talks; family days; concerts; formally organized educational programs; docent program; inter-museum loan; permanent, temporary & traveling exhibitions; workshops; classes; summer camps; tours and educational materials for people with physical & emotional challenges.
Publications: quarterly newsletter, Mosaic; exhibition catalogues & brochures; educational materials for children & adults.
Hours & Admission Prices: Tues.-Sat. 10-5, Sun. 1-5. Adults $12, senior citizens 65 & over $10; discounts to students & groups of 10 or more; AAM & MFA members, members, school groups, and children under 6 no charge. Closed New Year's Day; Martin Luther King Jr. Day; Independence Day; Thanksgiving; Christmas. ♿
Attendance: 98,290 (accurate)
Membership: Student $25; Educator $35; Individual $50; Dual $85; Family $95; Patron $150; Pelican Single $200; Pelican Dual $275; Fine Arts Sustainer $600. Support Groups: The Contemporaries for young professionals, & Friends of Decorative Arts $20 (in addition to museum membership); Friends of Photography $30; Marly Music Society $75; Collectors Circle $500.

THE PIER AQUARIUM, 800 Second Ave., N.E., Ste. 2001, Saint Petersburg, FL 33701-3503. Tel.: 727-895-7437. Fax: 727-894-1212.
E-mail: info@pieraquarium.org
Web Site: www.pieraquarium.org
Founded: 1988.
Congressional District: 10
Key Personnel: Pres., E. Howard Rutherford; Chm. (V), Mark Luther, Ph.D.; Museum Shop Mgr., Emily Stehle.
Personnel Profile: Full-Time Paid 5; Part-Time Paid 14; Part-Time Volunteers 200; Interns 2.
Governing Authority: Tax-exempt.
Aquarium.
Collections: marine environments from around the world; Tampa Bay touch tank.
Facilities: 2,000 sq. ft. aquarium; marine laboratory.
Activities: touch tank; fish feeding. Museum Sponsors: Fish-ful Saturday. Annual Events: Spa Beach Splash in March; Kids' Fishing Tournament in May; Fish Head Ball in October.
Publications: Fresh Fish Quarterly.
Hours & Admission Prices: Mon.-Sat. 10-8, Sun. 12-6. Adults $5, students 7 & over and seniors 65 & over $4; discounts on Sun.; children under 6 & members no charge. Tampa Bay Touch Tank: daily 1-4. Fish Feeding: daily 3pm. ♿
Attendance: 125,000 (accurate)
Membership: Student, Senior, & Volunteer Teacher $20; Adult $25; Couple $40; Family $50 ($5 each additional).

RANSOM VISUAL ARTS CENTER, Eckerd College, 4200 54th Ave. S., Saint Petersburg, FL 33711-4744. Tel.: 727-864-8340 & 8342.
Web Site: www.eckerd.edu/tour/index.php?f=arts3
Key Personnel: Dir., Arthur Skinner
Art Center.
Collections: works by students & local artists.
Facilities: 900 sq. ft. exhibit space.
Hours & Admission Prices: Mon.-Fri. 10-4:30. No charge.

ST. PETERSBURG MUSEUM OF HISTORY, 335 Second Ave., N.E., Saint Petersburg, FL 33701-3501. Tel.: 727-894-1052, ext. 207. Fax: 727-823-7276.
E-mail: george.banez@stpetemuseumofhistory.org
Web Site: www.spmoh.org
Founded: 1920.
Congressional District: 6
Key Personnel: Exec. Dir., George Banez; Pres. (V), Connie Kone; Vice Pres., Joan Karins; Dir. Mktg., Rinita Anderson; Cur. Education, Nevin Sitler; Administrative Asst., Tania Akl; Archivist, Ann Wikoff.
Personnel Profile: Full-Time Paid 4; Part-Time Paid 9; Part-Time Volunteers 100; Interns 2.
Governing Authority: nonprofit organization. Parent Institution: St. Petersburg Historical Society. Tax-exempt: 501(c)(3).
History Museum.
Collections: exhibits reflect St. Petersburg; the Pinellas Peninsula and Florida history.
Research Fields: St. Petersburg & Florida history; Pinellas Peninsula.
Facilities: learning/teaching center; archival center. Museum-related items for sale.
Activities: gallery tours; focused educational programs; lectures; exhibitions; outreach programs; evening rentals.
Publications: quarterly newsletter, The Sea Breeze.
Hours & Admission Prices: Wed.-Sat. 10-5, Sun. 1-5. Adults $12; discounts to students, seniors & teachers; members no charge ♿
Attendance: 35,000 (accurate)
Membership: Student $20; Individual $35; Family $50; Florida Settler $100; Archivist $500; Collector $1,000.

* **SALVADOR DALI MUSEUM,** 1000 Third St., S., Saint Petersburg, FL 33701-4901. Tel.: 727-823-3767. Fax: 813-894-6068.
Web Site: salvadordalimuseum.org
Founded: 1954.
Congressional District: 8
Key Personnel: Dir. & C.E.O., Dr. Charles Henri Hine; Chm. (V), Eleanor Morse; Pres. (V), Thomas James; Deputy Dir. Collections, Joan R. Kropf; Deputy Dir. Mktg., Kathy White; Cur. Exhibitions, William Jeffett; Museum Shop Mgr., Dianne Birmingham.
Personnel Profile: Full-Time Paid 30; Part-Time Paid 6; Part-Time Volunteers 200; Interns 4.
Governing Authority: nonprofit organization. Parent Institution: Salvador Dali Institute. Tax-exempt: 509(a).
Art Museum.

Collections: Salvador Dali oils, drawings, watercolors, graphics & sculpture.
Research Fields: Salvador Dali; surrealism.
Facilities: 5,000-vol. library of books by or about Dali available for use by private appointment.
Activities: lectures; permanent & traveling exhibitions; children's programs; film program; music programs.
Publications: books, Dali Draftsmanship Catalog; Dali Primer; Dali, A Panorama of his Art, 1974; Dali in Public Museum Collections, 1974; Poetic Homage to Dali, 1973; Dali-Picasso, A Study in their Similarities & Differences, 1973; Notes on the Paintings, Student Edition, 1973; The Dali Adventure, A Photo Album, 1973; Tragic Myth of Millett's Angelus by Dali; Dali in the Nude (Reprint); Passions of Salvador Dali; Dali's Animal Crackers; Dali, A Collection, 1972; exhibition catalogues, Dante Divine Comedy; Surrealist Drawings; Isidro Clott Sculpture catalog; Horses; Crucifixion (Corpus Hypercubus); Dali's Graphic Art; Kenny Scharf, Pop Surrealist; Dali, The Early Years; Andy Warhol at the Dali; Dali by Design; Man Ray's Paris Portraits 1921-1939; Surrealism in America During the 1930s & 1940s; Masson, Masterpieces of Surrealism; James Rosenquist: Paintings; James Rosenquist: Selects; A Disarming Beauty: The Venus de Milo in 20th Century Art; Salvador Dali: The Salvador Dali Museum Collection; Dali Objects/Dali Fetishes: Love and Death; Dali and Two French Writers; Dali and Miro c.1928; Persistence & Memory: New Critical Perspectives on Dali at the Centennial; Joan Fontcuberta: Imaginary Gardens; Jordi Colomer: Arabian Stars; Pollock To Pop: America's Brush with Dali.
Hours & Admission Prices: Mon.-Wed. & Fri.-Sat. 10-5:30, Thurs. 10-8, Sun. 12-5:30. Adults $17, senior citizens $14.50, students $12, children 5-9 $4; discounts to AAA, AAM & ICOM members, Hospitality Industry Association (H.I.A.) and Florida Attraction members with proper I.D.; children under 4 & members no charge. Closed Thanksgiving; Christmas. ♿
Attendance: 210,000 (estimated)
Membership: Student & Seniors $35; Individual $40; Zodiac Individual $60; Family $70; Zodiac Family $90. NARM: Individual $100; Family $300; Dadaist $250; Surrealist $500.

THE SCIENCE CENTER OF PINELLAS COUNTY, 7701 22nd Ave., N., Saint Petersburg, FL 33710-3899. Tel.: 727-384-0027. Fax: 727-343-5729.
E-mail: info@sciencecenterofpinellas.org
Web Site: www.sciencecenterofpinellas.com
Founded: 1959.
Congressional District: 10
Key Personnel: Chm., Willy Schwiekert; Dir., Joseph S. Cuenco; Dir. Education, Leah Heffner.
Personnel Profile: Full-Time Paid 10; Part-Time Paid 14; Part-Time Volunteers 21.
Governing Authority: private; nonprofit organization. Tax-exempt: 501(c)(3).
Science Center.
Collections: anatomy; anthropology; aquarium; archaeology; astronomy; botany; entomology; geology; herpetology; marine; medicine; natural history; paleontology; zoology; 600-gallon touch-tank; 16th century Indian Village.
Research Fields: all fields of science.
Facilities: science classrooms; planetarium with Minolta's Mediaglobe projector; 170-seat auditorium; computer facilities; observatory with Meade 16 inch LX200 telescope.
Activities: guided tours; lectures; films; formally organized educational programs; permanent exhibitions.
Publications: workshop brochures; newsletter, Flash.
Hours & Admission Prices: Mon.-Fri. 9-4, Sat. special events. Adults $5; discounts to ASTC & FAM members; members no charge. Closed New Year's Day; Thanksgiving; Christmas. ♿
Attendance: 52,000 (estimated)
Membership: Seniors $25; Individual $30; Family $55.

TED WILLIAMS MUSEUM AND HITTERS HALL OF FAME, One Tropicana Dr., Saint Petersburg, FL 33705-1703. Tel.: 888-326-7297.
E-mail: info@tedwilliamsmuseum.com
Web Site: www.tedwilliamsmuseum.com
Key Personnel: Exec. Dir., Dave McCarthy; Deputy Dir., John Papelbon.
Governing Authority: nonprofit. Tax-exempt: 501(c)(3).
Sports Museum.
Collections: history of baseball; Ted Williams' life & career; sculpture; photographs; personal artifacts; Hitters Hall of Fame.
Facilities: Museum-related items for sale.
Activities: tours; dinners; special events. Annual Event: Museum Induction Ceremony.
Hours & Admission Prices: During Tampa Bay Devil Rays games for game ticket purchasers.

Sanford

CENTRAL FLORIDA ZOO & BOTANICAL GARDENS, 3755 N.W. Hwy. 17-92, Sanford, FL 32771. Mailing Address: P.O. Box 470309, Lake Monroe, FL 32747-0309. Tel.: 407-323-4450, ext. 0. Fax: 407-321-0900.
E-mail: information@centralfloridazoo.org
Web Site: www.centralfloridazoo.org
Founded: 1971.
Congressional District: 7
Key Personnel: C.E.O., Joe Montisano; Chm. (V), Lena Wasserman; Dir. Mktg. & Public Rels., Shonna Green; Dir. Operations & Gen. Cur., Fred Antonio; Dir. Education, Sandi Linn; Dir. Guest Svcs., Jayna Fox; Dir. Accounting, Chuck Grimes; Dir. Devel., Linnette Padron-Boldig.
Personnel Profile: Full-Time Paid 37; Part-Time Paid 32; Part-Time Volunteers 100.
Governing Authority: private; nonprofit. Tax-exempt: 501(c)(3).
Zoo.
Collections: over 800 specimens (150 species) of mammals, birds, reptiles, amphibians & invertebrates; emphasis focuses on American Zoo and Aquarium (AZA) cooperative conservation programs for rare & endangered species; species emphasized include neotropical primates, small felids, soft-billed birds, large lizard species and tortoises.
Research Fields: behavioral, nutritional & reproductive biology; focal species include black howler monkey, black-footed cat, clouded leopard, wreathed hornbill and Grand Cayman Island rock iguana.
Facilities: 700-vol. library on natural sciences & ecology; educational facilities; nature/conservation center. Shirts, books & zoo-related items for sale.
Activities: docent program; guided tours; college credit internships; lectures; mobile vans; educational programs; community outreach programs; on-site special events. Annual Event: Black Tie on the Wild Side.
Publications: quarterly members' newsletter, ZooViews.
Hours & Admission Prices: Daily 9-5. Adults $10.95, seniors $8.95, children 3-12 $6.95; discounts to groups; children under 2 & members no charge. Closed Thanksgiving; Christmas. ♿
Attendance: 249,000 (accurate)
Membership: Single $45; Senior Plus $55; Single Plus $65; Family & Grandparent $70; Voting $125; Sustaining $250; Patron $500; Benefactor $1,000.

MUSEUM OF SEMINOLE COUNTY HISTORY, 300 Bush Blvd., Sanford, FL 32773-6135. Tel.: 407-665-2489. Fax: 407-665-5220.
Web Site: www.seminolecountyfl.gov/leisure/museum/
Founded: 1983.
Congressional District: 5
Key Personnel: Museum Coord., Karen Jacobs.
Personnel Profile: Full-Time Paid 2; Full-Time Volunteers 20; Part-Time Paid 1; Part-Time Volunteers 20.
Governing Authority: county; nonprofit. Tax-exempt.
History Museum.
Collections: artifacts from Civil War; Seminole wars; modern times; documents & photos; exhibits on the history of Seminole County & Central Florida.
Facilities: 200-vol. library on Florida & regional history available to the public; meeting room; 3,500 sq. ft. exhibit space; 173,500 sq. ft. (bldg 1); 2,400 sq. ft. (bldg. 2).
Activities: docent program; guided tours; lectures; loan & temporary exhibitions.
Publications: The Early Days of Seminole County; Touring Seminole County.
Hours & Admission Prices: Tues.-Fri. 1-5, Sat. 9-1. Adults $3, children 4-18 $1; children under 4 no charge. Closed New Year's Day; Martin Luther King Jr. Day; Memorial Day; Independence Day; Labor Day; Veterans Day; Thanksgiving & day after; Christmas. ♿
Attendance: 3,500 (accurate)
Membership: Single $15; Family $20; Patron $50; Life $250.

SANFORD MUSEUM, 520 E. First St., Sanford, FL 32771-1410. Mailing Address: P.O. Box 1788, Sanford, FL 32772-1788. Tel.: 407-688-5120 & 5198. Fax: 407-330-5666.
E-mail: clarkea@ci.sanford.fl.us
Founded: 1957.
Congressional District: 5
Key Personnel: Chm. (V) & Pres.(V), Patty Swann; Cur., Alicia Clarke.
Personnel Profile: Full-Time Paid 2; Part-Time Paid 3; Part-Time Volunteers 6.
Governing Authority: municipal; nonprofit. Parent Institution: City of Sanford. Tax-exempt.
Museum, Research Library & Archives.
Collections: photos; culture; local baseball history; library of 19th-century legal, diplomatic & government books, classics & periodicals; 1820-1890 portrait collection; 1823-1891 papers of H.S. Sanford; 19th-century decorative arts; local history.

Research Fields: local history; Henry S. Sanford; local architectural history & African-American history; diplomatic service; Congo; civil war; Florida; citrus.
Facilities: 2,700-vol. library, 55,000 papers & 149 microfilm; available to the public, microfilm available for inter-library loan; meeting room.
Activities: guided tours; lectures; temporary exhibitions.
Hours & Admission Prices: Tues.-Fri. 11-4, Sat. 1-4 & by appointment; No charge; donations accepted. Closed federal holidays; day after Thanksgiving. ♿
Attendance: 4,000
Membership: Affiliated Historical Society: Student $5; Single $10; Family $25; Patron $100; Corporate $500.

Sanibel

THE BAILEY-MATTHEWS SHELL MUSEUM, (M), 3075 Sanibel-Captiva Rd., Sanibel, FL 33957-3111. Mailing Address: P.O. Box 1580, Sanibel, FL 33957-1580. Tel.: 239-395-2233; 888-679-6450 (toll free). Fax: 239-395-6706.
E-mail: shell@shellmuseum.org
Web Site: www.shellmuseum.org
Founded: 1986.
Congressional District: 13
Key Personnel: Dir., Jose H. Leal, Ph.D.; Business Mgr., Mary Jo Bunnell; Public Rels Mgr., Kathleen Hoover; Museum Store Mgr., Kimberly Nealon.
Personnel Profile: Full-Time Paid 4; Part-Time Paid 5; Part-Time Volunteers 110.
Governing Authority: nonprofit organization. Parent Institution: The Shell Museum & Educational Foundation, Inc. Tax-exempt: 501(c)(3).
Natural History Museum.
Collections: mollusks; archives; malacological library.
Research Fields: malacology.
Facilities: 6,000-vol. library of popular to monographic works & scientific journals on mollusks; 150-seat auditorium; 5,000 sq. ft. exhibit space. Museum-related items, except shells, for sale.
Activities: video on shell life; Children's Learning Lab Center.
Publications: quarterly newsletter; books, Seashells Photo Postcards; Pliocene Mollusca of Southern Florida; Edge of the Fossil Sea; The Nautilus, Idea to Reality.
Hours & Admission Prices: Daily 10-5. Adults $7, youths 5-16 $4; discounts to AAM members; children 4 and under & members no charge. Closed major holidays. ♿
Attendance: 50,000 (estimated)
Membership: Periwinkle $40; Wentletrap $60; Golden Olive $100; Lion's Paw $250; Junonia $500; Angel Wing $1,000 & up.

SANIBEL-CAPTIVA CONSERVATION FOUNDATION, INC., 3333 Sanibel-Captiva Rd., Sanibel, FL 33957-3100. Mailing Address: P.O. Box 839, Sanibel, FL 33957-0839. Tel.: 239-472-2329. Fax: 239-472-6421.
E-mail: sccf@sccf.org
Web Site: www.sccf.org
Founded: 1967.
Congressional District: 14
Key Personnel: Exec. Dir., A. Erick Lindblad; Pres. (V), Bill Fenniman; Business Mgr., Wendy Cerdan; Legacy Funds Coord., Cheryl Giattini; Dir. Education, Kristie J. Seaman Anders; Landscaping for Wildlife Educator, Dee Century-Serage; Native Plant Nursery Mgr., Jenny Evans; Research Scientist, Dr. Eric Milbrandt; Member Rels. Dir., Marti Bryant; Dir. Wildlife Habitat Mgmt., Brad Smith.
Personnel Profile: Full-Time Paid 22; Part-Time Paid 1; Part-Time Volunteers 300; Interns 4.
Governing Authority: nonprofit organization. Tax-exempt: 501(c)(3).
Land Trust; Nature Center.
Collections: native plants of Florida; island butterflies; herbarium.
Research Fields: ecology of gopher tortoises on Sanibel; surface water management & eradication of exotic pest plants; sea turtle research & monitoring; restoration ecology; shorebird monitoring.
Facilities: 1,000-vol. library of barrier island flora & fauna material, available to members only; 60-seat auditorium; educational facilities; 1,300 sq. ft. exhibit space; field research station; nature center; native plant nursery; nature trails. Nature oriented items for sale.
Activities: docent program; formal educational programs; intern program for undergraduate or graduate college students; guided tours; lectures; participatory exhibits. Annual Events: Great Island Pickup; Beach Clean-up; Open House; Earth Day.
Publications: monthly newsletter, Update; book, Growing Native; book, A Natural Course; annual report.
Hours & Admission Prices: June-Sept. Mon.-Fri. 8:30-3; May-Oct. Mon.-Fri. 8:30-4; Dec.-April Mon.-Fri. 8:30-4, Sat. 10-3. Native Plant Nursery: May-Nov. Mon.-Fri. 8:30-5; Dec.-April Mon.-Fri. 8:30-5, Sat. 10-3. Adults $3; members & children under 17 no charge. Closed New Year's Day; Memorial Day; Independence Day; Labor Day; Thanksgiving; Christmas. ♿
Attendance: 15,000 (estimated)
Membership: Individual $25; Family $50; Corporate $100.

Sarasota

ART CENTER SARASOTA, INC, 707 N. Tamiami Tr., Sarasota, FL 34236-4050. Tel.: 941-365-2032. Fax: 941-366-0585.
E-mail: artsarasota@aol.com
Web Site: www.artsarasota.org
Formerly: Sarasota Visual Arts Center
Founded: 1926.
Congressional District: 8
Key Personnel: Exec. Dir., Fayanne Hayes; Pres., Kathleen McDonald.
Personnel Profile: Full-Time Paid 2; Full-Time Volunteers 10; Part-Time Paid 7; Part-Time Volunteers 30; Interns 2.
Governing Authority: nonprofit organization. Tax-exempt: 501(c)(3).
Art Gallery.
Collections: paintings; sculpture; graphics; photography.
Facilities: approx. 200-vol. library of art reference material available on premises.
Activities: guided tours; lectures; gallery talks; arts festivals; painting demonstrations; workshops; life-sketch groups; arts & crafts demonstrations; permanent & temporary exhibitions. Gallery Sponsors: The Sarasota County Public Schools Art Show; Annual Fund Drive for PBS T.V. WUSF as a collection point.
Publications: book, Sarasota Art Association Yearbook; monthly news bulletin; workshop brochures.
Hours & Admission Prices: Tues.-Sat. 10-4. Suggested Donation: adults $3. Closed on all major holidays. ♿
Attendance: 15,000 (estimated)
Membership: Single $50; Family & Sponsor $75; Associate $200; Patron $500; Life & Angel $1,500 minimum.

CROWLEY MUSEUM & NATURE CENTER, 16405 Myakka Rd., Sarasota, FL 34240-9192. Tel.: 941-322-1000. Fax: 941-322-1000.
E-mail: bcowdright@cmncfl.org
Web Site: www.cmncfl.org
Founded: 1974.
Congressional District: 13
Key Personnel: Exec. Dir., Bill Cowdright; Bd. Pres., Mary Anne Servian; Bd. Vice Pres., John Michel.
Personnel Profile: Full-Time Paid 2; Part-Time Paid 6; Part-Time Volunteers 25.
Governing Authority: nonprofit. Tax-exempt: 501(c)(3).
History Museum, Historic Building & Nature Center.
Collections: Florida pioneer lifestyles from late 1800s to early 1900s; blacksmith shop; replica homestead cabin; Victorian era home artifacts; general store; post office; Florida pioneer tools. Historic Buildings: 1892 Cracker House; sugar cane mill; sugar shack.
Research Fields: Crowley family; local Myakka area & Florida pioneers; Tatum Family.
Facilities: learning center; picnic pavilion; nature trails. Museum-related items for sale.
Activities: self-guided tours; lectures; workshops; organized educational programs; docent program; participatory exhibits. Museum Sponsors: Southwest Florida Heritage Festival in January.
Publications: e-newsletter.
Hours & Admission Prices: May-Sept. Thurs.-Sun. 8-2; Oct.-April Thurs.-Sun. 10-4. Adults $7, children 5-12 $3; members no charge. Closed New Year's Day; Independence Day; Thanksgiving; Christmas. ♿
Attendance: 6,100 (accurate)
Membership: Student $15; Individual $30; Family $40; Patron $100; Donor $500.

GULFCOAST WONDER AND IMAGINATION ZONE, DBA G.WIZ, (M), 1001Boulevard of the Arts, Sarasota, FL 34236. Tel.: 941-309-4949. Fax: 941-906-7292.
E-mail: cheryl@gwiz.org
Web Site: www.gwiz.org
Founded: 1990.
Congressional District: 13
Key Personnel: Dir., Molly Demeulenaere; Pres. Bd. (V), Chris Mencies; Museum Shop Mgr., Sherry Simons.
Personnel Profile: Full-Time Paid 12; Part-Time Paid 14; Part-Time Volunteers 125.
Governing Authority: private; nonprofit organization. Tax-exempt: 501(c)(3).
Interactive Science Center.

Collections: interactive science exhibits including physical science, life science & technology.
Facilities: teacher resource area; educational facilities; 35,000 sq. ft. exhibit space; classrooms; outdoor science playground; intermuseum hook-up; 70-seat theater. Museum-related items for sale.
Activities: informal education programs; guided tours; lectures; traveling & participatory exhibits.
Publications: e-newsletter (every two weeks); volunteer e-newsletter.
Hours & Admission Prices: Mon.-Sat. 10-5, Sun. 12-5. Adults $9, senior citizens $8, children 3-18 $6; discounts to ASTC reciprocal; members & children 2 and under no charge. Closed New Year's Day; Easter; Memorial Day; Independence Day; Thanksgiving; Christmas. ♿
Attendance: 150,000 (accurate)
Membership: Family $75; Family Plus $100; Edison Society $150; Bell Society $250; Fulton Society $500; Explorers $1,000.

* **JOHN AND MABLE RINGLING MUSEUM OF ART, (M),** 5401 Bay Shore Rd., Sarasota, FL 34243-2161. Tel.: 941-359-5700. Fax: 941-359-7704. TDD: 941-359-5700.
Founded: 1927.
Congressional District: 13
Key Personnel: Exec. Dir., Dr. John Wetenhall; Chm. (V), Frank J. Rief, III; Cur. Circus Museum & Archivist, Deborah Walk; Head Librarian, Linda McKee; Chief Conservator, Michelle Scalera; C.O.O., Chip Willis; Chief Mktg. & Communications, Pam Fendt; Chief Security, Events/Rentals & Facilities, Russell Pillifant; Information Technology Mgr., Beth Wallace; Mgr. Human Resources, Cindy Clenney; Registrar, Francoise Hack; Sr. Dir. Major Gifts, Suellen Field; Cur. Asolo Theater, Dwight Currie; Asst. Cur. European Art, Dr. Virginia Brilliant; Asst. Cur. European Art, Alexandra Libby; Assoc. Cur. Asian Art, Dr. Chang Qing; Museum Shop Mgr., Bill Wort.
Personnel Profile: Full-Time Paid 126; Part-Time Paid 115; Part-Time Volunteers 725; Interns 10.
Governing Authority: state. Parent Institution: Florida State University. Tax-exempt.
Art Museum & Estate.
Collections: Art Museum: Old Master paintings from the Renaissance through the 19th century including Venetian Baroque and Rubens; American paintings, sculpture, prints, drawings & photographs from 12th to 20th centuries; Asian art; decorative arts; archaeological material from Cyprus & the ancient Mediterranean. Circus Museum: circus memorabilia; wagons; costumes; miniatures; posters. Tibbals Learning Center: a miniature circus. Historic Asolo Theater: late 18th-century Italian theater. Ca'd'Zan Mansion: John & Mable Ringling's furnished 1920s residence; gardens.
Research Fields: Baroque art; circus history; 20th-century art; Chinese ceramics.
Facilities: 70,000-vol. library; archives; gardens; 260-seat theater; classrooms; restaurant. Books, prints, decorative objects, jewelry, furnishings, statuary & other museum-related items for sale.
Activities: guided tours; lectures; gallery talks; education programs; inter-museum loan, permanent, temporary & traveling exhibitions; volunteer & members events; daily theater performances.
Publications: quarterly, Ringling Museum Newsletter; books, The John & Mable Ringling Museum of Art; Museum Once Forgotten: The Rebirth of The John and Mable Ringling Museum; John Ringling, Dreamer, Builder, Collector; The John and Mable Ringling Museum of Art Guide to the Collections; The Circus in Miniature: The Howard Bros. Circus Model; exhibition catalogs; catalogue, The Italian Paintings Before 1800, Italian Collection, Great Paintings from the John & Mable Ringling Museum of Art; catalogue, The Flemish & Dutch Paintings: 1400-1900 Ringling Collection.
Hours & Admission Prices: Daily 10-5:30. Adults $25, seniors 65 & over $20, students & children 6-17 $10; discounts to groups & AAM members; members & children under 6 no charge. Call to confirm. ♿
Attendance: 360,000 (estimated)
Membership: Friend $75; Associate $100; Contributor $175; Sponsor $500; Colleague $1,000; Patron $5,000.

* **THE MARIE SELBY BOTANICAL GARDENS, INC.,** 811 S. Palm Ave., Sarasota, FL 34236-7995. Tel.: 941-366-5731. Fax: 941-366-9807.
E-mail: contactus@selby.org
Web Site: www.selby.org
Founded: 1973.
Congressional District: 8
Key Personnel: C.E.O., Tom Buchter; Chm. (V), Thomas B. Luzier, Esq.; Mktg. Dir., Debby Steele; Museum Shop Mgr., Amy Sullivan.
Personnel Profile: Full-Time Paid 37; Part-Time Paid 14; Part-Time Volunteers 450; Interns 4.
Governing Authority: nonprofit organization. Tax-exempt: 501(c)(3).
Arboretum & Botanical Garden: original building & grounds of Marie & William Selby.
Collections: herbarium of over 60,000 mounted & accessioned specimens in orchidaceae, gesneriaceae, araceae & bromeliaceae; tropical epiphytic plants; live plant collection of 8,000 documented, largely wild-collected epiphytes, including 4,500 orchidaceae.
Major Exhibits: Batiks Botanicos, 1/8/10-2/23/10; Ikebana Exhibit, 2/27/10-2/28/10; Rainforest Masks 2010, 3/5/10-4/24/10; 30th Annual Juried Photographis Exhibition, 4/30/10-6/6/10; 5th Annual Selby Instructors' Summer Showcase, 6/10/10-9/26/10; Holiday Mansion Exhibit, 12/3/10-1/2/10.
Research Fields: taxonomical research related to epiphytic plants; canopy biology.
Facilities: 5,000-vol. library of books primarily epiphytic botany & less extensive in general taxonomic botany, tropical display house; outdoor gardens; 75-seat auditorium. Plants, books & gifts associated with plants for sale.
Activities: guided tours; lectures; films; concerts; arts festivals; docent program or council; formally organized education programs for undergraduate & graduate college students; changing exhibits; elementary school science program.
Publications: annual journal, Selbyana; membership magazine, Tropical Dispatch.
Hours & Admission Prices: Daily 10-5. Adults $17, children 6-11 $6; children 5 & under and members no charge. Closed Christmas. ♿
Attendance: 200,000 (accurate)
Membership: Gardens Friend $60; Gardens Family $90; Contributing $125; Sustaining $250; Sponsor $500; Stewards of the Earth $1,000.

MOTE MARINE LABORATORY/AQUARIUM, 1600 Ken Thompson Pkwy., Sarasota, FL 34236-1096. Tel.: 941-388-4441, ext. 332. Fax: 941-388-4312.
E-mail: info@mote.org
Web Site: www.mote.org
Founded: 1955.
Congressional District: 13
Key Personnel: Pres., Dr. Kumar Mahadevan; Pres. (V), Joseph Mathis; Chm. Bd., Arthur L. Armitage; Administrative Dir., Dena J. Ayers; Cur., Dan Bebak; Archivist, Susan Stover; Grants, Ellen Vandernoot; Public Rels., Martha Wells; Security, Earl Stockton; Gift Shop Mgr., Joyce Gaffney.
Personnel Profile: Full-Time Paid 30; Part-Time Paid 2; Part-Time Volunteers 570; Interns 5.
Governing Authority: nonprofit organization. Parent Institution: Mote Marine Laboratory. Tax-exempt: 501(c)(3).
Marine Laboratory Museum.
Collections: marine animals; papers of MML.
Research Fields: marine biology; environmental assessment; aquatic chemistry; coastal engineering; physical oceanography; marine biomedicine & immunology; coastal ecology; marine fisheries; aquaculture; sharks; sea turtles; sea mammals.
Facilities: 22,000-vol. library automated with marine-related research available for inter-library loan; 25,000 sq. ft. exhibit space; 385-seat auditorium; marine educational resource center; field research station; nature center. Marine-related items for sale.
Activities: docent program; films; formal education programs; guided tours; mobile exhibit. Annual Events: Open House; Dinners; Lecture Series.
Publications: quarterly magazine, Mote Magazine; Mote Technical Reports; Collected Papers from Mote Marine Laboratory.
Hours & Admission Prices: Daily 10-5. Adults $17, youth 4-12 $12. ♿
Attendance: 364,647 (accurate)
Membership: Student $25; Duo $50; Friend $90; Sponsor $125; Sustaining $300; Patron $500; Benefactor $1,000; Captain $2,500; Research Association $5,000; Laboratory Partner $10,000.

RINGLING COLLEGE OF ART AND DESIGN, SELBY GALLERY, (M), 2700 N. Tamiami Trail, Sarasota, FL 34234-5895. Tel.: 941-359-7563. Fax: 941-309-1969.
E-mail: selby@ringling.edu
Web Site: www.ringling.edu/selbygallery
Founded: 1986.
Congressional District: 13
Key Personnel: Dir., Kevin Dean; Asst. Dir., Laura Avery; Gallery Asst., Candise Curlee.
Personnel Profile: Full-Time Paid 3; Part-Time Paid 1; Part-Time Volunteers 2; Interns 1.
Governing Authority: private college; nonprofit. Parent Institution: Ringling College of Art and Design, Sarasota. Tax-exempt: 501(c)(3).
Art Museum.
Collections: 20th-century prints.
Major Exhibits: Real(ists), 1/15/10-2/16/10; Perestroika(n) Restructuring: The

Glass Sculpture of Kathleen Mulcahy, Ron Desmett & Martin Prekop, 2/26/10-3/31/10; Best of Ringling: Annual Juried Student Exhibitions, 4/9/10-4/26/10; Ringling College Senior Thesis Exhibitions, 4/30/10-5/8/10; Annual Community Exhibitions: Suncoast Watercolor Society & Robert Hodgell, 5/14/10-5/28/10; David Budd: A 40-Year Retrospective, 6/25/10-7/28/10.
Facilities: 150-seat auditorium; 3,000 sq. ft. exhibit space.
Activities: lectures; gallery talks; panel discussions; outreach.
Publications: catalogues for select exhibitions.
Hours & Admission Prices: Mon. & Wed.-Sat. 10-4, Tues. 10-7. No charge; donations accepted. Closed school holidays. ♿
Attendance: 28,000 (estimated)

SARASOTA CLASSIC CAR MUSEUM, 5500 N. Tamiami Trail, Sarasota, FL 34243-2199. Tel.: 941-355-6228.
E-mail: info@sarasotacarmuseum.org
Web Site: www.sarasotacarmuseum.org
Founded: 1953.
Key Personnel: Pres., Martin Godbey.
Personnel Profile: Full-Time Paid 1; Part-Time Paid 12; Part-Time Volunteers 60; Interns 2.
Governing Authority: private; nonprofit organization. Tax-exempt: 501(c)(3).
Classic Car Museum.
Collections: John & Mable Ringling automobile collection; horseless carriages; automotive history from war & post-war periods to the present; vintage, antique & classic automobiles; antique game arcade.
Facilities: library; 60,000 sq. ft. exhibit space. Museum-related items for sale.
Activities: docent program; formal education programs for children; guided tours; rental gallery; study clubs. Museum Sponsors: Antique Car Auction; Soap Box Derby.
Publications: quarterly newsletter, Friends of Classic Cars.
Hours & Admission Prices: Daily 9-6. Adults 13-61 $8.50, seniors 62 & over $7.50, children 6-12 $6.50; discounts to groups; children 5 & under no charge. Closed Christmas. ♿
Attendance: 42,000 (estimated)
Membership: Children $16; Senior Citizens $18; Adults $20.

THE TURNER MUSEUM AND THOMAS MORAN GALLERIES, 930 N. Tamiami Trail, Sarasota, FL 34236-4063. Mailing Address: P.O. Box 11073, Sarasota, FL 34278-1073. Tel.: 941-365-1649 & 343-3728.
E-mail: turnermuseum@turnermuseum.org
Web Site: turnermuseum.org
Founded: 1973.
Congressional District: 13
Key Personnel: C.E.O., Pres. (V) & Dir., Douglass Montrose-Graem; Pres. (V) & Museum Shop Mgr., Isis Graham; Bd. Sec., Katherine Vaggalis.
Personnel Profile: Full-Time Volunteers 3; Part-Time Volunteers 55; Interns 2.
Governing Authority: nonprofit organization. Tax-exempt: 501(c)(3).
Art Center.
Collections: works of J.M.W. Turner & Thomas Moran including engravings, ranging from preliminary etchings to reprints, watercolors, touched proofs & drawings.
Major Exhibits: J.M.W. Turner & Italy, 11/09-12/10; J.M.W. Turner & The Sublime, 11/09-12/10; Henri Matisse & J.M.W. Turner, 11/09-12/10; Hokusai & J.M.W. Turner, 11/09-12/10; J.M.W. Turner & Renoir, 11/09-12/10.
Research Fields: J.M.W. Turner; Thomas Moran; Hokusai; Renoir.
Facilities: 1,000-vol. library of material relating to J.M.W. Turner & Thomas Moran, available for inter-library loan. Prints, books & other material relating to the artists for sale.
Activities: guided tours; lectures; gallery talks; live concerts combined with dinners/buffets; TV & radio programs; permanent, temporary & traveling exhibitions; monthly meetings; appraisals. Breakfasts, Luncheons, Duchess' High Teas (English Style) & candle-lit dinners served by appointment.
Publications: catalogue, Turner & Moran; Turner's Cosmic Optimism; Turner's Angels; Turner's Rainbows; Turner's Children; Turner's Powerful Allegories.
Hours & Admission Prices: By appointment only. Adults $15; discounts to seniors, and AAM & ICOM members. ♿
Attendance: 100,000 (estimated)
Membership: Children $1; Student $5; Junior $10; Family $25; Senior $50; Associate $100; Life Candidate $250; Business $500; Life $1,000; Corporate $5,000.

Sebring

CHILDREN'S MUSEUM OF THE HIGHLANDS, 219 N. Ridgewood Dr., Sebring, FL 33870-7204. Mailing Address: P.O. Box 1243, Sebring, FL 33871-1243. Tel.: 863-385-5437.
E-mail: linda@childrensmuseumhighlands.com
Web Site: www.childrensmuseumhighlands.com
Founded: 1990.
Congressional District: 16
Key Personnel: Dir., Linda Crowder.
Governing Authority: nonprofit organization.
Children's Museum.
Collections: hands-on exhibits.
Activities: field trips; birthday parties; programs & special events; summer classes.
Hours & Admission Prices: Tues.-Wed. & Fri.-Sat. 10-5, Thurs. 10-8. Admission $3, Thurs. after 5 $1; members no charge.
Attendance: 20,000 (estimated)

HIGHLANDS ART LEAGUE, 1989 Lakeview Dr., Sebring, FL 33870-7931. Tel.: 863-385-5312. Fax: 863-385-5336.
E-mail: info@highlandsartleague.com
Web Site: highlandsartleague.org/
Formerly: Highland Museum Of The Arts
Founded: 1969.
Key Personnel: Exec. Dir, Alice Stroppel; Pres. (V), Jeri Wohl; Office Asst., Samantha Miller.
Personnel Profile: Full-Time Paid 1; Part-Time Paid 2; Part-Time Volunteers 15.
Governing Authority: private; nonprofit organization. Parent Institution: Highlands Art League, Inc. Tax-exempt: 501(c)(3).
Art Museum: located in the Alan Altwater Civic Complex.
Collections: paintings; photographs; sculpture.
Activities: competitions; receptions; permanent exhibitions.
Publications: newsletter, Artistically Speaking.
Hours & Admission Prices: Call for hours. No charge; donations accepted. Closed major holidays.
Attendance: 1,500 (estimated)
Membership: Individual $50; Family $75.

HIGHLANDS HAMMOCK STATE PARK/CIVILIAN CONSERVATION CORPS MUSEUM, 5931 Hammock Rd., Sebring, FL 33872-7408. Tel.: 863-386-6094. Fax: 863-386-6095.
E-mail: dorothy.l.harris@dep.state.fl.us
Web Site: www.floridastateparks.org
Founded: 1994.
Congressional District: 10
Key Personnel: Pres. (V), Larry Levey; Park Mgr., Peter Anderson; Asst. Park Mgr., Jeanne Parks; Park Specialist, Dorothy Harris.
Personnel Profile: Full-Time Paid 12; Part-Time Paid 2; Part-Time Volunteers 30.
Governing Authority: state. Dept. of Environmental Protection, Div. of Recreation & Parks, 3900 Commonwealth Blvd., Commonwealth Bldg., Tallahassee, FL 32303. Tax-exempt.
Park Museum: housed in 1930s building constructed of heavy native timbers, lumber cut & fabricated on site by the Civilian Conservation Corps.
Collections: CCC memorabilia; photographs; tools; printed documents; life in the 1930s & 1940s; Florida land boom; bust; Great Depression; civilian conservation corps; World War II.
Facilities: nature trails; bicycle paths; campgrounds; bicycle rentals; camp store/restaurant
Activities: permanent, nature & CCC era exhibitions; guided tours; seasonal campfire programs. Museum Sponsors: CCC Era Festival in November.
Publications: interpretive booklet for the nature trails; checklist of birds & other vertebrates; technical listing of plants available for the serious student.
Hours & Admission Prices: Daily 8-sundown. Park entrance fee: $4 per vehicle (2-8 passengers), $3 per vehicle (1 passenger), pedestrians & bicycles $1. Call ranger station for tour bus rates. Entrance to museum is included in regular entrance fees. Museum hours: daily 9-4. Annual State Park Entrance Pass available. ♿
Attendance: 15,000 (estimated)

Seminole

PANAMA CANAL MUSEUM, (M), 7985 113th St., Ste. 100, Seminole, FL 33772-4785. Tel.: 727-394-9338. Fax: 727-394-2737.
E-mail: pankee@aol.com
Web Site: www.panamacanalmuseum.org
Key Personnel: Contact, Elizabeth Neily
History Museum.
Collections: Panama Canal history; documents; photographs.
Hours & Admission Prices: Mon.-Sat. 10-4; other times by appointment. Admission $3.

Stuart

ELLIOTT MUSEUM, 825 N.E. Ocean Blvd., Stuart, FL 34996-1696. Tel.: 772-225-1961. Fax: 772-225-2333.
E-mail: info@elliottmuseumfl.org
Web Site: www.elliottmuseumfl.org.
Founded: 1961.
Congressional District: 12
Key Personnel: Chm. (V), Scott Baratta; C.E.O., Robin Hicks-Connors; Dir. Devel., Amy Christensen; Dir. Visitor Svcs. & Museum Shop Mgr., Heidi May; Cur., Janel Hendrix.
Personnel Profile: Full-Time Paid 6; Part-Time Paid 5; Part-Time Volunteers 70.
Governing Authority: nonprofit organization. Parent Institution: Historical Society of Martin County. Branch Museum: House of Refuge Museum at Gilbert's Bar. Tax-exempt: 501(c)(3).
General Museum.
Collections: contemporary art gallery; furniture; costumes; antique cars; Indian artifacts; Americana; period rooms.
Research Fields: Florida & Martin County history.
Facilities: art gallery available for private functions by rental agreement. Gifts & books for sale.
Activities: permanent & temporary exhibitions.
Publications: History of Martin County.
Hours & Admission Prices: Museum: Mon.-Sat. 10-4, Sun. 1-4; school or other educational groups by appointment. Adults $8, children 5-12 $2; children under 5 & members no charge. Closed major holidays. ♿
Attendance: 25,000 (accurate)
Membership: Individual $35; Family $50; Sponsor $75; Patron $125; Car Club $150.

FLORIDA OCEANOGRAPHIC COASTAL CENTER, 890 N.E. Ocean Blvd., Hutchinson Island, Stuart, FL 34996-1627. Tel.: 772-225-0505.
Web Site: www.floridaoceanographic.org
Formerly: Coastal Science Center at Hutchinson Island
Key Personnel: Exec. Dir., Mark Perry
Maritime Museum.
Collections: marine artifacts; aquariums; replica of Saballariid reef.
Facilities: Museum-related items for sale.
Activities: videos.
Hours & Admission Prices: Mon.-Sat. 10-5, Sun. 12-4. Adults $8, children 3-12 $4; children under 3 & members no charge. Closed New Year's Day; Easter; Thanksgiving; Christmas.

HOUSE OF REFUGE MUSEUM, 301 S.E. MacArthur Blvd., Stuart, FL 34996. Tel.: 772-225-1875. Fax: 772-225-2333.
E-mail: info@elliottmuseumfl.org
Web Site: elliottmuseumfl.org/houseofrefuge/index.html
Formerly: Gilbert's Bar House of Refuge
Founded: 1875.
Congressional District: 12
Key Personnel: Keeper, Barbara Dewhirst.
Personnel Profile: Full-Time Paid 3; Part-Time Paid 2; Part-Time Volunteers 20.
Governing Authority: society. Parent Institution: Historical Society of Martin County, Stuart. Tax-exempt.
Historic House Museum: four room furnished house representing the period 1890-1904. National Register of Historic Places.
Collections: archives; life saving equipment.
Facilities: Gift items for sale.
Activities: special events.
Publications: History of Martin County.
Hours & Admission Prices: Mon.-Sat. 10-4, Sun. 1-4. Adults $6, children 5-12 $3; children under 5 no charge. Closed major holidays. ♿
Attendance: 17,000
Membership: Individual $35; Family $50; Sponsor $75; Patron $125; Car Club $150.

STUART HERITAGE MUSEUM, 161 S.W. Flagler Ave., Stuart, FL 34994-2139. Tel.: 772-220-4600. Fax: 772-781-3416.
Founded: 1988.
Key Personnel: Exec. Dir., Christine K. Sawicki; Mgr., Sally S. Glassburn.
Personnel Profile: Part-Time Paid 1; Part-Time Volunteers 12.
Governing Authority: Tax-exempt: 501(c)(3).
Local County History Museum: built in 1901.
Collections: 10,000 period artifacts including photographs, furnishings, period clothing, county artifacts, maps & books.
Activities: monthly meeting.
Publications: monthly members newsletter; Martin County, Our Heritage; Stuart Heritage Museum Activity Book; Stuart Heritage Cookbook; Stuart Heritage Commemorative Album.
Hours & Admission Prices: Daily 10-3. No charge; donations accepted. Closed New Year's Day; Thanksgiving; Christmas. ♿
Attendance: 4,995 (accurate)
Membership: Single $10; Family $20; Sponsor $50; Sustaining $100; Lifetime $500.

Tallahassee

ALFRED B. MACLAY GARDENS STATE PARK, 3540 Thomasville Rd., Tallahassee, FL 32309-3413. Tel.: 850-487-4556 & 4115. Fax: 850-487-8808.
E-mail: ginger.nichols@dep.state.fl.us
Web Site: www.floridastateparks.org/maclay
Founded: 1953.
Congressional District: 2
Key Personnel: Park Mgr., Beth Weidner.
Personnel Profile: Full-Time Paid 11; Full-Time Volunteers 1; Part-Time Paid 5; Part-Time Volunteers 50.
Governing Authority: state. Parent Institution: Florida Dept. of Environmental Protection. Subsidiary Institution: Division of Recreation & Parks. Tax-exempt.
Historic House Museum & Gardens: c.1909 Maclay House.
Collections: gardens containing plant life native to the Florida Panhandle; camellias; azaleas; dogwoods; mixed hardwood & pine forest; historic house.
Facilities: library; 28 acres of ornamental gardens; 17-acre recreation area; nature trail; rental picnic pavilion; banquet facilities; 2.8 mile hiking, bicycle & horse trail. Museum-related items for sale.
Activities: guided tours; lectures; organized education programs; docent program. Gardens' Sponsors: Pops in the Gardens; Tour of Gardens.
Publications: Maclay Gardens: a seasonal newsletter provided by Friends of Maclay Gardens.
Hours & Admission Prices: Maclay House & Gardens: daily 9-5. Park: 8am to sundown. House & Gardens: Jan.-April adults $6, children under 12 $3. Gardens: May-Dec. $6 per car (8 people); park fee includes gardens; bicyclers, walkers, extra persons in vehicle $2 per person; members 1st Sat. of each month no charge. ♿
Attendance: 147,000 (accurate)
Membership: Gardener $25; Garden Family $50; Patron $100; Sponsor $250; Donor $500.

FLORIDA ASSOCIATION OF MUSEUMS, (M), 459 Cedar Hill Rd, Tallahassee, FL 32312-1046. Mailing Address: P.O. Box 10951, Tallahassee, FL 32302-2951. Tel.: 850-222-6028. Fax: 850-222-6112.
E-mail: Fam@flamuseums.org
Web Site: www.flamuseums.org
Founded: 1986.
Congressional District: 2
Key Personnel: Exec. Dir., Malinda Horton; Pres. (V), Russell S. Daws.
Personnel Profile: Full-Time Paid 1; Part-Time Paid 2.
Governing Authority: nonprofit state association. Tax-exempt.
State Museum Association.
Publications: FAM Annual Directory.
Membership: Individual $30; Vendor & Affiliate $75; Institutional $250 or .1% of annual operating budget.

* **FLORIDA STATE UNIVERSITY MUSEUM OF FINE ARTS, (M),** Fine Arts Building, Rm. 250, Tallahassee, FL 32306-0001. Mailing Address: 530 W. Call St., P.O. Box 3061140, Tallahassee, FL 32306-1140. Tel.: 850-644-6836 & 1254. Fax: 850-644-7229.
E-mail: apalladinocraig@fsu.edu
Web Site: www.mofa.fsu.edu
Founded: 1950.
Congressional District: 2
Key Personnel: C.E.O. & Dir., Allys Palladino-Craig.
Personnel Profile: Full-Time Paid 5; Part-Time Paid 6; Part-Time Volunteers 30; Interns 2.
Governing Authority: state. Parent Institution: Florida State University. Subsidiary Institution: College of Visual Art, Theatre & Dance. Tax-exempt.
Art Museum.
Collections: The Victor & Mary Carter Collection of Peruvian Art, European Art, Asian Art & contemporary art; glass; graphics; photography; the Mary Lewis American Basketry Collection.
Major Exhibits: The Kids' Guernica, 1/10; Faculty Annual, 2/10-3/10; In Company With Angels (T), 2/10-3/10; Graduating Artists - Spring, 4/10; Artists' League Summer Annual, 6/10-7/10; Tallahassee International, 8/10-9/10; Graduating Artists - Fall, 11/10-12/10; Arts & Antiques Fair, 12/10.

Research Fields: contemporary art & art historical topics, subject to guest curatorial publications, Thematic.
Facilities: lecture room; lounge; sculpture garden.
Activities: lectures; gallery talks; formally organized education programs for graduate students; inter-museum loan, temporary & traveling exhibitions; performing arts events; theatre; music & dance; community outreach program.
Publications: brochures; exhibitions catalogues; art history journal, Athanor; curatorial publications, Thematic.
Hours & Admission Prices: May-Aug. Mon.-Fri. 9-4; Sept.-April Mon.-Fri. 9-4, Sat.-Sun. 1-4. No charge. Closed university holidays. ♿
Attendance: 36,628 (accurate)
Membership: Artist's League, Student & Senior Citizen $15; Individual $25; Family $35; Supporting $50; Century Club $100; Business $250; Westcott Society $500; Benefactor $1,000; Angel $1,000 & up.

FLORIDA'S HISTORIC CAPITOL, (M), 400 S. Monroe St., Tallahassee, FL 32399-6536. Tel.: 850-487-1902. Fax: 850-410-2233.
E-mail: info@flhistoriccapitol.gov
Web Site: www.flhistoriccapitol.gov
Key Personnel: Cur., John B. Phelps
History Museum.
Collections: local history & culture relating to Florida's legislative history; oral papers; photographs.
Hours & Admission Prices: Mon.-Fri. 9-4:30, Sat. 10-4:30, Sun. & holidays 12-4:30. No charge; donations accepted.Closed Thanksgiving; Christmas.

FOSTER-TANNER FINE ARTS GALLERY, Florida A&M University, Foster Tanner Arts Bldg., 1630 Pinder Dr., Tallahassee, FL 32307-0001. Tel.: 850-599-3161. Fax: 850-599-8761.
E-mail: harriswiltsher@famu.edu
Key Personnel: Dir., Harris Wiltsher
Art Museum.
Collections: African American & Native American artists.
Hours & Admission Prices: Jan. 3-Dec. 13 Mon.-Fri. 11-5. No charge; donations accepted.

GOODWOOD MUSEUM AND GARDENS, 1600 Miccosukee Rd., Tallahassee, FL 32308-5166. Tel.: 850-877-4202. Fax: 850-877-3090.
E-mail: director@goodwoodmuseum.org
Web Site: www.goodwoodmuseum.org
Key Personnel: Exec. Dir., Larry Paarlberg
Historic House: built c.1840.
Collections: period furnishings; personal artifacts.
Facilities: 16 acres. Museum-related items for sale.
Hours & Admission Prices: House: Mon.-Fri. 10-4, Sat. 10-2; groups by appointment. Gardens: Mon.-Fri. 9-5, Sat. 10-2. House: admission $6; children under 3 no charge. Gardens: no charge. Closed New Year's Eve & Day; Thanksgiving; Christmas Eve, Day & week.

KNOTT HOUSE MUSEUM, 301 E. Park Ave., Tallahassee, FL 32301-1513. Tel.: 850-922-2459 & 245-6400. Fax: 850-413-7261.
E-mail: bwcotellis@dos.state.fl.us
Web Site: www.flheritage.com/museum/sites/knotthouse
Founded: 1992.
Congressional District: 2
Key Personnel: Site Mgr., Beatrice Cotellis; Educator, June E. Finnegan, Ph.D.; Educator, Cynthia M. Bellacero, M.A.
Personnel Profile: Full-Time Paid 2; Part-Time Paid 1; Part-Time Volunteers 32; Interns 1.
Governing Authority: state. Parent Institution: Museum of Florida History, R.A. Gray Bldg., 500 S. Bronough St., Tallahassee, FL 32399-0250. Tax-exempt: 501(c)(3).
History Museum: housed in 1843 colonial revival house.
Collections: original furnishings; personal effects; books; cards; poems written by Mrs. Knott; documents, receipts & correspondence interpreting life in Tallahassee during 1928-1941.
Research Fields: women's history; 1930s in Florida; 1930 Florida gardens; Florida politics.
Facilities: classroom; 380 sq. ft. exhibit space. Museum-related items for sale.
Activities: art event; concerts; films; formal education programs; guided tours; participatory & temporary exhibitions; theater; teenage workshop; poetry readings; swing dance; walking tours; scout programs; lectures. Museum Sponsors: Emancipation Day.
Publications: Tales of Tallahassee, Twice Told and Untold.
Hours & Admission Prices: Sept.-July Museum: Tues.-Sat. 10-4. Tours: Wed.-Fri. 1, 2 & 3, Sat. on the hour from 10-3. No charge; donations encouraged. Group Tours: $1 per person. Closed Thanksgiving; Christmas. ♿

Attendance: 5,000 (estimated)

LAKE JACKSON MOUNDS ARCHAEOLOGICAL STATE PARK, 3600 Indian Mounds Rd., Tallahassee, FL 32303-2300. Tel.: 850-922-6007. Fax: 850-488-0366.
Web Site: www.floridastateparks.org
Founded: 1970.
Congressional District: 2
Key Personnel: Park Mgr., Barry A. Burch; Administrative Asst., Shirley Deal.
Personnel Profile: Full-Time Paid 2.
Governing Authority: state; nonprofit; Parent Institution: State of Florida, Dept. of Environmental Protection. Division of Recreation & Parks. Tax-exempt.
Archaeological Site: 1200-1500 ceremonial center of the Fort Walton period.
Collections: local history & culture; 1800s grist mill.
Facilities: library of printed references to artifact types, animal & plant species available to the public.
Activities: guided tours; self-guided trail; lectures; slides.
Publications: site specific brochure.
Hours & Admission Prices: Daily 8-sunset. $3 per car, $2 for pedestrians and bikers. Donations accepted. ♿
Attendance: 16,464 (estimated)

LEMOYNE CENTER FOR THE VISUAL ARTS, 125 N. Gadsden, Tallahassee, FL 32301-1507. Tel.: 850-222-8800. Fax: 850-224-2714.
E-mail: director@lemoyne.org
Web Site: www.lemoyne.org
Formerly: LeMoyne Art Foundation, Inc.
Founded: 1964.
Congressional District: 2
Key Personnel: Exec. Dir., Hillary Brett; Pres. (V), Kelly Dozier; Vice Pres., Eva B. Armstrong; Volunteer Coord. & Museum Shop Mgr., Betty Bayes Lessinger; Dir. Education, Anna Myers; Education Coord., Amanda Wilke; Education Coord., Jennifer Infinger; Cur., Lesley Marchessault; Events Coord., Sheri Sanderson.
Personnel Profile: Full-Time Paid 3; Part-Time Paid 6; Part-Time Volunteers 50; Interns 2.
Governing Authority: nonprofit organization. Tax-exempt: 501(c)(3).
Art Center: housed in 1852 wooden structure used as hospital during Civil War.
Collections: contemporary art; sculpture garden.
Research Fields: history; collect books & prints related to LeMoyne.
Facilities: educational facility. Gift items for sale.
Activities: guided tours; lectures; films; gallery talks; rental gallery; TV & radio programs; formally organized education programs; docent program or council, inter-museum loan, permanent, temporary & traveling exhibitions.
Publications: newsletter to members; exhibition catalogs.
Hours & Admission Prices: Tues.-Sat. 10-5. Adults $2; discounts to AAM & ICOM members; students & members no charge. Fees charged only for special exhibits. Closed major holidays. ♿
Attendance: 115,000 (estimated)
Membership: Regular: Individual $30; Family $50; Patron $120; Donor $250; Fellow $500; Benefactor $1,000; Life $5,000. Business: Patron $250; Contributing $500; Donor $1,000; Fellow $2,500; Benefactor $5,000; Life $10,000.

THE MARY BROGAN MUSEUM OF ART AND SCIENCE, (M), 350 S. Duval St., Tallahassee, FL 32301-1711. Tel.: 850-513-0700, ext. 221 & 232. Fax: 850-513-0143.
E-mail: cbarber@thebrogan.org
Web Site: www.thebrogan.org
Formerly: Odyssey Science Center/Museum of Art/Tallahassee
Founded: 1990.
Congressional District: 2
Key Personnel: Exec. Dir., Chucha Barber; C.O.O., Trish Hanson; Mgr. Public Rels., Kallen Lunt; Dir. Art Collections & Registrar, Michelle Smith Grindberg.
Personnel Profile: Full-Time Paid 23; Part-Time Paid 4; Part-Time Volunteers 200; Interns 8.
Governing Authority: Tax-exempt.
Art & Science Museum.
Collections: visual arts; hands-on science exhibits.
Facilities: classrooms; 6,500 sq. ft. exhibit space. Museum-related items for sale.
Activities: guided tours; lectures; docent program; MOA Corps; participatory & traveling exhibitions; field trips; birthday parties; summer camp. Museum Sponsors: Saturday at the Science Center; Odyssey Explorers; Star Lab; That Art Group.
Publications: catalogues; newsletters; annual report.
Hours & Admission Prices: Mon.-Sat. 10-5, Sun. 1-5. Adults $10, children

3-17, students, senior citizens 60 & over and military $5; discounts to groups, AAA & AAM members; ASTC members, children 2 & under, and museum members no charge. ♿
Attendance: 85,000 (accurate)
Membership: Individual $25; Membership for Two $35; Family $50; Smithsonian Affiliate $75; Pacesetter $150; Visionary $350; Champion $1,200.

* **MUSEUM OF FLORIDA HISTORY, (M),** 500 S. Bronough St., Tallahassee, FL 32399-6504. Tel.: 850-245-6400. Fax: 850-245-6433.
E-mail: jbrunson@dos.state.fl.us
Web Site: www.museumoffloridahistory.com
Founded: 1967.
Congressional District: 2
Key Personnel: Bureau Chief, Dr. Jeana Brunson; Chm., Frank Jameson; Cur. Historic Sites & Education, K.C. Smith; Cur. Research & Collections, Lea Ellen Thornton; Cur. Design & Fabrication, Charity Wood; Public Rels., Wanda Richey; Museum Shop Mgr., Susan Stratton.
Personnel Profile: Full-Time Paid 22; Part-Time Paid 8; Interns 3.
Governing Authority: state. Parent Institution: Florida Dept. of State. Tax-exempt: 501(c)(3).
History Museum.
Collections: historical material reflecting the history & culture of the State, including archaeological materials, Spanish numismatics & maritime objects; artifacts from citrus industry & steamboat era; early tourist memorabilia. Historic Building: 1843 restored Knott House Museum.
Research Fields: museology; Florida history; archaeology; Florida government.
Facilities: 49,000 sq. ft. exhibit space; 240-seat auditorium; cafe. Museum-related gifts for sale.
Activities: permanent, temporary & traveling exhibitions; formally organized education programs; statewide services. Museum Sponsors: State History Fair.
Publications: newsletter, Historically Speaking; site brochures, education guide; Heritage Education program guides.
Hours & Admission Prices: Mon.-Fri. 9-4:30, third Thurs. of month 9-8, Sat. 10-4:30, Sun. & holidays 12-4:30. No charge; donations accepted. Closed Thanksgiving; Christmas. ♿
Attendance: 56,727 (accurate)
Membership: Student $15; Senior & Teacher $25; Individual $35; Senior Family $50; Family $60.

RILEY HOUSE MUSEUM OF AFRICAN AMERICAN HISTORY & CULTURE, (M), 419 E. Jefferson St., Tallahassee, FL 32301-1817. Tel.: 850-681-7881. Fax: 850-386-4368.
E-mail: staff@rileymuseum.org
Web Site: www.rileymuseum.org; www.faahph.com
Founded: 1996.
Congressional District: 2
Key Personnel: Exec. Dir. & C.E.O., Althemese Barnes; Chm. (V), Dr. David Jackson; Chm., Gwendolyn Spencer; Program Coord., Maggie Lewis Butler; Mktg., Publicity Dir. & Museum Shop Mgr., Quenita White.
Personnel Profile: Full-Time Paid 2; Full-Time Volunteers 2; Part-Time Paid 2; Part-Time Volunteers 38; Interns 2.
Governing Authority: private; nonprofit organization. Parent Institution: John G. Riley Foundation Inc. Tax-exempt.
Historic House Museum: housed in home of John Gilmore Riley, first African American principal of Lincoln High School in Tallahassee, Florida; built in 1890.
Collections: grassroots African American Florida history; black abolitionists papers; American Missionary Society papers; Thelma Thurston Gorham collection; Black history books.
Research Fields: African American education in Florida 1865-1968; tenant farming & midwifery history in northwest Florida 1865-1950s; African American burial sites; Black abolitionist & American Missionary Society.
Facilities: 900 sq. ft. exhibit space. Museum-related items for sale.
Activities: formal educational programs; guided tours; loan, temporary, traveling & participatory exhibitions; school loan service; training programs for professional museum workers; broadcast & cable programs. Museum Sponsors: Members Reception; Statewide Conference; Emancipation Activity; Holiday Event.
Publications: quarterly newsletter, Out of the Past... A Noble Witness; Paths To Freedom.
Hours & Admission Prices: Jan. 3-Dec. 21 Mon., Wed. & Fri. 10-4; scheduled groups on Tues. & Thurs. Adults $2, members $1.50; discounts to AAM & ICOM members. Closed New Year's Day; Martin Luther King, Jr. Day; Easter weekend; Memorial Day; Independence Day; Thanksgiving & day before; Christmas. ♿
Attendance: 5,206 (accurate)
Membership: Individual $30; Contributor $100; Benefactor $250; Founder $1,000; Corporate $2,500.

TALLAHASSEE AUTOMOBILE MUSEUM, 6800 Mahan Dr., Tallahassee, FL 32308-1402. Mailing Address: P.O. Box 120, Hosford, FL 32334-0120. Tel.: 850-942-0137.
Formerly: Antique Car Museum
Founded: 1996.
Automobile Museum.
Collections: period automobiles; collectibles; Smoky Mountain trains.
Hours & Admission Prices: Mon.-Fri. 8-5, Sat. 10-5, Sun. 12-5; Thanksgiving & Christmas by appointment. Adults $16, 2 adults $13.50, students $10.75, children 5-9 $7.50; discounts to groups. Train Museum: $6 per person. ♿

* **TALLAHASSEE MUSEUM, (M),** 3945 Museum Dr., Tallahassee, FL 32310-6325. Tel.: 850-575-8684. Fax: 850-574-8243.
E-mail: rdaws@tallahasseemuseum.org
Web Site: www.tallahasseemuseum.org
Formerly: Tallahassee Museum of History and Natural Science
Founded: 1957.
Congressional District: 2
Key Personnel: C.E.O. & Exec. Dir., Russell S. Daws; Pres. (V), Susan Baldino; Facilities Mgr., Mike Sullivan; Dir. Finance, Theresa Davis; Cur. Collections & Exhibits, Linda Deaton; Cur. Animals, Mike Jones; Education Dir., Jennifer Golden; Museum Store Mgr., Theresa Davis.
Personnel Profile: Full-Time Paid 16; Part-Time Paid 63; Part-Time Volunteers 515; Interns 4.
Governing Authority: nonprofit organization. Tax-exempt: 501(c)(3).
General Museum.
Collections: 19th-century regional history & natural history; agricultural implements; household artifacts; textiles; clothing; native Florida wildlife. Historic Buildings: 1840s plantation house; African-American church & schoolhouse; caboose; 1880s farmstead.
Research Fields: regional history related to restored buildings; participants in Red Wolf captive breeding program; Florida Panther Recovery Program.
Facilities: natural habitat zoo; nature trails; discovery center; food service; meeting room. Museum-related items for sale.
Activities: formally organized educational programs; traveling, permanent & temporary exhibitions; school loan service; preschool; 19th-century crafts & skills demonstrations. Museum Sponsors: Arts & Crafts Festival; Music Festivals; Folklife Festival; summer camp.
Publications: bimonthly, Museum News.
Hours & Admission Prices: Mon.-Sat. 9-5, Sun. 12:30-5. Adults $9, seniors & college students $8.50, children $6; discounts to AAM & FAM members; members & children 3 & under no charge. Closed New Year's Day; Thanksgiving; Christmas Eve & Day. ♿
Attendance: 124,970 (accurate)
Membership: Individual $50; Family & Grandparent $60; Contributing $90-$179; Habitat Club $180 & up; Corporate $300.

Tampa

AMERICAN VICTORY MARINERS MEMORIAL & MUSEUM SHIP, 705 Channelside Dr., Tampa, FL 33602-5600. Tel.: 813-228-8766.
Maritime History Museum: housed on a 1940s-era merchant cargo ship.
Collections: maritime culture & industry; photographs; medals & documents; personal artifacts; navigational equipment; weaponry; hands-on exhibits.
Activities: ship tours; hands-on exhibits.
Hours & Admission Prices: Tues.-Sat. 10-5, Sun. 12-5. Adults $10, children $4; children 3 & under no charge.

CRACKER COUNTRY, 4800 N. Hwy. 301, Tampa, FL 33680. Mailing Address: P.O. Box 11766, Tampa, FL 33680-1766. Tel.: 813-627-4225. Fax: 813-740-3518. TDD: 813-621-7821.
Web Site: www.crackercountry.org
Founded: 1979.
Congressional District: 9
Key Personnel: Dir., Rip Stalvey; Maintenance Supt., Ron Tarlton; Mgr. Museum Experiences, Dan Marshall; Supvr. Store, Linda Mahoney; Supvr. Museum Programs, Susan Obarski.
Personnel Profile: Full-Time Paid 5; Part-Time Volunteers 150; Interns 3.
Governing Authority: state. Parent Institution: Florida State Fair Authority. Tax-exempt.
Historic Village & Museum: 12 turn-of-the-century buildings, 1870-1912, located on the Florida State Fairgrounds in a section known as Cracker Country.
Collections: all of the buildings are furnished with period furnishings; old Lionel train collection in Depot; collection of oil portraits of Florida's Governors beginning with Andrew Jackson; rural Florida late 1800s, early 1900s.
Facilities: Museum-related items for sale.
Activities: education programs for children; grade school tours; docent program. Annual Events: Florida State Fair in February; Discover the Past March to January.

Publications: brochure, Cracker Country; monthly newsletter, Traditions.
Hours & Admission Prices: Grade School Tours: March-May & Sept.-Dec. Tues.-Fri. Admission $5. Discover the Past: March-Jan. 1st Sat. of month 10-4. Adults $6, seniors & children 6-12 $5; children 5 & under no charge. ♿
Attendance: 300,000 (estimated)

FLORIDA AQUARIUM, 701 Channelside Dr., Tampa, FL 33602-5614. Tel.: 813-273-4000.
Web Site: www.flaquarium.org
Aquarium.
Collections: over 10,000 aquatic plants & animals.
Facilities: cafe. Museum-related items for sale.
Hours & Admission Prices: Daily 9:30-5. Adults $19.95, seniors 60 & over $16.95, children under 12 $14.95; children 2 & under no charge. Closed Thanksgiving; Christmas.

FLORIDA MUSEUM OF PHOTOGRAPHIC ARTS, (M), 200 N. Tampa St., Ste. 130, Tampa, FL 33602-5161. Tel.: 813-221-2222.
Web Site: www.fmopa.org
Formerly: Tampa Gallery of Photographic Art
Founded: 2001.
Key Personnel: Museum Mgr., Heather Trubee; Chm. (V), Carol Gaynor; Museum Shop Mgr., Jonathan Bykowski.
Personnel Profile: Full-Time Paid 1; Full-Time Volunteers 1; Part-Time Volunteers 50; Interns 3.
Governing Authority: Tax-exempt.
Art Museum.
Collections: works by national & international photographic artists.
Major Exhibits: August Sander & Jules Aarons, 1/10-3/10; Portraits of the Artists: Selections from the Collection of Robert Sanchez, 3/10-5/10; Shai Kremer, 3/10-5/10; Annual Members Show, 9/10.
Activities: children's literacy through photography program; photography classes & workshops.
Hours & Admission Prices: Tues.-Sat. 10-5. Adults $4; members no charge. Closed New Year's Day; Independence Day; Thanksgiving; Christmas. ♿
Attendance: 5,500 (estimated)
Membership: Student & Senior $25; Individual $30; Family $50; Friend $100; Donor $300; Contributor $500; Benefactor $1,000; Silver $2,500; Gold $5,000.

* **HENRY B. PLANT MUSEUM, (M),** 401 W. Kennedy Blvd., Tampa, FL 33606-1450. Tel.: 813-258-7301. Fax: 813-258-7272.
E-mail: cgandee@ut.edu
Web Site: www.plantmuseum.com
Founded: 1933.
Congressional District: 7
Key Personnel: C.E.O., Cynthia Gandee; Pres. Trustee (V), Renee Williams Vaughn; Pres. Volunteer Council (V), Cindy Xenick; Pres. Museum Society (V), Brenda Ketchey; Cur. & Registrar, Susan Carter; Operations & Membership, Heather Brabham; Museum Store Mgr., Sue Gauthier; Museum Rels., Sally Shifke; Curatorial Asst., Scott Waltz; Cur. Education, Gianna Russo.
Personnel Profile: Full-Time Paid 7; Part-Time Paid 2; Part-Time Volunteers 85; Interns 3.
Governing Authority: municipal. Parent Institution: The University of Tampa. Tax-exempt: 170(b)(1)(A).
History & Decorative Arts Museum: housed in 1891 Tampa Bay Hotel.
Collections: original furnishings & objects of the Gilded Age from 1891 Tampa Bay Hotel; Plant System railroad; steamship & hotel artifacts; Spanish-American War collection.
Major Exhibits: Gasparilla: A Tampa Tradition, 1/10-2/10; Victorian Christmas Stroll, 12/10.
Research Fields: decorative arts; The Tampa Bay Hotel; local history; Plant System railroads, steamships & hotels; early Florida tourist industry; Spanish-American War.
Facilities: library of reference materials relating to the collection available for use on the premises.
Activities: guided tours; outside lectures; school programs; special events; music programs; monthly antique evaluation clinics; audio wand tour. Museum Sponsors: Victorian Christmas Stroll. Theater: Upstairs/Downstairs at the Tampa Bay Hotel.
Publications: booklets, An Architectural Guide to the Tampa Bay Hotel, A Walking Tour of the Gardens, Moments in Time: The Tampa Bay Hotel, Its History & Glory 1891-1931; video, The Tampa Bay Hotel: Florida's First Magic Kingdom; video, Dateline Tampa 1898: Florida and the Spanish American War, narrated by General H. Norman Schwarzkopf. Henry Bradley Plant: The 19th century King of Florida; If Our Hotel Could Talk; Maggie and Max at the Museum.
Hours & Admission Prices: Tues.-Sat. 10-4, Sun. 12-4. Suggested Donation: adults $5, children $3; discounts to AAM members; members no charge. Closed Thanksgiving; Christmas. ♿
Attendance: 55,000 (accurate)
Membership: Friend $35; Family $60; Patron $200; Veranda Circle $500; Crescent Club $1,000; 1891 Landmark Society $5,000.

* **MUSEUM OF SCIENCE AND INDUSTRY, (M),** 4801 E. Fowler Ave., Tampa, FL 33617-2099. Tel.: 813-987-6300. Fax: 813-987-6310.
E-mail: shanij@mosi.org
Web Site: www.mosi.org
Founded: 1955.
Congressional District: 7
Key Personnel: Pres., Wit Ostrenko; Chm. (V), Harry F. Sheraw; Exec. Vice Pres., Vicki Ahrens; Vice Pres. Exhibits, Dave Conley; Vice Pres. Education, Anthonette Carregal; Vice Pres. Facilities, Donald D. Toeller; Vice Pres. Finance, Kathy Prossick; Vice Pres. Research & Institutional Devel., Dr. Judith L Lombana; Sr. Vice Pres. Advancement, Alicia Slater-Haase; Vice Pres. Mktg. & Corp. Rels., Tanya Vomacka; Vice Pres. Human Resources, Kelly Cunngton; Volunteer Coord., Joel Bates; Media Rels. Specialist, Shani Jefferson; Mgr. Planetarium Sr. Programs, Steve Nipper; Museum Shop Mgr., Laurel Jacobs.
Personnel Profile: Full-Time Paid 250; Part-Time Paid 132; Part-Time Volunteers 248.
Governing Authority: county. Parent Institution: Museum of Science & Industry Foundation. Tax-exempt.
Science, Industry & Technology Center.
Collections: science; technology; industry; human history.
Research Fields: relative to collections & geographic area.
Facilities: library; 74-acre site; 340-seat IMAX dome theater; 400,000 sq. ft. exhibit area; 400-seat auditorium; planetarium; natural water treatment facility with Butterfly Habitat; 30-acre natural habitat; 120-seat science demonstration theater; Verizon Challenger Learning Center; classrooms; Head Start Center; 40,000 sq. ft. children's science center; cafe. Museum-related science items for sale.
Activities: permanent & changing exhibits; science demonstrations; classes & group programs; community outreach activities; Headstart program; summer camps.
Publications: newsletter; annual report; magazine, MOSI Matters; Summer Science Camp catalog, guidebook to group programs.
Hours & Admission Prices: Daily 9-5. Adults 13-59 $20.95, seniors 60 & over $18.95, children 2-12 $16.95 (combo-MOSI, IMAX & MOSI); discounts for AAM, ASTC, & FDEP members; members no charge. Parking no charge. Call to confirm. ♿
Attendance: 630,993 (accurate)
Membership: Student & Individual $55; Dual $75; Family & Grandparents $99. IMAX: Individual $55; Dual $105; Family & Grandparent $150; Galaxy Circle $1,000 & up.

SCARFONE/HARTLEY GALLERY, 310 N. Blvd., Tampa, FL 33606-1403. Mailing Address: 401 W. Kennedy, Tampa, FL 33606-1450. Tel.: 813-253-3333 & 6217. Fax: 813-258-7497.
E-mail: dcowden@ut.edu
Web Site: www.ut.edu
Founded: 1977.
Congressional District: 7
Key Personnel: Dir., Dorothy C. Cowden.
Personnel Profile: Full-Time Paid 1; Part-Time Paid 10; Part-Time Volunteers 20; Interns 2.
Governing Authority: university. University of Tampa, 401 W. Kennedy, Tampa, FL 33606. Tax-exempt: 501(c)(3).
Fine Arts Gallery.
Collections: contemporary 3-D & 2-D sculpture; prints; paintings; drawings; ceramics.
Facilities: teaching gallery; lecture facility.
Activities: guided tours; lectures; films; concerts; dance performances; arts festivals; drama; training programs for professional museum workers; visual art exhibitions.
Publications: brochures for events & special exhibitions; catalogs for special events.
Hours & Admission Prices: Aug.-May Tues.-Fri. 10-4, Sat. 1-4. No charge; donations accepted. Closed national holidays. ♿
Attendance: 12,000 (estimated)
Membership: Friends of the Gallery: General $35; Patron $125-$1,000.

TAMPA BAY HISTORY CENTER, INC., (M), 801 St. Pete Times Forum Dr., Tampa, FL 33602-5411. Mailing Address: 801 Old Water St., Tampa, FL 33602-5418. Tel.: 813-228-0097. Fax: 813-223-7021.
E-mail: info@tampabayhistorycenter.org

Web Site: www.tampabayhistorycenter.org
Founded: 1989.
Congressional District: 7
Key Personnel: Chm., Marsha Rydberg; Pres. & C.E.O., C.J. Roberts; Vice Pres., Advancement, Grant Martin; Vice Pres. Programs, Elizabeth L. Dunham; Cur., Rodney Kite Powell; Cur. Education, Julie Matus; Assoc. Dir. Devel., Deborah Wagner; Dir. Mktg., Ashleigh Slyker; Vice Pres. Finance & Operations, Susan Casper; Mgr. Collections, Travis Puterbaugh; Accountant, Maria Steijlen; Exec. Asst., Kathy Williams; Administrative Asst., Judy Miller.
Personnel Profile: Full-Time Paid 19; Part-Time Paid 5; Part-Time Volunteers 80; Interns 3.
Governing Authority: private; nonprofit. Tax-exempt: 501(c)(3).
History Museum.
Collections: Florida, Hillsborough County & the Tampa Bay region from prehistoric era to present.
Research Fields: history, archaeology & multicultural heritage of Hillsborough County and the Tampa Bay region.
Facilities: 3,000-vol. library of regional history; 17,000 sq. ft. exhibit space; educational facilities.
Activities: lectures; guided tours; formal educational programs.
Publications: quarterly newsletter, Cotanchobee; Tampa Bay Frontier Series (12 vol.); journal, Tampa Bay History.
Hours & Admission Prices: Daily 10-5. Adults $12; discounts to FAM, AAM & ICOM members; members no charge. Closed Thanksgiving; Christmas. ♿
Attendance: 100,000 (estimated)
Membership: Student & Teacher $25; Individual $50; Companion $65; Family $75; Supporter $125; Sponsor $250; Patron $500; Benefactor $1,000; Founder $12,500 ($2,500 per year for 5 years).

*** TAMPA MUSEUM OF ART, (M),** 120 Gasparilla Dr., Tampa, FL 33602. Tel.: 813-274-8130. Fax: 813-274-8732.
Web Site: www.tampamuseum.org
Founded: 1979.
Congressional District: 7
Key Personnel: Chm. (V), Ray Ifert; Exec. Dir., Todd D. Smith; C.O.O., John Wren; Richard E. Perry Cur. Greek & Roman Art, Seth D. Pevnick; Registrar, Devon Dargan; Deputy Dir. Programming, Dawn Johnson.
Personnel Profile: Full-Time Paid 20; Part-Time Paid 8; Part-Time Volunteers 125.
Governing Authority: bd. of trustees. Parent Institution: Tampa Museum of Art, Inc. Subsidiary Institution: Tampa Museum of Art Foundation. Tax-exempt.
Art Museum.
Collections: 19th-century to contemporary paintings, sculpture & works on paper; Greek & Roman antiquities; C. Paul Jennewein collection of sculpture; photography.
Major Exhibits: A Celebration of Henri Matisse (T), 2/4/10-4/18/10; Jesper Just: Romantic Delusions (T), 5/8/10-9/5/10; American Impressionism and the Garden (T), 9/24/10-1/3/11.
Research Fields: 19th- to 20th-century American art; Greek and Roman antiquities, 2500 B.C.-300 A.D.
Activities: community outreach programs; special lectures; monthly events; workshops & programs.
Publications: member newsletter; exhibition catalogues for major TMA-organized exhibitions; gallery guides for some smaller exhibitions; educational collateral.
Hours & Admission Prices: Opening early 2010. Daily. Closed major holidays. ♿
Membership: Student $25; Senior $30; Individual $35; Senior Household $45; Household $50; Sustaining $100; Patron $250; Silver Patron $500; Gold Patron $1,000; Benefactor $2,500. Director's Circle $5,000 & up; President's Circle $10,000 & up.

TAMPA'S LOWRY PARK ZOO, 1101 W. Sligh Ave., Tampa, FL 33604-5958. Tel.: 813-935-8552. Fax: 813-935-9486.
E-mail: information@lowryparkzoo.com
Web Site: www.lowryparkzoo.com
Founded: 1957.
Congressional District: 11
Key Personnel: Chm. (V), Catherine Lowry Straz; Acting C.E.O. & Deputy Dir., Craig Pugh; Museum Shop Buyer & Mgr., Kim Gefre.
Personnel Profile: Full-Time Paid 140; Part-Time Paid 165; Part-Time Volunteers 1,800; Interns 6.
Governing Authority: society; nonprofit. Parent Institution: Lowry Park Zoological Society of Tampa, Inc. Tax-exempt: 501(c)(3).
Zoo.
Collections: over 2,000 animals & their habitats.
Facilities: library; children's zoo; aquarium; botanical garden; cafeteria; environmental education center; 2 amphitheaters; nature & conservation center. Museum-related items for sale.
Activities: arts festivals; concerts; docent program; formal educational programs; lectures; study clubs. Museum Sponsors: Annual Karamu, ZooFari; Summer Safari Night; ZooBoo; Wild Wonderland; Wild Australia; River Odessey Eco-Tour; Safari Africa; WaZoo; Fiesta Zoo.
Publications: newsletter quarterly; triannual newsletter, Zoo Chatter; quarterly education program guide; annual report.
Hours & Admission Prices: Daily 9:30-5. Adults $19.95, senior citizens $17.95, children $14.95; discounts to AZA member & groups; members no charge. Closed Thanksgiving; Christmas. ♿
Attendance: 1,104,280 (accurate)
Membership: Guest Pass $40; Individual $45; Dual $85; Single Parent $90; Family & Grandparent $125; Family Plus $180.

UNIVERSITY OF SOUTH FLORIDA BOTANICAL GARDEN, 4202 E. Fowler Ave., NES 107, Tampa, FL 33620-9951. Tel.: 813-974-2329. Fax: 813-974-4808.
E-mail: lwalker@mail.cas.usf.edu
Web Site: www.cas.usf.edu/garden
Key Personnel: Dir., Laurie Walker; Coord. Special Events, Kim Hutton; Mgr. Plant Shop, Valerie Nye; Sr. Agricultural Asst., David Ropp
Botanical Garden.
Collections: plants.
Facilities: Museum-related items for sale.
Activities: research; education programs.
Hours & Admission Prices: Mon.-Fri. 9-5, Sat. 9-4, Sun. 12-4. Adults $5. Closed major holidays.

*** UNIVERSITY OF SOUTH FLORIDA CONTEMPORARY ART MUSEUM, (M),** 4202 E. Fowler Ave., Tampa, FL 33620-9951. Mailing Address: 3821 Holly Dr., Tampa, FL 33620-7360. Tel.: 813-974-4133. Fax: 813-974-5130.
E-mail: caminfo@arts.usf.edu
Web Site: www.usfcam.usf.edu/CAM/cam_about.html
Founded: 1968.
Congressional District: 7
Key Personnel: Dir., Margaret A. Miller; Assoc. Dir., Alexa Favata; Collections Cur., Peter Foe; Exhibitions Supvr., Tony Palms; Dir. Public Art, Vincent Ahern; Security, David Waterman; Program Asst., Victoria Billig; New Media Cur., Don Michael Fuller; Business Coord. & Museum Shop Mgr., Randall West.
Personnel Profile: Full-Time Paid 11; Part-Time Paid 3; Part-Time Volunteers 3; Interns 6.
Governing Authority: university. Parent Institution: University of South Florida. Tax-exempt.
Contemporary Art Museum.
Collections: contemporary graphics; photography; public art commissions.
Research Fields: graphics; public art.
Facilities: Museum-related items for sale.
Activities: guided tours; lectures; films; gallery talks; formally organized education programs for undergraduate & graduate college students affiliated with University of South Florida; inter-museum loan, temporary & traveling exhibitions; art bank exhibition loan service.
Publications: exhibition catalogs; newsletters; posters; public art videos.
Hours & Admission Prices: Museum: Mon.-Fri. 10-5, Sat. 1-4. No charge. Closed university holidays. ♿
Attendance: 58,000 (estimated)
Membership: Student & Senior $15; Individual $25; Dual (2) $45; Benefactor $250; Patron $1,500; Corporate $2,500-$100,000.

YBOR CITY MUSEUM STATE PARK, 1818 Ninth Ave. E., Tampa, FL 33605-3818. Tel.: 813-247-6323. Fax: 813-233-3343.
E-mail: douglas.kinder@dep.state.fl.us
Web Site: www.ybormuseum.org
Formerly: Ybor City State Museum
Founded: 1980.
Key Personnel: Dir., Chantal Hevia; Park Mgr., Kimbelee Tennille; Asst. Park Mgr., Bobby Tootacker; Pres. (V), Rich Simmons; Park Ranger, Nancy Garrison; Park Svcs. Specialist, Alex Kinder; Museum Shop Mgr., Cookie Ginex.
Personnel Profile: Full-Time Paid 2; Part-Time Volunteers 38; Interns 1.
Governing Authority: state. Parent Institution: Dept. of Environmental Protection, Div. of Recreation & Parks. Tax-exempt.
Industrial Museum: 1923 Bakery Building; original brick commercial ovens. Complex also contains c.1895 restored & furnished house, originally rented to workers.
Collections: exhibits & artifacts interpreting the cigar industry in Tampa's Latin District, Ybor City; cigar-making tools.

Major Exhibits: Spain and the Creation of Modern Tampa, Fall 2009-Spring 2010.
Research Fields: cigar industry in Ybor City; various Latin ethnic groups.
Facilities: 2,800 sq. ft. exhibit space; garden available for rental. Museum-related items for sale.
Activities: docent program; museum/LaCasita tours; cigar rolling demonstrations.
Hours & Admission Prices: Daily 9-5. Adults $4; children under 6 no charge. LaCasita: daily 10-3 depending on docent availability. Closed New Year's; Thanksgiving; Christmas. ♿
Attendance: 29,714 (estimated)
Membership: Senior & Student $25; Museum Friend $35; Museum Family $50; Y.M. Ybor Patron $100; LaCasita Society $250; Latin Quarter Club $500; 1886 Founders Circle $1,000.

Tarpon Springs

LEEPA-RATNER MUSEUM OF ART AT ST. PETERSBURG COLLEGE, (M), 600 Klosterman Rd., Tarpon Springs, FL 34689-1299. Mailing Address: P.O. Box 1545, Tarpon Springs, FL 34688-1545. Tel.: 727-712-5762.
Web Site: www.spcollege.edu/central/museum/
Key Personnel: Dir., R. Lynn Whitelaw; Public Rels., Michelle Weyant
Art Museum.
Collections: paintings; photographs.
Hours & Admission Prices: Tues.-Wed. & Fri.-Sat. 10-5, Thurs. 10-9, Sun. 1-5. Adults $5, seniors $4, children, students, members & Sun. no charge.

SAFFORD HOUSE HISTORIC HOUSE MUSEUM, 23 Parkin Court, Tarpon Springs, FL 34689-3235. Tel.: 727-937-1130. Fax: 727-938-2429.
E-mail: tbucuvalas@ci.tarpon-springs.fl.us
Web Site: www.tarponarts.org/info_venues_safford.html
Founded: 1995.
Congressional District: 9
Key Personnel: Cur., Tina Bucuvalas.
Personnel Profile: Part-Time Paid 1; Part-Time Volunteers 10.
Governing Authority: municipal. Parent Institution: City of Tarpon Springs, P.O. Box 5004, Tarpon Springs, FL 34688. Tax-exempt.
Historic House Museum: home of Anson P.K. Safford from 1883-1891.
Collections: Safford family history; life in west central Florida during late 19th century; period furnishings.
Research Fields: Safford family; late Victorian life in Florida; late 19th century medical practice.
Facilities: 20-vol. library. Museum-related items for sale.
Activities: concerts; docent program; guided tours. Annual Events: Holiday Candlelight Tour in December.
Hours & Admission Prices: Wed. & Fri. 11-3; other times by appointment. Adults & students $5; discounts to Florida Association of Museums and AAM & ICOM members; children no charge. Closed New Year's Day; Memorial Day; Independence Day; Labor Day; Thanksgiving & day after; Christmas. ♿
Attendance: 986 (accurate)

TARPON SPRINGS AREA HISTORICAL SOCIETY - DEPOT MUSEUM, 160 E. Tarpon Ave., Tarpon Springs, FL 34689-3452. Tel.: 727-943-4624.
E-mail: tarpon.historical@verizon.net
Founded: 1976.
Congressional District: 9
Key Personnel: Pres., Carol Mountain; Treas., Ellen Scheible; Cur., Judith LeGath; Museum Shop Mgr., Margaret Rayner; Museum Shop Mgr., Yasmin Pianese.
Personnel Profile: Part-Time Paid 1; Part-Time Volunteers 35.
Governing Authority: private; nonprofit organization. Tax-exempt: 501(c)(3).
Historical Society Museum.
Collections: Tarpon Springs artifacts & archives from mid 19th century to present.
Research Fields: oral town histories; impact of railroad on the town.
Facilities: 47-vol. library. Museum-related items for sale.
Activities: docent program; films; lectures. Museum Sponsors: Historic House Tour. Annual Events: Cemetery Tour; Remembrance Tea.
Publications: monthly newsletter, Newsletter.
Hours & Admission Prices: Tues.-Sat. 11:30-4. No charge; donations accepted. Closed New Year's Day; Memorial Day; Independence Day; Thanksgiving; Christmas. ♿
Attendance: 4,670 (accurate)
Membership: Individual $20; Family $30; Sustaining $50; Contributing $100; Life $200.

TARPON SPRINGS CULTURAL CENTER, 101 S. Pinellas Ave., Tarpon Springs, FL 34689-3631. Tel.: 727-942-5605. Fax: 727-938-2429.
E-mail: bpoteat1@ci.tarpon-springs.fl.us
Founded: 1987.
Congressional District: 9
Key Personnel: Dir., Dr. Kathleen Monahan; Mktg., Gen Haley; Cur., Tina Bucuvalas, Ph.D.; Box Office Mgr., Lisa Cobb; Site Mgr., Billie Poteat; Office Asst., Alice Miller.
Personnel Profile: Full-Time Paid 4; Part-Time Paid 2; Part-Time Volunteers 40.
Governing Authority: municipal government. Parent Institution: City of Tarpon Springs. Tax-exempt.
Cultural Center: housed in a c.1915 city hall, national register listed building.
Collections: concentration on historical, artistic & ethnographic material relating to Tarpon Springs; photos.
Research Fields: Greek-American culture in Tarpon Springs; local & regional history.
Facilities: 35-vol. library; 90-seat theater. Florida folk crafts for sale.
Activities: concerts; dance recitals; films; formal education programs for children; guided tours; workshops; lectures; loan, participatory, temporary & traveling exhibitions; theater.
Hours & Admission Prices: Mon.-Fri. 9-4, Sat. 12-4. No charge; donations accepted. Closed New Year's Day; Independence Day; Veterans Day; Thanksgiving; Christmas. ♿
Attendance: 6,726 (accurate)
Membership: Senior $30; Individual $35; Senior Family $40; Family $45; Bronze $65; Silver $135; Gold $195; Platinum $295; Ruby $575; Diamond $1,295.

TARPON SPRINGS HERITAGE MUSEUM, 100 Beekman Lane, Tarpon Springs, FL 34689-3555. Mailing Address: P.O. Box 5004, Tarpon Springs, FL 34688-5004. Tel.: 727-937-0686 & 0699. Fax: 727-937-0657.
E-mail: info@tarponarts.org
Web Site: www.tarponarts.org
Founded: 2001.
Congressional District: 9
Key Personnel: Dir., Dr. Kathleen Monahan; Public Rels., Gen Haley; Cur., Judy LeGath.
Personnel Profile: Full-Time Paid 3; Part-Time Paid 1; Part-Time Volunteers 1.
Governing Authority: municipal. Parent Institution: City of Tarpon Springs. Tax-exempt.
History Museum.
Collections: period photographs; Greek American history; Christopher Still murals.
Hours & Admission Prices: Mon.-Fri. 10-4. Adults $3; children no charge. Closed public holidays. ♿
Attendance: 2,377 (accurate)

Tavares

LAKE COUNTY HISTORICAL MUSEUM, (M), Lake County Historic Courthouse, 317 W. Main St., Tavares, FL 32778-3813. Mailing Address: P.O. Box 7800, Tavares, FL 32778-7800. Tel.: 352-343-9600. Fax: 352-343-9696.
E-mail: dkamp@co.lake.fl.us
Founded: 1965.
Key Personnel: Dir., Dr. Diane D. Kamp.
Personnel Profile: Full-Time Paid 1; Part-Time Paid 1; Part-Time Volunteers 50.
Governing Authority: municipal. Tax-exempt.
County Museum.
Collections: history of Lake County; Native American artifacts; Spanish relics.
Activities: hands-on exhibits.
Publications: Gallery Guide; Lake Kids Do History Fast Facts.
Hours & Admission Prices: Mon.-Fri. 8:30-5. No charge. ♿
Attendance: 50,500 (accurate)

Tequesta

LIGHTHOUSE CENTER FOR THE ARTS, Gallery Square North, 373 Tequesta Dr., Tequesta, FL 33469-3027. Tel.: 561-746-3101. Fax: 561-746-3241.
Web Site: www.lighthousearts.org
Founded: 1965.
Key Personnel: Exec. Dir., Katie Deits.
Personnel Profile: Full-Time Paid 6; Part-Time Paid 2; Part-Time Volunteers 35; Interns 1.
Governing Authority: board of directors. Tax-exempt.
Art Gallery.
Collections: paintings; photographs; sculpture.
Facilities: Museum-related items for sale.

Activities: art classes; lectures; permanent & temporary exhibitions; jazz concerts; luncheon series.
Publications: newsletters.
Hours & Admission Prices: Sept.-May Mon.-Fri. 10-4:30. ♿
Attendance: 39,000 (estimated)
Membership: Individual $75; Family $150.

Titusville

AMERICAN POLICE HALL OF FAME AND MUSEUM, 6350 Horizon Dr., Titusville, FL 32780-8002. Tel.: 321-264-0911.
Founded: 1960.
Key Personnel: C.E.O., Donna Shepherd; C.F.O., Debra Chitwood; Exec. Dir., Barry Shepherd.
Governing Authority: Parent Institution: National Association of Chiefs of Police. Tax-exempt.
Police Museum.
Collections: Hall of Fame inductees; American law enforcement history; weapons; photographs; memorials; gangsters; future of law enforcement; cars; motorcycles.
Activities: indoor firing range; air tours.
Publications: Police Family News; The Chief of Police.
Hours & Admission Prices: Daily 10-6. Adults $12, seniors, military, & children 4-12 $8; discounts to AAA members & military; members, law enforcement & family survivors no charge. Closed New Year's Day; Thanksgiving; Christmas. ♿
Attendance: 25,000 (accurate)

NORTH BREVARD HISTORICAL MUSEUM, 301 S. Washington Ave., Titusville, FL 32796-3539. Mailing Address: P.O. Box 5265, Titusville, FL 32783-5265. Tel.: 321-269-3658.
Web Site: www.nbbd.com/godo/history
Founded: 1989.
Key Personnel: Pres. (V), Edmund M. Kindle.
Personnel Profile: Part-Time Volunteers 75.
Governing Authority: Operated by Historical Society of North Brevard. Tax-exempt.
Historical Museum.
Collections: personal artifacts; photographs; records; clothing; local history.
Activities: group tours.
Publications: newsletter.
Hours & Admission Prices: Tues.-Sat. 10-3. No charge; donations accepted.
Attendance: 2,500 (estimated)
Membership: Individual $15; Family $25; Associate & Business $50; Lifetime $500.

UNITED STATES ASTRONAUT HALL OF FAME, 6225 Vectorspace Blvd., Titusville, FL 32780-8040. Tel.: 321-455-7000 & 269-6100.
Web Site: www.kennedyspacecenter.com
Hall of Fame.
Collections: astronaut hall of fame; personal artifacts; space suits & equipment; photographs.
Hours & Admission Prices: Daily 10-6:30. Adults $17, children 3-11 $13.

VALIANT AIR COMMAND WARBIRD AIR MUSEUM, 6600 Tico Rd., Titusville, FL 32780-8009. Tel.: 321-268-1941. Fax: 321-268-5969.
E-mail: vacwarbirds@bellsouth.net
Web Site: www.vacwarbirds.org
Founded: 1977.
Key Personnel: Commander, Lloyd Morris.
Governing Authority: nonprofit. Tax-exempt: 501(c)(3).
Aviation History Museum.
Collections: aviation history; military aircraft.
Facilities: 30,000 sq. ft. exhibit space. Museum-related items for sale.
Activities: tours; airshow.
Publications: newsletter.
Hours & Admission Prices: Daily 9-5. Adults $12, senior citizens & military $10, children 5-12 $5; discounts to groups. Closed New Year's Day; Thanksgiving; Christmas.
Attendance: 60,000 (estimated)
Membership: Single $75; Family $100; Lifetime $500, $750 & $1,000.

Valparaiso

HERITAGE MUSEUM OF NORTHWEST FLORIDA, 115 Westview Ave., Valparaiso, FL 32580-1387. Tel.: 850-678-2615. Fax: 850-678-4547.
Web Site: heritage-museum.org
Founded: 1970.
Congressional District: 1
Key Personnel: Dir., Michelle Severino; Chm. (V), Ken Bailey.
Personnel Profile: Full-Time Paid 2; Part-Time Paid 4; Part-Time Volunteers 25; Interns 2.
Governing Authority: nonprofit; society. Parent Institution: Heritage Museum Association, Inc. Tax-exempt: 501(c)(3).
History Museum.
Collections: Northwest Florida history from prehistoric times to mid-20th century.
Major Exhibits: Vietnam Veteran Wall Memorial Exhibit (T), 6/17/10-6/20/10.
Research Fields: genealogy; agricultural history; turpentine industry; lumbering; railroading & fishing.
Facilities: 1,500-vol. library; classrooms. Handcrafted items for sale.
Activities: guided tours; lectures; gallery talks; heritage crafts classes; formally organized education programs for children; docent program or council; permanent & temporary exhibitions.
Publications: newsletter; monographs on local history.
Hours & Admission Prices: Tues.-Sat. 10-4. Adults $2; discounts to AAM members; members & children under 4 no charge. Closed legal holidays. ♿
Attendance: 17,000 (accurate)
Membership: Senior Citizen & Student $15; Individual $35; Family & Dual $50; Advocate $100; Sustaining $250; Benefactor $500; Heritage Circle $1,000 & up. Business memberships available.

Vero Beach

THE HERITAGE CENTER AND INDIAN RIVER CITRUS MUSEUM, 2140 14th Ave., Vero Beach, FL 32960-3432. Tel.: 772-770-2263. Fax: 772-770-2131.
E-mail: veroheritage@bellsouth.net
Web Site: www.veroheritage.org
Founded: 1991.
Personnel Profile: Full-Time Paid 1; Part-Time Paid 6; Part-Time Volunteers 5.
Governing Authority: Tax-exempt: 501(c)(3).
History Museum.
Collections: citrus industry history; period tools & artifacts; photographs.
Facilities: Museum-related items for sale.
Hours & Admission Prices: Tues.-Fri. 10-4. No charge; donations accepted. ♿
Attendance: 3,000 (estimated)
Membership: Individual $25; Family $35; Corporate $75; Trailblazer $125; Benefactor $250; Homesteader $1,000.

MCKEE BOTANICAL GARDEN, (M), 350 U.S. Hwy. 1, Vero Beach, FL 32962-2906. Tel.: 772-794-0601. Fax: 772-794-0602.
E-mail: info@mckeegarden.org
Web Site: www.mckeegarden.org
Founded: 1932.
Congressional District: 15
Key Personnel: Pres., Alma Lee Loy; Dir., Christine Hobart; Museum Shop Mgr., Gail Galbraith.
Personnel Profile: Full-Time Paid 6; Part-Time Paid 8; Part-Time Volunteers 125.
Governing Authority: private; nonprofit organization. Tax-exempt: 501(c)(3).
Botanical Garden: listed on the National Register of Historic Places.
Collections: plants; trees; flowers.
Major Exhibits: Return of the Dinosaur Invasion (T), 11/09-3/10.
Facilities: botanical garden. Museum-related items for sale.
Activities: formal educational programs for adults; lectures; seasonal events & activities.
Publications: newsletter 3 times a year, News from McKee Botanical Garden.
Hours & Admission Prices: Tues.-Sat. 10-5, Sun. 12-5. Adults $9, seniors $8, children 3-12 $5; reciprocal admission to American Horticultural Society; members no charge. Closed major holidays. ♿
Attendance: 35,000 (accurate)
Membership: Individual $35; Family $50; Sustaining $100; Patron $500; Associate $1,000; Gatekeeper $1,500.

MCLARTY TREASURE MUSEUM, 13180 Highway N. 1A, Part of the Sebastian Inlet State Park, Vero Beach, FL 32963-9400. Tel.: 772-589-2147. Fax: 321-984-4854.
Web Site: www.myflorida.com
Founded: 1970.
Congressional District: 16
Key Personnel: Dir., Ed Perry; Pres. (V), Fred Marshall; Park Mgr., Ronald N. Johns; Gift Shop Mgr., Barbara Kmack.
Personnel Profile: Full-Time Paid 1; Full-Time Volunteers 14; Part-Time Volunteers 20.
Governing Authority: state. Dept. of Environmental Protection (DEP), Div. of Recreation & Parks, 3900 Commonwealth Blvd., Tallahassee, FL 32303. Tax-exempt.
History and Film Museum: built on 1715 site of Spanish salvage campsite adjacent to shipwreck in Atlantic Ocean.

Collections: a portion of the State's share of the treasures & artifacts (worked metals, ceramics, glass) of the Spanish Fleet Shipwrecks of 1715.
Facilities: Books of local historical information for sale.
Activities: DVD presentation of A&E The Queen's Jewels & the 1715 Fleet; artifacts on display; observation deck overlooking shipwreck sites.
Publications: brochures.
Hours & Admission Prices: Daily 10-4:30; last film showing 3:15. Admission $2 per person; children under 6 no charge. ♿
Attendance: 14,690 (accurate)

* **VERO BEACH MUSEUM OF ART, INC., (M),** 3001 Riverside Park Dr., Vero Beach, FL 32963-1874. Tel.: 772-231-0707. Fax: 772-231-0938.
E-mail: info@verobeachmuseum.org
Web Site: www.verobeachmuseum.org
Founded: 1979.
Congressional District: 12
Key Personnel: Chm. Bd., Edward A. Michael; Exec. Dir., Lucinda H. Gedeon; Dir. Devel., Robyn P. Orzel; Dir. Education, J. Marshall Adams; Cur. Collections & Exhibitions, Jennifer Bailey Forbes; Registrar, J'Laine Newcombe; Coord. Public Rels., Joe Ellis; Dir. Facilities, Greg Kingsley; Dir. Security & Technical Svcs., John Janssen; Asst. to Exec. Dir., Diane E. Tilton; Museum Shop Mgr., Jo Anne Miller.
Personnel Profile: Full-Time Paid 27; Part-Time Paid 63; Part-Time Volunteers 519.
Governing Authority: nonprofit organization. Tax-exempt: 501(c)(3).
Art Museum.
Collections: 20th-century American art; 21st-century American & International art.
Major Exhibits: Luis Montoya and Leslie Ortiz, 12/09-5/10; Ships and Shorelines: 19th Century American Marine Paintings, 1/10-5/10; John Bisbee, 1/10-6/10; William Wegman: Fay, 10/10-1/11.
Research Fields: American art.
Facilities: 5,000-vol. library pertaining to general art history, materials & techniques available for reference; 250-seat auditorium; museum art school including sculpture foundry; sculpture park; lecture hall; cafe. Museum-related items for sale.
Activities: multi-disciplinary art instructional studios; museum school; temporary & permanent exhibitions; art festivals; guided tours; lectures; films; concerts.
Publications: newsletter; exhibition catalogues; annual report; quarterly magazine; public programs brochure; class schedule; e-newsletter.
Hours & Admission Prices: Memorial Day to Labor Day Tues.-Sat. 10-4:30, Sun. 1-4:30; Sept.-May Mon.-Sat. 10-4:30, Sun. 1-4:30. Call for admission prices; discounts to AAM & ICOM members; North American & Southeastern reciprocal museum privileges. Closed New Year's Day; Memorial Day; Independence Day; Labor Day; Thanksgiving; Christmas Day. ♿
Attendance: 72,229 (accurate)
Membership: Individual $35; Household $50; Benefactor & Business Benefactor $125; Donor $375; Business Patron $500; Patron $625; Chairman's Club $1,500; Corporate Partners Club $2,000; Chairman's Circle $2,500; Chairman's Council $5,000.

Weirsdale

FLORIDA CARRIAGE MUSEUM AND RESORT, 3000 Marion County Rd., Weirsdale, FL 32195-5168. Tel.: 352-750-5500. Fax: 352-750-1764.
E-mail: info@fcmr.org
Web Site: www.fcmr.org
Formerly: Austin Carriage Museum
Founded: 1995.
Key Personnel: Dir., Gloria Austin; Historian, Stephanie Sutch; Coord. (V), Inis Mendenhall; Museum Shop Mgr., Carol Martin.
Governing Authority: Tax-exempt.
Transportation Museum.
Collections: over 150 European & American carriages; period horse-related artifacts; horse drawn fire equipment.
Activities: Annual Events: Carriage & Horse Festival; Golden Carriage Tea; Pleasure Driving Competition.
Hours & Admission Prices: Tues.-Sat. 10-4, Sun. 12-4; groups by appointment. Adults $10, students 5-18 $5; children 4 & under no charge. Closed holidays. ♿

West Palm Beach

THE ARMORY ART CENTER, 1700 Parker Ave., West Palm Beach, FL 33401-7042. Tel.: 561-832-1776. Fax: 561-832-0191.
Web Site: www.armoryart.org
Formerly: The Robert & Mary Montgomery Armory Art Center
Founded: 1987.
Congressional District: 22
Key Personnel: Chief Exec., Sandra Barghini; Chm., Linda Silpe; Pres., James Swope; Dir. Mktg., Kati Erickson; Dir. Programs, Ann Fay Rushforth.
Personnel Profile: Full-Time Paid 11; Part-Time Paid 1; Part-Time Volunteers 100; Interns 6.
Governing Authority: private; nonprofit organization. Tax-exempt: 501(c)(3).
Art Center: housed in Historic Palm Beach County National Guard Armory.
Collections: works by contemporary artists.
Major Exhibits: Crafted Melodies, 1/15/10-2/4/10; Native to Florida, 1/15/10-2/4/10; Larry Leach Solo, 1/15/10-2/26/10; Muriel Kaplan Retrospective, 2/12/10-3/6/10; Mad Hatter's Teapot Invitational, 3/2/10-3/13/10; National Association Women in Arts, 3/19/10-4/8/10; Armory Annual Student Show, 3/19/10-4/8/10; Annual Armory Artists-in-Residence Exhibition, 4/16/10-5/8/10; Fibers & Printmaking Studio Exhibition, 5/14/10-6/5/10; Glass & Jewelry Studio Exhibition, 6/11/10-7/3/10.
Facilities: 3,000-vol. art history & practice library available to the public; 5,200 sq. ft. exhibit space; studio classrooms.
Activities: traveling exhibits; formal educational programs; guided tours; lectures; art classes; film series; demonstrations.
Publications: quarterly newsletter, Armory Artnews; exhibition catalogues.
Hours & Admission Prices: Mon.-Fri. 9-4. Receptions: adults $5; members no charge. Closed New Year's Day; Memorial Day; Independence Day; Labor Day; Thanksgiving; Christmas. ♿
Attendance: 25,000 (accurate)
Membership: Youth $35; Individual $75; Family $100; Patron $500; Studio Guild $750; Gallery Patron $1,000.

HISTORICAL SOCIETY OF PALM BEACH COUNTY, (M), 300 N. Dixie Hwy., West Palm Beach, FL 33401-4605. Mailing Address: P.O. Box 4364, West Palm Beach, FL 33402-4364. Tel.: 561-832-4164. Fax: 561-832-7965.
E-mail: info@historicalsocietypbc.org
Web Site: www.historicalsocietypbc.org
Founded: 1937.
Congressional District: 22
Key Personnel: C.E.O. & Pres., Loren Mintz; Chm., Mark B. Elhilow; Cur. Collections & Exhibits, Steven F. Erdmann; Cur. Education, Tony Marconi; Dir. Research & Archives, Debi Murray; Office Mgr., Margaret W. Tamsberg; Dir. Devel., Kae Jonsons; Asst. Dir. Public Rels., Special Events & Retail, Paula Martin; Volunteer Coord., Paula Marcus.
Personnel Profile: Full-Time Paid 8; Part-Time Paid 1; Part-Time Volunteers 60; Interns 1.
Governing Authority: nonprofit organization. Subsidiary Institution: The Richard & Pat Johnson Palm Beach County History Museum. Tax-exempt: 501(c)(3).
History Museum.
Collections: furniture; American Indian artifacts; sheet music; maps; vertical clipping file; photographic archive; Addison Mizner furniture & architectural drawings; Treanor & Fatio original architectural drawings & manuscript collection; microfilm of early Palm Beach County newspapers.
Major Exhibits: Civil Air Patrol, 2/9/10-7/16/10; Shipwreck! A Story of Treasure, 9/10-1/11.
Research Fields: Palm Beach County; South Florida; Caribbean.
Facilities: 3,000-vol. library of books, newspapers & pamphlets of the history of the Palm Beach area & on the state of Florida available on premises; research room.
Activities: lectures; traveling exhibits; collaborations with other museums; fund-raising dinner. Historical Society Sponsors: Yours Friends Events.
Publications: quarterly newsletter.
Hours & Admission Prices: Museum: Tues.-Sat. 10-5. No charge. Research by appointment. Research Fee $20; discounts to AAM & ICOM members; members no charge. ♿
Attendance: 50,000 (accurate)
Membership: Individual $50; Family $75; Barefoot Mailman $125; Mizner Circle $250; Flager Circle $500; Pioneer Circle $1,000.

MOUNTS BOTANICAL GARDEN, 531 N. Military Trail, West Palm Beach, FL 33415-1311. Tel.: 561-233-1757. Fax: 561-233-1723.
Web Site: www.mounts.org
Founded: 1954.
Key Personnel: Dir., Allen Sistrunk; Pres. (V), Mike Zimmerman; Head Horticulture, Heather Grzybek; Dir. Devel., Steven J. Reyer
Botanical Garden.
Collections: tropical & subtropical plants from six continents; Florida's plants, trees, tropical fruit, herbs, citrus & palms.
Facilities: Museum-related items for sale.
Publications: quarterly magazine, The Leaflet.
Hours & Admission Prices: Mon.-Sat. 8-4, Sun. 12-4. Suggested Donation: $5. Closed New Year's Day; Thanksgiving; Christmas Eve & Day.
Membership: Individual $35; Family & Friends $50; Donor $100; Sustaining $250; Patron $500; Gardening Angel $1,000.

* **NORTON MUSEUM OF ART, (M),** 1451 S. Olive Ave., West Palm Beach, FL 33401-7162. Tel.: 561-832-5196. Fax: 561-659-4689.
E-mail: museum@norton.org
Web Site: www.norton.org
Founded: 1940.
Congressional District: 22
Key Personnel: Interim Dir. & Chair, Cur. Dept. & Cur. European Art, Roger Ward; Dir. Finance, Lucy Bukewski; Chm. Bd., William Sned; Dir. Admin., Jane Pangborn; Human Resources Mgr., Jane Wattick; Cur. Contemporary Art, Cheryl Brutvan; Cur. Photography, Charlie Stainback; Dir. Membership, Graham Russell; Cur. Education, Glenn Tomlinson; Cur. Chinese Art, Laurie Barnes; Registrar, Pamela Parry; Assoc. Cur. Education, Carole Gutterman; Dir. Mktg. & Public Rels., Kipper Lance; Dir. Advancement, Larry Rosensweig; Museum Shop Mgr., Katherine Kress.
Personnel Profile: Full-Time Paid 77; Part-Time Paid 11; Part-Time Volunteers 400; Interns 9.
Governing Authority: nonprofit corporation. Tax-exempt: 501(c)(3).
Art Museum.
Collections: 19th & 20th century American paintings & sculpture; 15th - 20th century European paintings & sculpture; Chinese jades, bronzes, ceramics & Buddhist sculpture; contemporary art after 1970; photography.
Major Exhibits: George Segal: Street Scenes, 11/09-12/09; New York, New York: The 20th Century, 11/09-12/09; William Kentridge: Five Themes, 11/09-1/10; Habsburg Treasures: Renaissance Tapestries from Vienna (T), 1/10-4/10; Avedon Fashion 1944-2000 (T), 2/10-5/10; Reclaimed: Paintings from the Collection of Jacques Goudstikker (T), 2/10-5/10; RFK Funeral Train Rediscovered, 2/10-12/10; Here Comes the Sun: Warhol and Art after 1960 at the Norton, 2/10-12/10; Annie Leibovitz: WOMEN, 5/10-8/10; On the Silk Road and High Seas, 8/10-11/10.
Facilities: 4,000-vol. library of art history; reference materials; art periodicals; 112,500 sq. ft. exhibit space; 33 galleries; 3 gardens; education wing; 200-seat auditorium; cafe. Museum-related items for sale.
Activities: guided tours; lectures; films; gallery talks; concerts; formally organized educational programs; docent program; permanent, temporary & traveling exhibitions; teacher enrichment programs; school tours; community outreach; special events.
Publications: catalogs of the permanent collections; calendars; exhibition catalogs; posters; postcards of major works in permanent collection; member newsletter, annual report; books.
Hours & Admission Prices: Tues.-Sat. 10-5, Sun. 1-5. Adults $8, students $3; discounts to AAM & ICOM members; children under 13 & members no charge. Additional charge for special exhibitions. Closed major holidays. ♿
Attendance: 200,000 (estimated)
Membership: Student $25; Individual $70; Household $100; Supporter $125; Young Friends $200; Contributor $250; Patron $1,000; Founder's Circle $1,750-$10,000.

PALM BEACH PHOTOGRAPHIC CENTRE, 415 Clematis St., West Palm Beach, FL 33401-5319. Tel.: 561-276-9797. Fax: 561-276-1932.
E-mail: info@workshop.org
Web Site: www.workshop.org
Key Personnel: Exec. Dir., Fatima NeJame; Mng. Dir., Art NeJame
Photography Museum.
Collections: photographs.
Activities: photography classes; community programs; workshops; educational activities; seminars.
Hours & Admission Prices: Mon.-Sat. 9-6.

PALM BEACH ZOO, 1301 Summit Blvd., West Palm Beach, FL 33405-3098. Tel.: 561-547-9453. Fax: 561-585-6085.
E-mail: info@palmbeachzoo.org
Web Site: www.palmbeachzoo.org
Founded: 1969.
Congressional District: 23
Key Personnel: Pres., Luis Fernandez; Dir. Living Collections, Keith Lovett; C.O.O., W. Garrett Hambuechen; C.F.O., Kathleen Breland; Dir. Mktg., Claudia Harden; Dir. Education, Kristen Cytacki; Museum Shop Mgr., Lyn Monnette.
Personnel Profile: Full-Time Paid 79; Full-Time Volunteers 24; Part-Time Paid 21; Part-Time Volunteers 100; Interns 13.
Governing Authority: society; nonprofit Parent Institution: Zoological Society of the Palm Beaches. Tax-exempt: 501(c)(3).
Zoo.
Collections: over 1,700 animals from around the world.
Research Fields: husbandry & breeding of endangered species.
Facilities: 5,000-vol. library for staff use; botanical garden; 23 acres exhibit space. Museum-related items for sale.
Activities: volunteer & docent program; formal education programs for children; lecture & presentation series; wildlife rescue & rehabilitation; interactive fountain.
Publications: monthly e-newsletter, Zoo Bytes; quarterly magazine, Palm Beach Zoo.
Hours & Admission Prices: Daily 9-5. Adults $12.95, senior citizens $9.95, children 3-12 $8.95; discounts to groups, AAA & AZA members; children under 3 & zoo members no charge. Closed Thanksgiving; Christmas. ♿
Attendance: 250,000 (estimated)
Membership: Senior $55; Individual Plus $60; Family $85; Friends of the Zoo $150; Big Cat Society $1,000.

SOUTH FLORIDA SCIENCE MUSEUM, 4801 Dreher Trail N., West Palm Beach, FL 33405-3017. Tel.: 561-832-1988. Fax: 561-833-0551.
E-mail: media@sfsm.org
Web Site: www.sfsm.org
Founded: 1959.
Congressional District: 11
Key Personnel: C.E.O., Mary Sellers; Chm. Bd., Rhys Williams; Treas., Dan Fountain; Vice Pres. Education, Holly Hughes; Vice Pres. Operations, Derek Morell; Museum Shop Mgr., Pat Breitenbach; Vice Pres. Finance, Marcia Arseneault; Vice Pres. Institutional Advancement, Dr. Rachel Doceilal; Dir. Public Rels., Elizabeth Dashiell; Cur. Aquarium, Lee Dashiell.
Personnel Profile: Full-Time Paid 35; Part-Time Paid 7; Part-Time Volunteers 300.
Governing Authority: nonprofit organization. Tax-exempt: 501(c)(3); 170(b)(1)(a)(vi).
Science Museum.
Collections: natural history; paleontology; archaeology; astronomy; geology; concology.
Research Fields: shark tagging; coral surveys; aquatic plants; aquaculture.
Facilities: planetarium; discovery room; observatory; aquarium; auditorium; exhibit hall; outdoor science trails; Egypt gallery.
Activities: lectures; films; formally organized educational programs; traveling, permanent & temporary exhibits; science theater; teacher in-services.
Publications: annual report; Teacher's Guide; magazine.
Hours & Admission Prices: Mon.-Fri. 10-5, Sat. 10-6, Sun. 12-6. Adults $9, seniors $7.50, children 3-12 $6; discounts to groups, AAM, AAA, ICOM & ASTC members; children under 3 & members no charge. Call for information on Planetarium & Laser Light shows. Closed Thanksgiving; Christmas. ♿
Attendance: 117,000 (accurate)
Membership: Teacher $20; Dual Explorers $50; Galaxy & Space Traveler $70; Cygnus $250; Centarus $500; Draco $1,000; Phoenix $2,500; Orion $5,000; Canis Major $10,000.

YESTERYEAR VILLAGE, (M), 9067 Southern Blvd., South Florida Fairgrounds, West Palm Beach, FL 33411-3625. Mailing Address: P.O. Box 210367, West Palm Beach, FL 33421-0367. Tel.: 561-793-0333; 800-640-3247. Fax: 561-753-2124.
Founded: 1990.
Congressional District: 23
Key Personnel: C.E.O. & Dir., Richard Vymlatil; Devel., Vicki Chouris; Chm. (V), Dare Peterson; Chm. (V), Becky Kobussen; Public Rels., John Picano; Treas., Matt Wallsmith; Cur., Jennifer L. Irsay; Security, Frank Walker.
Personnel Profile: Full-Time Paid 2; Part-Time Volunteers 576.
Governing Authority: Tax-exempt.
History Museum.
Collections: 30 restored buildings including blacksmith shop; working sawmill; general store.
Facilities: Museum-related items for sale.
Activities: education programs; birthday parties; rental facility; school outings.
Hours & Admission Prices: Tues.-Sun. 10-5. Adults $5, seniors $4, children $3; children under 5 no charge.

White Springs

STEPHEN FOSTER FOLK CULTURE CENTER STATE PARK, U.S. 41 N., White Springs, FL 32096-0435. Mailing Address: P.O. Drawer G, White Springs, FL 32096-0435. Tel.: 386-397-2733. Fax: 386-397-4262.
E-mail: morris.cook@dep.state.fl.us
Web Site: www.floridastateparks.org/stephenfoster
Founded: 1939.
Congressional District: 4
Key Personnel: Pres. (V), Khrys Kantarze; Park Mgr., Benjamin Faure; Information Specialist, Mitzi Nelson; Museum Shop Mgr., Kelli Pipkins.
Personnel Profile: Full-Time Paid 15; Part-Time Volunteers 80.
Governing Authority: state. Parent Institution: Dept. of Environmental Protection, Div. of Recreation and Parks, 3900 Commonwealth Blvd., Commonwealth Bldg., Tallahassee, FL 32303. Tax-exempt: 170(b)(1)(A).
Folk Culture Museum: located on the Suwannee River at White Springs, FL.

Collections: Howard Chandler Christy paintings; musical instruments; minstrel show material; manuscripts; Stephen Foster's folk songs.
Research Fields: life & works of Stephen C. Foster; the Folk Arts; Suwannee River Life & History; Florida folklife.
Facilities: Florida crafts & museum-related gifts for sale.
Activities: guided tours; concerts; cultural festivals; formally organized education programs for children; workshops; craft demonstrations permanent exhibitions; Jeanie auditions & scholarship program; Christmas programs. Museum Sponsors: Stephen Foster Day in January; Florida Folk Festival.
Publications: books, Suwannee River & Biography of Stephen C. Foster; American Troubadour; single sheets, Biography of Stephen C. Foster.
Hours & Admission Prices: Daily 9-5. $5 per vehicle (up to 8 people), $1 per person over 8; motorcoach rates available. ♿
Attendance: 44,822 (accurate)
Membership: Annual fee $20.

Winter Garden

CENTRAL FLORIDA RAILROAD MUSEUM, 101 S. Boyd St., Winter Garden, FL 34787-3500. Mailing Address: P.O. Box 770567, Winter Garden, FL 34777-0567. Tel.: 407-656-0559.
Web Site: www.cfcnrhs.org/
Founded: 1981.
Key Personnel: Pres. (V), Phil Cross; Cur., Ken Murdock; Museum Shop Mgr., Denise Wurster.
Governing Authority: Parent Institution: Winter Garden Heritage Foundation. Subsidiary Institution: Central Florida Chapter, NRHS. Tax-exempt.
Historical Railroad Museum.
Collections: railroading history in Central Florida; railroad china; 1938 Fairmont motor car; Clinchfield caboose.
Publications: monthly newsletter, The Flatwheel; Outline History of Florida Railroads.
Hours & Admission Prices: Daily 1-5. No charge; donations accepted.
Membership: Annual $42.

WINTER GARDEN HERITAGE MUSEUM, (M), 1 N. Main St., Winter Garden, FL 34787-2824. Mailing Address: P.O. Box 770657, Winter Garden, FL 34777-0657. Tel.: 407-656-3244. Fax: 407-656-0110.
E-mail: museumdirector@wghf.org
Web Site: www.wghf.org
Founded: 1998.
Personnel Profile: Full-Time Paid 4; Part-Time Paid 5; Part-Time Volunteers 80.
Governing Authority: Tax-exempt.
Heritage History Museum.
Collections: Winter Garden history; architecture; photographs; Native American artifacts; citrus labels.
Hours & Admission Prices: Daily 1-5. No charge.
Attendance: 20,000 (estimated)

Winter Park

ALBIN POLASEK MUSEUM AND SCULPTURE GARDENS, 633 Osceola Ave., Winter Park, FL 32789-4429. Tel.: 407-647-6294. Fax: 407-647-0410.
Web Site: www.polasek.org/
Founded: 1961.
Art Museum.
Collections: sculptures; paintings.
Major Exhibits: Maidens and Monsters-The Art of Science Fiction, Adventure and Fantasy, 11/24/09-4/18/10; Winter Park Paint Out and Paint Out Exhibit, 4/27/10-5/16/10.
Facilities: gardens.
Activities: weddings; special events.
Hours & Admission Prices: Sept.-June Tues.-Sat. 10-4, Sun. 1-4; groups by appointment. Adults $5, seniors $4, students $3; members & children under 12 no charge. ♿
Membership: Individual $40; Student/Teacher/Senior 60 & over $30; Family or Dual $60; Participating $100. Friends of the Polasek: Contributing $200; Supporting $350; Sustaining $500; Corporate & Benefactor $1,000; Grand Benefactor $2,500; Preservationist $5,000; Lifetime $25,000 & up.

THE CHARLES HOSMER MORSE MUSEUM OF AMERICAN ART, (M), 445 N. Park Ave., Winter Park, FL 32789-3212. Tel.: 407-645-5311, 5316 & 5324. Fax: 407-647-1284.
Web Site: www.morsemuseum.org
Founded: 1942.
Congressional District: 9
Key Personnel: Dir., Dr. Laurence J. Ruggiero; Cur. & Mgr. Collections, Jennifer Thalheimer; Dir. Public Affairs, Catherine Hinman; Bldg. Mgr., Tom Mobley; Museum Shop Mgr., Ava Maxwell; Cur., Donna Climenhage; Cur. Education, Betsy Peters.
Personnel Profile: Full-Time Paid 23; Part-Time Paid 13; Part-Time Volunteers 75; Interns 2.
Governing Authority: nonprofit organization. Parent Institution: Charles Hosmer Morse Foundation, 445 N. Park Ave., Winter Park, FL 32789. Tax-exempt.
American Art Museum.
Collections: windows, lamps, blown glass, jewelry, pottery & paintings by Louis Comfort Tiffany & other turn-of-the-century masters; late 19th and early 20th-century American paintings; art pottery; exhibits include Tiffany's 1893 Chapel for the World's Columbian Exposition, windows, furniture and other objects designed by Tiffany for his personal use & from his Long Island home, Laurelton Hall.
Research Fields: American art 1850s-1930s.
Facilities: galleries. Museum-related items for sale.
Activities: guided docent tours; lectures; interpretive programs.
Publications: American Art Pottery; The Tiffany Chapel at the Morse Museum.
Hours & Admission Prices: May-Oct. Tues.-Sat. 9:30-4, Sun. 1-4; Nov.-April Tues.-Thurs. & Sat. 9:30-4, Fri. 9:30-8, Sun. 1-4; guided tours by appointment. Adults $3, students $1; children 12 and under, Fri. 4-8 & members no charge. Closed New Year's Day; Memorial Day; Labor Day; Thanksgiving; Christmas. ♿
Attendance: 57,563 (accurate)
Membership: Student & Teacher $5; Individual $15; Family $25; Contributing $50; Benefactor $100; Sustaining $1,000; Corporate $10,000 & up.

* **THE GEORGE D. AND HARRIET W. CORNELL FINE ARTS MUSEUM, (M),** Rollins College, 1000 Holt Ave., Winter Park, FL 32789-4499. Tel.: 407-646-2526. Fax: 407-646-2524.
E-mail: stodd@rollins.edu
Web Site: www.rollins.edu/cfam
Founded: 1978.
Congressional District: 8
Key Personnel: Dir., Kenneth Scearce; Registrar & Collection Mgr., Linda Ehmen; Cur. Academic Initiatives, Dr. Matthew McLendon; Education Coord., Tracy Gore; Exec. Asst., Sandy Todd; Membership Coord. & Museum Shop Mgr., Dana Thomas.
Personnel Profile: Full-Time Paid 6; Full-Time Volunteers 110; Part-Time Paid 6; Part-Time Volunteers 96; Interns 1.
Governing Authority: college. Parent Institution: Rollins College. Tax-exempt: 501(c)(3).
Art Museum.
Collections: 5,000 objects from the 14th to 21st centuries: European paintings of the Renaissance through contemporary; American & European paintings; bronzes; sculptures; prints; drawings; posters; photographs; Native American art; Kress Collection; Smith Watch Key Collection; decorative arts: furniture, glass, ceramics.
Research Fields: American & European art.
Facilities: college art museum.
Activities: temporary, loan & traveling exhibitions; lectures; films; workshops; guided tours.
Publications: permanent collection handbook, Treasures of the Cornell Fine Arts Museum; newsletter; exhibition catalogues; museum brochures; post cards; exhibition schedule brochures; posters; education brochure.
Hours & Admission Prices: Tues.-Fri. 10-4, Sat.-Sun. 12-5. Adults $5; discount to AAM members; students with ID, children & members no charge. Closed major holidays. ♿
Attendance: 25,000 (estimated)
Membership: Student $30; Friend $50; Dual $75; Patron $150; Collector $300; Salon $500; Benefactor $1,000; Corporate $2,000 & up.

Zephyrhills

ZEPHYRHILLS DEPOT MUSEUM, 39110 South Ave., Zephyrhills, FL 33542-5255. Tel.: 813-780-0067.
Key Personnel: Dir., Vicki S. Elkins
History Museum: housed in the restored 1927 Atlantic Coast Line Railroad Depot.
Collections: history of trains, local area, & culture; personal artifacts; photographs; school memorabilia; railroad artifacts.
Facilities: Museum-related items for sale.
Hours & Admission Prices: Tues.-Sat. 10-2. No charge. ♿
Attendance: 6,000 (estimated)

Zolfo Springs

CRACKER TRAIL MUSEUM, 2822 Museum Dr., Zolfo Springs, FL 33890-9433. Tel.: 863-735-0119.
E-mail: sandy.scott@hardeecounty.net
Founded: 1966.

Key Personnel: Supt. Bldg. & Grounds, Daniel Weeks; Cur., Sandy Scott.
Personnel Profile: Full-Time Paid 1; Part-Time Paid 1.
Governing Authority: county. Tax-exempt.
Park Museum.
Collections: aeronautics; agriculture; anthropology; archaeology; archives; paintings; decorative arts; circus costumes; history; Indian artifacts; industrial; medical; natural history; textiles; transportation; old train; old-time blacksmith shop.
Facilities: zoo; campgrounds.
Activities: guided tours; permanent & temporary exhibitions.
Hours & Admission Prices: Tues.-Sat. 9-5. Suggested Donation: $1 per person; discounts to school groups. ♿
Attendance: 6,809 (accurate)

GEORGIA

(271 listings)

Albany

ALBANY CIVIL RIGHTS MOVEMENT MUSEUM AT OLD MT. ZION CHURCH, (M), 326 Whitney Ave., Albany, GA 31701-2861. Mailing Address: P.O. Box 6036, Albany, GA 31706-6036. Tel.: 229-432-1698. Fax: 229-432-2150.
E-mail: iturner@acrmm.org
Web Site: albanycivilrights.org
Formerly: Mt. Zion Albany Civil Rights Movement Museum, Inc.
Founded: 1994.
Congressional District: 2
Key Personnel: Admin., Irene L. Turner; Pres., Kenneth Cutts; Sec., Geraldine Hudley.
Personnel Profile: Part-Time Paid 5; Part-Time Volunteers 10; Interns 1.
Governing Authority: private; nonprofit organization. Tax-exempt: 501(c)(3).
History Museum.
Collections: photographs; artifacts; archives.
Research Fields: civil rights movement in Albany & southwest Georgia; history of Mount Zion Baptist Church in Albany GA; the significance of music in the civil rights movement.
Facilities: library.
Activities: temporary exhibitions.
Hours & Admission Prices: Tues.-Sat. 10-4. Adults $6, senior citizens, students 5th-12th grade, military & college students $5, children 1st-4th grade $3, pre-school $2; members & children under 4 no charge. Closed holidays. ♿
Attendance: 6,000 (accurate)
Membership: Student & Senior Citizen $25; Individual $45; Family $65; Nonprofit Organization $325; Corporation & Business $625.

* **ALBANY MUSEUM OF ART, (M),** 311 Meadowlark Dr., Albany, GA 31707-5704. Tel.: 229-439-8400. Fax: 229-439-1332.
E-mail: info@albanymuseum.com
Web Site: www.albanymuseum.com
Founded: 1964.
Congressional District: 2
Key Personnel: Exec. Dir., Nick Nelson; Chm. (V), Bonny Dorough.
Personnel Profile: Full-Time Paid 4; Full-Time Volunteers 2; Part-Time Paid 2; Part-Time Volunteers 300.
Governing Authority: nonprofit organization. Tax-exempt: 501(c)(3).
Art Museum.
Collections: African art; 16th- to 17th-century European drawings; American paintings & works on paper since 1945; American & European decorative arts; folk art; Southern art.
Research Fields: 20th-century American art; American & European paintings & graphics; African objects.
Facilities: classrooms; auditorium; preparatory space; hands-on children's gallery.
Activities: guided tours; lectures; curriculum & lesson plan packets for teachers; art classes; children's membership programs; birthday parties; children's art fair; auction; education programs; docent program; loan, permanent, temporary & traveling exhibitions; community loan service; outreach programs.
Publications: bimonthly newsletter, ARTalk.
Hours & Admission Prices: Tues.-Sat. 10-5. Adults $4; discounts to SEMC, AAM & ICOM members; members & Thurs. no charge. Closed major holidays. ♿
Attendance: 20,000 (estimated)
Membership: Individual $25; Family $35; Young Patron $100; Individual Patron $125; Young Patron Couple $250; Benefactor $500; Sponsor $1,000.

FLINT RIVER QUARIUM, 101 Pine Ave., Albany, GA 31701-2593. Mailing Address: 117 Pine Ave., Albany, GA 31701-2593. Tel.: 229-639-2650. Fax: 229-639-2707.
Web Site: www.flintriverquarium.com
Founded: 2004.
Key Personnel: Dir., Scott W. Loehr; Chm. (V), Emily McAfee; Devel. & Public Rels., Wendy Bellacomo; Education, Melissa Martin; Cur., Richard Brown; Accounts Mgr., Vonda Hancock; Operations Mgr., Kathy Batson; Imagination Theater Mgr., Vashion Milledge; Membership & Guest Svcs. Mgr., Vicki Churchman; Aquarist, Kelly Putnam; Aquarist, Melissa Scott; Aquarist, Amanda Margraves.
Personnel Profile: Full-Time Paid 18; Part-Time Paid 10; Part-Time Volunteers 92; Interns 2.
Governing Authority: private; nonprofit organization. Tax-exempt: 501(c)(3).
Natural Science Museum.
Collections: local flora & fauna; aquatic animals.
Facilities: aquarium; aviary; educational facilities; 28,000 sq. ft. exhibit space; 103-seat large format theater. Gift items for sale.
Activities: docent program; films; guided tours; participatory exhibits; rental gallery; theater.
Publications: quarterly newsletter, The Blue Hole Banner.
Hours & Admission Prices: Mon.-Fri. 9-5, Sat. 10-6, Sun. 1-5. School Groups: Sept.-May 14 Mon.-Fri. 9-12. Adults $9, senior citizens $8, children $6, students $4.50; discounts to groups of 15 or more; members no charge. Closed Thanksgiving; Christmas. ♿
Attendance: 65,390 (accurate)
Membership: Individual $49; Family Plus $79; Family Adventure $99; Friend $149; Contributor $349; Blue Hole Society $1,000-$10,000.

THRONATEESKA HERITAGE FOUNDATION, INC., 100 W. Roosevelt Ave., Albany, GA 31701-2325. Tel.: 229-432-6955. Fax: 229-435-1572.
E-mail: info@heritagecenter.org
Web Site: www.heritagecenter.org
Founded: 1974.
Congressional District: 2
Key Personnel: C.E.O. & Exec. Dir., Tommy Gregors; Pres. (V), Ron Simpson; Museum Shop Mgr., Cheryl Jones.
Personnel Profile: Full-Time Paid 2; Full-Time Volunteers 1; Part-Time Paid 5; Part-Time Volunteers 40; Interns 1.
Governing Authority: nonprofit corporation. Tax-exempt.
History Museum.
Collections: costumes; pioneer tools; rocks; minerals; shells; historic artifacts; Indian artifacts; Nelson Tift furnishings; antique carriages; Confederate War Items; local artifacts of the history of Southwest Georgia area; railroad cars with model train exhibit; 1911 steam locomotive; manuscripts. Historic Buildings: 1913 Union Station; 1857 depot; 1919 Railway Express Bldg; science discovery center.
Research Fields: planetarium; local history.
Facilities: children's discovery room. Wetherbee planetarium; community meeting room; science technology center; history gallery.
Activities: guided tours; hobby workshops; formally organized education programs; temporary exhibits.
Publications: quarterly newsletter; annual, Journal of South Georgia History.
Hours & Admission Prices: Thurs.-Sat. 10-4; other times by appointment. No charge. Planetarium: Thurs.-Fri. 2:45, Sat. 12:30, 1:30 & 2:30. Admission $3.50; members no charge. Closed New Year's Day; Martin Luther King Jr. Day; Memorial Day; Independence Day; Labor Day; Thanksgiving; Christmas. ♿
Attendance: 21,271 (accurate)
Membership: Conductor $25; Station Master $35; Signalman $50; Brakeman $100; Steward $250; Engineer $500; Locomotive $1,000.

Americus

RYLANDER THEATER, 310 W. Lamar St., Americus, GA 31709-3543. Mailing Address: P.O. Box 864, Americus, GA 31709-0864. Tel.: 912-931-0001. Fax: 912-928-2466.
Web Site: www.rylander.org
Key Personnel: Gen. Dir., Norman S. Easterbrook
Historic Building: restored working theatre built in 1921.
Collections: art exhibits; classic movies.
Facilities: theater.
Activities: guided tours; stage performances.
Hours & Admission Prices: Tours: by appointment. Performances: call for hours. Closed New Year's Day & day after; Memorial Day; Independence Day; Thanksgiving & day after; Christmas Eve, Day & day after.

Andersonville

* **ANDERSONVILLE NATIONAL HISTORIC SITE, (M),** 496 Cemetery Rd., Andersonville, GA 31711-4040. Tel.: 229-924-0343. Fax: 229-924-1086.
Web Site: www.nps.gov/ande
Founded: 1971.
Congressional District: 2
Key Personnel: Supt., Brad Bennett; Chief of Interpretation & Resource Mgmt., Kim Humber; Museum Shop Mgr., Rene Frye.
Personnel Profile: Full-Time Paid 24; Part-Time Paid 2; Part-Time Volunteers 147; Interns 2.
Governing Authority: federal. Parent Institution: National Park Service, Dept. of the Interior. Tax-exempt: 170(b)(1)(A).
National Park & Historic Site: Civil War P.O.W. camp.
Collections: items related to the Andersonville prison; items related to P.O.W. camps; Civil War & later conflicts; 1890-1910 monuments & sculptures. Historic Buildings: 1877 Cemetery Sexton's residence; 1908 Cemetery chapel.
Research Fields: P.O.W.'s in Andersonville; Civil War; P.O.W.'s in other wars.
Facilities: 3,000-vol. library, official records of the War of the Rebellion, general Civil War, Civil War prisons, Andersonville prison & later P.O.W. camps & woman's relief corps journals available for research on premises only. Books, postcards & slides for sale.
Activities: guided tours; lectures; slide shows; permanent & temporary exhibitions.
Publications: brochure; bulletin, P.O.W. Site.
Hours & Admission Prices: Visitors Center: daily 8:30-5. Park: daily 8-5. No charge; donations accepted. Visitor Center closed New Year's Day; Thanksgiving; Christmas. Grounds open. ♿
Attendance: 160,000 (accurate)
Membership: Friends of Andersonville: Senior Citizen $10; Individual $15; Family $25; Corporate & Business $100.

Athens

CHURCH-WADDEL-BRUMBY HOUSE MUSEUM & ATHENS WELCOME CENTER, 280 E. Dougherty St., Athens, GA 30601-2611. Tel.: 706-353-1820. Fax: 706-353-1770.
E-mail: athenswc@negia.net
Web Site: www.athenswelcomecenter.com
Founded: 1968.
Congressional District: 10
Key Personnel: Dir., Evelyn Reece.
Personnel Profile: Full-Time Paid 1; Part-Time Paid 2; Part-Time Volunteers 10; Interns 2.
Governing Authority: nonprofit organization. Administered by Athens-Clarke Heritage Foundation, Firehall No. 2, 489 Prince Ave., Tel.: 706-353-1801, Fax: 706-552-0753. Tax exempt: 501(c)(3).
Historic House: housed in c.1820 Church-Waddel-Brumby House.
Collections: photographs; period furnishings.
Research Fields: local history.
Facilities: Gift items for sale.
Activities: daily guided tours & self-guided tours.
Hours & Admission Prices: Mon.-Sat. 10-5, Sun. 12-5. No charge. Closed New Year's Day; Thanksgiving; Christmas. No charge; donations accepted. ♿
Attendance: 13,000 (accurate)

CIRCLE GALLERY/COLLEGE OF ENVIRONMENT & DESIGN - UNIVERSITY OF GEORGIA, G14 Caldwell Hall, Athens, GA 30602-0001. Mailing Address: 609 Caldwell Hall, Athens, GA 30602-0001. Tel.: 706-542-8292. Fax: 706-542-4485.
E-mail: rds@uga.edu
Web Site: www.sed.uga.edu/gallery
Formerly: SED Gallery/School of Environmental Design - University of Georgia
Founded: 1993.
Congressional District: 11
Key Personnel: C.E.O., Rene D. Shoemaker.
Personnel Profile: Full-Time Paid 1; Part-Time Paid 7; Interns 1.
Governing Authority: public university; nonprofit organization. Parent Institution: University of Georgia. Subsidiary Institution: College of Environment & Design.
General Museum.
Collections: architecture; landscape architecture; historic preservation; art.
Facilities: 6,000-vol. library.
Activities: lectures; loan & temporary exhibitions; receptions.
Hours & Admission Prices: Mon.-Fri. 8:30-6. No charge. Closed holidays. ♿
Attendance: 2,500 (estimated)

* **GEORGIA MUSEUM OF ART, UNIVERSITY OF GEORGIA, (M),** 90 Carlton St., Athens, GA 30602-1502. Tel.: 706-542-4662. Fax: 706-542-1051. TDD: 706-542-0447.
E-mail: collardj@uga.edu
Web Site: www.uga.edu/gamuseum/
Founded: 1948.
Congressional District: 10
Key Personnel: Dir., William U. Eiland; Deputy Dir., Annelies Mondi; Chm. (V), Carl Mullis, III; Pres. Friends of the Museum, Karen Benson; Coord. Public Rels., Jenny Williams; Chief Preparator, Todd Rivers; Preparator, Lanora Pierce; Editor, Hillary Brown; Asst. Editor, Mary Koon; Cur. American Art, Paul Manoguerra; Cur. Education, Cecelia Hinton; Business Mgr., Marge Massey; Art Handler, Larry Forte; Museum Shop Mgr., Amy Miller; Cur. Pierre Daura, Lynn Boland.
Personnel Profile: Full-Time Paid 30; Part-Time Paid 5; Part-Time Volunteers 150; Interns 14.
Governing Authority: state. Parent Institution: University of Georgia. Subsidiary Institution: Friends of the Museum. Tax-exempt: 170(B)(1)(A).
Art Museum.
Collections: 19th- to 20th-century American painting; Kress Study Collection of Italian Renaissance paintings; European, American and Japanese prints & drawings; contemporary American photographs; decorative arts.
Major Exhibits: Imprinting the South: Works on Paper From the Collection of Lynn Barstis Williams and Stephen J. Goldfarb (T), 11/09-1/2/10.
Research Fields: American paintings, drawings & prints; old master & European modern prints.
Facilities: library of art history books; 200-seat auditorium; studio classroom; A-V theater; cafe; teacher resource center. Museum-related items for sale.
Activities: guided tours; docent program; gallery talks for children & adults; internships; educational programs for children, adults, families, senior citizens & university students; lectures; statewide outreach, temporary & traveling exhibitions; regular film series.
Publications: Georgia Museum of Art Bulletin; quarterly newsletter; exhibition catalogs & brochures; gallery notes; docent newsletter; calendar, GMOA on the Move.
Hours & Admission Prices: Closed for renovation until early 2011. ♿
Attendance: 100,000 (accurate)
Membership: Student & Senior $15; Individual $30; Family $50; Contributing $100; Business $100-$200; Donating $250; Sustaining $500; Benefactor $5,000.

GEORGIA MUSEUM OF NATURAL HISTORY, Natural History Bldg., University of Georgia, Athens, GA 30602-1882. Tel.: 706-542-1663. Fax: 706-542-3920.
E-mail: musinfo@uga.edu
Web Site: museum.nhm.uga.edu
Founded: 1977.
Congressional District: 10
Key Personnel: Dir. & Cur. Zoology, Dr. B. Freeman; Pres. (V), Jean Porter; Cur. Zooarchaeology, Dr. E. Reitz; Cur. Mineralogy, Dr. P. Schroeder; Cur. Archaeology, Dr. D.J. Hally; Cur. Education & Outreach, Dr. C. Hoffman; Cur. Botany, Dr. D. Giannasi; Cur. Botany, Dr. W. Zomlefer; Cur. Entomology, Dr. J. McHugh; Cur. Economic Geology, Dr. D. Crowe; Cur. Mycology, Dr. R. Hanlin.
Personnel Profile: Full-Time Paid 17; Part-Time Paid 12; Part-Time Volunteers 3; Interns 26.
Governing Authority: university. Parent Institution: University of Georgia. Tax-exempt.
Natural History Museum.
Collections: archaeology; botany; entomology; economic geology; mycology; paleontology; zooarchaeology; palynology; mineralogy; mammalogy; herpetology; ornithology; ichthyology.
Research Fields: anthropology; archaeology; botany; entomology; geology; mycology; zoology.
Facilities: laboratories; classrooms.
Activities: educational outreach programs; science box program; tours; special exhibits; collections available to qualified researchers.
Hours & Admission Prices: By appointment. No charge. Closed holidays. ♿
Attendance: 10,000 (estimated)
Membership: Student & Senior Citizens $15; Individual $30; Family $40.

LYNDON HOUSE ARTS CENTER, 293 Hoyt St., Athens, GA 30601-2648. Tel.: 706-613-3623. Fax: 706-613-3627.
Founded: 1973.
Congressional District: 10
Key Personnel: Dir., Claire Benson; Cur., Nancy Lukasiewicz; Pres. (V) Lyndon House Arts Foundation, Rinne Allen; Museum Shop Mgr., Celia Brooks.
Personnel Profile: Full-Time Paid 4; Part-Time Paid 1; Part-Time Volunteers 500.

Governing Authority: municipal. A facility of Athens-Clarke County Dept. of Leisure Services.
Art Center: c.1850 Ware-Lyndon House, originally built by Dr. Edward R. Ware & later sold to Dr. Edward Smith Lyndon.
Collections: decorative arts; furnishings; personal artifacts; historic house.
Major Exhibits: Portraits & Self Portraits by Students of Clarke County School District K-12, 11/09-1/10; 35th Juried Exhibition, 2/10-5/10; Full House Exhibition - Works by Members of 15 Artist Organizations That Call LHAC Home, 6/10-9/10.
Facilities: library; studios; meeting room.
Activities: special events; guided tours; lectures; gallery talks; arts festivals; meetings & workshops for local art organizations; formally organized education & awareness programs for children, adults, specialized groups & general public; art courses in photography; clay painting, printmaking, weaving & youth art; stained glass, internships for students at the University of Georgia.
Publications: periodic catalogs; newsletter.
Hours & Admission Prices: Tues. & Thurs. 12-9, Wed. & Fri.-Sat. 9-5. No charge; donations accepted. Closed Thanksgiving; Christmas. ♿
Attendance: 70,000

THE STATE BOTANICAL GARDEN OF GEORGIA, 2450 S. Milledge Ave., Athens, GA 30605-1674. Tel.: 706-542-1244. Fax: 706-542-3091.
E-mail: garden@uga.edu
Web Site: www.uga.edu/botgarden
Founded: 1968.
Congressional District: 10
Key Personnel: Interim Dir., Shirley Berry; Pres. (V) Friends of the Garden, Pam Bracken; Chm. (V) Advisory Bd., Dr. W. Felton Norwood; Dir. Research, Dr. James Affolter; Horticulturist, Jeannette Coplin; Dir. Education, Anne Shenk; Administrative Coord., Shirley Berry; Visitor Center Mgr., William Tonks; Information Specialist, Lisa Kennedy; Museum Shop Mgr., Julie Villella; Plant Conservation Coord., Jennifer Ceska; Office Mgr., Jason Burdette; Administrative Sec., Beverly Morton.
Personnel Profile: Full-Time Paid 27; Part-Time Paid 10; Part-Time Volunteers 150; Interns 1.
Governing Authority: university. Parent Institution: University of Georgia. Subsidiary Institution: Friends of the Garden. Tax-exempt.
University Botanical Garden.
Collections: woody plant collections; native flora; native & adapted trees & shrubs including shade & ornamental trees.
Research Fields: horticulture; botany; natural history; ecology; plant conservation.
Facilities: 140-seat chapel; 125-seat auditorium; classrooms; nature trails; visitor center & conservatory of tropical plants; conference facilities for up to 300 people. Museum-related items for sale.
Activities: lectures; films; concerts; workshops; trail walks; temporary exhibition of botanical art; guided tours.
Publications: quarterly, Garden News.
Hours & Admission Prices: Grounds: April-Sept. daily 8-8; Oct.-March daily 8-6. Visitor Center: Tues.-Sat. 9-4:30, Sun. 11:30-4:30. Cafe: Tues.-Fri. 11-2, Sat.-Sun. 11:30-3. No charge; donations accepted. Closed University holidays. ♿
Attendance: 200,000 (estimated)
Membership: Student $15; Senior Citizen $20; Nonprofit Organization $25; Senior Couple $30; Individual $35; Family $45; Sponsor $100; Donor $250; Contributor $500; Patron $1,000; Ambassador $2,500; Life $5,000.

TAYLOR-GRADY HOUSE, 634 Prince Ave., Athens, GA 30601-2453. Tel.: 706-549-8688. Fax: 706-613-0860.
E-mail: jlathens@aol.com
Web Site: www.taylorgradyhouse.com
Founded: 1968.
Congressional District: 10
Key Personnel: Chm. (V), Jennifer Wooten.
Personnel Profile: Full-Time Paid 3.
Governing Authority: nonprofit organization. Junior League of Athens, Inc. Tax-exempt.
Historic House Museum: 1845 Henry W. Grady Home.
Collections: period furnishings.
Activities: guided tours; rental gallery.
Publications: pamphlet.
Hours & Admission Prices: Mon.-Fri. 9-1 & 2-5. Suggested Donation $3. Closed holidays. ♿
Attendance: 5,000 (estimated)

U.S. NAVY SUPPLY CORPS MUSEUM, U.S. Navy Supply Corps School, 1425 Prince Ave., Athens, GA 30606-2205. Tel.: 706-354-4111.
Founded: 1974.
Congressional District: 11
Personnel Profile: Full-Time Paid 1.
Governing Authority: federal. Parent Institution: U.S. Navy. Tax-exempt: 501(c)(3).
Naval Museum: housed in 1910 Carnegie Library.
Collections: artifacts relating to U.S. naval history & logistical functions: historic uniforms; navigational equipment; gallery gear; paintings; ship models; books; personal memorabilia; photo archives; official records; manuals; yearbooks; newsletters; scrapbooks; directories.
Research Fields: U.S. Navy; Supply Corps; naval logistical functions.
Facilities: garden area with fountains & gazebo; archives. Gift-related items for sale by Supply Corps Foundation Office 706-354-4111.
Activities: guided tours available; rotating, temporary & permanent exhibits.
Publications: museum brochure; handouts regarding history of U.S. Navy Supply Corps & Supply Corps School; base brochure.
Hours & Admission Prices: Mon.-Fri. 9-4, call to confirm. No charge. Closed federal holidays.

Atlanta

THE APEX MUSEUM, 135 Auburn Ave., N.E., Atlanta, GA 30303-2567. Tel.: 404-523-2739. Fax: 404-523-3248 (call first).
E-mail: apexmuseum@aol.com
Web Site: www.apexmuseum.org
Founded: 1978.
Congressional District: 5
Key Personnel: Pres., Dan Moore, Sr.; Gallery & Tour Coord., Michele Mitchell.
Personnel Profile: Full-Time Paid 4; Part-Time Volunteers 40; Interns 4.
Governing Authority: nonprofit organization. Parent Institution: Collections of Life & Heritage, Inc. Tax-exempt: 501(c)(3).
History Museum & Building: 1910 John Wesley Dobbs Building, former School Book Depository; entity of the Sweet Auburn historic Freedom Walk.
Collections: Sankoya wood & brass artifacts; collection represents 10 West African countries; permanent African-American art collection which includes pieces by nationally renowned artists.
Facilities: 7,500 sq. ft. exhibit space; 50-seat Trolley Theatre. Museum-related items for sale.
Activities: guided tours; lectures; films; theatre; rental gallery; loan & temporary exhibitions; school loan service; docent program; underground railroad trek; tribute to the ancestors.
Publications: bimonthly, The APEX Times.
Hours & Admission Prices: Feb. & June-Aug. Tues.-Sat. 10-5, Sun. 1-5; March-May & Sept.-Jan. Tues.-Sat. 10-5. Adults $4, senior citizens & students $3; discounts to groups; members & children under 4 no charge. ♿
Attendance: 65,000 (accurate)
Membership: Student & Senior Citizen $15; Individual Adults $30; Family of 4 $50; Patron $100; Donor $250; Life $500.

AMERICAN BAPTIST HISTORICAL SOCIETY, 3001 Mercer University Dr., Atlanta, GA 30341-4115. Tel.: 678-547-6680.
Web Site: abhsarchives.org/index.shtml
Founded: 1853.
Congressional District: 34
Key Personnel: Exec. Dir., Dr. Deborah Bigham-Van Broekhoven; Communications & Reader Svcs., Betsy Dunbar.
Governing Authority: church. Affiliated with American Baptist Churches in United States Valley Forge, PA. 19481. Tax-exempt: 501(c)(3).
Research Library.
Collections: archives; manuscripts; original records; books; pamphlets; photographs; paintings.
Research Fields: Baptist history; American religion.
Facilities: 60,000-vol. library of books pertaining to Baptistiana, archives & manuscripts collections available for use under staff supervision on premises.
Publications: quarterly magazine, American Baptist Quarterly; newsletter, The Primary Source.
Hours & Admission Prices: By appointment. ♿
Membership: Basic $25; Subscribers $40.

ATLANTA BOTANICAL GARDEN, 1345 Piedmont Ave., N.E., Atlanta, GA 30309-3366. Tel.: 404-876-5859. Fax: 404-876-7472.
E-mail: info@atlantabotanicalgarden.org
Web Site: www.atlantabotanicalgarden.org
Founded: 1976.
Congressional District: 5
Key Personnel: Exec. Dir., Mary Pat Matheson; Supt., Dorothy Chapman

Fuqua Conservatory, Ron Determann; Mktg. Dir., Danny Flanders; Horticulturist, Mildred Pinnell; Volunteer Coord., Mary Woehrel; Museum Shop Mgr., Mandy Horneber; Public Rels. Mgr., Geri Laufer; Visitor Svcs. Mgr., Susan Clark.
Personnel Profile: Full-Time Paid 60; Part-Time Paid 14; Part-Time Volunteers 600; Interns 2.
Governing Authority: nonprofit organization. Tax-exempt.
Arboretum & Botanical Garden.
Collections: 15 acres of Georgia's native plant material; 15 acres of annual, perennial & woody plants; tropical & desert collections in Fuqua Conservatory; Fuqua Orchid Center with high elevation orchid house; tropical orchid display house; children's garden.
Research Fields: native & tropical plant conservation programs; conservation breeding programs involving poison & tree frogs; micro-propagation techniques for endangered species.
Facilities: 5,000-vol. library of botany, horticulture & taxonomy books available for research to members & visitors on premises; orchid reference library; tissue culture lab; glass conservatory; classrooms; workshop; conservation greenhouses. Museum-related items for sale.
Activities: guided tours; lectures; adult & children's classes; seasonal children's camps; entertainment program for children in Children's garden; films; art shows; plant society exhibits; docent program; permanent exhibitions; off premises garden tours; festivals; social functions.
Publications: 3 member newsletter, Clippings; 3 volunteer newsletter, Digging In; annual report.
Hours & Admission Prices: April Tues.-Sun. 9-7; May-Oct. Tues.-Wed. & Fri.-Sun. 9-7, Thurs. 9am-10pm; Nov.-March Tues.-Sun. 9-5. Adults $15 senior citizens & children 3-17 $12; members, children under 3, Thurs. after 3:00 & members of reciprocating institutions no charge. Closed New Year's Day; Thanksgiving; Christmas. ♿
Attendance: 325,000 (accurate)
Membership: Individual $50; Family & Dual $75; Contributing $125; Supporting $250; Donor $300; Director's Club $1,000; Arbor Circle $2,500; Magnolia Circle $5,000; Orchid Circle $10,000.

ATLANTA CONTEMPORARY ART CENTER, 535 Means St., N.W., Atlanta, GA 30318-5729. Tel.: 404-688-1970. Fax: 404-577-5856.
E-mail: info@thecontemporary.org
Web Site: www.thecontemporary.org
Formerly: Nexus Contemporary Art Center
Founded: 1973.
Congressional District: 5
Key Personnel: Chm. (V), Jon Shils; Mng. Dir., Stacie Lindner; Dir. Institutional Advancement, Saskia Benjamin; Dir. Communications, Stan Woodard; Artistic Dir., Stuart Horodner; Membership & Events, Alana Wolf.
Personnel Profile: Full-Time Paid 6; Part-Time Paid 2; Part-Time Volunteers 5; Interns 5.
Governing Authority: nonprofit organization. Tax-exempt: 501(c)(3).
Contemporary Art Gallery & Civic Cultural Center.
Collections: works by contemporary artists.
Research Fields: contemporary experimental visual, performing & book arts; strong emphasis on socio-political contemporary.
Facilities: 6,000 sq. ft. exhibit space; theater; 5,000 sq. ft. sculpture court; educational facilities.
Activities: guided tours; lectures; theater; media programs; concerts; dance recitals; arts festivals; docent program; participatory, loan, temporary & traveling exhibitions; education programs for children; formally organized programs for undergraduate & graduate students; focused on contemporary culture & cultural issues; classes for adult artists & collectors. Annual Events: issue-oriented membership symposiums.
Publications: exhibition catalogues.
Hours & Admission Prices: Tues.-Wed. & Fri.-Sat. 11-5, Thurs. 11-8, Sun. 12-5. Adults $5, students & seniors $3; Thurs. & members no charge. ♿
Attendance: 70,000 (estimated)
Membership: Working Artist $25; Individual $35; Dual & Family $55; Contributing $100; Supporting $250; Sustaining $500; Benefactor & Avant-Garde Society $1,000; Curator's Circle $5,000.

THE ATLANTA CYCLORAMA, 800-C Cherokee Ave., S.E., Atlanta, GA 30315-1470. Tel.: 404-658-7625. Fax: 404-658-7045.
Web Site: www.atlantacyclorama.org
Founded: 1898.
Congressional District: 5
Key Personnel: Dir., Camille R. Love; Bookstore Mgr., Beverly D. Williams; Mktg. & Public Rels., Yakingma L. Robinson; Administrative Asst., Senior, Kimberly Johnson.
Personnel Profile: Full-Time Paid 6.
Governing Authority: city. Parent Institution: Atlanta Department of Parks, Recreation & Cultural Affairs. Tax-exempt.
Art & Civil War Museum: located in c.1921 structure, housing a 42-ft. high x 356 ft. in circumference, c.1886 Cyclorama that depicts the July 22, 1864 Battle of Atlanta.
Collections: Civil War artifacts.
Research Fields: cyclorama art form; Civil War history.
Facilities: visitor center; available for rental. Books & museum-related items for sale.
Activities: lectures; gallery talks; film festivals; living history; art exhibits.
Publications: brochure; fact sheet; book, The Battle of Atlanta-The Cyclorama.
Hours & Admission Prices: June-Labor Day daily 9:30-5:30; Sept.-May daily 9:30-4:30. Adults 13 & over $6, senior citizens & children 6-12 $4; discounts for military, college students, museum professionals, AAA members, AARP, groups of 10 & over and "Special Audience" & "Arts For All" (city of Atlanta Community Programs); children under 6 no charge. ♿
Attendance: 175,000

* **ATLANTA HISTORICAL SOCIETY, (M),** 130 W. Paces Ferry Rd., N.W., Atlanta, GA 30305-1380. Tel.: 404-814-4000. Fax: 404-814-2041. TDD: 404-814-4000.
E-mail: scilella@atlantahistorycenter.com
Web Site: www.atlantahistorycenter.com
Founded: 1926.
Congressional District: 5
Key Personnel: C.E.O. & Pres., Salvatore G. Cilella; Chm. (V), Catherine Manning; C.O.O., Casey Steadman; Exec. Vice Pres., Michael Rose; Vice Pres. Operations, Sean Thorndike; Vice Pres. Public Programs, Kate Whitman; Vice Pres. Devel., Kathy Egan, CFRE; Vice Pres. Capital Projects, Jackson McQuigg; Dir. Margaret Mitchell House and Museum, Diane Lewis; Vice Pres. Mktg., Hillary Hardwick; Museum Shop Mgr., Michael Mims.
Personnel Profile: Full-Time Paid 70; Part-Time Paid 90; Part-Time Volunteers 375; Interns 20.
Governing Authority: board of trustees. Parent Institution: Atlanta Historical Society, Inc. Tax-exempt: 501(c)(3).
History Museum.
Collections: history of Atlanta, the Civil War & African-American history: manuscripts; 1,500,000 photographs; maps; 19,000 books; 100,000 architectural drawings; Atlanta newspapers; Margaret Mitchell memorabilia; early 19th-century furniture & tools; extensive costume & textile collection; folklife collection; Civil War artifacts; decorative arts; gardens; confederate money; collections of George Washington, Thomas Jefferson, Robert E. Lee, Jefferson Davis, John Tyler, John C. Calhoun, Napoleon, Gen. Robert Toombs, F.D. Roosevelt & Hitler; Georgian & Confederate history; Coca-Cola artifacts; early Japanese Zero plane; early Chinese items; early glass, porcelains, bronzes & furniture; Eli Whitney gun collection & original cotton gin; sculpture; Indian artifacts. Historic Houses: 1845 Tullie Smith Farm; 1890 Victorian Playhouse; 1928 Swan House; 1920 Margaret Mitchell House.
Research Fields: local & state history; regional, Civil War, Black, urban & suburban histories; folklife & decorative arts.
Facilities: cafe; 33-acre property; gardens. Museum-related items for sale.
Activities: permanent & changing exhibitions; workshops; tours; lectures; seminars; festivals; formally organized programs; teacher training classes; active auxiliary groups for crafts; current affairs & educational support.
Publications: quarterly journal, Atlanta History: A Journal of Georgia & the South; quarterly newsletter.
Hours & Admission Prices: Museum: Mon.-Sat. 10-5:30, Sun. 12-5:30. Library: Tues.-Sat. 10-5. Adults $15, students 13 & over and seniors 65 & over $12, youth 4-12 $10; discounts to groups, ICOM & AAM members; members & children under 4 no charge. Additional charge for some special events. Closed New Year's Day; Thanksgiving; Christmas Eve & Day. ♿
Attendance: 152,000 (accurate)
Membership: Student $25; Individual $40; Family & Dual $60; Sustaining $125; Sponsor $250; Patron $500; Director's Roundtable $1,000.

ATLANTA VISITOR'S CENTER AND MONETARY MUSEUM, 1000 Peachtree St., N.E., Atlanta, GA 30309-4470. Tel.: 404-498-8777.
Money Museum.
Collections: artifacts & memorabilia pertaining to the history of money.
Hours & Admission Prices: Tours: Mon.-Fri. 9-4.

THE BREMAN JEWISH HERITAGE & HOLOCAUST MUSEUM, (M), 1440 Spring St., N.W., Atlanta, GA 30309-2832. Tel.: 678-222-3700. Fax: 404-881-4009.
E-mail: jleavey@atljf.org
Web Site: www.thebreman.org
Founded: 1996.
Congressional District: 5
Key Personnel: Dir., Jane Leavey; Pres., Tom Asher; Archivist & Registrar, Sandra K. Berman; Coord. Special Exhibitions & Programs, Jennifer N.

Campbell; Weinberg Center for Holocaust Educ., Carla Singer; Public Rels. & Mktg., Phyllis Lazarus.
Personnel Profile: Full-Time Paid 6; Part-Time Paid 5; Part-Time Volunteers 150; Interns 2.
Governing Authority: private; nonprofit organization. Parent Institution: Jewish Federation of Greater Atlanta, 1440 Spring St., Atlanta, GA 30309.
Jewish Heritage Museum.
Collections: concentration on Georgia Jewish history from 1845 to the present; Holocaust history with special emphasis on the experiences of Holocaust survivors who have made new lives in Atlanta; Georgia Jewish history.
Research Fields: Atlanta Jewish history; Holocaust history; Georgia Jewish history; Alabama Jewish History.
Facilities: library of southern Jewish history, Holocaust, genealogy and general Judaica books, available to the public; 8,000 sq. ft. exhibit space; 200-seat auditorium; educational facilities; 500-seat theatre. Museum-related items for sale.
Activities: docent programs; films; formal education programs for adults; guided tours; lectures; school loan service; temporary exhibitions; theatre; children & family hands-on workshops; Holocaust survivors speakers bureau.
Publications: exhibition catalogues, Creating Community: The Jews of Atlanta from 1845 to the Present; Absence of Humanity; The Holocaust Years; Historical Survey: 150 Years of Creating Community; catalogues, Seeking Justice: The Leo Frank Case Revisited; ZAP! POW! BAM! The Superhero, The Golden Age of Comic Books, 1938-1950.
Hours & Admission Prices: Mon.-Thurs. 10-5, Fri. 10-3, Sun. 1-5. Adults $10, senior citizens 62 & over $7, students $5, children 3-6 $2; discount to groups; children under 3 & members no charge. Closed New Year's Day; Independence Day; Thanksgiving; Jewish Holy Days. ♿
Attendance: 40,000 (estimated)
Membership: Student & Senior $36; Individual $50; Family $75; Donor $150; Patron $250; Sponsor $500; Benefactor $1,000; Chai $1,800; President's Council $5,000.

CDC/GLOBAL HEALTH ODYSSEY, (M), 1600 Clifton Rd., N.E., (at CDC Pkwy. -MS A14), Atlanta, GA 30329-4018. Tel.: 404-639-0830. Fax: 404-639-0834.
E-mail: global@cdc.gov
Web Site: www.cdc.gov/gcc/exhibit
Founded: 1996.
Congressional District: 4
Key Personnel: Dir., Judy M. Gantt; Collections Mgr., Mary Hilpertshauser; Educator, Trudi Bothma Ellerman; Cur., Louise Shaw.
Personnel Profile: Full-Time Paid 4; Part-Time Paid 1; Part-Time Volunteers 50.
Governing Authority: federal; nonprofit. Parent Institution: Centers for Disease Control & Prevention. Tax-exempt.
Medical Museum.
Collections: the history of Public Health Service & Centers for Disease Control & Prevention with emphasis on benefits to nation and world of CDC's work: protection of health & safety; credible information, and promotion of health in all stages of life.
Facilities: 150-seat cafeteria; 50-seat cafe. Museum-related items for sale.
Activities: guided tours; video presentations. Museum Sponsors: Yearly Disease Detective Camp.
Hours & Admission Prices: Mon.-Wed. & Fri. 9-5, Thurs. 9-7. No charge. Closed federal holidays
Attendance: 56,000 (accurate)

CALLANWOLDE FINE ARTS CENTER, 980 Briarcliff Rd., N.E., Atlanta, GA 30306-2650. Tel.: 404-872-5338. Fax: 404-872-5175.
E-mail: info@callanwolde.org
Web Site: www.callanwolde.org
Founded: 1973.
Congressional District: 4
Key Personnel: Exec. Dir., Samuel Goldman, Ph.D.; Chm. (V), Palmer Proctor; Gallery Dir., Laurie Allan; Gen. Mgr., Ray Tankersley; Art Shop Mgr., Carol Hale; Dir. Arts Education, Casey Parsons; Chief Registrar, Robin L. Van Horne.
Personnel Profile: Full-Time Paid 12; Part-Time Paid 5; Part-Time Volunteers 150.
Governing Authority: nonprofit organization; The Callanwolde Foundation, Inc. Tax-exempt: 501(c)(3).
Arts Center: housed in 1917-1920 Callanwolde, home of Charles Howard Candler, son of Asa Candler of Coca-Cola fame.
Collections: personal artifacts; 1920s Gothic mansion.
Facilities: classrooms; rental gallery. Paintings, prints, sculpture, woven items, pottery & jewelry for sale.
Activities: guided tours; concerts; dance recitals; arts festivals; drama; formally organized education programs; docent program or council; traveling exhibitions; workshops.
Publications: quarterly, Classes Publication; quarterly newsletter, Callanwolde Fine Art Center.
Hours & Admission Prices: Mon.-Fri. 10-8, Sat. 10-3. No charge. Closed legal holidays. ♿
Attendance: 25,000 (estimated)
Membership: Student & Senior Citizen $15; Individual $25; Family $50; Sustaining $125; Contributor $250; Patron $500; Bronze $1,500-$3,499; Silver $3,500; Gold $5,000; Platinum $7,500; Diamond $10,000.

CENTER FOR PUPPETRY ARTS, 1404 Spring St., N.W., Atlanta, GA 30309-2820. Tel.: 404-873-3089. Fax: 404-873-9907.
E-mail: info@puppet.org
Web Site: www.puppet.org
Founded: 1978.
Congressional District: 4
Key Personnel: Exec. Dir., Vincent Anthony; Chm. (V), John Chandler; Administration, Lisa Rhodes; Production, Kristin Jarvis; Museum Shop Mgr., Julie Coenson.
Personnel Profile: Full-Time Paid 37; Part-Time Paid 25; Part-Time Volunteers 32.
Governing Authority: nonprofit organization. Tax-exempt: 501(c)(3).
Puppetry Museum.
Collections: global collections of puppets; toy & poster collection; collection of books, videos, DVDs & films on puppetry.
Research Fields: puppetry.
Facilities: 2,000-vol. library of books & periodicals, including 950 videotapes, available to the public; 170-seat theater; 350-seat theater; 4,000 sq. ft. exhibit space; educational facilities. Puppets, books & clothing for sale.
Activities: guided tours; lectures; theater; organized education programs; docent program; participatory, loan, temporary & traveling exhibitions; films.
Publications: monthly e-newsletter, Center News; exhibit catalogs.
Hours & Admission Prices: Tues.-Fri. 9-3, Sat. 9-5, Sun. 11-5. Museum: adults $8, seniors & students $7, children $6; discounts to groups, AAM & ICOM members; children under 2 & members no charge. Museum, Show & Workshop: adults $16, members $9. Closed New Year's Day; Easter; Memorial Day; Independence Day; Labor Day; Thanksgiving; Christmas. ♿
Attendance: 65,000 (estimated)
Membership: Individual $45-$74; Dual & Family $75-$149; Sponsor $150-$249; Sustainer $250-$499; Benefactor $500-$999; Impressario $1,000-$2,499.

CHATTAHOOCHEE RIVER NATIONAL RECREATION AREA, 1978 Island Ford Pkwy., Atlanta, GA 30350-3432. Tel.: 678-538-1200 & 1280. Fax: 770-399-8087.
Web Site: www.nps.gov/chat
Founded: 1978.
Congressional District: 5, 6 & 9
Key Personnel: Acting Supt., Rick Slade; Chief of Admin., Riana Bishop; Chief Ranger, Scott M. Pseninger; Chief Resource Education, Nancy Walther.
Personnel Profile: Full-Time Paid 32; Part-Time Volunteers 35; Interns 6.
Governing Authority: federal. Parent Institution: National Park Service, S.E. Region, 75 Spring St., S.W., Atlanta, GA 30303. Tax-exempt.
Natural & Cultural Area.
Collections: prehistoric village sites, rock shelters & fish weirs; historic Indian village sites & Civil War remains. Historic Structures: 1850 Allenbrook; 1850 ruins of Akers Mill-Marietta Paper Mill; 1840 Ivy (Laurel) Mill Ruins.
Research Fields: cultural resource inventory; archaeology; historic resources; natural resource base inventory.
Facilities: visitor contact areas; trails; open activity fields; picnic areas; concessions; cooperative association operations; collective research documents on natural & cultural history.
Activities: recreational & educational opportunities; guided walks; lectures; canoe, kayak & raft rentals; shuttle service; skill instructional clinics; horseback riding; 3-mile fitness trail with exercise stations; 50-mile hiking trails
Publications: brochures; trail maps.
Hours & Admission Prices: Daily 9-5. No charge. Parking Fee: daily $3, annual $25. Closed Christmas. ♿
Attendance: 2,800,000 (accurate)

CLARK ATLANTA UNIVERSITY ART GALLERIES, Trevor Arnett Hall, 2nd Fl., Atlanta, GA 30314. Mailing Address: 223 James P. Brawley Dr., S.W., Atlanta, GA 30314-4358. Tel.: 404-880-6102. Fax: 404-880-6968.
E-mail: tdunkley@cau.edu
Web Site: www.cau.edu/artgalleries
Founded: 1942.
Congressional District: 5
Key Personnel: Dir., Tina Dunkley; Curatorial Asst., Erikka Searles.
Personnel Profile: Full-Time Paid 2; Part-Time Volunteers 8; Interns 2.
Governing Authority: Parent Institution: Clark Atlanta University. Tax-exempt.
Art Galleries.
Collections: African-American art from 1942-1970; American & World art.
Activities: lectures; guided tours; films; gallery talks; permanent & temporary traveling exhibits; formal education program for children.
Hours & Admission Prices: Tues.-Fri. 11-4. No charge; donations accepted. ♿
Attendance: 10,000 (estimated)
Membership: Friends $25-$1,000.

DECORATIVE ARTS COLLECTION, INC. MUSEUM OF DECORATIVE PAINTING, (M), 650 Hamilton Ave., S.E., Ste. M, Atlanta, GA 30312. Mailing Address: P.O. Box 18028, Atlanta, GA 30316-0028. Tel.: 404-627-3662.
E-mail: dac@decorativeartscollection.org
Web Site: www.decorativeartscollection
Founded: 1982.
Key Personnel: Dir., Andy Jones; Chm. (V), Peggy Harris; Coord. Art Collection, Bette Marken.
Personnel Profile: Part-Time Paid 2; Part-Time Volunteers 20.
Governing Authority: Tax-exempt.
Art Museum.
Collections: historic & contemporary decorative painting; early American folk art from around the world.
Major Exhibits: Painted Quilts, 11/09-1/10.
Research Fields: appraisal, historical value of each piece as well as monetary worth.
Facilities: 1,375-vol. library on decorative art; classroom. Gift items for sale.
Activities: guided tours; loan, temporary & traveling exhibitions.
Publications: exhibition catalogues, Fathers of American Decorative Painting; Sentimental Collection of Roses; Celebrate St. Nicholas; The Book of Painted Quilts.
Hours & Admission Prices: Mon.-Fri. 11-4; other times by appointment. No charge; donations accepted. ♿
Attendance: 600 (estimated)
Membership: Friend $40; Contributor $100; Sponsor $250; Patron $500; Benefactor $1,000; Silver Benefactor $2,500; Gold Benefactor $5,000.

DELTA AIR TRANSPORT HERITAGE MUSEUM, (M), Delta World Headquarters, 1060 Delta Blvd., B-914, Atlanta, GA 30354. Mailing Address: 1060 Delta Blvd., Bldg. B, Dept. 914, Atlanta, GA 30354-1989. Tel.: 404-715-7886 (Office) & 773-1219 (Store).
Web Site: www.deltamuseum.org
Founded: 1995.
Key Personnel: Chm. (V), Harold Bevis; Dir., Tiffany Meng; Mgr. Archives, Marie Force; Museum Shop Mgr., Judy Bean.
Personnel Profile: Full-Time Paid 3; Part-Time Paid 2; Part-Time Volunteers 20; Interns 1.
Governing Authority: Parent Institution: Delta Air Lines. Tax-exempt.
Corporate History Museum.
Collections: Delta history; aircraft; airline uniforms; photographs; films; 2 1940s aircraft maintenance hangars.
Research Fields: Delta Air Lines history.
Facilities: Museum-related items for sale.
Hours & Admission Prices: Mon.-Thurs. 9-4 by appointment. No charge; donations accepted.
Attendance: 15,000 (estimated)

* **FERNBANK MUSEUM OF NATURAL HISTORY, (M),** 767 Clifton Rd., N.E., Atlanta, GA 30307-1274. Tel.: 404-929-6300 & 6400 (tickets). Fax: 404-929-6405 & 6406.
Web Site: www.fernbankmuseum.org
Founded: 1992.
Congressional District: 4
Key Personnel: C.E.O. & Pres., Susan E. Neugent; Bd. Chm., Hampton Morris; Vice Pres. Devel., Leslie Marlowe; Vice Pres. Education, Christine Bean; Museum Shop Mgr., Linda Gerber.
Personnel Profile: Full-Time Paid 77; Part-Time Paid 30; Part-Time Volunteers 350; Interns 6.
Governing Authority: private; nonprofit organization. Parent Institution: Fernbank, Inc. Tax-exempt: 501(c)(3).
Natural History Museum.
Collections: geology; paleontology; zoology; anthropology; archaeology; ethnography.
Major Exhibits: Gold, 11/09-1/3/10; Nature Unleashed: Inside Natural Disasters, 2/6/10-5/2/10; Geckos: Tails to Toepads, Summer and Fall 2010.
Research Fields: archaeology.
Facilities: 181-seat auditorium; 150-seat cafe; 60,000 sq. ft. exhibit space; 315-seat IMAX theatre; children's discovery rooms; facility rentals for private events.
Activities: lectures; loan, temporary, participatory & traveling exhibitions; volunteer program; summer camp; summer archaeology educational/research program; school programs; after-school program in partnership with Atlanta Public Schools; Urban Watch Atlanta; children's programming; special exhibitions; Martinis & IMAX(R) theatre; facilities rental.
Hours & Admission Prices: Mon.-Sat. 10-5, Sun. 12-5. Museum: adults $15, senior citizens & students $14, children 12 & under $13; discount to groups & ASTC members; members no charge. IMAX: adults $13, seniors & students $12, children $11, members $8. Closed Thanksgiving; Christmas. ♿
Attendance: 402,412 (accurate)
Membership: Individual $60; Family & Dual $85; Contributing $135; Family Advantage $150; Patron Circle $250; Benefactor's Circle $500.

FERNBANK SCIENCE CENTER, 156 Heaton Park Dr., N.E., Atlanta, GA 30307-1398. Tel.: 678-874-7102. Fax: 678-874-7110.
E-mail: fernbank@fernbank.edu
Web Site: www.fsc.fernbank.edu
Founded: 1967.
Congressional District: 4
Key Personnel: Dir., Douglas J. Hrabe.
Personnel Profile: Full-Time Paid 71; Part-Time Volunteers 30.
Governing Authority: public school district. Parent Institution: DeKalb County (GA) Bd. of Education. Tax-exempt: 501(c)(3).
Science Museum, Planetarium & Observatory.
Collections: skins; hides; entomology; ornithology; herbarium; geology; skeletal; gems; minerals; birds; mammals; insects.
Research Fields: life & physical sciences with emphasis on astronomy & ecology.
Facilities: 26,000-vol. library of biological & physical science books for reference only; planetarium; classrooms; forest; observatory; greenhouses; slide sets.
Activities: classes in nature & science; guided tours; formally organized education programs; formally organized education programs for undergraduate college students affiliated with Emory University; permanent, traveling & temporary exhibitions; children's programs; public programs for adults & children. Center Sponsors: classes for the handicapped.
Publications: Primarily for Understanding Science; Just for Understanding Science; Ready for Understanding Science.
Hours & Admission Prices: Mon.-Wed. 8:30-5, Thurs.-Fri. 8:30am-10pm, Sat. 10-5, Sun. 1-5; groups by appointment. Museum: no charge. Planetarium: adults $4, students & seniors $3; discounts to AAM & ICOM members; members no charge. ♿
Attendance: 850,000 (estimated)

FOX THEATRE, 660 Peachtree St., N.E., Atlanta, GA 30308-1929. Tel.: 404-881-2100 & 688-3353 (Tours). Fax: 404-872-2972.
Governing Authority: nonprofit organization. Parent Institution: Atlanta Landmarks.
Historic Building: built c.1920. A National Historic Landmark.
Collections: theatre history & architecture; films; performances.
Facilities: 4,678 auditorium. Museum-related items for sale.
Activities: performances; special events; outreach & educational programs; workshops; summer film series.
Hours & Admission Prices: Tours by appointment: Mon. & Wed.-Thurs. 10am, Sat. 10am & 11am. Adults $10, students & seniors $5.

GEORGIA AQUARIUM, 225 Baker St., Atlanta, GA 30313-1809. Tel.: 404-581-4000.
Web Site: www.georgiaaquarium.org
Founded: 2005.
Key Personnel: Dir. & Pres., Anthony Godfrey; Chm. (V), Bernie Marcus; Pres. (V), Debbie Meeks.
Personnel Profile: Full-Time Paid 220; Part-Time Paid 200; Part-Time Volunteers 1,800.
Governing Authority: Tax-exempt.
Aquarium.
Collections: aquatic animals representing 500 species from around the world; photographs; videos.

Research Fields: whale sharks; belugas; sea turtles; coral; dolphins.
Facilities: theater; cafe; ballroom; catering. Museum-related items for sale.
Activities: special events; tours; rental facilities; birthday parties; school programs; jazz; sleepovers; scuba & swim programs.
Publications: Bringing the Ocean to Atlanta.
Hours & Admission Prices: Sun.-Fri. 10-5, Sat. 9-6; see website for additional hours. Adults $26, seniors 65 & over $21.50, children 3-12 $19.50; discounts to groups & military. Annual Pass: $65. ♿
Attendance: 2,600,000 (accurate)

GEORGIA CAPITOL MUSEUM, (M), 206 Washington St., Atlanta, GA 30334. Mailing Address: 2 Martin Luther King Dr., Ste. 820, Atlanta, GA 30334-9000. Tel.: 404-656-2846; 463-4536 (tours). Fax: 404-657-3801.
E-mail: tfrilingos@sos.state.ga.us
Web Site: www.sos.georgia.gov/archives/state_capitol
Founded: 1895.
Congressional District: 4 & 5
Key Personnel: Mgr., Timothy Frilingos.
Personnel Profile: Full-Time Paid 3; Interns 1.
Governing Authority: state. Parent Institution: State of Georgia. Tax-exempt.
General Museum.
Collections: Georgia history; the Capitol building; portraits; sculpture; historic flags.
Activities: permanent exhibitions.
Publications: State Capitol pamphlets.
Hours & Admission Prices: Mon.-Fri. 8-5. No charge. Closed legal holidays. ♿
Attendance: 60,000 (estimated)

GEORGIA STATE UNIVERSITY SCHOOL OF ART & DESIGN GALLERY, 10 Peachtree Center Ave., Atlanta, GA 30303-3003. Mailing Address: P.O. Box 4107, Atlanta, GA 30302-4107. Tel.: 404-413-5221. Fax: 404-651-1779.
E-mail: artgallery@gsu.edu
Founded: 1970.
Congressional District: 5
Key Personnel: Dir., Waduda Muhummad; Cur. Visual Resources, Ann England.
Personnel Profile: Full-Time Paid 1; Part-Time Paid 2; Part-Time Volunteers 2; Interns 2.
Governing Authority: university. Parent Institution: Georgia State University. Subsidiary Institution: School of Art & Design. Tax-exempt: 170(b)(1)(A).
University Art Gallery.
Collections: American contemporary paintings, prints, photographs & crafts.
Research Fields: contemporary art issues.
Facilities: 3,000-vol. library of books, 100,000 slides, catalogues & specialized art publications available for research by special permission; reading room; 400-seat auditorium; classrooms; 400-seat cafeteria.
Activities: lectures; films; artist talks; symposiums; special programs; loan, temporary & traveling exhibitions.
Hours & Admission Prices: Mon.-Fri. 10-6. No charge. Closed school holidays; New Year's Day; Independence Day; Labor Day; Thanksgiving. ♿
Attendance: 6,000 (estimated)

GOVERNOR'S MANSION, 391 W. Paces Ferry Rd., N.W., Atlanta, GA 30305-1001. Tel.: 404-261-1776.
E-mail: mansionevents@gov.state.ga.us
Historic Home: home of current Governor Sonny Perdue.
Collections: 19th century neoclassical furnishings; paintings; porcelain; personal artifacts; photographs.
Hours & Admission Prices: Tours: Tues.-Thurs. 10 & 11:30.

HAMMONDS HOUSE MUSEUM, , 503 Peeples St., SW, Atlanta, GA 30313-1815. Tel.: 404-612-0500.
E-mail: myrna.anderson@fultoncountyga.gov
Web Site: hammondshouse.org
Key Personnel: Exec. Dir., Myrna Anderson-Fuller; Cur., Kevin Sipp; Communications Mgr. & Exec. Admin., Y'na Snipes; Facilities Mgr./Security, Byron Simmons
Art Museum: former home of late Dr. Otis Thrash Hammonds, built around 1872.
Collections: more than 350 art works from the mid-19th century; Haitian paintings, African sculptures & masks.
Hours & Admission Prices: Tues.-Fri. 10-6, Sat.-Sun. 1-5. Adults $4, senior citizens, students & children $2; members no charge. Closed national holidays.

THE HERNDON HOME, 587 University Pl., N.W., Atlanta, GA 30314-4126. Tel.: 404-581-9813. Fax: 404-588-0239.
E-mail: hhinfo@herndonhome.org
Web Site: www.herndonhome.org
Historic Home: former home of the Alonzo Herndon family, built in 1910. A National Historic Landmark.
Collections: family history; personal artifacts; period furnishings.
Hours & Admission Prices: Tours: by appointment. Adults $5, students $3.

* **THE HIGH MUSEUM OF ART, (M),** 1280 Peachtree St., N.E., Atlanta, GA 30309-3549. Tel.: 404-733-HIGH. Fax: 404-733-4529.
E-mail: highmuseum@woodruffcenter.org
Web Site: www.high.org
Founded: 1905.
Congressional District: 5
Key Personnel: Dir., Michael E. Shapiro; C.O.O., Philip Verre; Dir. Museum Advancement, Linda McNay; C.F.O., Rhonda Matheison; Dir. Mktg. & Communications, Susan Clark; Mgr. Exhibitions, Jody Cohen; Dir. Collections & Exhibitions, David Brenneman; Cur. Wieland Family Modern & Contemporary Art, Jeffrey Grove; Cur. Media Arts, Linda Dubler; Cur. Photography, Julian Cox; Cur. Folk Art, Susan Crawley; Cur. Fred & Rita Richman African Art, Carol Thompson; Consulting Cur. African American Art, Michael Harris; Margaret and Terry Stent Cur. American Art, Stephanie Heydt; Eleanor McDonald Storza Dir. Education, Pat Rodewald; Assoc. Chm. Education, Virginia Shearer; Head Museum Interpretation, Julia Forbes; Head School Programs, Lisa Hooten; Exhibitions Designer, Jim Waters; Sr. Devel. Mgr., Woodie Wisebram; Devel. Officer of Foundations & Government Support, Corinne Anderson; Louvre Atlanta Sponsor Mgr., Jennifer de Castro; Mgr. Individual Support, Ruth Richardson Kelly; Mgr. Wine Auction, Elizabeth Harris; Sr. Mgr. Membership, Billy Fong; Sr. Mgr. Public Rels., Cassandra Streich; Registrar, Frances Francis; Mgr. Publications, Kelly Morris; Mgr. Graphics Design, Angela Jaeger; Controller, Amy Arant; Mgr. Facilities & Logistics, Kevin Streiter; Head Retail Operations, Lacey Hauser; Chief Security, Al Holland.
Personnel Profile: Full-Time Paid 254; Part-Time Paid 5; Part-Time Volunteers 1,000.
Governing Authority: nonprofit organization. Parent Institution: Robert W. Woodruff Arts Center, Inc. Tax-exempt: 501(c)(3).
Art Museum.
Collections: 19th-20th century American art; European paintings & decorative art; African American art; modern & contemporary art; photography; Southern artists; folk & self-taught art.
Research Fields: permanent collection; exhibition programs.
Facilities: 10,000-vol. art reference library; reading room; 226-seat auditorium; classrooms. Museum-related items for sale.
Activities: annual film series & festivals; guided tours; lectures; films; gallery talks; concerts; dance recitals; arts festivals; study clubs; formally organized educational programs; docent program or council; inter-museum loan, temporary, traveling & permanent exhibitions. Museum Sponsors: community outreach program; Friday Jazz monthly.
Publications: monthly calendars; exhibition catalogues; newsletter; periodic institutional reports.
Hours & Admission Prices: Tues.-Wed. & Fri.-Sat. 10-5, Thurs. 10-8, Sun. 12-5. Adults $18, senior citizens & college students $15; children 6-17 $11, discounts to groups of 10 or more; children under 6 & members no charge. Closed New Year's Day; Martin Luther King, Jr. Day; Independence Day; Labor Day; Thanksgiving; Christmas. Friday Jazz 3rd Fri. of month 5-10. ♿
Attendance: 400,000 (estimated)
Membership: Student $35; Associate $50; Senior & Educator $55; Individual $65; Senior Dual, Educator Dual, & Family $80; Dual & Family $90; Young Patron $95; Young Patron Dual & Contributing $150.

HISTORIC OAKLAND CEMETERY, Historic Oakland Foundation, 248 Oakland Ave., S.E., Atlanta, GA 30312-2220. Tel.: 404-688-2107. Fax: 404-658-6092.
E-mail: oaklandcemetery@mindspring.com
Web Site: www.oaklandcemetery.com
Founded: 1850.
Key Personnel: Exec. Dir., David S. Moore; Chm. (V), May B. Hollis; Museum Shop Mgr., Claudia Hahn; Museum Shop Mgr., Sally Smith.
Personnel Profile: Full-Time Paid 3; Part-Time Paid 6; Part-Time Volunteers 100; Interns 1.
Governing Authority: private; nonprofit organization. Parent Institution: City of Atlanta. Tax-exempt.
Historical Society: office is located in the 1899 Bell Tower building (Norman).
Collections: Victorian funerary sculpture, monuments & architecture; Jewish, African-American & Confederate sections.
Activities: gardening; tours; picnicking; jogging; photography; landscape painting.

Publications: members newsletter, The Oakland Herald.
Hours & Admission Prices: Office: Mon.-Fri. 9-5. Tours: Sat. 10, 2 & 6:30, Sun. 2 & 6:30; other times by appointment. Cemetery no charge. Walking Tours: family $26, adults $10, seniors, students & children $5; members and children 6 & under no charge. ♿
Attendance: 65,000 (estimated)
Membership: Individual $40; Couple & Family $65; Friends $125; Historic Circle $300; Restoration Society $500; Preservation League $1,000; Grand Gatekeeper $2,500.

IMAGINE IT! THE CHILDREN'S MUSEUM OF ATLANTA, 275 Centennial Olympic Park Dr., N.W., Atlanta, GA 30313-1827. Tel.: 404-659-5437. Fax: 404-223-3675.
E-mail: askme@childrensmuseumatlanta.org
Web Site: www.imagineit-cma.org
Founded: 2003.
Key Personnel: Exec. Dir., Jane Turner; Museum Shop Mgr., Melissa Boggan
Children's Museum.
Collections: hands-on exhibits.
Hours & Admission Prices: Mon.-Fri. 10-4, Sat.-Sun. 10-5. Admission 2 & over $12.50; children under 2 & members no charge. Closed Thanksgiving; Christmas.
Attendance: 207,000 (estimated)
Membership: $75; $125; $250; $500.

IVAN ALLEN JR. BRAVES MUSEUM & HALL OF FAME/TURNER FIELD TOURS, 755 Hank Aaron Dr., Atlanta, GA 30315-1120. Tel.: 404-614-2311.
Web Site: atlanta.braves.mlb.com/atl/ballpark/museum.jsp
Sports Museum.
Collections: over 600 Braves artifacts; photographs.
Hours & Admission Prices: April-Sept. Mon.-Sat. 9-3, Sun. 1-3; Oct.-March Mon.-Sat. 10-2. Non-game Days: adults $5. Game Days: adults $2. Turner Field Tours & Braves Museum: adults $12, children 13 & under $7.

JIMMY CARTER LIBRARY AND MUSEUM, (M), 441 Freedom Pkwy., Atlanta, GA 30307-1497. Tel.: 404-865-7100. Fax: 404-865-7102.
E-mail: carter.library@nara.gov
Web Site: www.jimmycarterlibrary.gov
Founded: 1986.
Congressional District: 5
Key Personnel: Dir., Dr. Jay E. Hakes; Deputy Dir., David Stanhope; Cur., Sylvia Mansour Naguib; Museum Shop Mgr., James E. Stewart.
Personnel Profile: Full-Time Paid 28; Part-Time Paid 3; Part-Time Volunteers 39; Interns 3.
Governing Authority: federal. A unit of the National Archives and Records Administration, Washington, DC 20408. Tax-exempt: 170(b)(1)(A).
Presidential Library.
Collections: personal papers; government records; still photographs; motion picture films; audio & video tapes; sound recordings; head of state gifts; gifts from private citizens; political campaign items; personal & family memorabilia.
Research Fields: life, times, career & presidential administration of President Carter.
Facilities: research archives of materials from the Carter White House, including textual & audiovisual resources; research room; 25,000 sq. ft. exhibit space; two auditoriums & seminar room. Museum-related items for sale.
Activities: guided tours; lectures; films; permanent, temporary & traveling exhibitions; organized education programs for children, adults, undergraduate & graduate students.
Publications: list of holdings; general information brochure; museum store catalog.
Hours & Admission Prices: Mon.-Sat. 9-4:45, Sun. 12-4:45. Adults $8, senior citizens, students & military $6; discounts to AAM members; children under 16 & members no charge. Closed New Year's Day; Thanksgiving; Christmas. ♿
Attendance: 82,757 (accurate)
Membership: Friends of the Jimmy Carter Library: Individual $25; Family $40; Associate $75; Sustaining $150; Patron $400.

THE MARGARET MITCHELL HOUSE & MUSEUM, 990 Peachtree St., Atlanta, GA 30309-3901. Tel.: 404-249-7015. Fax: 404-249-7118.
Web Site: www.gwtw.org
Founded: 1990.
Personnel Profile: Full-Time Paid 10; Part-Time Paid 5; Part-Time Volunteers 25; Interns 2.
Governing Authority: Parent Institution: Atlanta Historical Society, Inc. Tax-exempt.
Historic House: the former home of Margaret Mitchell where she wrote the Pulitzer prize-winning novel, Gone With The Wind.
Collections: Mitchell's apartment in 1899 house restored to its original condition; Gone With the Wind movie memorabilia; Southern literature.
Facilities: visitor center. Museum-related items for sale.
Activities: individual & group tours; fundraising & promotional events; book signings; author programs; adult & youth writing workshops.
Publications: brochures.
Hours & Admission Prices: Mon.-Sat. 10-5:30, Sun. 12-5:30. Adults $12, seniors over 65 & students with ID $9, children 4-12 $5; discounts to groups, AAA, AAM & ICOM members; members & children under 4 no charge. Closed New Year's Day; Thanksgiving; Christmas Eve & Day. ♿
Attendance: 50,000 (accurate)
Membership: Individual $50; Dual $65; Family $75; Sustaining $125; Sponsor $250; Patron $500; Roundtable $1,000.

MARTIN LUTHER KING, JR. CENTER FOR NONVIOLENT SOCIAL CHANGE, INC., 449 Auburn Ave., N.E., Atlanta, GA 30312-1503. Tel.: 404-526-8900. Fax: 404-526-8932.
E-mail: information@thekingcenter.org
Web Site: www.thekingcenter.org
Founded: 1968.
Congressional District: 5
Key Personnel: C.E.O. & Co Pres., Isaac Newton Farris, Jr.; Acting Mng. Dir., Eric Tidwell.
Personnel Profile: Full-Time Paid 20; Part-Time Paid 5.
Governing Authority: nonprofit organization. Tax-exempt.
History Museum, Educational Center & Archives: located at the Martin Luther King, Jr. National Historic Site.
Collections: King family's furnishings & personal effects; artwork; manuscripts; memorabilia; works of art executed by artists in memory of Dr. King. Historic House: 1895 Dr. Martin Luther King birthplace. Historic Site: tomb of Dr. King.
Research Fields: life of Dr. King; American Civil Rights Movement.
Facilities: 5,000-vol. library; archival & museum materials pertaining to Dr. King, Black history & civil rights movement; reading room; reflecting pool; chapel; screening room. Books, recordings & other museum-related items for sale.
Activities: guided tour; permanent & temporary exhibitions.
Publications: brochures.
Hours & Admission Prices: Summer: Mon.-Fri. 9-6; Winter: Mon.-Fri. 9-5. No charge; donations accepted. Closed legal holidays. ♿
Attendance: 650,000

MARTIN LUTHER KING, JR. NATIONAL HISTORIC SITE AND PRESERVATION DISTRICT, 450 Auburn Ave., N.E., Atlanta, GA 30312-1504. Tel.: 404-331-5190 & 6922. Fax: 404-730-3112.
Web Site: www.nps.gov/malu
Founded: 1980.
Congressional District: 5
Key Personnel: Supt., Judy Forte; Administrative Officer, Tonya Perkins; Chief Interpretation, Faye Walmsley; Historian, Dean Rowley; Chief Ranger, Clark Moore.
Personnel Profile: Full-Time Paid 34; Part-Time Volunteers 3; Interns 1.
Governing Authority: federal. National Park Service. Tax-exempt.
Historic Site & District: neighborhood in which Dr. Martin Luther King, Jr. grew up, includes birthplace, boyhood home, church & gravesite.
Collections: historic photos; local & oral history; historic furnishings; African-American history.
Research Fields: African-American history; Civil Rights Movement; Dr. Martin Luther King, Jr.
Facilities: library; restored historic houses.
Activities: interpretive programs; talks on the community & the Civil Rights Movement; film presentation; tours of Dr. King's birthplace; walking tour of historic site.
Publications: catalog of historic structures; general management plan; book, Sweet Auburn-The Thriving Hub of Black Atlanta.
Hours & Admission Prices: Tours: mid-June to mid-Aug. daily 9:30-6; mid-Aug. to mid-June daily 10-5:30 by appointment. No charge; donations accepted. Closed New Year's Day; Thanksgiving; Christmas. ♿
Attendance: 900,000 (accurate)

* **MICHAEL C. CARLOS MUSEUM, (M), (I),** Emory University, 571 S. Kilgo St., Atlanta, GA 30322-0001. Tel.: 404-727-4282 & 0573. Fax: 404-727-4292. TDD: 404-727-8017.
Web Site: www.emory.edu/carlos
Founded: 1920.
Congressional District: 4
Key Personnel: Dir., Bonnie Speed; Assoc. Dir., Catherine Howett Smith; Co Chm. (V), Charles S. Ackerman; Co Chm. (V), Eleanor Ridley; Cur.

Egyptian, Nubian & Near Eastern Art, Dr. Peter Lacovara; Cur. Greek & Roman Art, Dr. Jasper Gaunt; Cur. Ancient American Art, Dr. Rebecca Rollins Stone; Assoc. Cur. African Art, Jessica Stephenson; Assoc. Cur. Works on Paper, Margaret Shufeldt; Dir. of Education, Elizabeth Hornor; Dir. Exhibitions & Collections, Nancy Roberts; Coord. Patron Rels., Gail Habif; Conservator, Renee Stein; Mgr. Budget & Personnel, Darlene Hayes; Public Rels. & Mktg., Priyanka Sinha; Registrar, Todd Lamkin; Museum Shop Mgr., Mark Burell.
Personnel Profile: Full-Time Paid 30; Full-Time Volunteers 72; Part-Time Paid 8; Part-Time Volunteers 100; Interns 6.
Governing Authority: Parent Institution: Emory University. Tax-exempt: 501(c)(3).
Art & Archaeology Museum.
Collections: fine art works on paper, photographs & painting: Mediterranean, Egyptian, Near Eastern, Mesoamerican, Central & South American, North American, ethnographic; African, Oceanic & Asian.
Facilities: university & sectional library.
Activities: special exhibitions; lectures; docent-led tours; gallery talks; films; storytelling; camps; concerts.
Publications: exhibition catalogs; newsletter; educational materials; catalogue, Surrealist Vision & Technique; handbook, Michael C. Carlos Museum.
Hours & Admission Prices: Tues.-Sat. 10-4, Sun. 12-4. Suggested Donation: adults $8, students, seniors & children 6-17 $6; discounts to AAM & ICOM members; members no charge. ♿
Attendance: 160,000 (estimated)
Membership: Teacher & University student, faculty or staff $30; Individual $40; Dual $60; Family $75; Doric $150; Ionic $250; Corinthian $500; Curator's Council $1,000; Collector's Council $2,500; Director's Council $5,000; Carlos Partnership $10,000.

MOUNT WILSON OBSERVATORY & MUSEUM, c/o CHARA, Georgia State Univ., One Park Pl., S. #720, Atlanta, GA 30303. Mailing Address: P.O. Box 1909, Atlanta, GA 30301-1909. Tel.: 404-413-5484. Fax: 404-413-5481.
Web Site: www.mtwilson.edu/index.php
Key Personnel: Dir., Dr. Harold McAlister; Deputy Dir., Dr. Arthur Vaughan
Science Museum.
Collections: astronomy; photographs.
Facilities: observatory; 256-seat auditorium.
Activities: summer lecture series.
Hours & Admission Prices: April-Nov. daily 10-4; weather permitting.

THE MUSEUM OF CONTEMPORARY ART OF GEORGIA (MOCA GA), 75 Bennett St., #A2, Atlanta, GA 30309-1275. Tel.: 404-367-8700. Fax: 404-367-1477.
E-mail: info@mocaga.org
Web Site: www.mocaga.org
Founded: 2000.
Key Personnel: C.E.O. & Pres., Annette Cone-Skelton; Chm. (V), Betty Edge.
Personnel Profile: Full-Time Paid 6; Part-Time Paid 4; Part-Time Volunteers 35; Interns 6.
Governing Authority: private; nonprofit organization. Tax-exempt: 501(c)(3).
Art Museum.
Collections: works by Georgia artists including paintings; prints; photographs; sculpture; video.
Research Fields: contemporary Georgia artists.
Facilities: library; resource center.
Activities: workshops; lectures; temporary exhibitions; films; guided tours. Annual Events: ArtMerge; MOCA Gala Art Auction Fundraiser; Movers & Shakers; Off-the-Wall Pin Up Show & Sale; Art for Everyone.
Publications: exhibition catalogues.
Hours & Admission Prices: MOCA GA: Tues.-Sat. 10-5. Adults $5; members no charge. Closed New Year's Day; Martin Luther King Jr. Day; Memorial Day; Independence Day; Labor Day; Thanksgiving; Christmas. ♿
Attendance: 6,000 (estimated)
Membership: Artist $25; Individual $35; Dual $55; Family $60; Friend $100; Contributor $250; Patron $500; Supporting Patron $1,000; Benefactor $2,500; Supporting Benefactor $5,000; Founder's Circle $10,000 & up.

MUSEUM OF DESIGN ATLANTA, 285 Peachtree Center Ave., Garden Level, Marquis Two Tower, Atlanta, GA 30303-1229. Tel.: 404-979-6455. Fax: 404-521-9311.
E-mail: info@museumofdesign.org
Web Site: www.museumofdesign.org
Formerly: Atlanta International Museum of Art and Design
Founded: 1989.
Congressional District: 5
Key Personnel: Exec. Dir., Brenda Galina, Ph.D.; Chm. (V), Angelyn Chandler; Dir. Programs & Operations, Raja Schaar; Devel. Officer, Daaimah Jones; Museum Shop Mgr., Esther Jensen.
Personnel Profile: Full-Time Paid 2; Part-Time Paid 3; Part-Time Volunteers 2; Interns 2.
Governing Authority: nonprofit. Affiliated with the Washington based Smithsonian Institution. Tax-exempt.
Design Museum.
Collections: architecture, industrial & product design.
Major Exhibits: Atlanta: Beyond Bricks & Sticks (T), 11/09-12/10; Love Nests, 2/12/10-7/10; Emerging Voices 2010, 8/10/10-8/28/10; Contemporary Ichiyo Ikebana, 9/7/10-9/25/10; Speed Dream, 10/19/10-12/22/10.
Facilities: Museum-related items for sale.
Activities: lectures; workshops; film screenings; home tours; summer camp.
Publications: e-newsletter.
Hours & Admission Prices: Tues.-Sat. 11-5. Adults $8; members no charge. ♿
Attendance: 45,000 (estimated)
Membership: Student $25; Avant Guard $50; Apprentice $50-$99; Journeyman $100-$249; Artisan $250-$499; Craftsman $500-$999; Master $1,000.

NATIONAL MUSEUM OF PATRIOTISM, (M), 275 Baker St,. N.W., Atlanta, GA 30313. Tel.: 404-524-0755; 877-276-1692 (toll free). Fax: 404-875-0415.
E-mail: info@museumofpatriotism.org
Web Site: www.museumofpatriotism.org
Key Personnel: Exec. Dir., Pat Stansbury; Dir. Operations, Jeffery Clark; Mgr. Education, Heather Wicker.
Governing Authority: nonprofit organization.
History Museum.
Collections: history of patriotism; photographs; sculptures; symbols of America; Hall of Patriots; Liberty Bell replica.
Facilities: theater.
Activities: educational programs for students; seminars; lectures; facility rental; group tours; films.
Hours & Admission Prices: Mon.-Fri. 10-5, Sat. 10-6, Sun. 1-5. Adults $15, students $12; discounts to groups; active military & children under 7 no charge.

OGLETHORPE UNIVERSITY MUSEUM OF ART, (M), 4484 Peachtree Rd., N.E., Atlanta, GA 30319-2797. Tel.: 404-364-8555. Fax: 404-364-8556.
E-mail: museum@oglethorpe.edu
Web Site: museum.oglethorpe.edu
Founded: 1993.
Key Personnel: Dir., Lloyd Nick; Asst. Dir. & Gift Shop Mgr., Betsy Ayers.
Personnel Profile: Full-Time Paid 2; Part-Time Paid 10; Part-Time Volunteers 6; Interns 1.
Governing Authority: private university; not-for-profit. Parent Institution: Oglethorpe University. Tax-exempt: 501(c)(3).
University Museum.
Collections: focus on representational & figurative artwork which is often international, spiritual & metaphysical.
Major Exhibits: Henri Matisse: A Celebration of French Poets and Poetry (T), 1/10-5/10; Southeastern Pastel Society International, 6/10-7/10.
Facilities: 3,500 sq. ft. exhibit space. Museum-related items for sale.
Activities: guided tours; lectures; docent program; music recitals; Argentine tango classes.
Publications: catalogs.
Hours & Admission Prices: Tues.-Sun. 12-5. Adults $5; children under 12 & members no charge. Closed major holidays; Christmas-New Year's week. ♿
Attendance: 10,000 (estimated)
Membership: Senior $20; Student $25; Individual $35; Family $55; Patron $100 and up.

PARKS, RECREATION & HISTORIC SITES DIVISION, GEORGIA DEPT. OF NATURAL RESOURCES, (M), 2 Martin Luther King Jr. Dr. E., Ste. 1352, Atlanta, GA 30334-9000. Tel.: 404-656-2770, ext. 5335. Fax: 404-651-5871.
Web Site: www.gastateparks.org
Founded: 1925.
Congressional District: 5
Key Personnel: Commissioner, Chris Clark; Dir., Becky Kelley; Chief Operations, Walley Woods; Interpretation, Dr. Debbie Wallsmith.
Governing Authority: state. Parent Institution: State of Georgia. Subsidiary Institution: Dept. of Natural Resources. Branch Museums: Vann House, Chatsworth; Historic Traveler's Rest, Toccoa; New Echota, Calhoun; Etowah Mounds Archaeological Area, Cartersville; Fort McAllister, Richmond Hill; Fort King George, Darien; Dahlonega Courthouse Gold Museum, Dahlonega; New Lapham-Patterson House, Thomasville, Jarrell Plantation, Juliette; Wormsloe, Savannah; Robert Toombs House, Washington; Fort Morris Historic Site, Midway; Alexander H. Stephens Memorial;

Liberty Hall & the Confederate Museum, Crawfordville; Hofwyl-Broadfield Plantation, Darien; Sweetwater Creek Park; Stephen C. Foster State Park Museum, Fargo; Panola Mountain State Park Museum; Providence Canyon State Park Museum, Lumpkin; Elijah Clark State Park Museum, Lincolnton; Pickett's Mill Battlefield, Dallas; Indian Springs Museum, Indian Springs; Kolomoki Mounds Museum, Blakely; Hamburg State Park Museum, Mitchell; Georgia Veterans Memorial, Cordele; Fort Yargo State Park, Winder; F.D. Roosevelt's Little White House, Warm Springs; Jefferson Davis Memorial Historic Site. Tax-exempt.
State Historic Agency.
Collections: general history; archaeology; marine; preservation project; Indian artifacts; mineralogy; medicine; military; politics; domestic; historical markers; agriculture; geological; fossils.
Research Fields: archaeology; general history; Georgia natural resources; marine; preservation; politics; agriculture; Georgia military history.
Facilities: 600-vol. library of research books available on premises. Publications & postcards for sale.
Activities: guided tours; gallery talks; permanent exhibitions; audiovisual programs.
Publications: brochures.
Hours & Admission Prices: Mon.-Fri. 8-6, Sat.-Sun. 9-5. Adults $1.50, children 6-17 $.75; discounts to handicapped veterans; children under 6 no charge. Office: Mon.-Fri. 8-4:30. Roosevelt's Little White House: adults $4, children 6-18 $2; children 5 & under no charge. Parking $2. Closed Thanksgiving; Christmas. ♿
Attendance: 2,356,821 (accurate)

PHOTOGRAPHIC INVESTMENTS GALLERY, 3977 Briarcliff Rd., N.E., Atlanta, GA 30345-2647. Tel.: 404-320-1012. Fax: 404-320-3465.
E-mail: ecsymmes@aol.com
Founded: 1979.
Key Personnel: Dir., Edwin C. Symmes, Jr.
Governing Authority: individual operation.
Photography Art Gallery.
Collections: 19th-century photography representing all processes & images worldwide; 19th-century & earlier Oriental Scrolls.
Facilities: original 19th-century photography & Oriental original paintings for sale.
Activities: guided tours; gallery talks; loan, permanent, temporary & traveling exhibitions.
Publications: catalogs.
Hours & Admission Prices: Daily by appointment. No charge. Closed legal holidays.

RHODES HALL, 1516 Peachtree St., N.W., Atlanta, GA 30309-2908. Tel.: 404-885-7800. Fax: 404-875-2205.
Web Site: www.georgiatrust.org/historic_sites/rhodes_hall.htm
Historic House: former home of Rhodes Furniture founder, Amos Rhodes.
Collections: period artifacts & memorabilia.
Hours & Admission Prices: Tues.-Fri. 11-4, Sat. 10-2. Behind-the Scenes Tour: adults $4. 1st Floor Tour: adults $5, senior citizens, students & children 6-12 $4; Georgia Trust members & children under 6 no charge.

ROBERT C. WILLIAMS PAPER MUSEUM, (M), Institute of Paper Science & Technology, 500 10th St., N.W., Atlanta, GA 30318. Mailing Address: Institute of Paper Science & Technology, Mail Code 0620, Georgia Tech, Atlanta, GA 30332-0620. Tel.: 404-894-7840. Fax: 404-894-4778.
E-mail: cindy.bowden@ipst.gatech.edu
Web Site: www.ipst.gatech.edu/amp
Formerly: Robert C. Williams American Museum of Papermaking at Georgia Tech
Founded: 1936.
Congressional District: 5
Key Personnel: C.E.O. & Museum Dir., Cindy Bowden; Chm. (V), Steve Miller; Program Coord., Juan Chevere; Cur. Education, Fran Rottenberg; Registrar, George Atkins; Cur., Teri Williams; Asst. Cur., J.D. Foote Marvin Greer; Membership, Brian Callahan.
Personnel Profile: Full-Time Paid 3; Part-Time Paid 2; Interns 7.
Governing Authority: Parent Institution: Georgia Institute of Technology. Tax-exempt: 501(c)(3).
History, Art & Technology Museum.
Collections: artifacts pertaining to the evolution of papermaking from 200 BC to modern times technology; included are watermarks, paper molds, wood blocks, prints, photographs, parchment & vellum; historic books; early papermaking machines; pre-paper artifacts.
Research Fields: pulp, paper & related science & technology; history papermaking & recycling; art of paper.
Facilities: 2,000-vol. library pertaining to the making of paper by hand & machine available for use on premises.
Activities: traveling exhibitions; papermaking for kids; video products.
Publications: newsletter; brochures; 75th Anniversary Book; From Appleton to Atlanta - The Institutes First 75 Years.
Hours & Admission Prices: Mon.-Fri. 9-5. No charge; donations requested. Closed holidays. ♿
Attendance: 25,000 (estimated)
Membership: Student $30; Individual $50; Family $60; Company & Institution $120; Patron $250; Sustaining $500; Life Membership $1,000.

THE SALVATION ARMY SOUTHERN HISTORICAL CENTER & MUSEUM, 1032 Metropolitan Pkwy., S.W., Atlanta, GA 30310-3488. Tel.: 404-752-7578 & 753-4166. Fax: 404-753-1932.
E-mail: historical_center@uss.salvationarmy.org
Web Site: www.salvationarmyhistory.org
Founded: 1986.
Key Personnel: Dir. & Archivist, Michael Nagy; Museum & Archival Asst., Andrea Troxclair.
Personnel Profile: Full-Time Paid 2.
Governing Authority: denominational group; nonprofit organization. Parent Institution: The Salvation Army-USA Southern Territory. Tax-exempt.
Religious Museum.
Collections: Salvation Army's movement from England to the southern U.S.; development & history in the south; photos; artifacts; microfilm; costumes; films; video & audio interviews; personal papers; musical instruments; music; flags.
Research Fields: history & methodology of various aspects of the Salvation Army's work in the southern states.
Facilities: Hicks Memorial Library, 20,000-vol. library of secular, religious & Salvation Army material available for inter-library loan & to the public; educational facilities; 4,670 sq. ft. exhibit space; theatres; research center; archives.
Activities: guided tours; lectures; seminars.
Publications: occasional brochures.
Hours & Admission Prices: By appointment. No charge; donations accepted. Closed New Year's Day; Good Friday; Easter; Memorial Day; Independence Day; Labor Day; Thanksgiving; Christmas. ♿
Attendance: 650 (accurate)

SAVANNAH COLLEGE OF ART & DESIGN-ATLANTA GALLERIES, Woodruff Arts Center, 1280 Peachtree St., N.E., Atlanta, GA 30309. Mailing Address: P.O. Box 3146, Savannah, GA 31402-3146. Tel.: 404-815-2931.
Web Site: www.acagallery.org
Formerly: Atlanta College of Art
Founded: 1905.
Congressional District: 5
Key Personnel: Chm. (V), John W. Spiegel; Pres., Paula S. Wallace; Vice Pres. Business Affairs, Timothy Spaeth; Asst. Dir. Conf. & Exhibitions, Katy Barnes.
Personnel Profile: Full-Time Paid 68; Part-Time Paid 95.
Governing Authority: college. Parent Institution: R.W. Woodruff Arts Center. Tax-exempt.
Art Gallery.
Collections: artists' books.
Research Fields: issues related to fine art & design.
Facilities: 30,000-vol. library of fine arts books available for inter-library loan during regular library hours; studios; classrooms. Art supplies for sale.
Activities: guided tours; lectures; films; traveling exhibitions; granting of BFA degree; continuing education courses.
Publications: catalogues for BFA degrees program & continuing education courses; annual news report magazine; exhibition brochures.
Hours & Admission Prices: Tues.-Thurs. 11-5, Fri. 11-8, Sat.-Sun. 12-5. No charge; donations accepted. Closed holidays. ♿
Attendance: 12,000 (estimated)

SOUTHERN ARTS FEDERATION, 1800 Peachtree St., N.W., Ste. 808, Atlanta, GA 30309-2512. Tel.: 404-874-7244. Fax: 404-873-2148. TDD: 404-876-6240.
Web Site: www.southarts.org
Founded: 1975.
Congressional District: 5
Key Personnel: Exec. Dir., Gerri Combs; Chm. Bd. Dirs., Todd Lowe; Traditional Arts & ADA Programs, Teresa Hollingsworth; Contemporary Arts, Allen Bell; Program Asst., Jenna Knight.
Personnel Profile: Full-Time Paid 12; Part-Time Paid 2; Part-Time Volunteers 2; Interns 3.
Governing Authority: private; nonprofit organization. Tax-exempt: 501(c)(3).
Arts Federation: a regional arts agency dedicated to providing leadership & support to affect positive change in the arts throughout the south.

Activities: folk arts & southern culture traveling exhibitions.
Publications: Directory of Southern Visions Traveling Exhibits.
Hours & Admission Prices: Mon.-Fri. 9-5. No charge. ♿
Attendance: 100,000 (estimated)

SPELMAN COLLEGE MUSEUM OF FINE ART, 350 Spelman Lane, S.W., Atlanta, GA 30314-4399. Mailing Address: Box 1526, Atlanta, GA 30314-4399. Tel.: 404-270-5607. Fax: 404-270-5980.
E-mail: museum@spelman.edu
Web Site: www.museum.spelman.edu
Founded: 1996.
Congressional District: 5
Key Personnel: Dir., Andrea D. Barnwell; Cur. Collections, Anne Collins Smith.
Personnel Profile: Full-Time Paid 3; Part-Time Paid 1; Part-Time Volunteers 54; Interns 4.
Governing Authority: private college. Parent Institution: Spelman College. Tax-exempt: 501(c)(3).
Art Museum.
Collections: 19th & 20th century American, African American & European works; African sculpture; textiles; crafts; works by & about women.
Research Fields: contemporary African American.
Facilities: 500-vol. library of art books not available to the public; conservation/restoration lab; climate controlled storage area; video viewing room. Museum-related items for sale.
Activities: formal education programs for undergraduate &r graduate college students; Directed Studies course for art majors: museum preparation & exhibition installation; temporary & traveling exhibitions.
Hours & Admission Prices: Tues.-Fri. 10-4, Sat. 12-4. Suggested Donation: $3 per person Closed Good Friday; all federal holidays & Spelman College breaks. ♿
Attendance: 7,000 (estimated)
Membership: Atlanta University Center Faculty & Staff & Students $25; Individual $35; Alumnae $50; Dual/Family $60; Contributor $100; Bronze $500; Silver $750; Gold $1,000; Platinum $3,000; Director's Circle $5,000.

SPRUILL GALLERY, 4681 Ashford-Dunwoody Rd., Atlanta, GA 30338-5501. Tel.: 770-394-4019. Fax: 770-394-3987.
Web Site: www.spruillarts.org
Formerly: Spruill Center for the Arts Gallery
Founded: 1975.
Congressional District: 4
Key Personnel: C.E.O. & Dir., Robert Kinsey; Chm. (V), Tania Armour Becker; Dir. Exhibitions, Hote Cohn; Exhibition Asst. & Museum Shop Mgr., Susannah Darrow.
Personnel Profile: Full-Time Paid 9; Part-Time Paid 2; Part-Time Volunteers 25; Interns 1.
Governing Authority: private; nonprofit organization. Parent Institution: Spruill Center for the Arts, 5339 Chamblee Dunwoody Rd., Atlanta, GA 30338. Tax-exempt: 501(c)(3).
Art Museum.
Collections: paintings; sculpture; photographs; drawings.
Facilities: 2,000 sq. ft. exhibit space. Museum-related items for sale.
Activities: lectures; workshops; arts festivals; formal education programs; guided tours; hobby workshops; participatory exhibits. Museum Sponsors: Members' Party; Fall Festival; Tree Lighting Ceremony; Holiday Artists' Market; Sidewalk Art Sales.
Publications: quarterly catalog, Catalog of Courses; quarterly newsletter, ARTicles; brochure with essay for each gallery exhibition.
Hours & Admission Prices: Jan. 12-Dec. 23 Wed.-Sat. 11-5. No charge; donations accepted. Closed Memorial Day; Independence Day; Labor Day. ♿
Attendance: 25,000 (estimated)
Membership: Senior $20; Individual $30; Family $60.

VSA ARTS OF GEORGIA - ARTS FOR ALL GALLERY, The Healey Bldg., 57 Forsyth St., N.W., Ste. R-1, Atlanta, GA 30303-2226. Tel.: 404-221-1270. Fax: 404-221-1984.
E-mail: info@vsaartsga.org
Web Site: www.vsaartsga.org
Founded: 1974.
Key Personnel: Exec. Dir., Elizabeth Labbe-Webb, M.B.A.
Art Gallery.
Collections: works by area artists who may be disabled or economically disadvantaged.
Activities: special programs & events.
Hours & Admission Prices: Mon.-Fri. 10-4. No charge. ♿
Attendance: 5,000 (estimated)

WORLD OF COCA-COLA PAVILION, 121 Baker St., N.W., Atlanta, GA 30313-1807. Tel.: 404-676-5151; 800-676-2653.
Web Site: www.worldofcoca-cola.com
History Museum.
Collections: Coke history & memorabilia; Dr. John Pemberton's handwritten formula book; photographs.
Facilities: theater. Museum-related items for sale.
Activities: sample soft drinks from around the world.
Hours & Admission Prices: Call for hours. Adults 13-64 $15, seniors 65 & over $13, youth 3-12 $10; children 2 & under no charge. Closed Easter; Thanksgiving; Christmas.

WREN'S NEST, 1050 Ralph David Abernathy Blvd., S.W., Atlanta, GA 30310-1812. Tel.: 404-753-7735, ext. 1. Fax: 404-753-8535.
E-mail: info@wrensnestonline.com
Web Site: www.wrensnestonline.com
Founded: 1909.
Congressional District: 5
Key Personnel: Interim Bd. Pres., Lain Shakespeare.
Personnel Profile: Full-Time Paid 1; Part-Time Paid 4; Part-Time Volunteers 40; Interns 1.
Governing Authority: nonprofit. Parent Institution: Joel Chandler Harris Association Inc. Tax-exempt.
Historic House: 1881 home of Joel Chandler Harris, creator of Uncle Remus & chronicler of stories about Br'er Rabbit.
Collections: original furnishings belonging to the Harris family; personal artifacts of Mr. Harris including his typewriter, hat, umbrella & rolltop desk which he used while employed at the Atlanta Constitution and where the Uncle Remus stories were introduced; photographs & memorabilia related to Harris, his family & the Uncle Remus stories.
Research Fields: literature, history; 19th century homes & furnishings; African-American Folktales; Turn-of-the-Century Journalism; Victorian furnishings & accessories.
Facilities: gardens; picnic grounds. Books & other museum related items for sale.
Activities: guided tours for adults & children; storytelling programs; permanent exhibits; special events.
Publications: periodic newsletters; brochures; pamphlets.
Hours & Admission Prices: Tues.-Sat. 10-2:30. Storytelling: Sat. 1pm. Adults $8, senior citizens & teens $7, children 4-12 $5; discounts for groups & AAM members; members no charge. Closed major holidays. ♿
Attendance: 9,850 (estimated)
Membership: Individual & Family $35; Br'er Fox $100; Br'er Bear $250; Br'er Rabbit $500; Br'er Patch Patron $1,000 & up.

ZOO ATLANTA, 800 Cherokee Ave., S.E., Atlanta, GA 30315-1470. Tel.: 404-624-5600.
E-mail: info@zooatlanta.org
Web Site: www.zooatlanta.org
Founded: 1889.
Congressional District: 5
Key Personnel: Pres. & C.E.O., Dr. David Allen; C.F.O., Kathy Heagney Williams; Vice Pres. Veterinary Svcs., Maria Crane, D.V.M.; Vice Pres. & C.O.O., Blythe Randolph; Sr. Vice Pres. Operations, Cary Burgess; Sr. Vice Pres. Animal Programs & Science, Dwight Lawson; Vice Pres. Mktg. & Sales, Marcus Margerum; Museum Shop Mgr., Greg Cain.
Personnel Profile: Full-Time Paid 172; Part-Time Paid 61; Part-Time Volunteers 275.
Governing Authority: nonprofit organization. Tax-exempt.
Zoo.
Collections: zoological collection.
Research Fields: primatology; herpetology; animal behavior.
Activities: summer classes; animal demonstrations; tours; educational programs.
Publications: guidebook; members' magazine, ZOOMagazine.
Hours & Admission Prices: April-Oct. Mon.-Fri. 9:30-4:30, Sat.-Sun. 9:30-5:30; Nov.-March Mon.-Fri. 9:30-4:30. Adults $18.99, seniors $14.99, children 3-11 $13.99; discounts to groups & reciprocal members; members & children under 3 no charge. Closed Thanksgiving; Christmas. ♿
Attendance: 710,000 (accurate)
Membership: Friend of Zoo Atlanta: Individual $59; Family $99; Serengeti $150; Patron $200; Keeper $300; Curator $500; (add a guest $20).

Augusta

* **AUGUSTA MUSEUM OF HISTORY,** 560 Reynolds St., Augusta, GA 30901-1430. Tel.: 706-722-8454. Fax: 706-724-5192.
E-mail: amh@augustamuseum.org
Web Site: www.augustamuseum.org
Formerly: Augusta Richmond County Museum

Founded: 1937.
Congressional District: 10
Key Personnel: Dir., Nancy J. Glaser; Pres. (V), Jefferson B.A. Knox, Sr.; Education Mgr., Heather Sellers; Dir. Operations, Kristine Hamilton; Exhibit Technician, Steve Walton; Registrar, Sean Todd; Visitor Svcs., W. Keith Bates; Cur., Guy C. Robbins; Bldgs. & Grounds, Larry Taylor.
Personnel Profile: Full-Time Paid 10; Part-Time Paid 8; Part-Time Volunteers 50; Interns 2.
Governing Authority: board of trustees. Branch Museum: Ezekiel Harris House, 1822 Broad St., Augusta. Tax-exempt: 501(c)(3).
History Museum presenting the past of Augusta, Georgia and its environs.
Collections: local & military history; regional archaeology; railroading artifacts; textiles; geology; costumes; early American artifacts. Historic House: 1797 Ezekiel Harris House.
Research Fields: local and regional history.
Facilities: research library & archives; classrooms; theatre. Museum-related items for sale.
Activities: guided tours; lectures; special events; permanent & traveling exhibitions; film series; adult & family programs.
Publications: quarterly newsletter; magazine.
Hours & Admission Prices: Museum: Tues.-Sat. 10-5, Sun. 1-5. House: Tues.-Fri. by appointment, Sat. 10-5. Museum: adults $4, seniors 65 & over $3, children 6-18 $2; discounts to AAM & ICOM members; children 5 & under and members no charge. House: adults $2, children $1; children under 5 no charge. ♿
Attendance: 52,100 (estimated)
Membership: Individual $30; Family & Dual $60; Friend $125; Contributor $250; Patron $500; Benefactor $1,000; Oglethorpe Society $10,000.

BOYHOOD HOME OF PRESIDENT WOODROW WILSON, (M), 419 Seventh St., Augusta, GA 30901-2317. Mailing Address: P.O. Box 37, Augusta, GA 30903-0037. Tel.: 706-722-9828. Fax: 706-724-3083.
E-mail: erick@historicaugusta.org
Web Site: www.wilsonboyhoodhome.org
Founded: 1991.
Congressional District: 12
Key Personnel: Exec. Dir., Erick D. Montgomery; Pres. (V), W. Tennent Houston; Museum Shop Mgr., Mary Bordeaux.
Personnel Profile: Part-Time Paid 2; Part-Time Volunteers 15.
Governing Authority: private; nonprofit organization. Parent Institution: Historic Augusta, Inc., Augusta, GA. Tax-exempt: 501(c)(3).
Historic House Museum: childhood home of President Woodrow Wilson 1860-1870.
Collections: original & period furniture; detached kitchen & service building; carriage house; 1860 decorative arts.
Research Fields: Woodrow Wilson; mid-19th century Augusta, GA; mid-19th century domestic decorative arts.
Facilities: 200-vol. library of Woodrow Wilson biographical material; rental space available. Museum-related items for sale.
Activities: docent program; guided tours; costumed interpretation. Annual Event: Woodrow Wilson Symposium; Historic Holiday Candlelight Tour.
Publications: book, Thomas Woodrow Wilson: Family Ties and Southern Perspectives.
Hours & Admission Prices: Tues.-Sat. 10-5 on the hour. Adults $5, senior citizens $4, students $3; discounts to groups. Closed New Year's Day; Thanksgiving; Christmas. ♿
Attendance: 4,500 (estimated)
Membership: Student $10; Single $30; Double & Nonprofit Institution $50; Lightfoot Society & Corporate $250.

GERTRUDE HERBERT INSTITUTE OF ART, 506 Telfair St., Augusta, GA 30901-2310. Tel.: 706-722-5495. Fax: 706-722-3670.
E-mail: ghia@ghia.org
Web Site: ghia.org
Founded: 1937.
Congressional District: 10
Key Personnel: Exec. Dir., Rebekah Henry; Chm. (V), Mickey Williford.
Personnel Profile: Full-Time Paid 3; Part-Time Paid 3; Part-Time Volunteers 40.
Governing Authority: board of trustees. Tax-exempt: 101(6).
Art Museum.
Collections: paintings; graphics; monthly changing exhibitions. Historic House: 1818 Ware's Folly.
Major Exhibits: Kristin Casaletto, 1/10-3/10; Sharon Lacey, 4/10-5/10; Raoul Pacheco, 6/10-7/10; 30th Annual Juried Exhibition, 9/10-10/10; Augusta State Univ. Art Faculty, 11/10-12/10.
Facilities: painting & drawing ateliers; sculptor's studio; potter's studio with kiln; education annex: photography studio, darkroom, printmaking studio.
Activities: lectures; formally organized education programs; exhibitions; outreach programs for artists.
Publications: information brochure; quarterly newsletter.
Hours & Admission Prices: Tues.-Fri. 10-5, Sat. by appointment. No charge; donations accepted. Closed holidays; Independence Day; Thanksgiving; Christmas Eve to New Year's Day. ♿
Attendance: 20,000 (estimated)
Membership: Student (18 & under) & Senior Citizen (65 & up) $20; Artist & Individual $30; Family $50; Donor $100; Sponsor $300; Patron $500; Benefactor $1,000.

LUCY CRAFT LANEY MUSEUM OF BLACK HISTORY AND CONFERENCE CENTER, (M), 1116 Phillips St., Augusta, GA 30901-2724. Tel.: 706-724-3576. Fax: 706-724-3576.
E-mail: info@lucycraftlaneymuseum.com
Web Site: www.lucycraftlaneymuseum.com
Founded: 1991.
Congressional District: 125
Key Personnel: Exec. Dir., Christine Miller-Betts.
Personnel Profile: Full-Time Paid 3; Part-Time Paid 1; Part-Time Volunteers 10.
Governing Authority: private; nonprofit organization. Parent Institution: Delta House, Inc. Tax-exempt 501(c)(3).
Art History Museum.
Collections: African Americans from the Augusta & Savannah River area who have made tremendous contributions to the areas of education, religion, science, sports, entertainment & medicine.
Research Fields: history of Augusta; local African American history.
Facilities: conference & children's center.
Activities: films; formal education programs for children; guided tours; lectures; temporary exhibitions; theater performances; art classes. Museum Sponsors: story telling & senior luncheons 1st Wed. August to June.
Publications: quarterly, Newsletter; brochures.
Hours & Admission Prices: Tues.-Fri. 9-5, Sat. 10-4; other times by appointment. Adults $5, senior citizens $3, students & children $2; discounts to military & seniors. Closed holidays. ♿
Attendance: 9,000 (estimated)
Membership: Friend $25-$99; Sponsor $100-$249; Supported $250-$499; Sustainer $500-$999.

MEADOW GARDEN MUSEUM, 1320 Independence Dr., Augusta, GA 30901-1038. Tel.: 706-724-4174.
Founded: 1900.
Congressional District: 10
Key Personnel: State Regent & Chm. Bd., Barbara Blakely Chastain; House Chm., Margaret Cagle; Chm., Susan Jackson.
Personnel Profile: Part-Time Paid 1; Part-Time Volunteers 40.
Governing Authority: Georgia State Society, NSDAR. Parent Institution: Georgia State Society, Daughters of the American Revolution. Tax-exempt.
Historic House: Meadow Garden, 1792-1804 residence of George Walton, youngest Georgia signer of the Declaration of Independence.
Collections: Walton memorabilia; 18th-19th century American & English furnishings; porcelains; paintings; early household equipment; 1700 medicinal herb garden; Weaver's Garden.
Activities: guided tours.
Hours & Admission Prices: Mon.-Fri. 10-4, Sat. by appointment. Adults $4, seniors $3.50, students 9-12 $2.50, students 4-8 $1, students K-3 $.50; discount to groups 10 & over. ♿
Attendance: 1,368 (accurate)
Membership: Friends & Supporters $10-$49; Patrons $50 & up; Society $100; Sons & Daughters of Liberty $250; Olivia's Legacy $500; George Walton Society $1,000; Meadow Garden Preservation Society $5,000.

MORRIS MUSEUM OF ART, (M), Tenth St., Augusta, GA 30901-1134. Tel.: 706-724-7501. Fax: 706-724-7612.
E-mail: mormuse@themorris.org
Web Site: www.themorris.org
Founded: 1985.
Congressional District: 10
Key Personnel: Exec. Dir., Kevin Grogan; Chm. (V), William S. Morris, III; Dir. Devel., Phyllis Giddens; Assoc. Cur. Education & Public Programs, Michelle Schulte; Cur. Education, David Tucker; Education Asst., Matt Porter; Creative Dir., Todd Beasley; Mktg. & Public Rels. Coord., Nicole McLeod; Coord. Membership, Lauren Powell; Registrar, Laura Pasch; Preparator & Exhibition Designer, Dwayne Clark; Chief of Security, Rex Bell; Finance Officer, Louis Gangarosa; Archivist & Librarian, Cary Wilkins; Special Events Coord., Janna Crane; Museum Shop Mgr., Kelly Catlett.
Personnel Profile: Full-Time Paid 16; Part-Time Paid 6; Part-Time Volunteers 50; Interns 4.
Governing Authority: private operating foundation. Tax-exempt: 501(c)(3).
Art Museum.

Collections: concentration on painting in the South; Antebellum portraiture to contemporary works.
Major Exhibits: Beverly Buchanan, 11/21/09-1/31/10; 'Deep Sea': Drawings by William Golding, 12/12/09-3/7/10; Regional Dialect: Paintings from The Susan and John Horseman Collection (T), 3/6/10-5/30/10; Homeplace: Photographs by Kay Duvernet, 3/20/10-6/13/10; Unhindered by Seriousness: Sculpture by Carl Blair, 6/26/10-9/19/10; Augusta Olscheig: Savannah Modernist, 10/2/10-12/31/10.
Research Fields: Art and artists of the American South, colonial era to the present.
Facilities: 14,000-vol. library; 120-seat auditorium; 18,000 sq. ft. exhibit space. Museum-related items for sale.
Activities: concerts; docent program; guided tours; lectures; loan, temporary & traveling exhibitions. Annual Events: gala.
Publications: newsletter; monographs; exhibition catalogues; gallery guides.
Hours & Admission Prices: Tues.-Sat. 10-5, Sun. 12:30-5. Adults $5, senior citizens, military & students $3; discount to groups, AAM, ICOM, SEMC, GAMG & Southeastern Art Museum Directors' Forum Members (SEAMD); children under 12, members & Sunday no charge. Closed New Year's Day; Easter; Independence Day; Thanksgiving; Christmas. ♿
Attendance: 36,000 (accurate)
Membership: Student $15; National, Teacher & Docent $30; Individual $40; Family $50; Supporter $100; Donor $250; Patron $500; Benefactor $1,000; Museum Society $2,500; Director's League $5,000; Chairman's Circle $10,000.

THE NATIONAL SCIENCE CENTER'S FORT DISCOVERY, One Seventh St., Augusta, GA 30901. Tel.: 800-325-5445; 706-821-0200 & 0648. Fax: 706-821-0269.
E-mail: info@www.nscdiscovery.org
Web Site: www.nationalsciencecenter.org
Founded: 1997.
Congressional District: 10
Key Personnel: C.E.O. & Pres. (V), Norwood R. (Rob) Dennis; C.O.O., David L. Keel; Dir. Mktg., Kathi Dimmock; Dir. Devel., Richard (Rich) Slaby; Education, Jim Frye; Museum Shop Mgr., Jeanette Nelson.
Personnel Profile: Full-Time Paid 50; Part-Time Paid 35; Part-Time Volunteers 180; Interns 1.
Governing Authority: private; nonprofit organization. Tax-exempt: 501(c)(3).
Science Center.
Collections: 250 interactive exhibits.
Facilities: 5,000-vol. library of texts, videos, software & kits available to teachers; 128,000 sq. ft. exhibit space; 200 hands-on exhibits; 250-seat large screen theater; 120-seat Power Station; 150-seat restaurant; classrooms. Museum-related items for sale.
Activities: virtual realities; demonstrations; Power Station & indoor lightning storm; hands-on kits; information & portable planetariums for teachers; traveling educational outreach programs; sponsored camps; arts festivals; education programs for adults; guided tours; hobby workshops; lectures; mobile vans; participatory exhibits; rental gallery; theater; traveling exhibitions; teleconferencing; TV programs.
Publications: quarterly newsletter, FOCUS; quarterly, Special Events Flyer.
Hours & Admission Prices: Thurs.-Sat. 10-5. Adults 18-54 $8, senior citizens 55 & over, students & children 4-17 $6; discounts to ASTC members, active duty personnel & groups; children under 4 no charge. Closed New Year's Day; Easter; Thanksgiving; Christmas. ♿
Attendance: 100,000 (estimated)
Membership: Individual $40; Grandparent $65.

1797 EZEKIEL HARRIS HOUSE, 1822 Broad St., Augusta, GA 30904-3918. Mailing Address: 560 Reynolds St., Augusta, GA 30901. Tel.: 706-722-8454. Fax: 706-737-2820.
E-mail: 1797EHarrisHouse@bellsouth.net
Web Site: www.augustamuseum.org/harris.htm
Founded: 1965.
Congressional District: 10
Key Personnel: Historic House Mgr., Benjamin E. Baughman.
Personnel Profile: Full-Time Paid 1; Part-Time Volunteers 5.
Governing Authority: city. Parent Institution: Augusta Museum of History. Managed by Augusta Museum of History. Tax-exempt.
Historic House: 1797 Ezekiel Harris House.
Collections: furnishings.
Activities: guided tours; gallery talks; permanent exhibitions; living history re-enactments.
Publications: brochure.
Hours & Admission Prices: Tues.-Fri. 1-5, Sat. 10-5 by appointment. Adults & seniors $2, children 6-18 $1; discounts to AAM members; members & children 5 and under no charge.
Attendance: 2,000 (accurate)
Membership: Student & Educator $20; Individual $25; Family & Dual $45; Friend $100; Contributor $250; Patron $500; Benefactor $1,000.

Bainbridge

FIREHOUSE CENTER & GALLERY, 119 W. Water St., Bainbridge, GA 39818-3620. Mailing Address: P.O. Box 35, Bainbridge, GA 39818-0035. Tel.: 229-243-1010.
Art Museum.
Collections: paintings; sculpture; photographs.
Activities: special events.
Hours & Admission Prices: Mon.-Fri. 12-4, Sat.-Sun. 1-5; groups by appointment.

Blairsville

UNION COUNTY HISTORICAL SOCIETY MUSEUM, (M), One Town Square, Blairsville, GA 30512. Mailing Address: P.O. Box 35, Blairsville, GA 30514-0035. Tel.: 706-745-5493. Fax: 706-781-1899.
E-mail: history1@windstream.net
Web Site: unioncountyhistory.org
Founded: 1976.
Congressional District: 9
Key Personnel: Pres. (V), Sam Ensley; Vice Pres., Ed Reed; Treas., Teresa Dorton; Research Asst. & Volunteer Coord., Jane Thompson; Admin., Edie Rich; Museum Shop Mgr., Frances Partin.
Personnel Profile: Part-Time Paid 3; Part-Time Volunteers 40.
Governing Authority: private; nonprofit organization. Parent Institution: Union Co. Historical Society. Tax-exempt: 501(c)(3).
Historical Society Museum: housed in old Union County Courthouse.
Collections: concentration on Union County and North Georgia history, 19th century to present. The holdings include the 1899 historic courthouse, a 1906 home and a 1860 log cabin as well as Margarita Morgan miniatures.
Major Exhibits: Military Tribute, 5/31/10-7/4/2010.
Facilities: 86-vol. library of genealogical materials.
Activities: guided tours; temporary exhibits. Annual Events: Mountain Gospel Music Convention 2nd weekend in May; Mountain Marketplace Heritage Festival in September; Bluegrass Festival 4th weekend in September; Halloween on the Square; Christmas on the Square.
Publications: quarterly newsletter; e-newsletter.
Hours & Admission Prices: May-Nov. Mon.-Sat. 10-4; Dec.-April Mon.-Fri. 10-4. Adults $2, students $1; members no charge. Closed New Year's Day; Labor Day; Christmas.
Attendance: 10,000 (estimated)
Membership: Individual $20; Family $30; Sustaining $100; Business $100-$250; Lifetime $350-$500.

Blakely

KOLOMOKI MOUNDS STATE PARK MUSEUM, Off U.S. Hwy. 27, follow signs for park, 205 Indian Mounds Rd., Blakely, GA 39823-4460. Tel.: 229-724-2150. Fax: 229-724-2152.
E-mail: kolomoki_park@dnr.state.ga.us
Web Site: www.gastateparks.org
Founded: 1938.
Congressional District: 2
Key Personnel: Park Mgr., Matt Bruner; Interpreter & Museum Shop Mgr., Billy Adams.
Personnel Profile: Full-Time Paid 6; Part-Time Paid 2; Part-Time Volunteers 4.
Governing Authority: state. Administered by Parks, Recreation & Historic Sites Div., Georgia Dept. of Natural Resources, 205 Butler St., S.E., Atlanta, GA 30334.
Historic Site: 13th-century Indian burial mound & village site.
Collections: archaeology; Indian artifacts; excavated mound; Mississippian mound complex.
Research Fields: Weeden Island period aboriginal occupation.
Facilities: nature trails.
Activities: guided tours; lectures; camping; swimming pool; playground.
Publications: report, Excavations at Kolomoki.
Hours & Admission Prices: Daily 8-5. Adults $3, children 6-18 $1.75, youth group $1.50; discounts to groups; children under 5 no charge. Historic Sites: adult $10, children $8, family $25 (up to 6 people). Closed New Year's Day; Thanksgiving; Christmas. ♿
Attendance: 20,000 (accurate)
Membership: Friends of Georgia State Parks & Historic Site $50.

Brunswick

HOFWYL-BROADFIELD PLANTATION STATE HISTORIC SITE, 5556 U.S. Hwy. 17 N., Brunswick, GA 31525-4651. Tel.: 912-264-7333. Fax: 912-262-3346.
Web Site: www.gastateparks.org/info/hofwyl/
Founded: 1974.
Congressional District: 1
Key Personnel: Park Ranger (Interpretation), Faye Cowart; Park Ranger (Interpretation), Andy Beckman.
Personnel Profile: Full-Time Paid 5; Part-Time Volunteers 3.
Governing Authority: state. Administered by Parks, Recreation & Historic Sites Div., Dept. of Natural Resources. Tax-exempt.
Historic House: c.1850 Hofwyl-Broadfield Plantation.
Collections: dairy equipment; rice tools; furnishings from the period 1790-1972.
Research Fields: rice culture; dairying; Georgia Coastal Life; Gullah/Geechee culture.
Facilities: trails; visitor center.
Activities: guided tours; audiovisual programs. Annual Events: Black History Program in February; Annual Plantation Christmas Program in December.
Publications: trail guide; postcards; brochures.
Hours & Admission Prices: Thurs.-Sat. 9-5, Sun. 2-5:30. Adults $5, senior citizens 62 & over $4.50, youth 6-18 $2.50; discount to groups. Closed New Years Day; Thanksgiving; Christmas. ♿
Attendance: 25,000 (accurate)

MARY MILLER DOLL MUSEUM, 209-211 Gloucester St., Brunswick, GA 31520-7008. Tel.: 912-267-7569. Fax: 912-267-7569.
Doll Museum.
Collections: 3,000 dolls, doll houses & toys from over 90 countries.
Hours & Admission Prices: Mon.-Fri. 11-4:30. Adults $2, children $1.50.

Buckhead

STEFFEN THOMAS MUSEUM OF ART, 4200 Bethany Rd., Buckhead, GA 30625-1729. Tel.: 706-342-7557. Fax: 706-342-4348.
E-mail: info@steffenthomas.org
Web Site: www.steffenthomas.org
Founded: 1998.
Key Personnel: Acting Dir., Lisa Conner; Pres., Marguerite Copelan; Vice Pres., Lee Glenn; Sec. & Treas., Todd Bearden; Office Administration, P. Tommany; Arts Outreach Program Coord., Lisa Conner; Visitor Svcs., Sadie Carter; Visitor Svcs., Ashley Myers.
Personnel Profile: Full-Time Paid 1; Full-Time Volunteers 1; Part-Time Paid 3.
Governing Authority: private; nonprofit organization. Tax-exempt: 501(c)(3).
Visual Arts Museum.
Collections: works by Steffen Thomas; sculpture; paintings; mosaics; furniture; works on paper.
Facilities: 100-vol. library; 8,000 sq. ft. exhibit space. Museum-related items for sale.
Activities: seminars; workshops; formal education programs; guided tours; loan, temporary & traveling exhibitions. Annual Events: Outdoor Spring Festival; Founder's Day in summer; Wine Tasting & Art Auctions in fall; Literary Arts Program in winter.
Publications: quarterly newsletter, STMA News.
Hours & Admission Prices: Tues.-Sat. 11-4. Adults $5, senior citizens & students $3; members & children under 6 no charge. Closed New Year's Day; Martin Luther King, Jr. Day; Memorial Day; Independence Day; Labor Day; Thanksgiving Day; Christmas. ♿
Attendance: 5,000 (accurate)
Membership: Student $15; Senior $20; Individual $25; Family $50; Supporting $100; Sustaining $150; Partner $250 & up.

Calhoun

NEW ECHOTA STATE HISTORIC SITE, 1211 Chatsworth Hwy., N.E., Calhoun, GA 30701. Tel.: 706-624-1321. Fax: 706-624-1324.
Web Site: www.gastateparks.org
Formerly: New Echota State Historical Society
Congressional District: 9
Key Personnel: Supt., David Gomez.
Personnel Profile: Full-Time Paid 1.
Governing Authority: state. Parent Institution: Parks, Recreation & Historic Sites Div., Dept. of Natural Resources, 205 Butler St., S.E., Atlanta, GA 30334.
Preservation Project: 1825 capital town of Cherokee Nation.
Collections: Historic Buildings: 1828 Rev. Samuel Worcester's mission; Vann tavern; replica of Cherokee Council House & Cherokee Phoenix print shop; courthouse.
Research Fields: Cherokee genealogy; Trail of Tears; architecture.
Facilities: Publications & postcards for sale.
Activities: guided tours; gallery talks; permanent exhibitions.
Hours & Admission Prices: Thurs.-Sat. 9-5. Self-Guided Tours: Thurs.-Sat. Adults $5.00, seniors 62 & over $4.50, youth 6-17 $3.50; discount to AAA & AAM members and groups; children 5 & under no charge. Closed New Year's Day; Thanksgiving; Christmas. ♿
Attendance: 20,000 (estimated)

ROLAND HAYES MUSEUM, 212 S. Wall St., Calhoun, GA 30701-2499. Tel.: 706-629-2599. Fax: 706-602-2599.
Web Site: harrisartscenter.com/events/rolandhayes/tabid/67/default.aspx
Key Personnel: Interim Dir. Harris Arts Center, Toni Molleson
History Museum.
Collections: personal artifacts & memorabilia from Hayes' life; Hayes' piano; photographs.
Activities: rental facilities; tours. Museum Sponsors: Roland Hayes Birthday Celebration in June.
Hours & Admission Prices: Mon. 10-6, Tues.-Thurs. 10-4, Fri.-Sat. 10-2. No charge.

Cartersville

BARTOW HISTORY MUSEUM, 13 N. Wall St., Cartersville, GA 30120-3331. Tel.: 770-382-3818. Fax: 770-383-9314.
Web Site: www.bartowhistorymuseum.org
Founded: 1987.
Congressional District: 7
Key Personnel: Dir., Trey Gaines; Education Coord., Amanda Brown; Museum Shop Mgr., Elaine Popham.
Personnel Profile: Full-Time Paid 4; Part-Time Paid 4; Part-Time Volunteers 8; Interns 1.
Governing Authority: Parent Institution: Georgia Museums Inc. Tax-exempt: 501(c)(3).
History Museum.
Collections: personal artifacts; farming tools; furnishings; documents/archives; photographs; textiles.
Research Fields: Bartow County history; northwest Georgia.
Facilities: 4,000 sq. ft. exhibit space. Museum-related items for sale.
Activities: guided tours; lectures; broadcast programs; school loan service; temporary & loan exhibits; workshops; children's programs; summer day camp; staff development workshops for teachers.
Publications: Evolution of a Potter; The General, The Great Locomotive Dispute; Architecture of Bartow County; quarterly newsletter, Recollections .
Hours & Admission Prices: Mon.-Sat. 10-5. Adults $3, seniors $2.50, students $2; discounts to AAM & ICOM members; active military & members no charge. Southeastern Reciprocal Membership Program. Closed major holidays. ♿
Attendance: 10,575 (accurate)
Membership: Educator $20; Individual $25; Family $50; Friend $100; Bronze $250; Silver $500; Gold $1,000.

BOOTH WESTERN ART MUSEUM, 501 Museum Dr., Cartersville, GA 30120-3272. Mailing Address: P.O. Box 3070, Cartersville, GA 30120-1702. Tel.: 770-387-1300. Fax: 770-387-1319.
Web Site: www.boothmuseum.org
Founded: 2000.
Congressional District: 11
Key Personnel: Dir., Seth Hopkins; Devel., Tom Roberson; Education, Lisa Wheeler; Mktg., Kathy Lyles; Treas., Cathy Lee Eckert; Registrar, Nikki Morris; Cur., Jeff Donaldson; Librarian & Archivist, Liz Gentry; Museum Shop Mgr., Macra Adair; Security, Ken Wade.
Personnel Profile: Full-Time Paid 40; Part-Time Paid 9; Part-Time Volunteers 77; Interns 1.
Governing Authority: private; nonprofit organization. Parent Institution: Georgia Museums, Inc., Cartersville, GA. Tax-exempt: 501(c)(3).
Art Museum.
Collections: Western American art & culture; Presidential letters & portraits; Western movie posters; contemporary Civil War art; Western illustration.
Research Fields: American West art; presidential history; Civil War.
Facilities: 20,000-vol. library; 55,000 sq. ft. exhibit space; 140-seat theatre; cafe. Museum-related items for sale.
Activities: lectures; demonstrations; discussions; film screenings; family events; arts festivals; concerts; docent program; guided tours; loan, participatory, traveling & temporary exhibitions; theater.
Publications: quarterly newsletter, The Booth Bulletin.
Hours & Admission Prices: Tues.-Wed. & Fri.-Sat. 10-5, Thurs. 10-8, Sun. 1-5. Adults $8, seniors 65 & over $6, students $5; discounts to groups of 15 or more; military, children 12 & under and members no charge. ♿
Attendance: 39,789 (accurate)

Membership: Individual $40; Family $75; Friend $150; Museum Package $200; Donor $250; Sponsor $500; Patron $1,000; Collector's Circle $2,500; Director's Circle $5,000 & up.

ETOWAH INDIAN MOUNDS HISTORICAL SITE, 813 Indian Mounds Rd., S.W., Cartersville, GA 30120-6415. Tel.: 770-387-3747. Fax: 770-387-3972.
E-mail: etowah_mounds@dnr.state.ga.us
Web Site: www.gastateparks.org/info/etowah
Founded: 1953.
Congressional District: 7
Key Personnel: Site Mgr., Kenneth Akins; Interpretive Ranger, Steve McCarty; Interpretive Ranger, Thomas Bagby; Trades Craftsman, Buster Garland; Exhibit Attendant, Samantha Baker.
Personnel Profile: Full-Time Paid 5; Part-Time Paid 1; Part-Time Volunteers 12.
Governing Authority: state. Affiliated with Parks, Recreation & Historic Sites Div., Dept. of Natural Resources, Suite 1352, 205 Butler St., S.E., Atlanta, GA 30334.
Archaeology Museum.
Collections: archaeological excavations of prehistoric American Indian center.
Research Fields: archaeology.
Facilities: American Indian books & postcards for sale.
Activities: guided tours; gallery talks; permanent exhibitions; flint chipping; basket weaving. Annual Event: Torchlight Tour of an Ancient City in October.
Hours & Admission Prices: Thurs.-Sat. 9-5, Sun 2-5:30. Adults $5, seniors $3.50, children 6-18 $2.50; discount to groups of 15 or more with reservation; children under 6 no charge. Closed New Year's Day; Thanksgiving; Christmas. ♿
Attendance: 50,000 (accurate)
Membership: Individual $45; Family $70; Supporting $100; Patron $500; Trustee $5,000.

EUHARLEE COVERED BRIDGE AND HISTORIC MUSEUM, 116 Covered Bridge Rd., Cartersville, GA 30120. Mailing Address: P.O. Box 200397, Cartersville, GA 30120-9007. Tel.: 770-607-2017.
Historic Site: bridge built in 1886 by Washington W. King, a black contractor. Listed on the National Register of Historic Places.
Collections: local history; photographs; personal artifacts.
Activities: seasonal events.
Hours & Admission Prices: Museum: Tues.-Fri. 1-5.

HISTORIC DEPOT AT FRIENDSHIP PLAZA, One Friendship Plaza, Cartersville, GA 30120-3570. Tel.: 770-387-1357; 800-733-2280.
Historic Building: built in 1854.
Collections: local history; personal artifacts; photographs.
Hours & Admission Prices: Mon.-Fri. 9-5, Sat. 11-2, Sun. 1:30-4:30. ♿

ROSE LAWN MUSEUM, (M), 224 W. Cherokee Ave., Cartersville, GA 30120-3004. Tel.: 770-387-5162. Fax: 770-386-1527.
E-mail: roselawnga@comcast.net
Web Site: www.roselawnmuseum.com
Founded: 1973.
Congressional District: 7
Key Personnel: Dir., Jane Drew; C.E.O. & Commissioner, Clarence Brown.
Personnel Profile: Full-Time Paid 1; Part-Time Paid 3; Part-Time Volunteers 10.
Governing Authority: county; nonprofit. Parent Institution: Bartow County. Tax-exempt: 170(b)(1)(A).
Historic House: c.1880 Victorian mansion, former home of evangelist Samuel Porter Jones.
Collections: furniture; farm implements; documents; clothing & costumes; silver; memorabilia belonging to Samuel Porter Jones; documents & memorabilia belonging to Rebecca Latimer Felton, first woman U.S. Senator.
Research Fields: architecture; ministerial.
Facilities: reception facilities. Antiques & museum-related items for sale.
Activities: guided tours; concerts; arts festivals; Tea & Tour.
Publications: books, History of Bartow County (reprint); Thunderbolts (reprint); Life and Sayings of Sam P. Jones; Quit Your Meanness; Laughter in the Amen Corner.
Hours & Admission Prices: Tues.-Fri. 10-12 & 1-5; other times by appointment. Adults $4, students $2. Closed holidays. ♿
Attendance: 10,000 (accurate)

Cedartown

THE POLK COUNTY HISTORICAL SOCIETY, 205 N. College St., Cedartown, GA 30125. Mailing Address: P.O. Box 203, Cedartown, GA 30125-0203. Tel.: 770-749-0073.
Founded: 1974.
Congressional District: 6
Key Personnel: Pres. (V), Tom Lowe; Museum Shop Mgr., Ann White.
Personnel Profile: Part-Time Volunteers 3.
Governing Authority: society; nonprofit organization. Tax-exempt: 501(c)(3).
Historical Society Museum: housed in 1921 former Hawke's Children's Library.
Collections: local artifacts.
Research Fields: artifacts & local history of Polk County; genealogy.
Facilities: display area; 100-seat meeting room.
Activities: guided tours; art festivals; permanent & temporary exhibitions. Annual Event: Tour of Homes.
Publications: quarterly newsletter.
Hours & Admission Prices: Wed. 1:30-4, last Sun. of month 1-5. No charge; donations accepted.
Attendance: 300 (estimated)
Membership: Single $15; Couple $20; Family $25; Corporate $100.

Chatsworth

CHIEF VANN HOUSE HISTORIC SITE, 82 Hwy. 225 N., Chatsworth, GA 30705-6331. Tel.: 706-695-2598. Fax: 706-517-4255.
E-mail: vann_house_park@dnr.state.ga.us
Web Site: www.gastateparks.org
Founded: 1952.
Congressional District: 10
Key Personnel: Pres. & Chm. (V), Carolyn Luffman; Co-Chm., Jan McNeil; Museum Shop Mgr. & Site Supvr., Jeff Stancil; Seasonal, Tim Howard; Seasonal, Chase Parker.
Personnel Profile: Full-Time Paid 2; Part-Time Paid 4; Part-Time Volunteers 30.
Governing Authority: state. Administered by Georgia Dept. of Natural Resources, Parks & Historic Sites Div., Floyd Towers E., 205 Butler St., S.E., Atlanta, GA 30334. Tax-exempt.
Historic House Museum: housed c.1804 Vann House.
Collections: furniture; personal items.
Research Fields: Vann family genealogy; Cherokee Indian history.
Facilities: Publications & postcards for sale.
Activities: guided tours; permanent exhibitions.
Publications: Murray County's Indian Heritage; If the Vann House Could Speak; The Vann House Speaks Again.
Hours & Admission Prices: Thurs.-Sat. 9-5. Adults $5, youth $3.50, school groups $3; children under 6 & members no charge. Closed New Year's Day; Thanksgiving; Christmas. ♿
Attendance: 12,000 (accurate)
Membership: Individual $5; Family $10; Vann Partner $15-$25; Cherokee Trader $26-$50; Scots Brigade $51-$75; Road Builders $76-$100; Mission Associates $101-$200; Braves $201-$500; Chief's Council $501-$1,000; Principal People $1,000 and up.

FORT MOUNTAIN STATE PARK, 181 Fort Mountain Park Rd., Chatsworth, GA 30705-6669. Tel.: 706-422-1932. Fax: 706-422-1930.
Web Site: www.gastateparks.org
Founded: 1938.
Congressional District: 9
Key Personnel: Supt., Brian Ensley.
Governing Authority: state. Parent Institution: State of Georgia, Parks Recreation & Historic Sites Div., Dept. of Natural Resources. Tax-exempt.
State Park.
Collections: pre-historic stone wall.
Research Fields: Woodland period; ceremonial sites; fault zone geology.
Facilities: nature trails; tower overlook.
Activities: seasonal guided walks & naturalist programs; camping.
Publications: brochure.
Hours & Admission Prices: Park: daily 7am-10pm. Office: daily 8-5. Parking $5.

Chickamauga

WALKER COUNTY REGIONAL HERITAGE & MODEL TRAIN MUSEUM, 100 Gordon St., Chickamauga, GA 30707-1453. Tel.: 706-375-6801.
Historic Building: housed in a former train depot; built in 1890.
Collections: local history; war memorabilia; Native American artifacts; furniture; period guns; Lionel Old Gauge model trains.
Facilities: Museum-related items for sale.

Activities: summer train excursions.
Hours & Admission Prices: Mon.-Sat. 10-4. Admission: $2.

Cleveland

WHITE COUNTY HISTORICAL SOCIETY, White County Court House, Cleveland, GA 30528. Mailing Address: P.O. Box 1139, Cleveland, GA 30528-0022. Tel.: 706-865-3225.
Web Site: www.georgiamagazine.com
Founded: 1965.
Congressional District: 9
Key Personnel: Pres., Janet Cox; Vice Pres., Betty Highsmith; Sec., Shirley McDonald; Treas., Rev. Dean Head; Gen. Office Mgr., Mildred Brady; Museum Shop Mgr., Norma Holeman.
Personnel Profile: Part-Time Paid 2.
Governing Authority: membership. Parent Institution: White County Historical. Tax-exempt.
Local History Museum.
Collections: old newspapers; Civil War documents; diaries & letters; historic local pictures; historic papers of happenings & events in county. Historic Building: 1859-60 Courthouse; historic covered bridge in Sauter/Nacoochee Valley.
Research Fields: oral history; folklore.
Facilities: cemeteries; historic sites & buildings.
Activities: guided tours; lectures; gallery talks; hobby workshops; permanent & temporary exhibitions.
Publications: monthly newsletter.
Hours & Admission Prices: Thurs.-Sat. 10-3. No charge; donations accepted.
Membership: Individual $15; Family $20; Life $150; Family Life $200.

Columbus

COCA-COLA SPACE SCIENCE CENTER, 701 Front Ave., Columbus, GA 31901-2925. Tel.: 706-649-1470. Fax: 706-649-1478.
E-mail: info@ccssc.org
Web Site: www.ccssc.org
Key Personnel: Exec. Dir., Dr. Shawn Cruzen; Information Svcs., Rachel Hoogacker; Dir. Challenger Learning Center, Scott Norman; Dir. Planetarium, Lance Tankersley
Science Center.
Collections: science; mathematics; technology.
Facilities: omnisphere theatre; Mead Observatory; Challenger Center.
Hours & Admission Prices: Mon.-Thurs. 10-4, Fri. 10-8, Sat. 10:30-8. Adults $6, military & seniors $5, children $4, additional shows & CSU ID card $3.

* **THE COLUMBUS MUSEUM, (M),** 1251 Wynnton Rd., Columbus, GA 31906-2899. Tel.: 706-748-2562. Fax: 706-748-2570.
Web Site: www.columbusmuseum.com
Founded: 1953.
Congressional District: 3
Key Personnel: Dir., Charles T. Butler; Asst. to Dir., Patricia Butts; Pres. Bd. of Trustees (V), Kenneth H. Callaway; Graphic Designer, Marcolm Tatum; Cur. Collections & Exhibitions, Kristen Miller Zohn; Assoc. Cur. History, Mike Bunn; Registrar, Aimee Brooks; Asst. Registrar, Mellda Alexander; Asst. Cur. Art, Deb Wiedel; Exhibit Designer, Roger Reeves; Art Handler, Chris Land; Art Preparator, Matt Albrecht; Cur. Education, Tim Brown; Coord. School & Educator Svcs., Kaci Kelly; Coord. Youth & Family Programs, Brena Meadows; Tour Coord. & Administrative Asst., Melinda Durham; Dir. Devel., Alaina Barnett; Membership and Art & Antique Show Coord., Lane Riley; Coord. Special Events, Wren Gilliam; Coord. Public Rels., Frank Etheridge; Devel. Programs Asst., Laura Narr; Deputy Dir. Operations, Kimberly Beck; Bookkeeper, Deborah Danford; Information Asst., Mary Goff; Front Desk Receptionist, Amy Kelly; Museum Shop Mgr. & Volunteer Coord., Jennifer Morgan; Weekend Receptionist, April Kitchens; Security Officer, John Stephens; Security Officer, Jimmie Reed; Security Deputy, Glenn Sparks; Building Engineer, Bruce Griffin.
Personnel Profile: Full-Time Paid 32; Part-Time Paid 2; Part-Time Volunteers 500; Interns 3.
Governing Authority: nonprofit corporation; board of trustees. Tax-exempt: 501(c)(3).
Art & History Museum.
Collections: American paintings; sculpture; drawings; archaeology; decorative arts; southern history; ethnology; costumes; folk art; crafts.
Research Fields: American art; regional history & culture.
Facilities: library of art, art reference books, special exhibition catalogs, collection catalogs & periodicals available for research on premises.
Activities: guided tours; films; gallery talks; formally organized education programs; inter-museum loan, permanent, temporary & traveling exhibitions.
Publications: quarterly newsletter; exhibition catalogs; occasional reports & scientific papers; annual report.
Hours & Admission Prices: Tues.-Wed. & Fri.-Sat. 10-5, Thurs. 10-9, Sun. 1-5. No charge; donations accepted. Closed legal holidays. ♿
Attendance: 65,000 (estimated)
Membership: Individual $35; Family $45; Contributing $125; Patron $300; Sustaining $600; Master's Circle $1,000 & up; Collector's Circle $2,500 & up; Director's Circle $5,000 & up.

HISTORIC COLUMBUS FOUNDATION, INC., 1440 Second Ave., Columbus, GA 31901-2124. Mailing Address: P.O. Box 5312, Columbus, GA 31906-0312. Tel.: 706-322-0756. Fax: 706-576-4760.
E-mail: hcfinc@historiccolumbus.com
Web Site: www.historiccolumbus.com
Founded: 1966.
Congressional District: 3
Key Personnel: Bd. Chm., George G. Flowers; Pres., Jack B. Key, III; Exec. Dir., Elizabeth K. Barker; Membership, Jane Etheridge; Dir. Mktg., Carroll Hudson; Office Mgr., Debbie Lipscomb; Dir. Planning & Devel., Justin Krieg; Dir. Cultural Outreach, Ridley Stallings.
Personnel Profile: Full-Time Paid 5; Part-Time Paid 2.
Governing Authority: nonprofit organization. Tax-exempt.
Historic Foundation: five house museums including c.1870 first brick house in original residential part of city.
Collections: early 1800s-late Victorian furniture & furnishings; Coca-Cola collectibles & memorabilia. Historic Houses: 1860 The Rankin House; 1828 The Walker-Peters-Langdon House; 1870 700 Broadway House; 1840 Pemberton House; 1840s Farm House; c.1820 log cabin.
Research Fields: Columbus' history; Blacks in the history of Columbus.
Facilities: interpretive center. Gift items for sale.
Activities: guided tours; lectures. Foundation Sponsors: heritage balls; trips.
Publications: quarterly, HCF Newsletter; Images; Our Town: An Introduction to the History of Columbus, Georgia; Architectural Styles of Our Town: Col. 6A; Heritage Park - The Industrial Heritage of Columbus, GA.
Hours & Admission Prices: Office: Mon.-Fri. 9-5. Tour of Houses: Wed.-Sat. 2. Adults: $5, students $1; members no charge.
Attendance: 3,000 (estimated)
Membership: Individual $40; Family $60; Business $100; Friend $125; Patron $250; Landmark $400; Corporate $500; Sponsor $600; Benefactor $1,000; Heritage $2,500.

NATIONAL CIVIL WAR NAVAL MUSEUM AT PORT COLUMBUS, 1002 Victory Dr., Columbus, GA 31901-3429. Tel.: 706-327-9798. Fax: 706-324-7225.
E-mail: cwnavy@portcolumbus.org
Web Site: www.portcolumbus.org
Founded: 1962.
Key Personnel: C.E.O. & Exec. Dir., Bruce Smith; Museum Shop Mgr., Susan Egram.
Personnel Profile: Full-Time Paid 4; Full-Time Volunteers 7; Part-Time Paid 3; Part-Time Volunteers 14.
Governing Authority: Consolidated Govt. Columbus & Muscogee County, Ga. Tax-exempt.
Naval Museum.
Collections: Civil War naval operations history; Confederate naval gunboats; CSS Jackson & CSS Chattahoochee on display; exhibits pertaining to U.S. & Confederate Navies.
Research Fields: design & construction of American Civil War era warships.
Facilities: Publications & museum-related items for sale.
Activities: guided tours; permanent exhibitions.
Publications: newsletter, Port City Ram.
Hours & Admission Prices: Daily 9-5. Adults $6.50, active military and seniors 65 & over $5.50, students $5; members no charge. Closed Christmas. ♿
Attendance: 28,000 (accurate)
Membership: Shipmate $25; Lieutenant $50; Commander $100; Captain $250; Commodore $500; Admiral $1,000.

NATIONAL INFANTRY MUSEUM, 3800 S. Lumpkin Rd., Columbus, GA 31903. Tel.: 706-545-2958. Fax: 706-545-5158.
E-mail: zachary.f.hanner@conus.army.mil
Web Site: www.infantry.army.mil/museum
Founded: 1959.
Congressional District: 3
Key Personnel: Cur. & Dir., Z. Frank Hanner; Registrar, Edward Annable; Museum Shop Mgr., Andrea Jones.
Personnel Profile: Full-Time Paid 8.
Governing Authority: U.S. Army. Parent Institution: Center of Military History, Washington, DC. Tax-exempt.
Military History Museum.
Collections: militaria; weapons; military art; photograph archives; firearms including experimental U.S. items; presidential collection.

Facilities: 6,000-vol. library of Army manuals, books on infantry weapons, uniforms, equipment & history; 250,000 photos; 100-seat auditorium.
Activities: permanent & temporary exhibitions.
Hours & Admission Prices: Mon.-Sat. 9-5, Sun. 11-5. ♿
Attendance: 77,493 (accurate)
Membership: Friend of the Infantry Museum $50. National Infantry Foundation, P.O. Box 2823, Columbus, GA 31902-2823.

Cordele

GEORGIA VETERANS MEMORIAL MUSEUM, 2459-A Hwy. 280 W., Cordele, GA 31015-9511. Tel.: 229-276-2371. Fax: 229-276-2711.
Founded: 1962.
Congressional District: 2
Key Personnel: Mgr., Keith Fleming; Interpretive Ranger, Mike Goodwin.
Personnel Profile: Full-Time Paid 1.
Governing Authority: state. Administered by the Parks, Recreation and Historic Sites Div., Georgia Dept. of Natural Resources, 270 Washington St. S.W., Atlanta, GA 30334. Tax-exempt.
Military Museum.
Collections: historic aircraft; fighting vehicles; uniforms; weapons; accoutrements.
Activities: self-guided tours; permanent exhibits.
Hours & Admission Prices: Daily 8-5. Museum: no charge. Park: $5 per vehicle. Closed Christmas. ♿
Attendance: 3,243 (accurate)

Crawfordville

CONFEDERATE MUSEUM, 456 Alexander St., Crawfordville, GA 30631-2903. Mailing Address: P.O. Box 310, Crawfordville, GA 30631-0310. Tel.: 706-456-2221 (Museum) & 2602 (Park Office). Fax: 706-456-2396.
Founded: 1952.
Congressional District: 10
Key Personnel: Dir., Andre McLenton.
Personnel Profile: Full-Time Paid 1; Part-Time Volunteers 1.
Governing Authority: state. Administered by Parks, Recreation & Historic Sites Div., Georgia Dept. of Natural Resources, Floyd Tower E., Suite 1352, 205 Butler St., S.E., Atlanta, GA. Tax-exempt.
History Museum.
Collections: arms & memorabilia of Civil War; furnishings; servants quarters & outbuildings. Historic House: 1875 Liberty Hall, home of Alexander H. Stephens.
Research Fields: political history of Civil War; life of A. H. Stephens.
Facilities: Gift items for sale.
Activities: permanent exhibitions; guided tours; audiovisual.
Hours & Admission Prices: Wed.-Sun. 9-5. Adults $4, senior citizens $3.50, children 6-18 $2; discounts to groups; children 5 & under no charge. Closed New Year's Day; Thanksgiving; Christmas. ♿
Attendance: 92,000

Dahlonega

DAHLONEGA GOLD MUSEUM STATE HISTORIC SITE, #1 Public Square, Dahlonega, GA 30533-1210. Tel.: 706-864-2257. Fax: 706-864-8370.
E-mail: dahlonega@dnr.state.ga.us
Web Site: www.gastateparks.org
Formerly: Historic Lumpkin County Courthouse
Founded: 1966.
Congressional District: 9
Key Personnel: Site Mgr., David Foot; Interpretive Ranger, Teresa Krummel; Interpretive Ranger, Robin Glass.
Personnel Profile: Full-Time Paid 5; Part-Time Paid 2; Part-Time Volunteers 2.
Governing Authority: state. Affiliated with Georgia Dept. of Natural Resources, State Parks & Historic Sites, Floyd Towers E., 205 Butler St., S.E., Atlanta, GA 30334. Tax-exempt.
Historic Building: housed in c.1836 Lumpkin County Courthouse.
Collections: Dahlonega's Gold Rush history; native Georgian gold & Dahlonega Mint coins; mining equipment; photographs.
Research Fields: Georgia gold mining history.
Facilities: Mining publications & other museum related items for sale.
Activities: guided tours; permanent exhibitions; 27-minute film.
Publications: book, History of Georgia's Gold Museum.
Hours & Admission Prices: Mon.-Sat. 9-5, Sun. 10-5. Adults $5, senior citizens 62 & over $4.50, children 6-18 $3.50; discount to groups with reservation; children 5 & under no charge. Annual Pass available. Closed New Year's Day; Thanksgiving; Christmas. ♿
Attendance: 60,000 (accurate)

Dalton

CREATIVE ARTS GUILD, 520 W. Waugh St., Dalton, GA 30720-3474. Mailing Address: P.O. Box 1485, Dalton, GA 30722-1485. Tel.: 706-278-0168. Fax: 706-278-6996.
E-mail: terryt@creativeartsguild.org
Web Site: www.creativeartsguild.org
Founded: 1963.
Congressional District: 9
Key Personnel: Chm. (V), Cindy McCreery; Guild Mgr., Leanne Lawson.
Personnel Profile: Full-Time Paid 4; Part-Time Paid 20; Part-Time Volunteers 1.
Governing Authority: nonprofit organization. Tax-exempt.
Art Commission & Gallery.
Collections: various types of art media.
Major Exhibits: Annual American Flag Show, 6/28/10-7/30/10; Festival of Fine Arts & Crafts, 8/13/10-9/19/10.
Facilities: classrooms; galleries; studios.
Activities: guided tours; lectures; concerts; dance recitals; arts festivals; drama; docent programs; permanent, temporary & traveling exhibitions; performing arts events; intercultural activities.
Publications: monthly bulletin, CAG; monthly class brochures.
Hours & Admission Prices: Mon.-Thurs. 9-6, Fri. 9-4:30. No charge; donations accepted. Closed New Year's Day; Memorial Day; Independence Day; Labor Day; Thanksgiving; Christmas. ♿
Attendance: 200,000
Membership: Senior Citizen $30; Standard $45; Family $50; Art Lovers & Friends of the Arts $100; Growth Partner $250; Founder's Circle $1,000.

HERITAGE CENTER MUSEUM, 215 Clisby Austin Rd., Dalton, GA 30755-9335. Mailing Address: P.O. Box 6177, Dalton, GA 30722-6177. Tel.: 706-876-1571.
Personnel Profile: Part-Time Paid 3.
History Museum.
Collections: history & heritage of Tunnel Hill; Native American; early settlers; 1850 railroad restoration; Civil War artifacts; personal artifacts; period furnishings.
Activities: school groups; tours.
Hours & Admission Prices: Mon.-Sat. 9-5. Adults $3, children under 12 $2; discounts to groups of 20 or more. Closed New Year's Day; Thanksgiving; Christmas Eve. ♿

PRATERS MILL FOUNDATION, 5845 Georgia Hwy. 2, Dalton, GA 30721-1282. Mailing Address: P.O. Drawer H, Varnell, GA 30756-1008. Tel.: 706-694-6455. Fax: 706-694-8413.
E-mail: info@pratersmill.org
Web Site: www.PratersMill.org
Founded: 1970.
Congressional District: 9
Key Personnel: Pres. (V), Judy Alderman; Treas., Melanie Ghapman.
Personnel Profile: Part-Time Paid 1.
Governing Authority: private; nonprofit organization. Subsidiary Institution: Varnell Heritage Center. Tax-exempt.
Historic Site Museum: housed in c.1855 grist mill & c.1898 Prater's Country Store.
Collections: horse-drawn farm implements.
Research Fields: Native American history of area; pioneer families, gristmills, music, dance, crafts, traditions & agriculture.
Facilities: library; nature trail; park; outdoor shed.
Activities: arts & crafts festivals; guided tours; temporary exhibitions. Museum Sponsors: Prater's Mill Foundation.
Publications: brochures; books; historical reviews.
Hours & Admission Prices: Call for hours. No charge. Annual Folk Festival: adults $5; discounts to groups; children no charge.
Attendance: 50,000 (estimated)

WHITFIELD-MURRAY HISTORY CENTER & ARCHIVES, 715 Chattanooga Ave., Dalton, GA 30720-8800. Mailing Address: P.O. Box 6180, Dalton, GA 30722-6180. Tel.: 706-278-0217.
E-mail: wmhs@optilink.us
Web Site: whitfield-murrayhistoricalsociety
Formerly: Crown Gardens and Archives
Founded: 1976.
Congressional District: 9
Key Personnel: Dir., Erik Gallman; Pres., Ellen Thompson.
Personnel Profile: Full-Time Paid 1; Part-Time Volunteers 40.
Governing Authority: society; nonprofit organization. Whitfield-Murray Historical Society. Tax-exempt: 501(c)(3).
Preservation Project & Historic Building: c.1890 Crown Cotton Mill office

building located in the Crown Mill Historic District; 1848 Blunt House; 1908 Wright Hotel-Chatsworth; 1840 John Hamilton House-Chatsworth Depot.
Collections: handmade tufted bedspreads; machines for making spreads; material; textiles; period furnishings; artifacts pertaining to the Black community; Sims Collection of hand-carved wooden objects; c.1890 furniture from the Loveman home; records of Mills; Whitfield Co. Census Indexes; Murray Co. Census Indexes; Civil War artifacts; antique apothecary jars-Hamilton Mountain and Dug Gap Battle Park; Civil War sites.
Research Fields: genealogy for the North Georgia area.
Facilities: 500-vol. library Robert Loveman Room; genealogical research material available for research on premises; archives; reading room; meeting room; banquet facilities; Indian & Civil War display. Books, recipe books & other museum-related items for sale.
Activities: exhibits; historical society meetings.
Publications: magazine, The quarterly of Whitfield-Murray Historical Society; books, Official History of Whitfield County, Georgia; Murray County Heritage.
Hours & Admission Prices: Tues.-Fri. 10-5, Sat. 9-1. Crown Gardens: no charge; donations accepted. Hamilton House & Blunt House: $5; discount to groups. Closed New Year's Day; Independence Day week; Thanksgiving; Christmas week. ♿
Attendance: 7,000 (estimated)
Membership: Student $10; Individual $20; Family $30.

Darien

FORT KING GEORGE HISTORIC SITE, 302 McIntosh Rd., S.E., Darien, GA 31305. Mailing Address: P.O. Box 711, Darien, GA 31305-0711. Tel.: 912-437-4770. Fax: 912-437-5479.
E-mail: ftkgeo@darientel.net
Web Site: www.gastateparks.org/fortkinggeorge
Founded: 1961.
Congressional District: 1
Key Personnel: Historic Site Supt., Steven Smith; Interpreter, Jason Baker.
Personnel Profile: Full-Time Paid 3; Part-Time Paid 1; Part-Time Volunteers 37.
Governing Authority: state. Administered by Parks, Recreation & Historic Sites Div., Dept. of Natural Resources, 2 Martin Luther King Dr., S.E., Atlanta, GA 30334. Tax-exempt.
History Museum & Historic Site.
Collections: Aboriginal & Spanish artifacts; reproductions of uniforms, weapons & accoutrements of British garrison.
Research Fields: coastal Georgia Indians; European exploration & colonization of the Southeast; early Georgia history; Darien & McIntosh county; history of early sawmilling in Georgia.
Facilities: Publications, postcards & gifts for sale.
Activities: tours of reconstructed 18th-century fort & blockhouse; permanent & changing exhibits; interpretive programs; slide presentations.
Publications: Fort King George-Step One to Statehood; Garrison Newsletter.
Hours & Admission Prices: Tues.-Sat. & Mon. holidays 9-5, Sun. 2-5:30. Adults $5, senior citizens $4.50, youths $2.50; discount to groups of 15 or more. Closed New Year's Day; Thanksgiving; Christmas. ♿
Attendance: 48,000 (estimated)

Decatur

DALTON GALLERIES, Agnes Scott College, Dana Fine Arts Bldg., 141 E. College Ave., Decatur, GA 30030-5361. Tel.: 404-471-5361. Fax: 404-471-5369.
E-mail: daltongallery@agnesscott.edu
Web Site: daltongallery.agnesscott.edu
Founded: 1957.
Key Personnel: Chm., Dr. Donna Sadler.
Personnel Profile: Full-Time Paid 1; Part-Time Paid 1.
Governing Authority: college; nonprofit organization. Tax-exempt: 170(b)(1)(A).
Art Gallery.
Collections: Harry L. Dalton collection; Steffen Thomas collection; Ferdinand Warren collection; Clifford Clarke collection.
Facilities: theater; classrooms.
Activities: drama; permanent & temporary exhibitions.
Hours & Admission Prices: During academic school year: Mon.-Fri. 10-4:30, Sat.-Sun.12-4. No charge. ♿
Attendance: 1,500 (estimated)

DEKALB HISTORY CENTER MUSEUM, 101 E. Court Sq., Decatur, GA 30030-2544. Tel.: 404-373-1088. Fax: 404-373-8287.
E-mail: dhs@dekalbhistory.org
Web Site: www.dekalbhistory.org
Formerly: DeKalb Historical Society Museum
Founded: 1947.
Congressional District: 4
Key Personnel: Exec. Dir., Melissa Forgey; Treas., Melvin Bettis.
Personnel Profile: Full-Time Paid 2; Full-Time Volunteers 50; Part-Time Paid 2; Part-Time Volunteers 100; Interns 3.
Governing Authority: society; nonprofit organization. Tax-exempt: 501(c)(3).
History Museum: housed in the Old Courthouse on Decatur Square.
Collections: six exhibit rooms containing memorabilia of DeKalb 1822-1922; Civil War memorabilia; manuscripts. Historic Buildings: 1830-40 Benjamin Swanton House; 1825 Thomas-Barber Cabin; 1822 John Biffle Cabin.
Research Fields: local history.
Facilities: 1,500-vol. library on historical subjects & private collections of classics available for research on premises only; reading room. Books & photographs for sale.
Activities: guided tours; lectures; films; oral history programs; formally organized education programs; loan & permanent exhibitions.
Publications: monthly newsletter, DeKalb Historical Society; books, The History of DeKalb County 1822-1900, The Story of Decatur, Life in Dixie During the War; postcards of DeKalb; tour guides.
Hours & Admission Prices: Museum: call for hours. Swanton House & Biffle Cabin: open by appointment. Closed county & national holidays. ♿
Attendance: 3,600 (estimated)
Membership: Student $20; Individual $30; Family $50; Patron $75; Sustaining $125.

Douglas

HERITAGE STATION MUSEUM, 219 W. Ward St., Douglas, GA 31533-3501. Tel.: 912-389-3461.
History Museum.
Collections: railroad history; Georgia's cultural heritage; Native American; business & industry; education; medical; early 1900s clothing; photography.
Facilities: library. Museum-related items for sale.
Activities: rental facilities; group tours; school groups; temporary exhibits.
Hours & Admission Prices: Thurs.-Sat. 10-4. No charge; donations accepted.

Douglasville

CULTURAL ARTS COUNCIL OF DOUGLASVILLE/DOUGLAS COUNTY, 8652 Campbellton St., Douglasville, GA 30134-1825. Mailing Address: P.O. Box 2018, Douglasville, GA 30133-2018. Tel.: 770-949-2787. Fax: 770-949-5788.
E-mail: cultureom@earthlink.net
Web Site: www.artsdouglas.org
Founded: 1986.
Congressional District: 13
Key Personnel: Exec. Dir., Laura Lieberman
Cultural Arts Center: housed in the historic Roberts/Mozley house, built in 1901. Listed on the National Register of Historic Places.
Collections: works by local & regional artists including sculptures & paintings.
Major Exhibits: Contemporary Cuban Artists, 1/10; Jacob Lawrence, 2/10; Youth Art Month, 3/10; Gazing at the Contemporary World, 6/10-7/10; Douglasville Celebrates Photography, 10/10; 24th National Juried Show, 11/10; Holiday Card Contest, 12/10.
Research Fields: local artists from Georgia.
Activities: classes; rental facilities; special events; meetings; performances.
Publications: quarterly newsletters; annual, Atlanta Celebrates Photography & Festival Guide; National Juried Fine Arts Exhibition; annual report.
Hours & Admission Prices: Jan. 3-Dec. 21 Mon.-Fri. 9-5. No charge; donations accepted. ♿
Attendance: 15,000
Membership: Student & Senior Citizen $10; Individual $20; Family $30; Friend $50; Patron & Business $100; Sponsor $500; Angel $1,000.

DOUGLAS COUNTY MUSEUM OF HISTORY AND ART, 6754 W. Broad St., Old Douglas County Courthouse, Douglasville, GA 30134-1711. Tel.: 770-949-4090.
E-mail: info@douglascountymuseum.com
Web Site: douglascountymuseum.com
History Museum: housed in the Old Douglas County Courthouse.
Collections: mid-20th century artifacts; personal artifacts; cocktail shakers; school lunchboxes; children's phonographs; Coca Cola memorabilia.
Hours & Admission Prices: Call for hours.

Dublin

DUBLIN-LAURENS MUSEUM, 311 Academy Ave., Dublin, GA 31021-5219. Mailing Address: P.O. Box 1461, Dublin, GA 31040-1461. Tel.: 478-272-9242.
E-mail: museum@laurenshistory.org

Founded: 1979.
Congressional District: 8
Key Personnel: Dir., Scott Thompson, Sr.; Mgr., Betty Page.
Personnel Profile: Part-Time Paid 1; Part-Time Volunteers 15.
Governing Authority: society; nonprofit. Parent Institution: The Laurens County Historical Society. Tax-exempt.
Historical Society Museum: housed in 1904 restored Carnegie Library.
Collections: textiles; photographs; farm tools & implements; art memorabilia; genealogy; Indian artifacts.
Research Fields: local history.
Facilities: 2,000 sq. ft. exhibit space.
Activities: guided tours; lectures; TV programs; permanent & temporary exhibitions; field trips.
Publications: quarterly newsletter, Laurens Co. Historical Society.
Hours & Admission Prices: Tues.-Fri. 1-4:30; other times by appointment. No charge; donations accepted. ♿
Attendance: 4,000 (estimated)
Membership: Individual $15; Family $20; Patron, Institutional, School Libraries & Museums $25; Sustaining $50; Sponsor $100; Benefactor $200.

Duluth

GWINNETT COUNTY PARKS & RECREATION - MCDANIEL FARM PARK, 3251 McDaniel Rd., Duluth, GA 30096-4605. Mailing Address: 75 Langley Dr., Lawrenceville, GA 30045-6936. Tel.: 770-814-4920. Fax: 770-814-4922.
E-mail: mark.patterson@gwinnettcounty.com
Web Site: www.gwinnettcounty.com
Formerly: Lanier Museum of Natural History
Founded: 2005.
Congressional District: 9
Key Personnel: Dir., Dr. Mark A. Patterson.
Personnel Profile: Full-Time Paid 1; Part-Time Paid 4; Part-Time Volunteers 6; Interns 2.
Governing Authority: county; nonprofit organization. Gwinnett County Parks & Recreation, 75 Langley Dr., Lawrenceville, GA 30045. Tax-exempt: 501(c)(3) & 701(b)(1)(A).
Historic Site.
Collections: period artifacts; birds; mammals; fish; butterflies & insects; rocks; minerals; fossils; shells; snakes; hands-on exhibits; journals; historic buildings.
Research Fields: natural history; science; cultural & historical local history.
Facilities: reference center.
Activities: guided tours; films; study & hobby workshops; formally organized education programs; docent program; changing exhibit areas.
Publications: quarterly journal, The Eyrie.
Hours & Admission Prices: Fri.-Sat. 10-4, Sun. 12-4. Admission $1; discounts to AAM & ICOM members; members & Gwinnett History Museum members no charge.
Attendance: 40,000 (estimated)
Membership: Student, Educator, Senior Citizen 55 & over $10; Individual $15; Families $25.

JACQUELINE CASEY HUDGENS CENTER FOR THE ARTS, 6400 Sugarloaf Pkwy., Bldg. 300, Duluth, GA 30097-7419. Tel.: 770-623-6002. Fax: 770-623-3555.
E-mail: info@thehudgens.org
Web Site: www.thehudgens.org
Formerly: Gwinnett Fine Arts Center
Founded: 1981.
Congressional District: 10
Key Personnel: C.E.O., Stan Hall; Interim Dir., Teresa Osborn; Dir. Mktg., Kelly Olson; Dir. Education, Angela Nichols; Museum Shop Mgr., Jane Roach.
Personnel Profile: Full-Time Paid 7; Full-Time Volunteers 1; Part-Time Paid 8; Part-Time Volunteers 250; Interns 1.
Governing Authority: nonprofit. Parent Institution: Gwinnett Council for the Arts. Tax-exempt: 501(c)(3).
Art & Children's Art Museum.
Collections: works by noted Georgia artists in all medias & styles since 1920; also works by Picasso, Kandinsky, Litchtenstein, Miro & Rauschenberg.
Facilities: botanical & sculpture garden; educational facilities; 6,000 sq. ft. exhibit space; 21,000 sq. ft. children's art museum; The Glass Pyramid. Gift items for sale.
Activities: arts festivals; concerts; docent program; films; formal education programs; guided tours; lectures; loan, temporary & traveling exhibitions; puppet theater; black box theater.
Publications: quarterly newsletter, Artsline; monthly newsletters, Arts Clips & Sketches.
Hours & Admission Prices: Tues.-Sat. 10-5. Donations Requested: adults $5, seniors & students $3; children 2 & under no charge. Closed New Year's Day; Martin Luther King Jr. Day; Memorial Day; Independence Day; Labor Day; Thanksgiving; Christmas. ♿
Attendance: 45,000 (estimated)
Membership: Student & Senior $15; Individual $20; Organization & Family $35; Sustaining $50; Contributing $100; Sponsor Patron $250; Donor Patron $500; Benefactor Patron $1,000; Grand Patron $2,000; Premier Patron $5,000.

SOUTHEASTERN RAILWAY MUSEUM, 3595 Buford Hwy., Duluth, GA 30096. Mailing Address: P.O. Box 1267, Duluth, GA 30096-0023. Tel.: 770-476-2013. Fax: 770-573-3754.
E-mail: admin@southeasternrailwaymuseum.org
Web Site: www.srmduluth.org
Founded: 1968.
Congressional District: 10
Key Personnel: Admin., Randy Pirkle; Pres. (V), John Pollock; Operations Mgr., Dale Grice; Preservation Mgr. & Librarian, Nick Whitehouse; Museum Shop Mgr., Lallie Morris.
Personnel Profile: Part-Time Paid 2; Part-Time Volunteers 50.
Governing Authority: society; nonprofit organization. Parent Institution: National Railway Historical Society. Affiliated with the Atlanta Chapter of the National Railway Historical Society, P.O. Box 1267, Duluth, GA 30096. Tax-exempt: 501(c)(3).
Railway Museum.
Collections: over 90 pieces of railroad rolling stock including Pullmans, steam locomotives & wooden freight cars; business records; blueprints; maps; books; magazines; trade journals & house organs; newspaper articles.
Facilities: 4,000-vol. library of railroad-related history available for research by appointment; over 30 pieces of rolling stock open for touring. Railroad-related gifts for sale.
Activities: special events; restored caboose rides on steam & diesel 1940s locomotives.
Publications: quarterly newsletter, Milepost 613.
Hours & Admission Prices: Jan.-March Sat. 10-5; April-Dec. Thurs.-Sat. 10-5. Adults $8, seniors 65 & over $6, children 2-12 $4; children under 2 no charge. ♿
Attendance: 15,150 (accurate)
Membership: Youth $20; Senior $35; Adult $45; Family $90.

Eatonton

UNCLE REMUS MUSEUM, 360 Oak St., Hwy. 441 S., Eatonton, GA 31024. Mailing Address: P.O. Box 3184, Eatonton, GA 31024-3184. Tel.: 706-485-6856.
Founded: 1963.
Congressional District: 11
Key Personnel: C.E.O., J. Marshal; Dir. & Museum Shop Mgr., Lanelle Frost; Pres. (V), Mona Betzel.
Personnel Profile: Full-Time Paid 5.
Governing Authority: nonprofit organization.
Historic House: c.1820 slave cabin.
Collections: furniture; personal artifacts; agriculture & wood working; books of Joel Chandler Harris, author of The Uncle Remus stories; Civil War; 3 slave cabins.
Facilities: Volumes of the Uncle Remus stories & related items for sale.
Activities: guided tours; lectures; loan & permanent exhibitions.
Hours & Admission Prices: March to mid-Nov. Mon.-Sat. 10-5, Sun. 2-5; mid-Nov. to Feb. Mon. & Wed.-Sat. 10-5. Adults $1, children under 8 & school groups $.50. Closed New Year's Day; Mother's Day; Independence Day; Christmas.
Attendance: 12,000 (estimated)
Membership: Individual $1; Life $50.

Elberton

ELBERTON GRANITE MUSEUM & EXHIBIT, 1 Granite Plaza, Elberton, GA 30635. Mailing Address: P.O. Box 640, Elberton, GA 30635-0640. Tel.: 706-283-2551. Fax: 706-283-6380.
E-mail: granite@egaonline.com
Web Site: www.egaonline.com/egaassociation/museum
Founded: 1981.
Congressional District: 10
Key Personnel: Exec. Vice Pres. & Dir., Doyle "Doye" G. Johnson.
Personnel Profile: Part-Time Paid 3.
Governing Authority: trade association. Affiliated with Elberton Granite Assn., Inc., P.O. Box 640, Elberton, GA 30635. Tax-exempt.
Granite Museum.
Collections: historical exhibits; artifacts; educational displays; granite monuments.
Facilities: classrooms.
Activities: guided tours for groups by prior arrangement; lectures; films.

Hours & Admission Prices: Mon.-Sat. 2-5; call for additional hours. No charge. Closed holidays.
Attendance: 3,885 (accurate)

Ellijay

GILMER ARTS AND HERITAGE ASSOCIATION, 207 Dalton St., Ellijay, GA 30540-9000. Tel.: 706-635-5605. Fax: 706-636-5606.
E-mail: gaha@ellijay.com
Web Site: www.gilmerarts.org
Key Personnel: Pres., John Mahan.
Personnel Profile: Full-Time Paid 1.
Governing Authority: tax-exempt.
Art Association, Heritage.
Collections: works by regional & national artists; Gilmer County artifacts.
Publications: newsletter.
Hours & Admission Prices: Mon.-Fri. 9-4:30. No charge.
Attendance: 500 (estimated)

Fairburn

OLD CAMPBELL COUNTY MUSEUM, Intersection of E. Broad St. & Cole St., Fairburn, GA 30213. Mailing Address: c/o OCCHS, P.O. Box 342, Fairburn, GA 30213-0342. Tel.: 770-964-6007.
E-mail: info@oldcampbellcountyhistoricalsociety.com
Web Site: www.oldcampbellcountyhistoricalsociety.com/homepage.html
Historical Society Museum.
Collections: artifacts & memorabilia pertaining to Campbell County.
Hours & Admission Prices: Tues. 11-4; other times by appointment. No charge.

Fairmount

SUNRISE PLANETARIUM & SCIENCE MUSEUM, 1427 Slate Mine Rd., Fairmount, GA 30139-2835. Tel.: 706-337-2775.
Planetarium & Science Museum.
Collections: anthropology; archaeology; astronomy; entomology; ethnology; geology.
Hours & Admission Prices: Oct.-May 1 Sun. 3; other times by appointment. No charge.

Fargo

STEPHEN C. FOSTER STATE PARK, 17515 Hwy. 177, Fargo, GA 31631-5004. Tel.: 912-637-5274. Fax: 912-637-5587.
Web Site: www.gastateparks.org/info/scfoster
Founded: 1954.
Congressional District: 8
Key Personnel: Mgr., Travis Griffin.
Personnel Profile: Full-Time Paid 12.
Governing Authority: state. Parent Institution: Georgia Dept. of Natural Resources. Administered by: State Parks & Historic Sites. Tax-exempt.
State Park Museum.
Collections: natural history of Okefenokee Swamp; lumbering; turpentining.
Research Fields: natural & cultural history of Okefenokee Swamp.
Facilities: canoe, boat & walking trails; boardwalk; camping; cottages.
Activities: tours; boat tours & educational programs.
Publications: Trail Guide; postcards.
Hours & Admission Prices: Park: 7am-10pm. Suwannee River Center: Wed.-Sun. 8-5. Office: Fall & Winter: daily 8-5; Spring & Summer: daily 7-6. National Park Pass: $5 per vehicle. Boat tours: adults $10, children $6; children under 4 no charge. ♿
Attendance: 65,000 (estimated)

Fayetteville

HOLLIDAY-DORSEY-FIFE HOUSE MUSEUM, 140 Lanier Ave., W., Fayetteville, GA 30214-1606. Tel.: 770-716-5332. Fax: 770-460-3906.
E-mail: jlynch@fayetteville-ga.gov
Web Site: hdfhouse.com
Key Personnel: House Mgr., John Lynch
History Museum.
Collections: historic artifacts & treasures of Fayette County, including Gone with the Wind memorabilia; relics & documents from the War Between the States.
Hours & Admission Prices: Thurs.-Sat. 10-5. Adults $5, senior citizens $4.

Fitzgerald

BLUE AND GRAY MUSEUM, 116 N. Johnston St., Fitzgerald, GA 31750-2475. Mailing Address: P.O. Box 1285, Fitzgerald, GA 31750-1285. Tel.: 229-426-5069; 800-386-4642.
Key Personnel: Dir., Al Strom; Asst. Dir., Charlotte Nelms; Dir. Tourism, Alesia Biggers.
Personnel Profile: Part-Time Paid 1; Part-Time Volunteers 12.
History Museum.
Collections: history of Fitzgerald; photographs; household artifacts; film documentary; life of General Raymond Davis, USMC (Ret.); period clothing; china; glassware; cooking utensils; American Civil War artifacts; oral histories; African American history; Southern Cross of Honor medal; Congressional Medal of Honor.
Activities: film.
Hours & Admission Prices: Tues.-Sat. 10-4, Sun. 1-5. Adults $3, students $1; discounts to AAM members, seniors & groups of 10 or more. Closed New Year's; Memorial Day; Independence Day; Labor Day; Thanksgiving & day after; Christmas. ♿
Membership: Individual $25; Couple $35; Business Club & Family $50; Benefactor $100-$250; Guardian $500, $750 & 1,000.

Flovilla

INDIAN SPRINGS STATE PARK MUSEUM, Hwy. 42, 5 mi. S. of Jackson, Flovilla, GA 30216. Mailing Address: 678 Lake Clark Rd., Flovilla, GA 30216-2309. Tel.: 770-504-2277. Fax: 770-504-2178.
Web Site: www.georgiastateparks.org
Founded: 1825.
Congressional District: 3
Key Personnel: Mgr., Ken Lalumiere.
Personnel Profile: Full-Time Paid 6; Part-Time Paid 1; Part-Time Volunteers 2.
Governing Authority: state. Administered by Parks, Recreation & Historic Sites Div., Georgia Dept. of Natural Resources, Floyd Towers E., 205 Butler St., Atlanta, GA 30334. Tax-exempt: 170(b)(1)(A).
History Museum.
Collections: photographs of local historical hotels, Civilian Corps., Hoard Mullis Amusement Park; pictures of local Creek Indians; treaties; replica of traditional Indian apparel; pottery; items that reflect stages of Indian civilization.
Research Fields: Creek Indians in Georgia.
Facilities: cottages; group camp facilities; fishing; picnicking; camping; beach; pedal boats; fishing boats; mini-golf. Gift items for sale.
Hours & Admission Prices: Memorial Day-Labor Day Sat.-Sun. 12-4. Museum: no charge. Parking $3. ♿
Attendance: 400,000 (accurate)

Fort Gaines

SUTTONS CORNER FRONTIER STORE MUSEUM, 115 S. Washington St., Fort Gaines, GA 31751. Mailing Address: P.O. Box 787, Fort Gaines, GA 39851-0787. Tel.: 229-768-2312.
History Museum: built c.1850.
Collections: local history & culture; period artifacts; wooden cash registers; grist mill; photographs; personal artifacts.
Hours & Admission Prices: Thurs. -Sat. 10-3 by appointment. No charge; donations accepted. Closed Thanksgiving; Christmas. ♿

Fort Gordon

U.S. ARMY SIGNAL CORPS MUSEUM, 504 Chamberlain Ave., Bldg. 29807, Fort Gordon, GA 30905-5735. Tel.: 706-791-2818 & 3856. Fax: 706-791-6069.
E-mail: atzh-pom-m@gordon.army.mil
Web Site: www.gordon.army.mil/ocos/Museum/
Founded: 1965.
Congressional District: 10
Key Personnel: Dir., Robert Anzuoni.
Personnel Profile: Full-Time Paid 3.
Governing Authority: federal government; U.S. Army. Parent Institution: Center of Military History. Tax-exempt.
Military/Science & Technology Museum.
Collections: U.S. Army signal corps history; c.1860-present signal flags; weapons; equipment; communication, science & technology; Signal Corps; uniforms & swords; 10th Armored Division artifacts.
Research Fields: Signal Corps equipment.
Facilities: 10,000-vol. library pertaining to Signal Corps equipment available to the public by appointment.
Activities: guided tours; films; training programs for professional museum workers; temporary & traveling exhibitions; school loan service; science & history classes for military and K-12; living history demonstrations.

Publications: Code Talker brochure; Story of Wig-Wag brochure; Signaling Souls brochure; The Korean War Brochure; Signal Camp of Instruction; Hello Girls; V-Mail; Junior Signalier; Army Values.
Hours & Admission Prices: Tues.-Fri. 8-4, Sat. 10-4. No charge; donations accepted. Closed federal holidays. ♿
Attendance: 34,000 (accurate)

Fort McPherson

NATIONAL MUSEUM OF THE ARMY RESERVE, 1401 Deshler St., S.W., Fort McPherson, GA 30330-1040. Tel.: 404-464-8465.
Web Site: www.usar.army.mil
Founded: 1999.
Key Personnel: Dir., Dr. Lee S. Hanford, Jr.; Chief Cur., Chris Kolakowski.
Personnel Profile: Full-Time Paid 3.
Governing Authority: Parent Institution: US Army Reserve Command.
Military Museum.
Collections: U.S. military history; uniforms; weapons; photographs; personal artifacts.
Research Fields: US Army Reserve history.
Activities: Museum Sponsors: Living History - War of 1812 & Civil War.
Publications: Warrior - Citizens of America.
Hours & Admission Prices: Mon.-Fri. 7:30-5 by appointment. No charge. Closed Federal holidays. ♿

Fort Oglethorpe

CHICKAMAUGA AND CHATTANOOGA NATIONAL MILITARY PARK, 3370 LaFayette Rd., Fort Oglethorpe, GA 30742. Mailing Address: P.O. Box 2128, Fort Oglethorpe, GA 30742-0128. Tel.: 706-866-9241.
Web Site: www.nps.gov/chch
Founded: 1890.
Congressional District: 9
Personnel Profile: Full-Time Paid 24; Part-Time Paid 8; Part-Time Volunteers 40; Interns 1.
Governing Authority: federal. Parent Institution: U.S. Government Dept. of Interior. Subsidiary Institution: National Park Service. Tax-exempt.
Military Museum.
Collections: Civil War artifacts; Fuller gun collection of American military shoulder arms. Historic Houses: 1866 Cravens House; 1850s & 1860s Brotherton, Snodgrass & Kelley Cabins.
Research Fields: Civil War History.
Facilities: 2,000-vol. library of books on Civil War history available on premises by appointment; 150-seat auditorium at Chickamauga.
Activities: seasonal guided tours & living history demonstrations; lectures; films & slides.
Publications: park brochure; trail map; self-guiding tour pamphlet.
Hours & Admission Prices: Daily 8:30-5. No charge; donations accepted. Closed Christmas. ♿
Attendance: 900,000 (accurate)

6TH CAVALRY MUSEUM, #2 Barnhardt Circle, Fort Oglethorpe, GA 30742-3646. Mailing Address: P.O. Box 2011, Fort Oglethorpe, GA 30742-0011. Tel.: 706-861-2860.
E-mail: info@6thcavalrymuseum.com
Web Site: www.6thcavalrymuseum.com
Founded: 1981.
Key Personnel: Dir., Christine McKeever; Chm. (V), Kyle Russell.
Personnel Profile: Full-Time Paid 1.
Governing Authority: Tax-exempt.
Military History Museum: listed on the National Register of Historic Places.
Collections: military artifacts; uniforms; weapons; photographs; Patton Tank and Cobra Gunship Helicopter.
Facilities: 6,500 sq. ft. exhibit space.
Hours & Admission Prices: Tues.-Sat. 9-12 & 1-4. Families $10, adults $3, students & seniors $2; discounts to groups; children under 5 no charge.
Attendance: 5,000 (estimated)

Fort Stewart

FORT STEWART MUSEUM, 2022 Frank Cochran Dr., Bldg. T904, Fort Stewart, GA 31314-4936. Tel.: 912-767-7885. Fax: 912-767-2121.
E-mail: walter.meeks@stewart.army.mil
Web Site: www.stewart.army.mil/ima/sites/about/history.asp
Founded: 1977.
Congressional District: 1
Key Personnel: Cur., Walter W. Meeks, III
Personnel Profile: Full-Time Paid 2.
Governing Authority: federal. Part of Army Museum System. Parent Institution: U.S. Army Center of Military History, Attn: DAMH-MD, 1099 14th St. N.W., Washington, DC 20005-3402. Tel. 202-761-5373. Tax-exempt.
Military Museum.
Collections: focuses on the history of 3rd Infantry Division, 24th Infantry Division & Fort Stewart follows history of units & the post Word War I, World War II, Korea & Desert Storm.
Research Fields: history, lineage & honors relating to the 3rd Infantry Division, 24th Infantry Division & Fort Stewart; the history of Fort Stewart; technical data on weapons, equipment & vehicles.
Facilities: 185-vol. library of hardback books, 91 paperback manuals, photo file of several hundred pieces on the history of division & its units, post, U.S. military history, general military history, historical data on arms & equipment available for research on premises & by special arrangement; displays.
Activities: guided tours; lectures; gallery talks; permanent & temporary exhibitions; staff rides.
Publications: brochure, 3rd Division History & Fort Stewart.
Hours & Admission Prices: Tues.-Sat. 10-4. No charge. Closed federal holidays. ♿
Attendance: 45,036 (accurate)

Fort Valley

A.L. FETTERMAN EDUCATIONAL MUSEUM, Massee Lane Gardens, 100 Massee Lane, Fort Valley, GA 31030-6974. Tel.: 478-967-2358. Fax: 478-967-2083.
E-mail: crichard@americancamellias.org
Web Site: www.americancamellias.org
Founded: 1989.
Congressional District: 8
Key Personnel: Operations Mgr., Celeste Richard; Pres., Roger Vinson; Museum Shop Mgr., Lesia Dortch.
Governing Authority: society; nonprofit. Parent Institution: American Camellia Society. Tax-exempt: 501(c)(3).
Library & Porcelain Museum.
Collections: two museum buildings with rare books, original paintings, prints; porcelain sculptures from Boehm, Connoisseur, Bronn, Cybis, Royal Worchester, Dorothy Doughty, Gunther Granget, Hummel & other art objects.
Research Fields: camellia cultivars & breeding.
Facilities: 1,500-vol. library of rare & current books relating to horticulture, with emphasis on camellias; 170-seat auditorium; botanical garden; banquet facilities available. Museum-related items for sale.
Activities: guided tours; lectures; organized education programs for adults; docent program; environmental day camp for children 6-11.
Publications: quarterly magazine, The Camellia Journal; annual, The Camellia Yearbook.
Hours & Admission Prices: Tues.-Sat. 10-4:30, Sun. 1-4:30. Adults $5, seniors 65 & over $4; ACS members & children under 12 no charge. Closed national holidays. ♿
Attendance: 22,500 (estimated)
Membership: Single $25; Joint or Family $27.50; Sustaining $50; Patron $125; Single Life $500; Joint Life $550.

MASSEE LANE GARDENS, HOME OF AMERICAN CAMELLIA SOCIETY, 100 Massee Lane, Fort Valley, GA 31030-6974. Tel.: 478-967-2358. Fax: 478-967-2083.
E-mail: crichard@camellias-acs.com
Web Site: www.camellias-acs.com
Founded: 1945.
Congressional District: 8
Key Personnel: Pres., Judge Roger Vinson; Operations Mgr., Celeste Richard; Museum Shop Mgr., Leisa Dortch.
Personnel Profile: Full-Time Paid 5; Part-Time Paid 1; Part-Time Volunteers 12.
Governing Authority: society; nonprofit organization. Parent Institution: American Camellia Society. Branch Museums: A. L. Fetterman Educational Museum; Stevens-Taylor Gallery. Tax-exempt: 501(c)(3).
Horticultural Society.
Collections: rare books; original paintings & prints; Boehm porcelains; Boehm; Connoisseur; Cybis; Bronn; Royal Copenhagen; Hummel; gardens; S.E. United States camellias & plants; porcelains.
Research Fields: horticulture.
Facilities: 5,000-vol. library of books on horticulture available for research on site; botanical garden; greenhouse; rose garden; Japanese garden; reading room; environmental garden. Museum-related items for sale.
Activities: lectures; gallery talks; workshops.
Publications: quarterly magazine, The Camellia Journal; book, The American Camellia Yearbook.
Hours & Admission Prices: Tues.-Sat. 10-4:30, Sun. 1-4:30. Adults $5; discounts to senior citizens, groups, AAA, AAM & ICOM members; children under 12 & members no charge. ♿
Attendance: 35,000 (estimated)

Membership: Single $25; Joint $27.50; Patron $100; Life-Single $500; Life-Double $550.

Gainesville

BRENAU UNIVERSITY GALLERIES, BRENAU UNIVERSITY, 500 Washington St., S.E., Gainesville, GA 30501-3697. Tel.: 770-534-6263 (gallery). Fax: 770-538-4599.
E-mail: gallery@brenau.edu
Web Site: www.brenau.edu
Founded: 1985.
Congressional District: 9
Key Personnel: Dir. & Cur., Vanessa Grubbs; University Pres., Ed Schrader; Dir. Art & Design Dept., Mary Beth Looney.
Personnel Profile: Full-Time Paid 2; Part-Time Paid 6; Part-Time Volunteers 9; Interns 1.
Governing Authority: private university; nonprofit. Parent Institution: Brenau University. Tax-exempt: 501(c)(3).
University Art Gallery: three gallery spaces, 2 housed in adjacent buildings, one is in the main floor of the Simmons Visual Arts Center, a recently renovated 1914 structure; the other gallery space is outside the balcony area of Brenau's c.1880s restored Pearce Auditorium. The third is in the new John S. Burd Center for the Performing Arts.
Collections: American artists, particularly women, pop artists & historical styles; paintings; drawings; prints; sculpture; photos; craft works: glass, metals, clay & fiber.
Major Exhibits: Elegance & Strength: Coture Designs by Yuki Yao, 11/17/09-1/17/10; The History & Techniques of Printmaking, 2/2/10-3/21/10; Collected Impressions: Print Selections from the Brenau University Permanent Art Collection, 2/2/10-3/21/10; Melissa Harshman, 2/2/10-3/21/10; The 2010 Brenau Collaborative, 4/13/10-4/23/10.
Research Fields: pop art movement of the 1960s; women's art; 18th-19th century American/European painting.
Facilities: Simmons Visual Arts Center; the Presidents Gallery; the Leo Castelli Art Gallery; 700-seat auditorium; 300-seat theatre; studios; lecture & recital halls. Museum-related items for sale.
Activities: docent program; formal education programs; interdisciplinary events; workshops; guided tours; lectures; loan, participatory, temporary & traveling exhibitions; training program for professional museum workers through the Arts Management degree program. University Fine Arts & Humanities Department Sponsors: Firespark, a summer program in the arts for high school students.
Publications: exhibition catalogues & brochures.
Hours & Admission Prices: Simmons Visual Arts Center & President's Gallery: Tues.-Fri. 10-4, Sun. 2-5. Leo Costell Art Gallery: Tues.-Fri. 1-4. No charge; donations accepted. Closed Easter; spring break (early March); Memorial Day; Independence Day; Labor Day; Thanksgiving week; Christmas break. ♿
Attendance: 26,000 (estimated)
Membership: Individual $25; Family $50; Patron $100; Sponsor $250; Benefactor $500; Director's Circle $1,000; Corporate $5,000.

ELACHEE NATURE SCIENCE CENTER, 2125 Elachee Dr., Gainesville, GA 30504-7158. Tel.: 770-535-1976. Fax: 770-535-2302.
E-mail: elachee@elachee.org
Web Site: www.elachee.org
Founded: 1976.
Congressional District: 9
Key Personnel: Pres. & C.E.O., Andrea Timpone; Pres., R.K. Whitehead; Education, Peter Gordon; Devel. & Public Rels., Lavon Callahan; Museum Shop Mgr., Judy Stock.
Personnel Profile: Full-Time Paid 8; Part-Time Paid 25; Part-Time Volunteers 120.
Governing Authority: private; nonprofit organization. Tax-exempt: 501(c)(3).
Nature Science Center.
Collections: native amphibians; reptiles.
Research Fields: archaeology; water quality; plant & animal biodiversity inventory.
Facilities: museum center; hiking trails; picnic area. Gift items for sale.
Activities: Southern Association of Colleges and Schools (SACS) accredited education programs for children; public programs; summer & school-break camps.
Hours & Admission Prices: Mon.-Sat. 10-5. Adults $5, children $3; discounts to ANCA members; members & children under 2 no charge. Closed New Year's Day; Thanksgiving; Christmas. ♿
Attendance: 70,000 (estimated)
Membership: Individual $30; Family $45; Friend $100; Donor $250; Patron $500; Grand Patron $1,000.

NORTHEAST GEORGIA HISTORY CENTER AT BRENAU UNIVERSITY, 322 Academy St., N.E., Gainesville, GA 30501. Mailing Address: P.O. Box 1451, Gainesville, GA 30503-1451. Tel.: 770-297-5900. Fax: 770-297-5933.
Web Site: www.negahc.org
Formerly: Georgia Mountains History Museum at Brenau University
Founded: 1981.
Congressional District: 9
Key Personnel: C.E.O., Glen Kyle; Pres. (V), Dr. Patricia Burd.
Personnel Profile: Full-Time Paid 2; Part-Time Paid 1; Part-Time Volunteers 100; Interns 2.
Governing Authority: private; nonprofit organization. Branch Museums: Chief White Path, Gainesville, GA. Tax-exempt: 501(c)(3).
History Museum.
Collections: textile; poultry; medical; African-American; Indian; firefighting tools & equipment; 19th-century American arts & crafts; Gen. James Longstreet memorabilia; Ed Dodd & Mark Trail exhibit.
Facilities: library; 8,000 sq. ft. exhibit space; American Freedom Garden. Gift items for sale.
Activities: docent program; guided tours; traveling exhibitions. Annual Events: Taste of History luncheon; Spring Estate sale.
Publications: monthly newsletter.
Hours & Admission Prices: Tues.-Sat. 10-4. Adults $5, senior citizens, students & children $3; discounts to AAA members; members no charge. Closed New Year's Day; Independence Day; Christmas. ♿
Attendance: 6,000 (accurate)
Membership: Student $15; Individual $35; Family $70; Sponsor $100; Contributor $250; Curator $500; Friend $1,000. Partnership Levels: $1,500; $2,500; $5,000.

QUINLAN VISUAL ARTS CENTER, 514 Green St., N.E., Gainesville, GA 30501-3314. Tel.: 770-536-2575.
E-mail: info@quinlanartscenter.org
Web Site: www.quinlanartscenter.org
Founded: 1946.
Congressional District: 10
Key Personnel: Asst. Dir., Amanda Kroll; Asst. to Dir., Paula E. Lindner
Arts Center.
Collections: paintings; sculpture.
Facilities: classrooms; galleries. Museum-related items for sale.
Activities: educational programs; summer art camps; workshops.
Publications: quarterly class schedule, newsletter, workshop brochure.
Hours & Admission Prices: Mon.-Fri. 9-5, Sat. 10-4. No charge; donations accepted. Closed Memorial Day; Independence Day; Labor Day; Thanksgiving; Christmas. ♿
Attendance: 9,000 (estimated)
Membership: Senior Citizen, Student, Teacher & Artist $45; Individual $50; Family $90; Contributing Patron $150; Donor Patron $300; Sustaining Patron $500; Medallion Associate $1,000; Medallion Patron $2,500; Medallion Benefactor $5,000.

Glennville

TATTNALL MUSEUM, 211 S. Tillman St., Glennville, GA 30427-1737. Mailing Address: P.O. Box 607, Glennville, CA 30427-0607. Tel.: 912-654-5276. Fax: 912-538-3156.
Key Personnel: Museum Bd. Chm., Daine Bazemore.
Governing Authority: Parent Institution: city of Glennville.
Art, Science & History Museum.
Collections: art; science; local history.
Hours & Admission Prices: Mon.-Thurs. 8am-9pm. Closed national holidays.

Hawkinsville

HAWKINSVILLE/PULASKI COUNTY ARTS COUNCIL, 100 Lumpkin St., Hawkinsville, GA 31036-1518. Tel.: 912-783-1884. Fax: 912-783-2333.
E-mail: ArtsCouncil@cstel.net
Web Site: www.hawkinsvilleoperahouse.com
Key Personnel: Office Mgr., Julianna Stewart
Art Gallery.
Collections: works by Georgia artists.
Activities: cultural & educational activities; tours.
Hours & Admission Prices: Tours: Mon.-Fri. 10-4.

Hiawassee

BRASSTOWN BALD VISITOR CENTER, 2941 State Hwy. 180, Hiawassee, GA 30546. Mailing Address: P.O. Box 9, Blairsville, GA 30514-0009. Tel.: 706-745-6928 & 896-2556. Fax: 706-745-7494.
Web Site: www.fs.fed.us/conf

Founded: 1967.
Congressional District: 9
Key Personnel: Resource Asst., Alison Koopman.
Personnel Profile: Part-Time Paid 4; Part-Time Volunteers 4.
Governing Authority: federal. U.S. Dept. of Agriculture Forest Service, Southern Region.
Park Museum: located within the Chattahoochee National Forest.
Collections: natural history; exhibits pertaining to Man & the Mountain.
Facilities: rooftop observation deck; mountaintop theater; hiking trails; picnic area. Museum-related items for sale.
Activities: video programs.
Publications: brochure.
Hours & Admission Prices: mid-April to May Sat.-Sun. 10-5; Memorial Day to Veterans Day daily 10-5. Parking Fee: bus $30, van $10, car $3. Center: No charge; donations accepted. ♿
Attendance: 75,000 (estimated)

Jefferson

CRAWFORD W. LONG MUSEUM, 28 College St., Jefferson, GA 30549-1036. Tel.: 706-367-5307.
E-mail: info@crawfordlong.org
Web Site: www.crawfordlong.org
Founded: 1957.
Congressional District: 9
Key Personnel: Administrative Mgr., Vicki Starnes; Consultant, Lesa Campbell.
Personnel Profile: Part-Time Paid 2; Part-Time Volunteers 5.
Governing Authority: municipal; City of Jefferson, GA.
Medical Museum, History Museum & Historic Building & Site.
Collections: 19th-century medical artifacts; personal effects of Dr. C.W. Long; history of the discovery & development of anesthesia; documents; photographs; 1840s doctor's office & apothecary shop; 19th-century general store.
Research Fields: Dr. C.W. Long; history of anesthesia; medicine; local history.
Facilities: three climate-controlled buildings.
Activities: guided tours; temporary exhibits; lectures; workshops.
Hours & Admission Prices: Tues.-Sat. 10-5. Adults $5, children 4-12 $3; children 3 & under no charge. Closed New Year's Day; Martin Luther King, Jr. Day; Memorial Day; Independence Day; Labor Day; Thanksgiving; Christmas. ♿
Attendance: 1,032 (accurate)
Membership: Student $20; Individual $25; Family $35; Corporate $100; Patron $200; Benefactor $1000 & up.

Jekyll Island

THE GEORGIA SEA TURTLE CENTER, 214 Stable Rd., Jekyll Island, GA 31527-0844. Tel.: 912-635-4444.
E-mail: georgiaseaturtlecenter@jekyllisland.com
Web Site: www.georgiaseaturtlecenter.org
Key Personnel: Dir. & Veterinarian, Terry Norton; Marine Field Programs Coord., Stefanie Ouellette; Education Coord., Alicia Marin; Educator, Kelly O'Keefe; Educator, Sarah Eckert
Marine Museum.
Collections: exhibits on sea turtle conservation & rehabilitation.
Hours & Admission Prices: March Tues.-Sat. 10-6; April-Nov. Mon. 10-2, Tues.-Sun. 9-5; Dec.-Feb. Tues.-Sun. 9-5. Adults 13 & over $6, senior citizens 65 & over $5, children 4-12 $4; children 3 & under no charge. Closed New Year's Day; Christmas Eve & Day.

JEKYLL ISLAND MUSEUM, 100 Stable Rd., Jekyll Island, GA 31527-0870. Mailing Address: 381 Riverview Dr., Jekyll Island, GA 31527-0874. Tel.: 912-635-4036. Fax: 912-635-4420.
E-mail: jhunter@jekyllisland.com
Web Site: www.jekyllisland.com
Founded: 1954.
Congressional District: 1
Key Personnel: Dir., John S. Hunter; Cur., Gretchen Greminger; Programming, Andrea Marroquin; Tours, Shirley Martin.
Personnel Profile: Full-Time Paid 16; Part-Time Paid 10; Part-Time Volunteers 40; Interns 7.
Governing Authority: State Park Authority; Jekyll Island Authority. Subsidiary Institution: Jekyll Island Museum Associates. Tax-exempt.
Historic Site & Preservation Project.
Collections: furnishings; documents; photographs; clothing & memorabilia; Tiffany stained-glass window. Historic Houses: 1896 Moss Cottage, former Struthers-Macy home; 1907 Goodyear Cottage, former F. H. Goodyear home: 1897 Club House; 1917 Crane Cottage, former R.T. Crane, Jr. home; 1891 Hollybourne Cottage, former C.S. Maurice home; 1927 Villa Ospo, former W. Jennings home; 1904 Cherokee Cottage, former Shrady-James home; 1900 Mistletoe Cottage, former Porter-Claflin home; 1904 Faith Chapel; 1900 service facilities including Club Dock; 1930 Club indoor Tennis court; 1890 infirmary; Baker Crane Stable; boat engineer's house & servant quarters; 1742 tabby ruins of Major Horton House; 1884 DuBignon Cottage; 1898 Visitor Center, former Jekyll Island Club Stables; 1892 Indian Mound, former McKay-W. Rockefeller home; 1928 Villa Marianna, former F. M. Gould home.
Research Fields: The Jekyll Club era, 1886-1942; Colonial Georgia, 1500-1776; decorative art; natural history, barrier island.
Facilities: 120-seat theater; document & photograph archives. Museum-related books & gifts for sale.
Activities: formally organized educational programs; volunteer program; permanent & temporary exhibits; internships; guided tours.
Publications: The Jekyll Island Club Historic District, 100 Years; Jekyll Island Club Historic District Walking Tour.
Hours & Admission Prices: Daily 9-5. Passport to the Century Tour: two period furniture restored cottages. Adults $10, students 6-18 $6; children under 6 no charge. Call for tour hours. Closed New Year's Day; Christmas. ♿
Attendance: 37,246 (accurate)
Membership: Friends of Historic Jekyll Island, Inc: Individual $25; Family $50; Preservation Partner $100; Business & Sponsor $250; Patron $500; Benefactor $1,000.

Johns Creek

AUTREY MILL NATURE PRESERVE & HERITAGE CENTER, 9770 Autrey Mill Rd., Johns Creek, GA 30022-7168. Tel.: 678-366-3511. Fax: 678-366-3512.
E-mail: autreymill@bellsouth.net
Web Site: autreymill.org
Key Personnel: Dir., Ben Team
Nature Preserve.
Collections: local history & culture; period artifacts; live amphibians, reptiles & insects; farming equipment; chapel. Historic Buildings: Summerour House, c.1880; Old Warsaw Church, c.1860; Green Country Store; 1800s Tenant Farmhouse; 1942 Program Barn; 1860s tenant house.
Hours & Admission Prices: Park: daily 8am to dusk. Visitor Center: Mon.-Sat. 10-4.

Jonesboro

ROAD TO TARA MUSEUM, 104 N. Main St., Jonesboro, GA 30236-8315. Tel.: 770-478-4800; 800-662-7829.
Web Site: visitscarlett.com/roadtotaramuseum.html
History Museum: housed in 1867 Historic Train Depot.
Collections: Civil War & Gone with the Wind memorabilia.
Hours & Admission Prices: Mon.-Fri. 8:30-5:30, Sat. 10-4. Adults $7, senior citizens & children $6.

STATELY OAKS PLANTATION, 100 Carriage Lane, Jonesboro, GA 30237. Mailing Address: P.O. Box 922, Jonesboro, GA 30237-0922. Tel.: 770-473-0197; 866-793-1839. Fax: 770-473-9855.
E-mail: statelyoaks@historicaljonesboro.org
Web Site: historicaljonesboro.org
Historic House.
Collections: period artifacts & memorabilia.
Hours & Admission Prices: Mon.-Sat. 10-4. Adults $12, senior citizens 55 & over and military with ID $9, children under 11 & retired military $6.

Juliette

JARRELL PLANTATION GEORGIA STATE HISTORIC SITE, 711 Jarrell Plantation Rd., Juliette, GA 31046-2525. Tel.: 478-986-5172. Fax: 478-986-5919.
E-mail: jarrell_plantation_park@dnr.state.ga.us
Web Site: gastateparks.org/info/jarrell
Founded: 1974.
Congressional District: 8
Key Personnel: Mgr., Marty Fleming; Interpretive Ranger, Bretta Perkins.
Personnel Profile: Full-Time Paid 4; Part-Time Paid 3; Part-Time Volunteers 60.
Governing Authority: state. Parent Institution: Georgia Dept. of Natural Resources, 2 Martin Luther King, Jr. Dr., S.E., Ste. 1352, Atlanta, GA 30334.
Living Farm Historic Site.
Collections: tools; furnishings; clothing; implements; grist mill; cotton gin; planing mill; boiler & steam engines; syrup evaporators; cane mill; saw mill; blacksmith forge.
Research Fields: Georgia agriculture & farm life, 1840-1960.

Facilities: visitor center; barns; outbuildings; two dwellings. Publications & brochures for sale.
Activities: guided house tours; weekend folklife demonstrations; seasonal special events.
Hours & Admission Prices: Thurs.-Sat. 9-5. Admission: $3.50-$5; discount to groups of 15 or more with reservation; children under 6 no charge. Closed New Year's Day; Thanksgiving; Christmas; Open on federal holidays that fall on a Mon. ♿
Attendance: 12,000 (estimated)
Membership: Friends of Jarrell Plantation $25 & up.

Kennesaw

KENNESAW MOUNTAIN NATIONAL BATTLEFIELD PARK, 900 Kennesaw Mountain Dr., Kennesaw, GA 30152-4854. Tel.: 770-427-4686.
Web Site: www.nps.gov/kemo
Founded: 1917.
Congressional District: 6 & 7
Key Personnel: Park Supt., Dr. Stanley Bond; Chief Interpreter & Resource Mgr., Lloyd Morris; Cur., Retha Stephens; Historian, W.R. Johnson; Museum Shop Mgr., Mike Stoudemire.
Governing Authority: federal. Affiliated with National Park Service, U.S. Dept. of Interior. Tax-exempt.
Civil War History Museum: located on the site of a Civil War battlefield.
Collections: dress & weapons of Civil War soldiers. Historic House: 1836 Kolb Farm.
Research Fields: Atlanta Campaign of 1864.
Facilities: 1,200-vol. non-circulating library of Civil War books, papers & diaries available on premises; 98-seat auditorium; trails.
Activities: self-guided tours; auto tour; hiking tour; audiovisual program; Civil War soldier living history demonstrations June-Aug.
Publications: park mini-folder.
Hours & Admission Prices: Visitor Center: Daylight Savings: Mon.-Fri. 8:30-5, Sat.-Sun. 8:30-6; Oct.-April daily 8:30-5. Closed New Year's Day; Thanksgiving; Christmas. ♿

KENNESAW STATE UNIVERSITY ART MUSEUM & GALLERIES, (M), 1000 Chastain Rd., #2901, Kennesaw, GA 30144-5591. Tel.: 770-499-3223. Fax: 770-499-3345.
Web Site: www.kennesaw.edu/visual_arts/ksugalleries
Formerly: Sturgis Library Art Gallery at Kennesaw State University Fine Arts Gallery
Congressional District: 11
Key Personnel: Dir. & Cur., Will Hipps.
Personnel Profile: Full-Time Paid 2.
Governing Authority: Parent Institution: Kennesaw State University. Tax-exempt.
Art Gallery.
Collections: contemporary & traditional works of art.
Activities: demonstrations; lectures; permanent & temporary exhibitions.
Hours & Admission Prices: The Art Gallery, Sturgis Library: Mon.-Tues. 11-3, Wed.-Thurs. 11-3 & 7-9, Sat. 1-4. Fine Arts Gallery, Wilson Bldg.: Mon.-Tues. 11-3, Wed.-Thurs. 11-3 & 7-9. Don Russell Clayton Gallery: May-July by appointment; Aug.-April Mon.-Thurs. 12-4. Closed university & public holidays. ♿

THE SOUTHERN MUSEUM OF CIVIL WAR AND LOCOMOTIVE HISTORY, (M), 2829 Cherokee St., Kennesaw, GA 30144-2823. Tel.: 770-427-2117. Fax: 770-421-8485.
E-mail: hharris@kennesaw.ga.us
Web Site: www.southernmuseum.org
Formerly: Kennesaw Civil War Museum
Founded: 1972.
Congressional District: 16
Key Personnel: C.E.O., Dr. Jeffery Drobney; Cur., George Deeming; Archivist, Sallie Loy; Dir. Education, Jennifer Legates; Asst. Cur., Michael Bearrow; Museum Shop Mgr., Jane Pies.
Personnel Profile: Full-Time Paid 8; Part-Time Paid 8; Part-Time Volunteers 10.
Governing Authority: municipal. Parent Institution: Smithsonian Institution. Tax-exempt.
Civil War & Train Museum: located on the site where the Great Locomotive chase began.
Collections: Civil War memorabilia; history of Georgia railroads; graphic presentation of the Andrews Raid; locomotive history; replica of a 1910 locomotive manufacturing facility which is belt driven with all machinery, production line, pattern shop, offices, forge & laboratories; 2 locomotives on assembly line. Historic Structure: c.1875 railroad depot.
Facilities: library; archives; theater. Museum-related items for sale.
Activities: guided tours; lectures; films.
Publications: brochures; quarterly newsletter.
Hours & Admission Prices: Mon.-Sat. 9:30-5. Adults $7.50, senior citizens $6.50, children 4-12 $5.50; members & children under 3 no charge. ♿
Attendance: 60,000 (accurate)
Membership: Individual $50; Family Plus Smithsonian $75; Sustaining $150; Patron $250; Sponsor $500; Benefactor $1,000.

Kingston

KINGSTON WOMAN'S HISTORY CLUB MUSEUM, 13 E. Main St., N.W., Kingston, GA 30145-2307. Mailing Address: P.O. Box 261, Kingston, GA 30145-0261. Tel.: 770-546-3116.
Governing Authority: private; nonprofit corporation. Tax-exempt: 501(c)(3).
History Museum.
Collections: local history & culture; scrapbooks; photographs.
Major Exhibits: Women of the KWHC, Inc., 1/24/10-12/10.
Hours & Admission Prices: Sat.-Sun. 1-4; other times by appointment. No charge; donations accepted.
Membership: Associate $15; Active $25.

LaFayette

THE MARSH HOUSE, (M), 308 N. Main St., LaFayette, GA 30728-2422. Mailing Address: P.O. Box 722, LaFayette, GA 30728-0722. Tel.: 706-638-5187.
Founded: 2002.
Congressional District: 9
Key Personnel: Pres., Evelle Dana; Recording Sec., Dr. David P. Boyle; House Mgr., Marjorie Craig; Events Coord., Mary Smitherman; Docent Training, Jennie Chandler.
Personnel Profile: Part-Time Paid 1.
Governing Authority: Parent Institution: Walker County Historical Society. Tax-exempt.
Historic House: built in 1836.
Collections: local history & culture; period artifacts; furnishings.
Publications: quarterly, Walker County Historical Society.
Hours & Admission Prices: Tours by appointment. Adults $3; members no charge. ♿
Attendance: 500 (estimated)
Membership: General $10.

LaGrange

HILLS AND DALES ESTATE, 1916 Hills and Dales Dr., LaGrange, GA 30240-2958. Mailing Address: P.O. Box 790, LaGrange, GA 30241-0014. Tel.: 706-882-3242. Fax: 706-882-3464.
E-mail: cwood@hillsanddales.org
Web Site: www.hillsanddales.org
Founded: 1998.
Congressional District: 7
Key Personnel: Exec. Dir., Carleton Wood; Pres. Foundation, H. Speer Burdette, III; Treas. Foundation, Esther S. Rainey; Museum Shop Mgr., Carrie Mills.
Personnel Profile: Full-Time Paid 12; Part-Time Paid 9; Part-Time Volunteers 1.
Governing Authority: private; nonprofit organization. Parent Institution: Fuller E. Callaway Foundation. Tax-exempt: 501(c)(3).
Historic House Museum: housed in the former home of textile magnate Fuller E. Callaway Sr. and his family.
Collections: decorative arts & artifacts related to the Fuller E. Callaway family; Ferrell Gardens including boxwood plantings, fountains, herb garden & greenhouse.
Research Fields: history of Hills and Dales Estate and Ferrell Gardens.
Facilities: 35-acre estate; 1,500 sq. ft. exhibit space; theater; gardens. Museum-related items for sale.
Activities: formal education programs; guided tours.
Publications: biannual newsletter.
Hours & Admission Prices: Tues.-Sun. by appointment. Adults $10, students $6. Closed New Year's Day; Easter; Independence Day; Thanksgiving; Christmas Eve & Day. ♿
Attendance: 8,000 (accurate)
Membership: Individual $28; Family $40.

LAGRANGE ART MUSEUM, 112 Lafayette Pkwy., LaGrange, GA 30240-3209. Tel.: 706-882-3267. Fax: 706-882-2878.
E-mail: cvam@charter.net
Web Site: www.lagrangeartmuseum.org
Formerly: Chattahoochee Valley Art Museum
Founded: 1963.
Congressional District: 3
Key Personnel: Exec. Dir., Judy Freeman; Pres., Rick Waterhouse.

Personnel Profile: Full-Time Paid 2; Part-Time Paid 3; Part-Time Volunteers 3; Interns 1.
Governing Authority: nonprofit organization. Tax-exempt: 501(c)(3).
Art Museum: housed in 1892 Victorian structure, originally a county jail.
Collections: contemporary American works of art.
Research Fields: art history.
Facilities: classrooms; art resource center.
Activities: guided tours; lectures; gallery talks; workshops; formally organized education programs; temporary exhibitions. Museum Sponsors: annual Kaleidoscope-A Fair on the Square, art festival; LaGrange National; Biennial Competition.
Publications: Artsplace, quarterly schedule of classes & activity; newsletter; exhibition catalogues.
Hours & Admission Prices: Tues.-Fri. 9-5, Sat. 11-5, Mon. by appointment. No charge; donations accepted. Closed New Year's Day; Memorial Day; Independence Day; Thanksgiving; Christmas. ♿
Attendance: 20,077 (accurate)
Membership: Artist $25; Art Angel $35; Individual $40; Family $60; Friend $150; Patron $250; Silver Society $500; Gold $1,000; Platinum $2,500; Corporate $3,000.

LAMAR DODD ART CENTER, LAGRANGE COLLEGE, 302 Forrest Ave., LaGrange, GA 30240. Mailing Address: 601 Broad St., LaGrange, GA 30240-2955. Tel.: 706-880-8211. Fax: 706-880-8007.
E-mail: dmarrin@lagrange.edu
Web Site: lagrange.edu/academics/art/lamar.dodd.htm
Founded: 1982.
Congressional District: 3
Key Personnel: Dir., John Lawrence; College Comptroller, Marty Pirrman.
Personnel Profile: Full-Time Paid 5.
Governing Authority: private college; nonprofit. Parent Institution: LaGrange College. Tax-exempt: 501(c)(3).
College Art Museum.
Collections: Southwestern American Indian; Lamar Dodd paintings & drawings; 20th-century photography; Christ-Janer prints.
Activities: guided tours; LaGrange National juried art competition.
Publications: exhibition catalogues.
Hours & Admission Prices: Jan.-May & Sept.-Nov. Mon.-Fri. 8:30-4:30. No charge. ♿
Attendance: 20,000 (estimated)

LEGACY MUSEUM ON MAIN: A HISTORY MUSEUM FOR WEST GEORGIA, (M), 136 Main St., LaGrange, GA 30240-3218. Mailing Address: P.O. Box 1051, LaGrange, GA 30241-0019. Tel.: 706-884-1828. Fax: 706-884-1840.
E-mail: info@trouparchives.org
Web Site: www.trouparchives.org
Founded: 2008.
Congressional District: 8
Key Personnel: Exec. Dir., Kaye L. Minchew; Education, Barry Jackson; Historian, F.C. Johnson, III; Cur., Laurie Sedicino.
Personnel Profile: Full-Time Paid 2; Part-Time Paid 4; Part-Time Volunteers 4; Interns 1.
Governing Authority: private; nonprofit organization. Parent Institution: Troup County Historical Society. Subsidiary Institution: Troup County Archives. Tax-exempt: 501(c)(3).
History Museum.
Collections: concentration on West Georgia & East Alabama history from prehistoric to modern times including Creek Indians; early settlers; first railroads; founding of educational institutions.
Facilities: library; educational facilities. Museum-related items for sale.
Activities: guided tours; lectures; temporary exhibitions.
Publications: quarterly newsletter, Troup County Historical Society & Archives.
Hours & Admission Prices: Call for hours. ♿

Lawrenceville

GWINNETT HISTORICAL SOCIETY, 185 Crogan St., Lawrenceville, GA 30045-4941. Mailing Address: P.O. Box 261, Lawrenceville, GA 30046-0261. Tel.: 770-822-5174. Fax: 770-237-5616.
E-mail: ghs@gwinnetths.org
Web Site: www.gwinnetths.org
Founded: 1966.
Congressional District: 9
Key Personnel: Pres. (V) & C.E.O., Spencer Roberts; Vice Pres., Steven P. Starling; Trustee, J.W. Baughman; Librarian, Harriett Nicholls; Corresponding Sec., Paula Wall McGee; Recording Sec., Louise Wallace.
Personnel Profile: Full-Time Volunteers 18; Part-Time Volunteers 30.
Governing Authority: society, nonprofit organization. Tax-exempt.
Historical Society Museum.
Collections: photographs; farm tools; county newspapers 1872-1964; 1853 U.S. Navy sword & scabbard; family history files; cemetery card file; 120-vol. official records of the War of the Rebellion; manuscript collections; photo albums; documents; Civil War letters.
Research Fields: genealogy; local history; historic preservation.
Facilities: 1,000-vol. library pertaining to local history, genealogy & court records available for research on premises only; reading room; slide show Vanishing Gwinnett available for rent to schools & civic clubs. Museum-related items for sale.
Activities: lectures; changing monthly displays; formally organized education tours. Museum Sponsors: Winn Festival held at Elisha Winn House to raise funds for restoration of house.
Publications: quarterly publication, Gwinnett Historical Society Quarterly; The Heritage; books on local history.
Hours & Admission Prices: Mon.- Fri. 10-2. No charge; donations accepted. ♿
Attendance: 1,600 (estimated)
Membership: Student $10; Regular $25; Family $35; Lifetime $300.

GWINNETT HISTORY MUSEUM, (M), Lawrenceville Female Seminary Bldg., 455 S. Perry St., S.W., Lawrenceville, GA 30045-4836. Tel.: 770-822-5178. Fax: 770-237-5612.
E-mail: gwinnetthistorymuseum@gwinnettcounty.com
Founded: 1974.
Congressional District: 4
Key Personnel: Dir., Jennifer Collins; Outreach Coord., Kim Elmore; Outreach Coord., Jillian Waters Griffin.
Personnel Profile: Full-Time Paid 1; Part-Time Paid 2.
Governing Authority: county; nonprofit. Parent Institution: Gwinnett County. Gwinnett County Community Svcs., Parks & Recreation Dept. Tax-exempt.
History Museum: housed on the second floor of the c.1854 Lawrenceville Female Seminary, an all-girls school. Listed on the National Register of Historic Places.
Collections: artifacts related to the history of Gwinnett County & its people; exhibits include Farmlife, Textiles, Old School Days, Wartime Gwinnett, Shape-Note Singing and Old-Time Music.
Research Fields: shape-note singing; old time music; family history; Gwinnett County, GA.
Facilities: library; 1,090 sq. ft. exhibit space. Books of local historical interest, notecards, 19th-century toys, games, Civil War posters, coloring books & museum-related items for sale.
Activities: formal education programs; guided tours; hobby workshops; lectures; outreach programs to local schools. Annual Event: folk music festival. Museum Sponsors: three monthly organizational meeting; coffeehouse nights monthly.
Publications: quarterly newsletter, The Gwinnett Muse; monthly coffeehouse newsletter, Java Jottings.
Hours & Admission Prices: Mon.-Thurs. 10-4, Sat. by appointment. Adults $1; discounts to AAM members; members no charge. Closed New Year's Day; Memorial Day; Independence Day; Labor Day; Christmas; federal holidays.
Attendance: 12,000 (estimated)
Membership: Senior & Student $8; Individual $15; Nonprofit Organization $20 & up; Family $25; Pioneer Circle $100; Female Seminary Circle $200; Button Gwinnett Circle $500; Corporate Sponsor $1,000 & up.

Leslie

GEORGIA RURAL TELEPHONE MUSEUM, 135 Bailey Ave., Leslie, GA 31764-2601. Mailing Address: P.O. Box 187, Leslie, GA 31764-0187. Tel.: 229-874-4786.
Key Personnel: C.E.O., Tommy C. Smith.
Governing Authority: nonprofit organization.
Telephone Museum: housed in renovated 1920s cotton warehouse.
Collections: history of communications; 1876 to 21st century telephones; telephone memorabilia.
Hours & Admission Prices: Mon.-Fri. 9-12 & 1-3:30. Adults $5, seniors $4, children $2; discounts to groups. Closed Memorial Day; Independence Day; Labor Day; Thanksgiving & day after; Christmas Eve & Day.

Lincolnton

ELIJAH CLARK MEMORIAL MUSEUM, 2959 McCormick Hwy., Lincolnton, GA 30817-3909. Tel.: 706-359-3458. Fax: 706-359-5856.
E-mail: eclark@g-net.net
Web Site: gastateparks.org/info/elijah
Founded: 1961.
Congressional District: 10
Key Personnel: Dir., Nelson S. Noble.
Governing Authority: state. Administered by Parks, Recreation & Historic Sites Div., Georgia Dept. of Natural Resources, Floyd Towers E. 205 Butler St. S.E., Atlanta, GA 30334. Tax-exempt.
State Park Museum: housed in replica of the house of Elijah Clark.

Collections: archives; uniforms; history artifacts of 1770s; reconstructed log house & outbuildings.
Research Fields: colonial weaponry & life styles.
Activities: guided tours.
Hours & Admission Prices: April-Nov. 1 Sat.-Sun. 9-5; other times by appointment. No charge.

Lithia Springs

SWEETWATER CREEK STATE PARK, 1750 Mount Vernon Rd., Lithia Springs, GA 30122-3501. Mailing Address: P.O. Box 816, Lithia Springs, GA 30122-0816. Tel.: 770-732-5871. Fax: 770-732-5874.
E-mail: info@friendsofsweetwatercreek.org
Web Site: gastateparks.org
Founded: 1972.
Congressional District: 6
Key Personnel: Park Mgr., Phil Delestrez.
Personnel Profile: Full-Time Paid 9; Part-Time Paid 2.
Governing Authority: state. Administered by the Parks, Recreation & Historic Sites Div., Georgia Dept. of Natural Resources, 270 Washington St. S.W., Atlanta, GA 30334. Tax-exempt.
State Park: located at the site of the ruins of an 1842 textile mill burned in Gen. Sherman's Atlanta Campaign.
Collections: local & natural history; wildlife; historic building.
Facilities: nature trails.
Activities: self-guided & guided tours; permanent exhibits; boating; canoeing; hiking; picnicking.
Publications: brochure.
Hours & Admission Prices: Daily 7am-10pm. No charge. Parking: $5; Wed. no charge. ♿
Attendance: 600,000 (estimated)

Lumpkin

BEDINGFIELD INN MUSEUM, Cotton St. on the Square, Lumpkin, GA 31815. Mailing Address: P.O. Box 818, Lumpkin, GA 31815-0818. Tel.: 229-838-6419. Fax: 229-838-6134.
Web Site: www.bedingfieldinn.org
Founded: 1965.
Congressional District: 2
Key Personnel: Pres., Rhoda Averett; Vice Pres., Joanne Bowles; Treas., Frank Heard.
Personnel Profile: Full-Time Volunteers 20; Part-Time Volunteers 20.
Governing Authority: nonprofit organization. Parent Institution: Stewart County Historical Commission. Tax-exempt: 501(c)(3).
Historic Building Museum: 1836 Stagecoach Inn.
Collections: decorative arts.
Facilities: Books for sale.
Activities: guided tours; permanent exhibitions. Museum Sponsors: Candlelight Tour; Fair on the Square in October.
Publications: books, The Bedingfield Inn Cookbook; Inventory of Early Stewart County Furniture.
Hours & Admission Prices: By appointment. Adult $5, children $2; members no charge.
Attendance: 500 (estimated)
Membership: Individual $25; Family $48; Business $100.

HISTORIC WESTVILLE, INC., 1850 Martin Luther King, Jr. Dr., Lumpkin, GA 31815. Mailing Address: P.O. Box 1850, Lumpkin, GA 31815-1850. Tel.: 229-838-6310. Fax: 229-838-4000.
E-mail: info@westville.org
Web Site: www.westville.org
Formerly: Westville Historic Handicrafts
Founded: 1966.
Congressional District: 2
Key Personnel: Exec. Dir., Leo J. Goodsell; Chm. (V), Patti Rioux; Dir. Interpretation, Michelle Alexander; Museum Shop Mgr., Kathryn Morris; Mgr. Restaurant, Shirley Platt.
Personnel Profile: Full-Time Paid 10; Part-Time Paid 11; Part-Time Volunteers 346; Interns 3.
Governing Authority: nonprofit organization. Parent Institution: Westville, Inc. Tax-exempt: 501(c)(3).
Historic Village Museum: thirty-four buildings & houses c.1850.
Collections: early 19th-century decorative arts; 1825-1860 appropriate Georgia landscaping & gardens. 34 Historic Houses & Structures dating from 1800-1864: 1850 Randle-Morton Store; 1832 Stewart County Academy; 1842 Grimes-Feagin House; 1843 McDonald House; 1836 Cabinet Shop; 1838 Shoemakers Shop; 1838 Singer House; 1845 Doctor's Office; 1854 Chattahoochee County Courthouse; 1851 Climax Presbyterian Church; 1831 Bryan-Worthington House; 1840 Bagley Gin House; Log Cabins; Patterson-Marrett Farmhouse; Mule Barn; 1827 Wells House; 1850 Blacksmith Shop; c.1850 Carriage Shelter; Adam's Store; 1836 Lawson House; 1840 Yellow Creek Camp Meeting Tabernacle; 1840 Moye Whitehouse; Pottery Pug Mill; 1878 Damascus Methodist Church; c.1850s Caproni Outhouse.
Research Fields: celebrated events of 1850; history of the 1826 land cession of Georgia; 19th-century interior painting in the Deep South; genealogy of West Georgia; Indian history of West Georgia; Stewart County African-American heritage.
Facilities: 1,500-vol. library available for research on premises; reading room; 300-seat outdoor auditorium. Handcrafted items & other museum-related items for sale.
Activities: self-guided tours; formally organized education programs for adults & undergraduate students; permanent exhibitions; seasonal special events; school programs. Museum Sponsors: Spring Festival; Creek Indian War Reenactment; Independence Day Celebration; Labor Day Festivities; Fall Harvest Days; Candle Light Tours.
Publications: newsletter, The Westville Mirror; books, The Groaning Board; Pot Liquor, Magic and Mystery of Westville.
Hours & Admission Prices: March-Dec. Thurs.-Sat. 10-5, Sun. 1-5. Adults $10, senior citizens, college students & military $8, children grades K-12 $5; discounts to groups, AAM & ALHFAM members; members no charge. Closed New Year's Eve & Day; Thanksgiving; Christmas. ♿
Attendance: 22,000 (estimated)
Membership: Individual $25; Builder $50; Sustainer $100; Patron $250; Westville Society $500; Millennium Society $1,000.

PROVIDENCE CANYON STATE PARK, Rte. 1, Lumpkin, GA 31815-9730. Mailing Address: P.O. Box 158, Lumpkin, GA 31815-9730. Tel.: 229-838-4244; 800-864-7275 (reservations). Fax: 229-838-6735.
Web Site: www.gastateparks.org
Founded: 1971.
Congressional District: 2
Key Personnel: Mgr., Joy L. Joyner; Interpreter, Sherry Stephens; Interpreter, Thomas Wilson.
Personnel Profile: Full-Time Paid 5; Part-Time Paid 2.
Governing Authority: state. Administered by Parks, Recreation & Historic Sites Div., Dept. of Natural Resources. Tax-exempt.
State Park Natural History Museum.
Collections: natural history; erosion.
Research Fields: endangered wildflowers; erosion; natural history.
Facilities: nature trails; interpretive center; picnic shelter; group shelter.
Activities: guided tours; self-guided tours; wildflower audio-visual program; hiking trails; backpacking; pioneer campground for organized groups.
Hours & Admission Prices: Park: mid-Sept. to mid-April daily 7-6; mid-April to mid-Sept. 7am-9pm. Office: daily 8-5. Buses: more than 30 passengers $50; Vans: 13-30 passenger $20. Parking: $3 per vehicle; Wed. no charge. ♿
Attendance: 90,000 (accurate)

Macon

THE CANNONBALL HOUSE, 856 Mulberry St., Macon, GA 31201-6755. Tel.: 478-745-5982. Fax: 478-745-5944.
E-mail: cbhinfo@yahoo.com
Web Site: www.cannonballhouse.org
Founded: 1963.
Congressional District: 8
Personnel Profile: Full-Time Paid 1; Part-Time Paid 6; Part-Time Volunteers 1.
Governing Authority: Parent Institution: Friends of the Cannonball House, Inc. Tax-exempt.
History Museum: c.1853.
Collections: period furnishings & clothing; personal artifacts; quilts; Civil War uniforms, equipment & firearms; flags; servants quarters; Alpha Delta Pi & Phi Mu furnishings.
Hours & Admission Prices: Summer: Mon.-Sat. 10-5, Sun. by appointment; Winter: Mon.-Sat. 11-5. Adults $6, military and senior citizens 65 & over $5, students $2; discounts to AAA members & groups of 15 or more; children 6 & under & members no charge. Closed most major holidays.
Attendance: 10,000 (estimated)
Membership: Individual $35; Family $75; Patron $150; Grand Patron $250; Donor $500; Benefactor $1,000.

GEORGIA MUSIC HALL OF FAME, (M), 200 Martin Luther King Jr. Blvd., Macon, GA 31201-3490. Mailing Address: P.O. Box 870, Macon, GA 31202-0870. Tel.: 888-GA-ROCKS; 478-751-3334. Fax: 478-751-3100.
E-mail: ccreekmore@georgia.org
Web Site: www.georgiamusic.org
Founded: 1996.
Congressional District: 8

Key Personnel: Dir., Lisa Love; Chm., Eugene C. Dunwody, Jr.; Cur., Joseph Johnson; Music Store Coord., Melvina Spence; Public Rels. & Event Mgr., Katie Roberts; Asst. Cur. & Educator, Kristin Veline; Visitor Svcs. Mgr., Mary Stansfield; Visitor Svcs. Coord. & Volunteer Coord., Steven Fulbright; Administrative Operations Coord., Cissie Creekmore; Mgr. Facilities, A.B. Goel.
Personnel Profile: Full-Time Paid 9; Part-Time Paid 6; Part-Time Volunteers 4; Interns 4.
Governing Authority: state. Parent Institution: Georgia Department of Economic Development. Tax-exempt: 501(c)(3).
Music Museum.
Collections: history of Georgia music from pre-colonial to present.
Research Fields: Georgia musical artists; Georgia instrument makers; Georgia music industry leaders & personalities; Georgia musical folkways & related international traditions.
Facilities: 1,100-vol. library; banquet room; archives; reading room; 15,000 sq. ft. exhibit space. Museum-related items for sale.
Activities: concerts; exhibit openings; volunteer & intern programs; guided tours; school tours; hobby & educational workshops; lectures; films; rental facilities; participatory & temporary exhibitions.
Publications: magazine, Georgia Music.
Hours & Admission Prices: Tues.-Sat. 9-5. Adults $8, senior citizens, students, tour & family groups $6, children $3.50; discounts to AAA members; members no charge. Closed New Year's Day; Thanksgiving; Christmas & day after. ♿
Attendance: 45,000 (estimated)
Membership: Solo $30; Duet $50; The Band (family) $75; Manager $100; Agent (patron) $250; Promoter $500.

GEORGIA SPORTS HALL OF FAME, 301 Cherry St., Macon, GA 31201-3398. Mailing Address: P.O. Box 4644, Macon, GA 31208-4644. Tel.: 478-752-1585, ext. 100. Fax: 478-752-1587.
Web Site: www.gshf.org
Founded: 1999.
Congressional District: 8
Key Personnel: Dir., Jacquelyn Decell; Chm. (V), Bobby Pope; Treas., Sherry Price; Devel., Ben Sapp; Museum Shop Mgr., Roze Gray; Security, Eric Thomas.
Personnel Profile: Full-Time Paid 5; Part-Time Paid 2.
Governing Authority: state; nonprofit.
State Agency.
Collections: history of sports in Georgia; sports heritage of Georgia's athletes.
Facilities: library; 14,000 sq. ft. exhibit space; 205-seat auditorium; large screen theater. Museum-related items for sale.
Activities: dance recitals; films; guided tours; lectures; participatory exhibits; rental gallery; temporary & traveling exhibitions; theater.
Publications: quarterly newsletter, Sports Report.
Hours & Admission Prices: Tues.-Sat. 9-5. Adults $8, senior citizens, students & military with ID $6, children $3.50; discounts to groups; members no charge. Closed New Year's Day; Easter; Thanksgiving; Christmas & day after. ♿
Attendance: 14,544 (accurate)
Membership: Student $20; Individual $35; Family $75; Friend $100; Contributor $150; Corporate $250; Patron $500; Grant Patron $1,000.

HAY HOUSE MUSEUM, 934 Georgia Ave., Macon, GA 31201-6708. Tel.: 478-742-8155. Fax: 478-745-4277.
Web Site: www.georgiatrust.org; www.hayhouse.org
Founded: 1977.
Congressional District: 8
Key Personnel: Dir., Katey Brown; Chm., Bert Maxwell, IV; Chm. (V), Heidi Ream; Museum Store Mgr., Karen Norwood.
Personnel Profile: Full-Time Paid 2; Part-Time Paid 12; Part-Time Volunteers 50; Interns 1.
Governing Authority: nonprofit organization. Parent Institution: The Georgia Trust for Historic Preservation. Tax-exempt: 501(c)(3).
Historic House: 1855-59 Italian Renaissance Revival Mansion.
Collections: period furnishings; porcelains; decorative arts relative to house & region.
Research Fields: architecture; decorative arts; regional history.
Facilities: rental facilities.
Activities: guided tours; lectures; education programs for students; docent program; birthday parties; rental facilities. Annual Event: Cherry Blossom Festival in March; Macon Gardens, Mansions & Moonlight Home & Garden Tour in May; Christmas at Hay House November-December.
Publications: bimonthly newsletter, The Rambler, from the Georgia Trust for Historic Preservation.
Hours & Admission Prices: Jan.-Feb. & July-Aug. Tues.-Sat. 10-4; March-June & Sept.-Nov. Tues.-Sat. 10-4, Sun. 1-4; Dec. daily 10-4; last tour at 3pm. Adults $8, senior citizens $7, student $4; discounts to AAA members; children under 6 & members no charge. Closed major holidays. ♿
Attendance: 19,523 (accurate)

HISTORIC MACON FOUNDATION, INC. - SIDNEY LANIER COTTAGE HOUSE MUSEUM, Sidney Lanier Cottage, 935 High St., Macon, GA 31201. Mailing Address: P.O. Box 13358, Macon, GA 31208-3358. Tel.: 478-743-3851 & 742-5084.
Web Site: www.historicmacon.org
Formerly: Middle Georgia Historical Society, Inc.
Founded: 1964.
Congressional District: 8
Key Personnel: Exec. Dir., Josh Rogers; Dir. SLC, Janis I. Haley; Dir. Finance, Cantey Ayres.
Personnel Profile: Full-Time Paid 5; Part-Time Paid 5; Part-Time Volunteers 6; Interns 1.
Governing Authority: bd. of trustees. Tax-exempt: 501(c)(3).
Historic Site: c.1840 birthplace of poet Sidney Lanier.
Collections: documents & photographs; renovation & restoration of poet Sidney Lanier's birthplace; memorabilia of Sidney Lanier; books; musical instruments.
Facilities: archives.
Activities: guided house tours; lectures; poetry readings; trips.
Publications: quarterly bulletin; Butler's History of Macon & Central Georgia; Macon's Architectural & Historic Heritage; Macon, A Pictorial History; Our Town Macon Coloring Guide for children; Macon Sets A Fine Table; Eneas Africanus; Living Macon Style; DVDs of Sidney Laniers Life, Rosehill Cemetery & Indian Historical Tour; Historic Macon.
Hours & Admission Prices: Mon.-Sat. 10-4; groups by appointment. Adults $5, seniors $4, children 6-18 $3; discounts to AAA members, groups of 10 or more & military. Closed major holidays. ♿
Attendance: 10,000 (estimated)
Membership: Student $20; Individual $40; Family $60; Patron $150; Benefactor $250; Supporting $400; Sustaining $600; Historic Macon Club $1,000.

* **MUSEUM OF ARTS AND SCIENCES, (M),** 4182 Forsyth Rd., Macon, GA 31210-4869. Tel.: 478-477-3232. Fax: 478-477-3251.
E-mail: lfisher@masmacon.com
Web Site: www.masmacon.com
Founded: 1956.
Congressional District: 8
Key Personnel: Dir., Suzanne Harper; Cur. Collections, Eric O'Dell; Bd. Pres., Nancy Shurling; Cur. Education, Susan Mays; Cur. Planetarium, Jim Greenhouse; Museum Shop Mgr., Andy Weaver.
Personnel Profile: Full-Time Paid 13; Part-Time Paid 21; Part-Time Volunteers 287; Interns 1.
Governing Authority: private; nonprofit corporation. Tax-exempt: 501(c)(3).
General Museum.
Collections: archaeological artifacts; exotic moths & butterflies; zyghoriza fossil; rocks & minerals; living zoological specimens; toys; paintings; drawings; prints & sculpture primarily by regional, some American artists; ceramics. Historic House: c.1928 The Kingfisher Cabin.
Research Fields: art, science & history of clay.
Facilities: 200-vol. library of reference material available for use by special permission; nature trails; three galleries featuring changing exhibits in art, science & humanities; three story Discovery House, an interactive gallery focused on process of learning & its Back Yard a two-story habitat for live collections; observatory; planetarium; auditorium; classroom. Imported crafts, original art, books, notepaper & kits for sale.
Activities: guided tours; lectures; films; gallery talks; classes; field trips; hobby workshops; formally organized education programs; docent program or council; permanent, temporary & traveling exhibitions; school loan service.
Publications: quarterly newsletter, Museum Muse; program guide; exhibit catalogues; gallery guides.
Hours & Admission Prices: Museum: Tues.-Sat. 10-5, Sun. 1-5, last Fri. of month 10-8. Adults $8, seniors $6; discounts to military & Smithsonian affiliates; members no charge. Planetarium Programs: Tues.-Thurs. 4, Fri. 4 & 8, Sat. 12, 2 & 4, Sun. 2 & 4. Mini-Zoo Tours: Sun.-Fri. 3, Sat. 1 & 3. Closed New Year's Day; Easter; Memorial Day; Independence Day; Labor Day; Thanksgiving; Christmas Eve & Day. ♿
Attendance: 72,273 (accurate)
Membership: Student $15; Teacher & Senior $20; Individual $25; Individual Plus $40; Family $45; Family Plus $60; Friend $150; Patron $300; Benefactor $500; President's Roundtable $1,000.

OCMULGEE NATIONAL MONUMENT, 1207 Emery Hwy., Macon, GA 31217-4320. Tel.: 478-752-8257, ext. 10. Fax: 478-752-8259.
Web Site: www.nps.gov/ocmu
Founded: 1936.

Congressional District: 8
Key Personnel: Supt., James David; Museum Shop Mgr., Patty Ellis.
Personnel Profile: Full-Time Paid 11; Part-Time Volunteers 358; Interns 1.
Governing Authority: federal. Affiliated with National Park Service, U.S. Dept. of Interior, Washington, DC. Tax-exempt: 501(c)(3).
Park Museum.
Collections: Indian artifacts; archaeology representing six culture levels covering 10,000 years; anthropology; history; ethnology; British Colonial Trading Post; Lamar Type Site. Historic Building: 900-1100 A.D. Earth-lodge.
Research Fields: southeast archaeology; Ocmulgee site history; ten prehistoric Mississippian style mounds.
Facilities: 2,000-vol. library of books on anthropology, archaeology & history of southeastern United States available on premises to authorized archaeologists, historians & students; discovery lab; nature trails; picnic area. Publications & American Indian crafts for sale.
Activities: lectures; formally organized education programs for children & college students in discovery lab; permanent exhibitions; native craft demonstrations; school loan service; driving & self-guiding trails.
Hours & Admission Prices: Daily 9-5. No charge; donations accepted. Closed New Year's Day; Christmas. ♿
Attendance: 170,000 (accurate)
Membership: Cooperating Association Memberships available. Student & Senior Citizen $10; Individual $15; Family $25; Contributing $50; Sustaining $100; Patron $250; Corporate $500.

TUBMAN AFRICAN-AMERICAN MUSEUM, (M), 340 Walnut St., Macon, GA 31201-0515. Mailing Address: P.O. Box 6671, Macon, GA 31208-6671. Tel.: 478-743-8544. Fax: 478-743-9063.
E-mail: guestservices@tubmanmuseum.com
Web Site: www.tubmanmuseum.com
Founded: 1982.
Congressional District: 3
Key Personnel: Bd. Chm., Billy Pitts; Bd. Vice Chm., George McCanless; Bd. Pres., Mike Dyer; Bd. Vice Pres., Jo Wilbanks; Exec. Dir, Andy Ambrose; Dir. Education, Anita Ponder; Devel. Asst. & Guest Svcs., Adra Dudley; Dir. Exhibitions, Jeff Bruce; Guest Svcs. Asst., Antowan Thomas; Dir. Mktg. & Sales, Chris Spicer; Dir. Capital Campaign, Karen Briggs; Outreach & Tour Coord., Quinton Tard; Finance Dir., Cynthia Hammond.
Personnel Profile: Full-Time Paid 8; Part-Time Paid 20; Part-Time Volunteers 100; Interns 3.
Governing Authority: nonprofit.
History Museum.
Collections: African-American art, history & culture.
Facilities: 1,000-vol. library.
Publications: six catalogs annually.
Hours & Admission Prices: Mon.-Sat. 9-5. Adults $6, seniors & military with ID $5, children $4; discounts to AAM & ICOM members; museum members no charge. Closed New Year's Day; Memorial Day; Independence Day; Thanksgiving; Christmas. ♿
Attendance: 68,722 (accurate)
Membership: Senior Citizen & Student $15; Individual $25; Family $50; Friend $100; Patron $250; Grand Patron $500; Benefactor $1,000; Grand Benefactor $2,500.

Madison

THE BRUCE WEINER MICROCAR MUSEUM, 2950 Eatonton Rd., Madison, GA 30650-5028.
E-mail: 2009@microcarmuseum.com
Web Site: microcarmuseum.com
Governing Authority: nonprofit organization. Tax-exempt: 501(c)(3).
Transportation Museum.
Collections: Microcars from late 1940s to 1964 with engine sizes of 700cc or less.
Hours & Admission Prices: Tues.-Thurs. 1-4, Sat. 10-4 Admission $5. Closed Thanksgiving weekend; three weeks during Christmas.

MADISON-MORGAN CULTURAL CENTER, 434 S. Main St., Madison, GA 30650-1640. Tel.: 706-342-4743. Fax: 706-342-1154.
E-mail: info@mmcc-arts.org
Web Site: www.mmcc-arts.org
Founded: 1976.
Congressional District: 10
Key Personnel: Exec. Dir. & Cur. Visual Arts, Judy Barber; Chm., Lyn Hunt; Vice Chm., Sue Baldwin; Membership & Business Mgr. Special Events, Elsie Monk; Dir. Mktg., Patricia DuBose; Technical Dir., Bryan Nunnally.
Personnel Profile: Full-Time Paid 6; Part-Time Paid 3; Part-Time Volunteers 50.
Governing Authority: nonprofit organization. Parent Institution: Morgan County Foundation Inc. Tax-exempt: 501(c)(3).
Multi-disciplinary Cultural Center: housed in the 1895 Madison Graded School, in Madison Historic District.
Collections: artifacts, photographs, papers pertaining to the history of Madison, Morgan County & the Piedmont region of Georgia; decorative arts; costumes; architectural fragments; tools; household utensils; Civil War materials; school related artifacts & furnishings; history & local education exhibits; restored classroom.
Research Fields: Madison & Morgan County history & architecture; arts & crafts decorative arts.
Facilities: 395-seat auditorium; four galleries for changing art exhibits; restored turn-of-the-century school room; Member's Room. Literature pertaining to Madison & Morgan County, exhibit catalogs & gift items for sale.
Activities: guided tours; lectures; theatre; concerts; demonstrations; formally organized education programs; docent programs; loan, permanent & traveling exhibitions; residencies; workshops; classes; seminars. Center Sponsors: annual four-day arts festival.
Publications: quarterly newsletter, Madison-Morgan Cultural Center; periodic catalogs of specific exhibitions.
Hours & Admission Prices: Tues.-Sat. 10-5, Sun. 2-5. Adults $3, seniors $2.50, students $2; discounts to groups of 20 or more; children under 6, museum & AAM members no charge. Closed New Year's Day; Memorial Day; Independence Day; Labor Day; Thanksgiving; Christmas Eve & Day. ♿
Attendance: 20,000
Membership: Students $10; Individual $20; School $25; Friend & Family $30; Civic Club or Group $60; Sustainer $60-$99; Contributor $100-$249; Associate $250-$499; Patron $500-$999; Benefactor $1,000 and up.

MADISON MUSEUM OF FINE ART, (M), 290 Hancock St., Madison, GA 30650-1305. Mailing Address: P.O. Box 814, Madison, GA 30650. Tel.: 706-485-4530.
E-mail: mbechtell@prodigy.net
Web Site: madisonmuseum.org
Founded: 2003.
Key Personnel: C.E.O., Pres. (V) & Dir., Michele L. Bechtell; Sec., Sean Gallagher; Treas., Henry C. Ransom.
Personnel Profile: Full-Time Volunteers 1; Part-Time Volunteers 10.
Governing Authority: private; nonprofit organization. Tax-exempt: 501(c)(3).
Visual Art History Museum.
Collections: paintings; sculptures.
Facilities: 60-seat auditorium; botanical garden; educational facilities; 5,000 sq. ft. exhibit space; 60-seat theater. Museum-related items for sale.
Activities: concerts; docent program; films; arts festivals; lectures; loan & traveling exhibitions; theater; training programs; broadcast programs. Annual Events: Spring Art Walk; Twelfth Night Renaissance Supper.
Publications: quarterly newsletter.
Hours & Admission Prices: Mon.-Sat. 1-5. No charge; donations accepted. ♿
Attendance: 4,000 (estimated)
Membership: Individual $35; Family $50; Friend $150; Contributing $250; Corporate $500; Patron $1,000; Director's Circle $2,500.

Marietta

COBB COUNTY YOUTH MUSEUM, (M), 649 Cheatham Hill Dr., Marietta, GA 30064-5512. Mailing Address: P.O. Box 78, Marietta, GA 30061-0078. Tel.: 770-427-2563. Fax: 770-427-1060.
E-mail: youthmuseum@aol.com
Web Site: www.cobbcountyyouthmuseum.org
Founded: 1964.
Congressional District: 6
Key Personnel: Pres. (V), Joanne Elsey; Pres. Elect, Scott Gregory; Dir., Anita S. Barton; Museum Shop Mgr., Lisa Schneiderman; Sec., Bookkeeper & Museum Shop Mgr., Eleanor Watson.
Personnel Profile: Full-Time Paid 1; Part-Time Paid 7; Part-Time Volunteers 3.
Governing Authority: nonprofit organization. Supported by the Cobb County & Marietta School Boards. Tax-exempt.
Youth Museum.
Collections: jet trainer; caboose; street car stop; canoe.
Major Exhibits: America's Pathways to Independence, 11/09-12/10.
Activities: guided tours; docent program; puppet shows; speakers bureau; living history exhibits; summer program. Annual Event: BBQ & Silent Auction.
Hours & Admission Prices: Tours: Sept.-May Mon.-Fri. 9:30-1:30 by appointment. Admission $7. Closed school holidays. ♿
Attendance: 13,817 (accurate)

GONE WITH THE WIND MOVIE MUSEUM, 18 Whitlock Ave., Marietta, GA 30064-2346. Tel.: 770-794-5576.
E-mail: csutherland@mariettaga.gov
Web Site: www.mariettaga.gov/gwtw/
Key Personnel: Dir., Connie Sutherland
Movie Museum.
Collections: original costumes; posters; books; props; sketches; photographs.
Facilities: Museum-related items for sale.
Activities: video.
Hours & Admission Prices: Mon.-Sat. 10-5. Adults $7, seniors & students $6; discounts to groups of 15 or more.

MARIETTA/COBB MUSEUM OF ART, 30 Atlanta St., S.E., Marietta, GA 30060-1975. Tel.: 770-528-1444. Fax: 770-528-1440.
E-mail: smacaulaymcma@bellsouth.net
Web Site: www.mariettacobbartmuseum.org
Founded: 1989.
Congressional District: 7
Key Personnel: Dir., Sally Macaulay; Chm., Ray Worden; Asst. Dir., Jennifer Fox; Coord. Special Events, Nichole Alexander.
Personnel Profile: Full-Time Paid 2; Part-Time Paid 2; Part-Time Volunteers 50.
Governing Authority: nonprofit organization. Tax-exempt: 501(c)(3).
Art Museum: housed in 1909 Greek Revival Post Office Building.
Collections: 19th & 20th century American art; paintings; prints; drawings; watercolors; pastels; Ash Can School works; contemporary art, 1980s-present; Soho, New York.
Research Fields: 19th & 20th century art.
Facilities: educational facilities.
Activities: docent program; formal education programs for adults; guided tours; workshops; lectures; temporary exhibitions of museum's American collections; loan, participatory & traveling exhibitions; weddings; meetings. Museum Sponsors: Annual Children's Art Festival; Art Camp.
Publications: newsletter, MCMA Chronicle.
Hours & Admission Prices: Tues.-Fri. 11-5, Sat. 11-4. Adults $5, students & senior citizens $3; discounts to groups, AAA, AAM & ICOM members; members & children under 6 no charge. Closed major holidays. ♿
Attendance: 75,000 (estimated)
Membership: Student & Senior $25; Individual $35; Family Dual $50; Supporting $100; Contributing $250; Patron $500; Sustaining $1,000; Benefactor $5,000; Grand Benefactor $10,000.

MARIETTA FIRE MUSEUM, 112 Haynes St., Fire Station #1, Marietta, GA 30060-1973. Tel.: 770-794-5491.
Web Site: www.marietta.gov/departments/emergency/fire/museum.aspx
Fire-Fighting Museum.
Collections: late 1800s photographs; early fire helmets; helmets from around the world; period fire-fighting equipment, hoses, nozzles & bells; 1879 Silsby Steamer; 1921 American LaFrance pumper; 1929 Seagrave pumper; 1949 Pirsch ladder truck; 1952 Chevrolet panel truck.
Hours & Admission Prices: Mon.-Fri. 8-5, Sat.-Sun. by appointment. No charge.

MARIETTA MUSEUM OF HISTORY, (M), 1 Depot St., Ste. 200, Marietta, GA 30060-1905. Tel.: 770-794-5710. Fax: 770-794-5733.
E-mail: info@mariettahistory.org
Web Site: www.mariettahistory.org
Founded: 1996.
Key Personnel: C.E.O. & Founder, Dan Cox; Exec. Dir., Jan Galt.
Personnel Profile: Full-Time Paid 4; Part-Time Paid 2; Part-Time Volunteers 30; Interns 2.
Governing Authority: Tax-exempt.
History Museum.
Collections: Marietta & Cobb County Georgia history.
Hours & Admission Prices: Mon.-Sat. 10-4. Adults $5, seniors & students $3; members & children under 6 no charge. Closed New Year's Day; Independence Day; Thanksgiving; Christmas. ♿
Attendance: 10,049 (accurate)
Membership: Bronze $30; Silver $50; Gold $75; Platinum $150; Diamond $500.

THE ROOT HOUSE MUSEUM, Marietta Pkwy. & Polk St., Marietta, GA 30060. Mailing Address: 145 Denmead St., Marietta, GA 30060-1934. Tel.: 770-426-4982. Fax: 770-499-9540.
E-mail: clhs2@bellsouth.net
Web Site: cobblandmarks.com
Founded: 1972.
Key Personnel: Dir., Daryl Barksdale; Chm., Skip Harper; Cur., Mary Ellen Higginbotham.
Personnel Profile: Part-Time Paid 5; Part-Time Volunteers 33.
Governing Authority: Parent Institution: Cobb Landmarks & Historical Society, Inc. Tax-exempt.
Historic House Museum: built c.1845.
Collections: Historic Building: c.1845 William Root house.
Facilities: Museum-related items for sale.
Publications: monthly newsletter, Landmarker; book, The 1st 100 Years of Cobb County; articles, Historic Highlights of Cobb County; Cobb County in the 20th Century.
Hours & Admission Prices: Tues.-Sat. 11-4. Adults $4, senior citizens $3, children $2; members no charge. ♿
Attendance: 6,000 (estimated)
Membership: Student & Institutional $20; Annual $45; Patron $100; Business $150; Donor $ 250; Silver Sponsor $500; Gold Sponsor $1,000; Platinum Sponsor $2,500

Midway

DORCESTER ACADEMY MUSEUM OF AFRICAN-AMERICAN HISTORY, 8787 E. Oglethorpe Hwy., Midway, GA 31320. Mailing Address: P.O. Box 51, Midway, GA 31320-0051. Tel.: 912-884-2347.
Web Site: dorchesteracademy.com
History Museum.
Collections: local history & culture; period artifacts; early farming tools & equipment; guns.
Hours & Admission Prices: Tues.-Fri. 11-2, Sat.-Sun. 2-4.

FORT MORRIS STATE HISTORIC SITE, 2559 Fort Morris Rd., Midway, GA 31320-6205. Tel.: 912-884-5999. Fax: 912-884-5285.
E-mail: fortmorris@coastalnow.net
Web Site: gastateparks.org
Founded: 1978.
Congressional District: 1
Key Personnel: Site Mgr., Arthur C. Edgar, Jr.
Personnel Profile: Full-Time Paid 1; Part-Time Volunteers 15.
Governing Authority: state. Administered by Parks Recreation & Historic Sites Div. Georgia Dept. of Natural Resources. Tax-exempt.
Military Museum.
Collections: 1814 remains of revolutionary earthwork.
Research Fields: Colonial American revolution; Civil War; Georgia history.
Facilities: visitor center. Postcards, gifts & books for sale.
Activities: guided tours; monthly programs; summer youth activities; military encampments; living history demonstrations, cannon firings; film.
Hours & Admission Prices: Thurs.-Sat. & holidays 9-5. Adults $4, senior citizens $3.50, youth 6-18 $2.75; children under 5 no charge. Group Tours: adults $3.25, youth 6-18 $2.50, children 5 & under $1. Closed New Year's Day; Thanksgiving; Christmas. ♿
Attendance: 13,000 (estimated)

MIDWAY MUSEUM, INC., U.S. Hwy. 17, Midway, GA 31320. Mailing Address: P.O. Box 195, Midway, GA 31320-0195. Tel.: 912-884-5837. Fax: 912-884-5837.
E-mail: info@themidwaymuseum.org
Web Site: themidwaymuseum.org
Founded: 1957.
Congressional District: 1
Key Personnel: Chm. & Pres. (V), Otis Amason; Treas., Jack Waters; Cur., Joann Clark; Museum Shop Mgr., Dianne Behrens.
Personnel Profile: Full-Time Paid 2; Part-Time Volunteers 1.
Governing Authority: society. Tax-exempt.
History Museum.
Collections: 1700s-1800s furnishings.
Research Fields: local genealogy & history.
Facilities: Museum-related items for sale.
Activities: guided tours; permanent exhibitions.
Publications: brochures.
Hours & Admission Prices: Tues.-Sat. 10-4, Sun 2-4. Adults $6, senior citizens $5, children $2; discounts to groups by appointment only; children under 6 no charge. Closed holidays.
Attendance: 50,000 (estimated)
Membership: Annual $10.

SEABROOK VILLAGE, (M), 660 Trade Hill Rd., Midway, GA 31320-6215. Tel.: 912-884-7008. Fax: 912-884-3046.
E-mail: cynthia@seabrookvillage.org
Web Site: seabrookvillage.org
Founded: 1994.
Key Personnel: Administrative Mgr., Florence Tate-Roberts.
Personnel Profile: Full-Time Paid 2; Part-Time Paid 1; Part-Time Volunteers 25.

History Museum.
Collections: open air African-American village.
Hours & Admission Prices: Tues.-Sat. 10-2. Self-Guided Tours: adults $5, children under 12 $3; discounts to active military, military reserve, AASLH, Coastal Museum Assoc., groups & AAM members; members & children under 6 no charge. Closed holidays.
Attendance: 5,000 (estimated)
Membership: $10; $25; $100.

Milledgeville

BLACKBRIDGE GALLERY - GEORGIA COLLEGE & STATE UNIVERSITY DEPARTMENT OF ART, (M), S. Clarke St., Milledgeville, GA 31061. Mailing Address: Campus Box 94, Milledgeville, GA 31061. Tel.: 478-445-4572.
Web Site: www.gcsu.edu/art/blackbridgegallery.htm
Key Personnel: Dir., Carlos M. Herrera
Art Gallery.
Collections: photographs; paintings.
Hours & Admission Prices: Mon.-Fri. 9-5.

GEORGIA COLLEGE AND STATE UNIVERSITY MUSEUM, 221 N. Clarke St., Milledgeville, GA 31061. Mailing Address: Campus Box 43, Milledgeville, GA 31061. Tel.: 478-445-4391. Fax: 478-445-6847.
E-mail: museum@gcsu.edu
Web Site: library.gcsu.edu/museum
Formerly: Museum & Archives of Georgia Education
Founded: 1975.
Congressional District: 11
Key Personnel: Cur., Shannon Morris; Dean, Dr. Rachel Schipper.
Personnel Profile: Full-Time Paid 1; Interns 1.
Governing Authority: university. Parent Institution: Georgia College & State University. Tax-exempt.
History Museum.
Collections: Flannery O'Connor; Georgia College and State University history.
Research Fields: historical records of schools in the state; comparison of textbooks.
Facilities: 3,000-vol. library of textbooks prior to 1950; records of school systems; biographical information on computers of state's retired teachers available for research by special request; reading room.
Activities: guided tours; lectures; school & community outreach programs; permanent & temporary exhibitions.
Hours & Admission Prices: Mon.-Sat. 10-4; other times by appointment. No charge; donations accepted. ♿
Attendance: 2,500 (estimated)

GEORGIA'S OLD CAPITAL MUSEUM, 201 E. Greene St., Milledgeville, GA 31061. Mailing Address: P.O. Box 1177, Milledgeville, GA 31059-1177. Tel.: 478-453-1803. Fax: 478-453-4813.
E-mail: info@oldcapitalmuseum.org
Web Site: www.oldcapitalmuseum.org
Founded: 1993.
Key Personnel: Exec. Dir., Dr. Amy Wright.
Personnel Profile: Full-Time Paid 1; Full-Time Volunteers 1; Part-Time Paid 2.
Governing Authority: private; nonprofit organization. Tax-exempt: 501(c)(3).
History Museum.
Collections: area history.
Research Fields: cultural history.
Facilities: research library; 6,000 sq. ft. exhibit space. Museum-related items for sale.
Activities: formal education programs for adults; guided tours; lectures.
Hours & Admission Prices: Tues.-Fri. 10-4, Sat. 12-4. No charge; donations accepted. Closed legal holidays.
Attendance: 5,000 (accurate)
Membership: Student $15; Senior Citizen $20; Individual $25; Family $40; Organization $50; Friend $100; Business $150; Patron $250; Corporate Donor $500.

JOHN MARLOR ARTS CENTER, 201 N. Wayne St., Milledgeville, GA 31061-3437. Tel.: 912-452-3950. Fax: 912-452-3950.
E-mail: alliedarts@peachnet.campuscwix.net
Key Personnel: Exec. Dir., Randy Cannon
Art Center: housed in home built by John Marlor in 1830.
Collections: paintings.
Hours & Admission Prices: Mon.-Fri. 9-5. No charge; donations accepted.

STETSON-SANFORD HOUSE, 601 W. Hancock St., Milledgeville, GA 31061-3215. Mailing Address: 201 E. Green St., Milledgeville, GA 31061-3519. Tel.: 800-653-1804.
Governing Authority: Parent Institution: Old Capital Historical Society.
Historic House Museum: housed in a former hotel built for George T. Brown; purchased by merchant Daniel B. Stetson in 1857 whose daughter Elizabeth married Judge Daniel B. Sanford, Clerk of the Secession Convention.
Collections: family & local history; period furnishings; photographs.
Hours & Admission Prices: Tues. & Fri. 10am by appointment.

Mitchell

HAMBURG STATE PARK MUSEUM, 6071 Hamburg State Park Rd., Mitchell, GA 30820-2999. Tel.: 478-552-2393; 800-864-7275.
Web Site: gastateparks.org/info/hamburg
Founded: 1968.
Congressional District: 10
Key Personnel: Park Ranger, Earvin Cordry.
Personnel Profile: Full-Time Paid 5; Part-Time Paid 1; Part-Time Volunteers 2.
Governing Authority: state. Parent Institution: Georgia Dept. of Natural Resources, Parks & Historic Sites Division, 2 Martin Luther King Jr. Dr., S.E., Atlanta, GA 30334. Tax-exempt.
Industrial Museum: housed in 1920 water turbine powered gin & milling complex.
Collections: farm tools; ginning equipment; milling machinery; corn shellers; animal drawn farm equipment.
Facilities: Corn meal for sale.
Activities: self-guided tours; milling demonstrations; permanent exhibits; guided & self guided tours.
Hours & Admission Prices: Park: daily 7am-10pm. Museum: daily 8-5. No charge. Parking: $3; Wed. no charge. Closed Thanksgiving; Christmas. ♿
Attendance: 3,500 (estimated)

Moreland

ERSKINE CALDWELL BIRTHPLACE MUSEUM, Camp St., Moreland, GA 30259. Mailing Address: P.O. Box 207, Moreland, GA 30259-0207. Tel.: 770-254-8657.
Web Site: www.newnan.com/ec
Key Personnel: Pres. (V), Winston Skinner.
Personnel Profile: Part-Time Volunteers 6.
History Museum.
Collections: personal artifacts; photographs.
Activities: special events; rental facility; receptions; meetings.
Hours & Admission Prices: Sat.-Sun. 1-4; other times by appointment. Adults $2, children $1; members no charge. ♿

LEWIS GRIZZARD MUSEUM, 2769 US Hwy. 29 S., Moreland, GA 30259-2407. Tel.: 800-8COWETA.
Web Site: explorecoweta.com/lewisgrizzardmuseum.html
History Museum.
Collections: personal artifacts & memorabilia of syndicated newspaper columnist & author Lewis Grizzard.
Hours & Admission Prices: Call for hours.

OLD MILL MUSEUM, Downtown Moreland Sq., Moreland, GA 30259. Mailing Address: P.O. Box 128, Moreland, GA 30259-0128. Tel.: 770-254-2627. Fax: 770-254-2628.
History Museum.
Collections: local history; period farming equipment; WWII artifacts.
Hours & Admission Prices: Sat.-Sun. 1-4; other times by appointment. No charge; donations accepted.

Moultrie

COLQUITT COUNTY ARTS CENTER, 401 7th Ave., S.W., Moultrie, GA 31768-4633. Tel.: 912-985-1922. Fax: 912-890-6746.
E-mail: info@colquittcountyarts.com
Key Personnel: Exec. Dir., Jeffery Ophime
Arts Center: housed in the former Moultrie High School.
Collections: works by national & international artists.
Activities: educational programs; special events. Annual Events: theater productions.
Hours & Admission Prices: Mon.-Fri. 10-5:30, Sat. 10-2.

MUSEUM OF COLQUITT COUNTY HISTORY, 4th Ave. & 5th St., S.E., Moultrie, GA 31788. Mailing Address: P.O. Box 86, Moultrie, GA 31776-0086. Tel.: 229-890-1626.
E-mail: olreb@moultriega.net
History Museum.
Collections: local history; personal artifacts; photographs; period furnishings.
Activities: special events.
Hours & Admission Prices: Fri.-Sat. 10-5, Sun. 2-5; other times by appointment. No charge; donations accepted.

Mountain City

THE FOXFIRE MUSEUM & HERITAGE CENTER, 200 Foxfire Lane, Mountain City, GA 30562. Mailing Address: P.O. Box 541, Mountain City, GA 30562-0541. Tel.: 706-746-5828.
E-mail: foxfire@foxfire.org
Web Site: www.foxfire.org
Founded: 1966.
Congressional District: 9
Key Personnel: Dir. & Pres., Ann Moore; Chm. (V), Janet Rechtman; Museum Shop Mgr., Paulette Carpenter.
Personnel Profile: Full-Time Paid 2; Part-Time Paid 2.
Governing Authority: nonprofit organization. Parent Institution: The Foxfire Fund, Inc. Tax-exempt.
Appalachian Historic Buildings.
Collections: period artifacts; over 20 historic log cabins, some dating back to the early 1800s; pottery; folk art. Buildings: chapel; blacksmith shop; mule barn; wagon shed; single-room home; gristmill; smokehouse.
Facilities: Museum-related items for sale.
Activities: self-guided & guided tours; workshops.
Publications: Foxfire book series (1-12); Foxfire 40 Years; Aunt Arie, A Foxfire Portrait; Appalachian Cookery; Foxfire Book of Toys and Games; A Foxfire Christmas; Foxfire Magazine; book, Foxfire Book of Woodstove Cookery.
Hours & Admission Prices: Mon.-Sat. 8:30-4:30; groups & guided tours by appointment. Self-Guided Tour: adults $6; discounts to AAA & AARP members; children 10 & under no charge. Closed Thanksgiving; Christmas.
Attendance: 12,000 (accurate)

Newnan

NEWNAN-COWETA HISTORICAL SOCIETY - MALE ACADEMY MUSEUM, 30 Temple Ave., Corner of Temple Ave. & College St., Newnan, GA 30263-2066. Tel.: 770-251-0207. Fax: 770-683-0208.
E-mail: nchs@newnanbiz.net
Key Personnel: Admin., Tom Redwine; Asst. Admin., Carlisle Young
Historical Society Museum.
Collections: area cultural, historical & architectural heritage.
Activities: special events.
Hours & Admission Prices: Tues.-Sat. 10-12 & 1-3, Sun. 2-5. Adults $3, children under 12 $1.

Pine Mountain

CALLAWAY GARDENS, Hwy. 18, Pine Mountain, GA 31822-2000. Mailing Address: P.O. Box 2000, Pine Mountain, GA 31822-2000. Tel.: 706-663-2281. Fax: 706-663-5004.
E-mail: info@ callawaygardens.com
Web Site: www.callawaygardens.com
Founded: 1952.
Congressional District: 3
Key Personnel: C.E.O., Edward C. Callaway; Pres., C. Robert McElerey; Dir. Retail, Julie Hicks; Dir. Devel., John P. Byrne; Dir. Historic Preservation, Michael A. Anderson; Museum Shop Mgr., Kevin Bridges.
Personnel Profile: Full-Time Paid 117; Part-Time Paid 49; Part-Time Volunteers 700; Interns 6.
Governing Authority: nonprofit organization. Parent Institution: Ida Cason Callaway Foundation. Subsidiary Institution: Callaway Gardens Resort Inc. Tax-exempt: 501(c)(3).
Arboretum/Botanical Garden.
Collections: southeastern U.S. native plants. Historic House: 1799 Log Cabin.
Research Fields: applied horticulture.
Facilities: botanical garden; theater; classrooms; butterfly center; horticultural center; discovery center. Gift items for sale.
Activities: guided tours; lectures; films; concerts; art festivals; formally organized educational programs for children, adults, undergraduate & graduate college students; summer intern program for students in horticulture & natural history; slide lending library.
Publications: newsletter, Nature Naturally; newsletter, Foundation.
Hours & Admission Prices: Labor Day to March 13 daily 9-5; March 19 to Sept. daily 9-6. Fantasy in Lights 5-10. Adults $15, children 6-12 $7.50; discounts to groups & AABGA members; members and children 5 & under no charge. ♿
Attendance: 1,000,000 (accurate)
Membership: Child 6-12 $15; Senior $25; Adult 13 & up $30; Large Family Price Cap $100; Deluxe Adult $105; Deluxe Adult for Two $160; Azalea $250; Magnolia $500; Dogwood $750.

Plains

JIMMY CARTER NATIONAL HISTORIC SITE, 300 N. Bond St., Plains, GA 31780-5562. Tel.: 229-824-4104. Fax: 229-824-3441.
Web Site: www.nps.gov/jica
Key Personnel: Supt., Gary Ingram; Cur., Kate Funk
Presidential Museums.
Collections: Plains Depot: presidential campaign memorabilia. Plains High School: furnished classroom; principal's office; auditorium; Carters' lives; political & business careers, education, family, religion & post-presidency; audiovisual tour of Carters' house. Boyhood Farm: restored 1937 farm including Carters' boyhood home & commissary.
Facilities: trails.
Activities: audiovisual tour; walking trails.
Hours & Admission Prices: Plains High School Museum: daily 9-5. Plains Depot - 1976 Carter Presidential Campaign Headquarters Museum: daily 9-4:30. Jimmy Carter Boyhood Farm Museum: daily 10-5. No charge. Closed New Year's Day; Thanksgiving; Christmas. ♿

Pooler

MIGHTY EIGHTH AIR FORCE MUSEUM, 175 Bourne Ave., Pooler, GA 31322-9516. Mailing Address: P.O. Box 1992, Savannah, GA 31402-1992. Tel.: 912-748-8888. Fax: 912-748-0209.
E-mail: development@mightyeighth.org
Web Site: www.mightyeighth.org
Founded: 1996.
Congressional District: 12
Key Personnel: C.E.O. & Pres., Henry Skipper; Chm. (V), Dr. William Cathcart; Dir. Devel., Brenda Elmgren; Dir. Oral Histories, Vivian Rogers-Price; Dir. Education, Heather Theis; Mktg. & Public Rels., Mandy Livingston; Dir. Finance, Pam Sconyers; Security & Operations, Bruce Johnson; Museum Store Mgr., Felice Stelljes; Registrar, Jean Prescott; Memorial Gardens, Peggy Harden; Advanced Coord., Susan Eiseman.
Personnel Profile: Full-Time Paid 24; Part-Time Volunteers 102; Interns 3.
Governing Authority: private; nonprofit organization. Tax-exempt: 501(c)(3).
Military History Museum.
Collections: 8th Air Force history from WWII to present; military & veterans artifacts; vehicles & aircraft; archives & iconographic collections; oral histories.
Research Fields: 8th Air Force history; American air power and the science of flight.
Facilities: 10,000-vol. library of books; 125-seat restaurant; 37,000 sq. ft. exhibit space; 4 theaters; memorial garden; chapel; educational facilities; rental facilities. Museum-related items for sale.
Activities: docent program; formal education programs for children; guided tours; lectures; rental gallery; theater; art exhibits; workshops; loan, participatory, temporary & traveling exhibitions; school loan service; summer camp. Annual Events: Museum Anniversary Celebration; Golf Tournament; Warbirds Ball and Gala.
Publications: quarterly newsletter, Mighty Eighth Air Force Museum News.
Hours & Admission Prices: Daily 9-5. Adults $10, senior citizens & students $9, children $6; members and children 5 & under no charge. Closed New Year's Day; Easter; Thanksgiving; Christmas. ♿
Attendance: 84,222 (accurate)
Membership: Veteran, Student & Heir of the Eighth $25; Individual $35; Family $50; Honor Guard $100; Squadron Leader $500; Wing Commander $1,000.

Richmond Hill

FORT MCALLISTER, 3894 Fort McAllister Rd., Richmond Hill, GA 31324-4862. Tel.: 912-727-2339. Fax: 912-727-3614.
E-mail: ftmcallr@coastalnow.net
Web Site: www.fortmcallister.org
Founded: 1958.
Congressional District: 1
Key Personnel: Park Mgr., Daniel Brown.
Personnel Profile: Full-Time Paid 5.
Governing Authority: state. Parent Institution: Parks, Recreation & Historic Sites Div., Georgia Dept. of Natural Resources, 270 Washington St., S.W., Atlanta, GA 30334. Tax-exempt.
Preservation Project: located on the site of 1861 Confederate fort.
Collections: restored earthworks; military.
Research Fields: development of artillery; static defenses; ironclad ships.
Facilities: camping; nature trails. Publications & postcards for sale.
Activities: guided tours; permanent exhibitions; living history demonstrations during summer.
Hours & Admission Prices: Daily 8-5. Adults $5, seniors $4.50, children $3.50; discounts to groups; children under 5 no charge. Closed Thanksgiving; Christmas. ♿

Attendance: 140,000 (estimated)
Membership: Friends of GA $35.

Rincon

GEORGIA SALZBURGER SOCIETY MUSEUM, 2980 Ebenezer Rd., Rincon, GA 31326-3716. Tel.: 912-826-5629.
E-mail: info@georgiasalzburgers.com
Web Site: www.georgiasalzburgers.com
Founded: 1925.
Key Personnel: Pres. (V), Julian Heyman; Treas., Kerry Edwards; Chm. (V) & Museum Shop Mgr., Martha Zeigler.
Personnel Profile: Part-Time Volunteers 10.
Governing Authority: society. Tax-exempt: 501(c)(3).
General Museum.
Collections: tools; furniture; letters; books; Bibles; deeds; maps; records of early settlers or their descendants before or just after the Civil War; Indian artifacts; Boltzius Monument. Historic Structure: 1769 Jerusalem Lutheran church; frame cottage.
Research Fields: genealogy.
Activities: tours; meetings.
Publications: newsletters, Salzburger Genealogy; Salzburger Cook Book; book, The Salzburgers & Their Descendants.
Hours & Admission Prices: Wed. & Sat.-Sun. 3-5; other times by appointment. No charge; donations accepted.
Attendance: 564 (accurate)
Membership: Regular, Associate or Friend $20; Life $200.

Ringgold

OLD STONE CHURCH MUSEUM, GA Hwy. #2, Ringgold, GA 30736. Mailing Address: CCHS P.O. Box 113, Ringgold, GA 30736-0113. Tel.: 706-935-5232.
Historic Building: housed in a former church built c.1849.
Collections: local history; Civil War artifacts; personal artifacts.
Hours & Admission Prices: Thurs.-Sun. 1-5. No charge; donations accepted.

Rome

CHIEFTAINS MUSEUM/MAJOR RIDGE HOME, (M), 501 Riverside Pkwy., Rome, GA 30161-2903. Mailing Address: P.O. Box 373, Rome, GA 30162-0373. Tel.: 706-291-9494. Fax: 706-291-2410.
E-mail: chmuseum@bellsouth.net
Web Site: www.chieftainsmuseum.org
Founded: 1969.
Congressional District: 7
Key Personnel: Exec. Dir., Claudia M. Oakes; Pres. (V), Marsha Welch; Programs Coord. & Museum Shop Mgr., Debby Brown.
Personnel Profile: Full-Time Paid 2; Part-Time Paid 1; Part-Time Volunteers 25.
Governing Authority: nonprofit organization. Parent Institution: Chieftains Museum, Inc. Tax-exempt.
History Museum: housed in 1790 log cabin, expanded in 1828, to a plantation house belonging to Cherokee leader Major Ridge.
Collections: items from Archaic Indian occupation to present time; trading post artifacts from archaeological dig; period furniture; costumes; photographs; paintings.
Major Exhibits: InDivisible (T), 4/10-6/10; Cherokee Carvers (T), 7/10-9/10; Homecoming at Chieftains, 10/10-12/10.
Research Fields: Ridge family history, Cherokee history & culture, architecture, archaeology.
Facilities: rotating exhibits.
Activities: guided tours; gallery talks; docent programs; occasional TV programs; loan, permanent & temporary exhibitions.
Publications: newsletter.
Hours & Admission Prices: Tues.-Fri. 9-3, Sat. 10-4. Adults $5, senior citizens 62 & over $3, children $2; discounts to AAM members, groups & school tours; members & Cherokee Nation registered members no charge. Closed major holidays. ♿
Attendance: 6,000 (accurate)
Membership: Individual $35; Family $50; Supporter $75; Friend $100; Sustainer $250; Patron $500; Benefactor $1,000; Chieftains $2,500.

OAK HILL AND THE MARTHA BERRY MUSEUM, 24 Veterans Memorial Hwy., Rome, GA 30161. Mailing Address: P.O. Box 490189, Mount Berry, GA 30149-0189. Tel.: 706-368-6789; 800-220-5504. Fax: 706-368-6787.
E-mail: oakhill@berry.edu
Web Site: www.berry.edu/oakhill
Founded: 1972.
Congressional District: 11
Key Personnel: Asst. Dir., Rebecca Roberts; Coord. Mktg., Patrice Shannon; Mgr. Operations & Museum Shop Mgr., Cheli Rouse; Ground Mgr., Kristin McNully; Horticulturalist, Heather Miller; Museum Asst., Rebecca Henry.
Personnel Profile: Full-Time Paid 3; Part-Time Paid 9.
Governing Authority: private college. Parent Institution: Berry College, 2277 Martha Berry Hwy., Mt. Berry, GA. Tax-exempt: 501(c)(3).
Historic House Museum: home and gardens of Martha Berry, Berry College founder. History Museum: maps the evolution of Berry College from an industrial and agricultural school to a liberal arts college.
Collections: period furnishings; china; silver; books; artifacts belonging to Martha Berry and her school; paintings; Italian & American arts.
Major Exhibits: Behind the Ropes, 3/10.
Facilities: 48-seat theater; public garden. Museum-related items for sale.
Activities: guided tours; lectures; temporary exhibitions. Museum Sponsors: Garden Events; Christmas Festival.
Publications: newsletter, The Oak Hill Gardener.
Hours & Admission Prices: Mon.-Sat. 10-5. Adults $5, children $3, tours & family group rates $4 per person; discounts to AAA members & senior citizens. Closed New Year's Day, Martin Luther King Jr. Day; Easter; Memorial Day; Independence Day; Labor Day; Christmas week. ♿
Attendance: 15,000 (estimated)

ROME AREA HISTORY MUSEUM, (M), 305 Broad St., Rome, GA 30161-3005. Tel.: 706-235-8051 & 292-9977 (store). Fax: 706-235-6631.
E-mail: lbarba@romehistorymuseum.com
Web Site: www.romehistorymuseum.com
Founded: 1996.
Key Personnel: Dir., Leigh Barba; Chm. (V), Gardner Wright; Pres. (V), Bill Temple; Cur., Cherry Johnson; Archivist, Russell McClanahan.
Personnel Profile: Full-Time Paid 1; Part-Time Paid 2; Part-Time Volunteers 8; Interns 2.
Governing Authority: Tax-exempt.
History Museum.
Collections: area history; Native Americans; early settlers through Civil War; culture; industries; documents; photographs; personal artifacts.
Activities: monthly lecture series; monthly afternoon tea; school programs.
Hours & Admission Prices: Tues.-Sat. 10-5. Adults $4, senior citizens $3, children 6-12 $2; children under 6 & members no charge. Closed New Year's Day; Independence Day; Labor Day; Thanksgiving; Christmas Eve & Day.
Attendance: 1,500 (estimated)
Membership: Student $15; Seniors over 60 $25; Individual $30; Family $50; Patron $100.

Rossville

THE CHIEF JOHN ROSS HOUSE ASSOC., 200 E. Lake Ave., Rossville, GA 30741. Mailing Address: 826 Chickamauga Ave., Rossville, GA 30741-1407. Tel.: 706-861-3954 & 866-5171. Fax: 706-861-3967.
Founded: 1797.
Congressional District: 7
Key Personnel: C.E.O. & Pres., W. Larry Rose.
Personnel Profile: Part-Time Paid 1.
Governing Authority: nonprofit organization. John Ross House Assoc. Tax-exempt.
Historic House: 1797 two-story log house of Chief John Ross.
Collections: Cherokee alphabet; arrowheads; pictures; letters; furniture; rugs & linens.
Research Fields: Cherokee Indian records.
Activities: guided tours; arts festivals; permanent exhibitions; special events.
Publications: brochures.

Hours & Admission Prices: June-Aug. Sat.-Sun. 10-2; groups by appointment. Adults $2; children under 12 no charge.
Attendance: 3,000 (estimated)
Membership: Individual $5; Family $10; Corporate $25; Chieftain $50 & up.

Roswell

ARCHIBALD SMITH PLANTATION HOME, 935 Alpharetta St., Roswell, GA 30075-3827. Tel.: 770-641-3978. Fax: 770-641-3974.
Founded: 1845.
Congressional District: 6
Key Personnel: Dir., Chuck Douglas.
Governing Authority: Tax-exempt.
History Museum.
Collections: personal artifacts; period furnishings; outbuildings; servants quarters; smoke house; corn crib; carriage house.
Hours & Admission Prices: Mon.-Sat. 10-3, Sun. 1-3. Adults $8, seniors 65 & over $7, students & children 6-18 $6; discounts to AAA members; members & children under 6 no charge. Closed major holidays. ♿
Attendance: 6,677 (accurate)
Membership: Individual $25; Family $50; Patron $100; Business $200; Sustainer $250; Benefactor $500 & up.

BULLOCH HALL, (M), 180 Bulloch Ave., Roswell, GA 30075-4420. Mailing Address: P.O. Box 1309, Roswell, GA 30077-1309. Tel.: 770-992-1731 & 1951. Fax: 770-587-1840.
E-mail: info@bullochhall.org
Web Site: www.bullochhall.org
Founded: 1978.
Congressional District: 5
Key Personnel: Dir., Pam Billingsley; Chm. (V), Bill W. Gray; Vice Chm., Tom Campbell; Asst. Site Coord., Janice Metzler.
Personnel Profile: Full-Time Paid 1; Part-Time Paid 8; Part-Time Volunteers 40.
Governing Authority: municipal. Tax-exempt.
Historic House: c.1839 Antebellum Greek Revival House & Cottage.
Collections: period furnishings; family photos; manuscripts.
Research Fields: Bulloch family; local history.
Facilities: archives.
Activities: guided tours; lectures; docent program & council; craft guilds; heritage craft classes.
Publications: quarterly newsletter, The Hallmark.
Hours & Admission Prices: Mon.-Sat. 10-3, Sun. 1-3; tours on the hour. Adults $8, seniors $7, children 6-18 $6; members & children under 6 no charge. Closed New Year's Eve & Day; Martin Luther King Jr. Day; Easter; Memorial Day; Independence Day; Labor Day; Thanksgiving; Christmas Eve & Day. ♿
Attendance: 11,000 (estimated)
Membership: Individual $25; Family $35; Business $50; Patron $100; Donor-Patron $500; Benefactor $1,000.

CHATTAHOOCHEE NATURE CENTER, 9135 Willeo Rd., Roswell, GA 30075-4723. Tel.: 770-992-2055.
E-mail: marketing@chattnaturecenter.org
Nature Center.
Collections: reptiles; amphibians; birds of prey; native & endangered plants.
Facilities: Museum-related items for sale.
Activities: adult programs; birthday parties; scout groups; special events.
Hours & Admission Prices: Mon.-Sat. 9-5, Sun. 12-5. Adults $8, seniors $6, children 3-12 $5; children 2 & under no charge. Closed New Year's Day; Thanksgiving; Christmas.

ROSWELL FIRE & RESCUE MUSEUM, 1002 Alpharetta St., Roswell, GA 30075-3661. Tel.: 770-641-3730.
Web Site: www.roswellgov.com/index.aspx?NID=208
Fire-Fighting Museum.
Collections: local history & culture; fire-related photographs; Atlanta's fire history; 1947 Ford American LaFrance Pumper.
Hours & Admission Prices: Call for hours.

ROSWELL VISUAL ARTS CENTER & GALLERY, 10495 Woodstock Rd., Roswell, GA 30075-2941. Mailing Address: 38 Hill St., Ste. 100, Roswell, GA 30075. Tel.: 770-594-6122.
E-mail: rrpd@ci.roswell.ga.us
Web Site: www.roswellgov.com
Key Personnel: Arts Supvr., Jan Gibbons.
Governing Authority: Branch: Roswell Art Center West, 1355 Woodstock Rd., Roswell, GA 30075. Tel.: 770-641-3990.
Art Gallery.
Collections: works by regional, local & international artists; drawings; paintings; printmaking; sculpture; ceramics; fiber; photography; mixed media.
Facilities: Museum-related items for sale.
Activities: special events; classes.
Hours & Admission Prices: Mon.-Fri. 9:30-6, Sat. 9-1. Roswell Art Center West: Wed.-Sat. 10-6. No charge. ♿

Royston

TY COBB MUSEUM, 461 Cook St., Royston, GA 30662-4003. Tel.: 706-245-1825. Fax: 706-245-1831.
Founded: 1998.
Congressional District: 9
Key Personnel: Cur., Julie Ridgway.
Personnel Profile: Full-Time Paid 1; Part-Time Paid 3; Part-Time Volunteers 1.
Sports Museum.
Collections: baseball & Ty Cobb history; art; memorabilia; books; video; film; personal artifacts; photographs.
Facilities: theater.
Activities: special events.
Hours & Admission Prices: Mon.-Fri. 9-4, Sat. 10-4; call to confirm. Adults $5, seniors 62 & over $4, students $3; discounts to groups of 10 or more; children under 5 & active military no charge.

Saint Marys

CUMBERLAND ISLAND NATIONAL SEASHORE, 129 Osborne St., Saint Marys, GA 31558-8416. Mailing Address: P.O. Box 806, Saint Marys, GA 31558-7109. Tel.: 912-882-4336 & 4335. Fax: 912-882-6284.
E-mail: john_a_mitchell@nps.gov
Web Site: www.nps.gov/cuis
Founded: 1972.
Congressional District: 1
Key Personnel: Supt., Fred Boyles; Cur., John A. Mitchell.
Governing Authority: federal. National Park Service, Southeast Region.
Historical Museum.
Collections: Historic Site: 2000 B.C. American Indian village site & Dungeness ruins. Historic Houses: c.1880-1910 Plum Orchard Mansion; Ice House Museum; outbuildings.
Research Fields: historic research appropriate to Cumberland Island; natural history; sea turtle research; bird tagging; family genealogy, history of island & region, natural history, pre-historic life-ways, architecture; majority of museum is in storage & needs special advance admission for research purposes.
Facilities: nature & visitor center; separate laboratory operation; small exhibit (historical) in Museum Ice House on Cumberland Island; historic buildings & ruins; natural fauna & flora.
Activities: guided tours; lectures; films; formally organized educational programs for children, adults, undergraduate & graduate students.
Publications: park mini-folder.
Hours & Admission Prices: Office: daily 8-4:30. Ferry: March-Nov. daily 9 am & 11:45 am; Dec-Feb. Mon. & Thurs.-Sun. 9 am & 11:45 am. Round trip: adults $17, senior citizens 65 & over $15; children 12 & under $12. Day use fee $4 per person; call office for reservations 912-673-7747. ♿
Attendance: 40,000 (estimated)

ST. MARYS SUBMARINE MUSEUM, 102 St. Marys St. W., Saint Marys, GA 31558-4945. Tel.: 912-882-2782. Fax: 912-882-2748.
E-mail: submus@tds.net
Web Site: www.stmaryssubmuseum.com
Founded: 1995.
Key Personnel: Pres., Doug Cooper; Museum Shop Mgr., John Crouse.
Personnel Profile: Full-Time Paid 1; Part-Time Paid 2.
Governing Authority: Tax-exempt.
Military & Submarine Museum.
Collections: submarine artifacts, history & memorabilia; photographs.
Research Fields: quarterly newsletter; submarine history.
Facilities: Gift items for sale.
Activities: submarine periscope look out. Museum Sponsors: U.S. Subvets WWII Annual Memorial Service.
Publications: quarterly newsletter; quarterly Georgia submarine veterans newsletter; submarine history CD.
Hours & Admission Prices: Tues.-Sat. 10-4, Sun. 1-5. Adults 19-62 $4, senior citizens 63-99 & military $3, children 6-18 $2; children under 6 & members no charge. Closed New Year's Eve, Day & week; Easter; Thanksgiving; Christmas week. ♿
Attendance: 10,000 (estimated)
Membership: Children $5; Individual $15; Family $25

Saint Simons Island

THE ARTHUR J. MOORE METHODIST MUSEUM, Arthur Moore Dr., Saint Simons Island, GA 31522. Mailing Address: P.O. Box 24081, Saint Simons Island, GA 31522-7081. Tel.: 912-638-4050. Fax: 912-638-9050.
E-mail: methmuse@bellsouth.net
Web Site: www.mooremethodistmuseum.org/
Founded: 1965.
Congressional District: 1
Key Personnel: Dir., Judi Fergus.
Personnel Profile: Full-Time Paid 2; Part-Time Volunteers 10.
Governing Authority: church. Parent Institution: South Georgia Annual Conference of the U.M.C. Affiliated with the South Georgia Methodist Conference Epworth by the Sea, Inc. Tax-exempt.
Religious Museum: near the site of Oglethorpe, John and Charles Wesley's activities in 1736.
Collections: John & Charles Wesley memorabilia, letters, land grants; Nativities from around the world.
Research Fields: history of Methodist churches.
Facilities: 6,000-vol. library of religious material available for research; reading room.
Activities: guided tours; docent program or council; temporary exhibitions.
Publications: brochure, Historical Highlights.
Hours & Admission Prices: Tues.-Sat. 10-4. No charge; donations accepted. Closed New Year's Day; Independence Day; Thanksgiving; Christmas. ♿
Attendance: 15,000 (estimated)

FORT FREDERICA NATIONAL MONUMENT, 6516 Frederica Rd., Saint Simons Island, GA 31522. Tel.: 912-638-3639. Fax: 912-634-5357.
E-mail: denise_spear@nps.gov
Web Site: www.nps.gov/fofr
Founded: 1936.
Congressional District: 1
Personnel Profile: Full-Time Paid 11; Part-Time Paid 2; Part-Time Volunteers 35.
Governing Authority: Parent Institution: Dept. of the Interior. Tax-exempt.
Park Museum: visitor center.
Collections: study collection of artifacts found at Fort Frederica and town of Frederica. Historic Sites: 1736-1758 ruins of English barracks, fort and house foundations.
Research Fields: Frederica archeological reports; Frederica's early settlers.
Facilities: library; auditorium. Historical books & historical reproductions for sale.
Activities: talks; permanent & temporary exhibitions; 25-min. film on Frederica history; tours; living history; children's program; Wayside exhibits. Museum Sponsors: Frederica Festival; Theatrical digital tour.
Publications: pamphlet, Fort Frederica National Monument; booklet, Fort Frederica Color Book; books, The Bloody Summer of 1742: A Colonial Boy's Journal; Voyage to Georgia; The First Families of Frederica; Phoebe's Secret Diary: Daily Life and First Romance of a Colonial Girl.
Hours & Admission Prices: Visitor Center: daily 9-5. Adults $3, annual park pass $10; children under 16, Golden Age & Access Pass holders no charge. Closed Christmas. ♿
Attendance: 292,505 (accurate)

THE GLYNN ART ASSOCIATION, INC., 319 Mallery St., Saint Simons Island, GA 31522-4718. Tel.: 912-638-8770. Fax: 912-634-2787.
E-mail: glynnart@bellsouth.net
Web Site: www.glynnart.org
Founded: 1953.
Congressional District: 1
Key Personnel: Pres. (V), Keith Crusan; Vice Pres., Joyce Ledingham.
Personnel Profile: Full-Time Paid 1; Part-Time Paid 1; Part-Time Volunteers 40.
Governing Authority: nonprofit organization. Glynn Art Association, Inc. dba Coastal Alliance for the Arts. Tax-exempt: 509(a)(2), 501(c)(3).
Art Gallery.
Collections: series, Yesterday's Golden Isles, early primitive paintings of the area; pottery; works represent 160 artists.
Facilities: library of general art books available for research upon request; reading room; classrooms. Museum replicas, arts & craft items for sale.
Activities: guided tours; lectures; films; gallery talks; concerts; dance recitals; arts festivals; drama; study clubs; TV programs; formally organized education programs; docent program; traveling exhibitions.
Publications: newsletter; Sapelo.
Hours & Admission Prices: Tues.-Sat. 9-5. No charge; donations accepted. Closed New Year's Day; Independence Day; Labor Day; Thanksgiving; Christmas. ♿
Attendance: 10,000 (estimated)
Membership: Individual $25; Family $35; Donor $50; Patron $75; Sponsor $125; Friend $250; Benefactor $500 & up.

MARITIME MUSEUM AT HISTORIC COAST GUARD STATION, 4201 First St., Saint Simons Island, GA 31522-3902. Mailing Address: P.O. Box 21136, Saint Simons Island, GA 31522-0636. Tel.: 912-638-4666. Fax: 912-638-6609.
E-mail: ssi1872@comcast.net
Founded: 2006.
Congressional District: 1
Key Personnel: Dir., Patricia Morris; Pres., Cesar Rodriguez; Treas., David Fox; Devel. & Public Rels., Jerri Hager; Cur., Jenny Herring; Museum Shop Mgr., Michele Collins.
Personnel Profile: Full-Time Paid 7; Part-Time Paid 6; Part-Time Volunteers 100; Interns 2.
Governing Authority: private; nonprofit organization. Parent Institution: Coastal GA Historical Museum. Tax-exempt: 501(c)(3).
Coast Guard & Natural History Museum.
Collections: Coast Guard & military history; coastal Georgia's natural history; military artifacts; structures; photographs; personal artifacts.
Facilities: outdoor classroom; nature center. Museum-related items for sale.
Hours & Admission Prices: Mon.-Sat. 10-5, Sun. 1:30-5. Adults $6, children $3; discounts to groups; members no charge. Closed New Year's Day; Easter; Thanksgiving; Christmas Eve & Day. ♿
Attendance: 40,000 (estimated)

* **ST. SIMONS ISLAND LIGHTHOUSE MUSEUM, (M),** 101 12th St., Saint Simons Island, GA 31522-4821. Mailing Address: P.O. Box 21136, Saint Simons Island, GA 31522-0636. Tel.: 912-638-4666. Fax: 912-638-6609.
E-mail: ssi1872@comcast.net
Web Site: saintsimonslighthouse.org
Founded: 1965.
Congressional District: 1
Key Personnel: C.E.O. & Pres. (V), Cesar Rodriguez; Dir., Pat Morris; Museum Shop Mgr., Michele Collins.
Personnel Profile: Full-Time Paid 6; Part-Time Paid 6; Part-Time Volunteers 100; Interns 2.
Governing Authority: nonprofit organization. Affiliated with the Coastal Georgia Historical Society, P.O. Box 21136, St. Simons Island, GA. Tax-exempt: 501(c)(3).
Historical Society Museum: located near the site of Colonial Fort St. Simons & Fort Brown, a Civil War site.
Collections: artifacts; books; journals; manuscripts; photographs; slides; graphic arts; audio-visual material of the coastal Georgia area from 1788-present. Historical Structures: c.1872 lighthouse; 1890 oil house; 1872 lightkeepers' dwelling & archives complex.
Research Fields: all aspects of coastal history, crafts & lifestyles from the Spanish period to the present.
Facilities: 500-vol. library on coastal history available for use on premises. Books & museum-related items for sale.
Activities: guided tours for groups; lectures; docent program; exhibitions; craft demonstrations; historical excursions; seminars.
Publications: quarterly newsletter; book, Historic Glimpses of St. Simons; pamphlet, Ghost Stories and Superstitions of Old St. Simons; Lighthouses of Georgia.
Hours & Admission Prices: Mon.-Sat. 10-5, Sun. 1:30-5. Adults $6, children under 12 $3; discounts to groups, AAM, ICOM, SEMC & museum members; military & children under 6 no charge. Closed New Year's Day; Easter; Thanksgiving; Christmas Eve & Day. ♿
Attendance: 90,000 (accurate)
Membership: Basic $35; Membership Plus $50; Second Asst. to Keeper $175; First Asst. to Keeper $300; Business $500; Keeper of Light $1,000.

Sandersville

THE BROWN HOUSE MUSEUM, 268 N. Harris St., Sandersville, GA 31082. Mailing Address: P.O. Box 6088, Sandersville, GA 31082-6088. Tel.: 478-552-1965 & 2963.
Founded: 1999.
Congressional District: 10
Key Personnel: Dir., Mary Alice Jordan; Pres. Society, Ed Jordan.
Personnel Profile: Full-Time Volunteers 18.
Governing Authority: Parent Institution: Washington County Historical Society.
History Museum: housed in c.1850 house, headquarters for General Sherman in 1864.
Collections: Washington County history.
Hours & Admission Prices: Tues. & Thurs. 2-5; other times by appointment. No charge; donations accepted. Closed holidays. ♿

THE CHARLES EDWARD CHOATE EXHIBIT, 131 W. Haynes St., Ste. B, Sandersville, GA 31082-1737. Mailing Address: P.O. Box 582, Sandersville, GA 31082-0582. Tel.: 478-552-3288. Fax: 478-552-1449.
E-mail: wacocofc@sandersville.net
Web Site: www.washingtoncounty-ga.com
Founded: 1996.
Congressional District: 12
Governing Authority: Parent Institution: Washington County Chamber of Commerce.
Art Museum.
Collections: Sterling Everett paintings; photographs.
Activities: self guided tours.
Hours & Admission Prices: Mon.-Fri. 9-12 & 1-5. No charge. Closed holidays. ♿
Attendance: 50 (estimated)

GENEALOGY RESEARCH CENTER AND OLD JAIL MUSEUM, 129 Jones St., Sandersville, GA 31082-1768. Mailing Address: P.O. Box 6088, Sandersville, GA 31082-6088. Tel.: 478-552-6965.
E-mail: wacogrc@nctv.com
Web Site: www.rootsweb.com/gawashin/genweb/
Formerly: Washington County Museum
Founded: 1978.
Congressional District: 10
Key Personnel: Dir. & Chm. (V), Loretta Cato; C.E.O., Ed Jordan.
Personnel Profile: Part-Time Volunteers 20.
Governing Authority: private; nonprofit organization. Branch Museums: The Brown House Museum, 268 N. Harris St., Sandersville, GA 31082. Tel. 912-552-1965. Genealogy Research Center and Museum, 129 Jones St., Sandersville, GA 31082. Tel. 912-552-6965. Tax-exempt.
History Museum: housed in c.1891 sheriffs' house with attached jail.
Collections: Washington County history; genealogy.
Research Fields: genealogy.
Publications: quarterly newsletter.
Hours & Admission Prices: Tues. & Thurs. 2-5. No charge; donations accepted. Closed holidays. ♿
Attendance: 400 (estimated)
Membership: Adult $12; Family $15.

Sandy Springs

SANDY SPRINGS HISTORIC SITE & MUSEUM, 6075 Sandy Springs Circle, Sandy Springs, GA 30328-3841. Mailing Address: P.O. Box 720213, Sandy Springs, GA 30358-2213. Tel.: 404-851-9111. Fax: 404-851-9807.
Key Personnel: Exec. Dir., Carol Thompson
Historic House: housed in the Williams-Payne house; built in 1869.
Collections: period artifacts; photographs; books; oral histories; maps; manuscripts.
Hours & Admission Prices: House: by appointment. Park: daily dawn to 8pm. No charge.

Sautee

SAUTEE-NACOOCHEE CENTER, (M), 283 Hwy. 255 N., Sautee, GA 30571-2606. Mailing Address: P.O. Box 460, Sautee, GA 30571-0460. Tel.: 706-878-3300. Fax: 706-878-1395.
Web Site: www.snca.org
Formerly: Sautee-Nacoochee Community Association
Founded: 1982.
Key Personnel: C.E.O. & Dir., Kathy Blandin, Ph.D.; Chm., John Erberle; Cur., Sam Schultz; Cur. Folk Pottery, John Burrison.
Personnel Profile: Full-Time Paid 3; Part-Time Paid 8; Part-Time Volunteers 312; Interns 2.
Governing Authority: private; nonprofit organization. Branch Museums: History Museum of Sautee-Nacoochee; The Center Gallery. Tax-exempt.
Art & History Museum.
Collections: paintings; pottery; glass; jewelry.
Major Exhibits: LQ Meaders Family Pottery Tradition, 11/09-9/10.
Research Fields: folk pottery.
Hours & Admission Prices: Office: Mon.-Fri. 9-5. Museum & Gallery: Sat. 10-5, Sun. 1-5. Adults $5. ♿
Attendance: 22,300 (estimated)
Membership: Student $28; Senior Individual $38; Individual $53; Senior Family $58; Family $83; Patron $150.

Savannah

ANDREW LOW HOUSE, 329 Abercorn St., Savannah, GA 31401-4634. Tel.: 912-233-6854. Fax: 912-233-9239.
E-mail: support@gapcdr.com
Web Site: www.andrewlowhouse.com
Founded: 1927.
Congressional District: 1
Key Personnel: Chm., Mrs. Samuel Zemurray; Pres., Mrs. Albert Esby Carlyle; Dir., Stephen Bohlin; Registrar, Jessica Mumford.
Personnel Profile: Full-Time Paid 1; Part-Time Paid 18; Part-Time Volunteers 60.
Governing Authority: private; nonprofit organization. Tax-exempt: 501(c)(3).
Historic Site: housed in the former home of Andrew Low, a wealthy Savannah cotton factor.
Collections: Andrew Low history; 19th-century decorative arts, 1800-1850.
Research Fields: building archaeology.
Facilities: 1,000-vol. library; botanical garden. Museum-related items for sale.
Activities: guided tours.
Publications: annual report, The Low Exchange.
Hours & Admission Prices: Mon.-Sat. 10-4, Sun. 12-4. Adults $8, students & children $6; discounts to groups of 10 or more. Closed Labor Day; Thanksgiving; Christmas.
Attendance: 21,078 (accurate)

ARCHIVES MUSEUM, TEMPLE MICKVE ISRAEL, Monterey Square, Savannah, GA 31401. Mailing Address: P.O. Box 816, Savannah, GA 31402-0816. Tel.: 912-233-1547. Fax: 912-233-3086.
E-mail: mickveisr@aol.com
Web Site: www.mickveisrael.org
Founded: 1733.
Congressional District: 12
Key Personnel: Rabbi, Arnold Belzer; Pres., Steve Gordon; Chm. (V), Eileen Lobel; Chm. (V), Alan Gaynor; Vice Pres., Neil Brecker; Gift Shop Mgr., Glenda McNew; Temple Admin., Anne Maner.
Personnel Profile: Full-Time Paid 5; Part-Time Volunteers 10.
Governing Authority: nonprofit organization. Tax-exempt.
Religious Museum: housed in c.1876 Gothic style, Congregation Mickve Israel Synagogue.
Collections: 18th-20th century artifacts of Jewish life.
Research Fields: archival records for research on Jews in Savannah, Georgia & the South from 1733-present day.
Facilities: 20,000-vol. library pertaining to Jewish studies available for research by special permission. Ceremonial objects, books & jewelry for sale.
Activities: guided tours; permanent exhibitions; heritage tours.
Publications: bimonthly newsletter, Contact; biweekly event newsletter.
Hours & Admission Prices: Mon.-Fri. 10-1 & 2-4, call to confirm. Adults $5; children under 12 & members no charge. Closed holidays. ♿
Attendance: 8,000 (estimated)

DAVENPORT HOUSE MUSEUM, 324 E. State St., Savannah, GA 31401-3411. Tel.: 912-236-8097. Fax: 912-233-7938.
E-mail: info@davenporthousemuseum.org
Web Site: davenporthousemuseum.org
Founded: 1955.
Congressional District: 12
Key Personnel: Pres. (V), Ann Koontz; C.E.O. Historic Savannah Foundation, Daniel Carey; Dir., Jamie Credle; Museum Assoc., Jeff Freeman; Volunteer Coord., Dottie Kraft; Museum Shop Mgr., Ben Head; Maintenance Technician, Raleigh Marcell.
Personnel Profile: Full-Time Paid 2; Part-Time Paid 15; Part-Time Volunteers 75.
Governing Authority: board of trustees. Parent Institution: Historic Savannah Foundation. Tax-exempt: 501(c)(3).
Historic House Museum.
Collections: period furniture based on the 1828 probate court inventory; Federal furniture; Kennedy pharmacy.
Research Fields: paint analysis; historic preservation; 19th century decorative arts; heritage education; antebellum social history.
Facilities: garden; meeting facilities. Museum-related items for sale.
Activities: guided tours; docent program; junior interpreter program; living history; holiday evening tours; Madeira traditions experience; tea program.
Publications: books: Savannah; Historic Savannah Survey Book; The Davenport House Museum: Savannah's Beacon of Preservation; tour book; monthly volunteer newsletter; semiannual newsletter, Friends.
Hours & Admission Prices: Mon.-Sat. 10-4, Sun. 1-4; tours on the half hour; special and group tours available upon request. Adults $8, students 6-18 $5; discount to AAM, AAA, Coastal Museum Assoc. members & National Trust Partner Place members; members & children under 6 no charge. Closed New Year's Day; St. Patrick's Day; Easter; Independence Day; Thanksgiving; Christmas Day.
Attendance: 28,508 (accurate)
Membership: Annual Giving Levels: Brick Mason $1-$49; Carpenter $50-$149; Master Builder $150-$249; Alderman $250-$599; Fire Warden $600-$999; McKinnon Circle $1,000.

FORT PULASKI NATIONAL MONUMENT, U.S. Hwy. 80 E., Savannah, GA 31410. Mailing Address: P.O. Box 30757, Savannah, GA 31410-0757. Tel.: 912-786-5787. Fax: 912-652-4232.
E-mail: june_devisfruto@nps.gov
Web Site: www.nps.gov/fopu/
Founded: 1924.
Congressional District: 1
Key Personnel: Supt., Randy Wester; Museum Shop Mgr., Patty Sevenheuser.
Personnel Profile: Full-Time Paid 15; Part-Time Paid 8; Part-Time Volunteers 30.
Governing Authority: federal. National Park Service, Dept. of the Interior, Washington, DC 20240. Tax-exempt.
History Museum & Park.
Collections: Civil War cannon and projectiles; uniform accessories; personal effects of soldiers; bottle collection; c.1862 period & replica room furnishings; c.1890 battery Horace Hambright.
Research Fields: garrison life of Federal and Confederate soldiers; heavy seacoast artillery; seacoast defenses of the U.S.
Facilities: 1,200-vol. library of general reference books & specialized research on Civil War, cultural & natural resource management, 1934-1940, historic preservation of Cockspur Island, Coastal Georgia & South Carolina on premises only with two weeks advance reservation; visitor center; history & nature trails; picnic area. Handbooks on various historic sites, natural history field guides, post cards & mementoes relating to Fort Pulaski for sale.
Activities: tours; lectures; costumed presentations; permanent & temporary exhibitions.
Publications: guidebooks; pamphlets.
Hours & Admission Prices: Labor Day-Memorial Day daily 9-5; call for extended summer hours. Adult 16 & over $3; children 15 & under no charge. Golden Age, Eagle & National Park Pass accepted. Closed Thanksgiving; Christmas. ♿
Attendance: 382,870 (accurate)

GEORGIA HISTORICAL SOCIETY, 501 Whitaker St., Savannah, GA 31401-4889. Tel.: 912-651-2125. Fax: 912-651-2831.
E-mail: ghs@georgiahistory.com
Web Site: www.georgiahistory.com
Founded: 1839.
Congressional District: 12
Key Personnel: Pres., Dr. W. Todd Groce; Chm., Bill Jones, III; Exec. Vice Pres., Laura Garcia-Culler; Dir. Library & Archives, Nora Lewis; Sr. Historian, Dr. Stan Deaton.
Personnel Profile: Full-Time Paid 17; Part-Time Paid 2; Part-Time Volunteers 19; Interns 4.
Governing Authority: society. Tax-exempt: 501(c)(3).
Historical Society Museum: housed in 1874-1875 building designed by Detlief Lienau.
Collections: Georgia history & culture; books; manuscripts; maps; photographs; prints; newspapers; paintings; portraits; period artifacts.
Research Fields: 18th, 19th & 20th-century Georgia manuscripts; southern history; genealogy.
Facilities: 25,000-vol. library of books on Georgia & American history; reading room.
Activities: lectures; temporary exhibitions; historical marker program; technical services & programming for local historical societies & museums; teacher institutes; educational programs for school children; historical tours.
Publications: quarterly magazine, Georgia Historical Quarterly; occasional volume, Collections of the Georgia Historical Society; quarterly newsmagazine, Georgia History Today.
Hours & Admission Prices: Tues.-Sat. 10-5. Adults $5; members no charge. Closed national & state holidays. ♿
Attendance: 35,000 (accurate)
Membership: Student $25; Individual $50; Family $60; Library $75; Sponsor $100; Benefactor $250; Corporate & Sustainer $500; John MacPherson Berrien Circle $1,000-2,499; William Brown Hodgson Circle $2,500 & up; 1839 Society $5,000.

JULIETTE GORDON LOW BIRTHPLACE, (M), 10 E. Oglethorpe Ave., Savannah, GA 31401-3707. Tel.: 912-233-4501. Fax: 912-233-4659. TDD: 912-233-4501.
E-mail: info@juliettegordonlowbirthplace.org
Web Site: www.girlscouts.org/birthplace
Founded: 1956.
Congressional District: 1
Key Personnel: C.E.O. & Dir., Fran Powell Harold; Cur., Sherry Lang; Program Mgr., Katherine Keena; Museum Shop Mgr., Linda LeFurgy.
Personnel Profile: Full-Time Paid 12; Part-Time Paid 55; Part-Time Volunteers 100; Interns 2.
Governing Authority: nonprofit organization. Parent Institution: Girl Scouts of the U.S.A., 420 5th Ave., New York, NY 10018. Tax-exempt.
Historic House Museum: 1818-1821 Wayne-Gordon House.
Collections: 19th-century memorabilia, art & furniture of Juliette Gordon Low & the Gordon family; Girl Scouts of the U.S.A.
Research Fields: Juliette Gordon Low; history of Wayne-Gordon House; founding & early years, 1912-1915, of Girl Scouts of the U.S.A.; 19th-century lifestyles.
Facilities: Museum-related items for sale.
Activities: guided tours; formally organized education programs for Girl Scouts, school groups & others; permanent & temporary exhibitions; special events.
Publications: Birthplace Bound.
Hours & Admission Prices: March-Oct. Mon.-Sat. 10-4, Sun. 11-4; Nov.-Feb. Mon.-Tues. & Thurs.-Sat. 10-4, Sun. 11-4. Adults $8; Girl Scout adults & students 6-20 $7, Girl Scouts 6-18 $6; children 5 & under no charge. Closed New Year's Day; St. Patrick's Day; Easter; Thanksgiving; Christmas Eve & Day; first two weeks in Jan. & Wed. Nov.-Feb. ♿
Attendance: 65,000 (accurate)
Membership: Girl Scouts of U.S.A.: Annual $10; the Birthplace Circle of Friends: Annual Green Level $50-$249; Silver Level $250-$499; Gold Level $500-$999; Platinum Level $1,000 & up.

OATLAND ISLAND WILDLIFE CENTER, 711 Sandtown Rd., Savannah, GA 31410-1019. Tel.: 912-395-1212 & 1500. Fax: 912-898-3983.
Web Site: www.oatlandisland.org
Formerly: Oatland Island Education Center
Founded: 1974.
Congressional District: 1
Key Personnel: Education, Heather Merbs; Education, Pam Keener; Education, Dan Genrich; Education, Annie Quinting; Education, Max McKelvey; Administrative Sec., Shirley Calhoun; Naturalist, Pam Hewatt; Naturalist, Michele Mazzei.
Personnel Profile: Full-Time Paid 12; Part-Time Volunteers 50; Interns 2.
Governing Authority: public school district. Parent Institution: Chatham-Savannah Board of Education, 208 Bull St., Savannah, GA 31406. Tel.: 912-234-2541. Tax-exempt.
Environmental Education Nature Center.
Collections: wild animals indigenous to state of Georgia; Phillips barn; Martin Cane mill. Historic Houses: 1835 Delk-Dawson House; 1835 Wayne County Cabin.
Facilities: 1,500-vol. library of natural science books available for research; zoological park; nature center; auditorium; classrooms; observatory.
Activities: guided tours; formally organized education programs for children, adults & undergraduate college students.
Publications: brochure; trail guide; program guide; newsletter.
Hours & Admission Prices: Daily 10-4. Adults $5, seniors, children 4-17 & military $3; members no charge. Closed New Year's Day; St. Patrick's Day; Easter; Memorial Day; Independence Day; Labor Day; Thanksgiving; Christmas. ♿
Attendance: 36,000 (estimated)
Membership: Student $15; Individual $25; Family $35; Supporter $50; Donor $100; Patron $250; Sponsor $1,000; Benefactor $2,000.

OLD FORT JACKSON, 1 Ft. Jackson Rd., Savannah, GA 31404-1039. Tel.: 912-232-3945. Fax: 912-236-5126.
E-mail: oldfortjackson@chsgeorgia.org
Web Site: www.chsgeorgia.org/jackson
Founded: 1975.
Congressional District: 1
Key Personnel: Site Mgr., Marty Liebschner.
Personnel Profile: Full-Time Paid 6; Part-Time Paid 4; Part-Time Volunteers 25.
Governing Authority: board of directors. Parent Institution: Coastal Heritage Society. Tax-exempt.
American Military Museum.
Collections: artifacts relating to the military history of Savannah including the American Revolution, the War of 1812 & the Civil War.
Research Fields: U.S. military in Savannah, 1800-1877; history of Deptford Tract where Fort Jackson now stands; history of construction technology; Savannah Naval Forces & CSS Georgia.
Facilities: picnic area. Museum-related items for sale.
Activities: daily self-guided tours with canon firing demonstrations & uniformed interpreters; holiday programs; special school & adult programs.
Publications: quarterly newsletter; book, Tide Craft.
Hours & Admission Prices: Daily 9-5. Adults $4.25, students, senior citizens & military (past & present) $3.75; discounts to AAA & CHS members; children 6 & under no charge. Closed New Year's Day; Thanksgiving; Christmas. ♿
Attendance: 75,000 (estimated)

Membership: Student $15; Basic $25; Patron $50; Contributing $100; Sustaining $250; Sponsor $500; Turnbull $1,000.

RALPH MARK GILBERT CIVIL RIGHTS MUSEUM, 460 Martin Luther King, Jr. Blvd., Savannah, GA 31401-4800. Tel.: 912-231-8900. Fax: 912-234-2577.
E-mail: nancyeand@yahoo.com
Web Site: www.sip.armstrong.edu/CivilRightsMuseum/Civilindex.html
History Museum: named in honor of the late Dr. Ralph Mark Gilbert, father of Savannah's civil rights movement & NAACP leader.
Collections: civil rights history; photographs.
Hours & Admission Prices: Tues.-Sat. 9-5. Museum Tours: adults $8, senior citizens 65 & over $6, students $4; discounts to groups of 10 or more; members no charge.

SAVANNAH COLLEGE OF ART AND DESIGN GALLERIES, (M), 201 E. Broughton St., Savannah, GA 31401-3401. Mailing Address: P.O. Box 3146, Savannah, GA 31402-3146. Tel.: 912-525-4735. Fax: 912-525-4952.
E-mail: exhibitions@scad.edu
Web Site: www.scad.edu
Formerly: Pinnacle Gallery
Founded: 1979.
Key Personnel: Exec. Dir., Laurie Ann Farrell.
Personnel Profile: Full-Time Paid 18; Part-Time Paid 5.
Governing Authority: Parent Institution: Savannah College of Art and Design (SCAD). Tax-exempt.
Art Museum.
Collections: work of prominent artists & emerging Savannah College of Art and Design alumni.
Publications: exhibition catalogs.
Hours & Admission Prices: Mon.-Fri. 10-6, Sat. 10-5, Sun. 1-4. No charge; donations accepted. ♿
Attendance: 25,000 (estimated)

SAVANNAH HISTORY MUSEUM, 303 Martin Luther King Jr. Blvd., Savannah, GA 31401-4217. Tel.: 912-651-6825 & 238-1779.
Web Site: www.chsgeorgia.org/shm/
Governing Authority: nonprofit organization. Tax-exempt: 501(c)(3).
History Museum: housed in the old Central of Georgia Railway passenger shed, built 1850-1860s.
Collections: Savannah's history from 1733 to present; Revolutionary War Battle of Savannah; dugout canoes; 19th & 20th-century women's fashions; Forest Gump's bench; weapons; military uniforms; Savannah's railway history.
Facilities: theater. Museum-related items for sale.
Activities: film presentations; programs.
Hours & Admission Prices: Mon.-Fri. 8:30-5, Sat.-Sun. 9-5. Call for admission prices.

SCAD MUSEUM OF ART, (M), 227 Martin Luther King Jr. Blvd., Savannah, GA 31401-4242. Mailing Address: P.O. Box 3146, Savannah, GA 31402-3146. Tel.: 912-525-7191 & 7199.
Web Site: www.scad.edu
Founded: 2002.
Congressional District: 12
Key Personnel: Dir., Maureen Burke, Ph.D.
Personnel Profile: Full-Time Paid 5; Part-Time Volunteers 1; Interns 2.
Governing Authority: college. Parent Institution: Savannah College of Art and Design. Subsidiary Institution: Earle W. Newton Center for British and American Studies; Walter O. Evans Center for African American Studies. Tax-exempt.
Art Museum.
Collections: paintings including 17th-19th century British & colonial American portaits; prints from the Newton collection; photographs including the 19th-20th century Rhoades collection; African American art from the Evans collection; 20th-21st century costumes including the C.Z. Guest collection.
Research Fields: British & American art; African-American art.
Activities: temporary & permanent exhibitions; group tours; gallery talks; lectures; special events.
Hours & Admission Prices: Mon.-Fri. 10-5, Sun. 1-5; groups by appointment. No charge; donations accepted.
Attendance: 12,000 (estimated)

SHIPS OF THE SEA MARITIME MUSEUM/WILLIAM SCARBROUGH HOUSE, (M), 41 Martin Luther King Blvd., Savannah, GA 31401-2435. Tel.: 912-232-1511. Fax: 912-234-7363.
E-mail: contact@shipsofthesea.org
Web Site: www.shipsofthesea.org
Founded: 1966.
Key Personnel: C.E.O., Tony Pizzo; Asst. Dir., Karl DeVries; Museum Shop Mgr., Eileen Lewis.
Personnel Profile: Full-Time Paid 3; Part-Time Paid 6.
Governing Authority: private; nonprofit organization. Tax-exempt: 501(c)(3).
Maritime Museum.
Collections: 18th-19th century large scale ship models, paintings & maritime antiques; navigational instruments; seafaring artifacts; video presentations.
Facilities: botanical garden; educational facilities. Museum-related items for sale.
Activities: formal educational programs for children; guided tours; lectures; instrument-making; boatbuilding.
Publications: book, Flotsam and Jetsam; William Scarbrough's House; Savannah Line; Savannah & The Civil War at Sea.
Hours & Admission Prices: Tues.-Sun. 10-5 (last admission 4:30). Family $20, adults $8, senior citizens & students $6; discounts to groups of 10 or more. Closed New Year's Eve & Day; St. Patrick's Day; Easter; Memorial Day; Labor Day; Thanksgiving & day after; Christmas Eve & Day.
Attendance: 20,000 (estimated)

* **TELFAIR MUSEUM OF ART, (M),** Telfair Academy of Arts & Sciences, 121 Barnard St., Savannah, GA 31401. Mailing Address: P.O. Box 10081, Savannah, GA 31412-0281. Tel.: 912-232-1177, ext. 16. Fax: 912-232-6954.
E-mail: hadaways@telfair.org
Web Site: www.telfair.org
Founded: 1875.
Congressional District: 1
Key Personnel: Dir., Steven S. High; Chm. (V) & Pres. (V), Cathy Solomons; Financial Officer, Shelly Cannady; Registrar, Jessica Mumford; Designer & Preparator, Milutin Pavlovic; Sr. Cur. Education, Harry H. DeLorme; Admin., Sandra S. Hadaway; Cur. Fine Arts & Exhibitions, Hollis K. McCullough; Cur. Owens-Thomas House, Tania J. Sammons; Asst. Cur., Elizabeth Moore; Asst. Cur., Courtney McGowan; Education Asst., Sara Ward; Studio Coord., Torrey Stifel; Volunteer & Special Events Mgr., Mikaela Green; Dir. Devel., Anne J. Bone; Dir. Membership, Pam Jones; Grants Mgr., Dustin Deal; Editor, Kate Hoernle; Dir. Mktg. & Public Rels., Kristin Boylston; Museum Shop Mgr., Lisa Ocampo.
Personnel Profile: Full-Time Paid 48; Part-Time Paid 35; Part-Time Volunteers 900; Interns 10.
Governing Authority: board of trustees; nonprofit. Subsidiary Institution: Owens-Thomas House; Jepson Center for the Arts, 207 W. York St., Savannah, GA. Tax-exempt: 501(c)(3).
Art Museum & Historic House: housed in 1819 Regency mansion, Telfair Academy building & Owens-Thomas House, designed by architect William Jay; 1883 wing added by architect Detlef Lienau.
Collections: Regency mansion contains many Telfair family objects from late 18th & early 19th century, including pieces commissioned from Duncan Phyfe and Thomas Cooke; Savannah-made silver; portraits. Art museum wing contains 18th-20th century American & European paintings; prints; drawings; sculptures; porcelain; costumes; collection of works by Kahlil Gibran; decorative arts; sculpture; prints; drawings; graphic arts; African American art.
Research Fields: pertaining to the collections: American painting, decorative arts; architecture.
Facilities: Jepson Center for the Arts; educational facilities. Museum-related items for sale.
Activities: docent tours; guided tours; special guided tours in French, Italian & Spanish available upon request; lectures; films; gallery talks; concerts; school & docent programs; education programs; permanent & temporary exhibitions.
Publications: books, Christopher P.H. Murphy: A Retrospective; The Octagon Room: Classical Savannah: Fine & Decorative Arts 1800-1840; Looking Back: Art in Savannah 1900-1960; Nostrums for Fashionable Entertainments: Dining in Georgia, 1800-1850.
Hours & Admission Prices: Sun. 1-5, Mon. & Wed.-Sat. 10-5. Adults $15, senior citizens & military $12, college students $5, children 6-12 $4; discounts to AAA, AAM, Southeast Reciprocal Museum Program, & members Gibbes Art Gallery, Charleston; members & children under 5 no charge. Closed holidays. ♿
Attendance: 186,999 (accurate)
Membership: Artist & Teacher $35; Individual $45; Senior & Dual $65; Family $75; Friend $150; Donor $500; Patron $1,000; Grand Patron $1,500; Sponsor $2,500; Benefactor $5,000.

WORMSLOE STATE HISTORIC SITE, 7601 Skidaway Rd., Savannah, GA 31406-6449. Tel.: 912-353-3023. Fax: 912-353-3023.
E-mail: wormsloe@bellsouth.net
Web Site: www.gastateparks.org
Founded: 1973.
Congressional District: 1

Key Personnel: Mgr., Chris Floyd; Interpretive Ranger, Lane Harris; Museum Shop Mgr., Kathy Morris.
Personnel Profile: Full-Time Paid 4; Part-Time Paid 2; Part-Time Volunteers 15.
Governing Authority: state. Parent Institution: Parks, Recreation & Historic Sites Div., Dept. of Natural Resources. Tax-exempt.
Historic Site: ruins of 1739 fortified house.
Collections: archaeological artifacts from period c.1733-1850.
Research Fields: Georgia cultural & natural history.
Facilities: interpretive center; audiovisual room; living history area.
Activities: guided & self-guided touring walks; audiovisual; special programs.
Hours & Admission Prices: Tues.-Sun. 9-5; groups by appointment. Adults $5, senior citizens & tour groups of 15 or more $4.50, children 6-17 $3.50, youth groups of 15 or more $3; children 5 & under no charge. Closed New Year's Day; Thanksgiving; Christmas. ♿
Attendance: 100,000 (estimated)
Membership: Child $10; Adult $15; Family $30.

Smyrna

SMYRNA MUSEUM, 2861 Atlanta Rd., S.E., Smyrna, GA 30080-3657. Tel.: 770-435-7549 & 431-2858.
E-mail: smyrnamuse@aol.com
Web Site: www.rootsweb.ancestry.com/~gashgs
Historical Society Museum.
Collections: photographs; publications; historical & genealogical research materials.
Hours & Admission Prices: Mon.-Sat. 10-4; other times by appointment. No charge.

Statesboro

* **GEORGIA SOUTHERN UNIVERSITY MUSEUM, (M),** Rosenwald Bldg., Statesboro, GA 30460-1000. Mailing Address: P.O. Box 8061, Statesboro, GA 30460-1000. Tel.: 912-478-5444. Fax: 912-478-0729.
E-mail: btharp@georgiasouthern.edu
Web Site: ceps.georgiasouthern.edu/museum/
Founded: 1980.
Congressional District: 1
Key Personnel: Dir., Dr. Brent W. Tharp; Asst. Dir., Debbie Gleason; Administrative Sec., Susan Shryock; Cur. Education, Ruby Ashley; Outreach Sec., Candace Green; Design Specialist, Deborah Harvey; Cur. Paleontology, Dr. Jonathan Geisler.
Personnel Profile: Full-Time Paid 7; Part-Time Paid 15; Part-Time Volunteers 20.
Governing Authority: university; nonprofit. Tax-exempt.
University Museum.
Collections: natural, cultural & geological history; fossil skeletons; 26-foot Mosasaur; 20-foot Middle-Eocene archaeocete whale; fossil vertebrates of Coastal Georgia; Southeastern Indians; fossil oysters; fish; Wiss cutlery, scissors & shears; dolphin & Bryde's whale skeletons.
Major Exhibits: Mad Scientist Laboratory: Earth Science, 11/09-5/10; Portraits in Bray (T), 11/09-12/09; Glyphs & Scripts: Writing Systems of the World, 1/10-4/10; Games & Bubbles, 5/10-8/10.
Research Fields: paleontology; geology; anthropology; technology.
Facilities: lecture hall; nature trail.
Activities: guided tours; lectures; films; broadcast programs; organized education programs adults, children & undergraduate or graduate college students; participatory, temporary & traveling exhibitions; science & social studies kit program & teacher training.
Publications: annual brochure, Georgia Southern Museum; occasional papers.
Hours & Admission Prices: Academic Year: Mon.-Fri. 9-5, Sat.-Sun. 2-5; Summer: Mon.-Fri. 10-5. No charge; donations accepted. Closed New Year's Day; Easter; Memorial Day; Independence Day; Labor Day; Thanksgiving; Christmas; academic breaks. ♿
Attendance: 35,000 (accurate)
Membership: Student $15; Individual $30; Family $50; Curator $100; Patron $250; Director $500; Monasaur Society $1,000; Georgiacetus Society $5,000.

Stockbridge

PANOLA MOUNTAIN STATE CONSERVATION PARK, 2600 Hwy. 155, S.W., Stockbridge, GA 30281-5250. Tel.: 770-389-7801. Fax: 770-389-7925.
E-mail: panola_mountain@mail.dnr.state.ga.us
Web Site: www.gastateparks.org/info/panolamt
Founded: 1974.
Congressional District: 6
Key Personnel: Resource Mgr., Jody Rice.
Personnel Profile: Full-Time Paid 6; Part-Time Paid 2; Part-Time Volunteers 4.
Governing Authority: state. Parks, Recreation & Historic Sites Div., Dept. of Natural Resources. Tax-exempt.
State Conservation Park.
Collections: granite monadnock; granite outcrop ecology; butterflies; moths; skippers; live reptiles; observation beehive; mounted mammal collection; live bats.
Research Fields: field ecology.
Facilities: visitor center; trails; scenic vistas; picnic area; playground.
Activities: teacher workshops; guided walks; audiovisual programs; environmental education programs.
Publications: newsletter.
Hours & Admission Prices: Park: Sept. 15-April 14 daily 7-6; April 15-Sept. 14 daily 7am-9pm. Interpretive Center: daily 8:30-5. $3 per vehicle; vans $20. Annual Pass: $30. ♿
Attendance: 201,000 (accurate)

Stone Mountain

ART STATION, 5384 Manor Dr., Stone Mountain, GA 30083-3067. Tel.: 770-469-1105.
E-mail: info@artstation.org
Web Site: www.artstation.org
Key Personnel: Founder, Pres. & Artistic Dir., David Thomas
Art Museum.
Collections: photographs; paintings.
Facilities: classrooms; studios; theater; rental facilities. Museum-related items for sale.
Activities: programs; performances; classes.
Hours & Admission Prices: Tues.-Fri. 10-5, Sat. 10-3. ♿

GEORGIA'S STONE MOUNTAIN PARK, Hwy. 78, Stone Mountain, GA 30086. Mailing Address: P.O. Box 778, Stone Mountain, GA 30086-0778. Tel.: 770-498-5690. Fax: 770-498-5735. TDD: 770-498-5702 (available through switchboard).
E-mail: smpmarketing@stonemountainpark.com
Web Site: www.stonemountainpark.com
Founded: 1958.
Congressional District: 55
Key Personnel: Gen. Mgr., Gerald Rakestraw; Coord. Mktg., Mike Duchock.
Personnel Profile: Full-Time Paid 18; Interns 1.
Governing Authority: Parent Institution: Silver Dollar City. state. Tax-exempt: 501(c)(3).
General Museum.
Collections: Indian artifacts; Civil War; preservation projects; Revolutionary War Colonial; early automobiles; musical instruments; 19th-century band organs; c.1830 Georgia-made furniture; 18th- & 19th-century English & American furniture. Historic Houses: 1790 Thornton House; 1845 Kingston House; 1845 Dickey House; 1845 Clayton House; 1869 grist mill; 1892 covered bridge.
Research Fields: Indian artifacts; geology; flora.
Facilities: botanical garden; nature trails.
Activities: school services; educational materials; guided tours; films; lectures. Park Sponsors: Yellow Daisy Festival and special events.
Hours & Admission Prices: Visitors Center: daily 8:30-5:30. One Day Adventure Pass: adults 12 & up $26, senior & military $23, children 3-11 $21. Closed Christmas. ♿
Attendance: 6,000,000 (accurate)

Thomasville

BIRDSONG NATURE CENTER, 2106 Meridian Rd., Thomasville, GA 31792-0417. Tel.: 229-377-4408; 800-953-BIRD (2473). Fax: 229-377-8723.
E-mail: birdsong@birdsongnaturecenter.org
Web Site: www.birdsongnaturecenter.org
Founded: 1986.
Congressional District: 2
Key Personnel: Exec. Dir., Kathleen D. Brady; Pres. (V), Robert Pando; Chm. (V), Bailey White.
Personnel Profile: Full-Time Paid 3; Part-Time Paid 8; Part-Time Volunteers 100.
Governing Authority: private; nonprofit organization. Tax-exempt: 501(c)(3).
Nature Center: former plantation; farmhouse & 1880s barn.
Collections: widely varying habitats; plants & wildlife; field, pine & hardwood forests; ponds; swamps.
Research Fields: bluebird breeding study; plant & animal inventory; prescribed burning; ecological management.
Facilities: nature center. Books, birdfeeders & museum-related items for sale.
Activities: guided tours; lectures; formal education programs for adults, children & tailored programs for undergraduate & graduate students.

Annual Events: Fall Festival; Winter Solstice Celebration; Butterfly Festival; Nature Writers Event; ongoing seasonal programs on weekends.
Publications: bimonthly newsletter & calendar of events, Birdsong Nature Center.
Hours & Admission Prices: Wed. & Fri.-Sat. 9-5, Sun. 1-5; groups by appointment. Adults $5, children $2.50; discount to groups; Association of Nature Center Administrators members no charge. Closed New Year's Day; Christmas.
Attendance: 3,700 (accurate)
Membership: Individual Friend $25; Family Friends $35; Friends of the Cardinal $50; Friends of the Chicadee $100; Friends of the Bluebird $500; Birdsong Naturalist $1,000; Corporate Friends $100-$1,000.

LAPHAM-PATTERSON HOUSE, 626 N. Dawson St., Thomasville, GA 31792-4449. Tel.: 229-225-4004. Fax: 229-227-2419.
E-mail: lphouse@rose.net
Web Site: www.gastateparks.org/info/lapham
Founded: 1974.
Congressional District: 2
Key Personnel: C.E.O. & Cur., Cheryl Walters; Interpretive Ranger, Voncile Jones; Chm. (V), John Wood.
Personnel Profile: Full-Time Paid 2; Part-Time Paid 2; Part-Time Volunteers 14.
Governing Authority: state. Affiliated with the Parks, Recreation & Historic Sites Div., Georgia Dept. of Natural Resources Parks & History Sites, 205 Butler St., S.E., Suite 1352, Atlanta, GA 30334. Tax-exempt.
Historic House: c.1884 Lapham-Patterson House, Victorian home.
Collections: furnishings; period rooms.
Research Fields: Victorian architecture.
Facilities: library.
Activities: guided tours; permanent & temporary exhibitions; community programs.
Publications: post cards; books.
Hours & Admission Prices: Temporarily closed. ♿
Attendance: 5,000 (accurate)
Membership: Individual $10; Family $15; Business $25; Corporate $250; Sustaining $500; Benefactor $1,000.

PEBBLE HILL PLANTATION, 1251 U.S. 319 S., Tallahassee Rd., Thomasville, GA 31792. Mailing Address: P.O. Box 830, Thomasville, GA 31799-0830. Tel.: 229-226-2344. Fax: 229-227-0095.
E-mail: swhite@pebblehill.com
Web Site: www.pebblehill.com
Founded: 1983.
Congressional District: 2
Key Personnel: Chm. (V), Warren Bicknell; Gen. Mgr., Wallace Goodman; Public Rels. & Asst. Gen. Mgr., Sue White; Museum Shop Mgr., Jed Wall.
Personnel Profile: Full-Time Paid 15; Part-Time Paid 12; Part-Time Volunteers 5.
Governing Authority: nonprofit organization. Parent Institution: Pebble Hill Foundation, Inc.
Historic Site & Buildings.
Collections: 18th- to 19th-century furniture; 18th- to 20th-century sporting art; photograph collections; decorative arts.
Research Fields: support research; site & family research related to interpretation; decorative arts.
Facilities: 3,600-vol. library of books. Gift items for sale.
Activities: guided tours; docent program; temporary exhibitions; special events.
Hours & Admission Prices: Tues.-Sat. 10-5, Sun. 1-5; last tour of the Main House begins at 3:45. Gate: adults $5, children 2-12 $2. House: adults $10, children 6-12 $4; children under 6 not admitted; discounts to groups of 18 & up with advance reservations. Closed New Year's Day; Thanksgiving; Christmas Eve & Day. ♿
Attendance: 20,000 (estimated)
Membership: Yearly membership $30.

THOMASVILLE CULTURAL CENTER, INC., 600 E. Washington St., Thomasville, GA 31792-4648. Mailing Address: P.O. Box 2177, Thomasville, GA 31799-2177. Tel.: 229-226-0588. Fax: 229-226-0599.
E-mail: info@thomasvilleculturalcenter.org
Web Site: www.thomasvilleculturalcenter.org
Founded: 1978.
Congressional District: 2
Key Personnel: C.E.O. & Exec. Dir., Tricia Collins; Pres. (V), Peggy Rich; Dir. Devel., Susan O'Neal; Dir. Finance, Kelly Swan; Dir. Education & Outreach, Mary Oglesby; Coord. Visual Arts, Amy Wheeler; Member Svcs. & Communications Coord., Rachael Fink; Dir. PWAF, Sharlene Celaya Cannon; Asst. Dir. PWAF, Holly Jarvis; Mgr. Bldg. & Grounds, Herbert Brinson; Administrative Asst., Casie Vela.
Personnel Profile: Full-Time Paid 10; Part-Time Paid 1; Part-Time Volunteers 197; Interns 1.
Governing Authority: nonprofit organization. Tax-exempt: 501(c)(3) and 170(b)(1)(A).
Cultural Center: housed in 1915 East Side School.
Collections: American and European paintings; wildlife art; over 800 ceramic objects; sculpture.
Major Exhibits: Winter Exhibition, 1/10-2/10; Youth Arts Show, 3/10; A Few of Our Favorite Things, 4/10-5/10; Summer Showcase & Invitational, 6/10-8/10; Fall Exhibition, 9/10-10/10.
Facilities: 550-seat auditorium; 4 exhibition galleries; instructional studio; educational facilities. Artwork on consignment & gifts of local interest for sale.
Activities: temporary & permanent exhibits; concerts; lectures; music & visual art classes for children & adults; guided tours; annual arts festivals.
Publications: newsletter, Plantation Wildlife; Arts Festival Magazine.
Hours & Admission Prices: Office: Tues.-Fri. 9-5. Gallery: Tues.-Fri. 9-5, Sat. 1-5. No charge; donations accepted. Closed New Year's Eve & Day; Martin Luther King Jr. Day; Easter; Memorial Day; Independence Day; Labor Day; Thanksgiving; Christmas Eve & Day. ♿
Attendance: 63,781 (estimated)
Membership: Individual $25-$50; Household $50-$100; Business $500; Artist's Guild (additional $10 at any level).

Thomson

HICKORY HILL, (M), 502 Hickory Hill Dr., Thomson, GA 30824-7655. Tel.: 706-595-7777; 877-595-9777 (toll free). Fax: 706-595-7177.
Web Site: www.hickory-hill.org
Founded: 2004.
Congressional District: 9
Key Personnel: Pres., Tad Brown; Chm. (V), Byron Attridge; Cur., Michelle Zupan.
Personnel Profile: Full-Time Paid 3; Part-Time Paid 2; Part-Time Volunteers 1; Interns 3.
Governing Authority: private; nonprofit organization. Parent Institution: The Watson Brown Foundation. Tax-exempt: 501(c)(3).
Historic House Museum: housed in the home of Thomas E. Watson.
Collections: personal artifacts; clothing; furniture; documents; photographs; 12 historic buildings; gardens.
Research Fields: Tom Watson's publishing plant, The Jeffersonian; Thomas Watson; populism.
Facilities: library; 256 acres; walking trails; gardens. Museum-related items for sale.
Activities: formal education programs; guided tours; scholar's forums; public history event. Annual Events: Tom Watson Watermelon Festival; Dig History Archaeology Camp; Sticks & Stones.
Publications: quarterly newsletter, Legacy; biannual, reprints of Tom Watson's books.
Hours & Admission Prices: Mon.-Fri. 10-5, Sat. by appointment. Adults $3, senior citizens $2, children $1; discounts AAM, ICOM & AASLH members & groups. Closed major holidays; Hickory Hill Forum. ♿
Attendance: 4,800 (estimated)

Tifton

AGRIRAMA, GEORGIA'S LIVING HISTORY MUSEUM & VILLAGE, Interstate 75 Exit 63B at 8th St., Tifton, GA 31793. Mailing Address: P.O. Box 736, Tifton, GA 31793-0736. Tel.: 229-386-3344; 800-767-1875. Fax: 229-386-3386.
E-mail: market@agrirama.com
Web Site: www.agrirama.com
Founded: 1972.
Congressional District: 2
Key Personnel: Dir., James Higgins; Chm. (V), George Lee; Mktg., Sherry Miley; Cur., John Johnson; Maintenance & Restoration, David King.
Personnel Profile: Full-Time Paid 15; Part-Time Paid 12; Part-Time Volunteers 4.
Governing Authority: state. Parent Institution: Georgia Agrirama Board of Authority. Tax-exempt.
19th-Century Living History Museum.
Collections: agriculture equipment; printing & typesetting equipment; furniture & furnishings of the period; naval stores implements; medical & dental equipment. Historic Buildings: 1896 farmhouse; 1886 log cabin; 1895 one-room school; 1890 sawmill; 1879 grist mill; 1885 printing office; 1899 railroad depot; 1887 doctor's office; 1882 church; 1879 commissary. Historic Reconstructions: 1890 turpentine still & cooper's shed; c.1890 cotton gin; c.1890 drug store; c.1900 variety works; 1877 log house; 1887 Victorian house.

Research Fields: 18th, 19th & early 20th century rural & agricultural history.
Facilities: 250-seat conference facility; full service kitchen; RV park; snack bar; picnic area; outdoor theatre. Gift items for sale.
Activities: tours; workshops; expositions; permanent & temporary exhibits; entertainment; fishing lake.
Publications: biannual newsletter, AgriRamblins; historic newspaper, Georgia Recorder.
Hours & Admission Prices: Tues.-Sat. 9-4:30. Adults $7, senior citizens $6, children 5-16 $4; discounts for AAM members & groups of 20 or more; children under 5 no charge. Closed New Year's Day; Thanksgiving; Christmas week. ♿
Attendance: 40,000 (accurate)
Membership: Individual $25; Family $50; Contributing $100; Sustaining $250; Individual Life $1,000.

Toccoa

TRAVELER'S REST STATE HISTORIC SITE, 4339 Riverdale Rd., Toccoa, GA 30577-8341. Tel.: 706-886-2256. Fax: 706-886-6860.
Web Site: www.gastateparks.org/info/travelers
Founded: 1955.
Congressional District: 9
Key Personnel: Mgr., Robert Emery.
Personnel Profile: Part-Time Paid 1.
Governing Authority: state. Parent Institution: Parks, Recreation & Historic Sites Div., Georgia Dept. of Natural Resources, 270 Washington St., S.W., Atlanta, GA 30334. Tax-exempt.
Historic Building: housed in a former stagecoach inn; built 1815.
Collections: furnishings; documents; historic house.
Research Fields: history of transportation, agriculture, & slavery.
Activities: guided tours; permanent exhibitions, special annual events; pioneer skills demonstrations; living history.
Publications: Traveler's Rest and the Tugaloo Crossroads.
Hours & Admission Prices: 1st Sat. of month; call for additional hours. Adults $4, senior citizens 62 & over $3.50, children 6-17 $2.75; discounts to groups of 15 or more. Closed New Year's Day; Thanksgiving; Christmas.
Attendance: 4,000 (accurate)

Tybee Island

TYBEE ISLAND LIGHT STATION AND TYBEE MUSEUM, 30 Meddin Dr., Tybee Island, GA 31328-9733. Mailing Address: P.O. Box 366, Tybee Island, GA 31328-0366. Tel.: 912-786-5801. Fax: 912-786-6538.
E-mail: tybeelh@bellsouth.net
Web Site: www.tybeelighthouse.org
Formerly: Tybee Museum and Lighthouse
Founded: 1960.
Congressional District: 1
Key Personnel: Dir., Cullen Chambers; Pres. (V), Jim Kluttz; Dir. Operations, Sarah Jones; Museum Shop Mgr., Candy Carter.
Personnel Profile: Full-Time Paid 11; Part-Time Paid 2; Part-Time Volunteers 56.
Governing Authority: board of directors. Parent Institution: Tybee Island Historical Society; Affiliated with Tybee Museum Association. Tax-exempt.
History Museum: housed in old Spanish-American War Coastal Defense Battery; c.1867 Tybee Island lighthouse & cottages.
Collections: guns & pistols; antique dolls; railroad memorabilia; military artifacts; lighthouse items.
Research Fields: U.S. coastal defense 1897-1946; U.S. Lighthouse Service 1789-1939.
Facilities: grounds adjacent to beach.
Activities: tours; lectures by appointment only.
Publications: books, Historic Tybee Island, Tybee Island Recipe Book, Fort Screven 1897-1945.
Hours & Admission Prices: Wed.-Mon. 9-5:30. Adults $7, seniors, military & children 6-17 $5; children under 6 no charge. Last ticket sold at 4:30. Closed New Year's Day; St. Patrick's Day; Thanksgiving Day; Christmas Day.
Attendance: 100,000 (accurate)
Membership: Single $35; Couple $45; Household $50; 2nd Asst. Keepers $100; 1st Asst. Keepers $150; Head Keeper $200; Lifetime $1,000.

Valdosta

THE CRESCENT, VALDOSTA GARDEN CENTER, INC., 904 N. Patterson St., Valdosta, GA 31601-4531. Mailing Address: P.O. Box 2423, Valdosta, GA 31604-2423. Tel.: 229-244-6747. Fax: 912-242-1005.
Founded: 1951.
Congressional District: 2
Key Personnel: Pres., Betty Becton.
Governing Authority: nonprofit. Parent Institution: The Garden Center, Inc. Tax-exempt.
Nature Center & Historic House: 1898 mansion, home of former U.S. Sen. William S. West.
Collections: period furniture; Day Lily, perennial & annuals gardens.
Research Fields: restoration; landscaping & flower arranging.
Facilities: 200-vol. library of books pertaining to gardening, landscaping & flower arranging available to view on premises; reading room; botanical garden; garden; field research station; 200-seat auditorium. Museum-related items for sale.
Activities: guided tours; lectures; films; study clubs; formally organized education programs. Museum Sponsors: Christmas Open House; Flower Show; Antique Shows.
Publications: yearbook.
Hours & Admission Prices: Mon.-Fri. 2-5; other times by appointment when not rented. No charge; donations accepted. ♿
Attendance: 4,286 (accurate)

LOWNDES COUNTY HISTORICAL SOCIETY AND MUSEUM, (M), 305 W. Central Ave., Valdosta, GA 31601-5404. Mailing Address: P.O. Box 56, Valdosta, GA 31603-0056. Tel.: 229-247-4780. Fax: 229-247-2840.
E-mail: history@valdostamuseum.org
Web Site: www.valdostamuseum.org
Founded: 1967.
Congressional District: 2
Key Personnel: Interim Dir., Donald Davis; Pres., Patsy Giles; Financial Dir., Redden Hart.
Personnel Profile: Full-Time Paid 2; Part-Time Paid 3; Part-Time Volunteers 10; Interns 1.
Governing Authority: private; nonprofit organization. Tax-exempt: 501(c)(3).
History Museum: housed in 1913 Carnegie Library.
Collections: artifacts, documents & photographs concerning Lowndes County Georgia; Doc Holliday exhibit.
Facilities: 500-vol. library of city directories, phone books, genealogical research, History of Georgia & Counties; 3,000 sq. ft. exhibit space.
Activities: formal education programs for children; guided tours; lectures. Museum Sponsors: History 100 Dinner, annual fundraiser.
Publications: monthly newsletter, Yesterday & Today; Doc Holliday Book; Way Back When Vol. I, II, III.
Hours & Admission Prices: Mon.-Fri. 10-5, Sat. 10-2. No charge; donations accepted. Closed New Year's Day; Sat. before Easter; Memorial Day; Independence Day; Labor Day; Thanksgiving; Christmas to New Year's Day. ♿
Attendance: 26,000 (accurate)
Membership: Student $10; Annual $25; Family $30; Organization & Business $50; Contributing $100; Patron $250; Life $1,000.

VALDOSTA STATE UNIVERSITY FINE ARTS GALLERY, Fine Arts Bldg., Rm 107, 1500 N. Patterson St., Valdosta, GA 31698-0001. Tel.: 229-333-5835. Fax: 229-259-5121.
E-mail: apearce@valdosta.edu
Web Site: valdosta.edu/art
Founded: 1906.
Congressional District: 8
Key Personnel: Gallery Dir., Julie Bowland.
Personnel Profile: Full-Time Paid 1; Part-Time Volunteers 25.
Governing Authority: board of regents; college. Affiliated with Valdosta State College. Tax-exempt.
Art Gallery.
Collections: The Lamar Dodd Collections.
Facilities: library; planetarium; reading room; auditorium; theater; classrooms.
Activities: guided tours; lectures; films; gallery talks; concerts; docent program or council; formally organized education programs for undergraduate college students.
Publications: exhibition catalogs; posters; postcards.
Hours & Admission Prices: Mon.-Thurs. 10-4, Fri. 10-3, Sat.-Sun, evenings open for performing events. No charge; donations accepted. Closed school holidays. ♿
Attendance: 10,000

Vidalia

ALTAMA MUSEUM OF ART & HISTORY, 611 Jackson St., Vidalia, GA 30474-4721. Mailing Address: P.O. Box 33, Vidalia, GA 30475-0033. Tel.: 912-537-1911.
E-mail: altama@bellsouth.net
Key Personnel: Dir., Rebecca Smelser.
Personnel Profile: Part-Time Paid 1.
Art Museum: housed in 1911 Brazell House.
Collections: porcelain; prints; wood sculptures; Girl Scout memorabilia; paintings; local history; Staffordshire porcelain.
Activities: art celebration for kids; workshops.

Hours & Admission Prices: Jan.-June & Sept.-Nov. Mon.-Tues. & Thurs.-Fri. 11-4. No charge. ♿
Membership: Individual $15; Family $25; Sponsor $50; Patron $100; Benefactor $250; Angel $500.

Vienna

GEORGIA STATE COTTON MUSEUM, 1321 E. Union St., Vienna, GA 31092-7540. Mailing Address: P.O. Box 309, Vienna, GA 31092-0309. Tel.: 229-268-2045. Fax: 229-268-3664.
Web Site: www.historicvienna.org
Founded: 1994.
Congressional District: 3
Key Personnel: Pres. (V), Diane Couch; Treas., Beth English; Cur., Margaret Hegidio.
Personnel Profile: Full-Time Paid 1; Part-Time Paid 2; Part-Time Volunteers 5.
Governing Authority: private; nonprofit organization. Tax-exempt: 501(c)(3).
History Museum.
Collections: period farm implements; cotton patch; history & production of cotton.
Facilities: library; 1,600 sq. ft. exhibit space; 20-seat theater. Museum-related items for sale.
Activities: formal education programs for children; guided tours; hobby workshops; loan exhibitions; theater. Annual Events: Christmas Open House; book signings & receptions; awards night.
Publications: monthly newsletter, VHPS News.
Hours & Admission Prices: Mon.-Sat. 9-4. Large Group Tours: $2 per person. Closed New Year's Day; Martin Luther King Jr. Day; Memorial Day; Independence Day; Labor Day; Thanksgiving; Christmas. ♿
Attendance: 3,000 (estimated)
Membership: Individual $10; Family $25; Cotton Club $50; George Club $100; Cheek Trust $1,000.

WALTER F. GEORGE LAW OFFICE MUSEUM, 106 N. 4th St., Vienna, GA 31092-1115. Mailing Address: 1321 E. Union St., Vienna, GA 31092-7540. Tel.: 229-268-3663. Fax: 229-268-3664.
Web Site: www.historicvienna.org
Founded: 1991.
Key Personnel: Pres. (V), Diane Couch; Public Rels., Janet Joiner; Treas., Beth English.
Personnel Profile: Full-Time Paid 1; Part-Time Volunteers 5.
Governing Authority: private; nonprofit organization. Tax-exempt: 501(c)(3).
History Museum: housed in U.S. Senator George's first law office in 1902.
Collections: artifacts & memorabilia pertaining to the life of U.S. Senator Walter F. George.
Research Fields: local history; genealogy.
Facilities: 450 sq. ft. exhibit space. Museum-related items for sale.
Activities: formal education programs for children; guided tours. Annual Events: Christmas Open House; awards night.
Publications: monthly newsletter, VHPS News.
Hours & Admission Prices: Mon.-Fri. 9-4 by appointment. No charge; donations accepted. Closed New Year's Day; Martin Luther King Jr. Day; Memorial Day; Independence Day; Labor Day; Thanksgiving; Christmas.
Attendance: 800 (accurate)
Membership: Individual $10; Family $25; Cotton Club $50; George Club $100; Cheek Trust $1,000.

Warm Springs

ROOSEVELT'S LITTLE WHITE HOUSE STATE HISTORIC SITE, 401 Little White House Rd., Warm Springs, GA 31830-2157. Tel.: 706-655-5870. Fax: 706-655-5872.
Web Site: www.gastateparks.org
Founded: 1946.
Congressional District: 10
Key Personnel: Site Mgr., Robin Glass; Asst. Mgr., Mary F. Thrash; Museum Shop Mgr., Diane Crane.
Personnel Profile: Full-Time Paid 19; Part-Time Paid 1; Part-Time Volunteers 3.
Governing Authority: state. Parent Institution: Georgia Department of Natural Resources. Tax-exempt.
Historic Buildings Museum: 1932 Georgia home of Pres. Roosevelt, where he died April 12, 1945.
Collections: personal items; gifts to Pres. Roosevelt from individuals, states and foreign countries; personal & official correspondence.
Research Fields: geology; prehistory & history of Warm Springs; historical significance of Franklin D. Roosevelt.
Facilities: research library; theater. Museum-related gifts for sale.
Activities: tours; films; permanent exhibitions.
Hours & Admission Prices: Daily 9-4:45. Adults $7, seniors over 62 $6, children 6-18 $4; discount to groups of 15 or more. Closed New Year's Day; Thanksgiving; Christmas. ♿
Attendance: 100,000 (estimated)

Warner Robins

* **MUSEUM OF AVIATION AT ROBINS AIR FORCE BASE, GA,** 1942 Heritage Blvd., Robins AFB, Warner Robins, GA 31099. Mailing Address: P.O. Box 2469, Warner Robins, GA 31099-2469. Tel.: 478-926-6870. Fax: 478-926-5566.
E-mail: kenneth.emery@robins.af.mil
Web Site: www.museumofaviation.org
Founded: 1984.
Key Personnel: Dir., Kenneth Emery; Pres. & C.O.O. Museum Foundation, Pat Bartness; Chm. Bd. Directors Museum Foundation, Marlan Nichols; Cur., Mike Rowland; Retail Shops Mgr., Sarah Bedgood.
Personnel Profile: Full-Time Paid 28; Part-Time Paid 29; Part-Time Volunteers 83.
Governing Authority: nonprofit organization. Parent Institution: U.S. Air Force. Subsidiary Institution: Robins Air Force Base, GA. Tax-exempt: 501(c)(3).
Aviation Museum.
Collections: World War II-present, aviation memorabilia; over 100 historic aircraft; missiles.
Facilities: library; 250-seat auditorium; 40-seat cafeteria; 200,000 sq. ft. exhibit space; 51 acre site. Aviation-related items for sale.
Activities: docent program; films; guided tours; Georgia Youth Science & Technology Center; 6 axis motion simulator. Museum Sponsors: Young Astronaut Day; Georgia Aviation Hall of Fame induction.
Publications: History of Robins Air Force Base; book, God is My Co-Pilot - 1943.
Hours & Admission Prices: Daily 9-5. No charge; donations accepted. Closed New Year's Day; Thanksgiving; Christmas. ♿
Attendance: 540,000 (estimated)
Membership: Students 18 & under $10; Individual $35; Silver Eagle Individual $100; Silver Eagle Club & Business $150; Gold Eagle Individual $500; Sustaining $1,000.

Washington

ROBERT TOOMBS HOUSE, 216 E. Robert Toombs Ave., Washington, GA 30673-2037. Mailing Address: P.O. Box 605, Washington, GA 30673-0605. Tel.: 706-678-2226. Fax: 706-678-7515.
E-mail: robert_toombs@dnr.state.ga.us
Web Site: www.gastateparks.org
Founded: 1982.
Congressional District: 10
Key Personnel: Interpretive Ranger, Marcia Campbell.
Personnel Profile: Full-Time Paid 2; Part-Time Paid 1; Part-Time Volunteers 3.
Governing Authority: state. Parks, Recreation & Historic Sites Div., Dept. of Natural Resources. Tax-exempt.
Historic House Museum.
Collections: historic house; outbuildings; furniture & furnishings from the period c.1840-1900; Toombs family artifacts.
Research Fields: life of Toombs; Civil War; politics.
Activities: tours; film on R. Toombs; school programs; living history programs.
Hours & Admission Prices: Tues.-Sat. & Mon. if federal holiday 9-5, Sun. 2-5. Adults $3, senior citizens over 62 $2.50, children 6-18 $1.75; discount to groups; children 5 & under no charge. Closed New Year's Day; Thanksgiving; Christmas.
Attendance: 3,000 (estimated)
Membership: Individual $45; Family $70; Supporting $100; Patron $500.

WASHINGTON HISTORICAL MUSEUM, 308 E. Robert Toombs Ave., Washington, GA 30673-2038. Tel.: 706-678-2105. Fax: 706-678-3752.
E-mail: historical@washingtonwilkes.org
Founded: 1959.
Congressional District: 10
Key Personnel: Coord., Stephanie Macchia.
Personnel Profile: Full-Time Paid 1; Part-Time Paid 4; Part-Time Volunteers 15.
Governing Authority: municipal. Parent Institution: City of Washington, GA. Subsidiary Institution: Washington-Wilkes Historical Foundation. Tax-exempt.
Historical Museum: 1836 Barnett-Slaton House, built by Albert Gallatin Semmes.
Collections: Confederate & Wilkes County history.
Research Fields: local Civil War & Wilkes County history.
Facilities: Music, publications & postcards for sale.
Activities: guided tours; permanent exhibitions.
Publications: books relating to Washington-Wilkes.

Hours & Admission Prices: Tues.-Sat. 10-5, Sun. 12:30-3:30. Adults $3, children 6-12 $2; discount to groups of 15 or more with advance reservations. Closed major holidays. ♿
Attendance: 2,400 (accurate)

Watkinsville

EAGLE TAVERN MUSEUM, 26 N. Main St., Watkinsville, GA 30677. Mailing Address: P.O. Box 959, Watkinsville, GA 30677-0021. Tel.: 706-769-5197. Fax: 706-310-1682.
E-mail: aford@oconee.ga.us
Web Site: www.visitoconee.ga.us
Founded: 1966.
Congressional District: 13
Key Personnel: Dir. Tourism & Cur., Peggy Holcomb.
Personnel Profile: Full-Time Paid 1; Part-Time Volunteers 5; Interns 1.
Governing Authority: county. Oconee County Bd. of Commissioners. Tax-exempt.
Historic Building: tavern stage coach stop.
Collections: late 18th-19th century furnishings.
Activities: guided tours; permanent exhibitions.
Publications: brochures pertaining to the state of Georgia & Eagle Tavern.
Hours & Admission Prices: Tours: Tues.-Fri. 10-4. Adults & seniors $2, children 6-15 $1; children under 6 no charge. ♿
Attendance: 7,000

Waycross

OKEFENOKEE HERITAGE CENTER, 1460 N. Augusta Ave., Waycross, GA 31503-4954. Tel.: 912-285-4260. Fax: 912-283-2858.
Web Site: www.okefenokeeheritagecenter.org/
Founded: 1975.
Congressional District: 8
Key Personnel: Dir. & Cur., Steven Bean; Chm. (V), Patty Baugh; Museum Shop Mgr., Betty Callahan.
Personnel Profile: Full-Time Paid 1; Part-Time Paid 2.
Governing Authority: nonprofit organization. Tax-exempt: 501(c)(3).
History Museum/Art Center.
Collections: regional art & history of Okefenokee Swamp & areas surrounding the swamp; renovated 1912 train, including steam engine & tender, 1 baggage car, 1 baggage/postal car, passenger car & caboose. Historic Buildings: 1900s Depot; c.1832 General Thomas Hilliard House; late 1800s print shop; 10,000 B.C. to 1840 A.D. Native Indian artifacts.
Research Fields: local history; arts; oral history.
Facilities: classrooms; conference room. Gifts items for sale.
Activities: tours; art classes; art shows; performances; special events.
Publications: newsletter; exhibition catalogues; brochures.
Hours & Admission Prices: Tues.-Sat. 10-4:30. Adults $3, children 4-18 $2; discounts to groups of 10 or more, senior citizens, military, AAA members & museum professionals; members no charge. Closed New Year's Day; Thanksgiving; Christmas. ♿
Attendance: 13,000 (estimated)
Membership: Individual $30; Family $50; Heritage Club $200; Business $300; Corporate $500.

SOUTHERN FOREST WORLD, 1440 N. Augusta Ave., Waycross, GA 31503-4954. Tel.: 912-285-4056. Fax: 912-283-2858.
Founded: 1981.
Congressional District: 8
Key Personnel: Chm. (V), Patricia Pearson.
Personnel Profile: Full-Time Paid 1; Part-Time Paid 1; Part-Time Volunteers 10.
Governing Authority: nonprofit organization. Tax-exempt: 501(c)(3).
Forestry Museum.
Collections: artifacts & specimens relating to the history & development of forestry in the South, including a 38' tall model of a Loblolly Pine; a cross-section of the nation's largest Slash Pine; 1905 steam powered logging locomotive; naval stores tools & cups; giant Cypress; working scale model of a turpentine still; 22' fire tower; 1900 logging cart.
Research Fields: forestry.
Facilities: permanent exhibitions. Gift items for sale.
Activities: youth programs; tree plantings; association seminars.
Hours & Admission Prices: Tues.-Fri. 12-4:30. Closed New Year's Day; Easter; Independence Day; Labor Day, Thanksgiving; Christmas. ♿
Attendance: 6,000 (estimated)
Membership: Individual $20; Family $30; Donor $50; Sponsor $100; Sustaining $250; Friend $500; Patron $1,000; Business & Corporate $100-$10,000.

Waynesboro

BURKE COUNTY MUSEUM, 536 Liberty St., Waynesboro, GA 30830. Mailing Address: 241 E. 6th St., Waynesboro, GA 30830-1480. Tel.: 706-554-4889.
E-mail: bcmuseum@bellsouth.net
Web Site: my.att.net/p/s/community.dll?ep=16&groupid=196378&ck=
Key Personnel: Cur., Robert L. Hammond
History Museum.
Collections: county history & culture; photographs; personal artifacts.
Hours & Admission Prices: Mon.-Fri. 8-4, Sat.-Sun. & holidays by appointment.

White

TELLLUS: NORTHWEST GEORGIA SCIENCE MUSEUM, 100 Tellus Dr., White, GA 30184. Mailing Address: P.O. Box 3663, Cartersville, GA 30120-1712. Tel.: 770-386-0576. Fax: 770-386-0600.
E-mail: joe@tellusmuseum.org
Web Site: www.tellusmuseum.org
Formerly: Weinman Mineral Museum
Founded: 1983.
Congressional District: 11
Governing Authority: private; nonprofit organization. Parent Institution: Georgia Museums Inc. Tax-exempt: 501(c)(3).
Science Museum.
Collections: minerals; fossils; gems; mining artifacts; rocks; Georgia mining heritage; books & magazines; period vehicles; space artifacts.
Research Fields: Georgia minerals, geology & mining; astronomy; transportation technology.
Facilities: planetarium; 32,000 sq. ft. exhibit space; lecture hall; classrooms; cafe; banquet facilities. Museum-related items for sale.
Hours & Admission Prices: Daily 10-5. Adults $12, seniors 65 & over $10, children 3-17 & students $8; active military no charge. ♿

Winder

FORT YARGO STATE PARK, 210 S. Broad St., Winder, GA 30680-2059. Tel.: 770-867-3489. Fax: 770-867-7517.
E-mail: fort_yargo_park@dnr.state.ga.us
Web Site: www.gastateparks.org
Founded: 1954.
Congressional District: 9
Key Personnel: Supt., Eric Bentley.
Governing Authority: state. Administered by the Parks, Recreation and Historic Sites Div., Georgia Dept. of Natural Resources, Floyd Tower E., Ste. 1352, 2 Martin Luther King, Jr. Dr., Atlanta, GA 30334. Tax-exempt.
Historic Building: restored blockhouse used during the Creek Indian Wars.
Collections: Historic House: 1792 Timber Blockhouse.
Research Fields: Georgia frontier.
Facilities: picnic & camping facilities.
Activities: conducted tours.
Hours & Admission Prices: Daily 7am-10pm. Old Fort Tours: by appointment. Park Pass: daily $5 per vehicle; Annual $50 per vehicle, senior citizens $25. ♿
Attendance: 400,000

Winterville

CARTER-COILE COUNTRY DOCTORS MUSEUM, 111 Marigold Lane, Winterville, GA 30683. Mailing Address: P.O. Box 306, Winterville, GA 30683-0306. Tel.: 706-742-8600. Fax: 706-742-5476.
E-mail: winterville@charter.net
Web Site: www.cityofwinterville.com/doctor_museum.html
Founded: 1971.
Congressional District: 11
Key Personnel: Municipal Clerk, Wendy Martin.
Governing Authority: nonprofit organization. Parent Institution: City of Winterville. Tax-exempt.
Medical Museum: housed in 1874 frame building used as an office by Dr. Warren Carter & Dr. Frank Coile.
Collections: medical equipment, furnishings, instruments, books, & special anatomy exhibits received from medical & other health personnel chiefly used in Clarke, GA & adjacent counties in the late 1800s & early 1900s & from Loree Florence, first women graduate of University of Georgia Medical School, 1926.
Research Fields: Winterville area physicians & their families; architecture.
Activities: guided tours; permanent exhibitions.
Hours & Admission Prices: Call for appointment. No charge; donations accepted.

Woodbine

WOODBINE INTERNATIONAL FIRE MUSEUM, 100 Bedell Ave., Woodbine, GA 31569-0058. Mailing Address: P.O. Box 58, Woodbine, GA 31569-0058. Tel.: 912-576-5351.
Founded: 1991.
Key Personnel: Dir., Jodie G. Briese; Cur., Robert J. Briese.
Personnel Profile: Part-Time Volunteers 2.
Governing Authority: private; nonprofit organization.
General Museum.
Collections: fire fighting equipment from Revolution to present from all over the world.
Research Fields: fire history & disasters.
Facilities: 300-vol. library.
Activities: guided tours; lectures.
Hours & Admission Prices: Mon.-Fri. 9:30-4, Sun. 11:30-4. No charge; donations accepted. Closed most major holidays.
Attendance: 2,700 (estimated)

Woodstock

AIR ACRES MUSEUM, 376 Air Acres Way, Woodstock, GA 30188-2910. Tel.: 770-517-6090.
Military Aircraft Museum.
Collections: period military aircraft.
Activities: Annual Event: Low Country Broil.
Hours & Admission Prices: Tues.-Sat.

HAWAII

(94 listings)

Captain Cook

AMY B.H. GREENWELL ETHNOBOTANICAL GARDEN, 82-6188 Mamalahoa Hwy., Captain Cook, HI 96704. Mailing Address: P.O. Box 1053, Captain Cook, HI 96704-1053. Tel.: 808-323-3318. Fax: 808-323-2394.
Web Site: www.bishopmuseum.org/greenwell
Founded: 1974.
Congressional District: 2
Key Personnel: Mgr., Peter Van Dyke; Cur., Brian Kiyabu.
Personnel Profile: Full-Time Paid 3; Part-Time Volunteers 20; Interns 4.
Governing Authority: private; nonprofit organization. Parent Institution: Bishop Museum, Honolulu, HI. Tax-exempt: 501(c)(3).
Botanical Garden.
Collections: native plants; Hawaiian crops.
Facilities: library; botanical garden; archaeology site. Museum-related items for sale.
Activities: docent program; formal education programs; guided tours; hobby workshops; lectures; school outreach program. Annual Events: Horticultural Festival; Seed Exchange; Arbor Day.
Hours & Admission Prices: Mon.-Fri. 8:30-5. No charge; donations accepted. Closed New Year's Day; Presidents' Day; Memorial Day; King Kamehameha Day; Independence Day; Labor Day; Thanksgiving & day after; Christmas.
Attendance: 16,000 (estimated)

KONA HISTORICAL SOCIETY - H.N. GREENWELL STORE, Hwy. 11, Captain Cook, HI 96704. Mailing Address: Kona Historical Society, P.O. Box 398, Captain Cook, HI 96704-0398. Tel.: 808-323-3222. Fax: 808-323-2398.
Web Site: www.konahistorical.org
Founded: 1976.
Governing Authority: nonprofit organization.
Historical Society Museum: housed in a restored general store; built c.1875. Listed on the National Register of Historic Places.
Collections: local history & culture; period general store merchandise.
Activities: interpretive programs.
Hours & Admission Prices: Mon.-Thurs. 10-2. Adults $7, children 5-12 $3; discounts to AAM & ICOM members; members & children under 5 no charge. ♿
Attendance: 6,000

Fort DeRussy

U.S. ARMY MUSEUM OF HAWAII, Battery Randolph, Kalia Rd., Fort DeRussy, HI 96815. Mailing Address: P.O. Box 8064, Honolulu, HI 96830-0064. Tel.: 808-438-2821. Fax: 808-438-2819.
Founded: 1976.
Congressional District: 1
Key Personnel: Cur., Judith Bowman.
Personnel Profile: Full-Time Paid 3; Part-Time Paid 1; Part-Time Volunteers 17.
Governing Authority: federal; nonprofit. Parent Institution: U.S. Army Garrison, Hawaii. Tax-exempt: 501(c)(3).
Military History Museum: housed in Battery Randolph, a Taft Period coast artillery battery; located at Fort DeRussy, one of the earliest military posts established by the U.S. Army in Hawaii.
Collections: military materials, domestic & foreign, associated with the history of the U.S. Army in the Pacific; Hawaiian military history.
Research Fields: military history of Hawaii & the role played by Hawaii & Hawaiians in the nation's defense.
Facilities: permanent exhibitions.
Activities: research assistance; school & group tours. Annual Event: Living History Day.
Hours & Admission Prices: Tues.-Sun. 9-5. No charge; donations accepted. ♿
Attendance: 100,000 (accurate)

Haleiwa

NORTH SHORE SURF AND CULTURAL MUSEUM, 66-250 Kamehameha Hwy., Ste. G100, Haleiwa, HI 96712-1491. Tel.: 808-637-8888.
Surf Museum.
Collections: local history & culture; period surfboards; photographs; movies.
Facilities: theater.
Hours & Admission Prices: Call for hours.

WAIMEA ARBORETUM AND BOTANICAL GARDEN IN WAIMEA VALLEY, 59-864 Kamehameha Hwy., Haleiwa, HI 96712-9406. Tel.: 808-638-7766. Fax: 808-638-7776.
E-mail: jhoh@waimeavalley.net
Web Site: waimeavalley.net
Formerly: Waimea Arboretum and Botanical Garden in Waimea Valley Audubon Center
Founded: 1973.
Congressional District: 2
Key Personnel: Dir., Gail Chew; Chm. (V), Cybil Rawlins; Propagator, Linda Bard; Botanical Mgr., Josephine Hoh; Museum Shop Mgr., Gail Cabalce.
Personnel Profile: Full-Time Paid 10; Interns 1.
Governing Authority: Parent Institution: Hi'ilei Aloha LLC. Subsidiary Institution: Hi'ipaka LLC. Tax-exempt.
Living Plant Museum, Arboretum & Botanical Garden.
Collections: living plant collection with scientific field data, arranged by genera, family or geographical region; collections of ancient Hawaiian strains of economic plants; seed collection; endangered bird species; herbarium collections of plants & seedlings; flora of the Mascarene & Ogasawara Islands.
Research Fields: propagation & preservation of rare & endangered tropical & sub-tropical plants; cultivation techniques of a wide range of plant species; excavation of historical sites; Hawaiian ethnobotany section, medicinal, food & useful plants; recreated Hawaiian living area.
Facilities: 2,000-vol. library & herbarium of books available upon request on premises only; botanical garden; nature center; 400-seat restaurant. Museum-related items for sale.
Activities: guided tours; formally organized education programs for children.
Hours & Admission Prices: Daily 9-5. Out-of-State Residents: adults $10. Hawaii Residents: adults $5, children 4-12 $3; children under 4 no charge. Closed New Year's Day; Christmas. ♿
Attendance: 250,000 (estimated)
Membership: Waimea Valley Audubon Center $25.

Hana, Maui

HANA CULTURAL CENTER, 4974 Uakea Rd., Hana, Maui, HI 96713. Mailing Address: P.O. Box 27, Hana, Maui, HI 96713-0027. Tel.: 808-248-8622. Fax: 808-248-7898.
E-mail: mail@hanaculturalcenter.org
Web Site: www.hanaculturalcenter.org
Founded: 1971.
Key Personnel: Gen. Operations Mgr., Meiling Hoopai; Pres., Esse Sinenci; Vice Pres., Malia Henderson; Chm. (V), Jackie Kahula; Program Mgr., Leinaala Estrella; Receptionist, Sydney Shamblin.
Personnel Profile: Full-Time Paid 1; Full-Time Volunteers 1; Part-Time Paid 3; Part-Time Volunteers 2.
Governing Authority: private; nonprofit organization. Tax-exempt: 501(c)(3).
Cultural Center.
Collections: Hawaiian articles.
Facilities: library; botanical garden. Museum-related items for sale.
Activities: guided tours; hobby workshops. Museum Sponsors: craft demonstrations June-August.

Publications: annual newsletter; brochures.
Hours & Admission Prices: Mon.-Fri. 10-4. Adults $3; members no charge. Closed New Year's Day; Easter; Thanksgiving; Christmas. ♿
Attendance: 26,510 (estimated)
Membership: Annual $25; Ohana $60; Life $250.

Hanalei

WAIOLI MISSION HOUSE MUSEUM, 4050 Nawiliwili Rd., Hanalei, HI 96714. Mailing Address: P.O. Box 1631, Lihue, HI 96766-5631. Tel.: 808-245-3202.
Historic House: housed in an 1837 missionary house. Listed on the National Register of Historic Places.
Collections: period furnishings; personal artifacts.
Hours & Admission Prices: Call for hours.

Hawaii Volcanoes National Park

HAWAII VOLCANOES NATIONAL PARK, KILAUEA VISITOR CENTER, Headquarters Bldg. #1, Crater Rim Dr., Hawaii Volcanoes National Park, HI 96718. Mailing Address: P.O. Box 52, Hawaii National Park, HI 96718-0052. Tel.: 808-985-6000. Fax: 808-967-8186.
Web Site: www.nps.gov/havo/
Founded: 1916.
Congressional District: 2
Key Personnel: Chief Cultural Resources, Laura C. Schuster.
Governing Authority: federal. Dept. of the Interior, National Park Service.
Visitor Center.
Collections: Hawaii artifact; natural history material; paintings; geological specimens; birds; archaeology; anthropology; ethnology; photographs.
Research Fields: Hawaiiana; park natural history.
Facilities: 2,500-vol. library available to on-site researchers by prearrangement; nature & conservation center; 210-seat auditorium. Books for sale.
Activities: guided tours; lectures; films; formally organized educational programs; temporary exhibitions.
Publications: Hawaii Natural History Association.
Hours & Admission Prices: Visitor Center: daily 7:45-5. Park open 24 hours. $10 entrance fee per car, $5 per pedestrian, good for seven days. ♿
Attendance: 1,500,000 (estimated)

Hilo

EAST HAWAII CULTURAL CENTER, 141 Kalakaua St., Hilo, HI 96720-2807. Tel.: 808-961-5711.
E-mail: arts@ehcc.org
Web Site: www.ehcc.org
Key Personnel: Acting Chm., Kay Yokoyama; Exec. Dir., Dennis Taniguchi
Art Gallery.
Collections: works by local, national & international artists.
Facilities: theater. Museum-related items for sale.
Activities: performances; meetings.
Hours & Admission Prices: Call for hours. Gallery: Mon.-Sat. 10-4. No charge; donations accepted.

* **LYMAN MUSEUM, (M),** 276 Haili St., Hilo, HI 96720-2978. Tel.: 808-935-5021. Fax: 808-969-7685.
E-mail: info@lymanmuseum.org
Web Site: www.lymanmuseum.org
Founded: 1931.
Congressional District: 2
Key Personnel: Pres. & Exec. Dir., Dr. Marie D. Strazar; Chm. (V), Richard Henderson.
Personnel Profile: Full-Time Paid 10; Part-Time Paid 2; Part-Time Volunteers 20; Interns 2.
Governing Authority: nonprofit organization. Tax-exempt: 501(c)(3).
General Museum: depicting the natural & cultural history of Hawaii.
Collections: early 19th- & 20th-century Hawaiian artists; Hawaiian & missionary artifacts; native & immigrant people of Hawaii and local culture; World Class minerals; manuscripts; Chinese art; worldwide seashells; Hawaii land shells; Flora & Fauna; natural history of Hawaii including it's volcanic origins. Historic Mission House: built in 1839 by missionaries from New England.
Research Fields: Hawaiiana & local history.
Facilities: 3,500-vol. library on Hawaiiana available for research on premises; 20,000 photo library of Old Hawaii; 200 blueprints; charts, daguerreotypes; glassplates; journals; letters; newsletters; 660 New England newspapers; 390 prints & maps; 508 rare newspapers; 2,500 ephemera collection. Museum-related items for sale.
Activities: guided tours; permanent and special exhibitions; lectures; workshops; Elderhostel programs.
Publications: books, The Lymans of Hilo; Hilo 1825-1925: A Century of Paintings & Drawings; The Private Japanese Hospital: An Unique Social Phenomenon on Hawaii, 1907-1960; Japanese Painting, Calligraphy & Lacquer; A Record of the Descendants of David Belden Lyman & Sarah Joiner Lyman of Hawaii 1832-1933; The Lymans of Hawaii Island. Educational Outreach Booklets: 'Ohe Kapala: Bamboo Printing; Kane, Kanaloa, Ku & Lono: Na Akua Nui O Hawai'i, (Four Major Gods of Hawaii); Early Hawaiian Musical Instruments; Ku'i I Ke Kalo: Pounding Taro; Gourds in the Garden at Work and in the Writings (of Old); Na Mea Nui O Na Ali'i Hawai'i: Symbols of Royalty. Museum newsletter; booklet, Lyman Mission House; books, Sarah Joiner Lyman of Hawaii: Her Own Story; Crystals of the Lyman Museum.
Hours & Admission Prices: Mon.-Sat. 10-4:30. Adults $10, senior citizens $8, children 6-17 $3; discounts to AAA, AAM, AASLH & Hawaii Museums Association members; members no charge. Closed New Year's Day; Memorial Day; Independence Day; Labor Day; Thanksgiving; Christmas. ♿
Attendance: 15,600 (accurate)
Membership: University Student $10; Individual $25; Family $35; Sustaining $100; Contributing $250; Lifetime $1,000.

NANI MAU GARDENS, 421 Makalika St., Hilo, HI 96720-5899. Tel.: 808-959-3500. Fax: 808-959-3501.
E-mail: corp@hottours.us
Web Site: www.nanimaugardens.com
Gardens.
Collections: tropical flowers & plants; orchids; palms & tropical fruit orchards.
Facilities: restaurant. Museum-related items for sale.
Activities: garden tours.
Hours & Admission Prices: Daily 9-4:30. Gardens: adults $10, children 4-10 $5. Garden & Tram Tour: adults $17, children 4-10 $10.

PACIFIC TSUNAMI MUSEUM, (M), 130 Kamehameha Ave., Hilo, HI 96720-2833. Tel.: 808-935-0926. Fax: 808-935-0842.
E-mail: tsunami@tsunami.org
Web Site: www.tsunami.org
Founded: 1994.
Key Personnel: Dir., Donna W. Saiki; Pres., Jim D. Wilson; Treas., Jill Jacunski; Cur. & Archivist, Barbara J. Muffler; Administrative Asst., Colleen DeSa.
Personnel Profile: Full-Time Paid 3; Full-Time Volunteers 1; Part-Time Paid 2; Part-Time Volunteers 18; Interns 1.
Governing Authority: private; nonprofit organization. Tax-exempt: 501(c)(3).
Natural History Museum.
Collections: tsunami photographs; 1946 tsunami in Hilo.
Facilities: classrooms; 7,250 sq. ft. exhibit space. Museum-related items for sale.
Activities: guided tours; lectures; participatory exhibits; docent program; formal education programs for children. Annual Event: Tsunami Story Festival.
Publications: biannual newsletter; Driving & Walking Tour of Historical Tsunami Sties in East Hawaii; Tsunami Education: A Blueprint for Coastal Communities.
Hours & Admission Prices: Mon.-Sat. 9-4. Adults $8, senior citizens & Kama'aina $7, children 6-17 $4; members and children 3 & under no charge. Closed New Year's Day; Independence Day; Thanksgiving; Christmas Eve & Day. ♿
Attendance: 19,925 (accurate)
Membership: Individual $15; Family $35; Supporting $50; Associate $100; Affiliate $250; Patron $500; Supporter $1,000; Benefactor $2,000.

PANAEWA RAINFOREST ZOO, Mamaki St., (one mile off Hwy. 11), Hilo, HI 96720. Mailing Address: Friends of the Zoo, P.O. Box 738, Kea'au, HI 96749-0738. Tel.: 808-959-9233. Fax: 808-961-8411.
E-mail: foz@hilozoo.com
Web Site: www.hilozoo.com
Zoo.
Collections: 80 animal species including the endangered Nene (Hawaii State Bird); white Bengal Tiger.
Facilities: 12 acres. Museum-related items for sale.
Activities: tiger feeding daily.
Hours & Admission Prices: Daily 9-4. Petting Zoo: Sat. 1:30-2:30. No charge. Closed New Year's Day; Christmas.

WAILOA CENTER FOR CULTURE AND ARTS, 200 Piopio St., Wailoa State Park, Hilo, HI 96720. Mailing Address: P.O. Box 936, Hilo, HI 96721-0936. Tel.: 808-933-0416. Fax: 808-933-0417.
E-mail: wailoa@yahoo.com
Founded: 1967.
Key Personnel: C.E.O. & Dir., Codie M. King.

Personnel Profile: Full-Time Paid 1; Part-Time Volunteers 18.
Governing Authority: Parent Institution: State of Hawaii. Subsidiary Institution: Department Land & Natural Resources, State Parks Division.
Art Museum.
Collections: works by local artists; Big Island history & culture.
Facilities: library; visitors center.
Activities: demonstrations; seminars; workshops; classes; school tour & outreach programs; films; concerts; live performances.
Hours & Admission Prices: Mon.-Tues. & Thurs.-Fri. 8:30-4:30, Wed. 12-4:30. No charge. Closed holidays. ♿
Attendance: 30,000 (estimated)

Honolulu

BATTLESHIP MISSOURI MEMORIAL, 63 Cowpens St., Honolulu, HI 96818-5006. Tel.: 808-423-2263.
Web Site: www.ussmissouri.com
Military Museum: housed on the USS Missouri, built in 1941.
Collections: battleship history; military artifacts & equipment; personal artifacts; photographs.
Facilities: Museum-related items for sale.
Activities: school group tours.
Hours & Admission Prices: Daily 9-5. Adults $16, children $8 (tickets available at the USS Bowfin Submarine Museum & Park). Closed New Year's Day; Thanksgiving; Christmas.

BERNICE PAUAHI BISHOP HERITAGE CENTER, THE KAMEHAMEHA SCHOOLS, 1887 Makuakane St., Honolulu, HI 96817-1800. Tel.: 808-842-8635. Fax: 808-842-8603.
Founded: 1988.
Key Personnel: Cur., Nuulani Atkins
Heritage Center: school founded by Bernice Pauahi Bishop & her husband, Charles Reed Bishop.
Collections: Bishop's furniture & personal artifacts.
Hours & Admission Prices: Call for hours.

* **BISHOP MUSEUM, (M),** 1525 Bernice St., Honolulu, HI 96817-2704. Tel.: 808-847-3511. Fax: 808-841-8968.
E-mail: museum@bishopmuseum.org
Web Site: www.bishopmuseum.org
Founded: 1889.
Congressional District: 19
Key Personnel: Chm. Bd., Charman J. Akina, M.D.; C.E.O. & Pres., Timothy Johns; Vice Pres. Science, Allen Allison, Ph.D.; Vice Pres. Strategic Initiatives, Elizabeth Tatar, Ph.D.; Senior Vice Pres. & C.O.O., Blair Collis; Vice Pres. Institutional Advancement, Amy Marvin; Vice Pres. Cultural Resources, Betty Lou Kam; Dir. Governmental Affairs, Jenny Chock Wooton; Personnel Officer, Corey Nakamoto; Plant Operations Mgr., Wayne Castro; Chm. Natural Sciences, Neal Evenhuis; Dir. Education, Michael Shanahan; Museum Shop Mgr., Maria Young.
Personnel Profile: Full-Time Paid 166; Part-Time Paid 70; Part-Time Volunteers 398; Interns 11.
Governing Authority: private charitable corporation. Subsidiary Institution: Hawaii Maritime Center. Tax-exempt: 501(c)(3), 170(b)(1)(A), 509(a)(1).
Cultural & Natural History Museum.
Collections: culture & natural history of Hawaii & the Pacific; anthropology; archaeology; archives; botany; entomology; ethnology; geology; herpetology; ichthyology; malacology; zoology; herbarium; philatelic; photographs; invertebrate zoology; mammalogy; ornithology; maps; motion picture film; art on paper & canvas; living ethnobotanical; pamphlets; manuscripts.
Research Fields: anthropology; archaeology; botany; entomology; ethnobotany; history; malacology; vertebrate & invertebrate zoology.
Facilities: 100,000-vol. library; 55,000 sq. ft. exhibit space; 12-acre campus on Oahu; 15-acre gardens on Hawaii Island; planetarium; 70-seat theatre. Books, handicrafts, jewelry, reproductions & video tapes for sale.
Activities: educational classes; school group visits; lectures; films; docent program; changing & traveling exhibitions; volunteer program; special events; planetarium programs; observatory telescope viewing; excursions. Museum Sponsors: Family Sundays.
Publications: four bulletins, anthropology, botany, entomology, zoology; occasional papers; monograph, Insects of Micronesia; handbooks, WAU Ecology; Indo-Pacific Fishes; special publications; miscellaneous publications; calendars; guidebooks; newsletter.
Hours & Admission Prices: Daily 9-5. Adult non-resident $15.95, senior citizens over 65 $11.95, adult resident $7.95, youth 4-12 $6.95; discounts for senior citizens, active military & AAM members; members & children under 4 no charge. Library & Archives: Tues.-Fri. 12-4, Sat. 9-12. Closed Christmas. ♿
Attendance: 327,967 (accurate)
Membership: Friend & Senior $35; Dual $50; Family & Friends $65; Patron $100; Benefactor $250; Visionary $500.

THE CONTEMPORARY MUSEUM, (M), 2411 Makiki Heights Dr., Honolulu, HI 96822-2547. Tel.: 808-526-1322. Fax: 808-536-5973.
E-mail: info@tcmhi.org
Web Site: www.tcmhi.org
Founded: 1961.
Congressional District: 1
Key Personnel: Dir., Georgianna Lagoria; Pres. (V), Violet Loo; Pres. Friends, Marge Ziffrin; Deputy Dir. Exhibitions & Collections, James Jensen; Cur. Exhibitions, Inger Tully; Coord. Membership, Rujunko Pugh; Mgr. Finance & Operations, John Talkington; Registrar, Tae Kitakata; Chief Preparator, John Koga; Cur. Education, Quala-Lynn Young; Volunteer & Special Events Coord., Sheryl Kramer; Mgr. Retail Operations, Bob Madison; Asst. to Dir., Gordon Wong; Exec. Chef, Scott Sakagucui; Facility Mgr., Garry Ka'aihue; Dir. Museum Advancement, Charlie Aldinger.
Personnel Profile: Full-Time Paid 18; Part-Time Paid 5; Part-Time Volunteers 150; Interns 2.
Governing Authority: public; nonprofit organization. Tax-exempt: 501(c)(3).
Art Museum.
Collections: regional, national & international art from 1940 to present; contemporary art.
Facilities: 3.5-acre site with gardens & outdoor sculpture; 6 exhibition galleries; cafe. Museum-related items for sale.
Activities: guided tours; gallery talks; permanent, temporary & traveling exhibitions; one-man & group shows by contemporary artists; workshops.
Publications: exhibition brochures; catalogues; newsletter.
Hours & Admission Prices: Makiki Museum: Tues.-Sat. 10-4, Sun. 12-4. One-day introductory membership: adults $5, senior citizens & students $3; discounts to AAM, Western Museum Group & North American Reciprocal Membership Program members; children 12 & under, members & third Thurs. of month no charge. Closed major holidays. ♿
Attendance: 85,216 (estimated)
Membership: Student $15; Out of State $20; Individual $45; Dual $75; Sponsor $125; Associate $250; Partner $500; Contemporary Circle $1,000; President's Circle $2,500; Director's Circle $5,000; Champion's Circle $10,000.

THE CONTEMPORARY MUSEUM AT FIRST HAWAIIAN CENTER, 999 Bishop St., Honolulu, HI 96813-4423. Mailing Address: 2411 Makiki Heights Dr., Honolulu, HI 96822-2547. Tel.: 808-526-1322. Fax: 808-536-5973.
E-mail: itully@tcmhi.org
Web Site: www.tcmhi.org
Founded: 1996.
Congressional District: 1
Key Personnel: Dir., Georgianna Lagoria; Pres.(V), Violet Loo; Volunteer & Special Events Coord., Sheryl Kramer; Assoc. Dir. & Chief Cur., James Jensen; Cur. Exhibitions, Inger Tully; Cafe Mgr. & Mgr. Retail Operations, Bob Madison; Membership Coord., Rujunko Pugh; Dir. Museum Advancement, Charlie Aldinger; Bldg. & Grounds Mgr., Garry Ka'aihue; Chief Preparator, John Koga; Cur. Education, Quala Lynn Young; Mgr. Finance & Operations, John Talkington; Asst. to Dir., Gordon Wong; Registrar, Tae Kitakata; Mgr. Cafe Kitchen, Scott Sakaguchi; Security Mgr., Michael Chock.
Personnel Profile: Full-Time Paid 15; Part-Time Paid 10; Part-Time Volunteers 200; Interns 3.
Governing Authority: public; nonprofit organization. Parent Institution: The Contemporary Museum Board of Trustees. Tax-exempt: 501(c)(3).
Art Museum.
Collections: art of local artists who live and/or work in the state of Hawaii, or were born & moved from the island, or who came to the island and produced work in the state.
Major Exhibits: Hiroki, Setsuko & Miho Morinoue, 11/09/09-2/19/10; Ray Yoshida Memorial, 3/12/10-6/18/10; Allyn Bromley Retrospective, 6/12/10-8/15/10; TCM Biennial of Hawaii Artists (T), 9/10/10-11/14/10.
Facilities: 3,500 sq. ft. in the main banking hall & designated gallery at The First Hawaiian Center building, downtown Honolulu.
Activities: guided tours; gallery talks; temporary exhibitions; one man & group shows by contemporary artists.
Publications: exhibition brochures; newsletter; catalogues.
Hours & Admission Prices: Mon.-Thurs. 8:30-4, Fri. 8:30-6. No charge. Reciprocal memberships. Closed bank holidays. ♿
Attendance: 85,216 (estimated)
Membership: Student $15; Nonresident $20; Individual $45; Dual $75; Sponsor $125; Associate $250; Partner $500; Contemporary Circle & Patron $1,000; President's Circle & Leader $2,500; Director's Circle & Benefactor $5,000; Champion's Circle $10,000.

DORIS DUKE FOUNDATION FOR ISLAMIC ART - SHANGRI LA, (M), 4055 Papu Circle, Honolulu, HI 96816-4850. Mailing Address: 4224 Waialae Ave., #412, Honolulu, HI 96816-5330. Tel.: 808-734-1941. Fax: 808-732-4361.
Web Site: www.shangrilahawaii.org
Founded: 1998.
Congressional District: 1
Key Personnel: Exec. Dir., Deborah Pope.
Personnel Profile: Full-Time Paid 22; Part-Time Paid 6; Part-Time Volunteers 1; Interns 2.
Governing Authority: Parent Institution: Doris Duke Charitable Foundation. Tax-exempt.
Art & History Museum: housed in the seasonal home of Doris Duke; built in 1937.
Collections: Islamic art & culture; period furnishings; religious works of art; 17th-19th centuries decorative arts.
Research Fields: Islamic art & culture.
Facilities: 5-acre waterfront property.
Activities: guided tours; lectures; symposia; scholarly research; educational programs and field studies; permanent & temporary exhibitions.
Publications: Doris Duke's Shangri La.
Hours & Admission Prices: Wed.-Sat. by appointment. Out-of-State $25; In-State $20. ♿
Attendance: 13,312 (accurate)

EAST-WEST CENTER, 1601 East-West Rd., Honolulu, HI 96848-1601. Tel.: 808-944-7111. Fax: 808-944-7376.
E-mail: ewcinfo@eastwestcenter.org
Web Site: www.eastwestcenter.org
Founded: 1961.
Key Personnel: Pres. & C.E.O., Charles Morrison; Arts Coord., William Feltz; Cur., Michael Schuster, Ph.D.
Personnel Profile: Full-Time Paid 3; Part-Time Volunteers 10; Interns 1.
Governing Authority: nonprofit. Tax-exempt.
General Museum.
Collections: art, ethnography & history exhibits.
Hours & Admission Prices: Mon.-Fri. 8-5, Sun. 12-4. No charge; donations accepted. Closed federal holidays. ♿
Attendance: 6,000

442ND VETERANS CLUB ARCHIVES, 933 Wiliwili St., Honolulu, HI 96826. Mailing Address: 933 Wiliwili St., Apt. 102, Honolulu, HI 96826-2766. Tel.: 808-945-0032 & 949-7997. Fax: 808-949-1539.
E-mail: 442veterans@hawaiiantel.net
Formerly: 442nd Veterans Archives & Learning Center
Key Personnel: Pres., William Thompson.
Personnel Profile: Part-Time Paid 2; Part-Time Volunteers 1.
Governing Authority: archives & exhibits of the 442nd combat team.
Military Museum.
Collections: personal artifacts.
Hours & Admission Prices: Mon.-Fri. 8-3; call to confirm. No charge; donations accepted.

HAROLD L. LYON ARBORETUM, 3860 Manoa Rd., Honolulu, HI 96822-1198. Tel.: 808-988-0456. Fax: 808-988-0462.
E-mail: lyonarb@hawaii.edu
Web Site: www.hawaii.edu/lyonarboretum
Founded: 1918.
Congressional District: 1
Key Personnel: Dir., Christopher Dunn, Ph.D.; Pres. Lyon Arboretum Assoc., Mrs. Emmy Seymour; Junior Researcher, Nelli Sugii; Horticulturalist, Elizabeth Huppman; Research Assoc. II, Karen Shigematsu; Research Assoc. IV, Ray Baker; Educational Specialist, Jill Laughlin; Research Technician, Carol Nakamura; Maintenance Worker I, Kenneth Seamon; Arborist, Leon Marcus; Sec., Tokiko Murakami; Research Affiliate, D.W. Arthur Whistler; Research Affiliate, Dr. George Staples, III; Research Affiliate, Dr. John Moody; Research Affiliate, Dr. Rich Criley.
Personnel Profile: Full-Time Paid 10; Part-Time Volunteers 350.
Governing Authority: state; not-for-profit organization. Parent Institution: University of Hawaii. Tax-exempt: 501(c)(3).
Botanical Garden & Arboretum.
Collections: native & endemic plants of Hawaii & tropics; Hawaiian, southeast Asian & Pacific ethnobotanical plants; germplasm of ornamental & economic plants.
Research Fields: taxonomy of native & endemic plants of Hawaii; taxonomy of tropical plants; ethnobotany of Pacific, Southeast Asian & Asian peoples; propagation & horticulture of tropical plants; propagation by micropropagation; culture; ecosystem restoration; rare Hawaiian plants conservation & biology; seed storage & conservation.
Facilities: botanical garden; classrooms; greenhouses; herbarium; laboratory; craft center; micropropagation facilities. Museum-related items for sale.
Activities: guided tours; hiking trails; lectures; docent program; temporary exhibits; formally organized education programs for children, adults, undergraduate & graduate college students affiliated with the University of Hawaii & private universities in Hawaii.
Publications: occasional periodical, Lyonia; annual periodical, Harold L. Lyon Arboretum Lecture; educational series; occasional pamphlets; books through Univ. of Hawaii Press; quarterly newsletter, The Kukui Leaf
Hours & Admission Prices: Mon.-Fri. 9-4, Sat. 9-3; other times by appointment. Suggested Donation: $5 per person. Closed holidays. ♿
Attendance: 30,000 (estimated)
Membership: Student $10; Senior Citizen-Kupuna 65 & over $20; Individual $25; Family (one household) $35; Kukui $50; Niu $100; Koa $250; 'Ohi'a $1,000.

HAWAII CHILDREN'S DISCOVERY CENTER, 111 Ohe St., Honolulu, HI 96813-5517. Tel.: 808-524-5437. Fax: 808-524-5400.
E-mail: info@discoverycenterhawaii.org
Web Site: www.discoverycenterhawaii.org
Founded: 1985.
Key Personnel: C.E.O., Chm. & Pres. (V), Loretta Yajima; Treas., Arthur Tokin; Dir. Exhibits & Programs, Museum Shop Mgr., Liane Usher.
Personnel Profile: Full-Time Paid 4; Full-Time Volunteers 1; Part-Time Paid 13; Part-Time Volunteers 50.
Governing Authority: not-for-profit organization. Tax-exempt: 501(c)(3).
Children's Museum.
Collections: hands-on exhibits.
Facilities: 38,000 sq. ft. exhibit space.
Activities: outreach activities including a children's fun run & other special events; spring, summer & winter day camps for children; weekly toddler classes & other special events.
Publications: quarterly newsletter; annual report; membership brochures.
Hours & Admission Prices: Tues.-Fri. 9-1, Sat.-Sun. 10-3. Adults $10, seniors 62 & over $6; children under one & members no charge. Closed New Year's Day; Easter; Thanksgiving; Christmas. ♿
Membership: Senior Citizen 62 & over $50; Individual & Grandparent $60 ($25 each grandchild); Family $100 & up.

HAWAII MARITIME CENTER, 1525 Bernice St., Honolulu, HI 96817-2704. Tel.: 808-523-6151. Fax: 808-536-1519.
Web Site: www.bishopmuseum.org
Founded: 1988.
Key Personnel: C.E.O., Tim Johns; Dir. Sales & Event Planning, Linda Chalk.
Personnel Profile: Full-Time Paid 3; Part-Time Paid 2; Part-Time Volunteers 32.
Governing Authority: private; nonprofit. Parent Institution: Bishop Museum. Tax-exempt: 501(c)(3).
Maritime Museum.
Collections: focus on maritime history of Hawaii from the time of the arrival of the Polynesians to the present; history; maritime commerce; recreational activities; historic vessel.
Hours & Admission Prices: Daily 9-5. Adults $7.50, children 6-17 $4.50; discounts to active duty military, tour groups & local residents; children under 6 & members no charge. Closed Christmas Day. ♿
Attendance: 68,400 (accurate)
Membership: Individual $35; Family $45; Navigator & Mate $60; Captain $100; Commodore $250.

HAWAII NATURE CENTER, 2131 Makiki Heights Dr., Honolulu, HI 96822-2520. Tel.: 808-955-0100; 888-955-0104.
E-mail: hawaiinaturecenter@hawaiirr.com
Web Site: www.hawaiinaturecenter.org
Key Personnel: Exec. Dir., Gregory D. Dunn; Dir. Oahu Operations, Casey Carmichael; Dir. Philanthropy, Kathryn A. Currier; Dir. Grants & Contract Admin., Mike Lee
Nature Center.
Collections: island environment, culture, & history; wildlife; plants.
Hours & Admission Prices: Daily 8-4:30. Grounds no charge. Closed New Year's Day; Thanksgiving; Christmas.

HAWAII PACIFIC UNIVERSITY GALLERY, 1164 Bishop St., Ste. 1111, Honolulu, HI 96813-2882. Tel.: 808-544-0287. Fax: 808-544-0852.
E-mail: jphilpott@hpu.edu
Web Site: www.hpu.edu
Founded: 1983.
Congressional District: 1
Key Personnel: C.E.O., Chatt G. Wright; Chm. (V), William E. Aull; Dir., Sanit Khewhok.

Personnel Profile: Part-Time Paid 1; Part-Time Volunteers 10.
Governing Authority: private; nonprofit organization. Parent Institution: Hawaii Pacific University. Tax-exempt.
Art Gallery.
Collections: paintings; sculpture; photographs.
Facilities: 2,000 sq. ft. exhibit space.
Activities: Annual Events: six exhibitions per academic year August to June.
Hours & Admission Prices: Mon.-Sat. 8-5. No charge. Closed New Year's Eve & Day; Thanksgiving; Christmas. ♿
Attendance: 7,000 (estimated)

HAWAII STATE CAPITOL, 415 S. Beretania St., Honolulu, HI 96813-2477. Mailing Address: 415 S. Beretania St., Rm 415, Honolulu, HI 96813-2407. Tel.: 808-586-0178 & 0146. Fax: 808-586-0046.
History Museum.
Collections: Hawaii history; photographs.
Activities: group & school tours.
Hours & Admission Prices: Mon.-Fri. 7:45-4:30. Tours: Mon., Wed. & Fri. 1:30. No charge. Closed holidays.

HAWAII STATE FOUNDATION ON CULTURE & THE ARTS AND HAWAII STATE ART MUSEUM, (M), 250 S. Hotel St., 2nd Fl., Honolulu, HI 96813-2831. Tel.: 808-586-0300. Fax: 808-586-0308.
E-mail: ken.hamilton@hawaii.gov
Web Site: www.hawaii.gov/sfca
Founded: 1965.
Congressional District: 1
Key Personnel: Exec. Dir., Ronald Yamakawa; Gallery Dir., Denise H. Kosaka; Dir. Art Public Places Program, David de la Torre; Public Information Officer, Ken Hamilton.
Personnel Profile: Full-Time Paid 27; Part-Time Volunteers 9.
Governing Authority: state government; nonprofit. Tax-exempt.
Art Museum.
Collections: over 5,000 works by Hawaiian contemporary artists from 1967 to present.
Research Fields: historical records of ethnic organizations in Hawaii; traditional Hawaiian arts & music.
Activities: arts festivals; concerts; broadcast programs; temporary off-site exhibits; training programs for professional museum workers; grants/funding program; technical assistance to other museums & organizations.
Publications: bimonthly newsletter, ARTREACH; annual report; small books related to specific projects.
Hours & Admission Prices: Offices: Mon.-Fri. 7:45-4:30. Museum: Tues.-Sat. 10-4. Closed state holidays. ♿
Attendance: 20,000 (accurate)
Membership: Student $15; Individual $30; Dual/Supporter $50; Contributor $75; Sponsor $100; Associate $250; Donor $500; Patron $1,000 & up.

HAWAIIAN HISTORICAL SOCIETY, 560 Kawaiaha'o St., Honolulu, HI 96813-5023. Tel.: 808-537-6271. Fax: 808-537-6271.
E-mail: bedunn@lava.net
Web Site: www.hawaiianhistory.org
Key Personnel: Administrative Dir. and Librarian, Barbara Dunn.
Governing Authority: nonprofit organization.
Historical Society Museum.
Collections: historical documents; newspapers; photographs; manuscripts.
Facilities: library.
Activities: research; history conferences; lectures; special events; membership meetings. Annual Event: Open House in December.
Publications: book, The Hawaiian Journal of History; newsletter, Na Mea Kahiko.
Hours & Admission Prices: Tues.-Fri. 10-4. No charge.
Membership: Student $20; Senior $30; Individual $40; Family $50.

* **HONOLULU ACADEMY OF ARTS, (M), (I),** 900 S. Beretania St., Honolulu, HI 96814-1495. Tel.: 808-532-8700. Fax: 808-532-8787.
Web Site: www.honoluluacademy.org
Founded: 1922.
Congressional District: 1
Key Personnel: Dir., Stephen Little; Chm. (V), Lynne Johnson; Deputy Dir., Robert Saarnio; Head Finance, Darin Mijo; Dir. Devel., Karen Sumner; Cur. Asian Art, Shawn Eichman; Mgr. Textiles, Sara Oka; Cur. European & American Art, Theresa Papanikolas; Cur. Education, Betsy Robb; Cur. Art Center, Vince Hazen; Cur. Film, Gina Caruso; Registrar, Collections, Pauline Sugino; Registrar, Exhibitions, Cynthia Low; Visitor & Volunteer Svcs., Vicki Reisner; Head Operational Svcs., Robert White; Museum Shop Mgr., Kathee Hoover; Cafe Mgr., Mike Nevin; Librarian, Ronald F. Chapman.
Personnel Profile: Full-Time Paid 101; Part-Time Paid 23; Part-Time Volunteers 404; Interns 6.
Governing Authority: nonprofit organization. Tax-exempt: 501(c)(3).
Art Museum: housed in c.1927 building designed by Bertram G. Goodhue Associates.
Collections: art from ancient to modern times including painting, sculpture, ceramics, bronzes, lacquer & furniture from China, Japan, India, Indonesia, Korea, the Philippines, & Southeast Asia; James A. Michener Japanese prints; European & American painting, prints, sculpture & decorative arts; Kress collection of Italian Renaissance painting; traditional arts of Oceania, the Americas & Africa; traditional & modern Hawaiian art; Islamic art.
Major Exhibits: From Whistler to Warhol: Modernism on Paper, 2/18/10-5/2/10; Masterpieces from the Richard Lane Collection, 3/4/10-5/23/10; Margaret Brewer Fowler Collection, 3/4/10-6/6/10; Men in Lace, 7/10-10/10/10; Old Master Paintings & Drawings in the HAA Collection, 9/10-12/10.
Research Fields: Asian, European and American art.
Facilities: 45,000-vol. library of art books available for use by members & scholars; reading room; 24,000 sq. ft. Art Center Studio Program; 300-seat auditorium; classrooms; restaurant; Mediterranean & Asian gardens. Art books, reproductions, museum replicas, slides, cards, folk art & crafts for sale.
Activities: permanent & temporary exhibitions; guided tours; lectures; films; gallery talks; art classes for children & adults; concerts; dance recitals; arts festivals; formally organized education programs; inter-museum loan, school loan service.
Publications: exhibition catalogs; books; pamphlets; Calendar News.
Hours & Admission Prices: Tues.-Sat. 10-4:30, Sun. 1-5. Adults $10, seniors, military & students with ID $5; discounts to AAM & ICOM members; children under 12, members & first Wed. of each month no charge. Closed New Year's Day; Independence Day; Labor Day; Thanksgiving; Christmas. ♿
Attendance: 237,922 (estimated)
Membership: Student $20; National & International $40; Individual $55; Family $95; Subscriber $150; Contributor $350; Sponsor $700; Guardian $1,500; Benefactor $2,500; Patron $5,000; Director's Circle $10,000.

HONOLULU BOTANICAL GARDENS, 50 N. Vineyard Blvd., Honolulu, HI 96817-3759. Tel.: 808-522-7060. Fax: 808-522-7050.
E-mail: hbg@honolulu.gov
Founded: 1931.
Key Personnel: Dir., Winifred Singeo; Education, Joyce Spoehr; Orchid Horticulturist, Scot Mitamura; Horticulturist, Joshlyn Sand; Community Gardens, Nathan Wong; Parks Grounds Supvr., Derrick Miyasaki; Botanist, Naomi Fenstenmacher.
Personnel Profile: Full-Time Paid 31; Part-Time Paid 8; Part-Time Volunteers 100.
Governing Authority: Parent Institution: Dept. of Parks & Recreation. Branch Museums: Foster Botanical Garden, Honolulu, HI; Wahiawa Botanical Garden, Wahiawa, HI; Ho'omaluhia Botanical Garden, Kaneohe, HI; Koko Crater Botanical Garden, Honolulu, HI; Lili'uokalani Botanical Garden, Honolulu, HI.
Botanical Gardens.
Collections: Hawaiian, Polynesian & tropical plants; hybrids; orchids.
Research Fields: cooperator: chemical & biological controls of invasive flora and fauna.
Facilities: botanical garden; visitor centers; educational facilities. Museum-related items for sale.
Activities: arts festivals; concerts; docent program; guided tours; lectures. Annual Event: Midsummer Night's Gleam.
Hours & Admission Prices: Foster, Ho'omaluhia & Wahiawa daily 9-4. Lili'uokalani daily 7-5. Koko Crater daily sunrise to sunset. Foster: adults $5, students 6-12 $3; children 5 & under no charge. Ho'omaluhia, Wahiawa, Lili'uokalani & Koko Crater no charge. Closed New Year's Day; Christmas. ♿
Attendance: 165,000 (estimated)

HONOLULU POLICE DEPARTMENT LAW ENFORCEMENT MUSEUM, 801 S. Beretania St., Honolulu, HI 96813-5790. Tel.: 808-529-3605. Fax: 808-529-3028.
E-mail: hpd@honolulupd.org
Web Site: www.honolulupd.org/community/cas/stationtours.htm
Founded: 1984.
Key Personnel: Cur. & Community Affairs Section Commander, Officer Eddie Croom.
Governing Authority: Parent Institution: Honolulu Police Department.
History Museum.
Collections: department history; Harley Davidson police motorcycle; uniforms; early 911 switchboard; Wall of Chiefs; documents; photos; weapons;

restraint devices; police call box; a 1904 arrest log; other items that document the 19th & 20th century Hawaii social & urban history.
Hours & Admission Prices: Mon.-Fri. 9-3:30. No Charge. Closed state & federal holidays. ♿
Attendance: 8,100 (estimated)

HONOLULU ZOO, 151 Kapahulu Ave., Honolulu, HI 96815-4096. Tel.: 808-971-7171 & 7174. Fax: 808-971-7173.
Web Site: www.honzoosoc.org
Founded: 1947.
Congressional District: 1
Key Personnel: Dir., Ken Redman; Asst. Dir., Tommy Higashino; Volunteer Coord., Barbara Thacker; Administrative Asst., Lois Yoshikawa; Museum Shop Mgr., Kim Borges.
Personnel Profile: Full-Time Paid 66; Part-Time Paid 8; Part-Time Volunteers 120.
Governing Authority: municipal; county. Parent Institution: City & County of Honolulu. Subsidiary Institution: Dept. of Enterprise Services. Tax-exempt.
Zoo.
Collections: live animals & plants from Africa, Asia, Oceania & Central/South America.
Research Fields: wild animal husbandry; propagation.
Facilities: 200-vol. zoological library available for staff and volunteer use only; children's zoo; education pavilion.
Activities: guided tours; docent program; summer concert series; adoption program; elephant encounters; keeper talks; educational programs. Museum Sponsors: Vacation Adventures for children; Zoo by Moonlight; Breakfast with a Keeper.
Publications: quarterly newsletter, Honolulu Zoological Society.
Hours & Admission Prices: Daily 9-4:30. Adults $8, children 6-12 $1; children 5 & under no charge. Residents & military stationed in Hawaii with local ID: adults $4, children 6-12 $1. ♿
Attendance: 495,184 (accurate)
Membership: Senior Citizen & Student $15; Individual $20; Family $25 (basic) & $35 (premium); Supporting $75; Patron $125; Benefactor $175.

IOLANI PALACE, (M), 364 S. King St., Honolulu, HI 96813-2900. Mailing Address: P.O. Box 2259, Honolulu, HI 96804-2259. Tel.: 808-522-0822. Fax: 808-532-1051.
E-mail: info@iolanipalace.org
Web Site: www.iolanipalace.org
Founded: 1966.
Congressional District: 1
Key Personnel: Exec. Dir., Kippen de Alba Chu; Pres., Edwina (Puchi) Romig; Cur., Stuart W. H. Ching; Museum Shop Mgr., Darrell Chun.
Personnel Profile: Full-Time Paid 27; Part-Time Paid 3; Part-Time Volunteers 113; Interns 1.
Governing Authority: state. Tax-exempt: 501(c)(3).
Historic Building: Iolani Palace c.1882 erected as state residence for Hawaii's last king, Kalakaua; Iolani Barracks c.1871 housed Royal Guard; Coronation Pavilion c.1883; 11-acre grounds with many original plantings.
Collections: furnishings & artifacts of the Hawaiian Royal Family from the period of the late 19th-century Hawaiian Monarchy, 1882-1893.
Research Fields: Hawaiian Monarchy period; decorative arts; local history.
Facilities: Museum-related items for sale.
Activities: guided tours of Iolani Palace; teacher workshops; lectures.
Publications: quarterly newsletter; books, Iolani Palace Guidebook; Iolani Palace Cookbook; The Queen's Quilt.
Hours & Admission Prices: Guided Tours: Tues.-Sat. 9-11:15, reservations required. Audio Tours: Tues.-Sat. 11:45-4. Galleries: Tues.-Sat. 9-5. Guided Tour: adults $20, children 5-12 $5; children under 5 not admitted. Audio Tours: adults $12, children 5-12 $5. Galleries: adults $6, children 5-12 $3; children under 5 welcome; residents with state I.D. first Sun. of month no charge. Closed New Year's Day; Independence Day; Thanksgiving; Christmas. ♿
Attendance: 76,622 (accurate)
Membership: Na Keiki 12 & under $10; Na Haumana (full-time students) $15; Na Kukui (active palace volunteers) $20; Na Kupuna (Seniors 65 & up) $25; Na Kakoo (Individuals) $35; Nonprofit Organizations $50; Na Ohana (Family) $100; Na Koa (Soldiers) $250; Na Kahu (Attendants) $500; Chamberlain's Circle $1,000; King's Royal Order $2,500; Kaulana Na Pua (Life) $5,000.

JAPANESE CULTURAL CENTER OF HAWAII, 2454 S. Beretania St., Honolulu, HI 96826-1524. Tel.: 808-945-7633. Fax: 808-944-1123.
E-mail: info@jcch.com
Web Site: www.jcch.com
Founded: 1987.
Congressional District: 1
Key Personnel: Pres. & Exec. Dir., Lenny Yajima Andrew; Chm. (V), Susan Yamada; Museum Shop Mgr., Barbara Ishida.
Personnel Profile: Full-Time Paid 9; Part-Time Paid 3; Part-Time Volunteers 200.
Governing Authority: private; nonprofit. Tax-exempt: 501(c)(3).
History Museum.
Collections: Japanese-American history in Hawaii from 1885 to contemporary times; 4,000 books; periodicals; pamphlets; newspapers; literature on the Japanese in Hawaii & Japan; Japanese on the mainland.
Facilities: 8,000-vol. library on Japanese American history & Japanese culture; education facilities; 5,000 sq. ft. exhibit space. Museum-related items for sale.
Activities: educational panels; forums; lectures. Annual Events: New Year's Ohana Festival; Shi Chi Go; San Kodomo no Hi: Keiki Fun Fest; Celebration of Leadership and Achievement Dinner.
Publications: newsletter, Legacies.
Hours & Admission Prices: Tues.-Sat. 10-4. Adults $7; discounts to senior citizens & school groups; members no charge. Parking validated. Gift Shop: Wed.-Sat. 10-3. ♿
Attendance: 15,000 (estimated)
Membership: Student $15; Regular $35; Family $50; Contributing $125; Nonprofit Organization $200; Supporting $250; Premier I $500; Premier II $750; Imperial $1,000.

JOHN YOUNG MUSEUM OF ART, Univ. of Hawaii at Manoa, Krauss Hall, 2500 Dole St., Honolulu, HI 96822-2349. Tel.: 808-956-3634.
Web Site: www.outreach.hawaii.edu/jymuseum
Art Museum.
Collections: Asian, Pacific & African art; art books.
Facilities: library.
Hours & Admission Prices: Tues. 10-1, Fri. 12-3, Sun. 1-4; groups by appointment. No charge; donations accepted. Parking: Tues. & Fri. $3; Sun. no charge.

KING KAMEHAMEHA V-JUDICIARY HISTORY CENTER, 417 S. King St., Honolulu, HI 96813-2943. Tel.: 808-539-4999. Fax: 808-539-4996.
E-mail: jhchawaii@yahoo.com
Web Site: jhchawaii.org
Founded: 1989.
Congressional District: 1
Key Personnel: Exec. Dir., Matt Mattice.
Personnel Profile: Full-Time Paid 3; Part-Time Paid 2; Part-Time Volunteers 14.
Governing Authority: executive board; nonprofit. Tax-exempt.
History Museum: housed in Ali'iolani Hale (1874), the Hawaii Supreme Court Building.
Collections: reproductions of artwork; court memorabilia; jury chair; dioramas; restored 1913 courtroom; artifacts, manuscripts; documents relating to Hawaii's legal & judicial history.
Research Fields: translation of 19-century court minute books from Hawaiian to English; oral history of jurists; biographical information on 19th- to 21st-century lawyers & judges; statistical information on 19th-century court cases.
Facilities: 45-seat theater; 5,000 sq. ft. exhibit space.
Activities: guided tours; theater; organized education programs for students; teacher workshops; docent program; temporary exhibitions; exhibits interpreting the transition from Hawaiian law to Western law; Hawaii under martial law.
Publications: semiannual newsletter, Kaulike; books, Kaahumanu, Molder of Change; Ali'iolani Hale, A Sentinel in Time; Curriculum Guide; Trial of a Queen: 1895 Military Tribunal; Judges in the Classroom; Hawaii Under Martial Law, 1941-1944; Annual Report.
Hours & Admission Prices: Mon.-Fri. 9-4, group & school tours by reservation. No charge; donations accepted. Closed state & federal holidays. ♿
Attendance: 51,596 (estimated)
Membership: Student & Senior Citizen $15; Individual $25; Family $50; Contributing $100; Corporate $300; Associate $500; Patron $1,000.

MANOA HERITAGE CENTER, (M), 2859 Manoa Rd., Honolulu, HI 96822-1752. Tel.: 808-988-1287.
E-mail: manoaheritagecenter@hawaiiantel.net
Web Site: www.manoaheritagecenter.org
Key Personnel: Educ. Dir., Margo Vitelli.
Governing Authority: nonprofit organization.
History Museum: listed on the National Register of Historic Places.
Collections: stone heiau/sacred site; native plants. Historic House: Ku'ali'i.
Hours & Admission Prices: Tues.-Sat. by appointment. Adults $7; seniors, students, military, educators and children 12 & under no charge.

*** MISSION HOUSES MUSEUM, (M),** 553 S. King St., Honolulu, HI 96813-3002. Tel.: 808-531-0481. Fax: 808-545-2280.
E-mail: info@missionhouses.org
Web Site: www.missionhouses.org
Founded: 1920.
Congressional District: 1
Key Personnel: Dir., David J. de la Torre; Pres. (V), Robert Becker, III; Head Librarian, Carol White; Devel. Dir., Mary Ann Lentz; Society Rels. Dir., Susie Goodbody-Murphy; Tour & Volunteer Coord., Mike Smola; Senior Resident Historian, Peter Salter; Sr. Cur., Elizabeth Nosek; Museum Shop Mgr., Lilith Samson.
Personnel Profile: Full-Time Paid 16; Part-Time Paid 2; Part-Time Volunteers 12.
Governing Authority: nonprofit organization. Parent Institution: Hawaiian Mission Children's Society.
Historic House Museum.
Collections: missionary & Polynesian artifacts including domestic artifacts & household furnishings; archival collections of missionary & Hawaiian church records; Hawaiian language materials; working replica of Ramage printing press; manuscripts. Historic Houses: 1821 frame mission house; 1831 Chamberlain House; 1841 printing office.
Research Fields: Protestant mission in Hawaii & the Pacific; 19th-century local history & cultural contact; daily life & material culture in 19th-century Hawaii; missionary-Hawaiian trade & exchange; archaeology.
Facilities: 12,000-vol. research library. Museum-related gifts for sale.
Activities: walking tours of historic Honolulu; guided tours; seasonal family programs; living history programs; permanent & temporary exhibitions; workshops & lectures; educational programs for primary, secondary & college level students; quarterly community festivals; premier juried holiday craft fair in the islands.
Publications: books, Missionary Album; Voyages to Hawaii Before 1860; The Hawaii Journals of the New England Missionaries 1813-1894; A Guide to the Holdings of the HMCS Library; The Journals of Cochran Forbes c.1831-1864; Mission Houses Museum Guidebook, 2001.
Hours & Admission Prices: Tues.-Sat. 10-4. Adults $10, Kama'aina, military & seniors $8, students 6 to college $6, school tours $2-$5 per student; members and children 5 & under no charge. Closed New Year's Day; Easter; Thanksgiving; Christmas. ♿
Attendance: 19,500 (estimated)
Membership: Student $25; Individual $40; Family $100; Friend $125; Contributor $250; Patron $500; Silver Circle $1,000; Gold Circle $2,500; Platinum Circle $5,000; Diamond $10,000.

MOANALUA GARDENS FOUNDATION, 1352 Pineapple Place, Honolulu, HI 96819-1796. Tel.: 808-839-5334. Fax: 808-839-3658.
E-mail: mgf-hawaii@hawaii.rr.com
Web Site: mgf-hawaii.com
Founded: 1970.
Key Personnel: Exec. Dir., Marilyn Schoenke.
Personnel Profile: Full-Time Paid 12; Part-Time Paid 2; Part-Time Volunteers 125.
Governing Authority: nonprofit organization. Tax-exempt: 501(c)(3).
Historic Foundation.
Collections: native & ethnic flora & fauna.
Research Fields: Hawaiian natural & cultural history.
Facilities: 3,000-vol. library of books, videotapes, & maps; reading room; nature center.
Activities: guided tours; lectures; formally organized educational program; docent program; slide show; field trips; hula festival; teacher training; distance learning program; CD-ROM tropical marine environments; neighbor island field trips; service trips.
Publications: quarterly newsletter, Na Makani O Moanalua; workbooks; field-site guides; view-plane guides; curricula manuals; videotape.
Hours & Admission Prices: By reservation: Mon.-Fri. 8-4. Guided Tours: $5 donation requested; fees for lectures & trips. Requested donations for Prince Lot Hula Festival. Closed state holidays.
Membership: Individual $25; Family $35; Friend $100; Supporter $250; Sustainer $1,000; Steward $5,000; Protector $10,000.

PACIFIC AVIATION MUSEUM - PEARL HARBOR, (M), Hangar 37, Ford Island, 319 Lexington Blvd., Honolulu, HI 96818-5004. Tel.: 808-441-1000. Fax: 808-441-1019.
E-mail: info@pacificaviationmuseum.org
Web Site: www.pacificaviationmuseum.org
Founded: 1997.
Key Personnel: C.E.O., Richard Beckerman; Chm. (V), Adm. Ronald Hays; Pres. (V), Clinton Churchill; Treas., Harvey Gray; Dir. Devel., Lauren Avery; Mktg., Public Rels., & Business Devel., Jean Navarra; Dir. Education, K.T. Budde-Jones; Restoration & Curatorial, Syd Jones; Museum Shop Mgr., Sue Reynolds.
Personnel Profile: Full-Time Paid 16; Full-Time Volunteers 2; Part-Time Paid 2; Part-Time Volunteers 70.
Governing Authority: private; nonprofit organization. Tax-exempt.
Military Aviation Museum.
Collections: U.S. military aviation in the Pacific from 1913 to present with emphasis on WWII, Korea & Vietnam.
Research Fields: WWII aircraft crash sites in Pacific region.
Facilities: 600-vol. library; aerospace education center; 217,000 sq. ft. exhibit space; 140-seat large screen theater; food court. Museum-related items for sale.
Activities: formal education programs; lectures; theater; tours. Annual Events: Annual Donor Dinner; member events.
Publications: bimonthly newsletter, Pacific Aviation Museum Newsletter.
Hours & Admission Prices: Daily 9-5. Adults $14, children $7; discounts to AAM & ICOM members; members no charge. Closed New Year's Eve & Day; Thanksgiving; Christmas. ♿
Attendance: 150,000
Membership: Individual $50; Family $100; Sponsor $500; Advocate $1,000; Patron $5,000.

QUEEN EMMA SUMMER PALACE, 2913 Pali Hwy., Honolulu, HI 96817-1417. Tel.: 808-595-3167. Fax: 808-595-4395.
E-mail: doh1903@hawaii.rr.com
Web Site: www.daughtersofhawaii.org
Founded: 1903.
Congressional District: 1
Key Personnel: Regent, Dale Bachman; Museum Shop Mgr., Marty Sczesny; Public Rels., Heidi Johnson.
Personnel Profile: Full-Time Paid 13; Part-Time Paid 4; Part-Time Volunteers 50.
Governing Authority: society. Parent Institution: Daughters of Hawaii. Branch Museum: 1837-38, Hulihee Palace, 75-5718 Alii Dr., Kailua-Kona, HI 96740. Tax-exempt: 501(c)(3).
Historic House Museum: c.1847 former home of Queen Emma & King Kamehameha IV, located on site where King Kamehameha I assembled his army, 1795 prior to conquering the island of Oahu & bringing the islands of the Hawaiian group under one head.
Collections: household furnishings & personal effects of Queen Emma & her family; period pieces; portraits; photographs; Hawaiian artifacts; tapa; feather work; Hawaiian quilts.
Research Fields: history of the collection; era presented; ancient Hawaiian history Queen Emma's era; history of Hawaiian quilts.
Facilities: meeting room with stage & kitchen; terraced area. Museum-related items for sale.
Activities: guided tours; special exhibits; demonstrations of dance, arts, crafts of ancient Hawaii; audiovisual programs; Hawaiian crafts; school programs; craft classes; choral group; language; hula classes.
Publications: Daughters of Hawai'i publications: Amos Starr Cooke & Juliette Montague Cooke 'Emalani; Hawaiian Furniture & Hawaii's Cabinetmakers; Liholiho & Emma; Memories of Majesty; Na Lani Kaumaka-A Century of Historic Preservation; Queen Emma & the Bishop; Reflections of Royalty; Stories of Long Ago; Treasures of the Hawaiian Kingdom (English & Japanese versions). Videos: Hulihe'e Palace-Treasure of the Hawaiian Kingdom; Queen Emma Summer Palace-A Royal Retreat.
Hours & Admission Prices: Daily 9-4. Adults $6, senior citizens $4, youth 17 & under $1; discounts to groups; members no charge. Closed holidays. ♿
Attendance: 13,394 (accurate)
Membership: Calabash Cousins: Individual $40; Family $60; Patron $110; Life $800; Family Life $1,200.

ROYAL MAUSOLEUM STATE MONUMENT, 2261 Nuouanu Ave., Honolulu, HI 96817-1713. Tel.: 808-536-7602.
Key Personnel: Cur., William Maioho
Historic Building: burial site of the Kamehameha & Kalahaua royal families; built in 1865.
Collections: royal family history; burial grounds; chapel.
Hours & Admission Prices: Mon.-Fri. 8-4; guided tours by appointment. No charge.

TENNENT ART FOUNDATION GALLERY, 203 Prospect St., Honolulu, HI 96813-1738. Tel.: 808-531-1987.
Founded: 1954.
Congressional District: 1
Governing Authority: nonprofit organization; board of trustees. Tax-exempt.
Art Gallery.
Collections: Madge Tennent oils, watercolors & drawings.
Facilities: 300-vol. library of art books available for use on premises; reading room.

Activities: guided tours; lectures; gallery talks; permanent exhibitions; school loan service.
Publications: quarterly newsletter, Prospectus.
Hours & Admission Prices: Tues.-Sat. 10-12, Sun. 2-4; other times by appointment. No charge; donations accepted.
Attendance: 1,000 (estimated)
Membership: Friends of the Tennent Gallery: Student $5; Individual $15; Family $25; Benefactor $100; Life $500; Patron $1,000.

UNIVERSITY OF HAWAII ART GALLERY, 2535 McCarthy Mall, Honolulu, HI 96822-2233. Tel.: 808-956-6888. Fax: 808-956-9659.
E-mail: gallery@hawaii.edu
Web Site: www.hawaii.edu/artgallery
Founded: 1976.
Key Personnel: Dir., Lisa Yoshihara; Assoc. Dir., Sharon Tasaka; Exhibition Design Asst., Wayne Kawamoto.
Personnel Profile: Full-Time Paid 3; Part-Time Paid 14; Part-Time Volunteers 20; Interns 4.
Governing Authority: university. Parent Institutions: University of Hawaii; Dept. of Art. Tax-exempt: 170(b)(1)(A).
Art Museum.
Collections: works by national & international artists.
Major Exhibits: The 10th International Shoebox Sculpture Exhibition (T), 1/10-1/11; Graduate Art Exhibition, 1/17/10-2/5/10; Eternal Blinking: Contemporary Art of Korea, 2/21/10-4/9/10; BFA Exhibition, 4/25/10-5/14/10; Edward Gorey Exhibition, 9/19/10-12/5/10.
Research Fields: Asian & Pacific art history.
Facilities: 300-seat auditorium; classrooms; two galleries.
Activities: guided tours; lectures; films; gallery talks; arts festivals; traveling & temporary exhibitions.
Publications: Pranas Domsaitis; The Art of Korea; Egyptian Antiquities from the Charles Pankow Collection; A Tradition of Excellence; Shoebox Sculpture Exhibition catalogues; Glass: Another View; First Impressions: Japanese Prints of Foreigners; Symbol and Surrogate: The Picture Within; The Art of Asian Costume; Sum of the Parts; Naked Truths; Huc Luquien's Hawaii: Prints 1918-1950; Crossings '97: France/Hawaii; Jose Guadalupe Posada: My Mexico; Crossing 2003: Korea/Hawaii; Making Connections: Treasures from the University of Hawaii Libraries; Painting with Threads: The Art of Japanese Embroidery; Reconstructing Memories; Excelling the Work of Heaven: Personal Adornment from China; Writing With Thread: Traditional Textiles of Southwest Chinese Minorities; exhibition catalogues; brochures.
Hours & Admission Prices: late Aug. to mid-May Mon.-Fri. 10:30-5, Sun. 12-5. No charge; donations accepted. Closed holidays. ♿
Attendance: 50,000 (estimated)

USS ARIZONA MEMORIAL, #1 Arizona Memorial Pl., Honolulu, HI 96818-3103. Tel.: 808-422-2771. Fax: 808-483-8608.
Web Site: nps.gov/usar
Founded: 1980.
Key Personnel: Dir. Pacific Area, Frank Hays; Historian, Daniel Martinez; Cur., Scott Pawlowski.
Governing Authority: federal. Dept. of the Interior, National Park Service, Washington, DC & the Arizona Memorial Museum Association.
Park Visitor Center & Military Museum; Historic Site & World War II Memorial Museum.
Collections: American & Japanese preparations for Pearl Harbor amidst two years of World War prior to U.S. entry; history of war time Hawaii & the attacks on Oahu's military sites; salvage & repair of ships; administrative history of the development of the memorial; History WWII Pacific through battle of Midway; USS Arizona (BB-39) and its crew; Pearl Harbor survivors & facilities.
Research Fields: martial law & wartime conditions in Hawaii; internment camps; pre war preparations & World War II in the Pacific through the Battle of Midway; military & civilian history; USS Arizona (BB-39); ships and military units on Oahu on Dec. 7, 1941.
Facilities: research library relating to Pearl Harbor history & World War II available for use on premises only. Books, video tape programs & other museum-related items for sale.
Activities: film presentation; shuttle boat to the Memorial; formally organized education programs for children; permanent & temporary exhibitions.
Publications: catalog; brochures.
Hours & Admission Prices: Daily 7:30-5. Shuttle Boat: 8-3. No charge; donations accepted. Closed New Year's Day; Thanksgiving; Christmas. ♿
Attendance: 1,420,000
Membership: Brass $25; Copper $50; Bronze $100; Silver $250; Gold $500.

USS BOWFIN SUBMARINE MUSEUM & PARK, 11 Arizona Memorial Dr., Honolulu, HI 96818-3104. Tel.: 808-423-1341. Fax: 808-422-5201.
E-mail: info@bowfin.org
Web Site: www.bowfin.org
Founded: 1978.
Congressional District: 1
Key Personnel: C.E.O. & Pres., Gerald Hofwolt; Chm. (V), Radm Gus Gustavson; Cur. Artifacts, Nancy Richards; Museum Shop Mgr., Shelly Gandall; Dir. Security & Operations, Bob Burt; Education & Outreach, Charles Hinman.
Personnel Profile: Full-Time Paid 46; Part-Time Paid 3; Part-Time Volunteers 1.
Governing Authority: nonprofit association. Parent Institution: Pacific Fleet Submarine Memorial Association. Tax-exempt.
Military Museum.
Collections: WWII submarine, USS Bowfin (SS-287); submarine related artifacts; assorted missile & torpedo displays; WWII patrol reports; files on submarines; files include foreign & domestic submarines & a variety of related topics; publications on submarines; A-1 Polaris missile & A-3 Polaris missile; periscope viewing structure; USS Parche conning tower; Japanese one-man suicide torpedo, Kaiten; C3 Poseidon missile.
Research Fields: submarines; rescue & salvage; deep sea diving; WWII naval history.
Facilities: 2,000-vol. research library; 10,000 item archives; WWII Waterfront Memorial; park.
Activities: self-guided tours; digital audio tours; permanent exhibitions.
Publications: semi-annual newsletter; book, On Eternal Patrol.
Hours & Admission Prices: Daily 8-5; guided tours by appointment. Adults $10, military not in uniform & dependents $7, children 4-12 $4; discounts to senior citizens & Hawaii residents with ID; military in uniform, children under 4 no charge in museum (not permitted on submarine for safety reasons).
Attendance: 222,448 (accurate)
Membership: Associate $25; Life $1,000.

WAIKIKI AQUARIUM, 2777 Kalakaua Ave., Honolulu, HI 96815-4027. Tel.: 808-923-9741. Fax: 808-923-1771.
E-mail: director@waquarium.org
Web Site: www.waquarium.org
Founded: 1904.
Congressional District: 1
Key Personnel: Dir., Dr. Andrew Rossiter; Chm. (V), Jennifer Isobe; Dir. Operations, Jerry Crow; Dir. Education, Sara Pelleteri; Museum Shop Mgr., Indahwati Soediamto.
Personnel Profile: Full-Time Paid 33; Part-Time Paid 22; Part-Time Volunteers 200.
Governing Authority: state. Parent Institution: University of Hawaii. Tax-exempt: 501(c)(3).
Marine Aquarium.
Collections: Hawaiian & Western tropical Pacific Ocean marine fauna, flora: living fishes, corals, jellyfish, mollusks, crustaceans, echinoderms, Hawaiian monk seals, Hawaiian coastal plants; influence of the ocean on early Hawaiian culture.
Research Fields: husbandry, behavior of aquarium specimens; nautilus husbandry, reproduction, propagation; husbandry, propagation, conservation of corals; Hawaiian monk seal behavior, digestive efficiency and interactions with humans; ID, treatment, prevention of diseases of captive marine life; propagation and biology of Pacific giant clams.
Facilities: rental facilities. Books & other marine-related items for sale.
Activities: formally organized education programs for school groups (pre-K to college); enrichment programs for families, children, adults; permanent exhibitions; study tours; lecture series; rental facilities.
Publications: quarterly newsletter, Kilo i'a.
Hours & Admission Prices: Daily 9-5. Adults $9, Hawaii residents, military & seniors over 60 $6, youths 13-17 $4, juniors 5-12 $2; children 4 & under, schools, approved institutions & FOWA members no charge. Closed Christmas Day. ♿
Attendance: 310,745 (accurate)
Membership: Friends of Waikiki Aquarium: Plus One $25 (add one person to existing membership); Senior $30; Individual $40; Grandparents & Family $60; Family Plus $85. Corporate Membership: Coral Reef Circle $500; Nautilus Circle $1,000; Mahimahi Circle $2,500; Mano Circle $5,000; Hawaiian Monk Seal $10,000.

WASHINGTON PLACE, 320 S. Beretania St., Honolulu, HI 96813-2420. Tel.: 808-586-0248.
Historic House: built in 1847 by Capt. John Dominis; home of Queen Lili'uokalani, Hawaii's last monarch & daughter in-law of Dominis.
Collections: Dominis period furnishings; the Queen's personal artifacts including her koa wood piano & Victorian furnishings.

Hours & Admission Prices: Tours: Mon.-Fri. by appointment. No charge; donations accepted. Closed holidays. ♿
Attendance: 9,000 (estimated)

Kahului

MAUI ARTS AND CULTURAL CENTER, One Cameron Way, Kahului, HI 96732-1137. Tel.: 808-242-2787. Fax: 808-244-4665.
E-mail: info@mauiarts.org
Web Site: www.mauiarts.org
Key Personnel: Pres. & C.E.O., Karen A. Fischer; Gallery Dir., Neida Bangerter
Art Gallery.
Collections: national & international artists; paintings; sculpture.
Activities: cultural programs.
Hours & Admission Prices: Mon.-Fri. 9-5. No charge.

Kahului Central Maui

PAPER AIRPLANE MUSEUM AND THE TIN CAN MAN OF MAUI, Kahului Central Maui, HI 96768. Mailing Address: 433 Nihoa St., Kahului, HI 96732-1108. Tel.: 808-244-4667. Fax: 808-244-4667.
E-mail: raytcm@webtv.net
Web Site: www.bcair.com/pam/index.htm
Founded: 1996.
Key Personnel: Owner, Pres. & Museum Shop Mgr., Ray Roberts.
Governing Authority: Tax-exempt.
Maui's Aviation, Railroad & Military History Museum.
Collections: over 2,000 paper model airplanes; photographs; Hawaiian Islands' aviation history from 1910 to present; tin can airplanes, cars, boats, trains, dinosaurs & ukuleles; tapes.
Facilities: Museum-related items for sale.
Activities: Mon.-Sat. No charge; donations accepted.
Hours & Admission Prices: Temporarily closed for relocation.

Kailua

HAWAII LOVES BARBIE DOLLS MUSEUM, 222 Hualani St., Kailua, HI 96734-2122. Mailing Address: P.O. Box 86, Kailua, HI 96734-0086. Tel.: 808-262-9138 & 1065. Fax: 808-262-1065.
Founded: 1980.
Key Personnel: Owner, Florence Marton
Doll Museum.
Collections: over 5,000 Barbie dolls.
Hours & Admission Prices: By appointment. No charge; donations accepted.

Kailua-Kona

ASTRONAUT ELLISON S. ONIZUKA SPACE CENTER, Keahole-Kona International Airport, Kailua-Kona, HI 96745. Mailing Address: P.O. Box 833, Kailua-Kona, HI 96745-0833. Tel.: 808-329-3441. Fax: 808-326-9752.
E-mail: tashima@aloha.net
Key Personnel: Cur., Nancy Tashima
Space Museum: dedicated to the memory of Hawaii's first astronaut who perished in the 1986 Challenger space shuttle disaster.
Collections: personal artifacts; moon rock; Apollo 13 space suit; gravity well; interactive rock-propulsion exhibit.
Facilities: library; 45-seat theater. Museum-related items for sale.
Activities: interactive exhibits.
Hours & Admission Prices: Daily 8:30-4:30. Adults & seniors $3, children 12 & under and students $1. Closed New Year's Day; Thanksgiving; Christmas.

HULIHEE PALACE, 75-5718 Alii Dr., Kailua-Kona, HI 96740-1702. Tel.: 808-329-1877 & 9555. Fax: 808-329-1321.
E-mail: doh1903@hawaiirr.com
Web Site: www.huliheepalace.org
Founded: 1928.
Congressional District: 2
Key Personnel: Palace Admin., Fanny Au Hoy; Office Mgr., Anita Okimoto.
Personnel Profile: Full-Time Paid 3; Part-Time Paid 3; Part-Time Volunteers 3.
Governing Authority: society. Parent Institution: Daughters of Hawaii. Tax-exempt.
Historic House Museum: c.1838 vacation residence for Hawaiian royalty, built by Gov. Kuakini, recently restored to the Kalakaua period.
Collections: Hawaiian artifacts; household furnishings; portraits; furniture; tapa; featherwork; Hawaiian quilts.
Research Fields: era presented; ancient Hawaiian artifacts.
Facilities: meeting room with kitchen. Museum-related items for sale.
Activities: guided tours; pageants & concerts by the sea; hula demonstrations; crafts.
Publications: Treasures of the Hawaiian Kingdom; books, Hawaiian Furniture & Hawaii's Cabinet; Stories of Long Ago; pamphlet, Emma & Liholiho.
Hours & Admission Prices: Wed.-Sat. 10-3. Adults $6, senior citizens & Kama'aina $4, students & children $1. Closed holidays. ♿
Attendance: 26,000 (accurate)
Membership: Support Group $30; Individual $45.

Kalaheo

KOKEE NATURAL HISTORY MUSEUM, Kokee State Park, Kalaheo, HI 96741. Mailing Address: P.O. Box 100, Kekaha, Kauai, HI 96752-0100. Tel.: 808-335-9975.
Natural History Museum.
Collections: local flora, fauna, & natural history; shells; Hawaiian artifacts; photographs.
Hours & Admission Prices: Daily 10-4. No charge; donations accepted.

NATIONAL TROPICAL BOTANICAL GARDEN, 3530 Papalina Rd., Kalaheo, HI 96741-9599. Tel.: 808-332-7324, ext. 203. Fax: 808-332-9765.
E-mail: members@ntbg.org
Web Site: www.ntbg.org
Founded: 1964.
Congressional District: 2
Key Personnel: C.E.O. & Dir., Chipper Wichman; Chm., Merrill L. Magowan; Museum Shop Mgr., Angela Whitlatch.
Personnel Profile: Full-Time Paid 110; Part-Time Paid 10; Part-Time Volunteers 250; Interns 8.
Governing Authority: board of trustees; nonprofit. Parent Institution: Organization Headquarters & main research center, Lawai, HI. Garden Sites: McBryde Garden, Allerton Garden (managed by NTBG), Lawai, HI; Limahuli Garden & Preserve, Haena, HI; Kahanu Garden, Hana, HI; Preserves, Big Island of HI; The Kampong, Coconut Grove, FL. Tax-exempt: 501(c)(3).
Tropical Botanical Garden.
Collections: 15,000-vol research library including the Loy McCandless Marks Botanical Library collection of books; thousands of living plants including rare & endangered species; plants of medicinal & nutritional value; tropical fruits; spices, palms; flowering trees; erythrinas; gingers; breadfruit, coconut; taro; bananas; vanilla; tropical ornamentals; ethnobotanical plants; ancient taro terraces; natural preserves; herbarium: 56,000 specimens, including native naturalized & cultivated plants of Kauai & other Hawaiian islands; vouchers of NTBG plants; 6,500 botanical prints; 17,000 photographic slides; culturally significant structures, objects & plants; sculptured gardens; water features. Allerton Gardens: former estate of Robert Allerton, managed by NTBG; McBryde Garden: scientific & conservation collections; Limahuli Garden: native Hawaiian plants, ancient taro terraces; Kahanu Garden: Polynesian ethnobotanical plants (including world's largest breadfruit collection), Piilanihale Heiau, Historical Landmark; The Kampong: former home horticulturist David Fairchild, tropical fruit cultivars, register historic places.
Research Fields: tropical plants; conservation of rare & endangered species; systematics & taxonomy, restoration ecology, evolutionary & floristic studies on flora of Hawaii & Polynesia; flora of Fiji; flora of the Marquesas Islands & Samoa; nutrition (breadfruit cultivars)medicinal & ethnobotanical plants of Polynesia; plants important to medicine, nutrition, conservation, horticulture & preservation; Florida: plants of the New and Old World tropics; tropical fruit cultivars; Pacific Islands.
Facilities: Headquarters: conservation center; botanical research center; lecture hall. Lawai Valley & Limahuli visitor centers. Museum-related items for sale.
Activities: lectures; workshops; educational tours; graduate & post-graduate courses; cooperation education with State Dept. of Education & University of Hawaii; in-school curriculum focusing on native plants; active collaborative relationship with Hawaii botanical & horticultural organizations, focusing on conservation of native plants; Florida horticultural classes University-level, horticultural organizations.
Publications: regional floras of Hawaii & Fiji; Polynesian medicinal plants manual; taxonomic revisions & monographs; an annotated botanical bibliography: Allertonia (scientific journal); Hawaii: A Natural History; members magazine; pamphlets & brochures; occasional papers; evolutionary studies.
Hours & Admission Prices: Reservations required. Allerton (guided), McBryde (self guided), call 808-742-2623; Limahuli Garden (guided & self guided), call 808-826-1053; Kahanu Garden (self guided), call 808-248-8912; The Kampong (guided), call 305-442-7169. Call for admission fees. Closed holidays. ♿
Attendance: 96,000 (estimated)
Membership: Individual $50; Family $150; Supporting $500; Silver Fellow $1,000; Fellow $1,500.

Kalaupapa

KALAUPAPA NATIONAL HISTORICAL PARK, 7 Puahi St., Kalaupapa, HI 96742. Mailing Address: P.O. Box 2222, Kalaupapa, HI 96742-0040. Tel.: 808-567-6802. Fax: 808-567-6729.
Web Site: www.nps.gov/kala/gov
Founded: 1980.
Congressional District: 2
Key Personnel: Supt., Stephen Prokop.
Governing Authority: federal. Parent Institution: National Park Service, U.S. Dept. of the Interior. Tax-exempt.
National Park: site of the 1886-present Molokai Island leprosy settlement.
Collections: history artifacts; areas related to early Hawaiian settlement; scenic & geologic resources; habitats for rare & endangered species.
Research Fields: natural sciences; historical archaeology; early 20th-century historical Hawaiian architecture.
Hours & Admission Prices: Park: Mon.-Fri. 7-3:30. Tours: Mon.-Sat. Call Damien Tours, 808-567-6171, for tour of the park.

Kamuela

ANNA RANCH HERITAGE CENTER, 65-1480 Kawaihae Rd., Kamuela, HI 96743-8554. Tel.: 808-885-4426.
E-mail: info@annaranch.org
Web Site: www.annaranch.org
Historic House: former home of Anna Leialoha Lindsey Perry-Fiske. Listed on the Hawaii State Register of Historic Places.
Collections: pa'u costumes, hats, boots & saddles; fine china.
Hours & Admission Prices: Call for hours.

PARKER RANCH HISTORIC HOMES & GARDENS, 671435 Manelahoa Hwy., Kamuela, HI 96743-8433. Tel.: 808-885-5433. Fax: 808-885-5889.
E-mail: info@parkerranch.com
Web Site: www.parkerranch.com
Key Personnel: Mgr. Sales & Operations, Anthony Roberts.
Governing Authority: Parent Institution: Parker Ranch Foundation Trust/Parker Ranch Inc.
Historic Homes: housed in Mana Hale, the home of founder John Palmer Parker and Puuopelu, the Parker Hawaiian Victorian Estate from 1879 to 1992.
Collections: Mana Hale: native koa wood interiors; handmade furniture; Hawaiian quilts. Puuopelu: period furnishings; French impressionist art; Asia figurines; gardens.
Activities: rental facilities; tours.
Hours & Admission Prices: Tues.-Sat. 10-5. Adults $10; discounts to seniors & children.

Kaneohe

SENATOR FONG'S PLANTATION & GARDENS, 47-285 Pulama Rd., Kaneohe, HI 96744-5026. Tel.: 808-239-6775. Fax: 808-239-6469.
E-mail: info@fonggarden.com
Web Site: www.fonggarden.net
Key Personnel: Mgr., Patsy Fong
Plantation & Garden Museum.
Collections: palms; fruit & nut trees; ferns; flowers.
Facilities: 725-acre garden. Museum-related items for sale.
Activities: walking tours; weddings; receptions; parties; luncheons; lei classes.
Hours & Admission Prices: Daily 10-2. Tours: 10:30am & 1pm. Adults $14.50, senior citizens 65 & over $13, children 5-12 $9; discounts to military, AAA members & groups. Closed New Year's Day; Christmas.

Kapaa

KAUAI CHILDREN'S DISCOVERY MUSEUM, 4-831 Kuhio Hwy. #332, Kapaa, HI 96746-1580. Mailing Address: 6458-B Kahuna Rd., Kapaa, HI 96746-9128. Tel.: 808-823-8222. Fax: 808-821-2558.
Web Site: www.kcdm.org
Founded: 1994.
Congressional District: 13
Key Personnel: Exec. Dir., Mari Y. de Moya; Pres. (V), Jean Camp; Devel. Dir., Danielle Engen.
Personnel Profile: Full-Time Paid 3; Part-Time Paid 5; Part-Time Volunteers 150; Interns 2.
Governing Authority: Tax-exempt.
Children's Museum & Science Center.
Collections: hands-on museum concentrating on the arts, science, cultures, technology & nature.
Activities: guided tours; workshops; vacation camps; special events.
Hours & Admission Prices: Tues.-Sat. 9-5. Adults 18 & over $5, children 1-17 $4; discounts to AAM & ICOM members; members no charge.
Attendance: 20,205 (accurate)
Membership: Individual $25; Family $45; Benefactor $100.

Kauai

KOKE'E NATURAL HISTORY MUSEUM, Kokee State Park, Kauai, HI 96752. Mailing Address: P.O. Box 100, Kekaha, Kauai, HI 96752-0100. Tel.: 808-335-9975. Fax: 808-335-6131.
E-mail: kokeemuseum@earthlink.net
Web Site: www.kokee.org
Founded: 1952.
Key Personnel: Exec. Dir., Marsha Erickson; Museum Shop Mgr., Paulette Burnter.
Personnel Profile: Full-Time Paid 3; Part-Time Paid 2.
Governing Authority: private; nonprofit organization. Parent Institution: Hui o Laka. Tax-exempt.
Natural History Museum.
Collections: Kaua'i's ecology, geology; climatology.
Activities: interpretive programs; exhibitions; festivals; school programs.
Hours & Admission Prices: Daily 10-4. No charge; donations accepted. ♿
Attendance: 200,000 (estimated)
Membership: Maile Lauli'ili'i $5; Mokihana $15; Hapu'u $25; Ohi'a Lehua $50; Koa $100; Iliahi $250; Kauila $500; Lama $1,000.

Kaumakani

GAY & ROBINSON SUGAR PLANTATION VISITOR CENTER, 2 Kaumakani Ave., Kaumakani, HI 96747. Mailing Address: P.O. Box 440, Kaumakani, HI 96747-0440. Tel.: 808-335-2824. Fax: 808-335-6852.
Web Site: www.hawaiimuseums.org/mc/iskauai_gayandrobinson.htm
Visitor Center.
Collections: company history; local culture; period artifacts; photographs; sugar politics; field & factory operations.
Hours & Admission Prices: Mon.-Fri. 8-4. Plantation Tour: adults $30, children $21. Olokele Tour: adult $60, children $45. Visitor's Center: no charge. Reservation required for tours. Closed plantation holidays.

Kilauea

KILAUEA POINT NATIONAL WILDLIFE REFUGE, Kilauea Point, Kilauea, HI 96754. Mailing Address: P.O. Box 1128, Kilauea, HI 96754-1128. Tel.: 808-828-1413. Fax: 808-828-1414.
Wildlife Refuge.
Collections: seabirds; native plants; marine mammals; lighthouse.
Facilities: nature trails.
Activities: hiking; hands-on environmental programs.
Hours & Admission Prices: Daily 10-4.

Kohala

PUUKOHOLA HEIAU NATIONAL HISTORIC SITE, 62-3601 Kawaihae Rd., Kohala, HI 96743-9720. Mailing Address: 62-3601 Kawaihae Rd., Kamuela, HI 96743-9720. Tel.: 808-882-7218. Fax: 808-882-1215.
Web Site: www.nps.gov/puhe
Founded: 1972.
Congressional District: 2
Key Personnel: Supt., Daniel Kawaiaea.
Personnel Profile: Full-Time Paid 9; Full-Time Volunteers 9; Part-Time Paid 4.
Governing Authority: federal. Administered by National Park Service, U.S. Dept. of the Interior. Tax-exempt.
Park Museum: ruins of Puukohola Heiau, Temple on the Hill of the Puukohola Whale, war temple built 1790-1791 by King Kamehameha the Great.
Collections: archaeological excavations & findings.
Facilities: visitor center.
Activities: hiking trails. Annual Events: National Park Week in April; Asian/Pacific American Heritage Day in May; Hawaiian Flag Day in July; Hawaiian Cultural Festival in August.
Publications: park information folder.
Hours & Admission Prices: Daily 7:30-5. No charge; donations accepted. ♿
Attendance: 256,639 (accurate)

Kualapua

MOLOKAI MUSEUM AND CULTURAL CENTER, Kala'e Hwy., Kualapua, HI 96757. Mailing Address: P.O. Box 269, Kualapua, HI 96757-0269. Tel.: 808-567-6436. Fax: 808-567-6624.
Key Personnel: Exec. Dir., Noelani Keliikipi
Historic Site: housed on the site of the former R.W. Meyer Sugar Mill, built in 1878. Listed on the National Register of Historic Places.
Collections: restored sugar mill; sugar cane maker; photographs.

Facilities: Museum-related items for sale.
Activities: guided hikes; seminars; rental facilities; dance performances.
Hours & Admission Prices: Mon.-Sat. 10-2. Adults $3.50, students 5-18 $1. Closed New Year's Day; Thanksgiving; Christmas.

Kurtistown

FUKU-BONSAI CULTURAL CENTER & HAWAII STATE BONSAI REPOSITORY, 17-656 Olaa Rd., Kurtistown, HI 96760. Mailing Address: P.O. Box 6000, Kurtistown, HI 96760-6000. Tel.: 808-982-9880. Fax: 808-982-9883.
Web Site: www.fukubonsai.com
Nature Center.
Collections: Hawaiian, Japanese, & Chinese bonsai; cultural artifacts; sculpture.
Hours & Admission Prices: Mon.-Sat. 8-4. No charge; donations accepted.

Lahaina

LAHAINA RESTORATION FOUNDATION, 120 Dickenson, Lahaina, HI 96761-1224. Tel.: 808-661-3262. Fax: 808-661-9309.
E-mail: info@lahainarestoration.org
Web Site: www.lahainarestoration.org
Founded: 1962.
Congressional District: 2
Key Personnel: Exec. Dir., Theo Morrison; Pres., David Allaire.
Personnel Profile: Full-Time Paid 4; Part-Time Paid 9; Part-Time Volunteers 4.
Governing Authority: nonprofit organization. Tax-exempt: 501(c)(3).
History Museums.
Collections: marine; archives; medical; history; architecture; period furniture; art; Hawaiian stone artifacts & tools; manuscripts; microfilm; 19th-century ship logs & journals; Maui's Humpback whales & the undersea world of Hawaii; Chinese artifacts; working Taoist Altar; Lahaina life during the Hawaiian Monarchy 1820-1893. Historical Houses; 1835 Baldwin Home; 1834 Masters Reading Room; 1837 Hale Pai Printing House; 1900 Wo Hing Chinese Temple; Hale Paahao Prison; Hale Aloha Church.
Research Fields: local history; ethnic & anthropological studies.
Facilities: 500-vol. library of early Hawaiiana available on premises by request; reading room; botanical garden. Books, microfilms, artifact reproductions & prints for sale.
Activities: guided tours; lectures; films; dance recitals; permanent & temporary exhibitions; films. Museum Sponsors: ethnic & cultural development & preservation programs for children.
Publications: quarterly newspaper; walking tour map.
Hours & Admission Prices: Daily 10-4. Baldwin: family $5, adults $3, senior citizens $2; Wo Hing Temple $1; members, school groups, children accompanied by parents no charge. Closed Thanksgiving; Christmas. ♿
Attendance: 240,000 (estimated)
Membership: Student $5; Individual $25; Ohana $35; Supporting $75; Business $100; Historian $250; Preservationist $500; Patron $1,000; Heritage Partner $2,500; Heritage Leader $5,000.

Lahaina, Maui

WHALERS VILLAGE MUSEUM, 2435 Ka'anapali Pkwy., Bldg. H-6, Lahaina, Maui, HI 96761-1980. Tel.: 808-661-4567.
E-mail: info@whalersvillage.com
Web Site: www.whalersvillage.com/museum/museum.htm
Whaling Museum.
Collections: Lahaina's whaling era, 1825-1860; photo murals; recreated whaling ship forecastle; period ornaments & utensils made from whale ivory and bone; 19th century scrimshaw.
Facilities: Museum-related items for sale.
Activities: self-guided audio tours; short videos.
Hours & Admission Prices: Daily 9am-10pm. No charge.

Laie

POLYNESIAN CULTURAL CENTER, 55-370 Kamehameha Hwy., Laie, HI 96762-1113. Tel.: 808-293-3005. Fax: 808-293-3022.
E-mail: internetrez@polynesia.com
Web Site: www.polynesia.com
Cultural Center.
Collections: people & cultures of Polynesia including Hawaii, Samoa, Aotearoa, Fiji, the Marquesas, Tahiti, and Tonga.
Facilities: IMAX theater. Museum-related items for sale.
Activities: shows.
Hours & Admission Prices: Mon.-Sat. 12:30-6:30. Call for admission prices. ♿

Lanai City

LANAI CULTURE & HERITAGE CENTER, 730 Lanai Ave., Rm. 126, Lanai City, HI 96763. Mailing Address: P.O. Box 631500, Lanai City, HI 96763-1305. Tel.: 808-565-7177.
Web Site: www.lanaichc.org
History Museum.
Collections: local heritage & culture; photographs; ranching; plantation history.
Activities: research.
Hours & Admission Prices: Mon.-Fri. 9-3. No charge.

Laupahoehoe

LAUPAHOEHOE TRAIN MUSEUM, 36-2377 Mamalahoa Hwy., Laupahoehoe, HI 96764. Mailing Address: P.O. Box 358, Laupahoehoe, HI 96764-0358. Tel.: 808-962-6300. Fax: 808-963-6957.
E-mail: laupahoehoetrainmuseum@yahoo.com
Web Site: www.thetrainmuseum.com
Founded: 1998.
Key Personnel: Pres. (V), Lisa Barton.
Governing Authority: Tax exempt.
History Museum.
Collections: islands history of railroads, plantations & local cultures; photographs; video.
Facilities: Museum-related items for sale.
Hours & Admission Prices: Mon.-Fri. 9-4:30, Sat.-Sun. 10-2; groups by appointment. Adults $4, seniors $3, children $2; discounts to AAM members. ♿
Attendance: 7,000 (estimated)
Membership: Grand Dancer $25; Brakeman $40; Fireman $100; Conductor $500; Engineer $1,000.

Lihue

GROVE FARM MUSEUM, Hwy. 58, Lihue, HI 96766. Mailing Address: P.O. Box 1631, Lihue, HI 96766-5631. Tel.: 808-245-3202. Fax: 808-245-7988.
E-mail: grovefarm@hawaiiantel.net
Key Personnel: Dir., Robert J. Schleck
Sugar Plantation: listed on the National Register of Historic Places.
Collections: sugar plantation history; period furnishings; historic buildings.
Activities: guided tours.
Hours & Admission Prices: Mon. & Wed.-Thurs. 10am & 1pm by appointment. Adults $10, children 5-12 $5.

KAUAI HISTORICAL SOCIETY, 4396 Rice St., Ste. 101, Lihue, HI 96766-1371. Mailing Address: P.O. Box 1778, Lihue, HI 96766-5778. Tel.: 808-245-3373. Fax: 808-245-8693.
E-mail: info@kauaihistoricalsociety.org
Web Site: www.kauaihistoricalsociety.org
Founded: 1914.
Key Personnel: Dir., Mary Requilnan.
Personnel Profile: Full-Time Paid 1; Part-Time Paid 1; Part-Time Volunteers 12.
Governing Authority: nonprofit organization. Tax-exempt.
Historical Society Museum & Archive.
Collections: period furniture; art; manuscripts; maps; photographs.
Facilities: library.
Activities: guided & school tours; permanent exhibits; historical programs; classes; workshops; performances; monthly lectures. Annual Event: The Royal Pa'ina in April.
Hours & Admission Prices: Office: Mon.-Fri. 8-4. Archives: by appointment. No charge; donations accepted.
Membership: Senior & Student $25; Individual $35; Family $50; Small Business $100 & up; Supporting $125; Contributing $250; Patron & Corporation $500.

KAUAI MUSEUM, 4428 Rice St., Lihue, HI 96766-1338. Mailing Address: P.O. Box 248, Lihue, HI 96766-0248. Tel.: 808-245-6931. Fax: 808-245-6864.
E-mail: robbie@kauaimuseum.org
Web Site: kauaimuseum.org
Founded: 1960.
Congressional District: 2
Key Personnel: Exec. Dir., Robbie Kaholokula; Pres., John Constantino; Cur., Chris Faye; Education & Art Mezzanine Gallery, Lyah Kama-Drake; Museum Shop Mgr., Jan DeLa Vega; Volunteer Coord., Chacha Kaluahine.
Personnel Profile: Full-Time Paid 4; Part-Time Paid 3; Part-Time Volunteers 75.
Governing Authority: nonprofit corporation. Tax-exempt: 501(c)(3)

History & Art Museum: housed in early 20th-century Wilcox building designed by Hart Wood.
Collections: Hawaiiana collection with particular emphasis on items dealing with the island of Kauai; Kauai photographs; school art exhibits; ethnic & heritage displays; paintings; dolls; textiles; WWII memorabilia; furnishings; weapons; scrimshaw.
Major Exhibits: King Kaumuali'i and the Russians, 11/09-3/22/10; Kauai's Industrial Revolution - Steam Power & Other Innovations, 11/09-4/26/10; The Kekaha Train Robbery, 4/3/10-9/27/10; 50th Anniversary Exhibit, 10/10-12/10.
Research Fields: Hawaiiana, particularly the Island of Kauai.
Facilities: 1,000-vol. library of books; pamphlets; photographs dealing with the history of the Island of Kauai available on premises. Hawaiiana books Niihau shell leis prints & handicrafts from the South Pacific for sale.
Activities: guided tours; films; arts festivals; permanent & temporary exhibitions.
Publications: Hawaiian Quilting on Kauai; Early Kauai Hospitality 1820-1920: A Family Book of Receipts; Amelia: a novel of midcentury Hawaii; Moki Learns to Count: a children's book; Kauai, The Separate Kingdom; Kauai Museum Quilt Collection.
Hours & Admission Prices: Mon.-Fri. 9-4, Sat. 10-4. Adults $10, seniors 65 & over $8, youths 13-17 $6, children 6-12 $2; discounts for members' guests, Western Museum Assoc. & Hawaii Museum members; 1st Sat. each month, member adults & children 5 & under no charge. Closed New Year's Day; Independence Day; Memorial Day; Labor Day; Thanksgiving; Christmas. ♿
Attendance: 25,175 (estimated)
Membership: Individual $25; Family $45; Contributing $75; Sustaining $100; Patron $250; Corporate $500 & up.

KILOHANA PLANTATION, 3-2087 Kaumualii Hwy., Lihue, HI 96766-9505. Mailing Address: P.O. Box 3121, Lihue, HI 96766-6121. Tel.: 808-245-5608. Fax: 808-245-7818.
E-mail: kilohana@hawaiilink.net
Web Site: www.kauaikilohana.com
Historic House: housed in the former home of sugar baron, Gaylord Parke Wilcox; built in 1936.
Collections: period furnishings; personal artifacts.
Hours & Admission Prices: Mon.-Sat. 9:30am-9:30pm, Sun. 9:30-4. No charge.

Maalaea

MAUI OCEAN CENTER, 192 Maalaea Rd., Maalaea, HI 96793-5931. Tel.: 808-270-7000. Fax: 808-270-7070.
E-mail: info@mauioceancenter.com
Web Site: www.mauioceancenter.com
Founded: 1998.
Key Personnel: Gen. Mgr., Kate Zolezzi; Controller, Bridget Reardon; Education, Ka'au Abraham; Sales & Mktg., Lori Mellenbruch; Cur., John Gorman; Museum Shop Mgr., Tapani Vuori.
Governing Authority: Parent Institution: Coral World International.
Aquarium.
Collections: Hawaiian marine life & cultural artifacts; living coral; reef fish; invertebrates; sharks; stingrays; sea turtles.
Facilities: aquarium; 200-seat restaurant. Museum-related items for sale.
Activities: lectures. Annual Events: Earth Day; World Ocean Day; Shark Week.
Hours & Admission Prices: July-Aug. daily 9-6; Sept.-May daily 9-5. Adults $25, senior citizens $22, children $18; discounts to groups; members no charge. ♿
Attendance: 350,000 (estimated)
Membership: Children $37; Senior $45; Adult $50; Family (2 adults & 2 children) $150.

Makawao, Maui

HUI NO'EAU VISUAL ARTS CENTER, 2841 Baldwin Ave., Makawao, Maui, HI 96768-9642. Tel.: 808-572-6560, ext. 34. Fax: 808-572-2750.
E-mail: info@huinoeau.com
Web Site: www.huinoeau.com
Founded: 1934.
Key Personnel: C.E.O., John Z. Lofgren; Exec. Dir., Deborah Michaels; Chm. Bd. (V), John Hoxie; Devel., Deborah Peterson; Registrar, Kate Stackhouse; Facility Mgr., Omega Reyes; Mng. Dir., Caroline Killhour; Program Mgr., Anne-Marie Forsythe.
Personnel Profile: Full-Time Paid 12; Part-Time Paid 3; Part-Time Volunteers 200; Interns 1.
Governing Authority: private; nonprofit organization.
Visual Arts Center: housed in 1917 Mediterranean-style home.
Collections: artifacts of Harry & Ethel Baldwin & their daughter Francis Cameron.
Facilities: library of historical references of art history, art magazines & books available to members; botanical garden; educational facilities; solarium; lecture & slide room; art studios. Museum-related items for sale.
Activities: docent program; guided tours; lectures. Museum Sponsors: Christmas House; Art Affair; Open House.
Publications: quarterly newsletter, Hui News.
Hours & Admission Prices: Exhibit Gallery & Gift Shop: Mon.-Sat. 10-4. Administrative Offices: Mon.-Fri. 8-5. No charge; donations accepted. ♿
Attendance: 30,000 (estimated)
Membership: Senior $30; Individual $40; Family $60; Sponsor $100-$249; Supporter $250-$499; Patron $500-$999; Benefactor $1,000-$2,499; President's Circle $2,500 & up.

Paia

MAUI CRAFTS GUILD, 43 Hana Way, Paia, HI 96779. Mailing Address: P.O. Box 790609, Paia, HI 96779-0609. Tel.: 808-579-9697. Fax: 808-579-8694.
E-mail: info@mauicraftsguild.com
Web Site: www.mauicraftsguild.com
Art Museum.
Collections: works by local artists including ceramics, sculpture, prints, textiles, photographs, baskets.
Hours & Admission Prices: Daily 10-6.

Papaikou

HAWAII TROPICAL BOTANICAL GARDEN, 27-717 Old Mamalahoa Hwy., Papaikou, HI 96781-7746. Mailing Address: P.O. Box 80, Papaikou, HI 96781-0080. Tel.: 808-964-5233. Fax: 808-964-1338.
E-mail: htbg@ilhawaii.net
Web Site: www.htbg.com
Founded: 1974.
Governing Authority: nonprofit. Tax-exempt: 501(c)(3).
Botanical Garden.
Collections: tropical & subtropical plants; palms; heliconias; gingers; bromeliads.
Facilities: 40-acres.
Hours & Admission Prices: Garden: daily 9-5. Gift Shop: daily 8:30-5. Adults $15, children 6-16 $5; children under 6 no charge. Closed New Year's Day; Thanksgiving; Christmas.
Attendance: 70,000

Puunene

ALEXANDER & BALDWIN SUGAR MUSEUM, (M), 3957 Hansen Rd., Puunene, HI 96784. Mailing Address: P.O. Box 125, Puunene, HI 96784-0125. Tel.: 808-871-8058. Fax: 808-871-4321.
E-mail: sugarmus@maui.net
Web Site: sugarmuseum.com
Founded: 1980.
Key Personnel: Pres. (V), Douglas Sheehan; Contact, Darla Palmer; Museum Shop Mgr., Sandra Nordstrom.
Personnel Profile: Full-Time Paid 2; Part-Time Paid 6; Part-Time Volunteers 20.
Governing Authority: private; nonprofit organization. Tax-exempt.
Agriculture Museum: housed in 1902 former sugar factory superintendent's residence, located across the way from Hawaii's largest sugar mill.
Collections: focus on sugar industry & plantation life on the island of Maui from 1850s to 1950s; emphasis on native cultures of various ethnic groups brought to Hawaii as labor.
Research Fields: sugar industry on island of Maui, 1850-1950; Hawaiian plantation life.
Facilities: 1,800 sq. ft. exhibit space. Hawaiian sugar-based food products, local craft items & other museum-related items for sale.
Activities: docent programs; educational programs for children; traveling exhibits.
Publications: newsletter.
Hours & Admission Prices: Feb.-April & July-Aug. daily 9:30-4:30; May-June & Sept.-Jan. Mon.-Sat. 9:30-4:30. Adults $7, children $2; discounts to AAM members. Closed New Year's Day; Easter; Thanksgiving; Christmas. ♿
Attendance: 38,453 (accurate)

Schofield Barracks

TROPIC LIGHTNING MUSEUM, Directorate of Plans, Training, Mobilization and Security, Bldg. #361, Waianae Ave., Schofield Barracks, HI 96857-5000. Mailing Address: Directorate of Plans, Training, Mobilization & Security, 742 Santos Dumont Ave., Rm. 306, Bldg. 108, Wheeler Army Airfield, Schofield Barracks, HI 96857-5026. Tel.: 808-655-0438.
Founded: 1958.
Military History Museum.
Collections: history of the 25th Infantry Division from 1941 to present; Wheeler Army Airfield; military equipment & uniforms; artillery guns; military vehicles; Schofield Barracks.
Hours & Admission Prices: Tues.-Sat. 10-4. No charge; donations accepted. Closed holidays. ♿
Attendance: 14,000 (estimated)

Volcano

VOLCANO ART CENTER GALLERY, 19-4074 Old Volcano Rd., Volcano, HI 96785. Mailing Address: P.O. Box 129, Volcano, HI 96785-0129. Tel.: 808-967-7565. Fax: 808-967-7511.
E-mail: gallery@volcanoartcenter.org
Web Site: www.volcanoartcenter.org
Founded: 1974.
Congressional District: 2
Key Personnel: Exec. Dir., Phyllis Segawa; Gallery Mgr., Fia Mattice; Bd. Pres. (V), Jim Wilson; Bd. Treas., Donald Hasenyager; Bd. Vice Pres., Tad Sewell; Dir. Education, Susan McGovern; Education Coord., Marsha Hee; Education Coord., Rob McGovern; Education Coord., Julie Mitchell; Office Mgr. & Bookkeeper, Jane Buchholz.
Personnel Profile: Full-Time Paid 10; Part-Time Paid 7; Part-Time Volunteers 300.
Governing Authority: not-for-profit organization. Offices: 19-4074 Old Volcano Rd., Volcano, HI 96785. Tax-exempt: 501(c)(3).
Cultural Center & Gallery: housed in a home built in 1877.
Collections: paintings; photographs; prints; ceramics; wood; glass.
Facilities: 300-seat theatre; classrooms; 7.4 acre rainforest site with nature trails.
Activities: concerts; dance recitals; guided tours; workshops; lectures; theatre. Museum Sponsors: Christmas in the Country; Love the Arts.
Publications: bimonthly, newsletter, Volcano Gazette.
Hours & Admission Prices: Daily 9-5. No charge; donations accepted. Closed Christmas. ♿
Attendance: 250,000 (estimated)
Membership: Students & Seniors $20; Individual $35; Dual & Family $50; Contributor $100; Supporting $250; Sponsor $500; Patron $1,000; Benefactor $2,500.

Wailuku

BAILEY HOUSE MUSEUM - MAUI HISTORICAL SOCIETY, 2375A Main St., Wailuku, HI 96793-1661. Tel.: 808-244-3326. Fax: 808-244-3920.
E-mail: baileyhousemuseum@clearwire.net
Web Site: www.mauimuseum.org
Founded: 1951.
Congressional District: 2
Key Personnel: Exec. Dir., Nicole McMullen; Pres. (V), Don Reeser.
Personnel Profile: Full-Time Paid 3; Part-Time Paid 2; Part-Time Volunteers 20; Interns 2.
Governing Authority: nonprofit organization. Parent Institution: Maui Historical Society. Tax-exempt: 501(c)(3) & 170(b)(1)(A).
Historic House: c.1833-1850 Bailey House; ancient Hawaiian site.
Collections: native Hawaiian artifacts of stone, wood shell, feathers; furniture; clothing of missionary era; paintings by E. H. Bailey; Kaho'olawe Island artifacts; gardens; photographs.
Research Fields: local history; archaeology of Maui County; ancient Hawaiian history missionary era.
Facilities: Books, clothing, jewelry, cards, stationery & Hawaiian crafts for sale.
Activities: guided tours; lectures; inter-museum loan, permanent & temporary exhibitions.
Publications: Hawaii Nei; Maui Remembers; Index to the Maui News; Maui, A Guide to Resources.
Hours & Admission Prices: Mon.-Sat. 10-4. Adults $7, seniors $5, children 6-12 $2; discounts to seniors 60 & over; active military, members & travel professionals no charge. Closed holidays.
Attendance: 12,500 (estimated)
Membership: Student & Senior Citizen $25; Individual $35; Family $50; Preservationist $3,000.

HAWAII NATURE CENTER, MAUI, 875 Iao Valley Rd., Wailuku, HI 96793-3009. Tel.: 808-244-6525.
E-mail: bookmaui@hawaiinaturecenter.org
Web Site: www.hawaiinaturecenter.org
Founded: 1992.
Key Personnel: Museum Shop Mgr., Dee Dee Santos
Nature Center.
Collections: island environment, culture, & history; wildlife; plants.
Activities: educational programs; school group tours; hiking.
Publications: quarterly newsletter; brochures.
Hours & Admission Prices: Daily 10-4. Adults $6; members no charge.
Membership: Individual $25; Family $50; Contributing $250; Sustaining $500; Steward $1,000.

MAUI OKINAWA CULTURAL CENTER, 688 Nukuwai Place, Wailuku, HI 96793-1340. Mailing Address: P.O. Box 1884, Wailuku, HI 96793-6884. Tel.: 808-242-1560. Fax: 808-242-5952.
Art Museum.
Collections: Okinawan culture; pottery; textiles; lacquerware; bingata; calligraphy.
Hours & Admission Prices: Mon.-Fri. 8:30-11:30; other times by appointment. No charge; donations accepted.

Waimanalo

SEA LIFE PARK HAWAII, 41-202 Kalanianaole Hwy., Ste. 7, Waimanalo, HI 96795-1897. Tel.: 866-393-5158 (Toll Free).
Nature Center.
Collections: marine mammals including dolphins, sea lions, rays, & penguins.
Facilities: theater; restaurant. Gift items for sale.
Activities: interactive programs; swim with dolphins.
Hours & Admission Prices: Daily 9:30-5. Adult $29, children 4-12 $19.

Waimea

FAYE MUSEUM, Waimea Plantation Cottages, 9400 Kaumualii Hwy., Waimea, HI 96796. Mailing Address: P.O. Box 1178, Waimea, HI 96796-1178. Tel.: 808-338-1625.
E-mail: waimeasugar@hawaiilink. net
Key Personnel: Cur., Chris Faye
History Museum: a pioneer sugar planter in West Kauai, H.P. Faye helped form Kekaha Sugar, incorporated in 1898.
Collections: local history; sugar industry; personal artifacts; photographs.
Hours & Admission Prices: Open Year Round: Mon.-Fri. 9-5. No charge.

GALLERY WEST, Waimea Plantation Cottages, 9400 Kaumualii Hwy., Waimea, HI 96796. Mailing Address: P.O. Box 1178, Waimea, HI 96796-1178. Tel.: 808-338-1625 & 2340.
Key Personnel: Mgr., Kathleen Miguel
Art Gallery.
Collections: works by local artists.
Hours & Admission Prices: Call for hours.

WAIMEA SUGAR MILL CAMP MUSEUM, 9400 Kaumualii Hwy., Waimea, HI 96796. Mailing Address: P.O. Box 1178, Waimea, HI 96796-1178. Tel.: 808-337-1005. Fax: 808-337-9449.
History Museum.
Collections: local history & culture.
Hours & Admission Prices: Tues., Thurs. & Sat. 9am by appointment.

WEST KAUAI TECHNOLOGY & VISITOR CENTER, 9565 Kaumualii Hwy., Waimea, HI 96796. Tel.: 808-338-1332.
History Museum.
Collections: area culture & history; science; technology.
Activities: multimedia presentations; demonstrations; walking tour; special events.
Hours & Admission Prices: Mon.-Fri. 9:30-5.

Waipahu

HAWAII OKINAWA CENTER, 94-587 Ukee St., Waipahu, HI 96797-4214. Tel.: 808-676-5400. Fax: 808-676-7811.
Cultural Center.
Collections: local history & culture; Okinawa crafts including pottery, doll making, & fabrics; early plantation & immigration.
Hours & Admission Prices: Mon.-Fri. 8:30-5, Sat. 9-3. Closed New Year's Day; Presidents' Day; Memorial Day; Independence Day; Labor Day; Thanksgiving; Christmas.

HAWAII'S PLANTATION VILLAGE, 94-695 Waipahu St., Waipahu, HI 96797-2601. Tel.: 808-677-0110. Fax: 808-676-6727.
E-mail: hpv.waipahu@hawaiiantel.net
Web Site: www.hawaiiplantationvillage.org
Founded: 1973.
Congressional District: 2
Key Personnel: Pres., Faith P. Evans; 1st Vice Pres., Deanna Espinas; 2nd Vice Pres., Loretta Pang; 3rd Vice Pres., Richard Oshiro; Sec., Robert Castro; Treas., Glenn Ifuku.
Personnel Profile: Full-Time Paid 6; Part-Time Paid 18; Part-Time Volunteers 120.
Governing Authority: private; nonprofit organization. Tax-exempt: 501(c)(3).
General Museum.
Collections: 1900-1940 Hawaii plantation family personal artifacts; ethnic & cultural materials related to the 8 major ethnic groups to work on the plantations.
Research Fields: plantation history; Oahu sugar records.
Facilities: 200-vol. library of Hawaii plantation & ethnic history books; 100 sq. ft. exhibit space; educational facilities. Museum-related items for sale.
Activities: docent program; guided tours; lectures; temporary exhibitions; ethnic heritage events.
Publications: quarterly newsletter, Plantation News.
Hours & Admission Prices: Office: Mon.-Sat. 8-4:30. Guided Tours: Mon.-Sat. 10-2. Adults $13, seniors 62 & over $10, Kama'aina & military $7, youth 4-11 $5. Closed New Year's Day; Good Friday; Memorial Day; Independence Day; Labor Day; Thanksgiving; Christmas. ♿
Attendance: 60,000 (estimated)
Membership: Youth $10; Student $15; Double Seniors $20; Individual $25; Family $40; Family Plus $55; Hoe Hana $100-$249; Wai Hana $250-$499; Luna $500-$749; Manager $750-$999; Sustainer $1,000 & up.

IDAHO

(119 listings)

Almo

CITY OF ROCKS NATIONAL RESERVE, 3035 Elba Almo Rd., Almo, ID 83312. Mailing Address: P.O. Box 169, Almo, ID 83312-0169. Tel.: 208-824-5519.
Park Museum.
Collections: local history; geology; flowers; trees; plants.
Facilities: visitor center.
Hours & Admission Prices: Park: daily. Visitor Center: April 17-Oct. 23 daily 8-4:30; Oct. 24-April 11 Mon.-Fri. 8-4:30.

American Falls

MASSACRE ROCKS STATE PARK, 3592 Park Lane, American Falls, ID 83211-5556. Tel.: 208-548-2672. Fax: 208-548-2671.
E-mail: mas@idpr.state.id.us
Web Site: parksandrecreation.idaho.gov/parks/massacrerocks.aspx
Founded: 1967.
Congressional District: 2
Key Personnel: Park Mgr., L. Max Newlin.
Personnel Profile: Full-Time Paid 3.
Governing Authority: state. Tax-exempt.
Park Museum.
Collections: Indian artifacts; natural history; pioneer & Oregon Trail history.
Research Fields: Oregon trail history.
Facilities: information center.
Activities: guided nature walks; evening campfire programs; Oregon trail tours.
Publications: Geology of Massacre Rocks; Jane A. Gould Journal; The Oregon Trail Revisited; Historic Sites along the Oregon Trail; maps.
Hours & Admission Prices: Visitor Center: May 15-Sept. 15 daily 7:30am-9pm. Park: Summer: daily 8:30-8:30; Sept.-June daily 7-3:30. $4 per vehicle. ♿
Attendance: 50,000

Arco

CRATERS OF THE MOON NATIONAL MONUMENT, 18 mi. S.W. of Arco on Hwy. 26, Arco, ID 83213. Mailing Address: P.O. Box 29, Arco, ID 83213-0029. Tel.: 208-527-1300. Fax: 208-527-3073.
Web Site: www.nps.gov/crmo
Founded: 1924.
Congressional District: 2
Key Personnel: Acting Supt., Doug Neighbor.
Personnel Profile: Full-Time Paid 1; Part-Time Paid 1.
Governing Authority: federal. Parent Institution: National Park Service. Tax-exempt.
Natural History Museum.
Collections: local geology; history; herbarium; manuscripts.
Facilities: 500-vol. library on natural science. Books for sale.
Activities: guided tours; campfires during summertime; films; permanent exhibitions.
Publications: Around the Loop; Geological Map of Craters of the Moon; pocket flower guide; Unearthly Landscape, Craters of the Moon-official handbook (published by the supporting Natural History Association).
Hours & Admission Prices: Memorial Day-Labor Day daily 8-6; Sept.-May daily 8-4:30. Visitor Center: no charge; donations accepted. Park: $8 per vehicle. Closed winter holidays. ♿
Attendance: 217,000 (accurate)

Ashton

HESS HERITAGE MUSEUM, 3411 E. 1200 N. on Reclamation Rd., Ashton, ID 83420. Mailing Address: P.O. Box 809, Ashton, ID 83420-0809. Tel.: 208-652-7353.
Key Personnel: Dir., Tom Hess; Dir., Tom Howell
Pioneer Farm Museum.
Collections: pioneer history; period farm equipment; mural depicting the history of agriculture; land, snow & air travel; carriage house; one-room schoolhouse; wildlife; blacksmith shop; period furnishings; military artifacts.
Facilities: 250-acre pioneer farm.
Hours & Admission Prices: mid-April to mid-Oct. Mon.-Wed. & Fri.-Sat. by appointment. Adults $5, children under 12 $3; discounts to groups.

Athol

FARRAGUT STATE PARK, 13550 E. Hwy. 54, Athol, ID 83801. Tel.: 208-683-2425.
State Park.
Collections: natural history; wildlife; local history.
Facilities: visitor center; naval training center. Museum-related items for sale.
Activities: hiking; biking; camping; guided walks; educational programs; model airplane flyer's field.
Hours & Admission Prices: Daily.

Atlanta

ATLANTA HISTORICAL SOCIETY, Middle Fork Rd., Atlanta, ID 83601. Mailing Address: P.O. Box 53, Atlanta, ID 83601.
Governing Authority: nonprofit. Tax-exempt: 501(c)(3).
Historical Society Museum.
Collections: local history; period artifacts; photographs; pioneer life. Historic Buildings; 1910 jail; c.1870 cabin.
Hours & Admission Prices: Summer: daily 10-9; other times by appointment. No charge.

Blackfoot

BINGHAM COUNTY HISTORICAL MUSEUM, 190 N. Shilling Ave., Blackfoot, ID 83221-2848. Tel.: 208-785-8065.
Key Personnel: Head Bd. Dirs., Lola Summers
Historic House Museum.
Collections: period dolls; Native American artifacts.
Hours & Admission Prices: Thurs.-Sat. 10-3. No charge; donations accepted.

IDAHO POTATO MUSEUM, 130 N.W. Main St., Blackfoot, ID 83221-0801. Mailing Address: P.O. Box 801, Blackfoot, ID 83221-0801. Tel.: 208-785-2517. Fax: 208-785-7974.
Founded: 1984.
Agriculture Museum.
Collections: potato industry history; period farming equipment.
Facilities: Museum-related items for sale.
Activities: video.
Hours & Admission Prices: April-Sept. Mon.-Sat. 9:30-5; Oct.-March Mon.-Fri. 9:30-3. Adults $3, seniors 55 & over $2.50, children 6-12 $1; discounts to AAA members.

Boise

BASQUE MUSEUM & CULTURAL CENTER, 611 Grove St., Boise, ID 83702-5971. Tel.: 208-343-2671. Fax: 208-336-4801.
E-mail: info@basquemuseum.com
Web Site: www.basquemuseum.com
Founded: 1985.
Key Personnel: Dir., Patty Miller; Cur., Michael J. Vogt
Culture & History Museum.

Collections: area history & culture; photographs; personal artifacts.
Facilities: library. Museum-related items for sale.
Activities: tours; special events; educational programs.
Hours & Admission Prices: Tues.-Fri. 10-4, Sat. 11-3. Adults $4, students & seniors $3, children $2; members no charge. Closed holidays.
Membership: Seniors $25; Individual $35.

*** BOISE ART MUSEUM, (M),** 670 Julia Davis Dr., Boise, ID 83702-7646. Tel.: 208-345-8330, ext. 10. Fax: 208-345-2247.
Web Site: www.boiseartmuseum.org
Founded: 1931.
Congressional District: 1
Key Personnel: Exec. Dir., Melanie Fales; Pres. Bd. of Trustees, Esther Oppenheimer; Dir. Devel., Brandi Staudt; Cur. Art, Sandy Harthorn; Registrar, Kathy Bettis; Cur. Education, Terra Feast; Assoc. Cur. Education, Drew Williams; Curatorial Asst., Catherine Rakow; Museum Store Mgr., Jenaleigh Kiebert; Preparator, Ronald Walker; Financial Mgr., Mary Schaefer; Asst. Preparator, Todd Newman; Events & Rental Coord., Michelle Darcy; Coord. Membership & Donor Rels., Hana Van Huffel.
Personnel Profile: Full-Time Paid 13; Part-Time Paid 15; Part-Time Volunteers 280; Interns 3.
Governing Authority: nonprofit organization. Parent Institution: Boise Art Museum, Inc. Tax-exempt.
General Art Museum.
Collections: 20-century American Art; Northwest artists; international ceramics; international prints & photographs; James Castle collection; Asian & African objects & adornments.
Major Exhibits: A Survey of Gee's Bead Quilts (T), 11/09-1/17/10; Patchwork: Historic Quilts, 11/09-4/10; The Dorothy & Herbert Vogel Collection - Fifty Works for Fifty States, 1/30/10-5/2/10; Robots: Evolution of a Cultural Icon (T), 2/6/10-5/16/10; Nick Cave: Tondos & Sound Suits (T), 5/10-8/15/10; John James Audubon: American Artist and Naturalist (T), 6/5/10-8/22/10.
Facilities: 10,000-vol. art reference library available on premises by permission; 3,000 exhibition catalogs; reading room; 34,800 sq. ft. building; 2,800 sq. ft. indoor sculpture court; 16,000 sq. ft. gallery space. Crafts by Northwest artists, books & postcards for sale in the museum store.
Activities: children's programming, guided tours; lectures; films; gallery talks; performances; educational programs; docent program; temporary & traveling exhibitions; annual fundraising events.
Publications: quarterly, calendar; 2007 Idaho Triennial Catalog; exhibition catalogs: 100 Years of Idaho Art; James Barsness; Fabricated Nature; Jack Dollhausen: A 30 Year Start; Gary Hill: Language Willing; John Grade: Sculpture and Drawings; James Castle: Drawings, Constructions and Books; Collection of the Boise Art Museum; Twice Removed: Deborah Oropallo; Unraveled: Hildur Bjarnadottir; American Art: Wilfred Davis Fletcher Collection; Scott Fife: Big Trouble; Kendall Buster: New Growth; Lead Pencil Studio: After Devorah Sperber: Threads of Perception.
Hours & Admission Prices: Tues.-Sat. 10-5 (1st Thurs. 10-9), Sun. 12-5. Adults $5, college students with ID & senior citizens $3, children grades K-12 $1; discounts to museum professionals & 1st Thurs. of month; members & children under 6 no charge. Closed New Year's Day; Martin Luther King Jr. Day; Presidents' Day; Memorial Day; Independence Day; Labor Day; Columbus Day; Thanksgiving; Christmas. ♿
Attendance: 55,466 (accurate)
Membership: Student & Senior Citizen $35; Individual $45; Family $60; Advocate $125; Contributor $250; Sustainer $500; Patron $1,000; Benefactor's Circle $2,500 & up.

THE DISCOVERY CENTER OF IDAHO, 131 Myrtle St., Boise, ID 83702-7652. Tel.: 208-343-9895. Fax: 208-343-0105.
E-mail: dcifilter@gmail.com
Web Site: www.scidaho.org
Founded: 1986.
Congressional District: 2
Key Personnel: Exec. Dir., Janine Boire; Pres. (V), Mark Solon; Dir. Exhibits, Bill Molina; Exhibit Builder, Mike Twitchell; Business Mgr., Jane Baird; Senior Sec. & Museum Shop Mgr., Joanne Beall; Dir. Public Programs, Susan Dittus; Coord. Education, Kris Allison; Dir. Personnel, Sally Stivison-Dunne.
Personnel Profile: Full-Time Paid 9; Full-Time Volunteers 150; Part-Time Paid 2; Part-Time Volunteers 200.
Governing Authority: not-for-profit organization. Tax-exempt: 501(c)(3).
Science Museum.
Collections: hands-on exhibits including science, math, & technology.
Facilities: educational facilities; portable, inflatable planetarium. Scientific tools, toys, games, books & charts for sale.
Activities: docent program; formal education programs for children; lectures; loan, participatory & traveling exhibitions; teacher workshops for credit; speaker series.
Publications: quarterly newsletter, Discovery News.
Hours & Admission Prices: Winter: Tues.-Thurs. 9-5, Fri. 9-7, Sat. 10-5, Sun. 12-5; Summer: Mon.-Thurs. 9-5, Fri. 9-7, Sat. 10-5, Sun. 12-5. Adults 13 & over $6.50, senior citizens 60 & over $5.50, children 3-17 $4; discounts to groups & ASTC affiliate members; members and children 2 & under no charge. Closed New Year's Day; Easter; Thanksgiving; Christmas. ♿
Attendance: 98,700 (accurate)
Membership: Individual $25; Grandparent $40; Family & Grandparent Plus $50; Family Plus $60; Adventurer $100; Sir Isaac Newton Society $250 & up.

IDAHO BLACK HISTORY MUSEUM, 508 Julia Davis Dr., Boise, ID 83702-7694. Tel.: 208-433-0017.
E-mail: museum@ibhm.org
Web Site: www.ibhm.org
Key Personnel: Pres., Cherie Buckner-Webb
History Museum.
Collections: history & culture of Idaho blacks.
Activities: lectures; workshops; musical presentations; permanent exhibitions.
Publications: newsletter.
Hours & Admission Prices: Sat. 11-4; groups by appointment. ♿
Membership: Student & Senior $15; Individual $30; Family $50; Friend $100; Associate $250; Patron $500; President's Circle $1,000; Corporate $2,500; Benefactor $5,000.

IDAHO BOTANICAL GARDEN, 2355 N. Penitentiary Rd., Boise, ID 83712. Tel.: 208-343-8649. Fax: 208-343-3601.
E-mail: info@idahobotanicalgarden.org
Web Site: www.idahobotanicalgarden.org
Founded: 1984.
Congressional District: 2
Key Personnel: Exec. Dir., Julia Rundberg; Pres. (V), Christopher Pooser; Educator, Elizabeth Dickey; Events, Doreen Martinek; Archivist, Sally Clark; Museum Shop Mgr., Connie Fledderjohann; Head Horticulture, Rod Burke; Gardener, Tim Szofran; Gardener, Rebecca Needles.
Personnel Profile: Full-Time Paid 8; Full-Time Volunteers 1; Part-Time Paid 10; Part-Time Volunteers 585; Interns 2.
Governing Authority: private; nonprofit organization. Tax-exempt: 501(c)(3).
Botanical Garden.
Collections: Gardens: herb; rose; butterflies & hummingbirds; Alpine; cactus; peony; native plants; Sacajawea monument.
Facilities: library; botanical garden. Museum-related items for sale.
Activities: weddings; community events; school tours; special events; concerts; docent tours; formal education programs; guided tours; hobby workshops; lectures. Annual Events: plant sale; Great Gatsby Garden Party; Great Garden Escape in summer; Bug Day; Mad Hatter Tea Party; Oktoberfest; Winter Garden aGlow.
Publications: quarterly newsletter, Garden Thymes.
Hours & Admission Prices: Summer: Mon.-Thurs. 9-5, Fri. 9-8, Sat.-Sun. 10-6. Winter: Mon.-Fri. 9-5, Sat.-Sun. 12-4. Adults $4, seniors $3, children 6-12 $2; discounts to groups of 20 or more; members no charge. ♿
Attendance: 85,000 (estimated)
Membership: Senior $25; Individual $35; Family $50; Contributing $75; Sustaining $150; Sponsoring $300; Patron $500; Director's $1,000.

IDAHO MILITARY HISTORY MUSEUM, 4748 Lindbergh St., Bldg. 924, Boise, ID 83705. Mailing Address: 4040 W. Guard St., Boise, ID 83705-5004. Tel.: 208-272-4841.
Web Site: museum.mil.idaho.gov
Founded: 1995.
Key Personnel: Pres., Russ Trebby; Museum Shop Mgr., Steve Bonde.
Personnel Profile: Full-Time Paid 1.
Governing Authority: nonprofit organization. Tax-exempt: 501(c)(3).
Military History Museum.
Collections: area military history & artifacts; Idaho National Guard; WWII; Vietnam War; photographs; 1857 Napoleon civil War era cannon; armored vehicles; Korean War; WWI; Medal of Honor; Navy; Marines' Air Force; Air National Guard; Gowen Field; Paul Gowen.
Activities: school & group tours.
Publications: newsletter, Pass In Review.
Hours & Admission Prices: Tues.-Sat. 12-4; other times by appointment. No charge; donations accepted. Closed New Year's Day; Easter; Thanksgiving; Christmas.
Membership: Individual: Student & Associate $10; Senior (60 & over) $15; General $25; Lifetime $375. Organizational: Bronze $50; Silver $100; Gold $250; Platinum $500.

IDAHO MUSEUM OF MINING AND GEOLOGY, 2455 Old Penitentiary Rd., Boise, ID 83712-8254. Tel.: 208-368-9876.
Web Site: www.idahomuseum.org

Founded: 1989.
Personnel Profile: Part-Time Volunteers 10.
Governing Authority: private; nonprofit organization. Tax-exempt: 501(c)(3).
Mining & Geology Museum.
Collections: displays of Idaho's geologic features; historic photographs & artifacts from 19th-20th century Idaho mining towns; mineral collection.
Activities: educational earth science activities; school tours & gold panning demos; lecture series; field trips.
Hours & Admission Prices: April-Oct. Wed.-Sun. 12-5. No charge; donations accepted. ♿
Attendance: 5,000 (estimated)
Membership: Junior Geologist $5; Individual $25; Family $35; Life $375.

IDAHO STATE CAPITOL, 700 W. Jefferson, Boise, ID 83720-0002. Mailing Address: P.O. Box 83720, Boise, ID 83720. Tel.: 208-334-2100.
Historic Building: built in 1886.
Collections: local & state government, history & political leaders; official portraits; personal artifacts; period furnishings; paintings; photographs; architecture; flags; statues.
Activities: guided tours.
Hours & Admission Prices: Closed for renovations until 2010.

* **IDAHO STATE HISTORICAL MUSEUM, (M),** 610 N. Julia Davis Dr., Boise, ID 83702-7646. Tel.: 208-334-2120. Fax: 208-334-4059.
E-mail: jody.ochoa@ishs.idaho.gov
Web Site: www.idahohistory.net/museum.html
Founded: 1881.
Congressional District: 2
Key Personnel: Admin., Museum & Historic Sites, Jody Ochoa; Dir. Idaho State Historical Society, Steve Guerber; Cur., Joe Toluse; Museum Shop Mgr., Karen Scheider.
Personnel Profile: Full-Time Paid 8; Part-Time Paid 6; Part-Time Volunteers 30; Interns 3.
Governing Authority: state. Parent Institution: Idaho State Historical Society. Tax-exempt: 501(c)(3).
History Museum.
Collections: historical objects pertaining to Idaho & Pacific Northwest history including mining, ranching, timber industry, transportation & the Oregon Trail; Indian artifacts; Chinese artifacts; manuscripts; archives; maps; photographs; books; newspapers.
Research Fields: history of Idaho & Pacific Northwest.
Facilities: research library available for on premises use; 13,000 sq. ft. exhibit space; auditorium; classroom. Gift items for sale.
Activities: guided tours; lectures; films; workshops; TV & radio programs; formally organized education programs; training programs for museum workers & college students; inter-museum loans; permanent, temporary & traveling exhibitions; school loan service.
Publications: quarterly magazine, Idaho Yesterdays; children's magazine, Prospector; quarterly newsletter, Mountain Light; miscellaneous short research papers on Idaho history.
Hours & Admission Prices: May-Sept. Tues.-Sat. 9-5, Sun. 1-5; Oct.-April Tues.-Fri. 9-5, Sat. 11-5. Adults $5, seniors $4, children & students with ID $3; discounts to AAM members; members & children under 6 no charge. Call for group rates. Closed New Year's Day; Thanksgiving; Christmas. ♿
Attendance: 190,000 (accurate)
Membership: Full-time Student & Senior Citizen (65 & over) $15; Senior Couple $25; Individual $35; Family $50; Contributing $75; Friend $150; Sponsoring $300; Patron $500; Benefactor $1,000; Director's Club $5,000.

MORRISON KNUDSEN NATURE CENTER, 600 S. Walnut St., Boise, ID 83712-7729. Tel.: 208-334-2225.
Nature Center.
Collections: local history; wildlife including fish, birds, waterfowl, & mammals; plants; trees; flowers.
Activities: guided tours; educational programs.
Hours & Admission Prices: Park: daily sunrise to sunset. Visitors Center: Tues.-Fri. 9-5, Sat.-Sun. 11-5.

OLD IDAHO PENITENTIARY STATE HISTORIC SITE, 2445 Old Penitentiary Rd., Boise, ID 83712-8254. Tel.: 208-334-2844. Fax: 208-334-3225.
Web Site: www.idahohistory.net/oldpen.html
Governing Authority: Parent Institution: Idaho State Historical Society. Tax-exempt.
Historic Building Museum: built in 1870, the penitentiary received over 13,000 convicts while in operation for more than a century. Listed on the National Register of Historic Places.
Collections: prison history; notorious inmates; daily prison life; Solitary Confinement; Death Row; the Gallows; period weapons.
Activities: education programs.
Hours & Admission Prices: Memorial Day to Labor Day daily 10-5; Sept.-May daily 12-5. Adults $5, seniors $4, children 6-12 $3; discounts for groups of 10 or more. Closed state holidays.
Attendance: 23,539 (accurate)

WORLD CENTER FOR BIRDS OF PREY, 5668 W. Flying Hawk Lane, Boise, ID 83709-7289. Tel.: 208-362-8687. Fax: 208-362-2376.
Formerly: Velma Morrison Interpretive Center
Key Personnel: Dir., Jack Cafferty.
Governing Authority: Tax-exempt.
Nature Center.
Collections: birds of prey.
Activities: raptor presentations; hands-on exhibits; falconry tours; educational programs.
Hours & Admission Prices: March-Oct. daily 9-5; Nov.-Feb. Tues.-Sun. 10-4. Adults 17 & over $7, seniors 62 & over $6, children 4-16 $5; members & children under 4 no charge.

WORLD SPORTS HUMANITARIAN HALL OF FAME, 1910 University Dr., Boise, ID 83725-0001. Mailing Address: P.O. Box 9324, Boise, ID 83707-3324. Tel.: 206-262-7301. Fax: 208-343-0831.
E-mail: mike.mcquaid@sportshumanitarian.com
Web Site: www.sportshumanitarian.com
Founded: 1994.
Key Personnel: Pres., Larry Maneely; Founder, Myron Finkbeiner; Dir., Mike McQuaid
Hall of Fame.
Collections: history of world-class; humanitarian athletes; photographs; personal artifacts; Hall of Fame Inductees.
Hours & Admission Prices: Mon.-Fri. 9-4. No charge.

ZOO BOISE, 355 Julia Davis Dr., Boise, ID 83702-7670. Tel.: 208-384-4260. Fax: 208-384-4059. TDD: 208-384-4240.
E-mail: zooboise@cityofboise.org
Web Site: www.zooboise.org
Key Personnel: Dir., Steve Burns; Registrar, Corinne Pickett
Zoo.
Collections: over 200 animals representing 80 species.
Facilities: cafe. Museum-related items for sale.
Hours & Admission Prices: Daily 10-5. Adults $ $6.50, senior citizens 62 & over $4, children 4-11 $3.75; children under 4 no charge; discount on Thurs. Closed New Year's Day; Thanksgiving; Christmas.

Bonners Ferry

BOUNDARY COUNTY HISTORICAL SOCIETY AND MUSEUM, (M), 7229 Main St., Bonners Ferry, ID 83805. Mailing Address: P.O. Box 808, Bonners Ferry, ID 83805-0808. Tel.: 208-267-7720.
Founded: 1969.
Key Personnel: Pres., Jill Nystrom; Sec., Gini Woodward; Treas., Orrin Everhart; Cur. & Collections Mgr., Sue Kemmis.
Personnel Profile: Part-Time Paid 1; Part-Time Volunteers 20.
Governing Authority: private; nonprofit organization.
History Museum.
Collections: local history; photographs; period tools; dishes; clothing.
Major Exhibits: MoMS Smithsonian Journey Stories (T), 5/28/10-7/10/10.
Publications: History of Boundary County, Vol. 1; cookbook, Family Favorites.
Hours & Admission Prices: May-Sept. Tues.-Sat. 10-4; Oct.-April Fri.-Sat. 10-3. No charge; donations accepted. ♿
Attendance: 3,000 (estimated)

KOOTENAI NATIONAL WILDLIFE REFUGE, 287 Westside Rd., Bonners Ferry, ID 83805-5172. Tel.: 208-267-3888. Fax: 208-267-5570.
Key Personnel: Mgr., Dianna Ellis
Wildlife Refuge.
Collections: over 300 species of wildlife.
Hours & Admission Prices: Refuge: daily dawn to dusk. Office: Mon.-Fri. 7:30-4.
Attendance: 20,000

Burley

CASSIA COUNTY MUSEUM, E. Main & Hiland Ave., Burley, ID 83318. Mailing Address: P.O. Box 331, Burley, ID 83318-0331. Tel.: 208-678-7172.
E-mail: cassiamuseum@cassiacounty.org
Founded: 1972.

Key Personnel: Pres., Rod Smith; Financial Dir. & Treas., Joel Robins; Cur., Valerie Bowen.
Personnel Profile: Full-Time Paid 1; Part-Time Volunteers 5.
History Museum.
Collections: schoolhouse; general store; cabin; train car; farm machinery; county covered wagon.
Activities: guided tours; Museum Sponsors: History Alive Days for county 4th graders.
Hours & Admission Prices: April-Oct. Tues.-Sat. 10-5. No charge; donations accepted. Closed Independence Day. ♿
Attendance: 1,750 (estimated)
Membership: Individual $10; Family $25.

Caldwell

KIWANIS VAN SLYKE MUSEUM FOUNDATION INC., Caldwell Municipal Park, Harrison St., Caldwell, ID 83605. Mailing Address: 411 Blaine St., Caldwell, ID 83605-3619. Tel.: 208-455-3011.
Founded: 1958.
Congressional District: 1
Key Personnel: Head of Kiwanis Committee, Mac McCann; Chm. City Hall, Susan Miller; Kiwanis Pres., Tracy Wharfield.
Personnel Profile: Part-Time Volunteers 5.
Governing Authority: nonprofit organization. Parent Institution: Caldwell, ID Kiwanis Club, P.O. Box 925, Caldwell 83605.
Park Museum & Visitors Center.
Collections: farm implements; agriculture; history. Historic Houses: 1864 McKenzie log cabin; 1864 Johnston Brothers log cabin.
Research Fields: Pioneer tools & equipment used to convert an arid sagebrush land to the now highly productive agriculture community of today.
Facilities: fenced-in compound in city park.
Activities: guided tours.
Hours & Admission Prices: By appointment only. No charge; donations accepted. ♿
Attendance: 350 (estimated)

ORMA J. SMITH MUSEUM OF NATURAL HISTORY, The College of Idaho, 2112 Cleveland Blvd., Caldwell, ID 83605-4432. Tel.: 208-459-5507.
E-mail: bclark@collegeofidaho.edu
Web Site: www.collegeofidaho.edu/campus/community/museum
Founded: 1976.
Congressional District: 1
Key Personnel: Dir., Adjunct Prof. of Biology, Cur. Invertebrates, & Bd. Member, William H. Clark; Asst. to Dir., JoAnn Bellon; Research Assoc., Dr. Paul Blom; Cur. Lepidoptera, Dr. Paul Castrovillo; Research Assoc., Robert Chehey; Archaeologist, Cur. Ethnology, Janet L. Summers Duffy; Cur. Paleontology, Howard Emry; Research Assoc., Mammology & Bd. Member, Dr. Sean Farley; Cur. Paleontology, Research Assoc., Paleobotany, Dr. Patrick F. Fields; Cur. Entomology, Dr. Alan R. Gillogly; Cur. Mollusca, Stephen J. Lysne; Research Assoc., John Keebaugh; Cur. Ethnography, Bill Nance; Asst. to Dir., Research Assoc. & Bd. Member, James Pike; Cur. Entomology, Dr. James K. Ryan; Assoc. Cur. Mollusca, Richard A. Salisbury; Cur. Fossil Fishes, Dr. Gerald R. Smith; Facilities & Bd. Member, Leland Thames; Asst. Prof. Biology, Assoc. Cur. Fishes & Bd. Member, Dr. Chris Walser; Gen. Entomology, Dr. David Ward; Cur. Mexican Plants & Research Assoc., Dr. Ronald R. Weedon; Research Assoc., Librarian & Cur. Invertebrates, Jerry Wood; Prof. Biology, Cur. Mammals, Biology Dept. Coord. of Museum Affairs & Bd. Member, Dr. Eric Yensen; Cur. Fishes, Donald W. Zaroban; Bd. Member, Dr. Ron Bitner; Bd. Member, Barry Fujishin.
Personnel Profile: Full-Time Paid 1; Part-Time Paid 1; Part-Time Volunteers 40; Interns 3.
Governing Authority: Parent Institution: The College of Idaho. Tax-exempt.
Natural History Museum.
Collections: entomology; anthropology; Native American artifacts; paintings; mammals; fossils; natural history; mollusca including snails & bivalves; birds; reptiles & amphibians.
Major Exhibits: Dienstbier African Mammal Exhibit, 1/10-12/10; Insects, 1/10-12/10; Local Archaeology, 1/10-12/10; Local Fossils, 1/10-12/10.
Research Fields: entomology (arthropods of Baja California, Mexico).
Facilities: research library.
Activities: education programs; scientific workshops; fundraisers. Museum Sponsors: Monthly Museum Volunteer Workdays; BioBlitz in summer; Bug Day in August.
Publications: museum brochures; staff & curator's research publications.
Hours & Admission Prices: By appointment. No charge. ♿
Attendance: 3,000 (accurate)

ROSENTHAL GALLERY OF ART, The College of Idaho, 2112 Cleveland Blvd., Caldwell, ID 83605-4432. Tel.: 208-459-5321 & 5209. Fax: 208-459-5885.
E-mail: gclaassen@collegeofidaho.edu
Founded: 1891.
Key Personnel: Dir., Garth Claassen.
Governing Authority: college. Parent Institution: College of Idaho. Tax-exempt: 501(c)(3).
Art Exhibition Gallery.
Collections: prints; paintings; sculptures.
Activities: guided tours; lectures; films; gallery talks; concerts; dance; poetry readings; inter-museum loan; permanent, temporary & traveling exhibitions.
Publications: annual brochures on exhibits.
Hours & Admission Prices: Mon.-Fri. 10-5; Sat.-Sun. by appointment. No charge; donations accepted. Closed academic holidays & breaks. ♿
Attendance: 1,500

WHITTENBERGER PLANETARIUM, Boone Science Hall, The College of Idaho, 2112 Cleveland Blvd., Caldwell, ID 83605. Mailing Address: 2112 Cleveland Blvd., Caldwell, ID 83605-4432. Tel.: 208-459-5211. Fax: 208-459-5175.
E-mail: atruksa@collegeofidaho.edu
Web Site: www.collegeofidaho.edu/media/phonebooks/default.asp?dpt=PLAN
Key Personnel: Dir., Amy Truksa; Administrative Asst., JoAnn Bellon
Planetarium.
Collections: astronomy; geological.
Activities: fieldtrips; public shows; Astronomy Day activities.
Hours & Admission Prices: Call for hours. Adults $4, students $2; discount to groups.

Cambridge

CAMBRIDGE MUSEUM, 15 N. Superior, Cambridge, ID 83610. Mailing Address: P.O. Box 35, Cambridge, ID 83610-0035. Tel.: 208-257-3485.
E-mail: shansen@ctcweb.net
History Museum.
Collections: local history; geological; farming; Native American; pioneer artifacts.
Facilities: genealogy & research library.
Publications: book, A Saga & A History Revisited.
Hours & Admission Prices: June-Aug. Wed.-Sat. 10-4; call to confirm. No charge; donations accepted. ♿
Attendance: 1,200 (accurate)

Cataldo

COEUR D'ALENES OLD MISSION STATE PARK, I-90, Exit 39, Cataldo, ID 83810. Mailing Address: P.O. Box 30, Cataldo, ID 83810-0030. Tel.: 208-682-3814. Fax: 208-682-4032.
E-mail: old@idpr.state.id.us
Web Site: www.idahoparks.org
Key Personnel: Park Mgr., Lonnie Johnson; Museum Shop Mgr., Marianne Warren.
Personnel Profile: Full-Time Paid 2; Part-Time Paid 3.
Governing Authority: state; not-for-profit organization. Tax-exempt.
Historic Building: built by the Coeur d'Alene Tribe & Jesuit missionaries in 1850.
Collections: structure & furnishings; tools & equipment; religious artifacts; artworks; cultural artifacts.
Hours & Admission Prices: June-Aug. daily 8-6; Sept.-May daily 9-5. Motor vehicle entry fee $4 per vehicle; tour buses $25. Closed New Year's Day; Thanksgiving; Christmas. ♿
Attendance: 90,000 (estimated)

Challis

NORTH CUSTER MUSEUM, 1201 E. Main Ave., Challis, ID 83226. Mailing Address: P.O. Box 776, Challis, ID 83226-0776. Tel.: 208-879-2846.
Founded: 1998.
Congressional District: 2
Key Personnel: Pres. (V), John Rose.
Personnel Profile: Part-Time Volunteers 4.
Governing Authority: Parent Institution: North Custer Historical Society.
History Museum.
Collections: local history & culture; personal artifacts; photographs.
Publications: annual newsletter.
Hours & Admission Prices: Memorial Day-Oct. 1 Fri.-Sun. 10-4. No charge; donations accepted. ♿
Attendance: 525 (accurate)

Membership: Individual $5; Family $10; Business $25.

THE SHOOTING GALLERY WILDLIFE MUSEUM, 25341 Hwy. 93, Challis, ID 83226. Tel.: 208-879-5999. Fax: 208-879-5998.
Web Site: www.rainbowsendbb.com
Wildlife Museum.
Collections: world-record trophies; sculptures; bullet drawings; period advertisements & artifacts; photographs; mounted animals; bronze sculptures.
Activities: 1914 Smith working shooting gallery; fly fishing.
Hours & Admission Prices: Summer: daily 9-7; Winter: daily 9-5. Adults $10, students $5; children under 12 no charge.

Coeur d'Alene

THE ART SPIRIT GALLERY, 415 Sherman Ave., Coeur d'Alene, ID 83814-2728. Tel.: 208-765-6006.
E-mail: steve@theartspiritgallery.com
Web Site: www.theartspiritgallery.com
Founded: 1997.
Key Personnel: Dir., Steven J. Gibbs.
Personnel Profile: Part-Time Paid 3.
Art Gallery.
Collections: paintings; drawings; sculpture; pottery.
Facilities: 2,500 sq. ft. exhibition space.
Activities: permanent & temporary exhibitions; receptions.
Hours & Admission Prices: June-Sept. Fri. 11-9, Sat.-Thurs. 11-6; Oct.-May Tues.-Thurs. & Sat. 11-6, Fri. 11-9. No charge. ♿

MUSEUM OF NORTH IDAHO, (M), 115 N.W. Blvd., Coeur d'Alene, ID 83814-2798. Mailing Address: P.O. Box 812, Coeur d'Alene, ID 83816-0812. Tel.: 208-664-3448.
E-mail: dd@museumni.org
Web Site: www.museumni.org
Founded: 1968.
Congressional District: 1
Key Personnel: Dir., Dorothy Dahlgren; Pres., Scott MacPhee; Sales Shop Mgr., Helen Naslund.
Personnel Profile: Full-Time Paid 1; Part-Time Volunteers 30.
Governing Authority: nonprofit organization. Branch Museum: Fort Sherman Museum, Coeur D'Alene. Tax-exempt: 501(c)(3).
Local History Museum.
Collections: exhibits of Coeur d'Alene region's history from early explorers to present; logging, mining, & transportation materials; Forest Service; textiles; firearms; Native American artifacts; photographs. Annex: logging equipment; history of Fort Sherman.
Facilities: library pertaining to history of Coeur d'Alene Region. Museum-related items for sale.
Activities: traveling exhibitions; school loan service.
Publications: newsletter, Museum of North Idaho Newsletter; books: In All the West No Place Like This: North Fork of the Coeur d' Alene River: White Pine Route: A Pictorial History of the Coeur d'Alene Region; Wildflowers of the Inland Northwest; The Milwaukee Road In Idaho: A Guide to Sites & Locations; Up the Swiftwater: A Pictorial History of the Colorful St. Joe Country; The Milwaukee Road Olympian, A Ride to Remember; Swiftwater People; From Hell to Heaven: Death Related Mining Accidents in North Idaho; Lookout Cookbook; The Milwaukee Road's Western Extension: The Building of a Transcontinental Railroad.
Hours & Admission Prices: Museum of North Idaho: April-Oct. Tues.-Sat. 11-5. Fort Sherman: May-Sept. Tues.-Sat. 1-5. Library: by appointment. Adults $3, children 6-16 $1; discounts to AAM & ICOM members; members no charge. Closed Independence Day. ♿
Attendance: 5,500 (accurate)
Membership: Amelia Wheaton $25; Flyer $50; Idaho $100; Georgie Oakes $100 & up.

Coolin

PRIEST LAKE STATE PARK, 314 Indian Creek Park Rd., Coolin, ID 83821-9769. Tel.: 208-443-2200. Fax: 208-443-3893.
State Park.
Collections: natural history; wildlife.
Facilities: nature trails.
Activities: camping; fishing; hiking; educational programs; guided walks.
Hours & Admission Prices: Daily.

Cottonwood

THE HISTORICAL MUSEUM AT ST. GERTRUDE, 465 Keuterville Rd., Cottonwood, ID 83522-5183. Tel.: 208-962-2050. Fax: 208-962-2059.
E-mail: museum@stgertrudes.org
Web Site: www.historicalmuseumatstgertrude.org
Formerly: St. Gertrude's Museum
Founded: 1931.
Congressional District: 1
Key Personnel: Dir. & Dir. Displays, Lyle Wirtanen; Cur. & Registrar, Mary Cay Henry; Museum Technician, Sister M. Bernice Wessels, O.S.B.
Personnel Profile: Full-Time Paid 2; Part-Time Paid 1; Part-Time Volunteers 22.
Governing Authority: nonprofit organization. Parent Institutions: Monastery of St. Gertrude; Idaho Corp. of Benedictine Sisters. Subsidiary Institution: St. Gertrude's Museum. Tax-exempt: 501(c)(3).
History Museum.
Collections: local history; Indian artifacts; old books; textiles; paintings; chinaware; tools; mineralogical & biological displays; dated medical equipment; war accoutrements; turn of the century music makers; cultural items from various foreign countries; Winifred Rhoads Emmanuel Collection (Oriental art); Polly Bemis Collection; Buckskin Bill Collection; photographs.
Research Fields: local Idaho history.
Facilities: library containing maps, manuscripts & books on local history & mineralogy; photographic lab; storage rooms.
Activities: guided tours for groups; lectures on local history. Museum Sponsors: Big Band Dinner Dance; Raspberry Festival & quilt show in August.
Publications: Pioneer Days in Idaho County, Volumes I & II; Idaho Chinese Lore; Polly Bemis; coloring book, Old Idaho; museum newsletter, Rediscover; museum journal, Echoes of the Past.
Hours & Admission Prices: Tues.-Sat. 9:30-4:30. Adults $5; members no charge. ♿
Attendance: 7,000 (estimated)
Membership: Individual $15; Couple $25; Family $50; Associate $100; Lifetime & Memorial $1,000.

Council

COUNCIL VALLEY MUSEUM, Galena St., Council, ID 83612. Mailing Address: P.O. Box 252, Council, ID 83612-0252. Tel.: 208-253-4582.
Founded: 1972.
Congressional District: 1
Key Personnel: Chm. (V), Dale Fisk.
Personnel Profile: Part-Time Volunteers 4.
Governing Authority: city. Tax-exempt.
History Museum.
Collections: local history; photographs; personal artifacts.
Hours & Admission Prices: Memorial Day to Labor Day Tues.-Sat. 10-4, Sun. 1-4. ♿
Attendance: 1,000 (estimated)

Donnelly

VALLEY COUNTY MUSEUM, 13131 Farm to Market Rd., Donnelly, ID 83615. Mailing Address: P.O. Box 444, Donnelly, ID 83615-0444. Tel.: 208-325-8628.
E-mail: lvps@ctcweb.net
Formerly: Long Valley Museum
Key Personnel: Dir. & Chm. (V), Phyllis Bulgin; Museum Shop Mgr., Sandra Cottrell.
Personnel Profile: Part-Time Paid 2.
Governing Authority: Parent Institution: Long Valley Preservation Society. Tax-exempt.
Historical Museum.
Collections: local history & culture; photographs; historic buildings; early 1900s town site & artifacts; period farm equipment.
Research Fields: genealogy; social history.
Facilities: research center.
Activities: research; rental facilities; concerts. Museum Sponsors: Music Festival; Arts & Crafts Show; Ice Cream Social.
Publications: newsletter.
Hours & Admission Prices: May & Oct. Sun. 1-5; June-Sept. Sat.-Sun. 1-5; other times by appointment. No charge; donations accepted.
Attendance: 10,500 (estimated)
Membership: Individual $8; Family $15; Life $100; Patron $500; Benefactor $1,000.

Dubois

HERITAGE HALL MUSEUM, 110 S. Reynolds, Dubois, ID 83423. Mailing Address: P.O. Box 253, Dubois, ID 83423-0253.
Founded: 1969.
Key Personnel: Chm. (V), Conni Owen; Pres. (V), Barbara Kidd.
Governing Authority: city. Tax-exempt.
Historical Society Museum.

Collections: local history & culture; photographs; personal artifacts.
Facilities: Museum-related items for sale.
Hours & Admission Prices: Memorial Day to Labor Day Fri.-Sat. 2-6; other times by appointment. No charge; donations accepted.
Attendance: 300 (estimated)

Elk River

ELK RIVER HISTORICAL MUSEUM, Community Center, Second & Main, Elk River, ID 83827. Mailing Address: P.O. Box 63, Elk River, ID 83827-0063. Tel.: 208-826-3390.
History Museum.
Collections: local history & culture; photographs; news articles; period furnishings; personal artifacts.
Hours & Admission Prices: Summer: Sat. 10 to noon; other times by appointment.

Emmett

GEM COUNTY HISTORICAL VILLAGE MUSEUM, 501 E. 1st St., Emmett, ID 83617-3005. Tel.: 208-365-9530 & 4340.
E-mail: gemcohs@bigskytel.com
Web Site: www.gemcohs.org
Formerly: Gem County Historical Society and Museum
Founded: 1974.
Key Personnel: Pres. Bd. (V), Kathleen Derig; Dir. Museum Shop Mgr., Meg Davis.
Personnel Profile: Part-Time Paid 1; Part-Time Volunteers 4.
Governing Authority: Parent Institution: Gem County Historical Society.
Historical Society Museum.
Collections: area history; Native American artifacts; trapping; mining; transportation; lumber; military; firearms; photographs; personal artifacts; medical; ranching.
Research Fields: Gem County history.
Activities: tours; meetings; special programs. Annual Events: Fundraising Chuckwagon Supper in September; Historical Reenactment in October.
Publications: quarterly newsletter.
Hours & Admission Prices: Wed. & Sat. 1-5, Thurs.-Fri. 10:30-5; tours by appointment. No charge; donations accepted. ♿
Attendance: 1,000 (accurate)
Membership: Individual $10; Family $15; Benefactor $25.

Filer

TWIN FALLS COUNTY HISTORICAL MUSEUM, 21337A Hwy. 30, Filer, ID 83328-5513. Tel.: 208-736-4675. Fax: 208-736-4675.
E-mail: tfcountymuseum@msn.com
Founded: 1957.
Congressional District: 24
Key Personnel: Pres., Susan Waters; Vice Pres., Alex Kunkel; Dir., S. Darleen Porter.
Personnel Profile: Part-Time Volunteers 28.
Governing Authority: nonprofit organization. Tax-exempt: 501(c)(3).
History Museum & Visitor Center: housed in the former Union School built in 1914.
Collections: period clothing; phonographs; musical instruments; schoolhouse display; pictures; sewing machines; wagons; gas pumps; farm machinery; washing machines; period rooms; steam engine; picture gallery; doctors equipment; blacksmith shop.
Research Fields: local history; agriculture; family history.
Activities: guided tours; programs; events.
Publications: newsletter, The Union School Report Card.
Hours & Admission Prices: Tues.-Sat. 10-5. No charge; donations accepted. Closed holidays. ♿
Attendance: 2,649 (accurate)
Membership: Student & Senior Citizens $10; Adult $15; Family $25; Nonprofit $50; Centennial $100; Sustaining & Lifetime $500; Millenial $1,000.

Fort Hall

SHOSHONE-BANNOCK TRIBAL MUSEUM, Simplot Rd., Fort Hall, ID 83203. Mailing Address: Box 306, Fort Hall, ID 83203-0306. Tel.: 208-237-9791. Fax: 208-237-0797.
Key Personnel: Mgr., Coord. & Museum Shop Mgr., Rosemary Devinney.
Governing Authority: Parent Institution: Shoshone-Bannock Tribes.
Tribal Museum.
Collections: Shoshone-Bannock history; culture; art; ceremonial clothing; photographs; Wrensted collections 1895-1912.
Facilities: Museum-related items for sale.
Activities: tours.
Hours & Admission Prices: June-Aug. daily 9:30-5; Sept.-May Mon.-Fri. 9:30-5. Adults $2.50, youth 6-18 $1; Native American Indians with Tribal ID no charge. Closed Tribal Holidays.

Glenns Ferry

GLENNS FERRY HISTORICAL MUSEUM, 211 W. Cleveland Ave., Glenns Ferry, ID 83623. Tel.: 208-366-2192.
Historic Building: housed in a former school; built in 1909. Listed on the National Register of Historic Places.
Collections: local history & culture; photographs; period furnishings; personal artifacts.
Activities: permanent & temporary exhibits.
Hours & Admission Prices: June-Sept. Sat.-Sun. 12-5; other times by appointment. No charge; donations accepted.

Gooding

GOODING COUNTY HISTORICAL SOCIETY MUSEUM, Euskadi Lane, Gooding, ID 83330. Mailing Address: P.O. Box 580, Gooding, ID 83330-0580. Tel.: 208-934-5135. Fax: 208-934-4885.
Historical Society Museum.
Collections: local history; photographs; personal artifacts; furnishings.
Facilities: Museum-related items for sale.
Activities: workshops; educational programs.
Hours & Admission Prices: By appointment. Adults $2, children $.50.

Grangeville

BICENTENNIAL HISTORICAL MUSEUM, Hwy. 95 @ Pine St., Grangeville, ID 83530. Mailing Address: P.O. Box 212, Grangeville, ID 83530-0212. Tel.: 208-983-2104 & 2277.
History Museum.
Collections: local history & culture; photographs; period furnishings; personal artifacts; clothing.
Hours & Admission Prices: June-Sept. Wed.-Fri. 1-5; other times by appointment. No charge; donations accepted.

Hagerman

HAGERMAN FOSSIL BEDS NATIONAL MONUMENT, 221 N. State St., Hagerman, ID 83332. Mailing Address: P.O. Box 570, Hagerman, ID 83332-0570. Tel.: 208-837-4793. Fax: 208-837-4857.
History Museum.
Collections: horse fossils; local history & culture; photographs.
Hours & Admission Prices: Memorial Day to Aug. 25 daily 9-6; Aug. 26 to May Thurs.-Mon. 9-5. Closed New Year's Day; Thanksgiving; Christmas.

HAGERMAN VALLEY HISTORICAL SOCIETY, Hagerman State Bank, 100 S. State St., Hagerman, ID 83332. Mailing Address: P.O. Box 86, Hagerman, ID 83332-0086. Tel.: 208-837-6288.
Key Personnel: Pres. (V), Peter Remmen.
Personnel Profile: Part-Time Volunteers 15.
Historical Society Museum.
Collections: local history; photographs; fossilized Hagerman horse replica.
Hours & Admission Prices: April-Oct. Wed.-Sun. 1-4. No charge.
Attendance: 1,500 (estimated)
Membership: Single $15; Couple $25.

Hailey

BLAINE COUNTY HISTORICAL MUSEUM, 218 N. Main St., Hailey, ID 83333. Mailing Address: P.O. Box 124, Hailey, ID 83333-0124. Tel.: 208-788-1801 & 4210. Fax: 208-788-1801.
E-mail: macleodssv@msn.com
Web Site: bchistoricalmuseum.org
Founded: 1964.
Congressional District: 2
Key Personnel: Chm. & C.E.O., Bob MacLeod; Dir., Teddie Daley.
Personnel Profile: Full-Time Volunteers 12; Part-Time Paid 3; Part-Time Volunteers 12.
Governing Authority: independent. Parent Institution: Blaine County. Subsidiary Institution: City of Hailey, ID. Tax-exempt: 501(c)(3).
History Museum: housed in an 1880 old armory & social center.
Collections: 5,000 political buttons & items donated by Joseph W. Fuld; replica of a mine tunnel; kitchen; living room; school; office; sewing room displays; antiques; first Idaho switchboard telephone; Ezra Pound exhibit, Poetry & Politics; photographs; biographical & historical items and data from Mallory Collection; journals dating to mid-1800s; legal documents; cameras; some military uniforms from first and second world wars.
Research Fields: Hailey, birthplace of Ezra Pound; genealogy; history.

Facilities: library.
Activities: Annual Events: Open House; Living History Day; Blaine County Heritage Court.
Publications: newsletter.
Hours & Admission Prices: Memorial Day weekend to Oct. daily 11-5. No charge; donations accepted. ♿
Attendance: 1,500 (accurate)

Harrison

CRANE HISTORICAL SOCIETY MUSEUM, 201 Coeur d'Alene Ave., Harrison, ID 83833. Mailing Address: P.O. Box 152, Harrison, ID 83833-0152. Tel.: 208-689-3111.
Founded: 1984.
Congressional District: 5
Key Personnel: Pres. (V), Berti Arnzen.
Personnel Profile: Part-Time Volunteers 8.
Governing Authority: Tax-exempt.
Historical Society Museum.
Collections: local history & culture; photographs; period furnishings; personal artifacts; 1920 town jail; logging; saw mill; early 1900s equipment.
Hours & Admission Prices: Memorial Day to Labor Day Sat.-Sun. & holidays 12-4; other times by appointment. No charge; donations accepted.
Attendance: 554 (accurate)
Membership: Single $10; Sawyer $25; Foreman $50; Mill Owner $75; Life $250.

Idaho City

BOISE BASIN MUSEUM, 503 Montgomery St., Idaho City, ID 83631. Mailing Address: P.O. Box 358, Idaho City, ID 83631-0358. Tel.: 208-392-9551. Fax: 208-392-9905.
History Museum.
Collections: local history; photographs; personal artifacts; Gold Rush; pioneer life.
Facilities: Museum-related items for sale.
Activities: rental facilities; tours.
Hours & Admission Prices: May & Sept. Sat.-Sun.; Memorial Day to Labor Day Mon.-Sat. 11-4, Sun. 1-4; tours by appointment. Adults $2, seniors & students $1.50; children under 6 no charge.

IDAHO CITY VISITOR CENTER, 100 Main St., Ste. A, Idaho City, ID 83631. Mailing Address: P.O. Box 350, Idaho City, ID 83631-0350. Tel.: 208-392-6040. Fax: 208-392-9512.
Visitor Center.
Collections: local history & culture; photographs.
Hours & Admission Prices: Daily 10-4.

Idaho Falls

THE ART MUSEUM OF EASTERN IDAHO, (M), 300 S. Capital Ave., Idaho Falls, ID 83402-3952. Tel.: 208-524-7777. Fax: 208-529-6666.
Formerly: Eagle Rock Art Museum and Education Center
Founded: 2002.
Congressional District: 2
Key Personnel: Exec. Dir., Christine Hatch; Administrative Asst., Ellie Hampton; Dir. Education, Alexa Stanger; Dir. Public Rels., Miyai Abe Griggs.
Personnel Profile: Full-Time Paid 4; Part-Time Paid 2; Part-Time Volunteers 30.
Governing Authority: Tax-exempt.
Art Museum.
Collections: works by Idaho artists including paintings; sculpture & photographs.
Facilities: Museum-related items for sale.
Activities: facility rental; adult programs; art education outreach program in public schools.
Publications: quarterly newsletter, MuseNews.
Hours & Admission Prices: Tues.-Sat. 11-5. Adults $4, youth 6-18 $2; children under 6 no charge. ♿
Attendance: 30,000 (estimated)
Membership: $50-$1,000.

COLLECTORS' CORNER MUSEUM, 900 John Adams Pkwy., Idaho Falls, ID 83401-4049. Tel.: 208-528-9900.
Web Site: idahofallsidaho.net
Founded: 2003.
Key Personnel: Co Dir., Nida Gyorfy; Co Dir., Jim Gyorfy.
Personnel Profile: Full-Time Volunteers 2; Part-Time Volunteers 10.
Collectors Museum.
Collections: local history & culture; personal artifacts; period furnishings; photographs; dolls; tools.
Major Exhibits: Honoring All Veterans, 10/10-11/15/10; Holiday Ornaments, 11/10-12/10.
Hours & Admission Prices: Tues.-Sat. 10-5. Adults $4, senior citizens & students $3, youth 4-7 $2; children 3 & under no charge. Closed holidays. ♿

LDS TEMPLE VISITOR CENTER, 1000 Memorial Dr., Idaho Falls, ID 83402. Tel.: 208-523-4504.
Religious Museum.
Collections: temple history; local culture; religious artifacts & furnishings; paintings; photographs; films.
Hours & Admission Prices: Center: daily 9-9. Temple Grounds: Summer daily. Temple interior closed to public.

MUSEUM OF IDAHO, (M), 200 N. Eastern Ave., Idaho Falls, ID 83402-4029. Tel.: 208-522-1400. Fax: 208-524-5060.
E-mail: kelseysalsbery@museumofidaho.org
Web Site: www.museumofidaho.org
Founded: 1985.
Key Personnel: Exec. Dir., David Pennock, Ph.D.; Chm. (V), Fred Goodworth; Chm. (V), Dr. James Harris; Dir. Devel., Nick Gailey; Education, Tevye Waite; Dir. Curatorial Affairs, Kirsten Hansen; Dir. Business Affairs, Mandy Gunderson; Dir. Exhibitions, Rod Hansen; Dir. Mktg., Kelsey Salsbery; Maintenance Supvr., Greg Stoddard; Museum Store Mgr., Sally Glass.
Personnel Profile: Full-Time Paid 10; Part-Time Paid 4; Part-Time Volunteers 250; Interns 5.
Governing Authority: private; nonprofit organization. Parent Institution: Bonneville County Historical Society. Tax-exempt.
History Museum.
Collections: regional natural history; cultural history; personal artifacts; furnishing; archaeological.
Major Exhibits: Wolf to Woof (T), 1/10-9/10; Olde Fashioned Christmas, 12/10-1/11.
Facilities: Museum-related items for sale.
Hours & Admission Prices: Mon.-Tues. 9-8, Wed.-Sat. 9-5. Adults $7, senior citizens 62 & over $6, children 4-17 $5; discounts to groups, family, AAM members & military; children under 4 no charge. ♿
Attendance: 100,000 (accurate)
Membership: Senior & Student $25; Adult $30; Dual $55; Family $100.

TAUTPHAUS PARK ZOO, 2725 Carnival Way, Idaho Falls, ID 83405. Mailing Address: P.O. Box 50220, Idaho Falls, ID 83405-0220. Tel.: 208-612-8552. Fax: 208-528-6256.
E-mail: ifzoo@idahofallszoo.org
Founded: 1935.
Key Personnel: Dir., William Gersonde.
Personnel Profile: Full-Time Paid 12; Part-Time Paid 14; Part-Time Volunteers 60.
Governing Authority: Parent Institution: City of Idaho Falls. Subsidiary Institution: Parks & Recreation Division.
Zoo.
Collections: over 400 animals.
Activities: educational programs.
Hours & Admission Prices: mid-April to Sept. daily 9-4; Memorial Day to Labor Day Mon. 9-8, Tues.-Sun. 9-5. Adults 13 & over $5, seniors 62 & over $3.50, children 4-12 $2.50; children 3 & under no charge. ♿
Attendance: 110,000 (estimated)

WILLARD ARTS CENTER/CARR GALLERY, 498 A St., Idaho Falls, ID 83402-3617. Tel.: 208-522-0471.
E-mail: jbarnes@idahofallsarts.org
Web Site: www.idahofallsarts.org
Key Personnel: Interim Exec. Dir. & Operations Mgr., Jill Barnes; Carr Gallery Cur., Nathan Barnes; Technical Dir., Brad Higbee; Visual Arts. & Educational Dir., Catherine Smith; Dir. Devel., Gaylene Verdoorn
Art Gallery.
Collections: artwork by local artists.
Hours & Admission Prices: Carr Gallery: Mon.-Fri. 11-5, Sat. 10-4. No charge.

Island Park

JOHNNY SACK'S CABIN, Big Springs, Hwy. 20, Island Park, ID 83429. Mailing Address: Ashton/Island Park Ranger District, Box 858, Ashton, ID 83420. Tel.: 208-652-7442.
Governing Authority: Parent Institution: U.S. Forest Service.
Historic House: housed in the hand-built former home of German immigrant, Johnny Sack; built in 1939. Listed on the National Register of Historic Places.

Collections: Johnny Sack's life & history; personal artifacts; handmade furnishings.
Hours & Admission Prices: mid-June to Labor Day daily 10-4. No charge; donations accepted.

Jerome

JEROME COUNTY HISTORICAL SOCIETY, INC. AND IDAHO FARM & RANCH MUSEUM, 220 N. Lincoln, Jerome, ID 83338-2325. Mailing Address: P.O. Box 50, Jerome, ID 83338-0050. Tel.: 208-324-5641. Fax: 208-324-7694.
E-mail: info@historicaljeromecounty.com
Web Site: www.historicaljeromecounty.com
Founded: 1981.
Congressional District: 2
Key Personnel: C.E.O., Ed Robertson; Treas., Shonna Fraser; Asst. Cur., Marguerite Roberson.
Personnel Profile: Part-Time Paid 1; Part-Time Volunteers 10.
Governing Authority: private; nonprofit organization. Tax-exempt: 501(c)(3).
General Museum.
Collections: antique farm machinery; historic structures; agricultural artifacts; history of Jerome County including World War II relocation camp.
Facilities: library.
Activities: Annual Event: Live History Day at Idaho F.A.R.M. in June.
Publications: monthly newsletter.
Hours & Admission Prices: Museum in Jerome Tues.-Sat. 1-5. Idaho Farm & Ranch Museum by appointment (under construction). No charge; donations accepted. Closed legal holidays. ♿
Attendance: 750 (estimated)
Membership: Regular $15; Family & 1001 Club $25; Supporting $75; Life $500.

Kellogg

CRYSTAL GOLD MINE MUSEUM, 51931 Silver Valley Rd., Kellogg, ID 83837. Mailing Address: P.O. Box 510, Kellogg, ID 83837-0510. Tel.: 208-783-4653. Fax: 208-783-4653.
Natural History Museum: housed in an 1880s underground gold mine.
Collections: gold mine history; gold mining.
Facilities: Museum-related items for sale.
Activities: guided underground tour; seasonal gold-panning.
Hours & Admission Prices: April & Oct. daily 10-4; May-Sept. daily 9-6; Nov.-March Sat.-Sun. 10-4. Adults $12, senior citizens $11, children 4-17 $8.50; children under 4 no charge.

SHOSHONE COUNTY MINING AND SMELTING MUSEUM D/B/A THE STAFF HOUSE MUSEUM, 820 McKinley Ave., Kellogg, ID 83837-2525. Mailing Address: P.O. Box 783, Kellogg, ID 83837-0783. Tel.: 208-786-4141.
Founded: 1986.
Key Personnel: Pres. (V), Robert Dunsmore.
Personnel Profile: Full-Time Volunteers 1; Part-Time Paid 3; Part-Time Volunteers 3.
Governing Authority: bd. of directors. Tax-exempt.
Mining & Smelting Museum: housed in the historic home of Stanley A. Easton, manager of Bunker Hill & Sullivan Mining & Concentrating Company; later converted to a residence for single Bunker Hill staff members.
Collections: mining; smelting; historic & cultural artifacts related to the history & industry of the area; scouting memorabilia.
Major Exhibits: 1910 Fire, 5/10-9/10; Sunshine Mine Fire, 5/10-9/10.
Facilities: Museum-related items for sale.
Hours & Admission Prices: May-Sept. daily 10-6; other times by appointment. Suggested: adults $4, seniors 55 & over $3, children 6-18 $1; discounts to groups; members & children under 6 no charge.
Attendance: 2,600 (accurate)
Membership: Single $15; Couple $20; Family $25; Business $30-$100; Golden $100; Life $500.

Ketchum

KETCHUM/SUN VALLEY HISTORICAL SOCIETY, 180 1st Ave. E., Ketchum, ID 83340. Mailing Address: P.O. Box 2746, Ketchum, ID 83340-2746. Tel.: 208-726-8118.
Web Site: www.ksvhistoricalsociety.org
Historical Society Museum.
Collections: local history & culture; photographs; personal artifacts.
Facilities: Museum-related items for sale.
Hours & Admission Prices: Mon.-Fri. 1-5, Sat. 1-4.

* **SUN VALLEY CENTER FOR THE ARTS, (M),** 191 5th St. E., Ketchum, ID 83340. Mailing Address: P.O. Box 656, Sun Valley, ID 83353-0656. Tel.: 208-726-9491. Fax: 208-726-2344.
Web Site: www.sunvalleycenter.org/arts
Key Personnel: Pres., Trina Peters; Vice Pres., Larry Helzel
Art Museum.
Collections: works by national & international artists; photographs; paintings.
Activities: special events; lectures.
Hours & Admission Prices: Summer: Mon.-Fri. 9-5, Sat. 11-5; Winter: Mon.-Fri. 9-5. No charge.

Kooskia

LOCHSA HISTORICAL RANGER STATION, US Hwy. 12, Kooskia, ID 83539. Mailing Address: 502 Lowry St., Kooskia, ID 83539. Tel.: 208-926-4274. Fax: 208-926-6450.
Historic Building: housed in a former forest service ranger station used during the 1920s & 1930s.
Collections: local history; period furnishings; personal artifacts; photographs.
Facilities: nature trails.
Activities: hiking.
Hours & Admission Prices: Memorial Day to Labor Day daily 9-5. No charge.

Lava Hot Springs

SOUTH BANNOCK COUNTY HISTORICAL CENTER, (M), 110 E. Main St., Lava Hot Springs, ID 83246. Mailing Address: P.O. Box 387, Lava Hot Springs, ID 83246-0387. Tel.: 208-776-5254. Fax: 208-776-5228.
E-mail: lavamus@dcdi.net
Founded: 1980.
Congressional District: 2
Key Personnel: C.E.O. & Pres., Janie Linford; Dir., Ruth Ann Olson; Sec., Grantwriter & Dir. Special Projects, Cathy Sheh; Treas., Janet Berreth; Cur. & Clerk, Lavenna Long; Cur. & Clerk, Jolene Ketchum; Museum Shop Mgr., Debbie Fagnant; Cur. & Clerk, Anna Hooper; Cur. & Clerk, Mary Avery; Custodian, Robert Kowaliw.
Personnel Profile: Part-Time Paid 6; Part-Time Volunteers 4.
Governing Authority: society; board of directors. Tax-exempt: 501(c)(3).
Historical Society.
Collections: artifacts; photographs; documents; family histories; Native American.
Research Fields: local, area & state history; genealogical; individual & family history.
Facilities: research center.
Activities: temporary & permanent exhibits; slide presentations; walking tours upon request.
Publications: walking tour guide; bimonthly newsletter; biographical sketches, Charley, The Virginian; Bob Dempsey-The Greatest Trader on the Immigrant Trail; Trails, Trappers, Trains & Travelers; A Century of Transition 1890-1990.
Hours & Admission Prices: Daily 12-5; other times by appointment. No charge; donations accepted. ♿
Attendance: 16,123 (accurate)
Membership: Single $10; Couple $15; Business $30.

Lewiston

LEWIS-CLARK STATE COLLEGE CENTER FOR ARTS & HISTORY, 500 8th Ave., Lewiston, ID 83501-2698. Mailing Address: 415 Main St., Lewiston, ID 83501-1821. Tel.: 208-792-2243. Fax: 208-792-2850.
Web Site: www.lcsc.edu/museum/contactus/default.htm
Art & History Museum: housed in the former Vollmer Great Bargain Store designed by architect, Kirtland Cutter; built in 1884. Listed on the National Register of Historic Places.
Collections: local history; visual arts.
Activities: special events.
Hours & Admission Prices: Tues.-Sat. 11-4.

NEZ PERCE COUNTY HISTORICAL SOCIETY AND MUSEUM, 0306 Third St., Lewiston, ID 83501-1860. Tel.: 208-743-2535. Fax: 208-743-2535.
E-mail: registrar@npchistsoc.org
Web Site: www.npchistsoc.org
Formerly: Luna House Museum
Founded: 1960.
Congressional District: 1
Key Personnel: Pres. (V), Richard Riggs; Registrar, Lora Feucht.
Personnel Profile: Full-Time Paid 1; Part-Time Paid 2; Part-Time Volunteers 1.
Governing Authority: board of directors; Nez Perce County Historical Society. Tax-exempt: 501(c)(3).
History Museum.

Collections: artifacts & photographs depicting Nez Perce County history from 1800 to present. Historic Building: Heritage House.
Research Fields: Nez Perce County, ID.
Facilities: library; archives.
Activities: temporary exhibits; educational programs; special lectures.
Publications: The Golden Age, journal of the Nez Perce County Historical Society (published semiannually); A Walking Tour of Historical Downtown Lewiston; annual historical photographic calendar; Lewiston Country, An Armchair History.
Hours & Admission Prices: March-Dec. Tues.-Sat. 10-4. No charge; donations accepted. Closed major federal holidays. ♿
Attendance: 4,000 (accurate)
Membership: Member $30-$49; Friend $50-$99; Sponsor $100-$499; Patron $500-$999; Lifetime $1,000 & up.

Mackay

LOST RIVER MUSEUM, 312 Capitol St., Mackay, ID 83251. Tel.: 208-588-3148.
History Museum: housed in a former church; built c.1900.
Collections: local history & culture; mining equipment & implements; railroad memorabilia; early printing equipment; personal artifacts; period clothing; household utensils; photographs.
Hours & Admission Prices: Memorial Day to Sept. Sat.-Sun. 1-5; other times by appointment.

MOOSE CENTER LEARNING LAB, 610 W. Custer, Mackay, ID 83251. Mailing Address: P.O. Box 30, Mackay, ID 83251-0030. Tel.: 208-588-2939. Fax: 208-588-2980.
Formerly: North American Moose Foundation
Founded: 2001.
History Museum.
Collections: North American moose head mounts; photographs; art; hides; antlers; moose scientific journals.
Activities: listen to recorded moose callings.
Hours & Admission Prices: Call for hours.
Membership: Seniors & Students $15; Individual $30; Family $50; Outfitters & Guides $75; Charter $100; Lifetime $1,000.

Malad

ONEIDA COUNTY PIONEER MUSEUM, 27 Bannock St., Malad, ID 83252-1240. Tel.: 208-766-4847.
Web Site: www.maladidaho.org/museum/museum.htm
History Museum: built in 1914.
Collections: period artifacts & furnishings.
Hours & Admission Prices: Tues.-Sat. 1-5; other times by appointment. No charge; donations accepted.

McCall

CENTRAL IDAHO CULTURAL CENTER, 1001 State St., McCall, ID 83638-3705. Tel.: 208-634-4497.
Historic Site: built in 1937 by the Civilian Conservation Corps. Listed on the National Register of Historic Places.
Collections: local history; personal artifacts; period furnishings; photographs. Historic Buildings: fire warden's house; crew quarters; machine shop; pump house.
Hours & Admission Prices: Memorial Day to Labor Day Wed.-Sat. 11-4; Winter: call for hours. Adults $2, youth 12-18 & seniors $1; children under 12 no charge.

Melba

CELEBRATION PARK, 5000 Victory Lane, Melba, ID 83641-5275. Tel.: 208-495-2745.
Park Museum.
Collections: local history; archaeology; Native American art & artifacts; photographs.
Facilities: visitor center.
Hours & Admission Prices: Daily 9-4. Closed major holidays.

Montpelier

NATIONAL OREGON/CALIFORNIA TRAIL CENTER, 320 N. 4th St., Montpelier, ID 83254-1256. Mailing Address: P.O. Box 323, Montpelier, ID 83254-0323. Tel.: 208-847-3800; 866-847-3800 (toll free). Fax: 208-847-1863.
E-mail: info@oregontrailcenter.org
Web Site: www.oregontrailcenter.org
Key Personnel: Dir., Becky Smith; Pres., Al Harrison; Vice Pres., Sherri Brown; Sec. & Treas., Andrea Mattson
History Museum.
Collections: pioneer history & heritage; early settlers; paintings.
Facilities: Museum-related items for sale.
Activities: simulated wagon train.
Hours & Admission Prices: May Mon.-Sat. 10-3; Memorial Day to Sept. Sun.-Tues. 9-5, Fri.-Sat. 9-6; Oct. Mon.-Fri. 10-2; Nov. call for hours.

Moscow

THE APPALOOSA MUSEUM AND HERITAGE CENTER, (M), 2720 W. Pullman Rd., Moscow, ID 83843-4024. Tel.: 208-882-5578, ext. 279. Fax: 208-882-8150.
E-mail: museum@appaloosa.com
Web Site: www.appaloosamuseum.org
Founded: 1973.
Congressional District: 1
Key Personnel: Pres. (V), King Rockhill.
Personnel Profile: Full-Time Paid 1; Part-Time Paid 2; Part-Time Volunteers 5; Interns 1.
Governing Authority: board of directors; nonprofit organization. Associated with the Appaloosa Horse Club, Inc., P.O. Box 8403, Moscow 83843. Tax-exempt.
History Museum.
Collections: equipment, photographs & art work relative to the history of the Appaloosa horse & the Nez Perce Indians who bred the Appaloosa horse.
Research Fields: the Appaloosa horse in European & U.S. history.
Facilities: 6,000 sq. ft. facility. Museum-related items for sale.
Activities: guided tours; lectures. Museum Sponsors: Annual Holiday Open House; Annual Trail Ride.
Publications: quarterly newsletter.
Hours & Admission Prices: Mon.-Fri. 10-5, Sat. 10-4. Suggested Donation: adults $2. Closed legal holidays. ♿
Attendance: 5,000 (estimated)
Membership: The Spurs $25; Roping Club $50; Bridle Club $100; Saddle Club $500; Patron $1,000; Benefactor $5,000.

IDAHO FOREST FIRE MUSEUM, 310 N. Main St., Moscow, ID 83843-2629. Tel.: 208-882-4767. Fax: 208-882-0373.
E-mail: smokey@smokeybeargists.com
Forest Fire Museum.
Collections: Smokey Bear history & memorabilia; forest firefighting; 1910 forest fires of northern Idaho & Western Montana; Edward Pulaski history; northwest art; photographs.
Hours & Admission Prices: Mon.-Fri. 9-5:30, Sat. 11-5:30. No charge; donations accepted.

MCCONNELL MANSION, 110 S. Adams, Moscow, ID 83843-2829. Mailing Address: 327 E. Second St., Moscow, ID 83843-2819. Tel.: 208-882-1004. Fax: 208-882-0759.
E-mail: lchslibrary@latah.id.us
Web Site: users.moscow.com/lchs
Founded: 1968.
Congressional District: 1
Key Personnel: Dir., Daniel Crandall; Pres. (V), Brian Magelky; Cur., Ann Catt.
Personnel Profile: Part-Time Paid 2; Part-Time Volunteers 30.
Governing Authority: board of trustees. Latah County Historical Society. Tax-exempt.
Local History Museum: housed in 1886 Governor McConnell Mansion.
Collections: concentration on the history of Latah County, Idaho, including interpretation of lifestyles in rural area Pacific Northwest from 1870-present; archives; photographs; oral history transcriptions.
Research Fields: lumber industry; railroads; oral history; local businesses & families; social history; conservation; historic preservation & restoration; agricultural history.
Facilities: research facilities.
Activities: guided tours; school tours; classroom instruction; speaker's series; workshops; interpretive exhibits; ice cream social; slide programs; hands-on exhibits & artifacts; treasure hunt for children; educational program.
Publications: books on local history; annual journal, Latah Legacy; newsletter; exhibit brochures.
Hours & Admission Prices: May-Sept. Tues.-Sat 1-5; Oct.-April Tues.-Sat. 1-4; other times by appointment. Suggested Donation: family $4, adults $2; members & children under 16 no charge.
Attendance: 3,500 (estimated)
Membership: Individual $25; Cultivator $35; Prospector $50; Builder $100; Engineer $250; Founder $500 & up.

Mountain Home

MOUNTAIN HOME HISTORICAL MUSEUM, 180 S. 3rd E., Mountain Home, ID 83647-3019. Tel.: 208-587-6847.
Historic Building: housed in the former Carnegie Public Library; built in 1908. Listed on the National Register of Historic Places.
Collections: local history; cultural heritage; mining; agriculture; railroad memorabilia; Native American artifacts; WWI & WWII.
Hours & Admission Prices: Mon.-Fri. 10-4, Sat. 12-4. No charge.

Mullan

CAPTAIN JOHN MULLAN MUSEUM, 229 Earle St., Mullan, ID 83846. Mailing Address: P.O. Box 675, Mullan, ID 83846-0675. Tel.: 208-744-1155 (June-Aug.) & 1557 (Sept.-May).
Founded: 1985.
Congressional District: 1
Key Personnel: Pres. & Chm. (V), Catherine Hendryx.
Personnel Profile: Part-Time Volunteers 16.
Governing Authority: Parent Institution: Mullan Historical Society. Tax-exempt.
History Museum: housed in the old Liberty Theater.
Collections: Mullan history; period furnishings; clothing; photographs; newspapers; mining artifacts; sports memorabilia; logging equipment; drugstore artifacts.
Research Fields: area history; genealogy.
Hours & Admission Prices: June-Aug. 10-4; other times by appointment. No charge; donations accepted. Closed holidays.
Attendance: 850
Membership: Yearly $10; Sustaining $25.

Murphy

OWYHEE COUNTY HISTORICAL MUSEUM, 17085 Basey St., Murphy, ID 83650. Mailing Address: P.O. Box 67, Murphy, ID 83650-0067. Tel.: 208-495-2319. Fax: 208-495-9824.
E-mail: info@owyheemuseum.org
Web Site: www.owyheemuseum.org
Founded: 1960.
Congressional District: 1
Key Personnel: Exec. Dir., Dr. Thomas Couch; Pres. (V), Brenda Richards; Office Mgr., Vivian Good; Librarian/Archivist, Joan Bachman; Museum Shop Mgr., Jan Alexander.
Personnel Profile: Full-Time Paid 1; Part-Time Paid 2; Part-Time Volunteers 31; Interns 1.
Governing Authority: society. Parent Institution: Owyhee County Historical Society. Subsidiary Institution: Owyhee County Museum. Tax-exempt.
Historical Society Museum.
Collections: schoolhouse; Owyhee County historical items; agriculture; Indian artifacts; general; geology; archives; mining; oral history; Owyhee county artist; Owyhee County artifacts.
Major Exhibits: Lawmen of Owyhee County, 11/09-6/11.
Research Fields: agriculture; Indian artifacts; archives; mining.
Facilities: Gifts & books for sale.
Activities: guided tours; lectures; field trips; temporary & permanent exhibits; activities & lectures for local school children.
Publications: annual magazine, Owyhee Outpost; Owyhee County Blue Book 1898; Sketches of Owyhee County; Outpost: A Journal of Owyhee County History.
Hours & Admission Prices: Tues.-Sat. 10-4. Adults $2; discounts to AAM & ICOM members & Owyhee County Residence; members no charge. Closed holidays. ♿
Attendance: 14,321 (accurate)
Membership: Senior & Student $10; Individual $15; Family $25; Supporting $50; Associate $250; Life $500.

Nampa

CANYON COUNTY HISTORICAL SOCIETY & MUSEUM, 1200 Front St., Nampa, ID 83651-3931. Mailing Address: P.O. Box 595, Nampa, ID 83653-0595. Tel.: 208-467-7611.
E-mail: info@canyoncountyhistory.com
Web Site: www.canyoncountyhistory.com
Founded: 1976.
Key Personnel: Dir., Wendy W. Miller; Chm. (V), Pati Sweet; Museum Shop Mgr., Thora Brown.
Personnel Profile: Full-Time Paid 1; Part-Time Paid 3; Part-Time Volunteers 4.
Governing Authority: Branch Museum: Our Memories Indian Creek Museum, 1122 Main St., Caldwell, ID 83605. Tax-exempt: 501(c)(3).
Historical Society Museum.
Collections: area history; period artifacts including cider press & cast iron stove; bottles; 1915 Edison phonograph; caboose phone & tools. Our Memories Museum: local history; c.1920s dental office; c.1940s operating room; period artifacts.
Facilities: Museum-related items for sale.
Activities: tours; research; special events. Museum Sponsors: Fund-raiser Tea & Style Show in March; Canyon County Historical Home Tour in August; Christmas Open House in December.
Publications: quarterly newsletter, Rivers, Rails, and Trails.
Hours & Admission Prices: May-Oct. Tues.-Fri. 11-5, Sat. 10-3; Nov.-April Tues.-Fri. 11-5, Sat. 11-3. Our Memories Indian Creek Museum: Tues. & Fri. 11-4, Sat. 11-3. Adults $2, children $1.
Attendance: 5,000
Membership: Individual $10; Couple $15; Family $18; Contributing $25; Sustaining $50; Sponsor $100; Business $250; Corporate $500; Founder $1,000.

DEER FLAT NATIONAL WILDLIFE REFUGE, 13751 Upper Embankment Rd., Nampa, ID 83686-8046. Tel.: 208-467-9278. Fax: 208-467-1019.
Founded: 1909.
Congressional District: 1
Personnel Profile: Full-Time Paid 5.
Wildlife Refuge.
Collections: wildlife & their habitats; birds; fish; plants.
Facilities: nature trails; visitor center.
Activities: hiking; hands-on activities; viewing platforms & blind; environmental education.
Hours & Admission Prices: Park: daily. Visitor Center: Mon.-Fri. 8-4, Sat. 10-4. No charge. Closed Federal holidays. ♿
Attendance: 170,000 (estimated)

WARHAWK AIR MUSEUM, 201 Municipal Dr., Nampa, ID 83687-8582. Tel.: 208-465-6446. Fax: 208-465-6232.
E-mail: admin@warhawkairmuseum.org
Web Site: warhawkairmuseum.org
Founded: 1989.
Congressional District: 1
Key Personnel: Exec. Dir., Sue Paul; Museum Shop Mgr., Tammy John; Administrative Asst., Carri King.
Governing Authority: Tax-exempt.
Military Museum.
Collections: WWI & WWII artifacts; WWII fighter airplanes including Curtiss P-40 & P-51C Mustang; 1940s survival gear & equipment; NASA.
Facilities: library. Museum-related items for sale.
Activities: special events; tours.
Publications: newsletter, Flight Line.
Hours & Admission Prices: April-Sept. 30 Tues.-Sat. 10-5, Sun. 11-4; Oct.-April Tues.-Fri. 10-4, Sat. 10-5. Adults $8; members no charge.
Membership: Individual $35; Family $60; Sponsorship $250; Sponsorship II $500, $1,000, $5,000 & $10,000.

Oakley

OAKLEY VALLEY HISTORICAL MUSEUM, 140 W. Main St., Oakley, ID 83346. Mailing Address: P.O. Box 239, Oakley, ID 83346-0239. Tel.: 208-862-7890.
Founded: 2000.
Congressional District: 2
Key Personnel: Pres., Robert Fehlman.
Governing Authority: Parent Institution: City of Oakley. Tax-exempt.
History Museum: listed on the National Register of Historic Places.
Collections: area history; historic buildings.
Hours & Admission Prices: Summer: Fri.-Sat. 1-4; other times by appointment. No charge; donations accepted.

Orofino

CLEARWATER HISTORICAL MUSEUM, 315 College Ave., Orofino, ID 83544. Mailing Address: P.O. Box 1454, Orofino, ID 83544-1454. Tel.: 208-476-5033.
E-mail: chmuseum@clearwater.net
Web Site: www.clearwatermuseum.org
Founded: 1960.
Congressional District: 1
Key Personnel: Pres., Nick Albers; Vice Pres., Mike McHone; Sec., Bruce Anderson; Treas., Selah Legus; Museum Dir., Bernice Pullen.
Personnel Profile: Part-Time Paid 1; Part-Time Volunteers 2.
Governing Authority: state & county. Parent Institution: Clearwater Historical Society. Tax-exempt.
History Museum.
Collections: books; Nez Perce Indian artifacts; photographs; logging equip.

used with horsepower; tapes of oral history; county artifacts; clippings from newspapers; Lewis-Clark histories & early mining days in Pierce City, Idaho.
Research Fields: history of Clearwater County & early family records.
Facilities: library of Idaho & County history, taped oral history & photograph collection; reading room. Local history books for sale.
Activities: guided tours; group tours; permanent & temporary exhibitions.
Publications: quarterly newspaper.
Hours & Admission Prices: June-Sept. Tues.-Sat. 12:30-5:30; Oct.-May Tues.-Sat. 1:30-4:30. No charge; donations accepted. Closed holidays. ♿
Attendance: 1,500 (estimated)
Membership: Individual $5; Life $100.

Paris

PARIS TABERNACLE HISTORICAL SITE, 109 S. Main St., Paris, ID 83261. Tel.: 208-945-2072.
Historic Building: housed in the Church of Jesus Christ of Latter Day Saints; built by Mormon pioneers in 1889. Listed on the National Register of Historic Places.
Collections: local history & culture; religious artifacts & furnishings; paintings.
Activities: organ recitals.
Hours & Admission Prices: Guided Tours: Memorial Day to Labor Day daily 9:30-5:30. No charge.

Parma

OLD FORT BOISE REPLICA AND MUSEUM, 20847 Old Fort Boise Rd., Parma, ID 83660. Mailing Address: P.O. Box 942, Parma, ID 83660-0942. Tel.: 208-722-5138.
History Museum.
Collections: local history & culture; photographs; period furnishings; personal artifacts.
Hours & Admission Prices: June-Aug. Fri.-Sun. 1-3; other times by appointment. No charge; donations accepted. ♿
Attendance: 450 (estimated)

Payette

PAYETTE COUNTY MUSEUM, 90 S. 9th St., Payette, ID 83661. Mailing Address: P.O. Box 696, Payette, ID 83661-0696. Tel.: 208-642-4883.
Founded: 1973.
Governing Authority: Parent Institution: Payette County Historical Society.
History Museum: housed in a former church.
Collections: local history & culture; period furnishings; 1861 Confederate Civil War Cannon barrel.
Hours & Admission Prices: Summer: Wed.-Sun. 12-4; Winter: Wed.-Sat. 12-4; other times by appointment. No charge; donations accepted. ♿

Pierce

J. HOWARD BRADBURY MEMORIAL LOGGING MUSEUM, 101 S. Main St., Pierce, ID 83546. Mailing Address: P.O. Box 378, Weippe, ID 83553-0378. Tel.: 208-464-2531 & 435-4670.
Logging History Museum.
Collections: logging industry history; photographs; tools.
Hours & Admission Prices: mid-June to mid-Oct. Fri.-Sat. 12-4; other times by appointment.

Pocatello

BANNOCK COUNTY HISTORICAL MUSEUM, 3000 Alvord Loop (Upper Level of Ross Park), Pocatello, ID 83201. Mailing Address: P.O. Box 253, Pocatello, ID 83204-0253. Tel.: 208-233-0434.
Founded: 1963.
Congressional District: 2
Key Personnel: Society Pres., Fred Dykes; Dir., Cur. & Society & Museum Account & Museum Shop Mgr., Margaret Barrett; Sec., Marvin McColl.
Personnel Profile: Full-Time Paid 1; Part-Time Paid 1; Part-Time Volunteers 3.
Governing Authority: society. Parent Institution: Bannock County Historical Society. Tax-exempt: 501(c)(3).
History Museum.
Collections: Wrensted collection; Indian photographs; Peake collection; Larsen collection; railroad photographs; farm equipment.
Activities: guided tours; permanent & temporary exhibitions.
Publications: annual newsletter.
Hours & Admission Prices: Memorial Day to Labor Day daily 10-6; Sept.-May Tues.-Sat. 10-2; other times by appointment. Adults $1, children 6-12 $.50; children under 6 & members no charge. Closed legal holidays. ♿
Attendance: 2,500 (estimated)
Membership: Individual $10.

FORT HALL REPLICA, 3002 Alvord Loop, Upper Level Ross Park, Pocatello, ID 83201. Tel.: 208-234-1795. Fax: 208-234-6578.
Web Site: www.forthall.net
History Museum: housed in a replica of the historic facility that served pioneers along the Oregon Trail.
Collections: Oregon Trail history; pioneer life & culture; covered wagon; tepee; period furnishings & artifacts; photographs.
Hours & Admission Prices: April 11-May 27 Tues.-Sat. 10-2; May 28-Sept. 6 daily 10-6; Sept. 7-Sept. 30 daily 10-2. Adults $2.50, seniors $2, youth 12-17 $1.50, children 3-11 $1; discounts to school groups.

IDAHO MUSEUM OF NATURAL HISTORY, (M), 5th & Dillon, Pocatello, ID 83209-0001. Mailing Address: 921 S. 8th Ave., Stop 8096, Pocatello, ID 83209-0002. Tel.: 208-282-3317. Fax: 208-282-5893.
E-mail: imnh@isu.edu
Web Site: imnh.isu.edu
Founded: 1934.
Congressional District: 2
Key Personnel: Dir. & Cur. Anthropology, Dr. Skip Lohse; Store Mgr., Bill Angle; Vertebrate Paleontology Cur., Dr. William Akersten; Earth Sciences Cur., Dr. Leif Tapanila; Education Resource Coord. & Education Cur., Rebecca Thorne-Ferrel; Life Sciences Cur., Dr. Rick Williams; Southeast Idaho Repository Mgr., Amy Commendador; Anthropology Cur., Dr. Herb Maschner; Registrar, Lynn Murdoch; Office Admin., Mary Moses.
Personnel Profile: Full-Time Paid 3; Part-Time Paid 16; Part-Time Volunteers 20; Interns 3.
Governing Authority: state. Administrative Authority: Idaho State University. Tax-exempt: 170(b)(1)(A).
Natural History Museum.
Collections: Great Basin collections in archaeology & ethnology; vertebrate fossils from the Intermountain West, specializing in Pleistocene; Crabtree flintworking; manuscripts & photographs of north Rocky Mountains region; major herbarium holdings; modern osteol; modern vertebrate; ornithology; mammalogy.
Research Fields: archaeology; botany; ethnography; herpetology; ornithology; recent vertebrates; historical photographs & documents; vertebrate paleontology; pertaining to the Great Basin & northern Rocky Mountains.
Facilities: library.
Activities: guided gallery tours; films; formally organized education programs; adult lectures; classes; field trips; temporary & permanent exhibitions; field work in anthropology & paleontology; summer programs for children & adults; self-guided ISU Tree Walk; Discovery Room; ScienceTrek sleepover; Natural History Academy; Pint-sized Science Academy; Forays into the Field; summer science snack.
Publications: Tebiwa, Journal of the Idaho Museum of Natural History; special publications; occasional papers series; booklets & pamphlets.
Hours & Admission Prices: Tues.-Sat. 10-5. Adults $5, senior $4, students with valid ID $3, children 4-11 $2; discounts to AAM members; children under 4 & members no charge. Closed holidays. ♿
Attendance: 8,829 (accurate)
Membership: Student $15; Senior 65 & over $20; Individual $25; Duo $35; Family $60; Enhanced Family $100; Sponsor $250; Donor $500; Collector's Circle, Educator's Circle & Researcher's Circle $750; Founder's Circle $1,000.

THE MUSEUM OF CLEAN, (M), 711 S. Second Ave., Pocatello, ID 83201-6520. Mailing Address: P.O. Box 6169, Pocatello, ID 83205-6169. Tel.: 208-241-4855 & 232-3535. Fax: 208-235-5481.
E-mail: rpb1963@gmail.com
Web Site: www.aslett.com/damc/
Formerly: Don Aslett's Cleaning Museum
Founded: 2007.
Congressional District: 2
Key Personnel: Interim Dir., Reed Phillips; C.E.O., Don Aslett.
Personnel Profile: Full-Time Paid 1; Part-Time Paid 1.
Governing Authority: Parent Institution: Don Aslett Clean World Foundation. Tax-exempt.
History Museum.
Collections: cleaning techniques, products, implements & machines.
Research Fields: environmental protection history; home living.
Hours & Admission Prices: Closed until May 2010. ♿

POCATELLO ZOO, 3101 Ave. of the Chiefs, Pocatello, ID 83204-2135. Tel.: 208-234-6264.
E-mail: sransom@pocatellor.us
Web Site: www.pocatellozoo.org

Key Personnel: Zoo Dir., Scott Ransom; Cur. Education, Bonnie Jakubos Zoo.
Collections: wildlife native to North America's Intermountain West.
Hours & Admission Prices: April 15-April 30 Sat.-Sun. 9-5; May-June 15 daily 9-5; June 16 to Labor Day daily 10-6; Sept.-Oct. Sat.-Sun. 10-4. Adults 12-59 $4.25, seniors 60 & over $3, children 3-11 $2.25; children 2 & under no charge.

Priest Lake

PRIEST LAKE MUSEUM, 38 W. Lakeshore Dr., Priest Lake, ID 83856. Mailing Address: P.O. Box 44, Coolin, ID 83821-0044. Tel.: 208-443-2676.
Web Site: www.thepriestlakemuseum.org
Founded: 1990.
Key Personnel: Pres. (V), Tom Weitz.
Governing Authority: Tax-exempt.
Historic Building Museum: housed in a former forest ranger cabin; c.1930s.
Collections: local history & culture; period furnishings; personal artifacts; photographs.
Publications: Pioneer Voices.
Hours & Admission Prices: Memorial Day to Labor Day Tues.-Sun. 10-4. No charge; donations accepted. ♿
Attendance: 3,000 (accurate)
Membership: $5-$500.

Priest River

KEYSER HOUSE TIMBER MUSEUM, 301 Montgomery St., Priest River, ID 83856. Mailing Address: Priest River Chamber of Commerce, P.O. Box 929, Priest River, ID 83856-0929. Tel.: 208-448-2721.
Historic House Museum: housed in the former home of Henry and Elizabeth Keyser; built in 1895.
Collections: local history & culture; pioneer life; Keyser family artifacts; timber industry; period furnishings; photographs; quilts; tools.
Hours & Admission Prices: Call for hours.

Rexburg

LEGACY FLIGHT MUSEUM, Rexburg Airport, 435 Airport Rd., Rexburg, ID 83440. Mailing Address: P.O. Box 122, Rexburg, ID 83440-0122. Tel.: 208-359-5905. Fax: 208-356-7989.
E-mail: legacyflightmuseum@hotmail.com
Founded: 2002.
Military History Museum.
Collections: military aircraft history; personal artifacts; photographs.
Hours & Admission Prices: Memorial Day to Labor Day Mon.-Sat. 9-5; Sept.-May Sat. 9-5.

TETON FLOOD MUSEUM, 51 N. Center St., Rexburg, ID 83440-1539. Mailing Address: P.O. Box 280, Rexburg, ID 83440-0280. Tel.: 208-359-3063. Fax: 208-359-9556.
E-mail: kristyg@rexburg.org
Key Personnel: Dir., Cur. & Museum Shop Mgr., Jill Spencer.
Personnel Profile: Part-Time Paid 1; Part-Time Volunteers 6.
Governing Authority: city. Tax-exempt.
History Museum: the disaster of the Teton Dam collapse on June 5, 1976.
Collections: personal artifacts; video of actual dam break; photographs; pioneer; western artifacts; war memorabilia.
Activities: tour of the actual dam; video of the break; temporary & permanent exhibitions.
Hours & Admission Prices: May-Sept. Mon. 10-7, Tues.-Sat. 10-5; Oct.-April Mon. 11-7, Tues.-Sat. 11-4. Adults $2, youth 12-18 $1, children under 12 $.50. ♿

UPPER SNAKE RIVER VALLEY HISTORICAL SOCIETY, 51 N. Center St., Rexburg, ID 83440-1539. Mailing Address: P.O. Box 244, Rexburg, ID 83440-0244. Tel.: 208-356-9100.
E-mail: usrvhistsoc@hotmail.com
Web Site: rexburghistoricalsociety.com
Founded: 1965.
Congressional District: 2
Key Personnel: C.E.O., Dir. & Cur., Louis Clements; Pres., Harvey Jackman; Vice Pres., Harold Forbush.
Personnel Profile: Full-Time Volunteers 1; Part-Time Volunteers 20.
Governing Authority: society. Branch Museums: Fremont County Museum, St. Anthony, ID; Teton Valley Museum, Driggs, ID; Jefferson County Museum, Rigby, ID; Bonnville County Museum, Idaho Falls, ID; Teton Flood Museum, Rexburg, ID. Tax-exempt: 170(b)(1)(A).
Local Historic Museum.
Collections: emphasis on Idaho & local history for teaching & information purposes; Teton flood collection; guns; agriculture; period artifacts; manuscripts.
Research Fields: Idaho history; local history; Teton flood.
Facilities: 200-vol. library of Idaho & local history available for inter-library loan & for research; reading room. Western history books for sale.
Activities: guided tours; lectures; films; gallery talks; TV & radio programs; formally organized education programs for children; inter-museum loan, permanent, temporary & traveling exhibitions. Institute Sponsors: History Fair, an annual gathering of artifact displays from over the state.
Publications: magazine, Snake River Echoes.
Hours & Admission Prices: April-Aug. Mon.-Sat. 10-5; Sept.-May Mon.-Fri. 11-4. Adults $2, children 14 & under $1. Closed national holidays. ♿
Attendance: 18,791 (accurate)
Membership: Individual $10; Life $200.

Rigby

JEFFERSON COUNTY HISTORICAL MUSEUM, 118 West 1st South, Rigby, ID 83442-1303. Mailing Address: P.O. Box 284, Rigby, ID 83442-0284. Tel.: 208-745-8423.
Web Site: www.blacksmithinn.com/museum.html
Founded: 1975.
Congressional District: 2
Key Personnel: Pres. (V), Gary Spaulding; Sec. & Treas., Kathryn McLain; Cur., Marjorie T. Scott.
Personnel Profile: Full-Time Volunteers 5; Part-Time Volunteers 23.
Governing Authority: Parent Institution: Jefferson County Historical Society. Tax-exempt.
History Museum.
Collections: area history; Philo Farnsworth, inventor with over 125 patents; photographs; Native American.
Activities: tours.
Hours & Admission Prices: Tues.-Sat. 1-5. Requested Donation: adults $2, children 6-17 $1; children under 6 no charge. ♿
Attendance: 1,500 (estimated)
Membership: Jefferson County Historical Society $10; Lifetime $100.

Rupert

MINIDOKA COUNTY HISTORICAL MUSEUM, 99 E. Baseline Rd., Rupert, ID 83350. Mailing Address: Box 21, Rupert, ID 83350-0021. Tel.: 208-436-0336.
Web Site: www.minidoka.id.us
Founded: 1970.
Key Personnel: Pres. (V), Arlo P. Lloyd; Museum Shop Mgr., Anne Schenk.
Personnel Profile: Part-Time Paid 1; Part-Time Volunteers 10.
History Museum.
Collections: local history; Native American artifacts; early 1900s marble soda fountain; over 600 bottles & jars; horse drawn farm equipment; Russell steam engine tractor; wooden wheeled carts; 1906 railroad depot history; photographs; Ice Age bones; newspapers from 1905 to present; 1940 fire engine; early 1900 wooden fire carts; 1906 HPPR Depot.
Facilities: research library.
Hours & Admission Prices: Call for hours. No charge; donations accepted. ♿
Attendance: 900
Membership: Youth 13-18 $$4; Single $10; Couple $15; Lifetime $100.

MINIDOKA NATIONAL WILDLIFE REFUGE, Rte. 4, 961 E. Minidoka Dam, Rupert, ID 83350-9414. Tel.: 208-436-3589.
Wildlife Refuge.
Collections: wildlife including swans; white pelicans; songbirds; mule deer; beaver; muskrat; coyote.
Facilities: nature trails.
Activities: hiking.
Hours & Admission Prices: Call for hours.

Saint Maries

HISTORICAL HUGHES HOUSE, 538 Main Ave., Saint Maries, ID 83861-2061. Tel.: 208-245-3212.
Historic House Museum: housed in a former men's club and later a doctor's office; built in 1902.
Collections: local history & culture; photographs; period furnishings; personal artifacts.
Hours & Admission Prices: Call for hours.

Salmon

LEMHI COUNTY HISTORICAL MUSEUM, 210 Main, Salmon, ID 83467-4111. Tel.: 208-756-3342.
E-mail: llemhi@centurytel.net
Web Site: www.lemhimuseum.org
Founded: 1963.
Congressional District: 2
Key Personnel: Pres. (V), Hope Benedict; Vice Pres., Laurie Rugierro; Sec., Dallas Lewis; Cur., Clair Wiley.
Personnel Profile: Part-Time Paid 1; Part-Time Volunteers 15.
Governing Authority: society; nonprofit organization.
History Museum.
Collections: local history & culture; Indian artifacts; mining; ranching; Lemhi Shoshoni artifacts; Asian artifacts including lost-wax bronzes & Ming Dynasty vases.
Publications: map, Lewis & Clark Route through Pass to Bitterroot; Madame Charbonneau.
Hours & Admission Prices: May 15 to mid-Oct. Mon.-Sat. 10-5. Admission 12 & over $2; children under 12 no charge. ♿
Attendance: 5,500 (estimated)
Membership: Individual $10.

SACAJAWEA INTERPRETIVE, CULTURAL & EDUCATIONAL CENTER, 60 Hwy. 28, Salmon, ID 83467-5340. Mailing Address: 200 Main St., Salmon, ID 83467-4111. Tel.: 208-756-1188.
Web Site: www.sacajaweacenter.org
Key Personnel: Dir., Angela Hurley
History Museum.
Collections: Sacajawea's life & cultural history; Sacajawea monument; wildlife; tipi encampment.
Facilities: learning center; visitor center; outdoor amphitheater; picnic areas; garden; interpretive trail; nature trail; low ropes challenge course.
Activities: special events; demonstrations; interpretive presentations; hands-on primitive living skills; classes; outdoor & environmental education; concerts.
Hours & Admission Prices: Park: daily. Visitor Center: May-Oct. Family $12, adult $5.

Sandpoint

BONNER COUNTY HISTORICAL MUSEUM, 611 S. Ella Ave., Sandpoint, ID 83864-1100. Tel.: 208-263-2344.
E-mail: bchs@verizon.net
Web Site: www.bonnercountyhistory.org
Founded: 1972.
Congressional District: 1
Key Personnel: Dir. & Cur., Ann M. Ferguson; Pres. (V), Barbara Botsch.
Personnel Profile: Part-Time Paid 1; Part-Time Volunteers 25.
Governing Authority: society; nonprofit organization. Parent Institution: Bonner County Historical Society, Inc. Tax-exempt.
Local History Museum.
Collections: local history; early Americana; geology; American Indian artifacts; forest history; logging; sawmilling; oral history; photographs; railroads.
Research Fields: historical site survey; local history.
Facilities: research library; photo display area; arboretum.
Activities: oral history program; historical site survey program; field trips; evening historical programs.
Publications: membership newsletter; Beautiful Bonner Vol. I & Vol. II.
Hours & Admission Prices: Summer: Tues.-Sat. 10-4; Winter: call for hours. Family $5, adults $3, students $1; members & children under 6 accompanied by adult no charge. ♿
Attendance: 5,000 (estimated)
Membership: Senior & Student $15; Individual $20; Family $25; Supporting $30; Professional $50; Association $100; Patron $500.

Shoshone

SHOSHONE INDIAN ICE CAVES, 1561 N. Hwy. 75, Shoshone, ID 83352-5246. Tel.: 208-886-2058.
History Museum.
Collections: local history; geology; lava ice case; Native American artifacts; minerals; gems.
Activities: guided tours.
Hours & Admission Prices: May-Sept. daily 8-7:15. Adults $7.50, seniors $6.50, children 4-12 $4; discounts to groups; children 3 & under no charge.

Spalding

NEZ PERCE NATIONAL HISTORICAL PARK, 39063 U.S. Hwy. 95, Spalding, ID 83540-9715. Mailing Address: P.O. Box 1000, Lapwai, ID 83540-1000. Tel.: 208-843-7001. Fax: 208-843-7003.
E-mail: bob_chenoweth@nps.gov
Web Site: www.nps.gov/nepe
Founded: 1965.
Congressional District: 1
Key Personnel: Supt., Gary Somers; Cur., Bob Chenoweth; Museum Shop Mgr., Mary Lou Tiede; Archivist & Library Technician, Robert Applegate; Museum Technician, Linda J. Paisano.
Personnel Profile: Full-Time Paid 27; Part-Time Paid 1; Part-Time Volunteers 2; Interns 1.
Governing Authority: federal. Parent Institution: National Park Service, Dept. of Interior, Washington DC 20240. Tax-exempt.
Park Museum: located on a site of prehistoric occupation & early mission.
Collections: Nez Perce ethnological; prehistoric lithics; Western Americana; local pioneer & historical documents & memorabilia; 4,000 photos on the Nez Perce Indians & the local region; Big Hole National ethnographic, historic & archeological related to the battlefield; Lake Roosevelt National Recreation area archeological & historical items associated with Fort Spokane; City of Rock National Reserve archeological material.
Research Fields: Nez Perce Indian culture; early mission activity; local historical events pertaining to park sites & westward American expansion.
Facilities: 2,500-vol. library of books about Nez Perce Indian & Pacific Northwest history available at research center; requests for legitimate study collections access should be made in advance; Visitor Center & Museum at Spalding, ID; Park Interpretive Shelters at Kamiah & White Bird, ID; 24 Wayside Interpretive Sites in ID on or near the Nez Perce Indian Reservation including Indian-U.S. military battle sites, other historical & Nez Perce cultural sites. Books, postcards & handcrafts for sale.
Activities: Nez Perce Indian craft demonstrations & cultural programs each summer; slide & film programs; guided tours; special events.
Publications: interpretive & information brochures; site bulletins.
Hours & Admission Prices: Winter: daily 8-4:30; Summer: daily 8-5:30. No charge. Closed New Year's Day; Thanksgiving; Christmas. ♿
Attendance: 152,393 (accurate)

Stanley

LAND OF THE YANKEE FORK HISTORIC ASSOCIATION MUSEUM, 350 Yankee Fork Rd., Stanley, ID 83274. Mailing Address: 201 Ashe Dr., Brigham City, UT 84302-2748. Tel.: 435-734-9857 & 730-5113.
E-mail: poundersinperth@hotmail.com
Formerly: Custer Museum
Founded: 1961.
Congressional District: 26
Key Personnel: District Forest Ranger, Russ Camper; Pres. (V), Jack Pounder; Museum Shop Mgr., Margaret Pounder.
Personnel Profile: Full-Time Volunteers 4; Part-Time Paid 4; Part-Time Volunteers 6.
Governing Authority: federal. Parent Institution: U.S. Department of Agriculture, Forest Service. Subsidiary Institution: Idaho Parks & Recreation. Tax-exempt: 501(c)(3).
History Museum: located on site of Custer Gold Mining Town.
Collections: gold rush mining equipment; household artifacts; Chinese personal items pertaining to mining; photographs; freighting equipment; school books & supplies. Historic Buildings: 1900 Custer School House; 1890 Custer Saloon & Doctor's Office; Brockman Cabin; McKenzie House.
Facilities: 40-vol. library of school books, hotel ledgers, 1880-1900 business records available on premises.
Activities: printed guide tours; lectures; permanent exhibitions; slide shows. Annual Event: Custer Day Celebration in July.
Publications: pamphlets, Custer, A Walking Tour of Custer Idaho; Land of the Yankee Fork Historic Area.
Hours & Admission Prices: Memorial Day weekend to Labor Day daily 10-5. No charge; donations accepted. ♿
Attendance: 10,000 (accurate)
Membership: Individual $5; Family $7.50; Lifetime $100.

Terreton

MUD LAKE HISTORICAL SOCIETY, City Bldg., Terreton, ID 83450. Mailing Address: P.O. Box 124, Terreton, ID 83450-0124. Tel.: 208-663-4376.
Key Personnel: Pres. (V), Orvin Twitchey
Historical Society Museum.
Collections: period artifacts; photographs.
Hours & Admission Prices: 2nd Mon. and 1st & 3rd Thurs. of month 2-4; other times by appointment. No charge; donations accepted. ♿

Twin Falls

*** HERRETT CENTER FOR ARTS & SCIENCE, FAULKNER PLANETARIUM AND CENTENNIAL OBSERVATORY, (M),** 315 Falls Ave., College of Southern Idaho, Twin Falls, ID 83301-3367. Mailing Address: P.O. Box 1238, Twin Falls, ID 83303-1238. Tel.: 208-732-6655. Fax: 208-736-4712.
E-mail: herrett@csi.edu
Web Site: herrett.csi.edu/
Founded: 1952.
Congressional District: 2
Key Personnel: Dir., James C. Woods; Collections Mgr., Phyllis Oppenheim; Exhibits Mgr. & Graphic Designer, Joey Heck; Art Gallery Mgr., Milica Popovic; Facility, Display & Planetarium Technician, Robert (Nick) Peterson; Office Mgr. & Museum Shop Mgr., Carolyn Browning; Planetarium Mgr., Rick Greenawald; Mktg. Coord, Doug Maughan; Education Facilitator, Darcy Thornborrow; Planetarium Production Specialist, Chris Anderson; Facilities Specialist & Special Events Coord., Kristi Cederstrom.
Personnel Profile: Full-Time Paid 8; Part-Time Paid 6; Part-Time Volunteers 5.
Governing Authority: Junior College District. Parent Institution: College of Southern Idaho. Tax-exempt.
Arts & Science Museum, Planetarium & Observatory.
Collections: Americas & European archaeology; natural history; modern paintings & sculptures.
Research Fields: Lithic technology.
Facilities: 5,000-vol. library of books available to students for research; art gallery; planetarium (Digistar II); observatory.
Activities: presentations for classes of students; permanent, temporary & traveling exhibitions.
Hours & Admission Prices: Tues. & Fri. 9:30-9, Wed.-Thurs. 9:30-4:30, Sat. 1-9. Planetarium: call for show times. Adults $4.50, senior $3.50, students $2.50; discounts to AAM members; children under 2 no charge. Observatory: call for hours. Closed holidays. ♿
Attendance: 40,535 (accurate)

Wallace

NORTHERN PACIFIC DEPOT RAILROAD MUSEUM, 219 6th St., Wallace, ID 83873-2283. Mailing Address: P.O. Box 469, Wallace, ID 83873-0469. Tel.: 208-752-0111. Fax: 208-753-9361.
Founded: 1986.
Railroad Museum: listed on the National Register of Historical Places.
Collections: depot & railroading history; 13 ft. glass map.
Activities: Annual Event: Classic Car Show & Festival in May.
Hours & Admission Prices: April-May & Sept.-Oct. 15 Mon.-Sat. 10-3; June-Aug. daily 9-7.

SIERRA SILVER MINE TOUR, 420 5th St., Wallace, ID 83873-2212. Tel.: 208-752-5151.
Geology Museum.
Collections: local history; mining equipment & tools; geology.
Activities: guided tours; demonstrations.
Hours & Admission Prices: May & Sept. daily 10-2; June-Aug. daily 10-4. Adults $12, seniors 60 & over $11, children 4-16 $8.50; discounts to groups; children under 4 no charge.

WALLACE DISTRICT MINING MUSEUM, 509 Bank St., Wallace, ID 83873-2224. Mailing Address: P.O. Box 469, Wallace, ID 83873-0469. Tel.: 208-556-1592. Fax: 208-556-1592.
Founded: 1956.
Congressional District: 1
Key Personnel: Exec. Dir., Jim McReynolds; Pres., Dale Lavigne; Sec., Dennis O'Brien.
Personnel Profile: Full-Time Paid 2; Part-Time Paid 4; Part-Time Volunteers 2.
Governing Authority: nonprofit. Tax-exempt.
Mining Museum.
Collections: mining exhibits.
Research Fields: Various records, maps & directories.
Facilities: Brochures, membership stock certificates & other museum-related items for sale.
Activities: permanent & temporary exhibitions.
Publications: brochure; booklet, Gold Strikes & Silver Linings.
Hours & Admission Prices: May-Sept. daily 9-5; Oct.-April Mon.-Fri. 10-5, Sat.-Sun. 10-3. Families $5, adults 16-54 $2, members & senior citizens 55 & over $1.50, children 6-15 $.50. Closed New Year's Day; Martin Luther King Jr. Day; Presidents' Day; Independence Day; Thanksgiving; Christmas. ♿
Attendance: 49,000 (estimated)
Membership: Sustaining $20; Contributing $50; Patron $100; Life $500.

Weippe

WEIPPE DISCOVERY CENTER, 204 Wood St., Weippe, ID 83553. Mailing Address: P.O. Box 435, Weippe, ID 83553-0435. Tel.: 208-435-4058. Fax: 208-435-4374.
E-mail: discovery@weippe.com
Web Site: www.weippelibrary.org
Key Personnel: Dir., Terri Summerfield
History Museum.
Collections: Lewis & Clark history; painted murals; life-size map of trail & campsites; Nex Perce artifacts.
Hours & Admission Prices: Mon. & Thurs.-Fri. 10-5, Tues.-Wed. 10-7, Sat. 10-1. No charge; donations accepted. ♿

WEIPPE HILLTOP HERITAGE MUSEUM, 105 N. 1st St. E., Weippe, ID 83553. Mailing Address: P.O. Box 279, Weippe, ID 83553-0279. Tel.: 208-435-4200.
Founded: 1999.
Congressional District: 1
Key Personnel: Pres. (V), Everet Martin; Dir., Lorna D. Hubler.
Personnel Profile: Part-Time Volunteers 1.
Governing Authority: Tax-exempt.
History Museum.
Collections: local history & culture; personal artifacts; photographs; period furnishings.
Publications: children's book, The Weippe Story.
Hours & Admission Prices: Wed. 10-4; other times by appointment. No charge; donations accepted. ♿
Attendance: 600 (estimated)
Membership: Individual $5; Family $20; Business $50.

Weiser

SNAKE RIVER HERITAGE CENTER, 2295 Paddock Ave., Weiser, ID 83672-1195. Mailing Address: P.O. Box 307, Weiser, ID 83672-0307. Tel.: 208-549-0205.
Founded: 1962.
Congressional District: 1
Key Personnel: Pres. (V), Lynn Isaacson.
Personnel Profile: Part-Time Paid 1; Part-Time Volunteers 12.
Governing Authority: private; nonprofit organization. Tax-exempt; 170(b)(1)(A).
Cultural Center & Museum: housed in 1899-1933 preparatory school.
Collections: music; costumes; folklore; glass; geology; Alumni Room with memorabilia of former institute students. Historic Buildings: 1880 Harper Cabin; 1923 Hooker Hall.
Research Fields: city, county & regional history.
Facilities: newspapers, pamphlets, letters, & photographs available for research on premises; 300-seat auditorium. Museum-related gifts for sale.
Activities: guided tours; drama; demonstrations; historical slide show presentation.
Publications: annual newsletter.
Hours & Admission Prices: Memorial Day-Labor Day Thurs.-Sat. 1-4; tours by appointment. No charge; donations accepted.
Attendance: 1,000 (estimated)
Membership: Individual, Couple & Family $15; Contributing $60; Patron $150.

Winchester

WOLF EDUCATION & RESEARCH CENTER, 518 Joseph Ave., Winchester, ID 83555. Mailing Address: P.O. Box 217, Winchester, ID 83555. Tel.: 888-422-1110, ext. 3.
Key Personnel: Coord. Education, Randy Stewart
Nature Center.
Collections: wolves & their habitats; natural artifacts; photographs.
Facilities: 300-acre sanctuary. Museum-related items for sale.
Activities: educational programs; tours.
Hours & Admission Prices: May & Sept. Self-Guided Tours: Sat.-Sun. 9-4; Guided Tours: call for appointment. Memorial Day to Labor Day Self-Guided Tours: daily 9-5; Guided Tours: daily 7:30-7; other times by appointment.

ILLINOIS

(389 listings)

Aledo

ESSLEY-NOBLE MUSEUM: MERCER COUNTY HISTORICAL SOCIETY, 1406 S.E. 2nd Ave., Aledo, IL 61231-2504. Mailing Address: P.O. Box 269, Aledo, IL 61231-0269. Tel.: 309-582-2280 & 584-4820.
Founded: 1959.
Congressional District: 19
Key Personnel: Pres., Mr. Bill Bertrand; Cur., Mrs. Shirley Crawford.
Personnel Profile: Part-Time Paid 1; Part-Time Volunteers 15; Interns 1.
Governing Authority: society; nonprofit organization. Parent Institution: Mercer County Historical Society. Tax-exempt: 501(c)(3).
Historical & Preservation Society: housed in the Essley-Noble Memorial Building.
Collections: local history; c.1900 kitchen; pearl button cutting lathe; old farming tools; Civil War items; Lincoln desk; 1880 parlor room; original Mercer county court house flag; showcase of early American toys; New Boston Millstone; Roosevelt Military academy; photographs; newspapers on microfilm; one room country school; genealogy; machine shed with farming tools & implements; William & Vashti College artifacts.
Research Fields: genealogy; local history & lore; county census-microfilm newspapers.
Facilities: 8-vol. library of Mercer County DAR cemetery records & various county genealogy material available for research on premises.
Activities: guided tours; permanent & temporary exhibitions; spring & fall meeting open to public with program. Annual Event: ice cream social open to public in August.
Publications: quarterly newsletter.
Hours & Admission Prices: April-Oct. Wed. & Sat.-Sun. 1-5; Nov.-March Sat. 12-4; school & groups by appointment. No charge; donations accepted.
Attendance: 1,200 (estimated)
Membership: Individual $15; Life $300.

Alton

ALTON MUSEUM OF HISTORY AND ART, INC., 2809 College Ave., Alton, IL 62002-4743. Tel.: 618-462-2763.
E-mail: altonmuseum@yahoo.com
Web Site: altonmuseum.com
Founded: 1971.
Congressional District: 12
Key Personnel: Pres., Dr. Norman Showers; 1st Vice Pres., Brian Combs; 2nd Vice Pres., Patti Culp; 3rd Vice Pres., Don Lobbig; Pres. Emeritus & Office Mgr., Charlene Johnson; Black Pioneer Committee, Marilyn Bradford; Koenig House Hostess & Museum Shop Mgr., Lois Lobbig.
Personnel Profile: Full-Time Volunteers 1; Part-Time Volunteers 65; Interns 1.
Governing Authority: nonprofit organization. Branch Museum: Koenig House, 829 E. 4th St., Alton, IL 62002. Tax-exempt: 501(c)(3).
History & Art Museum: c.1890 Victorian historic home; c.1832 educational building and museum.
Collections: river memorabilia; local paintings, sculptures, industry display; artifacts from local railroads, industries & business places; model trains; photographs; Freedom collection, including Elijah Lovejoy, Abraham Lincoln & Lyman Trumbull; Lovejoy print shop; underground railroad; Robert Wadlow, the world's tallest recorded man; fine arts; Black pioneers.
Research Fields: Alton Civil War prison; Black Pioneers; historic characters of region; underground railroad; Elijah Lovejoy; early education & transportation.
Facilities: 2,500 sq. ft. exhibit space. Art prints of local artists, books & other museum-related items for sale.
Activities: guided tours; lectures; arts festivals; organized educational programs; training programs for professional museum workers; participatory & temporary exhibitions; film; tours at Koenig House. Museum Sponsors: Christmas Tea; annual membership meeting; Miles Davis Jazz Celebration in May; Annual Guardian of History Award; Margaret Davis Weber Award; heirloom evaluation days; antique auction; Alton Landing Festival; Home & history house tour.
Publications: brochure; annual report; historic reprints; quarterly newsletter.
Hours & Admission Prices: Wed.-Sat. 10-4, Sun. 1-4. Adults $3, children $1; discounts to seniors on Wed.; members no charge. Closed Easter; Independence Day; Thanksgiving; Christmas.
Attendance: 11,000 (accurate)
Membership: Youth $5; Senior $20; Active (Single) $25; Family $30; History Loner $40; Patron of the Arts $50; Business $100; Life $1,000; Benefactor $5,000.

Arcola

ILLINOIS AMISH INTERPRETIVE CENTER, 111 S. Locust St., Arcola, IL 61910. Tel.: 888-452-6474. Fax: 217-268-4810.
History Museum.
Collections: Amish culture & history; Arthur Amish settlement; personal artifacts.
Facilities: Museum-related items for sale.
Activities: tours.
Hours & Admission Prices: Center: Mon.-Sat. 9-5. Adults $5, seniors 62 & over $4, children 6-11 $3; children under 6 no charge.

RAGGEDY ANN & ANDY MUSEUM, 110-114 E. Main St., Arcola, IL 61910. Mailing Address: P.O. Box 183, Arcola, IL 61910-0183. Tel.: 217-268-4908. Fax: 217-268-4708.
E-mail: tom@raggedyann-museum.org
Web Site: www.raggedyann-museum.org
Key Personnel: Co Dir., Joni Wannamaker; Co Dir., Tom Wannamaker
Toy Museum.
Collections: history of Johnny Gruelle, the author & illustrator of Raggedy Ann; product line from 1915 to present.
Hours & Admission Prices: Tues.-Sat. 10-4:30. Suggested Donation: $1.

Arlington Heights

ARLINGTON HEIGHTS HISTORICAL MUSEUM, (M), 110 W. Fremont St., Arlington Heights, IL 60004-5912. Tel.: 847-255-1225. Fax: 847-255-1570.
Web Site: www.ahmuseum.org
Founded: 1957.
Congressional District: 10th & 12th
Key Personnel: Pres., Tom Hahn; Museum Admin., Kristina Christie; Devel. Coord., Kristine Lundstrom; Cur., Mickey Horndasch; School Scout Coord., Bev Ottaviano; Program Coord., Cathy Robertson; Asst. Coord., Teri Ozawa.
Personnel Profile: Full-Time Paid 1; Part-Time Paid 9; Part-Time Volunteers 100.
Governing Authority: nonprofit organization. Parent Institution: Arlington Heights Historical Society. Subsidiary Institutions: Arlington Heights Park District; Village of Arlington Heights; Arlington Heights Memorial Library. Tax-exempt: 501(c)(3).
History Museum.
Collections: local history 1836-present. Heritage Gallery: temporary exhibits. Historic Buildings: c.1836 replica log cabin; c.1882 Muller house; c.1908 Banta house; c.1900 coach house; c.1906 soda pop factory building.
Research Fields: local history.
Facilities: library of clippings, photographs & archival material relating to Arlington Heights available for use by public. Heritage Gallery: museum-related items for sale.
Activities: guided tours; formally organized educational programs for school & scout children; permanent & temporary exhibitions; exhibit receptions & programs; craft workshops; family programs; special events.
Publications: bimonthly newsletter, The Dunton Post.
Hours & Admission Prices: Tours: Sat.-Sun. 2 & 3; other times & groups by appointment. Adults $4, children $2; discount to AAM members; members no charge. Heritage Gallery: Fri.-Sun. 1:30-4:30. No charge; donations accepted. Closed national holidays.
Attendance: 14,000 (estimated)
Membership: Individual $20; Family $40; Non-Profit $75; Patron $100; Individual Life $500; Business Memberships available.

Atlanta

ATLANTA LIBRARY & MUSEUM, 100 S.E. Race St., Atlanta, IL 61723-7526. Mailing Address: P.O. Box 568, Atlanta, IL 61723. Tel.: 217-648-2003.
Historic Building: built in 1908. Listed on the National Register of Historic Places.
Collections: local history; period high school photographs, plaques, & trophies; tools; personal artifacts.
Hours & Admission Prices: Tues.-Wed. & Fri. 12:30-4:30, Thurs. 12:30-8, Sat. 9-1.

Aurora

AURORA HISTORICAL SOCIETY, Cedar & Oak Sts., Aurora, IL 60506. Mailing Address: P.O. Box 905, Aurora, IL 60507-0905. Tel.: 630-906-0650. Fax: 630-906-0657.
E-mail: jjshanahan@aurorahistory.net
Web Site: www.aurorahistoricalsociety.org
Founded: 1906.

Congressional District: 4
Key Personnel: Exec. Dir., John R. Jaros; Pres., Jessica Byrne; Sr. Cur., Dennis Buck; Museum Shop Mgr., Jacqueline Shanahan.
Personnel Profile: Full-Time Paid 3; Part-Time Paid 4; Part-Time Volunteers 45.
Governing Authority: society; nonprofit organization. Affiliated with Aurora Historical Society. Tax-exempt.
Local History Museum: housed in 1857 mansion.
Collections: Indian and pioneer artifacts; mastodon bones; 19th & early 20th-century tools & household items; Victorian furnishings; timepieces; musical instruments; local photographs, books, documents; vehicles; locally manufactured goods; railroad items.
Research Fields: local history & genealogy.
Facilities: library; research room.
Activities: guided group tours; slide-lecture presentations; tour groups. Museum Sponsors: Fourth of July Bell-Ringing Ceremony; Christmas Open House.
Publications: booklets on history of Aurora; bimonthly newsletter; photos of museum.
Hours & Admission Prices: Tanner House: seasonal Mon. & Sat. 12-3. Art & History Center: Wed.-Sun. 12-4. Adults $3, students & seniors $1.50; members no charge.
Attendance: 10,000 (accurate)
Membership: Student & Senior Citizen $15; Individual $25; Family $35; Patron $100; Benefactor $250; Life $500; Business & Organization: $100, $250, $500 & $1,000.

AURORA PUBLIC ART COMMISSION, 20 E. Downer Place, Aurora, IL 60505-3302. Mailing Address: 44 E. Downer Place, Aurora, IL 60505-3302. Tel.: 630-906-0654. Fax: 630-906-6892.
E-mail: rchurch@aurora-il.org
Web Site: www.aurora-il.org
Founded: 1996.
Congressional District: 14
Key Personnel: Chm., Chris Hoban; Dir. & Cur., Rena J. Church.
Personnel Profile: Full-Time Paid 2; Part-Time Paid 3.
Governing Authority: municipal; nonprofit. Parent Institution: City of Aurora. Tax-exempt.
Art Commission: located in Stolp Island Historic District.
Collections: multi-dimensional in a variety of medium including oil, watercolor, intaglio, photography, as well as wooden & acrylic sculpture.
Activities: commission of major public pieces. Annual Events: photography competition & show; juried fine arts show; youth art program in summer.
Hours & Admission Prices: Wed.-Sun. 12-4. Adults $3, seniors & students $1.50; discounts to AAM members; children under 12 no charge. ♿
Attendance: 9,000 (accurate)

AURORA REGIONAL FIRE MUSEUM, (M), New York Ave. & Broadway, Aurora, IL 60507. Mailing Address: P.O. Box 1782, Aurora, IL 60507-1782. Tel.: 630-892-1572.
E-mail: arfminfo@aol.com
Web Site: www.auroraregionalfiremuseum.org
Founded: 1990.
Key Personnel: Mgr., Deborah Davis; Cur., David Lewis.
Personnel Profile: Full-Time Paid 2; Part-Time Volunteers 12.
Governing Authority: private; nonprofit organization. Tax-exempt: 501(c)(3).
Firefighting Museum: housed in the 1894 Old Central Fire Station.
Collections: firefighting history in Aurora & surrounding communities.
Facilities: library; 50-seat auditorium; 15,000 sq. ft. exhibit space; theater. Museum-related items for sale.
Activities: films; formal education programs; lectures. Annual Event: Fire Engine Muster.
Publications: quarterly newsletter, Fire Museum News.
Hours & Admission Prices: Thurs.-Sat. 1-4; groups by appointment. Adults $3.50, seniors & firefighters $2.50, children 12 & under $2. Closed all major holidays.
Attendance: 3,000 (estimated)
Membership: Student & Senior $10; Individual $15; Family $25; Patron $50; Institution $100; Life $500.

BLACKBERRY FARM'S PIONEER VILLAGE, 100 S. Barnes Rd., Aurora, IL 60506-8118. Tel.: 630-892-1550. Fax: 630-892-1597.
E-mail: ssmith@fvpd.net
Web Site: www.foxvalleyparkdistrict.org
Founded: 1969.
Congressional District: 15
Key Personnel: Exec. Dir., Steve Messerli; Mgr., Sandy Smith; Bd. Pres., Rose Smilays; Seasonal Cur., Amy Zillman; Supvr., Laureen Baumgartner.
Personnel Profile: Full-Time Paid 2; Part-Time Paid 40; Part-Time Volunteers 3.
Governing Authority: nonprofit organization. Parent Institution: Fox Valley Park District, 712 S. River St., Aurora, IL 60507. Tel.: 708-897-0516. Branch Museum: Red Oak Nature Center, Batavia, IL. Tax-exempt.
Village Museum.
Collections: restored carriages; 19th-century farm equipment; contents of 11 stores; decorative arts. Historic Buildings: stave silo; late 19th-century Big Rock train station; 1840s post and beam house built by John Wagner, Aurora, IL.
Research Fields: agricultural history of northern Illinois; c.1830-1910 one-room school in the late 19th century.
Facilities: botanical garden; classroom; food service. Gift items for sale.
Activities: guided tours; arts festivals; craft workshops; daily craft demonstrations; formally organized educational programs; permanent & temporary exhibitions.
Publications: brochure.
Hours & Admission Prices: May to Labor Day Mon.-Fri. 9:30-3:30, Sat.-Sun. 11-5; Sept. Sat.-Sun. 11-5; Oct. call for hours. Adults $7, children $6; discounts to members. ♿
Attendance: 72,500 (accurate)
Membership: Fox Valley Park District: Resident $25; Nonresident $30.

SCHINGOETHE CENTER FOR NATIVE AMERICAN CULTURES, Dunham Hall - Lower Level, 1400 Marseillaise Place (corner Marseillaise & Randall Rd.), Aurora, IL 60506-4892. Mailing Address: c/o Aurora University, 347 S. Gladstone Ave., Aurora, IL 60506-4892. Tel.: 630-844-7843. Fax: 630-844-6529.
E-mail: museum@aurora.edu
Web Site: www.aurora.edu/museum
Founded: 1989.
Congressional District: 14
Key Personnel: Exec. Dir. & Chief Cur., Meg Bero; Aurora Univ. Pres., Rebecca Sherrick; Finance Dir., Beth Reisenweber; Asst. Cur., Dave Spencer.
Personnel Profile: Full-Time Paid 3; Part-Time Paid 4; Part-Time Volunteers 12.
Governing Authority: private university; not-for-profit. Parent Institution: Aurora University. Tax-exempt.
Native American Museum.
Collections: Native American art; cultural materials of North, Central & South American peoples from prehistoric times to the present.
Major Exhibits: Frida Kahlo: Through the Eyes of Nickolas Muray (T), 1/31/10-3/28/10; IndVisible (T), 12/18/10-2/27/11.
Research Fields: cultural history; visual arts; intercultural contact; pedagogy; material culture studies.
Facilities: 3 exhibit galleries; research library of Native American art & culture, Native American periodicals, rare books, newspapers of Native American origin & pamphlet file available to the public; educational facilities through the university.
Activities: docent program; films; formal education programs for children & undergraduate or graduate college students; guided tours; lectures; loan & temporary exhibitions; school loan service; art & craft presentations by Native Americans; in-service programs for teachers. Annual Events: Native American film series.
Hours & Admission Prices: Academic Year: Tues. 10-7, Wed.-Fri. 10-4, Sun. 1-4; Summer: Tues.-Fri. 10-4. Suggested Donation: adults $3, students & seniors $2, children under 12 $1. Closed university holidays. ♿
Attendance: 9,912 (accurate)
Membership: Student $15; Individual $25; Family $45; Patron & Contributor $100; Benefactor $500.

SCITECH HANDS ON SCIENCE CENTER, 18 W. Benton, Aurora, IL 60506-6013. Tel.: 630-859-3434, ext. 218. Fax: 630-859-8692.
E-mail: joyce@scitechmuseum.org
Web Site: www.scitechmuseum.org
Founded: 1988.
Congressional District: 14
Key Personnel: Exec. Dir., Dr. Shawn Carlson, Ph.D.; Chm. (V), Dr. David James; Pres. (V), John Gudenas; Deputy Dir., David Alexander; Museum Shop Mgr., Teresa Lentz.
Personnel Profile: Full-Time Paid 6; Part-Time Paid 12; Part-Time Volunteers 1; Interns 1.
Governing Authority: nonprofit organization. Tax-exempt: 501(c)(3).
Science & Technology Museum: housed in historic former Aurora Post Office Building.
Collections: science & technology hands on exhibits on weather, light & color, heat, mathematics, sound & music, magnets & electricity, physics, chemistry, biology, astronomy & nuclear physics.
Facilities: outdoor science park. Science-related materials for sale.

Activities: informal educational programs for children; field trips; camps; overnights; parties.
Publications: newsletter.
Hours & Admission Prices: Summer: Mon.-Sat. 10-5, Sun. 12-5. Winter: Tues.-Fri. 10-3, Sat. 10-5, Sun. 12-5. Admission $8, seniors 60 & over $7; discount to ASTC members; children 3 & under no charge. Closed New Year's Eve; Memorial Day; Independence Day; Thanksgiving. ♿
Attendance: 52,000 (accurate)
Membership: Single $60; Family $75; Business Member $300; Life Member $1,500.

Barrington

THE BARRINGTON AREA HISTORICAL SOCIETY, 212 W. Main St., Barrington, IL 60010-3011. Tel.: 847-381-1730. Fax: 847-381-1766.
Founded: 1969.
Congressional District: 12
Key Personnel: C.E.O. & Pres., Michael J. Harkins; Coord., Dee Larson.
Governing Authority: nonprofit organization. Tax-exempt: 501(c)(3).
History Museum: housed in two Folk Victorian Houses.
Collections: early farm tools & equipment; blacksmith & harness making tools; clothing & furniture; memorabilia from community & surrounding areas; Barrington area history including photos & maps; blacksmith shop.
Research Fields: historic sites in area; history of Barrington & Cuba Townships.
Facilities: meeting room.
Activities: guided tours; permanent & changing exhibitions; school programs; slide lectures; community programs; genealogy series.
Publications: monthly newsletter; annual report.
Hours & Admission Prices: Tues.-Fri. 10-4, Sat. 10-1. Tours by appointment. Blacksmith Shop: Sat. 12-4. ♿
Membership: Senior Citizen $10; Senior Citizen Couple $15; Individual $25; Family $35; Business & Organization $50; Annual Contributing $100; Patron $250; Benefactor $500; Annual Friend $1,000.

CRABTREE NATURE CENTER, 3 Stover Rd., Barrington, IL 60010-5342. Tel.: 847-381-6592.
Founded: 1971.
Congressional District: 8
Governing Authority: Parent Institution: Forest Preserve District of Cook County. Tax-exempt.
Nature Center.
Collections: wildlife & their habitats; native plants.
Facilities: nature trails.
Activities: group talks; educational programs.
Publications: monthly program guide; trail maps.
Hours & Admission Prices: March to late Oct. Sat.-Thurs. 9-4:30; late Oct. to Feb. Sat.-Thurs. 9-3:30. No charge; donations accepted. Closed New Year's Day; Thanksgiving; Christmas.

Batavia

BATAVIA DEPOT MUSEUM, 155 Houston St., Batavia, IL 60510-1924. Tel.: 630-406-5274. Fax: 630-593-5202.
E-mail: carlah@bataviaparks.org
Web Site: bataviahistoricalsociety.org
Founded: 1960.
Congressional District: 14
Key Personnel: C.E.O. & Dir., Carla Hill; Pres., Richard A. Benson; Vice Pres. & Program Chm., Patty Rosenberg; Recording Sec., Chris Winter.
Governing Authority: society, municipal; nonprofit organization. Parent Institution: Batavia Historical Society & the Batavia Park District. Tax-exempt: 501(c)(3).
Historical Society Museum: housed in 1854 Batavia Depot, one of the oldest railroad station on the Burlington Line.
Collections: local history; clothing; tools; railroad; windmills; pioneer; genealogical; photographs of local historic houses; Mary Todd Lincoln display; manuscripts.
Research Fields: local genealogy; windmills; Newton Wagons; Mary Todd Lincoln.
Facilities: library of historical books & manuscripts.
Activities: guided tours; permanent & temporary exhibitions; lectures.
Publications: quarterly circular, Newsletter of Historical Society; books, Batavia Past & Present; Historical Batavia; Little Town In A Big Woods (grade school level).
Hours & Admission Prices: Wed. & Fri.-Mon. 2-4; other times by appointment. No charge; donations accepted. ♿
Membership: Individual $3; Family & School $5; Life $50.

RED OAK NATURE CENTER, 2343 S. River St., Batavia, IL 60510-9664. Tel.: 630-897-1808.
Nature Center.
Collections: hands-on exhibits; natural history; wildlife & their habitats; plants.
Facilities: nature trails.
Activities: educational programs; special events.
Hours & Admission Prices: Mon.-Fri. 9-4:30, Sat.-Sun. 10-3. No charge.

Belleville

LABOR AND INDUSTRY MUSEUM, 123 N. Church St., Belleville, IL 62220-1418. Tel.: 618-222-9430.
E-mail: laborandindustry@yahoo.com
Web Site: www.laborandindustrymuseum.org
Founded: 1996.
Key Personnel: Chm. (V), Pat Schmeder; Coord. Collections, Judy Belleville.
Governing Authority: Tax-exempt.
History Museum.
Collections: Illinois' labor & industry history; photographs.
Facilities: archives; learning center.
Hours & Admission Prices: Sat. 10-4; tours by appointment.

ST. CLAIR COUNTY HISTORICAL SOCIETY, 701 E. Washington St., Belleville, IL 62220-3846. Tel.: 618-234-0600. Fax: 618-234-3060.
Founded: 1905.
Congressional District: 57
Key Personnel: Pres., Daphne Sumner; Treas., Drew Awsumb; Museum Shop Mgr., Norma Walker.
Personnel Profile: Part-Time Paid 1; Part-Time Volunteers 10.
Governing Authority: society; board of directors. Branch Museum: 1830, The Kunz House, 602 Fulton St., Belleville, IL 62221. Tax-exempt.
Historical Museum: housed in 1866, Victorian home.
Collections: period furniture; costumes; tools; memorabilia; manuscript collections.
Research Fields: historical records of St. Clair County.
Facilities: research library; meeting room.
Activities: guided tours; permanent exhibitions; landmark & historic site awards; lectures. Annual Events: Annual Fashion Promenade and Luncheon; Candlelight House Tour in December.
Publications: monthly newsletter; annual journal.
Hours & Admission Prices: Mon.-Fri. 10-2; other times by appointment. Adults $2, children $1; discounts to AAM members; members no charge. Closed national holidays. ♿
Attendance: 1,500 (estimated)
Membership: Student $5; Individual $25; Family $40; Business $75; Life $500.

WILLIAM & FLORENCE SCHMIDT ART CENTER, (M), 2500 Carlyle Ave., Belleville, IL 62221-5859. Tel.: 618-222-5278; 800-222-5131, ext. 5278.
Founded: 2002.
Congressional District: 12
Key Personnel: Exec. Dir., Libby Reuter; Asst. Cur. & Registrar, Christina Cosio
Art Center.
Collections: works by contemporary artists.
Hours & Admission Prices: Academic Year: Tues.-Wed. & Fri.-Sat. 11-5, Thurs. 11-8; Summer: Tues.-Wed. & Fri. 11-5, Thurs. 11-8, Sat. 10-2. No charge.

Bellflower

BELLFLOWER HISTORICAL AND GENEALOGICAL SOCIETY, 210 N. Latcha St., Bellflower, IL 61724. Mailing Address: 407 W. Center St., Bellflower, IL 61724-9506. Tel.: 309-722-3757 & 3467.
Founded: 1976.
Congressional District: 22
Key Personnel: Co-Pres. (V), Dorothy Woliung; Co-Pres. (V), Phyllis Kumler.
Personnel Profile: Part-Time Volunteers 6.
Governing Authority: nonprofit. Tax-exempt.
Historic Building: early 1900 Illinois Central Railroad Depot.
Collections: local memorabilia.
Activities: guided tours; permanent & temporary exhibitions.
Publications: Highlights.
Hours & Admission Prices: By appointment. No charge; donations accepted.
Attendance: 128 (accurate)
Membership: Single $2; Couple $3; Family $4.

Belvidere

BOONE COUNTY HISTORICAL MUSEUM, 311 Whitney Blvd., Belvidere, IL 61008-3609. Tel.: 815-544-8391. Fax: 815-547-1691.
E-mail: info@boonecountyhistoricalmuseum.org
Web Site: www.boonecountyhistoricalmuseum.org
Founded: 1968.
Congressional District: 16
Key Personnel: Dir., Mary Hale; Pres., Carol Rowe; Research, Lonna Bentley.
Personnel Profile: Full-Time Paid 1; Part-Time Paid 2; Part-Time Volunteers 25.
Governing Authority: nonprofit organization. Subsidiary Institution: Leader Building 1890 Collection. Library: 121 E. Locust, Belvidere, IL 61008. Tel: 815-544-2580. Tax-exempt: 501(c)(3).
Historical Society Museum.
Collections: Civil War; sewing machines; washing machines; 19th-century Duxstad Log House; Newton natural history of Boone County; Chrysler automobiles; manuscripts; Native American arrow-heads, hatchets, axes; farm tools; archival files with photographs, letters & records of Boone County; photos; genealogy; pioneer artifacts; toys; vindex; Judy Ford (former Miss America) exhibit; 1906 Elridge Runabout, artifacts from the National Sewing Machine Company; vintage clothing from 1830's to present.
Research Fields: pertaining to collections, people, houses, land, genealogy, & events.
Facilities: 100-vol. library of history pertaining to Boone County for use on premises only; chapel. Books for sale.
Activities: guided tours; lectures; films; genealogy, maps; weddings.
Publications: books, Landmarks, The Story of Boone County; Then & Now; quarterly society newsletter; reprint, 95th Illinois Regiment.
Hours & Admission Prices: Museum: June Tues.-Fri. 9-4, Sat. 9-3; July-May Mon.-Fri. 9-4, Sat. 9-3; other times by appointment. No charge; donations accepted. Library: Tues.-Fri. 9-3. ♿
Attendance: 4,000 (estimated)
Membership: Senior 55 & over and Student $10; Individual $25; Grandpass $35; Family $50; Organizations & Small Business $100; Business (21 plus employees) $250.

Bement

BRYANT COTTAGE, 146 E. Wilson Ave., Bement, IL 61813-1250. Mailing Address: P.O. Box 41, Bement, IL 61813-0041. Tel.: 217-678-8184.
Web Site: www.bement.com/bryant.htm
Founded: 1925.
Congressional District: 15
Key Personnel: Site Mgr., Marilyn L. Ayers.
Personnel Profile: Full-Time Paid 1.
Governing Authority: Parent Institution: Illinois Historic Preservation Agency. Tax-exempt: 501(c)(3).
Historic House Museum: 1856 Bryant Cottage where the Lincoln-Douglas Debates were verbally agreed to be part of the 1858 Senate campaigns.
Collections: original & period furnishings.
Research Fields: 1850s lifestyle; local history; Lincoln & Douglas.
Activities: guided tours; lectures; permanent exhibitions; school program.
Publications: Historic Illinois; brochures.
Hours & Admission Prices: Call for hours. Donations accepted. Closed New Year's Day; Martin Luther King Jr. Day; President's Day; Thanksgiving; Christmas. ♿

Bishop Hill

BISHOP HILL HERITAGE MUSEUM, Steeple Building, 103 N. Bishop Hill St., Bishop Hill, IL 61419. Mailing Address: P.O. Box 92, Bishop Hill, IL 61419-0092. Tel.: 309-927-3899. Fax: 309-927-3010.
E-mail: bhha@winco.net
Web Site: www.bishophill.com
Founded: 1962.
Congressional District: 17
Key Personnel: Pres. (V), Warren Schulz; Vice Pres., Don Loveall; Dir., Michael D. Wendel; Museum Shop Mgr., Sally R. Smith.
Personnel Profile: Full-Time Paid 2; Part-Time Paid 4; Part-Time Volunteers 30; Interns 1.
Governing Authority: nonprofit organization. Parent Institution: Bishop Hill Heritage Association. Tax-exempt: 501(c)(3).
History Museum: housed in 1854 Steeple Building, located in Bishop Hill, a Swedish communal settlement founded in 1846 by religious dissenters.
Collections: artifacts of Bishop Hill Colony; manuscript collections; photograph collections. Historic Buildings: 1857 blacksmith shop; 1853 Bishop Hill Colony store; 1854 steeple; 1855 dairy building.
Research Fields: history of Swedish immigration; history of Bishop Hill Colony.
Facilities: 400-vol. library of archival materials on Bishop Hill Colony & Swedish immigration available in Steeple building by appointment; reading room. Swedish imports, folk & designer crafts for sale.
Activities: lectures; craft workshops; demonstrations of traditional folk crafts; formally organized education programs for adults; Bishop Hill documentary; costume guided tours.
Publications: quarterly news bulletin.
Hours & Admission Prices: Jan.-March daily 10-4; April-Oct. Sun. 12-5, Mon.-Sat. 10-5. No charge; donations accepted. ♿
Attendance: 100,000 (estimated)
Membership: Sustaining $100-$249; Patron $250-$499; Benefactor $500 & up.

BISHOP HILL STATE HISTORIC SITE, 304 S. Bishop Hill St., Bishop Hill, IL 61419-0104. Mailing Address: P.O. Box 104, Bishop Hill, IL 61419-0104. Tel.: 309-927-3345. Fax: 309-927-3343.
E-mail: bishophill@winco.net
Web Site: www.bishophill.com
Founded: 1946.
Congressional District: 17
Key Personnel: C.E.O., Maynard Crossland; Pres. Bd. Trustees, Julie Cellini; Site Mgr., Martha Downey.
Personnel Profile: Full-Time Paid 5; Part-Time Paid 3; Part-Time Volunteers 30.
Governing Authority: state. Parent Institution: State of Illinois, Illinois Historic Preservation Agency, Division of Historic Sites, Old State Capitol, Springfield, IL 62701. Tax-exempt.
History Museum: complex consists of 1848 Colony Church, located on the site of a Swedish communal settlement, and 1850s Bjorklund Hotel.
Collections: paintings pertaining to Bishop Hill colony by Olof Krans; artifacts & furniture from Bishop Hill colony during 1846-1861. Historic Building: 1852 Bjorklund Hotel operated by the Bishop Hill colony; 1988 Bishop Hill Museum.
Research Fields: restoration & immigrant history 1840-1860; Illinois history 1845-1870; Illinois Folk Art.
Facilities: picnic area.
Activities: guided tours; permanent exhibitions.
Hours & Admission Prices: March-April Wed.-Sun. 9-5; May-Oct. daily 9-5; Nov.-Feb. Wed.-Sun. 9-4. Suggested Donation: adults $2, children 17 & under $1. Closed New Year's Day; Martin Luther King Jr. Day; Presidents' Day; Columbus Day; Veterans Day; Thanksgiving; Christmas. ♿
Attendance: 79,381 (accurate)

Blandinsville

BLANDIN HOUSE MUSEUM, 215 S. Chestnut St., Blandinsville, IL 61420. Mailing Address: 755 W. Adams, Blandinsville, IL 61420-9169. Tel.: 309-652-3673.
Founded: 1970.
History Museum.
Collections: local history & culture; period artifacts; photographs.
Hours & Admission Prices: Mon.-Fri. call for hours.
Membership: Annual $10.

Bloomington

THE DAVID DAVIS MANSION, 1000 E. Monroe Dr., Bloomington, IL 61701-3333. Tel.: 309-828-1084. Fax: 309-828-3493.
E-mail: davismansion@yahoo.com
Web Site: www.davismansion.org
Founded: 1960.
Congressional District: 15
Key Personnel: Site Mgr., Marcia Young; Asst. Mgr., Jeannie Riordan; Cur., Jeff Saulsbery; Museum Shop Mgr., Bekah Litchfield.
Personnel Profile: Full-Time Paid 3; Part-Time Paid 2; Part-Time Volunteers 80; Interns 4.
Governing Authority: Parent Institution: Illinois Historic Preservation Agency. Tax-exempt.
Historic House: 1872 David Davis' Second Empire Italianate brick mansion. David Davis was the campaign manager for Abraham Lincoln who appointed him as a judge of the U.S. Supreme Court.
Collections: furnishings; decorative arts; textiles; 19th-century mechanical systems; barn artifacts.
Research Fields: 19th century cultural, social & political history; decorative arts; architectural history.
Facilities: visitor center.
Activities: guided tours; special events; educational programs.
Publications: David Davis Mansion Newsletter; Clover Lawn Souvenir booklet; Sarah's Garden; Managing Clover Lawn: A Guide to the Kitchen of Sarah Davis and the Life That Filled It.

Hours & Admission Prices: Wed.-Sun. 9-4. No charge; donations accepted. Closed New Year's Day; Thanksgiving; Christmas; state holidays. ♿
Attendance: 30,000 (estimated)
Membership: Individual $35; Family $50.

MCLEAN COUNTY ARTS CENTER, 601 N. East St., Bloomington, IL 61701-3094. Tel.: 309-829-0011. Fax: 309-829-4928.
E-mail: info@mcac.org
Web Site: www.mcac.org
Founded: 1922.
Congressional District: 15
Key Personnel: C.E.O. & Exec. Dir., Douglas Johnson; Cur., Alison Hatcher; Education Coord., Tony Preston-Schreck.
Personnel Profile: Full-Time Paid 2; Part-Time Paid 3; Part-Time Volunteers 8; Interns 4.
Governing Authority: nonprofit organization. Tax-exempt.
Arts Center.
Collections: permanent collection of McLean County Art Association.
Facilities: sales & rental gallery; rotating exhibits. Art works for sale.
Activities: gallery talks; permanent & temporary collections; educational program; monthly shows; trips to various museums.
Publications: quarterly newsletter, ART'S ALIVE!
Hours & Admission Prices: Tues. 10-7, Wed.-Fri. 10-5, Sat. 12-4. No charge; donations accepted. Closed national holidays. ♿
Attendance: 12,548 (accurate)
Membership: Individual $30; Family $50; Sponsor $100; Patron $250; Benefactor $500; Major Benefactor $1,000.

* **MCLEAN COUNTY MUSEUM OF HISTORY, (M),** 200 N. Main, Bloomington, IL 61701-3912. Tel.: 309-827-0428. Fax: 309-827-0100.
E-mail: mcmh@mchistory.org
Web Site: www.mchistory.org
Founded: 1892.
Congressional District: 15
Key Personnel: Exec. Dir., Greg Koos; Pres., Robert Watkins; Treas., Pete Borowski; Mgr. Devel. Operations, Graham Cowger; Cur., Susan Hartzold; Librarian & Archivist, William Kemp; Dir. Mktg., Jeff Woodord; Dir. Education, Candace Summers; Volunteer Coord., Mary Anne Scheirman.
Personnel Profile: Full-Time Paid 8; Part-Time Paid 5; Part-Time Volunteers 298; Interns 6.
Governing Authority: society; nonprofit. Parent Institution: McLean County Historical Society. Tax-exempt: 501(c)(3).
Historic Building: 1904 courthouse.
Collections: McLean County from prehistoric to present; textiles; costumes; settlement period collections; Civil War artifacts; 19th-century material culture; archives.
Major Exhibits: A Turbulent Time: Perspectives of the Vietnam War, 11/09-8/7/10; Come & Get It! The Way We Ate 1830-2008, 11/09-8/6/11.
Research Fields: local history.
Facilities: 10,000-vol. library pertaining to local history & genealogy; archives; discovery room. Books for sale.
Activities: guided tours; docent programs; organized education programs for children & undergraduate or graduate college students affiliated with Illinois State University & Illinois Wesleyan University; research services; permanent, traveling & temporary exhibit.
Publications: books, The Illustrated History of McLean County; The Heart of the Cornbelt: An Illustrated History of Corn Farming in McLean County, Illinois; Places of Pride: The Work & Photography of Clara Brian; A Matter of Life & Death: Health Illness & Medicine in McLean County; Prairie Roots: A Guide to Illinois Genealogy; History of African-Americans in McLean County, Illinois 1835-1975; Irish Immigrants in McLean County, Illinois; It Is Begun: The Pantagraph Reports The Civil War; Lincoln's Bloomington and Normal Illinois: A Tour Narrated by Abraham Lincoln; Gifts to the Prairie: The Work of Pioneer Nurserymen and the Art of the Prestele Family.
Hours & Admission Prices: June-Aug. Mon. & Wed.-Sat. 10-5, Tues. 10-9; Sept.-May Mon. & Wed.-Sat. 10-5, Sun. 1-5. Adults $5; discounts to Time Travelers, AAM & ICOM members; students & society members no charge. Closed national holidays. ♿
Attendance: 29,902 (accurate)
Membership: Student/Senior $15; Primary $30; Allin $50; Davis $100; Fell $250; Fifer $500; Stevenson $750; Lincoln $1,000.

MILLER PARK ZOO, 1020 S. Morris Ave., Bloomington, IL 61701-6307. Tel.: 309-434-2250. Fax: 309-434-2823.
E-mail: jtobias@cityblm.org
Web Site: www.millerparkzoo.org
Founded: 1891.
Key Personnel: Supt., John Tobias; Museum Shop Mgr., Jennifer Rogers.
Personnel Profile: Full-Time Paid 10.
Zoo.
Collections: big cats; Wallaby Walk-About & Rain Forest exhibits; children's zoo; bald eagles; wolves; owls; animals of Asia.
Hours & Admission Prices: Zoo: daily 9:30-4:30. Grounds: Memorial Day-Labor Day daily 9-6; Labor Day-Memorial Day 9-5. Adults 13-59 $4.50, senior citizens 60 & over and children 3-12 $3.50; children under 3 no charge. Closed Thanksgiving; Christmas Day. ♿
Attendance: 113,641 (accurate)
Membership: Senior $10; Individual $25; Family & Grandparent $50; Extended Family $75.

PRAIRIE AVIATION MUSEUM, 2929 E. Empire St., Bloomington, IL 61704-5452. Tel.: 309-663-7632. Fax: 309-663-8411.
Web Site: www.prairieaviationmuseum.org
Founded: 1984.
Personnel Profile: Part-Time Volunteers 100.
Governing Authority: Tax-exempt.
Aviation History Museum.
Collections: aviation history; aircraft; personal artifacts; photographs.
Activities: special events.
Hours & Admission Prices: Tues.-Sat. 11-4, Sun. 12-4. Adults $4, children 6-11 $2; children 5 & under and members no charge. Closed New Year's Day; Thanksgiving; Christmas.
Attendance: 3,000 (estimated)
Membership: Individual $30.

Bourbonnais

EXPLORATION STATION....A CHILDREN'S MUSEUM, 459 N. ennedy Dr., Bourbonnais, IL 60914-1970. Tel.: 815-933-9905. Fax: 815-928-6054.
E-mail: sarahw@btpd.org
Web Site: www.exploration-station.org
Founded: 1987.
Congressional District: 11
Key Personnel: Treas., Mileen Joines; Museum Shop Mgr., Cathy Gagnon.
Personnel Profile: Full-Time Paid 3; Part-Time Paid 15; Part-Time Volunteers 75.
Governing Authority: nonprofit. Bourbonnais Township Park District. Tax-exempt.
Children's Museum.
Collections: aircraft & NASA replicas.
Activities: guided tours; lectures; participatory & traveling exhibitions; study clubs; storytelling; art & science workshops; workshops for toddlers; Sat. specials; hands-on interactive exhibits for children. Annual Events: A Night in Sleepy Hollow.
Publications: quarterly newsletter; seasonal brochure.
Hours & Admission Prices: April-Aug. Mon., Wed. & Fri.-Sat. 10-5, Tues. & Thurs. 10-5:30; Sept.-March Tues. & Thurs. 10-5:30, Wed. & Fri.-Sat. 10-5. Adults $5, children & senior citizens $4; discounts to members. ♿
Attendance: 39,000 (accurate)
Membership: Single Parent $45; Family & Grandparent $60.

Brookfield

CHICAGO ZOOLOGICAL SOCIETY/BROOKFIELD ZOO, 3300 Golf Rd., Brookfield, IL 60513-1060. Tel.: 708-688-8400. Fax: 708-485-3532. TDD: 708-485-0360.
E-mail: webmaster@czs.org
Web Site: www.czs.org
Founded: 1921.
Congressional District: 3
Key Personnel: Chm. (V), W. C. Kunkler; Women's Bd. Pres., Jill Javors; C.E.O. & Pres., Stuart D. Strahl, Ph.D.; Sr. Vice Pres. Finance & Administration, Ken Kaduk; Sr. Vice Pres. Institutional Advancement, Cindy Zeigler; Sr. Vice Pres. Conservation, Education, & Training, Alejandro Grajal, Ph.D.; Sr. Vice Pres. Animal Programs, Dan Wharton, Ph.D.
Personnel Profile: Full-Time Paid 407; Part-Time Paid 1,221; Part-Time Volunteers 600; Interns 45.
Governing Authority: Managed by Chicago Zoological Society & owned by Cook County Forest Preserve District. Tax-exempt: 501(c)(3).
Zoo.
Collections: butterflies; scorpion; spider; salamander; frogs; tortoises; lizards; snakes; alligator; dwarf crocodile; chameleon; ostrich; emu; cassowary; heron; egret; ibis; stork; trumpeter swan; waterfowl; Humboldt penguin; wood stork; roadrunner; Andean condor; bald eagle; hawks; owls; peacock; tern; dove; touraco; keel-billed toucan; trumpeter hornbill; green-winged macaw; Mitchell's cockatoo; lorikeet; woodpecker; kookaburra; Micronesian kingfisher; hummingbirds; Bali mynah; red bird-of-paradise; tanagers; echidna; wombat; kangaroo; shrew; flying fox; bats; lemurs; capuchin;

mangabey; mandrill; colobus; tamarins; gibbon; orangutan; gorilla; sloth; anteater; mole-rat; porcupine; bottle-nosed dolphin; wolves; fox; African wild dog; sloth bear; brown bear; polar bear; otters; binturong; mongoose; meerkat; aardwolf; lion; caracal; leopard; tiger; seal; sea lion; aardvark; African elephant; rock hyrax; zebra; tapir; rhinoceros; hippopotamus; warthog; red river hog; camel; giraffe; okapi; bison; duiker; topi; kudu; addax; waterbuck; klipspringer; domesticated animals.
Research Fields: animal behavior; behavioral endocrinology; wildlife endocrinology; animal welfare science; ecological & evolutionary processes; molecular genetics; population genetics; population biology (restricted and/or captive populations); conservation biology; contraception & reproduction in animals; aging in animals; animal physiology; environmental physiology (UV light research); status of free-ranging populations; amphibian decline; marine mammal research; conservation medicine; disease dynamics & patterns; pathology; conservation psychology; visitor & other audience research.
Facilities: 10,000-vol. library of books & 210 scientific journals on biology, animal medicine, zoology, pathology, ecology, behavioral science & photography available for inter-library loan & use on premises; aquarium; restaurants; banquet facility; picnic area. Science books & animal art novelties for sale.
Activities: outdoor interactive game; carousel; college experiential learning opportunities; community outreach; docent & volunteer programs; educational programs; inter-museum loan & permanent exhibitions; outreach programs for underserved audiences; playgrounds; school of environmental education for high school students; Share the Care; special events; Splash Pad; subscription programs; tram tours; wild encounters; zoo camp.
Publications: quarterly member magazine, Gateways; biweekly member email; opt-in animal email; annual report.
Hours & Admission Prices: Memorial Day-Labor Day Mon.-Sat. 9:30-6, Sun. 9:30-7:30; Sept.-May daily 10-5. Adults $12, senior citizens 65 & over and children 3-11 $8; members, active military, reservists, Jan.-Feb. Tues., Thurs. & Sat.-Sun. & Oct.-Dec. Tues. & Thurs. no charge. Parking: buses $10.75, cars $8. Additional fees for shows & special areas. ♿
Attendance: 2,076,048 (accurate)
Membership: Senior $50; Individual $56; One Plus $62; Family $85; Family Plus $101; Supporting $195; Sustaining $395.

Buffalo Grove

RAUPP MEMORIAL MUSEUM, 901 Dunham Lane, Buffalo Grove, IL 60089. Tel.: 847-459-2318. Fax: 847-459-3148.
History Museum.
Collections: local history; period artifacts; photographs.
Hours & Admission Prices: Sun. 1-4, Mon.-Thurs. 11-4:30.

Cahokia

CAHOKIA COURTHOUSE STATE HISTORIC SITE, 107 Elm St., Cahokia, IL 62206-1014. Tel.: 618-332-1782. Fax: 618-332-1737.
Founded: 1940.
Congressional District: 12
Key Personnel: Site Supt., Molly McKenzie.
Personnel Profile: Full-Time Paid 3; Part-Time Paid 2; Part-Time Volunteers 60; Interns 1.
Governing Authority: state, nonprofit. Parent Institution: State of Illinois, Illinois Historic Preservation Agency, Historic Sites Div. Old State Capitol, Springfield, IL 62706. Tax-exempt: 501(c)(3).
History Museum: housed in 1737 residence.
Collections: artifacts; furniture. Historic Buildings: 1810 Jarrot Mansion; 1799 Holy Family Church; 1790 Martin-Boismenue House.
Research Fields: local history; French colonial architecture; territorial state government; American government in the old Northwest Territory; French colonial & American frontier lifeways.
Facilities: visitors center.
Activities: guided tours; lectures; permanent exhibitions; special events; living history programs.
Publications: bimonthly newsletter, Historic Illinois.
Hours & Admission Prices: Tues.-Sat. 9-5. No charge. Jarrot Mansion, Martin-Boismenue, Holy Family Church: by appointment. Closed major holidays. ♿
Attendance: 25,600 (estimated)

Cairo

MAGNOLIA MANOR, 2700 Washington Ave., Cairo, IL 62914-1458. Mailing Address: P.O. Box 286, Cairo, IL 62914-0286. Tel.: 618-734-0201. Fax: 618-734-0201.
Founded: 1952.
Congressional District: 24
Key Personnel: C.E.O. & Pres., Charles McGinness; Vice Pres., Elizabeth Morin; Cur. & Museum Shop Mgr., Tim Slapinski.
Personnel Profile: Full-Time Paid 1; Part-Time Volunteers 25.
Governing Authority: nonprofit organization. Owned & operated by Cairo Historical Association. Tax-exempt: 501(c)(3).
Historic House Museum: 1869 Magnolia Manor.
Collections: 19th-century furnishings; Cairo history; Civil War items.
Activities: guided tours. Museum Sponsors: Victorian Christmas.
Publications: cookbook; history book.
Hours & Admission Prices: Summer: Mon.-Sat. 9-4:30, Sun. 1-4:30. Adults $6, children $2. Closed New Year's Eve & Day; Easter; Independence Day; Thanksgiving; Christmas Eve, Day & week.
Attendance: 2,500 (estimated)
Membership: Individual $20.

Carbondale

THE SCIENCE CENTER, University Mall, 1237 E. Main Space C-8, Carbondale, IL 62901-5830. Tel.: 618-529-5431. Fax: 618-529-5431.
E-mail: thesciencecenter@hotmail.com
Web Site: yoursciencecenter.org
Founded: 1994.
Congressional District: 12
Key Personnel: C.E.O., Pamela Madden; Pres. (V), Gerard V. Smith; Financial Dir., Kristyn Pass.
Personnel Profile: Full-Time Paid 1; Full-Time Volunteers 1; Part-Time Paid 3; Part-Time Volunteers 20; Interns 2.
Governing Authority: private; nonprofit organization. Tax-exempt.
Children's Science Museum.
Collections: hands-on interactive exhibits based on scientific concepts for children 3-13 & their parents.
Facilities: educational facilities; 2,200 sq. ft. exhibit space. Museum-related items for sale.
Activities: docent program; education programs for children; loan exhibitions; summer camps; camp-ins.
Publications: quarterly newsletter, Discover Us.
Hours & Admission Prices: Mon.-Thurs. 10-6, Fri.-Sat. 10-7, Sun. 12-5:30. Admission $3.50; discount to ASTC members; children under 4 & members no charge. Closed Easter; Thanksgiving; Christmas. ♿
Attendance: 28,000 (accurate)

* **UNIVERSITY MUSEUM, (M),** Southern Illinois University Carbondale, 1000 Faner Dr., MC 4508, Carbondale, IL 62901-4328. Tel.: 618-453-5388. Fax: 618-453-7409.
E-mail: museum@siu.edu
Web Site: www.museum.siu.edu
Founded: 1869.
Congressional District: 22
Key Personnel: Dir. Museum & Museum Studies, Dona R. Bachman; Dir. Museum Education, Robert De Hoet; Cur. Collections, Lorilee C. Huffman; Cur. Exhibits, Nathaniel Steinbrink; Adjunct Cur. Geology, Harvey Henson; Sec., Joan Martin.
Personnel Profile: Full-Time Paid 5; Part-Time Paid 24; Part-Time Volunteers 75; Interns 8.
Governing Authority: state; university. Parent Institution: Southern Illinois University. Tax-exempt: 501(c)(3).
General Museum.
Collections: European & American paintings, drawings, prints from 13th to 20th century with emphasis on 19th & 20th centuries; 20th-century photography; 20th-century sculpture, metals, ceramics; musical instruments; extensive Oceanic collection; natural history; archaeology; geology; decorative arts; costumes; various Asiatic holdings; Southern Illinois history; Native American artifacts; WPA artifacts.
Major Exhibits: Ansel Adams (T), 1/10-3/10; Herbert Gentry, 1/10-3/10; Emmett Till (T), 1/10-3/10; Gary Kolb & Jay Needham, 3/10-5/10; Ed Shay Retrospective, 8/10-10/10.
Research Fields: history; geology; anthropology; archaeology; ethnology; museology; textiles; costumes; oral history; folklore; ethnomusicology.
Facilities: reference library; auditorium; laboratories; computer lab; galleries; sculpture garden; Japanese garden. Museum-related items for sale.
Activities: guided tours; lectures; films; inter-museum loans; temporary & traveling exhibitions; public outreach programs; volunteer program; museum studies program; museum student group.
Publications: catalogs for special exhibits; annual report; scholarly reports; museum newsletter.
Hours & Admission Prices: Tues.-Fri. 10-4, Sat.-Sun. 1-4; pre-arranged group tours available. No charge; donations accepted. Closed university & national holidays. ♿
Attendance: 15,000 (estimated)
Membership: Student $20; Individual $25; Family $50; Patron $100; Gold Patron $500; Corporate Patron $1,000.

Carmi

WHITE COUNTY HISTORICAL SOCIETY, 203 N. Church St., Carmi, IL 62821. Mailing Address: P.O. Box 121, Carmi, IL 62821-0121. Tel.: 618-382-8425.
Web Site: www.rootsweb.com/~ilwcohs
Founded: 1957.
Congressional District: 19
Key Personnel: Chm. (V), Lecta Hortin; Pres. (V), Henry Lewis.
Personnel Profile: Part-Time Paid 1; Part-Time Volunteers 40.
Governing Authority: society. Subsidiary Institution: Mary Smith Fay Genealogy Library. Branch Museums: Robinson-Stewart House, Main Cross St., Carmi, IL 62821; L. Haas Store Museum, E. Main St., Carmi, IL; Ratcliff Inn Museum, E. Main St., Carmi, IL; Matsel Cabin, Robinson St., Carmi, IL. Tax-exempt.
History Museum.
Collections: letters written by U.S. Senator John M. Robinson (1792-1843) & other pioneers. Historic Houses: 1814 Robinson-Stewart House; 1828 Ratcliff Inn; historic store: 1896 L. Haas Store; c.1850-1870 Matsel cabin; log house; pioneer cemetery.
Major Exhibits: Navy Harmonies - A Smithsonian Exhibit (T), 5/23/10-7/11/10.
Research Fields: genealogy.
Facilities: genealogy non-lending library. The 4 museums are located within a 1 1/2 block area. Historical cemetery, restored one-room school, several heritage homes & 1883 White County Court House are in the same close area.
Activities: guided tours; lectures; films; permanent exhibitions; dinner meetings with programs for membership & public.
Publications: members newspaper, White County Historian; Heritage Houses of White Co, IL; A Sketch of Crossville, IL in the Early Part of the 20th Century; Centennial History of Crossville and Phillips Township; books, Marriages from White County Illinois Vols. I-IV; Cemeteries of White County Illinois, Vols. I-II; Hamilton County Illinois Cemeteries & Probate Index; Early Land Grants of White County Illinois; White County Illinois Wills, 1816-1916; Index to White County Illinois Court Papers Vols. I-II; Original Land Grants, White County Illinois.
Hours & Admission Prices: Special events & other openings by appointment. Ratcliff Inn; Robinson-Stewart House; L. Haas Store Museum; Matsel Cabin; Genealogy Library: Tues.-Sat. 10-2. No charge; donation accepted. Closed national holidays.
Attendance: 1,500 (estimated)
Membership: Individual $25; Family $35; Sustaining $50; Patron $100; Corporate $500; Life $1,000.

Carterville

JOHN A. LOGAN COLLEGE MUSEUM, (M), 700 Logan College Rd., Carterville, IL 62918-2501. Tel.: 618-985-2828, ext. 8287. Fax: 618-985-2248. TDD: 618-985-2752.
E-mail: museum@jalc.edu
Web Site: www.jalc.edu/museum/index.html
Founded: 1983.
Congressional District: 12
Key Personnel: Dir., Adrienne Barkley Giffin.
Personnel Profile: Part-Time Paid 1; Part-Time Volunteers 10.
Governing Authority: public college. Parent Institution: John A. Logan College. Tax-exempt.
College Museum.
Collections: contemporary regional art & craft; wildlife art; historical memorabilia relating to the life of General John A. Logan. Historic Building: c.1860 one-room schoolhouse.
Facilities: 300-seat auditorium.
Activities: one room school, spring & fall sessions.
Hours & Admission Prices: During regular college hours: Mon.-Fri. 8-9, Sat. 9-5. No charge. ♿
Attendance: 40,000 (estimated)

Carthage

HANCOCK COUNTY HISTORICAL SOCIETY, 306 Walnut, Carthage, IL 62321-1354.
Founded: 1968.
Key Personnel: Pres., Larry Coleman; Vice Pres., Susan Cheney; Sec., Barbara Cochran; Treas., June Huff.
Personnel Profile: Part-Time Volunteers 15.
Governing Authority: society; nonprofit organization. Tax-exempt.
Historical Society: housed in Kibbe Museum at Carthage site.
Collections: personal artifacts; history books; genealogy books; census microfilm; area newspaper microfilm; obituary books; DAR books.
Research Fields: local history; genealogy.
Facilities: 250-vol. library of history books, atlases, directories, bound newspapers & genealogical material available for research on premises; 1830-1950, genealogical card index of early Hancock County families.
Activities: guided tours; lectures; radio programs; formally organized educational programs.
Publications: books, Pictorial History of Hancock County Illinois; Families of Hancock County Illinois, A Biographical History; I'll Be Seeing You World War II 1941-1945.
Hours & Admission Prices: Mon.-Fri. 9-3. No charge; donations accepted. Closed holidays. ♿
Attendance: 1,000 (estimated)
Membership: Active & Family $10; Life $125.

Champaign

CHAMPAIGN COUNTY HISTORICAL MUSEUM, (M), 102 E. University Ave., Champaign, IL 61820-4111. Tel.: 217-356-1010. Fax: 217-356-1478.
E-mail: director@champaignmuseum.org
Web Site: www.champaignmuseum.org
Founded: 1972.
Congressional District: 15
Key Personnel: Pres. (V), Hal Balbach; Treas., Sue Wood; Sec., Sandy Roberts.
Personnel Profile: Part-Time Volunteers 5.
Governing Authority: nonprofit organization. Tax-exempt: 501(c)(3).
County History Museum: housed in the Cattle Bank; built in 1858. Listed on the National Register of Historic Places.
Collections: period furnishings & furniture; documents; clothing; textiles; books; Champaign County history.
Research Fields: Champaign County history, including oral history; information on the built environment, the natural environment, agriculture & urban and rural community developments.
Facilities: 500-vol. library of books available for use on premises by appointment; reading room; classrooms. Books & gift items in keeping with historical theme for sale.
Activities: guided tours of local historic properties; lectures; concerts; temporary & traveling exhibitions; formally organized programs for children.
Publications: quarterly newsletter, Champaign County Historical Museum Newsletter; tour guide, Historic Sites in Champaign-Urbana; tour booklet, Historic Sites in Champaign County; booklets, Grass Roots Preservation; J.O. Cunningham; Views of the City of Champaign and the University of Illinois, 2009; essays, Historical Geography of Champaign County.
Hours & Admission Prices: Sat.-Sun. 12-5; other times by appointment; groups by appointment. No charge; donations accepted.
Attendance: 2,400 (estimated)
Membership: Student $5; Individual $25; Family $35; Business $100; Sustaining $100; Donor $250; Patron $500; Benefactor $1,000.

* **KRANNERT ART MUSEUM AND KINKEAD PAVILION, (M),** 500 E. Peabody Dr., University of Illinois, Champaign, IL 61820-6913. Tel.: 217-333-1861. Fax: 217-333-0883.
E-mail: kam@illinois.edu
Web Site: www.kam.illinois.edu
Founded: 1961.
Congressional District: 19
Key Personnel: Dir., Kathleen Harleman; Assoc. Dir., Chris Grant; Dir. Mktg. & Publications, Diane Schumacher; Dir. Education, Anne Sautman; Cur., Tumelo Mosaka; Cur., Allyson Purpura; Registrar, Kathleen Jones; Dept. Sec., Chris Schaede; Exhibition Designer, Eric Lemme; Exhibition Designer, Walter Wilson; Account Technician, Mona Sherman Dye; Security Chief, Don Matejowsky; Coord. Education Center., Virginia Erickson.
Personnel Profile: Full-Time Paid 18; Part-Time Paid 13; Part-Time Volunteers 155; Interns 3.
Governing Authority: university. Parent Institution: University of Illinois at Urbana-Champaign. Tax-exempt: 501(c)(3) & 170(c).
Art Museum.
Collections: Krannert Art Museum's collection of over 9,000 works of art represents the cultures of Africa, Asia, Europe and the Americas. In addition to the permanent collection, the Museum offers outstanding temporary exhibitions throughout the year.
Major Exhibits: Paradise on Earth: The Works of Reverend Howard Finster (T), 1/10-3/10; Baggage Allowance (T), 1/10-5/10; The Strange Life of Objects: The Art of Annette Lemieux (T), 10/10-12/10.
Research Fields: European & American art.
Facilities: auditorium; lecture room; cafe.
Activities: guided visits; lectures; gallery discussions; formally organized education programs; instructional materials loaned; inter-museum loan; permanent, temporary & traveling exhibitions; concerts & dance performances.
Publications: exhibition catalogs; brochures; biannual newsletter.

Hours & Admission Prices: Tues.-Wed. & Fri.-Sat. 9-5, Thurs. 9-9, Sun. 2-5. No charge; donations accepted. Closed national holidays. ♿
Attendance: 138,156 (accurate)
Membership: Student $15; Individual $45; Family & Dual $80; Benefactor $150; Patron $500; Director's Circle $1,000.

ORPHEUM CHILDREN'S SCIENCE MUSEUM, 346 N. Neil St., Champaign, IL 61820-3614. Tel.: 217-352-5895. Fax: 217-352-8160.
E-mail: orpheumkids@gmail.com
Web Site: www.orpheumkids.com
Founded: 1994.
Congressional District: 15
Key Personnel: C.E.O., Carolyn Knepp; Pres., James Quisenberry; Museum Shop Mgr., Susan Kitson.
Personnel Profile: Part-Time Paid 5; Part-Time Volunteers 113.
Governing Authority: Tax-exempt.
Children's Museum.
Collections: hands-on science exhibits.
Activities: school field trips; summer science camps; special events. Museum Sponsors: Weekend Wizards.
Publications: quarterly newsletter.
Hours & Admission Prices: Tues. 9-6, Wed.-Sun. 1-6; other times by appointment. Adults $3, children 2-18 $2; discounts to ACM & ASTC members; members no charge. Closed New Year's Day; Easter; Christmas. ♿
Attendance: 13,658 (accurate)
Membership: Child $20; Family & Sponsor $40; Family Plan $60; Super Family $100; Supporting $250.

PARKLAND COLLEGE ART GALLERY, 2400 W. Bradley Ave., Champaign, IL 61821-1899. Tel.: 217-351-2485 & 2200. Fax: 217-373-3899.
E-mail: lcostello@parkland.edu
Web Site: www.parkland.edu/gallery
Founded: 1980.
Congressional District: 15
Key Personnel: Dir., Lisa Costello; Chm. (V), Prof. Chris Berti; Exhibits Coord., Ricki Moore.
Personnel Profile: Full-Time Paid 1; Part-Time Paid 7; Part-Time Volunteers 35.
Governing Authority: college; nonprofit. Parent Institution: Parkland College. Tax-exempt.
Art Gallery.
Collections: contemporary art by regional & national artists: drawings; paintings; photography; crafts; sculpture; ethnic arts.
Major Exhibits: Indirect Objects: Captured Identities, 11/30/09-2/6/10; Parkland College Art & Design Juried Exhibition, 4/12/10-5/8/10; State of The Art 2010: National Biennial Ceramics Invitational, 4/15/10-3/30/10; Graphic Design: Student & Professional Juried Exhibition, 5/17/10-6/17/10.
Activities: lectures; loan & traveling exhibitions; TV & radio programs. Annual Events: Art Faculty Exhibit; National Drawing Invitational; Art Student Exhibit; High School Art Seminar. Biennial Events: State of the Art National Watercolor Invitational; Ceramics Invitational.
Publications: national watercolor catalogue; national biennial ceramics catalogue.
Hours & Admission Prices: Mon.-Thurs. 10-3 & 6-8, Fri. 10-3, Sat. 12-2. Summer: Mon.-Thurs. 10-3 & 6-8. No charge; donations accepted. Closed college & major holidays. ♿
Attendance: 10,000 (estimated)
Membership: Friend $25; Patron $50; Champion $50; Fellow $250; Guardian $500.

SOUSA ARCHIVES AND CENTER FOR AMERICAN MUSIC, Harding Band Bldg., Second Fl., 1103 S. Sixth St., Univ. of Illinois at Urbana-Champaign, Champaign, IL 61820. Tel.: 217-244-9309. Fax: 217-333-2868.
Web Site: www.library.uiuc.edu/sousa
Formerly: John Philip Sousa Museum
Founded: 1994.
Congressional District: 15
Key Personnel: Archivist Music & Fine Arts, Scott Schwartz; Asst. Archivist Music & Fine Arts, Adriana Cuervo.
Personnel Profile: Full-Time Paid 2; Part-Time Paid 3; Part-Time Volunteers 3.
Governing Authority: Parent Institution: University of Illinois. Tax-exempt.
American Music Museum.
Collections: original music compositions & arrangements by John Philip Sousa; 20th century electronic & avant-garde music; ethnomusicological research papers; period band uniforms; musical instruments; sound recording devices.
Major Exhibits: Roslyn Rensch: Harp Carvings and Irish Crosses, 11/09-12/09; The Women of the Marching Orange and Blue, 11/09-4/15/10; Beyond the Home: Women Redefining American Musical Life, 11/09-5/15/10; On The Road with the Women's Air Force Band, 11/09-6/15/10; Lady in White: The Virginia Root Story, 11/09-8/15/10.
Research Fields: musicology; ethnomusicology.
Activities: Museum Sponsors: American Music Month in November.
Hours & Admission Prices: Mon.-Fri. 8:30-12 & 1-5. No charge. ♿
Attendance: 2,508 (accurate)

WILLIAM M. STAERKEL PLANETARIUM, Parkland College, 2400 W. Bradley Ave., Champaign, IL 61821-1806. Tel.: 217-351-2568.
Planetarium.
Collections: Carl Zeiss M1015 Star Projecter.
Activities: special events; rental facilities; sky shows; children's programs; films.
Hours & Admission Prices: Aug.-May call for hours. Adults $4, children, seniors, & students $3; members no charge.

Charleston

* **TARBLE ARTS CENTER, EASTERN ILLINOIS UNIVERSITY, (M),** S. 9th St. at Cleveland Ave., Charleston, IL 61920. Mailing Address: 600 Lincoln Ave., Charleston, IL 61920-3011. Tel.: 217-581-2787. Fax: 217-581-7138.
E-mail: tarble@eiu.edu
Web Site: www.eiu.edu/~tarble
Founded: 1982.
Congressional District: 19
Key Personnel: Dir., Michael Watts; Pres., Thomas LeVeck; Interim Dean, Jeffrey P. Lynch; Cur. Education, Kit Morice.
Personnel Profile: Full-Time Paid 4; Part-Time Paid 9; Part-Time Volunteers 50.
Governing Authority: university. Parent Institution: Eastern Illinois University. Tax-exempt: 501(c)(3).
University Art Center.
Collections: late 20th century Illinois folk arts; contemporary U.S. works on paper; American Scene prints; Paul T. Sargent paintings.
Research Fields: folk arts of eastern & central Illinois.
Facilities: library containing audio & video tapes, slides of contemporary central & southern Illinois folk artists & artisans; classroom; sales & rental gallery; outdoor sculpture court; 6,400 sq. ft. modular exhibition space. Gift items for sale.
Activities: changing exhibitions; visiting artists & scholars; lectures & residencies; tours, enrichment & educational programs; classes; workshops; demonstrations; chamber music series; film & video; special events; docent program. Museum Sponsors: annual Celebration arts & humanities festival in April.
Publications: monthly newsletter, semesterly schedule of exhibitions & events; exhibition catalogues & brochures.
Hours & Admission Prices: late Aug. to mid-May Tues.-Fri. 10-5, Sat. 10-4, Sun. 1-4; mid-May to mid-Aug. Tues.-Sat. 10-4, Sun. 1-4. No charge; donations accepted. Closed major holidays. ♿
Attendance: 16,000 (estimated)
Membership: Friend $50; Sponsor $100; Patron $250; Benefactor $500; Associate $1,000.

Chatham

CHATHAM RAILROAD MUSEUM, 100 N. State St., Chatham, IL 62629-1350. Tel.: 217-483-7792.
Key Personnel: Pres., William Shannon
Railroad Museum: housed in 1902 era depot.
Collections: history of area & national railroads; passenger & freight railroad transportation from mid-1800s.
Hours & Admission Prices: 2nd & 4th Sun. 2-4. No charge; donations accepted. Closed holidays.

Chester

RANDOLPH COUNTY ARCHIVES AND MUSEUM, 1 Taylor St., Chester, IL 62233-1970. Tel.: 618-826-2667. Fax: 618-826-3750.
Founded: 1795.
Congressional District: 12
Key Personnel: Dir., Emily Lyons.
Personnel Profile: Part-Time Paid 1; Part-Time Volunteers 4.
Governing Authority: Parent Institution: Randolph County. Tax-exempt.
History Museum.
Collections: county history; photographs; documents.
Hours & Admission Prices: Mon.-Fri. 9-4; other times by appointment. No charge; donations accepted. Closed holidays.

Attendance: 800 (accurate)

Chicago

A. PHILIP RANDOLPH PULLMAN PORTER MUSEUM, 10406 S. Maryland Ave., Chicago, IL 60628-3090. Mailing Address: P.O. Box 6276, Chicago, IL 60680-6276. Tel.: 773-928-3935. Fax: 773-928-8372.
Web Site: www.aphiliprandolphmuseum.com
Key Personnel: Dir., Lyn Hughes.
Governing Authority: nonprofit organization. Tax-exempt: 501(c)(3).
African American History Museum.
Collections: A. Philip Randolph's life & history; labor history of African-Americans in America.
Activities: Museum Sponsors: Black History Events in February.
Hours & Admission Prices: April-Dec. 1 Thurs. 1-4, Fri.-Sat. 11-4; other times by appointment. General admission $5.

* **ADLER PLANETARIUM & ASTRONOMY MUSEUM, (M),** 1300 S. Lake Shore Dr., Chicago, IL 60605-2489. Tel.: 312-922-7827. Fax: 312-322-9909. TDD: 312-322-0995.
E-mail: museum@adlerplanetarium.org
Web Site: www.adlerplanetarium.org
Founded: 1930.
Congressional District: 7
Key Personnel: Chm. (V), Bryan Cressey; Pres., Dr. Paul Knappenberger, Jr.; Exec. Vice Pres. & C.O.O., Margaret A. Marek; Vice Pres. Research, Dr. Lucy Fortson; Dir. Astronomy, Dr. Geza Gyuk; Sr. Vice Pres. Finance & Admin. & C.F.O., Michael Lo Presti; Collections Mgr., Devon Pyle-Vowles; Dir. Museum Communications, Molly O'Connell; Dir. Foundation & Government Rels., Paula Pergament; Vice Pres. External Affairs, Charles L. Katzenmeyer; Dir. Campaign, Ginevra Ranney; Cur. Emerita, Marjorie K. Webster; Dir. Exhibits & Theaters, Susan Harrison; Vice Pres. Exhibits & Programs, Dr. Susan Wagner; Dir. Astronomy History, Dr. Marvin Bolt; Dir. Operations, William J. Wilhelm; Dir. Human Resources, Marguerite E. Dawson; Cur., Dr. Bruce Stephenson; Dir. Education, Karen Carney; Dir. Corporate Rels., Ave Costa; Dir. Sales & Private Events, Julie Bishop; Dir. Information Systems, Kenneth P. Kobus; Museum Shop Mgr., Linda Stucky.
Personnel Profile: Full-Time Paid 104; Part-Time Paid 107; Part-Time Volunteers 155; Interns 5.
Governing Authority: independent; nonprofit corporation. Tax-exempt: 501(c)(3).
Planetarium, History & Science Museum.
Collections: early scientific instruments in astronomy; time-keeping devices; navigation & engineering; rare books dealing with astronomy & related sciences; photographs related to scientific instruments; space exploration & related artifacts.
Research Fields: astronomy; astrophysics; history of science.
Facilities: 193-seat Star Rider Theater; 280-seat Zeiss Planetarium; 280-seat KROC Universe theatre; classrooms; restaurant; 18-unit computer classroom; distance learning studio.
Activities: family programs; demos; private events; public lectures; formal & informal education programs; permanent & temporary exhibitions; monthly public observing sessions with video hook-up to 20-inch computer-controlled Cassegrain telescope with charge-coupled device. Planetarium Sponsors: Astro-Science Workshop for high ability high school students; astronomy outreach programs with local schools & community groups; astronomy-related travel programs to global locations.
Publications: quarterly member's newsletter; gallery guides.
Hours & Admission Prices: Mon.-Fri. 9:30-4:30, Sat.-Sun. 10-4:30. Adults $10, seniors over 65 $8, children 3-14 $6; discounts to Chicago residents, AAM & ICOM members; members no charge. Closed Thanksgiving; Christmas. ♿
Attendance: 400,000 (estimated)
Membership: Student & Senior $45; Individual $60; Family $80; Mercury $150; Venus $250; Mars $500; Shepard Society $1,000.

ARC GALLERY (ARTISTS, RESIDENTS OF CHICAGO), 832 W. Superior St., Ste. 204, Chicago, IL 60622. Tel.: 312-733-2787. Fax: 312-733-2787.
E-mail: arcgallery@yahoo.com
Web Site: www.arcgallery.org
Founded: 1973.
Key Personnel: Administrative Dir., Brooke Demos; Mng. Dir., Charlotte Segal; Treas., Mirjana Ugrinov; Co-Treas., Deva Suckerman; Co-Treas., Melanie Adcock.
Personnel Profile: Full-Time Volunteers 15; Part-Time Paid 1; Part-Time Volunteers 20; Interns 2.
Governing Authority: not-for-profit organization. Tax-exempt: 501(c)(3).
Art Gallery.
Collections: contemporary Chicago artists exhibits.
Research Fields: emerging Chicago artists; women's issues.
Facilities: media room; special events gallery.
Activities: lectures. Annual Events: Members & Affiliates Show; panel discussions.
Publications: biannual Raw Space catalog; quarterly newsletter; members catalog; book show catalog; Poetic Dialogue exhibition catalog.
Hours & Admission Prices: Wed.-Sat. 12-6, Sun. 12-4. No charge; donations requested. Closed all major holidays. ♿
Attendance: 6,200 (estimated)
Membership: Arc Angel Artist members $25 per year, yearly juried exhibitions fees waived; Artist members who operate non-profit space $60 per month.

* **THE ART INSTITUTE OF CHICAGO, (M),** 111 S. Michigan Ave., Chicago, IL 60603-6492. Tel.: 312-443-3600. Fax: 312-443-0849. TDD: 312-443-3890.
Web Site: www.artic.edu
Founded: 1879.
Congressional District: 1
Key Personnel: Chm. (V), Thomas J. Pritzker; Dir., Pres. & C.E.O., James Cuno; Exec. Vice Pres., Julia E. Getzels; Sr. Vice Pres. Finance, Eric Anyah; Chm. African & Amerindian Art, Richard F. Townsend; Cur. African Art, Kathleen Bickford-Berzock; Chm. American Arts, Judith A. Barter; Cur. American Arts, Sarah E. Kelly; Asst. Cur. American Art, Ellen E. Roberts; Asst. Cur. American Art, Brandon K. Ruud; Chm. Architecture & Design, Joseph G. Rosa; Cur. Architecture & Design, Zoe J. Ryan; Cur. Ancient Art, Karen Manchester; Cur. Indian & Islamic Art, Madhuvanti Ghose; Assoc. Cur. Chinese Art, Elinor L. Pearlstein; Assoc. Cur. Japanese Art, Janice Katz; Asst. Cur. Ancient Art, Mary C. Greuel; Chm. Contemporary Art, James Rondeau; Asst. Cur. Contemporary Art, Lisa B. Dorin; Chm. European Decorative Arts, Christopher P. Monkhouse; Cur. European Decorative Arts, Ghenete Zelleke; Chm. Med-Mod European Paint & Sculpture and Chm. Prints & Drawings, Douglas Druick; Cur. Modern Painting & Sculpture, Stephanie D'Alessandro; Cur. European Painting Before 1750, Martha Wolff; Cur. European Painting, Gloria Groom; Asst. Cur. Medieval Art, Christina M. Nielsen; Chm. Photography, Matthew S. Witkovsky; Conservator, Photography, Douglas G. Severson; Assoc. Cur. Photography, Elizabeth Siegel; Asst. Cur. Photography, Katherine A. Bussard; Cur. Prints & Drawings, Suzanne McCullagh; Cur. Prints & Drawings, Martha Tedeschi; Conservator Prints & Drawings, Harriet Stratis; Assoc. Cur. Prints & Drawings, Mark Pascale; Cur. Prints & Drawings, Peter Zegers; Cur. Textiles, Odile V. Joassin; Conservator, Textiles, Lauren K. Chang; Exec. Dir., Conservation, Frank Zuccari; Sr. Conservator, Objects, Barbara Hall; Conservator, Objects, Suzanne Schnepp; Conservator, Paintings, Kristin Lister; Conservator, Paintings, Faye Wrubel; Assoc. Conservator, Objects, Emily D. Heye; Exec. Dir. Libraries, Jack P. Brown; Archivist, Bart Ryckbosch; Exec. Dir. Museum Education, Robert Eskridge; Dir. Administration & Interpretive Media Museum Education, David Stark; Dir. Adult Programs, Jeffery Nigro; Dir. Interpretive Exhibitions & Family Programs Museum Education, Jean Sousa; Exec. Dir. Publications, Robert V. Sharp; Dir. Publications, Sarah E. Guernsey; Assoc. Dir. Publication, Gregory Nosan; Deputy Dir. & C.O.O., Meredith Mack; Vice Pres., Auxiliary Operations, Elizabeth Grainer; Dir. Shop Operations, Daniel Sherry; Exec. Dir. Museum Registration, Patricia Loiko; Vice Pres. Collection Management & Technology, Samuel Quigley; Sr. Registrar Loans & Exhibitions, Darrell Green; Sr. Registrar Permanent Collections, Sally-Ann Felgenhauer; Registrar Permanent Collection, Gregory Tschann; Vice Pres. Exhibitions & Museum Administration, Dorothy Schroeder; Vice Pres. Museum Finances, Jeanne M. Ladd; Assoc. Vice Pres. Physical Plant, William D. Caddick; Assoc. Vice Pres. Protection Svcs., Michelle Lehman Jenness; Vice Pres. Mktg., Carrie Heinonen; Exec. Dir. Graphic Design & Communication Svcs., Lyn DelliQuadri; Vice Pres. Museum Devel., Mary J. Drews; Dir. Business & Civic Rels., Warren Davis; Vice Pres. Human Resources, Michael Nicolai; Vice Pres. Information Svcs. & CIO, Eugene B. Adams, Jr.
Personnel Profile: Full-Time Paid 534; Part-Time Paid 26; Part-Time Volunteers 600; Interns 60.
Governing Authority: nonprofit organization. Branch Institutions: School of the Art Institute, Columbus Dr. & Jackson Blvd. Tax-exempt: 501(c)(3).
Art Museum: housed in 1892-93 building designed by Shepley, Rutan and Coolidge & additional buildings.
Collections: all periods of European & American painting; sculpture; prints; drawings; decorative arts; textiles; Chinese, Japanese, Indian & Middle Eastern art; European medieval art; classical art; photography; African, pre-Hispanic & Native American art; architectural drawings & fragments; arms & armor.
Major Exhibits: Apostles of Beauty: Arts and Crafts from Britain to Chicago, 11/7/09-1/10; Modern American Works on Paper, 1/30/10-4/4/10; Democratic Camera, Photographs and Video 1958-2008 (Organized by the Whitney Museum of American Art), 2/20/10-5/16/10; Photographs of

Stanley Greenberg, 3/10-6/10; Fischli & Weiss Questions, 3/19/10-6/13/10; Matisse and the Methods of Modern Construction (T), 3/20/10-6/6/10; Contemporary Drawings, 4/24/10-9/6/10; Rodney Graham: Torqued Chandalier Release, 7/2/10-9/26/10; Richard & Mary Gray Collection, 9/25/10-1/2/11; Focus: Richard Hawkins, 10/22/10-1/17/11.
Research Fields: pertaining to collections.
Facilities: 341,679-vol. library of monographs, periodicals, exhibition catalogs, 490,000 slide images, photographs, color prints, architectural drawings, plans, manuscripts available for inter-library loan, to university faculty, staff of other museums & for use on premises by request; reading room; 4 auditoriums; theater; restaurants; education center. Books, reproductions, slides, postcards, jewelry, original decorative items & games for sale.
Activities: public lectures; tours; subscription programs; formally organized education programs for children, families & adults; outreach programs, workshops for teachers & paraprofessionals; permanent, temporary & traveling exhibitions; volunteer programs in all areas; subscription programs.
Publications: bimonthly bulletin; The Art Institute of Chicago Annual Report; semiannual, Museum Studies.
Hours & Admission Prices: Mon.-Wed. & Fri. 10:30-5, Thurs. 10:30-8, Sat.-Sun. 10-5. Adults $18, children, students & senior citizens 65 & over $12; children under 14 & members no charge. Closed Thanksgiving; Christmas. ♿
Attendance: 1,395,285 (accurate)
Membership: Student $40; Member $80; Member Plus $125; Premium Member $175.

BALZEKAS MUSEUM OF LITHUANIAN CULTURE, 6500 S. Pulaski Rd., Chicago, IL 60629-5136. Tel.: 773-582-6500. Fax: 773-582-5133.
E-mail: info@balzekasmuseum.org
Web Site: ww.balzekasmuseum.org
Founded: 1966.
Congressional District: 23
Key Personnel: Pres., Stanley Balzekas, Jr.; Exec. Dir., Rita Janz; Genealogist & Editor, Karile Vaitkute; Head Library, Robert Balzekas; Dir. Periodicals Collection, Irene Norbut; Cur. Cartography Dept., Edward Pocius; Librarian, Irena Pumputiene; Cur. Folk Art, Frank Zapolis; Mgr. Membership & Collections, Regina Vasiliauskiene; Dir. Intl. Programs, Rasa Rudzykte; Chm. Numismatic Dept., Frank Passic; Office Mgr., Rita Striegel.
Personnel Profile: Full-Time Paid 4; Full-Time Volunteers 5; Part-Time Paid 5; Part-Time Volunteers 5.
Governing Authority: nonprofit organization. Tax-exempt: 501(c)(3).
Lithuanian Culture Museum.
Collections: Lithuanian memorabilia & art; numismatics; philately; Lithuanian hagiology; rare books & maps; textiles; armor & period weapons; genealogy; Lithuanian art; folklore; ethnology; costumes; amber exhibit; photography; audiovisual, cartography; art archives.
Research Fields: Lithuanian & Eastern European history & folklore, Lithuanian immigration to the U.S.; genealogy; Lithuanian art.
Facilities: 75,000-vol. library of books written in all languages pertaining to Lithuania & 50,000-item archive on Eastern European history; manuscript division; 1,600 periodical titles; numismatics, armor, Center for the Study of U.S. Presidents & antique weapons available for inter-library loan & for use on premises. Amber, coins, stamps, folk art & miscellaneous items for sale.
Activities: guided tours; lectures; films; gallery talks; hobby workshops; discussion panel; formally organized educational programs; docent program or council; inter-museum loan, permanent, temporary & traveling exhibitions; school loan service. Museum Sponsors: folk art & art classes.
Publications: quarterly newsletter, Lithuanian Museum Review; genealogy.
Hours & Admission Prices: Daily 10-4. Adults $5, senior citizens & students $4, children 12 & under $1; discounts to AAM & ICOM members; members no charge. Closed New Year's Day; Easter; Christmas. ♿
Attendance: 44,000 (estimated)
Membership: Individual $30; Family $40; Supporting $50; Genealogy $75; Patron $100; Organization $250; Benefactor $500; Sponsor $1,000; Life $5,000.

BRONZEVILLE CHILDREN'S MUSEUM, 9301 S. Stony Island Ave., Chicago, IL 60617-3644. Tel.: 773-721-9301. Fax: 773-721-9303.
E-mail: bcm@bronzevillechildrensmuseum.org
Web Site: www.bronzevillechildrensmuseum.com
Key Personnel: Pres., Peggy A. Montes
Children's Museum.
Collections: hands-on exhibits.
Facilities: Museum-related items for sale.
Hours & Admission Prices: Tues.-Sat. 10-4. Admission $5.

CAMBODIAN AMERICAN HERITAGE MUSEUM AND KILLING FIELDS MEMORIAL, 2831 W. Lawrence Ave., Chicago, IL 60625-3619. Tel.: 773-878-7090. Fax: 773-878-5299.
Key Personnel: Dir., Charles Daas; Museum Archivist, Ty Tim
Cambodian Heritage Museum.
Collections: Cambodian history & culture; photographs.
Hours & Admission Prices: Museum & Memorial: Mon.-Fri. 10-4, Sat. by appointment. Community Center: Mon.-Fri. 9-5. No charge; donations accepted.

CHARNLEY-PERSKY HOUSE MUSEUM, (M), 1365 N. Astor St., Chicago, IL 60610-2144. Tel.: 312-915-0105 & 573-1365. Fax: 312-573-1141.
E-mail: psaliga@sah.org
Web Site: www.sah.org
Founded: 1998.
Key Personnel: C.E.O., Pauline Saliga; Pres. (V), Barry Bergdoll.
Personnel Profile: Part-Time Paid 1; Part-Time Volunteers 15.
Governing Authority: nonprofit educational organization. Parent Institution: Society of Architectural Historians. Tax-exempt.
Historic House Museum: 1891-92 Charnley-Persky house designed by Louis Sullivan & Frank Lloyd Wright.
Collections: historic house.
Activities: tours.
Hours & Admission Prices: Tour of House: Wed. 12 noon, Sat. 10:00 & 1:00. Suggested Admission $15; Wed. no charge.
Attendance: 1,354 (accurate)

CHICAGO ARCHITECTURE FOUNDATION, 224 S. Michigan Ave., Chicago, IL 60604-2505. Tel.: 312-922-3432, ext. 245. Fax: 312-922-2607.
E-mail: losmond@architecture.org
Web Site: www.architecture.org
Founded: 1966.
Congressional District: 7
Key Personnel: Pres. & C.E.O., Lynn Osmond; Chm., John DiCiurcio; C.F.O., Shari Massey; Vice Pres. Devel., Charles Stanford; Santa Fe Shop & Tour Center Mgr., Lynn Davis.
Personnel Profile: Full-Time Paid 40; Part-Time Paid 13; Part-Time Volunteers 460; Interns 7.
Governing Authority: nonprofit foundation. Tax-exempt: 501(c)(3).
Architecture Museum & Center.
Collections: sculptures; architecture.
Research Fields: Chicago architecture; urban planning & design, sustainability & infrastructure.
Facilities: Chicago Architecture Center; City Space; lecture facility; permanent exhibition space; education studios; Shop & Tour Orientation.
Activities: architectural tours of Chicago; lectures; permanent & temporary exhibits; docent training; teacher training, in-school & community youth programs, Newhouse Architecture Program.
Publications: annual tour announcements; books, A Walk Through Graceland Cemetery, A View From the River; tour brochure; A.I.A. guide to Chicago; quarterly newsletter, InSites; The Architecture Handbook: A Student Guide to Understanding Buildings; Schoolyards to Skylines - Teaching with Chicago's Amazing Architecture; Chicago Architecture: 1885 to Today; annual report.
Hours & Admission Prices: Mon.-Sat. 9-7, Sun. 9-6. Tours: Bus $40; River Cruise Mon.-Fri. $28, Sat.-Sun. $32; Walking $15. Closed New Year's Day; Memorial Day; Independence Day; Labor Day; Thanksgiving & day after; Christmas. ♿
Attendance: 476,000 (estimated)
Membership: Student $35; Senior & National $40; International $47; Individual $55; Senior Household & Household National $60; Household International $67.

CHICAGO CHILDREN'S MUSEUM, Navy Pier, 700 E. Grand Ave., Suite 127, Chicago, IL 60611-3577. Tel.: 312-527-1000. Fax: 312-527-9082.
E-mail: generalinquiries@chicagochildrensmuseum.org
Web Site: www.chicagochildrensmuseum.org
Founded: 1982.
Congressional District: 9
Key Personnel: Chm. Bd. & Dir, Gigi Pritzker Pucker; Pres. & C.E.O., Jennifer Farrington; Vice Pres. Planning & External Affairs, Jim Law; Vice Pres. Mktg., Communications & Guest Svcs., Betsey Grais; Vice Pres. Exhibits, Louise Belmont-Skinner; Vice Pres. Educ. & Community Connections, Natalie Bortoli; Vice Pres. Finance & I.T., Dana Thomas; Vice Pres. Human Resources, Catherine Patyk; Volunteer & Intern Resources Coord., Sarah Williams; Assoc. Vice Pres. Exhibit & Bldg. Operations, Peter Williams.
Personnel Profile: Full-Time Paid 53; Part-Time Paid 28; Part-Time Volunteers 254; Interns 27.
Governing Authority: nonprofit organization. Tax-exempt: 501(c)(3).

Children's Museum.
Collections: hands-on exhibits.
Facilities: 30,000 sq. ft. exhibit space. Gift items for sale.
Activities: hands-on permanent, temporary & traveling exhibits for children & their families; school & group, family travel & trunk shows; teacher & parent training; community outreach programs; paid programming; free family night; membership activities; performances. Special Events: annual meeting; Family Benefit; museum sponsored events.
Publications: quarterly newsletter, Handprint.
Hours & Admission Prices: Sun.-Wed. & Fri. 10-5, Thurs. & Sat. 10-8. Admission $9; discount to groups; children under 1, Thurs. evenings 5-8 & members no charge. Closed Thanksgiving; Christmas. ♿
Attendance: 773,000 (accurate)
Membership: Family (2 People) $60; Family (4 People) $90; Explorers $125; Corporate $5,000 & up.

CHICAGO CULTURAL CENTER, 78 E. Washington St., Chicago, IL 60602-4801. Tel.: 312-744-6630. Fax: 312-744-2089. TDD: 312-744-2947.
E-mail: culture@cityofchicago.org
Web Site: www.chicagoculturalcenter.org
Founded: 1897.
Congressional District: 7
Key Personnel: Commissioner, Chicago Dept. Cultural Affairs, Lois Weisberg; Deputy Commissioner Visual Arts, Gregory Knight; Cur. Exhibitions, Lanny Silverman; Exhibitions Designer & Preparator, Greg Lunceford.
Personnel Profile: Full-Time Paid 59; Part-Time Volunteers 150.
Governing Authority: Parent Institution: City of Chicago. Subsidiary Institution: Dept. of Cultural Affairs. Tax-exempt.
Art Museum & Cultural Center.
Collections: paintings; photographs; sculpture.
Major Exhibits: Angel Otero: New Paintings, 1/10-3/10; Hollis Sigler: Expect the Unexpected (T), 1/10-4/10; Graphic Works by Romare Bearden (T), 4/10-6/10; Diane Simpson: Sculpture & Drawing, 4/10-7/10; Stranger in Paradise: The Works of Howard Finster (T), 7/10-9/10; Jazz Loft: W. Eugene Smith (T), 7/10-9/10.
Research Fields: modern & contemporary art.
Facilities: 2 theaters; 2 concert halls; civic reception halls & performing arts areas; dance studio; Chicago Office of Tourism Visitor Information Center; cafe. Museum-related items for sale.
Activities: changing exhibitions on wide range of subjects: contemporary art; crafts; cultural traditions; musical concerts; dance; theater; lectures; film series; special exhibits & programs for children; literary arts program; group tours; building tours.
Publications: exhibition brochures; catalogs & educational brochures related to special exhibitions; performing arts brochures; self-guided tour of the Chicago Cultural Center brochure with map; book, The People's Palace: The Story of the Chicago Cultural Center; monthly calendar; building brochure; public art guides; tourism brochures.
Hours & Admission Prices: Cultural Center: Mon.-Thurs. 8-7, Fri. 8-6, Sat. 9-6, Sun. 10-6. No charge. Closed holidays. ♿
Attendance: 875,000 (estimated)
Membership: MOSAIC Membership: Student $25; Senior Individual $40; Individual $55; Senior Household $60; Household $75; Gem $125; Pillar $250; Tiffany $500; Luminary $1,000.

* **CHICAGO HISTORY MUSEUM, (M),** 1601 N. Clark St., Chicago, IL 60614-6038. Tel.: 312-642-4600 & 5035. Fax: 312-266-2077. TDD: 800-526-0857.
Web Site: www.chicagohistory.org
Formerly: Chicago Historical Society
Founded: 1856.
Congressional District: 9
Key Personnel: Pres., Gary T. Johnson; Exec. Vice Pres. & Chief Historian, Russell Lewis; Chm. (V), Sharon Gist Gilliam; Vice Pres. Interpretation & Education, Phyllis Rabineau; Chief Cur., Olivia Mahoney; Dir. Corporate Events, Barb Siska; Dir. Research & Access and Chief Librarian, Deborah Vaughan; Dir. Education, The Elizabeth F. Cheney, D. Lynn McRainey; Vice Pres. Finance, Cheryl Obermeyer; Dir. Exhibitions, Tamara Biggs; Dir. Properties, Larry Schmitt; Dir. Mktg. & Sponsorship, Melissa Hayes; Dir. Accounting, Leigh Stevenson; Dir. Technology, Don Pasqualini; Vice Pres. Administration & Human Resources, Bobbie Carter; Dir. Print & Multimedia Publications, Rosemary Adams; Dir. Merchandising & Museum Shop Mgr., Elizabeth Hubbartt; Dir. Visitor Svcs., Virginia Fitzgerald; Dir. Collections, Andrew W. Mellon, Kathleen Plourd; Museum Shop Mgr., Jennifer Vlna.
Personnel Profile: Full-Time Paid 132; Part-Time Paid 13; Part-Time Volunteers 99; Interns 12.
Governing Authority: nonprofit organization. Parent Institution: Chicago Historical Society. Tax-exempt: 501(c)(3).
History Museum.
Collections: American history, 1760-1865 including: Revolutionary War; westward expansion; Civil War; Lincoln. Chicago & Illinois history 1690-present includes: fur trade; railroad; industrialization; urban culture & society; archives; manuscripts; architectural drawings; models; fragments; paintings; sculpture; decorative & industrial arts; costumes; prints; photographs.
Major Exhibits: Lincoln Transformed, 11/09-4/10; Benito Juarez and the Making of Modern Mexico, 11/09-4/10; Lincoln Park Block by Block, 11/09-9/10; Chinatown, 12/09-7/10; Weddings, 5/10-1/11.
Research Fields: Chicago & Illinois history; urban history; post-1945 Chicago history; Lincoln; Civil War; race & ethnicity, fashion.
Facilities: research center; auditorium; meeting rooms; rental facility; outdoor plaza. Postcards, books, pamphlets, colored slides & reproductions of photos for sale.
Activities: guided tours; lectures; films; gallery talks; concerts; study clubs; docent program; inter-museum loan, permanent, temporary & traveling exhibitions.
Publications: quarterly journal, Chicago History; quarterly newsletter; calendar; catalogues; monographs related to research fields; encyclopedia of Chicago (online version).
Hours & Admission Prices: Galleries: Mon.-Sat. 9:30-4:30, Sun. 12-5. Audio Tours: adults $14, senior citizens 65 & over and students 13-22 $12; discounts for groups of 10 or more, AAM & ICOM members; DuSable Museum & the National Museum of Mexican Art members, members, children 12 and under & Mon. no charge. Research Center: Tues.-Thurs. 1-4:30, Fri.-Sat. 10-4:30. Annual $15, daily $5; members no charge. Closed New Year's Day; Thanksgiving; Christmas. ♿
Attendance: 265,991 (accurate)
Membership: Senior Citizen & Student $35; Individual $40; Senior Family $45; Family $50.

CHICAGO MARITIME SOCIETY, (M), 310 S. Racine, 6th Fl., Chicago, IL 60607-2841. Tel.: 312-421-9096.
Founded: 1982.
Congressional District: 7
Key Personnel: Pres. (V), Jerry H. Thomas, Ph.D.; Museum Shop Mgr., Don Glasell.
Personnel Profile: Full-Time Volunteers 1; Part-Time Volunteers 3; Interns 3.
Governing Authority: Tax-exempt.
Maritime Museum.
Collections: maritime history & artifacts; photographs; personal artifacts.
Facilities: Museum-related items for sale.
Activities: outreach programs; research; educational programs.
Publications: books, From Lumber Hookers to the Hooligan Fleet, A Treasury of Chicago Maritime History; Images of America - Maritime Chicago; Schooner Passage; Chicago Maritime - An Illustrated History.
Hours & Admission Prices: Call for hours.
Attendance: 300 (estimated)
Membership: Regular $35; Supporting $100; Sponsor $1,000; Director $2,000; Patron $5,000.

CHICAGO PUBLIC LIBRARY, 400 S. State St., Harold Washington Library Center, Special Collections & Preservation Div., Chicago, IL 60605-1216. Mailing Address: 9N-10, Special Collections & Preservation Div., 400 S. State St., Chicago, IL 60605. Tel.: 312-747-4883 & 4875.
E-mail: eholland@chipublib.org
Web Site: www.chipublib.org
Founded: 1872.
Congressional District: 7
Key Personnel: Commissioner, Mary Dempsey.
Personnel Profile: Full-Time Paid 11; Part-Time Paid 3; Part-Time Volunteers 1; Interns 1.
Governing Authority: municipal. Parent Institution: City of Chicago. Tax-exempt: 501(c)(3).
History Museum: general exhibition site housed in the Chicago Public Library, Harold Washington Library Center.
Collections: artifacts; books; manuscripts; photographs; graphics; art; archives.
Research Fields: Civil War; Chicago literary, cultural & social history; book arts.
Facilities: 18,000-vol. library pertaining to the Civil War & Chicago history; 390-seat auditorium; three exhibition spaces; special collections reading room.
Activities: lectures; films; concerts; organized educational programs; temporary & traveling exhibitions.
Publications: brochures; bibliographies & exhibitions catalogs.
Hours & Admission Prices: Library: Mon.-Thurs. 9-9, Fri.-Sat. 9-5, Sun. 1-5. Special Collections: Mon.-Thurs. 12-6, Fri.-Sat. 12-4. No charge. ♿
Attendance: 182,489 (estimated)

CHICAGO STATE UNIVERSITY, PRESIDENT'S GALLERY, 9501 S. King Dr., Cook Admin. Bldg., 3rd Fl., Chicago, IL 60628-1598. Tel.: 773-995-3905.
Key Personnel: Cur., Joyce Owens Anderson
Art Gallery.
Collections: paintings; photographs.
Activities: lectures; demonstrations; workshops; special events.
Hours & Admission Prices: Mon.-Fri. 8:30-5. No charge.

CHINESE-AMERICAN MUSEUM OF CHICAGO, 238 W. 23rd St., Chicago, IL 60616-1904. Tel.: 312-949-1000. Fax: 312-949-1001.
Web Site: www.ccamuseum.org
Founded: 2005.
Key Personnel: Pres. (V), Dr. Kim K. Tee.
Governing Authority: Parent Institution: Chinatown Museum Foundation, Chicago. Tax-exempt.
Chinese-American Museum.
Collections: local history & culture; documents; photographs; period artifacts; clothing; paintings; ceramics.
Major Exhibits: Chinese @ Play, 11/09-11/10; Great Wall to the Great Lakes, 2/10-2/16.
Facilities: Museum-related items for sale.
Activities: lectures; educational programs.
Publications: newsletter.
Hours & Admission Prices: Fri. 9:30-1:30, Sat.-Sun. 10-5. Suggested Donation: adults $2, seniors & students $1; members no charge.
Membership: Student $5; Individual $25; Family $50; Corporate $150; Honorary $200

CITY GALLERY AT THE HISTORIC WATER TOWER, 806 N. Michigan Ave., Chicago, IL 60611-2103. Tel.: 312-744-2400 & 742-0808.
Photography Gallery: housed in the historic Chicago Water Tower; built in 1869. Listed on the National Register of Historic Places.
Collections: Chicago-themed photographs by Chicago photographers.
Hours & Admission Prices: Mon.-Sat. 10-6:30, Sun. 10-5. No charge.

* **CLARKE HOUSE MUSEUM, (M),** 1827 S. Indiana Ave., Chicago, IL 60616-1308. Tel.: 312-745-0040. Fax: 312-745-0077.
E-mail: info@clarkehousemuseum.org
Web Site: www.clarkehousemuseum.org
Founded: 1984.
Congressional District: 7
Key Personnel: Commissioner Dept. Cultural Affairs, Loise Weisberg.
Personnel Profile: Full-Time Paid 2; Full-Time Volunteers 120; Part-Time Paid 1; Part-Time Volunteers 150.
Governing Authority: municipal government. Owned and operated by City of Chicago. Subsidiary Institution: Dept. of Cultural Affairs. Furnished by The National Society of Colonial Dames of America in The State of Illinois. Tax-exempt: 501(c)(3).
Historic House Museum: 1836 Greek Revival building, oldest home in Chicago.
Collections: period rooms; domestic life in Chicago, 1836-1860; 19th-century decorative arts; early urban development of Chicago.
Research Fields: early Chicago; domestic technology.
Facilities: 300-vol. library of books on 19th-century history, decorative arts & architecture.
Activities: guided tours; lectures; organized education programs for children; docent program. Museum Sponsors: Film Festival in summer; candlelight holiday tours.
Hours & Admission Prices: Wed.-Sun. 12-3, tours depart at 12 & 2. Adults $10, senior citizens & children $9; discounts to AAM & ICOM members; Wed. no charge. Closed New Year's Day; Easter; Memorial Day; Independence Day; Labor Day; Thanksgiving; Christmas Eve & Day. ♿
Attendance: 5,000 (accurate)

COLUMBIA COLLEGE CHICAGO CENTER FOR THE BOOK & PAPER ARTS, 1104 S. Wabash, 2nd Fl., Chicago, IL 60605-2334. Tel.: 312-369-6630. Fax: 312-369-8082.
E-mail: bookandpaper@colum.edu
Web Site: www.colum.edu/book_and_paper
Key Personnel: Dir., Dr. Steve Woodall
Art Gallery.
Collections: papermaking studio; letterpress studio; hot stampers; Vandercook and Chandler & Price presses; over 800 drawers of type.
Activities: lectures; special events.
Hours & Admission Prices: Gallery: Mon.-Fri. 10-6. Office: Mon.-Fri. 9:30-5. No charge.

DEPAUL UNIVERSITY ART MUSEUM, (M), 2350 N. Kenmore, Chicago, IL 60614-3210. Tel.: 773-325-7506 & 7593. Fax: 773-325-4506.
E-mail: lfatemi@depaul.edu
Web Site: www.museumsdepaul.edu
Founded: 1987.
Congressional District: 9
Key Personnel: Dir., Louise Lincoln; Asst. Dir., Laura Fatemi; Asst. Cur., Chris Mack.
Personnel Profile: Full-Time Paid 3; Part-Time Paid 10; Part-Time Volunteers 2; Interns 2.
Governing Authority: private university; nonprofit. Parent Institution: DePaul University. Tax-exempt: 170(b)(1)(A).
University Art Museum.
Collections: paintings; photographs; sculpture.
Activities: temporary, traveling & loan exhibitions; lectures.
Publications: gallery notes; exhibition catalogs.
Hours & Admission Prices: Mon.-Thurs. & Sat. 11-5, Fri. 11-7, Sun. 12-5. No charge; donations accepted. Closed university holidays. ♿
Attendance: 15,000 (accurate)

DUSABLE MUSEUM OF AFRICAN-AMERICAN HISTORY, INC., (M), 740 E. 56th Place, Chicago, IL 60637-1495. Tel.: 773-947-0600, ext. 246. Fax: 773-947-0677.
E-mail: AWright@dusablemuseum.org
Web Site: www.dusablemuseum.org
Founded: 1961.
Congressional District: 1
Key Personnel: C.E.O. & Pres., Antoinette D. Wright; Chief Cur., Charles E. Bethea; Dir. Education, Stephanie Davenport, Ph.D.; Facility Rental Mgr., Tracey Williams; Dir. Visitor Svcs., Josephine Phillips.
Personnel Profile: Full-Time Paid 21; Part-Time Paid 21; Part-Time Volunteers 40; Interns 12.
Governing Authority: nonprofit organization. Tax-exempt: 501(c)(3).
History Museum.
Collections: archives; African, Afro-American art; memorabilia; historical artifacts; sculpture; photographs; books.
Research Fields: African-American art history; Chicago & Illinois history.
Facilities: approx. 6,000-vol. library of African & Afro-American books, tapes, phonograph records, pictures, slides, biographical & vertical files available for use in library; reading room; auditorium; exhibition galleries. Curios, sculpture, prints, artifacts & publications for sale.
Activities: guided tours; lectures; traveling exhibitions; classes; film program; annual school oratorical; essay contests; after-school program.
Publications: Heritage Calendar; book of poems, What Shall I Tell My Children Who Are Black; books, Black Power in Old Alabama; The Birth & The Building of the Dusable Museum; Figures in Black History; Poetry of Prison.
Hours & Admission Prices: Mon.-Sat. 10-5, Sun. 12-5; groups by appointment. Adults $3, students & senior citizens $2, children 6-12 $1; discounts to AAM & ICOM members; children under 6 & Sun. no charge. Closed New Year's Eve & Day; Easter; Independence Day; Thanksgiving; Christmas. ♿
Attendance: 150,000 (accurate)
Membership: Seniors & Students $15; General $25; Family $35; Annual Sponsor $100; Corporate $500 & up; Corporate Donors $1,000.

FASHION COLUMBIA STUDY COLLECTION, (M), Columbia College Chicago, 618 S. Michigan Ave., 8th Fl., Chicago, IL 60605-1901. Tel.: 312-369-6283. Fax: 312-369-8422.
E-mail: aleblanc@colum.edu
Web Site: www.colum.edu/fashion_collection
Founded: 1989.
Key Personnel: Acting Collections Mgr., Anna Mary LeBlanc.
Governing Authority: Parent Institution: Columbia College Chicago. Tax-exempt.
Fashion Museum.
Collections: 6,000 items of dress including European, American & Japanese fashion designers; period artifacts; ethnic clothing.
Facilities: library.
Hours & Admission Prices: By appointment. No charge. ♿

* **FIELD MUSEUM OF NATURAL HISTORY, (M),** 1400 S. Lake Shore Dr., Chicago, IL 60605-2496. Tel.: 312-922-9410. Fax: 312-922-0741. TDD: 312-341-9299.
Web Site: www.fieldmuseum.org
Founded: 1893.
Congressional District: 7
Key Personnel: C.E.O. & Pres., John W. McCarter, Jr.; Bd. Chm. (V), John A. Canning; Exec. Vice Pres., J.W. Croft; Vice Pres. & Gen. Counsel, Joe Brennan; Vice Pres. Institutional Advancement, Sheila Cawley; Sr. Vice Pres. Collections & Research, Lance Grande; Vice Pres. Bd. Rels. & Sr. Dir.

Institutional Advancement, Melissa Hilton; Vice Pres. Admin., Shawn VanDerziel; Sr. Vice Pres. Environment, Culture & Conservation, Debra Moskovits; Sr. Vice Pres. Museum Enterprises, Laura M. Sadler.
Personnel Profile: Full-Time Paid 460; Part-Time Paid 32; Part-Time Volunteers 450; Interns 10.
Governing Authority: board of trustees; nonprofit organization. Tax-exempt: 501(c)(3) & 170(b)(1)(A).
Natural History Museum.
Collections: anatomy; anthropology; archaeology; archives; botany; costumes; entomology; ethnology; geology; herbarium; herpetology; Indian; mineralogy; natural history; paleontology; science; textiles; zoology.
Research Fields: archaeology; botany; geology; zoology; anthropology; environmental & conservation programs.
Facilities: 250,000-vol. library of natural history material available for inter-library loan & use on premises; full scale replica of a Pawnee Earth Lodge; Place for Wonder, natural & cultural artifacts; reading room; theater; classrooms; restaurant. Gift items, books & cards for sale.
Activities: guided tours; lectures; films; performances; demonstrations; adult education courses; formally organized education programs for children & graduate students affiliated with Northwestern University, University of Chicago & University of Illinois at Chicago, Northern Illinois University; one-day environmental field trips for adults & families; museum-wide volunteer program; docent program or council; training programs for professional museum workers; permanent, temporary & special exhibitions; school loan service.
Publications: monographs, Fieldiana Anthropology; Fieldiana Botany; Fieldiana Geology; Fieldiana Zoology; bimonthly periodical, In the Field.
Hours & Admission Prices: Daily 9-5. Adults $15, senior citizens 65 & over and students with ID $12, children 3-11 $10; discounts to Chicago residents, AAM & ICOM members; members, military personnel, individual teachers, children under 3 & groups of 10 or more with appointment no charge. Closed New Year's Day; Christmas. ♿
Attendance: 1,212,475 (accurate)
Membership: Student & Senior $30; Individual $40; Family $50; Contributor $100-$249: Adventurer $250-$499; Naturalist $500-$999; Explorer $1,000-$1,499; Founders' Council $1,500.

FIRE MUSEUM OF GREATER CHICAGO, (M), 52nd & Western, Chicago, IL 60609. Mailing Address: 5218 S. Western Ave., Chicago, IL 60609-5433. Tel.: 877-225-7491; 773-771-9976.
Web Site: www.firemuseumofgreaterchicago.org
Founded: 1997.
Key Personnel: Pres., William Kugelman
Fire History Museum.
Collections: Chicago fire & firefighting history; photographs; firefighting equipment; helmets; badges; uniforms; toys.
Facilities: library.
Hours & Admission Prices: Open House: 1st & 3rd Sat. of month; groups by appointment. No charge; donations accepted.
Membership: Basic $30; Founding $100; Corporate $1,000.

FREDERICK C. ROBIE HOUSE, 5757 S. Woodlawn Ave., Chicago, IL 60637-1698. Mailing Address: 411 Harrison St., Oak Park, IL 60304. Tel.: 708-848-1976 & 773-834-1847. Fax: 708-848-1248.
E-mail: info@gowright.org
Web Site: gowright.org
Founded: 1996.
Congressional District: 1
Key Personnel: C.E.O. & Pres., Joan B. Mercuri; Chm., Mike Poirier.
Personnel Profile: Full-Time Paid 7; Part-Time Paid 18; Part-Time Volunteers 105.
Governing Authority: private; nonprofit organization. Parent Institution: Frank Lloyd Wright Preservation Trust, Oak Park, IL. Tax-exempt: 501(c)(3).
Historic House Museum: 3-story residence designed by Frank Lloyd Wright, c.1908.
Collections: structures, furniture & decorative arts designed by Frank Lloyd Wright; Japanese art & decorative materials collected by Wright; drawings; prairie style architecture.
Research Fields: Frank Lloyd Wright's life & work from 1889-1916.
Facilities: 5,040 sq. ft. exhibit space. Museum-related items for sale.
Activities: docent program; formal education programs; guided tours; lectures; neighborhood walk; special events. Annual Events: Robie House Centennial Celebration in April; Wright Plus Housewalk in May.
Publications: quarterly newsletter, Wright Angles; books, The Oak Park Home & Studio of Frank Lloyd Wright; Frank Lloyd Wright and the Prairie; Building a Legacy: The Restoration of Frank Lloyd Wright's Home and Studio; Frank Lloyd Wright's Fifty Views of Japan; In Wright's Shadow: Artists and Architects in the Oak Park Studio; Hometown Architect: The Complete Buildings of Frank Lloyd Wright in Oak Park and River Forest; The Wright Family Library.
Hours & Admission Prices: Tours: Thurs.-Mon. 11-5; groups by reservation, call 800-514-3849. Book Shop: daily 10-5. Adults $12; discount to members & groups of 10 or more. Closed New Year's Day; Thanksgiving; Christmas.
Attendance: 33,000 (estimated)
Membership: Individual $50; Family $65; Prairie Society $125; Octagon Society $250; Inglenook Society $500; Skylight Society $1,000; Cornerstone Society $2,500; Wright Society $5,000.

GARFIELD PARK CONSERVATORY, 300 N. Central Park Ave., Chicago, IL 60624-1945. Tel.: 312-746-5100. Fax: 773-638-1777.
E-mail: donorservices@garfieldpark.org
Web Site: www.garfield-conservatory.org
Founded: 1908.
Congressional District: 7
Key Personnel: Dir. Conservatories, Mary Eysenbach; Gen. Foreman, Miguel del Valle; Foreman, Matthew Barrett; Foreman, Thomas Costanza; Foreman, Koch Unni; Horticulturist, John Raffetto.
Personnel Profile: Full-Time Paid 23; Part-Time Paid 2; Part-Time Volunteers 120.
Governing Authority: municipal; nonprofit. Parent Institution: Chicago Park District, 541 N. Fairbanks, Chicago, IL 60611. Subsidiary Institution: Garfield Park Conservatory Alliance. Tax-exempt.
Horticultural Conservatory.
Collections: botanical collection; tropicals; deserts; urban demonstration gardens; palms; aroids; ferns; cycads; perennials; children's garden; sensory garden.
Facilities: nature center; botanical garden; greenhouse; demonstration garden.
Activities: education programs; workshops; tours; permanent & temporary exhibitions; summer gardens; family programs. Museum Sponsors: Holiday Show; Spring Show; Tropical Show.
Publications: member magazine, Chicago Greenscapes; brochures; maps.
Hours & Admission Prices: Wed. 9-8, Thurs.-Tues. 9-5. No charge; donations accepted. ♿
Attendance: 143,000 (accurate)
Membership: Seedling $25; Flower $50; Fern $100; Palm $250; Director $500; Jensen Club $1,000 & up.

* **GLESSNER HOUSE MUSEUM, (M),** 1800 S. Prairie Ave., Chicago, IL 60616-1320. Tel.: 312-326-1480. Fax: 312-326-1397.
E-mail: glessnerhouse@sbcglobal.net
Web Site: www.glessnerhouse.org
Founded: 1994.
Congressional District: 7
Key Personnel: Exec. Dir., William Tyre; Pres., Rolf Achilles; Museum Shop Mgr., Oksana Paluch.
Personnel Profile: Full-Time Paid 2; Part-Time Paid 2; Part-Time Volunteers 60; Interns 4.
Governing Authority: nonprofit organization. Tax-exempt: 501(c)(3).
Historic House: 1887 home designed by H.H. Richardson.
Collections: English arts & crafts; aesthetic movement furniture; decorative arts; period furniture; glass; ceramics; engravings; books; photographs.
Research Fields: Arts & Crafts Movement; Aesthetic Movement; H.H. Richardson. Glessner family; Chicago architecture; Prairie Avenue Historic District; late 19th century, urban home designed by HH Richardson on Prairie Ave.
Activities: guided tours; lectures; educational programs; docent program.
Publications: membership newsletter, The Glessner Journal.
Hours & Admission Prices: Wed.-Sun. Tours: 1 & 3. Adults $10, senior citizens & students $9, children 5-12 $6; discounts to AAM, AAA & Public Broadcasting members; AASLH members, children under 5 & members no charge. Closed New Year's Eve & Day; Easter; Memorial Day; Independence Day; Labor Day; Thanksgiving; Christmas Eve & Day.
Attendance: 5,000 (estimated)
Membership: Student & Senior $25; Individual $35; Family $45; Friend $100; Patron $250; Curator $500; Prairie Avenue Circle $1,000 & up.

HELLENIC MUSEUM & CULTURAL CENTER, (M), 801 W. Adams, 4th Fl., Chicago, IL 60607-3034. Tel.: 312-655-1234. Fax: 312-655-1221.
E-mail: info@hellenicmuseum.org
Web Site: www.hellenicmuseum.org
Founded: 1983.
Congressional District: 7
Key Personnel: Pres. (V), Aristotle Halikias; Exec. Dir., Stephanie A. Vlahakis; Dir. Operations, Katherine K. Smith; Collections, Allison Heller; Librarian, Antonia B. Lekas; Media, Publicity & Public Rels., Peter Georgalan; Account Mgr., Nick Pangere; Dir. Education & Oral History, Vivian Haritos; Dir. Devel., Helen Alexander; Mgr. Oral History, Tom Tzouras.

Personnel Profile: Full-Time Paid 6; Part-Time Paid 3; Part-Time Volunteers 50; Interns 6.
Governing Authority: nonprofit. Tax-exempt.
Greek History, Art & Folk Art Museum focus on the history & experiences of the Greek-American immigrant.
Collections: Greek immigration; life of contemporary Greek-American; period artifacts.
Activities: children's programs & tours.
Publications: newsletter; brochures.
Hours & Admission Prices: Tues.-Fri. 10-4, Sat. 11-4. Admission $5; discounts to AAM & ICOM members; members no charge, except for special events. Closed New Year's Day; Easter; Memorial Day; Independence Day; Labor Day; Thanksgiving; Christmas. ♿
Attendance: 6,000 (estimated)
Membership: Senior $25; Individual $40; Family $65; Sustaining $100; Friends $250; Philos $500; Heritage Council $1,000.

HISTORIC PULLMAN FOUNDATION, Visitor Center & Museum, 11141 S. Cottage Grove Ave., Chicago, IL 60628-4614. Mailing Address: 614 E. 113th St., Chicago, IL 60628-5100. Tel.: 773-785-8181, 3828 (Tours) & 8901 (Visitor Center). Fax: 773-785-8182.
E-mail: foundation@pullmanil.org
Web Site: www.pullmanil.org
Founded: 1973.
Congressional District: 2
Key Personnel: Pres. (V), Michael Shymanski; Past Pres. (V), Cynthia McMahon; Tour & Visitor Svcs., Dee Dee Fabris.
Personnel Profile: Part-Time Paid 2; Part-Time Volunteers 35.
Governing Authority: nonprofit organization. Tax-exempt: 501(c)(3).
Historic District: 1880-84 built by Pullman's Palace Car Co.; first planned model industrial community.
Collections: Historic Buildings: 1881 Hotel Florence; 1881 The Historic Pullman Center; 1892 The Pullman Market Hall; 1883 Arcade Site & Pullman Visitor Center; 1882-5 various North Pullman Row Houses.
Research Fields: Pullman's history.
Facilities: Historic Pullman Foundation Visitor Center; archives. Museum-related items for sale.
Activities: guided tours; year-round educational tour program. Museum Sponsors: annual House tour in October; Historic Preservation Programs Bus Tour; Candlelight House Walk & Buffet Dinner in Dec.
Publications: quarterly newsletter, Update.
Hours & Admission Prices: Tours: May-Oct. 1st Sun. of month 1:30. Visitor Center: Feb. 12-Dec. Sat. 11-3, Sun. 12-3. Groups by appointment. Adults $7, seniors $5, students $4; children 12 & under no charge when accompanied by an adult. Closed national holidays. ♿
Attendance: 475,000 (estimated)
Membership: Pullman Resident $15; General $20; Associate $30; Supporting $50; Friend of the Foundation $100; Donor $500; Pullman Patron $1,000; Benefactor $2,500.

HYDE PARK ART CENTER, 5020 S. Cornell Ave., Chicago, IL 60615-3016. Tel.: 773-324-5520. Fax: 773-324-6641.
E-mail: info@hydeparkart.org
Web Site: hydeparkart.org
Founded: 1939.
Congressional District: 1
Key Personnel: Exec. Dir., Chuck Thurow; Chm. (V), Lawrence Furnstahl.
Personnel Profile: Full-Time Paid 9; Part-Time Paid 40; Part-Time Volunteers 65; Interns 12.
Governing Authority: nonprofit. Tax-exempt: 501(c)(3).
Art Gallery & School.
Collections: Chicago-rooted, national & international artists.
Major Exhibits: Close Encounters, 11/8/09-1/24/10; Works by Josue Pellot & Angel Otero, 5/10-8/10; The Spatial City: The Architecture of Idealism, 5/23/10-8/8/10; Emerging Chicago Artist, 8/10-10/10; Not Just Another Pretty Face, 11/10-3/11.
Facilities: classrooms; ceramics studio; art resource center.
Activities: education programs for children & adults with a hands-on focus; guided gallery tours; one day workshops; panel discussions; temporary exhibitions; community outreach program; artist & curator talks; family days; monthly creative events. Annual Events: benefit auction; student & faculty show; special benefits.
Publications: quarterly newsletter, News; quarterly school calendar; occasional exhibition catalogues.
Hours & Admission Prices: Mon.-Thurs. 9-8, Fri.-Sat. 9-5, Sun. 12-5. No charge; donations accepted. ♿
Attendance: 45,000 (estimated)
Membership: Student, Senior Citizen & Artist $30; Individual $45; Family $55; Sponsor $100; Patron $300; Benefactor $500; Ruth's Circle $1,000; Creative Leader $5,000.

ILLINOIS STATE MUSEUM, CHICAGO GALLERY, 100 W. Randolph, Ste. 2-100, Chicago, IL 60601-3921. Tel.: 312-814-5322. Fax: 312-814-3471.
Web Site: www.museum.state.il.us/ismsites/chicago/
Formerly: State of Illinois Art Gallery
Founded: 1985.
Congressional District: 7
Key Personnel: Dir., Kent Smith; Assoc. Cur., Jane Stevens; Assoc. Cur., Judith Burson Lloyd; Asst. Cur., Douglas Stapleton.
Personnel Profile: Full-Time Paid 3; Part-Time Paid 1; Part-Time Volunteers 2; Interns 2.
Governing Authority: state. Parent Institution: Illinois State Museum. Tax-exempt.
Art Gallery.
Collections: historic & contemporary Illinois art including paintings, drawings, printmaking, video, ceramics, photography & textiles.
Major Exhibits: Pathways & Portals (T), 1/25/10-5/7/10; Focus 5 (T), 6/7/10-9/3/10; Patinas of Age (T), 10/12/10-1/6/11.
Research Fields: Illinois artists.
Facilities: 3,200 sq. ft. exhibition space.
Activities: guided tours; lectures; organized educational programs; changing exhibitions.
Publications: brochures; catalogs; handouts.
Hours & Admission Prices: Mon.-Fri. 9-5. No charge. Closed national holidays. ♿
Attendance: 41,762 (accurate)
Membership: Artist $20; Individual $35; Family $50; Contributing $100; Sustaining $300; Life $500.

INDO-AMERICAN HERITAGE MUSEUM, 6328 N. California Ave., Chicago, IL 60659.
E-mail: info@iahmuseum.org
Web Site: www.iahmuseum.org
Heritage Museum.
Collections: Indian cultural heritage; immigrant history; photographs; personal artifacts.
Activities: educational programs & activities; special events.
Hours & Admission Prices: Mon.-Sat. 1-5.

INTERNATIONAL MUSEUM OF SURGICAL SCIENCE, (M), 1524 N. Lake Shore Dr., Chicago, IL 60610-1651. Tel.: 312-642-6502, ext. 3130. Fax: 312-642-9516.
E-mail: leonard@imss.org
Web Site: www.imss.org
Founded: 1953.
Congressional District: 7
Key Personnel: Pres. (V), Raymond Dieter, M.D.; Cur., Lindsey Thieman; Museum Shop Mgr., Lynnea Smith.
Personnel Profile: Full-Time Paid 2; Part-Time Paid 1; Part-Time Volunteers 10; Interns 2.
Governing Authority: nonprofit organization. Parent Institution: International College of Surgeons, 1516 N. Lake Shore Dr., Chicago, IL 60610. Tax-exempt: 501(c)(3).
Medical Museum: housed in 1917 Howard Van Doren Shaw Mansion.
Collections: medical collection showing the growth & perfection of many surgical specialties such as obstetrics & gynecology, orthopedics, urology, radiology, X-ray, heart research & acupuncture; manuscript collections; extensive collection of medical artifacts & art.
Facilities: 2,000-vol. library: books dealing with various fields of medicine; 80-seat auditorium.
Activities: self-guided tours; lectures; loan, permanent, temporary & traveling exhibitions.
Publications: quarterly newsletter, MuseLetter.
Hours & Admission Prices: May-Sept. Tues.-Sun. 10-4; Oct.-April Tues.-Sat. 10-4. Adults $10, senior citizens & students $6; discounts to AAM & ASTC members; members & Tues. no charge. Closed New Year's Day; Independence Day; Thanksgiving; Christmas. ♿
Attendance: 15,000 (accurate)
Membership: Student $15; Individual $25; Family $50; Director's Club $100; Chairman's Club $500; Founder's Club $1,000. Corporate & Business Membership: Sponsor $100; Director's Circle $1,000; Chairman's Circle $5,000; Founder's Circle $10,000.

INTUIT: THE CENTER FOR INTUITIVE AND OUTSIDER ART, 756 N. Milwaukee Ave., Chicago, IL 60642-5939. Tel.: 312-243-9088. Fax: 312-243-9089.
E-mail: intuit@art.org
Web Site: www.art.org
Founded: 1991.

Congressional District: 5
Key Personnel: C.E.O. & Dir., Cleo F. Wilson; Devel. & Membership, Kerry Schneider; Education & Museum Shop Mgr., Amanda Curtis; Pres. (V), William Swislow; Public Rels. & Security, Bryan Preston; Treas., Gary Zickel; Registrar & Archivist, Farris Wahbeh; Cur., Jan Petry.
Personnel Profile: Full-Time Paid 3; Full-Time Volunteers 5; Part-Time Paid 2; Part-Time Volunteers 2; Interns 2.
Governing Authority: private; nonprofit organization. Tax-exempt: 501(c)(3).
Art Museum.
Collections: art brut; non-traditional folk art; self-taught art; visionary art.
Research Fields: art & artists from the genres of art brut, non-traditional folk art, self-taught art, and/or visionary art; art environments, art & psychiatry, and the role of Chicago in the movement of folk & outsider art in America.
Facilities: library.
Activities: 75-seat auditorium; 1,300 sq. ft. exhibit space; films; formal education programs; guided tours; lectures; loan, temporary & traveling exhibitions. Museum-related items for sale. Annual Event: The Intuit Show of Folk and Outsider Art.
Publications: quarterly newsletter, The Outsider.
Hours & Admission Prices: Tues.-Wed. & Fri.-Sat. 11-5, Thurs. 11-7:30. No charge; donations accepted. Closed national holidays.
Attendance: 5,000 (estimated)
Membership: Student $25; Individual $40; Family & Partner $60; Associate $100-$249; Enthusiast $250-$499; Patron $500-$1,199; Benefactor $1,200-$2,499; Leadership Circle $2,500-$3,499; Visionary Circle $3,500 & up.

IRISH AMERICAN HERITAGE CENTER, 4626 N. Knox Ave., Chicago, IL 60630-4035. Tel.: 773-282-7035.
Web Site: irish-american.org
Key Personnel: Exec. Dir., Tim McDonald
Heritage Center.
Collections: Irish history & culture; furniture; personal artifacts; Irish lace; late 19th century piano; Belleek Parian china; period maps.
Activities: special events; temporary exhibits.
Hours & Admission Prices: Wed.-Sat. by appointment.

JAMES P. FITZGIBBONS HISTORICAL MUSEUM, 9801 Ave. G, Calumet Park Fieldhouse, Chicago, IL 60617. Tel.: 312-721-7948.
Key Personnel: Pres. (V), Bernard Janecki.
Governing Authority: Parent Institution: Southeast Chicago Historical Society.
Historical Society Museum.
Collections: local history & culture; personal artifacts; photographs.
Hours & Admission Prices: Thurs. 1-4, 1st Sun. of month 12-3.

JANE ADDAMS HULL-HOUSE MUSEUM, UNIVERSITY OF ILLINOIS CHICAGO, (M), 800 S. Halsted, (M/C 051), Chicago, IL 60607-7017. Tel.: 312-413-5353. Fax: 312-413-2092.
E-mail: jahh@uic.edu
Web Site: www.uic.edu/jaddams/hull/
Founded: 1967.
Congressional District: 7
Key Personnel: Dir., Lisa Yun Lee; Facilities Mgr. & Head Docent, Dan Portincaso.
Personnel Profile: Full-Time Paid 4; Part-Time Paid 6.
Governing Authority: university. Parent Institution: University of Illinois at Chicago. Tax-exempt.
Historic House Site: 1856 Hull Mansion occupied by Jane Addams in 1889; serving as the first settlement building of Hull House complex; 1907 Resident's Dining Hall.
Collections: structures; paintings; photographs; documents; artifacts; memorabilia; furniture; paintings & other artwork; books; papers, letters, clipping & manuscripts relating to history of Hull House, Jane Addams & the surrounding neighborhood.
Research Fields: history of settlement house movement in Chicago; life of Jane Addams; local history; history of social welfare reform; immigration & ethnic history.
Activities: guided tours; lectures; permanent & temporary exhibitions; audio-visual programs.
Publications: brochure.
Hours & Admission Prices: Tues.-Fri. 10-4, Sun. 12-4. No charge. Closed major holidays.
Attendance: 13,000 (accurate)

JOHN G. SHEDD AQUARIUM, 1200 S. Lake Shore Dr., Chicago, IL 60605-2490. Tel.: 312-939-2438. Fax: 312-939-8069.
E-mail: contactus@sheddaquarium.org
Web Site: www.sheddaquarium.org
Founded: 1924.
Congressional District: 7
Key Personnel: Pres. & C.E.O., Ted A. Beattie; Chm. (V), Sarah Nava Garvey; Sr. Vice Pres. Operations & Facilities, Brad Popovich; Vice Pres. Special Projects & Animal Legislation, Jim Robinett; Vice Pres. Planning & Design, Michael Delfini; Vice Pres. Education Conservation, Cheryl Mell; Vice Pres. Devel., Chris Jabin; Vice Pres. Human Resources, Nancy Anschel; Exec. Vice Pres., Debra Fassnacht; Exec. Vice Pres. & C.F.O., Joyce Simon; Exec. Vice Pres. Mktg., Public Rels. & Guest Experiences, Amy Ritter Cowen; Exec. Vice Pres. Animal Collections & Training, Ken Ramirez; Dir. Public Rels., Roger Germann; Museum Shop Mgr., Roy Schlegel.
Personnel Profile: Full-Time Paid 270; Part-Time Paid 115; Part-Time Volunteers 600.
Governing Authority: nonprofit organization. Parent Institution: Shedd Aquarium Society. Tax-exempt: 501(c)(3).
Aquarium.
Collections: 32,500 animals representing more than 1,500 species; invertebrates; fish; birds; reptiles; amphibians; mammals; 90,000-gallon Caribbean exhibit; Oceanarium: features whales, dolphins, sea otters, sea lions & penguins in re-creations of natural habitats; Amazon Rising features 14 floor-to-skylight habitats; Indo-Pacific shark & coral reef exhibit features shark, coral, & other marine life; Wild Reef includes 25 sharks & live coral.
Research Fields: marine mammals; coral reefs; wetlands; tropical marine fish propagation; snails; iguanas.
Facilities: 15,000-vol. library; 400 periodicals; auditorium; restaurant; cafeteria; classrooms; amphitheater. Educational materials & gift items for sale.
Activities: educational programs & materials for school groups; college credit courses; evening & weekend classes for adults & children; special exhibits on aquatic topics presented semiannually; nature films; lectures; performances; aquarium orientation; volunteer training programs; marine mammal shows; caribbean feeding; natural history trips.
Publications: WaterShedd; annual report.
Hours & Admission Prices: Memorial Day to Labor Day daily 9-6; Sept.-May Mon.-Fri. 9-5, Sat.-Sun. 9-6. Total Experience Pass (Waters of the World, Amazon Rising, Wild Reef, Oceanarium, Polar Play Zone, & one 4-D Experience): adults $28.95, youth $21.95. Shedd Pass (Waters of the World, Amazon Rising, Wild Reef, Oceanarium, & Polar Play Zone): adults $24.95, youth $17.95. Aquarium only: adults $8, youth $6; members no charge. Closed Christmas. ♿
Attendance: 2,000,000 (estimated)
Membership: Individual $80; Family $115; Family Plus $130; Partner $175-$249; Associate $250-$499; Sponsor $500-$1,499.

LATVIAN FOLK ART MUSEUM, 4146 N. Elston Ave., Chicago, IL 60618-1828. Tel.: 773-588-2085. Fax: 773-588-3405.
Founded: 1978.
Key Personnel: Pres. (V), Dace Kezbers.
Personnel Profile: Part-Time Volunteers 2.
Governing Authority: Tax-exempt.
Folk Art Museum.
Collections: textiles; ceremonial costumes; musical instruments.
Hours & Admission Prices: By appointment. No charge; donations accepted. Closed holidays.

LINCOLN PARK CONSERVATORY, 2391 N. Stockton Dr., Chicago, IL 60614-3419. Mailing Address: Garfield Park Conservatory, 300 N. Central Park Ave., Chicago, IL 60624. Tel.: 312-742-7736 & 746-5995. Fax: 312-742-5619.
Web Site: www.chicagoparkdistrict.com
Founded: 1890.
Congressional District: 9
Key Personnel: Dir. Conservatories, Mary Eysenbach; Gen. Foreman, Miguel del Valle; Foreman, Don Fuller; Foreman, Rose Bialis; Horticulturalist, Steve Meyer.
Personnel Profile: Full-Time Paid 16; Part-Time Paid 1; Part-Time Volunteers 250.
Governing Authority: municipal. Parent Institution: Chicago Park District, 541 N. Fairbanks, Chicago, IL 60611. Tax-exempt.
Horticultural Conservatory: housed in 1892 Lincoln Park Conservatory.
Collections: botanical collection; cycads; fern grotto; epiphytes including orchids and bromeliads; tropicals including palms, fruit trees, shrubs and ground covers; orchids.
Facilities: conservatory; outdoor gardens; greenhouses.
Activities: annual flower shows; outdoor summer gardens.
Publications: brochures; on-site map.
Hours & Admission Prices: Daily 9-5; guided tours by appointment. No charge; donations accepted. ♿
Attendance: 400,000 (estimated)

LINCOLN PARK ZOOLOGICAL GARDENS, 2001 N. Clark St., Chicago, IL 60614-4757. Mailing Address: P.O. Box 14903, Chicago, IL 60614-0903. Tel.: 312-742-2000. Fax: 312-742-2137.
E-mail: lpz@lpzoo.org
Web Site: www.lpzoo.org
Founded: 1868.
Congressional District: 5
Key Personnel: Zoo Dir., Pres. & C.E.O., Kevin J. Bell; Bd. Chair, Dave Bolger; Sr. Vice Pres. Operations, Troy Baresel; Sr. Vice Pres. Conservation Programs, Steven Thompson, Ph.D.; Vice Pres. Devel., Christine Zrinsky; Vice Pres. Conservation, Dominic Travis, D.V.M.; Vice Pres. Human Rels. & Administration, Donna Curtis; Vice Pres. Education, Rachel Bergren; Vice Pres. Communications & Public Affairs, Marybeth Johnson; Cur. Large Mammals and Carnivores, Dave Bernier; Cur. Small Mammals & Reptiles, Diane Mulkerin; Gen. Cur., Megan Ross, Ph.D.; Cur. Birds, Colleen Lynch; Asst. Cur. Primates, Maureen Leahy; Veterinarian, Kathryn Gamble, D.V.M.; Museum Shop Mgr., Marla Molinelli.
Personnel Profile: Full-Time Paid 181; Part-Time Paid 78; Part-Time Volunteers 750; Interns 40.
Governing Authority: society. Parent Institution: Lincoln Park Zoological Society. Branch Park: Indian Boundary Park Zoo, Chicago, IL. Tax-exempt: 501(c)(3).
Zoo.
Collections: 1,275 specimens of mammals, birds, reptiles, amphibians, invertebrates.
Research Fields: zoo medicine; animal nutrition; reproduction; comparative pathology; primatology; small population biology; epidemiology; field conservation; small population management; endocrinology.
Facilities: 2,000-vol. library of animal-related books available for use on premises; children's zoo; farm in zoo.
Activities: guided tours; volunteer programs on grounds; formally organized education programs for children, adults, students & teachers (K-12) website and distance learning programs; traveling zoo outreach program.
Publications: quarterly, Lincoln Park Zoo Magazine; quarterly, public programs mailer; brochure, group sales; catalogue, fall & winter/spring programs.
Hours & Admission Prices: Winter: daily 9-5; Summer: Mon.-Fri. 9-6, Sat.-Sun. & holidays 9-7. No charge. ♿
Attendance: 3,000,000 (estimated)
Membership: Lincoln Park Zoological Society: Individual $50; Household $70; Zoologist $120; Curator $250; Explorers' Circle $500; Conservator's Circle $1,500.

THE LITHUANIAN MUSEUM, 5600 S. Claremont Ave., Chicago, IL 60636-1039. Tel.: 773-434-4545. Fax: 773-434-9363.
E-mail: info@lithuanianresearch.org
Web Site: www.lithuanianresearch.org
Founded: 1989.
Congressional District: 3
Key Personnel: Pres., John A. Rackauskas, Ph.D., Litt.D.; Chm. (V), Vytautas Bielianskas, Ph.D.; Dir., Skirmante Miglinas; Financial Dir., Robert Vitas, Ph.D.; Dir. Medical Museum, Milda Budrys, M.D.; Public Rels., D. Petrulis, M.A.; Dir. Technical Svcs., Thomas R. Miglinas.
Governing Authority: nonprofit organization. Parent Institution: The Lithuanian Research & Studies Center, Inc. Subsidiary Museum: Lithuanian Museum of Medicine. Tax-exempt: 501(c)(3).
Lithuanian History Museum.
Collections: arts & crafts; history; militaria; music; medicine; coins; stamps; biography; posters; costumes; textiles; crosses; art; graphics; amber jewelry & objects.
Research Fields: Lithuanian art, culture & history; Lithuanian immigration to the U.S.
Facilities: 100,000-vol. library of books & periodicals available for use by public; educational facilities; 2,000 sq. ft. exhibit space.
Activities: guided tours; loan, temporary & traveling exhibitions.
Publications: books, Lithuanian-American Medical Directory; Lithuania & the United States: The Establishment of State Relations; Lithuanica Collections in European Research Libraries: A Bibliography; The Samogitian Crusade; journal reprint, Varpas, 1889-1905; The Baltic Crusade, second revised & enlarged edition; Samogitian Crusade; Tannenberg and After; Livonian Crusade.
Hours & Admission Prices: Tues.-Fri. 9:15-3:30, Sat. 9:15-2. No charge; donations accepted.
Attendance: 6,000 (estimated)
Membership: Individual $50; Supporter $100; Honorary $500; Perpetual $1,000.

LOYOLA UNIVERSITY MUSEUM OF ART, (M), 820 N. Michigan Ave., Chicago, IL 60611-2147. Tel.: 312-915-7600. Fax: 312-915-6388.
Web Site: www.luc.edu/luma
Founded: 2004.
Congressional District: 42
Key Personnel: Dir. Cultural Affairs, Pamela E. Ambrose; Advancement Coord., Corp. & Foundation Rels., Erika Cornelisen; Devel., Lisa Torgerson; Public Rels., Philip Hale; Cur., Jonathan Canning; Cur. Education, Ann M. Meehan; Mgr. Visitor Svcs., Emily Grimm; Mgr. Exhibitions, Andrew Cunningham.
Personnel Profile: Full-Time Paid 7; Part-Time Paid 15; Part-Time Volunteers 27; Interns 4.
Governing Authority: private university. Tax-exempt: 501(c)(3).
Art Museum.
Collections: Martin D'Arcy collection of Medieval, Renaissance & Baroque art; LUMA modern & contemporary art.
Major Exhibits: Moholy-Nagy: Education of the Senses, 2/10/10-5/9/10; Pilgrimages, 8/20/10-11/14/10; Art and Faith of the Creche, 11/27/10-1/16/11.
Facilities: library of art & architecture books; 25,000 sq. ft. exhibit space; lecture hall; children's gallery. Museum-related items for sale.
Activities: concerts; docent program; films; formal education programs; guided tours; lectures; loan, traveling & temporary exhibitions; study clubs; internships; special events.
Publications: quarterly newsletter, LUMANARY.
Hours & Admission Prices: Tues. 11-8, Wed.-Sun. 11-6. Adults $6, senior citizens $5; discounts to military, groups, AAM, NARM & ICOM members; students, children, members & Tues. no charge. Closed major holidays. ♿
Attendance: 27,000 (accurate)
Membership: Individual $50; Family $100; Supporter $250; Contributor $500; Sustainer $1,000; Patron $5,000; Benefactor $10,000.

MUSEUM OF BROADCAST COMMUNICATIONS, State & Kinzie Sts., Chicago, IL 60654-3709. Mailing Address: 676 N. LaSalle St., Ste. 424, Chicago, IL 60654. Tel.: 312-245-8200. Fax: 312-245-8207.
Broadcast History Museum.
Collections: American radio & television history.
Facilities: cafe. Museum-related items for sale.
Activities: view vintage shows; tape a newscast in the television studio.
Hours & Admission Prices: Temporarily closed for relocation.

*** MUSEUM OF CONTEMPORARY ART, (M),** 220 E. Chicago Ave., Chicago, IL 60611-2644. Tel.: 312-280-2660. Fax: 312-799-3510. TDD: 312-397-4006.
E-mail: webmaster@mcachicago.org
Web Site: www.mcachicago.org
Founded: 1967.
Congressional District: 7
Key Personnel: Dir. Pritzker, Madeleine Grynsztejn; Chm., Mary Ittelson; Deputy Dir. & C.O.O., Janet Alberti; C.F.O., Peter Walton; Dir. Mktg., Angelique Power; Dir. Admin., Helen Dunbeck; Dir. Collections & Exhibitions, Jennifer Draffen; Senior Cur., Elizabeth Smith; Dir. Facilities Management, Don Meckley; Dir. Performance Programs, Peter Taub; Dir. Retail Operations, Mark Millmore; Dir. Education, Erika Varricchio Hanner; Dir. Media, Karla Loring; Dir. Devel., Lisa Key; Dir. Security, Eddie Sallie.
Personnel Profile: Full-Time Paid 95; Part-Time Paid 70; Part-Time Volunteers 200; Interns 85.
Governing Authority: private; nonprofit organization; board of trustees. Tax-exempt: 501(c)(3).
Art Museum & Center.
Collections: post-World War II painting; sculpture; graphics; photography; mixed media; artists' conceptual works; artists' books; videos.
Major Exhibits: Liam Gillick: Three Perspectives and A Short (T), 11/09-1/10/10; Liam Gillick Curates the MCA Collection, 11/09-1/10/10; Daria Martin: Minotaur (T), 11/09-2/7/10; Italics: Italian Art Between Tradition and Revolution 1968-2008, 11/14/09-2/14/10; Production Site: The Artist's Studio Inside and Out, 2/6/10-5/23/10; Alexander Calder and Contemporary Art: Form, Balance, Joy, 6/19/10-10/10/10; Urban China, Fall 2010; Mathias Poledna: Crystal Palace, Fall 2010; Luc Tuymans (T), 10/2/10-1/9/11.
Facilities: 16,000-vol. library; artist files; catalogues; educational facilities; video orientation space; cafe. Books & gift items for sale.
Activities: temporary exhibitions & rotating installations of the permanent collection of contemporary art & photography; film series; performance art; lecture series; tours; educational outreach program; seminars; teacher workshops; children's art programs.
Publications: exhibit catalogs; gallery guides; quarterly calendar of events; museum brochure.
Hours & Admission Prices: Tues. 10-8, Wed.-Sun. 10-5. Adults $12, members $7, students & seniors $6; discounts to AAM & ICOM members; children under 12 no charge. Closed New Year's Day; Thanksgiving; Christmas. ♿

Attendance: 300,000
Membership: Student & Out of Town $30; Senior $40; Individual $60; Household $75.

*** MUSEUM OF CONTEMPORARY PHOTOGRAPHY, COLUMBIA COLLEGE CHICAGO, (M),** 600 S. Michigan Ave., Chicago, IL 60605-1900. Tel.: 312-663-5554. Fax: 312-369-8067.
E-mail: mocp@colum.edu
Web Site: www.mocp.org
Founded: 1976.
Congressional District: 7
Key Personnel: C.E.O., Alan Turner; Pres., Warrick L. Carter; Chm. (V), Lawrence K. Snider; Treas., R. Michael DeSalle; Chm. Photography, Bob Thall; Dir. & Cur., Rod Slemmons; Assoc. Dir., Natasha Egan; Mgr. Exhibitions, Stephanie Conaway.
Personnel Profile: Full-Time Paid 7; Part-Time Paid 4; Part-Time Volunteers 1; Interns 12.
Governing Authority: college; nonprofit organization. Parent Institution: Columbia College Chicago. Tax-exempt: 501(c)(3).
Photography Museum.
Collections: works of contemporary American photographers, including Zeke Berman, Ruth Bernhard, Dawoud Bey, Marsha Burns, Harry Callahan, Carl Chiarenza, Larry Clark, Linda Connor, Eileen Cowin, Barbara Crane, Louise Dahl-Wolfe, Bruce Davidson, Roy DeCarava, Elliott Erwitt, Walker Evans, Lee Friedlander, Emmet Gowin, Robert Heinecken, Barbara Kasten, Mark Klett, Dorothea Lange, Danny Lyon, Susan Meiselas, Ray Metzker, Nicholas Nixon, Anne Noggle, Irving Penn, Aaron Siskind, Mike & Doug Starn, Ruth Thorne-Thomsen, Jerry N. Uelsmann, James Van Der Zee, Carrie Mae Weems, William Wegman, Minor White, Garry Winogrand, Joel-Peter Witkin.
Research Fields: contemporary photography.
Facilities: classrooms; print study room; research & viewing center.
Activities: guided tours; lectures & symposia; traveling exhibitions originated by the museum; video, computer & participatory programs; publications; membership benefits; fine print program.
Publications: annual exhibition catalogues.
Hours & Admission Prices: Mon.-Wed. & Fri.-Sat. 10-5, Thurs. 10-8, Sun. 12-5. No charge; donations accepted. Closed Martin Luther King Jr. Day; Memorial Day; Independence Day; Labor Day; Thanksgiving weekend; Christmas Eve to New Year's Day. ♿
Attendance: 72,500 (accurate)
Membership: Student $20 Individual $35; Dual $50; Group Photo $100; Scholar $300; Collector $500; Director's Circle $1,000.

MUSEUM OF HOLOGRAPHY, 1134 W. Washington Blvd., Chicago, IL 60607-2021. Tel.: 312-226-1007. Fax: 312-829-9636.
Art Museum.
Collections: over 200 3D laser-generated images.
Hours & Admission Prices: Wed.-Sun. 12:30-5.

*** MUSEUM OF SCIENCE AND INDUSTRY, (M),** 5700 S. Lake Shore Dr., Chicago, IL 60637-2003. Tel.: 773-684-1414. Fax: 773-684-7141. TDD: 773-684-3323.
Web Site: www.msichicago.org
Founded: 1926.
Congressional District: 1
Key Personnel: Pres. & C.E.O., David R. Mosena; Asst. to Pres., Eileen M. Cabrera; Chm., Robert S. Morrison; Vice Pres. Exhibits & Collections, Kurt Haunfelner; Vice Pres. Finance & Administration, Bob Fisher; Vice Pres. Capital Campaign, Shannon Alexander; Vice Pres. Mktg. & Public Rels., Valerie Waller; Vice Pres. Education & Guest Svcs., Andrea Ingram; Dir. Temporary Exhibits, Anne Rashford; Dir. Business Operations, Andy Zakrajsek; Dir. Membership, Susan Rawls.
Personnel Profile: Full-Time Paid 287; Part-Time Paid 73; Part-Time Volunteers 605.
Governing Authority: nonprofit organization. Tax-exempt: 501(c)(3).
Science & Technology Museum: housed in classic Greek structure constructed as the Palace of Fine Arts for the World's Fair Columbian Exposition of 1893 in Chicago, located on the site of the Exposition in Jackson Park.
Collections: U-505 submarine; hands-on exhibits; aviation; scientific principles, technological applications & social implications; industry; Spirit of America; Empire 999; Pioneer Zephyr; Apollo 8 capsule.
Facilities: restaurants. Books & other museum-related items for sale.
Activities: guided tours; lectures; films; children & family classes; science fairs; arts festivals; inter-museum loan, permanent, temporary & traveling exhibitions; live science experiences; teacher development programs; student learning labs & video conferencing programs; group tours.
Publications: e-newsletters; member magazine, Momentum; teacher education guides; annual education calendars.
Hours & Admission Prices: Summer: Mon.-Sat. 9:30-5:30, Sun. 11-5:30; Winter: Mon.-Sat. 9:30-4, Sun. 11-4. Adults $13, seniors $12, children 3-11 $9; discounts to Chicago residents, and AAM & ICOM members; Illinois teachers, active military, police & fire personnel, members & children under 3 no charge. Omnimax Theater: adults $8, seniors $7, children 3-11 $6; children under 3 (on adult's lap) no charge. Combination tickets available. Closed Christmas. ♿
Attendance: 1,675,109 (accurate)
Membership: Associate Senior & Student $55; Bachelors Individual $70; Masters Family $105; Doctorate Family $175.

NATIONAL ITALIAN AMERICAN SPORTS HALL OF FAME, 1431 W. Taylor St., Chicago, IL 60607-4625. Tel.: 312-226-5566. Fax: 312-226-5678.
E-mail: george@niashf.org
Web Site: www.niashf.org/
Founded: 1977.
Key Personnel: Founder & Chm., George Randazzo.
Personnel Profile: Full-Time Paid 6; Full-Time Volunteers 1; Part-Time Paid 3; Interns 1.
Governing Authority: nonprofit. Tax-exempt.
Sports Museum.
Collections: history & heritage of Italian Americans in sports.
Facilities: rental facilities. Museum-related items for sale.
Activities: special events; boxing matches; guest speakers. Annual Event: NIASHF Induction and Awards Ceremony.
Publications: quarterly magazine, Red, White and Green; quarterly newsletter, NIASHF News.
Hours & Admission Prices: Mon.-Fri. 9-5, Sat.-Sun. 11-4; other times by appointment. Adults $5, seniors, children & groups over 15 $3. ♿

*** NATIONAL MUSEUM OF MEXICAN ART, (M),** 1852 W. 19th St., Chicago, IL 60608-2706. Tel.: 312-738-1503. Fax: 312-738-9740.
E-mail: carlos@nationalmuseumofmexicanart.org
Web Site: www.nationalmuseumofmexicanart.org
Formerly: Mexican Fine Arts Center Museum
Founded: 1982.
Congressional District: 1
Key Personnel: C.E.O., Pres. & Founder, Carlos Tortolero; Vice Pres., Juana Guzman; Vice Pres. & C.F.O., Martin Sandoval; Chm., Martin R. Castro; Cur. Permanent Collections, Rebecca D. Meyers; Dir. Devel., Randy Adamsick; Chief Cur. & Dir. Visual Arts, Cesareo Moreno; Performing Arts Dir., Jorge Valdivia; Museum Shop Mgr., Raquel Rios.
Personnel Profile: Full-Time Paid 38; Part-Time Paid 35; Part-Time Volunteers 32; Interns 11.
Governing Authority: nonprofit organization. Tax-exempt: 501(c)(3).
Art Museum.
Collections: Mexican art, folk art & culture as it manifests itself inside and outside of Mexico; photography; graphic arts; contemporary art.
Major Exhibits: Translating Revolution, 1/10-8/10; Dia De Los Muertos, 9/10-12/10.
Facilities: 48,000 sq. ft. exhibit space; educational facilities; 11,000 sq. ft. building off-site which houses a youth museum and WRTE-FM Radio Arte, a youth run radio station. Gift items for sale.
Activities: guided tours; lectures; arts festivals; organized education programs for children; participatory, loan, temporary & traveling exhibitions; performing arts events.
Publications: catalogues.
Hours & Admission Prices: Tues.-Sun. 10-5. No charge; donations accepted. Closed major holidays. ♿
Attendance: 168,000 (accurate)
Membership: Students & Senior Citizens $20; Individual $35; Family $55.

NATIONAL VIETNAM VETERANS ART MUSEUM, 1801 S. Indiana Ave., Chicago, IL 60616-1308. Tel.: 312-326-0270. Fax: 312-326-9767.
E-mail: info@nvvam.org
Web Site: www.nvvam.org
Key Personnel: Gen. Mgr. & Cur. Traveling Exhibits, Jerry Kykisz; Chief Cur. & Head Art Committee, Michael Helbing; Cur. & Project Devel., Ted Stanuga; Dir. Education & Outreach, Jennifer Komorowski
Military Art Museum.
Collections: paintings; photographs; sculpture.
Facilities: cafe. Museum-related items for sale.
Publications: newsletter, Artifacts.
Hours & Admission Prices: Tues.-Sat. 10-5. Adults $10, students $7; discounts to groups; members no charge.

ORIENTAL INSTITUTE MUSEUM, UNIVERSITY OF CHICAGO, 1155 E. 58th St., Chicago, IL 60637-1569. Tel.: 773-702-9520. Fax: 773-702-9853.
E-mail: oi-museum@uchicago.edu

Web Site: oi.uchicago.edu
Founded: 1894.
Congressional District: 1
Key Personnel: Dir., Gil Stein; Chm. (V), Terry Friedman; Chm. (V), Cathy Duenas; Head Museum Education & Pub. Programs, Carole Krucoff; Conservator, Laura D'Alessandro; Archivist, John Larson; Registrar & Cur., Helen McDonald; Gift Shop Mgr., Denise Browning; Asst. Conservator, Alison Whyte; Security Supvr., Adam Lubin.
Personnel Profile: Full-Time Paid 12; Part-Time Paid 22; Part-Time Volunteers 107; Interns 1.
Governing Authority: university. Parent Institution: University of Chicago, 5801 Ellis Ave. Tax-exempt: 501(c)(3).
Archaeology, Ancient History & Art Museum.
Collections: art & archaeology of the Ancient Near East, Egypt, Iraq, Iran, Israel, Syria, Cyprus, Palestine, Turkey, Nubia, Early Christian, Islamic material; manuscript collections.
Research Fields: Ancient Near Eastern archaeology & history, sculpture, decorative arts; Ancient Near Eastern languages; Islamic languages & civilization.
Facilities: 25,000-vol. research library; archives of Oriental Institute field expeditions; 65,000 photos; 8,600 slides of the ancient near East; 275-seat auditorium; classrooms. Books & other museum-related items for sale.
Activities: guided tours; lectures; films; formally organized education programs for adults, children, undergraduate & graduate students affiliated with University of Chicago; docent program; inter-museum loan, permanent & temporary exhibitions.
Publications: guide; occasional pamphlets; exhibition catalogs; museum brochure.
Hours & Admission Prices: Tues. & Thurs.-Sat. 10-6, Wed. 10-8:30, Sun. 12-6. No charge; donations accepted. ♿
Attendance: 60,113 (accurate)
Membership: Students $20 p.a. (USA only); Seniors, UC Faculty or Staff & Long-distance members $40 p.a.; Basic $50 p.a.; Sustaining $75 p.a.; Supporting $100 p.a.; Contributing $250 p.a.; Sponsoring $500 p.a.; Breasted Patron $1,000 p.a.; Director's Circle $2,500 p.a.

THE PALETTE & CHISEL, 1012 N. Dearborn, Chicago, IL 60610-2804. Tel.: 312-642-4400. Fax: 312-642-4317.
E-mail: fineart1012@sbcglobal.net
Web Site: www.paletteandchisel.org
Founded: 1895.
Key Personnel: Exec. Dir., William Ewers; Pres. (V), Dayle Sazonoff; Vice Pres., Leslie Outten; Treas., Christine Sauser; Corporate Sec., Christine Jones; Corresponding Sec., Barbara Graefen.
Personnel Profile: Full-Time Paid 1; Part-Time Paid 2; Part-Time Volunteers 2.
Governing Authority: nonprofit organization. Tax-exempt: 501(c)(3).
Art Academy: housed in c.1875 double bay Italianate mansion.
Collections: club archives 1895-present; c.1900-present artwork from members.
Facilities: library of donated art books; painting & sculpture classrooms.
Activities: arts festivals; formal education programs for adults; guided tours; lectures; temporary exhibitions. Annual Events: auction; juried shows; workshops & lectures; all day modeling marathons on New Year's Day, Labor Day & Memorial Day.
Publications: quarterly newsletter, The Cowbell.
Hours & Admission Prices: Mon.-Fri. 1-5; other times by appointment. No charge for exhibitions; fees for classes; workshops & lectures; discounts for members. Office closed New Year's Day; Memorial Day; Independence Day; Labor Day; Thanksgiving; Christmas Eve & Day.
Attendance: 750 (estimated)
Membership: Patron $50, $125, $1,000; Non-Resident Artist (Basic) $45; Non-Resident Artist (Workshop) $150; Resident Artist $360.

*** THE PEGGY NOTEBAERT NATURE MUSEUM, (M),** 2430 N. Cannon Dr., Chicago, IL 60614-2874. Tel.: 773-755-5100. Fax: 773-755-5199.
Web Site: naturemuseum.org
Formerly: The Chicago Academy of Sciences Peggy Notebaert Nature Museum
Founded: 1857.
Congressional District: 9
Key Personnel: Pres. Emeritus & Academy Counselor, Dr. Paul G. Heltne; Pres. & C.E.O., Donna Gustafsson; Chm. (V), Stephen R. Ferrara; C.F.O., Michael Bauman; Dir. Education, Rafael Rosa; Cur. Biology, Dr. Douglas Taron; Museum Shop Mgr., Cindy Prokop.
Personnel Profile: Full-Time Paid 65; Part-Time Paid 16; Part-Time Volunteers 220; Interns 29.
Governing Authority: nonprofit organization. Parent Institution: Chicago Academy of Sciences. Tax-exempt: 501(c)(3).
Natural Science Museum.
Collections: birds; mammals; herpetology; geology; paleontology; malacology; botany; entomology; zoology; photography.
Research Fields: natural sciences; effective role of museums in teacher professional development; ecology of urban wildlife; conservation biology of North American butterflies; conservation biology of midwestern freshwater & terrestrial mollusks; headstart program for Blanding's turtle; coordinator of the Illinois Butterfly Monitoring Network.
Facilities: 25,000 sq. ft. exhibit space; 6.2 acres of botanical communities; children's gallery; meeting rooms; cafe. Museum-related items for sale.
Activities: youth summer camps; volunteer & intern opportunities; science & nature lectures; early childhood classes; onsite workshops & classes; teacher professional development workshops; permanent & temporary exhibitions; public programs; school & community science, technology & nature outreach; teen college preparedness & job skill training.
Publications: quarterly newsletter; annual report.
Hours & Admission Prices: Mon.-Fri. 9-4:30, Sat.-Sun. 10-5. Adults $9, seniors & students $7, children 3-12 $6; discounts to Chicago residents, AAM, ICOM & ASTC members; members & groups of 10 or more with reservations & Thurs. no charge. Closed New Year's Day; Thanksgiving; Christmas Day. ♿
Attendance: 208,849 (accurate)
Membership: Individual $42; Senior $47; Senior Family $55; Family $60; Premier $130; President's Club $600.

POLISH MUSEUM OF AMERICA, 984 N. Milwaukee Ave., Chicago, IL 60642-4101. Tel.: 773-384-3352 & 3731. Fax: 773-384-3799.
E-mail: pma@polishmuseumofamerica.org
Web Site: www.polishmuseumofamerica.org
Founded: 1935.
Congressional District: 4
Key Personnel: Chm., Wallace M. Ozog; Dir., Mr. Jan M. Lorys; Pres. (V), Maria Ciesla; Asst. Cur., Bohdan Gorczynski; Archivist, Halina Misterka; Sec., Sabina Logisz; Treas., Camille Kopielski; Librarian, Malgorzata Kot; Museum Shop Mgr., Ms. Mary Jane Robles.
Personnel Profile: Full-Time Paid 6; Part-Time Paid 2; Part-Time Volunteers 8; Interns 2.
Governing Authority: nonprofit. Parent Institution: Polish Roman Catholic Union. Subsidiary Institution: PRCUA. Tax-exempt.
Ethnic Museum.
Collections: 1,400 originals of Polish & Polish American artists insignia & drawings of Polish kings; costumes; religious artifacts; Polish military memorabilia; memorabilia of T. Kosciuszko; Kossak paintings; memorabilia of Paderewski; folk art; sculptures; manuscripts; periodicals; medals; coins; large part of Polish pavilion from the 1939 New York World's Fair.
Research Fields: Polish & Polish American culture.
Facilities: 62,000-vol. library of publications pertaining to Poland, by American-Polish authors & by Polish-American publishing firms; slides, strips, maps, photos & phono records available for research on the premises only.
Activities: art contests; guided tours; rotating exhibitions; Polish classical concerts; lectures.
Publications: quarterly periodical, Polish Museum of America; newsletter.
Hours & Admission Prices: Museum: Fri.-Wed. 11-4. Library: Mon.-Tues. & Fri.-Sat. 10-4, Wed. 1-7. Donation Requested: adults $5, students & senior citizens $4, children under 12 $3. ♿
Membership: Individual $25; Family $40; Contributing $50; Supporting $100; Sustaining $500; Lifetime $1,000.

THE PRITZKER MILITARY LIBRARY, (M), 610 N. Fairbanks Ct., 2nd Fl., Chicago, IL 60611-4898. Tel.: 312-587-0234. Fax: 312-587-0536.
E-mail: info@pritzkermilitarylibrary.net
Web Site: www.pritzkermilitarylibrary.net
Key Personnel: Exec. Dir., Ryan Yantis; Exec. Producer, Ed Tracy; Deputy Dir., Mary Spurr; Digital Collections Librarian, Leighton Shell, MLIS; Senior Librarian, Theresa A.R. Embrey, MLIS; Program Dir., Andrew Edeker
Library & Gallery.
Collections: books, videos, posters, uniforms, rare coins, medals & stamps relating to military history.
Facilities: library.
Hours & Admission Prices: Mon.-Fri. 8:30-4:30. No charge.

THE RENAISSANCE SOCIETY AT THE UNIVERSITY OF CHICAGO, 5811 S. Ellis Ave., Chicago, IL 60637-1404. Tel.: 773-702-8670. Fax: 773-702-9669.
E-mail: haberman@uchicago.edu
Web Site: www.renaissancesociety.org
Founded: 1915.
Congressional District: 1
Key Personnel: Dir. & Cur., Susanne Ghez; Pres. (V), Jennifer Levine; Dir.

Devel., Lori Bartman; Dir. Education & Assoc. Cur., Hamza Walker; Registrar & Dir. Publications, Karen Reimer; Preparator, Robert Bain; Dir. Mktg., Mia Ruyter; Office Mgr., Lise Haberman.
Personnel Profile: Full-Time Paid 6; Part-Time Paid 2; Part-Time Volunteers 2; Interns 3.
Governing Authority: board of directors. University of Chicago, 5811 Ellis Ave., Chicago, IL 60637. Tax-exempt.
Contemporary Art Museum.
Collections: works by contemporary artists.
Activities: guided tours; lectures; films; gallery talks; inter-museum loan; concerts; temporary & traveling exhibitions.
Publications: catalogs; checklists.
Hours & Admission Prices: Sept.-June Tues.-Fri. 10-5, Sat.-Sun. 12-5. No charge. Closed national holidays. ♿
Attendance: 20,000 (estimated)
Membership: Student $25; Member $50; Friend $100; Contributor $250; Supporter $500; Patron $1,000; Benefactor $2,500; Director's Circle $5,000.

SCHOOL OF THE ART INSTITUTE OF CHICAGO, SULLIVAN GALLERIES, 33 S. State St., 7th Fl., Chicago, IL 60603-2809. Mailing Address: Sullivan Galleries, 33 S. State St., 7th Fl., Chicago, IL 60603. Tel.: 312-629-6635. Fax: 312-629-6636.
Web Site: www.saic.edu/exhibitions
Founded: 1984.
Key Personnel: Exec. Dir., Mary Jane Jacob.
Personnel Profile: Full-Time Paid 6; Part-Time Paid 2; Interns 30.
Governing Authority: private college; nonprofit. Subsidiary Institution: Art Institute of Chicago, IL. Tax-exempt: 501(c)(3).
College Art Gallery.
Collections: paintings; photographs; sculpture.
Activities: temporary exhibitions; performances; lectures; screenings by SAIC students, faculty & professional artists.
Hours & Admission Prices: Tues.-Sat. 11-6. No charge. Closed holidays. ♿
Attendance: 118,401 (accurate)

* **SMART MUSEUM OF ART, (M),** University of Chicago, 5550 S. Greenwood Ave., Chicago, IL 60637-1506. Tel.: 773-702-0200 & 834-1778. Fax: 773-702-3121.
E-mail: smart-museum@uchicago.edu
Web Site: smartmuseum.uchicago.edu
Founded: 1974.
Congressional District: 1
Key Personnel: Dir. Dana Feitler, Anthony G. Hirschel; Dir. Education, Kristy Peterson; Dir. Collections & Exhibitions, Stephanie Smith; Senior Cur., Richard A. Born; Cur. & Mellon Program Coord., Anne Leonard; Mgr. Education Programs, Lauren Boylan; Outreach Education Technical Coord., Melissa Holbert; Asst. Dir. Devel., Justin Glasson; Mgr. Devel. Operations, Kate Kennedy; Dir. Finance & Admin., Peg Liput; Chief Preparator, Rudy Bernal; Assoc. Registrar, Natasha Derrickson; Preparation Asst., Ray Klemchuck; Public Rels. & Mktg. Mgr., C.J. Lind; Events & Retail Mgr., Sarah Polachek; Asst. Facilities & Security Supvr., Paul Dougherty; Security Supvr., Paul Bryan; Asst. Cur. Contemporary Art, Jessica Moss; Mgr. Devel. Communications, Kate Nardin; Business Mgr., Joyce Norman; Asst. for Leadership Support, Emilia Pappas; Consulting Cur., Wu Hung.
Personnel Profile: Full-Time Paid 16; Part-Time Paid 5; Interns 11.
Governing Authority: university. Parent Institution: University of Chicago, 5801 S. Ellis Ave., Chicago. Tax-exempt: 501(c)(3).
University Art Museum.
Collections: painting, sculpture, decorative arts, drawings, prints, photography & East Asian art ranging from ancient to modern.
Major Exhibits: Heartland (T), 11/09-1/17/10; The Darker Side of Light (T), 2/11/10-6/13/10; Mid-Century Design, 7/8/10-9/5/10; Echoes of the Past (T), 9/30/10-1/23/11.
Research Fields: related to the permanent collection; special exhibitions.
Facilities: Exhibition catalogues, scholarly monographs in art & art history, posters, slides, postcards & stationery items for sale.
Activities: guided tours; lectures; gallery talks; symposia; colloquia; educational programs; permanent collection; special exhibitions.
Publications: Smart Museum Bulletin; exhibition catalogues; collection handbook.
Hours & Admission Prices: mid-June to Sept. Tues.-Fri. 10-4, Sat.-Sun. 11-5; Oct. to mid-June Tues.-Wed. & Fri. 10-4, Thurs. 10-8, Sat.-Sun. 11-5. No charge; donations accepted. Closed holidays. ♿
Attendance: 66,397 (accurate)
Membership: University of Chicago Students, Faculty & Staff $35; Smart $50; Fellow $150; Patron $300; Sustaining Fellow $500; Director's Council $1,000 & up.

SMITH MUSEUM OF STAINED GLASS WINDOWS, Navy Pier, 600 E. Grand Ave., Chicago, IL 60611-3419. Tel.: 312-595-5024.
Web Site: www.navypier.com
Key Personnel: Cur., Rolf Achilles
Stained Glass Museum.
Collections: over 150 stained glass windows including secular & religious art.
Hours & Admission Prices: Daily Sun.-Thurs. 10-8, Fri.-Sat. 10-10. Tours: Thurs. 2pm. No charge.

SPERTUS MUSEUM, 610 S. Michigan Ave., Chicago, IL 60605-1901. Tel.: 312-322-1747 & 1700. Fax: 312-922-3934.
E-mail: museum@spertus.edu
Web Site: www.spertus.edu
Founded: 1968.
Congressional District: 20
Key Personnel: Pres. & C.E.O., Howard A. Sulkin, Ph.D.; Dir., Rhoda Rosen; Registrar & Collections Mgr., Arielle Weininger; Asst. Registrar, Tom Gengler; Sr. Cur., Staci Boris; Sr. Judaica Cur., Felicitas Heimann-Jelinek; Educator, Amanda Friedeman; Dir. Design, Mark Akgulian; Designer, Tracy Kostenbader; Design Asst., Tony Doyle; Exhibition Coord., Sheila Cronin; Museum Shop Mgr., Alana Aldort; Asst. Cur., Sarah Nelson; Asst. Cur. Judaica, Ilana Segal.
Personnel Profile: Full-Time Paid 11; Part-Time Paid 10; Part-Time Volunteers 30; Interns 2.
Governing Authority: college. Parent Institution: Spertus Institute of Jewish Studies. Tax-exempt: 501(c)(3).
Cultural, Art & Children's Museum.
Collections: archives; archaeology; art library; fine arts; Jewish ceremonial arts; ethnology; folklore; contemporary art.
Research Fields: Judaica & pertinent fine arts; Jewish culture & civilization.
Facilities: 1,000-vol. library of books, catalogs & folios relating to Jewish art, graphics & historic material available for research by public; theater; rental facilities; classrooms; cafe. Museum-related items for sale.
Activities: guided tours; lectures; gallery talks; films; musical programs; workshops; docent programs; family programs; community-based outreach programs; formally organized education programs for graduate students; inter-museum loan, permanent & temporary exhibitions.
Publications: exhibition catalogue, The New Authentics.
Hours & Admission Prices: Sun.-Wed. 10-5, Thurs. 10-6, Fri. 10-3. Adults $7, students & seniors $5; children under 5, Tues. 10-12 & Thurs. 2-6 no charge. Closed Jewish & national holidays. ♿
Attendance: 50,000 (accurate)
Membership: SpertusNet $30-$55; Senior $40-$70; Basic $50-$90; Household $65-$120; Associate $150; Fellow $250; Patron $500; Benefactor $1,000; Angel $5,000.

STEPHEN A. DOUGLAS TOMB, 636 E. 35th St., Chicago, IL 60616-4196. Tel.: 312-225-2620. Fax: 312-225-7855.
Founded: 1865.
Congressional District: 1
Key Personnel: Site Supt., Michael Carson.
Governing Authority: state. Parent Institution: Illinois Historic Preservation Agency. Tel.: 312-814-2070. Tax-exempt.
Historic Site: 1866-1881 Stephen A. Douglas Tomb designed by Leonard W. Volk. Listed on the National Register of Historic Places.
Collections: monument; sculpture; Senator Douglas' life history & tomb.
Activities: guided tours; lectures.
Publications: bimonthly, newsletter, Historic Illinois.
Hours & Admission Prices: Wed.-Sun. 9-5. No charge. Closed New Year's Day; Thanksgiving; Christmas. ♿
Attendance: 15,000 (estimated)

SWEDISH AMERICAN HISTORICAL SOCIETY, 3225 W. Foster Ave., Chicago, IL 60625-4823. Mailing Address: 3225 W. Foster Ave., Box 48, Chicago, IL 60625-4823. Tel.: 773-538-5722.
E-mail: info@swedishamericanhist.org
Web Site: www.swedishamericanhist.org
Founded: 1948.
Congressional District: 5
Key Personnel: Chm. (V), Kevin Proescholdt; Pres. (V), Philip J. Anderson.
Personnel Profile: Part-Time Paid 1.
Governing Authority: society. Tax-exempt: 501(c)(3).
Historical Society Archives.
Collections: books; periodicals; manuscripts; microfilm; oral histories.
Research Fields: archives; religion; education; journalism; fine arts; government; science; business; industry from 1840 to present day of Swedes in the United States.
Facilities: 3,000-vol. library of ethnic history available on premises. Books for sale.

Activities: annual & spring meetings; tours.
Publications: journal; The Swedish American Historical Quarterly; book.
Hours & Admission Prices: Mon.-Fri. by appointment. No charge. Closed legal holidays. ♿
Membership: Student $10; Annual $25; Sustaining $50; Donor $100; Benefactor $250; Life $1,000.

SWEDISH AMERICAN MUSEUM, (M), 5211 N. Clark St., Chicago, IL 60640-2101. Tel.: 773-728-8111. Fax: 773-728-8870.
E-mail: museum@samac.org
Web Site: www.swedishamericanmuseum.org
Founded: 1976.
Congressional District: 9
Key Personnel: Exec. Dir., Karin Moen Abercrombie; Pres., Kerstin Nicholson; Chm. (V), Annika Jaspers; Museum Shop Mgr., Ann Cutler.
Personnel Profile: Full-Time Paid 5; Part-Time Paid 1; Part-Time Volunteers 54.
Governing Authority: nonprofit organization. Tax-exempt: 170(b)(1)(A).
Swedish History Museum.
Collections: paintings, tools & artifacts describing the emigration of the Swedish people to the United States; special displays featuring famous Swedes in this country; furniture & woodcarvings by Swedish Americans; models; 1910 organ.
Research Fields: Swedish pioneer life; contributions of Swedes to development of America.
Facilities: classroom. Museum-related items for sale.
Activities: formally organized educational programs; loan, permanent & traveling exhibitions; concerts; lectures.
Publications: newsletter, Flaggan.
Hours & Admission Prices: Tues.-Fri. 10-4, Sat.-Sun. 11-4. Adults $4; members no charge. Children's Museum of Immigration: Tues.-Fri. 1-4, Sat.-Sun. 11-4. ♿
Attendance: 45,000 (estimated)
Membership: Student & Senior $15; Senior Couple $25; Individual $35; Family $50; Nonprofit Organization & Sustaining $75; Sandburg $100-$249; Linnaeus $250-$520; 521 Club $521-$999; Three Crowns $1,000.

UKRAINIAN INSTITUTE OF MODERN ART, 2320 W. Chicago Ave., Chicago, IL 60622-4722. Tel.: 773-227-5522.
Web Site: www.uima-art.org
Founded: 1971.
Key Personnel: Chm., Lalyssa Reifel; Pres., Orysia Cardoso; Cur., Stanisliv Gredo
Art Museum.
Collections: works by Chicago artists & Ukrainian sculptors & painters.
Activities: film screenings; music recitals; literary events; concerts; lectures; cultural events.
Hours & Admission Prices: Wed.-Sun. 12-4. Suggested Donation: $5.

UKRAINIAN NATIONAL MUSEUM, INC., 2249 W. Superior St., Chicago, IL 60612-1327. Tel.: 312-421-8020. Fax: 773-772-2883.
E-mail: president@ukrainiannationalmuseum.org
Web Site: www.ukrainiannationalmuseum.org
Founded: 1952.
Congressional District: 7
Key Personnel: C.E.O. & Pres. (V), Jaroslaw J. Hankewych; Sec., Irene Subota; Admin., Anna Chychula.
Personnel Profile: Full-Time Paid 2; Full-Time Volunteers 1; Part-Time Paid 1; Part-Time Volunteers 25.
Governing Authority: nonprofit organization. Tax-exempt: 501(c)(3).
Folk Art Museum.
Collections: Ukrainian folk art; textiles; woodworking; embroideries; beadwork; weaving exhibits; historical exhibits; Ukrainian artists paintings & sculptures; local & national archives relating to Ukrainian subjects; organizational archives; rare book collection; photos; music; history of Ukrainian immigration to America, particularly Chicago.
Major Exhibits: Tkaczenko, Aleksander, 3/10; Podlevskyj/Mojsejeva, 4/10; Monastereckyj, Wolodymyr, 11/10.
Facilities: 16,320-vol. Ukrainian & East European subjects available for public use.
Activities: guided tours; lectures; hobby workshops; organized education programs for children; loan & temporary exhibitions.
Publications: quarterly newsletter, Museum Chronicle.
Hours & Admission Prices: Thurs.-Sun. 11-4, Mon.-Wed. by appointment only. Adults $5, students & children $2; tours require advanced notice. Closed New Year's Day; Easter; Independence Day; Labor Day; Thanksgiving; Christmas. ♿
Attendance: 4,200 (accurate)
Membership: Seniors $15; Regular $25; Supporting $100; Benefactors $500; Founders $1,000; Patrons $5,000.

WOMAN MADE GALLERY, 685 N. Milwaukee Ave., Chicago, IL 60642-8021. Tel.: 312-738-0400. Fax: 312-738-0404.
E-mail: gallery@womanmade.org
Web Site: www.womanmade.org
Key Personnel: Exec. Dir., Beate Minkovski; Gallery Coord., Amy Galpin
Art Gallery.
Collections: works by women artists.
Facilities: Museum-related items for sale.
Activities: rental facilities; special events.
Publications: quarterly newsletter.
Hours & Admission Prices: Wed.-Fri. 12-7, Sat.-Sun. 12-4. No charge.

Chicago Heights

UNION STREET GALLERY, 1527 Otto Blvd., Chicago Heights, IL 60411-3442. Tel.: 708-754-2601.
Art Gallery.
Collections: works by regional & national artists; paintings; photographs; sculpture.
Activities: special events.
Hours & Admission Prices: Wed.-Sat. 12-4, 2nd Fri. of month 12-4 & 6-9. No charge; donations accepted.

Cicero

HAWTHORNE WORKS MUSEUM, (M), Morton College, 3801 S. Central Ave., Cicero, IL 60804-4300. Tel.: 708-656-8000, ext. 320.
E-mail: jennifer.butler@morton.edu
Web Site: www.morton.edu/museum/index.html
Founded: 2008.
Key Personnel: Pres., Dr. Leslie Navarro; Dir., Jennifer Butler.
Personnel Profile: Full-Time Paid 1; Full-Time Volunteers 1; Part-Time Paid 1; Part-Time Volunteers 1.
Governing Authority: Parent Institution: Morton College, Cicero, IL. Tax-exempt.
Local Industrial History Museum.
Collections: local industrial history; 20th-century American history; photographs; communications artifacts; papers; Western Electric's Hawthorne Works, 1906-1986.
Research Fields: telephone & communication history; computer technology; local industry; immigrants; women's history.
Activities: classes; community outreach.
Publications: newsletter, Hawthorne Works Museum.
Hours & Admission Prices: Call for hours. No charge; donations accepted. Closed Martin Luther King Jr. Day; Presidents' Day; Pulaski's Birthday; spring & winter break; Memorial Day; Columbus Day; Thanksgiving & weekend after. ♿
Attendance: 1,000 (estimated)

Clinton

C.H. MOORE HOMESTEAD, 219 E. Woodlawn St., Clinton, IL 61727-1052. Tel.: 217-935-6066. Fax: 217-935-0553.
E-mail: chmoorehomestead@verizon.net
Web Site: chmoorehomestead.org
Founded: 1967.
Congressional District: 21
Key Personnel: C.E.O. & House Chm., Shirley Strange; Cur. Farm & Railroad Museum, Robert McMath; Treas., Connie Durbin.
Personnel Profile: Full-Time Paid 1; Part-Time Paid 2.
Governing Authority: nonprofit organization. Parent Institution: De Witt County Museum Association. Tax-exempt: 501(c)(3).
General Museum: housed in c.1867 C.H. Moore home, remodeled & expanded in 1876 & 1887.
Collections: clothing; dolls; agriculture; railroad; period furnishings.
Facilities: Gift items for sale.
Activities: guided tours; lectures; permanent & temporary exhibitions. Museum Sponsors: apple & pork festival; ice cream social; quilt show; Christmas tea.
Publications: booklet, The Homestead; annual newsletter.
Hours & Admission Prices: April-Dec. Tues.-Sat. 10-5, Sun. 1-5. Adults $3, children 12-18 $1; children under 12 no charge.
Attendance: 5,000 (estimated)
Membership: Individual $15; Family $20; Business $30; Supporting $50. DeWitt County: Landmark $100; Patron $500; Settler $1,000; Pioneer $10,000.

Coal Valley

NIABI ZOO, 12908 Niabi Zoo Rd., Coal Valley, IL 61240-9467. Tel.: 309-799-3482 & 5107. Fax: 309-799-5761.
E-mail: ask@niabizoo.com
Web Site: www.niabizoo.com
Founded: 1964.
Key Personnel: Dir., Tom Stalf; Pres. (V), Scott Lohman; Treas., Brian Neff; Asst. Dir. & Museum Shop Mgr., Jennifer Ryan; Public Rels. & Devel., Shayla Kiddoo; Education Dir., Sharon Freedman; Registrar, Amanda Reffett; Cur., Colleen Stalf.
Personnel Profile: Full-Time Paid 18; Part-Time Paid 20; Part-Time Volunteers 50; Interns 12.
Governing Authority: county. Tax-exempt: 501(c)(3).
Zoo.
Collections: animals from North America, Asia, Africa & Australia.
Facilities: snack bar; educational facilities; zoological park. Museum-related items for sale.
Activities: formal education programs for children; train rides; endangered species carrousel. Annual Events: Elephants' Birthday; Zoofari Ball; Boo at the Zoo.
Publications: quarterly newsletter, Zoonooz.
Hours & Admission Prices: Spring & Summer: daily 9:30-5; Fall: Mon.-Fri. 11-4, Sat.-Sun. 9:30-5; Winter: Sat.-Sun. 11-4. Adults $5, senior citizens $4.50, children $4; members no charge. ♿
Attendance: 200,000 (estimated)
Membership: Children $5, Senior Citizen & Student $25; Adult $30, additional Adult $15.

Collinsville

CAHOKIA MOUNDS STATE HISTORIC SITE, 30 Ramey St., Collinsville, IL 62234-7617. Tel.: 618-346-5160. Fax: 618-346-5162.
E-mail: cahokia.mounds@sbcglobal.net
Web Site: www.cahokiamounds.org
Founded: 1930.
Congressional District: 23
Key Personnel: C.E.O. Cahokia Mounds Museum Society, Leah Joyce; Pres. (V) Cahokia Mounds Museum Society, Terry Norris; Site Mgr., Mark Esarey; Asst. Site Mgr., Matt Migalla; Asst. Site Mgr. & Dir. Public Rels., William Iseminger; Volunteer Coord., Steve Riddle; Site Interpreter, Marilyn Harvey; Museum Shop Mgr. Cahokia Mounds Museum Society, Linda Krieg; Site Technician, Kevin Fernandez; Site Technician, Michael Nance; Site Technician, Gene Stratmann; Site Technician, Joseph Seago.
Personnel Profile: Full-Time Paid 12; Part-Time Paid 2; Part-Time Volunteers 120; Interns 2.
Governing Authority: state. Parent Institution: Illinois Historic Preservation Agency, Old State Capitol, Springfield, IL 62701. Tel.: 217-785-1584. Tax-exempt: 501(c)(3).
Archaeology Museum & Site: 800-1500 A.D., site of largest prehistoric Indian city in North America.
Collections: prehistoric Indian artifacts.
Research Fields: archaeology.
Facilities: 2,000-vol. library of books on archaeology, anthropology & American Indians available for research on premises; 150-seat orientation theatre; 265-seat auditorium. Museum-related items for sale.
Activities: guided tours; lectures; slides; formally organized educational programs; permanent & traveling exhibitions; school loan service. Special Events: Kid's Day & Contemporary Indian Art Show; Indian Powwow; Archaeology Day; Indian Market.
Publications: quarterly newsletter, Cahokian.
Hours & Admission Prices: Wed.-Sun. 9-5. Suggested Donations: families $10, adults $4, children $2. Closed most holidays. ♿
Attendance: 330,000 (estimated)
Membership: Cahokia Mounds Museum Society: Senior & Student $25; Individual & Family $35; Institution & Sustaining $75; Contributor $100; Donor $500; Patron (Annual) $1,000.

Cypress

ILLINOIS DEPARTMENT OF NATURAL RESOURCES, CACHE RIVER STATE NATURAL AREA, BARKHAUSEN CACHE RIVER WETLANDS CENTER, 8885 State Rte. 37 S., Cypress, IL 62923-2323. Tel.: 618-657-2064.
Web Site: www.dnr.state.il.us
Founded: 2005.
Governing Authority: state. Tax-exempt.
Wetlands Center.
Collections: cultural & natural history; flowers; plants; trees; wildlife.
Facilities: 2,000 sq. ft. exhibit space; nature trails; visitors center.
Activities: wildlife viewing area; orientation video; hiking.
Hours & Admission Prices: Wed.-Sun. 9-4. Closed New Year's Day; Lincoln's Birthday; Veterans Day; Thanksgiving & day after; Christmas. ♿
Attendance: 15,000 (estimated)

Danville

VERMILION COUNTY MUSEUM SOCIETY, 116 N. Gilbert St., Danville, IL 61832-8506. Tel.: 217-442-2922. Fax: 217-442-2001.
E-mail: vermilioncounty@att.net
Web Site: www.vermilioncountymuseum.org
Founded: 1964.
Congressional District: 15
Key Personnel: Pres. (V), Donald Richter; Museum Shop Mgr., Susan Richter.
Personnel Profile: Full-Time Paid 2; Part-Time Paid 2; Part-Time Volunteers 37.
Governing Authority: society. Tax-exempt: 501(c)(3).
History Museum: housed in 1855 Dr. Fithian Home, doctor's residence, often visited by Abraham Lincoln.
Collections: costumes; paintings; sculpture; graphics; decorative arts; herbarium; natural history; 1857 Mann's Chapel; 1860s Doctor Office; 1890s Parlor, Lincoln Room; 1920 Dental Office. New Museum Building contains recreations of: coal mine tunnel; main street Danville c.1929; Lincoln/Lamon law office; one room school.
Major Exhibits: New Harmonies: Celebrating American Roots Music (T), 4/10/10-5/23/10; Living Colours - APNQ Quilt Exhibit (T), 6/10; 28th Annual Midwest Heritage Quilt Show, 7/10.
Research Fields: costumes; natural history; paintings; sculpture; graphics; decorative arts; herbarium; county history.
Facilities: 300-vol. library of material on Lincoln, Civil War & history of area; reading room. Gifts for sale.
Activities: guided tours; lectures; arts festivals; permanent, temporary & traveling exhibitions.
Publications: quarterly magazine, Heritage of Vermilion County.
Hours & Admission Prices: Tues.-Sat. 10-5. Adults: $2.50 one site, $4 two sites, children 13-17 $1; discounts to AAA members; members & children under 13 no charge. Closed Independence Day; Thanksgiving; Christmas.
Attendance: 9,208 (accurate)
Membership: Student & Senior Citizen, Organizational & Contributing $15; Individual $20; Family $25; Sustaining $50; Patron $75; Business $100; Life $250.

VERMILION COUNTY WAR MUSEUM, 307 N. Vermilion, Danville, IL 61832-4769. Tel.: 217-431-0034.
E-mail: info@vcwm.org
Web Site: vcwm.org
Founded: 1997.
Military History Museum.
Collections: military history from the Revolutionary War to present.
Hours & Admission Prices: Tues.-Fri. 12-3, Sat. 10-4. No charge; donations accepted. ♿

DeKalb

THE ANTHROPOLOGY MUSEUM, (M), Northern Illinois University, Department of Anthropology, DeKalb, IL 60115. Tel.: 815-753-0230. Fax: 815-753-7027.
E-mail: awparsons@niu.edu
Web Site: www.niu.edu/anthro_museum
Founded: 1964.
Congressional District: 14
Key Personnel: Exec. Dir., Winifred Creamer, Ph.D.; Dir., Ann Wright-Parsons, MA
Personnel Profile: Full-Time Paid 1; Part-Time Paid 10; Part-Time Volunteers 10; Interns 2.
Governing Authority: university. Parent Institution: Northern Illinois University. Tax-exempt: 170(b)(1)(A).
Anthropology & Archaeology Museum.
Collections: ethnographic materials from Plains, Southwest & Northwest coasts & eastern North America, Mexico, South America, Pacific Islands, Southeast Asia, Africa & Greece; North America archaeology material; human & non-human primate skeletal material; pathological human skeletal material.
Research Fields: archaeology; ethnography; physical anthropology.
Facilities: separate lab operation; classrooms.
Activities: guided tours; lectures; gallery talks; permanent & temporary exhibitions; outreach program.
Publications: Archaeological Site Reports.
Hours & Admission Prices: Mon.-Fri. 9-5. No charge. Closed school holidays. ♿
Attendance: 2,000 (estimated)

ELLWOOD HOUSE MUSEUM, (M), 509 N. First St., DeKalb, IL 60115-3232. Tel.: 815-756-4609. Fax: 815-756-4645.
E-mail: ellwoodhouse@tbcnet.com
Web Site: www.ellwoodhouse.org
Founded: 1965.
Congressional District: 14
Key Personnel: Pres. (V), Jill Olson; Dir., Gerald J. Brauer; Cur. Education & Exhibits, Rebecca Nickels; Coord. Visitor & Volunteer Svcs., Donna Gable.
Personnel Profile: Full-Time Paid 2; Part-Time Paid 2; Part-Time Volunteers 50; Interns 1.
Governing Authority: nonprofit corporation. Parent Institution: Ellwood House Association in conjunction with DeKalb Park District. Tax-exempt: 501(c)(3).
Historic House Museum: housed in 1879 Victorian mansion Ellwood House.
Collections: Victorian furnishings; figural Staffordshire; costume collections; barbed wire history; horse drawn vehicles; buggies; cutters; private collections of books belonging to the Ellwood family. Historic Structures: c.1890 Victorian Play House; c.1905 Museum House; c.1880 Stone Water Tower.
Research Fields: barbed wire industry; Ellwood Family history; DeKalb County history; decorative arts.
Facilities: education & visitor center; 120-seat meeting room; park; gardens; wildflower study area. Museum-related items for sale.
Activities: guided tours; permanent & temporary exhibitions; docent program; special seasonal events; school outreach programs. Museum Sponsors: Art Fair; Ice Cream Social; Victorian Christmas; Decorative Arts Lecture Series.
Publications: quarterly bulletin, Ellwood House Herald; booklets, Ellwood House: An Estate of the Gilded Age; brochures.
Hours & Admission Prices: Museum: March to mid-Dec. Tues.-Sun. 1-5. Tours: Tues.-Fri. 1 & 3, Sat.-Sun. 1, 2 & 3; other times by appointment. Visitors Center: call for hours. Adults $8, youth 6-17 $3; discounts to AAM members; members no charge. ♿
Attendance: 8,000 (estimated)
Membership: Adult $25; Family $35; Contributing $50; Sustaining $100.

JACK OLSON GALLERY - NORTHERN ILLINOIS UNIVERSITY, (M), School of Art, 200 Visual Arts Bldg., DeKalb, IL 60115. Tel.: 815-753-4521. Fax: 815-753-7701.
E-mail: pvanael@niu.edu
Web Site: www.olsongallery.niu.edu
Key Personnel: Gallery Coord., Peter Van Ael
Art Gallery.
Collections: works by students & faculty.
Activities: lectures.
Hours & Admission Prices: Sept.-early May Mon.-Fri. 10-4. No charge; donations accepted. ♿

NIU ART MUSEUM, (M), Northern Illinois University, Altgeld Hall, DeKalb, IL 60115-2825. Tel.: 815-753-1936. Fax: 815-753-7897.
E-mail: jburke2@niu.edu
Web Site: www.niu.edu/artmuseum
Founded: 1970.
Congressional District: 14
Key Personnel: Dir., Jo Burke; Asst. Dir., Peter Olson; Coord. Mktg. & Education, Diana Arntzen.
Personnel Profile: Full-Time Paid 2; Part-Time Paid 8; Interns 1.
Governing Authority: public university. Parent Institution: Northern Illinois University. Tax-exempt.
University Art Museum.
Collections: contemporary works on paper; original prints, drawings & photographs; Burmese art.
Major Exhibits: Cannonball Press, 1/19/10-3/5/10; Midwest Blab!, 1/19/10-3/5/10; This Great Nation Will Endure, 4/8/10-5/28/10; Coming of Age: WPA Prints/America, 4/8/10-5/28/10; Autumn Leaves: A Century of Fall Fashion, 8/25/10-10/9/10; Burma Collections, 10/19/10-12/4/10.
Research Fields: Burmese art; contiguous southeast Asian countries; contemporary art.
Facilities: 4,000 sq. ft. exhibit space.
Activities: formal education programs for undergraduate or graduate students affiliated with Northern Illinois Univ.; guided tours; lectures; workshops for teachers; loan, temporary & traveling exhibitions; training programs for professional museum workers; school tours; programs in schools.
Publications: exhibition catalogs.
Hours & Admission Prices: Sept. to mid-May Tues.-Fri. 10-5, Sat. 12-4; group tours by appointment. No charge. ♿
Attendance: 9,000 (estimated)
Membership: Student $10; Senior $15; Individual $25; Dual $40; Sponsor $100; Patron $250.

Decatur

BIRKS MUSEUM, (M), Millikin University, 1184 W. Main, Decatur, IL 62522-2039. Tel.: 217-424-6337. Fax: 217-424-3992.
E-mail: ewalker@mail.millikin.edu
Web Site: www.millikin.edu/birks
Founded: 1981.
Congressional District: 20
Key Personnel: Cur., Ed Walker.
Personnel Profile: Part-Time Paid 1; Interns 2.
Governing Authority: college; nonprofit. Parent Institution: Millikin University. Tax-exempt: 501(c)(3).
China & Glass Museum.
Collections: 17th- to 20th-century ceramics & glass from Europe, America & China; American & European decorative arts; Millikin University memorabilia.
Facilities: 160-vol. library pertaining to ceramics, glass & decorative arts available for research on premise only.
Activities: guided tours; lectures; organized education programs for children, adults & undergraduate or graduate students affiliated with Millikin University; loan, temporary & traveling exhibitions.
Publications: brochure, The Birks Museum.
Hours & Admission Prices: Sept.-May daily 1-4. No charge; donations accepted.
Attendance: 1,700 (estimated)

CHILDREN'S MUSEUM OF ILLINOIS, 55 S. County Club Rd., Decatur, IL 62521-4470. Tel.: 217-423-KIDS.
E-mail: info@cmofil.com
Web Site: www.cmofil.com
Key Personnel: Dir., Melinda Shaw
Children's Museum.
Collections: hands-on exhibits.
Facilities: Museum-related items for sale.
Hours & Admission Prices: mid-June to mid-Aug. Mon.-Fri. 9:30-4:30, Sat. 10-5, Sun. 1-5; mid-Aug. to mid-June Tues.-Fri. 9:30-4:30, Sat. 10-5, Sun. 1-5. Admission $4; children one & under and members no charge. Closed major holidays. ♿
Attendance: 60,000 (accurate)
Membership: Family & Grandparent $60; Fun Family $135; Support $250; Life $1,000.

GALLERY 510 ARTS GUILD, 160 E. Main St., Ste. 100, Decatur, IL 62523-1283. Tel.: 217-422-1509.
E-mail: info@gallery510.org
Web Site: www.gallery510.org
Key Personnel: Exec. Dir., Barbara J. Dove.
Governing Authority: nonprofit organization.
Art Gallery.
Collections: works by local artists.
Facilities: Museum-related items for sale.
Hours & Admission Prices: Call for hours.

HIERONYMUS MUELLER MUSEUM, 420 W. Eldorado St., Decatur, IL 62522-2189. Tel.: 217-423-6161.
E-mail: muellermuseum@aol.com
Key Personnel: Mgr., Mike Deatherage
History Museum.
Collections: photographs; early Mueller family & company history.
Hours & Admission Prices: Thurs.-Sat. 1-4. Adults $2, children under 18 $1.50.

MACON COUNTY HISTORY MUSEUM, 5580 N. Fork Rd., Decatur, IL 62521-1859. Tel.: 217-422-4919. Fax: 217-422-4773.
E-mail: info@mchsdecatur.org
Web Site: www.mchsdecatur.org
Founded: 1916.
Congressional District: 21
Key Personnel: Exec. Dir., Patrick McDaniel; Pres. (V), Karen Anderson.
Personnel Profile: Full-Time Paid 1; Part-Time Paid 1; Part-Time Volunteers 60.
Governing Authority: society; Macon County Historical Society; nonprofit organization. Tax-exempt: 501(c)(3).
Historical Society Museum.
Collections: 1820-present, historical artifacts from Macon County & Central Illinois including photographs, tools, clothing, late Victorian & early 20th-century mass-produced decorative art; farm & kitchen paraphernalia; Lincoln's life & career; Civil War; Grand Army of the Republic. Historic

Buildings: 1855 log home; 1863 Salem Rural School; 1870s Gazebo; 1880s Depot; 1830s Lincoln Courthouse; The Lincoln Connection.
Research Fields: historical research in Decatur, Macon County & Central Illinois.
Facilities: 2,000-vol. library; permanent & rotating galleries & exhibits.
Activities: guided tours; school program; quarterly meetings for members.
Publications: bimonthly newsletter.
Hours & Admission Prices: Tues.-Sat. & 4th Sun. 1-4. Adults $2. ♿
Attendance: 5,000 (estimated)
Membership: Regular $25; Couple $40; Family $50; Donor $100; Patron $500; Benefactor $1,000; Founder $5,000.

PERKINSON GALLERY, Millikin University, 1184 W. Main St., Decatur, IL 62522-2039. Tel.: 217-424-6253. Fax: 217-424-3993.
E-mail: jschietinger@millikin.edu
Web Site: www.millikin.edu/art/galleries.asp
Founded: 1969.
Key Personnel: Dir., James Schietinger; Asst. Dir., Lyle J. Salmi.
Governing Authority: university. Parent Institution: Millikin University, 1184 W. Main St., Decatur, IL 62522. Tax-exempt.
Art Museum.
Collections: 19th- & 20th-century art: graphics, decorative art, paintings, sculpture.
Facilities: 2,000-seat auditorium; theater; classrooms.
Activities: concerts; dance recitals; arts festivals; drama; formally organized education programs for undergraduate college students affiliated with Millikin University; invitational exhibitions.
Hours & Admission Prices: Gallery: Mon.-Fri. 12-5. No charge; donations accepted. Closed university holidays. ♿
Attendance: 20,000

SCOVILL ZOO, 71 S. Country Club Rd., Decatur, IL 62521-4470. Tel.: 217-421-7435. Fax: 217-422-7330.
Web Site: www.scovillzoo.com
Personnel Profile: Full-Time Paid 11; Part-Time Paid 25; Part-Time Volunteers 60; Interns 2.
Zoo.
Collections: zoological.
Facilities: Museum-related items for sale.
Activities: petting zoo.
Hours & Admission Prices: April 10-May 22 & Aug. 17-Oct. 12 Mon.-Fri. 10-4, Sat.-Sun. 10-6:30; May 23-Aug. 16 daily 10-7. Adults $4.50, seniors 65 & over $3.50, children 2-12 $3; children under 2 no charge. Z.O. & O Express Train: adults $2, seniors 65 & over and children 2-12 $1.50; children under 2 no charge. Carousel Ride: $1.50. ♿
Attendance: 98,000 (accurate)
Membership: Individual $30; Family $50.

Des Plaines

DES PLAINES HISTORY CENTER, (M), 781 Pearson St., Des Plaines, IL 60016-4506. Tel.: 847-391-5399. Fax: 847-297-4741.
E-mail: contact@desplaineshistory.org
Web Site: desplaineshistory.org
Formerly: Des Plaines Historical Museum
Founded: 1967.
Congressional District: 6
Key Personnel: Dir., Joy A. Matthiessen; Pres. (V), John Burke; Mgr. Archives, Shari Caine; Program Mgr., Susan Golland; Mgr. Collections, Jennifer Galida; Sec., Liz Feltmann.
Personnel Profile: Full-Time Paid 4; Part-Time Paid 3; Part-Time Volunteers 100.
Governing Authority: society. Parent Institution: Des Plaines Historical Society. Tax-exempt: 501(c)(3).
Historic House Museum: located in 1906-1907 Kinder House.
Collections: furnishings; items of local significance; costumes; photographs; pioneer tools.
Research Fields: history of city of Des Plaines & Maine Township, Cook County, Illinois.
Facilities: library of monographs, biographies, histories, manuscripts, documents, transparencies, 10,000 photographs; history and visitor center. Post cards, stationery, Historical Society related items & hand-made items for sale.
Activities: guided tours; lectures; formally organized education programs for children; docent program; permanent & temporary exhibitions; monthly public programs; historic sites recording; slide programs.
Publications: newsletter, Cobweb; guidebooks for house & historic sites in community; Greetings From Des Plaines: A Community History Through Postcards.
Hours & Admission Prices: Mon.-Fri. 9-4, Sun. 1-4; other times by appointment. No charge; donations accepted. ♿
Attendance: 10,600 (estimated)
Membership: Student $7.50; Senior Citizen $10; Individual $17; Family $23; Patron $50; Business & Organization $100; Life $500.

KOEHNLINE MUSEUM OF ART, Oakton Community College, 1600 E. Golf Rd., Des Plaines, IL 60016-1234. Tel.: 847-635-2633. Fax: 847-635-1764.
E-mail: nharpaz@oakton.edu
Web Site: www.oakton.edu/museum
Key Personnel: Mgr. & Cur., Nathan Harpaz
Art Museum.
Collections: contemporary art; sculpture park.
Hours & Admission Prices: June-Aug. Mon.-Thurs. 10-7; Sept.-May Mon.-Fri. 10-6, Sat. 11-4.

MCDONALD'S #1 STORE MUSEUM, 400 N. Lee St., Des Plaines, IL 60016-4610. Mailing Address: McDonald's Corp., 2111 McDonald's Dr., Oak Brook, IL 60523. Tel.: 847-297-5022.
Web Site: www.mcdonalds.com/corp/about/museum_info.html
General Museum: a recreation of the first McDonald's Restaurant opened in Des Plaines, Illinois by founder, Ray Kroc, on April 15, 1955.
Collections: Speedee road sign; period equipment; mannequins representing the all male crew dressed in the 1955 uniform; photographs; early advertising.
Activities: video presentation.
Hours & Admission Prices: Call for hours. No charge.

Dixon

JOHN DEERE HISTORIC SITE, 8334 S. Clinton St., Main, Grand Detour, Dixon, IL 61021-9499. Tel.: 815-652-4551. Fax: 815-652-3835.
E-mail: timmermanlynna@johndeere.com
Web Site: johndeereattractions.com
Founded: 1953.
Congressional District: 35
Key Personnel: Dir. & Pres., James H. Collins; Site Mgr., Lynn A. Timmerman.
Personnel Profile: Full-Time Paid 3; Part-Time Paid 7.
Governing Authority: company organized for profit, The John Deere Foundation, Deere & Co., John Deere Rd., Moline, IL 61265. Tax-exempt.
Historic Site: 1836 Deere House.
Collections: archaeology exhibit; blacksmith shop; Deere house.
Facilities: Museum-related items for sale.
Activities: guided tours.
Hours & Admission Prices: May-Oct. Wed.-Sun. 9-5; Winter: tours by appointment only. Adults $5; children under 12 no charge. ♿
Attendance: 22,000 (accurate)

RONALD REAGAN BOYHOOD HOME, 816 S. Hennepin Ave., Dixon, IL 61021-3646. Mailing Address: Ronald Reagan Home Foundation, P.O. Box 816, Dixon, IL 61021-0816. Tel.: 815-288-5176. Fax: 815-288-3642.
E-mail: reagan1@grics.net
Web Site: www.ronaldreaganhome.com
Founded: 1980.
Congressional District: 14
Key Personnel: Exec. Dir., Connie G. Lange; Pres., Jim Burke.
Personnel Profile: Full-Time Paid 1; Part-Time Paid 1; Part-Time Volunteers 40.
Governing Authority: private; nonprofit organization. Tax-exempt.
Historic House: boyhood home of 40th U.S. President Ronald Reagan.
Collections: 1920s furnishings.
Facilities: library available to scholars & researchers; visitors center. Museum-related items for sale.
Activities: guided tours.
Hours & Admission Prices: April-Oct. 31 Mon.-Sat. 10-4, Sun. 1-4. Adults 12 & over $5. Closed Easter.
Attendance: 10,547 (accurate)
Membership: Friends of Ronald Reagan Boyhood Home: Lifeguard League $40-$124; Sportscaster Society $125-$249; Actor's Guild $250-$499; Governor's Group $500-$999; President's Circle $1,000-$4,999; World Leaders Alliance $5,000 & up.

Downers Grove

THE DOWNERS GROVE PARK DISTRICT MUSEUM, (M), 831 Maple Ave., Downers Grove, IL 60515-4904. Tel.: 630-963-1309. Fax: 630-963-0496.
E-mail: cchristensen@dgparks.org

Web Site: www.dgparks.org (click museum)
Founded: 1969.
Congressional District: 13
Key Personnel: Pres. Bd. of Park Commissioners, Robert Gelwicks; Vice Pres. Bd. of Park Commissioners, Ron Smith; Sec. Bd. of Park Commissioners, Katheryn Engel-Accettura; Treas. Bd. of Park Commissioners, Cathy Mahoney; Commissioner Bd., Janet Barr; District Admin., Dan Cermak; Dir. Recreation, Sandy Divon; Museum Supvr., Christa Christensen; Sec., David Docekal; Weekend Mgr., Carol Wandschneider; Asst. Weekend Mgr., David Roberts; Mgr. Collections, Sarah Ebel; Custodian, Karen Kurey.
Personnel Profile: Full-Time Paid 1; Part-Time Paid 5; Part-Time Volunteers 40.
Governing Authority: Parent Institution: Downers Grove Park District. Tax-exempt: 501(a).
Local History.
Collections: period furniture; decorative arts; textiles; vintage clothing; toys; tools; home paraphernalia; photographs; personal documents.
Major Exhibits: Linedrives & Lipstick: The Untold Story of Women's Baseball (T), 4/6/10-5/25/10.
Research Fields: historic homes; genealogy; local history.
Activities: organized education programs; docent program; temporary exhibitions. Museum Sponsors: special events.
Publications: monthly newsletter, The Plank.
Hours & Admission Prices: Public Tours: Sun.-Fri. 1-3. Group Tours: Mon.-Fri. 9-1 & 3-4:30 by appointment only. Office & Research: Mon.-Fri. 8:30-4:30. No charge; donations accepted. Closed holidays. ♿
Attendance: 2,800 (estimated)

Dundee

DUNDEE TOWNSHIP HISTORICAL SOCIETY, INC., 426 Highland Ave., Dundee, IL 60118-1225. Mailing Address: 437 Highland Ave., Dundee, IL 60118-1277. Tel.: 847-428-6996.
Web Site: www.northstarnet.org/dukhome/DTHS
Founded: 1964.
Congressional District: 33
Key Personnel: Programs Chm., Marge Edwards; Pres. (V), Kristie Benedik; Museum Co-Chm., Nancy Wendt; Museum Co-Chm., Jack Wendt; Library Volunteer, Audrey Falese; Library Volunteer, Mary Lamp; Library Volunteer, Louise Osada; Library Volunteer, Lana Graf; Library Volunteer, Sally Hane; Library Volunteer, Connie Kashub; Library Volunteer, Marge Edwards.
Governing Authority: society. Tax-exempt: 501(c)(3).
Historical Society.
Collections: local history; manuscript collections; exhibits highlighting Allen Pinkerton; exhibit featuring local industries & early settlers.
Research Fields: local history; genealogy.
Facilities: 1,000-vol. library of historical & biographical books, Illinois legislative records 1824-present, township census, cemetery records, genealogies, photographs, newspaper files on microfilm & magazines available for research by appointment; meeting room. Museum-related items for sale.
Activities: historical bus tours with slides for students, Scouts, & organizations available by appointment; permanent & semi-annual changing exhibits. Society Sponsors: bus tour in April; house walk in September; cemetery walk in October; Dickens in Dundee in December.
Publications: bimonthly society newsletter, The Informer; book, Dundee Township, 1835-1985.
Hours & Admission Prices: Wed. & Sun. 2-4; other times by appointment. Adults $1; members no charge.
Attendance: 1,000 (estimated)
Membership: Senior Citizens & Youth $7.50; Individual $10; Couple & Family $17.50; Sustaining Individual & Family $40; Business & Organization $60; Life $250.

East Alton

NATIONAL GREAT RIVERS MUSEUM, 2 Lock & Dam Way, East Alton, IL 62024-2406. Mailing Address: P.O. Box 337, Alton, IL 62002-0337. Tel.: 618-462-6979, ext. 7807. Fax: 618-462-7650.
E-mail: kimberly.g.rea@usace.army.mil
Web Site: www.mvs.usace.army.mil/rivers
Founded: 2000.
Key Personnel: Dir., Kimberly G. Rea.
Personnel Profile: Full-Time Paid 4; Part-Time Paid 1; Part-Time Volunteers 25.
Governing Authority: federal government; nonprofit.
History Museum.
Collections: history of the Mississippi River; history and workings of the locks & dams system.
Facilities: 7,000 sq. ft. exhibit space; educational facilities; aquarium; 100-seat theater. Museum-related items for sale.
Activities: formal educational programs.
Hours & Admission Prices: Daily 9-5; groups of 10 or more by appointment. Tour of Lock & Dam at 10, 1 & 3. No charge; donations accepted. Closed New Year's Day; Thanksgiving; Christmas. ♿
Attendance: 75,000 (accurate)

East Saint Louis

KATHERINE DUNHAM DYNAMIC MUSEUM, 1005 Pennsylvania Ave., East Saint Louis, IL 62201-1407. Mailing Address: P.O. Box 6, East Saint Louis, IL 62202-0006. Tel.: 618-874-8560. Fax: 618-874-8562.
E-mail: kdcahgloria@sbcglobal.net
Web Site: www.kdcah.com
Founded: 1978.
Key Personnel: Chm. (V), Riley Owens; Museum Shop Mgr., Gloria Atkins.
Personnel Profile: Part-Time Paid 2; Part-Time Volunteers 1; Interns 1.
Governing Authority: Parent Institution: Katherine Dunham Center for Arts & Humanities. Tax-exempt.
General Museum.
Collections: Katherine Dunham's writings, films, & works of visual arts; over 250 African & Caribbean art objects from around the world; tapestries; paintings; sculpture; musical instruments; ceremonial costumes; photographs; programs; awards & mementos from Miss Dunham's career; furniture; instruments.
Activities: seminar; training program for children.
Hours & Admission Prices: Mon.-Tues. & Thurs.-Sat. 10-4. No charge; donations accepted.
Attendance: 500 (estimated)

Edwardsville

MADISON COUNTY HISTORICAL MUSEUM & ARCHIVAL LIBRARY, (M), 715 N. Main St., Edwardsville, IL 62025-1111. Tel.: 618-656-7562 (museum) & 7569 (library). Fax: 618-659-3457.
E-mail: mchm@co.madison.il.us
Founded: 1924.
Congressional District: 21
Key Personnel: MCHS Bd. Pres (V), Joyce Williams; MCHS Bd. Vice Pres., Sharon Helms; MCHS Bd. Vice Pres., Marilyn Sule; Dir. Museum & Library, Suzanne Dietrich; Cur. Objects & Textiles, Mary Louise Brown; Mgr. Operations, Mary Westerhold; Archivist, Marion Sperling; Archivist, Carol Frisse.
Personnel Profile: Full-Time Paid 1; Part-Time Paid 5; Part-Time Volunteers 25.
Governing Authority: society & county government. Parent Institution: Madison County Historical Society & Madison County Government. Subsidiary Institution: Friends of the Madison County Museum. Tax-exempt: 501(c)(3).
Historical Society Museum: housed in 1836 John H. Weir home. Listed on the National Register of Historic Places.
Collections: Native American Indian & pioneer artifacts; books; manuscripts; furniture; clothing; tools; documents; maps; eight-room restored home; land grants.
Research Fields: genealogy; local history; industries; historic houses.
Facilities: 2,500-vol. library on Illinois & Madison County history; 40-seat meeting room. Books, gift items for sale.
Activities: school & scout field trips; guided tours; lectures; permanent & changing seasonal exhibits of historic costumes, quilts, needlework, Christmas decorations & highlights of Madison County history.
Publications: biannual, Museum Progress Report; biannual newsletter.
Hours & Admission Prices: Wed.-Fri. 9-4, Sun. 1-4. No charge; donations recommended. Closed holidays.
Attendance: 2,777 (accurate)
Membership: Student $15; Individual $35; Family $50; James Madison $100; Edward Coles $250; Elijah Lovejoy $500; John Weir M.D. $1,000.

THE UNIVERSITY MUSEUM, (M), Southern Illinois University at Edwardsville, Edwardsville, IL 62026-0001. Mailing Address: Box 1150, Southern Illinois University at Edwardsville, Edwardsville, IL 62026. Tel.: 618-650-2996. Fax: 618-650-2995.
E-mail: ebarnet@siue.edu
Founded: 1959.
Congressional District: 19
Key Personnel: Dir., Eric B. Barnett; Museum Exhibit Designer, Jerry L. Fahey.
Personnel Profile: Full-Time Paid 3; Part-Time Paid 4.
Governing Authority: state; university. Parent Institution: Southern Illinois University Edwardsville. Tax-exempt.
General Museum.

Collections: Stroup Korean Pottery Collection; Milton K. & Doris T. Harrington Collection; MFA at Edwardsville Collection; Nelson-Wagner Collection; Olin Collection; Sullivan Ornament Collection; University Drawing Collection; Nause & Graf Collection; Anthropology Teaching Museum; Folklore Archive; musical instruments.
Research Fields: architectural ornament restoration.
Facilities: classrooms.
Activities: guided tours; lectures; gallery talks; arts festivals; formally organized education programs for undergraduate & graduate students; training programs for professional museum workers; loan, permanent, temporary & traveling exhibitions.
Publications: catalogue, Louis H. Sullivan Architectural Ornament Collection.
Hours & Admission Prices: Mon.-Fri. 9-4:30. No charge; donations accepted. ♿
Attendance: 30,000 (estimated)
Membership: Senior & Student $20; Basic $35.

Elgin

ELGIN AREA HISTORICAL SOCIETY, (M), 360 Park St., Elgin, IL 60120-4455. Tel.: 847-742-4248. Fax: 847-931-6199.
E-mail: elginhistory@foxvalley.net
Web Site: www.elginhistory.org
Founded: 1961.
Congressional District: 14
Key Personnel: Dir., Elizabeth Marston; Pres. (V), Mary Hill; Museum Shop Mgr., Mary Pierce; Treas., Bill Briska; Registrar, Fran Alft; Researcher, David Siegenthaler; Educator, Lucy Elliott.
Personnel Profile: Part-Time Paid 3; Part-Time Volunteers 75; Interns 1.
Governing Authority: private; nonprofit organization. Tax-exempt: 501(c)(3).
History Museum: housed in c.1856 Greek Revival landmark building.
Collections: local city history; Elgin National Watch Company; Elgin photos & images; Elgin road races; local architecture; Courier News photo negatives, 1936-1983; Elgin businesses.
Major Exhibits: Deep Roots, Green Future: City Planning in Elgin (T), 2/10-9/10.
Facilities: 450-vol. library; 3,000 sq. ft. exhibit space. Museum-related items for sale.
Activities: docent program; films; formal education programs; guided tours; lectures; radio programs; loan, temporary & participatory exhibitions. Annual Events: Cemetery Walk; Holiday Tea; annual meeting.
Publications: bimonthly newsletter, Crackerbarrel.
Hours & Admission Prices: Wed.-Sat. 12-4. Adults $3, students $1; discounts to AAM, ICOM, AASLH & AMM members; members and children 6 & under no charge. Closed New Year's Day; Independence Day; Thanksgiving; Christmas Eve & Day. ♿
Attendance: 5,000 (estimated)
Membership: Student $10; Adult $25; Family $40; Sponsor $60; Century $100; Donor $500; Life $1,000.

ELGIN PUBLIC MUSEUM, (M), 225 Grand Blvd., Elgin, IL 60120-4278. Tel.: 847-741-6655. Fax: 847-931-6787.
E-mail: epm@cityofelgin.org
Web Site: www.elginpublicmuseum.org
Founded: 1904.
Congressional District: 12
Key Personnel: Exec. Dir., Margaret (Peggie) Stromberg; Pres. (V), Marty Kellams; Education Coord., Sara Russell.
Personnel Profile: Part-Time Paid 4; Part-Time Volunteers 20.
Governing Authority: nonprofit organization. Tax-exempt: 501(c)(3).
Natural History Museum: housed in 1907, Neo-Classical building with 30 ft. sky-lighted ceiling.
Collections: natural history specimens; botany; zoology; geology; anthropology; paleontology; endangered & extinct species including passenger pigeon, California condor, eagles, owls, hawks & skeletal material of the Irish deer; Native American objects; ornithology collection; interpretive collections including Illinois wildlife, fish of Illinois, butterflies, insects & fossils.
Research Fields: experiential teaching materials; natural history education for youth & cross-cultural understanding.
Facilities: 500-vol. natural history research library available on a limited basis to qualified researchers & students; 5,600 sq. ft. exhibit space.
Activities: guided tours; lectures; hobby workshops; organized educational programs; participatory, loan, temporary, permanent & traveling exhibitions; school loan service.
Publications: bimonthly newsletter, EPM News; booklets.
Hours & Admission Prices: June-Sept. 1 Tues.-Sat. 12-4; Sept. 2-May Sat.-Sun. 12-4; school programs by reservation. No charge; donations accepted. Closed most major holidays. ♿
Attendance: 20,000 (estimated)
Membership: Student & Senior Citizen $15; Individual $25; Family $35; Contributing $50; Sustaining $75; Patron $150.

Elk Grove Village

THE SCHUETTE BIERMANN FARMHOUSE MUSEUM, (M), 399 Biesterfield Rd., Elk Grove Village, IL 60007-3381. Tel.: 847-439-3994 & 690-1440.
E-mail: sdenninger@elkgroveparks.org
Web Site: www.elkgroveparks.org
Founded: 1975.
Key Personnel: Dir. & Cur., Sandy Denninger; Chm. (V), Gail Santroch.
Personnel Profile: Full-Time Paid 1; Part-Time Paid 2; Part-Time Volunteers 6; Interns 1.
Governing Authority: municipal government; nonprofit. Parent Institution: Elk Grove Park Dist., 499 Biesterfield Rd., Elk Grove Village, IL 60007. Tax-exempt: 170(b)(1)(A).
Farmhouse Museum: housed in an 1856 2-story vernacular frame house.
Collections: concentration on Elk Grove Township & village history from Native American-present; museum specific to mid 19th century farm life; artifacts specific to 1850-1900.
Major Exhibits: History of Jarosch Bakery, 3/10-6/10.
Research Fields: farm families 1830s to present; buildings; pictures.
Facilities: classroom; 1,200 sq. ft. exhibit space; 1880 horse barn; reproduction of 1910 one-room schoolhouse. Museum-related items for sale.
Activities: hobby workshops; lectures; participatory exhibits; docent program; formal education programs for children; guided tours; badge-related programs for scout groups. Annual Events: Spring Planting in May; Ice Cream Social in July; Pioneer Days in September.
Publications: quarterly newsletter/calendar, The Historian.
Hours & Admission Prices: June-Aug. Wed. 2:30-5:30, Fri. 9-12, Sat. 11-2; Sept.-May Wed. 2:30-5:30, Sat. 11-2; other times by appointment. Adults $1; members no charge. Closed major holidays.
Attendance: 3,500 (estimated)
Membership: Student & Senior $8; Adult $15; Family $20.

Ellis Grove

PIERRE MENARD HOME STATE HISTORIC SITE, 4230 Kaskaskia St., Ellis Grove, IL 62241-1718. Tel.: 618-859-3031. Fax: 618-859-3031.
Web Site: www.illinoishistory.gov/hs/pierre_menard.htm
Founded: 1927.
Key Personnel: C.E.O., Robert Coomer; Dir., Jan Grimes; Site Svcs. Specialist, Andrew Cooperman; Asst. Site Mgr., Dennis Thomas.
Personnel Profile: Full-Time Paid 1; Part-Time Paid 1; Part-Time Volunteers 4.
Governing Authority: state. Parent Institution: Illinois Historic Preservation Agency, 313 S. Sixth St., Springfield, IL 62701. Tax-exempt: 501(c)(3).
Historic House Museum: c.1815-1820 home of Pierre Menard, the first Lt. Governor of Illinois and U.S. Agent of Indian Affairs.
Collections: original furniture & artifacts; furnishings of the period; separate kitchen; smokehouse; springhouse.
Research Fields: political & business history; Menard family history; the French in Illinois.
Facilities: picnic areas; campground adjoining historic site at Ft. Kaskaskia.
Activities: orientation video; guided tours; special events.
Publications: bimonthly newsletter, Historic Illinois.
Hours & Admission Prices: Wed.-Sun. 9-5. No charge; donations requested. Closed New Year's Day; Martin Luther King Jr. Day; Thanksgiving; Christmas. ♿
Attendance: 6,000 (accurate)

Elmhurst

AMERICAN MOVIE PALACE MUSEUM, 152 N. York Rd., 2nd Fl., Elmhurst, IL Tel.: 630-782-1800.
Web Site: www.historictheatres.org
Theater History Museum.
Collections: American theater history; large scale-model of Chicago's 1927 Avalon Theatre; photographs; books; blueprints; memorabilia.
Activities: videos; special events.
Hours & Admission Prices: Tues.-Fri. 9-4, 3rd Sat. of month 9:30-1:30; groups by appointment. No charge; donations accepted.

ELMHURST ART MUSEUM, (M), 150 Cottage Hill Ave., Elmhurst, IL 60126-3329. Mailing Address: P.O. Box 23, Elmhurst, IL 60126-0023. Tel.: 630-834-0202. Fax: 630-834-0234.
E-mail: info@elmhurstartmuseum.org
Web Site: www.elmhurstartmuseum.org
Founded: 1981.
Congressional District: 6
Key Personnel: Pres., Blanche Hill; Dir., D. Neil Bremer; Asst. Dir., Stephanie

Grow; Cur., Melissa Ganje Dahlquist; Coord. Devel. & Mktg., Stuart Henn; Visitor Svcs. Coord., Jeff Francik; Controller, Heather Pastore; Coord. Education, Amy Janken; Museum Shop Mgr., Kellyn Ryan.
Personnel Profile: Full-Time Paid 7; Part-Time Paid 2; Part-Time Volunteers 20; Interns 2.
Governing Authority: private; not-for-profit organization. Tax-exempt: 501(c)(3).
Art Museum.
Collections: artwork by regional American and European artists - 20th century.
Activities: guided tours; lectures; participatory & traveling exhibits; broadcast programs of exhibits. Annual Event: Art in the Park Fine Arts Festival.
Publications: quarterly newsletter, Start with Art!
Hours & Admission Prices: Tues., Thurs. & Sat. 10-4, Wed. 1-8, Fri. & Sun. 1-4. Adults $4, seniors $3, students $2; discounts to AAM members; Tues. & children under 12 no charge. Closed national holidays. ♿
Attendance: 35,000 (accurate)
Membership: Individual $30; Family $45; Century $100.

ELMHURST HISTORICAL MUSEUM, (M), 120 E. Park Ave., Elmhurst, IL 60126-3420. Tel.: 630-833-1457. Fax: 630-833-1326.
E-mail: ehm@elmhurst.org
Web Site: www.elmhursthistory.org
Founded: 1952.
Congressional District: 6
Key Personnel: Dir., Brian F. Bergheger; Pres. Foundation (V), Val Stewart; Cur. Collections, Nancy Wilson; Cur. Exhibits, Lynne Jenco.
Personnel Profile: Full-Time Paid 4; Part-Time Paid 4; Part-Time Volunteers 40; Interns 2.
Governing Authority: municipal. Parent Institution: City of Elmhurst, IL. Tax-exempt.
History Museum: housed in 1892 Glos Mansion.
Collections: local history artifacts; manuscripts; literature on local history; photographs; slides; history of town & citizens; U.S. & state census; local newspapers.
Major Exhibits: Dwellings: A Study of Residential Architecture, 11/09-5/23/10; Beyond Baseball - The Roberto Clemente Story (T), 2/13/10-4/11/10; Magical History Tour, 6/15/10-9/19/10.
Research Fields: German-American settlement, architecture; 19th- to 20th-century Midwest history; suburbanization.
Facilities: over 500-vol. library of local history & museum administration; genealogy, archival, manuscript & iconographic holdings.
Activities: school services; lectures; performances; guided tours; workshops; special events.
Publications: books, Elmhurst Prairie to Tree Town; Old Elmhurst; Elmhurst: Origin of Names; Elmhurst: Trails From Yesterday; Elmhurst: Scenes from Yesterday; Visionary: An Elmhurst Retrospective.
Hours & Admission Prices: Tues.-Sun. 1-5. No charge; donations accepted. ♿
Attendance: 15,000 (accurate)

LIZZADRO MUSEUM OF LAPIDARY ART, (M), 220 Cottage Hill Ave., Elmhurst, IL 60126-3351. Tel.: 630-833-1616.
E-mail: info@lizzadromuseum.org
Web Site: www.lizzadromuseum.org
Founded: 1962.
Congressional District: 6
Key Personnel: Exec. Dir., John S. Lizzadro; Dir., Dorothy J. Asher; Museum Shop Mgr., Laura McCall.
Personnel Profile: Full-Time Paid 2; Part-Time Paid 12; Part-Time Volunteers 2; Interns 1.
Governing Authority: nonprofit organization. Tax-exempt: 501(c)(3).
Lapidary Arts Museum.
Collections: lapidary art; jade; ivory; hard-stone carvings; gemstones; gem materials; crystals; mineral specimens; mineralogy; paleontology; geology; archaeology.
Research Fields: areas pertaining to collections.
Facilities: 1,000-vol. library pertaining to lapidary arts, history of jades, archaeology, paleontology, mineralogy & geology available for research by members only; 100-seat auditorium. Stone carvings, minerals, fossils & jewelry items with natural stones for sale.
Activities: guided tours; lectures; films; gallery talks; formally organized educational programs; permanent, temporary & traveling exhibitions; field trips.
Publications: quarterly newsletter, Lizzadro Museum; book, The Lizzadro Collection-Chinese Jades & Other Hard Stone Carvings.
Hours & Admission Prices: Tues.-Sat. 10-5, Sun. 1-5. Adults $4, senior citizens $3, students $2, children 7-12 $1; discounts to AAM members; children under 7, museum members, active members of the armed forces & Fridays no charge. Closed New Year's Day; Easter; Independence Day; Thanksgiving; Christmas. ♿
Attendance: 29,011 (accurate)

Membership: Annual $30; Two-year $55; Sustaining $100; Life $1,000; Benefactor $2,500 & up.

Elsah

VILLAGE OF ELSAH MUSEUM, 26 LaSalle, Elsah, IL 62028. Mailing Address: P.O. Box 28, Elsah, IL 62028-0028. Tel.: 618-374-1041. Fax: 618-374-2625.
E-mail: voemayor@empowering.com
Web Site: www.elsah.org
Founded: 1978.
Congressional District: 17
Key Personnel: C.E.O., Marjorie A. Doerr.
Personnel Profile: Part-Time Paid 2; Part-Time Volunteers 4.
Governing Authority: municipal. Tax-exempt.
History Museum: housed in 1887 village hall.
Collections: local historical memorabilia including archaeological, geological, photographic, social & industrial components.
Research Fields: local history.
Facilities: 40-vol. library of local history & Illinois periodicals available for research on consultation with the director. Gift items for sale.
Activities: permanent exhibitions. Annual Event: Local Area Photography Contest July to September.
Publications: biannual newsletter; guide book, Historic Elsah.
Hours & Admission Prices: April-Oct. Fri.-Sun. 1-4. No charge; donations accepted. ♿
Attendance: 1,200 (accurate)

Evanston

EVANSTON ART CENTER, 2603 Sheridan Rd., Evanston, IL 60201-1776. Tel.: 847-475-5300. Fax: 847-475-5330.
Web Site: www.evanstonartcenter.org
Founded: 1929.
Congressional District: 9
Key Personnel: Exec. Dir., Alan Leder; Pres. (V), Harold Bauer.
Personnel Profile: Full-Time Paid 7; Full-Time Volunteers 50; Part-Time Paid 50; Part-Time Volunteers 5; Interns 4.
Governing Authority: nonprofit organization. Tax-exempt: 501(c)(3).
Contemporary Art Center.
Collections: works by regional & national artists.
Research Fields: emerging regional & contemporary artists; painting; sculpture & installation.
Facilities: studios; classrooms.
Activities: art classes; workshops; demonstrations; lectures; performances; youth outreach programs; outdoor sculpture installations; exhibitions program; curated exhibitions.
Publications: Art Center schedule of classes brochures; exhibition catalogs; quarterly newsletter, Concentrics; annual report.
Hours & Admission Prices: Mon.-Thurs. 10am-10pm, Fri.-Sat. 10-4, Sun. 1-4. Suggested donation: $3. Closed legal holidays. ♿
Attendance: 25,000 (estimated)
Membership: Senior Citizen $25; Student $30; Individual $35; Family $40; Contributing $50; Sponsor $100; Contemporary Circle $250; President's Roundtable $500; Patron $1,000; Benefactors $2,000; Sustaining Benefactors $5,000.

EVANSTON ENVIRONMENTAL ASSOCIATION/EVANSTON ECOLOGY CENTER, 2024 McCormick Blvd., Evanston, IL 60201-3055. Tel.: 847-448-8256. Fax: 847-448-8805.
E-mail: ecologycenter@cityofevanston.org
Web Site: www.laddarboretum.org
Founded: 1975.
Congressional District: 9
Key Personnel: Ecology Center Coord., Linda Lutz; Environmental Educator, Karen Taira; Environmental Education, Ellen Fierer; Coord. Garden, Becky Kass; Office Mgr., Elizabeth Cullen.
Personnel Profile: Full-Time Paid 4; Part-Time Paid 4; Part-Time Volunteers 16.
Governing Authority: nonprofit organization. Parent Institution: City of Evanston. Branch Museums: Ladd Arboretum & Ecology Center, 2024 McCormick, Evanston, IL 60201; Grosse Point Lighthouse, Nature Center, Central & Sheridan Rd., Evanston, IL. Tax-exempt: 501(c)(3).
Environmental Education Center & Arboretum.
Collections: natural history of region; history of Grosse Pointe Lighthouse; native wildflowers; alternative energy demonstration projects. Historic Building: 1874, Grosse Pointe Lighthouse Station.
Research Fields: natural landscaping; interpretive services; greenhouses; environmental studies.
Facilities: 450-vol. library of books relating to general public interest & environmental concerns available for research on premises; botanical

garden; solar greenhouse; classrooms; nature center; arboretum; demonstration energy systems. Booklets & pamphlets relating to environmental concerns for sale.
Activities: guided tours; lectures; films; workshops; formally organized educational programs; docent program; permanent exhibitions.
Publications: quarterly newsletter, Futures.
Hours & Admission Prices: Summer: Mon.-Fri. 9-4:30; Labor Day-Memorial Day Mon.-Sat. 9-4:30. No charge. Closed national holidays; Memorial Day; Independence Day weekend; Labor Day weekend. ♿
Attendance: 8,000 (estimated)
Membership: Individual $25; Family $50; Nonprofit, School & Contributing $100; Sustaining $250; Life $500; Corporate $1,000.

EVANSTON HISTORICAL CENTER AND CHARLES GATES DAWES HOUSE, (M), 225 Greenwood St., Evanston, IL 60201-4713. Tel.: 847-475-3410. Fax: 847-475-3599.
E-mail: evanstonhs@northwestern.edu
Web Site: www.evanstonhistorycenter.org
Founded: 1898.
Congressional District: 10
Key Personnel: Pres. (V), Robert Barr.
Personnel Profile: Full-Time Paid 2; Part-Time Paid 5; Part-Time Volunteers 45; Interns 1.
Governing Authority: private; nonprofit organization. Tax-exempt: 501(c)(3).
Historic House Museum: restored 1894 home of former Vice Pres. & Nobel laureate Dawes: 28-room mansion. National Historic Landmark.
Collections: Gen. Charles G. Dawes memorabilia; historical Evanston artifacts; archival material; costumes; photograph & newspaper archives; 1920s furnished rooms.
Research Fields: genealogical; Evanston history & architecture.
Facilities: 1.8 acre lakefront property.
Activities: tours of house; permanent & rotating exhibits; lectures; holiday events; special events. Annual Events: Mother's Day House Walk; Fall Ice Cream Social.
Publications: biannual membership newsletter, TimeLines.
Hours & Admission Prices: Tours: Fri.-Sun. 1-5. Tours: adults $5, students & seniors $3; discounts to AAM members; members no charge. Research: Tues., Thurs., Sat. 1-4 $5; members & students no charge. Closed legal holidays. ♿
Attendance: 6,000 (accurate)
Membership: Individual $30; Family & Dual $45; Sustainer $100; Patron $250; Currey Club Conservator $500; Curry Club Circle $1,000.

FRANCES WILLARD HOUSE MUSEUM, 1730 Chicago Ave., Evanston, IL 60201-4502. Mailing Address: Frances Willard Historical Assoc., 1730 Chicago Ave., Evanston, IL 60201. Tel.: 847-328-7500. Fax: 847-328-7500.
E-mail: info@franceswillardhouse.org
Web Site: www.franceswillardhouse.org
Formerly: The Willard House (WCTU Museum)
Founded: 1900.
Congressional District: 10
Key Personnel: Pres. (V), Liora Cobin.
Personnel Profile: Part-Time Volunteers 15.
Governing Authority: nonprofit organization. Parent Institution: Woman's Christian Temperance Union. Subsidiary Institution: Frances Willard Historical Assoc. Tax-exempt: 501(c)(3).
Historic House: home of Frances E. Willard (1865-1898).
Collections: period furniture; books; costumes; pictures; maps; items from around the world gathered by Frances Willard.
Activities: guided tours.
Hours & Admission Prices: 1st Sun. of each month 1-4; other times by appointment only. Adults $5; discounts to AAM & ICOM members; members no charge.
Attendance: 400 (estimated)
Membership: Gladys membership (children 18 & older) $5; Frances Willard Historical Association & Individual $15; Household $30; Supporter $50; Friend $100; Museum Council $250.

LEVERE MEMORIAL TEMPLE, 1856 Sheridan Rd., Evanston, IL 60201-3837. Mailing Address: P.O. Box 1856, Evanston, IL 60204-9918. Tel.: 847-475-1856; 800-233-1856. Fax: 847-475-2250.
Web Site: www.sae.net
Founded: 1929.
Congressional District: 9
Key Personnel: Dir., Steven K. Priepke, Esq.; Pres. (V), Thomas Z. Hayward, Jr.
Personnel Profile: Part-Time Paid 1.
Governing Authority: nonprofit organization. Parent Institution: Sigma Alpha Epsilon Foundation. Tax-exempt: 501(c)(3).
Preservation Society.
Collections: books; letters; fraternity jewelry & artifacts; early fraternity life & customs; manuscripts; Tiffany stained glass windows depicting fraternity & U.S.A. history; Fraternity Hall of Fame; restored Tiffany sketches, 70 chapel stained glass window templates; murals.
Facilities: library; 325-seat chapel.
Activities: guided tours; permanent exhibitions.
Publications: quarterly magazine for fraternity members, The Record; The Phoenix.
Hours & Admission Prices: Memorial Day to Labor Day Mon.-Thurs. 9-4:30, Fri. 9 to noon, Sat.-Sun. by appointment; Sept.-May Mon.-Fri. 9-4:30, Sat.-Sun. by appointment only. No charge; donations accepted. Closed New Year's Eve & Day; Presidents' Day; Easter; Memorial Day; Independence Day; Labor Day; Thanksgiving & day after; Christmas Day & week.
Attendance: 700 (estimated)

*** MARY AND LEIGH BLOCK MUSEUM OF ART, NORTHWESTERN UNIVERSITY,** 40 Arts Circle Dr., Evanston, IL 60208-2410. Tel.: 847-491-4001. Fax: 847-491-2261.
E-mail: block-museum@northwestern.edu
Web Site: www.blockmuseum.northwestern.edu
Founded: 1980.
Congressional District: 9
Key Personnel: Dir., David Alan Robertson; Chm., James Elesh; Dir. Devel., Helen Hilken; Business Admin. & Museum Shop Mgr., Carole Towns; Dir. Education Programs, Sheetal Prajapati; Grants Mgr., Nicole Druckman; Communications Mgr., Burke Patten; Collections & Exhibitions Asst., Elizabeth Wolf; Block Cinema, Will Schmenner; Sr. Cur., Debora Wood; Assoc. Cur., Corinne Granof; Registrar, Kristina Bottomley; Mgr. Exhibitions & Facilities, Dan Silverstein; Asst. to Dir., Julia Csikesz; Security Coord., James Foster; Security Asst., Aaron Chatman.
Personnel Profile: Full-Time Paid 13; Part-Time Paid 83; Part-Time Volunteers 88; Interns 4.
Governing Authority: nonprofit; university. Northwestern University, 633 Clark St., Evanston, IL 60208. Tax-exempt: 501(c)(3) & 170(b)(1)(A).
University Art Museum.
Collections: 15th-21st century prints, drawings, & photographs; architectural renderings by Walter Burley and Marion Mahony Griffin; textiles by Theo Leffman; modernist artist including Arp, Moore, Miro, Hepworth & more in outdoor sculpture garden.
Major Exhibits: A Room of Their Own: Bloomsbury Artists in American Collections, 1/10-3/10.
Research Fields: history of prints; sculpture.
Activities: lectures & symposia with artists and scholars; film series; guided exhibition tours; gallery talks; education programs for schools, children & families; classes and resources for graduate & undergraduate students affiliated with Northwestern University.
Publications: exhibition catalogues & guides; quarterly newsletter, Around the Block; quarterly exhibition & programming calendar; annual report.
Hours & Admission Prices: Tues. 10-5, Wed.-Fri. 10-8, Sat.-Sun. 12-5. No charge; donations accepted. ♿
Attendance: 35,000 (accurate)
Membership: Student $15; Individual $40; Family $60; Patron $100; Sustainer $250; Benefactor $500; Block Circle $1,000.

MITCHELL MUSEUM OF THE AMERICAN INDIAN, (M), 3001 Central St., Evanston, IL 60201-1102. Tel.: 847-475-1030. Fax: 847-475-0911.
Web Site: www.mitchellmuseum.org
Founded: 1977.
Congressional District: 9
Key Personnel: Exec. Dir., Lisa Cushing Davis; Chm. (V), Glennis Lundberg; Cur. Education, Penelope Berlet.
Personnel Profile: Full-Time Paid 3; Part-Time Volunteers 30.
Governing Authority: nonprofit organization. Tax-exempt.
Native American Museum.
Collections: 10,000 North American Indian artifacts from cultures of the Woodlands, Plains, Arctic, Southwest & Northwest coast
Research Fields: Native America
Facilities: 5,000-vol. library pertaining to American Indians; 500 video tapes.
Activities: guided tours; lectures; performances; workshops; school loan boxes; hands-on exhibits; family programs; permanent & temporary exhibits.
Publications: brochure; newsletter.
Hours & Admission Prices: Tues.-Wed. & Fri.-Sat. 10-5, Thurs. 10-8, Sun. 12-4. Adults $5, students, children & senior citizens $2.50; discounts to AAM, ICOM, AAA & AASLH members. Closed New Year's Day; Independence Day; Thanksgiving; Christmas. ♿
Attendance: 11,000 (estimated)
Membership: Individual $35; Family $50.

NOYES CULTURAL ARTS CENTER, 927 Noyes St., Evanston, IL 60201-6206. Tel.: 847-448-8260.
Art Gallery.
Collections: paintings; sculpture.
Activities: theatrical performances; special events.
Hours & Admission Prices: Mon.-Sat. 10-7, Sun. 10-6. No charge. ♿

THE PREHISTORIC LIFE MUSEUM, 704 Main St., Evanston, IL 60202-1702. Tel.: 847-866-7374. Fax: 847-866-6854.
Paleontology Museum.
Collections: dinosaur footprints; fossils; bones; dinosaur egg; insects; cave bear skeleton.
Facilities: Museum-related items for sale.
Hours & Admission Prices: Mon.-Tues. & Thurs.-Fri. 10:30-5:30, Sat. 10-5.

Fairbury

FAIRBURY ECHOES MUSEUM, 126 W. Locust, Fairbury, IL 61739-1549. Tel.: 815-692-2191.
E-mail: museum@bloomingtonnormal.net
Founded: 1979.
Key Personnel: Pres. (V), Diane Pawlowski.
Governing Authority: Tax-exempt.
History Museum.
Collections: history of Fairbury & local area; photographs; personal artifacts.
Publications: quarterly newsletter.
Hours & Admission Prices: Thurs.-Fri. 1-4:30, Sat. 9-11:30. No charge; donations accepted.

Fairfield

HANNA HOUSE MUSEUM, 101 E. Center, Fairfield, IL 62837-2101. Mailing Address: 300 S.E. 2nd St., Fairfield, IL 62837-2127.
Founded: 1953.
Key Personnel: Pres. (V), Judith Puckett.
Personnel Profile: Part-Time Volunteers 12.
Governing Authority: Parent Institution: Wayne County Historical Society. Tax-exempt.
Historic House Museum.
Collections: local history including prohibition-era gangland figures; oil boom; medicine; funeral equipment; education; military; sports; Lions' memorabilia.
Research Fields: Wayne County.
Publications: bimonthly membership newsletter.
Hours & Admission Prices: March-Oct. Sat.-Sun. 12:30-4:30. No charge; donations accepted. Closed holidays.
Attendance: 800 (estimated)
Membership: Annual $10; Lifetime $100.

Freeport

FREEPORT ART MUSEUM, (M), 121 N. Harlem Ave., Freeport, IL 61032-3845. Tel.: 815-235-9755. Fax: 815-235-6015.
E-mail: director@freeportartmuseum.org
Web Site: www.freeportartmuseum.org
Founded: 1975.
Congressional District: 16
Key Personnel: C.E.O. & Dir., Jennifer Kirker; Pres. (V), John Graff.
Personnel Profile: Full-Time Paid 4; Part-Time Paid 2; Part-Time Volunteers 55; Interns 2.
Governing Authority: private; nonprofit organization. Tax-exempt: 501(c)(3).
Art Museum & Center.
Collections: European artifacts including 19th century paintings, sculptures, prints & Florentine mosaics from the W.T. Rawleigh collection; Near & Far East artifacts including jewelry; glass; mummy case & other artifacts from Ancient Egypt, China & S.E. Asia; Native American artifacts including Sioux beadwork, Pueblo pottery (including pieces by Nampeyo & Martinez), Kachina dolls & pre-Columbian artifacts; Oceanic art including masks, ceremonial pieces, Indonesian textiles, pottery & musical instruments; works by contemporary artists such as Richard Boschulte, Dan Edler, Winn Jones, Andrew Langoussis, Michael Johnson, Jeanette Sloan, Roland Poska & Duane Smith; student art.
Research Fields: late 1800s & early 1900s paintings; ethnographic art; Egyptian, Oceanic, Greek & Roman antiquities; Native American artifacts.
Facilities: library; classrooms; meeting space.
Activities: guided tours; inter-museum loan & permanent exhibitions; area arts development programs-school artists in residence; extension exhibits; dance school, instructional classes; performances; concerts; poetry readings; festivals; family programs.
Publications: newsletter; catalogs.
Hours & Admission Prices: Tues.-Fri. 10-5, Sat. 12-5. No charge; donations accepted. Closed holidays. ♿
Attendance: 11,000 (accurate)
Membership: Senior Citizen, Teacher & Student $20; Individual $25; Family $40; Sponsor $70; Rilling Circle $100; Parvin Circle $250; Dedrick Circle $500; 121 Club $1,000; Rawleigh Circle $5,000 & up.

HIGHLAND COMMUNITY COLLEGE ARBORETUM, 2998 Pearl City Rd., Freeport, IL 61032-9341. Tel.: 815-235-6121. Fax: 815-235-6130. TDD: 815-235-9584.
E-mail: pete.willging@highland.edu
Founded: 1970.
Congressional District: 16
Key Personnel: Pres. (V), Joe Kanofsky; Business Officer, Pam Schleich; Dir. Public Rels., Pete Willging; Dir. Physical Plant & Maintenance, Rich Eads.
Personnel Profile: Full-Time Paid 2; Part-Time Paid 4.
Governing Authority: college. Parent Institution: Highland Community College Foundation. Tax-exempt: 170(b)(1)(A).
Arboretum.
Collections: 3,000 plantings representing over 300 different species of ground coverings, trees & shrubs.
Research Fields: hican & pecan cultivation.
Facilities: library; 150-seat auditorium; 400-seat theater; classrooms; cafeteria. Textbooks, instructional supplies, school & art supplies for sale.
Activities: guided tours.
Hours & Admission Prices: Daily 7-7. No charge; donations accepted. Closed legal holidays. ♿
Attendance: 5,000 (estimated)

SILVERCREEK MUSEUM, (M), 2954 S. Walnut Rd., Freeport, IL 61032-9528. Tel.: 815-235-7329 & 2198.
E-mail: jkayklever@verizon.net
Web Site: www.thefreeportshow.com
Founded: 1988.
Congressional District: 12
Key Personnel: Pres. (V), Larry Buttel; Vice Pres., Kay Klever; Sec., Cindy Drye; Treas., Kris McNames; Dir., Mary Scofield-Swanson; Dir., Bill Stimpert; Dir., Ed Keech.
Personnel Profile: Part-Time Volunteers 50.
Governing Authority: nonprofit. Stephenson County Antique Engine Club. Tax-exempt.
General Museum: housed in 1906 county poor farm.
Collections: 450 pieces of red wing pottery; W.T. Rawleigh Collection; brass; agricultural implements; art.
Activities: guided tours; temporary exhibitions; antique steam train rides. Annual Events: Pancake Supper in March & November; Ice Cream Social in May; Art Show in June; Quilt Show in July; Christmas Tea in December.
Hours & Admission Prices: Memorial Day to mid-Oct.11-4. Adults $3. ♿
Attendance: 5,000 (estimated)
Membership: Stephenson County Antique Engine Club: Family $20.

STEPHENSON COUNTY HISTORICAL SOCIETY, 1440 S. Carroll Ave., Freeport, IL 61032-6530. Tel.: 815-232-8419. Fax: 815-297-0313.
E-mail: director@stephcohs.org
Web Site: stephcohs.org
Founded: 1944.
Congressional District: 16
Key Personnel: C.E.O., Edward F. Finch; Pres. (V), Harvey Wilhelms; Museum Shop Mgr., Lorraine Slater.
Personnel Profile: Full-Time Paid 1; Part-Time Volunteers 30.
Governing Authority: society. Tax-exempt: 501(c)(3).
History Museum: housed in 1857 house built by Oscar & Malvina Taylor, listed on National Register of Historic Sites.
Collections: Lincoln-Douglas debate material; industrial items connected with county industries; 1843 log cabin; arboretum; Jane Addams collection; arcade toys. Historic Building: 1900-1915 one-room schoolhouse; Farm Museum, farmlife items in the horsepower age 1850-1910.
Facilities: 100-vol. library of local history available on premises by request; arboretum.
Activities: guided tours; lectures; study clubs; formally organized education programs for children; permanent & temporary exhibitions.
Publications: Roads of Stephenson County; Indians of Stephenson County; Looking Back: History of Stephenson County; Looking Back Vol. 1, 2 & 3; African-American History of Stephenson County; Ghost Stories of Stephenson County.
Hours & Admission Prices: Jan. by appointment only; Feb.-April & Nov.-Dec. Fri.-Sun. 12-4; May-Oct. Wed.-Sun. 12-4. Adults $3; members no charge. Closed holidays. ♿
Attendance: 3,500 (accurate)

Membership: Student $10; Individual $25; Family $35; Tutty $50; Addams $100; Lincoln $250; Taylor $500.

Galena

GALENA-JO DAVIESS COUNTY HISTORICAL SOCIETY & MUSEUM, 211 S. Bench St., Galena, IL 61036-2203. Tel.: 815-777-9129. Fax: 815-777-9131.
E-mail: info@galenahistorymuseum.org
Web Site: www.galenahistorymuseum.org
Founded: 1938.
Congressional District: 16
Key Personnel: Pres. (V), Marge Cooke; Exec. Dir., Nancy Breed; Asst. Dir., Colleen Yonda.
Personnel Profile: Full-Time Paid 2; Part-Time Paid 3; Part-Time Volunteers 25.
Governing Authority: nonprofit organization. Subsidiary Institution: Old Blacksmith Shop. Tax-exempt: 501(c)(3).
Historical Society Museum: housed in 1858 Daniel A. Barrows house.
Collections: regional artifacts & manuscripts of the upper Mississippi lead mine region; 1830s mine shaft; 19th-century mining tools; farm implements; costumes; industries in Galena; Civil War artifacts. Historic Building: 1858 U.S. Grant Leather Store; geology.
Research Fields: oral history; lead mining; steamboating; architecture; U.S. Grant; Civil War; upper Mississippi River.
Facilities: 1,000-vol. library of photographs, manuscripts, newspapers & publications relating to the area available for research on premises by appointment. Museum-related items for sale.
Activities: guided tours; lectures; gallery talks; formally organized educational programs; permanent & temporary exhibitions; school loan service; tours of Galena's historic district.
Publications: posters; books; exhibit catalogs; quarterly newsletter.
Hours & Admission Prices: Daily 9-4:30. Call for admission prices. Closed New Year's Eve & Day; Easter; Thanksgiving; Christmas Eve & Day.
Attendance: 13,945 (accurate)
Membership: Seniors $15; Single $20; Family $30; Sustaining $100; Patron $250; Benefactor $500; Guardian $1,000.

OLD MARKET HOUSE STATE HISTORIC SITE, Market Square, Galena, IL 61036. Mailing Address: 307 Decatur St., P.O. Box 333, Galena, IL 61036-0333. Tel.: 815-777-3310. Fax: 815-777-3310.
E-mail: granthome@granthome.com
Founded: 1947.
Congressional District: 16
Key Personnel: Site Mgr., Terry J. Miller.
Personnel Profile: Full-Time Paid 5; Part-Time Paid 7; Part-Time Volunteers 15.
Governing Authority: state. Illinois Historic Preservation Agency, Div. of Historic Sites, Old State Capitol, Springfield, IL 62701. Tax-exempt.
Historic House Museum: c.1845 Greek Revival-style Market House.
Collections: Galena artifacts; President Ulysses S. Grant artifacts.
Research Fields: history; architecture.
Facilities: meeting hall; market square.
Activities: guided tours; lectures; inter-museum loan exhibitions; permanent exhibitions. Museum Sponsors: weekly Galena farmers' market May to October.
Publications: bimonthly newsletter, Historic Illinois; brochure, Market House.
Hours & Admission Prices: Wed.-Sun. 9-12 & 1-5; Winter: 10-12 & 1-4. Donations suggested.
Attendance: 32,395 (accurate)

U.S. GRANT'S HOME STATE HISTORIC SITE, 500 Bouthillier St., Galena, IL 61036-2704. Mailing Address: 307 Decatur St., P.O. Box 333, Galena, IL 61036-0333. Tel.: 815-777-3310. Fax: 815-777-3310.
E-mail: granthome@granthome.com
Web Site: www.granthome.com
Founded: 1932.
Congressional District: 16
Key Personnel: Site Mgr., Terry J. Miller.
Personnel Profile: Full-Time Paid 5; Part-Time Paid 7; Part-Time Volunteers 15.
Governing Authority: state. Parent Institution: Illinois Historic Preservation Agency, Div. of Historic Sites, Old State Capitol, Springfield, IL 62701. Tax-exempt.
Historic House Museum: 1860 Italianate bracketed style house presented to Gen. Grant in 1865.
Collections: Grant mementos; Victorian furnishings; pictorial exhibit on Grant's life & Galena. Historic Buildings: c.1850 Greek Revival row house; 1844-1860 Elihu B. Washburne House State Historic Site; two 1840s log houses; 1891 frame house; 1838 frame house; c.1838 log house.
Research Fields: U.S. Grant; Galena & regional history.
Facilities: 300-vol. library of material on Grant & local history, 1828-1931 Galena newspapers.
Activities: permanent exhibitions. Special Event: Lamplight Tour in December.
Publications: bimonthly newsletter, Historic Illinois; brochure, Grant's Home.
Hours & Admission Prices: March-Oct. Wed.-Sun. 9-4:45; Nov.-Feb. Wed.-Sun. 9-4. Suggested Donation: adults $4, children under 18 $2. Closed New Year's Day; Martin Luther King Jr. Day; Presidents' Day; Election Day; Veterans Day; Thanksgiving; Christmas. ♿
Attendance: 84,770 (accurate)

Galesburg

CARL SANDBURG STATE HISTORIC SITE, 313 E. 3rd St., Galesburg, IL 61401-6021. Mailing Address: P.O. Box 108, Galesburg, IL Tel.: 309-342-2361. Fax: 309-342-2141.
E-mail: carl@sandburg.org
Web Site: www.sandburg.org
Founded: 1945.
Congressional District: 17
Key Personnel: Site Supt., Martha Downey.
Personnel Profile: Part-Time Paid 1; Part-Time Volunteers 3.
Governing Authority: state. Parent Institution: Illinois Historic Preservation Agency.
Historic Home Museum: c.1870 immigrant railroad worker's cottage.
Collections: period furniture; family pieces of the Sandburgs; Sandburg publications & memorabilia; memorial garden. Historic Site: Remembrance Rock where Sandburg's ashes were buried; 1858 house used as Visitor Center.
Facilities: garden; gravesite.
Activities: guided tours; permanent exhibits; video presentations.
Publications: newsletter, Inklings and Idlings.
Hours & Admission Prices: May-Oct. Thurs.-Sun. 9-5. Suggested Donations: family $10, adults $4, children 17 & under $2. Closed New Year's Day; Thanksgiving; Christmas. ♿
Attendance: 16,000 (estimated)

DISCOVERY DEPOT CHILDREN'S MUSEUM, 128 S. Chambers St., Galesburg, IL 61401-4966. Tel.: 309-344-8876.
E-mail: discoverydepot@grics.net
Web Site: www.discoverydepot.org
Governing Authority: nonprofit organization.
Children's Museum.
Collections: hands-on exhibits.
Facilities: Museum-related items for sale.
Activities: birthday parties; special programs.
Hours & Admission Prices: July-Aug. Mon.-Sat. 10-5, 3rd Fri. of month 10-7, Sun. 1-5; Sept.-June Tues.-Sat. 10-5, 3rd Fri. of month 10-7, Sun. 1-5. Admission $3.50.

GALESBURG CIVIC ART CENTER, 114 E. Main St., Galesburg, IL 61401-4601. Tel.: 309-342-7415.
E-mail: info@galesburgarts.org
Web Site: www.galesburgarts.org
Founded: 1923.
Congressional District: 17
Key Personnel: C.E.O., Heather L. Norman; Pres. (V), William Morris; Office Mgr., Lynn Miller; Archivist, Joanne Goudie.
Personnel Profile: Part-Time Paid 2; Part-Time Volunteers 100.
Governing Authority: nonprofit organization. Parent Institution: Galesburg Civic Art League. Tax-exempt.
Art Gallery & Civic Center: housed in c.1897 building.
Collections: W.P.A. prints including Thomas Hart Benton, Raphael Soyer, M. Albright; regional landscape paintings, including Harold Gregor; paintings from national competitions since 1965; works by Joe Bujnowski, J. Butler, H. Gerardia & Salvador Dali, Clare Smith.
Major Exhibits: Kid's Month, 1/23/10-1/30/10; Tom Foley, 2/5/10-3/6/10; Galex 44, 3/13/10-4/10/10; Merging Into the Future 10, 4/16/10-5/1/10; Dist. 205 Permanent Collection, 5/7/10-5/22/10; Susan Foley/Delores Fortuna, 5/28/10-6/26/10; Vesna Jovanovic/Gregory Page, 7/3/10-7/31/10; Members & Friends, 8/6/10-9/3/10; Les Barta/Dennis Belcher, 9/10/10-10/8/10; Joshua Dixon/Tanya Pshenychny, 10/15/10-11/12/10.
Research Fields: W.P.A. prints; regional central & central western Illinois.
Facilities: Museum-related items for sale.
Activities: lectures; loan & temporary exhibitions; educational programs. Annual Events: Galex National Exhibit; Art-in-the-Park fair; Studios Midwest Residency Program; The Black Earth Film Festival.
Publications: Artifacts Newsbulletin; brochures.
Hours & Admission Prices: Tues.-Fri. 10:30-4:30, Sat. 10:30-3; tours by appointment. No charge; donations accepted. Closed all holidays.
Attendance: 8,000 (estimated)

Membership: Senior & Student $20; Individual $40; Family $60; Patron-of-the-Arts $150; Muse $300; Art Champion $500; Benefactor $1,000 & up.

GALESBURG RAILROAD MUSEUM, 211 S. Seminary St., Galesburg, IL 61401-4955. Tel.: 309-342-9400.
History Museum.
Collections: railroad history & artifacts; memorabilia; 1930 passenger train; Pullman parlor car; caboose; tools; photographs; uniforms; utensils; books; magazines; china.
Hours & Admission Prices: April-Nov. Tues.-Sat. 10-4, Sun. 12-4.

ILLINOIS CITIZEN SOLDIER MUSEUM, 1001 Michigan Ave., Galesburg, IL 61401-6481. Tel.: 309-342-1181.
Founded: 1988.
Congressional District: 17
Key Personnel: Bldg. Mgr. & Museum Shop Mgr., Jim Verheyen; Pres. (V) & Treas., Mike Lummis.
Personnel Profile: Full-Time Volunteers 1; Part-Time Volunteers 5.
Governing Authority: veterans organization; nonprofit. Parent Institution: V.F.W. 2257. Tax-exempt.
Military Museum: housed in Admiral James Stockdale building, home of Veterans of Foreign Wars Post 2257.
Collections: Admiral James Stockdale memorabilia; artifacts & military memorabilia of Illinois service men and women from Spanish American War to present.
Facilities: 50-vol. library on miscellaneous military subjects; educational facilities; 1,300 sq. ft. exhibit space.
Activities: guided tours; lectures; loan, participatory & temporary exhibitions; school loan service; study clubs; broadcast programs.
Hours & Admission Prices: Mon.-Fri. 9-1:30, Sat. 9-4. No charge; donations accepted. Closed New Year's Day; Christmas; federal holidays. ♿
Attendance: 1,000 (estimated)

NATIONAL RAILROAD HALL OF FAME, 200 E. Main St., Galesburg, IL 61401-4707. Tel.: 309-345-4634.
E-mail: info@nrrhof.org
Web Site: www.nrrhof.org
Key Personnel: Exec. Dir., Julie King
Railroad Museum.
Collections: railroad history; Hall of Fame inductees.
Hours & Admission Prices: By appointment. No charge.

Geneva

FABYAN VILLA MUSEUM, 1511 S. Batavia Ave., Geneva, IL 60134. Mailing Address: P.O. Box 903, St. Charles, IL 60174-0903. Tel.: 630-377-6424. Fax: 630-377-6424.
E-mail: fabyanvilla@ppfv.org
Web Site: www.ppfv.org/fabyan.htm
Formerly: Fabyan Villa Museum, Dutch Windmill & Japanese Gardens
Founded: 1941.
Congressional District: 14
Key Personnel: Dir., Lynn Dransoff; Museum Asst., Amber Hare.
Personnel Profile: Part-Time Paid 3; Part-Time Volunteers 23.
Governing Authority: nonprofit. Kane County. Parent Institution: Forest Preserve District of Kane County. Tax-exempt.
Forest Preserve & Historic House: c.1907 home of Col. George Fabyan, re-designed by Frank Lloyd Wright, located in forest preserve, land formerly the estate of Col. Fabyan.
Collections: Asian aesthetic & cultural artifacts; historic photographs; Frank Lloyd Wright architecture & mission-style furniture; natural history specimens; scientific equipment; WW1 documents & cryptology apparatus; Silvio Silvestri sculptures; Japanese garden. Historic Structures: 19th-century Dutch windmill; lighthouse.
Major Exhibits: Japan's Rising Sun, 11/09-5/11; Finding Frank Lloyd Wright, 11/09-9/11.
Research Fields: local history; military history.
Facilities: gardens.
Activities: guided tours; lectures; slide show; kids programs; adult education programs; concerts.
Publications: The Preservation Advocate.
Hours & Admission Prices: Museum: May & Sept. to mid-Oct. Wed. & Sat.-Sun. 1-4:30; June-Aug. Wed.-Thurs. 1-4, Sat.-Sun. 1-4:30. Japanese Gardens: mid-May to mid-Oct. Sun. & Wed. 1-4. Adults $2, seniors & children $1.
Attendance: 5,000 (accurate)
Membership: Individual $25; Family $35.

Glen Ellyn

STACY'S TAVERN MUSEUM AND GLEN ELLYN HISTORICAL SOCIETY, (M), 557 Geneva Rd., Glen Ellyn, IL 60137-3728. Mailing Address: P.O. Box 283, Glen Ellyn, IL 60138-0283. Tel.: 630-858-8696.
Web Site: www.gehs.org
Founded: 1969.
Congressional District: 6
Key Personnel: C.E.O. & Dir., Janice L. Langford; Pres. (V), William B. Peterson; Museum Shop Mgr., Pat O'Connor.
Personnel Profile: Full-Time Paid 1; Part-Time Paid 1; Part-Time Volunteers 90; Interns 2.
Governing Authority: society; nonprofit organization. Affiliated with the Glen Ellyn Historical Society & the Village of Glen Ellyn. Tax-exempt: 170(b)(1)(A).
Historic House: 1846 Moses Stacy House & Inn; local Glen Ellyn Historical Exhibition & Archives.
Collections: pre-1850 American country furnishings; photographs; Glen Ellyn historical & archival collections.
Research Fields: local history; genealogy.
Facilities: library available for research on premises. Gift items & local history books for sale.
Activities: guided tours; lectures; films; arts festivals; docent program or council; temporary & traveling exhibitions.
Publications: quarterly newsletter; book series: Stories from Glen Ellyn's Past (Vol. I, 2009)
Hours & Admission Prices: Tues.-Wed. & Sun. 1:30-4:30; other times by appointment. No charge; donations accepted; special tours by arrangement. Closed New Year's Eve & Day; Easter; Mother's Day; Independence Day; Thanksgiving; Christmas. ♿
Attendance: 3,500 (accurate)
Membership: Senior $15; Individual $20; Family $30; Patron $100.

Glencoe

* **CHICAGO BOTANIC GARDEN, (M),** 1000 Lake Cook Rd., Glencoe, IL 60022-1169. Tel.: 847-835-5440, ext. 0. Fax: 847-835-4484. TDD: 847-835-0790.
E-mail: mschuler@chicagobotanic.org
Web Site: www.chicagobotanic.org
Founded: 1965.
Congressional District: 10
Key Personnel: Chm. Bd. (V), William J. Hagenah; Pres. & C.E.O., Sophia Siskel; Exec. Vice Pres. & Dir., Kris S. Jarantoski; Treas. & Sr. Vice Pres. Finance & Administration, Thomas J. Nissly; Vice Pres. Visitor Experience & Business Devel., Harriet Resnick; Vice Pres. Communications, Rich Bartecki; Vice Pres. Facilities & Planning, William W. Brown; Vice Pres. Community Education Programs, Patsy Benveniste; Dir. Community Gardening, Angela Mason; Dir. Center Teaching & Learning, Jennifer Shwarz Ballard, Ph.D.; Dir. Horticulture, Timothy D. Johnson; Dir. Plant Science & Conservation, and Medard & Elizabeth Welch Dir. Plant Conservation Science, Kayri Havens, Ph.D.; Dir. Environmental Horticulture, James A. Ault, Ph.D.; Dir. Plant Collections, Galen D. Gates; Dir. Living Plant Documentation, Boyce Tankersley; Dir. Restoration Ecology & Cur. Aquatic Plant & Urban Lake Studies, Robert Kirschner; Exec. Dir. BGCI-US, Andrea T. Kramer; Dir. Sustainable Operations, Stephen Bell; Dir. Government Affairs, Ginny Hotaling; Dir. Bd. Rels. & Governance, Lynn Abrahamson; Dir. Membership & Annual Fund, Anne Boynton; Dir. Foundation & Government Rels., Melissa Matterson; Dir. Interpretive Programs, Kristen P. Webber; Dir. Visitor Programs & Events, Jodi Zombolo; Dir. Corp. Rels., Steve Ball; Sr. Advancement Officer, Patricia M. Shanahan; Sr. Devel. Officer, Vivienne Jones; Dir. Lenhardt Library, Leora Siegel; Dir. Human Resources, Jerry Baker; Dir. Visitor Operations, Darren Bochat; Mgr. Volunteer Svcs., Judith M. Cashen; Dir. Information Svcs., Laura Altergott; Dir. Finance, Rob Pollack; Dir. Maintenance, Gregory L. Detlie.
Personnel Profile: Full-Time Paid 250; Part-Time Paid 45; Part-Time Volunteers 1,000; Interns 29.
Governing Authority: managed by the Chicago Horticultural Society. Parent Institution: The Forest Preserve District of Cook County. Tax-exempt.
Botanic Garden.
Collections: 2,300,000 living plants; 9,414 taxa including prairie, woodland & riparian, aquatic native plants, bulbs, edible plants, dwarf conifers, tropical & desert plants, annuals, perennials, roses, ornamental grasses, trees, shrubs, vines & ground covers. Scientific: National Tallgrass Prairie Seed Bank; herbarium. Fine & Decorative Arts: porcelains; prints; paintings; photographs; sculpture; oriental decorative arts; 23 specialty gardens; habitat areas.
Research Fields: Horticulture: environmental horticulture; ornamental plant breeding; plant evaluation & introduction; Chicagoland Grows(R); Plant Science and Conservation: invasive plant science and policy, plant biology;

economic botany; plant systematics; plant conservation; habitat fragmentation; climate change; land management; restoration genetics; rare plant restoration; Project Budburst; seed banking; restoration ecology; lake, prairie, river and woodland ecosystems; soil ecology.
Facilities: library; 200-seat auditorium; classrooms; herbarium; events pavilion; cafe. Gifts items for sale.
Activities: guided tram & walking tours; lectures; carillon concerts; formally organized education programs; narrated tram rides; workshops; demonstrations; art exhibits; plant society shows; seasonal plant sales; cultural events; certificate program; bachelors, masters & doctoral programs; community gardening programs; after school & camp programs; scout programs; wellness & lifestyle programs; horticultural therapy; public festivals.
Publications: quarterly newsletter, Member Magazine; brochures; Plant Evaluation Notes; Plant Facts; educational publications; The Sunflower Family in the Upper Midwest, The Chicago Botanic Garden Encyclopedia of Gardens: History & Design; Garden for Life; A Journey to Nine Islands; Wonderland Express; seasonal garden guide; seasonal visitor guides, Spring/Summer & Fall/Winter.
Hours & Admission Prices: June to Labor Day daily 7am-9pm. Garden: no charge. Parking: $15 car. Grand Tram Tours: April-Oct. Mon.-Fri. 10-4, Sat.-Sun. 10-5. Bright Encounters Tours: Mon.-Fri. 10:15-3:15, Sat.-Sun. 10:15-5:15. Adults $5, seniors $4, children 3-12 $3; discounts to groups of 15 & over. Closed Christmas Day. ♿
Attendance: 760,000
Membership: Individual $65; Family/Dual $80; Family Plus $105; Friends Circle $150-$249. National Membership: Individual $52; Family $64.

GLENCOE HISTORICAL SOCIETY AT THE EKLUND HISTORY CENTER & GARDEN, (M), 377 Park Ave., Glencoe, IL 60022-1551. Mailing Address: P.O. Box 457, 377 Park Ave., Glencoe, IL 60022-0457. Tel.: 847-835-0040.
E-mail: info@glencoehistoricalsociety.org
Web Site: glencoehistoricalsociety.org
Historical Society Museum.
Collections: items pertaining to the Village of Glencoe.
Hours & Admission Prices: Museum: Jan.-July & Sept.-Dec. Wed. 10-3, Sun. 1-4.

Glenview

GLENVIEW AREA HISTORICAL SOCIETY, 1121 Waukegan Rd., Glenview, IL 60025-3036. Tel.: 847-724-2235. Fax: 847-724-2235.
E-mail: berdaw@juno.com
Web Site: www.glenviewhistory.org
Founded: 1965.
Congressional District: 10
Key Personnel: Pres., A. C. Realie; Librarian, Beverly Dawson.
Personnel Profile: Part-Time Volunteers 25.
Governing Authority: society. Tax-exempt: 501(c)(3).
Historical Society Museum: housed in original 1864 farm house.
Collections: local history; clothing; furniture & furnishings; pictures; papers; Naval Air Station Glenview photographs & written material.
Research Fields: local history.
Facilities: 100-vol. Coach House Historical Library containing books on local history, available for research by prior arrangement; reading room.
Activities: guided tours; illustrated lectures; docent program.
Publications: G.A.H.S. newsletter.
Hours & Admission Prices: Museum: Sun. 1-4; other times by appointment. Library: Tues. 1-4. No charge; donations accepted. Closed holidays.
Attendance: 750 (estimated)
Membership: Individual $25; Business $25-$50; Household $50; Contributing Life $400.

THE GROVE, 1421 Milwaukee Ave., Glenview, IL 60025-1436. Tel.: 847-299-6096. Fax: 847-299-0571.
Web Site: glenviewparks.org
Founded: 1976.
Congressional District: 10
Key Personnel: Dir., Stephan Swanson; Museum Shop Mgr., Kris VanVoorhis.
Personnel Profile: Full-Time Paid 10; Part-Time Paid 27; Part-Time Volunteers 53; Interns 1.
Governing Authority: municipal. Affiliated with the Glenview Park District, 1930 Prairie St., Glenview, IL 60025. Tel. 847-724-5670. Tax-exempt.
Natural History Museum: housed in 1856 Kennicott House, site of original grounds.
Collections: Kennicott family papers; Donald Culross Peattie books; manuscripts; functioning blacksmith shop.
Research Fields: botanical gardens; natural history research; ecological studies.
Facilities: 400-vol. library of Kennicott Family history available for research on premises; botanical garden; nature conservation center; field research station; classrooms; Redfield Cultural Center; Interpretive Center.
Activities: guided tours; lectures; formally organized education programs; docent program; permanent exhibitions.
Publications: monthly newsletter, The Rustlings.
Hours & Admission Prices: Mon.-Fri. 8-4:30, Sat.-Sun. 9-5. No charge; donations accepted. Closed New Year's Day; Independence Day; Christmas. ♿
Attendance: 75,000 (estimated)
Membership: Individual $20; Family $40; Organization & Business $100; Contributing $250; Sustaining $500; Life $1,000.

HARTUNG'S AUTO AND LICENSE PLATE MUSEUM, 3623 W. Lake St., Glenview, IL 60026-1269. Tel.: 847-724-4354.
Founded: 1971.
Key Personnel: C.E.O. & Owner, Lee Hartung.
Governing Authority: individual operation.
Automotive Museum.
Collections: license plates; police badge collection; 100 period autos, trucks, tractors & motorcycles; hub caps; radiator emblems; mascots; spark plugs; watch fobs; tools; clocks; toys & farm machinery.
Activities: guided tours; permanent exhibitions.
Hours & Admission Prices: April-Nov. most weekends; call for hours. Donations accepted.

ILLINOIS PGA GOLF HALL OF FAME MUSEUM, 2901 W. Lake Ave., Glenview, IL 60026-1264. Tel.: 847-724-7272 & 729-5700, ext. 100.
Golf History Museum.
Collections: golf history; Hall of Fame inductees; golf memorabilia & equipment; photographs.
Activities: hands-on exhibits.
Hours & Admission Prices: Daily. No charge.

KOHL CHILDREN'S MUSEUM OF GREATER CHICAGO, 2100 Patriot Blvd., Glenview, IL 60026-8018. Tel.: 847-832-6600. Fax: 847-724-6469.
E-mail: info@kohlchildrensmuseum.org
Web Site: www.kohlchildrensmuseum.org
Founded: 1985.
Congressional District: 29
Key Personnel: C.E.O. & Pres., Sheridan Turner; Chm., W. Fritz Sonder; Controller, Howard Fox; Vice Pres. Programs, Mary Pinon; Vice Pres. External Affairs, Shana Hayes; Communications Mgr., Dave Judy; Vice Pres. Business Affairs, Bill Sanders; Museum Shop Mgr., Liz Berwanger.
Personnel Profile: Full-Time Paid 35; Part-Time Paid 35; Part-Time Volunteers 200; Interns 5.
Governing Authority: nonprofit organization. Tax-exempt: 501(c)(3).
Children's Museum.
Collections: 16 interactive hands-on exhibits including a child-sized supermarket; hands-on house; music; art studio; 2-acre outdoor exhibit area; sculpture trail.
Major Exhibits: Pizza: Any Way You Slice It (T), 1/10-5/10; Watch Us Grow: Eggs to Chicks, 3/10-5/10; Smokey Bear & Woodsy Owl: Home Sweet Home (T), 6/10-9/10; Watch Us Grow: Monarch Butterflies, 8/10-10/10; Curious George: Let's Ge Curious! (T), 10/10-2/11.
Activities: daily activities; Focus Field Trips; in-school programs; early childhood connections.
Publications: monthly calendar of activities; quarterly newsletter, Learning to Grow.
Hours & Admission Prices: Mon. 9:30-12, Tues.-Sat. 9:30-5, Sun. 12-5. Adults & children $7.50, senior citizens $6.50; discounts ACM reciprocal program members & children under one no charge. Closed New Year's Day; Independence Day; week of Labor Day; Thanksgiving; Christmas Eve & Day. ♿
Attendance: 332,000 (accurate)
Membership: Kids Club Grand $80; Kids Club $90; Kids Club Plus $110.

NAVAL AIR STATION GLENVIEW MUSEUM, (M), 2040 Lehigh Ave., Glenview, IL 60026-1619. Tel.: 847-657-0000.
E-mail: wam51@comcast.net
Web Site: www.hangarone.org/museum.asp
Key Personnel: Pres., Bill Marquardt
Naval Air Museum.
Collections: naval aviation history; models of aircraft; photographs; military uniforms & equipment.
Hours & Admission Prices: Sat. 10-5, Sun. 12-5; other times by appointment. Closed major holidays.

Grayslake

ROBERT T. WRIGHT COMMUNITY GALLERY OF ART, Library, College of Lake County, 19351 W. Washington St., Grayslake, IL 60030-1148. Tel.: 847-543-2240.
E-mail: sjones@clcillinois.edu
Web Site: gallery.clcillinois.edu/
Founded: 1981.
Congressional District: 8
Key Personnel: Dir., Steven Jones; Museum Shop Mgr., Christina Rasmussen.
Personnel Profile: Full-Time Paid 1; Part-Time Paid 1.
Art Gallery.
Collections: works by local, national & international artists; outdoor sculptures.
Hours & Admission Prices: Mon.-Thurs. 8am-9pm, Fri. 8-4:30, Sat. 9-4:30, Sun. 1-5. No charge. ♿
Membership: Student $15; Friend of Gallery & Artist $30.

Great Lakes

GREAT LAKES NAVAL MUSEUM, Bldg. 42, Naval Station Main Gate, Great Lakes, IL 60088-3607. Mailing Address: P.O. Box 886307, Great Lakes, IL 60088-6307. Tel.: 847-688-3154. Fax: 847-688-3169.
E-mail: therese.gonzalez@navy.mil
Web Site: www.nsgreatlakes.navy.mil/museum
Key Personnel: Cur., Therese Gonzalez
Military Museum.
Collections: boot camp training in the U.S. Navy; uniforms; photographs; U.S. Navy sailor.
Hours & Admission Prices: Fri. 1-4, Sat.-Sun. 7-3 (military ID required). No charge.

Greenville

HOILES-DAVIS MUSEUM, 318 W. Winter St., Greenville, IL 62246-1722. Mailing Address: P.O. Box 376, Greenville, IL 62246-0376. Tel.: 618-664-1590.
Founded: 1955.
Congressional District: 55
Key Personnel: Pres., Sharon Grimes; Vice Pres., Kathy Brewer; Treas., John S. Coleman; Historian, Dean Anthony; Historian, Nelda Anthony; Sec., June Wise.
Personnel Profile: Interns 1.
Governing Authority: society. Tax-exempt.
Historical Society Museum.
Collections: personal artifacts; books; newspaper articles; period furnishings; Bond County memorabilia from 1818-1960; WWI posters; vintage business items; one room school display; cemetery & original voters records of Bond County.
Major Exhibits: Lincoln in Greenville, 11/09-10/10; Civil War, 11/09-10/10.
Activities: temporary exhibitions.
Publications: pamphlet, History of Bond County.
Hours & Admission Prices: Sat. 1-3, Sun. 2-4. No charge; donations accepted. ♿
Attendance: 700 (estimated)
Membership: $15.

Hanna City

WILDLIFE PRAIRIE STATE PARK, 3826 N. Taylor Rd., Hanna City, IL 61536-9467. Tel.: 309-676-0998. Fax: 309-676-7783.
Web Site: www.wildlifeprairiestatepark.org
Founded: 1978.
Congressional District: 18
Key Personnel: Exec. Dir., Jeff Rosecrans; Gen. Mgr., Linda Prescott; Cur. Animals, Nancy Ream; Mktg. & Public Rels. Coord., Kelly Stickelmair; Controller, Maureen Lee; Security, Alan Burgett.
Personnel Profile: Full-Time Paid 25; Full-Time Volunteers 1; Part-Time Paid 20; Part-Time Volunteers 210; Interns 3.
Governing Authority: nonprofit organization. Parent Institution: Forest Park Foundation, 5823 N. Forest Park Dr., Peoria, IL 61614. Tax-exempt.
Wildlife Park.
Collections: animals & plants native to the prairie; pioneer farmstead.
Research Fields: animal behavior.
Facilities: botanical garden; zoological park; nature & conservation center; 650-seat capacity banquet hall; catering facilities; overnight lodging; train ride; pioneer farmstead. Gift items for sale.
Activities: guided tours; lectures; films; formally organized education programs for children, adults & undergraduate college students; docent program; train ride.
Publications: members newsletter, Outlook; facilities guide; tourism & lodging brochures; animal guide.
Hours & Admission Prices: mid-March to April & Oct. to mid-Dec. 9-4:30; May-Sept. 9-6:30. Adults $6.50, children 4-12 $4.50; discounts to groups; members and children 3 & under no charge. ♿
Attendance: 150,000 (accurate)
Membership: Individual $40; Family & Grandparent $50; Keepers Club $250-$499; Explorers Club $500-$999; Naturalist Club $1,000-$2,499; Director's Club $2,500-$4,999; Benefactor's Club $5,000-$9,999; Rutherford Society $10,000 & up.

Harvard

GREATER HARVARD AREA HISTORICAL SOCIETY, 308 N. Hart Blvd., Harvard, IL 60033-3018. Mailing Address: P.O. Box 505, Harvard, IL 60033-0505. Tel.: 815-943-6141.
Founded: 1977.
Congressional District: 33
Key Personnel: C.E.O. & Pres., Brian Schultz; Cur., Elaine Fiducci; Sec., Elzora Stoxen; Treas., Jim Finke.
Personnel Profile: Part-Time Volunteers 12.
Governing Authority: municipal.
History Museum & Historic Building.
Collections: military uniforms & artifacts; G.A.R. records; Woman's Relief Corps records; country school records; 1890-1950s clothing; WMCW original radio broadcasting equipment; original patents, financial records, catalogs from Starline Company; milk testing equipment; Milk Day memorabilia; toys; early small farm equipment; city tax & Justice of Peace records; early kitchen & household furnishings; period drugstore & doctors' equipment; model schoolroom with textbooks; early hospital records; Future Farmers of America high school records & farm tools
Research Fields: genealogical & local history.
Facilities: local history books, newspapers, documents available for research.
Activities: temporary exhibits; school visitations; programs for membership & the public; class reunions.
Publications: membership letters; brochure, G.H.A. Historical Society; historic walking tour guide; reprinted Harvard History Book; curators' report.
Hours & Admission Prices: May-Oct. Wed. 9:30-12, Sun. 1:30-4; or by appointment, call 815-943-3561. No charge; donations accepted.
Attendance: 800 (estimated)
Membership: Individual $9; Family of 3 or more $18; Organizations & Business $25; Sustaining $30; Annual Contributor $100 & up; Life $150.

Highland Park

HIGHLAND PARK HISTORICAL SOCIETY, 326 Central Ave., Highland Park, IL 60035-2611. Mailing Address: P.O. Box 56, Highland Park, IL 60035-0056. Tel.: 847-432-7090. Fax: 847-432-7307.
E-mail: hphistorical@sbcglobal.net
Web Site: www.highlandparkhistory.com
Founded: 1966.
Congressional District: 10
Key Personnel: Pres. (V), Elliott L. Miller; Dir. Program & Devel., Linda Marshall.
Personnel Profile: Full-Time Volunteers 1; Part-Time Paid 2; Part-Time Volunteers 50.
Governing Authority: society. Branch Museums: Jean Butz James Museum, 326 Central Ave., Highland Park, IL; Stupey Log Cabin, 1700 Block of St. Johns Ave., Highland Park, IL; Walt Durbahn Tool Museum, 326 Central Ave., Highland Park, IL; Bob Robinson Bandstand, Laurel & Prospect, Highland Park, IL. Tax-exempt: 170(b)(1)(A).
Local History Museum: housed in 1871 brick Victorian House.
Collections: local history; slides; period artifacts; tools; Ravinia Festival history. Historic House: 1847 Stupey cabin.
Major Exhibits: Antique Train Show, 11/09-2/10.
Research Fields: local history.
Facilities: 300-vol. library of books on local history available on premises by appointment.
Activities: guided tours; lectures; permanent & temporary exhibitions; meetings.
Publications: bimonthly newsletter; quarterly, Lamplighter.
Hours & Admission Prices: Feb. 15-Dec. 15 Wed.-Fri. 1-4, Sun. 2-4. Cabin: spring & summer only. No charge; donations accepted. Closed holidays. ♿
Attendance: 2,300 (estimated)
Membership: Family $35; Supporting $50; Sustaining $100; Benefactor $250; History Patron $500; Life Benefactor $1,000.

WALTER E. HELLER NATURE CENTER, 2821 Ridge Rd., Highland Park, IL 60035-1533. Mailing Address: 636 Ridge Rd., Highland Park, IL 60035-4361. Tel.: 847-433-6901 & 831-3810. Fax: 847-433-8856.
E-mail: heller@pdhp.org
Web Site: www.hellernaturecenter.org
Founded: 1980.

Congressional District: 10
Key Personnel: Exec. Dir., Ralph Volpe; Pres., Stacy Weiss; Site Mgr., Jeff Smith; Naturalist, Therese Greinig; Naturalist, Liza Fischel.
Personnel Profile: Full-Time Paid 4; Part-Time Paid 6.
Governing Authority: municipal. Parent Institution: Park District of Highland Park. Tax-exempt.
Nature Center & Preserve.
Collections: living botanical collections; wildflowers.
Research Fields: prairie vegetation cultivation.
Facilities: library of natural history, environmental education, plant & animal guides & Illinois animal life available for research on premises; nature center; classrooms; 100 acre site; 3 miles of trails.
Activities: guided tours; lectures; environmental & outdoor educational programs.
Publications: quarterly newsletter.
Hours & Admission Prices: Mon.-Sat. 8:30-5. No charge; donations accepted. Closed national holidays. ♿
Attendance: 17,000 (estimated)

Hinsdale

HINSDALE HISTORICAL SOCIETY, 15 S. Clay St., Hinsdale, IL 60521-3244. Mailing Address: P.O. Box 336, Hinsdale, IL 60522-0336. Tel.: 630-789-2600.
E-mail: info@hinsdalehistory.org
Web Site: www.hinsdalehistory.org
Founded: 1981.
Key Personnel: Mgr., Anne Swenson; Pres., Shannon Weinberger; Treas., Sharon Tayler; Cur., Susan Olsson; Archivist, Janet Miller; Membership, Penny Bohnen.
Personnel Profile: Part-Time Paid 1; Part-Time Volunteers 100; Interns 1.
Governing Authority: private; nonprofit organization. Tax-exempt.
Historical Society Museum: housed in a fully restored 1874 middle class residence.
Collections: concentration on local history with special emphasis on the Village of Hinsdale.
Research Fields: residential construction dates; village structures.
Facilities: 70-vol. library; garden. Museum-related items for sale.
Activities: docent program; guided tours; hobby workshops; lectures; temporary exhibitions; scout programs; adult & children's programs. Annual Event: Christmas Open House.
Publications: bimonthly newsletter.
Hours & Admission Prices: Fri.-Sat. 10-2; other times by appointment. Suggested Donation: adults $2; members no charge.
Attendance: 1,000 (accurate)
Membership: Individual $25; Family $40; Corporate $50; Friend $100; Lifetime $500.

ROBERT CROWN CENTER FOR HEALTH EDUCATION, 21 Salt Creek Lane, Hinsdale, IL 60521-2902. Tel.: 630-325-1900. Fax: 630-325-3970.
E-mail: rcche@robertcrown.org
Web Site: www.robertcrown.org
Founded: 1958.
Congressional District: 13
Key Personnel: C.E.O., Kathleen M. Burke; Chm. (V), Ross Forbes; Mgr. Chicago Campus, Tierra Johnson; Mgr. Aurora Campus, Althea Motley; Dir. Strategic Mktg., Jon Scoles.
Personnel Profile: Full-Time Paid 15; Part-Time Paid 5; Part-Time Volunteers 86; Interns 1.
Governing Authority: nonprofit. Tax-exempt: 501(c)(3).
Health Education Center.
Collections: human body; health; healthy living.
Facilities: education facilities.
Activities: general health education programs; family living & sex education; drug abuse prevention; summer camps; evening programs; classroom & outreach programs.
Publications: puberty education booklets; reality check newsletters; annual report.
Hours & Admission Prices: School Groups: mid-Sept. to mid-June Mon.-Fri. 9-2:30 by appointment. Admission $5; teachers no charge. Outreach: $7 per person. Closed national holidays. ♿
Attendance: 120,000 (accurate)

Ingleside

ARTWORKS CHILDREN'S MUSEUM, 130 Washington St., Ingleside, IL 60041-9236. Tel.: 847-587-7882.
E-mail: artworks4kids1@gmail.com
Web Site: www.artworks4kids.org
Key Personnel: Dir., Sharon White
Children's Museum.
Collections: hands-on exhibits.
Activities: birthday parties; special events; art classes.
Hours & Admission Prices: Call for hours. Children 1-18 $5; discounts to groups of 15 or more; adults & infants no charge.
Membership: Individual $25; Family $50; Supporting $100; Silver $250; Gold $500; Platinum $1,000.

Jacksonville

DAVID STRAWN ART GALLERY, (M), 331 W. College Ave., Jacksonville, IL 62650-2474. Mailing Address: P.O. Box 1213, Jacksonville, IL 62651-1213. Tel.: 217-243-9390.
Founded: 1873.
Congressional District: 18
Key Personnel: Pres., Ginny Fanning.
Personnel Profile: Part-Time Paid 3; Part-Time Volunteers 100.
Governing Authority: society. Parent Institution: The Art Association of Jacksonville.
Art Gallery: housed in 1915 former home of Dr. David Strawn.
Collections: early Mississippi Indian pottery; Miriam Cougar Allen collection of antique & collectible dolls; Charles Prentice Thompson classical collection.
Major Exhibits: Wildlife/Landscape Photographs by Robert McKemmie, 1/9/10-1/31/10; Posters by David Garrison & Cecile Houel, 2/6/10-2/28/10; Mixed Media by Br. Brian Zampier, 3/6/10-3/28/10; Photojournalists Steve & Tiffany Warmowski, 4/3/10-4/25/10; Watercolor Paintings by Sandy Meyer, 5/1/10-5/30/10.
Activities: formally organized education programs.
Publications: pamphlet, Pre-Columbian pottery; books, Strawn Family and Home History; The Art Association of Jacksonville History.
Hours & Admission Prices: Sept.-May Tues.-Sat. 4-6, Sun. 1-3. No charge. Closed holidays. ♿
Attendance: 5,974 (estimated)
Membership: Student & Associate (lives more then 50 miles away) $20; Single $35; Family $50; Sustaining $100; Individual Life $600; Couple Life $1,000.

Joliet

JOLIET AREA HISTORICAL MUSEUM, (M), 204 N. Ottawa St., Joliet, IL 60432-4007. Tel.: 815-723-5201. Fax: 815-723-9039.
E-mail: t.contos@jolietmuseum.org
Web Site: www.jolietmuseum.org
Formerly: Joliet Area Historical Society
Founded: 1999.
Congressional District: 4
Key Personnel: Exec. Dir., Anthony B. Contos; Museum Shop Mgr., Elaine Stonich.
Personnel Profile: Full-Time Paid 5; Part-Time Paid 5; Part-Time Volunteers 50; Interns 1.
Governing Authority: nonprofit. Tax-exempt: 501(c)(3).
Local History Museum.
Collections: Joliet industries, businesses, schools & citizens; photos; advertising items.
Facilities: orientation theater; 800 sq. ft. exhibit space.
Activities: lectures; temporary exhibitions; public programs; bus tours; guided tours; fundraisers.
Publications: quarterly newsletter, Legacy.
Hours & Admission Prices: Tues.-Sat. 10-5, Sun. 12-5. Adults $6, senior citizens 60 & over $5, youth 4-17 $3; discounts to AAM members; members no charge. Closed New Year's Eve & Day; Good Friday; Easter; Memorial Day; Independence Day; Labor Day; Thanksgiving; Christmas Eve & Day. ♿
Attendance: 16,605 (accurate)
Membership: Senior $20; Senior Family, Student & Teacher $25; Individual $35; Family $45.

LAURA A. SPRAGUE ART GALLERY, Joliet Junior College Main Campus, 1215 Houbolt Rd., Spicer-Brown Hall, Joliet, IL 60431-8938. Tel.: 815-280-2423 & 2223.
Web Site: www.jjc.edu/dept/finearts/laurasspraguegallery.htm
Key Personnel: Gallery Dir., Joe Milosevich
Art Gallery.
Collections: paintings.
Hours & Admission Prices: Mon.-Fri. 8-8.

RIALTO SQUARE THEATRE, 15 E. Van Buren St., Joliet, IL 60432-4211. Tel.: 815-726-7171.
Historic Building Museum: housed in a former movie theatre; built in 1926.

Collections: theatre history & culture; photographs; period furnishings; personal artifacts.
Facilities: theatre.
Activities: rental facilities; tours; children's programs; performances; shows; concerts.
Hours & Admission Prices: Tours: Tues. 1:30; other times by appointment. $5 per person.

SLOVENIAN WOMEN'S UNION HERITAGE MUSEUM, 431 N. Chicago St., Joliet, IL 60432-1785. Tel.: 815-727-1926. Fax: 815-723-0670.
E-mail: swvhome@swva.org
Web Site: www.swua.org
Heritage Museum.
Collections: Slovenian history & culture; period clothing; musical instruments; religious articles; photographs; art; furniture.
Facilities: 1,000-vol. library.
Hours & Admission Prices: Mon.-Fri. 10-2. No charge; donations accepted.

Kampsville

CENTER FOR AMERICAN ARCHEOLOGY, Hwy. 100, Kampsville, IL 62053. Mailing Address: P.O. Box 366, Kampsville, IL 62053-0366. Tel.: 618-653-4316. Fax: 618-653-4232.
E-mail: caa@caa-archeology.org
Web Site: www.caa-archeology.org
Formerly: Kampsville Archeological Museum
Founded: 1970.
Congressional District: 20
Key Personnel: Pres. (V), Jane E. Buikstra, Ph.D.; Museum Shop Mgr., Mary Pirkl.
Personnel Profile: Full-Time Paid 10; Part-Time Paid 3; Interns 3.
Governing Authority: nonprofit organization; board of directors. Tax-exempt: 501(c)(3).
Archaeology Museum.
Collections: archaeological materials representing cultures dating back to 10,000 BC.
Research Fields: archaeology research.
Facilities: archaeology library of books available for research with special permission from director; research station; separate laboratory operation.
Activities: guided tours; lectures; formally organized education programs for children, adults, undergraduate & graduate students.
Publications: archaeology books; Research Series; Technical Report Series.
Hours & Admission Prices: May-Oct. Tues.-Fri. 10-5, Sat. 10-4, Sun. 12-4. No charge; donations accepted. Fee for tours. ♿
Attendance: 3,000 (estimated)
Membership: $25; $45; $50; $75; $100; $250; $500; $1,000 & up.

Kankakee

KANKAKEE COUNTY MUSEUM, (M), 801 South Eighth Ave., Kankakee, IL 60901-4744. Tel.: 815-932-5279. Fax: 815-932-5204.
Web Site: www.kankakeecountymuseum.com
Formerly: Kankakee County Historical Society Museum
Founded: 1906.
Congressional District: 11
Key Personnel: C.E.O. & Museum Shop Mgr., Norman S. Stevens; Pres. (V), Larry Nolan; Research Asst., Jorie Walters; Office Mgr., Linda Stevens; Museum Asst., Loretta Mason; Museum Asst., Robin LaVoie; Cur. Collections, Sarah Faford.
Personnel Profile: Full-Time Paid 2; Part-Time Paid 4; Part-Time Volunteers 30.
Governing Authority: nonprofit organization; board of directors. Subsidiary Institution: KanKaKee County Historical Society. Tax-exempt.
County Historical Museum.
Collections: Native American artifacts; household objects; firearms; textiles; framed objects; decorative arts; agricultural items; toys; political item tools; edge weapons; approximately 75 plaster & marble studies of the sculptor George Grey Barnard; 1855 home of Dr. A.L. Small; boyhood home of Illinois Gov. Len Small 1921-1929; 1904 one room schoolhouse.
Research Fields: genealogy.
Facilities: 5,000-vol. library of history & genealogy. Traditional gift items & books on county history for sale.
Activities: guided tour groups; lectures; slide programs; interpretive programs; research for fee; traveling & special exhibits by appointment; lecture series; temporary exhibits. Special Events: Rhubarb Fest in May; Civil War encampment in October; Gallery of Trees Christmas event in December.
Publications: brochure, Kankakee County Historical Society Museum; museum newsletter; museum journal; magazine, Kankakee County History.
Hours & Admission Prices: May-Oct. 1 Mon.-Thurs. 10-4, Sat.-Sun. 1-4; Nov.-April Mon.-Thurs. 10-4, Sun. 1-4. Adults $3. Closed holidays. ♿
Attendance: 25,000 (estimated)
Membership: Annual $20; Life $250.

Kenilworth

THE KENILWORTH HISTORICAL SOCIETY, 415 Kenilworth Ave., Kenilworth, IL 60043-1134. Tel.: 847-251-2565. Fax: 847-251-2565.
E-mail: kenilworthhistory@sbcglobal.net
Web Site: www.kenilworthhistory.org
Founded: 1922.
Congressional District: 10
Key Personnel: Pres., Carol M. Schulz; Vice Pres., Sheila Mitchell; Treas., Peter Tyor; Sec., Rachel Noel; Cur., Melinda F. Kwedar.
Personnel Profile: Part-Time Paid 3; Part-Time Volunteers 15.
Governing Authority: nonprofit. Tax-exempt: 501(c)(3).
Historical Society Museum.
Collections: displays materials related to village & residents; house histories; costumes; local documents & artifacts; heirloom needlepoint rug; photographs; architectural & personal archival materials related to architect George W. Maher and other Kenilworth families & organizations.
Major Exhibits: Artists in Living: A History of Creativity in Kenilworth, 11/09-10/10.
Research Fields: histories of homes; biographical material of Kenilworth residents since 1882.
Facilities: library pertaining to books about Kenilworth & its residents for in-house use.
Activities: organized education programs for children; temporary exhibitions. Annual Events: Christmas Open House; Memorial Day Open House.
Publications: Kenilworth Tree Stories; George Washington Maher in Kenilworth; Joseph Sears & His Kenilworth; Jens Jensen in Kenilworth.
Hours & Admission Prices: Mon. 9-4:30, Thurs. 9-12; other times by appointment. No charge; donations accepted. ♿
Attendance: 750 (estimated)
Membership: Regular $35; Sustaining $100; Contributor $200; Life $1,000; Life Benefactor $5,000.

Knoxville

KNOX COUNTY MUSEUM, c/o City Hall, 45 N. Public Square, Knoxville, IL 61448-1378. Tel.: 309-289-2814. Fax: 309-289-8825.
Web Site: www.kville.org
Founded: 1953.
Congressional District: 47
Key Personnel: C.E.O. & Pres. (V), Peg Bivens; Cur., Sally Hutchcroft.
Personnel Profile: Part-Time Paid 1; Part-Time Volunteers 1.
Governing Authority: Affiliated with Knox County Historical Sites, Inc.
Historical Society Museum.
Collections: Abingdon pottery. Historic Buildings: 1839 Knox County Court House; 1845 Knox County Jail; 1832 John G. Sanburn Log Cabin.
Facilities: Gift items for sale.
Activities: guided tours.
Hours & Admission Prices: May-Sept. Sun. 2-4; Oct.-April tours by appointment. No charge. ♿
Attendance: 1,000 (estimated)
Membership: Annual $10; Lifetime $100.

La Grange

LA GRANGE AREA HISTORICAL SOCIETY, (M), 444 S. LaGrange Rd., La Grange, IL 60525-2448. Tel.: 708-482-4248. Fax: 708-482-4248.
E-mail: lagrangehistory@sbcglobal.net
Historical Society Museum: housed in the Vial House, built in 1874.
Collections: local history & culture; period furnishings; personal artifacts; photographs; costumes.
Hours & Admission Prices: Open House: last Sun. each month 1-4. Research: Wed. 9:30-12:30; other times by appointment.

LaFox

GARFIELD FARM MUSEUM, 3N016 Garfield Rd., LaFox, IL 60147-0403. Mailing Address: P.O. Box 403, LaFox, IL 60147-0403. Tel.: 630-584-8485. Fax: 630-584-8522.
E-mail: info@garfieldfarm.org
Web Site: garfieldfarm.org
Founded: 1977.
Congressional District: 14
Key Personnel: Dir., Jerome Martin Johnson; Site Mgr., Thomas Hillier; Asst. Site Mgr., William Wolcott; Pres. C.H.A.L. Inc., Helen Bauer; Treas. C.H.A.L. Inc., Donald Swanson; Pres. G.H.S. Inc., Keith Letsche; Treas. G.H.S. Inc., Susan Stillinger.
Personnel Profile: Full-Time Paid 4; Part-Time Paid 1; Part-Time Volunteers 200.

Governing Authority: nonprofit. Parent Institution: Campton Historic Agricultural Land, Inc. Subsidiary Institution: Garfield Heritage Society Inc. Tax-exempt: 501(c)(3).
Living Historic Farm & Inn Museum.
Collections: over 2,000 19th-century documents, diaries & artifacts of the Garfield and Mighell families; 600 photographs; family furnishings & tools; manuscript collections. Historic Structures: 1842 hay barn; 1846 inn; 1849 horse barn; 1890s granary; 1906 dairy barn; reconstructed chicken house; 1840s Burr family farmhouse; 1859 Edward Garfield/Mongerson Brothers Farmstead.
Research Fields: 1830-1850, Northern Illinois settlement, farm, tavern & rural life history.
Facilities: 370 acres farmland with prairie.
Activities: guided tours; lectures; rental gallery; docent program; organized education programs for children, undergraduate & graduate college students; training programs for professional museum workers. Museum Sponsors: Fall Festival in October.
Publications: biannual brochure; newsletter, Fairfield-Campton Crier; booklet, Garfield Farm: Setting the Benchmark; Prairie Messenger.
Hours & Admission Prices: June-Sept. Wed. & Sun. 1-4; other times by appointment only. Adults $3, youth groups under 13 $2; members no charge. Closed Thanksgiving; Christmas. ♿
Attendance: 10,000 (estimated)
Membership: Individual $20; Family $30; Patron $75; Commercial $100; Life $1,000.

Lake Forest

LAKE FOREST-LAKE BLUFF HISTORICAL SOCIETY, (M), 361 E. Westminster, Lake Forest, IL 60045-2255. Tel.: 847-234-5253. Fax: 847-234-5236.
E-mail: info@lflbhistory.org
Web Site: www.lflbhistory.org
Founded: 1972.
Congressional District: 10
Key Personnel: Exec. Dir., Janice Hack; Cur., Laurie Stein.
Personnel Profile: Part-Time Paid 3; Part-Time Volunteers 75; Interns 1.
Governing Authority: private; nonprofit organization. Tax-exempt: 501(c)(3).
Historical Society Museum.
Collections: concentration on Lake Forest & Lake Bluff history.
Facilities: 1,000-vol. library; 1,000 sq. ft. exhibit space. Museum-related items for sale.
Activities: lectures; temporary exhibitions; tours.
Publications: quarterly newsletter, The Heritage Timepiece; Lake Forest Day: 100 Years of Celebration; Walter Frazier: Homes of Chicago's North Shore 1940-1970.
Hours & Admission Prices: Memorial Day to Labor Day Tues.-Thurs. 1-4; Sept.-May Tues.-Thurs. & Sun. 1-4. No charge. Closed major holidays.
Attendance: 1,500 (estimated)
Membership: Individual $30; Family $50; Silver $100; Gold $250; Platinum $500; Museum $1,000.

Lerna

LINCOLN LOG CABIN STATE HISTORIC SITE, 402 S. Lincoln Hwy. Rd, Lerna, IL 62440. Tel.: 217-345-1845. Fax: 217-345-6472.
E-mail: hpa.lincolnlog@illinois.gov
Web Site: www.lincolnlogcabin.org
Founded: 1929.
Congressional District: 19
Key Personnel: Site Mgr., Matthew Mittelstaedt; Museum Shop Mgr., Patti Gutierrez.
Personnel Profile: Full-Time Paid 9; Part-Time Paid 15; Part-Time Volunteers 200.
Governing Authority: state. Affiliated with the State of Illinois Historic Preservation Agency, Old State Capitol, Springfield, IL 62701. Tax-exempt: 501(c)(3).
Historic Houses & Site: reconstructed cabin and farm of Thomas and Sara Lincoln on original site.
Collections: period furnishings.
Research Fields: Lincoln family; Pioneer farm life.
Facilities: visitor center; picnic areas.
Activities: guided tours; permanent exhibitions. Museum Sponsors: living history in summer months.
Publications: bimonthly, newsletter, Historic Illinois; site brochure.
Hours & Admission Prices: Daily 9-5. No charge; donations accepted. Closed New Year's Day; Thanksgiving; Christmas. ♿
Attendance: 126,000 (accurate)
Membership: $25; $50; $110; $250; $500; $1,000; $2,500.

REUBEN MOORE HOME STATE HISTORIC SITE, 400 S. Lincoln Hwy. Rd., Lerna, IL 62440-2840. Mailing Address: 400 S. Lincoln Hwy. Rd., P.O. Box 100, Lerna, IL 62440-0100. Tel.: 217-345-1845. Fax: 217-345-6472.
E-mail: hpa.lincolnlog@illinois.gov
Web Site: www.lincolnlogcabin.org
Founded: 1929.
Congressional District: 19
Key Personnel: Site Supt., Matthew Mittelstaedt.
Personnel Profile: Part-Time Paid 2.
Governing Authority: state. A part of the State of Illinois, Illinois Historic Preservation Agency, Old State Capitol, Springfield, IL 62701. Tax-exempt: 501(c)(3).
Historic House Museum: mid-19th century home of Reuben & Matilda Moore, daughter of Sara Lincoln and stepsister of Abraham Lincoln.
Collections: period furnishings.
Research Fields: 1850s-70s rural village life in east central Illinois.
Activities: permanent exhibitions.
Publications: bimonthly newsletter, Historic Illinois; brochure.
Hours & Admission Prices: June-Aug. Wed.-Sun.; Sept.-May by appointment only. No charge. Closed New Year's Day; Thanksgiving; Christmas. ♿
Attendance: 4,326 (accurate)

Lewistown

DICKSON MOUNDS MUSEUM, (M), 10956 N. Dickson Mounds Rd., Lewistown, IL 61542-9112. Tel.: 309-547-3721. Fax: 309-547-3189. TDD: 217-782-9175.
E-mail: wiant@museum.state.il.us
Web Site: www.museum.state.il.us/ismsites/dickson/
Founded: 1927.
Congressional District: 17
Key Personnel: Dir. Dickson Mounds Museum, Dr. Michael D. Wiant; Assoc. Cur., Dr. Michael Conner; Asst. Cur., Alan D. Harn; Exhibits Preparator, Kelvin Sampson; Museum Shop Mgr., Karen Fisk; Office Mgr., Kim Dunnigan.
Personnel Profile: Full-Time Paid 10; Part-Time Paid 1; Part-Time Volunteers 5.
Governing Authority: state. Parent Institution: Illinois State Museum, 502 S. Spring St., Springfield, IL 62706. Tax-exempt.
Anthropology Museum & Site.
Collections: archaeological materials from West Central Illinois; Mississippian & Middle Woodland sites on grounds; American Indian cultures of Illinois; Paleo-Indian to historic periods. Historic Buildings: 1839 school; 1850 Toll House & 1907 school.
Research Fields: archaeology; anthropology; local & state history.
Facilities: discovery center; resource center; archaeology laboratories & sites; picnic grounds; auditorium; outdoor stage; coffee shop. Museum-related items for sale.
Activities: guided tours; formally organized educational programs; workshops; demonstrations; performances; conferences; festivals; participatory programs; permanent & special exhibits; audiovisual programs.
Publications: quarterly newsletter, Fieldnotes; Dickson Mounds Museum Anthropological Studies.
Hours & Admission Prices: Daily 8:30-5. No charge; donations accepted. Closed New Year's Day; Thanksgiving; Christmas. ♿
Attendance: 38,874 (accurate)
Membership: Individual $35; Family $50; Contributing $100; Sustaining $300.

Libertyville

LIBERTYVILLE-MUNDELEIN HISTORICAL SOCIETY, INC., 413 N. Milwaukee Ave., Libertyville, IL 60048-2247. Tel.: 847-362-2330. Fax: 847-362-0006.
Founded: 1955.
Congressional District: 10
Key Personnel: Pres. (V), Jerrold L. Schulkin; Chm. Acquisitions Committee, Beverly Schar.
Personnel Profile: Part-Time Volunteers 35.
Governing Authority: nonprofit organization. Parent Institution: Cook Memorial Public Library District. Tax-exempt: 501(c)(3).
History Museum: housed in 1878 Ansel B. Cook home; listed on The National Register of Historic Places.
Collections: pioneer artifacts; Civil War items; historical books, pictures, maps & papers from pioneer families of the area.
Research Fields: history & artifacts of the Libertyville-Mundelein & Lake County areas.
Facilities: 500-vol. library of papers, pamphlets & books on local history available for use on premises to members & their guests; reading room.
Activities: guided tours of Victorian home. Museum Sponsors: Victorian period Christmas.

Publications: monthly newsletter.
Hours & Admission Prices: Summer: Sun. 2-4; Winter: call Faith Sage 847-362-3992 for appointment. Adults $2, students & seniors $1. ♿
Attendance: 1,100 (accurate)
Membership: Junior under 18 & Senior Citizens over 65 $5; Individual $8; Family $15; Contributor $25; Sponsor $50; Life $100.

Lincoln

LINCOLN HERITAGE MUSEUM, 300 Keokuk St., Lincoln, IL 62656-1699. Tel.: 217-732-3155, ext. 295.
E-mail: rkeller@lincolncollege.edu
Web Site: www.lincolncollege.edu/museum
Formerly: Lincoln College Museum
Founded: 1942.
Congressional District: 18
Key Personnel: Dir. & Cur., Ron Keller.
Personnel Profile: Full-Time Paid 1; Full-Time Volunteers 1; Interns 1.
Governing Authority: Parent Institution: Lincoln College.
History Museum.
Collections: Lincoln's life, heritage & history; personal artifacts; Presidential artifacts; photographs; period furnishings.
Facilities: Museum-related items for sale.
Activities: educational outreach; temporary exhibits; special programs.
Publications: newsletter, The Lincoln.
Hours & Admission Prices: Mon.-Fri. 9-4, Sat. 1-4. No charge; donations accepted. Closed Federal holidays except Lincoln's Birthday. ♿
Attendance: 4,000 (estimated)

POSTVILLE COURTHOUSE STATE HISTORIC SITE, 914 Fifth St., Lincoln, IL 62656-2308. Mailing Address: P.O. Box 355, Lincoln, IL 62656-0355. Tel.: 217-735-4977 & 737-0979. Fax: 217-735-4626.
E-mail: shirleyb@ccaonline.com
Founded: 1953.
Key Personnel: Pres. (V) & Museum Shop Mgr., Shirley R. Bartelmay.
Personnel Profile: Full-Time Volunteers 1; Part-Time Paid 2; Part-Time Volunteers 40.
Governing Authority: state. Parent Institution: Illinois Historic Preservation Agency, Old State Capitol, Springfield, IL 62701. Tax-exempt: 501(c)(3).
History Site/Museum.
Collections: replica of the first Logan County Illinois Court House; part of old 8th Judicial Circuit from 1839-48 where Abraham Lincoln practiced law; period furnishings including Lincoln's rocker; Mary Lincoln's garden; well.
Research Fields: Lincoln; the Illinois 8th Judicial Circuit; local history.
Facilities: garden.
Activities: guided tours; lectures; organized tours for schoolchildren & tour buses. Special Events: 1800s Craft Fair; Abe Lincoln's Birthday; Christmas Open House; Quilt Show.
Publications: bimonthly newsletter, Historic Illinois; brochure; event publications
Hours & Admission Prices: April-Sept. Tues.-Sat. 12-5; Oct.-March Tues.-Sat. 12-4; other times by appointment. No charge; donations accepted. Closed New Year's Day; Lincoln's Birthday; Veterans Day; Independence Day; Thanksgiving; Christmas.
Attendance: 6,000 (accurate)

Lisle

JURICA-SUCHY NATURE MUSEUM, Benedictine University, 5700 College Rd., Lisle, IL 60532-2851. Tel.: 630-829-6545. Fax: 630-829-6547.
E-mail: TSUCHY@ben.edu
Web Site: alt.ben.edu/resources/J_Museum/index.htm
Founded: 1970.
Congressional District: 14
Key Personnel: Pres., Dr. William Carroll; Chief Cur., Rev. Theodore D. Suchy, OSB
Personnel Profile: Part-Time Paid 2; Part-Time Volunteers 2.
Governing Authority: college. Tax-exempt.
Natural History Museum.
Collections: invertebrate; vertebrate; mammals, reptiles, fish, insects, birds; plants; skeletons of fossils; bird eggs; corals; crustaceans; minerals; American Indian artifacts; large mounted animals.
Facilities: library; reading room; classrooms; laboratory.
Activities: guided tours; formally organized education programs for elementary, high school & college students; permanent & temporary exhibitions.
Hours & Admission Prices: Mon.-Fri. 1-5, Sun. 2-4; groups by advance arrangement. No charge; donations accepted. Closed school vacations. ♿
Attendance: 6,000 (accurate)

THE MORTON ARBORETUM, (M), 4100 Illinois Rte. 53, Lisle, IL 60532-1293. Tel.: 630-968-0074. Fax: 630-719-2433.
E-mail: trees@mortonarb.org
Web Site: www.mortonarb.org
Founded: 1922.
Congressional District: 13
Key Personnel: Pres. & C.E.O., Dr. Gerard T. Donnelly; Volunteer Coord., Sally Kenaston; Museum Shop Mgr., Jacqueline Fucilla.
Personnel Profile: Full-Time Paid 140; Part-Time Paid 110; Part-Time Volunteers 940; Interns 2.
Governing Authority: nonprofit foundation. Tax-exempt: 501(c)(3).
Arboretum.
Collections: herbarium & botanical artifacts including 186,000 plant specimens representing 4,100 kinds of plants; trees, shrubs & woody plants arranged by taxonomic, geographic, special habitat, horticultural, rare & endangered collections.
Research Fields: tree health; tree improvement; woodland conservation.
Facilities: library; education center; visitor center; children's garden; restaurant; rental facilities; 1,700 acres site. Museum-related items for sale.
Activities: education programs for youth, family, schools & adults; special events & exhibits; guided tours; outdoor concerts; theater-hikes; 5K run; plant sale; bicycling; self-guided visits over 16 miles of trails & 9 miles of roads. Annual Events: Arbor Day Celebration; Fall Color Festival.
Publications: members newsletter; education program; plant information brochures; members e-mail; annual report (web-based).
Hours & Admission Prices: Grounds: daily 7-7 or sunset (whichever is earlier). Buildings: call for hours. Adults $11, seniors $10, children 3-17 $8; discounts on Wed; children 2 & under and members no charge. ♿
Attendance: 786,000 (accurate)
Membership: Individual $65; Family $100; Family Plus $135; Friend $250; Partner $500; Thornhill Society $1,000 & up.

THE MUSEUMS AT LISLE STATION PARK, 921 School St., Lisle, IL 60532-1951. Tel.: 630-968-0499.
Web Site: www.lisleparkdistrict.org
Founded: 1978.
Congressional District: 13
Key Personnel: Cur., Rose Mary Hose.
Personnel Profile: Part-Time Paid 1; Part-Time Volunteers 70.
Governing Authority: regional government. Parent Institution: Lisle Park District, 1825 Short St., Lisle 60532. Tax-exempt.
History Museum.
Collections: focuses on the history of the Lisle community from the settlement period of the 1830s-present; history of the CB&Q railroad in Lisle. Historic Structures: 1874 CB&Q depot with living quarters; 1881 CB&Q caboose; 1830s Beaubien Tavern; 1850s Greek Revival farmhouse; 19th century style blacksmith shop.
Facilities: 1,200 sq. ft. exhibit space; facility rental available. Handcrafted items for sale.
Activities: formal educational programs; guided tours; lectures; temporary & traveling exhibitions. Annual Events: Lisle Depot Days in September; Lights of Lisle & Once Upon A Christmas in December.
Publications: seasonal newsletter, Lisle Heritage Society Newsletter.
Hours & Admission Prices: April-Dec. Tues., Thurs. & Sat. 1-4; group tours by appointment. No charge; donations accepted. Closed New Year's Eve & Day; Good Friday to Easter; Memorial Day weekend; Independence Day; Labor Day weekend; Thanksgiving weekend; Christmas Eve & Day. ♿
Attendance: 8,000 (estimated)

Lockport

GAYLORD BUILDING HISTORIC SITE, 200 W. 8th St., Lockport, IL 60441-2878. Tel.: 815-838-9400.
Web Site: www.gaylordbuilding.org
Historic Building: housed in the former building that stored construction materials for the Illinois & Michigan Canal; built in 1838.
Collections: I&M Canal history; photographs; period artifacts.
Facilities: visitor center; restaurant.
Activities: special events.
Hours & Admission Prices: Tues.-Sat. 11-5, Sun. 12-5. No charge.

ILLINOIS STATE MUSEUM/LOCKPORT GALLERY, 201 W. 10th St., Lockport, IL 60441-2987. Tel.: 815-838-7400. Fax: 815-838-7448.
E-mail: jzimmer@museum.state.il.us
Web Site: www.museum.state.il.us/ismsites/lockport/
Founded: 1987.
Congressional District: 13
Key Personnel: Dir., Jim L. Zimmer; Cur. Art, Jennifer Jaskowiak.
Personnel Profile: Full-Time Paid 2; Part-Time Volunteers 3.
Governing Authority: Parent Institution: Illinois State Museum.

Art Museum.
Collections: fine, decorative & ethnographic arts of Illinois.
Research Fields: art & artists of Illinois.
Hours & Admission Prices: Mon.-Fri. 9-5, Sun. 12-5. No charge; donations accepted. Closed state holidays. ♿
Attendance: 16,437 (accurate)
Membership: Individual $35; Family $50; Contributing $100; Sustaining $300; Life $500.

WILL COUNTY HISTORICAL SOCIETY, (M), 803 S. State St., Lockport, IL 60441-3433. Tel.: 815-838-5080. Fax: 815-838-4547.
E-mail: info@willcountyhistory.org
Web Site: www.willcountyhistory.org
Formerly: Illinois and Michigan Canal Commissioners Office Museum
Founded: 1964.
Congressional District: 4
Key Personnel: Exec. Dir., Lynne Mickle Smaczny; Pres. (V), Richard C. Dystrup.
Personnel Profile: Full-Time Paid 1; Part-Time Paid 1; Part-Time Volunteers 50.
Governing Authority: nonprofit organization. Tax-exempt: 501(c)(3).
History Museum.
Collections: Will County history including governmental record books & original documents from the Illinois & Michigan Canal. Historic Building: I & M Canal Office, built 1837.
Research Fields: history & genealogy.
Activities: guided tours; permanent & temporary exhibitions; school, scout & family programs.
Publications: bimonthly newsletter, Rudder; quarterly journal, Quarterly.
Hours & Admission Prices: Museum: mid-Feb. to mid-Nov. Tues.-Sun. 12-4. Suggested Donations: adults $3; members no charge. Closed major holidays.
Attendance: 4,500 (estimated)
Membership: Student, Military & Seniors $7.50; Senior Plus $10; Individual $15; Family $25; Organization $40; Business $50; Contributing $100; Sustaining $500 & up.

Lombard

LILACIA PARK-LOMBARD PARK DISTRICT, 227 W. Parkside Ave., Lombard, IL 60148-2592. Tel.: 630-627-1281. Fax: 630-627-1286.
E-mail: info@lombardparks.com
Web Site: www.lombardparks.com
Congressional District: 6
Key Personnel: Pres., Char Roberts; Exec. Dir., Paul Friedrichs; Horticulturist, Jerry Budd; Museum Shop Mgr., Jackie Brzezinski.
Personnel Profile: Full-Time Paid 45; Part-Time Volunteers 125.
Governing Authority: municipal. Tax-exempt.
Horticultural Park.
Collections: 1,100 lilacs; 8-1/2 acres of lilac plantings. Historic House: 1888 Coach House.
Research Fields: botanical.
Facilities: botanical garden; picnic & food area; Coach House information center; country store. Gift items for sale.
Activities: children's entertainment; concerts; lilac planting & care seminars; family events; Lilac Queen coronation; tour program.
Publications: annual brochures, Lilac Time in Lombard.
Hours & Admission Prices: Daily 9-9. First two weeks of May (Lilac Time). No charge; donations accepted. ♿
Attendance: 14,000 (accurate)

LOMBARD HISTORICAL MUSEUM, (M), 23 W. Maple, Lombard, IL 60148-2512. Tel.: 630-629-1885. Fax: 630-629-9927.
Web Site: lombardhistory.org
Founded: 1970.
Key Personnel: Dir., Jeanne Schultz Angel; Pres. (V), Corinne Flemm; Treas., Richard Anstee; Membership, Barb Madigan.
Personnel Profile: Full-Time Paid 1; Part-Time Paid 3; Part-Time Volunteers 25; Interns 2.
Governing Authority: municipal. Parent Institution: Lombard Historical Society. Tax-exempt.
Local History Museum: housed in a historic home; features lifestyle of a middle class family in Lombard during the 1870s.
Collections: pre-1880 artifacts; Victorian crafts; photographs, artifacts & archives of Lombard history.
Research Fields: Victorian decorative arts; Lombard history.
Facilities: 525-vol. local history, archives & library available to the public by appointment.
Activities: guided tours; films; docent program; temporary exhibitions; walking tours; education program. Museum Sponsors: Holiday Programs, Ice Cream Social.
Publications: quarterly newsletter.
Hours & Admission Prices: Jan. to mid-Dec. Wed. & Sun. 1-4; other times by appointment. No charge; donations accepted. ♿
Attendance: 2,700 (accurate)
Membership: Students $5; Senior Individual $7.50; Senior Family $12.50; Individual $15; Family $25; Commercial $40; Supporting Individual $50; Supporting Commercial $100; Life $150; Life Family $200.

SHELDON PECK HOMESTEAD, 355 E. Parkside, Lombard, IL 60148-2776. Mailing Address: Lombard Historical Society, 23 W. Maple, Lombard, IL 60148. Tel.: 630-629-1885. Fax: 630-629-9927.
E-mail: lombardhistory@att.net
Web Site: lombardhistory.org
Founded: 1999.
Key Personnel: Dir., Jeanne Schultz Angel; Pres., Corinne Flemm; Treas., Richard Anstee; Museum Shop Mng., Janet Luberda.
Personnel Profile: Full-Time Paid 1; Part-Time Paid 1; Part-Time Volunteers 65; Interns 1.
Governing Authority: private; nonprofit organization. Parent Institution: Lombard Historical Society, 23 W. Maple, Lombard, IL 60148. Tax-exempt: 501(c)(3).
Historic House Museum: housed in an 1840s restored farmhouse; underground railroad site.
Collections: reproduction artwork of Sheldon Peck; 19th century furniture.
Research Fields: underground railroad.
Facilities: Museum-related items for sale.
Activities: docent program; guided tours; hobby workshops; lectures; loan & temporary exhibitions; broadcast programs. Annual Event: ice cream social in summer.
Hours & Admission Prices: Tues., Thurs. & Sun. 1-4. No charge; donations accepted. Closed holidays. ♿
Attendance: 2,300 (accurate)
Membership: Student $5; Senior Individual $7.50; Senior Family $12.50; Individual & Organization $15; Family $25; Commercial $40; Supporting $50; Supporting Commercial $100; Life $150; Life Family $200.

Macomb

WESTERN ILLINOIS UNIVERSITY ART GALLERY, (M), 1 University Circle, Macomb, IL 61455-1390. Tel.: 309-298-1587. Fax: 309-298-2400.
E-mail: JR-Graham@wiu.edu
Web Site: www.wiu.edu/artgallery
Founded: 1899.
Congressional District: 17
Key Personnel: Cur. Exhibits, John R. Graham.
Personnel Profile: Full-Time Paid 1; Part-Time Paid 3; Part-Time Volunteers 4.
Governing Authority: state. Parent Institution: Western Illinois University. Tax-exempt: 501(c)(3).
Art Museum.
Collections: contemporary graphics; paintings; sculpture; glass; jewelry; ceramics; Native American pottery; WPA graphics & paintings.
Major Exhibits: Master Prints from the Permanent Collection, 1/10-2/10; Paul Guzzardo, Jesse Codling and David Walczyk: The Cartographer's Dilemma, 1/10-2/10; Exploring Media, 2/10-3/10; Robert Middaugh: Paintings and Constructions, 3/10-4/10; Eleanor Spiess-Ferris: Sorrows of Swans Paintings of a Suffering Environment, 3/10-4/10; Senior B.F.A. Exhibitions, 4/10-5/10; Annual Juried Student Awards Show, 4/10-5/10; Senior B.F.A. Exhibitions, 12/10; Student Talent Grant Awards Show, 12/10.
Research Fields: WPA; contemporary prints & drawings.
Facilities: three galleries; preservation lab.
Activities: gallery talks & presentations; traveling exhibitions; exhibitions organized by university faculty; visiting artist lecture series; docent gallery talks & presentations.
Publications: exhibition catalogues.
Hours & Admission Prices: School Year Mon. & Wed.-Fri. 9-4, Tues. 9-4 & 6-8; other times by appointment. No charge. Closed university vacations. ♿
Attendance: 6,958 (accurate)

Mahomet

* **EARLY AMERICAN MUSEUM, (M),** 600 N. Lombard, Mahomet, IL 61853. Mailing Address: P.O. Box 1040, Mahomet, IL 61853-1040. Tel.: 217-586-2612. Fax: 217-586-3491.
E-mail: early@earlyamericanmuseum.org
Web Site: www.earlyamericanmuseum.org
Founded: 1967.
Congressional District: 15

Key Personnel: Dir., Cheryl Kennedy; Cur. History, Barbara Oehlschlaeger-Garvey.
Personnel Profile: Full-Time Paid 3; Part-Time Paid 5; Part-Time Volunteers 100; Interns 1.
Governing Authority: county. Parent Institution: Champaign County Forest Preserve. Tax-exempt: 170(b)(1)(A).
History Museum.
Collections: tools, implements, furniture, lighting devices & household items dating from c.1850-1920; one-room schoolhouse; town hall.
Facilities: reference library; discovery room. Early American gift items for sale.
Activities: lectures; events; changing displays; formally organized educational programs; permanent exhibitions.
Publications: brochures; newsletters.
Hours & Admission Prices: March-May & Sept.-Dec. daily 1-5; June-Aug. Mon.-Sat. 10-5, Sun. 1-5. Fee applies to special programs only. ♿
Attendance: 18,000 (estimated)

MABERY GELVIN BOTANICAL GARDEN, 109 S. Lake of the Woods Rd., Mahomet, IL 61853. Mailing Address: P.O. Box 1040, Mahomet, IL 61853. Tel.: 217-586-4389 & 4630. Fax: 217-586-6852.
E-mail: hq@ccfpd.org
Botanical Garden.
Collections: plants; trees; flowers.
Activities: rental facilities.
Hours & Admission Prices: Daily 7 am to sundown. No charge.

Makanda

GIANT CITY STATE PARK, 235 Giant City Rd., Makanda, IL 62958-3207. Tel.: 618-457-4836.
Park Museum.
Collections: natural & cultural history of the park; geology; plants; wildlife; film; Native American artifacts.
Facilities: nature trails; visitor center; observation deck. Museum-related items for sale.
Activities: film; hiking; camping.
Hours & Admission Prices: Call for hours.

Marion

CRAB ORCHARD NATIONAL WILDLIFE REFUGE, 8588 Rte. 148, Marion, IL 62959-5822. Tel.: 618-997-3344.
Wildlife Refuge.
Collections: migratory waterfowl; fish; endangered wildlife.
Facilities: nature trails; visitor center.
Activities: hiking trails; picnicking; wildlife observation; youth camps.
Hours & Admission Prices: Daily: $2 per vehicle; Weekly: $5 per vehicle.

WILLIAMSON COUNTY HISTORICAL SOCIETY, 105 S. Van Buren, Marion, IL 62959-2509. Tel.: 618-997-5863 (Thurs. 9-3).
Web Site: www.thewchs.com
Founded: 1976.
Key Personnel: Pres. (V), Bob Jackson; Cur., Mary Jean DeMattie; Membership Chm., Dolores Thetford.
Personnel Profile: Part-Time Volunteers 10; Interns 1.
Governing Authority: nonprofit organization. Tax-exempt.
County Historical Society Museum: housed in 1913 former county jail & sheriff's home.
Collections: genealogy records; military; bank; drug store; jail cell; grocery store; Native American room with arrowheads, stone tools & other artifacts.
Research Fields: history; genealogy.
Activities: programs during meetings of society; tours.
Publications: quarterly for members, Footprints in Williamson County; area history subject books.
Hours & Admission Prices: March to late Nov. Thurs. 9-3, third Thurs. of the month 9-8, last tour at 2, or by appointment; call for information on tours. Research Library: March-Nov. Requested Tour Donation: adults $2, children under 12 $1; discounts to students; members no charge. Closed Thanksgiving.
Attendance: 600 (estimated)
Membership: Annually $18.

Marshall

CLARK COUNTY MUSEUM, 402 S. 4th St., Marshall, IL 62441-1030. Mailing Address: P.O. Box 207, Marshall, IL 62441-0207. Tel.: 217-826-2252.
Founded: 1969.
Congressional District: 22
Key Personnel: Pres., Charles Gamm.
Governing Authority: society. Parent Institution: the Clark County Historical Society. Tax-exempt: 501(c)(3).
Local History Museum.
Collections: articles relating to Clark County history; china; furniture; photos & documents; primitive kitchen equipment; quilts; hand tools; microfilm copies of local paper 1870-1986.
Facilities: genealogical library south of courthouse for family research.
Activities: guided tours; special exhibits; marking historical sites.
Publications: annual, Clark County Museum Newsletter.
Hours & Admission Prices: Sun. 2-4; other times by appointment. No charge; donations accepted.
Attendance: 125 (accurate)
Membership: Annual $5.

Maywood

WEST TOWN MUSEUM OF CULTURAL HISTORY, 104 S. 5th Ave., Maywood, IL 60153-1308. Tel.: 708-343-3554. Fax: 708-343-3557.
Key Personnel: Pres., Northica H. Stone
Cultural History Museum.
Collections: Maywood history & culture; underground railroad history.
Hours & Admission Prices: Wed. 9:30-3; other times by appointment. Adults $5, children under 13 $3.

Metamora

METAMORA COURTHOUSE HISTORIC SITE, 113 E. Partridge, Metamora, IL 61548-7021. Mailing Address: P.O. Box 628, Metamora, IL 61548. Tel.: 309-367-4470.
E-mail: metcourt@mtco.com
Founded: 1845.
Congressional District: 15
Key Personnel: Cur., Jean Myers.
Personnel Profile: Full-Time Paid 1; Part-Time Volunteers 6.
Governing Authority: state. Tax-exempt: 501(c)(3).
History Museum: housed in a restored 1845 Greek Revival courthouse located in the 8th Judicial Circuit that Abraham Lincoln traveled as a circuit lawyer.
Collections: pioneer items used in Woodford County during the Lincoln era; 8th Judicial Circuit exhibit.
Activities: guided tours.
Publications: bimonthly newsletter, Historic Illinois; brochure.
Hours & Admission Prices: April-Oct. Tues.-Sat. 1-5; Nov.-March Tues.-Sat. 12-4; groups by appointment. No charge; donations accepted. Closed New Year's Day; Martin Luther King Jr. Day; Presidents' Day; Veterans Day; Election Day; Thanksgiving; Christmas. ♿
Attendance: 6,869 (accurate)

Metropolis

FORT MASSAC STATE PARK AND HISTORIC SITE, 1308 E. 5th St., Metropolis, IL 62960-2380. Tel.: 618-524-9321 & 4712. Fax: 618-524-9321.
E-mail: dnr.r5parks@illinois.gov
Founded: 1908.
Congressional District: 59
Key Personnel: Site Supt., Terry Johnson.
Personnel Profile: Full-Time Paid 4; Part-Time Volunteers 32.
Governing Authority: state. Parent Institution: Illinois Dept. of Natural Resources, One Natural Resource Way, Springfield, IL 62702. Tax-exempt: 501(c)(3).
History Museum: located on the site of 1756-1814, Military Post.
Collections: artifacts & reconstructed period buildings.
Research Fields: U.S. military history 1790-1820.
Activities: guided tours; lectures.
Publications: site brochure; calendar of events.
Hours & Admission Prices: Daily 9-4. No charge. Closed Thanksgiving; Christmas. ♿
Attendance: 1,604,115 (accurate)

Moline

DEERE & COMPANY, ADMINISTRATIVE CENTER, One John Deere Place, Moline, IL 61265-8098. Tel.: 800-765-9588.
Web Site: www.deere.com/en_us/attractions/worldhq/index.html
Founded: 1837.
Key Personnel: Dir. Community Affairs, James H. Collins; Mgr. Library Svcs., Betty S. Hagberg; Archivist, Vicki L. Eller.
Governing Authority: profit-making organization.
History Museum.
Collections: agriculture; archives; industrial; archaeology.

Research Fields: agriculture; archives.
Facilities: 25,000-vol. library of agricultural research & reference books, magazines, equipment catalogs & advertising literature available for use by appointment on the premises.
Activities: guided tours; permanent exhibitions.
Hours & Admission Prices: Daily 9-5. No charge. Closed national holidays.

JOHN DEERE PAVILION, 1400 River Dr., Moline, IL 61265. Tel.: 309-765-1000.
Agricultural History Museum.
Collections: agricultural history; John Deere equipment; hands-on exhibits.
Activities: rental facilities.
Hours & Admission Prices: Mon.-Fri. 9-5, Sat. 10-5, Sun. 12-4. Closed Good Friday; Memorial Day; Independence Day; Labor Day.

ROCK ISLAND COUNTY HISTORICAL SOCIETY, 822 11th Ave., Moline, IL 61265-1221. Tel.: 309-764-8590. Fax: 309-764-4748.
E-mail: richs@netexpress.net
Web Site: www.richs.cc
Founded: 1905.
Congressional District: 17
Key Personnel: Pres., Robert Pettit.
Personnel Profile: Part-Time Volunteers 50.
Governing Authority: society. Tax-exempt.
Historical Society Museum: housed in c.1877 Victorian three story house.
Collections: folklore; military; agriculture; costumes; Indian artifacts; carriage house.
Research Fields: local history of Rock Island County.
Facilities: 10,000-vol. library of books, leaflets, clippings, papers, diaries available for research on premises.
Activities: guided tours; lectures; Jr. Historian Jamboree-4th & 5th grade selected students workshop. Museum Sponsors: Open House.
Publications: quarterly newsletter.
Hours & Admission Prices: House Museum & Carriage House: by appointment. Library: Wed.-Sat. 9-4. No charge; donations accepted. ♿
Attendance: 5,000 (estimated)
Membership: Household & Business $25; Contributing $50-$99; Patron $100-$499; President's Circle $500 & up.

Monmouth

BUCHANAN CENTER FOR THE ARTS, 64 Public Square, Monmouth, IL 61462-1756. Tel.: 309-734-3033. Fax: 309-734-3554.
E-mail: bca2@frontiernet.net
Web Site: bcaarts.org
Founded: 1990.
Congressional District: 17
Key Personnel: Dir., Susan Twomey; Museum Shop Mgr., Karen Gillen.
Personnel Profile: Full-Time Paid 2.
Governing Authority: nonprofit. Tax-exempt.
Art Museum & Arts Agency.
Collections: furnishings; personal artifacts; drawings; paintings; decorative arts; costumes; textiles.
Facilities: 2400 sq. ft. gallery & studio. Museum-related items for sale.
Activities: classes; workshops.
Publications: Artscoop.
Hours & Admission Prices: Mon.-Fri. 9-5, Sat. 9-2. No charge; donations accepted. Closed major holidays. ♿
Attendance: 12,170 (accurate)
Membership: Friend $15 & up; Family & Organization Member $30; Grantor & Partner $50 & up; Sponsor & Associate $100 & up; Sustainer & Principal $250 & up; Benefactor & Advocate $500 & up; Patron $1,000 & up; Guarantor $2,500 & up; Founder $5,000 & up.

WYATT EARP BIRTHPLACE HOME, 406 S. 3rd St., Monmouth, IL 61462-1435. Tel.: 309-734-6771; 641-420-4407.
E-mail: wyattearpbirthp@aol.com
Web Site: www.earpmorgan.com/wyattearpbirthplacewebsite.html
Founded: 1986.
Congressional District: 47
Key Personnel: Pres. (V), Charles Holmes; Chm. (V) & Museum Shop Mgr., Audie Durand.
Personnel Profile: Full-Time Volunteers 1; Part-Time Volunteers 20.
Governing Authority: nonprofit organization. Parent Institution: Wyatt Earp Birthplace, Inc. Tax-exempt: 501(c)(3).
Historic House: built c.1841. Listed on the National Register of Historic Places.
Collections: photographs; news items; 1840-1880 furnishings; memorabilia of Wyatt Earp; genealogy; books.
Research Fields: life of Wyatt Earp.
Facilities: library; period furnished rooms. Books & museum-related items for sale.
Activities: guided tours; film & slide shows; reenactments; portrayals. Museum Sponsors: Birthday Celebration including TV's Wyatt Earp - Hugh O'Brian; talks by Earp authors & researchers.
Publications: brochures; annual newsletter; books, The Wyatt Earp Birthplace: A Review; Part I; Part II; Wyatt Earp, Native Son.
Hours & Admission Prices: Summer: 2-4; call for additional hours. Special Tours: adults $3, children 6-12 $1; discounts to AAM & ICOM members; members no charge. ♿
Attendance: 500 (accurate)
Membership: Local Student $1; Individual $5; Supporter $10; Sponsor $25, $50, $75, $100, $250, $500, $750, $1,000.

Monticello

ALLERTON PARK AND RETREAT CENTER, 515 Old Timber Rd., Monticello, IL 61856-8279. Tel.: 217-333-3287 & 762-7011. Fax: 217-762-3742.
Historic House & Park.
Collections: family history; personal artifacts; period furnishings; photographs.
Facilities: visitor center.
Hours & Admission Prices: Visitor Center: Staffed: April-Nov. Sat.-Sun. 9-5; Unstaffed: Dec.-March daily 9-5. Closed New Year's Day; Thanksgiving; Christmas.

MONTICELLO RAILWAY MUSEUM, Interstate 72 at Exit 166, Market St., Monticello, IL 61856. Mailing Address: P.O. Box 401, Monticello, IL 61856-0401. Tel.: 217-762-9011; 877-762-9011.
E-mail: info@mrym.org
Web Site: www.mrym.org
Founded: 1966.
Congressional District: 15
Key Personnel: Supt. Locomotives, Kent McClure; Pres. (V), Donna McClure; Vice Pres., Doug Butzow; Chm. (V), John Sciutto; Sec., Derek Kouzmanoff; Treas. & Gen. Mgr., Sylvester Keller; Museum Shop Mgr., Arthur Purchase.
Personnel Profile: Full-Time Volunteers 2; Part-Time Volunteers 40.
Governing Authority: nonprofit organization. Tax-exempt: 501(c)(3).
Railway Museum.
Collections: late 1890-1950 steam locomotives; diesel locomotives; freight & passenger cars. Historic Buildings: restored c.1920 Illinois Central Depot; 1899 Wabash Depot.
Facilities: Gift shop with railroad-related items for sale.
Activities: train rides May-Oct. Sat.-Sun. & holidays; Throw Momma on the Train; Father's Day; caboose trains; The Little Engine That Could(R); railroad days; ghost train; Throttle Time.
Publications: The Second Section; Iron Horse Times.
Hours & Admission Prices: May-Oct. Sat.-Sun. Museum: no charge. Train Rides: adults $9, senior citizens $8, youth 2-12 $6; discount to Illinois Central Railroad employees, AAA members & groups of 20 or more; children under 2 & members no charge. Write for schedule of events. ♿
Attendance: 16,730 (accurate)
Membership: Youth $18; Annual $30.

PIATT COUNTY MUSEUM, 315 W. Main, Monticello, IL 61856-1862. Tel.: 217-762-4731.
Web Site: www.piattmuseum.org
Founded: 1965.
Congressional District: 19
Key Personnel: Pres. (V), T.J. Shambaugh, IV; Trustee, Lorin I. Nevling, Ph.D.; Dir. Devel., Peg Bargon.
Personnel Profile: Part-Time Volunteers 15.
Governing Authority: nonprofit organization. Tax-exempt: 501(c)(3).
General Museum.
Collections: Fine arts; Civil War relics; model railroad & miniature city; WWI to WWII relics; agriculture.
Activities: Annual Event: Barn Tour in October.
Publications: newsletters.
Hours & Admission Prices: Call for hours.
Attendance: 600 (estimated)
Membership: Individual Patron $25; Family $35; Organization $75.

Morrison

MORRISON'S HERITAGE MUSEUM, 202 E. Lincoln Way, Morrison, IL 61270-2825. Mailing Address: P.O. Box 1, Morrison, IL 61270-0001. Tel.: 815-772-8889 & 3224.
Key Personnel: Pres., Jack Ottoson

History Museum.
Collections: manufacturing history; military artifacts; religious; American Indian; train models.
Facilities: Museum-related items for sale.
Hours & Admission Prices: April-Nov. Fri.-Sun. 1-4 by appointment. No charge; donations accepted. ♿
Membership: Single $10; Family $20.

Morton Grove

MORTON GROVE HISTORICAL MUSEUM/HAUPT-YEHL HOUSE, (M), 6240 Dempster St., Morton Grove, IL 60053. Mailing Address: 6834 N. Dempster, Morton Grove, IL 60053-2631. Tel.: 847-965-0203 & 1200. Fax: 847-965-7484.
E-mail: gomgpd@mortongroveparks.com
Web Site: www.mortongroveparks.com
Founded: 1984.
Congressional District: 9
Key Personnel: Cur., Mary Busch.
Personnel Profile: Part-Time Paid 3; Part-Time Volunteers 25.
Governing Authority: nonprofit. Parent Institution: Morton Grove Park District. Tax-exempt: 501(c)(3).
Historical Society Museum: housed in c.1888 farm home.
Collections: photographs; local memorabilia & artifacts; furniture & furnishings.
Research Fields: maps; printed material on local history; oral histories.
Activities: guided tours.
Publications: bimonthly newsletter, Historical Highlights.
Hours & Admission Prices: Sun. 2-4, Wed. 1-3; other times tours of 10 persons or more by appointment. No charge; donations accepted. Closed national holidays.
Attendance: 2,234 (accurate)
Membership: Student $1; Senior $5; Individual $7.50; Family $15; Sponsor $25; Individual Life $50; Family Life $100.

Mount Carmel

WABASH COUNTY MUSEUM, 320 N. Market St., Mount Carmel, IL 62863. Mailing Address: P.O. Box 512, Mount Carmel, IL 62863-0512. Tel.: 618-262-8774.
History Museum.
Collections: local history & culture; photographs; period furnishings; personal artifacts.
Facilities: library.
Activities: research.
Hours & Admission Prices: Tues., Thurs. & Sun. 2-5. Closed Easter; Thanksgiving; Christmas. ♿

Mount Prospect

MOUNT PROSPECT HISTORICAL SOCIETY MUSEUMS, 101 S. Maple, Mount Prospect, IL 60056-3229. Tel.: 847-392-9006.
Web Site: www.yourcentralschool.org
Founded: 1968.
Congressional District: 12
Key Personnel: Pres. (V), Marilyn Genther; Exec. Dir., Greg Peerbolte; Financial Dir., Frank Corry; Administrative Asst., Cindy Brok.
Personnel Profile: Full-Time Paid 1; Part-Time Paid 2; Part-Time Volunteers 63; Interns 2.
Governing Authority: nonprofit. Parent Institution: Dietrich Friedrichs House, 101 S. Maple, Mount Prospect, IL 60056. Tax-exempt: 501(c)(3).
Local History Museum: housed in a c.1906 home.
Collections: early 20th century domestic life in Mt. Prospect; exhibits relating to the history of Mt. Prospect; decorative arts; photographs; costumes; archives.
Major Exhibits: "They Felt it had Prospects for the Future", 11/09-4/11.
Research Fields: rural town life; history of Mt. Prospect; history of Illinois schooling; economic development; 20th-century suburban development; immigration history.
Facilities: library of local history materials; education center. Books, historic afghans & stationery items for sale.
Activities: guided tours; lectures; docent program; temporary exhibitions; educational programs; cemetery walk; pie contest. Museum Sponsors: Story Telling Festival; House Walk.
Publications: quarterly newsletter; History Book of Mt. Prospect; Mt. Prospect: Where Town & Country Met; Images of America: Mount Prospect; Lost Mount Prospect.
Hours & Admission Prices: Tours: Mon.-Fri. 11-6, Labor Day 12-6. Donations accepted. Closed New Year's Day; Independence Day; Thanksgiving; Christmas. ♿
Attendance: 5,000 (estimated)
Membership: Senior $20; Single $25; Family $30; Sponsor $75; Benefactor $150; Patron $250; Life $1,000.

Mount Pulaski

MT. PULASKI COURTHOUSE STATE HISTORIC SITE, 113 S. Washington, Mount Pulaski, IL 62548. Mailing Address: P.O. Box 171, Mount Pulaski, IL 62548-0171. Tel.: 217-792-3919.
Founded: 1936.
Congressional District: 18
Personnel Profile: Part-Time Paid 1; Part-Time Volunteers 16.
Governing Authority: state. Parent Institution: Illinois Historic Preservation Agency, Old State Capitol, Springfield, IL 62701. Tax-exempt: 501(c)(3).
Historic Building: 1848 Greek Revival County Court House; part of Illinois 8th Judicial Circuit where Abraham Lincoln practiced law.
Collections: furnishings.
Research Fields: history of area; Abraham Lincoln & the 8th Judicial Circuit.
Activities: guided tours; school programs.
Publications: bimonthly newsletter, Historic Illinois; brochure.
Hours & Admission Prices: Tues.-Sat. 12-4. No charge. Closed most holidays.
Attendance: 4,000

MOUNT PULASKI HISTORIC SOCIETY AND MUSEUM, 104 E. Cooke St., Mount Pulaski, IL 62548. Mailing Address: P.O. Box 181, Mount Pulaski, IL 62548-0181. Tel.: 217-792-5430.
Historical Society Museum.
Collections: local history, culture, & business; Abraham Lincoln's life & family; personal artifacts; period furnishings; photographs.
Facilities: library. Museum-related items for sale.
Publications: quarterly newsletter.
Hours & Admission Prices: April-Nov. Tues.-Fri. 12-4, Sat. by appointment. No charge; donations accepted. Closed New Year's Day; Martin Luther King's Birthday; Presidents' Day; Veterans Day; General Election Day; Thanksgiving; Christmas.

Mount Vernon

CEDARHURST CENTER FOR THE ARTS, 2600 Richview Rd., Mount Vernon, IL 62864. Mailing Address: P.O. Box 923, Mount Vernon, IL 62864-0019. Tel.: 618-242-1236. Fax: 618-242-9530.
E-mail: mitchellmuseum@cedarhurst.org
Web Site: cedarhurst.org
Formerly: Mitchell Museum at Cedarhurst
Founded: 1973.
Congressional District: 22
Key Personnel: Exec. Dir., Sharon Bradham; Craft Fair Coord., Linda Wheeler; Interim Dir. Visual Arts, Tracy Schilling; C.F.O., Heather Owens; Dir. Communications, Sarah Sledge; Interim Dir. Devel., Vonda Rister; Dir. Education, Jennifer Sarver; Dir. Operations, Greg Hilliard; Museum Shop Mgr. & Historian, Sarah Lou Bicknell.
Personnel Profile: Full-Time Paid 16; Part-Time Paid 2; Part-Time Volunteers 25.
Governing Authority: nonprofit organization. Parent Institution: John R. & Eleanor R. Mitchell Foundation. Tax-exempt: 501(c)(3).
Art Museum & Sculpture Park.
Collections: late 19th & early 20th-century American paintings; contemporary sculpture & art from the Midwest.
Research Fields: 19th & 20th-century American painting; contemporary sculpture & art from the Midwest.
Facilities: 1,900-vol. library; nature trails; bird sanctuary; children's gallery; 90-acre Cedarhurst Sculpture Park; Cedarhurst Art Center for art classes.
Activities: guided tours; sculpture walks; chamber music series; dinner theater; children's theater; summer concerts; docent program; temporary, traveling & juried exhibitions. Museum Sponsors: Annual Cedarhurst Craft Fair in September; Collector's Club.
Publications: newsletter; brochures; exhibition catalogues; annual report.
Hours & Admission Prices: Tues.-Sat. 10-5, Sun. 1-5. No charge; donations accepted. Closed national holidays. ♿
Attendance: 50,000 (estimated)
Membership: Individual $50; Family $75; Patron $150; Sponsor $250; Benefactor $500; Guarantor $1,000.

Murphysboro

GENERAL JOHN A. LOGAN MUSEUM, (M), 1613 Edith St., Murphysboro, IL 62966-2542. Mailing Address: P.O. Box 563, Murphysboro, IL 62966-0563. Tel.: 618-684-3455. Fax: 618-684-3569.
E-mail: johnaloganmuseum@globaleyes.net
Web Site: www.loganmuseum.org
Founded: 1989.
Congressional District: 12

Key Personnel: Dir., P. Michael Jones; Pres. (V), Michael J. McNerney.
Personnel Profile: Full-Time Volunteers 1; Part-Time Paid 4; Part-Time Volunteers 10.
Governing Authority: Tax-exempt.
Military History Museum.
Collections: life of General John A. Logan; 19th & early 20th century American history; Civil War; personal artifacts; photographs.
Hours & Admission Prices: June-Aug. Tues.-Sat. 10-4, Sun. 1-4; Sept.-May Tues.-Sun. 1-4; groups by appointment. No charge; donations accepted. Closed New Year's Eve; Christmas Eve; holidays. ♿
Attendance: 3,500 (accurate)

Naperville

DUPAGE CHILDREN'S MUSEUM, 301 N. Washington St., Naperville, IL 60540-4537. Tel.: 630-637-8000. Fax: 630-637-1276.
E-mail: admin@dupagechildrensmuseum.org
Web Site: www.dupagechildrensmuseum.org/index.html
Founded: 1987.
Congressional District: 13
Key Personnel: Museum Shop Mgr., Linda Miller
Children's Museum.
Collections: hands-on exhibits.
Facilities: Museum-related items for sale.
Activities: special programs; birthday parties; rental facilities; exhibit activities, science & art residencies; classes Just For Grown-Ups programs; Third Thursday; Tiny Great Performances (TM).
Publications: quarterly DCM newsletter; the DCM blog: www.thechildrensmuseumblog.blog-city.com; eNews Club.
Hours & Admission Prices: Mon. 9-1, Tues.-Thurs. & Sat. 9-5, third Thurs. of month & Fri. 9-8, Sun. 12-5. Admission 1-59 $8.50, seniors 60 & over $7.50; members & children under 1 no charge. Closed New Year's Eve & Day; Easter; Memorial Day; Independence Day; Labor Day; Thanksgiving; Christmas Eve & Day. ♿
Attendance: 300,000 (accurate)

* **NAPER SETTLEMENT, (M),** 523 S. Webster St., Naperville, IL 60540-6517. Tel.: 630-420-6010. Fax: 630-305-5255. Event Hotline: 630-305-5555.
E-mail: towncrier@naperville.il.us
Web Site: www.napersettlement.museum
Founded: 1969.
Congressional District: 41
Key Personnel: Exec. Dir., Peggy Frank; Pres., Christopher Birck; Dir. Preservation Svcs., Debbie Grinnell; Dir. Institutional Advancement, John Buckley; Cur., Louise Howard; Dir. Organization Resources, Harriet Pistorio; Dir. Visitor Svcs., Donna Sack; Mktg. Communications Mgr., Jody Ellyne; Education Mgr., Nancy Smith; Facilities Mgr., Sharon Bennett Hinkle; Business Mgr., Joleen Dimond; Museum Shop Coord., Jan Vorel.
Personnel Profile: Full-Time Paid 24; Part-Time Paid 29; Part-Time Volunteers 1,700; Interns 2.
Governing Authority: municipal, City of Naperville. Parent Institution: Naperville Heritage Society. Tax-exempt.
Historic Museum.
Collections: furnishings; costumes; dolls; glass; manuscripts; china; folk paintings; interactive displays; historical artifacts. Historic Buildings: 1883 Martin Mitchell Mansion & Carriage House; 1864 Century Memorial Chapel; c.1840s Halfway House; Conestoga Wagon; c.1860s Fire House; late 19th century Stonecarver's Shop; 1833 Paw Paw Post Office; 1841 Meeting House; c.1880s working Print Shop; c.1860 recreated Blacksmith Shop; c.1840 recreated one-room schoolhouse; c.1832 recreated fort.
Major Exhibits: Architecture: Old Forms, New Construction, 2/10.
Research Fields: history of Naperville, including as it relates to history in Midwest; genealogy.
Facilities: research library open to the public; 12-acre grounds with 30 historic structures; 2 permanent exhibits and 1 changing gallery; 7 landscaped gardens; rental facilities. Museum-related items for sale.
Activities: guided & self-guided tours; school programs; adult & children's programs; lecture series; geocaching; group outings; volunteer programs; special events. Annual Events: Civil War Days; Naper Days; Naperville Summer Nights; Dinner on the Town; All Hallows Eve: A 19th Century Halloween.
Publications: magazine, Treasures; brochures; calendar of events; annual report; CD's, Movin' In Building a Town; Trading in Time; Memories of the Past; Sharing Moments Through History; Tidbits of the Past, A Fun Collection of Historic Brainteasers; postcard & notecard series of current and historic photographs.
Hours & Admission Prices: Summer: April-Oct. Tues.-Sat. 10-4, Sun. 1-4. Adults $8, senior citizens $7, youth 4-17 $5.50; members no charge. Audio Tour: $3; geocache GPS unit $1; discounts to AAA members. Winter: Nov.-March Mon.-Fri. 10-4. Adults $4.25, senior citizens $3.75, youths 4-17 $3, audio tour included; discounts to AAA members; members no charge. Closed New Year's Day; Thanksgiving; Christmas. ♿
Attendance: 125,000 (estimated)
Membership: Individual (resident) $25; Individual (nonresident) $30; Family (Naperville resident) $50; Family (nonresident) $60; Sustaining Member $100-$500.

Nauvoo

JOSEPH SMITH HISTORIC SITE, 865 Water St., Nauvoo, IL 62354. Mailing Address: P.O. Box 338, Nauvoo, IL 62354-0338. Tel.: 217-453-2246. Fax: 217-453-6416.
E-mail: jshs@frontiernet.net
Web Site: cofchrist.org/js/
Founded: 1918.
Congressional District: 19
Key Personnel: C.E.O., Joyce A. Shireman, Ph.D.
Personnel Profile: Full-Time Paid 4; Full-Time Volunteers 12; Part-Time Paid 1; Part-Time Volunteers 10; Interns 10.
Governing Authority: church. Parent Institution: Community of Christ. Subsidiary Institution: Historic Sites Division. Tax-exempt: 501(c)(3).
Historic Sites & Buildings: 1803 & 1840 Joseph Smith Homestead; 1842 Joseph Smith Red Brick Store; 1843 Joseph Smith Mansion House.
Collections: original 19th-century furnishings, structures & recovered artifacts.
Research Fields: historic archaeology; Mormon history.
Facilities: library. Museum-related items for sale.
Activities: guided tours; summer kitchen-activities of daily living-1840s: cooking; carding wood; spinning candle making; herb garden; games.
Hours & Admission Prices: May-Oct. Mon.-Sat. 9-5, Sun. 1-5; Nov.-Dec. Tues.-Sat. 10-4. Summer Kitchen: Memorial Day to mid-Aug. daily 10-4. Guided Tour: $2 per person. ♿
Attendance: 90,000 (estimated)
Membership: $120, $300, $420 & $600; Heritage Club $1,000.

NAUVOO HISTORICAL SOCIETY MUSEUM, 980 S. Bluff St., Nauvoo, IL 62354. Mailing Address: P.O. Box 426, Nauvoo, IL 62354-0426. Tel.: 217-453-2512. Fax: 217-453-2512.
Founded: 1953.
Congressional District: 17
Key Personnel: Chm. & Pres. (V), Mary Reed; Site Supt., Regan Ramsey; Maintenance Supvr., Michael Locke; Site Tech, Mike Middendorf.
Personnel Profile: Part-Time Paid 3; Part-Time Volunteers 3.
Governing Authority: state; nonprofit organization. Affiliated with State of Illinois, Div. of Natural Resources, 600 N. Grand Ave. W, Springfield, IL 62706. Tax-exempt.
Historical Society Museum.
Collections: geology; history; American Indian artifacts; 1850 wine cellar & grape arbor.
Research Fields: Icarian period.
Facilities: wine cellar; 2 acre grape arbor.
Activities: guided tours; permanent exhibitions.
Publications: bimonthly newsletter, Historic Illinois; brochure.
Hours & Admission Prices: May to mid-Oct. daily 1-5. No charge; donations accepted. ♿
Attendance: 5,000 (estimated)
Membership: Individual $2; Family $5.

Newton

NEWTON PUBLIC LIBRARY AND MUSEUM, 100 S. Vanburen, Newton, IL 62448-1559. Tel.: 618-783-8141. Fax: 618-783-8149.
Founded: 1928.
Key Personnel: Head Librarian, Connie Davidson.
Personnel Profile: Full-Time Paid 2; Part-Time Paid 2.
Governing Authority: municipal. Tax-exempt.
Local History Museum.
Collections: military; early household wares; Indian artifacts; farm implements; uniforms; early German books & Bibles.
Facilities: 14,435-vol. library of reference material, children's books, adult fiction & genealogical material available for research on premises.
Activities: art exhibits; summer reading programs for children; adult book club.
Hours & Admission Prices: Mon.-Fri. 10-5, Sat. 10-1. No charge. Closed national holidays.

Nokomis

BOTTOMLEY-RUFFING-SCHALK BASEBALL MUSEUM, 121 W. State St., Nokomis, IL 62075-1658. Mailing Address: P.O. Box 75, Nokomis, IL 62075-0075. Tel.: 217-563-8807. Fax: 217-324-6616.
E-mail: info@brsmuseum.org
Web Site: brsmuseum.org

Key Personnel: Treas., Steve Johnson
Sports Museum.
Collections: Bottomley, Ruffing & Schalk personal artifacts & career history; baseball memorabilia.
Hours & Admission Prices: Mon. & Wed.-Fri. 9am-11am, Tues. 9am-11am & 6pm-9pm; other times by appointment. April-Oct. no charge.

Normal

CHILDREN'S DISCOVERY MUSEUM, 101 E. Beaufort, Normal, IL 61761-3026. Tel.: 309-433-3444. Fax: 309-451-3614.
E-mail: museum@normal.org
Web Site: childrensdiscoverymuseum.net
Founded: 1994.
Congressional District: 15
Key Personnel: Museum Mgr., Shari Spaniol Buckellew; Dir. Community Rels., Heather Young; Chm. (V), Holly Houska; Education Coord., Bethany Thomas.
Personnel Profile: Full-Time Paid 9; Part-Time Paid 40; Part-Time Volunteers 400; Interns 5.
Governing Authority: municipal. Parent Institution: Town of Normal. Tax-exempt.
Children's Museum.
Collections: hands-on exhibits; agriculture; environmental; imagination & creative play; art; climbing structure.
Research Fields: parent & child interaction in a cultural and educational setting.
Facilities: classrooms; birthday party rooms; 12,000 sq. ft. exhibit space; hands on exhibits; vending machines. Museum-related items for sale.
Activities: formal education programs for children; participatory exhibits.
Publications: quarterly newsletter; seasonal flyers; educators guide.
Hours & Admission Prices: Jan.-May & Sept.-Dec. Tues.-Wed. & Sat. 9-5, Thurs.-Fri. 9-8; June-Aug. Mon.-Wed. & Sat. 9-5, Thurs.-Fri. 9-8. Admission $6, field trips $4; ASTC, ACM, members & children under 2 no charge. Closed New Year's Day; Easter; Labor Day; Thanksgiving; Christmas. ♿
Attendance: 140,000 (accurate)
Membership: Family $85; ASTC & ACM $115.

North Chicago

FEET FIRST: THE SCHOLL STORY, ROSALIND FRANKLIN UNIVERSITY, 3333 Green Bay Rd., North Chicago, IL 60064-3037. Tel.: 847-578-8417 & 3000. Fax: 847-775-6521.
E-mail: david.mckay@rosalindfranklin.edu
Web Site: www.rosalindfranklin.edu
Founded: 1993.
Key Personnel: C.E.O., Terrence Albright, D.P.M.; Pres. Emeritus & College Historian, G.B. Geppner, D.P.M.
Personnel Profile: Part-Time Paid 2.
Governing Authority: private college; nonprofit. Parent Institution: Scholl College of Podiatric Medicine. Tax-exempt.
Podiatry Museum: housed in the Dr. William M. Scholl School of Podiatry.
Collections: photographs; period shoes; memorabilia from life of Dr. William Scholl; catalogs; shoe fluoroscope; exhibits to educate the public about the foot.
Research Fields: life of Dr. Scholl and his company; history of the institution.
Activities: guided tours for schools & groups.
Publications: Dr. Scholl: Man or Myth?; Dr. Scholl: Foot Doctor to the World.
Hours & Admission Prices: Daily 9-4. No charge; donations accepted. ♿
Attendance: 11,000 (accurate)

Oak Brook

GRAUE MILL AND MUSEUM, 3800 York Rd., Oak Brook, IL 60523-2738. Tel.: 630-655-2090 & 920-9720. Fax: 630-920-9721.
Web Site: www.grauemill.org
Founded: 1950.
Congressional District: 13
Key Personnel: Exec. Dir., Sandra Brubaker; Pres. (V), George Mueller.
Personnel Profile: Full-Time Paid 1; Part-Time Paid 23; Part-Time Volunteers 50.
Governing Authority: nonprofit corporation. Tax-exempt.
History Museum: housed in 1852 restored waterwheel gristmill.
Collections: Civil War; farm implements & vehicles; dolls; period furnishings; artifacts. Historic Buildings: c.1859 Miller's Home.
Facilities: fresh stoneground cornmeal in old-fashioned cloth bags for sale.
Activities: spinning & weaving demonstrations.
Publications: brochures, The Story of The Old Graue Mill; Field Trip Guide; children's book, Discover Graue Mill.
Hours & Admission Prices: mid-April to mid-Nov. Tues.-Sun. 10-4:30. Adults $3.50, senior citizens $3, children 3-15 $1.50; discounts to groups of 20 or more; members & children under 3 no charge. ♿
Attendance: 40,000 (estimated)
Membership: Individual: $25; Family: $40; Sustaining: $100-$249; Sponsor: $250-$499; Benefactor: $500-$999; Foundation: $1,000.

MAYSLAKE PEABODY ESTATE, 1717 W. 31st St., Oak Brook, IL 60523-1701. Tel.: 630-850-2363.
Historic House Museum: housed in the former home of Francis Stuyvesant Peabody, a coal baron & national figure in Democratic politics; built in 1921.
Collections: Francis Stuyvesant Peabody's life & family history; personal artifacts; period furnishings; photographs.
Activities: special events; theatrical performances; cultural events; educational programs; rental facilities.
Hours & Admission Prices: Guided Tours: mid-Jan. to mid-Dec. Wed. 11 & 12:30, Sat. 9:30, 10, 11, & 11:30; other times by appointment. $5 per person.

Oak Lawn

CHILDREN'S MUSEUM IN OAK LAWN, (M), 5100 Museum Dr., Oak Lawn, IL 60453-7005. Tel.: 708-423-6709. Fax: 708-423-6723.
E-mail: general.information@cmoaklawn.org
Web Site: www.cmoaklawn.org
Founded: 2001.
Key Personnel: Dir., Adam Woodworth; Pres. (V), Cathy Cepican.
Personnel Profile: Full-Time Paid 3; Part-Time Paid 2; Part-Time Volunteers 40; Interns 1.
Governing Authority: Tax-exempt.
Children's Museum.
Collections: hands-on exhibits.
Activities: birthday parties; special events; educational programs.
Hours & Admission Prices: Wed. 8:30-3, Thurs.-Sat. 10-3. Adults 17 & over $3.50, children 1-16 $3. Closed Christmas. ♿
Attendance: 20,000
Membership: Child $25; Family $55; Grand $65; All-in-the-Family $100.

Oak Park

* **FRANK LLOYD WRIGHT HOME AND STUDIO, (M),** 951 Chicago Ave., Oak Park, IL 60302-2007. Mailing Address: 931 Chicago Ave., Oak Park, IL 60302-2097. Tel.: 708-848-1976. Fax: 708-848-1248.
E-mail: info@gowright.org
Web Site: gowright.org
Founded: 1974.
Congressional District: 7
Key Personnel: C.E.O. & Pres., Joan B. Mercuri; Chm., Mike Poirier.
Personnel Profile: Full-Time Paid 9; Part-Time Paid 15; Part-Time Volunteers 375.
Governing Authority: private; nonprofit organization. Parent Institution: Frank Lloyd Wright Preservation Trust, Oak Park, IL. Tax-exempt: 501(c)(3).
Historic House Museum: 1889-1909 residence & office of Frank Lloyd Wright; birthplace of prairie-style architecture.
Collections: structures, furniture & decorative arts designed by Frank Lloyd Wright; Japanese Art & decorative materials collected by Wright; drawings; prairie style architecture.
Research Fields: Frank Lloyd Wright's life & work, 1889-1916.
Facilities: library; 8,223 sq. ft. exhibit space. Museum-related items for sale.
Activities: docent program; formal education programs; guided tours; lectures; walking tours; bus tours; workshops. Annual Event: Wright Plus Housewalk in May.
Publications: quarterly newsletter, Wright Angles; books, The Oak Park Home and Studio of Frank Lloyd Wright; Frank Lloyd Wright and the Prairie; Building a Legacy: The Restoration of Frank Lloyd Wright's Home and Studio; Frank Lloyd Wright's Fifty Views of Japan; In Wright's Shadow: Artists and Architects in the Oak Park Studio; Hometown Architect: The Complete Buildings of Frank Lloyd Wright in Oak Park and River Forest; The Wright Family Library.
Hours & Admission Prices: Tours: Memorial Day to Labor Day Mon.-Wed. & Fri. 11-3:20, Thurs. 11-6, Sat.-Sun. 11-4; Sept.-May Mon.-Fri. 11-3:20, Sat.-Sun. 11-4; groups by appointment, call 708-848-1978. Book Shop: daily 10-5. Adults $15, seniors & youth 4-17 $12; children 3 & under no charge. Closed New Year's Day; Thanksgiving; Christmas.
Attendance: 64,000 (accurate)
Membership: Individual $50; Family $65; Prairie Society $125; Octagon Society $250; Inglenook Society $500; Skylight Society $1,000; Cornerstone Society $2,500; Wright Society $5,000.

THE HEMINGWAY MUSEUM AND THE ERNEST HEMINGWAY BIRTHPLACE, 200 N. Oak Park Ave., Oak Park, IL 60302-2128. Mailing Address: P.O. Box 2222, Oak Park, IL 60303-2222. Tel.: 708-848-2222. Fax: 708-386-2952.
E-mail: ehfop@sbcglobal.net
Web Site: www.ehfop.org
Founded: 1990.
Congressional District: 7
Key Personnel: Chm. (V), Allan Baldwin; Vice Chm., Virginia R. Cassin; Archivist, Barbara Ballinger; Museum Shop Mgr., Conni Irwin.
Personnel Profile: Part-Time Paid 2; Part-Time Volunteers 200; Interns 1.
Governing Authority: private; nonprofit organization. The Ernest Hemingway Birthplace, 339 N. Oak Park Ave., Oak Park, IL 60302. Tax-exempt: 501(c)(3).
History Museum: housed in the birthplace of Ernest Hemingway.
Collections: Hemingway Museum: personal artifacts including high school papers & letters, studies in world languages, movie posters. Birthplace: Queen Ann Victorian style house contains artifacts depicting the life & development of Ernest Hemingway.
Research Fields: Hemingway's Oak Park years.
Facilities: archives; public lecture area. Museum-related items for sale.
Activities: arts festivals; docent program; films; guided tours; lectures; loan, temporary & traveling exhibitions; study clubs; broadcast programs. Annual Events: Hemingway birthday colloquist & lecture; Hemingway Birthplace Boxing Day.
Publications: monthly volunteer newsletter, At The Front; quarterly member newsletter, The Hemingway Despatch.
Hours & Admission Prices: Sun.-Fri. 1-5, Sat. 10-5. Adults $8, senior citizens & students $6; discounts to AAA members & tour groups of 10 or more; members & children 5 & under no charge. Closed New Year's Day; Martin Luther King Jr. Day; Easter; Memorial Day; Independence Day; Labor Day; Thanksgiving; Christmas. ♿
Attendance: 6,976 (estimated)
Membership: Student & Senior Citizen $30; Individual $45; Family $60.

HISTORICAL SOCIETY OF OAK PARK & RIVER FOREST, 217 Home Ave., Oak Park, IL 60302-3101. Mailing Address: P.O. Box 771, Oak Park, IL 60303-0771. Tel.: 708-848-6755. Fax: 708-848-0246.
E-mail: oprfhistorian@sbcglobal.net
Web Site: oprf.com/oprfhist
Founded: 1968.
Congressional District: 7
Key Personnel: Exec. Dir., Frank Lipo; Pres. (V), Laurel McMahon; Treas., Jim Taglia; Public Rels., Jean Guarino.
Personnel Profile: Full-Time Paid 2; Part-Time Volunteers 30; Interns 1.
Governing Authority: nonprofit organization. Tax-exempt: 501(c)(3).
Historical Society Museum: housed in 1897 Prairie style mansion.
Collections: Oak Park & River Forest history, 1830-present; exhibit on Edgar Rice Burroughs, creator of Tarzan; costumes; photographs; books; archives; artifacts.
Research Fields: local history.
Facilities: 800-vol. library of local history books & local newspapers; 700 sq. ft. exhibit space. Postcards & books on local sites & history for sale.
Activities: formal education programs for children; lectures; temporary exhibitions.
Publications: quarterly newsletter, Village Yesteryears; book, Ernest Hemingway as Recalled by his High School Contemporaries; Guidebook to Forest Home Cemetery; Grace Wilson Trout biography.
Hours & Admission Prices: Museum: Thurs.-Sun. 12:30-3:30; group tours by appointment. Office: Tues. & Thurs. 1-5. Adults $5, children 18 & under $3; Fri. & members no charge. Closed New Year's Day; Easter; Christmas.
Attendance: 5,000 (accurate)
Membership: Senior Citizen & Student $15; Individual $25; Family $35; Patron $50; Individual Life $500.

THE OAK PARK CONSERVATORY, 615 Garfield St., Oak Park, IL 60304-2001. Tel.: 708-386-4700. Fax: 708-386-3221.
Web Site: www.oakparkparks.com
Founded: 1929.
Congressional District: 3
Key Personnel: Mgr., Henrietta Yardley.
Personnel Profile: Full-Time Paid 3; Part-Time Paid 2; Part-Time Volunteers 20.
Governing Authority: municipal. Parent Institution: Park District of Oak Park, 218 Madison St., Oak Park, 60302. Tel.: 708-383-0002. Subsidiary Institution: Friends of the Oak Park Conservatory.
Conservatory.
Collections: cacti & succulent collection; exotic tropical plants; subtropical plants; seasonal flora; culinary, medicinal, scented & dye herbs; botanical art.
Facilities: library of horticultural publications, books & catalogs available for research by special request; conservatory center; kitchenette for rent; prairie garden with native Illinois species; herb garden; classrooms.
Activities: guided tours; lectures; films; hobby workshops; radio programs; formally organized education programs for children, adults & undergraduate college students; training programs; permanent & temporary exhibitions; plant clinic.
Publications: brochure; quarterly members newsletter, Conservatory Conversations.
Hours & Admission Prices: Mon. 2-4, Tues.-Sun. 10-4, holidays 10-3. Suggested Donations: adult $1, children $.50. ♿
Attendance: 34,105 (accurate)
Membership: Individual $25; Family & Dual $40; Associate $75; Premier $150; Sustaining $300.

WONDER WORKS, 6445 W. North Ave., Oak Park, IL 60302-1009. Tel.: 708-383-4815.
E-mail: info@wonder-works.org
Web Site: www.wonder-works.org
Children's Museum.
Collections: hands-on exhibits.
Activities: birthday parties; educational programs.
Hours & Admission Prices: Wed.-Sat. 10-5, Sun. 12-5. Admission $5; children under one & members no charge. Closed New Year's Day; Memorial Day; Independence Day; Labor Day; Thanksgiving; Christmas.

Oakbrook Terrace

LAKE VIEW NATURE CENTER, 17W063 Hodges Rd., Oakbrook Terrace, IL 60181-4505. Tel.: 630-941-8747. Fax: 630-941-3558.
E-mail: lvnc@obtpd.org
Web Site: www.obtpd.org
Founded: 1994.
Congressional District: 6
Key Personnel: Dir., Liane Knight.
Personnel Profile: Full-Time Paid 1; Part-Time Paid 5; Part-Time Volunteers 4.
Governing Authority: municipal. Parent Institution: Oakbrook Terrace Park District. Tax-exempt.
Nature Center.
Collections: regional flora, fauna & natural history.
Facilities: 800-vol. library; native botanical garden; nature center; 1,500 sq. ft. exhibit space.
Activities: formal environmental education programs; participatory exhibits. Annual Event: Spring Celebration in May; Fall Open House in November.
Publications: newsletter, Lake View's Nature News.
Hours & Admission Prices: Mon.-Fri. 9-4, Sat.-Sun. 12-4. No charge; donations accepted. Closed 1st Mon. each month; New Year's Eve & Day; Good Friday; Easter weekend; Memorial Day; Independence Day; Labor Day; Thanksgiving & day after; Christmas Eve & Day. ♿
Attendance: 16,300 (accurate)

Oglesby

STARVED ROCK STATE PARK, 2568 E. 950th Rd., Oglesby, IL 61348. Mailing Address: P.O. Box 509, Utica, IL 61373-0509. Tel.: 815-667-4906 & 5356. Fax: 815-667-5354.
E-mail: starvedrockv@ivnet.com
Web Site: dnr.state.il.us
Founded: 1911.
Congressional District: 15
Key Personnel: Supt., Tom Levy; Site Interpreter, Tobias Miller.
Governing Authority: state. A part of Illinois Dept. of Natural Resources, Div. of Land Management, 1 Natural Resources Way, Springfield, IL 62702. Tax-exempt.
Historic Park & Museum: located on the sites of former Indian village of Illinois Indians; 1673-1760 French occupation and 1683 French Fort St. Louis.
Collections: cultural & natural history; archeological; geological.
Research Fields: Indian & French history; biology.
Facilities: interpretive center, lodge with overnight accommodations & dining room; 15 miles of hiking trails; seasonal concessions.
Activities: guided tours; lectures; films; formally organized educational programs; permanent exhibitions; camping.
Publications: brochure, Starved Rock State Park.
Hours & Admission Prices: Park: daily 5am-9pm. Interpretive Center: daily 9-4. No charge; donations accepted. ♿
Attendance: 216,869 (accurate)

Ottawa

OTTAWA SCOUTING MUSEUM, (M), 1100 Canal St., Ottawa, IL 61350-4940. Mailing Address: P.O. Box 2241, Ottawa, IL 61350-6841. Tel.: 815-431-9353.
E-mail: scouter07@hotmail.com
Web Site: www.ottawascoutingmuseum.org
Founded: 1992.
Congressional District: 11
Key Personnel: C.E.O., Cur. & Public Rels., Mollie Perrot; Pres. & Museum Shop Mgr., Christine Hasty; Financial Dir., Joseph Martin; Archivist, Bruno Polli; Security, Steve Perrot.
Personnel Profile: Full-Time Volunteers 1; Part-Time Volunteers 30.
Governing Authority: private; nonprofit. Tax-exempt: 501(c)(3).
Scouting Museum.
Collections: artifacts; camping gear; uniforms; badges; patches; awards; medals; handbooks; Native American display; W.D. Boyce display; literature dating from the early days of scouting to the present.
Research Fields: Native American culture, nature & conservation as they relate to scouting; Ottawa, IL history.
Facilities: 2,800-vol. library; 60-seat auditorium; nature center; 2,700 sq. ft. exhibition space. Museum-related items for sale.
Activities: docent program; hobby workshops; temporary exhibitions; adult programs. Annual Events: Founder's Day; Preservation of Ottawa History group meetings, 4th Tuesday of each month.
Publications: quarterly newsletter, Memory Lane.
Hours & Admission Prices: Thurs.-Mon. 10-4. Adults $3, students & children $2; discount to groups of 10 or more; members no charge. Closed New Year's Eve & Day; Easter; Independence Day; Labor Day; Thanksgiving; Christmas Eve & Day. ♿
Attendance: 3,000 (accurate)
Membership: Youth $3; Adult $10; Family $15; Contributing $25; Patron $50; Benefactor $100; Guarantor $1,000.

Paris

BICENTENNIAL ART CENTER & MUSEUM, 132 S. Central Ave., Paris, IL 61944-1729. Tel.: 217-466-8130. Fax: 217-466-8130.
E-mail: susans@parisartcenter.com
Web Site: www.parisartcenter.com
Founded: 1975.
Congressional District: 19
Key Personnel: Dir., Susan Stafford.
Personnel Profile: Part-Time Paid 1; Part-Time Volunteers 100.
Governing Authority: nonprofit. Tax-exempt: 501(c)(3).
Art Museum.
Collections: paintings in oils & watercolors; drawings; sculpture; photography.
Facilities: 240-vol. library available for public use; classrooms.
Activities: formal education programs; classes & workshops; visual arts; participatory exhibits; monthly exhibits of professional artists. Museum Sponsors: County Schools Art Show; Fall Art Exhibit; Town & Country, Photography Show; annual Paint Illinois Exhibit (juried-open to all IL artists).
Publications: bimonthly newsletter.
Hours & Admission Prices: Tues.-Fri. 10-4. No charge. Closed New Year's Eve & Day; Easter; Independence Day; Thanksgiving & day after; Christmas Eve & Day. ♿
Attendance: 5,456 (accurate)
Membership: Student $5; Individual $20; Family $25-$49; Sponsor $50-$99; Benefactor $100-$150; Sustaining $200-$500; Life $1,000 & up.

EDGAR COUNTY HISTORICAL MUSEUM, 408 N. Main, Paris, IL 61944-1549. Tel.: 217-463-5305.
Founded: 1969.
Congressional District: 53
Key Personnel: Pres. (V), Kay Wolfe.
Personnel Profile: Part-Time Volunteers 24.
Governing Authority: society. Affiliated with Edgar County Historical Society, 408 N. Main St., Paris, IL 61944-1549. Tax-exempt: 170(b)(1)(A).
Historical Society Museum: housed in 1876 Arthur House. Listed on the National Register of Historic Places.
Collections: artifacts from Edgar County 19th-century family life; natural history; period clothing & furniture.
Research Fields: genealogical & historical.
Facilities: display areas apart from museum.
Activities: guided tours; lectures; films; docent program or council; field trips; permanent & temporary exhibitions.
Publications: quarterly, Edgar County Historical Society Newsletter.
Hours & Admission Prices: Wed.-Fri. 9-4. No charge; donations accepted. ♿
Attendance: 1,200 (estimated)
Membership: Single $10; Family $15; Individual Life $100; Couple Life $150.

Park Forest

TALL GRASS ARTS ASSOCIATION, 367 Artist Walk, Park Forest, IL 60466-2059. Tel.: 708-748-3377. Fax: 708-748-9132.
E-mail: tallgrass367@sbcglobal.net
Web Site: www.tallgrassarts.org
Founded: 1955.
Key Personnel: Exec. Dir., Roger Paris; Chm. (V), Janet Muchnic.
Personnel Profile: Part-Time Paid 3.
Governing Authority: Tax-exempt.
Art Gallery.
Collections: paintings; fine art.
Facilities: Museum-related items for sale.
Activities: art classes.
Publications: newsletter.
Hours & Admission Prices: Call for hours. No charge; donations accepted. ♿
Attendance: 10,000 (estimated)
Membership: $40, $75; $150; $250.

Park Ridge

WOOD LIBRARY-MUSEUM OF ANESTHESIOLOGY, 520 N. Northwest Hwy., Park Ridge, IL 60068-2538. Tel.: 847-825-5586. Fax: 847-825-1692.
E-mail: wlm@asahq.org
Web Site: www.woodlibrarymuseum.org
Founded: 1950.
Key Personnel: Pres., William D. Hammonds, M.D.; Librarian, Patrick Sim, MLS; Asst. Librarian, Karen Bieterman, MLIS; Cur., Hon. George S. Bause, M.D.; Collections Supvr., Judith Robins; Library Asst., Margaret Jenkins.
Personnel Profile: Full-Time Paid 4; Full-Time Volunteers 1; Part-Time Volunteers 1.
Governing Authority: American Society of Anesthesiologists. Tax-exempt: 501(c)(3).
Medical Museum.
Collections: medical & anesthesiology history; anesthesiology equipment; manuscripts; video oral history; current anesthesia books & journals.
Research Fields: medical & anesthesiology history.
Facilities: 13,000-vol. library of anesthesiology available for inter-library loan & for use on the premises; reading room.
Activities: annual Wood Library-Museum Fellowships; annual historical lectureship; quadriannual election of historian-laureate.
Publications: history of anesthesiology & education in anesthesiology publications; Living History of Anesthesiology (videotaped interviews).
Hours & Admission Prices: Mon.-Fri. 9-4:30. No charge. Closed holidays. ♿
Attendance: 200 (estimated)
Membership: Friends $40; Friends for Life $500.

Paxton

FORD COUNTY HISTORICAL SOCIETY, 145 S. Market St., Paxton, IL 60957-1284. Mailing Address: P.O. Box 115, Paxton, IL 60957-0115. Tel.: 217-379-3723.
E-mail: fordcohistsoc@hotmail.com
Web Site: www.rootsweb.com/~ilford
Founded: 1967.
Congressional District: 15
Key Personnel: Chm. (V), Cynthia Swanson; Chm. (V), Judith Ondercho; Pres. (V), Ed F. Karr.
Personnel Profile: Part-Time Volunteers 4.
Governing Authority: society; nonprofit organization. Parent Institution: Ford County Historical Society. Tax-exempt: 501(c)(3).
Historical Museum: housed in County Court House.
Collections: Indian artifacts of county; pioneer tools; Civil War memorabilia.
Research Fields: local history.
Facilities: library.
Activities: tours.
Publications: Ford County Histories; Prairie Farmer Directory; Ford County History 1985; book, A Ticket to the Best, a socioeconomic history of Paxton, IL 1989; bimonthly newsletter, Ford County Historical; book reprint, Remembrances of a Pioneer; atlases and biographical records for 1876, 1884, 1892, 1901 & 1916; Remembrances of A Pioneer - Autobiography of Jane Patton.
Hours & Admission Prices: Mon.-Fri. 9-5. No charge; donations accepted. Closed national holidays. ♿
Attendance: 3,000 (estimated)
Membership: Regular $5; Life $100.

Peoria

GEORGE L. LUTHY MEMORIAL BOTANICAL GARDEN, 2218 N. Prospect Ave., Peoria, IL 61603-2126. Tel.: 309-686-3362. Fax: 309-685-6240.
Web Site: peoriaparks.org
Founded: 1951.
Congressional District: 18
Key Personnel: Dir., Bonnie Noble; Business Officer, Jan Budzynski; Mgr., Bob Streitmatter; Museum Shop Mgr., Mary Mulay.
Personnel Profile: Full-Time Paid 4; Part-Time Paid 15; Part-Time Volunteers 63; Interns 1.
Governing Authority: municipal. Branch of Peoria Park District. Tax-exempt.
Botanical Garden.
Collections: tropical plants; orchids; woodland garden; rose garden; herb garden; perennial garden; numerous woody ornamentals; spring & fall borders; Hosta Glade.
Facilities: botanical garden; conservatory. Small plants, books & supplies for sale.
Activities: guided tours; lectures; concerts; art shows; study clubs; hobby workshops; formally organized educational programs; permanent & temporary exhibitions; landscape consulting.
Publications: quarterly newsletter, Leaves From The Garden.
Hours & Admission Prices: Conservatory & Gift Shop: Tues.-Sat. 10-5, Sun. 12-5. Admission $2. Outdoor Collections: daily 8:30am to dusk. No charge; donations accepted. ♿
Attendance: 135,000 (estimated)
Membership: Individual $20; Family $30; Contributing $50; Donor $100; Patron $250; Corporate $350 & up.

* **LAKEVIEW MUSEUM OF ARTS AND SCIENCES, (M),** 1125 W. Lake Ave., Peoria, IL 61614-5985. Tel.: 309-686-7000. Fax: 309-686-0280.
E-mail: kathleen@lakeview-museum.org
Web Site: www.lakeview-museum.org
Founded: 1965.
Congressional District: 18
Key Personnel: Pres. & C.E.O., James J. Richerson; Chm. (V), Jim Vergon; Vice Pres. Education, Sheldon Schafer; Vice Pres. Collections, Kristan H. McKinsey; Vice Pres. Devel., Nikki Cole; Vice Pres. Communications, Kathleen Woith; Dir. Exhibitions, Cory Tibbits; Dir. Education, Ann Schmitt; Dir. Preschool, Sherry Woessner; Museum Store Mgr., Linda Gouvia.
Personnel Profile: Full-Time Paid 21; Part-Time Paid 19; Interns 5.
Governing Authority: nonprofit organization. Tax-exempt: 501(c)(3).
General Museum.
Collections: 18th-20th century European & American paintings, sculpture, works on paper, decorative arts; Illinois folk art & duck decoys; Western African, Pre-columbian, Native American, Asian art & artifacts; natural sciences collections including entomological, mineral & fossil collections.
Research Fields: Illinois related artists; collection areas.
Facilities: research library; permanent exhibition area; three changing galleries; planetarium; art & science education wing; enriched preschool; performing arts auditorium; children's discovery center; school loan center; sculpture garden; community solar system model. Illinois Folk Art Gallery. Art objects & used books for sale.
Activities: guided tours; lectures; gallery talks; video; public planetarium shows; workshops & demonstrations; educational programs for children & adults in the arts, sciences & humanities; art, science & ethnic activities; permanent & temporary exhibitions; recycled book sales; school tours; picture person program; school loans.
Publications: monthly newsletter.
Hours & Admission Prices: Museum: Tues.-Sat. 10-4, Sun. 12-4. Adults $6, seniors 60 & over $5, children 3-17 $4; AAM members, members, children 3 & under no charge. Planetarium: adults $4, senior citizens & children 4-17 $3.50; discounts to AAM members. Combo tickets available. Closed major holidays. ♿
Attendance: 139,867 (accurate)
Membership: College Student $28; Individual $40; Grandpass & Family $60; Patron $100; Renaissance $1,000.

THE PEORIA ART GUILD, 203 Harrison St., Peoria, IL 61602-1536. Tel.: 309-637-2787, ext. 2.
Web Site: www.peoriaartguild.org
Contemporary Art Museum.
Collections: contemporary art.
Facilities: Museum-related items for sale.
Activities: studio school. Annual Event: Fine Art Fair.
Hours & Admission Prices: Mon.-Thurs. 10-6, Fri.-Sat. 10-5.

PEORIA HISTORICAL SOCIETY, 611 S.W. Washington St., Peoria, IL 61602-5104. Tel.: 309-674-1921. Fax: 309-674-1882.
Web Site: www.peoriahistoricalsociety.org
Founded: 1934.
Congressional District: 18
Key Personnel: Pres., Marilyn Leyland; Vice Pres., Sid Ruckriegel; Exec. Dir., Amy Kelly; Dir. Collections, Robert Killion.
Personnel Profile: Part-Time Paid 3; Part-Time Volunteers 100; Interns 4.
Governing Authority: incorporated by State of Illinois. Subsidiary Institution: Flanagan House & Pettengill-Morron House. Tax-exempt: 501(c)(3).
Historical Society: housed in c.1837 Flanagan House & 1868 Pettengill-Morron House.
Collections: Pettengill-Morron House, c.1868: furniture; silver; china; glassware; paintings; Oriental rugs; jewelry. Flanagan House, c.1837: carpenter shop with tools; pre-Civil War bedroom; period kitchen; local history artifacts.
Research Fields: local history of industry, recreation, architecture; oral histories; ethnic influences, including Native American, French, African American.
Facilities: library of histories, portrait and biographical albums, journals, legal documents & manuscripts, available for research on the premises; Bradley University Library, available to general public for research; reading room.
Activities: guided tours; lectures; arts festivals; temporary exhibitions; historic bus tours of Peoria. Museum Sponsors: historical lectures; school programs; Christmas season open house and tour.
Publications: bimonthly newsletter, Timeline.
Hours & Admission Prices: Sat. by appointment only. Adults $5, students 15 & under $2; members no charge. Closed holidays.
Attendance: 1,700 (estimated)
Membership: Student $10; Individual $25; Family $35; Contributor $50; Sustainer $100; Patron $250; Sponsor $500; Benefactor $1,000; Distinguished Benefactor $2,500; Director's Circle $5,000.

PEORIA ZOO AT GLEN OAK ZOO, 2218 N. Prospect Rd., Peoria, IL 61603-2126. Tel.: 309-686-3365. Fax: 309-685-6240.
E-mail: info@peoriazoo.org
Web Site: www.peoriazoo.org
Founded: 1955.
Congressional District: 47 & 93
Key Personnel: Dir., Yvonne Strode; Exec. Dir. Parks, Bonnie Noble.
Personnel Profile: Full-Time Paid 18; Part-Time Paid 32; Part-Time Volunteers 60; Interns 5.
Governing Authority: municipal. Parent Institution: Peoria Park District. Tax-exempt.
Zoo.
Collections: over 270 animals including mammals, birds, reptiles, amphibians, fish, & invertebrates representing 110 species.
Facilities: Gift items for sale.
Activities: guided tours; lectures; formally organized educational programs; docent program or council; traveling exhibitions; workshops; rental facilities.
Publications: newsletter, Zoo Tales.
Hours & Admission Prices: Daily 10-5. Adults $7.95, seniors $7.50, children 3-12 $4.25; PZS, AZA, other zoo members and children 2 & under no charge. Closed New Year's Eve & Day; Thanksgiving; Christmas Eve & Day. ♿
Attendance: 181,410 (accurate)
Membership: Individual $40; Joint $60; Grandparent & Family $75; Grandparent & Family Plus $100; Booster $150; Benefactor $300; Patron $500; Pride $1,000.

WHEELS O' TIME MUSEUM, 11923 N. Knoxville Ave., Peoria, IL 61612. Mailing Address: P.O. Box 9636, Peoria, IL 61612-9636. Tel.: 309-243-9020. Fax: 309-243-5616.
E-mail: wotmuseum@aol.com
Web Site: wheelsotime.org
Founded: 1977.
Congressional District: 19
Key Personnel: Pres., Gary O. Bragg; Treas., Fred Roland; Public Rels., Bobbie Rice; Museum Shop Mgr., Janice M. Bragg.
Personnel Profile: Part-Time Paid 2; Part-Time Volunteers 40.
Governing Authority: company organized for profit. Parent Institution: Wheels O' Time, Inc.
Transportation & Mechanical Museum.
Collections: airplanes; vintage & classic automobiles; barber shop with singing quartet; circus; clocks; gas & steam engines; fire engines & equipment; grandma's kitchen; military; tools; toys; tractors; model & full scale trains; washing machines; historical displays.
Facilities: 2,500-vol. library; 18,700 sq. ft. exhibit space. Museum-related items for sale.

Activities: guided tours; loan exhibitions; temporary exhibitions of your own collections; school group tours.
Publications: brochures; quarterly newsletter.
Hours & Admission Prices: May-Oct. Wed.-Sun. 12-5; other times by appointment. Call for admission prices; discounts to AAA members, groups over 20 & handicapped. ♿
Attendance: 6,000

Petersburg

LINCOLN'S NEW SALEM STATE HISTORIC SITE, 15588 History Lane, Petersburg, IL 62675-6010. Tel.: 217-632-4000. Fax: 217-632-4010.
E-mail: newsalemhpa@illinois.com
Web Site: www.lincolnsnewsalem.com
Founded: 1917.
Key Personnel: Site Supt., David Hedrick; Pres., Carol Jenkins; Treas., Ken Costa; Account Clerk, Michele Tella.
Personnel Profile: Full-Time Paid 14; Part-Time Paid 30; Part-Time Volunteers 350; Interns 6.
Governing Authority: state. State of Illinois, Historic Preservation Agency, R.R. 1, Petersburg, IL 62675. Subsidiary Institution: New Salem Lincoln League. Tax-exempt: 501(c)(3).
Village Museum: site of New Salem Village, in the 1830s where Lincoln lived as a young man. Structures are reconstructed.
Collections: twelve timber houses; Rutledge Tavern; 10 shops; stores; industries; school; period artifacts; furnishings; farm tools.
Research Fields: Lincoln & New Salem; local history; pioneer community life; agriculture in 1830s.
Facilities: picnic grounds; campgrounds. Museum-related items for sale.
Activities: self-guided tours; staffed cabins; permanent exhibitions; summer outdoor dramas.
Publications: bimonthly newsletter; brochures.
Hours & Admission Prices: March-April 15 & Sept.-Oct. Wed.-Sun. 9-5; April 16 to Labor Day daily 9-5; Nov.-Feb. Wed.-Sun. 8-4. No charge; donations accepted. Closed New Year's Day; Thanksgiving; Christmas. ♿
Attendance: 600,000
Membership: Annual $15.

STARHILL FOREST ARBORETUM, 12000 Boy Scout Tr., Petersburg, IL 62675-6034. Tel.: 217-632-3685. Fax: 217-632-3685.
E-mail: guy@starhillforest.com
Web Site: www.starhillforest.com
Founded: 1976.
Congressional District: 18
Key Personnel: Owner, Guy Sternberg; Owner, Edie Sternberg.
Personnel Profile: Full-Time Paid 1.
Governing Authority: Parent Institution: Illinois College. Tax-exempt.
Arboretum & Botanical Gardens.
Collections: living plant collections: natural forms & native species of woody arborescent plants; national oak collection for the North American Plant Collections Consortium.
Research Fields: ornamental horticulture; forestry; land architecture; ecology.
Facilities: 1,000-vol. reference library pertaining to horticulture & ecology for use on location only; botanical garden; field research station.
Activities: guided tours; lectures.
Publications: reports; brochures.
Hours & Admission Prices: By appointment only. No charge; donations accepted. ♿
Attendance: 200 (estimated)

Pontiac

CATHERINE V. YOST MUSEUM & ARTS CENTER, 298 W. Water, Pontiac, IL 61764-1757. Mailing Address: 115 W. Howard, Pontiac, IL 61764-1819. Tel.: 815-844-6574 & 5847 (Pontiac tourism).
Key Personnel: Cur., Carol Gardner
Historic House Museum: housed in Queen Anne-style home.
Collections: Yost family furnishings & personal artifacts.
Hours & Admission Prices: May-Dec. by appointment. Admission $2.

LIVINGSTON COUNTY WAR MUSEUM & DAL ESTES EDUCATION CENTER, 321 N. Main St., Pontiac, IL 61764-1929. Tel.: 815-842-0301.
Web Site: www.warmuseum.us
Founded: 2004.
Congressional District: 15
Key Personnel: Pres., Jack Murphy.
Personnel Profile: Full-Time Volunteers 6; Part-Time Volunteers 20.
Governing Authority: bd. dirs.
Military History Museum.
Collections: WWI to present; personal artifacts; uniforms.
Publications: quarterly newsletter.
Hours & Admission Prices: Tues.-Sat. 10-4, Sun. 12-4; other times by appointment. No charge. ♿
Attendance: 10,000
Membership: Annual $20; Life $100.

ROUTE 66 ASSOCIATION HALL OF FAME & MUSEUM, 110 W. Howard St., Pontiac, IL 61764-1820.
History Museum.
Collections: Route 66 history; photographs; plaques; personal artifacts; Hall of Fame inductees.
Hours & Admission Prices: Summer: Mon.-Fri. 9-5, Sat.-Sun. 10-4; Winter: Mon.-Fri. 11-3, Sat.-Sun. 10-4.

Prairie du Rocher

FORT DE CHARTRES STATE HISTORIC SITE & MUSEUM, Fort de Chartres Historic Site, 1350 State Rt. 155, Prairie du Rocher, IL 62277. Tel.: 618-284-7230. Fax: 618-284-7230.
E-mail: ftdchart@htc.net
Founded: 1913.
Congressional District: 22
Key Personnel: Site Mgr., Darrell Duensing; Asst. Mgr., Dennis Thomas; Museum Shop Mgr., Deb Horne.
Personnel Profile: Full-Time Paid 3; Part-Time Paid 4.
Governing Authority: Owned & operated by the State of Illinois Historic Preservation Agency, Old State Capitol, Springfield, IL 62701. Affiliated with Illinois Dept. of Conservation, Bureau of Land & Historic Sites, 405 E. Washington, Springfield, IL 62706. Tax-exempt: 501(c)(3).
State Park Museum & History Museum: located on the original site of the French Fort de Chartes built in 1753.
Collections: historical texts; archaeology; military; tools; weapons; utensils; artifacts; reconstructed period buildings. Historic Building: 1753 powder magazine.
Research Fields: archaeology; French, colonial & military life in North America during the 18th century.
Facilities: 85-vol. library of historical text of the 1720-1772 period available on premises; over 500-vol. non-lending research library open to public with microfilm & microfiche available.
Activities: self-guided tours; lectures; visitor center; permanent exhibitions. Museum Sponsors: annual Traders' Rendezvous; 18th-century kid's weekend; French & Indian War Assemblage.
Publications: brochure.
Hours & Admission Prices: Memorial Day to Labor Day daily 9-4; Sept.-May Wed.-Sun. 9-4. No charge; donations accepted. Closed New Year's Day; Thanksgiving; Christmas. ♿
Attendance: 65,000 (estimated)

Princeton

BUREAU COUNTY HISTORICAL SOCIETY MUSEUM, 109 Park Ave., W., Princeton, IL 61356-1927. Tel.: 815-875-2184.
E-mail: bchsmuseum@yahoo.com
Web Site: www.bureaucountymuseum.com
Founded: 1911.
Congressional District: 17
Key Personnel: Pres., Curt Johnson; Dir., Pam Lange.
Personnel Profile: Full-Time Paid 1; Part-Time Paid 6; Part-Time Volunteers 14.
Governing Authority: nonprofit. Tax-exempt.
Historical Society Museum.
Collections: local lore; family information & photographs of early residents.
Research Fields: genealogy, local county history.
Facilities: 500-vol. library of local history available on premises. Locally made & published books for sale.
Activities: guided tours; permanent exhibitions.
Publications: newsletter.
Hours & Admission Prices: March-Dec. Wed.-Sat. 1-5; group tours by advance reservation. Requested Donation: adults $3, children $1. Closed Easter; Mother's Day; Independence Day; Labor Day; Thanksgiving.
Attendance: 3,358 (accurate)
Membership: Annual $15; Life $150.

Quincy

ALL WARS MUSEUM, Illinois Veterans Home, 1707 N. 12th St., Quincy, IL 62301-1355. Tel.: 217-222-8641, ext. 380. Fax: 217-222-9621.
Key Personnel: Dir., Rick Gengenbacher; Cur., Bob Craig
Military History Museum.
Collections: U.S. military history from the Revolutionary War to present;

military artifacts; photographs; personal artifacts; M60 tank; M5 Stuart Tank; weapons; WWII-Korean War ambulance; jeeps.
Hours & Admission Prices: March-Dec. 1 Tues.-Sat. 9-12 & 1-4, Sun. 1-4. No charge; donations accepted.

THE GARDNER MUSEUM OF ARCHITECTURE & DESIGN, 332 Maine St., Quincy, IL 62301-3929. Tel.: 217-224-6873. Fax: 217-224-0006.
E-mail: gardnermuseum@sbcglobal.net
Web Site: www.gardnermuseumarchitecture.org
Founded: 1974.
Congressional District: 20
Key Personnel: Pres., Susan Deege; Museum Coord., Vicki Ebbing.
Personnel Profile: Full-Time Paid 2; Part-Time Paid 1; Part-Time Volunteers 30.
Governing Authority: nonprofit. Tax-exempt.
Architecture & Design Museum: housed in 1889, Richardsonian Romanesque style Old Public Library.
Collections: architectural artifacts from Quincy & Adams County; stained glass; architectural drawings; historic photographs; files on historic buildings in Quincy & Adams County; stone sculpture yard.
Major Exhibits: Builders & Manufacturers of Quincy, 11/09-8/10; Martin J. Geise - Architect, 11/09-8/10; The Architecture of the Mississippi River, 3/10-12/12.
Research Fields: regional history; regional architecture; state & local architects; the building arts.
Facilities: 600-vol. library pertaining to American architecture, design and architectural preservation.
Activities: guided tours; lectures; permanent, temporary & traveling exhibitions; living history program; walking tours; children's programming.
Publications: bimonthly newsletter; local and regional tour guides; exhibit brochures & catalogues; museum brochures.
Hours & Admission Prices: Gallery & Store: Wed.-Sun. 1-4. Offices & Library: Mon.-Fri. 9-4. Adults $3, children $1.50; members no charge. ♿
Attendance: 5,000 (estimated)
Membership: Individual $20; Family $35; Participating $50; Contributing $100; Supporting $200; Sustaining $500; Benefactor $1,000.

HISTORICAL SOCIETY OF QUINCY AND ADAMS COUNTY, 425 S. 12th St., Quincy, IL 62301-4303. Tel.: 217-222-1835. Fax: 217-222-8212.
E-mail: hsqac@sbcglobal.net
Web Site: www.adamscohistory.org
Founded: 1896.
Congressional District: 17
Key Personnel: Exec. Officer, Judith Winkelmann; Pres. (V), Dave Dulaney; Treas., Ann Busse; Museum Shop Mgr., Joe Winkelmann.
Personnel Profile: Part-Time Paid 5; Part-Time Volunteers 65; Interns 1.
Governing Authority: private; nonprofit organization. Tax-exempt: 501(c)(3).
Historic House Museum: 1835 home of former Governor of Illinois, John Wood, also founder of Quincy.
Collections: items relating to the history of Quincy & Adams County.
Research Fields: local & state history.
Facilities: 1,200-vol. library of history of the Midwest especially Illinois & local area; 80-seat meeting facility; 3,000 sq. ft. exhibit space. Museum-related items for sale.
Activities: guided tours; lectures; temporary exhibits; educational programs; community outreach. Annual Event: Christmas Candlelight tours of Gov. John Wood Mansion.
Hours & Admission Prices: Tours: April-Oct. Tues.-Sat. 10-2. Office: Mon.-Fri. 10-2. Adults $3, children $1.50; members no charge. Closed holidays.
Attendance: 5,500 (estimated)
Membership: Individual $20; Family $35; Sponsor $100; Patron $150; Sustaining $300; Life $1,000.

QUINCY ART CENTER, (M), 1515 Jersey St., Quincy, IL 62301-4250. Tel.: 217-223-5900. Fax: 217-223-6950.
E-mail: jnelson@quincyartcenter.org
Web Site: quincyartcenter.org
Founded: 1923.
Congressional District: 20
Key Personnel: Exec. Dir. & Cur., Julie D. Nelson; Pres., Kevin Curran.
Personnel Profile: Full-Time Paid 2; Part-Time Paid 4; Part-Time Volunteers 96; Interns 4.
Governing Authority: nonprofit organization. Tax-exempt: 501(c)(3).
Art Museum: housed in 1887 carriage house designed by Joseph Lyman Silsbee, mentor of Frank Lloyd Wright.
Collections: paintings; prints; drawings.
Major Exhibits: Jin Lee: Floating World, 1/10-3/10; Pat Badami: Recent Video-based Work, 1/10-3/10; Stephanie Dean: Modern Groceries, 1/10-3/10; 35th Annual High School Student Art Competition, 4/10-5/10; Muddy River Calligraphy Competition, 5/10-7/10; River Shore and Timber Birds: Patrick Gregory and Steve Quiram, 5/10-7/10; Class and Workshop Exhibition, 7/10-8/10; Quincy Artists Guild 58th Annual Show & Sale, 7/10-8/10; Permanent Collection Choices, 7/10-8/10.
Facilities: classroom & studio space including printmaking shop & ceramics studio. Gift items for sale (featuring work by Illinois artists & others).
Activities: temporary exhibits; two annual juried competitions, one serves artists within a 50 mile radius, the other artists residing in Illinois, Iowa, Missouri & Indiana; annual High School Competitive Exhibit; class & workshop program for children & adults; guided tours; tour & hands-on program with area schools; artist demonstration; gallery talks; community outreach program, Art on a cArt.
Publications: calendar of exhibits; exhibition announcements; juried exhibit catalog; Mary S. Oakley Area Artists Showcase brochure; class & workshop flyers.
Hours & Admission Prices: Tues.-Fri. 12-4, Sat.-Sun. 1-4. Adults $3, seniors, students & children $1; discounts to AAM members; members no charge. ♿
Attendance: 14,500 (estimated)
Membership: Senior Citizen $25; Individual $30; Household $40, $75, $100, $150, $250, $500 & up; Business $150, $250, $500, $1,000 & up.

THE QUINCY MUSEUM, (M), 1601 Maine St., Quincy, IL 62301-4264. Tel.: 217-224-7669. Fax: 217-224-9323.
Web Site: thequincymuseum.com
Founded: 1965.
Congressional District: 20
Key Personnel: C.E.O., Barbara Wilkinson; Pres. (V), Andrew Cashman; Volunteer Coord., Jane Hagler; Collections, Jane Huelsmeyer; Exhibits, Floyd Lish.
Personnel Profile: Full-Time Paid 2; Part-Time Paid 7; Part-Time Volunteers 20.
Governing Authority: nonprofit. Parent Institution: The Quincy Museum, Inc. Tax-exempt: 501(c)(3).
Natural History Museum.
Collections: fossils; minerals; oil paintings; Victorian era furnishings; firearms from Revolution to World War II; American Indian artifacts; natural history artifacts; dinosaurs; archaeological; ethnographical; decorative arts.
Research Fields: natural history of the Mississippi River Valley; archaeology; Victorian life.
Facilities: 1,500-vol. library.
Activities: education programming, lectures, field trips, hands-on activities for children.
Publications: monthly newsletter.
Hours & Admission Prices: Tues.-Sun. 1-5. Adults $3, children 5-18 & college students $2; members & children under 5 no charge. ♿
Attendance: 12,700 (accurate)
Membership: Individual $20; Family $35; Patron $100; Business $150 & up; Friend $500; Life $5,000.

Rantoul

CHANUTE AIR MUSEUM, (M), 1011 Pacesetter Dr., Rantoul, IL 61866-3672. Tel.: 217-893-1613. Fax: 217-892-5774.
E-mail: director@aeromuseum.org
Web Site: www.aeromuseum.org
Formerly: Octave Chanute Aerospace Museum
Founded: 1992.
Congressional District: 15
Key Personnel: Dir., Hal Loebach; Pres., Bill Geibel; Vice Pres., Justin Kneeland; Cur., Mark Hanson; Administrative Asst., Robyn York.
Personnel Profile: Full-Time Paid 3; Part-Time Paid 4; Part-Time Volunteers 110.
Governing Authority: private; nonprofit organization.
Aerospace Museum.
Collections: 30 fighter, bomber & training aircraft used by USAAF, USAF & Navy; replicas of JN4D Jenny & Chanute Glider; 3000 artifacts related to air flight, USAAF, USAF & Navy history; ICBM training silos; 100,000 photographs, slides & negatives.
Research Fields: Chanute Air Force Base history from 1917-1993; Illinois aviation; Octave Chanute; aerospace history; military aviation.
Facilities: research library available by appointment; 126,000 sq. ft. exhibit space.
Activities: formally organized education programs for grade & high school students; guided tours; summer camps.
Publications: biannual newsletter; brochure; web site listings.
Hours & Admission Prices: Mon.-Sat. 10-5, Sun. 12-5. Adults $10, senior citizens & retired military $8, students K-8 $5; tours & family groups; children 4 & under and members no charge. Closed New Year's Day; Easter; Thanksgiving; Christmas. ♿
Attendance: 17,000 (estimated)

Membership: Military, Student, Educator & Senior $30; Individual $35; Family $50; Business Crew Chief $100; Patron $250; Family Lifetime $1,000. Business: Pilot $500; Flight Commander $1,000; Operations Officer $2,000; Squadron Commander $3,000; Group Commander $4,000; Wing Commander $5,000.

River Grove

CERNAN EARTH & SPACE CENTER, Triton College, 2000 N. 5th Ave., River Grove, IL 60171-1907. Tel.: 708-456-0300, ext. 3372. Fax: 708-583-3153.
E-mail: cernan@triton.edu
Web Site: www.triton.edu/cernan
Founded: 1974.
Congressional District: 6
Key Personnel: Dir., Bart Benjamin; Production Asst., Dan Troiani; Financial & Membership Coord., Karen Pieranunzi; Technician, Joe Schultz.
Personnel Profile: Full-Time Paid 3; Part-Time Paid 9; Part-Time Volunteers 8.
Governing Authority: college. Parent Institution: Triton College. Tax-exempt: 501(c)(3).
Planetarium.
Collections: meteorites; space hardware of historical interest.
Research Fields: educational uses of media.
Facilities: planetarium; classrooms. Gift items for sale.
Activities: lectures; films; concerts; laser light show; loan & permanent exhibitions.
Publications: bimonthly newsletter; teacher guides; promotional literature.
Hours & Admission Prices: Mon.-Thurs. 9-5, Fri. 9-1 & 6:30-9:30, Sat. 6pm-9:30pm, Sun. 1:30-4:30. Earth and Sky Show: adults $8, children & senior citizens $4. Laser Show: adults $10, children & senior citizens $5. Closed major holidays. ♿
Attendance: 18,854 (accurate)
Membership: Mars $40; Venus $50; Saturn $75; Jupiter $100.

Rock Island

AUGUSTANA COLLEGE ART MUSEUM, 7th Ave. & 38th St., Art & Art History Dept., Rock Island, IL 61201-2296. Mailing Address: 639 38th St., Rock Island, IL 61201-2273. Tel.: 309-794-7231. Fax: 309-794-7678.
E-mail: sherrymaurer@augustana.edu
Web Site: www.augustana.edu/arts/artmuseum
Founded: 1983.
Congressional District: 17
Key Personnel: C.E.O., Steven Bahls; Dir., Sherry C. Maurer; Devel. & Membership, Lynn Jackson; Preparator & Registrar, Al Bieg; Public Rels., Eric Page.
Personnel Profile: Full-Time Paid 1; Part-Time Paid 8; Part-Time Volunteers 2.
Governing Authority: college. Parent Institution: Augustana College. Tax-exempt: 501(c)(3).
Art Museum.
Collections: Swedish-American art; 19th & 20th-century works; Inkstands from Schonstedt collection; Olson-Brandelle North American Indian art.
Major Exhibits: The Olson-Brandelle North American Indian Art Collection, 8/10-10/10.
Research Fields: Swedish-American art; Southwestern Native American Indian art; inkwells
Facilities: 3,310 sq. ft. exhibit space.
Activities: guided tours; lectures; films; concerts; organized education programs for adults & undergraduate college students; loan, temporary & traveling exhibitions.
Publications: annual museum calendar.
Hours & Admission Prices: Sept.-May Tues.-Sat. 12-4. No charge. Closed college holidays. ♿
Attendance: 35,959 (accurate)

BLACK HAWK STATE HISTORIC SITE: HAUBERG INDIAN MUSEUM, 1510 46th Ave., Rock Island, IL 61201-6853. Tel.: 309-788-9536. Fax: 309-788-9865.
E-mail: haubergmuseum@aol.com
Web Site: www.blackhawkpark.org/
Founded: 1927.
Congressional District: 19
Key Personnel: Site Supt., Scott Roman; Museum Dir., Elizabeth Carvey-Stewart.
Personnel Profile: Full-Time Paid 4; Part-Time Volunteers 4.
Governing Authority: state; nonprofit. Parent Institution: Illinois Historic Preservation Agency, Old State Capital, Springfield, IL 62701. Tax-exempt.
State Historic Site Museum: 1740-1831 site of the main villages of the Sauk & Fox Nations.
Collections: dioramas containing life-size figures of Sauk & Fox Indians; depicting daily life in an Indian village; Sauk & Fox material culture; 1933-1935 Civilian Conservation Corps camp photographs & video.
Research Fields: Sauk & Fox Indians; site research.
Facilities: lodge with banquet & meeting rooms.
Activities: guided tours; lectures; changing exhibitions; seminars.
Publications: bimonthly newsletter, Historic Illinois; brochure.
Hours & Admission Prices: March-Oct. daily 9-12 & 1-5; Nov.-Feb. daily 9-12 & 1-4. No charge; donations accepted. Closed New Year's Day; Thanksgiving; Christmas. ♿
Attendance: 32,344 (accurate)

COLONEL DAVENPORT HISTORICAL FOUNDATION, Hillman St. and Mississippi River, Rock Island Arsenal, Rock Island, IL 61299-0001. Mailing Address: P.O. Box 4603, Rock Island, IL 61204-4603. Tel.: 309-786-7336.
E-mail: peterson1@mchsi.com
Web Site: www.davenporthouse.org
Founded: 1978.
Congressional District: 17
Key Personnel: Pres. (V), John Norton; Membership, Kim Yarbrough.
Personnel Profile: Part-Time Volunteers 50.
Governing Authority: society; nonprofit. Tax-exempt: 501(c)(3).
Historical House Museum: George Davenport Home.
Collections: period furniture; personal artifacts.
Research Fields: Col. George Davenport; Native Americans, regional history.
Activities: guided tours; lectures; films; organized educational programs.
Publications: quarterly newsletter, The Cornucopia; periodic historical monographs.
Hours & Admission Prices: May-Oct. Thurs.-Sun. 12-4; Nov.-April by appointment. Families $10, adults $5, students & children $3; senior citizens $3; discounts to YPN Hot Spot, AAA, CDHF & WQPT members. ♿
Attendance: 1,500 (estimated)
Membership: Student $15; Senior Citizen $20; Single $25; Family $30; Patron $50; Sustaining $100; Benefactor $500; Life $2,000.

FRYXELL GEOLOGY MUSEUM, Swenson Hall of Geosciences, Augustana College, 38th St., Rock Island, IL 61201-2296. Tel.: 309-794-7318. Fax: 309-794-7564.
E-mail: glhammer@augustana.edu
Web Site: www.augustana.edu/academics/geology/department/fryxell.htm
Founded: 1929.
Congressional District: 19
Key Personnel: Dir., William R. Hammer.
Personnel Profile: Part-Time Paid 2; Part-Time Volunteers 1.
Governing Authority: college. Parent Institution: Dept. of Geology, Augustana College, Rock Island, IL.
Geology Museum.
Collections: paleontology; fossils; minerals; geology; remote sensing exhibits.
Research Fields: Triassic Antarctic vertebrates.
Facilities: college library is available for museum use.
Activities: guided tours; formally organized education programs; permanent & temporary exhibitions.
Publications: booklet, Fryxell Geology Museum; teacher's tour guide, Discovery Trip to the Fryxell Geology Museum.
Hours & Admission Prices: Sept.-May Mon.-Fri. 8-4:30, Sat.-Sun. 1-4. No charge. Closed holidays. ♿
Attendance: 8,000 (estimated)

JOHN DEERE PLANETARIUM, Augustana College, 639 38th St., Rock Island, IL 61201-2210. Tel.: 309-794-7327, 7000 & 7318. Fax: 309-794-7564.
E-mail: leecarkner@augustana.edu
Web Site: helios.augustana.edu/astronomy
Founded: 1969.
Congressional District: 17
Key Personnel: Dir., Lee Carkner; Sec., Gail Parsons.
Personnel Profile: Part-Time Paid 2; Part-Time Volunteers 1.
Governing Authority: university. Parent Institution: Augustana College, 639-38 St. Tax-exempt.
Planetarium.
Collections: meteorites; space materials.
Research Fields: meteorites.
Facilities: planetarium; 200-seat auditorium; classrooms.
Activities: lectures; films; formally organized education programs for elementary through college students; permanent exhibitions.
Hours & Admission Prices: Gallery: Sept.-May Mon.-Fri. 8-4. Planetarium: by reservation only. No charge. ♿
Attendance: 6,000 (estimated)

ROCK ISLAND ARSENAL MUSEUM, Bldg. 60, Rock Island Arsenal, Rock Island, IL 61299-5000. Mailing Address: 1 Rock Island Arsenal, Attn: IMNE-RIA-PLT, Rock Island, IL 61299-5000. Tel.: 309-782-5021. Fax: 309-782-3598.
E-mail: kris.leinicke@us.army.mil
Web Site: riamwr.com
Formerly: John M. Browing Memorial Museum
Founded: 1905.
Congressional District: 19
Key Personnel: Dir., Kris G. Leinicke; Cur. Collections, William E. Johnson; Registrar, Jodie Creen Wesemann; Resource Center Mgr., Jennifer M. Malone; Cur. Education, Jodean Rousey Murdock; Museum Shop Mgr., Linda Casel; Archives Technician, James L. Jones.
Personnel Profile: Full-Time Paid 6; Part-Time Volunteers 37.
Governing Authority: federal. Parent Institution: U.S. Army Center of Military History. Subsidiary Institution: Rock Island Arsenal Historical Society. Tax-exempt.
Military Museum.
Collections: weapons; equipment.
Research Fields: history of Arsenal Island; military production & development.
Facilities: resource center; theater. Books & museum-related items for sale.
Activities: lectures; inter-museum loan exhibitions.
Publications: books, The Spanish - American War: Its Impact on the Rock Island Arsenal; A Short History of the Rock Island Prison Barracks; An Illustrated History of the Rock Island Arsenal and Arsenal Island.
Hours & Admission Prices: Tues.-Sun. 10-4. No charge; donations accepted. Closed major holidays. ♿
Attendance: 26,886 (accurate)

Rockford

ANDERSON JAPANESE GARDENS, 318 Spring Creek Rd., Rockford, IL 61107-1035. Tel.: 815-229-9390.
Japanese Gardens.
Collections: Japanese plants, flowers, & trees; sculpture.
Facilities: 14-acre site; restaurant; visitors center; nature trails. Museum-related items for sale.
Activities: tours.
Hours & Admission Prices: May-Oct. Mon.-Thurs. 9-5, Fri. 9 am to sunset, Sat. 9-4, Sun. 10-4; Nov.-April call for hours. Adults $7, seniors 62 & over $6, students $5; children 4 & under no charge.

BURPEE MUSEUM OF NATURAL HISTORY, (M), 737 N. Main St., Rockford, IL 61103-6966. Tel.: 815-965-3433. Fax: 815-965-2703.
E-mail: info@burpee.org
Web Site: www.burpee.org
Founded: 1942.
Congressional District: 16
Key Personnel: Chm. (V), Fred Wham; Exec. Dir., Dr. Alan Brown; Dir. Education, Sheila Rawlings; Business Mgr., Rebecca Rydell; Collection Mgr., Scott Williams; Museum Shop Mgr., Holly Ni.
Personnel Profile: Full-Time Paid 11; Part-Time Paid 8.
Governing Authority: nonprofit corporation. Harry & Della Burpee Museum Association. Parent Institution: Rockford Park District. Tax-exempt: 501(c)(3).
Natural History Museum: housed in 1893 Victorian mansion, the Fletcher Barnes home.
Collections: natural history; zoology; geology; science; paleontology; mineralogy; archaeology; anthropology; American Indian; herpetology; herbarium; biology.
Research Fields: invertebrate paleontology.
Facilities: 500-vol. library of reference books, journals & files of publications pertaining to local natural history available on premises or by special arrangements; 42,000 sq. ft. Robert H. Salem wing; picnic area; meeting areas. Books, booklets, specimens, rocks, minerals, shells & miniature models for sale.
Activities: guided tours; lectures; films; study clubs; permanent & temporary exhibitions; pre-school animal adventures hour; natural history classes; field trips; birthday parties; environmental education programs; Dino-digs expeditions.
Publications: triannual newsletter.
Hours & Admission Prices: Mon.-Sat. 10-5, Sun. 12-5. Adults $5; discounts to ASTC members; members no charge. Closed New Year's Day; Easter; Christmas. ♿
Attendance: 111,401 (accurate)
Membership: Individual $50; Families & Grandparents $60.

DISCOVERY CENTER MUSEUM, 711 N. Main St., Rockford, IL 61103-7204. Tel.: 815-963-6769. Fax: 815-968-0164.
E-mail: sarahw@discoverycentermuseum.org
Web Site: www.discoverycentermuseum.org
Founded: 1981.
Congressional District: 16
Key Personnel: Pres. Bd., Harlan Barkley; Exec. Dir., Sarah Wolf; Exhibits Coord., Bruce Quast; Mktg. Mgr., Ann Marie Walker; Operations Mgr., Nancy Blank; Dir. Education & Programs, Corinne Sosso; Education Specialist, Christopher Bernd; Education Specialist, Mike Rathbon; Dir. Devel., Lynn Momberger; Dir. Early Childhood Education, Gloria Svanda; Museum Shop Mgr., Joyce Mazzola.
Personnel Profile: Full-Time Paid 10; Part-Time Paid 18; Part-Time Volunteers 90.
Governing Authority: nonprofit organization. Tax-exempt: 501(c)(3).
Children's Science Museum.
Collections: hands-on exhibits.
Facilities: 400-vol. library of children's science books, available to the public; planetarium; 5,000 sq. ft. auditorium; classrooms; 18,000 sq. ft. exhibit space; 8,000 sq. ft. exhibit space for outdoor science park; working replica of TV news studio. Museum-related items for sale.
Activities: guided tours; formally organized education programs for children; participatory & traveling exhibitions; outreach programs.
Publications: quarterly newsletter, Discover.
Hours & Admission Prices: Mon.-Sat. 10-5, Sun. 12-5. Adults $6, children $5; discount to ASTC & ACM member; members no charge. Closed New Year's Day; Easter; Thanksgiving; Christmas. ♿
Attendance: 136,500 (accurate)
Membership: Grand Pass $55; Family $60; Family Super Pass $100.

THE ERLANDER HOME MUSEUM, (M), 404 S. 3rd St., Rockford, IL 61104-2013. Tel.: 815-963-5559.
E-mail: museum@swedishhistorical.org
Web Site: www.swedishhistorical.org
Founded: 1951.
Congressional District: 16
Key Personnel: Pres., David Peterson.
Personnel Profile: Part-Time Volunteers 150.
Governing Authority: Parent Institute: Swedish Historical Society. Tax-exempt.
Historic House Museum.
Collections: Swedish-American cultural history; Rockford-made furniture; Charlotte Weibull dolls; Swedish immigration to northern Illinois; area Swedish heritage.
Activities: special events; cultural programs.
Publications: monthly, Nyheter; annual, Swedish Heritage.
Hours & Admission Prices: Tues.-Thurs. 1-4, Sun. 2-4.
Attendance: 5,000 (estimated)
Membership: Student $15; Senior $25; Individual $30; Family $40; Life $1,000.

ETHNIC HERITAGE MUSEUM, 1129 S. Main St., Rockford, IL 61101. Mailing Address: P.O. Box 382, Rockford, IL 61105-0382. Tel.: 815-962-7402 & 877-2287. Fax: 815-962-7402.
E-mail: ehm1129@comcast.net
Founded: 1989.
Congressional District: 16
Key Personnel: C.E.O., Pres. & Dir. (V), Sue Lewandowski; Vice Pres. Devel., Shirley DeBenedetto; Education, Marge Price; Education, Rose Costello; Treas., Joanne Baylis; Asst. Cur., Genevieve Sandona; Bldg. & Grounds, John Gagliano.
Personnel Profile: Full-Time Volunteers 4; Part-Time Volunteers 15; Interns 1.
Governing Authority: private; nonprofit organization. Tax-exempt: 501(c)(3).
History Museum.
Collections: 1st settlers of the southwest banks of the Rock River which include African American, Irish, Polish, Italian, Lithuanian & Latino cultures; photographs; folk art; costumes; oral histories.
Major Exhibits: Black History Month and Women's History Month, 2/10-3/10; Easter Tradition - Ethnic Groups Present, 4/10-5/10; Music Festival (Instruments - Folk), 6/10-8/10; Early History of Southwest Rockford, 9/10-10/10; Honoring Community Leaders, 10/10-11/10; Folk Holiday Traditions, 12/10-1/11.
Research Fields: The Crusader, African American newspaper, 1953-1973; oral history of family settlers; The South Rockford News: 1932-1942; Italian history; genealogy.
Facilities: library; 1,500 sq. ft. exhibit space; computer lab. Museum-related items for sale.
Activities: arts festivals; docent program; guided tours; hobby workshops; lectures; participatory & temporary exhibits; girl scouts program (West Annex Bldg.); Head Start program-City Source; genealogy research &

services. Annual Events: Black History Events in February; Celebrating Rockford's Women in March; Italian, Polish & Lithuanian Folk Art workshop in April; International Music Festival in June; Holiday & Christmas Event in December.
Publications: quarterly newsletter.
Hours & Admission Prices: Feb.-Dec. Sun. 2-4; other times by appointment. Special Events: family $5, individual $3; discounts to AAM & ICOM members. Closed New Year's Day & day after; Mother's Day; Memorial Day; Father's Day; Independence Day; Labor Day; Christmas Day & day after. ♿
Attendance: 1,900 (estimated)
Membership: Individual $15; Family $25; Trail Blazers $50 & up; Settlers $100; Pioneer $500; Discoverer $1,000.

KLEHM ARBORETUM & BOTANIC GARDEN, 2715 S. Main St., Rockford, IL 61102-3925. Tel.: 815-965-8146. Fax: 815-965-5914.
E-mail: jsnively@klehm.org
Web Site: www.klehm.org
Formerly: Northern Illinois Botanical Society
Founded: 1989.
Key Personnel: Dir., Jane Snively; Pres. (V), John Richards.
Personnel Profile: Full-Time Paid 5; Part-Time Paid 6; Part-Time Volunteers 3.
Governing Authority: Tax-exempt.
Arboretum & Botanical Garden.
Collections: fountain garden; children's garden; butterfly garden; demonstration garden; over 400 species of trees.
Facilities: library; classrooms; education center.
Activities: guided tours; horticultural programs & classes; concerts; rental facilities.
Hours & Admission Prices: April-Oct. Sun.-Thurs. 9-4, Fri.-Sat. 9-6; Nov.-March Mon.-Sat. 9-4. Adults $6, seniors 65 & over, children 3-18 and students $3; members & Mon. no charge. Closed New Year's Eve & Day; Thanksgiving; Christmas Eve & Day. ♿
Attendance: 75,000 (estimated)
Membership: Senior $20; Individual $30; Senior Family $40; Family $50.

MIDWAY VILLAGE MUSEUM, (M), 6799 Guilford Rd., Rockford, IL 61107-2613. Tel.: 815-397-9112. Fax: 815-397-9156.
E-mail: info@midwayvillage.com
Web Site: www.midwayvillage.com
Founded: 1970.
Congressional District: 16
Key Personnel: Chm., Jan Jones; Pres., David Byrnes; Administrative Asst., Deb Nau; Coord. Special Events, Jessica MacDonald; Mgr. Site & Operations, Shawn Baxter; Mgr. Customer Svc., Fran Hogan; Cur. Collections, Laura Bachelder; Cur. Education, Mark Herman; Asst. Cur., Carol Nordbrook; Educator, Lydia Cassinelli; Volunteer Coord., Gina Moseley; Business Mgr., Nancy McIntosh; Garden Historian, Tari Rowland; Dir. Mktg., Lonna Converso; Dir. Devel., Ann Hunt; Museum Shop Mgr., Susan Johnson.
Personnel Profile: Full-Time Paid 10; Full-Time Volunteers 250; Part-Time Paid 29; Part-Time Volunteers 370.
Governing Authority: nonprofit. Midway Village. Branch Museum: Old Dolls' House Museum. Tax-exempt: 170(b)(1)(A).
History Village Museum: 26 historic turn-of-the-century buildings located on 137 acres.
Collections: Camp Grant military artifacts; industrial building with machines & display of local industries; artifacts & research materials relevant to local history; plumbing shop; hospital; hotel; period artifacts; gardens. Historic Buildings: 1874, Harlem Town Hall; 1892, Holcomb Bank; 1870 farmhouse; 1902 Stone School; 1880 Church; 1900s blacksmith shop; 1860s Breckenridge House; 1855 jail; hardware store; general store; millhouse; fire station; print shop; police station; 1850, 1902 barns; 1910 barn silo; 1922 water tower; 1838 Marsh house; 1890s Pepper house; 1910 Ralston house; 1840s Mowry Brown house; 1860 Chamberlain Hotel.
Research Fields: exhibit projects.
Facilities: library; classrooms; banquet facilities. Museum-related items for sale.
Activities: guided tours; 1890 school enrichment program for children; formally organized education programs for children, adults & college students affiliated with Rock Valley College; lecture series; field trips; rental facilities; reenactments; docent program or council; Visions of the Past living history program; Summer Camps for Kids. Special Events: All Hallows Eve; Baseball & Barbershop; Bikes & Kites; Sock Monkey Madness Festival; World War II reenactment; Model Train Show; Vintage Baseball play by 1850s rules; Chautauqua; Scarecrow Harvest Festival; Holiday Traditions; Mystery Dinners; Victorian Wedding; Victorian Teas.
Publications: quarterly newsletter, Artifacts; Goldenrod Series of books for use in schoolhouse.
Hours & Admission Prices: Museum Center, Mill House & Old Dolls' House Museum: Jan.-April & Sept.-Dec. Tues.-Fri. 10-4, Sat. 10:30-4, May-Aug. Tues.-Fri. 10-4, Sat.-Sun. 10:30-4. Village: May Thurs.-Sun. 11-4; June-Aug. Tues.-Sun. 11-4; Sept.-April by appointment. Office: Mon.-Fri. 8:30-5. Adults $6, children 3-17 $4; discounts to senior citizens & AAM members; members no charge. Special Events: adults $6, children 3-17 $4; members no charge. Closed major holidays. ♿
Attendance: 306,929 (accurate)
Membership: Senior $25; Individual $30; Senior Family $50; Family $55; Kent Society $500-$999; 1834 Society $1,000 & up.

ROCKFORD ART MUSEUM, (M), 711 N. Main St., Rockford, IL 61103-7204. Tel.: 815-968-2787. Fax: 815-316-2179.
E-mail: staff@rockfordartmuseum.org
Web Site: www.rockfordartmuseum.org
Founded: 1913.
Congressional District: 16
Key Personnel: Pres., Lisa Lindman; Exec. Dir., Linda Dennis; Office Mgr., Nancy Sauer; Coord. Education, Stacey Sauer; Dir. Education, Elizabeth Dailing; Coord. Communications, Dave Dixon; Community Rels. Coord., Sarah McNamara; Registrar, Jeremiah Blankenbaker; Customer Svc. Coord., Carrie Johnson.
Personnel Profile: Full-Time Paid 8; Part-Time Paid 2; Part-Time Volunteers 450.
Governing Authority: nonprofit organization. Tax-exempt: 501(c)(3).
Art Museum.
Collections: American masters; American photography; contemporary glass art; modern & contemporary art; outsider art; history of art slide collection.
Research Fields: 19th- & 20th-century American art; photography; glass; outsider art.
Facilities: library of books & periodicals dealing with all aspects of the visual arts available for use by appointment; 17,000 sq. ft. exhibit space; classrooms; auditorium. Museum-related items for sale.
Activities: guided tours; educational programs; permanent, temporary & traveling exhibitions; lectures; special openings. Museum Sponsors: annual Greenwich Village Art Fair; Young Artist Show; Art in the Garden and Evergreen Ball; fundraising galas.
Publications: exhibition announcements; brochures; exhibition catalogs; quarterly, members publication; educator's guide, Year in Review.
Hours & Admission Prices: Mon.-10-5, Sun. 12-5. Adults $6, seniors & students $3; children under 12, members & Tues. no charge. Closed New Year's Day; Thanksgiving; Christmas. ♿
Attendance: 42,380 (accurate)
Membership: Student $20; Individual $35; Family $50; Contributor $100; Benefactor $250; Sustainer $500; Patrons' Circle $1,000.

ROCKFORD COLLEGE ART GALLERY/CLARK ARTS CENTER, 5050 E. State St., Rockford, IL 61108-2393. Tel.: 815-226-4105. Fax: 815-394-5167.
E-mail: cwatters@rockford.edu
Founded: 1847.
Congressional District: 16
Key Personnel: Dir., Carey Watters.
Governing Authority: Rockford College. Tax-exempt: 501(c)(3).
College Art Gallery.
Collections: 20th century paintings; prints; photography; ceramics; drawings; installations, assemblage; ethnographic art; prints by modern & contemporary masters.
Facilities: 1,400 sq. ft. exhibit space.
Activities: guided tours; lectures; organized education programs for college students; loan, temporary & traveling exhibitions.
Publications: art exhibition catalogs: Hollis Sigler, Breast Cancer Journal: Walking with the Ghosts of My Grandmothers; The New Woman in Chicago, 1910-1945: Paintings from Illinois Collections; No Feathers: Manifest Destiny Indicted; Prodigal Daughter; Studio Faculty, Rockford College Art Dept.; To Print Magnificently: Early Modern & Contemporary prints from the Rockford College Collection; Judy Chicago: Thinking About Trees.
Hours & Admission Prices: Sept.-May Tues. 12-3, Wed. 6pm-8pm, Thurs.-Sun. 3-6. No charge; donations accepted. ♿

TINKER SWISS COTTAGE MUSEUM, (M), 411 Kent St., Rockford, IL 61102-2915. Tel.: 815-964-2424. Fax: 815-964-2466. TDD: 815-963-3323.
E-mail: info@tinkercottage.com
Web Site: www.tinkercottage.com
Founded: 1943.
Congressional District: 16
Key Personnel: Dir. & Museum Shop Mgr., Beverly Broyles; Cur., Donna Langford; Visitor Svcs., Steve Litteral.
Personnel Profile: Full-Time Paid 3; Part-Time Paid 2; Part-Time Volunteers 76.

Governing Authority: not-for-profit; volunteer board of trustees; Rockford Park district. Tax-exempt: 990(a) & 501(c)(3).
Historic House Museum: 1865 Swiss-style home built by Robert H. Tinker.
Collections: original Tinker household furnishings, art, manuscripts & ephemera; reconstructed 1891 suspension bridge.
Research Fields: Robert Tinker diaries, personal letters, records & correspondence.
Facilities: education/visitor center; rose garden. Museum-related items for sale.
Activities: guided tours. Museum Sponsors: Ice Cream Social; Victorian Christmas guided tours; workshops; programs for schools, seniors, families & civic groups.
Publications: brochure; quarterly newsletter, Tinker Topics; general brochure; grounds tour brochure.
Hours & Admission Prices: Tours: Jan.-Feb. by appointment; March-Dec. Tues.-Sun. 1, 2 & 3; groups of 8 or more by appointment. Adults $5, senior citizens 65 & up $4, children 5-17 $2; discounts to Time Traveler, AASLH, AAA, AAM & ICOM members; members & children 5 & under no charge. Closed New Year's Day; Good Friday; Easter; Memorial Day; Independence Day; Labor Day; Thanksgiving; Christmas Eve & Day. ♿
Attendance: 10,000 (estimated)
Membership: Senior Citizen $15; Individual $20; Family $35; Patron $60; Donor & Business $100; Sustainer $200; Silver Plate Club $500.

Rockton

MACKTOWN, A LIVING HISTORY EDUCATION CENTER, 2221 Freeport Rd., Rockton, IL 61072-1817. Mailing Address: P.O. Box 566, Rockton, IL 61072-0566. Tel.: 815-624-4200. Fax: 815-624-4200.
E-mail: macktown1@verizon.net
Web Site: www.macktownlivinghistory.com
Founded: 1952.
Congressional District: 16
Key Personnel: Pres. (V) Macktown, A Living History Education Center, Ray Ferguson; Pres. Rockton Historical Society, Marilyn Mohring.
Personnel Profile: Full-Time Volunteers 2; Part-Time Volunteers 30.
Governing Authority: county; society. Parent Institution: Winnebago County Forest Preserve District. Affiliated with Rockton Township Historical Society. Tax-exempt.
Historic Houses: 1839 Stephen Mack House, two-story farm house, home to one of the first white settlers in Winnebago County; 1846 Whitman Trading Post, limestone building.
Collections: period artifacts & furnishings; cradle made by Stephen Mack; early wooden woodworking tools; 1830s heritage garden.
Research Fields: new archaeological dig.
Facilities: garden.
Activities: school programs; permanent exhibitions; archaeology digs; tours; cultural programs; workshops; special programs & events. Museum Sponsors: pre-1850s reenactment in April; Antiques Roadshow; Mother-Daughter Tea; 1830s Christmas Breakfast.
Publications: semiannual newsletter.
Hours & Admission Prices: Fri.-Sat. 10-2, Sun. 12-4. No charge; donations accepted.
Attendance: 6,500 (estimated)
Membership: Pioneer $25; Frontiersman $50; Trader $100; Corporate $500; Lifetime $1,000.

Romeoville

ISLE A LA CACHE MUSEUM, 501 E. Romeo Rd., Romeoville, IL 60446-1538. Tel.: 815-886-1467.
Web Site: www.fpdwc.org/isle.cfm
Founded: 1983.
Personnel Profile: Full-Time Paid 5; Part-Time Volunteers 15.
Governing Authority: Parent Institution: Forest Preserve District at Will County. Tax-exempt.
History Museum.
Collections: exhibits of the French fur trade; birch bark canoe; Native American artifacts including metal, beads & cloth.
Hours & Admission Prices: Tues.-Sat. 10-4, Sun. 12-4. ♿

Roscoe

HISTORIC AUTO ATTRACTIONS, 13825 Metric Dr., Roscoe, IL 61073-7607. Tel.: 815-389-9999. Fax: 800-779-6461.
Web Site: www.historicautoattractions.com
Founded: 2001.
Congressional District: 16
Key Personnel: Dir., Wayne Lensing; Treas., Cathy Ellis.
Personnel Profile: Full-Time Paid 1.
Governing Authority: private.
History Museum.
Collections: presidential & world leaders' cars & limousines; Kennedy artifacts; WWII history; Hollywood, crime & Western memorabilia; racing & television artifacts.
Research Fields: presidential history; American political history in relation to the White House.
Facilities: Museum-related items for sale.
Activities: Annual Events: Lensing Autumn Classic Car Show; Annual Motorcycle Show.
Hours & Admission Prices: Memorial Day to Labor Day Tues.-Sat. 10-5, Sun. 11-4; Sept.-Nov. Sat. 10-5, Sun. 11-4. Adults $10, senior citizens $8, students $6; children under 6 no charge. Season Pass: $25. ♿
Attendance: 6,000 (estimated)

Rosemont

DONALD E. STEPHENS MUSEUM OF HUMMELS, 5555 N. River Rd., Rosemont, IL 60018. Tel.: 847-692-4000.
E-mail: stephensmuseum@rosemont.com
Web Site: www.stephenshummelmuseum.com
General Museum.
Collections: over 1,000 M.I. Hummel figurines & ANRI woodcarvings.
Facilities: Museum-related items for sale.
Activities: tours.
Hours & Admission Prices: Call for hours. No charge.

Roxana

WOOD RIVER REFINERY HISTORY MUSEUM, Rte. 111, Roxana, IL 62084. Mailing Address: P.O. Box 76, Roxana, IL 62084-0076. Tel.: 618-255-3718.
Governing Authority: nonprofit organization.
History Museum.
Collections: refinery history; period artifacts; early cars; photographs.
Hours & Admission Prices: Wed.-Thurs. 10-4.

Rushville

SCHUYLER JAIL MUSEUM, 200 S. Congress St., Rushville, IL 62681-1410. Tel.: 217-322-6975.
Founded: 1968.
Key Personnel: Pres., Lillian Hoover; Cur., Maryjane Busby.
Governing Authority: nonprofit organization. Parent Institution: Schuyler-Brown Historical & Genealogical Society, Congress & Madison Sts., Rushville, IL 62681. Tax-exempt.
Historical Society Museum: housed in 1857-58 Schuyler Jail.
Collections: local memorabilia of Schuyler County; genealogy.
Research Fields: genealogy.
Facilities: library of genealogical books available for members of society; reading room.
Activities: guided tours.
Publications: quarterly magazine, The Schuylerite.
Hours & Admission Prices: April-Nov. daily 1-5; Dec.-March Sat.-Sun. 1-5. No charge; donations accepted. Closed major holidays. ♿
Membership: Individual $15.

Russell

RUSSELL MILITARY MUSEUM, 43363 Old Hwy. 41, Russell, IL 60075. Tel.: 847-395-7020. Fax: 847-395-7025.
E-mail: ksonday@db3mail.com
Web Site: www.russellmilitarymuseum.com
Formerly: Kenosha Military Museum
Founded: 1986.
Key Personnel: Dir., Mark Sonday; Museum Shop Mgr., Joyce Sonday.
Governing Authority: Tax-exempt.
Military Museum.
Collections: Ch-54 Skycranes; C-130 Hercules; WWI French howitzer; WWII Higgins boat; M-4 Sherman tanks; M-48 bridge layer; M-41 Walker Bulldog tank; Vietnam era river patrol boat; Huey helicopters; experimental hovercraft.
Facilities: Museum-related items for sale.
Activities: auction; birthday parties; school, scout & group specials.
Hours & Admission Prices: March-May & Sept.-Jan. Tues.-Sun. 10-5; Memorial Day to Labor Day daily 10-5. Adults 13 & over $7.50, children & seniors $5; children 2 & under no charge. ♿
Attendance: 20,000 (estimated)

Saint Charles

BEITH HOUSE MUSEUM, 8 W. Indiana St., Saint Charles, IL 60174-2829. Mailing Address: c/o PPFV, P.O. Box 903, Saint Charles, IL 60174-0903. Tel.: 630-377-6424. Fax: 630-377-6424.
E-mail: info@ppfv.org
Web Site: www.ppfv.org/beith.htm
Key Personnel: Dir., Elizabeth Safanda
Historic House Museum: housed in the home of Kane County stone mason, William Beith, built in 1850.
Collections: period furnishings; personal artifacts; photographs; archaeological remains.
Major Exhibits: Kids Dig Archaeology, 11/09-12/10; Is He or Isn't She?, 11/09-1/11.
Facilities: library of historical research & conservation resources.
Activities: Museum Sponsors: Old House Mysteries; Archaeology Dig; Is He or Isn't She Challenge.
Publications: preservation partners of the Fox Valley's Advocate.
Hours & Admission Prices: May-Oct. Tues. 1-4; other times by appointment. Suggested Donations: $1 per person, $3 per family.

DURANT HOUSE MUSEUM, 37W370 Dean St., Saint Charles, IL 60175. Mailing Address: P.O. Box 903, Saint Charles, IL 60174-0903. Tel.: 630-377-6424. Fax: 630-377-6424.
E-mail: info@ppfv.org
Web Site: www.ppfv.org/durant.htm
Historic House Museum: farmstead built in 1843.
Collections: period furnishings; personal artifacts; period tools & equipment.
Major Exhibits: Summer Frolic, 7/10; Pickling Party, 8/10; Bread & Butter, 9/10; Autumn Frolic, 10/10; Christmas on the Prairie, 12/10.
Activities: seasonal programs; educational programs by appointment.
Publications: preservation partners of the Fox Valley's Advocate.
Hours & Admission Prices: June-Aug. Thurs. & Sun. 1-4; Sept.-Oct. Sun. 1-4. Suggested Donation: adults $2, children $1.

ST. CHARLES HERITAGE CENTER, (M), 215 E. Main St., Saint Charles, IL 60174-2040. Tel.: 630-584-6967. Fax: 630-584-6077.
E-mail: info@stcmuseum.org
Web Site: www.stcmuseum.org
Founded: 1933.
Key Personnel: Pres., Laura Haule; Registrar, Julie Bunke.
Personnel Profile: Full-Time Paid 2; Part-Time Paid 1; Part-Time Volunteers 40; Interns 3.
Governing Authority: society; nonprofit. Subsidiary Institution: Dunham-Hunt Museum. Tax-exempt.
Historical Museum: housed in 1920s era gas station & a c.1840 historic house.
Collections: local history from Native American occupation to present; local history archive; Percheron horse archive materials; 1841 Sheldon Peck painting.
Research Fields: local history.
Facilities: library; 2,500 sq. ft. exhibit space.
Activities: guided tours; lectures; organized educational programs; permanent & temporary exhibitions; architectural quest; living history events.
Publications: quarterly newsletter, The Charlemagne Newsletter; booklets, Celebrating History-A Pictorial Essay of St. Charles; Reflections of St. Charles; The Potawatomi, A Native American Legacy; St. Charles In The Civil War; City Lights.
Hours & Admission Prices: Call for hours. No charge; donations accepted. Closed most holidays. ♿
Attendance: 6,000 (estimated)
Membership: St. Charles Junior Historical Society Age 9-14 $10; Individual $25; Family $40; Patron $125; Corporate $250; Sponsor $500; Benefactor $1,000.

Sandwich

SANDWICH HISTORICAL SOCIETY/STONE MILL MUSEUM, 315 E. Railroad, Sandwich, IL 60548-2241. Mailing Address: P.O. Box 82, Sandwich, IL 60548-0082. Tel.: 815-786-2513.
Founded: 1969.
Congressional District: 14
Key Personnel: Pres. (V), Pat Clapper.
Personnel Profile: Part-Time Volunteers 20.
Governing Authority: society; nonprofit. Parent Institution: Sandwich Historical Society. Tax-exempt.
Historical Society Museum: housed in an 1856 mill.
Collections: Indian artifacts; barbwire collection; local artifacts; manuscript collection; blacksmith tools; oldtime fire equipment; toys; military memorabilia; patent models; kitchen; dental parlor; bedroom; parlor; children's playroom clothes closet; farm machines; tools; c.1909 Regal touring car; early equipment manufactured in Sandwich; local artifacts.
Research Fields: Indian artifacts; farm machinery; carpenter & blacksmith tools.
Facilities: library of newspapers from Sandwich used for genealogy, reading room. Gifts for sale.
Activities: guided tours.
Hours & Admission Prices: April-Oct. Sun. 1-4; other times by appointment. No charge; donations accepted. Closed holidays.
Attendance: 1,500 (estimated)
Membership: Individual $10; Family $20.

Schaumburg

SPRING VALLEY NATURE CENTER & HERITAGE FARM, (M), 1111 E. Schaumburg Rd., Schaumburg, IL 60194-3648. Tel.: 847-985-2100. Fax: 847-985-9692.
Web Site: www.parkfun.com
Formerly: Spring Valley Nature Sanctuary & Volkening Heritage Farm
Founded: 1983.
Key Personnel: Exec. Dir., Jean Schlinkmann; Conservation Svcs. Mgr., David Brooks.
Personnel Profile: Full-Time Paid 10; Part-Time Paid 20; Part-Time Volunteers 250.
Governing Authority: municipal; nonprofit. Parent Institution: Schaumburg Park District. Tax-exempt.
Natural History Museum & Sanctuary; Living History Farm.
Collections: 1848 house; c.1875 dairy barn; c.1880 summer kitchen & smokehouse.
Research Fields: taxonomical study.
Facilities: 1,000-vol. library for public use; 8,500 sq. ft. earth-sheltered, passive solar interpretive center; 135 acres total; 3.5 miles handicapped accessible trails; native habitat greenhouse; Discovery Niches; meeting room. Honey, maple syrup, nature books, pamphlets, animal puppets & bird feeders for sale.
Activities: guided tours; lectures; films; study clubs; hobby workshops; organized education programs; docent program; participatory exhibits; outreach environmental education program. Museum Sponsors: Maple Syrup Fair; Autumn Pioneer Festival; Christmas In the Valley; Backyards for Nature Fair; Halloween Ghost Jaunt; Junior Girl Scout Badge Workshops.
Publications: bimonthly newsletter, Natural Enquirer; brochures, Spring Valley Nature Sanctuary; trail map; self-guiding trail book; Group Venture Program; Step Into the Wild Volunteer Program.
Hours & Admission Prices: Grounds: April-Oct. daily 8-8; Nov.-March daily 8-5. Visitors Center: daily 9-5. Farm Site: April-Oct. Tues.-Fri. 9-2, Sat.-Sun. 10-4; special events & groups by appointment. No charge; donations accepted. Closed New Year's Day; Thanksgiving; Christmas. ♿
Attendance: 85,000 (estimated)
Membership: Spring Valley Nature Club: Student & Senior Citizen $5; Family $10; Contributing $15; Supporting $25; Life $100; Sponsoring $1,000.

Skokie

SKOKIE HERITAGE MUSEUM & LOG CABIN, (M), 8031 Floral Ave., Skokie, IL 60077-3605. Tel.: 847-674-1500, ext. 3000; 677-6672.
Web Site: www.skokieparkdistrict.org
Founded: 1992.
Key Personnel: Facility Mgr., Amanda Hanson.
Personnel Profile: Full-Time Paid 1; Part-Time Paid 3; Part-Time Volunteers 3.
Governing Authority: Parent Institution: Skokie Park District. Subsidiary Institution: Skokie Historical Society. Tax-exempt.
History Museum.
Collections: period furnishings; fire department equipment. Historic Buildings: Engine House; 1847 log cabin.
Activities: classes; educational school programs; special events.
Hours & Admission Prices: Museum: Thurs.-Fri. 12-4, Sat.-Sun. 10-2. Log Cabin: by appointment. No charge; donations accepted. ♿
Attendance: 4,740 (estimated)

South Elgin

FOX RIVER TROLLEY MUSEUM/FOX RIVER TROLLEY ASSOCIATION, 361 S. La Fox (IL Rte. 31), South Elgin, IL 60177. Mailing Address: P.O. Box 315, South Elgin, IL 60177-0315. Tel.: 847-697-4676.
E-mail: info@foxtrolley.org
Web Site: www.foxtrolley.org
Founded: 1958.
Congressional District: 14
Key Personnel: Pres. (V), Edward J. Konecki; Public Rels., Don MacBean; Museum Shop Mgr., Laura Taylor.

Personnel Profile: Part-Time Volunteers 300.
Governing Authority: private; nonprofit organization.
Trolley Museum.
Collections: 25 cars & 2 diesel locomotives; maintain & operate 2.5 miles of trolley track.
Research Fields: interurban & street cars of the Greater Chicago area.
Facilities: Museum-related items for sale.
Activities: hobby workshops. Museum Sponsors: Caboose Day in Spring & Fall; Trolley Fest in late August; Pumpkin & Haunted Trolley in October.
Publications: quarterly newsletter, Fox River Lines; annual visitor's guide, Trolley Times.
Hours & Admission Prices: May 11-June 27 & Sept. Sun. 11-5; June 28-Aug. Sat.-Sun. 11-5; Oct. Sun. 11-5, Sat. call for hours. One Ride: adult $3.50, senior 65 & up and child 3-11 $2, each additional ride $.50. All day ticket: $7 per person; discount to groups of 20 or more.
Attendance: 10,500 (accurate)
Membership: Associate $25; Family $40.

South Holland

SOUTH HOLLAND HISTORICAL SOCIETY, 16250 Wausau Ave., South Holland, IL 60473-2199. Mailing Address: Box 48, South Holland, IL 60473-0048. Tel.: 708-596-2722.
Founded: 1969.
Congressional District: 3
Key Personnel: Pres. (V), Robin Scheldberg; Vice Pres., Bill Paarlberg; Sec., Carol Strand; Treas., Joyce Becker; Acting Cur., Edward Smith.
Personnel Profile: Part-Time Volunteers 20.
Governing Authority: society; nonprofit organization. Tax-exempt.
Historical Society Museum: housed in Village Library.
Collections: clothing; jewelry; books; tools; military; local memorabilia; diorama of South Holland in the 1920s. Historic Houses: 1869 Paarlberg Farm; 1858 Van Oostenbrugge Homestead.
Research Fields: local family histories.
Facilities: library of church books & newspaper clippings available for research on premises.
Activities: guided tours.
Publications: newsletter, The Onionskin.
Hours & Admission Prices: Sat. 1-4. Adults $1, children $.50; members no charge. ♿
Attendance: 300 (estimated)
Membership: Regular $10; Business $25; Life $100.

Springfield

ABRAHAM LINCOLN PRESIDENTIAL LIBRARY & MUSEUM, 212 N. 6th St., Springfield, IL 62701-1004. Tel.: 1-800-610-2094.
E-mail: HPA.info@illinois.gov
Web Site: www.presidentlincoln.org
Founded: 2005.
Key Personnel: Exec. Dir., Jan Grimes; Deputy Dir., Jennifer Tirey; State Historian, Thomas Schwartz, II; Cur. Lincoln, James Cornelius; Dir. Library Svcs., Kathryn M. Harris; ALPLM Foundation, Rene Brethorst; Dir. Guest Svcs., Clare Thorpe; Dir. Research & Collections, Thomas Schwartz; Education Program, Randy Wiseman; Volunteer Svcs. Coord., Linda Bee; Museum Shop Mgr., Amy Miller.
Governing Authority: Parent Institution: State of Illinois. Subsidiary Institution: Illinois Historic Preservation. Tax-exempt.
Historical Library & Museum.
Collections: Abraham Lincoln; Illinois history; genealogy; Illinois newspapers; Civil War; books; maps; manuscripts; photographs; Lincolniana.
Major Exhibits: Team of Rivals, 10/10-8/11.
Facilities: library; restaurant; Union Station Visitors Center. Museum-related items for sale.
Activities: Union Square Park: outdoor performances & events.
Publications: Foundation newsletter, Four Score and Seven.
Hours & Admission Prices: Library: Mon.-Fri. 9-5. Museum: daily 9-5. Research: call for appointment. Adults 16-61 $10, students, military and seniors 62 & over $7, children 5-15 $4; discounts to AAA members; children under 5 no charge. Closed New Year's Day; Thanksgiving; Christmas. ♿
Attendance: 600,000 (accurate)
Membership: Basic & National Associate $60; Family $75; Family Plus $100; Circuit Rider $300; Railsplitter $500; Presidents' Cabinet $1,000.

THE DANA-THOMAS HOUSE STATE HISTORIC SITE, 301 E. Lawrence Ave., Springfield, IL 62703-2232. Tel.: 217-782-6776 & 6773. Fax: 217-788-9450.
E-mail: dthf@warpnet.net
Web Site: dana-thomas.org
Founded: 1981.
Congressional District: 20
Key Personnel: Foundation Exec. Dir., Regina Albanese.
Personnel Profile: Full-Time Paid 3; Part-Time Paid 6; Part-Time Volunteers 110; Interns 1.
Governing Authority: state. Parent Institution: The Illinois Historic Preservation Agency. Tax-exempt: 501(c)(3).
Historic House Museum: 1902 Frank Lloyd Wright prairie period house.
Collections: original Wright-designed oak furniture; zinc-camed art glass; historic photographs; family documents; decorative arts; archival building documents.
Research Fields: turn-of-the-century arts & crafts; household arts; period architecture.
Facilities: 250-vol. library pertaining to Frank Lloyd Wright & architectural material available to the public; 45-seat orientation auditorium. Bookshop with Dana House, Frank Lloyd Wright & architecture-related material available.
Activities: guided tours; lectures; films; concerts; organized educational programs; docent program.
Publications: quarterly, Dana-Thomas House Foundation Newsletter, Wright in Springfield; monthly, Volunteer Interpreter Newsletter.
Hours & Admission Prices: Wed.-Sun. 9-5; last tour at 4. Suggested Donation: adults $5, children 3-17 $3; school classes no charge. Closed some state holidays.
Attendance: 40,000 (accurate)
Membership: The Dana-Thomas House Foundation: Supporter $35; Contributor $50; Donor $75-$125; Sponsor $250; Patron $500; Lifetime Individual $2,500.

HENSON ROBINSON ZOO, 1100 E. Lake Dr., Springfield, IL 62712-5536. Tel.: 217-753-6217. Fax: 217-529-8748.
E-mail: hrzoodir@aol.com
Web Site: www.hensonrobinsonzoo.org
Founded: 1970.
Key Personnel: Dir., Talon J. Thornton; Gift Shop Mgr., Kim Davis; Education, Emily McEvoy; Asst. Dir. & Cur., Jackie Peeler.
Personnel Profile: Full-Time Paid 16; Part-Time Paid 15; Part-Time Volunteers 80.
Governing Authority: municipal; not-for-profit. Parent Institution: Springfield Park District. Tax-exempt: 501(c)(3).
Zoo.
Collections: zoological.
Research Fields: reproductive biology with lemurs & felines; endangered species survival programs for lemurs, tamarins, cheetahs & red wolves.
Facilities: 125-vol. zoological related library; zoological park. Plush animals & zoo-related items for sale.
Activities: guided tours. Annual Events: Spring Opening Festival; Fall Closing Festival; Safe Halloween at Zoo.
Publications: quarterly newsletter, Cougar Chronicle.
Hours & Admission Prices: April-Oct. Mon.-Fri. 10-5, Sat.-Sun. 10-6; Nov.-March daily 10-4. Adults $4.00, seniors over 62 $2.50, children 3-12 $2.25; members and children 2 & under no charge. ♿
Attendance: 103,546 (accurate)
Membership: Individual $25; Family $35; Donor $60; Patron $100; President's Club $250-$499; Life $500.

ILLINOIS STATE MILITARY MUSEUM, Dept. of Military Affairs, 1301 N. MacArthur, Springfield, IL 62702-2317. Tel.: 217-761-3910. Fax: 217-761-3709.
Key Personnel: Dir., Mark Whitlock
Military History Museum.
Collections: military vehicles, aircraft, weapons, uniforms & equipment; flags; photographs; documents.
Facilities: library.
Activities: outreach programs.
Hours & Admission Prices: Tues.-Sat. 1-4:30; other times by appointment.

* **ILLINOIS STATE MUSEUM, (M),** 502 S. Spring St., Springfield, IL 62706-5000. Tel.: 217-782-7387. Fax: 217-782-1254. TTY: 217-782-9175.
E-mail: webmaster@museum.state.il.us
Web Site: www.museum.state.il.us
Founded: 1877.
Congressional District: 20
Key Personnel: Museum Dir., Dr. Bonnie W. Styles; Bd. Chm. Illinois State Museum Board, Dr. R-Lou Barker; Assoc. Dir., Karen A. Witter; Dir. Resource Allocation, C.F.O. & Human Resources Dir., Charlotte A. Montgomery, CPA; Dir. Art, Kent Smith; Asst. Dir. Art, Robert Sill; Exhibits Design, Joe Hennessy; Exhibits Prep., Paul Countryman; Education Chair, Beth Shea; Asst. Cur. Education, Nina Walthall; Anthropology Chair, Dr. Terry Martin; Cur. Anthropology, Dr. Robert Warren; Cur.

Anthropology, Dr. Jonathan Reyman; Geology Chair, Dr. Jeffrey J. Saunders; Cur. Geology, Dr. Chris Widga; Botany Chair, Dr. Eric Grimm; Assoc. Cur. Botany, Dr. Hong Qian; Zoology Chair, Dr. Everett D. Cashatt; Asst. Cur. Zoology, Dr. Meredith Mahoney; Asst. Cur. Zoology, H. David Bohlen; Librarian, Pat Burg; Assoc. Cur. Technology, Dr. Erich Schroeder; Dickson Mounds Museum Dir., Dr. Michael Wiant; Assoc. Cur. Dickson Mounds Museum, Dr. Michael Conner; Illinois Artisans Program Dir., Carolyn Patterson; Lockport Gallery Dir., Jim Zimmer; Illinois State Museum Chicago Gallery Asst. Gallery Admin., Jane Stevens; Southern Illinois Art & Artisans Center, Mary Lou Galloway; Southern Illinois Art Gallery Assoc. Cur., Debra Tayes; Museum Shop Mgr., Cheryl Staley.

Personnel Profile: Full-Time Paid 89; Full-Time Volunteers 21; Part-Time Paid 32; Part-Time Volunteers 122; Interns 15.

Governing Authority: state. Parent Institution: Illinois Dept. of Natural Resources. Branch Museums: Dickson Mounds Museum, Lewistown, IL 61542; Illinois State Museum Chicago Gallery, Chicago, IL 60601; Illinois State Museum Lockport Gallery, Lockport, IL 60441; Southern Illinois Art & Artisans Center, Whittington, IL 62897. Tax-exempt.

Natural History & Art Museum.

Collections: anthropology; archaeology; botany; geology; zoology; entomology; herbarium; herpetology; natural history; paleontology; fine art; decorative arts; art history of Illinois.

Research Fields: anthropology; archaeology; botany; ethnography; geology; paleobotany; paleoecology; paleontology; vertebrate paleontology; zoology; arts in Illinois.

Facilities: 10,000-vol. library of primarily scientific reference books & reports pertaining to the collections, publications & reprints by museum staff; laboratory center for study of prehistoric culture & environments.

Activities: guided tours; films; lectures; gallery talks; formally organized education programs; inter-museum loan, permanent, temporary, & traveling exhibitions; docent program; archaeological & paleontological field expeditions.

Publications: quarterly magazine, The Living Museum; quarterly periodical, Transactions of the Illinois State Academy of Science; quarterly periodical, Impressions; occasional popular & scientific publications.

Hours & Admission Prices: Mon.-Sat. 8:30-5, Sun. 12-5. No charge; donations accepted. Closed New Year's Day; Thanksgiving; Christmas. ♿

Attendance: 355,097 (accurate)

Membership: Individual $35; Family $50; Contributing $100; Sustaining $300; Life $500.

ILLINOIS STATE POLICE HERITAGE FOUNDATION MUSEUM, 4000 N. Peoria Rd., Springfield, IL 62702-1033. Tel.: 217-525-1922.

Founded: 2000.

Key Personnel: Pres., Joe Davis.

Governing Authority: Tax-exempt.

Police History Museum.

Collections: automobiles; police equipment & uniforms; photographs.

Publications: newsletter; brochure.

Hours & Admission Prices: Thurs. & Sat. 10-2. Suggested Donation: $1. Closed holidays. ♿

Attendance: 200 (estimated)

KOREAN WAR NATIONAL MUSEUM, 303 N. 5th St., Springfield, IL 62705-0299. Mailing Address: P.O. Box 299, Springfield, IL 62705-0299. Tel.: 888-295-7212.

E-mail: kwnm@kwnm.org

Web Site: www.kwnm.org

Founded: 1997.

Congressional District: 15

Key Personnel: C.E.O., Larry Sassorossi; Pres., Wes Stapleton; Treas., Merle Sims; Sec., Neil D. Hurley; Exec. Sec., Sharon Corum.

Personnel Profile: Full-Time Paid 3; Part-Time Volunteers 8.

Governing Authority: private; nonprofit organization. Tax-exempt: 501(c)(3).

Military & War Museum.

Collections: Korean War memorabilia; photographs; documents; books; artifacts.

Major Exhibits: POW/MIA's of Korean War, 1/10-6/10.

Research Fields: unit histories; Korean War; casualty documentation.

Facilities: library of books related to Korean War.

Activities: lectures.

Publications: newsletter, The Forgotten Voices; brochure.

Hours & Admission Prices: Tues.-Sat. 9-5, Sun. 1-5. Office: Mon.-Fri. 8-5. Suggested donation $3. Closed major holidays. ♿

Attendance: 20,000 (estimated)

Membership: Veteran $25; Veteran Family $30; General Public $35; General Public Family $40; Corporate Civic $50; Sponsor $100; Life $300.

LINCOLN DEPOT, 930 Monroe St., Springfield, IL 62701-1612. Tel.: 217-544-8695 & 788-1356.

Historic Building: housed in the former depot from which Lincoln left Springfield to start his inaugural journey to Washington DC. on Feb. 11, 1861.

Collections: Lincoln history; personal artifacts; period furnishings; photographs.

Hours & Admission Prices: May-Aug. daily 10-4.

LINCOLN HERDON LAW OFFICES STATE HISTORIC SITE, 112 N. Sixth St., Springfield, IL 62701. Mailing Address: Old State Capitol Complex, Springfield, IL 62701. Tel.: 217-785-7289. Fax: 217-557-0282.

Web Site: www.illinoishistory.gov

Founded: 1970.

Congressional District: 20

Key Personnel: Mgr., Justin Blanford; Foundation Chm., Sandy Pecori; Volunteer Coord., Sandy Temple; Museum Shop Mgr., Ron Hohman; Museum Shop Mgr., Dana Hohman.

Personnel Profile: Full-Time Paid 8; Full-Time Volunteers 50; Part-Time Paid 8; Part-Time Volunteers 50.

Governing Authority: state agency. Parent Institution: Illinois Historic Preservation Agency. Tax-exempt.

State Historic Site: located in 1840-1841 three-story commercial Greek Revival building built by Springfield merchant Seth M. Tinsley across from the 1839 Illinois Statehouse, now the Old State Capital Historic Site.

Collections: 19th-century law office & Federal Court Complex furnishings; 1841-1849 recreated Post Office; Lincoln's legal career historic site.

Facilities: Museum-related items for sale.

Activities: annual Illinois Statehood Day - Dec. 3rd.

Hours & Admission Prices: Sat. 9-4; last tour leaves 45 minutes before closing. Requested Donations: adults $2, children $1. Closed New Year's Eve & Day; Martin Luther King Jr. Day; Presidents' Day; Veterans' Day; Thanksgiving; Christmas; any general election day. ♿

Attendance: 30,000 (accurate)

Membership: Old State Capitol Complex Foundation (Support Group) $15; $40; $100; $250; $500.

LINCOLN HOME NATIONAL HISTORIC SITE, 413 S. 8th St., Springfield, IL 62701-1905. Tel.: 217-492-4241, ext. 221. Fax: 217-492-4673. TDD: 217-492-4244.

Web Site: www.nps.gov/liho

Founded: 1972.

Congressional District: 20

Key Personnel: Park Supt., James A. Sanders; Cur., Susan M. Haake; Historian, Timothy P. Townsend; Chief Operations, Kathleen DeHart; Museum Shop Mgr., David Mull.

Personnel Profile: Full-Time Paid 41; Part-Time Paid 30; Part-Time Volunteers 30; Interns 2.

Governing Authority: federal. Parent Institution: National Park Service, Dept. of the Interior, Washington, DC. Tax-exempt.

Historic District & Historic House Museum: Home of Abraham Lincoln, 16th President of the United States.

Collections: house furnishings; artifacts relating to & associated with the Lincoln family; architecture; archeology; archives.

Research Fields: historic structure report; historic landscape plan; historic furnishings plan.

Facilities: visitor center. Publications & museum-related items for sale.

Activities: guided tours & walks; dramatizations; lectures; films; audio-visual programs; formally organized educational programs; costumed interpretation programs; street theater.

Publications: brochure; information sheet; books; quarterly newsletter.

Hours & Admission Prices: Daily 8:30-5. tickets to entrance available on first-come, first serve basis at Visitor's Center. No charge; donations accepted. Closed New Year's Day; Thanksgiving; Christmas. ♿

Attendance: 259,948 (accurate)

LINCOLN MEMORIAL GARDEN AND NATURE CENTER, 2301 E. Lake Dr., Springfield, IL 62712-8908. Tel.: 217-529-1111. Fax: 217-529-0134.

E-mail: lmg2301@comcast.net

Web Site: www.lmgnc.org

Founded: 1935.

Congressional District: 20

Key Personnel: Exec. Dir., Jim Matheis; Pres., Joan Walters; Education Dir. & Naturalist, Betsy Irwin; Museum Shop Mgr., Jackie Carey.

Personnel Profile: Full-Time Paid 4; Part-Time Paid 5; Part-Time Volunteers 100; Interns 1.

Governing Authority: nonprofit organization. Tax-exempt: 501(c)(3).

Arboretum & Nature Center.

Collections: living flora & fauna native or naturalized to central Illinois.
Research Fields: prairie propagation; prairie & native Illinois landscape restoration; protection & propagation of endangered species; maintaining Jens Jensen designed landscape.
Facilities: 300-vol. library of books on plant & animal taxonomy, general information & natural science interpretation available for research; botanical garden; nature center; 110 acres; 5 miles of trails. Hand crafted nature-related items & science books for sale.
Activities: guided tours; lectures; formally organized education programs for children, adults, undergraduate & graduate college students affiliated with University of Illinois at Springfield; temporary exhibitions.
Publications: newsletter, Nature Center News.
Hours & Admission Prices: Tues.-Sat. 10-4, Sun. 1-4. No charge; donations accepted. Building: closed Easter; Independence Day; Thanksgiving; Christmas week. ♿
Attendance: 50,000 (estimated)
Membership: Senior Citizen $25; Individual $30; Family $50; Business $75; Railsplitter $100; Life $300; Life Couple $500.

LINCOLN TOMB STATE HISTORIC SITE, Oak Ridge Cemetery, Springfield, IL 62702. Mailing Address: 1500 Monument Ave., Springfield, IL 62702-2500. Tel.: 217-782-2717. Fax: 217-524-3738.
Founded: 1874.
Congressional District: 20
Key Personnel: Site Mgr., Nan L. Wynn; Site Service Specialist, Mikle Sierre; Site Interpreter, Luke Cummins; Maintenance, James Thompson.
Personnel Profile: Full-Time Paid 4; Part-Time Paid 4; Part-Time Volunteers 5.
Governing Authority: state. A part of the State of Illinois, Illinois Historic Preservation Agency, Old State Capitol, Springfield, IL 62701. Tax-exempt.
Historic Site: 1874, the tomb of Abraham Lincoln.
Collections: c.1865, public vault where Lincoln's body first lay; burial place of Abraham Lincoln, Mary Todd Lincoln, Edward Baker Lincoln, William Wallace Lincoln, Thomas Lincoln.
Research Fields: President Lincoln's funeral train; funeral services; public reaction.
Activities: oral presentations; flag ceremonies; memorial services; veterans and fraternal organization ceremonies; Boy Scout Pilgrimage. Site Sponsors: Tuesday evening formal flag lowering ceremonies & troop inspections by the 114th Regiment of the Illinois Volunteer Infantry June-August.
Publications: bimonthly newsletter, Historic Illinois; brochure.
Hours & Admission Prices: Tues.-Sat. 9-5. No charge. Closed New Year's Day; Martin Luther King Jr. Day; Presidents' Day; Veterans' Day; General Election Day; Thanksgiving; Christmas. ♿
Attendance: 345,000 (accurate)

MUSEUM OF FUNERAL CUSTOMS, 215 S. Grand Ave. W., Springfield, IL 62704-3838. Tel.: 217-544-3480. Fax: 217-544-3484.
E-mail: funeralmuseum@ifda.org
Web Site: www.funeralmuseum.org
Founded: 2000.
Congressional District: 18
Key Personnel: Dir., Jon N. Austin; Pres. (V), Paula Staab Polk.
Personnel Profile: Full-Time Paid 2; Part-Time Paid 1; Part-Time Volunteers 7; Interns 2.
Governing Authority: private; nonprofit organization. Tax-exempt: 501(c)(3).
History Museum.
Collections: American funeral & mourning customs; history of undertaking & funeral directing from 1840 to present; art & science of embalming; funeral rite, coffin & casket styles; memorialization; interment; grief & mourning.
Research Fields: U.S. Patents related to undertaking.
Facilities: 1,000-vol. library; 3,600 sq. ft. exhibit space. Museum-related items for sale.
Activities: guided tours; lectures; loan & temporary exhibitions. Annual Events: Symposium in October; poetry reading in March.
Publications: seven themed brochures related to funeral history and mourning.
Hours & Admission Prices: Tues.-Sat. 10-4, Sun. 1-4. Adults $4, senior citizens $3, students $2; discounts to AAM members; members and children 5 & under no charge. Closed New Year's Day; Independence Day; Thanksgiving & day after; Christmas. ♿
Attendance: 7,685 (accurate)

OLD STATE CAPITOL, Fifth at Adams Sts., 1 Old State Capitol Plaza, Springfield, IL 62701-1507. Mailing Address: Illinois Historic Preservation Agency, 112 N. Sixth St., Springfield, IL 62701-1310. Tel.: 217-785-7960. Fax: 217-557-0282. TDD: 217-524-7128.
E-mail: hpa.info@illinois.gov
Web Site: www.illinoishistory.gov
Founded: 1969.
Congressional District: 20
Key Personnel: C.E.O., Justin A. Blanford; Chm. Support Group (V), Sandy Pecori; Volunteer Coord., Sandy Temple; Museum Shop Mgr., Ron Homann; Museum Shop Mgr., Dana Homann.
Personnel Profile: Full-Time Paid 8; Full-Time Volunteers 50; Part-Time Paid 8; Part-Time Volunteers 50.
Governing Authority: state. Parent Institution: Illinois Historic Preservation Agency: Subsidiary Institution: Historic Sites Division. Tax-exempt.
Historic Building: 1839-1876, Illinois's fifth Statehouse.
Collections: period & original furnishings.
Research Fields: Lincolniana.
Facilities: Museum-related items for sale.
Activities: guided tours; costumed interpreters on Fri.-Sat.; first person interpretation & third person. Special Events: candlelight tours; statehood day in Dec.; naturalization ceremonies; Holocaust Observance; youth outreach.
Publications: Old State Capitol brochure; elementary school study guide; quarterly newsletter.
Hours & Admission Prices: Tues.-Sat. 9-5. Old State Capitol: no charge; donations requested. Lincoln Herndon Law Offices State Historic Site: Sat. 9-4 (217-785-7289). Adults $2, children 3-17 $1. Closed New Year's Day; Martin Luther King Jr. Day; Washington's Birthday; Veterans Day; Thanksgiving; Christmas. ♿
Attendance: 108,000 (accurate)
Membership: Old State Capitol Foundation (Support Group) $15; $40; $100; $250; $500.

THE PEARSON MUSEUM, 801 N. Rutledge, Springfield, IL 62702-4910. Mailing Address: S.I.U. School Medicine, P.O. Box 19635, Springfield, IL 62794-9635. Tel.: 217-545-8017 & 4261. Fax: 217-545-7903.
E-mail: probertson@siumed.edu
Web Site: www.siumed.edu/medhum/pearson
Founded: 1974.
Congressional District: 20
Key Personnel: Dir. & Devel. Dir., Phillip V. Davis, Ph.D.; Registrar, Allona Beasley Mitchell; Business Mgr., Patricia Robertson, M.A.
Personnel Profile: Part-Time Paid 3.
Governing Authority: university. Parent Institution: Southern Illinois University. Subsidiary Institution: School of Medicine. Tax-exempt: 501(c)(3).
University Medical Science Museum.
Collections: medical, dental & pharmaceutical artifacts; graphic art; photographs; slides.
Research Fields: 19th & early 20th-century medicine, dentistry & pharmacy practice in the upper Mississippi River basin area.
Facilities: auditorium; classrooms; teaching theatre; laboratory.
Activities: guided tours; permanent, temporary & traveling exhibitions.
Hours & Admission Prices: Tues 8:30-4:30; group tours by appointment. No charge; donations accepted. ♿
Attendance: 6,000 (estimated)
Membership: Friends of the Pearson Museum $50 & up.

SHEA'S GAS STATION MUSEUM, 2075 Peoria Rd., Springfield, IL 62702-1837. Tel.: 217-522-0475.
History Museum.
Collections: station history; gas pumps; signs; photographs; service station memorabilia; personal artifacts.
Hours & Admission Prices: Tues.-Sat. 7-4; other times by appointment. Admission $2.

SPRINGFIELD ART ASSOCIATION, 700 N. Fourth St., Springfield, IL 62702-5232. Tel.: 217-523-2631. Fax: 217-523-3866.
E-mail: office@springfieldart.org
Web Site: www.springfieldart.org
Founded: 1913.
Congressional District: 17
Key Personnel: Pres. (V), Jane Locascio; Education Coord., Katie Rasmussen; Exec. Dir., Betsy Dollar; Admin. Asst., Megan Metzger; Library Dir., Jan Dungey; Librarian, Mark Jenkins; Asst. Dir. & Cur., Amanda Gleason.
Personnel Profile: Full-Time Paid 4; Part-Time Paid 2; Part-Time Volunteers 150; Interns 3.
Governing Authority: nonprofit organization. Tax-exempt: 501(c)(3).
Historic Home: c.1833.
Collections: 19th & 20th-century paintings; African sculptures; Oriental artifacts: ceramic, bronze, glass, jewelry; eight rooms of 19th-century & early American furniture.
Major Exhibits: Scholastic Art Exhibit, 1/10-2/10.
Research Fields: Asian collection; African sculpture; George Peter Alexander Healy, portrait painter.
Facilities: art library; classrooms.
Activities: guided tours; lectures; films; gallery talks; arts festivals; formal

organized educational programs for children, adults & undergraduate college students; permanent & temporary exhibitions; art outreach program with local schools.
Publications: quarterly bulletin; exhibitions & collections catalogues.
Hours & Admission Prices: House Tours: Tues.-Sat. 11-2. Library: Mon.-Fri. 9-5, Sat. 10-3. Gallery: Mon.-Fri. 10-5, Sat. 10-3. No charge; donations accepted. Closed New Year's Day; President's Day; Columbus Day; Labor Day; Thanksgiving & day after; Christmas Eve, Day & week. ♿
Attendance: 1,000 (estimated)
Membership: College Student $35; Art Educator $40; Individual $55; Family & Dual $75; Patron $150; Sustainer $250; Benefactor $500; Thomas Condell Circle $750; Edwards Place Society $1,000 & up.

STATE OF ILLINOIS-HISTORIC PRESERVATION AGENCY, HISTORIC SITES DIVISION, (M), 313 S. 6th St., Springfield, IL 62701-1805. Tel.: 217-785-1584. Fax: 217-785-8117.
E-mail: hpa.info@illinois.gov
Web Site: www.illinoishistory.gov
Founded: 1985.
Congressional District: 20
Key Personnel: Dir., Jan Grimes; Chm. (V), Julie Cellini; Acting Supt. Historic Sites, Karen Everingham; Capital Projects, Jane Rhetta; Exhibits, Steve Leonard; Collections, Linda Norbut Suits; Historian, Mark Johnson; Conservator, Malcolm Brown.
Governing Authority: state. Branch Museums: Albany Mounds; Bishop Hill; Black Hawk; Bryant Cottage; Buel House; Cahokia Courthouse; Cahokia Mounds; Campbell's Island Memorial; Carl Sandburg Birthplace; Dana Thomas House; David Davis Mansion; Douglas Tomb; Emerald Mound; Fort de Chartres; Fort Kaskaskia; Governor Bond Memorial; Governor Coles Memorial; Governor Horner Memorial; Grand Village of the Illinois; Halfway Tavern; Hofmann Tower; Illinois Vietnam Veterans Memorial; Jarrot Mansion; Jubilee College; Kaskaskia Bell Memorial; Kincaid Mounds; Korean War Memorial; Lewis and Clark Memorial; Lincoln-Herndon Law Offices; Lincoln Log Cabin; Lincoln Monument Memorial; Lincoln Tomb; Lincoln Trail Memorial; Lincoln's New Salem; Lovejoy Memorial; Martin/Boismenue House; Metamora Courthouse; Moore Home; Mt. Pulaski Courthouse; Norwegian Settlers Memorial; Old Market House; Old State Capitol; Pierre Menard Home; Postville Courthouse; Pullman; Rose Hotel; Shawneetown Bank; U.S. Grant Home; Vachel Lindsay Home; Vandalia Statehouse; Washburne House; Wild Bill Hickok Memorial; Apple River Fort. Tax-exempt.
State Agency.
Collections: period furnishings; buildings; art; artifacts; primary source materials.
Research Fields: state & local history.
Activities: guided tours; lectures; restoration; interpretation; special events; audiovisual presentations; living history; outreach interpretive programs.
Publications: brochures for individual sites; bimonthly newsletter, Historic Illinois.
Hours & Admission Prices: Call for hours & admission information. No charge; donations accepted. ♿
Attendance: 2,800,000 (accurate)

VACHEL LINDSAY HOME STATE HISTORIC SITE, 603 S. Fifth St., Springfield, IL 62703-1604. Tel.: 217-524-0901. Fax: 217-557-0282.
Web Site: www.illinois-history.gov
Founded: 1946.
Congressional District: 20
Key Personnel: Mgr. Old State Capitol Complex, Justin Blandford; Admin., Jennie Battles.
Personnel Profile: Full-Time Paid 1; Part-Time Volunteers 10.
Governing Authority: nonprofit organization. Parent Institution: Illinois Historic Preservation Agency. Tax-exempt.
Historic House: 1846 home of Vachel Lindsay.
Collections: drawings; letters; manuscripts; books; paintings; sculpture; videotapes.
Facilities: library of poetry, prose & records of the poet. Museum-related items for sale.
Activities: lectures; gallery talks; resource & referral service; poetry & music programs.
Publications: book, City Is Not Builded in a Day; DVD, Look Into Your Heart: The Challenge of Vachel Lindsay, available through The Vachel Lindsay Association.
Hours & Admission Prices: Tours: Tues.-Sat. 12-4; groups of 10 or more by appointment. Suggested Donations: adults $4, students $2.
Attendance: 1,956 (estimated)
Membership: The Vachel Lindsay Association: Individual $25; Family $35; Patron $50; Sustaining $100; Benefactor $250; Life $2,500.

WASHINGTON PARK BOTANICAL GARDEN, 1740 W. Fayette, Springfield, IL 62704-2356. Tel.: 217-753-6228. Fax: 217-546-0257.
E-mail: chad@springfieldparks.org
Founded: 1972.
Congressional District: 20
Key Personnel: Exec. Dir., Michael Stratton; Superintendent Botanical Garden, Chad Scaife; Park Bd. Pres., Leslie Sgro.
Personnel Profile: Full-Time Paid 6; Part-Time Paid 6; Part-Time Volunteers 5.
Governing Authority: municipal. Parent Institution: Springfield Park District. Tax-exempt.
Botanical Garden.
Collections: tropical plants; roses; iris; cacti; trees; perennials.
Major Exhibits: Rainforest Festival, 2/10-3/10; Spring Floral Show, 3/10-4/10; Photography Displays, 5/10; Photography Displays, 8/10-9/10; Prairie Festival, 9/10-10/10; Winter Holiday & Poinsettia Show, 12/10.
Facilities: 162-vol. library pertaining to horticulture & botany; conservatory; educational facilities; alphabet garden; butterfly garden.
Activities: guided tours; lectures; organized educational programs. Annual Events: seasonal shows.
Publications: quarterly newsletter, The Washington Park Botanical Garden News.
Hours & Admission Prices: Mon.-Fri. 12-4, Sat.-Sun. 12-5; tours by appointment. No charge; donations accepted. Closed Thanksgiving; Christmas Eve & Day. ♿
Attendance: 110,000 (estimated)
Membership: Individual $5; Family $8.

Sterling

STERLING-ROCK FALLS HISTORICAL SOCIETY MUSEUM, 1005 E. 3rd. St., Sterling, IL 61081-2813. Mailing Address: 1005 E. Third St., P.O. Box 65, Sterling, IL 61081-2813. Tel.: 815-622-6215.
E-mail: srfhs@comcast.net
Web Site: www.svonline.net/~srfhs
Founded: 1959.
Congressional District: 15
Key Personnel: Dir. & Cur., Terence Buckaloo; Pres. (V), David B. Lowe.
Personnel Profile: Full-Time Paid 1; Part-Time Volunteers 20; Interns 1.
Governing Authority: nonprofit. Parent Institution: Sterling-Rock Falls Historical Society. Tax-exempt: 501(c)(3).
Historical Society Museum.
Collections: local general history; Indian & pioneer heritage; rare books; military; archives; paintings; industrial.
Major Exhibits: Lincoln in the Rock River Valley, 11/09-12/10; Ronald Regan in Whiteside County, 8/10-12/11.
Research Fields: local history; Indian & pioneer heritage; genealogy; historical structures.
Activities: guided tours; gallery talks; formally organized education programs for children.
Hours & Admission Prices: Tues., Thurs. & Sat. 10-12 & 1-4, Sun. 1-5. No charge; donations accepted. ♿
Attendance: 2,700 (accurate)
Membership: Individual $15; Family $25; Sustaining $50; Business $100; Life $300.

Stockton

STOCKTON HERITAGE MUSEUM, 107 W. Front Ave., Stockton, IL 61085-1317. Mailing Address: P.O. Box 93, Stockton, IL 61085-0093. Tel.: 815-947-9144.
Key Personnel: Dir. & Cur., Bobbi Reagan; Pres. (V), Melody Heidenreich.
Personnel Profile: Part-Time Volunteers 28.
Governing Authority: Tax-exempt: 501(c)(3).
History Museum.
Collections: local history; Kraft Cheese; Chicago Great Western Railroad.
Publications: quarterly newsletter.
Hours & Admission Prices: May-Dec. Sat. 9-1. No charge; donations accepted. ♿
Attendance: 450 (estimated)
Membership: Students $5; Seniors $10; Couple $20; Family $25.

Stone Park

ITALIAN CULTURAL CENTER OF CASA ITALIA, 1621 N. 39th Ave., Stone Park, IL 60165-1186. Tel.: 708-345-3842. Fax: 708-345-3891.
Web Site: www.casaitaliachicago.net
Key Personnel: Chm., Leonardo S. DeFranco; Dir. Exhibits, Josetta Mentesana Weber
Italian Heritage Museum.
Collections: contemporary art; local history.
Facilities: library.

Hours & Admission Prices: Mon.-Fri. 10-4; group tours by appointment.

Sugar Grove

AIR CLASSIC INC. MUSEUM OF AVIATION, 43W624 U.S. 30, Sugar Grove, IL 60554. Tel.: 630-466-0888.
Web Site: www.airclassicsmuseum.org
Congressional District: 14
Key Personnel: Pres., Mike Luman; Vice Pres., Lawrence Matt
Aviation & Military Museum.
Collections: planes from the Korean War II to Desert Storm.
Hours & Admission Prices: Tues.-Sun. 10-3; other times by appointment. Adults $5, seniors $4, children 6-18 $3; children under 6 no charge. Closed major holidays.
Attendance: 3,000 (estimated)
Membership: Student $15; Individual $30; Family $45.

Sycamore

MIDWEST MUSEUM OF NATURAL HISTORY, 425 W. State St., Sycamore, IL 60178-1410. Tel.: 815-895-9777; 866-895-6664 (Toll Free). Fax: 815-899-2552.
E-mail: questrelations@mmnh.org
Web Site: www.mmnh.org
Key Personnel: Exec. Dir., Chris Brodnicki
Natural History Museum.
Collections: preserved animals from around the world.
Facilities: classroom; cafeteria.
Activities: hands-on exhibits; school group programs.
Hours & Admission Prices: Mon.-Sat. 9-5, Sun. 12-5. Adults $5, seniors & children $4; discounts to groups of 20 or more; children 2 & under no charge.

SYCAMORE HISTORICAL SOCIETY & MUSEUM, 308 W. State St., Sycamore, IL 60178. Mailing Address: P.O. Box 502, Sycamore, IL 60178-0502. Tel.: 815-895-5762.
E-mail: sychist@tbc.net
Web Site: sycamorehistory.org
Founded: 1999.
Key Personnel: Dir., Michelle Donahoe; Pres. (V), Tom Oestreicher.
Governing Authority: Tax-exempt.
History Museum.
Collections: Sycamore's history & culture; photographs.
Research Fields: local history.
Activities: walking tours in summer; school groups; scouts. Museum Sponsors: monthly Brown Bag Lunch; Cemetery Walk in October.
Publications: newsletter.
Hours & Admission Prices: April-Oct. Tues., Thurs. & Sat. 10-1; Nov-March Tues. & Thurs. 10-1; other times by appointment. No charge; donations accepted. ♿
Attendance: 2,400 (estimated)
Membership: Student $5; Individual $15; Couple & Family $25; Life $150.

Teutopolis

TEUTOPOLIS MONASTERY MUSEUM, Rte. 40, & S. Garrott St., Teutopolis, IL 62467-1161. Tel.: 217-857-3586.
Founded: 1975.
Congressional District: 54
Key Personnel: Pres. (V), Ray Vahling; Vice Pres., Mary Angela Runde; Treas., Henry Hawickhorst; Sec. & Helping Tour Chm., Joyce Vahling; Helping Tour Chm., Eleanor Gebben.
Personnel Profile: Part-Time Volunteers 15.
Governing Authority: church; nonprofit organization. St. Francis Church. Tax-exempt.
Local History Museum: housed in 1862 Franciscan Novitiate.
Collections: furniture used by the Franciscan order; religious items & books; early pioneer artifacts; family portraits; clocks; archives.
Facilities: library of religious material; Teutopolis history; books in 21 languages. Gift items & books for sale.
Activities: guided tours.
Hours & Admission Prices: April-Nov. first Sun. of month 12:30-4; tours by appointment. Adults $3, children $1.
Attendance: 500 (estimated)

Tinley Park

TINLEY PARK HISTORICAL SOCIETY, (M), 6727 W. 174th St., Tinley Park, IL 60477-3529. Mailing Address: P.O. Box 325, Tinley Park, IL 60477-0325. Tel.: 708-429-4210. Fax: 708-444-5099. TDD: 708-444-5000.
E-mail: bbettenh@tinleypark.org
Founded: 1974.
Congressional District: 3
Key Personnel: Chm. (V), Brad L. Bettenhausen; Treas., Marian Block.
Personnel Profile: Part-Time Volunteers 8.
Governing Authority: private; nonprofit organization. Tax-exempt: 501(c)(3).
Historical Society Museum: housed in an 1884 frame church in Prairie Gothic style.
Collections: concentration on history of the Village of Tinley Park & surrounding area integral to its growth & development; ethnic heritage (German) of community & Rock Island Railroad.
Research Fields: history of community until 1900.
Facilities: 40-vol. library of local newspapers; 1,300 sq. ft. exhibit space; 175-person capacity church/meeting room; 90-person capacity kitchen/meeting room.
Activities: docent program; guided tours; temporary exhibitions. Annual Event: Christmas at the Landmark in December.
Publications: quarterly newsletter, New Bremen News.
Hours & Admission Prices: Wed. 10-2; other times by appointment. No charge; donations accepted. Closed federal & state holidays. ♿
Membership: Senior & Student $15; Adult $25; Institutional & Business $50; Supporting $100; Life $250; Founders Circle $500.

Union

DONLEY'S WILD WEST TOWN MUSEUM, 8512 S. Union Rd., Union, IL 60180-9661. Tel.: 815-923-9000. Fax: 815-923-2253.
Web Site: www.wildwesttown.com
Founded: 1975.
History Museum.
Collections: Wild West history & artifacts; cowboy memorabilia including wooly chaps, gun belts, guns, spurs, lariats, & boots; death masks; handcuffs; badges; mining tools & equipment; Civil War; period furnishings including music boxes & phonographs.
Hours & Admission Prices: April-May 24 & Sept. 5-Oct. Sat.-Sun. 10-6; May 25-Sept. 4 daily 10-6. Adults $15; children 2 & under no charge. (museum included in Wild West Town admission).

ILLINOIS RAILWAY MUSEUM, 7000 Olson Rd., Union, IL 60180. Mailing Address: P.O. Box 427, Union, IL 60180-0427. Tel.: 815-923-4391, ext. 404. Fax: 815-923-2006.
E-mail: nkallas@irm.org
Web Site: www.irm.org
Founded: 1953.
Congressional District: 12
Key Personnel: Exec. Dir., Nick Kallas; Pres. (V), Jim Nauer; Museum Shop Co-Mgr., Jennifer Kolanowski.
Personnel Profile: Full-Time Paid 3; Full-Time Volunteers 5; Part-Time Paid 8; Part-Time Volunteers 75.
Governing Authority: nonprofit organization. Tax-exempt: 501(c)(3).
Railway Museum: housed in c.1851 Marengo, Illinois rail depot.
Collections: steam, diesel & electric locomotives; passenger cars; streetcars; interurban cars; rapid transit cars; electric work equipment; box motors & freight; trolley buses; freight cars; motor buses; steam railroad work equipment; signal tower; railroad neon signs. Historic Buildings: 1851 railroad station; 1910 Chicago L Station; O'Mahoney Roadside Diner.
Research Fields: railway technology.
Facilities: 5,000-vol. library of technical railway materials available by request. Books & rail-oriented items for sale.
Activities: films; workshops; inter-museum loan, permanent & temporary exhibitions; rides.
Publications: quarterly newsletter, Rail and Wire.
Hours & Admission Prices: Memorial Day-Labor Day daily 10-4; Spring & Fall Sat.-Sun. 10-5. Admission & rides: adults $12, children $8; discounts to AAM & ICOM members & groups; members no charge.
Attendance: 67,057 (accurate)
Membership: Associate $40; Family $65.

MCHENRY COUNTY HISTORICAL SOCIETY AND MUSEUM, (M), 6422 Main St., Union, IL 60180. Mailing Address: Box 434, Union, IL 60180-0434. Tel.: 815-923-2267. Fax: 815-923-2271.
E-mail: info@mchsonline.org
Web Site: www.mchsonline.org
Founded: 1963.

Congressional District: 8 & 16
Key Personnel: C.E.O., Nancy J. Fike; Pres. (V), Dan Ring; Museum Shop Mgr., Jean Nigbor.
Personnel Profile: Full-Time Paid 3; Part-Time Volunteers 300.
Governing Authority: society. Tax-exempt: 501(c)(3).
Historical Society Museum.
Collections: papers; records of early settlers & the history of McHenry County. Historic Houses: 1847 log cabin; 1867 limestone one-room school house on original site; 1885 Town Hall; 1895 one-room schoolhouse; 1898 country church; 1949 modern tourist cabin; traveling history museum bus, The James.
Major Exhibits: Arrival-The 1890s, 11/09-10/11.
Research Fields: local history; local genealogy.
Facilities: 2,000-vol. library of original land grants; early text books; newspapers; biography files; business, governmental & organization records; diaries & maps available for research; photographs.
Activities: area meetings; special lecture & history programs; formally organized educational programs & tours for adults & students; historic plaque-ing program; traveling history bus.
Publications: quarterly newsletter, The Tracer and Society's Page.
Hours & Admission Prices: May & Oct. Tues.-Fri. & Sun. 1-4; June-Sept. Tues.-Fri. & Sun. 1-4. Adults $5, children & senior citizens 60 and over $3; discounts to AAM members & those who bring nonperishable goods; veterans & members no charge. Closed holidays. ♿
Attendance: 5,500 (estimated)
Membership: Seniors & Students $10; Individual $20; Organizations $25; Couple & Family (includes children in school) $30; Business $100; Life $500.

University Park

NATHAN MANILOW SCULPTURE PARK, GOVERNORS STATE UNIVERSITY, (M), 1 University Pkwy., University Park, IL 60484-3165. Tel.: 708-534-4486. Fax: 708-534-8399. TDD: 708-534-8650.
E-mail: g-bates@govst.edu
Web Site: www.govst.edu/sculpture
Founded: 1969.
Congressional District: 11
Key Personnel: Dir. & Cur., Geoffrey Bates; Chm. (V), Susan Ormsby.
Personnel Profile: Full-Time Paid 1; Part-Time Paid 1.
Governing Authority: public university. Parent Institution: Governors State University. Tax-exempt.
Sculpture Park.
Collections: over 20 works of sculpture.
Facilities: library.
Activities: guided group tours; educational programming; special events.
Publications: brochure; catalog; newsletter.
Hours & Admission Prices: Dawn to dusk. No charge; donations accepted.
Attendance: 15,000 (estimated)

Urbana

* **SPURLOCK MUSEUM, UNIVERSITY OF ILLINOIS AT URBANA-CHAMPAIGN, (M),** 600 S. Gregory St., Urbana, IL 61801-3759. Tel.: 217-333-2360 & 244-3355. Fax: 217-244-9419.
E-mail: ksheahan@illinois.edu
Web Site: www.spurlock.illinois.edu
Founded: 1912.
Congressional District: 19
Key Personnel: Dir., Wayne Pitard; Pres. (V), Clark Cunningham; Collections Mgr., Christa Deacy-Quinn; Asst. Collections Mgr., John Holton; Coord. Collections, Melissa Sotelo; Registrar, Jennifer White; Asst. Registrar, Amy Heggemeyer; Asst. Registrar, Cheri Vitez; Dir. Education, Tandy Lacy; Asst. Dir. Education, Kim Sheahan; Coord. Education, Beth Watkins; Coord. Learning Center, Julia Robinson; Coord. Education Program, Brook Taylor; Information Technology, Jack Thomas; Business Mgr. & Asst. to Dir., Dee Robbins; Program Coord., Karen Flesher; Coord. Special Events, Brian Cudiamat; Cur. Asia, Chiou-Peng TzeHuey; Cur. Africa, Mahir Saul; Cur. Ancient Near East, Wayne Pitard; Cur. East Asia, Kai Wing Chow; Cur. Oceania, Janet Keller; Cur. South America, Norman Whitten; Cur. East Asia, Yu Wang; Security Supvr., Harold Bush; Lead Guard, Cipriano Martinez; Guard, Michael Albert; Guard, Larry Booth; Guard, Kathy Johnston; Guard, Thomas Yu.
Personnel Profile: Full-Time Paid 19; Part-Time Paid 50; Part-Time Volunteers 24.
Governing Authority: university. Affiliated with the University of Illinois at Urbana-Champaign. Tax-exempt.
World Cultures Museum.
Collections: archaeology; art; history; numismatics; glass; pottery; bronzes; textiles; cast reproductions; classical & medieval sculpture; anthropology; American Indian; cuneiform tablets; Canelos Quichua ceramics; Amazonian bark cloth.
Major Exhibits: The Transforming Arts of Papua New Guinea, 1/10; Korean Funerary Figures: Companions for the Journey to the Other World (T), 3/10-7/10; Siyazama: Traditional Arts, Education, and AIDS in South Africa (T), 8/10-12/10.
Research Fields: cuneiform tablets; ancient pottery; Merovingian jewelry; American Indian artifacts.
Facilities: auditorium; reception facilities available; educational resource center; multipurpose learning center.
Activities: guided tours; lectures; gallery talks; permanent & temporary exhibitions; special events; dance; theatre; outreach programs; storytelling.
Publications: annual magazine, Spurlock; newsletter.
Hours & Admission Prices: Tues. 12-5, Wed.-Fri. 9-5, Sat. 10-4, Sun. 12-4. No charge; donations accepted. Closed university holidays. ♿
Attendance: 22,253 (accurate)
Membership: Museum Friends: Individual $25; Family $35; Sustaining $50; Donor $100; Sponsor $500; Patron $1,000; Benefactor $5,000; Founder $10,000.

WANDELL SCULPTURE GARDEN, Meadowbrook Park, Vine St., Urbana, IL 61801. Tel.: 217-367-1536. Fax: 217-367-1391.
Sculpture Garden.
Collections: oak, stainless steal, bronze, & concrete sculptures.
Hours & Admission Prices: Daily dawn to dusk.

Utica

LASALLE COUNTY HISTORICAL SOCIETY MUSEUM, (M), 101 E. Canal, Utica, IL 61373. Mailing Address: P.O. Box 278, Utica, IL 61373-0278. Tel.: 815-667-4861. Fax: 815-310-7613.
E-mail: lchsmuseum@gmail.com
Web Site: lasallecountymuseum.org
Founded: 1907.
Congressional District: 11
Key Personnel: Pres. (V), Andrew Svihra.
Personnel Profile: Part-Time Paid 4; Part-Time Volunteers 100; Interns 4.
Governing Authority: society. Parent Institution: LaSalle County Historical Society; CB&Q #4978 engine; herb & prairie plant gardens. Branch Historical Sites: Artesian Well House, Ottawa; blacksmith shop, Utica; Aitken School House (one-room); barn. Tax-exempt: 501(c)(3).
History Museum: housed in 1848 pre-Civil War stone warehouse along the Illinois Michigan canal.
Collections: American Indian artifacts; furnishings of early pioneer homes; clothing; farm tools; pioneer implements; Lincoln carriage.
Facilities: approx. 800-vol. library of books on the history of LaSalle County available for use on premises; reading room. Museum-related items for sale.
Activities: guided tours; lectures; radio programs; permanent & temporary exhibitions. Museum Sponsors: land cruises; Burgoo Festival.
Publications: bulletin, The Society Story; booklet, Focus on the Past; booklet, The First Kaskaskia; reprints of old LaSalle County books; Pioneers, Powwows & Prairie Playgrounds.
Hours & Admission Prices: Wed.-Fri. 10-4, Sat.-Sun. 12-4; other times by appointment. No charge; donations accepted. Closed major holidays. ♿
Attendance: 12,000 (estimated)
Membership: Student $2; Individual $20; Family $25; Sustaining $40; Organization $100; Life $250.

Vandalia

THE LITTLE BRICK HOUSE, 621 Saint Clair St., Vandalia, IL 62471. Mailing Address: Vandalia Historical Society, Inc., 105 S. 4th, Vandalia, IL 62471-2809. Tel.: 618-283-4866.
Founded: 1960.
Congressional District: 55
Key Personnel: Dir., Dale Timmermann.
Governing Authority: individual operation. Parent Institution: Vandalia Historical Society, Inc.
Historic House Museum: 1840-1860 James W. Berry property.
Collections: furniture; china; portraits; engravings; original buildings from 1825-1895; manuscripts by Vandalia authors; pictures of James Hall's family; books of early settlers; autographed books by Vandalia authors; sketches of Capital day leaders; Lincoln memorabilia.
Research Fields: frontier history; Abraham Lincoln; James Hall; capital leaders; 1820s-1840s culture.
Facilities: 100-vol. library of early Illinois & frontier period history available for research only. Antiques, books on Illinois history & other museum related items for sale.
Activities: guided tours; lectures; temporary exhibitions.
Publications: books, Seven Stories; European Journey; James Hall of Lincoln's Frontier World; Vandalia: Wilderness Capital of Lincoln's Land.
Hours & Admission Prices: By appointment only. Suggested Donations: adults $3, children 12 yrs. & under $1.

Attendance: 150 (estimated)

VANDALIA STATEHOUSE STATE HISTORIC SITE, 315 W. Gallatin St., Vandalia, IL 62471-2820. Tel.: 618-283-1161.
Founded: 1836.
Congressional District: 19
Key Personnel: Dir. IHPA, Jan Grimes; Site Supt., Mary Cole.
Personnel Profile: Full-Time Paid 2.
Governing Authority: state. Affiliated with Illinois Historic Preservation Agency, Old State Capitol, Springfield, IL 62701. Tax-exempt.
Historic Site: 1836 Vandalia Statehouse is the oldest Capitol building in the state of Illinois.
Collections: period furnishings.
Activities: guided tours; lectures; craft demonstrations. Museum Sponsors: Father's Day weekend; Grande Levee Candlelight Open House; candlelight tour second Saturday in December.
Publications: bimonthly newsletter, Historic Illinois.
Hours & Admission Prices: March-Oct. Tues.-Sat. 9-5; Nov.-Feb. Tues.-Sat. 9-4. Suggested Donations: adults $4, children $2. Closed New Year's Day; Thanksgiving; Christmas. ♿
Attendance: 35,000 (accurate)

Vernon Hills

CUNEO MUSEUM & GARDENS, 1350 N. Milwaukee, Vernon Hills, IL 60061-1540. Tel.: 847-362-3042 & 3054. Fax: 847-362-4130.
E-mail: padams@cuneomuseum.org
Web Site: www.cuneomuseum.org
Founded: 1991.
Congressional District: 10
Key Personnel: C.E.O. & Pres., John F. Cuneo; Exec. Dir., Pam Adams.
Personnel Profile: Full-Time Paid 25; Part-Time Paid 5; Part-Time Volunteers 40.
Governing Authority: bd. of directors; nonprofit. Parent Institution: Cuneo Foundation. Tax-exempt.
Historic House & Garden: 1914 Cuneo Mansion.
Collections: Renaissance paintings; 17th-century tapestries; period oriental rugs & furnishings.
Facilities: garden; conservatory; banquet facilities; 3,000 sq. ft. exhibit space.
Activities: arts festivals; concerts; docent program; organized education programs for adults; guided tours; lectures.
Publications: newsletter, CuneoGram.
Hours & Admission Prices: Feb.-Dec. Tues.-Sun. 10-5. Adults $12, seniors $11, students with ID $7; discounts to groups; members no charge. Closed New Year's Day; Thanksgiving; Christmas. ♿
Attendance: 30,000 (estimated)
Membership: Individual $45; Family $75; Director's Circle $150; Charter $250.

Volo

VOLVO AUTO MUSEUM ATTRACTION, 27582 W. Volo Village Rd., Volo, IL 60073-9613. Tel.: 815-385-3644. Fax: 815-385-0703.
E-mail: cyndis@volocars.com
Web Site: www.volocars.com
Formerly: Volo Antique Auto Museum and Village
Founded: 1961.
Key Personnel: C.E.O. & Owner, Greg Grams; Dir., Cyndi Sarabia; Devel. & Museum Shop Mgr., Myra Grams.
Personnel Profile: Full-Time Paid 8; Part-Time Paid 2.
Governing Authority: company organized for profit.
Automobile Museum.
Collections: approximately 250 vintage & collector automobiles including 60s TV series Batmobile replica; Boothill Express, funeral coach used for Bob Younger (the Jesse James outlaw gang); K.I.T.T., replica of Michael Knight's car from Knight Rider; General Lee, from Dukes of Hazzard.
Facilities: restaurant; banquet hall. Gift items for sale.
Hours & Admission Prices: Memorial Day to Labor Day Mon.-Fri. 10-5. Adults $10, senior citizens & military $7, children 5-12 $5; members no charge. Closed Thanksgiving; Christmas. ♿
Attendance: 500,000
Membership: Single $45; Family $65; Lifetime $500.

Watseka

IROQUOIS COUNTY HISTORICAL SOCIETY, 103 W. Cherry St., Watseka, IL 60970-1524. Tel.: 815-432-2215. Fax: 815-432-2215.
E-mail: ichs2215@mchsi.com
Web Site: www.oldcourthousemuseum.org
Founded: 1967.
Congressional District: 15
Key Personnel: Pres., Rolland Light; Vice Pres., Jean Hiles; Sec., Marilyn Wilken; Treas., Bob Ficke; Office Mgr., Judy Ficke.
Personnel Profile: Full-Time Paid 1; Part-Time Paid 4; Part-Time Volunteers 5.
Governing Authority: society; nonprofit. Subsidiary Institution: Iroquois Co. Genealogical Society. Tax-exempt: 501(c)(3).
General Museum: housed in 1866 Old Iroquois County Courthouse.
Collections: art; archaeology; geology; mineralogy; medical; apothecary; natural history; agriculture; antiques; architecture; costumes; furniture; guns; hobbies; horology; industrial; lapidary; numismatics; musical instruments; toys; dolls; military quilts.
Research Fields: genealogy; historic sites.
Facilities: library of county records, historical books & old school books available for use under the supervision of genealogy society members; reading room; 145-seat auditorium. Novelties, museum plates & books for sale.
Activities: guided tours; concerts; hobby workshops; rental gallery; permanent, temporary & traveling exhibitions; auctions; garden walk. Museum Sponsors: Golden Wedding anniversary celebration for senior citizens; Christmas Tree Lane; Harvest Daze; Christmas House Walk.
Publications: quarterly, Iroquois County Historical Society Newsletter; quarterly magazine, Iroquois Stalker; numerous centennial histories of towns in the county plus hardbound history books. Write for complete listing.
Hours & Admission Prices: Mon.-Fri. 10-4. Suggested Donations: adults $2, children $.50; members no charge. Closed major holidays. ♿
Attendance: 5,000 (estimated)
Membership: Individual $15; Family $40; Life $150; Commercial Life $300.

Wauconda

* **LAKE COUNTY DISCOVERY MUSEUM, (M),** Rte. 176, Fairfield Rd. & Lakewood Forest Preserve, Wauconda, IL 60084. Mailing Address: 27277 N. Forest Preserve Dr., Wauconda, IL 60084-2016. Tel.: 847-968-3400. Fax: 847-526-0024.
E-mail: LCMuseum@co.lake.il.us
Web Site: www.lakecountydiscoverymuseum.org
Founded: 1976.
Congressional District: 12
Key Personnel: C.E.O., Bonnie Thomson Carter; Chm., Susan Loving Gravenhorst; Pres. (V), Joan Hammel; Dir., Katherine Hamilton-Smith; Devel. Officer, Barb Vicory, CFRE; Collections Coord., Diana Dretske; Visitor Svcs. Mgr., Andrew Osborne; Mgr. Historical Resources, Christine Pyle; Exhibits Developer, Steve Furnett; Researcher, Debra Gust.
Personnel Profile: Full-Time Paid 9; Part-Time Paid 5; Part-Time Volunteers 500; Interns 4.
Governing Authority: county; nonprofit. Parent Institution: Lake County Forest Preserve District. Tax-exempt: 501(c)(3).
General Museum.
Collections: decorative arts; clothing; vehicles; household & farming equipment; regional history archives: documents; photographs; diaries; ledgers; Curt Teich Postcard Archives: view & advertising cards; photographic prints & negatives, 1898-1974; Lake County history in relation to Chicago; history & significance of postcards.
Research Fields: regional history; 20th-century North America.
Facilities: 1,500-vol. library pertaining to local history for use on premises; archives; 6,000 sq. ft. exhibit gallery; education space.
Activities: guided tours; lectures; films; workshops; organized education programs for children; volunteer program; organized intern program for undergraduate or graduate college students; participatory exhibits.
Publications: quarterly, Image File; Lake County Historian.
Hours & Admission Prices: Mon.-Sat. 11-4:30, Sun. 1-4:30. Adults $6, students $2.50; discounts to AAM members; members & pre-schoolers no charge. Closed New Year's Day; Thanksgiving; Christmas. ♿
Attendance: 70,000 (accurate)
Membership: Friends of the Lake County Museum & Curt Teich Archives: Individual $30; Family $45; Individual 2 years $55; Family Plus $75; Family 2 years $85; Discovery Circle $150; Mastodon Club $500.

WAUCONDA TOWNSHIP HISTORICAL SOCIETY, 711 Main St., Wauconda, IL 60084. Mailing Address: P.O. Box 256, Wauconda, IL 60084-0256. Tel.: 847-526-9303.
Founded: 1973.
Congressional District: 8
Key Personnel: Pres., Lynn McAlister; Treas., Roberta Francisco; Archivist, Registrar & Sec., Dale Buttolph.
Personnel Profile: Part-Time Volunteers 20.
Governing Authority: society; nonprofit organization. Affiliated with Wauconda Township Historical Society. Tax-exempt: 170(b)(1)(A).
Historical Society Museum: housed in c.1840 brick farm home of Andrew C. Cook.
Collections: farm equipment of area; toys; quilts; furnishings of 1860s; dolls;

Civil War cavalry equipment; books; photographs; fans; cameras; china; kitchen utensils & cow bells.
Research Fields: genealogy & history of Wauconda Township.
Facilities: library of books ranging from cookbooks to poetry available for research on premises. Museum-related items for sale.
Activities: guided tours; lectures; films; permanent & temporary exhibitions; open houses.
Publications: brochure, Andrew C. Cook Residence; Memory Books, interviews with long-time residents of the area.
Hours & Admission Prices: May-Sept. Sun. 1-4; other times by appointment. No charge; donations accepted. ♿
Attendance: 150 (estimated)
Membership: Student $2; Individual $10; Life $150.

Waukegan

WAUKEGAN HISTORY MUSEUM, WAUKEGAN HISTORICAL SOCIETY, 1917 N. Sheridan Rd., Bowen Park, Waukegan, IL 60087-5131. Tel.: 847-336-1859 & 360-4749. Fax: 847-662-6190.
E-mail: museum@waukeganhistorical.org
Web Site: www.waukeganhistorical.org
Formerly: Haines Museum, Waukegan Historical Society
Founded: 1968.
Congressional District: 31
Key Personnel: Pres. (V), Sara Griffin; Supvr., Ty Rohrer; Librarian, Beverly Millard.
Personnel Profile: Full-Time Paid 1; Part-Time Volunteers 20; Interns 1.
Governing Authority: nonprofit organization. Subsidiary Institution: Waukegan Park District. Tax-exempt.
Local History Museum.
Collections: artifacts of the Waukegan area; John Raymond Memorial Research Library; Lincoln Room; Civil War artifacts; furnishings; clothing; more than 8,000 photos of local & county historic landmarks; Indian artifacts.
Research Fields: genealogy; city of Waukegan; near north historical district; Waukegan landmarks; restoration of historic buildings; library resource center.
Facilities: library of material on Waukegan & Lake County history available for use on premises; reading room.
Activities: speakers bureau, slides of old Waukegan; walking, bicycle & automobile tours; lectures; school tours; inter-museum loan, permanent & temporary exhibitions. Museum Sponsors: annual tour of homes; restoration of historic buildings.
Publications: quarterly newsletter; brochure on museum; brochure, Near North Historic District; Waukegan's Legacy, Our Landmarks; Waukegan: A History.
Hours & Admission Prices: Tues., Thurs. & Sat. 10-4; other times by appointment. No Charge; donations accepted. Closed all major holidays. ♿
Attendance: 1,500 (estimated)
Membership: Student & Senior Citizen $7; Individual $15; Family $25; Patron $50; Individual Lifetime $100; Couple Lifetime $150; Corporate $500.

West Chicago

KLINE CREEK FARM, County Farm between North & Geneva Rds., West Chicago, IL 60185. Mailing Address: P.O. Box 5000, Wheaton, IL 60189-5000. Tel.: 630-876-5900. Fax: 630-293-9421.
E-mail: kcf@dupageforest.com
Web Site: www.dupageforest.com
Founded: 1989.
Congressional District: 6
Key Personnel: Pres., D. (Dewey) Pierotti, Jr.; Supvr., Keith R. McClow; Agricultural Specialist, Mark Johnson; Coord. Collection, Carol Nardbrook; Staff Asst., Sue Clark; Heritage Interpreter, Patricia Walton; Heritage Interpreter, Chris Gingrich; Heritage Interpreter, Wayne Hill; Heritage Interpreter, Howard Seargent; Heritage Interpreter, Elizabeth Smid.
Personnel Profile: Full-Time Paid 5; Part-Time Paid 5; Part-Time Volunteers 63; Interns 5.
Governing Authority: county; nonprofit. Parent Institution: Forest Preserve District, DuPage County, Inc. Tax-exempt: Illinois State Statute 96.5.
Living History Museum: re-creation of a turn-of-the-century farm in northeast Illinois.
Collections: 1890s farm equipment & household furnishings; purebred livestock. Historic Buildings: barn; house; summer kitchen; ice house; smoke house.
Research Fields: 1890s rural life; social customs; turn-of-the-century building methods; Victorian era interior decorating; farming methods & equipment; period clothing; purebred livestock.
Facilities: picnic areas.
Activities: guided tours; organized programs; farming demonstrations. Museum Sponsors: Ice Harvest; Maple Sugaring; Country Fair; Memorial Day Remembered; Holiday on the Farm.
Hours & Admission Prices: Thurs.-Mon. 9-5. No charge; donations accepted. Closed New Year's Eve & Day; Independence Day; Thanksgiving; Christmas Eve & Day. ♿
Attendance: 51,850 (estimated)

KRUSE HOUSE MUSEUM, 527 Main St., West Chicago, IL 60185-2842. Mailing Address: P.O. Box 246, West Chicago, IL 60186-0246. Tel.: 630-231-0564 & 2329.
E-mail: krusehouse@earthlink.net
Web Site: www.krusehousemuseum.org
Founded: 1976.
Congressional District: 14
Key Personnel: Pres. (V), Lance Conkright; Museum Shop Mgr., Donna Orlandini.
Personnel Profile: Part-Time Volunteers 30.
Governing Authority: society. West Chicago Historical Society. Tax-exempt.
Historical Society Museum: housed in 1917 Kruse House.
Collections: c.1920 household items & costumes belonging to railroad family.
Facilities: Museum & gift-related items for sale.
Activities: guided tours; special exhibits.
Publications: bimonthly newsletter.
Hours & Admission Prices: May-Sept. Sat. 11-3; tours by appointment. No charge; donations accepted.
Attendance: 520 (estimated)
Membership: Individual $15; Family $25; Organization $50; Individual Life $150; Family Life & Organization Life $250.

WEST CHICAGO CITY MUSEUM, (M), 132 Main St., West Chicago, IL 60185-2835. Tel.: 630-231-3376 & 293-2266. Fax: 630-293-2943.
E-mail: museum@westchicago.org
Web Site: www.westchicago.org
Founded: 1976.
Congressional District: 14
Key Personnel: Dir., LuAnn Bombard; Archivist, Sally DeFauw.
Personnel Profile: Full-Time Paid 2; Part-Time Volunteers 30; Interns 1.
Governing Authority: municipal. Parent Institution: City of West Chicago. Subsidiary Institution: CB & Q Rail Depot. Tax-exempt.
History Museum: housed in the former Town Hall & Fire Station; Chicago, Burlington & Quincy Station; c.1860. Listed on the National Register of Historic Places.
Collections: C&NW, CB&Q, CA&E Railroad; woodworking, 1880-1920; domestic tools & tools from various crafts; farm items; documents & photographs pertaining to local history & Illinois railroad history; genealogy files; manuscripts. Historic Railroad Park: mid 19th century CB&Q Station; 1880s standpipe.
Research Fields: Illinois railroad history; local history & genealogy; John W. Gates; tools.
Facilities: 200-vol. library of books & maps on local & Illinois railroad history available by appointment; microfilm reels of local newspapers; genealogical material for 11,000 former residents.
Activities: guided tours; lectures; formally organized educational programs for schools; school loan service; A/V presentations.
Publications: History of West Chicago; Historic Homes of West Chicago; History of an Old Railroad Town; Tales Tombstones Tell, Stirring Up History.
Hours & Admission Prices: Tues.-Fri. 10:30-3:30, Sat. 11-3; other times by appointment. Research: by appointment. No charge; donations accepted. ♿
Attendance: 3,000 (estimated)

West Frankfort

FRANKFORT AREA HISTORICAL MUSEUM, 2000 E. St. Louis St., West Frankfort, IL 62896-1647. Tel.: 618-932-6159.
Founded: 1972.
Congressional District: 25
Key Personnel: Pres., Sylvia Tharp; Vice Pres., Winona Harris; Sec., Mary Ellen Maragni; Treas., Dean Tharp; Asst. Dir. & Cur. Veteran's Museum, Robert Rogers; Librarian, Shirley Payne; Asst. Dir., Sue Rogers; Museum Shop Mgr., Sibyl Gossett.
Personnel Profile: Part-Time Volunteers 40.
Governing Authority: society; nonprofit organization. Tax-exempt: 501(c)(3).
Historical Building: housed in a former school building; built c.1916.
Collections: Southern Illinois history; farm utensils; tools; furnishings; toys; literature; war memorabilia; food preparation & preserving; methods of holiday celebration; one room school; coal mining. Historic Building: early 1900s home.
Research Fields: local history; genealogy.
Facilities: 10,000-vol. library of rare books on genealogy, local history & town records for research on premises only; maps; newspapers; microfilms;

slides; tapes; periodicals; 60-capacity auditorium; educational facilities; tea room. Homemade crafts & other museum-related items for sale.
Activities: guided tours; lectures; films; hobby workshops; TV & radio programs; docent program; organized education programs children, adults & undergraduate or graduate college students affiliated with Southern Illinois University, John A. Logan College & Rend Lake College; training programs for museum workers; participatory, loan, temporary & traveling exhibitions; school loan service. Museum Sponsors: Victorian Spring Luncheon; Ladies Spring Luncheon; Autumn High Tea; area Quilt Show in July; area Flea Market in September; Holiday House in December.
Publications: books, History of West Frankfort; Cooking With Kindness Vol. 1 & 2; brochures; Franklin County History Book.
Hours & Admission Prices: Wed.-Thurs. 9-3. No charge; donations accepted. Closed New Year's Day; Easter; Independence Day; Thanksgiving; Christmas. ♿
Attendance: 9,000 (estimated)
Membership: Friend $10; Patron $20; Associate $30; Partner $50; Executive $100; Benefactor $1,000.

VETERANS DEPOT MUSEUM, 101 W. Main St., West Frankfort, IL 62896-2317. Mailing Address: 2000 E. St. Louis, West Frankfort, IL 62896-1647.
Key Personnel: Dir., Robert Rogers; Chm. (V), Dwight Tharp.
Personnel Profile: Part-Time Volunteers 4.
Governing Authority: Subsidiary Institution: Frankfort Area Historical Museum. Tax-exempt.
Military Museum.
Collections: Civil War, WWI, WWII, Korean War, Vietnam War & Gulf War memorabilia; books; videos; WW radio equipment; military memorabilia.
Activities: guided tours; loan exhibitions. Annual Event: Veterans Day Ceremonies.
Hours & Admission Prices: March-Nov. Sun. 1-4; Dec.-Feb. by appointment. No charge; donations accepted. Closed national holidays.
Attendance: 400 (estimated)

Western Springs

WESTERN SPRINGS HISTORICAL SOCIETY, 4211 Grand Ave., Western Springs, IL 60558-1435. Mailing Address: P.O. Box 139, Western Springs, IL 60558-0139. Tel.: 708-246-9230.
Founded: 1967.
Congressional District: 4
Key Personnel: Pres., Kimberly Knake; Vice Pres., David Barritt; Cur. Res. & Artifacts, Betty L. Howard.
Personnel Profile: Part-Time Volunteers 12.
Governing Authority: society; nonprofit organization. Tax-exempt.
General Museum: housed in 1892 Old Water Tower.
Collections: history of Western Springs; records; books; manuscripts; maps; photographs.
Research Fields: history; genealogy; government; education.
Facilities: library of research aids, books, genealogy aids, classified local interests & history available for research on premises.
Activities: guided tours; films; training programs; permanent & temporary exhibitions. Museum Sponsors: Preservation Awards (homes).
Publications: books, Western Springs: A Centennial History of the Village, 1886-1986; 19th-Century Houses in Western Springs; Western Springs: The Story of Village Leadership; Walking tour of Western Springs.
Hours & Admission Prices: Call for hours. No charge.
Attendance: 1,000 (estimated)
Membership: Individual $10; Family $25; Business $30; Sustaining $50; Patron $100; Life $500.

Wheaton

BILLY GRAHAM CENTER MUSEUM, 500 E. College Ave., Wheaton, IL 60187-5534. Tel.: 630-752-5909, ext. 0. Fax: 630-752-5916.
E-mail: BGCMus@wheaton.edu
Web Site: www.billygrahamcenter.org/museum
Founded: 1975.
Congressional District: 14
Key Personnel: Museum Coord., Christian Sawyer; Dir. Resources, Paul Ericksen.
Personnel Profile: Full-Time Paid 3; Part-Time Paid 4.
Governing Authority: college. Affiliated with Wheaton College. Tax-exempt: 501(c)(3).
Religious Museum.
Collections: materials related to the history of evangelism, revival & missions in America; contemporary Christian art.
Research Fields: American church history; emphasis on evangelism, revival & missions.
Facilities: 65,000-vol. library of books & 130,000 microforms relating to missions, evangelism, church history & general theology available for research through Wheaton College; reading room; 500-seat auditorium; classrooms. Books for sale.
Publications: booklet, The Collections at the Billy Graham Center; Researching Modern Evangelicalism, A Guide to the Holdings of the Billy Graham Center, With Information on Other Collections.
Hours & Admission Prices: Mon.-Sat. 9:30-5:30, Sun. 1-5. No charge; donations accepted. ♿

CENTER FOR HISTORY, 315 W. Front St., 2nd Fl., Wheaton, IL 60187-5015. Mailing Address: P.O. Box 373, Wheaton, IL 60187-0373. Tel.: 630-871-6601. Fax: 630-871-6651.
E-mail: info@wheatonhistory.com
Web Site: www.wheatonhistory.org
Formerly: Wheaton History Center
Founded: 1986.
Key Personnel: Pres. & C.E.O., Alberta Adamson, CFRE; Chm., Ed Ewoldt; Museum Shop Mgr., Jane Rio.
Personnel Profile: Full-Time Paid 2; Part-Time Paid 1; Part-Time Volunteers 5.
Governing Authority: nonprofit organization. Parent Institution: Wheaton Historic Preservation Council. Branch Museum: 606 N. Main St., Wheaton, IL 60187. Tax-exempt: 501(c)(3).
History Museum.
Collections: golf collection including artifacts, publications & archives; slave artifacts & documents; oral histories; WWII; S.S. Eastland; local history.
Major Exhibits: Disaster in the Chicago River, 1/10-12/10; Fairways, Greens & Clubs, 1/10-12/10; Wheaton National Hall of Fame, 1/10-12/10.
Research Fields: Civil War; WWII; slavery; abolition; architecture; S.S. Eastland; Wheaton history; golf.
Activities: Community Outreach; facility rental; interpretation; lectures; research library & archives; school-based curriculum. Museum Sponsors: Housewalk; Architecture Tours; S.S. Eastland Reunion.
Publications: Recollections of the War of the Rebellion.
Hours & Admission Prices: Mon.-Sat. 10-5; tours, programs & research by appointment. Adults $7.50, seniors 60 & over $6.50, students $5.50; discounts to AAM members; members and children 8 & under no charge. Closed New Year's Day; Easter; Memorial Day; Labor Day; Thanksgiving; Christmas. ♿
Attendance: 15,000 (accurate)
Membership: Individual $30; Family $50; Corporate $100.

DUPAGE COUNTY HISTORICAL MUSEUM, (M), 102 E. Wesley St., Wheaton, IL 60187-5321. Tel.: 630-665-4710. Fax: 630-665-5880.
Web Site: www.dupagemuseum.com
Founded: 1965.
Congressional District: 14
Key Personnel: Dir., Mike Benard; Cur., Sara Arnas; Educator, Sara Buttita.
Personnel Profile: Full-Time Paid 2; Part-Time Volunteers 8; Interns 2.
Governing Authority: Parent Institution: Wheaton Park District and DuPage County. Subsidiary Institution: Du Page County Museum Association. Tax-exempt.
History Museum.
Collections: 19th, 20th & 21st-century material culture & archives pertaining to DuPage County; Colonial Coverlet Guild collection; costumes; model railroad.
Major Exhibits: The Covenet: Secrets Revealed, 1/10-12/10; DuPage County and the Civil War, 1/10-12/10.
Research Fields: county history; early families; home history research; textiles; 19th, 20th & 21st-century material culture; genealogy.
Facilities: 2,000-vol. library of county & local histories; city directories & archives available for research on premises. Local history books for sale.
Activities: monthly family programs; organized education programs for children; adult lectures & seminars; permanent & changing exhibits; research services; interactive exhibits; landscaped HO gauge model railroad depicting Chicago & Northwestern, Chicago, Aurora & Elgin, and Burlington Northern railroads, operates 3rd & 5th Sat. 1:30-3:30.
Publications: brochures; newsletter; quarterly calendar of events.
Hours & Admission Prices: Mon.-Fri. 8:30-4:30, Sat.-Sun. 12-4. No charge; donations accepted. Closed New Year's Eve & Day; Memorial Day; Independence Day; Labor Day; Thanksgiving; Christmas Eve & Day. ♿
Attendance: 8,669 (accurate)

THE FIRST DIVISION MUSEUM AT CANTIGNY, (M), 1s151 Winfield Rd., Wheaton, IL 60189-3353. Tel.: 630-260-8185. Fax: 630-260-9298.
E-mail: info@firstdivisionmuseum.org
Web Site: www.FirstDivisionMuseum.org
Founded: 1960.
Congressional District: 14
Key Personnel: Exec. Dir., Paul H. Herbert, Ph.D.; Dir. Museum Operations,

Keith R. Gill; Dir. Research Center, Eric Gillespie; Mgr. Public Programs, Michael Goodale; Dir. Information Management, Steve Hawkins; Cur. Collections, Terri Navratil; Asst. Cur. Collections, Carrie Tarasuk; Mgr. Exhibits, Teri Bianchi; Museum Educator, Melissa Neumann; Collections Mgr., Christopher Zielinski; Librarian, Tracy Cirar; Research Historian, Andrew Woods; Graphic Designer & Editor, Rebecca Tharp; Registrar, John Maniatis; Conservation & Exhibits, Al Potyen; Archivist, Kate Kleiderman.
Personnel Profile: Full-Time Paid 20; Part-Time Paid 2; Part-Time Volunteers 51; Interns 5.
Governing Authority: nonprofit; self-financing; Cantigny First Division Foundation. Parent Institution: Robert R. McCormick Foundation. Tax-exempt: 501(c)(3).
Military Museum: located on the grounds of The Robert R. McCormick Estate, Cantigny. (See separate listing).
Collections: story of 1st Infantry Div. from World War I to present; archives; outdoor display of military vehicles.
Research Fields: 1st Infantry Division; 1917-present; American military history; freedom of the press; publishing & journalism history; Chicago area history.
Facilities: 12,000-vol. library of books; 41,000 photographs; 73,000 documents & manuscripts; 12,000 artifacts pertaining to U.S. military history.
Activities: guided tours; lectures; audio-visual programs; educational programs; temporary exhibits; patriotic events; conferences & symposia.
Publications: Cantigy Military History Series, books; Bridgehead Sentinel, 1st Division Veterans' newspaper; conference reports; historical monographs; memoirs; bibliographies; videos; brochures.
Hours & Admission Prices: Feb. Fri.-Sun. 10-4; March-May & Sept.-Dec. Tues.-Sun. 10-4; Summer: Tues.-Sun. 10-5. Gardens & Grounds: dawn-dusk. $5 per car parking fee & road use Tues.-Sun. Closed New Year's Day; Thanksgiving; Christmas. ♿
Attendance: 106,000 (accurate)

ROBERT R. MCCORMICK MUSEUM AT CANTIGNY, (M), 1 S. 151 Winfield Rd., Wheaton, IL 60189-3353. Tel.: 630-260-8159. Fax: 630-260-8160.
E-mail: dgutenkauf@cantigny.org
Web Site: www.cantigny.org
Founded: 1955.
Congressional District: 14
Key Personnel: Dir., Diane Gutenkauf; C.E.O., David Hiller; Asst. Dir., William Buhlig; Exec. Dir. Cantigny Foundation, Matt Lafond; Tour Coord., Jeff Anderson; Museum Shop Mgr., Angelica Lopez.
Personnel Profile: Full-Time Paid 3; Part-Time Paid 8; Part-Time Volunteers 10.
Governing Authority: private; self-financing, nonprofit organization. Parent Institution: Cantigny Foundation. Tax-exempt: 501(c)(3).
Historic House: 1896, country home of Joseph Medill, editor of the Chicago Tribune built by architect C.A. Coolidge; house enlarged in 1932 for Col. Robert R. McCormick (grandson of Medill) editor & publisher of the Chicago Tribune.
Collections: furnishings; books & memorabilia of Col. Robert McCormick.
Facilities: 5,000-vol. library of books & documents; movie theater; gardens; small picnic area; Scout camp grounds; The First Division Museum (see separate listing).
Activities: guided tours; lectures; chamber music; patriotic celebrations; outdoor concerts.
Publications: Brochure.
Hours & Admission Prices: Feb. Fri.-Sun. 10-4; March-May & Sept.-Dec. Tues.-Sun. 10-4; Memorial Day to Labor Day Tues.-Sun. 10-5. Parking/road usage fee $5 per car; $70 per bus; $55 annual parking pass. Grounds: daily 7am to sunset. Closed New Year's Eve & Day; Thanksgiving & day after; Christmas Eve & Day. ♿
Attendance: 51,303 (accurate)

White Hall

GREGORY HOUSE MUSEUM, Rte. 1, White Hall, IL 62092. Mailing Address: Rte. 1, Box 94, White Hall, IL 62092-0094. Tel.: 217-374-6715.
Founded: 1993.
Key Personnel: Cur., Emily B. Esarey
Historic House Museum.
Collections: Gregory family history & personal artifacts; local agricultural, political & community history; paperweights.
Activities: Museum Sponsors: Greene County Days in September.
Hours & Admission Prices: By appointment. No charge; donations accepted. Closed Thanksgiving; Christmas. ♿
Attendance: 150 (estimated)

Whittington

SOUTHERN ILLINOIS ART & ARTISANS CENTER, 14967 Gun Creek Trail, Whittington, IL 62897-1000. Tel.: 618-629-2220. Fax: 618-629-2704.
E-mail: mgalloway@museum.state.il.us
Web Site: www.museum.state.il.us
Founded: 1990.
Key Personnel: Dir., Mary Lou Galloway; Cur., Debra Tayes; Museum Shop Mgr., Romaula Coleman.
Personnel Profile: Full-Time Paid 6; Part-Time Paid 5.
Governing Authority: state; nonprofit. Parent Institution: Illinois State Museum, 502 S. Spring St., Springfield, IL 62706. Tax-exempt: 501(c)(3).
Art & Artisans Center.
Collections: works by members of the Illinois Artisans Program.
Facilities: visitors center. Museum-related items for sale.
Activities: arts festivals; guided tours; craft workshops; lectures; temporary & traveling exhibitions; artisan demonstrations & workshops; outdoor festivals & special events. Annual Events: Children's Festival; Art & Wine Festival; Illinois Art & Fine Craft.
Publications: annual brochure, Calendar of Events & Programs.
Hours & Admission Prices: Daily 9-5. No charge. Closed New Year's Day; Easter; Thanksgiving; Christmas. ♿
Attendance: 39,741
Membership: Artist & Student $20; Individual $35; Family $50; Contributing $100; Life $500.

Williamsville

DIE CAST AUTO SALES, 117 N. Elm St., Williamsville, IL 62693-7503. Tel.: 217-566-3898.
History Museum: housed in a former 1930s service station.
Collections: die-cast cars; Coca Cola collectibles; Route 66 artifacts.
Hours & Admission Prices: Call for hours.

ROUTE 66 DREAM CAR MUSEUM, 530 W. Main St., Williamsville, IL 62693. Tel.: 217-566-3799.
Car Museum.
Collections: period cars; automobile history.
Activities: special events.
Hours & Admission Prices: Call for hours.

Wilmette

WILMETTE HISTORICAL MUSEUM, (M), 609 Ridge Rd., Wilmette, IL 60091-2441. Tel.: 847-853-7666. Fax: 847-853-7706.
E-mail: museum@wilmette.com
Web Site: www.wilmettehistory.org
Founded: 1949.
Congressional District: 10
Key Personnel: Dir., Kathy Hussey-Arntson.
Personnel Profile: Full-Time Paid 1; Part-Time Paid 2.
Governing Authority: municipal. Tax-exempt: 501(c)(3).
Local History Museum.
Collections: local history archives; costumes; history.
Research Fields: pertaining to collection.
Facilities: library; archives including photographs relating to Wilmette, Gross Point & vicinity available for research.
Activities: guided tours; lectures; formally organized education programs.
Publications: quarterly newsletter.
Hours & Admission Prices: Sun.-Thurs. 1-4:30. No charge; donations accepted. Closed national holidays. ♿
Attendance: 6,000 (estimated)

Winnetka

WINNETKA HISTORICAL SOCIETY, Museum & Research Center, 411 Linden, Winnetka, IL 60093. Mailing Address: P.O. Box 365, Winnetka, IL 60093-0365. Tel.: 847-446-0001. Fax: 847-501-3221.
E-mail: winnetka411@comcast.net
Web Site: www.winnetkahistory.org
Founded: 1932.
Congressional District: 10
Key Personnel: Pres., Laurie Petersen; Exec. Dir., Patti Van Cleave; Cur., Katherine Macica; Cur. Costume, Elizabeth Carlson.
Personnel Profile: Part-Time Paid 3; Part-Time Volunteers 15; Interns 1.
Governing Authority: nonprofit. Branch Museum: Schmidt-Burnham Log House, 1140 Willow Rd., Winnetka, IL 60093. Tax-exempt: 501(c)(3).
Local History Museum and Archives.
Collections: history of Winnetka & surrounding area; photographs; costumes; paintings; documents; artifacts. Historic House: c.1837 log house.
Research Fields: local, Chicago & Illinois history; authors from Winnetka.

Facilities: 900-vol. library of general & local history available to the public; reception area. Museum-related items for sale.
Activities: guided tours; lectures; educational programs for children & adults. Museum Sponsors: parties; benefit.
Publications: book, Winnetka Architecture: Where Past is Present; semiannual newspaper Winnetka Historical Society Gazette.
Hours & Admission Prices: Call for hours. Museum & participants of Time Travelers: no charge. Log House: call for admission prices. ♿
Attendance: 1,200 (estimated)
Membership: Friendship Pass (2 adults) $35; Family Pass (2 adults & children under 18) $50.

Zion

PLATEN PRESS PRINTING MUSEUM, 3051 Sheridan Rd., Zion, IL 60099-3243. Tel.: 847-746-8170.
Printing Museum.
Collections: printing; bindery equipment; addressograph machines; metal casting; letterpress; bookbinding.
Hours & Admission Prices: Call for hours.

ZION HISTORICAL SOCIETY, 1300 Shiloh Blvd., Zion, IL 60099-2622. Tel.: 847-746-2427 & 872-4566.
E-mail: tr91752@sbcglobal.net
Web Site: www.zionhs.com
Founded: 1967.
Congressional District: 10
Key Personnel: Pres., Carol Ruesch; Vice Pres., Lorna Yates.
Personnel Profile: Part-Time Volunteers 12.
Governing Authority: society. Tax-exempt: 501(c)(3).
Historic House Museum: 1902 Shiloh House, the residence of the founder of the city of Zion.
Collections: original furnishings: antiques; religious artifacts; manuscripts.
Facilities: library of religious & historical books available for use on premises. Gift items & local crafts for sale.
Activities: guided tours; lectures; films; inter-museum loan, permanent & temporary exhibitions.
Hours & Admission Prices: Memorial Day-Labor Day Sun. 2-5; other times by appointment. Adults $5, children $2.
Attendance: 150 (estimated)
Membership: Individual $7.50; Family $15; Contributing $25; Sustaining $35; Life $150.

INDIANA

(280 listings)

Albion

OLD JAIL MUSEUM, 215 W. Main St., Albion, IN 46701-1115. Mailing Address: P.O. Box 152, Albion, IN 46701-0152. Tel.: 260-636-3929.
Web Site: www. noblehistoricalsociety.org
Founded: 1968.
Congressional District: 4
Key Personnel: Vice Pres., Bill Landon; Dir., Richard Recker; Dir., Carol Kirsch; Pres., Bill Shultz; Bd. Directors, Mary Stolte; Treas., Judy Richter; Dir. & Museum Shop Mgr., Margaret Ott; Bd. Directors, Sondra Luke; Sec., Sarah Knopp.
Personnel Profile: Part-Time Volunteers 30; Interns 3.
Governing Authority: society; nonprofit organization. Tax-exempt.
Historic Building: 1876 Noble County Old Jail & sheriff's residence.
Collections: furnishings; artifacts; documents.
Facilities: library of old books & magazines. Gift items for sale.
Activities: guided tours; permanent exhibitions.
Publications: quarterly letter, Pioneer Echoes.
Hours & Admission Prices: Memorial Day to 3rd week in Sept. Sat.-Sun. 1:30-4:30; group tours by appointment. Adults $3, school children $1; members no charge.
Attendance: 325 (accurate)
Membership: Student $1.50; Individual $10; Life $100.

Anderson

THE ANDERSON CENTER FOR THE ARTS, (M), 32 W. Tenth St., Anderson, IN 46016-1409. Mailing Address: P.O. Box 1218, Anderson, IN 46015-1218. Tel.: 765-649-1248. Fax: 765-649-0199.
E-mail: info.taca@sbcglobal.net
Web Site: www.andersonart.org
Formerly: Anderson Fine Arts Center
Founded: 1966.
Congressional District: 2
Key Personnel: Dir., Deborah McBratney-Stapleton; Pres., Oz Morgan; Administrative Asst., Viki Jones.
Personnel Profile: Full-Time Paid 4; Part-Time Paid 3; Part-Time Volunteers 2; Interns 3.
Governing Authority: private; nonprofit organization. Tax-exempt: 501(c)(3).
Fine Arts Center.
Collections: paintings, sculpture, drawings and prints by Midwestern and Indiana artists & 20th-century American artists; crafts; pottery; metalsmithing.
Research Fields: American art.
Facilities: classroom; conference & meeting space.
Activities: guided tours; lectures; films; festivals; art classes; workshops; organized education programs; docent program; temporary & traveling exhibitions; outreach programs.
Hours & Admission Prices: Tues.-Fri. 12-5, Sat. 10-5, Sun. 2-5. Families $5, adults $2, seniors $1.50, children & students $1; discounts to AAM members; Tues., 1st. Sun. of each month, members & children under 4 no charge. Closed national holidays. ♿
Attendance: 35,000 (estimated)
Membership: Student K-12 $10; Individual $40; Family $60; Patron $125; Sustaining $250; Benefactor $500; Master $1,000 & up. Corporate: Friend $50; Patron $125; Sustaining $250; Sponsor $500; Master $1,000 & up.

GRUENEWALD HISTORIC HOUSE, 626 Main St., Anderson, IN 46016-1514. Tel.: 765-648-6875.
Web Site: www.gruenewaldhouse.com
Founded: 1976.
Congressional District: 6
Key Personnel: Dir., Jean Whitsell-Sherman.
Personnel Profile: Part-Time Paid 1; Part-Time Volunteers 12.
Governing Authority: Tax-exempt.
Historic House Museum.
Collections: personal artifacts; 1890s Victorian-style furnishings; gardens.
Activities: Museum Sponsors: History Awareness Series.
Publications: members' newsletters.
Hours & Admission Prices: April-Dec. Tues.-Fri. 10-3. Adults $5; discounts to AAA members; students & members no charge. Closed Thanksgiving; Christmas.
Attendance: 750 (estimated)
Membership: Individual $35; Family $50; Corporate $100.

GUSTAV JEENINGA MUSEUM OF BIBLE AND NEAR EASTERN STUDIES, Theology Bldg., 1123 Anderson University Blvd., Anderson, IN 46012-3495. Mailing Address: 1100 E. 5th St., Anderson, IN 46012-3462. Tel.: 765-641-4526. Fax: 765-641-3005.
E-mail: dlneidert@anderson.edu
Web Site: www.anderson.edu/campus/museum/index.html
Founded: 1963.
Congressional District: 6
Key Personnel: Dir., David Neidert.
Governing Authority: university. Parent Institution: Anderson University, Inc. Tax-exempt: 501(c)(3).
Archaeological Museum.
Collections: archaeological objects related to biblical & Near Eastern studies.
Activities: formally organized education programs for undergraduate & graduate students.
Publications: biannual newsletters, Illumination.
Hours & Admission Prices: Mon.-Fri. 9-5. No charge. ♿
Attendance: 2,000 (estimated)
Membership: Active $5; Family $10; Contributing $25; Sustaining $50.

WILSON GALLERIES, Anderson University, 1100 E. 5th St., Anderson, IN 46012-3462. Tel.: 800-428-6414.
Key Personnel: Dir., Robin Davis
Art Gallery.
Collections: over 140 works by Warner Sallman.
Hours & Admission Prices: Mon.-Fri. 10-5. No charge.

Angola

TRINE UNIVERSITY, GENERAL LEWIS B. HERSHEY MUSEUM, Ford Hall, 318 S. Darlilng St., Angola, IN 46703. Mailing Address: 1 University Ave., Angola, IN 46703-1764. Tel.: 260-665-4162 & 4100. Fax: 260-665-4283.
E-mail: brewerk@trine.edu
Web Site: www.trine.edu
Founded: 1970.
Congressional District: 4
Key Personnel: C.E.O. & Cur., Dr. Earl D. Brooks, II

Personnel Profile: Part-Time Volunteers 1.
Governing Authority: university. Tax-exempt: 170(b)(1)(A).
Military Museum.
Collections: memorabilia of General Lewis B. Hershey; service memorabilia since Civil War.
Facilities: classrooms.
Publications: Today - an alumni & friends publication.
Hours & Admission Prices: Mon.-Fri. 8-4:30; other times upon request. No charge; donations accepted. Closed national holidays. ♿

Auburn

* **AUBURN CORD DUESENBERG AUTOMOBILE MUSEUM, (M),** 1600 S. Wayne St., Auburn, IN 46706-3509. Mailing Address: P.O. Box 271, Auburn, IN 46706-0271. Tel.: 260-925-1444. Fax: 260-925-6266.
Web Site: acdmuseum.org
Founded: 1973.
Congressional District: 3
Key Personnel: Pres. (V), Robert Pass; Chm. (V), Jeffrey Turner; Exec. Dir., Laura Brinkman; Operations Dir., Kendra Klink; Exec. Vice Pres., Matt Short; Museum Store Mgr., Marcia Doell.
Personnel Profile: Full-Time Paid 11; Part-Time Paid 25; Part-Time Volunteers 120; Interns 1.
Governing Authority: nonprofit organization. Parent Institution: Auburn Automotive Heritage, Inc. Tax-exempt: 501(c)(3).
Transportation Museum: located in original 1930 Administration Building of the Auburn Automobile Co. Listed on the National Register of Historic Places; a National Historic Landmark.
Collections: over 100 period & classic cars; photographs; literature & memorabilia on cars manufactured in or associated with the City of Auburn & their impact on American culture.
Research Fields: automobile manufacturing operations based in Auburn, IN, from 1900 to 1937.
Facilities: archives of original photographs, sales manuals, technical data, & news articles related to automobiles built in Auburn, IN, available for inspection & research; catering & banquet facilities. Museum & automotive-related items for sale.
Activities: lectures; films; archives.
Publications: semiannual newsletter, The Accelerator; annual report.
Hours & Admission Prices: Daily 9-5. Adults $10, students $6; discounts to groups, AAM, ICOM & AAA members or any member of a recognized car club; children under 6 & members no charge. Closed New Year's Day; Thanksgiving; Christmas. ♿
Attendance: 52,611 (accurate)
Membership: Individual & Senior Citizens $35; Individual $45; Family $50; Patron $100; Sustaining $250; Life $1,500.

NATIONAL AUTOMOTIVE & TRUCK MUSEUM OF THE UNITED STATES, INC. (NATMUS), 1000 Gordon M. Buehrig Place, Auburn, IN 46706-3525. Tel.: 260-925-9100. Fax: 260-925-8695.
E-mail: info@natmus.com
Web Site: www.natmus.org
Founded: 1988.
Congressional District: 4
Key Personnel: Pres., Barry Gerig; Exec. Dir., Donald Grogg; Business Mgr., Audra Wilcoxson.
Personnel Profile: Part-Time Paid 5; Part-Time Volunteers 160.
Governing Authority: not-for-profit organization. Tax-exempt: 501(c)(3).
Automotive & Truck Museum: housed in c.1920 former Service Building & 1928 former L29 Cord/Experimental Building of the Auburn Automobile Company.
Collections: automobiles; trucks; models; toys; automobilia; automotive library; gas & oil pumps; pedal cars.
Research Fields: automotive, truck & business history; automotive and truck-related toys & models.
Facilities: 1,000-vol. library of automotive & truck literature; 112,000 sq. ft. exhibit space; meeting room.
Activities: guided tours; loan exhibitions.
Publications: occasional newsletter, Pastlane; National Automotive & Truck Newsletter.
Hours & Admission Prices: Daily 9-5. Adults $7, children 6-12 $4; discount to AAA & AAM members; children 5 & under and NATMUS members no charge. Closed New Year's Day; Thanksgiving; Christmas. ♿
Attendance: 11,500
Membership: Student & Senior Citizen $25; Family $30; Contributing $100; Sustaining $250; Classic $500; Life $1,000; Corporation $1,500; Patron $5,000; Heavy Hitter $10,000.

NATIONAL MILITARY HISTORY CENTER, 5634 County Rd. 11A, Auburn, IN 46706. Mailing Address: P.O. Box 1, Auburn, IN 46706-0001. Tel.: 260-927-9144. Fax: 260-927-8043.
Web Site: www.militaryhistorycenter.org
Formerly: World War II Victory Museum
Founded: 2003.
Key Personnel: Exec. Dir., Robert E. Krafft; Pres. (V), Dean V. Kruse; Museum Shop Mgr., Dianne Wineland.
Personnel Profile: Full-Time Paid 9; Part-Time Paid 6; Part-Time Volunteers 125; Interns 2.
Governing Authority: Parent Institution: Dean V. Kruse Foundation, Inc. Tax-exempt.
Military Museum.
Collections: WWII history; military artifacts; uniforms; equipment; personal artifacts; photographs; vehicles; weapons.
Facilities: library.
Activities: Annual Events: Memorial Day Celebration; Veterans Day Celebration; History Fest.
Publications: newsletter, The Salute.
Hours & Admission Prices: Mon.-Sat. 9-5, Sun. 12-5. Adults $10, seniors 55 & over $8, children 7-12 $6; discounts to groups; children under 7 & WWII veterans no charge. ♿
Attendance: 50,000 (estimated)
Membership: Senior $45; Individual $50; Family $100; Corporate $500; Lifetime $2,000.

Aurora

HILLFOREST HOUSE MUSEUM, (M), 213 Fifth St., Aurora, IN 47001-1211. Mailing Address: P.O. Box 127, Aurora, IN 47001-0127. Tel.: 812-926-0087. Fax: 812-926-1075.
E-mail: hillforest@embarqmail.com
Web Site: www.hillforest.org
Founded: 1956.
Congressional District: 9
Key Personnel: Pres. (V), Robert Powell; Dir., Cindy Schuette; Volunteer Coord., Suzanne Ullrich.
Personnel Profile: Full-Time Paid 1; Part-Time Paid 3; Part-Time Volunteers 30.
Governing Authority: nonprofit organization. Parent Institution: Hillforest Historical Foundation, Inc. Tax-exempt: 501(c)(3).
Victorian House Museum: 1852-91 Hillforest, Victorian Ohio River Valley mansion.
Collections: household furnishings & cultural items; archival materials; genealogical information.
Research Fields: regional & local history; local industry; Thomas Gaff & family.
Facilities: food service. Museum-related items for sale.
Activities: guided tours; lectures; docent program; historical & cultural programs; formally organized education programs for docents; educational outreach programs; youth day camps.
Publications: quarterly newsletter; annual calendar of events; brochure; cookbook; souvenir booklet; annual report.
Hours & Admission Prices: April-Dec. Tues.-Sun. 1-5. Adults $5, students 7-13 $3; discounts to groups & AAA members; children 6 & under and members no charge. Closed major holidays. ♿
Attendance: 3,000 (estimated)
Membership: Junior Historian $5; Individual $25; Family $40; Contributor $60; Sponsor $125; Patron $300; Benefactor $500; Life $5,000.

Battle Ground

HISTORIC PROPHETSTOWN, 3549 Prophetstown Tr., Battle Ground, IN 47920-7018. Mailing Address: P.O. Box 331, Battle Ground, IN 47920-0331. Tel.: 765-567-4700. Fax: 765-567-4736.
E-mail: farmdirector@prophetstown.org
Web Site: www.prophetstown.org
Formerly: The Museums At Prophetstown
Founded: 1996.
Congressional District: 7
Key Personnel: C.O.O., Dris Abraham; Pres., Gene Hatke; Treas., Kevin Niebrugge; Sec., Becky Stuckey.
Personnel Profile: Full-Time Paid 3; Part-Time Paid 4; Part-Time Volunteers 20.
Governing Authority: bd. of directors. Tax-exempt: 501(c)(3).
Agriculture Museum.
Collections: 1875-1930 agriculture; personal artifacts; art; botanical; outdoor living history; Native American village; 1920's farmstead; prairie re-creation.
Research Fields: Agriculture & lifestyles.
Activities: field trips programs; supper programs. Special Events: Plow Days;

Planting Days; Father's Day; Wheat Harvest; Threshing Show; Corn Husking; 1920s Country Fair; Armistice Day; Barn Dance.
Publications: newsletter, Prophetstown Dispatch.
Hours & Admission Prices: Call for hours & reservations. Car $6, adults $5, school children $3; members & state park entry holders no charge. ♿
Attendance: 15,000 (estimated)
Membership: Individual $45; Family $60; Friend $100; Benefactor $200; Patron $500.

TIPPECANOE BATTLEFIELD, 200 Battle Ground Ave., Battle Ground, IN 47920-7026. Mailing Address: c/o Tippecanoe County Hist. Assoc., 1001 South St., Lafayette, IN 47901. Tel.: 765-567-2147. Fax: 765-567-2149.
Web Site: www.tcha.mus.in.us
Founded: 1972.
Congressional District: 7
Key Personnel: Pres. (V), Del Bartlett.
Personnel Profile: Part-Time Paid 2; Part-Time Volunteers 6.
Governing Authority: private; nonprofit. Parent Institution: Tippecanoe County Historical Association. Tax-exempt: 501(c)(3).
Park Museum & Visitor Center: housed in Old Battle Ground Hotel, located on 1850s Methodist Church campground site of battle of Tippecanoe.
Collections: material pertaining to the Battle of Tippecanoe & the election of 1840; prehistoric Indian artifacts collection.
Research Fields: Wabash Valley; United Methodist Church history, re: frontier era, 1850 active campground years; Battle of Tippecanoe; Tecumseh; Wm. H. Harrison.
Facilities: retreat center; chapel; picnic grounds. Gifts for sale.
Activities: guided tours; lectures; education programs for children; living history interpretation.
Publications: newsletter; history & nature trail brochures.
Hours & Admission Prices: May-Dec. daily 10-5, call for winter hours. Adults $4, seniors, children, AAM & AAA members $2; members no charge. Closed New Year's Day; Easter; Thanksgiving; Christmas. ♿
Attendance: 35,000 (accurate)
Membership: Basic $35.

Bedford

LAWRENCE COUNTY HISTORICAL AND GENEALOGICAL SOCIETY, 929 15th St., Bedford, IN 47421-3813. Tel.: 812-278-8575. Fax: 812-278-8583.
E-mail: lchgs@hpcisp.com
Web Site: www.lawrencecountyhistory.org
Founded: 1928.
Congressional District: 9
Key Personnel: Pres., Rowena Cross-Najafi; Dir. Library, Joyce Shepherd; Museum Shop Mgr., Kenneth White.
Personnel Profile: Full-Time Paid 1; Part-Time Paid 1.
Governing Authority: county. Tax-exempt.
General Museum.
Collections: pioneer items; Civil War artifacts; genealogy; books & literature on Lawrence County.
Research Fields: genealogy.
Activities: guided tours; lectures; films; audiovisual programs; formally organized education programs for children.
Publications: newsletter; quarterly, Seedling Patch.
Hours & Admission Prices: Tues.-Fri. 9-4, Sat. 9-3. No charge; donations accepted. ♿
Attendance: 3,500 (accurate)
Membership: Student $5; Individual $15; Couple $20; Family $25; Sustaining $100-$249; Contributor $250-$499; Patron $500.

Berne

SWISS HERITAGE VILLAGE & MUSEUM, 1200 Swiss Way, Berne, IN 46711. Mailing Address: P.O. Box 88, Berne, IN 46711-0088. Tel.: 260-589-8007.
Web Site: www.swissheritage.org
Founded: 1985.
Key Personnel: Exec. Dir., Gretchen Lehman
Historic Buildings: late 1800s & early 1900s village.
Collections: local history, culture & heritage; period furnishings; photographs.
Activities: educational programs.
Hours & Admission Prices: Call for hours. Adults $6, seniors 65 & over $5, children 6-18 $3; children under 6 no charge.

Beverly Shores

DEPOT MUSEUM, 525 Broadway, Beverly Shores, IN 46301. Mailing Address: P.O. Box 305, Beverly Shores, IN 46301-0305. Tel.: 219-871-0832.
History Museum.
Collections: local history & culture; photographs; period furnishings; personal artifacts; paintings; maps.
Facilities: Museum-related items for sale.
Hours & Admission Prices: April-Nov. Fri.-Sun. 11:30-3:30. No charge; donations accepted.

Bloomington

ELIZABETH SAGE HISTORIC COSTUME COLLECTION, Memorial Hall E. 232, Indiana University, Bloomington, IN 47405. Mailing Address: Memorial Hall E. 232, 1021 E. 3rd St., Bloomington, IN 47405-7005. Tel.: 812-855-4627. Fax: 812-855-0362.
E-mail: ksrichar@indiana.edu
Web Site: www.indiana.edu/~sagecoll/index.html
Founded: 1935.
Congressional District: 7
Key Personnel: Exec. Dir., Nelda M. Christ; Cur., Kathleen L. Rowold; Asst. Cur., Kelly Richardson.
Personnel Profile: Full-Time Paid 1; Part-Time Paid 1; Part-Time Volunteers 4; Interns 1.
Governing Authority: university. Parent Institution: Indiana University. Tax-exempt: 170(b)(1)(A).
Textile & Costume Museum.
Collections: 19th & 20th-century Western European & American clothing; accessories.
Research Fields: 19th & 20th-century fashions; systematic methods of categorizing & identification of clothing items; by appointment only.
Facilities: 100-vol. library pertaining to fashion plates & advertising material related to 19th & 20th-century fashion available for research on premises by appointment only.
Activities: research & tours of storage by appointment only; off-site lectures & films; formally organized education program for graduate & undergraduate college students; temporary exhibits.
Publications: semiannual newsletter, Historic Costume News; brochure.
Hours & Admission Prices: By appointment only. No charge; donations accepted.
Membership: Friends of Elizabeth Sage: Associate Annual $25; Patron Annual $50; Contributor Annual $100; Life Single $500; Memorial Single $1,000; Corporate $1,000 & up.

HILLTOP GARDEN AND NATURE CENTER, 2367 E. 10th St., Bloomington, IN 47408-3900. Tel.: 812-855-2799 & 8808. Fax: 812-855-2799.
E-mail: hilltop@indiana.edu
Web Site: www.indiana.edu/~hilltop
Founded: 1948.
Congressional District: 7
Key Personnel: Dir., Greg Speichert; Pres. (V), Judith Granbois.
Personnel Profile: Full-Time Paid 1; Part-Time Paid 2.
Governing Authority: state; college; nonprofit organization. Parent Institution: Indiana University. Subsidiary Institution: Dept. Recreation & Park Administration. Tax-exempt.
Youth Garden & Nature Center.
Collections: plants: woody & herbaceous; daffodil test gardens; dwarf iris; hemerocallis collection; peonies; display garden; heirloom seed varieties.
Research Fields: teaching science to boys & girls; curriculum development for resource management sustainable development/organic production; people-plant relations; environmental education.
Facilities: library of nature study & horticulture books available to university students enrolled in horticulture & science education; nature center; reading room; classrooms; 20-acre wooded nature preserve.
Activities: guided tours; lectures; films; formally organized education programs for children, adults, undergraduate & graduate college students; leadership training; nature study; community projects. Museum Sponsors: special Open House; Spring Plants for sale; Home to Bloomington Water Garden Club, Bonsai; Japanese Floral Arranging & Southern Indiana Daylily, Hosta, Iris & Daffodil Society; seasonal festivals.
Publications: newsletters; publications in horticulture journals.
Hours & Admission Prices: Mon.-Fri. 9-5. Greenhouse Tours: call for appointment. ♿
Attendance: 2,000 (estimated)

* **INDIANA UNIVERSITY ART MUSEUM, (M),** 1133 E. Seventh St., Bloomington, IN 47405-7509. Tel.: 812-855-5445. Fax: 812-855-1023.
E-mail: iuam@indiana.edu

Web Site: www.artmuseum.iu.edu
Founded: 1941.
Congressional District: 7
Key Personnel: Dir., Adelheid M. Gealt; Chm. (V), Tony Morarec; Assoc. Dir. Editorial Svcs., Linda Baden; Assoc. Dir. Devel., Jeremy Hatch; Assoc. Dir. Curatorial Svcs., Diane Pelrine; Assoc. Dir. Administration, David Tanner; Museum Shop Mgr., Murat Candiler.
Personnel Profile: Full-Time Paid 38; Part-Time Paid 46; Part-Time Volunteers 64; Interns 10.
Governing Authority: state. Parent Institution: Indiana University. Tax-exempt: 501(c)(3).
Art Museum.
Collections: ancient Egyptian, Greek, Roman sculpture; vases; jewelry; coins & glass; 14th through 21st-century European & American paintings, sculpture, prints, drawings, photography, decorative arts; African, Oceanic, pre-Columbian, Japanese, Chinese, S.E. Asian paintings, sculpture, prints, ceramics, decorative arts.
Research Fields: ancient art; African art; Renaissance decorative arts; modernism; German expressionism; American regionalism.
Facilities: laboratories; cafe. Museum-related items for sale.
Activities: inter-museum loan, permanent, temporary & traveling exhibitions; gallery talks; museum education tours by arrangement; concerts.
Publications: exhibition catalogs; guide to the collections; occasional papers; annual reports; monthly calendars.
Hours & Admission Prices: Tues.-Sat. 10-5, Sun. 12-5. No charge; donations accepted. Closed New Year's Day; Memorial Day; Independence Day; Labor Day; Thanksgiving; Christmas. ♿
Attendance: 40,883 (accurate)

* **MATHERS MUSEUM OF WORLD CULTURES, (M),** 416 N. Indiana Ave., Bloomington, IN 47408-3742. Mailing Address: 601 E. Eighth St., Bloomington, IN 47408-3812. Tel.: 812-855-6873. Fax: 812-855-0205.
E-mail: mathers@indiana.edu
Web Site: www.mathers.indiana.edu
Formerly: William Hammond Mathers Museum
Founded: 1963.
Congressional District: 9
Key Personnel: Dir., Geoffrey Conrad; Asst. Dir., Judith Kirk; Registrar, Theresa Harley-Wilson; Conservator, Judith Sylvester; Business Mgr. & Museum Shop Mgr., Sandra Warren; Cur. Collections, Ellen Sieber; Cur. Education, Deeksha Nagar; Exhibits Co-Cur., Elaine Gaul; Security Coord., Kelly Wherley; Exhibits Co-Cur., Matthew Sieber.
Personnel Profile: Full-Time Paid 8; Part-Time Paid 2; Part-Time Volunteers 30.
Governing Authority: Indiana University. Tax-exempt: 170(b)(1)(A).
General Museum.
Collections: archaeological; ethnological; historical collections from North America, Latin America, Europe, Africa, Asia & Oceania.
Research Fields: anthropology; folklore & history.
Facilities: 1,000-vol. library relating to collections available on premises; classrooms.
Activities: guided tours; lectures; films; gallery talks; docent program; discovery kits; formally organized education programs for undergraduate & graduate students affiliated with Indiana University; rotating exhibits.
Publications: Wm. Hammond Mathers Museum Annual Report; Monograph Series: Occasional Papers; Interpreting Our Past; Photographs as Research Documents.
Hours & Admission Prices: Tues.-Fri. 9-4:30, Sat.-Sun. 1-4:30. No charge; donations accepted. Closed national holidays. ♿
Attendance: 45,272 (accurate)

MONROE COUNTY HISTORICAL SOCIETY, (M), 202 E. Sixth St., Bloomington, IN 47408-3518. Tel.: 812-332-2517. Fax: 812-355-5593.
E-mail: director@monroehistory.org
Web Site: www.monroehistory.org
Founded: 1980.
Congressional District: 8
Key Personnel: C.E.O., Jill Lesh; Pres. (V), Glenda Murray; Cur., Erica Kendall; Office Admin., Dara May; Education, Lisa Simmons; Museum Shop Mgr., Mary Lee Deckard.
Personnel Profile: Full-Time Paid 3; Part-Time Paid 2; Part-Time Volunteers 90.
Governing Authority: society; nonprofit organization. Parent Institution: Monroe County Historical Society, Inc. Tax-exempt.
Historical Society & History Museum: housed in the former Carnegie Library Building.
Collections: objects & documents related to the history of Monroe County; natural history specimens; tools; clothing; items relating to limestone & local industries; household items.
Research Fields: local history; material culture; folklore; limestone industry; architectural history.
Facilities: genealogy library. Gift & museum-items for sale.
Activities: guided tours; docent program; lectures; workshops; outreach program; permanent & temporary exhibitions.
Publications: newsletter; books; local history & cemetery records.
Hours & Admission Prices: Tues.-Sat. 10-4. Adults $2, children 4-18 $1; discounts to AAM, AAA & AASLH members; members no charge. Closed major holidays. ♿
Attendance: 12,000 (accurate)
Membership: Basic $35; Friend $60; Sustaining $100; Contributing $250; Patron $500; Corporate: Level 1 $100-$249; Level 2 $250-$499; Level 3 $500-$999; Level 4 $1,000 & up.

SCHOOL OF FINE ARTS GALLERY, INDIANA UNIVERSITY, (M), 1201 E. 7th St., Bloomington, IN 47405-5501. Tel.: 812-855-8490. Fax: 812-855-7498.
E-mail: sofa@indiana.edu
Web Site: www.indiana.edu/~sofa/
Founded: 1987.
Congressional District: 8
Key Personnel: Dir., Betsy Stirratt.
Personnel Profile: Full-Time Paid 2; Part-Time Paid 10; Part-Time Volunteers 2.
Governing Authority: public university; nonprofit. Tax-exempt: 170(b)(1)(A).
Art Gallery.
Collections: paintings; sculpture; photographs.
Activities: national & regional artist exhibitions; student exhibitions.
Publications: exhibition catalogs
Hours & Admission Prices: Tues.-Fri. 12-4, Sat. 1-4. No charge; donations accepted. Closed spring break; Thanksgiving; Christmas. ♿
Attendance: 20,000 (estimated)
Membership: Student $35; Basic $100; FAB $500; Deluxe $1,000; Primo $5,000.

WONDERLAB MUSEUM OF SCIENCE, HEALTH AND TECHNOLOGY, 308 W. Fourth St., Bloomington, IN 47404-5120. Tel.: 812-337-1337.
Web Site: www.wonderlab.org/
Founded: 1995.
Governing Authority: private; nonprofit organization. Tax-exempt: 501(c)(3).
Children's Museum.
Collections: hands-on exhibits.
Facilities: Museum-related items for sale.
Activities: special events.
Publications: science feature for newspapers, WonderPage.
Hours & Admission Prices: Tues.-Sat. 9:30-5, Sun. 1-5. Adult $7, children 1-17 $6; discounts to groups of 10 or more with reservation; children under 1, members & ASTC Passport members no charge. ♿
Attendance: 71,000 (accurate)

WYLIE HOUSE MUSEUM, 307 E. 2nd St., Bloomington, IN 47401-4799. Mailing Address: 317 E. 2nd St., Bloomington, IN 47401-4701. Tel.: 812-855-6224.
E-mail: libwylie@indiana.edu
Web Site: www.indiana.edu/~libwylie
Founded: 1960.
Key Personnel: Dir., Jo Burgess; Outdoor Interpreter, Sherry Wise; Cur. Education, Bridget Edwards.
Personnel Profile: Full-Time Paid 3; Part-Time Volunteers 12; Interns 1.
Governing Authority: public university; nonprofit. Parent Institute: Indiana University. Tax-exempt: 501(c)(3).
Historic House Museum: housed in 1835 home of Indiana University's first president.
Collections: a few original Wylie furnishings; personal artifacts; garden containing 19th-century varieties of flowers, herbs & vegetables which are raised for seeds to sell.
Research Fields: daily life activities & furnishing of 1840s; Andrew Wylie biography; Theophilus Wylie Family.
Facilities: 175-vol. library of books available for use on premises; botanical garden; 4,000 sq. ft. exhibit space. Museum-related items for sale.
Activities: concerts; docent program; guided tours. Annual Events: Spring Seed Sale in March; Fall Garden Fair in September; Candlelight Tour in December.
Publications: semiannual newsletter, Wylie House.
Hours & Admission Prices: March-Nov. Tues.-Sat. 10-2. No charge; donations accepted. Closed major holidays.
Attendance: 2,000 (accurate)

Bluffton

WELLS COUNTY HISTORICAL MUSEUM, 420 W. Market St., Bluffton, IN 46714. Mailing Address: P.O. Box 143, Bluffton, IN 46714-0143. Tel.: 260-824-9956.
E-mail: jcsturgeon@adamswells.com
Web Site: www.parlorcity.com
Founded: 1935.
Congressional District: 4
Key Personnel: Pres., James Sturgeon; 1st Vice Pres., Connie Brubaker; Sec., Marcia Hotopp; Treas., Greg Waters.
Governing Authority: society. Parent Institution: Wells County Historical Society. Tax-exempt.
Local History Museum.
Collections: items pertaining to Wells County history, culture & industry.
Research Fields: County site & structure survey; genealogy; family history.
Facilities: library of material on Wells County history available for use on premises; reading room.
Activities: guided tours; permanent exhibitions.
Publications: quarterly newsletters; Wells County History; Architectural Atlas of Wells County, Indiana; Wells County, Indiana - A Pictorial History 1999; Wells County Towns & Townships.
Hours & Admission Prices: April-May & Sept.-Nov. Sun. 1-4; June-Aug. Wed. & Sun. 1-4. No charge; donations accepted.
Attendance: 610 (estimated)
Membership: Individual $10; Family $15; Patron $25; Life $150.

Boonville

WARRICK COUNTY MUSEUM, INC., (M), 217 S. First St., Boonville, IN 47601-1701. Mailing Address: P.O. Box 581, Boonville, IN 47601. Tel.: 812-897-3100. Fax: 812-897-6104.
E-mail: wcmuseum@aol.com
Web Site: www.warrickcountymuseum.org
Founded: 1976.
Congressional District: 8
Key Personnel: Dir., Pres. & Chm. (V), Mark Gentry; Treas., Jeffrey Byrne; Museum Shop Mgr., Susan Decker; Museum Shop Mgr., Justin Green.
Personnel Profile: Part-Time Volunteers 15.
Governing Authority: private; nonprofit. Tax-exempt.
History Museum: located in 1901 Ella Williams School, in historic district.
Collections: life in Warrick County from the early 1800s.
Research Fields: Black Heritage underground railroad (Freedom Trails) sites.
Facilities: 3,000 sq. ft. exhibit space.
Activities: guided tours; temporary & loan exhibitions. Annual Events: The Boonville Downtown Square Flare; Christmas in Boon-Village.
Publications: Warrick County Sites, Scenes and Citizens; Warrick County Atlases 1880 and 1899; The Keith Murder Trial; Gold Fillings.
Hours & Admission Prices: March-Dec. Sun.-Wed. 1-4; tours by appointment. Adults $2, members $1. Closed holidays.
Attendance: 1,250 (accurate)
Membership: Student & Senior Citizen $10; Individual $15; Family $30; Business $50; Hemenway $100; Lincoln $250.

Bristol

BONNEYVILLE MILL, 53373 County Rd. 131, Bristol, IN 46507. Mailing Address: 211 W. Lincoln Ave., Goshen, IN 46526-3218. Tel.: 574-825-9324.
E-mail: info@elkhartcountyparks.org
Web Site: www.elkhartcountyparks.org/properties_locations/bonneyville_mill.htm
History Museum: housed in mid-1830s mill.
Collections: working mill grinds corn, wheat, rye & buckwheat.
Facilities: Museum-related items for sale.
Hours & Admission Prices: May-Oct. daily 10-5; guided tours by appointment. No charge.

ELKHART COUNTY HISTORICAL MUSEUM, (M), Rush Memorial Center, 304 W. Vistula St. (St. Rd. 120), Bristol, IN 46507. Mailing Address: P.O. Box 434, Bristol, IN 46507-0434. Tel.: 574-848-4322. Fax: 574-848-5703. TDD: 574-535-6420.
E-mail: museum@elkhartcountyparks.org
Web Site: elkhartcountyparks.org
Founded: 1896.
Congressional District: 3
Key Personnel: Pres. (V) Historical Society, Dean Hupp; Museum Dir., Nicholas Hoffman; Park Dir., Dan Seltenright; Asst. Museum Dir., Diana Zornow; Interpretation Coord., Gary Richards.
Personnel Profile: Full-Time Paid 4; Part-Time Paid 6; Part-Time Volunteers 40.
Governing Authority: county. Parent Institution: Elkhart County Park Dept. Subsidiary Institution: Elkhart County Historical Society. Tax-exempt.
General Museum: 1st consolidated school in Elkhart County; listed on the National Register.
Collections: agriculture; railroad history; home furnishings; apparel; one-room school; military artifacts & Native American artifacts.
Research Fields: Elkhart County history & genealogy.
Facilities: 1,500-vol. library of books; archives.
Activities: guided tours; lectures. Historical Society Programs: A Crystal Ball.
Publications: newsletter.
Hours & Admission Prices: Feb.-Dec. 1 Tues.-Fri. 10-4, Sun. 1-5. No charge; donations accepted. Closed federal holidays. ♿
Attendance: 5,500 (estimated)
Membership: Individual $10; Family $15; Lifetime Individual $150.

Brook

GEORGE ADE MEMORIAL ASSOCIATION INC., Hwy. #16, Brook, IN 47922. Mailing Address: P.O. Box 221, Brook, IN 47922-0221. Tel.: 219-275-6161.
Founded: 1961.
Congressional District: 5
Key Personnel: Cur., Richard Gerts.
Governing Authority: nonprofit organization. Tax-exempt.
Historic House Museum: home of George Ade, humorist, author & playwright.
Collections: objects of art & interest collected by George Ade during his trips at the turn of the century; furniture; mementos.
Activities: guided tours; permanent exhibitions; social functions.
Hours & Admission Prices: Call for hours. No charge; donations accepted. ♿

Brookville

FRANKLIN COUNTY SEMINARY AND MUSEUM, 5th & Mill St., Brookville, IN 47012. Mailing Address: P.O. Box 342, Brookville, IN 47012-0342. Tel.: 765-647-5182.
E-mail: beneker@verizon.net
Founded: 1969.
Congressional District: 9
Key Personnel: Pres., Franklin County Historical Society, Pamela Beneker; Museum Shop Mgr., Martha Shea.
Personnel Profile: Part-Time Volunteers 5.
Governing Authority: nonprofit organization. Parent Institution: The Franklin County Historical Society. Tax-exempt: 170(b)(1)(A).
Local History Museum: housed in c.1828-30 original Franklin County Seminary building.
Collections: records & artifacts of early Franklin County. Historic Houses: 1812 Little Cedar Grove Baptist Church; 1820-21 Old Brick Church & cemetery.
Hours & Admission Prices: By appointment only. No charge; donations accepted.
Membership: Society $8.

Buckskin

HENAGER "MEMORIES AND NOSTALGIA" MUSEUM AND NATIONAL VETERANS MEMORIAL, Hwy. 57, Buckskin, IN 47613. Mailing Address: 8837 S. State Rd. 57, Elberfeld, IN 47613-8445. Tel.: 812-795-2230.
Founded: 1996.
Key Personnel: Chm. (V), James G. Henager.
Governing Authority: Tax-exempt.
History & Military Museum: the National Veterans Memorial headquarters.
Collections: pop culture; WWI & II, Korean and Vietnam veterans; Roy Rodgers; the Beatles; Smokey Bear history & collectibles; woodworking art & history; Santa's workshop; scouting; automotive heritage; military artifacts including flags, mess kits, medals, headgear & photographs; veterans memorabilia; TV movies; heroes & legends; American music; veterans memorial.
Hours & Admission Prices: June-Aug. Mon.-Thurs. 8-7, Fri. 8-5, Sat. 8-4; Sept.-May Mon.-Fri. 8-5, Sat. 8-4. Adults $6, children $3; discounts to members & AAA members.
Membership: Retired & Active Duty $25; Individual $30; Family $65.

Cambridge City

HUDDLESTON FARMHOUSE INN MUSEUM, 838 National Rd., Mt. Auburn, Cambridge City, IN 47327. Mailing Address: P.O. Box 284, Cambridge City, IN 47327-0284. Tel.: 765-478-3172. Fax: 765-478-3410.
E-mail: huddleston@historiclandmarks.org
Web Site: www.historiclandmarks.org
Founded: 1977.

Congressional District: 2
Key Personnel: Museum Dir., Karen Trent; Pres., Marsh Davis; Program Assoc., James Orr.
Personnel Profile: Part-Time Paid 2; Part-Time Volunteers 12.
Governing Authority: nonprofit organization. Parent Institution: Historic Landmarks Foundation of Indiana, 340 W. Michigan, Indianapolis, IN 46202. Tax-exempt: 501(c)(3).
Historic Building: c.1840 federal style brick, 3-story farmhouse.
Collections: farmhouse; outbuildings complex; 1840-1860 period furnishings; farm implements; Huddleston family records; history of travelers & residents along National Road in Indiana; Quaker history.
Research Fields: architectural history; local history; preservation technology; National Road history; middle 19th-century life.
Facilities: 400-vol. preservation resource library; architectural slide & photo collection (eastern Indiana); meeting facilities.
Activities: tours daily; seasonal special events; school programs; group tours; summer camps for children; hearth dinners; lectures; Civil War encampment.
Hours & Admission Prices: Closed for renovations until 2011. ♿
Attendance: 3,633 (accurate)
Membership: Active $20; Contributing & Nonprofit Organization $30; Sponsoring $50; Sustaining $100; Fellow $250; Patron $500; Landmark Member $1,000.

MUSEUM OF OVERBECK ART POTTERY, Cambridge City Public Library, 33 W. Main St., Cambridge City, IN 47327-1117. Tel.: 765-478-3335. Fax: 765-478-6144.
E-mail: ccitypl@yahoo.com
Web Site: www.overbeckmuseum.org
Key Personnel: Dir., Phyllis Wurl; Dir. Library, Vicki Melek.
Governing Authority: bd. of directors. Parent Institution: Cambridge City Public Library. Tax-exempt.
Art Museum.
Collections: Overbeck sisters' art.
Hours & Admission Prices: Mon.-Sat. 10-12 & 2-5. No charge.
Attendance: 100 (estimated)

Carmel

THE MUSEUM OF MINIATURE HOUSES AND OTHER COLLECTIONS, INC., (M), 111 E. Main St., Carmel, IN 46032-1823. Tel.: 317-575-0240. Fax: 317-575-9466.
E-mail: mmhaoc@aol.com
Web Site: www.museumofminiatures.org
Founded: 1991.
Key Personnel: Dir., Suzanne Moffett; Treas. & Museum Shop Mgr., Suzanne H. Landshof.
Personnel Profile: Full-Time Volunteers 3; Part-Time Paid 1; Part-Time Volunteers 36.
Governing Authority: private; nonprofit organization. Tax-exempt: 501(c)(3).
Decorative Arts Museum.
Collections: miniatures; dollhouses.
Facilities: library. Museum-related items for sale.
Activities: guided tours; hobby workshops; special events.
Hours & Admission Prices: Wed.-Sat. 11-4, Sun. 1-4. Adults $4, children under 10 $2; members no charge. Closed New Year's Day; Easter; Memorial Day; Independence Day; Labor Day; Thanksgiving; Christmas. ♿
Attendance: 5,000 (accurate)
Membership: Friend $20; Family $35; Patron $100; Donor $250; Benefactor $1,000.

NATIONAL ASSOCIATION OF MINIATURE ENTHUSIASTS, 130 N. Rangeline Rd., Carmel, IN 46032-1743. Mailing Address: P.O. Box 69, Carmel, IN 46082-0069. Tel.: 317-571-8094. Fax: 317-571-8105.
E-mail: name@miniatures.org
Web Site: www.miniatures.org
Founded: 1972.
Congressional District: 10
Key Personnel: Pres., Karen Barone; Program Coord., Toni Cochran.
Personnel Profile: Full-Time Paid 3; Part-Time Paid 3.
Governing Authority: private; nonprofit organization.
Arts & Crafts/Hobby Museum.
Facilities: 110-vol. library of NAME publications, videos & slide programs; 1,000 sq. ft. exhibit space. Logo merchandise & NAME items for sale.
Activities: guided tours; hobby workshops; loan & participatory exhibits; arts festivals; study clubs. Museum Sponsors: national convention; annual business meeting; regional conventions.
Publications: quarterly, Miniature Gazette.
Hours & Admission Prices: Mon.-Fri. 9-4, Sat.-Sun. by appointment only. No charge; donations accepted. Closed New Year's Eve & Day; Labor Day; Thanksgiving & day after; Christmas Eve, Day & week. ♿

Attendance: 500 (estimated)
Membership: Additional Family Members $10; Individual $25; Foreign $30; Shop Membership $100.

Cedar Lake

LAKE OF THE RED CEDARS MUSEUM, 7408 Constitution Ave., Cedar Lake, IN 46303-9186. Mailing Address: P.O. Box 421, Cedar Lake, IN 46303-0421. Tel.: 219-374-6157. Fax: 219-374-6157.
Founded: 1977.
Congressional District: 1
Key Personnel: C.E.O. & Pres. (V), Robert Carnahan; Dir., Anne Zimmerman.
Personnel Profile: Part-Time Volunteers 20.
Governing Authority: nonprofit organization. Parent Institution: Cedar Lake Historical Association Inc. Tax-exempt: 501(c)(3).
Local History Museum: housed in 1920s 60-room hotel.
Collections: Cedar Lake history & the surrounding area; Chicago, IL history as it pertains to Cedar Lake history; prehistoric-modern artifacts; domestic collections; photographs; industrial artifacts; farming artifacts; archives.
Research Fields: ice industry; Mr. Samuel Bartlett.
Facilities: 8,150 sq. ft. exhibit space. Gift items for sale.
Activities: docent program; films; guided tours; hobby workshops; lectures; temporary & participatory exhibits. Museum Sponsors: Ice Cream Social; Bird House Bash; HoBo Dinner in November.
Publications: monthly newsletter.
Hours & Admission Prices: May-Oct. Thurs.-Sun. 1-4; other times by special arrangement for groups. Adults $2, children $1. ♿
Attendance: 1,000 (estimated)
Membership: Senior & Student $5; Senior Couple $7; Educator $8; Adult $10; Family $20; Patron & Sustaining $25; Benefactor $100.

Centerville

MODEL T MUSEUM, 119 W. Main St., Centerville, IN 47330. Mailing Address: P.O. Box 126, Centerville, IN 47330-0126. Tel.: 765-855-2008.
Automobile Museum.
Collections: Model T automobiles; photographs.
Hours & Admission Prices: Tues.-Sun. 10-5. No charge; donations accepted.

Charlestown

THOMAS DOWNS HOUSE, 1045 Main St., Charlestown, IN 47111-1223. Mailing Address: 8524 State Rd. 403, Charlestown, IN 47111.
Key Personnel: Cur., Donna Hart
History Museum.
Collections: period furnishings.
Hours & Admission Prices: Call for hours.

Chesterton

WESTCHESTER TOWNSHIP HISTORY MUSEUM, 700 W. Porter Ave., Chesterton, IN 46304-2205. Tel.: 219-983-9715. Fax: 219-926-1813.
Founded: 1998.
History Museum.
Collections: local history & culture; photographs; personal artifacts.
Hours & Admission Prices: Wed.-Sun. 1-5; other times by appointment. No charge.

Clarksville

FALLS OF THE OHIO STATE PARK, 201 W. Riverside Dr., Clarksville, IN 47129-3148. Tel.: 812-280-9970, ext. 400. Fax: 812-280-7110.
E-mail: park@fallsoftheohio.org
Web Site: www.fallsoftheohio.org
Founded: 1994.
Congressional District: 9
Key Personnel: Park Mgr., Steve Knowles; Registrar & Interpretive Naturalist, Alan Goldstein; Public Rels. & Interpretive Naturalist, Bett Etenohan.
Personnel Profile: Full-Time Paid 8; Part-Time Paid 6; Part-Time Volunteers 104.
Governing Authority: state; nonprofit. Tax-exempt.
Historic Site: State Park includes the George Rogers Clark homesite.
Collections: 200 acre Middle Devonian fossil beds in the Ohio River, known since the 18th-century. Historic House: log cabin representing George Rogers Clark's home, 1803-1809.
Research Fields: new methods of paleontology education for students & teachers; Silurian & Devonian paleontology & stratigraphy; pre-history at the Falls of the Ohio, bird populations.
Facilities: 1,000-vol. library of books related to ornithology, geology, paleontology, Ohio River history & life sciences; 2 marine & 1 freshwater

aquariums; classroom; 2,000 sq. ft. exhibit space; nature/conservation center; 122-seat theater. Fossils, minerals, jewelry, books, T-shirts & gift items with nature themes for sale.
Activities: docent program; films; formal education programs for teachers, children & college students; guided hikes; lectures; temporary exhibitions; theater; orientations for teachers bringing their classes to the park. Annual Events: Falls Fossil Festival; Raptor Day; Earth Day; Archaeology Day; Family Fun Fair; Clark Festival.
Publications: quarterly, Friends of the Falls Volunteer Newsletter; semiannual, Falls of the Ohio Newsletter; brochures about park-related themes, fossils, wildlife & trails; Educator's Handbook (most available through website).
Hours & Admission Prices: Mon.-Sat. 9-5, Sun. 1-5. Mon.-Thurs. adults $4; Fri.-Sun. & holidays adults $5, children 3-18 $2; children under 3 no charge. Parking: $2 per day. Closed Thanksgiving; Christmas. ♿
Attendance: 30,129 (accurate)
Membership: Friend $25; Associate $50; Sponsor $100; Patron $200. Corporate: $500; $1,000; $ 2,500; $5,000.

Columbia City

WHITLEY COUNTY HISTORICAL MUSEUM, 108 W. Jefferson, Columbia City, IN 46725-1744. Tel.: 260-248-3100. Fax: 260-244-6384.
E-mail: wcmuseum@whitleynet.org
Web Site: www.whitleynet.org/historical/
Founded: 1963.
Congressional District: 4
Key Personnel: Dir., Daney Tipman; Cur., Susan Richey; Bulletin Editor, Nicole Harris; Registrar, Jane Studebaker.
Personnel Profile: Full-Time Paid 1; Part-Time Paid 5; Part-Time Volunteers 12; Interns 1.
Governing Authority: state. Parent Institution: Whitley Co. Historical Society. Subsidiary Institution: Whitley County. Tax-exempt: 501(c)(3).
Historic Home & History Museum: housed in c.1875-1908 Vice Pres. Thomas R. Marshall home.
Collections: artifacts of prehistory & early history of Whitley County; early courthouse records; furniture belonging to Thomas R. Marshall; Marshall memorabilia; natural history displays.
Research Fields: genealogy; archaeology; pioneer.
Facilities: genealogy library; educational center.
Activities: children's programming. Museum Sponsors: Whitley County Historical Society; Old Settlers week special events; pioneer crafts; amateur archaeology association; nursing home programs; Christmas series; special Sunday displays & programs; spring & fall lecture series.
Publications: quarterly, Whitley County Historical Bulletin.
Hours & Admission Prices: Mon.-Thurs. 9-3, Fri. 9-12; other times by appointment. No charge; donations accepted. ♿
Attendance: 9,400 (estimated)
Membership: Individual & Family $15

Columbus

BARTHOLOMEW COUNTY HISTORICAL SOCIETY, 524 Third St., Columbus, IN 47201-6724. Tel.: 812-372-3541. Fax: 812-372-3113.
E-mail: bchs@tls.net
Web Site: barthist.com
Founded: 1921.
Congressional District: 2
Key Personnel: Exec. Dir., Julie Hughes; Pres. (V), Jeff Baker.
Personnel Profile: Full-Time Paid 1; Part-Time Paid 1; Part-Time Volunteers 40.
Governing Authority: private corp. Tax-exempt: 501(c)(3).
Local History Museum.
Collections: archives; Bartholomew County; manuscripts. Historic Houses: c.1867 McEwen-Samuels-Marr Home; c.1870 Henry Breeding Farm Home.
Research Fields: local history; genealogy services.
Facilities: 600-vol. library of manuscripts & material relating to Bartholomew County available for research on premises.
Activities: permanent & temporary exhibits; special programs for children; public events; quarterly meetings. Annual Event: Reeves Festival.
Publications: newsletter; county history; 1879, Atlas & reprints.
Hours & Admission Prices: Tues.-Fri. 9-4; other times by appointment. Adults $4; members no charge. ♿
Attendance: 4,000 (estimated)
Membership: Curator $50; Preserver $100; Heritage Builder $250; Founder (Life) $1,000.

COLUMBUS MUSEUM OF ART AND DESIGN, 390 The Commons, Columbus, IN 47201-6764. Tel.: 812-376-2597. Fax: 812-375-2726.
E-mail: admin@cmadart.org
Web Site: www.cmadart.org
Formerly: Indianapolis Museum of Art Columbus Gallery
Founded: 1974.
Congressional District: 2
Key Personnel: Pres. (V), Beth Stroh; Interim Dir., Jenny Simms.
Personnel Profile: Full-Time Paid 2; Part-Time Paid 3; Part-Time Volunteers 90.
Governing Authority: nonprofit organization.
Art Museum.
Collections: paintings; photographs; sculpture.
Activities: guided tours; lectures; temporary exhibitions; organized education programs for children.
Hours & Admission Prices: Currently closed. ♿
Attendance: 9,079 (accurate)

Connersville

FAYETTE COUNTY HISTORICAL MUSEUM, 103 S. Vine St., Connersville, IN 47331-2649. Mailing Address: P.O. Box 197, Connersville, IN 47331. Tel.: 765-825-5325.
Congressional District: 6
Key Personnel: Pres. (V) & Museum Shop Mgr., Paulette Hayes.
Personnel Profile: Part-Time Volunteers 12.
Governing Authority: Parent Institution: Historic Connersville, Inc. Tax-exempt.
History Museum.
Collections: local history; Civil War artifacts; photographs; personal artifacts; 4 locally-made automobiles.
Activities: monthly membership programs.
Publications: Pictorial History of Connersville; The Lexington Automobile.
Hours & Admission Prices: Thurs. 10-1, Sun. 1-4 by appointment. No charge. ♿
Attendance: 400
Membership: Single $15; Couple $25.

WHITEWATER VALLEY RAILROAD MUSEUM, 455 Market St., Connersville, IN 47331-2073. Mailing Address: P.O. Box 406, Connersville, IN 47331-0406. Tel.: 765-825-2054. Fax: 765-825-4550.
Railroad Museum.
Collections: diesel locomotives; open window coaches; local history; railroad history, transportation & equipment.
Activities: 19 mile scenic train rides; educational programs.
Hours & Admission Prices: May-Oct. daily 9-5. Train Rides: adults $14, children 2-12 $7.

Corydon

CORYDON CAPITOL HISTORIC SITE, 126 E. Walnut St, Corydon, IN 47112-1516. Tel.: 812-738-4890. Fax: 812-738-4904.
E-mail: corydoncapitol@seidata.com
Founded: 1930.
Congressional District: 9
Key Personnel: Cultural Admin., Bec Riley; Senior Interpreter, Nancy Snyder.
Personnel Profile: Full-Time Paid 3; Part-Time Paid 5.
Governing Authority: state. Parent Institution: Indiana Dept. of Natural Resources. Subsidiary Institution: Museum & Historic sites. Tax-exempt.
Historic Site: 1816, first State Capitol Building; Gov. William Hendricks headquarters 1822-1825.
Collections: period furnishings.
Research Fields: early Indiana government.
Activities: guided tours.
Hours & Admission Prices: April to mid-Dec. Tues.-Sat. 9-5, Sun. 1-5; mid-Dec. to March call for hours. Adults $3.50, seniors $3, children $2, students $1; discounts to groups; children under 3 no charge. Closed New Year's Day; Easter; Veterans Day; Columbus Day; Election Day; Thanksgiving; Christmas.
Attendance: 87,800 (estimated)

Crawfordsville

GENERAL LEW WALLACE STUDY & MUSEUM, 200 Wallace Ave., Crawfordsville, IN 47933-2546. Mailing Address: P.O. Box 662, Crawfordsville, IN 47933-0662. Tel.: 765-362-5769. Fax: 765-362-5769.
E-mail: study@ben-hur.com
Web Site: www.ben-hur.com
Formerly: Ben-Hur Museum (Gen. Lew Wallace Study)
Founded: 1905.
Congressional District: 7
Key Personnel: Dir., Larry Paarlberg; Pres., Dale Petrie; Assoc. Dir., Amanda Wesselmann; Visitor Svcs. Rep., Kara Edie; Grounds Mgr., Deb King.
Personnel Profile: Full-Time Paid 2; Part-Time Paid 2; Part-Time Volunteers 30; Interns 1.

Governing Authority: municipal. Parent Institution: City of Crawfordsville Park & Rec. Dept. Subsidiary Institution: Lew Wallace Study Preservation Society. Tax-exempt.
History Museum.
Collections: personal effects of Gen. Wallace, including artwork & inventions; items relating to the movies & Broadway play of Ben-Hur; Civil War & World War I items.
Major Exhibits: Agents of Deterioration, 3/10-12/10.
Research Fields: local history; Civil War; World War I; Ben-Hur movies & Broadway play; American literature; political history.
Facilities: 3 1/2-acre grounds; picnic area. Museum-related items for sale.
Activities: guided & self-guided tours; temporary & permanent exhibitions; video presentation; structured educational programming.
Publications: brochures; newsletter.
Hours & Admission Prices: Feb. to mid-Dec. Wed.-Sat. 10-5, Sun. 1-5; groups by appointment. Adults $3, students $1; discounts to AAM, AAA & AASLH members; LWS Preservation Society members & children under 6 no charge. Closed holidays. ♿
Attendance: 7,000 (accurate)
Membership: Lieutenant $25; Major General $50; Governor $100; Ambassador $250; Ben-Hur Club $500.

LANE PLACE, 212 S. Water St., Crawfordsville, IN 47933-2535. Mailing Address: P.O. Box 127, 212 S. Water St., Crawfordsville, IN 47933-0127. Tel.: 765-362-3416.
E-mail: mchs@accelplus.net
Web Site: www.lane-mchs.org
Founded: 1911.
Congressional District: 7
Key Personnel: Exec. Dir., Tamara Hemmerlein; Asst. Dir., Ann Harvey; Cur., Alison Wright.
Personnel Profile: Part-Time Paid 3; Part-Time Volunteers 26.
Governing Authority: society. Parent Institution: Montgomery County Historical Society. Tax-exempt.
Historic House: c.1845 home of Henry S. Lane, governor & senator of Indiana.
Collections: oil paintings; china; dolls; period furnishings; Lincoln memorabilia.
Research Fields: Abraham Lincoln; birth of Republican Party.
Activities: guided tours; temporary exhibitions; special & seasonal events.
Publications: annual local history book.
Hours & Admission Prices: March-Nov. Tues.-Sun. 1-4. Adults $3, children under 12 $1; members no charge. Closed all holidays.
Attendance: 2,000 (estimated)
Membership: Individual $15; Family $20.

THE ROTARY JAIL MUSEUM, (M), 225 N. Washington, Crawfordsville, IN 47933-1737. Mailing Address: Montgomery County Cultural Foundation, Inc., P.O. Box 771, Crawfordsville, IN 47933-0771. Tel.: 765-362-5222. Fax: 765-362-5222.
E-mail: oldjailmuseum@accelplus.net
Web Site: www.oldjailmuseum.net
Formerly: The Old Jail Museum
Founded: 1975.
Congressional District: 7
Key Personnel: Dir., Tamara Hemmerlein; Pres. (V), Carrie Sosbe.
Personnel Profile: Part-Time Paid 4; Part-Time Volunteers 30.
Governing Authority: nonprofit organization. Parent Institution: Montgomery County Cultural Foundation, Inc. Tax-exempt: 501(c)(3).
Historic Building: 1882 Old Jail only remaining rotating circular jail still in working condition.
Collections: Native American artifacts, clothing, furniture, books, toys, textiles, photos, tools; history & culture of Montgomery County, Indiana & the Midwest as a cultural whole.
Research Fields: relating to the exhibits.
Facilities: 111-vol. library available for use upon request; three exhibit rooms in former living quarters of the sheriff. Museum-related items for sale.
Activities: guided tours; docent program; temporary exhibitions; adult & youth art classes.
Publications: quarterly newsletter; biannual newsletter.
Hours & Admission Prices: March to mid-Dec. Wed.-Sat. 10-5, Sun. 1-5. Adults $3; members no charge. Closed holidays.
Attendance: 4,000 (estimated)
Membership: Individual $10; Family $15; Patron $25; Contributing $50; Sustaining $100; Benefactor $250.

Dale

DR. TED'S MUSICAL MARVELS, 11896 S. U.S. 231, Dale, IN 47523. Mailing Address: 911 Hickory Dr., Huntingburg, IN 47542. Tel.: 812-937-4250. Fax: 812-937-4250.
E-mail: mmarvels@psci.net
Web Site: drted.com
Formerly: House of Mechanical Music Machines
Founded: 1984.
Congressional District: 9
Key Personnel: Dir., Theodore Waflart, M.D.; Chm. (V), Mike Schum; Pres. (V), Mary Kay Waflart; Museum Shop Mgr., Millie Schum.
Personnel Profile: Part-Time Volunteers 4.
Governing Authority: private.
Musical Instrument Museum.
Collections: self-playing musical instruments from 1800s to mid-1900s.
Hours & Admission Prices: By appointment for groups of 15 or more. ♿
Attendance: 1,500 (estimated)

Dana

ERNIE PYLE STATE HISTORIC SITE, 120 W. Briarwood Ave., Dana, IN 47847-0338. Mailing Address: P.O. Box 338, Dana, IN 47847-0338. Tel.: 765-665-3633. Fax: 765-665-9312.
E-mail: erniepyle@abcs.com
Founded: 1976.
Congressional District: 7
Key Personnel: Tour Guide, Janice Duncan; Tour Guide, Joanie Rumple.
Personnel Profile: Full-Time Paid 1; Part-Time Paid 2.
Governing Authority: state. Branch of the Indiana State Museum System, Div. of the Dept. of Natural Resources, Indiana State Museum, 650 W. Washington St., Indianapolis, IN 46204. Tax-exempt.
Visitor Center & Historic House.
Collections: Visitor Center: two World War II-era Quonset huts; WWII uniforms, weapons & gear; Ernie Pyle memorabilia; photographs. Historic House: 1851 farmhouse, birthplace of noted WWII journalist Ernie Pyle was born in 1900.
Research Fields: life & writings of Ernie Pyle; World War II.
Facilities: visitor center. Museum-related items for sale.
Activities: audio & video stations; guided tours; permanent exhibits.
Hours & Admission Prices: May 3-Nov. 17 Thurs.-Sat. 10-5, Sun. 1-5. Closed Easter; Columbus Day; Election Day; Thanksgiving.
Attendance: 8,000 (estimated)

Decatur

ADAMS COUNTY HISTORICAL MUSEUM, 420 W. Monroe St., Decatur, IN 46733-1622. Mailing Address: P.O. Box 262, Decatur, IN 46733-0262. Tel.: 260-724-3493.
Founded: 1965.
Congressional District: 10
Key Personnel: Pres., Herbert Myers; Sec. & Treas., Linda Balsinger.
Governing Authority: society; nonprofit organization. Parent Institution: Adams County Historical Society. Tax-exempt: 501(c)(3).
Historical Society Museum: housed in c.1903 Charles Dugan Home.
Collections: local historical items.
Activities: guided tours; lectures.
Publications: newsletter, The Trumpeter; The History of Adams Co., Indiana, Vol. I & II.
Hours & Admission Prices: June-Sept. Sun. 1-4; other times by appointment only. No charge; donations accepted.
Attendance: 3,000 (estimated)
Membership: Single $10; Family $15; Sustaining $25; Life Single $250; Life with Spouse $350.

Delphi

CARROLL COUNTY HISTORICAL MUSEUM, 101 W. Main St., Ground Fl., Court House, Delphi, IN 46923-1566. Mailing Address: P.O. Box 277, Delphi, IN 46923-0277. Tel.: 765-564-3152. Fax: 765-564-6161.
E-mail: phyllismoore@ffni.com
Web Site: www.carrollcountymuseum.org
Founded: 1924.
Key Personnel: Cur., Phyllis Davis Moore.
Personnel Profile: Full-Time Paid 1; Part-Time Volunteers 8.
Governing Authority: Parent Institution: Carroll County Historical Society. Tax-exempt.
History Museum.
Collections: local history; cultural heritage; Conestoga wagon; period tools; dolls; paintings; genealogy.

Activities: research.
Publications: Carroll County Indiana Legacy, 1824-2005.
Hours & Admission Prices: Tues. & Thurs.-Fri. 10-4; other times by appointment. No charge; donations accepted. Closed holidays. ♿
Attendance: 6,500 (estimated)
Membership: Junior $3; Patron $15; Life $150.

Dugger

DUGGER COAL MUSEUM, 1080 S. Section St., Dugger, IN 47848. Mailing Address: P.O. Box 501, Dugger, IN 47848-0501.
Founded: 1980.
Key Personnel: Pres. (V), Beth Secrest; Cur., Martha Marlow.
Personnel Profile: Part-Time Volunteers 4.
Governing Authority: private; nonprofit organization. Tax-exempt.
Coal Mine Museum.
Collections: history & artifacts from deep coal mines & strip mines; manuals; equipment models; photographs; news clippings; miners tools; miniature electric drugline model; working model of a mine tipple; clothing; protective gear; hard hats; soft caps; all varieties of miners' lights; old mining reports; paychecks & old letters by & about miners; operators control station for an 8900 dragline.
Facilities: Museum-related items for sale.
Activities: Museum Sponsors: Alumni Banquet in September; Coal Festival in September.
Hours & Admission Prices: Coal Festival: Sept. daily 9-9; other times by appointment. No charge; donations accepted.
Attendance: 500 (estimated)
Membership: Individual $4; Lifetime $100.

Dunkirk

THE GLASS MUSEUM, 309 S. Franklin, Dunkirk, IN 47336-1209. Tel.: 765-768-6872. Fax: 765-768-6872.
Web Site: www.dunkirkpubliclibrary.com
Founded: 1979.
Congressional District: 4
Key Personnel: Pres. (V), Roy Sneed; Exec. Dir., Ailesia Franklin; Cur., Mary Newsome.
Personnel Profile: Part-Time Paid 2; Part-Time Volunteers 10.
Governing Authority: nonprofit organization. Parent Institution: Dunkirk Public Library. Tax-exempt: 501(c)(3).
Glass Museum: housed next to the Dunkirk library.
Collections: 8,500 pieces of glassware; Depression; Vaseline; Custard; Albany; hand blown glass; hand painted machine-pressed; handcrafted glassware; glass bottles; glass canes; Indiana glass; patterns & items from Indiana & 115 other glass factories from around the world; cup plates Cambridge glass; Fenton glass.
Activities: guided tours; lectures; rotating, permanent & temporary exhibits. Annual Event: Glass Days Festival in June.
Publications: brochures; annual newsletter.
Hours & Admission Prices: May-Oct. Tues.-Fri. 10-4, Sat. 10-2; Sun. by appointment only. Adults $2; discounts to AAA members & Enjoy Indiana cardholders; children no charge. Closed Memorial Day; Independence Day; Labor Day. ♿
Attendance: 1,200 (accurate)
Membership: Friend Club $5.

Edinburgh

CAMP ATTERBURY MUSEUM, 509C Schoolhouse Rd., Bldg. 427, Edinburgh, IN 46124. Mailing Address: P.O. Box 5000, Bldg. 427, Edinburgh, IN 46124-5000. Tel.: 812-526-1744.
E-mail: diana.hazelwood@us.army.mil
Web Site: www.campatterbury.in.ng.mil
Founded: 1998.
Key Personnel: Cur., Diana Hazelwood.
Personnel Profile: Full-Time Paid 1; Part-Time Volunteers 20.
Military Museum.
Collections: photographs; WWII artifacts; military equipment; POW Chapel.
Activities: veteran activities. Annual Events: POW reunion; former land owners picnic; Memorial Ceremony.
Hours & Admission Prices: Wed. & Sat.-Sun. 1-4; other times by appointment. No charge; donations accepted.

Elkhart

THE CTS HERITAGE ROOM, 905 West Blvd., N., Elkhart, IN 46514-1875. Tel.: 574-523-3800. Fax: 574-293-6146.
E-mail: turnermuseum@ctscorp.com
Web Site: www.ctscorp.com
Formerly: CTS Turner Museum
Founded: 1979.
Congressional District: 3
Key Personnel: Internal Dir., Joseph Carlson; C.E.O., Vinod Khilani.
Governing Authority: CTS Corporation.
Company & Technology Museum.
Collections: telephones; 1896-1940 switchboards; 1926-present electronic components.
Activities: guided tours.
Hours & Admission Prices: By appointment only. No charge.

MIDWEST MUSEUM OF AMERICAN ART, (M), 429 S. Main St., Elkhart, IN 46516-3210. Mailing Address: P.O. Box 1812, Elkhart, IN 46515-1812. Tel.: 574-293-6660. Fax: 574-293-6660 (call first).
E-mail: mdwstmsmam@aol.com
Web Site: www.midwestmuseum.us
Founded: 1978.
Congressional District: 2
Key Personnel: Chm. (V), Dr. Rick Burns; Dir., Jane Burns; Cur., Brian Byrn; Administrative Asst., Stacy Jordan; Museum Shop Mgr., Gertrude Basquin.
Personnel Profile: Full-Time Paid 1; Full-Time Volunteers 1; Part-Time Paid 1; Part-Time Volunteers 54; Interns 1.
Governing Authority: nonprofit organization. Tax-exempt: 501(c)(3).
Art Museum.
Collections: American Impressionists, Regionalists & Abstract Expression Illustrators; Chicago & Pop Art; prints, drawings, sculpture & photography; works by Robert Reid, Charles Hawthorne, Earnest Lawson, John Singer Sargent, Grandma Moses, Grant Wood & Thomas Hart Benton.
Major Exhibits: Samara: Frank Lloyd Wright Usonian Home (T), 1/8/10-2/21/10; Ray Howlett: The Art of Diachroic Glass (T), 4/4/10-5/30/10; The Unbroken Thread: Paintings by Phillip Koch (T), 6/4/10-9/5/10; Frank Dudky: Painter of the Indiana Dunes, 12/10/10-2/27/11.
Research Fields: American folk painting & American Art Movements.
Facilities: Museum-related items for sale.
Activities: guided tours; lectures; films; gallery talks; concerts; formally organized education programs; docent programs; permanent, temporary, loan & traveling exhibitions.
Publications: catalogue, Panorama of American Art; bulletin, Midwest Museum; bimonthly, Art News; catalogues, Midwest Photo 80; Midwest Photo 81; catalogue, Midwest Museum of American Art Permanent Collection.
Hours & Admission Prices: Tues.-Fri. 10-4, Sat.-Sun. 1-4. Adults $4, senior citizens $3, students $2; discounts to AAM, ICOM, AAA & Mobil Guide members; Sun. & members no charge. Closed New Year's Day; Memorial Day; Independence Day; Labor Day; Thanksgiving; Christmas. ♿
Attendance: 20,000 (accurate)
Membership: Student & Senior $10; Individual $20; Family $60; Junior Society $100; Society of Associates $150; Patrons $250; Benefactor $500; Sustainer $1,000; Guarantor $2,000; Endower $5,000.

NATIONAL NEW YORK CENTRAL RAILROAD MUSEUM, 721 S. Main St., Elkhart, IN 46516-3715. Mailing Address: P.O. Box 1708, Elkhart, IN 46515-1708. Tel.: 574-294-3001. Fax: 574-295-9434.
E-mail: info@nycrrmuseum.org
Web Site: www.nycrrmuseum.org
Founded: 1987.
Congressional District: 2
Key Personnel: Exec. Dir., Ron Troyer; Pres., Al Troyer.
Personnel Profile: Full-Time Paid 1; Part-Time Paid 3; Part-Time Volunteers 15; Interns 2.
Governing Authority: municipal government; nonprofit. Parent Institution: City of Elkhart. Tax-exempt.
Transportation Museum: housed in c.1885-1906 New York Central Freight-house complex.
Collections: the New York Central railroad, its predecessor & successor lines and their relationship to Elkhart, Indiana; National Railroad Adjustment Board annals; Engine House crew books; rules & regulations for railroad operation; steam & diesel engine equipment; personal papers & correspondence.
Research Fields: immigrants & the railroad; oral & video histories of ex-New York Central employees.
Facilities: 345-vol. library; 6,000 sq. ft. exhibit space. Railroad-oriented items for sale.
Activities: docent program; guided tours; lectures; loan, participatory, temporary & traveling exhibitions; school loan service; broadcast programs.
Publications: quarterly newsletter, New York Central News.
Hours & Admission Prices: Tues.-Sat. 10-4, Sun. 12-4. Adults $5, senior citizens & children $4. Closed New Year's Day; Easter; Independence Day; Thanksgiving; Christmas. ♿
Attendance: 20,000 (accurate)
Membership: Regular $25; Preferred $40; Life $500; VIP-Life $1,000.

RV/MH HERITAGE FOUNDATION, INC., 21565 Executive Pkwy., Elkhart, IN 46514-9693. Tel.: 574-293-2344; 800-378-8694. Fax: 574-293-3466.
E-mail: rvmhhall@aol.com
Web Site: rv-mh-hall-of-fame.org
Founded: 1972.
Congressional District: 3
Key Personnel: Pres., Carl A. Ehry; Chm. (V), Lon Larson.
Personnel Profile: Full-Time Paid 2; Part-Time Paid 2; Part-Time Volunteers 20.
Governing Authority: private; nonprofit organization. Subsidiary Institution: RV/MH Hall of Fame. Tax-exempt: 501(c)(3).
Industrial Museum.
Collections: publications, images & records of the recreational vehicle and manufactured housing industries; travel trailers, motorized units, manufactured equipment & supplies of the industries.
Research Fields: advent, growth & development of the recreational vehicle and manufactured housing industries; manufacturing technology, techniques & distribution; retailing; recreational & practical use of industry's product.
Facilities: 10,000-vol. library of industry & consumer publications; educational facilities; 14,000 sq. ft. exhibit space.
Activities: guided tours.
Publications: Heritage Happenings.
Hours & Admission Prices: Mon.-Fri. 9-5, Sat. 9-3; other times by appointment. Adults $8, seniors $6, youth 6-16 $3; discounts to groups. ♿
Attendance: 8,000 (estimated)
Membership: Bronze Patron $250; Silver Patron $500; Gold Patron $1,000; Star Patron $2,500.

RUTHMERE MUSEUM, 302 E. Beardsley Ave., Elkhart, IN 46514-2719. Tel.: 574-264-0330; 888-287-7696. Fax: 574-266-0474.
Web Site: www.ruthmere.org
Founded: 1973.
Congressional District: 3
Key Personnel: Founding Dir., Robert Beardsley; Chm. (V), George Freese; Exec. Dir., Laurel Spencer Forsythe; Librarian & Archivist, Marilou Ritchie; Bldg. & Grounds Mgr., Ronald Wolschlager.
Personnel Profile: Full-Time Paid 1; Part-Time Paid 12; Part-Time Volunteers 16.
Governing Authority: bd. of trustees; nonprofit organization. Tax-exempt: 501(c)(3).
Historic House Museum: c.1910.
Collections: Louis XV revival furniture; Dresden & Sevres porcelain; Wedgwood pottery; art glass by Steuben & Tiffany Studios; sculpture by A. Rodin, C. Claudel, W.O. Partridge; paintings by Samuel F.B. Morse, Alma-Tadema & other 19th-century American and European artists & craftsmen.
Research Fields: architect E. Hill Turnock; American Midwestern material culture 1910-1945.
Facilities: 1,875-vol. reference library of American decorative arts & domestic architecture.
Activities: guided tours; public programs.
Publications: quarterly newsletter.
Hours & Admission Prices: April-Dec. Tours: Tues.-Sat. 10am, 11am, 1pm, 2pm & 3pm, Sun. 1pm, 2pm & 3pm; group tours & Mon. by appointment. Adults $8, senior citizens over 62 $7, college students $5, students K-12 $3; discounts to AAM & ICOM members; children under 5 no charge.
Attendance: 7,000
Membership: Individual $25; Family $50; Patron $100; Bronze Patron $250; Silver Patron $500; Gold Patron $1,000.

Evansville

ANGEL MOUNDS STATE HISTORIC SITE, 8215 Pollack Ave., Evansville, IN 47715-6231. Tel.: 812-853-3956. Fax: 812-858-7686.
E-mail: angelmoundsshs@dnr.in.gov
Web Site: www.angelmounds.org
Founded: 1946.
Congressional District: 8
Key Personnel: C.E.O., Historic Site Cur. & Site Mgr., Mike Linderman; Pres. (V), Gary Bush; Sectional Archaeology Program Developer, Haley Tallman; Museum Shop Mgr., Patrick Thomas.
Personnel Profile: Full-Time Paid 6; Part-Time Paid 1; Part-Time Volunteers 30; Interns 2.
Governing Authority: state. Parent Institution: Indiana State Museums & Historic Sites. Tax-exempt.
Archaeology Museum and Pre-Historic Site: Middle Mississippian Indian Site.
Collections: Middle Mississippian Indian artifacts; Angel Mounds' excavation photographs; reconstructed village.
Research Fields: archaeology of Middle Mississippian Indians.
Facilities: 70-seat auditorium.
Activities: orientation video; permanent & temporary exhibits; lectures; tours; organized education programs for adults & students; special events.
Publications: historic site brochure & walking tour map.
Hours & Admission Prices: Tues.-Sat. 9-5, Sun. 1-5. Adults $4, senior citizens $3.50, children $2, school groups $1; members no charge. ♿
Attendance: 49,000 (estimated)
Membership: Friends Group: Individual $10; Family $15; Contributor $25; Supporting $50; Patron $100; Corporate $250.

EVANSVILLE AFRICAN AMERICAN MUSEUM, 579 Lincoln Ave., Evansville, IN 47713. Mailing Address: P.O. Box 3124, Evansville, IN 47731-3124. Tel.: 812-423-5188.
Web Site: www.evansvilleaamuseum.com
Founded: 1997.
Congressional District: 8
Key Personnel: Pres. (V), Lana Burton.
Personnel Profile: Part-Time Paid 2.
History Museum: housed in one of the nation's first housing projects, Lincoln Gardens; built in 1938.
Collections: African American culture & history; personal artifacts; photographs.
Activities: Museum Sponsors: Fabulous First Fridays monthly.
Hours & Admission Prices: Tues.-Sat. 10-5. Adults $5, children $3. Closed New Year's Day; Martin Luther King, Jr. Day; Memorial Day; Independence Day; Labor Day; Thanksgiving; Christmas. ♿
Attendance: 1,200
Membership: Individual $25; Family $60; Sustaining $100; Corporation $500; Lifetime $1,500.

*** EVANSVILLE MUSEUM OF ARTS HISTORY & SCIENCE, (M),** 411 S.E. Riverside Dr., Evansville, IN 47713-1098. Tel.: 812-425-2406. Fax: 812-421-7509.
Web Site: www.emuseum.org
Founded: 1926.
Congressional District: 8
Key Personnel: Dir., John W. Streetman, III; Pres., Robert Zimmermann, Sr.; Cur. Collections, Mary McNamee Bower; Registrar, Liz Fuhrman Bragg; Cur. History, Thomas R. Lonnberg; Dir. Koch Science Center & Planetarium, Mitchell Luman; Dir. Devel., Jane Ress Kline; Dir. Mktg. & Membership, Susan Washburn; Cur. Education, Stephanie Gerhardt; Science Educator, Gena Garrett; Museum Shop Mgr., Pati Hoskins.
Personnel Profile: Full-Time Paid 16; Full-Time Volunteers 1; Part-Time Paid 18; Part-Time Volunteers 50; Interns 10.
Governing Authority: nonprofit organization. Tax-exempt: 501(c)(3).
Arts, History & Science Museum.
Collections: painting; sculpture; prints & drawings; decorative arts; transportation; arms & armor; steam locomotive & cars; science displays; anthropology.
Facilities: 3,500-vol. library & archives related to art, history & science; planetarium; classroom; science center. Gift items for sale
Activities: guided tours; lectures; special programs; gallery talks; musicals; formally organized education programs; docent program; student volunteer program; demonstrations; inter-museum loans; permanent, temporary & traveling exhibitions; camp-ins.
Publications: quarterly members magazine, The COPIA; books: Architectural Heritage of Evansville; The Eye & the Heart: Watercolors of John Stuart Ingle; Simplicity, A Grace: Jacob Maentel in Indiana; A Charmed Vision: The Art of Carolyn Plochmann; Art School: A Homage to the Masters, Paintings by George Deem; T.C. Steele: An American Master of Light; catalogs of special exhibits; biennial catalogs of Mid-States Craft Exhibition & Mid-States Art Exhibition.
Hours & Admission Prices: Tues.-Sat. 10-5, Sun. 12-5. Suggested Donation: adult $4, child $2. Closed national holidays. ♿
Attendance: 72,500 (accurate)
Membership: Friend $35-$69; Contributor $70-$124; Patron $125-$249; Donor $250-$499; Director's Associate $500-$999; President's Circle $1,000-$2,499; Founder's Society $2,500 & up.

KOCH FAMILY CHILDREN'S MUSEUM OF EVANSVILLE, 22 S.E. 5th St., Evansville, IN 47708-1604. Mailing Address: P.O. Box 122, Evansville, IN 47701-0122. Tel.: 812-464-2663. Fax: 812-477-4339.
E-mail: info@cmoekids.org
Web Site: www.cmoekids.org
Formerly: Hands On Discovery
Founded: 1994.
Key Personnel: Exec. Dir., Carol R. Young; Pres. (V), Patrick Koontz.
Personnel Profile: Full-Time Paid 7; Part-Time Paid 19; Interns 3.
Governing Authority: nonprofit organization. Tax-exempt: 501(c)(3).
Children's Museum.

Collections: hands-on exhibits.
Hours & Admission Prices: Tues.-Sat. 10-5, Sun. 12-5. Admission 18 months & over $6; discount to ACM Reciprocal members; members no charge.
Attendance: 65,575 (accurate)
Membership: Family $99; Family Plus $129; Grandparents $139.

MESKER PARK ZOO & BOTANIC GARDEN, 1545 Mesker Park Dr., Evansville, IN 47720-8206. Tel.: 812-435-6143. Fax: 812-435-6140.
E-mail: zooservices@meskerparkzoo.com
Web Site: www.meskerparkzoo.com
Founded: 1929.
Congressional District: 8
Key Personnel: Dir., Dan McGinn; Pres. (V), Beck Kasha; Gen. Cur., Erik Beck; Visitor Svcs. Cur., Stephanie Sanderson; Education Cur., Diana Barber; Animal Cur., Brad Fichter; Registrar, Dana Duke; Botanic Cur., Paul Bouseman.
Personnel Profile: Full-Time Paid 35; Part-Time Paid 42; Part-Time Volunteers 450.
Governing Authority: municipal. A branch of Evansville Park Dept. & Recreation Dept. Civic Center. Evansville Zoological Society. Tax-exempt.
Zoo.
Collections: animal exhibits; 200 species of mammals, birds, reptiles; over 650 specimens.
Facilities: 500-vol. library of zoological books available for use on premises; 50 acre grounds; children's zoo. Museum-related items for sale.
Activities: lectures; permanent exhibitions; narrated safari train tour; day camp.
Publications: quarterly magazine; quarterly members newsletter, Mesker Messenger.
Hours & Admission Prices: Daily 9-5. Adults $7, children 3-12 $6; discounts to AAZPA & other zoo society members; members & children under 3 no charge. ♿
Attendance: 140,019 (accurate)
Membership: Senior $25; Individual $29; Couple $39; Family $49.

REITZ HOME MUSEUM, 224 S.E. First St., Evansville, IN 47713-1002. Mailing Address: P.O. Box 1322, Evansville, IN 47706-1322. Tel.: 812-426-1871. Fax: 812-426-2179.
E-mail: reitz@evansville.net
Web Site: www.reitzhome.evansville.net
Founded: 1974.
Congressional District: 8
Key Personnel: Pres., Dennis Lamey; Vice Pres., Rebecca Alcorn; Treas., Joan Evans; Sec., Alvin Basham; Cur., Pam Guthrie; Museum Shop Mgr., Anne Blake.
Personnel Profile: Full-Time Paid 3; Part-Time Paid 1; Part-Time Volunteers 250; Interns 2.
Governing Authority: private; nonprofit organization. Parent Institution: The Reitz Home Preservation Society. Tax-exempt: 501(c)(3).
Victorian Historic House: located in the Riverside Historic District, the 1871 house was built by hardwood lumber magnate John Augustus Reitz.
Collections: Victorian furniture & decorative arts from the 1871-1920 period.
Research Fields: original wall coverings & house history.
Facilities: educational facilities; 18,255 sq. ft. exhibit space. Museum-related items for sale.
Activities: docent program; formal education programs; guided tours; participatory exhibits. Annual Events: Mystery Event; Wine Dive; Victorian Christmas; Victorian Gala.
Publications: quarterly newsletter.
Hours & Admission Prices: Tues.-Sat. 11-3:30, Sun. 1-3:30. Adults $7.50, students $2.50, children 12 & under $1.50; discounts available to groups, schools & AAM members; Reitz Home members no charge. ♿
Attendance: 12,000 (accurate)
Membership: Student $10; Basic $25-$49; Family Circle $50-$99; 224 Club $100-$249; Patron Circle $250-$499; Victorian Society $500 & up; Presidents' Circle $1,000 & up.

WESSELMAN PARK NATURE CENTER, 551 N. Boeke Rd., Evansville, IN 47711-5923. Tel.: 812-479-0771.
Nature Center.
Collections: wildlife & their habitats; natural history.
Activities: special events; educational programs.
Hours & Admission Prices: Tues.-Sun. 8-6.

Fairmount

FAIRMOUNT HISTORICAL MUSEUM & GIFT SHOP, 203 E. Washington St., Fairmount, IN 46928-1700. Mailing Address: P.O. Box 92, Fairmount, IN 46928-0092. Tel.: 765-948-4555.
Web Site: www.jamesdeanartifacts.com/index.php
Founded: 1975.
Congressional District: 5
Key Personnel: Fairmount Historian, Ann Warr; Vice Pres., Gale Hikade; Chm. (V), Robert McManaman.
Governing Authority: Tax-exempt.
History Museum.
Collections: local history; photographs; personal artifacts of James Dean & his family; Jim Davis, creator of Garfield.
Activities: Museum sponsors: Fairmount Museum Day Remembering: James Dean in September
Publications: annual membership newsletter.
Hours & Admission Prices: March-Nov. Mon.-Sat. 10-5, Sun. 12-5; other times by appointment. No charge; donations accepted. Closed Easter; Thanksgiving. ♿
Attendance: 7,000 (accurate)
Membership: Annual $6; 6 Years $30; 10 Years $50; Life $100.

Fishers

* **CONNER PRAIRIE INTERACTIVE HISTORY PARK, (M),** 13400 Allisonville Rd., Fishers, IN 46038-4499. Tel.: 317-776-6000; 800-966-1836. Fax: 317-776-6014.
E-mail: rosenthal@connerprairie.org
Web Site: www.connerprairie.org
Founded: 1964.
Congressional District: 6
Key Personnel: Pres. & C.E.O., Ellen Rosenthal; Chm. Museum Bd., Gay Dwyer; Chm. Foundation Bd., Berkley Duck; C.F.O., Kyle Wenger; C.O.O., Ken Bubp; Deputy Dir. Museum Experience, Tim Crumrin; Mgr. Public Rels., Angela Tuell; Vice Pres. Devel., Cameron McGuire; Dir. Experience, Dan Freas; Dir. Mktg. Communications, Michelle Runzer; Dir. Human Resources, Susan Johnson; Dir. Facilities, John Spicklomine; Dir. Festivals & Special Events, Kelly Oles; Museum Shop Mgr., Elaine Molin; Dir. Corporate & Foundation Rels., Joe Hammer.
Personnel Profile: Full-Time Paid 87; Part-Time Paid 173; Part-Time Volunteers 488.
Governing Authority: Tax-exempt: 501(c)(3).
Interactive History Park & Museum.
Collections: microfilm of relevant magazines & newspapers; pioneer artifacts; 1859 balloon voyage & related artifacts; early aviation history; modern balloon flight. Historic Buildings: 1836 rural settlement with houses, store, blacksmith shop, pottery, carpenter shop, inn, schoolhouse, barns & other outbuildings; 1823 William Conner home; barn & supporting structures; loomhouse; 1886 Quaker Meeting house; covered bridge; district school and working farm; 1816 Lenape Indian Village.
Research Fields: Indiana & midwestern history, science, technology & environment.
Facilities: 3,500-vol. library of material relating to rural living, crafts, local & Indiana history and science available for research on premises; welcome center; picnic pavilions; restaurant; 800 acres; amphitheater; rental facilities. Park-related items for sale.
Activities: interactive exhibits; organized education programs; permanent exhibitions; lectures; special programs; costumed staff doing seasonal tasks; period craft programs; weddings; harvests; agricultural fairs; Underground Railroad program; play & learning area for young children. Annual Events: Hearthside Suppers January to March; Civil War Days in May; Fourth of July Celebration; County Fair in September; Headless Horseman Fall Festival; 1880s Agricultural Fair; Candlelight Tours in December; Indiana Festival.
Publications: member magazine, Closer Look.
Hours & Admission Prices: April Thurs.-Sat. 10-5, Sun. 11-5; May-Sept. Tues.-Sat 10-5, Sun. 11-5; Oct. Wed.-Sat. 10-5, Sun. 11-5; Nov.-March call for special programs & hours. Adults $12, senior citizens 65 & over $11, youth 2-12 $8; discounts to AAM & ICOM members; children 2 & under and members no charge. Closed Easter; Thanksgiving; Christmas Eve & Day. ♿
Attendance: 315,455 (accurate)
Membership: Individual $45; Family & Grandparent $65; Family & Grandparent Plus $95; Heritage $100-$249; Prairietown Citizen $250-$499; Golden Eagle $500-$999; Conner Society $1,000; Conner Society Silver $2,000; Conner Society Gold $5,000 & up.

Fort Wayne

AFRICAN-AMERICAN HISTORICAL MUSEUM, 436 E. Douglas Ave., Fort Wayne, IN 46802-3539. Tel.: 260-420-0765. Fax: 260-426-9773.
Founded: 1999.
Congressional District: 4
Key Personnel: Dir., Hana L. Stith; Pres. (V), Rubin L. Brown; Museum Shop Mgr., Patsy Brewer
History Museum.

Collections: African-American history & culture; photographs; personal artifacts; furnishings.
Hours & Admission Prices: Tues.-Fri. 9-1, Sat. 12-4, Sun. by appointment. Adults $3, children $2. Closed holidays.

ARTLINK, 437 E. Berry St., Fort Wayne, IN 46802-2817. Tel.: 260-424-7195. Fax: 260-424-8453.
Web Site: www.artlinkfw.com
Founded: 1978.
Key Personnel: Exec. Dir., Deb Washler; Bd. Pres., Theresa Stumpf; Education, Suzanne Galazka.
Personnel Profile: Full-Time Paid 2; Part-Time Paid 2.
Governing Authority: private; nonprofit organization. Tax-exempt: 501(c)(3).
Art Gallery.
Collections: paintings.
Major Exhibits: Just Desserts, 1/22/10-2/24/10; Regional University Exhibit, 5/5/10-4/7/10; 30th Annual National Print Exhibit, 4/16/10-5/26/10; Organic Prospective, 6/4/10-7/7/10; The Members' Show, 7/16/10-8/11/10; Landscapes - Urban & Rural, 8/20/10-10/6/10; Toyes and Book Illustration, 10/15/10-12/1/10.
Facilities: 2,000 sq. ft. exhibit space.
Activities: workshops. Annual Events: National Print Exhibition; Biannual Wet Paint Auction.
Publications: quarterly newsletter, Genre.
Hours & Admission Prices: Tues.-Thurs. 12-5, Fri.-Sat. 12-9, Sun. 1-5. Adults $2; members no charge. Closed New Year's Day; Memorial Day; Independence Day; Labor Day; Thanksgiving; Christmas Eve & Day. ♿
Attendance: 15,000 (estimated)
Membership: Student $10; Senior $15; Individual $20; Family $30; Contributor $50; Patron $100; Benefactor $200.

CATHEDRAL MUSEUM, Archbishop Noll Catholic Center, 915 S. Clinton St., Fort Wayne, IN 46801. Mailing Address: P.O. Box 390, Fort Wayne, IN 46801. Tel.: 260-422-4611, ext. 3337. Fax: 260-744-1972.
Web Site: www.diocesefwsb.org
Founded: 1980.
Congressional District: 3
Key Personnel: Dir., Rev. Phillip A. Widmann; Chm. (V), Margaret Venderley.
Personnel Profile: Part-Time Volunteers 21.
Governing Authority: Parent Institution: Diocese of Fort Wayne, South Bend. Tax-exempt.
Catholic Church Museum.
Collections: northern Indiana Catholic church history; wood carvings; sacred vessels; church vestments; paintings; religious artifacts, relics; books.
Facilities: Books & gift items for sale.
Activities: special events.
Publications: newsletter.
Hours & Admission Prices: Tues.-Fri. 10-2; other times by appointment. No charge; donations accepted. Parking: no charge. ♿
Attendance: 6,500 (accurate)

DIEHM MUSEUM OF NATURAL HISTORY, 600 Franke Park Dr., Fort Wayne, IN 46808. Mailing Address: 3411 Sherman Blvd., Fort Wayne, IN 46808-1522. Tel.: 260-427-6708.
Natural History Museum.
Collections: natural history; geology; wildlife dioramas.
Hours & Admission Prices: April 25-Oct. 15 Sat.-Sun. 12-5. Adults $2, children $1.

FOELLINGER-FREIMANN BOTANICAL CONSERVATORY, 1100 S. Calhoun St., Fort Wayne, IN 46802-3007. Tel.: 260-427-6440. Fax: 260-427-6450.
Web Site: www.botanicalconservatory.org
Founded: 1983.
Key Personnel: Dir., Mitch Sheppard; Museum Shop Mgr., Jane Ford; Business Devel., Linda Miller.
Personnel Profile: Full-Time Paid 11; Part-Time Paid 6; Part-Time Volunteers 200.
Governing Authority: city. Parent Institution: Fort Wayne Parks and Recreation Department. Tax-exempt.
Botanical Garden.
Collections: orchids; palm trees; cacti; tropical specimens; midwest trees & shrubs.
Major Exhibits: Three Faces of St. Paul's, 12/19/09-1/10; Build A City, 1/10; Downtown Landmarks, 1/2/10-4/4/10; Butterflies & Fairies, 4/10/10-6/27/10; Greek Odyssey, 7/3/10-11/14/10; Candyland, 11/20/10-1/2/11.
Facilities: Gift items for sale.
Activities: field trips; group tours; special events; horticultural workshops; plant sales; plant shows; plant swaps; art displays; summer day camp; garden weddings.
Publications: event brochure; quarterly program guide; volunteer newsletter.
Hours & Admission Prices: Tues.-Wed. & Fri.-Sat. 10-5, Thurs. 10-8, Sun. 12-4. Adults $5, children 3-17 $3; discount to AAA members & AHS reciprocal program members; members and children 2 & under no charge. Closed New Year's Day; Christmas. ♿
Attendance: 70,000 (accurate)
Membership: Add A Guest $15; Individual $35; Family $50; Friend $75; Booster $125; Patron $250; Advocate $500; Manager's Circle $1,000 & up.

FORT WAYNE CHILDREN'S ZOO, 3411 Sherman Blvd., Fort Wayne, IN 46808-1594. Tel.: 260-427-6800. Fax: 260-427-6820.
Web Site: www.kidszoo.org
Founded: 1965.
Congressional District: 3
Key Personnel: Dir., Jim Anderson; Animal Cur., Mark Weldon; Education, Cheryl Piropato; Devel., Kelly Hagerman; Veterinarian, Joe Smith; Operations, Jim McGowin; Finance, Dave Thomas.
Personnel Profile: Full-Time Paid 60; Part-Time Paid 100; Part-Time Volunteers 400; Interns 15.
Governing Authority: nonprofit. Subsidiary Institution: Fort Wayne Zoological Society. Tax-exempt: 501(c)(3).
Zoo.
Collections: African, Australian, & Indonesian animals; Indo-pacific fish & sharks.
Research Fields: Australian animals; native rattlesnakes.
Facilities: 2.000-vol. library of materials on natural history; food service available. Gift items for sale.
Activities: formal education programs; guided tours; lectures; mobile vans; participatory exhibits.
Publications: magazine, Zoo to You; newsletters, Zoo to You Extra; Kangaroo Pouch; z-mail electronic newsletter.
Hours & Admission Prices: late April to mid-Oct. daily 9-5. Adults $12, seniors $10, children 2-14 $8; discounts to reciprocal zoos; children under 2 no charge. ♿
Attendance: 600,000 (estimated)
Membership: Add-A-Guest $25; Individual $67; Single Parent $79; Family & Grandparent $85; Zoo Friend $110; Zoo Booster $150; Safari Club $250; Director's Circle $500; King of the Jungle $1,000.

FORT WAYNE FIREFIGHTERS MUSEUM, 226 W. Washington Blvd., Fort Wayne, IN 46802-3021. Tel.: 260-426-0051.
Web Site: www.fortwaynefiremuseum.com/Museum%20Web%20Site/
Founded: 1974.
Key Personnel: Pres. (V), Joel Degitz; Financial Dir., Ron Brockmyer; Devel., Education & Museum Shop Mgr., Dennis Giere.
Personnel Profile: Part-Time Paid 8; Part-Time Volunteers 10.
Governing Authority: private; nonprofit organization. Tax-exempt: 501(c)(3).
Fire-Fighting Museum: housed in an 1893 structure.
Collections: history of the Fort Wayne Fire Department dating back to 1800s; apparatus; equipment; patch collection.
Facilities: 200-vol. library. Museum-related items for sale.
Activities: guided tours; formal education for adults & children; temporary exhibitions.
Hours & Admission Prices: Mon.-Fri. 10-4, Sat. 10-3. Adults $4, senior citizens & students $3; discounts to groups with reservations; members and children 5 & under no charge. Closed New Year's Day; Memorial Day; Independence Day; Labor Day; Thanksgiving; Christmas.
Attendance: 3,113 (accurate)
Membership: Student 18 & under and Seniors 60 & over $15; Individual $20; Family (2 Adults) $25; Rookie $25-$99; Firefighter $100-$299; Hoseman $300-$499; Tillerman $500-$999; Fire Chief $1,000 & up.

* **FORT WAYNE MUSEUM OF ART, (M),** 311 E. Main St., Fort Wayne, IN 46802-1997. Tel.: 260-422-6467. Fax: 260-422-1374.
E-mail: mail@fwmoa.org
Web Site: www.fwmoa.org
Founded: 1922.
Congressional District: 4
Key Personnel: Pres., Leonard Helfrich; Vice Pres., Ben Eisbart; Business Mgr. & Museum Shop Mgr., Lon R. Braun; Dir., Charles A. Shepard, III; Dir. External Affairs, Linda Dykhuizen; Cur. Children & Family Education, Max Meyer; Cur. Exhibitions & Programs, Sarah Aubrey; Registrar, Leah Reeder.
Personnel Profile: Full-Time Paid 18; Part-Time Paid 1; Part-Time Volunteers 200.
Governing Authority: nonprofit organization. Tax-exempt: 501(c)(3).

Art Museum.
Collections: 19th- & 20th-century American prints & paintings; sculpture; works on paper; contemporary art.
Major Exhibits: ACRES Exhibit, 1/10-10/10; Scholastics Art & Writing Exhibition, 2/13/10-4/4/10; Wyeth: An American Art Legacy, 3/27/10-5/2/10; Expansion: Building the New Fort Wayne Museum of Art, 3/27/10-5/2/10; Japanese Prints from the FWMoA Collection, 3/27/10-5/2/10; Terry Ratliff: Fort Wayne Impressionist, 4/10/10-6/6/10; The Sweet Life: Sculpture by Ya Ya Chou, 5/14/10-8/15/10; Through the Glass Nightly: Photographs by Cara Lee Wade, 5/14/10-8/22/10; 1934: A New Deal for Artists, 5/22/10-8/22/10; Midwest Self Portraiture, 6/12/10-8/8/10.
Research Fields: 20th-century contemporary art.
Facilities: library; auditorium; classroom. Museum-related items for sale.
Activities: guided tours; gallery talks; films; lectures; education programs.
Publications: trimonthly newsletters; catalogs for special exhibits; biennial report.
Hours & Admission Prices: Tues.-Sat. 10-5, Sun. 12-5. Adults $5; discounts to AAM members; members, Wed. & 1st Sun. of each month no charge. Closed New Year's Day; Easter; Memorial Day; Independence Day; Labor Day; Thanksgiving; Christmas. ♿
Attendance: 80,000 (estimated)
Membership: Individual $35; Dual $50; Family $65; Donors: Bronze $100-$249; Silver $250-$499; Gold $500-$749; Platinum $750-$999; Director's Circle: Founder $1,000-$1,499; Sustainer $1,500-$2,499; Ambassador $2,500-$4,999; Visionary $5,000 & up.

GREATER FORT WAYNE AVIATION MUSEUM, Fort Wayne International Airport, Lt. Paul Baer Terminal, 3801 W. Ferguson Rd., Fort Wayne, IN 46809-3142. Tel.: 260-478-7146.
Web Site: www.fwairport.com/air-museum.aspx
Founded: 1984.
Congressional District: 3
Key Personnel: Chm. (V) & Cur., Roger Myers.
Personnel Profile: Part-Time Volunteers 12.
Governing Authority: Tax-exempt.
Aviation Museum.
Collections: area aviation history; military, commercial & general aviation; photographs; personal artifacts.
Facilities: 6,000 sq. ft. exhibit space.
Activities: group tours; scholarship granted to an Allen County high school senior.
Publications: quarterly newsletter, Contact.
Hours & Admission Prices: Daily 6am-7pm. No charge; donations accepted. ♿
Attendance: 3,000 (estimated)

THE HISTORY CENTER, 302 E. Berry St., Fort Wayne, IN 46802-2708. Tel.: 260-426-2882. Fax: 260-424-4419.
E-mail: histsociety@fwhistorycenter.com
Web Site: www.fwhistorycenter.com
Formerly: Allen County-Fort Wayne Historical Society Museum
Founded: 1921.
Congressional District: 4
Key Personnel: Pres. (V), Vincent Backs; Exec. Dir., Todd Maxwell Pelfrey; Cur., Walter Font; Community & Project Coord., Robert Nern; Museum Shop Mgr., Kathy Baker; Exhibitor, Randy Elliott; Devel. Coord., Sara Gabbard; Program Coord., Jamia Alexander.
Personnel Profile: Full-Time Paid 5; Part-Time Paid 4; Interns 2.
Governing Authority: nonprofit organization. Parent Institution: Allen County-Fort Wayne Historical Society. Subsidiary Institution: Old City Hall Museum & Chief Richardville House, 5705 Bluffton Rd., Fort Wayne, IN. Tax-exempt: 501(c)(3).
History Museum: housed in c.1893 Fort Wayne City Hall.
Collections: manuscripts & archives pertaining to Fort Wayne, Allen County & northeastern Indiana; 19th & 20th century clothing; c.1790-1820 military artifacts; paintings; toys; china; glass; maps; tools; Indian artifacts; industrial products & equipment; law enforcement artifacts. Historic House: Chief Richardville House c.1827.
Major Exhibits: Festival of Gingerbread, 11/26/10-12/12/10.
Research Fields: 19th & 20th century local history.
Facilities: library of Allen County history, manuscripts covering Fort Wayne history, 200 rolls of National Archives microfilm on military & Indian affairs & 25,000 photographs of locality available for use by public on premises. Books on local & Indiana history & historically oriented items for sale.
Activities: guided tours; lectures; formally organized education programs; docent program on permanent & temporary exhibitions; interactive exhibits; Native American study groups.
Publications: magazine, Old Fort News; brochures; newsletter.
Hours & Admission Prices: Mon.-Fri. 10-5, Sat. & 1st Sun. of month 12-5. Adults $5, seniors & students $3; members & children 5 and under no charge. Chief Richardville House: May-Nov. 1st Sat. of month 1-4. Adults $7, senior citizens & students $5; members no charge. New Year's Day; Memorial Day; Independence Day; Labor Day; Thanksgiving; Christmas. ♿
Attendance: 20,000 (estimated)
Membership: Senior $30; Senior Couple & Individual $35; Family $50; Hamilton $100; Anthony Wayne $250; Kekionga $500; Chief Richardville $1,000.

MACEDONIAN TRIBUNE MUSEUM, 124 W. Wayne St., Fort Wayne, IN 46802-2500. Tel.: 260-422-5900. Fax: 260-422-1348.
Web Site: www.macedonian.org
Founded: 1986.
Congressional District: 3
Key Personnel: Pres. (V), Andrea Andrioff; Museum Shop Mgr., Lois Eubank.
Personnel Profile: Part-Time Paid 3; Part-Time Volunteers 7.
Governing Authority: Parent Institution: Macedonian Patriotic Organization. Tax-exempt.
History Museum.
Collections: Macedonian history, art, religion & culture; costumes; personal artifacts; photographs.
Facilities: Museum-related items for sale.
Activities: special events; educational programs.
Publications: Macedonian Tribune.
Hours & Admission Prices: Tues. & Thurs.-Fri. 11-1:30; other times by appointment. Adults $3, youth 13-19 $2; members and children 12 & under no charge. Closed Federal holidays; Christmas week; Thanksgiving & Day after; snow emergencies.
Attendance: 521 (accurate)
Membership: Senior & Student $20; Individual $25; Family $45; St. Naum $50; St. Clement $100; St. Cyril $250; St. Methodius $500; Mother Teresa $1,000.

SCIENCE CENTRAL, 1950 N. Clinton St., Fort Wayne, IN 46805-4049. Tel.: 260-424-2400.
Web Site: www.sciencecentral.org
Founded: 1995.
Congressional District: 3
Key Personnel: Exec. Dir., Martin S. Fisher.
Personnel Profile: Full-Time Paid 14; Part-Time Paid 25; Part-Time Volunteers 50.
Governing Authority: Tax-exempt.
Science Museum.
Collections: hands-on science, math & technology exhibits.
Major Exhibits: Art: Morph, 11/09-12/09; Hubble Space Telescope (T), 1/10-3/10.
Activities: field trips; outreach; summer, spring, & winter science camps; teacher workshops; scout programs; birthday parties.
Publications: member newsletter.
Hours & Admission Prices: June-Aug. Tues.-Sat. 10-5, Sun. 12-5; Sept.-May Wed.-Sat. 10-5, Sun. 12-5. Admission $7; discounts to ASTC members; members and children 2 & under no charge. Closed New Year's Day; Easter; Memorial Day; Independence Day; Labor Day; Thanksgiving; Christmas Eve & Day. ♿
Attendance: 65,000 (accurate)
Membership: Family & Grandparent $65.

SWINNEY HOMESTEAD, 1424 W. Jefferson Blvd., Fort Wayne, IN 46802-4111. Tel.: 260-424-7212.
Web Site: www.settlersinc.org
Founded: 1971.
Key Personnel: Pres. (V), Linda H. Huge; Museum Shop Mgr., Kate Ferguson.
Governing Authority: bd. of directors.
Historic House Museum: housed in the former home of Thomas & Lucy Swinney, built in 1844. Listed on the National Register of Historic Places.
Collections: period artifacts & furnishings. Historic Building: 1849 log house.
Facilities: herb garden.
Activities: open houses; living history program; in-school activities; Hand Arts Series; special events.
Publications: The Broadside.
Hours & Admission Prices: Groups by appointment. ♿
Membership: General $25; Hand-Arts-Series $50.

Fountain City

LEVI COFFIN HOUSE, 113 U.S. 27 North, Fountain City, IN 47341. Mailing Address: Box 77, Fountain City, IN 47341-0077. Tel.: 765-847-2432. Fax: 765-847-2498.
E-mail: coffinhs@earthlink.com
Web Site: www.waynet.org

Founded: 1967.
Congressional District: 2
Key Personnel: Pres. (V), Janice McGuire; Museum Shop Mgr., Saundra Jackson.
Personnel Profile: Part-Time Volunteers 35.
Governing Authority: society; nonprofit organization. Parent Institution: Levi Coffin House Association through an operating agreement with the Indiana Dept. of Natural Resources, Div. of Museums & Memorials, 650 W. Washington St., Indianapolis, IN 46204. Tax-exempt.
Historic House: 1839 Levi Coffin House.
Collections: furnishings & furniture of the period.
Activities: guided tours; volunteer program.
Publications: History Booklet.
Hours & Admission Prices: June-Aug. Tues.-Sat. 1-4; Sept.-Oct. Sat. 1-4; school groups by appointment only. Adults $2, students & school groups $1. Closed Independence Day.
Attendance: 6,000 (estimated)
Membership: Student $5; Individual $10; Family $20; Contributing $35; Patron $75; Corporate $150.

Frankfort

CLINTON COUNTY MUSEUM, 301 E. Clinton St., Frankfort, IN 46041-1908. Tel.: 765-659-2030 & 4079. Fax: 765-654-7773.
E-mail: cchsm@geetel.net
Web Site: www.cchsm.org; www.oldstoney.org
Founded: 1980.
Congressional District: 5
Key Personnel: Pres. Bd., Dr. Mark Griffith; Vice Pres., Neil Conner; C.E.O. & Dir., Nancy Hart; Treas., Steve Beets; Sec., Joe Palmer; Bd. Member, Dr. Roger Robison; Bd. Member, Audrey Branagin; Bd. Member, Gloria Ponton; Bd. Member & Newsletter Editor, Donna Harmon; Archivist & Librarian, Joan Cox Bohm; Clinton County Historian, James Miller; Sec., Fay Gilbert.
Personnel Profile: Full-Time Volunteers 12; Part-Time Volunteers 16.
Governing Authority: nonprofit organization. Branch of Clinton County Historical Society. Tax exempt: 501(c)(3).
Local History Museum: housed in c.1892 Old Stoney, former Frankfort High School building.
Collections: 19th-century costumes; journals; manuscripts; rare books; novels & classic literature; photographs; post cards; letters; cut glass; period artifacts; quilts; agricultural tools; transportation objects; 1890s classroom interior objects; local art; medical tools; ornithology; general store; parlor; kitchen; bedroom & military displays following all wars; performance recordings & journals from tours of Freddie Shaffer's All Girl Band; Zerna Sharp's personal papers & photos; Pop Stairs' flight instructor papers, maps & photos; blacksmith shop; outhouse; train room; church; 1905 dental office; archives 1830-1925. Historic Building: 1859 log cabin.
Research Fields: local history; oral history; genealogy; business & industry; schools; post offices; transportation & communication; Freddie Shaffer's All Girl Band, USO tours 1940-1953, members of band were Clinton County natives until the last 2 years of the band.
Facilities: 1,000-vol. library of Indiana history, local high school yearbooks & city directories available for research in presence of museum volunteers on premises by appointment; reading room. Publications & museum-related items for sale.
Activities: guided tours; docent program or council; loan, permanent, temporary & traveling exhibitions; monthly DAR meetings. Museum Sponsors: America Blooms, We Partner With Main Street; Annual Armed Forces Day Program; Clinton County Gem in March, May, August & October; Christmas Open House.
Publications: quarterly newsletter, Clinton County Historical Society & Museum News; books, Dick & Jane, and the Lady Responsible for Their Being; Zerna Sharp, A Clinton County Native; Historical Notes; Pictorial History; Life in the Early 1900's; Civil War Soldiers from County; When Basketball was King & Everett Case; Pictorial - Clinton Co.; I Ran Away with an All Girl Band.
Hours & Admission Prices: Mon.-Fri. 9-4, 3rd Sat. of month 1-4. No charge; donations accepted. Closed holidays. ♿
Attendance: 1,563 (accurate)
Membership: General $20; Life $200; Business $500; Industry $1,000.

Franklin

JOHNSON COUNTY MUSEUM OF HISTORY, (M), 135 N. Main St., Franklin, IN 46131-1720. Tel.: 317-736-4655. Fax: 317-736-5451.
E-mail: srogers@cojohnson.in.us
Web Site: www.johnsoncountymuseum.org
Founded: 1931.
Congressional District: 2
Key Personnel: Dir., Sarah Rogers; Pres., Craig Moorman; Cur., Brenda Curdiff; Librarian, Linda Talley.
Personnel Profile: Full-Time Paid 3; Part-Time Paid 1; Part-Time Volunteers 20.
Governing Authority: society. Subsidiary Institution: Johnson County Historical Society. Tax-exempt.
History Museum.
Collections: textiles; costumes; furniture; decorative accessories; tools; artifacts; period rooms include Pioneer, Civil War, & Victorian artifacts; 1940s & 1950s artifacts; military.
Facilities: library of genealogy & public records area available for research.
Activities: guided tours; lectures; formally organized education programs for children; research.
Publications: quarterly magazine, Nostalgia News.
Hours & Admission Prices: Mon.-Fri. 9-4, 2nd Sat. of each month 10-3. Donation Requested $2. ♿
Attendance: 14,000 (accurate)
Membership: Student $10; Individual $20; Family $35; Life $500; Family Life $750.

French Lick

BODY REFLECTIONS SALON & HAIR MUSEUM, 448 S. Maple St., French Lick, IN 47432-1083. Tel.: 812-936-7008.
Founded: 1985.
Congressional District: 62
Key Personnel: Dir., Tony Kendall
Hair Museum.
Collections: hair styling history; cosmetology industry; period razors, shears, combs, hairbrushes, hair tonics, curling irons & permanent wave machines; hair; 1800s hair wreath; period hair dryers; bottles; photographs; magazines; hair jewelry.
Activities: Annual Event: Fall Hair & Trade Show.
Hours & Admission Prices: Tues.-Fri. 9-7, Sat. 9-2. No charge.

INDIANA RAILWAY MUSEUM, Hwy. 56, French Lick, IN 47432. Mailing Address: P.O. Box 150, French Lick, IN 47432-0150. Tel.: 800-74-TRAIN.
E-mail: info@indianarailwaymuseum.org
Web Site: www.indianarailwaymuseum.org
Railway Museum.
Collections: railroad history; photographs.
Activities: train rides.
Hours & Admission Prices: Museum: April-Oct. Mon.-Fri. 8:30-4, Sat.-Sun. 9-6; Nov. Mon.-Fri. 8:30-4, Sat.-Sun. 11-3. No charge. Train: April-May Sat.-Sun. 10, 1 & 4; June-Oct. Tues. & Thurs. 1pm, Sat.-Sun. 10, 1 & 4; Nov. Sat.-Sun. 1pm. Adults $14, children 3-11 $7; children 2 & under no charge. ♿

Garrett

GARRETT HISTORICAL MUSEUM, Heritage Park, 300 N. Randolph St., Garrett, IN 46738. Mailing Address: P.O. Box 225, Garrett, IN 46738-0225. Tel.: 260-357-5575 & 4812.
E-mail: jmohre@mchsi.com
Web Site: garretthistoricalsociety.org
Founded: 1971.
Congressional District: 4
Key Personnel: Pres. & C.E.O., John Mohre; Cur., Cleo Talley; Museum Shop Mgr., Katrina Custer.
Personnel Profile: Part-Time Volunteers 10.
Governing Authority: nonprofit organization. Tax-exempt.
History Museum.
Collections: railroad memorabilia; local history; caboose; 3 railroad signals; HO scale model railroad; railway post office car; 1875 B & O freight house; diesel locomotive.
Research Fields: railroad history; local history.
Facilities: railroad research library. Photos of old engines, post cards & museum-related items for sale.
Activities: guided tours.
Publications: quarterly newsletter, The Dispatcher.
Hours & Admission Prices: March-Dec. Sat.-Sun. 1-4; Winter: by appointment. No charge; donations accepted. ♿
Attendance: 4,400 (estimated)
Membership: Single $10; Family $25; Sponsor $50; Lifetime $500.

Geneva

LIMBERLOST STATE HISTORIC SITE, 200 6th St., Geneva, IN 46740-1004. Mailing Address: P.O. Box 356, Geneva, IN 46740-0356. Tel.: 260-368-7428. Fax: 260-368-7007.
E-mail: limberlost368@embarqmail.com

Web Site: www.genestrattonporter.net
Founded: 1947.
Congressional District: 6
Key Personnel: Pres. (V), Dave Cramer; Cur. & Site Mgr., Randy Lehman; Rgnl. Ecologist, Ken Brunswick; Museum Shop Mgr., Fran Austin.
Personnel Profile: Full-Time Paid 1; Part-Time Paid 2; Part-Time Volunteers 4; Interns 1.
Governing Authority: state. Parent Institution: Indiana State Museums & Historic Sites, 650 W. Washington St., Indianapolis, IN 46204. Branch of Indiana State Museum System, Div. of the Dept. of Natural Resources Indiana State Museum, 202 N. Alabama St., Indianapolis, IN 46204. Tax-exempt.
Historic House: Home of Gene Stratton-Porter 1895-1913, author & naturalist.
Collections: period furnishings; memorabilia of Gene Stratton Porter; Loblolly Marsh Wetland Preserve.
Research Fields: the works of Gene Stratton-Porter.
Facilities: Museum-related items for sale.
Activities: guided tours; special programming; outreach; tours of former wetland, a bird sanctuary; school programming. Museum Sponsors: Christmas Open House.
Publications: pamphlet on Gene Stratton-Porter; newsletter.
Hours & Admission Prices: April to late Dec. Wed.-Sat. 9-5, Sun. 1-5; other times by appointment. Adults $3.50, seniors $3, children $2; members no charge. Closed national holidays. ♿
Attendance: 6,000 (accurate)
Membership: Senior Citizen & Limited Income $10; Individual $20; Family $35; Business $50; Lifetime $1,000.

Greencastle

PUTNAM COUNTY MUSEUM, 1105 N. Jackson St., Greencastle, IN 46135-1072. Tel.: 765-653-8419.
Founded: 2000.
Key Personnel: Exec. Dir., Anne Lovold; Asst. Dir., Tanis Monday; Pres. Bd., Diana Laviolette; Education, Susan Parsons.
Personnel Profile: Full-Time Paid 1; Part-Time Paid 1; Part-Time Volunteers 60; Interns 1.
Governing Authority: private; nonprofit organization. Tax-exempt: 501(c)(3).
History Museum.
Collections: Putnam County history; natural & cultural artifacts; hands-on exhibits.
Facilities: 3,000 sq. ft. exhibit space.
Activities: guided tours; participatory & temporary exhibitions; presentations; formal education programs for children; DePauw University winter course; activity boxes for schools. Museum Sponsors: Roast-A-Relic Fundraiser; Annual Dinner & Meeting; Walk/Run Fundraiser.
Publications: quarterly newsletter, Putnam Past, Present and Future.
Hours & Admission Prices: Tues.-Fri. 1-4, Sat. 10-4; other times by appointment. No charge; donations accepted. Closed Memorial Day; Independence Day; Labor Day; Thanksgiving; Christmas. ♿
Attendance: 3,000 (accurate)
Membership: Student $10; Collectible $25-$49; Keepsake $50-$99; Artifact $100-$249; Antique $250-$499; Treasure $500-$999; Heirloom $1,000-$4,999; Partner $5,000 & up.

RICHARD E. PEELER ART CENTER, (M), 10 W. Hanna St., Greencastle, IN 46135-1911. Mailing Address: DePauw University, 10 W. Hanna St., Greencastle, IN 46135. Tel.: 765-658-4336. Fax: 765-658-6552.
E-mail: kajohnson@depauw.edu
Web Site: www.depauw.edu/galleries
Founded: 2002.
Congressional District: 7
Key Personnel: Dir. & Cur. University Galleries, Museums & Collections, Kaytie Johnson; Registrar Univ. Exhibitions & Collections, Christie Anderson.
Personnel Profile: Full-Time Paid 2; Part-Time Paid 3.
Governing Authority: private university. Parent Institution: DePauw University. Tax-exempt: 501(c)(3).
Art Museum.
Collections: contemporary art.
Major Exhibits: How Soon Is Now: Contemporary Art From the Permanent Collection, 2/10-5/10; The Veil: Visible and Invisible Spaces (T), 9/10-12/10.
Facilities: 8,000 sq. ft. exhibit space; 90-seat auditorium; educational facilities.
Activities: lectures; loan, traveling, temporary & participatory exhibits.
Publications: Mind Storm: Contemporary American Folk Art from the Arient Family Collection; Sally Heller: Material Minutiae; 2005 DePauw Biennial: Contemporary Art in the Midwest; Skirting the Line: Conceptual Drawing; Chuck Ramirez: Deeply Superficial.
Hours & Admission Prices: Tues.-Fri. 10-4, Sat. 11-5, Sun. 1-5. No charge. Closed university holidays & breaks. ♿
Attendance: 6,000 (estimated)

WILLIAM WESTON CLARKE EMISON MUSEUM OF ART, 204 E. Seminary St., Greencastle, IN 46135-1665. Mailing Address: DePauw University, Greencastle, IN 46135. Tel.: 765-658-4336. Fax: 765-658-6552.
Web Site: www.depauw.edu/museum
Founded: 2005.
Congressional District: 7
Key Personnel: Dir. & Cur. University Galleries, Museum & Collections, Kaytie Johnson; Registrar University Exhibitions & Collections, Christie Anderson; Exhibitions & Collections Asst., Peter Nguyen.
Personnel Profile: Full-Time Paid 3; Part-Time Paid 4; Interns 1.
Governing Authority: private university; nonprofit. Parent Institution: DePauw University. Tax-exempt: 501(c)(3).
Art Museum.
Collections: regional art of 19th & 20th centuries; African, Asian, Ethnographic, & American art.
Activities: temporary exhibitions.
Hours & Admission Prices: Tues.-Fri. 10-4, Sat. 11-5, Sun. 1-5. No charge. Closed during university holidays & breaks. ♿
Attendance: 3,000 (estimated)

Greenfield

JAMES WHITCOMB RILEY BIRTHPLACE & MUSEUM, Riley Home, 250 W. Main St., Greenfield, IN 46140. Mailing Address: Greenfield Parks and Recreation, 280 N. Apple St., Greenfield, IN 46140-2656. Tel.: 317-462-8539 & 477-4340 (Park Office). Fax: 317-477-4341.
E-mail: parks_rec@greenfieldin.org
Web Site: www.greenfield.org
Founded: 1937.
Congressional District: 10
Personnel Profile: Part-Time Paid 10; Part-Time Volunteers 16.
Governing Authority: municipal. Parent Institution: City of Greenfield. Subsidiary Institution: Riley Old Home Society. Tax-exempt.
Historic House & Museum: housed in 1849 birthplace of James Whitcomb Riley.
Collections: furniture; relics; manuscripts; period books; paintings; china; crafts; furniture made by Reuben Riley; John A. Riley poems; James Whitcomb Riley mementos; scrapbooks; local history; newspapers; yearbooks; Will Vawter paintings.
Research Fields: costumes; home decorating of period 1849-1864; literature; local & county history.
Facilities: library. Books, reproductions of John Singer Sargent portrait of Riley & other museum-related items.
Activities: guided tours; permanent exhibitions; special programs. Museum Sponsors: Little Orphan Annie; Pixy Magic Gardens; Happy Birthday to Riley; Annual Riley Days celebration in October; Christmas at the Riley Home.
Publications: brochures.
Hours & Admission Prices: April-Nov. 8 Mon.-Sat. 10-4. House: adults $3.50, children 6-18 $1.25, school groups $.75. ♿
Attendance: 4,118 (accurate)

OLD LOG JAIL AND CHAPEL MUSEUMS, Rte. 40 & Apple St., Greenfield, IN 46140. Mailing Address: P.O. Box 375, Greenfield, IN 46140-0375. Tel.: 317-462-7780 & 0631.
Founded: 1966.
Congressional District: 6
Key Personnel: C.E.O. & Pres. (V), Greg Roland; Cur. & Museum Shop Mgr., Jim Arthur.
Personnel Profile: Part-Time Paid 2; Part-Time Volunteers 9.
Governing Authority: society. Parent Institution: Hancock County Historical Society, P.O. Box 375, Greenfield, IN 46140. Tax-exempt.
Historic Buildings: 1853 Log Jail; 1856 Wooden Chapel.
Collections: Tom's Indian arrowhead collection; coverlets of the mid 1800s; pictures of local family, business & agriculture of 1870-1917; Knoop-Bodkin collection of Indian artifacts. Historic Building: 1856 Philadelphia Church.
Research Fields: jails of the mid 1800s.
Facilities: 50-vol. library. Museum-related items for sale.
Activities: guided tours; lectures; temporary exhibitions; school loan service.
Publications: newsletter, Log Chain.
Hours & Admission Prices: April-Oct. Sat.-Sun. 1-5; other times by appointment. Adults $2, children $1.
Attendance: 800
Membership: Junior $1; Adult $10; Life $100.

Greentown

GREENTOWN GLASS MUSEUM, INC., 112 N. Meridian, Greentown, IN 46936-0161. Mailing Address: P.O. Box 161, Greentown, IN 46936-0161. Tel.: 765-628-6206.
Web Site: www.eastern.k12.in.us/gpl/newgreentownglass.htm
Founded: 1969.
Congressional District: 5
Key Personnel: C.E.O. & Pres. (V), Jim Teter; Vice Pres., Merrill Swisher; Sec., Sally Mower; Head Cur., Norma Jean David; Treas., Gary Buckley.
Personnel Profile: Part-Time Paid 5; Part-Time Volunteers 18.
Governing Authority: nonprofit organization. Parent Institution: Greentown Glass Museum. Tax-exempt: 501(c)(3).
Glass Museum.
Collections: glassware manufactured by the Indiana Tumbler & Goblet Co. of Greentown, 1894-1903; Chocolate glass from other factories poured by Jacob Rosenthal, developer of Chocolate glass at Greentown; tools & materials used in the making of glassware; Holly Amber (Golden Agate), Chocolate & Nile Green Glassware collections.
Research Fields: history of the town at the time of the glassworks; history of the glassworks & the people working there; glassware poured at the Indiana Tumbler & Goblet Co.
Facilities: library of material relating to the Indiana Tumbler & Goblet Co. & the glassware manufactured there. Books & museum-related items for sale.
Activities: guided tours; lectures; films; arts festivals; temporary exhibitions. Annual Event: Fundraiser in April.
Publications: brochures.
Hours & Admission Prices: March-May 14 & Nov. Sat.-Sun. 1-4; May 15-Oct. 31 Mon.-Fri. 10-12 & 1-4, Sat.-Sun. 1-4. No charge; donations accepted. Closed Easter. ♿
Attendance: 20,000 (estimated)
Membership: Share $25.

Hagerstown

NETTLE CREEK CULTURAL CENTER, 96 1/2 E. Main, Hagerstown, IN 47346-1213. Mailing Address: Box 126, Hagerstown, IN 47346-0126. Tel.: 765-489-4005.
Formerly: Nettle Creek Valley Museum
Personnel Profile: Part-Time Paid 1; Part-Time Volunteers 25.
Governing Authority: Parent Institution: Historic Hagerstown, Inc. Tax-exempt.
Historic Building: built in 1880.
Collections: local history & culture; murals; industry; works by local artists.
Facilities: Museum-related items for sale.
Hours & Admission Prices: Wed. 9am-12pm, Fri.-Sun. 1-7; groups by appointment. No charge; donations accepted.
Membership: Student $15; Individual $20; Family 25; Business $30; Friend $50-$100; Patron $100-$300; Supporter $301-$500; Benefactor $501 & up.

WILBUR WRIGHT BIRTHPLACE & INTERPRETIVE CENTER, 1525 N. Co. Rd. 750 E., Hagerstown, IN 47346. Mailing Address: 15159 Hoover Rd., Hagerstown, IN 47346-9687. Tel.: 765-332-2495. Fax: 765-332-2805.
E-mail: wilbur@nltc.net
Web Site: www.wwbirthplace.com/pages/contact.php
Founded: 1929.
Congressional District: 2
Key Personnel: Co-Chm. (V), Dan Comway; Co-Chm. (V), Dan Bowman; Treas., Ed McConnell; Dir. Mktg., Martha Hall Bowman; Museum Shop Mgr., Shondae Yocum.
Personnel Profile: Full-Time Paid 1; Part-Time Volunteers 30.
Governing Authority: Wilbur Wright Birthplace Preservation Society. Tax-exempt.
Historic House: c.1867 re-created birthplace of Wilbur Wright.
Collections: period furniture; replica of 1903 Wright Flyer; F-84F jet fighter plane; local history, Brethren Church associations with The Wright Family.
Facilities: picnic area; conference room. Museum-related items for sale.
Activities: tours.
Publications: newsletter.
Hours & Admission Prices: House & Museum: Tues.-Sat. 10-5, Sun. 1-5. Family $7, adults $4, seniors $3, students $2; members no charge. ♿
Attendance: 10,000 (estimated)
Membership: Adults $4; Seniors $3; Students $2.

Hammond

SUZANNE G. LONG LOCAL HISTORY ROOM, 564 State St., Hammond, IN 46320-1532. Tel.: 219-931-5100, ext. 306. Fax: 219-931-3474. TDD: 219-852-2232.
E-mail: lytler@hammond.lib.in.us
Web Site: www.hammond.lib.in.us
Formerly: Hammond Historical Society
Founded: 1960.
Congressional District: 1
Key Personnel: Dir. &. C.E.O., Margaret Evans; Librarian, Richard Lytle.
Personnel Profile: Full-Time Paid 1; Part-Time Paid 1.
Governing Authority: nonprofit organization. Affiliated with Hammond Public Library. Tax-exempt: 501(c)(3).
Historical Society Museum.
Collections: books; photographs; tapes on Hammond & Calumet region history; video cassettes; scrapbooks; maps; documents.
Research Fields: regional & local history; early settlement; business; education; architectural history.
Facilities: 250-vol. library of books, newspaper negatives & pamphlets, including 150 cassettes of programs & tours; photocopies of print material by request; reading room.
Activities: temporary exhibitions.
Publications: 8 issues, newsletter, Hammond Historical Society.
Hours & Admission Prices: Tues. & Thurs.-Fri. 1-5, Wed. 1-9, Sat. 9-5. No charge. ♿
Attendance: 1,500
Membership: Individual $10; Life $100.

Hartford City

BLACKFORD COUNTY HISTORICAL SOCIETY, 321 N. High St., Hartford City, IN 47348. Mailing Address: P.O. Box 264, Hartford City, IN 47348-0264.
Historical Society Museum.
Collections: local history & culture; photographs; personal artifacts; period furnishings.
Hours & Admission Prices: April-Nov. Sun. 1-4.

Hobart

HOBART HISTORICAL SOCIETY MUSEUM, 706 E. Fourth St., Hobart, IN 46342-4411. Mailing Address: P.O. Box 24, Hobart, IN 46342-0024. Tel.: 219-942-0970.
Founded: 1968.
Congressional District: 1
Key Personnel: Pres., Elin Christianson; Business Officer, Robert Green.
Personnel Profile: Part-Time Volunteers 12.
Governing Authority: nonprofit organization. Parent Institution: Hobart Historical Society, Inc. Tax-exempt.
Historical Society Museum: housed in c.1914-1915 Carnegie Library Building. Listed on the National Register of Historic Places.
Collections: local history & culture. Ballantyne Gallery: wheelwright & woodworking tools; a replica of blacksmith shop & print shop; agricultural implements.
Research Fields: local history; local genealogy.
Facilities: 1,500-vol. library on the Calumet area and Hobart history available for inter-library loan or on-site research; c.1891 to present microfilms of local newspapers; 1840-1920 microfilm of Hobart Township census; reading room.
Activities: guided tours; lectures; films; gallery talks; permanent, temporary, loan & traveling exhibitions; school loan service.
Publications: quarterly newsletter, Hobart History News; books, George Earle & Family of Hobart Indiana; Along the Route: History of Hobart Post Office; The Old Settlers Cemetery (1975); The Nine Day Wonder and The One Month Doodlebug (2002); Growing Up in Hobart (1994); Hobart Memories (1996); Lake County Communities Past & Present (2001); periodical newspaper, Hobart History Advocate; Hobart's Historic Buildings (2002).
Hours & Admission Prices: Sat. 10-12; other times by appointment. No charge; donations accepted.
Attendance: 1,500 (accurate)
Membership: Senior Citizens $1; Personal $5; Contributing $25; Institutional $50; Century Club $100.

WOOD'S HISTORIC GRIST MILL, 9410 Old Lincoln Hwy., Hobart, IN 46342-7049. Tel.: 219-947-1958. Fax: 219-947-7105.
Founded: 1979.
Key Personnel: Museum Shop Mgr., Joanna Shearer
Historic Building: grist mill built late 1800s.
Collections: local history; period artifacts; photographs.
Facilities: nature trails.
Activities: demonstrations; hiking; picnicking.
Publications: Pathfinder.
Hours & Admission Prices: May-Oct. daily 10-5. No charge; donations accepted. ♿

Huntington

HUNTINGTON COUNTY HISTORICAL SOCIETY MUSEUM, 315 Court St., Huntington, IN 46750-2862. Tel.: 260-356-7264. Fax: 219-356-7264.
E-mail: info@huntingtonhistoricalmuseum.org
Web Site: www.huntingtonhistoricalmuseum.org
Founded: 1932.
Congressional District: 5
Key Personnel: Dir. & Museum Shop Mgr., Patricia Bergdall; Pres. (V), Mark Anson; Cur., Debra Gardner.
Personnel Profile: Part-Time Paid 1; Part-Time Volunteers 25.
Governing Authority: society. Tax-exempt.
Historical Society Museum.
Collections: county items; Indian stones & arrowheads.
Major Exhibits: They Served Proudly, 11/09-6/10.
Facilities: 8,500 sq. ft. exhibit space.
Activities: permanent exhibitions.
Publications: bimonthly newsletter.
Hours & Admission Prices: Feb.-Dec. Tues.-Fri. 10-4, Sat. 1-4. No charge; donations accepted. Closed Independence Day; Thanksgiving; Christmas.
Attendance: 1,800 (accurate)
Membership: Student $5; Individual $10; Family $15; Sustaining $50; Life $150.

ROBERT E. WILSON GALLERY, Huntington University, 2303 College Ave., Huntington, IN 46750-1237. Tel.: 260-356-6000.
E-mail: bmichel@huntington.edu
Web Site: www.huntington.edu/mca/gallery/default.htm
Key Personnel: Gallery Dir., Barb Michel.
Governing Authority: Tax-exempt.
Art Museum.
Collections: contemporary paintings, prints & sculptures.
Hours & Admission Prices: Feb. 4-Dec. 11 Mon.-Fri. 9-5; other times by appointment. No charge. ♿
Attendance: 3,000

SHEETS WILDLIFE MUSEUM, 200 Safari Trail, Huntington, IN 46750-8049. Tel.: 260-356-9453.
Founded: 2005.
Key Personnel: Dir., Shirley M. Schug.
Personnel Profile: Full-Time Paid 1.
Wildlife Museum.
Collections: animals & fish from around the world; shell art.
Facilities: theater. Museum-related items for sale.
Publications: quarterly, Museum Messenger.
Hours & Admission Prices: Tues.-Sat. 10-4. Adults $7, seniors 55 & over $6, children 4-15 $4; discounts to groups; children under 4 no charge. ♿

U.S. VICE PRESIDENTIAL MUSEUM AT THE DAN QUAYLE CENTER, (M), 815 Warren St., Huntington, IN 46750-2151. Mailing Address: P.O. Box 856, Huntington, IN 46750-0856. Tel.: 260-356-6356. Fax: 260-356-1455.
E-mail: info@quaylemuseum.org
Web Site: www.quaylemuseum.org
Formerly: The Dan Quayle Center & Museum
Founded: 1993.
Congressional District: 4
Key Personnel: C.E.O., Daniel Johns; Pres. (V), Darlene Stanley.
Personnel Profile: Full-Time Paid 1; Part-Time Paid 1; Part-Time Volunteers 25.
Governing Authority: private; nonprofit organization. Tax-exempt.
History Center: housed in 1919 former Christian Scientist Church; focus on the Vice Presidency & its challenges.
Collections: life of Dan Quayle from birth until the end of his vice presidency of the United States; history of four other Vice Presidents from Indiana, and the artifacts relating to all U.S. Vice Presidents.
Research Fields: history of the U.S. Vice Presidency; Vice Presidents from Indiana; Dan Quayle's life.
Facilities: 4,000 sq. ft. exhibit center.
Activities: seminars; lectures.
Publications: quarterly newsletter.
Hours & Admission Prices: Mon.-Fri. 9:30-4:30. Adults $3, children 7-17 $1; children under 6 & members no charge. Closed New Year's Day; Easter; Independence Day; Thanksgiving; Christmas Eve & Day. ♿
Attendance: 6,000 (accurate)
Membership: Grass Roots $30; Contributing $50; Sustaining $100; Supporting $250; Dan's Circle $1,000; Builder's Club $2,500; Founder's Club $5,000.

Indianapolis

* **BENJAMIN HARRISON PRESIDENTIAL SITE, (M),** 1230 N. Delaware St., Indianapolis, IN 46202-2531. Tel.: 317-631-1888. Fax: 317-632-5488.
Web Site: www.pbhh.org
Formerly: President Benjamin Harrison Home
Founded: 1966.
Congressional District: 11
Key Personnel: Pres. & C.E.O., Phyllis Geeslin; Education, Roger Hardig; Education, David Pleiss; Cur., Jennifer Capps; Dir. (V), Jo Baize; Financial Admin., Margaret Sallee; Dir. Devel., Erin Trisler.
Personnel Profile: Full-Time Paid 6; Part-Time Paid 3; Part-Time Volunteers 65; Interns 2.
Governing Authority: nonprofit corporation. Tax-exempt: 501(c)(3).
Historic House Museum: c.1874-75 President Benjamin Harrison home.
Collections: furniture; furnishings; books; election campaign items; inaugural Bible & other memorabilia; gifts to the president; law library; rare books; personal papers; women suffrage materials.
Research Fields: sponsored Harrison biographies by Fr. Harry J. Sievers, S. J.; materials on Benjamin Harrison, his grandfather, Wm. H. Harrison, Mary Lord Dimmick Harrison & Caroline Scott Harrison; Belva Lockwood; Arthur Jordan.
Facilities: library of books, general literature & court records of the Harrison collection available for use on premises; meeting & banquet rooms. Gift shop with postcards, books, pamphlets & notepaper, reproduction White House china for sale.
Activities: guided tours; docent program; educational programs & special events; changing exhibitions; Live from Delaware Street.
Publications: quarterly newsletter, The Statesman.
Hours & Admission Prices: Feb.-May & Aug.-Dec. Mon.-Sat. 10-3:30; June-July Mon.-Sat. 10-3:30, Sun. 12:30-3:30. Adults $8, seniors $6, students $3; discounts for groups, AAM & AAA members; members no charge. Closed New Year's Day; Easter; 500 Race Weekend; Memorial Day; Labor Day; Thanksgiving; Christmas Eve & Day. ♿
Attendance: 26,000 (accurate)
Membership: Voters (Individuals) $25; Electors (Family) $35; Delegates $50; Representatives $100; Senators $250; Justices $500; Cabinet $1,000 & up.

BROAD RIPPLE GALLERY, 714 E. 65th St., Indianapolis, IN 46220-1610. Tel.: 317-253-5340. Fax: 317-253-5468.
E-mail: info@hoosiersalon.org
Web Site: www.hoosiersalon.org
Formerly: Hoosier Salon Gallery
Founded: 1925.
Congressional District: 10
Key Personnel: Exec. Dir., Donnae Dole.
Personnel Profile: Full-Time Paid 1; Part-Time Paid 2; Part-Time Volunteers 30.
Governing Authority: nonprofit organization. Parent Institution: Hoosier Salon Patrons Association, Inc. Tax-exempt: 501(c)(3).
Art Gallery.
Collections: paintings; sculpture; prints.
Research Fields: Hoosier (Indiana) artists.
Activities: gallery talks; permanent, temporary & traveling exhibitions; community events. Gallery Sponsors: annual juried exhibition of living Indiana artists; artist seminar; spring & fall community tours; celebration of Hoosier artists.
Publications: quarterly, Hoosier Salon Newsletter; book, A Grand Tradition: The Art and Artists of the Hoosier Salon, 1925-1990.
Hours & Admission Prices: Tues.-Fri. 11-5, Sat. 11-3; other times by appointment. No charge. ♿
Attendance: 35,000 (estimated)
Membership: Artist $30; Patron $65; Business Patron, Contributing & Sustaining Business $100; Sustaining Patron $250; Corporate Sponsor $500; Lifetime Patron $2,000.

* **THE CHILDREN'S MUSEUM OF INDIANAPOLIS, (M),** 3000 N. Meridian St., Indianapolis, IN 46208-4716. Mailing Address: P.O. Box 3000, Indianapolis, IN 46206-3000. Tel.: 317-334-3322. Fax: 317-921-4019. TDD: 317-920-2020.
E-mail: customerservice@childrensmuseum.org
Web Site: www.childrensmuseum.org
Founded: 1925.
Congressional District: 10
Key Personnel: Chm. Trustees (V), Yvonne Shaheen; Pres. (V), Jeffrey H. Patchen; Vice Pres. Finance, Karen Kennelly; Dir. Education, David Cassady; Dir. Community Svcs., Janet Boston; Dir. Investments Management, John Grogan; Dir. Health, Safety & Security, Clarence Taylor; Museum Shop Mgr., Robert Tate.

Personnel Profile: Full-Time Paid 180; Part-Time Paid 200; Part-Time Volunteers 1,575.
Governing Authority: nonprofit corporation. Tax-exempt: 501(c)(3).
Children's Museum.
Collections: archaeology; ethnology; geology; history; natural history; paleontology; transportation with exhibits on railroading; natural science; physical science; prehistory; ancient Egypt; leisure time pursuits; operating Dentzel carousel; operating toy train layout; early toy trains; model trains; toys; dolls; folk art; objects from around the world; seasonal displays.
Research Fields: how children learn in informal environments.
Facilities: 4,000-vol. library related to collections for use on premises & inter-library loan; resource center; 130-seat planetarium; 350-seat theater; orientation classroom; meeting rooms; restaurant; theater. Gift items for sale.
Activities: guided tours; lectures; films; permanent & temporary exhibits; planetarium programs; gallery talks & demonstrations; science & computer festivals; drama; formally organized education programs for children & adults; craft classes; nature field trips; nature walks; performing arts including concerts, theater, dance & puppetry; mobile performing stage; science demonstrations; teacher workshops; Scout badge classes; hands-on exhibits.
Publications: monthly newsletter; quarterly report; souvenir booklet; annual report; gallery guides; teachers' guides; docent training manuals; pamphlets, museum history.
Hours & Admission Prices: March to Labor Day daily 10-5; Sept.-Feb. Tues.-Sun. 10-5. Adults $13.50, seniors $12.50, children 2-17 $8.50; 1st Thurs. of month 4-8 & members no charge. Closed Easter; Thanksgiving; Christmas. ♿
Attendance: 1,200,000 (accurate)
Membership: Individual $40; Family $55; Grandparents $60; Family Plus $75.

CRISPUS ATTUCKS CENTER MUSEUM, 1140 Dr. Martin Luther King Jr. St., Indianapolis, IN 46202-2221. Tel.: 317-226-2430. Fax: 317-226-4611.
E-mail: museumca@ips.k12.us
Web Site: www.crispusattucksmuseum.ips.k12.in.us/
Founded: 1998.
Key Personnel: Dir., Pat Payne; Cur., Robert Chester.
Personnel Profile: Full-Time Paid 2; Part-Time Paid 1; Part-Time Volunteers 5.
History Museum.
Collections: African American history; school history; Tuskegee Airmen; Crispus Attucks High School memorabilia.
Hours & Admission Prices: Mon.-Fri. 9-5, Sat. 12-5; guided tours by appointment. Adults $5, senior citizens 65 & over, college students & youth 6-13 $2; discount to groups of 15 & over.
Attendance: 5,000 (estimated)

*** EITELJORG MUSEUM OF AMERICAN INDIANS AND WESTERN ART, (M),** 500 W. Washington, Indianapolis, IN 46204-2775. Tel.: 317-636-9378, ext. 0. Fax: 317-264-1724.
Web Site: www.eiteljorg.org
Founded: 1985.
Key Personnel: Pres. & C.E.O., John Vanausdall; Chm., Betsey Harvey; Vice Pres. & Chief Cur. Officer, James H. Nottage; Vice Pres. Devel., Susie Maxwell; Vice Pres. Administration & C.F.O., Susan Lewis; Vice Pres. Public Programs & Visitor Svcs., Martha Hill; Vice Pres. Facilities & Security, Jim Fulton; Dir. Communications & Mktg., Tamara Winfrey Harris; Cur. Contemporary Art, Jennifer Complo; Dir. Collections, Amy McKune; Gund Cur. Western Art History & Culture, Suzan Campbell; Museum Shop Mgr., Judy Kirkwood.
Personnel Profile: Full-Time Paid 51; Part-Time Paid 19; Part-Time Volunteers 806; Interns 9.
Governing Authority: nonprofit organization. Tax-exempt: 501(c)(3).
Art Museum.
Collections: paintings, drawings, & bronzes relating to the American West; Native American art & cultural artifacts.
Research Fields: Native American cultures; artists & artwork of the West.
Facilities: library of printed material; 120-seat theater. Gift items for sale.
Activities: guided tours; lectures; films; organized education programs; docent program; loan, temporary & traveling exhibitions; school loan service; artist in-residence program; rental facilities.
Publications: quarterly newsletter; exhibition catalogs.
Hours & Admission Prices: Mon.-Sat. 10-5, Sun. 12-5; groups by appointment. Adults $8, senior citizens 65 & over $7, children 5-17 & full-time students $5; discount to AAM members, military & groups; members, IUPUI students, and children 4 & under no charge. Closed New Year's Day; Thanksgiving; Christmas Eve & Day. ♿
Attendance: 113,447 (accurate)
Membership: Teacher Plus Guest $45; Individual Plus Guest $50; Dual & Teacher Family $55; Family & Grandparent $60; Contributing $100; Sustaining $250; Patron $500; Eagle $1,500; Golden Eagle $2,500; Presidents Society $5,000.

EMIL A. BLACKMORE MUSEUM OF THE AMERICAN LEGION, 700 N. Pennsylvania St., Indianapolis, IN 46204-1129. Mailing Address: P.O. Box 1055, Indianapolis, IN 46206-1055. Tel.: 317-630-1356 & 1200. Fax: 317-630-1241.
E-mail: library@legion.org
Web Site: www.legion.org/library.htm
Founded: 1967.
Key Personnel: Natl. Adjutant, Daniel S. Wheeler; Librarian & Cur., Howard Trace.
Governing Authority: nonprofit organization. Parent Institution: The American Legion. Tax-exempt: 501(c)(3).
Military History Museum.
Collections: 20th-century U.S. military history & American Legion development.
Hours & Admission Prices: Mon.-Fri. 8-4. No charge. Closed New Year's Eve & Day; Martin Luther King Jr. Day; Presidents' Day; Good Friday; Memorial Day; Independence Day; Labor Day; Veterans Day; Thanksgiving & day after; Christmas. ♿

THE ENDOWMENT FUND OF THE PHI KAPPA PSI FRATERNITY-HERITAGE HALL, 5395 Emerson Way, Indianapolis, IN 46226-1415. Tel.: 317-632-1852. Fax: 317-637-1898.
E-mail: info@pkpfoundation.org
Web Site: www.phikappapsi.com
Founded: 1978.
Congressional District: 10
Key Personnel: Exec. Dir., Shawn M. Collingsworth; Chm., Wayne W. Wilson; Pres., Paul R. Wineman.
Personnel Profile: Full-Time Paid 2; Part-Time Volunteers 1.
Governing Authority: society; nonprofit. Affiliated Organization: Phi Kappa Psi Fraternity. Tax-exempt.
General Museum: housed in c.1876 two-story brick Italianate home.
Collections: decorative arts; period furniture.
Facilities: 1,200-vol. library.
Activities: guided tours.
Publications: quarterly magazine, The Shield.
Hours & Admission Prices: Mon.-Fri. 1-4. No charge. Closed national holidays.
Attendance: 750 (estimated)

FREETOWN VILLAGE LIVING HISTORY MUSEUM, 625 Indiana Ave., Indianapolis, IN 46202-3133. Mailing Address: P.O. Box 1041, Indianapolis, IN 46206-1041. Tel.: 317-631-1870. Fax: 317-631-0224.
E-mail: freetown_info@freetownvillage.org
Web Site: www.freetown.org
Founded: 1982.
Congressional District: 7
Key Personnel: Dir., Ophelia Wellington; Program Dir., Mirriam A. Umar
History Museum.
Collections: Indiana's African American history & culture.
Activities: programs; workshops; special events.
Publications: The Freetown Villager.
Hours & Admission Prices: Mon.-Fri. 10-5. No charge; donations accepted. Closed major holidays. ♿
Attendance: 17,500 (estimated)
Membership: Individual $15; Family $35; Village Elder $100; Corporate Elder $500; Heritage Builder $1,000.

HISTORIC LANDMARKS FOUNDATION OF INDIANA, 340 W. Michigan St., Indianapolis, IN 46202-3254. Tel.: 317-639-4534. Fax: 317-639-6734.
Web Site: www.historiclandmarks.org
Founded: 1960.
Congressional District: 10
Key Personnel: Pres., Marsh Davis; Exec. Vice Pres., Tina Connor; Honorary Chm., Randall T. Shepard; Chm., Jerry Fuhs; Dir. Devel., Andra Walters; Vice Pres. Preservation Svcs., Mark Dollase; Dir. Southern Rgnl. Office, Greg Sekula; Vice Pres., Mary Burger; Dir. Northern Rgnl. Office, Todd Zieger; Dir. Eastern Rgnl. Office, Wayne Goodman; Dir. Western Rgnl. Office, Tommy Kleckner; Admin. Morris-Butler House, Gwendolen Raley; Dir. Library & Education, Suzanne Stanis.
Personnel Profile: Full-Time Paid 39; Part-Time Paid 8; Part-Time Volunteers 40; Interns 3.
Governing Authority: nonprofit organization. Branch Museums: 1865 Morris-Butler House Museum, Indianapolis; 1840 Huddleston Farmhouse Inn Museum, Cambridge City; Veraestau Historic Site, Aurora. Tax-exempt: 501(c)(3).

Historic Preservation Foundation: housed in the Charles J. Kuhn House; c. 1879.
Collections: period furnishings; paintings by early Indiana artists.
Research Fields: nineteenth-century art, architecture & culture; architecture of Indiana; restoration & preservation techniques; community conservation; historic buildings survey.
Facilities: 2,000-vol. library on architecture, architectural history, restoration & renovation techniques, journals & periodicals, over 13,000 slides, black & white photo archives, historic buildings survey material, press clippings & archives on historic Indiana buildings available for use on premises by members; reading room.
Activities: guided tours; lectures; films; slide talks; formally organized education programs; docent program; permanent & temporary exhibitions; statewide revolving loan fund for restoration activities; preservation and design consultation; publications; resource centers; architectural survey; restoration projects; operation of museums; grants programs.
Publications: bimonthly magazine, Indiana Preservationist; technical leaflets; preservation bulletins; museum brochures; special publications.
Hours & Admission Prices: Office: Mon.-Fri. 8:30-5. No charge; donations accepted. Closed legal holidays. ♿
Membership: Student & Senior $20; Individual $35; Nonprofit Organization $40; Household $50; Portico $100; Business $125; Cornerstone $250; Newel $500; Pillar $1,000; Cornice $2,500; Pinnacle $5,000.

HOOK'S HISTORICAL DRUG STORE AND PHARMACY MUSEUM, Indiana State Fairgrounds, 1202 E. 38th St., Indianapolis, IN 46205-2807. Tel.: 317-924-1503.
Key Personnel: Chm., Bob Hunt.
Governing Authority: Parent Institution: Greenfield Museum Initiative.
History Museum: built in 1849.
Collections: American pharmacy artifacts; soda fountain memorabilia; period furnishings.
Hours & Admission Prices: Tues.-Sat. 11-8, Sun. 12-4.

IUPUI CULTURAL ARTS GALLERY, 420 University Blvd., Ste. 278, Indianapolis, IN 46202-5147. Tel.: 317-278-8511. Fax: 317-278-0828.
E-mail: maxwell@iupui.edu
Web Site: www.life.iupui.edu/campcntr
Key Personnel: Graphic Artist, Pamela Mullons.
Governing Authority: public university.
Art Museum.
Collections: paintings; sculpture.
Hours & Admission Prices: Mon.-Sat. 10-7, Sun. 1-7. No charge. ♿
Attendance: 18,000 (estimated)

* **IMA - INDIANAPOLIS MUSEUM OF ART, (M),** 4000 Michigan Rd., Indianapolis, IN 46208-4196. Tel.: 317-923-1331. Fax: 317-931-1978.
E-mail: ima@imamuseum.org
Web Site: www.imamuseum.org
Founded: 1883.
Congressional District: 7
Key Personnel: Chm., Myrta Pulliam; Vice Chm., John Krauss; Vice Chm., Stephen Russell; C.O.O., Jack Leicht; Dir. & C.E.O. The Melvin & Bren Simon, Maxwell L. Anderson; Dir. Public Affairs, Katie Zarich; The Ruth Lilly Dir. Environmental & Historic Preservation, Mark Zelonis; Dir. Lilly House, Bradley Brooks; Dir. Human Resources, Laura McGrew; C.F.O. & Dir. Institutional Resources, Anne Munsch; Chief Designer, David Russick; Wood-Pulliam Distinguished Sr. Cur. Painting & Sculpture 1800-1945, Ellen W. Lee; Cur. American Painting & Sculpture 1800-1945, Harriet G. Warkel; Cur. Asian Art, Dr. John T. Teramoto; Sr. Cur. Contemporary Art, Dr. Lisa Freiman; Asst. Cur. Contemporary Art, Sarah Green; Assoc. Cur. Prints, Drawings & Photographs, Annette Schlagenhauff; Cur. Prints, Drawings & Photographs, Martin F. Krause, Jr.; Cur. Textile & Fashion Arts, Niloo Imami-Paydar; Sr. Cur. European Painting & Sculpture before 1800, Ronda J. Kasl; Dir. Education, Linda Duke; Chief Information Officer, Robert Stein; Dir. Exhibitions & Publications, David Chalfie; Dir. Devel., Fred Duncan; Dir. New Media, Daniel Incandela; Chief Registrar, Katie Haigh; Deputy Dir. Collections & Programs, Sue Ellen Paxson; Dir. Protection & Visitor Svcs., Pam Godfrey; Cur. Design Arts, R. Craig Miller; Dir. Retail, Jenny Geiger.
Personnel Profile: Full-Time Paid 220; Part-Time Paid 27; Part-Time Volunteers 500; Interns 27.
Governing Authority: nonprofit. Tax-exempt: 501(c)(3).
Art Museum & Historic Site: Lilly House - former home of J.K. Lilly, Jr., the late Indianapolis businessman, collector & philanthropist. National Historic Landmark.
Collections: European & American paintings & sculpture; African, American, Asian, European, contemporary & decorative art, including paintings, sculpture, prints, drawings, photographs, textiles & costumes; Asian art; textiles; costumes; decorative arts; pre-Columbian art; Clowes Fund collection; J.M.W. Turner collection; the Holliday collection of Neo-Impressionist art; Eiteljorg collection of African & South Pacific Art; manuscripts; Josefowitz collection of Gauguin and the School of Pont-Aven. Japanese Edo-period paintings. Oldfields - Lilly House & Gardens: 22-room mansion on a 26-acre estate.
Facilities: reference library; educational resource center; gardens; 175-seat lecture hall & auditorium; educational resource center; restaurant; 500-seat special events pavilion; 600-seat theater. Museum-related items for sale.
Activities: guided tours; lectures; films; gallery talks; concerts; arts festivals; formally organized education programs; docent program or council; permanent, temporary & traveling exhibitions.
Publications: monthly email newsletter; catalogs of permanent collection & exhibitions; brochures; bimonthly member magazine.
Hours & Admission Prices: Gardens & Grounds: daily dawn to dusk. Museum & House: Tues.-Wed. & Sat. 11-5, Thurs.-Fri. 11-9, Sun. 12-5. Fee for special exhibitions only. Closed New Year's Day; Thanksgiving; Christmas. ♿
Attendance: 462,000 (accurate)
Membership: Student $25; Individual $50; Family $75; Sustaining $100; Associate $150; Advocate $250; Patron $500.

INDIANA HISTORICAL SOCIETY, (M), Eugene and Marilyn Glick Indiana History Center, 450 W. Ohio St., Indianapolis, IN 46202-3269. Tel.: 317-232-1882; 800-447-1830. Fax: 317-234-0079. TDD: 317-233-6615.
E-mail: welcome@indianahistory.org
Web Site: www.indianahistory.org
Founded: 1830.
Key Personnel: C.E.O. & Pres., John A. Herbst; Chm. (V), Thomas G. Hoback; Exec. Vice Pres., Stephen L. Cox; Sr. Dir. Collections, Steve Haller; Mgr. Media Rels., Amy Lamb; Vice Pres. Devel. & Membership, Linda Pratt; Vice Pres. Business & Operations, Jeff Matsuoka; Sr. Dir. Human Resources, April Kerber; Vice Pres. Mktg. & Public Rels., Jeanne Scheets; Controller, Kathleen A. Grothe, CPA; Sr. Dir. IHS Press, Paula Corpuz; Sr. Dir. Conservation, Ramona Duncan-Huse; Sr. Dir. Special Events, Mark Szobody; Sr. Dir. Public Programs, Trina Nelson Thomas.
Personnel Profile: Full-Time Paid 65; Part-Time Paid 35; Part-Time Volunteers 213; Interns 6.
Governing Authority: nonprofit organization. Tax-exempt: 501(c)(3).
Historical Society & Archives.
Collections: history of Indiana & the Old Northwest Territory; archives; photographs; manuscripts; books; printed items; artifacts.
Major Exhibits: You Are There: 1945 Hoosier Homefront, 3/10-12/10; You Are There: 1924 Tool Guys and Tin Lizzies, 3/10-2/11.
Research Fields: Indiana & Old Northwest history.
Facilities: library; 4,500 sq. ft. exhibit space; 300-seat theatre; cafe; conservation & microfilming labs; classrooms; music room. Museum-related items for sale.
Activities: lectures; educational programs; arts & cultural programs; loan, temporary & traveling exhibitions; field services; Jr. Historical Society programs; concerts; performances; workshops. Museum Sponsors: history conferences; landing the "Indiana Experience" in March 2010.
Publications: bimonthly newsletter; quarterly popular history magazine, Traces of Indiana and Midwestern History; semi-annual, The Hoosier Genealogist: Connections; various special interest newsletters; books.
Hours & Admission Prices: Tues.-Sat. 10-5. Adults $7; discount to AAM & ICOM members; members & library no charge. Closed New Year's Day; Independence Day; Thanksgiving; Christmas. ♿
Attendance: 139,785 (estimated)
Membership: Student $20; Individual $40; Family & Dual $50; Sustaining $100; Benefactor $250; History Patron $500.

INDIANA MEDICAL HISTORY MUSEUM, (M), 3045 W. Vermont St., Indianapolis, IN 46222-4943. Tel.: 317-635-7329. Fax: 317-635-7349.
E-mail: edenharter@imhm.org
Web Site: www.imhm.org
Founded: 1969.
Congressional District: 10
Key Personnel: Dir., Virginia L. Terpening; Pres. (V), Richard Feldman, M.D.
Personnel Profile: Part-Time Paid 3; Part-Time Volunteers 7; Interns 1.
Governing Authority: nonprofit organization. Tax-exempt: 501(c)(3).
Medical Museum: housed in c.1896 pathology laboratory.
Collections: over 15,000 medical artifacts & health care artifacts which include surgical & dental equipment; diagnostic instruments; nursing uniforms; pharmaceutical bottles; quack devices; health care history.
Research Fields: late 19th century & early 20th-century medicine in Indiana.
Facilities: 3,000-vol. library pertaining to late 19th & early 20th-century medicine.
Activities: guided tours; presentations; temporary exhibits; educational programs; research; rental facilities.
Publications: quarterly newsletter.

Hours & Admission Prices: Thurs.-Sat. 10-4. Adults $5, university students $3, students 18 & under $1; discounts to AAM members; members & children under 6 no charge. Closed New Year's Day; Independence Day; Thanksgiving & day after; Christmas. ♿
Attendance: 8,000 (estimated)
Membership: Annual $25.

* **INDIANA STATE MUSEUM, (M),** 650 W. Washington St., Indianapolis, IN 46204-2185. Tel.: 317-232-1637 & 5599. Fax: 317-232-7090. TDD: 317-234-2447.
E-mail: museumcommunication@dnr.state.in.us
Web Site: www.indianamuseum.org
Formerly: Indiana State Museums and Historic Sites
Founded: 1869.
Congressional District: 1-10
Key Personnel: C.E.O. & Pres., Barry Dressel; Chm. Bd., Gregory Pemberton; Dir. Collections & Interpretation, Rex Garniewicz; Dir. Education, Colleen Smyth; Dir. Exhibits, Jennifer Spitzer; Vice Pres. Mktg. & Communications, Janet Chronic; Chief Cur. Cultural History, Dale Ogden; Chief Cur. Natural History, Ron Richards; Cur. Historic Archaeology, Bill Wepler; Cur. Geology, Margaret Fisherkeller; Cur. Biology, Damon Lowe; Cur. Fine Arts, Rachel Perry; Cur. Social History, Mary Jane Teeters-Eichacker; Cur. Agriculture, Industry & Technology, Todd Stockwell; Mgr. New Media, Leslie Lorance; Mgr. Security, James Toler; Facility Mgr., Ron Tolan; Vice Pres. State Historic Sites, Kathleen McLary; Vice Pres. Human Resources & Finance, Arlene Phillips; Museum Shop Mgr., Kristin Peterson.
Personnel Profile: Full-Time Paid 110; Full-Time Volunteers 1,230; Part-Time Paid 25; Part-Time Volunteers 200; Interns 10.
Governing Authority: state; bd. of trustees. Parent Institution: State of Indiana. Branch Museums: Angel Mounds, Evansville; 1813 Corydon Capitol, Corydon; Culbertson Mansion, New Albany; 1844 Lanier Mansion, Madison; 1895 Limberlost, Geneva; c.1820 New Harmony; 1914 Gene Stratton Porter Home, Rome City; 1900 Ernie Pyle Birthplace; 1910 T.C. Steele Home & Studio, Nashville; c.1840 Whitewater Canal, Metamora; 1839 Levi Coffin Home, Fountain City; Vincennes, c.1810-1838; Indiana State Museum, Indianapolis. (Check individual listings for hours & further information). Tax-exempt.
General Museum.
Collections: period furnishings; art; science; culture; artifacts; natural history specimens; music; political; primary source material; prints; drawings; graphic arts; sculpture.
Major Exhibits: Lincoln Bicentennial: With Malice Toward None (T), 2/10-4/10.
Research Fields: Indiana natural & cultural history; art.
Facilities: orientation theatre; auditorium; meeting rooms; two restaurants; IMAX theater. Museum-related items for sale.
Activities: lectures; restoration; slide, film & tape presentations; formally organized education programs; special events; festivals; special traveling exhibits.
Publications: brochures for individual sites; member publications.
Hours & Admission Prices: Mon.-Sat. 9-5, Sun. 11-5. Adults $7; ASTC members & members no charge. Closed Thanksgiving; Christmas. ♿
Attendance: 325,000 (accurate)
Membership: Individual $39; Individual Premier $49; Family & Grandparent $59; Patron $100.

INDIANA STATE POLICE YOUTH EDUCATION AND HISTORICAL CENTER, 8500 E. 21st St., Indianapolis, IN 46219-2562. Tel.: 317-899-8293. Fax: 317-899-8289.
History Museum.
Collections: police vehicles & firearms; photographs; personal artifacts; uniforms; cars; equipment.
Hours & Admission Prices: Tours: Mon.-Fri. 8-4 by appointment.

INDIANA WAR MEMORIALS, 431 N. Meridian St., Indianapolis, IN 46204-1711. Tel.: 317-232-7615. Fax: 317-233-4285.
E-mail: iwm@iwm.in.gov
Web Site: www.in.gov/iwm/
Founded: 1927.
Congressional District: 10
Key Personnel: Pres. Commission, Brian Regan; Exec. Dir., Gen. J. Stewart Goodwin; Administrative Dir., Danyetta Powers; Museum Dir., Ethan Wright; Museum Specialist Collections, Donna M. Schmink; Museum Specialist, Chase Brazel; Museum Specialist, Ari Kaufman; Physical Plant Dir., Donald Hickey.
Personnel Profile: Full-Time Paid 17; Part-Time Volunteers 2.
Governing Authority: state commission. Indiana War Memorials Commission: maintains: Indiana War Memorials; Soldiers & Sailors Monument, Colonel Eli Lilly Civil War Museum, Monument Circle. Tax-exempt.
Historic Commission & Military Museum: housed in 1927 Indiana War Memorial.
Collections: uniforms, weapons, battle flags, pictures, helicopter, jeep, missile, cannon, from Revolutionary War to Operation Enduring Freedom.
Facilities: library of books, pictures & combat maps available for research on premises; auditorium.
Activities: permanent exhibitions.
Hours & Admission Prices: Wed.-Sun. 10-5. Memorial: no charge; donations accepted. Observatory: $1.00. Closed New Year's Day; Thanksgiving; Christmas. ♿
Attendance: 250,000 (accurate)

INDIANAPOLIS ART CENTER, 820 E. 67th St., Indianapolis, IN 46220-1199. Tel.: 317-255-2464. Fax: 317-254-0486.
E-mail: info@indplsartcenter.org
Web Site: www.indplsartcenter.org
Founded: 1934.
Congressional District: 6
Key Personnel: Pres. & C.E.O., Carter Wolf; Chm. (V), Tanya Stuart Overdorf; Office Mgr., Jennifer Collins; Dir. Operations, Pamela Rosenberg; Dir. Devel., Kelly Lamb; Dir. Exhibitions, David Kwasigroh; Exhibitions Asst., Patrick Flaherty; Dir. Outreach, Laura Alvarado; Vice Pres. & Dir. Programs, David S. Thomas; Education Assoc., Megan Perry; Dir. Special Events, Iris Dillon; Dir. Mktg., Lisa DeHayes; Dir. Finance, Doug Halman; Business Mgr., Alisia Morales; Facilities Mgr., Brett Sommers; Museum Shop Mgr., Melanie Reckas.
Personnel Profile: Full-Time Paid 40; Part-Time Paid 8; Part-Time Volunteers 4.
Governing Authority: nonprofit. Tax-exempt: 501(c)(3).
Studio Art Teaching Center & Exhibitions.
Collections: contemporary visual arts.
Research Fields: Indiana & 250 mi. radius of artists.
Facilities: 1,100-vol. library dedicated to arts related subjects, slides & videos of over 2,000 regional artists; 13 studio classrooms; 224 seat auditorium; 40,000 sq. ft. exhibition space; resource center; wildflower & sculpture garden.
Activities: over 300 different art classes; art education for all ages & skill levels; community arts resource center; local & regional artist exhibitions; programming for culturally diverse audiences including lectures, concerts & films; fine art day camp for children; art tours; outreach programs to youth in underserved areas.
Publications: newsletter; schedule of events & classes; occasional exhibition catalogues & posters; monthly event postcard.
Hours & Admission Prices: Mon.-Fri. 9am-10pm, Sat. 9-6, Sun. 12-6; hours may vary when classes are not in session. No charge; donations accepted. Closed New Year's Day; Memorial Day; Independence Day; Labor Day; Thanksgiving; Christmas. ♿
Attendance: 293,311 (estimated)
Membership: Student & Senior Citizen $30; Individual $40; Family $50.

INDIANAPOLIS FIREFIGHTERS MUSEUM & HISTORICAL SOCIETY, 748 Massachusetts Ave., Indianapolis, IN 46204-1609. Tel.: 317-262-5161. Fax: 317-262-5163.
Founded: 1996.
Congressional District: 7
Governing Authority: Parent Institution: Indianapolis Metropolitan Professional Firefighters Local 416. Tax-exempt.
Fire-Fighting Museum.
Collections: Indiana fire department & firefighting history; 1921 Stutz engine; 1921 Stutz ladder truck; horse drawn steam pumper; hose cart; badges; photographs.
Hours & Admission Prices: Mon.-Fri. 8:30-3. No charge; donations accepted. Closed holidays. ♿
Attendance: 5,000 (estimated)

INDIANAPOLIS MOTOR SPEEDWAY HALL OF FAME MUSEUM, (M), 4790 W. 16th St., Indianapolis, IN 46222-2573. Mailing Address: P.O. Box 24152, Speedway, IN 46224-0152. Tel.: 317-492-6784. Fax: 317-492-6449.
E-mail: ebireley@brickyard.com
Web Site: www.indianapolismotorspeedway.com
Founded: 1956.
Congressional District: 11
Key Personnel: Dir., Ellen K. Bireley.
Personnel Profile: Full-Time Paid 9; Part-Time Paid 26; Interns 1.
Governing Authority: nonprofit organization. Tax-exempt: 501(c)(3).
Transportation Museum.
Collections: racing-related cars; period & classic passenger cars; racing & automotive memorabilia; art; trophy collection.
Facilities: library of books on motor racing, antique & classic cars available for research by special request. Gift items for sale.

Activities: permanent & temporary exhibitions.
Hours & Admission Prices: May call for extended hours; June-April daily 9-5. Museum: Adults $3, youth 6-15 $1; children 6 & under no charge. Bus ride around track when not in use: adults $3, youth 6-15 $1; discounts to AAM & ICOM members; children 5 & under no charge. Closed Christmas. ♿
Attendance: 350,000 (estimated)

INDIANAPOLIS MUSEUM OF CONTEMPORARY ART, 340 N. Senate Ave., Indianapolis, IN 46204-1708. Tel.: 317-634-6622. Fax: 317-634-1977.
Web Site: www.indymoca.org
Founded: 2001.
Key Personnel: Dir., Katherine Nagler; Chm. & Cur., Jeremy Efroymson; Pres., Brandon Judkin; Vice Pres., Jennifer Boehm; Asst. Dir., Shauta Marsh; Education, Elizabeth Mix.
Personnel Profile: Full-Time Paid 2; Part-Time Paid 1; Part-Time Volunteers 100.
Governing Authority: nonprofit. Tax-exempt: 501(c)(3).
Art Museum.
Collections: works by contemporary artists.
Facilities: 1,200 sq. ft. exhibit space. Museum-related items for sale.
Activities: concerts; films; formal education programs; lectures; participatory & temporary exhibitions.
Hours & Admission Prices: Thurs.-Sat. 11-6, Sun. 12-3. No charge. Closed holidays.
Attendance: 25,000 (accurate)
Membership: Individual $30; Dual $50; Family $70; Sustaining $100; Friend $150.

* **INDIANAPOLIS ZOO,** 1200 W. Washington St., Indianapolis, IN 46222-4500. Tel.: 317-630-2001. Fax: 317-630-5153.
E-mail: info@indyzoo.com
Web Site: www.indianapoliszoo.com
Formerly: Indianapolis Zoological Society
Founded: 1964.
Congressional District: 11
Key Personnel: C.E.O. & Pres., Michael I. Crowther; Chm. (V), Mike Wells; Deputy Dir. & Senior Vice Pres., Paul Grayson; Senior Vice Pres. & C.F.O., Claudia Willis; Senior Vice Pres. External Rels., Karen Burns; Vice Pres. Operations, Tim Savona; Vice Pres. Internal Rels., Mary Jane Bennett; Vice Pres. Programs, David Merritt.
Personnel Profile: Full-Time Paid 215; Part-Time Paid 28; Part-Time Volunteers 1,200; Interns 40.
Governing Authority: nonprofit organization. Subsidiary Institution: Indianapolis Zoo & White River Gardens. Tax-exempt: 170(b)(1)(A); 501(c)3.
Zoo, Aquarium, & Botanical Garden.
Collections: live animals & plants from around the world.
Research Fields: reproduction in endangered & threatened species & nutritional studies.
Facilities: zoological park; 200-seat auditorium-theater; classrooms; concession stand; restaurant; aquarium; botanical garden with conservatory. Gift items for sale.
Activities: lectures; gallery talks; concerts; hobby workshops; family workshop; TV & radio programs; formally organized education programs for children, adults, undergraduate & graduate college students affiliated with Indiana University, Butler University, Ball State University, University of Indianapolis, Anderson College; docent program or council; training programs; permanent & temporary exhibitions; day camps; pre-school programs; volunteer council; cooperative programming with other agencies; train, pony, coaster & carousel rides; animal demonstrations in performance area; special events for families & children.
Publications: quarterly members magazine, Indianapolis Zoo Magazine; quarterly to donors, Inside the Zoo.
Hours & Admission Prices: Zoo & Gardens: Jan.-Feb. Wed.-Sun. 9-4; March 1-13 & Nov.-Dec. 4 daily 9-4; March 14-May 22 & Sept. 2-Oct. Mon.-Thurs. 9-4, Fri.-Sun. 9-5; May 23-Sept. 1 Mon.-Thurs. 9-5, Fri.-Sun. 9-6; Dec. 5-Dec. 30 daily 12-9. Adults $14; members no charge. Closed New Year's Day; Thanksgiving; Christmas Eve & Day. ♿
Attendance: 1,200,000 (accurate)
Membership: Individual Plus One $85; Family & Grandparents $105; Family Plus 2 & Grandparent Plus 2 $145.

J.I. HOLCOMB OBSERVATORY AND PLANETARIUM, 4600 Sunset Ave., Indianapolis, IN 46208-3443. Tel.: 317-940-8333.
E-mail: holcombobservatory@butler.edu
Web Site: www.butler.edu/holcomb
Founded: 1954.
Key Personnel: Dir., Dr. Brian Murphy; Assoc. Dir., Richard Brown.
Personnel Profile: Full-Time Paid 1; Part-Time Paid 1.
Governing Authority: university. Parent Institution: Butler University. Subsidiary Institution: Dept. of Physics & Astronomy. Tax-exempt: 501(c)(3).
Planetarium & Observatory.
Collections: astronomical tables; journals & books on astronomy & astrophysics.
Research Fields: astronomy.
Facilities: 250-vol. library of astronomical tables, research papers & ephemerides available for inter-library loan & by arrangement with Butler University Library; planetarium; classrooms.
Activities: guided tours; lectures; films; formally organized education programs for children & undergraduate college students.
Hours & Admission Prices: June-July Fri.-Sat. 9:15 & 10:15; Sept.-May Fri.-Sat. 7 & 8:15 pm. Adults $3, senior citizens & children over 4 $2.

JAMES WHITCOMB RILEY MUSEUM HOME, (M), 528 Lockerbie St., Indianapolis, IN 46202-3617. Tel.: 317-631-5885. Fax: 317-955-0619.
E-mail: rileyhome@rileykids.org
Founded: 1922.
Key Personnel: Dir., Sandra L. Crain.
Personnel Profile: Full-Time Paid 3; Part-Time Paid 1.
Governing Authority: philanthropic organization. Parent Institution: Riley Children's Foundation. Tax-exempt: 501(c)(3).
Historic House Museum: 1872 home of James Witcomb Riley.
Collections: art works; books; furnishings.
Facilities: 1,000-vol. library of general books. Books by James Whitcomb Riley & other memorabilia for sale.
Activities: guided tours.
Hours & Admission Prices: Tues.-Sat. 10-4. Adults $3, children 7-17 $.50. Closed major holidays.
Attendance: 7,500 (accurate)

MILITARY LIBRARY AND MUSEUM, 10801 N. College Ave., Indianapolis, IN 46280. Mailing Address: c/o Clay Township Trustee, 10701 N. College Ave., Indianapolis, IN 46280. Tel.: 317-582-0507.
Military History Museum.
Collections: local history; genealogy; archives; photographs.
Facilities: library.
Activities: research.
Hours & Admission Prices: Call for hours.

* **MORRIS-BUTLER HOUSE MUSEUM, (M),** 1204 N. Park Ave., Indianapolis, IN 46202-2638. Tel.: 317-636-5409. Fax: 317-636-2630.
E-mail: mbhouse@historiclandmarks.org
Web Site: www.historiclandmarks.org
Founded: 1969.
Congressional District: 10
Key Personnel: Chm. (V) Advisory Committee, Bradley Brooks; Pres., Marsh Davis; Museum Admin., Gwendolen Raley; Program Coord., Aimee Rose Forno.
Personnel Profile: Full-Time Paid 2; Part-Time Paid 1; Part-Time Volunteers 45; Interns 2.
Governing Authority: nonprofit organization. Parent Institution: Historic Landmarks Foundation of Indiana. Tax-exempt: 501(c)(3).
Historic House: 1864 Morris-Butler House.
Collections: c.1850-1886 Victorian decorative arts; theme rooms.
Major Exhibits: Victorian Foodways, 2/17/10-12/22/10.
Research Fields: decorative arts; local & social history; interior preservation.
Facilities: meeting room; banquet facilities.
Activities: guided tours; lectures; gallery talks; formally organized education programs for children; inter-museum loan; workshops; special events.
Publications: brochures; exhibit-related booklets.
Hours & Admission Prices: Wed.-Sat. 10-3; other times by appointment for groups. Tours on the hour; last tour 3pm. Adults $5, students $3; discounts to groups & AAM members; members no charge. ♿
Attendance: 6,000 (accurate)
Membership: Senior 60 & over $20; Individual $35; Household $50; Portico $100; Founder's Club $250-$500; President's Circle $1,000-$2,500; Chairman's Council $5,000 & up.

NATIONAL ART MUSEUM OF SPORT, INC., (M), University Place, IUPUI 850 W. Michigan St., Indianapolis, IN 46202-2800. Tel.: 317-274-3627 & 2700. Fax: 317-274-3878.
E-mail: arein@iupui.edu
Web Site: www.namos.iupui.edu
Founded: 1959.
Congressional District: 7
Key Personnel: Chm. (V), John D. Short; Pres., Shaun Healy Clifford; Exec. Dir., Ann M. Rein.
Personnel Profile: Part-Time Paid 1; Part-Time Volunteers 10.

Governing Authority: nonprofit corporation. Indiana charter, board of governors with an operating board of governors. Tax-exempt: 501(c)(3).
Sports Art Museum.
Collections: paintings; sculpture; graphics; photographs of sporting subjects.
Research Fields: Sport art & artists who incorporated sporting subjects into their work; photography & sport history; social issues & influences on sporting art.
Facilities: library pertaining to sporting art & cataloged works of sports world-wide; 10,500 sq. ft. exhibit space.
Activities: docent guided tours; permanent & temporary exhibitions; collaborative projects with other agencies.
Publications: exhibition catalogs; newsletter, Score Board.
Hours & Admission Prices: Mon.-Fri. 8-5. No charge. Closed major holidays. ♿
Attendance: 136,000 (estimated)
Membership: Sustaining & Benefactor $150; Germaine G. Glidden Society $1,000; 21st Century Society $2,000.

NCAA HALL OF CHAMPIONS, One NCAA Plaza, 700 W. Washington, Indianapolis, IN 46204-2710. Tel.: 800-735-NCAA (toll free); 317-916-HALL (local). Fax: 317-916-4254.
E-mail: hocmail@ncaa.org
Web Site: ncaahallofchampions.org
Key Personnel: Dir., Damon Schoening; Public & Media Rels., Gail Dent
Sports Museum.
Collections: photographs; sports memorabilia.
Facilities: theater. Museum-related items for sale.
Hours & Admission Prices: Tues.-Sat. 10-5, Sun. 12-5. Adults $5, senior citizens 65 & over and youth 6-18 $3; under under 6 no charge.

RHYTHM! DISCOVERY CENTER, 110 W. Washington St., Ste. A, Indianapolis, IN 46204-3423. Tel.: 317-974-4488. Fax: 317-974-4499.
Web Site: www.rhythmdiscoverycenter.org
Formerly: Percussive Arts Society Museum
Key Personnel: C.E.O., Michael Kenyon
Musical Instruments Museum.
Collections: percussion instruments; scores; recorded music; cultural, historical & modern use of drums & percussion around the world; hands-on exhibits; Gerhardt Marimba Xylophone cylinder recordings.
Facilities: library. Museum-related items for sale.
Activities: concerts; clinics; classes; labs; workshops; panels & presentations.
Hours & Admission Prices: Tues.-Sun. 10-5. Adults $8. ♿

Jamestown

JACKSON TOWNSHIP HISTORICAL SOCIETY, 41 W. Main St., Jamestown, IN 46147. Mailing Address: P.O. Box 297, Jamestown, IN 46147-0297. Tel.: 765-676-5891.
Historical Society Museum.
Collections: local history & culture; personal artifacts; period furnishings; photographs.
Hours & Admission Prices: Call for hours.

Jasper

INDIANA BASEBALL HALL OF FAME, Vincennes Univ. - Jasper Ruxer Student Ctr., 851 College Ave., Jasper, IN 47546. Mailing Address: 1436 Leopold St., Jasper, IN 47546-2117. Tel.: 812-482-2262. Fax: 812-482-1982.
Founded: 1977.
Congressional District: 63
Hall of Fame.
Collections: Hall of Fame inductees including pro-players, high school, college, & pro coaches and managers; photographs; personal artifacts; baseballs; gloves; uniforms; bats.
Hours & Admission Prices: mid-May to mid-Aug. daily 11-3; mid-Aug. to mid-May Thurs.-Sun. 11-3. Adults 13 & over $4, children 5-12 $3, senior citizens 60 & over $2; children 4 & under no charge.

KREMPP GALLERY, 951 College Ave., Jasper, IN 47546-9382. Tel.: 812-482-3070. Fax: 812-634-6997.
Web Site: www.jasperarts.org
Founded: 1975.
Congressional District: 9
Key Personnel: Dir., Kit Miracle.
Personnel Profile: Full-Time Paid 3; Part-Time Paid 8; Part-Time Volunteers 300; Interns 2.
Governing Authority: city. Tax-exempt.
Art Center.
Collections: paintings.
Major Exhibits: University of Southern Indiana Faculty Show, 1/10; Barbara Cade: Search for Serenity, 2/10; Youth Art Month - Local Schools, 3/10; Arthur Wang: Fleeing Dream, 4/10; Anissa Lewis, Narrative Images, 5/10; Robert Bean, Urban Images, 6/10; Dubois County Art Guild, 7/10-8/10; 17th Annual Juried Show, 9/10; Lawrence Rudolech, Capturing Indiana, 10/10; Mike Mergen & Alexandra Lee, 11/10.
Activities: lecture; workshop; art classes.
Publications: gallery cards; bi-annual newsletter; annual brochure.
Hours & Admission Prices: Mon.-Wed. & Fri. 10-5, Thurs. 10-7, Sun. 12-3. No charge; donations accepted. ♿

Jeffersonville

HOWARD STEAMBOAT MUSEUM AND MANSION, 1101 E. Market St., Jeffersonville, IN 47130-4333. Mailing Address: P.O. Box 606, Jeffersonville, IN 47131-0606. Tel.: 812-283-3728. Fax: 812-283-6049.
E-mail: hsmsteam@aol.com
Web Site: www.steamboatmuseum.org
Formerly: Howard Steamboat Museum, Inc.
Founded: 1958.
Congressional District: 9
Key Personnel: Pres. (V), David Reinhardt; Admin. & Museum Shop Mgr., Yvonne Knight.
Personnel Profile: Full-Time Paid 1; Part-Time Paid 6; Part-Time Volunteers 5; Interns 1.
Governing Authority: nonprofit organization; bd. of directors. Parent Institution: Clark County Historical Society. Tax-exempt: 501(c)(3).
Historic House Museum: 1894 home of Edmonds J. Howard, son of James E. Howard, founder of the Howard Shipyards 1834.
Collections: original 1893 furnishings; steamboat artifacts & models; photographs; half-breadth models; tools.
Research Fields: steamboat architecture & design; Ohio River history.
Facilities: Steamboat prints, books & museum-related items for sale.
Activities: guided tours; lectures; permanent exhibitions. Annual Event: Spring Festival: A Victorian Chautauqua in May.
Publications: brochures; semiannual newsletter; book, Scenes From Memory; booklet, 57.1 ft. The 1937 Flood Remembered.
Hours & Admission Prices: Tues.-Sat. 10-4, Sun. 1-4. Adults $5; discounts to groups, students, seniors, AARP, AAA, AIM, & AAM members; under 6 & members no charge. Closed most holidays.
Attendance: 10,000 (estimated)
Membership: Annual Personal Memberships: Student or Senior Citizen 65 & over $10; Individual $15; Family $25; Contributor $26-$99; Friend $100-$199; Benefactor $200-$499; James E. & Loretta Howard Society $500 & up.

Kendallville

MID-AMERICA WINDMILL MUSEUM, 732 S. Allen Chapel Rd., Kendallville, IN 46755-3220. Mailing Address: P.O. Box 5048, Kendallville, IN 46755-5048. Tel.: 260-347-2334.
Key Personnel: Dir., Sarah Hobson
Technology Museum.
Collections: windmills; history of wind power & windmills; photographs.
Facilities: library.
Activities: rental facilities; weddings; special events; video.
Hours & Admission Prices: April-Nov. Tues.-Fri. 10-4, Sat. 10-5, Sun. 1-4. Adults $4, senior citizens $3.50, students $1.50; children under 6 no charge.

Kokomo

AUTOMOTIVE HERITAGE MUSEUM, 1500 N. Reed Rd., U.S. 31 N., Kokomo, IN 46901-2592. Tel.: 765-454-9999. Fax: 765-454-9956.
E-mail: jp@automotiveheritagemuseum.com
Web Site: www.automotiveheritagemuseum.com
Key Personnel: Gen. Mgr., James Parsons
Automobile Museum.
Collections: over 100 period vehicles from 1895 to 1970s.
Activities: facility rental.
Hours & Admission Prices: Tues.-Sun. 10-4; groups by appointment. Adults $5, seniors $4, children 7-14 $2.

ELWOOD HAYNES MUSEUM, 1915 S. Webster St., Kokomo, IN 46902-2040. Tel.: 765-456-7500.
Founded: 1967.
Congressional District: 5
Key Personnel: Cur., Kay J. Frazer; Cur., Nancy Kennedy.
Personnel Profile: Full-Time Paid 1; Part-Time Paid 1.
Governing Authority: municipal; operated by the city Park Dept. Tax-exempt.
Industrial Museum: housed in 1915 home of Elwood Haynes.
Collections: automobiles, stainless steel & stellite invented by Elwood Haynes;

industrial products of the city of Kokomo; sculptures; photographs; period clothing; personal artifacts.
Facilities: 40-seat auditorium.
Activities: guided tours; films; formally organized education programs for children; permanent exhibitions.
Publications: books, Elwood Haynes 1857-1925; The Complete Motorist; Alloys & Automobiles, the Life of Elwood Haynes.
Hours & Admission Prices: Tues.-Sat. 11-4, Sun. 1-4. No charge; donations accepted. Closed most holidays.
Attendance: 4,000 (estimated)

HOWARD COUNTY HISTORICAL MUSEUM, (M), 1200 W. Sycamore St., Kokomo, IN 46901-4386. Tel.: 317-452-4314. Fax: 765-452-4581.
E-mail: director@howardcountymuseum.org
Web Site: howardcountymuseum.org
Founded: 1916.
Congressional District: 5
Key Personnel: C.E.O. & Museum Shop Mgr., Kelly Karickhoff; Pres., Dave Broman.
Personnel Profile: Full-Time Paid 3; Part-Time Paid 5; Part-Time Volunteers 100; Interns 2.
Governing Authority: nonprofit organization. Parent Institution: Howard County Historical Society. Subsidiary Institution: Howard County Museum. Tax-exempt.
History Museum & Historic House.
Collections: ethnological; archaeology; military; agriculture; glass & manufacturing. Historic Houses: Seiberling Mansion; c.1890 Elliott House.
Major Exhibits: Monroe Seiberling's Mansion, 2/10-12/10.
Research Fields: Howard County history, archaeology; Howard County inventions & manufacturing.
Facilities: research library; rental facilities.
Activities: children's educational programs; weddings, reunions. Museum Sponsors: Christmas at the Seiberling.
Publications: Museum Hi-Lites; newsletter.
Hours & Admission Prices: Feb.-Dec. Tues.-Sun. 1-4. Adults $4; discounts to seniors on tour buses, AAM & ICOM members; members no charge. Closed national holidays. ♿
Attendance: 20,000 (accurate)
Membership: Annual $20; Family $25; Contributing $50; Centennial $100; Corporate $250; Benefactor $500; Patron $1,000.

INDIANA UNIVERSITY KOKOMO ART GALLERY, 2300 S. Washington St., Kokomo, IN 46902-3557. Tel.: 765-455-9523.
E-mail: gsteel@iuk.edu
Web Site: www.iuk.edu/~koart/
Art Gallery.
Collections: works by local, regional, national & international artists; new media.
Activities: lectures; workshops; demonstrations; special events.
Hours & Admission Prices: Mon.-Tues. & Thurs. 10-4, Wed. 10-8, Sat. 12-4, Sun. 1-5. No charge.

KAA ART CENTER, 525 W. Ricketts St., Kokomo, IN 46902-2029. Tel.: 765-457-9480.
Web Site: www.kokomoartassociation.org
Formerly: Kokomo Art Center
Founded: 1987.
Key Personnel: Chm. (V) & Volunteer Coord., Elaine Wanke; Pres., K. Celeste Seay.
Governing Authority: Sponsored By: Kokomo Parks Dept. Subsidiary Institution: Artworks Gallery. Tax-exempt.
Art Center.
Collections: Hoosier art & artists; Norman Rockwell signed prints from Tom Sawyer book.
Major Exhibits: Permanent Collection - Latest Acquisitions, 2/10; Photography Show & Competition, 3/10; Celebrate Our Own Show, 4/10; Spring Show, 5/10; Aspiring Artists, 6/10; Celebrate Our Own Photography Show, 7/1/10-7/15/10; Hippensteel Award Winner, 7/16/10-7/31/10; Art Camp and Artworks Kids Show, 8/1/10-8/15/10; Photo Show Winner Show, 8/15/10-8/31/10; Fall Show Competition, 9/10.
Activities: classes; workshops; seminars; summer kid's art camp.
Publications: bimonthly newsletter, Art Strokes; annual directory, KAA Artists' Directory.
Hours & Admission Prices: House Tours: Feb.-Nov. Tues.-Sat. 1-4. No charge; donations accepted. Closed Labor Day; Memorial Day; Independence Day; Thanksgiving. ♿
Attendance: 400 (accurate)
Membership: Student $10; Single $25; Lifetime $1,000.

La Porte

LA PORTE COUNTY HISTORICAL SOCIETY MUSEUM, 2405 Indiana Ave., Ste. 1, La Porte, IN 46350-6063. Tel.: 219-324-6767. Fax: 219-324-9029.
E-mail: info@laportecountyhistory.org
Web Site: www.laportecountyhistory.org
Founded: 1906.
Congressional District: 13
Key Personnel: Pres. (V), Arnold Bass; Cur., James Rodgers; Asst. Cur. & Museum Shop Mgr., Susie Richter.
Personnel Profile: Full-Time Paid 2; Part-Time Paid 1; Part-Time Volunteers 10.
Governing Authority: society. Tax-exempt.
History Museum.
Collections: local history; Jones collection of firearms; manuscripts; Kesling Automobiles.
Research Fields: LaPorte County history; genealogical research.
Facilities: research library; meeting room.
Activities: guided tours; lectures; permanent exhibitions. Museum Sponsors: Annual Classic Car Show in July.
Publications: quarterly newsletter, Old Letter; book, The Belle Gunness Story; pamphlets on La Porte County history; reprints of county history & plat books; LaPorte and Environs.
Hours & Admission Prices: Tues.-Sat. 10-4:30. Adults: Out-of-County $5, In-County $3; members & Time Travelers no charge. Closed national holidays. ♿
Attendance: 7,634 (accurate)
Membership: Student $2.50; Active $10; Sustaining $20; Patron $35.

LaPorte

HESSTON STEAM MUSEUM, 1201 E. 1000 N., LaPorte, IN 46350-8642. Tel.: 219-778-2783.
Web Site: www.hesston.org
Governing Authority: nonprofit. Parent Institution: LaPorte County Historical Steam Society. Tax-exempt: 501(c)(3).
History Museum.
Collections: steam locomotives; steam powered saw mill; 92 ton railroad steam crane; electric power plant; steam traction engines.
Activities: Museum Sponsors: Hesston Steam & Power Show in September; Halloween Ghost Train in October; Santa's Candy Cane Express in December.
Hours & Admission Prices: Museum: Sat.-Sun. & holidays 11:30-5. No charge. Train Rides: Memorial Day to Labor Day Sat.-Sun. & holidays 12-5. Adults $5, children over 3 $3; children under 3 no charge.

Lafayette

*** ART MUSEUM OF GREATER LAFAYETTE, (M),** 102 S. 10th St., Lafayette, IN 47905-1173. Tel.: 765-742-1128. Fax: 765-742-1120.
E-mail: ksmith@glmart.org
Web Site: www.artlafayette.org
Formerly: Greater Lafayette Museum
Founded: 1909.
Congressional District: 7
Key Personnel: Exec. Dir., Kendall Smith, II; Museum Admin., Glenda McClatchey; Cur. Collections & Exhibitions, Michael Atwell.
Personnel Profile: Full-Time Paid 2; Part-Time Paid 2; Part-Time Volunteers 100.
Governing Authority: nonprofit organization. Tax-exempt: 501(c)(3).
Art Museum.
Collections: 19th & 20th-century American paintings, prints & drawings; historical and contemporary Indiana art; Latin American prints; American art pottery.
Research Fields: Indiana art.
Facilities: 3,000 sq. ft. exhibition gallery; classrooms. Museum-related items for sale.
Activities: guided tours of exhibitions & studios; national & regional temporary exhibits; children's activities; lecture series; education program; studio art classes.
Publications: quarterly, newsletter; class schedules.
Hours & Admission Prices: Tues.-Sat. 11-4. No charge; donation accepted. Closed New Year's Day; Martin Luther King. Jr. Day; Presidents' Day; Memorial Day; Independence Day; Labor Day; Thanksgiving; Christmas Eve & Day. ♿
Attendance: 15,000 (accurate)
Membership: Student $20; Individuals $35; Family $50; Friend $100; Advocate $250; Patron $500; Sustainer $1,000; Benefactor $2,500; Founder $5,000; Director's Circle $10,000.

COLUMBIAN PARK ZOO, 1915 Scott St., Lafayette, IN 47904-2929. Tel.: 765-807-1540. Fax: 765-807-1547.
E-mail: claufman@city.lafayette.in.us
Web Site: www.lafayette.in.gov/zoo
Founded: 1908.
Congressional District: 7
Key Personnel: Zoo Dir. & Zoo Gift Shop, Claudine Laufman; Asst. Zoo Dir., Dana Rhodes.
Personnel Profile: Full-Time Paid 7; Part-Time Paid 6; Part-Time Volunteers 27; Interns 2.
Governing Authority: municipal. Branch of Lafayette Board of Parks & Recreation, 1915 Scott St., Lafayette, IN 47904. Tel.: 765-807-1500. Tax-exempt: 501(c)(3).
Zoo.
Collections: exotic mammals; birds; reptiles; native wildlife.
Facilities: zoological park. Gift items for sale.
Activities: formally organized education programs for children; docent program or council; traveling exhibitions.
Publications: program guide, Funformation.
Hours & Admission Prices: Summer: daily 10-4:30. ♿
Attendance: 75,000 (estimated)
Membership: Individual $25; Family $40; Patron $50; Associate $75; Sustaining $100; Benefactor $250; Zoo Club $500; Zoo Fellow $1,000.

TIPPECANOE COUNTY HISTORICAL ASSOCIATION, 1001 South St., Lafayette, IN 47901-1571. Tel.: 765-476-8411. Fax: 765-476-8414.
Web Site: www.tcha.mus.in.us
Formerly: Tippecanoe County Historical Museum
Founded: 1925.
Congressional District: 2
Key Personnel: Pres. (V), Joseph D. Barlett.
Personnel Profile: Full-Time Paid 2; Part-Time Paid 4; Part-Time Volunteers 20; Interns 1.
Governing Authority: society. Branch Museums: Tippecanoe County Historical Museum; Battle of Tippecanoe Museum; Fort Ouiatenon; McCollough Archives & Research Center. Tax-exempt: 501(c)(3).
House Museum: housed in 1851-1852, Moses Fowler Home & site of 1811 battlefield. Interpretive museum located near the site of 1717-91, Fort Ouiatenon, the first fortified European settlement in Indiana.
Collections: pre-contact Native American artifacts & archaeology collections from the sites of Fort Ouiatenon & the Battle of Tippecanoe; personal artifacts including manuscripts, household goods & toys; agricultural, commercial, industrial, educational, social & military history of the county & region; newspapers; artworks & manuscripts by Indiana artist George Winter; local documents, photographs; negatives; county governmental records.
Research Fields: genealogy; 18th-century artifacts; local history; French Colonial archaeology; Tippecanoe Battlefield archaeology.
Facilities: 4,000-vol. library of books on history of Tippecanoe County & Indiana available in association's library across the street. Books & handcrafted items for sale.
Activities: guided tours; lectures; films; gallery talks; markers program; preservation awards; fall re-enactment festival; formally organized education programs for children; docent program or council; permanent & temporary exhibitions.
Publications: newsletter, TCHA News; leaflet series, Tippecanoe Tales; Books, Tippecanoe County Cartoonist; Historical Map of Tippecanoe County; Battle of Tippecanoe: Conflict of Cultures; Ouabache Potpourri; 100 Years of the Courthouse; The House That Moses Fowler Built; 1894 Bird's Eye View, Lafayette; Old Lafayette, 1825-1854; Old Lafayette, Vol. II, 1854-1876; Grist Mills of Tippecanoe County.
Hours & Admission Prices: Mon.-Fri. 8-5. Adults $3; discounts to AAM & Association of Indiana Museum members; members no charge. Closed legal holidays. ♿
Attendance: 150,000 (estimated)
Membership: Basic $35; Sustaining $250.

Lagrange

LAGRANGE COUNTY HISTORICAL SOCIETY, INC., Machan House Museum, 405 S. Poplar St. 4H Fair Grounds, Lagrange, IN 46761. Mailing Address: P.O. Box 134, Lagrange, IN 46761-0134. Tel.: 260-593-2593; 350-0606 (cell).
E-mail: 1kilowat@earthlink.net
Founded: 1966.
Congressional District: 4
Key Personnel: Pres. (V), Izara Miller.
Governing Authority: private; nonprofit. Tax-exempt.
Historical Society Museum.
Collections: historical papers; local artifacts. Historic Structure: log cabin; period clothing.
Research Fields: local history; genealogy.
Facilities: library of local histories, pamphlets, newspapers, clippings, pictures, cemetery records, war records, family records, & old & abandoned school records available for research by appointment.
Activities: formally organized education programs for adults; log cabin tours; picture & paper research.
Publications: History of LaGrange County, 1936; 1882, LaGrange County Histories; cemeteries of LaGrange County Indiana, 1832-1982; My Town, Your Town-LaGrange, 1836-1986.
Hours & Admission Prices: By appointment only. No charge; donations accepted.
Attendance: 500 (estimated)
Membership: Annual Single $10; Couple $20; Family $25; Contributing $50; Life $250.

Lebanon

CRAGUN HOUSE, 404 W. Main St., Lebanon, IN 46052. Mailing Address: P.O. Box 141, Lebanon, IN 46052-0140. Tel.: 765-483-9414.
Governing Authority: Parent Institution: Boone County Historical Society.
Historic House: built in 1893.
Collections: local history & culture; period furnishings; personal artifacts; photographs.
Facilities: rental facilities.
Activities: research.
Hours & Admission Prices: Mon.-Tues. 1-4; other times by appointment.

Liberty

UNION COUNTY HISTORICAL MUSEUM, 156 E. County Rd. 300 S., Liberty, IN 47353. Mailing Address: P.O. Box 143, Liberty, IN 47353-0143. Tel.: 765-458-5500.
Founded: 1929.
Congressional District: 5
Key Personnel: Pres. (V), Virginia Bostick.
Personnel Profile: Part-Time Volunteers 1.
Governing Authority: Parent Institution: Union County Historical Society.
History Museum.
Collections: local history & culture; photographs; personal artifacts.
Publications: annual newsletter.
Hours & Admission Prices: Call for hours. No charge; donations accepted. ♿
Attendance: 300 (accurate)
Membership: Individual $5; Family $10.

Ligonier

LIGONIER HISTORICAL MUSEUM, 300 S. Main St., Ligonier, IN 46767-1812. Tel.: 260-894-4511.
Web Site: www.nccvb.org/attract/lhm.htm
History Museum.
Collections: Ligonier's history; Jewish artifacts.
Hours & Admission Prices: May-Oct. Tues. & Sat.-Sun. 1-4:30; other times by appointment. Regular Hours: no charge. By appointment: $2 per person.

STONE'S TAVERN, State Rd. 5 & U.S. 33, Ligonier, IN 46767-9603. Mailing Address: 4946 N. State Rd. 5, Ligonier, IN 46767-9603. Tel.: 260-856-2871.
E-mail: sweeneyjanet@hotmail.com
Web Site: www.stonestrace.com
Founded: 1964.
Congressional District: 4
Key Personnel: Pres., Dick Hursey.
Governing Authority: society; nonprofit organization. Tax-exempt: 501(c)(3).
Historic Building Museum: 1839 Stone's Tavern.
Collections: archives.
Activities: permanent exhibitions. Museum Sponsors: Pioneer Crafts Festival in September.
Hours & Admission Prices: June-Sept. Sun. afternoons; other times by appointment. No charge; donations accepted. Sept. Crafts Festival Sat.-Sun. after Labor Day 10-5. Adults $4; children under 12 no charge.
Attendance: 1,000
Membership: Individual $3; Family $5.

Lincoln City

LINCOLN BOYHOOD NATIONAL MEMORIAL, 3027 E. South St., Lincoln City, IN 47552. Mailing Address: P.O. Box 1816, Lincoln City, IN 47552-1816. Tel.: 812-937-4541. Fax: 812-937-9929. TDD: 812-937-4541.
E-mail: libo_superintendent@nps.gov
Web Site: www.nps.gov/libo

Founded: 1962.
Congressional District: 9
Key Personnel: Chief of Interpretation & Resource Management, Mike Capps; Supt., Randy Wester.
Personnel Profile: Full-Time Paid 11; Part-Time Paid 7; Part-Time Volunteers 3.
Governing Authority: federal. U.S. Dept. of Interior, National Park Service. Tax-exempt.
Park History Museum.
Collections: Lincoln-related books; pioneer artifacts; Lincoln Living Historical Farm; reproduction of pioneer period cultural items. Historic Sites: Memorial Building; Nancy Hanks Lincoln Gravesite; Cabinsite Memorial; Trail of Twelve Stones; Lincoln Spring.
Research Fields: pioneer history of southern Indiana; Lincoln 1816-1830; Lincoln & Hanks genealogy.
Facilities: 1,000-vol. library of books on subjects related to Lincoln, family history, Spencer county, state & pioneer life available for research on premises; Lincoln Living Historical Farm; Lincoln Boyhood Trail; Trail of Twelve Stones; auditorium; visitor center. Museum-related items for sale.
Activities: guided tours; self-guided walks; historical interpretation; research; living history; environmental educational programs; loaning of various Lincoln films; on-site school group programs; off-site interpretive services.
Publications: brochures; teachers' packets.
Hours & Admission Prices: Daily 8-5. Family $5, adults $3. Closed New Year's Day; Thanksgiving; Christmas. ♿
Attendance: 150,000 (accurate)
Membership: Lifetime Golden Access Passport no charge; Lifetime Nationwide Golden Age Passport 62 & over or Lincoln Boyhood Pass $10; Nationwide Golden Eagle Passport $50.

LINCOLN STATE PARK & COLONEL JONES HOME, Hwy. 162, Lincoln City, IN 47552. Mailing Address: Lincoln State Park, P.O. Box 216, Lincoln City, IN 47552-0216. Tel.: 812-937-4710 & 2802. Fax: 812-937-4833.
E-mail: mcrews@dnr.in.gov
Web Site: www.in.gov/dnr/parklake/parks/lincoln.html
Formerly: Colonel William Jones State Historic Site/Lincoln State Park & Colonel Jones Home
Founded: 1976.
Congressional District: 8
Key Personnel: Site Mgr., Michael Crews.
Personnel Profile: Full-Time Paid 1; Part-Time Paid 3; Part-Time Volunteers 6.
Governing Authority: state. Parent Institution: Indiana Department of Natural Resources. Subsidiary Institution: Division of Parks and Reservoirs. Tax-exempt.
Historic House: c.1834 Colonel William Jones House & property.
Collections: house furnishings; papers & mementoes relating to house history.
Research Fields: Colonel William Jones family history; relationship of Colonel Jones & Abraham Lincoln.
Facilities: 100 acres of forests.
Activities: guided tours by docents in costume; annual festival.
Publications: folder, house history; Friends' group newsletter.
Hours & Admission Prices: May 10-Oct. Sat.-Sun. 11-4; other times by appointment. Suggested Donation: adults $2.
Attendance: 2,000 (accurate)

Linden

LINDEN RAILROAD MUSEUM, 520 N. Main St., Linden, IN 47955-0061. Mailing Address: P.O. Box 154, Linden, IN 47955-0154. Tel.: 765-339-7245; 877-643-6371. Fax: 765-339-4896.
Web Site: www.lindenrailroadmuseum.com
Founded: 1986.
Congressional District: 4
Key Personnel: Pres., Bob Strew; Vice Pres., Jim Davis; Treas., Joe Weaver; Sec. & Dir. Devel., Bob Straw.
Personnel Profile: Part-Time Paid 5; Part-Time Volunteers 12; Interns 1.
Governing Authority: nonprofit organization. Parent Institution: Historic Linden, Inc. Subsidiary Institution: Railway Heritage Trust. Tax-exempt: 501(c)(3).
Railroad Museum & Railroad History Resource Center.
Collections: memorabilia & records of railroads, 1800s-present.
Research Fields: Montgomery Co. (IN) railroads; Monon Railroad; Cloverleaf Railroad (Frankfort, IN-St. Louis, MO)
Facilities: 500-vol. library of railroad company records, available for use by the public & inter-library loan.
Activities: lectures; participatory, loan, temporary & traveling exhibitions; school loan service; annual awards series.
Publications: semiannual newsletter, Railway Heritage News; annual report, Annotated Activity Annual.
Hours & Admission Prices: May-Sept. Wed.-Sun. 1-5. Adults $2, children 13-18 $1, children 6-12 $.50; children under 6 no charge.
Membership: Railway Heritage Associate $10.

Logansport

CASS COUNTY HISTORICAL SOCIETY, (M), 1004 E. Market St., Logansport, IN 46947-3560. Tel.: 574-753-3866. Fax: 574-722-9267.
E-mail: cchistoricalsoc@verizon.net
Web Site: www.casshistory.com
Founded: 1907.
Congressional District: 5
Key Personnel: Pres., Burton Reed; Vice Pres., Harry Rodkey; Sec., Andrea Perrone; Treas., Linda Lantz.
Personnel Profile: Full-Time Paid 1; Part-Time Volunteers 19.
Governing Authority: county. Tax-exempt: 501(c)(3).
Historical Society: housed in 1853 Jerolaman-Long House.
Collections: lustre ware; glass; natural history; oral history transcriptions; regional art; Civil War room; log cabin; 1920 ReVere car; genealogy.
Research Fields: Civil War; Indians; Cass County history; genealogy.
Facilities: 5,000-vol. library of Civil War & general history books available for use on premises; reading room.
Activities: guided tours; lectures.
Publications: newsletter; book of early photographs, Where Two Rivers Meet; oral history transcriptions, Airing Cass County: Memories of the Old Times; History of Cass County IN 1913-2002.
Hours & Admission Prices: Jan.-Feb. by appointment; March-Dec. Tues.-Sat. 1-5. No charge; donations accepted. Closed legal holidays.
Attendance: 2,500 (estimated)
Membership: Junior $10; Regular $20; Sustaining $25; Patron $45; Life $500.

COLE CLOTHING MUSEUM, 900 E. Broadway, Logansport, IN 46947-3162. Tel.: 574-753-4058.
Clothing Museum.
Collections: period clothing from late 1800s to 1970s.
Activities: tea & style shows.
Hours & Admission Prices: By appointment.

Madison

HISTORIC MADISON, INC., (M), 500 West St., Madison, IN 47250-3399. Tel.: 812-265-2967.
E-mail: hmihmfi@seidata.com
Web Site: www.historicmadisoninc.com
Founded: 1960.
Congressional District: 9
Key Personnel: Exec. Dir., John M. Staicer; Pres., John E. Galvin.
Personnel Profile: Full-Time Paid 4; Part-Time Paid 4; Part-Time Volunteers 100.
Governing Authority: nonprofit organization. Subsidiary Institution: Historic Madison Foundation Inc. Branch Museums: 1818 Jeremiah Sullivan House; 1843 Dr. Wm. Hutchings Office & Hospital; The Talbott-Hyatt Pioneer Garden; 1835 HMI Auditorium; 1850 Francis Costican House; 19th century Saddletree Factory; 1839 St. Michael The Archangel Church; 1850 AME Church. Tax-exempt: 501(c)(3).
Preservation Project and Historic House Museum.
Collections: house furnishings, original & period; office & hospital furnishings of early 19th-century; woodworking & metalworking tools; transportation equipment & artifacts.
Research Fields: 19th-century architecture; 19th-century floriculture, horticulture, handcrafts; period house furnishings; urban development; industrial history - saddletree manufacturing; underground railroad.
Activities: guided tours; lectures; gallery talks; docent program or council; permanent exhibitions.
Publications: brochures; booklets, Jeremiah Sullivan House; A Horse & Buggy Doctor in Southern Indiana; Madison and the Garber Family: A Community and Its Newspaper 1837-1992; book, The Early Architecture of Madison, Indiana; video: Remembering Madison, 1961.
Hours & Admission Prices: Sullivan House & Dr. Wm. Hutchings Office: May-Oct. Sun. & Tues.-Thurs. 1-4:30, Mon. & Sat. 10-4:30. Francis Costigan House: May-Oct. Mon. 10-4:30, Sat.-Sun. 1-4:30. Schroeder Saddletree Factory Museum: May-Oct. Mon. 10-4:30, Sat.-Sun. 1-4:30. Adults $3; students & members no charge.
Membership: Annual $10; Family $15; Participating $25; Sustaining $50; Living Endowment $100; Patron $250; Benefactor $1,000.

JEFFERSON COUNTY HISTORICAL SOCIETY, INC., 615 W. First St., Madison, IN 47250-3731. Tel.: 812-265-2335. Fax: 812-273-5023.
E-mail: jchs@seidata.com
Web Site: www.jchshc.net

Founded: 1850.
Congressional District: 9
Key Personnel: Pres., Joseph D. Carr; Museum Shop Mgr., Diana Hand.
Personnel Profile: Full-Time Paid 1; Part-Time Paid 3; Part-Time Volunteers 80; Interns 2.
Governing Authority: nonprofit organization; society. Tax-exempt: 501(c)(3).
County History Museum & Madison Railroad Station: built in 1895.
Collections: artifacts reflecting history of the region from prehistory to 1980s; textiles; GAR memorabilia; county & city archives; caboose.
Research Fields: Ohio valley history.
Facilities: Museum-related items for sale.
Activities: guided tours; lectures; arts festivals; organized education programs for adults; docent program; participatory, loan, traveling & temporary exhibitions; rental facilities. Society Sponsors: Madison in Bloom garden tour; Chautauqua of the Arts.
Publications: quarterly newsletter, Composite Columns; Beloved Madison, a 300 color photo book of walking tours of historic district.
Hours & Admission Prices: Mon.-Sat. 10-4:30, Sun. 1-4. Adults $4; AAM & museum members no charge. Closed Thanksgiving; Christmas. ♿
Attendance: 18,000 (accurate)
Membership: Individual $25; Family $35; Sustaining $50; Sponsor $100; Donor $250; Patron $500; Corporate Benefactor $1,000.

LANIER MANSION STATE HISTORIC SITE, 601 W. First St., Madison, IN 47250-3731. Tel.: 812-273-0556. Fax: 812-273-0556.
E-mail: greilly@dnr.in.gov
Web Site: www.state.in.us/ism/sites/lanier
Formerly: Lanier State Historic Site
Founded: 1925.
Congressional District: 9
Key Personnel: C.E.O. & Dir., Gerry Reilly; Pres. (V), Sally Wurtz; Cultural Administrator, Phyllis Stephens.
Personnel Profile: Full-Time Paid 6; Part-Time Paid 1; Part-Time Volunteers 25.
Governing Authority: state. Parent Institution: Indiana Dept. of Natural Resources. Subsidiary Institution: Division of Indiana State Museum & Historic Sites. Tax-exempt.
Historic House and Site: 1844 Greek revival home of J.F.D. Lanier.
Collections: period furnishings; early to mid-Victorian Southern Indiana life.
Research Fields: 1817-1850 Indiana history.
Facilities: Museum-related items for sale.
Activities: guided tours; lectures; educational programs; special events.
Hours & Admission Prices: Daily 9-5; last tour begins at 4. Adults $4, seniors 60 & over $3.50, children 6-16 $2; discount to school groups; members no charge. Closed most state holidays.
Attendance: 11,162 (accurate)
Membership: Individual $25; Family & Grandparent $40; Patron $100; Partner $1,000.

SCHOFIELD HOUSE, 217 W. Second, Madison, IN 47250-3722. Mailing Address: P.O. Box 243, Madison, IN 47250-0243. Tel.: 812-265-4759.
Historic Tavern House: c.1816.
Collections: period furnishings; personal artifacts.
Hours & Admission Prices: April-Nov. Mon.-Sat. 9:30-4, Sun. 12:30-4. Adult $3; children no charge.

Marengo

MARENGO CAVE, 400 E. State Rd. 64, Marengo, IN 47140. Mailing Address: P.O. Box 217, Marengo, IN 47140-0217. Tel.: 888-702-2837; 812-365-2705.
Web Site: www.marengocave.com
Key Personnel: Owner, Gary Roberson
Natural History Museum.
Collections: natural history.
Facilities: cafe. Museum-related items for sale.
Activities: camping cabins; walking tours; pan for gemstones; cave simulator.
Hours & Admission Prices: Memorial Day to Labor Day Mon.-Fri. 9-6, Sat.-Sun. 9-6:30; Sept.-May daily 9-5. Adults $13-$20.50, children $7-$9; children 3 & under no charge. Closed Thanksgiving; Christmas.

Marion

MARION PUBLIC LIBRARY MUSEUM, Carnegie Bldg., 600 S. Washington St., Marion, IN 46953-1963. Tel.: 765-668-2900, ext. 150. Fax: 765-668-2911. TDD: 765-668-2907.
E-mail: jfelton@marion.lib.in.us
Web Site: www.marion.lib.in.us
Founded: 1884.
Congressional District: 5
Key Personnel: Dir., Mary Eckerle; Head of Indiana History & Genealogy Svcs., Rhonda Stoffer; Cur., June Felton.
Personnel Profile: Full-Time Paid 1; Part-Time Volunteers 1.
Governing Authority: public library district; not-for-profit municipal corporation. Parent Institution: Marion Public Library. Tax-exempt.
General Museum & History Museum: housed in renovated 1902 Carnegie library building.
Collections: concentration on the history of Marion & Grant County.
Research Fields: history & genealogy of Marion and Grant County.
Facilities: 4,000-vol. library of local history & genealogy; auditorium.
Activities: guided tours; docent program. Annual Events: Quilt Show; Archaeology/Paleontology Day in September.
Publications: bimonthly newsletter, Special Edition.
Hours & Admission Prices: Summer: Mon., Wed. & Fri. 9-5:30, Tues. & Thurs. 9-8, Sat. 9-5; Sept.-May Mon., Wed. & Fri. 9-5:30, Sat. 9-5, Sun. 1-4. No charge; donations accepted. Closed New Year's Eve & Day; Martin Luther King Jr. Day; Good Friday; Easter; Memorial Day; Independence Day; Labor Day; Thanksgiving; Christmas Eve & Day. ♿
Attendance: 8,000 (estimated)

THE QUILTERS HALL OF FAME, INC., 926 S. Washington St., Marion, IN 46953-1969. Mailing Address: P.O. Box 681, Marion, IN 46952-0681. Tel.: 765-664-9333. Fax: 765-664-9333.
E-mail: quiltershalloffame@sbcglobal.net
Web Site: quiltershalloffame.net
Founded: 1979.
Congressional District: 20
Key Personnel: Bd. Pres. & Public Rels., Karen Alexander; Treas., Karen Behnke; Archivist, Christine Blazina; Devel., Rosalind Perry; Public Rels., Lisa Iversen; Museum Shop Mgr., Becky Faulstich.
Personnel Profile: Full-Time Paid 2; Part-Time Paid 2; Part-Time Volunteers 5.
Governing Authority: nonprofit organization. Tax-exempt.
History Museum: housed in the former home of Marie D. Webster, a nationally known quilt designer of the early 20th century.
Collections: works & accomplishments of Hall of Fame inductees including quilts & patterns; quilting history.
Facilities: library; garden.
Activities: guided tours; workshops; lectures; temporary exhibits. Annual Event: Annual Celebration in July.
Publications: biannual newsletter; Celebration Program Booklet.
Hours & Admission Prices: March-Dec. Wed.-Sat. 10-4. Adults $4, seniors 65 & over $3; members no charge. Closed Independence Day; Christmas.
Attendance: 3,000 (estimated)
Membership: Senior $20; Individual $30; Associate $50; Donor $75; Sponsor & Quilt Guild $100; Patron $250; Benefactor $500.

Merrillville

MERRILLVILLE COMMUNITY PLANETARIUM, Clifford Pierce Middle School, 199 E. 70th Ave., Merrillville, IN 46410-3679. Tel.: 219-650-5486. Fax: 219-650-5470.
E-mail: info@mcpstars.org
Web Site: www.mcpstars.org
Founded: 1973.
Key Personnel: Planetarium Dir., Gregg Williams; Gift Shop Mgr., Pam Powell; Show Presenter, Linda Charnetzky; Show Presenter, Pam Gower; Show Presenter, Lou Brenan.
Personnel Profile: Full-Time Paid 1; Part-Time Paid 4; Part-Time Volunteers 40.
Governing Authority: Parent Institution: Merrillville Community School Corp. Tax-exempt.
Planetarium.
Collections: Spitz model 512 star projector; Sky-Skan DigitalSky system.
Facilities: 64-seat theater. Museum-related items for sale.
Activities: group programs; public shows; private group shows.
Hours & Admission Prices: School Days: 7:30-3:30; private shows by appointment. Adults $3, children $2. ♿
Attendance: 31,000 (accurate)

Metamora

WHITEWATER CANAL STATE HISTORIC SITE, 19083 Clayborn St., Metamora, IN 47030. Mailing Address: P.O. Box 88, Metamora, IN 47030-0088. Tel.: 765-647-6512. Fax: 765-647-2734.
E-mail: wwcshs@dnr.in.gov
Founded: 1845.
Congressional District: 2
Key Personnel: Historic Site Cur., Jay Dishman.
Personnel Profile: Full-Time Paid 6; Part-Time Paid 7.
Governing Authority: state. Parent Institution: Indiana State Museum System,

Div. of the Dept. of Natural Resources Indiana State Museum, 650 W. Washington St., Indianapolis, IN 46204. Tax-exempt.
Historic Site & Buildings.
Collections: milling machinery; early transportation & industrial development; early tools. Historic Structures: 1900 operative grist mill, c.1840 restored working canal locks, boat & aqueduct.
Research Fields: Whitewater Canal History; general canal history; local & regional history; grist mill history.
Facilities: picnic grounds; hiking trails.
Activities: milling operations; horse-drawn boat trip along the canal; guided tours.
Hours & Admission Prices: Grist Mill: Wed.-Sun. 9-5. No charge; donations accepted. Ben Franklin III Canal Boat: adults $4, seniors 55-89 $3.50, children 3-12 $2; discounts to school groups; over 90 & children under 3 no charge. Closed New Year's Day; Easter; Thanksgiving; Christmas. ♿
Attendance: 131,896 (accurate)

Michigan City

BARKER MANSION, 631 Washington St., Michigan City, IN 46360-3419. Tel.: 219-873-1520. Fax: 219-873-1520.
E-mail: c_zubler@comcast.net
Web Site: emichigancity.org
Key Personnel: Dir., Cecelia Zubler
Historic House Museum: housed in the former home of John H. Barker owner of Haskell & Barker Railroad Car Company, later known as Pullman-Standard.
Collections: books; paintings; family artifacts; furnishings; portraits.
Hours & Admission Prices: June-Oct. Mon.-Fri. 10, 11:30 & 1, Sat.-Sun. 12 & 2; Nov.-May Mon.-Fri. 10, 11:30 & 1. Adults $4, children under 12 $2. ♿

GREAT LAKES MUSEUM OF MILITARY HISTORY, 360 Dunes Plaza, Michigan City, IN 46360-7342. Tel.: 219-872-2702; 800-726-5912.
E-mail: info@militaryhistorymuseum.org
Web Site: www.militaryhistorymuseum.org/
Founded: 1993.
Key Personnel: C.E.O., Terrye Mansfield; Chm. (V), Ruth Mokrycki.
Personnel Profile: Part-Time Paid 2; Part-Time Volunteers 1.
Governing Authority: nonprofit organization. Tax-exempt: 501(c)(3).
Military Museum.
Collections: military heritage; military memorabilia from the Revolutionary War to present.
Activities: Annual Events: black-tie event honoring veterans; Military Vehicle Show
Publications: newsletter, The Bugler
Hours & Admission Prices: Memorial Day to Labor Day Tues.-Fri. 9-4, Sat. 10-4, Sun. 12-4; Sept.-May Tues.-Fri. 9-4, Sat. 10-4. Adults $3, seniors & veterans $2, children 8-18 $1; discounts to AIM members; children under 8 & active military no charge. Closed New Year's Eve & Day; Thanksgiving; Christmas Eve & Day. ♿
Attendance: 2,500 (estimated)

LUBEZNIK CENTER FOR THE ARTS, (M), 101 W. 2nd St., Michigan City, IN 46360-3225. Tel.: 219-874-4900. Fax: 219-872-6829.
E-mail: artinfo@lubeznikcenter.org
Web Site: www.lubeznikcenter.org
Formerly: John G. Blank Center for the Arts
Founded: 1977.
Congressional District: 3
Key Personnel: Exec. Dir. & Museum Shop Mgr., Carolyn Saxton; Pres. (V), Suzanne Cohan Lange; Dir. Exhibits & Education, Edwin Shelton.
Personnel Profile: Full-Time Paid 5; Part-Time Paid 4; Part-Time Volunteers 50; Interns 2.
Governing Authority: nonprofit. Tax-exempt: 501(c)(3).
Art Museum.
Collections: contemporary graphics, paintings, ceramics; photographs.
Research Fields: pertaining to collection.
Facilities: Museum-related items for sale.
Activities: art classes; tours; special presentations; facility rentals. Museum Sponsors: Annual Lakefront Art Festival in August.
Publications: newsletter, Artifacts; annual report; exhibit catalogues.
Hours & Admission Prices: Tues.-Fri. 10-5, Sat.-Sun. 11-4. Suggested Donation: $3 per person; discounts to group tours; members no charge. Closed legal holidays; New Year's Eve & Day; Christmas. ♿
Attendance: 9,800 (estimated)
Membership: Senior Individual $25; Individual $35; Family $50; Sustaining $100; Donor $300; Patron $500; Corporate $1,000; Benefactor $1,500.

OLD LIGHTHOUSE MUSEUM, Heisman Harbor Rd., Washington Park, Michigan City, IN 46360. Mailing Address: P.O. Box 512, Michigan City, IN 46361-0512. Tel.: 219-872-6133.
Web Site: www.oldlighthousemuseum.org
Founded: 1973.
Congressional District: 1
Key Personnel: Pres. (V), Fred Devries; Museum Shop Mgr., Jacqueline Glidden.
Personnel Profile: Part-Time Paid 1; Part-Time Volunteers 17.
Governing Authority: society. Parent Institution: Michigan City Historical Society, Inc. Tax-exempt: 501(c)(3).
Maritime & History Museum: housed in 1858 keepers dwelling.
Collections: lighthouse service artifacts; boat builder's tools; shipwreck artifacts; local Indian artifacts; local historical articles.
Research Fields: local history; maritime.
Facilities: 300-vol. library of material on county & area history, lakefront & shipping available for use in museum library by appointment. Postcards, historical maps, pamphlets & books for sale.
Activities: guided tours; lectures; docent council; permanent & temporary exhibitions.
Publications: quarterly newsletter, Old Lighthouse Museum News; booklets, Abijah Bigelow, Revolutionary Soldier, History of Michigan City, the Life of a Town; Great Lakes' First Submarine, L.D. Phillips; Fool Killer; U.S. Life Saving/Coast Guard 1889-1989; Michigan City's First Hundred Years; Little Bit of History Series; #1-Tribute to G.C. Calvert - Michigan City History; #2-History of the Trail Creek Region; #3-Two Speeches of the Mayor Martin T. Krueger; #4-Memories of Early Michigan City; #5-Memories of the Michigan City Lighthouse; #6-Eddyville & Eddyville school.
Hours & Admission Prices: April-Nov. Tues.-Sun. 1-4; other times by appointment. Adults $3, grades 9-12 $1, children under 12 $.50. Lantern Room: additional $1. Closed New Year's Day; Good Friday; Easter; Memorial Day; Independence Day; Thanksgiving; Christmas.
Attendance: 5,000 (estimated)
Membership: Individual $8; Family $10; Patron $25; Sponsor $50; Life $150.

WASHINGTON PARK ZOOLOGICAL GARDENS, 115 Lakeshore Dr., Michigan City, IN 46360-3256. Tel.: 219-873-1510. Fax: 219-873-1540.
E-mail: jmartinez@washingtonparkzoo.com
Web Site: www.washingtonparkzoo.com
Founded: 1928.
Key Personnel: Zoo Dir., Johnny Martinez; Asst. Dir., Jamie Huss; Cur., Elizabeth Emerick; Office Mgr., Shawne Sheldon.
Personnel Profile: Full-Time Paid 7; Part-Time Paid 6; Part-Time Volunteers 15; Interns 1.
Governing Authority: municipal. Tax-exempt.
Zoological Gardens & Nature Center.
Collections: 35 species mammals, 91 specimens; 25 species birds, 59 specimens; 23 species reptiles, 37 specimens; Children's Castle; Monkey Island; Petting Barn.
Facilities: zoological park. Zoological-related items for sale.
Activities: lectures; films; study clubs; TV & radio programs; formally organized education programs; docent program; loan, permanent, temporary & traveling exhibitions; school loan service.
Publications: quarterly newsletter.
Hours & Admission Prices: April-Oct. daily 10-5. Adults $5.50, seniors $4, children 3-11 $3.50; discounts reciprocal with member zoos; children 2 & under no charge. ♿
Attendance: 63,000 (accurate)
Membership: Individual $30; Family & Grandparent $40; Family Plus $50; Zookeeper $50.

Middletown

VERA'S LITTLE RED DOLLHOUSE MUSEUM, 4385 W. County Rd. 850, N., Middletown, IN 47356-9462. Tel.: 765-533-3453.
Doll Museum.
Collections: dolls; stuffed animals.
Hours & Admission Prices: Call for hours. ♿

Mishawaka

HANNAH LINDAHL CHILDREN'S MUSEUM, 1402 S. Main St., Mishawaka, IN 46544-5241. Tel.: 574-254-4540. Fax: 574-254-4585.
E-mail: pmarker@hlcm.org
Web Site: www.hlcm.org
Founded: 1946.
Congressional District: 3
Key Personnel: Pres. (V), Eva Jojo; Dir. & Cur., Peggy Marker.
Personnel Profile: Full-Time Paid 1; Part-Time Volunteers 30; Interns 1.
Governing Authority: public school district. Tax-exempt: 170(b)(1).

Local History & Children's Museum.
Collections: Indian artifacts; ethnic culture of Mishawaka; ethnic articles & period clothing; archaeology finds; military items; tools; books; natural history displays; Japanese house & gardens; airplane model collection; c.1800, Mishawaka village; Survive Alive House teaching fire safety; student projects.
Major Exhibits: A Look at Mishawaka 175 Years, 11/09-6/10; Trunks and Treasures, 2/10-3/10; Let's Talk, 4/10-12/10.
Research Fields: ethnic cultures of Mishawaka.
Facilities: library; arboretum. Gift items for sale.
Activities: guided tours; demonstrations; inter-school & inter-museum loans; changing exhibit windows.
Publications: quarterly newsletter.
Hours & Admission Prices: June Tues.-Thurs. 10-2; Sept.-May Tues.-Fri. 9-4. Adults $2; members no charge. Closed school holidays. ♿
Attendance: 8,500 (estimated)
Membership: First Time Family $10; Friend $20; Donor $35; Benefactor $50; Sponsor $75; Reciprocal $100; Corporate $150.

MISHAWAKA SPORTS MUSEUM, 109 Lincoln Way E., Mishawaka, IN 46544-2016. Tel.: 574-257-0039.
Founded: 1995.
Key Personnel: Museum Shop Mgr., Larry La Cluyse
Sports Museum.
Collections: early 1900s sports equipment; programs; autographs; period artifacts; photographs; magazines; books; Notre Dame memorabilia.
Hours & Admission Prices: Mon.-Fri. 11-5. No charge; donations accepted. Closed holidays.

OTIS BOWEN MUSEUM & ARCHIVES, 1001 W. McKinley Ave., Mishawaka, IN 46545-2232. Tel.: 219-259-8511. Fax: 219-257-3499.
History Museum.
Collections: Gov. Otis Bowen's personal artifacts & documents; photographs.
Hours & Admission Prices: By appointment.

Mitchell

PIONEER VILLAGE & VIRGIL GRISSOM MEMORIAL AT SPRING MILL STATE PARK, 3333 State Rd. 60 E., Mitchell, IN 47446. Mailing Address: P.O. Box 376, Mitchell, IN 47446-0376. Tel.: 812-849-4129. Fax: 812-849-4004. TDD: 812-849-4129.
E-mail: springmillstatepark@dnr.in.gov
Web Site: www.in.gov/dnr/parklake/2968.htm
Formerly: Spring Mill State Park Pioneer Village & Grissom Memorial
Founded: 1927.
Congressional District: 8
Key Personnel: Chm. (V), Coletta Prewitt; Property Mgr., Mark Young; Asst. Property Mgr., Jon Winne; Interpretive Naturalist, Jill Vance.
Personnel Profile: Full-Time Paid 16; Part-Time Paid 47; Part-Time Volunteers 162.
Governing Authority: state. Parent Institution: Dept. of Natural Resources. Div. of State Parks, 402 W. Washington, Rm. W298, Indianapolis, IN 46204. Tax-exempt.
Village Museum: housed in 1817 Grist Mill, & other restored buildings, located on the site of a flourishing pioneer village in the 1800s.
Collections: over 1,000 artifacts from the 1800s period of the village; early pioneer garden; Gemini III space capsule & suite; pioneer cemetery; mementoes of the life of Virgil I. (Gus) Grissom, pioneer in America's exploration of outer space & the second American astronaut to go into space.
Research Fields: botanical; history of the area.
Facilities: nature center; picnic areas; nature trails.
Activities: guided tours; candlelight tours; cave boat rides; craft demonstrations; naturalist programs; special events; fishing; mountain bikes; hayrides.
Publications: Gristmill Gazette; The Village That Slept Awhile; Pioneer Garden; Village coloring book; garden coloring book.
Hours & Admission Prices: Pioneer Village: May-Oct. Sun.-Thurs. 9-5, Fri.-Sat. 9-7. In-state car: Mon.-Thurs. $4, Fri.-Sun. & holidays $5; Out-of-state car $7; annual pass available. Grissom Memorial: daily 8:30-4. Nature Center: daily 9-4:30. ♿
Attendance: 670,000 (estimated)

Monticello

WHITE COUNTY HISTORICAL SOCIETY MUSEUM, 101 S. Bluff St., Monticello, IN 47960-2308. Tel.: 574-583-3998.
E-mail: wcmuseum@sugardog.com
Founded: 1911.
Congressional District: 2
Key Personnel: Dir., Judith Baker; Pres., Julie Gutwein; Vice Pres., Jack Ward.
Personnel Profile: Part-Time Paid 1; Part-Time Volunteers 6.
Governing Authority: nonprofit organization. Tax-exempt.
Historical Society Museum.
Collections: people & history of White County, Indiana.
Research Fields: family history; White County history.
Facilities: library available for use on premises.
Activities: guided tours; lectures; formally organized education programs for children; permanent & temporary exhibitions; research.
Publications: Museum Musings.
Hours & Admission Prices: Wed.-Fri. 10-4; other times by appointment. No charge; donations accepted.
Membership: Single $15; Family $25; Business $100; Life $150, Business Life $500.

Mooresville

ACADEMY OF HOOSIER HERITAGE, 250 N. Monroe St., Mooresville, IN 46158-1551. Tel.: 317-831-9001.
E-mail: abmuseum@scican.net
Web Site: www.academymuseum.org
History Museum.
Collections: community heritage & history; photographs; personal artifacts.
Activities: special events; temporary & permanent exhibits; educational programs.
Hours & Admission Prices: Mon., Wed. & Fri. 1-5; groups by appointment.

Muncie

ACADEMY OF MODEL AERONAUTICS/NATIONAL MODEL AVIATION MUSEUM, 5151 E. Memorial Dr., Muncie, IN 47302-9252. Tel.: 765-287-1256. Fax: 765-281-7904.
E-mail: michaels@modelaircraft.org
Web Site: www.modelaircraft.org/museum/museuminfo.aspx
Founded: 1936.
Congressional District: 2
Key Personnel: Pres. (V), Dave Mathewson; Archivist, Jackie Shalberg; Registrar, Maria VanVreede; Museum Dir., Michael Smith; Librarian, Rich LaGrange; Museum Shop Mgr., Sheila Tweedy.
Personnel Profile: Full-Time Paid 4; Part-Time Paid 1; Part-Time Volunteers 12; Interns 2.
Governing Authority: private; nonprofit organization. Parent Institution: Academy of Model Aeronautics. Tax-exempt.
Aeronautics Museum.
Collections: concentration on the developmental history of flying model/miniature aircraft; plans; photographs.
Research Fields: aviation & model aviation history.
Facilities: library & archive of books & magazines covering all aspects of aviation & model aviation; classroom; theater. Clothing, accessories, books, videotapes & items related to model aviation for sale.
Activities: docent program; guided tours; educational make-and-fly programming.
Publications: monthly magazine, Model Aviation; quarterly newsletter, Cloud Nine.
Hours & Admission Prices: April to late Nov. Mon.-Fri. 8-4:30, Sat.-Sun. 10-4; call for holiday hours; late Nov. to March Mon.-Fri. 8-4:30, Sat. 10-4. Adults $2, children 6-17 $1; discounts to group of 10 or more; members no charge. ♿
Attendance: 5,709 (accurate)
Membership: Patron $25; Supporter $100; Sustaining $500; Life $1,000.

* **BALL STATE UNIVERSITY MUSEUM OF ART, (M),** Riverside Ave. at Warwick Rd., Muncie, IN 47306-0001. Tel.: 765-285-5242 & 5270. Fax: 765-285-4003.
Web Site: www.bsu.edu/artmuseum
Founded: 1936.
Congressional District: 10
Key Personnel: Dir., Peter F. Blume; Assoc. Dir., Carl Schafer; Cur. Education, Tania Said; Preparator & Exhibition Designer, Randy Salway.
Personnel Profile: Full-Time Paid 4; Part-Time Paid 16; Part-Time Volunteers 25.
Governing Authority: state. Parent Institution: Ball State University. Tax-exempt: 170(b)(1)(A).
Art Museum.
Collections: Italian Renaissance art; 17th- to 19th-century European art; 19th- & 20th-century American art; Chinese art; Indian art; African art; art of ancient cultures.
Research Fields: pertaining to collections.
Facilities: 17,735 sq. ft. exhibit space.
Activities: guided tours for children & adults; lectures; gallery talks; inter-museum loan, permanent, temporary & traveling exhibitions.
Publications: catalogs for special exhibitions; annual report; newsletter.

Hours & Admission Prices: Mon.-Fri. 9-4:30, Sat.-Sun. 1:30-4:30. No charge; donations accepted. Closed holidays. ♿
Attendance: 25,000 (estimated)
Membership: Student $15; Individual $25; Family & Dual $50; Sponsor $100-$249; Patron $250-$499; Sustaining $500-$999; Benefactor $1,000-$1,999; Philanthropist $2,000 & up; Connoisseur, accumulated giving of $50,000 & up.

EMILY KIMBROUGH HOUSE, 715 E. Washington St., Muncie, IN 47305-2532. Mailing Address: 704 E. Main St., Muncie, IN 47305-2511. Tel.: 317-282-1550.
Historic House Museum: housed in the childhood home of author, Emily Kimbrough. Listed on the National Register of Historic Places.
Collections: period furnishings.
Hours & Admission Prices: Call for hours.

MINNETRISTA, (M), 1200 N. Minnetrista Pkwy., Muncie, IN 47303-2925. Tel.: 765-282-4848. Fax: 765-741-5110.
Web Site: www.minnetrista.net
Formerly: Minnetrista Cultural Center
Founded: 1988.
Congressional District: 2
Key Personnel: Pres. & C.E.O., Betty Brewer; Chm. (V), Terri Matchett; Vice Pres. Visitor Experience, Rebecca Holmquist; Vice Pres. Finance & Operations, Bill Buchanan; Vice Pres. Philanthropy, Bob Scott; Dir. Collections, Karen Vincent; Dir. Education & Experience, George Buss; Retail Mgr., Theresa Coy.
Personnel Profile: Full-Time Paid 43; Part-Time Paid 22; Part-Time Volunteers 401; Interns 6.
Governing Authority: nonprofit. Subsidiary Institution: Minnetrista Cultural Foundation, Inc. Tax-exempt: 501(c)(3).
General Museum.
Collections: artifacts documenting the heritage of East Central Indiana including documents, manuscripts, photographs, fruit jars, industrial products, clothing, quilts & coverlets, furniture, fine & decorative arts, military, toys, dolls, games, transportation; historic & contemporary gardens; 4 historic buildings.
Major Exhibits: Enchanted Museum (T), 11/09-2/7/10; Eyes on Earth (T), 1/30/10-5/9/10; Disease Detectives (T), 2/13/10-5/30/10; Minnetrista Annual Juried Art Show, 2/20/10-5/2/10; Ball Jars Revisited, 5/22/10-9/26/10; Quilt Art 20 (T), 6/12/10-8/29/10; Climate Change (T), 6/19/10-9/19/10; Open Space: Art About the Land, 9/10/10-10/10/10; Jazz in Black and White (T), 10/16/10-1/16/11; Survivor Jamestown, 10/23/10-1/24/11.
Research Fields: history, environment art & industry of east central Indiana.
Facilities: 2,500-vol. library of local history materials; 12,500 sq. ft. exhibit space; educational facilities; 6.3 acre nature area. Museum-related items for sale.
Activities: guided tours; lectures; films; concerts; arts festivals; study clubs organized educational programs; docent program; participatory, loan, traveling & temporary exhibits; distance learning; seasonal events.
Publications: quarterly, Columns Magazine; annual calendar.
Hours & Admission Prices: Mon.-Sat. 9-5:30, Sun. 11-5:30. Adults $7, senior citizens over 64 $6, children 3-18 & college students $4; discounts to groups, AAA & AAM members; members no charge; donations accepted. Gift Shops: The Center Shop: Mon.-Sat. 10-5, Sun. 12-5; Minnetrista Orchard Shop: Mon.-Sat. 10-4, Sun. 12-4. Closed New Year's Day; Easter; Thanksgiving; Christmas. ♿
Attendance: 70,000 (estimated)
Membership: Individual $30; Dual $50; Family $70; Premier $125; Maplewood Circle $250; Nebosham Circle $500; Oakhurst Circle $1,000.

THE MOORE-YOUSE HOME MUSEUM, 122 E. Washington St., Muncie, IN 47305-1734. Tel.: 765-282-1550.
E-mail: museum@the-dchs.org
Web Site: www.the-dchs.org/moore-youse_home_museum.htm
Governing Authority: Parent Institution: Delaware County Historical Society.
Historic House Museum.
Collections: Muncie history; furnishings; paintings; documents; photographs.
Hours & Admission Prices: March-Nov. 1st Sun. of month 1-4; other times by appointment. No charge.

MUNCIE CHILDREN'S MUSEUM, 515 S. High St., Muncie, IN 47305-2376. Mailing Address: P.O. Box 544, Muncie, IN 47308-0544. Tel.: 765-286-1660. Fax: 765-286-1662.
E-mail: museum@munciemuseum.com
Web Site: www.munciechildrensmuseum.com
Founded: 1977.
Congressional District: 2
Key Personnel: Exec. Dir., Mary Slafkosky; Chm. (V), James Borgmann; Pres. (V), Mike Musal; Museum Shop Mgr., Kynda Rinker.
Personnel Profile: Full-Time Paid 6; Full-Time Volunteers 200; Part-Time Paid 8; Part-Time Volunteers 200; Interns 1.
Governing Authority: nonprofit organization. Tax-exempt: 501(c)(3).
Children's Museum.
Collections: hands-on exhibits.
Facilities: 3 education classrooms. Educational items for sale.
Activities: guided tours; lectures; concerts; workshops; formally organized educational programs; docent program; permanent, temporary & loan exhibitions.
Publications: newsletter.
Hours & Admission Prices: Tues.-Sat. 10-5, Sun. 1-5. Adults $6; discounts to ASTC members. Closed major holidays. ♿
Attendance: 37,850 (accurate)
Membership: Family $70; Extended Family $100.

Munster

SOUTH SHORE ARTS, 1040 Ridge Rd., Munster, IN 46321-1876. Tel.: 219-836-1839, ext. 100. Fax: 219-836-1863.
Web Site: southshoreartsonline.org
Formerly: Northern Indiana Arts Association
Founded: 1969.
Congressional District: 1
Key Personnel: Exec. Dir., John Cain; Pres., Liz Valavanis; Administrative Asst., Shari Pettis; Dir. Finance & Administration, Susan Anderson; Gallery Mgr., Mary McClelland; Dir. Mktg. & Devel., Tricia Hernandez; Dir. Education, Linda Eyermann; Education Coord., Kimberly McKinley; Special Projects Mgr., Jennifer Vinovich; Museum Shop Mgr., Jackie Wicklund; Asst. Museum Shop Mgr., Andrea Miller.
Personnel Profile: Full-Time Paid 7; Part-Time Paid 3; Part-Time Volunteers 4; Interns 1.
Governing Authority: nonprofit. Tax-exempt: 501(c)(3).
Art Association Museum.
Collections: works by regional artists.
Facilities: library of reference, visual art & arts management material available to the public for use on premises; 370-seat auditorium; 5,000 sq. ft. exhibit space; educational facilities. Art museum-related gift items for sale.
Activities: guided tours; lectures; concerts; arts festivals; theater; organized education programs; docent program. Museum Sponsors: Salon Show; Elementary, Junior High & High School Art Shows; regional, national & international exhibits.
Publications: quarterly newsletter.
Hours & Admission Prices: Mon.-Fri. 10-5, Sat. 10-4, Sun. 12-4. Adults $3, students $2; members no charge. ♿
Membership: Student $25; Artist $40; Individual $45; Family $65; Patron $125; Sponsor $250; Benefactor $500; Life $1,000.

Nappanee

AMISH ACRES, 1600 W. Market St., Nappanee, IN 46550. Tel.: 800-800-4942; 574-773-4188.
Historic Farm Museum.
Collections: local history & culture; period furnishings & equipment; personal artifacts. Historic Buildings: farmhouse; two room house; barn; wagon shed; ice house; cider mill; one room schoolhouse.
Hours & Admission Prices: May-Oct. Tues.-Sat. 10-7, Sun. 10-6.

Nashville

BROWN COUNTY ART GALLERY AND MUSEUM, #1 Artist Dr., Nashville, IN 47448-8101. Mailing Address: P.O. Box 443, Nashville, IN 47448-0443. Tel.: 812-988-4609.
E-mail: brncagal@att.net
Web Site: www.browncountyartgallery.org
Founded: 1926.
Congressional District: 9
Key Personnel: Pres., Lyn Letsinger-Miller; Vice Pres., Cheryl Eyed.
Personnel Profile: Full-Time Paid 1; Full-Time Volunteers 17; Part-Time Paid 2; Part-Time Volunteers 12.
Governing Authority: Parent Institution: Brown County Art Gallery Foundation. Tax-exempt.
Art Association Gallery.
Collections: oil paintings & pastels by Glen Cooper Henshaw; memorial collection of artwork by prominent early Indiana artists & deceased artist members; paintings; etchings; prints; exhibits of contemporary artist members.
Activities: gallery talks; study clubs; annual exhibit; school & youth program; classes in fine & performing arts. Annual Events: Spring Patron Art Show in May; Indiana Heritage Arts Show in June; Neophytes Art Show in

August; Brown County Artists Today in September; Collector's Showcase in October; Christmas Art Show & Sale in November-December.
Publications: annual catalogue.
Hours & Admission Prices: Mon.-Sat. 10-5, Sun. 12-5. No charge; donations accepted. Closed New Year's Day; Thanksgiving; Christmas. ♿
Attendance: 7,500 (estimated)
Membership: Student $10; Single $25; Family $30; Patron & Group $40; Century Club & Corporate $100; Life $1,000.

BROWN COUNTY HISTORICAL SOCIETY PIONEER MUSEUM, Museum Lane, Nashville, IN 47448. Mailing Address: Box 668, Nashville, IN 47448-0668. Tel.: 812-988-6089.
E-mail: bcarchive@hotmail.com
Web Site: browncountyhistory.info
Formerly: Brown County Museum
Founded: 1957.
Congressional District: 9
Key Personnel: Pres. (V), Ivan Lancaster; 1st Vice Pres., Pete Sebert; Vice Pres. & Museum Shop Mgr., Ada M. Jones; Genealogist, Jeanette Richart; Archives, Rob Coulter; Treas., Gloria Berryman; Recording Sec., Pauline Hoover; Corresponding Sec., Nel Hamilton.
Personnel Profile: Part-Time Volunteers 60.
Governing Authority: society; nonprofit. Parent Institution: Brown County Historical Society. Subsidiary Institution: Pioneer Women's Club. Affiliated with the Indiana State Historical Society, Indianapolis, IN. Tax-exempt.
Historical Society Museum Village.
Collections: furnishings & furniture; completely equipped early doctor's office; weaving & spinning collections; pioneer artifacts. Historic Structures: log cabin; barn; log jail; doctor's office; blacksmith shop.
Research Fields: archaeology of Brown County.
Facilities: library of genealogical material & archives available for use by permission of archivist or genealogist on premises only.
Activities: guided tours; temporary exhibitions; spinning; weaving; blacksmith; woodworking; fireplace cooking; candle dipping; fabric dyeing.
Publications: quarterly newsletter; annual genealogy records; History of County Reprints.
Hours & Admission Prices: May-Oct. Sat.-Sun. 1-5. Suggested Donation: adults $1.50; discounts to AAM members; group school tours & members no charge.
Attendance: 1,500 (estimated)
Membership: Student $5; Annual $15; Sustaining $20; Business $25; Life $500.

T.C. STEELE STATE HISTORIC SITE, 4220 T.C. Steele Rd., Nashville, IN 47448-9586. Tel.: 812-988-2785. Fax: 812-988-8457.
E-mail: tcsteele@bloomington.in.us
Web Site: www.state.in.us/ism
Founded: 1945.
Congressional District: 9
Key Personnel: Pres. (V), Stephanie Dean; Historic Site Mgr., Andrea Smith DeTarnowsky.
Personnel Profile: Full-Time Paid 2; Part-Time Paid 4; Part-Time Volunteers 50.
Governing Authority: State of Indiana, Dept. of Natural Resources, Div. of Museums & Historic Sites, 650 W. Washington St., Indianapolis, IN 46204. Tax-exempt.
Historic Site.
Collections: Steele paintings; period furnishings; books; fine & decorative art. Historic Buildings: c.1907 T.C. Steele Home; c.1916 Studio.
Facilities: 5 hiking trails; over 3 acres of gardens; state nature preserve.
Activities: self-guided & guided tours; nature trails.
Hours & Admission Prices: Tues.-Sat. 9-5, Sun. 1-5. Adults $3.50, seniors 65 & over $3, children 12 & under $2; discounts to National Trust for Historic Preservation members & groups; Friends Group & Indiana State Museum Society members no charge. Closed most holidays. ♿
Attendance: 9,071 (accurate)
Membership: Individual $25; Family $40; Supporting $100; Sponsor $200; Patron $500; Lifetime $1,000.

New Albany

CARNEGIE CENTER FOR ART & HISTORY, (M), 201 E. Spring St., New Albany, IN 47150-3422. Tel.: 812-944-7336. Fax: 812-981-3544.
E-mail: snewkirk@carnegiecenter.org
Web Site: carnegiecenter.org
Founded: 1971.
Congressional District: 9
Key Personnel: Dir., Sally Newkirk; Cur., Karen Gillenwater; Dir. Mktg. & Outreach, Laura Wilkins; Public Rels. Assoc., Delesha Thomas; Maintenance, Paris Brock.
Personnel Profile: Full-Time Paid 4; Part-Time Paid 1; Part-Time Volunteers 15.
Governing Authority: nonprofit. NA-FC Public Library. Tax-exempt.
History Museum & Art Gallery: housed in 1904 Carnegie Library.
Collections: Underground Railroad history; local history & culture; works by regional artists.
Major Exhibits: Form, Not Function: Contemporary Quilt Art at the Carnegie, 1/8/10-3/6/10; Paintings by Susan Gorsen, 3/12/10-4/23/10; Contemporary Glass, 5/21/10-7/17/10.
Activities: tours, lectures; art & craft workshops for adults & children. Annual Event: National Juried Exhibition of Contemporary Quilt Art.
Publications: newsletter, Musings.
Hours & Admission Prices: Tues.-Sat. 10-5:30. No charge. Closed major holidays. ♿
Attendance: 13,000 (accurate)

CULBERTSON MANSION STATE HISTORIC SITE, 914 E. Main St., New Albany, IN 47150-5841. Tel.: 812-944-9600. Fax: 812-949-6134.
E-mail: culbertsonmansionshs@dnr.in.gov
Web Site: www.indianamuseum.org/shs
Founded: 1976.
Congressional District: 9
Key Personnel: Pres. (V), Eleene Metcalf; Historic Site Cur., Joellen Bye; Museum Shop Mgr., Jamie Mauch.
Personnel Profile: Full-Time Paid 2; Part-Time Paid 2; Part-Time Volunteers 110.
Governing Authority: state. Branch of Indiana State Museum System, Div. of the Dept. of Natural Resources Indiana, 650 West Washington St., Indianapolis, IN 46204. Tax-exempt.
Historic House: 1867 W.S. Culbertson Home, a 25-room Victorian mansion.
Collections: period furnishings.
Research Fields: mid-Victorian & Southern Indiana life.
Activities: guided tours; lectures.
Publications: semi-annually, The Culbertson Newsletter.
Hours & Admission Prices: April to mid-Dec. Tues.-Sat. 9-5, Sun. 1-5. Adults $3.50, seniors $3, children under 12 $2; discounts to groups with appointment; children 3 & under no charge. Closed Election Day; Veterans Day; Thanksgiving, Christmas. ♿
Attendance: 20,000 (accurate)
Membership: Student & Seniors 55 & over $5; Individual $10; Family $20; Sponsor $25; Patron $50; Benefactor $100; Life $1,000.

New Castle

ART ASSOCIATION OF HENRY COUNTY, INC., 218 S. 15th St., New Castle, IN 47362-3201. Mailing Address: P.O. Box 842, New Castle, IN 47362-0842. Tel.: 765-529-2634.
E-mail: aahc@nltc
Web Site: www.henrycountyarts.org
Key Personnel: Pres., Debby Weidert
Art Association.
Collections: paintings; photography.
Facilities: Museum-related items for sale.
Activities: classes; workshops; children's summer art day.
Hours & Admission Prices: Tues.-Fri. 9-4, Sat. 9-3, Sun. 1-4. No charge.
Attendance: 2,000
Membership: Student $5; Individual $25; Family & Club $40; Supporting $100; Sustaining $200; Benefactor $300; Corporate $500.

HENRY COUNTY HISTORICAL SOCIETY, 606 S. 14th St., New Castle, IN 47362-3339. Tel.: 765-529-4028.
E-mail: hchisoc@kiva.net
Web Site: www.kiva.net/~hchisoc/museum.htm
Founded: 1887.
Congressional District: 10
Key Personnel: Pres., Gene Ingram; Cur., Marianne Hughes.
Personnel Profile: Part-Time Paid 3; Part-Time Volunteers 2.
Governing Authority: county. Tax-exempt.
Historic House: 1870 home of Civil War General William Grose. Listed on the National Register of Historic Places.
Collections: archives; furniture; tools; china; glass; silver; county cemetery records; natural history; Indian relics; dolls.
Research Fields: genealogical; local history.
Facilities: 1,000-vol. library of books on local, state & Civil War history & biographical & genealogical materials available for use on premises; reading room.
Activities: guided tours; permanent exhibitions.
Publications: newsletter, Historicalog.
Hours & Admission Prices: Wed.-Sat. 1-4:30. Adults $2, students $1; children & members no charge. Closed holidays. ♿

Attendance: 1,200 (estimated)
Membership: Family $20.

INDIANA BASKETBALL HALL OF FAME, 408 Trojan Lane, New Castle, IN 47362. Mailing Address: One Hall of Fame Ct., New Castle, IN 47362-2941. Tel.: 765-529-1891. Fax: 765-529-0273.
Web Site: www.hoopshall.com
Founded: 1965.
Congressional District: 10
Key Personnel: C.E.O., Roger Dickinson; Pres. (V), Dr. Philip Eskew, Jr.; Museum Shop Mgr., Becky Beavers.
Personnel Profile: Full-Time Paid 3; Part-Time Paid 4; Part-Time Volunteers 100.
Governing Authority: nonprofit. Tax-exempt: 501(c)(3).
Sports Museum.
Collections: sports equipment; uniforms; photos; films; videos; newspapers.
Research Fields: sports history; history of Indiana high schools.
Facilities: 250-vol. library containing information on rules, strategy & history monographs; reading room; theater.
Activities: tours; tournaments; awards banquet.
Publications: quarterly newsletter, IBHF News; quarterly magazine, Indiana Basketball History.
Hours & Admission Prices: Sun. 1-5, Mon.-Sat. 10-5. Adults $5; discounts to AAM members; members no charge. Closed major holidays. ♿
Attendance: 10,000 (accurate)
Membership: Regular Member $100; Benefactor $250; Patron $500; Lifetime $3,000.

New Harmony

HISTORIC NEW HARMONY, (M), 603 West St., New Harmony, IN 47631. Mailing Address: P.O. Box 579, New Harmony, IN 47631-0579. Tel.: 812-682-4488. Fax: 812-682-4313.
E-mail: harmony@usi.edu
Web Site: www.newharmony.org
Founded: 1974.
Congressional District: 8
Key Personnel: Dir. Historic New Harmony, Connie Weinzapfel; Chm. (V), Karen Walker; Devel. & Public Rels. Mgr., Samantha Brown; Education Coord., Jan Kahle; Collections Mgr., Daniel Goodman; Collections Asst., Amanda Bryden; Group Sales, Sara Brown; Sr. Sales Asst., Rebecca Conner; Museum Shop Mgr., Christine Crews.
Personnel Profile: Full-Time Paid 9; Part-Time Paid 37; Part-Time Volunteers 6; Interns 1.
Governing Authority: nonprofit organization. Parent Institution: Univ. of Southern Indiana. Subsidiary Institution: USI/New Harmony Foundation. Tax-exempt: 501(c)(3).
History Museum & Preservation Project: located on the site of two early utopian experiments-George Rapp's 1814-1825 Harmony Society & Welsh-born social reformer & industrialist Robert Owen's New Harmony; it is also the site of the early headquarters of the U.S. Geological Survey; it provided many of the earliest collections of the Smithsonian Institution.
Collections: 1814-1834 house museums of the Harmonist & Owen periods; geological & natural science collections of the earliest geological surveys; early theatre; manuscripts; 81 hand-colored Maximilian-Bodmer lithographs. Historic Buildings: approx. 12 c.1814-1824 structures; 20 c.1830-1920 structures.
Research Fields: geology; archaeology; decorative arts; communal studies; architecture.
Facilities: archives; 250 & 427-seat auditorium; 200-seat theater; visitor's center. Books, prints & museum-related items for sale.
Activities: guided tours; films on history; gallery talks; concerts; drama; workshops; educational programs; dance recitals; arts festivals; drama; formally organized education programs for adults & undergraduate college students; permanent & traveling exhibitions.
Publications: biannual newsletter.
Hours & Admission Prices: March 15-Dec. 30 daily 9:30-5; Dec. 30-March 14 groups by appointment. Family $25, adults $10, children 7-17 $5; discounts to groups, AAM, ICOM & AAA members. ♿
Attendance: 21,183 (accurate)
Membership: Donor Categories: Historian $25; Educator $50; Naturalist $100; Preservationist $250; Philanthropist $500; Golden Raintree $1,000; Door of Promise $2,000.

NEW HARMONY GALLERY OF CONTEMPORARY ART, 506 Main St., New Harmony, IN 47631. Mailing Address: P.O. Box 627, New Harmony, IN 47631-0627. Tel.: 812-682-3156. Fax: 812-682-3870.
E-mail: emyersbro@usi.edu
Web Site: www.nhgallery.com
Founded: 1975.
Congressional District: 8
Key Personnel: Asst. Dir., Erika Myers-Bromwell.
Personnel Profile: Full-Time Paid 1; Part-Time Paid 2.
Governing Authority: nonprofit organization. University of Southern Indiana. Tax-exempt: 501(c)(3).
Contemporary Art Gallery.
Collections: changing exhibits; contemporary art.
Activities: lectures; workshops; monthly exhibitions.
Publications: catalogs.
Hours & Admission Prices: Jan.-March Tues.-Sat. 10-5; April-Dec. Tues.-Sat. 10-5, Sun. 12-4. No charge. ♿
Attendance: 40,000 (estimated)
Membership: Student $20; Individual $25; Family $40; Associate $100; Donor $200; Benefactor $500; Patron of the Arts $1,000.

NEW HARMONY STATE HISTORIC SITE/HISTORIC NEW HARMONY, Atheneum/Visitors Center, North & Arthur Sts., New Harmony, IN 47631. Mailing Address: P.O. Box 579, New Harmony, IN 47631-0579. Tel.: 800-231-2168. Fax: 812-682-4281.
E-mail: newharmonyshs@dynasty.net
Web Site: www.usi.edu/hnh/index2.asp
Founded: 1937.
Congressional District: 8
Personnel Profile: Full-Time Paid 8; Part-Time Volunteers 25.
Governing Authority: Parent Institution: Indiana State Museum. Subsidiary Institution: University of Southern Indiana. Tax-exempt.
Historic Site: site of two early utopian experiments, the communal societies of New Harmony.
Collections: documents relating to New Harmony. Historic Buildings and Sites: c.1820, 1840-1860 Fauntleroy House, containing Owen period furniture, memorabilia from scientific community and the Minerva Society; c.1822 Harmonist Dormitory #2, containing interpretative exhibits of education, printing in New Harmony; c.1824, 1857, 1888 Thrall's Opera House; c.1816, 1939 restored Harmonist Labyrinth; c.1820 Harmonist cemetery; c.1820 Scholle House.
Research Fields: communal societies of New Harmony and the later periods of the town.
Facilities: 250-seat opera house.
Activities: guided tours; formally organized education programs; permanent exhibits; changing exhibits of regional art & history.
Publications: quarterly newsletter, In Harmony.
Hours & Admission Prices: March-Dec. daily 9:30-5. Adults $10, children 7-17 $5; children under 6 no charge. ♿
Attendance: 26,000 (accurate)

WORKING MEN'S INSTITUTE, 407 W. Tavern St., New Harmony, IN 47631. Mailing Address: P.O. Box 368, New Harmony, IN 47631-0368. Tel.: 812-682-4806.
Web Site: www.newharmonywmi.lib.in.us
Formerly: New Harmony Working Men's Institute
Founded: 1838.
Congressional District: 8
Key Personnel: Dir., Sherry Graves.
Personnel Profile: Full-Time Paid 1; Part-Time Paid 2.
Governing Authority: Tax-exempt. 501(c)(3).
19th Century Museum & Library.
Collections: natural history; local history; portraits; books; textiles; education; teaching tools.
Publications: book, New Harmony Story.
Hours & Admission Prices: Tues.-Sat. 10-4:30, Sun. 12-4. No charge; donations accepted. Closed New Year's Eve & Day; Easter; Independence Day; Thanksgiving; Christmas Eve & Day.
Attendance: 7,000 (estimated)

Noblesville

INDIANA TRANSPORTATION MUSEUM, 825 Park Ave., Noblesville, IN 46060-0083. Mailing Address: P.O. Box 83, Noblesville, IN 46061-0083. Tel.: 317-773-6000 & 776-7881 & 7887. Fax: 317-773-5530.
E-mail: nkp587@iquest.net
Web Site: www.itm.org
Founded: 1960.
Congressional District: 5
Key Personnel: Chm., David Wilcox; Dir. Rail Operations, Ron Gaertner; Treas., Thomas H. Hicks, CPA; Sec., Peter McConnachie; Museum Shop Mgr., Eleanor Wilcox.
Personnel Profile: Full-Time Paid 1; Full-Time Volunteers 4; Part-Time Paid 1; Part-Time Volunteers 200.
Governing Authority: nonprofit organization. Tax-exempt: 501(c)(3).
Rail Transportation and Technology Museum: office housed in 1930 railroad station from Hobbs, IN.

Collections: early 20th century railway & trolley equipment; steam, diesel & electric railway equipment, timetables, photographs, blueprints, other transportation artifacts.
Research Fields: Industrial History & Technology.
Facilities: library of railroad material; picnic area. Museum-related items for sale.
Activities: permanent exhibitions; guided tours daily by appointment; steam and diesel train excursions to various cities; 1-1/2 mile electric trolley ride; machinery demonstration area.
Publications: quarterly & monthly newsletter, The Inside Track.
Hours & Admission Prices: April-Oct. Sat.-Sun. 11-4. Adults $3, children 3-12 $2; children 2 & under and members no charge. Excursion fares: call for information.
Attendance: 40,000 (estimated)
Membership: Individual $20; Family $35; Sustaining $50; Contributing $100; 20th Century $250; Patron $500; Benefactor $1,000.

North Manchester

MANCHESTER COLLEGE ART COLLECTION, 604 E. College Ave., North Manchester, IN 46962. Tel.: 260-982-5000.
Art Gallery.
Collections: paintings; drawings; sculpture.
Hours & Admission Prices: Call for hours.

Notre Dame

MUSEUM OF BIODIVERSITY AND GREENE-NIEUWLAND HERBARIUM, Dept. of Biological Sciences, Univ. of Notre Dame, Notre Dame, IN 46556-0369. Tel.: 574-631-6684. Fax: 574-631-7413.
E-mail: Barbara.J.Hellenthal.2@nd.edu
Founded: 1876.
Congressional District: 3
Key Personnel: Dir. Museum of Biodiversity, Ronald A. Hellenthal; Guest Dir. Herbarium, Richard J. Jensen; Cur., Barbara J. Hellenthal.
Personnel Profile: Full-Time Paid 1; Part-Time Volunteers 1.
Governing Authority: university. Parent Institution: University of Notre Dame. Tax-exempt.
Herbarium Museum.
Collections: 600,000 specimens; Edward Lee Greene collection includes 5,000 type of specimens from western North American plants; Nieuwland collection from around the world.
Research Fields: plant taxonomy; plant geography; ecology; entomology; parasitology; vertebrate biology.
Activities: formally organized education programs for undergraduate & graduate college students; inter-museum loan for research; Greene Herbarium searchable database of 67,000 specimens.
Publications: American Midland Naturalist.
Hours & Admission Prices: By appointment only. No charge. ♿
Attendance: 2,000 (accurate)

* **THE SNITE MUSEUM OF ART, UNIVERSITY OF NOTRE DAME, (M),** University of Notre Dame, 100 M. Krause Cir., Notre Dame, IN 46556-0368. Mailing Address: P.O. Box 368, Notre Dame, IN 46556-0368. Tel.: 574-631-5466. Fax: 574-631-8501.
Web Site: www.nd.edu/~sniteart
Founded: 1842.
Congressional District: 3
Key Personnel: Dir., Charles R. Loving; Assoc. Dir., Ann M. Knoll; Cur. Ethnographic Arts, Douglas E. Bradley; Cur. Photography, Stephen R. Moriarty; Mktg. & Public Affairs Specialist, Gina Costa; Exhibition Designer, John Phegley; Cur. Education, Academic Programs, Diana Matthias; Cur. Education, Public Programs, Jacqueline H. Welsh; Chief Preparator, Gregory Denby; Exhibit Coord., Ramiro Rodriguez; Cur. Native American Art, Joanne Mack; Registrar, Robert Smogor; Coord. Friends of the Snite Museum, Heidi Williams; Staff Accountant, Carolyn Niemier.
Personnel Profile: Full-Time Paid 21; Part-Time Paid 20; Part-Time Volunteers 100; Interns 3.
Governing Authority: religious order; Congregation of Holy Cross. Parent Institution: University of Notre Dame. Tax-exempt: 501(c)(3).
Art Museum.
Collections: Italian Renaissance paintings and sculpture; pre-Columbian sculptures, textiles; ceramics; 15th-20th century drawings and prints; Kress study collection; 17th & 18th century Italian, Dutch, Flemish and English paintings; 19th century French oil sketches, drawings, & paintings; 20th century paintings, photography & sculpture; paintings; sculpture; furniture; ceramics; glass; Mestrovic sculpture.
Research Fields: history & provenance of paintings; sculpture; drawings; prints; photographs; objects of art; pre-Columbian, Native American, Old Master drawings; French oil sketches.
Facilities: catalogue & reference library.
Activities: guided tours; lectures; films; gallery talks; concerts; formally organized education programs; permanent, temporary & traveling exhibitions; symposia.
Publications: catalogs, Victor Higgins: An American Master; Master Drawings from the Reilly Collection; White Swan: Crow Indian, Warrior and Painter; Ivan Mestrovic; Rembrandt Etchings; Selected Works from the Snite Museum of Art; University of Notre Dame Master Drawings: The Wisdom-Reilly Collection; Taos Artists and Their Patrons, 1898-1950; A Gift of Light: Photographs in the Janos Scholz Collections; handbook, Selected Works Collection; Nineteenth Century French Drawings.
Hours & Admission Prices: Tues.-Wed. 10-4, Thurs.-Sat 10-5, Sun. 1-5. No charge; donations accepted. Closed major holidays. ♿
Attendance: 58,136 (accurate)
Membership: Senior Citizen $25; Active $40; Family $60; Sustaining $100; Supporting $250; Patron $500; Benefactor $750; Donor $1,000; Director's Circle $5,000; Premium $10,000.

Parker City

ME'S ZOO, 12441 W. County Rd. 300 S., Parker City, IN 47368. Tel.: 765-468-8559. Fax: 765-468-9014.
Web Site: www.meszoo.com
Zoo.
Collections: over 300 animals.
Facilities: Museum-related items for sale.
Activities: petting zoo. Museum Sponsors: Holiday Lights in November & December.
Hours & Admission Prices: April 14-Sept. Tues.-Thurs. & Sat. 10-5, Sun. 12-5; Nov.-Dec. call for hours. Adults $6.50, children 1-12 $5.50; discounts on Wed. ♿

Peru

CIRCUS CITY FESTIVAL MUSEUM, 154 N. Broadway, Peru, IN 46970-2234. Tel.: 765-472-3918. Fax: 765-472-2826.
E-mail: perucirc@perucircus.com
Web Site: www.perucircus.com
Founded: 1959.
Key Personnel: Pres. & Vice Pres. Bldg. & Property, Kurt Krauskopf; Exec. Vice Pres., Bruce Embrey; Vice Pres. Publicity & Public Rels., Steve Ailes; Vice Pres. Museum & Exhibits, Timothy Bessignano; Vice Pres. Festival, Kevin Gallahan; Exec. Sec. & Office Mgr., Linda Cawood; Pres. Circus & Recording Sec., Sylvia Miller; Treas., Kenneth Hasselkus.
Personnel Profile: Full-Time Paid 1; Part-Time Paid 1; Part-Time Volunteers 200.
Governing Authority: nonprofit organization. Parent Institution: Circus City Festival, Inc. Tax-exempt: 501(c)(3).
Circus Museum.
Collections: circus history; circus lithographs; photographs; uniforms & costumes of famous performers; trapeze; rigging; harness; guns; mouthpieces & other such items; furniture from The Wallace Circus Train, The Ben Wallace Home, The Mugivan Home; wild animal cage used at the Old Circus Winter Quarters; miniature circus wagons & scale circuses; paintings; 1894 Sicilian donkey cart.
Facilities: Gifts, circus & other museum-related items for sale.
Activities: guided tours; lectures; films.
Publications: newsletter.
Hours & Admission Prices: July call for hours; Aug.-June Mon.-Fri. 9-1 & 2-4. No charge; donations accepted. Closed holidays. ♿
Membership: Youth $5; Annual & Adult Member $10; Circus Family Membership $20; Contributing $25; Sustaining $50; Century Club $100; Donor $250; Patron $500; Life $1,000.

GRISSOM AIR MUSEUM, 1000 W. Hoosier Blvd., Peru, IN 46970-3723. Tel.: 765-689-8011. Fax: 765-689-9288.
E-mail: info@grissomairmuseum.com
Web Site: www.grissomairmuseum.com
Founded: 1981.
Congressional District: 5
Key Personnel: Dir., Roger Bitzer; Mgr. Facilities & Aircraft, Richard Muchler.
Personnel Profile: Full-Time Paid 2; Part-Time Paid 3; Part-Time Volunteers 30.
Governing Authority: private; nonprofit. Subsidiary Institution: Indiana State Museum & Historic Sites, Indianapolis, IN. Tax-exempt: 501(c)(3).
Military & Space Museum: located adjacent to Grissom Air Reserve Base. An Indiana State Historic Site.
Collections: aircraft; equipment; memorabilia ranging from World War II to the present; B-17 Flying Fortress; B-58 nuclear bomber; aviation art; 25 aircraft.

Research Fields: history of the aircraft, personnel & organizations related to the adjacent Air Base, which initially opened as Bunker Hill Air Station in 1942.
Facilities: 1,200-vol. library of technical aircraft manuals and aviation-related magazines, books & newspapers; 28-seat auditorium; 6,000 sq. ft. exhibit space; 20 acres of outdoor displays. Aviation-related books, art & clothing for sale.
Activities: aviation art shows; model shows; guest speakers; guided tours; loan & temporary exhibitions; theater.
Publications: quarterly newsletter, Grissom Air Museum Times.
Hours & Admission Prices: Feb.-May & Sept. to mid-Dec. Tues.-Sat. 10-4, Sun. 12-4; Memorial Day to Labor Day daily 10-4. Adults $4, seniors 55 & over, veterans & students 7-18 $3; members and children 6 & under no charge. Closed most major holidays. ♿
Attendance: 30,000 (accurate)
Membership: Cadet $20; Wingman $50; Century $100; Patriot $250; Liberator $500; Eagle $1,000.

INTERNATIONAL CIRCUS HALL OF FAME & MUSEUM, 3076 E. Circus Lane, Peru, IN 46970-7133. Tel.: 800-771-0241.
Circus History Museum.
Collections: circus life, history & professionals; posters; wagons; models; miniature 1934 Hagenbeck Wallace Circus replica; Hall of Fame; photographs.
Hours & Admission Prices: May-June & Aug.-Oct. Mon.-Fri. 10-4; July Mon.-Sat. 10-4, Sun. 12-4.

MIAMI COUNTY MUSEUM, (M), 51 N. Broadway, Peru, IN 46970-2237. Tel.: 765-473-9183. Fax: 317-473-3880.
E-mail: admin@miamicountymuseum.com
Web Site: www.miamicountymuseum.com
Founded: 1916.
Congressional District: 5
Key Personnel: Pres., John Kennedy; Cur., Mildred Kopis; Asst. Cur. & Registrar, Betty Wilson; Archivist, Nancy Masten; Museum Shop Mgr., Ellen Wilson.
Personnel Profile: Full-Time Paid 3; Full-Time Volunteers 0; Part-Time Paid 1; Part-Time Volunteers 57.
Governing Authority: society. Miami County Historical Society, 51 N. Broadway, Peru, IN 46970. Tax-exempt.
General Museum.
Collections: local history items; Miami & American Indian artifacts; pioneer items; circus memorabilia; transportation vehicles; archives & research; microfilm; Victorian rooms & stores; Cole Porter display & his 1955 Fleetwood Cadillac.
Research Fields: local history; railroad; Miami Indian; Cole Porter; Civil War; circus; Wabash & Erie Canal; local history, genealogy.
Facilities: library of local newspapers 1837-1938 available for research. Museum-related items for sale.
Activities: tours; lectures; temporary & permanent exhibitions; outreach programs.
Publications: monthly bulletin (newsletter); books & leaflets pertaining to Miami County history; 1996 Pictorial History Book of Miami County.
Hours & Admission Prices: Tues.-Sat. 9-5, Sun. by appointment. No charge; donations accepted. Closed holidays. ♿
Attendance: 12,000 (estimated)
Membership: General $25; Museum One Hundred $100.

Plymouth

MARSHALL COUNTY HISTORICAL MUSEUM, 123 N. Michigan St., Plymouth, IN 46563-2132. Tel.: 574-936-2306. Fax: 574-936-9306.
E-mail: mchistory@mchistoricalsociety.org
Web Site: www.mchistoricalsociety.org
Founded: 1957.
Congressional District: 13
Key Personnel: Dir. & C.E.O., Linda Rippy; Bd. Pres. (V), Dr. Ronald Liechty.
Personnel Profile: Full-Time Paid 2; Part-Time Paid 2; Part-Time Volunteers 40.
Governing Authority: nonprofit organization. Parent Institution: Marshall County Historical Society, Inc., Plymouth, IN. Tax-exempt: 501(c)(3).
History Museum.
Collections: local county history artifacts; tools; furniture; household items; local genealogy; photos; Indian artifacts; clothing; books.
Research Fields: local history; family genealogy.
Facilities: 150-vol. library of books on local history & genealogy, also publications & newspapers available for use on premises.
Activities: guided tours; lectures; permanent & temporary exhibitions.
Publications: quarterly newsletter; quarterly journal.
Hours & Admission Prices: Tues.-Sat. 10-4. No charge; donations accepted. Closed county holidays. ♿
Attendance: 5,000 (estimated)
Membership: Annual $25; Annual Business $50; Five Year $100; Ten Year $200.

Portage

PORTAGE COMMUNITY HISTORICAL SOCIETY, 5250 U.S. Hwy. 6, Portage, IN 46368. Mailing Address: P.O. Box 305, Portage, IN 46368-0305. Tel.: 219-762-8349.
Web Site: www.geocities.com/portagehistorical society
Formerly: Al Goin Historical Museum
Founded: 1988.
Key Personnel: Pres. (V), Lois J. Mollick; Newsletter, Kathy Heckman.
Personnel Profile: Part-Time Volunteers 25; Interns 1.
Governing Authority: Subsidiary Institution: Portage City Park Dept. Tax-exempt.
Local History.
Collections: city history; tools & farm equipment; Indian artifacts; school history; early settlers; period fire truck. Historic Buildings: farmhouse; barn; stagecoach.
Activities: genealogy research. Museum Sponsors: Historical Festival in June; Christmas Open House in December.
Publications: bimonthly newsletter; books, Township History, 2003; Historic Homes, 2005.
Hours & Admission Prices: March to early Dec. Fri.-Sat. 11-3. No charge; donations accepted. Closed Independence Day. ♿
Attendance: 2,500 (estimated)
Membership: Individual $18; Family $48; Business $58; Lifetime $109.

Porter

INDIANA DUNES NATIONAL LAKESHORE, 1100 N. Mineral Springs Rd., Porter, IN 46304-1225. Tel.: 219-926-7561, ext. 225. Fax: 219-926-7561.
Web Site: www.nps.gov/indu
Founded: 1970.
Congressional District: 2
Key Personnel: Historian, Janice Slupski; Supt., Dale B. Engquist; Asst. Supt., Garry Traynham; Chief, Interpretation & Education, Julia Holmaas; Program Mgr., Bruce Rowe; Visitor Svcs. Mgr., Laura Gundrum; Education Specialist, Kim Holsen.
Personnel Profile: Full-Time Paid 130; Part-Time Paid 55; Part-Time Volunteers 595.
Governing Authority: federal. Parent Institution: National Park Service, Dept. of the Interior, Washington DC. Tax-exempt.
Park Visitor Center.
Collections: prehistoric cultural collection; fur trade items; 19th-century farming & settlement; natural history. Historic Structures: 19th-century, Bailly Homestead; 19th-century Chellberg Farm; 1933 World's Fair Houses.
Research Fields: air & water quality; plant & animal ecology.
Facilities: 1,600-vol. park library & study collection available for research; two visitor centers; herbarium. Books & items related to park themes for sale.
Activities: guided tours; interpretive programs; audiovisual; formally organized educational programs; overnight educational programs.
Publications: English & Spanish brochure; guides; handbooks.
Hours & Admission Prices: Park: daily. $4 parking fee at West Beach. Visitor Center: daily 8-5, call for extended summer hours. No charge; donations accepted. ♿
Attendance: 1,834,435 (estimated)

Portland

MUSEUM OF THE SOLDIER, 510 E. Arch St., Portland, IN 47371-1525. Mailing Address: P.O. Box 518, Portland, IN 47371-0518. Tel.: 260-726-2967.
Web Site: www.museumofthesoldier.com/
Governing Authority: nonprofit organization. Tax-exempt: 501(c)(3).
Military Museum.
Collections: military uniforms, weapons & equipment; personal artifacts.
Activities: lectures; banquets; temporary & permanent exhibits.
Hours & Admission Prices: 1st & 3rd Sat.-Sun. 12-5; other times by appointment. Adults $2, students & seniors $1; members and children 10 & under no charge.

Rensselaer

LILIAN FENDIG ART GALLERY, 301 N. Van Rensselaer St., Rensselaer, IN 47978-2630. Tel.: 219-866-5278. Fax: 219-866-5278.
E-mail: prairie@nwiis.com
Web Site: www.liljasper.com/pac/
Founded: 1993.
Key Personnel: Staff Dir., Amy Byrd.
Personnel Profile: Full-Time Paid 1; Part-Time Volunteers 22; Interns 2.
Governing Authority: Parent Institution: Prairie Arts Council, Inc. Tax-exempt.
Art Gallery.
Collections: paintings; archives.
Facilities: archives.
Activities: Museum Sponsors: ARTCAMP; Junior Art Club; dance program; Taste of Rensselaer; Holiday Art Show & Sale.
Publications: exhibition brochures; catalogs; newsletters; annual report.
Hours & Admission Prices: Mon.-Fri. 10-2. No charge; donations accepted. ♿
Attendance: 12,000 (estimated)
Membership: Student $10; Individual $25; Family $35; Sponsor & Organization $50; Patron $100-$249; Sustaining $250-499; Benefactor $500-$999.

Richmond

GAAR MANSION AND FARM MUSEUM, 2593 Pleasant View Rd., Richmond, IN 47374-2050. Tel.: 765-966-1262 & 935-8687.
Historic Building: built in 1876. Listed on the National Register of Historic Places.
Collections: period furnishings; personal artifacts.
Activities: rental facility.
Hours & Admission Prices: June-Aug. 1st & 3rd Sun. 1-4; Dec. 1st 3 Sun. 1-4; tours by appointment. Adults $6, children 18 & under $2.

HAYES ARBORETUM, 801 Elks Rd., Richmond, IN 47374-2526. Tel.: 765-962-3745. Fax: 765-966-1931.
E-mail: stephenhayes13@yahoo.com
Web Site: www.hayesarboretum.org
Founded: 1959.
Congressional District: 10
Key Personnel: C.E.O., Stephen H. Hayes.
Personnel Profile: Full-Time Paid 1; Part-Time Paid 1; Part-Time Volunteers 20.
Governing Authority: nonprofit. The Stanley W. Hayes Research Foundation Inc., P.O. Box 1404, Richmond, IN 47374. Tax-exempt: 501(c)(3), 4942(J)(3).
Arboretum & Nature Center.
Collections: 10-acre native woody plant preserve, including one specimen of each species of native woody plant indigenous to the Whitewater Drainage Basin of Indiana & Ohio, incorporating 10 counties of Indiana & 4 counties in Ohio.
Research Fields: arboricultural; botanical; taxonomical.
Facilities: science related library available for on-site use; arboretum; nature & conservation center; reading room; 100-seat auditorium; classrooms.
Activities: guided tours; children's summer classes; cooperative programs with Ball State, Miami University & Earlham College; permanent & temporary exhibitions.
Publications: brochures, Welcome; Auto Tour Guide.
Hours & Admission Prices: March-Oct. Tues.-Sat. 9-5. No charge; donations accepted. ♿
Attendance: 20,000 (estimated)

INDIANA FOOTBALL HALL OF FAME, 815 N. A St., Richmond, IN 47374-3119. Mailing Address: P.O. Box 1035, Richmond, IN 47375-1035. Tel.: 765-966-2235.
E-mail: joyce@indiana-football.org
Web Site: www.geocities.com/indfoothall/
Sports Museum.
Collections: Hall of Fame inductees; football history; photographs; high school helmets; scholarship wall; uniforms.
Hours & Admission Prices: May-Sept. daily 10-4; Oct.-April daily 10-2; other times by appointment.

JOSEPH MOORE MUSEUM, Earlham College, 801 National Rd. W., Richmond, IN 47374. Tel.: 765-983-1303. Fax: 765-983-1497.
E-mail: johni@earlham.edu
Web Site: www.earlham.edu
Founded: 1887.
Congressional District: 10
Key Personnel: Dir., Dr. John B. Iverson; Coord. Educational Outreach, Carol Stocksdale.
Personnel Profile: Full-Time Paid 1; Part-Time Paid 3; Part-Time Volunteers 2; Interns 20.
Governing Authority: college. Parent Institution: Earlham College. Tax-exempt: 501(c)(3).
Natural History Museum.
Collections: skins of birds & mammals; dried & liquid-preserved insects; live & preserved reptiles; vertebrate & invertebrate fossils; Indian artifacts; natural history.
Research Fields: mammalogy; ornithology; entomology; paleoecology; herpetology; paleontology.
Facilities: research library; planetarium. Museum-related items for sale.
Activities: guided tours; permanent & temporary exhibitions; natural history workshops.
Hours & Admission Prices: June-Aug. Sun. 1-5; Sept.-May Sun.-Mon., Wed. & Fri. 1-5; tours by appointment only. No charge; donations accepted. ♿
Attendance: 4,500 (estimated)

LEEDS GALLERY - EARLHAM COLLEGE, 801 National Rd. W., Richmond, IN 47374-4095. Tel.: 765-983-1410.
Art Gallery.
Collections: paintings; photographs; sculpture; drawings; ceramics.
Hours & Admission Prices: Mon.-Fri. 9-8, Sat.-Sun. 1-8.

RICHMOND ART MUSEUM, (M), 350 Hub Etchison Pkwy., Richmond, IN 47374-5339. Tel.: 765-966-0256. Fax: 765-973-3738.
E-mail: shaund@rcs.k12.in.us
Web Site: www.richmondartmuseum.org
Formerly: Art Association of Richmond
Founded: 1898.
Congressional District: 2
Key Personnel: Exec. Dir., Shaun Dingwerth; Pres., Barry Jonston.
Personnel Profile: Full-Time Paid 3; Part-Time Paid 1; Part-Time Volunteers 75.
Governing Authority: board of trustees; nonprofit organization. Tax-exempt.
Art Museum.
Collections: American paintings; sculpture; graphics; decorative arts; Indiana artists; Richmond School; Hoosier group art pottery; Overbeck.
Research Fields: art education; Indiana & Richmond artists.
Facilities: 1,200-vol. library of art available on premises; archives; reading room; 525-seat auditorium.
Activities: guided tours; lectures; films; gallery talks; art classes for children; education programs; docent program or council; inter-museum loan, permanent, temporary & traveling exhibitions; school loan service; juried professional & amateur artists competition.
Publications: newsletter, 1898-1978 Art in Richmond; Richmond Art Museum History and Permanent Collection.
Hours & Admission Prices: Tues.-Fri. 10-4, Sun. 1-4. No charge; donations accepted. Closed national & school holidays. ♿
Attendance: 12,500 (estimated)
Membership: Individual $35; Family $50; Supporting $75; Sustaining $100; Friends of the Museum $250; Sustaining Business $300; Museum Advocate & Patron & Contributing Business $500; Benefactor & Corporate Sponsor $1,000; Donor $1,500.

RONALD GALLERY - EARLHAM COLLEGE, 801 National Rd. W., Richmond, IN 47374-4095. Tel.: 765-983-1410.
Key Personnel: Cur., Julia May
Art Gallery.
Collections: over 3,000 paintings, prints & sculptures.
Hours & Admission Prices: Mon.-Thurs. 8am to midnight, Fri. 8am-10pm, Sat. 10-10, Sun. noon to midnight.

WAYNE COUNTY HISTORICAL MUSEUM, (M), 1150 N. A St., Richmond, IN 47374-3298. Tel.: 765-962-5756. Fax: 765-939-0909.
Web Site: www.waynecountyhistoricalmuseum.com
Founded: 1930.
Congressional District: 10
Key Personnel: C.E.O. & Museum Shop Mgr., James Harlan; Pres. (V), Marilyn Martus.
Personnel Profile: Full-Time Paid 2; Part-Time Paid 1; Part-Time Volunteers 60.
Governing Authority: society; nonprofit organization. Affiliated with Wayne County Historical Society. Tax-exempt: 501(c)(3).
General Museum: housed in 1864 Hicksite Friends Meeting House.
Collections: china; glass; silver; apothecary; agriculture; architecture; fire-fighting equipment; guns; hobbies; musical instruments; toys and dolls; transportation; Wooten desk; 1929 Davis plane; early Richmond-made autos; C. Francis Jenkins (radiovision) collection; Starr-Gennett jazz history; Gaar-Scott steam engines; 3,000 yr. old Egyptian Mummy &

related artifacts; textile collection - clothing, quilts, coverlets. Historic Houses: 1823 Soloman Dickinson Log House.
Facilities: 500-vol. library of county histories, scrapbooks & newspapers available for use on premises. Historical reproductions & museum-related items for sale.
Activities: guided tours; lectures; arts festivals; hobby workshops; docent program or council; permanent exhibitions.
Publications: quarterly newsletter.
Hours & Admission Prices: Jan.-Feb. Mon.-Fri. 9-4, Sat. 1-4; March-Dec. Mon.-Fri. 9-4, Sat.-Sun. 1-4. Adults $5, seniors $4, students 6-18 $2; discounts to groups, AAA, AAM & ICOM members; children under 6 & members no charge. Closed national holidays. ♿
Attendance: 10,987 (accurate)
Membership: Student $20; Individual $30; Family $40; Contributing $100; Patron $150; Business $250; Life $1,000; Corporate Sponsorship $2,500.

Rochester

FULTON COUNTY HISTORICAL SOCIETY MUSEUM, 37 E. 375 N., Rochester, IN 46975-9718. Tel.: 574-223-4436. Fax: 574-224-4436.
E-mail: fchs@rtcol.com
Web Site: www.icss.net/~fchs
Founded: 1963.
Congressional District: 5
Key Personnel: Pres. Emerita, Shirley Willard; Dir., Melinda Clinger; Pres., Lois Ulerick; Treas., Lola Riddle.
Personnel Profile: Full-Time Paid 1; Part-Time Paid 3; Part-Time Volunteers 90; Interns 1.
Governing Authority: nonprofit organization. Tax-exempt: 501(c)(3).
Living History Village & History Museum: 35-acre village including 13 buildings.
Collections: furniture; farm equipment; photos; tools; literature; artifacts; Elmo Lincoln's first Tarzan films & posters; reconstructed 1924 round barn which houses farm machinery; 1971 caboose from Norfolk & Western; boxcar; 160 ft. track. Historic Structures: Loyal, Indiana; 1832 William Polke House/Stagecoach Inn; 1874 Rochester Depot; 1860s Pioneer Woman's Log Cabin; 1910 Dr. Shafer's office; 1920 general store; 1915 small red round barn/granary; replica blacksmith shop, 1920s print shop, windmill, 1920s footbridge made by Rochester Bridge Co.; 1940 round chicken house; 1912 jail; 1900 cider mill; 1961 octagonal corn crib; 1930s railcar & garage.
Research Fields: genealogy; local history; Trail of Death removal of Potowatomi Indians in 1838.
Facilities: 1,500-vol. library of old school texts, histories, county newspapers 1858 to present, Civil War diaries, Bibles & newspapers available for use on premises. Handcrafts, Indian jewelry & local history books for sale.
Activities: guided tours; lectures; films; permanent & temporary exhibitions; manuscript collections; school loan service. Museum Sponsors: Living History Fair in March; Redbud Trail Rendezvous in April; Historical Power Show in June; Potawatomi Trail of Death from Indiana to Kansas; Cruzin for History in August; Trail of Courage Living History Festival in September; Toy Show in October; Haunted Woods Walk in October; Farmers Market November to May; Christmas Crafts & Open House in December.
Publications: magazine, Fulton County Images; books, Fulton County Folks, Volumes 1 & 2; Historical Atlas of Fulton County 1883 reprint; Home Folks-Tales of Old Settlers of Fulton County 1910 reprint; Wagoner Family History, 1941 reprint; 1935 Shields Genealogy reprint; semiannual genealogical newsletter, Fulton County Folk Finder; semiannual newsletter, Potawatomi Trail of Death Association; bimonthly, Fulton County Historical Power News; Historical Society Newsletter; book, Potawatomi Trail of Death 1838 Indiana to Kansas, Hollywood Indian - Chief White Eagle.
Hours & Admission Prices: Mon.-Sat. 9-5. No charge; donations accepted. Closed holidays. ♿
Attendance: 35,000 (accurate)
Membership: Individual $20; Family $30; Sponsor $50; Club $100; Corporation $250; Benefactor $500; Life $750.

Rockville

BILLIE CREEK VILLAGE, INC., 65 S. Billie Creek Rd., Rockville, IN 47872. Mailing Address: P.O. Box 357, Rockville, IN 47872-0357. Tel.: 765-569-0252. Fax: 765-569-3582.
E-mail: billiecreekvillage@billiecreekvillage.org
Web Site: www.billiecreekvillage.org
History Museum.
Collections: recreated turn-of-the-century village & farmstead; 38 buildings.
Hours & Admission Prices: Village: daily 11-4. General Store: Mon.-Sat. 10-4, Sun. 12-4. Admission $3. Special Events: $5.

Rome City

GENE STRATTON-PORTER STATE HISTORIC SITE, 1205 Pleasant Point, Rome City, IN 46784-9644. Tel.: 260-854-3790. Fax: 260-854-9102.
E-mail: genestrattonportershs@dnr.in.gov
Web Site: indianamuseum.org
Founded: 1946.
Congressional District: 4
Personnel Profile: Full-Time Paid 2; Part-Time Paid 3; Part-Time Volunteers 25.
Governing Authority: state. Branch of Indiana State Museum System, Div. of the Dept. of Natural Resources, Indiana State Museum, 202 N. Alabama St., Indianapolis, IN 46204. Tax-exempt.
Historic House: c.1920 home of Gene Stratton Porter.
Collections: period furnishings; Gene Stratton Porter photographs & memorabilia.
Facilities: 125-acres of grounds; 3 miles of walking trails & scenic paths; formal gardens; arboretum; picnic area; bird sanctuary.
Activities: guided tours; lectures.
Publications: newsletter, Gene Stratton-Porter Memorial Society.
Hours & Admission Prices: Carriage House Visitor Center: Tues.-Sat. 10-5, Sun. 1-5. No charge. Cabin Tours: Tues.-Sat. 10-4, Sun. 1-4. Adults $3.50, seniors 55 & over $3, children 12 & under $2; discounts to groups. Closed New Year's Day; Memorial Day; Independence Day; Labor Day; Thanksgiving; Christmas. ♿
Attendance: 60,000 (estimated)
Membership: Single $10; Family $15; Sustaining $20; Nonprofit $25; Business $50; Life Single $100; Husband & Wife $150.

Salem

STEVENS MUSEUM, 307 E. Market St., Salem, IN 47167-2119. Tel.: 812-883-6495.
E-mail: jhc@blueriver.net
Web Site: www.stevensmuseum.com
Founded: 1897.
Congressional District: 9
Key Personnel: Pres. (V), Willie Harlen; Sec., Katherine Simpson; Treas., Clara Marie Burns; Museum Shop Mgr., Kathy Wade.
Personnel Profile: Full-Time Paid 2; Part-Time Paid 2; Part-Time Volunteers 10.
Governing Authority: bd. of directors. Parent Institution: Washington County Historical Society. Subsidiary Institution: John Hay Center. Tax-exempt: 501(c)(3).
Local History, 1824 John Hay birthplace, Pioneer Village & Depot Museum.
Collections: manuscripts; newspapers; period furnishings; coverlets & quilts; furniture; farm tools; educational; church; costumes; dentistry; medical; pioneer; Indians; wars; guns; dishes; textiles.
Research Fields: genealogy; history; wars; school; cemetery; period furniture & furnishings; church.
Facilities: 5,000-vol. genealogy library available on premises; reading room; 125-seat auditorium.
Activities: guided tours; lectures; permanent & temporary exhibitions.
Publications: quarterly newsletter.
Hours & Admission Prices: Tues.-Sat. 9-5. Genealogy research: Tues.-Sat. 9-5. Museum: adults $2; members & children under 6 no charge. Library: $3. Closed New Year's Day; Easter; Mother's Day; Memorial Day; Father's Day; Independence Day; Labor Day; Thanksgiving; Christmas. ♿
Attendance: 30,000
Membership: Individual $15; Life $200; Couple Life $250.

Scottsburg

SCOTT COUNTY HERITAGE CENTER AND MUSEUM, 1050 S. Main St., Scottsburg, IN 47170-6663. Mailing Address: P.O. Box 122, Scottsburg, IN 47170-0122. Tel.: 812-752-1050.
Governing Authority: Parent Institution: Preservation Alliance, Inc. Tax-exempt.
History Museum.
Collections: local history & culture; personal artifacts; photographs.
Hours & Admission Prices: Mon.-Fri. 9-5, Sat. 9-1. No charge. ♿

Shelbyville

LOUIS H. & LENA FIRN GROVER MUSEUM, 52 W. Broadway, Shelbyville, IN 46176-1256. Tel.: 317-392-4634.
E-mail: director@grovermuseum.org
Web Site: www.grovermuseum.org
Founded: 1980.
Congressional District: 2
Key Personnel: Dir., Candace Miller; Staff Asst., Teresa Tungate.

Personnel Profile: Full-Time Paid 2; Part-Time Volunteers 10.
Governing Authority: society. Parent Institution: Shelby County Historical Society. Tax-exempt: 501(c)(3).
Historical Society Museum.
Collections: agricultural implements; medical; photographs; documents; tools; toys; textiles; model railroad - trains & buildings; street scene - 30 buildings and artifacts from 1900-1910; Shelby County archaeological artifacts. Historical House: 1820 Thomas Hendricks Boyhood Home.
Research Fields: local history topics.
Facilities: 100-seat auditorium; classrooms. Books, pictures & postcards for sale.
Activities: formally organized education programs for adults; temporary exhibitions; heritage skills classes. Annual Events: Quilt Show & Luncheon; Bear Paw Quilt Guild; Fall Street Fair; Christmas Tree & Tea in November & December.
Publications: quarterly newsletter, Echoes of Old Shelby.
Hours & Admission Prices: Tues.-Sat. 9-4, Sun. 1-4. No charge; donations accepted. Closed holidays. ♿
Attendance: 7,600 (accurate)
Membership: Single $20; Family $30; Sustaining $40.

Shipshewana

HOSTETLER'S HUDSON AUTO MUSEUM, (M), 760 S. Van Buren St., Shipshewana, IN 46565-8611. Tel.: 260-768-3021.
Auto Museum.
Collections: period Hudson-produced cars, trucks, & utility vehicles.
Activities: rental facilities.
Hours & Admission Prices: Memorial Day to Labor Day Mon.-Tues. 9-8, Wed.-Sun. 9-5; Sept.-May daily 9-5; groups by appointment. Adults $8, seniors 60 & over $7, students 6-17 $4; discounts to groups; children under 5 no charge.

Shoals

MARTIN COUNTY MUSEUM, 220 Capitol, Shoals, IN 47581-0564. Mailing Address: P.O. Box 564, Shoals, IN 47581-0564. Tel.: 812-247-1133.
Personnel Profile: Part-Time Volunteers 7.
History Museum.
Collections: period artifacts; tax records; assessment records; marriages; school records; scrapbooks; photographs.
Publications: newsletters.
Hours & Admission Prices: Mon., Wed. & Fri. 10-4. No charge; donations accepted. ♿
Attendance: 500 (estimated)
Membership: Individual $10; Family $25.

South Bend

COLLEGE FOOTBALL HALL OF FAME, 111 S. Saint Joseph St., South Bend, IN 46601-1901. Tel.: 800-440-FAME. Fax: 574-235-5720.
E-mail: lisa.malin@collegefootball.org
Web Site: www.collegefootball.org
Founded: 1951.
Key Personnel: Exec. Dir, Lisa Malin; Pres., Steve Hatchell; Chm. (V), Archie Manning; Dir. Mktg., Katie Berrettini; Sales Mgr., Jeney Anderson; Public Rels. Mgr., Kristen Pflipsen; Volunteer Coord., Laurie Cayia; Financial Svcs. Coord., Patti Glascoe; AV Coord., Richard Allen; Collections Mgr., Kent Stephens; Dir. Operations, Mark Maurer; Museum Shop Mgr., Laura Holaway.
Personnel Profile: Full-Time Paid 9; Part-Time Paid 7; Part-Time Volunteers 126; Interns 7.
Governing Authority: company. Parent Institution: National Football Foundation & College Football Hall of Fame, 22 Maple Ave., Morristown, NJ 07960. Tax-exempt.
Sports Museum.
Collections: football history, equipment & memorabilia; photographs; manuscripts; personal artifacts; Hall of Fame inductees.
Facilities: 230-seat auditorium; theater; 70-seat restaurant; 400-seat banquet facility. Museum-related gifts for sale.
Activities: films; loan, permanent & temporary exhibitions; photograph reproduction service; luncheons; autograph sessions; Festival-film transfer.
Hours & Admission Prices: Memorial Day-Nov. Mon.-Thurs. 10-5, Fri.-Sat. 9-6, Sun. 8-5, Thanksgiving to Memorial Day daily 10-5. Adults $12, St. Joseph County resident adults $9, students 13 yrs.-college & senior citizens $8, children 5-12 $5; discounts to groups of 20 or more, ICOM & AAA members; children under 4 no charge. Closed New Year's Day; Thanksgiving; Christmas. ♿
Attendance: 70,000 (estimated)

COPSHAHOLM HOUSE MUSEUM & HISTORIC OLIVER GARDENS, Northern Indiana Center for History, 808 W. Washington, South Bend, IN 46601-1439. Tel.: 574-235-9664. Fax: 574-235-9059.
E-mail: director@centerforhistory.org
Web Site: www.centerforhistory.org
Founded: 1990.
Congressional District: 3
Key Personnel: C.E.O., Randy W. Ray; Cur., David S. Bainbridge; Dir. Public Programs, Stephanie McCune; Dir. Mktg., Marilyn Thompson; Dir. Facilities & Grounds, Tom Rapach; Registrar, Jennifer Johns; Dir. Education, Travis Childs; Visitor Svcs. Dir., Ken Cencelewski; Dir. Devel., Karen Shirk; Finance Mgr., Marilyn Jurgonski; Volunteer Coord., Debra Neumann.
Personnel Profile: Full-Time Paid 16; Part-Time Paid 14; Part-Time Volunteers 120.
Governing Authority: nonprofit organization. Parent Institution: Northern Indiana Historical Society. Tax-exempt.
Historic House; 1895-1896 38-room Oliver Family mansion.
Collections: original mid-17th to mid-20th century furnishings; furniture; decorative arts; household objects; works of art; costumes; archival collection includes business ledgers & papers of South Bend Iron Works, Oliver Chilled Plow Works, Oliver Farm Equipment Company, personal papers, letters, diaries, photos, blueprints & plans for Copshaholm & gardens.
Research Fields: history of America's industrial midwest in late 19th & early 20th centuries; the Oliver Family & companies; historic American gardens, architecture, decorative arts & household lifestyles.
Facilities: visitor center. Museum-related items for sale.
Activities: guided tours; lectures; classes; workshops; docent program; student designed tours.
Publications: newsletter; docent manual; publications related to Copshaholm.
Hours & Admission Prices: Mon.-Sat. 10-5, Sun. 12-5; last tour leaves at 2. Adults $8, seniors $6.50, children $5; children under 5, staff of other museums, AAM, ICOM & NIHS members no charge. Closed major holidays.
Attendance: 25,000 (accurate)
Membership: Student & Senior $30; Individual $40; Family $60; Sustainer $125; Sponsor $250.

HEALTHWORKS! KIDS' MUSEUM, Memorial Leighton Healthplex, 111 W. Jefferson St., Ste. 2000, South Bend, IN 46601-1994.
Web Site: www.qualityoflife.org/healthworks
Founded: 1999.
Children's Health Museum.
Collections: hands-on exhibits.
Activities: special events; school programs.
Hours & Admission Prices: Memorial Day to Labor Day Mon.-Fri. 9-4; Sept.-May Mon.-Fri. 9-4, Sat. 12-4. Admission $4; members, ACM & children under 2 no charge. Closed New Year's Day; Thanksgiving; Christmas. ♿
Attendance: 70,000 (estimated)
Membership: Best Buddy $50; Awesome Amigo $100; Precious Pal $250; Fantastic Friend $500; Spectacular Sponsor $1,000.

NORTHERN INDIANA CENTER FOR HISTORY, (M), 808 W. Washington, South Bend, IN 46601-1439. Tel.: 574-235-9664. Fax: 574-235-9059.
E-mail: director@centerforhistory.org
Web Site: www.centerforhistory.org
Founded: 1867.
Congressional District: 3
Key Personnel: C.E.O. & Exec. Dir., Randy W. Ray; Pres. (V), Linda Doshl; Cur., David S. Bainbridge; Dir. Visitor Svcs., Ken Cencelewski; Dir. Public Programs, Stephanie McCune; Dir. Education, Travis Childs; Dir. Devel., Janine Andrysiak; Dir. Mktg., Marilyn Thompson; Dir. Facilities & Grounds, Tom Rapach; Registrar, Jennifer Johns; Finance Mgr., Marilyn Jurgonski; Volunteer Coord., Debra Neumann.
Personnel Profile: Full-Time Paid 18; Part-Time Paid 14; Part-Time Volunteers 120; Interns 2.
Governing Authority: nonprofit organization. Parent Institution: Northern Indiana Historical Society. Tax-exempt: 501(c)(3).
History Museum & Children's Interactive Museum.
Collections: local history & culture from the prehistoric era to the present; pioneer; Native American; works of art; decorative art; military; industrial; costume; toys; dolls; games; transportation; ethnic; political; textile; sports; All-American Girls Professional Baseball League artifacts; tools; Archives includes fur trading journals, regional newspapers from 1830-1960s, court documents & records from St. Joseph County, genealogical manuscripts, diaries, letters, bound volumes on regional & Indiana history, photographs, sheet music, military, ethnic.

Major Exhibits: Lincoln, 11/09-2/10; Life on the Lake, 4/10-10/10; Liberty on the Border (T), 11/10-3/11.
Research Fields: prehistoric era to present including pioneer, Native American, works of art, decorative art, military, industrial, costume, toys, dolls, games, transportation, ethnic, political, textile, sports; All-American Girls Professional Baseball League; fur trading; genealogy & history of St. Joseph County & state of Indiana.
Facilities: research library; auditorium; amphitheatre. Museum-related items for sale.
Activities: self-guided tours; guided tours; lectures; classes; workshops; docent program; films; historical archaeology programs; weekly newspaper article; off-site exhibitions; treasure hunt; experiential classroom kits; living history programs; historical competitions; publications; children's hands-on history exhibits.
Publications: newsletters, volunteer corps newsletter; historical calendar; books; pamphlets; reprints.
Hours & Admission Prices: Mon.-Sat. 10-5, Sun. 12-5. Adults $8, seniors $6.50, children $5; discounts to staff of other museums, AAM & ICOM members; members & children under 6 no charge. ♿
Attendance: 45,250 (accurate)
Membership: Student & Senior $30; Individual $40; Family $60; Patron & Sustainer $125; Sponsor $250.

POTAWATOMI ZOO, 500 S. Greenlawn Ave., South Bend, IN 46615-1341. Mailing Address: P.O. Box 1746, South Bend, IN 46634. Tel.: 574-288-4639. Fax: 574-289-3776.
E-mail: info@potawatomizoo.org
Web Site: potawatomizoo.org
Founded: 1902.
Congressional District: 3
Key Personnel: Zoo Dir., Terry DeRosa; Society Dir., Marcy Dean; Veterinarian, Dr. Carol Bradford; Office Mgr., Pat Fenters.
Personnel Profile: Full-Time Paid 20; Part-Time Paid 12; Part-Time Volunteers 35; Interns 3.
Governing Authority: municipal. Parent Institution: City of South Bend, South Bend, IN 46617. Tel.: 574-284-9401. Tax-exempt: 501(c)(3).
Zoo.
Collections: animals from around the world; mammals; birds; reptiles.
Facilities: 23-acre zoological park; butterfly house; classroom; concessions. Museum-related items for sale.
Activities: guided tours; educational classes; camps; special events; zoo train.
Publications: newsletter, UPROAR.
Hours & Admission Prices: April to late Nov. daily 10-5. Adults $7.50, children & seniors $5.50; discount to school groups; children 2 & under, AZA, & zoo society members no charge. ♿
Attendance: 185,000 (accurate)
Membership: Senior Citizen $25; Individual $35; Grandparents $55; Family $60; Patron $100; Contributor $250.

* **SOUTH BEND REGIONAL MUSEUM OF ART, (M),** 120 S. St. Joseph St., South Bend, IN 46601-1902. Tel.: 574-235-9102. Fax: 574-235-5782.
E-mail: info@southbendart.com
Web Site: sbrma.org
Founded: 1947.
Congressional District: 3
Key Personnel: Exec. Dir., Susan R. Visser; Pres. Bd. Trustees (V), June H. Edwards; Dir. Devel., Melanie Zeitler; Cur. Collections & Exhibitions, Kim Hoffmann; Cur. Exhibitions & Education, Jason Lahr; Cur. Education, Jessica Lentych; Mktg. Mgr., Amy Kleinert; Business Mgr., Bill Seybold; Devel. Mgr. & Membership Coord., Claudia Maskowski.
Personnel Profile: Full-Time Paid 9; Part-Time Paid 9; Part-Time Volunteers 40; Interns 3.
Governing Authority: municipal. Parent Institution: South Bend Art Association. Tax-exempt: 501(c)(3).
Art Museum.
Collections: historic & contemporary Midwestern artists; 19th-20th century American paintings & works on paper.
Research Fields: historic & contemporary American and Indiana art.
Facilities: classroom; special children's studio; activity rooms for films, lectures & meetings. Museum-related items for sale.
Activities: lectures; films; gallery talks; formally organized education programs; studio art program for adults & children; docent training; inter-museum loan; family programs; traveling exhibitions; scholarships to talented and underprivileged students. Museum Sponsors: outdoor jazz & sculpture events, Meet Me On the Island; Day of the Dead Celebration.
Publications: quarterly newsletter; exhibition announcements; checklists; catalogues; class brochures.
Hours & Admission Prices: Office: Mon.-Fri. 9-5. Galleries & Retail: Tues.-Fri. 11-5, Sat.-Sun. 12-5. No charge; donations accepted. Closed New Year's Day; Easter; Christmas. ♿
Attendance: 45,000 (estimated)
Membership: Students & Senior Citizens $30; Individual $40; Household $60; Sustaining $100; Supporting $250; Donor $500; Benefactor $1,000.

* **STUDEBAKER NATIONAL MUSEUM, INC., (M),** 201 S. Chapin St., South Bend, IN 46601-2521. Tel.: 574-235-9714; 888-391-5600. Fax: 574-235-5522.
E-mail: info@studebakermuseum.org
Web Site: www.studebakermuseum.org
Founded: 1977.
Congressional District: 3
Key Personnel: Exec. Dir., Rebecca Bonham; Pres. Bd. Trustees, Mark McDonnell; Business Mgr., Bonnie Oswald; Administrative Asst., Susan Cook; Cur. Collections, Anthony Smith; Archivist, Andrew Beckman; Mgr. Mktg. & Asst. Dir., Peggy Soderberg; Museum Shop Asst., Susan Boocher; Exhibit Designer & Facilities Mgr., Don Filley.
Personnel Profile: Full-Time Paid 8; Part-Time Paid 7; Part-Time Volunteers 30.
Governing Authority: bd. of trustees; nonprofit corporation. Tax-exempt: 501(c)(3).
Automobile Museum.
Collections: 1824-1966 Studebaker historic vehicles including carriages, wagons & automobiles; products manufactured in South Bend & Mishawaka, Indiana from 1830 to the present.
Major Exhibits: Lincoln: The Man You Didn't Know, 11/09-2/10; Harley Davidson: Building A Legend, 11/09-3/10; National Treasures, 11/09-3/10; Life on the Lakes, 4/10-9/10; Chills, Thrills, & Grilles, 10/10; A Studebaker Family Christmas, 11/10-12/10.
Research Fields: South Bend area industrial & commercial history; Studebaker & Packard records of production & history.
Facilities: archives. Museum-related items for sale.
Activities: guided tours; lectures; docent program; education programs; permanent, temporary & traveling exhibits; inter-museum loans.
Publications: quarterly newsletter; annual report.
Hours & Admission Prices: Mon.-Sat. 10-5, Sun. 12-5. Archives: Mon.-Thurs. 10-4; other times by appointment. Museum: adults $8, senior citizens over 60 & student over 18 $6.50, children 6-18 $5; discounts to groups and AAM & AAA members; members & children under 6 no charge. Campus: adults $12, seniors over 60 & student over 18 $10, youth 6-18 $7; discounts to groups; members no charge. Museum: closed New Year's Day; Easter; Thanksgiving; Christmas Eve & Day. ♿
Attendance: 38,000 (accurate)
Membership: Museum: Senior Citizen over 60 $30; Individual $40; Dual $50; Family $60. Campus: Senior over 60 $45; Individual $60; Dual $75; Family $90. Corporate $1,000 & up.

Syracuse

SYRACUSE-WAWASEE HISTORICAL MUSEUM, 1013 N. Long Dr., Syracuse, IN 46567-1060. Tel.: 574-457-3599.
History Museum.
Collections: local history & culture; photographs; period artifacts.
Activities: educational programs.
Hours & Admission Prices: Summer: Wed.-Sat. 1-5; Winter: Thurs.-Fri. 1-5; other times by appointment. No charge; donations accepted.

Terre Haute

CANDLES HOLOCAUST MUSEUM AND EDUCATION CENTER, 1532 S. Third St., Terre Haute, IN 47802-1012. Tel.: 812-234-7881. Fax: 812-478-2824.
E-mail: candles@candlesholocaustmuseum.org
Web Site: www.candlesholocaustmuseum.org
Founded: 1984.
Holocaust Museum.
Collections: Holocaust history; Mengele twins; photographs.
Activities: lectures.
Hours & Admission Prices: Tues.-Sat. 1-4. No charge; donations accepted. ♿

CLABBER GIRL MUSEUM, 900 Wabash Ave., Terre Haute, IN 47807-3208. Mailing Address: P.O. Box 150, Terre Haute, IN 47808-0150. Tel.: 812-232-9446. Fax: 812-478-7181.
E-mail: mmorgan@clabbergirl.com
Web Site: www.myclabbergirl.com
Founded: 2003.
Key Personnel: Cur., Meegan Morgan; Museum Shop Mgr., Lisa Yowell
Historic Building: housed in the former home of Herman Hulman & his sons; built by them in 1892 and where they founded their family wholesale grocery business.

Collections: Hulman family history; wholesale grocery business; history of baking; history of automobile racing & wheels in motion.
Major Exhibits: 1916 Baby Interstate Race Car, 11/09-5/10; 1954 Dean Van Lines Race Car, 11/09-5/10.
Facilities: Museum-related items for sale.
Activities: culinary tour packages, Rex Roasting Co. (coffee roasting company); interactive culinary classes.
Publications: quarterly newsletter.
Hours & Admission Prices: Mon.-Fri. 10-6, Sat. 9-3; guided tours by appointment. No charge. Closed holidays. ♿

EUGENE V. DEBS HOME, 451 N. Eighth St., Terre Haute, IN 47807-3006. Mailing Address: P.O. Box 9454, Terre Haute, IN 47808-9454. Tel.: 812-232-2163 & 237-3443.
E-mail: cking6@isugw.indstate.edu
Web Site: eugenevdebs.com
Founded: 1962.
Congressional District: 8
Key Personnel: Pres. (V), Michael J. Sullivan; Exec. Vice Pres., Noel Beasley; Treas., Mick Love; Cur. & Museum Dir., Karon Brown; Sec., Charles King.
Personnel Profile: Full-Time Paid 1.
Governing Authority: nonprofit organization. Parent Institution: Eugene V. Debs Foundation. Tax-exempt.
Historic House: c.1890 home of Eugene V. Debs.
Collections: period furnishings; mementos of Debs' labor activism and his campaigns for the presidency; historical photographs.
Research Fields: labor; socialism; social reform.
Activities: guided tours; permanent exhibitions.
Publications: semi-annual newsletter.
Hours & Admission Prices: Wed.-Sun. 1-4:30. No charge; donations accepted. Closed national holidays.
Attendance: 1,305 (accurate)
Membership: Student $5; Regular $10; Supporting $25; Sustaining $100; Life $250.

NATIVE AMERICAN MUSEUM, 5170 E. Poplar St., Terre Haute, IN 47803-9313. Tel.: 812-877-6007. Fax: 812-232-7313.
Founded: 1994.
Congressional District: 7
Key Personnel: Cur., Amanda Smith.
Personnel Profile: Full-Time Paid 1; Part-Time Paid 4.
Governing Authority: municipal; nonprofit. Tax-exempt.
Museum of Native American Cultures.
Collections: Indiana history from prehistoric to modern times with special emphasis on the native tribes of western Great Lakes, Wabash River Valley & Ohio's Lower River Valley; wigwam; longhouse; tools & materials for cooking; clothing; basketry; weapons; dolls.
Facilities: 320-vol. library of books on native peoples culture; 2,600 sq. ft. exhibit space; botanical garden; educational facilities.
Activities: guided tours; hobby workshops; lectures; loan & temporary exhibitions. Annual Events: Buffalo Chip Throwing Contest; Archaeology Week; Museum Day.
Hours & Admission Prices: Mon.-Sat. 9-5, Sun. 12-5. No charge; donations accepted. Closed New Year's Day; Martin Luther King Jr. Day; Presidents' Day; Abraham Lincoln's Birthday; Good Friday; Easter; Memorial Day; Independence Day; Labor Day; Election Day; Thanksgiving; Christmas. ♿
Attendance: 13,000 (estimated)

PAUL DRESSER MEMORIAL BIRTHPLACE, First & Farrington Sts., Terre Haute, IN 47802. Mailing Address: Fairbanks Park, Dresser Dr., Terre Haute, IN 47802. Tel.: 812-235-9717. Fax: 812-235-9717.
Founded: 1967.
Congressional District: 7
Key Personnel: Exec. Dir., Marylee Hagan; Asst. Dir., Barbara Carney.
Personnel Profile: Full-Time Paid 1; Part-Time Paid 1; Part-Time Volunteers 1.
Governing Authority: nonprofit organization. Vigo County Historical Society. Branch Museums: Historical Museum of the Wabash Valley, Terre Haute, IN. Tax-exempt: 501(c)(3).
Historic House Museum: c.1850 Paul Dresser Birthplace.
Collections: furniture; household items; period artifacts.
Research Fields: local history.
Activities: tour groups.
Publications: quarterly pamphlets, Leaves of Thyme.
Hours & Admission Prices: May-Sept. Sun. 1-4. Museum: Tues.-Sun. 1-4; other times by appointment, weather permitting. No charge; donations accepted. Closed holidays.
Attendance: 15,000 (estimated)
Membership: Individual $30; Household $50; Patron $100; Sustaining $150; Business Sponsor $500; Life $1,000.

* **SWOPE ART MUSEUM, (M),** 25 S. 7th St., Terre Haute, IN 47807-3692. Tel.: 812-238-1676. Fax: 812-238-1677.
E-mail: info@swope.org
Web Site: www.swope.org
Founded: 1942.
Congressional District: 7
Key Personnel: Dir., Brian Whisenhunt; Pres. Bd. Mgrs. (V), Rick Shagley; Pres. Bd. Overseers, Ralph Fowler; Mgr. Communications, Kristi Finley; Cur., Elizabeth Petrulis; Mgr. Collection, Stephanie Standish; Visitor Svcs., Mary Lou Jennings; Membership, Jenna Auterson.
Personnel Profile: Full-Time Paid 4; Part-Time Paid 7; Part-Time Volunteers 20; Interns 1.
Governing Authority: nonprofit organization. Tax-exempt: 501(c)(3).
Art Museum: housed in 1901 Renaissance Revival building.
Collections: 19th- to 20th-century American paintings, sculpture & works on paper.
Major Exhibits: small architecture BIG LANDSCAPES, 2/5/10-3/13/10; Print Shop/Screenprint, 2/12/10-3/26/10; 43rd Annual Student Art Exhibition, 4/10/10-5/15/10; 66th Annual Wabash Valley Juried Exhibition, 7/10/10-9/4/10; Frank Lloyd Wright's Usonian-Samara House, 10/8/10-12/10.
Research Fields: 19th & 20th Century American art.
Activities: guided tours; lectures; gallery talks; art classes; formally organized education programs; docent program; inter-museum loan; permanent, temporary & traveling exhibitions.
Publications: descriptive brochure; semiannual newsletter; special exhibition catalogs; class schedule; Brown Bag schedule.
Hours & Admission Prices: Tues.-Fri. 10-5, Sat. 12-5. No charge; donations accepted. Closed national holidays. ♿
Attendance: 13,000 (accurate)
Membership: Individual $40; Dual & Family $65; N.A.R.M. $125; Sponsor $250; Patron $500; Benefactor $1,000; Director's Circle $2,500.

TERRE HAUTE CHILDREN'S MUSEUM, 523 Wabash Ave., Terre Haute, IN 47807-3217. Tel.: 812-235-5548.
E-mail: info@terrehautechildrensmuseum.com
Web Site: www.terrehautechildrensmuseum.com
Founded: 1988.
Children's Museum.
Collections: hands-on exhibits.
Hours & Admission Prices: Tues.-Fri. 10-5, Sat. 10-4. Adults $4, seniors & children 3-12 $3; children under 3 no charge.

UNIVERSITY ART GALLERY, INDIANA STATE UNIVERSITY, Center for Performing & Fine Arts, N. 7th & Chestnut St., Terre Haute, IN 47809-0001. Mailing Address: Dept. of Art, FA 108, Terre Haute, IN 47809-0001. Tel.: 812-237-3720 & 3787. Fax: 812-237-4359.
E-mail: mvandenberg@isugw.indstate.edu
Web Site: www.indstate.edu/artgallery
Founded: 1939.
Congressional District: 7
Key Personnel: Interim Dir., Erin Caldwell; Interim Chm., Dr. Steven K. Pontius; Pres., Dr. Lloyd Benjamin.
Personnel Profile: Full-Time Paid 1; Part-Time Paid 6; Part-Time Volunteers 2; Interns 1.
Governing Authority: university. Parent Institution: Indiana State University. Tax-exempt.
Art Gallery.
Collections: paintings; sculpture; prints; ceramics.
Facilities: 2,600 sq. ft. exhibition space.
Activities: regional, national & international contemporary art exhibitions; educational programs for undergraduate & graduate studies.
Publications: 2 selected catalogs for special exhibits per year.
Hours & Admission Prices: Mon.-Wed. & Fri. 11-4, Thurs. 11-8. No charge. Closed holidays. ♿
Attendance: 18,000 (estimated)

VIGO COUNTY HISTORICAL MUSEUM, 1411 S. 6th St., Terre Haute, IN 47802-1114. Tel.: 812-235-9717. Fax: 812-235-4998.
E-mail: vchs@vigohistory.com
Web Site: www.vigo
Founded: 1958.
Congressional District: 7
Key Personnel: C.E.O. & Exec. Dir., Marylee Hagan; Pres., Ken Warner; Asst. Dir., Barbara Carney.
Personnel Profile: Full-Time Paid 1; Part-Time Paid 2; Part-Time Volunteers 25.
Governing Authority: society; owned & operated by Vigo County Historical Society, Inc. Branch Museums: Paul Dresser Memorial Birthplace. Tax-exempt: 501(c)(3).

General Museum: housed in 1868 brick two story Italianate building.
Collections: textiles; archaeology; costumes; military; restored Victorian rooms & country store; schoolroom; dressmakers shop; Coca Cola bottle memorabilia.
Research Fields: local history.
Facilities: library; 50-seat meeting room. Museum-related items for sale.
Activities: guided tours; lectures; films; formally organized education programs; docent program; permanent & temporary exhibitions.
Publications: Four annual pamphlets, Leaves of Thyme.
Hours & Admission Prices: Tues.-Sun. 1-4. No charge; donations accepted. Closed national holidays.
Attendance: 15,000 (estimated)
Membership: Individual $30; Household $50; Patron $100; Sustaining $150; Business Sponsor $500; Life $1,000.

Thorntown

THORNTOWN HERITAGE MUSEUM, 124 W. Main St., Thorntown, IN 46071-1128. Tel.: 765-436-2202.
History Museum.
Collections: local history & culture; photographs; period furnishings; personal artifacts.
Hours & Admission Prices: May-Sept. Fri. 4-7, Sat. 11-5, Sun. 1-4.

Tipton

TIPTON COUNTY HERITAGE CENTER, 323 W. South St., Tipton, IN 46072-2068. Tel.: 765-675-5828.
History Museum.
Collections: local history & culture; period documents; photographs.
Hours & Admission Prices: Tues.-Sat. 1-5.

Union City

ART ASSOCIATION OF RANDOLPH COUNTY, INC., 115 N. Howard, Union City, IN 47390-1435. Tel.: 765-964-7227. Fax: 765-964-4569.
E-mail: jan@artsdepot.org
Web Site: www.artsdepot.org
Founded: 1955.
Key Personnel: Exec. Dir., Jan Roestamadji; Pres. (V), Don Stocksdale.
Personnel Profile: Full-Time Paid 1.
Governing Authority: private; nonprofit organization. Tax-exempt: 501(c)(3).
Art Museum.
Collections: local artists from east central Indiana.
Facilities: 250-vol. library; 80-seat auditorium; educational facilities.
Activities: formal education programs; concerts; guided tours; hobby workshops; lectures; loan & participatory exhibits; rental gallery; dinners. Annual Events: Art Show; Photograph Show; Quilt Show.
Publications: quarterly newsletter, Artracks.
Hours & Admission Prices: Tues.-Fri. 10-4; other times by appointment. No charge; donations accepted. Closed major holidays. ♿
Attendance: 5,000 (estimated)
Membership: Student $10; Single $20; Family $30; Friend of Art $100; Patron $250; Partner $500; Angel $1,000.

Valparaiso

BRAUER MUSEUM OF ART, (M), Valparaiso University Center for the Arts, Valparaiso, IN 46383-6349. Mailing Address: Valparaiso University Center for the Arts, 1709 Chapel Dr., Valparaiso, IN 46383-4519. Tel.: 219-464-5365. Fax: 219-464-5244.
E-mail: gregg.hertzlieb@valpo.edu
Web Site: www.valpo.edu/artmuseum
Founded: 1953.
Congressional District: 5
Key Personnel: Dir. & Cur., Gregg Hertzlieb; Asst. Cur. & Registrar, Gloria Ruff.
Personnel Profile: Full-Time Paid 2; Part-Time Volunteers 8; Interns 4.
Governing Authority: university. Tax-exempt: 501(c)(3).
Art Museum.
Collections: 19th, 20th, & 21st century American Art; paintings, drawings, sketchbooks & archival material by Junius Sloan; world religious art.
Research Fields: American & religious art.
Facilities: Arts Center: theatre; recital hall; arts instructional spaces.
Activities: lectures; permanent, temporary & traveling exhibitions; guided tours; gallery talks; inter-museum loans; virtual exhibitions available on web site; receptions.
Publications: Exhibition brochures; Inaugural booklet.
Hours & Admission Prices: Academic year: Tues. & Thurs.-Fri. 10-5, Wed. 10-8:30, Sat.-Sun. 12-5. Academic recess & summer: Tues.-Sun. 12-5. No charge; donations accepted. Closed New Year's Eve & Day, Good Friday; Easter; Independence Day; Thanksgiving; Christmas Eve & Day. ♿
Attendance: 10,000 (estimated)
Membership: Apprentice $25; Craftsman $50; Artist $100; Mentor $250; Master $500; Curator $1,000.

INDIANA AVIATION MUSEUM, 4601 Murvihill Rd., Valparaiso, IN 46383-6957. Tel.: 219-548-3123. Fax: 219-929-1349.
Aviation Museum.
Collections: Planes: 1941 PT-17 Stearman; 1945 P-51D Mustang; 1952 AT-6G Texan; 1953 DHC 1 MK22 Chipmunk; 1955 T-28B Trojan; 1957 T-34B Mentor; 1943 L-2 Grasshopper; 1967 A-37A Dragonfly; 1991 Van's Aircraft RV-4; Engines: R-2800 Double Wasp; Rolls-Royce Merlin.
Hours & Admission Prices: May-Oct. Sat. 10-4, Sun. 1-4; other times by appointment. Adults $5, seniors $4; children 12 & under no charge.

THE MEMORIAL OPERA HOUSE, 104 Indiana Ave., Valparaiso, IN 46383-5603. Tel.: 219-548-9137.
Key Personnel: Dir., Brian Schafer.
Governing Authority: Parent Institution: Porter County.
Historic Building: built in 1893. Listed on the National Register of Historic Places.
Collections: theater history; period furnishings; photographs.
Facilities: 364-seat theatre.
Activities: performances; concerts; films; special events; tours.
Hours & Admission Prices: Mon.-Sat. 10-2; groups by appointment. No charge; donations accepted.

PORTER COUNTY MUSEUM & HISTORICAL SOCIETY, 153 S. Franklin St., Valparaiso, IN 46383-5631. Tel.: 219-465-3595.
E-mail: info@portercountymuseum.org
Web Site: portercountymuseum.org
Formerly: Old Sail Museum
Founded: 1912.
Congressional District: 1
Key Personnel: Chm. (V), Michael Spudic; Exec. Dir., Kevin Matthew Pazour.
Personnel Profile: Full-Time Paid 1; Part-Time Paid 1; Interns 1.
Governing Authority: society. Parent Institution: Historical Society of Porter County. Tax-exempt: 35-6042748.
Local History Museum.
Collections: mastodon bones found in county; relics from pioneer families & Indians; period photographs.
Research Fields: old histories & naturalization records for schools & genealogy.
Facilities: library of county history & genealogy books available for use only on premises; War of the Rebellion Collection records library.
Activities: guided tours; education programs for children.
Publications: newsletters.
Hours & Admission Prices: Fri.-Sun. 1-4. No charge: donations accepted. Closed some national holidays.
Attendance: 4,000 (estimated)
Membership: Friend of the Museum $25; Family $50; Historical Society Supporter $100; Board of Directors $250; 1912 Society $500.

Veedersburg

FOUNTAIN COUNTY WAR MUSEUM, INC., 116 E. First St., Veedersburg, IN 47987-1402. Tel.: 765-793-2321.
Founded: 1995.
Congressional District: 7
Key Personnel: Dir. & Pres. (V), Willard Williams; Chm. (V), Tye Auter; Treas., Dorothy Williams.
Personnel Profile: Part-Time Volunteers 8.
Governing Authority: private; nonprofit organization. Tax-exempt.
War Museum.
Collections: military artifacts; personal artifacts; photographs.
Facilities: library.
Activities: guided tours; lectures; temporary exhibitions. Annual Event: festival.
Hours & Admission Prices: first Sun. of month 2-4; other times by appointment. No charge; donations accepted. ♿
Attendance: 500 (estimated)

Versailles

RIPLEY COUNTY, INDIANA, HISTORICAL SOCIETY MUSEUM, Water & Main, Versailles, IN 47042. Mailing Address: Box 525, Versailles, IN 47042-0525.
Founded: 1930.
Congressional District: 9
Key Personnel: Dir. & Treas., Owen Menchhofer; Pres. & Acting Cur., Cheryl Welch.

Personnel Profile: Part-Time Volunteers 23.
Governing Authority: society; bd. of directors. Tax-exempt.
Historical Society Museum.
Collections: Civil War artifacts; Native American artifacts; books; primitive tools; costumes & textiles.
Research Fields: cemeteries; genealogies; local history.
Facilities: archives.
Activities: permanent exhibitions. Museum Sponsors: Pumpkin Show.
Publications: cemetery records; quarterly bulletin; Ripley County History, 1818-1988, Vol. I.
Hours & Admission Prices: Museum: Memorial Day-Labor Day Sun. 2-4. Library: Mon.-Fri. 1-4. No charge; donations accepted. Library Research: nonmembers $3; members no charge. ♿
Attendance: 1,000 (estimated)
Membership: Annual $10.

Vevay

LIFE ON THE OHIO RIVER HISTORY MUSEUM, 208 E. Market St., Vevay, IN 47043-1233. Mailing Address: P.O. Box 201, Vevay, IN 47043-0201.
Founded: 2004.
Congressional District: 9
Key Personnel: Dir., Martha Bladen; Pres. (V), Janet Hendricks; Treas., Ruth Osborn; Sec., Wanda Benzing; Coord. Collections, Ann Farnsley.
Personnel Profile: Full-Time Paid 1; Part-Time Paid 3; Part-Time Volunteers 5; Interns 1.
Governing Authority: Parent Institution: Switzerland County Historical Society. Tax-exempt.
History Museum.
Collections: river history; steamboat models; pilot wheel; photos; documents.
Research Fields: Ohio River history.
Facilities: genealogy library.
Activities: riverboat cruises during the Swiss Wine Festival in August.
Publications: newsletter, Grapevine; postcards.
Hours & Admission Prices: April-Oct. daily 10-5; Nov.-March daily 12-4. Adults $3; members no charge; donations accepted. Closed Christmas Eve & Day. ♿
Attendance: 2,000 (estimated)
Membership: Basic $10; Contributing $20; Supporting $30; Sustaining $50; Life $200.

SWITZERLAND COUNTY HISTORICAL MUSEUM, 208 Main & Market Sts., Vevay, IN 47043. Mailing Address: P.O. Box 201, Vevay, IN 47043-0201. Tel.: 812-427-3560.
E-mail: swcomuseums@embarqmail.com
Web Site: www.switzcomuseums.org
Founded: 1924.
Congressional District: 9
Key Personnel: Dir., Martha Bladen; Pres. (V), Janet Hendricks; Recording Sec., Wanda Benzing.
Personnel Profile: Full-Time Paid 1; Part-Time Paid 3; Interns 1.
Governing Authority: Parent Institution: Switzerland County Historical Society. Tax-exempt.
County History Museum.
Collections: costumes; pioneer relics; documents; Indian artifacts; textiles & quilts; dolls; first piano in Indiana. Historic Building: 1860 Presbyterian Church located in Vevay.
Research Fields: genealogy.
Facilities: genealogy library.
Activities: monthly programs; summer garden tour; storyfest; Christmas tour of homes; permanent & temporary exhibits.
Publications: newsletter, The Grapevine; Harraman's History of Switzerland County; The American Vine-Dresser's Guide; The Vevay Cook Book.
Hours & Admission Prices: April-Oct. daily 10-5; Nov.-March daily 12-4. Adults $3; members no charge. Closed Easter; Christmas Eve & Day. ♿
Attendance: 3,500 (estimated)
Membership: Individual $10; Family $15; Contributing $20; Business & Supporting $30; Sustaining $50; Lifetime $200.

Vincennes

GEORGE ROGERS CLARK NATIONAL HISTORICAL PARK, 401 S. Second St., Vincennes, IN 47591-1001. Tel.: 812-882-1776, ext. 110. Fax: 812-882-7270.
E-mail: gero_ranger_activities@nps.gov
Web Site: www.nps.gov/gero
Founded: 1967.
Congressional District: 8
Key Personnel: Supt., Dale K. Phillips.
Personnel Profile: Full-Time Paid 11.
Governing Authority: federal. Dept. of the Interior, National Park Service. Tax-exempt.
Park Museum.
Collections: British & American frontier weapons, uniforms, clothing, accoutrements; French Canadian household items; flat work; maps, diagrams & interpretive texts; oil murals; bronze statue of George Rogers Clark.
Research Fields: American Revolutionary War in the West; Old Northwest Territory.
Facilities: 600-vol. library of books, journals, maps on Revolutionary War in the West, early settlement of Old Northwest & evolution from territory status to statehood.
Activities: self-guided tours; movie; rifle & musket demonstrations; museum talks.
Publications: handbook.
Hours & Admission Prices: Daily 9-5. Adults 17 & over $3. Closed New Year's Day; Thanksgiving; Christmas. ♿
Attendance: 129,950 (accurate)

INDIANA MILITARY MUSEUM INC., 2074 N. Old Bruceville Rd., Vincennes, IN 47591-8922. Tel.: 812-882-8668.
Web Site: www.indianamilitarymuseum.org
Founded: 1983.
Key Personnel: Dir., Jim R. Osborne.
Personnel Profile: Part-Time Volunteers 36.
Governing Authority: Tax-exempt.
Military Museum.
Collections: military memorabilia, vehicles, artillery, uniforms & equipment from the Civil War to Desert Storm.
Hours & Admission Prices: April-Oct. daily 12-4; Winter: by appointment. Adults $3, children $1; discounts to groups; members no charge. Closed New Year's Day; Thanksgiving; Christmas. ♿
Attendance: 3,500 (estimated)
Membership: Single $10; Family $20; Life $200.

MICHEL BROUILLET HOUSE & MUSEUM, 509 N. 1st St., Vincennes, IN 47591-1401. Mailing Address: P.O. Box 1979, Vincennes, IN 47591. Tel.: 812-882-7422. Fax: 812-882-0928.
Founded: 1975.
Congressional District: 8
Key Personnel: Chm. Bd., Jimmy Morrison; Cur., Richard Day; Pres., P.R. Sweeney; Mgr. Vincennes Historic Sites, Bruce Beesley.
Governing Authority: nonprofit. Parent Institution: The Old Northwest Corporation. Tax-exempt: 501(c)(3).
History Museum: housed in 1806 restored French Pioneer Home.
Collections: furnishings; fur traders exhibit; Stone Age implements; Indian weapons; domestic utensils; dioramas; fossils.
Research Fields: early French settlement of Vincennes; prehistoric period in Wabash Valley.
Activities: lectures; guided tours; special shows.
Publications: monthly newsletter, Old Northwest Corporation Newsletter.
Hours & Admission Prices: By appointment. Adults $2, children $1.
Membership: Individual $10; Family $15; Business $25; Corporate $100.

OLD CATHEDRAL LIBRARY & MUSEUM, 205 Church St., Vincennes, IN 47591-1133. Tel.: 812-882-5638.
Founded: 1794.
Personnel Profile: Part-Time Volunteers 5.
Governing Authority: Parent Institution: St. Francis Xavier Church. Tax-exempt.
Religious Museum.
Collections: books; church records; Simon Brute de Remur collection; St. Francis Xavier Church, Vincennes records 1749 to present; theology, Bibles & Biblical works; historical civil & religious works.
Facilities: over 10,000-vol. library.
Hours & Admission Prices: June to mid-Aug. Mon.-Fri. 1-4; other times by appointment. Adults $1, children 12 & under $.50.

VINCENNES STATE HISTORIC SITE, INDIANA TERRITORY, First & Harrison Sts., Vincennes, IN 47591. Mailing Address: P.O. Box 81, Vincennes, IN 47591-0081. Tel.: 812-882-7422. Fax: 812-882-0928.
Web Site: www.state.in.us/ism/sites/vincennes/
Founded: 1949.
Congressional District: 8
Key Personnel: Cur., Bruce A. Beesley; Asst. Cur., Richard Day.
Personnel Profile: Full-Time Paid 4; Part-Time Volunteers 5.
Governing Authority: state. Parent Institution: Indiana Dept. of Natural Resources. Subsidiary Institution: Indiana State Museum. Tax-exempt.
Historic Site: c.1805 Territory Capitol Building.

Collections: period furnishings; printing equipment; replica 1804 print shop; replica 1801 schoolhouse.
Activities: guided tours; lectures.
Hours & Admission Prices: April-Nov. Mon.-Sat. 9-5. Adults $3.50, seniors $3, children $2. Closed state holidays. ♿
Attendance: 33,000 (accurate)

VINCENNES STATE HISTORIC SITE, OLD STATE BANK, 114 N. Second St., Vincennes, IN 47591-1217. Mailing Address: P.O. Box 81, Vincennes, IN 47591-0081. Tel.: 812-882-7422. Fax: 812-882-0928.
Web Site: www.state.in.us/ism/sites/vincennes/
Founded: 1838.
Congressional District: 8
Key Personnel: Historic Site Cur., Bruce Beesley; Asst. Cur., Richard Day.
Personnel Profile: Full-Time Paid 4; Part-Time Volunteers 5.
Governing Authority: government. State of Indiana. Subsidiary Institution: Ind. Dept. of Natural Resources. Tax-exempt.
1838 State Bank Building.
Collections: local history & culture; period artifacts.
Activities: tours/interpretation.
Publications: newsletters.
Hours & Admission Prices: By appointment. Adults $3.50. ♿
Attendance: 5,000 (estimated)

WILLIAM HENRY HARRISON MANSION, GROUSELAND, 3 W. Scott St., Vincennes, IN 47591-1433. Tel.: 812-882-2096. Fax: 812-882-7626.
E-mail: grouseland@sbcglobal.net
Web Site: grouselandfoundation.org
Founded: 1911.
Congressional District: 8
Key Personnel: Pres., James Corridan; Treas., Winifred Berry; Cur., Robert Stevens; Admin., Dennis Latta.
Personnel Profile: Full-Time Paid 1; Part-Time Paid 4; Part-Time Volunteers 25.
Governing Authority: private; nonprofit organization. Parent Institution: Grouseland Foundation, Inc. Tax-exempt: 501(c)(3).
History Museum: Presidential Home. A National Historic Landmark.
Collections: the life of William Henry Harrison from his birth in Virginia to his death in the White House; personal artifacts; early 19th century furnishings.
Research Fields: William Henry Harrison genealogy & artifacts.
Facilities: Museum-related items for sale.
Activities: guided tours; school loan service; temporary exhibitions. Annual Events: Candlelight tours in May & December; Quilt Show in October.
Hours & Admission Prices: Jan.-Feb. daily 11-4; March-Dec. Mon.-Sat. 9-4, Sun. 1-4. Family $10, adults $5, seniors $4, students $3, children 5-12 $2; children under 5 no charge. Closed New Year's Day; Easter; Thanksgiving; Christmas Eve & Day.
Attendance: 11,500 (accurate)
Membership: Student $25; Individual $40; Family $75; Grouseland Patron $100; Governor's Society $250; President's Society $500; Harrison's Cabinet $1,000.

Wabash

CHARLEY CREEK GARDENS, 551 N. Miami St., Wabash, IN 46992. Mailing Address: P.O. Box 454, Wabash, IN 46992-0454. Tel.: 260-563-1020.
Key Personnel: Dir., Kelly Smith
Gardens.
Collections: native & foreign plants; horticulture.
Facilities: gardens.
Activities: educational programs; research; guided tours; rental facilities.
Hours & Admission Prices: Gardens: daily dawn to dusk. Center: by appointment.

DR. JAMES FORD HISTORIC HOME, (M), 177 W. Hill St., Wabash, IN 46992-3049. Tel.: 260-563-8686.
Web Site: jamesfordmuseum.org
Historic House Museum: housed in a 19th century physician's home; built 1841.
Collections: mid- to late 19th century furnishings; 19th century surgeon's office.
Research Fields: Ford family.
Facilities: library; gardens. Museum-related items for sale.
Activities: special events; lectures; recitals; festivals.
Publications: newsletter, Faith, Family, Posterity.
Hours & Admission Prices: Fri. 12-5, Sat.-Sun. 10-5; groups by appointment. Adults $3, children 14 & under $2.

HONEYWELL CENTER, 275 W. Market St., Wabash, IN 46992-3057. Tel.: 260-563-1102. Fax: 260-563-0873.
Web Site: www.honeywellcenter.org
Key Personnel: Exec. Dir., Tod Minnich; Gallery Mgr., Bonnie McKee
Art Gallery.
Collections: works by local & national artists; sculpture.
Facilities: 1,500-seat theater.
Activities: traveling exhibitions.
Hours & Admission Prices: Daily 9am-10pm. No charge.

WABASH COUNTY HISTORICAL MUSEUM, (M), 36 E. Market St., Wabash, IN 46992-3124. Tel.: 260-563-9070.
Key Personnel: Dir., Tracy Stewart; Chm. (V), Jim Ridenour.
Personnel Profile: Full-Time Volunteers 1; Part-Time Paid 5; Part-Time Volunteers 25.
Governing Authority: Tax-exempt.
History Museum.
Collections: county history & culture; photographs.
Major Exhibits: Stephen Douglas, 2/10-7/10.
Facilities: archives; 32-seat theater.
Hours & Admission Prices: Tues.-Sat. 10-4. Adults $5, children 6-12 and seniors 60 & over $3; discounts to groups; museum associates and children 5 & under no charge. ♿
Attendance: 6,000 (estimated)
Membership: Individual $25; Grandparent $40; Family $45.

Wakarusa

BIRD'S EYE VIEW MUSEUM OF MINIATURES, 325 S. Elkhart St., Wakarusa, IN 46573-9727. Tel.: 574-862-2367.
History Museum.
Collections: 215 miniature models of Indiana landmarks.
Activities: guided tours.
Hours & Admission Prices: Mon.-Fri. 8-5, Sat. 8am to noon. No charge; donations accepted.

Warsaw

KOSCIUSKO COUNTY HISTORICAL SOCIETY, Corner of Main & Indiana Sts., Warsaw, IN 46581. Mailing Address: P.O. Box 1071, Warsaw, IN 46581-1071. Tel.: 574-269-1078.
Governing Authority: nonprofit organization.
Historical Society Museum.
Collections: local history & culture; photographs.
Activities: special programs.
Publications: newsletter.
Hours & Admission Prices: Thurs.-Fri. 9-4, Sat. 10-4. Closed major holidays.

Washington

DAVIESS COUNTY HISTORICAL SOCIETY MUSEUM, 212 1/2 E. Main St., Washington, IN 47501. Mailing Address: P.O. Box 2341, Washington, IN 47501-0981. Tel.: 812-444-9360. Fax: 812-257-0301.
E-mail: dchistory@sbcglobal.net
Web Site: www.daviesscountyhistory.net
Formerly: Daviess County Museum
Founded: 1966.
Congressional District: 8
Key Personnel: Dir., Vincent A. Sellers; Pres. (V), Dean Dorrell.
Personnel Profile: Full-Time Paid 1; Part-Time Volunteers 10.
Governing Authority: Tax-exempt: 501(c)(3).
History Museum.
Collections: local history & culture; photographs; personal artifacts; coal; farming; Amish; B&O railroad; Wabash & Erie Canal.
Facilities: meeting facilities.
Activities: quarterly programs.
Publications: quarterly newsletter.
Hours & Admission Prices: Mon.-Fri. 10-4, Sat. 9-12. Adults $2; members no charge. ♿
Attendance: 1,500
Membership: Student $10; Basic $20; Family $35; Sustaining $100; Benefactor $250.

West Lafayette

THE ARTHUR & KRIEBEL HERBARIA, PURDUE UNIVERSITY, 915 W. State St., Dept. of Botany & Plant Pathology, West Lafayette, IN 47907-2054. Tel.: 765-494-4651. Fax: 765-494-0363.
E-mail: herbaria@purdue.edu
Web Site: www.btny.purdue.edu/Herbaria/herbaria.html

Founded: 1873.
Congressional District: 7
Key Personnel: Dir., Gregory Shaner.
Personnel Profile: Part-Time Paid 1.
Governing Authority: university. Parent Institution: Purdue University. Subsidiary Institution: Dept. Botany & Plant Pathology.
Herbarium.
Collections: rust plant parasitic fungi; plants; fungi.
Research Fields: taxonomy & ecology of plant parasitic fungi, mainly rust fungi worldwide; plants & mushrooms of Indiana.
Facilities: lab.
Activities: formally organized education programs for graduate, undergraduate & grade school students; public exhibitions; talks & excursions.
Hours & Admission Prices: Mon.-Fri. 9-5. No charge. Closed state & national holidays. ♿
Attendance: 150 (estimated)

PURDUE UNIVERSITY GALLERIES, Yue-Kong Pao Hall, 552 W. Wood St., West Lafayette, IN 47907-2002. Tel.: 765-494-3061. Fax: 765-496-2817.
E-mail: galleries@purdue.edu
Web Site: www.purdue.edu/galleries
Founded: 1978.
Congressional District: 7
Key Personnel: Dir., Craig Martin; Asst. Dir., Michal Hathaway; Asst. to Dir., Mary Ann Anderson.
Personnel Profile: Full-Time Paid 3; Part-Time Paid 20; Part-Time Volunteers 6.
Governing Authority: university. Parent Institution: Purdue University. Tax-exempt: 501(c)(3).
University Art Gallery.
Collections: More than 5,200 objects are in the permanent collection: 3,000 historic to contemporary prints, photographs, and works on paper; Art of the Americas, including Native American baskets, Pre-Columbian textiles and ceramics. Paintings, drawings and prints by the Mexican Modernists.
Major Exhibits: Dream Deferred, 1/11/10-2/21/10; 60 Square Inches: 17th Biennial North American Small Print Exhibition, 3/8/10-4/25/10.
Research Fields: pertaining to collections.
Activities: guided tours; lectures; films; loan, temporary & traveling exhibitions; hands-on relief printmaking activity.
Publications: newsletter.
Hours & Admission Prices: Mon.-Wed. & Fri.-Sat. 10-5, Thurs. 10-8, Sun. 1-5. No charge. Closed university holidays. ♿
Attendance: 24,797 (accurate)

Whiting

WHITING-ROBERTSDALE HISTORICAL MUSEUM, 1610 119th St., Whiting, IN 46394-1702. Tel.: 219-659-1432.
History Museum.
Collections: local history & culture; photographs; personal artifacts.
Hours & Admission Prices: Tues.-Wed. & Sat. 1-4.

Winchester

RANDOLPH COUNTY HISTORICAL MUSEUM, 416 S. Meridian, Winchester, IN 47394-2028. Tel.: 317-584-1334.
E-mail: rchsin2@comcast.net
Founded: 1968.
Congressional District: 2
Key Personnel: Pres. (V), Marjorie Birtwhistle; Vice Pres., Saundra Jackson; Treas., Sharon Smith; Sec. & Museum Shop Mgr., Monisa Wisener.
Personnel Profile: Full-Time Volunteers 1; Part-Time Volunteers 5.
Governing Authority: society; nonprofit. Parent Institution: Randolph County Historical Society. Tax-exempt: 170(b)(1)(A).
Genealogy & History Museum: housed in 1858 brick home built by Carey Goodrich.
Collections: clothes; dishes; photos; tools; books; furniture & furnishings of the period.
Research Fields: genealogy; school records; history books & maps.
Facilities: research library of genealogical & historical information. Museum-related items for sale.
Activities: guided tours; lectures; permanent exhibitions.
Publications: newsletter; book, 1818-1990 Randolph County History; reprint, 1882 History Randolph County; 1895 & 1918 Atlas (Randolph County).
Hours & Admission Prices: Mon.-Fri. 10-12:30 & 1:30-5; other times by appointment. No charge; donations accepted. ♿
Membership: Annual $15.

Winona Lake

BILLY SUNDAY HOME MUSEUM AND VISITORS CENTER, 1101 Park Ave., Winona Lake, IN 46590-1062. Tel.: 574-268-0660.
Web Site: www.villageatwinona.com
Key Personnel: Dir., Bill Firstenberger.
Personnel Profile: Full-Time Paid 1; Part-Time Volunteers 50; Interns 2.
Governing Authority: Parent Institution: Village at Winona. Tax-exempt.
Historic Site: housed in former home of professional baseball player turned evangelist, Billy Sunday.
Collections: personal artifacts; furnishings; paintings; needlework; folk art; needlecrafts; baseball memorabilia.
Research Fields: Billy Sunday; art & crafts design.
Facilities: visitors center.
Hours & Admission Prices: Tues.-Sat. 10-5. Visitors Center: donations accepted. Sunday Home Tour: adults $4; discounts to groups with appointment; children 12 & under no charge. Closed New Year's Day; Good Friday; Thanksgiving; Christmas. ♿
Attendance: 7,000 (estimated)

Wolcott

HISTORIC WOLCOTT HOUSE, 500 N. Range St., Wolcott, IN 47995-8276. Fax: 219-279-2561.
Key Personnel: Pres., Ann Cain
Historic House Museum.
Collections: period furnishings.
Hours & Admission Prices: By appointment. No charge; donations accepted.

Zionsville

P.H. SULLIVAN MUSEUM AND GENEALOGY LIBRARY, 225 W. Hawthorne St., Zionsville, IN 46077-1620. Tel.: 317-873-4900.
Web Site: www.sullivanmunce.org
Founded: 1973.
Congressional District: 6
Key Personnel: Pres. Bd. Dir. (V), Lee Ann Schiller; Exec. Dir., Janet Campbell Baker; Pres. Museum Women's Guild (V), Ann Van Horn.
Personnel Profile: Full-Time Paid 2; Part-Time Paid 2; Part-Time Volunteers 30.
Governing Authority: nonprofit organization. Parent Institution: P.H. Sullivan Foundation. Branch Museums: Munce Art Center. Tax-exempt: 501(c)(3).
Local History Museum.
Collections: Boone County & Indiana history.
Research Fields: United States genealogy.
Facilities: 4,500-vol. library of material on Boone County, Indiana & other states available on premises; reading room; permanent & temporary exhibitions.
Activities: lectures; workshops; temporary exhibitions; artist-in-residence program.
Hours & Admission Prices: Tues.-Sat. 10-4. No charge; donations accepted. Closed New Year's Day; Thanksgiving; Christmas. ♿
Attendance: 7,000 (estimated)
Membership: $25; $50; $100; $250; $500; $1,000.

SULLIVANMUNCE CULTURAL CENTER, 205-225 W. Hawthorne St., Zionsville, IN 46077-1620. Tel.: 317-873-4900. Fax: 317-873-6862.
E-mail: cynthiayoung@sullivanmunce.org
Web Site: www.sullivanmunce.org
Formerly: Munce Art Center
Founded: 1981.
Congressional District: 6
Key Personnel: Exec. Dir., Janet C. Baker; Pres., Stan Evans; Pres. (V), Linda Weintraut; Museum Dir., Marianne Doyle; Art Center Dir., Cynthia Young; Mktg. Coord., Lynne Manning; Museum Shop Mgr., Kay Cunningham.
Personnel Profile: Full-Time Paid 3; Part-Time Paid 1.
Governing Authority: nonprofit organization. Parent Institution: P.H. Sullivan Foundation. Tax-exempt: 501(c)(3).
History and The Arts.
Collections: local & early Indiana art.
Facilities: library of art books & genealogical records; archives; classrooms.
Activities: classes; temporary exhibitions.
Publications: quarterly, class schedule; tri-annual, newsletter.
Hours & Admission Prices: Tues.-Sat. 10-4. No charge; donations accepted. Closed holidays. ♿
Attendance: 11,000 (estimated)
Membership: $25 & up.

IOWA

(217 listings)

Ackley

ACKLEY HERITAGE CENTER, 208 State St., Ackley, IA 50601-1545. Tel.: 641-847-2201.
E-mail: ackleyhc@mchsi.com
Web Site: www.ackleyheritagecenter.com
History Museum.
Collections: local history & culture; photographs; personal artifacts.
Hours & Admission Prices: Tues. & Thurs.-Fri. 1:30-4:30; other times by appointment.

Albert City

ALBERT CITY HISTORICAL MUSEUM, 212 2nd St., N., Albert City, IA 50510-1210. Tel.: 712-843-5684.
History Museum.
Collections: military room; grocery store; tool shop; early 1900s cars, music boxes, glassware figurines, railroad memorabilia; medical instruments; period furnishings. Historic Buildings: 1900s home; 1875 schoolhouse.
Hours & Admission Prices: Sun. 2-5; other times by appointment.

Algona

CAMP ALGONA POW MUSEUM, 114 S. Thorington St., Algona, IA 50511-2616. Mailing Address: P.O Box 174, Algona, IA 50511-0174. Tel.: 515-395-2267 & 295-3719.
E-mail: yocumcampalgona@netamumail.com
Web Site: www.pwcamp.algona.org
Key Personnel: Pres., Nick Scholer; Vice Pres., Bill Fjetland; Sec. & Treas., Don Hansen
History Museum: former camp for German POW's from 1944-1946.
Collections: weapons; World War II uniforms & artifacts; poetry; paintings; woodcarvings.
Hours & Admission Prices: April-Dec. Sat.-Sun. 1-4; other times by appointment. Adults $3. ♿
Attendance: 2,000 (accurate)
Membership: Individual $10.

Allison

BUTLER COUNTY HISTORICAL SOCIETY, 219 1/2 S. Main St., Allison, IA 50602-9507. Mailing Address: Box 14, Allison, IA 50602-0014. Tel.: 319-267-2664 & 2255.
Formerly: Butler County Historical Museum-Little Yellow Schoolhouse
Founded: 1956.
Congressional District: 3
Key Personnel: C.E.O. & Pres. (V), Deb Bochmann; Vice Pres., Ruth Haan; Sec., Anita Hardy; Treas., Judi Poppen.
Personnel Profile: Part-Time Volunteers 10.
Governing Authority: nonprofit. Branch Museum: Little Yellow School House; Log Cabin; Hall of Fame; Butler County Museum; Anna Pals House. Tax-exempt.
Historical Society Museum: residing on the Butler County Fairgrounds.
Collections: agriculture; history; preservation project. Historic Buildings: 1888 Little Yellow Schoolhouse - one room country school; Hall of Fame includes accomplishments of Butler County residents; 1850s Log Cabin reproduction; restored home of Anna Pal.
Facilities: 200-vol. library.
Activities: guided tours; permanent & temporary exhibitions.
Publications: booklet, History of the Little Yellow School House.
Hours & Admission Prices: June-Sept. by appointment. No charge; donations accepted. ♿
Attendance: 850 (estimated)
Membership: Individual $10; Lifetime $100.

Amana

AMANA HERITAGE MUSEUM, 705 44th Ave., Amana, IA 52203-0081. Mailing Address: P.O. Box 81, Amana, IA 52203-0081. Tel.: 319-622-3567. Fax: 319-622-6481.
E-mail: amherit@juno.com
Web Site: www.amanaheritage.org
Formerly: Museum of Amana History
Founded: 1969.
Congressional District: 3
Key Personnel: Dir., Lanny Haldy; Pres. (V), Allyn Neubauer; Cur., Jennifer Engelkemier; Museum Shop Mgr., Brandi Jones.
Personnel Profile: Full-Time Paid 3; Part-Time Paid 20.
Governing Authority: nonprofit organization. Parent Institution: Amana Heritage Society. Tax-exempt: 501(c)(3).
Historical Society Museum: housed in 1865 & 1870 buildings.
Collections: artifacts pertaining to Amana (Community of True Inspiration) history; crafts; costumes; decorative arts; archives; photographs; furnishings; textiles.
Research Fields: local history; history of Community of True Inspiration; German immigration; Pietism.
Facilities: library; 85-seat auditorium; 5,000 sq. ft. exhibit space. Books for sale.
Activities: guided tours; lectures; organized education programs for children; temporary exhibitions; guided walking tours of village of Amana.
Publications: quarterly newsletter.
Hours & Admission Prices: April-Oct. 30 Mon.-Sat. 10-5, Sun. 12-5. Adults $7; discount to groups; children, students & members no charge. ♿
Attendance: 25,000 (accurate)
Membership: Contributing $25; Silver Heritage $75; Gold Heritage $200.

Ames

* **BRUNNIER ART MUSEUM, (M),** University Museums, Iowa State University, 290 Scheman Bldg., Ames, IA 50011-0001. Tel.: 515-294-3342. Fax: 515-294-3342.
Web Site: www.museums.iastate.edu
Founded: 1975.
Key Personnel: Dir. & Chief Cur., Lynette L. Pohlman; Collections Mgmt. & Communications Coord., Allison Juull; Interpretive Specialist, Amanda Hall; Devel. Sec., Sue Olson; Educator, Visual Literacy & Learning, Nancy Gebhart; Administrative Specialist & Museum Shop Mgr., Angela Shippy.
Governing Authority: state. Parent Institution: University Museums, Iowa State University. Tax-exempt.
Decorative & Fine Arts Museum.
Collections: decorative arts including glass, dolls, ceramics, jade.
Research Fields: decorative arts; glass; ceramics.
Facilities: library of reference books available for research on premises; reading room. Catalogues & slides for sale.
Activities: guided tours; gallery talks; docent program; permanent, temporary & traveling exhibitions. Annual Events: Brunnier Bash; Brunnier in Bloom.
Publications: quarterly newsletter, News from University Museums.
Hours & Admission Prices: Tues.-Fri. 11-4, Sat.-Sun.1-4. No charge; donations accepted. Closed Memorial Day; Independence Day; Labor Day; Thanksgiving; Christmas; university holidays. ♿
Attendance: 15,000 (estimated)
Membership: College Student $10; Household $50; Sustained $100; Pacesetter $250; Director's Guild $500; Benefactor $1,000; Patron $2,500; Curator's Associate (Lifetime) $10,000; Curators $15,000.

CHRISTIAN PETERSEN ART MUSEUM, Morrill Hall, Iowa State University, Ames, IA 50011-0001. Mailing Address: University Museums, Iowa State University, 290 Scheman Bldg., Ames, IA 50011-0001. Tel.: 515-294-9500. Fax: 515-294-3342.
Founded: 2007.
Key Personnel: Dir. & Chief Cur., Lynette Pohlman; Collections Mgmt. & Communications Coord., Allison Juull; Interpretive Specialist, Amanda Hall; Devel. Sec., Sue Olson; Educator, Visual Literacy & Learning, Nancy Gebhart; Administrative Specialist & Museum Shop Mgr., Angela Shippy.
Governing Authority: state; nonprofit. Parent Institution: University Museums, Iowa State University, Ames, IA. Tax-exempt: 501(c)(3).
Art Museum.
Collections: 20th century & contemporary art; works by Christian Petersen.
Research Fields: American regionalism; campus public art.
Facilities: 200-vol. library; 5,060 sq. ft. exhibit space; classroom.
Activities: films; formal education programs for college students; guided tours; lectures; temporary & traveling exhibitions.
Publications: quarterly newsletter, News From University Museums.
Hours & Admission Prices: Mon.-Fri. 11-4. No charge; donations accepted. Closed major holidays; semester breaks. ♿
Attendance: 15,000 (estimated)
Membership: College Student $10; Household $50; Sustained $100; Pacesetter $250; Director's Guild $500; Benefactor $1,000; Patron $2,500; Curator's Associate (Lifetime) $10,000; Curators $15,000.

FARM HOUSE MUSEUM, Farm House Ln., Iowa State University, Ames, IA 50011-0001. Mailing Address: University Museums, Iowa State University, 290 Scheman Bldg., Ames, IA 50011-0001. Tel.: 515-294-7426. Fax: 515-294-3342.
Web Site: www.museums.iastate.edu
Founded: 1974.
Key Personnel: Dir. & Chief Cur., Lynette Pohlman; Collections Mgmt. &

Communications Coord., Allison Juull; Interpretive Specialist, Amanda Hall; Devel Sec., Sue Olson; Educator, Visual Literacy & Learning, Nancy Gebhart; Administrative Specialist & Museum Shop Mgr., Angela Shippy.
Governing Authority: state; nonprofit. Parent Institution: University Museums, Iowa State University. Tax-exempt.
Historic Site: c.1860-1864 The Farm House.
Collections: c.1860-1910 decorative arts; period furnishings.
Research Fields: historical objects; Iowa & Iowa State University history.
Facilities: 4,080 sq. ft. exhibit space.
Activities: guided tours; gallery talks; docent program; loan, permanent, temporary & traveling exhibitions. Annual Event: Haunted Iowa State.
Publications: quarterly newsletter, News From University Museums.
Hours & Admission Prices: Mon.-Fri. 12-4 by appointment only. No charge; donations accepted. Closed university holidays; semester breaks. ♿
Attendance: 6,000 (estimated)
Membership: College Student $10; Household $50; Sustained $100; Pacesetter $250; Director's Guild $500; Benefactor $1,000; Patron $2,500; Curator's Associates (Lifetime) $10,000; Curators $15,000.

OCTAGON CENTER FOR THE ARTS, 427 Douglas Ave., Ames, IA 50010-6281. Tel.: 515-232-5331. Fax: 515-232-5088.
E-mail: gallery@octagonarts.org
Web Site: www.octagonarts.org
Founded: 1966.
Congressional District: 4
Key Personnel: Acting Exec. Dir. & Cur., Heather Johnson; Pres., Mark Peterson; Vice Pres., Alan Johnson; Octogan Shop Mgr., Ruth Wiedemeier; Educ. Dir., Beth Weninger.
Personnel Profile: Full-Time Paid 6; Part-Time Paid 8; Part-Time Volunteers 75; Interns 3.
Governing Authority: nonprofit organization. Tax-exempt: 501(c)(3).
Art Center.
Collections: traditional & contemporary international masks; Feinberg Mask collection.
Research Fields: traditional & contemporary crafts.
Facilities: 150-seat auditorium; educational facilities. Art work for sale.
Activities: guided tours; lectures; concerts; arts festivals; theater; organized education programs; loan, temporary, & traveling exhibitions; exhibitions geared towards children; internships for undergraduate & graduate college students; outreach programming to schools, organizations & agencies. Museum Sponsors: Annual national juried show.
Publications: monthly, The Octagon Center for the Arts Newsletter; exhibition catalogues; quarterly, class schedules.
Hours & Admission Prices: Gallery: Tues.-Fri. 10-5, Sat.-Sun. 1-5. Office: Mon.-Fri. 8-5. Shop: Mon.-Wed. & Fri. Sat. 10-5, Thurs. 10-8. Gallery: no charge; donation suggested. Fees for classes & special events. Closed major holidays. ♿
Attendance: 30,000 (estimated)
Membership: Student $15; Senior Citizen $25; Individual $35; Family $50; Sustaining $75-$200; Founder's Club $300; Sponsorships $300 & up.

Anamosa

ANAMOSA STATE PENITENTIARY MUSEUM, 406 N. High St., Anamosa, IA 52205-1199. Mailing Address: P.O. Box 144, Anamosa, IA 52205-0144. Tel.: 319-462-2386.
E-mail: aspmuseum@mchsi.com
Web Site: www.asphistory.com/museum
Founded: 2001.
Personnel Profile: Part-Time Volunteers 15.
Governing Authority: Tax-exempt.
Penitentiary Museum.
Collections: Iowa's 132 year prison history; prison life; photographs; cell replica; video.
Facilities: Museum-related items for sale.
Activities: video.
Hours & Admission Prices: Memorial Day to Oct. Fri.-Sun. 12-4; other times by appointment. Adults $3; members no charge. ♿
Attendance: 1,700 (accurate)
Membership: Annual $10; Lifetime $125.

GRANT WOOD ART GALLERY, 124 E. Main St., Anamosa, IA 52205-1879. Tel.: 319-462-4267.
E-mail: grantwoodartgallery@grantwoodgallery.org
Web Site: www.grantwoodartgallery.org
Founded: 1973.
Key Personnel: Chm. (V) & Museum Shop Mgr., Jon D. Hatcher.
Personnel Profile: Part-Time Volunteers 25.
Governing Authority: Tax-exempt.
Art Gallery.
Collections: Grant Wood's life & paintings; prints; photography; murals.
Facilities: Museum-related items for sale.
Hours & Admission Prices: Jan.-March Sun. 1-4; April-Dec. Mon.-Sat. 10-4, Sun. 1-4. No charge.

NATIONAL MOTORCYCLE MUSEUM, 200 E. Main St., Anamosa, IA 52205-1806. Mailing Address: P.O. Box 405, Anamosa, IA 52205-0405. Tel.: 319-462-3925. Fax: 319-462-3982.
E-mail: museum@nationalmcmuseum.org
Web Site: www.nationalmcmuseum.org
Founded: 1989.
Governing Authority: nonprofit.
Motorcycle Museum.
Collections: motorcycle industry history; vintage bikes; photographs; Hall of Fame.
Facilities: Museum-related items for sale.
Hours & Admission Prices: April-Oct. Mon.-Sat. 9-5, Sun. 10-4; Nov.-March Mon.-Fri. 9-5, Sat. 10-4, Sun. 11-4. Adults $7, seniors $6; children 12 & under no charge. ♿
Membership: Annual $50; Sustaining $100; Lifetime $500.

Ankeny

ANKENY ART CENTER, 1520 S.W. Ordnance Rd., Ankeny, IA 50023-2510. Tel.: 515-965-0940. Fax: 515-963-1009.
E-mail: ankenyarts@ankenyartcenter.com
Web Site: www.ankenyartcenter.com
Key Personnel: Dir., Barb Vaske.
Governing Authority: nonprofit organization.
Art Center.
Collections: works by Iowa artists.
Activities: classrooms; outdoor events; education programs; special events; summer art camps.
Hours & Admission Prices: Tues.-Wed. & Fri. 9-1, Thurs. 4-7, Sat. 9-12. No charge.

Armstrong

ARMSTRONG HERITAGE MUSEUM, 425 Sixth St., Armstrong, IA 50514. Tel.: 712-868-3669 & 865-3562.
Web Site: www.armstrongiowa.net/libmus.php
History Museum.
Collections: local history & culture.
Hours & Admission Prices: By appointment.

Arnolds Park

ABBIE GARDNER STATE SITE, 34 Monument Dr., Arnolds Park, IA 51331. Mailing Address: P.O. Box 74, Arnolds Park, IA 51331-0074. Tel.: 712-332-7248. Fax: 515-282-0502.
Founded: 1856.
Congressional District: 6
Key Personnel: Dir., Mike Koppert
Historic House Museum: housed in log cabin built in 1856; located on the site of the Spirit Lake Massacre in 1857. Listed on the National Register of Historic Places.
Collections: period furnishings; personal artifacts.
Hours & Admission Prices: Memorial Day to Labor Day daily 12-4; Sept. Sat. 12-4. No charge; donations accepted. ♿
Attendance: 15,000

IOWA GREAT LAKES MARITIME MUSEUM, (M), 243 W. Broadway, Arnolds Park, IA 51331-7779. Mailing Address: P.O. Box 726, Arnolds Park, IA 51331-0726. Tel.: 712-332-5264. Fax: 712-332-7714.
Web Site: www.arnoldspark.com
Founded: 1987.
Key Personnel: Gen. Mgr., Scott Pyle; Cur., Mary Kennedy.
Personnel Profile: Part-Time Paid 1; Part-Time Volunteers 10.
Governing Authority: private; nonprofit organization. Tax-exempt: 501(c)(3).
Maritime Museum.
Collections: wooden boats from the Iowa Great Lakes area of Northwest Iowa; personal artifacts; photographs.
Facilities: 1,850-vol. library; 6,000 sq. ft. exhibit space; 150-seat theater.
Activities: films; formal education programs for adults; guided tours; lectures; temporary exhibitions; theater.
Publications: biannual newsletter, The Steam Whistle.
Hours & Admission Prices: Daily 10am, closing time varies. No charge; donations accepted. Closed Easter; Thanksgiving; Christmas. ♿
Attendance: 75,000 (estimated)
Membership: Captain $35; Rear Admiral $75; Commander $150; Fleet $250; Wish List $1,000.

IOWA ROCK 'N ROLL MUSIC ASSOCIATION MUSEUM, 91 Lake St., Arnolds Park, IA 51331. Mailing Address: P.O. Box 557, Arnolds Park, IA 51331-0557. Tel.: 712-332-6540. Fax: 712-332-7714.
Founded: 1997.
Governing Authority: nonprofit organization.
Music Museum: housed on the site of the Roof Garden Ballroom.
Collections: rock 'n roll history; Iowa music, entertainers, radio stations, ballrooms & promoters; photographs; recording studio.
Hours & Admission Prices: mid-May to mid-Sept. daily 11-7; mid-Sept. to mid-May Tues.-Sat. 12-4. Adults 13 & over $1; IRRMA members and children 12 & under no charge. Closed New Year's Day; Veterans Day; Thanksgiving; Christmas. ♿
Membership: Silver $30; Bronze $50; Gold $100; Platinum $500.

Ashton

DEBOER GROCERY MUSEUM AND LITTLE HOUSE MUSEUM, 320 Third St., Ashton, IA 51232. Tel.: 712-724-6239.
Founded: 1996.
Congressional District: 5
Governing Authority: Parent Institution: Osceola County Historical Society. Tax-exempt.
History Museum.
Collections: original grocery store shelving; fruit & vegetable counters; walk-in meat cooler; scales; early cash register.
Hours & Admission Prices: Memorial Day-Labor Day 1st & 3rd Sun. 10-2; other times by appointment. No charge; donations accepted.
Attendance: 200 (estimated)
Membership: Individual $15; Family $25.

Battle Creek

BATTLE HILL MUSEUM OF NATURAL HISTORY, Hwy. 175 E., Battle Creek, IA 51006. Mailing Address: 231 Ida St., Battle Creek, IA 51006-9439.
Natural History Museum.
Collections: rocks; fossils; shells; dioramas; antlers & horns; skeletons & skulls; wildlife mounts; hides.
Activities: petting zoo; school groups.
Hours & Admission Prices: June-Aug. 1st Sun. of month 1-5, call to confirm; other times by appointment.

Bettendorf

* **FAMILY MUSEUM,** 2900 Learning Campus Dr., Bettendorf, IA 52722-7710. Tel.: 563-344-4106. Fax: 563-344-4164.
E-mail: familymuseum@bettendorf.org
Web Site: www.familymuseum.org
Founded: 1974.
Congressional District: 1
Key Personnel: Dir., Tracey K. Kuehl; Program Mgr., Rachel Demaris; Exhibits Mgr., Tom Stanger; Coord. Group Svcs., Becky Ortner; Coord. Events, Glenn Boyles; Coord. Public Rels., Elly Gerdts; Business Devel. Mgr., Jeff Reiter; Mgr. Guest Svcs. & Museum Shop Mgr., Kathy Brown; Volunteer Coord., Cindy Bales; Dance Coord., Jessica Halfhill.
Personnel Profile: Full-Time Paid 13; Part-Time Paid 12; Part-Time Volunteers 180; Interns 1.
Governing Authority: municipal. Parent Institution: City of Bettendorf. Tax-exempt.
Children's Museum.
Collections: hands-on exhibits.
Facilities: multi-purpose room; meeting room; theatre.
Activities: guided tours; permanent & temporary exhibitions; classes; special events; birthday parties.
Publications: brochure; class catalogs; weekly member e-mail.
Hours & Admission Prices: Memorial Day-Labor Day: Mon.-Sat. 9-5, Sun 12-5; Sept.-May: Mon.-Thurs. 9-8, Fri.-Sat. 9-5, Sun. 12-5. Adults $6, seniors 60 & over $4; discounts to AAM, ASTC & ACM members; children under 2 & members no charge. Closed major holidays. ♿
Attendance: 92,960 (estimated)
Membership: Individual $30; 1 + 1 & Grandparent $60; Family $85; Family Plus $110.

Boone

BOONE COUNTY HISTORICAL CENTER, 602 Story St., Boone, IA 50036-2832. Tel.: 515-432-1907.
E-mail: bchs@opencominc.com
Web Site: www.boonecountyhistory.org
Founded: 1990.
Congressional District: 4
Key Personnel: Dir., Charles Irwin; Chm. (V), Rita Knight; Sec., Janet Tait; Treas., Troy Thompson.
Personnel Profile: Full-Time Paid 1; Part-Time Paid 1; Part-Time Volunteers 35.
Governing Authority: nonprofit. Parent Institution: Boone County Historical Society, 602 Story St., Boone, IA 50036. Tax-exempt: 501(c)(3).
Cultural Center & Museum: housed in 1907 Masonic Temple.
Collections: Boone County & Iowa's natural, military, domestic, agricultural & industrial history.
Research Fields: local history; Iowa history.
Facilities: archival material available to the public; 150-seat auditorium; classrooms; conference & meeting rooms.
Activities: cultural festivals; concerts; docent programs; films; guided tours; formal education program for children; loan, temporary & traveling exhibitions; genealogical & historical research.
Publications: biannual historical journal, Trail Tales; biannual newsletter, History Page.
Hours & Admission Prices: Mon.-Fri. 1-4; other times by appointment. Adults $3; discount to groups; children & members no charge. Closed New Year's Day; Easter; Thanksgiving; Christmas. ♿
Attendance: 5,150 (accurate)
Membership: Individual & Family $35; Business & Organizational $100; Life $600.

IOWA RAILROAD HISTORICAL SOCIETY, 225 10th St., Boone, IA 50036-2004. Mailing Address: P.O. Box 603, Boone, IA 50036-0603. Tel.: 515-432-4249, ext. 10; 800-626-0319. Fax: 515-432-4253.
E-mail: info@bsvrr.com
Web Site: www.scenic-valleyrr.com
Founded: 1983.
Congressional District: 5
Key Personnel: C.E.O., Fenner Stevenson; Chm. (V) & Cur., Loren Karr; Pres. (V), Dean Briley; Financial Dir., Gary Stasko; Museum Shop Mgr., Jim Barkwill.
Personnel Profile: Full-Time Paid 7; Full-Time Volunteers 5; Part-Time Paid 3; Part-Time Volunteers 200.
Governing Authority: private; nonprofit organization. Subsidiary Institution: Boone & Scenic Valley Railroad. Tax-exempt: 501(c)(3).
Historical Railroad Museum.
Collections: full-sized railroad cars & engines; switch keys; photographs; railroad history.
Research Fields: history of railroading in Iowa.
Facilities: 2,000 sq. ft. exhibit space. Railroad-related items for sale.
Activities: train rides; guided tours; participatory & temporary exhibitions. Annual Events: Pufferbilly Days; day out with Thomas event; Pumpkin Trains; Santa Express(TM) Trains.
Publications: quarterly newsletter, Keeping Track.
Hours & Admission Prices: Memorial Day to Oct. Mon.-Fri. 8:30-4:30, Sat.-Sun. 10-6; Nov.-May Mon.-Fri. 8:30-4:30. Adults $16, children $5. Closed New Year's Day; Thanksgiving; Christmas. ♿
Attendance: 50,799 (accurate)
Membership: Individual $25; Bronze $125; Silver $250; Gold $500; Platinum $1,000.

KATE SHELLEY RAILROAD MUSEUM, 1198 - 232nd St., Boone, IA 50036-7118. Mailing Address: 602 Story St., Boone, IA 50036-2832. Tel.: 515-432-1907.
E-mail: bchs@opencominc.com
Web Site: www.boonecountyhistory.org
Founded: 1976.
Congressional District: 4
Key Personnel: Dir., Charles W. Irwin; Chm. (V), Rita Knight; Treas., Troy Thompson; Sec., Janet Tait.
Personnel Profile: Full-Time Paid 1; Part-Time Paid 1.
Governing Authority: nonprofit. Parent Institution: Boone County Historical Society, 602 Story St., Boone 50036. Tax-exempt: 501(c)(3).
Historic Site & Railroad Depot.
Collections: artifacts relating to railroad heroine Kate Shelley's life; recreated 19th century railroad passenger station; rail passenger car on adjacent track; working telegraph system; railroad memorabilia.
Facilities: small theater in the railroad passenger car.
Activities: guided tours; video presentation on the Kate Shelly story.
Publications: biannual journal, Trail Tales; biannual newsletter, History Page.
Hours & Admission Prices: Call for hours. No charge for general admission; bus tours: $1 per person.
Attendance: 2,000 (accurate)
Membership: Boone County Historical Society $35; Business & Organizational $100; Life $600.

MAMIE DOUD EISENHOWER BIRTHPLACE, 709 Carroll St., Boone, IA 50036. Mailing Address: 602 Story St., Boone, IA 50036-2832. Tel.: 515-432-1896; 1907.
E-mail: bchs@opencominc.com
Web Site: mamiesbirthplace.homestead.com
Founded: 1970.
Congressional District: 5
Key Personnel: Exec. Dir., Charles Irwin.
Personnel Profile: Full-Time Paid 1; Part-Time Paid 2; Part-Time Volunteers 50.
Governing Authority: nonprofit organization. Tax-exempt: 501(c)(3).
Historic House: c.1890 Mamie Doud Eisenhower birthplace.
Collections: chronology of Mamie Doud Eisenhower in memorabilia; photographs; newspapers; campaign & inaugural items; gifts from Mrs. Eisenhower; Doud & Carlson family history; manuscripts; period furniture & furnishings; books; video & audio tapes; magazines; political cartoons; awards to Mamie Doud Eisenhower. Historic Automobiles: 1962 Plymouth Valiant once owned by Mamie Doud Eisenhower; 1949 Chrysler Windsor.
Research Fields: Doud, Carlson & Eisenhower family history; Boone County history.
Facilities: 2,000-vol. library of books, magazines, newspapers, photographs, papers & letters of Mamie Doud Eisenhower, Dwight D. Eisenhower & their families available for research on premises & by special arrangement; reading room. Books, publications & other museum-related articles for sale.
Activities: guided tours; lectures; docent program or council; loan, permanent & temporary exhibitions; slide programs.
Publications: brochures; books; newspapers; newsletter.
Hours & Admission Prices: Mon.-Fri. 1-5; other times by appointment. Adults $4, children 6-17 $1; discounts to AAM & ICOM members; children under 6, members, museum professionals & researchers no charge.
Attendance: 6,000 (estimated)
Membership: Single $15; Couple $30; Sponsor $50; Patron $100; Sustaining $500-$1,000.

Burlington

ART GUILD OF BURLINGTON, INC., 620 Washington St., Burlington, IA 52601-5145. Tel.: 319-754-8069. Fax: 319-754-4731.
E-mail: arts4living@aol.com
Web Site: www.artguildofburlington.org
Founded: 1966.
Congressional District: 3
Key Personnel: Exec. Dir., Ann Distelhorst; Education, Lillian Rubin.
Personnel Profile: Part-Time Paid 2; Interns 1.
Governing Authority: private; nonprofit organization. Tax-exempt: 501(c)(3).
Art Gallery.
Collections: fine art & crafts by regional artists.
Facilities: library; classroom; 175-seat auditorium; 2,400 sq. ft. exhibit space; sculpture garden. Museum-related items for sale.
Activities: arts festivals; concerts; dance recitals; films; formal education program; guided tours; hobby workshops; lectures; temporary, loan & traveling exhibitions. Annual Events: member exhibit; Snake Alley Art Fair in June.
Publications: monthly newsletter; annual report.
Hours & Admission Prices: No charge; donations accepted. ♿
Attendance: 10,000 (estimated)
Membership: Student $15; Individual $30; Family $50; Sustaining $100; Patron $250.

HAWKEYE LOG CABIN, 2915 S. Main St., Crapo Park, Burlington, IA 52601-5117. Mailing Address: c/o Des Moines County Historical Society, 501 N. Fourth St., Burlington, IA 52601. Tel.: 319-753-5880.
E-mail: dmcohist@interl.net
Founded: 1971.
Congressional District: 1
Key Personnel: Chm. (V), Randy Bloomberg; Pres. (V), Judy Johnson; Treas., Terri Dowell; Exec. Sec., Debra Olson; Museum Shop Mgr., Mary Krohlow.
Personnel Profile: Part-Time Paid 2; Part-Time Volunteers 25.
Governing Authority: nonprofit. Parent Institution: Des Moines Co. Historical Society. Branch Museums: Phelps House; The Apple Trees Museum. Tax-exempt: 509(A)(54); 509(A)(87).
History Museum; Historic House: 1909 log cabin.
Collections: pioneer tools & furnishings.
Facilities: Gift items for sale.
Activities: guided tours.
Publications: monthly newsletter; annual report; yearbook.
Hours & Admission Prices: May-Sept. Sat.-Sun. 1:30-4:30. Admission $2 for special arranged tours; call 319-753-5981. No charge; donations accepted. ♿
Attendance: 1,654 (accurate)
Membership: Student $2; Individual $10; Sustaining $20; Business, Professional & Patron $50.

PHELPS HOUSE, 521 Columbia, Burlington, IA 52601-5117. Tel.: 319-753-5880.
E-mail: dmchs.jhunt@yahoo.com
Founded: 1974.
Congressional District: 1
Key Personnel: Pres. (V), Judy Johnson; 1st Vice Pres., Martha Wilson; 2nd Vice Pres., Lyle Magneson; Phelps House Chm., Barb Bonnett; Treas., Terri Dowell; Publications & Public Rels. Dir., Debra Olson; Museum Shop Mgr., Mary Krohlow.
Personnel Profile: Part-Time Paid 2; Part-Time Volunteers 20.
Governing Authority: nonprofit. Parent Institution: Des Moines County Historical Society. Branch Museums: Log Cabin Museum; The Des Moines County Heritage Center, 501 N. 4th St., Burlington, IA. Tax-exempt: 504(A)(54); 504(A)(87).
Historical Preservation of Historic House: 1851 Victorian Mansion.
Collections: period furniture & furnishings; medical museum artifacts.
Facilities: Museum-related items for sale.
Activities: group guided tours by appointment. Annual Event: Victorian Christmas Open House in December.
Publications: Membership/Program Yearbook; monthly newsletter; annual report; town meeting publicity.
Hours & Admission Prices: May-Oct. Sat.-Sun. 1:30-4:30; group tours by appointment. Adults $3; members and children 14 & under no charge.
Attendance: 754 (accurate)
Membership: Individual $15; Family & Grandparents $30; Sponsor $50; Benefactor $100; Sho Quo Quon Society $500; Grimes-Saller Society $1,000. Corporate: Contributing $50; Supporting $75; Sustaining $100.

Burr Oak

LAURA INGALLS WILDER PARK & MUSEUM, INC., 3603 236th Ave., Burr Oak, IA 52101-7889. Tel.: 563-735-5916. Fax: 563-735-5464.
E-mail: museum@lauraingallswilder.us
Web Site: www.lauraingallswilder.us
Founded: 1976.
Congressional District: 3
Key Personnel: Dir. & Museum Shop Mgr., Steve Luse; Pres. Bd., Kristina Falck; Vice Pres., Michelle Bloom; Treas., Carol Thumberg.
Personnel Profile: Part-Time Paid 7; Part-Time Volunteers 6.
Governing Authority: nonprofit organization. Tax-exempt: 501(c)(3).
Park & Museum.
Collections: restored hotel; furniture of the 1800 period; Laura Ingalls Wilder's personal artifacts; 2 historic buildings.
Facilities: picnic shelter.
Activities: guided tours; hands-on activities; educational programming.
Publications: book, Laura Ingalls Wilder: The Iowa Story.
Hours & Admission Prices: April-May & Sept.-Oct. Tues.-Sat. 10-4, Sun. 12-4; Memorial Day to Labor Day Mon.-Sat 9-5, Sun. 12-4. Adult $7, children 6-17 $5; members no charge. ♿
Attendance: 8,000 (accurate)
Membership: Half Pint $20; Trailblazer $30; Family $50; Settler $100; Homesteader $200; Pioneer $350.

Cedar Falls

CEDAR FALLS HISTORICAL SOCIETY, 308 W. 3rd St., Cedar Falls, IA 50613-2745. Tel.: 319-266-5149. Fax: 319-268-1812.
E-mail: cfhistory@cfu.net
Web Site: www.cedarfallshistorical.org
Founded: 1962.
Congressional District: 1
Key Personnel: Exec. Dir., Jeffrey J. Kurtz.
Personnel Profile: Full-Time Paid 2; Part-Time Paid 2; Part-Time Volunteers 275; Interns 1.
Governing Authority: society. Branch Museums: Victorian Home & Carriage House Museum, 308 W. 3rd St., Cedar Falls, IA; Ice House & Little Red School House, First & Clay Sts., Cedar Falls, IA 50613; Wyth House & Viking Pump Museum, 303 Franklin, Cedar Falls, IA 50613; William J. Lenoir Model Train Collection, 308 W. 3rd St., Cedar Falls, IA; Behrens-Rapp Service Station Museum, 1st & Clay Sts., Cedar Falls, IA. Tax-exempt.
Local History Museums.
Collections: 50 year file of Cedar Falls Record newspaper; clothes; taped interviews; local historic photographs; aviator John H. Livingston trophies & files; novelist Bess Streeter Aldrich books; ice industry; local archives; William Lenoir model trains; agriculture-related items; genealogy & cemetery records; horse drawn transportation artifacts.

Research Fields: local history; natural ice industry; late 19th-century agriculture; art deco.
Facilities: reading room.
Activities: guided tours; films; gallery talks; permanent & temporary exhibitions; open houses; local history slide presentations; newspaper column. Museum Sponsors: George Wyth House special events.
Publications: quarterly newsletter.
Hours & Admission Prices: Victorian Home: Wed.-Sat. 10-4, Sun. 1-4. Little Red School & Ice House Museum: May-Oct. Wed. & Sat.-Sun. 2-4:30. George Wyth House: May-Oct. 3rd Sat-Sun. of month 12-4; other times by appointment. No charge; donations accepted. ♿
Attendance: 17,944 (accurate)
Membership: Individual $20; Family $45; Business or Organization $75.

HARTMAN RESERVE NATURE CENTER, 657 Reserve Dr., Cedar Falls, IA 50613-4723. Tel.: 319-277-2187. Fax: 319-277-4420.
E-mail: hartmanreserve@co.black-hawk.ia.us
Web Site: www.hartmanreserve.org
Founded: 1976.
Congressional District: 3
Key Personnel: Dir., Ed Gruenwald; Pres., Greg Greco; Program Coord., Chris Anderson; Dir. Devel., Anne Duncan.
Personnel Profile: Full-Time Paid 6; Part-Time Paid 3; Interns 4.
Governing Authority: county. Black Hawk County Conservation Board, 2410 W. Lone Tree Rd., Cedar Falls, IA 50613. Tax-exempt.
Nature Center.
Collections: insects; mammal skins; animal parts; mounted birds & mammals; amphibians.
Research Fields: ecological monitoring of woodland.
Facilities: 150-vol. library on nature study, environmental education & nature-related periodicals; nature & conservation center; classroom; nature trails.
Activities: guided tours; lectures; organized education programs; school field trips; in-service training; teacher workshops; special programs for organizations & other groups; temporary exhibitions.
Publications: quarterly newsletter; annual informational brochures.
Hours & Admission Prices: March-May & Sept.-Oct. Mon.-Fri. 8-4:30, Sun. 1-5; June-Aug. & Nov.-Feb. Mon.-Fri. 8-4:30. No charge; donations accepted. Fees charged for specific programs. ♿
Attendance: 51,000 (estimated)
Membership: Student $10; Senior $20; Individual $25; Family $35; Contributor $50; Developer $100; Sustainer $250; Champion $500; Founder $1,000; Life $2,500.

ICE HOUSE MUSEUM, Franklin St., (at W. 1st St.), Cedar Falls, IA 50613. Mailing Address: Cedar Falls Historical Society, 308 W. 3rd St., Cedar Falls, IA 50613-2745. Tel.: 319-266-5149.
Key Personnel: Exec. Dir., Jeff Kurtz
History Museum: listed on the National Register of Historic Places.
Collections: cutting, harvesting, storing, selling & uses of natural ice; tools & cutting implements; photographs; ice-boxes; ice wagon; horse drawn vehicles.
Hours & Admission Prices: May-Sept. Wed. & Sat.-Sun. 2-4:30. No charge; donations accepted. ♿
Attendance: 6,340 (accurate)

JAMES & MERYL HEARST CENTER FOR THE ARTS AND HEARST SCULPTURE GARDEN, (M), 304 W. Seerley Blvd., Cedar Falls, IA 50613-4050. Tel.: 319-273-8641. Fax: 319-273-8659.
E-mail: mary.huber@cedarfalls.com
Web Site: www.hearstartscenter.com
Founded: 1989.
Congressional District: 2
Key Personnel: Pres. Bd. (V), Santha Kerns; Dir., Mary Huber; Education Coord., Todd Kern; Cur., Emily Drennan; Svcs. Coord., Gail LeFlore; Devel. Coord., Vicki Simpson; Museum Shop Mgr., Abby Haigh.
Personnel Profile: Full-Time Paid 2; Part-Time Paid 16; Part-Time Volunteers 74; Interns 3.
Governing Authority: municipal; nonprofit. Parent Institution: City of Cedar Falls. Subsidiary Institution: Friends of the Hearst. Tax-exempt.
Art Museum, Sculpture Garden & Community Public Art Collections.
Collections: two & three dimensional works by regional artists; book illustrations by Gary Kelley; special collections; public art; sculpture garden; children's book illustration.
Major Exhibits: Selections from the Permanent Collection, 3/13/10-3/28/10; Developing Expressions: Student Art from Cedar Falls Community Schools, 4/11/10-5/9/10; Prints from the Permanent Collection, 5/20/10-7/11/10; Hearst Competitive Exhibit, 5/20/10-8/22/10; Tom Peterson's Collection, 7/11/10-9/3/10; Society of Illustrators (T), 9/4/10-11/21/10; The Legend of Sleepy Hollow, 10/8/10-11/28/10; Children's Book Illustrators: Society of Illustrators, 10/8/10-11/28/10; The River Series, 12/8/10-1/30/11.
Research Fields: regional artists.
Facilities: auditorium; 3 classrooms; meeting rooms; sculpture garden.
Activities: guided tours; lectures; concerts; dance recitals; arts festival; study clubs; organized education programs; loan exhibitions; internship; temporary & traveling exhibitions. Museum Sponsors: activities at Sturgis Falls Festival; College Hill Art Festival; Cedar Trails Festival & Main Street Art Fair and Festival.
Publications: exhibition catalogs; quarterly brochure; volume of poetry, Selected Poems by James Hearst; volume of photographs, Platinum Scenes: Photographs by Irving Herman; The Complete Poetry of James Hearst.
Hours & Admission Prices: Tues. & Thurs. 8-9, Wed. & Fri. 8-5, Sat.-Sun. 1-4. No charge; donations accepted. Closed New Year's Day; Easter weekend; Memorial Day; Independence Day; Labor Day weekend; Thanksgiving weekend; Christmas. ♿
Attendance: 56,200 (estimated)
Membership: Student & Senior $20; Individual $25; Family $35; Supporter $50; Sponsor $100; Benefactor $500; Collector $1,000.

MARSHALL CENTER SCHOOL, 3219 Hudson Rd., Cedar Falls, IA 50614-0001. Tel.: 319-273-2188. Fax: 319-273-6924.
E-mail: doris.mitchell@uni.edu
Web Site: www.uni.edu/museum/mcs/index.html
Key Personnel: Dir., Dr. Sue Grosboll
Historic Building Museum.
Collections: period furnishings & artifacts.
Hours & Admission Prices: Fri.-Sat. 2-4. No charge.

UNI GALLERY OF ART, UNIVERSITY OF NORTHERN IOWA, (M), 1601 W. 27th St., 104 Kamerick Art Bldg., Cedar Falls, IA 50614-0362. Tel.: 319-273-3095. Fax: 319-273-7333.
E-mail: galleryofart@uni.edu
Web Site: www.uni.edu/artdept/gallery/
Founded: 1978.
Congressional District: 3
Key Personnel: Head Dept. Art, Jeffery Byrd; Dir. Gallery, Darrell Taylor.
Personnel Profile: Full-Time Paid 1; Part-Time Paid 11; Interns 1.
Governing Authority: university. Parent Institution: University of Northern Iowa, Cedar Falls, IA 50614. Tax-exempt: 170(b)(1)(A).
Art Gallery.
Collections: 20th century American & European; contemporary artists.
Research Fields: 20th century European & American Art.
Activities: guided tours; lectures; films; gallery talks; formally organized education programs for children & undergraduate college students; permanent, temporary & traveling exhibitions.
Publications: Contemporary Chicago Painters; De Kooning 1969-78; Standards by Allan Kaprow; Reuben Nakian; Leda & The Swan; Art for Public Spaces; University of Northern Iowa Dept. Art Faculty Exhibition-1982; 75th Anniversary Alumni Invitational-1982; 1985 Art Faculty Exhibition; The Contemporary American Potter: Recent Vessels; Jose de Creeft 1884-1982, works from the Collection of Nina de Creeft Ward & William de Creeft; David Delafield: A Retrospective of An Iowa Artist; Philip Pearlstein Painting to Watercolors; Art Nouveau Glass & Pottery from the Syracuse University Art Collections; Juane Quick-to-see Smith & George Longfish: Personal Symbols; Walter Dusenbery: Classical Echoes; Born In Iowa: 29 Artists; John Page: A Retrospective Exhibition in Three Parts; Magic Silver Catalog; exhibition catalogs, A Question of Faith (juror: Eleanor Heartney), Residue of Silence (essay: Matthew Baigell), Figured Ceramics; Rie Hachiyanagi: A Retrospective; David Delafield Retrospective; Mary Snyder Behrens: New Work; Transformations in the Nervepool: The Rituals & Zoacodes of Ebon Fisher; Creating Our World: Russian/American Children's Art Exhibition; Justice Illuminated: The Art of Arthur Szyk; Quiet Village: Recent Works by Michael Krueger and Jenny Schmid; George Longfish - A Retrospective; Dean and Gunnar Schwarz: Pottery Form and Inherent Expression; Marguerite Wilderhain; World Views: Photographs by Tina Barney, Linda Conner, Andrew Moore, and JoAnn Verburg; New Polyphonies: Contemporary Art from Portugal; Highlights from the Collection; Body Prop - New Works by Nick Dong, Erica Duffy, Lauren Kalman, and Deb Todd Wheeler; Frje Echeverria: Four Decades of Working Beside Students; Love Me or Die: Cat Chow.
Hours & Admission Prices: Academic Year: Mon.-Thurs. 9-9, Fri. 9-5, Sat.-Sun. 12-5; Summer: Mon.-Fri. 9:30-4:30, Sat.-Sun. 12:30-4:30. No charge. Closed holidays; when classes are not in session. ♿
Attendance: 12,000 (accurate)

*** UNIVERSITY OF NORTHERN IOWA MUSEUMS & COLLECTIONS, (M),** 3219 Hudson Rd., Cedar Falls, IA 50614-0199. Mailing Address: Univ. of Northern Iowa, Cedar Falls, IA 50614-0199. Tel.: 319-273-2188. Fax: 319-273-6924.
E-mail: doris.mitchell@uni.edu
Web Site: www.uni.edu/museum
Founded: 1892.
Congressional District: 3
Key Personnel: Dir., Dr. Sue Grosboll; Collections Mgr., Kim Taylor; Public Affairs Coord., Jori Wade-Booth; Education Coord., Diane Schupbach; Exhibit Preparator, Connie Svoboda; Museum Shop Mgr., Barb MacDonald.
Personnel Profile: Full-Time Paid 3; Part-Time Paid 14; Part-Time Volunteers 40; Interns 20.
Governing Authority: state. Parent Institution: University of Northern Iowa. Tax-exempt: 170(c)(1).
Natural & Human History Museum.
Collections: minerals; rocks; fossils; mammals; birds; reptiles; fish; marine invertebrates; ethnological pieces from Africa, Asia & the Americas; university & education history. Historic Building: Historic School House.
Major Exhibits: Coffee: The World In Your Cup, 2/10-5/10; Playing Around: Games Across the Globe, 6/10-8/10; Art & Artifact, 9/10-12/10.
Facilities: 1,450-vol. library; meeting room.
Activities: permanent & temporary exhibitions; hands-on activities; guided tours; lectures; films; workshops; club meetings; internships; field trips; research; traveling trunks.
Publications: newsletter.
Hours & Admission Prices: University Museum: Mon.-Fri. 9-4:30, Sat. 1-4. Marshall Center School: Fri.-Sat. 2-4; other times by appointment. No charge; donations accepted. Closed holidays. ♿
Attendance: 57,000
Membership: Student $20; Explorer $35; Naturalist $60; Researcher $125; Conservator $250; Curator $500; Director $1,000.

Cedar Rapids

AFRICAN AMERICAN HISTORICAL MUSEUM & CULTURAL CENTER OF IOWA, (M), 55 12th Ave., S.E., Cedar Rapids, IA 52401-2202. Mailing Address: P.O. Box 1626, Cedar Rapids, IA 52406-1626. Tel.: 319-862-2101. Fax: 319-862-2105.
E-mail: information@blackiowa.org
Web Site: blackiowa.org
Founded: 1994.
Key Personnel: Exec. Dir., Thomas Moore.
Personnel Profile: Full-Time Paid 10; Part-Time Paid 3; Interns 1.
Governing Authority: private; nonprofit organization. Tax-exempt: 501(c)(3).
History Museum.
Collections: African American history of Iowa.
Facilities: library; educational facilities; 4,200 sq. ft. exhibit space; celebration hall. Museum-related items for sale.
Activities: docent program; formal education programs; guided tours; lectures; loan, participatory, temporary & traveling exhibitions. Annual Events: Juneteenth; golf outings; banquet; Kwanza.
Publications: quarterly newsletter, Griot.
Hours & Admission Prices: Mon.-Sat. 10-4. Adults $4, children $2.50; discounts to groups; members no charge. Closed New Year's Day; Martin Luther King Jr. Day; Memorial Day; Independence Day; Labor Day; Thanksgiving; Christmas. ♿
Attendance: 10,772 (accurate)
Membership: Youth $5; Individual $25; Family $50; Golden $100; Century $200; Corporate $250 & up.

BRUCEMORE, 2160 Linden Dr., S.E., Cedar Rapids, IA 52403-1748. Tel.: 319-362-7375. Fax: 319-362-9481.
E-mail: mail@brucemore.org
Web Site: www.brucemore.org
Founded: 1981.
Congressional District: 1
Key Personnel: Exec. Dir., James Kern; Pres. (V), Mark Long; Bldg. & Grounds Supt., Roger Johnson; Asst. Dir., Maura Pilcher; Gardener, Deb Engmark; Administrative Asst., Kandi Allison; Museum Shop Mgr., Gayle Stone; Asst. Gardener, David Morton; Collections Care Technician & Maintenance Technician, Tara Marsh; Accountant, Kelly Costello.
Personnel Profile: Full-Time Paid 12; Part-Time Paid 8; Part-Time Volunteers 240; Interns 4.
Governing Authority: nonprofit organization. Parent Institution: National Trust for Historic Preservation, 1785 Massachusetts Ave., N.W., Washington, DC 20036. Tax-exempt: 501(c)(3).
Historic Site & Community Cultural Center: housed in a 21-room Queen Anne-style Mansion; 26 acre historic estate; c.1886.
Collections: furnishings, archives, archaeology, historic structures.
Research Fields: family history; Midwest social history.
Facilities: 3,000-vol. library; archives; formal gardens; orchard.
Activities: guided tours; lectures; concerts; docent program or council; outdoor theater. Museum Sponsors: Garden & Landscape Show; Opera.
Publications: quarterly newsletter.
Hours & Admission Prices: Tours: March-Dec. Tues.-Sat. 10-3, Sun. 12-3; other times by appointment. Adults $7, students $3; members, Brucemore & National Trust members no charge. ♿
Attendance: 42,350 (accurate)
Membership: Individual $35; Grandparent & Household $50; Patron $100; Donor $250; Benefactor $500; Trustees Club $1,000; The George and Irene Douglas Circle $2,500; The Howard and Margaret Hall Heritage Club $5,000.

THE CARL & MARY KOEHLER HISTORY CENTER, 615 First Ave., SE, Cedar Rapids, IA 52401-1315. Tel.: 319-362-1501. Fax: 319-362-6790.
E-mail: history@historycenter.org
Web Site: www.historycenter.org
Formerly: Linn County Historical Society and Museum
Founded: 1969.
Congressional District: 1
Key Personnel: Exec. Dir., Melanie Alexander; Pres., Marv Houg; Asst. to Dir., Beth Miller.
Personnel Profile: Full-Time Paid 1; Full-Time Volunteers 1; Part-Time Paid 2; Part-Time Volunteers 140.
Governing Authority: private; nonprofit organization. Tax-exempt: 501(c)(3).
History Museum.
Collections: Linn County, Iowa history from prehistoric-present; history of Cedar Rapids.
Research Fields: business, social & cultural history of Linn County, prehistoric-1859; history of Cedar Rapids during the 1865 period & at the turn-of-the century, 1960.
Facilities: library; archives; research facilities; 5,000 sq. ft. exhibit space.
Activities: guided tours; adult & children's programs.
Publications: quarterly newsletter, Linn County Time Lines.
Hours & Admission Prices: Tues., Thurs. & Sat. 10-4. Adults $3, students $1; discounts to AAM & ICOM members; members no charge. Closed New Year's Day; Memorial Day; Labor Day; Thanksgiving; Christmas. ♿
Attendance: 18,000 (accurate)
Membership: Individual $25; Family $50; Contributor $100-$499; Benefactor $500 & up.

*** CEDAR RAPIDS MUSEUM OF ART, (M),** 410 Third Ave, S.E., Cedar Rapids, IA 52401-1620. Tel.: 319-366-7503. Fax: 319-366-4111.
E-mail: info@crma.org
Web Site: www.crma.org
Founded: 1905.
Congressional District: 2
Key Personnel: Exec. Dir., Terence Pitts; Devel., Kelly Leusch; C.F.O. & Business Mgr., Deanna Clemens Pedersen; Registrar, Teri Van Dorston; Preparator, Judy Frauenholtz; Cur., Sean Ulmer; Coord. Communications, Kristan Hellige; Education Coord., Andrea Jilovec; Special Events Coord., Beth Roof; Bldg. Supvr., Carlis Faurot; Museum Shop Mgr., Casey Dunagan; Security, Tom Kluth; Security, Robin Hines.
Personnel Profile: Full-Time Paid 10; Part-Time Paid 10; Part-Time Volunteers 55; Interns 5.
Governing Authority: nonprofit corporation. Tax-exempt: 501(c)(3).
Art Museum.
Collections: 20th century modern and regionalist paintings; works by Grant Wood, Marvin Cone, James Swann, Malvina Hoffman, Bertha Jaques, Mauricio Lasansky; 19th & 20th century sculpture, paintings, prints, photographs; ancient Roman portrait busts.
Major Exhibits: Norman Rockwell: Fact & Fiction, 11/09-1/10; Less is More: The Vogel Collection, 1/10-5/10; From Monet to Picasso: The Riley Collection, 5/10-9/10.
Research Fields: local regionalist artists.
Facilities: classrooms; auditorium.
Activities: guided tours; lectures; films; gallery talks; concerts; Grant Wood Studio tours; workshops; temporary & traveling exhibitions.
Publications: newsletters; catalogs; selected exhibitions.
Hours & Admission Prices: Tues.-Wed. & Fri.-Sat. 10-4, Thurs. 10-8, Sun. 12-4. Adults $5, students & senior citizens $4; discounts to AAM & AAA members; children 18 & under, members & North American Reciprocal Museum Program members no charge. Closed national holidays. ♿
Attendance: 55,000 (estimated)
Membership: Student, Educator & Senior Citizen $30; Individual & Senior Couple $40; Family $60; Patron $125; Benefactor $250; Conewood Society $500; Turner Society $1,000 & up.

COE COLLEGE ART GALLERIES, 1220 1st Ave., N.E., Cedar Rapids, IA 52402-5092. Tel.: 319-399-8647. Fax: 319-399-8557.
Key Personnel: Dir., Mariah Dekkenger
Art Gallery.
Collections: paintings; photographs; sculpture.
Hours & Admission Prices: Daily 3-5. No charge.

IOWA MASONIC LIBRARY AND MUSEUM, 813 1st Ave., S.E., Cedar Rapids, IA 52402-5001. Mailing Address: P.O. Box 279, Cedar Rapids, IA 52406-0279. Tel.: 319-365-1438. Fax: 319-365-1439.
E-mail: librarian@gl-iowa.org
Web Site: www.gl-iowa.org
Founded: 1845.
Congressional District: 1
Key Personnel: Grand Sec. & Librarian, William R. Crawford; Asst. Librarian, William R. Kreuger.
Personnel Profile: Full-Time Paid 1; Part-Time Volunteers 10.
Governing Authority: nonprofit organization. Affiliated with Grand Lodge of Iowa, A.F. & A.M., The Free Masons' Lodges in Iowa. Tax-exempt.
Library & History Museum.
Collections: Masonic collection; Swab collection; manuscripts.
Research Fields: Free masonry; Iowa history; religion.
Facilities: 100,000-vol. library of Masonic history, Iowa history, biography, poetry & literature, Burnisiana & Lincolniana; microfilms of Cedar Rapids newspapers available for inter-library loan; reading room.
Activities: guided tours; lectures; films; permanent exhibitions.
Publications: Grand Lodge Bulletin.
Hours & Admission Prices: Mon.-Fri. 8-12 & 1-5. No charge; donations accepted. Closed national holidays.
Attendance: 1,300 (accurate)

SCIENCE STATION, 427 1st St., S.E., Cedar Rapids, IA 52401-1808. Mailing Address: Lindale Mall, 444 First Ave., NE, Cedar Rapids, IA 52402. Tel.: 319-363-4629. Fax: 319-366-4590.
E-mail: john@sciencestation.org
Web Site: www.sciencestation.org
Founded: 1986.
Congressional District: 1
Key Personnel: Exec. Dir., John Swanson; Pres. (V), Todd Bergen; Education Coord., Stacey Brooks; Business Mgr., Terri Breheny.
Personnel Profile: Full-Time Paid 9; Part-Time Paid 20; Part-Time Volunteers 50.
Governing Authority: nonprofit organization. Tax-exempt: 501(c)(3).
Science Museum: housed in c.1917 Fire Station building.
Collections: hands-on science exhibits emphasizing light & perception, sound, motion & energy.
Facilities: classrooms; IMAX theater. Science kits & laboratory supplies for sale.
Activities: films; organized education programs; participatory & traveling exhibitions.
Hours & Admission Prices: Temporarily located at Lindale Mall, 4444 First Ave., NE, Cedar Rapids, IA. June-Aug 30. Mon.-Sat. 10-5, Sun. 12-5; Aug. 31-May Tues.-Sat. 10-5, Sun. 12-5. Family $10, adults & preschoolers $3; members no charge. Closed major holidays. ♿
Attendance: 90,000 (accurate)
Membership: Dual $60; Family $80.

Charles City

FLOYD COUNTY HISTORICAL MUSEUM, (M), 500 Gilbert St., Charles City, IA 50616-2738. Tel.: 641-228-1099. Fax: 641-228-1157.
E-mail: fchs@fiai.net
Web Site: www.floydcountymuseum.org
Founded: 1961.
Congressional District: 2
Key Personnel: Co-Pres. (V), Jody Flint; Co-Pres. (V), Art White; Dir., Mary Ann Townsend; Office Asst. & Receptionist, Elaine Mead.
Personnel Profile: Full-Time Paid 1; Part-Time Paid 2; Part-Time Volunteers 20.
Governing Authority: society; board of trustees. Parent Institution: Floyd County Historical Society. Tax-exempt.
History Museum.
Collections: archaeology; medical; pharmacology; military; 1850-1900 period rooms; model railroad club; quilts; archives; Hart-Parr, Oliver & White tractors; horse drawn conveyances; 1910 Cretors Popcorn Wagon; Salsbury's Veterinary Laboratories; 1856 Mutchlar log cabin; 1873 Legel's Drugstore.
Research Fields: Hart-Parr & Oliver Tractor company archives; agricultural equipment; Carrie Lane Chapman Catt; Floyd County history.
Facilities: library of 1858-1937 newspaper files, documents & history books available for use on premises. Museum-related items for sale.
Activities: guided & unguided tours; films; permanent exhibitions; short term exhibits.
Publications: quarterly newsletter, Floyd County Heritage; Hart-Parr, Oliver & White Farm Equipment manuals.
Hours & Admission Prices: June-Aug. Mon.-Fri. 9-4:30, Sat.-Sun. 1-4; Sept.-May Mon.-Fri. 9-4:30. Adults $4, children 10-18 $2; members & children under 10 no charge. Closed New Year's Day; Thanksgiving; Christmas. ♿
Attendance: 5,500 (accurate)
Membership: Single $10; Family $20.

Cherokee

* **SANFORD MUSEUM AND PLANETARIUM, (M),** 117 E. Willow St., Cherokee, IA 51012-1854. Tel.: 712-225-3922. Fax: 712-225-0446.
E-mail: sanfordmuseum@iowatelecom.net
Web Site: sanfordmuseum.org
Founded: 1951.
Congressional District: 6
Key Personnel: Dir., Linda Burkhart; Asst. Dir., Michele Deiber Kumm; Educator & Museum Shop Manager, Kerisa Pingel; Cur. Archaeology, Jason Titcomb.
Personnel Profile: Full-Time Paid 4; Part-Time Paid 4.
Governing Authority: Tiel Sanford Memorial Fund. Tax-exempt: 501(c)(3).
General Museum.
Collections: archaeology; history; geology; paleontology; zoology; ethnology; archives.
Research Fields: archaeology; history; paleontology.
Facilities: 5,000-vol. library of research materials in archaeology, geology & general works available for inter-library loan & on request; reading room. Reproductions, books, rocks, fossils, shells & collecting equipment for sale.
Activities: guided tours; lectures; films; gallery talks; drama; formally organized education programs; inter-museum loan, permanent, temporary & traveling exhibitions; planetarium demonstrations; monthly astronomy night programs (observation of night sky, weather permitting); monthly art displays; annual archaeology field school.
Publications: newsletter, Northwest Chapter Iowa Archaeological Society.
Hours & Admission Prices: Museum: Mon.-Fri. 9-5, Sat.-Sun. 12-5. No charge. Planetarium programs: by appointment or last Sun. of month 2 p.m. Closed major holidays. ♿
Attendance: 20,000 (estimated)
Membership: Sanford Museum Association Membership: Contributing $10; Sustaining $25; Associate $50; Patron $100.

Clarion

4-H SCHOOLHOUSE MUSEUM, Central Ave. W., Clarion, IA 50525. Tel.: 515-532-3453. Fax: 515-532-2511.
E-mail: clchamb@goldfieldaccess.net
Web Site: www.clarion-iowa.com
Founded: 1955.
Congressional District: 6
Key Personnel: Chm. (V), Yvonne Stevens.
Governing Authority: municipal; nonprofit organization. Parent Institution: City of Clarion. Subsidiary Institution: 4-H Museum.
History Museum: birthplace of the 4-H emblem.
Collections: 4-H memorabilia; history of 4-H movement; early 1900s school artifacts; clothing.
Facilities: 225-vol. library.
Activities: guided tours.
Hours & Admission Prices: June-Aug. Tues. & Thurs. 1-4, Sat. 9-12; other times by appointment. No charge; donations accepted.
Attendance: 1,200 (accurate)

HEARTLAND MUSEUM, Hwy. 3 W. & 9th St., S.W., Clarion, IA 50525. Mailing Address: P.O. Box 652, Clarion, IA 50525-0652. Tel.: 515-602-6000.
Web Site: www.heartlandmuseum.org
Founded: 1999.
Key Personnel: Pres. (V), George Boyington.
Personnel Profile: Full-Time Volunteers 5; Part-Time Volunteers 8.
Governing Authority: bd. of directors. Tax-exempt.
History Museum.
Collections: agricultural machinery including farm tractors & construction machinery; horse drawn wagons, carriages, & sleighs; toys; local history & cultures; hats; international teddy bears; Victorian Era streetscapes; 1930s doctor's office.
Research Fields: genealogy.
Facilities: Museum-related items for sale.

Activities: Museum Sponsors: Spring Fling in May; Country Western Jam Sessions in summer; Trial Reenactments in July; Historical Society Cemetery Walk in August; Folk Fair in September; Festival of Trees in December.
Publications: brochure, Heartland News; newsletters, Teddy Bear; Hat Parlor.
Hours & Admission Prices: May-Sept. Sat. 1-4; other times by appointment. Adults $6, children 11 & under $3. ♿
Attendance: 4,100 (estimated)
Membership: Child $10; Senior $14; Adults $16; Family $35.

Clear Lake

KINNEY PIONEER MUSEUM AND HISTORICAL SOCIETY OF NORTH IOWA, 9184 G 265th St., Clear Lake, IA 50428-8507. Mailing Address: P.O. Box 421, Mason City, IA 50402-0421. Tel.: 641-423-1258.
Founded: 1964.
Congressional District: 3
Key Personnel: Pres., Richard Peterson; Dir., Bonnie Frenz; Sec., Suzanne Kisner; Treas., Paul Pirkl.
Personnel Profile: Part-Time Paid 2; Part-Time Volunteers 25.
Governing Authority: society; nonprofit organization. Tax-exempt.
Historical Society Museum.
Collections: local historical items; Indian artifacts; furniture & furnishings; fossil collection; handmade implements; old dolls & toys; hand-drawn fire engine; milk wagon; harp. 1911 Colby Car made in Mason City. 1906 Ford Model N; 1923 Model T Ford; 1929 Model A Ford Sedan; Barbie doll collection; Regina Orchestra Corona. Historic Buildings: 1900 schoolhouse; 1856 log cabin.
Facilities: Museum-related items for sale.
Activities: guided tours; permanent & temporary exhibitions.
Publications: Memories of Old Cerro Gordo: First Person and Contemporary Tales; Gone But Not Forgotten Wheelwood, IA; The Dougherty Fighting Irish.
Hours & Admission Prices: May-Sept. Tues.-Sun. 1-5. Adults $3, children $.75; members no charge. Season Pass: family $20, adult $10. ♿
Attendance: 3,000 (estimated)
Membership: Individual $10; Family $20.

Clermont

MONTAUK, 26223 Harding Rd., Clermont, IA 52135-8600. Mailing Address: P.O. Box 372, Clermont, IA 52135-0372. Tel.: 563-423-7173. Fax: 563-423-7378.
E-mail: montauk@acegroup.cc
Founded: 1968.
Congressional District: 2
Key Personnel: Acting Mgr., Nadine West.
Personnel Profile: Full-Time Paid 2; Part-Time Paid 6; Part-Time Volunteers 2.
Governing Authority: state. State Historical Society of Iowa, Dept. of Cultural Affairs, Capitol Complex, Des Moines, IA 50319. Tel. 515-281-7650. Branch Museum: Clermont Museum. Tax-exempt.
Historic House: 1874 home of William Larrabee, Iowa's 12th Governor.
Collections: household furnishings, clothing & memorabilia of the Larrabee family; small art; natural science; manuscripts; history collections of the Clermont Museum. Historic Building: 1857 Union Sunday School.
Research Fields: Victorian furnishings; Iowa political history.
Activities: guided tours; concerts; temporary exhibitions; special events.
Publications: Iowa Heritage Illustrated.
Hours & Admission Prices: Memorial Day-Oct. daily 12-4. No charge; donations accepted. ♿
Attendance: 4,500 (accurate)

Clinton

BICKELHAUPT ARBORETUM, 340 S. 14th St., Clinton, IA 52732-5432. Tel.: 563-242-4771. Fax: 563-243-0385.
E-mail: bickarb@clinton.net
Web Site: www.bickarb.org
Founded: 1970.
Congressional District: 2
Key Personnel: Exec. Dir., Francie B. Hill; Vice Pres., Frances K. Bickelhaupt.
Personnel Profile: Full-Time Paid 3; Part-Time Paid 2; Part-Time Volunteers 88.
Governing Authority: nonprofit organization. Tax-exempt: 501(c)(3).
Arboretum.
Collections: woody plants; perennial herbaceous plants; eastern Iowa & northwestern Illinois native plants.
Facilities: 600-vol. library of books & periodicals pertaining to horticulture available for inter-library loan; 65-seat education center; 70-seat outdoor amphitheatre; indoor plant conservancy.
Activities: guided tours; lectures; formally organized education programs.
Publications: annual report.
Hours & Admission Prices: Daily dawn-dusk. No charge; donations accepted. ♿
Attendance: 31,000 (estimated)

CLINTON COUNTY HISTORICAL SOCIETY, 601 S. 1st St., Clinton, IA 52732-4118. Mailing Address: P.O. Box 2435, Clinton, IA 52733-2435. Tel.: 563-242-1201.
Founded: 1965.
Congressional District: 1
Key Personnel: Pres., Don Dethmann; Treas., Janice Hansen.
Personnel Profile: Part-Time Volunteers 20.
Governing Authority: private; nonprofit organization. Tax-exempt: 501(c)(3).
Historical Society Museum.
Collections: Clinton County, city & area history.
Facilities: library; 5,000 sq. ft. exhibit space.
Activities: guided tours; lectures.
Publications: bimonthly members newsletter.
Hours & Admission Prices: Wed. & Sun. 1-4; other times by appointment. No charge. ♿
Attendance: 2,000 (estimated)
Membership: Individual $10; Family $15; Supporting $25; Patron $100.

FELIX ADLER MEMORIAL ASSOCIATION, INC., Felix Adler Children's Discovery Center, 332 Eighth Ave. S., Clinton, IA 52732. Mailing Address: P.O. Box 346, Clinton, IA 52733-0346. Tel.: 563-243-3600. Fax: 563-243-3600.
E-mail: discoverycenter@qwestoffice.net
Formerly: Children's Discovery Center
Founded: 1993.
Congressional District: 1
Key Personnel: Dir., Chm. (V) & Museum Shop Mgr., Theo Smith.
Personnel Profile: Full-Time Volunteers 2; Part-Time Paid 1; Part-Time Volunteers 30.
Governing Authority: Subsidiary Institution: Felix Adler Children's Discovery Center. Tax-exempt.
Children's Museum.
Collections: hands-on exhibits.
Activities: special events; educational programs; miniature golf course; early out reading program; after school mentor program. Museum Sponsors: Felix Adler Day Celebration in June.
Publications: newsletter; school event flyers.
Hours & Admission Prices: Wed.-Sat. 10-4, Sun. 1-4. Adults $4, senior citizens 65 & over $3; discounts to AAM & ICOM members; members & children under 2 no charge. ♿
Attendance: 250 (estimated)
Membership: Individual $30; Grandparent $40; Family $50; Reciprocal $100.

Colfax

TRAINLAND U.S.A., 3135 Hwy. 117 N., Colfax, IA 50054-7534. Tel.: 515-674-3813. Fax: 515-674-3813.
E-mail: red@trainlandusa.com
Web Site: www.trainlandusa.com
Founded: 1981.
Congressional District: 4
Key Personnel: Pres. (V), Leland Atwood; Museum Shop Mgr., Judy Smith-Atwood.
Personnel Profile: Part-Time Paid 6.
Governing Authority: private.
Toy Museum.
Collections: 1916-1987 Lionel toy trains & accessories; steam & diesel railroads.
Major Exhibits: Calamus C&NW Depot, 6/10.
Facilities: 4,400 sq. ft. exhibit space. Train-related items for sale.
Activities: guided tours; lectures; hobby workshops; organized educational programs for children.
Hours & Admission Prices: Memorial Day-Labor Day daily 10-6. Adults $5, senior citizens over 55 $4.50, children 2-12 $3; discounts to groups; children under 2 no charge. ♿
Attendance: 15,000 (estimated)

Coralville

ANTIQUE CAR MUSEUM OF IOWA, 860 Quarry Rd., Coralville, IA 52241-2226. Tel.: 319-354-3310. Fax: 319-354-3310.
Web Site: www.acmoi.com
Founded: 2006.
Key Personnel: Pres., Dean Oakes.
Personnel Profile: Part-Time Volunteers 12.

Governing Authority: bd. of directors. Tax-exempt: 501(c)(3).
Car Museum.
Collections: 90 automobiles from 1899 to present.
Major Exhibits: Abernathy Boys, 11/09-6/10.
Facilities: 28,000 sq. ft. exhibit space.
Activities: guided tours.
Hours & Admission Prices: Tues.-Sat. 10-5, Sun. 12-5. No charge; donations accepted. ♿
Attendance: 6,300 (estimated)

THE IOWA CHILDREN'S MUSEUM, 1451 Coral Ridge Ave., Coralville, IA 52241-2802. Tel.: 319-625-6255.
Web Site: www.theicm.org/
Key Personnel: Exec. Dir., Deb Dunkhase; Dir. Devel. & Mktg., Fran Jensen; Dir. Visitor Experience, Jordan Hougham; Coord. Special Programs, Julie Thomas; Exhibit Fabricator, Leonid Stepanov.
Personnel Profile: Full-Time Paid 5; Full-Time Volunteers 1; Part-Time Paid 15; Part-Time Volunteers 125; Interns 3.
Governing Authority: nonprofit organization. Tax-exempt: 501(c)(3).
Children's Museum.
Collections: hands-on exhibits.
Facilities: Museum-related items for sale.
Activities: make your own video; interactive exhibits; birthday parties; field trips; special programs.
Hours & Admission Prices: June to mid-Sept. Mon.-Thurs. & Sat. 10-6, Fri. 10-8, Sun. 11-6; Sept.-May Tues.-Thurs. & Sat. 10-6, Fri. 10-8, Sun. 11-6. Admission $6, seniors 60 & over $5; discounts to groups of 10 or more; children under 1 & members no charge. Closed major holidays.
Attendance: 90,000 (accurate)
Membership: Family Circle $90; Family Circle Plus $100; Grandparent Circle $125.

JOHNSON COUNTY HISTORICAL SOCIETY, (M), 860 Quarry, Coralville, IA 52241-2226. Mailing Address: P.O. Box 5081, Coralville, IA 52241-5081. Tel.: 319-351-5738. Fax: 319-351-5310.
E-mail: questions@johnsoncountyhistory.org
Web Site: www.jchsiowa.org
Formerly: Johnson County Heritage Museum
Founded: 1973.
Congressional District: 1
Key Personnel: Pres. (V), Dee Weber.
Personnel Profile: Full-Time Paid 2; Part-Time Volunteers 125.
Governing Authority: society. Tax-exempt: 501(c)(3).
Historical Society Museum: located in 1876 two-story school.
Collections: photographs; local advertising; tools; glassware; textiles; costumes; books; toys; furnishings.
Research Fields: Johnson County history.
Facilities: Museum-related items for sale.
Activities: guided tours; lectures; organized education programs; docent program; loan & temporary exhibitions.
Publications: brochure, Heritage Museum; bimonthly newsletter; exhibit-related catalogues.
Hours & Admission Prices: Tues.-Sat. 10-5, Sun. 12-5. No charge; donations accepted. Bus tours welcome. Closed major holidays.
Attendance: 6,200 (estimated)
Membership: Sustaining Individual $25; Household $35.

Correctionville

CORRECTIONVILLE MUSEUM, Fifth and Driftwood Sts., Correctionville, IA 51016-7732. Mailing Address: City of Correctionville, P.O. Box 46, Correctionville, IA 51016-0046. Tel.: 712-372-4791.
E-mail: cville@ruralwaves.us
History Museum: housed in old Merchants State Bank.
Collections: local history & culture.
Hours & Admission Prices: Memorial Day-Labor Day Sat. 10-1, Sun. 2-4.

Corydon

PRAIRIE TRAILS MUSEUM OF WAYNE COUNTY, Hwy. 2 E., Corydon, IA 50060. Mailing Address: P.O. Box 104, Corydon, IA 50060-0104. Tel.: 641-872-2211. Fax: 641-872-2211.
E-mail: ptmuseum@grm.net
Web Site: www.prairietrailsmuseum.org
Founded: 1942.
Congressional District: 4
Key Personnel: Pres. (V), Hal Greenlee.
Personnel Profile: Part-Time Paid 1; Part-Time Volunteers 30.
Governing Authority: society. Parent Institution: Wayne County Historical Society. Tax-exempt.
General Museum.
Collections: agriculture; paintings; Native American artifacts; natural history; machinery; cars; Mormon Trail; family & household artifacts.
Facilities: library of genealogical research books.
Activities: Museum Sponsors: Freedom Ring in July; Pioneer Festival in October.
Publications: quarterly newsletter, Wayne County Historical Society Newsletter.
Hours & Admission Prices: April-May & Sept.-Oct. Mon.-Fri. 1-5; June-Aug. Mon.-Fri. 10-5, Sat.-Sun. 1-5; call for additional hours. Family $15, adults $5, college $3, students 7th-12th grade $2, children K-6th grade $1; members with card no charge. Tour: $4. ♿
Attendance: 2,500 (accurate)
Membership: Individual $10; Life $100.

Council Bluffs

HISTORIC GENERAL DODGE HOUSE, 605 3rd St., Council Bluffs, IA 51503-6614. Mailing Address: 621 3rd St., Council Bluffs, IA 51503-6614. Tel.: 712-322-2406 & 3504. Fax: 712-322-3504.
E-mail: generaldodgehouse@windstream.net
Web Site: www.dodgehouse.org
Founded: 1964.
Congressional District: 5
Key Personnel: Exec. Dir., Kori L. Nelson; Pres., Dick Miller; Vice Pres., Kim McKeown; Museum Shop Mgr., Cathy Born.
Personnel Profile: Full-Time Paid 2; Part-Time Paid 15; Part-Time Volunteers 50.
Governing Authority: municipal; nonprofit. Tax-exempt.
Historic House: 1869 Victorian 14-room home of General Grenville M. Dodge. Victorian Arts, RR history, Civil War history.
Collections: Victorian furnishings; 1869-1916 artifacts.
Research Fields: Victorian period costumes & furniture; Dodge's involvement in the Civil War & Iowa 4th Infantry troop; early railroad construction, especially the Union Pacific.
Facilities: Museum-related items for sale.
Activities: guided tours; films; docent program; organized educational programs for students; special annual events.
Publications: quarterly newsletter.
Hours & Admission Prices: Feb.-Dec. Tues.-Sat. 10-5, Sun. 1-5. Adults $7, seniors 62 & over $5, children 6-16 $3; discounts to groups of 20 or more & AAA members; children under 6 & members no charge. Closed some holidays.
Attendance: 11,000 (accurate)
Membership: Individual $25; Dual $40; Family $55; Sustainer $75; Century $100; Donor Circle $250. Business memberships available.

UNION PACIFIC RAILROAD MUSEUM, (M), 200 Pearl St., Council Bluffs, IA 51503-0825. Tel.: 712-329-8307. Fax: 712-323-4973.
E-mail: andi@uprrmuseum.org
Web Site: www.uprrmuseum.org
Founded: 1921.
Congressional District: 5
Key Personnel: Dir., Beth Lindquist; Dir. Historic Programs, John Bromley; Outreach Coord., Patricia LaBounty; Museum Shop Mgr., Andi Hodge.
Personnel Profile: Full-Time Paid 3; Part-Time Volunteers 100.
Governing Authority: private; nonprofit. Tax-exempt: 501(c)(3).
History Museum.
Collections: western railroad history to modern technology; American history 1850s to present; artifacts, archives & photographs.
Facilities: 700-vol. library; 18,000 sq. ft. exhibit space; theater. Museum-related items for sale.
Activities: temporary & participatory exhibits.
Publications: quarterly newsletter, Golden Spike.
Hours & Admission Prices: Tues.-Sat. 10-4. No charge; donations accepted. Closed New Years Eve & Day; Presidents Day; Good Friday; Memorial Day; Independence Day; Labor Day; Thanksgiving; Christmas Eve & Day. ♿
Attendance: 25,030 (accurate)
Membership: Switchman $25; Brakeman $50; Conductor $100; Engineer $250; Dispatcher $500; Magnate $1,000.

Creston

UNION COUNTY HISTORICAL COMPLEX, McKinley Park, 116 W. Adams St., Creston, IA 50801. Tel.: 641-782-8220.
Web Site: unioncountyiowatourism.com/sites.html
Founded: 1966.
Key Personnel: Dir., Mark Huff.
Personnel Profile: Part-Time Paid 4; Part-Time Volunteers 25.
Governing Authority: nonprofit organization. Tax-exempt.

Village Museum.
Collections: Historic Buildings: schoolhouse; depot; log cabin; barn; church; country store (replica); railroad watch tower; railroad caboose & house; barber shop; leather & blacksmith shop; 2 machine sheds.
Facilities: library of books available for research by appointment.
Activities: guided tours by appointment only; rental facilities; school groups.
Hours & Admission Prices: June to Labor Day daily 1-5. No charge; donations accepted.
Attendance: 1,000 (estimated)
Membership: Regular $1; Senior Citizen Life $20; Life $25.

Dakota City

HUMBOLDT COUNTY HISTORICAL ASSOCIATION MUSEUM, 905 1st Ave., N., Dakota City, IA 50529-5134. Mailing Address: P.O. Box 162, Humbolt, IA 50548-0162. Tel.: 515-332-5280.
Founded: 1962.
Congressional District: 6
Key Personnel: Dir., Connie Overby; Pres. (V), Norm Caldwell; Vice Pres. (V), Bill Fort.
Personnel Profile: Part-Time Paid 1.
Governing Authority: nonprofit organization. Tax-exempt: 501(c)(3).
County Historical Museum.
Collections: local history & culture; Native American artifacts; manuscripts. Historic Structures: 1879 Mill Farm house; 1883 Norway No. 6 District School; 1883 Hardy Methodist Church; red barn; Rutland Jail; 1875 chickenhouse; log cabin; kettle shed.
Research Fields: state & local county history.
Facilities: 100-vol. library of Humboldt County & Iowa history books available for use by special arrangement. Handmade articles for sale.
Activities: guided tours; lectures; permanent & temporary exhibitions; meeting programs throughout the year; tapes of interviews of old residents. Museum Sponsors: special displays & demonstrations during the summer.
Publications: book, History of the City of Humboldt-First 100 Years; Gotch: Biography of World's Champion Wrestler, Frank Gotch.
Hours & Admission Prices: June-Sept. Mon.-Tues. & Thurs.-Sat. 10-4, Sun. 1:30-4:30; special tours by appointment. General admission: $5.
Attendance: 2,000 (estimated)
Membership: Annual $10; Lifetime $200.

Davenport

FEJERVARY ZOO, Fejervary Park, 1800 W. 12th St., Davenport, IA 52804. Tel.: 563-326-7812.
Founded: 1952.
Congressional District: 1
Key Personnel: Dir. Parks & Recreation, Seve Ghose; Park Mgr., Steve Ehrler.
Governing Authority: privately owned. Tax-exempt.
Zoo.
Collections: birds; mammals; North American animals.
Facilities: children's garden.
Activities: wildlife interpretive program.
Publications: brochure.
Hours & Admission Prices: Memorial Day to Labor Day Tues.-Sat.10-5, Sun. 12-5; Sept.-Oct. Sat. 10-5, Sun. 12-5. Adults $3, youth 12-17 $2.50, seniors 62 & over and youth 3-11 $2; children 2 & under no charge.
Attendance: 20,000 (estimated)
Membership: Student & Senior $10; Individual $15; Family $35.

* **FIGGE ART MUSEUM, (M),** 225 W. 2nd St., Davenport, IA 52801-1804. Tel.: 563-326-7804. Fax: 563-326-7876.
E-mail: clerk@figgeartmuseum.org
Web Site: figgeartmuseum.org
Formerly: Davenport Museum of Art
Founded: 1925.
Congressional District: 1
Key Personnel: Exec. Dir., Dr. Sean O'Harrow; C.F.O., Todd Woeber; Cur. Education, Ann Marie Hayes Hawkinson; Assoc. Cur., Dr. Rima Girnius; Registrar, Andrew Wallace; Outreach Coord., Lynn Gingrass-Taylor; Business Mgr., Sue O'Malley; Dir. Museum Svcs., Jennifer Brooke; Dir. Devel., Dan McNeil; Devel. & Membership, Susan Horan; Museum Shop Mgr., Chris Sweeney.
Personnel Profile: Full-Time Paid 18; Part-Time Paid 9; Part-Time Volunteers 113; Interns 13.
Governing Authority: private. Subsidiary Institutions: Volunteer Guild. Tax-exempt.
Art Museum.
Collections: American, European, Haitian, Mexican Colonial & Asian art; Grant Wood & the Regionalists.
Major Exhibits: Branching Out: The Art of Wood, 11/09-2/14/10; Visions of Iowa: Arthur Geisert Country Road: A Farming ABC, 2/27/10-5/31/10; Mercedes Matter: A Retrospective, 4/24/10-8/22/10; The Dance of Death, 9/18/10-11/28/10.
Research Fields: Haitian art of the native tradition; Mexican-Colonial Art; American Art.
Facilities: 6,000-vol. library of art reference; auditorium; classrooms. Museum-related items for sale.
Activities: guided tours; lectures; gallery talks; concerts; arts festivals; formally organized education programs for children, adults & undergraduate college students; docent program or council; inter-museum loan, permanent & temporary exhibitions.
Publications: quarterly newsletter; invitations; biennial report; books, exhibition catalogues.
Hours & Admission Prices: Tues.-Wed. & Fri.-Sat. 10-5, Thurs. 10-9, Sun. 12-6. Adults $7; members no charge. ♿
Attendance: 60,000 (estimated)
Membership: Senior, Student & Educator $40; Individual $50; Household $75.

GERMAN AMERICAN HERITAGE CENTER, 712 W. Second St., Davenport, IA 52802-1410. Tel.: 563-322-8844. Fax: 563-322-2687.
E-mail: director@gahc.org
Web Site: www.gahc.org
Cultural Heritage Museum.
Collections: German American cultural heritage; photographs; personal artifacts.
Activities: special events & programs.
Hours & Admission Prices: Tues.-Sat. 10-4, Sun. 12-4; other times by appointment. Adults $5, senior citizens $4, children 5-17 $3; children under 5 & members no charge. ♿

PALMER MUSEUM OF CHIROPRACTIC HISTORY, 1000 Brady St., Davenport, IA 52803. Tel.: 563-884-5404. Fax: 563-884-5616.
Founded: 1997.
Key Personnel: Dir., Alana Callender; Education, Dr. Roger Hynes; Public Rels., Julie Arnold.
Personnel Profile: Full-Time Paid 2; Part-Time Paid 1.
Governing Authority: private college.
History Museum.
Collections: chiropractic history from 1895 to present; chiropractic table & technique tools.
Activities: guided tours; loan exhibitions.
Hours & Admission Prices: Jan. 4-Dec. 21 Mon.-Fri. 8-4, Sat.-Sun. by appointment. No charge; donations accepted.
Attendance: 400 (estimated)

* **PUTNAM MUSEUM OF HISTORY & NATURAL SCIENCE, (M),** 1717 W. 12th St., Davenport, IA 52804-3597. Tel.: 563-324-1933 & 1054. Fax: 563-324-6638.
E-mail: museum@putnam.org
Web Site: www.putnam.org
Founded: 1867.
Congressional District: 1
Key Personnel: C.E.O. & Pres., Kim Findlay; Chm., Dana Waterman; C.F.O., Kim Nickels; Chief Cur., Eunice Schlichting; Cur. History, Christina Kastell; Dir. Education, Donna Murray; Cur. Natural Science, Christine Chandler; Dir. Theatre Operations, Dean K. Fick; Dir. Mktg., Lori Arguello; Dir. Human Resources & Administration, Drue Curry; Dir. Facilities, Mike Murphy; Dir. Visitor Svcs., Beth Knaack; Retail Sales Mgr., Sue Folwell.
Personnel Profile: Full-Time Paid 24; Part-Time Paid 14; Part-Time Volunteers 101; Interns 21.
Governing Authority: nonprofit corporation. Tax-exempt: 501(c)(3).
History, Natural Science & Anthropology Museum.
Collections: regional history with emphasis on the Quad cities of Iowa & Illinois: geology; ethnology; archaeology; botany; paleontology; anthropology; zoology; archives & decorative arts.
Major Exhibits: Davenport Civil Rights, 12/09-2/10; Oceania (Working Title), 2/10-5/10; Aviation (Working Title), 7/10-9/10.
Research Fields: history & natural history of the Quad Cities of Iowa & Illinois.
Facilities: 5,000-vol. library of history, natural history & fine art books available for use by special request; classrooms; Heritage Theatre (R); scilab; 300-seat auditorium; discovery room; meeting rooms; 270-seat IMAX(R) 3D Theatre. Books, publications & gifts related to the museum for sale.
Activities: permanent & changing exhibits; IMAX films, lectures; concerts; classes; family workshops; school tours; school & community outreach programs; special events; World Adventure Travelogue Series.
Publications: brochures; proceedings of the Davenport Academy of Sciences; Vascular Plants of Scott & Muscatine Counties; The Indian Mounds at Albany, Illinois; Prehistoric Moundbuilders of the Mississippi Valley;

Watching the River, Walking the Land: A Natural History of Eastern Iowa and Western Illinois; The Nazca Pottery of Ancient Peru
Hours & Admission Prices: Mon.-Sat. 10-5, Sun. 12-5. Museum: $4-$6; discounts to members. IMAX: $6.50-$8.50; discounts to members. IMAX & Museum: $8-$10; discount to members. Closed Thanksgiving; Christmas. ♿
Attendance: 160,000 (estimated)
Membership: Individual $35; Adventurer $40; Duo $60; Grand & Family $80; IMAX $125; Triple $190.

VANDER VEER BOTANICAL PARK, Btw. Brady and Harrison Sts., Davenport, IA 52803. Mailing Address: 214 W. Central Park Ave., Davenport, IA 52803-1503. Tel.: 563-326-7818.
Botanical Garden.
Collections: plants & flowers including azaela, lily, daisy & fuchsia.
Hours & Admission Prices: Park: daily sunrise to sunset. The Conservatory and Park Store: Tues.-Sun. 10-4. Adults $1, children 15 & under no charge.

Decorah

FINE ARTS COLLECTION, LUTHER COLLEGE, 700 College Dr., Luther College Library, Decorah, IA 52101-1041. Tel.: 563-387-1195. Fax: 563-387-1657.
E-mail: kempjane@luther.edu
Web Site: finearts.luther.edu
Congressional District: 4
Key Personnel: Supvr., Jane Kemp; Gallery Coord., David Kamm.
Personnel Profile: Full-Time Paid 1; Part-Time Paid 1.
Governing Authority: private college; nonprofit. Parent Institution: Luther College. Tax-exempt: 501(c)(3).
Art Museum.
Collections: contemporary & historic prints, paintings & sculpture; Gerhard Marcks drawings & prints; Marguerite Wildenhain pottery & drawings; pre-Columbian pottery; Inuit sculpture; Scandinavian immigrant paintings.
Research Fields: Marguerite Wildenhain; Gerhard Marcks; pre-Columbian Panamanian ceramics; Inuit sculpture.
Facilities: 2,265 sq. ft. exhibit space.
Activities: student, temporary & traveling exhibits; gallery talks; scholarly research & education.
Publications: exhibition catalogs; brochures; flyers.
Hours & Admission Prices: Sept.-June Mon.-Fri. 8-10, Sat. 9-5, Sun. 12-10. No charge. Closed college holidays. ♿
Attendance: 10,000

GEOLOGY COLLECTION, LUTHER COLLEGE, 700 College Dr., Decorah, IA 52101-1045. Tel.: 563-387-1508.
E-mail: youngjea@luther.edu
Web Site: geology.luther.edu
Key Personnel: Cur., Jean Young
Geology Museum.
Collections: minerals; rocks; fossils.
Hours & Admission Prices: By appointment. No charge.

LUTHER COLLEGE ETHNOGRAPHIC AND ARCHAEOLOGICAL COLLECTIONS, 700 College Dr., Anthropology Lab, Decorah, IA 52101-1041. Tel.: 563-387-2156.
E-mail: landch01@luther.edu
Web Site: anthrophology.luther.edu
Founded: 1969.
Congressional District: 4
Personnel Profile: Full-Time Paid 1; Part-Time Paid 12.
Governing Authority: Parent Institution: Luther College. Tax-exempt.
History Museum.
Collections: North American & Midwest archaeology; Native American, Inupiat, African, Asian ethnographic artifacts; period Greek & Roman coins & numismatic collections; paper currency.
Hours & Admission Prices: Call for hours.

* **VESTERHEIM NORWEGIAN-AMERICAN MUSEUM, (M),** 523 W. Water St., Decorah, IA 52101-1733. Mailing Address: P.O. Box 379, Decorah, IA 52101-0379. Tel.: 563-382-9681. Fax: 563-382-8828.
Web Site: www.vesterheim.org
Founded: 1877.
Congressional District: 4
Key Personnel: Chm., Sonja Peterson; Interim Exec. Dir., Steve Johnson; Exec. Asst., Marcia McKelvey; Coord. Tours to Norway, Michelle Whitehill; Volunteer Coord., Martha Griesheimer; Membership Mgr., Peggy Sersland; Cur. Textiles, Laurann Gilbertson; Cur., Tova Brandt; Registrar & Archivist, Jennifer Johnston Kovarik; Editor, Charlie Langton; Office Mgr., Blythe Landsman; Technology Specialist, Faust Gertz; Devel. Officer, Kirsten Heine; Museum Shop Mgr., Ken Koop.
Personnel Profile: Full-Time Paid 9; Part-Time Paid 10; Part-Time Volunteers 459; Interns 3.
Governing Authority: nonprofit organization. Tax-exempt: 501(c)(3).
Ethnic Museum.
Collections: Norwegian, Norwegian immigrant & Norwegian-American artifacts; folk art; fine art; furnishings; tools & technology; clothing & personal artifacts; archives. Historic buildings; 1880 log schoolhouse; 1860 drying house; 1860 waterpower grain mill; 1851 grist mill; 1863 stone church; 1860 Norwegian house; 1850-1929 immigrant farmstead; 1855 Stovewood house; 1877 hotel; 1852 pioneer immigrant log home; 1859 pioneer immigrant log home; 1859 frame general store; 1879 northern plains frame house; 1905 northern plains frame church.
Major Exhibits: Sacred Symbols; Ceremonial Cloth, 11/09-2/10; Vesterheim's Featherlite Pioneer Immersion Program - Exhibit of Projects, 5/10; National Exhibition of Folk Art in the Norwegian Tradition, 7/10; 5th Biennial Vesterheim Auction, 9/10-10/10; Quilts, Fall 2010.
Research Fields: Norwegian American material culture.
Facilities: 10,000-vol. research library; reading room; classrooms. Museum-related items for sale.
Activities: guided tours; lectures; arts festivals; folk-art classes; formally organized education programs for adults & youth; inter-museum loan, permanent & temporary exhibitions. Museum Sponsors: special undergraduate internships for Luther College students; Nordic Fest; national juried exhibitions in traditional Norwegian arts & crafts; folk art tours in Norway.
Publications: newsletters; semiannual magazine; specialty newsletters, Rosemaling; books & pamphlets on Norwegian and Norwegian-American textiles, painting, woodcarving, silversmithing.
Hours & Admission Prices: May-Oct. Thurs. 8-8, Fri.-Wed. 9-5; Nov.-April Thurs. 10-8, Fri.-Wed. 10-4. Adults $7, seniors & youth 7-18 $5; discounts for families, groups, AAM & ICOM members; Thurs., children 6 & under and members no charge. Closed New Year's Day; Easter; Thanksgiving; Christmas. ♿
Attendance: 15,727 (accurate)
Membership: Individual $35; Family $50; Supporter $250; Sponsor $500; Sustaining Fellow $1,000.

Des Moines

ANDERSON GALLERY - DRAKE UNIVERSITY, Harmon Fine Arts Center, 25th St. & Carpenter Ave., Des Moines, IA 50311. Tel.: 515-271-1994. Fax: 515-271-2558.
E-mail: heatherskeens@drake.edu
Web Site: www.drake.edu/andersongallery
Founded: 1996.
Key Personnel: Dir., Heather Skeens
Art Gallery.
Collections: paintings; sculpture.
Activities: lectures; workshops.
Hours & Admission Prices: Tues.-Sun. 12-4. No charge.

BLANK PARK ZOO, 7401 S.W. 9th St., Des Moines, IA 50315-6667. Tel.: 515-285-4722. Fax: 515-974-2590.
E-mail: info@blankparkzoo.com
Web Site: www.blankparkzoo.com
Founded: 1963.
Key Personnel: Dir. Operations, Anne Shimerdla; C.E.O., Mark Vukovich; Dir. Animal Care & Conservation, Kevin Drees; Dir. Devel., Sarah Bonetas; Public Rels., Ryan Bickel; Museum Shop Mgr., Cindy Hutt.
Personnel Profile: Full-Time Paid 18; Part-Time Paid 17; Part-Time Volunteers 90; Interns 5.
Governing Authority: municipal. Parent Institution: Blank Park Zoo Foundation. Tax-exempt.
Zoo.
Collections: 104 animal species.
Facilities: library of books related to animals; cafeteria with outdoor seating. Animal-related items for sale.
Activities: mobile vans; day camp; annual events.
Publications: quarterly newsletter, Zootracks.
Hours & Admission Prices: March-April & Oct. daily 10-4; May-Sept. daily 10-5; Nov.-Feb. Wed.-Sun. 10-4. Adults $9.95, senior citizens $7.95, children 3-12 $4.95; members & children 2 & under no charge. ♿
Attendance: 380,000 (accurate)
Membership: One Plus One $59; Family & Grandparent $79.

DES MOINES ART CENTER, (M), 4700 Grand Ave., Des Moines, IA 50312-2099. Tel.: 515-277-4405. Fax: 515-271-0357.
E-mail: cdoolittle@desmoinesartcenter.org

Web Site: www.desmoinesartcenter.org
Founded: 1933.
Congressional District: 66
Key Personnel: Pres. Bd., Mary Kelly; Dir., Jeff Fleming; Dir. Studio Programs, Peggy Leonardo; Registrar, Rose Wood; Protection Svc. Dir., Michael O'Neal; Dir. Finance, Cheryl Larkin; Museum Shop Mgr., Christine Goodwin.
Personnel Profile: Full-Time Paid 60; Part-Time Paid 40; Part-Time Volunteers 100.
Governing Authority: nonprofit organization. Parent Institution: Edmunson Art Foundation. Tax-exempt: 501(c)(3).
Art Museum.
Collections: late 19th-21st-century European & American painting & sculpture; prints; African Art.
Facilities: 14,000-vol. research library; 220-seat auditorium; classrooms; studios; restaurant. Museum-related items for sale.
Activities: inter-museum loan; permanent, temporary & traveling exhibitions; lectures; gallery talks; performing arts programs; film programs; docent tours; educational programs; musical entertainment; guided tours. Museum Sponsors: Contemporary Collectors; Art Noir; Print Club; Arts After Hours monthly.
Publications: exhibition catalogs; bulletin, News; gallery handouts; program brochures; gallery guides; Visitor's Guide; class schedules.
Hours & Admission Prices: Tues.-Wed. & Fri.-Sat. 11-4, Thurs. 11-9, Sun. 12-4. No charge; donations accepted. Closed New Year's Eve & Day; Independence Day; Thanksgiving; Christmas. ♿
Attendance: 377,062 (accurate)
Membership: Individual $35; Household $50; Contributor $100; Sustainer $500; Patron $1,000.

DES MOINES BOTANICAL CENTER, 909 Robert D. Ray Dr., Des Moines, IA 50316-2897. Tel.: 515-309-2489. Fax: 515-323-6275.
E-mail: botanicalcenter@botanicalcenter.com
Web Site: www.botanicalcenter.com
Founded: 1979.
Congressional District: 4
Key Personnel: Exec. Dir., Mark Reed; Horticulture Mgr., Scott Atzen; Pres. (V), Amy Mills; Lead Gardener, Todd Monson; Facilities Mgr., Dawn Goodrich.
Personnel Profile: Full-Time Paid 15; Part-Time Paid 7; Part-Time Volunteers 210; Interns 3.
Governing Authority: municipal. Department of Parks & Recreation, 3226 University, Des Moines, IA 50311. Parent Institution: City of Des Moines. Tax-exempt.
Botanical Garden.
Collections: 2,250 tropical & semi-tropical plants; arid indoor; outdoor cactus; succulent garden; dwarf conifer collection; twenty seven Bonsai; medicinal, culinary & fragrance herb garden; butterfly garden; perennial garden; rock garden.
Research Fields: horticulture; ornamental horticulture.
Facilities: 1,000-vol. library of botanical, horticultural books & periodicals available for research on premises; botanical garden; reading room; garden cafe. Small plants, horticultural books & other museum-related items for sale.
Activities: guided tours; lectures; hobby workshops; formally organized education programs; temporary exhibitions.
Publications: quarterly, Botanical Center Newsletter; yearly events calendar; plant information fact sheets.
Hours & Admission Prices: Daily 10-5. Adults $4, senior citizens & children 6-17 $2; discount to groups of 10 or more, AABGA, American Heart Assoc., American Assoc. of Botanical Gardens, American Horticultural Society & Arboretum members; members & children under 5 no charge. Closed New Year's Day; Thanksgiving; Christmas. ♿
Attendance: 200,000 (estimated)
Membership: Senior Citizen & Student $20; Individual $30; One Plus One, Family & Grandparent $40; Cultivators: Seed $100; Sprout $250; Bud $500 & up; Flower $1,000 & up; Garden $2,500 & up.

FORT DES MOINES MUSEUM AND EDUCATION CENTER, 75 E. Army Post Rd., Des Moines, IA 50315-5866. Tel.: 888-828-FORT; 515-282-8060.
Key Personnel: Exec. Dir., Joe Nolte; Museum Shop Mgr., Diana Wheeland
History Museum.
Collections: African American men of WWI; Women's Army Auxiliary Corps; photographs; period art.
Activities: facilities rental; educational programs; weddings; receptions; meetings.
Hours & Admission Prices: Mon.-Sat. 10-4. Adults $2; members no charge. ♿
Attendance: 10,000 (accurate)
Membership: Individual $30; Family $60; Bronze $100; Silver $250; Gold $500.

HOYT SHERMAN PLACE, 1501 Woodland Ave., Des Moines, IA 50309-3283. Tel.: 515-244-0507. Fax: 515-237-3582.
Web Site: www.hoytsherman.org
Founded: 1907.
Congressional District: 4
Key Personnel: Exec. Dir., Carol Pollock.
Personnel Profile: Full-Time Paid 8; Part-Time Paid 1; Part-Time Volunteers 163; Interns 1.
Governing Authority: nonprofit. Parent Institute: Hoyt Sherman Place Foundation. Tax-exempt: 501(c)(3).
Art Museum Complex: comprised of 1877 House; 1907 Art Museum; 1923 Theater.
Collections: 17th- to 19th-century paintings; statuary; antique furniture; 16th century carved Swiss cabinets; decorative arts; artifacts.
Facilities: meeting rooms; 1,250-seat theater.
Activities: guided tours; lectures; docent program; participatory exhibits.
Publications: quarterly members newsletter.
Hours & Admission Prices: Mon.-Fri. 9-4. No charge. Guided Tours: $2 per person. ♿
Attendance: 90,000 (estimated)
Membership: Friend $25-$99; Supporting Cast $250-$499; Leading Role $500-$999; Center Stage $1,000-$2,499; Marquee VIP $2,500-$4,999; Encore VIP $5,000 & up.

IOWA DEPARTMENT OF NATURAL RESOURCES, 502 E. 9th St., Des Moines, IA 50319-0034. Tel.: 515-281-5918. Fax: 515-281-6794. TDD: 515-242-5967.
Web Site: www.iowadnr.gov
Founded: 1935.
Key Personnel: Dir., Richard Leopold.
Governing Authority: state. Tax-exempt.
State Park Museum.
Collections: Museum: Iowa Civilian Conservation Corps Museum At Backbone State Park, Delaware Co. Historic Houses: 1847 Ft. Atkinson grounds & museum; 1850 Wildcat Den State Park, 1847 Pine Creek old grist mill, one-room school building; 1951 Cedar Rock, home, boat house & grounds designed by Frank Lloyd Wright.
Publications: monthly, Iowa Conservationist.
Hours & Admission Prices: Museum: May-Oct. Sat.-Sun. 11-5. Wildcat Den Mill & School: park & grounds open year-round, buildings open only for special events. Fort Atkinson: mid-May to Oct. Tues-Sun. 1-5. Cedar Rock: May-Oct. Tues.-Sun. 11-5. No charge. ♿
Attendance: 35,000

IOWA HALL OF PRIDE, 330 Park St., Des Moines, IA 50309-1701. Tel.: 515-280-8969. Fax: 515-280-3211.
E-mail: shelly@iowahallofpride.com
Web Site: www.iowahallofpride.com
Key Personnel: Dir., Jack Lashier; Education & Group Coord., Shelly Johnson
History Museum.
Collections: state history; Iowa's sports legends, movie stars, scientists & heroes; art.
Facilities: theater.
Activities: special events; birthday parties; facility rental; school & scout groups.
Hours & Admission Prices: Mon.-Sat. 9:30-4:30, Sun. by appointment. Adults $5, out of state students $4; discounts to groups; Iowa children K-12 no charge. Closed major holidays. ♿

POLK COUNTY HERITAGE GALLERY, Polk County Office Bldg., 111 Court Ave., Des Moines, IA 50309-2218. Tel.: 515-286-2242. Fax: 515-286-3082. TDD: 515-286-2003.
E-mail: info@heritagegallery.org
Web Site: www.heritagegallery.org
Founded: 1980.
Congressional District: 7
Key Personnel: Pres. (V), Tom Green.
Personnel Profile: Full-Time Volunteers 1; Part-Time Volunteers 20.
Governing Authority: Parent Institution: Polk County Heritage Gallery Board. Tax-exempt.
Art Gallery: housed in 1908 post office. Listed on the National Register of Historic Places.
Collections: local history & culture; period furnishings; personal artifacts; photographs.
Research Fields: Postal History.
Activities: changing exhibits.

Hours & Admission Prices: Mon.-Fri. 11-4:30. No charge; donations accepted. Closed legal holidays. ♿
Attendance: 4,000 (accurate)

SALISBURY HOUSE & GARDENS, (M), 4025 Tonawanda Dr., Des Moines, IA 50312-2909. Tel.: 515-274-1777. Fax: 515-274-0184.
E-mail: contactus@salisburyhouse.org
Web Site: www.salisburyhouse.org
Founded: 1993.
Congressional District: 4
Key Personnel: Exec. Dir., Mark J. Heppner; Chm. (V), Mike Simonson.
Personnel Profile: Full-Time Paid 8; Part-Time Paid 2; Part-Time Volunteers 60.
Governing Authority: Tax-exempt: 501(c)(3).
Historic House Museum & Gardens: built 1923-28.
Collections: 14th to 20th-century furnishings & tapestries; manuscript collections; paintings; rare books.
Facilities: 2,100-vol. library of rare books available for use on premises. Brochures & postcards for sale.
Activities: guided tours; annual education & public programs; rental facilities; special events.
Publications: quarterly newsletter, Beneath the Rafters.
Hours & Admission Prices: Tours: March-Dec. Tues.-Fri. 1 & 2:30. Adults $7, seniors $6, children 6-12 $3; discounts to members & school groups sponsored by members. Closed most holidays. ♿
Attendance: 30,000 (estimated)
Membership: Individual $35; Family $50; Friend $100; Contributor $250; Patron $500; Benefactor $1,000.

* **SCIENCE CENTER OF IOWA, (M),** 401 W. Martin Luther King Jr. Pkwy., Des Moines, IA 50309-4776. Tel.: 515-274-6868, ext. 250. Fax: 515-274-3404.
E-mail: info@sciowa.org
Web Site: www.sciowa.org
Founded: 1965.
Congressional District: 4
Key Personnel: Pres. & C.E.O., Paul Jennings; Museum Shop Mgr., Derek Blessen.
Personnel Profile: Full-Time Paid 30; Part-Time Paid 45; Interns 14.
Governing Authority: nonprofit organization. Tax-exempt: 501(c)(3).
Science & Technology Museum.
Collections: rocks, minerals & fossils of Iowa; native Iowa animals; native animals; interactive exhibits.
Facilities: 110-seat auditorium; classrooms; preschool; IMAX Dome Theater; Star Theater with walk through planetarium; John Deere Adventure Theater; cafe. Telescopes, science kits, science books for sale.
Activities: demonstration; lectures; films; hobby workshops; formally organized education programs; statewide outreach program; docent program; temporary & traveling exhibitions; volunteer programs; small discoveries children 7 & under; live performances.
Publications: quarterly newsletter.
Hours & Admission Prices: Mon.-Wed. & Fri.-Sat. 9-5:30, Thurs. 9-8, Sun. 12-5:30. Science Center: adults $9, senior citizens 65 & over $8, children 2-12 $6; discounts to AAM members; members no charge. IMAX: adults $8-$11.25, senior citizens 65 & over $7-$10.25, children $6-$9.25. Closed Easter; Thanksgiving; Christmas. ♿
Attendance: 500,000 (accurate)
Membership: SCI: One Plus One $50; Family & Grand Pass $70; Family Plus Two $100; SCI & Zoo Family $119. Combination memberships available.

STATE HISTORICAL MUSEUM OF IOWA, 600 E. Locust St., Des Moines, IA 50319-1006. Tel.: 515-281-5111. Fax: 515-282-0502. TDD: 515-242-5147.
E-mail: deirdre.giesler@iowa.gov
Web Site: www.iowahistory.org
Formerly: State Historical Society of Iowa
Founded: 1892.
Congressional District: 4
Key Personnel: Interim Museum Dir. & Chief Cur., Michael O. Smith; Dir. Iowa Dept. Cultural Affairs, Cyndi Pederson; Interim Admin., Jerome Thompson; Chm. (V), Peggy Whitworth; Supvr. Libraries & Special Collections, Carol Kirsh; Cur. Natural History, William M. Johnson; Cur. History, John C. Lufkin; Conservator, Peter Sixbey; Exhibits Designer, Jerry Brown; Education Coord., Sarah Macht; Public Rels., Sarah Oltrogge; Registrar, Jodi Evans; Museum Theater, Maureen Korte; Mktg. & Public Rels., Jeff Morgan; Museum Shop Mgr., Laurie Craig.
Personnel Profile: Full-Time Paid 50; Part-Time Paid 5; Part-Time Volunteers 157.
Governing Authority: state. Affiliated with State Historical Society of Iowa, Historical Division. Parent Institution: Iowa Dept. of Cultural Affairs. Subsidiary Institution: Museum Bureau. Tax-exempt.
History Museum.
Collections: archaeology; ornithology; geology; paleontology; neontology; decorative arts; crafts; clothing; textiles; agricultural; tools & equipment; medical equipment; transportation; politics; social history.
Research Fields: textiles; furniture; military; social history.
Facilities: library of history, genealogy, manuscripts, state archives, Iowa census records, newspapers, historical sites & state historic preservation office.
Activities: guided tours.
Publications: Iowa Heritage Illustrated; Annals of Iowa; Iowa Historian.
Hours & Admission Prices: Tues.-Sat. 9-4:30, Sun. 12-4:30. No charge; donations accepted. Closed state holidays. ♿
Attendance: 51,000 (estimated)
Membership: Basic $50-$99; Enhanced $100-$249; Donor $250-$499; Patron $500-$749; Founding $750-$999; Sustaining $1,000-$2,499; Conserver $2,500-$4,999; Historian $5,000 & up.

TERRACE HILL HISTORIC SITE AND GOVERNOR'S MANSION, 2300 Grand Ave., Des Moines, IA 50312-5308. Tel.: 515-242-5841.
E-mail: brian.browning@iowa.gov
Web Site: www.terracehill.org
Founded: 1971.
Key Personnel: Admin., Brian Browning; Chm. Terrace Hill Commission, Jim Hubbell, III; Pres. Terrace Hill Society, Florence Buhr; Pres. Terrace Hill Commission, Mary Mamatt; Horticulturist, Montgomery Lovell; Coord. Communication & Programs, Erin Del Collo; Dir. Devel., Jacqueline Devine; Museum Shop Mgr., Chris Cameron; Maintenance, Tom O'Brien.
Personnel Profile: Full-Time Paid 8; Part-Time Volunteers 80.
Governing Authority: state government. Subsidiary Institution: Terrace Hill Foundation. Tax-exempt.
Historic Site: restored to the opulent Victorian lifestyle of the late 1880s-early 1900s, a mansion, carriage house & gardens are situated on 9 acres.
Collections: concentration on the Victorian era, late 1880s to early 1900s.
Facilities: 20-vol. library of Victorian information relating to decorating, gardening & entertaining; research & reference materials; educational facilities; 15,000 sq. ft. exhibit space; formal gardens. Historic Home: Victorian period. Museum-related items for sale.
Activities: docent program; internships; guided tours; lectures. Annual Events: Jazz in July; Victorian Christmas in December.
Publications: quarterly newsletter, Terrace Hill; annual magazine, Terrace Hill; books, Little Man with the Long Shadow; Our Governor's Mansions; cookbook, Fresh from Terrace Hill.
Hours & Admission Prices: March-Dec. Tues.-Sat. 10-1:30. Tours at 10:30, 11, 11:30, 12:30 & 1:30. Adults $5, children 6-12 $2. Terrace Hill Society members one free admission per year. Closed state holidays; Christmas Eve; New Year's Eve. ♿
Attendance: 17,921 (accurate)
Membership: Individual $15; Household $25; Supporting $50; Patron $100; Benefactor $250; Preservation Club $500 & up.

Dows

DOWS DEPOT WELCOME CENTER, 1896 Railroad St., Dows, IA 50071. Mailing Address: P.O. Box 287, Dows, IA 50071-0287. Tel.: 515-852-3595.
Web Site: www.dowsiowa.com/welcomecenter.html
Railroad Museum: Wright County's first depot built in 1896. Listed on the National Register of Historical Places.
Collections: railroad memorabilia; local period artifacts.
Facilities: Museum-related items for sale.
Hours & Admission Prices: Mon.-Sat. 9-5, Sun. 12-5. No Charge. Closed New Year's Day; Easter; Thanksgiving; Christmas.

QUASDORF BLACKSMITH AND WAGON MUSEUM, Railroad St., Dows, IA 50071. Tel.: 515-852-3595. Fax: 515-852-4326.
Web Site: www.dowsiowa.com/quasdorfmuseum.html
Historic House Museum: built in 1899. Listed on the National Register of Historic Places.
Collections: machines; tools; belt-driven & electric welding equipment; wagon wheels; blacksmithing artifacts; books.
Hours & Admission Prices: Mon.-Sat. 9-5, Sun. 12-5. Call for hours. No charge.

Dubuque

DUBUQUE ARBORETUM & BOTANICAL GARDENS, (M), 3800 Arboretum Dr., Dubuque, IA 52001-1040. Tel.: 563-556-2100. Fax: 563-556-2443.
E-mail: DubArbBotGardens@aol.com

Web Site: www.dubuquearboretum.com
Founded: 1980.
Congressional District: 2
Key Personnel: Pres. (V), Wylie Bledsoe; Financial Dir. & Museum Shop Mgr., Ms. Barbara Barton; Horticulturist, Mr. Jim Schwarz; Devel., Mr. Lloyd Streief; Rosarian, Mr. Marlyn Bausman.
Personnel Profile: Full-Time Volunteers 1; Part-Time Volunteers 360.
Governing Authority: private; nonprofit organization. Tax-exempt: 501(c)(3).
Arboretum & Botanical Garden.
Collections: All-American rose selections: hybrid, miniature, shrub & old garden roses; All-American annuals & perennials; Dwarf Conifer collections: Bill Walter collection, Hermsen collection; formal herb garden; Hostas: over 13,000 plants, 850 varieties; woodland wildflowers; water & shade gardens; prairie wildflowers & grasses; ornamental tree & shrub collections: viburnam, azalea, lilacs; displays: iris, peony, lily, day lily, chrysanthemum, dahlia, cactus; Japanese garden.
Research Fields: Japanese garden.
Facilities: 5,000-vol. library; botanical garden; educational facilities. Gift items for sale.
Activities: concerts; dance recitals; formal education programs; guided tours; hobby workshops; lectures; participatory exhibits; rental gallery; school loan service.
Publications: quarterly newsletter, Groundcover; yearly program, Programs & Events; yearly music program, Music in the Gardens; rose festival program.
Hours & Admission Prices: Arbor Day-Oct. 8am to sunset; Nov.-April Mon.-Fri. 9-5, Sat. 9-1. Gift Shop & Library: 9-6. No charge; donations accepted. Closed New Year's Day; Thanksgiving; Christmas. ♿
Attendance: 100,000 (estimated)
Membership: Individual $25; Family $50; Supporting $100.

*** DUBUQUE MUSEUM OF ART, (M),** 701 Locust St., Dubuque, IA 52001-6817. Tel.: 563-557-1851. Fax: 563-557-7826.
E-mail: info@dbqart.com
Web Site: www.dbqart.com
Founded: 1874.
Congressional District: 1
Key Personnel: Exec. Dir., Edwin Ritts, Jr.; Deputy Dir., Diane Sass; Pres. (V), Ms. Mantea Schmid; Dir. Education, Margaret Buhr; Mgr. Collections & Exhibitions, Stacy Gage.
Personnel Profile: Full-Time Paid 4; Part-Time Paid 4; Part-Time Volunteers 25; Interns 3.
Governing Authority: nonprofit. Tax-exempt: 501(c)(3).
Art Museum
Collections: state, national art.
Major Exhibits: Quiet Courage: Images of Women Edward Curtis, 12/8/09-3/28/10; Larry Schulte, 12/8/09-3/28/10; Ongoing Permanent Collection Grant Wood and More, 1/10-12/10; Citywide High School Exhibition, 4/13/10-5/9/10; Stephen Gassman & Carol Jean Carter, 5/25/10-8/15/10; Eagle Point Blueprints by Alfred Caldwell, 5/25/10-8/8/10; Mary Griep, 8/31/10-11/7/10; Joseph Walter Retrospective, 8/24/10-11/7/10; Teresa Paschke, 12/7/10-3/6/11; Biennial Juried Exhibition, 12/7/10-3/6/11.
Facilities: classrooms.
Activities: guided tours; lectures; gallery talks; concerts; arts festivals; formally organized education programs; temporary exhibitions. Museum Sponsors: bimonthly exhibits.
Publications: quarterly newsletter.
Hours & Admission Prices: Tues-Fri. 10-5, Sat.-Sun. 1-4. No charge; donations accepted. ♿
Attendance: 8,527 (accurate)
Membership: Student $15; Individual & Senior Citizens $40; Family $60; Partners $100; Donors $250; Benefactors $500; Director's Circle $1,000; Visionaries $2,000 & up.

*** MATHIAS HAM HOUSE HISTORIC SITE, (M),** 2241 Lincoln Ave., Dubuque, IA 52001-1424. Mailing Address: 350 E. 3rd St., Dubuque, IA 52001-2302. Tel.: 563-557-9545. Fax: 563-583-1241.
Web Site: www.rivermuseum.com
Founded: 1964.
Congressional District: 2
Key Personnel: Dir., Jerome A. Enzler; C.O.O., Alan Stache; Pres., Jeff Bertsch; Cur., Tacie N. Campbell; Program & Membership, Ginger Sakas; Program & Membership, Rosemary Hopkins; Dir. Mktg., John Sutter; Sales Mgr., Nate Brietsprecher; Office Mgr., Marilyn Snyder; Museum Shop Mgr., Mary Jo Gothard.
Personnel Profile: Full-Time Paid 1; Part-Time Paid 8; Part-Time Volunteers 100.
Governing Authority: private; nonprofit society. Parent Institution: Dubuque County Historical Society. Subsidiary Institution: Mississippi River Museum. Tax-exempt: 501(c)(3).
Historical Society Museum.
Collections: local history. Historic Buildings: c.1857 restored Victorian Mansion; c.1827 log cabin; c.1883 one-room schoolhouse; c.1840 granary.
Research Fields: local history; utilitarian & decorative arts.
Facilities: Museum-related gift items for sale.
Activities: guided tours; walking tours; preservation of buildings; architectural program for county schools; TV & radio programs; permanent, temporary & traveling exhibitions.
Publications: newsletters.
Hours & Admission Prices: May-Oct. daily 10-4:30. Adults $5, children 7-17 $3.50; discounts to Time Travelers, AAA & AAM members; members no charge. ♿
Attendance: 36,000 (accurate)
Membership: Individual $30; Family $75; Pilot $100; Chief Pilot $250; Captain $500; Commodore $1,000.

NATIONAL MISSISSIPPI RIVER MUSEUM & AQUARIUM, 350 E. 3rd St., Dubuque, IA 52001-2302. Tel.: 563-557-9545. Fax: 563-557-9545.
Web Site: www.rivermuseum.com
Founded: 1950.
Congressional District: 2
Key Personnel: C.E.O. & Dir., Jerome A. Enzler; Pres. & Chm. (V), Jeff Bertsch; Devel. Dir., Ginger Sakas; Devel. Asst., Vicki Sutter; Cur., Tacie N. Campbell; C.O.O., Alan Stache; Project Mgr., Mark Hantelmann; Group Tour Mgr., Nate Brietsprecher; Membership & Programs, Rosemary Hopkins; Administrative Asst., Marilyn Snyder; Exhibit Design, Wayne McDermott; Mktg. Dir., John Sutter; Archives, James Wall-Wild; Museum Shop Mgr., Mary Jo Gothard.
Personnel Profile: Full-Time Paid 30; Full-Time Volunteers 5; Part-Time Paid 70; Part-Time Volunteers 200; Interns 3.
Governing Authority: private; nonprofit society. Parent Institution: Dubuque County Historical Society. Subsidiary Institution: Mathias Ham House Historic Site. Tax-exempt: 501(c)(3).
Marine Museum & Aquarium.
Collections: upper Mississippi River & Rivers of America; canoes; flatboats; steamboats; artifacts of Upper Mississippi River Valley; steam engines; towboating; river history; National Rivers Hall of Fame. National Historic Landmark: 1934 riverboat, sidewheeler William M. Black, 1940 towboat Logsdon; 1901 renovated railroad freight house.
Research Fields: river history; especially Upper Mississippi River Valley; amphibian conservation.
Facilities: 18,000 item library & archives on river history; theatre. Museum-related items for sale.
Activities: guided tours; school programs; publications.
Publications: walking tours; newsletter; monographs; annual report.
Hours & Admission Prices: Daily 10-6. Adults $10.50, seniors $9.50, youth 7-17 $8, child 3-6 $4.50; discounts to AAA & AAM members; members no charge. Closed Thanksgiving; Christmas. ♿
Attendance: 265,000 (accurate)
Membership: Individual $30; Family $75; Pilot $100; Chief Pilot $250; Commodore $1,000.

Dyersville

FIELD OF DREAMS MOVIE SITE, 28995 Lansing Rd., Dyersville, IA 52040-8005. Tel.: 888-875-8404. Fax: 563-875-7253.
E-mail: fodbetty@aol.com
Web Site: www.fodmoviessite.com
Movie Site: Iowa farm used for the filming of Field of Dreams.
Collections: baseball field.
Facilities: concession stand. Museum-related items for sale.
Activities: play ball on baseball field.
Hours & Admission Prices: April-Nov. daily 9-6. No charge; donations accepted. ♿
Attendance: 60,000 (estimated)

NATIONAL FARM TOY MUSEUM, 1110 16th Ave. Ct., S.E., Dyersville, IA 52040-2374. Tel.: 563-875-2727. Fax: 563-875-8467.
E-mail: farmtoys@dyersville.com
Web Site: www.national/farmtoymuseum.com
Founded: 1986.
Key Personnel: Exec. Dir., Jacque Rahe; Chm. (V), Dave Bell; Membership Coord., Amanda Schwartz; Asst. Mgr. & Museum Shop Mgr., Ellen Hunt.
Personnel Profile: Full-Time Paid 2; Part-Time Paid 12; Part-Time Volunteers 1; Interns 1.
Governing Authority: Parent Institution: Dyersville Industries, Inc. Tax-exempt: 501(c)(3).
Farm Toy.
Collections: farm toys; tractors; trucks; life-size toy tractors; toy pedal tractors; toy manufacturers; collectors toys.
Hours & Admission Prices: Daily 8-6. Adults $5, seniors 65 & over $4, youth

6-17 $3; discounts to AAA & IMA members; children 5 & under no charge. Closed New Year's Day; Easter; Thanksgiving; Christmas. ♿
Attendance: 15,000 (estimated)
Membership: Individual $25; Family $50; Enthusiast $100; Collector $150.

Eldon

AMERICAN GOTHIC HOUSE CENTER, 300 American Gothic St., Eldon, IA 52554-9654. Tel.: 641-652-3352.
E-mail: aghc@iowatelecom.net
Web Site: www.theamericangothichouse.net
Founded: 2007.
Congressional District: 2
Key Personnel: Pres. (V), Pris Coffman; Admin., Jessica Strom.
Personnel Profile: Full-Time Paid 1; Part-Time Volunteers 30.
Governing Authority: county. Tax-exempt.
Historic House: housed next to the home used as the backdrop of Grant Wood's 1930 painting; built in 1882. Listed on the National Register of Historic Places.
Collections: Grant Wood's life & art; American Gothic history & parodies; video of Grant Wood.
Facilities: Museum-related items for sale.
Activities: take costumed photos in front of the house; video about Grant Wood; educational programs; rental facilities; childrens activities.
Hours & Admission Prices: May-Sept. Sun.-Mon. 1-4, Tues.-Sat. 10-5; Oct.-April Tues.-Fri. 10-4, Sat.-Mon. 1-4. No charge; donations accepted. Closed New Year's Day; Martin Luther King Jr. Day; Presidents' Day; Veterans Day; Thanksgiving & day after; Christmas Eve & Day. ♿
Attendance: 8,989 (accurate)

Eldora

HARDIN COUNTY FARM MUSEUM, 203 Washington St., Eldora, IA 50627. Mailing Address: P.O. Box 41, Eldora, IA 50627-0041. Tel.: 641-939-7107.
Web Site: eldoraiowa.com/pages/farm-museum
Founded: 1998.
Congressional District: 4
Farm Museum.
Collections: farm history & equipment; agriculture industry; farm life; round-roofed barn.
Activities: special events. Museum Sponsors: tractor pulls; threshing days; craft & antique shows; barn dance.
Hours & Admission Prices: By appointment. No charge; donations accepted.
Membership: Family $15.

Elk Horn

THE DANISH IMMIGRANT MUSEUM, (M), 2212 Washington St., Elk Horn, IA 51531. Mailing Address: P.O. Box 470, Elk Horn, IA 51531-0470. Tel.: 712-764-7001. Fax: 712-764-7002.
E-mail: info@danishmuseum.org
Web Site: www.danishmuseum.org
Founded: 1983.
Congressional District: 4
Key Personnel: Exec. Dir., John Mark Nielsen; Pres. (V), Marc Petersen; Treas., John Molgaard; Museum Shop Mgr., Joni Soe-Butts.
Personnel Profile: Full-Time Paid 9; Part-Time Paid 4; Part-Time Volunteers 100.
Governing Authority: private; nonprofit organization. Tax-exempt: 501(c)(3).
Danish Immigrant Museum.
Collections: 35,000 artifacts documenting the life, culture & diversity of Danish-American immigrants to North America & their descendants; period furnishings. Historic House: Bedstemor's turn-of-the-century home.
Major Exhibits: Anni Holm, 11/09-1/10; Evelyn Matthies, 1/10-7/10; Paul Solevad, 7/10-1/11.
Research Fields: Danish American material culture; transformations of Danish customs & traditions in an American setting.
Facilities: 13,000-vol. library; 10,000 sq. ft. exhibit space. Gift items for sale.
Publications: The America Letter.
Hours & Admission Prices: Museum: Mon.-Fri. 9-5, Sat. 10-5, Sun. 12-5. Bedstemor's House: May 15-Sept. 15 daily 1-4. Family History Center: May-Oct. Tues.-Wed. & Sat. 9-5; Nov.-April Tues.-Wed. & Fri. 10-4. Adults $5, children 8-17 $2; members no charge. Closed New Year's Day; Easter; Thanksgiving; Christmas. ♿
Attendance: 10,000 (estimated)
Membership: Active $30; National $50; Contributing & Business/Organization $100; Sustaining $250; Sponsoring $500; Benefactor $1,000; Patron $2,500 & up.

Emmetsburg

VICTORIAN ON MAIN, 1703 Main St., Emmetsburg, IA 50536-1653. Tel.: 712-852-3781.
Historic House: built in 1883.
Collections: period furnishings.
Hours & Admission Prices: Sun. 1-4; other times by appointment.

Estherville

H.G. ALBEE MEMORIAL MUSEUM, 1720 Third Ave., S., Estherville, IA 51334. Mailing Address: P.O. Box 101, Estherville, IA 51334-0101. Tel.: 712-362-2750.
Founded: 1964.
Congressional District: 6
Key Personnel: Pres., David Kaltved; Sec., Mary Gray; Treas., Mike Maloney.
Personnel Profile: Part-Time Paid 1; Part-Time Volunteers 60.
Governing Authority: nonprofit organization. Parent Institution: Emmet County Historical Society, Inc. Branch Museums: Restored Country School; Country Church. Tax-exempt: 501(c)(3).
Historical Society Museum.
Collections: general collection pertaining to Emmet County & country schools; horse drawn farm machinery; country church; blacksmith shop.
Research Fields: genealogy.
Facilities: 20-vol. library of photo books with captions, brief history & special events from each township in the county available for use on premises.
Activities: guided tours; permanent & temporary exhibitions.
Publications: Emmet County History, Vol. III.
Hours & Admission Prices: June-Aug. daily 2-5; other times by appointment. No charge; donations accepted.
Attendance: 1,200 (accurate)
Membership: Individual $5; Life $50.

Exira

AUDUBON COUNTY HISTORICAL SOCIETY, Courthouse Museum, Washington St., Exira, IA 50076. Mailing Address: 1745 160th St., Audubon, IA 50025-7483. Tel.: 712-563-3984.
Founded: 1960.
Congressional District: 5
Key Personnel: Pres., Carma Hutchins; Vice Chm. (V), William Roth.
Personnel Profile: Part-Time Paid 1; Part-Time Volunteers 20.
Governing Authority: society. Branch Museums: Nathaniel Hamlin Museum, Hwy. 71, Audubon, IA 50025; Old Court House Museum, Exira, IA. Tax-exempt.
History Museum.
Collections: Indian history; 1958 Audubon County flood memorabilia; painting; 100 ft. painted mural.
Major Exhibits: Military, 9/10-10/10.
Research Fields: development of hybrid corn.
Facilities: 50-vol. library of county maps & other items available for research by special appointment.
Activities: guided tours; permanent & temporary exhibitions. Museum Sponsors: Spring Festival in June; Fall Festival in October.
Publications: brochure; book, Mudroad Mac.
Hours & Admission Prices: Memorial Day-Labor Day Sun. 1:30-4:30. Adults $3, discounts to members; students no charge. ♿
Attendance: 1,500 (estimated)
Membership: Annual $2; Life $10.

Fairfield

CARNEGIE HISTORICAL MUSEUM, 114 S. Court, Fairfield, IA 52556. Mailing Address: P.O. Box 502, Fairfield, IA 52556-0009. Tel.: 641-472-6343.
Founded: 1870.
Congressional District: 3
Key Personnel: Pres., Gene Luedtke; Bd. Member, Dot Hellkamp; Bd. Member, Keith Dimmitt; Dir., Mark Shaffer; Treas., Scott Reneker.
Governing Authority: municipal. Tax-exempt.
General Museum: housed in Carnegie library building.
Collections: Indian artifacts; Iowa pioneer artifacts; period furnishings; mounted birds; mammals; rocks; period drug store.
Activities: guided tours; gallery talks.
Hours & Admission Prices: 1st & 3rd Sun. of the month 1-4; other times by appointment. No charge. ♿
Membership: Students $5; Individual $10; Family $15; Contributing & Business $25; Sustaining $50; Patron $100; Life $200.

FAIRFIELD ART ASSOCIATION, 200 N. Main, Fairfield, IA 52556-2835. Tel.: 641-472-2000. Fax: 641-472-7890.
E-mail: info@fairfieldacc.com
Web Site: www.fairfieldacc.com/artgallery.html
Founded: 1964.
Key Personnel: Pres. & Volunteer Dir., Suzan Kessel.
Governing Authority: nonprofit organization. Tax-exempt.
Arts & Convention Center.
Collections: paintings & sculptures by Iowa & Midwest artists.
Facilities: classrooms; gallery.
Activities: guided tours; lectures; films; gallery talks; arts festivals; formally organized education programs; temporary & traveling exhibitions.
Publications: monthly newsletter, Fairfield Art Association Newsletter.
Hours & Admission Prices: Mon.-Fri. 9-5; call for additional hours. No charge; donations accepted. ♿
Attendance: 1,000 (estimated)
Membership: Student $5; Individual $10; Family $15; Contributing $25; Friends $50; Patron $100.

Fort Dodge

* **BLANDEN MEMORIAL ART MUSEUM, (M),** 920 Third Ave., S., Fort Dodge, IA 50501-4723. Tel.: 515-573-2316. Fax: 515-573-2317.
E-mail: pkay@blanden.org
Web Site: www.blanden.org
Founded: 1930.
Congressional District: 5
Key Personnel: Dir., Margaret A. Skove; Pres., Dr. Kenneth Adams; Business Office, Pam Kay; Educator, Linda Flaherty; Maintenance & Security, Mark Jessen.
Personnel Profile: Full-Time Paid 4; Part-Time Volunteers 22; Interns 1.
Governing Authority: municipal. Parent Institution: City of Fort Dodge. Subsidiary Institution: Blanden Charitable Foundation. Tax-exempt: 501(c)(3).
Art Museum.
Collections: American & European paintings & sculpture; 16th- to 20th-century prints; drawings; 17th- to 20th-century Asian art; 19th- & 20th-century tribal art.
Major Exhibits: A Measure of Grace, 1/10-3/10; Paul Klee: Prints, 1/10-6/10; Urban Life: Paintings & Prints, 4/10-8/10; Gary Hallman: Photographs, 7/10-11/10; Shared Earth: Paintings & Prints, 9/10-1/11.
Research Fields: 19th & 20th-century European & American painting, prints & sculpture.
Facilities: 4,000-vol. non-circulating fine arts library available to public; studio art classrooms. Cards; jewelry; hand-blown glass & pottery items for sale.
Activities: permanent & traveling exhibitions; gallery talks; artist's lectures; guided tours; education program; community outreach program; concerts; outreach art education program; artist-in residence workshops; music & vocal performances.
Publications: triannual color magazine; exhibition catalogues; 76 Years of Collecting: Blanden Art Museum.
Hours & Admission Prices: Tues.-Sat. 11-5. No charge. Closed holidays. ♿
Attendance: 12,471 (accurate)
Membership: Blanden Charitable Foundation: Individual $25; Household $40; Contributing & Business $100-$249; Patron $250-$499; Benefactor $500; Conservator $1,000.

Fort Madison

NORTH LEE COUNTY HISTORICAL SOCIETY AND SANTA FE DEPOT MUSEUM COMPLEX, 814 10th St. & Ave. H, Fort Madison, IA 52627-0285. Mailing Address: Box 285, Fort Madison, IA 52627-0285. Tel.: 319-372-7661.
E-mail: nlchs@iowatelecom.net
Founded: 1962.
Congressional District: 2
Key Personnel: Pres., Andr Andrews.
Personnel Profile: Part-Time Paid 2; Part-Time Volunteers 6.
Governing Authority: board of trustees. Subsidiary Institution: North Lee County Historic Center. Tax-exempt 501(c)(3).
Historic Center: located in 1910 Santa Fe Railroad depot (National Register of Historic Buildings in historic district); caboose; 1870s country school; Brush College; 1993 Flood museum; Louis Koch Gallery of Historic Paintings; furniture.
Collections: Indian artifacts; old Fort Madison artifacts; Sheaffer Pen Co.; Prison; Mississippi River; Santa Fe Railway; Silsby Fire Engine Pumper; Civil War; Louis Koch Collection.
Research Fields: local history; artifacts; railroad history; firefighting lore; Sheaffer Fountain Pen history; Iowa territorial & pioneer days.
Facilities: Old Sante Fe Depot Museum & office building; historic district with railway express office building; Brush College Country School.
Activities: guided tours; formally organized education programs for children & schools. Museum Sponsors: annual flea market in September; car show in May.
Publications: yearly newsletter; museum brochure.
Hours & Admission Prices: Memorial Day-Labor Day Mon.-Sat. 10-4, Sun. 12-4; Sept.-Oct. Fri.-Sat. 10-2; other times by appointment. Adults $2, children $1; discounts to groups of 15 or more; members & children under 6 no charge. Brush College: by appointment only. ♿
Attendance: 4,000 (accurate)
Membership: Students $5; Adults $10; Immediate Family $25; Sponsor $30; Patron $40; Business $50.

Garnavillo

GARNAVILLO HISTORICAL MUSEUM, 205 N. Washington, Garnavillo, IA 52049-7220. Mailing Address: 508 Monroe, Garnavillo, IA 52049-9751. Tel.: 563-964-2607.
Founded: 1965.
Congressional District: 2
Key Personnel: Pres., Gertrude Brase.
Personnel Profile: Full-Time Volunteers 4; Part-Time Volunteers 25.
Governing Authority: society. Tax-exempt: 501(c)(3).
General Museum: housed in 1866 church.
Collections: archives; archaeology; anthropology; manuscripts; extensive genealogy file; general; history; Indian artifacts; restored furnished Log Cabin; 1860 Lodge Hall.
Research Fields: archaeology; local history; genealogy.
Facilities: 7,400 card reference file involving names & historical references; newspapers dating from 1800 available for research on the premises.
Activities: permanent exhibitions.
Publications: 1836-1876 history of Garnavillo; Garnavillo, Gem of the Prairie.
Hours & Admission Prices: Memorial Day-Labor Day Sat.-Sun. & holidays 1-4. No charge; donations accepted.
Attendance: 700 (estimated)
Membership: Annual $5; Life $25.

George

GEORGE BICENTENNIAL MUSEUM, 204 E. Michigan Ave., George, IA 51237. Tel.: 712-475-3612.
History Museum.
Collections: pioneer life & history; farm tools & equipment; household artifacts; musical instruments; military uniforms.
Hours & Admission Prices: June-Aug. Sun. 2-4; other times by appointment.

Glenwood

MILLS COUNTY HISTORICAL SOCIETY AND MUSEUM, Glenwood Lake Park, Glenwood, IA 51534. Mailing Address: P.O. Box 255, Glenwood, IA 51534-0255. Tel.: 712-527-9221 & 5038.
E-mail: carriemerritt@hotmail.com
Founded: 1959.
Congressional District: 4
Key Personnel: C.E.O. & Pres., Carrie Merrit.
Personnel Profile: Full-Time Volunteers 88; Part-Time Volunteers 92.
Governing Authority: society. Tax-exempt.
Local History Museum.
Collections: machinery hall; dolls; guns; household furniture; glass & china; pre-historic Indian artifacts; period furnishings; c.1900 metal toys; pioneer artifacts; Burlington train caboose. Historic Buildings: 1881 country schoolhouse; farm cottage.
Facilities: Indian earth lodge.
Activities: guided tours; permanent exhibitions; performances.
Hours & Admission Prices: May-Sept. Sat.-Sun. 1-4; other times by appointment. Adults $2, children 5-12 $1; discounts to school groups; children under 5 no charge.
Attendance: 2,015 (estimated)
Membership: Annual $5; Life $25.

Greenfield

IOWA AVIATION MUSEUM, Greenfield Municipal Airport, 2251 Airport Rd., Greenfield, IA 50849. Mailing Address: P.O. Box 31, Greenfield, IA 50849-0031. Tel.: 641-343-7184.
E-mail: aviation@iowatelecom.net
Web Site: www.flyingmuseum.com
Formerly: Iowa Aviation Preservation Center
Founded: 1990.
Congressional District: 4
Key Personnel: Exec. Dir. & Museum Shop Mgr., Lee Ann Nelson; Pres. (V), Ron Havens; Vice Pres., Gregory Schildberg.

Personnel Profile: Full-Time Paid 1; Part-Time Paid 2; Part-Time Volunteers 12.
Governing Authority: nonprofit organization. Parent Institution: Antique Preservation Association. Tax-exempt: 501(c)(3).
Aviation Museum.
Collections: Iowa aviation history; photographs; memorabilia; 1928-1946 airplanes; books & magazines.
Facilities: 1,500-vol. library of aviation books; 7,500 sq. ft. exhibit space. Museum-related items for sale.
Activities: guided tours; traveling exhibitions; pilot training courses; antique plane rides; public events. Annual Events: Hall of Fame banquet; Fly-In in summer & winter.
Publications: quarterly, APA Newsletter.
Hours & Admission Prices: May-Sept. Mon.-Sat. 10-5, Sun. 1-5; Oct.-April Mon.-Fri. 10-5, Sat.-Sun. 1-5. Motor coach tours $80, adults $3, seniors $2.50, children 5-12 $1.50; members & children 4 and under no charge. Closed New Year's; Easter; Thanksgiving; Christmas Eve & Day. ♿
Attendance: 2,363 (accurate)
Membership: Sponsoring $25; Sustaining $50; Supporting $100; Patron $500; Prestigious $1,000.

Grinnell

FAULCONER GALLERY AT GRINNELL COLLEGE, 1108 Park St., Grinnell, IA 50112-1643. Tel.: 641-269-4660. Fax: 641-269-4626.
E-mail: Strongdj@Grinnell.edu
Web Site: www.grinnell.edu/faulconergallery
Formerly: Faulconer Gallery
Founded: 1999.
Congressional District: 3
Key Personnel: Dir., Lesley Wright; Assoc. Dir. & Cur. Exhibitions, Daniel Strong; Cur. Collections, Kay Wilson; Cur. Academic & Community Outreach, Tilly Woodward; Exhibition Designer, Milton Severe.
Personnel Profile: Full-Time Paid 5; Part-Time Paid 19; Interns 3.
Governing Authority: private college. Parent Institution: Grinnell College. Tax-exempt: 501(c)(3).
College Art Museum.
Collections: c.1300 to present, art on paper, African ceramics.
Facilities: 7,500 sq. ft. gallery designed by Cesar Pelli; print & drawing study room.
Activities: temporary exhibitions; lectures; musical performances.
Publications: Sandy Skoglund: Raining Popcorn; Layers of Brazilian Art; John Wilson: A Retrospective; William Kentridge Prints; Scandinavian Photography 1: Sweden; Scandinavian Photography 2: Denmark; Austin Thomas: Perches and Drawings; Hin: The Quiet Beauty of Japanese Bamboo Art; Frank Breuer Photographs; Where Are You From: Contemporary Portuguese Art; Angela Strassheim: Left Behind; Works in Progress: Prints from Wildwood Press.
Hours & Admission Prices: Sat.-Wed. 12-5, Thurs.-Fri. 12-7. No charge; donations accepted. Closed holidays. ♿
Attendance: 10,000 (estimated)

GRINNELL HISTORICAL MUSEUM, 1125 Broad St., Grinnell, IA 50112. Mailing Address: 903 16th Ave., Grinnell, IA 50112-1106. Tel.: 641-236-7827.
E-mail: ghmuseum@ioloatelecom.net
Web Site: www.grinnellmuseum.org
Founded: 1954.
Key Personnel: Pres., Howard McDonough; Sec., Michele Parslow; Treas., Vera Cousins.
Personnel Profile: Part-Time Volunteers 12.
Governing Authority: private; nonprofit organization. Tax-exempt: 501(c)(3).
History Museum: housed in an 1895-1896 home.
Collections: history of Grinnell; period artifacts; photographs.
Research Fields: genealogical research.
Facilities: 2,000 sq. ft. exhibit space.
Activities: guided tours.
Hours & Admission Prices: June-Aug. Tues.-Sun. 2-4; Sept.-May Sat.-Sun. 2-4; groups by appointment. No charge; donations accepted. Closed New Year's Day; Independence Day; Christmas.
Attendance: 800 (estimated)

IOWA TRANSPORTATION MUSEUM, 927 Fourth Ave., Grinnell, IA 50112-2043. Tel.: 641-990-0752. Fax: 641-236-2626.
Key Personnel: Exec. Dir., Charles Brooke
Transportation Museum.
Collections: Iowa's transportation history.
Activities: special events; rental facilities.
Hours & Admission Prices: Call for hours.

Hampton

REA POWER PLANT MUSEUM, 1450 110th St., Hampton, IA 50441. Mailing Address: P.O. Box 442, Hampton, IA 50441-0442. Tel.: 641-456-5777.
History Museum.
Collections: Iowa's electric power history; farming.
Hours & Admission Prices: By appointment. No charge.

Harpers Ferry

EFFIGY MOUNDS NATIONAL MONUMENT, 151 Highway 76, Harpers Ferry, IA 52146-7519. Tel.: 563-873-3491. Fax: 563-873-3743.
E-mail: efmo_superintendent@nps.gov
Web Site: www.nps.gov/efmo
Founded: 1949.
Congressional District: 1 & 4
Key Personnel: Supt., Phyllis Ewing; Collections Mgr., Sharon Greener.
Personnel Profile: Full-Time Paid 9; Part-Time Paid 7; Part-Time Volunteers 10.
Governing Authority: federal. Parent Institution: National Park Service, Dept. of the Interior, Washington, DC. Tax-exempt.
Archaeology Museum: located within visitors center.
Collections: Indian artifacts; ethnology; archaeological collections of mound excavations; manuscript collections.
Research Fields: archaeology.
Facilities: 500-vol. library on anthropology, Iowa geology & history with limited access to certified researches. Books, postcards & color slides for sale.
Activities: guided tours; interpretive talks; environmental films; education programs for children; permanent exhibitions.
Hours & Admission Prices: Daily 8-5. Annual Family Pass $10, $3 per person; April-Nov. $5 maximum per car; fee for education programs; children 15 & under no charge. Closed New Year's; Thanksgiving; Christmas. ♿
Attendance: 90,000 (estimated)

Hawarden

CALLIOPE VILLAGE, 19th St. & Ave. E, Hawarden, IA 51023. Mailing Address: City of Hawarden, 1150 Central Ave., Hawarden, IA 50123-1815. Tel.: 712-551-2403.
E-mail: happ@cityofhawarden.com
Village History Museum.
Collections: local history & culture; personal artifacts; period furnishings; photographs; church; log house. Historic Buildings: harness shop; 1872 school; medical building; bank; jail; 1878 cabin; barn; 1882 depot; 1886 Carlson home; 1881 general store; Shoemaker Museum.
Hours & Admission Prices: Memorial Day to Labor Day Sun. 1-4.

Independence

WAPSIPINICON MILL MUSEUM, 100 1st St. W., Independence, IA 50644-2601. Mailing Address: P.O. Box 321, Independence, IA 50644-0321. Tel.: 319-334-4616.
Web Site: www.buchanancountyhistory.com
Governing Authority: Tax-exempt.
Historic Building: housed in an 1870s grain mill. Listed on the National Register of Historic Places.
Collections: 1870s grain milling process; mill history.
Hours & Admission Prices: mid-May to mid-Sept. Tues.-Sun. 12-4; other times by appointment. Groups $3. ♿

Indianola

NATIONAL BALLOON MUSEUM AND HALL OF FAME, 1601 N. Jefferson Way, Indianola, IA 50125-1484. Mailing Address: P.O. Box 149, Indianola, IA 50125-0149. Tel.: 519-961-3714. Fax: 515-961-4243.
E-mail: balloonmuseum@bfa.net
Web Site: www.nationalballoonmuseum.com
Founded: 1973.
Key Personnel: Chm. (V), Beverly Koehlmoos; Pres. (V), Denis Frischmeyer; Cur., Becky Wigeland; Museum Shop Mgr., Pat Kelley
Balloon Museum & Hall of Fame.
Collections: ballooning & its history; ballooning hall of famers; photographs; balloon gondolas & memorabilia; gas balloons.
Major Exhibits: Karl & Lucy Stefan HOF, 2/10-6/10; First Hot Air Balloon to Fly Over English Channel, 2/10-12/10; Lake Tahoe Balloons, 2/10-12/10.
Facilities: research library. Museum-related items for sale.
Activities: ballooning events.
Publications: book, Indianola, Ballooning Capital of Iowa; newsletter.

Hours & Admission Prices: May-Dec. 23 Mon.-Fri. 9-4, Sat. 10-4, Sun. 1-4; Dec. 27-Dec. 30 & Feb.-April Mon.-Sat. 10-2, Sun. 1-4. Adults $3. Closed holidays. ♿
Attendance: 4,700 (estimated)
Membership: Balloon Watcher $25; Crew $50; Pilot $100; Captain $250; Aeronaut Explorer $500; Aeronaut Record Setter $1,000; Life $2,500.

SIMPSON COLLEGE/FARNHAM GALLERIES, 701 N. C St., Mary Berry Hall, 3rd Fl., Indianola, IA 50125-1202. Tel.: 515-961-1761; 800-362-2454. Fax: 515-961-1498.
E-mail: jnostra@simpson.edu
Web Site: www.simpson.edu/art/gallery
Founded: 1982.
Congressional District: 5
Key Personnel: Dir. & Chair, Art Dept., Justin Nostrala; Vice Pres. Business & Finance, Ken Birkenholtz.
Personnel Profile: Full-Time Paid 1; Part-Time Paid 2.
Governing Authority: college; nonprofit. Parent Institution: Simpson College. Tax-exempt.
Art Gallery.
Collections: paintings; sculpture; photographs.
Activities: formal education programs for college students; traveling exhibitions.
Hours & Admission Prices: Mon.-Fri. 8:30-4:30, weekends by appointment. No charge; donations accepted. ♿
Attendance: 300 (estimated)

Iowa City

OLD CAPITOL MUSEUM, The University of Iowa, 21 Old Capitol, Iowa City, IA 52242. Tel.: 319-335-0548. Fax: 319-353-2982.
E-mail: shalla-wilson@uiowa.edu
Web Site: www.uiowa.edu/~oldcap/
Founded: 1976.
Congressional District: 3
Key Personnel: Dir., Pamela Trimpe; Cur., Shalla Wilson.
Personnel Profile: Full-Time Paid 2; Part-Time Paid 8; Part-Time Volunteers 35.
Governing Authority: university. Affiliated with The University of Iowa. Tax-exempt.
Historic Building: Old Capitol, Iowa's last territorial capitol from 1842-46; first state capitol with the admission of Iowa to the Union in 1846.
Collections: furniture & furnishings of the period; original library collection.
Research Fields: pertaining to the structure & its contents & history.
Facilities: library.
Activities: self-guided tours; guided tours; discovery center; Iowa Humanities Gallery.
Publications: folders, Old Capitol; Old Capitol Tour Guide; booklet, Old Capitol.
Hours & Admission Prices: Tues.-Wed. & Fri. 10-3, Thurs. & Sat. 10-5, Sun. 1-5. No charge; donations accepted. Closed national holidays; Dec. 23-Jan. 13. ♿
Attendance: 30,000 (accurate)

PLUM GROVE HISTORIC HOME, 1030 Carroll St., Iowa City, IA 52240-4601. Mailing Address: Johnson County Historical Society, 310 5th St., Box 5081, Coralville, IA 52241-2421. Tel.: 319-337-6846 & 351-5738. Fax: 319-351-5310.
E-mail: questions@johnsoncountyhistory.org
Web Site: www.johnsoncountyhistory.org
Founded: 1944.
Congressional District: 1
Key Personnel: C.E.O., Shaner Magalhaes; Pres. (V), Dee Weber.
Personnel Profile: Part-Time Paid 2; Part-Time Volunteers 10.
Governing Authority: state. Parent Institution: State Historical Society of Iowa. Subsidiary Institution: Johnson County Historical Society. Tax-exempt.
Historic Building: 1844 home of Robert Lucas, first governor of Territory of Iowa.
Collections: period furnishings.
Activities: guided tours; formally organized education programs.
Publications: brochures.
Hours & Admission Prices: Memorial Day to mid-Oct. Wed.-Sun. 1-5. No charge; donations accepted. Closed Independence Day.
Attendance: 2,000 (accurate)

PROJECT ART-UNIVERSITY OF IOWA AND CLINICS, (M), 200 Hawkins Dr., Iowa City, IA 52242-1009. Tel.: 319-353-6417. Fax: 319-384-8141.
E-mail: adrienne-drapkin@uiowa.edu
Web Site: uihealthcare.com/projectart
Founded: 1978.
Congressional District: 1
Key Personnel: Dir., Adrienne Drapkin.
Personnel Profile: Full-Time Paid 2; Part-Time Paid 2; Part-Time Volunteers 8.
Governing Authority: state government. Parent Institution: University of Iowa Hospitals and Clinics, 200 Hawkins Dr., Iowa City, IA. Tax-exempt.
Art Museum.
Collections: original American art; contemporary Iowa and Midwest artists; Native American art in all media both historic and modern; contemporary glass by internationally recognized artists; weavings from early 20th-century Turkey.
Research Fields: fine art related to health issues, the body; Iowa based art; contemporary photography, glass.
Facilities: 200-seat restaurant; 2,000 sq. ft. exhibit space.
Activities: concerts; lectures; art instruction for patients; summer concert series. Annual Event: Festivals of World Cultures.
Hours & Admission Prices: Mon.-Fri. 8-5; permanent collection is on view 24 hours a day in the public corridors, lobbies & waiting rooms. No charge. ♿
Attendance: 40,000 (estimated)

UNIVERSITY OF IOWA HOSPITALS & CLINICS MEDICAL MUSEUM, 200 Hawkins Dr. 8014 RCP, Iowa City, IA 52242-1009. Mailing Address: UIHC Medical Museum, Iowa City, IA 52242. Tel.: 319-353-6417; 356-7106. Fax: 319-384-8141.
E-mail: adrienne-drapkin@uiowa.edu
Web Site: uihealthcare.com/medmuseum
Founded: 1989.
Key Personnel: Dir., Adrienne Drapkin.
Personnel Profile: Full-Time Paid 1.
Governing Authority: public university; nonprofit. Parent Institution: University of Iowa. Subsidiary Institution: University of Iowa Hospitals & Clinics. Tax-exempt: 501(c)(3).
Medical Museum.
Collections: instruments; artifacts; photographs; books; documents; uniforms; medical & healthcare history.
Research Fields: instrumentation; medical history; current medical procedures & technologies.
Facilities: 125-vol. library of 1850-1950s medical texts; College of Medicine notebooks & documentation; historical hospital records; 1,900 sq. ft. exhibit space.
Activities: guided tours; lectures; films; participatory & temporary exhibitions.
Publications: exhibition brochures & catalogues.
Hours & Admission Prices: Mon.-Fri. 8-5, Sat.-Sun. 1-4. No charge. Closed New Year's Day; Thanksgiving; Christmas. ♿
Attendance: 50,000 (estimated)

* **UNIVERSITY OF IOWA MUSEUM OF ART, (M),** 1375 Hwy. 1 W., 1840 Studio Arts, Iowa City, IA 52242-1789. Tel.: 319-335-1727. Fax: 319-335-3677.
E-mail: uima@uiowa.edu
Web Site: www.uiowa.edu/uima
Founded: 1967.
Congressional District: 1
Key Personnel: Interim Dir., Pamela J. White; Chief Cur., Kathleen Edwards; Dir. Education, Dale William Fisher; Mgr. Exhibitions & Collections, Jeff Martin; Research Cur., Christopher Roy.
Personnel Profile: Full-Time Paid 5; Part-Time Paid 18; Part-Time Volunteers 110.
Governing Authority: state. Parent Institution: University of Iowa. Tax-exempt: 501(c)(3).
Art Museum.
Collections: paintings; prints & drawings; African art; pre-Columbian art; metalwork & jewelry; photography; sculpture.
Activities: guided tours; lectures; concerts; educational programs; permanent & traveling exhibitions; special exhibitions; docent program; study tours; the Elliott Society.
Publications: exhibition catalogs; magazine.
Hours & Admission Prices: Temporarily closed. Collections temporarily located at Iowa Memorial Union & Figge Art Museum. ♿
Attendance: 40,000 (estimated)
Membership: Contributor $25; Benefactor $100; Elliott Society $150; Curator's Circle $250; Sponsor $500; Director's Circle $1,000; Patron $5,000.

UNIVERSITY OF IOWA MUSEUM OF NATURAL HISTORY, (M), 10 Macbride Hall, Iowa City, IA 52242-1322. Tel.: 319-335-0481. Fax: 319-335-0653.
E-mail: mus-nat-hist@uiowa.edu
Web Site: www.uiowa.edu/~nathist
Founded: 1858.
Congressional District: 3

Key Personnel: Dir., Pamela White; Asst. Dir., Shalla Wilson; Education & Outreach Coord. & Museum Shop Mgr., Sarah Horgen; Mgr. Collections, Cindy Opitz; Exhibits Preparator, Byron Preston.
Personnel Profile: Full-Time Paid 5; Part-Time Paid 8; Part-Time Volunteers 28; Interns 2.
Governing Authority: university. Parent Institution: University of Iowa. Tax-exempt: 501(c)(3).
Natural History Museum.
Collections: Iowa Hall gallery of state geology, archaeology, & ecology; Laysan Island cyclorama; major phyla of animal kingdom series; North American birds & mammals; marine invertebrate series; ethnographic materials from Philippines, North America, Africa, & New Zealand.
Research Fields: midwest archaeology; paleontology; botany; mammalogy; ornithology; environmental studies.
Facilities: reference library of natural history subjects; casting laboratory. Postcards, books & collection-related items for sale.
Activities: guided tours; public lecture & fieldtrip series; formally organized programs for children; school curriculum programming; formally organized museum studies program for undergraduate & graduate students affiliated with University of Iowa; training programs for professional museum workers; casting program for specimen reproduction & exchange; inter-museum loan, permanent & temporary exhibitions; school loan service.
Publications: series, University of Iowa Studies in Natural History; tour guides & brochures; ASC Featured Institution reprints; school curriculum materials.
Hours & Admission Prices: June-July. Tues.-Sat. 10-5, Sun. 1-5; Aug.-May Tues.-Wed. & Fri. 10-3, Thurs. & Sat. 10-5, Sun. 1-5. No charge; donations accepted. Closed national holidays. ♿
Attendance: 30,000 (estimated)

Iowa Falls

CALKINS NATURE AREA/FIELD MUSEUM, 18335 135th St., Iowa Falls, IA 50126-8512. Tel.: 641-648-9878. Fax: 641-648-9878.
E-mail: naturecenter@hardincountyconservation.com
Founded: 1890.
Congressional District: 3
Key Personnel: Exec. Dir., Wes Wiese; Chm. (V), William H. Schmidt; Museum Shop Mgr., Dick Larson.
Personnel Profile: Full-Time Paid 2; Part-Time Paid 3; Part-Time Volunteers 20.
Governing Authority: college. Parent Institution: Hardin County Conservation Board. Subsidiary Institution: Ellsworth College. Tax-exempt.
Natural Science & History Museum.
Collections: mounted bird & mammal specimens; Indian artifacts; eggs from 197 species of birds; fossils & minerals; shells; insects; other invertebrates.
Facilities: library; 100-seat multipurpose room; classroom.
Activities: guided tours; lectures; educational programs; permanent & temporary exhibits.
Publications: newsletter, Calkins Nature Notes; book, The History of the Ellsworth College Museum.
Hours & Admission Prices: Interpretive Center: Mon.-Fri. 8-4; Summer Sat.-Sun. 1-4. No charge; donations accepted. ♿
Attendance: 4,700
Membership: Student $5; Individual $10; Family $15; Donor $25; Sustaining $50; Patron $100; Benefactor $200; Founder $500.

Jefferson

JEFFERSON TELEPHONE MUSEUM, 105 W. Harrison, Jefferson, IA 50129-2105. Mailing Address: P.O. Box 269, Jefferson, IA 50129-0269. Tel.: 515-386-4141. Fax: 515-386-2600.
Founded: 1958.
Key Personnel: Gen. Mgr., James Daubendiek.
Governing Authority: company; nonprofit.
Technology Museum.
Collections: telephones & related telephone equipment; history & evolution of telephony.
Activities: guided tours.
Hours & Admission Prices: Mon.-Fri. 9-4. No charge. Closed major holidays.
Attendance: 100 (estimated)

Johnston

IOWA GOLD STAR MILITARY MUSEUM, 7105 N.W. 70th Ave., Johnston, IA 50131-1824. Tel.: 515-252-4531. Fax: 515-727-3107.
E-mail: goldstarmuseum@iowa.gov
Web Site: www.iowanationalguard.com
Military Museum.
Collections: Iowa veterans; Iowa military history; photographs; personal artifacts.
Activities: group tours.
Hours & Admission Prices: Mon.-Sat. 8:30-4:30. Closed holidays. No charge. ♿

Kellogg

KELLOGG HISTORICAL SOCIETY, 218 High St., Kellogg, IA 50135. Mailing Address: P.O. Box 295, Kellogg, IA 50135-0295.
Founded: 1980.
Congressional District: 3
Key Personnel: Pres. (V), Bill Steenhoek; Financial Dir., Jenna Shine.
Personnel Profile: Part-Time Volunteers 9.
Governing Authority: private; nonprofit organization. Tax-exempt: 501(c)(3).
Historical Society Museum.
Collections: 1,100 piece pitcher collection; 150 nativity sets; artifacts; farm-related items; military display. Historic Buildings: two-story agricultural building; restored country church & school; furnished factory & bank; machine shed & blacksmith shop with equipment & tools.
Facilities: library of genealogy & cemetery records. Museum-related items for sale.
Activities: guided tours. Historical Society Sponsors: biennial 2 day Down Home Christmas Celebration in December.
Publications: quarterly newsletter, The Kellogg Enterprise.
Hours & Admission Prices: Memorial Day weekend to Sept. 1 Mon.-Fri. 9-4, Sun. 1:30-5, Sat. by appointment. Donations requested. Closed all holidays. ♿
Attendance: 1,000 (estimated)
Membership: Annual $15.

Keokuk

KEOKUK RIVER MUSEUM, 117 S. Water St., Keokuk, IA 52632. Mailing Address: P.O. Box 400, Keokuk, IA 52632-0400. Tel.: 319-524-4765. Fax: 319-524-2642.
Web Site: geomverity.org
Founded: 1962.
Congressional District: 1
Key Personnel: Chm. (V), Charles R. Pietscher.
Personnel Profile: Part-Time Volunteers 5.
Governing Authority: municipal. Parent Institution: City of Keokuk. Tax-exempt: 170(b)(1)(A).
Maritime Museum: housed in 1927 Geo. M. Verity Mississippi River Steamboat.
Collections: river transportation; marine.
Research Fields: Upper Mississippi river boats.
Facilities: Museum-related items for sale.
Activities: Civil War re-enactment on hospital boat.
Hours & Admission Prices: April-Oct. Mon. & Thurs.-Fri. 9-12 & 4-6, Sat.-Sun. 9-6. Adults $3, children $1.50; special group rates for 12 or more.
Attendance: 6,000 (accurate)

Keosauqua

VAN BUREN COUNTY HISTORICAL SOCIETY, 1st. St., Keosauqua, IA 52565. Mailing Address: P.O. Box 236, Keosauqua, IA 52565-0236. Tel.: 319-293-3088.
E-mail: dorissecor@netins.net
Web Site: www.villagesofvanburen.com
Founded: 1960.
Congressional District: 1
Key Personnel: Pres., Marvin Danneil; Sec., Doris Secor; Treas., Joe Stump.
Personnel Profile: Part-Time Volunteers 12; Interns 1.
Governing Authority: society. Tax-exempt: 501(c)(3).
Historical House Museum.
Collections: local history & culture; guns; military equipment; personal artifacts; photographs; period furnishings. Historical Buildings: c.1845 Pearson House; 1855 Aunty Green Hotel, Bonaparte; restored log cabins, Selma & Keosauqua; country schoolhouse, sheds; c.1870 Twombly Building.
Facilities: 40-vol. library of maps; atlases; 100 rolls microfilm; census; county newspapers; documents; scrapbooks & books on local history & genealogies available for use on premises. Museum-related items for sale.
Activities: guided tours; formally organized education programs for children; permanent exhibitions.
Publications: books, History of Bonaparte, Iowa; History of Selma-Douds; History of Milton; History of Stockport; History of Birmingham; History of Cantril; Four Seasons-Life on a Pioneer Van Buren County Farm.
Hours & Admission Prices: Society: June to mid-Oct. Sun. & holidays 1-4; other times by appointment. No charge; donations accepted. Pearson House May-Oct. Sun. 1-4. Suggested Donation: adults $2; students $1. Closed holidays.

Attendance: 325 (accurate)
Membership: Van Buren Historical Society: Individual $10.

Knoxville

NATIONAL SPRINT CAR HALL OF FAME & MUSEUM, One Sprint Capital Pl., Knoxville, IA 50138. Mailing Address: P.O. Box 542, Knoxville, IA 50138-0542. Tel.: 641-842-6176. Fax: 641-842-6177.
E-mail: bbaker@sprintcarhof.com
Web Site: www.sprintcarhof.com
Founded: 1986.
Congressional District: 3
Key Personnel: Exec. Dir., Bob Baker; Pres. (V), Mike Brooks; Cur., Tom Schmeh; Devel., Vickie Agan; Mktg. Mgr., Chuck Stowe; Education, Sherry Turner; Registrar & Museum Shop Mgr., Lori DeMoss; Security, Joel Frascht.
Personnel Profile: Full-Time Paid 4; Part-Time Paid 5; Part-Time Volunteers 25.
Governing Authority: private; nonprofit organization. Tax-exempt: 501(c)(3).
Sports Museum.
Collections: history of sprint car racing from early 1900s; open wheel racers to super-modified & big car racing to its present form of winged & non-winged sprint cars.
Major Exhibits: Salute to the 50th Annual Knoxville Nationals, 11/09-8/10.
Facilities: library; 18,000 sq. ft. exhibit space; 40-seat theater; suites & skyboxes. Museum-related items for sale.
Activities: films; guided tours; hobby workshops; mobile vans; theater; traveling exhibitions. Annual Events: Induction Banquet; golf tourneys; auctions; film festival; autograph sessions; trade show.
Publications: bimonthly newsletter, Hallmarks; annual program, NSCHOF Induction Program.
Hours & Admission Prices: Mon.-Fri. 10-5, Sat.-Sun. 12-5. Adults $4; discounts to AAA & ISHA members; members no charge. Closed New Year's Day; Easter; Thanksgiving; Christmas. ♿
Attendance: 9,468 (accurate)
Membership: Supporter $25; International $40; Family $50; Team $100; Friend of the Hall $500; Patron $1,000.

Lake City

CENTRAL SCHOOL MUSEUM, 211 S. Center St., Lake City, IA 51449-2003. Tel.: 712-464-8639.
E-mail: csp1884@hotmail.com
History Museum: housed in a restored 1884 schoolhouse. Listed on the National Historic Register.
Collections: local history & culture; photographs; period furnishings.
Hours & Admission Prices: Daily 9:30-11:30 & 1-5; other times by appointment.

Lamoni

LIBERTY HALL HISTORIC CENTER, 1138 W. Main St., Lamoni, IA 50140-1273. Tel.: 641-784-6133.
E-mail: libhall@grm.net
Founded: 1976.
Congressional District: 5
Key Personnel: C.E.O., Lach Mackay; Pres., Jeff Naylor; Museum Site Dir., Martha McKain.
Personnel Profile: Full-Time Volunteers 1; Part-Time Volunteers 5.
Governing Authority: nonprofit. Parent Institution: Community of Christ. Tax-exempt: 501(c)(3).
Historic House: 1881 building; 1876 schoolhouse.
Collections: period furnishings, textiles, clothing; quilt collections; emphasis on Community of Christ.
Research Fields: biographic research; archaeological dig.
Activities: lectures; organized education programs for children, adults & undergraduate or graduate college students affiliated with Graceland University. Annual Events: teas; Christmas Festival.
Publications: quarterly, Restoration Trail Forum; semi-annual, Community of Christ Historic Sites Foundation Newsletter.
Hours & Admission Prices: March-Dec. 20 Tues.-Sat. 10-4, Sun. 1:30-4. No charge, donations accepted; group tours by appointment, call 641-784-6133.
Attendance: 2,500 (estimated)

Laurens

POCAHONTAS COUNTY IOWA HISTORICAL SOCIETY MUSEUM, 271 N. 3rd St., Laurens, IA 50554-1274. Mailing Address: P.O. Box 148, Laurens, IA 50554-0148. Tel.: 712-841-2577.
Founded: 1977.
Congressional District: 4
Key Personnel: C.E.O., Ann Beneke; Chm. (V) & Pres. (V), Marcia Leu; Financial Dir., Kristy Mather; Cur., Joseph Sobotka; Archivist, Jane Kirchner.
Personnel Profile: Part-Time Volunteers 11.
Governing Authority: society; nonprofit. Tax-exempt.
Historical Society Museum: housed in Carnegie library.
Collections: medical instruments & records of early local physicians; Native American artifacts; World War I uniforms; surveying instruments; farm tools; stereoscope & slides; household items; furnishings; school trophies; costumes; toys; Civil War books. Historic Site: c.1900, Wiegert Farm; two-story farmhouse; barn; smokehouse; hoghouse; machinery building; one-room schoolhouse; church; garden.
Research Fields: county farmsteads.
Facilities: 2,500 sq. ft. exhibit space. Museum-related items for sale.
Activities: school class trips; guided tours; living history farm. Annual Event: farm festival in August.
Publications: quarterly newsletter; annual membership book.
Hours & Admission Prices: Memorial Day-Oct. every other Sun. 2-5, call for reservations. No charge; donations accepted. ♿
Attendance: 650 (estimated)
Membership: Annual $2.50; Life $25.

Le Claire

BUFFALO BILL MUSEUM OF LE CLAIRE, IOWA, INC., 199 N. Front St., Le Claire, IA 52753-7713. Mailing Address: P.O. Box 284, Le Claire, IA 52753-0284. Tel.: 563-289-5580 & 4603.
E-mail: ahlgren1@mchsi.com
Web Site: buffalobillmuseumleclaire.com
Founded: 1957.
Congressional District: 1
Key Personnel: Pres., Kristi Bailey; Exec. Dir., Mary Ahlgren, Ph.D.; Vice Pres., Robert Schiffke; Sec., Debbie Smith; Treas., Betty Clemons.
Personnel Profile: Part-Time Paid 1; Part-Time Volunteers 25.
Governing Authority: nonprofit organization; board of trustees. Tax-exempt: 170(b)(1)(A).
Preservation Project.
Collections: Buffalo Bill Cody memorabilia; riverboat memorabilia; steamboat models; 1869 wooden hall coal fired work boat on the Mississippi River; Lone Star Steamboat; Indian & pioneer artifacts; airplane flight recorders & automobile safety models of Prof. James Ryan II; manuscripts; tax records; rapids pilots; Scott County & Le Claire records.
Research Fields: Cody family; rapids pilots; pioneer families.
Facilities: library. Gift items for sale.
Activities: guided tours; lectures; permanent exhibitions.
Publications: Le Claire, Iowa, A Mississippi River Town; National Historic District Guide to the City of Le Claire, Iowa; newsletter, River Pilot's Pier.
Hours & Admission Prices: Mon.-Sat. 9-5, Sun. 12-5. Adults $5, students & children 5-15 $1; discounts to tour groups of 10 or more, seniors 65 & over and AAM members; scout groups, school groups & members no charge. Closed New Year's Day; Thanksgiving; Christmas. ♿
Attendance: 15,000 (estimated)
Membership: Single $10; Couple $15; Family $20.

Le Mars

ICE CREAM CAPITAL OF THE WORLD VISITOR CENTER, Wells Dairy, Inc., 126 3rd St., S.W., Le Mars, IA 51031-2008. Tel.: 712-546-4090; 800-942-3800, ext. 4090.
E-mail: kmfaber@bluebunny.com
Web Site: welldairy.com
General Museum: home of Blue Bunny Ice Cream.
Collections: history of ice cream & Wells Dairy; simulated production.
Hours & Admission Prices: May-Sept. Mon.-Sat. 10-4, Sun. 1-4; Oct. April Tues.-Sat. 10-4. Adults 13 & over $3, youth 5-12 $1; children 4 & under no charge.

PLYMOUTH COUNTY HISTORICAL MUSEUM, 335 1st Ave., S.W., Le Mars, IA 51031-2000. Tel.: 712-546-7002.
E-mail: pchm@lemarscomm.net
Web Site: plymouthcountymuseum.homestead.com/museum.html
Key Personnel: Admin., Judy Bowman; Registrar & Exhibit Mgr., Jill Titcomb
History Museum. Listed on the National Register of Historic Places.
Collections: local history & culture relating to Plymouth County.
Hours & Admission Prices: Tues.-Sun. 1-5. No charge.

Logan

MUSEUM OF RELIGIOUS ARTS, 2697 Niagara Trail, Logan, IA 51546-6015. Tel.: 712-644-3888.
E-mail: museum@loganet.net
Web Site: www.mrarts.org
Founded: 1995.
Key Personnel: Pres. (V), Kris Haase; Dir., Rhonda McHugh.
Personnel Profile: Full-Time Paid 2; Part-Time Paid 3; Part-Time Volunteers 17.
Governing Authority: nonprofit organization. Tax-exempt: 501(c)(3).
Religious Museum.
Collections: religious history, arts, tradition & culture; statues; Biblical scenes; illuminate films; 44 life-size wax figures.
Facilities: library; chapel; hospitality room; meeting room; theater. Museum-related items for sale.
Activities: chapel rental; tours; films.
Hours & Admission Prices: Tues.-Fri. 9-4, Sat. 10-4, Sun. 12-4. Adults $5; discounts to AAM members; children 15 & under no charge. Sun. pay what you wish. Closed New Year's Day, Easter, Memorial Day, Independence Day, Labor Day, Thanksgiving & Christmas. ♿
Attendance: 12,000 (estimated)
Membership: Single $25; Family $40.

Long Grove

DAN NAGLE WALNUT GROVE PIONEER VILLAGE, 18817 290th St., Long Grove, IA 52756-9615. Tel.: 563-328-3283.
E-mail: conservation@scottcountyiowa.com
Web Site: www.scottcountyiowa.com/conservation
Governing Authority: Parent Institution: Scott County Conservation.
Historic Buildings.
Collections: 18 Historic Buildings: c.1890 Walnut Grove Bank; c.1870 Donahue Train Depot; farm machinery building; barber shop; Bison Saloon; blacksmith shop; carpenter shop; doctor's office; Donahue Train Depot; firehouse; Keppy & Nagle General Store; school; soda fountain shop; telephone office.
Hours & Admission Prices: April-Oct. daily 9-6. No charge; donations accepted.

Lucas

JOHN L. LEWIS MINING & LABOR MUSEUM, 102 Division St., Lucas, IA 50151-7700. Mailing Address: P.O. Box 3, Lucas, IA 50151-0003. Tel.: 641-766-6831. Fax: 641-766-6831.
E-mail: danallen@coalmininglabormuseum.com
Web Site: www.coalmininglabormuseum.com
Governing Authority: nonprofit organization.
Mining & Labor Museum.
Collections: coal mining & labor history; photographs; mine workers memorabilia; period coal mining equipment, tools & documents; John L. Lewis' personal artifacts; family history.
Facilities: theater.
Hours & Admission Prices: April 15-Oct. 15 Mon.-Sat. 9-3; groups by appointment. Adults $2, students 11 & over $1; children under 10 no charge. Closed holidays. ♿
Membership: Individual $5.

Maquoketa

CLINTON ENGINES MUSEUM, Maple & Clark Sts., Maquoketa, IA 52060. Mailing Address: P.O. Box 1245, Maquoketa, IA 52060-1245. Tel.: 563-652-5020. Fax: 563-652-5020.
E-mail: museum@jciahs.com
Web Site: www.clintonengines.com
Key Personnel: C.E.O. & Chm., Asher Schroeder; Cur., Bonnie W. Mitchell
History Museum.
Collections: corporation history & artifacts; gasoline engines; hands-on exhibits.
Facilities: research library; meeting rooms.
Activities: tours.
Publications: Clinton Engines - 1950-1959, The Don Thomas Years; The Maquoketa I Remember; Maquoketa, One of a Kind.
Hours & Admission Prices: Tues.-Fri. 10-4, Sat.-Sun. 12-4. Adults $5. Closed major holidays.

JACKSON COUNTY HISTORICAL MUSEUM & RESEARCH LIBRARY, (M), 1212 E. Quarry, Fairgrounds, Maquoketa, IA 52060. Mailing Address: P.O. Box 1245, Maquoketa, IA 52060-1245. Tel.: 563-652-5020. Fax: 563-652-5020.
E-mail: museum@jciahs.com
Web Site: www.jciahs.com
Founded: 1964.
Congressional District: 2
Key Personnel: C.E.O. & Pres. (V), Asher Schroeder; Cur., Bonnie W. Mitchell.
Personnel Profile: Part-Time Paid 6; Part-Time Volunteers 100.
Governing Authority: historical society board. Parent Institution: Jackson County Historical Society. Subsidiary Institution: Clinton Engines Corporation. Iowa Orphan Train Association Headquarters. Tax-exempt.
History Museum.
Collections: horse-drawn farm machinery; dolls; books; township history; genealogical research material; crafts; spinning; quilting; carpentry tools; transportation; small farm tools; local paintings; country school; printing shop; business & professional; postal; log cabin; firearms; 1914 Case Steam Engine; reproduction of a McCormack Reaper; military artifacts; early cameras & radios; period tractors & agricultural equipment; general store; textiles; wildlife; phones; photographs.
Research Fields: genealogy & township histories of Jackson county; textile information; railroad; lime kilns.
Activities: school, club & tourist tours; tours of local attractions; open houses & demonstrations. Museum Sponsors: Brown Bag Lunch every Tuesday; monthly programs on various topics; garage sale second week of June; Pioneer Day, first Sunday in October; Heritage Dinner, first Sunday in November; Holiday Basket Auction, second Tuesday evening in December.
Publications: quarterly historical society newsletter, Timelines; local interest history books, Ghost Towns of Jackson County; Old Creameries; Agriculture; Country Schools; Cemetery Tours; Couple Dozen in All; Vigilantes; Clinton Engines - 1950-1959, The Don Thomas Years; The Maquoketa I Remember; Maquoketa, One of a Kind.
Hours & Admission Prices: Tues.-Fri. 10-4, Sat.-Sun. 12-4. Adults $5. Closed major holidays. ♿
Attendance: 6,000 (estimated)
Membership: Individual $20; Family $30; Contributor $50.

Marion

MARION HERITAGE CENTER, 590 Tenth St., Marion, IA 52302-4409. Mailing Address: P.O. Box 753, Marion, IA 52302-0753. Tel.: 319-477-6377; 6376.
E-mail: Marionheritage@marion-historical-society.org
Founded: 2000.
Key Personnel: Center Coord., Karen Clark-Hansen; Pres. (V), Marjorie Reynolds.
Personnel Profile: Part-Time Paid 1.
Governing Authority: municipal. Parent Institution: Marion Historical Society. Tax-exempt.
History Museum.
Collections: local history.
Facilities: Museum-related items for sale.
Activities: tours; special events.
Hours & Admission Prices: Wed.-Sun. 1-4. Adults $3, children $1; members no charge. ♿
Attendance: 5,000 (estimated)
Membership: Individual $30; Family $50; Sustaining $100; Silver $250; Gold $500; Platinum $1,000.

MARION HISTORICAL MUSEUMS, INC. - GRANGER HOUSE, 970 Tenth St., Marion, IA 52302-3572. Mailing Address: P.O. Box 753, Marion, IA 52302-0753. Tel.: 319-377-6672.
E-mail: grangerhouse@marian-historical-society.org
Web Site: marion-historical-society.org
Founded: 1973.
Key Personnel: Pres. (V), Marjorie Reynolds.
Personnel Profile: Part-Time Paid 1.
Governing Authority: Parent Institution: Marion Historical Museum Inc., d/b/a Marion Historical Society. Tax-exempt.
Historic House & Site.
Collections: Victorian furnishings; period time pieces; wagon; small carriage house; buggy.
Research Fields: local history.
Facilities: Museum-related items for sale.
Activities: tours; workshops; special events. Museum Sponsors: Ice Cream Social.
Hours & Admission Prices: May-Sept. & late Nov. to early Jan.Thurs.-Sun. 1-4; other times by appointment. Adults $3, children $1; members no charge.
Attendance: 1,500 (estimated)
Membership: Individual $30; Family $50; Sustaining $100.

*** NATIONAL CZECH & SLOVAK MUSEUM & LIBRARY, (M),** 1 Research Center, Marion, IA 52302-5868. Mailing Address: Lindale Mall, 4444 First Ave., NE, Cedar Rapids, IA 52402. Tel.: 319-362-8500. Fax: 319-447-5540.
Web Site: www.ncsml.org
Founded: 1974.
Congressional District: 1
Key Personnel: C.E.O. & Pres., Gail Naughton; Chm. (V), Gary Rozek; Cur., Stefanie Kohn; Librarian, David Muhlena; Volunteer Coord., Patricia Hikiji; Dir. Operations & Education, Janet L. Stoffer; Dir. Devel., Jason Wright; Museum Shop Mgr., Shirley Rosencrans.
Personnel Profile: Full-Time Paid 9; Part-Time Volunteers 200.
Governing Authority: nonprofit organization. Tax-exempt: 501(c)(3).
Heritage Center; Ethnic Museum; Czech and Slovak history and culture. Historic Building: 1880-1900, restored Czech immigrant home.
Collections: folk costumes from the Czech Republic & Slovakia; glass; ceramics; porcelain; ethnic dolls; handwork; wood-carved items; painting & prints; maps & graphic materials; folk, decorative & fine arts; farm tools & implements.
Research Fields: Czech and Slovak history and culture.
Facilities: 20,000-vol. library: Czech & Slovak history & culture. Ethnic glass, ceramics, books & instructional booklets, music & language tapes for sale.
Activities: guided tours; out-reach programs; arts & crafts demonstration; special exhibits; educational programs.
Publications: museum brochure; museum newsletter; journal, Slovo.
Hours & Admission Prices: Temporary location: Lindale Mall, 4444 First Ave., NE Cedar Rapids, IA. Mon.-Sat. 10-5, Sun. 12-5. ♿
Attendance: 34,000 (accurate)
Membership: Individual $35; Family $45; Contributing $100; Sustaining $250.

Marshalltown

CENTRAL IOWA ART ASSOCIATION, Fisher Community Center, Marshalltown, IA 50158. Mailing Address: 709 S. Center St., Marshalltown, IA 50158-2876. Tel.: 641-753-9013.
E-mail: ciaa@iowatelecom.net
Web Site: www.centraliowaartassociation.com
Founded: 1946.
Congressional District: 3
Key Personnel: Pres. (V), William Flowers; Museum Shop Mgr., Jeanne Newton-Schoborg.
Governing Authority: nonprofit organization. Tax-exempt: 501(c)(3).
Impressionist & Ceramics Museum.
Collections: Sisley, Van Dongen, Bonnard, Signac, Henner, Vlaminck, Minaux, Buffet, Utrillo, Degas, Monticelli, Vuillard, Mattisse, Cassatt, Pissarro, Fisher Gallery, ceramics study collection.
Facilities: 500-vol. library of art books available for research to members; studio. Paintings, prints, ceramics, art supplies & jewelry for sale.
Activities: lectures; films; gallery talks; arts festivals; hobby workshops; rental gallery; formally organized education programs; permanent & temporary exhibitions; school loan service; classes & workshops; field trips; local artists gallery. Museum Sponsors: monthly art exhibits.
Publications: monthly newsletter.
Hours & Admission Prices: Mon.-Fri. 11-5. No charge; donations accepted to view art collection only. Closed holidays. ♿
Attendance: 4,000 (estimated)
Membership: Military Veterans $15; High School & College $25; Individual $35; Family $55; Scholarship Fund $100; Arts Angel $200; Painter's Silver $400; Painter's Gold $600; Painter's Platinum $1,000.

MATTHEW EDEL BLACKSMITH SHOP, 202 E. Church St., Marshalltown, IA 50158-2943. Tel.: 641-752-6664 & 475-3299.
History Museum: listed on the National Register of Historic Places.
Collections: early 20th-century blacksmithing.
Hours & Admission Prices: Memorial Day to Labor Day daily 12-4. No charge.

Mason City

*** CHARLES H. MACNIDER MUSEUM, (M),** 303 2nd St., S.E., Mason City, IA 50401-3988. Tel.: 641-421-3666. Fax: 641-422-9612.
E-mail: blanchard@macniderart.org
Web Site: www.macniderart.org
Founded: 1964.
Congressional District: 2
Key Personnel: Dir., Edith M. Blanchard; Pres., Jay Hansen; Coord. Education, Linda Willeke; Registrar & Curatorial Asst., Mara Linskey.
Personnel Profile: Full-Time Paid 7; Part-Time Paid 3.
Governing Authority: municipal. Parent Institution: City of Mason City, IA. Tax-exempt: 170(b)(1)(A).
American Art Museum.
Collections: American and Iowa art including paintings, prints, drawings & pottery; ceramics; puppets, marionettes & related items created & collected by the late master puppeteer Bil Baird.
Major Exhibits: Iowa Crafts: 39, 11/19/09-2/7/10; Running Out of Time, 3/4/10-5/2/10; 30th Annual Cerro Gordo Photo Show, 4/15/10-6/27/10; Iowa Crafts: 39 Best in Show Award Winner Solo Exhibition, 7/8/10-8/29/10.
Research Fields: American & Iowa art.
Facilities: 1,500-vol. library of books on art history, techniques & biographical with emphasis on American art available for use on premises; reading room; classrooms. Paintings, drawings, pottery, jewelry, prints & sculpture for sale.
Activities: guided tours; lectures; films; gallery talks; concerts; arts festivals; drama; rental gallery; formally organized education programs; docent program; permanent, temporary & traveling exhibitions.
Publications: quarterly newsletter; exhibit catalogs; annual report.
Hours & Admission Prices: Tues. & Thurs. 9-9, Wed. & Fri.-Sat. 9-5, Sun. 1-5. No charge; donations accepted. Closed national holidays. ♿
Attendance: 19,482 (estimated)
Membership: Student $25; Individual $30 & up; Household $40 & up; Bronze $100 & up; Silver $250 & up; Gold $500 & up; Platinum $1,000 & up.

Maxwell

COMMUNITY HISTORICAL MUSEUM, Main St., Maxwell, IA 50161. Mailing Address: 11311 W. 124 St., Collins, IA 50055-8505. Tel.: 641-385-2376.
E-mail: jlengeli@iowatelecom.net
Founded: 1964.
Congressional District: 4
Key Personnel: Pres. & Cur., Robert Swanson; Vice Pres., Max Swalwell; Historian, Mrs. Mildred McIntosh.
Personnel Profile: Part-Time Volunteers 10.
Governing Authority: society. Tax-exempt: 501(c)(3).
General Museum.
Collections: agriculture; costumes; history; Indian artifacts; children's museum; transportation; textiles.
Facilities: 600-vol. library of Iowa history books available for use on premises; archives; reading room.
Activities: permanent, temporary & traveling exhibitions.
Publications: Maxwell Centennial History
Hours & Admission Prices: April-Sept. Sun., holidays & by appointment. No charge; donations accepted. ♿
Attendance: 1,350 (accurate)
Membership: Annual $5; Life & Memorials $25.

Middle Amana

COMMUNAL KITCHEN AND COOPERSHOP MUSEUM, 1003 26th Ave., Middle Amana, IA 52203. Mailing Address: Amana Heritage Society, P.O. Box 81, Amana, IA 52203-0081. Tel.: 319-622-3567.
Web Site: www.amanaheritage.org
History Museum.
Collections: period kitchen artifacts; cooper trade tools; restored 1930s communal kitchen.
Hours & Admission Prices: Call for hours. Adults $4, children 8-17 $1; children 7 & under no charge.

Milford

CLARK MUSEUM OF LAKES AREA AND IOWA HISTORY, 2151 213th Ave., Milford, IA 51351-7200. Tel.: 712-338-2147.
E-mail: ijclark1@msm.com
History Museum.
Collections: local & state history and culture; historic photographs; period farm equipment; early furnishings, restaurant & lodging memorabilia; personal artifacts; period advertising; signs; horse-drawn school bus; gas engines; calvary wheels.
Hours & Admission Prices: April-Oct. Tues.-Sat. 10-6, Sun. 11-6. No charge; donations accepted.

Minburn

THE VOAS NATURE AREA/VOAS MUSEUM, 1930 Lexington Rd., Minburn, IA 50167-8148. Mailing Address: 14581 K Avenue, Perry, IA 50220-6379. Tel.: 515-465-3577. Fax: 515-465-3579.
Founded: 1991.
Congressional District: 4
Key Personnel: C.E.O., Mike Wallace; Cur., Archivist & Education, Pete Malmberg.
Personnel Profile: Full-Time Paid 2; Part-Time Paid 1; Part-Time Volunteers 10.

Governing Authority: county. Parent Institution: Dallas County Conservation, 1477 K Ave., Perry, IA 50220. Tax-exempt.
Geological Museum.
Collections: rocks; fossils; minerals; rare native elements; quartz specimens.
Facilities: 265 acre recreation & conservation area; natural resource center; wetland restoration area; woodland & trails; 2,000 sq. ft. exhibit space; botanical garden.
Activities: formal education programs; guided tours.
Publications: triannual newsletter, Raccoon River Greenbelt Newsletter.
Hours & Admission Prices: May-Oct. Sat.-Sun. 1-4 when volunteers are available; other times by appointment; Nov.-April by appointment only. No charge; donations accepted.
Attendance: 1,000 (estimated)

Missouri Valley

STEAMBOAT BERTRAND COLLECTION, DeSoto National Wildlife Refuge, 1434 316th Lane, Missouri Valley, IA 51555-7033. Tel.: 712-642-2772 & 4121. Fax: 712-642-5427.
E-mail: r3bertrand@fws.gov
Web Site: refuges.fws.gov/generalinterest/steamboatbertrand.html
Founded: 1969.
Congressional District: 4
Key Personnel: Refuge Mgr., Tom Cox; Cur., Dean Knudsen.
Personnel Profile: Full-Time Paid 2; Part-Time Volunteers 1.
Governing Authority: federal. Parent Institution: U.S. Fish & Wildlife Service, Dept. of Interior, Washington, DC. Tax-exempt.
Park Museum Center & Historic Site: excavation of the 1865 steamboat Bertrand.
Collections: excavated items from the Bertrand; 1865 sunken steamboat cargo; tools; hardware; textiles; clothing & shoes; armaments; patent medicine; bottled & canned food; housewares; mining, lumbering, farming & building supplies.
Research Fields: steamboat construction; mercantile packing & shipping; tools; hardware; clothing; textiles; food preservation; bottle & can manufacture; bitters; wines; Missouri River transportation; Civil War-era civilian frontier material culture.
Facilities: 1,300-vol. library pertaining to cultural history, western river navigation, steamboating & nature available for research on premises by appointment; nature & conservation center; 80-seat auditorium; theater; visitor center. Historical & nature books, prints & craft items for sale.
Activities: films; formally organized education programs for children; volunteer program; loan & permanent exhibitions.
Publications: guidebook; books, The Steamboat Bertrand; The Bertrand Stores.
Hours & Admission Prices: Daily 9-4:30. $3 per vehicle. Bus: 20 people or less $20; over 20 people $30. Federal Golden Age Passport, Federal Golden Access Passport, Federal Golden Eagle Passport, Federal Duck Stamp no charge. Closed New Year's Day; Thanksgiving; Christmas. ♿
Attendance: 60,000 (accurate)

Mount Pleasant

HARLAN-LINCOLN HOUSE, 101 W. Broad St., Mount Pleasant, IA 52641-1337. Mailing Address: Iowa Wesleyan College, 601 N. Main St., Mount Pleasant, IA 52641. Tel.: 319-385-6215. Fax: 319-385-6324.
E-mail: iwcarch@iwc.edu
Web Site: iwc.edu
Founded: 1959.
Congressional District: 1
Key Personnel: C.E.O., Lynn Ellsworth; Chm. (V), Elizabeth Garrels.
Personnel Profile: Part-Time Paid 1; Part-Time Volunteers 15.
Governing Authority: college. Affiliated with Iowa Wesleyan College, N. Main St. Tax-exempt: 501(c)(3).
Historic House: housed in retirement home of U.S. Senator James Harlan (1876-1899); the summer home of the Robert Todd Lincoln Family (1876-1907).
Collections: original furnishings and memorabilia of the Harlan & Lincoln families; objects of same period.
Activities: guided tours.
Publications: newsletter, Friends of the Harlan-Lincoln House.
Hours & Admission Prices: By appointment only. Adults $2; members no charge. ♿
Attendance: 1,000 (accurate)
Membership: Individual $30; Family $50; Ambassador $100-$249; Cabinet $250-$499; Senator $500-$999; Harlan Society $1,000-$4,999.

MIDWEST OLD SETTLERS & THRESHERS ASSOCIATION, INC., 405 E. Threshers Rd., Mount Pleasant, IA 52641-2584. Tel.: 319-385-8937. Fax: 319-385-0563.
E-mail: admin@oldthreshers.org
Web Site: www.oldthreshers.org
Founded: 1950.
Congressional District: 1
Key Personnel: C.E.O., Lennis Moore; Pres. (V), Bob Gilchrist; Cur. Theatre, Dr. Mike Kramme; Pub. Rels. Coord., Terry McWilliams; Museum Shop Mgr., Linda Dovenspike.
Personnel Profile: Full-Time Paid 7; Full-Time Volunteers 4; Part-Time Paid 2; Part-Time Volunteers 497; Interns 4.
Governing Authority: nonprofit organization. Parent Institution: Midwest Old Threshers. Branch Museum: Museum of Repertoire Americana, Mt. Pleasant, IA. Tax-exempt: 501(c)(3).
Agricultural History Museum.
Collections: steam traction engines, stationary steam, agricultural implements; transportation; folk theatre; antiques. Historic Buildings: authentic railroad depot; narrow gauge railroad; trolleys; log houses; country church; schoolhouse; barber shop; bandstand.
Research Fields: agricultural history; Chautauqua & repertoire theater.
Facilities: research library; theater. Museum-related items for sale.
Activities: guided tours; lectures; films; TV & radio programs; formally organized education programs; permanent, temporary & traveling exhibitions; repertoire theater; docent program. Museum Sponsors: Bussey Doll Convention; Printers' Fair; Midwest Haunted Rails; Thrashers' House of Terror.
Publications: quarterly newspaper, Threshers Chaff; annual, Threshers Review.
Hours & Admission Prices: Office: Mon.-Fri. 8-5. Museum: call for hours. Adults $5; children 14 & under no charge. Theatre museum, $3 per person. ♿
Attendance: 5,127 (estimated)
Membership: Annual $20.

Mount Vernon

MCWETHY HALL, LUCE GALLERY, CORNELL COLLEGE, 600 1st St. W., Mount Vernon, IA 52314-1098. Tel.: 319-895-4491. Fax: 319-895-4519.
E-mail: scoleman@cornellcollege.edu
Web Site: www.cornellcollege.edu
Formerly: Armstrong Gallery, Cornell College
Founded: 1853.
Congressional District: 1
Key Personnel: Pres., Les Garner; Dept. Chm., Tony Plant; Interim Dean, Chris Carlson; Business Officer, Tom Church; Exhibitions Coord., Susan Coleman; Dir. Public Information, DeeAnn Rexroat.
Personnel Profile: Full-Time Paid 1; Interns 2.
Governing Authority: college. Parent Institution: Cornell College. Tax-exempt.
College Museum.
Collections: Sonnenschein Collection of baroque drawings; drawings & prints of Thomas Nast; Whiting Collection of Phoenician glass; Karel Appel painting; Roy Lichtenstein litho. prints; Grant Wood lithographs; Charles Atherton Cummings paintings; Richard Anuskiewicz; Larry Rivers painting; Henry A Mills paintings.
Major Exhibits: Group Show Paintings by Steve Erickson, 1/10/10-2/7/10; Three for a Dime, Maxine Payne, 2/21/10-3/21/10; Senior Shows, 4/11/10-5/19/10; Homecoming Exhibition, 9/10-10/10.
Activities: lectures; formally organized education programs for undergraduate college students; temporary & traveling exhibitions.
Hours & Admission Prices: Academic Year: Mon.-Fri. 9-4, Sun. 2-4; Summer: by appointment only. No charge; donations accepted. Closed school holidays. ♿
Attendance: 5,000 (estimated)

Muscatine

* **MUSCATINE ART CENTER, (M),** 1314 Mulberry Ave., Muscatine, IA 52761-3429. Tel.: 563-263-8282. Fax: 563-263-4702.
E-mail: art@ci.muscatine.ia.us
Web Site: www.muscatineartcenter.org
Founded: 1965.
Congressional District: 1
Key Personnel: Dir., Barbara C. Christensen; Friends Pres., Kristin McHugh-Johnston; Education Coord., Maria Norton; Registrar, Virginia Cooper; Office Coord., Lynn Bartenhagen; Office Asst., Patricia Carver; Technician, Andrew Tabor; Technician, Julie Lear.
Personnel Profile: Full-Time Paid 2; Part-Time Paid 5; Part-Time Volunteers 20.
Governing Authority: municipal. Tax-exempt: 501(c)(3).
Art Center: housed in 1908 Edwardian style Musser Mansion & 1976 Stanley Gallery.
Collections: 19th & 20th century American art; paintings; sculpture; prints;

drawings; oriental rugs; textiles; decorative arts; historical artifacts of Iowa & Muscatine; antique glass paperweights; children's toys.
Research Fields: related to art collection, emphasizing the Great River Collection of works documenting the Mississippi River.
Facilities: 1,000-vol. library of art history, period furnishings, decorative arts, available for research on premises only; 100-seat auditorium; classrooms; gallery.
Activities: guided tours; lectures; films; gallery talks; concerts; formally organized education programs; docent program; permanent & temporary exhibitions.
Publications: bimonthly newsletter; catalogues of exhibitions.
Hours & Admission Prices: Tues., Wed. & Fri. 10-5, Thurs. 10-7, Sat. & Sun. 1-5. No charge. Closed national holidays. ♿
Attendance: 16,000
Membership: Individual $30; Family $50; Contributing $100; Sustaining $500; Benefactor $1,000.

MUSCATINE HISTORY & INDUSTRY CENTER/PEARL BUTTON MUSEUM, (M), 117 W. Second St., Muscatine, IA 52761-3714. Tel.: 563-263-1052.
E-mail: malexander@machlink.com
Web Site: www.muscatinehistory.org
Founded: 1992.
Key Personnel: Exec. Dir., Melanie K. Alexander; Pres., Clyde Evans; Treas., Mark Huddleston.
Personnel Profile: Full-Time Paid 1; Part-Time Paid 1; Part-Time Volunteers 15; Interns 1.
Governing Authority: private; nonprofit organization. Parent Institution: Historic Muscatine, Inc., 117 W. 2nd St., Muscatine, IA 52761. Tax-exempt: 501(c)(3).
History Museum.
Collections: 1890-1960s pearl button memorabilia & machinery; history of the freshwater pearl button industry in Muscatine, IA; local business artifacts.
Research Fields: clamming history; history of button manufacturing.
Facilities: Museum-related items for sale.
Activities: guided tours; temporary exhibitions. Annual Events: Button Workers' Reunion; Historic Preservation Awards.
Publications: quarterly newsletter, Pearl Button Bulletin.
Hours & Admission Prices: Tues.-Sat. 10-4. Suggested Donation: adults $4, students $2.
Attendance: 10,000 (accurate)
Membership: Senior $25; Individual $35; Household $50; Corporate $500 & up.

PINE CREEK GRIST MILL, Wildcat Den State Park, 1884 Wildcat Den Rd., Muscatine, IA 52761-9479. Tel.: 319-263-4337. Fax: 319-264-8329.
E-mail: jim.ohl@dnr.state.ia.us
Web Site: www.pinecreekgristmill.com
Historic Building: built in 1848 by Benjamin Nye. Listed on the National Register of Historic Places.
Collections: structure; 19th-century milling industry.
Activities: educational programs for students.
Hours & Admission Prices: May & Sept. 26-Oct. 11 Sat.-Sun. 12:30-4:30; June-Sept. 20 Wed.-Sun. 12:30-4:30

Nashua

CHICKASAW COUNTY HISTORICAL SOCIETY BRADFORD PIONEER VILLAGE MUSEUM, 2729 Cheyenne Ave., Nashua, IA 50658-9611. Tel.: 641-435-2567.
E-mail: cchs@myclearwave.net
Web Site: www.chickasawtrails.com
Founded: 1953.
Congressional District: 2
Key Personnel: Pres., Ben Scholl; Vice Pres., Dick Schilling; Sec., Marilyn Randall; Treas., Ruth Rosauer; Museum Shop Mgr., Karen Wilson.
Personnel Profile: Full-Time Paid 1; Part-Time Paid 1; Part-Time Volunteers 10.
Governing Authority: nonprofit organization. Tax-exempt: 170(b)(1)(A).
General Museum: located on site of 1859 original Bradford village.
Collections: pioneer farm machinery; Indian artifacts; arts & crafts; clothing; Victorian cottage & furniture; Dr. Pitts Medical Office; depot & railroad museum; caboose & railroad track; 2 log homes; country store; laundry; blacksmith shop; agriculture building; heritage house; toy shop; country school; old jail.
Research Fields: genealogy.
Facilities: old school texts & medical books available for use by appointment. Gifts & handicrafts for sale.
Activities: guided tours; lectures; permanent exhibitions.
Publications: pamphlet; annual report; newsletter; guide book tours.
Hours & Admission Prices: May-Oct. Mon.-Sat. 9-5, Sun. 12-5; groups by appointment only. Adults $5, children K-12 $3; members no charge.
Attendance: 3,000 (estimated)
Membership: Annual $20.

New London

DOVER HISTORICAL MUSEUM, 213 W. Main St., New London, IA 52645-1337. Tel.: 877-468-7700.
Web Site: www.dovermuseum.org
Founded: 1994.
Key Personnel: Pres. (V), Gwen Moore.
Personnel Profile: Part-Time Volunteers 20.
Governing Authority: Tax-exempt.
Historic Building: listed on the National Register of Historic Places.
Collections: local history; genealogy; rocks & minerals; quilts; early businesses; Masons & Eastern Star; one-room school; agriculture; military.
Major Exhibits: Plank Road (T), 1/10-12/10.
Activities: demonstrations for children.
Hours & Admission Prices: May-Dec. Sat.-Sun. 1-4. No charge; donations accepted. ♿
Attendance: 1,700 (estimated)
Membership: Student $1; Individual $10; Family $15; Friend $50-$99; Sustaining $100-$249; Supporting $250-$499; Benefactor $500-$999; Sponsor $1,000 & up.

Oakland

NISHNA HERITAGE MUSEUM, 117 Main St., Oakland, IA 51560. Mailing Address: P.O. Box 324, Oakland, IA 51560-0324. Tel.: 712-482-6802.
Web Site: www.nishnaheritagemuseum.com
Founded: 1975.
Congressional District: 5
Key Personnel: Pres., Gayle Perkins; Finance Dir., Wilson Pechacek; Trustee, Jo Kates.
Personnel Profile: Full-Time Volunteers 1; Part-Time Volunteers 6.
Governing Authority: society; nonprofit organization. Parent Institution: Oakland Historical Society. Tax-exempt: 501(c)(3).
Heritage Museum: housed in 1905 general store; 1907 hardware store.
Collections: thimbles; sewing machines; washing machines; keys; buttons; buckles; ladies combs; irons; clothing; fruit jars; lighting fixtures; ice making machinery; furnishings; local artifacts; household items; old conveyances; soda fountain, ice cream table & chairs; dolls; model Conestoga wagon. Historic Building: 1907 hardware store; archaeology bones of 1 to 64 million years ago; history of printing artifacts; salesman models.
Research Fields: c.1900 artifacts.
Activities: guided tours; lectures; organized education programs for children.
Publications: weekly columns; newspaper.
Hours & Admission Prices: Mon.-Fri. 11-3, Sun. 12-3. Adults $5. ♿
Attendance: 500 (estimated)
Membership: Annual $10.

Odebolt

ODEBOLT HISTORICAL MUSEUM, 2nd & Maple Sts., Odebolt, IA 51458. Mailing Address: P.O. Box 196, Odebolt, IA 51458-0196. Tel.: 712-668-2264 & 2766.
E-mail: cklarson@netins.net
Web Site: www.odebolt.net/museum.html
Key Personnel: Pres. & Cur., Kathy Larson; Vice Pres., Mary Schroeder; Sec., Eleanor Peterson; Treas., Renae Babcock
History Museum.
Collections: military artifacts; household items; farming tools & equipment; Buffalo Bill's buffalo robe; photographs.
Hours & Admission Prices: Memorial Day & Odebolt Creek Days in June; other times by appointment. No charge; donations accepted.

Oelwein

OELWEIN AREA HISTORICAL SOCIETY MUSEUM, 900 2nd Ave., S.E., Oelwein, IA 50662-3055. Mailing Address: P.O. Box 445, Oelwein, IA 50662-0445. Tel.: 319-283-4203.
Historical Society Museum.
Collections: local history & culture; photographs; personal artifacts.
Hours & Admission Prices: June-Sept. Sun. 1-4; Oct.-May by appointment. Adults $2, students $1; discounts to groups; children under 12 no charge.

Ogden

HICKORY GROVE RURAL SCHOOL MUSEUM, Baltin Chapel Complex, Junction of E 41 & J Ave., Ogden, IA 50212. Mailing Address: 602 Story St., Boone, IA 50036-2832. Tel.: 515-432-1907.
E-mail: bchs@opencominc.com
Founded: 1972.
Congressional District: 4
Key Personnel: Dir., Charles Irwin; Chm. (V), Rita Knight; Sec., Janet Tait; Treas., Troy Thompson.
Personnel Profile: Full-Time Paid 1; Part-Time Paid 1; Part-Time Volunteers 10.
Governing Authority: nonprofit organization. Parent Institution: Boone County Historical Society, 602 Story St., Boone, IA 50036. Tax-exempt: 501(c)(3).
Historic House & Museum: housed in an 1889 restored rural school.
Collections: original double desks; stage curtain; pot-bellied stove; angle lamps; pump organ; photographs; documents; teacher's & children's costumes.
Research Fields: rural school history of Boone County & Iowa.
Facilities: 200-vol. library of rural school textbooks; adjacent park with fishing, golfing & camping available.
Activities: guided tours; organized educational programs for children; video tape presentation.
Publications: biannual journal, Trail Tales; biannual newsletter, History Page.
Hours & Admission Prices: Call for hours. No charge; donations accepted.
Attendance: 400 (estimated)
Membership: Boone County Historical Society: Individual & Family $35; Business & Organization $100; Life $600.

Okoboji

THE HIGGINS MUSEUM, (M), 1507 Sanborn Ave., Okoboji, IA 51355. Mailing Address: P.O. Box 258, Okoboji, IA 51355-0258. Tel.: 712-332-5859. Fax: 712-332-5859.
E-mail: ladams@thehigginsmuseum.org
Web Site: www.thehigginsmuseum.org
Founded: 1978.
Congressional District: 5
Key Personnel: Bd. Pres. & Chm. (V), Dean Oakes; Cur., Larry Adams.
Personnel Profile: Full-Time Paid 1; Part-Time Paid 1; Part-Time Volunteers 5.
Governing Authority: private; nonprofit organization.
History & Numismatics Museum.
Collections: national bank notes from 1863-1935; concentrating on Iowa & adjoining states (MN, NE, WI, IL, MO, SD) with representation from all issuing states; 20,000 real photos, turn of the century Iowa postcards; security printing.
Research Fields: national banks in Iowa, Minnesota, South Dakota, Nebraska, Missouri & other states.
Facilities: 2,500-vol. library of numismatics; 7,000 sq. ft. exhibit space. Museum-related items for sale.
Activities: guided tours; temporary exhibitions. Annual Event: coin, paper money & post card show in August.
Hours & Admission Prices: May-Sept. Tues.-Sun. 11-5:30. No charge; donations accepted. ♿
Attendance: 1,020 (accurate)

PEARSON LAKES ART CENTER, 2201 Hwy. 71, Okoboji, IA 51355-0255. Mailing Address: P.O. Box 255, Okoboji, IA 51355-0255. Tel.: 712-332-7013. Fax: 712-332-7014.
E-mail: info@lakesart.org
Web Site: www.lakesart.org
Founded: 1965.
Key Personnel: C.E.O., Tom Tourville; Dir. Visual Arts, Lissa Potter; Dir. Performing Art, Danielle Clouse; Dir. Education, Katie Meyer.
Personnel Profile: Full-Time Paid 3; Part-Time Paid 4.
Governing Authority: Tax-exempt.
Art Center.
Collections: hands-on exhibits; works by international & national artists.
Major Exhibits: Hiromi Okumura, 4/23/10-6/26/10; Managed Collections, 4/23/10-7/17/10; Bill Hamilton, 5/7/10-7/10/10; Dennis Dykema, 7/2/10-10/2/10; Barbara Brandel/Tony Winchester, 7/16/10-10/9/10; Schminke/Krause/Lhotka, 7/23/10-11/6/10; Plein Air Exhibition, 10/8/10-12/4/10; Bill Lieb, 10/15/10-12/31/10; Wanda J. Skogerboe Juried Exhibition, 12/11/10-3/5/11.
Activities: festivals; film series; readings; educational programs; musical & theatrical events.
Hours & Admission Prices: June-Aug. Mon.-Wed. & Fri.-Sat. 10-4, Thurs. 10-9, Sun. 12-3; Sept.-May Tues.-Wed. & Fri.-Sat. 10-4, Thurs. 10-9. No charge; donations accepted. ♿
Attendance: 20,000 (accurate)
Membership: Senior $35; Single $45; Family $65; Sustainer $125; Supporter $165; Patron $250; Associate $500; Benefactor $1,000; Corporate $5,000.

Onawa

MONONA COUNTY HISTORICAL MUSEUM, 47 12th St., Onawa, IA 51040. Mailing Address: Box 382, Onawa, IA 51040-0382. Tel.: 712-423-3452.
Key Personnel: Pres. (V), Phyllis Mander.
Personnel Profile: Full-Time Volunteers 1; Part-Time Volunteers 15.
Governing Authority: Parent Institution: Loess Hills Historical Society. Tax-exempt.
History Museum: birthplace of the Eskimo Pie.
Collections: Eskimo Pie company history; dipping machine & equipment; farm implements; period furnishings.
Hours & Admission Prices: Memorial Day to Labor Day Sat.-Sun. 1-4:30; other times by appointment. No charge; donations accepted. ♿
Attendance: 1,000 (estimated)
Membership: Individual $5; Senior Citizen $25; Family $50.

MONONA COUNTY VETERAN'S MEMORIAL MUSEUM, 203 12th St., Onawa, IA 51040. Mailing Address: P.O. Box 418, Onawa, IA 51040-0418. Tel.: 712-423-2411.
Founded: 2000.
Key Personnel: Cur., William Wonder; Cur., Duane Miller
Military Museum.
Collections: M60 armored tank; A7D Corsair II fighter jet; Vietnam ear UH-1 Huey helicopter; photographs; uniforms; personal artifacts; 105 Howitzer; '42 Ford Jeep; Danforth ship's anchor; military weapons.
Hours & Admission Prices: May-Sept. Sat.-Sun. 1-4; other times by appointment. No charge; donations accepted. ♿
Attendance: 2,750 (accurate)

Osage

CEDAR VALLEY MEMORIES, 1 1/2 Mile W. Hwy. 9, Osage, IA 50461. Mailing Address: Cedar Valley Memories c/o Mitchell County Historical Society, P.O. Box 51, Osage, IA 50461-0051. Tel.: 641-732-1269.
Governing Authority: county. Parent Institution: Mitchell County Historical Society. Tax exempt: 501(c)(3).
History Museum.
Collections: 5 vintage steam engines including 1922 32 H.P. Advence-Rumley, 1912 Reeves 40-140 Cross Compound, 1878 Blumentrit, two cylinder; first gas running car built in Osage, 1901; agricultural items.
Activities: Museum Sponsors: Cedar Valley Memories Power Show in August.
Hours & Admission Prices: Memorial Day to Labor Day Sat.-Sun. 1-4; other times by appointment. No charge.

MITCHELL COUNTY HISTORICAL MUSEUM, (M), N. 6th, Osage, IA 50461. Mailing Address: P.O. Box 297, Riceville, IA 50466-0297. Tel.: 515-732-1269.
Founded: 1965.
Congressional District: 4
Key Personnel: Chm., Merri Cross; Pres. (V), Krista Koschmeder.
Personnel Profile: Part-Time Paid 2; Part-Time Volunteers 50; Interns 2.
Governing Authority: county. Parent Institution: Mitchell County Historical Society. Tax-exempt: 501(c)(3).
History Museum: housed in 1869 Cedar Valley Seminary.
Collections: clothing; guns; tools; household items; books; portraits; documents; mail wagon, covered wagon; musical instruments; medical instruments; spinning wheels; original beauty shop equipment; Indian artifacts; Hamlin Garland.
Research Fields: genealogy; cemeteries of the county; rural school records; Pioneer Club; Century Farms; county history.
Facilities: 2,000-vol. library; reading room. Museum-related items for sale.
Activities: guided tours; lectures; study clubs; spinning wheel demonstrations.
Publications: cookbook, Heritage from the Kitchen; History of David, Iowa.
Hours & Admission Prices: Memorial Day-Labor Day Sat.-Sun. 1-4. No charge; donations accepted.
Attendance: 400 (estimated)
Membership: Individual $15.

Oskaloosa

NELSON PIONEER FARM AND MUSEUM, 2211 Nelson Lane, Oskaloosa, IA 52577-9609. Mailing Address: Mahaska County Historical Society, P.O. Box 578, Oskaloosa, IA 52577-0578. Tel.: 515-672-2989.
E-mail: nelsonpioneerfarm@pcsia.net
Web Site: www.nelsonpioneer.org
Founded: 1942.

Key Personnel: Pres., Joe Crookham; Vice Pres., Dale Van Veldhuizen; Cur. & Museum Shop Mgr., Pamela Howard.
Personnel Profile: Full-Time Paid 1; Part-Time Paid 2; Part-Time Volunteers 3.
Governing Authority: society; nonprofit educational institution. Owned and operated by Mahaska County Historical Society. Tax-exempt.
General Museum: housed in 1853 Daniel & Margaret Nelson Home & 1856 Nelson barn; located on 1844 homestead.
Collections: agriculture; Indian artifacts; archaeology; farm machinery exhibit. Historic Houses: 1853 Prine Schoolhouse; 1861 Littler Log Cabin; Spring Creek Voting House; 1915 W.L. Mott & Son General Store; 1865 Buffalo farm scale & Scale House; 1864 Coal Creek Friends meeting house; Wright, Iowa Post Office; Kalbach Lumberyard first office; blacksmith shop; Hopewell building.
Research Fields: agriculture.
Facilities: 1,000-vol. library of books, scrap books, folders & clippings available for use on premises. Gift items for sale.
Activities: guided tours; permanent exhibitions. Museum Sponsors: Fall Festival Day in September.
Publications: quarterly newsletter, News Bulletin.
Hours & Admission Prices: mid-May to mid-Oct. Tues.-Sat. 10-4, Sun. 12-5. Tours 10-3; bus tours by special arrangement. Adults $7, students 5-16 $2; children under 5 & society members no charge. ♿
Attendance: 3,537 (accurate)
Membership: Individual $10; Family $18; Lifetime $100; Lifetime Couple $175.

Ottumwa

AIRPOWER MUSEUM INC., 22001 Bluegrass Rd., Ottumwa, IA 52501-8569. Tel.: 641-938-2773. Fax: 641-938-2093.
E-mail: antiqueairfield@sirisonline.com
Web Site: www.antiqueairfield.com
Founded: 1965.
Congressional District: 3
Key Personnel: Chm. & C.E.O., Robert L. Taylor; Treas., Brent Taylor; Graphics Editor, Cindy Reis.
Governing Authority: nonprofit organization. Tax-exempt: 501(c)(3).
Aeronautics Museum.
Collections: period airplanes; model airplanes; aviators clothing; manuscripts; medals; trophies; 57 full-size aircraft; 150 aircraft models; 50 aircraft engines; miscellaneous items related to aviation history.
Research Fields: aviation history; historical technical information.
Facilities: library of books on aviation history; reading room. Books & gift items for sale.
Activities: loan & permanent exhibitions.
Publications: quarterly magazine, Airpower Museum (APM); bulletin.
Hours & Admission Prices: Mon.-Fri. 9-5, Sat. 10-5, Sun. 1-5. No charge; donations accepted. Closed New Year's Day; Independence Day; Labor Day; Thanksgiving; Christmas. ♿
Attendance: 6,500 (estimated)

WAPELLO COUNTY HISTORICAL MUSEUM, 210 W. Main, Ottumwa, IA 52501-2500. Tel.: 641-682-8676. Fax: 641-682-8676.
E-mail: wcha@pcsia.net
Founded: 1959.
Congressional District: 1
Key Personnel: Pres., George Israel; Vice Pres., Harold Gipson; Sec., Carole Parcel; Treas., Cathy Penniston; Registrar & Coord., Sue Parrish; Cur., Rusty Cordor.
Personnel Profile: Full-Time Paid 1; Part-Time Paid 2; Part-Time Volunteers 37.
Governing Authority: society. Parent Institution: Wapello Co. Historical Society. Tax-exempt.
History Museum.
Collections: artifacts from all aspects of life in Wapello County from prehistory to present; records of early industries; old blacksmith, carpenter & stonemason tools; detailed scale model of 1890-1891 Ottumwa Coal Palace Industrial Exhibit Hall; old kitchen utensils; early furniture; costumes; telecommunications.
Research Fields: local & county history; early Iowa Indian Territory.
Facilities: 200-vol. library of state, county & local history, available for use on premises.
Activities: guided tours; lectures; permanent exhibitions; special events.
Publications: quarterly newsletter; local history brochures & pamphlets.
Hours & Admission Prices: Tues.-Fri. 10-4, Sat. 12-4. Adults $3, children under 12 $1; scheduled student tours & members no charge. ♿
Attendance: 1,423 (accurate)
Membership: Individual $15; Family $25; Life $250; Corporate $500.

Pella

PELLA HISTORICAL VILLAGE, 507 Franklin St., Pella, IA 50219-1671. Mailing Address: P.O. Box 145, Pella, IA 50219-0145. Tel.: 641-628-4311. Fax: 515-628-9192.
E-mail: pellatuliptime@iowatelecom.net
Web Site: www.pellatuliptime.com
Founded: 1965.
Key Personnel: C.E.O., Jeff Bollard; Dir., Patsy Sadler.
Personnel Profile: Full-Time Paid 2; Part-Time Paid 6.
Governing Authority: society. Parent Institution: Pella Historical Society. Tax-exempt: 170(b)(1)(A).
Ethnic (Dutch) Museum Complex: located in 20 historic buildings.
Collections: archives; ethnology; industrial; preservation project; authentic Dutch costumes; Dutch bakery; complete set of newspapers printed in Pella. Historic Buildings: 1851 Wyatt Earp boyhood home; 1843 pioneer log cabin; 1853 Van Spankeren store; 1874 Amsterdam school; 1850 Dutch windmill.
Research Fields: archives; ethnology; industrial; preservation project.
Facilities: Items from the Netherlands for sale.
Activities: guided tours; films; arts festivals.
Publications: annual brochure, Tulip Time in Pella; quarterly newsletter, Historic Village Newsletter.
Hours & Admission Prices: March-Dec. Mon.-Sat. 9-4. Adults $8, K-12 $2; members no charge. Closed national holidays. ♿
Attendance: 20,000 (estimated)
Membership: Individual $35; Silver $55; Family $65; Gold $105.

SCHOLTE HOUSE MUSEUM, 728 Washington, Pella, IA 50219-1523. Tel.: 641-628-3684.
Founded: 1982.
Key Personnel: Chm. (V), Arlys Verdoorn; Cur., Shirley J. Rudd; Archivist, Susan Miller; Museum Shop Mgr., Kathy Jaarsma-Tripp.
Personnel Profile: Full-Time Volunteers 1; Part-Time Volunteers 14.
Governing Authority: private; nonprofit organization. Parent Institution: Pella Historical Society. Tax-exempt.
Historic House Museum: home of the founding father of the town of Pella, Dominie Henry Peter Scholte c.1847.
Collections: furnishings and art belonging to Dominie Scholte and his family.
Facilities: library of books written by Dominie Scholte. Museum-related items for sale.
Activities: concerts; teas; self-guided tours; workshops for volunteers.
Publications: brochures.
Hours & Admission Prices: March-Dec. Mon.-Sat. 1-4; appointments available. Adults $5, students & children $1; discounts to AAA members; Pella district & Central College students no charge. Windmill Historical Village & Scholte House: adults $11. Closed New Year's Day; Easter; Memorial Day; Independence Day; Labor Day; Thanksgiving; Christmas Eve & Day. ♿
Attendance: 3,000 (estimated)

Perry

CARNEGIE LIBRARY MUSEUM, 1123 Willis Ave., Perry, IA 50220. Tel.: 515-465-7713; 3511 (hotel). Fax: 515-465-7714.
Governing Authority: city of Perry.
Library Museum: built in 1904. Listed on the National Register of Historic Places.
Collections: books including midwest literature, women's fiction, children's books, & books on literacy and libraries; early life of area women; town's former courthouse.
Hours & Admission Prices: Call for hours.

FOREST PARK MUSEUM AND ARBORETUM, (M), 14581 K Ave., Perry, IA 50220-6379. Tel.: 515-465-3577. Fax: 515-465-3579.
E-mail: conservation@co.dallas.ia.us
Web Site: www.conservation.co.dallas.ia.us
Founded: 1953.
Congressional District: 4
Key Personnel: C.E.O., Mike Wallace; Cur., Archivist & Education, Pete Malmberg.
Personnel Profile: Full-Time Paid 1; Part-Time Paid 1; Part-Time Volunteers 10; Interns 1.
Governing Authority: county. Parent Institution: Dallas County Conservation Department, Perry, IA 50220. Subsidiary Institution: The Voas Nature Area/Voas Museum, Minburn, IA. Tax-exempt.
History Museum.
Collections: early transportation; farm machinery; small hand tools; railroading; blacksmith shop.

Research Fields: archaeological excavations; early farmstead; cultural resource surveys & mapping.
Facilities: 100-vol. library Perry Newspapers; 6,500 sq. ft. exhibit space; arboretum; visitor center; picnic area; county conservation headquarters.
Activities: arts festivals; concerts; formal education programs; historical programs; guided tours; lectures; loan & temporary exhibitions. Museum Sponsors: Arboretum Accolades - concert; Scenic History Drive; Pioneer Heritage Day - festival; antique roadshows (evaluations); family fun days; old fashioned Christmas.
Publications: quarterly newsletter.
Hours & Admission Prices: May-Oct. Mon.-Fri. 9-4:30, Sat.-Sun. 1-4:30; Nov.-April by appointment only. No charge.
Attendance: 2,000 (estimated)

Peterson

PRAIRIE HERITAGE CENTER, 4931 Yellow Ave., Peterson, IA 51047-7528. Tel.: 712-295-7200.
E-mail: occb@iowatelecom.net
Web Site: prairieheritagecenter.org
History Museum.
Collections: exhibits & artifacts relating to the prairie.
Hours & Admission Prices: Wed.-Fri. 9-4, Sat.-Sun. 1-4.

Pomeroy

THE KALEIDOSCOPE FACTORY, 104 S. Main St., Pomeroy, IA 50575-7736. Tel.: 712-468-2420.
E-mail: chelp@ncn.net
Web Site: kaleidoscopefactory.com
Key Personnel: Head Kaleidoscope Maker, Leonard Olson
History Museum.
Collections: hand-krafted kaleidoscopes, dippers & spurtles.
Facilities: Museum-related items for sale.
Activities: woodturning demonstrations.
Hours & Admission Prices: Tours: Tues. & Thurs. 1-9, Sat. 10-5; other times by appointment. No charge.

Prairie City

NEIL SMITH NATIONAL WILDLIFE REFUGE PRAIRIE LEARNING CENTER, 9981 Pacific St., Prairie City, IA 50228-7820. Mailing Address: P.O. Box 399, Prairie City, IA 50228-3400. Tel.: 515-994-3400.
E-mail: buffalo@tallgrass.org
Web Site: www.tallgrass.org
Key Personnel: Pres. Friends of Prairie Learning Center, Mark Lyle; Park Ranger, Al Murray; Park Ranger, Hallie Runeussen
Wildlife Refuge.
Collections: bison & elk; interactive exhibits; photographs; film.
Facilities: nature trails. Museum-related items for sale.
Activities: film.
Hours & Admission Prices: Mon.-Sat. 9-4, Sun. 12-5. No charge. Closed New Year's Day; Thanksgiving; Christmas. ♿

Prescott

KLINE MUSEUM, 2280 6th Ave., Prescott, IA 50859.
History Museum.
Collections: local history; period vehicles including 1911 Carter Car, 1929 Ford Model A fire truck; Ford Model T truck; farm machinery; local memorabilia.
Hours & Admission Prices: Memorial Day to Labor Day Sun. 1-4; other times by appointment.

Princeton

BUFFALO BILL CODY HOMESTEAD, 28050 230th Ave., Princeton, IA 52768-9713. Mailing Address: 14910 110th Ave., Davenport, IA 52804-9020. Tel.: 563-225-2981. Fax: 563-381-2805.
Web Site: www.scottcountyiowa.com
Founded: 1970.
Congressional District: 1
Key Personnel: C.E.O., Roger Kean; Museum Shop Mgr., Marilyn McCool.
Personnel Profile: Full-Time Paid 1; Part-Time Paid 2.
Governing Authority: county. Parent Institution: Scott County Conservation Bd. Tax-exempt: 501(c)(3).
Historic House: 1847 boyhood home of Buffalo Bill Cody.
Collections: middle 19th-century furnishings; photos; Indian artifacts; farm implements; buffalo.
Facilities: Gift items for sale.
Activities: guided tours.
Hours & Admission Prices: April-Oct. daily 9-5. Adults $2; children 16 & under no charge.
Attendance: 7,000 (estimated)

Rock Rapids

LYON COUNTY HISTORICAL SOCIETY MUSEUM COMPLEX, 110 1/2 N. Story St., Rock Rapids, IA 51246-1526. Tel.: 712-472-3101.
History Museum: housed in the former Rock Island Depot.
Collections: local history & culture; caboose; livery stable; windmill; Victorian house; photographs; personal artifacts.
Hours & Admission Prices: Memorial Day-Labor Day Sun. & holidays 2-5; other times by appointment.

Rockwell City

CALHOUN COUNTY MUSEUM, 150 E. High St., U.S. Hwy. 20, Rockwell City, IA 50579. Mailing Address: 2314 310th St., Rockwell City, IA 50579-7657. Tel.: 712-297-8139, 8307 & 8302.
Founded: 1956.
Congressional District: 6
Key Personnel: Pres., Weston Thompson; 1st Vice Pres., Marlene Johnson; Sec., Marjorie Hepp; Treas., Toni Kerns; Museum Shop Mgr., JoAnn Maguire.
Personnel Profile: Part-Time Paid 1; Part-Time Volunteers 25.
Governing Authority: bd. of directors. Tax-exempt: 501(c)(3).
General Museum.
Collections: farming & period farm machinery; medical & dental equipment; clothing; irons; bottles; typewriters; books; dishes; pioneer equipment; photographic equipment; period furnishings; 1,000 salt & pepper shakers; 100 birds & small animals; local genealogical records; manuscripts; scrapbooks; musical instruments; period carpenter's tools; Mickey Mouse; quilts.
Research Fields: county history; preservation of artifacts; genealogy.
Facilities: 1,450-vol. library of books from early homes & schools available for research; 600 books of tax records.
Activities: guided tours; permanent & temporary exhibitions; pioneer crafts for sixth grade classes; tour & pioneer history of county for second, third & fourth grade classes.
Publications: cemetery booklets, County Tours; book, Calhoun County History, Sesquicentennial.
Hours & Admission Prices: May-Oct. Tues. & Sat.-Sun. 1-4. No charge; donations accepted. ♿
Attendance: 2,500 (estimated)
Membership: Annual $5; Life $50.

Ruthven

LOST ISLAND PRAIRIE WETLAND NATURE CENTER, 3259 355th Ave., Ruthven, IA 51358-8521. Tel.: 712-837-4866. Fax: 712-837-4831.
E-mail: info@paccb.org
Web Site: paccb.org
Key Personnel: Dir., Stephen Pitt; Naturalist, Miriam Patton; Office Mgr., Mary Barrick
Nature Center.
Collections: wildlife & their habitats.
Hours & Admission Prices: Jan.-Feb. Wed.-Fri. 9-12, Sat.-Sun. 1-4; March-Dec. Wed.-Fri. 9-4, Sun. 1-4.

Sac City

SAC CITY MUSEUM, 1301 W. Main St., Sac City, IA 50583. Tel.: 712-662-7383.
E-mail: shirely@sccountyiowa.com
Web Site: saccountyiowa.com
History Museum.
Collections: costumes; period artifacts; farm tools & equipment. Historic Village: country store, doctor's office, post office; hardware store.
Hours & Admission Prices: Memorial Day-Labor Day Sat.-Sun. 2-4:30.

Shell Rock

SHELL ROCK COMMUNITY HISTORICAL MUSEUM, 127 E. Adair St., Shell Rock, IA 50670-9713. Mailing Address: P.O. Box 57, Shell Rock, IA 50670-0057. Tel.: 319-885-4478 & 6687.
Founded: 2007.
Congressional District: 3
Key Personnel: Chm. (V), Sherri Willey; Museum Shop Mgr., Linda McCann.
Personnel Profile: Part-Time Volunteers 40.

Governing Authority: Parent Institution: Shell Rock Community Historical Society. Tax-exempt.
Historic House Museum: housed in a 1920s craftsman-style home.
Collections: period furnishings; maps; personal artifacts; Shell Rock High School artifacts.
Publications: quarterly newsletter, Shell Rock Historical Society.
Hours & Admission Prices: May-Oct. Sat.10-2; other times by appointment. No charge; donations accepted. ♿
Attendance: 200 (accurate)
Membership: Single $15; Family $25.

Sibley

MCCALLUM MUSEUM & BRUNSON HERITAGE HOME, 5th St. & 8th Ave., Sibley, IA 51249. Mailing Address: 724 3rd Ave, Sibley, IA 51249-1606. Tel.: 712-754-3882.
E-mail: jstoff@hickorytech.net
Web Site: www.osceolacountyia.com/info/museums.htm
Founded: 1956.
Congressional District: 6
Key Personnel: Dir., Jan Stofferan; Pres. (V), Shirley Swenson.
Personnel Profile: Part-Time Paid 1; Part-Time Volunteers 10.
Governing Authority: municipal. Parent Institution: Osceola County Historical Association. Subsidiary Institution: Tracy House, Ocheyedan, IA; DeBoer Museum, Ashton, IA. Tax-exempt.
History Museum.
Collections: Civil War guns, swords, bayonets, ammunition cases & uniforms; World War I & II items; china; glass; farm & household equipment; furniture; agriculture; Indian artifacts; paintings; dolls; photos; books; 1908 auto buggy; sleigh, surrey; quilts. Historic Buildings: Brunson Heritage House; Rogers House.
Research Fields: Civil War; Osceola County History.
Facilities: 75-vol. library.
Activities: guided tours; permanent exhibitions.
Hours & Admission Prices: May-Sept. Sun. 1:30-4:30; other times by appointment. No charge; donations accepted. Closed holidays. ♿
Attendance: 1,000 (estimated)
Membership: Individual $15; Family $25; Benefactor $25; Patron $50; Contributor $100; Corporate $200.

Sioux City

DOROTHY PECAUT NATURE CENTER, 4500 Sioux River Rd., Sioux City, IA 51109-1657. Tel.: 712-258-0838. Fax: 712-258-1261.
E-mail: dsnyder@sioux-city.org
Web Site: www.woodburyparks.com
Nature Center.
Collections: Loess Hills natural history; live native reptile & fish; hands-on exhibits.
Hours & Admission Prices: Tues.-Sat. 9-5, Sun. 1-5. Closed New Year's Day; Thanksgiving; Christmas Eve & Day.

LOREN D. CALLENDAR GALLERY, City Hall, 405 6th St., Sioux City, IA 51101-1255. Tel.: 712-279-6174. Fax: 712-252-5615.
Web Site: www.siouxcitymuseum.org
Governing Authority: Parent Institution: Sioux City Public Museum.
Art Gallery.
Collections: photographs; Sioux City history.
Hours & Admission Prices: Mon.-Fri. 8-4:30. No charge. Closed holidays.

SERGEANT FLOYD MUSEUM & WELCOME CENTER, 1000 Larsen Park Rd., Sioux City, IA 51103-4914. Tel.: 712-279-0198. Fax: 712-279-6934.
E-mail: scpm@sioux-city.org
Web Site: www.siouxcitymuseum.org
Governing Authority: Parent Institution: Sioux City Public Museum. Tax-exempt.
Maritime History Museum.
Collections: Siouxland maritime history; 1932 Army Corps of Engineers work boat; photographs.
Facilities: Museum-related items for sale.
Hours & Admission Prices: March-Oct. daily 10-5; Nov.-Feb. Wed.-Sun. 10-5. No charge; donations accepted. Closed New Year's Day; Easter; Thanksgiving; Christmas. ♿
Attendance: 26,583 (accurate)

* **SIOUX CITY ART CENTER,** 225 Nebraska St., Sioux City, IA 51101-1712. Tel.: 712-279-6272, ext. 208. Fax: 712-255-2921.
E-mail: jcollins@sioux-city.org
Web Site: www.siouxcityartcenter.org
Founded: 1914.
Congressional District: 6
Key Personnel: Dir., Al Harris-Fernandez; Pres. (V), Kent Vriezelaar; Chm. (V), Margot Chesebro; Registrar, Shannon Sargent; Sec., Kjersten Welch.
Personnel Profile: Full-Time Paid 11; Part-Time Paid 8; Part-Time Volunteers 460; Interns 2.
Governing Authority: municipal. Parent Institution: City of Sioux City. Subsidiary Institution: Art Center Assoc. of Sioux City. Tax-exempt: 501(c)(3).
Art Museum.
Collections: work by contemporary regional, national & international artists.
Research Fields: Upper Midwest artists.
Facilities: permanent collection gallery; 4 temporary exhibition halls; children's hands-on gallery; 6 studios; non-lending library. Museum-related items for sale.
Activities: inter-museum loan; permanent & temporary exhibitions; lectures; film series; gallery talks; formally organized education programs; docent program; tours. Museum Sponsors: ARTSPLASH Festival of the Arts, Labor Day weekend arts festival.
Publications: quarterly bulletin; catalogs for exhibitions & special programs; announcements.
Hours & Admission Prices: Tues.-Wed. & Fri.-Sat. 10-4, Thurs. 10-9, Sun. 1-4. No charge; donations accepted. Closed holidays. ♿
Attendance: 55,497 (accurate)
Membership: Senior Citizen $15; Individual $35; Household $50; Donor $100; Charter $250; Leader $500; Renaissance Society $1,000 & up.

THE SIOUX CITY LEWIS & CLARK INTERPRETIVE CENTER, 900 Larsen Park Rd., Sioux City, IA 51103-4916. Tel.: 712-224-5242. Fax: 712-224-5244.
E-mail: mpoole@siouxcitylcic.com
Web Site: www.siouxcitylcic.com
Key Personnel: Exec. Dir., Marcia Poole; Business Mgr., Russell Movall
History Museum.
Collections: artifacts & memorabilia pertaining to Lewis & Clark.
Hours & Admission Prices: Tues.-Sat. 9-5, Sun. 12-5. Closed New Year's Day; Easter; Thanksgiving; Christmas.

* **SIOUX CITY PUBLIC MUSEUM, (M),** 2901 Jackson St., Sioux City, IA 51104-3697. Tel.: 712-279-6174. Fax: 712-252-5615.
E-mail: scpm@sioux-city.org
Web Site: www.siouxcitymuseum.org
Founded: 1886.
Congressional District: 5
Key Personnel: C.E.O., Steven D. Hansen; Chm. (V), Ray Krigsten; Cur. History, Grace Linden; Cur. Education, Theresa Weaver-Basye; Exhibits Designer, Matt Anderson; Devel. Coord., Mary Green-Warnstadt; Welcome Center Supvr., Kathy Meisner; Administrative Asst., Deanna Mayo.
Personnel Profile: Full-Time Paid 6; Part-Time Paid 8; Part-Time Volunteers 66; Interns 3.
Governing Authority: municipal. Parent Institution: City of Sioux City, IA. Subsidiary Institution: Sioux City Museum & Historical Association. Tax-exempt.
General Museum: housed in early c.1890s, Peirce Mansion; Sergeant Floyd River Museum & Welcome Center; Loren D. Callendar Gallery; Pearl Street Research Center.
Collections: Indian artifacts; national, state & local history; archives; archaeology; mineralogy; paleontology; military; costumes.
Research Fields: local history.
Facilities: 2,000-vol. library on state & local history available for use on premises; archives; classroom. Cards, pottery, jewelry, wood carvings & books for sale.
Activities: oral history program; lectures; films; hobby workshops; formally organized education programs; inter-museum loan, permanent, temporary & traveling exhibitions; school loan service.
Publications: book, Sioux City, A Pictorial History; Sioux City History, 1980-2002.
Hours & Admission Prices: Museum: Tues.-Sat. 9-5, Sun. 1-5. Sergeant Floyd River Museum & Welcome Center daily 9-5. Pearl Street Research Center: Wed.-Fri. 12-5. No charge; donations accepted. Closed holidays. ♿
Attendance: 50,741 (accurate)
Membership: Senior Citizen $15; Individual $20; Family $30; Supporting $50; Patron & Business $100.

South Amana

COMMUNAL AGRICULTURE MUSEUM, 505 P St., South Amana, IA 52334. Mailing Address: Amana Heritage Society, P.O. Box 81, Amana, IA 52203-0081. Tel.: 319-622-3567.
Web Site: www.cr.nps.gov/nr/travel/amana/agr.htm

Agriculture Museum.
Collections: period agricultural implements; photographs.
Hours & Admission Prices: May-Sept. Mon.-Sat. 10-5, Sun. 12-5.

Spencer

PARKER HISTORICAL MUSEUM, 300 E. Third St., Spencer, IA 51301-5111. Mailing Address: P.O. Box 91, Spencer, IA 51301-0091. Tel.: 712-262-3304. Fax: 712-262-3304.
Historic House: built in 1916.
Collections: local history & culture; photographs; personal artifacts.
Hours & Admission Prices: Tues.-Fri. 11:30-3:30; other times by appointment. No charge; donations accepted.

Spillville

BILY CLOCK MUSEUM/ANTONIN DVORAK EXHIBIT, 323 S. Main, Spillville, IA 52168. Mailing Address: P.O. Box 258, Spillville, IA 52168-0258. Tel.: 563-562-3569.
E-mail: bilyclocks@mchsi.com
Web Site: www.bilyclocks.org
Founded: 1923.
Congressional District: 2
Key Personnel: Dir. & Museum Shop Mgr., Georgiann Eckheart.
Personnel Profile: Full-Time Paid 1; Part-Time Paid 5; Part-Time Volunteers 1.
Governing Authority: municipal. Tax-exempt.
Clock Museum.
Collections: hand carved clocks. Historic Building: c.1859 former home of composer Antonin Dvorak; summer of 1893.
Activities: guided tours; permanent exhibitions.
Hours & Admission Prices: March-April & Nov. Sat.-Sun. 10-4; May-Oct. daily 9-5; call for other times. Family $16, adults $6, seniors over 65 $5, children 7-18 $4; special school & group rates; discount to AAM & AAA members; children under 7 & members no charge. Closed New Year's Day; Easter; Thanksgiving; Christmas. ♿
Attendance: 14,000 (estimated)
Membership: Individual $30; Seniors $40; Dual $50; Lifetime $500; Business $1,000.

State Center

WATSON'S GROCERY STORE MUSEUM, 106 W. Main St., State Center, IA 50247. Tel.: 641-483-3002 & 485-3959.
Key Personnel: Dir., Everett Halsted; Pres. (V), Mike Riemenschneider.
Governing Authority: Parent Institution: State Center Development Association. Tax-exempt.
Historic Building: housed in an 1886 general store.
Collections: period furnishings & artifacts; photographs.
Hours & Admission Prices: Memorial Day to Labor Day Sat.-Sun. 1-4; other times by appointment. No charge; donations accepted.
Attendance: 2,000 (estimated)

Storm Lake

WITTER GALLERY, 609 Cayuga St., Storm Lake, IA 50588-2239. Tel.: 712-732-3400.
E-mail: wittergallery@yahoo.com
Web Site: thewittergallery.org
Founded: 1972.
Congressional District: 6
Key Personnel: Gallery Dir., Ron Stevenson.
Personnel Profile: Part-Time Paid 2; Part-Time Volunteers 100; Interns 2.
Governing Authority: nonprofit organization. Tax-exempt.
Art Gallery.
Collections: oil paintings by Ella Witter; woodcuts; lithographs by Dorothy Skewis.
Activities: lectures; workshops; instructional art classes; programs for children; performances; artists receptions; temporary & traveling exhibitions.
Publications: monthly newsletter; exhibition catalogs.
Hours & Admission Prices: Summer: Tues.-Wed. & Fri. 1-5, Thurs. 1-6, Sat. 10-2; Winter: Tues.-Wed. & Fri. 1-5, Thurs. 1-7, Sat. 10-2. No charge, donations accepted. Closed national holidays. ♿
Attendance: 11,000 (accurate)
Membership: Active $25; Sustaining $50; Supporting $100; Sponsor $250; Benefactor $500; Patron $1,000 & up.

Strawberry Point

WILDER MEMORIAL MUSEUM, 123 W. Mission, Strawberry Point, IA 52076. Mailing Address: Box 206, Strawberry Point, IA 52076-0206. Tel.: 563-933-4615.
E-mail: manager@wildermuseum.org
Web Site: www.wildermuseum.org
Founded: 1970.
Congressional District: 1
Key Personnel: Pres. (V), Linda Lenz; Mgr., Angela Beenken.
Personnel Profile: Part-Time Paid 5.
Governing Authority: municipal; nonprofit. Tax-exempt.
Historical Museum.
Collections: Victorian furniture & art glass; hanging lamps; 800 period dolls; period furnishings; military artifacts from Revolutionary War; prairie farming.
Activities: guided tours.
Publications: brochures.
Hours & Admission Prices: May & Sept.-Oct. Sat.-Sun. 10-4; Memorial Day-Labor Day Mon.-Fri. 11-4, Sat.-Sun. 10-4; other times by appointment. Family $10, adults $4, students $2; discounts for senior citizens on Wed., AAA members & groups of 10 or more adults; pre-school & members no charge. ♿
Attendance: 1,000 (estimated)
Membership: Life $50.

Swedesburg

SWEDISH AMERICAN MUSEUM, 107 James Ave., Swedesburg, IA 52652. Tel.: 319-254-2317.
Founded: 1991.
Congressional District: 2
Key Personnel: Pres. (V), William Tolander; Museum Shop Mgr., Norma Lindeen
Swedish American Museum.
Collections: Swedish heritage, culture, & history; personal artifacts; photographs.
Facilities: library. Museum-related items for sale.
Activities: audio tours.
Publications: newsletter.
Hours & Admission Prices: Mon.-Tues. & Thurs.-Sat. 9-4. No charge; donations accepted. Closed New Year's Day; Thanksgiving; Christmas. ♿
Membership: Annual $5.

Toledo

TAMA COUNTY HISTORICAL MUSEUM, 200 N. Broadway, Toledo, IA 52342-1308. Tel.: 641-484-6767. Fax: 515-484-6767.
E-mail: tracers@pcpartner.net
Founded: 1942.
Congressional District: 3
Key Personnel: Pres., Joyce Wiese; Vice Pres., Christine Draisey; Treas., Karlene Foreman; Exec. Sec., Wilma Parizek.
Personnel Profile: Full-Time Volunteers 12; Part-Time Volunteers 6.
Governing Authority: society. Tax-exempt.
Local History Museum: housed in 1869 former Tama County Jail.
Collections: pioneer & Indian artifacts; Mesquakie Indian clothing & tools; county newspapers on micro-film, county records & census rolls; genealogies; extensive genealogical collection of Tama County, state of Iowa and beyond; one room schoolhouse; music room; patriotic room; military room; professional room; 1870 one-room schoolhouse. Historic Building: 1860s loghouse.
Research Fields: genealogy; county history; Indians.
Facilities: 2,000-vol. genealogical library with microfilms of newspapers, county records & census of all counties of Iowa; reading room.
Activities: guided tours; lectures; preservation of Tama County pioneer artifacts; permanent exhibitions.
Publications: quarterly, Tama County Museum News.
Hours & Admission Prices: Tues.-Sat. 1-4:30; other times by appointment. Bus tours available. No charge; donations accepted. Closed holidays. ♿
Attendance: 1,750
Membership: Individual $15; Family & Business $25.

Traer

TRAER HISTORICAL MUSEUM, 514 2nd St., Traer, IA 50675-1139. Mailing Address: 705 Mill St., Traer, IA 50675-1439. Tel.: 319-478-2744.
History Museum: highlights the life of "Tama Jim" Wilson, U.S. Secretary of Agriculture.
Collections: Wilson's career & family history; northern Tama County & Traer history.

Hours & Admission Prices: Wed.-Sun. 2-4. No charge.

Urbandale

LIVING HISTORY FARMS, 2600 111th St., Urbandale, IA 50322-3792. Tel.: 515-278-5286. Fax: 515-278-9808.
E-mail: info@lhf.org
Web Site: www.livinghistoryfarms.org
Founded: 1967.
Congressional District: 3
Key Personnel: C.E.O. & Pres., Ruth Haus; Chm., Craig Thomson; Devel., Jim Dietz-Kilen; Treas., Don Brush; Dir. Interpretation, Janet Clair Dennis; Dir. Mktg. & Communications, Jennie Deerr; Asst. Dir., Nancy Wente; Finance & Museum Shop Mgr., Elaine Raleigh.
Personnel Profile: Full-Time Paid 35; Part-Time Paid 70; Part-Time Volunteers 1,302; Interns 27.
Governing Authority: nonprofit.
Living History Museum.
Collections: pioneer artifacts; farm machines; quilt collection; 1875 businesses & stores; Victorian Flynn House, barn & Tangen home; farm implement dealer.
Research Fields: midwestern agriculture & rural life.
Facilities: visitor center; 1700 Iowa Indian farm; 1850 & 1900 working farms; 1875 town of Walnut Hill including working trades; Henry Wallace Exhibit Center; William Murray Conference Center; picnic shelter. Museum-related items for sale.
Activities: organized education programs for children; hands-on activities; farming at 1700, 1850 & 1900 farms; special events; organized education programs for undergraduate or graduate college students.
Publications: annual brochures; quarterly newsletter, Almanack; members newsletter, The Advocate.
Hours & Admission Prices: May-Oct. call for hours. Adults $11, senior citizens $10, children $6; discounts to AAM & ICOM members; members & museum professionals with prior arrangements no charge. ♿
Attendance: 142,112 (accurate)
Membership: Individual $50; One Plus One $60; Grandparent & Family $70; Family Plus $95.

Van Meter

BOB FELLER MUSEUM, 310 Mill St., Van Meter, IA 50261. Mailing Address: P.O. Box 95, Van Meter, IA 50261-0095. Tel.: 515-996-2806; 866-996-2806. Fax: 515-996-2952.
E-mail: info@bobfellermuseum.org
Web Site: www.bobfellermuseum.org/
Founded: 1995.
Key Personnel: Mgr., Scott Havick
Sports Museum: housed in the hometown of Cleveland Indians pitcher, Bob Feller, 1936-1956; member of the Baseball Hall of Fame.
Collections: personal artifacts; photographs; baseball memorabilia.
Facilities: Museum-related items for sale.
Activities: autograph signings; special events.
Publications: newsletter.
Hours & Admission Prices: Oct.-March Tues.-Sat. 10-3, Sun. 12-4; April-Sept. Tues.-Sat. 10-5, Sun. 12-4. Adults $5, seniors & school-aged children $3; discounts to groups with appointment.

Vinton

FRANK G. RAY HOUSE, 912 First Ave., Vinton, IA 52349-1712. Mailing Address: Benton County Historical Society, P.O. Box 22, Vinton, IA 52349.
Historic House Museum: built in 1893. Listed in the National Register of Historical Places.
Collections: Victorian architecture with Queen Anne features; carriage house.
Hours & Admission Prices: June-Aug. Sat.-Sun. 1-4.

HORRIDGE HOUSE, 612 First Ave., Vinton, IA 52349-1705. Mailing Address: PO Box 22, Vinton, IA 52349-0022. Tel.: 319-472-4574. Fax: 319-472-4574.
Historic House Museum: c.1860.
Collections: period furnishings & artifacts.
Hours & Admission Prices: Library: June-Aug. Wed. & Sat.-Sun. 1-4; Sept.-May Wed. 1-4.

Walcott

IOWA 80 TRUCKING MUSEUM, I-80 Exit 284, Walcott, IA 52773. Mailing Address: 505 Sterling Dr., Walcott, IA 52773. Tel.: 563-468-5500. Fax: 536-284-6475.
Web Site: www.iowa80truckingmuseum.com
Trucking Museum.
Collections: trucking history; period trucks; toy trucks; trucking memorabilia.
Facilities: Museum-related items for sale.
Activities: view truck restorations.
Hours & Admission Prices: Wed.-Sat. 10-6, Sun. 12-5. Donations requested.

Waterloo

* **GROUT MUSEUM DISTRICT: GROUT MUSEUM OF HISTORY AND SCIENCE, BLUEDORN SCIENCE IMAGINARIUM, RENSSELAER RUSSELL HOUSE MUSEUM, SNOWDEN HOUSE, (M),** 503 South St., Waterloo, IA 50701-1517. Tel.: 319-234-6357. Fax: 319-236-0500.
Web Site: www.groutmuseumdistrict.org
Founded: 1933.
Congressional District: 1
Key Personnel: Exec. Dir., Billie K. Bailey; Chm. & Pres. (V), Roger Olesen; Cur. Exhibits, Robin Venter; Dir. Devel. & Mktg., Cyd McHone; Mktg. Asst., Kathy Meyer; Mgr. Collections, Lorraine Ihnen; Devel. & Visitor Service Asst., Nancy Kinter; Russell House Mgr. & Museum Shop Mgr., Judith Slaikeu; Imaginarium Mgr., Alan Sweeney; Mgr. Operations, Wendy Zitterich; Archivist, Catreva Manning; Coord. Veterans Project, Bob Neymeyer; Education Asst., Jane Ryan; Exhibit Technician, William Bisbee; Coord. Outreach, Erin Hogan.
Personnel Profile: Full-Time Paid 16; Part-Time Paid 8; Part-Time Volunteers 20; Interns 8.
Governing Authority: nonprofit organization. Subsidiary Institution: Rensselaer Russell House Museum; Carl A. & Peggy J. Bluedorn Imaginarium Science Museum. Tax-exempt: 501(c)(3).
General Museum.
Collections: early Native American artifacts; industrial history; textiles, costumes; Pioneer Hall historical dioramas including log cabin, toolshed, carpenter shop, blacksmith shop, country store, apothecary shop; genealogy; anthropology; paleontology; geology; astronomy; manuscript collections. Physical Sciences: Bluedorn Science Imaginarium. Historic House: Rensselaer Russell House.
Facilities: 950-vol. library; planetarium; 200-seat conference room. Museum-related items for sale.
Activities: tours; formally organized education programs; permanent & temporary exhibitions; planetarium programs; history & science traveling trunk program; hands-on discovery zone; science demonstrations. Annual Events: Winter Welcome Candlelight Walk; cemetery walk; garden tour; tour of homes.
Publications: Museum Calendar; newsletter; membership brochure; general brochure; Teacher's Guide to Programs; summer activities guide; group tour manual; annual report; visitors guide.
Hours & Admission Prices: Tues.-Sat. 9-5. Adults $4.50, children 12 & under $3; discounts to AAM members; members no charge. ♿
Attendance: 33,630 (accurate)
Membership: Individual $36; Family $48.

WATERLOO CENTER FOR THE ARTS, 225 Commercial St., Waterloo, IA 50701-1313. Tel.: 319-291-4490. Fax: 319-291-4270.
E-mail: museum@waterloo-ia.org
Web Site: www.waterloocenterforthearts.org
Formerly: Waterloo Museum of Art
Founded: 1947.
Congressional District: 3
Key Personnel: Dir., Cammie V. Scully; Chm. Cultural & Arts Commission (V), Tom Langlas; Pres. Friends of the Art Center (V), Barb Krizek; Visitor Svcs. Mgr., Maureen Newbill; Education Dir., Bonnie Winninger; Cur., Kent Shankle; Registrar, Marlene Ackerman; Digital Arts Mgr., Chawne Paige; Building Mgr., Mike Guild; Coord. Public Programs, Chad Allen; Finance Mgr., Paulette Hawkenson; Develop & Marketing Dir., Shannon Farlow; Maintenance Supvr., Lonzo Coleman; Sec., Maureen Hastings; Sec., Nita Hodapp.
Personnel Profile: Full-Time Paid 8; Part-Time Paid 45; Part-Time Volunteers 100; Interns 2.
Governing Authority: municipal; nonprofit. Parent Institution: City of Waterloo Cultural & Arts Commission. Tax-exempt.
Art Museum.
Collections: midwest regionalists; American decorative arts; Caribbean Art; Haitian Art; Grant Wood collection.
Research Fields: midwest regionalists art; Haitian & Caribbean art; international folk art; American decorative art.
Facilities: 2,000-vol. library of American art & art of the Midwest material available to the public by appointment; 385-seat theater; 60-seat theater; 250 to 300-seat auditorium; ceramics classroom; art classroom; youth pavilion. Museum-related items for sale.
Activities: guided tours; lectures; films; concerts; arts festival; theater; study clubs; hobby workshops; education programs; docent program; loan,

traveling, & temporary exhibitions; school programs K-8 grades; Northeast Iowa Print Club; youth hands-on learning experiences. Museum Sponsors: Annual Holiday Arts Festival; Rooftop Jazz & Blues; Performing Arts series; Arti Gras.

Publications: Exhibition & program announcements; exhibition catalogues; quarterly newsletter; class brochures; monthly calendars.

Hours & Admission Prices: Tues.-Sat. 10-5, Sun. 1-5. No charge; donations accepted. Closed New Year's Day; Memorial Day; Independence Day; Labor Day; Veterans Day; Thanksgiving & day after; Christmas Day & day after. ♿

Attendance: 100,000 (estimated)

Membership: Student & Senior $30; Individual $40; Family & Dual $50; Supporting $75; Contributing $100; Corporate $200-$1,000; Sustaining $250; Patron $500; Benefactor $1,000.

West Branch

HERBERT HOOVER NATIONAL HISTORIC SITE, 110 Parkside Dr., West Branch, IA 52358. Mailing Address: P.O. Box 607, West Branch, IA 52358-0607. Tel.: 319-643-2541. Fax: 319-643-7864.

Web Site: www.nps.gov/heho

Founded: 1965.

Congressional District: 2

Key Personnel: Eastern Natl. Book Store Mgr., Bonnie Blaford.

Governing Authority: federal. National Park Service. Tax-exempt.

Historic Site: birthplace of Herbert Hoover and graves of President & Mrs. Hoover.

Collections: Herbert Hoover's childhood; late 19th century Americana; blacksmithing & related trades; prairie environment & management; National Park system resources & management; cultural & natural history. Historic House & Buildings: 1871 Hoover Birthplace; 1856 Friend's Meetinghouse; 1853 School House; late 19th & early 20th-century homes.

Research Fields: Herbert Hoover's childhood.

Facilities: 430-vol. library 1874-1885; reading room; picnic area. Publications, national park themes & products of demonstration from the blacksmith shop for sale.

Activities: guided tours; lectures; films; concerts; formally organized education programs for children, adults & undergraduate college students; loan, permanent & temporary exhibitions.

Publications: brochure; guidebook.

Hours & Admission Prices: Daily 9-5. No charge. Closed New Year's Day; Thanksgiving; Christmas. ♿

Attendance: 125,000 (accurate)

HERBERT HOOVER PRESIDENTIAL LIBRARY-MUSEUM, (M), 210 Parkside Dr., West Branch, IA 52358-9685. Mailing Address: P.O. Box 488, West Branch, IA 52358-0488. Tel.: 319-643-5301. Fax: 319-643-6045.

E-mail: hoover.library@nara.gov

Web Site: www.hoover.archives.gov

Founded: 1962.

Congressional District: 2

Key Personnel: Dir., Timothy Walch; Cur., Maureen Harding; Asst. Cur., Marcus Eckhardt; Education Specialist, Mary Evans; Registrar, Jennifer Pedersen; Photo Archivist, Lynn Smith; Outreach Archivist, Matthew Schaefer; Internet Archivist, Craig Wright; Museum Shop Mgr., Pamela Hinkhouse.

Personnel Profile: Full-Time Paid 15; Part-Time Paid 5; Part-Time Volunteers 35; Interns 3.

Governing Authority: federal. Parent Institution: National Archives & Records Admin., Washington, DC. Subsidiary Institution: Hoover Presidential Library Assoc. Tax-exempt: 170(b)(1)(a).

Presidential Library.

Collections: personal papers; government records; photographs; motion picture films; audio & video tapes; sound recordings; head of state gifts; gifts from private citizens; political campaign items; personal & family memorabilia; journalism; atomic energy; civil aviation; public administration.

Research Fields: life, times, career & presidential administration of President Hoover & associates.

Facilities: 25,000-vol. library; 180-seat auditorium. Documents, slides, prints, posters, books, exhibit catalogs & other museum-related items for sale.

Activities: guided tours; lectures; films; permanent, temporary & traveling exhibitions; organized educational programs for children, adults, undergraduate & graduate students; scholarly conferences.

Publications: brochure; exhibition catalogs; books.

Hours & Admission Prices: Daily 9-5. Adults $6, senior citizens $3; children under 16 no charge. Closed New Year's; Thanksgiving; Christmas. ♿

Attendance: 70,000 (estimated)

Membership: Hoover Association $40 & up.

West Des Moines

THE BENNETT SCHOOL, 4001 Fuller Rd., West Des Moines, IA 50061. Mailing Address: West Des Moines Historical Society, 2001 Fuller Rd., West Des Moines, IA 50265-5528. Tel.: 515-225-1286.

Web Site: thejordanhouse.org

Governing Authority: Parent Institution: West Des Moines Historical Society.

Historical Society Museum: housed in c.1926 one room school.

Collections: period furnishings; photographs.

Activities: tours.

Hours & Admission Prices: Call for hours. Adults $3, children $1; discounts to groups with reservation; members no charge.

THE JORDAN HOUSE, 2001 Fuller Rd., West Des Moines, IA 50265-5528. Tel.: 515-225-1286.

E-mail: jordanhouse@dwx.com

Web Site: thejordanhouse.org

Governing Authority: Parent Institution: West Des Moines Historical Society. Subsidiary Institution: Bennett School, Fuller Rd. & 50th St., West Des Moines, IA.

Historic House Museum: housed in the former home of James Jordan, the founder of Valley Junction (later renamed West Des Moines); the home served as a station on the Underground Railroad. National Register of Historic Places.

Collections: period furnishings; personal artifacts; Underground Railroad.

Activities: rental facilities; special events.

Hours & Admission Prices: May-Sept. Wed. & Sat. 1-4, Sun. 2-5; groups of 10 or more by appointment. Adults $3, children $1; members no charge.

West Union

FAYETTE COUNTY HELPERS CLUB & HISTORICAL SOCIETY, 100 N. Walnut St., West Union, IA 52175-1347. Tel.: 563-422-5797.

Founded: 1975.

Congressional District: 2

Key Personnel: Genealogy Coord. & Pres. (V), Ruth Brooks; Pres., Frances Bowden; Admin., Frances Graham.

Personnel Profile: Full-Time Volunteers 3; Part-Time Volunteers 9.

Governing Authority: nonprofit organization. Tax-exempt.

Historical & Preservation Society.

Collections: materials & artifacts relating to the history & heritage of Fayette County, Iowa; cemetery records; genealogical materials & records; manuscript collections. Historic Building: Pleasant Ridge #5 Schoolhouse.

Research Fields: Fayette County history & genealogy.

Facilities: 200-vol. library, 1850-present, Fayette County historical material & typed census records by townships available for use by prior arrangement; reading room; microfilm reader & printer; meeting facilities.

Activities: lectures; temporary exhibitions.

Publications: quarterly, letter to members; calendars, historical.

Hours & Admission Prices: Mon.-Fri. 10-4; other times by appointment. No charge: donations accepted. ♿

Attendance: 3,000 (estimated)

Membership: Individual $10; Life $100.

Winfield

WINFIELD HISTORICAL SOCIETY AND MUSEUM, 114 S. Locust St., Winfield, IA 52659-9586. Mailing Address: P.O. Box 184, Winfield, IA 52659-0184. Tel.: 319-257-6974.

Historical Society Museum.

Collections: local history & culture; photographs; personal artifacts; newspaper press; Senator William Carden memorabilia.

Hours & Admission Prices: Mon. 10-2; other times by appointment. No charge.

Winterset

BIRTHPLACE OF JOHN WAYNE, 216 S. 2nd St., Winterset, IA 50273-1910. Tel.: 515-462-1044. Fax: 515-462-3289.

E-mail: director@johnwaynebirthplace.org

Web Site: www.johnwaynebirthplace.org

Founded: 1981.

Congressional District: 5

Key Personnel: Pres., Lynn Ochiltree; Exec. Dir., Brian Downes; Dir. & Museum Shop Mgr., Carolyn Wilson; Treas., Randy Lee; Vice Pres., Joe Zuckschwerdt; Sec., Wayne Davis.

Personnel Profile: Part-Time Paid 16.

Governing Authority: nonprofit. Tax-exempt: 501(c)(3).

Historic House & Preservation Project: c.1907 frame house, birthplace of film star John Wayne.

Collections: John Wayne memorabilia; family photographs.

Activities: guided tours.
Publications: brochures.
Hours & Admission Prices: Daily 10-4:30. Adults $6, seniors $5, children $2; babies in arms no charge. ♿
Attendance: 40,000
Membership: Supporting $35; Starring Role $100.

MADISON COUNTY HISTORICAL SOCIETY, 815 S. 2nd Ave., Winterset, IA 50273-2108. Mailing Address: P.O. Box 15, Winterset, IA 50273-0015. Tel.: 515-462-2134. Fax: 515-462-4531.
E-mail: mchistory@i-rule.net
Web Site: www.historyonthehill.com
Founded: 1904.
Congressional District: 5
Key Personnel: Pres. (V), Bob Young; Vice Pres., Sally Oldham; Treas., Tim Waddingham.
Personnel Profile: Full-Time Paid 1; Part-Time Paid 5; Part-Time Volunteers 139.
Governing Authority: nonprofit. Tax-exempt: 701(b)(1)(A).
Historic Society Museum Complex.
Collections: articles belonging to Madison County settlers; Indian artifacts; uniforms; tools; clothing; furniture; large mineral & rock collection; new barn structure housing farm equipment. Historic Structures: 1850 log school; 1850 log post office; 1880 church; 1850 brick house; 1850 stone barn; depot; 1920s country schoolhouse; neighborhood store; attorney's office.
Activities: guided tours.
Publications: newsletter; The Delicious Apple; Three River Country; Scenic Madison County, Iowa; George Washington Carver.
Hours & Admission Prices: May-Oct, Mon.-Sat. 11-4, Sun. 1-5. Museum: adults $3. House: adults $3. Combination Ticket: $5, group rate $4; children under 12 no charge if accompanied by an adult. ♿
Attendance: 10,000 (estimated)
Membership: Annual $10; Life $150.

WINTERSET ART CENTER, 224 S. John Wayne Dr., Winterset, IA 50273. Mailing Address: P.O. Box 325, Winterset, IA 50273-0325. Tel.: 515-210-3286.
E-mail: wacjnarland@aol.com
Web Site: www.wintersetartcenter.org
Founded: 1958.
Congressional District: 5
Key Personnel: Chm., Jerrold Narland; Sec., Ethel Lee Osborne; Public Rels., Joe Held.
Governing Authority: nonprofit. Tax-exempt: 170(b)(1)(A).
Art Museum: housed in c.1854 building used as an Underground Railway stop during the Civil War.
Collections: various medias of art.
Research Fields: history relative to George Washington Carver.
Activities: arts festivals; hobby workshops; organized education programs; temporary exhibitions.
Hours & Admission Prices: Mon.-Sat. 10-4 & by appointment. No charge; donations accepted.
Attendance: 3,000 (estimated)
Membership: Junior & Student $10; Regular $20; Family $45.

KANSAS

(255 listings)

Abilene

DICKINSON COUNTY HERITAGE CENTER, (M), 412 S. Campbell St., Abilene, KS 67410-2905. Tel.: 785-263-2681. Fax: 785-263-0380.
E-mail: heritagecenterdk@sbcglobal.net
Web Site: heritagecenterdk.com
Founded: 1928.
Congressional District: 2
Key Personnel: Dir. & C.E.O., Jeff Sheets; Pres. (V), Thelma Lexow; Museum Shop Mgr., Twila Jackson.
Personnel Profile: Full-Time Paid 1; Part-Time Paid 5; Part-Time Volunteers 50; Interns 1.
Governing Authority: nonprofit organization. Parent Institution: Dickinson County Historical Society. Tax-exempt: 501(c)(3).
History Museum.
Collections: agriculture; cattle drive memorabilia; toys; carnivals; household items; musical instruments.
Research Fields: early settling of the West; county & state history; genealogy.
Facilities: county archives; newspapers & photographic collections; cemetery surveys; census records; Outdoor Museum including a 1901 C.W. Parker Carousel, pioneer log cabin, 1900 telephone exchange building and Blacksmith shop.
Activities: guided tours; summer lecture series. Museum Sponsors: annual Heritage Day; Pioneer camp; Christmas in the Cabin; annual quilt show.
Publications: quarterly magazine, Gazette.
Hours & Admission Prices: Mon.-Sat. 10-3, Sun. 1-5. Extended hours Memorial Day to Labor Day. Adults $4, children 2-15 $2; discounts to AAM members & telephone pioneers. Carousel Rides $2. Closed New Year's Day; Thanksgiving; Christmas. ♿
Attendance: 14,000 (accurate)
Membership: Individual $15; Family $25; Institutional $50; Contributing $50-$999; Life $1,000.

DWIGHT D. EISENHOWER LIBRARY-MUSEUM, 200 S.E. 4th St., Abilene, KS 67410-2900. Tel.: 785-263-6700. Fax: 785-263-6718.
E-mail: eisenhower.library@nara.gov
Web Site: www.eisenhower.archives.gov
Founded: 1962.
Congressional District: 1
Key Personnel: Dir., Karl Weissenbach; Cur., Dennis H.J. Medina.
Personnel Profile: Part-Time Volunteers 5.
Governing Authority: federal. Parent Institution: National Archives and Records Administration, Washington, DC 20408. Tax-exempt: 170(b)(1)(A).
Presidential Library & Museum.
Collections: personal papers; government records; photographs; motion picture films; audio & video tapes; sound recordings; head of state gifts; gifts from private citizens; political campaign items; personal & family memorabilia; 35,000 serials. Historic House: 1887 Eisenhower family home.
Major Exhibits: Gem on the Plains, 1/10-2/21/10; The Working White House (T), 3/20/10-4/10; Holocaust, 6/10-1/11.
Research Fields: life, times, career & presidential administration of President Eisenhower.
Facilities: 25,000-vol. library; 2 auditoriums. Document facsimiles, slides; prints; posters; books, exhibit catalogs & museum object reproductions for sale.
Activities: guided tours; lectures; films; permanent, temporary & traveling exhibitions; organized educational programs for children, adults and undergraduate & graduate students.
Publications: general information brochure; newsletter, Overview.
Hours & Admission Prices: Memorial Day-Labor Day daily 9-6; Sept.-May daily 9-4:45. Museum: adults $8, seniors $6.50, children 7-16 $1. Closed New Year's Day; Thanksgiving; Christmas. ♿
Attendance: 89,500 (accurate)
Membership: Friends of the Eisenhower Library Foundation: One Star up to $50; Two Star $51-$100; Three Star $101-$500; Four Star $501-$1,000; Five Star $1,001-$10,000; Presidential $10,000 & up.

GREYHOUND HALL OF FAME, 407 S. Buckeye, Abilene, KS 67410-2925. Tel.: 785-263-3000. Fax: 785-263-2604.
E-mail: info@greyhoundhalloffame.com
Web Site: greyhoundhalloffame.com
Founded: 1963.
Congressional District: 1
Key Personnel: Dir., Edward Scheele; Pres., Vey O. Weaver; Exec. Asst., Kathryn Lounsbury.
Personnel Profile: Full-Time Paid 3; Part-Time Paid 2.
Governing Authority: nonprofit organization. Tax-exempt: 501(c)(3).
Sports Museum.
Collections: historic items relating to the sport of greyhound racing & the greyhound animal.
Research Fields: history.
Facilities: 800-vol. library of statistics & history available for use on premises; theater. Books, gifts & museum-related items for sale.
Activities: guided tours; films; permanent & temporary exhibitions.
Hours & Admission Prices: Daily 9-5. No charge; donations accepted. Closed New Year's Day; Thanksgiving; Christmas. ♿
Attendance: 50,000 (estimated)
Membership: Hall of Fame Club: Assoc. $100; Full $250.

MUSEUM OF INDEPENDENT TELEPHONY, 412 S. Campbell, Abilene, KS 67410-2905. Tel.: 785-263-2681. Fax: 785-263-0380.
Web Site: www.heritagecenterdk.com
Founded: 1973.
Congressional District: 2
Key Personnel: C.E.O. & Dir., Jeff Sheets.
Personnel Profile: Full-Time Paid 2; Part-Time Volunteers 50.

Governing Authority: Parent Institution: Dickinson County Historical Society. Tax-exempt: 501(c)(3).
Telephonic History Museum.
Collections: early artifacts of communications; telephones from the primitive to the modern; old telephone business office; old phone booths; switchboards; sheet music; photographs; interactive exhibits.
Research Fields: telephone company history & the history of independent telephone companies.
Facilities: 1,000-vol. library of books on telephone history; outdoor museum, 1927 Mack Line Truck.
Activities: guided tours; lectures; films; gallery talks; permanent & traveling exhibitions.
Publications: Tales of Telephony.
Hours & Admission Prices: Memorial Day-Labor Day Mon.-Fri. 9-4, Sat. 9-8; Winter: Mon.-Fri. 9-3, Sat. 10-5, Sun. 1-5. Adults 16 & over $4, seniors 62 & over $3, children 2-15 $2; discounts to groups, AAA & AAM members. Closed New Year's Day; Thanksgiving; Christmas. ♿
Attendance: 10,904 (estimated)
Membership: Individual $10; Family $15; Corporate $100.

THE SEELYE MANSION & PATENT MEDICINE MUSEUM, 1105 N. Buckeye Ave., Abilene, KS 67410-1942. Mailing Address: P.O. Box 337, Abilene, KS 67410-0337. Tel.: 785-263-1084.
E-mail: terryt@access-one.com
Web Site: www.seeleymansion.org
Historic House: former home of Dr. and Mrs. A.B. Seelye; built in 1905.
Collections: Mansion: period artifacts & furnishings. Medicine Museum: A.B. Seeyle Medical Company artifacts.
Hours & Admission Prices: Mon.-Sat. 10-6, Sun. 1-5. Adults $10, children 6-12 $5. Closed Christmas.

VINTAGE FASHION MUSEUM, 212 N. Broadway, Abilene, KS 67410. Mailing Address: 309 N. Buckeye Ave., Abilene, KS 67410-2527. Tel.: 785-263-7997.
Fashion Museum.
Collections: fashions from 1870s to 1970s.
Activities: temporary exhibits; educational programs.
Hours & Admission Prices: Mon.-Sat. 10-4, Sun. 1-4. Closed New Year's Day; Thanksgiving; Christmas.

Alden

AT & SF DEPOT, Alden, KS 67512-0158. Mailing Address: P.O. Box 158, Alden, KS 67512-0158. Tel.: 620-534-2425.
E-mail: prflrcraft@aol.com
Founded: 1970.
Congressional District: 1
Key Personnel: Dir., Sara Fair Sleeper.
Governing Authority: county. Parent Institution: Rice County Historical Museum. Subsidiary Institution: Coronado Quivira Museum. Tax-exempt.
Transportation Museum: housed in c.1872 Atchison, Topeka & Santa Fe railroad building & contents.
Collections: railroad items.
Activities: tours.
Hours & Admission Prices: By appointment only. No charge.
Attendance: 4 (estimated)

Alma

WABAUNSEE COUNTY HISTORICAL MUSEUM, 227 Missouri, Alma, KS 66401. Mailing Address: P.O. Box 387, Alma, KS 66401-0387. Tel.: 785-765-2200.
Founded: 1968.
Congressional District: 5
Key Personnel: Pres. (V), John Gehrt; Cur., Alan Winkler; Asst. Cur., Linda Maas.
Personnel Profile: Part-Time Paid 2; Part-Time Volunteers 6.
Governing Authority: society. Tax-exempt: 501(c)(3).
Historical Society Museum: housed in 100-year old native stone building.
Collections: Gen. Lewis Walt's display; Native American artifacts; old time school room display; old time doctor's office; photos; guns; buggies; clothes, costumes; Main Street U.S.A.; general store; barber shop; shoe & harness shop; 1923 REO fire truck; post office; blacksmith shop; ladies mercantile shop; railroad depot; Cane collection; farm machinery; genealogy.
Research Fields: oral history project; school records.
Facilities: library.
Activities: guided tour of museum; lectures; permanent & temporary exhibitions; fall historical tour of Wabaunsee County; annual meeting historical speaker.
Publications: quarterly newsletter; pamphlets.
Hours & Admission Prices: March-Nov. Tues.-Sat. 10-12 & 1-4, Sun. 1-4; Dec.-Feb. Tues.-Wed. 10-12 & 1-4. Suggested Donations: adults 22-64 $2; seniors & students no charge. Closed major holidays. ♿
Attendance: 1,100 (accurate)
Membership: Individual $25; Family $50; Donor $75.

Argonia

SALTER MUSEUM, 220 W. Garfield, Argonia, KS 67004. Mailing Address: P.O. Box 126, Argonia, KS 67004-0126. Tel.: 620-435-6376.
Founded: 1961.
Congressional District: 4
Key Personnel: Pres. Argonia & Western Sumner Historical Society, Troy Bookless; Docent, Carol Pearce; Chief Cur., Mary Beth Bookless.
Governing Authority: nonprofit organization. Affiliated with Argonia and Western Sumner County Historical Society. Tax-exempt.
Historic House Museum: 1884 home of America's first woman mayor, Mrs. Susanna M. Salter.
Collections: 19th-century home furnishings. Historic Building: 1924 church building.
Research Fields: Sumner County history.
Activities: guided tours.
Publications: brochure.
Hours & Admission Prices: By appointment. No charge; donations accepted. ♿
Membership: Annual $5; Life $100.

Arkansas City

CHEROKEE STRIP LAND RUSH MUSEUM, (M), 31639 US 77, Arkansas City, KS 67005. Mailing Address: P.O. Box 778, Arkansas City, KS 67005-0778. Tel.: 620-442-6750. Fax: 620-441-4332.
E-mail: hferguson@arkansascityks.gov
Web Site: www.arkansascityks.gov
Founded: 1966.
Congressional District: 5
Key Personnel: City Mgr., Steve Archer; Chm., Jerry Hooley; Dir., Heather Ferguson.
Personnel Profile: Full-Time Paid 1; Part-Time Paid 1; Part-Time Volunteers 10.
Governing Authority: nonprofit organization. Tax-exempt.
History Museum.
Collections: Cherokee Strip Land Rush of Sept. 16, 1893; historical artifacts from 1800s-1920s; Indian & military artifacts; Bryson Paddock Wichita Indian archaeological site replica (1700-1753). Historic Buildings: Hardy Jail; Bland Schoolhouse.
Research Fields: Cherokee Strip Run; Cherokee Outlet; Chilocco Indian School.
Facilities: 100-vol. library of books on the Cherokee Strip available for research; Cowley County Genealogical Society Collection. Western & Indian items for sale.
Activities: guided tours; lectures; traveling exhibitions. Annual Events: Mountain Man Living History Encampment; Pioneer Festival and Western Heritage Days.
Publications: Between the Rivers, Vols. 1-3; Images of America Cherokee Strip Land Rush; Arkansas City - Images of America Series.
Hours & Admission Prices: Tues.-Sat. 10-5. Adults $4.50, senior citizens $3.50, children 6-12 $2; discount to AAM & AAA members & senior citizens; children under 6 & members no charge. Closed major holidays. ♿
Attendance: 10,428 (accurate)
Membership: Individual $15; Family $25; Extended Family $30; Benefactor $50; Business $100; Corporate $200.

Arma

SCOTTY'S CLASSIC CAR MUSEUM, 302 N. 9th St., Arma, KS 66712-9520. Tel.: 620-347-8387. Fax: 620-249-5555.
E-mail: memrylane@yahoo.com
Web Site: www.scottysclassiccars.com
Key Personnel: Owner, Scotty Bitner
History Museum.
Collections: classic & period automobiles.
Hours & Admission Prices: Tues.-Sat. 11-5; other times by appointment.

Ashland

PIONEER-KRIER MUSEUM, 430 W. 4th, Ashland, KS 67831. Mailing Address: P.O. Box 862, Ashland, KS 67831-0862. Tel.: 620-635-2227. Fax: 620-635-2227 (call first).
E-mail: pioneer@ucom.net

Web Site: www.pioneer-krier.com
Founded: 1966.
Congressional District: 1
Key Personnel: Pres., Don Howell; Vice Pres., Jim Baker; Cur. & Admin., Tony Maphet; Treas., Milton Hughes.
Personnel Profile: Part-Time Paid 1; Part-Time Volunteers 25.
Governing Authority: society. Parent Institution: Clark County Historical Society. Tax-exempt: 501(c)(3).
Pioneer & Aerobatic Museum.
Collections: dishes, glassware & other kitchen equipment; dolls & toys; bits & spurs; guns; pre-1900 musical instruments; blacksmith shop; furniture; handcrafts; military memorabilia; pioneer pictures; church furniture; farm machinery; pioneer era saddles & tack; fossils from local area; Indian artifacts; display of aerobatic airplanes & trophies; musical instruments; pioneer doctor & hospital equipment; business office of pioneer undertaker & abstractor; early day bank; general store; barbed wire; manuscripts.
Research Fields: old cattle trails; prehistoric fossils; pioneer graves; pioneer life; cattle industry.
Facilities: 750-vol. library of books on genealogy, Kansas history, family records & collection of 1884-1991; reading room. Books & museum-related items for sale.
Activities: school study tours; permanent & temporary exhibitions.
Publications: books, 6-vol., Notes on Early Clark County, Kansas; booklets, Souvenir of Ashland & Clark County, 1884-1909; Kings & Queens of the Range; Pictures of Trail Drives & Ranches, 1894-1904; Cattle Ranching South of Dodge City - the Early Years 1870-1920.
Hours & Admission Prices: Tues.-Fri. 10-12 & 1-5. No charge; donations accepted. Closed New Year's Day; Thanksgiving; Christmas. ♿
Attendance: 2,000 (accurate)
Membership: Life $25.

Atchison

AMELIA EARHART BIRTHPLACE MUSEUM, 223 North Ter., Atchison, KS 66002-2525. Mailing Address: 609 Meridian Rd., Chester, NE 68327-7004. Tel.: 913-367-4217.
E-mail: aemuseum@lvnworth.com
Web Site: ameliaearhartmuseum.org
Founded: 1984.
Congressional District: 2
Key Personnel: Chm. (V), Carole Sutton; Museum Shop Mgr., Jan Coyle.
Personnel Profile: Full-Time Paid 1; Part-Time Paid 1; Part-Time Volunteers 40.
Governing Authority: private; nonprofit organization. Parent Institution: The Ninety-Nines, Inc., 4300 Amelia Earhart Rd., Will Rogers Airport, Oklahoma City, OK 73159. Tax-exempt: 501(c)(3).
Historic House: 1861 Gothic Revival cottage, birthplace of Amelia Earhart.
Collections: period furnishings & memorabilia; life of Amelia Earhart & other women pilots.
Research Fields: Amelia Earhart & other women pilots, past & present.
Facilities: 500-vol. library of books on aviation & women aviators. Museum-related items for sale.
Activities: docent program; guided tours; lectures; participatory exhibits. Museum Sponsors: Women in History Month; Amelia Earhart Festival & Birthday Celebration; seasonal open houses.
Publications: annual Amelia Earhart picture calendar; Amelia Earhart cookbook.
Hours & Admission Prices: Feb. 16-Dec. 14 Mon.-Fri. 9-4, Sat. 10-4, Sun. 1-4; Dec. 15-Feb. 15 Wed.-Sat. 10-4, Sun. 1-4. Adults $3, children 12 & under $.50. Closed New Year's Day; Christmas. ♿
Attendance: 12,000 (estimated)

ATCHISON COUNTY HISTORICAL SOCIETY, (M), 200 S. 10th St., Atchison, KS 66002-2772. Mailing Address: P.O. Box 201, Atchison, KS 66002-0201. Tel.: 913-367-6238.
E-mail: gowest@atchisonhistory.org
Web Site: www.atchisonhistory.org
Founded: 1967.
Congressional District: 2
Personnel Profile: Full-Time Paid 1; Part-Time Volunteers 2; Interns 1.
Governing Authority: society; nonprofit organization. Branch Museum: Independence Creek Lewis and Clark Historic Site, 19917 314th Rd., P.O. Box 201, Atchison, KS 66002. Tax-exempt: 501(c)(3).
Historical Society Museum: housed in c.1880 Santa Fe Depot.
Collections: county history & culture; firearms from Revolutionary War & Civil War-modern era; military items; childhood memorabilia, clothing from Amelia Earhart; Lewis & Clark artifacts.
Research Fields: Atchison County, Kansas.
Facilities: small group meeting facilities.
Activities: guided tours; lectures; study clubs.
Publications: bimonthly newsletter, Go West.
Hours & Admission Prices: Mon.-Fri. 8-5, Sat. 9-5, Sun. 12-5. No charge; donations accepted. ♿
Attendance: 24,000 (estimated)
Membership: Scout $5; Pony Express $10; Overland Stage & Pioneer $15; Homesteader $25; Gov. Glick $50; AT & SF $100; Lewis & Clark $1,000; Senator J.J. Ingalls $5,000.

EVAH C. CRAY HISTORICAL HOME MUSEUM, 805 N. 5th St., Atchison, KS 66002-1807. Tel.: 913-367-3046.
Historic House: housed in a 25-room Victorian era mansion; built in 1882.
Collections: local history & culture; Victorian furnishings; personal artifacts; photographs; carriage house.
Facilities: theater. Museum-related items for sale.
Hours & Admission Prices: April 10-4; May-Oct. Mon.-Sat. 10-4, Sun. 1-4; Nov. 27-Dec. 17 Fri.-Mon. call for hours.

THE MUCHNIC GALLERY, 704 N. 4th St., Atchison, KS 66002-1924. Tel.: 913-367-4278. Fax: 913-367-2939.
E-mail: atchart@ponyexpress.net
Founded: 1970.
Congressional District: 2
Key Personnel: Dir. & Cur., Gloria Davis; Pres. (V), Patty Boldridge.
Personnel Profile: Part-Time Paid 1.
Governing Authority: nonprofit organization. Parent Institution: Atchison Art Association. Tax-exempt.
Art Gallery: housed in 1885 Victorian brick residence.
Collections: paintings & lithographs of John Falter, John S. Curry, Jim Hamil, Thomas Hart Benton, Robert Sudlow & Jack O'Hara; furniture & paintings of the Muchnic family.
Activities: guided tours; permanent & traveling exhibitions.
Publications: brochure, Tour Guide of Home.
Hours & Admission Prices: Gallery: Wed. 10-5, Sat.-Sun. 1-5, Special Exhibits: Sat.-Sun. 1-5; special tours available. No charge.
Attendance: 1,500 (accurate)

Augusta

AUGUSTA HISTORICAL MUSEUM & GENEALOGY, 303 State, Augusta, KS 67010-1103. Tel.: 316-775-5655.
E-mail: augustahm@aol.com
Web Site: www.augustahistoricalsociety.net
Founded: 1938.
Congressional District: 5
Key Personnel: Pres., Eldon Foreman; Dir., Rachelle Meinecke.
Personnel Profile: Full-Time Paid 1; Part-Time Paid 1; Part-Time Volunteers 7.
Governing Authority: county. Tax-exempt.
General Museum.
Collections: pioneer relics; items from late 1800s settlements. Historic Building: 1868 log house.
Research Fields: genealogy.
Activities: permanent exhibitions.
Publications: Cabin Chronicle.
Hours & Admission Prices: Mon.-Fri. 11-3, Sat.-Sun. 1-4. No charge; donations accepted. Closed holidays.
Attendance: 8,500 (accurate)
Membership: Pioneer $25; Settler $50; Patron $100.

KANSAS MUSEUM OF MILITARY HISTORY, 135 S. Hwy. 77, Augusta, KS 67010-7681. Tel.: 316-775-1425.
E-mail: info@kmmh.org
Web Site: www.kmmh.org
Key Personnel: Museum Dir. & Pres., John Lara
Military Museum.
Collections: aviation & military artifacts & memorabilia.
Hours & Admission Prices: April-Sept. daily 1-5; Oct.-March Sat.-Sun. 1-5.

Baldwin City

OLD CASTLE MUSEUM, 511 Fifth St., Baldwin City, KS 66006. Mailing Address: Baker University, P.O. Box 65, Baldwin City, KS 66006-0065. Tel.: 785-594-8380. Fax: 785-594-2522.
E-mail: brenda.day@bakeru.edu
Founded: 1953.
Congressional District: 2
Key Personnel: Pres. of Baker University, Dan Lambert; Dir., Brenda Day.
Governing Authority: Parent Institution: Baker University, 515 5th, Baldwin City, KS 66006. Tax-exempt: 170(b)(1)(A).
Historic Buildings Complex: 1857 original Santa Fe Trail Post Office; 1857 replica of Kibbee cabin; 1858 3-story stone structure.
Collections: Midwest Native American display; Southwest Native American

pottery; pioneer artifacts; 19th century print shop; early dentist & doctor exhibit; ironstone china pieces; silver & pewter items.
Research Fields: Santa Fe Trail.
Facilities: library.
Activities: individual & group tours by appointment.
Publications: pamphlets, Old Castle Museum; Kibbee Cabin; Palmyra Post Office.
Hours & Admission Prices: Mon.-Fri. 8-12; other times by appointment. No charge; donations accepted.
Attendance: 5,436 (accurate)

QUAYLE RARE BIBLE COLLECTION, Collins Library-Spencer Quayle Wing, 518 8th St., Baldwin City, KS 66006-0065. Mailing Address: Collins Library, P.O. Box 65, Baldwin City, KS 66006-0065. Tel.: 785-594-8393. Fax: 785-594-6721.
E-mail: quayle@bakeru.edu
Web Site: www.bakeru.edu/library
Founded: 1925.
Congressional District: 3
Key Personnel: Dir., Kay Bradt.
Personnel Profile: Part-Time Paid 2; Part-Time Volunteers 7.
Governing Authority: Baker University. Tax-exempt.
Rare Bible Museum.
Collections: 600 rare Bibles or portions thereof, including illuminated manuscripts & incunabula.
Facilities: 100-vol. library of books by William A. Quayle & reference materials on items in the collection available for use by special permission of the director; reading room.
Activities: guided tours with advance notice of 2 weeks; lectures; gallery talks; formally organized education programs for undergraduate college students affiliated with Baker University; permanent & temporary exhibitions.
Publications: book, The Catalog of The William Alfred Quayle Bible Collection; flyers; exhibit booklet.
Hours & Admission Prices: Sat.-Sun. 1-4; other times by appointment. No charge; donations accepted. Closed university holidays. ♿
Attendance: 450 (estimated)

Baxter Springs

BAXTER SPRINGS HERITAGE CENTER AND MUSEUM, 740 East Ave., Baxter Springs, KS 66713. Mailing Address: P.O. Box 514, Baxter Springs, KS 66713-0514. Tel.: 620-856-2385.
E-mail: heritagectr@embarqmail.com
Web Site: www.baxterspringsmuseum.org
Founded: 1962.
Congressional District: 14
Key Personnel: Pres. (V), Phyllis Abbott; Treas., Earleene Spaulding.
Personnel Profile: Full-Time Paid 1; Full-Time Volunteers 2; Part-Time Volunteers 100.
Governing Authority: private; nonprofit organization. Tax-exempt: 501(c)(3).
History Museum.
Collections: Civil War; 1863 Baxter Springs Massacre; school & education; Native American; mining; industry & business; domestic life; WWI & WWII.
Research Fields: historical Civil War battle site.
Facilities: Museum-related items for sale.
Activities: docent program; guided tours; lectures.
Publications: quarterly newsletter, Cassion Tracks.
Hours & Admission Prices: April-Oct. Mon.-Sat. 10-4:30, Sun. 1-4:30; Nov.-March Thurs.-Sat. 10-4:30, Sun. 1-4:30; other times by appointment. No charge; donations accepted. ♿
Attendance: 4,000 (estimated)
Membership: Yearly $5; Life Single $40; Life Couple $70.

Belleville

REPUBLIC COUNTY HISTORICAL SOCIETY MUSEUM, 615 28th St., Belleville, KS 66935. Mailing Address: P.O. Box 218, Belleville, KS 66935-0218. Tel.: 785-527-5971.
E-mail: repcomuse@nckcn.com
Web Site: www.nckcn.com/homepage/repcomuse/home.htm
Founded: 1985.
Key Personnel: C.E.O., Cur. & Archivist, Sherrie Larson; Pres. (V), Nancy Holt; Treas., David Bowersox; Asst. Cur., Vicki Kolarso.
Personnel Profile: Full-Time Paid 1; Part-Time Paid 1; Part-Time Volunteers 6.
Governing Authority: historical society. Tax-exempt: 501(c)(3).
Historical Society Museum.
Collections: pioneer historical artifacts; tool collection; railroad caboose. Historic Buildings: rural schoolhouse; log cabin; country church.
Facilities: 300-vol. library of history & genealogy.
Activities: Museum Sponsors: Soup Supper in January; Ice Cream Social in July.
Publications: newsletter 3 times per year, Illumination.
Hours & Admission Prices: Jan.-April Mon.-Fri. 1-5; May-Dec. Mon.-Fri. 1-5, Sun. 1:30-4:30. Adults $3; members & children under 10 no charge. Closed major holidays. ♿
Attendance: 1,440 (estimated)
Membership: Individual $10; Family $15; Business $25.

Beloit

LITTLE RED SCHOOLHOUSE-LIVING LIBRARY, Roadside Park, N. Walnut & Hwy. 24, Beloit, KS 67420. Mailing Address: P.O. Box 582, 123 N. Mill, Beloit, KS 67420-0582. Tel.: 785-738-2717.
Founded: 1976.
Congressional District: 106
Key Personnel: Chm. (V), Mildred Peterson.
Governing Authority: nonprofit. Parent Institution: City of Beloit. Subsidiary Institution: Alpha Pi Chapter of Delta Kappa Gamma. Tax-exempt: 501(c)(3)(6).
Education Museum: housed in 1874 one-room schoolhouse.
Collections: early school books & rhythm band instruments; manuscripts; recitation bench; country school desks; pot belly stove; teaching materials; bells; slate boards; globes; maps; water pails; dipper; dinner buckets; syrup pails; dunce stool; pictures; piano; library shelves; teacher's desk.
Research Fields: early day schools of Mitchell Co.
Facilities: 323-vol. library of old classroom texts & early day children's books. Pamphlets, postcards & other museum-related items for sale.
Activities: guided tours; retired teachers (many who taught in one-room schools) hold sessions for field trips; activities as they were done in the late 1800s & early 1900s; inter-museum loan & temporary exhibitions; meetings; parties; clubs.
Hours & Admission Prices: May 1-Oct. 1 Fri.-Mon. 1:30-4:30; other times by appointment. No charge; donations accepted.
Attendance: 379 (accurate)

Bonner Springs

THE NATIONAL AGRICULTURAL CENTER & HALL OF FAME, 630 N. 126th St., Bonner Springs, KS 66012-9045. Tel.: 913-721-1075. Fax: 913-721-1202.
E-mail: info@aghalloffame.com
Web Site: www.aghalloffame.com
Founded: 1958.
Congressional District: 3
Key Personnel: Exec. Dir., Tim Daugherty; Chm. (V), Robert Carlson; Pres. (V), Joel Ebbertt; Cur., Kate Alexander; Dir. Education, Lee Sigley; Museum Shop Mgr., Angela Cannizzano.
Personnel Profile: Full-Time Paid 4; Part-Time Paid 15; Part-Time Volunteers 15; Interns 1.
Governing Authority: nonprofit organization. Tax-exempt: 501(c)(3).
Agriculture Museum.
Collections: harvesting & planting equipment; steam traction engines; rural living items; farm equipment & tools; buggies, wagons & trucks; National Farmers Memorial; Farm Town including one-room school, train depot, museum & blacksmith shop.
Facilities: 200-seat auditorium; nature trail; early 1900s rural village replica. Museum-related items for sale.
Activities: arts festivals; guided tours; formal education programs for children; permanent & temporary exhibitions. Annual Events: threshing exhibition; Antique Tractor Pull; Artist-of-the-Month; Santa's Express.
Publications: quarterly newsletter, Update.
Hours & Admission Prices: mid-March to Nov. Tues.-Sat. 9-5, Sun. 1-5. Adults $7, senior citizens over 62 $6, children 5-16 $3; discounts for individual programs, groups, AAA, AAM & ICOM members and Newcomer's Packets; members & children under 5 no charge. ♿
Attendance: 25,000 (estimated)
Membership: Booster Club $25; Honorary Farmer $100; Honor Acre $200; Sustaining $1,000; Sponsoring $5,000; Foundation $50,000.

WYANDOTTE COUNTY MUSEUM, (M), 631 N. 126th St., Bonner Springs, KS 66012-9046. Tel.: 913-721-1078. Fax: 913-721-1394.
E-mail: krs@kckcvb.org
Formerly: Wyandotte County Historical Society and Museum
Founded: 1889.
Congressional District: 6
Key Personnel: C.E.O. & Dir., Trish Schurkamp; Cur., Jennifer Laughlin.
Personnel Profile: Full-Time Paid 3; Part-Time Volunteers 3.
Governing Authority: Unified government of Wyandotte County and Kansas City, Kansas. Tax-exempt: 501(c)(3).
History Museum.

Collections: Emigrant Tribal material; textiles and crafts; photographs; costumes pertaining to Wyandotte County; decorative arts; manuscript collections; archives.
Research Fields: Wyandotte County & adjacent areas; genealogy.
Facilities: library; 100-seat auditorium. Museum-related items for sale.
Activities: guided tours; lectures; permanent exhibitions; fourth grade education program.
Hours & Admission Prices: Mon.-Sat. 10-4. No charge; donations accepted. Closed holidays. ♿
Attendance: 300 (accurate)

Burlingame

BURLINGAME SCHUYLER MUSEUM, 117 S. Dacotah, Burlingame, KS 66413-1225. Mailing Address: P.O. Box 74, Burlingame, KS 66413-0074. Tel.: 785-654-3170.
E-mail: museum@burlingamemuseum.org
Web Site: www.burlingamemuseum.org
Founded: 2001.
Key Personnel: Pres. (V), David Prescott.
Personnel Profile: Part-Time Volunteers 75.
Governing Authority: Parent Institution: Burlingame Historical Society. Tax-exempt.
History Museum: former home of The Schuyler Grade School, built in 1902.
Collections: local history & culture; arrowheads; Native American artifacts; military artifacts; coal mining.
Research Fields: genealogy.
Facilities: Museum-related items for sale.
Hours & Admission Prices: Wed., Fri. & Sun. 1-4, Sat. 10-4. No charge; donations accepted. Closed occasional holidays. ♿
Attendance: 1,500 (estimated)
Membership: Individual $20; Family & Business $25.

Burlington

THE COFFEY COUNTY HISTORICAL MUSEUM, (M), 1101 Neosho St., Burlington, KS 66839-1656. Tel.: 620-364-2653. Fax: 620-364-8933.
Web Site: coffeycountymuseum.org
Key Personnel: Exec. Dir., Deborah Kennamore; Chm. (V), Kelly Hull; Education & Cur., Shirley Gorge; Treas., Brenda Grace Klubeck; Museum Shop Mgr., Erin Petterson.
Personnel Profile: Full-Time Paid 3; Part-Time Paid 2; Part-Time Volunteers 38.
Governing Authority: private; nonprofit organization. Tax-exempt: 501(c)(3).
Historical Society Museum.
Collections: Kansas history; Coffey County history; pioneer history.
Research Fields: genealogy; personal histories.
Facilities: library.
Activities: guided tours; hobby workshops; lectures; rental gallery; traveling exhibitions.
Publications: quarterly newsletter, Timelines.
Hours & Admission Prices: Mon.-Fri. 10-5, Sat.-Sun. 1-4. No charge; donations accepted. Closed national & state holidays.
Attendance: 7,000 (estimated)
Membership: Adult $5; Business $25; Lifetime $100.

Caney

CANEY VALLEY HISTORICAL SOCIETY, 310 W. 4th St., Caney, KS 67333. Mailing Address: P.O. Box 354, Caney, KS 67333-0354. Tel.: 620-879-5131. Fax: 620-879-5131.
Founded: 1984.
Congressional District: 4
Key Personnel: Pres. (V), Nancy Roe.
Governing Authority: Tax-exempt: 501(c)(3).
General Museum.
Collections: education; medical; post office; military; municipal; religious; industry; organizations; domestic; early businesses; meeting room with kitchen & genealogy room; photographs; Osage Indian artifacts; 28 ft. wall mural; farming tools.
Research Fields: early community events history; genealogy.
Facilities: Museum-related items for sale.
Activities: temporary exhibitions; children's programs; banquet. Museum Sponsors: Christmas Program.
Publications: quarterly newsletter.
Hours & Admission Prices: Mon.-Fri. 9-12 & 12:30-3. No charge; donations accepted. Closed New Year's Eve & Day; Memorial Day; Independence Day; Christmas Eve & Day. ♿
Attendance: 550 (estimated)
Membership: Individual $10.

Chanute

MARTIN AND OSA JOHNSON SAFARI MUSEUM, 111 N. Lincoln Ave., Chanute, KS 66720-1819. Tel.: 620-431-2730. Fax: 620-431-2730.
E-mail: osajohns@safarimuseum.com
Web Site: www.martinandosa.com
Founded: 1961.
Congressional District: 5
Key Personnel: Pres. Bd. Trustees, Kim Rutter; Dir., Conrad G. Froehlich; Cur., Jacqueline L. Borgeson; Store & Office Mgr., Shirley Rogers-Naff.
Personnel Profile: Full-Time Paid 3; Part-Time Volunteers 40.
Governing Authority: private. Tax-exempt: 501(c)(3).
Biographical Museum: located in historic Santa Fe Train Depot.
Collections: Johnson Collection: films, photographs, manuscripts & artifacts of Martin & Osa Johnson; ethnological collections from West Africa, East Africa, Borneo & South Pacific; natural history library; natural history art collection, originals & hand colored lithographs.
Research Fields: ethnology; anthropology; natural history; exploration; African art; photographic & film resources of E. Africa, South Pacific, Borneo 1917-1936.
Facilities: 10,000-vol. natural history & exploration library available on premises; Johnson Archives. Museum-related items for sale.
Activities: guided tours; film showings; education programs. Annual Events: Film Festival in April.
Publications: I Married Adventure; Four Years in Paradise; quarterly newsletter, Martin & Osa Johnson Safari Museum(R) Wait-A-Bit News.
Hours & Admission Prices: Mon.-Sat. 10-5, Sun. 1-5. Adults $4, senior citizens & students over 12 $3, children 6-12 $2; discounts to prearranged bus tours, KMA, ICOM, AASLH, AAM, MPMA and AAA members; children under 6 accompanied by adult no charge. Closed New Year's Day; Easter; Independence Day; Thanksgiving; Christmas. ♿
Attendance: 6,000 (accurate)
Membership: Single $25; Family $45; Wanderer $70; Adventurer & Business $100; Explorer $250 & up.

Chapman

KANSAS AUTO RACING MUSEUM, 1205 Manor Rd., Chapman, KS 67431. Mailing Address: P.O. Box 549, Chapman, KS 67431. Tel.: 785-922-6644.
Founded: 1998.
Congressional District: 2
Key Personnel: Dir., Doug Thompson.
Governing Authority: Tax-exempt.
Auto Racing Museum.
Collections: auto racing history & cars; first NASCAR trophy; photographs; personal artifacts; first NHRA trophy.
Hours & Admission Prices: Mon.-Sat. 9-5, Sun. by appointment. Adults $5. Closed New Year's Day; Easter; Thanksgiving; Christmas. ♿
Attendance: 4,000 (accurate)

Chetopa

CHETOPA HISTORICAL MUSEUM, 419 Maple St., Chetopa, KS 67336. Mailing Address: P.O. Box 648, Chetopa, KS 67336-0648. Tel.: 620-236-7121.
Founded: 1881.
Congressional District: 5
Key Personnel: Dir., Cur. & Museum Shop Mgr., Fannie Bassett.
Governing Authority: society. Affiliated with the Labette County Historical Society, Parsons, 67357. Tax-exempt: 501(c)(3).
History Museum.
Collections: local history; local papers on microfilm from 1869-2005.
Hours & Admission Prices: April-Oct. Mon.-Wed. & Fri. 10-4. No charge; donations accepted. ♿
Attendance: 450 (estimated)
Membership: Individual $2.

Clifton

CLIFTON COMMUNITY HISTORICAL SOCIETY, 105 Clifton St., Clifton, KS 66937-9780. Mailing Address: P.O. Box 5, Clifton, KS 66937-0005.
Founded: 1976.
Key Personnel: Pres. (V), Mary Veesart; Treas., Erma Bouley.
Governing Authority: private; nonprofit organization. Tax-exempt.
General Museum: housed in Old Missouri Pacific Depot & Caboose.
Collections: period artifacts from Clifton & surrounding areas including military & scout clothing; 19th century photos; country school records; china; tools; newspapers; film of Clifton, Kansas newspapers from start to June 24, 1993.

Research Fields: genealogy from old newspapers.
Facilities: 10-vol. family genealogy library available to the public; school corner. Museum-related items for sale.
Activities: guided tours. Museum Sponsors: Christmas Party-meal.
Publications: quarterly newsletter, Courier.
Hours & Admission Prices: By appointment. No charge; donations accepted. Closed New Year's Day; Easter; Independence Day; Thanksgiving; Christmas. ♿
Attendance: 62 (estimated)
Membership: Family & Business $5; Life $100.

Coffeyville

BROWN MANSION, 2019 S. Walnut, Coffeyville, KS 67337-6819. Mailing Address: P.O. Box 843, Coffeyville, KS 67337-0843. Tel.: 620-251-0431. Fax: 620-251-5448.
Web Site: www.brownmansion.com
Founded: 1904.
Congressional District: 4
Key Personnel: Pres., Nancy Garton; Vice Pres., Darla Thornburg; Mansion Mgr., Woody De Pontier; Cur., Doris Scism.
Personnel Profile: Full-Time Volunteers 10.
Governing Authority: nonprofit society. Parent Institution: Coffeyville Historical Society. Tax-exempt.
Historic House.
Collections: period furniture, carpets, china & silver; leaded Tiffany glass accents; Tiffany chandelier.
Facilities: Museum-related items for sale.
Activities: guided tours.
Hours & Admission Prices: March-Dec. Sun. 1-4, Mon.-Tues. & Thurs.-Sat. 10-4. Adults $6; children 6 & under no charge. Closed Easter; Thanksgiving; Christmas; during special events.
Attendance: 7,500 (estimated)

DALTON DEFENDERS MUSEUM, 113 E. 8th, Coffeyville, KS 67337-5803. Mailing Address: P.O. Box 843, Coffeyville, KS 67337-0843. Tel.: 620-251-5944.
E-mail: chamber@coffeyville.com
Web Site: www.daltondefendersmuseum.com
Founded: 1954.
Congressional District: 4
Key Personnel: Pres., Nancy Garton; Vice Pres., Darla Thornburg; Museum Mgr., John Alvey; Museum Mgr., Wendy Alvey.
Personnel Profile: Full-Time Volunteers 15.
Governing Authority: nonprofit. Parent Institution: Coffeyville Historical Society. Tax-exempt.
History Museum.
Collections: mementos from the Dalton Raid and from Dalton Gang members; Wendell Willkie mementos; Walter Johnson mementos; Native American artifacts; artifacts & photographs from the early history of Coffeyville.
Facilities: Museum-related items for sale.
Activities: guided tours.
Hours & Admission Prices: Daily 10-4; other times by appointment. Adults $6, children $3; discounts to AAA members; children 7 & under no charge. Closed Easter; Thanksgiving; Christmas.
Attendance: 9,000 (estimated)

Colby

THE PRAIRIE MUSEUM OF ART & HISTORY, (M), 1905 S. Franklin, Colby, KS 67701-3710. Tel.: 785-460-4590. Fax: 785-460-4592.
E-mail: prairiem@st.tel.net
Web Site: www.prairiemuseum.org
Founded: 1959.
Congressional District: 1
Key Personnel: Dir., Sue Ellen Taylor.
Personnel Profile: Full-Time Paid 4; Part-Time Paid 4; Part-Time Volunteers 20.
Governing Authority: society; nonprofit organization. Thomas County Historical Society. Tax-exempt: 501(c)(3).
Historical Society Museum & Archives.
Collections: articles relating to the area's history from the period of the homesteaders who lived in sod homes to World War II; the Kuska Collection, containing 2,000 dolls; signed Tiffany & Sevres, Capo De Monte, Royal Vienna, Satsuma, Ridgway, Wedgwood, Limoge & Meissen; glass including cut, Redford, Steigel, Stuben, Galle & Cameo; furniture; textiles; silver; books; memorabilia.
Research Fields: pertaining to the collection.
Facilities: library of books, manuscripts, documents & photography pertaining to Thomas County; reading room. Books, arts & crafts of the area & museum-related items for sale.
Activities: guided tours; lectures; films; gallery talks; formally organized education programs; docent program; loan, permanent & temporary exhibitions; hobby workshops. Museum Sponsors: Sam White Day; folk artists; Horse Powered Harvest.
Publications: quarterly newsletter, Prairie Winds; books, Land of the Windmills; Golden Jubilee; Golden Heritage of Thomas County Kansas; A History of Thomas County, Kansas, 1885-1964.
Hours & Admission Prices: April-Oct. Mon.-Fri. 9-5, Sat.-Sun. 1-5; Nov.-March Tues.-Fri. 9-5, Sat.-Sun. 1-5. Adults $5, senior citizens $2.50, children 6-16 $2; members & Sun. no charge. Closed New Year's Day; Easter; Thanksgiving; Christmas. ♿
Attendance: 15,000 (accurate)
Membership: Individual $15; Family $25; Lifetime $500.

Concordia

CLOUD COUNTY HISTORICAL SOCIETY MUSEUM, 635 Broadway, Concordia, KS 66901-2914. Tel.: 785-243-2866.
Founded: 1959.
Congressional District: 1
Key Personnel: Pres., Dana Brewer; Sec., Aline Luecke; Treas., Mary Dean Nelson.
Personnel Profile: Part-Time Paid 1; Part-Time Volunteers 14; Interns 1.
Governing Authority: county. Parent Institution: Cloud County Historical Society. Tax-exempt.
Historical Society Museum: housed in 1908 Andrew Carnegie Library.
Collections: prisoner of war camp, military casket flags; clothing; dolls; medical, architectural, royal families, dental & school textbooks; Indian artifacts; household goods; farm tools; books; pictures & photographs; early undertaking equipment; long distance telephone switchboard; PBX cordboard; telephone memorabilia; barbed wire collection; absorption type wavemeter; 1936 amateur radio WGWXY; 1928 Lincoln-Page biplane with 90 HP. Curtis engine; horse drawn farm machinery including 1898 horseless carriage; 1903 Holsman car; printing presses; linotype; railroad nails; candy making equipment; period toys; toothpick holders; gem & mineral collection; Concordia Daily Kansas 1900-1918; 1870-2005 microfilm of Concordia Blade-Empire; newspaper microfilm: Jamestown 1881-1985, Miltonvale 1882-2001, Clyde 1878-2003, Glasco 1883-2001; Concordia Kansas 1918-1983.
Research Fields: Cloud County history; genealogy.
Activities: guided tours of county interest areas; quarterly meetings. Annual Events: Open House; dinner meeting with elected officers in October.
Publications: quarterly newsletter, Cloud Comments.
Hours & Admission Prices: Tues.-Sat. 1-5; other times by appointment. No charge; donations requested. ♿
Attendance: 4,000 (accurate)
Membership: Annual $5; Life $15-$150.

Cottonwood Falls

CHASE COUNTY HISTORICAL SOCIETY, INC., 301 Broadway, Cottonwood Falls, KS 66845. Mailing Address: Box 375, Cottonwood Falls, KS 66845-0375. Tel.: 620-273-8500.
E-mail: cchistorical@bulldognet.com
Web Site: skyways.lib.ks.us/genweb/society/cottonwd/
Founded: 1934.
Key Personnel: Pres., David Croy; Financial Dir., Joyce Blount; Cur., Christine Kabler.
Personnel Profile: Part-Time Paid 1; Part-Time Volunteers 3.
Governing Authority: county government; nonprofit. Tax-exempt.
Historical Museum.
Collections: old tools; household items; obituaries; marriage licenses, cemetery records.
Research Fields: genealogy.
Facilities: 4-vol. library of Chase Co. Historical Sketches; 16,000 sq. ft. exhibit space.
Activities: guided tours; annual meeting.
Publications: Chase County Historical Sketches, Vols. 1, 2, 3, 4.
Hours & Admission Prices: Tues.-Sat. 12-4. No charge; donations accepted. Closed New Year's Day; Memorial Day; Independence Day; Thanksgiving; Christmas.
Attendance: 2,000 (estimated)
Membership: Lifetime $25.

RONIGER MEMORIAL MUSEUM, 315 Union St., Cottonwood Falls, KS 66845. Mailing Address: P.O. Box 70, Cottonwood Falls, KS 66845-0070. Tel.: 620-273-6310 & 6412. Fax: 620-273-6335.
E-mail: deroy10@sbcglobal.net
Founded: 1959.
Key Personnel: Pres. & Cur., David E. Croy; Sec. & Treas., John Roniger.
Personnel Profile: Full-Time Paid 1.

Governing Authority: county. Tax-exempt.
History Museum: located on lawn of 100-year old courthouse.
Collections: Indian artifacts; stuffed native animals; local historical mementoes.
Hours & Admission Prices: Tues.-Sun. 1-5; other times by appointment only. No charge; donations accepted. ♿
Attendance: 2,000

Council Grove

KAW MISSION STATE HISTORIC SITE, (M), 500 N. Mission, Council Grove, KS 66846-1433. Tel.: 620-767-5410. Fax: 620-767-5816.
E-mail: kawmission@kshs.org
Web Site: www.kawmission.org
Founded: 1951.
Congressional District: 5
Key Personnel: Historic Site Admin., Mary Honeyman; Pres. (V), Jeremiah Hershberger.
Personnel Profile: Full-Time Paid 1; Part-Time Paid 1; Part-Time Volunteers 35.
Governing Authority: state. Parent Institution: Kansas State Historical Society, 6425 S.W. Sixth St., Topeka, KS 66615. Tel. 913-296-3251. Tax-exempt: 501(c)(3).
Historical Society Museum: 1850-1851, 2-story building.
Collections: 19th century America; Plains Indians.
Research Fields: History of Kaw or Kansas Native American Indian Tribe, Santa Fe Trail & Council Grove.
Facilities: reconstructed Indian hut; meeting room; education center.
Activities: guided tours; permanent exhibitions. Museum Sponsors: Annual Wah-Shun-Gah days activities in June; Kaw Nation Inter-tribal Pow-wow; Kaw Councils, education program series.
Publications: quarterly newsletter, Toh-Po-Ska.
Hours & Admission Prices: March-Nov. Wed.-Sat. 9-5, Sun. 1-5; Dec.-Feb. Thurs.-Sat. 10-5. Adults $2, students $1; children under 5 & members no charge. Closed state holidays. ♿
Attendance: 7,500 (accurate)
Membership: Individual $10; Business & Family $30; Benefactor $50; Sustaining $100.

Dighton

LANE COUNTY HISTORICAL MUSEUM, 333 N. Main St., Dighton, KS 67839. Mailing Address: P.O. Box 821, Dighton, KS 67839-0821. Tel.: 620-397-5652. Fax: 620-397-5652.
E-mail: lchm@st-tel.net
Founded: 1976.
Congressional District: 1
Key Personnel: Pres., Mark West; Chm., Mary Waugh; Cur., Virginia Johnston.
Personnel Profile: Full-Time Volunteers 12; Part-Time Paid 2; Part-Time Volunteers 8.
Governing Authority: society; nonprofit. Parent Institution: Lane County Historical Society. Tax-exempt.
History Museum.
Collections: early Lane County photos; articles used in Lane County; manuscript collections. Historic House: sod house.
Research Fields: local history.
Facilities: 50-vol. library of books pertinent to Lane County available for use within the library; reading room; workroom; meeting room; machinery park; temporary exhibit room. Handcrafted items & books for sale.
Activities: guided tours; lectures; films; gallery talks; arts festivals; hobby workshops; permanent, temporary & traveling exhibitions; school loan service.
Publications: quarterly newsletter, Friends of Museum.
Hours & Admission Prices: Memorial Day to Labor Day Tues.-Sat. 1-5, Sun. 2-5; Sept.-May Tues.-Sat. 1-5. No charge; donations accepted. Closed legal holidays. ♿
Attendance: 1,200 (estimated)
Membership: Individual & Contributing $10; Business $15; Lifetime $100.

Dodge City

BOOT HILL MUSEUM, INC., (M), Front St., Dodge City, KS 67801. Tel.: 620-227-8188. Fax: 620-227-7673.
Web Site: www.boothill.org
Founded: 1947.
Congressional District: 1
Key Personnel: Gen. Mgr., Lara Brehm; Chm. Bd. Dir., Pat Hamit; Chief Cur., Karen Pankratz; Asst. Cur., Kathie Bell.
Personnel Profile: Full-Time Paid 8; Part-Time Paid 150; Part-Time Volunteers 100.
Governing Authority: nonprofit. Subsidiary Institution: Boot Hill Museum Store. Tax-exempt: 501(c)(3).
Western History Museum: located on Boot Hill.
Collections: 19th-century business & home furnishings, equipment; tools; agricultural equipment; weapons. Historic Buildings: 1878 cattleman's home; 1880 carriage shop; 1865 Fort Dodge jail; 1917 school; 1931 depot.
Research Fields: 19th-century business & social life in southwest Kansas; decorative arts; historic preservation; history of Dodge City.
Facilities: 1,200-vol. library of historical books & documents on Dodge City available for use on premises; photographic collections; theater. Museum-related items for sale.
Activities: permanent & temporary exhibits; school loan service; craft demonstrations; inter-museum loans; formally organized education programs for children; docent program; Long Branch Saloon Revue & medicine shows.
Publications: brochure; exhibit catalog; gallery guides; book, Dodge City: Up Through A Century in Story & Pictures.
Hours & Admission Prices: Winter: Mon.-Sat. 9-5, Sun. 1-5; Memorial Day to Labor Day daily 8-8. Summer: adults $8, seniors & students $7.50; children 6 & under no charge. Off-Season: adults $7, senior citizens 62 and over & students $6.50; discounts to AAA members; children 6 & under and members no charge. New Year's Day; Thanksgiving; Christmas. ♿
Attendance: 76,791 (accurate)
Membership: Senior 62 & over $40; Single $45; Senior Family $60; Family $65; Marshal (Business) $250.

HOME OF STONE (THE MUELLER-SCHMIDT HOUSE 1881), A FORD COUNTY MUSEUM, CURATED BY FORD COUNTY HISTORIC SOCIETY, (M), Ave. A & Vine St., Dodge City, KS 67801. Mailing Address: P.O. Box 131, Dodge City, KS 67801-0131. Tel.: 620-227-6791.
E-mail: georgedcks@yahoo.com
Web Site: www.skyways.org/orgs/fordco
Founded: 1965.
Congressional District: 116
Key Personnel: Pres. (V), George Laughead, Jr.; Financial Dir., Jim Sherer; Archivist, Ann Warner; Museum Shop Mgr., Janice Klein.
Personnel Profile: Full-Time Volunteers 2; Part-Time Paid 5; Part-Time Volunteers 10.
Governing Authority: private; nonprofit organization. Parent Institution: Ford County Historical Society. Tax-exempt: 501(c)(3).
Historic House.
Collections: original kerosene lamps, clocks & winding walnut staircase; Pioneer Mother Room; picture collection.
Facilities: 500-vol. library; 1,200 sq. ft. exhibit space. Museum-related items for sale.
Activities: guided tours; temporary exhibitions. Annual Events: Victorian Christmas Tea; Spring Open House.
Publications: monthly newsletter, Ford County Historical Society, Inc.
Hours & Admission Prices: Memorial Day to Labor Day Mon.-Sat. 9-5, Sun. 2-4. Adults $3.
Attendance: 4,000 (accurate)
Membership: Individual $10; Lifetime $50.

THE KANSAS TEACHERS' HALL OF FAME, 603 5th St., Dodge City, KS 67801-1674. Mailing Address: P.O. Box 1674, Dodge City, KS 67801-1674. Tel.: 620-225-7311.
E-mail: kthof@kthof.org
Web Site: www.kthof.org
Founded: 1977.
Key Personnel: Dir., Nancy Tramer; Pres. (V), Carol J. Swinney.
Personnel Profile: Part-Time Volunteers 5.
Governing Authority: private; nonprofit organization.
Outstanding Teachers Museum.
Collections: pictures of outstanding teachers inducted into the Hall of Fame; textbooks & other items pertinent to early day classrooms.
Facilities: library of textbooks available for use on premises. Museum-related items for sale.
Activities: Annual Events: induction ceremony & banquet.
Hours & Admission Prices: April-May & Sept.-Oct. Mon.-Sat. 11-4, Sun. 1-5; Memorial Day-Labor Day Mon.-Sat. 8:30-6, Sun. 1-5. No charge; donations accepted. ♿
Attendance: 7,500 (estimated)

Douglass

DOUGLASS HISTORICAL MUSEUM, 318 S. Forest, Douglass, KS 67039. Mailing Address: P.O. Box 95, Douglass, KS 67039-0095. Tel.: 316-746-2319 & 747-2166.
Founded: 1950.
Congressional District: 5
Key Personnel: Dir. & Cur., Frances Renfro.
Personnel Profile: Part-Time Volunteers 6.
Governing Authority: society. Tax-exempt.

Pioneer Museum.
Collections: Indian artifacts; tools; costumes; kitchen display; school-room; church display; Victorian sitting room; millinery & dress shop; doctors office; photographs; cookbooks; farming tools; medical items; toys; family history files.
Research Fields: town, business & people of Douglass.
Facilities: library of local & pioneer history books, photographs, cemetery maps & 1884-1984 microfilm of Douglass Tribune available for use on premises; Osage hunting grounds.
Activities: guided tours; temporary exhibitions.
Publications: The Douglass Story; cookbook, Family Favorites.
Hours & Admission Prices: Mon., Wed. & Fri. 9-11 & 1-3; other times by appointment. No charge; donations accepted. Closed New Year's Eve & Day; Christmas Eve, Day & week. ♿
Attendance: 750 (estimated)
Membership: Patron $25; Life Time $500.

Edna

EDNA HISTORICAL MUSEUM, 100 S. Delaware, Edna, KS 67342. Mailing Address: P.O. Box 368, Edna, KS 67342-0368.
Founded: 1978.
Congressional District: 2
Key Personnel: Pres. (V), Kenneth E. Cary; Treas., Hazel Stone; Cur., Ronald Neidigh.
Personnel Profile: Part-Time Volunteers 6.
Governing Authority: private; nonprofit organization. Tax-exempt: 501(c)(3).
History Museum: housed in the old First National Bank building.
Collections: early Edna history; newspapers on microfilm; area family histories.
Activities: guided tours.
Hours & Admission Prices: May-Oct. Fri. 1-4, Sat. 9-12; other times by appointment. No charge; donations accepted. Closed all holidays.
Attendance: 100 (estimated)
Membership: Annual $1.

El Dorado

BUTLER COUNTY HISTORY CENTER & KANSAS OIL MUSEUM, 383 E. Central Ave., El Dorado, KS 67042-2133. Tel.: 316-321-9333. Fax: 316-321-3619.
E-mail: history@kansasoilmuseum.org
Web Site: www.kansasoilmuseum.org
Founded: 1956.
Congressional District: 5
Key Personnel: Chm. (V), Richard King; Exec. Dir., Teresa Bachman; Cur. Collections, Mindy Tallent; Cur. Education, Lisa Cooley.
Personnel Profile: Full-Time Paid 3; Part-Time Paid 1; Part-Time Volunteers 70.
Governing Authority: nonprofit organization. Parent Institution: Butler County Historical Society. Subsidiary Institution: Kansas Oil Museum. Tax-exempt: 501(c)(3).
History Museum.
Collections: Butler County & Kansas oil history; objects & documents related to the history of the Kansas oil industry; oil field equipment & restored buildings; objects related to county development by ranching & farming; Flint Hills flora & fauna. Historic Structures: 1858 Conner Log Cabin; 1930s oil field lease house; oil tank car; 1930s cable tool drilling rig; 1950 rotary drilling rig; late 1920s reconstructed grocery store, doctor's office & print shop; 1917 lease house; 1890s one-room schoolhouse.
Research Fields: petroleum & local history.
Facilities: 4,500-vol. library pertaining to petroleum, technology & local history available for use on premises only; nature conservation center; reading room. Museum-related items for sale.
Activities: guided tours; lectures; films; permanent, temporary & traveling exhibitions; educational programs; special events.
Publications: newsletter, The Crownblock; books related to county history; Illustrated Directory of Kansas Oilmen; Stone Arch Bridges of Southern Butler County; video, Oil in Kansas.
Hours & Admission Prices: May-Sept. Mon.-Sat. 9-5; Oct.-April Tues.-Fri. 9-5, Sat. 12-5. Adults $4; members no charge. Closed major holidays. ♿
Attendance: 9,897 (accurate)
Membership: Individual $25; Family $35; Benefactor $75; Business $120; Corporate $300.

COUTTS MEMORIAL MUSEUM OF ART, INC., 110 N. Main St., El Dorado, KS 67042-2016. Mailing Address: P.O. Box 1, El Dorado, KS 67042-0001. Tel.: 316-321-1212. Fax: 316-321-1215.
E-mail: coutts@coutts.kscoxmail.com
Web Site: couttsmuseum.org
Founded: 1970.
Congressional District: 4
Key Personnel: Pres. Bd., Connie Walton; Co Dir., Rhoda Hodges; Co Dir., Terri Scott; Sec., Bill Kloeblen.
Personnel Profile: Full-Time Paid 2; Part-Time Paid 1; Part-Time Volunteers 35.
Governing Authority: nonprofit organization. Tax-exempt: 501(c)(3).
Fine Art Museum: housed in 1917 bank building.
Collections: paintings; sculptures; items of historical interest.
Research Fields: historical sites.
Activities: talks; tours; organizational meetings; art shows, concerts & promotions.
Publications: quarterly newsletter.
Hours & Admission Prices: Mon., Wed. & Fri. 1-5, Tues. & Thurs. 9-12 & 1-5, Sat. 12-4; tours arranged for groups of 12 or more by appointment. No charge; donations accepted. Closed federal & state holidays. ♿
Attendance: 7,200 (estimated)
Membership: Single $25; Couple & Patron $50; Underwriter $100; Benefactor $500 & up.

Ellis

WALTER P. CHRYSLER BOYHOOD HOME AND MUSEUM, 102 W. 10th, Ellis, KS 67637. Mailing Address: P.O. Box 229, Ellis, KS 67637-0229. Tel.: 785-726-3636. Fax: 785-726-3653.
E-mail: chrysler55@eaglecom.net
Web Site: www.chryslerboyhoodhome.com
Founded: 1954.
Key Personnel: Dir., Dr. Cline; Pres. (V), Michael Downing; Treas., John Barker.
Personnel Profile: Part-Time Paid 3.
Governing Authority: private; nonprofit organization. Tax-exempt: 501(c)(3).
History Museum.
Collections: personal artifacts; jewelry; books; photographs.
Facilities: Museum-related items for sale.
Activities: guided tours.
Hours & Admission Prices: Memorial Day to Labor Day Tues.-Sat. 10-4; Sept.-May Tues.-Sat. 11-3. Adults 16 & up $3, senior citizens 62 & up $2.50, children 8-15 $1; children under 7 no charge. Closed New Year's Day; Easter; Thanksgiving; Christmas.
Attendance: 1,200 (estimated)

Ellsworth

HODGDEN HOUSE MUSEUM COMPLEX, 104 W. South Main, Ellsworth, KS 67439-3232. Mailing Address: P.O. Box 144, Ellsworth, KS 67439-0144. Tel.: 785-472-3059.
E-mail: echs@eaglecom.net
Formerly: Ellsworth County Museum Complex
Founded: 1961.
Congressional District: 1
Key Personnel: C.E.O., Phyllis Dolenzal; Museum Shop Mgr., Georgia Smith.
Personnel Profile: Full-Time Paid 1; Part-Time Paid 2; Part-Time Volunteers 6.
Governing Authority: society. Parent Institution: Ellsworth County Historical Society. Tax-exempt.
Museum Complex.
Collections: folklore; Indian; agriculture; archaeology; costumes. Historic Buildings: 1876 Hodgden house; livery stable; country schoolhouse; church; Union Pacific caboose; log cabin; Ft. Harker Guardhouse and officer's house; 2 train depots; jail.
Facilities: 200-vol. library of local newspapers, file books & books used by pioneers available for use on microfilm. Books & pamphlets for sale.
Activities: Annual Event: Cowtown Days in September.
Publications: Sharing History; brochure
Hours & Admission Prices: Tues.-Sat. 9-5, Sun. 1-5. Adults $3 (includes entrance to Fort Harker Museum Complex). Closed New Year's Day; Easter; Thanksgiving; Christmas. ♿
Attendance: 3,000 (estimated)
Membership: Individual $10; Family $20; Business $25; Life $200.

ROGERS HOUSE MUSEUM GALLERY, 102 E. Main St., Ellsworth, KS 67439. Tel.: 785-472-5674.
Founded: 1968.
Congressional District: 1
Key Personnel: Dir., Robert Rogers.
Governing Authority: individual operation.
Art Museum: housed in 1870, American House, cowboy hotel.
Collections: original paintings; prints; art.
Facilities: original paintings & fine art prints for sale.
Activities: permanent & temporary exhibitions.
Publications: books, The Great West; Quill of the Kansan; Country Neighbor; Art Observations.

Hours & Admission Prices: Open by appointment; call for information. No charge; donations accepted. ♿

Emporia

DAVID TRAYLOR ZOO OF EMPORIA, 75 Soden Rd., Emporia, KS 66801-8702. Mailing Address: P.O. Box 928, Emporia, KS 66801-0928. Tel.: 620-341-4365. Fax: 620-341-4367.
E-mail: emporiazoo@emporia-kansas.gov
Web Site: www.emporiazoo.org
Founded: 1934.
Congressional District: 5
Key Personnel: Interim Dir. & Mgr. Animal Collection, Lisa Keith; Chm. (V), Angela Anderson; Pres., Mike Turnbull; Museum Shop Mgr., Lori Heavener.
Personnel Profile: Full-Time Paid 3; Part-Time Paid 3; Part-Time Volunteers 21.
Governing Authority: municipal. Parent Institution: City of Emporia. Tax-exempt.
Zoo: located in Soden's Grove Park, one of Emporia's earliest parks.
Collections: native & exotic hoofed stock; Cinereous vultures; mountain lion; eagles; bobcat; lemurs; tamarins; waterfowl; birds of prey; wallabies; small animals; birds; badgers; prairie dogs; bison; llamas; mule deer; cranes.
Research Fields: waterfowl propagation.
Facilities: zoological park.
Activities: guided tours & animal presentations for groups & organizations by appointment.
Publications: newsletter, Keeping In Touch.
Hours & Admission Prices: Winter: daily 10-4:30; Summer: Mon.-Tues. & Thurs.-Sat. 10-4:30, Wed. & Sun. 10-8. No charge; donations accepted. ♿
Attendance: 64,518 (accurate)
Membership: Emporia Friends of the Zoo: Individual $20; Family $30; Sponsor $50; Patron $100; Benefactor $500; Endowment $1,000.

EMPORIA STATE UNIVERSITY JOHNSTON GEOLOGY MUSEUM, 1200 Commercial St., Emporia, KS 66801-5087. Mailing Address: ESU Cram Science Hall, 14th and Merchant St., Emporia, KS 66801. Tel.: 620-341-5330. Fax: 620-341-6055.
Web Site: www.emporia.edu/earthsci/museum/museum.htm
Formerly: Emporia State University Geology Museum
Founded: 1983.
Key Personnel: Dir., Dr. Michael Morales.
Governing Authority: public university; nonprofit.
Geology Museum.
Collections: Kansas vertebrate & invertebrate fossils; materials collected from the Hamilton Quarry, which includes fossil flora, insects, fish & amphibians from one layer of Pennsylvanian strata.
Facilities: 1,800 sq. ft. exhibit space.
Hours & Admission Prices: School in session: Mon.-Fri. 8am-10pm, Sat. 8-12. No charge; donations accepted. Closed holidays.
Attendance: 750 (estimated)

LYON COUNTY HISTORICAL SOCIETY AND MUSEUM, (M), 118 E. 6th Ave., Emporia, KS 66801-3922. Tel.: 620-340-6310.
E-mail: lycomu@osprey.net
Founded: 1937.
Congressional District: 5
Key Personnel: Exec. Dir., J. Greg Jordon; Pres. (V), Lisa Goldstein; Chm. (V), Annette Rice; Education Coord., Laura Dodge; Registrar, Jake Dalton; Asst. Registrar, Clerk & Museum Store Mgr., Carolyn Eckstrom.
Personnel Profile: Full-Time Paid 1; Part-Time Paid 4; Part-Time Volunteers 30; Interns 1.
Governing Authority: society. Parent Institution: Lyon County Historical Society. Subsidiary Institution: Lyon County Historical Museum. Tax-exempt: 501(c)(3).
County General History Museum: housed in 1904 Carnegie Library.
Collections: costumes; local, county archives & artifacts; State archives & documents; Gilson scrapbook collection; manuscripts; family histories; photographs.
Research Fields: Lyon County history; genealogical research.
Facilities: library & archives available for use on premises; research room. Kansas artists' work, Kansas made & museum-related articles for sale.
Activities: lectures; tours; multi-media & slide & VCR presentations; rotating exhibits; participatory education programs; research service.
Publications: Lyon County Lines; Lyon County Historical Society Happenings.
Hours & Admission Prices: Tues.-Sat. 1-5; other times by appointment. Adults $2, children over 6 $1; children under 6 no charge. Closed major holidays. ♿
Attendance: 10,000 (estimated)
Membership: General $15; Contributing $25; Sustaining $50; Benefactor $100.

NORMAN R. EPPINK ART GALLERY, EMPORIA STATE UNIVERSITY, 1200 Commercial, Emporia, KS 66801-5057. Tel.: 620-341-5246. Fax: 316-341-6246.
E-mail: reichenb@emporia.edu
Web Site: www.emporia.edu/m/www/art/eppink.htm
Founded: 1939.
Congressional District: 5
Key Personnel: C.E.O., Michael Lane; Dir., Roberta Eichenberg.
Personnel Profile: Full-Time Paid 1; Part-Time Paid 4.
Governing Authority: state. Parent Institution: Emporia State University. Tax-exempt: 170(b)(1)(A).
University Art Gallery.
Collections: contemporary drawings & prints; artifacts; paintings; sculpture.
Facilities: library; nature center; field research station; reading room; 400-seat auditorium; theater; classrooms; cafeteria.
Activities: guided tours; lectures; gallery talks; TV & radio programs; formally organized education programs for undergraduate & graduate students affiliated with Emporia State University; loan, temporary & traveling exhibitions.
Publications: annual, National Invitational Drawing Exhibition Catalog; annual, Art Faculty Exhibition catalog.
Hours & Admission Prices: Mon.-Fri. 9-4. No charge; donations accepted. Closed university holidays. ♿
Attendance: 11,000 (estimated)

RICHARD H. SCHMIDT MUSEUM OF NATURAL HISTORY, 1200 Commercial St., Emporia State Univ., Emporia, KS 66801-5057. Mailing Address: Dept. of Biological Sciences, Box 4050, Emporia State Univ., Emporia, KS 66801. Tel.: 620-341-5311. Fax: 620-341-5607.
E-mail: wjensen1@emporia.edu
Web Site: www.emporia.edu/smnh/
Founded: 1959.
Congressional District: 5
Key Personnel: Dir., Dr. William Jensen.
Governing Authority: state. Affiliated with Emporia State University. Tax-exempt: 501(a).
Natural History Museum.
Collections: skins & mounted specimens of birds, mammals; ornithology; mammalogy; ichthyology; herpetology.
Research Fields: ornithology; mammalogy.
Facilities: nature center; field research station.
Activities: guided tours; lectures; formally organized education programs for children & undergraduate college students; permanent, temporary & traveling exhibitions.
Publications: Kansas School Naturalist.
Hours & Admission Prices: Mon.-Fri. 8am-10pm, Sat. 8-12. No charge. Closed school holidays. ♿

WILLIAM ALLEN WHITE STATE HISTORIC SITE, 927 Exchange St., Emporia, KS 66801-3040. Tel.: 620-342-2800.
Governing Authority: Parent Institution: Kansas Historical Society.
Historic House: housed in the former home of William Allen White, nationally known newspaperman & author.
Collections: family history; personal artifacts; period furnishings; photographs.
Hours & Admission Prices: Wed.-Sat. 9:30-5, Sun. 1-5. Adults $3, students $1; discounts to groups; members, active military & children 5 and under no charge.
Attendance: 1,750 (estimated)

Erie

MEM-ERIE HISTORICAL MUSEUM, 225 S. Main St., Erie, KS 66733. Mailing Address: 421 S. Main, Erie, KS 66733-1440. Tel.: 620-244-3309.
E-mail: lhoppas@cox.net
Founded: 1994.
Key Personnel: Pres. (V), Ruth McKinney; Sec. & Treas., Lavon Hoppas.
Personnel Profile: Part-Time Paid 1; Part-Time Volunteers 12.
Governing Authority: private; not-for-profit organization. Tax-exempt.
Historical Society Museum: site of first Masonic Hall in 1860s.
Collections: furnishings, photographs, personal artifacts & documents dating from founding of Erie in 1860s; recreational artifacts; books on Erie family history; men's & women's military suits; World War I & II GAR roster; Santa Fe & Kay railroad artifacts.
Research Fields: houses; jail; businesses; genealogy.
Facilities: library; educational facilities for grade school children. Pencils & books for sale.

Activities: guided tours; educational programs for grade school children; study clubs; temporary exhibits. Annual Event: Old Soldiers & Sailors Reunion.
Publications: newspaper; newsletter.
Hours & Admission Prices: Feb.-Nov. Fri.-Sat. 1-5; other times by appointment. No charge; donations accepted. ♿
Attendance: 160 (accurate)
Membership: Single $10; Family $25.

Eureka

GREENWOOD COUNTY HISTORICAL SOCIETY & MUSEUM, 120 W. 4th St., Eureka, KS 67045-1445. Tel.: 620-583-6682.
E-mail: gwhistory@sbcglobal.net
Founded: 1973.
Congressional District: 4
Key Personnel: Pres., Barbara Robison; Vice Pres., Francis Campbell; Sec., Hazel Russell; Treas., Sue Williams; Historian, Margaret Osmundson.
Personnel Profile: Full-Time Paid 1; Part-Time Volunteers 6.
Governing Authority: nonprofit organization. Tax-exempt.
Historical Society Museum.
Collections: dolls; tools; pictures; 1868-2007, newspapers; furniture; dishes; bottles; genealogy.
Research Fields: genealogy; town & county history.
Facilities: 450-vol. library; 3,100 sq. ft. exhibit space.
Activities: guided tours. Museum Sponsors: Open House.
Publications: semi-annual newsletter.
Hours & Admission Prices: Mon.-Fri. 10-12 & 1-4, Sat. by appointment only. No charge; donations accepted. Closed national holidays. ♿
Attendance: 1,100 (estimated)
Membership: Single $10; Couple & Corporate $15; Sustaining $25; Life $200.

Florence

HARVEY HOUSE MUSEUM, 221 Marion, Florence, KS 66851-1263. Mailing Address: P.O. Box 147, Florence, KS 66851-0147. Tel.: 620-878-4296.
Web Site: www.florenceks.com
Founded: 1971.
Congressional District: 5
Key Personnel: Pres., Judy Mills; Vice Pres., Sarah Cope; Treas., Twilah Williams; Sec., Marjorie Jackson; Trustee, Neva Robinson.
Personnel Profile: Part-Time Volunteers 10.
Governing Authority: nonprofit organization. Parent Institution: Florence Historical Society. Subsidiary Institution: City of Florence, KS. Tax-exempt: 501(c)(3).
Historic Building: 1878 first Fred Harvey Restaurant-Hotel.
Collections: period furniture; pictures; dishes; tools; Santa Fe Way Car (caboose); baggage wagon.
Research Fields: Santa Fe railroad; Harvey Houses; local history.
Activities: guided tours; permanent exhibitions; limited number of dinners served annually.
Publications: booklets, Harvey House; Century of Pride; newsletter, Florence Historical Society News; book, Florence Historical Society Cookbook.
Hours & Admission Prices: Daily 2-5; other times by appointment. No charge; donations accepted. Closed New Year's Day; Easter; Thanksgiving; Christmas. ♿
Attendance: 700 (estimated)
Membership: Member $10; Life $100.

Fort Leavenworth

FORT LEAVENWORTH HISTORICAL SOCIETY, Gift Shop-Post Museum, 100 Reynolds Ave., Fort Leavenworth, KS 66027. Mailing Address: P.O. Box 3356, Fort Leavenworth, KS 66027-0356. Tel.: 913-651-7440 & 684-3327.
E-mail: flhsgs@kc.rr.com
Founded: 1950.
Congressional District: 2
Key Personnel: Museum Shop Mgr., Lois Kaftner.
Personnel Profile: Full-Time Paid 3; Part-Time Paid 2.
Governing Authority: society; nonprofit organization. Parent Institution: United States Army, Ft. Leavenworth. Tax-exempt: 501(c)(3).
Historical Society.
Collections: local history; period artifacts; photographs.
Research Fields: local history.
Facilities: Museum-related items for sale.
Activities: guided tours; programs.
Publications: monographs on the history of Fort Leavenworth.
Hours & Admission Prices: Mon.-Sat. 9-4, Sun. 12-4. No charge; donations accepted. ♿
Attendance: 50,000 (accurate)
Membership: Family & Individual $5 annually.

* **FRONTIER ARMY MUSEUM, (M),** 100 Reynolds Ave., Fort Leavenworth, KS 66027-2334. Tel.: 913-684-3767. Fax: 913-684-3192.
E-mail: leav-fam@conus.army.mil
Web Site: usacac.army.mil/CAC2/CSI/FrontierArmyMuseum.asp
Founded: 1938.
Key Personnel: Dir., Stephen J. Allie; Exhibit Mgr., George Moore; Collection Mgr., Russ Ronspies; Museum Shop Mgr., Lois Kaftner.
Personnel Profile: Full-Time Paid 4; Part-Time Volunteers 200.
Governing Authority: federal. Administered by United States Army. Parent Institution: Center of Military History. Tax-exempt: 170(b)(1)(A).
Military Museum: located at Fort Leavenworth.
Collections: evolution of military technology; 19th-20th century Fort Leavenworth; military uniforms & equipment 1804-present; military horse-drawn vehicles; evolution of military education.
Research Fields: history of Fort Leavenworth & the U.S. Army in the development of the trans-Mississippi West.
Facilities: 1500-vol. library of books & other research material related to Museum mission available for use on premises only. Museum-related items for sale.
Activities: guided tours; traveling & temporary exhibits; living history programs; multi-media history presentations.
Publications: pamphlets: Frontier Army Museum; Self-Guided Tours of Fort Leavenworth.
Hours & Admission Prices: Mon.-Fri. 9-4, Sat. 10-4. No charge; donations accepted. Closed federal holidays. ♿
Attendance: 25,000 (estimated)

Fort Riley

FIRST TERRITORIAL CAPITOL OF KANSAS, Bldg. 693, Huebner Rd., K-18, Fort Riley, KS 66442. Mailing Address: Box 2122, Fort Riley, KS 66442-0122. Tel.: 785-784-5535 & 238-1666.
Web Site: www.kshs.org
Founded: 1928.
Congressional District: 2
Key Personnel: Cur., Ron Tedder.
Personnel Profile: Part-Time Paid 1; Part-Time Volunteers 20.
Governing Authority: state. Parent Institution: Kansas History Center, 6425 S.W. 6th Ave., Topeka, KS 66615-1099. Tax-exempt.
Historic House Museum: 1855 two-story stone structure that served as the first territorial capitol of Kansas.
Collections: local history items; Civil War calvary accoutrements; weapons; Indian artifacts; photographs; early Pawnee city & pre-civil war artifacts; 1858 Bogus Law Book.
Research Fields: local & political history.
Facilities: nature trails. Museum-related items for sale.
Activities: lectures; films; slide programs; nature trail activities; special school student history days. Special Events: living history festival weekend; Buffalo Soldiers event.
Publications: The Five Day Capitol.
Hours & Admission Prices: Summer: Thurs.-Sat. 10-5, Sun. 1-5; Winter: call for hours. No charge; donations accepted. Closed major holidays. ♿
Membership: Student & Senior $10; Individual $12; Family $20; Business & Organization $50; Sustainer $100; Benefactor $500.

U.S. CAVALRY MUSEUM, Bldg. 205, Fort Riley, KS 66442. Mailing Address: Bldg. 205, Fort Riley, KS 66442. Tel.: 785-239-2737. Fax: 785-239-6243.
E-mail: mckalew@riley.army.mil
Web Site: www.uscavalry.org/
Founded: 1957.
Congressional District: 2
Key Personnel: C.E.O., William McKale; Exhibit Specialist, Don Rush.
Personnel Profile: Full-Time Paid 6; Part-Time Volunteers 33.
Governing Authority: federal. Parent Institution: U.S. Army. Tax-exempt.
Military Museum: housed in 1855 building used as a hospital, 1855-1890 & as post headquarters 1890-1948.
Collections: 1776-1950 historical artifacts of U.S. Cavalry.
Research Fields: 1776-1950 U.S. Cavalry.
Facilities: 4,500-vol. library of books on the Cavalry & the U.S. Army available for use on premises; reading room.
Activities: guided tours; lectures.
Publications: quarterly newsletter, Bugle Notes.
Hours & Admission Prices: Mon.-Sat. 9-4:30, Sun. 12-4:30. No charge; donations accepted. Closed New Year's Day; Easter; Thanksgiving; Christmas. ♿
Attendance: 35,000 (estimated)

Fort Scott

FORT SCOTT NATIONAL HISTORIC SITE, Old Fort Blvd., Fort Scott, KS 66701. Mailing Address: P.O. Box 918, Fort Scott, KS 66701-0918. Tel.: 620-223-0310. Fax: 620-223-0188.
E-mail: fosc_superintendent@nps.gov
Web Site: www.nps.gov/fosc
Founded: 1978.
Congressional District: 2
Key Personnel: Supt., Betty Boyko; Chief Interpretation & Resource Management, Kelley Collins; Program Coord., Galen Ewing; Cooperating Assoc. Coord., Barak Geertsen.
Personnel Profile: Full-Time Paid 13; Part-Time Paid 22; Part-Time Volunteers 360; Interns 4.
Governing Authority: federal. National Park Svc. Tax-exempt.
Historic Site: 1842 restored & reconstructed Fort Scott.
Collections: Historic Buildings: 1842-53 Officers Quarters; Post Hospital; Barracks; Post Headquarters; Stable; Guardhouse; Magazine; Bakery; Quartermaster Storehouse; Well Canopy.
Research Fields: Fort Scott as a frontier military post; Bleeding Kansas; Civil War; Kansas railroad years 1865-1873.
Facilities: library. Books, pamphlets & postcards for sale.
Activities: self-guided tours; living history demonstrations; special events; weekend conducted activities during the summer.
Publications: booklet, Fort Scott on the Indian Frontier.
Hours & Admission Prices: April-Nov. daily 8-5; Dec.-March daily 9-5. Adults $3; children under 16 no charge. Closed New Year's Day; Thanksgiving; Christmas. ♿
Attendance: 26,175 (accurate)

Fredonia

STONE HOUSE GALLERY, 320 N. 7th St., Fredonia, KS 66736-1337. Mailing Address: P.O. Box 355, Fredonia, KS 66736-0355. Tel.: 620-378-2052.
E-mail: stonehouse320@embarqmail.com
Founded: 1967.
Congressional District: 2
Key Personnel: Pres. (V), Celia Harris; Admin., Gail Harshaw.
Personnel Profile: Part-Time Paid 1; Part-Time Volunteers 18.
Governing Authority: society; nonprofit organization. Parent Institution: Fredonia Arts Council, Inc. Tax-exempt: 501(c)(3).
Art Museum: housed in 1872 Stone House.
Collections: visual art collection.
Activities: monthly art exhibits; guided tours; gallery talks; hobby workshops; formally organized education programs; docent program or council; loan, temporary & traveling exhibitions.
Publications: monthly newsletter.
Hours & Admission Prices: Summer: Mon.-Fri. 9-2; Winter: Mon.-Fri. 12:30-4:30; other times by appointment. No charge; donations accepted. Closed New Year's Day; Independence Day; Thanksgiving; Christmas. ♿
Attendance: 1,000 (estimated)
Membership: Friend $10; Member $25; Contributor $50; Supporter $100; Patron $250; Benefactor $500.

WILSON COUNTY HISTORICAL SOCIETY MUSEUM, 420 N. 7th, Fredonia, KS 66736-1315. Tel.: 620-378-3965.
Founded: 1961.
Congressional District: 5
Key Personnel: C.E.O. & Pres. (V), Emma Crites; Vice Pres., Joan Richardson; Sec., Mary Jean Browne; Treas., Lucille Doyle; Genealogist, Margery Pickell; Historian, Irene Gudde; Museum Shop Mgr., E. Nadine Dishman.
Personnel Profile: Full-Time Paid 2; Part-Time Volunteers 8.
Governing Authority: society. Tax-exempt.
General Museum: located in old county jail.
Collections: pioneer relics related to farming, industry, schools, churches, household; quilts; American Indian artifacts; costumes; children's toys, books & clothing; photographs; archives; taped interviews; programs; glass; special war commemorative displays; manuscript collections: obituary notebooks & card file index, county cemetery indexes, birth & marriage records, family genealogies; 1930 Federal Census.
Research Fields: archives; local history; American Indian artifacts; genealogy.
Facilities: 425-vol. library on history; Civil War records; genealogy; maps available for use on premises.
Activities: guided tours; lectures; films; permanent & temporary exhibitions.
Publications: newsletter; book, Fredonia Cemetery Index; Wilson County 1881/1890 Atlas; 1930 Federal Census.
Hours & Admission Prices: Mon.-Fri. 1-4:30. No charge; donations accepted. Closed national holidays.
Attendance: 550 (accurate)
Membership: Historical Society $15; Historical & Genealogical Society $19.

Galena

GALENA MINING & HISTORICAL MUSEUM, 319 W. Seventh St., Galena, KS 66739-1211. Mailing Address: P.O. Box 372, Galena, KS 66739-0372. Tel.: 620-783-2192.
Founded: 1984.
Congressional District: 2
Key Personnel: Pres. (V), Gene Russell; Treas., Don Noe.
Personnel Profile: Part-Time Volunteers 4.
Governing Authority: private; nonprofit organization.
Mining Museum: housed in the old Katy Train Depot.
Collections: lead & zinc mine artifacts; tools; lamps; pictures; paintings; mineral specimens; locomotive; caboose; helicopter; tank.
Facilities: Museum-related items for sale.
Activities: guided tours.
Hours & Admission Prices: Mon.-Sat. 9-11:30 & 1-3:30; Winter: reduced hours in the afternoon. No charge; donations accepted. Closed New Year's Day; Memorial Day; Independence Day; Labor Day; Thanksgiving; Christmas.
Attendance: 1,200 (estimated)
Membership: Yearly Adult $10; Lifetime $100.

Garden City

FINNEY COUNTY KANSAS HISTORICAL SOCIETY, INC., Finnup Park, 403 S. 4th, Garden City, KS 67846. Mailing Address: P.O. Box 796, Garden City, KS 67846-0796. Tel.: 620-272-3664. Fax: 620-272-3662.
E-mail: fico.historical@gcnet.com
Web Site: www.finneycounty.org/history.asp
Founded: 1948.
Congressional District: 1
Key Personnel: Dir., Mary Regan; Pres., Lynn Lightner; Asst. Dir., Laurie Oshel; Mgr. Collections, Yadira Hernandez; Education & Museum Shop Mgr., Chevelle Thomas.
Personnel Profile: Full-Time Paid 4; Part-Time Paid 8; Part-Time Volunteers 10.
Governing Authority: society. Tax-exempt: 170(b)(1)(A).
History Museum.
Collections: newspaper clippings; farm & agricultural equipment; pioneer pictures; photographs of Finney County; 19th- & 20th-century Western Kansas artifacts; extensive photograph collection; textile & clothing collection; new permanent exhibit on history of cattle industry in Finney County; repository for information on local participation in Ford Foundation study on new immigration.
Research Fields: pioneer history; sugar beet & cattle industry of Finney County; immigration.
Facilities: 1,000-vol. library of the history of Southwest Kansas.
Activities: guided tours; permanent & temporary exhibitions; children's history workshops; oral history projects; media presentations; film series; exhibit programs.
Publications: quarterly bulletin, The Sequoyan; Finney Co. History Vol. 1 & 2. Conquest of Southwest Kansas; book, Constant Frontier, The Continuing History of Finney County, Kansas; Those Who Served...Finney County Veterans; Buffalo Jones: Citizen of the Kansas Frontier.
Hours & Admission Prices: Winter: daily 1-5; Summer: Mon.-Sat. 10-5, Sun. 1-5. No charge; donations accepted. ♿
Attendance: 24,000 (accurate)
Membership: Individual $15; Family $25; Business $50.

FINNUP PARK AND LEE RICHARDSON ZOO, 312 E. Finnup Dr., Garden City, KS 67846-6561. Tel.: 620-276-1250. Fax: 316-276-1259.
E-mail: zoo@garden-city.org
Web Site: www.garden-city.org/zoo
Founded: 1927.
Congressional District: 1
Key Personnel: Dir., Kathy Sexson; Society Pres., Rich Taylor; Deputy Dir., Kristi Newland.
Personnel Profile: Full-Time Paid 25; Part-Time Paid 8; Part-Time Volunteers 33; Interns 1.
Governing Authority: municipal. Parent Institution: City of Garden City. Subsidiary Institution: Friends of the Lee Richardson Zoo. Tax-exempt.
Zoo, Arboretum & Nature Center.
Collections: over 300 animals; birds; reptiles; aviary.
Facilities: 1,200-vol. library of zoology, conservation & horticulture books; 125-seat auditorium; botanical garden; snack bar; classrooms; conservation center. Museum-related items for sale.
Activities: guided tours; lectures; loan, permanent, traveling & participatory exhibitions; docent program; formal education programs; mobile vans; school loan service; broadcast programs; summer zoo camp; monthly coffee hour; weekly children's story hour. Annual Events: Animal Attractions (Valentine Dinner); Boo at the Zoo; A Wild Affair; Tumbleweed Festival.

Publications: quarterly newsletter, Zoo Gnus.
Hours & Admission Prices: April 11-Sept 7 daily 8-6:30; Sept. 8-March daily 8-4:30. Vehicle $3. AZA reciprocal members. Closed New Year's Day; Thanksgiving; Christmas. ♿
Attendance: 198,000 (estimated)
Membership: Individual $25; Family $35; Business $100; Sustaining $225; Corporate $300; Lifetime $1,000.

Garnett

ANDERSON COUNTY HISTORICAL MUSEUM, 406 W. 4th Ave., Garnett, KS 66032. Mailing Address: P.O. Box 183, Garnett, KS 66032. Tel.: 785-867-2966 & 448-5740.
Founded: 1968.
Congressional District: 5
Key Personnel: Chm. & Pres., Dorothy L. Lickteig.
Personnel Profile: Full-Time Volunteers 7; Part-Time Volunteers 10.
Governing Authority: society; county. Tax-exempt.
Local History Museum: 1886 home & carriage house of Dr. Harris; Longfellow school building.
Collections: guns; history of early settlers; Indian artifacts; furniture; church & school items; farm tools; genealogy records; early diggings; local histories; family stories & books; clothing; military artifacts; country store.
Research Fields: pertaining to collections; genealogy; church, marriage, birth & census records; town & it's citizens.
Facilities: 500-vol. library.
Activities: guided tours; formally organized education programs for adults; permanent & temporary exhibitions.
Publications: quarterly newsletter, Regional Museum News.
Hours & Admission Prices: Oct.-May Tues.-Sat. 1-4. No charge; donations accepted. ♿
Attendance: 1,800 (accurate)
Membership: Individual $5; Lifetime $50.

THE WALKER ART COLLECTION OF THE GARNETT PUBLIC LIBRARY, 125 W. 4th Ave., Garnett, KS 66032-1313. Mailing Address: Library, 125 W. 5th Ave., Garnett, KS 66032. Tel.: 785-448-5496. Fax: 913-448-3936 & 5555.
Web Site: www.garnettks.net
Founded: 1965.
Congressional District: 5
Key Personnel: Chm. (V), Terry J. Solander.
Personnel Profile: Full-Time Paid 1; Part-Time Paid 6; Part-Time Volunteers 5.
Governing Authority: municipal. Parent Institution: City of Garnett. Tax-exempt: 501(c)(3).
Art Gallery.
Collections: 19th-20th century oil paintings & works on paper; regional artists.
Facilities: library.
Activities: guided tours; lectures; docent program; participatory & loan exhibitions; school loan service; slide & audio tour of the collection.
Hours & Admission Prices: Mon.-Tues. & Thurs. 10-8, Wed. & Fri. 10-5:30, Sat. 10-4. No charge; donations accepted. Closed New Year's Day; Presidents' Day; Memorial Day; Independence Day; Labor Day; Veterans Day; Thanksgiving; Christmas. ♿
Attendance: 15,000 (estimated)
Membership: Family $5.

Girard

HISTORICAL MUSEUM OF CRAWFORD COUNTY, 300 S. Summit St., Girard, KS 66743-1543. Tel.: 620-724-6450.
Web Site: skyways.lib.ks.us/towns/Girard/museum.html
History Museum: housed in the former St. John's Episcopal Church. Listed on the National Historic Register.
Collections: local history & culture; period clothing; personal artifacts; photographs.
Hours & Admission Prices: Sun. 2-4; other times by appointment.

Glasco

OSBORNE COUNTY HISTORICAL MUSEUM, 929 N. 2nd St., Glasco, KS 67445. Mailing Address: P.O. Box 572, Glasco, KS 67445-0572. Tel.: 785-346-2881 & 2798.
History Museum.
Collections: county history & culture; photographs.
Hours & Admission Prices: Memorial Day to Labor Day Mon.-Thurs. 2-4; other times by appointment.

Goddard

LAKE AFTON PUBLIC OBSERVATORY, 25,000 W. 39th St., S., (Mac Arthur Rd.), Goddard, KS 67052. Mailing Address: 1845 Fairmont, Wichita, KS 67260-9700. Tel.: 316-978-3191. Fax: 316-978-3350.
E-mail: observatory@wichita.edu
Web Site: webs.wichita.edu/lapo
Founded: 1980.
Congressional District: 4
Key Personnel: Dir., Greg Novacek; Program Mgr., Robert Henry.
Personnel Profile: Part-Time Paid 4; Part-Time Volunteers 6.
Governing Authority: nonprofit organization. Tax-exempt: 501(c)(3).
Astronomy Museum.
Collections: telescopes; astronomy exhibits of celestial objects & concepts.
Research Fields: photometry of variable stars.
Facilities: observation room; outdoor observing pad; classrooms.
Activities: guided tours; computer games; lectures; organized educational programs for children, undergraduate & graduate college students affiliated with Wichita State University; participatory exhibits; school loan service.
Publications: annual brochures; public & school programs.
Hours & Admission Prices: March-Sept. Fri.-Sat. call for hours; Oct.-Feb. Fri.-Sat. 7:30 pm-10 pm. Adults 13 & over $4, children 6-12 $3; children under 6 & members no charge. Closed New Year's Eve & Day; Christmas Eve, Day & week. ♿
Attendance: 4,500 (estimated)
Membership: Student & Senior $15; Individual $20; Family $30.

Goessel

MENNONITE HERITAGE & AGRICULTURAL MUSEUM, 200 N. Poplar St., Goessel, KS 67053. Mailing Address: P.O. Box 231, Goessel, KS 67053-0231. Tel.: 620-367-8200.
E-mail: mhmuseum@mtelco.net
Web Site: skyways.lib.ks.us/museums/goessel
Founded: 1974.
Congressional District: 5
Key Personnel: Pres. & Chm. (V), Donavon Schmidt; Dir., Cur. & Museum Shop Mgr., Marjorie J. Shoemaker; Treas., Aileen Esau.
Personnel Profile: Part-Time Paid 4; Part-Time Volunteers 20.
Governing Authority: nonprofit; board of directors. Affiliated with the Mennonite Immigrant Historical Foundation. Tax-exempt.
History Museum.
Collections: late 1800s & early 1900s Kansas agriculture; Mennonite immigrants; manuscripts; clothing; household goods; books; farm machinery including threshing machines of various periods; machinery related to wheat industry. Historic Buildings: 1906 The Preparatory School; 1910-1935 The Goessel State Bank; 1911 Friesen House; 1875 South Bloomfield School (one-room); 1875 Krause House; 1902 Schroeder Barn; 1874 Immigrant House replica.
Research Fields: history of the German Russian Mennonites.
Facilities: Books, wheat weaving & museum-related items for sale.
Activities: guided tours; lectures; quilt shows; country threshing days; permanent & temporary exhibitions.
Publications: quarterly newsletter; Church Book of the Alexanderwohl Mennonite Church; Church Records of Old Flemish or Groningen Mennonisten Societaet in West Prussia; In Earlier Days: A History of Goessel, Kansas; From Pluma Moos to Pie Cookbook; They Sought a New Land; A Country Midwife.
Hours & Admission Prices: March-April & Oct.-Nov. Tues.-Sat. 12-4; May-Sept. Tues.-Sat. 10-5, Sun. 1-5; groups of 10 or more by appointment. Adults $4, children 7-12 $2; discounts to AAM & ICOM members; members no charge. Closed major holidays. ♿
Attendance: 1,500 (estimated)
Membership: Single $10; Couple $30; Family $40; Life $500.

Goodland

HIGH PLAINS MUSEUM, (M), 1717 Cherry, Goodland, KS 67735-3200. Tel.: 785-890-4595.
E-mail: museumsir@goodlandks.us
Founded: 1959.
Congressional District: 1
Key Personnel: Dir., Linda Holton.
Personnel Profile: Full-Time Paid 1; Part-Time Paid 3.
Governing Authority: municipal. Tax-exempt: 501(c)(3).
History Museum.
Collections: Plains Indians artifacts; pioneer life; Rock Island History in Sherman County; Sherman County History; farming tools; 1902 rope-driven automobile; first patented helicopter in America; six local history dioramas.

Research Fields: aviation history in Northwest Kansas; rainmaking in the Great Plains; Rock Island railroad.
Facilities: 3,000 sq. ft. exhibit space. Local handcrafts & books for sale.
Activities: guided tours; lectures; participatory & temporary exhibitions.
Publications: brochures.
Hours & Admission Prices: June-Aug. Sun. 1-4, Mon.-Fri. 9-5, Sat. 9-4; Sept.-May Mon.-Fri. 9-5, Sat. 9-4. No charge; donations accepted. Closed major holidays. ♿
Attendance: 3,000 (accurate)

Great Bend

BARTON COUNTY HISTORICAL MUSEUM & VILLAGE, 85 S. Hwy. 281, Great Bend, KS 67530. Mailing Address: P.O. Box 1091, Great Bend, KS 67530-1091. Tel.: 620-793-5125. Fax: 620-793-5125 (call first).
E-mail: director@bartoncountymuseum.org
Web Site: www.bartoncountymuseum.org
Formerly: Barton County Historical Society Village & Museum
Founded: 1963.
Congressional District: 1
Key Personnel: C.E.O. & Chm., Beverly Komarek; Pres. (V), Marion Lightfoot; Registrar, Frances Wasson; Museum Shop Mgr., Irene Pommerenke.
Personnel Profile: Part-Time Paid 3; Part-Time Volunteers 35; Interns 1.
Governing Authority: society; nonprofit organization. Tax-exempt.
Historic Village.
Collections: dolls; wedding dresses; photographs; Civil War & other military items; farm implements; period artifacts; general store; barber & beauty shop; telephone switchboard; quilt shop; blacksmith shop; Santa Fe National Historic Trail. Historic Buildings: 1875 stone house; 1898 church; c.1900 schoolhouse; c.1900 post office; 1910 railway depot; furnished 1950 Lustron House.
Research Fields: county history.
Facilities: 400-vol. library available to public; 1,600-vol. research library; classroom; 15,000 sq. ft. exhibit space; research area; conservation center; interpretive facility. Museum-related items for sale.
Activities: guided tours; lectures; organized education programs; docent program; participatory & temporary exhibitions.
Publications: quarterly newsletter, The Village Crier.
Hours & Admission Prices: Tues.-Fri. 10-5, Sat.-Sun. 1-5. Adults $2; members no charge. Closed most major holidays. ♿
Attendance: 5,000 (estimated)
Membership: Annual $15; Family $25; Contributor $100-$499; Benefactor $500.

SHAFER GALLERY - BARTON COUNTY COMMUNITY COLLEGE, (M), 245 N.E. 30 Rd., Great Bend, KS 67530-9107. Tel.: 800-722-6842; 620-792-9342.
Key Personnel: Dir., Megan Benitz
Art Gallery.
Collections: sculpture; paintings; bronzes.
Facilities: 7,709 sq. ft. exhibit space.
Hours & Admission Prices: Mon.-Fri. 10-5, Sun. 1-4; groups by appointment. No charge; donations accepted. Closed college-related holidays. ♿
Attendance: 7,000 (estimated)

Greensburg

BIG WELL, 315 S. Sycamore, Greensburg, KS 67054-1758.
Founded: 1937.
Key Personnel: Museum Shop Mgr., Rich Stephenson.
Personnel Profile: Full-Time Paid 1; Part-Time Paid 5.
Governing Authority: Parent Institution: Greensbury Chamber of Commerce.
General Museum.
Collections: local history; Pallasite meteorite; hand dug well c.1887.
Facilities: Museum-related items for sale.
Activities: guided tours upon request.
Hours & Admission Prices: Memorial Day to Labor Day 8-8; Winter: Mon.-Sat. 9-5, Sun. 1-5. Adults $2, children $1.50. Closed Thanksgiving; Christmas.
Attendance: 42,672 (accurate)

Halstead

KANSAS LEARNING CENTER FOR HEALTH, 505 Main St., Halstead, KS 67056-2233. Mailing Address: P.O. Box 288, Halstead, KS 67056-0288. Tel.: 316-835-2662. Fax: 316-835-2755.
Web Site: www.learningcenter.org
Founded: 1965.
Congressional District: 4
Key Personnel: C.E.O. & Dir., Brenda S. Sooter; Pres. (V), Vernon Nikkel; Museum Shop Mgr., Debbie Nightingale.
Personnel Profile: Full-Time Paid 2; Part-Time Paid 6; Part-Time Volunteers 12.
Governing Authority: nonprofit organization. Tax-exempt: 501(c)(3).
Health Museum.
Collections: displays depicting the human body & the way it functions.
Facilities: 61-seat auditorium. Health education materials for sale.
Activities: guided tours; lectures; films; gallery talks; formally organized education programs; permanent & temporary exhibitions; school assemblies; professional development workshops.
Publications: quarterly newsletter.
Hours & Admission Prices: Mon.-Fri. 9-4. Full Day Program: $7. Half Day Program $4. Self-Guided Tour: $2. Closed New Year's Day; Easter; Memorial Day; Independence Day; Labor Day; Thanksgiving; Christmas. ♿
Attendance: 22,000 (accurate)

Hanover

HOLLENBERG STATION STATE HISTORIC SITE, 2889 23rd Rd., Hanover, KS 66945-8901. Tel.: 785-337-2635. Fax: 785-337-2635.
E-mail: hollenberg@kshs.org
Web Site: www.history.cc.ukans.edu/heritage/kshs/places/howlenbg
Formerly: Hollenberg Pony Express Station Museum
Congressional District: 1 & 2
Key Personnel: Cur., Duane R. Durst.
Personnel Profile: Full-Time Paid 1; Part-Time Paid 2; Part-Time Volunteers 16.
Governing Authority: state. Parent Institution: Kansas History Center, 6425 S.W. 6th Ave., Topeka, KS 66615-1099. Tax-exempt.
Historic Building: 1857 Pony Express station, comprised of general store, tavern & stage station.
Collections: period items; Oregon trail period; Pony Express items; tools; cart maps; biographical data on Gerat Hollenberg 1823-74; weaponry; pioneer items; furnished 1860 kitchen; bar room.
Research Fields: Pony Express; Oregon & California trails.
Facilities: visitors center.
Activities: tours. Museum Sponsors: Pony Express Festival in August.
Publications: pamphlet.
Hours & Admission Prices: April-Aug. Wed.-Sat. 9:30-5. Adults $3, seniors & students $2, school groups $1; discounts to other groups. Closed all holidays. ♿
Attendance: 22,500 (estimated)

Harper

HARPER CITY HISTORICAL SOCIETY, 804 E. 12th St., Harper, KS 67058-1804. Mailing Address: 1002 Oak, Harper, KS 67058-1233. Tel.: 620-896-2115.
Founded: 1959.
Congressional District: 5
Key Personnel: Pres., Mickey Bowen; Sec. & Treas., Mary Helen Baker.
Personnel Profile: Part-Time Volunteers 5.
Governing Authority: society. Parent Institution: The Kansas Historical Society. Tax-exempt: 170(b)(1)(A).
Historical Society Museum: housed in 1887 German Apostolic Church.
Collections: furniture; period artifacts; early kitchen; tools; Bibles; square grand piano; clothing. Historic Building: c.1889 Runnymede Church.
Facilities: library of Harper Advocate newspapers & quarterlies of Kansas Historical Society of Topeka available by request.
Activities: guided tours; permanent exhibitions.
Publications: annual newsletter.
Hours & Admission Prices: By appointment. No charge; donations accepted.
Attendance: 300 (estimated)
Membership: Individual & Business $10.

Hays

ELLIS COUNTY HISTORICAL SOCIETY, 100 W. 7th St., Hays, KS 67601-4429. Tel.: 785-628-2624. Fax: 785-628-0386.
E-mail: office@elliscountyhistoricalsociety.org
Web Site: www.elliscountyhistoricalmuseum.org
Founded: 1971.
Congressional District: 1
Key Personnel: Pres., Tom Drees; Treas., Brad Boyer; Cur., Elisha Beck; Archivist & Dir., Janet Johannes; Dir. & Museum Shop Mgr., Sharon Behrman.
Personnel Profile: Full-Time Paid 4; Part-Time Paid 3; Part-Time Volunteers 10.
Governing Authority: private; nonprofit organization. Tax-exempt: 501(c)(3).
History Museum.
Collections: archives; photographs; area history from 1867 to present; history

of Wild West; Volga-German & other immigrant groups; agriculture & business; personal articles. Historic Building: chapel.
Research Fields: early settlement; wild west period; Volga-German history; local history.
Facilities: library; 4,000 sq. ft. exhibit space; archives. Museum-related items for sale.
Activities: Annual Events: Independence Day Celebration; Oktoberfest; Christmas Open House; annual meeting; Pioneer Day.
Publications: quarterly newsletter, Homesteader.
Hours & Admission Prices: June-Aug. Tues.-Fri. 10-5, Sat. 1-5; Sept.-May Tues.-Fri. 10-5. Adults $4; members no charge.
Attendance: 3,000 (accurate)
Membership: Student under 18 $3; College Student $10; Single $15; Family $25; Friend $75; Homesteader $200; Sponsorship $250; Settler: Lifetime $500, Couple $750.

FORT HAYS STATE HISTORIC SITE, 1472 Hwy. 183 Alt., Hays, KS 67601-9212. Tel.: 785-625-6812. Fax: 785-625-6812.
E-mail: thefort@kshs.org
Web Site: www.kshs.org/places/forthays/index.htm
Founded: 1965.
Congressional District: 1
Key Personnel: Exec. Dir. KSHS, Jennie Chinn; Pres. (V), Terry Mannell; Supt., Robert Wilhelm; Museum Shop Mgr., Connie Schmeidler.
Personnel Profile: Full-Time Paid 1; Part-Time Paid 2; Part-Time Volunteers 45.
Governing Authority: state. Parent Institution: Kansas State Historical Society, 6425 S.W. 6th, Topeka, KS 66615. Tel. 785-272-8681. Tax-exempt.
Military Museum; Visitors & Tourist Information Center.
Collections: uniforms; accoutrements; utensils; Indian artifacts; weapons; excavated bottles & tools; insignias. Historic Structures: 1872 furnished Guardhouse; 1867 Blockhouse; 1867 two officers' quarters.
Research Fields: fort history.
Facilities: library of Fort Hays records & documents on microfilm available for viewing on premise only; 40 acres of native grassland. Museum-related items for sale.
Activities: guided tours; lectures; films; docent programs; formally organized education programs for undergraduate college students; folk art workshops; permanent exhibitions. Museum Sponsors: living history demonstration in summer; Fort Hays Anniversary Celebration; Christmas Program.
Publications: quarterly newsletter, Post Returns; brochures, Bugle Calls at Fort Hays, Buffalo Soldiers at Fort Hays, Fort Hays, Conflict on the Plains; Educational Programs at Fort Hays.
Hours & Admission Prices: Tues.-Sat. 9-5. Adults $3, students and seniors 60 & over $2; KSHS and Society of Friends of Historic Fort Hays and children 5 & under no charge. Closed legal holidays. ♿
Attendance: 20,000 (estimated)
Membership: Society of Friends of Historic Fort Hays: Student $10; Individual $15; Family $20; Organization & Business $30; Life $250 & up.

STERNBERG MUSEUM OF NATURAL HISTORY, (M), Fort Hays State University, 3000 Sternberg Dr., Hays, KS 67601-2006. Tel.: 785-628-5516. Fax: 785-628-4518.
E-mail: jchoate@fhsu.edu
Web Site: www.fhsu.edu/sternberg/
Founded: 1926.
Congressional District: 1
Key Personnel: C.E.O. & Cur. Mammals, J.R. Choate; Cur. Plants, J.R. Thomasson; Asst. Cur. Birds, G. Farley; Asst. Cur. Insects, R. Packauskas; Museum Educator, C. Liggett; Chief Cur. & Cur. Vertebrate Paleontology, R.J. Zakrzewski; Collection Mgr., M. Eberle; Exhibits Dir., G. Walters; Office Mgr., A. Klein; Reservations Mgr. & Volunteer Program Coord., M. Kellerman; Operations Mgr., James Helget; Education Asst., Thea Haugen; Exhibit Technician, S. Moses; Mgr. Visitor Svcs., Brad Penka; Cur. Emeritus, Gene Fleharty; Cur. Emeritus, H. Reynolds; Assoc. Cur. Herptiles, T. Taggart; Assoc. Cur. Herptiles, C. Schmidt; Adjunct Cur. Herptiles, Joe Collins; Adjunct Cur. Vertebrate Paleontology, Mike Everhart; Adjunct Cur. Mammals, D. Kaufman; Adjunct Cur. Mammals, G. Kaufman; Adjunct Cur. Birds & Mammals, E. Finck; Adjunct Cur. Vert Paleontology, K. Shimada; Adjunct Cur. Vert Paleontology, B. Schumacher; Adjunct Cur. Paleontology, G. Liggett; Asst. Cur. Fishes, W. Stark; Adjunct Cur. Spiders, H. Guarisco; Building Maintenance, G. Beilman.
Personnel Profile: Full-Time Paid 9; Part-Time Paid 6; Part-Time Volunteers 175.
Governing Authority: Parent Institution: Fort Hays State University. Subsidiary Institution: Sternberg Museum Foundation. Tax-exempt: 501(c)(3).
Natural History Museum.
Collections: natural history of the Great Plains; herbarium; insects; birds; amphibians & reptiles; mammals; fossils; fish.
Research Fields: ornithology; mammalogy; herpetology; paleobotany; plant taxonomy; entomology; ichthyology; paleontology.
Facilities: 15,000-vol. research library; separate laboratory operation; classrooms; scanning electron microscope.
Activities: guided tours; lectures; training programs; docent program; discovery room; field trips; education programs for children & teachers.
Publications: infrequent, processed material, Occasional Papers of the Sternberg Museum of Natural History; periodical, Fort Hays Studies; annual report.
Hours & Admission Prices: Tues.-Sat. 9-7, Sun. 1-7. Adults $6, seniors & children $4; discounts to ICOM & ASTC members; members no charge. ♿
Attendance: 35,050 (accurate)
Membership: Student & Senior Citizens $15; Individual $25; Family $50; Sponsor & Corporate Sponsor $100-$249; Curator Club & Corporate Curator Club $250-$999; Director Club & Corporate Director Club $1,000 & up.

Herington

HERINGTON HISTORICAL SOCIETY & MUSEUM, INC. - SE DICKINSON COUNTY, 800 S. Broadway, Herington, KS 67449-3060. Tel.: 785-258-2842.
E-mail: trimusda@access-one.com
Formerly: Tri-County Historical Society & Museum, Inc.
Founded: 1975.
Congressional District: 74
Key Personnel: Dir., Museum Shop Mgr. & Membership Chm., Jolene Bradford; Pres., Richard Nielsen; Vice Pres., Paul Cohan; Sec., Helen Mitchell; Treas., Pat Miller.
Personnel Profile: Part-Time Paid 1; Part-Time Volunteers 10.
Governing Authority: society; nonprofit corporation. Parent Institution: Kansas State Historical Society. Subsidiary Institution: Dickinson County Historical Society. Tax-exempt: 501(c)(3).
General & Rock Island Railroad History Museum.
Collections: agricultural & historical artifacts; archives; genealogy books; Herington collection; military uniform collections; Rock Island railroad collection; slides; photographs; Herington Times newspapers back to 1884 on micro-film; Herrington Sun newspapers May 13, 1920-Dec. 31, 1931 on microfilm; Hope, KS Dispatch 1885-1979.
Research Fields: genealogy; historical data for the public & for writers; city history; World War II Herington Army air field; Rock Island depot history; Herington Times newspaper, May 1920 to Dec. 1931; Herington Cemetery record; Dickinson, Morris & Marion counties Federal census, 1865-1920; Herington High school history, graduates' addresses; Herington's Sunset Hill Cemetery records; Clark's Creek Cemetery records; St. Paul Lutheran Church cemetery records, Ramona, Kansas; St. Paul Lutheran Church records, Shadybrook, KS; St. John's Catholic Church cemetery records, Herington; St. Johns Lyon Creek church records 1861-present.
Facilities: 25-vol. family genealogy books, 9-vol. community history books; 8-vol. area church history booklets, 10-vol. area church history, 42-vol. club scrapbooks & minutes all available to the public. Gift items for sale.
Activities: guided tours; lectures; docent program. Museum Sponsors: annual banquet; special displays; 4-H Fair & Carnival; tours of the Rock Island railroad baggage car annex & caboose.
Publications: quarterly newsletter, Tri-County Newsletter.
Hours & Admission Prices: Tues.-Fri. 1-5. No charge; donations accepted. ♿
Attendance: 1,000 (estimated)
Membership: Student $5; Individual $10; Family $15; Life $200; Commercial $250.

Hiawatha

AG MUSEUM & WINDMILL LANE, 301 E. Iowa St., Hiawatha, KS 66434-9826. Tel.: 785-742-3702.
E-mail: bchsdirector@yahoo.com
Web Site: www.bckshistory.com
Key Personnel: Dir. & Cur., Eric Oldham
Historical Society Museum.
Collections: horse-drawn combine; buggy; tractors; period cars; the first Brown County post office; sleigh; Brown County artifacts.
Hours & Admission Prices: Tues.-Fri. 10-4.

MEMORIAL AUDITORIUM, 611 Utah St., Hiawatha, KS 66434-2319. Tel.: 785-742-3330.
E-mail: bchsdirector@yahoo.com
Web Site: www.bckshistory.com
Historical Society Museum.
Collections: period artifacts & clothing.
Hours & Admission Prices: Mon.-Fri. 10-12 & 1-3.

Hillsboro

HILLSBORO MUSEUMS, 501 S. Ash St., Hillsboro, KS 67063-1531. Tel.: 620-947-3775.
E-mail: hillsboro_museums@yahoo.com
Web Site: www.hillsboro-museums.com
Formerly: Hillsboro Historical Society & Museum
Founded: 1958.
Congressional District: 1
Key Personnel: C.E.O., Stan R. Harder.
Personnel Profile: Full-Time Paid 3; Part-Time Paid 2; Part-Time Volunteers 20.
Governing Authority: municipal; nonprofit. Parent Institution: City of Hillsboro. Subsidiary Institution: The Mennonite Settlement Museum; The William F. Schaeffler House Museum; and the Hillsboro Museums Visitor Center. Tax-exempt.
History Museum.
Collections: agriculture; folklore; preservation project. Mennonite Settlement Museum: Russian & Polish Mennonite immigrant village life in Kansas. Historic Structures: Peter Paul Loewen House; Kreutziger Country Schoolhouse; William Schaeffler House; Jacob Friesen Dutch Flouring Windmill replica; Mennonite Settlement Museum.
Research Fields: Russian Mennonite immigration to North America.
Activities: guided tours to the Mennonite Settlement Museum and the William F. Schaeffler House Museum; special events. Museum Sponsors: Independence Day Celebration; Schaeffler House concerts; Weihrachtsfest.
Publications: periodic brochures & handbills; local histories; annual newsletter; centennial history publication, Hillsboro: City on the Prairie 1884-1984.
Hours & Admission Prices: March-Dec. Tues.-Fri. 10-12 & 1:30-4, Sat.-Sun. 2-4. Adults $3, students $1; discounts to AAM members. Closed holidays. ♿
Attendance: 3,000 (estimated)
Membership: Friends $5.

Holton

JACKSON COUNTY HISTORICAL SOCIETY, 216 New York Ave., Holton, KS 66436-1738. Tel.: 785-364-4991.
Founded: 1979.
Congressional District: 2
Key Personnel: Chm. (V), Anna Wilhelm.
Personnel Profile: Part-Time Volunteers 25.
Governing Authority: Tax-exempt.
Historical Society Museum.
Collections: local history & culture; personal artifacts; photographs; Victorian era clothing; lace.
Publications: quarterly newsletter, The Jacksonian.
Hours & Admission Prices: May-Oct. Fri.-Sat. 10-4, Sun. 2-4; other times by appointment. No charge; donations accepted. ♿
Attendance: 457 (accurate)
Membership: Individual $25; Family $40; Supporting & Business $75; Individual Life $400; Business Life $600.

Hugoton

STEVENS COUNTY GAS AND HISTORICAL MUSEUM, 905 S. Adams, Hugoton, KS 67951-2817. Mailing Address: P.O. Box 87, Hugoton, KS 67951-0087. Tel.: 620-544-8751.
E-mail: svcomus@pld.com
Founded: 1961.
Congressional District: 1
Key Personnel: Pres., Stanley McGill; Cur. & Museum Shop Mgr., Gladys Renfro.
Personnel Profile: Part-Time Paid 3.
Governing Authority: county. Tax-exempt: 501(c)(3).
History Museum Complex: 1913 original A.T.S.F. depot country store, including barber shop & grocery store.
Collections: period furnishings; American Indian artifacts; early furnishings; art; gas industry equipment; model drilling rigs; horse drawn machinery vehicles; active gas well; agricultural & automotive artifacts. Historic Buildings: 1888 schoolhouse; 1886-1887 house; 1905-1906 Second Methodist Church; first county jail; 1887 South Harmony School.
Research Fields: American Indian artifacts.
Activities: guided tours; school groups; meeting places for local clubs.
Publications: brochures, Sixty Years of Development of the Hugoton Fields; The Hugoton Stony Meteorite, Stevens County, Kansas; Buddy Heaton; single sheets of museum complex; postcards.
Hours & Admission Prices: June-Aug. Mon.-Fri. 9:30-11:30 & 1-5, Sat. 2-4, Sun. by appointment; Sept.-May Mon.-Fri. 1-5, Sat. 2-4, Sun. by appointment. No charge; donations accepted. Closed Easter; Memorial Day; Labor Day; Columbus Day; Veterans Day; Thanksgiving; Christmas. ♿
Attendance: 1,091 (accurate)
Membership: Annual $1; Life $10.

Humboldt

HUMBOLDT HISTORICAL MUSEUM, 416 N. Second, Humboldt, KS 66748-1402. Mailing Address: P.O. Box 63, Humboldt, KS 66748-0063. Tel.: 620-473-5055.
E-mail: rrthompson504@yahoo.com
Web Site: www.usd258.net~humbmuseum
Founded: 1966.
Key Personnel: Dir., Roland E. Thompson; Sec., Janice McCullough; Treas., Lois Squire.
Personnel Profile: Full-Time Volunteers 15; Part-Time Volunteers 5.
Governing Authority: Tax-exempt.
History Museum.
Collections: historic farm equipment; furnished kitchen, dining & bedroom displays; Civil War cannon; Humboldt's original jail cell; horse-drawn adult & infant hearse; collection of scale model horse-drawn wagons; clothing; quilts; toys; medical instruments; books; photographs; paintings.
Hours & Admission Prices: Open year round by appointment. No charge; donations accepted. ♿
Attendance: 1,865 (accurate)
Membership: Lifetime $10.

Hutchinson

HUTCHINSON ART CENTER, 405 N. Washington, Hutchinson, KS 67501-4852. Tel.: 620-663-1081. Fax: 620-663-6367.
E-mail: hutchart2@hac.kscoxmail.com
Web Site: hutchinsonartcenter.org
Founded: 1949.
Congressional District: 1
Key Personnel: Dir., Mark L. Rassette; Pres. (V), Ann Richardson.
Personnel Profile: Part-Time Paid 2; Part-Time Volunteers 2.
Governing Authority: private; nonprofit organization. Subsidiary Institution: Vignettes. Tax-exempt: 501(c)(3).
Art Museum.
Collections: 19th-20th century American & European art.
Facilities: 6,611 sq. ft. exhibit space; classroom; auditorium. Museum-related items for sale.
Activities: guided tours; lectures; loan exhibitions; arts and humanities events.
Publications: quarterly newsletter, Gallery Notes.
Hours & Admission Prices: Tues.-Fri. 9-5, Sat.-Sun. 1-5. No charge; donations accepted. ♿
Attendance: 5,000 (accurate)
Membership: Student & Senior Citizens $20; Individual $30; Artist $35; Family $40; Contributor $100; Business $200; Friend $250; Donor $500; Patron $1,000; Benefactor $5,000.

KANSAS COSMOSPHERE AND SPACE CENTER, (M), 1100 N. Plum, Hutchinson, KS 67501-1418. Tel.: 620-662-2305. Fax: 620-662-3693.
E-mail: info@cosmo.org
Web Site: www.cosmo.org
Founded: 1962.
Congressional District: 4
Key Personnel: C.E.O. & Pres., Christopher D. Orwoll; Chm. Bd., Mr. Kim Corcoran; Vice Chm., Bob Fee; Vice Pres. Devel., Marisa Honomichl; Controller, Steven Birdsall; Museum Retail Mgr., Phyllis Cole.
Personnel Profile: Full-Time Paid 30; Part-Time Paid 35; Part-Time Volunteers 87.
Governing Authority: public; nonprofit foundation. Tax-exempt: 501(c)(3).
Space Museum.
Collections: U.S. & Soviet space artifacts including Mercury, Gemini & Apollo spacecrafts; Vostok, Voskhod & Soyuz spacecraft; spacesuits; a lunar module; rocket engines; SR-71 Blackbird; German V-1 and V-2 rockets; actual Apollo 13 command module Odyssey; planetarium; Hall of Space Museum.
Research Fields: space sciences & related astronomy.
Facilities: theater with IMAX Dome; planetarium; classrooms; NASA Teacher Resource Center.
Activities: astronomy & scientific programs; teacher in-service programs; lectures; films; space science discovery workshops; tours; classes; Future Astronaut Training Program summer camps; elderhostel astronaut training program; adult astronaut adventure.
Hours & Admission Prices: Spring, Summer & Christmas Breaks: Mon.-Sat. 9-8, Sun. 12-8; Fall, Spring & Winter: Mon.-Thurs. 9-5, Fri.-Sat. 9-8, Sun. 12-5. All Day Mission Pass: adults $15, senior citizens 60 & over and children 3-12 $13; discounts to AAM members; children 2 & under no

charge. Single Venue: adults $8.50, senior citizens 60 & over and children 3-12 $8; discounts to AAM members. Closed Easter; Thanksgiving; Christmas. ♿
Attendance: 140,000 (accurate)
Membership: Senior 60 & over and Student $35; Individual $40; Senior Family 60 & over $65; Family $75; Mercury $125; Gemini $250; Apollo $500; Shuttle $1,000.

KANSAS UNDERGROUND SALT MUSEUM, 3504 E. Ave. G, Hutchinson, KS 67501-8284. Mailing Address: P.O. Box 1864, Hutchinson, KS 67504-1864. Tel.: 620-662-1425; 866-755-3450. Fax: 620-259-6134.
Web Site: www.undergroundmuseum.org
Key Personnel: Dir. Operations, Gayle Ferrell; Volunteer Coord., Tonya Gehring; Maintenance, Dave Unruh; Visitor Svcs. Coord., Colleen McCallister
Mining Museum.
Collections: mining equipment, artifacts & memorabilia.
Hours & Admission Prices: Tues.-Sat. 9-6, Sun. 1-6. Adults $14.35, seniors 60 & over, active military & AAA members $12.75; Reno County residents & children 4-12 $9.05.

RENO COUNTY MUSEUM, (M), 100 S. Walnut, Hutchinson, KS 67501-7406. Mailing Address: P.O. Box 664, Hutchinson, KS 67504-0664. Tel.: 620-662-1184. Fax: 620-662-0236.
Web Site: renocomuseum.org
Founded: 1961.
Congressional District: 1
Key Personnel: Exec. Dir., Linda Schmitt; Chief Cur., Jamin Landavazo; Administrative Asst., Heidi Martin.
Personnel Profile: Full-Time Paid 5; Part-Time Paid 6; Part-Time Volunteers 6.
Governing Authority: nonprofit organization. Parent Institution: Reno County Historical Society. Tax-exempt: 501(c)(3).
County History Museum.
Collections: artifacts relating to the history of Reno County, Kansas.
Research Fields: Reno County history.
Facilities: research library; meeting rooms. Museum-related items for sale.
Activities: permanent & temporary exhibits; special events; education programs.
Publications: quarterly journal, Legacy: The Journal of the Reno County Historical Society.
Hours & Admission Prices: Museum: Tues.-Sat. 9-5. Office: Mon.-Fri. 8-5. No charge; donations accepted. ♿
Attendance: 22,129 (accurate)
Membership: Pioneer $40; Salt Miner $100; Salt Soldier $150; Salt City Settler $250; Salt Tycoon $500; Salt Magnate $1,000. Corporate: Houston Whiteside $500; Jesse Reno $1,000; E. L. Meyer $2,500; C.C. Hutchinson $5,000; Emerson Carey $10,000 & up.

Independence

INDEPENDENCE HISTORICAL MUSEUM, (M), 123 N. 8th, Independence, KS 67301-3501. Mailing Address: P.O. Box 294, Independence, KS 67301-0294. Tel.: 620-331-3515.
E-mail: museum@comgen.com
Web Site: independencehistoricalmuseum.org
Formerly: Independence Museum
Founded: 1882.
Congressional District: 5
Key Personnel: Pres., Jannette Luthi; Dir., Sylvia Augustine.
Personnel Profile: Full-Time Paid 1; Part-Time Paid 1; Part-Time Volunteers 80.
Governing Authority: nonprofit. Parent Institution: Ladies Library & Art Association. Tax-exempt.
History & Art Museum.
Collections: coin glass; cigar store Indian; 12' statue of Miss Justice; 1850's barber shop; oil history room; military room; fishing room; school room; doctor's office; paintings; period clothing; general store; bedroom; kitchen; black pottery; blacksmith shop; early fire equipment; western room; 1869 log cabin.
Activities: concerts; arts festivals; study clubs; permanent, temporary & traveling exhibitions; private artists exhibits; quilt exhibits.
Publications: monthly newsletter.
Hours & Admission Prices: Tues.-Sat. 10-4. No charge; donations accepted. Call for special tours. Closed national holidays. ♿
Attendance: 2,500 (accurate)
Membership: Single $25; Couple $40; Business & Organization $50; Patron $100.

INDEPENDENCE SCIENCE AND TECHNOLOGY CENTER, 125 S. Pennsylvania, Independence, KS 67301-3525. Tel.: 620-331-1999; 800-882-3606.
Science Center.
Collections: science & physics exhibits.
Activities: educational programs.
Hours & Admission Prices: Daily 1-5. Adults $3.

LITTLE HOUSE ON THE PRAIRIE HISTORIC SITE, 2507 CR 3000, Independence, KS 67301-7265. Mailing Address: P.O. Box 110, Independence, KS 67301-0110. Tel.: 620-289-4238.
Web Site: www.littlehouseontheprairie.com
Historic House: official site of Little House on the Prairie from Laura Ingalls Wilder's books.
Collections: period artifacts & memorabilia.
Hours & Admission Prices: March 22-Oct. Mon.-Sat. 10-5, Sun. 1-5. No charge; donations accepted.

Ingalls

SANTA FE TRAIL MUSEUM, 204 S. Main St., Ingalls, KS 67853. Mailing Address: P.O. Box 74, Ingalls, KS 67853-0074. Tel.: 620-335-5220.
E-mail: dlmkwend@ucom.net
Founded: 1973.
Congressional District: 1
Key Personnel: Pres. (V), Kyleen Lacy; Sec., Crystal Denton; Treas., Linda Hirschler; Museum Shop Mgr., Debbie Milne.
Personnel Profile: Part-Time Paid 2; Part-Time Volunteers 5.
Governing Authority: nonprofit organization. Tax-exempt: 501(c)(3).
Historical Site & Local History Museum: housed in two Santa Fe railroad depot buildings.
Collections: exhibits pertaining to the area including: china; glass; silver; antiques; furniture; military & agricultural items; religious articles; old school textbooks; original pump from Soule Canal Irrigation project.
Activities: guided tours; loan exhibitions.
Hours & Admission Prices: May-Oct. Mon.-Sat. 9-11 & 1-4; other times by appointment; Nov.-April by appointment only. No charge; donations accepted.
Attendance: 256 (accurate)

Iola

ALLEN COUNTY HISTORICAL SOCIETY, 20 S. Washington Ave., Iola, KS 66749-3204. Tel.: 620-365-3051.
E-mail: achm@aceks.com
Web Site: www.frederickfunston.org
Founded: 1956.
Congressional District: 2
Key Personnel: Exec. Dir. & Cur., Clyde Toland; Pres. (V), Leon Smith.
Personnel Profile: Part-Time Paid 1.
Governing Authority: society, with county contract. Tax-exempt: 501(c)(3).
Local History Museum.
Collections: Allen County memorabilia; A.E. Gibson collection of negatives & photos. Historic Building: 1869 jail.
Research Fields: local history & gas boom in Kansas.
Facilities: 1869 jail building with cells & restored jailors quarters on top floor; museum room at the County Courthouse.
Activities: tours & special exhibits.
Publications: quarterly newsletter, Gaslight.
Hours & Admission Prices: May-Oct. Tues.-Sat. 12:30-4; Nov.-April Tues.-Sat. 2-4. No charge; donations accepted. ♿
Attendance: 1,300 (accurate)
Membership: Annual $10; Life $100.

THE MAJOR GENERAL FREDERICK FUNSTON BOYHOOD HOME AND MUSEUM, 14 S. Washington Ave., Iola, KS 66749-3204. Tel.: 620-365-3051.
E-mail: achm@aceks.com
Web Site: www.frederickfunston.org
Founded: 1995.
Congressional District: 2
Key Personnel: Exec. Dir. & Cur., Clyde Toland; Pres. (V), Leon Smith.
Governing Authority: private; nonprofit. Subsidiary Institution: Allen County Historical Society, Iola. Tax-exempt: 501(c)(3).
History Museum: housed in the c.1860 Frederick Funston childhood residence, originally located on a homestead approximately five miles north of Iola.
Collections: the home is restored in Victorian decor typical of the 1880s & 1890s; artifacts & furniture that were used during Frederick Funston's boyhood as well as items pertaining to his botanical explorations and military career.

Research Fields: life & career of Frederick Funston, his family & relations; the era during which he lived; Spanish American War; Philippines' Insurrection; 1906 San Francisco earthquake & fire.
Facilities: library; theater. Toys, postcards, clothing & local items for sale.
Activities: docent program; films; guided tours; lectures.
Publications: quarterly newsletter, Gaslight.
Hours & Admission Prices: May-Oct. Tues.-Sat. 12:30-4; Nov.-April Tues.-Sat. 2-4; other times by appointment. No charge; donations accepted. ♿
Attendance: 500 (accurate)
Membership: Annual $10; Lifetime $100.

Jewell

PALMER MUSEUM, 108 S. Washington, Jewell, KS 66949. Tel.: 785-428-3466 & 3335.
Founded: 1991.
Key Personnel: Chm. (V), Roberta Holbren.
Personnel Profile: Part-Time Volunteers 8.
Governing Authority: Chamber of Commerce. Parent Institution: Jewell Chamber of Commerce.
General Museum.
Collections: bound copies of the Jewell County Republican; printing machines; city history artifacts; high school trophies before 1964; 1872 wedding dress made in Scotland.
Activities: temporary exhibitions.
Hours & Admission Prices: By appointment. No charge; donations accepted.
Attendance: 480 (estimated)

Johnson

STANTON COUNTY MUSEUM, (M), 104 E. Highland, Johnson, KS 67855. Mailing Address: P.O. Box 806, Johnson, KS 67855. Tel.: 620-492-1526. Fax: 620-492-1785.
History Museum.
Collections: county history & heritage; personal artifacts; photographs; period artifacts.
Activities: educational programs; research.
Hours & Admission Prices: Memorial Day to Labor Day & Dec. Mon.-Fri. 10:30-12 & 1-5, Sun. 1-4; other times by appoitment.

Kanopolis

FORT HARKER MUSEUM COMPLEX, 309 W. Ohio St., Kanopolis, KS 67454. Mailing Address: P.O. Box 144, Ellsworth, KS 67439-0144. Tel.: 785-472-3059.
E-mail: echs@eaglecom.net
Founded: 1961.
Congressional District: 1
Key Personnel: Chm. (V) & Pres. (V), Phyllis Dolezal; C.E.O., Dir. & Museum Shop Mgr., Georgia Smith.
Personnel Profile: Full-Time Paid 1; Part-Time Paid 2; Part-Time Volunteers 6.
Governing Authority: society. Parent Institution: Ellsworth County Historical Society, Ellsworth, KS 67439. Tax-exempt.
Military Museum.
Collections: documents; files; 1870-present, guns & material; uniforms; Indian artifacts; train depot. Historic House: 1867 Fort Harker Guardhouse; Jr. & Commanding Officer's quarters.
Facilities: Pamphlets, papers & museum-related items for sale.
Activities: Museum Sponsors: Frontier Military Living History in July.
Publications: brochure, Sharing History.
Hours & Admission Prices: April & Oct. Tues.-Fri. & Sun. 1-5, Sat. 10-5; May-Sept. Tues.-Sat. 10-5, Sun. 1-5; Nov.-March Sat. 10-5, Sun. 1-5. Adults $3 (includes entrance to Hogden House Museum complex); discounts to groups; members no charge. Closed New Year's Day; Easter; Memorial Day; Independence Day; Labor Day; Thanksgiving; Christmas. ♿
Attendance: 3,000 (estimated)
Membership: Individual $10; Family $20; Business $25.

Kansas City

GRINTER PLACE STATE HISTORIC SITE, 1420 S. 78th St., Kansas City, KS 66111-3208. Tel.: 913-299-0373. Fax: 913-788-8046.
E-mail: grinter@kshs.org
Web Site: www.kshs.org
Formerly: Grinter Place Museum
Founded: 1971.
Congressional District: 2
Personnel Profile: Full-Time Paid 1; Part-Time Paid 2; Part-Time Volunteers 160.
Governing Authority: state. Parent Institution: Kansas State Historical Society. Tax-exempt.
Historic House: built by Moses Grinter.
Collections: 1860s-1890s household furnishings.
Research Fields: Delaware Indians in Kansas; interaction of cultures in 19th century Kansas including Europeans, Africans & Delaware Indians.
Activities: guided tours; crafts festivals; quilt show; school programs; outreach. Museum Sponsors: Apple Fest in Fall.
Publications: GPF News.
Hours & Admission Prices: March-Nov. Thurs.-Sat. 10-5; Dec.-Feb. Fri.-Sat. 10-5. Adults $2, seniors & students $1; members, military, and children 5 & under no charge. Closed state holidays. ♿
Attendance: 1,000 (estimated)
Membership: Individual $10; Family $15.

STRAWBERRY HILL ETHNIC MUSEUM & CULTURAL CENTER, 720 N. 4th St., Kansas City, KS 66101-2908. Tel.: 913-371-3264.
Web Site: strawberryhillmuseum.org
Founded: 1988.
Personnel Profile: Part-Time Volunteers 30.
Governing Authority: Tax-exempt.
History Museum.
Collections: period furnishings; culturally specific artifacts.
Publications: quarterly, Strawberry Hill Vine.
Hours & Admission Prices: Sat.-Sun. 12-5; other times by appointment. Adults $7, children 6-12 $3; children under 6 no charge. Closed New Year's Day; Easter; Mother's Day; Father's Day; Christmas. ♿
Attendance: 4,000
Membership: Associate $25-$99; Individual $100-$249; Patron $250-$499; Cultural $500-$999; Display $1,000-$4,999; Life $5,000 & up.

UNIVERSITY OF KANSAS MEDICAL CENTER, CLENDENING HISTORY OF MEDICINE LIBRARY AND MUSEUM, 3901 Rainbow Blvd., Kansas City, KS 66160-0001. Tel.: 913-588-7243. Fax: 913-588-7060.
E-mail: nhulston@kumc.edu
Web Site: clendening.kumc.edu
Founded: 1945.
Key Personnel: Dir., Nancy Hulston; Interim Chm., Christopher Crenner; Rare Book Librarian, Dawn McInnis.
Governing Authority: state. Parent Institution: University of Kansas.
Medical Museum.
Collections: microscopes; Egyptian amulets; surgical instruments; obstetrical forceps; brass acupuncture manikins; diagnostic doll; British touch pieces; 19th century American medical artifacts.
Facilities: 29,000-vol. library of medicine history available for inter-library loan except rare & fragile items which are to be used on premises only; reading room; research by appointment only.
Hours & Admission Prices: Museum: daily 8-4:30. Library: Mon. & Wed. 9-1, Tues. & Thurs. 12-4; other times by appointment. No charge. Closed New Year's Day; Martin Luther King Jr. Day; Easter; Memorial Day; Independence Day; Labor Day; Thanksgiving & day after; Christmas. ♿
Attendance: 1,000

Kingman

KINGMAN COUNTY HISTORICAL MUSEUM, 400 N. Main, Kingman, KS 67068-1304. Mailing Address: P.O. Box 281, Kingman, KS 67068-0281. Tel.: 620-532-2627 & 5274.
Founded: 1969.
Congressional District: 4
Key Personnel: C.E.O., Ted Giesert; Vice Chm., Frank Miller.
Personnel Profile: Part-Time Volunteers 12.
Governing Authority: nonprofit. Tax-exempt: 501(c)(3).
History Museum: housed in 1888 City Hall.
Collections: World War I books & uniforms; World War II uniforms; Indian artifacts; salt mine; farm tools; family histories; fire engines; dresses; one-room school; records of county; early days band music; musical instruments; hospital surgical instruments; early furniture; dental equipment; old Cessna airplane parts; mural of Cessna plane & stage coach; church organ; death & birth records.
Research Fields: anything pertaining to Kansas; Kingman County.
Facilities: approx. 150-vol. library of Kansas history, Kingman County history & records of early school teachers available for use on premises; reading room. Postcards, personalized notes, replicas of Kingman KS buildings & museum publications for sale.
Activities: guided tours; lectures; permanent & temporary exhibitions. Museum Sponsors: program talks to Rotary, school classes, Boy & Girl Scouts.
Publications: book, History of Kingman County; Centennial History of Kingman KS; Centennial Cookbook of Kingman KS.
Hours & Admission Prices: Fri. 9-4; other times by appointment. No charge; donations accepted. Closed Christmas.
Attendance: 2,500 (estimated)

Membership: Annual $25; Lifetime $150.

SANTA FE DEPOT FOUNDATION, 201 E. Sherman, Kingman, KS 67068-1906. Tel.: 620-532-2142.
E-mail: sfdepot@sbcglobal.net
Historic Building: built in 1910. Listed on the National Register of Historic Places.
Collections: depot & railroad history; HO gauge model trains.
Activities: rental facility.
Publications: guides to Kansas Depots & other railroad-related items.
Hours & Admission Prices: Mon.-Fri. 8:30-11:30; call for additional hours. No charge; donations accepted. ♿

Kinsley

EDWARDS COUNTY HISTORICAL MUSEUM, Hwy. 50 & 56, #183, Kinsley, KS 67547-0064. Mailing Address: P.O. Box 64, Kinsley, KS 67547-0064. Tel.: 620-659-2420.
Founded: 1967.
Congressional District: 1
Key Personnel: Pres. (V), Robert Cross; Cur., Ted Taylor.
Personnel Profile: Full-Time Paid 1; Part-Time Paid 1.
Governing Authority: nonprofit organization. Parent Institution: Edwards County Historical Society. Tax-exempt: 501(c)(3).
History Museum.
Collections: agriculture; costumes; Indian artifacts; farm implements; late 1880s period furnishings; sod house replicas.
Facilities: wood-framed church available for meetings & weddings. Museum-related items for sale.
Activities: guided tours; permanent & temporary exhibitions.
Hours & Admission Prices: May-Sept. Mon.-Sat. 9-5, Sun. 1-5; other times by appointment. No charge; donations accepted. ♿
Attendance: 2,695 (estimated)
Membership: Individual $5 & up.

La Crosse

BARBED WIRE MUSEUM, W. 1st St., La Crosse, KS 67548. Mailing Address: P.O. Box 578, La Crosse, KS 67548-0578. Tel.: 785-222-9900.
E-mail: barbedwiremuseum@rushcounty.org
Web Site: www.rushcounty.org/barbedwiremuseum
Founded: 1971.
Congressional District: 110
Key Personnel: C.E.O. & Pres. (V), Bradley R. Penka; Museum Mgr., Mary Herman; Museum Mgr., Raymond Georg.
Personnel Profile: Part-Time Paid 3; Part-Time Volunteers 10.
Governing Authority: Parent Institution: Kansas Barbed Wire Collectors Association. Tax-exempt.
Barbed Wire Museum.
Collections: more than 1,000 varieties of barbed wire; tools & items related to barbed wire; fencing tools.
Facilities: reference library; research center.
Publications: quarterly magazine, Kansas Wire Collector.
Hours & Admission Prices: mid-April to mid-Sept. Mon.-Sat. 10-4:30, Sun. 1-4:30. No charge; donations accepted. ♿
Attendance: 1,800 (estimated)
Membership: Individual $25; Family $50; Sustaining $100; Lifetime $1,000.

RUSH COUNTY HISTORICAL SOCIETY, INC., 202 W. 1st St., La Crosse, KS 67548. Mailing Address: P.O. Box 473, La Crosse, KS 67548-0473. Tel.: 785-222-2719 & 2478.
Formerly: Post Rock Museum
Founded: 1962.
Congressional District: 1
Key Personnel: Pres. (V), Lawrence Erbes; Sec. & Treas., Mary Ann Pechanec; Museum Shop Mgr., Lenore Reinhardt.
Governing Authority: society. Parent Institution: Rush County Historical Society Inc., La Crosse, KS 67548. Branch Museums: Rush County Historical Museum; Nekoma State Bank Museum; Post Rock Museum. Tax-exempt.
History Museum.
Collections: post rock products; quarrying tools; history of post rock; rolling pins; area historical memorabilia. Bank Museum: bank artifacts; teller stations. Historic Buildings: Post Rock House Train Depot.
Research Fields: stories & uses of the post rock.
Activities: permanent exhibitions.
Hours & Admission Prices: May 1 to mid-Sept. Mon.-Sat. 10-4:30, Sun. 1-4:30; other times by appointment. No charge; donations accepted. ♿
Attendance: 1,500 (estimated)
Membership: Rush County Historical Society Inc.: Annual $10; Life $25.

Lakin

KEARNY COUNTY HISTORICAL MUSEUM, 111 S. Buffalo, Lakin, KS 67860. Mailing Address: P.O. Box 329, Lakin, KS 67860-0329. Tel.: 620-335-7448.
History Museum.
Collections: county history; Santa Fe Trail; period artifacts. Historic Buildings: depot; schoolhouse; 1882 house.
Hours & Admission Prices: Tues.-Fri. 1-4. No charge; donations accepted. ♿
Membership: Life $20.

Lansing

LANSING HISTORICAL MUSEUM, (M), 115 E. Kansas Ave., Lansing, KS 66043-1667. Tel.: 913-250-0203.
E-mail: lphillippi@sbcglobal.net
Web Site: www.lansing.ks.us
Founded: 1992.
Congressional District: 2
Key Personnel: Site Supvr., Laura Phillippi.
Personnel Profile: Full-Time Paid 1.
Governing Authority: city of Lansing. Tax-exempt.
Historic Building: housed in the restored Atchison, Topeka & Santa Fe depot built in 1887.
Collections: area history; railroad artifacts; photographs; period farming equipment.
Hours & Admission Prices: Tues.-Sat. 10-5, Sun. 1-4. No charge; donations accepted. Closed federal holidays. ♿
Attendance: 1,100 (estimated)

Larned

CENTRAL STATES SCOUT MUSEUM, 815 Broadway, Larned, KS 67550-2525. Tel.: 620-285-8938 & 6427.
Scouting Museum.
Collections: scouting memorabilia; personal artifacts.
Activities: bunkhouse camping.
Hours & Admission Prices: Admission $1.

FORT LARNED NATIONAL HISTORIC SITE, Rte. 3, Larned, KS 67550. Mailing Address: 1767 KS Hwy. 156, Larned, KS 67550-9321. Tel.: 620-285-6911. Fax: 620-285-3571.
E-mail: george_elmore@nps.gov
Web Site: www.nps.gov/fols
Founded: 1964.
Congressional District: 1
Key Personnel: Supt., Kevin McMurry; Cur., George Elmore; Museum Shop Mgr., Mike Seymour.
Personnel Profile: Full-Time Paid 14; Part-Time Paid 10; Part-Time Volunteers 250; Interns 1.
Governing Authority: Parent Institution: U.S. Dept. of Interior. Subsidiary Institution: National Park Service, Washington, DC 20240. Tax-exempt.
Historic Site: historic fort on Santa Fe Trail.
Collections: military items of the period 1859-1878; 80,000 recovered artifacts. Historic Buildings: officers' quarters; quartermaster storehouse; commanding officer's quarters; two commissary storehouses; shops building containing the post bakery, carpenter, paint, saddlers, wheelwright and blacksmith shops; infantry barracks; combination barracks/post hospital; reconstructed blockhouse/guardhouse.
Research Fields: 1859-1878 U.S. Military; military uniforms, weapons, accoutrements; 1859-1878 fort furnishings; 1859-1878 history of Ft. Larned.
Facilities: 500-vol. library including photographs, slides, archival material, microfilm records for research on premises; visitor center with museum exhibits; picnic area; hiking trails. Books for sale.
Activities: guided & self-guided tours; lectures; exhibitions; history talks and living history demonstrations throughout the summer on weekends; self-guided history/nature trail; audio-visual program. Site Sponsors: Santa Fe Trail Days; Old Time Independence Day Celebration; Fall Candlelight Tour; Christmas Open House.
Publications: handbook, Fort Larned.
Hours & Admission Prices: Daily 8:30-4:30. No charge. Closed New Year's Day; Thanksgiving; Christmas. ♿
Attendance: 38,000 (accurate)

* **SANTA FE TRAIL CENTER, (M),** 1349 K-156 Hwy., Larned, KS 67550-5347. Tel.: 620-285-2054. Fax: 620-285-7491.
E-mail: museum@santafetrailcenter.org
Web Site: www.santafetrailcenter.org
Founded: 1974.
Congressional District: 1

Key Personnel: Pres. (V), Tom Seltmann; Dir., Ruth Olson Peters; Cur., Afton Eye; Digitization Project Archivist, Jennifer Farr; Office Mgr., Linda Revello; Supt. Bldgs. & Grounds, Kevin Wilson.
Personnel Profile: Full-Time Paid 4; Part-Time Paid 1; Part-Time Volunteers 317.
Governing Authority: society. Parent Institution: Fort Larned Historical Society, Inc. Tax-exempt: 501(c)(3).
History Museum.
Collections: prehistoric & historic artifacts. Historic Buildings: 1908 L'Dora School from Frizell, KS; 1929 Santa Fe Railroad Depot from Frizell, KS; c.1870 Stone Cooling House; 1906 Escue Chapel CME Church.
Research Fields: economics & history of the Santa Fe Trail; Pawnee County history & genealogy.
Facilities: 2,000-vol. library of books dealing with the Santa Fe Trail & Pawnee County, Kansas, available for use in library reading room; auditorium. Museum-related items for sale.
Activities: guided tours; lectures; films; gallery talks; formally organized education programs; docent program; permanent & temporary exhibitions.
Publications: newsletter, Trail Ruts; pamphlet.
Hours & Admission Prices: Memorial Day-Labor Day: daily 9-5; Sept.-May Tues.-Sun. 9-5. Adults $4, student 12-18 $2.50, children 6-11 $1.50; discounts to organized school groups; members no charge. Closed New Year's Day; Thanksgiving; Christmas. ♿
Attendance: 6,785 (accurate)
Membership: Student $10; Individual $30; Friend $50; Nonprofit & Civic Groups $100; Patron $100-$350; Business $250 & up; $1 A Day $365; Sustaining $370-$999; Benefactor $1,000 & up.

Lawrence

KU BIODIVERSITY INSTITUTE - KU NATURAL HISTORY MUSEUM, (M), The University of Kansas, 1345 Jayhawk Blvd., Dyche Hall, Lawrence, KS 66045-7505. Tel.: 785-864-4540. Fax: 785-864-5335.
E-mail: kunhm@ku.edu
Web Site: www.nhm.ku.edu
Founded: 1866.
Congressional District: 2
Key Personnel: Dir., Dr. Leonard Krishtalka; Chm. (V), Janet Martin McKinney; Assoc. Dir. Administration, Jordan Yochim; Asst. Dir. Informatics, James Beach; Cur. Mammalogy, Robert Timm; Cur. Mammalogy, Norman Slade; Cur. Ornithology, Townsend Peterson; Cur. Ornithology, Robert Moyle; Collection Mgr. Ornithology, Mark Robbins; Cur. Entomology, Caroline Chaboo; Cur. Entomology, Michael Engel; Cur. Entomology, Andrew Short; Museum Specialist Entomology, Jennifer Thomas; Collection Mgr. Entomology, Zack Falin; Cur. Invertebrate Paleontology, Bruce Lieberman; Collection Mgr. Invertebrate Paleontology, Talia Karim; Cur. Invertebrate Zoology, Daphne Fautin; Cur. Botany, Craig C. Freeman; Cur. Botany, Mark Mort; Collection Mgr. Botany, Caleb Morse; Cur. Herpetology, Linda Trueb; Cur. Herpetology, Rafe Brown; Museum Specialist Herpetology, Andrew Campbell; Cur. Ichthyology, E.O. Wiley; Collection Mgr. Ichthyology, Andy Bentley; Cur. Vertebrate Paleontology, Larry Martin; Collection Mgr. Vertebrate Paleontology, Desui Miao; Preparator, Vertebrate Paleontology, David Burnham; Cur. Paleobotany, Tom Taylor; Cur. Paleobotany, Edith Taylor; Collection Mgr. Paleobotany, Rudolph Serbet; Cur. Parasitology, Kirsten Jensen; Cur. Archaeology, Mary Adair; Research Scientist, Global Biodiversity Science, Jorge Soberon; Accountant, Don Shobe; Dir. Exhibits, Bruce Scherting; Exhibits Asst., Gregory Ornay; Dir. Education, Teresa MacDonald; Program Specialist Education, Dawn Kirchner; Coord. Visitor Svcs. & Museum Shop Mgr., Tristan Smith; Dir. Communications, Jen Humphrey; Asst. to Dir., Lori Schlenker.
Personnel Profile: Full-Time Paid 70; Part-Time Paid 20; Part-Time Volunteers 12.
Governing Authority: university. Parent Institution: The University of Kansas. Subsidiary Institution: R.L. McGregor Herbarium, 2045 Constant Ave., Univ. of Kansas, Lawrence, 785-864-4493; Entomology Div., 1501 Crestline Dr., Suite 140, Univ. of Kansas, Lawrence, 785-864-2234; Invertebrate Paleontology Div., 120 Lindley Hall, Univ. of Kansas, Lawrence, 785-864-2747; The Archaeology Research Center, 1340 Jayhawk Blvd., Spooner Hall, Lawrence, KS, 785-864-2675. Tax-exempt: 501(c)(3).
Natural History Museum: housed in c.1901 Romanesque Revival building, listed on National Register of Historic Places.
Collections: eight and a half million specimens pertaining to botany, paleobotany, invertebrate paleontology, entomology, mammalogy, ornithology, herpetology, ichthyology, vertebrate paleontology; Great Plains animals & habitats including panorama of North American plants & animals; 7th Cavalry horse Comanche; live snakes, & bees; endangered species; archaeology.
Research Fields: systematic & evolutionary biology; ecology; environmental informatics; ecological niche modeling.
Facilities: 50,000 sq. ft. exhibit space; 75,000 sq. ft. of research collections & associated office space.
Activities: lectures; films; organized education programs for adults, children & undergraduate or graduate college students affiliated with Univ. of Kansas; training programs for professional museum workers and elementary & secondary science teachers; summer workshops for young people.
Publications: papers; monographs; publications; Nature in Kansas series; newsletters.
Hours & Admission Prices: Tues.-Sat. 9-5, Sun. 12-5. Suggested Donations: adults $5, children 6-18 & seniors $3; museum members, KU students, staff & faculty and children under 6 no charge. Closed most federal holidays. ♿
Attendance: 46,000 (accurate)
Membership: Senior & Youth $20; Individual $30; Household $40; Patron $75; Contributor $150; Curator's Circle $300 & up.

THE ROBERT J. DOLE INSTITUTE OF POLITICS, 2350 Petefish Dr., Lawrence, KS 66045-7555. Tel.: 785-684-4900. Fax: 785-684-1414.
E-mail: doleinstitute@ku.edu
Web Site: www.doleinstitute.org/vistors.html
Key Personnel: Dir., William B. "Bill" Lacy; Assoc. Dir. Programming, Jonathan Earle; Assoc. Dir. Outreach, Barbara Ballard; Senior Archivist, Dole Archive, Morgan Davis; Dir. Facilities & Events, Lawrence D. Bush; Media & Exhibits Archivist, Judy Sweets; Communications & Events Coord., Cori Ast; Asst. to Dir., Maggie Mahoney; Friends of Dole Institute, Lori Hutfles; Asst. Archivist, Catherine (Cat) C. Riggs; Asst. Archivist, Robert Lay; Mktg., Alison Heath Carther; Dir. Devel., Shawn McDaniel
History Museum.
Collections: artifacts & memorabilia pertaining to Senator Robert Dole's life.
Hours & Admission Prices: Mon.-Sat. 9-5, Sun. 12-5. No charge; donations accepted. Closed New Year's Day; Thanksgiving; Christmas.

*** SPENCER MUSEUM OF ART, THE UNIVERSITY OF KANSAS, (M),** 1301 Mississippi St., Lawrence, KS 66045-7500. Tel.: 785-864-4710. Fax: 785-864-3112. TDD: 800-776-3777 (Kansas Relay).
E-mail: spencerart@ku.edu
Web Site: www.spencerart.ku.edu
Founded: 1928.
Congressional District: 2
Key Personnel: Dir., Saralyn Reece Hardy; Asst. Dir. & Museum Shop Mgr., Carolyn Chinn Lewis; Cur. European & American Arts, Susan Earle; Cur. Arts & Cultures of the Americas, Africa, & Oceania, Nancy Mahaney; Cur. Asian Art, Kris Ercums; Sr. Cur. Prints & Drawings, Stephen Goddard; Asst. Dir. Collections, Janet Dreiling; Exhibition Designer, Richard Klocke; Photographer, Robert Hickerson; Public Rels. Liaison, Bill Woodard; Dir. Museum Advancement, Margaret Perkins-McGuinness; Dir. Education, Kristina Walker; Head of Security, Cynthia Waterman.
Personnel Profile: Full-Time Paid 23; Part-Time Paid 10; Part-Time Volunteers 170; Interns 6.
Governing Authority: university. Parent Institution: The University of Kansas. Tax-exempt: 170(b).
Art Museum.
Collections: European & American painting, sculpture, prints, drawings, photographs, decorative arts; textiles; Japanese paintings & prints; Chinese paintings & sculpture; American & African art; ethnographic artifacts including Native American, African, Latin American & Australian cultures.
Major Exhibits: Transforming the Everyday, 11/09-2/10; C.A. Seward, 1/10-3/10; World War I: Machine in a Void, 3/10-5/10.
Research Fields: history of art in relation to teaching; use of permanent collections & exhibits.
Facilities: over 170,000-vol. library of art & architecture. Art books & museum-related items for sale.
Activities: guided tours; lectures; films; classes for children & adults; concerts; inter-museum loans, permanent, temporary & traveling exhibitions; international artist in residency program; interdisciplinary programs across the university.
Publications: annual journal, The Register of the Spencer Museum of Art; annual, Murphy Lecture in Art Series; exhibitions catalogues; collection catalogues; quarterly newsletter.
Hours & Admission Prices: Tues.-Wed. & Fri.-Sat. 10-4, Thurs. 10-8, Sun. 12-4. No charge; donations accepted. Discount to AAM members in bookstore. Closed holidays. ♿
Attendance: 142,000 (estimated)
Membership: Student $15; Senior Citizen $35; Friend $50-$199; Donor $200-$499; Patron $500-$999; Benefactor $1,000-$2,499; Fellow $2,500-$4,999; Cornerstone $5,000 & up. Corporate: Friend $150-$299; Donor $300-$499; Patron $500-$999; Benefactor $1,000-$1,499; Associate $1,500-$2,499; Fellow $2,500-$4,999; Cornerstone $5,000 & up.

WATKINS COMMUNITY MUSEUM OF HISTORY, (M), 1047 Massachusetts St., Lawrence, KS 66044-2961. Tel.: 785-841-4109. Fax: 785-841-9547.
Web Site: www.watkinsmuseum.org

Founded: 1972.
Congressional District: 3
Key Personnel: Interim Dir., Mike Wildgen; Archivist, Helen Krische-Dee.
Personnel Profile: Full-Time Paid 1; Full-Time Volunteers 2; Part-Time Paid 3; Part-Time Volunteers 59; Interns 1.
Governing Authority: nonprofit society. Parent Institution: Douglas County Historical Society. Tax-exempt: 170(b)(1)(A).
Local History Museum: housed in 1888 Richardsonian Romanesque building built by J.B. Watkins.
Collections: photographs & illustrations; documents including scrapbooks, maps & pamphlets; textile items including clothing, lace & quilts; toys, dolls & other personal items; tools & agricultural equipment; 1879 reconstructed children's playhouse; 1900 surrey; Mexican war cannon Old Sacramento.
Research Fields: county & local history and genealogy; Bleeding Kansas, Civil War & Quantrill's Raid; 19th-20th century history; social history, Native Americans, local culture.
Facilities: archives of local history for use on premises; temporary & permanent exhibits.
Activities: lecture series; youth programming; workshops; historical programs; walking tours.
Publications: quarterly newsletter.
Hours & Admission Prices: Museum: Tues.-Wed. & Fri.-Sat. 10-4, Thurs. 10-8. Research Room: Tues.-Fri. 10-4 & by appointment. No charge; donations accepted. Closed holidays. ♿
Attendance: 7,715 (accurate)
Membership: Junior $5; Individual $25; Family $40; Conservator $60; Preserver $100; Friend $250; Sponsor $500; Patron $1,000; Benefactor $5,000.

Leavenworth

C.W. PARKER CAROUSEL MUSEUM, 320 S. Esplanade, Leavenworth, KS 66048-1585. Tel.: 913-682-1331.
Web Site: www.firstcitymuseums.org/carousel_main.html
Key Personnel: Dir., Jerry Reinhardt
History Museum.
Collections: carousel artifacts & memorabilia.
Hours & Admission Prices: Feb.-Dec. Thurs.-Sat. 11-5, Sun. 1-5. Adults $5, children $3. Closed New Year's Eve & Day; Easter; Independence Day; Thanksgiving; Christmas Eve & Day.

CARROLL MANSION MUSEUM HOME OF LEAVENWORTH COUNTY HISTORICAL SOCIETY, 1128 5th Ave., Leavenworth, KS 66048-3213. Tel.: 913-682-7759. Fax: 913-682-7759.
E-mail: leavenworthhistory@sbcglobal.net
Web Site: www.leavenworthhistory.org
Founded: 1964.
Congressional District: 2
Key Personnel: Pres., Shirley Stieger; Interim Dir., Joanie Kepka; Museum Shop Mgr., Hazel May Fackler.
Personnel Profile: Full-Time Paid 1; Part-Time Paid 1; Part-Time Volunteers 50.
Governing Authority: county. Parent Institution: Leavenworth County Historical Society. Tax-exempt.
History Museum: housed in 1867 Carroll Mansion.
Collections: furniture; silver; china; costumes; baths; Victorian furnishings & local artifacts; local history.
Research Fields: Leavenworth County & Kansas history.
Activities: guided tours; city tours; lectures; school programs & tours.
Publications: quarterly, Historical Society Gazette.
Hours & Admission Prices: April-Nov. Tues.-Sat. 10:30-4:30; Dec.-March Tues.-Sat. 1-4:30. Adults $5, seniors $4, children 5-12 $3; discounts to AAM & AAFLH members; children under 5 & members no charge. Closed federal holidays.
Attendance: 12,000 (estimated)
Membership: Student $15; Individual $25; Family $40; Contributor $100; Patron $250 & up.

FIRST CITY MUSEUM, 743 Delaware St., Leavenworth, KS 66048-2472. Tel.: 913-682-1866. Fax: 913-682-1866.
E-mail: first_city_museum@yahoo.com
Web Site: www.firstcitymuseums.org
Founded: 1988.
Key Personnel: Chm. (V), C. H. VanOrden; Pres. (V), John D. Sanders; Museum Shop Mgr., Audrey Sanders.
Personnel Profile: Part-Time Volunteers 17.
Governing Authority: Parent Institution: Leavenworth Historical Museum Assoc. Tax-exempt.
History Museum.
Collections: local history; photographs.
Facilities: Books for sale.
Activities: Museum Sponsors; Open Houses.
Hours & Admission Prices: Thurs.-Sat. 9-11 & 1-4. No charge; donations accepted. ♿
Attendance: 335 (estimated)

NATIONAL FRED HARVEY MUSEUM, 624 Olive St., Leavenworth, KS 66048-2653. Tel.: 913-682-1866.
E-mail: fredharveymuseum@lvnworth.com
Web Site: www.firstcitymuseums.org/fredharvey_main.html
Historic House Museum.
Collections: Harvey family history; personal artifacts; period furnishings.
Hours & Admission Prices: Tours by appointment.

Lecompton

CONSTITUTION HALL, 319 Elmore, Lecompton, KS 66050. Mailing Address: P.O. Box 198, Lecompton, KS 66050-0198. Tel.: 785-887-6520.
Founded: 1986.
Personnel Profile: Full-Time Paid 1.
Governing Authority: Parent Institution: Kansas State Historical Society.
History Museum.
Collections: local history & culture; photographs; period furnishings; personal artifacts.
Facilities: Museum-related items for sale.
Activities: special events.
Hours & Admission Prices: Wed.-Sat. 9-5, Sun. 1-5; other times by appointment. Adults $2, students $1; members, active military and children 5 & under no charge. Closed state holidays. ♿

TERRITORIAL CAPITAL-LANE MUSEUM, 393 N. 1900 Rd., Lecompton, KS 66050-4119. Tel.: 785-887-6148 & 6285. Fax: 785-887-6148.
E-mail: lanemuseum@aol.com
Web Site: www.lecomptonkansas.com
Founded: 1969.
Congressional District: 2
Key Personnel: C.E.O. & Pres., Paul M. Bahnmaier; Chm. (V) & Education, Charlene Winter; Dir., Rich McConnell; Treas. & Gift Shop Mgr., Betty Leslie; Cur., Arlene Simmons; Archivist, Mae Holderman; Membership, Iona Spencer; Public Rels., Opal Goodrick; Registrar, Helen Norwood; Security, Bob Weeks.
Personnel Profile: Part-Time Paid 2; Part-Time Volunteers 60.
Governing Authority: Lecompton Historical Society, not-for-profit organization. Tax-exempt: 501(c)(3).
History Museum: located on foundation of proposed capitol building of Kansas.
Collections: Kansas territorial history through the Lane University era; quilts; early pioneer artifacts.
Research Fields: Lecompton history.
Facilities: 250-vol. library of territorial books & territorial maps of Kansas available to the public; Lane University chapel. Museum-related items for sale.
Activities: guided tours. Annual Event: Territorial Day in June.
Publications: quarterly newsletter, Bald Eagle.
Hours & Admission Prices: Wed.-Sat. 11-4, Sun. 1-5; tours by appointment; call 913-887-6285 for more information. No charge; donations accepted. ♿
Attendance: 5,300 (estimated)
Membership: Adult $10; Family $14; Life $100.

Lenexa

LEGLER BARN MUSEUM, 14907 W. 87th St., Pkwy., Lenexa, KS 66215-4135. Tel.: 913-492-0038.
Web Site: www.leglerbarn.org
Personnel Profile: Part-Time Paid 2.
Governing Authority: city. Parent Institution: Lenexa Historical Society. Tax-exempt.
Historic Building: housed in stone barn built by Adam Legler in 1864.
Collections: period furnishings; personal artifacts.
Hours & Admission Prices: Tues.-Fri. 10-4, Sat.-Sun. 1-4. Suggested Donation: adults $2, children $1. Closed holidays.

Liberal

MID-AMERICA AIR MUSEUM, 2000 W. 2nd St., Liberal, KS 67901. Mailing Address: P.O. Box 2199, Liberal, KS 67905-2199. Tel.: 620-624-5263. Fax: 316-624-5454.
E-mail: liberalcityam@swko.net
Web Site: www.liberalairmuseum.com
Formerly: Liberal Air Museum

Founded: 1987.
Congressional District: 1
Key Personnel: Exec Dir., Donald Westfall; Chm. (V), Thaine Weber; Museum Shop Mgr., Hellen Evans.
Personnel Profile: Full-Time Paid 4; Part-Time Paid 1; Part-Time Volunteers 50.
Governing Authority: Parent Institution: City of Liberal. Tax-exempt: 501(c)(3).
Aviation Museum.
Collections: aircraft & artifacts relating to military & civilian aviation; photographs; personal collections; Hall of Aviation Science featuring hands-on displays.
Facilities: 20-vol. library of aviation books; 1,000-vols. of aviation magazines, available for research; 250-seat auditorium; 80,000 sq. ft. exhibit space. Museum-related items for sale.
Activities: films; guided tours; traveling exhibitions.
Publications: monthly newsletter, Mid-America Air Museum News; quarterly newsletter, Flying Colors.
Hours & Admission Prices: Mon.-Fri. 8-5, Sat. 10-5, Sun. 1-5. Adults $7, senior citizens $5, children 6-18 $3; discounts for AAM members & groups of 10 or more; children 5 & under and members no charge. Closed New Year's Day; Thanksgiving; Christmas. ♿
Attendance: 12,000 (accurate)
Membership: Individual $25; Family $50; Sustaining $100; Patron $250; Donor $500.

SEWARD COUNTY HISTORICAL MUSEUM, (M), 567 E. Cedar, Liberal, KS 67901-3865. Tel.: 620-624-7624.
Key Personnel: Exec. Dir., JoAnne Mansell
History Museum.
Collections: county history; personal artifacts; period furnishings.
Hours & Admission Prices: Memorial Day to Labor Day Mon.-Sat. 9-6, Sun. 1-6; Sept.-May Tues.-Sat. 9-5, Sun. 1-5. Dorothy's House & Land of Oz: adults $5, senior citizens & children 6-18 $3.50; children 5 & under no charge.

Lincoln

KYNE HOUSE MUSEUM, 216 W. Lincoln Ave., Lincoln, KS 67455. Mailing Address: P.O. Box 85, Lincoln, KS 67455-0085. Tel.: 785-524-9997.
Founded: 1978.
Congressional District: 1
Key Personnel: Pres. (V), Kathy Lupfer-Nielsen.
Personnel Profile: Part-Time Paid 1; Part-Time Volunteers 14.
Governing Authority: Tax-exempt.
Historic House Museum: built in 1885.
Collections: Lincoln County history, artifacts, culture & events; farm equipment; dolls; Indian artifacts; military artifacts; blacksmith; a hotel lobby; period store; doctor's office; tack & saddle artifacts; undertaker's equipment; 1920s furniture; F.A. Cooper's paintings, life, drawings, & metal etchings; genealogical records.
Facilities: library; research room. Museum-related items for sale.
Activities: guided tours; loan & participatory exhibits; educational programs for Lincoln County 2nd & 5th graders. Museum Sponsors: Lincoln Day & Lincoln Look-A-Like Contest.
Hours & Admission Prices: Kyne House: Tues. & Thurs. 1-4, Sat. 10-1. Suggested Donation $2. Marshall-Yohe House: by appointment. Adults $5, groups $4. ♿
Attendance: 1,400 (estimated)
Membership: Individual $10; Family $15; Business & Institution $25.

LINCOLN COUNTY HISTORICAL SOCIETY, 216 W. Lincoln Ave., Lincoln, KS 67455-1920. Mailing Address: P.O. Box 85, Lincoln, KS 67455-0085. Tel.: 785-524-9997.
Founded: 1978.
Congressional District: 1
Key Personnel: Pres., Kathy Lupfer-Nielsen; Treas., Brenda Peterson.
Personnel Profile: Part-Time Paid 1; Part-Time Volunteers 14.
Governing Authority: private; nonprofit organization. Branch Institution: Marshall-Yohe House, Lincoln, KS 67455. Tax-exempt: 501(c)(3).
General Museum.
Collections: Lincoln County history, artifacts, culture & events; farm equipment; dolls; Indian artifacts; military artifacts; blacksmith display; a hotel lobby; old time store; doctors office; tack & saddle room; an undertaker's display; 1920s furniture; F.A. Cooper's paintings, life story, drawings & metal etchings.
Research Fields: brochures.
Facilities: library; research room. Museum-related items for sale.
Activities: guided tours; loan & participatory exhibits; educational programs for Lincoln County 5th graders at Marshall-Yohe House. Annual Events: Lincoln Day Brunch for Abe Lincoln look-alike contestants & judges in February; Secretary Week luncheon at Marshall-Yohe House in June; Topsy School Program.
Publications: annual newsletter.
Hours & Admission Prices: Kyne House Museum: Tues. & Thurs. 1-4, Sat. 10-1. Suggested Donation: $2. Marshall-Yohe House: by appointment. Adults $5, groups $4. ♿
Attendance: 1,400 (estimated)
Membership: Individual $10; Family $15; Business & Institution $25.

POST ROCK SCOUT MUSEUM, 161 E. Lincoln Ave., Lincoln, KS 67455-2050. Tel.: 785-524-5383.
Key Personnel: Owner, Kathie Crispin
Scout Museum.
Collections: scouting history; Girl Scout uniforms from 1918 to present; badges; photographs; personal artifacts.
Activities: youth project area.
Publications: semiannual newsletter.
Hours & Admission Prices: By appointment. No charge; donations accepted.
Attendance: 350 (estimated)
Membership: $10; $25; $50; $100; $500; $1,000.

Lindsborg

BIRGER SANDZEN MEMORIAL GALLERY, 401 N. 1st St., Lindsborg, KS 67456-1813. Mailing Address: P.O. Box 348, Lindsborg, KS 67456-0348. Tel.: 785-227-2220. Fax: 785-227-4170.
E-mail: fineart@sandzen.org
Web Site: www.sandzen.org
Founded: 1957.
Congressional District: 4
Key Personnel: Sandzen Foundation Pres. & C.E.O., Ruth Browne; Dir., Larry L. Griffis; Cur., Ron Michael; Dir. Devel., Clay Myers-Bowman; Sec., Muriel Gentine.
Personnel Profile: Full-Time Paid 3; Full-Time Volunteers 14; Part-Time Paid 1; Part-Time Volunteers 10.
Governing Authority: nonprofit. Tax-exempt: 501(c)(3).
Art Museum. Built in memory of Swedish-American painter and printmaker Birger Sandzen.
Collections: oils, watercolors, prints, archives of letters & papers by Birger Sandzen; family & contemporaries for research purposes; Henry Varnum Poor; Marsden Hartley; Doel Reed; Lester Raymer; Swedish-American artists; paintings, ceramics, sculpture & graphics by well-known artists; Carl Milles fountain; oriental art.
Major Exhibits: Contemporary Quilts, 1/8/10-2/10; 112th Annual Midwest Art Exhibition, 3/15/10-4/25/10; Kansas Collegiate Aesthetics, 5/8/10-6/27/10; Retrospective Exhibition - Betty Jo Houchen, 9/7/10-11/21/10; Paintings By James Borger, 11/7/10-12/26/10.
Facilities: library containing art books; gallery & recital area.
Activities: guided tours by appointment; lectures; gallery talks; concerts; loan exhibitions; college receptions.
Publications: book, Birger Sandzen: An Illustrated Biography; The Graphic Work of Birger Sandzen, by Charles Pelham Greenough, 3rd; a catalogue of the graphic work of Birger Sandzen; Sandzen and the New Land, an exhibition catalogue.
Hours & Admission Prices: Tues.-Sun. 1-5. No charge. Closed New Year's Day; Memorial Day; Independence Day; Thanksgiving; Christmas. ♿
Attendance: 17,227 (accurate)
Membership: Strom $30; Wallin $35, Jaderborg $50; Lofgren $100; Brase $250; Thorsen $500; Milles $1,000.

MCPHERSON COUNTY OLD MILL MUSEUM AND PARK, 120 Mill St., Lindsborg, KS 67456-2815. Mailing Address: P.O. Box 94, Lindsborg, KS 67456-0094. Tel.: 785-227-3595. Fax: 785-227-2810.
E-mail: oldmillmuseum@hotmail.com
Web Site: www.oldmillmuseum.org
Founded: 1959.
Congressional District: 4
Key Personnel: C.E.O. & Dir., Lorna Nelson; Museum Shop Mgr., Lenora Lynam.
Personnel Profile: Full-Time Paid 3; Full-Time Volunteers 2; Part-Time Paid 7; Part-Time Volunteers 75; Interns 1.
Governing Authority: county. Parent Institution: McPherson County. Tax-exempt.
History Museum & Historic Site.
Collections: history; agriculture; Native American artifacts; industrial; folklore; natural history; geology; archives. Historic Buildings: 1898 Smoky Valley Roller Mill; 1904 Swedish Pavilion.

Research Fields: local & regional history with emphasis on Swedish & Mennonite heritage of area.
Facilities: library of county & local history information available for use on premises; reading room.
Activities: Special Events: Millfest, guided tours of 1898 flour mill in May; Heritage Christmas in December.
Publications: brochures & Mill history booklet; McPherson County Genealogical resources Guide.
Hours & Admission Prices: Mon.-Sat. 9-5, Sun. 1-5. Adults $2, children 6-12 $1; discounts to school & group tours. Closed New Year's Day; Thanksgiving; Christmas. ♿
Attendance: 10,000 (estimated)

RED BARN STUDIO MUSEUM, 212 S. Main, Lindsborg, KS 67456-2614. Tel.: 785-227-2217.
Web Site: www.redbarnstudio.org/
Founded: 1988.
Congressional District: 1
Key Personnel: Dir., Marsha Howe; Pres. (V), Tim Johnson
Art Museum.
Collections: works by Lester Raymer; paintings; prints; ceramics; metalwork; woodcarving; furniture; jewelry.
Hours & Admission Prices: Tues.-Sun. 1-4; other times by appointment. No charge; donations accepted.
Attendance: 1,500 (accurate)
Membership: Student $15; Individual $25; Family $35; Friend $50; Donor $100; Sponsor $250; Patron $500; Benefactor $1,000.

Logan

DANE G. HANSEN MEMORIAL MUSEUM, (M), 110 W. Main St., Logan, KS 67646. Mailing Address: P.O. Box 187, Logan, KS 67646-0187. Tel.: 785-689-4846. Fax: 785-689-4892.
E-mail: hansenmuseum@ruraltel.net
Web Site: www.hansenmuseum.org
Founded: 1973.
Congressional District: 1
Key Personnel: Dir., Shirley A. Henrickson; Pres. Museum Bd., Deb Berg.
Personnel Profile: Full-Time Paid 2; Part-Time Paid 4.
Governing Authority: nonprofit organization. Tax-exempt: 501(c)(3).
Art Museum.
Collections: Oriental art; gun, coin & spoon collection; work by Kansas artists; Hansen Family memorabilia.
Major Exhibits: Sum of the Parts (T), 12/11/09-2/7/10; High School Art Show, 2/12/10-3/14/10; Ray Howlett (T), 3/19/10-5/2/10; Uncommon Threads (T), 5/7/10-6/20/10; Fragile Nature (T), 6/25/10-8/8/10; Super Croc (T), 8/13/10-11/7/10; Portraits from the Golden Age of Jazz (T), 11/12/10-12/12/10; Sean McLaren & Deb Pipes (T), 12/17/10-2/6/11.
Facilities: meeting space.
Activities: guided tours; arts festivals; permanent & traveling exhibitions.
Publications: quarterly newsletter; brochure, Hansen Family; brochure, Museum Plaza.
Hours & Admission Prices: Mon.-Fri. 9-12 & 1-4, Sat. 9-12 & 1-5, Sun. & holidays 1-5. No charge. Closed New Year's Day; Thanksgiving; Christmas. ♿
Attendance: 8,000 (estimated)
Membership: Benefactor $10; Patron $25; Sustaining $50.

Lucas

GARDEN OF EDEN AND CABIN HOME, 305 E Second St., Lucas, KS 67648. Tel.: 785-525-6395.
Web Site: www.garden-of-eden-lucas-kansas.com
Founded: 1907.
Key Personnel: Pres., Jon Blumb; Dir., John Hachmeister; Mgr., Lynn Schneider.
Personnel Profile: Part-Time Paid 6; Part-Time Volunteers 20.
Governing Authority: Parent Institution: Garden of Eden, Inc.
Historic House Museum: housed in the former home of S.P. Dinsmoor. Listed on the National Register of Historic Places.
Collections: concrete sculptures; limestone log cabin.
Facilities: picnic area.
Hours & Admission Prices: March-April daily 1-4; May-Oct. daily 10-5; Nov.-Feb. Sat.-Sun. 1-4. Adults $6, children 6-12 $1; discounts to groups; children 5 & under no charge. Closed major holidays.
Attendance: 10,000 (estimated)

Lyndon

OSAGE COUNTY HISTORICAL SOCIETY RESEARCH CENTER, 631 Topeka Ave., Lyndon, KS 66451. Mailing Address: P.O. Box 361, Lyndon, KS 66451-0361. Tel.: 785-828-3477.
E-mail: researchosagechs@embarqmail.com
Web Site: www.osagechs.org
Founded: 1963.
Congressional District: 5
Key Personnel: C.E.O. & Pres. (V), Eileen Matzek Davis; Vice Pres., Lester Arb; Treas., Jean Timm.
Personnel Profile: Part-Time Paid 1; Part-Time Volunteers 10.
Governing Authority: society. Parent Institution: Osage County Kansas. Tax-exempt.
History Museum & Genealogy Library.
Collections: Osage County historical items; mining & railroad artifacts; civil & criminal court cases; 1864-1930 newspapers; 1865-1925 census.
Research Fields: local history; genealogy.
Facilities: museum at Lyndon.
Activities: Museum Sponsors: genealogical workshop.
Publications: quarterly, Hedge Post; book, Stories of Osage County & Its Families; reprints, Annals of Lyndon: Early Days in Kansas; Along the Santa Fe & Lawrence Trails: Old Ridgeway; Council City 1854-55; Superior 1856; Burlingame 1856-64; County Atlas 1879; index, Probate County record; index, Osage County marriages & divorces; Osage County cemetery records; Osage County Murders; Sac & Fox Chief Keokuk in his Time; Mokohoko Chief of Sac & Fox Indians.
Hours & Admission Prices: Lyndon Museum & Research Center: April-Oct. Wed.-Sat. 1-5; other times by appointment. No charge; donations accepted. Closed holidays. ♿
Attendance: 850 (estimated)
Membership: Individual & Family $10; Business $15.

Lyons

CORONADO-QUIVIRA MUSEUM, (M), 105 W. Lyon, Lyons, KS 67554-2703. Tel.: 620-257-3941.
E-mail: cqmuseum@hotmail.com
Founded: 1927.
Congressional District: 5
Key Personnel: Exec. Dir., Janel Cook; Pres. (V), Charles Hayes; Museum Shop Mgr., Annabelle Hensley.
Personnel Profile: Full-Time Paid 2; Part-Time Paid 4; Part-Time Volunteers 15; Interns 1.
Governing Authority: society; nonprofit. Parent Institution: Rice County Historical Society, Inc. Branch Museum: Alden Santa Fe Depot Museum, Alden, KS 67512. Tax-exempt.
General Museum: housed in 1910-1911 Carnegie library building.
Collections: Coronado & Quiviran Indian artifacts; Wichita Indians; Santa Fe Trail; 1541 Coronado chain mail; pre-1934 pioneer artifacts; anthropology; archaeology; pioneer.
Research Fields: Coronado & Quiviran Indian artifacts; pioneers; Santa Fe Trail; Wichita Indians.
Activities: guided tours; lectures; films; permanent & temporary exhibitions; children's hands-on exhibits.
Publications: Chase (KS.) America; My One-Half Mile of the Santa Fe Trail; From the Little Arkansas to the Big Arkansas; The Quiviran Expert Ecologist.
Hours & Admission Prices: Mon.-Sat. 9-5, Sun. 1-5. Out of county visitors: ages 13 & up $2, children 6-12 $1; children under 6 no charge. ♿
Attendance: 4,000 (estimated)
Membership: Individual $10; Family $15; Business $25; Patron $30.

Manhattan

GOODNOW MUSEUM STATE HISTORIC SITE, 2301 Claflin Rd., Manhattan, KS 66502. Mailing Address: 2309 Claflin Rd., Manhattan, KS 66502-3421. Tel.: 785-565-6490. Fax: 785-565-6491.
Web Site: www.kshs.org
Founded: 1969.
Congressional District: 2
Key Personnel: Contact, D. Cheryl Collins.
Personnel Profile: Part-Time Volunteers 10.
Governing Authority: state. Parent Institution: Kansas State Historical Society, 6425 S.W. 6th Ave., Topeka, KS 66615. Tel.: 785-272-8681. Subsidiary Institution: Riley County Historical Society & Museum. Tax-exempt.
Historic House: home of pioneer Kansas educator, Isaac Tichenor Goodnow and his wife, Ellen Denison Goodnow.
Collections: artifacts relating to Goodnow family & early Kansas education programs, systems & schools.
Activities: guided tours.

Publications: brochure.
Hours & Admission Prices: Sat.-Sun. 2-5 & by appointment. No charge; donations accepted. Closed Easter; national holidays.
Attendance: 1,500 (estimated)

HAROLD M. FREUND AMERICAN MUSEUM OF BAKING, 1213 Bakers Way, Manhattan, KS 66502-4555. Mailing Address: P.O. Box 3999, Manhattan, KS 66505-3999. Tel.: 785-537-4750. Fax: 785-537-1493.
E-mail: info@aibonline.org
Web Site: www.aibonline.org
Founded: 1982.
Key Personnel: Asst. Cur., Tammy L. Popejoy.
Governing Authority: nonprofit. Parent Institution: American Institute of Baking, Manhattan, KS. Tax-exempt: 501(c)(3).
Baking Museum.
Collections: history of baking & milling.
Research Fields: bakery products; contributions by specific individuals & companies to the baking industry.
Facilities: library; 900 sq. ft. exhibit space.
Activities: group tours by appointment.
Hours & Admission Prices: Mon.-Thurs. 7:30-7, Fri. 7:30-6:30. No charge. Closed New Year's Day; Memorial Day weekend & Fri. before; Independence Day; Labor Day weekend & Fri. before; Thanksgiving & day after; Christmas Day.
Attendance: 900 (estimated)

HARTFORD HOUSE MUSEUM, 2309 Claflin Rd., Manhattan, KS 66502-3421. Tel.: 785-565-6490.
Web Site: www.rileycountyks.gov/museum
Founded: 1974.
Congressional District: 2
Key Personnel: Dir., D. Cheryl Collins; Pres. (V), Arlene Hopkins.
Personnel Profile: Part-Time Volunteers 100.
Governing Authority: society. Parent Institution: Riley County Historical Society & Museum, 2309 Claflin Rd., Manhattan, KS 66502. Tax-exempt.
Historic House: restored 1855 pre-fabricated house shipped on the Hartford Steamboat to Manhattan, KS.
Collections: Victorian period furnishings.
Publications: booklet; brochure.
Hours & Admission Prices: Tues.-Fri. 8:30-5 subject to availability of staff, Sat.-Sun. 2-5. No charge; donations accepted. Closed national holidays.
Attendance: 1,500 (estimated)

KANSAS STATE UNIVERSITY HERBARIUM, Div. of Biology, Ackert Hall, Manhattan, KS 66506-4900. Tel.: 785-532-6619. Fax: 785-532-6653.
E-mail: herbarium@ksu.edu
Web Site: www.ksu.edu/herbarium
Founded: 1875.
Congressional District: 2
Key Personnel: Dir., Carolyn Ferguson, Ph.D.
Personnel Profile: Full-Time Paid 1; Part-Time Paid 4.
Governing Authority: university. Tax-exempt.
Herbarium.
Collections: botany; 200,000 plant specimens.
Research Fields: systematic botany; plant evolution.
Facilities: 3,000-vol. library of books on systematic botany available on premises.
Activities: formally organized education programs for undergraduate & graduate college students affiliated with Kansas State University; specimen identification available to the public; research in systematic botany.
Hours & Admission Prices: Mon.-Fri. 8-5. No charge. Closed national holidays. ♿

THE KANSAS STATE UNIVERSITY INSECT ZOO, 1500 Denison Ave., Manhattan, KS 66506. Tel.: 785-532-2847.
E-mail: insect@ksu.edu
Web Site: www.k-state.edu/butterfly/index.htm
Insect Museum.
Collections: many species of tropical insects including tarantulas & spiders, scorpions & other arthropods.
Hours & Admission Prices: Tues.-Sat. 12-6; other times by appointment. Adults $2, senior citizens $1.50.

MANHATTAN ARTS CENTER, 1520 Poyntz Ave., Manhattan, KS 66502-4147. Tel.: 785-537-4420. Fax: 785-539-3356.
E-mail: director@manhattanarts.org
Web Site: www.manhattanarts.org
Founded: 1996.
Key Personnel: Dir., Penny Senften.
Personnel Profile: Part-Time Paid 4; Part-Time Volunteers 2.
Governing Authority: private; nonprofit organization. Tax-exempt.
Art Museum.
Collections: Gordon Parks photograph collection, From the Huge Silence: A Century of Life in a Small Kansas Town; Grandma Layton drawing; F. Remington sculpture, Bronco Buster; Remington cowboy.
Facilities: 125-seat auditorium; classroom; theatre.
Activities: concerts; lectures; rental gallery; temporary exhibitions; theater.
Publications: magazine, City Arts.
Hours & Admission Prices: Mon.-Fri. 10-5, Sat. 1-4. No charge; donations accepted. Closed Christmas. ♿
Attendance: 5,000 (estimated)
Membership: Student $10-$24; Friend $25-$49; Supporter $50-$99; Advocate $100-$249; Sponsor $250-$499; Benefactor $500-$999; Endower $1,000 & up.

* **MARIANNA KISTLER BEACH MUSEUM OF ART AT KANSAS STATE UNIVERSITY, (M),** 701 Beach Lane, Manhattan, KS 66506-0601. Tel.: 785-532-7718. Fax: 785-532-7498.
E-mail: beachart@ksu.edu
Web Site: www.beach.k-state.edu
Founded: 1996.
Congressional District: 2
Key Personnel: Dir., Lorne E. Render; Pres. (V), Charles Reagan; Sr. Cur., Bill North; Asst. Cur., Liz Seaton; Registrar & Collections Mgr., Sarah Price; Mgr. Business & Mktg., Martha Scott; Coord. Membership & Events, Ladonna Piper; Exhibitions Designer, Lindsay Smith; Sr. Educator, Katherine Walker Schlageck.
Personnel Profile: Full-Time Paid 10; Part-Time Paid 15; Part-Time Volunteers 25; Interns 5.
Governing Authority: nonprofit. Parent Institution: Kansas State University, Manhattan, KS. Tax-exempt: 501(c)(3).
Art Museum.
Collections: art of Kansas & the Mountain Plains region with emphasis on printmaking & painting; works by John Steuart Curry; 20th- & 21st-century American printmaking.
Major Exhibits: Following the Sun: The Art of Sue Jean Covacevich, 1905-1998, 1/10-5/10; Gail Gregg: The Album Series, 1/10-5/10; Teri Schmidt: 2010 Friends of the Beach Museum of Art Gift Print Artist, 4/10-7/10; Pieces of Time: Quilts from the KSU Historic Costume and Textile Museum, 5/10-9/10; Material Evidence, 10/10-1/11.
Research Fields: 20th-21st century art of Kansas & the Mountain Plains region; 20th-century Kansas printmaking; 20th-21st century American printmaking.
Facilities: 4,000-vol. library; 10,600 sq. ft. exhibit space; 100-seat auditorium; classroom. Museum-related items for sale.
Activities: docent program; formal education programs for children & undergraduate or graduate college students; guided tours; lectures; loan & traveling exhibitions; school loan service; pre-professional museum training; teachers workshops.
Publications: newsletter, In Sight; exhibition catalogues.
Hours & Admission Prices: Tues.-Sat. 10-5, Sun. 12-5. No charge; donations accepted. Closed major holidays. ♿
Attendance: 28,500 (estimated)
Membership: Student $20; Beach Buddies $25; Friend $40-$99; Supporter $100-$249; Benefactor $500-$999; Curator's Circle $1,000-$2,499; Director's Circle $2,500 & up.

PIONEER LOG CABIN, City Park, 11th & Poyntz, Manhattan, KS 66502. Mailing Address: 2309 Claflin, Manhattan, KS 66502-3421. Tel.: 785-565-6490. Fax: 785-565-6491.
Web Site: www.rileycountyks.gov/museum
Founded: 1914.
Congressional District: 2
Key Personnel: Pres. (V), Arlene Hopkins; Dir., D. Cheryl Collins.
Personnel Profile: Part-Time Paid 1.
Governing Authority: Society. Parent Institution: Riley County Historical Society. Tax-exempt: 501(c)(3).
History Museum: housed in log cabin.
Collections: farm & shop tools; log cabin pioneer home.
Activities: tours.
Publications: newsletter.
Hours & Admission Prices: April-Oct. Sun. 2-5; other times by appointment. No charge; donations accepted. ♿
Attendance: 500 (estimated)
Membership: Riley County Historical Society: Individual: Friend $10-$49; Sponsor $50-$74; Sustainer $75-$99; Patron $100 & up. Family: Friend $15-$54; Sponsor $55-$79; Sustainer $80-$110; Patron $110 & up.

RILEY COUNTY HISTORICAL MUSEUM, (M), 2309 Claflin Rd., Manhattan, KS 66502-3421. Tel.: 785-565-6490. Fax: 785-565-6491.
Web Site: www.rileycountyks.gov/museum
Founded: 1914.
Congressional District: 2
Key Personnel: Dir., D. Cheryl Collins.
Personnel Profile: Full-Time Paid 3; Part-Time Paid 5; Part-Time Volunteers 131; Interns 1.
Governing Authority: Parent Institution: Riley County and Riley County Historical Society. Branch Museums: Hartford House Museum; Goodnow House State Historic Site; Pioneer Log Cabin; Wolf House; Rocky Ford School; Randolph Jail. Tax-exempt: 501(c)(3).
History Museum.
Collections: household equipment, furniture, tools, weapons, musical instruments, toys, glass, china, school equipment, church equipment, doctor's & dentist's equipment; local Indian artifacts; dolls; transportation; hardware; pictures, photos, newspapers, books relating to local history; manuscript collections.
Research Fields: history of Riley County.
Facilities: 4,000-vol. library of county history. Prints of historic buildings, books, stationery & cards for sale.
Activities: guided tours; lectures; films; drama; formally organized education programs; docent program; permanent & temporary exhibitions; intern program.
Publications: newsletter; brochure; books on Riley County.
Hours & Admission Prices: Museum: Tues.-Fri. 8:30-5, Sat.-Sun. 2-5. Library: by appointment. No charge; donations accepted. Closed national holidays. ♿
Attendance: 10,000 (estimated)
Membership: Riley County Historical Society: Individual: Friend $10-$49; Sponsor $50-$74; Sustainer $75-$99; Patron $100 & up; Life $300. Family: Friend $15-$54; Sponsor $55-$79; Sustainer $80-$110; Patron $110 & up.

SUNSET ZOOLOGICAL PARK, 2333 Oak St., Manhattan, KS 66502-3824. Tel.: 785-587-2737. Fax: 785-587-2730.
E-mail: shoemaker@ci.manhattan.ks.us
Web Site: www.sunsetzoo.com
Founded: 1933.
Congressional District: 2
Key Personnel: C.E.O., Scott Shoemaker.
Personnel Profile: Full-Time Paid 15; Part-Time Paid 15; Part-Time Volunteers 160; Interns 10.
Governing Authority: municipal government. Parent Institution: City of Manhattan. Tax-exempt.
Zoo.
Collections: home to 220 animals representing 104 species from around the world featuring: red panda, snow leopard, chimpanzee, maned wolves, Caribbean flamingos & cheetahs.
Research Fields: conservation; Conservation Action Partnership (CAP) Paraguay.
Facilities: 48 acres; concession. Museum-related items for sale.
Activities: 14 special events each year.
Publications: quarterly magazine; annual report.
Hours & Admission Prices: April-Oct. daily 9:30-5; Nov.-March daily 12-5. Adults, senior citizens & students $4, children 3-12 $2; discounts to groups; members no charge. ♿
Attendance: 64,500 (accurate)
Membership: Senior Citizen $20; Individual $40; Individual Plus $45; Family $50; Zoo Buff $75; Director's Club Associate $250; Director's Club Patron $500; Director's Club Benefactor $1,000.

WOLF HOUSE MUSEUM, 630 Fremont, Manhattan, KS 66502-5820. Mailing Address: Riley County Historical Society, 2309 Claflin Rd., Manhattan, KS 66502. Tel.: 785-565-6490. Fax: 785-565-6491.
Web Site: www.rileycountyks.gov/museum
Founded: 1983.
Congressional District: 2
Key Personnel: Pres. (V), Arlene Hopkins; Dir., D. Cheryl Collins; Cur., Edna Williams.
Personnel Profile: Part-Time Paid 3; Part-Time Volunteers 50.
Governing Authority: society. Parent Institution: Riley County Historical Society. Tax-exempt.
Historic House: 1868 boarding house.
Collections: c.1830-1900 Wolf collection; 1880s artifacts.
Research Fields: 19th-century furniture; boarding houses.
Activities: Museum Sponsors: special events in late spring & Christmas.
Publications: brochure.
Hours & Admission Prices: Sat. 1-5, Sun. 2-5. No charge; donations accepted.
Attendance: 1,500 (estimated)
Membership: Riley County Historical Society: Individual: Friend $10-$49; Sponsor $50-$74; Sustainer $75-$99; Patron $100 & up; Life $300. Family: Friend $15-$54; Sponsor $55-$79; Sustainer $80-$110; Patron $110 & up.

Mankato

JEWELL COUNTY HISTORICAL MUSEUM, 118 N. Commercial St., Mankato, KS 66956-2207. Tel.: 785-545-6426.
E-mail: lkboden@ruraltel.net
Web Site: www.jewellcountyhistory.com
Founded: 1961.
Congressional District: 6
Key Personnel: C.E.O., Roger Fedde; Pres. (V), Leon Boden; Cur. & Museum Shop Mgr., Karen Boden.
Personnel Profile: Part-Time Paid 1; Part-Time Volunteers 3.
Governing Authority: nonprofit. Tax-exempt.
Agriculture Museum.
Collections: farm implements; county history; Federal & State census records, 1870-1920; political & military memorabilia; turn of the century period rooms; general store; post office; pharmacy; doctor's office; old limestone jail; blacksmith shop; geology; oral history recordings of county residents.
Facilities: library of county newspapers on microfilm.
Activities: quarterly education programs; guided tours; temporary exhibitions. Museum Sponsors: annual Antique Farm Machinery Show and Threshing Bee; Arts & Crafts Festival.
Publications: quarterly newsletter; family histories of people of the county.
Hours & Admission Prices: Thurs.-Fri. 1-5, Sat. 9-1; other times by appointment. No charge; donations accepted. Closed holidays.
Attendance: 488 (accurate)
Membership: Individual $5; Family $10; Life $100.

Marysville

DOLL HOUSE MUSEUM, 912 Broadway, Marysville, KS 66508-1805. Mailing Address: 1107 Pony Express Hwy., Marysville, KS 66508. Tel.: 785-562-3029. Fax: 785-562-2990.
E-mail: candcdoll@yahoo.com
Founded: 1997.
Key Personnel: Dir., Lois Cohorst.
Personnel Profile: Part-Time Volunteers 2.
Governing Authority: Tax-exempt: 501(c)(3).
Doll, Toy, & Indian Artifacts Museum.
Collections: dolls; toys; Native American artifacts; rocking horses; pedal toys; doll houses.
Major Exhibits: The Nativities, 12/09.
Activities: storytelling.
Hours & Admission Prices: By appointment. Suggested Donation: $3 per person. ♿
Attendance: 1,100 (estimated)

KOESTER HOUSE MUSEUM, 209 N. 8th, Marysville, KS 66508-1637. Tel.: 785-562-2417.
Historic House Museum: housed in the former home of banker, Charles F. Koester; c.1876.
Collections: period furnishings; personal artifacts; portraits; clothing; toys; books; white bronze sculptures.
Facilities: gardens.
Hours & Admission Prices: May-Nov. Tues.-Sun. 10-12 & 1-4:30; other times by appointment.

LEE DAM CENTER FOR FINE ART, 201 S. 9th St., Marysville, KS 66508-1909. Mailing Address: Marysville Chamber of Commerce, 101 N. Tenth, Hwy. 77 & 36, Marysville, KS 66508. Tel.: 785-562-2828.
Fine Art Center.
Collections: visual arts.
Activities: workshops; concerts; performances; cultural events; music & educational programs. Museum Sponsors: Christmas Fine Arts Show & Sale.
Hours & Admission Prices: Thurs. & Sat.-Sun. 1-4; other times by appointment.

MARSHALL COUNTY HISTORICAL SOCIETY, 1207 Broadway, Marysville, KS 66508-1845. Tel.: 785-562-5012.
Historic Building: housed in the county courthouse; built in 1891.
Collections: county history; books; photography.
Facilities: library.
Hours & Admission Prices: Museum: Memorial Day to Sept. 15 daily 1-4; Winter: Mon.-Fri. 1-4. Library: Mon.-Fri. 1-4.

PONY EXPRESS ORIGINAL HOME - STATION #1, 106 S. 8th St., Marysville, KS 66508-1832. Tel.: 785-562-3825.
Historic Building: built in 1859 by Joseph Cottrell; original home station along the Pony Express route.
Collections: Pony Express mail service history.
Hours & Admission Prices: April-Oct. Mon.-Sat. 10-5, Sun. 12-4.

McPherson

MCPHERSON MUSEUM & ARTS FOUNDATION, (M), 1130 E. Euclid, McPherson, KS 67460-4506. Tel.: 620-241-8464. Fax: 620-241-2676.
E-mail: mcmuseum@sbcglobal.net
Web Site: mcphersonmuseum.com
Founded: 1984.
Congressional District: 1
Key Personnel: Exec. Dir., Carla Barber; Pres., Mike Rausch.
Personnel Profile: Full-Time Paid 2; Part-Time Paid 4; Part-Time Volunteers 2; Interns 1.
Governing Authority: McPherson Museum & Arts Foundation. Tax-exempt: 501(c)(3).
General Museum: housed in 1921 F.A. Vaniman Home.
Collections: Oriental porcelains; Native American artifacts; Pleistocene fossils; rocks & minerals; meteorites; period furniture & clocks; pioneer farm tools & household goods; art.
Major Exhibits: Here's To Your Health, 1/19/10-2/20/10; The Story Behind the Roar: Leo, The MGM Lion, 3/9/10-5/8/10; Living Traditions: The Culture of Native Americans, 6/10-8/14/10; Art Exhibit: Photography by Ansley Simmons (T), 8/31/10-11/20/10.
Research Fields: local history; paleontology.
Facilities: Museum-related items for sale.
Activities: guided tours; lectures; gallery talks; permanent & temporary exhibitions; research; open microphone event for poetry, music & short stories; writers' workshop; student writers' competition.
Publications: newsletter, The Diamond; brochures.
Hours & Admission Prices: Tues.-Sat. 1-5. Adults $3; discounts to AAM members; members no charge. Closed legal holidays.
Attendance: 4,503 (estimated)
Membership: Railroader & Clubs $35; Bagpiper $50; Refiner $75; Light Capital Club $100; World Travelers' Club $250; Diamond Club $500; Director's Circle $501 & up.

Meade

DALTON GANG HIDEOUT, Pearlette St., Meade, KS 67864. Mailing Address: P.O. Box 515, Meade, KS 67864-0515. Tel.: 620-873-2731; 800-354-2743.
E-mail: daltonhideout@yahoo.com
Web Site: oldmeadecounty.com
Founded: 1941.
Congressional District: 1
Key Personnel: Museum Shop Mgr., Marc S. Ferguson.
Personnel Profile: Full-Time Paid 1.
Governing Authority: Parent Institution: Meade County Historical Society.
Historic House Museum: housed in the former home of Eva Dalton, sister of the Dalton Gang.
Collections: House: period furnishings. Barn: 95 ft. long tunnel to the house; period artifacts.
Facilities: Barn serves as entrance to the house. Museum-related items for sale.
Publications: Historical Society Newsletter.
Hours & Admission Prices: Mon.-Sat. 9-5, Sun. 1-5. Admission $4.
Attendance: 9,000 (accurate)

MEADE COUNTY HISTORICAL SOCIETY MUSEUM, 200 E. Carthage, Meade, KS 67864-6490. Mailing Address: P.O. Box 893, Meade, KS 67864-6490. Tel.: 620-873-2359. Fax: 620-873-2359.
E-mail: meademuseums@swko.net
Founded: 1969.
Congressional District: 1
Key Personnel: C.E.O., Norman Dye; Vice Chm., Glen Lauppe; Administration, Jennifer Conway; Asst., Paulette Vanderpool.
Personnel Profile: Full-Time Paid 2; Full-Time Volunteers 6; Part-Time Paid 2; Part-Time Volunteers 4.
Governing Authority: society; nonprofit. Tax-exempt.
General Museum.
Collections: American Indian artifacts; 400-600 year old artifacts from archaeological dig; general store; barber shop; harness shop; blacksmith shop; sod house; parlor, kitchen, bedroom of turn-of-the-century home; covered wagon; agricultural exhibits; photographer's studio; bank; doctor's office; school & chapel; Rock Island & Pacific Railroad; Livery Barn; county schoolhouse; farm machinery exhibit; 1925 Ford sedan; 1927 Ford truck.
Research Fields: Meade County history.
Facilities: 500-vol. library, to be used on premises; microfilms of all 1878-1986 county newspapers; reading room. County history books & other western history books for sale.
Activities: guided tours; formally organized education programs for children; permanent exhibitions.
Publications: annual newsletter.
Hours & Admission Prices: Mon.-Sat. 9-5, Sun. 1-5. Admission $3; children 5 & under no charge. Closed Thanksgiving; Christmas. ♿
Attendance: 5,000 (estimated)
Membership: Ranch Hands $25; Pioneer $100; Homesteaders $250; Trail Boss $500.

Medicine Lodge

CARRY A. NATION HOME MEMORIAL, 209 W. Fowler, Medicine Lodge, KS 67104-1536. Mailing Address: 104 Lisa Circle, Medicine Lodge, KS 67104-1605. Tel.: 620-886-3553.
Founded: 1950.
Congressional District: 7
Key Personnel: C.E.O. & Treas., Dorothy Reed; Museum Shop Mgr., Ann Bryan; Museum Shop Mgr., Janet Hindman.
Personnel Profile: Part-Time Paid 2; Part-Time Volunteers 4.
Governing Authority: society. Parent Institution: City of Medicine Lodge. Tax-exempt.
Historic House Museum: 1880-1903 home of Carry A. Nation.
Collections: furniture & original articles used by the Nations; Carry A. Nations' bed, organ, hat, dresser, valise and purse; stockade; period artifacts; old jail. Historic Building: 1877 log cabin.
Activities: guided tours.
Publications: pamphlet, A Short Biography of Carry A. Nation.
Hours & Admission Prices: Summer: 10:30-5; Winter: 1-4. Adults $5, senior citizens $4, children 6-17 $3; discounts to AAM members; children under 5 no charge.
Attendance: 500 (estimated)

Montezuma

STAUTH MEMORIAL MUSEUM, (M), 111 N. Aztec St., Montezuma, KS 67867-8801. Mailing Address: P.O. Box 396, Montezuma, KS 67867-0396. Tel.: 620-846-2527. Fax: 620-846-2810.
E-mail: stauthm@ucom.net
Web Site: stauthmemorialmuseum.org
Founded: 1996.
Congressional District: 1
Key Personnel: Dir., Financial Dir. & Public Rels., Kim Legleiter.
Personnel Profile: Full-Time Paid 1; Part-Time Paid 2.
Governing Authority: private; nonprofit organization. Tax-exempt: 501(c)(3).
Decorative Arts Museum.
Collections: decorative art, woodcarvings, sculpture, ivory carvings, musical instruments, real & ceremonial weapons, foreign coins & currency, fur wall hangings, animal hides, cloisonne & jewelry collected from around the world; over 10,000 slides; big game animal trophies from Canada, Alaska & Norway, as well as other parts of North America.
Facilities: 700-vol. library of National Geographic magazines; 9,000 sq. ft. exhibit space; 100-seat community room serves as an auditorium, classroom, theatre & meeting room.
Activities: films; guided tours; lectures; traveling & temporary exhibitions.
Publications: traveling exhibition schedule.
Hours & Admission Prices: Tues.-Sat. 9-12 & 1-4:30, Sun. 1:30-4:30. No charge; donations accepted. Closed New Year's Day; Easter; Independence Day; Thanksgiving; Christmas. ♿
Attendance: 4,589 (accurate)

Mulvane

MULVANE MUSEUM, 300 W. Main, Mulvane, KS 67110-1779. Mailing Address: P.O. Box 67, Mulvane, KS 67110-0067. Tel.: 316-777-4850.
History Museum.
Collections: local history; photographs; period artifacts.
Hours & Admission Prices: Tues.-Sat. 10-4. Closed holidays.

Neodesha

NORMAN #1 OIL WELL MUSEUM, 106 S. 1st St., Neodesha, KS 66757-1802. Tel.: 620-325-5316. Fax: 316-325-5316.
E-mail: norman1@terraworld.net
Founded: 1967.
Key Personnel: Pres., Dan Railsback; Dir., Jackie Clark.
Personnel Profile: Full-Time Paid 1; Part-Time Paid 1; Part-Time Volunteers 3.
Governing Authority: municipal; nonprofit organization. Tax-exempt.

Historical & Oil Museum: first commercial oil well in the mid-continent oil fields.
Collections: full sized derrick; oil well equipment; farming tools & equipment; clown clothing & props used by two former Neodesha High School graduates that have since retired from Ringling Bros. Circus; Indian tools & artifacts; WPA dolls, standard oil refinery Osage Indian artifacts.
Facilities: small chapel; RV park. Museum-related items for sale.
Activities: guided tours; formal education programs for children; temporary exhibitions.
Publications: Little Bear Tracks; Cho-O-Nee to High Iron.
Hours & Admission Prices: Tues.-Sat. 10-5. No charge; donations accepted. Closed Independence Day; holidays. ♿
Attendance: 1,000 (estimated)
Membership: Roughneck $15; Wildcats $25; Roustabout $50; Jughound $100; Swamper $250; Oil Tycoon over $250.

Ness City

NESS COUNTY HISTORICAL MUSEUM, 123 S. Pennsylvania, Ness City, KS 67560-1907. Tel.: 785-798-3298.
Founded: 1930.
Congressional District: 1
Personnel Profile: Part-Time Paid 1; Part-Time Volunteers 20.
Governing Authority: Tax-exempt.
History Museum.
Collections: county history; photographs; period furnishings; obituaries; tableware; quilts; tools.
Hours & Admission Prices: Tues.-Fri. 1-5; other times by appointment. Closed holidays.
Membership: Life $25.

Newton

HARVEY COUNTY HISTORICAL SOCIETY, 203 N. Main, Newton, KS 67114-3442. Mailing Address: P.O. Box 4, Newton, KS 67114-0004. Tel.: 316-283-2221. Fax: 316-283-2221.
E-mail: info@hchm.org
Web Site: www.hchm.org
Founded: 1962.
Congressional District: 4
Key Personnel: Dir., Debra Hiebert; Chm. (V), Thomas Sandwell; Archivist, Jane Jones; Cur., Kris Schmucker; Photo Technician, Linda Koppes; Office Mgr., Lana Myers.
Personnel Profile: Part-Time Paid 4; Part-Time Volunteers 30.
Governing Authority: board of directors. Tax-exempt.
Historical Society Museum: housed in 1903 Carnegie Library Building.
Collections: railroad artifacts; county records; pioneer artifacts; photographs; microfilm reader of Harvey County newspapers through 1946. Historic Building: 1873 Kellas school.
Major Exhibits: An Accomplished Young Lady, 1/10-12/6/10.
Facilities: 1,000-vol. library of books & documents of city & county history; reading room. Museum-related items for sale.
Activities: guided & self-guided tours; permanent & temporary exhibitions; educational programs; Speaker's Bureau programs; reunions.
Publications: quarterly newsletter.
Hours & Admission Prices: Wed.-Sun. 1-4. Adults $3, children 5-17 $2; members, children 5 & under no charge. Closed most major holidays.
Attendance: 1,200 (estimated)
Membership: Individual & Senior $15; Senior One Plus One $20; One Plus One, Couple & Family $25; Sustaining Member $50; Business $100.

North Newton

KAUFFMAN MUSEUM, Bethel College, 2801 N. Main, North Newton, KS 67117-1700. Tel.: 316-283-1612.
E-mail: kauffman@bethelks.edu
Web Site: www.bethelks.edu/kauffman
Founded: 1941.
Congressional District: 4
Key Personnel: Dir., Rachel K. Pannabecker; Pres. (V), Glen Ediger; Cur. Education, Andrea Schmidt Andres; Cur. Exhibits, Charles Regier; Prairie Coord., Dwight Platt; Graphic Designer, Robert Regier; Museum Technician, David Kreider.
Personnel Profile: Full-Time Paid 3; Part-Time Paid 6; Part-Time Volunteers 85; Interns 1.
Governing Authority: Parent Institution: Bethel College & Kauffman Museum Assoc. Tax-exempt.
Cultural & Natural History Museum.
Collections: 40,000 items with emphasis on the natural and cultural history of Central Plains.
Major Exhibits: Images of Paraguay, 3/10-5/10.
Research Fields: Mennonite history.
Facilities: 16,000 sq. ft. interpretation building; historic farmstead; 1.5 acre prairie reconstruction.
Activities: lectures, guided tours, exhibits, concerts; special & traveling exhibitions.
Publications: newsletter; exhibition catalogs.
Hours & Admission Prices: Tues.-Fri. 9:30-4:30, Sat.-Sun. 1:30-4:30. Adults $4, children 6-16 $2; members no charge. ♿
Attendance: 7,000 (estimated)
Membership: Individual $30; Family $50; Patron $100; Fellow $500; Benefactor $1,000; Founder $5,000.

MENNONITE LIBRARY AND ARCHIVES, Bethel College, 300 E. 27th St., North Newton, KS 67117-0531. Tel.: 316-283-2500 & 284-5304. Fax: 316-284-5843.
E-mail: mla@bethelks.edu
Web Site: www.bethelks.edu/mla
Founded: 1938.
Congressional District: 5
Key Personnel: Archivist, John D. Thiesen; Librarian, Barbara A. Thiesen; Asst. Archivist, James Lynch.
Personnel Profile: Part-Time Paid 3; Part-Time Volunteers 7.
Governing Authority: college; church. Parent Institution: Bethel College. Affiliated with Mennonite Church USA. Tax-exempt.
Religious Museum.
Collections: Anabaptist & Mennonite manuscripts, prints, paintings, lithographs; archives.
Research Fields: Anabaptist & Mennonite studies; peace studies; regional history.
Facilities: 35,000-vol. library of books on Mennonite & Anabaptist history, life & principles available for inter-library loan; reading room.
Activities: guided tours; lectures.
Publications: Mennonite Life.
Hours & Admission Prices: Mon.-Thurs. 10-12 & 1-5. No charge; donations accepted. Closed national holidays. ♿
Attendance: 927 (estimated)

Norton

NORTON COUNTY HISTORICAL SOCIETY & MUSEUM, 105 E. Lincoln, Norton, KS 67654. Mailing Address: P.O. Box 303, Norton, KS 67654-0303. Tel.: 785-877-5107.
Historical Society Museum.
Collections: county history; photographs; prehistoric animal bones; 1948 meteor strike history.
Hours & Admission Prices: Wed. & Sat. 2-4.

STATION 15, Water Tower Park, W. Hwy. 36, Norton, KS 67654-0097. Mailing Address: Norton Area Chamber of Commerce, 104 S. State, P.O. Box 97, Norton, KS 67654-0097. Tel.: 785-877-2501. Fax: 785-877-3300.
E-mail: nortoncc@ruraltel.net
Web Site: us36.net/nortonkansas
Founded: 1961.
Congressional District: 1
Key Personnel: Exec. Dir., Karla Reed; Chm. (V), Myron Veh.
Governing Authority: Norton Travel & Tourism.
Historic Site.
Collections: papier mache figures; replica of stagecoach & wagon train depot of 1859; costumed figures; Indian artifacts.
Publications: handouts, excerpts from Kansas Historical Quarterlies & writings of Horace Greeley and Albert Dean Richardson.
Hours & Admission Prices: Daily 24 hours. No charge. ♿

Oakley

FICK FOSSIL & HISTORY MUSEUM, 700 W. 3rd St., Oakley, KS 67748-1256. Tel.: 785-671-4839. Fax: 785-672-3497.
E-mail: fickmuseum@ruraltel.net
Web Site: www.DiscoverOakley.com
Founded: 1972.
Congressional District: 1
Key Personnel: Pres., Alice Lindeman; Dir., Janet Bean; Registrar, Ruth Clark; Tour Guide, Nadine Kuasnicka.
Personnel Profile: Full-Time Paid 1; Part-Time Paid 2; Part-Time Volunteers 3.
Governing Authority: municipal. Parent Institution: City of Oakley. Tax-exempt.
Geology, Paleontology & History Museum.
Collections: locally found fossils; fossil art; minerals; rocks; wood carvings; general store with period items; local history; historical photos; sod house; replica of Oakley 1886 Union Pacific Depot; military; depression glass.

Research Fields: Monument Rocks in Logan & Gove Counties of Kansas.
Facilities: 2,000 photographs showing 100 years of history.
Activities: guided tours; temporary exhibits.
Publications: brochure.
Hours & Admission Prices: Summer: Mon.-Sat. 9-5, Sun. 1-5; Winter: Mon.-Sat. 9-12 & 1-5. No charge; donations accepted. Closed holidays. ♿
Attendance: 10,000

Oberlin

DECATUR COUNTY LAST INDIAN RAID MUSEUM, 258 S. Penn Ave., Oberlin, KS 67749-2245. Tel.: 785-475-2712.
E-mail: lirm@sbcglobal.net
Web Site: skyways.lib.ks.us/museums/lirm
Founded: 1958.
Congressional District: 1
Key Personnel: Pres., Dana Marintzer; Vice Pres., Chris Koerperich; Cur., Sharleen Wurm; Sec. & Treas., Barbara Dehlinger.
Personnel Profile: Full-Time Paid 2; Part-Time Paid 1; Part-Time Volunteers 4.
Governing Authority: society; nonprofit organization. Tax-exempt.
History Museum: located near the site of 1878 last Indian raid on Kansas soil.
Collections: local history; manuscripts; Indian artifacts; Western art; dolls; quilts.
Research Fields: local history; Indian raid of 1878.
Facilities: Museum-related items for sale.
Activities: guided tours; lectures; hobby workshops; formally organized education programs; permanent collections.
Publications: weekly newspaper column; brochures on Indian Raid; quarterly newsletter.
Hours & Admission Prices: Museum: April-Nov. Tues.-Sat. 9:30-12 & 1-4:30. Office: Dec.-March Tues.-Thurs. 9:30-12 & 1-4:30. Adults $5, children 6-12 $3; children 6 & under and members no charge. Closed holidays. ♿
Membership: Individual $10; Family $20.

Olathe

DEAF CULTURAL CENTER AND WILLIAM J. MARRA MUSEUM, 455 E. Park St., Olathe, KS 66061-5436. Tel.: 913-782-5808.
E-mail: kefdcc0@sbcglobal.net
Web Site: www.kefdcc.org
Founded: 2005.
Key Personnel: Exec. Dir., Sandra Kelly; Pres., Terry Hostin; Treas., David Wilcox; Volunteer Coord., Arlene Kuschmider; Volunteer Coord., Vickie Baska; Museum Shop Mgr., Nancy Crews.
Personnel Profile: Part-Time Paid 10; Part-Time Volunteers 60.
Governing Authority: Parent Institution: Deaf Cultural Center Foundation. Tax-exempt.
History Museum.
Collections: history & culture of the deaf and hard of hearing; photographs.
Facilities: Museum-related items for sale.
Activities: classes; educational programs.
Publications: Hand Signs: A Broader Vision.
Hours & Admission Prices: Tues.-Fri. 10-4, Sat. 10-3. No charge; donations accepted. Closed New Year's Day; Independence Day; Thanksgiving; Christmas. ♿
Attendance: 2,000 (estimated)
Membership: Contributor $50; Supporter $100; Sponsor $250; Director $500; Patron $1,000; Underwriter $2,500; Benefactor $5,000; Benefactor Champion $10,000.

ENSOR PARK AND MUSEUM, 18995 W. 183rd St., Olathe, KS 66062-9278. Tel.: 913-592-4141.
E-mail: larrywohxs@yahoo.com
Web Site: www.ensorparkandmuseum.org
Formerly: Ensor Farmsite and Museum
Founded: 1975.
Personnel Profile: Full-Time Paid 1; Part-Time Paid 2.
Governing Authority: city. Tax-exempt.
Historic Buildings.
Collections: Ensor family history; period furnishing; handmade textiles; fabric art; radio artifacts; industrial arts; metal sculpture by Alexander Calder; period furnishings. Historic Buildings: 1890 barn; 1892 farmhouse.
Activities: school tours; special events.
Hours & Admission Prices: May-June & Sept.-Oct. Sat.-Sun. 1-5; other times by appointment. No charge; donations accepted.

ERNIE MILLER NATURE CENTER, 909 N. Hwy. 7, Olathe, KS 66061-4040. Tel.: 913-764-7759.
Web Site: www.erniemiller.com
Nature Center.
Collections: live animals; natural, cultural, & environmental history.
Facilities: nature trails; amphitheater.
Activities: educational programs; hiking; summer camp.
Hours & Admission Prices: Center: April-May & Sept.-Oct. Mon.-Sat. 9-12 & 1-5, Sun. 1-5; June-Aug. Mon.-Sat. 9-12 & 1-5; Nov.-March Mon.-Sat. 9-12 & 1-4:30, Sun. 12:30-4:30. Trails: daily dawn to dusk.

MAHAFFIE STAGECOACH STOP AND FARM HISTORIC SITE, 1200 E. Kansas City Rd., Olathe, KS 66061-3002. Tel.: 913-971-5111. Fax: 913-971-5114.
E-mail: mahaffie@olatheks.org
Web Site: www.mahaffie.org
Founded: 1977.
Congressional District: 3
Key Personnel: Site Mgr., Tim Talbott; Volunteer Coord., Wendy Burkett; Museum Shop Mgr., Alexis Radil.
Personnel Profile: Full-Time Paid 7; Part-Time Paid 13; Part-Time Volunteers 136.
Governing Authority: city government, Olathe, KS.
Historic Site & House: 1865 Mahaffie house and stagecoach stop on Santa Fe Trail.
Collections: furnishings; agricultural equipment & machinery.
Research Fields: stagecoaches; Oregon Trail; Santa Fe Trail; local & state history; Mahaffie family.
Facilities: 600-vol. library pertaining to history available for research; reading room.
Activities: guided tours; lectures; docent programs; educational programs; off-site programs & lectures; living history programs.
Publications: newsletter.
Hours & Admission Prices: April-May & Nov.-Dec. Wed.-Sat. 10-4, Sun. 12-4; June-Oct. Thurs.-Sat. 10-4; other times by appointment. Call for admission prices. ♿
Attendance: 38,000 (estimated)
Membership: Individual $35; Family $75.

Osawatomie

JOHN BROWN MUSEUM STATE HISTORIC SITE, 10th & Main Sts., Osawatomie, KS 66064. Mailing Address: Box 37, Osawatomie, KS 66064-0037. Tel.: 913-755-4384. Fax: 913-755-4164.
E-mail: adaircabin@kshs.org
Formerly: John Brown State Historic Site
Founded: 1854.
Congressional District: 2
Key Personnel: Co Dir. & Site Cur., Grady Atwater; Co Dir. & Site Admin., Andrea Renick-Bell; Chm. (V), Lorene Hydorn; Service Asst., Ben Mainer.
Personnel Profile: Full-Time Paid 1; Part-Time Paid 1; Part-Time Volunteers 2.
Governing Authority: state. Parent Institution: Kansas State Historical Society & City of Osawatomie. Tax-exempt.
Historic House & Site: 1854 Adair Cabin, used as headquarters by John Brown 1855-58; 1856 Battle of Osawatomie; Underground Railroad stop.
Collections: weapons; pictures; antiques; fireplace cooking equipment.
Research Fields: abolitionists; slavery; Civil War; Bleeding Kansas.
Facilities: city park.
Activities: tours. Museum Sponsors: Annual reenactment of the Battle of Osawatomie; John Brown Jamboree in June; Christmas Program; Railroad Day in fall.
Publications: yearly program series, Border War Brochures; Safe Passages in Perilous Times; Territorial Kansas Heritage Alliance-John Brown Brochure.
Hours & Admission Prices: Tues.-Sat. 10-5, Sun. 1-5. No charge; donations accepted. Closed national holidays. ♿
Attendance: 5,000 (estimated)

Oskaloosa

OLD JEFFERSON TOWN, 703 Walnut, Hwy. 59, Oskaloosa, KS 66066. Mailing Address: P.O. Box 146, Oskaloosa, KS 66066-0146. Tel.: 785-863-2070.
Founded: 1966.
Congressional District: 2
Key Personnel: Pres. (V), Paul Flower; Cur., Marilyn Sharkey.
Personnel Profile: Part-Time Paid 1; Part-Time Volunteers 200.
Governing Authority: nonprofit. Jefferson County Historical Society. Tax-exempt.
Preservation Society: housed in seven c.1880 buildings, relocated to Old Jefferson Town.
Collections: country store, chapel & school with original furnishings; 1906 replica Jefferson County Courthouse bandstand; city jail; blacksmith shop. Historic House: 1880 Nincehelser House with original furnishings; John Stewart Curry, famous artist, boyhood home with art gallery.
Research Fields: local & family history.

Facilities: library containing records of families, census, cemeteries, churches, schools & files of newspapers pertinent to early history of Jefferson County. Crafts & museum-related items for sale.
Activities: guided tours; kids' workshop; craft demonstrations.
Publications: quarterly newsletter; semiannual history journal, Yesteryears.
Hours & Admission Prices: Museum: May-Nov. Sat. 1-5, Sun. 1:30-5. Library: April-Nov. Sat. 1-5, Sun. 1:30-5; Dec.-March Sat. 1-5. Tours by appointment. Suggested Donation: adults $2. ♿
Attendance: 4,000 (estimated)
Membership: Annual $15; Life $225.

Oswego

OSWEGO HISTORICAL MUSEUM, INC., 410 Commercial St., Oswego, KS 67356-2018. Tel.: 620-795-4500.
E-mail: historyatoswego@oswego.net
Founded: 1967.
Congressional District: 2
Key Personnel: Pres. (V), Cheryl L. Lewis; Treas., Eleanor Monroe.
Personnel Profile: Part-Time Paid 2; Part-Time Volunteers 4.
Governing Authority: county; nonprofit. Tax-exempt.
History Museum.
Collections: paintings; photographs; furnishings; personal artifacts; genealogy.
Facilities: 100-vol. library. Museum-related items for sale.
Activities: docent program; formal education programs for children; guided tours; school loan service; temporary exhibitions.
Hours & Admission Prices: June-Oct. Mon.-Fri. 1-5. No charge; donations accepted. ♿
Attendance: 859 (estimated)

Ottawa

OLD DEPOT MUSEUM, 135 W. Tecumseh, Ottawa, KS 66067. Mailing Address: P.O. Box 145, Ottawa, KS 66067-0145. Tel.: 785-242-1250. Fax: 785-242-1267.
E-mail: history@old.depot.museum
Web Site: www.old.depot.museum
Founded: 1963.
Congressional District: 2
Key Personnel: C.E.O. & Dir., Deborah Barker; Pres., Geoff Hanson; Treas., Greg Gilroy; Archivist, Ann Shepheard; Registrar, Laura Miller; Museum Asst., Phyllis Foster; Museum Shop Mgr., Kim Hanson.
Personnel Profile: Full-Time Paid 1; Part-Time Paid 4; Part-Time Volunteers 27; Interns 1.
Governing Authority: private; nonprofit organization. Subsidiary Institution: Dietrich Cabin, 5th & Main, Ottawa, KS 66067. Tax-exempt: 501(c)(3).
Historical Society Museum.
Collections: period rooms display local manufacturing items & furniture, clothing & accessories. Historic Sites: c.1888 limestone passenger depot; c.1859 walnut cabin.
Research Fields: Underground Railroad through the area; emigrant tribes of Native Americans; 19th century school discrimination case.
Facilities: 22,000-vol. library; 7,000 sq. ft. exhibit space. Museum-related items for sale.
Activities: guided tours; loan & temporary exhibitions. Museum Sponsors: Kansas Day; Christmas Event; Esoteric and Terrible Order of Pie Eaters Conclave.
Publications: bimonthly newsletter, The Headlight.
Hours & Admission Prices: Tues.-Sat. 10-4, Sun. 1-4. Adults $3, students $1; discounts to groups; members & preschoolers no charge. Closed New Year's Day; Easter; Thanksgiving; Christmas. ♿
Attendance: 2,879 (accurate)
Membership: Individual $15; Family $35; 1937 $50; A.P. Elder $100; Ben Park $250; Jacob Dietrich $500; Train Master $1,000.

Overland Park

NERMAN MUSEUM OF CONTEMPORARY ART, (M), 12345 College Blvd., Overland Park, KS 66210-1283. Tel.: 913-469-3000. Fax: 913-469-2348.
E-mail: awilso78@jccc.edu
Web Site: www.nermanmuseum.org
Formerly: Johnson County Community College, Gallery of Art
Founded: 1969.
Congressional District: 3
Key Personnel: Pres. (V), Dr. Terry Calaway; Dir., Bruce Hartman; Dir. Devel., Joe Sopcich; Dir. College Information, Julie Haas; Supvr. Security, Gus Ramirez.
Personnel Profile: Full-Time Paid 6; Part-Time Paid 16; Part-Time Volunteers 30.
Governing Authority: college. Parent Institution: Johnson County Community College. Tax-exempt.
Contemporary Art Museum.
Collections: contemporary paintings; ceramics; works on paper; photography; Oppenheimer collection.
Research Fields: contemporary art.
Facilities: 12,000 sq. ft. exhibition space; 110-seat cafe; 200-seat auditorium; 2 classrooms. Museum-related items for sale.
Activities: docent guided tours; lectures; visiting artists; film series; children's studio classes; theatre; broadcast programs; organized education programs for children, adults & undergraduate students affiliated with Johnson County Community College; temporary, permanent, loan & traveling exhibitions.
Publications: exhibition & collection catalogues.
Hours & Admission Prices: Tues.-Thurs. & Sat. 10-5, Fri. 10-9, Sun. 12-5. No charge. Closed major holidays. ♿
Attendance: 100,000 (accurate)
Membership: Student $15; Individual $50; Friend $75; Contributor $125; Patron $250; Sponsor $500; Underwriter $1,000; Benefactor $5,000.

Paola

SWAN RIVER MUSEUM, 12 E. Peoria, Paola, KS 66071-1707. Mailing Address: P.O. Box 123, Paola, KS 66071-0123. Tel.: 913-294-4940. Fax: 913-294-5040.
History Museum.
Collections: Miami County history; military artifacts; Native American & pioneer artifacts; period clothing; furniture; toys; fishing; sports equipment.
Hours & Admission Prices: Mon.-Sat. 10-4. No charge. Closed holidays.

Parker

PARKER HISTORICAL MUSEUM, 207 W. Main, Parker, KS 66072. Mailing Address: Parker Community Historical Society, P.O. Box 173, Parker, KS 66072-0173. Tel.: 913-898-4781.
Key Personnel: Pres., John Riggs.
Governing Authority: Parent Institution: Parker Community Historical Society.
Historic Buildings.
Collections: Parker history; newspapers.
Facilities: Museum-related items for sale.
Activities: special events. Museum Sponsors: PRHS Alumni Banquet in April.
Hours & Admission Prices: By appointment.

Parsons

PARSONS HISTORICAL COMMISSION MUSEUM, 401 S. 18th St., Parsons, KS 67357-4220. Tel.: 620-421-7000 & 3694.
Formerly: Parsons Historical Society Museum
Founded: 1969.
Congressional District: 2
Key Personnel: Chm. (V), Lewis Hevel; Financial Dir., Betty Olmsted.
Personnel Profile: Part-Time Paid 9; Part-Time Volunteers 15.
Governing Authority: private; nonprofit organization. Owned by City of Parsons. Operated by bd. directors. Tax-exempt.
Historical Society Museum.
Collections: Parsons history from 1870 to present with an emphasis on MKT Railroad; local historic memorabilia.
Facilities: 300-vol. library; 7,000 sq. ft. exhibit space.
Activities: guided tours.
Hours & Admission Prices: May-Oct. Fri.-Sun. 1-4. No charge; donations accepted. ♿
Attendance: 1,200 (estimated)
Membership: Individual $1; Life $20.

Peabody

PEABODY HISTORICAL MUSEUM, 106 E. Division, Peabody, KS 66866. Mailing Address: 1556 E. 59, Peabody, KS 66866-9485. Tel.: 620-983-2174.
Founded: 1961.
Key Personnel: Hostess, Gwen Gaines.
Governing Authority: bd. of directors. Tax-exempt.
History Museum.
Collections: period history; photographs. Historic Buildings: 1874 library; 1881 newspaper editor's home; 1920 printing building; 1904 barn.
Publications: biannual newsletter.
Hours & Admission Prices: Call for hours. Adults $5; members no charge. ♿
Membership: Individual $10; Family $15; Lifetime $100.

Phillipsburg

FORT BISSELL MUSEUM, 501 Fort Bissell Ave., Phillipsburg, KS 67661-7116. Tel.: 785-543-6212.
Web Site: www.phillipsburgks.us
Formerly: Old Fort Bissell
Founded: 1961.
Congressional District: 1
Key Personnel: Pres., Setul Parikh; Chm. (V) & Sec., Shelly Lare; Vice Pres., Stephanie Ausein; Treas., Kathy Beard.
Personnel Profile: Part-Time Paid 2.
Governing Authority: society. Parent Institution: Phillips County Historical Society, Inc. Tax-exempt.
Historical Society Museum.
Collections: artifacts from 1740 to present, guns; McDowell saddle & chaps. Historic Buildings: 1872 two log cabins; 1885 store; sod house; 1879 railroad depot; 1882 schoolhouse.
Major Exhibits: I Do - Antique Wedding Dresses, 6/10; Trinkets, Baubbles & Bling - Antique Jewelry, 7/10; Saddles, Chaps & Spurs, 8/10.
Research Fields: historical artifacts.
Activities: guided tours; permanent exhibitions.
Publications: brochures.
Hours & Admission Prices: Memorial Day to Labor Day Tues. & Thurs.-Fri. 8-4, Wed. 8-8, Sat. 10-4; tours by appointment. No charge; donations accepted. Closed Independence Day. ♿
Attendance: 1,500 (estimated)
Membership: Individual $5; Family $10; Business Institutions $15; Sustaining $25; Life $100.

Pittsburg

CRAWFORD COUNTY HISTORICAL MUSEUM, 651 S. Hwy. 69, Pittsburg, KS 66762-8600. Tel.: 620-231-1440.
Founded: 1968.
Congressional District: 5
Key Personnel: C.E.O., Alan Ross; Treas., Denny Davidson.
Personnel Profile: Part-Time Volunteers 10.
Governing Authority: county; society. Operated by the Crawford County Historical Society, Inc. Tax-exempt: 501(c)(3).
General Museum.
Collections: art; decorative arts; clothing; farming; government; household; industry; transportation; primitive; education; biology; taped local history collections; 1922 Marion steam shovel. Historic Buildings: 1902 grocery store; one-room schoolhouse.
Facilities: library of historical documents.
Activities: Museum Sponsors: annual Ice Cream Social; Open House in June.
Hours & Admission Prices: Wed.-Sun. 1-5. No charge; donations accepted. ♿
Attendance: 2,895 (accurate)
Membership: Individual $6; Contributing $10; Sustaining $20; Donor $25; Patron $100.

Pleasanton

LINN COUNTY MUSEUM/GENEALOGY LIBRARY, 307 E. Park (Dunlap Park), Pleasanton, KS 66075. Mailing Address: P.O. Box 137, Pleasanton, KS 66075-0137. Tel.: 913-352-8739. Fax: 913-352-8739.
Formerly: Linn County Museum
Founded: 1973.
Congressional District: 5
Key Personnel: Pres., Ola May Earnest.
Personnel Profile: Full-Time Volunteers 2; Part-Time Volunteers 5.
Governing Authority: nonprofit. Linn County Historical Society. Tax-exempt.
History Museum.
Collections: panels containing pictures, maps, copies of documents, and explanations of events of Linn County history; artifacts from 1850-early 1900s; four period rooms; paintings by Linn County artists; authentic country store; genealogy library.
Research Fields: genealogy; county history.
Facilities: library of books on Linn County history; microfilm copies of all existing Linn County newspapers; display area emphasizing Linn County history; genealogy center with microfilm reader; 1920's era car museum & R.R. depot with related items. Books & other related items for sale.
Activities: guided tours; bus tours of historic sites in Pleasanton area; narrated school bus trips to historic sites.
Publications: newsletter, Heritage; books, From Pioneering to the Present, Vols. I, II, III; reprint of 1928 Linn County History; booklets, Historic Linn County; Border Warfare in Southeastern Kansas; Linn County Cemeteries.
Hours & Admission Prices: June-Sept. Tues.-Sun. 1-5; Oct.-May Tues. & Thurs. 9-4, Sat.-Sun. 1-5 & by appointment. No charge; donations accepted. ♿
Attendance: 3,000 (estimated)
Membership: Annual $5; Life $25.

MINE CREEK BATTLEFIELD, 20485 Kansas Hwy. 52, Pleasanton, KS 66075-9549. Tel.: 913-352-8890.
Governing Authority: Parent Institution: Kansas State Historical Society.
Historic Site: location of the Civil War battle fought on Oct. 25, 1864.
Collections: Civil War history; personal artifacts; period furnishings & clothing; weapons; photographs.
Facilities: Museum-related items for sale.
Hours & Admission Prices: March-Nov. Wed.-Sat. 9-5, Sun. 1-5; Dec.-Feb. Fri.-Sat. 9-5, Sun. 1-5; other times by appointment. Adults $2, seniors & students $1; members, active military and children 5 & under no charge. Closed state holidays. ♿

Pratt

KANSAS DEPARTMENT OF WILDLIFE & PARKS, 512 S.E. 25th Ave., Pratt, KS 67124-8174. Tel.: 620-672-5911, ext. 108 & 0708. Fax: 620-672-6020.
E-mail: miker@wp.state.ks.us
Web Site: www.kdwp.state.ks.us
Founded: 1903.
Congressional District: 4
Key Personnel: C.E.O., Mike Rader; Caretaker, Chris Shrack.
Personnel Profile: Full-Time Paid 1; Part-Time Paid 2.
Governing Authority: state. Tax-exempt.
Nature Center.
Collections: live display of fish & reptiles species of Kansas; exhibits of birds & animals of Kansas; hands-on displays.
Facilities: aquarium.
Activities: school & group tours available upon request for museum & fish hatchery.
Publications: Kansas Wildlife & Parks Magazine; ON T.R.A.C.K.S.; The Field Glass; self-guided museum tour brochures.
Hours & Admission Prices: Mon.-Fri. 8-5. No charge; donations accepted. ♿
Attendance: 4,300 (estimated)

PRATT COUNTY HISTORICAL SOCIETY MUSEUM, 208 S. Ninnescah St., Pratt, KS 67124-2715. Tel.: 620-672-7874.
E-mail: pchsmuseum@sctelcom.net
Web Site: prattcountymuseum.org/
Founded: 1967.
Congressional District: 1
Key Personnel: Pres. (V), Marvin Proctor; Vice Pres., Ross Hoener; Treas., Linda Brehm; Bd. Sec., Ulanda Stiebben; Office Mgr., Sandra Hettrick; Cur., Marsha Brown.
Personnel Profile: Part-Time Paid 1; Part-Time Volunteers 40.
Governing Authority: private; nonprofit organization. Tax-exempt: 501(c)(3).
General Museums.
Collections: fossils; Plains Indian artifacts; Pratt County pioneer period rooms; Miss Kansas display; military artifacts; turn-of-the-century general store, jail, carpenter shop, post office; 1890s Main St; railroad history.
Research Fields: family histories; history of business buildings & homestead land owners.
Facilities: 2,218-vol. library; 2,200 sq. ft. exhibit space. Museum-related items for sale.
Activities: formal education programs for children; guided tours; temporary & loan exhibitions; school loan service. Museum Sponsors: Open House in Fall; Miss KS Pageant week open house; Christmas Open House; historical programs 4 times a year.
Publications: newsletter, Pratt County Historical Society.
Hours & Admission Prices: Mon.-Fri. 1-4, Sat.-Sun. 1-3; other times by appointment. No charge; donations accepted. Closed New Year's Day; Easter; Memorial Day; Independence Day; Labor Day; Thanksgiving; Christmas. ♿
Attendance: 3,000 (estimated)
Membership: Annual $10; Life $75.

Randolph

WONDER WORKSHOP CHILDREN'S MUSEUM, 12324 Main Rd., Randolph, KS 66554-9062. Tel.: 785-776-1234.
E-mail: wonder@kansas.net
Web Site: www.kansas.net/~wonder/
Children's Museum.
Collections: hands-on exhibits.
Activities: workshop; special events; after-school programs.
Hours & Admission Prices: Mon.-Sat. 10-2. Admission $2.50; children 2 & under no charge.

Republic

PAWNEE INDIAN VILLAGE STATE HISTORIC SITE, 480 Pawnee Trail, Republic, KS 66964-8057. Tel.: 785-361-2255. Fax: 785-361-2255.
E-mail: piv@kshs.org
Web Site: www.kshs.org
Founded: 1967.
Congressional District: 1
Key Personnel: Historic Property Cur., Richard Gould; Chm. (V), Narveen Brzon; Pres. (V), Beth Carlgren.
Personnel Profile: Full-Time Paid 1; Part-Time Paid 3; Part-Time Volunteers 2.
Governing Authority: state. Admin. by Kansas State Historical Society, 6425 S.W. 6th Ave., Topeka, KS 66615-1099. Tel.: 785-272-8681. Tax-exempt: 501(c)(3).
Archaeology Museum: located on the preserved Pawnee Site.
Collections: original lodge floor; hearth; stone; metal tools & implements; bone hoe blades made from the scapula of a bison; trade gun; artifacts to illustrate Pawnee life & customs; dioramas.
Research Fields: Pawnee Indians.
Facilities: nature walk; picnic grounds.
Activities: guided tours.
Hours & Admission Prices: March-Nov. Wed.-Sat. 9-5, Sun. 1-5; Dec.-Feb. Wed.-Sat. 10-5; other times by appointment. Adults $3, seniors & students $2; members, military, and children 5 & under no charge. Closed major holidays. ♿
Attendance: 15,000 (accurate)
Membership: Kansas State Historical Society: Student $15; Individual $25; Family $35.

Russell

DEINES CULTURAL CENTER, 820 N. Main St., Russell, KS 67665-1932. Tel.: 785-483-3742. Fax: 785-483-4397.
E-mail: deinescenter@russellcity.org
Founded: 1990.
Congressional District: 1
Key Personnel: Dir., Nancy Selbe.
Personnel Profile: Part-Time Paid 3; Part-Time Volunteers 6.
Governing Authority: municipal. Parent Institution: City of Russell. Tax-exempt.
Art Center.
Collections: E. Hubert Deines wood engravings; 20th-century art.
Activities: temporary & traveling exhibitions.
Hours & Admission Prices: Tues.-Sun. 12:30-5:30. No charge; donations accepted. ♿
Attendance: 2,500 (estimated)
Membership: Supporting $25; Patron $50; Sustaining $100; Advocate $500; Benefactor $1,000.

OIL PATCH MUSEUM, 100 Edwards Ave., Russell, KS 67665. Tel.: 785-483-6640.
Web Site: www.rchs.russellks.net
Oil History Museum.
Collections: western Kansas oil history; oil storage tank; drilling & pumping equipment.
Hours & Admission Prices: June-Aug. daily 4-8; Winter: by appointment. Suggested Donation $2.

RUSSELL COUNTY HISTORICAL SOCIETY/FOSSIL STATION MUSEUM, 331 Kansas St., Russell, KS 67665-2019. Mailing Address: Main Building, P.O. Box 245, Russell, KS 67665-0245. Tel.: 785-483-3637.
E-mail: rchs@russellks.net
Web Site: www.rchs.russellks.net
Founded: 1969.
Congressional District: 1
Key Personnel: Pres., Kay Homewood; Vice Pres., Lila Schmitt.
Personnel Profile: Part-Time Paid 1; Part-Time Volunteers 4.
Governing Authority: county government; nonprofit. Subsidiary Institutions: Gernon House, 818 Kansas St., Russell, KS 67665; Oil Patch Museum. Jct. I-70 & U.S. 281, Russell, KS 67665; Heym Oliver House, 503 Kansas St., Russell, KS 67665. Tax-exempt: 501(c)(3).
Historical Society.
Collections: Native American artifacts; historic furniture & household items from 1850-1930; cable tool & rotary oilfield equipment from 1900-1965.
Research Fields: arts & entertainment history of Russell County history.
Facilities: 50-vol. genealogical library; 1,500 sq. ft. exhibit space.
Activities: guided tours; loan, travel & temporary exhibits; school loan service.
Hours & Admission Prices: Memorial Day to Labor Day Sun. 1-4, Mon.-Sat. 12-5; other times by appointment. No charge; donations accepted.
Attendance: 358 (estimated)
Membership: Life $25.

Russell Springs

BUTTERFIELD TRAIL HISTORICAL MUSEUM, 515 Hilts, Russell Springs, KS 67764. Tel.: 913-751-4242.
Founded: 1964.
Congressional District: 1
Key Personnel: Pres., Jarett Haremza; Museum Shop Mgr., Andrea Plummer.
Governing Authority: nonprofit. Sponsored by The Butterfield Trail Association & Historical Society of Logan County, Kansas, Inc. Tax-exempt.
History Museum: housed in 1887 Logan County Courthouse & Jail.
Collections: period furniture; artifacts relating to the passage through & settlement of the High Plains; fossils; Indian relics; dishware; agricultural implements; family heirlooms.
Research Fields: Logan County history; Butterfield Overland Dispatch & the Smoky Hill Trail.
Facilities: 250-vol. library of Kansas law books, periodicals, old local newspapers & county records available for use on the premises; reading room. Curios, books by local authors & newspaper reprints on local history for sale.
Activities: guided tours; permanent exhibitions. Museum Sponsors: annual Butterfield Trail Ride; annual Old Settlers Picnic & Butterfield Day.
Publications: semiannual newsletter, Butterfield Happenings.
Hours & Admission Prices: May to Labor Day Tues.-Sat. 9-12 & 1-5, Sun. 1-5. No charge; donations accepted.
Attendance: 1,000 (accurate)
Membership: Annual $10; Life $100.

Sabetha

ALBANY HISTORICAL SOCIETY, INC., 415 Grant, Sabetha, KS 66534-2317. Tel.: 785-284-3446 & 3529.
Web Site: www.albanydays.org
Founded: 1965.
Congressional District: 2
Key Personnel: Pres., Daryl Bechtelhermer; Vice Pres., Paul Huffman; Sec., Alex Dawdy.
Personnel Profile: Part-Time Volunteers 20.
Governing Authority: society. Tax-exempt.
General Museum: housed in 1867 two-story stone schoolhouse.
Collections: period vehicles; agricultural machinery; train equipment; military; two airplanes. Historic Buildings: 1866-1867 Albany School; Berwick School wood structure; Rock Island Depot; Union Pacific Caboose; 1866 frame dwelling; c.1870 Most House; machinery building; car building; shelter house; two-story log cabin; post office; operative blacksmith shop; sawmill.
Research Fields: local history.
Facilities: 500-vol. library of school books, histories & magazines available for use on premises under supervision of director.
Activities: guided tours; permanent exhibitions. Society Sponsors: Threshing Bee; Arts & Crafts.
Publications: book, History of Albany; Recipes & Remembrances.
Hours & Admission Prices: Memorial Day-Labor Day Sat.-Sun. 2-5; other times by appointment. No charge; donations accepted. ♿
Attendance: 3,000
Membership: Active $2.50; Contributing $5; Sustaining & Business $15; Life $100.

Saint Francis

CHEYENNE COUNTY MUSEUM, U.S. Hwy. 36 W., Saint Francis, KS 67756. Mailing Address: P.O. Box 611, Saint Francis, KS 67756-0611. Tel.: 785-332-2504.
History Museum.
Collections: county history; personal artifacts; furnishings.
Hours & Admission Prices: Mon.-Fri. 1-4; other times by appointment.

Saint John

ST. JOHN SCIENCE MUSEUM, 312 N. Main St., Saint John, KS 67576-1733. Tel.: 620-549-3818.
Science Museum.
Collections: hands-on exhibits.
Activities: demonstrations; school groups.
Hours & Admission Prices: Call for hours; groups by appointment. No charge; donations accepted.

Saint Marys

INDIAN PAY STATION MUSEUM, 111 E. Mission, Saint Marys, KS 66536-1526. Mailing Address: Saint Marys Historical Society, P.O. Box 130, Saint Marys, KS 66536. Tel.: 785-437-6600.
Historic Building Museum: built in 1857 as an Indian Agency for the Pottawatomie; later used to receive payments for lands taken from them. Listed on the National Register of Historic Places.
Collections: early 1800 artifacts; recreated general store.
Hours & Admission Prices: Daily 1-4; other times by appointment.

Salina

ROLLING HILLS WILDLIFE ADVENTURE, 625 N. Hedville Rd., Salina, KS 67401-9764. Tel.: 785-827-9488.
E-mail: vickee@rollinghillswildlife.com
Web Site: www.rollinghillswildlife.com
Key Personnel: Dir., Kathy Tolbert; Cur., Sandy Walker; Dir. Operations, Jeff Parker; Dir. Education, Anita Butler; Dir. Devel. & Mktg., Vickee Spicer; Exec. Asst., Debra Preston; Group Sales Mgr. & Special Events, Debbie Tasker; Conference Center Mgr., Gail Vance
Zoo.
Collections: 105 species of animals.
Hours & Admission Prices: Summer: daily 8-5; winter: daily 9-5. Zoo: adults $10.95, senior citizens 65 & over $9.95, children 3-12 $5.95; children under 3 no charge. Museum: adults $9.95, senior citizens 65 & over $8.95, children 3-12 $4.95; children under 3 no charge. Combo: adults $13.95, senior citizens 65 & over $12.95, children 3-12 $7.95; children under 3 no charge. Closed New Year's Day; Christmas Eve & Day.

* **SALINA ART CENTER, (M),** 242 S. Santa Fe, Salina, KS 67401-3932. Mailing Address: Box 743, Salina, KS 67402-0743. Tel.: 785-827-1431. Fax: 785-827-0686.
E-mail: info@salinaartcenter.org
Web Site: www.salinaartcenter.org
Founded: 1978.
Congressional District: 1
Key Personnel: Pres., Sydney Soderberg; Exec. Dir. & Cur., Christopher Cook; Dir. Cinema, Heather Smith.
Personnel Profile: Full-Time Paid 5; Full-Time Volunteers 1; Part-Time Paid 5; Part-Time Volunteers 3; Interns 3.
Governing Authority: nonprofit organization. Tax-exempt: 501(c)(3).
Art Center.
Collections: temporary exhibitions.
Facilities: film theatre; classroom.
Activities: films; artist residencies; tours; lectures; concerts; outreach education; interdisciplinary adult & children's workshops & classes; hands-on Discovery Area; visual art exhibition; interactive exhibits.
Publications: exhibition catalogues; Exhibits & Programs guide; annual report.
Hours & Admission Prices: Wed.-Sat. 12-5, Sun. 1-5. No charge; donations accepted. Closed major holidays. ♿
Attendance: 29,331 (accurate)
Membership: Basic $50; Friend $100; Supporter $250; Patron $500; Sustainer $1,000; Advocate $2,500; Benefactor $5,000; Partner $10,000.

* **SMOKY HILL MUSEUM, (M),** 211 W. Iron Ave., Salina, KS 67401-2613. Mailing Address: P.O. Box 101, Salina, KS 67402-0101. Tel.: 785-309-5776. Fax: 785-826-7414.
E-mail: museum@salina.org
Web Site: www.smokyhillmuseum.org
Founded: 1983.
Congressional District: 1
Key Personnel: C.E.O., Connie Stewart; Co-Chm. (V), Lucy Larson; Dir., Susan Hawksworth; Registrar, Jennifer Toelle; Cur. Collections, Lisa Upshaw; Sec., Pauline Fallis; Vol. Coord., Haley Brown; Cur. Exhibits, Joshua Morris; Education Coord., Nona Miller; Museum Shop Mgr., Kay Carlson.
Personnel Profile: Full-Time Paid 6; Part-Time Paid 5; Part-Time Volunteers 160; Interns 2.
Governing Authority: city. Parent Institution: Salina Arts & Humanities Commission; City of Salina. Subsidiary Institution: Friends of the Smoky Hill Museum. Tax-exempt.
History Museum: housed in 1937 federal building.
Collections: history; archives.
Research Fields: history; archives.
Facilities: full size sod dugout; newly renovated permanent gallery.
Activities: tours; changing exhibitions; historical presentations; school programs.
Publications: newsletter, Heritage Express.
Hours & Admission Prices: Tues.-Fri. 12-5, Sat. 10-5, Sun. 1-5. Closed all major holidays. No charge. ♿
Attendance: 23,083 (accurate)
Membership: Friend $35; Participant $50; Patron $75-$199; Advocate $200-$499; Supporter $500-$999; Benefactor $1,000-$2,499; Partner $2,500-$4,999; Corporate $5,000 & up.

YESTERYEAR MUSEUM, 1100 W. Diamond Dr., Salina, KS 67401-9542. Tel.: 785-825-8473.
Governing Authority: nonprofit organization. Parent Institution: Central Kansas Flywheels.
History Museum.
Collections: American history & heritage; 1880s print shop; 1869 Swedish Bible; Boy Scout memorabilia; toys.
Activities: Museum Sponsors: By Gone Days in Spring; Antique Engine Show and Antique Tractor Pull in Fall.
Hours & Admission Prices: Call for hours.

Scandia

SCANDIA MUSEUM, 409 4th St., Scandia, KS 66966. Tel.: 785-335-2620.
Founded: 1947.
History Museum.
Collections: Scandinavian history & heritage; farm machinery; tools; buggies; war memorabilia; photographs; scrapbooks; genealogy.
Hours & Admission Prices: Memorial Day to Labor Day Mon.-Sat. 2-4; other times by appointment. No charge; donations accepted. ♿

Scott City

KEYSTONE GALLERY, 401 U.S. 83, Scott City, KS 67871-8013. Tel.: 620-872-2762.
Founded: 1991.
Congressional District: 1
Key Personnel: Dir., Barbara Shelton; Chm., Charles Bonner
Fossils & Art Gallery.
Collections: Kansas fossils; local history; paintings; monument rocks.
Research Fields: paleontological.
Facilities: Museum-related items for sale.
Activities: fossil hunts.
Hours & Admission Prices: Call for hours. No charge; donations accepted. Closed Thanksgiving; Christmas.
Attendance: 5,000 (estimated)

Sedan

EMMETT KELLY HISTORICAL MUSEUM, 202 E. Main, Sedan, KS 67361-1629. Tel.: 620-725-3470.
Web Site: www.emmettkellymuseum.com
Founded: 1967.
Congressional District: 5
Key Personnel: Chm. (V), Roger Floyd; Museum Shop Mgr., Darla Loyd.
Personnel Profile: Part-Time Paid 1; Part-Time Volunteers 35.
Governing Authority: municipal; museum board. Tax-exempt.
Clown & Historical Museum.
Collections: clowns; circus; decanters; county & historical items; quilts; period print shop; paintings of Chautauqua Co. artists; Civil War, World War I & II show cases; Native American artifacts; shell collection from Guam; 50 period radios & consoles.
Research Fields: circus; clowns local history.
Publications: brochures.
Hours & Admission Prices: April Tues.-Fri. 10-4, Sat. 10-12 & 1-5, Sun. 1-4; May-Oct. Tues.-Fri. 10-4, Sat. 10-12 & 1-5. No charge; donations accepted. ♿
Attendance: 1,500 (estimated)

Shawnee

JOHNSON COUNTY MUSEUM, (M), 6305 Lackman Rd., Shawnee, KS 66217-9740. Tel.: 913-715-2550. Fax: 913-715-2565. TDD: 913-782-7188.
E-mail: jcmuseum@jocogov.org
Web Site: www.jocomuseum.org
Founded: 1967.
Congressional District: 3
Key Personnel: Chm. Advisory Council (V), Nancy Wallerstein; Pres., Mindi C. Love; Cur. Collections & Exhibits, Kathy Daniels; Asst. Cur., Melissa Fisher Isaacs; Cur. Education, Erin Befort; Museum Shop Mgr., Tom McCabe; Site Mgr., Stephanie Clayton; Collections Mgr., Russ Czaplewski.
Personnel Profile: Full-Time Paid 7; Part-Time Paid 3; Part-Time Volunteers 50; Interns 3.

Governing Authority: county. Subsidiary Institution: Friends of Johnson County Museum; Museum of History; Lanesfield School Historic Site; 1950's All-Electric House. Tax-exempt.
History Museum.
Collections: Johnson County history 1820s-present; suburbia.
Research Fields: local history; suburban history.
Activities: tours; speakers; films; workshops; permanent & changing exhibits.
Publications: newsletter, The Album; book, Johnson County Kansas: A Pictorial History, 1825-2005.
Hours & Admission Prices: Tues.-Sat. 10-4:30, Sun. 1-4:30. Museum of History & Lanesfield School Historic Site: no charge; donations accepted. 1950s All-Electric House: adults $2, children 12 & under $1; discounts to Time Travelers & AASLH members. Closed legal holidays. ♿
Attendance: 54,904 (accurate)
Membership: Friend $25; Good Friend $50; Really Good Friend $100; Best Friend $250.

SHAWNEE TOWN, (M), 11501 W. 57th St., Shawnee, KS 66203-2225. Tel.: 913-248-2360. Fax: 913-248-2363.
E-mail: gclemenson@cityofshawnee.org
Web Site: www.shawneetown.org
Founded: 1966.
Congressional District: 3
Key Personnel: C.E.O., Gay L. Clemenson; Chm. (V), Les Palmer; Museum Shop Mgr., Royal Krueger.
Personnel Profile: Full-Time Paid 4; Part-Time Paid 5; Part-Time Volunteers 160.
Governing Authority: municipal. Parent Institution: City of Shawnee, Shawnee, KS. Tax-exempt.
History Museum.
Collections: history of Shawnee from 1840s to present.
Research Fields: local history.
Facilities: rental facilities for parties, meetings & weddings.
Activities: concerts; docent program; guided tours; permanent exhibit on the history of Shawnee, KS; youth & adult educational programs. Annual Events: Old Shawnee Days; Craft Fair; Barbecue Contest; Straw Hat Saturdays; Garden Party; Tomato Roll; Historical Hauntings; Christmas Around Town.
Hours & Admission Prices: March-Oct. Tues.-Sat. 10-4:30. Self-Guided Tours: adults & senior citizens $1, students $.50; discounts to AAM members & Time Travelers; members & children under 6 no charge. Closed Memorial Day; Independence Day; Labor Day. ♿
Attendance: 120,000 (estimated)
Membership: Friends $35; Business $100.

WONDERSCOPE CHILDREN'S MUSEUM OF KANSAS CITY, 5700 King, Shawnee, KS 66203-2708. Tel.: 913-287-8888. Fax: 913-268-4608.
E-mail: info@wonderscope.org
Web Site: www.wonderscope.org
Founded: 1989.
Key Personnel: C.E.O & Dir., Lauranne Hess; Chm. (V), Kevin Tubbesing.
Personnel Profile: Full-Time Paid 4; Part-Time Paid 10.
Governing Authority: Tax-exempt.
Children's Museum.
Collections: hands-on exhibits.
Activities: workshops; special events; educational programs; temporary & traveling exhibits.
Hours & Admission Prices: March-Aug. Mon.-Sat. 10-5, Sun. 12-5; Sept.-Feb. Tues.-Sat. 10-5, Sun. 12-5. Admission 3-63 $7, senior citizens 64 & over $6, children 1-2 $4; children under 1 & members no charge. Reciprocal admission to Association of Children's Museum members. Closed major holidays. ♿
Attendance: 79,398 (accurate)
Membership: Playtime $80; Wonderful $125.

Stafford

STAFFORD COUNTY HISTORICAL SOCIETY MUSEUM, 100 N. Main, Stafford, KS 67578-1343. Tel.: 620-234-5664.
E-mail: mjhathaway61@earthlink.net
Web Site: home.earthlink.net/~mjhathaway61
Founded: 1976.
Key Personnel: Pres. (V), Marion Hearn.
Personnel Profile: Full-Time Paid 1; Part-Time Volunteers 20.
Governing Authority: Tax-exempt.
Historical Society Museum & Library.
Collections: local history; personal artifacts; photographs; genealogy.
Facilities: library.
Publications: biannual newsletter, Reflections.
Hours & Admission Prices: Museum: Summer: Tues.-Thurs. 1:30-3:30, Sat. 1-3; Winter: Tues.-Thurs. 1:30-3:30; other times by appointment. Library: Mon.-Fri. 9-3:30. No charge; donations accepted.
Attendance: 919 (accurate)
Membership: Family $15; Sponsor $25; Donor $100; Contributor $250; Sustaining $500; Patron $1,000; Royal Patron $2,000.

Stockton

FRANK WALKER MUSEUM, 921 S. Cedar, Stockton, KS 67669. Tel.: 785-425-7217.
Governing Authority: Parent Institution: Rooks County Historical Society.
History Museum.
Collections: local history & culture; dolls; Lorenzo Fuller's instruments; medical equipment; farm tools; clothing; machinery.
Hours & Admission Prices: Tues., Thurs. & Sat. 10-4; other times by appointment. No charge; donations accepted.

Studley

COTTONWOOD RANCH, 14432 E. US Hwy. 24, Studley, KS 67740-4135. Mailing Address: Rte. 1, Box 57M, Studley, KS 67740. Tel.: 785-627-5866.
Governing Authority: Parent Institution: Kansas State Historical Society.
Historic Site: built by John Fenton Pratt from 1885-1896.
Collections: Pratt family history; photographs; personal artifacts; period furnishings.
Hours & Admission Prices: Jan. 5-Feb. Fri.-Sat. 10-4, Sun. 1-4; March-Nov. Wed.-Sat. 9-5, Sun. 1-5. Adults $2, seniors & students $1; active military & children under 5 no charge. Closed state holidays. ♿

Sublette

HASKELL COUNTY HISTORICAL SOCIETY, North Fairground Rd., Sublette, KS 67877. Mailing Address: P.O. Box 101, Sublette, KS 67877-0101. Tel.: 620-675-8344.
Formerly: The Haskell County Historical Museum
Founded: 1983.
Congressional District: 1
Key Personnel: Pres. (V), James Groth; Dir., Darlene Groth.
Personnel Profile: Full-Time Paid 1.
Governing Authority: private; nonprofit organization. Tax-exempt: 501(c)(3).
General Museum.
Collections: artifacts; rocks & minerals; American Indian artifacts.
Facilities: library; 10,000 sq. ft. exhibit space.
Activities: workshops; meetings.
Hours & Admission Prices: Tues.-Sat. 1-5. No charge; donations accepted. Closed major holidays ♿
Attendance: 650 (accurate)
Membership: Annual $5; Sustaining $15; Life $100.

Sylvan Grove

YESTERDAY HOUSE MUSEUM, 118 S. Main St., Sylvan Grove, KS 67481. Mailing Address: P.O. Box 68, Sylvan Grove, KS 67481. Tel.: 785-526-7270.
Governing Authority: Parent Institution: Sylvan Grove Historical Society.
History Museum.
Collections: local history & culture; photographs; period furnishings; barbed wire.
Hours & Admission Prices: May-Oct. Sat.-Sun. 1-5; other times by appointment.

Syracuse

HAMILTON COUNTY MUSEUM, Hwy. 50 & Gates St., Syracuse, KS 67878. Mailing Address: 102 N. Gates, P.O. Box 923, Syracuse, KS 67878-0923. Tel.: 620-384-7496.
E-mail: historic@pld.com
Founded: 1966.
Congressional District: 122
Key Personnel: Dir., Joanice Jantz.
Personnel Profile: Full-Time Paid 1.
Governing Authority: bd. Parent Institution: Hamilton County Historical Society.
History Museum.
Collections: local history & culture; photographs; period furnishings; personal artifacts; Native American; barber shop; general store; guns; military artifacts.
Hours & Admission Prices: Tues.-Sat. 9-12 & 1-4. No charge; donations accepted. Closed New Year's Day; Labor Day; Thanksgiving; Christmas.
Attendance: 1,000 (estimated)

Membership: Annual $5; Lifetime $100.

Tonganoxie

TONGANOXIE COMMUNITY HISTORICAL SOCIETY, 201 W. Washington St., Tonganoxie, KS 66086. Mailing Address: P.O. Box 785, Tonganoxie, KS 66086-0785. Tel.: 913-369-3835.
Founded: 1981.
Personnel Profile: Part-Time Volunteers 15.
Local History Museum.
Collections: local history & culture; photographs; period furnishings & clothing; personal artifacts.
Activities: educational programs.
Hours & Admission Prices: April-Oct. Wed. 9-12, Sun. 1-4. No charge; donations accepted. ♿
Attendance: 376 (estimated)
Membership: Single $10; Family $15; Life $100.

Topeka

ALICE C. SABATINI GALLERY-TOPEKA AND SHAWNEE COUNTY PUBLIC LIBRARY, (M), 1515 W. 10th, Topeka, KS 66604-1304. Tel.: 785-580-4515 & 4400. Fax: 785-580-4496.
E-mail: sbest@tscpl.org
Web Site: www.tscpl.org
Founded: 1870.
Congressional District: 2
Key Personnel: C.E.O., Gina Millsap; Coord., Kari Zimmerman; Gallery Dir., Sherry L. Best; Deputy Dir., Robert Banks; Museum Shop Mgr., Bobbie Pfeiffer.
Personnel Profile: Full-Time Paid 4; Part-Time Volunteers 11.
Governing Authority: municipal. Tax-exempt. 170(b)(1)(A).
Fine Arts Gallery.
Collections: period & contemporary glass paperweights; art Nouveau glass & ceramics; contemporary ceramics; American prints; Kansas paintings, drawings, photography, fiber, & sculpture; Topeka collectors: West African sculpture, East African beadwork, southwestern reliquary figures, Chinese pewters, & books as art; archives.
Major Exhibits: Africa Everyday, 1/10-2/10; Larry Peters & Barbara Waterman-Peters, 3/10-4/10; The Color of Water - Annual Art Exhibit for Children, 5/10-6/10; Convergence: Kansas Landscape, 7/10-9/10; The Painted Image 3, 10/10-1/11.
Research Fields: glass & ceramics.
Facilities: 30,000-vol. library on the arts; reading room.
Activities: lectures; 1/2-inch videotapes; gallery talks; concerts; inter-museum loan & temporary exhibitions.
Hours & Admission Prices: Memorial Day-Labor Day Mon.-Fri. 9-9, Sat. 9-6; Sept.-May Mon.-Fri. 9-9, Sat. 9-6, Sun. 12-9. No charge; donations accepted. Closed New Year's Day; Washington's Birthday; Memorial Day; Independence Day; Veterans Day; Christmas. ♿
Attendance: 28,000 (estimated)
Membership: General Reader $5; Avid Reader $10; Book Worm $25; Researcher $50; Library Friends $5-$100; Bibliophile $100; Life Member $2,000.

BROWN V. BOARD OF EDUCATION NATIONAL HISTORIC SITE, 1515 S.E. Monroe St., Topeka, KS 66612-1143. Tel.: 785-354-4273.
Web Site: www.nps.gov/brvb
Historic Site.
Collections: artifacts & memorabilia from the Supreme Court decision to end segregation.
Hours & Admission Prices: Daily 9-5. No charge; donations accepted. Closed New Year's Day; Thanksgiving; Christmas.

CHARLES CURTIS HOUSE MUSEUM, 1101 SW Topeka Blvd., Topeka, KS 66612-1602. Tel.: 785-597-5380 & 357-1371.
Web Site: www.charlescurtismuseum.com
Historic House: former home of Senator Charles Curtis; built in 1879.
Collections: Curtis family history; personal artifacts; period furnishings.
Hours & Admission Prices: Sat. 11-3; other times by appointment. Adults $5.

COMBAT AIR MUSEUM, INC., Forbes Field, J St., Hangar 602, Topeka, KS 66619. Mailing Address: P.O. Box 19142, Topeka, KS 66619-0142. Tel.: 785-862-3303. Fax: 785-862-3304.
E-mail: combatairmuseum@aol.com
Web Site: www.combatairmuseum.org
Founded: 1976.
Congressional District: 2
Key Personnel: Chm. & Pres., Gene Howerter.
Personnel Profile: Full-Time Paid 1; Part-Time Paid 1; Part-Time Volunteers 35.
Governing Authority: nonprofit organization. Tax-exempt: 501(c)(3).
Military Aviation Museum: 1942 Topeka Army Air Field-later Forbes AFB, now Forbes Field.
Collections: military aircraft, weapons, uniforms & vehicles; insignia; photographs; medals; period rooms. Historic Aircraft: JN-4D Jenny (replica); MIG-15; MIG-17; 1939 O-47B; C-47 Skytrain; Harvard MK IV; T-33A; F-86H Sabre; US-2A Tracker; EC-121T Super Constellation; F-84F Thunderstreak; F11F-1 Tiger, Blue Angel #5; F-101B Voodoo; RU-8D Seminole; F-4D Phantom; F3D Skyknight; UH-1H Iroquois Huey; UH-1M Iroquois Huey; CH-54 Tarhe Sky Crane; NCH-53 Sea Stallion; F-105D Thunderchief; TA-4J Skyhawk; Meyers OTW #1; SNB-5; UC-61K Forwarder; F9F-5 Panther; BF-109 Movie Mockup; 1914 Taube (1/2 scale replica); Hiller UH-12A; BT-13A Valiant; MiG-21.
Facilities: Gift items for sale.
Activities: guided tours.
Publications: bimonthly newsletter, Plane Talk.
Hours & Admission Prices: Jan.-Feb. daily 12-4:30; March-Dec. Mon.-Sat. 9-4:30, Sun. 12-4:30; last admission 3:30. Adults $6, active military & children 6-17 $4; children under 6 & members no charge. Closed New Year's Day; Easter; Thanksgiving; Christmas. ♿
Attendance: 10,000 (accurate)
Membership: Individual $30; Family $40; Lifetime $500.

THE GREAT OVERLAND STATION, 701 N. Kansas Ave., Topeka, KS 66608-1260. Mailing Address: P.O. Box 8792, Topeka, KS 66608-0792. Tel.: 785-232-5533. Fax: 785-232-6259.
E-mail: info@greatoverlandstation.com
Web Site: greatoverlandstation.com
Founded: 2000.
Congressional District: 2
Key Personnel: Exec. Dir., Bette Allen; Chm., Ray Harvey; Dir. Capital Campaign, Beth Fager; Museum Shop Mgr., Trisha Smith; Business Mgr., Jeannie Rose.
Personnel Profile: Full-Time Paid 2; Part-Time Paid 6; Part-Time Volunteers 40.
Governing Authority: private; nonprofit organization. Parent Institution: Railroad Heritage, Inc. Tax-exempt: 501(c)(3).
Railroad Heritage Museum: housed in historic railroad station.
Collections: people of the railroad; Oregon Trail & Santa Fe Railway history; local history; underground railroad; Vice President Charles Curtis.
Activities: rental facilities; tours; Harvey house luncheons & tours; member events. Museum Sponsors: Gala Event; Topeka Railroad Festival.
Publications: newsletter.
Hours & Admission Prices: Tues.-Sun. call for hours. Adults $4, seniors $3, children $2; discounts to military; members no charge. Closed holidays. ♿
Attendance: 20,000 (accurate)
Membership: Family $35; Bronze $100; Silver $250; Gold $500; Platinum $1,000; Diamond $2,500.

HOLLEY MUSEUM OF MILITARY HISTORY, The Ramada Hotel, 6th & Jefferson, Topeka, KS 66606. Mailing Address: 420 SE 6th Ave., Topeka, KS 66607-1181. Tel.: 785-272-6204. Fax: 785-224-5034.
Web Site: holleymuseum.org
Key Personnel: Cur., Jane Holley
Military History Museum.
Collections: military artifacts including WWI & WWII; U.S. Navy; Air Force One; Kansas war heroes.
Hours & Admission Prices: Daily 10-8.

* **KANSAS MUSEUM OF HISTORY, (M),** 6425 S.W. Sixth St., Topeka, KS 66615-1099. Tel.: 785-272-8681, ext. 401. Fax: 785-272-8682.
Web Site: www.kshs.org
Founded: 1875.
Congressional District: 2
Key Personnel: Exec. Dir. Kansas State Historical Society, Jennie Chinn; Chm. (V), Brian Moline; Pres. (V), Hal Ross; Museum Dir., Robert J. Keckeisen; Asst. Dir., Rebecca J. Martin; Cur., Blair D. Tarr; Cur., Laura Vannorsdel; Exhibits Dir., Chris Prouty; Education & Outreach Dir., Mary Madden; Registrar, Sarah Miller; Museum Shop Mgr., Julie Schloetzer.
Personnel Profile: Full-Time Paid 19; Part-Time Paid 2; Part-Time Volunteers 130; Interns 2.
Governing Authority: state. Parent Institution: Kansas State Historical Society. Branch Museums: 1851 Kaw Mission, Council Grove; 1855 First Territorial Capitol of Kansas, Fort Riley; 1857 Hollenberg Pony Express Station, Hanover; 1846 Native American Heritage Museum, Highland; 1838 Shawnee Mission, Kansas City; Pawnee Indian Village, Republic; 1865 Fort Hays & Frontier Historical Park, Hays; 1854 John Brown Memorial Park,

Osawatomie; 1870 Marais des Cygnes Massacre Memorial Park, Pleasanton; 1857 Grinter Place, Kansas City; 1860 Goodnow House, Manhattan; Cottonwood Ranch, Studley; Constitution Hall, Lecompton. Tax-exempt: 501(c)(3).
History Museum.
Collections: ethnological & archaeological materials; costumes; decorative arts; furniture; textiles; transportation vehicles; military equipage; agricultural implements; tools representing 19th-century trades, crafts, paintings, drawings & prints.
Research Fields: social, cultural, political, railroad & military history, material culture of Kansas & the West.
Facilities: Museum-related items for sale.
Activities: guided tours; permanent, temporary & traveling exhibitions; adult & youth workshops; field trips; lectures; school loan service; slide & tape programs; craft demonstrations; films; internship program with Kansas colleges & universities; traveling resource trunk program for schools.
Publications: occasional exhibit catalogs; culture essays.
Hours & Admission Prices: Museum: Tues.-Sat. 9-5, Sun. 1-5. Historic Sites: Tues.-Sat. 10-5, Sun. 1-5. Adults $5, seniors $4, students $3; members no charge. Closed New Year's Day; Thanksgiving; Christmas; state holidays. ♿
Attendance: 89,829 (accurate)
Membership: Student $15; Individual & Educational Institution $25; Family $35; Contributor $50; Sustainer $100; Sponsor $250; Benefactor $1,000 & up.

KANSAS STATE ARCHIVES, Center for Historical Research, Reference Dept., 6425 S.W. Sixth Ave., Topeka, KS 66615-1099. Tel.: 785-272-8681, ext. 117.
Archives.
Collections: local history & culture; genealogical records; photographs; newspapers; government & military records; maps.
Hours & Admission Prices: Call for hours.

*** MULVANE ART MUSEUM, (M),** 17th & Jewell Sts., Topeka, KS 66621-1150. Tel.: 785-670-1124. Fax: 785-670-1329.
E-mail: mulvane.info@washburn.edu
Web Site: www.washburn.edu/mulvane
Founded: 1922.
Congressional District: 2
Key Personnel: Dir., Cindi Morrison; Cur. Collections & Exhibitions, Carol Emert; Coord. Education, Brogan Lasley; Assoc. Education Coord., Kandis Barker; Preparator, Michael Hager; Office Asst., Delene VanSickel.
Personnel Profile: Full-Time Paid 6; Part-Time Paid 1; Part-Time Volunteers 150; Interns 1.
Governing Authority: university. Parent Institution: Washburn University of Topeka. Tax-exempt.
Art Museum.
Collections: 19th- to 21st-century American art; 16th- to 20th-century European prints; contemporary representational, figurative & narrative work; young & emerging eastern Kansas artists.
Research Fields: contemporary representational, figurative and narrative work in all media.
Facilities: William I. Koch Fine Arts Library located in university's Mabee Library; ArtLab. Museum-related items for sale.
Activities: lectures, gallery talks & guided tours; creative writing readings; music events; art after school & art in-school outreach programs; fall, spring & summer art classes for K-adult. Annual Events: Mountain Plains Fine Art Fair.
Publications: Exhibition catalogues; brochures; newsletter; annual report.
Hours & Admission Prices: Tues. 10-7, Wed.-Fri. 10-5, Sat.-Sun. 1-4. No charge; donations accepted. Closed major holidays. ♿
Attendance: 30,000 (accurate)
Membership: Student & Senior Citizen $25; Individual $35; Young Contemporaries $55-$75; Dual & Family $60; Director's Circle $125; Silver Circle $250; Gold Circle $500; Platinum Circle $1,000.

MUSEUM OF THE KANSAS NATIONAL GUARD, 6700 S.W. Topeka Blvd., Topeka, KS 66619-1401. Tel.: 785-862-1020.
E-mail: kngmuseum@aol.com
Web Site: www.kansasguardmuseum.org
Military Museum.
Collections: Kansas National Guard history & heritage; personal artifacts; period furnishings; military uniforms, weapons & equipment; medals; photographs.
Hours & Admission Prices: Tues.-Sat. 10-4.

OLD PRAIRIE TOWN AT WARD-MEADE HISTORIC SITE, 124 N.W. Fillmore, Topeka, KS 66606-1171. Tel.: 785-368-3888. Fax: 785-368-3890.
E-mail: sleeth@topeka.org
Web Site: www.topeka.org
Formerly: Historic Ward-Meade Park
Key Personnel: Exec. Dir., Sara Leeth.
Personnel Profile: Full-Time Paid 4; Part-Time Paid 7; Part-Time Volunteers 100.
Governing Authority: municipal; nonprofit. Parent Institution: City of Topeka.
History Museum.
Collections: clothing; toys; furniture; art work; mid-1800s to 1900s physician's & dentist's equipment; 1800s church; replica log cabin; drugstore; dentist & physician's office; general store. Historic Building: 1870s Victorian home.
Facilities: botanical garden; 35-seat soda fountain; visitor center. Museum-related items for sale.
Activities: docent program; guided tours. Annual Events: Apple Festival; A Night Under the Stars Campout; summer concert; Scary on the Prairie in October; Holiday Happenings.
Publications: bimonthly newsletter, Prairie Sun.
Hours & Admission Prices: Park: daily 8am to dusk. General Store & Drugstore: Mon.-Sat. 10-4, Sun. 12-4. Guided Tours: Mon.-Fri. 10, 12 & 2, Sat.-Sun. 12 & 2. Tours: adults $4.50, senior citizens $4, children 6-12 $2; discounts to school groups; children under 5 & botanical garden no charge. Stores closed federal holidays. ♿
Attendance: 70,000 (estimated)

TOPEKA ZOOLOGICAL PARK, 635 S.W. Gage Blvd., Topeka, KS 66606-2066. Tel.: 785-368-9180. Fax: 785-368-9152.
E-mail: zoo@topeka.org
Web Site: www.topeka.org/zoo
Founded: 1933.
Congressional District: 2
Key Personnel: Dir. Zoo, Michael D. Coker.
Personnel Profile: Full-Time Paid 36; Full-Time Volunteers 1; Part-Time Paid 2; Part-Time Volunteers 100; Interns 3.
Governing Authority: municipal. Parent Institution: City of Topeka. Tax-exempt: 170(b)(1)(A).
Zoo.
Collections: mammals; birds; reptiles; amphibians; fish; invertebrates; natural history collection of skulls; egg shells.
Research Fields: zoo animal nutrition, behavior & reproduction.
Facilities: 1,000-vol. reference library; tropical rain forest; great ape facility; small animal exhibit; classroom; concessions. Zoo-related items for sale.
Activities: guided tours; Discovery Carts; films; TV & radio programs; organized classes for children & adults; docent program; Explorer Post; audio-visual loans to teachers.
Publications: magazine published 3 times annually, Zooreka.
Hours & Admission Prices: Daily 9-5. Adults $5.25, senior citizens $4.25, children 3-12 $3.75; discounts to AZA members; members, other zoo societies, children 2 & under no charge. Closed New Year's Day; Christmas. ♿
Attendance: 180,000 (accurate)
Membership: Baby Sitter $12; Senior Citizen $20; Individual $30; Single Parents $35; Family $50; Special Friend $60; Zoo Buff $85; Super Zoo Buff $135;

Ulysses

GRANT COUNTY MUSEUM AKA HISTORIC ADOBE MUSEUM, (M), 300 E. Oklahoma, Ulysses, KS 67880-2542. Mailing Address: P.O. Box 906, Ulysses, KS 67880-0906. Tel.: 620-356-3009. Fax: 620-356-5082.
E-mail: ulyksmus@pld.com
Web Site: www.historicadobemuseum.org
Founded: 1978.
Congressional District: 1
Key Personnel: Dir. & Chm. (V), Ginger Anthony; Pres. (V), Sheryl Deyoe; Cur., Marlene Calhoun; Treas., Jim Hickok.
Personnel Profile: Full-Time Paid 3; Part-Time Paid 1; Part-Time Volunteers 1.
Governing Authority: county. private; nonprofit organization. Tax-exempt: 501(c)(3).
General Museum.
Collections: Indian artifacts; turn of the century furnishings; toys; clothing; quilts; local & family history.
Activities: guided tours; formal education programs for children.
Hours & Admission Prices: Mon.-Fri. 10-5, Sat.-Sun. 1-5. No charge; donations accepted. Closed holidays. ♿
Attendance: 9,000 (estimated)
Membership: Life $25.

Wakefield

WAKEFIELD MUSEUM ASSOCIATION, 604 Sixth St., Wakefield, KS 67487-9155. Mailing Address: 901 10th St., Wakefield, KS 67487-9155. Tel.: 785-461-5516.
E-mail: wakefieldmuseum@oz-online.net
Founded: 1973.
Key Personnel: Pres. & Cur., Lorraine Cowell; Treas., Barbara McGee.
Personnel Profile: Part-Time Paid 1; Part-Time Volunteers 58.
Governing Authority: private; nonprofit organization. Subsidiary Museums: Sunnyslope School, Wakefield, KS; Saints John & George Episcopal Church, Wakefield, KS; Republican Valley Farm Museum. Tax-exempt.
General Museum.
Collections: history of Wakefield; genealogy files; music; textiles; hats; toys; furniture; governor's desk & clothing; books; pictures; newspapers.
Research Fields: genealogy.
Facilities: library. Museum-related items for sale.
Activities: guided tours for children; temporary exhibitions. Annual Event: Christmas Bazaar.
Publications: winter newsletter, Christmas Bazaar; spring newsletter, Annual Newsletter.
Hours & Admission Prices: Jan.-March Sat.-Sun. 1-4; April-Dec. Wed.-Sun. 1-4. No charge; donations accepted. Closed New Year's Day; Thanksgiving; Christmas; Easter. ♿
Attendance: 841 (accurate)
Membership: Individual $7.50; Family $15.

Wamego

THE COLUMBIAN THEATRE, MUSEUM & ART CENTER, 521 Lincoln Ave., Wamego, KS 66547-1633. Tel.: 785-456-2029. Fax: 785-456-9498.
E-mail: boxoffice@columbiantheatre.com
Web Site: columbiantheatre.com/main.asp
Founded: 1990.
Congressional District: 2
Key Personnel: Foundation Pres., Lance White; Exec. Dir., Jim Ginavan.
Personnel Profile: Full-Time Paid 4; Part-Time Paid 25; Part-Time Volunteers 200.
Governing Authority: nonprofit organization. Tax-exempt: 501(c)(3).
Decorative Arts Museum; housed in 1895 building to display the 1893 Chicago World's Fair paintings bought by J.C. Rogers.
Collections: six historic 16' x 11' murals that hung in the rotunda of the government building at the 1893 Chicago World's Fair, representing the promise & prosperity of America at the end of the 19th century.
Research Fields:
Activities: workshops.
Hours & Admission Prices: Tues.-Fri. 10-5, Sat. 10-3. No charge; donations accepted. Closed New Year's Day; Easter; Thanksgiving; Christmas. ♿
Attendance: 60,000 (estimated)
Membership: Individual $40; Family $75; Columbian Assets $150; Corporate Eagles $250; Roger's Circle $500; Roger's Circle Patron $1,500.

OZ MUSEUM, 511 Lincoln, Wamego, KS 66547-1633. Tel.: 866-458-TOTO (toll free). Fax: 785-458-8687.
E-mail: ozmuseum@wamego.net
Web Site: www.ozmuseum.com
Founded: 2003.
Governing Authority: Parent Institution: The Columbian Theater Foundation. Tax-exempt: 501(c)(3).
Movie Museum.
Collections: over 2,000 artifacts from 1900 to present; Wizard of Oz memorabilia; early silent films; Baum books; Oz Parker Brothers board games.
Facilities: Museum-related items for sale.
Hours & Admission Prices: Mon.-Sat. 10-5, Sun. 12-5. Adults 13 & over $7, children 4-12 $4; discounts to groups & military; children 3 & under no charge.

Washington

WASHINGTON COUNTY HISTORICAL SOCIETY, 216 Ballard, Washington, KS 66968-1901. Mailing Address: P.O. Box 31, Washington, KS 66968-0031. Tel.: 785-325-2198.
Founded: 1982.
Key Personnel: Pres. (V), Jack Barley; Editor of Newsletter, Librarian & Genealogy, Jo Rippe; Treas., Arlene Dague; Archivist & Genealogy, Mary Alice Pacey.
Personnel Profile: Part-Time Volunteers 27.
Governing Authority: county. Tax-exempt: 501(c)(3).
Historical Society Museum.
Collections: artifacts from the 1860s to 2000s.
Research Fields: genealogy.
Publications: quarterly newsletter.
Hours & Admission Prices: Mon.-Fri. 9-4, Sun. 1-4. No charge; donations accepted. Closed New Year's Day; Thanksgiving; Christmas. ♿
Attendance: 2,500 (accurate)
Membership: Individual & Family $10; Life $100; Life Couple $150.

Wellington

CHISHOLM TRAIL MUSEUM, 502 N. Washington, Wellington, KS 67152-4061. Tel.: 620-326-3820 & 7466.
Founded: 1964.
Congressional District: 4
Key Personnel: Pres. (V), Richard M. Gilfillan; Sec., Nancy McNett; Treas., Colleen Carson; Cur. Archives & Librarian, Doris Dwyer.
Personnel Profile: Part-Time Volunteers 8.
Governing Authority: nonprofit. Tax-exempt: 170(b)(1)(A).
History Museum: housed in first hospital in Wellington.
Collections: china; glass; silver; folk art; costumes; toys & dolls; parlor; school room; old kitchen; barber shop; doctor's office; military; grandmother's room; woolly mammoth skull & bones; cattle trail artifacts & history.
Research Fields: genealogy.
Facilities: 600-vol. library of old & rare books; 8,000 genealogical & historical printed items about Wellington & Sumner County available on premises under supervision. Handwork, Kansas books & pioneer curios for sale.
Activities: guided tours; gallery talks; permanent & temporary exhibitions.
Hours & Admission Prices: mid-April to Memorial Day Sat.-Sun. 1-4; June-Oct. daily 1-4, Nov. Sat.-Sun 1-4. No charge; donations accepted.
Attendance: 2,000 (estimated)
Membership: Annual $10; Patron $100.

Wichita

BOTANICA, THE WICHITA GARDENS, 701 Amidon, Wichita, KS 67203-3199. Tel.: 316-264-0448. Fax: 316-264-0587.
E-mail: mmiller@botanica.org
Web Site: www.botanica.org
Founded: 1985.
Congressional District: 4
Key Personnel: C.E.O., Marty Miller; Pres. (V), Peter Salmeron; Cur., Pat McKernan; Public Rels., Mia Jenkins; Volunteer Coord., Carrie Greene; Facilities Coord., Linda Keller; Memberships, Kathy Scott; Dir. Finance, Paula Eaglert.
Personnel Profile: Full-Time Paid 13; Part-Time Paid 4; Part-Time Volunteers 350; Interns 3.
Governing Authority: municipal; nonprofit organization. Tax-exempt: 501(c)(3).
Botanical Gardens.
Collections: annual & perennial plants; sculptures.
Facilities: 2,700-vol. reference library available to public; 300-seat auditorium. Cards, china, tools, yard ornaments & jewelry for sale.
Activities: guided tours; lectures; organized education programs; summer concerts; docent program. Museum Sponsors: Christmas Display; Poster Contest; photo competition; River Festival Garden Party; Art Show & Dinner Gala in the Gardens.
Publications: newsletter; magazine.
Hours & Admission Prices: April-Oct. Mon.-Sat. 9-5, Sun. 1-5; Nov.-March Mon.-Fri. 9-5. Adults $6.50, seniors $5, students & children 2-12 $3; discounts to active military, American Horticultural Society & American Public Garden Assoc. members; children under 2 & members no charge. Closed New Year's Day; Thanksgiving; Christmas. ♿
Attendance: 106,000 (accurate)
Membership: Individual Plus One $45; Family $55; Family Plus One $70.

EXPLORATION PLACE, INC., 300 N. McLean Blvd., Wichita, KS 67203-5901. Tel.: 316-263-3373. Fax: 316-263-4545.
Web Site: www.exploration.org
Formerly: Exploration Place, Inc. dba the Children's Museum of Wichita
Founded: 1984.
Congressional District: 4
Key Personnel: Pres., Alberto C. Meloni; Chm., Vera Bothner; Dir. Communications, Christina Bluml; Dir. Devel., Dion Brown; Dir. Exhibits & Technical Svcs., Traci Kallhoff; Museum Shop Mgr., John Foote.
Personnel Profile: Full-Time Paid 32; Part-Time Paid 47; Part-Time Volunteers 185; Interns 3.
Governing Authority: private; not-for-profit organization. Tax-exempt: 501(c)(3).
Science Museum.
Collections: interactive exhibits.

Facilities: interactive exhibits and Presentation Theatre, KSN-TV WeatherLab; CyberDome Theatre; MiniGolf course; Exploration Park.
Activities: interactive exhibits.
Publications: quarterly, newsletter for annual Passport Holders.
Hours & Admission Prices: Sun.-Mon. 12-5, Tues.-Wed. 10-5, Thurs.-Sat. 10-8. Adults 16-64 $8, senior citizens 65 & over $7.50, youth 5-15 $6, children 2-4 $3. Minigolf, CyberDome Theater or Simulation Center: $2; discounts to groups of 15 or more. Closed Thanksgiving; Christmas. ♿
Attendance: 273,116 (accurate)
Membership: Individual Explorer Passports: Children 2-4 $7; Youth 5-15 $18; Seniors 65 & over $23; Adults 16-64 $25.

GREAT PLAINS TRANSPORTATION MUSEUM, 700 E. Douglas, Wichita, KS 67202-3506. Tel.: 316-263-0944.
Web Site: www.gptm.us
Founded: 1983.
Congressional District: 4
Key Personnel: Vice Pres., Steve Corp; Pres. (V), John Gries; Financial Dir., Gale Meek; Public Rels., Affairs & Devel., J. Harvey Koehn; Membership, Fred Tefft; Security, Norman Walters; Museum Shop Mgr., David Meek.
Personnel Profile: Part-Time Volunteers 20.
Governing Authority: private; nonprofit organization. Parent Institution: Wichita Chapter-National Railway Historical Society. Tax-exempt: 501(c)(3).
Transportation Museum.
Collections: locomotives; rolling stock; railroad prints, signs, lanterns, & tools.
Facilities: 2,000-vol. library of railroad history; 50,800 sq. ft. exhibit space. Museum-related items for sale.
Activities: guided tours; loan & temporary exhibitions. Museum Sponsors: Train Show with Model R.R. Hobiests.
Publications: monthly newsletter, Great Plains Dispatcher.
Hours & Admission Prices: April-Oct. Sat. 9-4, Sun. 1-4; Nov.-March Sat. 9-4. Adults $5, children 3-12 $3; children under 3 no charge. Closed Christmas.
Attendance: 2,979 (accurate)
Membership: Regular $20; Family $30.

THE KANSAS AFRICAN AMERICAN MUSEUM, 601 N. Water St., Wichita, KS 67203-3833. Tel.: 316-262-7651. Fax: 316-265-6953.
E-mail: tkaam1@aol.com
Web Site: tkaam.org
Founded: 1972.
Congressional District: 4
Key Personnel: Interim Exec. Dir., Lisa Dodson; Pres. (V), Carol Cole.
Personnel Profile: Full-Time Paid 2; Part-Time Paid 2.
Governing Authority: private; nonprofit organization. Tax-exempt.
Art & Culture Museum.
Collections: documents, programs & visual art forms of African American life & culture.
Facilities: 500-vol. library.
Hours & Admission Prices: Tues.-Fri. 10-5, Sun. 2-6. No charge; donations accepted. Guided tours: $2.
Attendance: 12,000 (estimated)
Membership: The Cradle Roll Club $20; The Live Wire Class $35; Mission Club $50; Friendship Club $100; Missionary Society $350; Calvary Club $500; Harmony Motion Club $1,000; Trustee Club $5,000.

KANSAS AVIATION MUSEUM, (M), 3350 George Washington Blvd., Wichita, KS 67210-2194. Tel.: 316-683-9242. Fax: 316-683-0573.
E-mail: ksaviation@kansasaviationmuseum.org
Web Site: www.kansasaviationmuseum.org
Founded: 1990.
Congressional District: 4
Key Personnel: Dir., Lon Smith; Pres. (V), Tim Bonnell, Sr.
Personnel Profile: Full-Time Paid 3; Part-Time Paid 1; Part-Time Volunteers 125.
Governing Authority: nonprofit organization. Tax-exempt: 501(c)(3).
Aviation Museum: housed in c.1935 art deco municipal air terminal administration building.
Collections: vintage airplanes manufactured in Kansas; photographic collection of early development of aviation industry.
Facilities: library of books, manuals & videos; 20,000 sq. ft. exhibit space. Museum-related items for sale.
Activities: guided tours. Museum Sponsors: Wright Brothers celebration in November.
Publications: quarterly newsletter; booklet, Prairie Runways; various brochures.
Hours & Admission Prices: Tues.-Sat. 9-5. Adults $7, seniors 60 & over and military $6, children 4-12 $5; discounts to AAA members; children under 3 no charge. Closed holidays.
Attendance: 12,000 (accurate)
Membership: Student $20; Individual $50; Family & Grandparent $80; Crew $100-$300; Co-Pilot $300-$1,000; Pilot $1,000-$3,000; Wing Leader $3,000-$5,000; Commander $5,000-$10,000.

KANSAS SPORTS HALL OF FAME, 238 N. Mead St., Wichita, KS 67202-2708. Tel.: 316-262-2038. Fax: 316-263-2539.
Web Site: www.kshof.org
Founded: 1961.
Key Personnel: Pres. & C.E.O., Ted Hayes; Office Mgr., Laura Hartley; Museum Mgr., Mark Kenny; Events & Communications Mgr., Neal Smith.
Personnel Profile: Full-Time Paid 3; Part-Time Paid 2.
Governing Authority: Tax-exempt.
Sports Museum.
Collections: Kansas sports heroes; sports history; photographs.
Activities: induction ceremony; rental facilities; virtual sports game.
Hours & Admission Prices: Tues.-Sat. 10-5, Sun. 1-5. Adults $7, students K-12 & seniors $6; discounts to members, AARP, AAA members & military; children under 6 no charge. Closed New Year's Day; Easter; Thanksgiving; Christmas. ♿
Attendance: 10,000 (accurate)
Membership: Individual $25; Family $75.

MID-AMERICA ALL INDIAN CENTER, 650 N. Seneca, Wichita, KS 67203-3204. Tel.: 316-262-5221. Fax: 316-262-4216.
Web Site: www.theindiancenter.org
Founded: 1975.
Congressional District: 4
Key Personnel: C.E.O., John DeAngelo; Chm. (V), Newman Washington; Dir. Operations, Chris Dendurent; Facilities Operational Dir., April Scott.
Personnel Profile: Full-Time Paid 1; Part-Time Volunteers 5.
Governing Authority: nonprofit organization. Parent Institution: City of Wichita. Tax-exempt: 170(b)(1)(A), 501(c)(3), 509(c)(2).
Native American Museum: located on the site of old Indian council grounds.
Collections: Native American art & artifacts from North America, specializing in traditional Plains artifacts & art, contemporary works & paintings.
Research Fields: Native American life, art & religion; life & works of Blackbear Bosin; life & works of other plains artists.
Facilities: 1,250-vol. library of books pertaining to Native Americans available for use on premises only; Blackbear Resource Center. Native American arts & crafts for sale.
Activities: guided tours; lectures; gallery talks; rental gallery; docent program.
Publications: The Keeper of the Plains.
Hours & Admission Prices: Tues.-Sat. 10-4. Adults $7, seniors 55 & over $5, children 6-12 $3, children under 6 no charge. Closed New Year's Eve & Day; Easter; Thanksgiving; Christmas. ♿
Attendance: 60,000 (estimated)
Membership: Individual $25; Family $35; Contributor $50; Friend $100; Patron $250; Benefactor $500 & up.

MIDWEST HISTORICAL AND GENEALOGICAL LIBRARY, 1203 N. Main, Wichita, KS 67203-3614. Mailing Address: P.O. Box 1121, Wichita, KS 67201-1121. Tel.: 316-264-3611.
Library.
Collections: local history & culture; genealogical records; books; magazines; manuscripts; photographs.
Hours & Admission Prices: Call for hours.

MUSEUM OF WORLD TREASURES, (M), 835 E. First, Wichita, KS 67202-2791. Tel.: 316-263-1311.
Web Site: www.worldtreasures.org/
Founded: 2001.
Key Personnel: Founder, Dr. Jon Kardatzke; Pres. & C.E.O., Mike Noller; Operations Mgr., Ken Reavis; Dir. Education, Danielle Ricklefs; Dir. Collections, LaWanda Smith; Dir. Business Devel., Stacey Boyd.
Personnel Profile: Full-Time Paid 5; Full-Time Volunteers 1; Part-Time Paid 8; Part-Time Volunteers 10; Interns 30.
Governing Authority: nonprofit organization. Tax-exempt.
General Museum.
Collections: prehistoric animals & cultures; early civilizations; meteorites & crystals; Presidents; European Royalty; Civil War to Vietnam War artifacts; Wichita Sports Hall of Fame; Old West; Hollywood celebrities.
Facilities: music room; youth activity center. Museum-related items for sale.
Activities: guided tours; birthday parties; club & business meetings; special events.
Hours & Admission Prices: Mon.-Sat. 10-5, Sun. 12-5. Adults 12-59 $8.95, seniors 60 & over $7.95, children 4-12 $6.95; discounts to AAM & ICOM members; children under 4 no charge. ♿
Attendance: 40,000 (accurate)

* **OLD COWTOWN MUSEUM, (M),** 1865 W. Museum Blvd., Wichita, KS 67203-3295. Mailing Address: 1871 Sim Park Dr., Wichita, KS 67203-3203. Tel.: 316-660-1871. Fax: 316-264-2937.
E-mail: cowtown@sedgwick.gov
Web Site: www.oldcowtown.org
Founded: 1950.
Congressional District: 4
Key Personnel: Pres., Jennifer Lee; Exec. Dir., David Flask; Cur. & Volunteer Focal, Amy Loch.
Personnel Profile: Full-Time Paid 9; Part-Time Volunteers 200; Interns 2.
Governing Authority: nonprofit corporation. Parent Institution: Historic Wichita Sedgwick County, Inc. Tax-exempt: 501(c)(3).
History Museum: 1865-1880 era of Wichita & Sedgwick County Kansas.
Collections: 1865-1880 history of Wichita & Sedgwick County; textiles; clothing; tools; agricultural & documentary artifacts; transportation & recreational artifacts; societal & ceremonial artifacts; packages & containers; natural specimens; architectural fragments; a study collection; archives.
Research Fields: commercial & social activities of groups in early Wichita & Sedgwick County; regional history.
Facilities: archives; microfilms of 1860-1880 Wichita & area newspapers; snack bar. Museum-related items for sale.
Activities: living history programs; special events; Teaching in a One-Room School program; 19th century blacksmithing demonstrations & workshops; re-enactments of 1870s County Fair & 1876 Independence Day; 1880s Living History Farm; interpretive tours; lecture series; Girl Scout living history summer program; formally organized education programs; membership & volunteer programs.
Publications: The Chronicle Newsletter; volunteer newsletter.
Hours & Admission Prices: Oct. Thurs.-Mon. 10-4, Sun. 11-4; Nov.-May Tues.-Sat. 10-4. Adults $7.75, senior citizens $6.50, youth 12-17 $6, children 4-11 $5.50; discounts to AAM & ICOM members & groups of 15 or more; children under 4 & member adults no charge. Closed New Year's Day; Thanksgiving; Christmas. ♿
Attendance: 51,890 (accurate)
Membership: Single $30; Companion $45; Family & Grandparent $55; Patron $75; Pioneer Society $100 & up.

SEDGWICK COUNTY ZOO, 5555 Zoo Blvd., Wichita, KS 67212-1643. Tel.: 316-660-9453. Fax: 316-942-3781.
E-mail: mreed@scz.org
Web Site: www.scz.org
Founded: 1971.
Congressional District: 4
Key Personnel: Dir., Mark C. Reed; C.F.O., Vickie Moore; Pres. (V), Steven A. Houlik; Asst. Dir., Jim Marlett; Visitor Svcs. Mgr., Steve Fairchild; Volunteer Coord., Bridget Landers.
Personnel Profile: Full-Time Paid 105; Part-Time Paid 50; Part-Time Volunteers 872; Interns 6.
Governing Authority: county; nonprofit. Parent Institution: County of Sedgwick & Sedgwick County Zoological Society, Inc. Tax-exempt: 501(c)(3).
Zoo.
Collections: animals; plants.
Research Fields: embryo transfer; reproductive studies.
Facilities: over 1,000-vol. library of reference & animal material; botanical garden; zoological park; educational facilities. Gift items for sale.
Activities: guided tours; lectures; films; organized education programs for children, adults & undergraduate or graduate students affiliated with Friends University or Wichita State University; docent program; participatory exhibits. Museum Sponsors: Zoobilee; Halloween Party; Kid's Zoobilee; other events all year long.
Publications: bimonthly newsletter, Zoo Tracks; annual report.
Hours & Admission Prices: Winter: daily 10-5; Summer: daily 8:30-5. Adults and children 12 & over $11, children 4-11 $6.50, school groups $4 each; discounts to AZA members; children under 3 & members no charge. ♿
Attendance: 584,076 (accurate)
Membership: Family $85; Household Plus $105; Sponsor $160; Associate & Contributing $350 & up.

* **ULRICH MUSEUM OF ART, (M),** Wichita State University, 1845 Fairmount St., Wichita, KS 67260-0046. Tel.: 316-978-3664. Fax: 316-978-3898.
E-mail: ulrich@wichita.edu
Web Site: www.ulrich.wichita.edu
Formerly: Edwin A. Ulrich Museum of Art
Founded: 1974.
Congressional District: 4
Key Personnel: Dir., Patricia McDonnell; Chm. (V), Carol Wilson; Cur. Modern & Contemporary Art, Emily Stamey; Exhibitions Cur., Kevin Mullins; Collection Mgr., Mark Janzen; Cur. Education, Aimee Geist; Asst. Dir. Finance & Mgmt., Linda Doll; Administrative Specialist, Angela Lentino; Mgr. Public Rels., Teresa Veazey.
Personnel Profile: Full-Time Paid 8; Part-Time Paid 5; Interns 2.
Governing Authority: nonprofit. Parent Institution: Wichita State University. Tax-exempt: 501(c)(3).
University Art Museum.
Collections: outdoor sculpture collection; 20th-21st century art, paintings, works on paper & electronic art; contemporary artists; new media works.
Major Exhibits: The Weight of Words: Artists Work with Language, 11/09-12/10; Make It New: Abstract Art from the Collection, 11/09-12/10; Crossroads: The Art of Gordon Parks, 1/23/10-4/11/10; Art of Our Time: Selections from the Ulrich Museum of Art Collection (T), 4/24/10-8/8/10.
Research Fields: modern & contemporary art.
Facilities: 10,000 sq. ft. exhibit space.
Activities: lectures; gallery talks; guided tours; organized education programs for undergraduate & graduate college students and adults 55 & over; artists-in-residence programs; hands-on workshops; films; conferences; docent program.
Publications: books: Not So Cute & Cuddly: Dolls and Stuffed Toys in Contemporary Art; The Sculptor's Clay, Sculpture by Duane Hanson, The John Philip Kassebaum Collection (ceramics); Tobi Kahn Correspondence; American Visions: The Paintings of Sandy Walker; Beyond the Museum Walls: The Martin H. Bush Outdoor Sculpture Collection; catalogues: Subversive Domesticity, Portrait Prints (1599-1641), Force I sculptures & paintings, The Persistence of Abstraction; David Reed - Leave Yourself Behind: Paintings and Special Projects, 1967-2005; Poets on Painters, 2006.
Hours & Admission Prices: Tues.-Fri. 11-5, Sat.-Sun. 1-5. No charge; donations accepted. Closed major & university holidays. ♿
Attendance: 19,405 (accurate)
Membership: WSU Students no charge; WSU Faculty, Staff, & Seniors 55 & over $30; Individual $50; Dual & Family $60-$99; Friend $100-$249; Supporter $250-$499; Sustainer $500-$749. Salon Circle: Curator $750-$2,499; Director $2,500-$4,999; Trustee $5,000-$9,999; Benefactor $10,000-$19,999; Grand Gallery $20,000 & up.

* **WICHITA ART MUSEUM, (M),** 1400 W. Museum Blvd., Wichita, KS 67203-3296. Tel.: 316-268-4921 & 4976. Fax: 316-268-4980.
E-mail: info@wichitaartmuseum.org
Web Site: www.wichitaartmuseum.org
Founded: 1935.
Congressional District: 4
Key Personnel: Chm. Bd. & Pres., Marni Vliet; Dir., Charles K. Steiner; Chief Cur., Stephen Gleissner; Dir. Education, Andrea Keppers; Registrar, Leslie Servantez; Museum Shop Mgr., Kevin Bishop.
Personnel Profile: Full-Time Paid 22; Full-Time Volunteers 1; Part-Time Paid 18.
Governing Authority: municipal. Subsidiary Institution: Friends of the Wichita Art Museum Inc. Tax-exempt.
Art Museum.
Collections: Roland P. Murdock Collection of American Art; John W. & Mildred L. Graves Collection; Paul Ross Charitable Foundation Collection of American Painting; L.S. & Ida L. Naftzger Collection of American & European Prints & Drawings; M. C. Naftzger collection of Charles M. Russell paintings, drawings & sculpture; Gwendolyn Houston Naftzger collection of Porcelain birds; Kurdian & Beren collection of Pre- Columbian Mexican artifacts; European porcelain & faience; Ablah collection of British watercolors; Misco collection of Art Works; F. Price Cossman collection of Steuben Glass.
Research Fields: American Art.
Facilities: 10,000-vol. library of books & magazines on art available on premises; restaurant. Art books, postcards, slides, museum reproductions & gift items for sale.
Activities: permanent, temporary & traveling exhibitions.
Publications: bimonthly magazine; exhibition catalogues & educational brochures.
Hours & Admission Prices: Adults $7, seniors & students $5, youth 5-17 $3; discount to AAM members; children under 4, Sat. & members no charge. Closed national holidays. ♿
Attendance: 46,700 (accurate)
Membership: Student $20; Individual $35; Family $60; Donor $150; Sponsor $350; Patron $600; Benefactor $1,000; Director's Circle $5,000.

WICHITA CENTER FOR THE ARTS, 9112 E. Central, Wichita, KS 67206-2506. Tel.: 316-634-2787. Fax: 316-634-0593.
E-mail: arts@wcfta.com
Web Site: www.wcfta.com
Founded: 1920.
Congressional District: 4
Key Personnel: Exec. Dir., Howard W. Ellington; Gallery Dir., Jana Durfee;

Chm., Carol Wilson; Dir. Education, Kathy Sweeney; Dir. Theatre, John Boldenow; Business Mgr., Shawna Thompson.
Personnel Profile: Full-Time Paid 12; Part-Time Paid 31; Interns 2.
Governing Authority: nonprofit organization. Tax-exempt: 501(c)(3).
Art Center.
Collections: paintings; drawings; fine prints; enamels; sculpture; pottery; porcelains; textiles; 20th-century decorative arts.
Research Fields: 20th-century American decorative art; works of Bruce Moore.
Facilities: 3,000-vol. library of art reference & magazines; school of theatre & performing arts; school of visual arts; professional community theater.
Activities: lectures; films; consultation service; concerts; professional community theatre for adults & children; formally organized education programs in performing & visual arts for children & adults; rotating schedule of permanent & temporary exhibitions; national competitive exhibitions.
Publications: bimonthly newsletter; exhibition catalogues; school of theatre & performing arts & school of visual arts catalogues; annual roster & report; activities; bulletins.
Hours & Admission Prices: Tues.-Fri. 10-5, Sat.-Sun. 1-5. No charge; donations accepted. Closed national holidays. ♿
Attendance: 53,484 (accurate)
Membership: Student $20; Individual $35; Family $60; Contemporaries $75; Patron $150; Sponsor $250; Associate $500; Donor $1,000; Benefactor $5,000 & up.

* **WICHITA-SEDGWICK COUNTY HISTORICAL MUSEUM ASSOCIATION, (M),** 204 S. Main, Wichita, KS 67202-3796. Tel.: 316-265-9314. Fax: 316-265-9319.
E-mail: wschm@wichitahistory.org
Founded: 1939.
Congressional District: 4
Key Personnel: Dir., Eric M. Cale; Pres., Alisa Arst.
Personnel Profile: Full-Time Paid 5; Part-Time Paid 2; Part-Time Volunteers 3.
Governing Authority: society. Tax-exempt: 501(c)(3).
History Museum: housed in 1892 old City Hall.
Collections: local history; costumes; Indian artifacts; industrial; toys; period rooms.
Research Fields: local business; transportation; cultural history.
Facilities: 1,000-vol. library of books on Wichita & Kansas history; reading room. Books & note paper for sale.
Activities: guided tours; lectures; films; gallery talks; docent program; permanent, temporary & traveling exhibitions.
Publications: biannual newsletter, Heritage.
Hours & Admission Prices: Tues.-Fri. 11-4, Sat.-Sun. 1-5. Adults $4, children $2; discounts to AAM & ICOM members; members no charge. Closed national holidays. ♿
Attendance: 8,900 (accurate)
Membership: Individual $25; Family $35; Donor $50; Contributing $75; Sustaining $150; Patron $250 & up.

Wilson

WILSON CZECH OPERA HOUSE CORPORATION, FOUNDATION, INC. & HOUSE OF MEMORIES MUSEUM, 415 27th St., Old Hwy. #40, Wilson, KS 67490-0271. Mailing Address: P.O. Box 271, Wilson, KS 67490-0271. Tel.: 785-658-3505 & 3343.
Founded: 1986.
Congressional District: 1
Key Personnel: C.E.O., Pres. & Chm., Libbie Sebesta; Vice. Pres., Laverne Libal; Dir. House of Memories Museum, Pres. (V), & Museum Shop Mgr., Jean T. Kingston; Treas., Ida Mae Goodman; Sec. & City Delegate, Joe E. Vocasek; Security, Bill Seifers; Security, Tim Heard; Asst. & Tour Guide Museum Shop Mgr., Una Joyce Podlena.
Personnel Profile: Full-Time Paid 1; Full-Time Volunteers 3; Part-Time Paid 1; Part-Time Volunteers 3.
Governing Authority: private; nonprofit organization. Parent Institution: Wilson Czech Opera House Corp. Subsidiary Institution: House of Memories Museum (Basement). Tax-exempt: 501(c)(3).
History Museum.
Collections: items from Czech heritage; trophies; memorabilia; hair wreath; 1st phone book; hand tools; glassware for Czechoslovakia; costumes.
Research Fields: House of Memories inventory.
Facilities: library; 450-seat auditorium; 200-seat restaurant; 1,500 sq. ft. exhibit space. Gift items for sale.
Activities: art festivals; films; formal education programs for college students; guided tours; hobby workshops; loan & temporary exhibitions; study clubs; theater; broadcast programs. Museum Sponsors: Czech Festival in July; Alumni Dinners; Foreign Exchange week.
Publications: brochure; History of Wilson; History of J.T. Hastings.
Hours & Admission Prices: Mon.-Sat. 10-12 & 1-4, Sun. 1-4. No charge; donations accepted. ♿
Attendance: 575 (estimated)
Membership: Individual $10.

Winfield

THE COWLEY COUNTY HISTORICAL SOCIETY, 1011 Mansfield St., Winfield, KS 67156-3557. Tel.: 620-221-4811.
E-mail: cchsm@kans.com
Web Site: www.cchsm.com
Founded: 1931.
Congressional District: 4
Key Personnel: Pres. (V), Jerry Aistrup; Museum Shop Mgr., Jane Reeves.
Personnel Profile: Full-Time Paid 1; Part-Time Paid 1; Part-Time Volunteers 10.
Governing Authority: society; nonprofit organization. Tax-exempt: 501(c)(3) & 170(b)(1)(A).
General Museum.
Collections: manuscripts; glassware; costumes; household equipment from pioneer days.
Research Fields: early history of the community.
Facilities: 5,000-vol. library of history books; reading room; period rooms; archives. Museum-related items for sale.
Activities: guided tours; lectures; slides; formally organized education programs for children; permanent & temporary exhibitions; oral history program.
Publications: newsletter.
Hours & Admission Prices: Tues.-Sun. 1-4. No charge; donations accepted. Closed New Year's Day; Easter; Memorial Day; Labor Day; Thanksgiving; Christmas. ♿
Attendance: 8,000 (accurate)
Membership: Active $15-$25; Sustaining $35; Organization $50; Life $200; Patron $500; Benefactor $1,000.

Yates Center

WOODSON COUNTY HISTORICAL SOCIETY, 208 W. Mary, Yates Center, KS 66783-1728. Mailing Address: 602 S. Kalida, Yates Center, KS 66783-1508. Tel.: 620-625-2626.
E-mail: rcall1@cox.net
Founded: 1965.
Congressional District: 5
Key Personnel: Pres., Ben Henry; Vice Pres., Pete Watts; Cur., Geri Town; Treas., Linda Call; Sec., Doris Horst.
Personnel Profile: Part-Time Paid 2; Part-Time Volunteers 3.
Governing Authority: society. Tax-exempt.
Historic Buildings: 1877 church; Country School; 1866 Log Cabin.
Collections: agriculture; Indian artifacts.
Activities: bimonthly dinner meeting.
Hours & Admission Prices: June-Sept. Mon.-Wed. & Fri.-Sat. 10-4. No charge; donations accepted. ♿
Attendance: 820 (accurate)
Membership: Annual $2; Life $25; Memorial Gifts (for name on plaque) $100.

KENTUCKY

(170 listings)

Ashland

HIGHLANDS MUSEUM & DISCOVERY CENTER, (M), 1620 Winchester Ave., Ashland, KY 41101-7639. Tel.: 606-329-8888. Fax: 606-324-3218.
E-mail: highlandsmuseum@yahoo.com
Web Site: www.highlandsmuseum.com
Founded: 1984.
Congressional District: 4
Key Personnel: C.E.O., Cur. & Registrar, Carolyn P. Warnock; Exec. Dir., Leigh Ann Heineman; Pres. (V), Pamela H. Potter; Treas., Lori Arthur; Museum Shop Mgr, Jennifer Criswell.
Personnel Profile: Full-Time Paid 4; Part-Time Paid 1; Part-Time Volunteers 125; Interns 5.
Governing Authority: private; nonprofit organization. Tax-exempt: 501(c)(3).
Children's & History Museum.
Collections: period clothing from 1850s to modern era; transportation; communication; industry; country music; medical & military from WWII to present; cultural & industrial heritage of the Highlands region of Appalachia.
Major Exhibits: John Carpenter: Hall of Champions, 11/09-1/10; A Step Ahead, 11/09-1/10; Beyond the Log Cabin (T), 11/09-2/19/10; KHS Quilt Posters (T), 3/10; Student Art Show, 4/17/10-5/8/10.
Facilities: educational facilities; 200-seat community hall; 15,000 sq. ft. exhibit space; portable planetarium; reception area. Museum-related items for sale.

Activities: concerts; dance recitals; docent program; formal education programs for children; guided tours; lectures; loan, participatory, temporary, traveling exhibitions; rental gallery. Annual Events: decorator showcase; auction; book & attic sale; Christmas House Tours.
Publications: monthly newsletter, The Highlander.
Hours & Admission Prices: Mon. by appointment, Tues.-Sat. 10-5, 1st Fri. of month 5-8. Adults $5.50, senior citizens & children $4.50; discounts to AAM members, ASTC reciprocal & groups; children under 2 & members no charge. Closed New Year's Day; Memorial Day; Independence Day; Labor Day; Thanksgiving; Christmas. ♿
Attendance: 26,000 (accurate)
Membership: Family $58; Century $100-$249; Horizon $250-$499; Heritage $500-$999; Highlands $1,000 & up.

Barbourville

DR. THOMAS WALKER STATE HISTORIC SITE, 4929 KY 459, Barbourville, KY 40906-7232. Tel.: 606-546-4400.
Key Personnel: Park Mgr., Andy Teasley
Historic Site.
Collections: replica of the first cabin built in Kentucky by Dr. Thomas Walker.
Hours & Admission Prices: Call for hours.

KNOX HISTORICAL MUSEUM, 196 Daniel Boone Dr., Barbourville, KY 40906-1162. Mailing Address: P.O. Box 1446, Barbourville, KY 40906. Tel.: 606-546-4300.
E-mail: khm1446@hotmail.com
Web Site: www.knoxcochamber.com/museum.asp
Founded: 1988.
Key Personnel: Pres. (V), Charles Reed Mitchell.
Personnel Profile: Part-Time Volunteers 3.
Governing Authority: Tax-exempt.
History Museum.
Collections: local history & culture.
Publications: quarterly, The Knox Countian.
Hours & Admission Prices: Wed. 10-4. No charge; donations accepted.
Membership: $15; $20; $30; $50; $100; $500.

Bardstown

MY OLD KENTUCKY HOME STATE PARK, 501 E. Stephen Foster Ave., Bardstown, KY 40004-2205. Mailing Address: P.O. Box 323, Bardstown, KY 40004-0323. Tel.: 502-348-3502; 800-323-7803. Fax: 502-349-0054. TDD: 502-348-3502.
Web Site: www.kystateparks.com
Founded: 1922.
Congressional District: 2
Key Personnel: Park Supt., Alice Heaton; Pres. (V), Dr. Harry Spalding; Museum Shop Mgr., Gail Downs.
Governing Authority: state. Parent Institution: Kentucky Dept. of Parks, Capital Plaza Tower, Frankfort, KY 40601. Tel. 502-564-2172. Subsidiary Institution: My Old Kentucky Home Foundation. Tax-exempt.
Historic House: 1818 home of Judge John Rowan, where Stephen Foster wrote My Old Kentucky Home.
Collections: original Rowan furniture; china.
Facilities: 200-vol. library of books available for research by special permission from Parks Commissioner; theater; visitor center. Crafts, glass & china for sale.
Activities: guided tours.
Hours & Admission Prices: Daily 9-5. Adults $5.50, children 6-12 $3.50. Closed New Year's Day; Thanksgiving; Christmas week. ♿
Attendance: 100,000 (estimated)

OSCAR GETZ MUSEUM OF WHISKEY HISTORY AND THE BARDSTOWN HISTORICAL MUSEUM, 114 N. Fifth St., Bardstown, KY 40004-1449. Tel.: 502-348-2999.
E-mail: whiskeymuseum@bardstowncable.net
Web Site: www.whiskeymuseum.com
Founded: 1984.
Congressional District: 2
Key Personnel: Chm. (V), Thomas C. Dawson; Cur., Mary Ellyn Hamilton.
Personnel Profile: Full-Time Paid 1; Part-Time Paid 3.
Governing Authority: nonprofit organization. Tax-exempt.
Local History Museum.
Collections: documentaries, exhibits, memorabilia, & artifacts pertaining to the history of the American whiskey industry since its beginnings in the mid-18th century, through the Prohibition Era.
Research Fields: old whiskey memorabilia.
Facilities: 50-vol. library of books on whiskey.
Activities: permanent exhibitions. Annual Events: On the Lawn - Wine & Cheese Tasting in June; Antique Bourbon Auction in September.
Publications: books, Pictorial History of Whiskey; Whiskey, An American Pictorial History.
Hours & Admission Prices: May-Oct. Mon.-Fri. 10-5, Sat. 10-4, Sun. 12-4; Nov.-April Tues.-Sat. 10-4, Sun. 12-4. No charge; donations accepted. Guided Group Tours: $3 per person. Call for holiday closings. ♿
Attendance: 10,040 (accurate)

Benham

KENTUCKY COAL MINING MUSEUM, 231 Main St., Benham, KY 40807. Tel.: 606-848-1530.
Founded: 1994.
Congressional District: 5
Key Personnel: Dir., Phyllis Sizemore; Pres. (V), Dr. W. Bruce Ayers.
Personnel Profile: Full-Time Paid 2; Part-Time Paid 3; Part-Time Volunteers 12.
Governing Authority: Tax-exempt.
Coal Mining Museum.
Collections: history of coal mining; two-ton block of coal; 1940s model electric locomotive; mining machinery; mining process; fossils; mining tools; photographs; Benham history; family histories.
Facilities: Museum-related items for sale.
Activities: video; tours.
Hours & Admission Prices: Tues.-Sat. 10-5; groups by appointment. Adults $6, senior citizens 62 & over $5, college students $4, children 3-12 $3. ♿
Attendance: 20,000 (estimated)

Berea

BEREA COLLEGE BURROUGHS GEOLOGICAL MUSEUM, Main St., Berea, KY 40404-0001. Mailing Address: CPO 2191, Berea, KY 40404-0001. Tel.: 859-985-3351 & 3893. Fax: 859-985-3303.
E-mail: larry_lipchinsky@berea.edu
Web Site: www.berea.edu
Founded: 1920.
Congressional District: 6
Key Personnel: Cur., Zelek L. Lipchinsky.
Personnel Profile: Full-Time Volunteers 1.
Governing Authority: college. Parent Institution: Berea College. Subsidiary Institution: Berea College Geology Dept. Tax-exempt: 501(c)(3).
Science Museum.
Collections: geological & archaeological specimens.
Facilities: gallery.
Activities: permanent exhibits; guided tours. Educational material for sale.
Hours & Admission Prices: Mon.-Fri. 9-5. No charge; donations accepted. ♿
Attendance: 2,000 (estimated)

BEREA COLLEGE, DORIS ULMANN GALLERIES, Corner of Chestnut & Elipse St., Berea, KY 40403. Mailing Address: CPO 2162, Berea, KY 40404-0001. Tel.: 859-985-3530.
E-mail: tina_mccalment@berea.edu
Web Site: www.berea.edu/art/dug/default.asp
Founded: 1975.
Congressional District: 6
Key Personnel: Chm. Art Dept., Lisa Kriner, MFA; Dir., Tina McCalment.
Personnel Profile: Full-Time Paid 1.
Governing Authority: college. Parent Institution: Berea College. Subsidiary Institution: Berea College Art Dept. Tax-exempt: 501(c)(3).
College Art Galleries.
Collections: crafts; paintings; Doris Ulmann photographs of Appalachian people & craftsmen; African art; European, Asian & American prints; 13 Kress paintings; C.C. Coyle paintings; Frank Long paintings; Chinese robes; contemporary prints.
Activities: intermuseum loan; temporary & traveling exhibitions.
Hours & Admission Prices: Fall-Spring Mon.-Thurs. 8-9, Fri. 8-5, Sun. 1-5. No charge. Closed college holidays. ♿

BEREA COLLEGE WEATHERFORD PLANETARIUM, Science Bldg., Berea, KY 40404-0001. Mailing Address: CPO 1872, Berea, KY 40404-0001. Tel.: 859-985-3277. Fax: 859-985-3303.
E-mail: amer_lahamer@berea.edu
Web Site: www.physics.berea.edu
Founded: 1985.
Congressional District: 6
Key Personnel: Chm., Amer S. Lahamer.
Governing Authority: college. Parent Institution: Berea College. Subsidiary Institution: Berea College Physics Dept. Tax-exempt: 501(c)(3).
Planetarium.
Collections: astronomy.
Activities: planetarium shows.

Hours & Admission Prices: Sept.-May Sun. 4 pm; other times by appointment. Adults $1, $10 per group (seats 50). ♿
Attendance: 1,000 (accurate)

Bowling Green

BRIMS - BARREN RIVER IMAGINATIVE MUSEUM OF SCIENCE, 1229 Center St., Bowling Green, KY 42101-3426. Mailing Address: P.O. Box 71, Bowling Green, KY 42102-0071. Tel.: 270-843-9779.
E-mail: b.r.i.m.s@insightbb.com
Founded: 1994.
Key Personnel: Dir., Charles Phillips; Chm. & Pres. (V), Doug Jenkins.
Governing Authority: nonprofit organization.
Science Museum.
Collections: sciences & technology.
Activities: special events.
Publications: quarterly newsletter.
Hours & Admission Prices: Thurs.-Sat. 10-3, Sun. 1-4; groups by appointment. Adults $5, students $4.
Attendance: 7,000
Membership: Annual $50.

HARDIN PLANETARIUM, Western Kentucky University, Dept. of Physics & Astronomy, 1906 College Heights Blvd., #11077, Bowling Green, KY 42101-1077. Tel.: 270-745-4044. Fax: 270-745-4255.
E-mail: roger.scott@wku.edu
Web Site: physics.wku.edu/planetarium.html
Founded: 1967.
Congressional District: 2
Key Personnel: Dir., Dr. Roger L. Scott.
Personnel Profile: Full-Time Paid 2; Part-Time Paid 1.
Governing Authority: state; university. Parent Institution: Western Kentucky University, Bowling Green, KY 42101. Tax-exempt.
Planetarium, Observatory & Astronomy Museum.
Collections: meteorite; astronomy photographs.
Facilities: 200-vol. library of astronomy books; 160-seat auditorium.
Activities: guided tours; lectures; films; formally organized programs for children, adults & undergraduate college students affiliated with Western Kentucky University; temporary, traveling & permanent exhibitions.
Hours & Admission Prices: Sept.-May Mon.-Fri. 8-4:30 during academic session. No charge. ♿
Attendance: 15,000

HISTORIC RAILPARK TRAIN MUSEUM - L&N DEPOT, 401 Kentucky St., Bowling Green, KY 42101-1260. Tel.: 877-337-6859; 270-745-7317.
Web Site: www.historicalrailpark.com
Key Personnel: Exec. Dir., Sharon Tabor
Railroad Museum.
Collections: vintage railroad equipment & artifacts.
Hours & Admission Prices: May-Oct. Mon.-Sat. 9-5, Sun. 1-4, Nov.-April Tues.-Sat. 9-5, Sun. 1-4. Adults $10, seniors 55 & over $8, children 4-10 $5; children 3 & under no charge.

THE KENTUCKY LIBRARY & MUSEUM, (M), 1906 College Heights Blvd. #11092, Bowling Green, KY 42101-1092. Tel.: 270-745-2592. Fax: 270-745-6264.
E-mail: timothy.mullin@wku.edu
Web Site: www.wku.edu/library/kylm
Formerly: The Kentucky Museum
Founded: 1939.
Congressional District: 2
Key Personnel: Dir., Timothy J. Mullin; Chm. (V), Ron Hatcher; Cur. Exhibits, Donna Parker; Registrar & Cur. Collections, Sandra Staebell; Education Cur., Christy Spurlock; Univ. Archivist, Suellyn Lathrop; Exhibits Technician, Tony Thurman; Cur. Books, Nancy Baird; Cur. Images, Nancy Richey; Special Collections, Sue Lynn McDaniel; Manuscripts, Jonathan Jeffrey; Artist-in-Residence, Lynne Ferguson; Devel. Officer, Josh Hawkins; Museum Asst., Lynn Claycomb; Museum Shop Mgr., Deborah Cole.
Personnel Profile: Full-Time Paid 16; Part-Time Paid 26; Part-Time Volunteers 8.
Governing Authority: bd. of Regents. Parent Institution: Western Kentucky University. Tax-exempt: 501(c)(3).
History Museum/Historic House.
Collections: period furniture; Shaker decorative arts; toys; traditional tools; musical instruments; anthropology; Kentucky, textiles; photographs; Civil War Center; manuscripts; folk life; University Archives; rare books; maps. Historic Building: log house.
Research Fields: genealogy; Kentucky history; Shaker history; Civil War history, upper south; folk life.
Facilities: 100,000-vol. library of books, manuscripts, sheet music & photos on Kentucky history & crafts available for use on premises; 4,000 sq. ft. Kentucky room for outside functions; 50,000 sq. ft. gallery space; 10,000 sq. ft. offsite storage; historic house.
Activities: guided tours; lectures; student research projects; permanent & temporary exhibits; workshops; children's activities; volunteer organization.
Publications: brochure; catalogues; newsletter, Collections and Connections.
Hours & Admission Prices: Mon.-Sat. 9-4, Sun. 1-4; groups by appointment. Adults $5, seniors 60 & over and children 6-16 $2.50; discounts to AAM, AASLH, AAA, & KAM members, regional & state museum associations & employees of museums; children 5 & under and members no charge. Closed major holidays. ♿
Attendance: 70,000 (accurate)
Membership: Individual $50; Donor $120; Patron $500; President's Club $1,000.

NATIONAL CORVETTE MUSEUM, 350 Corvette Dr., Bowling Green, KY 42101-9134. Tel.: 270-781-7973. Fax: 270-781-5286.
Web Site: www.corvettemuseum.org
Founded: 1994.
Congressional District: 2
Key Personnel: Dir., Wendell Strode; Museum Shop Mgr., Tammy Bryant.
Personnel Profile: Full-Time Paid 30; Part-Time Paid 43.
Governing Authority: nonprofit. Tax-exempt: 501(c)(3).
Automobile Museum.
Collections: over 70 Corvettes including classics, race cars, & design cars; photographs; movies & videos; advertisements; scale models; memorabilia.
Facilities: 165-seat theater. Museum-related items for sale.
Activities: school programs.
Publications: magazine, America's Sports Car.
Hours & Admission Prices: Daily 8-5. Museum: adults $8, children 6-16 $4.50; discounts to seniors, AAA members & GM employees; members and children 5 & under no charge. Plant: admission $5; active military no charge. Closed New Year's Day; Easter; Thanksgiving; Christmas Eve & Day. ♿
Attendance: 130,000
Membership: Individual $50; Family $100; Business $250; Lifetime $1,500; Business Lifetime $2,500.

RIVERVIEW AT HOBSON GROVE, 1100 W. Main Ave., Bowling Green, KY 42101-4894. Tel.: 270-843-5565. Fax: 270-843-5557.
E-mail: rivervw@bowlinggreen.net
Web Site: www.bgky.org/riverview/
Founded: 1972.
Congressional District: 2
Key Personnel: Interim Dir. & Museum Shop Mgr., Laura Southard; Chm. (V), Margaret Stein; Pres. (V), Angie Hoyle.
Personnel Profile: Full-Time Paid 1; Part-Time Paid 4; Part-Time Volunteers 50; Interns 1.
Governing Authority: municipal government; nonprofit. Tax-exempt: 501(c)(3).
Historic House Museum: housed in a c.1872 Italianate architecture home which was used to store Confederate munitions during the Civil War.
Collections: concentration on the Victorian family living in southern Kentucky during the 1860s-1890s; personal artifacts & decorative arts pieces.
Research Fields: 19th-century recreation, servant life and death & mourning customs; the life of Victorian women; Civil War.
Facilities: tea & luncheon committee caters by reservation. Museum-related items for sale.
Activities: docent program; formal education programs for children; guided tours; lectures; temporary exhibitions; children's Manners classes. The Other Victorians: 19th-Century Servant Life Tour; Riverview Chautauqua Series features monthly programs, activities, & exhibits related to the time period.
Publications: quarterly newsletter, The Riverview Observer.
Hours & Admission Prices: Feb.-Dec. Tues.-Sat. 10-4, Sun. 1-4. Families $10, adults $5, students $2.50; discount to groups, seniors, students, members & AAA members; children under 6 & AASLH members no charge. Closed at noon Good Friday. Closed Easter; Memorial Day; Independence Day; Labor Day; Thanksgiving; Christmas to New Year's Day.
Attendance: 3,600 (accurate)
Membership: Individual $15; Family $25; Contributor $50; Sustaining $100; Patron $101 & up.

WESTERN KENTUCKY UNIVERSITY GALLERY, Rm. 441 Ivan Wilson Center for Fine Arts, Bowling Green, KY 42101-1000. Mailing Address: 1906 College Heights Blvd., Art Dept., Bowling Green, KY 42101-1000. Tel.: 270-745-3944. Fax: 270-745-5932.
E-mail: brent.oglesbee@wku.edu

Web Site: www.wku.edu/art/
Congressional District: 13
Key Personnel: Dept. Head, Brent Oglesbee.
Governing Authority: university. Parent Institution: Western Kentucky University. Subsidiary Institution: Art Dept. Tax-exempt.
Art Gallery.
Collections: contemporary works.
Major Exhibits: WKU Faculty Biennial, 1/25/10-2/22/10; Jason Lee, In-Scape, 2/26/10-4/2/10; TEH Weatherplot, 4/9/10-5/21/10; WKU Graduating Seniors, 4/16/10-5/15/10; Cecelia Kane: Hand to Hand, 10/5/10-10/28/10.
Activities: gallery talks; temporary & traveling exhibitions.
Hours & Admission Prices: Mon.-Fri. 8-4:30. No charge. Closed between exhibitions. ♿
Attendance: 3,500 (estimated)

Burlington

DINSMORE HOMESTEAD FOUNDATION, 5656 Burlington Pike, Burlington, KY 41005-8668. Mailing Address: P.O. Box 453, Burlington, KY 41005-0453. Tel.: 859-586-6117. Fax: 859-334-3690.
Web Site: www.dinsmorefarm.org
Founded: 1986.
Congressional District: 4
Key Personnel: Exec. Dir., Marty McDonald; Chm., Susan Shuffert; Education Coord., Cathy Collopy; Homestead Asst., Sue Clare.
Personnel Profile: Full-Time Paid 1; Part-Time Paid 2; Part-Time Volunteers 40.
Governing Authority: private; nonprofit organization. Tax-exempt: 501(c)(3).
History Museum: housed in c.1842 Federal farmhouse.
Collections: furniture; books; photographs; paintings; textiles; family correspondence journals on microfilm; early Boone County history.
Research Fields: African-American slavery; local plant life; paint & wallpaper.
Facilities: library of microfilmed family papers; nature center; 1,500 sq. ft. exhibit space. Museum-related items for sale.
Activities: docent program; formal education programs; guided tours; hobby workshops.
Publications: quarterly newsletter, The Dinsmore Dispatch.
Hours & Admission Prices: April-Dec. 15 Wed. & Sat.-Sun. 1-5; other times by appointment. Adults $5, senior citizens $3, children 7-17 $2; members no charge.
Attendance: 3,500
Membership: Student & Senior Citizen $20; Individual $35; Family $60; Friend $100; Julia Dinsmore Society $250-$2,500.

Cadiz

JANICE MASON ART MUSEUM, 71 Main St., Cadiz, KY 42211-9101. Mailing Address: P.O. Box 303, Cadiz, KY 42211-0303. Tel.: 270-522-9056.
E-mail: jmam@bellsouth.net
Web Site: www.jmam.org
Founded: 1998.
Congressional District: 1
Personnel Profile: Part-Time Paid 2; Part-Time Volunteers 30.
Governing Authority: Tax-exempt.
Art Museum.
Collections: paintings; sculpture.
Major Exhibits: Aqueous 2009 (T), 3/5/10-3/21/10; Kentucky Women Photographers Network, 3/27/10-5/10/10; Mitchell Chamberlain - Paintings, 5/14/10-6/27/10.
Activities: classes; educational programs.
Hours & Admission Prices: Tues.-Sat. 10-4, Sun. 1-4. No charge; donations accepted. Closed holidays. ♿
Attendance: 5,000 (accurate)
Membership: Individual $35.

Campbellsville

JACOB HIESTAND HOUSE, 1075 Campbellsville Bypass, Campbellsville, KY 42718-8835. Tel.: 270-789-4343.
Founded: 1992.
Congressional District: 2
Key Personnel: Chm. (V), Betty Gorin; Pres. (V), Debbie Gilpin.
Governing Authority: Tax-exempt.
Historic House Museum: built in 1823.
Collections: period furnishings.
Hours & Admission Prices: Tues.-Sat. 10-3. Tours: $3; discounts to groups; children under 12 no charge. Closed New Year's Day; Memorial Day; Independence Day; Labor Day; Christmas. ♿
Membership: Annual $10.

THE FRIENDSHIP SCHOOLHOUSE, 300 Ingram Ave., Campbellsville, KY 42718-1625. Tel.: 270-465-5410, 5106, 2055.
Web Site: www.campbellsvilleky.com/historical.html
History Museum.
Collections: historic school memorabilia from 1918-1955.
Hours & Admission Prices: 1st Sun. of the month 1-4 or by appointment.

Carrollton

BUTLER-TURPIN STATE HISTORIC HOUSE, General Butler State Resort Park, 1608 Hwy. 227, Carrollton, KY 41008-8051. Tel.: 502-732-4384; 866-462-8853.
Key Personnel: Park Mgr., Eddie Moore
Historic House: former home of the Butler family, built in 1859.
Collections: military documents; furniture; objects; paintings.
Hours & Admission Prices: Tours by appointment.

Cave City

DINOSAUR WORLD, 711 Mammoth Cave Rd., Cave City, KY 42127-8437. Tel.: 270-773-4345. Fax: 270-773-5303.
E-mail: dinosaurworld@scrtc.com
Web Site: www.dinoworld.net
Natural History Museum.
Collections: over 150 life-size dinosaurs.
Hours & Admission Prices: Daily 8:30am to sunset. Adults $12.75, seniors over 60 $10.75, children 3-12 $9.75. Closed Thanksgiving; Christmas.

MAMMOTH CAVE WAX MUSEUM, Hwy. 70 W., 901 Mammoth Cave Rd., Cave City, KY 42127. Mailing Address: P.O. Box 678, Cave City, KY 42127-0678. Tel.: 270-773-3010.
Key Personnel: Dir., Wesley Odle
Wax Museum.
Collections: wax figures.
Hours & Admission Prices: Call for hours.

MAMMOTH CAVE WILDLIFE MUSEUM, 409 E. Happy Valley St., Cave City, KY 42127. Tel.: 270-773-2255.
Web Site: www.mammothcave.com/index.htm
Wildlife Museum.
Collections: tigers; lions; bears; leopards; Snow Leopard; deer; sheep; ox; marine life; birds.
Facilities: 14,000 sq. ft. exhibit space.
Activities: education programs.
Hours & Admission Prices: Call for hours.

Clay City

RED RIVER HISTORICAL SOCIETY MUSEUM, 4541 Main Street, Clay City, KY 40312. Mailing Address: Box 195, Clay City, KY 40312-0195. Tel.: 606-663-9930.
Founded: 1966.
Congressional District: 7
Key Personnel: Dir., Larry G. Meadows; Cur. Archaeology, John Faulkner; Cur. Photography, Steve Abner; Cur. History, Jim Spencer.
Governing Authority: nonprofit.
General Museum: located in 1889 National Bank.
Collections: general display of local articles.
Research Fields: local Indian archaeology.
Activities: guided tours; lectures; films.
Publications: Natural Bridge in the Kentucky Mountains.
Hours & Admission Prices: Sat.-Sun. & holidays 10-6 or by appointment (call 606-663-4000). No charge; donations accepted.
Attendance: 5,500
Membership: Annual $10.

Clermont

BERNHEIM ARBORETUM AND RESEARCH FOREST, Hwy. 245, Clermont, KY 40110. Mailing Address: P.O. Box 130, Clermont, KY 40110-0130. Tel.: 502-955-8512. Fax: 502-955-4039.
E-mail: nature@bernheim.org
Web Site: www.bernheim.org
Founded: 1929.
Congressional District: 2
Key Personnel: Exec. Dir., Mark Wourms, Ph.D.; Pres. Bd. Trustees, Frank B. Hower, III; Dir. Education, Claude Stephens; Dir. Horticulture, Dena Rae Garvue; Dir. Mktg., Margaret Zurkahlen; Dir. Operations, Roger Fauver; Museum Shop Mgr., Deborah P'Pool Midget.
Personnel Profile: Full-Time Paid 39; Part-Time Paid 10; Part-Time Volunteers 300; Interns 5.

Governing Authority: nonprofit organization. Parent Institution: Isaac W. Bernheim Foundation. Tax-exempt: 501(c)(3).
Nature Museum & Arboretum.
Collections: 4,000 varieties of plants in arboretum; exhibits on native flora & fauna; research forest.
Research Fields: study aids; university projects.
Facilities: 2,300-vol. library of horticulture & nature books; 14,000-acre wildlife refuge; arboretum; nature center; research forest.
Activities: planned walking lectures, workshops, seminars; planned school activities including fieldtrips, teacher workshops & a self-guided tour; art & cultural events.
Publications: Geology of Bernheim Forest; History of Bernheim Forest; Nature Trail Guide Sheet, Road & Trail Guide, cards; Wildflower Check List of Bernheim; Bird Check List; Plant Materials List.
Hours & Admission Prices: Daily. Admission: Sat.-Sun. & holidays $5 per vehicle; discounts to AAM, AABGA & AHS members under reciprocal visitation agreement; Mon.-Fri. & members no charge. Closed New Year's Day; Christmas. ♿
Attendance: 250,000 (accurate)
Membership: Individual $25; Family $35; Orchid Sponsor $50; Columbine Club $100; Holly Patron $500; Tuliptree Council $1,000; Oak Society $5,000; Director's Circle $10,000.

Clinton

HICKMAN COUNTY MUSEUM, 221 E. Clay St., Clinton, KY 42031-1224. Tel.: 270-653-6587.
Historic House Museum: housed in the former home of Captain Henry C. Watson of the Confederate 7th Kentucky Infantry Regiment; c.1870.
Collections: local history; period furnishings; medical & military artifacts; sports memorabilia; government; business; Native American artifacts.
Hours & Admission Prices: Wed.-Sat. 1-4; other times by appointment. No charge; donations accepted.

Columbus

COLUMBUS-BELMONT CIVIL WAR MUSEUM, Columbus-Belmont State Park, 350 Park Rd., Columbus, KY 42032. Mailing Address: P.O. Box 9, Columbus, KY 42032-0009. Tel.: 270-677-2327. Fax: 270-677-4013. TDD: 270-677-2327.
E-mail: cindy.lynch@.ky.gov
Web Site: www.kystateparks.com/agencies/parks/columbus.htm
Founded: 1934.
Congressional District: 1
Key Personnel: Park Mgr., Cindy Lynch.
Personnel Profile: Part-Time Paid 1.
Governing Authority: state. Parent Institution: the Kentucky Dept. of Parks, Capital Plaza Tower, Frankfort, KY 40601. Tax-exempt.
History Museum.
Collections: Civil War artifacts; pioneer relics of Old Columbus; Indian artifacts; audio-visuals; hospital artifacts.
Activities: school groups & organization visits.
Hours & Admission Prices: May-Sept. daily; Winter: by appointment only. Adults $2, child $1.50; discount to groups. ♿
Attendance: 6,000

Corbin

HARLAND SANDERS MUSEUM & CAFE, 688 US Hwy. 25W., Corbin, KY 40701. Tel.: 606-528-2163.
General Museum: housed in the original restaurant of Kentucky Fried Chicken; built in 1937. Listed on the National Register of Historic Places.
Collections: artifacts & memorabilia from the early days of Kentucky Fried Chicken.
Hours & Admission Prices: Daily 10-10.

Covington

BEHRINGER-CRAWFORD MUSEUM, 1600 Montague Rd., Devou Park, Covington, KY 41011-5648. Tel.: 859-491-4003. Fax: 859-491-4006.
E-mail: info@bcmuseum.org
Web Site: www.bcmuseum.org
Founded: 1950.
Congressional District: 4
Key Personnel: Exec. Dir., Laurie Risch; Asst. Dir., Sarah Siegrist; Chm., Rick Hampton; Pres. Bd., Gary L. Johnston; Dir. Education, Regina Siegrist; Museum Shop Mgr., Mary Ann Courtoy; Museum Svcs. Coord., Kathy Boemker.
Personnel Profile: Full-Time Paid 4; Part-Time Paid 3; Part-Time Volunteers 30; Interns 2.
Governing Authority: nonprofit organization. Tax-exempt: 501(c)(3).
History & Culture Museum.
Collections: northern Kentucky history & culture; transportation; paleontology; prehistoric & historic archaeology; mineralogy; textiles; costumes; glass; military artifacts; Ohio River heritage; taxidermy; fine, decorative, & folk art.
Research Fields: historic archaeology; transportation history; northern Kentucky history; Civil War; Ohio Valley.
Facilities: 860-vol. library; 12,500 sq. ft. exhibit space. Books & children's items for sale.
Activities: guided tours; lectures; radio programs; organized education programs; participatory, loan & temporary exhibitions.
Publications: quarterly newsletter; triannual program guide.
Hours & Admission Prices: Tues.-Fri. 10-5, Sat.-Sun. 1-5. Discount to AAM, SEMC & Kentucky Association of Museums members; members no charge. Closed holidays. ♿
Attendance: 20,000 (estimated)

JAMES A. RAMAGE CIVIL WAR MUSEUM, 409 Kyles Lane, Covington, KY 41011-3743. Tel.: 859-344-1145.
Civil War Museum.
Collections: Civil War history, artifacts, & memorabilia; Fort Wright history.
Activities: special events; group tours.
Hours & Admission Prices: Fri.-Sat. 10-5, Sun. 12-5. Closed holidays.

THE RAILWAY EXPOSITION CO., INC., 315 W. Southern Ave., Covington, KY 41015-1180. Mailing Address: 212 Wyoming Ave., Cincinnati, OH 45215-4308. Tel.: 513-761-3500.
Founded: 1975.
Congressional District: 4
Key Personnel: Vice Pres., William F. Sprague; Public Rels., Roberta Sprague; Museum Shop Mgr., Corrie Reade-Hale.
Personnel Profile: Part-Time Volunteers 50.
Governing Authority: nonprofit organization. Tax-exempt: 501(c)(3).
Railway Museum.
Collections: railroad passenger cars & locomotives; railroad memorabilia; paper items of railroad history.
Research Fields: passenger car restoration.
Facilities: library of early railroad records; 30-seat lecture area. Museum-related items for sale.
Activities: guided tours; lectures; films; participatory exhibits.
Publications: monthly newsletter, Trainsheet.
Hours & Admission Prices: May-Oct. Sun. 12:30-4:30; special tours by appointment. Adults $4, children $2; discounts to groups. Closed holiday weekends.
Membership: Regular $20; Family $25; Business $150; Life $200.

Cynthiana

CYNTHIANA - HARRISON COUNTY MUSEUM, 124 S. Walnut St., Cynthiana, KY 41031-1592. Mailing Address: P.O. Box 411, Cynthiana, KY 41031-0411. Tel.: 859-234-7179.
Founded: 1994.
History Museum.
Collections: local history & culture; military; agriculture; industry; religion; medical artifacts.
Facilities: Museum-related items for sale.
Publications: Chronicles of Cynthiana; Cromwell's Comments; This Old House.
Hours & Admission Prices: Fri.-Sat. 10-5; other times by appointment. No charge.

Danville

CONSTITUTION SQUARE STATE HISTORIC SITE, 134 S. Second St., Danville, KY 40422-1802. Tel.: 859-239-7089. Fax: 859-239-7894.
Web Site: www.ky.parks.ky.gov
Founded: 1937.
Congressional District: 6
Key Personnel: Park Mgr., Jack Bailey.
Personnel Profile: Full-Time Paid 3; Part-Time Paid 2; Part-Time Volunteers 5.
Governing Authority: state. Branch of Kentucky Dept. of Parks, Capital Plaza Tower, Frankfort, KY 40601. Tel.: 502-564-8110. Tax-exempt.
Historic Site.
Collections: personal items of Isaac Shelby, first Governor of Kentucky. Historic Buildings: c.1792 Post Office; 1785 Grayson's Tavern; c.1816-1817 Watts-Bell House; 1817 Fisher's Row houses with gallery & visitor center; replicas of original log courthouse, site of first 10 constitutional conventions; jail; Presbyterian meetinghouse; restored c.1820 brick schoolhouse; c.1820 Alban Goldsmith House.
Facilities: picnic area.

Activities: guided tours. Annual Events: Brass Band Festival in June; Historic Constitution Square Festival in Sept.
Hours & Admission Prices: March-Dec. Thurs.-Sat. 10-4. Call for admission prices & tours. ♿
Attendance: 60,000 (estimated)

THE GREAT AMERICAN DOLL HOUSE MUSEUM, 344 Swope Ave., Danville, KY 40422. Tel.: 859-583-8000.
E-mail: lori@thedollhousemuseum.com
Web Site: www.thedollhousemuseum.com
Key Personnel: Cur., Lori Kagan-Moore; Sculptor & Dollmaker, Nicola Cooper; Diversity Advisor, J.H. Atkins; Web Designer, Jon Sachs; Consultant Asian Design & History, Akiki Otake; Set Designer, Ruth Neeman
Doll Museum.
Collections: dollhouses displayed in a 1900s village setting.
Hours & Admission Prices: Tues.-Sat. 11-5. Adults $7, children $5.

MCDOWELL HOUSE MUSEUM, (M), 125 S. 2nd St., Danville, KY 40422-1801. Tel.: 859-236-2804. Fax: 859-236-2804 (press star twice).
E-mail: mcdhse@kih.net
Web Site: www.mcdowellhouse.org
Formerly: McDowell House and Apothecary Shop
Founded: 1939.
Congressional District: 5
Key Personnel: C.E.O., Dr. Charles Martin; Dir., Carol J. Senn; Asst. Dir., Alberta Moynahan; Museum Shop Mgr., Anna Ingram.
Personnel Profile: Part-Time Paid 4; Part-Time Volunteers 4; Interns 1.
Governing Authority: Parent Institution: McDowell House Museum, Inc. Tax-exempt.
Historic Building: housed in the former home & shop of pioneer surgeon, Ephraim McDowell; built from 1792-1820.
Collections: medical; herbarium; paintings; books.
Research Fields: herbarium; medical & social history.
Facilities: 200-vol. library concerning Ephraim McDowell & Jane Todd Crawford, early medical books & books printed before 1830 available for use on the premises. Literature, slides & postcards for sale.
Activities: guided tours; lectures; permanent exhibitions; special events.
Publications: annual newsletter; The Life & Times of Ephraim McDowell; historical data catalog; video tour of McDowell House for sale.
Hours & Admission Prices: March-Oct. Mon.-Sat. 10-12 & 1-4, Sun. 2-4 (last tour at 3:30); Nov.-Feb. Tues.-Sat. 10-12 & 1-4, Sun. 2-4. Adults $7, senior citizens 62 & over $5, students over 12 $3; discounts to prearranged groups of 10 or more & AAA members; children 5 & under and members no charge. Closed New Year's Day; Easter; Thanksgiving; Christmas.
Attendance: 1,595 (estimated)
Membership: Individual $25; Family $50; Sponsor $100; Jane Todd Crawford Circle $250-$500; Life $500; Ephraim McDowell Society $1,000; Corporate $1,000.

Dawson Springs

DAWSON SPRINGS MUSEUM AND ART CENTER, INC., 127 S. Main St., Dawson Springs, KY 42408-1713. Mailing Address: P.O. Box 107, Dawson Springs, KY 42408-0107. Tel.: 270-797-0909.
E-mail: thomas1958@bellsouth.net
Founded: 1986.
Congressional District: 1
Key Personnel: Pres., Kathy Lyon; Exec. Dir., Sylvia Lynn Thomas; Chm. (V), Shirley Menser.
Personnel Profile: Full-Time Volunteers 1; Part-Time Volunteers 40.
Governing Authority: private; nonprofit organization. Tax-exempt: 501(c)(3).
Art & History Museum: housed in the 1907 Romanesque style Commercial Bank.
Collections: history of Dawson Springs, which was a leading spa of the south from late 19th-century to the Depression era; cultural heritage: The Spa Days, The Outwood Days, History of the Dawson Springs Independent School System & The Coal Mining Days; Japanese art; woodblock prints; Kimono; 150 period cassette tapes; 1,200 photographs.
Facilities: 70-vol. history library; 535 sq. ft. exhibit space.
Activities: loan & traveling & temporary exhibitions.
Publications: brochure, The Dawson Springs Museum & Art Center.
Hours & Admission Prices: Feb.-Dec. Tues.-Fri. 1-4. No charge; donations accepted. Closed major holidays. ♿
Attendance: 2,200 (estimated)
Membership: Single $10; Family $15; Supporting $50.

Elizabethtown

HARDIN COUNTY HISTORY MUSEUM, 201 W. Dixie Ave., Elizabethtown, KY 42701-1533. Tel.: 270-763-8339.
E-mail: info@hardinkyhistory.org
Web Site: www.hardinkyhistory.org
History Museum.
Collections: artifacts, documents & other memorabilia relating to Hardin County.
Hours & Admission Prices: Call for hours.

SCHMIDT MUSEUM OF COCA-COLA MEMORABILIA, 109 Buffalo Creek Dr., Elizabethtown, KY 42701-7518. Tel.: 270-234-1100.
E-mail: schmidtmuseum@yahoo.com
Web Site: www.schmidtmuseum.com
Founded: 1976.
Congressional District: 2
Governing Authority: Tax-exempt: 501(c)(3).
History Museum.
Collections: Coca-Cola memorabilia.
Publications: newsletters.
Hours & Admission Prices: Mon.-Sat. 10-6, Sun. 1-5. Adults $5, seniors $4, students $2; discounts to military, groups, AAA & AARP members; preschoolers no charge. Closed major holidays. ♿
Attendance: 17,000 (accurate)

SWOPE'S CARS OF YESTERYEAR, 1100 N. Dixie Ave., Elizabethtown, KY 42701-2534. Tel.: 270-765-2181. Fax: 270-763-6187.
E-mail: bills13@juno.com
Web Site: www.swopemuseum.com
Founded: 1999.
Congressional District: 2
Key Personnel: Dir., Bill Swope; Cur., Sue Marski; Hostess, Judy Asbury; Hostess, Linda Snyder.
Personnel Profile: Part-Time Paid 3.
Governing Authority: Parent Institution: Swope Auto Center.
Auto Museum.
Collections: 56 period cars from 1910-1969.
Facilities: Cars for sale.
Hours & Admission Prices: Mon.-Sat. 10-5. No charge. Closed holidays. ♿

Elkhorn City

ELKHORN CITY RAILROAD MUSEUM, 100 Pine St., Elkhorn City, KY 41522. Mailing Address: P.O. Box 1497, Elkhorn City, KY 41522-1497. Tel.: 606-754-8300.
E-mail: elkhorncityrailroadmuseum@yahoo.com
Web Site: elkhorncityrrm.tripod.com
Railroad Museum.
Collections: railroad history; railroad artifacts & memorabilia.
Hours & Admission Prices: March.-Nov. Tues.-Sat. 10-4, Sun. 12-4.

Erlanger

ERLANGER HISTORICAL SOCIETY, 3319 Crescent Ave., Erlanger, KY 41018. Mailing Address: P.O. Box 18062, Erlanger, KY 41018-0062. Tel.: 859-727-2630.
Web Site: erlangerhistoricalsociety.org
Founded: 1990.
Congressional District: 4
Key Personnel: Chm. (V), Patricia A. Hahn; Pres. (V), John Scheben
Historic Building: built in 1877 by the Southern Railway Company.
Collections: railroad history; period artifacts.
Facilities: picnic area; playground.
Activities: rental facilities; arts & crafts vendors; music. Museum Sponsors: Heritage Day in September.
Publications: newsletter; history book.
Hours & Admission Prices: March-Nov. Sat. 12-4. No charge; donations accepted. ♿
Attendance: 5,000 (estimated)
Membership: Individual $10; Corporate $100.

Fairview

JEFFERSON DAVIS MONUMENT STATE PARK, Hwy. 68, Fairview, KY 42221. Mailing Address: Box 157, Fairview, KY 42221-0157. Tel.: 270-889-6100. Fax: 270-889-9369.
E-mail: mark.doss@ky.gov
Founded: 1924.
Congressional District: 1

Key Personnel: Site Supt., Mark Doss.
Governing Authority: state. Affiliated with the Kentucky Dept. of Parks, Capital Plaza Tower, Frankfort, KY 40601. Tax-exempt.
State Park Monument.
Collections: life of Confederate President, Jefferson Davis.
Facilities: Museum related items for sale.
Activities: guided tours; gallery talks.
Hours & Admission Prices: May-Oct. Tours: 9:30-4:30. Adults $4, children 12 & under $2.50. ♿
Attendance: 25,000 (estimated)

Fort Campbell

DON F. PRATT MEMORIAL MUSEUM, 5702 Tennessee Ave., Fort Campbell, KY 42223-5919. Mailing Address: P.O. Box 2133, Fort Campbell, KY 42223-2133. Tel.: 931-431-2619.
Web Site: www.fortcampbell.com/pratt.php
Founded: 1956.
Congressional District: 7
Key Personnel: Historian, Mr. John O'Brien, III; Dir. Mktg. & Public Rels., Sheryl Lowell; Tech., John Foley; Exhibits Specialist, Jim Spencer.
Personnel Profile: Full-Time Paid 4; Full-Time Volunteers 2; Part-Time Volunteers 9; Interns 3.
Governing Authority: federal. Affiliated with U.S. Army Museums System, Office of the Center of Military History, Department of Army, Washington, DC 20315: Tax-exempt.
Airborne Military Museum.
Collections: Fort Campbell, KY from 1942 to present; history of 101st ABN Division; 11th Airborne Division; 12th & 14th Armored Divisions; 173rd Airborne Brigade; U.S., German, Japanese, Iraqi & Vietnamese uniforms; equipment & documents relating to U.S. military heritage; WWII 20th Armored Division, U.S. Army.
Research Fields: U.S. Military; U.S. Airborne history; 101st Airborne Div. history.
Facilities: library of books & manuscripts pertaining to Fort Campbell Airborn, 101st & 11th Airborne Divisions history, 12th & 14th Armored Divisions & 173rd Airborne Brigade.
Activities: guided tours; lectures; films; student programs; loan, permanent & temporary exhibitions.
Publications: pamphlets, 101st Airborne Div. (Air Assault), Fort Campbell.
Hours & Admission Prices: Mon.-Sat. 9:30-4:30, guided tours of 10 or more by appointment. No charge; donations accepted. Closed New Year's Day; Christmas Day. ♿
Attendance: 55,000 (accurate)

Fort Knox

GENERAL GEORGE PATTON MUSEUM, 4554 Fayette Ave., Fort Knox, KY 40121-0208. Mailing Address: P.O. Box 208, Fort Knox, KY 40121-0208. Tel.: 502-624-3812. Fax: 502-624-2364.
E-mail: museum@knox.army.mil
Web Site: www.generalpatton.org
Formerly: Patton Museum of Cavalry and Armor
Founded: 1948.
Congressional District: 2
Key Personnel: Dir., Frank Jardin; Cur., C.R. Lemons; Librarian, Candace L. Fuller; Museum Shop Mgr., Bill Anderson.
Governing Authority: federal. Affiliated with U.S. Army Armor Center & Fort Knox. Tax-exempt.
Military Museum.
Collections: tanks; armored vehicles; firearms; medals & decorations; Gen. Patton memorabilia; paintings.
Research Fields: U.S. Army mechanized cavalry & armor; Gen. George S. Patton, Jr.; Fort Knox; armor units.
Facilities: library of material on U.S. & foreign fighting vehicle history & technology available for use on premises by personal application.
Activities: films; temporary exhibitions. Museum Sponsors: 4th of July World War II operational armor demonstration.
Hours & Admission Prices: Mon.-Fri. 9-4:30, Sat.-Sun. & holidays 10-4:30. No charge; donations accepted. Closed New Year's Eve & Day; Easter; Thanksgiving; Christmas Eve & Day. ♿
Attendance: 358,025 (accurate)

Fort Mitchell

VENT HAVEN MUSEUM, 33 W. Maple Ave., Fort Mitchell, KY 41011-2616. Tel.: 859-341-0461.
E-mail: venthaven@insightbb.com
Web Site: www.venthavenmuseum.net
Founded: 1973.
Congressional District: 4
Key Personnel: Cur., Jen Dawson.
Governing Authority: nonprofit organization. Tax-exempt.
Theater Museum.
Collections: 675 ventriloquial figures; library of rare books; manuscripts; films; records; play bills.
Activities: guided tours; permanent exhibitions; videotape presentation.
Hours & Admission Prices: May-Sept. by appointment only. Admission Donation: $5.
Attendance: 1,000

Frankfort

CAPITAL CITY MUSEUM, 325 Ann St., Frankfort, KY 40601-2803. Tel.: 502-696-9127.
Key Personnel: Cur., Nicky Hughes; Asst. Cur., Russ Hatter
History Museum: housed in the former Gayle Drug Store.
Collections: local history; period furnishings; personal artifacts; political memorabilia; whiskey distilling industry.
Hours & Admission Prices: Mon.-Sat. 10-4. No charge.

CLYDE E. BUCKLEY WILDLIFE SANCTUARY, 1305 Germany Rd., Frankfort, KY 40601-8257. Tel.: 859-873-5711. Fax: 859-873-5711.
E-mail: twilliams@audubon.org
Web Site: www.audubon.org
Founded: 1967.
Key Personnel: Sanctuary Mgr., Tim Williams.
Personnel Profile: Full-Time Paid 1; Interns 3.
Governing Authority: private; nonprofit society. Parent Institution: The National Audubon Society. Tax-exempt: 501(c)(3).
Wildlife Sanctuary & Nature Center.
Collections: various plants & animals native to the area, including birds, reptiles & amphibians; terrariums & aquariums; insects; collection of the prints of Ray Harm; hands-on exhibits & displays.
Research Fields: flora & fauna of the Inner Bluegrass area.
Facilities: 200-vol. library of books & magazines available for use on premises; nature & conservation center; Marion E. Lindsey Bird Blind, which has one-way windows to permit visitors to observe the feeding of the birds; nature trails; information area. Nature books, stationery & bird related items for sale.
Activities: guided tours; lectures; slide presentations; environmental workshops; organized education programs & activities for children & adults; permanent & temporary exhibitions; intern program.
Publications: sanctuary information & history brochure; internship brochure.
Hours & Admission Prices: Sanctuary: Wed.-Fri. 9-5, Sat.-Sun. 9-6. Museum: Sat.-Sun. 1-6; other times by appointment. Adults $4, children $3; members no charge. Closed holidays. ♿
Attendance: 10,000
Membership: Individual $35; Family $50; Patron $150 & up.

THE GOVERNOR'S MANSION, 704 Capitol Ave., Frankfort, KY 40601-3448. Tel.: 502-564-8004. Fax: 502-564-5022.
E-mail: ann.evans@ky.gov
Web Site: www.governorsmansion.ky.gov
Formerly: The Executive Mansion
Founded: 1914.
Congressional District: 6
Key Personnel: Exec. Dir., Ann Evans.
Governing Authority: state. Parent Institution: Finance & Administration Cabinet. Subsidiary Institution: Historic Properties. Tax-exempt.
Historic House: c.1914 Beaux-Arts style 25-room residence of 23 of Kentucky's governors.
Collections: furnishings; Kentucky paintings; period silver; Chinese porcelains.
Activities: guided tours.
Publications: brochure.
Hours & Admission Prices: Tues. & Thurs. 9-11. No charge; donations accepted. Closed legal holidays. ♿

KENTUCKY DEPARTMENT OF FISH & WILDLIFE RESOURCES-SALATO WILDLIFE EDUCATION CENTER, 1 Sportsman's Lane, Frankfort, KY 40601-3951. Tel.: 502-564-7863, ext. 459 & 4336; 1-800-858-1549. Fax: 502-564-6508.
Web Site: www.fw.ky.gov
Founded: 1947.
Congressional District: 4
Key Personnel: Commissioner, Dr. Jonathan W. Gossett.
Personnel Profile: Full-Time Paid 6; Part-Time Paid 8; Part-Time Volunteers 6.
Governing Authority: state. Parent Institution: Kentucky State Government. Subsidiary Institution: Kentucky Dept. Fish & Wildlife Resources, Frankfort, KY 40601. Tax-exempt.

Wildlife Museum.
Collections: live animals & birds; animal artifacts & native plants.
Research Fields: preserved specimens fish, amphibians.
Facilities: wildlife education center; zoological park; picnic area.
Activities: special programming; self-guided tours.
Publications: magazine, Kentucky Afield-The Magazine; technical papers on fish & wildlife; newsletter, Wildways.
Hours & Admission Prices: mid-Feb. to mid-Dec. Tues.-Fri. 9-5, Sat. 10-5. No charge. Closed state holidays. ♿
Attendance: 100,000 (accurate)

* **KENTUCKY HISTORICAL SOCIETY, (M),** 100 W. Broadway, Frankfort, KY 40601-1931. Tel.: 502-564-1792. Fax: 502-564-4701.
E-mail: KHS@ky.gov
Web Site: www.history.ky.gov
Founded: 1836.
Congressional District: 6
Key Personnel: Dir., Kent Whitworth; Museum Shop Mgr., Nina Elmore.
Personnel Profile: Full-Time Paid 69; Part-Time Paid 12.
Governing Authority: state. Branch Museums: Thomas D. Clark Center for Kentucky History; Kentucky Military History Museum (Old State Arsenal); Old State Capitol. Tax-exempt: 501(c)(3).
History Museum.
Collections: decorative arts; textiles; social & political history material related to Kentucky history; military artifacts.
Research Fields: genealogy; Kentucky history; military history.
Facilities: 80,000-vol. library of books, 3,000-vol. of genealogies, 10,000-reels of microfilm, a complete set of Kentucky legislative journals, manuscript collection & Kentucky tax records, available for use on premises only. Gift items for sale.
Activities: guided tours; interpretive programs & school activities by schedule; permanent, temporary & traveling exhibitions; local history; Historymobile.
Publications: quarterly, The Register; quarterly, Kentucky Ancestors; quarterly newsletter, The Chronicle.
Hours & Admission Prices: Center for Kentucky History, Old State Capitol & Library: Tues.-Sat. 10-4. Military Museum: closed for renovation. Adults $4, youth 6-18 $2; children 5 & under and members no charge. ♿
Attendance: 228,000 (estimated)
Membership: Student $20; Senior $35; Individual $40; Senior Household $45; Household & Institutional $50; Friend $100.

KENTUCKY MILITARY HISTORY MUSEUM, 128 E. Main St., Frankfort, KY 40601. Mailing Address: 100 W. Broadway, Frankfort, KY 40601-1931. Tel.: 502-564-3265. Fax: 502-564-4054.
Web Site: history.ky.gov
Founded: 1974.
Congressional District: 6
Key Personnel: Cur., Bill Bright.
Personnel Profile: Full-Time Paid 3; Part-Time Paid 1; Part-Time Volunteers 2; Interns 3.
Governing Authority: state. Parent Institution: Kentucky Historical Society. Subsidiary Institution: Kentucky Dept. of Military Affairs (Kentucky National Guard). Tax-exempt.
Military Museum: housed in 1850 State Arsenal, built for Kentucky Militia.
Collections: Kentucky-related ordnance; flags; uniforms; personal items; archival materials.
Research Fields: general Kentucky military history; history of Kentucky militia & national guard; Civil War; 20th century.
Activities: guided tours; hands-on programs for school groups; living history programs in schools; permanent, temporary & traveling exhibitions.
Publications: brochures; exhibit guides; calendar.
Hours & Admission Prices: Tues.-Sat. 10-5; call to confirm. Adults $4; members no charge. Closed New Year's Eve & Day; Easter; Thanksgiving; Christmas Eve & Day. ♿
Attendance: 15,000 (accurate)
Membership: Kentucky Historical Society: Student $20; Senior $35; Individual $40; Senior Family $45; Family & Institutional $50; Friend $100; Benefactor $250.

KENTUCKY STATE CAPITOL, Capital Ave., Frankfort, KY 40601. Mailing Address: Historic Properties, Berry Hill Mansion, 700 Louisville Rd., Frankfort, KY 40601-3304. Tel.: 502-564-3000 & (Tour Information) 564-3449. Fax: 502-564-6505.
E-mail: david.buchta@ky.gov
Web Site: www.historicproperties.ky.gov
Founded: 1910.
Congressional District: 6
Personnel Profile: Full-Time Paid 2; Part-Time Paid 1; Interns 2.
Governing Authority: state. Parent Institution: Finance & Administration Cabinet. Subsidiary Institution: Historic Properties.
Historic Building: c.1910 Kentucky's fourth Statehouse.
Collections: period furnishings; murals; early 20th-century decorative arts; First Ladies miniature collection.
Activities: guided tours; rotating exhibits; self-guided walking tour.
Publications: brochure.
Hours & Admission Prices: Mon.-Fri. 8-4:30. No charge. Closed New Year's Day; Easter; Thanksgiving; Christmas Eve & Day. ♿
Attendance: 100,000 (estimated)

LIBERTY HALL HISTORIC SITE, (M), 202 Wilkinson St., Frankfort, KY 40601-1826. Tel.: 502-227-2560; 888-516-5101. Fax: 502-227-3348.
Web Site: www.libertyhall.org
Founded: 1937.
Congressional District: 6
Key Personnel: Exec. Dir., Karla Nicholson; Coord. Education, Jennifer Koach; Cur., Beth Caffery.
Personnel Profile: Full-Time Paid 3; Part-Time Paid 2; Part-Time Volunteers 35; Interns 1.
Governing Authority: private; nonprofit organization. Parent Institution: Liberty Hall Inc. Tax-exempt: 501(c)(3).
Historic site consisting of Liberty Hall, a 1796 Georgian house, the Orlando Brown House, an 1835 Greek Revival house. The site is the home of Senator John Brown, Kentucky's first US senator.
Collections: late 18th- & 19th-century furniture; family portraits; china; silver; books; Brown family furnishings; art; decorative art; kitchen & household artifacts; family documents.
Research Fields: life in late 18th-century to early 19th-century Kentucky & slavery in this time period.
Facilities: 1,000-vol. library of history & genealogy books available for use by prior arrangement; garden wedding facilities; botanical garden.
Activities: guided tours; formal education programs; hobby workshops; lectures; loan, permanent & temporary exhibitions; 19th-century Christmas; docent program.
Publications: books, Liberty Hall & Orlando Brown; The Browns of Liberty Hall; Kentucky Courthouses; Kentucky Ante-Bellum Portraits; bimonthly newsletter, Liberty Hall Historic Site Gazette.
Hours & Admission Prices: Tours: March to mid-Dec. Tues.-Sat. 10:30, 12, 1:30, 3; Sun. 1:30, 3. Adults $4, seniors 60 & over $3, children 5-18 $1; discounts to AAM members; children 4 & under no charge. Closed New Year's Day; Independence Day; Thanksgiving; Christmas.
Attendance: 4,276 (accurate)

THE OLD GOVERNOR'S MANSION, (M), 420 High St., Frankfort, KY 40601-2175. Mailing Address: 700 Capitol Ave., Frankfort, KY 40601-3410. Tel.: 502-564-3449. Fax: 502-564-4099.
Founded: 1798.
Congressional District: 6
Key Personnel: Dir., David Buchta.
Personnel Profile: Full-Time Paid 4; Part-Time Paid 2; Part-Time Volunteers 4.
Governing Authority: state. Parent Institution: Finance & Administration cabinet, Historic Properties. Tax-exempt.
Historic Building: 1798 transitional Federal-Georgian style Old Governor's Mansion.
Collections: historic furniture & artifacts that belonged to former Governors; furniture; paintings; portraits; silver items.
Activities: guided tours.
Publications: brochure.
Hours & Admission Prices: Closed until October 2010. ♿
Attendance: 6,000 (estimated)

VEST-LINDSEY HOUSE, 401 Wapping St., Frankfort, KY 40601-2607. Tel.: 502-564-3000 & 6980. Fax: 502-564-6505.
Founded: 1978.
Congressional District: 6
Key Personnel: Dir. & Cur., David Buchta.
Personnel Profile: Full-Time Paid 2.
Governing Authority: state of Kentucky.
Historic House: c.1820 12-room home located in a four-block area of 28 historic homes & churches; official state meeting house.
Collections: early 1800s furnishings.
Activities: guided tours.
Publications: brochure.
Hours & Admission Prices: By appointment. No charge. Closed state & national holidays. ♿

Franklin

AFRICAN AMERICAN HERITAGE CENTER, 500 Jefferson St., Franklin, KY 42134-1728. Mailing Address: P.O. Box 353, Franklin, KY 42135-0353. Tel.: 270-586-0099. Fax: 270-586-5719.
E-mail: africanamericanh@bellsouth.net
Web Site: www.aahconline.org
History Museum: listed on the National Register of Historic Places.
Collections: local history & culture pertaining to African Americans in Simpson County.
Hours & Admission Prices: Mon.-Fri. 9-12 & 1-4:30, Sat. 9-11. Closed holidays.

SIMPSON COUNTY ARCHIVES & MUSEUM, 206 N. College St., Franklin, KY 42134-1826. Tel.: 270-586-4228. Fax: 270-586-4429.
E-mail: oldjail@comcast.net
History Museum: housed in the old jail and jailer's residence.
Collections: old scrapbooks; family Bibles; assorted manuscripts; census records; maps.
Hours & Admission Prices: Mon.-Fri. 9-4, Sat. 10-2; other times by appointment. Closed federal holidays.

Georgetown

GEORGETOWN COLLEGE ART GALLERIES, 400 E. College St., Georgetown, KY 40324-1628. Tel.: 502-863-8399.
E-mail: rachel_brewer@georgetowncollege.edu
Web Site: www.georgetowncollege.edu/art/gallery/gallery.htm
Key Personnel: Dir. & Cur. Collections, Rachel Brewer
Art Gallery.
Collections: art exhibitions.
Major Exhibits: Homeless: Telling Our Own Story, 1/21/10-2/19/10; Jamie McIntosh: Twisted Textiles, 2/25/10-4/9/10; Emily Howard, 2/25/10-4/28/10; Class of 2010 Senior Art Exhibit, 4/15/10-5/9/10; Virginia Woolf and the Natural World, 5/13/10-6/10/10.
Hours & Admission Prices: Mon.-Fri. 12-4:30; other times by appointment. No charge.

GEORGETOWN-SCOTT COUNTY MUSEUM, 229 E. Main St., Georgetown, KY 40324-1759. Tel.: 502-863-6201.
Key Personnel: Dir., John Toncray; Program Coord., Andrew Green
History Museum.
Collections: local history & culture; photographs; personal artifacts; video.
Activities: video.
Hours & Admission Prices: Mon.-Fri. 9-4, Sat. 10-4; other times by appointment.

WARD HALL, 1782 Frankfort Pike, Georgetown, KY 40324. Mailing Address: P.O. Box 1957, Georgetown, KY 40324-6957. Tel.: 859-879-9393.
Web Site: www.wardhall.net
Founded: 1979.
Congressional District: 6
Key Personnel: Chm., David Stuart.
Governing Authority: individual operation.
Historic House: 1853 Classical Greek Revival House.
Collections: period furnishings.
Research Fields: Bluegrass houses & traditions; antebellum houses.
Activities: guided tours.
Publications: booklet, Ward-Johnson Families of Central Kentucky; Scott County History Book; The Bluegrass of Kentucky; information sheets on architectural features of the house.
Hours & Admission Prices: By appointment only. No Charge.

Glasgow

SOUTH CENTRAL KENTUCKY CULTURAL CENTER, 200 W. Water St., Glasgow, KY 42141-1738. Tel.: 270-651-9792.
E-mail: sckculturalcenter@glasgow-ky.com
Web Site: www.kyculturalcenter.org
History Museum housed in the old Kentucky Pants factory.
Collections: local history & cultural pertaining to Barren County.
Hours & Admission Prices: Mon.-Fri. 9-4, Sat. 9-2.

Golden Pond

USDA FOREST SERVICE - LAND BETWEEN THE LAKES, 100 Van Morgan Dr., Golden Pond, KY 42211-9001. Tel.: 270-924-2000. Fax: 270-924-2060.
E-mail: rroby@fs.fed.us
Web Site: www.lbl.org
Formerly: Tennessee Valley Authority Land Between the Lakes
Founded: 1963.
Congressional District: 1
Key Personnel: Gen. Mgr., Bill Lisowsky.
Governing Authority: federal. USDA Forest Service
Historic Building & Site, Park & Nature Center, Planetarium & Natural History Museum.
Collections: period furnishings; farm tools. Historic Structures: 1850 The Homeplace, 16 structures comprising a living history farm.
Research Fields: regional & local history; recreation, cultural & natural resource management.
Facilities: Golden Pond Visitor Center; theatre; observatory; planetarium; The Nature Station; Homeplace-1850; The Elk & Bison Prairie.
Activities: guided group tours, scheduled on request; AV presentations; educational exhibits; information services; variety of programmed learning & skill-developing activities; trails for handicapped; special weekends; arts & crafts festival; group camps; horseback riding; student intern & apprentice programs; organized education programs for undergraduate & graduate college students; living history demonstrations.
Publications: Spring Wildflowers; Summer and Fall Wildflowers; Ancient Man; Amphibians and Reptiles of Land Between The Lakes; Lichens and Ferns of Land Between The Lakes; Trees and Shrubs of Land Between The Lakes; Mushrooms of Land Between the Lakes; 1850s Cookbook; Tennessee's Iron Industry Revisited: The Stewart County Story; leader guide.
Hours & Admission Prices: The Homeplace-1850: March & Nov. Wed.-Sat. 9-5, Sun. 10-5; April-Oct. Mon.-Sat. 9-5, Sun. 10-5. Adults $3, children 5-12 $2; discounts to groups; children 4 & under no charge. ♿
Attendance: 2,450,000 (accurate)
Membership: Land Between the Lakes Association: Sponsor $30; Sustaining $50; Patron $100; Business $250; Corporate $1,000.

Greenville

DUNCAN MUSEUM & ART GALLERY, 122 S. Cherry St., Greenville, KY 42345-1234. Mailing Address: P.O. Box 289, Greenville, KY 42345-0289. Tel.: 270-338-2605.
E-mail: duncan.museum@gmail.com
Web Site: www.duncanculturalcenter.com
Formerly: Duncan Cultural Center Museum and Art Gallery
Founded: 1989.
Congressional District: 15
Key Personnel: Dir., Shara Snodgrass; Chm. (V), Tommy Harrison.
Governing Authority: Tax-exempt.
History Museum & Art Gallery.
Collections: Duncan family history; period furnishings; personal artifacts; coal mining; Victorian artifacts; Native American.
Major Exhibits: History of the L & N Railroad (T), 2/10; Harlan Hubbard Collection (T), 8/10.
Activities: rental facilities; special events. Museum Sponsors: Mother's Day Victorian Tea in May; Mad Hatter Tea Party for Kids in May.
Publications: annual yearbook.
Hours & Admission Prices: Mon.-Fri. 11-4. No charge; donations encouraged. ♿
Attendance: 3,000
Membership: Annual $25; Life $500; Patron $500; Benefactor $1,000.

Hardinsburg

BRECKINRIDGE COUNTY HISTORICAL SOCIETY MUSEUM, 108 E. 3rd St., Hardinsburg, KY 40143. Tel.: 270-756-2867.
Founded: 1984.
Key Personnel: Pres., Rebecca J. Davis
Historical Society Museum: housed in Taylor house.
Collections: local history & culture; photographs; period artifacts.
Hours & Admission Prices: Sat. 9-12. No charge.
Membership: Individual $15; Lifetime $100.

Harrodsburg

MORGAN ROW MUSEUM AND HARRODSBURG-MERCER COUNTY RESEARCH LIBRARY, 220 S. Chiles St., Harrodsburg, KY 40330-1631. Mailing Address: P.O. Box 316, Harrodsburg, KY 40330-0316. Tel.: 859-734-5985.
Formerly: Morgan Row Museum and Research Center
Founded: 1907.
Key Personnel: Pres. (V), Jerry Sampson.
Governing Authority: society. Affiliated with Harrodsburg Historical Society. Tax-exempt.
Historic House: 1800s Row House built by Joseph Morgan.
Collections: an original Chester Harding portrait of Daniel Boone; antique furniture; displays of rifles; miniature furniture; examples of early glass,

china & silver; original documents & personal items related to the early history of Harrodsburg & Mercer County; Genealogy Library: family files, cemetery records, tax & census, newspapers, books of history, original documents of local families. Historical Building: 1800 Old Mud Meeting House, built for the first Dutch Reformed Church west of the Alleghenies.
Research Fields: genealogy; early Kentucky history.
Facilities: genealogical & research library of rare books, documents, maps, family & subject files, census records & material dealing with the early history of this area available for research on premises with a member of the society present; microfilm reader; meeting room.
Activities: permanent displays of portraits by Kentucky artists.
Publications: 4-vols. Mercer County Cemetery Records; 1831-1850 Mercer County Marriage Bonds & Consents; Old Mud Meeting House.
Hours & Admission Prices: Tues. 10-4, Wed.-Sat. 1-4. Museum: no charge; donations accepted. Library: $5.
Attendance: 900 (estimated)

OLD FORT HARROD STATE PARK MANSION MUSEUM, 100 S. College St., Harrodsburg, KY 40330-1508. Mailing Address: P.O. Box 156, Harrodsburg, KY 40330-0156. Tel.: 859-734-3314. Fax: 859-734-0794.
E-mail: fortharrod@ky.gov
Web Site: www.parks.ky.gov/findparks/recparks/fh
Founded: 1934.
Congressional District: 6
Key Personnel: Park Mgr., David Coleman.
Personnel Profile: Full-Time Paid 3; Part-Time Paid 16; Part-Time Volunteers 1.
Governing Authority: state. Parent Institution: Kentucky Department of Parks, Capital Plaza Tower, Frankfort, KY 40601.
Museum & Historic House: 1830 Greek revival mansion; replica of original fort built by James Harrod.
Collections: archaeology; archives; costumes; decorative arts; glass; history; Indian artifacts; music; President Abraham Lincoln memorabilia.
Activities: guided tours; permanent exhibitions; manuscript collections.
Hours & Admission Prices: Museum: mid-March to Oct. daily 9-5. Fort: Nov. to mid-March daily 9-4:30. Mid-March to Oct. adults $5, seniors $4, children $3; Nov. to mid-March adults $2, children $1. Closed New Year's Eve & Day; Christmas Eve, Day & week. ♿
Attendance: 30,000 (accurate)

SHAKER VILLAGE OF PLEASANT HILL, 3501 Lexington Rd., Harrodsburg, KY 40330-8846. Tel.: 859-734-1549. Fax: 859-734-7278.
E-mail: lcurry@shakervillageky.org
Web Site: www.shakervillageky.org
Founded: 1961.
Congressional District: 6
Key Personnel: C.E.O. & Pres., Madge B. Adams; Vice Pres. & Cur., Larrie Spier Curry; Chm. Bd. (V), James G. Kenan; Dir. Human Resources, Candace Parker; Mgr. Interpretation & Education, Susan Lyons Hughes; Mgr. Historic Farm, Ralph E. Ward; Mgr. Craft Store, Lorrin Ingerson; Mgr. Preservation, Mike McGinnis.
Personnel Profile: Full-Time Paid 86; Part-Time Paid 89; Part-Time Volunteers 45.
Governing Authority: nonprofit organization. Tax-exempt: 501(c)(3).
Historic Village Museum: over 2,900 acres former Shaker farmland includes 34 original 19th century buildings.
Collections: 34 historic early 19th-century buildings; furniture; artifacts of Shakers; tools & equipment for agriculture, woodworking & other 19th-century industries; textiles; manuscripts; photographs.
Research Fields: Shaker & Utopian social history of the 19th-century; 19th-century agriculture, trades & religious history.
Facilities: 1,500-vol. library of material relating to the history of the Shakers & 19th-century Utopian societies, 2,900 acres with 40 miles of multi-use trails; meeting & conference rooms; overnight accommodations & dining room. Shaker furniture reproductions & publications; handmade Kentucky crafts for sale.
Activities: self-guided & guided tours; lectures; films; music & dance interpretation; historic agriculture; interpreted horse-drawn carriage tours; crafts events; temporary & permanent exhibitions; hands-on exhibit; organized educational programs; workshops; hiking & horseback trails; nature hikes; riverboat excursions. Museum Sponsors: seasonal special events. Annual Events: craft fair; antique show & sale; Chamber Music Festival.
Publications: books, Pleasant Hill & Its Shakers; Welcome Back to Pleasant Hill; We Make You Kindly Welcome; Pleasant Hill in the Civil War; The Gift of Pleasant Hill; quarterly newsletter; annual calendar, Keepsake Art Calendar.
Hours & Admission Prices: April-Oct. daily 10-5. Village Tour: adults 13 & over $15, youth 6-12 $5. Riverboat Excursions: children 13 & over $10, youth 6-12 $5; discounts to groups; children under 6 accompanied by a parent & members no charge. Nov.-March tour hours & prices reduced.
Attendance: 58,072 (accurate)
Membership: member $50; Partner $100; Supporter $250; Contributor $500; Benefactor $1,000.

Hartford

THE BLUEGRASS MOTORCYCLE MUSEUM, 5608 US Hwy. 231 N., Hartford, KY 42347-9583. Tel.: 270-298-7764.
Key Personnel: Owner, Jack Embry; Owner, Nancy Embry
Motorcycle Museum.
Collections: period motorcycles.
Hours & Admission Prices: Tues.-Fri. 10-5, Sat. 10-3; other times by appointment.

Hazard

BOBBY DAVIS MUSEUM AND PARK, 234 Walnut St., Hazard, KY 41701-1852. Tel.: 606-439-4325.
Web Site: www.kaht.com/multiple/bobbydavis.htm
History Museum.
Collections: local history; photographs; historical documents; oral history tapes; period artifacts.
Hours & Admission Prices: Mon.-Fri. 8-4.

Henderson

JOHN JAMES AUDUBON MUSEUM, (M), 3100 U.S. Hwy. 41 N., Henderson, KY 42420-2055. Mailing Address: P.O. Box 576, Henderson, KY 42419-0576. Tel.: 270-826-2247. Fax: 270-826-2286. TDD: 270-826-2247.
E-mail: audubon@ky.gov
Web Site: parks.ky.gov/findparks/recparks/au/
Founded: 1938.
Congressional District: 1
Key Personnel: Cur., Alan Gehret.
Personnel Profile: Full-Time Paid 6; Part-Time Paid 2; Part-Time Volunteers 8.
Governing Authority: state. Affiliated with Kentucky Dept. of Parks, Capital Plaza Tower, Frankfort, KY 40601.
State Park Museum: located on migratory bird route.
Collections: works, prints & personal memorabilia of John James Audubon; exhibits about Audubon's life and work; archives; paintings; botany; costumes; history; natural history; manuscript collections.
Facilities: nature observatory; discovery room devoted to study of birds; nature trails. Wildlife prints, printed matter & works of wildlife artists for sale.
Activities: guided tours; lectures; gallery talks; arts festivals; nature trail tours; over-night lodging available; formally organized education programs for children; wildlife observation area.
Publications: The Warbler.
Hours & Admission Prices: March-Nov. daily 10-5; Dec.-Feb. Wed.-Sun. 8-4:30. Family $10, adults $4, children 6-12 $2.50; discounts to groups; members, Friends of Audubon members & children under 6 no charge. Closed New Year's Eve & Day; Martin Luther King Jr. Day; Thanksgiving & day after; Christmas week. ♿
Attendance: 12,000 (estimated)
Membership: Student $5; Individual $20; Family $35; Donor $100.

Highland Heights

MUSEUM OF ANTHROPOLOGY, (M), University Drive, Northern Kentucky Univ., 216 Landrum Academic Center, Highland Heights, KY 41099-0001. Tel.: 859-572-1569. Fax: 859-572-5566.
E-mail: voelkerjl@nku.edu
Web Site: anthropologymuseum.nku.edu
Founded: 1976.
Congressional District: 6
Key Personnel: Dir., Dr. Judy Voelker.
Personnel Profile: Part-Time Paid 2.
Governing Authority: Northern Kentucky University. Tax-exempt.
Anthropology Museum.
Collections: Ohio Valley archaeological materials; contemporary West Africa; contemporary Southwestern Indians; contemporary Southeastern Indians; contemporary Northwest Coast; Huichol Indians; New Guinea; Mexico; Latin America; hominid fossil casts; comparative vertebrate collection.
Research Fields: Ohio Valley archeology.
Facilities: 200-vol. library of archaeological reports, research manuals, journals available for research by special arrangement; field research station; separate laboratory operation; classrooms.
Activities: lectures; films; slide shows; demonstrations; guided tours; gallery talks; formally organized education programs for school & citizen groups; museum methods course for college students; loan, permanent & temporary exhibitions.

Publications: reports; contract archaeology.
Hours & Admission Prices: By appointment only. No charge. Closed university holidays; Christmas. ♿
Attendance: 800 (estimated)

NORTHERN KENTUCKY UNIVERSITY ART GALLERIES, Nunn Dr., Highland Heights, KY 41099-0001. Tel.: 859-572-5148 & 5421. Fax: 859-572-6501.
E-mail: knight@nku.edu
Web Site: www.nku.edu/~art/galleries.html
Founded: 1968.
Congressional District: 4
Key Personnel: Dir., David J. Knight.
Personnel Profile: Full-Time Paid 1; Interns 3.
Governing Authority: public university; nonprofit. Parent Institution: State of Kentucky. Tax-exempt.
Art Museum.
Collections: concentration on regional & national artists and varied media.
Facilities: library of various art exhibition catalogues; 2,700 sq. ft. exhibit space.
Activities: lectures; participatory & traveling exhibits.
Hours & Admission Prices: mid-Jan. to mid-Dec. Mon.-Fri. 9-9, other hours by appointment. No charge; donations accepted. Closed legal holidays; spring break. ♿
Attendance: 18,000 (estimated)

Hodgenville

ABRAHAM LINCOLN BIRTHPLACE NATIONAL HISTORIC SITE, 2995 Lincoln Farm Rd., Hodgenville, KY 42748-9707. Tel.: 270-358-3137. Fax: 270-358-3874.
E-mail: abli_superintendent@nps.gov
Web Site: www.nps.gov/abli
Founded: 1916.
Congressional District: 2
Key Personnel: Supt., Keith Pruitt.
Personnel Profile: Full-Time Paid 7; Full-Time Volunteers 2; Part-Time Paid 3; Part-Time Volunteers 3; Interns 1.
Governing Authority: federal. Parent Institution: National Park Service, Department of the Interior.
Historic Site: birthplace of Abraham Lincoln.
Collections: Lincoln family Bible; tools & household objects relating to pioneer living of the early 19th century; graphics. Historic Buildings: c.1911 memorial building; c.1840 cabin.
Research Fields: early life of Lincoln & the environment of his birth.
Facilities: 300-vol. library of books on Abraham Lincoln, Kentucky history & the Civil War available for use on application to the Superintendent; 80-seat auditorium.
Activities: self-guided tours; programs; films; permanent exhibitions; ranger guided tours.
Publications: folder covering basic park history.
Hours & Admission Prices: Memorial Day-Labor Day daily 8-6:45; Sept.-May daily 8-4:45. Visitor Center: call for hours. No charge; donations accepted. Closed New Year's Day; Thanksgiving; Christmas. ♿
Attendance: 235,000 (accurate)

THE LINCOLN MUSEUM, 66 Lincoln Sq., Hodgenville, KY 42748-1551. Tel.: 270-358-3163.
E-mail: abe@lincolnmuseum-ky.org
Web Site: www.lincolnmuseum-ky.org
History Museum.
Collections: 12 dioramas depicting Lincoln's life; paintings; photographs.
Hours & Admission Prices: Mon.-Sat. 8:30-4:30, Sun. 12:30-4:30.

Hopkinsville

PENNYROYAL AREA MUSEUM, 217 E. Ninth St., Hopkinsville, KY 42240-3448. Mailing Address: P.O. Box 1093, Hopkinsville, KY 42241-1093. Tel.: 270-887-4270. Fax: 270-887-4271.
E-mail: pennyroyal.museum@gmail.com
Founded: 1975.
Congressional District: 10
Key Personnel: Dir., Donna K. Stone; Education & Program Dir., Janet Bravard.
Personnel Profile: Full-Time Paid 2; Part-Time Paid 2; Part-Time Volunteers 25.
Governing Authority: municipal. Parent Institution: City of Hopkinsville, KY. Tax-exempt: 501(c)(3).
History Museum.
Collections: pioneer bedroom; household & farm tools; Black heritage objects; Mogul farm wagon; L & N railroad items; Railway Express Wagon; 1909 Model 10 Buick; 1926 Chevrolet Pumper Truck (fire); historic clothing; asst. room & business settings; Edgar Cayce artifacts; tobacco farming exhibit.
Research Fields: Kentuckian & Kentucky New Era Newspaper files.
Facilities: Locally-crafted items & Kentucky gift items for sale.
Activities: guided tours; lectures; formally organized education program for adults & undergraduate college students affiliated with Murray State University & Hopkinsville Community College, permanent & temporary exhibitions; school loan service.
Publications: booklet, Building of a Monument; Pennyroyal Rambler; Pictorial History of Hopkinsville & Christian County, Gateway II; Edgar Cayce's Hometown; Hopkinsville Postcard History; assortment of local genealogical research books, as available.
Hours & Admission Prices: Mon.-Fri. 8:30-4:30, Sat. 10-3. Adults $2, senior citizens & children $1; discounts for prearranged group tours & AAM members; members & prearranged museum professionals no charge. Closed New Year's Day; Memorial Day; Independence Day; Labor Day; Thanksgiving; Christmas. ♿
Attendance: 17,000 (accurate)
Membership: Individual $15; Senior Individual $12; Senior Couple $20; Family $25; Contributing & Sustaining $100; Lifetime $1,000.

Horse Cave

AMERICAN CAVE MUSEUM & HIDDEN RIVER CAVE, 119 E. Main St., Horse Cave, KY 42749-1112. Mailing Address: P.O. Box 409, Horse Cave, KY 42749-0409. Tel.: 270-786-1466. Fax: 270-786-1467.
E-mail: acca@cavern.org
Web Site: cavern.org
Founded: 1977.
Key Personnel: Exec. Dir., David G. Foster; Administrative Asst., Shannon L. Johnson; Mktg. & Community Outreach, Peggy A. Nims
Natural Science Museum.
Collections: prehistoric cave explorers; modern cave exploration; cave lighting; ground water in America; Cave County living; history of Mammoth & Horse Cave; cave wars; story of Floyd Collins.
Hours & Admission Prices: Memorial Day-Labor Day daily 9-7; Sept.-May daily 9-5. Adults 16 & over $15, youth 12-15 $10, children 3-11 $7; active military no charge. Closed New Year's Eve & Day; Thanksgiving; Christmas Eve & Day. ♿
Membership: Student $15; Regular $25; Family $35; Supporter $50; Sustainer $100; Guarantor $200; Benefactor $500; Patron $1,000.

KENTUCKY DOWN UNDER, 3700 L & N. Tpke. Rd., Horse Cave, KY 42749. Mailing Address: P.O. Box 189, Horse Cave, KY 42749-0189. Tel.: 800-762-2869; 270-786-2634.
E-mail: info@kdu.com
Web Site: www.kdu.com
Key Personnel: Dir., Judy Austin; Dir. Mktg., Melissa McGuire; Personnel Mgr., Karin Barnes; Animal Crew Mgr., April Hatcher; Bookkeeping, Vicki Fancher; Gift Shop Mgr., Courtney Eaton
Animal Park.
Collections: animals from Australia & the U.S. including Red Kangaroo, Emu, Kookaburra, Blue Tongue Skink, Papuan Frogmouth, Rainbow Lorikeet.
Hours & Admission Prices: March 14-April 2 & Sept. 11-Nov. 5 daily 9-4; April 3-May 21 & Aug. 7-Sept. 10 daily 8-5; May 22-Aug. 6 daily 8-6. Adults $22, seniors 62 & over $19.30, children 5-14 $13; discounts to AAA members; children 4 & under and active military with ID no charge.

Jackson

BREATHITT COUNTY MUSEUM, INC., 329 Broadway St., Jackson, KY 41339-1040. Tel.: 606-666-4159.
E-mail: breathittmuseum@bellsouth.net
Web Site: breathittmuseum.com
Founded: 1980.
Congressional District: 5
Key Personnel: Dir., Janie Griffith; Chm. & Pres. (V), Grace Warrix.
Personnel Profile: Full-Time Paid 1.
Governing Authority: Tax-exempt.
Appalachian History Museum.
Collections: county history & culture; photographs; personal artifacts; farming; mining; food preparation; textiles; logging; education; military.
Activities: classes.
Hours & Admission Prices: Mon., Wed. & Fri. 9-3:30. ♿

Jeffersontown

THE JEFFERSONTOWN HISTORICAL MUSEUM, 10635 Watterson Tr., Jeffersontown, KY 40299-3850. Tel.: 502-261-8290.
Web Site: www.jeffersontownky.com/Museum06.html
Key Personnel: Dir., Beth Wilder.
Personnel Profile: Full-Time Paid 2.
Governing Authority: city.
History Museum.
Collections: artifacts & photographs from the early times in Jeffersontown.
Hours & Admission Prices: Mon.-Fri. 10-5. No charge. ♿
Attendance: 5,000 (accurate)

La Grange

OLDHAM COUNTY HISTORY CENTER, (M), 106 N. Second Ave., La Grange, KY 40031-1102. Tel.: 502-222-0826. Fax: 502-222-7115.
E-mail: ochstryctr@aol.com
Web Site: oldhamcountyhistoricalsociety.org
Founded: 1958.
Congressional District: 4
Key Personnel: Exec. Dir., Nancy Theiss; Pres., Robert Martin.
Personnel Profile: Full-Time Paid 1; Part-Time Paid 4; Part-Time Volunteers 87.
Governing Authority: Tax-exempt.
History Museum & Center.
Collections: documents, books & maps pertaining to Oldham County; videos; interactive exhibits.
Facilities: archives.
Activities: lectures; school & family programs; archaeology programs.
Publications: Oldham County Kentucky: The First Century 1824-1924.
Hours & Admission Prices: Library & Archives: Tues.-Sat. 10-4. No charge; donations accepted. Museum: Tues.-Thurs. & Sat. 10-4, Fri. 10-8. No charge; donations accepted. Closed legal holidays. ♿
Attendance: 22,000 (accurate)
Membership: Individual $25; Family $50; Donor $100; Friend $250; Patron $500; Director's Circle $1,000.

Lexington

AMERICAN SADDLEBRED MUSEUM, 4083 Iron Works Pkwy., Lexington, KY 40511-8401. Tel.: 859-259-2746. Fax: 859-255-4909.
E-mail: museum@asbmuseum.org
Web Site: www.asbmuseum.org
Founded: 1962.
Key Personnel: Exec. Dir., Tolley Graves; C.E.O. & Pres. (V), Laurel P. Nelson; Museum Shop Mgr., Lynn Morris.
Personnel Profile: Full-Time Paid 3; Part-Time Paid 7; Part-Time Volunteers 25.
Governing Authority: nonprofit organization. Tax-exempt: 501(c)(3).
Natural History Museum.
Collections: development of the American Saddlebred Horse; paintings; trophies; saddles; doctor's buggy; photographs.
Research Fields: American Saddlebred Horse; registered horse breed.
Facilities: 3,000-vol. library. Museum-related items for sale.
Activities: permanent special & interactive exhibitions; multi-image theater presentation; videos.
Publications: Commitment.
Hours & Admission Prices: Memorial Day-Labor Day daily 9-6; Sept.-Oct. & mid-March to Memorial Day daily 9-5; Nov. to mid-March Wed.-Sun. 9-5. Adults $15 (includes Kentucky Horse Park); discounts to groups, Kroger Plus, AAA & AARP members; children under 6 & members no charge. ♿
Attendance: 30,000 (accurate)
Membership: Youth $10; Individual $35; Family $50; Contributing $125; Business/Farm/Association $150; Dual Contributing $200; Life $1,000.

* **THE ART MUSEUM AT THE UNIVERSITY OF KENTUCKY, (M),** Rose St. & Euclid Ave., Lexington, KY 40506-0001. Tel.: 859-257-5716. Fax: 859-323-1994.
Web Site: www.uky.edu/artmuseum
Founded: 1976.
Congressional District: 6
Key Personnel: Dir., Kathleen Walsh-Piper; Cur. Education, Deborah Borrowdale-Cox; Registrar, Barbara Lovejoy; Preparator, Hubert Burton; Budget Officer, Becky Hudson; Cur., Janie Welker; Mktg. & Membership, Kristine Craig; Devel. Coord., Amy Nelson; Publications & Public Rels., Dorothy Freeman.
Personnel Profile: Full-Time Paid 10; Part-Time Paid 7; Part-Time Volunteers 35; Interns 6.
Governing Authority: state. Parent Institution: University of Kentucky, Rose St., Lexington 40506. Tax-exempt.
Art Center.
Collections: 14th- to 20th-century painting, sculpture, works of art on paper; decorative arts; pre-Columbian, African & Asian art; photography; regional art.
Major Exhibits: Bluegrass Collects: The New English Arts Club, 1/24/10-4/11/10; Andre Pater Retrospective, 5/2/10-7/25/10; Hoofbeats and Heartbeats: The Horse in Americna Art, 8/22/10-11/21/10.
Research Fields: related to collections.
Activities: special loan exhibitions; educational activities related to collections & exhibitions.
Publications: newsletter, Educational Materials; exhibition catalogs.
Hours & Admission Prices: Tues.-Thurs. & Sat.-Sun. 12-5, Fri. 12-8. Fee charged for some special exhibitions. Closed university holidays. ♿
Attendance: 27,300 (estimated)
Membership: Faculty, Teacher, & Staff $30; Individual $45; Family $60; Supporting $100; Patron $250; Sustaining $500; Benefactor $1,000.

ASHLAND, THE HENRY CLAY ESTATE, 120 Sycamore Rd., Lexington, KY 40502-1842. Tel.: 859-266-8581. Fax: 859-268-7266.
E-mail: ahmichel@henryclay.org
Web Site: www.henryclay.org
Founded: 1926.
Congressional District: 6
Key Personnel: Exec. Dir., Ann Hagan-Michel; Pres., Richard DeCamp; Cur., Eric Brooks; Museum Shop Mgr., Judy Ogger.
Personnel Profile: Full-Time Paid 3; Part-Time Paid 7; Part-Time Volunteers 80.
Governing Authority: nonprofit organization. Parent Institution: Henry Clay Memorial Foundation. Tax-exempt: 501(c)(3).
Historic House: c.1806 estate of Henry Clay; c.1856 house of James Clay.
Collections: family furnishings.
Facilities: 17 acres of greenspace; 1/2 acre formal garden.
Activities: guided tours; lectures; videos; special events.
Publications: newsletter & Web site.
Hours & Admission Prices: Feb. by appointment; March-Dec. Tues.-Sat. 10-4, Sun. 1-4. Adults $7, children $4; discounts to AAA members & groups; members no charge. Closed major holidays.
Attendance: 14,000 (accurate)
Membership: Single $25; Family $45; Donor $50; Contributing $100; Supporting $500; Sustaining $1,000.

AVIATION MUSEUM OF KENTUCKY INC., (M), 4316 Hanger Dr., Blue Grass Airport, Lexington, KY 40510-9681. Tel.: 859-231-1219. Fax: 859-381-8739.
E-mail: emgarman@mac.com
Web Site: aviationky.org
Founded: 1995.
Congressional District: 6
Key Personnel: Chm. Bd., Dr. Ray Garman; Pres., Dr. G.M. Gumbert, Jr., M.D.; Archivist, Dennis Sparks.
Personnel Profile: Full-Time Volunteers 50; Part-Time Volunteers 60.
Governing Authority: private; nonprofit. Subsidiary Institution: The Kentucky Aviation Hall of Fame. Tax-exempt.
Aviation Museum.
Collections: early Kentucky aviation history; space & exploration; general aviation history; helicopter; Cessna 150; Navy A-4; Marine F-4; Air Force T-38; WACO RNF Biplane; Air Force RF-101; Navy F-14.
Research Fields: Navy F-14 Tomcat; Army Cobra helicopter.
Facilities: 1,000-vol. library; 75-seat auditorium; field research station. Museum-related items for sale.
Activities: docent program; formal education programs for children; guided tours; hobby workshops; lectures; loan, temporary & traveling exhibitions; participatory aircraft exhibits; flight simulator; TV & radio programs. Museum Sponsors: Aviation Camps for children 10-15 in June & July.
Publications: monthly newsletter, AMK News.
Hours & Admission Prices: Tues.-Sat. 10-5, Sun. 1-5. Adults $7, senior citizens $6, students $5; discounts to AAM members & groups. ♿
Attendance: 45,000 (estimated)
Membership: Student $15; Individual $30; Family $40.

BODLEY-BULLOCK HOUSE, 200 Market St., Lexington, KY 40507-1030. Tel.: 859-259-1266.
History Museum: built c.1814 for Lexington Mayor Thomas Pindell, shortly after sold to General Thomas Bodley, a veteran of the War of 1812. Served as headquarters for both Union and Confederate forces during the Civil War.
Collections: personal artifacts; furnishings.
Facilities: garden.
Activities: tours.
Hours & Admission Prices: By appointment. Closed holidays.

EXPLORIUM OF LEXINGTON, 440 W. Short St., Lexington, KY 40507-1206. Tel.: 859-258-3253. Fax: 859-258-3255.
E-mail: explore@ex
Web Site: www.explorium.com
Formerly: Lexington Children's Museum
Founded: 1990.
Congressional District: 6
Key Personnel: Exec. Dir., Mike Gilmore; Dir. Exhibits, Margaret Trafton.
Personnel Profile: Full-Time Paid 8; Part-Time Paid 10; Part-Time Volunteers 10; Interns 2.
Governing Authority: nonprofit organization. Tax-exempt: 501(c)(3).
Children's Museum: located in Victorian Square.
Collections: hands-on exhibits.
Facilities: 20,000 sq. ft. exhibit space; multi-use room: changing exhibits; fabrication shop. Museum-related items for sale.
Activities: participatory exhibits; weekend programs; demonstrations; workshops; performances.
Publications: monthly calendar of events; newsletter, News to Explore, Explorium of Lexington.
Hours & Admission Prices: Tues.-Sat. 10-5, Sun. 1-5. Admission $6; discounts to ACM, ASTC, KY Horse Park & Lexington Children's Theatre members; members & children under one no charge. Closed Easter; week after Labor Day; Thanksgiving; Christmas Eve & Day. ♿
Attendance: 90,000 (accurate)
Membership: Teachers $25; Grandparents $50; Family $75 & $125.

HEADLEY-WHITNEY MUSEUM, (M), 4435 Old Frankfort Pike, Lexington, KY 40510-9657. Tel.: 859-255-6653. Fax: 859-255-8375.
E-mail: hwmuseum@headley-whitney.org
Web Site: www.headley-whitney.org
Founded: 1968.
Congressional District: 6
Key Personnel: C.E.O., Sarah E. Henrich; Chm., Janet Craig; Graphic Designer, Sarai Steward; Educator, Amanda Harris; Cur., Amy Gundrum.
Personnel Profile: Full-Time Paid 7; Full-Time Volunteers 20; Part-Time Paid 8; Part-Time Volunteers 10; Interns 3.
Governing Authority: nonprofit organization. Subsidiary Institution: Smithsonian Affiliate. Tax-exempt: 501(c)(3).
Decorative Arts Museum.
Collections: Chinese porcelains; oriental textiles, ceramics & furniture; Asian, European & American textiles; glass & metalwork; Kentucky-made silver; jewelry & bibelots of founder/designer George W. Headley.
Facilities: 1,500-vol. library of Decorative art books, periodicals & catalogues; reading room; picnic area; 15 acres. Museum-related items for sale.
Activities: changing temporary exhibitions; lectures; concerts; education, travel, tour & volunteer programs; special cultural events; school outreach programs; Symposia; outreach programming; S.O.D.A. (Students of Decorative Art).
Publications: book, The Headley Treasure of Bibelots & Boxes; newsletter, The Jewel; regular exhibition catalogues; Stories of the Messengers.
Hours & Admission Prices: Feb.-Dec. Tues.-Fri. 10-5, Sat.-Sun. 12-5. Adults $7, seniors & students $5; discounts for AAM, AAA, KAM & SEMC members & University of KY employees. Closed New Year's Day; Memorial Day; Independence Day; Labor Day; Thanksgiving; Christmas. ♿
Attendance: 17,950 (accurate)
Membership: Individual $35; Family $65; Supporter $125; Benefactor $500; Patron $750; Directors Circle $1,000.

HUNT-MORGAN HOUSE, 201 N. Mill St., Lexington, KY 40507-1034. Mailing Address: 253 Market St., Lexington, KY 40507-1031. Tel.: 859-233-3290 & 253-0362. Fax: 859-259-9210.
E-mail: info@bluegrasstrust.org
Web Site: bluegrasstrust.org
Founded: 1955.
Key Personnel: Dir., Julie Good.
Governing Authority: nonprofit organization. Parent Institution: Blue Grass Trust. Tax-exempt: 501(c)(3).
Historic House: housed in a c.1814 Federal-style home located in Gratz Park historic district.
Collections: period furniture; decorative objects; portraits.
Activities: guided tours; docent program.
Hours & Admission Prices: March to mid-Dec. Wed.-Fri. & Sun. 1-5, Sat. 10-4. Adults $7, students & children 3 & up $4; members no charge. Closed major holidays.
Attendance: 5,000 (estimated)
Membership: Individual $50; Family $100; Hunt-Morgan Society $250; Clay Lancaster Society $500; Carolyn Reading Hammer Society $1,000.

INTERNATIONAL MUSEUM OF THE HORSE, (M), 4089 Iron Works Pkwy., Lexington, KY 40511-8483. Tel.: 859-259-4232. Fax: 859-225-4613. TDD: 859-233-4303.
E-mail: info@kyhorsepark.com
Web Site: www.kyhorsepark.com
Founded: 1978.
Congressional District: 6
Key Personnel: Dir., Bill Cooke; Art Dir., Gina Gibson; Cur. Collections, Jenifer Stermer; Cur. Asst., Shannon Leva; Registrar, Travis Robinson.
Personnel Profile: Full-Time Paid 9; Part-Time Paid 4; Part-Time Volunteers 3; Interns 1.
Governing Authority: Commonwealth of Kentucky. Parent Institution: Kentucky Horse Park Board of Management, 4089 Iron Works Pkwy., Lexington 40511. Tax-exempt.
Equine Museum.
Collections: equine history collection covering all breeds worldwide.
Research Fields: equine history.
Facilities: library of equine history available for in-house research during museum operating hours; reading room.
Activities: lectures; films; gallery tours; education program; docent programs; inter-museum loans; education packets for primary & secondary levels.
Publications: booklet, The International Museum of the Horse.
Hours & Admission Prices: March 15-Oct. daily 9-5; Nov.-March 14 Wed.-Sun. 9-5. Adults $15, children $8. ♿
Attendance: 200,000 (estimated)

THE LEXINGTON CEMETERY, 833 W. Main St., Lexington, KY 40508-2094. Tel.: 859-255-5522. Fax: 859-258-2774.
Web Site: www.lexcem.org
Founded: 1849.
Key Personnel: Pres. & Gen. Mgr., Daniel R. Scalf; Asst. Gen. Mgr., Mark C. Durbin.
Personnel Profile: Full-Time Paid 25; Part-Time Paid 6.
Governing Authority: private, nonprofit, non-sectarian corporation. Tax-exempt: 501(c)(13).
Union & Confederate Civil War Cemetery.
Collections: cemetery monuments from mid-1800's to present; Henry Clay Memorial.
Research Fields: genealogy; horticulture.
Facilities: botanical garden; arboretum; files open to public for genealogy research.
Activities: self-guided tours.
Publications: brochure, Self-Guided Historical Walking Tour; children's brochure, Self Guided Tree Tour.
Hours & Admission Prices: Cemetery: daily 8-5. Office: Mon.-Fri. 8-4, Sat. 8am-12pm. No charge. ♿

LEXINGTON HISTORY MUSEUM, (M), 215 W. Main St., Lexington, KY 40507-1305. Tel.: 859-254-0530.
E-mail: info@lexingtonhistorymuseum.org
Web Site: www.lexingtonhistorymuseum.org
Founded: 1999.
Congressional District: 6
Key Personnel: Pres. & C.E.O., J.K. Millard; Chm. (V), Dr. James F. Glenn; Vice Chm., Stephen G. Amato; Treas., Carl T. Cone; Museum Shop Mgr., Paige Prewitt.
Personnel Profile: Full-Time Paid 2; Part-Time Volunteers 42; Interns 2.
Governing Authority: private; nonprofit organization. Parent Institution: Lexington History Museum, Inc. Tax-exempt.
History Museum.
Collections: historical artifacts related to Lexington & the Bluegrass area from 1792 to present.
Major Exhibits: Lincoln and His Wife's Hometown, 1/1/10-10/3/10; For What I Do Not Know: The Reign of Terror in Civil War Ky, 2/1/10-10/31/10; Holiday Traditions of the Blue Grass, 11/10-12/10.
Facilities: 100-vol. library; rental facilities; 160-seat auditorium; 8,000 sq. ft. exhibit space. Museum-related items for sale.
Activities: docent program; films; formal education programs for adults; guided tours; hobby workshops; lectures; temporary exhibitions; rental facilities; family activities.
Publications: quarterly newspaper, The Bluegrass Historian; monthly postcard, Vidette.
Hours & Admission Prices: Sun.-Mon. & Fri. 12-4, Sat. 10-4. No charge; donations accepted. Closed major holidays. ♿
Attendance: 9,595 (accurate)
Membership: Student $10; Individual $38; Family $50; Weathervane Directors $100; Lafayette Circle $200; Phoenix Friends $500; Thomas D. Clark Society $1,000.

THE LIVING ARTS AND SCIENCE CENTER, INC., 362 N. Martin Luther King Blvd., Lexington, KY 40508-1889. Tel.: 859-252-5222 & 255-2284. Fax: 859-255-7448.
E-mail: info@lasclex.org
Web Site: www.lasclex.org
Founded: 1968.
Congressional District: 8
Key Personnel: Pres. (V), Yajaira Aich; Dir., Heather Lyons; Coord. Educational Outreach, Katherine Bullock; Cur., Elaine Quave; Art Education, Molly Wilson; Bookkeeper, LeAnn Jenkins.
Personnel Profile: Full-Time Paid 6; Part-Time Paid 33; Part-Time Volunteers 10.
Governing Authority: nonprofit organization. Affiliated with Lexington Arts & Cultural Council. Tax-exempt: 501(c)(3) & 170(b)(1)(A).
Children's Art and Science Center.
Collections: art & science exhibits; native Kentucky plants; butterfly garden.
Major Exhibits: The Art of Architecture, 11/09-5/30/10; The Emerald City, 1/5/10-2/1/10.
Facilities: 600-vol. library of books on art, environmental & natural science & education; classrooms.
Activities: art & science classes for children; outreach programs; loan, temporary & traveling exhibitions; teachers workshops; lectures; festivals; special education classes for underserved populations, at risk youth & special needs populations; traveling science kits; traveling Starlab Planetarium; field trip programs for K-12 in the arts & sciences.
Publications: exhibition brochures; teacher reference materials; quarterly schedule of classes; quarterly newsletter & program schedule, Imagine That!
Hours & Admission Prices: Academic Year: Mon.-Fri. 8:30-5, Sat. 10-2; Summer: Mon.-Fri. 8-5. No charge; donations accepted. Closed New Year's Day; Independence Day; Thanksgiving; Christmas. ♿
Attendance: 25,000 (estimated)
Membership: Individual $30; Family $50; Friend $100; Supporter $250; Patron $500.

MARY TODD LINCOLN HOUSE, 578 W. Main, Lexington, KY 40507-1642. Mailing Address: P.O. Box 132, Lexington, KY 40588-0132. Tel.: 859-233-9999. Fax: 859-252-2269.
E-mail: mtlhouse@windstream.net
Web Site: www.mtlhouse.org
Founded: 1968.
Congressional District: 6
Key Personnel: Dir., Gwen Thompson; Chm. (V), Priscilla Lynd; Museum Shop Mgr., Glenna Holloway.
Personnel Profile: Full-Time Paid 1; Part-Time Paid 8; Part-Time Volunteers 5.
Governing Authority: nonprofit organization. Parent Institution: Kentucky Mansions Preservation Foundation, Inc., 578 W. Main, Lexington, KY 40588. Tax-exempt.
Historical & Preservation Society Museum: housed in 1803-1806 Inn occupied by Todd family from 1832-1849.
Collections: Lincoln book collection; rare old leather bound books; personal articles of Mary Todd Lincoln & the Lincoln family; julep cup collections; furnishings & furniture of the period; family portraits.
Activities: guided tours.
Publications: The Courier Newsletter.
Hours & Admission Prices: March 15-Nov. 30 Mon.-Sat. 10-4, last tour at 3:15. Adults $7, children 6-12 $4; tours of 15 or more $5 per person; discounts to AAA, KMPF & AAM members. Closed holidays. ♿
Attendance: 9,609 (accurate)
Membership: Individual $25; Family $40; Voting Membership $125; Corporate $1,000.

PHOTOGRAPHIC ARCHIVES, University of Kentucky, Special Collections & Archives, M.I. King Library, 104 A King Bldg., Lexington, KY 40506-0001. Tel.: 859-257-2654. Fax: 859-257-6311.
E-mail: jasonf@.uky.edu
Web Site: www.uky.edu/libraries/special/av
Founded: 1978.
Congressional District: 6
Key Personnel: Photographic Archivist, Jason Flahardy.
Governing Authority: university. Parent Institution: University of Kentucky. Tax-exempt: 170(b)(1)(A).
Library of Photographic Material.
Collections: 100,000 photographs documenting the history of photography and the history of Kentucky, Appalachia and surrounding areas; manuscript collections.
Research Fields: history of photography, photographers; general history of city, state, region.
Facilities: 80,000-vol. library; manuscript materials available for qualified researchers upon request; reading room; 80-seat auditorium.
Activities: lectures; concerts; loan & temporary exhibitions.
Publications: exhibition catalogs.
Hours & Admission Prices: Mon.-Fri. 8-5. No charge. Closed legal & academic holidays. ♿
Attendance: 2,000

TRANSYLVANIA MUSEUM, 300 N. Broadway, Lexington, KY 40508-1797. Tel.: 859-233-8229. Fax: 859-233-8171.
E-mail: jday@transy.edu
Web Site: www.transy.edu/homepages/museum
Founded: 1802.
Key Personnel: Dir., Dr. James Day.
Governing Authority: university. Affiliated with the Transylvania University. Tax-exempt: 101.
Science Museum: housed in 1833 Greek Revival University Bldg.
Collections: early 19th-century scientific apparatus; equipment used in teaching 19th-century medicine; mounted bird skins. Historic Buildings: 1780 Patterson Cabin; 1833 Old Morrison.
Research Fields: early scientific instruments; natural history.
Activities: guided tours; formally organized education programs for students.
Hours & Admission Prices: By appointment. No charge. Closed national holidays. ♿
Attendance: 150

WAVELAND STATE HISTORIC SITE, 225 Waveland Museum Lane, Lexington, KY 40514-1618. Tel.: 859-272-3611. Fax: 859-272-4834.
E-mail: ron.bryant@ky.gov
Web Site: www.parks.ky.gov
Founded: 1957.
Congressional District: 6
Key Personnel: Park Mgr., Ron D. Bryant.
Personnel Profile: Full-Time Paid 4; Part-Time Paid 3; Part-Time Volunteers 2; Interns 1.
Governing Authority: state. Parent Institution: Kentucky Department of Parks, Capital Plaza Tower, Frankfort, KY 40601. Tax-exempt.
Historic Site & House: 1847 Greek Revival Mansion.
Collections: period furniture; portraits; china. Historic Buildings: servants' quarters with fully equipped fireplace kitchen; smokehouse; ice house.
Facilities: playground; picnic area.
Activities: guided tours; lectures; formally organized education programs for children; permanent & temporary exhibitions.
Hours & Admission Prices: Mon.-Sat. 10-5, Sun. 1-5. Adults $7, seniors $6, students $4; discount to groups; children under 6 no charge. ♿
Attendance: 4,000 (accurate)

London

MOUNTAIN LIFE MUSEUM, Levi Jackson Park, 998 Levi Jackson Mill Rd., London, KY 40744-8325. Tel.: 606-330-2130. Fax: 606-330-2123. TDD: 606-330-2130.
Web Site: www.kystateparks.com/agencies/parks/levijack.htm
Founded: 1929.
Congressional District: 5
Key Personnel: Dir., Recreational Parks, Museums and Shrines & Park Supt., William Meadors; Museum Supt., Ella Goodin.
Personnel Profile: Full-Time Paid 1; Part-Time Paid 3.
Governing Authority: state. Parent Institution: Kentucky Department of Parks, Capital Plaza Tower, Frankfort, KY 40601. Tax-exempt.
History Museum.
Collections: archives; manuscripts; costumes; decorative arts; folklore; glass; history; Indian artifacts; preservation project; textiles; transportation; primarily 1860s era farming tools & household implements.
Facilities: Mountain-made crafts for sale.
Activities: guided tours; permanent exhibitions.
Hours & Admission Prices: April-Oct. call for hours. Adults $3.50, children $2.50; discounts to groups; children 2 & under no charge.
Attendance: 10,967 (accurate)

Louisville

ALLEN R. HITE ART INSTITUTE, (M), Univ. of Louisville, Belknap Campus, Schneider Hall, Louisville, KY 40292-0001. Tel.: 502-852-4483. Fax: 502-852-6791.
E-mail: john.begley@louisville.edu
Web Site: www.art.louisville.edu
Founded: 1946.
Congressional District: 3
Key Personnel: Professor, Dir. & Chm., James Grubola; Professor Emeritus, William Morgan; Professor Emeritus, Donald R. Anderson; Professor Emeritus, Henry J. Chodkowski; Professor Emeritus, Suzanne Mitchell;

Professor Emeritus, Stephanie J. Maloney; Professor, John Whitesell; Asst. Professor, Che Rhodes; Assoc. Professor, Jay M. Kloner; Assoc. Professor, Linda Gigante; Professor, Lida Gordon; Assoc. Professor, Barbara Hanger; Professor, Steven Skaggs; Professor, Ying Kit Chan; Dir. Speed Art Museum, Peter Morrin; Assoc. Professor, Mark Priest; Asst. Professor, Mary Carothers; Asst. Professor, Mitch Eckert; Assoc. Professor, Stow Chapman; Assoc. Professor, Moon-He Baik; Gallery Dir. & Adjunct Professor, John Begley; Asst. Professor, Benjamin Hufbauer; Asst. Professor, Christopher Fulton; Art Librarian, Gail Gilbert; Professor Emeritus, Dario A. Covi; Assoc. Professor Emerita, Nancy L. Pearcy; Asst. Professor, Todd Burns; Asst. Professor, Scott Massey; Unit Business Mgr., Linda Rowley; Facilities Coord., Wesley Kent; Designer-in-Residence, Leslie Friesen; Asst. Professor, Susan Jarosi; Asst. Professor, Delin Lai.

Personnel Profile: Full-Time Paid 27; Part-Time Paid 16; Part-Time Volunteers 10.

Governing Authority: Parent Institution: University of Louisville. Subsidiary Institution: Hite Art Institute; Cressman Center for Visual Art, 1st St. at Main, Louisville. Tax-exempt: 101(6).

Art Institute.

Collections: University Art Collection; 15th- to 20th-century European & American prints, drawings & paintings; objects focused on Louisville area.

Facilities: 80,000-vol. library of art books available for inter-library loan; non-circulating reference library; 350,000 slide visual resources collection.

Activities: lectures; formally organized education programs for undergraduate & graduate college students; temporary exhibitions.

Publications: exhibition catalogues; graduate art history student journal, Parnassus.

Hours & Admission Prices: Mon.-Fri. 9-4:30, Sat. 10-2, Sun. 1-6. No charge; donations accepted. Closed national holidays. ♿

Attendance: 48,000 (estimated)

CONRAD-CALDWELL HOUSE MUSEUM, 1402 St. James Ct., Louisville, KY 40208-2127. Tel.: 502-636-5023. Fax: 502-636-1264.

E-mail: info@conradcaldwell.org

Web Site: www.conradcaldwell.org

Key Personnel: Dir., Deb Riall

Historic House Museum.

Collections: period furnishings; stained glass; personal artifacts.

Activities: tours.

Hours & Admission Prices: Sun. & Wed.-Fri. 12-4, Sat. 10-4; other times by appointment. Adults $5, senior citizens $4, students $3.

FARMINGTON HISTORIC PLANTATION, 3033 Bardstown Rd., Louisville, KY 40205-3019. Tel.: 502-452-9920. Fax: 502-456-1976.

E-mail: farmington@historichomes.org

Web Site: www.historichomes.org/farmington

Founded: 1958.

Congressional District: 3

Key Personnel: Exec. Dir., Andrea Pridham; Regent, Davis Boland; Treas., Amanda McWane.

Personnel Profile: Full-Time Paid 3; Part-Time Volunteers 75.

Governing Authority: nonprofit organization. Parent Institution: Historic Homes Foundation. Tax-exempt: 501(c)(3).

Historic Site: house built in 1816.

Collections: 1830 period furnishings; Lincoln artifacts.

Research Fields: Speed family history; Jeffersonian architecture; African-American slave community & oral history; 19th-century social history.

Facilities: visitor's center. Crafts & reproductions of decorative pieces for sale.

Activities: guided tours; education programs. Annual Events: Harvest Festival; Derby Breakfast; An Evening in the Garden; Home for the Holidays.

Publications: membership newsletter; Calendar of Special Events.

Hours & Admission Prices: Tues.-Sat. 10-4:30. Adults $9, senior citizens 60 & up and military $8, students 6-18 $4; discounts to groups with reservation & AAA members; children under 6 & members no charge. Closed New Year's Day; Easter; Mother's Day; Father's Day; Kentucky Derby Day; Independence Day; Thanksgiving; Christmas Eve & Day.

Attendance: 14,000 (estimated)

Membership: Individual $35; Family $50; Friend $100; Donor $250; Patron $500; Benefactor $1,000.

THE FILSON HISTORICAL SOCIETY, INC., (M), 1310 S. Third St., Louisville, KY 40208-5506. Tel.: 502-635-5083. Fax: 502-635-5086.

E-mail: markweth@filsonhistorical.org

Web Site: www.filsonhistorical.org

Formerly: Filson Club Historical Society, Inc.

Founded: 1884.

Congressional District: 3

Key Personnel: C.E.O. & Dir., Mark V. Wetherington; Pres. (V), Orme Wilson, III

Personnel Profile: Full-Time Paid 15; Part-Time Paid 5; Part-Time Volunteers 10; Interns 2.

Governing Authority: nonprofit. Parent Institution: The Filson Historical Society, Inc. Tax-exempt: 501(c)(3).

History Museum.

Collections: 50,000-vol. library; Kentucky, Ohio Valley & Upper South history; original manuscripts, portraits, landscapes, photographs & prints; genealogical materials; printed family histories; local business records; portraits by artists Matthew Harris Jouett, Chester Harding, John Wesley Jarvis, Joseph H. Bush, G.P.A. Healy, John J. Audubon, George Caleb Bingham & Nicola Marschall; frontier, Lewis and Clark expedition; antebellum; Civil War; sculpture.

Research Fields: history of Kentucky, Ohio River Valley & the Upper South; genealogy.

Facilities: 50,000-vol. library of books, pamphlets, maps, manuscripts, newspapers & microfilm available for use on premises.

Activities: lectures; exhibit openings; permanent & temporary exhibitions; self-guided tours; educational programs for school groups;

Publications: journal, Ohio Valley History; members' magazine, The Filson; book, Dear Brother, Letters of William Clark to Jonathan Clark; museum guides.

Hours & Admission Prices: House & Museum: Mon.-Fri. 9-5. No charge. Library: Mon.-Fri. 9-5, 1st Sat. of month 9-4. Adults $10; discount to members. Special Collections: Mon.-Fri. 9-5, 1st Sat. of month 9-4. Adults $10; discount to members. Closed national holidays. ♿

Attendance: 28,000 (estimated)

Membership: Student $25; Individual $50; Boone $100; Audubon $250; Clay $500; Shelby $1,000; Clark $2,500; Filson $5,000.

FRAZIER INTERNATIONAL HISTORY MUSEUM, (M), 829 W. Main St., Louisville, KY 40202-2619. Tel.: 502-753-5663; 866-886-7103. Fax: 502-412-8148.

E-mail: info@fraziermuseum.org

Web Site: www.fraziermuseum.org

Formerly: Frazier Historical Arms Museum

Founded: 2004.

Key Personnel: Exec. Dir., Madeleine H. Burnside, Ph.D.; Chm. (V), Owsley Brown Frazier; Vice Pres. Operations & Finance, Craig S. Mooney; Dir. Public Rels. & Mktg., Krista McHone

History Museum.

Collections: arms; armor; personal artifacts; history of Armouries.

Major Exhibits: WWII: 48 Local Stories That Changed the World, 11/09-3/10; The American Soldier (T), 4/10-9/10; Pirates (T), 5/10-10/10.

Facilities: 120-seat auditorium; 48-seat theater; cafe; rooftop garden. Gift items for sale.

Activities: audio tour; group tours; educational field trips.

Publications: newsletter, Compass.

Hours & Admission Prices: Mon.-Sat. 9-5, Sun. 12-5. Adults $9, seniors 60 & over $7, children under 14 & students $6; children under 5 no charge. Audio Tour: additional $3. Closed Thanksgiving; Christmas.

Membership: Teacher $45; Individual $50; Dual $65; Family & Grandparents $75; Contributing $100; Sustaning $250; Patron $500; The Legend's Society $1,000.

GHEENS SCIENCE HALL AND RAUCH PLANETARIUM, Univ. of Louisville, Belknap Campus, Louisville, KY 40292-0001. Mailing Address: Rauch Planetarium, University of Louisville, Louisville, KY 40292-0001. Tel.: 502-852-6664 & 7597. Fax: 502-852-0831.

E-mail: planet@louisville.edu

Web Site: www.louisville.edu/planetarium

Founded: 1962.

Congressional District: 3

Key Personnel: Dir., Rachel Connolly; Technical Coord., Drew Foster; Mktg., Dorothy J. Vittitow; Devel., Paula Campbell; Operations Mgr., Paula McGuffey.

Personnel Profile: Full-Time Paid 3; Part-Time Paid 2.

Governing Authority: state. Affiliated with University of Louisville. Tax-exempt: 501(c)(3).

Planetarium.

Collections: astronomy; space science.

Facilities: Books & gadgets pertaining to astronomy for sale.

Activities: lectures; films; formally organized education programs for children, adults & undergraduate college students.

Publications: quarterly newsletter.

Hours & Admission Prices: Tues.-Sat. call for hours. Adults $7, children, seniors & students $5; members no charge. ♿

Attendance: 91,000 (accurate)

Membership: Student & Senior $35; Individual $45; Family $75.

HISTORIC HOMES FOUNDATION, INC., 3110 Lexington Rd., Louisville, KY 40206-3002. Tel.: 502-899-5079. Fax: 502-899-5016.
E-mail: director@historichomes.org
Web Site: www.historichomes.org
Founded: 1957.
Congressional District: 3
Key Personnel: Pres. HHF, Patrick Sartor; Dir. Farmington Historic Plantation, Andrea Pridham; Dir. Thomas Edison House, Kristen Lutes; Dir. Whitehall House, Merrill Simmons; Bookkeeper, Terry Gassman.
Personnel Profile: Full-Time Paid 4; Part-Time Paid 5; Part-Time Volunteers 120; Interns 2.
Governing Authority: nonprofit organization. Subsidiary Institutions: Farmington, 3033 Bardstown Rd., Louisville, KY 40205; Thomas Edison House, 729 E. Washington St., Louisville 40202; Whitehall, 3110 Lexington Rd., Louisville. Tax-exempt: 501(c)(3).
Historic Houses.
Collections: Kentucky & Southern made furnishings. Historic Houses: 1810 Farmington; 1850s Thomas Edison house; 1860s Whitehall.
Research Fields: archaeology; local history; archaeology; historic landscapes; Abraham Lincoln; Thomas Edison.
Facilities: classrooms; meeting rooms; facilities for private parties. Gift items for sale.
Activities: guided tours; lectures; arts festivals; antique shows; formally organized education programs for adults & children; docent program or council; temporary exhibitions; garden tours. Foundation Sponsors: Derby Breakfast.
Publications: quarterly, newsletter; calendar.
Hours & Admission Prices: Farmington: Tues.-Sat. 10-4:30, Sun. 1:30-4:30; last tour 3:45. Adults $9, senior citizens $8, students $4; children 5 & under no charge. Whitehall Mon.-Fri. 10-2. Adults $5, senior citizens $4, students $3; children 5 & under no charge. Thomas Edison House: Tues.-Sat. 10-2 or by appointment. Adults $5, senior citizens $4, students $3; children under 5 no charge. Group Tours: minimum 25. $3 per person. Closed New Year's Day; Easter; Derby Day; Thanksgiving; Christmas Eve & Day. ♿
Attendance: 29,000 (estimated)
Membership: Individual $35; Family $50; Patron $60; Friend $100; Benefactor $200; Donor $250.

KENTUCKY DERBY MUSEUM, (M), 704 Central Ave., Gate 1, Churchill Downs, Louisville, KY 40208-1212. Tel.: 502-637-1111. Fax: 502-636-5855.
E-mail: info@derbymuseum.org
Web Site: www.derbymuseum.org
Founded: 1985.
Congressional District: 3
Key Personnel: Exec. Dir., Lynn Ashton; Pres. & Chm. (V), Barrett Nichols; Dir. Finance, Dennis Loomer; C.O.O., Sherry Crose; Museum Shop Mgr., Anne Westfall; Dir. Facilities, Dan Shomer; Museum Educator, Liz Williams; Dir. Public Rels., Wendy Trienan; Membership Coord., Carla Grego; Dir. Klein Family Learning Center, Jennifer Hoert.
Personnel Profile: Full-Time Paid 30; Part-Time Paid 30; Part-Time Volunteers 55.
Governing Authority: nonprofit organization. Tax-exempt: 501(c)(3).
Thoroughbred Racing & Equine Art, History & Science: located at Gate 1 of Churchill Downs, a National Historic Landmark.
Collections: Thoroughbred racing & equine artifacts; memorabilia; photographs; archives; artwork; trophies.
Major Exhibits: Student Art Exhibit, 1/10-3/10; Bill Shoemaker, 4/10-12/10.
Research Fields: Thoroughbred racing with emphasis on the Kentucky Derby.
Facilities: research library of books on horses; multimedia presentation facility; restaurant. Gift items for sale.
Activities: guided tours; formally organized education programs; permanent & changing exhibitions.
Publications: newsletter, The Inside Track; Churchill Downs, America's Most Legendary Racetrack.
Hours & Admission Prices: March 15- Nov. Mon.-Sat. 8-5, Sun. 11-5; Dec.-March 14 Mon.-Sat. 9-5, Sun. 11-5. Adults $12, senior citizens $11, children 3-11 $5; discounts to AAM members; members & children under 5 no charge. Insiders Tour: $10. Backside Track Tours: $10. Closed Oaks Day; Derby Day; Thanksgiving; Christmas. ♿
Attendance: 215,000 (accurate)
Membership: Call to Post $45; First Turn $125; Backstretch $250; Finish Line $500-$750; Farm $500-$1,000; Aristides $1,000-$2,000; Corporate: Oaks $750; Derby $1,250; Winners Circle $2,000.

KENTUCKY MUSEUM OF ART AND CRAFT, 715 West Main, Louisville, KY 40202-2633. Tel.: 502-589-0102. Fax: 502-589-0154.
E-mail: admin@kentuckyarts.org
Web Site: www.kentuckyarts.org
Formerly: Kentucky Museum of Arts & Design
Founded: 1981.
Congressional District: 3
Key Personnel: Chm. (V), Marlene M. Grissom; Pres. (V), Mary Stone; Dir., Kevin O'Brien; Deputy Dir. & Cur., Brion Clinkingbeard; Museum Shop Mgr., David McGuire.
Personnel Profile: Full-Time Paid 17; Part-Time Paid 3; Part-Time Volunteers 12; Interns 3.
Governing Authority: nonprofit organization. Tax-exempt: 501(c)(3).
Art & Craft Museum.
Collections: decorative arts.
Research Fields: contemporary crafts & folk art.
Facilities: educational workshop space. Crafts made by Kentucky artists for sale.
Activities: guided tours; lectures; arts festivals; loan, traveling & temporary exhibitions; annual craft conference; educational workshops.
Publications: annual newsletter; annual exhibition catalog.
Hours & Admission Prices: Mon.-Fri. 10-5, Sat. 11-5. Adults $5, seniors & military $4; members, students with ID & children under 12 no charge. Closed most public holidays; Derby Day. ♿
Attendance: 63,000 (accurate)
Membership: Individual $40; Family $75; Patron $150; Fellow $250; Benefactor $500.

* **LOCUST GROVE, (M),** 561 Blankenbaker Lane, Louisville, KY 40207-7100. Tel.: 502-897-9845. Fax: 502-897-0103.
E-mail: lghh@locustgrove.org
Web Site: www.locustgrove.org
Founded: 1964.
Congressional District: 3
Key Personnel: Dir., Carol Ely; Pres., Gwynne Potts; Treas., Preston Thomas; Programs, Mary Beth Williams; Museum Shop Mgr., Jennifer Jansen.
Personnel Profile: Full-Time Paid 3; Part-Time Paid 10; Part-Time Volunteers 140; Interns 2.
Governing Authority: Tax-exempt: 501(c)(3).
Historic Site: housed in the former home of the Croghan family & General George Rogers Clark; built 1790s.
Collections: early Kentucky furniture; textiles; tools; maps; surveying equipment. Historic Buildings: mansion; outbuildings.
Research Fields: 1778-1849 Clark & Croghan family, furniture & accessories; early Kentucky & regional history and lifestyle; American Revolution in the West; slave life in the upper south.
Facilities: visitors center. Museum-related items for sale.
Activities: guided tours; lectures; concerts; pioneer skills workshops; organized education programs for adults & children; docent program; permanent exhibitions; weekend events; video presentations. Museum Sponsors: 18th Century Market Fair.
Publications: newsletter; brochure; book, George Rogers Clark & Locust Grove.
Hours & Admission Prices: Mon.-Sat. 10-4:30, Sun. 1:30-4:30. Adults $8, seniors $7, children $4; discounts to National Trust, AAA, AASLH, ICOM & AAM members; members & children under 6 no charge. Closed New Year's Eve & Day; Easter; Derby Day; Thanksgiving; Christmas Eve & Day. ♿
Attendance: 22,050 (accurate)
Membership: Individual $35; Family $50.

LOUISVILLE SCIENCE CENTER, 727 W. Main St., Louisville, KY 40202-2681. Tel.: 502-561-6100. Fax: 502-561-6145.
E-mail: lscinfo@louisvilleky.gov
Web Site: www.louisvillescience.org
Founded: 1872.
Congressional District: 3
Key Personnel: C.E.O. & Dir., JoAnna Haas; Chm. (V), William G. Strench; Mng. Dir. Visitor Experiences, Theresa Mattei; Museum Shop Mgr., Toph Bryant.
Personnel Profile: Full-Time Paid 45; Full-Time Volunteers 750; Part-Time Paid 25; Part-Time Volunteers 886.
Governing Authority: private; nonprofit. Tax-exempt.
Science & Technology Center: housed in 1878 five-building structure.
Collections: archaeology findings; geology items; prehistory items; history artifacts; mineralogy; natural history exhibits; science technology; space science artifacts; clothing, costume & seashell collections; electricity, sound, light & color displays; dental health displays; Egyptian mummy & related artifacts.
Major Exhibits: Titanic: The Artifact Exhibition (T), 1/10-2/10.
Research Fields: education; archaeology; geology; paleontology; zoology; history.
Facilities: 1,000-vol. reference library available for use in building only; 40,000 sq. ft. exhibit space; IMAX theatre; video conferencing room;

classrooms; special function room; lunchroom; snack bar; restaurant. Science & math kits, books & science equipment & other museum-related items for sale.
Activities: guided tours; lectures; IMAX films; gallery talks; workshops; formally organized education programs for school children; family, group & adult training programs; volunteer programs; teacher institutes; permanent, temporary & traveling exhibitions; outreach kits; assembly programs; camp-ins; educational videoconferences.
Publications: quarterly newsletter; membership & guide brochures; educator's guides; summer program catalogue; special program announcements; tourism & promotional brochures; annual report.
Hours & Admission Prices: Mon.-Thurs. & Sun. 9:30-5, Fri.-Sat. 9:30-9. Museum/IMAX: adults $15, senior citizens & children 2-12 $12. IMAX only: adults $8, senior & children 2-12 $7, members $6. Museum only: adults $12, senior citizens & children 2-12 $10; discounts to ASTC members, sponsored groups, school groups; tourists & visitors with qualifying coupons; members & children under 2 no charge. Closed Thanksgiving; Christmas Eve & Day. ♿
Attendance: 500,000 (estimated)
Membership: Individual $69; Household $75; Super Scientist $99; Dual $140. Underwriter Membership: Benefactor $150; Patron $250; Supporter $500; Advocate $1,000.

LOUISVILLE SLUGGER MUSEUM & FACTORY, 800 W. Main St., Louisville, KY 40202-2637. Tel.: 502-585-5226. Fax: 502-585-1179.
E-mail: museum@slugger.com
Web Site: www.sluggermuseum.com
Founded: 1996.
Key Personnel: Exec. Dir., Anne Jewell; Museum Shop Mgr. & Retail Dir., Whitney Pfister; Dir. Operations, Deana Lockman.
Personnel Profile: Full-Time Paid 12; Part-Time Paid 20.
Governing Authority: private corporation. Parent Institution: Hillerich & Bradsby Co., 800 W. Main St., Louisville, KY.
Baseball Museum and Bat Factory.
Collections: valuable & rare baseball bats; baseball related artifacts.
Major Exhibits: Linedrives and Lipstick (T), 2/10-3/10; We are the Ship-Negro Leagues Baseball (T), 4/10-9/10; Merry Christmas, Charlie Brown, 11/10-12/10.
Research Fields: baseball.
Facilities: 15,000 sq. ft. exhibit space; 87-seat large screen theatre. Museum-related items for sale.
Activities: films; education programs for children; guided tours; lectures; loan, participatory & traveling exhibitions; theatre; broadcast programs; batting cages; interactive exhibits.
Hours & Admission Prices: Mon.-Sat. 9-5, Sun. 12-5. Adults $10, senior citizens $9, children $5; discounts to groups & AAM members. Closed New Year's Day; Thanksgiving; Christmas Day. ♿
Attendance: 220,000 (accurate)

LOUISVILLE VISUAL ART ASSOCIATION, 3005 River Rd., Louisville, KY 40207-1098. Tel.: 502-896-2146. Fax: 502-896-2148.
E-mail: shannon@louisvillevisualart.org
Web Site: www.louisvillevisualart.org
Founded: 1909.
Congressional District: 3
Key Personnel: Exec. Dir., Shannon Westerman; Pres. (V), W.W. Benton Clark; Vice Pres., John H. Clark, IV; Treas., Henry Hensley; Education Coord., Linda Sanders; Sec., Anne M. Braun; Exhibition Coord., Kay Grubola.
Personnel Profile: Full-Time Paid 4; Part-Time Paid 6; Interns 1.
Governing Authority: nonprofit organization.
Art Gallery: 1860 neo-classical building once housed public water systems first pumping station.
Collections: structures; contemporary art.
Research Fields: regional & national contemporary art.
Facilities: library of art publications, catalogues & magazines available to the public; classrooms.
Activities: tours; lectures; workshops; organized education programs for adults & children; internships with Louisville metro area institutions; loan & traveling exhibitions; slide registry & consultation service; temporary exhibitions.
Publications: newsletter; art auction calendar.
Hours & Admission Prices: Mon.-Fri. 9-5, Sun. 12-4. No charge; donations accepted. Closed New Year's Day; Easter; Independence Day; Thanksgiving; Christmas Eve & Day. ♿
Attendance: 150,000 (accurate)
Membership: Students $20; Individual $30; Family $45; Friend $100; Patron $300; Benefactor $500.

* **LOUISVILLE ZOOLOGICAL GARDEN,** 1100 Trevilian Way, Louisville, KY 40213-1559. Mailing Address: P.O. Box 37250, Louisville, KY 40233-7250. Tel.: 502-459-2181. Fax: 502-459-2196.
Web Site: www.louisvillezoo.org
Founded: 1963.
Congressional District: 3
Key Personnel: Exec. Dir., John Walczak; Senior Veterinarian, Dr. Roy Burns, D.V.M.; Society Pres., Thomas P. O'Brien, III; Foundation Pres., Mark F. Wheeler; Asst. Dir., Mark Zoeller; General Cur., Steven Wing; Dir. Communications, Deborah R. Sebree; Business. Mgr., Carol Miller; Mktg. Dir., Maureen Horrigan; Dir. Devel., Jill Gorsky; Education Cur., Marcelle Gianelloni; Museum Shop Mgr., Kathy Kline.
Personnel Profile: Full-Time Paid 135; Part-Time Paid 150; Part-Time Volunteers 1,427; Interns 3.
Governing Authority: municipal; city. Tax-exempt: 501(c)(3).
Zoo & Botanical Gardens.
Collections: 1,300 animals; birds; mammals; reptiles; amphibians; invertebrates; fish; exotic environmental habitats; plants; gardens; ornamental displays.
Research Fields: raptor rehabilitation program; exotic bird breeding; behavior studies with South American woolly monkeys; pioneered first successful transfer of an exotic equine, Grant's Zebra; embryo to a surrogate mother (quarter horse); artificial insemination research; Cuban crocodile; Timber rattlesnake; Blackfooted ferret breeding program 1991-present; breeding & husbandry of other exotic species; animal enrichment & behavioral training programs.
Facilities: 135 acres; HerpAquarium; zoo education center; restaurant. Museum-related items for sale.
Activities: interactive exhibits; lectures; festivals; organized education programs; docent programs; community presentations; special promotional events; seasonal scenic train & tram rides; permanent exhibitions; indoor & outdoor viewing; discovery trail; researcher's station; carousel; miniature train; formal education programs: in-house & outreach throughout the state; Backyard Action Hero & youth incentive.
Publications: quarterly newsletter, Trunkline; member e-mails; map inserts; Backyard Action Hero Guidebooks; education guides.
Hours & Admission Prices: March-Labor Day daily 10-5; Sept.-Feb. daily 10-4. Adults 12-59 $11.95, senior citizens 60 & over and children 3-11 $8.95; discounts to AZA, reciprocal Zoos & Aquaria members; children under 3 & members no charge. Closed New Year's Day; Thanksgiving; Christmas. ♿
Attendance: 810,546 (accurate)
Membership: Individual $45; Family $75; Keeper $95; Family Dual $140; Curator $150; Keeper Dual $180; Conservation Partner $350; Nature's Guardian $500; Wildlife Champion $1,000.

MUHAMMAD ALI CENTER, One Muhammad Ali Plaza, 144 N. Sixth St., Louisville, KY 40202-2939. Tel.: 502-584-9254. Fax: 502-589-4905.
E-mail: info@alicenter.org
Web Site: www.alicenter.org
Founded: 1997.
Congressional District: 3
Key Personnel: Dir., Gregory Roberts; Museum Shop Mgr., Sarah Risch.
Governing Authority: Tax-exempt.
History Museum.
Collections: Muhammad Ali's life & history; photographs; personal artifacts; poetry; drawings.
Facilities: library & archives; auditorium; classrooms; rental facility; theater. Museum-related items for sale.
Activities: education outreach; public programs & global initiatives.
Publications: membership newsletter, In Your Corner.
Hours & Admission Prices: Mon.-Sat. 9:30-5, Sun. 12-5. Adults $9, seniors 65 & over $8, military & students $5, children 6-12 $4; discounts to groups; members & children 5 & under no charge. Closed New Year's Day; Easter; Independence Day; Thanksgiving; Christmas. ♿
Attendance: 135,000 (accurate)
Membership: Student & Senior 65 & over $25; Adult $45; Family $75.

MUSEUM OF THE AMERICAN PRINTING HOUSE FOR THE BLIND, (M), 1839 Frankfort Ave., Louisville, KY 40206-3148. Tel.: 502-895-2405, ext. 365; 800-223-1839, ext. 365. Fax: 502-899-2363.
E-mail: museum@aph.org
Web Site: www.aph.org
Founded: 1994.
Congressional District: 3
Key Personnel: Dir., Micheal A. Hudson; Museum Assoc., Ann Rich.
Personnel Profile: Full-Time Paid 2; Part-Time Paid 3; Part-Time Volunteers 1.
Governing Authority: Parent Institution: American Printing House for the Blind. Tax-exempt.
History Museum.

Collections: artifacts & interpretive materials related to the history of the education of blind & visually impaired people; history of the American Printing House for the Blind (founded 1858); historical tactile books, tactile writing & printing equipment, education aids for visually impaired.
Research Fields: blindness education; printing history.
Facilities: 4,600 sq. ft. exhibition space; reception area; orientation room.
Activities: guided tours; interactive & hands-on exhibits; audio; print, and Braille descriptions; traveling exhibits; education programs.
Publications: brochures: Museum; a history of the American printing house for the blind.
Hours & Admission Prices: Mon.-Fri. 8:30-4:30, Sat. 10-3. Plant Tours: Mon.-Thurs. 10 & 2. No charge; donations accepted. Closed New Year's Day; Derby Day; Memorial Day; Independence Day; Labor Day; Thanksgiving; Christmas. ♿
Attendance: 5,000 (accurate)

NATIONAL SOCIETY OF THE SONS OF THE AMERICAN REVOLUTION, (M), 1000 S. Fourth St., Louisville, KY 40203-3292. Tel.: 502-589-1776. Fax: 502-589-1671.
Web Site: www.sar.org
Founded: 1876.
Key Personnel: Exec. Dir., Joe Harris.
Governing Authority: nonprofit organization. Parent Institution: National Society SAR. Subsidiary Institution: State Societies & chapters. Tax-exempt: 501(c)(3).
National Historical Society.
Collections: 18th-century memorabilia relating to the American Revolutionary War; 18th-century fine arts, prints, engravings, paintings, statuary; manuscripts.
Research Fields: American Revolutionary War; genealogy; fine arts relating to the 18th century.
Facilities: 28,000-vol. library of genealogy & history pertaining to the Revolutionary War available for researcher or student, for use on premises only; reading room; 150-seat auditorium. Items relating to history & S.A.R. memorabilia for sale.
Activities: guided tours; lectures; films; gallery talks; formally organized education programs for children & adults; docent programs; permanent, temporary & traveling exhibitions.
Publications: quarterly, The S.A.R. Magazine.
Hours & Admission Prices: Tues.-Sat. 9:30-5, Sun. 12-5. No charge; donations accepted. Closed New Year's Eve & Day; Independence Day; Thanksgiving; Christmas Eve & Day; national holidays. ♿
Attendance: 5,000 (estimated)
Membership: Individual $20.

THE NICOL & EISENBERG ARCHAEOLOGICAL COLLECTION, Southern Baptist Theological Seminary, 2825 Lexington Rd., Louisville, KY 40280-0001. Tel.: 502-897-4039. Fax: 502-897-4036.
E-mail: campinfo@sbts.edu
Web Site: www.sbts.edu
Formerly: The Joseph A. Callaway Archaeological Museum
Founded: 1963.
Key Personnel: Librarian, Bruce Keisling.
Governing Authority: college. Parent Institution: Southern Baptist Seminary. Tax-exempt: 501(c)(3) & 170(b)(1)(A).
Biblical Archaeology Museum.
Collections: archaeology; glass; textiles; sculpture; excavation materials from Jericho; Ai; Raddana; Machaerus; numismatics; pottery; papyri; Egyptian mummy.
Research Fields: archaeology; glass; textiles; sculpture; numismatics.
Facilities: 200,000-vol. library available for inter-library loan; reading room.
Activities: guided tours; films.
Hours & Admission Prices: Closed indefinitely. ♿
Attendance: 7,000 (estimated)

PORTLAND MUSEUM, 2308 Portland Ave., Louisville, KY 40212-1036. Tel.: 502-776-7678. Fax: 502-776-9874.
E-mail: pmuse@iglou.com
Web Site: www.goportland.org
Founded: 1978.
Congressional District: 3
Key Personnel: Exec. Dir., Nathalie Taft Andrews; Pres., Christian Trabue; Chm. (V), Sally Craven; Asst. to Dir & Museum Shop Mgr., Jessica Dawkins.
Personnel Profile: Full-Time Paid 3; Part-Time Paid 1; Part-Time Volunteers 25; Interns 1.
Governing Authority: nonprofit organization. Tax-exempt: 501(c)(3).
General Museum: housed in 1850 Beach Grove residence of William Skene.
Collections: local, historic & contemporary artifacts; children's photography; family home movie archive; historic photographs & documents related to Portland neighborhood.
Research Fields: local history; maritime history of the Western Waters; women's & family history.
Facilities: 10,000 sq. ft. exhibit space; 20-seat theater; educational facilities. Readers, workbooks, handmade crafts, hand-printed books & other gift items for sale.
Activities: guided tours; lectures; films; concerts; theater; broadcast programs; organized education programs for children & adults; school loan service; temporary exhibitions.
Hours & Admission Prices: Tues.-Fri. 10-4:30. Adults $7, senior citizens $6, students 6 & over $5; discounts to AAA & AAM members; donations accepted on Wednesday; children 5 & under no charge. ♿
Attendance: 5,000 (estimated)

RIVERSIDE, THE FARNSLEY-MOREMEN LANDING, 7410 Moorman Rd., Louisville, KY 40272-4572. Tel.: 502-935-6809. Fax: 502-935-6821.
E-mail: info@riverside-landing.org
Web Site: www.riverside-landing.org
Founded: 1993.
Congressional District: 3
Key Personnel: Dir. & Mgr., Patti Linn; Chm. (V), Reba Doutrick; Museum Shop Mgr., Heather French.
Personnel Profile: Full-Time Paid 4; Part-Time Paid 3; Part-Time Volunteers 60.
Governing Authority: private; nonprofit organization. Tax-exempt: 501(c)(3).
Historic House Museum.
Collections: Farnsley & Moremen families personal artifacts; 19th century Kentucky farm life; historic farm life on the Ohio River. Historic Building: 1837 Farnsley Moremen House.
Research Fields: Louisville, KY historical interiors & decorative arts, 1840s & 1880s.
Facilities: 250-vol. library; 200-seat auditorium; educational facilities; 3,000 sq. ft. exhibit space; 300 acre historic farm. Museum-related items for sale.
Activities: concerts; docent program; formal education programs; guided tours; lectures; temporary exhibitions. Annual Events: Ice Cream Social; Riverside Heritage Festival; Plant & Herb Sale; A Riverside Christmas.
Publications: quarterly newsletter, Riverside Review.
Hours & Admission Prices: Tues.-Sat. 10-4:30, Sun. 1-4:30. Family $15, adults $6, senior citizens $5, students & children $3; members no charge. Closed major holidays. ♿
Attendance: 25,000 (estimated)
Membership: Individual $20; Family $35.

SPECIAL COLLECTIONS, UNIVERSITY OF LOUISVILLE LIBRARIES, Ekstrom Library, University of Louisville, 2301 S. 3rd St., Louisville, KY 40292-0001. Tel.: 502-852-6752. Fax: 502-852-8734.
E-mail: special.collections@louisville.edu
Web Site: special.library.louisville.edu
Founded: 1967.
Congressional District: 3
Key Personnel: Dir. University Archives & Records Center, William J. Carner; Assoc. Cur., Amy Purcell; Cur. Rare Books, Delinda Buie.
Personnel Profile: Full-Time Paid 4; Part-Time Paid 2; Part-Time Volunteers 4.
Governing Authority: university. Parent Institution: University of Louisville. Affiliated with University of Louisville Libraries, Louisville, KY 40292. Tax-exempt.
Historic Research Institute.
Collections: 1,500,000 photographs; small equipment collection; fine art print collection; photographically illustrated books; manuscripts; fine prints.
Research Fields: history of photography; documentary photography; photography as a fine art; history of Louisville, KY.
Facilities: 75,000-vol. library; reading room; reference service.
Activities: lectures; temporary & traveling exhibitions.
Publications: book, For Love of Learning.
Hours & Admission Prices: Mon.-Fri. 9-5. No charge; donations accepted. ♿

* **THE SPEED ART MUSEUM, (M),** 2035 S. Third St., Louisville, KY 40208-1812. Tel.: 502-634-2700. Fax: 502-636-2899. TDD: 502-634-2706.
E-mail: info@speedmuseum.org
Web Site: www.speedmuseum.org
Founded: 1925.
Congressional District: 3
Key Personnel: Dir. & C.E.O., Charles L. Venable; Chief Advancement Officer, Paula Hale; Chm., Todd P. Lowe; Chief Cur., Ruth Cloudman; Registrar, Charles Pittenger; Dir. Education, Cynthia Moreno; C.F.O. & Business Mgr., David C. Knopf; Head Preparator, Bill Staley; Dir. Capital Campaign & Strategic Initiatives, Lisa Betson Resnik; Dir. Visitor Experience, Mindy Johnson.
Personnel Profile: Full-Time Paid 58; Part-Time Paid 45; Part-Time Volunteers 229; Interns 6.
Governing Authority: nonprofit organization. Tax-exempt: 501(c)(3).

Art Museum.
Collections: over 14,000 works from antiquity to the present of European & American decorative arts; paintings; sculpture; graphic arts; antiquities; African arts; Native American arts.
Major Exhibits: Karsh: A Bio in Images, Spring 2010 (T); 50 Years of Contemporary Glass, 4/10-8/10; Contemporary British Exhibition, Fall 2010; A Book of Prayers: The Medieval Bestseller, 10/10; Hattie Bishop Speed: Founder & Collector, 11/10-3/11.
Research Fields: paintings; sculpture; graphics.
Facilities: 13,000-vol. art library; art learning center; workshop; lecture rooms; restaurant; 350-seat auditorium. Books, reproductions & museum-related items for sale.
Activities: guided tours; lectures; films; gallery talks; concerts; family fests; school programs; teacher inservices; education programs for children & adults; docent program; inter-museum loan, permanent, temporary & traveling exhibitions. Museum Sponsors: The Alliance, Collectors groups.
Publications: annual report; Exhibition Catalogs; quarterly members' program guide; handbook.
Hours & Admission Prices: Tues.-Wed. & Fri. 10:30-4, Thurs. 10:30-8, Sat. 10:30-5, Sun. 12-5. Museum: no charge; donations accepted. Children's section $3.50. Closed New Year's Day; the first Sat. in March & May; Memorial Day; Independence Day; Labor Day; Christmas Day. ♿
Attendance: 100,879 (accurate)
Membership: Individual $50; Family & Dual $70; Reciprocal $130; Supporter $250. Patron Circle: Silver $500-$999; Gold $1,000-$2,499; Platinum $2,500-$4,999. Connoisseurs: Donor Circle $5,000-$9,999; Curator Circle $10,000-$24,999; Director Circle $25,000-$49,999; Artist Circle $50,000 & up. Corporate: Friends $250-$499; Patrons $500-$999; Trustees $1,000-$2,499; Sustainers $2,500-$4,999; Benefactors $5,000-$7,499; Guarantors $7,500-$9,999; Round Table $10,000 & up.

THOMAS EDISON HOUSE, 729-731 E. Washington St., Louisville, KY 40202-1050. Tel.: 502-585-5247. Fax: 502-585-5231.
E-mail: edisonhouse@historichomes.org
Web Site: www.historichomes.org
Founded: 1978.
Congressional District: 3
Key Personnel: Exec. Dir., Kristen Lutes; Chm. Bd., Tom Sherman.
Personnel Profile: Full-Time Paid 1; Part-Time Paid 1; Part-Time Volunteers 27; Interns 1.
Governing Authority: nonprofit organization. Parent Institution: Historic Homes Foundation, Inc. Tax-exempt.
Historic House.
Collections: Edison's inventions, including phonographs, kinetoscope & bulbs.
Research Fields: history, science & communication.
Facilities: Gift items for sale.
Activities: guided tours; films, interactive experiences.
Publications: foundation newsletter, The Foundation.
Hours & Admission Prices: Tues.-Sat. 10-2, or by appointment. Adults $5, senior citizens $4, students $3; discounts to AAA members; children under 5, Historic Homes Foundation & members no charge (not including special events). Closed New Year's Day; Thanksgiving; Christmas Eve & Day. ♿
Attendance: 5,500 (estimated)
Membership: Student $15; Individual $35; Family $50; Donor $100; Supporter $500; Benefactor $1,000.

Mammoth Cave

MAMMOTH CAVE NATIONAL PARK, U.S. Dept. Interior, 10 miles I65 exit 53, Mammoth Cave, KY 42259. Mailing Address: P.O. Box 7, Mammoth Cave, KY 42259-0007. Tel.: 270-758-2180 & 2181. Fax: 270-758-2447.
E-mail: maca_information@nps.gov
Web Site: www.nps.gov/maca/home.htm
Founded: 1941.
Congressional District: 2
Key Personnel: Supt., Patrick Reed; Education Coord., Cheryl Messenger; Cultural Resource Specialist, Bob Ward.
Governing Authority: federal. National Park Service, Dept. of the Interior, Washington, DC 20240. Tel.: 202-343-4621. Tax-exempt.
National Park: 52,000+ acre park with over 360 miles of underground passageways, some exposed for public viewing.
Collections: natural & cultural history collections with objects related to the prehistory, history & biological diversity of the park.
Research Fields: hydrology; geology; biology; archaeology; paleontology; ethnology; history; speleology; ecology; geomorphology; meteorology.
Facilities: 550-vol. library pertaining to natural history available for research on premises; visitor center; field research station; 188-seat auditorium; above surface 200-seat cafeteria & restaurant. Books & other museum related items for sale.
Activities: guided tours; formally organized education programs for children; hiking; underground cave tours.
Publications: brochures.
Hours & Admission Prices: March 12 to mid-June & Sept.-Oct. daily 8-6; mid-June to Labor Day daily 8-7; Nov.-March 11 8:45-5. Tours 1 to 6 hours long depending on time of year, call for information on reservations & fees at 877-444-6777 or www.recreation.gov. Discounts to children 6-12, groups of 12 or more, school groups, Golden Age/Access card holders. Closed Christmas Day.
Attendance: 1,800,000 (estimated)
Membership: Friends: Student $15; Troglobite $25; Caver $50; Lantern $100; Big Woods $250; Echo River $500; Mammoth $1,000.

Marion

BEN E. CLEMENT MINERAL MUSEUM, (M), 205 N. Walker St., Marion, KY 42064. Mailing Address: P.O. Box 391, Marion, KY 42064-0391. Tel.: 270-965-4263; 877-965-4263 (Toll Free).
E-mail: beclement@kynet.biz
Web Site: www.clementmineralmuseum.org
Founded: 1996.
Key Personnel: Dir. & Museum Shop Mgr., Tina Walker; Chm. (V), Bill Frazer.
Personnel Profile: Full-Time Paid 1; Part-Time Paid 2; Part-Time Volunteers 1.
Governing Authority: Tax-exempt.
Mineral Museum.
Collections: local history; minerals; geology; mining equipment.
Activities: educational & mineral digs.
Hours & Admission Prices: Wed.-Sat. 10-3; other times by appointment. Adults $5. Closed New Year's Day; Thanksgiving; Christmas. ♿
Attendance: 2,500 (estimated)

CRITTENDEN COUNTY HISTORICAL MUSEUM, 124 E. Bellville St., Marion, KY 42064-1410. Tel.: 270-965-9257.
Historic Building: housed in the first church in Marion, built in 1881.
Collections: local history & culture; military uniforms; 200 year old loom; spinning wheels; farm equipment; telephone switchboard; photographs; period clothing.
Hours & Admission Prices: April-Oct. Tues.-Sat. 10-3; other times by appointment. No charge.

Maysville

KENTUCKY GATEWAY MUSEUM CENTER, (M), 215 Sutton St., Maysville, KY 41056-1109. Tel.: 606-564-5865. Fax: 606-564-4372.
E-mail: museum@kygmc.org
Web Site: www.kentuckygatewaymuseumcenter.org
Formerly: Mason County Museum & Museum Center
Founded: 1878.
Congressional District: 4
Key Personnel: Pres. (V), Jim Clarke; Registrar, Mary V. Clarke; Dir., Dawn C. Browning; Cur. Books, Art & Artifacts, Sue Ellen Grannis; Business Mgr., Gayle McKay; Communications, Dir. Visitors Svcs. & Museum Shop Mgr., Lynn David; Researcher, Caye Chamness; Researcher, Myra Hardy; Accounting, Joyce Weigott; Cur. Education, James Shires, Ph.D.; Reference Registrar, Susan Feil; Reference Registrar, Anne Pollitt.
Personnel Profile: Full-Time Paid 5; Part-Time Paid 6; Part-Time Volunteers 60.
Governing Authority: nonprofit. Tax-exempt: 170(b)(1)(A).
Art Gallery, Genealogical & Historical Library & Museum: housed in 1881, restored library building.
Collections: paintings; geology & early Indian items; papers & documents; slides, photos & artifacts; dioramas of the earliest settlement; miniatures.
Research Fields: genealogy; Kentucky history; Civil War.
Facilities: 7,500-vol. library of genealogical & historical material for use on premises; reading room; theater. Books & museum-related items for sale.
Activities: guided tours; educational activities; loan, permanent, temporary & traveling exhibitions; pioneer life movies.
Publications: quarterly newsletter; books: Maysville, KY Its Past & Present; Towns of Mason County, KY; Bicentennial Minutes Maysville, KY 1787-1987.
Hours & Admission Prices: Tues.-Fri. 10-5, Sat. 10-4, Sun. 1-4, call to confirm. Museum: adults $10, students $2; discounts to AAA members; AASLH members no charge. Library: adults $5. Closed New Year's Day; Easter; Mother's Day; Father's Day; Independence Day; Thanksgiving; Christmas. ♿
Attendance: 5,000 (estimated)
Membership: Individual $30; Family $40; Wormald Society Individual $130; Wormald Society Family $140; Corporate Business $200-$500.

Middlesboro

CUMBERLAND GAP NATIONAL HISTORICAL PARK, U.S. 25 E. (1/4 mi. S. of Middlesboro), Middlesboro, KY 40965. Mailing Address: P.O. Box 1848, Middlesboro, KY 40965-3848. Tel.: 606-248-2817. Fax: 606-248-7276.
Web Site: www.nps.gov/cuga
Founded: 1959.
Congressional District: 5
Key Personnel: Supt., Mark H. Woods.
Governing Authority: federal. Affiliated with the U.S. Department of Interior, National Park Service. Tax-exempt.
History Museum.
Collections: Cumberland Gap history; botany; archaeology. Historic Houses: 1903-1951 Hensley Settlement.
Research Fields: westward expansion; Civil War; Appalachian culture.
Facilities: 1,500-vol. library of history & natural history books available for use on premises by appointment. Educational literature for sale.
Activities: Park wide lectures; films; permanent exhibitions; campfire programs; nature walks; on-site tours; sound/slide programs; loan films & sound/slide programs.
Hours & Admission Prices: Visitor Center and Pinnacle: daily 8-5. Park Gates: April-May & Sept.-Oct. 8-7; June-Aug. 8 am-9 pm; Nov.-March 8-5. Park: no charge. Wilderness Road Campground: user fee charged. Visitor Center closed: New Year's Day; Christmas. ♿

Monticello

WILLIAM CRENSHAW KENNEDY, JR. MEMORIAL MUSEUM, 75 N. Main St., Monticello, KY 42633-1439. Mailing Address: P.O. Box 67, Monticello, KY 42633-0067. Tel.: 606-340-2300.
Key Personnel: Dir. & Cur., Harlan Ogle
History Museum.
Collections: local history & culture relating to the heritage of Monticello & Wayne County.
Hours & Admission Prices: Tues.-Sat. 10-4; other times by appointment. No charge; donations accepted.

Morehead

THE KENTUCKY FOLK ART CENTER, (M), 102 W. First St., Morehead, KY 40351-1723. Tel.: 606-783-2204. Fax: 606-783-5034.
E-mail: g.barker@morehead-st.edu
Web Site: www.kyfolkart.org
Founded: 1994.
Congressional District: 6
Key Personnel: C.E.O., Garry G. Barker; Cur., Adrian Swain; Chm. (V), Jean M. Dorton; Museum Store Mgr., Tammy F. Stone.
Personnel Profile: Full-Time Paid 5; Part-Time Volunteers 50; Interns 2.
Governing Authority: private; nonprofit organization. Parent Institution: Kentucky Folk Art Center, Inc. Subsidiary Institution: Morehead State University. Tax-exempt.
Folk Art Museum.
Collections: contemporary folk art.
Facilities: 5,000 sq. ft. exhibit space.
Activities: lectures; films; workshops; outreach programs; organized education programs for children; traveling exhibitions.
Publications: annual report; newsletter.
Hours & Admission Prices: Mon.-Sat. 9-5. Adults 12 & over $3, seniors & children under 12 $2; members no charge. ♿
Attendance: 8,000 (estimated)
Membership: Senior Citizen & Student $15-$24; Individual $25-$34; Family $35-$99; Patron $100-$499; Sustaining $500-$999; Benefactor $1,000-$5,000; Live $5,000 & up.

Morganfield

CAMP BRECKINRIDGE MUSEUM & ARTS CENTER, 1116 N. Village Rd., Morganfield, KY 42437. Mailing Address: P.O. Box 60, Morganfield, KY 42437-0060. Tel.: 270-389-4420.
History Museum.
Collections: military history; murals; photographs; paintings.
Hours & Admission Prices: Tues.-Fri. 10-3, Sat. 10-4, Sun. 1-4.

Mount Olivet

BLUE LICKS PIONEER MUSEUM, Blue Licks Battlefield State Resort Park, Hwy. 68, Mount Olivet, KY 41064. Mailing Address: Blue Licks Battlefield State Resort Park, P.O. Box 66, Mount Olivet, KY 41064-0066. Tel.: 800-443-7008. Fax: 859-289-5409.
E-mail: bluelicks@ky.gov
Web Site: www.parks.ky.gov
Founded: 1928.
Congressional District: 7
Key Personnel: Resort Park Mgr., Stefanie Gaither; Business Mgr., Erik Unthank; Park Naturalist & Cur., Paul Tierney; Museum Shop Mgr., Jean Dillon.
Personnel Profile: Full-Time Paid 1; Part-Time Paid 3.
Governing Authority: state. Affiliated with Kentucky Dept. of Parks, Capital Plaza Tower, Frankfort, KY 40601. Tax-exempt.
History Museum.
Collections: Fort Ancient artifacts; fossils; mastodon & musk ox bones; pioneer tools & artifacts; folklore; Native American; Revolutionary War; natural history; geological; archaeology; archives; area history.
Facilities: 100-vol. library of history books available for use by special permission from State Dept. Gift items for sale.
Activities: guided tours; gallery talks; audiovisuals; special events & programs. Museum Sponsors: Guided Battlefield Walks in summer; Revolutionary War Reenactment & 18th Century Programs & Demonstrations in August.
Hours & Admission Prices: March 15-Nov. Mon.-Fri. 9-5. Adults $4, children 5-12 $3; discounts to groups; children 4 & under no charge. ♿
Attendance: 10,000 (estimated)

Munfordville

HART COUNTY HISTORICAL MUSEUM, 109 Main St., Munfordville, KY 42765. Mailing Address: P.O. Box 606, Munfordville, KY 42765-0606. Tel.: 270-524-0101.
E-mail: hartmuseum@scrtc.com
Web Site: www.hartcountymuseum.org
History Museum: housed in the historic 1893 Chapline Building.
Collections: historic artifacts, photographs & documents on the history of Hart County.
Hours & Admission Prices: Mon.-Fri. 9-4, Sat. 9-1. No charge; donations accepted. ♿

Murray

UNIVERSITY ART GALLERIES, MURRAY STATE UNIVERSITY, Price Doyle Fine Arts Center, 15th & Olive Sts., 6th Fl., Murray, KY 42071. Mailing Address: 604 Fine Arts Center, Murray, KY 42071-3342. Tel.: 270-809-3052 & 6734.
E-mail: becky.atkinson@murraystate.edu
Founded: 1971.
Congressional District: 1
Key Personnel: C.E.O. & Dir., Becky Atkinson.
Personnel Profile: Full-Time Paid 1; Part-Time Paid 1; Interns 5.
Governing Authority: university. Parent Institution: Art Department, Murray State University. Tax-exempt.
University Art Gallery.
Collections: 1,200-work permanent collection including Harry L. Jackson print Collection; Asian Cultural Exchange Foundation of Asian Art & artifacts; WPA print collection; MSU student art collection; magic silver photography collection.
Facilities: two lecture halls.
Activities: guided tours; lectures; gallery talks; formally organized education programs for children, adults & undergraduate & graduate students of Murray State University; loan, temporary & traveling exhibitions.
Publications: exhibition catalogues.
Hours & Admission Prices: Sept.-May Mon.-Fri. 8-5, Sat.-Sun. 1-4; Summer Mon.-Fri. 9-4. No charge. Closed university holidays. ♿
Attendance: 12,000 (accurate)

WRATHER WEST KENTUCKY MUSEUM, Murray State University, 100 Wrather Museum, Murray, KY 42071-3315. Tel.: 270-809-4771. Fax: 270-809-4485.
Web Site: www.murraystate.edu/info/wrather/wrather.htm
Founded: 1982.
Congressional District: 1
Key Personnel: C.E.O., Kate A. Reeves.
Personnel Profile: Full-Time Paid 1; Part-Time Volunteers 1; Interns 1.
Governing Authority: university. Parent Institution: Murray State University. Tax-exempt.
History Museum.
Collections: guns; period furniture & tools; Murray State University memorabilia.
Facilities: 260-seat auditorium.
Activities: permanent & traveling exhibitions.
Hours & Admission Prices: Mon.-Fri. 8:30-4, Sat. 10-1. No charge; donations accepted. Closed university holidays. ♿
Attendance: 20,200 (accurate)

Nancy

MILL SPRINGS BATTLEFIELD MUSEUM, 9020 W. Hwy. 80, Nancy, KY 42544. Mailing Address: Mill Springs Battlefield Association, P.O. Box 282, Nancy, KY 42544-0282. Tel.: 606-636-4045.
E-mail: info@millsprings.net
Web Site: www.millsprings.net/museum.htm
History Museum.
Collections: artifacts & exhibits pertaining to the Battle of Mill Springs.
Hours & Admission Prices: Tues.-Thurs. 10-4, Fri.-Sat. 10-6, Sun. 12-6. Adults $4, seniors & military $3, students $2; members no charge.

New Haven

KENTUCKY RAILWAY MUSEUM, INC., 136 S. Main St., New Haven, KY 40051-6355. Mailing Address: P.O. Box 240, New Haven, KY 40051-0240. Tel.: 800-272-0152; 502-549-5470. Fax: 502-549-5472.
E-mail: kyrail@bardstown.com
Web Site: kyrail.org
Founded: 1954.
Congressional District: 4
Key Personnel: Exec. Dir. & Pres., Greg Mathews; Chm. Bd. (V), Frank Bryan; Office Mgr., Kim Maupin; Marketing & Public Rels., Lynn Dawson; Maintenance, William Ward; Museum Store Mgr., Brooke Routt.
Personnel Profile: Full-Time Paid 5; Part-Time Paid 4; Part-Time Volunteers 60.
Governing Authority: county; nonprofit organization. Tax-exempt: 501(c)(3).
Railroad Transportation Museum.
Collections: railroad engines; steam & diesel; passenger & freight car; blueprints; memorabilia; special rail equip.; John B. Hundley model train collection; model trains; photographs; L & N steam wrecker; railroad related articles. Historic Railway Structures: c.1912, wooden L & N combine; c.1920, Pullman Solarium Car; Monon #32, BL-2 diesel locomotive; c.1905, Pacific, 4-6-2 L & N #152 steam locomotive; CF-7 Santa Fe locomotive; H12-44 Fairbanks-Morse diesel locomotive; two RS4-TC diesel locomotives; railroad records.
Research Fields: railroad history, equipment, restoration, operation, maintenance.
Facilities: library of Trains magazine, Railfan magazine, industrial publications pertaining to railroad history, Poor's manual & archives of L & N law records available for research on premises; technical & historical books. Railway & other museum-related items for sale.
Activities: 22-mile roundtrip rail excursions; permanent & temporary exhibitions. Museum Sponsors: Railway Banquet in April.
Publications: newsletter, The Station Lamp; annual report; brochures.
Hours & Admission Prices: Train Rides: March-May & Aug.-Dec. Sat. 11-2, Sun. 2; June-July Tues. & Fri. 1. Museum: adults $5, children 2-12 $2. Train Tickets: adults $15.50, children $10.50; discounts to AAA members; museum members no charge. Package rates available. ♿
Attendance: 40,000 (accurate)
Membership: Member $45; Family $60; Patron & Life $500.

Newport

NEWPORT AQUARIUM, One Aquarium Way, Newport, KY 41071-1679. Tel.: 859-261-7444. Fax: 859-261-5888.
Web Site: www.newportaquarium.com
Aquarium.
Collections: aquatic life from around the world.
Activities: educational programs; shows.
Hours & Admission Prices: Daily 10-6. Adults $20, children 2-12 $13; children under 2 no charge.

Olive Hill

NORTHEASTERN KENTUCKY MUSEUM, 1385 Carter Caves Rd., Olive Hill, KY 41164-8295. Tel.: 606-286-6012.
E-mail: nekymuseum@atcc.net
Web Site: www.kymuseum.org
Founded: 1972.
History Museum.
Collections: rocks & fossils; early native art & artifacts; pioneer tools & weapons; Civil War, World War I & II artifacts.
Hours & Admission Prices: Spring to Summer daily 9-5, Winter by appointment. No charge.

Owensboro

INTERNATIONAL BLUEGRASS MUSIC MUSEUM, 207 E. Second St., Owensboro, KY 42303-4201. Tel.: 270-926-7891. Fax: 270-689-9440.
E-mail: gabrielle@bluegrassmuseum.org
Web Site: www.bluegrassmuseum.org
Founded: 1992.
Congressional District: 2
Key Personnel: C.E.O. & Exec. Dir., Gabrielle Gray; Chm., Mary Tyler Doub; Dir. Operations, Michael Ricks; Asst. Dir., Mike Lawing.
Personnel Profile: Full-Time Paid 5; Part-Time Paid 5; Part-Time Volunteers 77; Interns 2.
Governing Authority: private; nonprofit. Tax-exempt: 501(c)(3).
Music Museum: housed in renovated c.1895 three-story brick Victorian storefront building attached to River Park Performing Arts Center.
Collections: artifacts; library & archival holdings; all tangible & recorded aspects of the history & development of bluegrass music; musical instruments; clothing; accessories; posters; flyers; recorded sound in all formats; fine art related to bluegrass music; radio & recording technology; bluegrass CD collection.
Research Fields: bluegrass professional musicians' oral histories; history of bluegrass music, c.1700-1985; interpretive presentation on bluegrass festivals, 1965-1985.
Facilities: 3,000-vol. library of books & periodicals relating to bluegrass & country music history under development; 20,000 sq. ft. exhibit space; classroom; auditorium. Recorded music & other museum-related items for sale.
Activities: open jam sessions; workshops; lectures; temporary & participatory exhibits; films; docent program; concerts; festival; video oral history program. Museum Sponsors: Bluegrass in the Schools.
Publications: quarterly newsletter, Bluegrass Legacy.
Hours & Admission Prices: Tues.-Sat. 10-5, Sun. 1-4; other times by appointment. Adult $5, children 16 & under $2; discounts to groups; members and children 6 & under no charge. ♿
Attendance: 20,000 (estimated)
Membership: Student $20; Base $40; Couple $75; Band & Organization $150; Silver Lifetime $1,000; Gold Lifetime $5,000.

OWENSBORO AREA MUSEUM OF SCIENCE & HISTORY, (M), 122 E. 2nd St., Owensboro, KY 42303-4108. Tel.: 270-687-2732. Fax: 270-687-2738.
E-mail: information@owensboromuseum.com
Web Site: owensboromuseum.com
Founded: 1966.
Congressional District: 2
Key Personnel: Exec. Dir., Kathy Olson; Education Dir., Jennifer Hunzinger; Chm., Clay Ford; Cur. Exhibits, Chris Norton; Government, Wendell H. Ford; Coord. Education Center, Ron Mayhew.
Personnel Profile: Full-Time Paid 5; Part-Time Paid 2; Part-Time Volunteers 50.
Governing Authority: public school district; nonprofit organization. Tax-exempt: 501(c)(3).
General Museum.
Collections: agricultural & industrial technology; social & natural history; paleontology; geology; physical science.
Research Fields: archaeology; local & state history; paleontology.
Facilities: 250-vol. library of natural science & history research material available to students on the premises; archive of photographs & manuscripts; hands-on science discovery center; nature center.
Activities: guided tours; lectures; films; gallery talks; arts festivals; temporary exhibitions; school loan service.
Publications: quarterly newsletter: Mammoth Happenings.
Hours & Admission Prices: Sun. 1-5, Mon. 10-8, Tues.-Sat. 10-5. Admission $3; discounts to ASTC, AAM, SEMC & KAM members; children 2 & under no charge. Closed New Year's Eve & Day; Thanksgiving; Christmas. ♿
Attendance: 70,000 (estimated)
Membership: Student $5; Single $20; Family $30; Contributing $50; Donor $100; Supporting $250; Patron $500; Sustaining $1,000.

OWENSBORO MUSEUM OF FINE ART, INC., 901 Frederica St., Owensboro, KY 42301-3052. Tel.: 270-685-3181. Fax: 270-685-3181.
E-mail: mail@omfa.museum
Web Site: www.omfa.museum
Founded: 1977.
Congressional District: 2
Key Personnel: C.E.O. & Dir., Mary Bryan Hood; Chm., B. Dean Stanley; Registrar, Anthony Hardesty; Dir. Operations, Jason Hayden; Business Mgr., Jacqueline Day; Gift Shop Mgr., Nancy Harper-Gardner.
Personnel Profile: Full-Time Paid 6; Part-Time Paid 10; Part-Time Volunteers 300.
Governing Authority: nonprofit organization. Tax-exempt: 501(c)(3).
Art Museum: listed on National Register of Historic sites.
Collections: 19th- & 20th-century American, English & French paintings, drawings, graphics & sculpture; 14th -through 18th-century American &

Asian decorative arts; contemporary American art; 19th-century German stained glass; 20th-century Appalachian Folk Art; 20th-century studio glass; Atrium Sculpture Court. Historic Buildings: 1905 Carnegie Library; pre-Civil War era mansion 1859.
Major Exhibits: Holidaze: 3 Dimensional Forms, 11/9/10-12/10.
Research Fields: 19th-20th century American artists & craftsmen with emphasis on Kentucky and the region through birth, education or residency; Appalachian Folk Art.
Facilities: sculpture court; outdoor sculpture park; classrooms. Museum-related items for sale.
Activities: guided tours; lectures; films; gallery talks; formally organized education program for children & adults; docent program; permanent, temporary & traveling exhibitions.
Publications: newsletter; exhibition catalogues & brochures.
Hours & Admission Prices: Tues.-Fri. 10-4, Sat.-Sun. 1-4. Suggested Donations: adult $2, children $1; discounts to AAM members. Closed New Year's Day; Memorial Day; Independence Day; Labor Day; Christmas. ♿
Attendance: 72,000 (estimated)

Paducah

NATIONAL QUILT MUSEUM, MUSEUM OF THE AMERICAN QUILTER'S SOCIETY, 215 Jefferson St., Paducah, KY 42001-0714. Mailing Address: P.O. Box 1540, Paducah, KY 42002-1540. Tel.: 270-442-8856. Fax: 270-442-5448.
E-mail: info@quiltmuseum.org
Web Site: www.quiltmuseum.org
Founded: 1991.
Congressional District: 1
Key Personnel: C.E.O. & Exec. Dir., May Louise Zumwalt; Pres. (V), Meredith Schroeder; Vice Pres., Lynn Loyd; Registrar & Cur. Collections, Judith Schwender; Museum Shop Mgr., Pam Hill.
Personnel Profile: Full-Time Paid 8; Part-Time Paid 8; Part-Time Volunteers 207.
Governing Authority: private; nonprofit organization. Tax-exempt: 501(c)(3).
Arts & Textile (Quilt) Museum.
Collections: contemporary quilting from 1980 to present.
Research Fields: contemporary quilt making.
Facilities: 20,000 sq. ft. exhibit space; classrooms. Quilt-related books & handcrafted gift items for sale.
Activities: docent program; formal education programs for adults & children with course credit from West Kentucky Community & Technical College; guided tours; lectures; loan, temporary & traveling exhibitions; hands-on activities; special events.
Publications: quarterly, Friends of Museum Newsletter; exhibit catalogues, Museum Quilts: The Founder's Collection.
Hours & Admission Prices: April-Oct. Sun. 1-5, Mon.-Sat. 10-5; Nov.-March Mon.-Sat. 10-5. Adults $8, seniors & students 13 & over $6; discounts to groups & seniors; K-12 school groups with reservation, children, & museum friend donors no charge. Closed New Year's Day; Easter; Thanksgiving; Christmas Eve & Day. ♿
Attendance: 39,000 (accurate)
Membership: Friends Program: Basic $30; Associate $50; Benefactor $100; Donor $250; Patron $500; President's Club $1,000; Program Sponsor $3,500-$10,000 & up.

RIVER DISCOVERY CENTER, (M), 117 S. Water St., Paducah, KY 42001-0787. Tel.: 270-575-9958. Fax: 270-444-9944.
E-mail: jharris@riverheritagemuseum.org
Web Site: www.riverdiscoverycenter.org
Formerly: River Heritage Museum
Founded: 1990.
Congressional District: 1
Key Personnel: Exec. Dir., Julie Harris; Chm., Alex Edwards; Education, E.J. Abell.
Personnel Profile: Full-Time Paid 3; Part-Time Paid 5; Part-Time Volunteers 5.
Governing Authority: private; nonprofit organization. Tax-exempt: 501(c)(3).
General Museum.
Collections: river & nautical memorabilia; Civil War artifacts; riverboat, steamboat, towboat & paddlewheel models.
Facilities: 148-seat auditorium; 2,300 sq. ft. exhibit space. Museum-related items for sale.
Activities: films; guided tours; participatory exhibits; rental gallery; school loan service. Annual Event: Marine Industry Day.
Publications: quarterly newsletter, The Anchor.
Hours & Admission Prices: April-Nov. Mon.-Sat. 9:30-5, Sun. 1-5. Adults $5, senior citizens $4.50, children $3; discounts to groups; members no charge. Closed Thanksgiving; Christmas Eve & Day. ♿
Attendance: 15,000 (accurate)
Membership: First Mate $50; Crew $100; Engineer $250; Pilot $500; Captain $1,000.

WHITEHAVEN TOURIST WELCOME CENTER, 1845 Lone Oak Rd., Paducah, KY 42001-7903. Tel.: 270-554-2077. Fax: 270-554-2077.
E-mail: kenstate@bellsouth.net
Founded: 1983.
Congressional District: 1
Key Personnel: Supvr., Rose Morgan.
Personnel Profile: Full-Time Paid 5.
Governing Authority: nonprofit. Parent Institution: Commonwealth of Kentucky. Subsidiary Institution: Dept. of Travel Devel. Tax-exempt: 501(c)(3).
Historic House: c.1860 Classical Revival Mansion.
Collections: memorabilia from home of Alben Barkley, Vice President of the United States, 1949-1953.
Activities: guided tours; organized education programs for children.
Publications: quarterly newsletter, Whitehaven.
Hours & Admission Prices: Daily 1-4; tours every half hour. No charge. Closed New Year's Eve & Day; Thanksgiving & day after; Christmas Eve & Day. ♿
Attendance: 23,000 (accurate)
Membership: Individual $15; Donor $50.

WILLIAM CLARK MARKET HOUSE MUSEUM, 121 S. 2nd St. in Market House Sq., Paducah, KY 42001-0789. Mailing Address: P.O. Box 12, Paducah, KY 42002-0012. Tel.: 270-443-7759.
E-mail: info@markethousemuseum.com
Web Site: markethousemuseum.com
Founded: 1968.
Congressional District: 1
Key Personnel: Exec. Dir., Penny Baucum Fields.
Personnel Profile: Full-Time Paid 1; Part-Time Paid 1; Part-Time Volunteers 22.
Governing Authority: nonprofit organization. Tax-exempt: 501(c)(3).
History Museum: built in 1905 the Market House was used as a farmers market.
Collections: complete two story Victorian Gingerbread woodwork interior of 1877 List Drug Store; 1913 American LaFrance Fire Truck; fire-related items; Irvin S. Cobb & Vice President Alben W. Barkley exhibits; silver service; wheel & fog bell from U.S.S. gunboat, Paducah; exhibits & artifacts of the War between the states; KY Orphan's Brigade exhibit; 1850 parlor set used by U.S. Grant; Native American artifacts.
Research Fields: Paducah & Kentucky history 1820-present.
Facilities: 4,800 sq. ft. exhibit space.
Activities: self or guided tours; temporary & rotating exhibitions.
Hours & Admission Prices: March to mid-Dec. Mon.-Sat. 12-4. Adults $4, children 6-11 $1; children under 6 no charge. Closed major holidays. ♿
Attendance: 10,000 (estimated)

YEISER ART CENTER, 200 Broadway, Paducah, KY 42001-0732. Tel.: 270-442-2453. Fax: 270-442-0828.
E-mail: info@theyeiser.org
Web Site: www.theyeiser.org
Founded: 1957.
Congressional District: 1
Key Personnel: Exec. Dir. & Museum Shop Mgr., Michael Crouse; Pres. (V), Robert Bloomingburg.
Personnel Profile: Part-Time Paid 2; Part-Time Volunteers 40.
Governing Authority: nonprofit organization. Tax-exempt: 501(c)(3).
Art Museum: housed in 1905 Market House.
Collections: European, American, Asian & African 19th & 20th century works of art.
Major Exhibits: Teen Spirit 2010, 1/10-2/10; M. Ben Cohan & Jake Wells, 2/10-3/10; Fantastic Fibers Competition, 4/10; Creatures Great & Small, 5/10-6/10; Paducah Photo 2010, 6/10-7/10; Travis Graves Solo Show, 8/10; Anne Bagby & Christina Bartsch, 9/10; Robert Bean Solo Show, 10/10-11/10; Yeiser Members Show, 12/10.
Facilities: Local & regional artworks, pottery, jewelry, weaving, glass and museum-related items for sale.
Activities: docent program; guided tours; lectures; participatory & temporary exhibitions. Annual Events: National Fiber Exhibit; national competition.
Publications: monthly newsletter; fiber catalog.
Hours & Admission Prices: Tues.-Sat. 10-4. No charge; donations accepted. Closed major holidays. ♿
Attendance: 10,000 (estimated)
Membership: Supporter $25; Friend $50; Patron $100; Sponsor $250; Partner $500; Big Time Friend $1,000; Benefactor $2,500.

Paris

HOPEWELL MUSEUM, (M), 800 Pleasant St., Paris, KY 40361-1734. Tel.: 859-987-7274. Fax: 859-987-7274.
E-mail: hopewellmuseum@yahoo.com

Web Site: www.hopewellmuseum.org
Founded: 1995.
Congressional District: 6
Key Personnel: Dir., Nancy Smith.
Personnel Profile: Full-Time Paid 1; Part-Time Volunteers 45.
Governing Authority: private; nonprofit. Parent Institution: Historic Paris-Bourbon County, Inc. Tax-exempt: 501(c)(3).
History & Art Museum: housed in a 1909 Beaux-Arts style post office building.
Collections: local, regional & state art, artists, art history and general history; art, artifacts & papers from Paris and Bourbon County, Kentucky within a state & national context.
Research Fields: local history; noted local artists; distilling; hemp; equine racing industries for history exhibits.
Activities: docent program; films; lectures; loan & temporary exhibitions.
Publications: bimonthly newsletter, Hopewell Museum Post.
Hours & Admission Prices: Wed.-Sat. 12-5, Sun. 2-4. Adults $3; students, children & members no charge. ♿
Attendance: 3,978 (accurate)
Membership: Senior 65 & over $30; Senior & Spouse or Individual $35; Family $45; Supporter & Corporation $100; Patron $250; Sponsor $500; Benefactor 1,000.

Perryville

PERRYVILLE BATTLEFIELD STATE HISTORIC SITE, 1825 Battlefield Rd., Perryville, KY 40468-0296. Tel.: 859-332-8631. Fax: 859-332-2440. TDD: 859-332-8631.
E-mail: joan.house@ky.gov
Web Site: www.perryvillebattlefield.org
Formerly: Perryville Battlefield Museum
Founded: 1965.
Congressional District: 6
Key Personnel: Park Supt., Kurt Holman; Program Coord., Joan House.
Personnel Profile: Full-Time Paid 4; Full-Time Volunteers 12; Part-Time Paid 4; Interns 1.
Governing Authority: state. Parent Institution: Kentucky Dept. of Parks, Capital Plaza Tower, Frankfort, KY 40601. Tax-exempt.
Civil War Museum.
Collections: artifacts from the Battle of Perryville.
Facilities: interpretive exhibits.
Activities: tours; self-guided walking tour; living history programs. Museum Sponsors: battle reenactment in October.
Hours & Admission Prices: Grounds: March-Dec. daily. Museum: daily 9-5. Adults $3.50, children under 12 $2.50; discount to groups of 10 or more.
Attendance: 186,000 (estimated)

Petersburg

CREATION MUSEUM, 2800 Bullittsburg Church Rd., Petersburg, KY 41080-9364. Mailing Address: P.O. Box 510, Hebron, KY 41048-0510. Tel.: 888-582-4253.
Web Site: creationmuseum.org
Natural History Museum.
Collections: life-sized dinosaur models; fossils; minerals; waterfalls; frogs; fish; turtles; bugs.
Facilities: 180-seat theater; nature trails; planetarium. Books for sale.
Activities: workshops; videos.
Hours & Admission Prices: Museum: March-Sept. Mon.-Thurs. 10-6, Fri. 10-9, Sat. 9-6, Sun. 12-6; Oct.-Feb. Mon.-Fri. 10-6, Sat. 9-6, Sun. 12-6. Petting Zoo: March-Sept. Mon.-Thurs. 10:30-6, Fri. 10:30-8, Sat. 9:30-6, Sun. 12-6; Oct.-Feb. Mon.-Fri. 10:30-6, Sat. 9:30-6, Sun.12-6. Admission 13-59 $21.95, seniors 60 & over $16.95, children 5-12 $11.95; fire, military, police, & children under 5 no charge. Closed Thanksgiving; Christmas.

Pikeville

BIG SANDY HERITAGE CENTER, (M), 773 Hambley Blvd., Pikeville, KY 41501-9078. Mailing Address: P.O. Box 1041, Pikeville, KY 41502-1041. Tel.: 606-218-6050.
E-mail: everett.johnson@bigsandyheritage.org
Web Site: www.bigsandyheritage.org
Key Personnel: Cur., Everett Johnson
History Museum.
Collections: local history & culture relating to Pike County & the region.
Hours & Admission Prices: Mon.-Fri. 10-5, Sat.-Sun. evenings by appointment. Adults $3, seniors & children $2.

Princeton

ADSMORE MUSEUM, 304 N. Jefferson St., Princeton, KY 42445-1551. Tel.: 270-365-3114. Fax: 270-365-3310.
E-mail: adsmore@vci.net
Web Site: www.adsmore.org
Founded: 1986.
Key Personnel: Cur., Ardell Jarratt; Museum Shop Mgr., Janis P'Pool.
Personnel Profile: Full-Time Paid 2; Part-Time Paid 8.
Governing Authority: nonprofit. PNC Bank Trust. Subsidiary Institution: Caldwell Co. Library Dist. Tax-exempt.
Living History Museum.
Collections: period furnishings; silver; china; linens; clothing; decorative accessories; photographs; letters; toys.
Research Fields: family history.
Facilities: 3,500 sq. ft. exhibit space. Museum-related items for sale.
Activities: concerts; guided tours; candlelight tours; teas.
Publications: brochure.
Hours & Admission Prices: Tues.-Sat. 11-4, Sun. 1:30-4. Adults $7, senior citizens 65 & over $6, children 6-12 $2; discounts to groups, AAA members & military and their families. Closed New Year's Day; Easter; Independence Day; Thanksgiving; Christmas Eve & Day. ♿
Attendance: 7,000 (estimated)

CALDWELL COUNTY RAILROAD MUSEUM, 116 Edwards St., Princeton, KY 42445-2217.
Railroad Museum.
Collections: railroad history; railroad artifacts & memorabilia.
Facilities: Museum-related items for sale.
Hours & Admission Prices: May-Dec. Wed.-Sun. 1-4; groups by appointment.

Renfro Valley

KENTUCKY MUSIC HALL OF FAME AND MUSEUM, 2590 Richmond Rd., Renfro Valley, KY 40473. Mailing Address: P.O. Box 85, Renfro Valley, KY 40473-0085. Tel.: 606-256-1000. Fax: 606-256-2989.
E-mail: info@kentuckymusicmuseum.com
Web Site: kentuckymusicmuseum.com
Key Personnel: Chm. Bd., Roy Martin; Exec. Dir., Robert Lawson
Music Museum.
Collections: Kentucky music history & heritage; instruments; photographs; costumes; Kentucky stars & entertainers.
Facilities: Museum-related items for sale.
Activities: educational programs; special events; induction ceremony.
Hours & Admission Prices: Wed.-Sat. 10-6, Sun. 9-3. Adults $7.50, seniors $7, children 6-12 $4.50; discounts to groups; children under 6 & teachers no charge.

Richmond

FORT BOONESBOROUGH MUSEUM, 4375 Boonesboro Rd., Richmond, KY 40475-9333. Tel.: 859-527-3131. Fax: 859-527-3328. TDD: 859-527-3131.
E-mail: phil.gray@ky.gov
Web Site: parks.ky.gov/findparks/recparks/fb
Founded: 1974.
Congressional District: 5
Key Personnel: Dir. Living History & Museum Shop Dir., Bill Farmer; Parks Mgr., Phil Gray; Cur., Jerry Raisor.
Personnel Profile: Full-Time Paid 12; Part-Time Paid 60.
Governing Authority: state. Affiliated with KY Dept. of Parks, Capital Plaza Tower, Frankfort, KY 40601. Tax-exempt.
History Museum.
Collections: objects & archives relating to the early Euro-American settlement of Kentucky; local Native American artifacts; Kentucky River history and navigation; indigenous plant species; history of Daniel Boone & the Transylvania Land Company; 1906 River Lock & Dam.
Research Fields: Kentucky River Valley history.
Facilities: river walk trails; children's theatre; interpretive center; living fort surrounding museum; campgrounds; picnic area; snack bar. Fort-made crafts & museum-related items for sale.
Activities: living history demonstrations & instruction; native botanical restorations; special events for school programs & educational seminars; guided tours.
Hours & Admission Prices: April-Oct. daily 9-5. Adults $7, children $5; discount to groups. ♿
Attendance: 60,000

WHITE HALL STATE HISTORIC SITE, 500 White Hall Shrine Rd., Richmond, KY 40475-9159. Tel.: 859-623-9178. Fax: 859-626-8489.
E-mail: whitehall@ky.gov

Web Site: parks.ky.gov/findparks/histparks/wh
Founded: 1971.
Congressional District: 6
Key Personnel: Dir., Kathleen White; Cur., Lashe Mullins.
Personnel Profile: Full-Time Paid 3; Part-Time Paid 7.
Governing Authority: state; Kentucky State Park System. Tax-exempt.
Historic House: 1798 Georgian style building, added to in 1861 in the Italianate style, with 44 rooms & eight levels. Home of Cassius M. Clay, Ambassador to Russia during the 1860's under Abraham Lincoln.
Collections: period furnishings; Kentucky history from late 1700s to early 1900s; Cassius M. Clay & the Clay family history.
Research Fields: Cassius M. Clay & the Clay family.
Facilities: picnic area. Museum-related items for sale.
Activities: guided tours; concerts; internships; temporary exhibitions. Annual Events: Halloween Ghost Walk; theater event in October.
Hours & Admission Prices: April to Labor Day Sat.-Sun. 9-4; Sept.-Oct. Wed.-Sun. 9-4; Nov.-Dec. 23 Wed.-Fri. 10, 12 & 2. Adults $6, children $3; discounts to Kentucky Junior Historical Society & groups of 10 or more.
Attendance: 5,000 (estimated)

Slade

KENTUCKY REPTILE ZOO, 200 L&E Railroad, Slade, KY 40376. Tel.: 606-663-9160. Fax: 606-663-6917.
E-mail: reptilezoo@bellsouth.net
Web Site: www.kyreptilezoo.org
Reptile Museum.
Collections: reptiles including a reticulated python, gaboon viper, desert tortoise & rattlesnakes.
Facilities: Museum-related items for sale.
Activities: venom extraction; outreach programs; internships; school field trips.
Hours & Admission Prices: March to mid-May & Labor Day-Oct. Fri.-Sun. 11-6; Memorial Day-Sept. daily 11-6. Adults $6, children 3-15 $4; discounts to AAA members, seniors & groups of 10 or more; children under 3 no charge.

South Union

SHAKER MUSEUM AT SOUTH UNION, (M), 850 Shaker Museum Rd., South Union, KY 42283. Mailing Address: P.O. Box 177, Auburn, KY 42206-0177. Tel.: 502-542-4167 & 7734. Fax: 502-542-7558.
E-mail: shakmus@logantele.com
Web Site: www.shakermuseum.com
Founded: 1960.
Congressional District: 3
Key Personnel: Pres., Thomas Moody; Dir. & Cur., Tommy Hines; Museum Shop Mgr., Sue Brooks.
Personnel Profile: Full-Time Paid 3; Part-Time Paid 6; Part-Time Volunteers 25; Interns 1.
Governing Authority: nonprofit; board of directors. Parent Institution: Shakertown Revisited, Inc. Tax-exempt.
Historic Site: located on the site of 1807 South Union Shaker Village.
Collections: Shaker furniture; tools; textiles; boxes; baskets; straw bonnets; wooden ware; photographs. Historic House & Buildings: 1824 Centre House, used by the church family; c.1834 preservatory; 1847 Steam House; 1869 tavern; 1846 Ministry Shop; 1875 Grain Barn; 1917 store.
Research Fields: records of South Union Colony; history of Shakers.
Facilities: Museum & Shaker-related gifts for sale.
Activities: guided tours; lectures for groups; festivals; permanent & temporary exhibitions.
Publications: newsletter, South Union Messenger.
Hours & Admission Prices: March-Nov. Sun. 1-5, Mon.-Sat. 9-5; Dec.-Feb. Tues.-Sat. 10-4. Adults $6, children 6-12 $2; discounts to AAA members; members & children under 6 no charge. Closed New Year's Eve & Day; Thanksgiving; Christmas Eve & Day.
Attendance: 10,000 (accurate)
Membership: Individual $25; North Family $50; West Family $100; East Family $250; Centre Family $500; Jasper Springs Society $1,000.

Springfield

LINCOLN HOMESTEAD STATE PARK, 5079 Lincoln Park Rd., Springfield, KY 40069-9504. Tel.: 859-336-7461. Fax: 859-336-0659. TDD: 606-336-7461.
Web Site: www.state.ky.us/agencies/parks/linchome.htm
Founded: 1936.
Congressional District: 2
Key Personnel: Museum Shop Mgr. & Park Mgr., Robert Bartholomai.
Personnel Profile: Part-Time Paid 1; Part-Time Volunteers 2.
Governing Authority: state. Affiliated with Kentucky Department of Parks, Division of Museums and Shrines, Capital Plaza Tower, Frankfort, KY 40601. Tax-exempt.
Park Museum.
Collections: archives; natural history. Historic Buildings: Francis Berry House; Lincoln Home; blacksmith shop.
Facilities: outdoor museum.
Activities: guided tours; lectures; permanent exhibitions.
Hours & Admission Prices: May-Sept. daily 10-5:30. Adults $2, children $1.50; discounts to groups of 10 or more. ♿
Attendance: 4,000 (estimated)

Stanford

WILLIAM WHITLEY HOUSE STATE HISTORIC SITE, 625 William Whitley Rd., Stanford, KY 40484-9770. Tel.: 606-355-2881. Fax: 606-355-2778.
Web Site: parks.ky.gov/statehistoricsites/ww/index.htm
Founded: 1938.
Congressional District: 5
Key Personnel: Park Mgr., Jack C. Bailey.
Personnel Profile: Full-Time Paid 3; Part-Time Paid 2; Part-Time Volunteers 2.
Governing Authority: state. Parent Institution: Kentucky Dept. of Parks, Capitol Plaza Tower, Frankfort, KY 40601. Tax-exempt.
Historic House: c.1792 William Whitley House, one of the first brick homes west of the Alleghenies.
Collections: period furnishings; gun powder horn & shoulder belt.
Facilities: picnic area; playground. Museum-related items for sale.
Activities: guided tours.
Publications: book, The William Whitley House.
Hours & Admission Prices: May-Dec. Wed.-Sat. 9-5, Sun. 12-6; other times by appointment. Closed Thanksgiving; Christmas. ♿
Attendance: 5,000 (estimated)

Stearns

MCCREARY COUNTY MUSEUM, 100 Henderson St., Stearns, KY 42647. Mailing Address: P.O. Box 452, 1 Henderson St., Stearns, KY 42647-0452. Tel.: 606-376-5730. Fax: 606-376-5332.
E-mail: museum@bsfsry.com
Web Site: www.mccrearycountymuseum.com
Formerly: Stearns Museum
Founded: 1988.
Congressional District: 5
Key Personnel: Dir., Amy Combs.
Personnel Profile: Full-Time Paid 1; Part-Time Volunteers 20.
Governing Authority: Parent Institution: McCreary County Heritage Foundation. Tax-exempt.
History Museum: housed in the old Stearns Coal and Lumber Company Corporate Headquarters, built in 1907.
Collections: historic documents; objects; photographs; replica bedroom & parlor from the early 1930's.
Publications: newsletter, Museum News.
Hours & Admission Prices: April & Nov. Thurs.-Sat. 9-4; May-Oct. Tues.-Sat. 9-4, Sun. 12-4. Adults 12-59 $5, seniors 60 & over $4, children 6-12 $3; discounts to local residents & school groups; members and children 5 & under no charge. Closed Thanksgiving. ♿
Attendance: 12,500 (estimated)
Membership: Individual $25; Dual $35; Family $50; Friend $100; Patron $200.

Tompkinsville

OLD MULKEY MEETINGHOUSE STATE HISTORIC SITE, 38 Old Mulkey Park Rd., Tompkinsville, KY 42167-6781. Tel.: 270-487-8481.
E-mail: sheila.rush@ky.gov
Key Personnel: Park Mgr., Sheila Rush
Historic Site: built in 1804.
Collections: local history & culture; period furnishings.
Hours & Admission Prices: April-Nov. daily 9-5. No charge.
Attendance: 15,000 (estimated)

Union

BIG BONE LICK STATE PARK MUSEUM, 3380 Beaver Rd., Union, KY 41091-8433. Tel.: 859-384-3522. Fax: 859-384-4775.
Web Site: www.parks.ky.gov
Founded: 1971.
Congressional District: 4
Key Personnel: Park Mgr., Bertie Lucas.
Personnel Profile: Full-Time Paid 7; Part-Time Paid 2.
Governing Authority: state. Branch of Kentucky Dept. of Parks, Capital Plaza Tower, Frankfort, KY 40601. Tel. 502-564-3811. Tax-exempt.
Historic Site.
Collections: mastodon & bison bones.

Research Fields: archaeology.
Facilities: theater. Crafts for sale.
Activities: gallery talks; formally organized education programs for children & adults.
Hours & Admission Prices: Grounds: dawn-dusk. Museum: Jan.-March Thurs.-Sun. 8-4:30; April-Dec. Mon.-Thurs. 8-4:30, Fri.-Sun. 9-5. No charge.
Attendance: 5,000 (estimated)

Van Lear

COAL MINERS' MUSEUM/VAN LEAR HISTORICAL SOCIETY, INC., 78 Miller's Creek Rd., Van Lear, KY 41265. Mailing Address: P.O. Box 369, Van Lear, KY 41265-0369. Tel.: 606-789-8540.
E-mail: thebankmule@yahoo.com
Web Site: www.vanlear.org
Founded: 1984.
Congressional District: 5
Key Personnel: Pres., Debra B. Music; Dir. & Vice Pres., Tina S. Webb.
Personnel Profile: Full-Time Volunteers 1; Part-Time Volunteers 12.
Governing Authority: private; nonprofit organization. Parent Institution: Van Lear Historical Society, Inc. Tax-exempt: 501(c)(3).
Historical Society Museum: housed in the former office building of The Consolidation Coal Company.
Collections: artifacts from 1908 to present; mining implements; recreation of doctor's office with original equipment; Van Lear country music room; Van Lear veterans room; Van Lear post office; restored town jail; Van Lear school-related memorabilia; 1950s store; early town diorama.
Facilities: library; resource center. Museum-related items for sale.
Activities: guided tours; mobile vans; teacher in-service program; history classes for Prestonsburg Community College. Annual Event: Van Lear Town Celebration; 7th Annual Haunted House; 7th Annual Breakfast with Santa.
Publications: quarterly newsletter, The Bankmule.
Hours & Admission Prices: Nov.-Oct. 9 by appointment. Adults $4, senior citizens $3; members and children 5 & under no charge. ♿
Attendance: 500 (estimated)
Membership: Annual $15.

Versailles

BLUEGRASS RAILROAD MUSEUM, 175 Beasley Rd., Versailles, KY 40383-8992. Mailing Address: P.O. Box 27, Versailles, KY 40383-0027. Tel.: 859-873-2476; 800-755-2476 (outside KY). Fax: 859-873-0408.
E-mail: thebgrm@yahoo.com
Web Site: www.bgrm.org
Founded: 1976.
Key Personnel: Exec. Dir. & Pres., John Penfield.
Personnel Profile: Full-Time Volunteers 4; Part-Time Volunteers 5.
Governing Authority: nonprofit organization.
Railroad Museum.
Collections: railroad history; railroad artifacts.
Activities: 7 mile round-trip train ride in period railroad coaches.
Publications: newsletter, The Connecting Rod.
Hours & Admission Prices: Call for hours. Train rides: Adults $10, senior citizens 65 & over $9, children 2-12 $8; members & children under 2 no charge.
Attendance: 5,500 (estimated)
Membership: Regular $30; Family $45.

JACK JOUETT HOUSE, 255 Craig's Creek Rd., Versailles, KY 40383-9649. Tel.: 859-873-7902.
E-mail: info@jouetthouse.org
Web Site: www.jouetthouse.org
Key Personnel: Exec. Dir., Michael Lynch.
Personnel Profile: Full-Time Paid 1; Part-Time Paid 2.
Governing Authority: Tax-exempt.
Historic House Museum: housed in a Federal-style house, built in 1797.
Collections: period furnishings; personal artifacts.
Hours & Admission Prices: April-Oct. Wed. & Sat.-Sun. 1-5; other times by appointment. No charge; donations accepted.

NOSTALGIA STATION TOY AND TRAIN MUSEUM, 279 Depot St., Versailles, KY 40383. Tel.: 859-873-2497.
Toy Museum: housed in a restored 1911 railroad station.
Collections: toys; railroad memorabilia; late 1950s Lionel store display; reproduction of a 1926 standard gauge Lionel store display.
Hours & Admission Prices: Wed.-Sat. 10-5, Sun. 1-5. Adults $3.50, seniors 62 & over $3, children $1; children 3 & under no charge. Closed major holidays.

WOODFORD COUNTY HISTORICAL SOCIETY MUSEUM, 121 Rose Hill, Versailles, KY 40383-1221. Tel.: 859-873-6786.
E-mail: woodford@qx.net
Web Site: www.woodfordkyhistory.org
Founded: 1966.
Key Personnel: Library Asst., Lorraine Bradenburg.
Personnel Profile: Part-Time Paid 2; Part-Time Volunteers 7.
Governing Authority: Tax-exempt.
History Museum.
Collections: Woodford County history; genealogy; Civil War memorabilia; quilts; clothing; furniture; spinning wheel; photographs; paintings.
Facilities: library.
Activities: research.
Hours & Admission Prices: Tues.-Sat. 10-4. No charge.

West Liberty

MEMORY HILL FOUNDATION MUSEUM, 89 Memory Hill Lane, West Liberty, KY 41472-8743. Tel.: 606-743-4482.
Web Site: www.kentuckytourism.com/listing/2063
History Museum.
Collections: eight restored & furnished log cabins; 20-room colonial home with furnishings of early Americana, Victorian & Empire eras.
Hours & Admission Prices: By appointment only.

Wickliffe

WICKLIFFE MOUNDS STATE HISTORIC SITE, 94 Green St., Wickliffe, KY 42087. Mailing Address: P.O. Box 155, Wickliffe, KY 42087-0155. Tel.: 270-335-3681.
E-mail: wickliffemounds@ky.gov
Web Site: www.parks.ky.gov
Founded: 1932.
Congressional District: 1
Key Personnel: Park Mgr., Carla Hildebrand.
Personnel Profile: Full-Time Paid 2; Part-Time Paid 1; Part-Time Volunteers 2.
Governing Authority: state government. Parent Institution: Commonwealth of Kentucky, Tourism, Arts and Heritage Cabinet, Department of Parks. Tax-exempt.
Archaeology Museum.
Collections: block excavations & artifact collections of Mississippian culture.
Research Fields: archaeology; anthropology.
Facilities: three exhibit buildings; reception area; lecture room.
Activities: self-guided tours; special events.
Hours & Admission Prices: April & Oct. call for hours; May-Sept. Tues.-Sun. 9-4:30. Adults $5, children 6-12 $4, children under 6 $1; discount to groups. Closed Christmas-New Year's. ♿
Attendance: 7,130 (accurate)

Williamsburg

CUMBERLAND INN & MUSEUM, 649 S. 10th St., Williamsburg, KY 40769-1647. Tel.: 800-315-0286; 606-539-3100.
E-mail: museum@cumberlandinn.com
Web Site: www.cumberlandinn.com/mus.htm
Key Personnel: Gen. Mgr., David Maggard
History Museum.
Collections: Cumberland College archives; stamps; arrowheads; coins; nutcrackers; Henkelmann Life Science; The Carl Williams Cross collection.
Hours & Admission Prices: Call for hours. Adults $4, seniors over 65 $3, children 6-12 $2, children 5-1 $1.

Winchester

BLUEGRASS HERITAGE MUSEUM, 217 S. Main St., Winchester, KY 40391-2455. Mailing Address: P.O. Box 147, Winchester, KY 40392-0147. Tel.: 859-745-1358.
E-mail: bgheritage@bellsouth.net
Web Site: www.bgheritage.com
Key Personnel: Dir., Sandy Stults; Pres., Gardner Wagers
History Museum.
Collections: area history; Bluegrass culture & history; Native American artifacts.
Facilities: Museum-related items for sale.
Hours & Admission Prices: Mon.-Sat. 12-4.

LOUISIANA

(183 listings)

Abbeville

ALLIANCE CENTER MUSEUM AND ART GALLERY, 200 N. Magdalen Square, Abbeville, LA 70510-4645. Tel.: 337-898-4114.
General Museum.
Collections: local history & culture; genealogy; photographs; documents; period artifacts; paintings.
Hours & Admission Prices: Tues. & Sat. 10-3, Wed.-Fri. 10-5.

Alexandria

* **ALEXANDRIA MUSEUM OF ART,** 933 Main St., Alexandria, LA 71301-8322. Mailing Address: P.O. Box 1028, Alexandria, LA 71309-1028. Tel.: 318-443-3458. Fax: 318-443-0545.
E-mail: boutlaw@themuseum.org
Web Site: www.themuseum.org
Founded: 1977.
Congressional District: 6 & 8
Key Personnel: Exec. Dir., Richard Gwartney; Pres. (V), Mike Young; Finance & Operations Mgr., Billy Outlaw; Cur. Art, Anne Reid; Visitor Svcs., Cherry Davis; Coord. Art Education, Natalie Walker.
Personnel Profile: Full-Time Paid 4.
Governing Authority: nonprofit organization. Tax-exempt: 501(c)(3).
Art Museum: housed in c.1900 Bank Building.
Collections: contemporary works in sculpture, on paper & painting; North Louisiana Folk crafts; contemporary Louisiana artists.
Research Fields: North Louisiana Folk Art; modern & contemporary American art.
Facilities: 3,500-vol. research library & archive; classroom; garden; multimedia auditorium. Museum-related items for sale.
Activities: guided tours; lectures; films; gallery talks; study clubs; formal education programs for children & adults; education programs for students affiliated with local & area colleges; temporary, loan & traveling exhibitions; school loan service; summer arts program.
Publications: exhibit catalogs; quarterly newsletters; annual report.
Hours & Admission Prices: Tues.-Fri. 10-5, Sat. 10-4. Adults $4, seniors, students & military $3, children under 12 $2; discounts to groups, AAM, SEMC & LAM members; members no charge. Closed legal holidays. ♿
Attendance: 4,913 (accurate)
Membership: Individual $25; Family $35; Patron $50; Sponsor $100; Sustainer $250; Bronze Circle $500; Silver Circle $1,000 & up.

ALEXANDRIA ZOOLOGICAL PARK, 3016 Masonic Dr., Alexandria, LA 71301-4240. Mailing Address: P.O. Box 6015, Alexandria, LA 71307-6015. Tel.: 318-473-1143, ext. 0. Fax: 318-473-1149.
E-mail: info@thealexandriazoo.com
Web Site: www.thealexandriazoo.com
Founded: 1926.
Key Personnel: Gen. Cur., Carla Oncay
Zoo.
Collections: over 600 animals.
Facilities: 33 acres.
Activities: train rides.
Hours & Admission Prices: Daily 9-5. Adults 13-64 $3, children 4-12 $2, seniors 65 & over $1.50; discounts to groups of 15 or more; children 3 & under and FOTAZ members no charge. Train Rides: $1.50; children under 1 no charge. Closed New Year's Day; Thanksgiving; Christmas.

ARNA BONTEMPS AFRICAN AMERICAN MUSEUM, 1327 Third St., Alexandria, LA 71301-8248. Tel.: 318-473-4692. Fax: 318-473-4675.
E-mail: admin@arnabontempsmuseum.com
Web Site: www.arnabontempsmuseum.com
Governing Authority: nonprofit organization.
Historic House Museum: housed in the boyhood home of poet, author, anthologist & librarian, Arna Bontemps. Listed on the National Register of Historic Places.
Collections: Bontemps family history; African American history & culture.
Activities: educational programs.
Hours & Admission Prices: Tues.-Fri. 10-4, Sat. 10-2. No charge; donations accepted.

KENT PLANTATION HOUSE, 3601 Bayou Rapides Rd., Alexandria, LA 71303-3629. Tel.: 318-487-5998. Fax: 318-442-4154.
E-mail: admin@kenthouse.org
Historic House Museum: built c.1796. Listed on the National Register of Historic Places.
Collections: period furnishings; photographs; personal artifacts.
Hours & Admission Prices: Mon.-Sat. 9-5. Adults $6, military, AAA members and seniors 65 & over $5, children 6-12 $2; discounts to groups; children 5 & under no charge.
Attendance: 12,000 (estimated)

T.R.E.E. HOUSE - THE RAPIDES EXPLORATORY EDUCATION HOUSE, 1403 Third St., Alexandria, LA 71301-8250. Tel.: 318-619-9394. Fax: 318-619-9395.
E-mail: questions@kidstreehouse.org
Web Site: www.kidstreehouse.org
Governing Authority: Tax-exempt: 501(c)(3).
Children's Museum.
Collections: hands-on exhibits.
Activities: educational programs.
Hours & Admission Prices: Tues.-Fri. 9-3, Sat. 9-4. Admission $3.50; members & children under 2 no charge. Closed major holidays.

Angola

LOUISIANA STATE PENITENTIARY MUSEUM, (M), Rte. 66, Angola, LA 70712. Mailing Address: General Delivery, Angola, LA 70712-9999. Tel.: 225-655-2592. Fax: 225-655-2842.
E-mail: lspmuseu@bellsouth.net
Web Site: angolamuseum.org
Key Personnel: Dir., Marsha Lindsey.
Governing Authority: nonprofit organization. Parent Institution: Louisiana State Penitentiary Museum Foundation.
Penitentiary Museum.
Collections: prison artifacts; clothing; newspapers; photographs; a jail cell; inmate weapons; farm tools & equipment; movie memorabilia.
Hours & Admission Prices: Mon.-Fri. 8-4:30, Sat. 9-5, Sun. 10-5. No charge; donations accepted. Closed New Year's Day; Easter; Independence Day; Thanksgiving; Christmas. Closed major holidays.

Avery Island

JUNGLE GARDENS, Hwy. 329, Avery Island, LA 70513. Tel.: 337-369-6243.
Garden & Bird Sanctuary.
Collections: plants & flowers; birds; deer; alligators; raccoons.
Facilities: 250-acre site; nature trails.
Hours & Admission Prices: Daily 9-5. Adults $6.25, children 12 & under $4.50. Island Toll: $1.

MCILHENNY COMPANY & VISITOR CENTER, Hwy. 329, Avery Island, LA 70513. Tel.: 800-634-9599; 337-365-8173.
Web Site: www.tabasco.com
Company Museum.
Collections: company history; Tabasco brand products; period advertisements & artifacts; photographs; bottling & packaging machines & equipment.
Facilities: visitor center. Museum-related items for sale.
Activities: pepper sauce factory tours.
Hours & Admission Prices: Daily 9-4. Island Toll: $1. Closed major holidays.

Baker

HERITAGE MUSEUM & CULTURAL CENTER, 1606 Main St., Hwy. 19, Baker, LA 70714. Mailing Address: P.O. Box 707, 1606 Main St., Baker, LA 70704-0707. Tel.: 225-774-1776. Fax: 225-775-5635.
E-mail: bakermuseum@bellsouth.net
Web Site: www.bakerheritagemuseum.org
Governing Authority: municipal government.
History Museum.
Collections: history & heritage of Baker; documents; railroad car. Buildings: restored 1906 Victorian Cottage; one room school; rural store; train depot; chapel; barn.
Activities: exhibit box program; cultural activities; speakers.
Publications: monthly newsletter, Musings.
Hours & Admission Prices: Mon.-Sat. 10-4. No charge; donations accepted.

Bastrop

SNYDER MUSEUM & CREATIVE ARTS CENTER, 1620 E. Madison Ave., Bastrop, LA 71220-4062. Tel.: 318-281-8760.
Founded: 1974.
Congressional District: 5
Key Personnel: Dir., Mary Hodgkins.
Personnel Profile: Part-Time Paid 2.
Governing Authority: nonprofit. Tax-exempt: 501(c)(3).

Local History Museum & Art Center.
Collections: Indian artifacts; Civil War items; archival materials; photograph collection; vintage clothing collection; farm implement collection; early home & store items.
Research Fields: local history.
Facilities: library.
Activities: guided tours; lectures; docent program; traveling, loan & temporary exhibitions. Museum Sponsors: Fundraiser; 8th grade tour.
Publications: quarterly newsletter, Museum Notes.
Hours & Admission Prices: Tues.-Fri. 9-4. No charge; donations accepted. Closed Easter; Memorial Day; Independence Day; Labor Day; Christmas. ♿
Attendance: 1,000 (estimated)
Membership: Individual $10; Family $25; Patron $50; Sustaining $100.

Baton Rouge

BATON ROUGE ZOO, 3601 Thomas Rd., Baton Rouge, LA 70807. Mailing Address: P.O. Box 60, Baker, LA 70704-0060. Tel.: 225-775-3877. Fax: 225-775-3931.
E-mail: info@brzoo.org
Web Site: www.brzoo.org
Formerly: BREC's Baton Rouge Zoo
Founded: 1970.
Congressional District: 6
Key Personnel: Dir., Phillip L. Frost; Dir. Mktg. & Devel., Mary Woods; Gen. Cur., Sam Winslow; Cur. Education, Felicia Johnson; Cur. Birds, Sam Moran; Cur. Hoofstock, John Marshall; Cur. Primates & Carnivores, Greg McCumsey; Cur. Fish & Reptiles, Danna Spayde; Volunteer Coord., Dodi Falcon; Administrative Svcs. Coord., Lois Cook; Vet. Tech., Holly Taylor; Receptionist & Librarian, Kim Lodrigue; Commissarian, Melissa Prisk; Zoo Veterinarian, Dr. Gordon Pirie; Souvenir Shop Mgr., Carroll Shirey; Guest Svcs. Mgr., Vicki Jones; Concessions Mgr., Gilda Conrad.
Personnel Profile: Full-Time Paid 67; Part-Time Paid 37; Part-Time Volunteers 57.
Governing Authority: municipal. Parent Institution: Baton Rouge Recreation & Parks Commission. Tax-exempt: 501(c)(3).
Zoological Park.
Collections: mammals; birds; reptiles; amphibians.
Research Fields: animal behavior work with LSU Vet. School; embryo transfer - Bongo, Asian elephant artificial insemination.
Facilities: 300-vol. library of encyclopedias on animals & books on vertebrate groups, specific orders & habitat, diet, medication & reproduction of animals & groups of animals represented at the zoo, available for research on premises only; auditorium. Zoo-related items for sale.
Activities: guided tours; lectures; slide shows; concerts; explorer scouts study clubs; formally organized education programs for children, adults & graduate students affiliated with LSU; mobile vans.
Publications: newsletter.
Hours & Admission Prices: Daily 9:30-5. Adults & teens $6, senior citizen 65 & over $5, children 2-12 $3; children 1 & under, AZA members & Friends of the Zoo no charge. Closed New Year's Day; Thanksgiving; Christmas Eve & Day. ♿
Attendance: 261,407 (accurate)
Membership: Individual $25; Household $40; Individual Plus 3 $50; Honorary Keeper $65; Safari Club $150; Director's Circle $250.

* **BREC'S MAGNOLIA MOUND PLANTATION, (M),** 2161 Nicholson Dr., Baton Rouge, LA 70802-8105. Tel.: 225-343-4955. Fax: 225-343-6739.
E-mail: information@magnoliamound.org
Web Site: www.magnoliamound.org
Formerly: Magnolia Mound Plantation
Founded: 1968.
Congressional District: 4
Key Personnel: Dir., Steven Fullen; Chm. (V), Jane Thomas; Museum Shop Mgr., Charlene Bertrand.
Personnel Profile: Full-Time Paid 5; Part-Time Paid 11; Part-Time Volunteers 85; Interns 4.
Governing Authority: municipal. Parent Institution: Baton Rouge Park & Recreation Commission. Tax-exempt: 501(c)(3).
Historic Houses: 1791-1830 plantation house & outbuildings.
Collections: furnishings dating from 1780-1830.
Research Fields: restoration; architecture; archaeology; family & social history; period cooking; Louisiana history.
Facilities: visitors center; interpretive exhibits. Gift items for sale.
Activities: guided tours; docent program; formally organized education programs for adults & children; open hearth & bake oven cooking demonstrations.
Publications: quarterly newsletter; docent manual; walking tour booklet; books, Magnolia Mound Kitchen Book; Magnolia Mound, a Louisiana River Plantation; A Year in the Garden; children's workbook.
Hours & Admission Prices: Mon.-Sat. 10-4, Sun. 1-4. Adults $8, senior citizens & students $6, children 5-17 $3; discounts to groups, LAM, BREC, military, AAA & AAM members; children under 5 no charge. Closed New Year's Day; Mardi Gras Day; Easter; Independence Day; Thanksgiving; Christmas. ♿
Attendance: 21,656 (accurate)
Membership: Friend $25; Family Friend $40; Sustainer $100; Contributor $250; Benefactor $500; Duplantier Society $1,000.

THE ENCHANTED MANSION, A DOLL MUSEUM, (M), 190 Lee Dr., Baton Rouge, LA 70808-4953. Mailing Address: 172 Lee Dr., Ste. 3, Baton Rouge, LA 70808-5088. Tel.: 225-769-0005. Fax: 225-766-6822.
E-mail: temansion@tem.brcoxmail.com
Web Site: www.enchantedmansion.org
Founded: 1995.
Congressional District: 6
Key Personnel: C.E.O., Rosemary Sedberry; Office Mgr. & Museum Shop Mgr., LuLu Ragusa.
Personnel Profile: Full-Time Paid 2; Part-Time Paid 4; Part-Time Volunteers 1.
Governing Authority: private; nonprofit organization. Tax-exempt.
Toy & Doll Museum.
Collections: a life-size Victorian doll house; doll collection.
Activities: birthday parties; workshops for children & adults; meeting room.
Hours & Admission Prices: Thurs.-Sat. 10-5. Adults $4.50, senior citizens $3.50, children under 15 $2; discount to groups of 15 or more; handicapped, children under 2 & members no charge. Closed Thanksgiving; Christmas. ♿
Attendance: 5,000 (estimated)
Membership: Baby Doll $20; Rag Doll $35; Teddy Bear $100; China Head $250; Queen Anne Doll $500; Angel $1,000.

LAURENS HENRY COHN, SR. MEMORIAL PLANT ARBORETUM, 12206 Foster Rd., Baton Rouge, LA 70811-1231. Mailing Address: 6201 Florida Blvd., Baton Rouge, LA 70806-4467. Tel.: 225-775-1006. Fax: 225-775-1006.
Founded: 1965.
Congressional District: 6
Key Personnel: Horticulture Foreman, Mike Hano; Mgr. Horticulture, K. Ed Morred.
Personnel Profile: Full-Time Paid 7; Part-Time Paid 4; Part-Time Volunteers 4.
Governing Authority: society. East Baton Rouge Parish Recreation & Park Commission, P.O. Box 15887, Baton Rouge, LA 70895. Tel. 504-272-9200.
Arboretum & Botanical Garden.
Collections: native plant collection; rare & unusual plants of the region; plants from other countries; herbs; herbs of fragrance; Japanese maple collection.
Research Fields: wildflowers; tropicals; adaptable species.
Facilities: classrooms; greenhouses.
Activities: guided tours; lectures; plant recording system; seed exchange program.
Publications: newsletter, Arbornotes; Plantnotes Flyer; Review & Prospectus; Guidenotes.
Hours & Admission Prices: Daily 8-5. No charge. ♿
Attendance: 13,257 (estimated)

* **LOUISIANA ART & SCIENCE MUSEUM - IRENE W. PENNINGTON PLANETARIUM, (M),** 100 River Rd. S., Baton Rouge, LA 70802-5730. Mailing Address: P.O. Box 3373, Baton Rouge, LA 70821-3373. Tel.: 225-344-5272 & 9478. Fax: 225-344-9477.
E-mail: lasm@lasm.org
Web Site: www.lasm.org
Founded: 1960.
Congressional District: 4
Key Personnel: Chm., Mike Anderson; Pres. & Exec. Dir., Carol S. Gikas; Asst. Dir., Sam Losavio; Dir. Mktg., Elizabeth Tadie; Dir. Planetarium, Jon Elvert; Dir. Devel., Pamela Sills; Museum Cur., Elizabeth Chubbuck Weinstein; Publications Mng. & Editor, Catherine McKenzie; Cur. Art Education, Tammy Johnston; Cur. Science Education, Nita Mitchell; Collections Mgr., Leslie Charleville; Chm. (V) & Special Events Coord., Cindy Verdin; Museum Shop Mgr., Paula Taylor; Membership Sec., Barbara Miller; Planetarium Mgr. & Technical Dir., David Kors; Planetarium Producer, Mike Smail; Operations Mgr., Lani Harris; Planetarium Educator, Chandra Weathers; Planetarium Educator, Sheree Westerhauge; Bldg. Supvr., Robert Gourgues; Asst. Dir. Devel., Katie Allen.
Personnel Profile: Full-Time Paid 25; Part-Time Paid 35; Part-Time Volunteers 75; Interns 2.
Governing Authority: nonprofit organization. Parent Institution: Louisiana Art & Science Museum. Tax-exempt: 501(c)(3).
Art & Science Museum: housed in renovated & expanded former Illinois Central Railroad Station; space theater.
Collections: Louisiana modern & contemporary art from 1900 to present;

American & European art from 18th-21st centuries including Ivan Mestrovic sculptures & drawings, Charles Burchfield, John Marin, Dale Chihuly; photographs; ethnographic art including Inuit, Tibetan, Native American, African, & pre-Colombian; antiquities including a Ptolemaic-era mummy; scientific artifacts including meteorites & star charts; hands-on children's exhibits.

Major Exhibits: Still Life Painting By Four Louisiana Artists, 12/26/09-2/21/10; The Curious World of Patent Models (T), 2/27/10-5/9/10; Almost Alice: Illustrations of Wonderland by Maggie Taylor (T), 5/15/10-6/18/10; Tradition/Innovation: American Masterpieces of Southern Craft and Traditional Art (T), 7/24/10-9/26/10; Keith Sonnier: Sculptor of Light, 10/9/10-1/9/10.

Research Fields: art history, particularly Louisiana modernists; American contemporary art; astronomy.

Facilities: planetarium; theatre; auditorium; classrooms. Museum-related items for sale.

Activities: permanent & temporary exhibitions; docent programs; art history lectures; artist talks; guided tours; films; sky shows; astronomy lectures; formally organized education programs for children; in-service workshops for teachers; public education programs.

Publications: LASM Quarterly; special exhibition catalogues.

Hours & Admission Prices: Tues.-Fri. 10-4, Sat. 10-5, Sun. 1-5. Planetarium: Tues.-Fri. 10-4, Sat. 10-8, Sun. 1-5. Galleries: adults $6; discounts to seniors, children, AAA & ASTC members; members no charge. Galleries Plus Theater: adults $8; discounts to members, seniors, children, AAA & ASTC members. Closed major holidays. ♿

Attendance: 209,000 (accurate)

Membership: Student & Teacher $25; Friend $50; Family I $75; Family II $100; Contributor $150; Patron $300; Supporting $500; Sustaining $1,000.

LOUISIANA MUD PAINTINGS, 16950 Strian Rd., Baton Rouge, LA 70816-1823. Tel.: 225-275-5126.

Art Gallery.

Collections: paintings by Henry Neubig using mud & clay found in Louisiana.

Hours & Admission Prices: Tues.-Sat. 10-5.

LOUISIANA NAVAL WAR MEMORIAL/U.S.S. KIDD, 305 S. River Rd., Baton Rouge, LA 70802-6220. Tel.: 225-342-1942. Fax: 225-342-2039.

E-mail: info@usskidd.com

Web Site: www.usskidd.com

Founded: 1981.

Congressional District: 6

Key Personnel: Exec. Dir. & Ship's Cur., H. Maury Drummond; Museum Shop Mgr., Monica Dugus; Administrative Asst., Tim Nessmith; Museum Shop Asst., Jenny Bennett.

Governing Authority: state; nonprofit. Affiliated with Louisiana State Department of Culture & Louisiana Naval War Memorial Commission & Foundation. Tax-exempt: 501(c)(3).

Maritime Museum & Historic Ship.

Collections: U.S. Navy shipboard destroyer operations including weapons, electronics, lifestyle, uniforms, books & documents; maritime history represented by ship models, paintings, photographs & various artifacts; CBI display featuring restored P-40 fighter plane; documents, photographs, & memorabilia associated with Flying Tigers. Historic Ship: 1942 USS KIDD-Fletcher Class; a replica of USS Constitution's gun deck, Old Iron Sides; Corsair A-7 aircraft in tribute to Vietnam Veterans.

Research Fields: destroyer operations; design & development.

Facilities: 500-vol. library of blueprints, documents, technical manuals, training manuals, publications & nautical charts relating to United States Navy destroyer; 100-seat theater; 30-seat snack bar. Museum-related items for sale.

Activities: guided tours; lectures; docent program; temporary, traveling & loan exhibitions; school loan service; shipboard overnight camping for youth groups.

Publications: quarterly newsletter, KIDD's Compass; book, U.S.S. KIDD (DD-661) Technical History; documentary, Fletcher Class destroyers.

Hours & Admission Prices: Daily 9-5. Ship & Museum: adults $7, senior citizens 60 & over $6, active military with ID $5, children 5-12 $4; discounts for groups of 20 or more; members & children 4 and under no charge. Museum only: adults $4, children 5-12 $3; children 4 & under no charge. Closed Thanksgiving; Christmas. ♿

Attendance: 53,303

Membership: Individual $25; Family Member & Sustaining $50; Century $100; Patron $500; President's Council $1,000; Honor Council $1,000 & up.

LOUISIANA STATE UNIVERSITY HERBARIUM, A257 Life Sciences Annex, LSU, Baton Rouge, LA 70803-1715. Mailing Address: 202 Life Sciences Building, Dept. of Biological Sciences, LSU, Baton Rouge, LA 70803-1715. Tel.: 225-578-8564. Fax: 225-578-2597.

E-mail: leu@lsu.edu

Web Site: www.herbarium.lsu.edu

Founded: 1869.

Congressional District: 6

Key Personnel: Dir., Lowell E. Urbatsch; Cur., Diane Ferguson.

Personnel Profile: Full-Time Paid 1; Part-Time Paid 4.

Governing Authority: university. Parent Institution: Louisiana State University. Subsidiary Institution: Dept. of Biological Sciences. Tax-exempt.

Herbarium.

Collections: vascular plants of Louisiana & U.S.; Asteraceae; Fabaceae; Poaceae; tropical America.

Research Fields: morphological & biosystematic studies of plants; monographic botany; Louisiana area flora; biochemical systematics; compositae; DNA systematics.

Facilities: library; plant specimen preparation & storage.

Activities: scientific studies; research; identification of vascular plants; classes in taxonomy & ecology; local field trips.

Hours & Admission Prices: Mon.-Fri. 8:30-4:30. No charge; donations accepted.

Attendance: 150 (estimated)

LOUISIANA STATE UNIVERSITY MUSEUM OF ART, (M), Shaw Center for the Arts, 100 Lafayette St., Baton Rouge, LA 70801-1201. Tel.: 225-389-7200. Fax: 225-389-7219.

E-mail: radam14@lsu.edu

Web Site: www.lsu.edu/lsumoa

Founded: 1959.

Congressional District: 6

Key Personnel: Exec. Dir., Thomas A. Livesay; Chm. (V), Sharon Field; Asst. Dir., Fran Huber; Asst. Dir. & Devel., Melissa Daly; Asst. Cur., Natalie Mault; Asst. Dir. Curatorial, Victoria Cooke; Cur. Education, Lara Gautreau; Dir. Mktg., Renee Payton; Administrative Asst., Becky Adams; Museum Shop Mgr., LeAnn Russo.

Personnel Profile: Full-Time Paid 12; Part-Time Paid 5; Part-Time Volunteers 25.

Governing Authority: state. Parent Institution: Louisiana State University. Tax-exempt: 501(c)(3).

Art Museum.

Collections: American contemporary art; decorative arts; fine arts; photography; prints; Asian, European & American art; 18th-20th century American & European ceramics, drawings, paintings; furniture; sculpture; Newcomb College ceramics; regional silver; Chinese jade; American photographers.

Major Exhibits: Of People and Places: Contemporary Art from the JP Morgan Chase Art Collection, 11/21/09-2/13/10; George Ohr Rising: The Emergence of an American Master (T), 3/10-8/1/10; Tribute: Eugene Martin, John T. Scott & Emerson Bell, and Frank Hayden, 8/27/10-11/12/10.

Research Fields: decorative arts; paintings; graphics; sculpture; works on paper; photography.

Facilities: 500-vol. library of material pertaining to paintings, prints, drawings & decorative arts.

Activities: guided tours; lectures; films; gallery talks; inter-museum loan, permanent, temporary & traveling exhibitions.

Publications: exhibit catalogs; Whispers From the Stone; The James R. & Ann A. Peltier Collection of Chinese Jade; ARTALK.

Hours & Admission Prices: Tues.-Wed. & Fri.-Sat. 10-5, Thurs. 10-8, Sun. 1-5. Adults $8; discounts to AAM members; members no charge. Closed New Year's Day; Mardi Gras; Easter; Thanksgiving; Christmas Eve & Day. ♿

Attendance: 32,500 (estimated)

Membership: Student $15; Individual $40; Dual & Family $60; Patron $100; Sustaining $250; Benefactor $500; Endowment Society $1,000; Corporate: $2,500; $5,000; $10,000.

* **LOUISIANA'S OLD STATE CAPITOL, (M),** 100 North Blvd., Baton Rouge, LA 70801-1502. Mailing Address: P.O. Box 94125, Baton Rouge, LA 70804-9125. Tel.: 225-342-0500; 800-488-2968. Fax: 225-342-0316.

E-mail: osc@sos.louisiana.gov

Web Site: www.sos.louisiana.gov/osc

Founded: 1994.

Congressional District: 6

Key Personnel: Dir., Mary Louise Prudhomme; Public Rels., Nancy Chesson; Museum Shop Mgr., Charlotte Wall; Security, James Wilson.

Personnel Profile: Full-Time Paid 21; Part-Time Paid 6.

Governing Authority: state. Parent Institution: Office of the Secretary of State, Baton Rouge, LA. Tax-exempt.

Political History Museum.

Collections: political & governmental history of Louisiana; memorabilia; audio & video tapes.
Research Fields: history, politics & government, 1780's-present.
Facilities: theater. Museum-related items for sale.
Activities: arts festivals; docent program; films; guided tours; lectures; loan, temporary, traveling, interactive & participatory exhibitions; formal education programs; rental gallery; theater; broadcast programs. Annual Events: Red Stick Animation Festival; Veterans Day; Santa in the Senate.
Hours & Admission Prices: Mon.-Sat. 9-4:30, Sun. 12-4:30. No charge. Closed most state holidays. ♿
Membership: Call for information.

MUSEUM OF AFRICAN AMERICAN HISTORY, 538 S. Boulevard, Baton Rouge, LA 70802-6442. Tel.: 225-343-4431.
E-mail: sadierobertsjoseph@yahoo.com
Founded: 2001.
Congressional District: 6
Key Personnel: Founder & Cur., Sadie Roberts-Joseph
History Museum.
Collections: minority inventors & inventions; African art; period artifacts.
Activities: Annual Events: Dr. Martin Luther King Jr. Holiday in January; State Juneteenth Celebration in June; Veterans Day Celebration in November.
Hours & Admission Prices: Mon.-Fri. 1-5; other times by appointment. Adults $4; discounts to AAM & ICOM members. Closed major holidays. ♿
Attendance: 1,500
Membership: Student $8; Individual $35; Friend $100; Life $200.

MUSEUM OF NATURAL SCIENCE, 119 Foster Hall, LSU, Baton Rouge, LA 70803-0001. Tel.: 225-578-2855. Fax: 225-578-3075.
E-mail: museum@lsu.edu
Web Site: appl003.lsu.edu/natsci/lmnh.nsf/index
Founded: 1936.
Congressional District: 6
Key Personnel: Dir., Dr. Frederick H. Sheldon; Cur. Fishes, Dr. Prosanta Chakrabarty; Cur. Birds, Dr. J.V. Remsen, Jr.; Cur. Paleontology, Dr. Judith A. Schiebout; Cur. Anthropology, Dr. Rebecca A. Saunders; Cur. Herpetology, Dr. Christopher C. Austin; Dir. Education, Dr. Sophie Warny; Cur. Animals, Dr. Mark Hafner; Cur. Genetic Resource, Dr Robb Brumfield.
Personnel Profile: Full-Time Paid 17; Part-Time Paid 6; Part-Time Volunteers 8.
Governing Authority: university. Parent Institution: Louisiana State University. Tax-exempt: 501(c)(3).
Natural History Museum.
Collections: ornithology; mammalogy; ichthyology; herpetology; frozen tissues; paleontology; archaeology; anthropology.
Research Fields: ornithology; mammalogy; ichthyology; herpetology; systematics; zoogeography; evolutionary biology; ecology; behavior; paleontology; archaeology; anthropology.
Facilities: vertebrate research collections; biochemical systematics laboratories; morphology analysis laboratory; karyology laboratory; sound analysis laboratory; computer laboratory; reprint library; classrooms; dermestid colony; paleontological collections; archaeological & anthropological collections.
Activities: research programs by staff & graduate students; permanent & temporary exhibits.
Publications: Occasional papers, Museum of Natural Science.
Hours & Admission Prices: Mon.-Fri. 8-4. No charge. Closed university holidays. ♿
Attendance: 32,000
Membership: Friends of the LSU Museum of Natural Science (Support group) $25.

OLD ARSENAL MUSEUM, Capitol Lake Dr., Baton Rouge, LA 70804. Mailing Address: P.O. Box 94125, Baton Rouge, LA 70804-9125. Tel.: 225-342-0401. Fax: 225-342-5577.
E-mail: arsenal@sos.louisiana.gov
Web Site: www.sos.louisiana.gov/oam
Formerly: Old Arsenal Powder Magazine Museum
Key Personnel: Dir., Gregory Leggio.
Personnel Profile: Full-Time Paid 1.
Governing Authority: state. Parent Institution: Louisiana Secretary of State, Baton Rouge, LA. Tax-exempt.
History Museum: built in 1838; used by the US military during the Mexican & Civil Wars. Listed on the National Register of Historic Places.
Collections: Louisiana heritage; military history; photographs.
Activities: guided group tours; participatory exhibits.
Hours & Admission Prices: Tues.-Sat. 9-4. No charge. Closed most state holidays. ♿

OLD LOUISIANA GOVERNOR'S MANSION, 502 N. Blvd., Baton Rouge, LA 70802. Tel.: 225-387-2464.
Historic Mansion: built in 1930. Listed on the National Register of Historic Places.
Collections: local history & culture; period furnishings; photographs; personal artifacts; political history & artifacts.
Hours & Admission Prices: Tours: Tues.-Fri. 10-4.

ROBERT A. BOGAN FIRE MUSEUM, 427 Laurel St., Baton Rouge, LA 70801-1810. Tel.: 225-344-8558. Fax: 225-344-7777.
E-mail: katherine@acgbr.com
Web Site: www.artsbr.org
Formerly: Old Bogan Firefighters Museum
Founded: 1924.
Congressional District: 6
Key Personnel: Deputy Dir., Katherine Scherer.
Personnel Profile: Part-Time Volunteers 5.
Governing Authority: nonprofit. Tax-exempt: 501(c)(3).
Fire-Fighting Museum.
Collections: fire helmets, extinguishers, alarms boxes & horns; trophies; 1919 Type 17 Motor Aerial Truck with 75 ft. ladder; original brass poles; photographs.
Activities: guided tours; organized education programs for children.
Hours & Admission Prices: Temporarily closed. ♿
Attendance: 3,000 (estimated)

RURAL LIFE MUSEUM & WINDRUSH GARDENS, 4560 Essen Lane, Baton Rouge, LA 70809-3424. Mailing Address: P.O. Box 80498, Baton Rouge, LA 70898-0498. Tel.: 225-765-2437. Fax: 225-765-2639.
E-mail: rurallife@lsu.edu
Web Site: rurallife.lsu.edu
Founded: 1970.
Congressional District: 6
Key Personnel: Exec. Dir., David Floyd; Interpretive Specialist, Catherine White; Registrar & Conservator, David Nicolosi; Mgr., Elizabeth McInnis; Devel. Dir., Tonja Normand.
Personnel Profile: Full-Time Paid 5; Part-Time Paid 5; Part-Time Volunteers 60; Interns 1.
Governing Authority: public university; nonprofit. Parent Institution: Louisiana State University. Tax-exempt: 501(c)(3).
History Museum.
Collections: local history exhibits; glass; ceramics; metalwares; farm equipment & tools; tools for various trades; textiles; furniture; medical items; lighting devices; logging, hunting, trapping, & fishing items; transportation; Civil War items; toys. Historic Buildings: c.1835 general store; c.1835 overseer's house; c.1855 kitchen; c.1830-1840 sick house; c.1853 schoolhouse; c.1835 blacksmith's shop; c.1835 slave cabins; c.1870 country church; c.1840 pioneer's cabin & corncrib; c.1870 dogtrot house; cane grinder & sugarhouse; grist mill; acadian house; shotgun house.
Facilities: 1,200-vol. library of books, periodicals & related material pertaining to Louisiana & the South available for use on premises only; botanical garden.
Activities: guided tours; lectures; organized education programs for children, undergraduate, & graduate students; docent program.
Publications: museum guidebook.
Hours & Admission Prices: Daily 8:30-5. Adults & children 12-61 $7, seniors 62 & over $6, children 5-11 $4; children under 5 no charge. Closed New Year's Day; Easter; Thanksgiving; Christmas Eve & Day. ♿
Attendance: 15,000 (accurate)

USS KIDD VETERANS MEMORIAL & MUSEUM, 305 S. River Rd., Baton Rouge, LA 70802-6220. Tel.: 225-342-1942. Fax: 225-342-2039.
Military Museum: housed on a U.S. Navy destroyer.
Collections: destroyer history; military equipment; personal artifacts; photographs.
Facilities: Museum-related items for sale.
Hours & Admission Prices: Call for hours. Ship & Museum: adults 13 & over $7, seniors 60 & over $6, children 5-12 $4; children 4 & under no charge. Museum: adults 13 & over $4, children 5-12 $3; children 4 & under no charge.

Belle Chasse

THE TULANE UNIVERSITY MUSEUM OF NATURAL HISTORY, 3705 Main St., Bldg. A-3, Belle Chasse, LA 70037-3001. Tel.: 504-394-1711. Fax: 504-394-5045.
E-mail: hank@museum.tulane.edu
Web Site: www.museum.tulane.edu
Key Personnel: Cur. Fish, Dr. Henry L. Bart; Collections Mgr., Nelson Rios; Adjunct Cur. Mammals, Dr. Craig Hood

Natural History Museum.
Collections: invertebrates; fish; amphibians; reptiles; birds; mammals; vertebrate fossils.
Hours & Admission Prices: Mon.-Fri. 8:30-5.

Bermuda

BEAU FORT PLANTATION HOME, 4078 Hwy. 494 & Hwy. 119, Bermuda, LA 71456. Mailing Address: 919 Parkway, Natchitoches, LA 71457-5533. Tel.: 318-352-9580 & 5340. Fax: 318-352-7280.
Founded: 1790.
Congressional District: 4
Key Personnel: C.E.O. & Owner Oper., Mrs. Jack O. Brittain; Guide, David Hooper; Guide, Janet LaCour; Guide, Lucile Hendrick.
Personnel Profile: Full-Time Paid 1; Full-Time Volunteers 2.
Governing Authority: privately owned.
Historic House: 1790 Creole one & one-half cottage type building, built with walls of bousillage.
Collections: Louisiana Creole period furnishings & furniture; ornaments dating to the Ching Dynasty; punkah; crystal; brass; paintings; enclosed courtyard & patio; piecrust table; sofa, Napoleonic era; Mallard, Seinueret, Belter, Chippendale pieces of furniture; 1790 French desk; 1830-1860 pieces of furniture, Haviland & Lemoges china.
Facilities: rental space available for receptions & parties.
Activities: formal or informal lunches, brunches & dinners served by appointment; wedding receptions; bed & breakfast.
Publications: brochure.
Hours & Admission Prices: Daily 1-4. Adults $6, high school students $3, children $2; discounts to groups of 20 or more; guide & bus driver no charge. ♿
Attendance: 15,000 (estimated)

Bernice

BERNICE DEPOT MUSEUM, Fourth and Louisiana St., Bernice, LA 71222. Mailing Address: P.O. Box 633, Bernice, LA 71222-0633. Tel.: 318-285-2433.
Key Personnel: Museum Shop Mgr., Gladys Harkins
Historic Building: built in 1899.
Collections: railroad history & memorabilia; period artifacts; tools; wooden ox yoke.
Activities: special events.
Hours & Admission Prices: Mon.-Fri. 10-12 & 1-3. No charge; donations accepted.

Broussard

ZOO OF ACADIANA, 5601 Hwy. 90 E., Broussard, LA 70518. Mailing Address: 116 Lakeview Dr., Broussard, LA 70518-8004. Tel.: 337-837-4325. Fax: 337-837-4253.
E-mail: wild@zoofacadiana.org
Key Personnel: Co Owner, George Oldenburg; Co Owner, Marleen Oldenburg
Zoo.
Collections: over 500 animals representing more than 125 species.
Facilities: Museum-related items for sale.
Activities: train rides; special events; school groups. Annual Events: Zoolebrate; Eggstravaganzoo; Boo at the Zoo; Safari of Lights.
Hours & Admission Prices: Jan.-Nov. daily 9-5; Dec. daily 9-4. Safari of Lights: Dec. 5pm-9pm. Adults 13-54 $9.25, seniors 55 & over $8.25, children 3-12 $5.50; children 2 & under no charge. Closed New Year's Day; Easter; Thanksgiving; Christmas.

Carville

NATIONAL HANSEN'S DISEASE MUSEUM, Bldg. 12, Carville Historic District, 5445 Point Clair Rd., Carville, LA 70721-2119. Mailing Address: 1770 Physicians Dr., Baton Rouge, LA 70816. Tel.: 225-642-1950. Fax: 225-642-1949.
E-mail: NHDPmuseum@hrsa.gov
Web Site: www.hrsa.gov/hansens/museum/default.htm
Founded: 1996.
Key Personnel: Interim Cur., Vicki Joseph.
Personnel Profile: Full-Time Paid 1; Part-Time Paid 1; Part-Time Volunteers 1.
Governing Authority: Parent Institution: National Hansen's Disease Programs. Tax-exempt.
History & Medical Museum.
Collections: medical & social history; photographs; PHS Hospital artifacts.
Publications: With Love in Their Hearts: 1896-1996 Daughters of Charity at Carville; 100 Years - Carville Centennial.
Hours & Admission Prices: Tues.-Sat. 10-4. No charge; donations accepted. Closed federal holidays. ♿
Attendance: 2,000 (accurate)

Charenton

CHITIMACHA MUSEUM, 3289 Chitimacha Trail, Charenton, LA 70523. Mailing Address: P.O. Box 661, Charenton, LA 70523-0661. Tel.: 337-923-4830.
Web Site: www.chitimacha.org
Native American Museum.
Collections: Chitimacha history & culture; Native American artifacts; baskets.
Activities: videos.
Hours & Admission Prices: Tues.-Sat. 9-4:30. No charge. ♿

Cloutierville

THE KATE CHOPIN HOUSE & BAYOU FOLK MUSEUM, 243 Hwy. 495, Cloutierville, LA 71416-2026. Mailing Address: P.O. Box 2248, Natchitoches, LA 71457-2248. Tel.: 318-379-2233. Fax: 318-379-0055.
Founded: 1965.
Congressional District: 5
Key Personnel: Chm., Sadie Newell; Dir., Amanda Chenault; Pres., Dr. Sue Weaver.
Personnel Profile: Full-Time Paid 1; Full-Time Volunteers 3; Part-Time Paid 2; Part-Time Volunteers 5.
Governing Authority: society. Subsidiary Institution: Assoc. for the Preservation of Historic Natchitoches. Tax-exempt.
Historic House: c.1800 home of Creole writer Kate Chopin from 1880-1884; national historic landmark.
Collections: furniture; furnishings; artifacts relating to the educational, religious, social & economic life of Creoles; agricultural tools; doctor's office & implements; blacksmith's shop.
Research Fields: family history; church history; Kate Chopin; 1800s-early 1900s clothing.
Facilities: library of books by Louisiana writers; scrapbooks; files; photographs; documents; family records.
Activities: guided tours; lectures for study groups; permanent exhibitions; dramatizations of Kate Chopin's works by The Bayou Folk Players.
Hours & Admission Prices: Tues.-Sun. 12-4. Adults $5, students 12-18 $3; discounts to senior citizen groups; children under 6 & members no charge. Tours by appointment. Closed New Year's Day; Easter; Thanksgiving; Christmas.
Attendance: 1,859 (accurate)
Membership: Assoc. for the Preservation of Historic Natchitoches: Annual $15.

Covington

INSTA-GATOR RANCH & HATCHERY, 23440 Lowe Davis Rd., Covington, LA 70435-6512. Tel.: 985-892-3669; 888-448-1560.
Alligator Farm.
Collections: over 2,000 alligators of all sizes & ages; Louisiana alligator industry; Cajun heritage & culture.
Facilities: Museum-related items for sale.
Activities: educational programs; guided tours; video
Hours & Admission Prices: Daily call for hours. Adults $16, military $14, children 12 & under $10; discounts to groups.

Crowley

CROWLEY ART ASSOCIATION & GALLERY, 220 N. Parkerson, Crowley, LA 70526-5003. Tel.: 337-783-3747. Fax: 337-783-3747.
E-mail: gallerythe@bellsouth.net
Web Site: www.crowleyartgallery.com
Founded: 1980.
Congressional District: 7
Key Personnel: C.E.O., Hurley Gautreaux; Vice Pres., Virgie LeBlue; Museum Shop Mgr., Becky Faulk.
Personnel Profile: Full-Time Paid 1; Full-Time Volunteers 50; Part-Time Paid 1; Part-Time Volunteers 20.
Governing Authority: nonprofit organization. Parent Institution: Crowley Art Association. Tax-exempt.
Art Association & Gallery.
Collections: pottery & crafts.
Facilities: library of art history & educational books, available for use by members only. Paintings in all media, crafts, jewelry, porcelain & needlework for sale.
Activities: guided tours; arts festivals; hobby workshops; formal education programs for children & adults; docent program; participatory exhibits. Association Sponsors: two outdoor arts & crafts shows; children's & adult workshops; poster contests; special exhibits & receptions; one outdoor show & one indoor show.

Publications: monthly, CAA Newsletter; annually, CAA Yearbook.
Hours & Admission Prices: Mon.-Fri. 10-4. No charge. Closed New Year's Day; Independence Day; Thanksgiving; Christmas week. ♿
Membership: Adult $20; Gallery $24; Family $25.

CRYSTAL RICE HERITAGE FARM, 6428 Airport Rd, Crowley, LA 70526-1604. Mailing Address: P.O. Box 1425, Crowley, LA 70527-1425. Tel.: 337-783-6417. Fax: 337-788-0123.
E-mail: dwrighth@cs.com
Web Site: www.crystalrice.com
Formerly: Crystal Rice Plantation
Founded: 1970.
Congressional District: 7
Key Personnel: C.E.O., Diane Hoffpauer; Treas., Elaine Wright; Dir. & Museum Shop Mgr., Redell Miller.
Governing Authority: nonprofit.
Classic Car Museum & Historical Society: c.1848 plantation home.
Collections: period furniture & implements; rice samples; pictures; dolls; classic cars.
Research Fields: rice industry; crawfish production.
Facilities: rice research station.
Activities: tours.
Hours & Admission Prices: Mon.-Fri. 10-3 by appointment. Adults $10, senior citizens $6, students $4.50; discounts to AAA members; members no charge. Closed all holidays.
Attendance: 1,000 (accurate)

RICE INTERPRETIVE CENTER AND J.D. MILLER RECORDING STUDIO MUSEUM, 425 N. Parkerson Ave., Crowley, LA 70526. Tel.: 337-783-0824.
History Museum.
Collections: local history & culture; photographs; videos; J.D. Miller's music & life; personal artifacts; early machinery; rice history, growing & production; recording equipment.
Activities: video; hands-on exhibits.
Hours & Admission Prices: Call for hours.

Darrow

HERMITAGE PLANTATION, 38308 Hwy. 942, River Rd., Darrow, LA 70725. Tel.: 225-473-1813.
E-mail: info@hermitageplantation.com
Historic House: built in 1812. Listed on the National Register of Historic Places.
Collections: local history & culture; period furnishings; personal artifacts; photographs; paintings.
Hours & Admission Prices: By appointment.

HOUMAS HOUSE PLANTATION AND GARDENS, 40136 Hwy. 942, Darrow, LA 70725-2302. Tel.: 225-473-9380. Fax: 225-473-7891.
Historic House.
Collections: local history & culture; period furnishings; personal artifacts. photographs; paintings.
Facilities: restaurant.
Activities: guided tours.
Hours & Admission Prices: Mon.-Tues. 9-5, Wed.-Sun. 9-7. Tours: Mansion & Gardens $20. Gardens & Grounds: $10.

Destrehan

DESTREHAN PLANTATION, 13034 River Rd., Destrehan, LA 70047-5202. Tel.: 985-764-9315; 877-453-2095. Fax: 985-725-1929.
Web Site: www.destrehanplantation.org
Key Personnel: Site Mgr., Nancy Robert
Plantation: a National Historic Landmark, established in 1787.
Collections: period furnishings; personal artifacts; photographs.
Hours & Admission Prices: Daily 9-4. Adults $10, children 6-16 $5. Closed major holidays.

Donaldsonville

RIVER ROAD AFRICAN AMERICAN MUSEUM, (M), 406 Charles St., Donaldsonville, LA 70346-3312. Mailing Address: P.O. Box 266, Donaldsonville, LA 70346-0266. Tel.: 225-474-5553.
E-mail: kathe@africanamericanmuseum.org
Web Site: www.africanamericanmuseum.org
Key Personnel: Dir., Kathe Hambrick
History Museum.
Collections: local African American history & culture; books; photographs; period artifacts; .
Hours & Admission Prices: Wed.-Sat. 10-5, Sun. 1-5; groups of 10 or more by appointment. Museum or School & Church Tour: adults $4. Heritage Tour: adults $25.

Erath

THE ACADIAN MUSEUM, 203 S. Broadway, Erath, LA 70533-4003. Tel.: 337-233-5832. Fax: 337-235-4382.
E-mail: info@acadianmuseum.com
Web Site: www.acadianmuseum.com
History Museum.
Collections: local history & culture; paintings; photographs; books; maps; artifacts.
Hours & Admission Prices: Mon.-Fri. 1-4; other times by appointment. No charge.

Eunice

EUNICE DEPOT MUSEUM, 220 S. C.C. Duson Dr., Eunice, LA 70535-7808. Tel.: 337-457-6540 & 2565.
Historic Site: housed in the building where C.C. Duson sold the first land sites & named the town after his wife Eunice; 1893-1894. Listed on the National Register of Historic Places.
Collections: town history; Cajun Mardi Gras & music; period toys; railroad artifacts; pioneer farming; Native American culture.
Facilities: Museum-related items for sale.
Activities: craft workshops.
Hours & Admission Prices: Tues.-Sat. 8-12 & 1-5. No charge.

Ferriday

DELTA MUSIC MUSEUM, 218 Louisiana Ave., Ferriday, LA 71334-2828. Mailing Address: P.O. Box 94125, Baton Rouge, LA 70804-9125. Tel.: 318-757-9999. Fax: 318-757-1973.
E-mail: deltamusic@sos.louisiana.gov
Web Site: www.sos.louisiana.gov/dmm
Founded: 2001.
Congressional District: 5
Key Personnel: Dir., Judith Bingham.
Personnel Profile: Full-Time Paid 1; Part-Time Paid 6.
Governing Authority: state. Parent Institution: Louisiana Secretary of State, Baton Rouge, LA. Tax-exempt.
Music Museum.
Collections: local & music history; Louisiana-Mississippi Delta region culture & music; mannequins; interactive music kiosks; Jerry Lee Lewis; Mickey Gilley; Jimmy Swaggart; Mississippi River Delta musicians including Leon (Pee Wee) Whittaker, Jimmie Davis, Conway Twitty, & Aaron Neville.
Facilities: theater. Museum-related items for sale.
Activities: loan, traveling & interactive exhibits; live performances; concerts; films; guided tours; theater; arts festivals; dance recitals; docent program; lectures. Annual Event: Delta Music Festival in April.
Hours & Admission Prices: Mon.-Sat. 9-4; student groups by appointment. No charge. Closed most state holidays. ♿
Membership: Call for information.

Folsom

GLOBAL WILDLIFE CENTER, 26389 Hwy. 40, Folsom, LA 70437. Tel.: 985-796-3585.
Founded: 1991.
Key Personnel: Museum Shop Mgr., Beth Kuhnau.
Governing Authority: Tax-exempt.
Wildlife Center.
Collections: over 4,000 animals from around the world.
Activities: birthday parties.
Hours & Admission Prices: Daily call for hours. Suggested Donations: adults $17, seniors $13, children $10; discounts to groups. ♿
Attendance: 350,000
Membership: Family $100; Family Plus $150; Lifetime $1,000.

Fort Polk

FORT POLK MUSEUM ACTIVITY, (M), Bldg. 917 S. Carolina Ave., Fort Polk, LA 71459. Mailing Address: P.O. Box 3916, Fort Polk, LA 71459-0916. Tel.: 337-531-7905 & 4840. Fax: 337-531-4202.
E-mail: binghamd@polk.army.mil
Formerly: Fort Polk Historical Holding Area
Founded: 1972.
Congressional District: 4
Key Personnel: Historian & Cur., David S. Bingham.

Personnel Profile: Full-Time Paid 1.
Governing Authority: federal. Tax-exempt.
Military Museum.
Collections: artifacts & memorabilia pertaining to the history of Camp/Fort Polk & Divisions stationed there since 1941; items from WWII, Korean War & Vietnam; 1940-1944 Louisiana Maneuvers; 7,000 military photographs; 2-acre outdoor park displaying: armor; helicopters; artillery; vehicles; missiles.
Research Fields: U.S. Army military history from WWII to present.
Facilities: 6,000-vol. library of books & publications on U.S. army history, military equipment data & museum professional publications available for research on premises; outdoor display park.
Activities: lectures upon request; permanent exhibitions.
Hours & Admission Prices: Wed.-Fri. 10-2, Sat.-Sun. 9-4. No charge. Closed New Year's Day; Thanksgiving; Christmas. ♿
Attendance: 15,000 (estimated)

Franklin

GREVEMBERG HOUSE MUSEUM, 407 Sterling Rd., Hwy. 322, Franklin, LA 70538-0400. Mailing Address: P.O. Box 400, Franklin, LA 70538-0400. Tel.: 337-828-2092. Fax: 337-828-2028.
E-mail: info@grevemberghouse.com
Web Site: www.grevemberghouse.com
Founded: 1972.
Congressional District: 3
Key Personnel: Pres., Fred Schwitz; Treas. & Public Rels., Didi Battle; Archivist, Margie Luke; Lead Interpreter, Craig Landry.
Personnel Profile: Part-Time Paid 2; Part-Time Volunteers 17.
Governing Authority: private; nonprofit organization. Tax-exempt: 501(c)(3).
Historical Society Museum: housed in c.1851 Greek-revival townhouse. Listed on National Register of Historic Places.
Collections: 1820-1870 furniture; 19th century life in south Louisiana; Civil War artifacts.
Research Fields: translation of Grevemberg family papers; period furnishings.
Facilities: 5,000 sq. ft. exhibit space.
Activities: guided tours. Annual Event: Victorian Christmas Celebration.
Publications: semiannual newsletter, Landmark Lagniappe.
Hours & Admission Prices: Daily 10-4. Adults $10, senior citizens & students 12-18 $8, children under 12 $5; discounts to groups of 20 or more; members no charge. Closed New Year's Day; Good Friday; Easter; Thanksgiving; Christmas Eve & Day. ♿
Attendance: 331 (accurate)
Membership: Foundation $35; Pillar (couple) $60; Conservator $75; Gothic $100; Victorian $250; Queen Anne $500; Corinthian $1,000-$1,499; Greek Revival $1,500-$1,999; Italianate $2,000-$3,999; Landmark $4,000 & up.

OAKLAWN MANOR, 3296 E. Oaklawn Dr., Franklin, LA 70538-3218. Tel.: 337-828-0434. Fax: 337-828-1930.
E-mail: oaklawnmanor@yahoo.com
Historic House Museum.
Collections: local history & culture; period furnishings; personal artifacts.
Hours & Admission Prices: Tues.-Sun. 10-4. Adults $10, students $6.

YOUNG SANDERS CENTER, 104 Commercial St., Franklin, LA 70538-5427. Mailing Address: P.O. Box 545, Franklin, LA 70538-0545.
E-mail: ysc1861@aol.com
Web Site: www.youngsanders.org
History Museum.
Collections: artifacts; documents; journals; period maps; photographs.
Hours & Admission Prices: Mon.-Fri. 9-5. ♿

Franklinton

WASHINGTON AREA MUSEUM FOUNDATION/VARNADO STORE MUSEUM, 936 Pearl St., Franklinton, LA 70438-1736. Mailing Address: P.O. Box 184, Franklinton, LA 70438-0184. Tel.: 985-795-0680. Fax: 985-795-0680.
E-mail: varnadostoremuseum@franklinton.net
Web Site: www.varanadostoremuseum.org
Founded: 1996.
Key Personnel: Pres. (V), Dianne Smith; Dir., Terry Seal.
Governing Authority: Tax-exempt.
History Museum.
Collections: local history & heritage.
Major Exhibits: Quilts-Old and New, 1/10-2/10; Vintage Clothing, 3/10; Green Gardening, 4/10-5/10; Tribute to the Military, 6/10-7/10; History of Education in Our Parish, 8/10; History of Washington Parish Fair, 9/10-10/10; Christmases Past-Festival, 11/10-12/10.
Facilities: Museum-related items for sale.
Activities: lectures; demonstrations; group tours; school field trips. Museum Sponsors: Street Fair in Spring; Christmas Festival in December.
Publications: members newsletter.
Hours & Admission Prices: Fri. by appointment, Sat. 10-4, Sun. 1-4. No charge; donations accepted. ♿
Attendance: 1,500 (estimated)
Membership: Student $5; Teacher's Circle & Individual $25; Family $35; Corporate, Institution & Organization $100; Bronze $300; Silver $500; Gold $1,000.

Frogmore

FROGMORE COTTON PLANTATION & GINS - COTTON THEN & NOW, 11054 Hwy. 84, Frogmore, LA 71334-4655. Tel.: 318-757-2453 & 3333. Fax: 318-757-6535.
Web Site: www.frogmoreplantation.com
History Museum.
Collections: plantation history; agriculture; industry; slave culture.
Hours & Admission Prices: March 8-May & Sept.-Nov. 15 Mon.-Fri. 9-3, Sat. 10-2; June-Aug. Mon.-Fri. 9-1; Winter: call for hours; other times by appointment. Historical Tour: adults 19 & over $10, students $5; children 5 & under no charge. Modern Tour: adults 19 & over and students $5; children 5 & under no charge. Complete Tour: adults 19 & over $12, students $5; children 5 & under no charge.

Garyville

SAN FRANCISCO PLANTATION, 2646 Hwy. 44 (River Rd.), Garyville, LA 70051. Mailing Address: P.O. Box 950, Garyville, LA 70051-0950. Tel.: 888-509-1756; 985-535-2341. Fax: 985-535-5450.
Web Site: www.sanfranciscoplantation.org
History Museum: plantation built in 1856.
Collections: period furnishings; personal artifacts; photographs.
Activities: rental facilities; special events.
Hours & Admission Prices: April-Oct. daily 9:30-5; Nov.-March daily 9-4:30. Adults $10, children $5; discounts to military & AAA members; children 5 & under no charge. Closed New Year's Day; Mardi Gras Day; Thanksgiving; Christmas.

Gibsland

BONNIE AND CLYDE AMBUSH MUSEUM, 2419 Main St., Gibsland, LA 71028. Mailing Address: P.O. Box 39, Gibsland, LA 71028. Tel.: 318-843-1934.
Web Site: www.bonnieandclydemuseum.com
Key Personnel: Owner, Colonel Charles Heard; Owner, Ken M. Holmes, Jr.
History Museum: housed in the former Ma Canfield's Cafe, the last place Bonnie Parker & Clyde Barrow visited before they were killed.
Collections: photographs; Clyde's Remington shotgun; Bonnie's red tam; ambush mural; bullet-ridden V-8 Ford replica used in the 1967 movie.
Hours & Admission Prices: Daily 10-6. Adults $7, seniors, active duty military & children 12 and under $5.

Gonzales

TEE JOE GONZALES MUSEUM, 217 W. Main St., Gonzales, LA 70737-2811. Mailing Address: 120 S. Irma Blvd., Gonzales, LA 70737-3604. Tel.: 225-647-9552. Fax: 225-647-9557.
E-mail: latuso@gonzalesla.com
History Museum.
Collections: early settlers; period furnishings; photographs; clothing.
Hours & Admission Prices: Mon.-Thurs. 10-12 & 1-5 or by appointment. No charge. Closed major holidays.

Homer

THE HERBERT S. FORD MEMORIAL MUSEUM, 519 S. Main St., Homer, LA 71040-3955. Mailing Address: P.O. Box 157, Homer, LA 71040-0157. Tel.: 318-927-9190.
E-mail: FordMuseum@bellsouth.net
Web Site: ford.claiborneone.org
Congressional District: 4
Key Personnel: Pres. (V), Darden Gladney; Project Dir., Linda Volentine.
Personnel Profile: Part-Time Paid 1.
History Museum.
Collections: history & culture of north central Louisiana; Herbert Ford's personal artifacts; period Native American artifacts; military artifacts; 1920s oil boom.
Hours & Admission Prices: Mon., Wed. & Fri. 9-12 & 1-4; other times by appointment. Families $5, adults $3, children $1.

Attendance: 1,350 (estimated)
Membership: Basic $10; Friend $25-$49; Supporting $50-$99; Sustaining $100-$149; Business $150-$499; Patron $500 & up.

Houma

BAYOU TERREBONNE WATERLIFE MUSEUM, 7910 Park Ave., Houma, LA 70364-3285. Tel.: 985-580-7200.
Web Site: www.houmaterrebonne.org/waterlife.asp
Key Personnel: Dir., Ann Picon
History Museum.
Collections: south Louisiana's cultural, industrial & ecological waterlife.
Hours & Admission Prices: Tues. & Thurs. 10-7, Wed. & Fri. 10-5, Sun. 12-4. Adults 14-65 $3, children 2-13 $2.

REGIONAL MILITARY MUSEUM, (M), 1154 Barrow St., Houma, LA 70360-5608. Mailing Address: P.O. Box 10247, Station 1, Houma, LA 70363-0247. Tel.: 985-873-8200.
E-mail: rmmuseum@triparish.net
Web Site: regionalmilitarymuseum.com
Key Personnel: Pres. & Chm. Bd., C.J. Christ; Vice Pres., Will Theriot; Sec., Kenneth Royston; Treas., Hymel "Sarge" Henry
Military Museum.
Collections: military armament; uniforms of the Vietnam era; photographs; paintings.
Hours & Admission Prices: Mon.-Fri. 9-5, Sat. 9-1.

SOUTHDOWN PLANTATION HOUSE/THE TERREBONNE MUSEUM, 1208 Museum Dr., Houma, LA 70360-6072. Mailing Address: P.O. Box 2095, Houma, LA 70361-2095. Tel.: 985-851-0154. Fax: 985-868-1476.
E-mail: info@southdownmuseum.org
Web Site: www.southdownmuseum.org
Formerly: Terrebonne Historical and Cultural Society
Founded: 1972.
Key Personnel: Pres. (V), Doug Holloway; Vice Pres, Dale Norred; Treas., Liz Bass; Sec., Barbara Morris; Exec. Dir., Karen Hart; Museum Shop Mgr., Melva Fournier.
Personnel Profile: Full-Time Paid 2; Part-Time Volunteers 100.
Governing Authority: private; nonprofit organization. Parent Institution: Terrebonne Historical & Cultural Society. Tax-exempt: 501(c)(3).
General Museum: housed in the Southdown plantation house.
Collections: history & culture of Terrebonne Parish, south Louisiana including Cajuns & Native Americans; sugar plantation history; 135 Boehm & Doughty porcelain birds; re-creation of U.S. Senator Allen J. Ellender's private office in Washington, D.C.; Minor family furniture; native people of Louisiana; art gallery; history & culture of South Louisiana residents including Cajuns & Native Americans.
Facilities: picnic area; outdoor pavilion. Gift items for sale.
Activities: docent program; guided tours; loan exhibitions. Annual Events: Marketplace Arts, Crafts & Food Festival in spring & fall.
Publications: quarterly, THACS Newsletter.
Hours & Admission Prices: Tues.-Sat. 10-4. Adults $6, senior citizens & college students $5, students $3; discounts to groups & AAM members; children under 6 & members no charge. Closed New Year's Eve & Day; Mardi Gras; Good Friday; Independence Day; Thanksgiving; Christmas Eve & Day. ♿
Attendance: 31,179 (accurate)
Membership: Individual $20; Family $35; Contributing $50; Donor $100; Supporting $150.

Jackson

PORT HUDSON STATE HISTORIC SITE, 236 Hwy. 61, Jackson, LA 70748-4217. Tel.: 225-654-3775; 888-677-3400 (Toll Free).
E-mail: porthudson@crt.state.la.us
Founded: 1982.
Personnel Profile: Full-Time Paid 8; Part-Time Paid 1; Part-Time Volunteers 6.
Governing Authority: Parent Institution: Louisiana State Parks.
Historic Site: a National Historic Landmark.
Collections: Civil War history; period artifacts & furnishings; military weapons & uniforms; photographs.
Facilities: nature trails.
Activities: guided tours; hiking; special events; demonstrations.
Hours & Admission Prices: Daily 9-5; groups by appointment. Adults $2; seniors 62 & over and children 12 & under no charge. Closed New Year's Day; Thanksgiving; Christmas. ♿
Attendance: 25,000 (estimated)

Jeanerette

JEANERETTE BICENTENNIAL PARK AND MUSEUM, 500 E. Main St., Jeanerette, LA 70544-3712. Mailing Address: P.O. Box 1011, Jeanerette, LA 70544. Tel.: 337-276-4408. Fax: 337-276-9557.
E-mail: jbpmuseum@bellsouth.net
Web Site: www.jeanerettemuseum.com
Founded: 1976.
History Museum.
Collections: local history; sugar can industry history; natural wildlife; period furniture; Black history; Mardi Gras; French embroidery & crochet; videos.
Facilities: library. Museum-related items for sale.
Activities: videos.
Hours & Admission Prices: Call for hours. Adults $3, children under 12 $1. ♿
Attendance: 1,938 (accurate)

Jennings

W.H. TUPPER GENERAL MERCHANDISE MUSEUM, 311 N. Main St., Jennings, LA 70546-5341. Tel.: 337-821-5532.
E-mail: tuppermuseum@cfweb.net
Web Site: www.tuppermuseum.com
History Museum.
Collections: period general store furnishings & merchandise including clothing, school supplies, tools, medicines, & toys; Native Indian basketry.
Hours & Admission Prices: Mon.-Fri. 9-5. Adults $3, students $1. Closed major holidays.

ZAM - ZIGLER ART MUSEUM, (M), 411 Clara St., Jennings, LA 70546-5235. Tel.: 337-824-0114. Fax: 337-824-0120.
E-mail: zigler-museum@charter.net
Web Site: www.ziglerartmuseum.com
Founded: 1963.
Congressional District: 7
Key Personnel: Dir., Dolores Spears; Chm. (V), Gregory Marcantel; Pres. (V), Harriet Shultz; Museum Shop Mgr., Jane Miller.
Personnel Profile: Full-Time Paid 1; Part-Time Paid 2; Part-Time Volunteers 10.
Governing Authority: nonprofit. Tax-exempt: 501(c)(3).
European & American Art.
Collections: art collection including work by Jean-Louis Vergne, Charles Sprague Pearce, Louis Jambor, George Inness, Helen Turner, Robert Rucker, John Constable, James McNeil Whistler, Albrecht Durer, Camille Pissaro, Maurice deVlaminck, Robert Henri, John James Audubon, Albert Bierstadt, R.A. Blakelock, Sir John Everette Millias, Sir Anthony Wan Dyck & Japanese Woodblock Prints (18th-19th century); wildlife & natural history art.
Major Exhibits: ZAM's Mardi Gras Exhibit, 1/15/10-2/18/10; Experiencing Katrina, 1/26/10-3/1/10; Exploring Clementine Hunter, 3/6/10-4/10/10; A Collector's Exhibit, 4/17/10-5/30/10; Mother & Daughter Exhibit, 6/12/10-7/17/10; Magnificent, Marvelous, Martele American Art Nouveau Silver Exhibit, 7/12/10-9/18/10; Louisiana Sat Night & Elton Louviere Exhibit, 10/4/10-11/13/10; Festival of Christmas, 11/27/10-12/22/10.
Research Fields: Chenier Culture Jefferson Davis Parish History.
Activities: tours; art-related workshops; monthly guest artist shows.
Publications: catalog of Zigler Museum's collection of works by William Tolliver.
Hours & Admission Prices: Tues.-Sat. 10-4, Sun. 1-4. Adults $5, children $2; discounts to tour groups and ICOM & AAM members; members no charge. Closed major holidays. ♿
Attendance: 4,385 (estimated)
Membership: Individual $20; Family $30; Supportive $50; Patron $100-$500; Corporate $500-$1,000; Lifetime $5,000.

Kenner

MARDI GRAS MUSEUM, 415 Williams Blvd., Rivertown, Kenner, LA 70062. Tel.: 504-468-7231.
Web Site: www.rivertownkenner.com
General Museum.
Collections: 150 years of history from New Orleans to Acadiana; videos & memorabilia depicting King Cake traditions, balls, parades, French Quarter & Mardi Gras.
Activities: float & costume-making demonstrations.
Hours & Admission Prices: Tues.-Sat. 9-5. Adult $3, senior citizen 60 & over $2.50, children 2-12 $2.

Lafayette

ACADIAN VILLAGE, 200 Greenleaf Dr., Lafayette, LA 70506-7400. Tel.: 337-981-2364; 800-962-9133. Fax: 337-988-4554.
E-mail: amanda@acadianvillage.org
Web Site: www.acadianvillage.org
Key Personnel: Dir., Amanda L. Toups
Folk Life and History Museum.
Collections: local history & culture; photographs; furnishings. Historic Homes: Bernard House c.1800; Billeaud House; Castille House c.1860; Leblac House, built between 1821 & 1856; St. John House c.1840; Thibodaux House c.1820. Doctor's Museum: office of the first resident dentist, Dr. Hypolite Salles.
Hours & Admission Prices: Daily 10-4. Adults 15-61 $8, seniors 62 & over $7, students 7-14 $5; children 6 & under no charge. Closed major holidays.

ALEXANDRE MOUTON HOUSE/LAFAYETTE MUSEUM, 1122 Lafayette St., Lafayette, LA 70501-6838. Tel.: 337-234-2208. Fax: 337-234-2208.
Founded: 1954.
Congressional District: 3
Key Personnel: Hostess & Guide, Phyllis Goff; Hostess & Guide, Joyce Boutin.
Personnel Profile: Part-Time Paid 2.
Governing Authority: nonprofit organization. Affiliated with the Lafayette Museum Assn. Tax-exempt: 501(c)(3).
Historic Building.
Collections: period furniture & textiles c.1850; historical documents; manuscripts; portraits; Civil War & Indian artifacts; Mardi Gras costumes.
Activities: guided tours; permanent & temporary exhibitions.
Publications: cookbooks, First You Make a Roux; Let Us Entertain You; illustrated brochure, The Lafayette Museum.
Hours & Admission Prices: Tues.-Sat. 10-4, Sun. 1-4. Adults $3, senior citizens $2, students $1; discounts to groups; school tours no charge. Closed New Year's Day; Mardi Gras; Easter; Independence Day; Christmas. ♿
Membership: $25-$99; $100-$249; $250-$499; $500 & up.

CATHEDRAL OF ST. JOHN THE EVANGELIST, 914 St. John St., Lafayette, LA 70501. Mailing Address: P.O. Drawer V, Lafayette, LA 70502-8022. Tel.: 337-232-1322 & 1325. Fax: 337-232-1379.
Religious Museum: built in 1916. Listed on the National Register of Historic Properties.
Collections: parish history; religious artifacts & furnishings; documents; photographs; statues; paintings; Italian Nativity.
Facilities: Museum-related items for sale.
Hours & Admission Prices: By appointment. Tours: Mon.-Fri. 9-12 & 1-4. Adults $3, senior citizens $2, children 12 & under $1; discounts to groups of 20 or more.

CHILDREN'S MUSEUM OF ACADIANA, 201 E. Congress, Lafayette, LA 70501-6919. Tel.: 337-232-8500. Fax: 337-232-8167.
Web Site: www.childrensmuseumofacadiana.com
Founded: 1990.
Congressional District: 7
Children's Museum.
Collections: hands-on exhibits.
Activities: performances; workshops.
Publications: newsletter.
Hours & Admission Prices: Tues.-Sat. 10-5. Admission $5; children one & under no charge. ♿
Attendance: 35,000 (accurate)
Membership: Individual $50; Grandparent $75; Basic $125; Family Plus $175.

LAFAYETTE SCIENCE MUSEUM, (M), 433 Jefferson St., Lafayette, LA 70501-7013. Tel.: 337-291-5544. Fax: 337-291-5464.
Web Site: www.lafayettesciencemuseum.com
Formerly: Lafayette Natural History Museum and Planetarium
Founded: 1969.
Congressional District: 7
Key Personnel: Dir., Mary Henderson; Pres. (V), David Andrus; Cur. Planetarium, David Hostetter; Cur. Collections, Dr. Deborah J. Clifton; Cur. Education, Dawn Edelen; Museum & Planetarium Technician, Dexter LeDoux; Asst. Planetarium Cur., Charlotte Guillot; Sec., Karen Miller; Tour Coord., Edi Gilbert; Exhibit Cur., Kevin Krantz; Exhibit Guide, Keith Richard; Receptionist, Robert Burleigh; Asst. Planetarium Technician, William Depa; Laborer II, Albert Davis; Cashier, Likassina Brown.
Personnel Profile: Full-Time Paid 13; Part-Time Paid 10; Part-Time Volunteers 23; Interns 3.
Governing Authority: municipal. Parent Institution: Lafayette Consolidated Government. Subsidiary Institution: Lafayette Science Museum Foundation. Tax-exempt: 501(c)(3).
Natural History Museum & Planetarium.
Collections: living & preserved floral & faunal specimens of Louisiana area in excess of 55,000 items; material-culture of Louisiana's Native Americans and other groups including Creole, Spanish, French & African-American including contemporary photographic documentation & present-day crafts; Louisiana Acadian Textile Collection.
Major Exhibits: Lizards & Snakes: Alive! (T), 1/10; Engineer It! (T), 2/10-5/10; Museum of Fear, 10/10; Star Wars: Where Science Meets Imagination (T), 10/10-1/11.
Research Fields: regional culture.
Facilities: 10,000 vol. library; 72-seat planetarium; 13,000 sq. ft. exhibit space; archives resources file; 150 seat auditorium; 2 classrooms.
Activities: guided tours; lectures; films; hands-on workshops; formally organized education programs for children & adults; permanent, temporary & traveling exhibitions; school loan service.
Publications: Checklist of the Vascular Flora of Louisiana; Checklist of the Birds of Louisiana; Checklist and Key to the Amphibians and Reptiles of Louisiana; Life in the Atchafalaya Swamp; Louisiana Ferns and Fern Allies; How Men Cook; exhibition catalogs; Travailler, C'est Trop Dur: The Tools of Cajun Music; Image of Lafayette Chitimacha Notebook; Craft Talk; Palmetto Braiding: The Folk Art of Elvina Kidder.
Hours & Admission Prices: Tues.-Fri. 9-5, Sat. 10-6, Sun. 1-6. Adults $5, seniors $3, children & chaperon $2, school groups outside of Lafayette Parish $1 per student; discounts to AAM members. Closed Mardi Gras; Easter; Thanksgiving; Christmas. ♿
Attendance: 64,000 (accurate)
Membership: Student & Senior Citizen $30; Individual $35; Family & Grandparent $50; Patron $150; Group & Corporate $300; Benefactor $750; Lifetime $1,000.

PAUL AND LULU HILLIARD UNIVERSITY ART MUSEUM, UNIVERSITY OF LOUISIANA AT LAFAYETTE, (M), 710 E. St. Mary Blvd., Lafayette, LA 70503-2332. Mailing Address: P.O. Drawer 42571, Lafayette, LA 70504-0001. Tel.: 337-482-2278. Fax: 337-262-1268.
E-mail: artmuseum@louisiana.edu
Web Site: museum.louisiana.edu
Formerly: University Art Museum University of Southwestern Louisiana Campus; University Art Museum, University of Louisiana at Lafayette
Founded: 1968.
Congressional District: 7
Key Personnel: Dir., Mark A. Tullos, Jr.; Registrar, Joyce Penn; Visitor Svcs. & Volunteer Coord., Cindy Hamilton; Cur. Exhibitions & Collections, Dr. Lee Gray; Security, Jack Harrison; Security, Hugo Boute; Administrative Asst., Becky Berner.
Personnel Profile: Full-Time Paid 7; Part-Time Paid 4; Part-Time Volunteers 50; Interns 2.
Governing Authority: nonprofit organization. Parent Institution: University of Louisiana at Lafayette. Tax-exempt: 501(c)(3).
Art Museum.
Collections: The Louisiana Collection: 19th to 20th-century drawings, paintings, photographs & sculpture; Henry Botkin collection: paintings, drawings, collages 1928-1981; 19th to 20th-century Japanese prints; southern outsider art; naive art.
Major Exhibits: Neo-Pop: New China, 1/23/10-5/1/10; Faces & Stories by Mark Story, 1/23/10-5/22/10; Hunt Slonem (T), 5/15/10-9/4/10; Ajiaco: Cuban Artists, 7/15/10-12/18/10.
Research Fields: Louisiana photography; outsider art.
Facilities: 11,000 sq. ft. exhibit space; one acre sculpture garden.
Activities: guided tours; lectures; films; gallery talks; concerts; traveling exhibitions.
Publications: catalogues; calendars; retrospectives; books; seasonal newsletter.
Hours & Admission Prices: Tues.-Sat. 10-5. Adults $5, senior citizens $4, students 5-17 $3; discounts to NARM, AAM & ICOM members & groups of 20 or more; members no charge. Closed major holidays. ♿
Attendance: 30,000 (accurate)
Membership: Senior Citizen $25; Individual $40; Family $55; Donor $100; Patron $250; Contributing $500; Benefactor $1,000 & up.

VERMILIONVILLE, 300 Fisher Rd., Lafayette, LA 70508-2028. Tel.: 337-233-4077; 866-992-2968. Fax: 337-233-1694.
E-mail: vermil@vermilionville.org
Web Site: www.vermilionville.org
Folklife Park.
Collections: local history & culture; historic village containing six restored original homes.
Facilities: art gallery; restaurant. Museum-related items for sale.
Hours & Admission Prices: Tues.-Sun. 10-4. Adults $8, seniors 65 & over $6.50, students 6-18 $5; children under 6 no charge. Closed New Year's Eve

& Day; Martin Luther King Day; Mardi Gras Day; Memorial Day; Labor Day; Thanksgiving; Christmas Eve & Day.
Membership: Senior Citizen $20; Individual $25; Couple $45; Family & Grandparents $55; Vermilionaire $120.

Lafitte

LOUISIANA MARINE FISHERIES MUSEUM, 580 Jean Lafitte Blvd., Lafitte, LA 70067-5108. Tel.: 504-689-3497.
Cultural Heritage Museum.
Collections: 3,000 yr. old dugout canoe; Lafitte Skiff; trenasse digger; period boats; crawfish farming; hunting; cypress lumbering; moss picking; ranching & farming; period fishing & trapping implements; photographs.
Hours & Admission Prices: Wed.-Sun. 10-4. Admission $1.

Lake Charles

CHILDREN'S MUSEUM OF LAKE CHARLES, INC., 327 Broad St., Lake Charles, LA 70601-4223. Tel.: 318-433-9420. Fax: 318-433-0144.
E-mail: dan@child-museum.org
Web Site: www.child-museum.org
Founded: 1988.
Congressional District: 7
Key Personnel: Exec. Dir., Dan Ellender; Asst. Dir., Allyson Blackwell; Education & Program Dir., Erin Bentley.
Personnel Profile: Full-Time Paid 1; Part-Time Paid 6; Part-Time Volunteers 20.
Governing Authority: nonprofit organization. Tax-exempt: 501(c)(3).
Children's Museum.
Collections: hands on learning center including Kid's Town, USA.
Facilities: 9,000 sq. ft. exhibit area; nature center; computer lab; shadow room; art space. Museum-related items for sale.
Activities: guided tours; organized education programs for students; docent program; participatory, traveling & temporary exhibitions.
Publications: quarterly museum newsletter.
Hours & Admission Prices: Mon.-Sat. 10-5. Adults & children $6.50, senior citizens 55 & over and active duty military $5; discounts to groups of 10 or more with a reservation; children 2 and under & members no charge. Closed major holidays. ♿
Attendance: 24,000 (accurate)
Membership: Family $40; Family Plus & Grandparents $50.

IMPERIAL CALCASIEU MUSEUM, INC., (M), 204 W. Sallier St., Lake Charles, LA 70601-5844. Tel.: 337-439-3797. Fax: 337-439-6040.
E-mail: impmuseum@bellsouth.net
Web Site: www.imperialcalcasieumuseum.org
Founded: 1963.
Congressional District: 7
Key Personnel: Exec. Dir., Susan H. Reed.
Personnel Profile: Full-Time Paid 1; Part-Time Paid 9.
Governing Authority: nonprofit. Tax-exempt: 501(a).
Local History Museum.
Collections: Victorian period furnishings: parlor, kitchen, bedroom, country store; barber shop; pharmacy; dolls & toys; Audubon prints; Louisiana game bird exhibit; Civil War & World War I collection; historical photographs; paddleboat steering wheels; period musical instruments; Attakapa Indian artifacts; glass bottles; 16th-18th century apothecary jars; period shaving mugs.
Research Fields: historical, 5 parish area, comprising the original Imperial Calcasieu Land Grant.
Facilities: 300-vol. library of old school books & bibles; Gibson-Barham fine arts gallery; 100-seat auditorium. Cookbooks & sculpture for sale.
Activities: guided tours; permanent & temporary exhibitions. Museum Sponsors: special events for children June to August.
Hours & Admission Prices: Tues.-Sat. 10-5. Adults $2, children $1; members no charge. Closed major holidays. ♿
Attendance: 6,800 (estimated)
Membership: Family $50; Associate $100; Patron $300; Corporate $500 & up.

Lake Providence

LOUISIANA STATE COTTON MUSEUM, 7162 Hwy. 65 N., Lake Providence, LA 71254-5226. Mailing Address: P.O. Box 94125, Baton Rouge, LA 70804-9125. Tel.: 318-559-2041. Fax: 318-559-2217.
E-mail: cotton@sos.louisiana.gov
Web Site: www.sos.louisiana.gov/lscm
Founded: 1992.
Congressional District: 5
Key Personnel: Dir., John Ann Tyler.
Personnel Profile: Full-Time Paid 2; Part-Time Paid 2.
Governing Authority: state. Parent Institution: Louisiana Secretary of State, Baton Rouge, LA. Tax-exempt.
Cotton Museum.
Collections: history & heritage of cotton cultivation; cottons influence on life in Louisiana; photographs.
Facilities: Museum-related items for sale.
Activities: guided tours.
Hours & Admission Prices: Mon.-Fri. 9-4:30. No charge. Closed most state holidays. ♿
Membership: Call for information.

Leesville

MUSEUM OF WEST LOUISIANA, 803 S. Third St., Leesville, LA 71446-4703. Tel.: 337-239-0927.
Founded: 1987.
Key Personnel: Museum Shop Mgr., Mary Cleveland.
Personnel Profile: Full-Time Volunteers 1; Part-Time Paid 1.
Governing Authority: Parent Institution: Vernon Parish Police Jury. Subsidiary Institution: Museum Association of West Louisiana. Tax-exempt.
History Museum.
Collections: archaeological artifacts; logging implements; railroad memorabilia; P.O.W. paintings; WWII artifacts; toys; photographs; quilts; clothing; cooking; household items; furniture; history, culture, folk art, & resources of Vernon Parish and the West Central area of the Louisiana Territory; scale models of various buildings from 1800s.
Facilities: Museum-related items for sale.
Activities: picnics; special events; tours.
Hours & Admission Prices: Tues.-Sun. 1-5; other times by appointment. No charge; donations accepted. Closed major holidays. ♿
Attendance: 8,000 (accurate)
Membership: Student & Senior Citizen $10; Individual $15; Family $25; Patron $50; Benefactor $100; Corporate Donor $250; Angel $1,000.

Long Leaf

SOUTHERN FOREST HERITAGE MUSEUM, 77 Longleaf Rd., Long Leaf, LA 71448. Mailing Address: P.O. Box 101, Long Leaf, LA 71448-0101. Tel.: 318-748-8404. Fax: 318-748-8410.
E-mail: longleaf@centurytel.net
Web Site: www.forestheritagemuseum.org
Founded: 1992.
Congressional District: 5
Key Personnel: Dir., Robert (Bob) Carroll; Pres., James Barnett; Public Rels., Buck Vandersteen; Treas., Harold Elliott; Security, Charles Hudson.
Personnel Profile: Full-Time Paid 1; Part-Time Paid 7; Part-Time Volunteers 20.
Governing Authority: private; nonprofit organization. Tax-exempt: 501(c)(3).
History Museum.
Collections: early 20th-century sawmill town history; forestry & lumber history; tools; 1910 planer mill & sawmill; c.1915 machine shop; 3 steam locomotives; steam logging equipment including 1919 Clyde skidder & two 1919 McGiffert loaders; archives.
Facilities: 500-vol. library; 57-acre site; 7,500 sq. ft. exhibit space; 50-seat theater; arboretum; nature trail. Museum-related items for sale.
Activities: machine shop demonstrations; railroad ride; docent program; guided tours; participatory exhibits; theater. Annual Events: antique tractor pulls; Heritage Day.
Publications: quarterly newsletter, Edgings & Trimmings.
Hours & Admission Prices: Daily 9-4. Adults $8, students $4; discounts to members & groups. Closed Easter; Thanksgiving; Christmas. ♿
Attendance: 4,810 (accurate)
Membership: Senior & Teacher $20; Individual $25; Family $50; Contributing $100; Supporting $250; Sustaining $500; Wall of Honor $1,000 & up.

Madisonville

LAKE PONTCHARTRAIN BASIN MARITIME MUSEUM, 133 Mabel Dr., Madisonville, LA 70447-9301. Tel.: 985-845-9200. Fax: 985-845-9201.
E-mail: info@lpbmaritimemuseum.org
Web Site: www.lpbmaritimemuseum.org
Founded: 2001.
Key Personnel: Dir., Dr. Jay C. Martin; Educator, Kristen Garcia; Administrative Asst., Melanie Waddell.
Personnel Profile: Full-Time Paid 3; Part-Time Paid 4; Part-Time Volunteers 12; Interns 1.
Governing Authority: private; nonprofit organization. Tax-exempt: 501(c)(3).
Maritime Museum.
Collections: nautical & cultural heritage of Lake Pontchartrain Basin. Historic Buildings: Tchefuncte River lighthouse, c.1837; Tchefuncte River light-keepers cottage, c.1887.

Research Fields: shoreline erosion; maritime Louisiana history & culture.
Facilities: rental facilities.
Activities: boatbuilding classes; lightkeepers overnight program. Annual Event: Madisonville Wooden Boat Festival in October.
Publications: quarterly newsletter, Shipways.
Hours & Admission Prices: Tues.-Sat. 10-4, Sun. 12-4. Adults $5; discount to groups; members and children 12 & under no charge. Closed New Year's Day; Thanksgiving; Christmas Day. ♿
Attendance: 30,000 (estimated)
Membership: Family $25; Friend $100; Supporting $500.

MADISONVILLE MUSEUM, 201 Cedar St., Madisonville, LA 70477. Mailing Address: P.O. Box 160, Madisonville, LA 70447-0160. Tel.: 985-845-2100.
Founded: 1991.
Key Personnel: Dir., Ginger Stanga
History Museum.
Collections: local wildlife; Civil War; Native American artifacts.
Hours & Admission Prices: Sat.-Sun. 12-4. No charge; donations accepted.

OTIS HOUSE - FAIRVIEW-RIVERSIDE SATE PARK, 119 Fairview Dr., Madisonville, LA 70447. Tel.: 985-845-3318; 888-677-3247.
Park & Historic House: built in the 1880s. Listed on the National Register of Historic Places.
Collections: local history & culture; photographs; period furnishings; period artifacts.
Hours & Admission Prices: Wed.-Sun. 9-5. Adults $2; children 3 & under and seniors 62 & over no charge. Closed New Year's Day; Thanksgiving; Christmas.

Mansfield

MANSFIELD FEMALE COLLEGE MUSEUM, 101 Monroe St., Mansfield, LA 71052. Mailing Address: P.O. Box 94125, Baton Rouge, LA 70804-9125. Tel.: 318-871-9978. Fax: 318-871-9978.
E-mail: paula.flournoy@sos.louisiana.gov
Web Site: www.sos.louisiana.gov/mfcm
Founded: 2003.
Congressional District: 4
Key Personnel: Dir., Paula Flournoy.
Personnel Profile: Part-Time Paid 1.
Governing Authority: state. Tax-exempt.
History Museum.
Collections: history of women's education in northwest Louisiana & De Soto Parish; photographs; furnishings; personal artifacts.
Facilities: library.
Activities: docent program; guided tours; traveling exhibitions.
Hours & Admission Prices: Tues.-Fri. 10-4. No charge. Closed most state holidays. ♿

MANSFIELD STATE HISTORIC SITE - CIVIL WAR BATTLEFIELD, 15149 Hwy. 175, Mansfield, LA 71052-4774. Tel.: 318-872-1474; 888-677-6267. Fax: 318-871-4345.
E-mail: mansfield@crt.state.la.us
Web Site: www.crt.state.la.us
Formerly: Mansfield State Commemorative Area
Founded: 1957.
Congressional District: 4
Key Personnel: Historic Site Mgr., Steve Bounds.
Personnel Profile: Full-Time Paid 5; Part-Time Paid 2; Part-Time Volunteers 50.
Governing Authority: state. Parent Institution: Louisiana Office of State Parks. Tax-exempt.
Civil War Battlefield
Collections: documents; letters; pictures; diaries of soldiers; manuscript collections; Civil War artifacts & books; Civil War era cabin & winter camp.
Research Fields: history of the Civil War.
Facilities: 400-vol. library of books, letters, diaries & official records of Union & Confederate Armies available for use on the premises; picnic area; reading room; projection room; trails.
Activities: guided tours; school tours; lectures; formally organized education programs; film programs for students on school days by appointment; campaign movie; living history weekends; self guided battlefield tours.
Publications: brochures.
Hours & Admission Prices: Daily 9-5. Adults $2; school groups with reservations on school days, senior citizens over 61 & children under 12 no charge. Closed New Year's Day; Thanksgiving; Christmas.
Attendance: 11,850 (accurate)

Marksville

MARKSVILLE STATE HISTORIC SITE, 837 Martin Luther King Dr., Marksville, LA 71351-2478. Tel.: 318-253-8954; 888-253-8954.
E-mail: marksville@crt.state.la.us
Web Site: www.crt.state.la.us/parks/iMarksvle.aspx
Historic Site. Designated as a National Historic Landmark.
Collections: 3,300 ft. semi-circular earthwork.
Hours & Admission Prices: Daily 9-5. Adults $2; seniors 62 & over and children 12 & under no charge. Closed New Year's Day; Thanksgiving; Christmas.

TUNICA-BILOXI NATIVE AMERICAN MUSEUM, (M), 150 Melancon Rd., Marksville, LA 71351. Mailing Address: P.O. Box 1589, Marksville, LA 71351-1589. Tel.: 318-253-8174. Fax: 318-253-7711.
E-mail: ebarbry@tunica.org
Web Site: www.tunica.org
Founded: 1989.
Congressional District: 6
Key Personnel: C.E.O., Cur. & Archivist, Earl J. Barbry, Jr.; Treas., Doug Burke; Public Rels., Niki Jeter; Security, Harold Pierite, Sr.; Museum Shop Mgr., Juanita Ducote.
Personnel Profile: Full-Time Paid 5.
Governing Authority: Federally recognized Native American Tribal Council.
History Museum.
Collections: French & Indian artifacts.
Facilities: library; 1,500 sq. ft. exhibit space; 40-seat large screen theater. Museum-related items for sale.
Hours & Admission Prices: Temporarily closed.
Attendance: 2,400 (estimated)

Marrero

BARATARIA PRESERVE, JEAN LAFITTE NATIONAL HISTORICAL PARK AND PRESERVE, 6588 Barataria Blvd., Marrero, LA 70072-7526. Tel.: 504-589-2330, ext. 10. Fax: 504-589-2690.
Web Site: www.nps.gov/jela/
Founded: 1978.
Congressional District: 3
Key Personnel: Supervisory Park Ranger, Angela Rathle; Education Coord., Allyn Rodriguez; Volunteer Coord., Jack Henkels; Publications Coord., Kristy Wallisch; Bookstore Mgr., Julie Castille.
Governing Authority: federal. Administered by the National Park Service, Washington, DC 20240. Tax-exempt.
Park Visitor Center, Folkway & Natural History Museum.
Collections: artifacts; traps; fishing equipment; moss gathering equipment; pirogues; cypress logging industry.
Research Fields: folkways of S. Louisiana; natural history & environment of park; prehistoric Indians Resource management.
Facilities: 50-seat auditorium; boardwalk trails; observation decks in swamp & marsh; interpretive waysides; environmental education center.
Activities: guided tours; film; nature trails; picnic area; permanent exhibits; pre-registration for school group interpretation; canoe trails; fishing & hunting in season; curriculum based programs for K-3, 4-5, 6-8 & 9-12 grades.
Publications: trail brochure; site bulletins; newsletter, Park News.
Hours & Admission Prices: Daily 9-5. No charge; donations accepted. Closed Christmas; Mardi Gras. ♿
Attendance: 35,000

Marthaville

REBEL STATE HISTORIC SITE & LOUISIANA COUNTRY MUSIC MUSEUM, 1260 Hwy. 1221, Marthaville, LA 71450-3459. Tel.: 318-472-6255; 888-677-3600. Fax: 318-472-9315.
E-mail: rebel@crt.state.la.us
Web Site: www.crt.state.la.us
Formerly: Rebel State Commemorative Area Louisiana Country Music Museum
Founded: 1981.
Congressional District: 5
Personnel Profile: Full-Time Paid 3; Part-Time Paid 2.
Governing Authority: state. Louisiana Office of State Parks, P.O. 44426, Baton Rouge, LA 70804. Tel. 504-342-8105. Tax-exempt.
Louisiana Country Music Museum: housed in clef-note shaped building; Rebel State Historic Site; resting place of the Unknown Confederate Soldier.
Collections: Louisiana country music; musical instruments; costumes of performers; memorabilia & graphic representations of the history of music; juke boxes; victrolas.
Research Fields: folk traditions of popular & country music; gospel music.
Facilities: 1,500-capacity amphitheater.

Activities: guided tours; lectures; concerts; formally organized education programs for children; permanent & temporary exhibitions.
Hours & Admission Prices: Daily 9-5. Adults $2; seniors 62 & over, children 12 & under, school and church groups no charge. Closed New Year's Day; Thanksgiving; Christmas. ♿
Attendance: 10,923 (accurate)

Martinville

AFRICAN AMERICAN MUSEUM, 125 S. New Market St., Martinville, LA 70582. Mailing Address: P.O. Box 379, Saint Martinville, LA 70582-0379. Tel.: 337-394-2230. Fax: 337-394-2244.
History Museum.
Collections: African American history & culture; photographs; personal artifacts; period furnishings; mural.
Hours & Admission Prices: Daily 10-4:30. Adults $3; children 12 & under no charge.

Melrose

MELROSE PLANTATION HOME COMPLEX, Melrose Plantation Home Complex, Melrose General Delivery, Melrose, LA 71452. Mailing Address: Box 2248, Natchitoches, LA 71457-2248. Tel.: 318-379-0055. Fax: 318-379-0055 (call first).
Founded: 1970.
Congressional District: 5
Key Personnel: C.E.O. & Pres., Dr. Vicki Parrish; Museum Shop Mgr., Betty Metoyer; Cur., Scott Norton.
Personnel Profile: Full-Time Paid 1; Part-Time Paid 7; Part-Time Volunteers 21.
Governing Authority: society. Parent Institution: Association for the Preservation of Historic Natchitoches. Tax-exempt.
Historic House: 1833 early Louisiana type plantation home of Marie Therese Coin; Coin & her children freed slaves.
Collections: furnishings dating from 1796-early 1900s; plantation gardens. Historic Houses: c.1796 Yucca; c.1800 The African House; The Weaving House; The Bindery; The Writer's Cabin; c.1796 Ghana.
Facilities: library of books & crafts.
Activities: Museum Sponsors: annual Historical Tour of Natchitoches & the Cane River Country in Oct.; annual Melrose Arts & Crafts Show in June.
Publications: pamphlets.
Hours & Admission Prices: Tues.-Sun. 12-4; other times by appointment. Adults $7, students 13-17 $4, children 6-12 $3; discounts to groups of 22 or more by appointment; members no charge. For further information call Natchitoches Parish Tourist Commission, Tel. 800-259-1714. Closed Easter; Independence Day; Thanksgiving; Christmas. ♿
Attendance: 7,730 (accurate)
Membership: Annual $25; Couple $35; Contributing $50; Sponsor $100.

Monroe

BIEDENHARN MUSEUM & GARDENS, (M), 2000 Riverside Dr., Monroe, LA 71201-4268. Tel.: 318-387-5281; 800-362-0983. Fax: 318-387-8253.
E-mail: director@bmuseum.org
Web Site: www.bmuseum.org
Founded: 1971.
Congressional District: 5
Key Personnel: Pres., Murray Biedenharn; Exec. Dir., Ralph Calhoun; Museum Shop Mgr., Kathy Posey.
Personnel Profile: Full-Time Paid 13; Part-Time Paid 18; Part-Time Volunteers 4.
Governing Authority: private foundation. Parent Institution: Emy-Lou Biedenharn Foundation. Tax-exempt: 501(c)(3).
Historic House, Garden & Museum Complex: Bible Museum: c.1914 Southern house, home of Joseph A. Biedenharn, first bottler of Coca-Cola; 1946 formal Elsong Gardens; 1971 Biblical Museum; Coca-Cola Museum.
Collections: Biedenharn Home: marble statue of cherub musicians; fireplace with andirons & grate from Spain; 18th-century Meissen porcelain musicians; hand-woven rug from France; Steinway piano; portraits; miniatures; Waterford crystal chandeliers; high testered beds; 1700s silver collection; period artifacts; art objects; Coca-Cola memorabilia; Model T Coca-Cola delivery truck; reproduction soda fountain. Elsong Gardens: Italian Garden; Water Garden; cast iron statues; porcelain fountain of Catherine the Great. Bible Museum: Exhibition of texts & artifacts structured to demonstrate the contribution of biblical text to the enrichment of Western culture, with special emphasis upon the role of the Bible in American life. Elsong Garden: 1946, formal English gardens; Biblical garden; 1990 octagonal conservatory with its Victorian design.
Research Fields: Biblical topics.
Facilities: 2,000-vol. library of biblically related books & manuscripts; biblical garden; formal gardens & conservatory; 50-seat auditorium & 60-seat meeting room.
Activities: guided tours; lectures; garden symposia; concerts; permanent, traveling & temporary exhibits.
Publications: booklets, 1993: Elsong Garden; 1994: The Story of Joseph Augustus Biedenharn & The Bottling of Coca-Cola.
Hours & Admission Prices: Mon.-Sat. 10-5, Sun. 2-5; tours on the hour; groups of 10 or more by appointment. Adults $5; discounts to AAM members. Closed New Year's Day; Easter; Independence Day; Thanksgiving; Christmas Eve & Day. ♿
Attendance: 30,000 (estimated)

CHENNAULT AVIATION AND MILITARY MUSEUM, 701 Kansas Lane, Monroe, LA 71203-4775. Mailing Address: P.O. Box 94125, Baton Rouge, LA 70804-9125. Tel.: 318-362-5540. Fax: 318-362-5545.
E-mail: nell.calloway@sos.louisiana.gov
Web Site: www.sos.louisiana.gov/camm
Formerly: Aviation and Military Museum of Louisiana
Founded: 1995.
Congressional District: 5
Key Personnel: Dir., Nell Calloway.
Personnel Profile: Full-Time Paid 1; Part-Time Paid 3.
Governing Authority: state. Parent Institution: Louisiana Secretary of State, Baton Rouge, LA. Tax-exempt.
Military Museum.
Collections: aviation & military history; Delta Airlines history; Selman Field memorabilia.
Facilities: theater. Museum-related items for sale.
Activities: films; guided tours; lectures; loan, temporary & traveling exhibitions; theater. Annual Events: Veterans Day Program; Memorial Day Program.
Hours & Admission Prices: Mon.-Fri. 9-4:30, Sat.-Sun. 1-4:30. No charge. Closed most state holidays. ♿
Membership: Call for information.

LOUISIANA PURCHASE GARDENS AND ZOO, 1405 Bernstein Park Rd., Monroe, LA 71202-5545. Tel.: 318-329-2400.
E-mail: education@monroezoo.com
Web Site: www.monroezoo.org
Key Personnel: Cur. Education, Kimberly Bachus
Gardens & Zoo.
Collections: mammals; birds; reptiles; amphibians; fish; invertebrates; gardens.
Activities: special events; boat rides; rental facilities; birthday parties.
Hours & Admission Prices: Daily 10-5. Adults 13-64 $4.50, seniors 65 & over and children 3-12 $3; discounts to groups of 10 or more; children 2 & under no charge. Boat Rides: March 2-Oct. 10-4:30. Admission $2. Closed New Year's Day; Thanksgiving; Christmas.

MASUR MUSEUM OF ART, (M), 1400 S. Grand St., Monroe, LA 71202-2012. Tel.: 318-329-2237. Fax: 318-329-2847.
E-mail: info@masurmuseum.org
Web Site: www.masurmuseum.org
Founded: 1963.
Congressional District: 5
Key Personnel: Dir., Anne A. Dennington; Asst. Dir. & Chief Cur., Evelyn P. Stewart; Mgr. Mktg. & Communications, Gregory R. Hudgins, Jr.
Personnel Profile: Full-Time Paid 3; Part-Time Paid 4; Part-Time Volunteers 30.
Governing Authority: municipal; nonprofit organization. Parent Institution: City of Monroe. Subsidiary Institution: Twin City Art Foundation. Tax-exempt.
Art Museum.
Collections: paintings; prints; sculpture; photographs.
Research Fields: 20th-century art;19th-20th-century Louisiana art.
Facilities: classrooms.
Activities: permanent, temporary & traveling exhibitions; lectures; gallery talks; guided tours; films; studio art classes; docent program; drop-in activities for children; visiting curator program; artist-in-residence program.
Publications: monthly newsletter, Museum News; temporary exhibition brochures; catalogue for annual juried competition; monthly e-newsletter; exhibition catalogues; children's activity book.
Hours & Admission Prices: Tues.-Fri. 9-5, Sat. 12-5. No charge. Closed national holidays.
Attendance: 20,000 (estimated)
Membership: Student Artist $20; Individual $40; Family $60; Single Patron $95; Patron $150; Grand Patron $250; Donor $500. Corporate: Corporate

Member $300; Corporate Donor $500; Corporate Sponsor $1,000; Corporate Leader $2,500; Event Sponsor $5,000.

NSCDA IN LOUISIANA; ISAIAH GARRETT LAW OFFICE, 520 S. Grand St., Monroe, LA 71201-7314. Mailing Address: 2405 Pargoud Blvd., Monroe, LA 71201. Tel.: 318-387-5691.
Founded: 1840.
Congressional District: 5
Governing Authority: Parent Institution: The National Society of the Colonial Dames of America. Tax-exempt.
Historic House: built in 1840.
Collections: local history & culture; period furnishings; personal artifacts; photographs.
Hours & Admission Prices: By appointment.

NORTHEAST LOUISIANA CHILDREN'S MUSEUM, 323 Walnut St., Monroe, LA 71201-6711. Tel.: 318-361-9611. Fax: 318-361-9613.
E-mail: nelcm@nelcm.org
Web Site: www.nelcm.org
Key Personnel: Exec. Dir., Julia Bland
Children's Museum.
Collections: hands-on exhibits.
Facilities: Museum-related items for sale.
Activities: traveling & permanent exhibitions; monthly events; volunteering; birthday parties.
Hours & Admission Prices: Tues.-Fri. 9-2, Sat. 10-5. Admission 1 & over $5; discounts to groups of 15 or more.

NORTHEAST LOUISIANA DELTA AFRICAN AMERICAN HERITAGE MUSEUM, 503 Plum St., Monroe, LA 71202-2609. Mailing Address: P.O. Box 168, Monroe, LA 71210-0168. Tel.: 318-323-1167. Fax: 318-323-8954.
Web Site: www.nldaahm.com
Founded: 1994.
Congressional District: 34
Key Personnel: Exec. Dir., Lorraine Slacks; Sec., Patricia Hudson.
Governing Authority: Parent Institution: Ouachita African American Historical Society. Tax-exempt.
History Museum.
Collections: historical artifacts; African art; visual art; furniture.
Research Fields: History.
Activities: student workshops; films; lectures.
Publications: newsletter, Tall Talk.
Hours & Admission Prices: Tues.-Sat. 10-4. Adults $2. ♿
Attendance: 10,000 (estimated)
Membership: Senior Citizen $10; Family $25; Organization $100.

Natchitoches

FORT ST. JEAN BAPTISTE STATE HISTORIC SITE, 155 Jefferson, Natchitoches, LA 71457-4350. Tel.: 318-357-3101. Fax: 318-357-7055.
E-mail: fortstjean@crt.state.la.us
Web Site: www.crt.state.la.us
Formerly: Fort St. Jean Baptiste State Commemorative Area
Founded: 1982.
Congressional District: 5
Key Personnel: Cur., James Prud'Homme; Mgr., Rick Seale; Interpretive Ranger, Tommy Adkins; Interpretive Ranger, Rhonda Gauthier.
Personnel Profile: Full-Time Paid 6; Part-Time Paid 5; Part-Time Volunteers 10.
Governing Authority: state. The Dept. of Culture, Recreation & Tourism, Office of State Parks, Baton Rouge, LA 70821. Tel.: 504-342-8111.
Historical Fort: reconstruction of 1732 fort & related buildings.
Collections: barracks; guardhouse; servant & kitchen huts; officers' quarters; church; powder magazine; warehouse; bastion; videos.
Facilities: visitor center.
Activities: guided tours; videos. Museum Sponsors: daily living history activities; annual programs March & December.
Publications: pamphlet.
Hours & Admission Prices: Daily 9-5. Adults $2; children under 12 & senior citizens 62 & over no charge. Closed New Year's Day; Thanksgiving; Christmas. ♿
Attendance: 14,283 (accurate)

IMMACULATE CONCEPTION CATHOLIC CHURCH, 145 Church St., Natchitoches, LA 71457-4624. Mailing Address: 145 Church St., P.O. Box 13, Natchitoches, LA 71458-0013. Tel.: 318-352-3422. Fax: 318-352-3822.
Founded: 1728.
Congressional District: 31
Key Personnel: Rev. James FosterSec., Wanda McCain.
Personnel Profile: Part-Time Volunteers 5.
Governing Authority: church. Parent Institution: Immaculate Conception Church. Tax-exempt.
Historic Building & Museum: c.1856 Immaculate Conception Church and 1885 Rectory.
Collections: 1880 church bell; Austrian stained glass windows; French fittings & furnishings; chandeliers; spiral staircase with no center support; 18th-20th century church artifacts. Historic Buildings: 1885 Rectory; 1855 Old Seminary, now named the Bishop Martin Museum containing records; church artifacts; bells.
Hours & Admission Prices: Church: daily 9-4. Bishop Martin Museum: call 318-352-3422 for appointment. No charge; donations accepted.
Attendance: 500 (estimated)

THE LEMEE HOUSE, APHN Headquarters, 310 Jefferson St., Natchitoches, LA 71457-4355. Mailing Address: P.O. Box 2248, Natchitoches, LA 71457-2248. Tel.: 318-357-7907. Fax: 318-352-2415.
Founded: 1834.
Congressional District: 5
Key Personnel: Pres. (V), Dr. Vicki Parrish.
Personnel Profile: Full-Time Volunteers 1; Part-Time Volunteers 6.
Governing Authority: society. Parent Institution: The Association for the Preservation of Historic Natchitoches. Tax-exempt.
Historic House: c.1833 house bought by Alexis Lemee in 1849 to serve as his home & the Union Bank of New Orleans.
Collections: period furnishings & artifacts; paintings; lamps; 1792 map by French engineer J. F. Broutin; c.1805 Seth Thomas clock; Rena Phillips fountain.
Facilities: rental facilities.
Activities: meetings for APHN, Les Aimes & Leche organizations.
Publications: semi-annual, Calico Bells.
Hours & Admission Prices: Oct. call for hours. ♿
Attendance: 1,800 (estimated)
Membership: Individual $25; Couple $35; Group $100; Sponsor $500.

NATCHITOCHES NATIONAL FISH HATCHERY, 615 South Dr., Natchitoches, LA 71457-3056. Tel.: 318-352-5324. Fax: 318-352-8082.
E-mail: karen_kilpatrick@fws.gov
Founded: 1966.
Congressional District: 4
Key Personnel: Project Leader, Karen M. Kilpatrick; Deputy Project Leader, Dr. Jan Dean; Maintenance Mechanic, Dennis Scarbrough; Office Asst., Lana J. Litton.
Personnel Profile: Full-Time Paid 5.
Governing Authority: federal. Dept. of the Interior, U.S. Fish & Wildlife Service, Regional Office, Richard B. Russell Federal Bldg., 1875 Century Blvd., Atlanta, GA 30303, Tel. 404-679-4157. Tax-exempt.
Aquarium & Fish Hatchery.
Collections: live displays of fishes of the southeastern United States & Louisiana; reptile tank containing alligators & turtles.
Facilities: aquarium.
Activities: guided group tours; lectures; films & slides.
Publications: brochure.
Hours & Admission Prices: Daily 8-3, group tours: call for appointment. No charge. Closed all federal holidays. ♿
Attendance: 30,000

New Iberia

BAYOU TECHE MUSEUM, 131 E. Main St., New Iberia, LA 70560. Mailing Address: P.O. Box 14151, New Iberia, LA 70562-4151. Tel.: 337-369-2383. Fax: 337-369-2346.
E-mail: bayoutechemuseum@gmail.com
Founded: 1992.
Key Personnel: Dir., Tasha B. Dugas; Pres. (V), Larry Hensgens; Treas., Art Mixon; Public Rels., Paul Schexnayder.
Personnel Profile: Full-Time Volunteers 15; Part-Time Paid 1.
Governing Authority: private; nonprofit organization.
History Museum.
Collections: Iberia Parish history & culture; industry; period artifacts; paintings; photographs.
Research Fields: Spanish history related to Iberia Parish; early settlement.
Facilities: 12-seat theater.
Hours & Admission Prices: Thurs.-Sat. 10-4 by appointment. Adults $4, senior citizens $3, children $2. Closed major holidays. ♿

RIP VAN WINKLE GARDENS ON JEFFERSON ISLAND, 5505 Rip Van Winkle Rd., New Iberia, LA 70560-8167. Tel.: 337-359-8525. Fax: 337-359-8526.
E-mail: jislgdns@earthlink.net

Web Site: www.ripvanwinklegardens.com
Founded: 1978.
Key Personnel: Mgr., Michelle Richard.
Personnel Profile: Full-Time Paid 10.
Botanical Garden & Historic Houses: c.1870 house built by actor Joseph Jefferson; semi-tropical 25 acre landscape garden.
Collections: furniture; paintings; decorative accessories relating to Victorian lifestyle of 19th & 20th century occupants of the house.
Facilities: 600-vol. library of books pertaining to horticulture and Joseph Jefferson; 25-acre botanical garden; 15,000 sq. ft. exhibit space. Books on horticulture & Victorian lifestyle for sale.
Activities: guided tours; lectures.
Hours & Admission Prices: Daily 9-4. Adults $10, children & senior citizens $8; discounts to groups; children under 8 & members no charge. Closed New Year's Day; Thanksgiving, Christmas Eve & Day. ♿
Attendance: 40,000 (accurate)

THE SHADOWS-ON-THE-TECHE, 317 E. Main St., New Iberia, LA 70560-3728. Tel.: 337-369-6446. Fax: 337-365-5213.
E-mail: shadows@shadowsontheteche.org
Web Site: www.shadowsontheteche.org
Founded: 1961.
Congressional District: 3
Key Personnel: Chm. Property Council, Taylor Barras; Dir., Patricia Kahle; Administrative Asst., Michelle Meche; Cur. Education, Catherine T. Schramm; Curatorial Technician, Yvonne Leblanc.
Personnel Profile: Full-Time Paid 4; Part-Time Paid 6; Part-Time Volunteers 75.
Governing Authority: nonprofit organization. Property of the National Trust for Historic Preservation, 1785 Massachusetts Ave., N.W., Washington, DC 20036. Tax-exempt: 501(c)(3).
Historic House Museum: 1834 plantation home & restored landscape.
Collections: decorative arts; textiles & costumes; furnishings.
Research Fields: social history of pre-Civil War South & south central Louisiana; historic landscape.
Facilities: meeting space; gardens. Books & other museum-related items for sale.
Activities: guided tours; school programs; lectures; special events; summer interpreter program for high school students; teacher workshops; thematic tours & exhibits; living history programs.
Publications: The Shadows-on-the-Teche Cookbook; Shadows-on-the-Teche: Preserving a Picture of Life; Fine Things Are Without Value: Inside the Shadows.
Hours & Admission Prices: Mon.-Sat. 9-4:30, Sun. 12-4:30. Adults $10, senior citizens 65 & over $8, students 6-17 $6.50; discounts to groups, AAM & ICOM members; National Trust for Historic Preservation members; Friends of the Shadows & children under 6 no charge. Closed major holidays. ♿
Attendance: 17,592 (accurate)
Membership: Friends of the Shadows: Individual $25; Family $50; Sustaining $100; Contributing $250; Supporting $500; Donor $1,000; Patron $2,500; Benefactor $5,000. Corporate: $500, $1,000 & $1,500.

New Orleans

AFRICAN AMERICAN MUSEUM, 1418 Gov. Nicholls St., New Orleans, LA 70116-2344. Tel.: 504-566-1136.
Art and History Museum: housed in the Treme Villa, built in 1828-29.
Collections: African beadwork; costumes; masks; textiles; musical instruments; divination objects.
Hours & Admission Prices: Wed.-Sat. 11-4. Adults $5, students & seniors $3, children 6-12 $2. ♿

AMERICAN ITALIAN RENAISSANCE FOUNDATION, 537 S. Peters St., New Orleans, LA 70130-1628. Mailing Address: P.O. Box 2392, New Orleans, LA 70176-2392. Tel.: 504-522-7294. Fax: 504-522-1657.
Web Site: www.airf.org
Founded: 1978.
Key Personnel: Dir., Felicia Weinstein; Museum Shop Mgr., Mae Webb.
Personnel Profile: Full-Time Paid 1; Part-Time Volunteers 4.
Governing Authority: Tax-exempt.
History Museum.
Collections: history & culture of Italian Americans in the Southeast; photographs; articles; family histories; memorabilia; genealogy records.
Activities: Annual Event: Louisiana American Italian Sports Hall of Fame Induction Banquet.
Publications: quarterly digest, Italian American Digest.
Hours & Admission Prices: Wed.-Fri. 10-4. No charge; donations accepted. Closed holidays. ♿
Membership: Level I $55; Level 2 $75; Level 3 $150; Level 4 $250; Level 5 $500.

AMISTAD RESEARCH CENTER, INC., Tilton Hall-Tulane University, 6823 St. Charles Ave., New Orleans, LA 70118-5665. Tel.: 504-862-3222. Fax: 504-862-8961.
Web Site: www.amistadresearchcenter.org
Founded: 1966.
Key Personnel: Exec. Dir., Lee Hampton; Dir. Archives, Brenda B. Square; Dir. Reference & Library Svcs., Christopher Harter; Dir. Processing, Laura Thomson; Senior Processing Asst., Shannon Burrell; Archives & Library Asst., Andrew Salinas.
Personnel Profile: Full-Time Paid 6; Part-Time Paid 2; Part-Time Volunteers 2.
Governing Authority: Tax-exempt.
History Museum.
Collections: art; archives & manuscripts; photographs; digital archives.
Publications: Amistad Reports.
Hours & Admission Prices: Mon.-Fri. 8:30-4:30. No charge. ♿
Attendance: 1,443 (accurate)
Membership: Retiree & Student $20; Phillis Wheatly Club $40; Family & Sojourner Truth Club $55; Frederick Douglass Club $100; Carter G. Woodson Club $250; Harriet Tubman Club $500; Cinque Club $1,000; Clifton H. Johnson Club $5,000

AUDUBON AQUARIUM OF THE AMERICAS, 1 Canal St., New Orleans, LA 70130-1175. Mailing Address: P.O. Box 4327, New Orleans, LA 70178-4327. Tel.: 800-774-7394; 504-581-4629. Fax: 504-565-3010.
E-mail: mlee@audoboninstitute.org
Web Site: www.auduboninstitute.org
Founded: 1990.
Congressional District: 91
Key Personnel: C.E.O. & Pres., L. Ronald Foreman; Financial Dir., Larry Rivarde; Cur., John Hewitt; Public Rels., Melissa Lee; Security, Perry Gallon; Museum Shop Mgr., Laura Seiner.
Personnel Profile: Full-Time Paid 160; Part-Time Paid 118; Part-Time Volunteers 356.
Governing Authority: municipal; partnership; nonprofit organization. Parent Institution: Audubon Institute, P.O. Box 4327, New Orleans, LA 70178-4327. Tax-exempt: 501(c)(3).
Aquarium.
Collections: fresh & salt water fish; invertebrates; birds; reptiles; amphibians.
Research Fields: exotic animal behavior; endangered species preservation.
Facilities: library books on aquatic life, research & aquarium husbandry; 122,000 sq. ft. exhibit space; 354-seat, 3D Energy IMAX theatre; classrooms; restaurant. Museum-related and educational items for sale.
Activities: arts festivals; formal education programs for adults & children; mobile vans; traveling & participatory exhibits; training programs for professional museum workers.
Publications: quarterly membership magazine, Audubon Up Close; annual report.
Hours & Admission Prices: Tues.-Sun. 10-5. Aquarium: adults $13.50, senior citizens $10, children 2-12 $6.50. IMAX: Mon.-Sat. 10-7. Adults $7.75, senior citizens $6.75, children 2-12 $5. Closed Mardi Gras; Christmas Eve & Day. ♿
Attendance: 990,000 (accurate)
Membership: Individual $45, $65, $85; Individual plus one $55, $85, $105; Family $65, $95, $115; Family plus one $85, $125, $145. Prices depend on how many facilities are joined.

AUDUBON INSECTARIUM, 423 Canal St., New Orleans, LA 70130. Mailing Address: P.O. Box 4327, New Orleans, LA 70178. Tel.: 800-774-7394; 504-581-4629.
Nature Center.
Collections: insects; insect history; butterfly garden.
Facilities: theater.
Hours & Admission Prices: Tues.-Sun. 10-5. Adults 13-64 $15, seniors 65 & over $12, children 2-12 $10.

AUDUBON LOUISIANA NATURE CENTER, 5601 Read Blvd., Joe Brown Memorial Park, Nature Center Dr., New Orleans, LA 70127. Mailing Address: Audubon Zoo, 6500 Magazine St., New Orleans, LA 70118-4848. Tel.: 504-212-5197. Fax: 504-242-1889.
E-mail: alegaux@auduboninstitute.org
Web Site: www.auduboninstitute.org
Founded: 1980.
Congressional District: 1
Key Personnel: C.E.O., Amy LeGaux.
Governing Authority: nonprofit organization. Parent Institution: Audubon Nature Institute, P.O. Box 4327, New Orleans, LA 70178-4327. Tax-exempt: 501(c)(3).
Nature Center.

Collections: nature center; bottomland hardwood forest; outdoors wetland exhibit; teaching collections.
Hours & Admission Prices: Currently closed to the public.

AUDUBON ZOO, 6500 Magazine St., New Orleans, LA 70118-4848. Mailing Address: P.O. Box 4327, New Orleans, LA 70178-4327. Tel.: 504-861-2537. Fax: 504-865-7332.
E-mail: air@auduboninstitute.org
Web Site: www.auduboninstitute.org
Formerly: Audubon Park and Zoological Garden
Founded: 1914.
Congressional District: 89
Key Personnel: Pres. & C.E.O., L. Ronald Forman; Chm. (V), J. Kelly Duncan; Dir., Larry Rivarde; Financial Dir., Caroline Tierney; Cur., Rick Dietz; Devel., Laurie Conkerton; Public Rels., Sarah Burnette; Registrar, Adrienne Miller; Museum Shop Mgr., Debra McGuire.
Personnel Profile: Full-Time Paid 175; Part-Time Paid 150; Part-Time Volunteers 300.
Governing Authority: municipal; partnership; nonprofit organization. Parent Institution: Audubon Nature Institute, Inc., P.O. Box. 4327, New Orleans, LA 70178-4327. Tax-exempt: 501(c)(3).
Zoo and Park.
Collections: mammals; birds; reptiles; amphibians; fish; invertebrates.
Research Fields: exotic animal behavior; endangered species preservation.
Facilities: 2,125-vol. library; cafeteria. Museum-related items for sale.
Activities: arts festivals; formal education programs for adults and children; hobby workshops; lectures; mobile vans; participatory exhibits; training programs for professional museum workers. Annual Events: Zoo-to-Do; Earth Fest; Swamp Fest; Boo at the Zoo; Member Night Zoobilation.
Publications: quarterly membership magazine; annual report; education calendar; conservation report.
Hours & Admission Prices: Tues.-Sun. 10-4. Adults $12.50, senior citizens $9.50, children $7.50; members no charge. Closed Mardi Gras; Thanksgiving; Christmas. ♿
Attendance: 717,000 (estimated)
Membership: Individual $50; Individual Plus One $65; Family $80; Family Plus One $95; Safari Krewe $150.

BACKSTREET CULTURAL MUSEUM, 1116 St. Claude Ave., New Orleans, LA 70116-2330. Tel.: 504-522-4806.
E-mail: info@backstreetmuseum.org
Web Site: www.backstreetmuseum.org
Key Personnel: Exec. Dir., Sylvester Francis
Folk-Life and History Museum.
Collections: local history & culture; artifacts; exhibits; memorabilia; films & videos depicting Mardi Gras Indians.
Activities: Museum Sponsors: Treme Call Out and Dance; Mardi Gras Open House; All Saints Day Parade in November.
Hours & Admission Prices: Tues.-Sat. 10-5. Adults $5.

BEAUREGARD-KEYES HOUSE, (M), 1113 Chartres St., New Orleans, LA 70116-2504. Tel.: 504-523-7257. Fax: 504-523-7257.
Personnel Profile: Full-Time Paid 3; Part-Time Paid 2; Part-Time Volunteers 10.
Governing Authority: Parent Institution: Keyes Foundation.
Historic House Museum: home of wealthy auctioneer Joseph LeCarpentier, built in 1826.
Collections: period furnishings; personal artifacts; garden; period dolls; tea pots; folk costumes.
Facilities: Museum-related items for sale.
Activities: guided tours.
Publications: Beauregard-Keyes House; Lunch With Mrs. Keyes.
Hours & Admission Prices: Mon.-Sat. 10-3. Adults $8, students & senior citizens $7, children 6-12 $3; children under 6 no charge. Closed major holidays; Mardi Gras.

BLAINE KERN'S MARDI GRAS WORLD, 233 Newton St., New Orleans, LA 70114. Tel.: 800-362-8213; 504-361-7821.
General Museum.
Collections: Mardi Gras history, customs, costumes, & floats; float designing & building.
Activities: video.
Hours & Admission Prices: Daily 10-6. Adults $18, seniors $14, children $11; discounts to groups. ♿

CATHOLIC CULTURAL HERITAGE CENTER/OLD URSULINE CONVENT/ST. LOUIS CATHEDRAL, (M), 1100 Chartres St., New Orleans, LA 70116-2505. Tel.: 504-529-3040.
Founded: 2004.
Congressional District: 2
Key Personnel: Dir., Rev. Msgr. Crosby W. Kern; Museum Shop Mgr., Jolie Sekinger.
Personnel Profile: Part-Time Paid 1; Part-Time Volunteers 5.
Religious Museum: built in 1752.
Collections: religious artifacts; oil paintings; religious statues; bronze busts; manuscripts; drawings.
Major Exhibits: A Retrospective on the Art of Enrique Alferez, 1/10-6/10.
Facilities: archives; gardens.
Hours & Admission Prices: Tours: Tues.-Sun. 10-4. Adults $5, seniors $4, students $3; discounts to groups of 20 or more; members no charge. ♿
Attendance: 56,000 (accurate)

COLLINS C. DIBOLL ART GALLERY, 4th Fl. Monroe Library, 6363 St. Charles Ave., New Orleans, LA 70118-6143. Tel.: 504-864-7248.
E-mail: gallery@loyno.edu
Web Site: www.loyno.edu/dibollgallery
Key Personnel: Gallery Dir., Karoline Schleh
Art Gallery.
Collections: paintings.
Hours & Admission Prices: Mon.-Sat. 10-4. No charge.

CONFEDERATE MUSEUM, (M), 929 Camp St., New Orleans, LA 70130-3907. Tel.: 504-523-4522. Fax: 504-523-8595.
E-mail: memhall@aol.com
Web Site: www.confederatemuseum.com
Founded: 1891.
Congressional District: 1
Key Personnel: Cur., Pat Ricci.
Personnel Profile: Full-Time Paid 1; Full-Time Volunteers 5; Part-Time Paid 2; Part-Time Volunteers 1; Interns 1.
Governing Authority: nonprofit. Parent Institution: Memorial Hall, Inc. Tax-exempt.
Military Museum: housed in 1890 Memorial Hall.
Collections: pictures; paintings; weapons; silver; uniforms; flags; medical instruments; memorabilia of early Louisiana and Civil War history; personal effects of Jefferson Davis, Beauregard, Bragg, Lee & other Civil War leaders.
Research Fields: Louisiana history; Civil War.
Facilities: Books & other gift items for sale.
Activities: tours; permanent exhibitions; educational programs.
Publications: Louisiana Historical Association Books on Louisiana History & Civil War.
Hours & Admission Prices: Temporarily closed.
Attendance: 15,000

CONTEMPORARY ARTS CENTER, (M), 900 Camp St., New Orleans, LA 70130-3908. Tel.: 504-528-3805. Fax: 504-528-3828.
Web Site: www.cacno.org
Founded: 1976.
Congressional District: 2
Key Personnel: Exec. & Artistic Dir., Jay Weigel; Pres., Bennett Davis; Cur. Visual Arts, Dan Cameron.
Personnel Profile: Full-Time Paid 13; Part-Time Paid 8.
Governing Authority: private; nonprofit organization. Tax-exempt.
Arts Center.
Collections: contemporary art.
Facilities: theater; performance spaces.
Activities: music, dance & theatre performances; temporary exhibitions; educational programs for children & adults.
Hours & Admission Prices: Thurs.-Sun. 11-4. Adults $5, senior citizens & students $3; discounts to groups; members and children 15 & under no charge. Performance & special events prices may vary. Closed most major holidays. ♿
Attendance: 125,000 (estimated)
Membership: Student & Artist $25; Individual $35; Family & Couple $55; Friend $80; Collector's Club $175; Center Stage $250; Patron Now $500; Silver Circle $1,000; President's Council $5,000.

DEGAS HOUSE, 2306 Esplanade Ave., New Orleans, LA 70119-2502. Tel.: 504-821-5009.
Web Site: www.degashouse.com
Historic House: former home of the French Impressionist painter Edgar Degas.
Collections: paintings.
Hours & Admission Prices: Guided tours by appointment only. Suggested donations: adults $10, seniors $8, children & students $5.

FORT PIKE STATE HISTORIC SITE, 27100 Chef Menteur Hwy., New Orleans, LA 70129-3106. Mailing Address: P.O. Box 44426, Baton Rouge, LA 70804-4426. Tel.: 504-255-9171; 888-662-5703. Fax: 504-662-0147.
E-mail: fortpike_mgr@crt.state.la.us
Web Site: www.crt.state.la.us
Formerly: Fort Pike State Commemorative Area
Founded: 1934.
Congressional District: 1
Key Personnel: Historic Site Mgr., Michelle Lewis.
Personnel Profile: Full-Time Paid 4; Part-Time Paid 3; Part-Time Volunteers 10.
Governing Authority: state. Parent Institution: Office of State Parks, Louisiana. Tax-exempt: 501(c)(3).
Military Museum: housed in 1818-1827 fort built by U.S. government.
Collections: government relics and displays of armaments, dress and battle orders from the period 1812-1865; Louisiana history.
Research Fields: military history of War of 1812 & Civil War.
Facilities: picnic facilities; day-use recreation area.
Activities: guided tours; lectures; permanent exhibitions.
Publications: brochures.
Hours & Admission Prices: Thurs.-Mon. 9-5. Admission $2; seniors 62 & over and children 12 & under no charge. Closed New Year's Day; Thanksgiving; Christmas.
Attendance: 13,500 (estimated)

GALLIER HOUSE, 1132 Royal St., New Orleans, LA 70112. Mailing Address: P.O. Box 56836, New Orleans, LA 70156-6836. Tel.: 504-525-5661. Fax: 504-568-9735.
E-mail: hgrimagallier@aol.com
Web Site: www.hgghh.org
Key Personnel: Exec. Dir., Mamie Sterkx Gasperecz; Deputy Dir., Carolyn Bercier; Chm. Bd. The Woman's Exchange, Ashley Bright; C.F.O., Steven Smith; Pres. (V), E. Tiffany Adler; Dir. Devel., Lisa Samuels; Dir. Communications, Nadine Segari; Cur. Collections, Richard Scott; Asst. Cur. Collections, Betsy Kleinfelder; Museum Shop Mgr., Klara Hammer.
Personnel Profile: Full-Time Paid 6; Part-Time Paid 7; Part-Time Volunteers 30.
Governing Authority: Parent Institution: The Woman's Exchange. Branch Museum: Hermann-Grima, 820 St. Louis St., New Orleans, LA 70112. Tax-exempt: 501(c)(3).
Historic House: housed in the former home of architect, James Gallier, Jr.; built in 1857.
Collections: Gallier's life & family; personal artifacts; period furnishings; garden; slave quarters.
Research Fields: buildings; furnishings; gardens; life style, cooking methods during the period 1830-1860 in New Orleans; Creole foods & Christmas celebrations; social customs; urban archaeology; funeral practices; courtship & marriage customs; childhood; free blacks; urban slavery.
Facilities: Museum-related items for sale.
Activities: guided tours; lectures; education programs; docent programs; children's workshops; summer camp programs; special events.
Publications: Women Who Cared: The 100 Years of the Christian Woman's Exchange; quarterly newsletter; Creole cookery.
Hours & Admission Prices: Tours: Mon. & Fri. 10, 11, 12, 1 & 2, Sat. 12, 1, 2 & 3; other times by appointment. Adults $10, students, senior citizens & children 8-18 $8; discounts to AAM, ICOM, LAM, National Trust & SEMC members; members & children under 8 no charge. Closed major holidays.
Attendance: 9,000 (estimated)
Membership: Student & Senior Citizen $15; Individual $25; Family $50; Patron $100, $500, $1,000; Corporate $100, $500, $1,000, $5,000.

* **HERMANN-GRIMA, (M),** 820 St. Louis St., New Orleans, LA 70112-3416. Mailing Address: P.O. Box 56836, New Orleans, LA 70156. Tel.: 504-525-5661. Fax: 504-568-9735.
E-mail: hgrimagallier@aol.com
Web Site: www.hgghh.org
Founded: 1971.
Congressional District: 2
Key Personnel: Exec. Dir., Mamie Sterkx Gasperecz; Deputy Dir., Carolyn Bercier; Chm. Bd. The Woman's Exchange, Ashley Bright; Pres. (V), E. Tiffany Adler; C.F.O., Steven Smith; Cur. Collections, Richard Scott; Asst. Cur. Collections, Betsy Kleinfelder; Museum Shop Mgr., Klara Hammer; Dir. Devel., Lisa Samuels; Dir. Communications, Nadine Segari.
Personnel Profile: Full-Time Paid 6; Part-Time Paid 7; Part-Time Volunteers 30.
Governing Authority: Parent Institution: The Woman's Exchange. Branch Museum: Gallier House, 1132 Royal St., New Orleans, LA 70116. Tax-exempt: 501(c)(3).
Historic House: built in 1831
Collections: 1830-1860 furnishings; textiles; needlework; cooking implements; restored 1830 open-hearth kitchen.
Research Fields: buildings; furnishings; gardens; life style, cooking methods during the period 1830-1860 in New Orleans; Creole foods & Christmas celebrations; social customs; urban archaeology; funeral practices; courtship & marriage customs; childhood; free blacks; urban slavery.
Facilities: rental facilities. Gift items for sale.
Activities: guided tours; lectures; formally organized education programs for school groups & adults; internships; docent program; period cooking demonstrations; adult education programs; children's workshops; summer camp programs; rental facilities. Museum Sponsors: open hearth cooking October to May.
Publications: Women Who Cared: The 100 Years of the Christian Woman's Exchange; quarterly newsletter; Creole cookery.
Hours & Admission Prices: Tours: Mon.-Tues. & Thurs.-Fri. 10, 11, 12, 1 & 2, Sat. 12, 1, 2 & 3; other times by appointment. Adults $10, students, senior citizens & children 8-18 $8; discounts to AAM, ICOM, LAM, National Trust & SEMC members; members & children under 8 no charge. Closed major holidays. ♿
Attendance: 9,000 (estimated)
Membership: Student & Senior Citizen $15; Individual $25; Family $50; Patron $100, $500, $1,000; Corporate $100, $500, $1,000, $5,000.

* **THE HISTORIC NEW ORLEANS COLLECTION, (M),** 533 Royal St., New Orleans, LA 70130-2113. Tel.: 504-523-4662. Fax: 504-598-7108.
E-mail: wrc@hnoc.org
Web Site: www.hnoc.org
Founded: 1966.
Congressional District: 2
Key Personnel: Exec. Dir., Priscilla O'Reilly-Lawrence; Dir. Museum Programs, John H. Lawrence; Financial Dir., Kathy Slimp; Dir. Systems, Carol Bartels; Mgr. Mktg., Teresa Devlin; Mgr. Collections, Warren Woods; Dir. Research Center, Alfred Lemmon; Dir. Publications, Jessica Dorman; Museum Shop Mgr., Michelle Gaynor.
Personnel Profile: Full-Time Paid 61; Part-Time Paid 20; Part-Time Volunteers 50; Interns 4.
Governing Authority: nonprofit organization. Parent Institution: Kemper & Leila Williams Foundation. Branch Museum: The Williams Research Center, 410 Chartres St., New Orleans, LA. Tax-exempt: 501(c)(3).
History Museum & Research Center.
Collections: New Orleans, Louisiana & the Gulf South history & culture including books, pamphlets, manuscript materials, paintings, prints, drawings, maps, photographs, & period artifacts; historic buildings.
Major Exhibits: Between Colony and State: Louisiana in the Territorial Period, 1803-1812, 11/09-5/2/10; The Photographs of John T. Mendes, 12/09; Katrina Plus 5, 5/10-9/10; Mignon Faget: Forty Years, 9/10-1/11.
Research Fields: all aspects of Louisiana history & culture; architecture; river life; maps; French Quarter; Mardi Gras; Battle of New Orleans; Civil War; Louisiana artists; cemeteries; New Orleans imprints; land tenure; performing arts; plantation & family papers; jazz; literature.
Facilities: Research Center: library. Museum-related items for sale.
Activities: tours; gallery talks; docent program; temporary exhibitions; publishing; seminars; lectures; symposia; educational programming.
Publications: Historic New Orleans Collection Quarterly; Tennessee Williams Annual Review; books, Vaudechamp in New Orleans; Printmaking in New Orleans; Common Routes: St. Domingue, Louisiana; A British Eyewitness at the Battle of New Orleans: The Memoir of Royal Navy Admiral Robert Aitchison, 1808-1827; From Louis XIV to Louis Armstrong: A Cultural Tapestry; George L. Viavant: Artist of the Hunt; Charting Louisiana: Five hundred years of maps; Queen of the South: New Orleans, 1853-1862: The Journal of Thomas K. Wharton; Complementary Visions of LA Art: The Laura Simon Nelson at the Historic New Orleans Collection; Haunter of Ruins: The Photography of Clarence John Laughlin; Jazz Scrapbook: Bill Russell and Some Highly Musical Friends; Bibliography of New Orleans Imprints, 1764-1864; Vicksburg: Southern City Under Siege; Nelly Custis Lewis's Housekeeping Book; The Buildings of the Historic New Orleans Collection; Encyclopedia of New Orleans Artists, 1718-1918; Southern Travels: Journal of John H.B. Latrobe, 1834; Music in the Street: Photographs of New Orleans by Ralston Crawford; Josephine Crawford: An Artist's Vision.
Hours & Admission Prices: Tues.-Sat. 9:30-4:30, Sun. 10:30-4:30. Tours: 10, 11, 2, 3. Tour $5; discounts to AAM members; changing exhibitions & research areas no charge. Closed major holidays. ♿
Attendance: 35,000 (estimated)
Membership: Founder $35; Merieult Society $100; Mahalia Society $250; Jackson Society $500; Laussat Society $1,000; Bienville Circle $5,000.

HOUSE OF BROEL'S VICTORIAN MANSION AND DOLLHOUSE MUSEUM, 2220 St. Charles Ave., New Orleans, LA 70130. Tel.: 504-522-2220; 800-827-4325.
E-mail: info@houseofbroel.com
Historic Mansion: built c.1850.
Collections: local history & culture; dollhouses; period furnishings; Mardi Gras memorabilia; Asian art; photographs.
Activities: rental facilities.
Hours & Admission Prices: Mon.-Sat. 10-5. Adults $10, children $5.

THE JACKSON BARRACKS MILITARY MUSEUM, (M), 6400 St. Claude Ave., New Orleans, LA 70117-1456. Tel.: 504-278-8242.
E-mail: jbmuseum@la.ngb.army.mil
Web Site: www.la.ngb.army.mil
Key Personnel: Cur., Stan Amerski
Military Museum.
Collections: uniforms; honors & decorations dating back to the American Revolution; war letters, diaries & personal artifacts; tanks; fighter planes; helicopters; antiaircraft batteries; cannons.
Facilities: theater.
Activities: films; award ceremonies; concerts; historic society meetings; official functions.
Hours & Admission Prices: Mon.-Fri. 8-4, Sat. by appointment; group tours by appointment. No charge. Closed holidays.

JEAN LAFITTE NATIONAL HISTORICAL PARK & PRESERVE, (M), 419 Decatur St., New Orleans, LA 70130-1035. Tel.: 504-589-3882. Fax: 504-589-3851.
E-mail: kathy_lang@nps.gov
Web Site: www.nps.gov/jela
Founded: 1978.
Congressional District: 1
Personnel Profile: Full-Time Paid 1.
Governing Authority: federal. Administered by the National Park Service, Washington, DC 20240. Branch Units: Acadian, Chalmette, Barataria Preserve & New Orleans. Tax-exempt.
History Museum.
Collections: natural history; archaeology; military; furnishings; household items; tools & equipment; cultural & natural resources of the Mississippi Delta region; cultural resources related to the Acadian people. Historic House: c.1832 Malus Beauregard home.
Research Fields: Battle of New Orleans; War of 1812; historic & prehistoric archaeology in area; American Indians; ethnic groups of Mississippi Delta Region; environment of park; National Cemetery; natural history of area; history of French Quarter & New Orleans.
Facilities: 500-vol. library on Battle of New Orleans, historical military books, films, photos, maps & information on surrounding area & National Parks; photo files; archives; three Acadian Unit visitor centers: Lafayette, 150-seat theater; Eunice, 125-seat video area; Thibodaux, 200-seat theater, 25-seat video area; Bataria Preserve Visitor Center exhibits; 65-seat theater; New Orleans Visitor Center exhibits; 40-seat multipurpose area. Publications & gift items for sale.
Activities: canoe treks; videos; self-guided tours; dramatic presentation.
Publications: NPS handbooks.
Hours & Admission Prices: Daily 9-5. No charge. Closed New Year's Day; Mardi Gras; Christmas. ♿
Attendance: 1,315,000 (estimated)

* **LONGUE VUE HOUSE & GARDENS, (M),** 7 Bamboo Rd., New Orleans, LA 70124-1007. Tel.: 504-488-5488. Fax: 504-486-7015.
E-mail: lcosta@longuevue.com
Web Site: www.longuevue.com
Founded: 1980.
Congressional District: 1
Key Personnel: Admin., Ribby Ferguson; Chm. & Pres. (V), Rene Fransen; Cur., Lydia H. Schmalz; Accountant, Bridgit Miller; Special Events, Rebecca Schultz; Operations & Sales, Anna Bell Jones; Dir. Programs, Jennifer Gick.
Personnel Profile: Full-Time Paid 14; Part-Time Paid 21; Part-Time Volunteers 150; Interns 1.
Governing Authority: nonprofit organization. Parent Institution: Longue Vue Foundation.
Historic House & Gardens: 1939-42, Palladian style, Longue Vue, home of cotton broker Edgar Bloom Stern & Edith Rosenwald Stern, daughter of Sears Roebuck financier & philanthropist, Julius Rosenwald.
Collections: 17th to 20th-century European decorative arts; archival materials related to house & gardens; gardens designed by Ellen Biddle Shipman.
Research Fields: architecture; history; decorative arts; fine arts; horticulture & landscape gardening.
Facilities: 100-vol. library of horticulture, landscape architecture, architecture, decorative arts, archival design material, photographs & family papers available for research; 80-seat auditorium. Decorative arts, horticulture objects & publications related to the house & gardens for sale in museum shop.
Activities: guided tours; lectures; films; gallery talks; docent program or council; permanent & changing exhibitions.
Publications: exhibition catalogs; guide book; quarterly newsletter; rack cards.
Hours & Admission Prices: Mon.-Sat. 10-4:30, Sun. 1-5. House & Gardens: adults $10, children & students $5; discounts to senior citizens, students, tour groups, AABGA, AAA & AAM members; members no charge. Closed national holidays. ♿
Attendance: 45,000 (accurate)
Membership: Student & Senior Citizen $20; Individual $25; Dual $45; Family $50; Associate $75; Sustaining $100; Longuefellow $500; Long Viewer $1,000.

LOUISIANA CHILDREN'S MUSEUM, 420 Julia St., New Orleans, LA 70130-3606. Tel.: 504-523-1357. Fax: 504-529-3666.
E-mail: sseyler@lcm.org
Web Site: www.lcm.org
Founded: 1981.
Congressional District: 2
Key Personnel: Exec. Dir., Julia W. Bland; Dir. Education, Ruth Blum; Dir. Public Rels. & Mktg., Shannon Seyler.
Personnel Profile: Full-Time Paid 17; Part-Time Paid 15; Part-Time Volunteers 150; Interns 1.
Governing Authority: nonprofit. Tax-exempt: 501(c)(3).
Children's Museum.
Collections: hands-on exhibits.
Facilities: 40,000 sq. ft. exhibit space; educational facilities. Gift items for sale.
Activities: special weekend & summer programs; hobby workshops; organized education programs for children; participatory exhibits.
Publications: bimonthly newsletter, Hands-On; membership & visitor brochures; annual report.
Hours & Admission Prices: Winter: Tues.-Sat. 9:30-4:30, Sun. 12-4:30; Summer: Mon.-Sat. 9:30-5, Sun. 12-5. Admission $7.50; members no charge. ACM reciprocal member. Closed New Year's Day; Mardi Gras; Easter; Independence Day; Thanksgiving; Christmas. ♿
Attendance: 121,000 (accurate)
Membership: Family I $50; Family II $65; Family III $80; Magician $125; Wizard $250; Wonder Worker $500.

* **LOUISIANA STATE MUSEUM, (M),** 751 Chartres St., New Orleans, LA 70116-3205. Mailing Address: P.O. Box 2448, New Orleans, LA 70176-2448. Tel.: 800-568-6968. Fax: 504-568-4995.
E-mail: asmith@crt.state.la.us
Web Site: lsm.crt.state.la.us
Founded: 1906.
Congressional District: 2, 4 & 6
Key Personnel: Exec. Dir., Sam Rykels; Deputy Dir., Robert Wheat; Chm. (V), Rosemary Ewing; Dir. Interpretive Svcs., Whitney Babineaux; Dir. Collections, Greg Lambousey; Dir. Mktg. & Public Rels., Arthur Smith; Museum Historian, Dr. Karen Leathem; Museum Historian, Dr. Charles Chamberlain; Cur. Costumes & Textiles, Wayne Phillips; Dir. Curatorial Svcs., Jeff Rubin; Asst. Registrar, Jennae Biddiscombe; Cur. Visual Arts, Tony Lewis; Dir. Museum Div., Greg Lambousy; Registrar, Ann Woodruff; Dir. Museum Branch, Kathryn Delee; Dir. Museum Branch, William Stark.
Personnel Profile: Full-Time Paid 120; Full-Time Volunteers 30; Part-Time Volunteers 140; Interns 12.
Governing Authority: state. Parent Institution: Dept. of Culture, Recreation & Tourism, State of Louisiana. Tax-exempt: 170(b)(1)(A).
Historical Museum Complex: six National Historic Landmark buildings located in the New Orleans French Quarter, Baton Rouge, Patterson, Thibodaux & Natchitoches.
Collections: fine, decorative & folk art; costumes, textiles, jazz music; photographic & inventive arts of Louisiana; science & technology; military history; paintings & portraiture; 1704-1803 Louisiana Aviation Colonial Archives. Historic Houses: 1795 The Cabildo; 1791 The Presbytere; 1850 The Lower Pontalba Building; 1788 Madame John's Legacy; 1835 The New Orleans Branch of the U.S. Mint; 1842 Creole House; 1842 Jackson House; 1839 Old Arsenal; Old Courthouse Museum; The Louisiana State Museum, Patterson; E.D. White Historic Site.
Major Exhibits: From Tramps to Kings: 100 Years of LSU (T), 11/09-3/10; Unsung Heroes: The Secret History of Louisiana Rock N Roll (T), 11/09-5/10; Tokens of Love and Affection (T), 2/10-2/11; Race, 4/10-9/10; Newcomb Pottery, 9/10.
Research Fields: Louisiana history: social, cultural, science, economic, technology, religion, folklore, music, politics, ethnic, racial.

Facilities: 40,000-vol. historical research library & archives; curatorial research library; exhibition galleries; three auditoriums; museum learning center; rental space. Museum-related items for sale.
Activities: tours; lectures; educational programs; consultation to Louisiana historical agencies; special & traveling exhibitions; conservation; restoration.
Publications: special exhibition & collection catalogs; section in monthly magazine, Cultural Vistas; Louisiana Life.
Hours & Admission Prices: The Louisiana State Museum-Baton Rouge: Tues.-Sat. 9-5, Sun. 12-5. The Cabildo: Tues.-Sun. 10-4. Presbytere: Fri.-Sun. 10-4. Old U.S. Mint, 1850 House & Madame John's Legacy are temporarily closed. The Louisiana State Museum-Baton Rouge, The Cabildo & Presbytere: adults $6, students, seniors & active military $5; combination tickets to all LSM properties available. Louisiana State Museum-Patterson, the Old Courthouse Museum: adults $3, students, seniors & active military $2; discounts to Louisiana Association of Museums, Louisiana Museum Foundation, Friends of the Cabildo, AAM & ICOM members; children 12 & under, school tours & members no charge. Closed legal & state holidays. ♿
Membership: Friends of the Cabildo: Statewide $15; Individual $25; Family $35; Friend $50; Sustaining $75; Contributing $100; Louisiana Museum Foundation $2,000.

MUSEE CONTI WAX MUSEUM, 917 Rue Conti, New Orleans, LA 70112-3409. Tel.: 504-581-1993; 800-233-5405. Fax: 504-566-7636.
Web Site: www.get-waxed.com
Founded: 1963.
Wax Museum.
Collections: 154 life-size figures depicting New Orleans' history, legend & scandal.
Facilities: banquet facilities.
Activities: themed parties; receptions; dinners; tours; special events.
Hours & Admission Prices: Mon. & Fri.-Sat. 10-4. Adults $6.75, senior citizens $6.25, children 4-17 $5.75; discounts to groups & AAA members. Closed Mardi-Gras; Thanksgiving; Christmas Eve, Day & week. ♿

MUSEUM OF THE AMERICAN COCKTAIL, Riverwalk Marketplace, Ste. 169, 1 Poydras St., New Orleans, LA 70130-1657. Tel.: 504-569-0405.
Governing Authority: nonprofit organization.
History Museum: housed in an 1823 French Quarter town house.
Collections: liquor history; period liquor bottles; cocktail shakers & memorabilia; early swizzle sticks & Tiki cups; bartending; drink recipes; books; prohibition-era literature; glassware.
Activities: seminars.
Hours & Admission Prices: Mon.-Sat. 10-7, Sun. 12-6. Adults $10.

NATIONAL SHRINE OF BLESSED FRANCIS XAVIER SEELOS, 919 Josephine St., New Orleans, LA 70130. Tel.: 504-525-2495. Fax: 504-581-9181.
Web Site: www.seelos.org
Founded: 1959.
Key Personnel: Dir., Rev. Byron Miller, C.SS.R.; Museum Shop Mgr. & Admin., Joyce Bourgeois.
Governing Authority: Parent Institution: Redemptorists - Denver Province. Tax-exempt.
Religious Museum.
Collections: portrait of Father Seelos used in Rome for his beatification; religious paintings; tapestries; photographs; religious artifacts; Father Seelos' personal artifacts; life-sized bronze statue of Father Seelos; hand-carved wooden statues of saints from Germany; 1891 German organ.
Hours & Admission Prices: Shrine: Mon.-Fri. 9-3, Sat. 10:30-3:30, Sun. between masses. Shop: Mon.-Fri. 9-3, Sat. 10:30-3:30. Shrine: no charge; donations accepted. ♿
Attendance: 25,000

THE NATIONAL WORLD WAR II MUSEUM, 945 Magazine St., New Orleans, LA 70130-3813. Tel.: 504-527-6012. Fax: 504-527-6088.
E-mail: info@nationalww2museum.org
Web Site: www.nationalww2museum.org
Formerly: The National D-Day Museum
Founded: 1991.
Congressional District: 2
Key Personnel: C.E.O. & Pres., Dr. Gordon H. Mueller; Chm. (V), Philip G. Satre; Sr. Vice Pres. Institutional Advancement, Alma Jane Shepard; Dir. Sales, Michelle Mueller; Vice Pres. & C.F.O., Rebecca Mackie; Vice Pres. & C.O.O., Stephen Watson; Dir. Education, Kenneth Hoffman; Sr. Vice Pres. Capital Projects, Bob Farnsworth; Dir. Security, Dave Heidenthal; Mgr. Research, Seth Paridon; Dir. Facilities, Frankie Harelson; Visitor Svcs. Mgr., Barry Statia; Dir. Collections & Exhibitions, Thomas Czekanski; Assoc. Vice Pres. Operations, Cindy McCurdy; Assoc. Vice Pres. Mktg., Clem Goldberger; Dir. Museum Rentals, Karen Robichaux; Dir. Membership, Terri Burton; Dir. Museum Store, Louise Fletcher; Dir. Information Systems, Paul Parrie.
Personnel Profile: Full-Time Paid 90; Part-Time Paid 7; Part-Time Volunteers 150; Interns 6.
Governing Authority: private; nonprofit organization. Tax-exempt: 501(c)(3).
History Museum.
Collections: artifacts, archival and audio/visual materials relating to the American experience in WWII.
Research Fields: World War II history.
Facilities: educational facilities; 40,000 sq. ft. exhibit space; 240-seat theater; cafe. Museum-related items for sale.
Activities: docent program; films; formal education programs for adults, college students & children; guided tours; lectures; loan, traveling & temporary exhibitions; rental gallery; theater; training programs for professional museum workers.
Publications: quarterly newsletter, D-Days.
Hours & Admission Prices: Daily 9-5. Adults $20, seniors 65 & over, students with ID & US military $6, children 5-17 $5; discount to members; children under 5 & military in uniform no charge. Closed New Year's Day; Mardi Gras; Thanksgiving; Christmas. ♿
Attendance: 145,009 (accurate)
Membership: Student & Teacher $20; Friend $35; Friend Plus One $60; Family $70; Advocate $150; Sponsor $500; Patron $1,000 & up.

NEW ORLEANS FIRE DEPT. MUSEUM & EDUCATIONAL CENTER, 1135 Washington Ave., New Orleans, LA 70130-5632. Tel.: 504-658-4713. Fax: 504-896-4756.
Founded: 1992.
Key Personnel: C.E.O., Chief Warren E. McDaniels; Cur., Archivist & Museum Shop Mgr., Michael Williams; Public Rels., Capt. Norman Woodridge.
Personnel Profile: Full-Time Paid 1; Full-Time Volunteers 1.
Governing Authority: municipal. Tax-exempt: 501(c)(3).
Fire-Fighting Museum: c.1852 fire house.
Collections: history of fire fighting in New Orleans.
Facilities: 240-vol. library; 2,300 sq. ft. exhibit space; 30-seat theater; 30-seat auditorium. Museum-related items for sale.
Activities: guided tours; hobby workshops; loan & temporary exhibitions; safety programs; interactive exhibits.
Hours & Admission Prices: By appointment. No charge; donations accepted. Closed New Year's Eve & Day; Martin Luther King Jr. Day; Mardi Gras; Good Friday; Memorial Day; Independence Day; Thanksgiving; Christmas Eve & Day.
Attendance: 5,200 (accurate)
Membership: Institution $20.

* **NEW ORLEANS MUSEUM OF ART, (M),** One Collins Diboll Circle, New Orleans, LA 70124-4605. Mailing Address: P.O. Box 19123, New Orleans, LA 70179-0123. Tel.: 504-658-4100. Fax: 504-658-4199.
E-mail: jlsullivan@noma.org
Web Site: www.noma.org
Founded: 1910.
Congressional District: 1
Key Personnel: C.E.O. & Dir., E. John Bullard; Chm., Stephen A. Hansel; Chm. (V), Janet Frischhertz; Deputy Dir., Jacqueline L. Sullivan; Dir. Devel., Marilyn Dittmann; Facilities Mgr., Karl Oelkers; Mgr. Sculpture Garden, Pamela Buckman; Asst. Dir. Art, Lisa R. McCord; Asst. Dir. Education, AliceRae Yelen; Cur. African Art, William Fagaly; Cur. Decorative Arts, John Keefe; Controller, Gail Asprodites; Cur. Photography, Diego Cortez; Cur. Native American & Pre-Columbian Art & Registrar, Paul Tarver; Cur. Modern & Contemporary Art, Miranda Lash; Cur. Education, Marney Robinson; Cur. Prints & Drawings, George Roland; Graphics Coord. & Web Master, Aisha Champagne; Dir. Communications & Mktg., James Mulvihill; Arts Quarterly Editor, Caroline E. Goyette; Museum Shop Mgr., Patricia Trautman; Librarian, Shelia Cork; Registrar, Jennifer Ickes; Grants Officer, Julie Galstad.
Personnel Profile: Full-Time Paid 53; Full-Time Volunteers 2; Part-Time Paid 8; Part-Time Volunteers 150; Interns 4.
Governing Authority: municipal. Tax-exempt: 501(c)(3).
Art Museum.
Collections: Old Master paintings of various schools; Kress collection of Italian Renaissance & Baroque paintings; Chapman H. Hyams collection of Barbizon & Salon paintings; pre-Columbian masterworks from Mexico, Central & South America; Latin American & Spanish colonial paintings & sculptures; 20th-century English & European art, including Surrealism & School of Paris; Japanese Edo period paintings; African art; photography; graphics; Glass Collection; 19th- & 20th-century U.S. & Louisiana paintings & sculptures; Latter-Schlesinger collection of English & continental

portrait miniatures; collections of African, oceanic northwest coast American Indian & 20th-century European & American paintings & sculptures; The Matilda Geddings Gray Foundation collection of works by Peter Carl Faberge; Rosemunde E. & Emile Kuntz Federal & Louisiana period rooms; 16th to 20th-century French art; Sydney and Walda Besthoff Sculpture Garden, contemporary sculpture.
Major Exhibits: Dreams Come True: Art of the Classic Fairy Tales from the Walt Disney Studio, 11/15/09-3/14/10; Beyond the Blue: Reflections of African America in the Fine Arts Collection of the Amistad Research Center (T), 4/10/10-7/11/10; Andy to Jim: American Master Prints 1960-1980 (T), 7/24/10-10/24/10; Jacob Petit: Porcelain Master of the Second Empire (T), 11/14/10-1/23/11.
Research Fields: pre-Columbian; Ancient, European & American glass; 19th-century Louisiana painting; Latin American Spanish Colonial art; European art; African art; portrait miniatures; Japanese art; photography; contemporary art.
Facilities: 7,500-vol. library of general art, slide library available by appointment; 171,500 sq. ft. exhibition space; 5 acre sculpture garden; 220-seat auditorium; studio classrooms. Museum-related items for sale.
Activities: guided tours; lectures; films; gallery talks; adult art classes; arts festivals; formally organized education programs for children; concerts; docent program; inter-museum loan, permanent & temporary exhibitions; art therapy program in public schools.
Publications: Arts Quarterly; handbook of the permanent collection & special exhibition catalogs.
Hours & Admission Prices: Wed. 12-8, Thurs.-Sun. 10-5. Adults $8, senior citizens 65 & over and full-time students $7, children 3-17 $4; discounts to AAM & ICOM members; members, children under 3, NOMA, & LA residents with ID no charge. Closed legal holidays. ♿
Attendance: 114,431 (accurate)
Membership: General $60; Champions $100; Sustaining $125; Collector's Society $200; Delgado $500; Fellows $1,500; Patron's Circle $5,000; Director's Circle $10,000; President's Circle $20,000.

NEW ORLEANS PHARMACY MUSEUM, (M), 514 Chartres St., New Orleans, LA 70130-2110. Tel.: 504-565-8027. Fax: 504-565-8028.
E-mail: nopharmsm@aol.com
Web Site: www.pharmacymuseum.org
Founded: 1950.
Congressional District: 2
Key Personnel: Pres. (V) & C.E.O., Edward S. Bopp; Dir., Liz Good; Asst. Cur., Eboni Evans; Membership Sec., Patricia S. Bopp; Public Rels., Charlotte D'Angelo.
Personnel Profile: Full-Time Paid 1; Part-Time Paid 1; Part-Time Volunteers 3.
Governing Authority: municipal government; nonprofit. Friends of Historical Pharmacy. Tax-exempt: 501(c)(3).
Pharmacy & Medicine Museum: housed in 1823 building constructed for Louis Joseph Dufilho, Jr., first licensed pharmacist in the U.S.
Collections: history of pharmacy, medicine, & health care during the 19th century; apothecary bottles & jars; drugs & herbs; medical devices; trade journals; pharmacopoeias; Civil War surgical instruments; cosmetics; c.1855 soda fountain; archives; gris-a-gris potions used by voodoo practitioners.
Research Fields: pharmacology; history of voodoo, gris-gris & pharmacy; patent medicines; European, American, African & Asian approaches & contributions to the discipline of botanical medicine especially in the profession of pharmacy & medicine.
Facilities: garden with medicinal herbs; function areas for rental. Museum-related items for sale.
Activities: docent program; formal education programs for children, adults & undergraduate & graduate students; guided tours; lectures; loan exhibitions; rental gallery.
Publications: quarterly newsletter, RX News.
Hours & Admission Prices: Call for hours. Adults $5, senior citizens & students $4; discounts to AAM & AAA members; children under 6 & members no charge. Closed New Year's Day; Mardi Gras; Easter; Independence Day; Labor Day; Thanksgiving; Christmas Day.
Attendance: 55,000 (accurate)
Membership: Individual $50; Family $75; Lifetime & Corporate $500.

NEWCOMB ART GALLERY, (M), Woldenberg Art Center, Tulane University, New Orleans, LA 70118-5698. Tel.: 504-865-5328. Fax: 504-865-5329.
E-mail: smain@tulane.edu
Web Site: www.newcomb.tulane.edu/artindex.html
Founded: 1996.
Congressional District: 1
Key Personnel: Dir., Charles M. Lovell; Senior Cur., Sally Main; Coord. Education, Shelley Boles; Coord. Mktg. & Membership, Teresa Parker Farris; Registrar, Thomas Strider.
Personnel Profile: Full-Time Paid 5; Part-Time Volunteers 5; Interns 3.
Governing Authority: college. Parent Institution: Tulane University. Tax-exempt.
Art Museum.
Collections: Newcomb pottery & related crafts; paintings; sculpture; works on paper by Newcomb faculty & students; Tiffany windows. Tulane University Art Collection: 19th-20th century European & American paintings; sculpture; works on paper with emphasis on Louisiana artists.
Major Exhibits: Polaridad Complementaria: Recent Works from Cuba (T), 1/10-3/10; Joan Mitchell: Works on Paper, 3/10-6/10.
Facilities: library of fine arts available to public; slide library open to scholars & researchers in the fine arts field; art gallery.
Activities: gallery talks; symposia; workshops.
Publications: Newcomb Pottery and Crafts; Ida Kohlmeyer: Systems of Color; Carrie Mae Weems: The Louisiana Project; From Society to Socialism: The Art of Caroline Durieux; In Company with Angels: Seven Rediscovered Tiffany Windows; special exhibition catalogs.
Hours & Admission Prices: Tues., Thurs. & Fri. 10-6, Wed. 10-8, Sat.-Sun. 11-5. No charge. Closed New Year's Eve & Day; Mardi Gras; Thanksgiving; Christmas Eve & Day. ♿
Attendance: 10,000
Membership: Student $10; Individual $35; Family $50; Friend $100; Advocate $250; Patron $500; Title Sponsor $1,500; Corporate Sponsor $2,500.

THE OGDEN MUSEUM OF SOUTHERN ART, 925 Camp St., New Orleans, LA 70130-3907. Tel.: 504-539-9600. Fax: 504-539-9602.
E-mail: info@ogdenmuseum.org
Web Site: www.ogdenmuseum.org
Founded: 1994.
Key Personnel: Dir., J. Richard Gruber, Ph.D.; Chm. (V), Julia Reed; Treas., Lloyd Shields; Education, Kate Barron; Dir. Public Rels., Sue Strachan; Registrar & Archivist, Bradley Sumrall; Cur., David Houston; Security, Emmett Brown; Cur. Music, Libra LaGrone.
Personnel Profile: Full-Time Paid 12; Part-Time Paid 3; Interns 5.
Governing Authority: public university. Tax-exempt: 501(c)(3).
Art Museum.
Collections: visual art of 15 southern states & District of Columbia from 1733 to present.
Major Exhibits: Billie Ruth Suddeth (Craft: Baskets), 1/10; Give My Pour Heart Ease: Voices of the Mississippi Blues - William Ferris Photography, 4/10; Tom Rankin Photography, 8/10.
Facilities: library; theater. Museum-related items for sale.
Activities: docent program; guided tours; workshops; lectures; family programs. Museum Sponsors: Kohlmeyer Circle; Ogden After Hours; The Art of Giving; Southern Storytellers. Annual Events: Omazing Race; Sippin in Seersucker; O What A Night.
Hours & Admission Prices: Wed. & Fri.-Sun. 10-5, Thurs. 11-4 & 6pm-8pm. Adults $10, senior citizens 65 & over and college students $8, children 17 & under $5; discounts to groups; children under 5, members & Louisiana residents Thurs. 10-5 no charge. Closed New Year's Day; Mardi Gras; Memorial Day; Independence Day; Thanksgiving; Christmas. ♿
Attendance: 53,000 (estimated)
Membership: University of New Orleans Students $15; Individual $50; Family & Dual $75; Supporting $125-$249; Partners $250-$499; Curator's Circle $500-$999.

PITOT HOUSE MUSEUM, 1440 Moss St., New Orleans, LA 70119-2904. Tel.: 504-482-0312. Fax: 504-482-0363.
E-mail: info@louisianalandmarks.org
Web Site: www.louisianalandmarks.org
Founded: 1964.
Key Personnel: Pres. (V), Anne Morse; Chm. (V), Mercedes Whitecloud; Dir., Susan McClamroch.
Personnel Profile: Full-Time Paid 1; Part-Time Paid 3; Part-Time Volunteers 10.
Governing Authority: municipal; nonprofit. Parent Institution: Louisiana Landmarks Society. Tax-exempt.
Historic House: 1799 French West Indies Country house.
Collections: 1790-1840, Louisiana cultural history items.
Facilities: botanical garden.
Activities: guided tours; heritage education programs; service learning partnership with Tulane Univ. Preservation students; preservation technology workshops. Annual Events: Life on the Bayou; Vino on the Bayou with Cork & Bottle Wine.
Publications: quarterly newsletter, Preservation.
Hours & Admission Prices: Wed.-Sat. 10-3. Adults $7, senior citizens & children $5; discounts to groups & National Trust members; members no charge. Closed major holidays.
Attendance: 2,000 (estimated)

Membership: Loyalist $25; Advocate $35; Guardian $250-$499; Pitot Protector $500-$999; Sustainer $1,000-$4,999; Preserver $5,000-$9,000; Champion $10,000 & up.

PRESERVATION RESOURCE CENTER, 923 Tchoupitoulas St., New Orleans, LA 70130-3819. Tel.: 504-581-7032. Fax: 504-636-3073.
E-mail: prc@prcno.org
Web Site: www.prcno.org
Founded: 1974.
Congressional District: 2
Key Personnel: Exec. Dir., Patricia H. Gay; Pres. Bd. (V), Holly Sharp.
Personnel Profile: Full-Time Paid 30; Part-Time Paid 4; Part-Time Volunteers 250; Interns 10.
Governing Authority: Tax-exempt: 501(c)(3).
Historical & Preservation Society: housed in 1853 Gothic Revival style building designed by James H. Dakin.
Collections: archive, photograph & slide collection on architecture, historic preservation in historic districts in New Orleans.
Facilities: 44,000-entry cataloguing articles on landscape architecture & renovation available to members; meeting room.
Activities: guided tours; lectures; historic home tours; architecture symposium; home ownership & renovation seminars.
Publications: newspaper magazine 10 times annually, Preservation in Print; books, New Orleans: Life in an Epic City; New Orleans's Favorite Shotguns.
Hours & Admission Prices: Mon.-Fri. 9-5. No charge; donations accepted. ♿
Attendance: 2,500 (estimated)
Membership: Introductory $25-$39; Individual $40-$59; Dual $60-$84; Family $85-$199; Preserver $200-$349; Restorer $350-$499; Conservator $500-$999; Landmark $1,000 plus; President's Circle $5,000 plus.

SAINTS HALL OF FAME MUSEUM, The Superdome, 1500 Poydras St., New Orleans, LA 70112-1216. Mailing Address: 415 Williams Blvd., Kenner, LA 70062. Tel.: 504-450-9893.
Key Personnel: Dir., Ken Trahan
Sports Museum.
Collections: New Orleans team memorabilia, photographs & videos.
Hours & Admission Prices: NFL Game Days 3 hrs. before game until 30 minutes after; other times by appointment. Adult $7; discounts to groups of 20 or more. ♿

SOUTHERN FOOD AND BEVERAGE MUSEUM, 1 Poydras St., #169, New Orleans, LA 70130-1657. Tel.: 504-569-0405. Fax: 504-587-7944.
Founded: 2008.
Governing Authority: nonprofit organization.
Cultural History Museum.
Collections: southern culture & history of food & drink; cultural heritage; oral histories; videos; paintings; photographs.
Facilities: library.
Activities: special events; classes; tastings; videos; demonstrations; lectures; research.
Hours & Admission Prices: Call for hours.

New Roads

POINTE COUPEE MUSEUM, 8348 False River Rd., New Roads, LA 70760. Mailing Address: P.O. Box 555, New Roads, LA 70760-0555. Tel.: 225-638-3500. Fax: 225-638-9858.
Web Site: www.pcchamber.org
Historic Building.
Collections: local history & culture; period furnishings; personal artifacts.
Hours & Admission Prices: Daily 10-3; other times by appointment.

Oil City

LOUISIANA STATE OIL & GAS MUSEUM, (M), 200 S. Land Ave., Oil City, LA 71061. Mailing Address: P.O. Box 94125, Baton Rouge, LA 70804-9125. Tel.: 318-995-6845. Fax: 318-995-6848.
E-mail: oil@sos.louisiana.gov
Web Site: www.sos.louisiana.gov/lsoagm
Formerly: Caddo-Pine Island Oil & Historical Society Museum
Founded: 1965.
Congressional District: 4
Key Personnel: Dir., Coe Haygood.
Personnel Profile: Full-Time Paid 2; Part-Time Paid 1.
Governing Authority: nonprofit organization. Parent Institution: Louisiana Secretary of State Office. Tax-exempt: 501(c)(3) & 170(b)(1)(A).
Oil and Gas Museum.
Collections: local history & culture; Caddo Indians; oil field equipment.
Facilities: library. Museum-related items for sale.
Activities: guided tours; organized education programs for children.
Hours & Admission Prices: Mon.-Fri. 9-4. No charge; donations accepted. Closed major federal & state holidays.
Membership: Call for information.

Olla

CENTENNIAL CULTURAL CENTER, 2962 Front St., Olla, LA 71465. Mailing Address: P.O. Box 896, Olla, LA 71465-0896. Tel.: 318-495-7988. Fax: 318-495-7988.
E-mail: cultural@centurytel.net
Web Site: www.culturalcenter.us
Key Personnel: Dir., Shawna Cockerham.
Governing Authority: nonprofit organization. Tax-exempt: 501(c)(3).
History Museum.
Collections: Olla, Tullos, & Urania history; photographs; period artifacts; oral histories.
Hours & Admission Prices: Mon.-Fri. 9-1.

Opelousas

OPELOUSAS MUSEUM AND INTERPRETIVE CENTER, (M), 315 N. Main St., Opelousas, LA 70570-6201. Tel.: 337-948-2589. Fax: 337-948-2592.
E-mail: museum@cityofopelousas.com
Web Site: www.cityofopelousas.com
Founded: 1992.
Congressional District: 7
Personnel Profile: Full-Time Paid 2; Part-Time Paid 1; Part-Time Volunteers 4.
Governing Authority: municipal government; nonprofit. Parent Institution: City of Opelousas. Tax-exempt: 501(c)(3).
History Museum.
Collections: history & culture of the Opelousas area from prehistoric times to present.
Research Fields: zydeco music; medical & local history.
Facilities: 3,500 sq. ft. exhibit space. Books on the Opelousas area & musical & Cajun humor tapes for sale.
Activities: films; formal education programs for adults; guided tours; lectures; temporary exhibitions; broadcast programs. Annual Events: Birthday; Cultural A-Fair; Christmas Flower Show.
Publications: bimonthly, Dust & Cobwebs.
Hours & Admission Prices: Mon.-Sat. 9-5. Tour Buses: $3 per person; discounts to AAM & ICOM members. Closed Easter; Thanksgiving; Christmas. ♿
Attendance: 6,000 (estimated)
Membership: Friends of the Museum: Student 5 volunteer hours; Individual $10-$50; Business $75-$150; Corporate $200-$500.

Patterson

LOUISIANA STATE MUSEUM-PATTERSON, 118 Cotten Rd., Patterson, LA 70392. Mailing Address: P.O. Box 38, Patterson, LA 70392-0038. Tel.: 985-399-1268. Fax: 985-399-9910.
E-mail: kdelee@crt.state.la.us
Web Site: lsm.crt.state.la.us/
Formerly: Wedell Williams Memorial Aviation Museum
Founded: 1975.
Congressional District: 50
Key Personnel: Div. Dir., Kathryn DeLee.
Personnel Profile: Full-Time Paid 7.
Governing Authority: state; nonprofit. Subsidiary Institution: Wedell-Williams & Cypress Sawmill Foundation. Tax-exempt: 501(c)(3).
Aviation Museum.
Collections: 067 aircraft & aviation memorabilia, emphasizing Louisiana natives & industry.
Research Fields: aviation; cypress lumber industry.
Facilities: 24-seat theater.
Activities: guided tours; films; temporary & permanent exhibitions; 2nd Saturday children's programs; adult & family programs.
Publications: quarterly newsletter.
Hours & Admission Prices: Tues.-Sat. 9-5. Adults $3, students, seniors & active military $2; children under 12 & members no charge. Closed state holidays. ♿
Attendance: 10,000 (accurate)
Membership: Individual $25; Family $50; Supporter $100; Sponsor $250; Donor $500; Benefactor $1,000; Patron $5,000.

Plaquemine

IBERVILLE MUSEUM, 57735 Main St., Plaquemine, LA 70764-2564. Mailing Address: P.O. Box 701, Plaquemine, LA 70765-0701. Tel.: 225-687-7197. Fax: 225-687-3060.
E-mail: ibervillemuseum@yahoo.com
Key Personnel: Dir., Bethany Cardinal
History Museum: built in 1848. Listed in the National Register of Historic Places.
Collections: Iberville history & culture; photographs; America's wars; personal artifacts.
Hours & Admission Prices: Tues.-Sat. 10-4, Sun. by appointment. Adults 13 & over $2, children 6-12 $1; discounts to groups; teachers no charge.

PLAQUEMINE LOCK STATE HISTORIC SITE, 57730 Main St., Plaquemine, LA 70764-2530. Tel.: 225-687-7158; 877-987-7158.
E-mail: plaqlock@crt.state.la.us
Web Site: www.crt.state.la.us/parks/iplaqlock.aspx
Historic Site. Listed on the National Register of Historic Places.
Collections: local history & culture; photographs.
Hours & Admission Prices: Daily 9-5. Adults $2; seniors 62 & over and children 12 & under no charge. Closed New Year's Day; Thanksgiving; Christmas.

Port Allen

* **WEST BATON ROUGE MUSEUM, (M),** 845 N. Jefferson Ave., Port Allen, LA 70767-2417. Tel.: 225-336-2422. Fax: 225-336-2448.
E-mail: contact_us@wbrmuseum.org
Web Site: westbatonrougemuseum.com
Founded: 1968.
Congressional District: 6
Key Personnel: Dir., Julia Rose; Pres. (V), Helen Thibodeaux; Chm. (V), Gary Hubble; Vice Chm., Ellis Gauthier; Cur., Lauren Davis; Education Cur., Jeannie Luckett; Museum Shop Mgr., Lorry Trotter.
Personnel Profile: Full-Time Paid 4; Part-Time Paid 10; Part-Time Volunteers 146; Interns 2.
Governing Authority: nonprofit organization. West Baton Rouge Historical Association. Tax-exempt: 501(c)(3).
Regional History Museum.
Collections: 19th- & 20th-century lifestyles in a Louisiana sugar parish; West Baton Rouge artifacts and memorabilia; raw sugar production. Historic Buildings: c.1904 model raw sugar mill; c.1850 slave cabin; c.1830 French-Creole cottage; 1880 share cropper cabin; 20th century shore cropper cabin; 20th century shotgun house.
Major Exhibits: We Remember: Coretta Scott King (T), 1/10-2/10; Trench Art: WWII (T), 11/10-12/10.
Research Fields: sugar industry.
Activities: guided tours; lectures; education programs for children & adults; folklife and Louisiana artists exhibitions; festivals.
Publications: newsletter, Ecoutez.
Hours & Admission Prices: Tues.-Sat. 10-4:30, Sun. 2-5, Mon. by appointment. Adults $4, students, military & seniors $2; discounts offered to AAM, AAA, LAM members & other tourism coupon holders; WBR Historical Assoc. members, citizens of WBR parish & members no charge. Closed major holidays. ♿
Attendance: 170,000 (estimated)
Membership: Student $5; Member $10; Patron $35; Friends $100.

Ruston

LINCOLN PARISH MUSEUM & HISTORICAL SOCIETY, (M), 609 N. Vienna St., Ruston, LA 71270-3842. Tel.: 318-251-0018.
Founded: 1975.
Congressional District: 5
Key Personnel: C.E.O., Chm. (V) & Pres. (V), William Davis Green; Vice Pres., Johnnie Hogan; Dir., Hostess & Museum Shop Mgr., Margaret Anne Emory; Treas., Don Faust; Sec., Linda Graham.
Personnel Profile: Full-Time Paid 1.
Governing Authority: nonprofit organization. Subsidiary Institution: Absalom Autrey House Museum. Tax-exempt: 501(c)(3).
Historical Society Museum: housed in 1886 Victorian home.
Collections: artifacts reflecting the history & culture of North Central Louisiana from prehistoric to present. Historic House: 1849 Autrey House log cabin.
Research Fields: restoration of log houses; north Louisiana quilting; WPA textiles.
Facilities: 100-seat conference room; 4,000 sq. ft. exhibit space.
Activities: guided tours; arts festivals; temporary & traveling exhibitions; rental facilities.
Publications: biannual newsletter; monthly article in local newspaper; material on the Kidd-Davis House & The Absalom Autrey House.
Hours & Admission Prices: Tues.-Fri. 10-4. No charge; donations accepted. Closed New Year's Day; Independence Day; Thanksgiving; Christmas. ♿
Attendance: 2,500 (accurate)
Membership: Individual $15; Friend $25; Donor $50; Sponsor $100; Sustaining $250; Patron $500.

LOUISIANA MILITARY MUSEUM, (M), 201 Memorial Dr., Ruston, LA 71270-3955. Mailing Address: P.O. Box 94125, Baton Rouge, LA 70804-9125. Tel.: 318-251-5099. Fax: 318-251-5099.
E-mail: military@sos.louisiana.gov
Web Site: www.sos.louisiana.gov/lmm
Congressional District: 5
Key Personnel: Dir., Ernest Stevens.
Personnel Profile: Full-Time Paid 1; Part-Time Paid 2.
Governing Authority: state. Parent Institution: Louisiana Secretary of State, Baton Rouge, LA. Tax-exempt.
Military Museum.
Collections: military history from Civil War to present; period artifacts; military artifacts including weapons, uniforms, flags, banners, medals & badges.
Research Fields: area veterans.
Activities: guided tours; temporary exhibitions; special events.
Hours & Admission Prices: Mon.-Fri. 10-6:30, Sat. 10-5, Sun. 1-5. No charge. Closed most state holidays.

LOUISIANA TECH MUSEUM, Louisiana Tech University, Ruston, LA 71272-0001. Tel.: 318-257-2935 & 3660. Fax: 318-257-2579.
E-mail: pcarter@latech.edu
Founded: 1982.
Congressional District: 5
Key Personnel: Devel., Jonathan Donehoo; Education, Joan Marie Edinger; Public Rels., Sally R. Hollis; Archivist, Peggy Carter.
Personnel Profile: Part-Time Paid 2; Part-Time Volunteers 5.
Governing Authority: public university; nonprofit. Parent Institution: Louisiana Tech University, Ruston. Tax-exempt.
University Museum.
Collections: Indian artifacts; paleontologic & geologic collections; pre-World War II weapons; Roman & Egyptian archaeology.
Research Fields: Indian archaeology.
Facilities: 500 sq. ft. exhibit space.
Activities: formal education programs for children, undergraduate & graduate students; guided tours; lectures; loan exhibitions.
Hours & Admission Prices: Mon.-Fri. 8-4. No charge; donations accepted. Closed New Year's Day; Thanksgiving; Christmas; university holidays. ♿
Attendance: 400 (estimated)

Saint Bernard

LOS ISLENOS HERITAGE & CULTURAL SOCIETY, 1357 Bayou Rd., Saint Bernard, LA 70085. Mailing Address: 206 Decatur St., New Orleans, LA 70130-1016. Tel.: 504-682-0862.
History Museum.
Collections: Spanish heritage, culture, music & language; period furnishings; personal artifacts; photographs.
Activities: special events.
Hours & Admission Prices: Call for hours.

Saint Francisville

AUDUBON STATE HISTORIC SITE, 11788 Hwy. 965, Saint Francisville, LA 70775. Mailing Address: P.O. Box 546, Saint Francisville, LA 70775-0546. Tel.: 225-635-3739; 888-677-2838. Fax: 225-784-0578.
E-mail: audubon@crt.state.la.us
Web Site: www.crt.state.la.us
Formerly: Audubon State Commemorative Area
Founded: 1947.
Congressional District: 6
Key Personnel: Historic Site Mgr., John House.
Personnel Profile: Full-Time Paid 6; Part-Time Paid 6.
Governing Authority: state; nonprofit organization. Affiliated with Louisiana Office of State Parks, P.O. Drawer 1111, Baton Rouge, LA 70821. Tax-exempt.
State Park Museum: housed in 1806 Oakley House.
Collections: Federal Period furnishings; 1st edition Audubon prints; early American lighting devices.
Research Fields: archaeological program on the plantation complex; new archival work on house & grounds.
Facilities: library of books on life of Audubon available for use on the premises.

Activities: guided tours; lectures; permanent exhibitions.
Publications: brochure, Oakley.
Hours & Admission Prices: Oakley House & Grounds: daily 9-5. Adults $2; senior citizens 62 & over, children under 13 & school groups no charge. Closed New Year's; Thanksgiving; Christmas.
Attendance: 30,000 (accurate)

ROSEDOWN PLANTATION, 12501 Hwy. 10, Saint Francisville, LA 70775. Tel.: 888-376-1867; 225-635-3332.
Historic House.
Collections: local history; agriculture; period furnishings; photographs; gardens.
Facilities: gardens.
Hours & Admission Prices: Daily 9-5. Adults $10; senior citizens 62 & over $8; students 6-17 $4; children 5 & under no charge. Closed New Year's Day; Thanksgiving; Christmas.

Saint Martinville

LONGFELLOW EVANGELINE STATE HISTORIC SITE, 1200 N. Main St., Saint Martinville, LA 70582-3516. Tel.: 888-677-2900; 337-394-3754. Fax: 337-394-3553.
E-mail: longfellow@crt.state.la.us
Web Site: www.crt.state.la.us/Parks/ilongfell.aspx
Formerly: Oliver House & Interpretive Center
Founded: 1931.
Congressional District: 3
Key Personnel: Historic Site Mgr., Reinaldo Barnes; Cur., Suzanne Laviolette.
Personnel Profile: Full-Time Paid 8; Part-Time Paid 4.
Governing Authority: state; nonprofit. Parent Institution: Louisiana Culture Recreation & Tourism Office of State Parks P.O. Drawer 1111, Baton Rouge, LA. Tax-exempt.
History Museum.
Collections: 18th & 19th-century furniture; Acadian cypress looms; 19th-century textiles; woodworking tools; agricultural implements pertaining to cotton & sugar plantation; Spanish moss artifacts; 19th & 20th-century ironstone & porcelain.
Research Fields: 19th-century plantation life; sugar cane economy; Acadian & Creole culture; Acadian & French migration to southwest Louisiana.
Facilities: 150-acre state commemorative area along the Bayou Teche; visitor center; pavilions & picnic area; vegetable gardens; native plants; formal historic garden; education center; workshop area.
Activities: tours of plantation house & Acadian cabin; interpretive center; education center; demonstration.
Publications: brochure, Welcome to Longfellow-Evangeline State Commemorative Area.
Hours & Admission Prices: Daily 9-5. Adult $2; senior citizens over 62, children 12 & under no charge. Tours: 10-4 every hour on the hour. Closed New Year's Day; Thanksgiving; Christmas. ♿
Attendance: 27,000 (accurate)
Membership: Annual Permit $50 (good for day entrance to all state parks & commemorative area).

MUSEUM OF THE ACADIAN MEMORIAL, 121 S. New Market St., Saint Martinville, LA 70582. Mailing Address: P.O. Box 379, Saint Martinville, LA 70582-0379. Tel.: 337-394-2258. Fax: 337-394-2260.
History Museum.
Collections: local history & culture; personal artifacts; photographs; period furnishings; mural.
Activities: audio tour.
Hours & Admission Prices: Daily 10-4:30.

Scott

FLOYD SONNIER'S BEAU CAJUN ART GALLERY, 1010 St. Mary St., Scott, LA 70583. Mailing Address: P.O. Box 397, Scott, LA 70583. Tel.: 337-237-7104.
Art Gallery: built in 1918.
Collections: drawings; prints; period furnishings.
Publications: book, From Small Bits of Charcoal - The Life and Works of a Cajun Artist.
Hours & Admission Prices: Wed.-Fri. 10-5, Sat. 10-4; other times by appointment.

Shreveport

ARK-LA-TEX ANTIQUE & CLASSIC VEHICLE MUSEUM, 601 Spring St., Shreveport, LA 71101. Mailing Address: P.O. Box 5040, Shreveport, LA 71135-5040.
Founded: 1993.
Congressional District: 5
Key Personnel: C.E.O. & Devel., Francene Miller; Pres. (V), Bill Henderson; Financial Dir., Scott Massey.
Personnel Profile: Full-Time Paid 1; Full-Time Volunteers 4; Part-Time Paid 2; Part-Time Volunteers 10; Interns 2.
Governing Authority: private; nonprofit organization. Tax-exempt: 501(c)(3).
Automobile Museum.
Collections: period & classic vehicles; 25 vintage costumes; 21 historic sets; automotive art; automotive library.
Research Fields: historic & class automotive; development of seminars related to displays & hands-on educational tools for children & adults.
Facilities: 330-vol. library on automobiles; 24,000 sq. ft. exhibit space; theater; roof top area; special events showroom. Gift items for sale.
Activities: films; guided tours; participatory, loan & temporary exhibitions; rental gallery; vintage costume show & luncheons for guests. Annual Events: Krause 'N on the Red - vehicle auction show; Car shows in September; Santa's Transportation - Live Reindeer in November; Festival of Trees in November & December.
Publications: quarterly newsletter, Motoring Museum News.
Hours & Admission Prices: Tues.-Fri. 9-4:30, Sat. 9-5, Sun. 1-5. Adults $6, senior citizens & students 12-18 $5, children 6-12 $4; discount to groups of 10 or more, AAM & ICOM members; children 1-6 & members no charge. Closed New Year's Day; Christmas. ♿
Attendance: 70,000 (estimated)
Membership: Student $10; Individual $25; Couple $35; Family $40; Associate $100; Small Co. (100 employees) $250; Large Corporate $500.

LOUISIANA STATE EXHIBIT MUSEUM, (M), 3015 Greenwood Rd., Shreveport, LA 71109-4640. Mailing Address: P.O. Box 94125, Baton Rouge, LA 70804-9125. Tel.: 318-632-2020. Fax: 318-632-2056.
E-mail: lsem@sos.louisiana.gov
Web Site: www.sos.louisiana.gov/lsem
Founded: 1937.
Congressional District: 4
Key Personnel: Dir., Forrest Dunn; Education, Cynthia Grogan; Cur., Nita Cole; Security, Perry Smith.
Personnel Profile: Full-Time Paid 10; Part-Time Paid 7.
Governing Authority: state. Parent Institution: Louisiana Secretary of State, Baton Rouge, LA. Tax-exempt.
History & Art Museum.
Collections: murals; dioramas; period artifacts; agriculture; industrial; archaeology; glass; china; Native American artifacts; folk culture.
Research Fields: archaeology, prehistory, history; Louisiana Native American culture.
Facilities: auditorium.
Activities: permanent, temporary & traveling exhibitions; art workshops; films; concerts; formal education programs for children; rental gallery; lectures; guided tours.
Hours & Admission Prices: Mon.-Fri. 9-4, Sat.-Sun. 12-4. No charge. Closed most state holidays. ♿
Membership: Call for information.

* **MEADOWS MUSEUM OF ART OF CENTENARY COLLEGE, (M),** 2911 Centenary Blvd., Shreveport, LA 71104-3335. Tel.: 318-869-5169. Fax: 318-869-5730.
E-mail: ddufilho@centenary.edu
Web Site: www.centenary.edu
Founded: 1976.
Congressional District: 4
Key Personnel: C.E.O., Dr. Kenneth Schwab; Pres. (V), Grace Bareikis; Dir., Diane Dufilho; Cur., Bruce Allen; Museum Shop Mgr., Lorraine Soffer; Museum Education, Connie Blake; Collections Mgr., Kathy Brodnax; Student Registrar, Amanda Schiffner; Officer Mgr. & Internal Accountant, Neeta Kaji.
Personnel Profile: Full-Time Paid 3; Part-Time Paid 3; Part-Time Volunteers 90.
Governing Authority: college. Parent Institution: Centenary College of Louisiana. Tax-exempt.
Art Museum.
Collections: Indochina collection by French academic artist Jean Despujols features the people & lands of French Sado-China between 1936-37; paintings by George Grosz, Alfred Maurer, William Glackens, & Ernest Lawson; Latin American works on paper featuring Diego Rivera, David Sigueiros, Emilio Amero & Jose Clemente Orozco; American works on paper include Reginald Mavsh, Mary Cassatt & Isabel Bishop; African American, Haitian, Inuit & tribal works.
Research Fields: Southeast Asia 1900-1940; French artists 1915-1940.
Facilities: 8,500 sq. ft. exhibition space; art resource center. Museum-related items for sale.

Activities: guided tours; lectures; films; documentary films; gallery talks; concerts; docent program; permanent & temporary exhibitions.
Publications: booklet.
Hours & Admission Prices: mid-Aug. to July Tues.-Wed. & Fri. 12-4, Thurs. 12-5, Sat.-Sun. 1-4. No charge; donations accepted. Fee for some special exhibits. Closed New Year's Day; Easter; Memorial Day; Labor Day; Thanksgiving; Christmas. ♿
Attendance: 15,000 (estimated)
Membership: Individual $25; Family $40; Sustaining $100; Patron $250; Donor & Corporate $500.

PIONEER HERITAGE CENTER, LSU-SHREVEPORT, (M), One University Place, Shreveport, LA 71115-2301. Tel.: 318-797-5339. Fax: 318-797-5110.
E-mail: marty.young@lsus.edu
Web Site: www.lsus.edu/pioneer
Founded: 1977.
Congressional District: 4
Key Personnel: Dir., Marvin R. Young, II; Pres. (V), Dr. Vincent J. Marsala; Treas., Michael Ferrell.
Personnel Profile: Full-Time Paid 1; Part-Time Volunteers 5.
Governing Authority: state. Parent Institution: Louisiana State University in Shreveport. Tax-exempt: 501(c)(3).
History Museum Complex.
Collections: Northwest Louisiana & 19th-Century Red River regional history; medical implements; blacksmith & carpenter tools; period furnishings; textiles; clothing; books; archival documents & photographs; 300-pcs. 19th-century agricultural implements. Historic Structures: log single pen blacksmith shop; Thrasher House; log dogtrot; Caspiana House; plantation cottage; detached kitchen; doctor's office (shotgun house); Webb & Webb Plantation Commissary; blacksmith shop; riverfront mission.
Research Fields: folklife & history of Northwest Louisiana; history of medicine; humanities.
Facilities: library containing early medical books & plantation journals; 750-seat auditorium; educational facilities; classroom; conservation lab area in University Technology Center building; snack shop. University adjunct facilities available.
Activities: guided tours; lectures; films; broadcast programs; organized education programs for children, adults, undergraduate & graduate students; docent program; training programs for professional museum workers; participatory exhibits. Museum Sponsors: Suitcase museums: workshops for students & teachers; teaching packets; slide & tape presentations. Annual Events: Authors in April fundraiser; History Fair co-sponsored by LSU-Shreveport History Club.
Publications: annual brochure; teachers' packets; docent's manual; pamphlets; local history publications.
Hours & Admission Prices: Feb. to mid-Dec. Tues.-Fri. by appointment; other times for special events. Admission $2; discounts to AAM members; children under 5 no charge. Closed major holidays.
Attendance: 5,000 (accurate)
Membership: Pioneer Heritage Society $125; Sponsor $500 & up.

R.S. BARNWELL MEMORIAL GARDEN AND ART CENTER, 601 Clyde Fant Pkwy., Shreveport, LA 71101-3207. Tel.: 318-673-7703. Fax: 318-673-7707.
E-mail: director@barnwellcenter.com
Web Site: www.barnwellcenter.com
Founded: 1970.
Congressional District: 4
Key Personnel: Pres., Dr. Joe White; Museum Shop Mgr., Barbara White; Sec., Wendy Liles.
Personnel Profile: Full-Time Paid 3; Part-Time Volunteers 10.
Governing Authority: municipal. Parent Institute: City of Shreveport. Tax-exempt.
Garden & Art Center.
Collections: paintings & tropical environment for plants.
Activities: lectures; films; arts festivals; study clubs; hobby workshops; formally organized education programs; traveling exhibitions.
Publications: quarterly report, Barnwell Beacon.
Hours & Admission Prices: Tues.-Fri. 10-4, Sat. 10-5, Sun. 1-5. No charge; donation accepted. Closed New Year's Day; Martin Luther King, Jr. Day; Presidents' Day; Good Friday; Easter; Memorial Day; Independence Day; Labor Day; Thanksgiving; Christmas. ♿
Attendance: 30,000 (estimated)
Membership: Individual $15; Family $25; Organization $50; Supporting $100; Patron $200; Gold $500.

THE R.W. NORTON ART GALLERY, (M), 4747 Creswell Ave., Shreveport, LA 71106-1899. Tel.: 318-865-4201. Fax: 318-869-0435.
E-mail: gallery@rwnaf.org
Web Site: www.rwnaf.org
Founded: 1946.
Congressional District: 4
Key Personnel: C.E.O. & Pres. Bd. Control, M. Lewis Norton; Dir. Public Rels. & Sec. Bd., Jerry M. Bloomer; Bldg. & Grounds Supt., Gerry Ward.
Personnel Profile: Full-Time Paid 29; Part-Time Volunteers 1.
Governing Authority: nonprofit organization. Parent Institution: R.W. Norton Art Foundation. Tax-exempt: 501(c)(3).
Art Museum & Gallery.
Collections: American painting, sculpture, glass, silver, miniatures, including works by western artists Charles M. Russell & Frederic Remington; European paintings, sculpture, miniatures, tapestries; Wedgwood collection; dolls dressed in authentic fashions of Louisiana from 1720-1920; rare books; atlases including elephant folio edition of Audubon Birds of America; complete set of John Gould ornithology works; firearms collection.
Major Exhibits: Fantasies and Fairy-Tales: Maxfield Parrish and the Art of the Print, 1/26/10-4/11/10; Alex Dzigurski: Poet of the Land and Sea, 4/27/10-8/1/10; Under the Magnifying Glass: 50 Miniatures by Wes and Rachelle Siegrist, 5/4/10-7/25/10; Ansel Adams: The Masterworks, 8/17/10-12/10.
Research Fields: 19th- & early 20th-century American & European art.
Facilities: 12,000-vol. library of fine arts, history, literature, ornithology, genealogy; James M. Ownes Memorial Collection of Early Americana, available for use by public on premises. Exhibition catalogs for sale.
Activities: guided tours; lectures; films; gallery talks; formally organized education programs for children & adults; permanent, temporary & traveling exhibitions.
Publications: collection brochures; exhibition catalogs; catalogs of the Charles Russell & Wedgwood collections.
Hours & Admission Prices: Tues.-Fri. 10-5, Sat.-Sun. 1-5. Library: Tues.-Fri. 1-5. No charge; donations accepted. Closed national holidays. ♿
Attendance: 15,612 (accurate)

SCI-PORT DISCOVERY CENTER, 820 Clyde Fant Pkwy., Shreveport, LA 71101-3667. Tel.: 318-424-3466. Fax: 318-222-5592.
E-mail: egipson@sciport.org
Web Site: www.sciport.org
Founded: 1994.
Key Personnel: Pres. & C.E.O, Ann Fumarolo; Public Rels. Mgr., Eric Gipson; Museum Shop Mgr., Jacqui Brumley.
Personnel Profile: Full-Time Paid 39; Part-Time Paid 26; Part-Time Volunteers 70; Interns 1.
Governing Authority: nonprofit organization. Tax-exempt: 501(c)(3).
Science Museum.
Collections: science, math, & science hands-on exhibits.
Facilities: 67,000 sq. ft. exhibit space; classroom; 173-seat IMAX Dome Theater.
Activities: science teacher workshop, camp.
Publications: newsletter.
Hours & Admission Prices: Memorial Day to Labor Day Mon.-Sat. 10-6, Sun. 1-6; Sept.-May Mon.-Fri. 10-5 , Sat. 10-6, Sun. 1-6. Exhibits: adults $12, children 3-12 $9. Theater: adults $8.50, children 3-12 $7.50. Combo: adults $17, children $12; discounts to groups, AAA, AAM & ASTC members; museum members no charge. Closed Easter; Thanksgiving; Christmas. ♿
Attendance: 300,000 (estimated)
Membership: Discovery $70; Family Plus $85; Friend $125.

SHREVEPORT WATER WORKS MUSEUM, 142 N. Common St., Shreveport, LA 71101-2614. Mailing Address: P.O. Box 94125, Baton Rouge, LA 70804-9125. Tel.: 318-221-3388.
Web Site: www.sos.louisiana.gov/swwm
Formerly: McNeill Street Pumping Station Museum
Congressional District: 4
Key Personnel: Chm. (V), Dale Ward.
Personnel Profile: Part-Time Paid 2.
Governing Authority: state. Parent Institution: Louisiana Secretary of State, Baton Rouge, LA. Tax-exempt.
Water Works Museum.
Collections: period steam water pumping engines from 1898; community water development; water works history.
Activities: guided tours.
Hours & Admission Prices: Tues.-Sat. 10-3:30. No charge. Closed most state holidays.
Membership: Call for information.

SPRING STREET HISTORICAL MUSEUM, 525 Spring St., Shreveport, LA 71101-3231. Mailing Address: P.O. Box 94125, Baton Rouge, LA 70804-9125. Tel.: 318-424-0964. Fax: 318-424-0964.
E-mail: debra.helton@sos.louisiana.gov
Web Site: www.sos.louisiana.gov/sshm
Founded: 1977.
Congressional District: 4
Key Personnel: Dir., Debra M. Helton.
Personnel Profile: Full-Time Paid 2.
Governing Authority: state. Parent Institution: Louisiana Secretary of State, Baton Rouge, LA. Tax-exempt.
History Museum.
Collections: history of Shreveport & surrounding area; portraits of early settlers; maps; written documents; artifacts; newspaper illustrations; 19th century architecture; costumes & textiles.
Research Fields: women's suffrage; prohibition; the Depression; northwest Louisiana history.
Facilities: Museum-related items for sale.
Activities: docent program; guided tours; lectures; participatory, loan, temporary & traveling exhibitions.
Hours & Admission Prices: Tues.-Sat. 10-3:30; group tours by appointment. No charge. Closed most state holidays. ♿
Membership: Call for information.

STEPHENS AFRICAN-AMERICAN MUSEUM, 2810 Lindholm, Shreveport, LA 71108-2610. Tel.: 318-635-2147. Fax: 318-635-2147.
Founded: 1994.
Key Personnel: C.E.O., Chm. (V) & Pres. (V), Spencer Stephens; Museum Shop Mgr., Gwendolyn Frazier.
Personnel Profile: Part-Time Paid 2.
Governing Authority: private; nonprofit organization. Parent Institution: Spencer R. Stephens Foundation Inc. Tax-exempt: 501(c)(3).
Art Museum.
Collections: African-American art including paintings, sculptures, prints & drawings.
Facilities: library; 1,200 sq. ft. exhibit space; classrooms.
Activities: arts festival; formal education programs; guided tours; lectures; temporary exhibitions. Annual Event: Back to School Art Festival.
Publications: newsletter, African-American Museum.
Hours & Admission Prices: Tues.-Sat. 12-4. Adults $2, senior citizens $1.75, students & children $1; discounts to AAM & ICOM members; members no charge. Closed Independence Day; Easter; Christmas. ♿
Attendance: 15,000 (estimated)

WALTER B. JACOBS MEMORIAL NATURE PARK, 8012 Blanchard Furrh Rd., Shreveport, LA 71107-8310. Tel.: 318-929-2806. Fax: 318-929-3718.
E-mail: lraymond@caddo.org
Web Site: www.caddoparks.com/memorial.cfm
Founded: 1976.
Congressional District: 4
Key Personnel: Dir., Larry R. Raymond; Sr. Park Naturalist, Judith Sneed; Park Naturalist, Rachel Demascal; Park Naturalist, Kimberly Warren; Park Naturalist, Natalie Beebe.
Personnel Profile: Full-Time Paid 3; Part-Time Paid 2.
Governing Authority: county; nonprofit. Operated by the Caddo Parish Commission Parks & Recreation Dept. Tax-exempt.
Nature Park & Interpretive Center.
Collections: natural history of northwest Louisiana; leaves of woody plants; 52 taxidermy mounts of North American waterfowl; tanned skins & skulls of north Louisiana mammals; 1,000 pieces of large & small petrified wood; Pleistocene gravel; 5,000 reprints; 2,000 35mm slides.
Research Fields: plants & animals of the park; reproductive biology of local amphibians.
Facilities: library of natural history material including books, 100 magazines & 3,000 & more reprinted articles available for inter-library loan & to the public; 800 sq. ft. exhibit space; classroom facilities; pavilion workshop.
Activities: guided tours; lectures; films; slide shows; organized education programs; temporary & participatory exhibits; summer environmental day camp; discovery boxes available for loan to teachers: Earth Science Treasure Chest; Fantastic Fossils; Insects; The Bones Box; The Tree Trunk; Reptiles & Amphibians; Butterflies & Hummingbirds; Wetlands; The Wonder of Birds; Wildflowers; Dinosaurs; Mammal Tracks & Trails.
Hours & Admission Prices: Wed.-Sat. 8-5, Sun. 1-5. No charge; donations accepted. Closed New Year's Day; Easter; Thanksgiving; Christmas. ♿
Attendance: 15,956 (accurate)

Slidell

SLIDELL CULTURAL CENTER, 2055 Second St., Slidell, LA 70458-3430. Mailing Address: P.O. Box 828, Slidell, LA 70459-0828. Tel.: 985-646-4375. Fax: 985-646-4231.
E-mail: kbergeron@cityofslidell.org
Web Site: slidell.la.us
Founded: 1989.
Congressional District: 1
Key Personnel: Dir., Kim Bergeron.
Personnel Profile: Full-Time Paid 3; Part-Time Paid 2.
Governing Authority: municipal government; nonprofit. Parent Institution: City of Slidell. Subsidiary Institution: Dept. of Cultural & Public Affairs. Tax-exempt.
Art Center.
Collections: works by local & regional artists.
Facilities: 600-vol. library; 1,328 sq. ft. exhibit space; meeting room.
Activities: concerts; guided tours; traveling & temporary exhibitions; performing artists residency training. Annual Event: City Arts Awards.
Publications: quarterly newsletter, Bravo!
Hours & Admission Prices: Mon.-Fri. 10-12:30 & 1:30-4:30, Sat. 10-2. No charge; donations accepted. Closed New Year's Day; Martin Luther King Jr. Day; Mardi Gras; Good Friday; Memorial Day; Independence Day; Labor Day; Thanksgiving; Christmas Eve & Day. ♿
Attendance: 7,000 (estimated)

SLIDELL MUSEUM, 2020 First St., Slidell, LA 70458-3402. Mailing Address: P.O. Box 828, Slidell, LA 70459-0828. Tel.: 985-646-4380. Fax: 985-646-6107.
E-mail: cityslidell@charter.net
Web Site: www.slidell.la.us
Founded: 1987.
Key Personnel: Dir., Reinhard Dearing; Financial Dir., Sharon Howes; Cur., Priscilla Davis.
Personnel Profile: Part-Time Paid 3; Part-Time Volunteers 2.
Governing Authority: municipal.
History Museum: housed in the city's original town hall & jail built in 1907.
Collections: history of Slidell from its founding to present; war between the states; Louisiana's military leaders.
Facilities: 300-vol. library.
Activities: guided tours; traveling exhibitions; monthly artists' reception. Museum Sponsors: monthly Artist of the Month for Slidell Art League.
Hours & Admission Prices: Tues.-Sat. 9-4. No charge; donations accepted. Closed city holidays.
Attendance: 1,500 (accurate)

Sorrento

LOUISIANA POTTERY MUSEUM, 6470 Hwy. 22, Cajun Village, Sorrento, LA 70778. Tel.: 225-675-5572.
General Museum: housed in an Acadian style home; c.1830.
Collections: pottery; etchings; hand-blown glass; pine needle baskets; hand-carved wooden ducks & boats; books.
Activities: temporary exhibits; classes.
Hours & Admission Prices: Tues.-Sun. 10-5.

Sulphur

BRIMSTONE MUSEUM, (M), 900 S. Huntington St., Sulphur, LA 70663-4420. Tel.: 337-527-0357. Fax: 337-527-0359.
E-mail: trahan@brimstonemuseum.org
Web Site: www.brimstonemuseum.org
Founded: 1975.
Congressional District: 7
Key Personnel: Pres., Randall Broussard; Dir., Thomas Trahan.
Personnel Profile: Full-Time Paid 1; Part-Time Paid 1; Part-Time Volunteers 5.
Governing Authority: society; nonprofit. Parent Institution: Brimstone Historical Society. Tax-exempt: 501(c)(3).
History Museum: housed in 1915 railroad station.
Collections: sulphur mining by Frasch process; mid-1800 medical instruments; 1876 bell clock; 1800s clothing; sulphur mining photographs; renovated railway caboose.
Facilities: 1,950 sq. ft. exhibit space.
Activities: guided tours; permanent, temporary & traveling exhibitions, summer programming.
Hours & Admission Prices: Mon.-Fri. 10-12 & 1-5. No charge; donations accepted. Closed New Year's Eve & Day; Good Friday; Memorial Day; Independence Day; Labor Day; Thanksgiving weekend; Christmas Eve & Day. ♿
Attendance: 7,600 (accurate)

Membership: Student & Senior $10; Individual $20; Family $45; Sponsor $250; Friend $350; Patron $500; Historian $750; Curator $1,000; Founder $2,500 & up.

Tallulah

HERMIONE MUSEUM, 315 N. Mulberry, Tallulah, LA 71282-3828. Mailing Address: P.O. Box 268, Tallulah, LA 71284-0268. Tel.: 318-574-0082. Fax: 318-574-0082.
E-mail: hermionemuseum@bellsouth.net
Founded: 1994.
Congressional District: 5
Key Personnel: Pres. (V) & Dir., Geneva Williams; Chm. (V), Codie Ray; Museum Shop Mgr., Melvin Whitaker.
Personnel Profile: Full-Time Volunteers 1; Part-Time Volunteers 1; Interns 1.
Governing Authority: nonprofit. Parent Institution: Madison Historical Society, Inc. Tax-exempt.
Historic House Museum.
Collections: local history; aviation artifacts; Civil War.
Research Fields: local history archives.
Activities: special events.
Hours & Admission Prices: Tues.-Fri. 10-4. No charge; donations accepted.
Attendance: 1,000 (estimated)
Membership: Individual $15; Associate $50; Patron $100; Super Patron $500; Lifetime $750.

Tangipahoa

CAMP MOORE CONFEDERATE CEMETERY AND MUSEUM, 70640 Camp Moore Rd., Tangipahoa, LA 70465. Mailing Address: P.O. Box 25, Tangipahoa, LA 70465-0025. Tel.: 985-229-2438.
Key Personnel: Dir., H. Mike Neal, Jr.
Personnel Profile: Part-Time Paid 1; Part-Time Volunteers 6.
Governing Authority: Tax-exempt.
History Museum.
Collections: Camp Moore artifacts; soldiers' letters & journals; newspapers; photographs.
Facilities: library.
Activities: research. Annual Event: Camp Moore Reenactment in November.
Publications: quarterly newsletter.
Hours & Admission Prices: Tues.-Sat. 10-3. Adults $2, students $1; children under 6 no charge. Closed New Year's Day; Thanksgiving; Christmas.
Attendance: 1,500 (estimated)
Membership: Friends of Camp Moore: Individual $10; Family $30.

Vacherie

LAURA: A CREOLE PLANTATION, 2247 Hwy. 18, River Rd., Vacherie, LA 70090. Tel.: 888-799-7690; 225-265-7690.
Historic House: built in 1840.
Collections: Creole history & culture; period furnishings; personal artifacts; photographs; historic buildings.
Activities: guided tours.
Hours & Admission Prices: Guided Tours: daily. Adults $15, students 6-17 $5; children 5 & under no charge. Closed New Year's Day; Mardi Gras Day; Easter; Thanksgiving; Christmas.

OAK ALLEY PLANTATION, 3645 Hwy. 18, Vacherie, LA 70090. Tel.: 225-265-2151. Fax: 225-265-7035.
Historic Mansion.
Collections: local history & culture; period furnishings; personal artifacts; photographs.
Hours & Admission Prices: Mon.-Fri. 10-4, Sat.-Sun. 10-5. Adults 19 & over $15, students 13-18 $7.50, children 6-12 $4.50. Closed New Year's Day; Mardi Gras Day; Thanksgiving; Christmas.

ST. JOSEPH PLANTATION, 3535 Hwy. 18, Vacherie, LA 70090. Tel.: 225-265-4078.
Historic House.
Collections: local history & culture; personal artifacts; period furnishings; photographs.
Facilities: Museum-related items for sale.
Hours & Admission Prices: Mon.-Sat. 9:30-5. Adults $15, youth 13-18 $7, children 6-12 $5; children under 6 no charge. Closed New Year's Day; Easter; Independence Day; Labor Day; Thanksgiving; Christmas Eve & Day.

Ville Platte

LOUISIANA ARBORETUM, STATE PRESERVATION AREA, 4213 Chicot Park Rd., Ville Platte, LA 70586-7576. Tel.: 337-363-6289 & 888-677-6100. Fax: 337-363-5616.
E-mail: arboretum@crt.state.la.us
Web Site: www.crt.state.la.us/parks/iarbor.aspx
Founded: 1961.
Congressional District: 8
Key Personnel: Park Mgr., Jim Robinson; Interpretive Naturalist, Kenneth Johnson; Cur., Kim Hollier; Horticulturist, Brian Buller.
Personnel Profile: Full-Time Paid 4; Part-Time Paid 2.
Governing Authority: state. Affiliated with the Dept. of Culture, Recreation & Tourism, Office of State Parks.
Arboretum.
Collections: native Louisiana flora; herbarium.
Facilities: 2 outdoor classrooms; 3 miles of interpretive nature trails.
Activities: tours by appointment; 52 planned public interpretive programs.
Hours & Admission Prices: Daily 9-5. No charge. Closed New Year's Day; Thanksgiving; Christmas. ♿
Attendance: 7,500 (accurate)
Membership: Friends of the Arboretum $10.

Washington

WASHINGTON MUSEUM & TOURIST CENTER, 402 N. Main St., Washington, LA 70589. Mailing Address: P.O. Box 597, Washington, LA 70589-0597. Tel.: 337-826-3627.
E-mail: towtourism@bellsouth.net
Web Site: washington-la.org
Founded: 1972.
Congressional District: 7
Key Personnel: Dir. Tourism, Raynold Soileau; Cur., Debrah Joubert; Cur., Lienola Chelette.
Personnel Profile: Part-Time Paid 3.
Governing Authority: nonprofit organization. Parent Institution: Town of Washington. Tax-exempt.
History Museum.
Collections: artifacts; tools; 19th-century documents; ledgers; Indian baskets; fans; 19th-century stethoscope; photographs; firemen's hats.
Facilities: reading room.
Activities: guided tours.
Publications: brochures & maps of historic sites.
Hours & Admission Prices: Daily 8-12 & 1-4. No charge; donations accepted. ♿
Attendance: 5,000 (estimated)

Westwego

WESTWEGO HISTORICAL MUSEUM, 275 Sala Ave., Westwego, LA 70094-3650. Tel.: 504-341-3161. Fax: 504-341-2570.
Key Personnel: Museum Coord., Lori Guin
History Museum.
Collections: period furnishings; hardware store.
Hours & Admission Prices: Mon.-Fri. 9-4; groups by appointment. Adults $3, seniors & children under 12 $2; discounts to groups of 10 or more; society members no charge.

White Castle

NOTTOWAY, 31025 Louisiana Hwy. 1, White Castle, LA 70788. Tel.: 866-527-6884; 225-545-2730. Fax: 225-545-8632.
Historic House: built in 1859. Listed on the National Register of Historic Places.
Collections: local history & culture; period furnishings; personal artifacts; paintings; photographs.
Facilities: rental facilities; restaurant.
Activities: guided tours.
Hours & Admission Prices: Daily 9-4. Adults $15, children under 12 $6.

Winnfield

LOUISIANA POLITICAL MUSEUM AND HALL OF FAME, 499 E. Main St., Winnfield, LA 71483-3224. Tel.: 318-628-5928.
Web Site: www.lapoliticalmuseum.com
Political History Museum.
Collections: Louisiana politicians & politics; Hall of Fame inductees includes senators, congressmen & representatives.
Hours & Admission Prices: Mon.-Fri. 9-5, Sat. by appointment. No charge.

MAINE

(170 listings)

Alexander

ALEXANDER-CRAWFORD HISTORICAL SOCIETY, 216 Pokey Rd., Alexander, ME 04694-6012. Tel.: 207-454-7476.
Founded: 1980.
Congressional District: 2
Historical Society Museum.
Collections: area history & culture; genealogy; photographs.
Publications: newsletter.
Hours & Admission Prices: By appointment.
Membership: Annual $10.

Alna

WISCASSET, WATERVILLE & FARMINGTON RAILWAY MUSEUM, 97 Cross Rd., Alna, ME 04535. Mailing Address: P.O. Box 242, Alna, ME 04535-0242. Tel.: 207-563-2516.
E-mail: info@wwfry.org
Web Site: www.wwfry.org
Founded: 1989.
Congressional District: 1
Key Personnel: Pres., Stephen T. Zuppa; Membership Sec., Frank Knight; Treas., James Patten; Archivist, Bruce Wilson; Museum Shop Mgr., Linda Zollers.
Personnel Profile: Part-Time Volunteers 1,125.
Governing Authority: private; nonprofit organization. Tax-exempt: 501(c)(3).
Operating Narrow Gauge Railroad Museum.
Collections: two foot gauge railroad equipment; books; photographs; documents; period artifacts; steam locomotives.
Facilities: 300-vol. library; operating restored two foot gauge railroad; 5,000 sq. ft. exhibit space. Museum-related items for sale.
Activities: docent program; films; guided tours; training programs for professional museum workers. Annual Events: Picnic; Halloween Trains; Christmas Trains.
Publications: bimonthly, WW&F Newsletter; book, WW&F Musings; children's book, Harry's Train; The Twenty-Four Inch Gauge Railroad at Bridgton, Maine.
Hours & Admission Prices: Memorial Day to Columbus Day Sat.-Sun. 9-5; Oct.-May Sat. 9-5. Museum: no charge. Steam Train Rides: adults $6, seniors $5, children $4; children 3 & under no charge. ♿
Attendance: 5,500 (accurate)
Membership: Individual $30; Life $300.

Ashland

ASHLAND LOGGING MUSEUM, INC., 267 Garfield Rd., Ashland, ME 04732-5105. Mailing Address: P.O. Box 866, Ashland, ME 04732-0866. Tel.: 207-435-6679. Fax: 207-435-6579.
Web Site: www.townofashland.com/Ashland_Logging_Museum.htm
Founded: 1964.
Congressional District: 14
Key Personnel: Pres. (V), Robert Sawyer, V; Vice Pres., Robert Sawyer, IV; Cur., Ed Chase.
Governing Authority: nonprofit. Tax-exempt: 501(c)(3).
Logging Museum: housed in a reproduction of an early logging camp.
Collections: 1903 Lombard steam & gas log haulers; log hauler sleds; bateau; tote wagon; pine log with king's arrow mark; tamarack ship's knee; machinery & hand tools from past years of lumbering activity.
Facilities: two machine sheds; logging camp.
Hours & Admission Prices: Fri. 1-4; other times by appointment. No charge; donations accepted.
Attendance: 500

Auburn

ANDROSCOGGIN HISTORICAL SOCIETY, 2 Turner St. Unit 8, Auburn, ME 04210-5978. Tel.: 207-784-0586.
E-mail: androhs@verizon.net
Web Site: www.rootsweb.ancestry.com/~meandrhs
Founded: 1923.
Congressional District: 2
Key Personnel: Pres., David C. Young; Membership Sec., Bruce A. Hall; Treas., Susan F. Sturgis.
Personnel Profile: Part-Time Paid 1; Part-Time Volunteers 4.
Governing Authority: society. Tax-exempt.
Historical Society Museum.
Collections: pioneer items; early settlers; Indian artifacts; dishes; furniture; clothing; small household items; photographs; maps; manuscripts; diaries; early documents; local history & genealogy .
Research Fields: local family & town history.
Facilities: 3,900-vol. library of local, county & Maine history books.
Activities: guided & self guided tours; lectures; permanent exhibitions. Museum Sponsors: annual dinner.
Publications: newsletter of the Androscoggin Historical Society Inc.; Androscoggin History.
Hours & Admission Prices: Call for hours. No charge; donations accepted. Closed national holidays. ♿
Attendance: 200 (accurate)
Membership: Individual $15; Family $25; Life $150; Corporate Patron I $50; Corporate Patron II $100; Corporate Sponsor $150; Corporate Sustaining $250.

Augusta

BLAINE HOUSE, 192 State St., Augusta, ME 04330-6406. Tel.: 207-287-2121.
Congressional District: 1
Key Personnel: Residence Mgr., Sue J. Plummer.
Governing Authority: state.
Historic House: 1830-1833 Blaine House, governor's mansion of Maine.
Collections: furnishings; silver from the battleships USS Maine 1895-98, 1905-22.
Facilities: 300-vol. private library of James G. Blaine.
Activities: guided tours.
Publications: The Blaine House Brochure.
Hours & Admission Prices: Tues.-Thurs. 2-4; tours on the half-hour. No charge. Closed national holidays. ♿
Attendance: 10,500 (accurate)

CHILDREN'S DISCOVERY MUSEUM, 171 Capitol St., Augusta, ME 04330-4615. Tel.: 207-622-2209.
E-mail: info@childrensdiscoverymuseum.org
Web Site: www.childrensdiscoverymuseum.org
Children's Museum.
Collections: hands-on exhibits.
Hours & Admission Prices: Tues.-Thurs. 10-4, Fri.-Sat. 10-5, Sun. 11-4. Children $5, adults $4.

* **MAINE STATE MUSEUM, (M),** State House Complex, Cultural Bldg., Augusta, ME 04333-0083. Mailing Address: 83 State House Station, Augusta, ME 04333-0083. Tel.: 207-287-2301. Fax: 207-287-6633. TDD: 207-287-6740.
Web Site: www.mainestatemuseum.org
Founded: 1837.
Congressional District: 1
Key Personnel: Dir., Joseph R. Phillips; Asst. Dir., Sheila McDonald; Chm. (V), Margaret A. Kelley; Chief Scientist, David Work; Cur. Photography, Fine Arts & Archives, Deanna Bonner Ganter; Art Dir., Don Bassett; Operations Mgr., Scott Mosher; Chief Cur. History & Decorative Arts, Laurie LaBar; Cur. Historical Collections, Kate McBrien; Registrar, Paula Work; Chief Educator, Joanna Torow; Chief Archaeologist, Bruce Bourque; Museum Store Mgr., Michelle Lagueux.
Personnel Profile: Full-Time Paid 14; Part-Time Paid 12; Part-Time Volunteers 90; Interns 3.
Governing Authority: state; independent state agency. Subsidiary Institution: Friends of the Maine State Museum. Tax-exempt.
General Museum.
Collections: history; natural history; anthropology; ethnology; geology; marine; mineralogy; science; technology; art.
Major Exhibits: Uncommon Threads: Wabanaki Textiles, Clothing and Costume (T), 11/09-5/11.
Research Fields: Maine history; regional natural history; regional archaeology; paleontology.
Facilities: 2,600-vol. library of research materials available for use on premises; conservation center. Items and books relating to Maine and the region for sale.
Activities: guided tours; lectures; formally organized education programs for archaeological field schools, children & undergraduate college students; inter-museum loan; permanent & temporary exhibitions; school loan service.
Publications: quarterly newsletter, Broadside; books, pamphlets & reports relating to collections.
Hours & Admission Prices: Tues.-Fri. 9-5, Sat. 10-4. Adults $2; discounts to AAM members; members no charge. Closed holidays. ♿
Attendance: 59,203 (accurate)
Membership: Senior Citizen & Student $25; Individual $30; Family &

Household $40; Supporting $75; Sustaining $125; Contributing & Corporate $250; Curator's Circle $500; Director's Circle $1,000.

OLD FORT WESTERN, 16 Cony St., Augusta, ME 04330-5200. Tel.: 207-626-2385. Fax: 207-626-2304.
E-mail: oldfort@oldfortwestern.org
Web Site: www.oldfortwestern.org
Founded: 1922.
Congressional District: 1
Key Personnel: Dir. & Cur. Collections, Jay Adams; Chm., David H. Crockett; Cur. Education, Patricia A. Viotelte.
Personnel Profile: Full-Time Paid 2; Part-Time Paid 15; Part-Time Volunteers 25.
Governing Authority: board of trustees. Parent Institution: City of Augusta. Tax-exempt.
Historic House.
Collections: recreation of fort complex with 1922 blockhouses; 1754 main house with reproduction blockhouses & picket-work; watchboxes & palisade; 1754-1810 military, store & residential artifacts.
Research Fields: local history as it relates to the Kennebec Valley & New England, with emphasis on the 18th century.
Facilities: Gift items for sale.
Activities: tours; special events; demonstrations; lectures; pre-scheduled school & group programs.
Publications: occasional publications on research topics; booklet series on local history subjects; newsletter.
Hours & Admission Prices: Memorial Day to Labor Day daily 1-4; Sept.-Columbus Day Sat.-Sun. 1-4; other times by appointment. Adults $6, children 6-16 $4; discounts to AAM members, school groups, group tours & programs year-round; children under 6 & members no charge. ♿
Attendance: 24,000 (accurate)
Membership: The Beverly Hewins Society $25-$99; The Robert Hotelling Society $100-$299; Mary Maher McCarthy Society $300-$499; The Gannett Society $500 & up.

Bangor

BANGOR MUSEUM AND HISTORY CENTER, (M), 159 Union St., Bangor, ME 04401-6147. Tel.: 207-942-1900. Fax: 207-942-1910.
Web Site: www.bangormuseum.org
Formerly: Thomas A. Hill Historical House and Civil War Museum
Founded: 1864.
Congressional District: 2
Key Personnel: Collections Mgr., Dana Lippitt.
Personnel Profile: Full-Time Paid 1; Part-Time Paid 1; Part-Time Volunteers 10; Interns 1.
Governing Authority: society. Parent Institution: Bangor Historical Society. Tax-exempt: 501(c)(3).
History Museum.
Collections: restored 19th-century rooms; local history; portraits; manuscripts; photographs; Civil War artifacts. Historic House: Thomas A. Hill House & Civil War Museum.
Research Fields: history of Penobscot River area.
Facilities: 1,200-vol. library of Maine history.
Activities: lectures; permanent & temporary exhibitions; Mt. Hope Cemetery tour; candlelight ghost walks.
Publications: semiannual newsletter.
Hours & Admission Prices: June-Sept. Tues.-Fri. 10-4; other times by appointment. Adults $5, senior citizens $4; discounts to students, AAA, AAM & NEMA members; children & members no charge. Closed national holidays.
Attendance: 500 (estimated)
Membership: Friend $25; Household $50; River Driver $100; Master Mariner $250; Lumber Baron $500; Queen City Club $1,000 & up.

BANGOR POLICE MUSEUM, 240 Main, Bangor, ME 04401. Tel.: 207-947-7384.
Police History Museum.
Collections: police department history from 1700s to present; personal artifacts; uniforms; photographs; newspaper clippings; mobile one-person jail.
Hours & Admission Prices: Mon.-Fri. 8-5.

COLE LAND TRANSPORTATION MUSEUM, 405 Perry Rd., Bangor, ME 04401-6725. Mailing Address: 359 Perry Rd., Bangor, ME 04401-6723. Tel.: 207-990-3600. Fax: 207-990-2653.
E-mail: mail@colemuseum.com
Web Site: www.colemuseum.org
Founded: 1990.
Congressional District: 2
Key Personnel: Chm. (V), Garret E. Cole; Pres. (V), John I. Simpson.
Personnel Profile: Full-Time Paid 2; Part-Time Paid 6; Part-Time Volunteers 80.
Governing Authority: nonprofit organization. Tax-exempt.
Transportation Museum & the WWII, Korean & Vietnam Veterans Memorial.
Collections: period cars, trains, buses; military artifacts, equipment & vehicles.
Facilities: Books & pamphlets related to transportation & museum-related items for sale.
Activities: docent program; films; guided tours; participatory exhibits; TV programs.
Publications: books, As A Practical Matter: A Biography of Galen Cole, Allie Cole: A Maine Pioneer, The Cole Company: Started at Enfield Station in Maine, Allie Cole: The Man That Maine Made, Lest We Forget: A Pictorial History of Maine's Veterans, 1861-1995, The Collection - picture book of the major pieces in the museum; Quiet Courage - Stories of Maine Veterans.
Hours & Admission Prices: May-Nov. 11 daily 9-5. Adults $6, senior citizens $4; discounts to AAA members; students & children under 19 no charge. ♿
Attendance: 17,410 (accurate)

HOSE 5 FIRE MUSEUM, 247 State St., Bangor, ME 04401-5418. Tel.: 207-945-3229.
Web Site: www.bangormaine.gov/cs_ps_hose5museum.php
Fire Museum.
Collections: fire fighting artifacts; restored fire trucks including 1930 McCann Pumper, a 1917 Garford Pumper, a 1952 Mack LS Pumper, a 1947 Jeep, a 1939 Seagraves Pumper, Bangor's old Engine #2; fire gear; hand & breathing apparatus; alarm boxes; wooden water mains; photographs.
Activities: tours.
Hours & Admission Prices: Call for hours; tours by appointment. No charge; donations accepted.

MAINE DISCOVERY MUSEUM, 74 Main St., Bangor, ME 04401-6304. Tel.: 207-262-7200.
E-mail: astark@mainediscoverymuseum.org
Web Site: www.mainediscoverymuseum.org
Founded: 2001.
Congressional District: 2
Key Personnel: Exec. Dir., Andrea Stark.
Governing Authority: private; nonprofit organization. Tax-exempt: 501(c)(3).
Children's Museum.
Collections: hands-on exhibits.
Facilities: Museum-related items for sale.
Activities: educational programs.
Hours & Admission Prices: Winter: Tues.-Sat. 9:30-5, Sun. 12-5; Summer: call for extended hours; groups by appointment. Adults $7.50; discounts to groups; members and children one & under no charge. ACM reciprocal program & ASTC Passport program. ♿
Attendance: 65,000 (estimated)
Membership: You & Me $60; Grandparent $70; Household $90; Reciprocal $125.

UNIVERSITY OF MAINE MUSEUM OF ART, (M), 40 Harlow St., Bangor, ME 04401-5102. Tel.: 207-561-3350. Fax: 207-561-3351.
Web Site: www.umma.umaine.edu
Founded: 1946.
Congressional District: 2
Key Personnel: Asst. Museum Coord. & Membership Mgr., Kathryn Jovanelli; Exhibits Preparator, Stephen Ringle; Museum Dir., George Kinghorn; Education Coord., Gina Platt; Museum Technician, Aaron Pyle.
Personnel Profile: Full-Time Paid 5; Part-Time Volunteers 3; Interns 8.
Governing Authority: state. Parent Institution: University of Maine, Orono. Tax-exempt: 170(b)(1)(A).
Art Museum: housed in downtown Bangor's historic Norumbega Hall.
Collections: 18th to 20th-century American & European graphics & paintings; modern & historic Maine art; contemporary art.
Major Exhibits: Meg Chase, 1/15/10-4/3/10; Gerry Stecca Structures, 1/15/10-4/3/10; Bio-Permutation - Sculptures by David Isenhour, 1/15/10-4/3/10; I-95 Triennial Invitational Exhibition, 4/23/10-6/16/10.
Facilities: four galleries; classroom; fine art storage in Norumbega Hall.
Activities: modern & contemporary art exhibitions; guided tours; gallery talks; films; education programs for community; museums by mail; traveling exhibition service.
Publications: exhibition catalogues.
Hours & Admission Prices: Mon.-Sat. 10-5. Adults $3; discounts to AAM & NEMA members; University of Maine students & members no charge. Closed major holidays. ♿
Attendance: 25,000 (estimated)
Membership: Educator $35; Individual $50; Dual & Household $60; Patron $100; Sponsor $250; Benefactor $500; Corporate $1,000.

Bar Harbor

ABBE MUSEUM, (M), 26 Mount Desert St. & Sieur de Monts Spring, Acadia National Park, Bar Harbor, ME 04609. Mailing Address: P.O. Box 286, Bar Harbor, ME 04609-0286. Tel.: 207-288-3519. Fax: 207-288-8979.
E-mail: info@abbemuseum.org
Web Site: www.abbemuseum.org
Founded: 1928.
Congressional District: 2
Key Personnel: C.E.O., Cinnamon Catlin-Legutko; Pres. Bd., Sandy Wilcox, Ph.D.; Vice Pres., John Collier; Vice Pres., Barbara McLeod; Public Affairs, Jason K. Brown; Business Mgr., John Brown; Program Coord., Raney Bench; Collections Mgr., Julia Clark; Museum Shop Mgr. & Visitor Svcs. Mgr., Adrienne Redhair.
Personnel Profile: Full-Time Paid 7; Part-Time Paid 9.
Governing Authority: board of trustees; nonprofit organization. Branch Museum: 26 Mount Desert St., Bar Harbor, ME 04609. Tel.: 207-288-3519. Tax-exempt.
Archaeology, Anthropology & Ethnology Museum: located on site at Sieur de Monts Spring, within Acadia National Park and downtown Bar Harbor at 26 Mount Desert Street.
Collections: Maine Native American culture, history & archaeology; past & present Indian artifacts & handicrafts.
Research Fields: archaeology.
Facilities: 500-vol. library available for use within the museum by appointment. Bulletins & books related to artifacts of Mount Desert Island & the Frenchman Bay area for sale.
Activities: gallery talks; school programs; crafts classes & demonstrations; library; inter-museum loan, permanent & temporary exhibitions; archaeology field schools. Museum Sponsors: Native American Festival.
Publications: The Handycraft of The Modern Indians of Maine; Uses of Birchbark in the Northeast; Brief Description of Birchbark Canoe Building; Indian Games, Toys & Pastimes of Maine & The Maritime Indians; Island in Time; Dogs of the Northeastern Woodland Indians; The Indian Shell Heap: Archaeology of the Ruth Moore Site.
Hours & Admission Prices: Sieur de Monts: mid-May to mid-Oct. daily 9-4. Adults $3, children $1. Mount Desert St.: May 22-Nov. 2 daily 10-6; Nov. 6-May 21 Thurs.-Sat. 10-4. Adults $6, children $2; AAM & ICOM members, members, Native Americans, New England Museums Assoc. & Maine Archives no charge. ♿
Attendance: 23,741 (accurate)
Membership: Individual $40; Household $65; Sweetgrass Circle $125; Birchbark Circle $300; Brown Ash Circle $500; Quillwork Circle $1,500; Root Club Circle $2,500; Lifetime $5,000.

BAR HARBOR HISTORICAL SOCIETY, 33 Ledgelawn Ave., Bar Harbor, ME 04609-1303. Tel.: 207-288-0000 & 3807.
E-mail: bhhistorical@gwi.net
Web Site: barharborhistorical.org
Founded: 1946.
Congressional District: 2
Key Personnel: Pres. (V), Edwin Garrett; Cur., Debbie Dyer.
Personnel Profile: Part-Time Volunteers 6.
Governing Authority: historical society. Tax-exempt.
Local History Museum.
Collections: photographs; artifacts; maps; records; deeds; manuscripts; hotel registers; newspapers, 1881 to date; early business account books & records of '47 fire; scrapbooks; video cassette of early moving pictures & stereopticon views; microfilm of local newspapers 1850-present.
Research Fields: early history of town & area.
Facilities: research material available.
Activities: meetings; programs.
Publications: quarterly newsletter.
Hours & Admission Prices: mid-June to mid-Oct. Mon.-Sat. 1-4. No charge; donations accepted. Closed holidays.
Attendance: 1,500 (accurate)
Membership: Regular $20; Patron $50.

BAR HARBOR WHALE MUSEUM, (M), 52 West St., Bar Harbor, ME 04609-1858. Tel.: 207-288-0288.
E-mail: t.stephenson@coa.edu
Web Site: barharborwhalemuseum.org
Founded: 1991.
Key Personnel: Dir., Toby Stephenson; Museum Shop Mgr., Mindy Viechnicki.
Governing Authority: Parent Institution: College of the Atlantic. Tax-exempt.
Natural History Museum.
Collections: Gulf of Maine sea life and history.
Research Fields: marine studies.
Activities: educational programs.
Hours & Admission Prices: June & Sept.-Oct. daily 10-8; July-Aug. daily 9-9. No charge; donations accepted. ♿
Attendance: 70,000 (accurate)

GEORGE B. DORR MUSEUM OF NATURAL HISTORY, 105 Eden St., College of the Atlantic, Bar Harbor, ME 04609-1136. Tel.: 207-288-5395. Fax: 207-288-2917.
E-mail: museum@coa.edu
Web Site: www.coa.edu/dorr-museum-microsite.htm
Formerly: The Natural History Museum
Founded: 1982.
Congressional District: 2
Key Personnel: C.E.O. & College Pres., David Hales; Program Dir., Dianne Clendaniel; Dir., Dr. Stephen Ressel.
Personnel Profile: Part-Time Paid 3.
Governing Authority: College of the Atlantic; nonprofit. Tax-exempt.
Natural History Museum.
Collections: whale skeletons; taxidermy specimens; exhibits on relationships between people & the environment, mammals, birds & plants of Maine.
Research Fields: local natural history; exhibit preparation; design of interpretative programs.
Facilities: teaching area. Books & museum-related items for sale.
Activities: participatory programs for children & adults; lectures; slide shows; inter-museum loan, temporary & traveling exhibitions; summer field studies for children.
Publications: brochure; newsletter.
Hours & Admission Prices: Tues.-Sat. 10-5. No charge; donations accepted. ♿
Attendance: 10,000 (estimated)

MOUNT DESERT OCEANARIUM, 1351 State Rte. 3, Bar Harbor, ME 04609. Tel.: 207-288-5005.
E-mail: theoceanarium@earthlink.com
Web Site: theoceanarium.com
Founded: 1972.
Congressional District: 2
Key Personnel: C.E.O. & Dir., David K. Mills; Museum Shop Mgr., Audrey S. Mills.
Personnel Profile: Full-Time Paid 3; Part-Time Paid 2; Interns 8.
Oceanarium.
Collections: touch tank; lobster room; over 20 tanks of sea life from the coast of Maine; scallop tank; whale exhibit; sea exhibit including tides, waves, shells, sea salts, weather, survival, seaweeds, seagulls; fishing gallery; replica of wheelhouse; fishing gear diorama; lobster hatching process; harbor seals program; live salt marsh tours.
Research Fields: lobsters.
Facilities: aquarium. Books & sea related items for sale.
Activities: guided tours; lectures; organized education programs for children & college students affiliated with Kalamazoo College, Penn State University, Southampton College, Gordon College or Eastern Nazarene College; participatory exhibits; lobster & fishing programs. Museum Sponsors: unusual seafood festivals; Safety at Sea programs.
Publications: annual newsletter.
Hours & Admission Prices: Call for hours & admission prices. ♿

SIEUR DE MONTS SPRINGS NATURE CENTER, Acadia National Park, Rte. 233, Eagle Lake Rd., Bar Harbor, ME 04609. Mailing Address: P.O. Box 177, Bar Harbor, ME 04609-0177. Tel.: 207-288-3338. Fax: 207-288-8813.
E-mail: acadia_information@nps.gov
Founded: 1916.
Congressional District: 2
Key Personnel: Museum Cur., John McDade; Supt., Sheridan Steele; Museum Shop Mgr., Ann Cummings.
Personnel Profile: Full-Time Paid 1; Part-Time Paid 2; Part-Time Volunteers 1.
Governing Authority: federal. Parent Institution: National Park Service. Subsidiary Institution: Acadia National Park. Tax-exempt.
Nature Center & Botanical Gardens.
Collections: Acadia National Park & Mount Desert Island natural history specimens; William H. Proctor invertebrate collection; Ralph H. Long ornithological slides; Harold White Odonata collection.
Research Fields: natural history of Acadia National Park.
Facilities: Sieur de Monts Springs Nature Center; Wild Gardens of Acadia.
Activities: permanent & temporary exhibitions.
Hours & Admission Prices: May call for hours; June-Aug. 9-5; Sept. to early Oct. 9-4. No charge. ♿
Attendance: 65,500 (estimated)

WILLIAM OTIS SAWTELLE COLLECTIONS AND RESEARCH CENTER, Acadia National Park, Rte. 233, Eagle Lake Rd., Bar Harbor, ME 04609. Mailing Address: Acadia National Park, P.O. Box 177, Bar Harbor, ME 04609-0177. Tel.: 207-288-8729. Fax: 207-288-8709.
E-mail: john_mcdade@nps.gov
Web Site: www.nps.gov/acad/historyculture/collections.htm
Founded: 1916.
Congressional District: 2
Key Personnel: Supt., Sheridan Steele; Museum Cur., John McDade.
Personnel Profile: Full-Time Paid 1; Part-Time Volunteers 5.
Governing Authority: federal government. Parent Institution: National Park Service. Subsidiary Institution: Acadia National Park. Tax-exempt.
Research Center.
Collections: 1.5 million artifacts; archival documents, natural history specimens, & archeological materials pertaining to Acadia National Park; Saint Croix Island, International Historic Site; Town of Cranberry Isles; Naval Security Group Activity, Winter Harbor; Carroll family; Mount Desert Island; Maine; New France (Acadia).
Research Fields: genealogy; New France; History of Acadia National Park; natural history of Acadia National Park; Cranberry Isles; Saint Croix Island; archaeological; NSGA; Schoodic; Winter Harbor.
Facilities: collections & research center.
Activities: research.
Hours & Admission Prices: Tues.-Fri. 8:30-3:30 by appointment only. No charge. ♿
Attendance: 70 (accurate)

Bath

* **MAINE MARITIME MUSEUM, (M),** 243 Washington St., Bath, ME 04530-1638. Tel.: 207-443-1316. Fax: 207-443-1665.
E-mail: reservations@maritimeme.org
Web Site: mainemaritimemuseum.org
Founded: 1963.
Congressional District: 1
Key Personnel: Exec. Dir., Amy Lent; Dir. Finance, Jackie Berry; Cur., Dir. Library & Archivist, Nathan Lipfert; Cur. Exhibits, Chris Hall; Dir. Public Programs, Jason Morin; Volunteer Coord., Ann Harrison; Education Coord., James Nelson.
Personnel Profile: Full-Time Paid 12; Part-Time Paid 9; Part-Time Volunteers 200; Interns 2.
Governing Authority: nonprofit organization. Tax-exempt: 501(c)(3).
Maritime Museum & Historic Shipyard.
Collections: Maine maritime history: paintings; decorative & folk arts; photographs; ship plans; charts; maps; shipping & shipbuilding records; models; half models; tools; instruments; trade goods; seamen's possessions; small boats; Percy & Small shipyard historic structures; small craft center. Historic House: c.1880 Donnell House.
Research Fields: Maine maritime history; Percy & Small 19th-century shipyard with 5 original buildings.
Facilities: 10,000-vol. library on Maine & maritime history; Percy & Small 19th-century shipyard; Maine Coast & Lobstering Exhibit building. Museum-related items for sale.
Activities: tours; permanent & temporary exhibitions; school programs; visiting vessels & tall ships; annual symposium on maritime history; evening lecture & film series; shipyard crafts demonstrations; waterfront activities & Kennebec River cruises; volunteer program; wooden boat building classes.
Publications: quarterly newsletter; books, Maritime History of Bath & the Kennebec River Region; Half-hull Modeling, Lobstering & the Maine Coast; The Skolfields & Their Ships; The Tancook Whalers; The Wessaweskeag Thorndikes; boat plans; The Pattens of Bath; A Shipyard in Maine: Percy & Small and the Great Schooners; A Doryman's Day; Snow Squall.
Hours & Admission Prices: Daily 9:30-5. Adults $12, seniors $11, children 4-17 $9; discounts to groups, AAM, ICOM & CAMM members; children under 4, museum members & staff no charge. Closed New Year's Day; Thanksgiving & Christmas. ♿
Attendance: 40,000 (accurate)
Membership: Individual $35; Family $65; Sustaining $125; Shipwright $500; Downeaster $1,000.

Belfast

BELFAST HISTORICAL SOCIETY AND MUSEUM, 10 Market St., Belfast, ME 04915-6555. Tel.: 207-338-9229.
Web Site: belfastmuseum.org
Founded: 1955.
Historical Society Museum.
Collections: local maritime history; Percy Sanborn paintings; photographs; postcards; scrapbooks; maps.
Hours & Admission Prices: late June to Labor Day Tues.-Sat. 11-4. No charge; donations accepted.

Bethel

BETHEL HISTORICAL SOCIETY REGIONAL HISTORY CENTER, (M), 10-14 Broad St., Bethel, ME 04217-0012. Mailing Address: P.O. Box 12, Bethel, ME 04217-0012. Tel.: 207-824-2908; 800-824-2910. Fax: 207-824-0882.
E-mail: info@bethelhistorical.org
Web Site: www.bethelhistorical.org
Founded: 1966.
Congressional District: 2
Key Personnel: Pres. & Chm. Trustees, Susan Henling; Exec. Dir., Dr. Stanley Russell Howe; Registrar, Jane W. Hosterman; Museum Shop Mgr., Danna Nickerson.
Personnel Profile: Full-Time Paid 1; Part-Time Paid 2; Part-Time Volunteers 100; Interns 1.
Governing Authority: society; nonprofit organization. Parent Institution: Bethel Historical Society. Tax-exempt: 501(c)(3).
Regional History Center: housed in Robinson House; built in 1821.
Collections: early & mid-19th century furnishings; archival material relating to Oxford County & the White Mountains, Northern New England. Historic Building: 1813 federal style house.
Major Exhibits: To Improve the Farmer's Lot: The Grange in Maine, 11/09-12/10; White Mountain Club of Portland, 11/09-12/10.
Research Fields: Oxford County life; the White Mountains, Northern New England.
Facilities: 3,000-vol. library of books, pamphlets & journals relating to Oxford Co., Maine history & the White Mountains; technical library & research room available only on premises; 100-seat auditorium. Museum-related items for sale.
Activities: guided tours; lectures; films; gallery talks; formally organized educational programs; permanent & temporary exhibitions; training programs for professional museum workers; docent program; craft demonstrations; conferences; special events.
Publications: The Courier; The Broad Street Herald.
Hours & Admission Prices: July-Labor Day Tues.-Fri. 10-12 & 1-4, Sun. & holidays 1-4; Sept.-June Tues.-Fri. 10-12 & 1-4; other times by appointment. Adults $3, children under 12 $1.50; discounts to AAM, AAA & Mobil members; members no charge. ♿
Attendance: 5,000
Membership: Student $5; Senior $10; Sustaining $15; Contributing $25; Patron $35; Benefactor $45; Corporate & Business $100, $150, $200; Life Individual $150; Life Couple & Senior Life Individual $250; Senior Life Couple $350.

Blue Hill

BLUE HILL HISTORICAL SOCIETY, Water St., Blue Hill, ME 04614. Mailing Address: P.O. Box 710, Blue Hill, ME 04614-0710.
Web Site: www.bluehillhistory.org
Founded: 1902.
Historical Society Museum: housed in Holt House, built in 1815.
Collections: period furniture & clothing; photographs; records & memorabilia from the 18th-20th centuries.
Hours & Admission Prices: July-Sept. Tues.-Fri. 1-4, Sat. 11-2.

THE JONATHAN FISHER MEMORIAL, INC., 44 Mines Rd., Blue Hill, ME 04614. Mailing Address: P.O. Box 537, Blue Hill, ME 04614-0537. Tel.: 207-374-2459. Fax: 207-374-5082.
E-mail: info@jonathanfisherhouse.org
Web Site: www.jonathanfisherhouse.org
Formerly: Parson Fisher House
Founded: 1954.
Congressional District: 2
Key Personnel: Pres. (V), Brad Emerson.
Governing Authority: nonprofit corporation; Jonathan Fisher Memorial, Inc. Tax-exempt.
Historic House: 1814 Jonathan Fisher House.
Collections: paintings; woodcuts; art work & furniture made by Jonathan Fisher; diaries, journals & books; manuscripts.
Facilities: homestead of Jonathan Fisher.
Activities: guided tours; permanent exhibitions.
Publications: book, Scripture Animals by Jonathan Fisher; Jonathan Fisher-Maine Parson by Mary Ellen Chase.
Hours & Admission Prices: July 5-Oct. 15 Thurs.-Sat. 1-4; other times by appointment. No charge; donations accepted. ♿
Attendance: 350 (estimated)
Membership: Annual $30; Sustaining $50; Contributing $100; Life $1,000.

Boothbay

BOOTHBAY RAILWAY VILLAGE, (M), 586 Wiscasset Rd., Boothbay, ME 04537. Mailing Address: P.O. Box 123, Boothbay, ME 04537-0123. Tel.: 207-633-4727. Fax: 207-633-4733 (call first).
E-mail: staff@railwayvillage.org
Web Site: www.railwayvillage.org
Founded: 1962.
Congressional District: 1
Key Personnel: Dir., Robert Ryan; Sec. & Museum Shop Mgr., Maureen H. Stormont.
Personnel Profile: Full-Time Paid 7; Part-Time Paid 5; Part-Time Volunteers 6.
Governing Authority: nonprofit organization. Tax-exempt.
Transportation Museum.
Collections: antique auto display; railroad memorabilia; transportation; The Thorndike Railroad Station; Freeport Station; period engines; turn-of-the-century displays; vintage steam operated narrow gauge locomotives; period vehicles.
Facilities: Early New England gifts & books on period autos & railroads for sale.
Activities: temporary exhibitions. Museum Sponsors: Steam train rides; special events.
Publications: newsletter, The Village Dispatch.
Hours & Admission Prices: Memorial Day to mid-June Sat.-Sun. 9:30-5; mid-June to mid-Oct. daily 9:30-5. Adults $9, children $5; members no charge. ♿
Attendance: 25,000 (accurate)
Membership: Individual $50; Family & Grandparent $60; Patron $85; Supporting $125.

Boothbay Harbor

BOOTHBAY REGION ART FOUNDATION, INC., One Townsend Ave., Boothbay Harbor, ME 04538-1765. Mailing Address: P.O. Box 124, Boothbay Harbor, ME 04538-0124. Tel.: 207-633-2703.
E-mail: braf@boothbayartists.org
Web Site: www.boothbayartists.org
Founded: 1964.
Congressional District: 1
Key Personnel: Pres. (V), James Taliana.
Personnel Profile: Full-Time Paid 1; Part-Time Volunteers 30.
Governing Authority: nonprofit; board of trustees. Tax-exempt.
Art Gallery.
Collections: local artists.
Activities: art exhibits; school art show.
Hours & Admission Prices: Mon.-Sat. 10-5, Sun. 1-5. No charge; donations suggested.
Attendance: 10,000 (estimated)
Membership: Individual $45; Contributing $50; Exhibiting Artist $65; Patron $100 & up.

Bradley

MAINE FOREST AND LOGGING MUSEUM, 54 Government Rd., Bradley, ME 04411. Mailing Address: P.O. Box 456, Orono, ME 04473-0456. Tel.: 207-974-6278.
E-mail: info@leonardsmills.com
Key Personnel: Dir., John Daigle
History Museum.
Collections: late 18th century life & history; period furnishing & artifacts; photographs.
Activities: tours; educational programs.
Hours & Admission Prices: April-Oct. by appointment.

Brewer

BREWER HISTORICAL SOCIETY'S CLEWLEY MUSEUM, 199 Wilson St., Brewer, ME 04412-2029. Tel.: 207-989-5013. Fax: 207-989-2693.
Personnel Profile: Part-Time Volunteers 10.
Governing Authority: Tax-exempt.
History Museum.
Collections: local history & culture; Maine's Underground Railroad; Civil War; photographs.
Activities: groups tours; educational programs.
Hours & Admission Prices: Museum: Summer Tues. & 4th Sat. 1-4; Spring & Fall Tues. & 4th Sat. 10-1. Park: daily. No charge; donations accepted.
Membership: Individual $10; Family $25; Sustaining $100.

Bridgton

BRIDGTON HISTORICAL SOCIETY, Gibbs Ave., Bridgton, ME 04009. Mailing Address: P.O. Box 44, Bridgton, ME 04009-0044. Tel.: 207-647-3699 (Gibbs Ave. museum) & 9954 (Narramissic).
E-mail: info@bridgetonhistory.org
Web Site: www.bridgtonhistory.org
Founded: 1953.
Congressional District: 1
Key Personnel: Pres. (V), Ned Allen.
Personnel Profile: Part-Time Paid 2; Part-Time Volunteers 25; Interns 1.
Governing Authority: nonprofit corporation. Subsidiary Institutions: Gibbs Avenue Museum, Tel. 207-647-3699; Narramissic, the Historic Peabody Fitch Farm, Ingalls Rd., South Bridgton, Tel. 207-647-9954. Tax-exempt: 501(c)(3).
Historical Society Museum & Historic House Museum: housed in 1902 former firehouse.
Collections: artifacts; decorative arts; lumber & textile industries' mechanical implements; photographs; 18th- & 19th-century rural New England documents; narrow-gauge railway documents. Historic House: 1797 Narramissic.
Research Fields: genealogical; local architecture & industries; social history.
Facilities: library of local & state history, school records, maps, 1750s-present newspaper files & local archival records available for use by arrangement with the curator or librarian.
Activities: guided tours; films; craft demos & lectures.
Publications: book, Bridgton History: 1768-1968; Rediscover Brighton's Main Street.
Hours & Admission Prices: Call for hours & admission prices. ♿
Membership: Student & Retiree $10; Individual $15; Family $20; Contributing $30; Sustaining $50; Patron $100; Life $500.

THE RUFUS PORTER MUSEUM AND CULTURAL HERITAGE CENTER, 67 N. High St., Bridgton, ME 04009-1111. Mailing Address: P.O. Box 544, Bridgton, ME 04009-0544. Tel.: 207-647-2828.
Web Site: www.rufusportermuseum.org
Key Personnel: Pres., Carolyn Stanhope; Project Mgr., Nancy Smoak; Cur., Julie Lindberg
History Museum.
Collections: paintings by Rufus Porter.
Hours & Admission Prices: June-Oct. Wed.-Sat. 12-4; other times by appointment. Adults $5, students & groups over 15 $4; children 12 & under no charge.

Brunswick

* **BOWDOIN COLLEGE MUSEUM OF ART, (M),** Walker Art Bldg., Brunswick, ME 04011. Mailing Address: 9400 College Station, Brunswick, ME 04011-8494. Tel.: 207-725-3275. Fax: 207-725--3762.
E-mail: artmuseum@bowdoin.edu
Web Site: www.bowdoin.edu/art-museum
Founded: 1811.
Congressional District: 1
Key Personnel: Dir., Kevin Salatino; Asst. Dir. Operations, Suzanne K. Bergeron; Registrar, Laura J. Latman; Tech. & Prep., Jose L. Ribas; Museum Shop Mgr., Liza Nelson.
Personnel Profile: Full-Time Paid 8; Part-Time Paid 2; Part-Time Volunteers 45; Interns 1.
Governing Authority: college. Parent Institution: Bowdoin College. Tax-exempt: 101(6).
Art Museum: housed in 1894, Walker Art Building, designed by Charles Follen McKim, located on the campus of Bowdoin College.
Collections: Assyrian sculpture; Greek & Roman antiquities; European & American paintings, prints, drawings, sculpture & decorative arts; Kress Study collection; Molinari Medals & Plaquettes; Winslow Homer memorabilia; Far Eastern ceramics; African & pre-Columbian sculpture.
Research Fields: American & European art; Winslow Homer; medals & plaquettes.
Facilities: collections available for use by scholars. Catalogues of collections & special exhibitions, art books, postcards & posters for sale.
Activities: guided tours; lectures; gallery talks; formally organized education programs for adults & undergraduate college students; inter-museum loan, permanent, temporary & traveling exhibitions.
Publications: catalogues of the permanent collections & temporary exhibitions.
Hours & Admission Prices: Tues.-Wed. & Fri.-Sat. 10-5, Thurs. 10-8:30, Sun. 1-5. No charge; donations accepted. Closed holidays. ♿
Attendance: 45,000 (accurate)
Membership: Student $15; Individual $ 35; Dual/Family $60; Sponsor $100; Patron $250; Benefactor $500; Director's Circle $1,000 & up.

* **THE PEARY-MACMILLAN ARCTIC MUSEUM, (M),** Bowdoin College, 9500 College Station, Brunswick, ME 04011-8495. Tel.: 207-725-3416 & 3062. Fax: 207-725-3499.
Web Site: www.bowdoin.edu/arctic-museum
Founded: 1967.
Key Personnel: Dir., Dr. Susan A. Kaplan; Technician & Designer, David R. Maschino; Museum Outreach & Svcs. Coord., Amy Hawkes; Cur., Dr. Genevieve LeMoine; Sec. to Dir., Kristi Clifford; Asst. Cur., Anne Witty; Exhibit Tech., Steve Bunn.
Personnel Profile: Full-Time Paid 5; Part-Time Paid 2; Part-Time Volunteers 25; Interns 7.
Governing Authority: college. Parent Institution: Bowdoin College. Tax-exempt: 501(c)(3).
College Museum.
Collections: arctic exploration, ecology, anthropology, archeology; prehistoric & historic Inuit (Eskimo) artifacts; contemporary Inuit arts & crafts; arctic flora & fauna; exploration equipment; nautical equipment; archives; photographs.
Research Fields: archeology; cultural anthropology; ecology of Arctic North America & Scandinavia.
Facilities: 3,000-vol. library pertaining to arctic exploration & research. Inuit arts & crafts, books & other related items for sale.
Activities: guided tours; lectures; films; docent program; organized education programs for children, undergraduate & graduate students affiliated with Bowdoin College.
Hours & Admission Prices: Tues.-Sat. 10-5, Sun. 2-5. No charge; donations accepted. Closed national holidays.
Attendance: 15,437 (accurate)

PEJEPSCOT HISTORICAL SOCIETY, (M), 159 Park Row, Brunswick, ME 04011-2005. Tel.: 207-729-6606. Fax: 207-729-6012.
E-mail: pejepscot@suscom-maine.net
Web Site: www.community.curtislibrary.com/pejepscot.htm
Founded: 1888.
Congressional District: 1
Key Personnel: Exec. Dir., Brian Collins; Collections Management Specialist, John B. Briley.
Personnel Profile: Full-Time Paid 1; Part-Time Paid 1; Part-Time Volunteers 60; Interns 1.
Governing Authority: society. Branch Museums: Skolfield-Whittier House Museum, 161 Park Row, Brunswick; Joshua Chamberlain Museum, 226 Maine St., Brunswick. Tax-exempt: 501(c)(3).
Historical Society Museums.
Collections: regional history items; domestic artifacts; garments; early craft & industry items; local history archives; Joshua L. Chamberlain research collection. Historic Houses: 1858 Captain Alfred Skolfield-Whitter House; General Joshua Chamberlain House.
Research Fields: local history; Maine; Civil War & Joshua L. Chamberlain; Victorian period; industrial history; Franco-American history; women's history.
Facilities: archive room.
Activities: lectures; permanent & temporary exhibitions; tours; slide show talks; school programs; community outings.
Publications: newsletter.
Hours & Admission Prices: Skolfield-Whittier House: Memorial Day to Columbus Day Thurs.-Sat. Tours 11 & 2. Adults $5, children $2.50; discounts to AAM members; members no charge. Chamberlain House: Memorial Day to Columbus Day Tues.-Sat. 10-4. Adults $5, children $2.50; discounts to AAM members; members no charge. Combination tickets to both houses available. Pejepscot Museum: Tues.-Sat. 10-4. No charge; donations accepted. Closed holidays. ♿
Attendance: 12,000 (accurate)
Membership: Individual $35; Family $50; Contributing $75 & up.

Bryant Pond

WOODSTOCK HISTORICAL SOCIETY, 70 S. Main St., Bryant Pond, ME 04219-6424. Tel.: 207-665-2450.
Founded: 1979.
Key Personnel: Pres. (V), Olive Risko; Treas., Paul Billings; Cur., Larry Billings.
Personnel Profile: Full-Time Volunteers 1; Part-Time Volunteers 20.
Governing Authority: private; nonprofit. Tax-exempt: 501(c)(3).
Historical Society Museum.
Collections: paintings & artifacts from the town of Woodstock, Maine.
Facilities: library of books pertaining to items of local interest. Museum-related items for sale.
Activities: guided tours. Annual Event: History Day in August.
Hours & Admission Prices: Museum: June-Sept. Sat. 1-4. Meetings: 7pm second Sat. of each month. No charge; donations accepted.
Attendance: 250 (estimated)
Membership: Annual $2; Life (over 54) $15; Life (under 55) $25.

Bucksport

BUCKSPORT HISTORICAL SOCIETY, INC., 379 Main St., Bucksport, ME 04416. Mailing Address: P.O. Box 798, Bucksport, ME 04416-0798. Tel.: 207-469-0924.
Founded: 1964.
Congressional District: 2
Key Personnel: Vice Pres., Mrs. Arthur M. Joost.
Governing Authority: nonprofit. Tax-exempt: 501(c)(3).
General Museum: housed in 1874 Old Maine Central Railroad Station.
Collections: marine; military; naval; transportation; tools; toys; clothing; furniture; quilts; pictures; town history; newspapers; Admiral Perry collection; manuscripts.
Research Fields: local history.
Facilities: 200-vol. library of local history books & ship logs available for research by special request; reading room.
Activities: permanent & temporary exhibitions.
Publications: booklets, Did You Know?; Jonathan Buck of Bucksport; pamphlet, Bucksport Historical Society.
Hours & Admission Prices: July-Aug. Wed.-Fri. 1-4; other times by appointment. Admission $1; members no charge. ♿
Attendance: 350 (accurate)
Membership: Annual $5; Sustaining $10; Life $100.

NORTHEAST HISTORIC FILM, 85 Main St., Bucksport, ME 04416. Mailing Address: P.O. Box 900, Bucksport, ME 04416-0900. Tel.: 207-469-0924.
Web Site: www.ddfilm.org
Founded: 1986.
Key Personnel: Exec. Dir., David S. Weiss.
Personnel Profile: Full-Time Paid 2; Full-Time Volunteers 1; Part-Time Paid 8; Interns 2.
Governing Authority: Tax-exempt.
Historic Building: housed in a 1916 cinema, The Alamo Theatre.
Collections: motion picture history; cultural history of movie-going; videos; projectors; cameras; editing equipment; posters; photographs; theater seats; tickets; advertisements.
Facilities: library; study center. Museum-related items for sale.
Activities: group tours; shows current Hollywood features; research. Museum Sponsors: Film Symposium in summer; Northeast Silent Film Festival.
Publications: biannual, Moving Image Review.
Hours & Admission Prices: Mon.-Fri. 9-4; call for additional hours. ♿
Attendance: 15,000 (estimated)
Membership: $20; $35; $50; $60; $100; $150; $250; $500; $1,000.

Burlington

STEWART M. LORD MEMORIAL HISTORICAL SOCIETY, INC., Rte. 188, Burlington, ME 04417. Mailing Address: P.O. Box 307, Howland, ME 04448-0367. Tel.: 207-732-3129.
E-mail: info@smlmhs.org
Web Site: www.smlmhs.org
Founded: 1968.
Key Personnel: Cur., Fern P. Cummings.
Personnel Profile: Part-Time Volunteers 10.
Governing Authority: society.
History Museum.
Collections: pictures; documents; carriages; lumbering & household equipment of 1800s; Maine residents from 1800 to present; farming. Historical Buildings: 1850 general store, 1844 tavern; Page Building: wagons, surry boat; W.W. Building.
Research Fields: local history.
Activities: permanent & temporary exhibitions.
Publications: biannual newsletter.
Hours & Admission Prices: July-Labor Day Sun. 2-4; other times by appointment. No charge; donations accepted. ♿
Attendance: 145 (estimated)
Membership: Annual $5.

Camden

CONWAY HOMESTEAD AND CRAMER MUSEUM, U.S. Rte. 1, Camden-Rockport Lane, Camden, ME 04843. Mailing Address: P.O. Box 747, Rockport, ME 04856-0747. Tel.: 207-236-2257.
E-mail: info@conwayhousemuseum.org
Web Site: www.crmuseum.org
Founded: 1962.
Congressional District: 1
Key Personnel: Dir. & C.E.O., Marlene Hall; Pres., Brenda Barrett; Museum Shop Mgr., Brenda Richardson.

Personnel Profile: Full-Time Paid 2; Full-Time Volunteers 2.
Governing Authority: Camden-Rockport Historical Society. Tax-exempt: 501(c)(3).
Historical Society Museum Complex.
Collections: archives; paintings; books; photographs; costumes; folklore; local history; marine; musical instruments; manuscripts; homestead & agricultural artifacts; Mary Meeker Cramer Museum. Historic Buildings: c.1780 Conway House; barn; Blacksmith Shop; Herb Garden; 1820 Maple Sugar House.
Facilities: 500-vol. library of historical & genealogical books available for research on premises; reading room.
Activities: guided tours; permanent & temporary exhibitions; walking, bicycle & car tour of district. Museum Sponsors: Conway Day celebration; 1820 Maple Sugar Sunday; Heritage Day Camp for children; Coffee/Chat Lecture series.
Publications: book, History of Camden; Bicentennial edition of 1859 History of Camden; newsletter, Camden, Rockport Historical Society Newsletter.
Hours & Admission Prices: July-Aug. Tues.-Fri. 11-3; other times by appointment. Call for admission prices. ♿
Attendance: 1,724 (estimated)
Membership: Annual $15; Family $25; Supporting $50.

Caribou

THE NYLANDER MUSEUM OF NATURAL HISTORY, 657 Main St., Caribou, ME 04736-4431. Tel.: 207-493-4209. Fax: 207-498-3954.
E-mail: nylander@mainerr.com
Web Site: www.nylandermuseum.org
Founded: 1938.
Congressional District: 2
Key Personnel: Exec. Dir., Jeanie L. McGowan; Pres. Bd. Trustee, Deborah Nichols; Aide & Gift Shop Mgr., Liz Maifield.
Personnel Profile: Part-Time Paid 2; Part-Time Volunteers 15.
Governing Authority: municipal. Parent Institution: City of Caribou. Tax-exempt.
Natural History Museum.
Collections: fossils; shells; mineralogy; geology; early man artifacts; mounted birds; mounted mammals of Maine; wetlands; Native American medicinal herb garden
Research Fields: geology; conchology; paleontology; artifacts of early man.
Facilities: resource library with books pertaining to native wild flowers, fresh water mollusks, fossils in the area & Northeastern Native Americans available for use in the museum by reservation only. Museum-related items for sale.
Activities: guided tours; permanent, temporary & traveling exhibitions; pre-arranged school programs throughout the year; traveling kits for science education programs.
Hours & Admission Prices: May -Oct. Mon.-Sat. 12:30-4:30; Nov.-April Wed. 9-5, Tues. & Thurs. by appointment. No charge; donations accepted. ♿
Attendance: 701 (accurate)
Membership: Friend $20; Patron $50; Donor $100.

Castine

CASTINE SCIENTIFIC SOCIETY AKA WILSON MUSEUM, (M), 120 Perkins St., Castine, ME 04421. Mailing Address: P.O. Box 196, Castine, ME 04421-0196. Tel.: 207-326-9247. Fax: 207-326-9237.
E-mail: info@wilsonmuseum.org
Web Site: www.wilsonmuseum.org
Founded: 1921.
Congressional District: 2
Key Personnel: Dir., Patricia Hutchins; Administrative Asst., Debra Morehouse.
Personnel Profile: Full-Time Paid 2; Part-Time Paid 6; Part-Time Volunteers 20.
Governing Authority: nonprofit organization. Tax-exempt: 501(c)(3).
History Museum.
Collections: Historic Buildings: 1921 Wilson Museum; 1763-83 John Perkins House: furnished with heirlooms & period pieces; blacksmith shop: working smithy.
Research Fields: local history; geology.
Facilities: library pertaining to anthropology, archaeology & local history for use by appointment; 6,000 sq. ft. exhibit space.
Activities: guided tours; blacksmith & living history demonstrations; lectures; workshops; permanent exhibitions.
Publications: newsletter; Wilson Museum Bulletin.
Hours & Admission Prices: Perkins House & Blacksmith Shop: July-Aug. Wed. & Sun. 2-5. Perkins House: $5 per person; discounts to National Trust, NEMA Institutional staff, AAM & AAA members. Blacksmith Shop: no charge. Wilson Museum: May 27 to Sept. daily 2-5. No charge; donations accepted.
Attendance: 4,000 (estimated)
Membership: Active $25; Life $500.

Chebeague Island

MUSEUM OF CHEBEAGUE HISTORY, 137 South Rd., Chebeague Island, ME 04017-3100. Tel.: 207-846-5237.
E-mail: history@chebeague.net
Governing Authority: Parent Institution: Chebeague Island Historical Society.
History Museum: built in 1871.
Collections: local history & culture; photographs; furnishings; personal artifacts.
Hours & Admission Prices: Tues.-Sun. 1-6. No charge; donations accepted.

Columbia Falls

RUGGLES HOUSE SOCIETY, 1/4 mile off U.S. Rte. 1, 146 Main St., Columbia Falls, ME 04623. Mailing Address: 298 Tenan Lane, Cherryfield, ME 04622-4334. Tel.: 207-483-4637 & 546-7903.
Web Site: www.ruggleshouse.org
Founded: 1949.
Congressional District: 2
Key Personnel: Pres., Larry D. Smith; Sec., Ellen Tenan.
Personnel Profile: Part-Time Paid 3; Part-Time Volunteers 12.
Governing Authority: society; bd. dirs. Tax-exempt: 501(c)(3).
Historic House Museum: 1818 Ruggles House.
Collections: genealogical records; photographs; maps; news files; glass; hand-carved woodwork; period furniture; children's toys & furniture.
Activities: guided tours.
Publications: leaflet.
Hours & Admission Prices: June to mid-Oct. Mon.-Sat. 9:30-4:30, Sun. 11-4:30. Adults $5, children $2. ♿
Attendance: 1,800 (estimated)
Membership: $10 & up.

Corinth

CORINTH HISTORICAL SOCIETY, Old Grange Hall, Corinth, ME 04427. Mailing Address: P.O. Box 541, Corinth, ME 04427-0541. Tel.: 207-285-7885.
Key Personnel: Pres. (V), Sharon Buswell; Cur., Betty LaForge.
Personnel Profile: Part-Time Volunteers 8.
Governing Authority: private; nonprofit organization. Tax-exempt: 501(c)(3).
Historical Society Museum: built in 1907.
Collections: early plows & farm implements; period horse drawn fire wagon & hearse; trolley seats; period toys; school desks; military artifacts; WWI, WWII & Korean war uniforms; Civil War guns; period sewing machines, washing machines & kitchen items; quilts; handmade children's clothing & wedding dress.
Research Fields: Corinth history.
Facilities: library. Museum-related items for sale.
Activities: Annual Events: 4th Grade Children's History Day for Corinth Grade School; Quilt Show.
Publications: quarterly newsletter, Corinth Historical Society.
Hours & Admission Prices: June to 1st weekend Oct. Wed. 2-7. No charge; donations accepted. ♿
Attendance: 200 (estimated)
Membership: Junior $3; Individual $10; Benevolent Donor $25; Lifetime $100; Benefactor $500.

Deer Isle

DEER ISLE-STONINGTON HISTORICAL SOCIETY, 416 Sunset Rd., Rte. 15A, Deer Isle, ME 04627. Mailing Address: P.O. Box 652, Deer Isle, ME 04627-0652. Tel.: 207-348-6400.
Founded: 1959.
Congressional District: 2
Personnel Profile: Part-Time Volunteers 27.
Governing Authority: bd. of trustees; nonprofit. Tax-exempt.
History Museum.
Collections: preservation project; marine; archives; agriculture; costumes; manuscripts; Indian artifacts; basketry; genealogical. Historic House: 1830 Salome Sellers Home.
Research Fields: genealogy; local history; Americana.
Facilities: 350-vol. library of marine & historic books; family genealogies; reading room.
Activities: permanent & temporary exhibitions.
Publications: semi-annual newsletter; booklet, Salome Sellers; Images of America: Deer Isle and Stonington, Arcadia, 2004; Postcard History Series; Deer Isle and Stonington, Arcadia 2008.
Hours & Admission Prices: July-Sept. Wed. & Fri.-Sat. 1-4; Oct.-May Wed. & Fri. 1-4 for research only. No charge; donations accepted.

Attendance: 400 (estimated)
Membership: Individual $15; Family $35; Contributing $50.

Dennysville

DENNYS RIVER HISTORICAL SOCIETY, 9 King St., Dennysville, ME 04628. Mailing Address: P.O. Box 11, Dennysville, ME 04628-0011. Tel.: 207-726-3905.
Founded: 1987.
Congressional District: 2
Key Personnel: Pres., Ronald A. Windhorst; Treas., Richard H. Hobart; Dir. Programs & Devel., Colin J.C. Windhorst; Vice Pres. Public Rels., William Attick; Sec., Kathrine Attick; Cur., Melinda Jaques; Archivist & Editor, Rebecca Hobart.
Personnel Profile: Part-Time Volunteers 22.
Governing Authority: private; nonprofit organization. Tax-exempt: 501(c)(3).
History Museum.
Collections: history of Eastern Maine from prehistoric times to present; Native American artifacts; late 18th-19th century village history; photographs; furniture; costumes; rural industry & transportation; family papers; archives.
Research Fields: 19th century costumes; architectural & building history in Eastern Maine; documenting family archival collections on Dennys River; rural industry & commerce; WWI in rural Maine.
Facilities: 150-vol. library; reading room; 1,000 sq. ft. exhibit space.
Activities: formal education programs; guided tours; lectures & seminars; school loan service; study clubs; temporary exhibitions. Annual Event: Summer Historical Tours.
Publications: occasional monographs; quarterly newsletter, Dennys River Historical Society Newsletter.
Hours & Admission Prices: Tues.-Fri. 1-4. No charge; donations accepted. Closed national & state holidays.
Attendance: 450 (estimated)
Membership: Individual $15; Family $25.

Dexter

DEXTER HISTORICAL SOCIETY CAMPUS, 3 Water St. & 12 Church St., Dexter, ME 04930. Mailing Address: P.O. Box 481, Dexter, ME 04930-0481. Tel.: 207-924-5721.
E-mail: info@dexterhistoricalsociety.com
Web Site: dexterhistoricalsociety.com
Formerly: Dexter Historical Society Museum
Founded: 1966.
Congressional District: 2
Key Personnel: Dir. & Cur., Richard Whitney.
Personnel Profile: Part-Time Paid 1; Part-Time Volunteers 6; Interns 1.
Governing Authority: nonprofit. Tax-exempt.
General Museum: housed in 1854 Grist Mill, located on the site 1818 canal.
Collections: artifacts of local historical interest; pictures; manuscripts; antiques; genealogy. Historic Buildings: 1854 Grist Mill, 1825 Millers House, 1845 one room schoolhouse; 1836 former Town Hall (Woolen Mill Office) now Abbott Museum.
Research Fields: local history & genealogy.
Facilities: 1,000-vol. library. Museum-related gift items for sale.
Activities: arts festivals; permanent exhibitions; seasonal public displays; outreach programs.
Publications: Dexter: Spirit of An Age; Our Neighborly Neighbors, Rural Dexter 1800-2000; Bubbles in the Sun; Growing Up In Dexter, Maine.
Hours & Admission Prices: mid-June to Labor Day Mon.-Fri. 10-4, Sat. 1-4, Sun. & holidays by appointment. Abbott Museum: Memorial Day to Columbus Day Mon.-Sat. 10-4; Oct.-May Wed.-Fri. 1-4, Sat. 10-4. No charge; donations accepted. Closed Independence Day. ♿
Attendance: 2,000 (estimated)
Membership: Annual $10.

Dover-Foxcroft

BLACKSMITH SHOP MUSEUM, 103 Dawes Rd., Dover-Foxcroft, ME 04426-3732. Tel.: 207-564-8618.
E-mail: dlockwood3@verizon.net
Founded: 1963.
Key Personnel: Pres. (V), Mary Annis; Cur., Dave Lockwood; Treas., James Annis; Sec., Susan Burleigh.
Governing Authority: society. Affiliated with Dover-Foxcroft Historical Society. Tax-exempt.
Historic Building: 1863 Blacksmith Shop.
Collections: early blacksmith tools & equipment.
Research Fields: smithing in late 19th-century.
Activities: permanent exhibitions.
Publications: brochure.
Hours & Admission Prices: May-Oct. daily 8-8. No charge; donations accepted.
Attendance: 250 (estimated)
Membership: Individual $10.

Dresden

1761 POWNALBOROUGH COURTHOUSE, 23 Courthouse Rd., Rte. 128, Dresden, ME 04342. Mailing Address: P.O. Box 61, Wiscasset, ME 04578-0061. Tel.: 207-737-2504 & 882-6817.
E-mail: lcha@wiscasset.net
Web Site: www.lincolncountyhistory.org
Founded: 1954.
Congressional District: 1
Key Personnel: Exec. Dir., Jay Robbins; Court House Chm., Steve Eagles.
Personnel Profile: Full-Time Paid 1; Part-Time Paid 6; Part-Time Volunteers 15.
Governing Authority: nonprofit. Parent Institution: Lincoln County Historical Association, Inc. Federal St., Wiscasset, ME 04578. Tax-exempt.
Historic Building: 1761 Pownalborough Court House.
Collections: mid 1700s-1900, pre-Revolutionary War court room; original court room, family rooms, tavern & ice making.
Research Fields: archaeological; Fort Shirley; period cemetery; 1761 court house.
Facilities: nature trails; picnic area.
Activities: guided tours; special exhibits; ice making. Special Events: Memorial Day Observance; Fall & Winter lecture series.
Publications: newsletter, The Lincoln County Chronicle; brochure, The Pre-Revolutionary Pownalborough Court House; 19th Century Law and Order: The 1811 Old Jail and 1839 Jailer House Museum; Preserve Local History: The Lincoln County Historical Association.
Hours & Admission Prices: Memorial Day to June & Sept.-Columbus Day Sat. 10-4, Sun. 12-4; July-Aug. Tues.-Fri. 10-4. Adults $4; AAA members & children no charge.
Attendance: 1,000 (estimated)
Membership: Single $25; Family $35; Supporting $60; Sustaining $100.

Eastport

BORDER HISTORICAL SOCIETY, 74 Washington St., Eastport, ME 04631. Mailing Address: P.O. Box 95, Eastport, ME 04631-0095. Tel.: 207-853-2328.
E-mail: borderhistoricalsociety@yahoo.com
Web Site: borderhistoricalsociety.com
Key Personnel: Pres., Frances Raye
Historical Society Museum.
Collections: local history & culture; photographs.
Hours & Admission Prices: Call for hours. No charge; donations accepted.

Ellsworth

STANWOOD WILDLIFE SANCTUARY, Rte. 3 289 High St., Ellsworth, ME 04605. Mailing Address: P.O. Box 485, Ellsworth, ME 04605-0485. Tel.: 207-667-8460.
E-mail: birdsacre@hotmail.com
Web Site: www.birdsacre.com
Founded: 1959.
Key Personnel: Pres. (V), Stanley Richmond; Chm. (V), Donald Knowles; Museum Shop Mgr., Carmen Morse.
Personnel Profile: Full-Time Volunteers 1; Part-Time Volunteers 6; Interns 1.
Governing Authority: nonprofit. Tax-exempt: 501(c)(3).
Homestead Museum & Nature Center: home of Cordelia Stanwood, pioneer naturalist, photographer & conservationist.
Collections: Victorian furnishings; wood carvings; bird mounts; pioneer photography.
Facilities: library; bird rehabilitation facilities; bird shelters; picnic areas; trails. Gift items for sale.
Activities: museum tours; on & off site educational programs for children; natural history programs.
Publications: biannual newsletter, The Birdsacre Seasonal.
Hours & Admission Prices: Sanctuary: daily dawn-dark. Homestead Museum: mid-June to mid-Oct. Nature Center daily 10-4. No charge; donations accepted. Closed Independence Day; Labor Day. ♿
Attendance: 10,000 (estimated)
Membership: Support Categories: Sustaining $10; Supporting $25; Patron $50; Benefactor $100; Sponsor $500.

THE TELEPHONE MUSEUM, 166 Winkumpaugh Rd., Ellsworth, ME 04605-3035. Mailing Address: P.O. Box 1377, Ellsworth, ME 04605-1377. Tel.: 207-667-9491. Fax: 207-667-9491 (call first).
E-mail: switchboard@downeast.net

Web Site: www.thetelephonemuseum.org
Founded: 1983.
Key Personnel: Dir. & Pres. (V), Sandra Galley; Treas., David Thompson.
Personnel Profile: Full-Time Volunteers 2; Part-Time Volunteers 20.
Governing Authority: private; nonprofit organization. Tax-exempt: 501(c)(3).
Communications Museum.
Collections: history of communications; hands-on exhibits; electro-mechanical telephone switching systems; switchboards; telephone sets; central office equipment; outside plant equipment; technical documentation; archival material.
Research Fields: early telephone lines in Hancock County, Maine.
Facilities: library; 2,000 sq. ft. exhibit space.
Activities: guided tours; participatory & temporary exhibits. Annual Event: Family Day.
Publications: biannual newsletter, The Pole Line; annual membership directory, Subscriber Directory.
Hours & Admission Prices: June & Oct. by appointment only; July-Sept. Thurs.-Sun. 1-4. Adults $5, children $2.50. ♿
Attendance: 350 (estimated)
Membership: Individual $20; Family & Organization $35; Participating $100; Sustaining $250; Life $1,000.

WOODLAWN MUSEUM/THE BLACK HOUSE, 19 Black House Dr., Ellsworth, ME 04605-2320. Mailing Address: P.O. Box 1478, Ellsworth, ME 04605-1478. Tel.: 207-667-8671. Fax: 207-667-7950.
E-mail: director@woodlawnmuseum.org
Web Site: www.woodlawnmuseum.org
Formerly: Colonel Black Mansion
Founded: 1928.
Congressional District: 2
Key Personnel: Exec. Dir., Joshua C. Torrance; Chm. (V), Sandra Blake-Leonard.
Personnel Profile: Full-Time Paid 2; Part-Time Paid 3; Part-Time Volunteers 7; Interns 3.
Governing Authority: nonprofit organization. Parent Institution: Hancock County Trustees of Public Reservations. Tax-exempt.
Historic House: 1827 Black Family House.
Collections: original furnishings & outbuilding; formal garden; history; archives; paintings; decorative art.
Research Fields: social history of Down East, ME; local history; decorative & fine art; personal artifacts; ME lumbering history.
Facilities: 1,000-vol. library of Col. Black's personal books; 180-acre estate; 2 miles of walking trails & gardens.
Activities: guided tours; special events; workshops; lectures. Museum Sponsors: weekly teas on Wed. in July & August; Ellsworth Antiques show at Woodlawn; holiday tours in Dec.
Publications: newsletter; annual journal.
Hours & Admission Prices: May & Oct. Tues.-Sun. 1-4; June-Sept. Tues.-Sat. 10-5, Sun. 1-4. Tours every hour. Adults $10, children $3; discount to AAA & AAM members; members & public park no charge. Closed Independence Day.
Attendance: 10,000 (estimated)
Membership: Student $5; Individual $35; Household $40; Supporter $125; Sponsor $250; Patron $500; Benefactor $1,000.

Falmouth

THE FALMOUTH HERITAGE MUSEUM, 60 Woods Rd., Falmouth, ME 04105. Mailing Address: PMB 367, 190 US Rte. 1, Falmouth, ME 04105-1313. Tel.: 207-781-4727.
E-mail: falmouthhistorical@myfairpoint.net
Web Site: www.falmouthmehistory.org
Governing Authority: Parent Institution: Falmouth Historical Society.
Historical Society Museum.
Collections: local history & culture; photographs.
Hours & Admission Prices: Call for hours. No charge; donations accepted. ♿
Membership: Individual $15; Family $25; Supporting $50.

THE FALMOUTH HISTORICAL SOCIETY, 190 U.S. Rte. 1, PMB 367, Falmouth, ME 04105-1313. Tel.: 207-781-4727.
E-mail: falmouthhistorical@myfairpoint.net
Web Site: www.falmouthmehistory.org
Key Personnel: Pres., Carol I. Kauffman; Vice Pres., Mary Honan
Historical Society Museum.
Collections: local history & culture; photographs; personal artifacts.
Hours & Admission Prices: Call for hours.
Membership: Student $5; Individual $15; Family $25; Supporting $50 & up.

Farmington

NORDICA HOMESTEAD, 116 Nordica Lane, Farmington, ME 04938. Mailing Address: c/o Franklin County Savings Bank, P.O. Box 825, Farmington, ME 04938-0825. Tel.: 207-778-2042.
Web Site: www.lilliannordica.com
Founded: 1927.
Congressional District: 2
Key Personnel: C.E.O. & Pres. (V), Tom Sawyer; Vice Pres. & Publicity Dir., Marion Smith; Treas., Cindy Wright.
Personnel Profile: Full-Time Volunteers 2.
Governing Authority: society. Nordica Memorial Association, Inc. Tax-exempt.
Historical Society Museum: housed in c.1840 Nordica Homestead.
Collections: items relating to the life of Lillian Nordica, opera singer; opera & concert gowns by Worth; record containing all 14 recordings she is known to have made.
Research Fields: material related to Lillian Nordica.
Facilities: 300-vol. library of books, magazines & programs on Maine available by application to publicity director. Photographs, postcards, note paper, books, records & biography of Nordica for sale.
Activities: guided tours; permanent exhibitions.
Publications: brochure.
Hours & Admission Prices: June-Sept. 15 Tues.-Sat. 10-12 & 1-5, Sun. 1-5; Sept.16-Oct. 15 by appointment only. Adults $2, children $1; discounts to AAA members & school children groups; children under 6 no charge. ♿
Attendance: 700 (estimated)
Membership: Annual $5; Life $100; Patron $500.

Franklin

FRANKLIN HISTORICAL SOCIETY, Rte. 200, Sullivan Rd., Franklin, ME 04634. Mailing Address: P.O. Box 317, Franklin, ME 04634-0317. Tel.: 207-565-3635. Fax: 207-565-3323.
Founded: 1960.
Congressional District: 2
Key Personnel: Pres., Dania Stager-Snow; Vice Pres., William Robertson; Cur. & Museum Shop Mgr., Helen Cantor.
Governing Authority: society; nonprofit organization. Tax-exempt.
Historical Society Museum: housed in Old East Franklin Church.
Collections: clothing; uniforms; picture albums; farming tools; lumbering & shipbuilding items; granite-work tools; household artifacts.
Facilities: library; 120-seat auditorium.
Activities: guided tours; organized education programs for children. Annual Events: Antique Fair in July; scholarship drive; educational workshop, Franklin-Past, Present & Future in June & July.
Hours & Admission Prices: July-Labor Day Sat. 2-4. No charge; donations accepted. ♿
Attendance: 90
Membership: Individual $3.

Freeport

FREEPORT HISTORICAL SOCIETY, 45 Main St., Freeport, ME 04032-1212. Tel.: 207-865-3170.
E-mail: info@freeporthistoricalsociety.org
Web Site: www.freeporthistoricalsociety.org
Founded: 1969.
Congressional District: 1
Key Personnel: C.E.O., Randall Wade Thomas; Pres. (V), Bill Muldoon; Exec. Dir., Christine White.
Personnel Profile: Full-Time Paid 1; Part-Time Paid 2; Part-Time Volunteers 30.
Governing Authority: nonprofit organization. Tax-exempt: 501(c)(3).
Historical Society.
Collections: manuscripts; photographs; artifacts & furnishings. Historic Houses: 1830 Harrington House; 1810 Rodick/Pettengill Farm.
Research Fields: saltwater farming; Maine coastal life & natural history; Freeport history.
Facilities: local history archives.
Activities: interpretation of historic sites; exhibits; school programs; workshops & demonstrations; local art exhibits.
Publications: quarterly newsletter, Freeport Historical Society Newsletter; book, Tides of Change; maps & Freeport related books; local history publications; A Window Through Time: Pettengill Farm and the Soul of New England.
Hours & Admission Prices: Office: Mon.-Fri. 8:30-5. Archives: Mon. & Thurs.-Fri. 10-5, Sat. 10-2; other times by appointment. No charge; donations accepted.
Attendance: 3,000 (estimated)

Membership: Senior Citizen & Student $10; Individual $20; Family $30; Contributing & Business $50; Supporting $75; Corporate & Sustaining $150.

Fryeburg

FRYEBURG FAIR FARM MUSEUM, 113 N. Fryeburg Rd., Fryeburg, ME 04037. Tel.: 207-935-3268. Fax: 207-935-3662.
E-mail: info@fryeburgfair.org
Web Site: www.fryeburgfair.com
Founded: 1970.
Congressional District: 2
Key Personnel: Cur., Edward W. Jones; Asst. Cur., Diane L. Jones.
Governing Authority: nonprofit organization. Parent Institution: Oxford Agricultural Society, Fryeburg, ME. Tax-exempt.
Agricultural Museum: housed in 1832 barn & carriage house.
Collections: farming & related industries; period woodstove; farm tools & implements; carriages; barn; carriage shed; one room schoolhouse; blacksmith shop; smokehouse; tool shed.
Research Fields: identification & facts on old Fryeburg & surrounding area industries & crafts; identification of old tools & artifacts; safeguards.
Activities: guided tours by appointment; demonstrations; temporary exhibits; cider making.
Hours & Admission Prices: early Oct. during Fair Week daily 9-9; school tours by appointment. ♿
Attendance: 50,000

Gorham

BAXTER HOUSE MUSEUM, 67 South St., Gorham, ME 04038. Tel.: 207-839-3878. Fax: 207-839-7749.
Founded: 1908.
Congressional District: 1
Key Personnel: Guide, Chm. (V) & Pres. Bd. Library Trustees (V), Linda M. Frinsko.
Personnel Profile: Part-Time Paid 1; Part-Time Volunteers 16.
Governing Authority: municipal; Baxter Library Board & Town of Gorham. Tax-exempt: 501(c)(3).
Historic House: c.1797 Baxter House.
Collections: local history & culture; period furniture; early records.
Publications: brochure.
Hours & Admission Prices: June-Aug. Tues. & Thurs. 10-1; other times by appointment. No charge; donations accepted. ♿
Attendance: 300 (estimated)

USM ART GALLERY, 37 College Ave., Gorham Campus, Gorham, ME 04038-1032. Tel.: 207-780-5460 & 5008. Fax: 207-780-5759. TDD: 207-780-5646.
E-mail: ceyler@maine.edu
Web Site: www.usm.maine.edu/~gallery
Founded: 1965.
Key Personnel: Dir. Exhibits & Programs, Carolyn Eyler.
Personnel Profile: Full-Time Paid 1; Part-Time Volunteers 1; Interns 3.
Governing Authority: university. Parent Institution: University of Southern Maine. Tax-exempt: 501(c)(3).
Art Museum.
Collections: paintings; sculpture; graphics; photographs.
Research Fields: contemporary art.
Activities: lectures; films; gallery talks; concerts; arts festivals; inter-museum loan, temporary & traveling exhibitions.
Publications: exhibition catalogs.
Hours & Admission Prices: Academic Year: Tues.-Fri. 11-4, Sat.-Sun. 1-5. No charge; donations accepted. ♿

Greenville

MOOSEHEAD HISTORICAL SOCIETY, (M), 444 Pritham Ave., Greenville, ME 04441-1116. Mailing Address: P.O. Box 1116, Greenville, ME 04441-1116. Tel.: 207-695-2909.
Governing Authority: nonprofit organization.
Historical Society Museum.
Collections: local & regional heritage & history; military artifacts; period clothing & furnishings. Historic Houses: 1899 Victorian mansion; Eveleth-Crafts-Sheridan House.
Hours & Admission Prices: June-Sept. Wed.-Fri. 1-4. Adults $4.

MOOSEHEAD MARINE MUSEUM, 12 Lily Bay Rd., Greenville, ME 04441. Mailing Address: P.O. Box 1151, Greenville, ME 04441-1151. Tel.: 207-695-2716.
E-mail: katahdin2@myfairpoint.net
Web Site: katahdincruises.com
Founded: 1977.
Congressional District: 2
Key Personnel: Pres., Maynard Russell; Vice Pres., Richard McKeil; Museum Shop Mgr., Ardean Thornton.
Personnel Profile: Part-Time Paid 8; Part-Time Volunteers 8.
Governing Authority: nonprofit organization. Parent Institution: Moosehead Marine Museum, Inc. Tax-exempt.
Marine Museum.
Collections: steamboat memorabilia; photographs; Moosehead area history; Katahdin, a 115' 1914 steamboat converted to diesel.
Activities: Katahdin cruises; special events; weddings; charter cruises from late June to mid-Oct.
Hours & Admission Prices: Call for hours & cruise rates. Museum: no charge; donations accepted.
Attendance: 7,000 (accurate)
Membership: Single $25; Family $40.

Hallowell

HARLOW GALLERY, KENNEBEC VALLEY ART ASSOCIATION, 160 Water St., Hallowell, ME 04347-1315. Tel.: 207-622-3813.
E-mail: kvaa@harlowgallery.org
Web Site: harlowgallery.org
Founded: 1963.
Congressional District: 1
Key Personnel: C.E.O., Deborah Fahy; Vice Pres., Michael Hudak; Treas., Karen Johnson; Asst. Dir., Nancy Barron.
Personnel Profile: Part-Time Paid 4; Part-Time Volunteers 40; Interns 2.
Governing Authority: nonprofit. Tax-exempt.
Art Gallery.
Collections: works by Maine artists.
Activities: monthly exhibitions; gallery talks; poetry reading; art workshops.
Publications: monthly newsletter.
Hours & Admission Prices: Wed.-Thurs. & Sun. 12-4, Fri.-Sat. 12-6. No charge; donations accepted. Closed most holidays.
Attendance: 7,000
Membership: Student $10; Regular $30; Family $40; Sustaining $60; Patron $120.

Hinckley

L.C. BATES MUSEUM, (M), Good Will-Hinckley Home For Boys & Girls, Rte. 201, Hinckley, ME 04944-0159. Mailing Address: Good Will-Hinckley Home For Boys & Girls, P.O. Box 159, Hinckley, ME 04944-0159. Tel.: 207-238-4250. Fax: 207-238-4007.
E-mail: lcbates@gwh.org
Web Site: www.gwh.org/html/lcbatesmuseum.htm
Founded: 1889.
Congressional District: 2
Key Personnel: Exec. Dir., Cur. & Museum Shop Mgr., Deborah Staber; Chm. (V), Donald Marden; Museum Educator, Serena Sandborn; Museum Educator, Steve Lemieux.
Personnel Profile: Full-Time Paid 1; Part-Time Paid 3; Part-Time Volunteers 43; Interns 4.
Governing Authority: nonprofit organization. Parent Institution: Good Will-Hinckley Home Association. Tax-exempt.
General Museum.
Collections: Native American; natural history; archaeological stone; contemporary art; mineralogy; military artifacts; local pioneer artifacts; agricultural antiques; Good Will-Hinckley history & archives.
Research Fields: American social history; archives of Good Will-Hinckley.
Facilities: library of secondary school level scholastic books with emphasis on history & natural history available for research on premises; 250-seat auditorium; classrooms; trails in 2,400-acre wildlife area; arboretum.
Activities: guided tours; permanent exhibitions; nature trail; outreach programs. Museum Sponsors: Junior Naturalist programs, after school & summers.
Publications: book, The Record; newsletter, Beaver Paw Press.
Hours & Admission Prices: April-Nov. Wed.-Sat. 10-4:30, Sun. 1-4:30; Dec.-March Wed.-Sat. 10-4:30; other times by appointment. Adults $2.50, youth under 18 $1; discounts to AAM & AAA members, MEMA & group tours; members no charge.
Attendance: 14,000 (accurate)
Membership: Individual $15; Family $25-$50; Group $51-$100; Patron $101-$500; Benefactor $501-$1,000; Corporate $1,000 & up.

Indian Island

PENOBSCOT NATION MUSEUM, 12 Downstreet St., Indian Island, ME 04468. Tel.: 207-827-4153.
Native American Museum.
Collections: Native American history, culture, & artifacts; personal artifacts; photographs; baskets; woodcarvings; paintings.
Activities: tours.
Hours & Admission Prices: Mon.-Thurs. 9-2, Sat. 10-3.

Islesboro

ISLESBORO HISTORICAL SOCIETY AND MUSEUM, 388 Main Rd., Islesboro, ME 04848. Mailing Address: P.O. Box 301, Islesboro, ME 04848-0301. Tel.: 207-734-6733.
E-mail: info@islesborohistorical.org
Web Site: www.islesborohistorical.org
Founded: 1964.
Congressional District: 2
Key Personnel: Archivist, Bunny Logan.
Personnel Profile: Part-Time Paid 1; Part-Time Volunteers 51.
Governing Authority: society. Tax-exempt.
Historical & Preservation Society Museum: housed in 1894 Town Hall.
Collections: photographs; textiles; boats; vehicles; paintings & drawings; farm & household equipment; Islesboro artifacts including a phone exchange; two post office letter boxes; c.1900 telephone booth; 100-year old weaving loom; manuscripts; scrapbooks; arts; crafts.
Research Fields: 19th to early 20th century Maine.
Facilities: library; stage.
Activities: arts festivals; loan, permanent & temporary exhibitions; historical presentations; concerts; research.
Publications: books, History of Islesboro; History of Islesborough, Maine, 1764-1893; History of Islesboro, Maine 1893-1983; The Summer Cottages of Islesboro - 1890-1930.
Hours & Admission Prices: Society: by appointment. Museum: July-Aug. Sat.-Wed. 12:30-4:30. No charge; donations accepted.
Attendance: 654 (accurate)
Membership: Regular $10; Contributing $25; Sustaining $50; Patron $100.

SAILOR'S MEMORIAL MUSEUM, Grindle Point, Islesboro, ME 04848. Mailing Address: P.O. Box 76, Islesboro, ME 04848-0076. Tel.: 207-734-2253. Fax: 207-734-8394.
Founded: 1936.
Congressional District: 2
Key Personnel: Town Mgr., Damaris A. Diffin.
Personnel Profile: Part-Time Paid 1; Part-Time Volunteers 6.
Governing Authority: municipal. Tax-exempt.
Maritime Museum: housed in 1850 Lighthouse.
Collections: marine; history. Historic House: 1850, Grindle Point Keeper's House.
Activities: permanent exhibitions.
Hours & Admission Prices: mid-June to Labor Day Tues.-Sun. 10-4. No charge; donations accepted. ♿
Attendance: 1,500 (estimated)

Islesford

ISLESFORD HISTORICAL MUSEUM, Little Cranberry Island, Islesford, ME 04646. Mailing Address: Acadia National Park, P.O. Box 177, Bar Harbor, ME 04609-0177. Tel.: 207-288-8729. Fax: 207-288-8709.
E-mail: john_mcdade@nps.gov
Web Site: www.nps.gov/acad/planyourvisit/islesfordhistoricalmuseum.htm
Founded: 1919.
Congressional District: 2
Key Personnel: Supt., Sheridan Steele; Museum Cur., John McDade.
Personnel Profile: Full-Time Paid 1; Part-Time Paid 2; Part-Time Volunteers 2.
Governing Authority: federal government. Parent Institution: National Park Service. Subsidiary Institution: Acadia National Park. Tax-exempt.
History Museum.
Collections: artifacts & archival documents pertaining to the maritime history & settlement of the Cranberry Isles; ship models; genealogy of Cranberry Isles settlers.
Research Fields: genealogy; New France, maritime & town history.
Facilities: Islesford Historical Museum.
Activities: permanent & temporary exhibitions.
Publications: One Man's Museum: History of the Islesford Collection.
Hours & Admission Prices: mid-June to Sept. Mon.-Sat. 9-12 & 12:30-3:30, Sun. 10:45-12 & 12:30-3:30. No charge; donations accepted.
Attendance: 14,935 (accurate)

Kennebunk

*** BRICK STORE MUSEUM, (M),** 117 Main St., Kennebunk, ME 04043-7088. Tel.: 207-985-4802. Fax: 207-985-6887.
Web Site: www.brickstoremuseum.org
Founded: 1936.
Congressional District: 1
Key Personnel: Exec. Dir., Tracy L. Baetz; Pres. Bd. Trustees, Stephen P. Spofford; Archivist, Rosalind Magnuson; Registrar & Collections Mgr., Kathryn Hussey; Community Outreach, Cheryl Price.
Personnel Profile: Full-Time Paid 1; Full-Time Volunteers 2; Part-Time Paid 1; Part-Time Volunteers 90; Interns 2.
Governing Authority: nonprofit organization. Tax-exempt: 501(c)(3).
Local History Museum Complex: housed in 1825 William Lord's Brick Store building & three adjacent restored 19th-century buildings.
Collections: costumes; marine history; tools; early American utensils & decorative arts; manuscripts; documents; fine arts; photographs; Kenneth Roberts materials; Booth Tarkington materials; Abbott Graves, Thomas Badger & John Brewster paintings.
Research Fields: maritime; decorative arts; local history.
Facilities: 3,000-vol. library of books on history & genealogy. Publications for sale.
Activities: lectures; seminars; architectural tours; school programs; field trips; workshops.
Publications: newsletter; local history journal, Chapters in Local History; exhibit catalogs; books, Agreeable Situations: Society, Commerce & Art in South Maine 1780-1830; Sketch of An Old River: Shipbuilding On The Kennebunk; handbooks of architectural styles; An Anchor to Windward: The Maine Connection; Quiet, Well-Kept for Sensible People: The Development of Kennebunk Beach, 1860-1920; Trunks, Textiles and Transits: Manufacturing on the Mousan River.
Hours & Admission Prices: Tues.-Fri. 10-4:30, Sat. 10-1. Suggested Donation: $5; discounts to AAM, ICOM, NEMA & AAA members; members no charge. Closed holidays. ♿
Attendance: 5,696 (accurate)
Membership: Student & Senior Individual $20; Individual $30; Senior Couple $35; Family $40; Business Partner Program $150-$1,000.

Kennebunkport

KENNEBUNKPORT HISTORICAL SOCIETY, 125 North St., Kennebunkport, ME 04046. Mailing Address: P.O. Box 1173, Kennebunkport, ME 04046-1173. Tel.: 207-967-2751.
E-mail: kporths@gwi.net
Web Site: www.kporthistory.org
Founded: 1952.
Congressional District: 1
Key Personnel: Pres. (V) & Museum Shop Mgr., Lynne Longworth; Treas., Karen Duddy.
Personnel Profile: Part-Time Paid 2; Part-Time Volunteers 100.
Governing Authority: nonprofit organization. Tax-exempt: 501(c)(3).
Historic House & History Museum: housed in 1853 Greek Revival Nott House; c.1900 District 5 Schoolhouse.
Collections: local crafts, art, shipbuilding & archives; genealogy; manuscript collections; over 2,000 photographs; old gowns; Clark shipyard office maritime collection; period furnishings; original jail cells of town; Nott House Victorian gardens. Historic Buildings: 1900 schoolhouse; Clark shipbuilding office; Louis D. Norton artist studio.
Research Fields: genealogy; land titles; local history; shipbuilding & maritime history.
Facilities: research library in schoolhouse.
Activities: lectures; temporary exhibitions; local research; house tours; historic village walking tours. Annual Events: re-creation of Nott House gardens in spring; Christmas Prelude in December.
Publications: newsletter, The Log.
Hours & Admission Prices: Town House School: Research Wed. & Fri. 10-1. Pasco Exhibit Center: July-Sept. Tues.-Fri. 10-4, Sat. 10-1; Oct.-June Tues.-Fri. 10-4. No charge; donations accepted. Nott House: July-Aug. Thurs. 10-4 & 7-9, Fri. 1-4, Sat. 10-1; Sept. to Columbus Day Thurs. 10-4, Fri. 1-4, Sat. 10-1. Adults $7; children 17 & under and society members no charge. Closed holidays.
Attendance: 2,000 (estimated)
Membership: Individual $30; Household $40; Business $100; Life $1,000.

SEASHORE TROLLEY MUSEUM, (M), 195 Log Cabin Rd., Kennebunkport, ME 04046-1690. Mailing Address: P.O. Box A, Kennebunkport, ME 04046-1690. Tel.: 207-967-2712. Fax: 207-967-0867.
E-mail: carshop@gwi.net
Web Site: www.trolleymuseum.org
Founded: 1939.
Congressional District: 1

Key Personnel: Chm. (V), James D. Schantz; Pres. (V), Dann Chamberlin; Treas. & Comptroller, Jeffrey N. Sisson; Vice Pres. Business Administration, John Middleton; Museum Shop Mgr., Gayle Dion; Museum Shop Mgr., Donald Curry.
Personnel Profile: Full-Time Paid 5; Full-Time Volunteers 4; Part-Time Paid 3; Part-Time Volunteers 100.
Governing Authority: nonprofit organization. Owned by New England Electric Railway Historical Society, Inc. Subsidiary Institution: National Streetcar Museum at Lowell. Tax-exempt: 501(c)(3).
Electric Railway History & Technology Museum.
Collections: city trolley cars; interurban electric cars; early streetcars; rapid transit cars; trackless trolley coaches; buses; plows & sweepers; work cars; mail & express cars; locomotives; demonstration electric railway.
Research Fields: publications on equipment & corporate history.
Facilities: 10,000-vol. library of books, blueprints, photographs & documents; demonstration railway with 3 mile rides featuring different trolley cars; visitor center. Railroad & trolley related books & souvenirs for sale.
Activities: guided tours; lectures; films; workshops; training programs for professional museum workers; permanent & temporary exhibitions; educational ride on original trolley equipment; special events.
Publications: bimonthly newsletter: Dispatch; annual report.
Hours & Admission Prices: May & Oct. Sat.-Sun. 10-5; Memorial Day to Columbus Day daily 10-5. Adults $8, seniors 60 & over $6, children 6-16 $5.50; discounts to groups, AAM & ARM members; members and children 5 & under no charge. ♿
Attendance: 19,000 (estimated)
Membership: Students, Senior Citizens, Military & Handicapped $30; Regular $35; Family $50; Sustaining $60; Contributing $120; Life $900; Benefactor $1,200.

Kingfield

STANLEY MUSEUM, INC., 40 School St., Kingfield, ME 04947. Mailing Address: P.O. Box 77, Kingfield, ME 04947-0077. Tel.: 207-265-2729. Fax: 207-265-4700.
E-mail: maine@stanleymuseum.org
Web Site: www.stanleymuseum.org
Founded: 1981.
Congressional District: 2
Key Personnel: Pres., C.E.O. & Museum Shop Mgr., Bobby Brown; Chm. (V), Lynn Curry; Vice Chm., John Linderman; Archivist, Jim Merrick; Office Mgr., Kim Richmond White.
Personnel Profile: Full-Time Paid 3; Full-Time Volunteers 2; Part-Time Paid 3; Part-Time Volunteers 10; Interns 2.
Governing Authority: nonprofit organization. Branch Site: Stanley Museum in Lower Stanley Village, Estes Park, CO 80517. Tax-exempt: 501(c)(3).
History & Transportation Museum: housed in 1903 school designed by F.E. Stanley, inventor of the steam car.
Collections: steam cars; violins; painting; airbrush art; photography; historical materials documenting inventions & activity.
Research Fields: steam cars & photography; Northeast art; violins; airbrush.
Facilities: archive material pertaining to cars, photography & family history; educational facilities. Museum-related items for sale.
Activities: guided tours; lectures; films; concerts; arts festivals; hobby workshops; docent program; participatory, loan & temporary exhibitions; art classes; programs at the Stanley Hotel, Estes Park, CO.
Publications: quarterly magazine, The Stanley Museum; books, Historic Touring, Early Tale of Steam Travel; Reflections of Transportation & Communication, An Evening with R. Buckminister Fuller; Stanley Family Reunion: A Family History Transcript; The Genealogy of the Locomobile Steam Carriage; The Stanleys: Renaissance Yankees; Innovations in Industry & the Arts; Mr. Stanley of Estes Park, 2000; The Stanley Steamer: America's Legendary Steam Car, 2004; Bravo Stanley, 2006.
Hours & Admission Prices: June-Oct. Tues.-Sun. 1-4; Nov.-May Tues.-Fri. 1-4; other times by appointment. Adults $4, seniors $3, children $2; discounts to AAM, AAA, & ICOM members; museum members no charge. ♿
Attendance: 75,000 (accurate)
Membership: Individual $35; Family $50; Contributing $75; Supporting & Business $100; Associate $250; Founding $500; Benefactor $1,000.

Kittery

KITTERY HISTORICAL & NAVAL MUSEUM, 200 Rogers Rd. Ext., Kittery, ME 03904-1458. Mailing Address: P.O. Box 453, Kittery, ME 03904. Tel.: 207-439-3080. Fax: 207-439-3080.
E-mail: kitterymuseum@netzero.net
Web Site: kitterymuseum.com
Founded: 1976.
Congressional District: 1
Key Personnel: Dir., Wayne Manson; Museum Shop Mgr. & Program Chair, Barbara Estes.
Personnel Profile: Full-Time Volunteers 1; Part-Time Volunteers 20.
Governing Authority: nonprofit organization. Tax-exempt: 501(c)(3).
Naval & History Museum.
Collections: local history items; documents; ship models; decorative arts; crafts; regional archaeology finds; shipbuilding; maritime.
Research Fields: local maritime history; town history.
Facilities: library by appointment only; 3,000 sq. ft. exhibit space.
Activities: guided tours; lectures; organized educational programs.
Publications: quarterly newsletter, The Bosun's Pipe.
Hours & Admission Prices: June to Columbus Day Tues.-Sat. 10-4; Nov.-May Wed & Sat. 10-4 or by appointment. Adults $3, senior citizens $2, children 7-15 $1.50; discounts to groups, AAM, ICOM & AAA members; members no charge. ♿
Attendance: 1,200 (accurate)
Membership: Associate $15; Family $25; Contributing $50; Sustaining $100; Donor $250; Patron $500; Benefactor $1,000.

Lewiston

BATES COLLEGE MUSEUM OF ART, (M), 75 Russell St., Lewiston, ME 04240-6044. Tel.: 207-786-6158. Fax: 207-786-8335.
E-mail: museum@bates.edu
Web Site: www.bates.edu/museum.xml
Founded: 1986.
Congressional District: 2
Key Personnel: Dir., Mark H.C. Bessire; Cur., William Low; Cur. Education, Anthony Shostak.
Personnel Profile: Full-Time Paid 3; Part-Time Paid 2.
Governing Authority: college. Parent Institution: Bates College.
Art Museum.
Collections: Marsden Hartley Memorial Collection of drawings & memorabilia; European & American paintings, prints & sculptures.
Activities: gallery talks; inter-museum loan; permanent, temporary & traveling exhibitions.
Publications: catalogs: Ninety-Nine Drawings by Marsden Hartley; Eight Poems & One Essay by Marsden Hartley; Documenting China; Robert Indiana: The Hartley Elegies; Cryptozoology: Oct of Time Place Scale; Charlie Hewitt.
Hours & Admission Prices: Tues.-Sat. 10-5. No charge. Closed major holidays. ♿
Attendance: 19,200 (accurate)
Membership: Student $10; Member $30 & $50; Patron $100.

Liberty

THE DAVISTOWN MUSEUM, 58 Main St., Rte. 173, Liberty, ME 04949. Mailing Address: Hulls Cove Office, P.O. Box 144, Hulls Cove, ME 04644-0144. Tel.: 207-288-5126. Fax: 207-288-2725.
E-mail: curator@davistownmuseum.org
Web Site: www.davistownmuseum.org
Founded: 2000.
Key Personnel: C.E.O., Harold G. Brack.
Personnel Profile: Full-Time Volunteers 2; Part-Time Paid 2; Interns 1.
Governing Authority: Tax-exempt.
History & Art Museum.
Collections: history of tool making; New England's maritime culture; Native American history; sculpture; works of local & regional artists.
Facilities: library; garden.
Activities: special events; internships. Annual Event: Art Show.
Hours & Admission Prices: Summer: Wed.-Fri. & Sun. 11-5, Sat. 10-5; call for additional seasonal hours. No charge.
Attendance: 1,000 (estimated)
Membership: Student $10; Individual $25; Family $30; Associate $50; Contributing $100; Sustaining $500; Partner $1,000; Benefactor $5,000.

Lincolnville

SCHOOL HOUSE MUSEUM LINCOLNVILLE HISTORICAL SOCIETY, 33 Beach Rd. (Rte. 173), Lincolnville, ME 04849. Mailing Address: P.O. Box 204, Lincolnville, ME 04849-0204. Tel.: 207-789-5445.
E-mail: history@sent.com
Web Site: www.lincolnvillehistory.org/
Historical Society Museum: housed in a one room school built in 1892.
Collections: period furnishings; photographs; genealogy notebooks.
Hours & Admission Prices: June-Oct. Mon., Wed. & Fri.-Sat. 1-4. No charge.

Livermore

WASHBURN NORLANDS LIVING HISTORY CENTER, 290 Norlands Rd., Livermore, ME 04253-3807. Tel.: 207-897-4366. Fax: 207-897-4963.
E-mail: norlands@norlands.org
Web Site: www.norlands.org
Living History Museum.
Collections: Historic Buildings: the Mansion, Library, Meeting House & School House containing artifacts relating to 18th & 19th century rural Maine.
Hours & Admission Prices: Tours by appointment.

Lubec

QUODDY HEAD STATE PARK, 973 S. Lubec Rd., 4 miles off Rte. 189, Lubec, ME 04652-3676. Mailing Address: P.O. Box 1490, Lubec, ME 04652-3676. Tel.: 207-733-0911 (Park season) & 941-4014 (Off season).
Web Site: www.state.me.us/cgi-bin/doc/parks/find_one_name.pl?park_id=10
State Park Museum: located on the easternmost point of land in the U.S.
Collections: lighthouse; forests; bogs.
Facilities: 481 acres; hiking trails; picnic sites.
Activities: hiking; whale watching.
Hours & Admission Prices: May 15 to Oct. 15.

Machias

BURNHAM TAVERN MUSEUM, Rte. 192, Machias, ME 04654. Mailing Address: 2 Main St., Machias, ME 04654. Tel.: 207-255-6930.
E-mail: info@burnhamtavern.com
Web Site: www.burnhamtavern.com
Founded: 1910.
Congressional District: 2
Key Personnel: Dir. & Chm. (V), Ruth H. Ahrens, Ed.D.
Personnel Profile: Part-Time Volunteers 10.
Governing Authority: society. Affiliated with Hannah Weston Chapter, Daughters of the American Revolution. Tax-exempt.
Historic Building: c.1770 Burnham Tavern.
Collections: pre-1830 period furnishings; local history.
Research Fields: local history.
Facilities: library of period documents, journals & day books.
Activities: guided tours; permanent exhibitions.
Hours & Admission Prices: mid-June to Sept. Mon.-Sat. 9:30-4; other times by appointment. Adults $5, children $.25; children under 6 no charge.
Attendance: 1,000 (estimated)

Machiasport

GATES HOUSE, MACHIASPORT HISTORICAL SOCIETY, 344 Port Rd., Machiasport, ME 04655. Mailing Address: P.O. Box 301, Machiasport, ME 04655-0301. Tel.: 207-255-8461.
E-mail: franklf@midmaine.com
Founded: 1964.
Congressional District: 2
Key Personnel: C.E.O., Ray Foster; Recording Sec., James Sherman; Treas., Barbara Maloy.
Personnel Profile: Part-Time Volunteers 10.
Governing Authority: nonprofit organization. Tax-exempt.
Historic House: c.1810 Gates House.
Collections: marine artifacts; period furniture & clothing; genealogy; early post cards of local area; photographs; carpenter's tools.
Research Fields: local history & genealogy.
Facilities: library; reading room.
Activities: lectures; films; junior members history research classes.
Publications: booklet, The Whitneyville & Machiasport Railroad; descriptive brochures of Machiasport; biannual newspaper, The Tide; Sails to Rails & Beyond: A Brief Study of Transportation in the Machias Valley of Maine 1763-1983.
Hours & Admission Prices: July-Aug. Tues.-Fri. 12:30-4:30; other times by appointment. Suggested Donations: $2.
Attendance: 500 (estimated)
Membership: Annual $15; Life $300.

Madawaska

TANTE BLANCHE MUSEUM, U.S. #1, Madawaska, ME 04756-1165. Mailing Address: Madawaska Public Library, 393 Main St., Madawaska, ME 04756-1165. Tel.: 207-728-4649.
E-mail: ktheriault@madawaskahistorical.org
Web Site: madawaskahistorical.org
Founded: 1968.
Congressional District: 2
Key Personnel: Pres. (V), Darlene Coltart; Treas., Celine Lausier.
Governing Authority: society; nonprofit. Parent Institution: Madawaska Historical Society. Subsidiary Institution: Genealogical Research Center. Tax-exempt: 501(c)(3).
History Museum.
Collections: Acadian & French Canadian artifacts & records. Historic Structure: Acadian Cross Historic Shrine.
Research Fields: genealogy.
Facilities: library, for use on premises only.
Activities: guided tours; lectures; temporary exhibitions. Museum Sponsors: family reunions; Acadian festivals; educational scholarship.
Publications: annual newsletter.
Hours & Admission Prices: June to mid-Aug. Wed.-Sun. 12-4. No charge; donations accepted.
Attendance: 3,000 (estimated)

Milbridge

MILBRIDGE HISTORICAL MUSEUM, Main St., Milbridge, ME 04658. Mailing Address: P.O. Box 194, Milbridge, ME 04658-0194. Tel.: 207-546-4471.
History Museum.
Collections: town's shipbuilding history; local industries; historic buildings; genealogy; period artifacts.
Activities: group tours; special events.
Hours & Admission Prices: June to early Sept. Tues. & Sat.-Sun. 1-4. No charge; donations accepted.
Attendance: 329 (accurate)

Millinocket

NORTH LIGHT GALLERY, 256 Penobscot St., Millinocket, ME 04462-1510. Tel.: 207-723-4414.
Key Personnel: Founder, Marsha Donahue
Art Gallery.
Collections: paintings; drawings; sculpture.
Activities: special events; temporary & permanent exhibits.
Hours & Admission Prices: Mon.-Sat. 10-6; other times by appointment.

Milo

MILO HISTORICAL SOCIETY, 12 High St., Milo, ME 04463-1315. Tel.: 207-943-2268.
E-mail: bradeen@prexar.com
Web Site: www.milohistorical.org
Key Personnel: Cur., Gwen Bradeen
Historical Society Museum.
Collections: town history & heritage; photographs.
Activities: educational programs; group tours.
Hours & Admission Prices: June-Aug. Tues.-Fri. 1-3; other times by appointment.

Monhegan

THE MONHEGAN MUSEUM, (M), 1 Lighthouse Hill, Monhegan, ME 04852. Tel.: 207-596-7003.
E-mail: museum@monheganmuseum.org
Web Site: www.monheganmuseum.org
Founded: 1968.
Key Personnel: Pres., Edward Deci; Cur., Jennifer Pye; Cur., Emily Grey.
Personnel Profile: Part-Time Paid 3; Part-Time Volunteers 60.
Governing Authority: society. Parent Institution: Monhegan Historical & Cultural Museum Association, Monhegan, ME. Tax-exempt.
Art & History Museum: housed in 19th-century lighthouse & outbuildings.
Collections: fishing & lobster trapping gear & equipment; wildlife displays; topographical & ecological maps of the island; Indian artifacts; local historical memorabilia; Monhegan Art; lighthouse exhibits.
Major Exhibits: A Gift to the Island: Pictures from the Collection of Remak Ramsay, 7/10-9/10.
Research Fields: local history.
Activities: permanent & temporary exhibitions.
Hours & Admission Prices: July-Aug. daily 11:30-3:30; Sept. daily 1:30-3:30. No charge; donations requested. ♿
Attendance: 6,000 (estimated)
Membership: Student $1; Regular $5; Fellow $25; Sponsor $100; Patron $250; Benefactor $1,000.

Mount Desert

MOUNT DESERT ISLAND HISTORICAL SOCIETY, 373 Sound Dr., Mount Desert, ME 04660. Mailing Address: P.O. Box 653, Mount Desert, ME 04660-0653. Tel.: 207-276-9323. Fax: 207-276-4204.
Web Site: www.mdihistory.org
Founded: 1931.
Congressional District: 2
Key Personnel: Pres. (V), Kathleen W. Miller; Exec. Dir., Charlotte Singleton.
Personnel Profile: Full-Time Paid 1; Part-Time Paid 1; Part-Time Volunteers 86.
Governing Authority: society; board of directors. Tax-exempt.
Local History Museum.
Collections: period artifacts; books& genealogical records of early Mount Desert Island; furniture; deeds; 2 historic buildings.
Research Fields: genealogy of Mount Desert Island.
Facilities: library of old history books, Bibles & textbooks available for use upon request; research room.
Activities: guided tours; monthly programs; permanent exhibitions.
Publications: biannual newsletter; annual history journal; annual magazine, The Mount Desert Island Historical Society.
Hours & Admission Prices: Somesville Museum: July to mid-Sept. Tues.-Sat. 1-4. Sound School House: June-Aug. Tues.-Sat. 10-4; Sept.-May Mon.-Fri. 10-4. No charge; donations accepted.
Attendance: 3,000 (estimated)
Membership: Individual $25; Family $40; Artifact $60; Archivist $100; Curator's Circle $500; Heirloom Society $1000; Honor Roll $5000.

Naples

NAPLES HISTORICAL SOCIETY, On the Village Green, Rte. 302, Naples, ME 04055. Mailing Address: Town Office, Naples, ME 04055. Tel.: 207-693-4297.
E-mail: nhs@fairpoint.net
Web Site: www.napleshs.org
Founded: 1972.
Key Personnel: Cur., Merry Watson; Cur. Dillingham Collection, Richard Doyle.
Personnel Profile: Part-Time Volunteers 3.
Naples History Museum.
Collections: local history & culture; books; photographs; Native American artifacts.
Major Exhibits: The Dillingham Collection, 6/10-9/10.
Activities: Museum Sponsors: Wheels and Water Show in June; Wheels and Water Antique Transportation Show in June; Native American Pow Wow in September.
Publications: brochures, Cumberland and Oxford Canal; Bay of Naples Hotel, The Idol.
Hours & Admission Prices: Sept.-June. No charge; donations accepted. ♿
Attendance: 100 (estimated)
Membership: Individual $5.

New Gloucester

SHAKER MUSEUM, 707 Shaker Rd., New Gloucester, ME 04260-2652. Tel.: 207-926-4597.
E-mail: usshakers@aol.com
Web Site: www.shaker.lib.me.us
Founded: 1931.
Congressional District: 1
Key Personnel: Dir., Leonard L. Brooks; C.E.O., Sr. Frances Carr; Cur., Michael S. Graham; Librarian, Tina S. Agren.
Personnel Profile: Full-Time Paid 4; Part-Time Paid 7; Part-Time Volunteers 50.
Governing Authority: nonprofit organization. Parent Institution: United Society of Shakers. Tax-exempt: 501(c)(3).
Religious Museum & Library: located at an active Shaker religious community, comprising of 18 buildings on 1,900 acres dating from the 1760s to 1960s.
Collections: Shaker furniture; tinware; woodenware; folk art; decorative arts; tools; farm implements; Shaker books, manuscripts, ephemera books, manuscripts dealing with religious communities.
Research Fields: research into all aspects of Shakerism, information disseminated through The Shaker Quarterly & 17 publications; herbal medicine; The Koreshan Unity; Muggletonians; Free Will Baptists; Christian Israelitism.
Facilities: 3,000-vol. library available to the public of Shaker (8,000 MSS, 3,300 ephemera); 545-vol Koreshan Unity; 9,795-vol. religion, agriculture & herbs; botanical garden; 7,500 sq. ft. exhibit space. Gift items for sale.
Activities: guided tours; lectures; concerts; organized educational programs; craft workshops & demonstrations; loan & traveling exhibitions; nature walks. Annual Events: Friends of the Shakers Meeting; Apple Saturdays; Maine Festival of American Music; Maine Farm Day; Christmas Fair.
Publications: The Shaker Quarterly; Shaker Your Plate; Gift Drawing & Gift Song; The Sabbathday Lake Shakers; Holy Land; Poems & Prayers; Life in the Christ Spirit; All Things Anew; In The Eye of Eternity; Shakerism For Today; Ingenious & Useful; Growing Up Shaker.
Hours & Admission Prices: Memorial Day-Columbus Day Mon.-Sat. 10-4:30. Introductory Tour: adults $6.50, children $2; discounts to groups & NEMA members. ♿
Attendance: 9,082 (accurate)
Membership: Individual $25; Family $35; Sponsor $100; Patron $200; Life $1,000.

New Harbor

COLONIAL PEMAQUID, Colonial Pemaquid State Historical Site, New Harbor, ME 04554. Mailing Address: P.O. Box 117, New Harbor, ME 04554-0117. Tel.: 207-677-2423 (April-Oct); 207-624-6075 (Off-Season).
Web Site: www.friendsofcolonialpemaquid.org
Founded: 1970.
Congressional District: 1
Key Personnel: Mgr., Kelsie Tardif; Pres. (V), Bob Howell; Museum Shop Mgr., Carol Ring.
Personnel Profile: Full-Time Paid 6; Part-Time Volunteers 35.
Governing Authority: state. Affiliated with State of Maine, Bureau of Parks & Lands, Augusta, ME 04333. Tax-exempt.
Archaeological Dig Site.
Collections: Indian & Colonial artifacts; replica of 1692 Fort William Henry.
Research Fields: history; archeology.
Facilities: 70-vol. library of books pertaining to history of Pemaquid.
Activities: guided group tours; lectures; formally organized education programs for children; permanent exhibitions.
Hours & Admission Prices: Memorial Day to Labor Day daily 9-6. Adults $2; children under 12 & seniors over 65 no charge. ♿
Attendance: 100,000 (estimated)
Membership: Single $10; Family $25.

THE FISHERMEN'S MUSEUM, Lighthouse Park, End of Rte. 130, New Harbor, ME 04554. Mailing Address: P.O. Box 263, New Harbor, ME 04554-0263. Tel.: 207-677-2726.
Founded: 1972.
Key Personnel: Dir., John Allan; Pres., Robert Cushing; Chm. (V), Barbara Marshall.
Personnel Profile: Part-Time Paid 4; Part-Time Volunteers 20.
Governing Authority: nonprofit organization. Tax-exempt: 501(c)(3).
Historical & Preservation Society: housed in old 1827 lighthouse keeper's house.
Collections: artifacts; period pictures; charts; models of fishing boats.
Activities: permanent exhibitions.
Hours & Admission Prices: June to mid-Oct. Mon.-Sat. 10-5, Sun. 11-5. No charge; donations accepted. ♿
Attendance: 46,479 (accurate)

New Portland

NOWETAH'S AMERICAN INDIAN MUSEUM & STORE, 2 Colegrove Rd., New Portland, ME 04961-3821. Tel.: 207-628-4981.
Web Site: www.nowetahs.webs.com
Founded: 1969.
Key Personnel: Owner & Cur., Mrs. Nowetah Cyr.
Personnel Profile: Full-Time Volunteers 2.
Native American Museum.
Collections: American Indian art with emphasis on the Abenaki of Maine; over 600 Native sweetgrass & brown ash splint baskets; quill embroidered moccasins; bark moose calls & cradleboards; moose hair & quill embroidered pipe bags; hunting decoys; musical instruments including drums & flutes; dolls; carvings; peace-pipes; war bonnets; birch bark hunter canoe; 12 ft. long wood dug-out racing canoe.
Facilities: Museum-related items for sale.
Publications: books, The Indian Massacre of 1724 at Norridgewock, Maine; The History of Indian Wampum; How to Smoke Deerhide - The Old Indian Way; How to Weave an Indian Rug; The Ancient Wisdoms & Knowledge of the Abenaki Indians.
Hours & Admission Prices: Daily 10-5. No charge; donations accepted. Closed Thanksgiving; Christmas. ♿
Attendance: 4,000 (estimated)

New Sweden

LARS NOAK BLACKSMITH SHOP, LARSSON/OSTLUND LOG HOME & ONE-ROOM CAPITOL SCHOOL, Station Rd., New Sweden, ME 04762. Mailing Address: P.O. Box 50, New Sweden, ME 04762-0050. Fax: 207-896-3199.
E-mail: info@maineswedishcolony.info
Web Site: www.maineswedishcolony.info
Founded: 1989.
Congressional District: 2
Key Personnel: Pres. (V), William Duncan; Vice Pres., Matt Grandy; Dir., Allen Kampe; Dir., Linnea Helstrom; Dir., Ralph Ostlund; Sec., Jean Duncan; Treas., Alwin Espling; Correspondence Sec., Sylvia Kamps; Asst. Treas. & Museum Gift Shop Mgr., Rena Hultgren.
Personnel Profile: Full-Time Volunteers 2; Part-Time Volunteers 25.
Governing Authority: society; nonprofit. Parent Institution: Maine's Swedish Colony, Inc. Tax-exempt.
Historic Village.
Collections: blacksmith shop tools & equipment; woodworking & wheel-making equipment; period furnishings; c.1870 farm log home & buildings; one-room schoolhouse with furnishings & books; blacksmith shop.
Research Fields: history of Maine's Swedish Colony.
Facilities: Gift items for sale.
Activities: living museum activities.
Publications: newsletter to members; historical booklets; monographs; calendars; poetry.
Hours & Admission Prices: By appointment. ♿
Attendance: 4,500 (estimated)
Membership: Initiation Fee $50; Associate Membership $5; Life Membership $100.

NEW SWEDEN HISTORICAL SOCIETY, 116 Station Rd., New Sweden, ME 04762-3523. Mailing Address: P.O. Box 33, New Sweden, ME 04762. Tel.: 207-896-5240.
Web Site: www.maineswedishcolony.info
Founded: 1925.
Key Personnel: Pres., Debbie Eustis-Grandy; Sec., Janice McDougal; Treas. & Museum Shop Mgr., Gloria Ringdahl.
Personnel Profile: Part-Time Volunteers 20.
Governing Authority: society; nonprofit corporation. Tax-exempt.
Historical Society Museum: replica of original colony capital which burned in 1971.
Collections: historical collection, from life of early settlers of Maine's Swedish Colony in New Sweden, Maine founded 1870; household furnishings, textile equipment, farm equipment, photographs & portraits of immigrants; early furnishings; restored immigrant cottage, Lindsten Stuga.
Research Fields: family history & culture.
Facilities: picnic area.
Activities: Swedish language lessons. Museum Sponsors: Midsummer Celebration; Founder's Day Celebration; video series on Swedish-American topics in July.
Publications: newsletter.
Hours & Admission Prices: Memorial Day to Labor Day Mon.-Fri. 12-4, Sat.-Sun. 1-5; Sept.-May by appointment. No charge; donations accepted.
Attendance: 500 (estimated)
Membership: Individual $10; Family $20.

Newfield

19TH CENTURY WILLOWBROOK VILLAGE, (M), 70 Elm St., Newfield, ME 04056. Mailing Address: P.O. Box 28, Elm St., Newfield, ME 04056-0028. Tel.: 207-793-2784.
E-mail: director@willowbrookmuseum.org
Web Site: www.willowbrookmuseum.org
Founded: 1970.
Congressional District: 1
Key Personnel: C.E.O., Amelia E. Chamberlain; Chm. & Pres. (V), Donald Kopp; Museum Shop Mgr., Debbie Albert.
Personnel Profile: Full-Time Paid 1; Part-Time Paid 10; Part-Time Volunteers 35; Interns 1.
Governing Authority: individual operation. Tax-exempt.
History Museum.
Collections: arts & crafts; washing machines; churns; looms; shoe & harness making; carriages and sleighs; bicycles; gasoline engines; wheelrights; farm tools & equipment; costumes; musical instruments; toys; scales; barber shop; photo shop; country bank; print shop; carpenter shop; horse stock building; cooperage; boat shop. Historic Buildings: 1813 restored William Durgin Homestead; 1856 Dr. Isaac Trafton Homestead; 1810 schoolhouse; 1849 restored Concord stagecoach; 1894 restored Armitage-Herschell carousel powered by original steam engine.
Facilities: sandwich shop; ice cream parlor; country store; picnic area. Gift items for sale.
Activities: guided tours to organized educational groups; children's programs; demonstration & displays of heritage crafts & trades.
Publications: biannual newsletter, Willowbrook.
Hours & Admission Prices: Memorial Day to Oct. Thurs.-Mon. 10-5. Adults $9, seniors $7.50, students 6-18 $4; discounts to groups over 20, AAM members & local historical society members; children under 6 & members no charge. ♿
Attendance: 7,582 (accurate)
Membership: Individual $25; Dual $40; Family $50; Business/Library $100; Patron $250; Corporate $1,000.

Nobleboro

NOBLEBORO HISTORICAL SOCIETY, 198 Center St., Nobleboro, ME 04555. Mailing Address: P.O. Box 122, Nobleboro, ME 04555-0122. Tel.: 207-563-5376.
E-mail: sheldon@tidewater.net
Web Site: www.nobleborohistoricalsociety.org
Founded: 1978.
Congressional District: 1
Key Personnel: Pres. & Cur., Mary K. Sheldon; Treas., Eleanor O'Donnell.
Personnel Profile: Part-Time Volunteers 20.
Governing Authority: society; nonprofit. Tax-exempt.
Historical Society Museum: housed in an 1819 schoolhouse.
Collections: agricultural, forestry, Indians, sailing vessels, home utensils, schoolbooks, history books & industry artifacts; genealogical records; maps; cemeteries & town records.
Research Fields: local history; artifacts.
Facilities: 25-vol. library of local history books available to the public; 1,200 sq. ft. exhibit space; 40-seat auditorium; large screen theatre.
Activities: formal education for adults; temporary exhibitions. Annual Events: one day event for all school children; 5 society meetings.
Publications: biannual newsletter, Spring & Fall; brochure; news articles in weekly newspapers.
Hours & Admission Prices: July-Aug. Sat. 1:30-4:30 & for special exhibits; also by appointment. No charge; donations accepted.
Attendance: 450 (estimated)
Membership: Children $1; Single Adult $10; Family $15; Life $200.

North Amity

A.E. HOWELL WILDLIFE CONSERVATION CENTER & SPRUCE ACRES REFUGE, 101 Lycette Rd., North Amity, ME 04471-5114. Tel.: 207-532-6880. Fax: 207-532-6880 (call first).
E-mail: eagleman1008@earthlink.net
Web Site: www.spruceacresrefuge.org
Key Personnel: Vice Pres., Janet M. Easter; Dir., Kim Keehn
Wildlife Refuge.
Collections: native wildlife; plants.
Hours & Admission Prices: May-Oct. 15 Mon.-Sat. 10-4 by appointment. Adults $10; children under 16 no charge.

Northeast Harbor

GREAT HARBOR MARITIME MUSEUM, 124 Main St., Northeast Harbor, ME 04662. Mailing Address: P.O. Box 145, Northeast Harbor, ME 04662-0145. Tel.: 207-276-5262.
Formerly: Great Harbor Collection
Founded: 1982.
Congressional District: 5
Key Personnel: Co Chm. (V), Sydney Roberts Rockefeller; Co Chm. (V), Carl E. Kelley.
Personnel Profile: Part-Time Paid 1; Part-Time Volunteers 4.
Governing Authority: private; nonprofit organization. Tax-exempt: 501(c)(3).
Maritime Museum.
Collections: regional boats; harbors; boat builders; boat design; education; arts.
Major Exhibits: A Story of Morris Yachts, 6/10-9/10; Local Boat Models, 6/10-9/11.
Research Fields: oral history; lobstering; boat building; steamships; small boats.
Facilities: 2,700 sq. ft. exhibit space. Museum-related items for sale.
Activities: educational art programs; island exploration; lectures; arts festivals; films; formal education programs for children; participatory exhibits. Annual Event: exhibit openings with music.
Hours & Admission Prices: late June to mid-Oct. Tues.-Sun. 9-5. No charge; donations accepted. ♿
Attendance: 5,000 (estimated)

Oakfield

OAKFIELD RAILROAD MUSEUM, Station St., Oakfield, ME 04763. Mailing Address: Oakfield Historical Society, P.O. Box 176, Oakfield, ME 04763-0176. Tel.: 207-757-8575.
E-mail: oakfieldmuseum@pwless.net
Web Site: www.oakfieldmuseum.org
Railroad Museum.
Collections: early railroad transportation; photographs; period signs; signal lanterns; maps; telegraph equipment; newspapers; a Hand Car; Motor Car; C-66 caboose; small scale model railroad station.
Facilities: Museum-related items for sale.
Activities: tours; special events.
Hours & Admission Prices: late May to Labor Day Sat.-Sun. 1-4. No charge; donations accepted.

Oakland

MACARTNEY HOUSE MUSEUM, 25 Main St., Oakland, ME 04963. Mailing Address: P.O. Box 59, Oakland, ME 04963-0059. Tel.: 207-465-7549.
Founded: 1979.
Key Personnel: Pres. (V), Alberta Porter; Treas., Richard Lord; Cur., Ruth W. Wood.
Personnel Profile: Part-Time Volunteers 60.
Governing Authority: private; nonprofit organization.
History Museum.
Collections: Oakland area history; period furniture; artifacts.
Facilities: research library.
Publications: biannual newsletter.
Hours & Admission Prices: June-Aug. Wed. 1:30-4:30; other times by appointment. No charge; donations accepted.
Membership: Individual $5; Family $7.50; Life $50.

Ogunquit

OGUNQUIT MUSEUM OF AMERICAN ART, (M), 543 Shore Rd., Ogunquit, ME 03907-0815. Mailing Address: P.O. Box 815, Ogunquit, ME 03907-0815. Tel.: 207-646-4909. Fax: 207-646-6903.
E-mail: rcrusan@ogunquitmuseum.org
Web Site: ogunquitmuseum.org
Founded: 1952.
Congressional District: 1
Key Personnel: Dir., Ron Crusan; Pres. (V), Michael Kenslea; Coord. Visitor Svcs. & Museum Shop Mgr., Susan Joy Sager; Financial Operations & Membership Coord., Marsha Sibley.
Personnel Profile: Full-Time Paid 1; Part-Time Paid 6; Part-Time Volunteers 20; Interns 2.
Governing Authority: nonprofit organization. Tax-exempt: 501(c)(3).
Art Museum.
Collections: 19th-century to present American art.
Facilities: outside sculpture garden. Museum-related items for sale.
Activities: permanent exhibitions; individual & group shows.
Publications: annual illustrated catalog; museum bulletin.
Hours & Admission Prices: May-Oct. Mon.-Sat. 10-5, Sun. 1-5. Adults $7, seniors $5, students $4; children under 12 & members no charge. Closed Labor Day. ♿
Attendance: 16,000 (accurate)
Membership: Individual $35; Dual $60; Family $85; Associate $150; Supporting $250; Donor $500; Partner's Circle $1,000; Benefactor $5,000; Corporate $10,000.

Old Orchard Beach

OLD ORCHARD BEACH HISTORICAL SOCIETY, 4 Portland Ave., Old Orchard Beach, ME 04064-2212. Mailing Address: P.O. Box 464, Old Orchard Beach, ME 04064-0464. Tel.: 207-934-9319.
Key Personnel: Museum Trustee, Daniel Blaney; Pres., Arthur Guerin; Vice Pres., Charles Davis; Sec., Arlene Hanson; Treas., Priscilla Gallant; Cur., James Molloy; Projects Mgr. & Researcher, Evelyn Cooper
Historical Society Museum.
Collections: local history & culture; archives; photographs.
Activities: group tours.
Hours & Admission Prices: June 24 to Labor Day Tues.-Fri. 11-4, Sat. 9-12; other times by appointment.

Old Town

OLD TOWN MUSEUM, (M), 353 Main St., Old Town, ME 04468-1536. Mailing Address: P.O. Box 375, Old Town, ME 04468-0375. Tel.: 207-827-7256.
E-mail: eustis@infionline.net
Web Site: oldtownmuseum.com
Founded: 1976.
Congressional District: 2
Key Personnel: Exec. Bd. Member, Richard Eustis.
Personnel Profile: Part-Time Paid 1; Part-Time Volunteers 15.
Governing Authority: nonprofit. Tax-exempt: (501)(c)(3).
History Museum: housed in c.1928 former Church.
Collections: Civil War items; period telephones; costumes; glass ceramics; photographs; logging artifacts.
Facilities: Museum-related items for sale.
Activities: guided tours; lectures; films; organized educational programs for children; loan exhibitions.
Hours & Admission Prices: May-Oct. Wed.-Sun. 1-5. No charge. ♿
Attendance: 2,500 (accurate)
Membership: Regular $20; Civic Group & Corporate $100.

Orland

ORLAND HISTORICAL SOCIETY, Castine Rd., Orland, ME 04472. Mailing Address: P.O. Box 59, East Orland, ME 04431-0059. Tel.: 207-469-0077 & 7788. Fax: 207-469-0077.
E-mail: orland-historical@att.net
Founded: 1966.
Key Personnel: Pres. (V), Cindi Kimball; Treas., JoAnn Carlson.
Personnel Profile: Part-Time Volunteers 3.
Governing Authority: society. Tax-exempt.
General Museum: housed in 1800s store.
Collections: local historical artifacts.
Facilities: library of historical documents pertaining to early settlement of Orland available by appointment.
Activities: guided tours.
Publications: Orland Historical Highlights
Hours & Admission Prices: June-Sept. Wed. & Sat. 12-3; other times by appointment. No charge.
Attendance: 100 (estimated)
Membership: One Year $5; Two Years $10; Three Years $15; Five Years $20; Life $125.

Orono

THE FAY HYLAND BOTANICAL PLANTATION, 5751 Murray Hall, Univ. of Maine, Orono, ME 04469-0001. Tel.: 207-581-2540. Fax: 207-581-2537.
Founded: 1934.
Key Personnel: Chm., Dr. Christopher S. Campbell.
Governing Authority: university.
Arboretum.
Collections: trees & shrubs.
Research Fields: reproductive biology & biosystematics of woody plants.
Facilities: botanical garden; arboretum.
Activities: formally organized education programs for undergraduate college students.
Hours & Admission Prices: Daily dawn-dusk. No charge.

HUDSON MUSEUM, THE UNIVERSITY OF MAINE, 5476 Maine Center for the Arts, Orono, ME 04469-0001. Tel.: 207-581-1901. Fax: 207-581-1950.
E-mail: hudsonmuseum@umit.maine.edu
Web Site: www.umaine.edu/hudsonmuseum/
Founded: 1986.
Congressional District: 2
Key Personnel: Dir., Gretchen Faulkner; Registrar, Susan M. Smith; Museum Shop Mgr., Kathleen Maseychik.
Personnel Profile: Full-Time Paid 1; Part-Time Paid 2; Part-Time Volunteers 12; Interns 2.
Governing Authority: state government. Parent Institution: University of Maine. Tax-exempt.
Anthropology Museum.
Collections: ethnology collections from Oceania, Africa, Central, North & South America, Arctic, Asia; archaeological material from North, Central & South America.
Research Fields: ethnographic research in Northeastern United States.
Facilities: Publications in connection with exhibitions & museum-related items for sale.

Activities: guided tours; lectures; family program; collectors' workshop; intermuseum loans; permanent & temporary exhibitions. Annual Events: Maine Indian Basketmakers sale & demonstration.
Publications: gallery guides; Bibliographic Guide to the Native Peoples of Maine; newsletters, Totem; Realms.
Hours & Admission Prices: Mon.-Fri. 9-4. No charge; donations accepted. Closed federal & state holidays. ♿
Attendance: 67,427 (estimated)
Membership: Student, Educator & Senior $25; Basic $40; Contributor $100-$249; Supporter $250-$499; Palmer Circle $500 & up.

PAGE FARM & HOME MUSEUM - THE UNIVERSITY OF MAINE, Portage Rd., Orono, ME 04469-5787. Tel.: 207-581-4100.
Web Site: www.umaine.edu/pagefarm/
Key Personnel: Dir., Patricia Hemer
History Museum.
Collections: Maine farming history & cultural heritage.
Activities: special events.
Hours & Admission Prices: Tues.-Fri. 9-4, Sat.-Sun. 11-4. Closed holidays.

Orrington

CURRAN HOMESTEAD, Fields Pond Rd., Orrington, ME 04474. Mailing Address: P.O. Box 107, Orrington, ME 04474-0107. Tel.: 207-945-9311. Fax: 207-942-9914.
Living History Farm & Museum.
Collections: farm history; period furnishings; farm equipment & tools; photographs.
Activities: guided tours; demonstrations.
Hours & Admission Prices: Call for hours.

Owls Head

* **OWLS HEAD TRANSPORTATION MUSEUM, (M),** 117 Museum St., Rte. 73, Owls Head, ME 04854. Mailing Address: P.O. Box 277, Owls Head, ME 04854-0277. Tel.: 207-594-4418. Fax: 207-594-4410.
E-mail: info@ohtm.org
Web Site: www.ohtm.org
Founded: 1974.
Congressional District: 1
Key Personnel: Dir., Charles Chiarchiaro; Cur. & Dir. Education, Ethan Yankura; Chm., James S. Rockefeller, Jr.; Museum Shop Mgr., Michael Vilchinsky.
Personnel Profile: Full-Time Paid 12; Part-Time Paid 2; Part-Time Volunteers 200; Interns 2.
Governing Authority: nonprofit organization. Tax-exempt: 501(c)(3).
Transportation Museum.
Collections: pioneer air & ground vehicles.
Major Exhibits: Horse Power, 1/10-12/10.
Research Fields: evolution of transportation.
Facilities: library; reading room; nature park. Gift items for sale.
Activities: guided tours; lectures; films; gallery talks; TV & radio programs; formally organized education programs; operational weekend displays.
Publications: quarterly newsletter, The Strut and Axle; collections catalog; History of the Museum.
Hours & Admission Prices: Daily 10-5. Adults $10, seniors 65 & over $8; children under 18 & members no charge. Closed New Year's Day; Thanksgiving; Christmas. ♿
Attendance: 96,377 (accurate)
Membership: Individual $40; Family $60; Participating $100; Supporting $250; Sustaining $500; Benefactor $1,000; Life $5,000.

Paris

HAMLIN MEMORIAL LIBRARY & MUSEUM, Hannibal Hamlin Dr., Paris, ME 04271. Mailing Address: P.O. Box 43, Paris, ME 04271-0043. Tel.: 207-743-2980.
E-mail: hamlinstaff@hamlin.lib.me.us
Web Site: www.hamlin.lib.me.us
Historic Building: built in 1822.
Collections: portraits of members of early Paris families; Lincoln-Hamlin campaign artifacts; local minerals & gems; grandfather clock; friendship quilt.
Hours & Admission Prices: April 1-Nov. 1 Tues.-Thurs. 11-5, Sat. 10-3.

Patten

PATTEN LUMBERMEN'S MUSEUM, INC., 61 Shin Pond Rd., Patten, ME 04765. Mailing Address: P.O. Box 300, Patten, ME 04765-0300. Tel.: 207-528-2650. Fax: 207-528-2650.
E-mail: curator@lumbermensmuseum.org
Web Site: www.lumbermensmuseum.org
Founded: 1963.
Key Personnel: Dir. & Cur., Rhonda R. Brophy; Pres., Donald Shorey; Vice Pres., Bud Blumenstock.
Personnel Profile: Full-Time Paid 1; Full-Time Volunteers 40; Part-Time Paid 3; Part-Time Volunteers 30; Interns 1.
Governing Authority: nonprofit organization. Tax-exempt: 501(c)(3).
Logging & Lumbering History Museum.
Collections: lumberman, carpenter, wheelwright, cooper & blacksmith tools; horse drawn logging equipment; bateaux; Lombard loghaulers; photographs; paintings; working models of saw mills; early trucks; 1820 logging camp; double camp; single camp; blacksmith shop.
Facilities: reception center. Books, postcards & memorabilia for sale.
Activities: guided tours; permanent exhibitions. Annual Event: Bean Hole Bean Dinner in August.
Hours & Admission Prices: Memorial Day to June Fri.-Sun. 10-4; July-Oct. Tues.-Sun.10-4. Adults $8, seniors $5, children 7-12 $3; discounts to groups, AAM & AAA members; members & children under 6 no charge. ♿
Attendance: 3,800 (estimated)
Membership: Individual $10; Family $20; Friend $25; Steward $50; Supporter $75; Sustaining $100; Sponsor $150; Patron $200; Benefactor $500; Guardian $1,000.

Peaks Island

FIFTH MAINE REGIMENT MUSEUM, 45 Seashore Ave., Peaks Island, ME 04108-1311. Mailing Address: P.O. Box 41, Peaks Island, ME 04108-0041. Tel.: 207-766-3330. Fax: 207-766-5514.
E-mail: fifthmaine@juno.com
Web Site: www.fifthmainemuseum.org
Founded: 1954.
Congressional District: 1
Key Personnel: Pres. (V), William B. Zimmerman; Treas., Carol A. Kinney; Dir. & Cur., Kim Mac Isaac; Museum Shop Mgr., Joy Kilbourn; Museum Educator, Patricia Erikson.
Personnel Profile: Full-Time Paid 1; Part-Time Paid 1; Part-Time Volunteers 25; Interns 1.
Governing Authority: private; nonprofit. Tax-exempt: 501(c)(3).
Military Museum: housed in the Fifth Maine Regiment Memorial Hall, built in 1888 as a Civil War Memorial & Reunion Hall; listed in the National Register of Historic Places.
Collections: focuses on the Civil War with special emphasis on the Fifth Maine soldiers & Maine's role; Peaks Island history from c.1600 to present.
Research Fields: war time activities of the Fifth Maine Regiment; post-war lives of many of the Fifth Maine soldiers.
Facilities: library; resource room; 100-seat auditorium; 1,528 sq. ft. exhibit space; dining room. Civil War & local history books, maps, T-shirts and caps for sale.
Activities: concerts; docent program; formal education programs for children & college students; guided tours; lectures; temporary & permanent exhibitions. Annual Events: fair; Civil War reenactment.
Publications: biannual newsletter, Fifth Maine News; An Island at War: The Peaks Island Military Reservation 1942-1946.
Hours & Admission Prices: Mon.-Fri. 12-4, Sat.-Sun. 11-4. Suggested Donation: adults $5; discounts to New England Museum Association, Maine Archives & Museums, AASLH and Civil War Preservation Trust members. ♿
Attendance: 6,000 (accurate)
Membership: Individual $15; Family $30; Patron $50; Hundred Club $100; Corporate $250.

Phillips

PHILLIPS HISTORICAL SOCIETY, 8 Pleasant St., Phillips, ME 04966. Mailing Address: P.O. Box 216, Phillips, ME 04966-0216. Tel.: 207-639-3111.
Founded: 1959.
Congressional District: 2
Key Personnel: Pres., Dennis Atkinson.
Personnel Profile: Part-Time Volunteers 12.
Governing Authority: society. Subsidiary Institution: Sandy River & Rangeley Lakes R.R. Tax-exempt: 501(c)(3).
General Museum: housed in 1832 house owned by important local families connected with town's history.

TRUST FOR THE PRESERVATION OF MAINE INDUSTRIAL HISTORY AND TECHNOLOGY D/B/A MAINE NARROW GAUGE RAILROAD CO. & MUSEUM, 58 Fore St., Portland, ME 04101-4842. Tel.: 207-828-0814. Fax: 207-879-6132.
E-mail: info@mngrr.org
Web Site: www.mngrr.org
Founded: 1993.
Key Personnel: Dir., Susan S. Davis; Pres., Erving Bickford; Museum Shop Mgr., Allison Tivsh Zittel.
Personnel Profile: Full-Time Paid 3; Full-Time Volunteers 10; Part-Time Paid 3; Part-Time Volunteers 40.
Governing Authority: bd. of trustees.
Railroad Museum.
Collections: two-foot gauge trains; period rail cars; steam & diesel locomotives.
Facilities: Museum-related items for sale.
Activities: birthday parties; train rides; special events. Museum Sponsors: Polar Express in December.
Publications: Two Foot Flyer.
Hours & Admission Prices: Museum: Jan. 4-Feb. 11 Sat.-Sun. 10-3; Feb. 12-Dec. daily 10-4. Adults $2, seniors & children 3-12 $1. Train Rides: Feb. 13-May 28 Sat.-Sun. 11-3; May 29-June & Sept.-Oct. 11 daily 11-3; July 4 to Labor Day daily 11-4. Adults $10, senior citizens $9, children 3-12 $6; children under 2 no charge. Closed New Year's Day; Thanksgiving; Christmas. ♿
Attendance: 40,000 (estimated)
Membership: Students & Seniors $25; Individual $35; Family $65; Supporter $100-$249; Sponsor $250-$499; Benefactor $500-$999; Patron $1,000-$4,999; Lifetime $5,000.

UNIVERSITY OF NEW ENGLAND GALLERY OF ART, 716 Stevens Ave., University of New England, Westbrook College Campus, Portland, ME 04103-2693. Tel.: 207-221-4499. Fax: 207-523-1901.
E-mail: azill@une.edu
Web Site: www.une.edu/artgallery
Formerly: Payson Gallery
Founded: 1977.
Congressional District: 1
Key Personnel: Dir., Anne B. Zill.
Personnel Profile: Full-Time Paid 1; Part-Time Paid 3; Part-Time Volunteers 2; Interns 1.
Governing Authority: private university.
Fine Art Gallery.
Collections: 19th-20th century art; contemporary arts; photographs; paintings; prints; sculpture.
Activities: formal education programs for UNE, adults & children; lectures; loan & temporary exhibitions.
Hours & Admission Prices: Wed. & Fri.-Sun. 1-4, Thurs. 1-7. No charge; donations accepted. Closed Easter; Independence Day; Thanksgiving; Christmas.
Attendance: 10,000 (estimated)
Membership: $35; $50; $100; $500; $1,000.

VICTORIA MANSION, (M), 109 Danforth St., Portland, ME 04101-4504. Tel.: 207-772-4841. Fax: 207-772-6290.
E-mail: information@victoriamansion.org
Web Site: www.victoriamansion.org
Founded: 1941.
Congressional District: 1
Key Personnel: Pres. (V), Michael Stone; Dir., Robert Wolterstorff; Deputy Dir. Administration, Julia Kirby; Office Mgr., Timothy Brosnihan; Site Mgr. & Education Asst., Katie Worthing; Dir. Education, Tracy Quimby; Museum Shop Mgr., Alice Dwyer Ross.
Personnel Profile: Full-Time Paid 3; Part-Time Paid 10; Part-Time Volunteers 60.
Governing Authority: nonprofit organization. Tax-exempt: 501(c)(3).
Historic House Museum: National Historic Landmark.
Collections: the first and only known surviving commission of Gustave Herter, 1858-1860; original house contents including furniture, gas lighting fixtures, wall paintings, artworks, carpets, stained glass, porcelain, textiles & architecture.
Research Fields: 19th & early 20th-century material culture, architecture & the decorative arts & social history.
Facilities: Carriage House: gift-items for sale such as Victorian-era style items, Victorian Mansion memorabilia & books.
Activities: guided tours; temporary exhibitions; educational programs: lectures & displays. Museum Sponsors: special installations & tours in December.
Publications: newsletter 3 times per year; brochures; A Guide to Victoria Mansion.
Hours & Admission Prices: May-Oct. Mon.-Sat. 10-4, Sun. 1-5, group tours by appointment. Adults $15, children 6-17 $4; discounts to senior citizens, groups, AAM, AAA members; children under 6 & members no charge. ♿
Attendance: 17,759 (accurate)
Membership: Individual $35; Family & Household $65; Supporting $125; Herter Circle $125 & up; Hester Circle $250 & up; Morse Assoc. $1,000 & up.

Presque Isle

THE NORTHERN MAINE MUSEUM OF SCIENCE, UNIVERSITY OF MAINE, Folsom Hall, 181 Main St., Presque Isle, ME 04769-2844. Tel.: 207-768-9482. Fax: 207-768-9553.
Web Site: www.umpi.maine.edu/info/nmms/about.htm
Key Personnel: Dir., Dr. Kevin McCartney; Cur. Chemistry, Michael Knopp, Ph.D.; Cur. Herbarium, Robert J. Pinette, Ph.D.; Cur. Mathematics, Richard Kimball; Cur. Collections, Jeanie McGowan
Science Museum.
Collections: fresh-water sea shells; local forestry specimens; biology; geology; chemistry; physics; agriculture.
Activities: tours.
Hours & Admission Prices: Daily 7am-10pm. No charge. Closed university holidays & breaks.

PRESQUE ISLE AIR MUSEUM, Northern Maine Regional Airport, 650 Airport Dr., Ste. 4, Presque Isle, ME 04769. Tel.: 207-764-2542.
E-mail: piairmuseum@fcmail.com
Founded: 1999.
Congressional District: 1
History & Pictorial Museum.
Collections: historical artifacts & photographs relating to the 1930s, WWII, the Cold War & the Missile age.
Hours & Admission Prices: Call for hours. No charge; donations accepted. ♿
Attendance: 10,000 (estimated)

Prospect

FORT KNOX STATE HISTORIC SITE AND PENOBSCOT NARROWS OBSERVATORY, 711 Fort Knox Rd., Prospect, ME 04981-3125. Mailing Address: P.O. Box 456, Bucksport, ME 04416-0456. Tel.: 207-469-7719 & 6553. Fax: 207-469-6906.
E-mail: fofk1@aol.com
Web Site: fortknox.maineguide.com
Founded: 1923.
Congressional District: 2
Key Personnel: Exec. Dir., Leon Seymour; Pres. (V), Chris Popper; Mgr., Mike Wilusz.
Personnel Profile: Full-Time Paid 1; Part-Time Paid 8; Part-Time Volunteers 13.
Governing Authority: state. Affiliated with Bureau of Parks & Lands Augusta, ME 04333. Subsidiary Institution: Friends of Fort Knox. Tax-exempt.
Historic Site: 1844 Fort Knox.
Collections: 19th-century fort; Rodman cannons.
Facilities: picnic area; activity field.
Activities: guided tours; special tours by arrangement. Museum Sponsors: Civil War Reenactment; weekend special events.
Publications: folder, Maine Fort Histories.
Hours & Admission Prices: May-Oct. call for hours & admission prices. ♿
Attendance: 50,000 (estimated)
Membership: Individual $20; Vehicle (includes all occupants) $40.

Rangeley

RANGELEY LAKES REGION LOGGING MUSEUM, Rte. 16, Rangeley, ME 04970. Mailing Address: P.O. Box 154, Rangeley, ME 04970-0154. Tel.: 207-864-3939 & 5595.
E-mail: myocom@gmu.edu
Web Site: mason.gmu.edu/~myocom
Founded: 1979.
Congressional District: 2
Key Personnel: Pres. (V) & Dir., Rodney C. Richard, Sr.; Vice Pres., Ron Haines; Festival Coord., Stephen A. Richard; Public Rels., Cur. & Archivist, Dr. Margaret Yocom; Treas., Harry Simon.
Personnel Profile: Part-Time Paid 1.
Governing Authority: private; nonprofit organization. Tax-exempt: 501(c)(3).
Logging Museum.
Collections: logging in the western mountains of Maine; history & folk life of logging; tools; equipment; early photographs; woodcarving; paintings; textile arts.
Research Fields: history of local loggers; log driving; folk arts & related logging culture.
Facilities: 30-vol. library. Museum-related items for sale.

Activities: woodcarving; painting; knitting; storytelling; lectures; group tours. Annual Events: Logging Festival in July; Knit, Crochet, Craft Show & Sale; Auction; Apple Festival.
Publications: books, Logging in the Maine Woods: The Paintings of Alden Grant; Working the Woods.
Hours & Admission Prices: July to Labor Day Sat.-Sun. 11-2; other times by appointment. No charge; donations accepted. ♿
Attendance: 400 (estimated)
Membership: Individual $5.

WILHELM REICH MUSEUM - ORGONON, Dodge Pond Rd., Rangeley, ME 04970. Mailing Address: P.O. Box 687, Rangeley, ME 04970-0687. Tel.: 207-864-3443. Fax: 207-864-5156.
E-mail: wreich@rangeley.org
Web Site: www.wilhelmreichmuseum.org
Historic House Museum: housed in the home, laboratory & research center of physician & scientist, Wilhelm Reich, M.D.
Collections: Reich's life & work; inventions & scientific equipment; personal artifacts; paintings; sculptures.
Facilities: 175 acres; nature trails; Orgone Energy Observatory. Books for sale.
Activities: video. Annual Event: Summer Conferences.
Hours & Admission Prices: Conference Center: Mon.-Fri. 9-2. Observatory: July-Aug. Wed.-Sun. 1-5; Sept. Sun. 1-5; other times by appointment. Adults $6; children 12 & under no charge.

Richmond

CHTJ SOUTHARD HOUSE MUSEUM, 75 Main St., Richmond, ME 04357. Tel.: 207-737-8202 & 8772. Fax: 207-737-8772.
Founded: 1990.
Key Personnel: C.E.O. & Financial Dir., Frederic F. Case; Chm. (V), Wilber A. Cooper; Pres. (V) & Cur., Carolyn Cooper Case.
Personnel Profile: Part-Time Volunteers 6.
Governing Authority: nonprofit. Tax-exempt: 501(c)(3).
Historic House: housed in c.1870 Victorian building, restructured in 1886, located in the heart of historic district. Known as shipbuilding & ice-harvesting community at turn-of-the-century.
Collections: period agricultural & woodworking tools from 1700s to early 1900s; toys & dolls from 1800s to early 1900s; clothing, quilts & other textiles from late 1700s to early 1900s; local history & family life artifacts from 1800s to early 1900s.
Research Fields: local oral history; news items from local newspapers & town reports from 1800s to present available to public on a limited basis; construction & use of antique tools; indigenous flora & fauna; changing ecosystem & tidal lowlands.
Facilities: library; 6,000 sq. ft. exhibit space; educational facilities; field research station & observation tower with view of Kennebec River.
Activities: guided tours; study clubs. Annual Event: Open House: Richmond Days in June.
Hours & Admission Prices: Call for hours. Donations $1. No charge during Richmond Days.
Attendance: 550 (estimated)

Rockland

MAINE LIGHTHOUSE MUSEUM, One Park Dr., Rockland, ME 04841. Mailing Address: P.O. Box 1116, Rockland, ME 04841-1116. Tel.: 207-594-3301. Fax: 207-596-6549.
E-mail: info@mainelighthousemuseum.org
Web Site: www.mainelighthousemuseum.org
Formerly: Shore Village Museum
Founded: 2005.
Congressional District: 1
Key Personnel: Dir., Dorothy Black; Chm. (V), Paul Dilger; Visitor Svcs. Mgr., Julia Friese.
Personnel Profile: Full-Time Volunteers 2; Part-Time Paid 2; Part-Time Volunteers 25.
Governing Authority: Parent Institution: Maine Lighthouse Museum, Inc. Tax-exempt.
Maritime: Maine Lighthouse Museum.
Collections: lighthouse artifacts; related books; marine items from the U.S. Coast Guard including working foghorns, lights, lenses; scrimshaw lobster-ing tools; ship models; items of local historic interest; lighthouse lenses.
Research Fields: local history; documentation records dating from late 1860s.
Activities: guided tours; lectures; gallery talks; loan, permanent & temporary exhibitions; special programs for children.
Publications: newsletter.
Hours & Admission Prices: Mon.-Fri. 9-5, Sat.-Sun. 10-4. Adults $5; members & children under 12 no charge. ♿
Attendance: 12,000 (estimated)
Membership: Basic $25; Family $50; Supporting $100; Sustaining $250; Sponsor $500; Lightkeeper $1,000.

*** WILLIAM A. FARNSWORTH LIBRARY AND ART MUSEUM, INC. D/B/A FARNSWORTH ART MUSEUM,** 16 Museum St., Rockland, ME 04841-2867. Tel.: 207-596-6457. Fax: 207-596-0509.
E-mail: writeus@farnsworthmuseum.org
Web Site: www.farnsworthmuseum.org
Founded: 1948.
Congressional District: 1
Key Personnel: Interim Dir. & Chief Cur., Michael K. Komanecky; Trustee, Richard Aroneau; Business Mgr., Cathy Knowles; Cur. Historic Properties, Janice Kasper; Chief Cur., Michael Komanecky; Registrar, Angela Waldron; Dir. Operations, Jeffrey Charland.
Personnel Profile: Full-Time Paid 25; Part-Time Paid 24; Part-Time Volunteers 250.
Governing Authority: board of directors. Tax-exempt: 501(c)(3).
Art Museum.
Collections: 19th-20th century American art related to Maine; works by Andrew, N.C., James Wyeth, George Bellows, & Fitz Hugh Lane; Louise Nevelson; photographs; prints. Historic Houses: c.1850 Farnsworth Homestead; c.1820 Olson House.
Research Fields: Maine & American art.
Facilities: 4,250-vol. library; general art reference area; special archive collections; educational facilities. Museum-related items for sale.
Activities: guided tours; lectures; films; gallery talks; concerts; permanent, temporary & traveling exhibitions; artist residency program.
Publications: books; exhibition catalogs; annual reports.
Hours & Admission Prices: Memorial Day-Columbus Day daily 10-5. Winter Hours: Tues.-Sun. 10-5. Adults $12, senior citizens & students $10; discounts to AAM & ICOM members; members & New England Consortium of Museums members no charge. ♿
Attendance: 65,000 (accurate)
Membership: Student $30; Senior 65 & over $50; Individual $60; Senior Dual $75; Dual $85; Partner $150; Patron $250; Sustainer $500; Circle $1,000; Benefactor $2,500; Founder $5,000.

Rockport

CENTER FOR MAINE CONTEMPORARY ART, 162 Russell Ave., Rockport, ME 04856. Mailing Address: P.O. Box 147, Rockport, ME 04856-0147. Tel.: 207-236-2875, ext. 306. Fax: 207-236-2490.
E-mail: info@cmcanow.org
Web Site: www.cmcanow.org
Formerly: Maine Coast Artists
Founded: 1952.
Congressional District: 1
Key Personnel: Acting Exec. Dir. & Cur., Britta Konau; Mgr. Operations & Finance, Kat Richman; Chm., Penny Harris; Curatorial & Devel. Asst., Melissa Poulin; Dir. Education, Cathy Melio; Museum Shop Mgr., Barbara Michelena.
Personnel Profile: Full-Time Paid 5; Part-Time Paid 1; Part-Time Volunteers 80; Interns 2.
Governing Authority: nonprofit corporation. Tax-exempt.
Contemporary Art.
Collections: paintings; photographs; prints; sculpture.
Major Exhibits: Yvonne Jacquette: Works on Paper, 5/10-7/10; Post-Natural, 5/10-7/10; 2010 Biennial Juried Exhibition, 8/10-9/10; Dozier Bell, 10/10-12/10.
Research Fields: Maine artists & their work; current Maine artists.
Activities: workshops; lectures; temporary exhibitions; evening programs; art tours; works of Maine artists.
Publications: exhibition catalogs.
Hours & Admission Prices: Tues.-Sat. 10-5, Sun. 1-5. Adults $5; discounts to NARM members; children & members no charge. ♿
Attendance: 15,000 (estimated)
Membership: Artists $25; Individual $40; Family $60; Patron $125; Contributor $250; Supporter $500; Curator's Circle $1,000.

Saco

SACO MUSEUM, (M), 371 Main St., Saco, ME 04072-1520. Tel.: 207-283-3861. Fax: 207-283-0754.
E-mail: museum@sacomuseum.org
Web Site: www.sacomuseum.org
Formerly: York Institute Museum
Founded: 1867.
Congressional District: 1
Key Personnel: Dir., Jessica Routhier; Exec. Dir., Leslie Rounds; Collections Mgr., Marie O'Brien; Program & Education Mgr., Camille Smalley.
Personnel Profile: Full-Time Paid 2; Part-Time Paid 3; Part-Time Volunteers 13; Interns 2.

Governing Authority: nonprofit organization. Parent Institution: Dyer Library Association. Tax-exempt: 501(c)(3).
History & Art Museum.
Collections: Colonial & Federal period fine & decorative arts; regional paintings & furniture; works by John Brewster, Jr., Gibeon Elden Bradbury & Charles Henry Granger; historical & contemporary issues.
Major Exhibits: The Maine Art Educators Association, 1/15/10-3/20/10; The Mill-ennial: Celebrating the Art and Artists of the Cities on the Saco, 4/2/10-6/13/10; Making History: Art and Industry in the Saco River Valley, 5/29/10-12/10; In A Place By Himself: The Graphic World of Winslow Homer, 6/26/10-11/14/10; Festival of Trees, 11/26/10-12/10.
Research Fields: Maine history; 18th to 20th-century American Art; decorative arts research.
Activities: guided tours; inter-museum loan, permanent & temporary exhibitions; programs include Artist-in-Residence courses in fine arts, lecture series, teacher workshops & gallery talks.
Publications: occasional monographs.
Hours & Admission Prices: Tues.-Thurs. & Sun. 12-4, Fri. 12-8, Sat. 10-4. Adults $4, seniors $3, students & children $2; discounts to NEMA, AAA, AAM & ICOM members; members & Fri. 4-8 no charge. Closed legal holidays. ♿
Attendance: 9,675 (accurate)
Membership: Individual $25.

Saint George

MARSHALL POINT LIGHTHOUSE MUSEUM, Rte. 131 Port Clyde Rd., Saint George, ME 04860. Mailing Address: P.O. Box 247, Port Clyde, ME 04855-0247. Tel.: 207-372-6450.
Web Site: www.marshallpoint.org
Key Personnel: Chm., Bob Sierer; Dir., Jim Quinn; Museum Shop Mgr., Jan Smith
History Museum.
Collections: local quarry history; tool; photographs; fishing in St. George; miniature lobster trap buoys; lighthouse memorabilia; area history.
Facilities: Museum-related items for sale.
Hours & Admission Prices: May Sat.-Sun. 1-5; Memorial Day to Columbus Day Sun.-Fri. 1-5, Sat. 10-5.

Scarborough

SCARBOROUGH HISTORICAL MUSEUM, 649A U.S. Rte. 1 Dunstan, Scarborough, ME 04074. Mailing Address: P.O. Box 156, Scarborough, ME 04070-0156. Tel.: 207-883-3539.
Founded: 1961.
Congressional District: 1
Key Personnel: Pres. (V), Rodney Laughton.
Personnel Profile: Part-Time Volunteers 9.
Governing Authority: society. Parent Institution: Scarborough Historical Society, Inc. Tax-exempt: 170(b)(1)(A).
History Museum.
Collections: tools; colonial farmhouse memorabilia; old school records & pictures; old town valuation books & records.
Facilities: over 500-vol. library of books pertaining to local & state history, Scarborough town record books, bibles & old school books.
Activities: guided tours; lectures; permanent & temporary exhibitions.
Publications: quarterly newsletter, Owascoag Notes.
Hours & Admission Prices: Tues. 9-12; other times by appointment. No charge; donations accepted. ♿
Attendance: 225 (estimated)
Membership: Student $1; Individual $10; Sponsor $25; Life $75; Benefactor $100.

Seal Cove

THE SEAL COVE AUTO MUSEUM, (M), Pretty Marsh Rd., 1414 Tremont Rd., Seal Cove, ME 04674. Mailing Address: P.O. Box 45, Mount Desert, ME 04660. Tel.: 207-244-9242.
E-mail: info@sealcoveautomuseum.org
Web Site: www.sealcoveautomuseum.org
Founded: 1963.
Key Personnel: Exec. Dir., Roberto Rodriguez; Pres. (V), Peter Murray.
Personnel Profile: Full-Time Paid 2; Part-Time Paid 2.
Governing Authority: Tax-exempt.
Transportation Museum.
Collections: antique cars & motorcycles.
Activities: programs.
Hours & Admission Prices: Memorial Day to Columbus Day daily 10-5. Adults $5; discounts to AAM members. ♿
Attendance: 4,000 (estimated)
Membership: Individual $45; Family $65; Supporting $100.

Searsport

* **PENOBSCOT MARINE MUSEUM, (M),** 5 Church St., Searsport, ME 04974-3351. Mailing Address: P.O. Box 498, Searsport, ME 04974-0498. Tel.: 207-548-2529. Fax: 207-548-2520.
E-mail: museumoffices@pmm-maine.org
Web Site: www.penobscotmarinemuseum.org
Founded: 1936.
Congressional District: 1
Key Personnel: Exec. Dir., Niles Parker; Cur., Benjamin A.G. Fuller; Dir. Education, Betty Schopmeyer; Business Mgr., Matthew Timney.
Personnel Profile: Full-Time Paid 11; Full-Time Volunteers 1; Part-Time Paid 19; Part-Time Volunteers 18; Interns 1.
Governing Authority: nonprofit corporation. Tax-exempt: 501(c)(3).
Maritime Museum: housed in the homes of three former shipmasters and the original Town Hall.
Collections: paintings; prints; ship models; builders half models; small craft collection; shipbuilding tools; navigational instruments; charts; 19th-century American & Oriental furnishings; log books; manuscripts; genealogy; whaling memorabilia. Historic Houses: 1805/1837 Fowler House; 1845 Old Town Hall; 1860 Merithew House; 1880 Nichols House; 1843 Education Center.
Research Fields: Maine & regional maritime history.
Facilities: 12,000-vol. library on maritime history available for use on premises.
Activities: permanent & temporary exhibitions; guided tours; school loan service; inter-museum loans; special art exhibitions; degree programs with Univ. of Maine-Orono & Colby College. Annual Event: Fall Regional History Conference.
Publications: catalogs; annual report; newsletter, The Bay Chronicle.
Hours & Admission Prices: Mon.-Sat. 10-5, Sun. 12-5. Family $18, adults $8, children 7-15 $3; discounts to local guests of Inns, groups, AAM & CAMM members; children under 7 & members no charge. ♿
Attendance: 13,000 (accurate)
Membership: Friend $40; Supporter $65; Contributor $150; Sponsor $250; Patron $500; Benefactor $1,000; President's Circle $2,000.

Sedgwick

SEDGWICK-BROOKLIN HISTORICAL SOCIETY, 575 N. Sedgwick Rd., Sedgwick, ME 04676. Mailing Address: P.O. Box 171, Sedgwick, ME 04676-0063. Tel.: 207-359-4422.
Founded: 1963.
Congressional District: 2
Key Personnel: Pres. & Chm. (V), John Bishof; Dir., Elaine S. Trowbridge.
Personnel Profile: Part-Time Paid 1.
Governing Authority: board of trustees; nonprofit organization. Tax-exempt: 501(c)(3).
History Museum: housed in 1795 Rev. Daniel Merrill house.
Collections: archives; local history; tools; toys; photographs; horse-drawn hearses; barn; clothing; farm equipment. Historical Buildings: c.1795 Reverend Daniel Merrill House; 1793-1794 Sedgwick Town House & Common; 1821 Town Cattle Pound; Hearse House; 1798 rural cemetery; renovated barn using timber & boards from original structure.
Research Fields: archives; local history; genealogy.
Facilities: library of old account books, maps, genealogical material & local histories; reading room.
Activities: lectures; programs. Museum Sponsors: annual Ax Throwing Contest.
Publications: booklets, History of Brooklin, Maine, 1876; Our Tradition of Optimism; History of Sedgwick; map, Plan of Sedgwick (Township #4); The Cemeteries of Brooklin, Maine a Genealogist's Guide; Life and Times in a Coastal Village/Sedgwick, Maine 1789-1989; Sedgwick Cemeteries.
Hours & Admission Prices: July-Aug. Sun. 2-4; other times by appointment. No charge; donations accepted.
Attendance: 100 (estimated)
Membership: Single $10; Family $20; Enthusiastic $35; Stalwart $60; Committed $100.

Skowhegan

MARGARET CHASE SMITH LIBRARY, 56 Norridgewock Ave., Skowhegan, ME 04976-1204. Tel.: 207-474-7133.
E-mail: gpg@mcslibrary.org
Web Site: www.mcslibrary.org
Key Personnel: Dir., Gregory Gallant
Library & Archives.
Collections: life & career of Senator Margaret Chase Smith.
Facilities: library.
Activities: group tours; educational programs; research; educational programs.
Hours & Admission Prices: Mon.-Fri. 10-4.

SKOWHEGAN HISTORY HOUSE INC., 66 Elm St., Skowhegan, ME 04976-0832. Mailing Address: P.O. Box 832, Showhegan, ME 04976-0832. Tel.: 207-474-6632.
E-mail: skowheganhistoryhouse@hotmail.com
Web Site: skowhegan.maineusa.com/kb/historyh/index.htm
Founded: 1937.
Congressional District: 93
Key Personnel: Pres., Melvin Burnham; Sec., Margaret Reid; Treas., Patricia Horine; Cur., Lee Granville.
Personnel Profile: Part-Time Paid 1; Part-Time Volunteers 7.
Governing Authority: nonprofit organization. Parent Institution: Bloomfield Trust. Tax-exempt: 501(c)(3).
Local History Museum: built in 1839.
Collections: furnishings; toys; Civil War; guns; early town records.
Research Fields: local history; historic documents; family histories.
Facilities: 500-vol. library of books on local history available for use on premises.
Activities: Museum Sponsors: Annual Garden Party in June; Arts & Garden Tour in July.
Publications: association newsletter.
Hours & Admission Prices: mid-June to mid-Sept. Tues.-Fri. 1-5; school classes by appointment. No charge; donations accepted. Closed Independence Day.
Attendance: 490 (accurate)
Membership: Senior $15; Adult $25; Life $125.

South Berwick

HAMILTON HOUSE, 40 Vaughan's Lane, South Berwick, ME 03908-1711. Mailing Address: 141 Cambridge St., Boston, MA 02114-2702. Tel.: 207-384-2454; 617-227-3956 (Historic New England). Fax: 617-227-9204.
Web Site: www.historicnewengland.org
Founded: 1949.
Congressional District: 1
Key Personnel: Pres., Carl Nold; Site Mgr., Peggy Wishart.
Governing Authority: society; nonprofit organization. Parent Institution: Historic New England, 141 Cambridge St., Boston, MA 02114. Tel. 617-227-3956. Tax-exempt: 501(c)(3).
Historic House: c.1785 Hamilton House, Georgian estate overlooking the Salmon Falls River.
Collections: furniture & artifacts of the 18th & 19th centuries; colonial revival reproduction of wallpapers, personal & decorative objects belonging to Mrs. Tyson & her stepdaughter.
Facilities: garden.
Activities: guided tours; lectures & special events; concerts in the garden.
Publications: Historic New England Guide.
Hours & Admission Prices: June-Oct. 15 Wed.-Sun. 11-4. Adults $8; discounts to seniors, AAM, ICOM, AAA, WGBH members; members no charge.
Attendance: 4,334 (accurate)
Membership: National $35; Individual $45; Household $55; Garden & Landscape $75; Institutional $85; Contributing $100; Historic Homeowner $200; Supporting $250.

SARAH ORNE JEWETT HOUSE, 5 Portland St., South Berwick, ME 03908. Mailing Address: 141 Cambridge St., Boston, MA 02114-2702. Tel.: 207-384-2454; 617-227-3956 (Historic New England). Fax: 617-227-9204.
E-mail: jewetthouse@historicnewengland.org
Web Site: www.historicnewengland.org
Founded: 1931.
Key Personnel: Pres., Carl Nold; Site. Mgr., Peggy Wishart.
Governing Authority: society; nonprofit organization. Parent Institution: Historic New England, 141 Cambridge St., Boston, MA 02114. Tel.: 617-227-3956. Tax-exempt: 501(c)(3).
Historic House: 1774 Georgian residence of the celebrated regional author Sarah Orne Jewett.
Collections: furniture; artifacts; refurbished original wall paper & paneling.
Activities: guided tours; special events; lectures.
Publications: Guide to Historic New England.
Hours & Admission Prices: June-Oct. 15 Fri.-Sun. 11-5. Adults $5; discounts to seniors, AAM, ICOM, AAA, WGBH members; members no charge. Call for further information.
Attendance: 1,909 (accurate)
Membership: Historic New England: National $35; Individual $45; Household $55; Garden & Landscape $75; Institutional $85; Contributing $100; Historic Homeowner $200; Supporting $250.

Southport

HENDRICKS HILL MUSEUM, 417 Hendricks Hill Rd., Rte. 27, Southport, ME 04576. Mailing Address: P.O. Box 3, Southport, ME 04576-0003. Tel.: 207-633-1102.
Founded: 1988.
Congressional District: 1
Personnel Profile: Part-Time Volunteers 45.
Governing Authority: Tax-exempt: 501(c)(3).
History Museum: housed in 1810 farmhouse.
Collections: period furnishings; 1850-1960 fishing equipment; photographs; genealogical. Boatshop: boats, tools, ice harvesting equipment.
Activities: tours.
Publications: annual newsletter; local history books.
Hours & Admission Prices: July-Labor Day Tues., Thurs. & Sat. 11-3; Sept. by appointment. Donations accepted. ♿
Attendance: 400 (accurate)
Membership: $5; $10 & up.

Southwest Harbor

WENDELL GILLEY MUSEUM, (M), 4 Herrick Rd., Southwest Harbor, ME 04679-4431. Mailing Address: P.O. Box 254, Southwest Harbor, ME 04679-0254. Tel.: 207-244-7555. Fax: 207-244-5134.
E-mail: info@wendellgilleymuseum.org
Web Site: www.wendellgilleymuseum.org
Founded: 1979.
Congressional District: 2
Key Personnel: C.E.O. & Dir., Nina Z. Gormley; Pres., Eleanor T.M. Hoagland; Exec. Vice Pres., Paul F. Haertel; Carver-in-Residence, Steven L. Valleau; Member & Visitor Svcs. Mgr., Jennifer Linforth.
Personnel Profile: Full-Time Paid 2; Part-Time Paid 4; Part-Time Volunteers 6.
Governing Authority: nonprofit. Tax-exempt: 501(c)(3).
Folk Art & Woodcarving Museum.
Collections: over 200 Wendell Gilley's woodcarvings; decorative birds & decoys; Audubon Birds of America facsimile; prints; wildlife art; Carroll S. Tyson's Birds of Mount Desert Island prints; miniature waterfowl carvings by A. Elmer Crowell; study & mounted bird specimens.
Major Exhibits: Sculptures by Don Rambadt, 7/10-10/10.
Facilities: library of material relating to wildlife & art topics; bird carving patterns & work of Wendell Gilley available for research by request; solar energy heating system; reading room. Carving tools, books & other bird-related items for sale.
Activities: guided tours; lectures; films; formally organized educational programs; permanent, loan & temporary exhibitions; movie rental to schools loan service; carving demonstrations & classes.
Publications: brochures; biannual newsletter, The Eider.
Hours & Admission Prices: Jan.-April by appointment only; May & Nov.-Dec. Fri.-Sun. 10-4; June & Sept.-Oct. Tues.-Sun. 10-4; July-Aug. Tues.-Sun. 10-5. Adults $5, children 5-12 $2; discounts to groups, AAM & ICOM members; Maine Association of Museums & New England Museum Association members & members no charge. Closed national holidays. ♿
Attendance: 26,450 (accurate)
Membership: Individual $35; Family $50; Sustaining $100; Sponsor $250; Patron $500; Benefactor $1,000 and up.

Standish

MARRETT HOUSE, Rte. 25, Standish, ME 04084. Mailing Address: 141 Cambridge St., Boston, MA 02114-2702. Tel.: 207-882-7169. Fax: 617-227-9204.
Web Site: www.historicnewengland.org
Founded: 1944.
Key Personnel: Pres., Carl Nold; Regl. Mgr., Peggy Konitzky.
Governing Authority: society; nonprofit organization. Parent Institution: Historic New England, 141 Cambridge St., Boston, MA 02114. Tel.: 617-227-3956. Tax-exempt: 501(c)(3).
Historic House: 1789 late Georgian house externally remodeled in the later Greek Revival & 19th century styles.
Collections: furnishings & family memorabilia spanning 150 years.
Facilities: perennial flower & herb garden.
Activities: guided tours; plant sale.
Publications: Historic New England Guide.
Hours & Admission Prices: June-Oct. 15 1st & 3rd Sat. of month 11-4. Adults $5; discounts to seniors, children, AAM, ICOM, AAA & WGBH members; Historic New England members no charge.
Attendance: 1,175 (accurate)
Membership: Historic New England: Individual $45; Household $55; Contributing $100; Garden & Landscape $75; Institutional $85; Historic Homeowner $200; Supporting $250.

Stockholm

STOCKHOLM HISTORICAL SOCIETY MUSEUM, 280 Main St., Stockholm, ME 04783. Tel.: 207-896-5759.
E-mail: jhede@mfx.net
Web Site: aroostook.me.us
Founded: 1976.
Congressional District: 2
Key Personnel: Pres. (V), Albertine Dufour; Vice Pres., Sandra Hara; Vice Pres., Clayton Nelson; Sec., Rosemary Hede; Treas. and Librarian, Collection & Display, Linda Callison; Membership, John H. Hede.
Personnel Profile: Part-Time Paid 2; Part-Time Volunteers 7.
Governing Authority: society; nonprofit. Parent Institution: Stockholm Historical Society. Tax-exempt: 501(c)(3).
Historical Society Museum: housed in 1900 store & post office.
Collections: photographs; tapes; town reports; oral & centennial (1881-1981) histories; town books; household items; farm & lumber implements.
Research Fields: family & house histories; town history.
Facilities: library of books available for use on premises; reading room.
Activities: permanent & temporary exhibitions; historical & cultural programs; video tapes of community events available for viewing at museum or taken on loan.
Publications: annual, Stockholm Historical Society Newsletter.
Hours & Admission Prices: July to early Sept. Wed.-Sun. 1:30-4:30; other times by appointment. No charge; donations accepted. ♿
Attendance: 200 (estimated)
Membership: Student $1; Active $2; Contributing $5; Business $25; Life $100.

Thomaston

MONTPELIER-THE GENERAL HENRY KNOX MUSEUM, 30 High St., Thomaston, ME 04861. Mailing Address: P.O. Box 326, Thomaston, ME 04861-0326. Tel.: 207-354-8062. Fax: 207-354-3501.
Web Site: www.knoxmuseum.org
Founded: 1931.
Key Personnel: Chm. (V), Patrick Cardon; Dir., Douglas E. Winterich; Mgr., Susan H. Edmands; Museum Shop Mgr., Suzi Barbee; Cur. & Education Dir., Ellen S. Dyer.
Personnel Profile: Full-Time Paid 4; Full-Time Volunteers 20; Part-Time Volunteers 60; Interns 3.
Governing Authority: state. Subsidiary Institution: Maine State Preservation Comm. Tax-exempt.
Historic House: 1795 Montpelier home of Major General Henry Knox.
Collections: furniture & artifacts of Colonial & Federal periods; Knox family memorabilia.
Research Fields: Henry Knox; pre- & post-Revolutionary War American history; early settlements of Maine.
Activities: guided tours; lectures; encampments; family picnic. Special Events: concerts June to September; Knox birthday celebration in July; Revolutionary Encampment in August; Fall Harvest Weekend in October; Christmas Open House in December.
Publications: brochure, Montpelier-The General Henry Knox Museum; semi-annual newsletter, The Cannon.
Hours & Admission Prices: June-Oct. Tues.-Sat. 10-4; groups & other times by appointment. Family $18, adults $7, seniors $6, children 5-14 $4; discounts to groups of 10 or more, AAA & AARP members; children under 5 & members no charge.
Attendance: 2,500 (estimated)
Membership: Individual $25; Basic Family $40; Revere Circle $100; Knox Circle $250; Washington Circle $500; Patriot $1,000.

THOMASTON HISTORICAL SOCIETY, 80 Knox St., Thomaston, ME 04861-3714. Mailing Address: P.O. Box 384, Thomaston, ME 04861-0384. Tel.: 207-354-2295 & 2314.
E-mail: dallan@msad50.org
Web Site: www.thomastonhistoricalsociety.com
Founded: 1971.
Congressional District: 1
Key Personnel: C.E.O. & Pres., Dan Allan; Vice Pres., Carol Achterhof; Treas., Frances Hernandez; Acting Cur., Margaret McCrea; Sec., Alethe Donaldson; Security, Galo Hernandez; Finance, Blake Donaldson.
Personnel Profile: Part-Time Volunteers 8.
Governing Authority: society. Tax-exempt.
Historic House Museum: housed in Henry Knox farmhouse; built in 1797.
Collections: paintings; furniture; maps of the town of Thomaston; photographs; journals; logbooks; historical books; ship models; Jonathan Cilley letters 1820-1867 & family letters thru mid 1860s; Revolutionary War, Civil War, World Wars I & II documents & memorabilia; 19th-century political artifacts; artifacts from 19th-century shipbuilding & seafarers lives.
Research Fields: local genealogy; maritime history; photographic journals; ship's logs.
Facilities: lecture hall.
Activities: guided tours; monthly lectures. Annual Event: Knox Birthday Observance in July; Holiday House Tour in December.
Publications: annual newsletter; occasional, historical reprints: A Town That Went to Sea; History of Thomaston; Tall Ships, White Houses and Elms; A Thomaston Scrapbook; books, A Breach of Privilege: The Cilley Family Letters 1820-1867.
Hours & Admission Prices: June-Aug. Tues.-Thurs. 2-4; other tours by appointment. No charge; donations requested. ♿
Attendance: 380 (estimated)
Membership: Single $18; Family $25; Business $75.

Union

MATTHEWS MUSEUM OF MAINE HERITAGE, Union Fairgrounds, Union, ME 04862. Mailing Address: P.O. Box 582, Union, ME 04862-0582. Tel.: 207-563-1544. Fax: 207-785-3321.
E-mail: mmomh@matthewsmuseum.org
Web Site: matthewsmuseum.org
Founded: 1965.
Congressional District: 1
Key Personnel: Chm. & Pres. (V), George R. Gross; Cur., Irene Hawes; Museum Shop Mgr., Nick Santorineos.
Personnel Profile: Full-Time Volunteers 2; Part-Time Volunteers 30; Interns 1.
Governing Authority: society. Parent Institution: Knox Agricultural Society & Union Fair. Tax-exempt: 501(c)(3).
Heritage Museum: one-room Hodge Schoolhouse (1864-1954).
Collections: artifacts of early Maine settlers; Maine life; agricultural; movie memorabilia; Moxie bottle stand.
Research Fields: tracing local families & farms; history of Maine.
Facilities: 800-vol. library of old account, school & agriculture books & Civil War maps; picnic grounds by appointment only.
Activities: guided tours; hand-crafts exhibits; demonstrations; craft lessons; school field trips by appointment; Moxie bottle stand. Hodge School Sponsors: story readings for visiting children.
Publications: books, revision of The Two Hundred Years of Union, history of Union, Maine; Edward Matthews Horse & Buggy Days; The Life & Efforts of the Evangelist Rev. Edward Smith Ufford; The First Century Union Fair, 1869-1969; Come Spring by Ben Ames Williams; Sibley's History of Union.
Hours & Admission Prices: July-Labor Day Wed.-Sat. 12-4. Adults $3, senior citizens & children $1; discounts to groups; members no charge. ♿
Attendance: 4,000 (accurate)
Membership: Adult $5; Family $10; Business $25; Individual Life $100.

Van Buren

ACADIAN VILLAGE, 859 Main St., U.S. Rte. 1, Van Buren, ME 04785. Mailing Address: P.O. Box 165, Van Buren, ME 04785-0165. Tel.: 207-868-5042.
Founded: 1976.
Personnel Profile: Full-Time Volunteers 2; Part-Time Paid 3.
Historic Village: listed on the National Registry for the Preservation of Historical Landmarks.
Collections: Historic Houses: The Roy House & The Morneault House.
Major Exhibits: Native American Exhibit (T), 6/10-9/10.
Hours & Admission Prices: June 14-Sept. 15 daily 12-5. Adults $6, children $3; discount to AAM, ICOM & AAA members.
Attendance: 700 (estimated)
Membership: Yearly $5; Lifetime $30.

Vinalhaven

THE VINALHAVEN HISTORICAL SOCIETY MUSEUM, 41 High St., Vinalhaven, ME 04863. Mailing Address: P.O. Box 339, Vinalhaven, ME 04863-0339. Tel.: 207-863-4410.
E-mail: vhhissoc@myfairpoint.net
Web Site: www.vinalhavenhistoricalsociety.org
Founded: 1963.
Congressional District: 1
Key Personnel: Pres., William Chilles; Dir., Susan Rodley; Vice Pres., Wyman Philbrook; Treas., Jacob Thompson.
Personnel Profile: Full-Time Paid 1; Part-Time Volunteers 7.
Governing Authority: nonprofit organization. Parent Institution: Vinalhaven Historical Society. Tax-exempt.
History Museum: housed in 1838 church built in Rockland, moved to Vinalhaven Island in 1875.
Collections: granite industry; lobstering; fishing; sailboats; home appliances; farm & sea life; archives; costumes; folklore; manuscripts; Indian artifacts; genealogical records; 30 Microfilm rolls, 1872-1949 town property & poll tax books, 1884-1889 newspapers, 1850, 1860, 1870, 1880, 1900, 1910 &

1920 Vinalhaven census, 1787-1849 Penobscot-Castine district vessels; vital records 1789-1983; granite cutters union journal 1877-1939; Vinalhaven census 1930.
Facilities: library.
Activities: permanent & temporary exhibitions; school loan service.
Publications: annual spring newsletter, Vinalhaven Island (photographs) Arcadia, Images of America series.
Hours & Admission Prices: June 10-June & Sept. 1-Sept. 13 Tues.-Sat. 11-3; July-Aug. daily 11-3; other times by appointment. No charge; donations accepted.
Attendance: 1,600 (estimated)
Membership: Seniors 65 & over and Students $5; Individual $10; Family $15; Associate $30; Life $100.

Warren

WARREN HISTORICAL SOCIETY, 225 Main St., Warren, ME 04864. Mailing Address: P.O. Box 11, Warren, ME 04864-0011. Tel.: 207-273-2726.
Founded: 1964.
Congressional District: 1
Key Personnel: Pres., Bruce Thornton; Cur., Barbara Larson; Genealogist, Diana Sewell.
Personnel Profile: Part-Time Volunteers 5.
Governing Authority: society. Tax-exempt.
Regional History Museum.
Collections: history & growth of the Warren settlement & town; medical doctor's office; Warren archaeology artifacts; memorabilia & photos of wars; household furnishings; canal diagrams & history. Historic Buildings: c.1849 house & shed.
Research Fields: local history & traditions.
Facilities: 300-vol. library of historical material.
Activities: special events. Annual Event: Warren Day Celebration.
Publications: annual newsletter; Annals of Warren, 1605-1876; From Warren to the Sea, 1827-1852; Old Warren (photos), 1736-1936; Warren Cemeteries 1736-1985.
Hours & Admission Prices: Call for appointment. No charge; donations accepted.
Attendance: 300
Membership: Individual $5; Sustaining $10; Contributing $15 and over; Life $50.

Waterville

* **COLBY COLLEGE MUSEUM OF ART, (M),** 5600 Mayflower Hill, Waterville, ME 04901-8856. Tel.: 207-859-5600. Fax: 207-859-5606.
E-mail: museum@colby.edu
Web Site: www.colby.edu/museum
Founded: 1959.
Congressional District: 1
Key Personnel: Carolyn Muzzy Dir. & Chief Cur., Sharon Corwin; Chm. (V), Barbara Alfond; Asst. Dir. Operations, Gregory J. Williams; Asst. Dir. Admin. & Collections Mgmt., Patricia King; Mirken Cur. Education, Lauren Lessing; Lunder Cur. American Art, Elizabeth Finch; Administrative Sec., Karen Wickman; Curatorial Fellow, Isabelle Smeall; Coord. Education, Kim Brennan.
Personnel Profile: Full-Time Paid 6; Part-Time Paid 1; Part-Time Volunteers 27; Interns 5.
Governing Authority: college. Parent Institution: Colby College. Tax-exempt.
Art Museum.
Collections: American Heritage Collection; Helen Warren and Willard Howe Cummings collection of American folk art; 18th-century American portraits; 19th-century weathervanes and landscapes; Jette collection of American painters of the Impressionist Period; John Marin collection; Alex Katz collection & archive; Lunder collection; James McNeill Whistler prints; 20th century & contemporary American painting, sculpture, photography; Bernat collection of Oriental ceramics; Colville collection of early Chinese art; Terry Winters prints.
Major Exhibits: Art at Colby: Celebrating the 50th Anniversary of the Colby College Museum of Art, 11/09-2/21/10; Myths and Metamorphosis, 11/3/09-1/17/10; Puns and Rebuses in Chinese Art, 1/28/10-3/24/10; Experimental Geography (T), 2/21/10-5/30/10; Garry Mitchell, 3/19/10-4/10; Senior Exhibition, 5/6/10-5/23/10; Sharon Lockhart: Lunch Break, 7/10/10-10/17/10; Will Barnet: New York Drawings, 7/10/10-10/17/10; James McNeill Whistler, 7/10/10-12/10; Winslow Homer, 7/10/10-12/10.
Facilities: Museum-related items for sale.
Activities: guided tours; lectures; gallery talks; formally organized education programs for school children, adults & undergraduate college students; loan, permanent, temporary & traveling exhibitions.
Publications: Art at Colby Celebrating the Fiftieth Anniversary of the Colby College Museum of Art; With the Help of Friends The Colby College Museum of Art The First Fifty Years, 1959-2009; Colby Museum exhibition catalogs: Handbook of the Colby College Art Museum; Maine & Its Role in American Art; American Painters of the Impressionist Period; Maine Forms of American Architecture; Drawings from Maine Collections; Alex Katz at Colby College; 100 Works of the 20th Century at Colby; The John Marin Collection at the Colby College Museum of Art; Alex Katz: Collages; Currents1: Julianne Swartz; Currents2: Sam Van Aken; Currents3: Lihua Lei; The Skowhegan School of Painting and Sculpture: 60 Years.
Hours & Admission Prices: Tues.-Sat. 10-4:30, Sun. 12-4:30; tours by appointment. No charge. Closed holidays. ♿
Attendance: 19,517 (accurate)
Membership: Single $15; Family $25; Contributor $50; Sponsor $100; Subscriber $250; Benefactor $500; Patron $1,000.

REDINGTON MUSEUM, 62 Silver St., Unit B, Waterville, ME 04901-6524. Tel.: 207-872-9439.
Web Site: www.redingtonmuseum.org
Founded: 1903.
Congressional District: 2
Key Personnel: Pres. Historical Society (V), Frederic P. Johnson; Cur., Willard B. Arnold, III
Personnel Profile: Part-Time Paid 1; Part-Time Volunteers 25.
Governing Authority: society; nonprofit organization. Parent Institution: Waterville Historical Society. Tax-exempt.
Historical Society Museum: housed in 1814 residence of Asa Redington.
Collections: house furnishings; early 19th-century tools & utensils; early American apothecary; Apothecary Museum; local portraits; local scenic photos 1855 to present; maps; charts; Indian artifacts; manuscripts; early weapons; complete file of the Waterville Mail newspaper; early toys; clothing; period furniture.
Research Fields: local & Civil War history.
Facilities: 3,000-vol. library of history books, chiefly on Maine & imported collection of early schoolbooks available for use on premises.
Activities: guided tours; lectures; formally organized educational programs; permanent & temporary exhibitions; cooperative program at Colby College for student research in local history.
Publications: picture book, Old Waterville.
Hours & Admission Prices: Memorial Day-Labor Day Tues.-Sat. Tours: 10, 11, 1 & 2. Adults $3, children under 12 $2; members no charge. Closed holidays.
Attendance: 600 (estimated)
Membership: Single $20; Family $40; Friend $100; Sponsor $250; Patron $500; Benefactor $1,000.

Wells

HISTORICAL SOCIETY OF WELLS AND OGUNQUIT, Rte. 1, 938 Post Rd., Wells, ME 04090. Mailing Address: P.O. Box 801, Wells, ME 04090-0801. Tel.: 207-646-4775. Fax: 207-646-0832.
E-mail: wohistory@gwi.net
Web Site: www.historicalsocietyofwellsandogunquit.org
Founded: 1954.
Congressional District: 1
Key Personnel: Chm. (V), Lee Richheimer.
Personnel Profile: Part-Time Paid 1; Part-Time Volunteers 35.
Governing Authority: Tax-exempt: 501(c)(3).
Historic Structure: 1862 Meeting House in Wells.
Collections: costumes; paintings; crafts; decorative arts; archives; photographs; genealogy.
Research Fields: genealogical & historical records.
Facilities: 1,100-vol. library; 200-seat auditorium; area for educational presentations. History books for sale.
Activities: guided tours; lectures; concerts; organized educational programs; docent program.
Publications: annual programs; guide to historic sites; quarterly newsletter.
Hours & Admission Prices: Memorial Day to Columbus Day Tues.-Thurs. 10-4; Oct.-May Wed.-Thurs. 10-4; other times by appointment. Requested Donation: $5; discounts to AAM members. ♿
Attendance: 600 (estimated)
Membership: Senior & Student $10; Individual $25; Family $35; Sustaining $50; Supporting Business $75; Patron $100; Benefactor $250-$500; Life $1,000.

WELLS AUTO MUSEUM, 1181 Post Rd., Wells, ME 04090. Mailing Address: P.O. Box 196, Wells, ME 04090-0196. Tel.: 207-646-9064 (June-Sept.) & 5054 (off season).
E-mail: wellsauto@aol.com
Web Site: www.wellsautomuseum.com
Founded: 1954.
Key Personnel: Mgr., Kenneth E. Creed, III

Personnel Profile: Part-Time Paid 6.
Governing Authority: nonprofit corporation. Tax-exempt.
Automotive Museum.
Collections: period cars; fire engines; motorcycles; bicycles; license plates; toys; nickelodeons; picture machines.
Facilities: Museum-related items for sale.
Activities: antique car rides.
Hours & Admission Prices: late June to Labor Day daily 10-5. Adults $7, children 6-12 $4; discounts to groups & AAA members; children under 6 & members no charge. ♿
Attendance: 10,500 (accurate)
Membership: Individual $10; Family $15; Benefactor $50; Life $100.

Wiscasset

CASTLE TUCKER, 2 Lee St., Wiscasset, ME 04578-4121. Mailing Address: Historic New England, 141 Cambridge St., Boston, MA 02114-2702. Tel.: 207-882-7169; 617-227-3956 (Historic New England). Fax: 617-227-9204.
Web Site: www.historicnewengland.org
Founded: 1974.
Congressional District: 1
Key Personnel: Pres., Carl Nold; Site Mgr., Peggy Konitzy.
Governing Authority: society. Parent Institution: Historic New England.
Historic House: 1807 mansion overlooking Wiscasset Harbor.
Collections: mid-Victorian era furnishings & wallpaper typical of a wealthy sea-captain's home; free-standing elliptical staircase.
Research Fields: local history.
Activities: guided tours.
Publications: Guard to Historic New England.
Hours & Admission Prices: June-Oct. 15 Wed.-Sun. 11-5. Adults $5; discounts for seniors, AAA, AAM, WBGH & ICOM members; members no charge.
Attendance: 2,727 (accurate)
Membership: National $35; Individual $45; Household $55; Garden & Landscape $75; Institutional $85; Contributing $100; Historic Homeowner $200; Supporting $250.

THE 1811 LINCOLN COUNTY MUSEUM & OLD JAIL, 133 Federal St., Wiscasset, ME 04578. Mailing Address: P.O. Box 61, Wiscasset, ME 04578-0061. Tel.: 207-882-6817.
E-mail: lcha@wiscasset.net
Web Site: www.lincolncountyhistory.org
Founded: 1954.
Congressional District: 1
Key Personnel: Exec. Dir., Jay Robbins.
Personnel Profile: Full-Time Paid 1; Part-Time Paid 6; Part-Time Volunteers 15.
Governing Authority: nonprofit. Parent Institution: Lincoln County Historical Association, Inc. Tax-exempt.
Regional History Museum.
Collections: history; textiles; prints & photographic glass negatives of area. Historic Houses: 1809-1811 Old Lincoln County Jail; 1839 jailer's house.
Research Fields: jails; law; 19th century penal and criminal justice system; 19th century Wiscasset.
Facilities: reference library & regional histories; index of Maine design.
Activities: tours; lectures; workshops; school services; permanent & temporary exhibitions.
Publications: newsletter, The Lincoln County Chronicle; 18th Century Law & Order: 1761 Pownalborough Courthouse; 19th Century Law and Order: The 1811 Old Jail and 1839 Jailer House Museum; Preserve Local History; jail history brochure; The First Lincoln County Jail in Pownalborough; Histories of the Pownalborough Court House.
Hours & Admission Prices: Memorial Day to June & Sept. to Columbus Day Sat. 10-4, Sun. 12-4; July-Aug. Tues.-Fri. 10-4; other times by appointment. Adults $4; AAA members & children no charge.
Attendance: 2,000 (estimated)
Membership: Student $2; Single $25; Family $35; Supporting $60; Sustaining $100.

MAINE ART GALLERY, Warren St., Wiscasset, ME 04578. Mailing Address: P.O. Box 315, Wiscasset, ME 04578-0315. Tel.: 207-882-7511.
E-mail: info@maineartgallery.org
Web Site: www.maineartgallery.org
Founded: 1958.
Congressional District: 1
Key Personnel: Pres. (V), Merlin Smith; Vice Pres., Barbara Vanderbilt; Gallery Mgr., Michele Roberge.
Personnel Profile: Full-Time Paid 1; Part-Time Paid 3; Part-Time Volunteers 10.
Governing Authority: nonprofit. Tax-exempt.
Art Gallery.
Collections: paintings by Maine artists. Historic House: 1807 Old Academy.
Facilities: Art for sale.
Activities: guided tours; temporary exhibitions; monthly shows.
Publications: monthly catalog; newsletters; show announcements.
Hours & Admission Prices: Tues.-Sat. 10-4, Sun. 11-4. No charge; donations accepted.
Attendance: 1,600 (accurate)
Membership: Member $35; Couple $60; Sustaining $100; Patron $250.

MUSICAL WONDER HOUSE, 18 High St., Wiscasset, ME 04578-4118. Mailing Address: P.O. Box 604, Wiscasset, ME 04578-0604. Tel.: 207-882-7163. Fax: 207-882-6373.
Web Site: www.musicalwonderhouse.com/
Founded: 1963.
Key Personnel: Trustee & Founder, Danilo Konvalinka; Trustee, Joseph M. Villani.
Personnel Profile: Full-Time Paid 2; Part-Time Paid 1; Interns 1.
Governing Authority: individual operation.
Mechanical Musical Instrument Museum: housed in 1852 sea captain's home.
Collections: musical boxes; gramophones; player & crank pianos; player & crank organs; talking machines; mechanical musical instruments.
Research Fields: mechanical musical instruments; preservation of antique music boxes, gramophones, player & crank pianos and organs.
Facilities: library of books in the field of mechanical music, player-piano & player-organ catalogues, talking machine literature & musical box literature available for use on premises. Museum-related items for sale.
Activities: guided tours; lectures; TV programs; permanent exhibitions. Museum Sponsors: Head Start programs; blindness programs; Voice of America.
Publications: Musical Wonder House Recordings; brochures.
Hours & Admission Prices: Memorial Day to Oct. Mon.-Sat. 10-5, Sun. 12-5. Tours: $10; $20; $40; discounts to seniors & AAA members. ♿
Attendance: 5,000 (estimated)

NICKELS-SORTWELL HOUSE, 121 Main St., Rte. 1, Wiscasset, ME 04578. Mailing Address: 141 Cambridge St., Boston, MA 02114-2702. Tel.: 207-882-7169; 617-227-3956 (Historic New England). Fax: 617-227-9204.
Web Site: www.historicnewengland.org
Founded: 1958.
Key Personnel: Pres., Carl Nold; Site Admin., Jennie Weeks.
Governing Authority: society; nonprofit organization. Parent Institution: Historic New England, 141 Cambridge St., Boston, MA 02114. Tel.: 617-227-3956. Tax-exempt: 501(c)(3).
Historic House: 1807 mansion designed with an elliptical stairway, lit by a skylight; Colonial Revival furnishings.
Collections: Sortwell family furnishings.
Activities: guided tours; special events.
Publications: Historic New England, Historic New England Guide.
Hours & Admission Prices: June-Oct. 15 Fri.-Sun. 11-5. Adults $5; discounts to seniors, AAM, ICOM, AAA, WGBH members; Wicasset residents, SPNEA members no charge. Call for further information.
Attendance: 1,517 (accurate)
Membership: National $35; Individual $45; Household $55; Garden & Landscape $75; Institutional $85; Contributing $100; Historic Homeowner $200; Supporting $250.

Yarmouth

MUSEUM OF YARMOUTH HISTORY, (M), Merrill Memorial Library, 215 Main St., Yarmouth, ME 04096. Mailing Address: P.O. Box 107, Yarmouth, ME 04096-0107. Tel.: 207-846-6259. Fax: 207-846-2422.
E-mail: yarmouth-history@inetmail.att.net
Web Site: www.yarmouth.me.us
Founded: 1958.
Congressional District: 1
Key Personnel: Dir., Marilyn J. Hinkley; Chm. (V), Margaret Soule.
Personnel Profile: Full-Time Paid 2; Part-Time Paid 2; Part-Time Volunteers 12; Interns 1.
Governing Authority: board of trustees. Parent Institution: Yarmouth Historical Society. Tax-exempt: 501(c)(3).
Local History Museum.
Collections: local & maritime history; fine & decorative arts; business & domestic artifacts; organizational artifacts; photographs & documentary materials; historical recordings & literature. Historic Building: 1738 one-room Old Ledge Schoolhouse.
Research Fields: geology; genealogy; archaeology; sociology; industrial development; local history; social history; land use; architecture; maritime history.
Facilities: research room.
Activities: lectures & slide series; formally organized educational programs;

oral history recording program; field trips; permanent & temporary exhibitions; special events; research.
Publications: newsletter, Yarmouth Historical Society; brochures; annual report.
Hours & Admission Prices: July-Aug. Mon.-Fri. 1-5; Sept.-June Wed.-Fri. 1-5, Sat. 10-5. Closed holiday weekends. No charge; donations accepted. ♿
Attendance: 2,000 (estimated)
Membership: Students & Senior Citizens $10; Individual $20; Family $30; Historian $50; Archivist $100; Curator $200; Patron $500.

York

MUSEUMS OF OLD YORK, 207 York St., York, ME 03909-1044. Mailing Address: P.O. Box 312, York, ME 03909-0312. Tel.: 207-363-4974. Fax: 207-363-4021.
E-mail: oyhs@oldyork.org
Web Site: www.oldyork.org
Formerly: Old York Historical Society
Founded: 1984.
Congressional District: 1
Key Personnel: Pres., Charles Steedman; Dir., Scott Stevens; Dir. Devel., Erica Holthausen; Coord. Education, Zoe Keefer-Norris; Registrar, Cynthia Young-Gomes; Office Mgr., Frith Foss; Supvr. Bldgs. & Grounds, Jon Powers; Librarian, Virginia Spiller.
Personnel Profile: Full-Time Paid 6; Part-Time Paid 13; Part-Time Volunteers 300; Interns 4.
Governing Authority: nonprofit organization. Tax-exempt: 101(6); 501(c)(3).
Historic Building Complex.
Collections: American furniture; decorative arts; manuscripts; ceramic & glass collection; tools & maritime artifacts; textiles. Historic Buildings: 1742 Emerson-Wilcox House; 1754 Jefferds' Tavern; 1740 John Hancock Warehouse; 1870 Marshall Store; 1745 schoolhouse; 1730 Elizabeth Perkins house; 1719 Old Gaol; 1820 Ramsdell house; 1834 Remick barn.
Research Fields: local history; colonial revival; decorative arts; archaeology; architecture; crime & punishment; genealogy.
Facilities: library/archives; visitors center. Museum-related items for sale.
Activities: guided tours; lectures; films; permanent & changing exhibitions; educational programs; summer children's camp; fellowship program; special events.
Publications: quarterly newsletters; annual educational materials; annual Proceedings of Elizabeth Perkins Fellowship Symposium.
Hours & Admission Prices: Houses: June-Oct. Mon.-Sat. 10-5. Office: Mon.-Fri. 9-5. Family $20, adults $10, senior citizens $9, children 6-16 $5; discounts to AAA, AAM members & groups; members & children under 6 no charge. Library: Thurs.-Fri. 9-12 & 1-5, Sat. 10-4. Adults $5; members no charge. ♿
Attendance: 30,000 (estimated)
Membership: Individual $35; Family/Duel $60; Contributing & Business Friend $100; Sustaining & Business Associate $250; Business Patron $500; 1631 Partner & Business Partner $1,000.

York Harbor

SAYWARD-WHEELER HOUSE, Nine Barrell Lane Extension, York Harbor, ME 03911. Mailing Address: 141 Cambridge St., Boston, MA 02114-2702. Tel.: 207-384-2454; 617-227-3956. Fax: 617-227-9204.
Web Site: www.historicnewengland.org
Founded: 1977.
Key Personnel: Pres., Carl Nold; Site Mgr., Elizabeth Farish.
Governing Authority: society; nonprofit organization. Parent Institution: Historic New England, 141 Cambridge St., Boston, MA 02114. Tel.: 617-227-3956. Tax-exempt: 501(c)(3).
Historic House: c.1718 house built on a slope overlooking the York River.
Collections: Queen Anne & Chippendale furniture; family portraits; china.
Activities: guided tours.
Publications: Guide to Historic New England.
Hours & Admission Prices: Tours: June-Oct. 15 2nd & 4th Sat. of month 11-4. Adults $5; discounts to groups & seniors, ICOM, AAM, AAA & WGBH; Historic New England members no charge.
Attendance: 2,057 (accurate)
Membership: National $35; Individual $45; Household $55; Garden & Landscape $75; Institutional $85; Contributing $100; Historic Homeowner $200; Supporting $250.

MARYLAND

(228 listings)

Aberdeen Proving Ground

U.S. ARMY ORDNANCE MUSEUM, Aberdeen Blvd., Bldg. 2601, Aberdeen Proving Ground, MD 21005. Tel.: 410-278-3602 & 9096. Fax: 410-278-7473.
Web Site: www.goordnance.apg.army.mil/museum
Founded: 1919.
Congressional District: 2
Key Personnel: Dir., Joe Rainer, Ph.D.; Pres. (V), Gen. John G. Coburn, Ret.; Museum Shop Mgr., Joe Wurm; Cur., Roy E. Heasley.
Personnel Profile: Full-Time Paid 5; Part-Time Volunteers 2; Interns 1.
Governing Authority: federal. Affiliated with U.S. Army Center of Military History. Parent Institution: U.S. Army Ordnance Center & School. Tax-exempt.
History & Military Museum.
Collections: ordnance equipment from the principal powers with emphasis on WWI and WWII; foreign military equipment both captured and donated; small arms from 16th century to the present; ammunition; archives; outdoor collection of 250 pieces of artillery & tanks.
Research Fields: weaponry.
Facilities: 5,000-vol. library of books, pamphlets, field & technical manuals pertaining to ordnance material available for research on premises by appointment. Museum-related items for sale.
Activities: self-guided tours; permanent & temporary exhibitions.
Publications: brochure.
Hours & Admission Prices: Outdoor: daily dawn-dusk. Indoor: daily 9-4:45. No charge; donations accepted. Closed some federal holidays. ♿
Attendance: 75,000 (estimated)

Accident

DRANE HOUSE, Old Cemetery Rd., Accident, MD 21520. Mailing Address: P.O. Box 190, Accident, MD 21520. Tel.: 301-746-6346. Fax: 301-746-7376.
E-mail: accidenttownhall@verizon.net
Historic House: frontier plantation house; built late 1700s.
Collections: local history; period artifacts.
Hours & Admission Prices: By appointment. No charge; donations accepted.

Accokeek

THE ACCOKEEK FOUNDATION, INC., 3400 Bryan Point Rd., Accokeek, MD 20607-9676. Tel.: 301-283-2113. Fax: 301-283-2049.
E-mail: accofound@accokeek.org
Web Site: www.accokeek.org
Founded: 1957.
Congressional District: 4
Key Personnel: Chm., Patricia E. Williams; Pres., Wilton C. Corkern; Museum Shop Mgr., Annmarie Buckley.
Personnel Profile: Full-Time Paid 15; Part-Time Paid 16; Part-Time Volunteers 210; Interns 5.
Governing Authority: nonprofit. Tax-exempt: 501(c)(3).
Agriculture Museum.
Collections: outdoor living history museum of Colonial farming practices; sample crops, Indian corn & tobacco seed; preservation project; archaeology; botany; Native American artifacts; technology; entomology (nonliving)
Research Fields: historical research into 18th-century crops & their culture; genetic research on crops & animals of the 18th century, the development of a blight-resistant American Chestnut; colonial life; land use.
Facilities: 500-vol. library of history & agriculture available for inter-library loan & for use on premises; field research station.
Activities: guided tours; lectures; films; formally organized education programs for children & adults; permanent & temporary exhibitions; special events for Colonial crafts; daily activities of an 18th-century tobacco plantation.
Publications: newsletter.
Hours & Admission Prices: Park: dawn to dusk. Self-guided Tours: Mon.-Fri. Guided Tours: mid-Dec. to mid-March Sat.-Sun. 1 & 3. Adults $2, children under 12 $.50, $5 maximum per family; members no charge. Closed New Year's Day; Thanksgiving; Christmas.
Attendance: 30,000 (estimated)
Membership: Individual $25; Family $40.

Annapolis

ANNAPOLIS MARITIME MUSEUM, 723 Second St., Annapolis, MD 21403-3323. Mailing Address: P.O. Box 3088, 723 Second St., Annapolis, MD 21403-0088. Tel.: 410-295-0104. Fax: 410-295-2962.
E-mail: office@maritime.org
Web Site: www.amaritime.org
Founded: 1997.
Congressional District: 40
Key Personnel: Dir., Jeff Holland.
Personnel Profile: Full-Time Paid 3; Part-Time Volunteers 250.
Governing Authority: bd. of directors. Tax-exempt.
Maritime Museum.
Collections: maritime heritage of Annapolis & the Chesapeake Bay; maritime artifacts. Historic Structure: Thomas Point Shoal Lighthouse.
Major Exhibits: Legacy to the Bay, 11/09-12/09.
Activities: concerts; boat rides to lighthouse; lectures; educational programs; lighthouse tours; concerts.
Publications: quarterly newsletter.
Hours & Admission Prices: Museum: Thurs.-Sun. 12-4. Lighthouse Tours: call for hours. No charge; donations accepted. Boat Ride: adults 12 & over $70; children under 12 not admitted. ♿
Membership: Shipmate $35; Ensign $60; 1st Mate $100; Commander $500; Captain $1,000.

BANNEKER-DOUGLASS MUSEUM, (M), 84 Franklin St., Annapolis, MD 21401-2738. Tel.: 410-216-6180. Fax: 410-974-2553.
Web Site: www.bdmuseum.com
Founded: 1984.
Key Personnel: Exec. Dir., Joni Jones.
Personnel Profile: Full-Time Paid 5; Interns 2.
Governing Authority: Parent Institution: Governor's Office of Community Initiatives. Subsidiary Institution: MD Commission of African American History and Culture. Tax-exempt.
African American Heritage Museum.
Collections: African American culture & history; photographs; African American art; books.
Facilities: library.
Activities: lectures; workshops; performances; educational programs.
Hours & Admission Prices: Tues.-Sat. 10-4. No charge. ♿

CHARLES CARROLL HOUSE, 107 Duke of Gloucester St., Annapolis, MD 21401-2526. Tel.: 410-269-1737. Fax: 410-269-1746.
E-mail: info@charlescarrollhouse.com
Web Site: www.charlescarrollhouse.com
Historic House Museum: housed in the home of Charles Carroll, a signer of the Declaration of Independence in 1776.
Collections: personal artifacts; period furnishings; wine cellar.
Facilities: gardens; theater.
Activities: educational seminars; school programs; theater performances; wine events.
Hours & Admission Prices: Sat.-Sun. 12-4. No charge; donations accepted. Closed Easter; Thanksgiving; Christmas Eve & Day.

CHASE-LLOYD HOUSE, 22 Maryland Ave., Annapolis, MD 21401-8006. Tel.: 410-263-2723.
Founded: 1896.
Historic House Museum.
Collections: furnishings; personal artifacts.
Hours & Admission Prices: March-Dec. Mon.-Sat. 2-4. Admission $4; children under 6 no charge. Closed holidays.

THE CHESAPEAKE CHILDREN'S MUSEUM, 25 Silopanna Rd., Annapolis, MD 21403-1117. Tel.: 410-990-1993.
E-mail: info@theccm.org
Web Site: www.theccm.org/
Founded: 1992.
Congressional District: 1
Key Personnel: C.E.O. & Dir., Deborah Wood.
Governing Authority: Tax-exempt.
Children's Museum.
Collections: hands-on exhibits.
Facilities: nature trail; herb garden.
Activities: please visit website at www.theccm.org or call for current newsletter.
Publications: Long Ago is Closer Than You Think.
Hours & Admission Prices: Summer: Thurs.-Tues. 10-5, Wed. groups by appointment; Winter: Thurs.-Tues. 10-4, Wed. groups by appointment. Admission 1 & over $3. ACM reciprocal member. Closed New Year's Day; Christmas. ♿
Attendance: 20,000
Membership: Summer (June 1-Labor Day) $20; Basic $50; Reciprocal $110; Funded $150.

ELIZABETH MYERS MITCHELL ART GALLERY, ST. JOHN'S COLLEGE, (M), 60 College Ave., Annapolis, MD 21401-1687. Mailing Address: P.O. Box 2800, 60 College Ave., Annapolis, MD 21404-2800. Tel.: 410-263-2371 & 626-2556. Fax: 410-626-2886.
Web Site: www.stjohnscollege.edu
Founded: 1989.
Congressional District: 4
Key Personnel: C.E.O. & Pres., Christopher Nelson; Chm. & Pres. (V), Dennis Younger; Dir., Hydee Schaller; Treas., Bronte Jones; Financial Dir., Barbara Goyette; Security, Timon K. Linn; Security, Mike Boston; Membership Coord., Kathy Dulisse; Art Educator, Lucinda Dukes Edinberg.
Personnel Profile: Full-Time Paid 2; Part-Time Paid 7; Part-Time Volunteers 35; Interns 1.
Governing Authority: college; nonprofit. Parent Institution: St. John's College. Tax-exempt: 501(c)(3).
College Art Gallery.
Collections: 16th-century Italian art; 20th-century American art; 17th-century Dutch art; 20th-century Japanese art.
Major Exhibits: The Wine Dark Sea: Works by Joyce J. Scott & Friends, 1/10-2/10; The Grand Tour in 18th Century Venice and Rome, 3/10-4/10; Image & Imagination: Anne Arundel County Juried Exhibition, 5/27/10-6/10/10.
Facilities: 1,825 sq. ft. exhibit space; lecture room; studios.
Activities: lectures; family programs; group tours; exhibit related workshops; loan, temporary & traveling exhibitions; studio courses in painting, life-drawing, sculpture, ceramics & photography; poetry writing workshops & readings; interpretive music programs; docent program; art express lunch-time tours; docent tours.
Publications: exhibition programs, Artline (for Mitchell Gallery membership); exhibit brochures & exhibition catalogues.
Hours & Admission Prices: Academic Year: Tues.-Thurs. & Sat.-Sun. 12-5, Fri. 12-5 & 7-8, call for details. No charge. ♿
Attendance: 13,000 (accurate)
Membership: Teacher $40; Single $45; Dual & Family $75; Business $100 & up; Sponsor $100-$349; Patron $350-$999; Benefactor $1,000 & up.

HAMMOND-HARWOOD HOUSE ASSOCIATION, (M), 19 Maryland Ave., Annapolis, MD 21401-1626. Tel.: 410-263-4683. Fax: 410-267-6891.
E-mail: clively@hammondharwoodhouse.org
Web Site: www.hammondharwoodhouse.org
Founded: 1938.
Congressional District: 4
Key Personnel: Exec. Dir., Mr. Carter C. Lively; Pres., Barbara Goyette; Vice Pres., Anthony Christhilf.
Personnel Profile: Full-Time Paid 3; Full-Time Volunteers 3; Part-Time Paid 25; Part-Time Volunteers 270; Interns 2.
Governing Authority: nonprofit organization. Tax-exempt: 501(c)(3).
Historic House: 1774 Hammond-Harwood House.
Collections: 18th-century furniture; decorative arts; paintings.
Research Fields: 18th-century architecture; 18th-century American & English decorative arts; Maryland & Annapolis history.
Facilities: Gift items for sale.
Activities: guided tours; special events.
Publications: books, Maryland's Way; The Hammond-Harwood House Cookbook; Hammond-Harwood House: An Illustrated History and Guide.
Hours & Admission Prices: April-Oct. Tues.-Sun. 12-5; Nov.-March by appointment. Adults $6, senior citizens $5.50, children 6-11 & Students $3; discounts to groups, AAM & AAA members; children under 6 & members no charge. Closed New Year's Day; Thanksgiving; Christmas.
Attendance: 13,249 (estimated)
Membership: Individual $40; Contributor $50; Patron $100; Sponsor $250; Donor $500; Benefactor $1,000.

*** HISTORIC ANNAPOLIS FOUNDATION, (M),** 18 Pinkney St., Annapolis, MD 21401-1763. Tel.: 410-267-7619. Fax: 410-267-6189.
E-mail: info@annapolis.org
Web Site: www.annapolis.org
Founded: 1952.
Congressional District: 1
Key Personnel: Pres., John W. Guild; Vice Pres. Collections, Heather Ersts; Chm. (V), James P. Nolan; Vice Pres. Advancement, Carrie Kiewitt; Dir. Garden, Mollie Ridout.

Personnel Profile: Full-Time Paid 11; Part-Time Paid 28; Part-Time Volunteers 450; Interns 5.
Governing Authority: private; nonprofit organization. Tax-exempt: 501(c)(3).
Preservation & Education organization: housed in 5 historic sites.
Collections: architecture & decorative arts; Annapolis history. Historic Houses: 1765 William Paca House & Garden; c.1715 Shiplap House; barracks; waterfront warehouse; Historyquest at St. Clair Wright Center, c.1790.
Research Fields: Maryland & Annapolis history; 18th- & 19th-century architecture, household & business inventories.
Facilities: research center; history center. Museum-related items for sale.
Activities: guided tours; lectures; films; formally organized education program for children & adults; special events; architectural survey; audio walking tours of historic downtown Annapolis; research.
Publications: William Paca House & Garden; Archaeological Annapolis; Journal; tour guides.
Hours & Admission Prices: Adults $8; discounts to AAA & AAM members & senior citizens; members no charge. Closed New Year's Day; Thanksgiving; Christmas. ♿
Attendance: 428,000 (estimated)
Membership: Individual $50; Family & Patron $75; Sponsor & Small Business $125; Donor $250; Benefactor $500; Preservation Circle $1,000.

MARYLAND STATE ARCHIVES, (M), 350 Rowe Blvd., Annapolis, MD 21401-1686. Tel.: 410-260-6400. Fax: 410-974-3895. TDD: 800-735-2258.
E-mail: archives@mdsa.net
Web Site: www.msa.md.gov
Founded: 1935.
Congressional District: 4
Key Personnel: State Archivist, Edward C. Papenfuse; Dept. Archivist, Timothy Baker; Dir. Artistic Property, Elaine Rice Bachmann; Dir. Reference Svcs., Mike McCormick; Dir. Acquisition & Preservation, Kevin J. Swanson; Dir. Government Information Svc., Diane P. Evartt; Personnel, Richard Richardson; Dir. Special Collections, Rob Schoeberlein; Dir. Information Svcs., Wei Yang; Cur. Artistic Property, Alexander "Sasha" Lourie; Librarian, Christine Alvey; Registrar, Christopher Kintzel.
Personnel Profile: Full-Time Paid 100; Part-Time Volunteers 15; Interns 25.
Governing Authority: state. Tax-exempt.
State Archival Institution.
Collections: colonial & state executive, legislative & judicial government records from 1634 to present; county probate, land & court records; private papers; church records; business records; state publications & reports; newspapers; maps; photographs; paintings; decorative arts; sculpture.
Research Fields: Maryland history; genealogy; American portraiture; decorative & fine arts.
Facilities: 14,000-vol. library of books on Maryland history, genealogy, U.S. history, archival & manuscript repositories available for use on premises; 100,000 cu. ft. of public government records; research room.
Activities: research, digitizing of land & other records.
Publications: Archives of Maryland (new series); Maryland Manual (biennial); finding aids; scholarly editions; historical essays.
Hours & Admission Prices: Tues.-Sat. 8:30-4:30. No charge; donations accepted. Closed state holidays; holiday weekends; first Sat. each month. ♿

MARYLAND STATE HOUSE, 100 State Circle, Annapolis, MD 21401. Tel.: 410-974-3400.
E-mail: elaineb@masa.net
Founded: 1772.
Historic Building.
Collections: state history; paintings; John Shaw furniture; silver; statuary.
Hours & Admission Prices: Mon.-Fri. 9-5, Sat.-Sun. 10-9. Tours: 11 & 3. No charge. Closed New Year's Day; Thanksgiving; Christmas. ♿

UNITED STATES NAVAL ACADEMY MUSEUM, 118 Maryland Ave., Annapolis, MD 21402-5034. Tel.: 410-293-2108. Fax: 410-293-5220.
Web Site: www.usna.edu/Museum
Founded: 1845.
Congressional District: 4
Key Personnel: Dir., Dr. J. Scott Harmon; Assoc. Dir. & Senior Cur., James W. Cheevers; Cur. Ship Models, Donald R. Preul; Cur. Beverly R. Robinson Collection, Laura Arrington.
Personnel Profile: Full-Time Paid 7; Part-Time Paid 1; Part-Time Volunteers 14.
Governing Authority: federal. Affiliated with the United States Naval Academy. Tax-exempt.
Naval Museum: located at the U.S. Naval Academy.
Collections: paintings; prints; sculpture; historic ship models; naval uniforms; navigational instruments; naval weapons & gear; trophies of war; flags; china; silver; anthropological; numismatics; manuscripts & personal memorabilia of naval officers; over 6,000 naval battle & ship prints dating from 16th century to present; rare books; remains of John Paul Jones & artifacts.
Research Fields: naval history; naval & marine art; ship models; naval uniforms; instruments; equipment; weapons.
Facilities: 2,500-vol. library of books on U.S. Navy & Naval Academy history, marine architecture, naval flags, marine art & museology available for inter-library loan & on the premises.
Activities: hobby workshops; formally organized education programs for undergraduate students affiliated with USNA; permanent & temporary exhibitions.
Publications: various catalogs.
Hours & Admission Prices: Mon.-Sat. 9-5, Sun. 11-5. No charge; donations accepted. Closed New Year's; Thanksgiving; Christmas. ♿
Attendance: 170,000 (accurate)

Arnold

HERBARIUM AT ANNE ARUNDEL COMMUNITY COLLEGE, 101 College Pkwy., Arnold, MD 21012-1895. Tel.: 410-541-2260.
Herbarium.
Collections: plant specimens.
Facilities: library.
Activities: temporary exhibits.
Hours & Admission Prices: Mon.-Fri. by appointment.

Baltimore

THE ALBIN O. KUHN LIBRARY & GALLERY, UNIVERSITY OF MARYLAND-BALTIMORE COUNTY, 1000 Hilltop Cir., Baltimore, MD 21250-0001. Tel.: 410-455-2232. Fax: 410-455-1567.
E-mail: beck@umbc.edu
Web Site: www.umbc.edu/library
Founded: 1975.
Congressional District: 7
Key Personnel: Chief Cur., Tom Beck; Head Info Technology, May Chang.
Personnel Profile: Full-Time Paid 3; Part-Time Paid 4; Part-Time Volunteers 4; Interns 2.
Governing Authority: public university; nonprofit. Parent Institution: University of Maryland-Baltimore County. Tax-exempt: 501(c)(3).
University Museum.
Collections: over 1.5 million photographs, including 19th & 20th-century photographers Lewis Hine, Lotte Jacobi and photo-secessionists; Azriel Rozenfeld Science Fiction Research collection; Edward G. Howard collection of Marylandia; Merkle 18th & 19th-century English graphic satire; biological sciences archives including The American Society of Microbiology and The American Society of Cell Biology; rare books; manuscripts.
Research Fields: 19th and 20-century photographs; biological sciences; popular culture.
Facilities: 40,400-vol. library of books on photographs, microbiology and science fiction research; reading room; 4,420 sq. ft. exhibit space.
Activities: guided tours; formal education programs for the general public & campus community; loan, temporary & traveling exhibitions.
Publications: exhibition catalogues, Framing the Exhibition: Multiple Constructions; Eye of the Storm: Photographs by Mildred Grossman; Word & Image: Swiss Poster Design, 1955-1997; Visual Griots: Works by Four African-American Photographers; Fields of Vision: Women in Photography; Romantic Archaeologies: Some Images of the Age and Selected Women Writers; An American Vision: John G. Bullock and the Photo-Secession; A. Audrey Bodine; INTERMEDIA: The Dick Higgins Collection at UMBC; Typographically Speaking: The Art of Matthew Carter.
Hours & Admission Prices: Gallery: Sept-Dec. 13 Mon.-Wed. & Fri. 12-4, Thurs. 12-8, Sat.-Sun. 1-5. Library: Mon.-Thurs. 8:30-10:30, Fri. 8:30-6, Sat. 12-6, Sun. 12-10:30. No charge; donations accepted. Closed major holidays. ♿
Attendance: 12,000 (estimated)
Membership: Student $15; Associate $25; Patron $50; Contributor $100; Sponsor $500; Benefactor $1,000 & up.

AMERICAN VISIONARY ART MUSEUM, 800 Key Hwy., Baltimore, MD 21230-3940. Tel.: 410-244-1900. Fax: 410-244-5858.
E-mail: info@avam.org
Web Site: www.avam.org
Founded: 1995.
Congressional District: 3
Key Personnel: Dir., Rebecca Alban Hoffberger; Chairperson, Sandra Magsamen; Dir. Education & Design, Theresa Segreti; Dir. Communications, Pete Hilsee; C.F.O., Donna Katrinic; Registrar, Sarah Templin; Exhibition Design, Mark Ward; Admin. & Facility Rental, Alicia Karroll; Education & Volunteer Coord., Maggie Muth; Membership & Devel. Assoc., Katie Adams.
Personnel Profile: Full-Time Paid 18; Part-Time Paid 7; Interns 3.

Governing Authority: private; nonprofit. Tax-exempt.
Art Museum: located on 1.1 acre campus at Baltimore's Inner Harbor.
Collections: original works of art created by self-taught, intuitive artists; works range in scale from a 55 ft., 3 ton whirligig to mixed media assemblages, textiles, film & works on paper.
Research Fields: outsider art; visionary environments; Social Action and Art of Living.
Facilities: 1,000-vol. library of visionary, folk art & creativity reference books and visionary art catalogues; wildflower sculpture garden; permanent collection gallery & theater; Thou Art Creative classrooms; 7,500 sq. ft. conference party & space; 35,000 sq. ft. three-story main building, the former Baltimore Copper Paint Company offices; Tall Sculpture Barn with 45 ft. ceiling; 45,000 sq. ft. Jim Rouse Visionary Center; 1,000 seat outdoor movie theater; restaurant. Museum-related items for sale.
Activities: workshops conducted by visionary artists; films; guided tours; lectures; temporary exhibitions; performances; annual Kinetic Sculpture Race; conferences.
Publications: annual magazine, Visions Magazine, corresponding to thematic mega-exhibition which runs from October-September.
Hours & Admission Prices: Tues.-Sun. 10-6. Adults $14, senior citizens 60 & over $10, students & children $8; discounts to groups and AAM & ICOM members; children 6 & under no charge. Closed Thanksgiving; Christmas. ♿
Attendance: 60,000 (estimated)
Membership: Student $25; Senior $35; Single $50; Couple $75; Family $100.

THE BABE RUTH MUSEUM AND SPORTS LEGENDS AT CAMDEN YARDS, 216 Emory St., Baltimore, MD 21230-2235. Tel.: 410-727-1539. Fax: 410-727-1652.
E-mail: info@baberuthmuseum.com
Web Site: www.baberuthmuseum.com
Formerly: The Babe Ruth Birthplace & Museum
Founded: 1974.
Congressional District: 3
Key Personnel: Exec. Dir., Michael L. Gibbons; Chm. (V), Thomas Winstead; Cur., Shawn Herne; Deputy Dir., John Ziemann; Dir. Sales & Mktg., John Hein.
Personnel Profile: Full-Time Paid 15; Full-Time Volunteers 100; Part-Time Paid 5; Part-Time Volunteers 50; Interns 2.
Governing Authority: nonprofit organization. Parent Institution: Babe Ruth Birthplace Foundation, Inc. Tax-exempt: 501(c)(3).
Sports Museum.
Collections: 500 Home Run Club; life & career of Babe Ruth; autographed baseballs & bats; trophies; photographs; Baltimore Orioles & Baltimore Colts & Ravens memorabilia; Baltimore baseball history; Negro League exhibits; Maryland Baseball Hall of Fame; regional baseball archives for Maryland; video tapes of Baltimore Orioles Highlights; life of Babe Ruth film documentary; trophy collection; archives of Johnny Unitas; 714 Home Run.
Research Fields: Baltimore baseball statistics & history.
Facilities: library of scrapbooks, record books, clippings, newspapers, magazines, photographs, film, audio tapes & phonograph records; theatre. Museum & local sports-related items for sale.
Activities: permanent, temporary & traveling exhibitions; films; lectures; educational programs; speakers bureau. Annual Events: Babe Ruth's Birthday; Fall gala; Game Day events.
Publications: newsletter; brochures, education; Visit The Museum.
Hours & Admission Prices: April-Oct. daily 10-6; Nov.-March daily 10-5; when Orioles play at home 10-7. Museum: Adults $6, senior citizens $4, children 3-12 $3; discounts to military, AAA & AAM members. Sports Legends at Camden Yards: adults $8, senior citizens $6, children 3-12 $5. Closed New Year's; Thanksgiving; Christmas. ♿
Attendance: 70,000 (accurate)
Membership: Children 5-12 $15; Individual $35; Family & Dual $50; Heavy Hitter $100; Sultan of Swat $150; Corporate $250-$2500.

BALTIMORE AMERICAN INDIAN CENTER, 113 S. Broadway, Baltimore, MD 21231-1727. Tel.: 410-675-3535. Fax: 410-675-6909.
E-mail: info@baic.org
Web Site: www.baic.org
Key Personnel: Exec. Dir., John Simermeyer
History Museum.
Collections: Native American history & culture; sculpture; textiles; costumes; folk culture; archaeological artifacts; equipment; personal artifacts; tools.
Activities: Annual Events: Powwow in August.
Hours & Admission Prices: Mon.-Fri. 9:30-4.

BALTIMORE & OHIO RAILROAD MUSEUM, 901 W. Pratt St., Baltimore, MD 21223-2644. Tel.: 410-752-2490. Fax: 410-752-2499.
E-mail: info@borail.org
Web Site: www.borail.org
Formerly: The B&O Railroad Museum
Founded: 1953.
Congressional District: 7
Key Personnel: Chm. Bd., Francis X. Smyth; Exec. Dir., Courtney B. Wilson; Vice Pres., Gino Gemignani, Jr.; Vice Pres., Gregory A. Farno; Vice Pres., Greg C. Pinkard, CPM; C.O.O., Stef Fay; Dir. Corporate Sponsorship & Events, Kathy Hargest; Grants Writer, James Smolinksi; Dir. Museum Svcs., Dana Kirn; Dir. Facilities, Steven Johnson; Mgr. Group Sales & Membership, Kelly Flanagan; Acting Supt. Railroad Operations, Matt Couchenour; Chief Cur., Dave Shackelford; Dir. Operations, Tania Mansour; Museum Shop Mgr., Eileen Blinzley.
Personnel Profile: Full-Time Paid 30; Part-Time Paid 20; Part-Time Volunteers 100.
Governing Authority: nonprofit organization. Parent Institution: B&O Railroad Museum, Inc. Tax-exempt: 501(c)(3).
Transportation Museum: located on site of the historic Baltimore & Ohio Railroad's Mt. Clare Shops, site of the birthplace of American railroading.
Collections: over 120 locomotives & rolling stock; textiles; tools; lanterns; dining car china and silver; clocks & pocket watches; communication devices; signals; models; shop equipment; archival collections include corporate records; photographs; manuscripts; mechanical & engineering drawings; maps; artwork; rare books; audiovisual & film. Historic Buildings: 1884 Roundhouse; 1851 Mt. Clare Station; 1884 Annex; 1869 North Car Shop.
Major Exhibits: Thomas the Tank Engine, 4/23/10-4/25/10; Thomas the Tank Engine, 4/30/10-5/2/10.
Facilities: research library & archives; theater car; snack area. Museum-related items for sale.
Activities: living history, docent, & educational programs for all ages; scheduled programs; short-line excursion train ride on 1 mile track; 40' HO model train layout; seasonal outdoor family activity area containing G-Scale train layout and miniature train ride; special events; rental facilities.
Publications: The Roundhouse Review; monthly enewsletter, Train Mail.
Hours & Admission Prices: Mon.-Sat. 10-4, Sun. 11-4. Adults $14, senior citizens $12, children 2-12 $8; discount to groups of 20 or more with reservations, AAM & AAA members; members, children 2 & under no charge. Closed New Year's Day; Easter; Memorial Day; Independence Day; Labor Day; Thanksgiving; Christmas Eve & Day. ♿
Attendance: 90,000 (estimated)
Membership: Senior $45; Individual $50; Dual Senior $65; Dual $70; Grand Family $80; Family $85; Family & Friends $115; Lifetime: Society of the Iron Horse $5,000.

BALTIMORE CITY ARCHIVES, 2615 Mathews St., Baltimore, MD 21218-4705. Tel.: 410-396-0306.
History Museum.
Collections: Baltimore history; pamphlets; photographs; posters; brochures.
Hours & Admission Prices: Call for hours.

BALTIMORE CITY FIRE MUSEUM, Old Town Mall, 414 N. Gay St., Baltimore, MD 21202-4134. Tel.: 410-396-4686.
History Museum.
Collections: local firefighting history; furnishings; personal artifacts; fire equipment & tools; books; photographs; prints; drawings.
Facilities: Museum-related items for sale.
Hours & Admission Prices: Thurs. 9:30-12, Fri. 6:30pm-9:30pm, Sun. 1-4; other times by appointment.

BALTIMORE CIVIL WAR MUSEUM, 601 President St., Baltimore, MD 21202-4472. Tel.: 410-385-5188. Fax: 410-962-7058.
E-mail: museum_dept@mdhs.org
Web Site: www.mdhs.org
Founded: 1995.
Congressional District: 3
Key Personnel: Dir., Robert Rogers; Mgr. Museum, Frank Maurer; Chm., Henry Stansbury; Pres., Alex Fisher.
Personnel Profile: Full-Time Paid 1; Part-Time Volunteers 2; Interns 1.
Governing Authority: private; nonprofit organization. Parent Institution: Maryland Historical Society. Tax-exempt: 170(b)(1)(a).
History Museum: located in the c.1850 President Street Station.
Collections: artifacts relating to Baltimore's role in the Civil War; MD railroad history; station's role in the underground railroad.
Facilities: 1,500 sq. ft. exhibit space. Museum-related items for sale.
Activities: guided tours; lectures; living history; walking tours.
Publications: Baltimore Civil War Museum Guide Book; newsletter.
Hours & Admission Prices: Library: Wed.-Sat. 10-4:30. Museum: Wed.-Sun. 10-5. Adults $4, seniors, students with ID & children 13-18 $3; discounts to

AAM members; children under 12 & members no charge. Closed Thanksgiving; Christmas. ♿
Attendance: 14,129 (accurate)
Membership: $50-$1,000.

*** THE BALTIMORE MUSEUM OF ART, (M),** 10 Art Museum Dr., Baltimore, MD 21218-3827. Mailing Address: Public Relations, 10 Art Museum Dr., Baltimore, MD 21218-3898. Tel.: 443-573-1700. Fax: 443-573-1582. TDD: 410-396-4930.
E-mail: amannix@artbma.org
Web Site: www.artbma.org
Founded: 1914.
Congressional District: 3
Key Personnel: Dir., Doreen Bolger; Chm. (V), Stiles Colwill; Deputy Dir. Mktg. & Communications, Becca Seitz; Deputy Dir. Devel., Judith Gibbs; Deputy Dir. Operations & Capital Planning, Alan Dirican; Deputy Dir. Curatorial Affairs & Sen. Cur Prints, Drawings & Photographs, Jay Fisher; Senior Cur. Painting & Sculpture before 1900, Sona Johnston; Cur. Painting & Sculpture, Katherine Rothkopf; Cur. Textiles, Anita Jones; Librarian, Linda Tompkins-Baldwin; Dir. Communications, Anne Mannix; Dir. Retail Operations, Deana Karras; Dir. Security, Fred Venhuizen; Cur. Decorative Arts and American Painting & Sculpture, David Park Curry; Deputy Dir. Education & Interpretation, Anne Manning; Deputy Dir. Finance & Planning, Christine Dietz; Coord. Rights & Reproductions, Brianna Bedigian.
Personnel Profile: Full-Time Paid 127; Part-Time Paid 42; Part-Time Volunteers 550; Interns 11.
Governing Authority: municipal. Tax-exempt: 501(c)(3).
Art Museum: housed in 1929 building designed by John Russell Pope with later additions & adjoining sculpture gardens.
Collections: European paintings & sculpture from the Renaissance to present; 18th- to 20th-century American paintings; The Cone Collection, featuring works of Matisse & Picasso; west wing for Modern & Contemporary Art featuring 20th-century American & European paintings & sculpture; prints; drawings, especially 19th-century French (The George A. Lucas Collection); photographs; American, European & Asian decorative arts & textiles; Maryland furniture & silver; pre-Columbian, Native American, African & Oceanic arts; 1st- to 3rd-century mosaics from Antioch, Syria.
Major Exhibits: Cezanne and American (T), 2/10-5/10; Andy Warhol in the 1980s, 10/10-1/11.
Research Fields: pertaining to collections.
Facilities: library; inter-library loan of art reference books; auditorium; sculpture gardens; cafe; education classroom. Art books & museum-related articles for sale.
Activities: gallery guide programs; lectures; concerts; dance recitals; education program for children & teachers; scholarly symposia; permanent & temporary exhibitions; docent-led & self-guided gallery tours; special programs for senior citizens, singles & adolescents at risk; special services for visually & hearing impaired upon advance request.
Publications: bimonthly calendar; newsletters; miscellaneous brochures; exhibition & collection catalogs; posters; postcards; bookmarks; quarterly members magazine.
Hours & Admission Prices: Wed.-Fri. 10-5, Sat.-Sun. 11-6. No charge. Special ticketed exhibitions. Closed New Year's Day; Independence Day; Thanksgiving; Christmas. ♿
Attendance: 268,000 (estimated)
Membership: Seniors $40; Donor $50, $75, $150, $250; Patron $500, $750, $1,000, $1,500; Benefactor $2,500, $3,500, $5,000, $7,500 and up.

BALTIMORE MUSEUM OF INDUSTRY, (M), 1415 Key Hwy., Inner Harbor South, Baltimore, MD 21230-5100. Tel.: 410-727-4808, ext. 101. Fax: 410-727-4869.
E-mail: tours@thebmi.org
Web Site: www.thebmi.org
Founded: 1977.
Congressional District: 3
Key Personnel: Exec. Dir., Roland H. Woodward; Bd. Chm., Peter Macnab; Dir. Communications & Public Rels., Jessica Williams; Deputy Dir., Carole Baker; Dir. Public Programs, Lori Finkelstein; Cur. Collections & Exhibits, Shawn Gladden.
Personnel Profile: Full-Time Paid 22; Part-Time Paid 30; Part-Time Volunteers 100; Interns 2.
Governing Authority: nonprofit organization. Tax-exempt: 501(c)(3).
History & Industry Museum: housed in 1865 waterfront oyster cannery.
Collections: historical & modern industrial and business artifacts; tools; Maryland's popular culture; business records; manuscripts; photographs; films; tapes; books & serial publications; electric light bulb history from Edison's first installations in the 1880s; lamp from the Enola Gay; microscopic light bulb from a missile warhead; machine shop; blacksmith; print shop. Historic Vessel: 1906 S.T. Baltimore (steam tug).
Research Fields: industrial & business history; technology; labor & economic history; historical geography; Baltimore history.
Activities: docent guided tours; children's educational programs (Kids Cannery - role playing activity recreating 1883 oyster cannery workers; Children's Motor Works - children experience assembly line production while manufacturing toy model vehicle); temporary special exhibits; lectures; concerts; internship opportunities.
Publications: newsletter, Nuts & Bolts; annual report; e-newsletter.
Hours & Admission Prices: Tues.-Sat. 10-4, Sun. 11-4. Adults $10, seniors & students $6; discounts to AAM & ICOM members; children under 4 & members no charge. Closed New Year's Day; Thanksgiving; Christmas Eve & Day. ♿
Attendance: 160,000 (estimated)
Membership: Senior Citizen $25; Individual $35; Household $55; Supporter $100-$249.

BALTIMORE PUBLIC WORKS MUSEUM, INC., 751 Eastern Ave., Baltimore, MD 21202-4369. Tel.: 410-396-5565. Fax: 410-545-6781.
E-mail: mari.ross@baltimorecity.gov
Web Site: www.baltimorepublicworksmuseum.org
Founded: 1982.
Congressional District: 1
Key Personnel: C.E.O., David E. Scott; Exec. Dir., Mari B. Ross; Dir. Education & Programs, Vince Pompa.
Personnel Profile: Full-Time Paid 4; Part-Time Paid 1; Interns 1.
Governing Authority: nonprofit organization. Parent Institution: Baltimore Dept. of Public Works. Tax-exempt: 501(c)(3).
Urban Environmental History Museum: housed in restored c.1912 sewage pumping station.
Collections: approx. 2,000 c.1910 glass plate negatives documenting the construction of public works projects; c.1804 wooden water pipes; heavy equipment; gauges; meters; electrical material; tools; machinery.
Research Fields: Baltimore public works projects; urban environmental issues.
Facilities: library of books, journals & yearly reports on engineering & urban planning; 2,000 sq. ft. exhibit space. Gift items & books for sale.
Activities: guided tours; programs for high school & elementary school students; videos; internship programs; permanent exhibits.
Publications: Highlights in Public Works History.
Hours & Admission Prices: Tues.-Sun. 10-4. Adults $3, seniors, students & active military $2.50; discounts for groups of 10 or more & AAM members; Baltimore City public school students & members no charge. Closed holidays. ♿
Attendance: 20,000 (estimated)
Membership: Iron $150; Copper $450; Bronze $750; Silver $1,000; Gold $1,500.

BALTIMORE STREETCAR MUSEUM, INC., (M), 1901 Falls Rd., Baltimore, MD 21211. Mailing Address: P.O. Box 4881, Baltimore, MD 21211-0881. Tel.: 410-547-0264. Fax: 410-547-0264.
Web Site: www.baltimorestreetcar.org/
Founded: 1966.
Congressional District: 7
Key Personnel: Pres., John J. O'Neill; Exec. Vice Pres., Christopher M. McNally; Admin. Vice Pres., Edward M. Amrhein; Vice Pres. Engineering & Operations, John D. La Costa; Vice Pres. Cur., Mark E. Dawson; Treas., Christopher Howell; Comptroller, Paul W. Wirtz; Corp. Sec. & Recording Sec., Mark A. Hurley; Dir. Public Affairs, Andrew S. Blumberg; Museum Shop Mgr., Raymond L. Cannon.
Personnel Profile: Part-Time Volunteers 40.
Governing Authority: nonprofit organization. Tax-exempt: 501(c)(3).
Transportation Museum: located on site of the Maryland & Pennsylvania RR Terminal in Baltimore.
Collections: 1880-1944 Baltimore streetcars; 1859 & 1880 horsecars; 1913 crane; 1922 & 1940 trackless trolleys; 1945, 1947 & 1963 buses; 1952 line truck.
Research Fields: street railway & Baltimore history.
Facilities: library relating to Baltimore street railway history. Museum-related items for sale.
Activities: streetcar rides; guided tours; lectures; permanent exhibitions; video presentation.
Publications: newsletter, Live Wire; guide book; annual report; visitors' brochure.
Hours & Admission Prices: June-Oct. Sat.-Sun. 12-5; Nov.-May Sun. 12-5. Adults $7, children 4-11 & seniors 65 & over $5, maximum family $24; children under 4 no charge; valid passes issued by other Association of Railway Museums (ARM) honored for admission. Closed New Year's Day; Christmas. ♿
Attendance: 15,000 (estimated)
Membership: Senior Citizen $15; Student $17.50; Senior Family $20; Individual $30; Family $40.

BALTIMORE TATTOO MUSEUM, 1534 Eastern Ave., Baltimore, MD 21231-2330. Tel.: 410-522-5800. Fax: 410-522-4074.
Web Site: www.baltimoretattoomuseum.net/
Tattoo Art Museum.
Collections: original artwork; tattooing equipment; lithographs; tattoo history.
Hours & Admission Prices: Mon.-Sat. 10-9, Sun. 11-7. No charge.

BALTIMORE'S BLACK AMERICAN MUSEUM, 1767 Carswell St., Baltimore, MD 21218-4908. Tel.: 410-243-9600.
History Museum.
Collections: African American history & culture; photographs; personal artifacts.
Hours & Admission Prices: Sat. 8am-11pm, 1st Sun. of month 2-4; other times by appointment.

THE BENJAMIN BANNEKER PARK & MUSEUM, 300 Oella Ave., Baltimore, MD 21228-5416. Tel.: 410-887-1081. Fax: 410-203-2747.
Web Site: www.thefriendsofbanneker.org
Founded: 1998.
Congressional District: 7
Key Personnel: Dir., Steven Lee; Chm. (V), William Lambert; Museum Shop Mgr., Marilyn Cornish.
Personnel Profile: Full-Time Paid 1; Part-Time Paid 6; Part-Time Volunteers 20.
Governing Authority: private; nonprofit organization. Parent Institution: Baltimore County Government. Subsidiary Institution: The Friends of Banneker Historical Park. Tax-exempt: 501(c)(3).
Historical Park & Museum.
Collections: historical & archaeological artifacts & prints; historical & cultural books; videos; wildlife habitats. Historic Building: farmhouse; log cabin.
Major Exhibits: The Power of the Telescope 'Scope': From Galileo to Banneker to Hubble, 11/09-5/10.
Research Fields: early history of free African Americans & Native Americans; archaeology; the legacy of Benjamin Banneker; the natural environment native to our land; Colonial & early American history.
Activities: educational history tours & nature presentations; concerts; special events; permanent & temporary exhibitions.
Publications: newsletter, Banneker Journal.
Hours & Admission Prices: Tues.-Sat. 10-4. No charge; donations accepted. Charge for events & programs. Closed holidays. ♿
Attendance: 40,000 (estimated)
Membership: Full-Time Student & Senior Citizen $15; Individual $25; Family $40; Patron $75; Donor-Bronze $150; Donor-Silver $200; Donor-Gold $250.

CENTER FOR ART DESIGN AND VISUAL CULTURE, 1000 Hilltop Circle, Baltimore, MD 21250-0002. Tel.: 410-455-3188.
Governing Authority: nonprofit organization.
Art Museum.
Collections: paintings; sculpture; drawings; printmaking; graphic design; digital art; video; film; architecture; art history.
Facilities: 4,200 sq. ft. exhibit space.
Activities: outreach programs; permanent & temporary exhibitions.
Hours & Admission Prices: Tues.-Sat. 10-5. Closed New Year's Eve & Day; Christmas Eve, Day & week.

CONTEMPORARY MUSEUM, 100 W. Centre St., Baltimore, MD 21201-4502. Tel.: 410-783-5720. Fax: 410-783-5722.
E-mail: info@contemporary.org
Web Site: www.contemporary.org
Founded: 1989.
Congressional District: 7
Key Personnel: Exec. Dir., Irene Hofmann; Deputy Dir., Robert Haywood; Pres. (V), Pamela Berman; Sr. Admin. & Membership Dir., Johaniris M. Rivera Rodriguez.
Personnel Profile: Full-Time Paid 3; Part-Time Paid 4; Part-Time Volunteers 5; Interns 4.
Governing Authority: private; nonprofit organization. Tax-exempt: 501(c)(3).
Art Museum.
Collections: contemporary art.
Research Fields: national & international contemporary art.
Activities: temporary exhibitions; gallery talks; tours; lectures; symposia; artist residencies & fellowships.
Publications: quarterly newsletter.
Hours & Admission Prices: Administrative Offices: Mon.-Fri. 9-5. Galleries: Wed.-Sun. 12-5. Suggested Donations: adults $5, senior citizens, students & children $3. Closed federal holidays. ♿
Attendance: 12,000 (accurate)
Membership: Student $20; Individual $40; Family $60; Friend $100; Explorer $250; Supporter $ 500; Donor $1,000.

CYLBURN ARBORETUM, Cylburn Mansion, 4915 Greenspring Ave., Baltimore, MD 21209-4642. Tel.: 410-367-2217. Fax: 410-367-7112.
E-mail: info@cylburnassociation.org
Web Site: www.cylburnassociation.org
Founded: 1954.
Congressional District: 7
Key Personnel: Pres., Nell Strachan; Exec. Dir., Natalie Lopes; Nature Museum Dir., Patsy Perlman; Chief Horticulturist, William Vondrasek; Dir. Education, Nancy Hill.
Personnel Profile: Full-Time Paid 1; Full-Time Volunteers 2; Part-Time Paid 2; Part-Time Volunteers 200.
Governing Authority: municipal. Affiliated with Cylburn Arboretum, Inc. Tax-exempt: 501(c)(3).
Natural History Museum: housed in a Victorian mansion of Renaissance revival style, built of stone from a nearby chromite mine & 207 acre arboretum.
Collections: birds; mammals; insects; plants; local material; rocks; minerals; arboretum; trees; magnolias; viburnums; maples; conifers; hollies.
Facilities: 207 acre arboretum; junior museum; nature center; 85-seat auditorium; educational facilities.
Activities: guided tours; lectures; formally organized education programs for children; loan, permanent & temporary exhibitions; school loan service.
Publications: Association's newsletters, City Farms Newsletter; Trails Guide.
Hours & Admission Prices: Call for hours. No charge; donations accepted. ♿
Attendance: 15,000 (estimated)
Membership: Individual $25; Household $35; Group $50; Sustaining $100; Life $500.

DR. SAMUEL D. HARRIS NATIONAL MUSEUM OF DENTISTRY, (M), 31 S. Greene St., Baltimore, MD 21201-1504. Tel.: 410-706-0600. Fax: 410-706-8313.
E-mail: edunning@dentalmuseum.umaryland.edu
Web Site: www.dentalmuseum.org
Founded: 1996.
Congressional District: 7
Key Personnel: Chm. Bd. of Visitors, Leslie W. Seldin, D.D.S.; Dir. Operations, Elza Dunning; Dir. Education, Beth Cooper; Cur., Dr. Scott D. Swank.
Personnel Profile: Full-Time Paid 8; Part-Time Paid 2; Part-Time Volunteers 25; Interns 2.
Governing Authority: Parent Institution: University of Maryland, Baltimore. Tax-exempt.
Dentistry Museum.
Collections: early dental instruments; furniture; equipment; early dentures; artifacts; portraits.
Major Exhibits: Mouth Power (T), 11/09-8/10; Your Spitting Image (T), 11/09-8/10.
Research Fields: dental history.
Facilities: reading room; library; archives; meeting & reception space.
Activities: guided tours; reading room; permanent, traveling & temporary exhibitions; educational programs.
Publications: book, The Baltimore College of Dental Surgery: The Pioneer of Dental Education; The Articulator.
Hours & Admission Prices: Wed.-Sat. 10-4, Sun. 1-4. Adults $7, seniors & college students w/ID $5, children 3-18 $3; discounts to AAM & AAA members; members & children under 3 no charge. Closed most major holidays. ♿
Attendance: 10,000 (estimated)
Membership: Individual $50; Family $75; Dental Office $100.

EDGAR ALLAN POE HOUSE AND MUSEUM, 203 N. Amity St., Baltimore, MD 21223-2501. Mailing Address: 417 E. Fayette St., 8th Fl., Baltimore, MD 21202-3431. Tel.: 410-396-7932. Fax: 410-396-5662.
Web Site: www.eapoe.org/balt/poehse.htm
Founded: 1923.
Key Personnel: Dir., Kathleen Kotarba; Cur., Jeff Jerome.
Personnel Profile: Full-Time Paid 1; Part-Time Volunteers 5.
Governing Authority: municipal. Affiliated with the Baltimore City Preservation Commission.
Historic House: 1830 home of Edgar Allan Poe.
Collections: period artifacts; Poe artifacts; lamps.
Activities: guided tours; lectures; slide & audiovisual presentations.
Hours & Admission Prices: April-Nov. Wed.-Sat. 12-3:30. Adults $3; night tours of the Poe grave & catacombs by special arrangement: $4 per person in groups of 25 & over. Closed national holidays.
Attendance: 6,000 (estimated)

EUBIE BLAKE NATIONAL JAZZ INSTITUTE AND CULTURAL CENTER, 847 N. Howard St., Baltimore, MD 21201-4605. Tel.: 410-225-3130. Fax: 410-225-3139.
E-mail: info@eubieblake.org
Web Site: www.eubieblake.org
Founded: 1983.
Congressional District: 7
Key Personnel: Exec. Dir., Troy Burton; Chm., John Clark Mayden.
Personnel Profile: Full-Time Paid 3; Part-Time Paid 16; Part-Time Volunteers 10.
Governing Authority: nonprofit. Tax-exempt: 501(c)(3).
History Museum.
Collections: Eubie Blake memorabilia.
Activities: African-American heritage performance series.
Publications: quarterly newsletter, Ragtime.
Hours & Admission Prices: Wed.-Fri. 11-6, Sat. 11-3, Sun. by appointment. Admission $5. Closed federal holidays. ♿
Attendance: 10,000 (estimated)
Membership: Students $10; Individual $20; Family Members $50; Patrons $100

EVERGREEN MUSEUM & LIBRARY, JOHNS HOPKINS UNIVERSITY MUSEUMS, 4545 N. Charles St., Baltimore, MD 21210-2693. Tel.: 410-516-0341. Fax: 410-516-0864.
E-mail: evergreenmuseum@jhu.edu
Web Site: www.museums.jhu.edu
Founded: 1990.
Congressional District: 3
Key Personnel: Dir., James Archer Abbott; Chm. (V), James R. Garrett; Coord. Membership, Rosalie Parker; Coord. Mktg., Heather Egan Stalfort; Tour Coord., Nancy Powers; Coord. Special Events, Anna Papierniak.
Personnel Profile: Full-Time Paid 7; Part-Time Paid 2; Part-Time Volunteers 75; Interns 3.
Governing Authority: university; board of trustees; nonprofit. Parent Institution: Johns Hopkins University. Tax-exempt: 501(c)(3).
Historic House: housed in an 1850s Italianate mansion formerly owned by philanthropic Garrett family.
Collections: international art; French post-Impressionist paintings; furnishings; rare books; European & Oriental porcelain; Japanese Inro, Netsuke and Lacquer; Tiffany glass; carriage house.
Research Fields: rare books; Tiffany glass; oriental rugs & artifacts; American & English furniture; 20th century contemporary art.
Facilities: research library; theatre; formal gardens.
Activities: guided tours; Tea & Tour; concerts; symposia; lectures; meetings; temporary exhibitions; outdoor theatre productions; rental facility.
Publications: print & electronic newsletters, View From Evergreen; annual report.
Hours & Admission Prices: Tues.-Fri. 11-4, Sat.-Sun. 12-4; last tour 3pm. Adults $6, senior citizens $5, students with ID $3; discounts to groups, AAM & ICOM members, JHU faculty & staff; members & JHU students no charge. Closed holidays. ♿
Attendance: 11,600 (accurate)
Membership: Friend $50; Family $75; Supporter $125; Fellow $250; Patron $500; Benefactor $1,000.

FELLS POINT MARITIME MUSEUM, 1724 Thames St., Baltimore, MD 21231-3416. Tel.: 410-732-0278.
Web Site: www.mdhs.org
Maritime Museum.
Collections: maritime history & artifacts; medical; law; religion; furnishings; tools; photographs; documents.
Facilities: library. Museum-related items for sale.
Activities: lectures; special events.
Hours & Admission Prices: Thurs.-Mon. 10-5. Adults $4, children, students & seniors $3; children 12 & under no charge.

FORT MCHENRY NATIONAL MONUMENT AND HISTORIC SHRINE, 2400 E. Fort Ave., Baltimore, MD 21230-5390. Tel.: 410-962-4290. Fax: 410-962-2500. TDD: 410-962-4290.
E-mail: fomc_superintendent@nps.gov
Web Site: www.nps.gov/fomc
Founded: 1933.
Congressional District: 3
Key Personnel: Supt., Gay Vietzke; Historian, Scott Sheads; Chief Interpretation, Vince Vaise; Museum Shop Mgr., Karol Clark.
Personnel Profile: Full-Time Paid 25; Full-Time Volunteers 8; Part-Time Paid 15; Part-Time Volunteers 60; Interns 1.
Governing Authority: federal. Parent Institution: U.S. Dept. of Interior. Subsidiary Institution: National Park Service, Washington, DC 20240. Tax-exempt: 501(c)(3).
Historic Site: 1812 fort, site of the bombardment that inspired Francis Scott Key to write The Star-Spangled Banner, the National Anthem; fort also served during the American Civil War (1861-65) as a Union prison camp for Confederate soldiers and sympathizers, and as a hospital in WWI (1917-1925).
Collections: archives; military artifacts; U.S. Flags; Rodman Guns; Mrs. Reuben Ross Holloway manuscript collection relating to The Star-Spangled Banner becoming the National Anthem; Historic & Archaeological Research Project; c.1900 to the present, photographs. Historic Buildings: 1814 power magazine & guardhouse; 1830s soldiers' barracks.
Research Fields: Battle of Baltimore; War of 1812; U.S. flag; history of Fort McHenry; The Star-Spangled Banner.
Facilities: library of material relative to Fort's history, War of 1812 & National Park Service available on premises; visitor center; 81-seat auditorium. Publications & museum-related items for sale.
Activities: living history presentation; ranger programs; films; permanent exhibitions; research by appointment only; special events.
Publications: park folder, Fort McHenry National Monument & Historic Shrine.
Hours & Admission Prices: 1st weekend in June to Labor Day daily 8-8; Tues. after Labor Day to 1st weekend in June daily 8-5. Adults 16 & over $7; senior citizens 62 & over with Golden Age Passport/Senior Pass and children under 15 no charge. Research: by appointment. Closed New Year's Day; Thanksgiving; Christmas. ♿
Attendance: 600,000 (estimated)

GLENN L. MARTIN MARYLAND AVIATION MUSEUM, 701 Wilson Point Rd., Hangar 5, Ste. 531, Baltimore, MD 21220-4238. Mailing Address: P.O. Box 5024, Baltimore, MD 21220-0024. Tel.: 410-682-6122.
E-mail: info@marylandaviationmuseum.org
Web Site: www.marylandaviationmuseum.org
Personnel Profile: Part-Time Volunteers 45.
Governing Authority: private; nonprofit organization. Tax-exempt: 501(c)(3).
Aviation Museum.
Collections: Maryland's aviation history; aircraft & rocket models; aircraft; photographs.
Research Fields: Martin; Maryland aviation.
Facilities: archives by appointment.
Publications: quarterly newsletter.
Hours & Admission Prices: Wed.-Sat. 11-3. No charge. ♿
Membership: Senior & Student $15; Individual & Teacher $25; Family $45; Supporting $100; Patron $250; Lifetime $1,000. Corporate: Friend $1,000; Associate $2,500; Contributor $5,000; Benefactor $10,000; Leader $15,000.

GOLDSMITH MUSEUM OF CHIZUK AMUNO CONGREGATION, (M), 8100 Stevenson Rd., Baltimore, MD 21208-1899. Tel.: 410-486-6400.
Jewish Heritage Museum.
Collections: Jewish life, culture & history; religious artifacts.
Facilities: Museum-related items for sale.
Hours & Admission Prices: Call for hours.

THE HERITAGE MUSEUM, Hamlet Court, 4509 Prospect Circle, Baltimore, MD 21216-1615. Tel.: 410-664-6711. Fax: 410-664-6711.
Founded: 1991.
Key Personnel: C.E.O., Steven Lee.
Personnel Profile: Full-Time Paid 1; Part-Time Paid 2; Part-Time Volunteers 5.
Governing Authority: private; nonprofit organization. Tax-exempt: 501(c)(3).
Cultural, Historical & Environmental Museum.
Collections: traditional & contemporary art from Africa & the Americas; arboretum; rare & endangered, native & exotic plants.
Research Fields: early history of free African Americans & Native Americans; inventory & assessment of the natural resource of the Gwynns Falls wilderness park.
Facilities: 15,000-vol. library of history & culture of people of color; botanical garden; studio; field research station. Museum-related items for sale.
Activities: concerts; formal education programs for children; guided tours; lectures; temporary & traveling exhibitions; community programs.
Hours & Admission Prices: Mon.-Fri. 10-4:30. No charge; donations accepted. Charge for events & programs. Closed holidays.
Attendance: 800 (estimated)
Membership: Student & Seniors $20; Individual $25; Corporate $300.

HOMEWOOD MUSEUM, The Johns Hopkins Univ., 3400 N. Charles St., Baltimore, MD 21218-2608. Tel.: 410-516-5589. Fax: 410-516-7859.
E-mail: homewoodmuseum@jhu.edu
Web Site: www.museums.jhu.edu
Founded: 1987.
Congressional District: 7
Key Personnel: Dir., Winston Tabb; Pres. (V), Ross Jones; Cur., Catherine

Rogers Arthur; Program Coord., Judith L. Proffitt; Coord. Membership, Rosalie Parker; Coord. Mktg. & Communications, Heather Egan Stalfort.
Personnel Profile: Full-Time Paid 5; Part-Time Paid 3; Part-Time Volunteers 50; Interns 4.
Governing Authority: university; advisory council. Parent Institution: Johns Hopkins University. Tax-exempt: 501(c)(3).
Historic House Museum: 1801 Federal period home.
Collections: Federal period furnishings; porcelain; ceramics; tableware; textiles; furniture; prints; paintings; kitchen equipment; household items.
Research Fields: late 18th-to early 19th century domestic architecture; Carroll family history; late 18th- to early 19th century lifeways; 19th century games; Day in 1808, middle school program; slave/servant life in Baltimore; gardens & plants.
Facilities: 2,000-vol. research library, available to scholars. Museum-related items for sale.
Activities: guided tours; lectures; decorative arts workshops; volunteer program; membership program; holiday & seasonal events.
Hours & Admission Prices: Tues.-Fri. 11-4, Sat.-Sun. 12-4; last tour at 3:30. Adults $6, groups & senior citizens $5, students with ID $3; discounts to AAM & ICOM members and JHU faculty & staff; members & JHU students no charge. Closed holidays.
Attendance: 5,000 (accurate)
Membership: Friend $50; Supporter $125; Fellow $250; Patron $500; Benefactor $1,000.

JAMES E. LEWIS MUSEUM OF ART, MORGAN STATE UNIVERSITY, (M), 2201 Argonne Dr., Baltimore, MD 21251-0001. Mailing Address: The Carl J. Murphy Fine Arts Center, Rm. 242, 1700 E. Coldspring Lane, Baltimore, MD 21251-0001. Tel.: 443-885-3030 & 3333. Fax: 443-885-8258.
E-mail: gabriel.tenabe@morgan.edu
Web Site: www.jelma.org
Founded: 1951.
Congressional District: 3
Key Personnel: Dir. & Cur., Gabriel S. Tenabe; Cur., Aaron Bryant; Asst. Dir. Museum Studies & Historical Preservation, Robin Howard; Registrar, Deborah Johnson-Simon.
Personnel Profile: Full-Time Paid 4; Part-Time Paid 1; Part-Time Volunteers 10; Interns 4.
Governing Authority: university. Affiliated with Morgan State University. Tax-exempt: 170(b)(1)(A).
Fine Art Center.
Collections: 19th- & 20th-century American and European sculpture; graphics; paintings; decorative arts; archaeology; African & New Guinean sculpture.
Research Fields: European, American, African & Afro-American art.
Activities: lectures; gallery talks; temporary, traveling & permanent exhibitions; visiting artists.
Publications: catalogs of collections & temporary exhibitions.
Hours & Admission Prices: Tues.-Fri. 10-4, Sat. 11-4, Sun. 12-4. No charge; donations accepted. Closed New Year's Eve & Day; Easter; Thanksgiving; Christmas break. ♿
Attendance: 40,000 (accurate)

∗ **JEWISH MUSEUM OF MARYLAND, (M),** 15 Lloyd St., Baltimore, MD 21202-4606. Tel.: 410-732-6400. Fax: 410-732-6451.
E-mail: info@jewishmuseummd.org
Web Site: www.jewishmuseummd.org
Formerly: Jewish Historical Society of Maryland
Founded: 1960.
Congressional District: 7
Key Personnel: Exec. Dir., Avi Y. Decter; Pres., David B. Liebman; Assoc. Dir., Anita Kassof; C.F.O., Susan Press; Cur., Karen Falk; Collections Mgr., Jobi Zink; Dir. Education, Deborah Cardin; Research Historian, Deborah R. Weiner; Museum Shop Mgr., Esther Weiner.
Personnel Profile: Full-Time Paid 14; Part-Time Paid 7; Part-Time Volunteers 45; Interns 6.
Governing Authority: nonprofit organization. Tax-exempt: 501(c)(3).
History Museum: housed in a 3-building complex, including history museum & the Lloyd St. Synagogue, built in 1845 and the B'nai Israel Synagogue built in 1876.
Collections: manuscripts; documents; photographs; ceremonial art; business records; ephemera; costumes; textiles; paintings; fine art; folk art; furniture; 6,500 objects related to regional Jewish history; 100,000 photographs and negatives; rare books, microfilms & materials on Jewish genealogy. Historic Buildings: 1876 Moorish Revival style synagogue; 1845 Greek Revival Synagogue.
Major Exhibits: The Synagogue Speaks, 3/21/10.
Research Fields: Jewish life related to Maryland & surrounding region pertaining to European and other antecedents; immigration; settlement; religious; business; social and urban history; Jewish religious architecture; material culture; decorative art; general Jewish history, culture & art related to or ancestral to the Jewish experience in Maryland from the 18th century to the present.
Facilities: 3,000-vol. library of local and American Jewish history; 4,500 sq. ft. exhibit space; children's museum; educational facilities. Jewish art, ceremonial items, books & publications for sale.
Activities: gallery & historic building tours; walking tours; bus trips; lectures; films; concerts; study clubs; organized educational programs for children & adults; special public school programs; speakers' bureau; docent program; permanent, temporary & traveling exhibits.
Publications: exhibit catalogues; monographs; tri-annual newsletter, Museum Matters; annual magazine, Generations; books.
Hours & Admission Prices: Tues., Thurs. & Sun. 12-4; other times by appointment. Library & Archives by appointment. Adults $8, students $4, children 12 & under $3; discounts to groups, AAM, GBHA, AASLH & CAJM members; members no charge. Closed national & major Jewish holidays. ♿
Attendance: 12,330 (estimated)
Membership: Individual $36; Family $60; Sponsor $75; Patron $150; President's Circle $500.

THE JOHNS HOPKINS UNIVERSITY ARCHAEOLOGICAL COLLECTION, 129/130 Gilman Hall, 3400 N. Charles St., Baltimore, MD 21218-2608. Tel.: 410-516-7561 & 6717. Fax: 410-516-4848.
E-mail: emaguire@jhu.edu
Web Site: neareast.jhu.edu/archaeo/
Founded: 1884.
Key Personnel: Dir. Dept. Near Eastern Studies, Dr. Betsy Bryan; Cur., Dr. Eunice Daughterman-Maguire.
Governing Authority: university. Parent Institution: The Johns Hopkins University. Tax-exempt.
Art & Archaeology Museum.
Collections: Egyptian, Mesopotamian, Greek & Roman art objects & artifacts from c.4000 B.C.-500 A.D.
Activities: gallery talks on special request; loan, permanent & temporary exhibitions.
Publications: Ellen Reeder Williams, The Archaeological Collection of the Johns Hopkins University.
Hours & Admission Prices: Temporarily closed. ♿
Attendance: 700

LITHUANIAN HALL MUSEUM, 851-3 Hollins St., Baltimore, MD 21201-1003. Tel.: 410-685-5787.
Lithuanian Heritage Museum.
Collections: Lithuanian heritage, culture, & history; photographs; personal artifacts; replica of c.1890 Lithuanian house.
Hours & Admission Prices: By appointment.

LOVELY LANE MUSEUM AND ARCHIVES, 2200 St. Paul St., Baltimore, MD 21218-5805. Tel.: 410-889-4458. Fax: 410-889-1501.
E-mail: director@lovelylanemuseum.com
Web Site: www.lovelylanemuseum.com
Founded: 1955.
Congressional District: 3
Key Personnel: C.E.O. & Dir., James E. Reaves; Exec. Sec. (V), Rev. Edwin Schell; Pres. (V), Rev. Emora Brannan; Asst. Archivist, Wanda B. Hall.
Personnel Profile: Full-Time Paid 1; Part-Time Paid 1; Part-Time Volunteers 10; Interns 1.
Governing Authority: church. Parent Institution: Balto-Washington United Methodist Church. Subsidiary Institution: Strawbridge Shrine Assn. Inc. Tax-exempt.
Religious Museum.
Collections: Methodist history; archives; paintings; graphics; archaeology; manuscripts; genealogy; biography.
Research Fields: Methodist history; genealogy of Methodist preachers & church members.
Facilities: 4,300-vol. library of Methodist Church history books by appointment; reading room; archives.
Activities: guided tours; lectures; permanent, temporary & traveling exhibitions.
Publications: quarterly newsletter, Third Century Methodism; pamphlets; brochures.
Hours & Admission Prices: Thurs.-Fri. 10-4; other times by appointment. ♿
Attendance: 1,000 (estimated)
Membership: Associate $25; Partner $50; Ambassador $100; Life $300.

MARYLAND ART PLACE, Byrd, Baltimore, MD 21202-4015. Tel.: 410-962-8565. Fax: 410-244-8017. TDD: 1-800-735-2258.
E-mail: map@mdartpeace.org
Web Site: www.mdartplace.org

Founded: 1981.
Congressional District: 29
Key Personnel: Exec. Dir., Cathy Byrd; Chm. (V), Suzi Cordish; Pres. (V), Samuel Polakoff; Registry Coord., Sofia Rutka; Devel. Coord., Jessica D'Argenio; Programming Asst., Esther Sang-Ah Kim; Admin. Asst., Claud Vandernotte.
Personnel Profile: Full-Time Paid 2; Part-Time Paid 2; Part-Time Volunteers 80; Interns 5.
Governing Authority: nonprofit organization. Tax-exempt: 501(c)(3).
Art Museum.
Collections: temporary exhibitions of contemporary visual art & annual series of contemporary performing arts.
Facilities: 3,400 sq. ft. exhibit space; 120-seat theater.
Activities: participatory & traveling exhibitions; concerts; performances; films; guided tours; lectures; workshops. Annual Programs: Critics-in-Residence; Curator's Incubator.
Publications: quarterly newsletter; annual, Critics' Residency Catalog.
Hours & Admission Prices: Office: Tues.-Sat. 9-5. Gallery: Tues.-Sat. 11-5. No charge; donations accepted. Closed federal holidays. ♿
Attendance: 50,000 (estimated)
Membership: Artist $30; Individual $40; Dual $65; Contributor $100; Supporter $250.

MARYLAND HISTORICAL SOCIETY, (M), 201 W. Monument St., Baltimore, MD 21201-4674. Tel.: 410-685-3750. Fax: 410-962-7058.
E-mail: museum_dept@mdhs.org
Web Site: www.mdhs.org
Founded: 1844.
Congressional District: 7
Key Personnel: Dir., Robert W. Rogers; Pres., Alex Fisher; Chm., Henry Stansbury; Cur. Collections & Interpretation, Alexandra Deutsch; Chief Steward, Louise Brownell; Archivist, Francis O'Neil.
Personnel Profile: Full-Time Paid 47; Part-Time Paid 12; Part-Time Volunteers 50.
Governing Authority: nonprofit organization.
History Museum.
Collections: Maryland portraits & landscapes; furniture; silver; china; glass; costumes; clocks; uniforms; textiles; Chesapeake Bay maritime collection; maps; Civil War gallery; photographs, prints; architectural drawings; manuscripts including original draft of Star Spangled Banner; books; collections from the Baltimore City Life Museums.
Research Fields: Maryland history; material culture; maritime, architectural, fine & decorative arts.
Facilities: 60,000-vol. library of books; event spaces & meeting rooms. Pamphlets & books on Maryland history & gift items for sale.
Activities: guided tours; lectures; films; formally organized education programs; permanent & temporary exhibitions.
Publications: quarterly magazine, Maryland Historical Magazine; news bulletin, MdHS News, three times per year.
Hours & Admission Prices: Museum: Wed.-Sun. 10-5. Library: Wed.-Sat. 10-4:30. Museum: adults $4, senior citizens & students $3; members no charge. Library: $6. Closed New Year's Eve & Day; Martin Luther King Jr Day; Memorial Day; Labor Day; Thanksgiving; Christmas. ♿
Attendance: 12,000 (accurate)
Membership: Student, Teacher & Scholar $40; Individual $50; Household $65.

THE MARYLAND INSTITUTE, COLLEGE OF ART: DECKER, MEYERHOFF AND PINKARD GALLERIES, 1300 Mt. Royal Ave., Baltimore, MD 21217-4191. Tel.: 410-669-9200 & 225-2280. Fax: 410-225-2396.
Web Site: www.mica.edu
Founded: 1826.
Congressional District: 7
Key Personnel: Pres., Fred Lazarus, IV; Exhibitions Dir., Gerald Ross.
Governing Authority: board of trustees. Tax-exempt: 501(c)(3).
Art Galleries: housed in 1896 Mt. Royal Railroad Station & Fox Building, former Cannon Shoe Factory.
Collections: George A. Lucas collection of 19th-century paintings.
Research Fields: American and European paintings, drawings, prints.
Facilities: over 39,000-vol. library of books on art, art history, design, photography, crafts & fine arts; graduate studio; auditorium; classrooms.
Activities: lectures; concerts; tours of the station building & Fox Building; changing exhibitions; performances.
Publications: exhibition catalogs; bulletins; posters.
Hours & Admission Prices: Call for hours. No charge. ♿

MARYLAND SCIENCE CENTER, 601 Light St., Baltimore, MD 21230-3803. Tel.: 410-685-5225. Fax: 410-545-5973. TDD: 410-962-0223.
E-mail: kpattik@marylandsciencecenter.org
Web Site: www.marylandsciencecenter.org
Formerly: Maryland Academy of Sciences
Founded: 1797.
Congressional District: 39
Key Personnel: C.E.O., Van R. Reiner; Chm. (V), Edward A. St. John; Dir. Education, Pete Yancone; Senior Dir., Planetarium & IMAX, Jim O'Leary; Senior Dir. Mktg., Christopher Cropper; Vice Pres. Institutional Advancement, Toni Condon; C.O.O., Richard Hesse; Senior Dir. Visitor Svcs., Lori Blau; Dir. Facilities, Bruce Baldwin; Museum Shop Mgr., Donna Plitt.
Personnel Profile: Full-Time Paid 100; Part-Time Paid 86; Part-Time Volunteers 154; Interns 10.
Governing Authority: nonprofit. Parent Institution: Maryland Academy of Sciences. Tax-exempt: 501(c)(3).
Science & Technology Museum.
Collections: participatory exhibits on space; earth science; human body; early childhood education; science arcade; Hubble space telescope.
Facilities: 400-seat IMAX theater; 140-seat planetarium; 135-seat live theatre; classrooms; observatory; meeting rooms. Museum-related items for sale.
Activities: lectures; films; formally organized education programs for children & adults; informal workshops; scientific excursions; science demonstrations; traveling exhibitions; live demonstrations daily. Museum Sponsors: Student Science Seminars; scientific interest groups; career symposia.
Publications: education program catalogs & course descriptions; annual report; brochures; visitor map guide; monthly e-newsletter.
Hours & Admission Prices: Call or visit website for hours. Adults $14.95, senior citizens 60 & over $13.50, children 3-12 $10.95; discounts to AAM, ICOM & ASTC members; members & children under 3 no charge. Closed Thanksgiving; Christmas. ♿
Attendance: 700,000 (estimated)
Membership: Explorer $75; Voyager $100; Adventurer $125; Discoverer $150; Pioneer $200.

THE MARYLAND ZOO IN BALTIMORE, 1876 Mansion House Dr., Druid Hill Park, Baltimore, MD 21217. Tel.: 410-396-7102. Fax: 410-396-6464.
E-mail: info@marylandzoo.org
Web Site: www.marylandzoo.org
Formerly: The Baltimore Zoo
Founded: 1876.
Congressional District: 2
Key Personnel: C.E.O. & Pres., Donald Hutchinson; Vice Chm., Christopher Pope; Veterinarian, Dr. Ellen Bronson; C.O.O., Karl Kranz; Gen. Cur., Mike McClure; Vice Pres. Human Resources, Steve Devine; Dir. Volunteers, Kerrie Kovaleski; Exec. Vice Pres. Institutional Advancement, Terry Slade Young; Dir. Public Rels. & Mktg., Jane Ballentine; Vice Pres. Education, Kathy Foat.
Personnel Profile: Full-Time Paid 214; Part-Time Volunteers 100.
Governing Authority: society. Maryland Zoological Society Inc. Tax-exempt: 501(c)(3).
Zoo.
Collections: over 1,500 animals.
Research Fields: animal research, health, reproduction & behavior.
Facilities: 500-vol. library of zoo-oriented books available for research to qualified researchers; classrooms. Gift items for sale.
Activities: guided tours; lectures; films; formally organized education programs for children, adults & undergraduate college students; docent program or council.
Publications: quarterly, Zoogram; Events & Edventures; Penguin Press; School Services catalog; annual report.
Hours & Admission Prices: Daily 10-4. Adults $15, children 2-11 $12, seniors $10; discount on weekdays; members & children under 2 no charge. Closed Thanksgiving; Christmas. ♿
Attendance: 345,000 (estimated)
Membership: Individual $55; Senior $59; Individual Plus $65; Family $87; Family Plus $99.

MOTHER SETON HOUSE, 600 N. Paca St., Baltimore, MD 21201-1995. Tel.: 410-523-3443.
Religious Museum: housed in the home of Saint Elizabeth Ann Seton, the first American native-born canonized Saint of the Roman Catholic Church. Founder of Sisters of Charity of St. Joseph which later became the Daughters and Sisters of Charity in the US & Canada.
Collections: Mother Seton history; personal artifacts; period furnishings.
Hours & Admission Prices: Nov.-Feb. Sat.-Sun. 1-3; other times by appointment. No charge.

MOUNT CLARE MUSEUM HOUSE, 1500 Washington Blvd., Carroll Park, Baltimore, MD 21230. Tel.: 410-837-3262. Fax: 410-837-0251.
E-mail: info@mountclare.org
Web Site: www.mountclare.org

Founded: 1917.
Congressional District: 3
Key Personnel: Dir., Jane D. Woltereck; Pres. (V), Sally Johnston; Museum Shop Mgr., Marguerite Ayers.
Personnel Profile: Full-Time Paid 1; Part-Time Paid 5; Part-Time Volunteers 15; Interns 2.
Governing Authority: municipal; nonprofit organization. Affiliated with The National Society of the Colonial Dames of America in the State of Maryland, 2715 Que St., N.W., Washington, DC 20007. Tax-exempt: 501(c)(3).
Historic House: built in 1760.
Collections: 18th-century and early 19th-century silver; furniture; china; glassware; family portraits by Charles Willson Peale, Robert Feke, John Hesselius; many items original to mansion.
Research Fields: archaeological historical; 18th century topics & industries.
Facilities: 1,000-vol. library of genealogical books & records available on premises; Mount Clare Stable, available for meetings & parties, adjacent to mansion.
Activities: guided tours; permanent & temporary exhibits; lectures; educational programs; workshops; colonial camps; special exhibits. Museum Sponsors: Colonial Christmas Event.
Publications: quarterly newsletter, Notes From the Mount; booklet, Mount Clare; book, Mount Clare, Being an Account of the Seat Built by Charles Carroll, Barrister, Upon His Lands at Patapsco; Adventures, Cavaliers, Patriots; Mrs. Carroll's Favorite Receipts; Maryland's First Ladies of the White House.
Hours & Admission Prices: Tours: Tues.-Sat. 10-3. Adults $6, seniors $5, students $4; discounts to groups, tour operators, AAA & AAM members; members & children under 5 no charge. Closed major holidays.
Attendance: 5,700 (estimated)
Membership: Individual Friends $25-$49; Family $50-$99; Heritage $100-$249; Patrons $250-$749; Barrister $750 & up.

MUSEUM OF BALTIMORE LEGAL HISTORY, Clarence M. Mitchell Jr. Courthouse, 100 N. Calvert St., Rm. 243, Baltimore, MD 21202. Mailing Address: 101 W. Lombard St., Baltimore, MD 21201-2605. Tel.: 410-962-2820.
Founded: 1984.
Congressional District: 7
Key Personnel: Dir., Judge James F. Schneider
Legal History Museum.
Collections: artwork; books; photographs; furnishings; tools; 18th century memorabilia of judges & lawyers.
Hours & Admission Prices: Mon.-Fri. 12-1 by appointment. Closed holidays. ♿
Attendance: 5,000

NATIONAL AQUARIUM, 501 E. Pratt St., Pier 3, Baltimore, MD 21202-3103. Tel.: 410-576-3800. Fax: 410-576-8238. TDD: 410-727-3022.
E-mail: dpittenger@aqua.org
Web Site: www.aqua.org
Founded: 1981.
Congressional District: 3
Key Personnel: Exec. Dir., David M. Pittenger; Dept. Exec. Dir. Programs & Operations, and C.O.O., Paula Schaedlich; Deputy Exec. Dir. External Affairs, Kathy Sher; Chm., William R. Roberts; Deputy Exec. Dir. Finance, C.F.O. & Administration, Bruce Hoffberger; Senior Dir. Mktg., Denise Aranoff-Brown; Deputy Exec. Dir. Biological Programs, Dr. Brent Whitaker.
Personnel Profile: Full-Time Paid 250; Part-Time Paid 29; Part-Time Volunteers 797; Interns 55.
Governing Authority: nonprofit organization. Parent Institution: National Aquarium Institute. Tax-exempt: 501(c)(3).
Aquarium.
Collections: marine life: over 14,000 fish, birds, amphibian, invertebrates & mammals.
Major Exhibits: Jellies: Oceans Out of Balance, 11/09-6/12.
Research Fields: husbandry of aquatic animals; water quality & treatment; veterinary medicine.
Facilities: marine mammal pavilion; aquarium; auditorium; classrooms; restaurant. Gift items for sale.
Activities: members' programs & trips; lecture series; events; school tours & programs; teacher training; outreach programs; conservation activities.
Publications: quarterly, Watermarks; annual report.
Hours & Admission Prices: Call for hours & admission prices. ♿
Attendance: 1,431,077 (accurate)
Membership: Individual $74; Senior $80; Couples $104; Family & Grandparents $149; Family Plus $199; Stingray Club $250; Dolphin Club $500.

THE NATIONAL GREAT BLACKS IN WAX MUSEUM, INC., 1601-03 E. North Ave., Baltimore, MD 21213-1409. Tel.: 410-563-3404; 410-563-7809 (Exec. Office). Fax: 410-675-5040; 410-563-7806 (Exec. Office).
E-mail: jmartin@greatblacksinwax.org
Web Site: www.ngbiwm.com
Founded: 1983.
Congressional District: 7
Key Personnel: Co-Founder, Pres. & C.E.O., Dr. Joanne M. Martin; Deputy Dir. Operations, Jon Wilson; Devel. Dir., Karaleigh Henson; Public & Media Rels., Ginger Williams; Gift Shop Mgr., Michelle Sharp.
Personnel Profile: Full-Time Paid 9; Full-Time Volunteers 2; Part-Time Paid 6; Part-Time Volunteers 30; Interns 2.
Governing Authority: not-for-profit organization. Tax-exempt: 501(c)(3). Executive Office: 1649 E. North Ave., Baltimore, MD 21213.
History & Wax Museum.
Collections: African-American history from ancient Africa to the present; African artifacts; over 100 wax figures of African ancestored Americans.
Research Fields: African-American history.
Facilities: 250-seat auditorium. Gift items for sale.
Activities: films; formal education programs for children; guided tours; lectures; rental gallery; traveling exhibitions.
Publications: quarterly, GBIW Newsletter.
Hours & Admission Prices: March-June & Sept. Tues.-Sat. 9-6, Sun. 12-6; July-Aug. Mon.-Sat. 9-6, Sun. 12-6; Oct.-Jan. Tues.-Sat. 9-5, Sun. 12-5. Adults $12, senior citizens, college students & children 12-17 $11, children 3-11 $10; discount to AAM, ICOM, AAA members & groups of 10 or more; members & children under 3 no charge. Closed New Year's Day; Thanksgiving; Christmas. ♿
Attendance: 200,000 (estimated)
Membership: Senior & College Students $20; Individual $30; Mates $50; Great Walk Contributor $250.

NATIONAL LACROSSE HALL OF FAME/US LACROSSE, 113 W. University Pkwy., Baltimore, MD 21210-3301. Tel.: 410-235-6882, ext. 122 & 133. Fax: 410-366-6735.
E-mail: info@uslacrosse.org
Web Site: www.laxmagazine.com
Formerly: The Lacrosse Museum & National Hall of Fame/US Lacrosse
Founded: 1959.
Key Personnel: Museum & Gift Shop Mgr., Casey Culler.
Personnel Profile: Full-Time Paid 55; Part-Time Paid 6; Part-Time Volunteers 12; Interns 2.
Governing Authority: nonprofit organization. Parent Institution: US Lacrosse. Tax-exempt: 501(c)(3).
National Lacrosse Hall of Fame.
Collections: rare photographs & art; vintage equipment & uniforms; sculpture; trophies; memorabilia; artifacts; medals; prints; books; Hall of Fame plaques; periodicals; traces & documents oldest team sport native to the North American continent 500 years old from its roots in Native American religion to present day.
Research Fields: history of lacrosse.
Facilities: resource center. Books & museum-related items for sale.
Activities: Hall of Fame elections; magazine publishing; information & resource center. U.S. Lacrosse Sponsors: funding for U.S. National Team; National Development Center.
Publications: magazine published twelve times a year, Lacrosse Magazine.
Hours & Admission Prices: Feb.-May Tues.-Sat. 10-3; June-Jan. Mon.-Fri. 10-3. Adults $3, children $2; U.S. lacrosse members no charge. Please call for closing dates: 410-235-6882, ext. 122. ♿
Attendance: 6,000 (estimated)
Membership: Youth $25; High School $35; Adult $50.

NATIONAL MUSEUM OF CERAMIC ART AND GLASS, 2406 Shelleydale Dr., Baltimore, MD 21209-3242. Tel.: 410-764-1042. Fax: 410-764-1042.
Founded: 1989.
Congressional District: 3
Key Personnel: Chm. (V) & Education, Shirley B. Brown; Pres. (V), Richard Taylor; Vice Pres. & Membership, Paulyn Hyman; Financial Dir., Robert B. Brown; Devel., Bruce T. Taylor, M.D.
Personnel Profile: Full-Time Paid 1; Part-Time Paid 4; Part-Time Volunteers 1.
Governing Authority: nonprofit organization. Tax-exempt: 501(c)(3).
Ceramic Art Museum.
Collections: ceramics; glass.
Activities: lectures; films; concerts; hobby workshops; organized education programs for children & adults; seminars; temporary exhibitions; special events.
Publications: quarterly newsletter.
Hours & Admission Prices: Please call for hours & admission prices. ♿
Attendance: 11,500 (estimated)

Membership: Students $15; Donor $25; Contribution $50; Associate $100; Sustainer $250; Supporter $500; Benefactor $1,000.

NORMAN AND SARAH BROWN ART GALLERY, Jewish Community Center, 5700 Park Heights Ave., Baltimore, MD 21215-3930. Tel.: 410-542-4900, ext. 239.
Art Gallery.
Collections: paintings; prints; sculpture; photographs; documents; drawings; books.
Facilities: community center; classrooms; garden. Museum-related items for sale.
Activities: temporary exhibitions.
Hours & Admission Prices: Mon.-Tues. 11-5, Wed.-Thurs. 3-5, Fri. 12-2:30, Sun. 12-5.

OLD ST. PAUL'S CEMETERY, 737 W. Redwood St., Baltimore, MD 21201-1011. Mailing Address: Old St. Paul's Parish Office, 309 Cathedral St., Baltimore, MD 21201-4410. Tel.: 410-685-3404. Fax: 410-385-0186.
Cemetery.
Collections: cemetery monuments from early 1800's to early 1900s.
Hours & Admission Prices: Cemetery: by appointment. Office: Mon.-Fri. 11:30-1:30.

PORT DISCOVER CHILDREN'S MUSEUM, 35 Market Place, Baltimore, MD 21202-4002. Tel.: 410-727-8120. Fax: 410-864-2729; 410-727-3042. TDD: 410-823-2551.
E-mail: info@portdiscovery.org
Web Site: www.portdiscovery.org
Formerly: Port Discovery, The Children's Museum in Baltimore
Founded: 1977.
Congressional District: 3
Key Personnel: C.E.O. & Pres., Bryn Parchman.
Personnel Profile: Full-Time Paid 27; Part-Time Paid 49; Part-Time Volunteers 5; Interns 2.
Governing Authority: private; nonprofit organization. Tax-exempt.
Children's Museum.
Collections: hands-on exhibits.
Major Exhibits: Curious George Let's Get Curious (T), 2/10-6/10.
Publications: calendar; newsletter, DreamScene.
Hours & Admission Prices: Memorial Day-Labor Day Mon.-Sat. 10-5, Sun. 12-5; Sept. Fri. 9:30-4:30, Sat. 10-5, Sun. 12-5; Oct.-May Tues.-Fri. 9:30-4:30, Sat. 10-5, Sun 12-5. Admission $12.95; discounts for AAM members; passholders & children under 2 no charge. Closed Thanksgiving; Christmas. ♿
Attendance: 250,000 (estimated)
Membership: Family & Grandparent $99; Family Plus $129.

REGINALD F. LEWIS MUSEUM OF MARYLAND AFRICAN AMERICAN HISTORY AND CULTURE, (M), 830 E. Pratt St., Baltimore, MD 21202-4403. Tel.: 443-263-1800. Fax: 410-333-1138.
E-mail: emailus@maamc.org
Web Site: www.africanamericanculture.org
Founded: 1998.
Key Personnel: Exec. Dir., David Taft Terry, Ph.D.; Chm., Leslie King-Hammond, Ph.D.; Devel. & Membership, Zandra Carson; Dir. Education, Mirma Johnson; Dir. Admin. & Finance, Junius Randolph; Dir. Collections, Michelle J. Wilkinson, Ph.D.; Exhibits Mgr., Dawn Bennett; Mktg. & Public Rels., Cherrie Woods; Registrar, Kathryn Coney.
Governing Authority: private; nonprofit organization. Tax-exempt: 501(c)(3).
History Museum.
Collections: African American heritage; personal artifacts; folk culture; paintings; audiovisual & film; sculpture; photographs; decorative arts.
Facilities: 200-seat auditorium; restaurant; theater; resource center; distance learning center; recording & listening studio. Museum & gift-related items for sale.
Activities: concerts; dance recitals; docent program; films; formal educational programs; guided tours; lectures; loan, participatory & traveling exhibitions; theater training programs for professional museum workers. Museum Sponsors: fundraising gala.
Publications: quarterly members newsletter, Journeys.
Hours & Admission Prices: Wed.-Sat. 10-4. Cafe 10-4. Adults $8, senior citizens & students with valid I.D. $6, discount to groups; children under 6 & members no charge. Closed New Year's Day; Easter; Thanksgiving; Christmas. ♿
Membership: Student $20; Senior Charter $30; Individual Charter $35; Family $55; Directors' Circle $1,000; Chairman's Circle $5,000.

ROSENBERG GALLERY, GOUCHER COLLEGE, 1021 Dulaney Valley Rd., Baltimore, MD 21204-2780. Tel.: 410-337-6477. Fax: 410-337-6405. TDD: Maryland Relay System.
E-mail: laura.amussen@goucher.edu
Web Site: www.goucher.edu/rosenberg
Founded: 1885.
Congressional District: 2
Key Personnel: Dir. Exhibitions & Collection Coord., Laura Amussen.
Personnel Profile: Part-Time Paid 1.
Governing Authority: nonprofit. Parent Institution: Goucher College. Tax-exempt: 501(c)(3).
Art Gallery.
Collections: contemporary & modern art; photography; prints; Asian art; Mexican ceramics.
Facilities: 1,000-seat theater; 225-seat auditorium.
Activities: lectures; temporary exhibitions of contemporary art. Annual Event: multi-disciplinary panel discussion.
Publications: quarterly, exhibition catalog.
Hours & Admission Prices: mid-Jan. to May & Sept.-Dec. 24 Mon.-Fri. 9-5, evenings & weekends of performances. No charge. ♿
Attendance: 175,000 (estimated)

THE STAR-SPANGLED BANNER FLAG HOUSE, 844 E. Pratt St., Baltimore, MD 21202-4495. Tel.: 410-837-1793. Fax: 410-837-1812.
E-mail: info@flaghouse.org
Web Site: www.flaghouse.org
Founded: 1927.
Congressional District: 3
Key Personnel: Exec. Dir., Ann Beegle; Pres., David Gildea.
Personnel Profile: Full-Time Paid 3; Part-Time Paid 15; Part-Time Volunteers 15; Interns 1.
Governing Authority: board of directors; nonprofit organization. Parent Institution: The Star-Spangled Banner Flag House Association, Inc. Tax-exempt: 501(c)(3).
History Museum: The Flag House, a National Historic Landmark, home of Mary Pickersgill, who sewed the Star-Spangled Banner which inspired Francis Scott Key to write the poem that became the National Anthem.
Collections: collection of 19th-century American documents, paintings, prints, watercolors; early 20th-century photographs; 19th-century American decorative arts; textiles. The Star-Spangled Banner Museum: flags; Mary Pickersgill artifacts; War of 1812 artifacts.
Research Fields: history & art history.
Facilities: 200-vol. library of books on the War of 1812 & the History of the Flag available on the premises by appointment. Flags, maps, American crafts & other museum-related items for sale.
Activities: guided tours; slide lectures; permanent & temporary exhibitions; living history program.
Publications: newsletter, The Star; annual report.
Hours & Admission Prices: Tues.-Sat. 10-4; last tour 3:15. Adults $7, senior citizens $6, children & students $5; discount to AAM members & groups; members & children under 6 no charge. Closed major holidays. ♿
Attendance: 13,127 (accurate)
Membership: Individual $25; Family $35; Patron $50; Banner $100.

UNITED METHODIST HISTORICAL SOCIETY, 2200 St. Paul St., Baltimore, MD 21218-5805. Tel.: 410-889-4458.
Web Site: www.lovelylanemuseum.com
Historical Society Museum.
Collections: church history & heritage; religious artifacts; portraits.
Facilities: library. Museum-related items for sale.
Activities: research; tours.
Publications: newsletter.
Hours & Admission Prices: Thurs.-Fri. 10-4; other times by appointment.

UNIVERSITY OF MARYLAND SCHOOL OF NURSING MUSEUM, 655 W. Lombard St., Rm. 733B, Baltimore, MD 21201-1512. Tel.: 410-706-2822.
Web Site: nursing.umaryland.edu/offices/development/museum/index.htm
Formerly: University of Maryland School of Nursing Living History Museum
Founded: 1999.
Congressional District: 7
Key Personnel: Cur., Jennifer Ruffner.
Personnel Profile: Full-Time Paid 1; Part-Time Volunteers 20.
Governing Authority: Parent Institution: University of Maryland School of Nursing.
Nursing History Museum.
Collections: original nursing artifacts, historical photographs, letters & documents; audio & video presentations.
Hours & Admission Prices: Academic year: Mon.-Wed. 10-2; Winter & Summer breaks by appointment. No charge; donations accepted. ♿

Attendance: 1,000 (estimated)

USS CONSTELLATION MUSEUM & BALTIMORE MARITIME MUSEUM, (M), Pier 1, 301 E. Pratt St., Baltimore, MD 21202-3134. Tel.: 410-539-1797, ext 422. Fax: 410-539-6238.
E-mail: crowsom@historicships.org
Web Site: historicships.org
Founded: 1999.
Congressional District: 7
Key Personnel: Exec. Dir., Christopher Rowsom; Chm. (V), Herbert Frerichs, Jr.; Dir. Finance, Richard Goldstein; Membership, Dayna Aldridge; Education, Stan Berry; Public Rels., Laura Givens; Restoration Mgr., Paul Powichroski; Museum Shop Mgr., Audrey Monsberger.
Personnel Profile: Full-Time Paid 12; Full-Time Volunteers 1; Part-Time Paid 30; Part-Time Volunteers 180.
Governing Authority: private; nonprofit organization. Tax-exempt: 501(c)(3).
Military Museum: housed in a vessel that actively participated in the Civil War; the last all-sail warship built for the US Navy.
Collections: artifacts, photographs, documents & history related to the three ships that carry the name Constellation; personal artifacts; furnishings; U.S. Lighthouse Service, U.S. Navy & the U.S. Coast Guard artifacats. Historic Ships: U.S.C.G.C. Taney; U.S.S. Torsk; Light Ship Chesapeake.
Research Fields: Civil War; US Naval History; sailor life; naval ordnance; wooden shipbuilding; maritime navigation; naval medicine.
Facilities: 150-vol. library; classroom; 525 sq. ft. exhibit space. Museum-related items for sale.
Activities: tours; demonstrations; special programming; formal education programs; guided tours; lectures; participatory & temporary exhibitions.
Publications: quarterly newsletter, The Deck Log.
Hours & Admission Prices: May & Sept.-Oct. 14 daily 10-5:30; June-Aug. call for hours; Oct. 15-April 30 daily 10-4:30. Adults $10, senior citizens $8, children 6-14 $5; discount to groups, AAM & ICOM members; children 5 & under and members no charge. Closed New Year's Day; Thanksgiving; Christmas. ♿
Attendance: 100,000 (estimated)
Membership: Individual $30; Family $50; Sailing Master $100; Captain $250; Commodore $500; Admiral $1,000.

* **WALTERS ART MUSEUM, (M),** 600 N. Charles St., Baltimore, MD 21201-5185. Tel.: 410-547-9000 & 685-7823. Fax: 410-783-7969 & 752-4797 (curatorial) & 727-7591 (marketing).
E-mail: info@thewalters.org
Web Site: www.thewalters.org
Founded: 1931.
Congressional District: 7
Key Personnel: C.E.O. & Dir., Dr. Gary Vikan; Assoc. Dir. External Affairs & Operations, Kate Markert; Chm., Andrea B. Laporte; Pres., Peter L. Bain; Cur. Renaissance & Baroque Art, Dr. Joaneath Spicer; Dir. Intl. Curatorial Rels. & Cur. Ancient Art, Dr. Regine Schulz; Cur. 18th & 19th Century Art, Dr. Eik Kahng; Cur. Manuscripts & Rare Books, Dr. William Noel; Dir. Conservation & Technical Res., Terry Drayman-Weisser; Dir. Education, Jacqueline Tibbs Copeland; Dir. Devel., Joy Heyrman; Dir. Mktg., Mindy Riesenberg; Assoc. Dir. Collections & Exhibitions, Dr. Nancy E. Zinn; Dir. Finance & Admin., Harold Stephens; Registrar, Joan-Elisabeth Reid; Museum Shop Mgr., Alice McAuliffe.
Personnel Profile: Full-Time Paid 135; Part-Time Paid 13; Part-Time Volunteers 317; Interns 30.
Governing Authority: municipal. Tax-exempt: 170(b)(1)(A).
Art Museum.
Collections: arts from antiquity through 19th-century; decorative arts; paintings; sculpture; arms & armor; jewelry; manuscripts.
Major Exhibits: Heroes: Mortals and Myths in Ancient Greece (T), 11/09-1/10; Japanese Cloisonne Enamels, 2/10-5/10; Walter Wick: Games, Gizmos, & Toys, 9/10-1/11.
Research Fields: art history; archaeology; conservation & technical research of art objects.
Facilities: 80,000-vol. library of art history reference material available for inter-library loan & on premises by appointment; reading room; 400-seat auditorium; classrooms. Gift items for sale.
Activities: special exhibitions; guided tours; lectures; films; gallery talks; concerts; formally organized education programs; inter-museum loan, permanent, temporary & traveling exhibitions.
Publications: annual journal, The Journal of the Walters Art Museum; collection & exhibition catalogs; quarterly magazine for members; annual report.
Hours & Admission Prices: Wed.-Sun. 10-5. Fees for some special exhibitions. Closed Independence Day; Thanksgiving; Christmas Eve & Day. ♿
Attendance: 150,000 (estimated)
Membership: Individual $50; Dual & Family $75; Supporter $125-$249; Sustainer $250-$749; Patron $750-$1,499; Curator's Circle $1,500-$2,499; Director's Circle $2,500-$4,999; Henry & William Walker's Circle $5,000-$9,999; Founder's Circle $10,000-$24,999; Benefactor $25,000-$49,999; President's Club $50,000 & up.

Berlin

CALVIN B. TAYLOR HOUSE MUSEUM, 208 N. Main St., Berlin, MD 21811. Mailing Address: Berlin Heritage Foundation, Inc., P.O Box 351, Berlin, MD 21811-0351. Tel.: 410-641-1019.
E-mail: taylorhousemuseum@verizon.net
Web Site: www.taylorhousemuseum.org
Founded: 1981.
Congressional District: 1
Key Personnel: Pres. (V), Edward Hammond, Jr.
Personnel Profile: Part-Time Paid 1; Part-Time Volunteers 32.
Governing Authority: Parent Institution: Berlin Heritage Foundation, Inc. Tax-exempt.
Historic House Museum.
Collections: period furnishings; personal artifacts; local memorabilia.
Facilities: 20-seat meeting room.
Activities: concerts on the lawn; fundraising dinners.
Publications: quarterly newsletter.
Hours & Admission Prices: Memorial Day to Oct. Mon., Wed. & Fri.-Sat. 1-4; other times by appointment. No Charge; donations excepted.
Attendance: 2,000 (estimated)
Membership: Individual $10; Family $15; Corporate $25.

Bethesda

DEWITT STETTEN, JR., MUSEUM OF MEDICAL RESEARCH, NIH, Bldg. 45, Rm. 3An38, MSC 6330, Office of Intramural Research, Bethesda, MD 20892-0001. Tel.: 301-496-6610. Fax: 301-402-1434.
E-mail: history@nih.gov
Web Site: www.history.nih.gov
Founded: 1986.
Congressional District: 8
Key Personnel: Dir., Robert Martensen, M.D., Ph.D.; Deputy Dir., David Cantor, Ph.D.; Archivist, Barbara Harkins, M.L.S.; Cur., Michele Lyons, M.A.; Program Asst., Sharon Mathis; Exhibits & Education, Henry Grasso, M.A.
Personnel Profile: Full-Time Paid 5; Part-Time Paid 2; Part-Time Volunteers 3; Interns 4.
Governing Authority: federal government; nonprofit organization. Foundation for Advanced Education in the Sciences, Inc. Parent Institution: National Institutes of Health. Tax-exempt.
Medical Museum.
Collections: 20th-21st century biomedical research instruments & technologies; history of NIH; National Institutes of Health memorabilia; documents; photographs.
Research Fields: biomedical research.
Facilities: library of reference books, archives & museum collections available to public by appt.; educational facilities; 250-seat auditorium; 1,500-seat cafeteria. Must pass through NIH security gateway to enter campus.
Activities: guided tours; lectures.
Publications: brochures; books; articles.
Hours & Admission Prices: Clinical Center: daily 24 hours. Exhibits: daily 9-9. Campus access through security entrance. No charge. ♿
Attendance: 20,000 (estimated)

Big Pool

FORT FREDERICK STATE PARK, 11100 Fort Frederick Rd., Big Pool, MD 21711-1313. Tel.: 301-842-2155. Fax: 301-842-0028.
E-mail: park-ft-frederick@dnr.state.md.us
Web Site: www.dnr.state.md.us
Founded: 1922.
Congressional District: 6
Key Personnel: Park Mgr., Angie Hummer; Asst. Park Mgr., Ben Sanderson; Administrative Specialist, Sherian Hose; Park Sec., Betsy Mellott; Ranger, Steve Robertson; Maintenance Chief, Kevin Zeigler; Ranger, Andy Simmons; Maintenance Tech, Dean Smook.
Personnel Profile: Full-Time Paid 8; Part-Time Paid 25; Part-Time Volunteers 150.
Governing Authority: state. A facility of the Maryland Dept. of Natural Resources, Tawes Office Bldg., Annapolis, MD 21401. Tax-exempt.
Historic Building & Site.
Collections: Indian relics; artifacts; history of Fort Frederick; early firearms; Civil War rifle; Confederate bronze Napoleon cannon; household & farm equipment.
Research Fields: French & Indian War; Revolutionary War; Civilian Conservation Corps.

Facilities: visitor center; French & Indian war fort; Civilian Conservation Corps Museum.
Activities: guided tours; permanent exhibitions; living history programs; camping. Museum Sponsors: 18th Century Market Fair; French & Indian War Muster.
Publications: annual calendar of events.
Hours & Admission Prices: April-May & Sept.-Oct. Sat.-Sun. 9-5; Memorial Day-Labor Day daily 9-5. Adults $3, children $2. ♿
Attendance: 197,000 (accurate)
Membership: Friends of Fort Frederick State Park, Inc. Annual: Student $5; Individual $10; Couple $15; Family $20; Contributing $100; Life: Regular $500; Sustaining $1,000; Endowing $2,000.

Boonsboro

BOONSBOROUGH MUSEUM OF HISTORY, (M), 113 N. Main St., Boonsboro, MD 21713-1007. Tel.: 301-432-6969. Fax: 301-416-2222.
Founded: 1975.
Congressional District: 6
Key Personnel: Dir. & Owner, Douglas G. Bast.
Personnel Profile: Part-Time Volunteers 2.
Governing Authority: private; nonprofit organization.
History Museum.
Collections: local & state history; antique lighting; Russian icons; ceramics & glassware; dinosaur bones; Egyptian animal mummies; Civil War artifacts. Historic Buildings: cabinetmaker's shop; 19th century general store.
Activities: guided tours; temporary exhibitions.
Hours & Admission Prices: May-Sept. Sun. 1-5; tours by appointment. Adults $4, tours & groups $3, children $1.50; discounts to AAM & ICOM members; local school groups no charge.
Attendance: 750 (estimated)

WASHINGTON COUNTY RURAL HERITAGE MUSEUM, 7313 Sharpsburg Pike (Rte. 65), Boonsboro, MD 21713-2431. Tel.: 240-313-2839.
E-mail: eknight@washco-md.net
Web Site: www.ruralheritagemuseum.org
Founded: 2000.
Key Personnel: Pres. (V) & Museum Shop Mgr., Marge Peters.
Governing Authority: Parent Institution: Washington County Buildings, Grounds & Parks. Tax-exempt.
History & Rural Heritage Museum and Village.
Collections: farm kitchen; parlor; country church; modes of travel including a Conestoga wagon, sleighs & sleds; farming equipment & artifacts; butchering; dairying; log cabins; homestead; church.
Facilities: Museum-related items for sale.
Activities: special events: Spud Fest in August; Track Show and Pull in May.
Hours & Admission Prices: April-Dec. Sat.-Sun. 1-4; other times by appointment. No charge; donations accepted. ♿
Attendance: 3,500 (accurate)
Membership: Single $10; Family $15; Sustain $25; Contributor $50; Benefactor $100 & up; Corporate $250 & up.

Bowie

BELAIR MANSION, 12207 Tulip Grove Dr., Bowie, MD 20715-2340. Tel.: 301-809-3089. Fax: 301-809-2308.
E-mail: museums@cityofbowie.org
Web Site: www.cityofbowie.org/museum
Founded: 1968.
Congressional District: 5
Key Personnel: Dir., Pamela Williams; Chm. (V), Jean Lancaster.
Personnel Profile: Full-Time Paid 5; Part-Time Paid 7; Part-Time Volunteers 35; Interns 2.
Governing Authority: municipal; nonprofit. Parent Institution: City of Bowie Museums. Tax-exempt: 170(b)(1)(A).
Historic House Museum: housed in c.1745 Georgian plantation of Governor Samuel Ogle, and later country estate of William Woodward.
Collections: furniture & decorative arts c.1730-1957.
Research Fields: decorative & social history of Maryland plantation houses, 1745-1955.
Facilities: 100-vol. library of local history & decorative arts. Postcards, books, notecards & museum-related items for sale.
Activities: docent program; guided tours; lectures; loan & temporary exhibitions. Annual Events: Bowie Heritage Day; Candlelight Tour.
Publications: newsletter, Musings.
Hours & Admission Prices: Tues.-Sun. 12-4. No charge; donations accepted. Closed major holidays. ♿
Attendance: 5,400 (accurate)
Membership: Individual $20; Family $30; Club & Group $35; Patron $110; Life $500.

BELAIR STABLE MUSEUM, 2835 Belair Dr., Bowie, MD 20715. Mailing Address: 12207 Tulip Grove Dr., Bowie, MD 20715-2340. Tel.: 301-809-3089. Fax: 301-809-2308.
E-mail: museums@cityofbowie.org
Web Site: www.cityofbowie.org/museum
Founded: 1968.
Congressional District: 5
Key Personnel: Dir., Pamela Williams; Museum Facility Mgr., Russell Davies; Chm. (V), David Taft Terry.
Personnel Profile: Full-Time Paid 3; Part-Time Paid 1; Part-Time Volunteers 8; Interns 1.
Governing Authority: municipal; nonprofit. Parent Institution: City of Bowie Museums. Tax-exempt: 170(b)(1)(A).
History Museum.
Collections: Thoroughbred racing artifacts; farming implements; furnishings & carriage collection.
Research Fields: history of Thoroughbred racing in America.
Facilities: 500-vol. library of local history & decorative arts. Postcards, books, notecards & museum-related items for sale.
Activities: docent program; guided tours; lectures; loan & temporary exhibitions. Annual Event: Bowie Heritage Day.
Publications: newsletter, Musings.
Hours & Admission Prices: Tues.-Sun. 12-4. No charge; donations accepted. Closed major holidays. ♿
Attendance: 3,700 (accurate)
Membership: Student $10; Individual $15; Family $30; Club & Group $35; Patron $110; Life $500.

BOWIE HERITAGE WELCOME CENTER, 8606 Chestnut Ave., Bowie, MD 20715. Mailing Address: 12207 Tulip Grove Dr., Bowie, MD 20715-2340. Tel.: 301-575-2488.
Web Site: www.cityofbowie.org/museum
Founded: 2006.
Key Personnel: Dir., Pamela Williams; Facility Mgr., Ruth A. Murphy.
Personnel Profile: Full-Time Paid 1; Part-Time Paid 1.
Governing Authority: municipal; nonprofit. Parent Institution: City of Bowie Museums, Bowie, MD. Tax-exempt: 170(b)(1)(A).
Children's Museum.
Collections: Bowie social & business history.
Research Fields: African-American.
Facilities: Museum-related items for sale.
Activities: participatory exhibits. Annual Events: Spring Fling; Fall Fest; Kids' Kaboose.
Hours & Admission Prices: Tues.-Sun. 10-4. No charge; donations accepted. ♿
Attendance: 5,000 (estimated)

BOWIE RAILROAD STATION MUSEUM, 8614 Chestnut Ave., Bowie, MD 20715-3732. Mailing Address: 12207 Tulip Grove Dr., Bowie, MD 20715-2340. Tel.: 301-809-3089. Fax: 301-809-2308.
E-mail: museums@cityofbowie.org
Web Site: www.cityofbowie.org/museum
Founded: 1994.
Congressional District: 5
Key Personnel: Dir., Pamela Williams; Chm. (V), Robert Rapczinsky.
Personnel Profile: Full-Time Paid 1; Part-Time Paid 2; Part-Time Volunteers 20; Interns 1.
Governing Authority: municipal; nonprofit. Parent Institution: City of Bowie. Tax-exempt: 170(b)(1)(A).
History Museum.
Collections: railroad artifacts; history of Huntington section of Old Bowie. Historic Structures: c.1910-1933 Pennsylvania Railroad Station; tower; passenger shed; 1922 N&W R.R. caboose.
Research Fields: rail history & development of Huntington section of Old Bowie.
Facilities: Postcards, books, notecards & museum-related items for sale.
Activities: docent program; guided tours; lectures; loan & temporary exhibitions. Annual Events: Bowie Heritage Day; Spring Fling; Fall Antiques Street Fest; Kids Kaboose.
Publications: newsletter, Musings.
Hours & Admission Prices: Tues.-Sun. 10-4. No charge; donations accepted. Closed major holidays. ♿
Attendance: 3,000 (accurate)
Membership: Student $2; Individual $5; Family, Club & Group $10; Contributor $20; Supporting $50; Patron $100; Life $500.

CITY OF BOWIE MUSEUMS, (M), 12207 Tulip Grove Dr., Bowie, MD 20715-2340. Tel.: 301-809-3089. Fax: 301-809-2308.
E-mail: museums@cityofbowie.org

Web Site: www.cityofbowie.org/museum
Founded: 1968.
Congressional District: 5
Key Personnel: Dir., Pamela Williams; Cur., Jason D. Illari.
Personnel Profile: Full-Time Paid 5; Part-Time Paid 7; Part-Time Volunteers 35; Interns 3.
Governing Authority: municipal; nonprofit. Parent Institution: City of Bowie. Subsidiary Museums: Belair Mansion; Belair Stable Museum; Bowie Railroad Station; Bowie Heritage Children's Museum and Welcome Center. Subsidiary Institution: Prince George's Co. Genealogical Library; Radio-Television Museum. Tax-exempt: 170(b)(1)(A).
History Museums.
Collections: focus on Belair Estate, railroad & development of the City of Bowie.
Research Fields: decorative & social history of Maryland plantation houses, 1745-1955; development of Maryland railroad towns; history of Thoroughbred racing.
Facilities: 1,000-vol. library of local history & decorative arts.
Activities: Bowie Heritage Day.
Publications: quarterly newsletter, Musings; calendar of special events.
Hours & Admission Prices: Office: Mon.-Fri. 9-5. No charge; donations accepted. ♿
Attendance: 11,000 (accurate)

RADIO & TELEVISION MUSEUM, 2608 Mitchellville Rd., Bowie, MD 20716-1392. Tel.: 301-390-1020. Fax: 301-809-2308.
E-mail: radiobelanger@comcast.net
Web Site: www.radiohistory.org
Founded: 1999.
Congressional District: 5
Key Personnel: Exec. Dir. & Cur., Brian Belanger; Pres., Christopher Sterling.
Personnel Profile: Part-Time Paid 2; Part-Time Volunteers 25.
Governing Authority: municipal; nonprofit organization. Subsidiary Institution: Radio History Society, Inc. Tax-exempt.
History Museum.
Collections: radio & television equipment; broadcast history 1900-present.
Research Fields: history of radio & television development.
Publications: newsletter, Dials and Channels.
Hours & Admission Prices: Fri. 10-5, Sat.-Sun. 1-5. No charge; donations accepted. Closed major holidays.
Attendance: 1,800 (estimated)
Membership: Basic $25; Supporter $50; Benefactor $100; Patron $250; Corporate $1,000.

Brunswick

BRUNSWICK RAILROAD MUSEUM AND C&O CANAL VISITORS CENTER, 40 W. Potomac St., Brunswick, MD 21716-1111. Tel.: 301-834-7100.
E-mail: contact@brrm.net
Web Site: brrm.net
Founded: 1974.
Congressional District: 6
Key Personnel: Cur., Rebecca O'Leary.
Personnel Profile: Part-Time Paid 4; Part-Time Volunteers 40.
Governing Authority: private; nonprofit organization. Parent Institution: Brunswick-Potomac Foundation Inc. Tax-exempt: 501(c)(3).
Transportation & Social History Museum.
Collections: Ca 1880-1920 Baltimore & Ohio Railroad communications technology; small equipment; tools; vintage photographs; costume; ephemera; social history of town life in room dioramas; costume; baseball; medical & organizational exhibitions; African American railroad workers & wives of railroaders; interactive HO scale model of Baltimore & Ohio metropolitan branch line between DC & Brunswick; interactive telegraphy; Chesapeake & Ohio canal history, 1828-1924.
Research Fields: Baltimore & Ohio freight classification, roundhouse operations, communications & equipment; railroad social history & town life c.1880-1920.
Facilities: cafe; boutique; meeting rooms; children's activity room. Museum-related items for sale.
Activities: docent-led tours; canal hikes; lectures on railroad history; birthday parties. Special Events: Bell & History Days in April; Railroad Days in October; Victorian Christmas weekend following Thanksgiving.
Publications: newsletter, Rail Letter
Hours & Admission Prices: Fri. 10-2, Sat. 10-4, Sun. 1-4. Adults $6, senior citizens $5.40, children $3; discounts to groups, MD Passport Program, National Railway Historical Society & AAA members; children 3 & under, members and county docents no charge. Closed major holidays. ♿
Attendance: 8,000 (estimated)
Membership: Senior $20; Individual $25; Senior Partner $30; Partner $40; Family $60; Benefactor $75; Patron $125; Lifetime $1,500.

Burretsville

GATHLAND STATE PARK, 1 Mile West off Rte. 17, Burretsville, MD 20866. Mailing Address: c/o South Mountain Recreation Area, 21843 National Pike, Boonsboro, MD 21713-9535. Tel.: 301-791-4767. Fax: 301-791-0962. TDD: 301-974-3683.
Web Site: www.dnr.state.md.us/publiclands/western/gathland.html
Founded: 1958.
Key Personnel: Greenbrier Park Mgr., Dan Spedden; Shelter Mgr., Marge Magruder.
Personnel Profile: Full-Time Paid 2; Part-Time Paid 6; Part-Time Volunteers 270.
Governing Authority: state; nonprofit. Parent Institution: State Forest & Park Service. Subsidiary Institution: Friends of Gathland. Tax-exempt.
Park Museum: located on the estate of George Alfred Townsend.
Collections: photographs; architectural pieces; Civil War guns; Civil War Battle of South Mountain.
Activities: Civil War living history weekends.
Publications: The Arch: News & Happenings of the Friends of Gathland State Park.
Hours & Admission Prices: Daily 8-sunset. No charge. Closed Christmas. ♿
Attendance: 78,000 (estimated)
Membership: Individual $10; Family $25.

Cambridge

LAGRANGE PLANTATION, 902 LaGrange Ave., Cambridge, MD 21613-2009. Tel.: 410-228-7953. Fax: 410-228-2947.
E-mail: dchs@verizon.net
Web Site: dorchesterhistory.org
Formerly: Dorchester County Historical Society
Founded: 1953.
Congressional District: 1
Key Personnel: Chm., Mary Jo Papin; Pres., Ron Wade; Treas., Bruce Steele.
Personnel Profile: Part-Time Paid 1; Part-Time Volunteers 30.
Governing Authority: private; nonprofit organization. Tax-exempt: 501(c)(3).
Historical Society Museum.
Collections: Dorchester County history from prehistoric to modern times with emphasis on the agricultural & development of the county; historic house includes period furnishings, dolls, portraits & personal artifacts of notable persons from the county's past; local farming & Indian artifacts. Historic Buildings: c.1760 two and a half story brick Georgian building with Greek Revival alterations; c.1790 brick federal Goldsborough Stable; c.1750 stronghouse, log outbuilding.
Facilities: 500-vol. library on history & genealogy available to the public; 1,000 document files including wills & deeds; more than 90 rolls of microfilm; 5,280 sq. ft. exhibit space.
Activities: guided tours; lectures; temporary exhibitions; bus trips; social events; afternoon teas. Annual Event: Harvest Festival.
Publications: newsletter published four times annually; tombstone records of Dorchester County; Bible records of Dorchester County.
Hours & Admission Prices: Tues.-Sat. 10-4; other times by appointment. Adults $3; discounts to bus tours. Closed major holidays. ♿
Attendance: 3,000 (estimated)
Membership: Individual $25; Couple $40; Family $50; Patron $75; Benefactor $100; Life Single $500; Life Couple $1,000.

RICHARDSON MARITIME MUSEUM, 401 High St., Cambridge, MD 21613-1804. Mailing Address: P.O. Box 1198, Cambridge, MD 21613-5198. Tel.: 410-221-1871. Fax: 410-228-5471.
E-mail: info@richardsonmuseum.org
Web Site: www.richardsonmuseum.org/
Key Personnel: Dir. Ruark Boatworks, Harold Ruark; Cur., Melvin Hickman Maritime Museum.
Collections: life & work of James B. (Mr. Jim) Richardson; 50 Chesapeake Bay wooden boat models; watermen's equipment & gear; boatbuilding tools; photographs & artifacts from the George T. Johnson & Sons Shipyard.
Activities: special events.
Publications: newsletter.
Hours & Admission Prices: Wed. & Sun. 1-4, Sat. 10-4 or by appointment. Suggested Donation: $3. Closed New Year's Day; Easter; Independence Day; Thanksgiving; Christmas. ♿

Catonsville

SPRING GROVE HOSPITAL CENTER, ALUMNI MUSEUM, 55 Wade Ave., Garrett Bldg., Catonsville, MD 21228-4663. Tel.: 410-402-7786 & 6000. Fax: 410-402-7050.
Web Site: www.springgrove.com/history.html
Founded: 1995.

Congressional District: 7
Key Personnel: Chm. (V), Joseph Sanphilipo; Treas., Diane Johns.
Personnel Profile: Full-Time Volunteers 12; Part-Time Volunteers 15.
Governing Authority: state; nonprofit. Tax-exempt: 501(c)(3).
History Museum.
Collections: hand-made tools; furniture; artifacts; photographs dating back to 1897.
Facilities: library.
Activities: Annual Events: May Pole; Flea Market; Christmas party for patients.
Hours & Admission Prices: Thurs. 9am to noon; other times by appointment. No charge; donations accepted. Closed holidays.
Attendance: 132

Centerville

HISTORIC SITES CONSORTIUM OF QUEEN ANNE'S COUNTY, 124 S. Commerce St., Centerville, MD 21617. Mailing Address: P.O. Box 62, Centerville, MD 21617-0062. Tel.: 410-758-3010.
E-mail: qachistorical@comcast.net
Web Site: www.historicqac.org
Founded: 1995.
Key Personnel: Dir., Rebecca Marquardt.
Personnel Profile: Full-Time Paid 1; Part-Time Volunteers 55.
Governing Authority: Parent Institution: Queen Anne's County, MD. Tax-exempt.
Historic Sites Preservation Consortium.
Collections: regional cultural history & heritage; historic structures.
Hours & Admission Prices: Office: Wed. 10-1. Historic Sites: call for hours. No charge; donations accepted.
Attendance: 3,239 (accurate)

Chesapeake Beach

THE CHESAPEAKE BEACH RAILWAY MUSEUM, (M), 4155 Mears Ave., Chesapeake Beach, MD 20732. Mailing Address: P.O. Box 1227, Chesapeake Beach, MD 20732-1227. Tel.: 410-257-3892.
E-mail: cbrailway@co.cal.md.us
Web Site: www.cbrm.org
Founded: 1979.
Congressional District: 27
Key Personnel: Pres., Kristen Scott; Chief Cur., Harriet M. Stout; Administrative Asst., Correine E. Moore.
Personnel Profile: Full-Time Paid 2; Part-Time Paid 6; Part-Time Volunteers 35.
Governing Authority: society; county government; historical society. Calvert County Government; Calvert County Historical Society. Tax-exempt: 501(c)(3).
History Museum: housed in 1898-1899 Chesapeake Beach Railway Station.
Collections: archives; photographs; artifacts relating to the early railroad era of 1900-1935; artifacts relating to the resort, 1900-1971; local history; oral history collection.
Research Fields: history of the Chesapeake Beach Railway; local history; history of early Chesapeake resort town.
Facilities: 300-vol. library; archives; 1,000 sq. ft. exhibit space; study & research area; 20-seat AV area. Museum-related items & books for sale.
Activities: guided tours; lectures; films; concerts; organized education programs for children, adults & undergraduate or graduate college students; training programs for professional museum workers; temporary exhibitions. Museum Sponsors: Family Fun Day in Fall & Spring; Bay Breeze Summer Series June to September; Children's Summer Program Series June to August; Bayside Chats.
Publications: biannual, The Chesapeake Beach Railway Museum Newsletter, The Chesapeake Dispatcher.
Hours & Admission Prices: Mid-March & Nov Sat.-Sun. 1-4; April & Oct. daily 1-4; June-Aug. Sat.-Sun. 11-5; other times by appointment; call for groups & tours. No charge; donations accepted. Closed New Year's Day; Christmas. ♿
Attendance: 12,000 (accurate)
Membership: Individual $10; Family $15; Business $50; Life $100.

Chestertown

HISTORICAL SOCIETY OF KENT COUNTY, INC., (M), 101 Church Alley, Chestertown, MD 21620-1505. Mailing Address: P.O. Box 665, Chestertown, MD 21620-0665. Tel.: 410-778-3499. Fax: 410-778-3747.
E-mail: director@kentcountyhistory.org
Web Site: www.kentcountyhistory.org
Founded: 1936.
Congressional District: 1
Key Personnel: Pres., Robert L. Bryan, Jr.; Museum Shop Mgr., Karen L. Emerson.
Personnel Profile: Full-Time Volunteers 1; Part-Time Paid 3; Part-Time Volunteers 50; Interns 1.
Governing Authority: nonprofit organization. Tax-exempt: 501(c)(3).
History Museum.
Collections: Indian artifacts; furniture; paintings; maps; special exhibits. Historic House: c.1750 building.
Research Fields: history & limited genealogical assistance.
Facilities: library.
Activities: permanent & temporary exhibitions; special tours; lectures; social functions. Museum Sponsors: First Friday Happy Hours 4-6pm; Country Driving Tour in June; Walking Tour of 18th, 19th, & 20th century homes in October.
Publications: Historic Houses of Kent County (1998, 2008); The Rolling Year on Maryland's Upper Eastern Shore (1985) Trumpington.
Hours & Admission Prices: May-Oct. Tues.-Fri. 10-4, Sat. 1-4; Nov.-April Tues.-Fri. 1-4; group tours by appointment. Walking Tour: no charge. Historic Group Tours: Historic District $15; House $4.
Attendance: 4,000 (estimated)
Membership: Individual $30; Family $50; Century $100; Lifetime $1,000.

Chevy Chase

AUDUBON NATURALIST SOCIETY, 8940 Jones Mill Rd., Chevy Chase, MD 20815-4799. Tel.: 301-652-9188. Fax: 301-951-7179.
E-mail: contact@audubonnaturalist.org
Web Site: www.audubonnaturalist.org
Founded: 1897.
Congressional District: 8
Key Personnel: C.E.O. & Exec. Dir., Neal Fitzpatrick; Pres., Anne Cottingham; Vice Pres., Kathy Rushing; Sec., Lois Schiffer; Financial Dir., Fred Bailey.
Personnel Profile: Full-Time Paid 18; Part-Time Paid 14; Part-Time Volunteers 400; Interns 9.
Governing Authority: society. Tax-exempt: 501(c)(3).
Nature Center & Conservation Area: headquarters housed in c.1927 Georgian Revival brick and stone house, located on 40-acre Woodend Sanctuary.
Collections: marked tree specimens; Wilbur Fisk Banks Memorial collection of birds.
Research Fields: natural history; bird populations.
Facilities: 4,000-vol. non-circulating library containing natural history books & conservation materials; nature center; nature trails; educational facilities. Books, guides, bird feeders, optical equipment & related items for sale.
Activities: guided tours; lectures; organized education programs; self-guiding nature trails; teacher training programs in environmental education.
Publications: Audubon Naturalist News.
Hours & Admission Prices: Offices: Mon.-Fri. 9-5. Grounds: daily dawn-dusk. No charge; donations accepted. Closed federal holidays. ♿
Membership: Student $10; Individual & Senior Family $30; Family $40; Contributing $50; Sustaining $100; Supporting $150.

Clinton

SURRATT HOUSE MUSEUM, (M), 9118 Brandywine Rd., Clinton, MD 20735-2501. Mailing Address: P.O. Box 427, Clinton, MD 20735-0427. Tel.: 301-868-1121. Fax: 301-868-8177. TDD: 301-699-2544.
Web Site: www.surratt.org
Founded: 1976.
Congressional District: 4
Key Personnel: C.E.O., Dir. & Staff Historian, Laurie Verge; Pres. (V), Tom Buckingham; Museum Shop Mgr., Joan Chaconas.
Personnel Profile: Full-Time Paid 2; Part-Time Paid 5; Part-Time Volunteers 40.
Governing Authority: bi-county agency chartered under the State of Maryland. Maryland-National Capital Park & Planning Commission, Dept. of Parks & Recreation for Prince George's County, Natural & Historical Resources Div. Tax-exempt: 501(c)(3).
Historic House.
Collections: 1800-1865 furnishing & decorative arts; archival & photographic material relating to Lincoln assassination, Civil War era & mid-19th century life.
Major Exhibits: Remembering Mr. Lincoln, 1/10-12/10.
Research Fields: Lincoln assassination.
Facilities: 2,000-vol. library of books on the Civil War & Lincoln assassination available for use by the public in-house, National archives files available on microfilm & extensive vertical file materials. Gift items & books for sale.
Activities: guided tours; lectures; docent program; temporary exhibitions. Museum Sponsors: John Wilkes Booth Escape Route Tour in April & September.
Publications: monthly newsletter, Surratt Courier; occasional research materials.

Hours & Admission Prices: July-Aug. Wed.-Fri. 11-3, Sat.-Sun. 12-4; Sept.-June Thurs.-Fri. 11-3, Sat.-Sun. 12-4. Adults $3, senior citizens $2, students 5-18 $1; discounts to groups, Civil War Trust, National Historical Trust, AAA & AAM members; children under 5 & members no charge. Closed Easter; Independence Day; Thanksgiving; Christmas. ♿
Attendance: 10,414 (accurate)
Membership: Individual $7 (each additional family member $3); Life $125.

Cockeysville

HISTORICAL SOCIETY OF BALTIMORE COUNTY, 9811 Van Buren Lane, Cockeysville, MD 21030-5022. Tel.: 410-666-1878.
E-mail: info@hsobc.org
Web Site: www.hsobc.org
Founded: 1959.
Congressional District: 2
Key Personnel: Bd. Pres. (V), Glenn Johnston; Admin., Adam Youssi; Mgr. Collections, Melissa Heaver.
Personnel Profile: Full-Time Paid 1; Full-Time Volunteers 2; Part-Time Paid 1; Part-Time Volunteers 30; Interns 3.
Governing Authority: society. Tax-exempt: 501 (c)(3).
Historical Society Museum.
Collections: artifacts from early country homes & farms; manuscripts; agriculture; history; military; music; textiles; transportation; maps; photographs.
Research Fields: genealogy; mills; homes; cemetery transcriptions; manufacturing; land records; maps; 350 years of history.
Facilities: library of history books; archives.
Activities: guided tours; lectures; slides; permanent & temporary exhibitions; education trunks for schools.
Publications: quarterly pamphlet, History Trails; quarterly, newsletter.
Hours & Admission Prices: 2nd Wed. of month 6:30pm-8:30pm, Fri. 12-4, Sat. 10-2. Adults $5; members no charge. ♿
Attendance: 979 (accurate)
Membership: Senior $35; Senior Couple $45; Sustaining & Family $55; Contributor & Family Sustaining $65; Family Contributor $75; Benefactor $250; Corporate Bronze $500; Corporate Silver $1,000; Corporate Gold $1,500.

College Park

THE ART GALLERY AT THE UNIVERSITY OF MARYLAND, COLLEGE PARK, (M), 1202 Art-Sociology Building, University of Maryland, College Park, MD 20742-0001. Tel.: 301-405-2763. Fax: 301-314-7774.
E-mail: theartgallery@umd.edu
Web Site: www.artgallery.umd.edu
Founded: 1966.
Congressional District: 5
Key Personnel: Dir., John Shipman; Asst. Dir., Jennie Fleming; Mgr. Arts Admin., Jewell Watson.
Personnel Profile: Full-Time Paid 2; Part-Time Paid 10; Interns 2.
Governing Authority: Regents. Parent Institution: University of Maryland, College Park. Tax-exempt: 501(c)(3).
Art Gallery.
Collections: 20th-century American paintings & prints; WPA mural studies; African art; contemporary prints; Japanese prints; photography.
Research Fields: art history; art criticism & WPA murals.
Facilities: 40,000-vol. library; reference room.
Activities: lectures; gallery talks; inter-museum loan; temporary & traveling exhibitions.
Publications: Women Artists in Washington Collection, 1979; 350 Years of Art and Architecture in Maryland, 1984; Dreams, Lies, and Exaggerations: Photomontage in America, 1991; Sources: Multicultural Influences on Contemporary African American Sculptors, 1993; The Helen D. Ling Collection of Chinese Ceramics, 1995; Terra Firma, 1997; Willem de Looper: A Retrospective Exhibition 1966-1996, 1997; Russian Constructivist Roots: Present Concerns, 1997; Narratives of African American Art and Identity: The David C. Driskell Collection, 1998; Reframing Andy Warhol: Constructing American Myths, Heroes, and Cultural Icons, 1998; Close Enough: Photography by David Seymour (Chim), 1999; Handle with Care, Loose Threads in Fiber, 2000; Possible Futures: Science Fiction Art From The Frank Collection: Re-Reading Science Fiction Art, 2000; Prints by African American Artists from the Jean and Robert Steele Collection, 2002; Steven Cushner, Recent Paintings, 2002; Clarice Smith ReCollection 1978-2003, 2003; Andrew Dunnill, Extractions, 2005; Michael Platt, Just Above Water, 2006; Out of Place, 2007; Trajectories, Considering Time in Contemporary Art, 2008; Linn Meyers, Here Today, 2009.
Hours & Admission Prices: Aug.-May Mon.-Tues. & Thurs.-Sat. 11-4, Wed. 11-6. No charge; donations accepted. Closed national & university holidays. ♿
Attendance: 8,000 (accurate)

COLLEGE PARK AVIATION MUSEUM, 1985 Cpl. Frank Scott Dr., College Park, MD 20740-2000. Tel.: 301-864-6029. Fax: 301-927-6472.
Web Site: www.collegeparkaviationmuseum.com
Founded: 1982.
Congressional District: 5
Key Personnel: Dir., Catherine Allen; Cur. Programs, Warren Kasper; Asst. Program Cur., Kristen Jackson; Museum Educator, Jane Welsh; Museum Shop Mgr. & Librarian, William Herndon; Restoration Shop, John Liebl; Collection Mgr., Tiffany Davis.
Personnel Profile: Full-Time Paid 7; Part-Time Paid 14; Part-Time Volunteers 84; Interns 3.
Governing Authority: county. Parent Institution: Maryland-National Capital Park & Planning Commission. Subsidiary Institution: Natural & Historical Resources Division. Tax-exempt.
Aviation Museum: located on the grounds of College Park Airport.
Collections: photographs; College Park Airport history; models; art; interactive exhibits; World War I artifacts; uniforms; books; historic aircraft items; archaeology; footings & foundations of original hangars; original air mail hangar & compass rose; aircraft - repro. Wright B (1910); 1916 NJ4 Jenny; 1924 Berliner helicopter; 1932 Monocoupe; 1936 J2-Cub; Wright memorabilia; 1946 Ercoupe; 1941 Boeing Stearman; 1939 Taylorcraft; 1912 Bleriot; 1911 Curtiss pusher.
Research Fields: related to College Park Airport & its history; general aviation history; early WWI & pre WWI aviation history; early military aviation history.
Facilities: 2,000-vol. library; 15,000 sq. ft. exhibit space; auditorium. Museum-related items for sale.
Activities: films; intern program for college students; children programs; guided tours; lectures; loan & participatory exhibits; restoration & preservation; research; archival preservation; school, camp & scout tours; Wright Bros. Wing Rib Making (1909); federally legislated Veterans History Project partner.
Publications: book, Maryland Aloft.
Hours & Admission Prices: Daily 10-5. Adults $4, seniors & groups $3, children under 2-18 $2; members & children under 2 no charge. Closed major holidays. ♿
Attendance: 65,772 (accurate)
Membership: Individual $25; Family (up to 4) $75.

THE NATIONAL MUSEUM OF LANGUAGE, 7100 Baltimore Ave., College Park, MD 20740-3627. Tel.: 301-864-7071.
Web Site: www.languagemuseum.org
Founded: 1997.
Congressional District: 21
Key Personnel: Chm. (V), Dr. Amelia C. Murdoch.
Personnel Profile: Part-Time Paid 1; Part-Time Volunteers 20; Interns 1.
Governing Authority: Tax-exempt.
History Museum.
Collections: research materials relating to language.
Major Exhibits: Living Language, 1/10-2/10.
Publications: NML Newsletter.
Hours & Admission Prices: Tues. & Sat. 10-4, 1st & 3rd Sun. of month 1-4. No charge; donations accepted.
Attendance: 800 (estimated)
Membership: Student & Senior $20; Individual $50; Dual & Family $70; Contributing $100-$249; Supporting $250-$499; Institutional & Organizational $300; Sustainer $500-$999; Benefactor $1,000-$4,999; Corporate $2,500; Patron $5,000 & up.

NIXON PRESIDENTIAL MATERIALS STAFF, 8601 Adelphi Rd., Rm. 1360, College Park, MD 20740-6002. Tel.: 301-837-3290. Fax: 301-837-3202.
Web Site: nixon.archives.gov/index.php
Key Personnel: Dir., Tim Naftali; Deputy Dir., Marty McGann; Staff Cur., Edward R. Quick; Archivist, Shar Conway-Lanz.
Personnel Profile: Full-Time Paid 23; Part-Time Volunteers 3; Interns 3.
Governing Authority: federal.
Presidential Museum.
Collections: Nixon administration materials created & received by the White House from 1969-1974.
Facilities: library.
Activities: research.
Hours & Admission Prices: Research Room: Mon.-Tues. & Sat. 9-5, Wed.-Fri. 9-9. Closed federal holidays.

UNION GALLERY, 1220 Stamp Student Union, Adele Stamp Memorial Union, The University of Maryland, College Park, MD 20742-0001. Tel.: 301-314-8492.
E-mail: jmilad@umd.edu

Web Site: www.union.umd.edu/gallery
Key Personnel: Program Coord., Jackie Milad
Art Gallery.
Collections: photographs; paintings.
Hours & Admission Prices: Fall & Spring Mon.-Thurs. 10-8, Fri. 10-6, Sat. 11-4; Summer Mon.-Thurs. 10-6, Fri.-Sat. 11-4.

Colton's Point

* **ST. CLEMENTS ISLAND AND PINEY POINT MUSEUMS, (M),** 38370 Point Breeze Rd., Colton's Point, MD 20626-2011. Tel.: 301-769-2222. Fax: 301-769-2225.
Web Site: www.stmarysmd.com/recreate/museums
Founded: 1975.
Congressional District: 1
Key Personnel: Dir., Debra L. Pence; Chm. (V), Shirley L. Leyland; Historic Site Mgr., Lydia Wood; Site Supvr. SCI, Christina Barbour; Site Supvr. PPLM, April Havens; Mktg. & Programs, Kimberly Cullins; Exhibits Fabricator, Gregory Mora; Museum Shop Mgr., Carol Cribbs.
Personnel Profile: Full-Time Paid 7; Full-Time Volunteers 1; Part-Time Paid 10; Part-Time Volunteers 40.
Governing Authority: county government. Parent Institution: St. Mary's County Department of Recreation, Parks and Community Services. Tax-exempt: 501(c)(3).
Archaeology & History Museum: located on 1634 landing site of Maryland colonists; site of first Roman Catholic mass in English colonies.
Collections: Archaic & Woodland Period Native Americans; 17th- to 20th-century material culture; maritime collections; documents.
Research Fields: archaeology pertaining to early Maryland; marine surveys of Potomac River; architectural contributions of 18th & 19th centuries.
Facilities: 300-vol. library of Maryland & general history books & vertical files, available for inter-library loan & for use by public; 40 acre site on St. Clements Island; 4,000 sq. ft. exhibit space; nature center. Gift items & books for sale.
Activities: guided tours; lectures; organized education programs for children & adults; docent program; participatory, temporary & traveling exhibitions; school loan service. Museum Sponsors: Children's Waterfront Festival; Blessing of the Fleet; Maryland Day; Christmas Exhibit.
Publications: quarterly newsletter, Finer Points.
Hours & Admission Prices: March 25-Sept. daily 10-5; Oct.-March 24 Wed.-Sun. 12-4. Adults $3, students 6-18 $1; members & children under 6 no charge. Water Taxi Service: $5 per person. Closed New Year's Day; Thanksgiving; Christmas. ♿
Attendance: 17,000 (accurate)
Membership: Individual $25; Family $35; Heritage $100 Corporate $150.

Columbia

AFRICAN ART MUSEUM OF MARYLAND, 5430 Vantage Point Rd., Columbia, MD 21044-2642. Mailing Address: P.O. Box 1105, Columbia, MD 21044-0105. Tel.: 410-730-7106. Fax: 410-730-7105.
E-mail: africanartmuseum@aol.com
Web Site: www.africanartmuseum.org
Formerly: Maryland Museum of African Art
Founded: 1980.
Congressional District: 3
Key Personnel: Founder & Dir., Doris H. Ligon; Chm. Bd. (V), Jean W. Toomer.
Personnel Profile: Full-Time Volunteers 1; Part-Time Paid 1; Part-Time Volunteers 35.
Governing Authority: nonprofit organization. Subsidiary Institution: Baltimore/Washington Jazz Fest. Tax-exempt: 501(c)(3).
Art Museum.
Collections: African art, including sculpture, textiles, masks, jewelry; musical instruments; household items.
Research Fields: traditional African art.
Activities: guided tours; lectures; films; formally organized education programs for children; school outreach programs; temporary & traveling exhibitions; special events.
Publications: newsletter, Museum Memos; program booklets for major exhibitions; quarterly jazz journal, The Quartet.
Hours & Admission Prices: Tues.-Fri. 9-3, Sun. 12-4. Adults $2, children & seniors $1; discounts for AAA, AAM & ICOM members; members no charge. ♿
Attendance: 45,000 (estimated)
Membership: Students & Seniors $20; Individual $25; Senior Family $35; Family $40; Contributing $100; Community Organization/Non-Profit $75.

HOWARD COUNTY CENTER OF AFRICAN AMERICAN CULTURE, (M), 5434 Vantage Point Rd., Columbia, MD 21044-2644. Tel.: 410-715-1921. Fax: 410-715-8755.
E-mail: hccaacmd@juno.com
Web Site: www.nccaac.org
Founded: 1987.
Congressional District: 3
Key Personnel: Dir., Wylene Sims-Burch; Chm. (V), Everlene G. Cunningham; Museum Shop Mgr., Florence C. Smith.
Personnel Profile: Full-Time Volunteers 1; Part-Time Paid 6; Part-Time Volunteers 20.
Governing Authority: private; nonprofit organization. Tax-exempt.
History Museum.
Collections: artifacts; murals.
Research Fields: County Underground Railroad.
Facilities: 3,000-vol. library.
Activities: book club; poetry hour; African American Artists' Alliance.
Publications: newsletter, Compass.
Hours & Admission Prices: Tues.-Fri. 10-5, Sat. 10-4, Sun. by appointment. Adults $4, children $2; members no charge.
Attendance: 5,000 (estimated)
Membership: Junior $10; Friends $25; Contributor $50; Patron $100; Life $500; Corporate $1,500.

Crownsville

RISING SUN INN, 1090 Generals Hwy., Crownsville, MD 21032-1417. Tel.: 410-268-9249. Fax: 410-268-1994.
Key Personnel: Dir., Ellan Thorson.
Governing Authority: Tax-exempt. Parent Institution: Maryland Historical Trust.
Historic House Museum: housed in the chapter house of the Ann Arundel Chapter of the Daughters of the American Revolution; built c.1753. Listed on the National Register of Historic Places.
Collections: period artifacts; Colonial money & eyewear; pewter; cannonballs.
Hours & Admission Prices: 2nd Sun. of month 1-4; other times by appointment. Donation: $5.

Cumberland

ALLEGANY COUNTY HISTORICAL SOCIETY, INC., 218 Washington St., Cumberland, MD 21502-2827. Tel.: 301-777-8678. Fax: 301-777-8678.
E-mail: info@gordon-robertshouse.com
Web Site: www.gordon-robertshouse.com
Founded: 1937.
Congressional District: 1
Key Personnel: Dir., Sharon Nealis; Pres., Nadeane Gordon; Cur., Wilma Thompson; Museum Shop Mgr., Mickey Miller.
Personnel Profile: Full-Time Paid 3; Part-Time Paid 2; Part-Time Volunteers 50.
Governing Authority: society. Tax-exempt: 501(c)(3).
Historic House Museum: 1867 Second Empire-style home built by Josiah Hance Gordon.
Collections: American decorative arts from 1800-1930; dolls & toys.
Research Fields: genealogy; histories of Western Maryland.
Facilities: 2,000-vol. library of history & genealogy books available by appointment.
Activities: guided tours; monthly exhibits; educational program; docent group; lifestyle tour with costumed tour docents; Museum Explorer Tour for children.
Publications: members' quarterly newsletter.
Hours & Admission Prices: Wed.-Sat. 10-4; bus tours available. Adults $7, seniors 60 & over $ 6, children 12 & under $5. Closed major holidays.
Attendance: 8,000 (accurate)
Membership: Student $10; Individual $20; Joint $30; Family $35; Patron $100; Life Individual $300; Life Couple $450; Corporate $500.

ALLEGANY COUNTY MUSEUM, 81 Baltimore St., Cumberland, MD 21502. Tel.: 301-777-7200 & 724-4339.
History Museum.
Collections: local history & culture; period furnishings; personal artifacts; photographs.
Hours & Admission Prices: June-Nov. Tues.-Sun. 10-4.

F. BROOKE WHITING HOUSE MUSEUM, 632 Washington St., Cumberland, MD 21502-2711. Tel.: 301-777-7782.
E-mail: info@whitinghouse.com
Web Site: whitinghouse.org
Historic House: housed in the home of F. Brook Whiting I; built in 1911.
Collections: personal artifacts; oriental porcelains; artwork; period furnishings.

Hours & Admission Prices: Call for hours.

GEORGE WASHINGTON'S HEADQUARTERS, Greene St., Cumberland, MD 21502. Mailing Address: Parks/Recreation City Hall, P.O. Box 1702, Cumberland, MD 21501-1701. Tel.: 301-759-6636. Fax: 301-759-3223.
E-mail: djohnson@ci.cumberland.md.us
Founded: 1925.
Congressional District: 6
Key Personnel: Dir. Parks & Recreation, Diane Johnson; Dir., Cathy McKenny.
Governing Authority: municipal. Subsidiary Institution: Daughters of the American Revolution (DAR) Cresap Chapter. Tax-exempt.
Historic Building: 1755 log cabin built during the French & Indian War.
Collections: French & Indian War relics; early Allegany County history.
Activities: guided tours; lectures.
Hours & Admission Prices: by appointment only. No charge.

QUEEN CITY TRANSPORTATION MUSEUM, 210 S. Centre St., Cumberland, MD 21502-3010. Tel.: 301-777-1776.
E-mail: info@queencitytransportationmuseum.com
Web Site: www.queencitytransportationmuseum.com/index.html
Key Personnel: Dir., Jeff Nealis
Transportation Museum.
Collections: early transportation history; period automobiles & wagons.
Activities: children's programs.
Hours & Admission Prices: May-Oct. Tues.-Sun. 10-5; Nov.-April Tues.-Sat. 10-4. Adults $5, children $3; discount to groups; children under 6 no charge.

THE SAVILLE GALLERY, 9 N. Centre St., Cumberland, MD 21502. Tel.: 301-777-2787.
Art Gallery.
Collections: works by local, regional & national artists.
Hours & Admission Prices: mid-May to mid-Nov. Mon.-Fri. 9-5, Sat.-Sun. 11-4; mid-Nov. to mid-May Mon.-Fri. 9-5, Sat. 11-4. No charge. ♿

Denton

MUSEUM OF RURAL LIFE, 16 N. 2nd St., Denton, MD 21629-1004. Mailing Address: P.O. Box 514, Denton, MD 21629-0514. Tel.: 410-479-2055. Fax: 410-479-4513.
Key Personnel: Pres. Historical Society, J.O.K. Walsh; Dir. & Cur., Carol D. Stockley; Treas., Dorsey L. Wooters.
Personnel Profile: Part-Time Paid 1.
Governing Authority: private; nonprofit organization. Tax-exempt: 501(c)(3)
History Museum.
Collections: Caroline County, Maryland history; structures; furnishings; personal artifacts; photographs.
Research Fields: deeds; property; inventories; families of Caroline County, MD.
Facilities: 30-seat theater. Museum-related items for sale.
Activities: fund-raisers (approx. four per year); guided tours; lectures; rental gallery; temporary exhibitions of your own collection.
Publications: annual activities report, Museum Notes.
Hours & Admission Prices: Fri.-Sat. 10-3, Sun. 12-4. No charge; donations accepted.
Attendance: 400 (accurate)
Membership: Individual $20.

Easton

* **ACADEMY ART MUSEUM, (M),** 106 South St., Easton, MD 21601-2949. Tel.: 410-822-2787. Fax: 410-822-5997.
E-mail: Academy@goeaston.net
Web Site: www.academyartmuseum.com
Founded: 1958.
Congressional District: 1
Key Personnel: Exec. Dir., Christopher J. Brownawell; Chm., Patricia Roghe; Cur., Brian Young; Education Coord., Janet Hendricks; Asst. to Dir., Marie Bradley.
Personnel Profile: Full-Time Paid 7; Part-Time Paid 10; Part-Time Volunteers 225.
Governing Authority: nonprofit organization. Tax-exempt: 501(c)(3).
Art Museum.
Collections: paintings; sculpture; prints; photographs.
Facilities: 3,000-vol. library of books on painting, sculpture, architecture & graphics available for use; classrooms; sculpture courtyard.
Activities: lectures; films; gallery talks; concerts; formally organized education programs for children & adults; temporary exhibitions. Academy Sponsors: art appreciation programs in public schools.
Publications: exhibition catalogues; quarterly magazine, Academy.
Hours & Admission Prices: Mon.-Sat. 10-4. Adults $3; AAM members no charge. Closed New Year's Day; Easter; Memorial Day; Independence Day; Labor Day; Thanksgiving; Christmas. ♿
Attendance: 71,230 (accurate)
Membership: Individual $50; Family $65; Friend $100; Contributor $250; Sustaining $500; Patron $1,000; Benefactor $5,000.

HISTORICAL SOCIETY OF TALBOT COUNTY, 25 S. Washington St., Easton, MD 21601-3014. Tel.: 410-822-0773. Fax: 410-822-7911.
E-mail: director@hstc.org
Web Site: www.hstc.org
Founded: 1954.
Congressional District: 3
Key Personnel: Pres., Richard Tilghman; Dir., Eleanor K. Shriver Magee; Cur., Beth Hansen; Tharpe Consignments, Dorothy Moore; Office Mgr., Karen Clements.
Personnel Profile: Full-Time Paid 2; Part-Time Paid 4; Part-Time Volunteers 120.
Governing Authority: society. Tax-exempt.
Historical Society Museum.
Collections: costumes; furniture; china; documents; decorative arts. Historic Buildings: 1795 frame dwelling; 1880 stove store; 1810 Federal Period townhouse.
Major Exhibits: Town of Trappe, 11/09-8/10; Farm Life (T), 9/10-10/10.
Research Fields: local history.
Facilities: auditorium. Museum-related items for sale.
Activities: guided house tours; walking tours; family programs; vinntage baseball team.
Publications: quarterly newsletter.
Hours & Admission Prices: Mon.-Sat. 10-4. Tours: adults $5, children 6-12 $2; discounts to groups of 20 or more; members and children 6 & under no charge. Closed major holidays. ♿
Attendance: 7,382 (accurate)
Membership: Individual $40; Family $50; Business $100; Patron $250; Sustaining $500; James Neall Society $1,000.

Edgewater

HISTORIC LONDON TOWN AND GARDENS, 839 Londontown Rd., Edgewater, MD 21037-2120. Tel.: 410-222-1919. Fax: 410-222-1918.
E-mail: londontown@historiclondontown.org
Web Site: historiclondontown.org
Founded: 1971.
Congressional District: 4
Key Personnel: Exec. Dir., Donna M. Ware; Dir. Operations, Ken Schroeder; Chm. (V), Nicholas Cannistraro, Jr.; Horticulturist, Cathy Umphrey.
Personnel Profile: Full-Time Paid 2; Part-Time Paid 8; Part-Time Volunteers 100; Interns 3.
Governing Authority: Parent Institution: London Town Foundation. Tel. 410-222-1919. Tax-exempt: 501(c)(3).
Historic Building & Botanical Gardens: c.1760 Georgian mansion & 8-acre botanical garden; significant archaeological site.
Collections: mid-18th century furnishings appropriate for a rural Maryland home & tavern; country Queen Anne & early Chippendale furniture, pewter, creamware & Hogarth prints; plant collection of native & exotic species.
Research Fields: 18th-century history of Anne Arundel County, Maryland; horticulture; archaeology.
Facilities: botanical garden; archaeology dig; carpenter shop. Museum-related items for sale.
Activities: museum reproduction program; public archaeology; guided house tours; lectures; concerts; plant sales; education programs for children; rentals for private functions.
Publications: quarterly newsletter; London Town News.
Hours & Admission Prices: Tours: Jan.-Feb. Wed.-Fri. 10-4, Sun. 12-4; March-Dec. Wed.-Sat. 10-4, Sun. 12-4; other times by appointment. Gardens: Tues.-Sat. 10-3. Adults $10, senior citizens $9, children 7-18 $5; discounts to AAM members; members no charge. Additional fee for special events. Closed major holidays.
Attendance: 17,883 (accurate)
Membership: Individual $25; Family $50; Friend $100; Patron $250; Benefactor $500.

Elkton

HISTORICAL SOCIETY OF CECIL COUNTY, 135 E. Main St., Elkton, MD 21921-5955. Tel.: 410-398-1790.
E-mail: questions@cchistory.org
Web Site: www.cchistory.org
Founded: 1931.
Congressional District: 1

Key Personnel: Dir., Paula Newton.
Personnel Profile: Full-Time Volunteers 20; Part-Time Volunteers 20.
Governing Authority: society; board of officers & trustees. Tax-exempt.
History Museum.
Collections: genealogy; manuscripts; over 1,000 Cecil County photographs; Cecil County newspapers, 1838-1980; governmental records including road books, commissioners' minutes, tax assessment books & slave register. Historic Buildings: c.1799 school; log house.
Research Fields: genealogical; Cecil County & Maryland history.
Facilities: 1,800-vol. library on Cecil County history.
Activities: tours by appointment; permanent & temporary exhibitions.
Publications: triannual bulletin, The Historical Society of Cecil County.
Hours & Admission Prices: Mon. & Thurs. 10-4, Tues. 6pm-8:30pm, 1st & 4th Sat. of month 10-2. No charge. ♿
Attendance: 2,000 (accurate)
Membership: Student $10; Basic $20; Couple $25; Contributor $50; Benefactor $75; Curator's Circle $100; Director's Circle $200; Historian's Circle $300; Legacy Circle $500; Life $1,000.

Ellicott City

B&O RAILROAD MUSEUM: ELLICOTT CITY STATION, 2711 Maryland Ave., Ellicott City, MD 21043-4661. Tel.: 410-461-1945. Fax: 410-461-1944.
E-mail: ellicottcity@borail.org
Web Site: www.ecborail.org
Founded: 1976.
Congressional District: 6
Key Personnel: Site Mgr., Adele Air; Asst. Site Mgr., Travis Harry.
Personnel Profile: Full-Time Paid 2; Part-Time Paid 4; Part-Time Volunteers 85.
Governing Authority: nonprofit. Owner: Howard County Rec. & Parks. Subsidiary Institution: B&O Railroad Museum, Inc. Tax-exempt: 501(c)(3).
Transportation Museum: housed in 1831 B&O Railroad Station, first terminus in the United States; terminus is located at the end of the first 13 miles of track laid in the U.S.
Collections: 45 ft. long HO layout of the first 13 miles from Baltimore to Ellicott City; 1927 caboose; tools & transportation equipment.
Facilities: theater. Gift items for sale.
Activities: temporary & permanent exhibitions; presentations on history of railroading; living history program; special events; holiday train layouts. Museum Sponsors: Holiday Festival of Trains November to January.
Publications: biannual newsletter, Roundhouse Review.
Hours & Admission Prices: Wed.-Sun. 11-4. Adults $5, senior citizens $4, children 2-12 $3; discounts to AAM members; members no charge. Closed major holidays. ♿
Attendance: 25,000 (accurate)
Membership: Senior $45; Individual $50; Dual $70; Dual Senior $65; Grand Family Senior Member $80; Family $85; Family & Friends $115.

THE FIREHOUSE MUSEUM, 3829 Church Rd., Ellicott City, MD 21043. Mailing Address: Howard County Recreation & Park, 7120 Oakland Hills Rd., Columbia, MD 21046-1621. Tel.: 410-465-8500. Fax: 410-465-8817.
E-mail: jgalke@howardcountymd.gov
Web Site: www.howardcountymd.gov
Founded: 1991.
Key Personnel: Heritage Programs Supvr., Jacquelyn Galke.
Governing Authority: Parent Institution: Howard County Recreation & Park.
Firefighting Museum: 1889 Ellicott City fire station.
Collections: original fire equipment including a two-wheeled hose cart put into service in 1893; fallen heroes dedication; firefighting gear.
Hours & Admission Prices: April-Dec. Sat.-Sun. 1-4. Private tours year-round by appointment. No charge; donations accepted. ♿
Attendance: 2,000 (estimated)

HOWARD COUNTY HISTORICAL SOCIETY, (M), 8328 Court Ave., Ellicott City, MD 21043. Mailing Address: P.O. Box 109, Ellicott, MD 21041-0109. Tel.: 410-750-0370. Fax: 410-750-0370.
E-mail: info@hchsmd.org
Web Site: www.hchsmd.org
Founded: 1957.
Congressional District: 3
Key Personnel: Pres. (V), Shelley D. Wygant; Dir., Richard Flint; Cur., Karen Griffith.
Personnel Profile: Part-Time Paid 2; Part-Time Volunteers 15.
Governing Authority: private; nonprofit organization. Tax-exempt: 501(c)(3).
Historical Society Museum.
Collections: artifacts that reflect Howard County's history from 1700 to present; period furniture 1550-1890; weapons Revolution to Civil War.
Research Fields: Howard County history.
Facilities: library. Gift items for sale.
Activities: formal education programs for children & adults; guided tours on request; lectures. Annual Events: Dinner Dance, members & guests; Candlelight tour, members & guests; lectures, 4 times per year.
Publications: quarterly newsletter, The Legacy.
Hours & Admission Prices: Tues. & Sat. 1-4. No charge; donations accepted. Closed New Year's Day; Independence Day; Thanksgiving; Christmas.
Attendance: 1,400 (accurate)
Membership: Student $6; Single $15; Family $20; Sustaining $50; Corporate $100; Life $500.

Fort Meade

FORT GEORGE G. MEADE MUSEUM, 4674 Griffin Ave., Fort Meade, MD 20755-7047. Mailing Address: Attn: IMNE-MEA-M, Fort George G. Meade, MD 20755-5094. Tel.: 301-677-6966 & 7054. Fax: 301-677-2953.
E-mail: robert.johnson31@us.army.mil
Web Site: www.ftmeade.army.mil/museum/index.htm
Founded: 1963.
Congressional District: 6
Key Personnel: Cur., Robert S. Johnson; Pres. (V), (Ret) MAS David L. Burget; Exhibits Specialist, Barbara Taylor; Museum Technician, Richard Frank.
Personnel Profile: Full-Time Paid 3; Part-Time Volunteers 12.
Governing Authority: federal. Parent Institution: U.S. Army Center of Military History. Tax-exempt.
Military Museum.
Collections: uniforms; weapons & equipment of the U.S. Army from the Revolution to the present; photographs & graphics; World War I & II research collections.
Research Fields: history of Fort Meade.
Facilities: library of military books, journals & unit histories particularly related to World Wars I & II; research area.
Activities: guided tours; lectures; permanent & temporary exhibitions.
Publications: Illustrated History of Fort George G. Meade.
Hours & Admission Prices: Wed.-Sat. 11-4, Sun. 1-4; other times by appointment. No charge. Closed national holidays. ♿
Attendance: 23,741 (accurate)

NATIONAL CRYPTOLOGIC MUSEUM, (M), 9900 Colony 7 Rd., Fort Meade, MD 20755-6272. Mailing Address: P.O. Box 1682, Fort George G. Meade, MD 20755-9998. Tel.: 301-688-5849.
Founded: 1993.
Congressional District: 3
Key Personnel: Cur., Patrick Weadon.
Personnel Profile: Full-Time Paid 4; Part-Time Volunteers 15.
Governing Authority: federal government; nonprofit. Tax-exempt.
Cryptologic Museum.
Collections: cipher machines; cryptologic equipment; rare books; historical computers.
Research Fields: cryptologic history.
Facilities: library available to scholars & researchers. Gift items for sale.
Activities: guided tours; films; acoustiguide tour device; youth programs.
Publications: brochures.
Hours & Admission Prices: Mon.-Fri. 9-4, 1st & 3rd Sat. 10-2. No charge. Closed federal holidays. ♿
Attendance: 50,000 (estimated)
Membership: National Cryptologic Museum Foundation: Sustaine $25; Contributor $100; Donor $500; Sponsor $1,000; Patron $5,000; Benefactor $10,000.

Fort Washington

FORT WASHINGTON PARK, 13551 Fort Washington Rd., Fort Washington, MD 20744-7044. Tel.: 301-763-4600. Fax: 301-763-1389.
E-mail: nace_fort_washington_park@nps.gov
Web Site: www.nps.gov/fowa
Founded: 1940.
Congressional District: 4
Key Personnel: Supt., Gale Hazelwood; Asst. Supt., Alex Romero; Park Mgr., Bill Clark.
Personnel Profile: Full-Time Paid 4; Part-Time Paid 2; Part-Time Volunteers 125; Interns 1.
Governing Authority: federal. Parent Institution: National Capital Parks-East, National Park Svc., U.S. Dept. of Interior, 1900 Anacostia Dr. S.E., Washington, DC 20020. Tax-exempt.
Military Museum: housed in 1824 Fort Washington; 1817 Commandant's house.
Collections: military; history.
Facilities: research files on historic records available for use in office by request.

Activities: guided tours; lectures; living history demonstrations.
Publications: interpretive folder.
Hours & Admission Prices: Park: 8-sunset. Historic Fort & Visitor Center: 1st Sun. April to last Sat. Oct. daily 9-5; Nov.-March daily 9-4:30. Annual Pass $20; $5 per vehicle, buses & walk-in $3 per person. Closed New Year's Day; Thanksgiving; Christmas. ♿
Attendance: 297,000 (accurate)

Frederick

THE CHILDREN'S MUSEUM OF ROSE HILL MANOR PARK, 1611 N. Market St., Frederick, MD 21701-4304. Tel.: 301-600-1650 & 1646. Fax: 301-600-2749. TDD: 301-696-2936.
E-mail: parksandrecreation@fredco-md.net
Founded: 1972.
Congressional District: 7A
Key Personnel: Pres. Museum Council (V), Don Cornell; Museum Mgr., Kari Saavadra; Museum Shop Mgr., Shirley Swaim.
Personnel Profile: Full-Time Paid 1; Part-Time Paid 18; Part-Time Volunteers 22; Interns 1.
Governing Authority: county; nonprofit. Parent Institution: Frederick County Commissioners. Subsidiary Institution: Rose Hill Manor Park. Division of Parks & Recreation. Tax-exempt: 501(c)(3).
Children's Museum.
Collections: 19th-century house & farm.
Activities: seasonal weekend festivals.
Hours & Admission Prices: April-Oct. Mon.-Sat. 10-4, Sun. 1-4; Nov. Sat. 10-4, Sun. 1-4. Adults $5, senior citizens 55 & over & children 3-17 $4; discounts to AAM members; museum employees & volunteers no charge. ♿
Attendance: 20,000 (estimated)

FREDERICK COUNTY VOLUNTEER FIRE & RESCUE MUSEUM AND PRESERVATION SOCIETY, 527 N. Market St., Frederick, MD 21701-5242. Mailing Address: c/o Frederick County Volunteer Fire & Rescue Association, 340 Montevue Lane, Frederick, MD 21702-8214. Tel.: 301-631-3465. Fax: 301-694-6063.
E-mail: dsears@fredco-md.net
Web Site: www.fcvfra.com
Key Personnel: Pres., Mickey Fyock
Fire-Fighting Museum.
Collections: fire-fighting equipment; personal artifacts.
Hours & Admission Prices: April 7-Nov. daily 10-2. No charge.

*** THE HISTORICAL SOCIETY OF FREDERICK COUNTY, INC., (M),** 24 E. Church St., Frederick, MD 21701-5402. Tel.: 301-663-1188. Fax: 301-663-0526.
E-mail: hshoaf@hsfcinfo.org
Web Site: www.hsfcinfo.org
Founded: 1892.
Congressional District: 6
Key Personnel: Pres., Colleen Remsberg; Exec. Dir., Heidi Campbell-Shoaf; Treas., H. Mark Alexander; Cur., Kelly McCartney; Education Coord., Ellen Seagraves; Librarian, Marie Washburn; Museum Asst., Joyce Cooper; Site Mgr., Jennifer Winter; Asst. Dir., Duane K. Doxzen; Archivist, Brigette Kamsler.
Personnel Profile: Full-Time Paid 7; Part-Time Paid 2; Part-Time Volunteers 116; Interns 4.
Governing Authority: Parent Institution: Historical Society of Frederick County. nonprofit. Tax-exempt: 501(c)(3).
History Museum.
Collections: Frederick County history & culture; decorative & fine arts; historical artifacts; photographs; textiles; archives; genealogical artifacts. Historic Buildings: 1820s headquarters; 1790s home of Chief Justice Roger B. Taney.
Major Exhibits: In & Out of Frederick County: 300 Years of Travel & Tourism, 11/09-12/10.
Research Fields: Frederick County History.
Facilities: library; archives. Books for sale.
Activities: guided tours; lecture series; seminars; workshops; special exhibits; docent & intern programs; children's story hour; walking tours.
Publications: quarterly newsletter; semi-annual journal; e-newsletter.
Hours & Admission Prices: Museum: mid-Jan. to Dec. Museum: Mon.-Sat. 10-4, Sun. 1-4. Library: Mon.-Sat. 10-4. Taney House: April to mid-Dec. Sat. 10-4, Sun. 1-4. Adults $5; discounts to AAA members; members & children under 17 no charge. Closed Easter; Memorial Day; Independence Day; Labor Day; Thanksgiving; Christmas. ♿
Attendance: 6,100 (accurate)
Membership: Student $5; Regular $35; Family $50; Contributing $75; Patron $100; Business $250; Life $1,000.

MONOCACY NATIONAL BATTLEFIELD, 5201 Urbana Pike, Frederick, MD 21704-7303. Mailing Address: 4801 Urbana Pike, Frederick, MD 21704-7307. Tel.: 301-662-3515. Fax: 301-668-7437.
E-mail: cathy_beeler@nps.gov
Web Site: www.nps.gov/mono
Founded: 1991.
Congressional District: 6
Key Personnel: Facility Mgr., Al Kirkwood; Supt., Susan Trail; Administrative Officer, Kathy Snider; Park Ranger & Chief, Resource Education & Visitor Svcs., Cathy Beeler; Park Ranger & Collateral Curator, Tracy L. Shives; Museum Shop Mgr., Bob Casey; Security, Todd Stanton.
Personnel Profile: Full-Time Paid 14; Part-Time Paid 3; Part-Time Volunteers 5.
Governing Authority: federal. Tax-exempt.
Historic Site & Monument: dedicated to soldiers who fought in the Battle of Monocacy, July 9, 1864.
Collections: Civil War relics; battlefield artifacts; copy of Jedediah Hotchkiss map of Monocacy battlefield.
Research Fields: Civil War history, primarily Battle of Monocacy.
Facilities: 230-vol. library on Civil War history available for public use on premises only; walking trails. Museum-related items for sale.
Activities: ranger programs; living history programs.
Publications: leaflet & map, Monocacy National Battlefield; park brochure; auto-tour folder; Junior Ranger activity folder; various trail brochures.
Hours & Admission Prices: Daily 8:30-5. No charge. Closed New Year's Day; Thanksgiving; Christmas. ♿
Attendance: 30,000 (estimated)

*** NATIONAL MUSEUM OF CIVIL WAR MEDICINE, (M),** 48 E. Patrick St., Frederick, MD 21701-5628. Mailing Address: P.O. Box 470, Frederick, MD 21705-0470. Tel.: 301-695-1864. Fax: 301-695-6823.
E-mail: museum@civilwarmed.org
Web Site: www.CivilWarMed.org
Founded: 1990.
Congressional District: 3
Key Personnel: Exec. Dir., George Wunderlich; Chm. (V), Gordon E. Dammann, D.D.S.; Pres. (V), Betsy Estilow; Treas., Meredith Harshman; Museum Shop Mgr., Judy Candela.
Personnel Profile: Full-Time Paid 7; Part-Time Paid 7; Part-Time Volunteers 50; Interns 1.
Governing Authority: private; nonprofit organization. Branch Museum: Pry House Field Hospital Museum, 18906 Shepherds Town Pike, Antietam National Battlefield, Sharpsburg, MD 21782. Tax-exempt: 501(c)(3).
History Museum: housed in Carty Building, former 1832 furniture store & funeral home.
Collections: over 3,000 Union & Confederate Civil War artifacts & documents related to medical history of the Civil War including surgical instruments, stretchers, uniforms & insignia, books, documents, manuscripts and personal effects from doctors, nurses & patients.
Research Fields: Civil War medicine.
Facilities: 500-vol. library on medical history of Civil War. Museum-related items for sale.
Activities: special events; living history; guided & educational tours; outreach programs. Annual Event: Civil War Medicine Conference in October.
Publications: quarterly journal.
Hours & Admission Prices: Adults $6.50, seniors 60 & over $6, children 10-16 $4.50; members & children under 10 no charge. ♿
Attendance: 35,000 (accurate)
Membership: Medical Cadet (Student) $35; First Aid Station (Individual) $50; Ambulance (Family of 4) $75; Field Hospital $125; Brigade Hospital $250; General Hospital $500; Surgeon General $1,000; Corporate $5,000.

SCHIFFERSTADT ARCHITECTURAL MUSEUM, 1110 Rosemont Ave., Frederick, MD 21701-4127. Tel.: 301-663-3885.
E-mail: schifferstadtam@aol.com
Web Site: frederickcountylandmarksfoundation.org
Founded: 1974.
Congressional District: 6
Key Personnel: Pres. (V), Dean Fitzgerald; Dir., Liz Lipke; Museum Shop Mgr., Kathy Moyer.
Personnel Profile: Full-Time Volunteers 5; Part-Time Paid 2; Part-Time Volunteers 60; Interns 1.
Governing Authority: private; nonprofit organization. Parent Institution: Frederick County Landmarks Foundation. Tax-exempt: 501(c)(3).
Architecture Museum: housed in c.1758 German sandstone farmhouse; wattle & daub construction; hand-hewn oak beams pinned with wooden pegs.
Collections: farming tools & household implements; original 5-plate jamb stove, wrought iron hardware; archaeology; vaulted cellar; squirrel tail bake oven; stone dry sink; wishbone (divided) central chimney; hearth; summer kitchen.

Facilities: library.
Activities: guided tours; demonstrations; public events; temporary exhibitions.
Publications: quarterly newsletter.
Hours & Admission Prices: April to mid-Dec. Fri.-Sun. 12-4; other times by appointment. Adults $3, discounts to members, AAA, seniors & students; children 12 & under no charge.
Attendance: 20,000 (estimated)
Membership: Student & Senior $20; Individual $25; Family $35; Corporate $250; Life $500.

Frostburg

FROSTBURG MUSEUM, Hill & Oak St., Frostburg, MD 21532. Mailing Address: P.O. Box 92, Frostburg, MD 21532-0092. Tel.: 301-689-1195.
Web Site: frostmuseum.allconet.org
Key Personnel: Cur., Garry Ritchie
Historic Building: housed in the former Hill Street School; built in 1899.
Collections: local history; personal artifacts; photographs.
Hours & Admission Prices: Tues.-Sat. 12-5. No charge.

FROSTBURG STATE UNIVERSITY PLANETARIUM, Tawes Hall, Frostburg, MD 21532. Mailing Address: Dept. of Physics & Engineering, 101 Braddock Rd., Frostburg, MD 21532-1099. Tel.: 301-687-4270.
E-mail: rdoyle@frostburg.edu
Planetarium.
Collections: astronomy; space science.
Activities: educational programs.
Hours & Admission Prices: Call for hours.

THRASHER CARRIAGE MUSEUM, 19 Depot St., Frostburg, MD 21532-1309. Mailing Address: c/o Allegany County Historical Society, 210 S. Centre St., Cumberland, MD 21502-3010. Tel.: 301-689-3380. Fax: 301-689-3380.
E-mail: info@thethrashercarriagemuseum.com
Web Site: www.thethrashercarriagemuseum.com
Founded: 1992.
Congressional District: 1
Key Personnel: Exec. Dir., Sharon Nealis.
Personnel Profile: Full-Time Paid 1; Part-Time Paid 4; Part-Time Volunteers 12; Interns 2.
Governing Authority: county; nonprofit. Parent Institution: Allegany County Commissioners. Subsidiary Institution: Allegany County Historical Society. Branch Museum: Queen City Transportation Museum, 210 S. Centre St., Cumberland, MD 21502. Tax-exempt: 501(c)(3).
Transportation Museum: housed in a renovated 1800s era warehouse.
Collections: 100 horse-drawn conveyances; phaetons; landaus; wagons; carts; surreys; sleighs; delivery wagons; hearse; buckboards; saddles; harnesses; bridles; carriage tools; early automobiles.
Research Fields: museum collection; socio-economic factors of the carriage era specific to Allegany County, Maryland.
Facilities: 7,000 sq. ft. exhibit space. Museum-related items for sale.
Activities: docent program; guided tours; lectures; temporary exhibitions.
Publications: Horse Drawn Vehicles: Carriages and the Community.
Hours & Admission Prices: Jan.-April by appointment; May 2-Oct. Thurs.-Sun. 12-2; Nov. to mid-Dec. Sat.-Sun. 12-2. Adults $4, students $2; discount to groups; children under 6 no charge. Closed New Year's Day; Martin Luther King Jr. Day; Presidents' Day; Thanksgiving; Christmas. ♿
Attendance: 18,000 (accurate)
Membership: Students $5; Individuals $10; Family $25; Patron $100; Lifetime $2,000; Corporate $10,000.

Galesville

CARRIE WEEDON SCIENCE CENTER, 911 Galesville Rd., Galesville, MD 20765-3101. Tel.: 410-222-1625. Fax: 410-867-0588.
E-mail: fieldtrip@carrieweedon.org
Web Site: www.carrieweedon.org
Founded: 1988.
Congressional District: 4
Key Personnel: Dir. & Lead Teacher, Sharon Hartge Solbert; Pres., Dorothy Chaney.
Personnel Profile: Full-Time Volunteers 1.
Governing Authority: college; nonprofit organization. Parent Institution: Anne Arundel County Public Schools. Tax-exempt.
Natural History & Science Museum.
Collections: history of Anne Arundel County; freshwater aquaria; ornithology; horticultural gardens; insect collection; flora & fauna of the Chesapeake Bay.
Research Fields: estuarine biology.
Facilities: botanical garden; aquarium; classrooms.

Activities: formally organized education programs for children & undergraduate college students; permanent & traveling exhibitions; school loan service.
Hours & Admission Prices: Mon.-Fri. 8-4. Donations accepted. ♿
Attendance: 5,000 (estimated)
Membership: Family $25; Silver $50; Gold $100; Diamond $500; Lifetime $1,000; Benefactor $10,000 & up.

Glen Echo

* **CLARA BARTON NATIONAL HISTORIC SITE, (M),** 5801 Oxford Rd., Glen Echo, MD 20812-1201. Tel.: 301-320-1410. Fax: 301-320-1415.
E-mail: gwmp_clara_barton_nhs@nps.gov
Web Site: www.nps.gov/clba
Founded: 1975.
Congressional District: 8
Key Personnel: Museum Cur., Maria Angela Capozzi; Museum Technician, Kimberly Robinson.
Personnel Profile: Full-Time Paid 6; Part-Time Volunteers 12.
Governing Authority: federal. Parent Institution: U.S. Department of the Interior, National Park Service. Tax-exempt: 500.
Historic House Museum: 1897-1912 home of Clara Barton, founder of the American Red Cross.
Collections: Victorian furnishings; Clara Barton artifacts; archives.
Research Fields: Clara Barton; American Red Cross; Victorian America 1891-1912; women's history.
Facilities: 500-vol. research library; transcripts of Barton diaries & manuscripts available for use on premises. Bookstore items for sale.
Activities: Volunteer-in-Park program; guided tours of site; Park-as-Classrooms education program; interpretive special events; online Jr. Ranger program; online virtual tour.
Publications: park brochure.
Hours & Admission Prices: Daily 10-5. Tours: 10-4 on the hour; groups of 10 or more by appointment. No charge; donations accepted. Closed New Year's Day; Thanksgiving; Christmas.
Attendance: 17,000 (accurate)

Glenn Dale

MARIETTA HOUSE MUSEUM, 5626 Bell Station Rd., Glenn Dale, MD 20769-9120. Tel.: 301-464-5291. Fax: 301-464-5654. TDD: 301-699-2544.
E-mail: susan.reidy@pgparks.com
Web Site: www.pgparks.com
Founded: 1978.
Congressional District: 5
Key Personnel: Natural & Historical Div. Chief, Chris Wagnon; Facility Mgr., Susan Reidy.
Personnel Profile: Full-Time Paid 3; Part-Time Paid 4; Part-Time Volunteers 15.
Governing Authority: county. Parent Institution: Maryland National Capital Park & Planning Commission, Natural & Historical Resources Div., Greenlanding Rd., Upper Marlboro, MD. Tax-exempt: 501(c)(3).
Historic House: c.1815 Federal style brick home.
Collections: 19th-century decorative arts & furnishings; outbuildings; smokehouse; law office; root cellar.
Research Fields: county history; U.S. Supreme Court Associate Justice Gabriel Duvall; 19th-century history.
Facilities: educational facilities. Gift items for sale.
Activities: docent program; guided tours; lectures; living history encampment. Annual Events: Marching Through Time, A Multiperiod (from 1st century to 20th century) in April.
Hours & Admission Prices: Fri.-Sun. 12-4; group tours by appointment. Adults $3, senior citizens $2, students $1; discounts to groups; Metropolitan Washington Historic Houses Consortium & Prince George County History Consortium no charge. Closed major holidays. ♿
Attendance: 5,000 (accurate)

Grantsville

SPRUCE FOREST ARTISAN VILLAGE, 177 Casselman Rd., Grantsville, MD 21536. Tel.: 301-895-3332.
History & Art Museum.
Collections: paintings; pottery; sculpture. Historic Buildings: log cabins; 1800s grist mill.
Activities: special events; workshops; group tours.
Hours & Admission Prices: May-Dec. call for hours.

Greenbelt

GREENBELT MUSEUM, 15 Crescent Rd., Rm. 110, Greenbelt, MD 20770-0805. Mailing Address: P.O. Box 1025, Greenbelt, MD 20768. Tel.: 301-474-1936 & 507-6582. Fax: 301-441-8248.
E-mail: museum@greenbeltmd.gov
Web Site: www.greenbeltmuseum.org
Founded: 1987.
Congressional District: 5
Key Personnel: Cur. & Dir. Historical Programs, Megan Searing Young.
Personnel Profile: Full-Time Paid 1; Part-Time Volunteers 50; Interns 1.
Governing Authority: nonprofit organization. Parent Institution: City of Greenbelt. Subsidiary Institution: Friends of the Greenbelt Museum. Tax-exempt.
History Museum.
Collections: 1930s & 1940s furnishings & furniture; toys; glass & china; kitchen equipment; textiles; drawings & print materials; Lenore Thomas' replica sculpture of Mother & Child statuette; Greenbelt history book; depression era, era of the New Deal; material culture of the 1930s & planned communities; World War II homefront experience.
Research Fields: decorative arts of the 1930s & 1940s; Great Depression; social history of the 1930s, education, recreation, political affairs; domestic technology, women & domestic work.
Facilities: Video-related, note cards, post cards & museum-related items for sale.
Activities: guided tours; lectures; docent program; temporary exhibitions; special exhibits in community center rotating every 18 months.
Publications: quarterly newsletter for members; Greenbelt: History of a New Town 1937-1997.
Hours & Admission Prices: Sun. 1-5; other times by appointment. Community Center Exhibit Room: Mon.-Sat. 9-9, Sun. 9-7. Tours: adults $3, senior & children $2; members & children under 12 no charge. ♿
Attendance: 2,500 (estimated)
Membership: Individual $15; Family $25; Patron $50-$99; Donor $100-$499; Roosevelt Club $500 & up.

Hagerstown

BEAVER CREEK SCHOOL MUSEUM, 9702 Beaver Creek Church Rd., Hagerstown, MD 21740. Mailing Address: Washington County Historical Society, 135 W. Washington St., Hagerstown, MD 21740-4709. Tel.: 301-797-8782.
Historic Building: house in a former two-room school; built in 1904.
Collections: period furnishings; books; slates; tools; hats; musical instruments; glassware; clothing.
Hours & Admission Prices: April-Nov. Sun. 1-4.

CHESAPEAKE AND OHIO CANAL NATIONAL HISTORICAL PARK, 1850 Dual Hwy., Ste. 100, Hagerstown, MD 21740-6622. Tel.: 301-739-4200. Fax: 301-739-5275.
Web Site: www.nps.gov/choh
Formerly: Chesapeake & Ohio Canal Tavern Museum
Founded: 1971.
Congressional District: 6 & 8
Key Personnel: Supt., Kevin Brandt; Interpretation Chief, Bill Justice.
Personnel Profile: Full-Time Paid 135; Part-Time Volunteers 85; Interns 16.
Governing Authority: federal. Parent Institution: National Park Service, U. S. Department of the Interior. Branch Facilities: Georgetown Visitor Center, 1057 Thomas Jefferson St. N.W., Washington, DC 20007, Tel. 202-653-5190. Great Falls Tavern, 11710 MacArthur Blvd., Potomac, MD 20854, Tel. 301-767-3714. Brunswick Visitor Center, 40 W. Potomac St., Brunswick, MD 21716, Tel. 301-834-7100. Williamsport Visitor Center, 205 W. Potomac St., Williamsport, MD 21795, Tel. 301-582-0813. Hancock Visitor Center, 326 E. Main St., Hancock, MD 21750, Tel. 301-678-5463. Cumberland Visitor Center, Western Maryland Station, 13 Canal St., Cumberland, MD 21502, Tel. 301-722-8226.
Historic Canal between Georgetown, District of Columbia to Cumberland, Maryland.
Collections: artifacts relating to construction and operation of canal, 1828-1924, including navigation, commerce and domestic items; archaeological specimens; historic images. Historic Structures: over 1,300 including Great Falls Tavern, 1828-1830, Monocacy Aqueduct, 1829-1833 and Paw Paw Tunnel, 1836-1850.
Research Fields: archaeology; Potomac, Chesapeake and Ohio Canal (1785-1924); transportation & regional history (Washington D.C., Central & Western Maryland).
Facilities: visitor centers located in Georgetown, Great Falls, Brunswick, Williamsport, Hancock and Cumberland; hiking & biking towpath; camping facilities.
Activities: interpretive walks and programs; living history demonstrations; canal boat rides; audiovisual programs.
Publications: Chesapeake and Ohio Canal, Official National Park Handbook.
Hours & Admission Prices: Park daylight hours. Great Falls: $5 per vehicle; special rates for buses; National Parks Passes honored. ♿
Attendance: 3,100,000 (accurate)

CHRISTIAN HERITAGE MUSEUM, 14111 Pennsylvania Ave., Hagerstown, MD 21742-2346. Tel.: 877-313-9002.
History Museum.
Collections: English & American Bibles; religious art; documents; paintings; prints.
Facilities: Museum-related items for sale.
Hours & Admission Prices: By appointment.

CONTEMPORARY SCHOOL OF THE ARTS AND GALLERY, 4 W. Franklin St., Hagerstown, MD 21740. Tel.: 301-791-6191.
Web Site: www.csagi.org
Art Gallery.
Collections: paintings; sculpture.
Activities: after-school programs; classes.
Hours & Admission Prices: Mon.-Fri. 11-3, Sat.-Sun. 1-3.

DISCOVERY STATION AT HAGERSTOWN, 101 W. Washington St., Hagerstown, MD 21740-4709. Tel.: 301-790-0076; 877-790-0076 (Toll Free). Fax: 301-790-0045.
History & Science Museum.
Collections: hands-on exhibits; science; technology; history.
Activities: educational programs.
Hours & Admission Prices: June-Sept. Tues.-Sat. 10-4; Oct.-May Tues.-Sat. 10-4, Sun. 2-5. Adults $7, children 3-17 $6, seniors 55 & over $5; children under 3 no charge. Closed New Year's Day; Easter; Mother's Day; Father's Day; Independence Day; Thanksgiving; Christmas Eve, Day & day after.

HAGERSTOWN AVIATION MUSEUM, 101 W. Washington St., Hagerstown, MD 21740. Tel.: 717-377-3030 & 597-9695.
Aviation Museum.
Collections: aviation history & heritage; photographs; models; engines; equipment; electronics.
Hours & Admission Prices: Call for hours.

HAGERSTOWN RAILROAD MUSEUM AT CITY PARK, 501 Virginia Ave., Hagerstown, MD 21740. Tel.: 301-791-5076 & 739-8393.
Railroad Museum.
Collections: railroad history & memorabilia; steam locomotive 202; signs; signals; bells; tools; telephones; 1885 Pump Car; 1875 Velocipede; 8 cabooses.
Hours & Admission Prices: May-Oct. Tues.-Sat. 10-4, Sun. 1-5.

HAGERSTOWN ROUNDHOUSE MUSEUM, 300 S. Burhans Blvd., Hagerstown, MD 21740-5339. Mailing Address: P.O. Box 2858, Hagerstown, MD 21741-2858. Tel.: 301-739-4665. Fax: 301-739-5598.
Founded: 1990.
Key Personnel: Chm. (V), Blaine Snyder; Pres. (V), Rick Eyler; Museum Shop Mgr., Crystal Sprecher.
Personnel Profile: Part-Time Volunteers 150.
Governing Authority: Tax-exempt: 501(c)(3).
Railroading History.
Collections: local railroad history & culture; photographs; model trains; period railway equipment.
Major Exhibits: The Trains of Christmas, 11/20/09-2/10.
Activities: Annual Event: Railroad Heritage Days in June.
Hours & Admission Prices: Fri.-Sun. 1-5. Adults $4; discounts to groups of 20 or more; members no charge. Closed New Year's Day; Easter; Christmas.
Attendance: 10,000 (accurate)
Membership: Individual $25; Family $30.

HAGERSTOWN ROUNDHOUSE MUSEUM, 300 S. Burhans Blvd., Hagerstown, MD 21740. Mailing Address: P.O. Box 2858, Hagerstown, MD 21741-2858. Tel.: 301-739-4665.
Railroad History Museum.
Collections: photographs; period cabooses & locomotives; model railroads; railroad art.
Facilities: library. Museum-related items for sale.
Hours & Admission Prices: Fri.-Sun. 1-5. Adults $3.50, children 4-12 $.50; children 3 & under no charge.

JONATHAN HAGER HOUSE & MUSEUM, 110 Key St., Hagerstown, MD 21740-6253. Tel.: 301-739-8393.
E-mail: hagerhouse@hagerstownmd.org
Web Site: www.hagerhouse.org

Founded: 1962.
Congressional District: 6
Key Personnel: Cur., John Bryan.
Personnel Profile: Full-Time Paid 1; Part-Time Paid 2; Part-Time Volunteers 2.
Governing Authority: municipal. Parent Institution: City of Hagerstown. Tax-exempt.
Historic House: housed in 1739 Hager House constructed as a private frontier fort.
Collections: 18th-century furnishings; pottery; glass; china; 18th-century coins.
Research Fields: life of Jonathan Hager, founder of Hagerstown Maryland; private frontier forts in the mid-Atlantic.
Facilities: medical herbal gardens. Museum-related items for sale.
Activities: guided tours; formally organized education programs for children; craft demonstrations; concerts; Christmas celebration; permanent exhibitions.
Publications: booklet, Jonathan Hager, Founder; book, What God Does Is Well Done - The Jonathan Hager Files.
Hours & Admission Prices: April-Dec. Tues.-Sat. 10-4, Sun. by appointment. Adults $3, senior citizens & groups of 20 or more $2, children 6-12 $1; children under 6 no charge. Closed New Year's Day, Easter, Thanksgiving week & Christmas.
Attendance: 13,000 (estimated)

MANSION HOUSE ART CENTER, 501 Highland Way, Hagerstown, MD 21740. Tel.: 301-797-6813.
Art Gallery.
Collections: paintings; etchings; silk screen; lithographs; carvings;
Hours & Admission Prices: Fri.-Sat. 11-4, Sun. 1-5.

THE TRAIN ROOM AND MUSEUM, 360 S. Burhans Blvd., Hagerstown, MD 21740-5339. Tel.: 301-745-6681. Fax: 301-766-4697.
E-mail: conniemo@mris.com
Web Site: www.the-train-room.com
Founded: 1988.
Key Personnel: Museum Shop Mgr., Charle Lee Mozingo
Lionel Train & Toy Museum.
Collections: period Lionel & Marx trains; model railroading.
Facilities: Museum-related items for sale.
Hours & Admission Prices: Sun. 12pm-5pm, Mon. & Fri. 9-7, Tues., Thurs. & Sat. 9-5.
Attendance: 5,000 (estimated)

WASHINGTON COUNTY ARTS COUNCIL, 14 W. Washington St., Hagerstown, MD 21740-4804. Tel.: 301-791-3132.
Art Gallery.
Collections: works by regional artists.
Hours & Admission Prices; Tues.-Fri. 10-3, Sat. 10-2; other times by appointment.

WASHINGTON COUNTY HISTORICAL SOCIETY AND MILLER HOUSE MUSEUM, (M), 135 W. Washington St., Hagerstown, MD 21740-4709. Mailing Address: Box 1281, Hagerstown, MD 21741-1281. Tel.: 301-797-8782. Fax: 240-625-9498.
E-mail: histsoc@earthlink.net
Web Site: www.rootsweb.com/~mdwchs
Founded: 1911.
Congressional District: 6
Key Personnel: Exec. Dir., James D. Neville; Pres. (V), Bill Soulis; Treas., William Beard; Cur., Michael L. Kyne, Jr.
Personnel Profile: Full-Time Paid 2; Part-Time Paid 1; Part-Time Volunteers 21; Interns 1.
Governing Authority: private; nonprofit organization. Parent Institution: Washington County Historical Society. Branch Museums: Beaver Creek School Museum. Tax-exempt: 501(c)(3).
Antique Museum: housed in Miller House, an 1825 Federal style townhouse.
Collections: clocks; Bell pottery; dolls; period furniture; costumes & textiles; toys; period automobiles; Civil War exhibit. Historic Building: Beaver Creek School c.1904 two-room schoolhouse.
Research Fields: genealogy.
Facilities: 2,150-vol. library of material on genealogy, church records, local history, documents, deeds & photographs available for research on premises; 400 sq. ft. exhibit space.
Activities: lectures; guided tours; temporary exhibitions. Annual Events: Blues Fest Garden Party; Family Day/All Years' Reunion.
Publications: quarterly newsletter, The Legacy.
Hours & Admission Prices: Library: Tues.-Sat. 9-4. Beaver Creek: April 1-Nov 11 Sun. 1-4; other times by appointment. No charge, donations accepted. Miller House: April-Dec. Wed.-Sat. 1-4. Adults $5, senior citizens $3; members & children under 16 no charge. Closed major holidays.

Attendance: 2,500 (estimated)
Membership: Student & Senior $15; Single $20-$34; Family $35-$99; Supporters $100-$499; Patron $500 & up.

* **WASHINGTON COUNTY MUSEUM OF FINE ARTS, (M),** City Park, 91 Key St., Hagerstown, MD 21740-6271. Tel.: 301-739-5727. Fax: 301-745-3741.
E-mail: info@wcmfa.org
Web Site: www.wcmfa.org
Founded: 1929.
Congressional District: 6
Key Personnel: Dir., Rebecca Massie Lane; Pres., Thomas C. Newcomer; Vice Pres., Howard Kaylor; Vice Pres., Marjorie Hobbs; Sec., Mary Helen Strauch; Treas. Bd., Bradley Pingrey; Asst. Cur., Jennifer Smith; Educator, Amy Hunt; Registrar, Linda Dodson; Museum Shop Mgr., Phyllis Beard; Head Security, Bobby Frederick.
Personnel Profile: Full-Time Paid 8; Part-Time Paid 9; Part-Time Volunteers 150; Interns 1.
Governing Authority: private. Tax-exempt: 501(c)(3).
Art Museum.
Collections: American art with focus on 19th-20th century; collection of old masters; 19th century European paintings; Asian & African art.
Facilities: 4,500-vol. art reference library; music gallery; classrooms. Crafts, toys, museum replicas & jewelry for sale.
Activities: guided tours; lectures; concerts; education programs for children; art classes; inter-museum loan & permanent exhibitions.
Publications: quarterly, News Bulletin; special exhibition catalogs.
Hours & Admission Prices: Tues.-Fri. 9-5, Sat. 9-4, Sun. 1-5. No charge; donations accepted. Closed New Year's Eve & Day; Good Friday; Independence Day; Thanksgiving; Christmas Eve & Day. ♿
Attendance: 65,000 (accurate)
Membership: Individual $30; Dual $50; Family $60; Friend $150; Diana League or Business & Civic Association $500-$999; Decorative Arts Guild $1,000-$2,499; Federal Portrait Patron $2,500-$4,999; Singer's Sponsor $5,000-$9,999; Hudson River Society $10,000 & up.

WILLIAM M. BRISH PLANETARIUM, 820 Commonwealth Ave., Hagerstown, MD 21740-6836. Tel.: 301-766-2898.
Planetarium.
Collections: astronomy; space science.
Facilities: 70-seat planetarium.
Activities: educational programs.
Hours & Admission Prices: Sept.-May Tues. 7am-8pm. Adults $3, children & students $2; senior citizens no charge.

Havre de Grace

HAVRE DE GRACE DECOY MUSEUM, 215 Giles St., Havre de Grace, MD 21078-3661. Tel.: 410-939-3739. Fax: 410-939-3775. TDD: 410-939-3739 5x.
E-mail: mlelledge@verizon.net
Web Site: www.decoymuseum.com
Founded: 1983.
Congressional District: 2
Key Personnel: Pres., Ed Watts; Vice Pres., Patrick Vincenti; Sec., Charles Packard; Treas., Robert Bendler; Special Events Coord., Margaret Jones.
Personnel Profile: Full-Time Paid 1; Part-Time Paid 5; Part-Time Volunteers 80.
Governing Authority: nonprofit organization. Tax-exempt: 501(c)(3).
Folk Art Museum.
Collections: hunting accessories; primarily hunting decoys; firearms; watercraft; clothing; tools & equipment associated with decoy carving; photographs; a decoy maker's shop equipment.
Facilities: carving classroom; research library; meeting room. Museum-related items for sale.
Activities: guided tours; public education programs; carving instruction. Annual Events: Decoy Festival; Duck Fair.
Publications: quarterly news magazine, The Canvasback.
Hours & Admission Prices: Mon.-Sat. 10:30-4:30, Sun.12-4. Adults $6, senior citizens $5, children 9-18 $2; discounts to groups & AAA members; children under 8 no charge. Closed New Year's Day; Easter; Thanksgiving; Christmas. ♿
Attendance: 16,927 (accurate)
Membership: Student $15; Individual $25; Family $40; Business $100; Life $500.

HAVRE DE GRACE MARITIME MUSEUM, (M), 100 Lafayette St., Havre de Grace, MD 21078-3542. Tel.: 410-939-4800. Fax: 410-939-0019.
E-mail: museum@comcast.net
Web Site: www.hdgmaritimemuseum.org

Founded: 1988.
Congressional District: 34
Key Personnel: Exec. Dir., Brenda D. Guldenzopf; Pres. (V), Hurst Hessey; Cur., Ann Persson; Mgr. Collections, Keira Gruber; Public Rels., Iris Barnes.
Personnel Profile: Part-Time Paid 4; Part-Time Volunteers 30; Interns 2.
Governing Authority: bd. of directors. Tax-exempt.
History Museum.
Collections: local maritime heritage; regional history; Native American artifacts; lifeways from the 1600s to present day life; archaeology.
Research Fields: regional history & archaeology.
Facilities: library; archives; resource center; environmental center; boat building school; classroom; event pavilion. Museum-related items for sale.
Activities: lectures; workshops; classes; camps; guided tours; boat building; presentation series; festivals; special events; ecology.
Publications: monthly e-newsletter.
Hours & Admission Prices: June-Aug. daily 10-5; Sept.-May Wed. & Fri.-Mon. 10-5. Adults $3.50, seniors, students & military $2.50; children under 8 no charge. Closed major holidays. ♿
Attendance: 15,000 (estimated)
Membership: Student $15; Individual $25; Family $40; Lifetime $300; Family Lifetime $500; Friend $1,000; Corporate $1,500.

STEPPINGSTONE MUSEUM, 461 Quaker Bottom Rd., Havre de Grace, MD 21078-1329. Tel.: 410-939-2299; 888-419-1762. Fax: 410-939-2321 (pre-arranged time).
E-mail: steppingstonemuseum@msn.com
Web Site: www.steppingstonemuseum.org
Founded: 1970.
Congressional District: 35
Key Personnel: Exec. Dir. & Museum Shop Mgr., Linda M. Noll; Pres. (V), Don Osman.
Personnel Profile: Full-Time Paid 1; Part-Time Paid 2; Part-Time Volunteers 100; Interns 2.
Governing Authority: private; nonprofit corporation. Tax-exempt: 501(c)(3).
Arts & Crafts Museum: housed in late 18th-century two story stone dwelling.
Collections: 1880 to 1920 agricultural tools; 1880 to 1920 rural arts & crafts. Historic Buildings: 1771 Land of Promise historic house; c.1880 blacksmith shop.
Research Fields: agricultural history; rural arts & crafts; local history.
Facilities: outdoors rental facilities. Rural arts, crafts & other museum related items for sale.
Activities: guided tours; annual special programs; formally organized education programs for children; permanent & temporary exhibitions; school loan service; craft demonstrators to local colleges & churches; living history demonstrations.
Publications: newsletter, Steppingstones; booklet, The Land of Promise; The Rural Arts and Crafts of Harford County and Steppingstone Museum.
Hours & Admission Prices: May-Sept. Sat.-Sun. 1-4; other times by appointment. Adults $3; members & children under 12 no charge. Fee for special events vary. ♿
Attendance: 15,000 (estimated)
Membership: Single $15; Family $30; Sustaining $50; Corporate $150; Life $500.

SUSQUEHANNA MUSEUM OF HAVRE DE GRACE INC. AT THE LOCK HOUSE, (M), 817 Conesteo St., Havre de Grace, MD 21078. Mailing Address: P.O. Box 253, Harve de Grace, MD 21078-0253. Tel.: 410-939-5780. Fax: 410-939-5780.
Web Site: www.lockhousemuseum.org
Founded: 1970.
Congressional District: 34
Key Personnel: Pres., Gary Wasielewski; Vice Pres., Jim Sherring.
Personnel Profile: Part-Time Volunteers 60.
Governing Authority: private; nonprofit organization. Tax-exempt: 501(c)(3).
History Museum.
Collections: artifacts from mid-19th century to recent local history; Pivot Bridge over lock; Outlet Lock.
Research Fields: Revolutionary War.
Facilities: 200-vol. library; educational facilities; 1,000 sq. ft. exhibit space; 20-seat theater. Gift items for sale.
Activities: concerts; docent program; formal education programs for children; guided tours; lectures; school loan service; temporary exhibitions; training programs for volunteer professional museum workers. Annual Events: Pirate Gala Fundraiser; Candlelight Tour, Christmas tour of old homes decorated for the holidays; War of 1812 reenactment.
Publications: quarterly newsletter.
Hours & Admission Prices: Sat.-Sun. 1-5; group tours by appointment. No charge. ♿
Attendance: 9,000 (estimated)
Membership: Individual Adult $30; Family $40; Corporate $100; Corporate $200.

Highland Beach

FREDERICK DOUGLASS MUSEUM AND CULTURAL CENTER, 3200 Wayman Ave., Highland Beach, MD 21403. Mailing Address: Highland Beach Historical Commission, 3202 Wayman Ave., Highland Beach, MD 21403. Tel.: 410-268-2956 & 267-6960.
Key Personnel: Dir., Jean Langston
History Museum.
Collections: photographs; furniture; personal artifacts; documents newspaper & magazine articles; slides; films; videos.
Activities: temporary exhibits.
Hours & Admission Prices: By appointment.

Hollywood

SOTTERLEY PLANTATION, (M), 44300 Sotterley Lane off Rte. 245N., Hollywood, MD 20636. Mailing Address: Historic Sotterley, Inc., P.O. Box 67, Hollywood, MD 20636-0067. Tel.: 301-373-2280; 800-681-0850. Fax: 301-373-8474.
E-mail: officemanager@sotterley.org
Web Site: www.sotterley.org
Founded: 1961.
Congressional District: 1
Key Personnel: Exec. Dir., Nancy L. Easterling; Chm. Bd. Trustees & Pres. (V), Ellen Zahniser; Education Dir., Carolyn Hoey; Office Mgr., Kim Husick; Museum Shop Mgr., Kim Curry.
Personnel Profile: Full-Time Paid 6; Part-Time Paid 6; Part-Time Volunteers 165.
Governing Authority: board of trustees. Tax-exempt.
Historic House Museum: 1703 mansion & outbuildings illustrating Tidewater Plantation culture.
Collections: architecture, home furnishings; slave cabin; customs warehouse; smokehouse; formal gardens. Historic House: 1703 mansion.
Research Fields: architecture of buildings; archaeology of grounds; African-American experience.
Facilities: gardens; farm; estuarine site.
Activities: guided tours; colonial African-American history and environmental education for school groups; speaker series. Annual Events: Quilt & Needlework Show; garden symposium; Independence Celebration concert; Wine Festival; Ghost Tours; Holiday Candlelight Tours; Family Plantation Christmas.
Publications: pamphlet; newsletters, News From the Customs House & the Sotterley Times.
Hours & Admission Prices: Guided Manor House Tours: May 1-Oct. 31 Tues.-Sat. 10-4, Sun. 12-4. Adults $10, seniors $8, children 6-12 $5; discount to National Trust for Historic Preservation members; children 5 & under no charge. Self-guided grounds tour $3; Sotterley members with unlimited touring no charge. Please visit website for additional information. ♿
Attendance: 31,000 (accurate)
Membership: Individual $35; Family $55; Patron $150; Sponsor $300; Preserver $500; George Plater Society $1,200; Rousby Circle $2,500 & up.

Kennedyville

KENT COUNTY FARM MUSEUM, 13689 Turner's Creek Rd., Kennedyville, MD 21645. Mailing Address: P.O. Box 43, Kennedyville, MD 21645-0043. Tel.: 410-348-5543.
Web Site: www.kentcounty.com/farmmuseum
Farm Museum.
Collections: farming history; agriculture machinery; period artifacts; household items.
Hours & Admission Prices: May-Oct. 1st & 3rd Sat. 12-3; other times by appointment. No charge; donations accepted.

Lanham-Seabrook

HOWARD B. OWENS SCIENCE CENTER AND CHALLENGER LEARNING CENTER, 9601 Greenbelt Rd., Lanham-Seabrook, MD 20706-3397. Tel.: 301-918-8750. Fax: 301-918-8753.
Web Site: www.pgcps.org
Founded: 1978.
Congressional District: 14
Key Personnel: Program Admin., Scott Hangey; Planetarium Dir., Patty Seaton.
Governing Authority: Prince George's County Public School District. Tax-exempt: 170(b)(1)(A).
Science Museum & Planetarium.

Collections: interactive exhibits & instructional programs for the Prince George's County Public School System.
Research Fields: science education.
Facilities: 174-seat planetarium; classrooms; laboratory; demonstration area; Challenger Learning Center.
Activities: guided tours; lectures; formally organized education programs for children & adults; docent program; permanent & temporary exhibitions.
Publications: annual brochures; fliers.
Hours & Admission Prices: Call for information. ♿
Attendance: 90,000

Laurel

THE LAUREL MUSEUM, (M), 817 Main St., Laurel, MD 20707-3429. Tel.: 301-725-7975. Fax: 301-725-2675.
E-mail: director@laurelhistoricalsociety.org
Web Site: www.laurelhistoricalsociety.org
Founded: 1996.
Congressional District: 5
Key Personnel: Pres. (V), Jhanna Levin; Vice Pres., Lisa Losito; Dir., Lindsey Baker; Museum Shop Mgr., Frieda Weise.
Personnel Profile: Full-Time Paid 1; Part-Time Paid 1; Part-Time Volunteers 30.
Governing Authority: private; nonprofit. Parent Institution: Laurel Historical Society. Tax-exempt: 509(c).
History Museum: housed in an 1840 millworkers house.
Collections: concentration on Laurel history from local Native American times to present with emphasis on the social, financial, religious & cultural development of the city of Laurel and its people.
Facilities: library on local & Maryland history and genealogy; educational facilities. Books & video on Laurel history for sale.
Activities: guided tours; lectures; college internships for University graduate programs; temporary exhibitions.
Publications: bimonthly society newsletter, Laurel Light.
Hours & Admission Prices: Wed. & Fri. 10-2, Sun. 1-4; groups & other times by appointment. No charge. ♿
Attendance: 3,000 (estimated)
Membership: Seniors & Students $15; Individual $20; Family $25; Corporate $35; Lifetime $300.

MONTPELIER MANSION, (M), 9650 Muirkirk Rd., Laurel, MD 20708-2605. Tel.: 301-377-7817; 498-8486 (gift shop). Fax: 301-377-7818. TTY: 301-699-2544.
E-mail: mary.jurkiewicz@pgparks.com
Web Site: www.pgparks.com
Founded: 1976.
Congressional District: 5
Key Personnel: Pres. Volunteer Group, Friends of Montpelier, Helen Bailey; Chief, Natural & Historical Resources Div., Anthony Nolan; Dir., Mary Jurkiewicz; Museum Shop Mgr., Valerie Peacock.
Personnel Profile: Full-Time Paid 1; Part-Time Paid 6; Part-Time Volunteers 20.
Governing Authority: county. Parent Institution: Maryland-National Capital Park & Planning Commission, Natural & Historical Resources Div. Tax-exempt: 501(c)(3).
Historic House: 18th-century Georgian mansion.
Collections: 18th- & early 19th-century decorative arts & furnishings; replica early 19th-century kitchen.
Research Fields: 18th-19th century gardens & landscapes; 18th century, early domestic life.
Facilities: 333-vol. library of agriculture, historic preservation & restoration, 18th- to 19th-century domestic life, local & state history. Gift items for sale.
Activities: concerts; docent program; guided tours; lectures; loan exhibitions; afternoon tea by reservation. Annual Events: Needleart Exhibit; Christmas Candlelight; Herb & Arts Festival.
Publications: quarterly newsletter, The Fireback; annual brochure, Montpelier Mansion.
Hours & Admission Prices: Jan.-Feb. Sun. Tours: 1 & 2; March-Nov. Mon.-Thurs. 11-3; group tours by appointment. Adults $3, senior citizens over 62 & groups of 10 or more $2, children 5-18 $1; discounts to members of Consortium of Historic House Museums of Metropolitan Washington, DC & members of Friends of Montpelier; members no charge. Closed major holidays.
Attendance: 8,929 (accurate)
Membership: Annual $10; Life $200.

NATIONAL WILDLIFE VISITOR CENTER, PATUXENT RESEARCH REFUGE, 10901 Scarlet Tanager Loop, Laurel, MD 20708-4011. Tel.: 301-497-5763. Fax: 301-497-5765. TDD: 301-497-5779.
E-mail: patuxent@fws.gov
Web Site: www.fws.gov/northeast/patuxent
Founded: 1994.
Congressional District: 5
Key Personnel: Refuge Mgr., Brad Knudsen; Chm. Friends of Patuxent (V), Emmy Holdridge; Treas., Evelyn Adkins; Public Rels. & Education, Nell Baldacchino; Museum Shop Mgr. & Bookstore Mgr., Sally Bordeaux.
Personnel Profile: Full-Time Paid 22; Part-Time Paid 1; Part-Time Volunteers 100; Interns 2.
Governing Authority: federal. Parent Institution: Department of the Interior, US Fish & Wildlife Service.
Science & Environmental Education Center.
Collections: dioramas of gray wolves, sea otters, whooping cranes & canvas backs; endangered species; causes of decline; recovery efforts for extinct species; tools & equipment used by scientists in research studies & recovery techniques; impact of man on wildlife throughout the country.
Research Fields: environmental containments; endangered species recovery; wetlands & wildlife habitat management.
Facilities: 520-vol. library of natural history, zoology, biographies & children's books; 230-seat auditorium; conference facilities; meeting rooms; 4,000 sq. ft. exhibit space; wildlife observation; hiking trails. Museum-related items for sale.
Activities: films; guided tours; tram tours; participatory & traveling exhibitions; teacher workshops; environmental education programs for scouts, school classes & summer camp groups. Annual Events: Refuge Birthday Celebration; International Migratory Bird Day; Earth Day; Fishing Day; National Fishing & Hunting Day; Patuxent Wildlife Festival.
Hours & Admission Prices: Daily 9-4:30. Tram Tours: mid-March to mid-Nov. Sat.-Sun. & late June to late Aug. daily 9:30, 11am, 12:30, 2pm & 3:30. No charge. Closed federal holidays. ♿
Attendance: 100,000 (estimated)

Lavale

LAVALE TOLL GATE HOUSE, 14302 National Hwy., S.W., Rte. 40, Lavale, MD 21502. Tel.: 301-729-1681.
Historic Building: built in 1833.
Collections: local history; photographs; period furnishings; historic plaque indicating fees to use the road.
Hours & Admission Prices: May-Oct. Sat.-Sun. 1:30-4:30; other times by appointment.

Leonardtown

NORTH END GALLERY, 41652 Fenwick St., Leonardtown, MD 20650. Tel.: 301-475-3130.
E-mail: lindaepstein1@mac.com
Web Site: www.northendgallery.org
Art Gallery.
Collections: paintings; photographs; drawings; sculpture; jewelry.
Activities: Annual Event: Community Show in summer.
Hours & Admission Prices: Tues.-Sat. 11-6, Sun. 12-4.

Lexington Park

PATUXENT RIVER NAVAL AIR MUSEUM, 22156 Three Notch Rd., Lexington Park, MD 20653-2008. Tel.: 301-863-7418. Fax: 301-863-5048.
E-mail: director@paxmuseum.com
Web Site: www.paxmuseum.com
Key Personnel: Dir., Karen Hill; Pres., Adm. Gus Eggert, USN (Ret.); Museum Shop Mgr., Don House.
Personnel Profile: Full-Time Paid 4; Part-Time Paid 6; Part-Time Volunteers 6; Interns 3.
Naval Air Museum.
Collections: aircraft; photographs; art; documents; Naval aviation history & artifacts; Naval aircraft development & technology.
Research Fields: Naval aviation history.
Activities: flight simulators.
Hours & Admission Prices: Tues.-Sun. 10-5. No charge; donations accepted. ♿
Membership: Individual $35; Gold Corporate $1,000.

Linthicum

NATIONAL ELECTRONICS MUSEUM, (M), 1745 W. Nursery Rd., Linthicum, MD 21090-2906. Mailing Address: P.O. Box 1693, MS4015, Baltimore, MD 21203-1693. Tel.: 410-765-0230. Fax: 410-765-0240.
E-mail: nemuseum@gmail.com
Web Site: www.hem-usa.org
Formerly: Historical Electronics Museum
Founded: 1980.
Congressional District: 4
Key Personnel: Pres., Roland Anders; Dir., Michael Aurele Simons; Asst. Dir., Rebecca Glasby; Financial Dir., Larraine Clark.

Personnel Profile: Full-Time Paid 2; Part-Time Paid 3; Part-Time Volunteers 31; Interns 1.
Governing Authority: not-for-profit organization. Tax-exempt: 501(c)(3).
History & Technology Museum.
Collections: breakthroughs in advanced electronics technology, with emphasis on radar, countermeasures & communications; radar systems; transmitters; receivers; antennas; satellites; test equipment; archives; hands-on/interactive displays teaching the fundamental principles of electricity & electronics.
Facilities: library; 20,000 sq. ft. exhibit space.
Activities: guided tours; participatory exhibits; hands-on exhibits for children.
Publications: quarterly newsletter.
Hours & Admission Prices: Mon.-Fri. 9-3, Sat. 10-2. No charge; donations accepted. Closed major holidays. ♿
Attendance: 28,000 (accurate)
Membership: Student $15; Individual $25; Family $30; Supporting $100; Life $1,000.

Lutherville

FIRE MUSEUM OF MARYLAND, INC., 1301 York Rd., Lutherville, MD 21093-6035. Tel.: 410-321-7500. Fax: 410-769-8433.
E-mail: info@firemuseummd.org
Web Site: www.firemuseummd.org
Founded: 1971.
Congressional District: 2
Key Personnel: Dir. & Cur., Stephen G. Heaver, Jr.; Pres., W. Lee Smith, III; Registrar, Melissa M. Heaver; Museum Shop Mgr., Marilyn Smoot.
Personnel Profile: Full-Time Paid 2; Full-Time Volunteers 2; Part-Time Paid 7; Part-Time Volunteers 30; Interns 1.
Governing Authority: private; nonprofit corporation. Tax-exempt: 501(c)(3).
Fire Museum.
Collections: 50 pieces of period fire fighting apparatus, including hand-pulled, horse drawn & motorized from 1806-1957; period artifacts; photographs; operational fire alarm telegraph system; Great Baltimore fire of 1904.
Research Fields: fire-fighting apparatus & equipment; history of fire service; fire manufacturers.
Facilities: library of fire history, technical manuals, catalogs & annual reports; archives; children's discovery room; 25,000 sq. ft. exhibit area; movie theater; rental facilities; birthday parties. Museum-related items for sale.
Activities: guided tours by appointment; lectures; films; permanent & temporary exhibitions; active restoration of vehicles; audio tours.
Publications: apparatus catalog; color post cards; semi-annual newsletter; fire history books.
Hours & Admission Prices: May & Sept.-Nov. Sat. 10-4; June-Aug. Wed.-Sat. 10-4, Sun. 1-4; tours by appointment. Adults $10, firefighters & senior citizens $8, children 2-18 $5; discounts for group tours & AAM members; members & children under 2 no charge. Closed Independence Day; Christmas Eve & Day. ♿
Attendance: 14,974 (accurate)
Membership: Jr. Firefighter $10; Firefighter & Senior Citizen $20; Individual $25; Family $45; Engineer $60; Lieutenant $100.

Marbury

MATTAWOMAN CREEK ART CENTER, Smallwood State Park, Marbury, MD 20658. Mailing Address: P.O. Box 258, Marbury, MD 20658-0258. Tel.: 301-743-5159.
Governing Authority: Tax-exempt: 501(c)(3).
Art Gallery.
Collections: works by regional, national & international artists; paintings; sculpture.
Activities: workshops; lectures; demonstrations; films; seminars.
Hours & Admission Prices: Gallery: Fri.-Sun. 11-4. Office: Mon. & Wed.-Thurs. 9-1. Closed Memorial Day; Thanksgiving.

SMALLWOOD STATE PARK, 2750 Sweden Point Rd., Marbury, MD 20658-2102. Tel.: 301-743-7613; 888-432-2267. Fax: 301-743-9405. TTY: 866-804-7864.
E-mail: park-smallwood@dnr.state.md.us
Web Site: www.dnr.state.MD.us
Founded: 1954.
Congressional District: 1
Key Personnel: Asst. Park Mgr., Patrick Bright; Park Ranger, Nakia Johnson; Park Ranger, Stephen Youngkin.
Personnel Profile: Full-Time Paid 4; Part-Time Paid 12; Part-Time Volunteers 35.
Governing Authority: state. Parent Institution: Maryland Park Service, Dept. of Natural Resources, Tawes State Office Bldg., 580 Taylor Ave., Annapolis, MD 21401. Tax-exempt.
State Park Museum & Historic House: Gen. Smallwood's retreat.
Collections: 18th-century furniture; historic 18th-century home & kitchen; restored 19th-century tobacco barn.
Facilities: picnic areas; boating ramps; marina; playground equipment; hiking trails; information center; kitchen & herb gardens.
Activities: guided tours; lectures; nature walks; cooking demonstrations; candlemaking.
Hours & Admission Prices: May-Sept. Sun. 1-5; groups by appointment. Park Service Charge: April-Oct. Sat.-Sun. & holidays $3. ♿
Attendance: 10,000 (estimated)

Marion

ACCOHANNOCK INDIAN TRIBAL MUSEUM, 28325 Farm Market Rd., Marion, MD 21838. Mailing Address: Box 404, Marion, MD 21838-0404. Tel.: 410-623-2660.
E-mail: accohannock@verizon.net
Native American Indian Cultural Museum.
Collections: Native American culture, traditions & history; personal artifacts.
Facilities: Museum-related items for sale.
Activities: special programs; demonstrations.
Hours & Admission Prices: Mon.-Fri. call for hours. Suggested Donation: adults $3; children under 6 no charge.

Middletown

MIDDLETOWN VALLEY HISTORICAL SOCIETY, 305 W. Main St., Middletown, MD 21769-7928. Mailing Address: P.O. Box 294, Middletown, MD 21769-0294. Tel.: 301-371-7582. Fax: 301-371-7582.
E-mail: j.dwighthut@juno.com
Founded: 1976.
Congressional District: 6
Key Personnel: Pres. (V), Dave Myers; Museum Shop Mgr., Edna Alice Hoffman.
Personnel Profile: Part-Time Volunteers 20.
Governing Authority: private; nonprofit association. Tax-exempt: 501(c)(3).
Historical Society: housed in 1840 stone house.
Collections: local artifacts.
Facilities: genealogy research library for local families.
Hours & Admission Prices: May-Oct. Sun. 2-4; Nov.-April for special events only. No charge; donations accepted.
Attendance: 100 (estimated)
Membership: Single $15; Family $25; Life $200.

Monkton

LADEW TOPIARY GARDENS, 3535 Jarrettsville Pike, Monkton, MD 21111-1910. Tel.: 410-557-9570 (office) & 9466 (information). Fax: 410-557-7763.
E-mail: eemerick@ladewgardens.com
Web Site: www.ladewgardens.com
Founded: 1971.
Congressional District: 2
Key Personnel: C.E.O., Cur. House & Exec. Dir., Emily W. Emerick; Pres. (V), Dudley Mason; House Com., L.B. Boyce; Museum Shop Mgr., Betsey Barringer.
Personnel Profile: Full-Time Paid 13; Part-Time Paid 15; Part-Time Volunteers 400.
Governing Authority: nonprofit organization. Tax-exempt: 501(c)(3).
Topiary Gardens & Manor House Museum.
Collections: art; silver; period artifacts; fox hunting objects & memorabilia; 3 centuries of decor. Historic Building: Manor House.
Research Fields: horticultural.
Facilities: 22-acre botanical garden; nature walk; 75-seat auditorium; picnic grounds. Gift items for sale.
Activities: horticultural lecture series; concert series. Annual Event: Christmas Open House.
Publications: newsletter three times annually.
Hours & Admission Prices: mid-April to Oct. Mon.-Fri. 10-4, Sat.-Sun. 10:30-5; group tours by appointment. Garden: adults $10, students & senior citizens $8, children $2; members no charge. House: additional charge. ♿
Attendance: 30,000 (accurate)
Membership: Individual $35; Garden Contributor $65; Garden Friend $100; Garden Patron $250; Garden Benefactor $500; Garden Leader $1,000.

Mount Airy

SWETCHARNIK ART STUDIO, 7044 Woodville Rd., Mount Airy, MD 21771-7934. Tel.: 301-829-0137; 240-394-9294.
Web Site: www.swetcharnik.com
Founded: 1980.
Key Personnel: Dir. & Artist, William Swetcharnik; Project Coord. & Artist, Sara Morris Swetcharnik.

Governing Authority: private. Subsidiary Institutions: Latin American Art Resource Project; Art Resource Traditions.
Art Museum.
Collections: works by William & Sara Swetcharnik.
Facilities: educational facilities.
Activities: formal education programs; guided tours; lectures; loan, temporary & traveling exhibitions.
Hours & Admission Prices: By appointment. No charge; donations accepted.
Attendance: 5,000 (estimated)

Newark

QUEPONCO RAILWAY STATION MUSEUM, 8378 Patey Woods Rd., Newark, MD 21841. Mailing Address: P.O. Box 146, 2378 Patey Woods Rd., Newark, MD 21841-0146. Tel.: 410-632-0950 & 641-0067.
Web Site: www.octhebeach.com/museum/Queponco.html
Founded: 1910.
Congressional District: 3
Key Personnel: Pres. (V), Ralph L. Mason, Jr.
Governing Authority: Tax-exempt.
Railway Station Museum: housed in a 1910 depot.
Collections: railroad station history; period artifacts; railroad wrenches; hand car mover; scales; freight cart; locks; telegraph key; early telephone; hand carts; steamer trunk; strawberry crate; morse code.
Hours & Admission Prices: May-Oct. 1st & 3rd Sat. 1-4; other times by appointment. No charge; donations accepted. ♿
Attendance: 200
Membership: Single $25; Family $40; Corporate $100.

North East

UPPER BAY MUSEUM, Walnut St., North East Town Park, North East, MD 21901. Mailing Address: P.O. Box 275, North East, MD 21901-0275. Tel.: 410-287-2675.
History Museum.
Collections: local commercial & recreational fishing and hunting; decoys; period marine engines; photographs; personal artifacts.
Activities: Museum Sponsors: Decoy Show in spring.
Hours & Admission Prices: Memorial Day to Labor Day Sat. 10-3, Sun. 10-4; other times by appointment. Donation Requested. ♿

Oakland

GARRETT COUNTY HISTORICAL MUSEUM, 107 S. 2nd St., Oakland, MD 21550-1519. Tel.: 301-334-3226.
E-mail: gchsmuseum@verizon.net
Web Site: www.gchsmuseum.com
Founded: 1969.
Congressional District: 6
Key Personnel: Pres., Robert Boal; Vice Pres., Jim Ashby; Sec., Alice Eary; Cur., Eleanor Callis; Asst. Cur., Brenda Gnegy.
Personnel Profile: Part-Time Paid 2; Part-Time Volunteers 20.
Governing Authority: society. Affiliated with Garrett County Historical Society. Tax-exempt.
Historical Society Museum.
Collections: local Indian artifacts; period rooms; early cooking utensils; glassware; railroad exhibit; leather tools; weaving; bridal gowns; coal mining exhibit & tools; old dolls & carriages; U.S.S. Garrett County artifacts.
Research Fields: Garrett County.
Activities: guided tours by appointment; permanent & temporary exhibitions.
Publications: quarterly booklet, Glade Star.
Hours & Admission Prices: Mon.-Sat. 10-3. No charge; donations accepted. ♿
Attendance: 6,000 (estimated)
Membership: Single & Couple $20; Life $250.

HISTORIC B&O TRAIN STATION, 117 E. Liberty St., Oakland, MD 21550-1201. Tel.: 301-334-2691.
Historic Train Station: built in 1884.
Collections: depot history; period furnishings; photographs.
Hours & Admission Prices: Sat. 10-2, Sun. 12-4.

Ocean City

OCEAN CITY LIFE-SAVING STATION MUSEUM, 813 S. Atlantic Ave., Ocean City, MD 21842. Mailing Address: P.O. Box 603, Ocean City, MD 21843-0603. Tel.: 410-289-4991.
E-mail: curator@ocmuseum.org
Web Site: www.ocmuseum.org/
Founded: 1978.
Congressional District: 38
Key Personnel: Cur., Suzanne B. Hurley; Pres. (V), J.D. Quillin, III; Office Mgr., Diane Knuckles.
Personnel Profile: Full-Time Paid 3; Part-Time Paid 5; Part-Time Volunteers 20.
Governing Authority: Tax-exempt.
History Museum.
Collections: history of the United States Life-Saving Service on the Eastern Shore of Maryland, Delaware & Virginia; history & heritage of Ocean City, Maryland; miniature replicas of past boardwalk hotels; shipwreck artifacts; mermaids; period bathing suits; sands from around the world.
Facilities: Museum-related items for sale.
Hours & Admission Prices: April Sat.-Sun. 10-4, May & Oct. daily 10-4, call to confirm; June-Sept. daily 10-10; winter call for hours. Adults $3, children 6-12 $1; discounts to AAA members; members & children under 6 no charge.
Attendance: 19,003 (accurate)
Membership: Student $5; Individual $10; Family $30; Supporting $100; Sustaining $250; Benefactor $500.

OCEAN CITY LIFE-SAVING STATION MUSEUM, 813 S. Atlantic Ave., Ocean City, MD 21843. Mailing Address: P.O. Box 603, Ocean City, MD 21843-0603. Tel.: 410-289-4991.
E-mail: sandy@ocmuseum.org
Web Site: www.ocmuseum.org
Founded: 1978.
Congressional District: 10
History Museum.
Collections: exhibits relating to the history of the U.S. Life-Saving Service & Ocean City history; mermaid collection; shipwreck artifacts; sands of the world; bathing fashions.
Hours & Admission Prices: Jan.-April & Nov.-Dec. call for hours; May & Oct. daily 10-4, June-Sept. daily 10-10. Adults $3, children 6-12 $1; children under 6 & members no charge. ♿
Attendance: 18,007 (accurate)
Membership: Student $5; Individual $10; Family $30; Supporting $100; Sustaining $250; Keeper $500.

WHEELS OF YESTERDAY, 12708 Ocean Gateway, Ocean City, MD 21842-9542. Tel.: 410-213-7329.
Founded: 1997.
Key Personnel: Cur., Jack Jarvis
Transportation Museum.
Collections: period cars & fire engine; replica 1950s service station.
Facilities: Museum-related items for sale.
Hours & Admission Prices: Call for hours. Adults $5, children 12 & under $3; discounts to groups of 20 or more.

Oldtown

IRVIN ALLEN/MICHAEL CRESAP MUSEUM, 19015 Opessa St., S.E., Oldtown, MD 21555-9702. Tel.: 301-478-5848.
Historic House Museum: built in 1764.
Collections: local history; period furnishings; personal artifacts.
Hours & Admission Prices: May-Oct. by appointment.

Oxford

OXFORD MUSEUM, INC., Morris and Market Sts., Oxford, MD 21654. Mailing Address: P.O. Box 131, Oxford, MD 21654-0131. Tel.: 410-226-0191.
Web Site: www.oxfordmuseum.org
Founded: 1964.
Congressional District: 1
Key Personnel: Pres. Bd., Gordon Graves; Dir., Ellen Anderson.
Personnel Profile: Part-Time Paid 1; Part-Time Volunteers 75.
Governing Authority: nonprofit organization. Tax-exempt.
Local History Museum.
Collections: maritime.
Research Fields: Oxford & Talbot County history.
Activities: lectures; slides; multimedia productions.
Publications: Port of Entry (Oxford History); Oxford Treasures - Then & Now; walking tour brochure.
Hours & Admission Prices: late April to May & Oct. to mid-Nov. Mon. & Fri.-Sat. 10-4, Sun. 1-4; June-Sept. Mon., Wed. & Fri.-Sat. 10-4, Sun. 1-4. No charge; donations suggested. ♿
Attendance: 4,000 (estimated)
Membership: Annual $25-$250.

Oxon Hill

OXON COVE PARK, 6411 Oxon Hill Rd., Oxon Hill, MD 20745-1100. Mailing Address: 1900 Anacostia Dr., S.E., Washington, DC 20020-6722. Tel.: 301-839-1176. Fax: 301-763-1066. TDD: 301-839-1783.
E-mail: vanessa-molineaux@nps.gov
Web Site: www.nps.gov/oxhi
Founded: 1967.
Congressional District: 4
Key Personnel: Acting Dir., Lisa Mendelson-Lelmini; Supt., Gale Hazelwood; Asst. Supt., Alex Romero; Park Mgr., Sharon Vanessa Molineaux.
Governing Authority: federal. Parent Institution: National Capital Parks-East, National Park Service, U.S. Dept. of the Interior, 1900 Anacostia Dr., S.E., Washington, DC 20020. Tax-exempt.
Agriculture Museum: housed in c.1900 farm & farm outbuildings.
Collections: farming tools & implements; farm animals.
Research Fields: agriculture of 1900; equipment; techniques.
Facilities: picnic area.
Activities: self-guided tours; living history & farm chore demonstrations.
Publications: brochure; monthly news sheet, Farmer's Log & handbill.
Hours & Admission Prices: Daily 8-4:30. No charge; donations accepted. Closed New Year's Day; Thanksgiving; Christmas. ♿
Attendance: 100,000 (estimated)

Perryville

RODGERS TAVERN, 259 Broad St., Perryville, MD 21903-2816. Mailing Address: P.O. Box 322, Perryville, MD 21903-0322. Tel.: 410-642-6066. Fax: 410-642-6391.
E-mail: townhall@perryvillemd.org
Web Site: www.Perryvillemd.org
Founded: 1956.
Congressional District: 1
Key Personnel: Chm. (V), Barbara Brown.
Personnel Profile: Full-Time Volunteers 1; Part-Time Volunteers 12.
Governing Authority: society. Town of Perryville.
Historic House: pre-1743 building, operated by Rodgers family.
Collections: local history.
Activities: guided tours; fund-raising bazaars; annual meetings. Museum Sponsors: Spring Fling in May; Autumnfest in October; Colonial Christmas in December.
Publications: brochure, Historic Rodgers Tavern.
Hours & Admission Prices: Grounds: by appointment. Building: temporarily closed for renovation. No charge; donations accepted.
Attendance: 6,000 (estimated)
Membership: Individual & Institutional $5; Family $10.

Pikesville

MARYLAND STATE POLICE MUSEUM, 1201 Reisterstown Rd., Pikesville, MD 21208-3898. Tel.: 410-653-4278. Fax: 410-653-4559.
E-mail: mrichardson@mdsp.org
Web Site: www.mdsp.org
Key Personnel: Coord., Margaret Richardson
Police History Museum.
Collections: law enforcement history; weaponry; riot helmets; period uniforms; photographs; memorials.
Hours & Admission Prices: Mon.-Fri.

Pocomoke City

STURGIS ONE-ROOM SCHOOL MUSEUM, 209 Willow St., Pocomoke City, MD 21851. Mailing Address: P.O. Box 697, Pocomoke City, MD 21851-0697. Tel.: 410-957-1913.
E-mail: gatling144@verizon.net
Web Site: www.sturgismuseum.org
Key Personnel: Pres., James Gatling; Cur., Sudie Gatling
History Museum: housed in a one-room African American school house used for first through seventh grades until 1937.
Collections: schoolhouse furnishings.
Hours & Admission Prices: May-Oct. Tues.-Sat. 1-4; other times by appointment. Adults $3, children $1.

Poolesville

SENECA SCHOOLHOUSE MUSEUM, 16800 River Rd., Poolesville, MD 20837-0232. Mailing Address: Historic Medley District, Inc., P.O. Box 232, Poolesville, MD 20837-0232. Tel.: 301-972-8588.
E-mail: info@historicmedley.org
Web Site: www.senecaschoolhouse.com
Key Personnel: Dir., Patty Cooper
Historic Building Museum.
Collections: period furnishings & artifacts.
Facilities: Museum-related items for sale.
Activities: education programs; school groups.
Hours & Admission Prices: By appointment.

Port Deposit

PAW PAW MUSEUM, 98 N. Main St., Port Deposit, MD 21904-1210. Tel.: 410-378-4480.
E-mail: pawpawmuseum@gmail.com
Historic Building: housed in a former Methodist Church; built in 1821.
Collections: local history & culture; personal artifacts; photographs; clothing; yearbooks; Civil War artifacts.
Facilities: Museum-related items for sale.
Hours & Admission Prices: May-Oct. 2nd & 4th Sun. of month 1-5.

Port Tobacco

PORT TOBACCO ONE ROOM SCHOOL, 7215 Chapel Point Rd., Port Tobacco, MD 20677. Mailing Address: P.O. Box 2770, La Plata, MD 20646-2770. Tel.: 301-934-9483.
Key Personnel: Chm., Dale Cornette
History Museum: built in 1871.
Collections: schoolhouse furnishings; books; toys; period lunch pails.
Hours & Admission Prices: By appointment. No charge.

Princess Anne

THE SOMERSET COUNTY HISTORICAL SOCIETY, INC., Teackle Mansion, 11736 Mansion St., Princess Anne, MD 21853. Mailing Address: P.O. Box 181, Princess Anne, MD 21853-0181. Tel.: 410-651-2238.
E-mail: info@teackle.mansion.museum
Web Site: teackle.mansion.museum
Formerly: Olde Princess Anne Days, Inc.
Founded: 1958.
Congressional District: 1
Key Personnel: Pres., Robyn D. Zweig; Vice Pres., Dave Ridgway; Museum Shop Mgr., Linda Alder.
Personnel Profile: Part-Time Volunteers 68.
Governing Authority: nonprofit organization. Tax-exempt: 170(b)(1)(A).
General Museum: housed in 1801 Teackle Mansion, early 19th-century federal period building.
Collections: costumes; archives; decorative arts; furniture; paintings.
Facilities: 100-vol. library of historical books available for research by permission of directors; children's museum.
Activities: guided tours. Special Event: Olde Princess Anne Days in October, tour of Teackle Mansion & 20 local historic homes.
Hours & Admission Prices: April to mid-Dec. Wed. & Sat.-Sun. 1-3; mid-Dec. to March Sun. 1-3; tours by appointment. Adults $4, students $2; discounts to members; children under 12 accompanied by adult no charge.
Attendance: 742 (accurate)
Membership: Individual $20; Family $40.

Ridgely

ADKINS ARBORETUM, (M), 12610 Eveland Rd., Ridgely, MD 21660. Mailing Address: P.O. Box 100, Ridgely, MD 21660-0100. Tel.: 410-634-2847. Fax: 410-634-2878.
E-mail: info@adkinsarboretum.org
Web Site: www.adkinsarboretum.org
Founded: 1980.
Key Personnel: Dir., Ellie Altman
Arboretum.
Collections: native plants, trees, & wildflowers.
Facilities: 400-acre garden; nature trails.
Activities: educational programs.
Hours & Admission Prices: Daily 10-4. Adults $3, students 6-18 $1; members and children 5 & under no charge. Closed major holidays.
Attendance: 20,000
Membership: Individual $45; Family $60.

Riverdale Park

RIVERSDALE HOUSE MUSEUM, 4811 Riverdale Rd., Riverdale Park, MD 20737-1911. Mailing Address: 6005 48th Ave., Riverdale Park, MD 20737-2015. Tel.: 301-864-0420. Fax: 301-927-3498. TDD: 301-699-2544.
E-mail: riversdale@pgparks.com
Web Site: www.mncppcapps.org/pgparks/places/eleganthistoric/riversdale_intro.html

Founded: 1949.
Congressional District: 22
Key Personnel: Dir., Edward Day; Pres. (V), Patrick Gossett; Div. Chief, Anthony Nolan; Museum Shop Mgr., Renee Kidd.
Personnel Profile: Full-Time Paid 2; Part-Time Paid 11; Part-Time Volunteers 61.
Governing Authority: nonprofit organization. Parent Institution: The Maryland National-Capital Park & Planning Commission. Subsidiary Institution: Natural and Historical Resources Division. Tax-exempt.
National Historic Landmark. Historic House: 1803 five-part stucco covered brick plantation, blending Belgian & American architectural styles built by Henri Stier & occupied by his daughter, Rosalie & her husband George Calvert and inherited by their son Charles Benedict. Later influential residents included Senator Hiram Johnson (CA) & Senators Thaddeus & Hattie Caraway (AR).
Collections: personal & domestic artifacts; home furnishings; outbuildings.
Research Fields: home & life of Rosalie & George Calvert; early 1800s; African-American history; foodways; early 19th-century costume.
Facilities: visitors center.
Activities: guided tours; rental gallery; docent program; formal education programs; open-hearth cooking; garden & grounds tours; school groups; scout badge programs.
Publications: quarterly newsletter, The Riversdale Letter; quarterly, The Riversdale Docent.
Hours & Admission Prices: Sun. & Fri. 12:15-3:15; other times by appointment. Adults $3, senior citizens 60 & over $2, children $1; discounts to groups. Closed New Year's Day; Independence Day; Christmas. ♿
Attendance: 12,282 (accurate)
Membership: Riversdale Historical Society: Basic $25; Supporting $50.

Rock Hall

WATERMAN'S MUSEUM, 20880 Rock Hall Ave., Rock Hall, MD 21661-1407. Tel.: 410-778-6697.
Web Site: www.havenharbour.com/hhwatmus.htm
Key Personnel: Mgr., Jonathan Jones
History Museum.
Collections: oystering; crabbing; fishing; photographs; carvings; boats; shanty house replica.
Hours & Admission Prices: Daily 8-5. No charge; donations accepted.

Rockville

JANE L. AND ROBERT H. WEINER JUDAIC MUSEUM, The Gildenhorn/Speisman Center for the Arts, 6125 Montrose Rd., Rockville, MD 20852-4860. Tel.: 301-881-0100 & 230-3711. Fax: 301-881-5512. TDD: 301-881-0012.
Web Site: www.jccgw.org
Founded: 1969.
Congressional District: 17
Personnel Profile: Full-Time Paid 2; Part-Time Volunteers 90.
Governing Authority: nonprofit organization. Parent Institution: Jewish Community Center of Greater Washington. Tax-exempt.
Judaic Museum.
Collections: Judaica; ethnology; archaeology; art.
Facilities: library.
Activities: lectures; guided tours; films; concerts; dance recitals; workshops; organized education programs for children; inter-arts programs; inter-museum loans; permanent & traveling exhibitions.
Publications: exhibition notes & catalogue; Center Scene.
Hours & Admission Prices: Mon.-Thurs. 12-4 & 7:30 pm-9:30 pm, Sun. 2-5. No charge. Closed national & Jewish holidays. ♿
Attendance: 9,000 (estimated)

LATVIAN MUSEUM, 400 Hurley Ave., Rockville, MD 20850-3121. Mailing Address: P.O. Box 67, Fabius, NY 13063. Tel.: 301-340-1914. Fax: 301-340-8732.
Web Site: www.alausa.org
Founded: 1980.
Congressional District: 8
Key Personnel: Dir. & Cur., Lolita Bergs.
Personnel Profile: Part-Time Volunteers 12.
Governing Authority: nonprofit organization. Parent Institution: American Latvian Association in the United States. Subsidiary Institution: Latvian Institute. Tax-exempt: 501(c)(3).
Ethnic Museum: Latvian historic & cultural development from Ice Age to 20th Century.
Collections: textiles; costumes; farm implements; photographs; documents; folk art; military uniforms & medals; philately; numismatics.
Research Fields: Latvian history & culture; folk arts; political & military history.

Facilities: 1,200 sq. ft. exhibition space.
Activities: guided tours.
Publications: brochure.
Hours & Admission Prices: 1st Sun. of month 12-2; other times by appointment. No charge; donations accepted. ♿
Attendance: 2,000 (estimated)

THE MONTGOMERY COUNTY HISTORICAL SOCIETY, INC., (M), 103 W. Montgomery Ave., Rockville, MD 20850-4212. Mailing Address: 111 W. Montgomery Ave., Rockville, MD 20850-4212. Tel.: 301-340-2825 & 1492. Fax: 301-340-2871.
E-mail: info@montgomeryhistory.org
Web Site: www.montgomeryhistory.org
Founded: 1944.
Congressional District: 8
Key Personnel: Exec. Dir., Debbie Rankin; Pres. (V), Jack Devine; Dir. Waters House Site, Elizabeth Hickey; Education & Program Coord., Karen Yaffe Lottes; Librarian, Patricia Andersen; Museum Shop Mgr., Maureen Altobello; Cur., Millicent Gay; Collections Mgr., Joanna Church; Admin., Jennie Cottrell; School Program Coord., Emily Correll.
Personnel Profile: Full-Time Paid 3; Part-Time Paid 6; Part-Time Volunteers 100; Interns 2.
Governing Authority: society. Subsidiary Institution: Research Library, 42 W. Middle Lane, Rockville, MD 20850. Branch Museum: Waters House, 12535 Milestone Manor Lane, Germantown, MD 20876. Tax-exempt: 501(c)(3).
Historic House: 1815 Beall-Dawson House; 1852 Stonestreet Medical Museum.
Collections: 23,000 Montgomery County artifacts including archival records; photographs; maps; costumes; quilts; glass; furniture & medical instruments. Historic Buildings: c.1851 Stonestreet Medical Museum; Waters House, Germantown, MD.
Research Fields: Montgomery County history including genealogy, oral history, archaeology, historic preservation.
Facilities: 2,000-vol. library of books; 12,000 linear ft. of general history material on Maryland & Montgomery County available for use on premises; reading room. Museum-related items for sale.
Activities: guided tours; lectures; walking tours; research assistance; preservation workshops.
Publications: quarterly magazine, The Montgomery County Story; monthly newsletter; brochures; county history books; monographs.
Hours & Admission Prices: Museum: Tues.-Sun. 12-4. Library: Tues.-Sat. 10-4, Sun. 1-4. Adults $3, students & senior citizens $2; members & children under 13 no charge; use of library $2. Closed major holidays.
Attendance: 6,000 (accurate)
Membership: Genealogical Club Only $20; Basic $35; Century Circle $100; Heritage Circle $250.

Saint Leonard

JEFFERSON PATTERSON PARK & MUSEUM, (M), 10515 Mackall Rd., Saint Leonard, MD 20685-2433. Tel.: 410-586-8500. Fax: 410-586-0080. TDD: 800-735-2258 (Maryland Relay).
E-mail: jppm@mdp.state.md.us
Web Site: www.jefpat.org
Founded: 1983.
Congressional District: 3
Key Personnel: Exec. Dir., Michael A. Smolek; Chief Conservator, Betty Seifert; Fiscal Officer, Denise America; Admin. Education, Kimberley Popetz; Admin. Research, Edward E. Chaney; Mktg. & Devel. Coord., Megan Williams; Coord. Education, Kelly Cooper; Collections, Rebecca Morehouse; Museum Shop Mgr., Michele Parlett; Education & Archaeology Specialist, Kate Dinnel; Conservation Tech, Gareth McNair-Lewis; Sec., Sharon Raftery; Federal Cur., Sara Rivers-Cofield; Friends Sec., Lisa Starr; Maintenance Supvr., Dimitrios Papadakis; Maintenance Mechanic, Stephen Embrey; Maintenance Asst., William Wyatt.
Personnel Profile: Full-Time Paid 23; Part-Time Paid 18; Part-Time Volunteers 30; Interns 3.
Governing Authority: state government. Parent Institution: Maryland Historical Trust. Subsidiary Institution: Friends of JPPM, Inc. Tax-exempt.
Park & Museum.
Collections: life in the Chesapeake Bay area from prehistoric to historic times; prehistoric & historic artifacts; historic farm equipment & machinery; 75 archaeological sites on property; 560-acre waterfront park; Native American structures. Historic Structures: 1932 steer barn; 1936 tenant farmer complex.
Research Fields: prehistoric & historic archaeology; Southern Maryland history & agriculture; research & collections care; African American, European American & Native American rural life oral history research; War 1812.

Facilities: archaeology trail; visitor center; nature trail; Maryland Archaeological Conservation Laboratory; Family Discovery Room; archaeological teaching laboratory; gardens. Archaeology books, artifact replicas, farm toys & other related items for sale.
Activities: guided walking & wagon ride tours; lectures; films; concerts; organized education programs; docent program; public archaeology program. Museum Sponsors: Children's Day on the Farm; Celtic Festival; African-American Family Community Day; War of 1812 reenactment; American Indian Heritage Day; War of 1812 Tavern nights.
Publications: newsletter, Patterson Points; newsletter, MAC Lab; Popular Archaeology Series; annual report.
Hours & Admission Prices: April 15-Oct. 15 Wed.-Sun. 10-5. No charge; donations accepted. ♿
Attendance: 32,000 (accurate)
Membership: Individual $35; Family $50; Supporting $100; Associate $250; Sponsor $500; Sustaining $1,000; Patron $5,000; Founder $10,000.

Saint Mary's City

THE DWIGHT FREDERIC BOYDEN GALLERY, (M), St. Mary's College of Maryland, 18952 E. Fisher Rd., Saint Mary's City, MD 20686-3002. Tel.: 240-895-4246. Fax: 240-895-4958.
E-mail: mcbraun@smcm.edu
Web Site: www.smcm.edu/art/gallery
Founded: 1971.
Key Personnel: Dir., Mary E. Braun.
Personnel Profile: Full-Time Paid 1; Part-Time Paid 4; Interns 1.
Governing Authority: Saint Mary's College of Maryland. Tax-exempt.
Art Gallery.
Collections: 20th & 21st century paintings, sculpture, prints & drawings.
Facilities: 1,600 sq. ft. exhibit space.
Activities: lectures; loan & traveling exhibitions. Annual Event: Student Art Exhibit.
Hours & Admission Prices: Sept.-May Mon.-Fri. 11-5; Summer: call for hours. No charge; donations accepted. ♿
Attendance: 2,791

* **HISTORIC ST. MARY'S CITY, (M),** Rte. 5, Saint Mary's City, MD 20686. Mailing Address: P.O. Box 39, Saint Mary's City, MD 20686-0039. Tel.: 240-895-4990. Fax: 240-895-4968. TDD: 800-735-2258.
E-mail: hsmc@smcm.edu
Web Site: www.stmaryscity.org
Founded: 1966.
Congressional District: 1
Key Personnel: C.E.O., Regina Faden; Chm. (V), Richard Moe; Pres. (V), Patricia King Jackson; Dir. Research, Henry M. Miller; Dir. Communications & Mktg., Susan Wilkinson; Dir. Public Programs, Dorsey Bodeman; Museum Shop Mgr., Cheryl Stevenson.
Personnel Profile: Full-Time Paid 30; Part-Time Paid 30; Part-Time Volunteers 150; Interns 3.
Governing Authority: state. Parent Institution: State of Maryland. Tax-exempt: 170(b)(1)(A).
Outdoor Living History Museum.
Collections: archaeology; architecture; anthropology. Re-created Historic Houses: 1676 State House; 17th-century plantation & outbuildings; 17th-century inn. Historic Ship: Maryland Dove.
Research Fields: Maryland & Colonial history & architecture; archaeology.
Facilities: library of books on Maryland history, architectural history & archaeology available for research purposes. Museum-related items for sale.
Activities: living history interpretations & historical vignettes; craft demonstrations; archaeological field school; internships; permanent & temporary exhibitions; craft workshops; lectures; educational & outreach programs; sail-training program.
Publications: St. Mary's Research series; St. Mary's City Archaeology series; brochures; quarterly newsletters; annual report; visitor's guide.
Hours & Admission Prices: mid-March to Nov. Adults $10, senior citizens $8, students $6, children 6-12 $3.50; discounts to ICOM & AAM; children under 6 no charge. ♿
Attendance: 45,000 (estimated)
Membership: Individual $30; Dual & Family $50; Patron $100; Contributor $250; Benefactor $500.

Saint Michaels

* **CHESAPEAKE BAY MARITIME MUSEUM, (M),** 213 N. Talbot St., Saint Michaels, MD 21663-0636. Mailing Address: P.O. Box 636, Saint Michaels, MD 21663-0636. Tel.: 410-745-2916. Fax: 410-745-6088.
E-mail: info@cbmm.org
Web Site: www.cbmm.org
Founded: 1965.
Congressional District: 1
Key Personnel: Pres., Stuart L. Parnes; Chm. (V), Robert A. Perkins; Vice Chm., Alan Griffith; Dir., Center for Chesapeake Studies, Melissa McLoud; Cur. Collections, Ronald E. (Pete) Lesher; Vice Pres. Finances, Heather Moore; Vice Pres. Operations, William Gilmore; Vice Pres. Advancement, Kathleen Rattie; Dir. Devel., Julie Barnett; Coord. Special Events, Ida Heelan; Museum Shop Mgr., Mitch Anderson.
Personnel Profile: Full-Time Paid 32; Part-Time Paid 12; Part-Time Volunteers 210; Interns 4.
Governing Authority: private; nonprofit organization. Tax-exempt: 501(c)(3) & 170(6)(1)(A).
Regional Maritime History Museum.
Collections: art; small craft; tools of fisheries; waterfowling; boatbuilding; lighthouses; steamboats; shoreside trades; manuscripts; photographs; ship plans.
Major Exhibits: A Rising Tide, 3/10-4/11; Kuchter-Castilli Watercolors, 5/10-12/10.
Research Fields: Chesapeake Bay culture.
Facilities: 10,000-vol. library of books on maritime history & Chesapeake Bay area; 18 acre campus with 12 exhibit buildings; lighthouse; boatyard.
Activities: guided tours; lectures; permanent & temporary exhibits; year-round formally organized education & apprentice programs. Museum Sponsors: festivals; boat auction; outdoor concerts.
Publications: quarterly magazine, CBMM; monographs, A Heritage in Wood; Maryland's Oyster Navy; Lambert Wickes: Pirate or Patriot; Chesapeake Bay Sloops; Chesapeake Bay Crabbing Skiffs; Notes on Chesapeake Bay Skipjacks; booklets, Bay Sailing Craft; It's How You Pick the Crab: An Oral Portrait of Eastern Shore Crab Picking; Beacons of Hooper Strait; books, John M. Barbers Chesapeake; From Pot Pie to Hell and Damnation, An Illustrated Gazetteer of Talbot County; My Life as an Oyster.
Hours & Admission Prices: March 1-May 31 & Oct. 1-Nov. 13 daily 10-5; June 1-Sept. 30 daily 10-6; Nov. 14-Feb. 28 daily 10-4. Adults $13, seniors $9, seniors $10; children 6-17 $5; discounts to groups, AAA, AARP & AAM members, college students & military personnel; children under 6 & members no charge. Closed New Year's Day; Thanksgiving; Christmas. ♿
Attendance: 59,726 (accurate)
Membership: Introductory $55; Family $70; Contributor $100; Supporter $200; Benefactor $500; Sustaining $1,000; Life $2,500.

Salisbury

SALISBURY STATE UNIVERSITY GALLERIES, (M), 1101 Camden Ave., Salisbury, MD 21801-6837. Tel.: 410-548-2547 & 6000. Fax: 410-548-3002.
Web Site: salisbury.edu
Formerly: Salisbury State University Galleries
Founded: 1962.
Congressional District: 1
Key Personnel: Cur., Linda Shipp; Dir. Cultural Affairs, June Krell-Salgado.
Personnel Profile: Full-Time Paid 3; Part-Time Paid 6; Part-Time Volunteers 30; Interns 1.
Governing Authority: university; not-for-profit. Parent Institution: Salisbury State University. Affiliated with University of MD System. Tax-exempt: 170(b)(1)(A).
University Art Gallery.
Collections: Maryland regional artists; post-Impressionist prints & drawings; landscape photographs; 19th & 20th-century American sculpture; Japanese block prints.
Facilities: Fulton Hall Gallery and Atrium Gallery.
Publications: quarterly newsletter.
Hours & Admission Prices: Fulton Hall Gallery: Sept.-May Tues.-Fri. 10-4. Atrium Gallery: Sept.-May Mon.-Wed. 10-4. No charge; donations accepted. Closed major holidays. ♿
Attendance: 20,000 (accurate)
Membership: Individual $30; Family $50; Benefactor $100; Supporting $500.

THE SALISBURY ZOOLOGICAL PARK, 755 S. Park Dr., Salisbury, MD 21804-5600. Mailing Address: P.O. Box 2979, Salisbury, MD 21802-2979. Tel.: 410-548-3188. Fax: 410-860-0919.
E-mail: salisburyzooed@gmail.com
Web Site: www.salisburyzoo.org
Founded: 1954.
Congressional District: 1
Key Personnel: Dir., Joel Hamilton; Chm. (V), Ronald G. Alessi, Sr.; Cur. Education, Leonora Dillon; Membership & Museum Shop Mgr., Mary Seemann.
Personnel Profile: Full-Time Paid 14; Part-Time Paid 14; Part-Time Volunteers 50; Interns 4.
Governing Authority: Parent Institution: City of Salisbury. Subsidiary Institution: Salisbury Zoo Commission. Affiliated with the Dept. of Public Works, City of Salisbury, Government Bldg., Salisbury, MD 21801. Tel. 410-548-3170. Tax-exempt: 501(c)(3).

Zoo.
Collections: mammals; reptiles; waterfowl; several species of endangered animals.
Research Fields: ethology.
Facilities: 100-vol. library of books on animals available for educational reasons to people associated with the zoo.
Activities: guided tours; ZOO-TO-YOU program; lectures; films; formally organized education programs for children & undergraduate college students affiliated with Salisbury St. University; docent program; permanent exhibitions.
Publications: quarterly newsletter.
Hours & Admission Prices: Memorial Day-Labor Day daily 9-7:30; Sept.-May daily 9-4:30. No charge; donations accepted. Closed Thanksgiving; Christmas. ♿
Attendance: 192,000 (estimated)
Membership: Senior $20; Individual $30; Individual Plus $40; Family & Grandparent $45; Deluxe Family $70; Naturalist $100; Patron $500; Wildlife Benefactor $1,000.

THE WARD MUSEUM OF WILDFOWL ART, SALISBURY UNIVERSITY, (M), 909 S. Schumaker Dr., Salisbury, MD 21804-8722. Tel.: 410-742-4988, ext. 120. Fax: 410-742-3107.
E-mail: ward@wardmuseum.org
Web Site: www.wardmuseum.org
Founded: 1975.
Congressional District: 1
Key Personnel: Exec. Dir., Lora Bottinelli; Chm. Bd., John Maphis; Dir. Education, Kim Check; Events Coord., Helen Rogan; Membership & Mktg., Rose Taylor; Cur. & Folklorist, Dr. Cynthia Byrd; Dir. Volunteers, Renee Frederickson; Museum Shop Mgr., Judy Covey.
Personnel Profile: Full-Time Paid 12; Part-Time Paid 5; Part-Time Volunteers 200; Interns 4.
Governing Authority: nonprofit. Parent Institution: The Ward Foundation, Inc. DBA The Ward Museum of Wildfowl Art an affiliated Foundation of Salisbury University. Tax-exempt: 501(c)(3).
Art Museum.
Collections: decoys; decorative bird carvings; wildfowl paintings; fowling pieces & skiffs; hunting artifacts; documents & manuscripts; audiovisual archives.
Research Fields: folk art, history, maritime & art history; American historical economics; folklore & folklife.
Facilities: library; 31,000 sq. ft. exhibit space; theatre; education center; nature trails. Gift items for sale.
Activities: guided tours; lectures; films; gallery talks; arts festivals; workshops; formally organized education programs; loan, permanent & temporary exhibitions. Chesapeake Wildfowl Expo; Ward World Championship Wildfowl Carving Competition.
Publications: magazine, Wildfowl Art; documentary films; exhibit catalogues.
Hours & Admission Prices: Mon.-Sat. 10-5, Sun. 12-5. Families $17 on Sun., adults $7, seniors $5, children under 18 $3; preschoolers, members, Salisbury Univ. staff, students & faculty no charge. Closed New Year's Day; Thanksgiving; Christmas. ♿
Attendance: 35,000 (estimated)
Membership: Personal $35; Family $60; Sponsor $150; Contributor $250; Heritage $500; Heritage Gold $1,000; Benefactor $5,000. Foreign Members: Canada add $10; Other Countries add $25.

Sandy Spring

SANDY SPRING MUSEUM, (M), 17901 Bentley Rd., Sandy Spring, MD 20860-1001. Tel.: 301-774-0022. Fax: 301-774-8149.
Web Site: www.sandyspringmuseum.org
Founded: 1980.
Congressional District: 8
Key Personnel: Exec. Dir., Sharon Ann Holt; Pres. (V), Joseph Furey; Administrative Mgr., Ellen Hartge; Museum Shop Mgr., Kathy Polletto.
Personnel Profile: Full-Time Paid 1; Part-Time Paid 6; Part-Time Volunteers 20; Interns 5.
Governing Authority: nonprofit organization. Tax-exempt: 501(c)(3).
History Museum.
Collections: farm tools; china; costumes; domestic utensils; furniture; photographs; books; toys; documents; letters; barn; smithy.
Research Fields: local social & architectural history; 18th-century land patents; index of the Annals of Sandy Spring; genealogical research; historic homes; 18th & 19th century Quakers, education, slavery & emancipation.
Facilities: 1,300-vol. library containing 18th to 20th-century books & photographs for use on premises; rental facilities; performance space; garden.
Activities: guided tours; lectures; arts festivals; organized education programs for children & adults; docent program; children's summer craft program; summer art show; community service hours program; members' tours to area museums. Museum Sponsors: Strawberry Festival; Antique Show; Garden Club; Holiday Open House; Chamber music series; Greens Sale.
Publications: quarterly newsletter, The Sandy Spring Museum Legacy.
Hours & Admission Prices: Mon. & Wed.-Thurs. 9-4, Sat.-Sun. 12-4. Adults $5; members & children no charge. Closed New Year's Eve & Day; Labor Day; Christmas Eve, Day & week. ♿
Attendance: 10,000 (estimated)
Membership: Individual $40; Family $65; Educators $200; Collectors $500; Curators $1,000; Preservationists $2,500; Innovators $5,000; Historians $10,000; Stewards $25,000.

Shady Side

CAPTAIN SALEM AVERY HOUSE MUSEUM, SHADY SIDE RURAL HERITAGE SOCIETY, INC., (M), 1418 E.W. Shadyside Rd., Shady Side, MD 20764-9713. Mailing Address: P.O. Box 89, Shady Side, MD 20764-0089. Tel.: 410-867-4486. Fax: 410-867-4486.
E-mail: captainavery@verizon.net
Web Site: www.averyhouse.org
Founded: 1988.
Congressional District: 5
Key Personnel: Dir., Laurel Fletcher; Chm. (V), Susy Smith; Public Rels., Mavis Daly; Treas., Pat Freiberg; Museum Shop Mgr., Melanie Turner.
Personnel Profile: Full-Time Volunteers 2; Part-Time Paid 2; Part-Time Volunteers 150.
Governing Authority: nonprofit. Tax-exempt.
Historic House: 1860 waterman's house & 1920s fishing club.
Collections: furniture; tools; 1860-1920 boats; artifacts; photographs; oral history.
Research Fields: 1860-1890 life of watermen of Chesapeake; 20th century history; local community history.
Facilities: library of history & genealogy books available to the public; 600 sq. ft. exhibit space. Gift items for sale.
Activities: arts festivals; films; guided tours; lectures; participatory & temporary exhibitions. Annual Events: lecture series in winter; children's series in summer; Girl Scout & school programs.
Publications: Miss Ethel Remembers...; Capt. Salem Avery House Museum, Its History 1860-1990; Doc. The Life of Emily Hammond Wilson; Journey To Our Past; teachers activity guide, Seasons of a Chesapeake Bay Waterman.
Hours & Admission Prices: Museum: April-Dec. Sun. 1-4. Library: Mon. 12-3. Grounds & Outdoor Exhibits: daily dawn to dusk. No charge; donations accepted. ♿
Attendance: 7,179 (accurate)
Membership: Student & Older Adults (over 65) $15; Individual $20; Family $35; Sustaining $40; Donor $100; Patron $250; Benefactor $500.

Sharpsburg

ANTIETAM NATIONAL BATTLEFIELD-VISITOR CENTER, 5831 Dunker Church Rd., Sharpsburg, MD 21782. Mailing Address: P.O. Box 158, Sharpsburg, MD 21782-0158. Tel.: 301-432-5124. Fax: 301-432-4590. TDD: 301-432-5124.
Web Site: www.nps.gov/anti
Founded: 1890.
Congressional District: 6
Key Personnel: Supt., John Howard.
Governing Authority: federal. Affiliated with Dept. of the Interior National Park Service. Tax-exempt.
Historic Site: site of 1862 Civil War Maryland Campaign & battle of Antietam or Sharpsburg.
Collections: Civil War weapons; military uniforms & equipment; relics; documents; lithographs; photographs; military and personal papers of Henry Kyd Douglas; Captain James Hope paintings; Cope-Carman battlefield maps. Historic Houses: c.1840 Sherrick House; 1853 Dunker Church, rebuilt 1961; late 18th-century Piper House; Pry House, Gen. McClellan's headquarters; 19th-century Mumma Farm.
Research Fields: Civil War history.
Facilities: 1,200-vol. library of Civil War records & books relating to Maryland campaign & participants available for use on the premises; numerous monuments & markers. Publications for sale.
Activities: taped tours; films; firearm demonstrations; historical walks; living history programs; audiovisual programs; wayside exhibits.
Publications: leaflet & map, Antietam Battlefield.
Hours & Admission Prices: Jan-May daily 8:30-5; Summer: daily 8:30-7. 3 Day Pass: family $6, adults $4. Closed New Year's Day; Thanksgiving; Christmas. ♿
Attendance: 313,201 (accurate)
Membership: Annually $15.

BARRON'S C & O CANAL MUSEUM, 5632 Mose Circle, Synders Landing Rd., Sharpsburg, MD 21782-1408. Mailing Address: P.O. Box 356, Sharpsburg, MD 21782-1408. Tel.: 301-432-8726.
History Museum.
Collections: canal history; photographs; working boat model.
Research Fields: C & O Canal.
Hours & Admission Prices: Sat.-Sun. 9-5. No charge.

KENNEDY FARM HOUSE MUSEUM, 2406 Chestnut Grove Rd., Sharpsburg, MD 21782. Tel.: 202-537-8900.
Historic House Museum: housed in the farmhouse that served as a staging area for John Brown and his army as they prepared for the Harpers Ferry raid in the summer of 1859. A National Historic Landmark.
Collections: local history; period furnishings; personal artifacts.
Hours & Admission Prices: May-Oct. by appointment.

Silver Spring

GEORGE MEANY MEMORIAL ARCHIVES, 10000 New Hampshire Ave., Silver Spring, MD 20903-1706. Tel.: 301-431-5451. Fax: 301-431-5455.
E-mail: ldeloach@nlc.edu
Web Site: www.nlc.edu/archives/home.html
Founded: 1980.
Congressional District: 5
Key Personnel: Dir., Pat Greenfield; Archivist, Lynda DeLoach; Archivist, Sarah M. Springer.
Governing Authority: nonprofit. Parent Institution: The George Meany Center for Labor Studies. Tax-exempt.
History Museum: labor organizations.
Collections: George Meany permanent exhibit; records of AFL, CIO & AFL-CIO; labor arts.
Publications: journal, Labor's Heritage.
Hours & Admission Prices: Research by appointment: Mon.-Tues. & Fri. 8:30-5, Wed.-Thurs. 7:30-6. No charge. Closed federal holidays. ♿
Attendance: 3,000 (estimated)

NATIONAL CAPITAL TROLLEY MUSEUM, 1313 Bonifant Rd., Silver Spring, MD 20905-5955. Tel.: 301-384-6352. Fax: 301-384-2865.
Web Site: www.dctrolley.org
Founded: 1959.
Congressional District: 4
Key Personnel: C.E.O., Pres. (V) & Museum Shop Mgr., Ken Rucker; Treas., Charles Tirschman; Dir. Devel., Wesley Paulson.
Personnel Profile: Full-Time Volunteers 2; Part-Time Paid 3; Part-Time Volunteers 30.
Governing Authority: private; nonprofit organization.
Transportation Museum.
Collections: electric street cars; postal cards; photographs; trolley era ephemera; demonstration railway.
Facilities: 600-vol. of railway history books; 65-seat auditorium; 900 sq. ft. exhibit space. Museum-related items for sale.
Activities: docent program; films; formal education for children; participatory exhibits. Annual Events: Holly Trolley Fest; DC Transit Day; Cabin Fever Day; History Day.
Publications: bimonthly newsletter, The Headway Recorder; journal, NCTM Journal.
Hours & Admission Prices: Closed until late fall 2009.
Attendance: 15,155 (accurate)
Membership: Student $15; Individual $30.

Snow Hill

FURNACE TOWN LIVING HERITAGE MUSEUM, (M), 3816 Old Furnace Rd., Snow Hill, MD 21863-3420. Mailing Address: P.O. Box 207, Snow Hill, MD 21863-0207. Tel.: 410-632-2032. Fax: 410-632-1735.
Web Site: www.furnacetown.com/museum.htm
Founded: 1982.
Congressional District: 1
Key Personnel: Dir., Sarah Meyers; Bd. Pres. (V), John Malloy; Museum Shop Mgr., Elvira Jones; Treas., Larry Knudsen.
Personnel Profile: Full-Time Paid 1; Part-Time Paid 14.
Governing Authority: private; nonprofit organization. Tax-exempt: 501(c)(3).
Living Heritage Museum.
Collections: 1820-1850 village life; printing; broommaking; textile arts; blacksmithing; woodworking; gardening.
Research Fields: early 19th century iron manufacturing.
Facilities: 100-vol. library. Museum-related items for sale.
Activities: docent program; formal education programs for children; arts festivals; guided tours; lectures. Annual Event: Celtic Festival.
Publications: newsletter, Furnace Town Times.
Hours & Admission Prices: Buildings: April-Oct. daily 10-5. Grounds: daily 10-5. Adults $5, senior citizens over 60 & military with ID $4.50, children 2-18 $3; discount to AAA members. ♿
Attendance: 15,917 (accurate)
Membership: Individual $20; Family $35; Collier $50; Ironmaster $75; Corporate & Supporter $125.

JULIA A. PURNELL MUSEUM, 208 W. Market St., Snow Hill, MD 21863-1059. Tel.: 410-632-0515. Fax: 410-632-0515.
E-mail: mail@purnellmuseum.com
Web Site: www.purnellmuseum.com
Founded: 1942.
Congressional District: 1
Key Personnel: Dir., Claire Otterbein; Bd. Pres. (V), Joshua Fradel.
Personnel Profile: Full-Time Paid 2; Part-Time Paid 2; Part-Time Volunteers 50.
Governing Authority: board of directors; nonprofit. Parent Institution: Town of Snow Hill. Tax-exempt: 501(c)(3).
History Museum: housed in 1891 former Catholic Church.
Collections: area U.S. history; history of Worcester County; recreated general merchandise store; agricultural & domestic tools; Worcester County machinery; Victorian life; regional history of Pocomoke Indians of 16th century; fine & folk art.
Research Fields: material culture of Worcester County's place in U.S. & Maryland history; museum collection.
Facilities: 670-vol. library; 1,387 sq. ft. exhibit space; archives; conference area.
Activities: guided tours; docent program; formal education program for Salisbury State Univ. students; training programs for professional museum workers; concerts; participatory & temporary exhibitions; time travel trunk of cultural artifacts for children; heritage arts programs for adults & children; scavenger hunts; field trip programs; group tours; NYC excursions; summer concerts. Annual Events: Victorian Christmas; needlework show & contest; Del Marva Needle Art Show and Competition; Kids' Discovery Day; Julia Purnell's Birthday Party; Fiber Fest!
Publications: newsletter, The Sampler; children's artifacts coloring book; biography, Julia A. Purnell, A Life Embroidered with Love; People of the Pocomoke; Smoke on the Pocomoke; Historic Snow Hill Walking Tour; educators' packet; Snow Hill Calendar of Events.
Hours & Admission Prices: April-Oct. Tues.-Sat. 10-4, Sun. 1-4; Nov.-March by appointment. Adults $2, children $.50; discounts to AAM & ICOM members; members no charge. Package tours available for surrounding museums. Closed major holidays. ♿
Attendance: 4,000 (estimated)
Membership: Student $10; Individual $15; Family $25; Patron $50; Sponsor $100; Lifetime $500.

Solomons

ANNMARIE GARDEN, (M), 13480 Dowell Rd., Solomons, MD 20629. Mailing Address: P.O. Box 99, Dowell, MD 20629-0099. Tel.: 410-326-4640. Fax: 410-326-4887.
E-mail: gardeninfo@chesapeake.net
Web Site: www.annmariegarden.org
Key Personnel: Dir., Stacey Hann-Ruff
Sculpture Park & Arts Center.
Collections: outdoor sculpture; garden.
Facilities: nature trails.
Activities: educational programs; classes; workshops; special events.
Hours & Admission Prices: Park: daily 9-5. Arts Building: Tues.-Sun. 10-5. Adults $3, senior citizens & children 5-12 $2; children under 5 & AMG members no charge. Closed Independence Day; Thanksgiving; Christmas Eve & Day. ♿

* **CALVERT MARINE MUSEUM, (M),** 14200 Solomons Island Rd., Solomons, MD 20688. Mailing Address: P.O. Box 97, Solomons, MD 20688-0097. Tel.: 410-326-2042. Fax: 410-326-6691. TDD: 1-800-735-2258.
E-mail: information@calvertmarinemuseum.com
Web Site: www.calvertmarinemuseum.com
Founded: 1969.
Congressional District: 1
Key Personnel: Dir., C. Douglass Alves, Jr.; Chm. (V), RoxAnne Cumberland; Business Mgr., Lea Ann Smiley; Deputy Dir., Sherrod Sturrock; Cur. Estuarine Biology, Kenneth Kaumeyer; Cur. Paleontology, Stephen J. Godfrey; Cur. Maritime History, Richard Dodds; Cur. Exhibits, James Langley; Dir. Devel., Vanessa Gill; Maintenance Supvr., Kenny Heard; Boat Capt., Don Prescott; Museum Shop Mgr., Maureen P. Baughman; Librarian, Paul Berry.

Personnel Profile: Full-Time Paid 28; Full-Time Volunteers 1; Part-Time Paid 34; Part-Time Volunteers 200; Interns 5.
Governing Authority: Calvert Marine Museum Society. Parent Institution: Calvert County Government. Tax-exempt: 501(c)(3); 170(b)(1)(A).
Marine Museum.
Collections: maritime history; small craft; estuarine biological specimens; marine paintings, fossils. Historic Boat: 1899 log-built oyster boat. Historic Buildings: 1883 Drum Point Lighthouse on waterfront; 1934 seafood packing house; 1925 schoolhouse; 1828 Cove Point Lighthouse.
Research Fields: paleontology; maritime history; estuarine biology; southern Maryland; Chesapeake Bay.
Facilities: 8,000-vol. library; photographic & manuscript archives; commercial fisheries collections housed in seafood packing house. Local handicrafts, art, books, models & decorative items pertaining to museum's collection for sale.
Activities: guided tours; lectures; craft demonstrations; slide & film programs; field trips; formally organized educational programs; permanent & temporary exhibitions; boat rides.
Publications: quarterly newsletter, Bugeye Times.
Hours & Admission Prices: Daily 10-5. Adults $7, seniors & military $6, children $2; discount to AAM & CAMM members; members no charge. Closed New Year's Day; Thanksgiving; Christmas. ♿
Attendance: 72,222 (accurate)
Membership: Individual $35 & up; Family $50 & up; Sustaining $100 & up; Associate $250 & up; Patron $500 & up; Bugeye Society $1,000 & up. Corporate Dues: Sustaining $125 & up; Associate $250 & up; Patron $500 & up; Bugeye Society $1,000 & up.

Suitland

AIRMEN MEMORIAL MUSEUM, 5211 Auth Rd., Suitland, MD 20746-4339. Mailing Address: P.O. Box 50, Temple Hills, MD 20757-0050. Tel.: 301-899-8386 & 3500; 800-638-0594. Fax: 301-899-8136.
E-mail: staff@afsahq.org
Web Site: www.afsahq.org
Founded: 1986.
Congressional District: 4
Key Personnel: Exec. Dir. & C.E.O., Richard M. Dean.
Personnel Profile: Full-Time Paid 1.
Governing Authority: nonprofit. Parent Institution: Air Force Sergeants Association. Tax-exempt: 501(c)(3).
Military Museum.
Collections: personal items & equipment used by enlisted personnel during their service with the Army Air Corps, Army Air Forces, & U.S. Air Force; archival holdings from 1907 particular emphasis on World War II color photography.
Research Fields: contributions by enlisted men & women in the Army Air Corps, Army Air Forces, & modern day Air Force.
Facilities: library of material pertaining to enlisted personnel; 6,000 sq. ft. exhibit space.
Activities: magazine, SERGEANTS.
Publications: The Airmen Heritage Series, video histories & educational monographs.
Hours & Admission Prices: Mon.-Fri. 8-5. No charge; donations accepted. Closed federal holidays. ♿

Thurmont

CATOCTIN WILDLIFE PRESERVE & ZOO, 13019 Catoctin Furnace Rd., Thurmont, MD 21788-2134. Tel.: 301-271-4922 & 3180. Fax: 301-271-2673.
E-mail: administration@cwpzoo.com
Web Site: www.cwpzoo.com
Founded: 1933.
Key Personnel: Dir., Richard Hahn, C.A.P.; Pres. (V), Carole R. Brown; Vice Pres., Kelly Johnson; Gen. Cur., June Bellizzi; Museum Shop Mgr., Brandi Owens.
Personnel Profile: Full-Time Paid 24; Part-Time Paid 10; Part-Time Volunteers 12; Interns 2.
Governing Authority: corporation. Parent Institution: Global Wildlife Trust, Inc.
Zoological Park.
Collections: animals from around the world; natural history; reptiles.
Research Fields: reptilian propagation, primate propagation & conservation.
Facilities: outdoor stage; picnic pavilion; concession stand; classroom.
Activities: guided tours by appointment; lectures; sleepovers; birthday parties; 25-acre safari ride.
Publications: quarterly newsletter, Encounters.
Hours & Admission Prices: March & Nov. Sat.-Sun. 10-4 (weather permitting); April Mon.-Fri. 10-5, Sat.-Sun. 9-5; May daily 9-5; Memorial Day to Sept. Mon.-Fri. 9-5, Sat.-Sun. 9-6; Oct. daily 10-5. Adult $15.95, children $9.95; discounts for seniors, military & scheduled groups of 15 or more; members no charge. ♿
Attendance: 80,000 (estimated)
Membership: Child $27; Senior Citizen & Military $35; Adult $45.

Towson

ASIAN ARTS & CULTURE CENTER, TOWSON UNIVERSITY, (M), Asian Arts & Culture Center, Towson University, 8000 York Rd., Towson, MD 21252-0001. Tel.: 410-704-2807. Fax: 410-704-4032.
E-mail: sshieh@towson.edu
Web Site: www.towson.edu/asianarts
Founded: 1971.
Congressional District: 2 & 3
Key Personnel: Dir., Mrs. Suewhei Shieh; Pres. (V), Anthony Montcalmo.
Personnel Profile: Full-Time Paid 1; Part-Time Paid 5; Part-Time Volunteers 20; Interns 1.
Governing Authority: university; nonprofit. Parent Institution: Towson University. Tax-exempt: 501(c)(3).
University Arts Center.
Collections: concentration on Asian art from neolithic to modern times.
Major Exhibits: Furniture for the Divine: Selections from the Foo Collection, 11/09-12/09; Aesthetics of the Sacred: Buddhist Arts of Tibet India & Southeast Asia, 2/10-5/10.
Facilities: 100-vol. library on Asian art; 2,000 sq. ft. exhibit space.
Activities: lectures; arts festivals; workshops; concerts; dance recitals; films; temporary, permanent, loan & traveling exhibitions. Annual Events: craft show & sale.
Publications: biannual newsletter.
Hours & Admission Prices: Mon.-Fri. 11-4, Sat. 1-4; call to confirm hours. Exhibits: no charge. Special Events: adults $8-$15; discounts to senior citizens, students, & museum members. Closed Easter; Christmas; national holidays. ♿
Attendance: 10,000 (estimated)
Membership: Individual $35; Family & Dual $60; Crane Club $100-$249; Tiger $250-$499; Phoenix Circle $500-$999; Dragon Circle $1,000 & up; Jade Circle $2,500.

HAMPTON NATIONAL HISTORIC SITE, 535 Hampton Lane, Towson, MD 21286-1397. Tel.: 410-823-1309. Fax: 410-823-8394.
Web Site: www.nps.gov/hamp
Founded: 1948.
Congressional District: 1
Key Personnel: Supt., Laurie Coughlan; Gen. Supt., Gay Vietzke; Volunteer Mgr., Kirby Shedlowski; Cur., Gregory Weidman; Museum Shop Mgr., Eileen Kalinoski.
Personnel Profile: Full-Time Paid 9; Part-Time Paid 1; Part-Time Volunteers 45; Interns 2.
Governing Authority: federal. Parent Institution: National Park Service. Affiliated with U.S. Dept. of the Interior, National Park Service, Washington, DC 20240. Tax-exempt.
Historic House & Site: c.1783-1790 late Georgian Mansion including slave quarters located on agricultural-industrial complex.
Collections: furniture & decorative objects c.1760-1948; English landscape park & formal Italian gardens; specimen trees; 27 historic structures including dairy & slave quarters; archives; 5,000 historic photographs.
Research Fields: decorative arts; history; architecture; gardening; ethnography.
Facilities: mansion; stables & plantation dependencies; formal gardens; reconstructed Orangery. Museum-related items for sale.
Activities: guided tours; self-guided walking tour; lectures. Museum Sponsors: Second Sunday Programs.
Publications: brochure; cookbook; guidebook; walking tour guide of gardens & grounds; site bulletins.
Hours & Admission Prices: Mansion: daily 9-4. Grounds: daily 9-5. Tours: daily 9-4 (advanced reservation required for 10 or more). No charge; donations accepted. Closed New Year's Day; Thanksgiving; Christmas. ♿
Attendance: 30,000 (estimated)
Membership: Historic Hampton, Inc.: Senior Citizen $25; Individual $30; Family $45; Sponsor $100; Patron $250.

Union Bridge

WESTERN MARYLAND RAILWAY HISTORICAL SOCIETY, 41 N. Main St., Union Bridge, MD 21791-9100. Mailing Address: P.O. Box 395, Union Bridge, MD 21791-0395. Tel.: 410-775-0150.
Founded: 1967.
Key Personnel: Chm. (V), Stan Johnson; Pres. (V), Dennis Wertz; Museum Shop Mgr., Leo Armentroit
Historical Society Museum.
Collections: railroad history & artifacts; photographs.

Hours & Admission Prices: Sun. 1-4, Wed. 9-12 & 1-3; other times by appointment. No charge; donations accepted. Closed New Year's Day; Easter; Christmas.
Membership: U.S. $30; International $50.

Upper Marlboro

DARNALL'S CHANCE HOUSE MUSEUM, M-NCPPC, 14800 Gov. Oden Bowie Dr., Upper Marlboro, MD 20772-3073. Tel.: 301-952-8010. Fax: 301-952-1773.
E-mail: susan.reidy@pgparks.com
Web Site: www.pgparks.com
Founded: 1988.
Congressional District: 5
Key Personnel: Natural & Historical Resources Div. Mgr., Christopher Wagnon; Dir., Susan Reidy.
Personnel Profile: Full-Time Paid 1; Part-Time Paid 3; Part-Time Volunteers 10.
Governing Authority: county. Parent Institution: Maryland National Capital Park & Planning Commission. Subsidiary Institution: Natural & Historical Resources Div. Tax-exempt.
Historic House: 1742, 18th century home of James and Lettice Wardrop.
Collections: archaeological artifacts; c. 18th C. underground brick burial vault; period furniture.
Research Fields: archaeology; burial vaults; county history.
Facilities: rental facilities.
Activities: guided tours; lectures; permanent, temporary & loan exhibitions; rental facilities; weddings; meetings. Annual Events: Upper Marlboro Day; Colonial Tavern Dinners; Gingerbread House Contest & Show; Ghost Walk.
Hours & Admission Prices: Tues.-Thurs. tours by appointment, Fri. & Sun. 12-4. Call for additional information. Closed major holidays. ♿
Attendance: 4,647 (accurate)

MERKLE WILDLIFE SANCTUARY & VISITOR CENTER, 11704 Fenno Rd., Upper Marlboro, MD 20772-8179. Tel.: 301-888-1377; 800-784-5380.
Web Site: www.dnr.state.md.us/publiclands/merkletrails.html
Wildlife Sanctuary.
Collections: wildlife & their habitats; natural history; ecology.
Facilities: nature trails.
Activities: hiking; bird watching.
Hours & Admission Prices: Grounds: daily 7-sunset. Visitor Center: Sat.-Sun. 10-4.

THE PATUXENT RURAL LIFE MUSEUMS, Patuxent River Park, 16000 Croom Airport Rd., Upper Marlboro, MD 20772-8395. Mailing Address: 6706 Green Landing Rd., Upper Marlboro, MD 20772-7618. Tel.: 301-627-6074. Fax: 301-627-7085. TDD: 301-699-2544.
E-mail: mary.haley-amen@pgparks.com
Web Site: www.pgparks.com/places/eleganthistoric/patuxent_intro.html
Formerly: W. Henry Duvall Tool Museum
Founded: 1983.
Key Personnel: Dir., Mary Haley-Amen.
Personnel Profile: Full-Time Paid 1; Part-Time Paid 4; Part-Time Volunteers 10.
Governing Authority: county; nonprofit. Parent Institution: Patuxent River Park. Tax-exempt.
Tool Museum.
Collections: farm tools; dental office; hand tools; storekeeper's supplies; domestic items; carpenter tools.
Facilities: 20-vol. library of tool guides.
Activities: guided tours.
Hours & Admission Prices: April-Oct. Sat.-Sun. 1-4; other times by appointment. Guided Tours: by appointment. Sat.-Sun. no charge. ♿
Attendance: 2,158 (accurate)

Walkersville

FOUNTAIN ROCK NATURE CENTER, 8511 Nature Center Place, Walkersville, MD 21793-8325. Tel.: 301-898-1460.
Web Site: www.co.frederick.md.us/index.asp?nid=2934
Founded: 1990.
Key Personnel: Park Naturalist, Alice Nemitsas.
Personnel Profile: Full-Time Paid 1; Part-Time Paid 16; Part-Time Volunteers 40.
Governing Authority: county; nature council; nonprofit. Tax-exempt: 501(c)(3).
Nature Center.
Collections: wildlife mounts; working & observational honeybee hive; water spring; wetland, woodland & field habitats; 1872 battery of limestone kilns; hands-on exhibits; natural history; Native American artifacts; live animals including snakes, toads, turtles & insects.
Facilities: 22.5 acres in county park; nature trails.
Activities: nature programs; educational birthday parties.
Publications: The Recreater.
Hours & Admission Prices: 8am to sunset; groups by appointment. No charge. Nature Programs: adults $5, children $4. Closed holidays. ♿
Attendance: 10,000 (estimated)

WALKERSVILLE SOUTHERN RAILROAD MUSEUM, 34 W. Pennsylvania Ave., Walkersville, MD 21793-8505. Mailing Address: P.O. Box 651, Walkersville, MD 21793-0651. Tel.: 301-898-0899; 877-363-WSRR (toll free).
E-mail: musdir@wsrr.org
Web Site: www.wsrr.org/museum.htm
Founded: 1995.
Key Personnel: Dir., Paul Kovalcik
Railroad History Museum.
Collections: railroad history; model railroad; Pennsylvania Railroad magazine ads, timetables & documents. Historic Buildings: railroad station; freight house.
Activities: ride 1920s passenger car.
Hours & Admission Prices: Museum: call for hours. Train: May-June & Sept. Sat.-Sun. 11am & 2pm; Oct. Sat.-Sun. 11am, 1pm & 3pm; July-Aug. Sat. 11am & 2pm; additional special event hours. Adults $9, seniors over 55 $8, children $5; children under 3 no charge.

Warwick

OLD BOHEMIA HISTORICAL SOCIETY, Bohemia Church Rd., Warwick, MD 21912. Mailing Address: P.O. Box 61, Warwick, MD 21912. Tel.: 302-328-4803.
Founded: 1953.
Congressional District: 1
Key Personnel: Pres. & Museum Shop Mgr., Margaret Matyniak; Pastor, Rev. Steven B. Giuliano.
Personnel Profile: Part-Time Volunteers 10.
Governing Authority: society. Parent Institution: Catholic Diocese Foundation. Tax-exempt: 501(c)(3).
Historical Society Museum: 1704 Jesuit mission site, 1797 church, rectory with museum of religious artifacts (liturgical vessels, vestments, prayer books, devotional articles), barn with farm conveyances & tools, historic cemetery.
Collections: old furniture & church-related articles; patens; chalices; farm equipment; history & religious books; tools.
Facilities: restoration & maintenance of historic shrine.
Activities: religious & educational activities.
Hours & Admission Prices: Call for hours. No charge; donations accepted.
Attendance: 700 (estimated)
Membership: Annual $15; 3 yr. $40; Benefactor $100.

Westernport

WESTERNPORT HERITAGE SOCIETY, Maryland Ave., Westernport, MD 21562.
E-mail: westernport@mail.gcnet.net
Heritage Society Museum.
Collections: local history & heritage; photographs; G-scale train; HO-scale railcars.
Hours & Admission Prices: 2nd & 4th Sat.-Sun. 1-4.

Westminster

CARROLL COUNTY FARM MUSEUM, (M), 500 S. Center St., Westminster, MD 21157-5664. Tel.: 410-386-3880. Fax: 410-876-8544. TDD: 410-848-3017.
E-mail: ccfarm@ccg.carr.org
Web Site: www.carrollcountyfarmmuseum.org
Founded: 1965.
Congressional District: 6
Key Personnel: Admin., Dottie Freeman; Admin. Office Assoc., Susan Dell; Cur., Victoria Fowler; Museum Shop Mgr., Emma Beaver; Mktg., Jackie Koch; Events Coord., Sharon Martin.
Personnel Profile: Full-Time Paid 10; Part-Time Paid 5; Part-Time Volunteers 100.
Governing Authority: county; nonprofit. Parent Institution: Carroll County Government. Tax-exempt.
Agricultural & Historical Museum: housed in c.1852 historic building on 142 acres.

Collections: artifacts relating to the lifestyle of rural 19th-century Carroll County & rural America.
Facilities: 600-vol. library on agriculture, farm equipment, farm life & archives available for inter-library loan & to the public upon request; nature trail. Museum-related items for sale.
Activities: formal education programs for children; guided tours; artisan workshops; temporary exhibitions; weddings; receptions; reunions; picnics. Annual Events: Civil War Encampment; Fiddler's Convention; Old Fashioned July 4th Celebration; Spring Muster & Antique Fire Equipment Show; Living History Camp; Steam Show Days; The Maryland Wine Festival; Blacksmith Day; Fall Harvest Days; Holiday Visit; Specialty Teas; Learning Lunch Talks; Surf & Turf Festival.
Publications: calendar of events; fliers; brochures; rack cards.
Hours & Admission Prices: May-June & Sept.-Oct. Sat.-Sun. 12-5; July-Aug. Tues.-Fri. 10-4, Sat.-Sun. 12-5; group tours by reservation only. Adults $5, students 7-18 and senior citizens 60 & over $3; discounts to groups & AAM members; children 6 & under & members no charge. ♿
Attendance: 100,000 (accurate)
Membership: Individual $30; Family $60; Lifetime $300.

HISTORICAL SOCIETY OF CARROLL COUNTY, (M), 210 E. Main St., Westminster, MD 21157-5225. Tel.: 410-848-6494. Fax: 410-848-3596.
E-mail: hscc@carr.org
Web Site: hscc.carr.org
Founded: 1939.
Key Personnel: Exec. Dir., Timatha S. Pierce; Chm. (V), David H. Roush; Treas., Arthur Palaia; Mgr. Operations, Linda Cunfer; Cur., Cathy Baty; Administrative Asst., Donna Hewitt.
Personnel Profile: Full-Time Paid 3; Part-Time Paid 1; Part-Time Volunteers 150.
Governing Authority: private; nonprofit organization. Tax-exempt: 501(c)(3).
Historical Society Museum: housed in Kimmey House; c.1800
Collections: history & culture of Carroll County; photographs; clothing; quilts; ceramics & glass; furniture; clocks. Historic Houses: c.1807 Sherman-Fisher-Shellman House, contains personal artifacts depicting the life of a Pennsylvania German family; c.1820 Cockey's Tavern.
Facilities: 1,000-vol. library; 1,200 sq. ft. exhibit space; learning center. Museum-related items for sale.
Activities: docent program; guided tours; lectures; broadcast programs; temporary exhibits; monthly box lunch talks. Annual Events: County Birthday Celebration; Maryland in the Civil War seminar; Antiques Appraisal Day.
Publications: quarterly newsletter, Carroll Courier; various books available related to local history; Carroll History Journal.
Hours & Admission Prices: Office: Mon.-Fri. 8:30-5. Library: Tues.-Fri. 9:30-12:30 & 1-4, 2nd & 4th Sat. 9-12. Gallery: Tues.-Fri. 12:30-4:30, Sat.-Sun. by appointment. No charge; donations accepted. Sherman-Fisher Shellman House Museum: adults $3; members no charge. Closed New Year's Day; Martin Luther King Jr. Day; Presidents' Day; Good Friday; Memorial Day; Independence Day; Labor Day; Thanksgiving Day & day after; Christmas Day & day after. ♿
Attendance: 3,000 (estimated)
Membership: Senior Individual & Student $25; Individual $40; Senior Couple $45; Family $60; Business $250.

UNION MILLS HOMESTEAD & GRIST MILL, 3311 Littlestown Pike, Westminster, MD 21158-2137. Tel.: 410-848-2288.
E-mail: ejss61@aol.com
Web Site: www.unionmills.org
Founded: 1797.
Congressional District: 6
Key Personnel: Dir. & Museum Shop Mgr., Jane S. Sewell; Pres. Bd., Dr. Brian Lockard.
Personnel Profile: Full-Time Paid 1; Part-Time Paid 2; Part-Time Volunteers 40.
Governing Authority: nonprofit foundation; Union Mills Homestead Foundation. Administered for Carroll County Commissioners. Tax-exempt: 501(c)(3).
Historic House Museum: 1797 Shriver Homestead and Mill.
Collections: 18th-century mill & homestead containing original household & agricultural items.
Research Fields: Shriver family archives; social, industrial, political & architectural history surrounding the homestead.
Facilities: library of 19th-century books, periodicals & photographs available for research by personal request. Local craft items, cards & other museum-related items for sale.
Activities: classroom presentations; hands-on exhibits; guided tours; flower & plant market; grist mill grinding corn, wheat & buckwheat. Museum Sponsors: Flower Plant Market in May; Old Fashioned Ice Cream Sundae Social in July; Old-fashioned Corn Roast in August; Microbrewery Festival in September; fund-raiser events.
Publications: quarterly newsletter; pamphlet & booklet.
Hours & Admission Prices: May & Sept. Sat.-Sun. 12-4; June-Sept. 1 Tues.-Fri. 10-4, Sat.-Sun. 12-4; bus tours by appointment. Adults $5, children 6-12 $3; discounts to groups & senior citizens; members no charge. Combination ticket for house & mill: adults $5, children 6-12 $3. Closed Independence Day.
Attendance: 10,000 (estimated)
Membership: Individual $20; Husband & Wife $25; Family & Institutional $30; Life $200.

Wheaton

BROOKSIDE GARDENS, 1800 Glenallan Ave., Wheaton, MD 20902-1369. Tel.: 301-962-1400. Fax: 301-962-7878.
Web Site: www.brooksidegardens.org
Founded: 1969.
Key Personnel: Dir., Stephanie Oberle; Mgr. Plant Collection, Philip Normandy; Supvr., Joe Krout; Supvr. Enterprise, Ellen Hartranft.
Personnel Profile: Full-Time Paid 28; Part-Time Paid 25; Part-Time Volunteers 300.
Governing Authority: county. Affiliated with The Maryland National Capital Park & Planning Commission, 8787 Georgia Ave., Silver Spring, MD 20910. Tel.: 301-495-4500. Tax-exempt: 170(b)(1)(A).
Botanical Garden.
Collections: flower gardens; hardy trees & shrubs; display conservatories.
Research Fields: testing & evaluation of plant collection from Japan.
Facilities: 3,000-vol. reference library of books, periodicals, handouts & catalogs available for research on premises; botanical gardens.
Activities: guided tours; lectures; formally organized education programs for children & adults; bus & van trips to regional horticultural institutions; special events.
Publications: horticulture information handouts, Adult Education Programs.
Hours & Admission Prices: Visitor Center: daily 9-5. North Conservatory: daily 10-5. Gardens: sunrise-sunset. No charge; donations accepted. Closed Christmas Day. ♿
Attendance: 320,000 (estimated)

Wye Mills

WYE GRIST MILL, 900 Wye Mills Rd., Wye Mills, MD 21679. Mailing Address: P.O. Box 277, Wye Mills, MD 21679-0277. Tel.: 410-827-3850.
E-mail: oldwyemill@atlanticbbn.net
Web Site: oldwyemill.org
History Museum.
Collections: Maryland's agricultural heritage; milling equipment; farm equipment. Historic Structure: working water-powered grist mill.
Research Fields: eastern shore agriculture; milling.
Hours & Admission Prices: mid-April to mid-Nov. Mon.-Sat. 10-4, Sun. 1-4. Tours: by appointment. Suggested Donation: $2.

MASSACHUSETTS

(394 listings)

Abington

DYER MEMORIAL LIBRARY, 28 Centre Ave., Abington, MA 02351-2228. Mailing Address: P.O. Box 2245, Abington, MA 02351-0745. Tel.: 781-878-8480.
E-mail: info@dyerlibrary.org
Web Site: www.dyerlibrary.org
Founded: 1932.
Congressional District: 11
Key Personnel: Dir., Joice Himawan; Librarian, Pamela Whiting.
Personnel Profile: Full-Time Paid 1; Part-Time Paid 3.
Governing Authority: trust. Tax-exempt: 501(c)(3).
General Museum.
Collections: local history & genealogy.
Research Fields: local history; genealogy.
Facilities: 15,000-vol. library of local history books & genealogy available for research on premises only; reading room.
Activities: guided tours; lectures; slides; formally organized educational programs; school loan service.
Publications: Old Abington in the American Revolution; The North Abington Riot; Heritage Trail.
Hours & Admission Prices: Tues.-Fri. 1-5, 2nd & 4th Sat. 12-4; other times by appointment. No charge; donations accepted. Closed holidays.
Attendance: 1,200 (estimated)

Acton

THE DISCOVERY MUSEUMS, 177 Main St., Acton, MA 01720-3647. Tel.: 978-264-4200. Fax: 978-264-0210.
Web Site: www.discoverymuseums.org
Founded: 1982.
Congressional District: 5
Key Personnel: Pres. Bd. (V), Lees Stuntz; Exec. Dir., Neil H. Gordon; Dir. Education Science Discovery Museum, Denise LeBlanc; Assoc. Dir. Education Science Discovery Museum, Margaret Wimikates; Dir. Education, Amy Spencer; Dir. Finance & Business Admin., Kavita Katti; Dir. Devel. & Communications, Claudia Veitch; Dir. School Programs, Jill Foster; Dir. Mktg., Vicki Greene; Dir. Exhibits, Steve Roake.
Personnel Profile: Full-Time Paid 12; Part-Time Paid 55; Part-Time Volunteers 50; Interns 3.
Governing Authority: nonprofit organization. Parent Institution: The Discovery Museums, Inc. Subsidiary Institutions: The Children's Discovery Museum; The Science Discovery Museum. Tax-exempt: 501(c)(3).
Children's Museums: consisting of The Children's Discovery Museum, housed in a 10-room Victorian house, and The Science Discovery Museum.
Collections: Children's Museum: hands-on interactive exhibit rooms including: Train Room, Discovery Ship, Bessie's Play Diner, & Sensations. Science Museum: interactive exhibits with scientific themes including Inventor's Workshop, Math Room, Light & Color Room, Water Room, Earth Science, Sound & Communication, Electricity, Magnets and Nature Balcony.
Facilities: 4 acres of wooded land; woodland path abutted by 200 acres of conservation land; discovery classroom; birthday parties; corporate events.
Activities: self-guided tours; organized education programs for children; teacher training; school outreach; participatory exhibits; collaborative partnerships with schools & universities; day camp in July & August; after-school discovery programs; workshops; Scout programs; weekly science drop-in workshops; science classes.
Publications: quarterly newsletter, Discovery Digest; flyer.
Hours & Admission Prices: Call for hours. One Museum: $9 per person; Two Museums: $13 per person; discount to groups; members, children under 1, museum staff plus one guest no charge. Closed Independence Day; Labor Day; Thanksgiving Eve & Day; Christmas Eve & Day. ♿
Attendance: 140,000 (estimated)

Agawam

AGAWAM HISTORICAL & FIRE HOUSE MUSEUM, 35 Elm St., Agawam, MA 01001-2407. Mailing Address: P.O. Box 552, Agawam, MA 01001-0552. Tel.: 413-786-4631.
Fire-Fighting Museum.
Collections: antique fire engines & apparatus; photographs.
Hours & Admission Prices: Call for hours.

Amesbury

THE BARTLETT MUSEUM, (M), 270 Main St., Amesbury, MA 01913. Mailing Address: P.O. Box 692, Amesbury, MA 01913-0016. Tel.: 978-388-4528.
E-mail: museum@bartlettmuseum.org
Web Site: bartlettmuseum.org
Founded: 1968.
Congressional District: 6
Key Personnel: Pres. (V), Richard Gale; Treas. (V), Steven Klomps; Dir., Hazel Kray.
Personnel Profile: Part-Time Paid 1.
Governing Authority: nonprofit organization. Tax-exempt.
History Museum: housed in 1870 Old Victorian School House.
Collections: local artifacts; natural history; carriage trade; Victorian schoolroom; bird collection; Indian artifacts; old tools & implements; paintings of early Amesbury residents. Historic Building: c.1880 Salisbury Point Waiting Station.
Research Fields: genealogy; area sites.
Facilities: 100-vol. library of books written by local personages available by special permission only. Books, leaflets, brochures & maps for sale.
Activities: guided tours; lectures; films; concerts; arts festivals; hobby workshops; sound slide shows pertaining to carriages & churches of Amesbury; formally organized education programs; inter-museum loan, permanent & temporary exhibitions. Museum Sponsors: Genealogy Group.
Publications: quarterly newsletter.
Hours & Admission Prices: Memorial Day weekend to Labor Day Fri. & Sun. 1-4, Sat. 10-4; other times by appointment. Adults $3, children & senior citizens $1; AAM & museum members no charge.
Attendance: 1,000 (estimated)
Membership: Student $1; Adult $10; Family $20; Sustaining $25 & up.

LOWELL'S BOAT SHOP, 459 Main St., Amesbury, MA 01913-4207. Tel.: 978-834-0050.
E-mail: info@lowellsboatshop.com
Web Site: www.lowellsboatshop.com
Founded: 1793.
Congressional District: 6
Key Personnel: Exec. Dir. & Museum Shop Mgr., Pam Bates; Chm., George O'Dell; Chm., Steven Batchelder; Pres., Sally McKay.
Personnel Profile: Full-Time Paid 1; Full-Time Volunteers 4; Part-Time Paid 1; Part-Time Volunteers 30; Interns 2.
Governing Authority: Parent Institution: Lowell's Maritime Foundation. Tax-exempt.
Historic Buildings: housed in 19th century boat building shop.
Collections: fleet of dories; patterns; handtools; business papers; working shop.
Research Fields: wooden boatbuilding of lower Merrimac Valley; relationship & impact of dories on Gulf of Maine fisheries.
Facilities: working 19th century shop & equipment; education center; river landing site.
Activities: boat building, on-the-water educational programs; dory model classes; seasonal rowing; tours.
Hours & Admission Prices: May-Oct. Tues.-Fri. 11-4, Sat.-Sun. 12-4; Nov.-April Tues.-Fri. 11-4. Office: Mon.-Fri. 10-5. Adults 15 & over $8, children 7-14 $6; discounts to members; children under 7 no charge. ♿
Attendance: 1,340 (estimated)
Membership: Single $35; Crew $60; Centennial $100; Quartermaster $250; Steward $500.

WHITTIER HOME ASSOCIATION, (M), 86 Friend St., Amesbury, MA 01913. Mailing Address: P.O. Box 632, Amesbury, MA 01913-0014. Tel.: 978-388-1337. Fax: 978-388-1337.
E-mail: whittierhome@verizon.net
Web Site: www.whittierhome.org
Formerly: John Greenleaf Whittier Home
Founded: 1898.
Congressional District: 6
Key Personnel: Pres. (V), Cynthia C. Costello; Museum Shop Mgr., Dianne Cole.
Personnel Profile: Part-Time Paid 1.
Governing Authority: nonprofit organization. Tax-exempt.
Historic House: 1820 home of poet & abolitionist John Greenleaf Whittier.
Collections: manuscripts; books; pictures; original furniture & furnishings.
Research Fields: 19th century literature & poetry; life & work of J. G. Whittier; inventory of Whittier's works; local history.
Facilities: approx. 1,000-vol. library of literature & history books available on premises by appointment; garden. Postcards & books for sale.
Activities: guided tours; permanent exhibitions.
Publications: brochure.
Hours & Admission Prices: May-Oct. Wed. & Sat. 11-4; last tour 3:30; other times by appointment. Adults $6, seniors & students $5, children 7-17 $3; discounts to AAM & ICOM members & groups; members & children under 7 no charge. Closed Thanksgiving; Christmas.
Attendance: 400 (accurate)
Membership: Active $25.

Amherst

AMHERST COLLEGE MUSEUM OF NATURAL HISTORY, Amherst College, 11 Barrett Hill Rd., Amherst, MA 01002-5000. Tel.: 413-542-2165. Fax: 413-542-2713.
E-mail: llthomas@amherst.edu
Web Site: www.amherst.edu/mm/44872
Formerly: Pratt Museum of Natural History
Founded: 1848.
Key Personnel: Dir., Tekla Harms; Mgr. Collections, Kate Wellspring; Coord. Education, Steve Sauter.
Personnel Profile: Full-Time Paid 1; Part-Time Paid 3; Part-Time Volunteers 4; Interns 1.
Governing Authority: college. Parent Institution: Amherst College. Tax-exempt.
Natural History Museum.
Collections: paleontology; geology; ostcology; mineralogy; taxidermy; anthropology; ichnology.
Research Fields: vertebrate & invertebrate paleontology; ichnology; geology.
Facilities: library; laboratory.
Activities: prearranged guided group tours; formally organized education programs; permanent exhibitions.
Publications: self-guided tour sheets for Vertebrate Fossil & Mineral Exhibits; brochure; postcard.
Hours & Admission Prices: Academic Year: Tues.-Wed. & Fri.-Sun. 11-4, Thurs. 11-4 & 6-10; Summer: Sat. 10-4, Sun. 12-5. No charge. Closed holidays. ♿

Attendance: 25,000 (accurate)

AMHERST HISTORY MUSEUM AT THE STRONG HOUSE - AMHERST HISTORICAL SOCIETY, 67 Amity St., Amherst, MA 01002-2214. Tel.: 413-256-0678. Fax: 413-256-0672.
E-mail: amhersthistory@yahoo.com
Web Site: www.amhersthistory.org
Founded: 1899.
Key Personnel: Dir., Pat Lutz; Pres., Arthur Kinney.
Personnel Profile: Full-Time Paid 1; Part-Time Volunteers 25; Interns 4.
Governing Authority: society; nonprofit. Parent Institution: Amherst Historical Society. Tax-exempt: 501(c)(3).
History Museum/History Site: housed in c.1750 Strong house. Listed on the National Register of Historic Places.
Collections: decorative arts; textiles; photographs; period clothing; household tools; folk arts; furniture; weaponry; tools; local history artifacts.
Facilities: 18th-century garden. Museum-related items for sale.
Activities: guided tours; lectures; organized programs for children; temporary exhibitions; school loan service. Museum Sponsors: Garden Tour; Victorian Christmas House; House Tour.
Publications: quarterly newsletter.
Hours & Admission Prices: May-Nov. Wed.-Sat. 12-4. Adults $5, seniors, students & children $3; discounts to AAM members; children 6 & under and Amherst Historical Society members no charge.
Attendance: 2,400 (estimated)
Membership: Senior & Student $18; Individual $20; Family $35; Donor & Business $50-$149; Patron $150 & up.

EMILY DICKINSON MUSEUM: THE HOMESTEAD AND THE EVERGREENS, (M), 280 Main St., Amherst, MA 01002-2349. Tel.: 413-542-8161. Fax: 413-542-2152.
E-mail: info@emilydickinsonmuseum.org
Web Site: www.emilydickinsonmuseum.org
Formerly: Dickinson Homestead
Founded: 2003.
Congressional District: 1
Key Personnel: Exec. Dir., Jane H. Wald; Dir. Interpretation & Programming, Cindy Dickinson; Chm. (V), Kent W. Faerber.
Personnel Profile: Full-Time Paid 2; Part-Time Paid 30; Part-Time Volunteers 10; Interns 2.
Governing Authority: private college; nonprofit. Parent Institution: Amherst College. Tax-exempt: 501(c)(3).
Historic Houses: The Dickinson Homestead c.1813, birthplace & home of poet Emily Dickinson; The Evergreens 1856, home of the poet's brother Austin & sister-in-law Susan.
Collections: 19th-century furniture; decorative arts related to the Dickinson family.
Facilities: Books & postcards for sale.
Activities: docent program; guided tours; school programs; special programs; landscape tour Museum Sponsors: poetry walk in May; poetry garden series in July; birthday open house & birthday lecture in December.
Publications: Emily Dickinson: The Poet at Home c.2000; electronic newsletter.
Hours & Admission Prices: March-May & Sept.-Dec. Wed.-Sun. 11-4; June-Aug. Wed.-Sun. 10-5. Guided Tours: call for information. Closed major holidays. ♿
Attendance: 12,000 (accurate)

THE ERIC CARLE MUSEUM OF PICTURE BOOK ART, 125 W. Bay Rd., Amherst, MA 01002-3357. Tel.: 413-658-1145 & 1100. Fax: 413-658-1139.
Web Site: www.carlemuseum.org
Founded: 2001.
Key Personnel: Exec. Dir., Alexandra Kennedy; Chief Cur., H. Nichols B. Clark; Chm. (V), Chris Milne; Dir. Devel., Rebecca Miller Goggins; Cur. Education, Rosemary Agoglia; Dir. Finance & Administration, Andrea Powers; Registrar, Heidi O'Neill; Mgr. Facilities, John Stark; Mgr. Mktg., Sandy Soderberg; Museum Shop Mgr., Andrew Laties.
Personnel Profile: Full-Time Paid 14; Part-Time Paid 9; Part-Time Volunteers 25; Interns 4.
Governing Authority: private; nonprofit organization. Tax-exempt: 501(c)(3).
Art Museum.
Collections: original picture book art from around the world.
Major Exhibits: 80/40 Continuing the Celebration and Exploring the Undersea World with Eric Carle's Mister Seahorse and A House for Hermit Crab, 11/09-3/21/10; Golden Legacy: Original Art from 65 Years of Golden Books, 11/24/09-2/10; Mother Goose in an Air Ship: McLoughlin Bros. 19th Century Children's Books from the Liman Collection, 11/24/09-4/18/10; Into the Wood: Antonio Frasconi's Art for Children, 3/23/10-6/13/10; Eric Carle/Recent Acquisitions, 4/6/10-9/5/10; Leo Lionni: Geraldine, The Music Mouse, 5/4/10-11/28/10; Lisbeth Zwerger, 7/6/10-9/26/10; Eric Carle/Recent Acquisitions, 9/21/10-3/20/11; Monsters and Miracles: A Journey Through Jewish Picture Books (T), 10/26/10-1/23/11; The Carle Collection, 12/14/10-5/1/11.
Research Fields: picture book art & artists; connection between visual & verbal literacy.
Facilities: 3,800-vol. library; 137-seat auditorium; 60-seat cafeteria; art studio; 6,000 sq. ft. exhibit space. Museum-related items for sale.
Activities: arts festival; concerts; dance recitals; docent program; films; formal education programs; guided tours; lectures; loan, participatory, traveling & temporary exhibitions; theater; training programs; studio classes; teacher training. Annual Event: Summer Reading Festival With the Western Massachusetts Illustrators Guild; The Carle Honors Awards Event in the Field of Picture Book Art.
Publications: newsletter, Sowing the Seeds.
Hours & Admission Prices: July-Aug. & MA School Vacation Weeks Mon.-Fri. 10-4, Sat. 10-5, Sun. 12-5; Sept.-June Tues.-Fri. 10-4, Sat. 10-5, Sun. 12-5. Adults $9, senior citizens & children $6; discount to groups & AAM members; members no charge. Closed New Year's Day; Independence Day; Thanksgiving; Christmas Eve & Day. ♿
Attendance: 47,860 (accurate)
Membership: Student $20; Senior $30; Teacher, Librarian & National Associate $35; Individual $45; Family $65; Art Associate & Organizational $125; Studio Sponsor $250; Picture Book Patron $500; Founder's Society $1,000; Director's Guild $2,500; Chairman's Circle $5,000.

* **MEAD ART MUSEUM, (M),** Amherst College, Amherst, MA 01002. Mailing Address: Amherst College, P.O. Box 5000, Amherst, MA 01002-5000. Tel.: 413-542-2335. Fax: 413-542-2117.
E-mail: mead@amherst.edu
Web Site: www.amherst.edu/museums/mead
Founded: 1821.
Congressional District: 1
Key Personnel: Dir. & Chief Cur., Elizabeth Barker; Pres. Amherst College, Anthony W. Marx; Preparator, Timothy Gilfillan; Accounting, Mktg. & Web Mgr., Karen Cardinal; Collections Mgr., Stephen S. Fisher; Asst. to Dir., Teddy O'Connor.
Personnel Profile: Full-Time Paid 9; Part-Time Paid 42; Part-Time Volunteers 1; Interns 2.
Governing Authority: college. Parent Institution: Amherst College. Tax-exempt: 501(c)(3).
Art Museum.
Collections: American paintings; sculpture; prints & photos; drawings & watercolors; decorative arts; additional works: Asian; Ancient Pre-Columbian; Mexican; African.
Major Exhibits: Selected Objects from the Mead's Permanent Collection, 11/09-12/10.
Research Fields: art history.
Facilities: auditorium.
Activities: lectures; films; formally organized education programs for undergraduate college students affiliated with Amherst, University of Massachusetts, Smith, Mt. Holyoke & Hampshire Colleges; inter-museum loan & temporary exhibitions.
Publications: occasional catalogs, brochures, calendars.
Hours & Admission Prices: Academic Season: Tues.-Thurs. & Sun. 9am to midnight, Fri.-Sat. 9-5. Academic Recess: Tues.-Sun. 9-5, 1st Thurs. of month 9-8. No charge; donations accepted. ♿
Attendance: 36,000 (estimated)

NATIONAL YIDDISH BOOK CENTER, Harry & Jeanette Weinberg Bldg., 1021 West St., Amherst, MA 01002-3375. Tel.: 413-256-4900. Fax: 413-256-4700.
E-mail: yiddish@bikher.org
Web Site: www.yiddishbookcenter.org
Founded: 1980.
Congressional District: 1
Key Personnel: Pres., Aaron Lansky; Chm. (V), Lief D. Rosenblatt; Dir. Visitors Center, Jane Gronau.
Personnel Profile: Full-Time Paid 21; Part-Time Paid 2; Part-Time Volunteers 10; Interns 18.
Governing Authority: Tax-exempt.
Jewish Cultural Organization.
Collections: Eastern European Jewish history & culture, with the focus on Yiddish literature.
Facilities: 1,000,000-vol. library. Books for sale.
Activities: films; lectures; concerts; performances; exhibits; tours.
Publications: magazine, English-language magazine, Pakn Treger; English-language brochures.
Hours & Admission Prices: Mon.-Fri. 10-4, Sun. 11-4. No charge; donations accepted. Closed Jewish & national holidays. ♿

Attendance: 11,000 (accurate)
Membership: Member $36.

NATURAL HISTORY COLLECTIONS, Univ. of Massachusetts, Rm. 146 Morrill 2, 622 N. Pleasant St., Amherst, MA 01002-1526. Mailing Address: 611 N. Pleasant St., Amherst, MA 01003. Tel.: 413-577-2303. Fax: 413-545-3243.
E-mail: bdumont@bio.umass.edu
Web Site: bcrc.bio.umass.edu/ummnh
Formerly: Museum of Zoology
Founded: 1863.
Congressional District: 1
Key Personnel: Dir., Elizabeth Dumont; Cur. Amphibians & Reptiles, Alan Richmond; Collection Mgr., Katherine Doyle.
Governing Authority: university. Affiliated with University of Massachusetts.
Zoology Museum.
Collections: preserved animals of all groups.
Research Fields: anatomy; ecology; systematics.
Activities: formally organized education programs for undergraduate & graduate college students; loan exhibitions.
Hours & Admission Prices: Call for appointment. No charge. Closed state & national holidays. Exhibits not open to public. ♿

UNIVERSITY GALLERY, UNIVERSITY OF MASSACHUSETTS AT AMHERST, (M), University Gallery, Fine Arts Center, University of Massachusetts, 151 Presidents Drive, Office 2, Amherst, MA 01003-9331. Tel.: 413-545-3670. Fax: 413-545-2018.
E-mail: ugallery@acad.umass.edu
Web Site: www.umass.edu/fac/universitygallery
Founded: 1975.
Congressional District: 1
Key Personnel: Dir., Loretta Yarlow; Communications, Thonsey Keopanya; Education Cur., Eva Fierst; Gallery Mgr., Craig Allaben; Collections Registrar & Preparator, Justin Griswold.
Personnel Profile: Full-Time Paid 3; Part-Time Paid 2; Part-Time Volunteers 2; Interns 3.
Governing Authority: university. Parent Institution: Univ. of Massachusetts. Tax-exempt.
University Art Gallery.
Collections: 20th-century American photography, prints & drawings.
Research Fields: 20th-century prints, drawings, photographs, sculpture & painting.
Facilities: 6,533 sq. ft. exhibit space.
Activities: guided tours; lectures; films; gallery talks; formally organized education programs for undergraduate & graduate university students; temporary, traveling & loan exhibitions.
Publications: exhibition catalogues: Critical Perspectives in American Art, 1976; Selections From the Chase Manhattan Bank Art Collection, 1981; Bilge Friedlaender, 1976; Richard Fleischner, 1977; Late 19th Century American Drawings & Watercolors, 1977; Criticism of Photography, 1978; The Class of 1928 Photography Collection, 1978; Antonakos: Neons for the University of Massachusetts, 1978; Sam Gilliam: Indoor & Outdoor Paintings 1967-1978; John Walker, 1979; Al Souza: Photoworks 1974-1979; Sculpture on the Wall: Relief Sculpture of the Seventies, 1980; Jackie Ferrara, 1981; George Trakas, 1981; The Prints of Barnett Newman, 1983; Martin Puryear 1983; Mauro Staccioli, 1984; Domestic Tales, 1984; Ten, 1985; Mel Kendrick, 1985; Anish Kapoor 1987; Jeffrey Brosk: Prairie Dance, 1987; Beyond Light: Infrared Photography by Six New England Artists, l987; Daniel Buren, 1988; Francesc Torres: Belchite/South Bronx, 1988; Allen Wexler: Dining Rooms & Furniture for the Typical House, l989; Cristos Gianakos: Rampworks, 1989; In Site: Five Conceptual Artists from the Bay Area, 1991; brochure, Rita Myers: Phantom Cities, 1991; Ellen Phelan: From the Lives of Dolls, 1992; George Wardlaw: Exodus II; Alumni III, 1993; Traditional Artifacts from the South Pacific, 1993; Shirazeh Houshiary: Turning Around the Centre, 1994; Jin Soo Kim, 1994; Michele Blondel, 1994; In Vivo, 1995; Daisy Youngblood, 1996; Socks on my spoons: Ursula von Rydingsvard, 1996; The Thin Veneer: The Peoples of Bosnia & Their Disappearing Cultural Heritage, 1997; Something Else to See: Improvisational Bordering Styles in African-American Quilts, 1997; The Lois Beurman Torf Collection for the University of Massachusetts, 1997; Alumni IV, 1999; Primary Source: Roger Ackling, Dove Bradshaw & Sandy Gellis, 1999; Head to Toe: Impressing the Body, 2000; Soft White: Lighting Designs by Artists, 2000; Rolf Julius Black (Red), 2001; Natalie Alper, 2001; Brenda Zlamany, 2001; The Culture of Violence, 2002; Mandrake Tango, 2002.
Hours & Admission Prices: Feb. to mid-May & mid-Sept. to mid-Dec. Tues.-Fri. 11-4:30, Sat.-Sun. 2-5. No charge. ♿
Attendance: 12,600 (estimated)

Andover

ADDISON GALLERY OF AMERICAN ART, (M), Phillips Academy, Andover, MA 01810-4161. Mailing Address: 180 Main St., Andover, MA 01810-4166. Tel.: 978-749-4015. Fax: 978-749-4025.
E-mail: addison@andover.edu
Web Site: www.addisongallery.org
Founded: 1931.
Congressional District: 5
Key Personnel: Dir., Brian T. Allen; Assoc. Dir. & Cur., Susan Faxon; Cur., Allison Kemmerer; Dir. Education, Julie Bernson; Registrar, Denise J.H. Johnson.
Personnel Profile: Full-Time Paid 14; Part-Time Paid 9; Interns 2.
Governing Authority: nonprofit. Parent Institution: Phillips Academy. Tax-exempt.
Art Museum.
Collections: American art; paintings; sculpture; drawing; prints; 17th century-present photography; ship models.
Major Exhibits: Addison Reopening, 4/10-7/10; Sheila Hicks: Fifty Years (T), 11/10-2/11.
Research Fields: secondary school art education.
Activities: temporary exhibitions; lectures; films.
Publications: catalogs, Carroll Dunham Prints; Ipswich Days: Arthur Wesley Dow; William Wegman: Funney/Strange; Jennifer Bartlett: Early Plate Work; Sol Lewitt, 25 years of Wall Drawings 1968-1993; 1/4 in. scale models of American Sailing Ships; Addison Gallery of American Art: 65 years; Arthur Dove: A Retrospective; Joel Shapiro, 1971-1997; Terry Winters: Paintings, Drawings & Prints 1994-2004; Reinventing the West: The Photographs of Ansel Adams and Robert Adams; Riding 1st Class on the Titanic: Photographs by Nathan Lyons; Trisha Brown: Art and Dance in Dialogue; John O'Reilly; Miracle in the Scrap Heap: The Sculpture of Richard Stankiewicz; The Treasures of the Addison Gallery of American Art; Richard Serra.
Hours & Admission Prices: Reopening April 30. Sept.-July Tues.-Sat. 10-5, Sun. 1-5. No charge; donations accepted. ♿
Attendance: 30,000 (estimated)
Membership: Friends: $50; $100; $250; $500; $750; Director's Circle: $1,000; $2,500; $5,000; $10,000.

* **ANDOVER HISTORICAL SOCIETY, (M),** 97 Main St., Andover, MA 01810-3803. Tel.: 978-475-2236. Fax: 978-470-2741.
E-mail: info@andoverhistorical.org
Web Site: www.andoverhistorical.org
Founded: 1911.
Congressional District: 5
Key Personnel: Exec. Dir., Elaine Clements; Pres., Donald Robb; Museum Educator, Sarah Sycz.
Personnel Profile: Full-Time Paid 1; Part-Time Paid 5; Part-Time Volunteers 120.
Governing Authority: board of directors; nonprofit organization. Tax-exempt: 501(c)(3).
Local History Museum: c.1818-19 house & barn.
Collections: American & imported furnishings; costumes; textiles; household, agricultural & trade implements; photographs; genealogy & local history research materials. Historic House: c.1818 house & barn.
Research Fields: local history; architecture & decorative arts; genealogy.
Facilities: 3,500-vol. research library & archives, including Andover imprints, local & regional histories & documents, photographs, maps, architectural drawings, reference books & periodicals.
Activities: guided tours; lectures; educational programs; permanent & temporary exhibitions; workshops, outreach programs.
Publications: booklets, Andover A Century of Change: 1896-1996, The Townswoman's Andover, Historic Andover 325th Anniversary, Andover, Massachusetts 1946-1971; quarterly newsletter; walking tour brochures; catalog, Addison B. LeBoutillier: Andover Artist and Craftsman.
Hours & Admission Prices: Museum: Tues.-Sat. 1-4. Library: Tues.-Sat. 10-4 & by appointment. Office: Tues.-Fri. 10-4. No charge; donations accepted. Closed national holidays.
Attendance: 3,900 (accurate)
Membership: Student & Senior $20; Individual $25; Family & Dual $40; Contributor $75; Sustaining $100; Patron $250; Benefactor $500; Blanchard Circle $1,000.

ROBERT S. PEABODY MUSEUM OF ARCHAEOLOGY, (M), 175 Main St., Andover, MA 01810. Mailing Address: Phillips Academy, Andover, MA 01810-4161. Tel.: 978-749-4490. Fax: 978-749-4495.
E-mail: rspeabody@andover.edu
Web Site: www.andover.edu/rspeabody/
Founded: 1901.
Congressional District: 5

Key Personnel: Dir., Malinda S. Blustain; Chm. (V), Peabody Awborg; Chm. (V), Marshall P. Cloyd; Registrar & Sr. Collection Mgr., Bonnie Sousa; Honorary Cur., Eugene C. Winter; Educator, Donald Slater; Educator, Lindsay Randall; Asst. Collection Mgr., Marla Taylor.
Personnel Profile: Full-Time Paid 3; Part-Time Paid 2; Part-Time Volunteers 10; Interns 4.
Governing Authority: nonprofit organization. Parent Institution: Phillips Academy. Tax-exempt: 170(b)(1)(A).
Archaeology Museum.
Collections: archaeology of North America, emphasis on Northeast, Southeast, Midwest, Southwest, Mexico & the Arctic; collections from Maine, Massachusetts, Etowah, GA., Yukon, Mexico & Pecos, NM; Highland Maya & North America ethnology; anthropology.
Research Fields: American archaeology; social organization; acculturation.
Facilities: 5,000-vol. library of books on archaeology, ethnology & physical anthropology.
Activities: speakers for both Phillips Academy & general public; permanent & temporary exhibits.
Publications: Papers of The R.S. Peabody Foundation (Inactive).
Hours & Admission Prices: by appointment only. No charge; donations accepted. Closed New Year's Day; Memorial Day; Independence Day; Labor Day; Thanksgiving; Christmas.
Attendance: 6,800 (estimated)

Arlington

THE ARLINGTON HISTORICAL SOCIETY, 7 Jason St., Arlington, MA 02476-6410. Tel.: 781-648-4300.
E-mail: contact@arlingtonhistorical.org
Web Site: www.arlingtonhistorical.org
Founded: 1897.
Congressional District: 8
Key Personnel: Pres. (V), Robert L. Fredieu; Museum Admin., Doreen Stevens.
Personnel Profile: Part-Time Paid 2; Part-Time Volunteers 25.
Governing Authority: nonprofit corporation. Branch Museums: Jason Russell House & George Abbot Smith History Museum. Tax-exempt.
Museum & Historic Building & Site.
Collections: photographic archives; archives; 17th to 19th-century furnishings; textiles; dolls; weaponry; regional & local history; historic house.
Research Fields: regional & local history.
Facilities: archives of books, photographs & documents; meeting space.
Activities: guided tours; changing exhibits; monthly programs; education program.
Publications: books; newsletter.
Hours & Admission Prices: April-Oct. Sat.-Sun. 1-4; other times by appointment. Adults $3, children under 12 $1; discounts to AAM, members of Lexington Historical Society & Massachusetts Teacher's Association; society members no charge.
Attendance: 700 (estimated)
Membership: Student $10; Adult $20; Family $40; Sustaining $75; Life $450; Donation $600.

CYRUS E. DALLIN ART MUSEUM, INC., 1 Whittemore Park, Arlington, MA 02474-1105. Tel.: 781-641-0747.
Web Site: www.dallin.org
Founded: 1995.
Congressional District: 7
Key Personnel: Co Chm., Roland Chaput; Co Chm., Heather Leavell.
Governing Authority: Tax-exempt.
Art Museum.
Collections: plaster models; plaster & bronze sculptures; C.E. Dallin archival material; silver & bronze medals.
Activities: group tours; elementary school outreach program. Museum Sponsors: Town Day, Art on the Green.
Publications: Cyrus E. Dallin and His Native American Work; Cyrus E. Dallin, Sculptor Frontier to Fame; Walking Tour of Dallin Sculptures.
Hours & Admission Prices: Tues.-Sun. 12-4. No charge; donations accepted. ♿

THE OLD SCHWAMB MILL, 17 Mill Lane, Arlington, MA 02476-4189. Tel.: 781-643-0554. Fax: 781-643-0640.
Web Site: www.oldschwambmill.org
Founded: 1969.
Congressional District: 8
Key Personnel: Site Admin., Ed Gordon.
Personnel Profile: Part-Time Paid 2; Part-Time Volunteers 21.
Governing Authority: nonprofit. Parent Institution: The Schwamb Mill Preservation Trust. Tax-exempt: 501(c)(3).
Industrial History Museum: housed in 1860 The Old Schwamb Mill, the waterpowered mill site at the Foot of the Rocks.
Collections: working 19th-century assembly of belt-driven shaft & pulley operated woodworking machinery for production of oval & circular picture frames; woodworking hand tools; Hercules water turbine, sluice gates, stone bearings for water wheel & other parts of obsolete waterpower system; business & genealogical records of the five-generation German Schwamb Family & their Yankee & English Puritan predecessors over 350 years on the site; six historic wall paintings by Jonathan D. Poor, 1830. Historic Buildings: three 19th-century mill buildings.
Research Fields: architectural & business history recorded by Historic American Engineering Record of the U.S. Dept. of the Interior; local history; mill families' genealogy; history of picture frames; historic waterpowered mill sites' markers along rails to trails bicycle path paralleling Mill Brook in Arlington and Lexington.
Facilities: Shaker workshops reproduction wooden furniture & made to order museum-quality carved picture frames for sale.
Activities: guided tours by appointment; PBS-TV nationally aired programs: Norm Abram's New Yankee Workshop, Boyhood of John Muir & This Old House; 19th century woodworking machinery demonstrations; MA Dept. of Education, Technology Summer Institute for public school teachers K-12.
Publications: brochure, Old Schwamb Mill; semiannual newsletter.
Hours & Admission Prices: Tues. & Sat. 11-3. No charge; donations accepted. Tour groups (6-10 people) $35; members no charge. Closed legal holidays.
Attendance: 1,000 (estimated)
Membership: Individual $30; Family $40; Sustaining $300 & up.

Ashfield

ASHFIELD HISTORICAL SOCIETY, 457 Main St., Ashfield, MA 01330. Mailing Address: P.O. Box 277, Ashfield, MA 01330-0277. Tel.: 413-428-4541.
E-mail: grace240@verizon.net
Web Site: www.ashfieldhistorical.org
Key Personnel: Pres. (V), Alden Gray; Cur., Grace Lesure; Museum Shop Mgr., Suzi Day
Historic Building: built in 1830.
Collections: glass plate negatives; early Ashfield industries; 19th century period furnishings; military artifacts.
Activities: special events.
Hours & Admission Prices: June-1st weekend in Oct. Sat.-Sun. 11-1; other times by appointment.

Ashland

ASHLAND HISTORICAL SOCIETY, INC., 2 Myrtle St., Ashland, MA 01721-1106. Mailing Address: P.O. Box 145, Ashland, MA 01721-0145. Tel.: 508-881-8183.
Web Site: ashlandhistsociety.com
Founded: 1909.
Congressional District: 4
Key Personnel: Pres. (V), Clifford Wilson.
Governing Authority: society. Tax-exempt.
History Museum.
Collections: genealogy; early books; newspapers; furniture; implements; portraits; glassware; china; household goods; manuscripts; school & town records. Historic House: 1748 house.
Research Fields: genealogy & vital record files.
Facilities: manuscripts on local history, Bibles, old school books, hymnals, microfilms of newspapers, 1869-1914 Ashland Advertiser & 1914-1915 Ashland Tribune available for use on premises; reading room.
Activities: guided tours; formally organized education programs for children; temporary exhibitions; public talks; presentations. Museum Sponsors: Open Houses.
Publications: books, History of Ashland, 1942; reprint maps; monthly newsletter.
Hours & Admission Prices: Wed. 7-9 by appointment. No charge. ♿
Attendance: 450 (estimated)
Membership: Annual $10.

Ashley Falls

COL. ASHLEY HOUSE, Cooper Hill Rd., Ashley Falls, MA 01222. Mailing Address: P.O. Box 792, Stockbridge, MA 01262-0792. Tel.: 413-298-3239, ext. 3000. Fax: 413-298-5239.
E-mail: wgarrison@ttor.org
Web Site: www.thetrustees.org
Founded: 1972.
Congressional District: 1
Key Personnel: Exec. Dir., Andrew Kendall; Western Rgnl. Historic Resources Mgr., Will Garrison.

Personnel Profile: Part-Time Paid 3.
Governing Authority: privately-administered. Parent Institution: The Trustees of Reservations, 572 Essex St., Beverly, MA 01915. Tax-exempt.
Historic House: 1735 oldest house in Berkshire County.
Collections: colonial furnishings; pottery; tools; African-American history.
Activities: guided tours.
Publications: illustrated booklet on Ashley family and house, 1982.
Hours & Admission Prices: mid-May to Columbus Day Sat.-Sun. 10-5. Adults $5, children 6-12 $3; discounts to AAM members; members no charge.
Attendance: 800 (accurate)
Membership: Individual $45; Family $65.

Attleboro

ATTLEBORO AREA INDUSTRIAL MUSEUM, INC., 42 Union St., Attleboro, MA 02703-2948. Tel.: 508-222-3918.
E-mail: info@industrialmuseum.com
Web Site: www.industrialmuseum.com
Founded: 1975.
Congressional District: 3
Key Personnel: Exec. Dir., George Shelton.
Personnel Profile: Part-Time Paid 2; Part-Time Volunteers 24; Interns 6.
Governing Authority: Tax-exempt.
Industrial Museum.
Collections: local history.
Research Fields: jewelry industry; local industry.
Facilities: research library.
Activities: jewelry studio classes; museum school classes.
Publications: A Bit of Nostalgia.
Hours & Admission Prices: Thurs.-Fri. 10-4; groups by appointment. Adults $6, children $4. Closed Independence Day week. ♿
Attendance: 3,000 (estimated)
Membership: Member $25; Family $35; Sponsor $50; Patron $100; Corporate Sponsor $200.

ATTLEBORO ARTS MUSEUM, 86 Park St., Attleboro, MA 02703-2335. Tel.: 508-222-2644. Fax: 508-226-4401.
E-mail: office@attleboroartsmuseum.org
Web Site: www.attleboroartsmuseum.org
Formerly: Attleboro Museum, Center for the Arts
Founded: 1929.
Key Personnel: Pres. Bd. of Trustees, Nancy Aleo; Exec. Dir., Mim Fawcett; Museum Shop Mgr., Marion Volterra; Community Resource/Volunteer Coord., Lucrecia Sosa.
Personnel Profile: Full-Time Paid 2; Part-Time Paid 2; Part-Time Volunteers 50; Interns 3.
Governing Authority: nonprofit organization. Tax-exempt: 501(c)(3).
Art Museum & Cultural Center.
Collections: American art & craft; prints; costumes; decorative arts; ceramics; photographs; paintings; Civil War flags, swords, medals.
Research Fields: regional art.
Activities: arts festivals; concerts; dance recital; classes for adults & children; visiting artist's workshops; offsite school arts program; lectures; participatory & temporary exhibitions.
Publications: quarterly newsletter; announcements; quarterly museum school brochure.
Hours & Admission Prices: Summer: June-Aug. Tues.-Sat. 10-4; Sept.-May Tues.-Sat. 10-5. No charge; donations accepted. Closed national holidays & holiday weekends. ♿
Attendance: 10,000 (estimated)
Membership: Senior Citizen & Student $25; Artist & Individual $35; Family & Household $50; Associate $75; Supporting $125; Benefactor $250; Patron $500; Cornerstone $1,000.

CAPRON PARK ZOO, 201 County St., Attleboro, MA 02703-3510. Tel.: 774-203-1840. Fax: 508-223-2208.
E-mail: zoo@cityofattleboro.us
Web Site: www.capronparkzoo.com
Key Personnel: Dir., Jean Benchimol; Cur. Education, Mel Stoehrer
Zoo.
Collections: animals from around the world.
Activities: educational programs; recreational activities.
Hours & Admission Prices: April to early Oct. daily 10-5; Oct. Mon.-Fri. 10-4, Sat.-Sun. 10-5; Nov.-March daily 10-4. Adults $5.50, children & seniors $3.75; discounts to military & Attleboro residents; children under 3 no charge. ♿

WOMEN AT WORK MUSEUM, Rte. 123, Attleboro, MA 02703. Mailing Address: P.O. Box 355, 35 County St., Attleboro, MA 02703-0006. Tel.: 508-222-4430.
E-mail: info@womenatworkmuseum.org
Web Site: www.womenatworkmuseum.org
Key Personnel: Pres., Nancy Young; Treas., Kelly Fox.
Personnel Profile: Part-Time Paid 2; Interns 1.
Governing Authority: Tax-exempt.
History Museum.
Collections: achievements of women around the world; paintings; quilts; photographs.
Activities: special events; educational programs.
Hours & Admission Prices: Sat. 11-4. ♿
Membership: Senior Citizen & Youth $20; Adult $35; Family $50; Supporting $100; Sustaining $250 & up.

Barnstable

OLDE COLONIAL COURTHOUSE, TALES OF CAPE COD, INC., Olde Colonial Courthouse, Rondezvous Lane & Rt. 6A, Barnstable, MA 02630. Mailing Address: P.O. Box 41, Barnstable, MA 02630-0041. Tel.: 508-362-8927. Fax: 508-362-9056.
Web Site: talesofcapecod.org
Founded: 1949.
Congressional District: 12
Key Personnel: Pres., Lilla Robinson; Vice Pres., Judith Arsenault; Treas., Ken Robinson.
Personnel Profile: Part-Time Volunteers 20.
Governing Authority: board of trustees. Tax-exempt: 170(b).
Historic Site Museum & Olde Colonial Courthouse: Sachem Iyanough's gravesite dedicated to early Indians who befriended Pilgrims.
Collections: folklore; history; archaeology; Indian artifacts; films & slides of Cape Cod scenes; videotaped interviews.
Research Fields: oral & video folk tale recordings.
Facilities: collections of recordings of Cape Cod residents available for use in Cape Cod Room, Cape Cod Community College.
Activities: community cable TV show. Museum Sponsors: summer historic lecture series in July & August.
Publications: rare photographs; Cape Cod stories; legends; anecdotes; Cape Cod Trivia; Cape Cod Historical Almanac; Indian Rocks on Cape Cod; Henry's Cape Cod; Vikings to Vonnegut.
Hours & Admission Prices: By appointment only. Donations accepted. Lecture Series: July-Aug. Tues. 7:30pm.
Attendance: 1,250 (estimated)
Membership: Individual $15; Couple & Family $30; Sustaining $50; Life $200.

STURGIS LIBRARY, 3090 Main St., Barnstable, MA 02630. Mailing Address: Box 606, Barnstable, MA 02630-0606. Tel.: 508-362-6636. Fax: 508-362-5467.
Web Site: www.sturgislibrary.org
Founded: 1867.
Congressional District: 10
Key Personnel: Dir., Lucy Loomis; Pres. Bd. Trustees, Ellie Claus.
Personnel Profile: Full-Time Paid 3; Part-Time Paid 7; Part-Time Volunteers 30.
Governing Authority: nonprofit. Tax-exempt.
Historic Building: housed in 1644 Rev. Lothrop House.
Collections: genealogy & local history; maritime history; Cape Cod History.
Research Fields: maritime history; Barnstable family genealogy; Cape Cod history.
Facilities: 65,000-vol. library includes Cape Cod, maritime history & genealogy; reading room. Postcards, books & gifts for sale.
Activities: monthly & temporary exhibitions.
Publications: quarterly newsletter; books, The History of the Sturgis Library; Nineteenth Century Literary Gentlemen.
Hours & Admission Prices: Mon., Wed. & Thurs.-Fri. 10-5, Tues. 1-8, Sat. 10-4. No charge; donations accepted. Closed holidays. ♿
Attendance: 45,000 (accurate)

TRAYSER MUSEUM GROUP DBA COAST GUARD HERITAGE MUSEUM, 3353 Main St., Barnstable, MA 02630. Mailing Address: P.O. Box 161, Barnstable, MA 02630-0161. Tel.: 508-362-8521.
E-mail: cgheritage@comcast.net
Web Site: coastguardheritagemuseum.org
Formerly: Donald G. Trayser Memorial Museum/Barnstable County Customs House
Founded: 2004.
Congressional District: 2
Key Personnel: Dir. Planning, Zoning & Historical Preservation, Tom Broadrick; Pres., William Collette.

Governing Authority: municipal. Town of Barnstable. Tax-exempt.
History Museum: housed in 1856 Old Customs House.
Collections: history; marine articles; ship models; Indian artifacts; Coast Guard artifacts; blacksmith shop. Historic Building: 1800s jail.
Research Fields: early Barnstable.
Hours & Admission Prices: May-Oct. Tues.-Sat. 10-3. Admission $5; active Coast Guard and children 10 & under no charge.
Attendance: 500 (estimated)

Barre

BARRE HISTORICAL SOCIETY, INC., 18 Common St., Barre, MA 01005. Mailing Address: P.O. Box 755, Barre, MA 01005-0755. Tel.: 978-355-4978.
Founded: 1955.
Congressional District: 2
Key Personnel: Pres., Daniel E. Stevens; Cur., Bertyne Smith; Treas., Phyllis K. Allen; Assoc. Treas., Margaret Frost; Sec., Lester W. Paquin.
Personnel Profile: Part-Time Volunteers 11.
Governing Authority: society. Tax-exempt: 501(c)(3).
Local History Museum: housed in 1839 home of Spencer Field; built by Elias Carter, architect.
Collections: 1763-1940 first parish records; 1823-1969 United Methodist Church records; papers of Willard Broad; papers of Marshall D. Eaton; Houghton papers; manuscripts; 1859 12 passenger stage coach.
Research Fields: town history; genealogy.
Facilities: library of local history & genealogy available on premises with supervision.
Activities: guided tours; permanent exhibitions.
Hours & Admission Prices: Thurs. 10-12; other times by appointment. No charge; donations accepted.
Attendance: 300 (estimated)
Membership: Individual $10; Family $25; Corporate $50; Life $100.

Becket

BECKET LAND TRUST HISTORIC QUARRY & FOREST, (M), Quarry Rd., Becket, MA 01223. Mailing Address: P.O. Box 44, Becket, MA 01223-0044. Tel.: 413-623-2100.
E-mail: landtrust@becketlandtrust.org
Web Site: www.becketlandtrust.org
Key Personnel: Dir., Dorothy Napp Schindel.
Governing Authority: nonprofit organization.
History Museum.
Collections: Hudson-Chester Quarry history; mining; period truck; blacksmith's shop; wooden derrick; mining equipment.
Facilities: 300-acre preserve; nature trails.
Activities: educational programs.
Hours & Admission Prices: Dawn-dusk. No charge.

Belchertown

THE STONE HOUSE MUSEUM, 20 Maple St., Belchertown, MA 01007-9416. Mailing Address: P.O. Box 1211, Belchertown, MA 01007-1211. Tel.: 413-323-6573.
E-mail: director@stonehousemuseum.org
Web Site: www.stonehousemuseum.org
Founded: 1903.
Congressional District: 1
Key Personnel: Pres. (V), Tom Stockton; Asst. Cur., Shirley Bock; Archivist, Cliff McCarthy.
Personnel Profile: Part-Time Volunteers 30; Interns 2.
Governing Authority: society. Parent Institution: The Belchertown Historical Assoc. Tax-exempt: 501(c)(3).
Historic House Museum: 1827 stone house.
Collections: china; furniture; household goods; costumes; fabrics & hand work; jewelry; pewter; shaker; farm equipment; old vehicles; Rogers groups; toys; musical instruments; archives; manuscript collections; printing office; stone barn; portraits; carriages; sleighs; stagecoach; print shop.
Research Fields: ceramics; local families; accounting books for local business; genealogy.
Facilities: 500-vol. library of local history; genealogy. Local authors & religious works available for use on the premises by appointment.
Activities: guided tours; permanent exhibitions; living history programs; interactive school programs.
Publications: newsletter; brochures; cookbook.
Hours & Admission Prices: mid-May to mid-Oct. Sat. 2-5 & by appointment. Adults $5, seniors $4; discounts to AAM, ICOM & MTA members; members no charge.
Attendance: 2,000 (estimated)
Membership: Student under 18 $5; Senior 65 & over $8; Individual $15; Family $30; Friend $50; Patron $100; Benefactor $250 & up.

Bellingham

WHATCOM CHILDREN'S MUSEUM, 121 Prospect St., Bellingham, MA 98225-4401. Tel.: 360-733-8769.
Children's Museum.
Collections: hands-on exhibits.
Hours & Admission Prices: Tues.-Wed. & Sun. 12-5, Thurs.-Sat. 10-5.

Berlin

BERLIN ART AND HISTORICAL COLLECTIONS, 4 Woodward Ave., Berlin, MA 01503. Mailing Address: P.O. Box 35, Berlin, MA 01503-0087. Tel.: 978-838-2502.
E-mail: historical@townofberlin.com
Web Site: www.townofberlin.com/historical
Founded: 1950.
Key Personnel: Pres. (V), Richard Wheeler.
Personnel Profile: Part-Time Volunteers 7.
Governing Authority: municipal. Parent Institution: Berlin Art & Historical Society.
General Museum.
Collections: archives; history; military; costumes; folklore; genealogy. Historic Houses: 1814 Powder House; 1870 Town Hall; 1805 Hearse House; 1790 Bullard House.
Research Fields: archives; history; military; costumes; folklore; genealogy.
Activities: lectures; temporary exhibitions; programs for historical society & schools.
Publications: newsletters, Heritage News; Berlin Historian.
Hours & Admission Prices: By appointment. No charge.
Membership: Junior $1; Adult $10.

Beverly

BEVERLY HISTORICAL SOCIETY AND MUSEUM, (M), 117 Cabot St., Beverly, MA 01915-5196. Tel.: 978-922-1186. Fax: 978-922-7387.
E-mail: info@beverlyhistory.org
Web Site: www.beverlyhistory.org
Founded: 1891.
Congressional District: 6
Key Personnel: Dir., Susan Goganian; Mgr. Collections, Darren Brown; Accountant, Jan Jefgood, CPA
Personnel Profile: Full-Time Paid 2; Part-Time Paid 1; Part-Time Volunteers 23; Interns 5.
Governing Authority: society. Branch Museums: John Balch House, 448 Cabot St., Beverly, MA; Rev. John Hale Farm, 39 Hale St., Beverly, MA. Tax-exempt: 501(c)(3).
Historical Society Museum: housed in 1781 John Cabot Mansion.
Collections: decorative art; portraits; military; maritime; transportation; toys; dolls; genealogy; railroad photographs. Historic Houses: 1636 John Balch House; 1694 Rev. John Hale House.
Research Fields: Beverly history; maritime history; genealogy; New England transportation.
Facilities: 5,000-vol. library & manuscripts, including extensive shipping papers & log books.
Activities: guided tours; permanent & temporary exhibitions.
Publications: quarterly newsletter; Beverly Historical Review; books, Ryal Side from Early Days of Salem Colony; The Old Planters of Beverly; booklets, Men in the War of Independence; Made in Beverly.
Hours & Admission Prices: Museum: Tues. & Thurs.-Sat. 10-4, Wed. 1-9. Research-Galloupe Library: Tues. & Wed. Museum: adults $5, students & seniors $4; discounts to AAM & NEMA members; members & children under 16 no charge. Library: adults $5 per hour; members no charge.
Attendance: 2,608 (estimated)
Membership: Students & Seniors $25; Individual $30; Family $40; Patron $100; Sponsor $250; Benefactor $500; Lifetime $1,000.

THE TRUSTEES OF RESERVATIONS, 572 Essex St., Beverly, MA 01915-1530. Mailing Address: Castle Hill, 290 Argilla Rd., Ipswich, MA 01938. Tel.: 978-921-1944. Fax: 978-921-1948.
E-mail: information@ttor.org
Web Site: www.thetrustees.org
Founded: 1891.
Key Personnel: Pres., Andrew Kendall; Chm. (V), Elliot M. Surkin; Vice Pres. Land Conservation Center, Wesley Ward; Dir. Devel., Ann Powell; Dir. Historic Resources, Susan C.S. Edwards; Dir. Finance & Admin., Marbella Haly.
Personnel Profile: Full-Time Paid 110; Part-Time Paid 200; Interns 5.
Governing Authority: nonprofit organization. Subsidiary Institution: Massachusetts Land Conservation Trust. Tax-exempt: 501(c)(3) & 701(b).
Open Space & Historic Preservation; Preservation Project: maintaining & protecting 87 properties in the state of Massachusetts.

Collections: The Trustees for Reservations is associated with various reservations and natural areas throughout Massachusetts. Historic Houses: 1735 Colonel John Ashley House, Ashley Falls; furniture & household objects from 18th & early 19th centuries. 1783 William Cullen Bryant Homestead, Cummington: contains much of Bryant's original furniture. Barn with early farm implements. 1928 The Crane Estate at Castle Hill, Ipswich: former home of industrialist Richard T. Crane, Jr.; gardens. 1739 Mission House, Stockbridge: built by Rev. John Sergeant, first missionary to Stockbridge Indians; period furniture; herb & perennial garden. 1885 Naumkeag, Stockbridge: former home of Joseph Hodges Choate; American & European decorative arts; gardens. 1770 The Old Manse, Concord: home of Nathaniel Hawthorne & Ralph Waldo Emerson; period furniture. 1918 Stevens-Coolidge Place, North Andover: remodeled Colonial Revival house; Chinese export porcelain, Anglo-Irish cut glass; American decorative arts; gardens; 1720 Paine House, Ipswich American decorative arts, 18th century dairy; The Folly 1965, Williamstown, designed by Ulnch Frauzen & interior furnishings also designed by him.
Research Fields: deer management; tern & piping, plover habitat & nesting; successful barrier beach management.
Facilities: vary by property.
Activities: guided tours; canoeing; cross-country skiing; fishing; hiking; picnicking; swimming; special events.
Publications: brochures; quarterly newsletter; annual report; topographical & trail maps.
Hours & Admission Prices: Office: Mon.-Fri. 9-5. Contact the Trustees of Reservations for details on hours & admissions for the various properties; members no charge to most properties.
Attendance: 1,000,000 (estimated)
Membership: Individual $40; Family $60; Contributing $100; Supporting $150; Sustaining $300; Sponsor $600; 1891 Society Member $1,000; The Charles Eliot Society $2,500.

Billerica

BILLERICA HISTORICAL SOCIETY, Clara Sexton House, Concord Rd., Billerica, MA 01821. Mailing Address: P.O. Box 381, Billerica, MA 01821-0381. Tel.: 978-667-7020.
E-mail: billericahistorical@verizon.net
Web Site: www.billericahistorical.com
Historical Society.
Collections: artifacts; photographs.
Hours & Admission Prices: Call for hours.

Bolton

BOLTON HISTORICAL SOCIETY, INC., Sawyer House, 676 Main St., Bolton, MA 01740. Mailing Address: P.O. Box 211, Bolton, MA 01740-0211. Tel.: 978-779-6392.
Founded: 1962.
Congressional District: 5
Key Personnel: Pres. (V), Tim Fiehler.
Personnel Profile: Part-Time Volunteers 8.
Governing Authority: board of directors of society. Tax-exempt.
General Museum: housed in c.1810 Sawyer House & farm/barn blacksmith shop.
Collections: early industrial work; post-war articles; records & articles used in early religious observances; family histories; early home articles; old farm tools & machinery; old blacksmith shop with tools; letters; diaries; documents; 18th & 19th century surveyors maps; 19th century medical instruments; barn.
Research Fields: town history.
Facilities: archives containing local records, town & school department reports, books & papers by local authors, genealogy, history & geographic material of the area available for use on premises; 50-seat auditorium.
Activities: guided tours by appointment; lectures; formally organized education programs for children; permanent & temporary exhibitions.
Publications: newsletters; program listings.
Hours & Admission Prices: Thurs. 1:30-3:30; tours by appointment. No charge; donations accepted.
Attendance: 300 (estimated)
Membership: Single $20; Family $35.

Boston

ANCIENT AND HONORABLE ARTILLERY COMPANY OF MASSACHUSETTS, 1 Faneuil Hall, Armory, Boston, MA 02109-1604. Tel.: 617-227-1638. Fax: 617-227-7221.
E-mail: ahac.curator@verizon.net
Web Site: www.ahac.us.com
Founded: 1638.
Congressional District: 9
Key Personnel: Commanding Officer, Cpt. Michael W. Downing; Cur., Lt. John F. McCauley.
Personnel Profile: Full-Time Paid 1.
Governing Authority: municipal. Tax-exempt: 501(c)(3).
Military Museum.
Collections: archives; historical paintings; portraits; relics of wars; military weapons.
Research Fields: 18th, 19th & 20th-century military history.
Facilities: 2,500-vol. library of military books & information available by appointment.
Activities: lectures to groups of 25 or more.
Publications: company history brochure.
Hours & Admission Prices: Call for information. No charge; donations accepted. ♿
Attendance: 40,000 (estimated)

ARNOLD ARBORETUM OF HARVARD UNIVERSITY, 125 Arborway, Boston, MA 02130-3500. Tel.: 617-524-1718. Fax: 617-524-1418.
E-mail: arbweb@arnarb.harvard.edu
Web Site: www.arboretum.harvard.edu
Founded: 1872.
Congressional District: 9
Key Personnel: Dir., Dr. Robert E. Cook; Finance & Admin., Andrea Nix.
Personnel Profile: Full-Time Paid 51; Part-Time Volunteers 100; Interns 14.
Governing Authority: university. Parent Institution: Harvard University. Tax-exempt: 501(c)(3).
Arboretum.
Collections: living collection of hardy trees & shrubs; herbarium; archives.
Research Fields: plant systematics; taxonomy; floristics.
Facilities: 40,000-vol. library of books on dendrology, botany, economic botany, history, monographs & herbarium available for use to recognized scholars or verified students.
Activities: guided tours; lectures; formally organized education programs for adults, children, undergraduate & graduate college students; permanent & temporary exhibitions. Museum Sponsors: Members Plant Sale in September; Lilac Sunday in May.
Publications: newsletter, Arnoldia.
Hours & Admission Prices: Visitor Center: Mon.-Fri. 9-4, Sat. 10-4, Sun. 12-4. Library: Mon.-Sat. 10-4. Closed holidays. Grounds: daily sunrise-sunset. No charge; donations accepted. ♿
Attendance: 250,000 (estimated)
Membership: Individual $35; Family $50; Sustaining $100; Sponsoring $200; Benefactor $1,000.

THE ART INSTITUTE OF BOSTON MAIN GALLERY, 700 Beacon St., Boston, MA 02215-2598. Tel.: 617-585-6656. Fax: 617-437-1226.
E-mail: robinson@aiboston.edu
Web Site: www.aiboston.edu
Founded: 1909.
Key Personnel: C.E.O., Bonnell Robinson.
Personnel Profile: Full-Time Paid 1; Part-Time Paid 1; Part-Time Volunteers 2; Interns 2.
Governing Authority: university. Tax-exempt.
Art Gallery.
Collections: paintings; sculpture; photographs.
Major Exhibits: Alessandra Sanguinetti, Spring 2010.
Research Fields: design; illustration; fine arts; photography; sculpture; ceramics.
Facilities: 1,600 sq. ft. exhibit space.
Activities: arts festivals; lectures; traveling & loan exhibitions.
Publications: exhibition posters; annual catalogues; postcards.
Hours & Admission Prices: Jan. 4-Dec. 23 Tues.-Fri. 12-6, Sat.-Sun. 12-5. No charge. Closed major holidays. ♿
Attendance: 8,200 (estimated)

THE BOSTON ATHENAEUM, 10 1/2 Beacon St., Boston, MA 02108-3777. Tel.: 617-227-0270. Fax: 617-227-5266.
Web Site: www.bostonathenaeum.org
Formerly: Boston Athenaeum Library
Founded: 1807.
Congressional District: 9
Key Personnel: Pres., G. Marshall Moriarty; Acting Dir. & Librarian, Paula Matthews; Assoc. Dir., John Lannon; Cur. Prints & Photographs, Catharina Slautterback; Cur. Art, David Dearinger; Cur. Rare Books, Stanley E. Cushing; Assoc. Cur. Paintings & Sculpture, Hina Hirayama; Conservator, James Reid-Cunningham; Cur. Manuscripts & Coord. Community Affairs, Stephen Nonack; Acquisition Librarian, Anthea Harrison Reilly; Head Technical Svcs., Robert Kruse.

Personnel Profile: Full-Time Paid 34; Part-Time Paid 7; Part-Time Volunteers 48; Interns 5.
Governing Authority: nonprofit organization. Tax-exempt: 501(c)(3).
Library with Art Collection: housed in 1847-49 library building.
Collections: paintings; sculpture; prints; drawings; photographs; daguerreotypes; architectural drawings; archives; rare & illustrated books; manuscripts.
Research Fields: American & European history; fine & decorative arts; prints & photographs.
Facilities: 700,000-vol. library of general books available for inter-library loan & to the public upon request; reading room.
Activities: permanent & temporary exhibitions; lectures; concerts.
Publications: annual report; exhibition catalogues; monographs; library newsletter.
Hours & Admission Prices: Late May to early Sept. Mon. & Wed. 8:30-8, Tues. & Thurs.-Fri. 8:30-5:30; Sept. 12-May 22 Mon. & Wed. 8:30-8, Tues. & Thurs.-Fri. 8:30-5:30, Sat. 9-4. No charge. Closed major holidays. ♿
Membership: Associate Membership: Individual $110; Family $165. Family Membership: Individual $220; Family $275. Life: Annual $275.

* **BOSTON CHILDREN'S MUSEUM, (M),** Children's Wharf, 300 Congress St., Boston, MA 02210-1034. Tel.: 617-426-6500. Fax: 617-426-1944. TDD: 617-426-5466.
E-mail: info@bostonchildrensmuseum.org
Web Site: www.bostonchildrensmuseum.org
Formerly: The Children's Museum, Inc.
Founded: 1913.
Congressional District: 9
Key Personnel: Chm. Bd., Jon Rounds; Exec. Vice Pres. & C.O.O., Neil Gordon; Sr. Vice Pres. & C.F.O., Amy Auerbach; Vice Pres. Human Resources, Jane Barry; Vice Pres. Devel., Judi Cantor; Vice Pres. Corporate Devel. & External Rels., Charlayne Murrell-Smith; Vice Pres. Exhibits & Production, Gail Ringel; Vice Pres. Family Learning & Early Childhood Programs, Jeri Robinson; Sr. Vice Pres. Research & Program Planning, Leslie Swartz; Vice Pres. Community Learning & Partnerships, Ginny Zanger; Dir. Mktg. & Public Rels., Jo-Anne Baxter.
Personnel Profile: Full-Time Paid 80; Part-Time Paid 64; Interns 5.
Governing Authority: nonprofit. Parent Institution: The Children's Museum. Tax-exempt: 501(c)(3).
Children's Museum.
Collections: 50,000 artifacts; Native American archaeological & cultural artifacts with a focus on Northeast Woodland Indians & contemporary arts; 19th century Japanese merchant's house; global cultural artifacts; international folk dolls; toys; dolls; dollhouses; Boston & American social history; regional natural history.
Major Exhibits: Top Secret: Mission toy (T), 1/10-5/10; Curious George (T), 2/10-6/10; Out on a Limb (T), 6/10-9/10; Keep Your Balance (T), 9/10-1/11.
Research Fields: pertaining to issues facing children & families in contemporary society; science; child development; multicultural education.
Facilities: 150-seat proscenium theater. Educational toys, games, books and museum-related items for sale.
Activities: educational programs; teacher, parent & student workshops and consulting services; neighborhood outreach; museum professional training; educational materials development; permanent, participatory, temporary & traveling exhibitions; Kit Rental: over 90 kits in social studies, physical sciences, natural history, & arts & crafts; Friday night performances; special events; KidStage, interactive theater.
Publications: newsletters; research reports; classroom kits; science books; multicultural books; audio tapes & teachers guides; books related to program areas; exhibit-related books, periodicals, & audiovisual materials.
Hours & Admission Prices: Fri. 10-9, Sat.-Thurs. 10-5. Adults $12, senior citizens 65 & over and children 1-15 $9; AAM members, other museum staff with ID, children under one, & members no charge. Closed Thanksgiving; Christmas. ♿
Attendance: 551,000 (estimated)
Membership: ACM Family (6 people) $125; ACM Plus Family (6 people) $250; Corporate $600-$10,000 & up; Library $335-$675.

BOSTON FIRE MUSEUM, 344 Congress St., Boston, MA 02210-1204. Tel.: 617-482-1344.
E-mail: info@bostonfiremuseum.com
Web Site: bostonfiremuseum.com
Founded: 1983.
Congressional District: 9
Key Personnel: Chm. (V), Daniel O'Neill; Pres. (V), Charles Holloran; Museum Shop Mgr., James Daly.
Personnel Profile: Part-Time Volunteers 20.
Governing Authority: not-for-profit organization. Parent Institution: Boston Sparks Association. Tax-exempt: 501(c)(3).
Fire-Fighting History and Education Museum: housed in 1891 Congress Street Fire Station, a National Historic Landmark Building.
Collections: fire photographs, newspapers, printed material; helmets, fire alarm equipments; c.1905 hand-drawn American LaFrance Hook and Ladder Truck; 1826 Hunneman hand-pump; 1882 Christie/Amoskeag steam pumper; 1966 American LaFrance pumper.
Research Fields: history of fire-fighting in the Boston area.
Facilities: 3,000 sq. ft. exhibit area. Museum-related items for sale.
Activities: tours for visitors to local fire stations; youth education.
Publications: monthly newsletter, The General Order.
Hours & Admission Prices: April-Oct. Fri. 10-4, Sat. 11-4; other times by appointment. No charge; donations accepted. ♿
Attendance: 3,500 (accurate)

BOSTON NATIONAL HISTORICAL PARK, Charlestown Navy Yard, Boston, MA 02129. Tel.: 617-242-5648 & 5620. Fax: 617-241-8650.
E-mail: marty_blatt@nps.gov
Web Site: www.nps.gov/bost/
Founded: 1974.
Congressional District: 8
Key Personnel: Chief of Cultural Resources, Martin Blatt; Supt., Terry Savage; Cur., David Vecchioli; Museum Specialist, Phillip Hunt.
Personnel Profile: Full-Time Paid 90; Part-Time Paid 80; Part-Time Volunteers 60; Interns 1.
Governing Authority: federal government. Parent Institution: National Park Service, U.S. Dept. of the Interior. Tax-exempt.
Historic Houses & Sites.
Collections: Historic Sites & Structures include Old North church; Charlestown Navy Yard; Bunker Hill monument; Paul Revere house; Faneuil Hall; Old South meeting house; Old State House; Dorchester Heights; U.S.S. Constitution Museum; U.S.S. Cassin Young.
Research Fields: Boston history; Boston National Historical Park Sites; Boston Naval Shipyard.
Facilities: library; archives; visitor center; national park area.
Activities: visitor information; films; talks; guided tours; self-guided tours; museum sales; special events; educational programs; lecture series.
Publications: brochures; hardbooks.
Hours & Admission Prices: Daily 9-5. No charge. ♿
Attendance: 2,700,000 (accurate)

BOSTON PUBLIC LIBRARY, 700 Boylston St., Boston, MA 02116-2813. Tel.: 617-536-5400. Fax: 617-236-4306. TDD: 617-536-7055.
E-mail: ask@bpl.org
Web Site: www.bpl.org
Founded: 1852.
Congressional District: 9
Key Personnel: Cur. Fine Arts, Janice Chadbourne; Keeper Special Collections, Susan L. Glover.
Governing Authority: municipal; board of trustees. Parent Institution: City of Boston. Tax-exempt: 501(c)(3).
Public Library with Art Collections.
Collections: mural decorations by Edwin A. Abbey, John Elliott, Pierre Puvis de Chavannes, John Singer Sargent; bronze doors by Daniel Chester French; sculptures by Frederick MacMonnies, Bela Pratt, Augustus & Louis Saint Gaudens, Francis Derwent Wood; paintings by Copley, Duplessis; dioramas depicting Dicken's London, Alice in Wonderland, Arabian Nights & famous printmakers at work; Albert H. Wiggin Collection of 18th & 19th-century French and English prints; Old Masters prints & drawings; 18th & 19th-century American historical prints; 19th-century American photography by Bell, O'Sullivan, W.H. Jackson; British printmakers; American posters of the 90s; contemporary American printmakers; modern German prints; early French lithography; Holt Collection of photographs relating to Boston architecture; architectural drawings by Peabody & Stearns Cram & Ferguson, William G. Preston, Maginnis & Walsh, Charles Bulfinch, Charles Strickland; Charles J. Connick Collections of gouaches, photographs; bronzes, medals & graphics on Joan of Arc; Society of Arts & Crafts; Boston archives; 19th & 20th-century costumes & stage designs.
Research Fields: art & art history; architecture; history of photography; decorative arts & crafts of all countries & periods; New England artists; printing history; fine bookbinding.
Facilities: 138,000-vol. library representing all fields of art, 200,000 mounted pictures, 10,000 mounted photographs, 650,000 unmounted photographs, 150,000 postcards, 75,000 original prints, 170,000 prints by New England artists & books on Boston architecture available for research on premises; Index to Boston Architecture; 500,000 architectural plans; late 19th-century city building documents; microfilm sets on art, architecture, photography & the decorative arts; vertical & clipping files; Boston Pictorial Archive.
Activities: guided tours; lectures; films; concerts; demonstrations; gallery talks; inter-museum loan; temporary & traveling exhibitions.
Publications: books, A Handbook to the Art & Architecture of the Boston

Public Library; A Survey of Boston Architectural Drawings & Photographs; Armstrong & Company: Artistic Lithographers; Etched in Sunlight: Fifty Years in the Graphic Arts (Samuel Chamberlain); The Lithographs of Stow Wengenroth, 1931-1972; Society of Arts & Crafts, Boston Exhibition Record 1897-1928; Afro-American Artists: A Bibliographical Directory; American Posters of the Nineties; Ralph Adams Cram, American Medievalist; The Work of Thomas W. Nason, N.A.; others in catalog of publications available upon request.
Hours & Admission Prices: June-Sept. Mon.-Thurs. 9-9, Fri.-Sat. 9-5; Oct.-May Sun. 1-5, Mon.-Thurs. 9-9, Fri.-Sat. 9-5. No charge. Closed national holidays. ♿
Attendance: 2,000,000

BOSTON UNIVERSITY ART GALLERY, (M), 855 Commonwealth Ave., Boston, MA 02215-1303. Tel.: 617-353-3329. Fax: 617-353-4509.
E-mail: gallery@bu.edu
Web Site: www.bu.edu/ART
Founded: 1960.
Congressional District: 8
Key Personnel: Dir., Marc Mitchell; Gallery Staff, Molly Scheu; Gallery Staff, Evelyn Cohen.
Personnel Profile: Full-Time Paid 2; Part-Time Paid 1; Interns 13.
Governing Authority: university; Boston University, Boston, MA 02215. Tax-exempt: 170(b)(1)(a).
Art Gallery.
Collections: paintings.
Research Fields: modern & contemporary art; New England art; history of photography.
Activities: lectures; gallery talks; concerts; formally organized education programs for undergraduate & graduate students affiliated with Boston University; training programs for professional museum workers; traveling exhibitions.
Publications: exhibition catalogues.
Hours & Admission Prices: mid-Jan. to mid-May & mid-Sept. to mid-Dec. Tues.-Fri. 10-5, Sat.-Sun. 1-5. No charge. Closed major holidays. ♿
Attendance: 7,450 (accurate)

BROMFIELD ART GALLERY, 450 Harrison Ave., Boston, MA 02118-2400. Tel.: 617-451-3605.
E-mail: gduehr@comcast.net
Web Site: www.bromfieldgallery.com
Founded: 1974.
Key Personnel: Pres. (V), Florence Montgomery; Gallery Mgr., Gary Duehr.
Personnel Profile: Part-Time Paid 1; Part-Time Volunteers 15; Interns 1.
Governing Authority: cooperative organization.
Cooperative Art Gallery.
Collections: paintings; drawings; sculpture; photographs.
Facilities: 800 sq. ft. exhibit space.
Activities: guided tours; lectures; performances; rental gallery; poetry readings; members exhibits.
Hours & Admission Prices: Wed.-Sat. 12-5. No charge; donations accepted. ♿
Attendance: 3,000 (estimated)

THE COMMONWEALTH MUSEUM, 220 William T. Morrissey Blvd., Boston, MA 02125-3314. Tel.: 617-727-9268. Fax: 617-825-3613.
E-mail: commonwealthmuseum@sec.state.ma.us
Web Site: www.sec.state.ma.us/mus/museum/index.htm
Founded: 1986.
Congressional District: 9
Key Personnel: Sec. of State, William Frances Galvin; Dir., Stephen Kenney, Ph.D.
Personnel Profile: Full-Time Paid 3; Part-Time Paid 2; Part-Time Volunteers 1; Interns 3.
Governing Authority: state. Parent Institution: Office of the Sec. of State. Tax-exempt: 170(c)(1).
State History Museum.
Collections: local history & culture; period furnishings; photographs; personal artifacts.
Research Fields: Massachusetts state & local history; archives.
Facilities: lecture & conference room.
Activities: rotating, loan, participatory, temporary & traveling exhibitions; public tours; lectures; school loan service; broadcast programs; special events.
Publications: biannual newsletter; exhibition guides; educational materials; curriculum materials for teachers.
Hours & Admission Prices: Mon.-Fri. 9-5. No charge. Closed major holidays. ♿
Attendance: 10,000 (estimated)

THE GIBSON SOCIETY, INC. DBA GIBSON HOUSE MUSEUM, 137 Beacon St., Boston, MA 02116-1504. Tel.: 617-267-6338. Fax: 617-267-6338.
E-mail: info@thegibsonhouse.org
Web Site: thegibsonhouse.org
Founded: 1957.
Congressional District: 8
Key Personnel: Exec. Dir., J. Charles Swift; Pres., Elizabeth T. Harbison; Treas., Robert S. Goodof; Museum Asst., Kyla Mackay-Smith; Consulting Cur., Wendy Swanton; Consulting Preservationist, Barbara Thibault.
Personnel Profile: Full-Time Paid 1; Part-Time Paid 5; Part-Time Volunteers 5; Interns 1.
Governing Authority: society. Subsidiary Institution: Victorian Society in America, New England Chapter. Tax-exempt: 501(c)(3).
Historic House Museum: 1859 Gibson House.
Collections: decorative arts; paintings; sculpture; photographs; clothing; Victorian period furniture.
Research Fields: Victorian decorative arts.
Facilities: meeting rooms.
Activities: guided tours; permanent exhibitions. Museum Sponsors: monthly lectures. Annual Events: Benefit Tea in March; Holiday Open House in December.
Publications: illustrated guide, Gibson House.
Hours & Admission Prices: Tours: Wed.-Sun. 1, 2 & 3. Adults $9, senior citizens & students $6, children $3; discount to Victorian Society (New England) & AAA members; members no charge. Closed national holidays.
Attendance: 3,500 (accurate)
Membership: Friend $50; Two Friends at the Same Address $75; Neighbor $100; Back Bay $150; Poet's Circle $250; Improper Bostonian $500; Proper Bostonian $1,000.

*** HISTORIC NEW ENGLAND, (M),** 141 Cambridge St., Boston, MA 02114-2799. Tel.: 617-227-3956. Fax: 617-227-9204.
Web Site: www.historicnewengland.com
Formerly: The Society for the Preservation of New England Antiquities, Harrison Gray Otis House
Founded: 1910.
Congressional District: 9
Key Personnel: Pres., Carl Nold; Site Mgr., Leah Walczak.
Governing Authority: nonprofit organization. Branch Museums: 1800 Barrett House, Forest Hall, Main Street, New Ipswich, NH; 1907-34 Beauport Sleeper-McCann House, 75 Eastern Point Blvd., Gloucester, MA; c.1690 Spencer-Peirce- Little Farm, Newbury, MA; 1846 Roseland Cottage, Rte. 169, Woodstock, CT; c.1740 Casey Farm, Rte. 1A, Saunderstown, RI; c.1740 Codman Estate, The Grange, Codman Rd., Lincoln, MA; c.1678 Coffin House, 14 High Rd., Rte. 1A, Newbury, MA; c.1938 Gropius House, 68 Baker Bridge Rd., Lincoln, MA; c.1785 Hamilton House, 40 Vaughan's Ln., South Berwick, ME; 1774 Sarah Orne Jewett House, 5 Portland St., South Berwick, ME; 1807 Castle Tucker, Lee St. at High St., Wiscasset, ME; c.1728 Cogswell's Grant. Spring St., Essex, MA; 1784 Governor John Langdon House, 143 Pleasant St., Portsmouth, NH; 1793 Lyman Estate, The Vale, 185 Lyman St., Waltham, MA; 1789 Marrett House, Rte. 25, Standish, ME; 1807 Nickels-Sortwell House, 121 Main St., Wiscasset, ME; 1796 Otis House, 141 Cambridge St., Boston, MA; 1807 Rundlet-May House, 364 Middle St., Portsmouth, NH; 1718 Sayward-Wheeler House, 9 Barrell Ln., York Harbor, ME; 1796 Watson Farm, 455 North Rd., Jamestown, RI; c.1780 Winslow-Crocker House, 250 King's Hwy., Rte. 6A, Yarmouthport, MA; 1664 Jackson House, 76 Northwest St., Portsmouth, NH; c.1750 Casey Farm; c.1821 Phillips House, 34 Chestnut St., Salem, MA. Historic New England also operates 13 properties that may be visited by appointment (617-227-3956) & are for architectural study. Tax-exempt: 501(c)(3).
History Museum: housed in 1796 Federal residence; the first of three houses in Boston designed by Charles Bulfinch.
Collections: New England architectural artifacts; decorative arts; textiles; wallpapers; ceramics; glass; photographs; architectural drawings; ephemera; manuscripts; material culture; regional transportation;
Research Fields: architectural history; photographic history; decorative arts; preservation & conservation techniques for buildings & furniture.
Facilities: archives of 1,000,000 photographs; architectural drawings & other primary materials; auditorium.
Activities: guided tours; special events; lectures; school programs.
Publications: visitors guide; exhibition catalogues; magazine, Historic New England.
Hours & Admission Prices: Offices: Mon.-Fri. 9-5. Archives: by appointment. Otis House: Wed.-Sun. Tours 11-4:30. Admission $8; discounts to senior citizens, ICOM, AAA, AAM, WGBH members; members no charge.
Attendance: 169,446 (accurate)
Membership: National $35; Individual $45; Household $55; Garden &

Landscape $75; Institutional $85; Contributing $100; Historic Homeowner $200; Supporting $250.

* **THE INSTITUTE OF CONTEMPORARY ART/BOSTON, (M),** 100 Northern Ave., Boston, MA 02210-1870. Tel.: 617-478-3100. TDD: 617-927-6622.
E-mail: info@icaboston.org
Web Site: www.icaboston.org
Founded: 1936.
Congressional District: 9
Key Personnel: Pres. (V), Charles A. Brizins; Chm. (V), Paul Buttenwieser; Dir., Jill Medvedow; Assoc. Cur., Randi Hopkins; Assoc. Cur., Jen Mergel; Dir. Media, Branka Bogdanov; Dir. External Rels., Paul Bessire; Exhibitions & Facilities Mgr., Tim Obetz; Museum Shop Mgr., Victor Oliveira; Dir. Mktg. & Communications, Donna Desrochers; Dir. Education, Monica Garza; Registrar, Janet Moore.
Personnel Profile: Full-Time Paid 46; Part-Time Paid 29; Part-Time Volunteers 8; Interns 13.
Governing Authority: nonprofit organization. Tax-exempt: 170(b)(1)(A).
Art Museum.
Collections: contemporary works in various media.
Major Exhibits: Roni Horn aka Roni Horn (T), 2/19/10-6/13/10; Dr. Lakra, 4/14/10-9/6/10; Momentum 16: Goshka Macuga, 4/14/10-9/6/10; Charles LeDray (T), 7/16/10-10/17/10; Foster Prize, 9/10-1/11.
Research Fields: 20th-21st century art.
Facilities: mediatheque; theater; art lab; digital studio. Museum-related items & exhibition videos for sale.
Activities: lecture series; poetry; literary readings; dance; theatre; performance; video & films; educational workshops.
Publications: books, Utopia Post Utopia: Configuration of Nature and Culture in Recent Sculpture and Photography; On the Passage of a Few People Through a Rather Brief Moment in Time: The Situationist International 1957-1972; Between Spring and Summer: Soviet Conceptual Art in the Era of Late Communism; Ulrike Rosenback: Video & Performance Art; Dissent: The Issue of Modern Art in Boston; The British Edge; Boston School; Inside the Visible; El Corazon Sangrante; Rachel Whiteread; Elvis and Marilyn: 2x Immortal; ICA Newsletter; Collectors Collect Contemporary 1990-99; Frieze; New Histories; Cornelia Parker Customized: Hot Rods, Low Riders & American Car; catalogues, Super Vision; Philip Lorca di Corcia; Anish Kapoor: Past, Present, Future; Tara Donovan; 20th Anniversary Limited Edition of Shepard Fairey: Supply & Demand; Damian Ortega: Do It Yourself.
Hours & Admission Prices: Tues.-Wed. & Sat.-Sun. 10-5, Thurs.-Fri. 10-9. Adults $15, students & senior citizens $10; discounts to AAM & ICOM members; children under 17, families on last Sat. of month, Thurs. after 5 & members no charge. Closed New Year's Day; Thanksgiving; Christmas. ♿
Attendance: 268,000 (accurate)
Membership: Individual $65; Dual & Family $95; Associate $125; Friend $250; Patron $500; Advocate $1,000. Director's Circle: Fellow $2,000; Leader $5,000; Ars Longa $10,000.

* **ISABELLA STEWART GARDNER MUSEUM, (M),** 280 The Fenway, Boston, MA 02115-5809. Mailing Address: Two Palace Rd., Boston, MA 02115-5807. Tel.: 617-566-1401 & 278-5156. Fax: 617-264-6096.
E-mail: information@isgm.org
Web Site: www.gardnermuseum.org
Founded: 1903.
Congressional District: 9
Key Personnel: Chm. (V), John L. Gardner; Pres. (V), Barbara Hostetter; Dir., Anne Hawley; Treas., William Poorvu; Cur. Education, Margaret Burchenal; C.O.O., Peter Bryant; Dir. Public Rels., Katherine Armstrong; Dir. Devel., Helena Hartnett; Cur. Collections, Alan Chong; Cur. Contemporary Art, Pieranna Cavalchini; Museum Shop Mgr., Beverly Shmeis; Dir. Music, Scott Nickrenz.
Personnel Profile: Full-Time Paid 68; Part-Time Paid 102; Part-Time Volunteers 108; Interns 7.
Governing Authority: nonprofit organization. Tax-exempt: 501(c)(3).
Art Museum: housed in 15th-century Venetian style palace.
Collections: paintings; sculpture; tapestries; stained glass; furniture; prints; textiles; decorative arts; music; horticulture installations; archives of letters to Founder.
Major Exhibits: Taro Shinoda: Lunar Reflections, 11/09-1/10; Terracotta Sculpture of the Italian Renaissance, 2/10-5/10.
Research Fields: pertaining to collections.
Facilities: library of books pertaining to the collections available by appointment only; cafe. Museum-related items for sale.
Activities: concerts; guided tours; lectures; scholarly symposia; educational programming; artist in residence program.
Publications: annual report; books; catalogues; e-newsletter.
Hours & Admission Prices: Tues.-Sun. 11-5. Adults $12, senior citizens $10, college students with current ID $5; discounts to AAM & ICOM members; children under 18, members, anyone named Isabella, & on your birthday no charge. Reservation for guided tours 3 weeks in advance. Closed Independence Day; Thanksgiving; Christmas. ♿
Attendance: 180,000 (accurate)
Membership: Student $25; Nonresident $50; Individual $60; Family & Dual $85; Sustainer $120; Supporter $250; Contributor $500; Courtyard Circle $1,000.

JOHN F. KENNEDY PRESIDENTIAL LIBRARY & MUSEUM, (M), Columbia Point, Boston, MA 02125. Tel.: 617-514-1600. Fax: 617-514-1652. TDD: 617-514-1573.
Web Site: www.jfklibrary.org
Founded: 1979.
Congressional District: 9
Key Personnel: Chm. (V), Paul Kirk; Pres. (V), Caroline Kennedy; Dir. Library & Museum, Tom Putnam; Treas., Marie Carbone; Cur., Stacey Bredhoff; Deputy Dir., James Roth; Devel., Sandra Sedacca; Education, Nancy McCoy; Public Rels., Rachel Day; Registrar, Kathryn Dodge; Archivist, Allan Goodrich; Museum Shop Mgr., Terri McGrath; Security, Norm Beland.
Personnel Profile: Full-Time Paid 52; Part-Time Paid 16; Part-Time Volunteers 20; Interns 20.
Governing Authority: federal. Parent Institution: National Archives and Records Administration, Washington, DC 20408. Tax-exempt: 170(b)(1)(A).
History & Presidential Library.
Collections: the life & times of John F. Kennedy; films; memorabilia; tape recordings; personal papers; government records; political campaign items; presidential manuscripts; 32 million documents; 150,000 photographs; 11,000 serials; papers of Ernest Hemingway.
Research Fields: life, times, career & presidential administration of John F. Kennedy; middle 20th-century American politics & government; life & work of Ernest Hemingway.
Facilities: 70,000-vol. library pertaining to mid-century American politics & government available on premises for research only; 38,000 sq. ft. exhibit space; cafeteria; educational facilities; 700-seat auditorium; two 230-seat theaters. Museum-related items for sale.
Activities: lectures; formal education programs for children; temporary exhibitions; films; public forum series; teacher education institutes. Annual Events: PEN/Hemingway Awards Ceremony; Profile in Courage Essay Contest; Profile in Courage Awards Ceremony.
Publications: brochure; guide to collections; biannual newsletter, JFK Library Foundation Newsletter.
Hours & Admission Prices: Daily 9-5; groups by appointment. Adults $12, senior citizens & college students with ID $10, children 13-17 $9; discounts to groups, museums of Boston, NEMA & AAM members; members & children under 12 no charge. Closed New Year's Day; Thanksgiving; Christmas. ♿
Attendance: 220,000 (accurate)
Membership: Friends of the Kennedy Library: Individual $40; Family $60; Contributor $100; Benefactor $250; Leadership Circle $500; President's Circle $1,000.

THE MARY BAKER EDDY LIBRARY FOR THE BETTERMENT OF HUMANITY, (M), 200 Massachusetts Ave., Boston, MA 02115-3017. Tel.: 617-450-7000; 888-222-3711. Fax: 617-450-7048.
E-mail: librarymail@marybakereddylibrary.org
Web Site: www.marybakereddylibrary.org
Founded: 2000.
Congressional District: 8
Key Personnel: Pres. & Exec. Mgr., Lesley Pitts; Chm., Dr. Mary Metzner Trammell; Reference Room Admin., Jonathan Eder; Art Dir., Mark Thayer; Mgr. Mktg., M.J. Pullins; Senior Cur., Alan K. Lester; Senior Researcher, Judith A. Huenneke.
Personnel Profile: Full-Time Paid 28; Part-Time Paid 4; Part-Time Volunteers 4.
Governing Authority: private; nonprofit organization. Branch Museums: 12 Broad St., Lynn, MA; 400 Beacon St., Chestnut Hill, MA. Tax-exempt: 501(c)(3).
History Museum.
Collections: books; manuscripts; letters & correspondence; personal artifacts; photographs; films; paintings.
Research Fields: spirituality & health; American women in religious leadership; ideas & life of Mary Baker Eddy; quest for spirituality today.
Facilities: 12,000-vol. library; 75-seat restaurant; 13,500 sq. ft. exhibit space.
Activities: docent program; guided tours; lectures; participatory exhibits. Annual Event: Summer SOULstice, arts educational program; First Night Boston.

Publications: quarterly magazine, The Mary Baker Eddy Library for the Betterment of Humanity.
Hours & Admission Prices: Tues.-Sun. 10-4. Adults $6, seniors, students, children & groups $4; children under 6 & members no charge. Closed New Year's Day; Martin Luther King Jr. Day; Patriots' Day; Memorial Day; Independence Day; Labor Day; Thanksgiving; Christmas. ♿
Attendance: 100,000 (estimated)

MASSACHUSETTS HISTORICAL SOCIETY, 1154 Boylston St., Boston, MA 02215-3695. Tel.: 617-536-1608. Fax: 617-859-0074.
E-mail: library@masshist.org
Web Site: www.masshist.org
Founded: 1791.
Congressional District: 9
Key Personnel: Pres., Dennis A. Fiori; Chm. Bd., William C. Clendaniel; Librarian, Peter Drummey; Editor in Chief, C. James Taylor.
Personnel Profile: Full-Time Paid 45; Part-Time Paid 4; Part-Time Volunteers 3; Interns 2.
Governing Authority: board of trustees. Tax-exempt: 501(c)(3).
Library.
Collections: archives; paintings; sculpture; American & New England history; manuscript collections.
Facilities: 400,000-vol. library of books & manuscripts relating to the history of the U.S., New England & Massachusetts available for research on the premises; reading room.
Activities: lectures; inter-museum loan, permanent & temporary exhibitions.
Publications: Massachusetts Historical Society Review; newsletter, Miscellany; books.
Hours & Admission Prices: Mon.-Wed. & Fri. 9-4:45, Thurs. 9-7:45, Sat. 9-4. No charge. Closed national holidays. ♿
Attendance: 5,000 (estimated)
Membership: Annual $150.

MUSEUM OF AFRICAN AMERICAN HISTORY, (M), 46 Joy St., Boston, MA 02114-4005. Mailing Address: 14 Beacon St., Ste. 719, Boston, MA 02108-3710. Tel.: 617-725-0022. Fax: 617-720-5225.
E-mail: history@maah.org
Web Site: www.maah.org
Founded: 1966.
Congressional District: 9
Key Personnel: Exec. Dir., Beverly Morgan-Welch; Chm. (V), James S. Hoyte.
Personnel Profile: Full-Time Paid 8; Part-Time Paid 7; Part-Time Volunteers 1; Interns 6.
Governing Authority: nonprofit organization. Tax-exempt: 501(c)(3).
History Museum.
Collections: artifacts & archival material relating to the history of Afro-Americans in New England; photographs; papers on civil rights & civic organizations; Black family papers; sculptures; Civil War artifacts; artworks. Historic Buildings: 1806 African meeting house, the oldest extant Black church in the U.S.; 1835 Abiel Smith School, the first publicly funded school for African Americans; the African Meeting House on Nantucket, 1820s; The Florence Higginbotham on Nantucket, 1845.
Research Fields: social history of African-American communities in New England; historic archaeology; oral history.
Facilities: 1,200-vol. library of literature on African American history available to students & faculty of Suffolk University & members; historic classroom.
Activities: gallery guided tours; lectures; films; guided walking tours of Black Heritage Trail (R); temporary exhibits; rental facilities.
Publications: electronic bulletin; occasional archaeology reports; brochure; Black Heritage Trail; guide, A Gathering Place for Freedom.
Hours & Admission Prices: Mon.-Sat. 10-4. No charge; donations requested. Closed major holidays. ♿
Attendance: 230,000 (estimated)
Membership: Eunice Ross Senior & Student $15; Lewis Hayden Individual $25; Susan Paul Family $50; National Trust Fund $125; Maria Stewart Society $500; Frederick Douglas Society $1,000; Legacy Society $5,000.

* **MUSEUM OF FINE ARTS, (M),** 465 Huntington Ave., Boston, MA 02115-5597. Tel.: 617-267-9300. Fax: 617-369-3064. TDD: 617-267-9703.
E-mail: webmaster@mfa.org
Web Site: www.mfa.org
Founded: 1870.
Congressional District: 9
Key Personnel: Dir., Malcolm Rogers; Deputy Dir., Katherine Getchell; Deputy Dir., Kim French; Chm. (V), Stokley P. Towles; Pres. (V), Barbara Alfond; Deputy Dir., Patricia B. Jacoby; Deputy Dir. & C.F.O., Mark Kerwin; Dir. Public Rels., Dawn Griffin; Dir. Membership & Visitor Svcs., Lisa Krassner; Chm. Prints, Drawings & Photographs, Clifford S. Ackley; Chm. Art of Asia, Oceania & Africa, Jane Portal; Chm. Art of the Americas, Elliot Davis; Chm. Art of Europe, George T.M. Shackelford; Chm. Ancient World, Rita Freed; Chm. Conservation & Collections Management, Mathew Siegal; Dir. Libraries & Archives and Museum Historian, Maureen Melton; Deputy Dir. & Dean, Deborah Dluhy; Dir. Exhibitions & Design, Patrick McMahon; Chm. Contemporary Art & MFA Programs, Edward Saywell; Dir. Human Resources, Jane O'Reilly; Dir. Intellectual Property & Publisher, Mark Polizzotti; Cur. Textiles & Fashion Arts, Pamela A. Parmal; Cur. Education, Barbara Martin; Cur. Musical Instruments, Darcy Kuronen; Museum Shop Mgr., Ellen Bragalone.
Personnel Profile: Full-Time Paid 577; Part-Time Paid 172; Part-Time Volunteers 1,213; Interns 150.
Governing Authority: nonprofit organization. Subsidiary Institution: School of the Museum of Fine Arts. Tax-exempt.
Art Museum & School.
Collections: Asiatic, Egyptian, Greek & Roman Near-Eastern art; Old Master European paintings, prints & drawings; French Impressionist & post-impressionist painting; American portraits & Impressionist paintings; French & Flemish tapestries; Peruvian & Coptic weavings; European & Near-Eastern embroideries, lace, printed fabrics, costumes, fashion, jewelry & accessories; American & European period furnishings; 18th & 19th century American arts; Colonial silver; early musical instruments; Chinese export porcelain; ship models; 20th century & contemporary art; 19th & 20th century photography; period American art; African & Oceanic art; Nubian; Japanese; American & European decorative arts & sculpture; Chinese; contemporary craft.
Major Exhibits: Contemporary Outlook: Seeing Songs, 11/09-2/21/10; L'eta di Courbet e Monet (T), 11/09-3/7/10; Villa Manin, Passariano de Codropio da Rembrandt a Gauquin a Picasso (T), 11/09-3/14/10; Rimini, Castel Sismondo The Secrets of Tomb 10A: Egypt 2000 BC, 11/09-5/16/10; Harry Callahan: American Photographer, 11/21/09-7/3/10; Albrect Durer: Virtuoso Printmaker, 11/21/09-7/3/10; Object, Image, Collector: African and Oceanic Art in Focus, 12/12/09-7/18/10; Luis Melendez: Master of the Spanish Still Life, 2/2/10-5/9/10.
Research Fields: art historical, archaeological & conservation science disciplines.
Facilities: 250,000-vol. library of art reference works available for inter-library loan & for use on the premises. Books, painting, sculpture, jewelry reproductions, postcards, note paper, miscellaneous gift items & reproductions of objects from the collections for sale.
Activities: guided tours; lectures; films; gallery talks; concerts; dance recitals; arts festivals; formally organized education programs; inter-museum loan, permanent, temporary & traveling exhibitions.
Publications: bimonthly, Preview; exhibition & permanent collection catalogues; annual report; art books.
Hours & Admission Prices: Museum: Mon.-Tues. & Sat.-Sun. 10-4:45, Wed.-Fri. 10-9:45. Gund Gallery closes 15 min. before museum. Adults $17, senior citizens & college students $15; members and children 17 & under after school no charge. Closed New Year's Day; Patriot's Day; Independence Day; Thanksgiving; Christmas. ♿
Attendance: 1,028,168 (accurate)
Membership: Individual $75; Dual/Family $100; Associate $170; Family Plus $175; Universal $350; Supporting $750; Sustaining $1,000; Patron Member $2,500; Patron Fellow $5,000; Patron Sponsor $10,000; Director's Circle $25,000 & Up.

* **MUSEUM OF SCIENCE, (M),** Science Park, Boston, MA 02114-1099. Tel.: 617-589-0100 & 0222. Fax: 617-742-2246 & 589-0454. TTY: 617-589-0417.
Web Site: www.mos.org
Founded: 1830.
Congressional District: 9
Key Personnel: C.O.O., Wayne Bouchard; Chm. (V), Richard Burnes; Dir. & Pres., Dr. Ioannis Miaoulis; Sr. Vice Pres. Strategic Initiatives, Larry Bell; Sr. Vice Pres. Advancement, Joan Hadly; Volunteer Service League Pres. (V), Irv Krause; Vice Pres. Education, Paul Fontaine; Vice Pres. Visitor Svcs. & Operations, Jonathan Burke; Vice Pres. Mktg. & External Affairs, Cynthia Mackey; Vice Pres. Human Resources, Britton O'Brien; Vice Pres. Finance & System Svcs., John Slakey; Dir. Current Science & Technology, David Rabkin; Vice Pres. Research, Christine Cunningham.
Personnel Profile: Full-Time Paid 348; Part-Time Paid 40; Part-Time Volunteers 659; Interns 50.
Governing Authority: nonprofit organization. Tax-exempt: 501(c)(3).
Science & Technology Museum.
Collections: mounted animal specimens; live animals; live plants; mineral, rock & gem specimens; fossils; paintings, prints & illustrations, scientific in context; sculptures; scientific instruments & inventions with a historical perspective; electrical devices & technological advancements; natural science & historical dioramas; models; transportation; botanical; human body organs & parts; photo & graphic panels detailing: bones, lungs, brain,

heart, teeth, human reproductive process, living cells & DNA and hip repair; archeological artifacts; astronomical devices & photos.
Facilities: 17,000-vol. library of science books available for inter-library loan & on premises; Charles Hayden Planetarium; Thomson Theatre of Electricity; ComputerPlace; Mugar Omni Theater; reading room; cafeteria. Books, hobby material & other museum-related items for sale.
Activities: lectures; films; demonstrations; formally organized educational programs; standing exhibits.
Publications: members newsletter, Sparks; Annual Report; Engineering is Elementary; museum magazine.
Hours & Admission Prices: July 5 to Labor Day Fri. 9-9, Sat.-Thurs. 9-7; Sept.-July 4 Fri. 9-9, Sat.-Thurs. 9-5. Omni Theater, Planetarium, Laser Shows: call for hours. Exhibit Halls: adults $21, seniors $19, children $18. Omni Theater, Planetarium & Laser: adults $9, seniors $8, children $7. Combo: adults $25.50, seniors $23, children $21.50; members no charge. Call 617-723-2500 or visit website for special holiday & vacation hours. Closed Thanksgiving; Christmas. ♿
Attendance: 1,565,840 (accurate)
Membership: Basic 2 $75; Basic 5 $105; Premier 2 $110; Basic 8 $135; Premier 5 $140; Premier 8 $170.

MUSEUM OF THE NATIONAL CENTER OF AFRO-AMERICAN ARTISTS, 300 Walnut Ave., Boston, MA 02119-1369. Tel.: 617-442-8614. Fax: 617-445-5525.
E-mail: bgaither@mfa.org
Web Site: www.ncaaa.org
Founded: 1969.
Congressional District: 9
Key Personnel: Co Chm., Margaret Burnham; Co Chm., Vivian Johnson, Ph.D.; Dir. & Cur., Edmund Barry Gaither; Asst. to Dir. & Registrar, Carol Murray.
Personnel Profile: Full-Time Paid 5; Part-Time Paid 5; Part-Time Volunteers 4.
Governing Authority: nonprofit. Parent Institution: National Center of Afro-American Artists, Boston, MA. Tax-exempt: 170(b)(1)(A).
Art Museum.
Collections: paintings; prints & graphics by Afro-American artists; African art. Historic House: 19th-century house.
Research Fields: Afro-American, African & Afro-Caribbean art.
Activities: guided tours; lectures; films; gallery talks; concerts; dance recitals; arts festivals; inter-museum loan, temporary & traveling exhibitions; educational school programs.
Publications: quarterly newsletter; annual report.
Hours & Admission Prices: Tues.-Sun. 1-5. Adults $4, students & senior citizens $3; members no charge.
Attendance: 10,000 (estimated)
Membership: Student $20; Individual $35; Family $55; Friend $85; Supporters $100; Donor $150; Contributor $250; Patron $500; Grand Patron $1,000.

* **NEW ENGLAND AQUARIUM CORPORATION,** Central Wharf, Boston, MA 02110-3399. Tel.: 617-973-5200, ext. 0. Fax: 617-720-5098. TDD: 617-973-0223.
Web Site: www.neaq.org
Founded: 1957.
Congressional District: 9
Key Personnel: Pres., Howard (Bud) Ris; Chm., William Burgess; Exec. Vice Pres., Walter Flaherty; Vice Pres. Programs & Exhibits, William Spitzer; Dir. Visitor Svcs., Deborah Bobeck; Vice Pres. Devel., Nancy Perkins; Vice Pres. Research, Scott Kraus; Vice Pres. Sales & Mktg., Jane Wolfson; Dir. & Gen. Cur., John Dayton; Cur. Mammals, Kathy Streeter; Cur. Fishes, Steve Bailey; Dir. Design, Jim Duffy; Dir. Education, John Anderson; Assoc. Vice Pres. Conservation, Heather Tausig; Dir. Foundation & Government Support, Susan Thompson; Dir. MIS, Barbara Waller; Dir. Media Rels., Tony Lacasse; Dir. Gift Shop, Kendra Forrand.
Personnel Profile: Full-Time Paid 199; Part-Time Paid 98; Part-Time Volunteers 500; Interns 61.
Governing Authority: nonprofit organization. Tax-exempt: 501(c)(3).
Aquarium.
Collections: live aquatic displays; maritime history; oceanography; fishing industry; seal exhibit; natural history.
Research Fields: aquatic marine biodiversity: marine mammals, fisheries bycatch, oceanic fishes & turtles; animal husbandry & telemetry.
Facilities: 2,700-vol. library of marine sciences available for use on the premises; education center with classrooms & wet lab; cafe. Aquarium-related items for sale.
Activities: films; formally organized educational programs; temporary & traveling exhibitions; Sleep with the Fish Programs; lecture series on-line information via homepage; giant ocean tank dives; whale watch.
Publications: quarterly newsletter, Blue; teachers newsletter, Schooling; children's books, aquatic forums.
Hours & Admission Prices: Summer: Mon.-Fri. 9-6, Sat.-Sun. 9-7; Winter: Mon.-Fri. 9-5, Sat.-Sun. 9-6. Adults $19.95, senior citizens $17.95, children 3-11 $11.95; discounts to groups; children under 3 & members no charge. Closed Thanksgiving; Christmas. ♿
Attendance: 1,300,000 (accurate)
Membership: Associate $75; Patron $125; Ambassador $175; Ocean Explorer $250; Conservation Society $500; Navigator Society $1,500.

NICHOLS HOUSE MUSEUM, (M), 55 Mount Vernon St., Boston, MA 02108-1330. Tel.: 617-227-6993. Fax: 617-723-8026.
E-mail: info@nicholshousemuseum.org
Web Site: www.nicholshousemuseum.org
Founded: 1961.
Congressional District: 8
Key Personnel: Exec. Dir., Flavia Cigliano; Pres., Lynne Rickabaugh.
Personnel Profile: Full-Time Paid 2; Part-Time Paid 3; Part-Time Volunteers 40; Interns 3.
Governing Authority: nonprofit organization. Tax-exempt: 501(c)(3).
Historic House Museum: housed in former Beacon Hill home of Rose Standish Nichols.
Collections: early 1800s furnishings; sculpture; decorative arts.
Research Fields: textiles, ceramics, landscape gardening.
Facilities: library of books available on site by application only.
Activities: guided tours; lectures; permanent exhibitions.
Publications: books: Rose Nichols As We Knew Her.
Hours & Admission Prices: April-Oct. Tues.-Sat. 11-4; Nov.-March Thurs.-Sat. 11-4. Adults $7; discounts to MA Teachers Assoc., AAA, AAM, WGBH & ICOM members; children under 12 & members no charge. Closed holidays.
Attendance: 4,260 (accurate)
Membership: Single $35; Family $55; Sponsor $100; Donor $250; Corporate $500.

OLD SOUTH MEETING HOUSE, (M), 310 Washington St., Boston, MA 02108-4616. Tel.: 617-482-6439. Fax: 617-482-9621.
Web Site: www.oldsouthmeetinghouse.org
Founded: 1877.
Congressional District: 9
Key Personnel: Exec. Dir., Emily Curran; Pres., William G. Constable; Dir. Education, Aliza Saivetz; Asst. Dir., Janine Fabiano; Visitor Svcs. & Museum Shop Mgr., Karen Costello; Mktg. & Events Mgr., Robin DeBlosi.
Personnel Profile: Full-Time Paid 5; Part-Time Paid 9; Interns 2.
Governing Authority: nonprofit organization. Parent Institution: Old South Association in Boston. Tax-exempt: 501(c)(3).
Historic Site: 1729 Old South Meeting House.
Collections: early American history; political & religious history related to Old South Meeting House.
Research Fields: historic preservation; issues involving freedom of speech; events leading to American Revolution, especially the Boston Tea Party.
Facilities: meeting hall; lecture hall; education room; 650-seat lecture & concert hall. Museum-related items for sale.
Activities: lectures; Music at the Meeting House Concert Series; forums; performances & walking tours; ongoing programs include Middays at the Meeting House weekly concert & lecture series; Summer Town Meeting reenactments; Partners in Public Dialogue public forum series; annual reenactment of the Boston Tea Party; wide array of educational programs for schools & community groups.
Publications: Old South Leaflets; newsletter; curriculum materials; An Architectural History of the Old South Meeting House.
Hours & Admission Prices: April-Oct. daily 9:30-5; Nov.-March daily 10-4. Adults $5, senior citizens 62 & over and students with ID $4, children 6-18 $1; members & children under 6 no charge. Closed New Year's Day; Thanksgiving; Christmas Eve & Day. ♿
Attendance: 78,000 (accurate)
Membership: Individual $35; Family $55; Old South Friend $100; Old South Donor $500; Phillis Wheatly Leadership Circle $1,000; Steeple Society $2,500; Boston Tea Party Patron $5,000.

OLD STATE HOUSE-THE BOSTONIAN SOCIETY, (M), 206 Washington St., Boston, MA 02109-1773. Tel.: 617-720-1713. Fax: 617-720-3289.
E-mail: adele@bostonhistory.org
Web Site: www.bostonhistory.org
Founded: 1881.
Congressional District: 9
Key Personnel: Exec. Dir., Brian Lemay; Bd. Chm. (V), Eric Hayes; Dir. The Old State House Museum, Rainey Tisdale; Dir. Finance & Admin., Linda Atlas; Collections Mgr., Marieke Van Damme; Devel., Gerrit Petersen; Office Mgr. & Collections and Library Asst., Adele Barbato; Mgr. Public Programs, Samantha Nelson; Visitor Svcs. Mgr., Erin Spencer; Facilities Mgr., Matthew Ottinger; Dir. Merchandising & Commercial Operations,

Chuck Gordon; Distribution Mgr., S. Mark Edwards; Office Asst., Ashley Martin; Museum Shop Mgr., Nick Trainor.
Personnel Profile: Full-Time Paid 12; Part-Time Paid 28; Part-Time Volunteers 11; Interns 2.
Governing Authority: society. Tax-exempt: 501(c)(3).
History Museum: 1713 Old State House.
Collections: Revolutionary & colonial artifacts; 19th century maritime & firefighting artifacts; domestic & commercial objects focusing on public life in Boston; paintings; manuscripts; photographs.
Research Fields: Boston history; architecture.
Facilities: 7,600-vol. library of Boston history books available to the public on a non-circulating basis; photo resource center; reading room. Museum-related items for sale.
Activities: lectures; gallery talks; walking tours.
Publications: pamphlets; newsletter.
Hours & Admission Prices: Daily 9-5. Adults $7, senior citizens & students $6, children 6-18 $3; discount to AAM members; MA school children, MA school teachers, NEMA members & active duty military no charge. Closed New Year's Day; Thanksgiving; Christmas.
Attendance: 105,538 (accurate)
Membership: Student $25; Senior Citizen $40; Individual $50; Family $80; Supporter $150; Benefactor $500; Life Benefactor $5,000.

* **PAUL REVERE HOUSE/PAUL REVERE MEMORIAL ASSOCIATION, (M),** 19 North Sq., Boston, MA 02113-2405. Tel.: 617-523-2338. Fax: 617-523-1775.
E-mail: staff@paulreverehouse.org
Web Site: www.paulreverehouse.org
Founded: 1907.
Congressional District: 9
Key Personnel: Exec. Dir., Nina Zannieri; Pres. (V), Paul Revere, Jr.; Cur., Edith Steblecki; Dir. Education, Emily Holmes; Dir. Research, Patrick Leehey; Interpretations & Visitor Svcs. Dir., Kristin Peszka.
Personnel Profile: Full-Time Paid 7; Part-Time Paid 15; Part-Time Volunteers 10; Interns 4.
Governing Authority: nonprofit organization. Parent Institution: Paul Revere Memorial Association. Branch Museum: The Pierce/Hichborn House, 29 N. Square, Boston, MA 02113. Tax-exempt: 501(c)(3).
History Museum & Historic Houses: c.1680 Paul Revere House, Boston's oldest house; c.1711 Pierce-Hichborn House.
Collections: furniture & artifacts of the 17th-19th centuries; Revere engravings, documents, silver, family items & memorabilia.
Research Fields: social & political history of Boston, 1680 to present; material culture of the 17th- to 19th-centuries; Revere's life & work; immigrant history of the North End.
Facilities: Books, pamphlets, cards & reproductions for sale.
Activities: guided tours; after-school & summer camp programs; neighborhood walking tours; special programs & events; permanent & temporary exhibitions; internship; research fellowship.
Publications: pamphlets; books; newsletter.
Hours & Admission Prices: Jan.-March Sun. & Tues.-Fri. 9:30-4:15; early April & Nov.-Dec. daily 9:30-4:15; mid-April to Oct. daily 9:30-5:15. Adults $3.50, college students & senior citizens $3, children $1; discounts to active military, museum professionals, AAM & ICOM members; members no charge. Closed New Year's Day; Thanksgiving; Christmas. ♿
Attendance: 264,841 (accurate)
Membership: Individual $20; Family $35; Supporting $50; Patron $100; Patriot $250.

PHOTOGRAPHIC RESOURCE CENTER, 832 Commonwealth Ave., Boston, MA 02215-1205. Tel.: 617-975-0600. Fax: 617-975-0606.
E-mail: prc@bu.edu
Web Site: www.prcboston.org
Founded: 1976.
Key Personnel: Exec. Dir., Jim Fitts; Pres. Bd. Dir., Cathy England.
Personnel Profile: Full-Time Paid 1; Part-Time Volunteers 12; Interns 3.
Governing Authority: nonprofit organization. Tax-exempt: 501(c)(3).
Photography Museum.
Collections: photographs.
Facilities: 3,250-vol. library of photo books & magazines.
Activities: lectures; temporary & traveling exhibitions; workshops. Annual Events: fundraising auctions.
Hours & Admission Prices: Tues.-Wed. & Fri. 9-6, Thurs. 9-8, Sat.-Sun. 12-5. Adults $3, student & senior citizens $2; discounts to CAA, AAM & ICOM members & other museum employees; children & members no charge. Closed major holidays. ♿
Attendance: 10,000 (estimated)
Membership: Student $25; Seniors $40; Individual $50; Family $75; Supporting $150; Contributor $250; Benefactor $500; Patron $1,000; Angel $2,000.

SHIRLEY-EUSTIS HOUSE, (M), 33 Shirley St., Boston, MA 02119-2725. Tel.: 617-442-2275. Fax: 617-442-2270.
E-mail: shirleyeustis@verizon.net
Web Site: www.shirleyeustishouse.org
Founded: 1913.
Congressional District: 9
Key Personnel: Exec. Dir., Andrea Taaffe; Pres. (V), Brian Pfeiffer; Treas., Dalton J. Avery.
Personnel Profile: Full-Time Paid 1; Part-Time Paid 1; Part-Time Volunteers 8; Interns 3.
Governing Authority: nonprofit organization. Parent Institution: Shirley-Eustis House Association. Tax-exempt: 501(c)(3).
Historic House: 1747 Georgian country house designed by Peter Harrison, built by Royal Governor William Shirley; restored to Federal appearance, 1800; furnished according to Gov. William Eustis inventory, 1825; 1806 Gardner Carriage House.
Collections: decorative arts; French & Federal furnishings.
Research Fields: history of Shirley Place & its inhabitants, especially Gov. Shirley & Gov. Eustis; decorative arts of the Federal period; Georgian & Federal gardens.
Facilities: 3,500 sq. ft. exhibit space.
Activities: guided tours; lectures; loan exhibitions.
Publications: newsletter, Shirley-Eustis Newsletter.
Hours & Admission Prices: June-Oct. 5 Thurs.-Sun. 12-4; other times by appointment. Adults $5, children & senior citizens $3; discounts to AAA, AAM & ICOM members; members no charge. Closed New Year's Day; Independence Day; Thanksgiving; Christmas.
Attendance: 2,000 (estimated)
Membership: Individual $25; Family $40; Business & Organization $100; Charter $250; Governors' Club $500.

THE SPORTS MUSEUM, TD Garden, 100 Legends Way, Boston, MA 02114-1300. Tel.: 617-624-1237. Fax: 617-624-1238.
E-mail: rsullivan@dncboston.com
Web Site: www.sportsmuseum.org
Formerly: The Sports Museum of New England
Founded: 1977.
Congressional District: 8
Key Personnel: C.E.O. & Exec. Dir., Rusty Sullivan; Cur., Richard Johnson; Assoc. Cur., Brian Codagnone; Education & Public Program Mgr., Michelle Gormley.
Personnel Profile: Full-Time Paid 4; Part-Time Paid 4; Part-Time Volunteers 6; Interns 2.
Governing Authority: nonprofit organization. Tax-exempt: 501(c)(3).
Sports Museum.
Collections: sports artifacts; films; documents archives; oral history; interactive exhibits.
Research Fields: sports history; sports media; sports equipment, uniforms, photos & video.
Facilities: 2,500-vol. library of general sport information; research archives.
Activities: special events.
Hours & Admission Prices: Daily 11, 12, 1, 2 & 3; call to confirm. Adults $6, seniors 60 & over and children 6-17 $4; discounts to AAM members & groups; children under 6 & members no charge. ♿
Attendance: 111,000 (estimated)
Membership: Individual & Senior Citizen $35; Family $75; Library $200.

* **USS CONSTITUTION MUSEUM, (M),** Boston National Historical Park, Charlestown Navy Yard, Boston, MA 02129. Mailing Address: P.O. Box 1812, Boston, MA 02129-0215. Tel.: 617-426-1812. Fax: 617-242-0496.
E-mail: getinvolved@ussconstitutionmuseum.org
Web Site: www.ussconstitutionmuseum.org
Founded: 1972.
Congressional District: 8
Key Personnel: Pres., Burt Logan; Chm., James Stokes; Exec. Vice Pres., Anne Grimes Rand; Vice Pres. & C.F.O., Adrian Bresler; Vice Pres. Institutional Advancement, Don Main; Dir. Retail Operations, Chris White; Dir. Exhibits, Robert Kiihne; Cur., Sarah Watkins.
Personnel Profile: Full-Time Paid 20; Full-Time Volunteers 2; Part-Time Paid 15; Part-Time Volunteers 46; Interns 6.
Governing Authority: private; nonprofit. Tax-exempt: 501(c)(3).
History Museum.
Collections: naval & maritime history; works of art & memorabilia relating to USS Constitution; archives; manuscripts.
Research Fields: American naval history; Maritime history; social history.
Facilities: research library; microfilm of naval documents. Books, slides & nautical items for sale.
Activities: special programs for school groups by appointment; school outreach kits; audiovisual program; permanent & temporary collections.

Publications: biannual Constitution Chronicle; monthly member e-news; quarterly general e-news.
Hours & Admission Prices: April-Oct. daily 9-6; Nov.-March daily 10-5; groups by appointment. No charge; donations accepted. Closed New Year's Day; Thanksgiving; Christmas. ♿
Attendance: 265,000 (accurate)
Membership: Basic: Crew Member (Individual) $30; Quartermaster (Family) $50; Midshipman $75. Captain's Circle: Captain John Percival Society $100; Captain Silas Talbot Society $250; Commodore Edward Preble Society $500; Commodore William Bainbridge Society $1,000; Commodore Isaac Hull Society $2,500.

VILNA SHUL BOSTON'S CENTER FOR JEWISH CULTURE, (M), 18 Phillips St., Boston, MA 02114-3711. Tel.: 617-523-2324. Fax: 781-459-2660.
E-mail: info@vilnashul.org
Web Site: www.vilnashul.org
Formerly: Boston Center for Jewish Heritage
Founded: 1995.
Key Personnel: Dir., Steven M. Greenberg; Pres. (V), Jack Swartz.
Personnel Profile: Full-Time Paid 2; Part-Time Volunteers 12; Interns 1.
Governing Authority: private; nonprofit organization. Tax-exempt.
Cultural Heritage Museum.
Collections: local Jewish culture, immigrants & diversity issues.
Research Fields: Jewish history of Boston; genealogy of Jewish Boston with a focus on the Vilna Shul.
Activities: concerts; docent program; films; guided tours; lectures; participatory exhibitions.
Publications: biannual newsletter, The Scribe.
Hours & Admission Prices: March-Nov. Wed.-Fri. 11-5, Sun. 1-5. No charge. Closed Jewish holidays.
Attendance: 8,000 (accurate)
Membership: Student & Senior $18; Individual $36; Family $72; Contributor $180; Chei Society $360; Shamos Society $1,080.

ZOO NEW ENGLAND, One Franklin Park Rd., Boston, MA 02121-3255. Tel.: 617-541-5466. Fax: 617-989-2025.
E-mail: info@zoonewengland.com
Web Site: www.zoonewengland.com
Formerly: Franklin Park Zoo
Founded: 1905.
Congressional District: 7
Key Personnel: C.E.O. & Pres., John Linehan; Chm. Commonwealth Zoological Corp., Grace Fey; Museum Shop Mgr., Donna Roberts.
Personnel Profile: Full-Time Paid 121; Part-Time Paid 4; Part-Time Volunteers 80; Interns 5.
Governing Authority: state; nonprofit. Parent Institution: Commonwealth Zoological Corporation, Boston, MA. Tax-exempt.
Zoo.
Collections: lions; western lowland gorillas; monkeys; baboons; giraffes; bali mynahs; Siberian cranes; zebras; camels; snow leopards; domestic animal farmyard; jaguars; African wild dogs; cougars; flamingos.
Research Fields: wildlife conservation.
Facilities: food service available. Gift items for sale.
Activities: education programs; guided tours.
Publications: newsletter, Wild Words.
Hours & Admission Prices: April-Sept. Mon.-Fri. 10-5, Sat.-Sun. 10-6; Oct.-March daily 10-4. Adults 16 & up $14, seniors 62 & over $12, children 2-12 $8; members & children under 12 no charge. ♿
Attendance: 495,000 (accurate)
Membership: Individual $40; Family $60; Friend $100; Curator $250; Founder $1,000.

Bourne

APTUCXET TRADING POST MUSEUM, (M), 24 Aptucxet Rd., Bourne, MA 02532-5434. Mailing Address: P.O. Box 3095, Bourne, MA 02532-0795. Tel.: 508-759-8167.
E-mail: bournehistoricalsociety@comcast.net
Web Site: www.bournehistoricalsoc.org
Founded: 1921.
Congressional District: 10
Key Personnel: C.E.O., Judith McAlister; Pres., Jack MacDonnell; Site Mgr., Eleanor A. Hammond; Museum Shop Mgr., Mary Reid.
Personnel Profile: Part-Time Paid 4; Part-Time Volunteers 100; Interns 1.
Governing Authority: nonprofit organization. Parent Institution: Bourne Historical Society, Inc. Tax-exempt: 501(c)(3).
Historic Building: trading post reconstructed on original 1627 site.
Collections: windmill; railroad station built for President Grover Cleveland; reconstruction of salt works; artifacts & written materials relating to the history of Bourne.
Research Fields: history; archaeology.
Facilities: picnic area. Books & museum-related items for sale.
Activities: guided tours; lectures; Maritime Week in May; Strawberry Festival in June; Cape Heritage Week in June; Colonial Day in July; Massachusetts Archaeology Week in autumn; Wampanoag Day in September.
Publications: newsletter, Post Scripts.
Hours & Admission Prices: Memorial Day to Columbus Day Tues.-Sat. 10-4, Sun. 2-5; other times by appointment. Adults $4, seniors $3.50, children 6-18 $2; discounts to groups, AAM members & member guests; members no charge. ♿
Attendance: 6,000 (estimated)
Membership: Individual $25; Family $35; Institutional $50; Contributor $100; Business Supporter $200; Business Benefactor $400; Life $1,000.

Boylston

* **WORCESTER COUNTY HORTICULTURAL SOCIETY/TOWER HILL BOTANIC GARDEN, (M),** 11 French Dr., Boylston, MA 01505-1008. Mailing Address: P.O. Box 598, Boylston, MA 01505-0598. Tel.: 508-869-6111 (hold or dial 10). Fax: 508-869-0314.
E-mail: thbg@towerhillbg.org
Web Site: www.towerhillbg.org
Founded: 1842.
Congressional District: 3
Key Personnel: Exec. Dir., John W. Trexler; Pres., Betsy DeMallie; Dir. Horticulture, Joann Vieira; Librarian, Susanna Haney; Dir. Mktg., Michael J. Arnum; Receptionist, Sue Southard; Dir. Bldgs., Steve Smith; Museum Shop Mgr., Gayle Farley; Dir. Finance, Sharon Chauvin.
Personnel Profile: Full-Time Paid 17; Part-Time Paid 11; Part-Time Volunteers 170; Interns 5.
Governing Authority: nonprofit organization; society. Tax-exempt.
Arboretum & Botanical Garden.
Collections: woody orchard 119 pre-20th century apple varieties; herbaceous & woody ornamentals suited to area, non-hardy plants in orangerie.
Facilities: 8,000-vol. library of books on horticulture available for use by the public.
Activities: symposia; educational lectures; workshops; tours; seasonal flower shows; formally organized education programs; temporary exhibitions; New England School of Gardening accredited program.
Publications: quarterly newsletter; program guide.
Hours & Admission Prices: Mon. holidays & Tues.-Sun. 10-5. Adults $10, seniors $7, children 6-18 $5; discounts to members of AAM, AABGA, MA Horticultural Society, WICN & groups; members & children under 6 no charge. Closed New Year's Day; Thanksgiving; Christmas Eve & Day. ♿
Attendance: 60,000 (accurate)
Membership: Individual $55; Family & Dual $70; Friend $100; Library & Organization $150; Contributing $250; Supporting $500; Patron $1,000; Benefactor $3,000. Corporate: Friend $250; Contributing $500; Patron $1,000; Sponsor $2,500; Benefactor $5,000.

Braintree

BRAINTREE HISTORICAL SOCIETY, INC., 31 Tenney Rd., Braintree, MA 02184-6512. Tel.: 781-848-1640. Fax: 781-380-0731.
E-mail: bhsinc@braintreehistorical.org
Web Site: www.braintreehistorical.org
Founded: 1930.
Congressional District: 11
Key Personnel: Pres., Paul Carr; Treas., Blaine Banker; Vice Pres., Military Archivist & Cur., James Fahey; Librarian & Archivist, Marjorie P. Maxham; Dir. Membership, Alan Weinberg; School Program, Gail Burns; Museum Shop Mgr., Ruth Powell.
Personnel Profile: Full-Time Paid 1; Part-Time Paid 1; Part-Time Volunteers 30.
Governing Authority: private; nonprofit organization. Subsidiary Museums: General Sylvanus Thayer Birthplace, 786 Washington St.; Gilbert Bean Museum; Watson Library and Research Center. Tax-exempt: 501(c)(3).
Historical Society Museum.
Collections: decorative arts (American); 17-19th century American furniture; American folk art; 18-20th century decorative fans; American costumes & textiles; 2 early American homes (early 17-18th century). Historic Home: 1785 birthplace of Sylvanus Thayer.
Research Fields: manufacture of American hand fans; genealogy of local families; history of Braintree; life of Thomas A. Watson.
Facilities: genealogy library; herb gardens. Museum-related items for sale.
Activities: formal education programs for children; guided tours; lectures; temporary exhibitions.
Publications: quarterly members newsletter, The Lantern; gallery guides; exhibit catalogs; History of Braintree & General Sylvanus Thayer.

Hours & Admission Prices: Gilbert Bean Museum & Research Library: Thurs.-Sat. 10-4. Thayer Birthplace: April-Nov. Wed.-Fri. 1-3; Dec.-March by appointment only. Adults $3, children $2; discounts to AAA & AAM members; members no charge. Closed major holidays. ♿
Attendance: 7,000 (accurate)
Membership: Single $25; Family $50; Sustaining $100; Patron $500; Life $1,000.

Brewster

CAPE COD MUSEUM OF NATURAL HISTORY, INC., (M), 869 Rte. 6A, Brewster, MA 02631-1056. Tel.: 508-896-3867. Fax: 508-896-8844.
E-mail: rdwyer@ccmnh.org
Web Site: www.ccmnh.org
Founded: 1954.
Congressional District: 10
Key Personnel: Chm. Bd. Trustees, John McNair; Exec. Dir., Robert F. Dwyer; Museum Shop Mgr., Donna Durkee.
Personnel Profile: Full-Time Paid 4; Part-Time Paid 13; Part-Time Volunteers 250.
Governing Authority: nonprofit organization. Tax-exempt: 501(c)(3).
Natural History Museum.
Collections: flora & fauna of Cape Cod; marine aquaria & displays; local archaeological collections; natural history exhibits; herbarium.
Research Fields: archaeology; flora & fauna of grounds; bird banding.
Facilities: 19,000-vol. library of natural sciences, conservation, natural history, ecology & reference books available to members of museum, teachers & children participating in educational programs; 3 nature trails; nature & conservation center; aquarium; 100-seat auditorium; classrooms. Prints, posters, cards, gift items & natural history books for sale.
Activities: guided tours; lectures; films; educational programs; permanent exhibitions; environmental science program; teacher workshops; field walks; consulting services; research; monthly art exhibits; off-site trips; PDP courses for teachers.
Publications: environmental education material.
Hours & Admission Prices: Jan. open for special programs only; Feb.-March Thurs.-Sun. 11-3; April-May & Oct.-Dec. Wed.-Sun. 11-3; June-Sept. daily 9:30-4. Additional hours during school vacation weeks. Adults $8, seniors 65 & over $7, children 3-12 $3.50; members & children under 3 no charge. Closed Federal holidays; Christmas Eve. ♿
Attendance: 31,000 (estimated)
Membership: Student $10; Individual $35; Family $60; Supporter $150; Sponsor $250; Patron $500; Benefactor $1,000; Visionary $5,000. Business: Good Neighbor $100; Corporate $250; Corporate Benefactor $500.

Brockton

BROCKTON FIRE MUSEUM, 216 N. Pearl St., Brockton, MA 02301-1712. Tel.: 508-583-1039.
Web Site: www.firemuseums.com
Founded: 1992.
Fire-Fighting Museum.
Collections: area fire fighting history; fire-fighting artifacts; 1941 Strand Theater disaster memorial.
Hours & Admission Prices: 1st & 3rd Sun. of month 2-4; other times by appointment. Adults $2; children under 12 no charge.
Membership: Individual $20; Family $30; Business & Supporting $100; Life $200; Family Life & Benefactor $300.

* **FULLER CRAFT MUSEUM, (M),** 455 Oak St., Brockton, MA 02301-1340. Tel.: 508-588-6000. Fax: 508-587-6191.
E-mail: communications@fullercraft.org
Web Site: www.fullercraft.org
Formerly: Fuller Museum of Art
Founded: 1969.
Congressional District: 11
Key Personnel: Exec. Dir., Wyona Lynch-McWhite; Dir. Emeritus & Chief Cur., Gretchen Keyworth; Guest Svcs. Mgr., Tom Bourne; Administrative Asst., Brianne O'Neil.
Personnel Profile: Full-Time Paid 12; Part-Time Paid 30; Part-Time Volunteers 50; Interns 10.
Governing Authority: nonprofit organization. Tax-exempt: 501(c)(3).
Craft Museum.
Collections: contemporary craft.
Research Fields: craft & art education.
Facilities: library; theater; art studios. Museum-related items for sale.
Activities: workshops; lectures; Meet the Maker weekends; tours; concerts; art classes; Family Days; outreach programs; docent program; inter-museum loan; temporary & traveling exhibitions.
Publications: newsletter; exhibition catalogues.
Hours & Admission Prices: Tues. & Thurs.-Sun. 10-5. Wed. 10-9. Adults $8, senior citizens & students $5; discounts to AAM members; members, children under 12 & Wed 5-9 no charge. Closed New Year's Day; Christmas. ♿
Attendance: 18,000 (estimated)
Membership: Senior Basic 1 $30; Basic 1 $40; Senior Basic 2 $45; Basic 2 & Senior Friends 1 $50; Friends 1 $60; Basic 4 & Senior Friends 2 $65; Friends 2 $75; Friends 4 $100; Contributor $125; Supporter $250; Partner $500; Benefactor $1,000.

Brookline

BROOKLINE HISTORICAL SOCIETY, 347 Harvard St., Brookline, MA 02446-2907. Tel.: 617-566-5747.
E-mail: brooklinehistory@gmail.com
Web Site: www.brooklinehistoricalsociety.org
Founded: 1901.
Key Personnel: Pres., Ken Liss.
Governing Authority: society. Branch Museum: 1768 Putterham School, Newton & Grove Sts., Larz Anderson Park, off Newton St. Tax-exempt.
Historical Society Museum: housed in c.1740 Edward Devotion House.
Collections: local furnishings; portraits; photos; Devotion family furniture; books; portraits; school furnishings.
Research Fields: local history.
Facilities: manuscripts pertaining to old Brookline, housed in the Brookline Public Library, available by consultation with accredited persons at the library.
Activities: guided tours; lectures; permanent exhibitions. Museum Sponsors: tours for schools.
Publications: pamphlet, Proceedings of the Brookline Historical Society.
Hours & Admission Prices: Call for hours. No charge; donations accepted.
Attendance: 500 (estimated)
Membership: Sponsor $30; Family $40; Friends of the Society $60.

FREDERICK LAW OLMSTED NATIONAL HISTORIC SITE, 99 Warren St., Brookline, MA 02445-5930. Tel.: 617-566-1689. Fax: 617-232-4073.
Web Site: www.nps.gov/frla
Founded: 1979.
Congressional District: 4
Key Personnel: Supt., Myra Harrison; Supervisory Park Ranger, Alan Banks; Site Mgr., Lee Farrow Cook.
Governing Authority: federal. Parent Institution: National Park Service, Dept. of the Interior, Interior Bldg., Washington, DC. Subsidiary Institution: Olmsted Center for Landscape Preservation. Tax-exempt.
Historic Site: 1810 home & office of Frederick Law Olmsted.
Collections: 1857-1980 archival collection of landscape architectural design documents including drawings, plans, planting lists, lithographs, photographs & related records created by Frederick Law Olmsted, his sons, partners & successors.
Research Fields: landscape architecture; urban planning.
Facilities: archives available for research on premises by appointment only.
Activities: guided tours; permanent exhibitions.
Hours & Admission Prices: Closed for renovation until 2010. ♿
Attendance: 4,500 (accurate)

JOHN FITZGERALD KENNEDY NATIONAL HISTORIC SITE, 83 Beals St., Brookline, MA 02446-6010. Tel.: 617-566-7937. Fax: 617-730-9884.
E-mail: frla_kennedy_nhs@nps.gov
Web Site: www.nps.gov/jofi
Founded: 1969.
Congressional District: 4
Key Personnel: Supt., Myra Harrison; Site Mgr., Lee Farrow Cook.
Personnel Profile: Full-Time Paid 1; Full-Time Volunteers 2; Part-Time Volunteers 3.
Governing Authority: federal. Parent Institution: National Park Service, U.S. Dept. of Interior, Washington DC 20240. Tax-exempt.
Historic House Museum: housed in c.1909 home of Joe & Rose Kennedy, birthplace of our 35th president, John F. Kennedy.
Collections: furnishings as Mrs. Rose Kennedy remembers as they appeared May 29, 1917, the date of John F. Kennedy's birth.
Facilities: Museum-related items for sale.
Activities: ranger-guided tour; special school programs; permanent exhibitions.
Hours & Admission Prices: May 22-Nov 1. Wed.-Sun. 10-4:30, house tours every half hour; school groups by appointment. Adults $3; children under 18, America the Beautiful, annual, senior & access passes no charge.
Attendance: 9,699 (accurate)

LARZ ANDERSON AUTO MUSEUM, 15 Newton St., Brookline, MA 02445-7406. Tel.: 617-522-6547. Fax: 617-524-0170.
Web Site: www.larzanderson.org
Formerly: Museum of Transportation
Founded: 1952.
Congressional District: 4
Key Personnel: Exec. Dir., Michael Iandoli; Asst. Dir., Tyler Burns; Pres. (V), Joseph S. Freeman; Cur., Evan Ide; Master Teacher, Sheldon Steele.
Personnel Profile: Full-Time Paid 5; Part-Time Volunteers 50.
Governing Authority: private; nonprofit. Tax-exempt: 501(c)(3), 509(a)(2).
Transportation Museum.
Collections: period automobiles manufactured prior to 1942; gas, electric & steam cars; horse-drawn carriages & sleighs from the last quarter of the 19th-century; boneshakers, highwheel safeties, ordinaries, tricycles, bicycles, dating to the pre-war period; early period motorcycles; personal artifacts of Larz & Isabel Anderson; French lithograph collection from the Montaut school; automobilia; Packard Co. materials; Anderson vehicle & estate photographs.
Major Exhibits: Style & Innovation of the American Automobile, 11/09-5/10.
Research Fields: historic & vintage autos (Edwardian, brass & nickel eras), 19th-century carriages & bicycles; Weld Garden, the estate of Larz & Isabel Anderson; Anderson collection of automobiles, carriages & sleighs.
Facilities: 1,400-vol. library & photographic archives focusing on pre-war automobiles available for research.
Activities: rotating exhibits; guided tours; education programs; vintage, classic & antique auto shows; evening lecture series; car show lawn events.
Publications: quarterly newsletter, Carnotes; e-newsletter.
Hours & Admission Prices: Tues.-Sun. 10-4. Adults $10, children, seniors, students, & military $5; discounts to groups, AAA, AARP, WGBH, AAM, ICOM & MTA members; children under 6 & members no charge. Closed New Year's Day; Easter; Patriot's Day; Independence Day; Labor Day; Thanksgiving; Christmas. ♿
Attendance: 34,000 (estimated)
Membership: Individual $30; Family $50; Contributing $100; Sponsoring $250; Patron $500. Car Club Membership: $100-$350.

Burlington

BURLINGTON HISTORICAL MUSEUM, 13 Bedford St., Burlington, MA 01803. Mailing Address: Town Hall, 29 Center St., Burlington, MA 01803-3058. Tel.: 781-272-1049 & 270-1600.
E-mail: archives@burlmass.org
Web Site: www.burlington.org
Founded: 1970.
Congressional District: 7
Key Personnel: C.E.O., Museum Guide & Museum Moderator, Joyce Fay; Co Chm. Burlington Historical Commission, Mike Tredeau; Co Chm. & Museum Guide, Toni Faria; Archivist, Daniel McCormack.
Personnel Profile: Full-Time Volunteers 7.
Governing Authority: municipal. Parent Institution: Town of Burlington. Tax-exempt.
History Museum.
Collections: primitive agriculture; archives; costumes; slide collection; school furnishings; dolls; furniture; World War I memorabilia; toys; paintings; farm tools; Town of Burlington history; RCA memorabilia. Historic Building: restored one room schoolhouse, West School.
Facilities: library of books of town history available for use for school projects. Museum-related items for sale.
Activities: temporary exhibitions; historical homes and sites tours; monthly meetings & programs; lectures; children's groups & school field trips.
Publications: historic house pamphlets; books, The History of Burlington, 1640-1950; Burlington, Part of a Greater Chronicle; Images of America-Burlington; Images of America-Burlington Firefighting; 1998-1999 Historic Preservation Survey of Burlington.
Hours & Admission Prices: Summer: Tues. & Sat. 10-2. Archives: 8-12 & 1-4:30. No charge.
Attendance: 600 (estimated)

Buzzards Bay

CAPTAIN CHARLES H. HURLEY LIBRARY, Massachusetts Maritime Academy, 101 Academy Dr., Buzzards Bay, MA 02532-3405. Tel.: 508-830-5034. Fax: 508-830-5074.
Web Site: www.maritime.edu; library.maritime.edu
Founded: 1891.
Congressional District: 12
Key Personnel: Dir., Susan S. Berteaux; Pres., Richard G. Gurnon.
Personnel Profile: Full-Time Paid 4.
Governing Authority: state. Massachusetts Maritime Academy, Academy Dr., Buzzards Bay, MA 02532. Tax-exempt: 501(c)(3).
Maritime Naval Museum & Library.
Collections: archives; manuscripts; 95 scaled models set in base representing the sea & panoramic background.
Facilities: 54,000-vol. library primarily in maritime transportation & engineering; reading rooms.
Activities: guided tours; lectures; formally organized education programs for undergraduate college students; permanent & temporary exhibitions.
Hours & Admission Prices: Academic Year: Sun. 3:30-10pm, Mon.-Thurs. 7:30-10pm, Fri. 7:30-4; extended hours during exams. No charge. Closed state & federal holidays. ♿
Attendance: 83,900 (accurate)

NATIONAL MARINE LIFE CENTER, 120 Main St., Buzzards Bay, MA 02532-3221. Mailing Address: P.O. Box 269, Buzzards Bay, MA 02532-0269. Tel.: 508-743-9888. Fax: 508-759-5477.
E-mail: nmlc@nmlc.org
Web Site: www.nmlc.org
Formerly: The National Marine Life Center's Marine Animal Discovery Center
Key Personnel: Pres. & Exec. Dir., Kathy Zagzebski, M.E.M.; Chm. (V), Sean Randall; Exec. Asst., Outreach Coord. & Museum Shop Mgr., Joanne Nicholson; Animal Care & Facilities Coord., Brian Moore; Science Dir. & Assoc. Veterinarian, Sea Rogers Williams, V.M.D.; Assoc. Veterinarian, Bridget Dunnigan.
Personnel Profile: Full-Time Paid 3; Part-Time Paid 5; Part-Time Volunteers 50; Interns 2.
Governing Authority: Tax-exempt.
Marine Museum.
Collections: marine animals including sea turtles & seals; care & rehabilitation; marine science; ocean conservation.
Research Fields: marine wildlife health & conservation.
Facilities: Museum-related items for sale.
Activities: educational programs.
Publications: newsletter, NewsSplash; e-newsletter, E-Splash.
Hours & Admission Prices: Memorial Day-Labor Day daily 10-5; call for additional hours. No charge; donations accepted. ♿
Attendance: 6,054 (accurate)

Cambridge

BOTANICAL MUSEUM OF HARVARD UNIVERSITY, 26 Oxford St., Cambridge, MA 02138-2902. Tel.: 617-495-3045. Fax: 617-495-5667.
E-mail: hmnh@oeb.havard.edu
Web Site: www.hmnh.harvard.edu
Founded: 1858.
Key Personnel: Cur. Paleobotany, Andrew H. Knoll.
Personnel Profile: Full-Time Paid 5; Part-Time Paid 2.
Governing Authority: university. Parent Institution: Harvard University. Tax-exempt.
Botanical Museum: located within Harvard Museum of Natural History.
Collections: narcotic & medicinal plants; rubber-yielding plants; pre-Columbian ethnobotany; economic botany; paleobotany; Blaschka glass models of plants; Hankins collection of fossil woods; taxonomic collection of orchids; Tina and Gordon Wasson ethnomycological collection; manuscripts.
Research Fields: economic botany, including ethnobotany; paleobotany; orchid taxonomy; conservation of tropical forests.
Facilities: 45,000-vol. library; tape tour of glass flowers.
Publications: technical leaflets, Botanical Museum of Harvard University; occasional books.
Hours & Admission Prices: Daily 9-5. Adults $9, seniors 65 & over and students $7, children 3-18 $6; Harvard students with ID no charge. Closed New Year's Day; Thanksgiving; Christmas Eve & Day. ♿
Membership: see Harvard Museum of Natural History for membership levels & prices.

CAMBRIDGE HISTORICAL SOCIETY, 159 Brattle St., Cambridge, MA 02138-3300. Tel.: 617-547-4252.
E-mail: info@cambridgehistory.org
Web Site: www.cambridgehistory.org
Founded: 1905.
Congressional District: 8
Key Personnel: Exec. Dir., Gavin Kleespies; Pres. (V), Jinny Nathans; Treas., Andrew Leighton; Asst. Dir., Cynthia Brennen.
Personnel Profile: Full-Time Paid 1; Part-Time Paid 2; Part-Time Volunteers 2; Interns 2.
Governing Authority: society; nonprofit. Tax-exempt: 501(c)(3).
Historical Society Museum: 1685 building remodeled in early Georgian period.
Collections: artifacts; printed material & manuscripts; period furnishings.
Research Fields: local history; historic house interpretation.

Facilities: 300-vol. library pertaining to local history available on premises. Publications & postcards for sale.
Activities: guided tours; lectures; organized educational programs; internship programs.
Publications: periodical, Proceedings of the C-H-S; occasional monographs of Cambridge history; newsletter, Newetowne Chronicle.
Hours & Admission Prices: Mon.-Fri. by appointment. Adults $5, senior citizens & children $3; discounts to AAM & ICOM members; members no charge. Closed major holidays.
Attendance: 2,000 (estimated)
Membership: Individual $35; Family $60; Fellow $100; Sponsor $250; Patron $500; Benefactor $750.

* **HARVARD ART MUSEUM,** 32 Quincy St., Cambridge, MA 02138-3845. Tel.: 617-495-9400, ext. 0.
Web Site: www.harvardartmuseum.org
Founded: 1895.
Congressional District: 8
Key Personnel: Dir., Thomas W. Lentz; Dir. Information Technology, Mary Gallagher; Deputy Dir., Jose Ortiz; Dir. Education, Ray Williams; Cur. Ancient Art, Susanne Ebbinghaus; Cur. Chinese Art, Robert D. Mowry; Cur. Islamic & Later Indian Art, Mary A. McWilliams; Cur. American Art, Theodore E. Stebbins; Cur. Busch-Reisinger Museum, Peter Nisbet; Cur. Paintings, Sculpture & Decorative Arts, Stephan Wolohojian; Cur. Drawings, William W. Robinson; Cur. Prints, Susan M. Dackerman; Cur. Photographs, Deborah Martin Kao; Dir. Collections Management, Maureen Donovan; Dir. Design & Publications, Katie Andresen; Dir. Institutional Advancement, Bradford Voigt; Dir. Facilities Planning & Management, John Seager; Dir. Visitor Svcs., Sanja Cvjeticanin; Dir. Straus Center for Conservation & Technical Studies, Henry Lie; Dir. Communications, Daron Manoogian; Dir. Budget & Finance, Stephanie Schilling; Dir. Human Resources, Holly Abernethy; Archaeological Exploration of Sardis, Turkey, Elizabeth Gombosi; Archives, Susan von Salis; Dir. Center for the Technical Study of Modern Art, Carol Mancusi-Ungaro; Mgr. Digital Imaging & Visual Resources, David Sturtevant; Cur. Modern & Contemporary Art., Helen Molesworth; Dir. Safety & Security, Michael Kirchner.
Personnel Profile: Full-Time Paid 167; Part-Time Paid 46; Part-Time Volunteers 24; Interns 6.
Governing Authority: university. Parent Institution: Harvard University. Constituent Museums: Arthur M. Sackler Museum, 485 Broadway, Cambridge. Founded: 1985; Busch-Reisinger Museum, 32 Quincy St., Cambridge. Founded: 1901. Fogg Museum, 32 Quincy St., Cambridge. Founded: 1891. Tax-exempt: 501(c)(3).
University Art Museums.
Collections: Fogg Museum: Western art from the Middle Ages to present with emphasis in Italian early Renaissance, British pre-Raphaelite, & 19th century French art; Wertheim collection; Grenville L. Winthrop collection including 19th century paintings, early Chinese art, & Buddhist sculptures. Busch-Reisinger Museum: art from Central & Northern Europe with emphasis on German-speaking countries; Austrian Secession art; Bauhaus materials; Willy & Charlotte Reber collection; Barbara & Peter Moore Fluxus collection. Arthur M. Sackler Museum: Asian, Islamic, Indian & period art; Chinese jades; Japanese surimono; Chinese bronzes; ceremonial weapons; Buddhist cave-temple sculpture; Chinese & Korean ceramics; Japanese woodblock prints; calligraphy; Mongol, Timurid, & Safavid Iran; Ottoman Turkey; Rajput & Mughal India; Greek, Roman, Egyptian, Near Eastern art; Greek & Roman sculpture; Greek vases; period coins.
Research Fields: all media of fine arts. Arthur M. Sackler Museum: ancient, Asian, Islamic & Indian art. Busch-Reisinger Museum: Bauhaus, Walter Gropius & Lyonel Feininger. Fogg Museum: prints; drawings; conservation; photography; all areas of Western art.
Facilities: Arthur M. Sackler Museum: 10,000 sq. ft. exhibit space; 275-seat lecture hall. Museum-related items for sale.
Activities: guided tours; lectures; gallery talks; seminars; concerts; permanent, loan & temporary exhibitions; formally organized education programs for undergraduate & graduate students affiliated with Harvard University; internships & fellowships for museum professionals; public education programs.
Publications: quarterly calendar; gallery guides & catalogues; annual report.
Hours & Admission Prices: Mon.-Sat. 10-5, Sun. 1-5. Adults $9, senior citizens $7, college students w/ID $6; discounts to AAM & ICOM members; children under 18, Sat. until noon, Harvard ID holders, members & Cambridge Public Library card holders no charge. The Fogg Museum & Busch-Reisinger Museum are closed for renovation. ♿
Attendance: 108,140 (accurate)
Membership: Student & Senior $45; Individual $55; Dual $75; Supporter $125; Contributor $250; Sustaining $500; Fellow $1,000 & up.

HARVARD MUSEUM OF NATURAL HISTORY, (M), 26 Oxford St., Cambridge, MA 02138-2932. Tel.: 617-495-3045. Fax: 617-496-8206.
E-mail: hmnh@oeb.harvard.edu
Web Site: www.hmnh.harvard.edu
Founded: 1995.
Congressional District: 8
Key Personnel: Exec. Dir., Elisabeth Werby; Deputy Dir., Vicki Boone; Dir. Education, Wendy Derjue-Holzer; Dir. Public Programs, Tom Scanlon; Dir. Exhibitions, Janis Sacco; Volunteer Coord., Carol Carlson; Dir. Communications, Blue Magruder; Dir. Travel Program, Lauren Brock; Dir. Devel., Hilton Jankelowitz; Assoc. Dir. Operations, Kevin Ebert.
Personnel Profile: Full-Time Paid 19; Part-Time Paid 21; Part-Time Volunteers 90; Interns 1.
Governing Authority: university. Parent Institutions: Harvard University; Herbaria; Mineralogic Museum; Museum of Comparative Biology. Tax-exempt: 501(c)(3).
Natural History Museum.
Collections: glass flowers; zoological; mineral; collections of The Museum of Comparative Zoology, The Mineralogical Museum & The Harvard University Hebaria.
Major Exhibits: Language of Color, 11/09-3/10; Evolution, 11/09-12/10; Domesticated: Photographs by Amy Stein, 1/10-3/10.
Facilities: educational facilities; 30,000 sq. ft. exhibit space. Museum-related items for sale.
Activities: docent program; formally organized educational programs; guided tours; lectures; rental gallery; temporary exhibitions; international travel program.
Publications: program & events calendar.
Hours & Admission Prices: Daily 9-5. Adults $9, senior citizens 65 & over and students $7, children 3-18 $6; discounts to AAM & ICOM members; MA residents, Harvard ID; Sept.-May Wed. 3-5, Sun. 9am-12, members & children under 3 no charge. Closed New Year's Day; Thanksgiving; Christmas Eve & Day. ♿
Attendance: 175,000 (accurate)
Membership: Student & Senior $35; Individual $50; Household $85; Sustaining $200; Patron $500.

THE HARVARD UNIVERSITY HERBARIA, 22 Divinity Ave., Cambridge, MA 02138-2020. Tel.: 617-495-2365. Fax: 617-495-9484.
E-mail: jmacklin@oeb.harvard.edu
Web Site: www.huh.harvard.edu
Founded: 1864.
Key Personnel: Dir. Herbaria, Robert E. Cook; Dir. Botany Libraries, Judith A. Warnement; Dir. Collections & Information, James Macklin.
Governing Authority: university. Affiliated with Harvard University.
Herbarium.
Collections: botany; flowering plants; gymnosperms; ferns; cryptogams.
Research Fields: evolutionary & systematic botany; population biology; bibliography; botanical history.
Facilities: 291,000-vol. library of botany & horticulture books available for use on premises by researchers & students affiliated with Harvard University.
Activities: formally organized education program for undergraduate & graduate college students; inter-museum loans.
Publications: journal, Harvard Papers in Botany; Gray Herbarium index.
Hours & Admission Prices: Mon.-Fri. 9-5. Closed university holidays. ♿

HARVARD UNIVERSITY SEMITIC MUSEUM, (M), 6 Divinity Ave., Cambridge, MA 02138-2020. Tel.: 617-495-4631. Fax: 617-496-8904.
E-mail: semiticm@fas.harvard.edu
Web Site: www.fas.harvard.edu/~semitic
Founded: 1889.
Key Personnel: Dir. & Cur., Prof. Lawrence E. Stager; Cur. Cuneiform Collections, Prof. Piotr Steinkeller; Asst. Dir., Joseph A. Greene; Asst. Cur. Collections, James A. Armstrong; Museum Admin., Dena S. Davis; Dir. Publication, M.D. Coogan.
Personnel Profile: Full-Time Paid 2; Full-Time Volunteers 2; Part-Time Paid 5; Part-Time Volunteers 11.
Governing Authority: Faculty of Arts & Sciences, Harvard University, University Hall, Cambridge. Tax-exempt.
Archaeological Museum: specializing in ancient Near East archaeology.
Collections: archaeology.
Research Fields: ancient Near Eastern languages & history; archaeology field work in Near East.
Activities: guided tours; lectures; special programs for groups by reservation; inter-museum loan, permanent, temporary & traveling exhibitions; White-Levy Program for Archaeological Publications: gives grants to publish terminated and unpublished archaeological field work from sites in the Levant, Mesopotamia, Aegean and Anatolia.
Publications: books, Harvard Semitic Series; Harvard Semitic Monographs,

Studies in the Archaeology and History of the Levant; members' association newsletter; exhibition catalogs.
Hours & Admission Prices: Mon.-Fri. 10-4, Sun. 1-4. No charge; donations accepted. Closed holidays.
Attendance: 5,000 (estimated)
Membership: Individual & Family $35; Donor $50; Contributing $100; Supporting $250; Sustaining $500; Benefactor $1,000.

LONGFELLOW NATIONAL HISTORIC SITE, 105 Brattle St., Cambridge, MA 02138-3499. Tel.: 617-876-4491. Fax: 617-497-8718.
Web Site: www.nps.gov/long
Founded: 1973.
Congressional District: 8
Key Personnel: Site Mgr., James M. Shea; Supervisory Park Mgr., Nancy Jones; Supt., Myra Harrison; Archives Specialist, Anita Israel; Museum Technician, Lauren Malcolm.
Personnel Profile: Full-Time Paid 5; Part-Time Paid 11; Part-Time Volunteers 2; Interns 1.
Governing Authority: federal. Administered by the National Park Service, U.S. Dept. of the Interior, Washington, DC. Tax-exempt.
Historic House & Site Museum: 1759 house, later home of Henry Wadsworth Longfellow; headquarters of George Washington, 1775-1776.
Collections: books; furnishings; paintings; works of art; manuscripts; letters; photographs; textiles; architectural fragments. Historic Building: 1844 Barn.
Research Fields: Henry Wadsworth Longfellow & family; 19th-century American social & cultural history; 19th-century domestic life; decorative arts; 18th-century architecture; colonial revival movement; George Washington in Cambridge 1775-1776.
Facilities: Longfellow's personal library, manuscripts of various Longfellow family members available to researchers by appointment. Verse folders & various Longfellow related material for sale.
Activities: guided house tours; summer garden concert series; summer poetry readings.
Publications: Commemorative Conference; Friends of the Longfellow House Newsletter.
Hours & Admission Prices: June-Oct. Wed.-Sun. 10-4:30. Adults $3; children 15 & under no charge. National park passes honored. ♿
Attendance: 38,000 (accurate)

* **MIT-LIST VISUAL ARTS CENTER, (M),** 20 Ames St., E15-109, Cambridge, MA 02142-1308. Tel.: 617-253-4680 & 4400. Fax: 617-258-7265.
Web Site: listart.mit.edu
Founded: 1950.
Congressional District: 8
Key Personnel: Dir., Jane Farver; Asst. Dir., David Freilach; Administrative Asst., Barbara Pine; Registrar, John Rexine; Gallery Mgr., Tim Lloyd; Cur., Joao Ribas; Educator & Public Rels. Officer, Marle Linga.
Personnel Profile: Full-Time Paid 7; Part-Time Paid 7; Interns 8.
Governing Authority: university. Parent Institute: Massachusetts Institute of Technology. Tax-exempt: 501(c)(3).
Art Gallery & Visual Arts Center.
Collections: MIT permanent collection: sculpture, paintings, works on paper, photographs, drawings & video.
Facilities: study archives.
Activities: changing exhibitions of contemporary art in all mediums; associated educational activities & publications.
Publications: exhibition catalogs & brochures; gallery guides.
Hours & Admission Prices: Oct.-July Tues.-Wed. & Fri.-Sun. 12-6, Thurs. 12-8. No charge; donations accepted. Closed holidays. ♿
Attendance: 18,000 (estimated)

* **MIT MUSEUM, (M),** 265 Massachusetts Ave., Cambridge, MA 02139-4307. Mailing Address: Bldg. N52, 2nd Fl., 265 Massachusetts Ave., Cambridge, MA 02139-4307. Tel.: 617-253-5927. Fax: 617-253-8994.
E-mail: museum@mit.edu
Web Site: web.mit.edu/museum
Founded: 1971.
Congressional District: 8
Key Personnel: Dir., John Durant; Chm. (V), Dr. David Ellis; Assoc. Dir., Mary Leen; Mgr. Exhibitions, Donald Stidsen; Dir. Public Rels., Josie Patterson; Dir. Technology, Allan Doyle; Dir. Cambridge Science Festival, P.A. d'Arboloff; Cur. Hart Nautical Collections, Kurt Hasselbalch; Cur. Science & Technology Collections, Deborah Douglas, Ph.D.; Collections Mgr. & Registrar, Joan Parks-Whitlow; Cur. Architecture & Design, Gary van Zante; Museum Shop Mgr., Claudia Majetich.
Personnel Profile: Full-Time Paid 23; Part-Time Paid 10; Part-Time Volunteers 10; Interns 5.
Governing Authority: university. Parent Institution: Massachusetts Institute of Technology, 77 Massachusetts Ave., Cambridge 02139. Branch Galleries: Francis Russell Hart Nautical Gallery, 55 Massachusetts Ave.; Margaret Hutchinson Compton Gallery, 77 Massachusetts Ave. Tax-exempt: 501(c)(3).
Science & Technology Museum.
Collections: Architecture & Design collection: 1873-1968 student theses & projects; 1840-1920 rare drawings by European & American architects. Hart Nautical Gallery: late 19th to early 20th century New England technical history of ship & small craft design, construction & propulsion. Holography collection: 1940s inception to current artistic & technical evolution. MIT general collection: artifacts, visual & written materials documenting history of MIT & its role in the development of science, technology & engineering. Science & Technology Collection: record of 19th-20th century innovation.
Facilities: holography lab.
Activities: temporary & traveling exhibition programs; hands-on family programs.
Publications: exhibition brochures.
Hours & Admission Prices: Main facility at 265 Massachusetts Ave.: daily 10-5. Adults $7.50, youth 5-18, college students & seniors $3; discount to AAM members; MIT Community members & Sun. 10 to noon no charge. Hart Nautical Galleries: daily 9-8. Compton Gallery: daily 10-5. No charge. Closed holidays. ♿
Attendance: 97,398 (accurate)

MUSEUM OF COMPARATIVE ZOOLOGY, 26 Oxford St., Cambridge, MA 02138-2902. Tel.: 617-495-2460. Fax: 617-496-8308.
E-mail: cweisel@oeb.harvard.edu
Web Site: www.mcz.harvard.edu
Founded: 1859.
Congressional District: 8
Key Personnel: C.E.O., James Hanken.
Personnel Profile: Full-Time Paid 60; Part-Time Paid 80; Part-Time Volunteers 50.
Governing Authority: private university. Parent Institution: Harvard University. Subsidiary Institution: Harvard Museum of Natural History (HMNH), Cambridge, MA. Tax-exempt: 501(c)(3).
Zoological Museum.
Collections: ornithology; herpetology; mammals; invertebrate zoology; invertebrate & vertebrate paleontology; entomology; marine biology; biological oceanography; population genetics; ichthyology; malacology.
Research Fields: entomology; invertebrate zoology; population genetics; invertebrate & vertebrate paleontology; herpetology; ichthyology; ornithology; marine biology; biological oceanography; malacology; mammalogy.
Activities: see Harvard Museum of Natural History listing for activities.
Publications: periodicals, Bulletin of the Museum of Comparative Zoology; Breviora of the Museum of Comparative Zoology.
Hours & Admission Prices: see Harvard Museum of Natural History for hours & admission. ♿
Membership: see Harvard Museum of Natural History listing for membership levels & prices.

* **PEABODY MUSEUM OF ARCHAEOLOGY & ETHNOLOGY, (M),** 11 Divinity Ave., Cambridge, MA 02138-2096. Tel.: 617-496-1027. Fax: 617-495-7535.
Web Site: www.peabody.harvard.edu
Founded: 1866.
Congressional District: 8
Key Personnel: Dir., Dr. William L. Fash; Deputy Dir. Administration, Catherine Cezeaux; Dir. Collections, Dr. Steven LeBlanc; Dir. External Rels., Dr. Pamela Gerardi; Deputy Dir. Curatorial Affairs, Dr. Jeffrey Quilter; Asst. Dir. Security, Dr. Lawrence Flynn; Registrar, Dr. Viva Fisher; Assoc. Cur., Dr. Castle McLaughlin; Assoc. Cur., Dr. Diana Loren; Assoc. Cur., Dr. Michele Morgan; Assoc. Cur., Dr. Patricia Capone; Collections Assoc., Susan Haskell; Head Conservator, T. Rose Holdcraft; Programs, Catherine Linardos; Senior Collections Mgr., David De Bono Schafer; Senior Archivist, India Spartz; Conservator, Scott Fulton; Bldg. Mgr., Eugene Ayres; Exhibit Designer & Coord., Samuel Tager; Librarian, Lynne M. Schmelz.
Personnel Profile: Full-Time Paid 40; Part-Time Paid 18; Part-Time Volunteers 14; Interns 15.
Governing Authority: university. Parent Institution: Harvard University. Tax-exempt: 501(c)(3).
Anthropology Museum.
Collections: five million objects; archaeological & ethnographic collections from most areas of the world mainly North, South & Middle America; Old World (especially Paleolithic), European Iron Age; Near East archaeology; ethnography of Africa, North America & Oceania; photographic archives of over 500,000 images; paintings, prints & drawings; archival materials.

Research Fields: archaeology; biological anthropology; social anthropology; ethnography; zooarchaeology.
Facilities: 225,260-vol. library of books on anthropology available for inter-library loan & for research on premises; classrooms; zooarchaeology lab; casting lab.
Activities: lectures; films; education programs for undergraduate & graduate students affiliated with Harvard University; inter-museum loan, permanent & temporary exhibitions; guided tours; preschool & youth education programs; workshops. Museum Sponsors: Annual Weekend of the Americas in October.
Publications: annual report; periodical monographs; scientific papers; memoirs; bulletins; exhibition catalogues; newsletter, Symbols.
Hours & Admission Prices: Daily 9-5. Adults $9, senior citizens & students with ID $7, children 3-18 $6; children under 3, Harvard students, members, Sun. 9-12, Sept.-May Wed. 3-5 no charge. Closed New Year's Day; Thanksgiving; Christmas Eve & Day. ♿
Attendance: 150,000 (estimated)
Membership: Senior & Student $25; Individual $40; Household & Dual $60; Sustaining $125; Supporting $250; Patron $500; Peabody Institute $1,000.

Canton

CANTON HISTORICAL SOCIETY, 1400 Washington St., Canton, MA 02021-2240. Tel.: 781-828-6957. Fax: 781-821-5780.
E-mail: historical@canton.org
Web Site: canton.org
Founded: 1893.
Key Personnel: Pres., Wallis Gibbs.
Governing Authority: nonprofit. Tax-exempt.
History Museum.
Collections: Indian relics; manuscripts; James Bazin collection; genealogies; musical instruments; photographs.
Facilities: 500-vol. library of county & local history available by appointment with president of society; conservation area; Indian burial ground; nature trails.
Activities: guided tours; lectures; formally organized educational programs; permanent & temporary exhibitions.
Hours & Admission Prices: Open select holidays & by request. No charge; donations accepted.
Attendance: 50
Membership: Annual $10; Life $100 or an outstanding contribution to the society.

MILTON ART MUSEUM, 900 Randolph St., Canton, MA 02021-1355. Tel.: 781-821-2222, ext. 2124.
E-mail: miltonmuseum@hotmail.com
Web Site: www.miltonartmuseum.org
Founded: 1986.
Key Personnel: Chm. (V), Ellyn Moller.
Governing Authority: Tax-exempt.
Art Museum.
Collections: Western & European prints; sculpture; lithographs; etchings; photography; Asian art.
Hours & Admission Prices: Mon.-Thurs. 8-6:30, Fri. 8-4:30; extended hours 1st week in Aug. No charge. ♿
Membership: Annual $25.

VISUAL ARTS CENTER AND MILDRED MORSE ALLEN WILDLIFE SANCTUARY, (M), 963 Washington St., Canton, MA 02021-2117. Tel.: 781-821-8853.
Key Personnel: Dir., Amy Montague
Nature Center & Art Gallery.
Collections: natural history art; photographs; wildflowers; hawks; meadow; forest; swamp.
Facilities: nature trails.
Activities: educational programs; permanent & temporary exhibitions.
Hours & Admission Prices: Gallery: Tues.-Sun. 1-5. Trail: Tues.-Sun. 9-5. Adults $4; members no charge.

Centerville

CENTERVILLE HISTORICAL MUSEUM, 513 Main St., Centerville, MA 02632-2913. Tel.: 508-775-0331. Fax: 508-862-9211.
E-mail: chsm@centervillehistoricalmuseum.org
Web Site: www.centervillehistoricalmuseum.org
Founded: 1952.
Key Personnel: C.E.O., Cur. & Devel., Randall Hoel; Pres., Royden Richardson; Treas., Don Vincent.
Personnel Profile: Full-Time Paid 1; Part-Time Volunteers 20.
Governing Authority: private; nonprofit organization. Tax-exempt: 501(c)(3).
19th century Cape Cod History Museum.
Collections: costumes; quilts; military artifacts & uniforms; marine artifacts; tools; toys; photographs; Dodge MacKnight watercolors; A.E. Crowell carved bird; decorative arts.
Research Fields: Civil War; Lt. Augustus D. Ayling.
Facilities: library. Museum-related items for sale.
Activities: concerts; docent program; films; guided tours; hobby workshops; lectures; temporary exhibitions; outreach programs. Annual Events: Open House Tours on holidays; Family Days; Old Home Week.
Publications: quarterly newsletter, Chequaquet Log.
Hours & Admission Prices: May-Dec. 15 Tues.-Sat. 12-4; other times by appointment. Adults $6, senior citizens & students $5; discounts to AAA & MTA members; members & children under 8 no charge. ♿
Attendance: 3,012 (accurate)
Membership: Individual $25; Family $40; Patron $75; Benefactor $125.

Charlestown

BUNKER HILL MUSEUM, 43 Monument Sq., Charlestown, MA 02129-3430. Mailing Address: Boston National Historic Park, Charlestown Navy Yard, Charlestown, MA 02129-4543. Tel.: 617-242-7275.
Web Site: www.nps.gov/bost/historyculture/bhmuseum.htm
Founded: 1975.
Congressional District: 8
Key Personnel: Pres. & C.E.O. (V), Arthur L. Hurley; Chm. (V) & Museum Shop Mgr., Terry Savage.
Personnel Profile: Part-Time Volunteers 5.
Governing Authority: society; nonprofit organization. Charlestown Historical Society. Tax-exempt.
History Museum: located across from the Bunker Hill Monument grounds.
Collections: local pottery; period gowns; history of Battle of Bunker Hill & community of Charlestown.
Research Fields: local history.
Facilities: 175-seat auditorium. Commemorative medals & crafts for sale.
Activities: guided tours; drama; inter-museum loan, permanent exhibitions.
Hours & Admission Prices: Daily 9-5. No charge; donations accepted. Closed New Year's Day; Thanksgiving; Christmas.
Membership: Individual $2; Family $15; Friend $50; Business $100.

Chatham

CHATHAM HISTORICAL SOCIETY, HOME OF ATWOOD HOUSE MUSEUM, (M), 347 Stage Harbor Rd., Chatham, MA 02633-2229. Mailing Address: P.O. Box 709, Chatham, MA 02633-0709. Tel.: 508-945-2493. Fax: 508-945-1205.
E-mail: info@chathamhistorical.org
Web Site: www.chathamhistoricalsociety.org
Founded: 1923.
Congressional District: 12
Key Personnel: Chm., Spencer Y. Grey; Dir. & Cur., Mark Wilkins; Museum Shop Mgr., Barbara Newberry.
Personnel Profile: Full-Time Paid 1; Part-Time Paid 2; Part-Time Volunteers 12; Interns 3.
Governing Authority: society. Parent Institution: Chatham Historical Society. Subsidiary Institution: Atwood House Museum. Tax-exempt: 501(c)(3).
Historical Museum: housed in 1752 Atwood House and additions.
Collections: archives; period artifacts; Crowell birds; Sandwich glass; Stallknecht murals; Parian Ware; sea shells; manuscripts & publications of Joseph C. Lincoln; paintings by Harold Brett; portraits of local sea captains & other local people by Frederick S. Wright; period tools; North Beach camp; herb garden; maritime paintings & artifacts; paintings & objects related to the China trade; commercial fishing history; Chatham's twin light lantern & Fresnel lens; maps & sea charts.
Research Fields: genealogy; local & maritime history.
Facilities: 300-vol. library of books & old reference books available for genealogical research available by appointment; research room; William Nickerson Wing.
Activities: guided tours; lectures; special & permanent exhibitions; summer children's programs; preserving your family papers classes. Museum Sponsors: Open House in June; Appraisal Day in June; Antiques Show mid September; Tree Festival With Chatham Garden Club in November; Hearth Warming in December.
Publications: pamphlets, Old Chatham Houses; Chatham Since the Revolution; The Nickerson North Beach Camp; books, W. C. Smith History of Chatham, Mass., 1981; The History of Weir Fishing; Beyond The Bar: The Perilous Journey (history of fishing industry), 2007; Chatham Vital Records Vol. 1 to 1865; 1994 Vital Records, Vol. II, 1866-1910; Days to Remember; A Home on the Rolling Deep; Home Song; Weathering a Century of Change, Chatham, MA 1900-2000; Picturing Chatham-American Landscape Painting 1880-1977.
Hours & Admission Prices: June & Sept.-Oct. Tues.-Sat. 1-4; July-Aug.

Tues.-Sat. 10-4. Adults $5, children 12 & up $3; discount to AAM members; children 11& under and members no charge. Closed Independence Day; Labor Day. ♿
Attendance: 3,700 (accurate)
Membership: Single $25-$34; Family $35-$74; Contributing $75-$149; Sustaining $150-$249; Sponsoring $250-$499; Patron $500-$999; Benefactor $1,000 & up.

Chestnut Hill

LONGYEAR MUSEUM, (M), 1125 Boylston St., Chestnut Hill, MA 02467-1811. Tel.: 617-278-9000. Fax: 617-278-9003.
E-mail: letters@longyear.org
Web Site: www.longyear.org
Founded: 1923.
Congressional District: 4
Key Personnel: Exec. Dir., Anne H. McCauley; Chm. (V), Gail Hewitt; Pres. (V), Robert B. Larsen; Dir. Cur., Stephen R. Howard; Dir. Activities, Sandra Houston; Dir. Devel., John Mitchell; Dir. Collections, Cheryl Moneyhun; Museum Shop Mgr., Amy Grier.
Personnel Profile: Full-Time Paid 33; Part-Time Paid 8; Interns 1.
Governing Authority: nonprofit organization; board of trustees. Parent Institution: Longyear Foundation. Branch Museums: Eight Mary Baker Eddy Historic Houses: 23 Paradise Rd., Swampscott, MA; Stinson Lake Rd., Rumney, NH; 133 Central St., Stoughton, MA; North Groton, NH; 277 Main St., Amesbury, MA; 62 N. State St., Concord, NH; 12 Broad St., Lynn, MA; 400 Beacon St., Chestnut Hill, MA. Tax-exempt: 501(c)(3).
Historical Museum.
Collections: artifacts; manuscripts, letters; photographs; portraits; paintings; books, houses & furniture pertaining to the life & achievements of Mary Baker Eddy, founder of Christian Science.
Research Fields: Mary Baker Eddy & the history of Christian Science dating from 1821-1910; the Baker family; the Longyear family; papers and reminiscences of Christian Scientists active prior to 1911; the Longyear Foundation.
Facilities: 5,000-vol. library; 350 cu. ft. of archival material available for use by qualified researchers. Museum-related items for sale.
Activities: workshops; children's programs; school programs; lectures; speakers' bureau; walking tours; domestic & foreign travel; programs; concerts; documentary films.
Publications: newsletter, Report to Members; books, Pioneers in Christian Science; Christian Science in Germany; The Stoughton Years; A Precious Legacy: Christian Science Comes to Japan; The Human Life, 1906-1907 articles on Mary Baker Eddy; A Most Agreeable Man: Lyman Brackett; Genesis of a Poem; A Chronological Reference to Mary Baker Eddy's Books: Miscellaneous Writings, 1883-1896 and the First Church of Christ, Scientist and Miscellany; films, The Onward and Upward Chain; Remember the Days of Old; "Who Shall Be Called?"; The Pleasant View Household: Working and Watching; books, Homeward Part I: Lynn; Homeward Part II: Chestnut Hill; Violet Hay.
Hours & Admission Prices: Longyear Museum: Mon. & Wed.-Sat. 10-4, Sun. 1-4. Historic Houses: call for hours. No charge; donations accepted. Closed holidays. ♿
Membership: Student $10; Individual $25; Family $50.

MCMULLEN MUSEUM OF ART, BOSTON COLLEGE, Devlin Hall, 140 Commonwealth Ave., Chestnut Hill, MA 02467-3800. Tel.: 617-552-8587. Fax: 617-552-8577.
E-mail: artmusm@bc.edu
Web Site: bc.edu/artmuseum
Founded: 1976.
Congressional District: 4
Key Personnel: Dir., Dr. Nancy Netzer; Chm. (V), C. Michael Daley; Devel., Simon Welsby; Devel., Catherine Concanon; Mgr. Exhibitions & Collections, Diana Larsen; Admin. & Collections, John McCoy; Publications & Exhibitions Admin., Margaret Neeley; Museum Shop Mgr., Chris Bergin.
Personnel Profile: Full-Time Paid 6; Part-Time Paid 6; Part-Time Volunteers 12; Interns 6.
Governing Authority: private college; nonprofit. Parent Institution: Boston College. Tax-exempt.
Art Museum.
Collections: 15th- to 17th-century European paintings, drawings, tapestries, prints, sculpture; Japanese prints; 19th- to 20th-century American paintings.
Facilities: 350-seat auditorium; educational facilities.
Activities: formal education programs for undergraduate & graduate students; guided tours; lectures; loan, temporary & traveling exhibitions.
Publications: triannual, Friends Newsletter; exhibition catalogs.
Hours & Admission Prices: Mon.-Fri. 11-4, Sat.-Sun. 12-5. No charge; donations accepted. Closed New Year's Day; Martin Luther King Jr. Day; Washington's Birthday; Good Friday; Easter; Memorial Day; Labor Day; Columbus Day; Christmas. ♿

Attendance: 75,000 (accurate)
Membership: Standard $50.

Clinton

MUSEUM OF RUSSIAN ICONS, (M), 203 Union St., Clinton, MA 01510-2903. Tel.: 978-598-5000. Fax: 978-598-5009.
Web Site: www.museumofrussianicons.org
Founded: 2006.
Key Personnel: Dir. & Pres. (V), Kent Russell; Chm. (V), Gordon B. Lankton; Cur. Asst., Jesse W. Rives; Admin. & Programs Coord., Laura Garrity-Arquitt.
Personnel Profile: Full-Time Paid 3; Full-Time Volunteers 2; Part-Time Paid 4; Part-Time Volunteers 15; Interns 2.
Governing Authority: private; nonprofit organization. Tax-exempt: 501(c)(3).
Art Museum.
Collections: works by Russian artists; paintings.
Research Fields: Russian history; Russian Icons.
Facilities: 200-vol. library; 20-seat restaurant; educational facility; 5,000 sq. ft. exhibit space. Museum-related items for sale.
Activities: arts festivals; concerts; dance recitals; films; docent program; educational programs; guided tours; workshops; lectures; loan, temporary, traveling & participatory exhibits; rental gallery; training programs for museum workers; broadcast programs.
Publications: quarterly newsletter, IcoNews.
Hours & Admission Prices: Tues.-Wed. & Fri. 11-3, Thurs. 11-7, Sat. 9-3; groups by appointment. Adults $5; discounts to groups; members, students & children no charge. Closed New Year's Day; Independence Day; Thanksgiving; Christmas. ♿
Attendance: 5,000
Membership: Senior & Student $15; Individual $30; Family & Dual $45; Cossack $100; Boyar $250; Prince $500; Czar $1,000.

Cohasset

CAPTAIN JOHN WILSON HOUSE, 4 Elm St., Cohasset, MA 02025-1829. Mailing Address: 106 S. Main St., P.O. Box 627, Cohasset, MA 02025-0627. Tel.: 781-383-1434.
E-mail: cohassethistory@yahoo.com
Web Site: www.cohassethistoricalsociety.org
Founded: 1928.
Congressional District: 10
Key Personnel: Pres., Kathleen O'Malley; Historian, David Wadsworth; Exec. Admin., Lynne DeGiacomo.
Personnel Profile: Part-Time Paid 2; Part-Time Volunteers 50.
Governing Authority: society. Parent Institution: Cohasset Historical Society. Tax-exempt.
Historic House Museum.
Collections: costumes; textiles; decorative arts; period furnishings.
Research Fields: decorative arts.
Activities: guided tours; permanent & temporary exhibits.
Publications: newsletter, Historical Highlights; Images of America/Cohasset.
Hours & Admission Prices: June-Sept. Tues.-Fri. 1-4, Sat. 10-2. No charge; donations accepted.
Attendance: 800 (estimated)
Membership: Individual $25; Family $35; Sustaining $50; Patron $500; Benefactor $1,000.

MARITIME MUSEUM - COHASSET HISTORICAL SOCIETY, 6 Elm St., Cohasset, MA 02025. Mailing Address: P.O. Box 627, Cohasset, MA 02025-0627. Tel.: 781-383-1434.
E-mail: cohassethistory@yahoo.com
Founded: 1956.
Congressional District: 10
Key Personnel: Pres., Kathleen O'Malley; Historian, David Wadsworth; Exec. Admin., Lynne DeGiacomo.
Personnel Profile: Part-Time Paid 2; Part-Time Volunteers 10.
Governing Authority: society. Parent Institution: Cohasset Historical Society. Tax-exempt: 501(c)(3).
Maritime Museum.
Collections: shipwreck; lifesaving equipment; 19th-century maritime artifacts; sailing ship models; paintings; early tools; Indian stone artifacts; local historic artifacts; mercantile; fishing; ship building; Cohasset seafaring history; Minot's Ledge Lighthouse.
Research Fields: maritime; military; local history.
Activities: guided tours; lectures; permanent exhibitions.
Publications: newsletter, Historical Highlights.
Hours & Admission Prices: June-Sept. Tues.-Fri. 1-4, Sat. 10-2. No charge; donations accepted.
Attendance: 800 (estimated)

Membership: Cohasset Historical Society: Individual $25; Family $35; Sustaining $50; Patron $500; Benefactor $1,000.

PRATT BUILDING - COHASSET HISTORICAL SOCIETY, 106 S. Main St., Cohasset, MA 02025-2097. Mailing Address: P.O. Box 627, Cohasset, MA 02025-0627. Tel.: 781-383-1434.
E-mail: cohassethistory@yahoo.com
Web Site: cohassethistoricalsociety.org
Founded: 1928.
Congressional District: 10
Key Personnel: Pres., Kathleen O'Malley; Historian, David Wadsworth; Exec. Admin., Lynne DeGiacomo.
Personnel Profile: Part-Time Paid 2; Part-Time Volunteers 50.
Governing Authority: Parent Institution: Cohasset Historical Society. Subsidiary Institution: Maritime Museum, Capt. John Wilson House. Tax-exempt.
History Museum.
Collections: maritime; costumes; town history; Native American artifacts.
Research Fields: Cohasset history; local architectural surveys; theatre, professional & amateur archives; maritime.
Activities: lectures; permanent & temporary exhibits; research.
Publications: newsletter, Historical Highlights; Images of America: Cohasset.
Hours & Admission Prices: Mon.-Fri. 10-4, Sat. call for hours. No charge; donations accepted. ♿
Attendance: 1,500 (estimated)
Membership: Cohasset Historical Society: Individual $25; Family $35; Sustaining $50; Patron $500; Benefactor $1,000.

Concord

CONCORD ART ASSOCIATION, (M), 37 Lexington Rd., Concord, MA 01742-2570. Tel.: 978-369-2578. Fax: 978-371-2496.
E-mail: gallery@concordart.org
Web Site: www.concordart.org
Founded: 1922.
Congressional District: 5
Key Personnel: Exec. Dir., Lili Ott; Dir. Education, Michele Kenna.
Personnel Profile: Full-Time Paid 1; Part-Time Paid 3; Part-Time Volunteers 80.
Governing Authority: nonprofit organization. Tax-exempt.
Art Gallery & Sculpture Garden: building built in 1760.
Collections: early American portraits; paintings; sculpture; graphics; decorative arts.
Facilities: garden; facilities for wedding receptions, programs, meetings & workshops.
Activities: arts festivals; outdoor sculpture exhibits; permanent & temporary exhibitions.
Publications: newsletter; catalogs.
Hours & Admission Prices: Tues.-Sat. 10-4:30, Sun. 12-4. No charge; donations accepted. Closed holidays. ♿
Attendance: 8,500 (estimated)
Membership: Senior $35; Artist & Individual $50; Family $75; Patron $100; Life $500; Corporate $1,000.

* **CONCORD MUSEUM, (M),** Cambridge Turnpike, at Lexington Rd., Concord, MA 01742-3711. Mailing Address: P.O. Box 146, Concord, MA 01742-0146. Tel.: 978-369-9763. Fax: 978-369-9660.
E-mail: cm1@concordmuseum.org
Web Site: www.concordmuseum.org
Founded: 1886.
Congressional District: 5
Key Personnel: Pres. (V), Jean Haley Hogan; Exec. Dir., Desiree Caldwell; Cur., David Wood; Dir. Devel., Rebecca Wright; Public Rels., Carol Haines; Museum Shop Mgr., David Hesel.
Personnel Profile: Full-Time Paid 8; Part-Time Paid 31; Part-Time Volunteers 250; Interns 2.
Governing Authority: society. Parent Institution: Concord Antiquarian Society. Tax-exempt: 501(c)(3).
History & Decorative Arts Museum.
Collections: American decorative arts; paintings & graphics; Ralph Waldo Emerson's study; Henry David Thoreau; Revolution artifacts, Native American stone tools.
Research Fields: American decorative arts; Middlesex County history; Concord history.
Facilities: 1,400-vol. library of decorative arts & New England history books available on premises. Museum-related items for sale.
Activities: seminars/symposia; lectures; films; concerts; trips; formally organized education programs; permanent, temporary & traveling exhibitions; education program serving 13,000 school children from 55 Massachusetts communities & 19 states.
Publications: book, Concord Museum: Climate for Freedom; catalogs, Two Towns, Concord & Wethersfield, A Comparative Exhibition of Regional Culture 1635-1850; Decorative Arts from a New England Collection; bulletin, The Newsletter; catalogue, Forms to Sett on: A Social History of Concord Seating Furniture; From Musketaquid to Concord; sourcebook, Native American Sourcebook: A Teacher's Resource on New England Native Peoples; catalog, Harry Little's Concord: Public and Domestic Architecture, 1914-1941; book, An Observant Eye: The Thoreau Collection at the Concord Museum.
Hours & Admission Prices: Jan.-March Mon.-Sat. 11-4, Sun. 1-4; April-May & Sept.-Dec. Mon.-Sat. 9-5, Sun. 12-5; June-Aug. daily 9-5. Adults $10, senior citizens & students $8, children $5; discounts to AAM, AAA & MTA members; members no charge. ♿
Attendance: 48,000 (accurate)
Membership: Individual $50; Family $65; Contributor $125; Patron $250; Benefactor $500.

MINUTE MAN NATIONAL HISTORICAL PARK, 174 Liberty St., Concord, MA 01742-1705. Tel.: 978-369-6993. Fax: 978-318-7800.
E-mail: mima_info@nps.gov
Web Site: www.nps.gov/mima
Founded: 1959.
Congressional District: 4 & 5
Key Personnel: Supt., Nancy Nelson; Cur., Teresa Wallace; Museum Shop Mgr., Steve Moore.
Personnel Profile: Full-Time Paid 25; Part-Time Volunteers 100.
Governing Authority: federal. National Park Service, U.S. Department of the Interior, Washington, DC 20240. Tax-exempt.
National Park & Historic Houses: located along 1775 battle road; 19th-century Wayside, Nathaniel Hawthorne & Alcott & Lothrop family home.
Collections: structures, furnishings, photographs & books; archaeology; Harriett M. Lothrop family papers.
Research Fields: American Revolutionary War period & 19th-century New England literature.
Facilities: 1,200-vol. library of history & ecology available for use on premises upon request; Colonial Living Interpretive Center. Pamphlets, booklets & other museum-related items for sale.
Activities: guided tours; lectures; permanent exhibitions; environmental study area; literary & patriotic 1883-1924; hiking on five-mile Battle Road Trail.
Publications: brochures.
Hours & Admission Prices: Park: daily sunrise to sunset. No charge; donations accepted. Wayside Historic Houses: late-May to early Nov. Wed.-Sun, call for hours. Admission $5. Closed New Year's Day; Thanksgiving; Christmas. ♿
Attendance: 1,000,000 (estimated)

THE OLD MANSE, 269 Monument St., Concord, MA 01742-1837. Mailing Address: P.O. Box 572, Concord, MA 01742-0572. Tel.: 978-369-3909. Fax: 978-287-6154.
E-mail: oldmanse@ttor.org
Web Site: www.thetrustees.org/places-to-visit/greater-boston/old-manse.html
Founded: 1939.
Congressional District: 5
Key Personnel: Historic Site Mgr., Tom Beardsley; Dir. Historic Resources, Susan C.S Edwards.
Personnel Profile: Full-Time Paid 1; Part-Time Paid 15; Part-Time Volunteers 24.
Governing Authority: society. The Trustees of Reservations, Long Hill - 572 Essex St., Beverly, MA 01915. Tel. 978-921-1944. Tax-exempt: 501(c)(3).
Historic House & Site: built in 1770 for Rev. William Emerson, town minister & patriot; located next to the North Bridge, site of the 1st major skirmish of the Revolutionary War, April 19, 1775. Later home to Emerson's grandson, Ralph Waldo, who drafted his first published work, Nature, here; home of Nathaniel & Sophia Hawthorne 1842-45.
Collections: original family furnishings.
Research Fields: American studies.
Facilities: Books for sale.
Activities: guided tours. Annual Events: Patriot's Day in April; Fall Festival in October; Halloween Event in October.
Hours & Admission Prices: mid-April to Oct. Mon.-Fri. 10-5, Sun. & holidays 12-5, last tour leaves at 4:30; other times by appointment. Adults $8, senior citizens & students $7, children 6-12 $5; discounts for groups of 10 or more & for AAA, MTA & WGBH members; Trustees members & children under 6 no charge. ♿
Attendance: 11,400 (accurate)
Membership: Senior & Student $35; Individual $45; Friends & Family $65; Contributing $100; Supporting $150; Sustaining $300; Sponsor $600.

ORCHARD HOUSE, (M), 399 Lexington Rd., Concord, MA 01742-3712. Mailing Address: P.O. Box 343, Concord, MA 01742-0343. Tel.: 978-369-4118. Fax: 978-369-1367.
E-mail: info@louisamayalcott.org
Web Site: www.louisamayalcott.org
Founded: 1911.
Congressional District: 5
Key Personnel: Exec. Dir., Jan Turnquist; Pres. (V), Beth Neeley Kubacki; Museum Shop Mgr., Sally Cody; Exec. Asst., Maria Powers; Education Dir., Lis Adams; Bldg. & Grounds Supt., Jay Powers.
Personnel Profile: Full-Time Paid 6; Part-Time Paid 35; Part-Time Volunteers 36.
Governing Authority: nonprofit organization. Parent Institution: Louisa May Alcott Memorial Association. Tax-exempt: 501(c) (3).
History Museum: house where Louisa May Alcott wrote Little Women, and also the site of Bronson Alcott's School of Philosophy.
Collections: memorabilia of the Alcotts; manuscripts & publications, particularly by Louisa May Alcott & Bronson Alcott; paintings by May Alcott. Historic Buildings: 18th-century Orchard House; 1880 School of Philosophy.
Research Fields: Louisa Alcott; Bronson Alcott; Transcendental Movement in Concord.
Facilities: Museum-related items for sale.
Activities: guided tours; living history programs; children's programs; lecture series in School of Philosophy; school of philosophy can be rented for events.
Publications: Story of the Alcotts; The Poetry of Louisa May Alcott; American Transcendentalism; The Concord Summer School of Philosophy.
Hours & Admission Prices: April-Oct. Mon.-Sat. 10-4:30, Sun. 1-4:30; Nov.-March Mon.-Fri. 11-3, Sat. 10-4:30, Sun. 1-4:30. Adults $9, senior citizens 62 and over & college students with ID $8, youth 6-17 $5; discounts to families, military, teachers, AAM & MTA members; members & children under 6 no charge. Closed Easter; Thanksgiving; Christmas.
Attendance: 48,910 (accurate)
Membership: Junior 17 & under $10; Student & Senior $25; Individual $40; Household $60; Supporting $125; Philosophers Group $250; Transcendentalist Club $500.

RALPH WALDO EMERSON HOUSE, 28 Cambridge Tpke., Concord, MA 01742-3700. Tel.: 978-369-2236.
Founded: 1930.
Key Personnel: Pres., Mrs. Nicholas Bancroft; Dir., Marie A. Gordinier.
Personnel Profile: Part-Time Paid 10.
Governing Authority: nonprofit organization. Parent Institution: Ralph Waldo Emerson Memorial Association. Tax-exempt: 501(c)(3).
Memorial Museum: housed in 1935 Ralph Waldo Emerson House. Ralph Waldo Emerson's home for the greater part of his life 1835 to his death in 1882.
Collections: preservation project of Emerson's personal belongings; portraits; books; furniture.
Activities: guided tours; permanent exhibitions.
Hours & Admission Prices: mid-April to Oct. Thurs.-Sat. 10-4:30, Sun. 1-4:30; group tours by appointment. Adults $8, seniors & students $6; discounts to groups & AAM members; children under 6 no charge.
Attendance: 3,454 (accurate)

Cotuit

CAHOON MUSEUM OF AMERICAN ART, (M), 4676 Falmouth Rd., Cotuit, MA 02635. Mailing Address: P.O. Box 1853, Cotuit, MA 02635-1853. Tel.: 508-428-7581. Fax: 508-420-3709.
E-mail: cmaa@cahoonmuseum.org
Web Site: www.cahoonmuseum.org
Founded: 1984.
Congressional District: 10
Key Personnel: C.E.O., Robert Gambone; Pres., Carl Scrivener; Museum Shop Mgr., Susan Quinlan-Brown.
Personnel Profile: Full-Time Paid 2; Part-Time Paid 4; Part-Time Volunteers 75.
Governing Authority: nonprofit organization. Tax-exempt: 501(c)(3).
Art Museum: housed in 1775 Cape Cod Colonial tavern used for overnight stops on Hyannis-Sandwich Stagecoach line.
Collections: 19th-21st century American paintings; primitive artists Ralph & Martha Cahoon.
Major Exhibits: Regional Exhibition: American Society of Maritime Artists (T), 4/10-5/10; Sam Barber: Cape Cod Impressionist, 7/10.
Research Fields: 19th to early 20th-century American & women artists; primitive painters, Ralph & Martha Cahoon.
Facilities: 1,500-vol. art library on American paintings specializing in artists of New England & American women artists. Notecards, prints, books & other art-related items for sale.
Activities: guided tours; lectures; artist demonstrations; art classes; special exhibitions; organized education programs; children's program.
Publications: quarterly newsletter, Spyglass; brochure; exhibition catalogue, American Paintings from Nature: Flower, Fruit & Leaf; Simple Pleasures: The Art of Martha Cahoon; Modern Primitives: Simple Art in a Complex Age; In the Beginning: The Decorated Furniture of Ralph and Martha Cahoon, 2005.
Hours & Admission Prices: Feb.-Dec. Tues.-Sat. 10-4, Sun. 1-4. Adults $5, seniors & students $4; discounts to teachers & AAM members; members & children under 12 no charge. Closed major holidays.
Attendance: 7,500 (estimated)
Membership: Individual $40; Family $60; Contributor $100; Associate $250; Sponsor $500; Patron $1,000; Cahoon Society $1,500; Benefactor $5,000 & up.

HISTORICAL SOCIETY OF SANTUIT AND COTUIT, 1148 Main St., Cotuit, MA 02635. Mailing Address: P.O. Box 1484, Cotuit, MA 02635-1484. Tel.: 508-428-0461.
E-mail: cotuithssc@verizon.net
Web Site: www.cotuithistoricalsociety.org
Founded: 1954.
Congressional District: 10
Key Personnel: Pres., Joyce Ginouves; Vice Pres., Stephen Whalen; Treas., Duke Bates; Cur., Marian Nicastro; Museum Shop Mgr., Scott Harvey.
Personnel Profile: Part-Time Volunteers 25.
Governing Authority: society. Tax-exempt: NZ 23-7177654.
Historic House: 1800-1850 restored home of village carpenter.
Collections: historic furnishings. Historical Building: Dottridge Homestead.
Research Fields: old houses in village.
Facilities: herb garden. Museum-related items for sale.
Activities: temporary & loan exhibitions; educational tours; docent tours. Annual Events: Strawberry Festival; Wine Festival; Harvest Festival; Christmas in Cotuit in December.
Publications: annual historical paper.
Hours & Admission Prices: Memorial Day to Labor Day Sat.-Sun. 1-5; Sept. to Columbus Day Sat. 1-5. No charge; donations accepted.
Attendance: 2,500 (estimated)
Membership: Individual $25; Family $35; Life $500.

Cummington

KINGMAN TAVERN HISTORICAL MUSEUM, 41 Main St., Cummington, MA 01026-9742. Mailing Address: P.O. Box 10, Cummington, MA 01026-0010. Tel.: 413-634-5527 & 8828 (administrative).
Web Site: hiddenhills.com/kingmantavern/
Founded: 1967.
Congressional District: 1
Key Personnel: Chm. (V), Carla Ness; Historic Commission, Stephanie Pasternak; Historic Commission, Stephen Howes; Historic Commission, Matthew Grallert; Historic Commission, Karen Westergaard.
Personnel Profile: Part-Time Paid 4; Part-Time Volunteers 8.
Governing Authority: municipal. Tax-exempt.
Historical Museum: housed in 1800 frame building used as a post office, Masonic Lodge meeting hall & tavern.
Collections: furniture & furnishings of earlier inhabitants of the town; tavern room; examples of early American stenciling; tools; toys; costumes; a collection of twenty miniature rooms made by Alice C. Steele; 17 room tavern; barn; cider mill; carriage house; general store; farm machinery.
Research Fields: town histories & family genealogical material.
Facilities: 25-vol. library of reference material on early American tools, furniture & equipment available for use in museum library during regular hours or by appointment. Miniatures & museum-related items for sale.
Activities: films; slides; implement demonstrations.
Publications: books, Only One Cummington; Alice C. Steele's Miniature Rooms; Childhood Memories; Olive Thayer's Remembering Cummington; Aunt Teeks in Memoryland; vital records of Cummington.
Hours & Admission Prices: July-Aug. Sat. 2-5; other times by appointment. No charge; donations accepted. ♿
Attendance: 150 (estimated)

WILLIAM CULLEN BRYANT HOMESTEAD, 207 Bryant Rd., Cummington, MA 01026-9639. Tel.: 413-634-2244. Fax: 413-634-0376.
E-mail: bryanthomestead@ttor.org
Web Site: www.thetrustees.org
Founded: 1928.
Congressional District: 11
Key Personnel: C.E.O., Andy Kendall; Rgnl. Dir. The Trustees of Reservation, Jocelyn Forbush; Supt., Jim Caffrey; Historic Site Admin., Ellice Gonzalez.
Personnel Profile: Full-Time Paid 1; Part-Time Paid 6; Part-Time Volunteers 15.

Governing Authority: nonprofit. Parent Institution: The Trustees of Reservations, Long Hill 572 Essex St., Beverly, MA 01915. Tel. 978-921-1944. Tax-exempt.
Historic House: 1789 boyhood home & adult summer residence of famed poet William Cullen Bryant.
Collections: 3 generations of Bryant family furnishings; 19th century European & Middle East exotic travel memorabilia; rural life artifacts.
Research Fields: literature; 19th-century travel; rural life.
Facilities: grounds available for special events. Museum-related items for sale.
Activities: guided tours; interpretive events.
Hours & Admission Prices: last week in June-Labor Day Fri.-Sun. & Mon. holidays 1-5; Sept.-Columbus Day Sat.-Sun. & Mon. holidays 1-5. Adults $5, children 6-12 $2.50; children under 6 & Trustees of Reservation members no charge. ♿
Attendance: 7,000 (estimated)
Membership: Membership in the Trustees of Reservations: Individual $45; Family $65.

Dalton

CRANE MUSEUM OF PAPERMAKING, Housatonic St. off Rte. 8 & 9, Dalton, MA 01226. Mailing Address: c/o Crane & Co., Inc., 30 South St., Dalton, MA 01226-1751. Tel.: 413-684-6481. Fax: 413-684-0817.
Web Site: www.crane.com
Governing Authority: Parent Institution: Crane & Co., Inc.
Historic Building: housed in the former papermaking business of Crane and Co.'s Old Stone Mill, built in 1844. Crane produces the rag paper that US currency is printed on.
Collections: papermaking company history; papermaking process; financial instruments; stationery.
Hours & Admission Prices: June to mid-Oct. Mon.-Fri. 1-5. No charge.
Attendance: 1,000 (estimated)

Danvers

DANVERS ARCHIVAL CENTER, 15 Sylvan St., Danvers, MA 01923-2735. Tel.: 978-774-0554. Fax: 978-762-0251.
Web Site: www.danverslibrary.org
Founded: 1972.
Congressional District: 6
Key Personnel: Town Archivist, Richard B. Trask.
Personnel Profile: Full-Time Paid 1; Part-Time Paid 1; Part-Time Volunteers 3.
Governing Authority: municipal government. Parent Institution: Peabody Institute Library of Danvers.
Town Archives: housed in 1892, Peabody Institute Library.
Collections: books; pamphlets; manuscripts; maps; broadsides; photographs; newspapers; printed or written media relating to the growth, development & history of Salem Village & Danvers.
Facilities: 7,000-vol. library on the history of witchcraft, Danvers, local history & biography available for use by the public; 130-seat auditorium. Gift items for sale.
Hours & Admission Prices: Mon. 1-7:30, Wed.-Thurs. & 1st. Sat. of month 9-12 & 1-5; 2nd & 4th Fri. of month 1-5. No charge. Closed state & national holidays. ♿
Attendance: 1,200 (estimated)

DANVERS HISTORICAL SOCIETY, (M), 11 Page St., Danvers, MA 01923-2813. Mailing Address: Box 381, Danvers, MA 01923-0681. Tel.: 978-777-1666. Fax: 978-777-5028.
E-mail: dhs@danvershistory.org
Web Site: www.danvershistory.org
Founded: 1889.
Congressional District: 6
Key Personnel: Chm. (V), Richard Moody; Dir. Operations, Cathy Gareri; Office Mgr., Paula Ruta.
Personnel Profile: Full-Time Paid 1; Part-Time Paid 5; Part-Time Volunteers 30.
Governing Authority: society. Tax-exempt: 501(c)(3).
Historical Society Museum.
Collections: furniture; tools; objects showing growth & development of town; archaeology; manuscripts; burial ground. Historic Houses: 1754 Jeremiah Page House, 11 Page St.; 1792 McIntyre Tea House; 1893 Glen Magna, 57 Forest St; 1850 Mrs. Day's Ideal Baby Shoe Shop; 17th century Israel Putnam birthplace, Maple Street.
Research Fields: local history.
Facilities: botanical garden; 130-seat auditorium. Books for sale.
Activities: guided tours; lectures; permanent & temporary exhibitions; school programs; community outreach & advocacy.
Publications: books, Danvers Historical Society Collections; Chronicles of Danvers; As The Century Turned: Photographic Glimpses of Danvers, Massachusetts, 1880-1910; On The Sands of Time: The Life of Charles Sutherland Tapley; The Devil Hath Been Raised: A Documentary History of the Salem Village Witchcraft Outbreak of March, 1692. Historical Glimpses of Danvers (2002).
Hours & Admission Prices: Society: Mon.-Fri. 9-1; other times by appointment. Donations accepted. Glen Magna & McIntyre Tea House: June-Labor Day Tues. & Thurs. 10-4; other times by appointment. Adults $5. ♿
Attendance: 11,500 (estimated)
Membership: Student (K-12) $10; Individual $20; Senior (65 & over) $18; Household $30; Sustaining $100; Benefactor $150.

REBECCA NURSE HOMESTEAD, 149 Pine St., Danvers, MA 01923-2693. Mailing Address: P.O. Box 456, Hathorne, MA 01937-0456. Tel.: 978-774-8799.
E-mail: president@rebeccanurse.org
Web Site: www.rebeccanurse.org
Founded: 1974.
Congressional District: 6
Key Personnel: Pres. & Bd. Chm., Marta Driscoll; Vice Pres., Jackson Tingle; Treas., William Quilnan; Clerk, Niamh Dolan; Bldg. Chm., Henry W. Rutkowski; Cur., Kathryn P. Rutkowski; Museum Shop Mgr., Candice Clemenzi.
Personnel Profile: Part-Time Paid 6; Part-Time Volunteers 20.
Governing Authority: society; nonprofit organization. Parent Institution: Danvers Alarm List Co., Inc. Tax-exempt: 501(c)(3).
Historic House: 1678 home of Rebecca Nurse, hanged as a witch in 1692.
Collections: Massachusetts artifacts from 1650-1780; 17th & 18th century furnishings; Old Salem Village including early 18th century Saltbox house; reproduction 1672 Salem Village meeting house; barn; Nurse family cemetery.
Research Fields: 17th & 18th century Salem Village and Danvers; 1692 witch hysteria; 1770s militia; architecture.
Facilities: Museum-related items for sale.
Activities: guided tours; craft; militia activities and demonstrations by the Danvers Alarm List Company, a recreation of an 18th century militia, courses; lectures; annual 18th Century Field Day & Muster.
Publications: book, Rebecca Nurse-Saint but Witch Victim; quarterly newsletter, Rebecca Nurse Homestead Preservation Society.
Hours & Admission Prices: June 15 to Labor Day Fri.-Sun. 10-4; Sept.-Oct. Sat.-Sun. 10-4; other times by appointment. Adults $6.50, seniors $5, children under 16 $4.50; discount to school groups; members no charge.
Attendance: 4,000 (estimated)
Membership: Individual $25; Family $50; Sponsor $100; Patron $250.

Dedham

DEDHAM HISTORICAL SOCIETY MUSEUM, (M), 612 High St., Dedham, MA 02026-1833. Mailing Address: P.O. Box 215, Dedham, MA 02027-0215. Tel.: 781-326-1385.
E-mail: society@dedhamhistorical.org
Web Site: dedhamhistorical.org
Founded: 1859.
Congressional District: 9
Key Personnel: Exec. Dir. & C.E.O., Ronald F. Frazier.
Personnel Profile: Full-Time Paid 1; Part-Time Paid 4; Part-Time Volunteers 65.
Governing Authority: society. Tax-exempt: 501(c)(3).
History Museum & Genealogy Library.
Collections: 16th to 20th-century furniture; portraits & paintings; regional historical & industrial artifacts; Dedham & Chelsea pottery; needlework & costumes; manuscripts, newspapers & photo archive; genealogies & family histories; Katharine Pratt Silver; Dedham & Chelsea pottery & decorative arts; artists: Alvan Fisher, Lilian & Philip Hale, Henry Hitchings, Charles Mills, Harry Spiers, James Frothingham, Gilbert Stuart, & Jacob Wagner. Historic House: 1766 powder house.
Research Fields: Norfolk County area history & New England genealogy.
Facilities: 20,000-vol. library of history & genealogical books & microform source materials, including partial IGI, available for use on premises; reading room.
Activities: museum tours; house tours; lecture series; educational programs for students; permanent & temporary exhibitions; courses on genealogy & antiques; special member events.
Publications: bimonthly newsletter; books, The Dedham Pottery & Earlier Robertson's Chelsea Potteries, Dedham reprinting; Dedham, 1635-1890; Building Dedham; Images of America, Dedham.
Hours & Admission Prices: Tues.-Fri. & even dated Sat. Adults $2, children $1. Library: $5; discounts for groups & AAM members; members no charge. Closed national & state holidays; Thanksgiving & day after; Christmas week.
Attendance: 2,000 (estimated)

Membership: Student $10; Individual $35; Family $50; Contributing $75; Life $750. Corporate: Contributor $150; Donor $250; Patron $500; Benefactor $1,200.

FAIRBANKS HOUSE, (M), 511 East St., Dedham, MA 02026-3060. Tel.: 781-326-1170. Fax: 781-326-2147.
E-mail: homestead@fairbankshouse.org
Web Site: www.fairbankshouse.org
Founded: 1903.
Congressional District: 11
Key Personnel: Pres., Al Blood; Treas., Lynn Fairbank; Dir. & Cur., Alex Service.
Personnel Profile: Full-Time Paid 1; Part-Time Paid 1; Part-Time Volunteers 12.
Governing Authority: nonprofit organization. Parent Institution: The Fairbanks Family in America. Tax-exempt: 501(c)(3).
Historic House: c.1641 Fairbanks House, oldest surviving timber frame house in North America, built for Jonathan & Grace Fairbanks and their family.
Collections: Fairbanks' family furnishings; personal artifacts.
Research Fields: 17th-century architectural research; Fairbanks family, allied families; life in America 1630-1905.
Facilities: Museum-related items for sale.
Activities: guided tours; lectures; docent program; formally organized education program for adults & school groups.
Publications: quarterly publication, Homestead Courier.
Hours & Admission Prices: Tues.-Sat. 10-5, Sun. 1-5. Tours given on the hour, last tour at 4pm. Adults $5, children 6-12 $2; discounts to AAM, AAA, MTA & NEMA members.
Attendance: 1,800 (estimated)
Membership: Regular $25; Life $500.

MUSEUM OF BAD ART, 580 High St., Dedham, MA 02026-1845. Mailing Address: 73 Parker Rd., Needham, MA 02494-2038. Tel.: 781-444-6757. Fax: 781-433-9991.
E-mail: moba@museumofbadart.org
Web Site: www.museumofbadart.org
Founded: 1993.
Key Personnel: Exec. Dir., Louise R. Sacco; Dir. Special Events, Garen Daley; Cur., Mike Frank.
Personnel Profile: Part-Time Volunteers 5.
Governing Authority: nonprofit corporation. Branch Institution: MOBA Gallery, 55 Davis Sq., Somerville, MA.
Art Museum.
Collections: bad works of art in all media.
Facilities: 1,500 sq. ft. exhibit space. Museum-related items for sale.
Activities: lectures; loan exhibitions; TV programs.
Publications: email newsletter, Museum of Bad Art News; book, Museum of Bad Art: Art Too Bad To Be Ignored.
Hours & Admission Prices: Sun.-Thurs. 2-9, Fri.-Sat. 1-10. No charge; donations accepted.
Attendance: 6,300 (estimated)

Deerfield

* **HISTORIC DEERFIELD, INC., (M),** 84B Old Main St., Deerfield, MA 01342. Mailing Address: P.O. Box 321, Deerfield, MA 01342-0321. Tel.: 413-774-5581. Fax: 413-775-7220.
E-mail: tours@historic-deerfield.org
Web Site: www.historic-deerfield.org
Founded: 1952.
Congressional District: 1
Key Personnel: Pres., Philip Zea; Vice Pres. Museum Affairs, Anne Digan Lanning; Chm. Curatorial Dept., Amanda E. Lange; Cur. Academic Programs, Joshua W. Lane; Vice Pres. Business Affairs, Susan Martinelli; Dir. Museum Education & Interpretation, Amanda Rivera Lopez; Librarian, David C. Bosse; Museum Shop Mgr., Kathleen McAndrews; Supt. Properties Maintenance, George Holmes.
Personnel Profile: Full-Time Paid 59; Part-Time Paid 110; Part-Time Volunteers 115; Interns 8.
Governing Authority: nonprofit organization. Tax-exempt: 501(c)(3).
Outdoor History Museum Village: consisting of 14 18th & 19th-century structures.
Collections: early New England Life; decorative arts; furniture; ceramics; silver; metalwork; 1998 Flynt Ctr of Early New England Life; textiles; costumes; paintings; 1814 Henry Needham Flynt Silver & Metalware. Historic Buildings: c.1760 Frary House; c.1733 Allen House; c.1733 Ashley House; c.1753 Sheldon House; c.1746 Wells-Thorn House; c.1799 Asa Stebbins House; c.1760-1800 Hall Tavern; c.1816 Hinsdale & Anna Williams House; c.1795 Barnard Tavern; c.1848 Rev. Johnson Farwell Moors House.
Research Fields: decorative arts; furniture; history; folklore; silver; ceramics; paintings; archaeology.
Facilities: 10,000-vol. library of history & decorative arts available on premises; reading room; restaurant. Publications, slides, needlework, postcards & museum reproductions for sale.
Activities: guided tours; lectures; films; elementary & secondary school tours; formally organized programs for college classes; workshops; forums; archaeological field school; family events; museum courses for adults.
Publications: books, Heritage Foundation Collection of Silver; Parson Ashley House; Early Settlement in the Connecticut Valley; booklets, Historic Deerfield: An Introduction; Five Colleges: Five Histories; In Debt to Shays: The Bicentennial of an Agrarian Rebellion; Historic Deerfield: A Portrait of Early America; Old Deerfield Massachusetts; Pursuing Refinement in Rural New England, 1750-1850, A Deerfield Sampler; record, Faded Memories: Songs of Deerfield; Delftware at Historic Deerfield, 1600-1800.
Hours & Admission Prices: April 17-Nov. 28 daily 9:30-4:30. Flynt Center of Early New England Life: Jan.-March Sat.-Sun. Adults $12, children $5; discounts to groups of 20 or more with reservations & AAM members; members no charge. Closed Thanksgiving; Christmas Eve & Day. ♿
Attendance: 30,000 (estimated)
Membership: Individual $40; Family $60; Active $100; Contributing $150; Associate $250; Patron $500; Asher Benjamin Society $1,000, $2,000 & $5,000; Life $10,000.

MEMORIAL HALL MUSEUM, POCUMTUCK VALLEY MEMORIAL ASSOC., 8 Memorial St., Deerfield, MA 01342. Mailing Address: Box 428, Deerfield, MA 01342-0428. Tel.: 413-774-7476, ext. 10. Fax: 413-774-5400.
E-mail: tneumann@deerfield.history.museum
Web Site: www.old-deerfield.org
Founded: 1870.
Congressional District: 1
Key Personnel: Dir., Timothy C. Neumann; Dir. Youth Programs, Lynne Manring; Pres., Carol Letson; Cur., Suzanne Flynt; Librarian, David Bosse; Museum Shop Mgr., Tom Mershon.
Personnel Profile: Full-Time Paid 11; Full-Time Volunteers 1; Part-Time Paid 25; Part-Time Volunteers 75.
Governing Authority: nonprofit organization. Affiliated with the Pocumtuck Valley Memorial Assn. Tax-exempt: 501(c)(3).
History & Decorative Arts Museum: housed in 1798 Deerfield Academy Building.
Collections: early American furniture; American & English pewter; iron; tin & woodenware; glass; ceramics; farm tools; craftsmen's tools; tavern signs; textiles; architectural fragments; American paintings; musical instruments; toys; military equipment; manuscripts; Native American artifacts.
Facilities: 12,000-vol. library of books on local history, imprints, periodicals, manuscripts, 380 account & day books, school materials & diaries available for use on premises only. Books for sale.
Activities: lectures; gallery talks; concerts; formally organized education programs for children; permanent & temporary exhibitions; chamber theater group.
Publications: books, History of Deerfield; Short History of Deerfield; The Boy Captive of Old Deerfield; The Boy Captive in Canada; Deerfield Embroidery; Gathered & Preserved; Hadley Chests; The Allen Sisters: Pictorial Photographs 1885-1920.
Hours & Admission Prices: May-Oct. daily 11-5. Adults $6, children & students 6-21 $3; discounts to AAM members; members no charge. Library: call for hours. ♿
Attendance: 52,292 (accurate)
Membership: Annual $40; Family $60.

Dennis

CAPE COD MUSEUM OF ART, (M), Rte. 6A, Dennis, MA 02638. Mailing Address: P.O. Box 2034, Dennis, MA 02638-5034. Tel.: 508-385-4477. Fax: 508-385-7933.
E-mail: info@ccmoa.org
Web Site: www.ccmoa.org
Formerly: Cape Museum of Fine Arts, Inc.
Founded: 1981.
Congressional District: 10
Key Personnel: Exec. Dir., Elizabeth Ives Hunter; Pres. (V), Thomas J. Lucey; Museum Shop Mgr., Martha Michalek.
Personnel Profile: Full-Time Paid 11; Full-Time Volunteers 1; Part-Time Paid 5; Part-Time Volunteers 200; Interns 3.
Governing Authority: nonprofit organization. Tax-exempt: 501(c)(3).
Art Museum & Center.
Collections: 20th-century fine & contemporary art.
Research Fields: archives on artists; fine art of Cape Cod.
Facilities: auditorium; educational facilities. Museum-related items for sale.
Activities: exhibition & museum tours; lectures; studio arts for children;

workshops; educational films; art & foreign film series; docent program; permanent & loan exhibitions; cultural travel program; art festival; Silent & Wet Art Auction; special events; volunteer & intern programs.
Publications: quarterly brochure; Art Matters; exhibition catalogs.
Hours & Admission Prices: Memorial Day to Columbus Day Mon.-Wed. & Fri.-Sat. 10-5, Thurs. 10-8, Sun. 12-5; Oct.-May Tues.-Wed. & Fri.-Sat. 10-5, Thurs. 10-8, Sun. 12-5. Adults $8; discounts to groups & AAM, ICOM, MASS, Teacher's Assoc., New England Consortium of Art Museums, & WGBH members; children & members no charge. Thurs. by donation. Closed New Year's Day; Thanksgiving; Christmas. ♿
Attendance: 35,885 (accurate)
Membership: Student, Artist & Teacher $30; Individual $50; Dual $75; Sponsor $150; Patron $250; Sustaining $500; Associate $1,000; Fellow $2,500; Benefactor $5,000.

Dover

CARYL HOUSE AND FISHER BARN, 107 Dedham St., Dover, MA 02030-2223. Mailing Address: P.O. Box 534, Dover, MA 02030-0534. Tel.: 508-785-1832. Fax: 508-785-0789.
Web Site: www.doverhistoricalsociety.org
Founded: 1920.
Congressional District: 9
Key Personnel: Dir., Elisha F. Lee, Jr.; Vice Pres., Priscilla P. Jones.
Personnel Profile: Part-Time Volunteers 20.
Governing Authority: historical society. Parent Institution: Town of Dover. Tax-exempt: 501(c)(3).
Historic House: built c.1777.
Collections: documents & artifacts of 1790s minister, doctor & families; restored barn, 1777; area agricultural artifacts.
Research Fields: history & culture of 1790s Dover & vicinity; early practice of medicine.
Hours & Admission Prices: April-June & Sept.-Nov. Sat. 1-4 & by appointment. No charge; donations accepted. Closed Sat. holidays.
Attendance: 500 (estimated)
Membership: Individual $25; Family $50.

DOVER HISTORICAL SOCIETY - SAWIN MUSEUM, 80 Dedham St., Dover, MA 02030. Mailing Address: P.O. Box 534, Dover, MA 02030-0534. Tel.: 508-785-1832.
Web Site: doverhistoricalsociety.org
Founded: 1895.
Congressional District: 9
Key Personnel: Pres., Elisha Lee; Vice Pres., Priscilla Jones; Cur. Sawin, Fay Bacher; Cur. Caryl, Barbara Palmer; Cur. Barn, Jack Hoehlen.
Personnel Profile: Part-Time Volunteers 15.
Governing Authority: nonprofit organization. Parent Institution: Dover Historical Society. Tax-exempt: 501(c)(3).
Historical Society Museum.
Collections: documents & artifacts of Dover & vicinity; manuscripts.
Facilities: 700-vol. library of history & school books available on premises.
Activities: permanent & temporary exhibitions.
Hours & Admission Prices: April-June & Sept.-Nov. Sat. 1-4 & by appointment. No charge; donations accepted. Closed Sat. holidays.
Attendance: 200 (estimated)
Membership: Single $40; Family $65; Supporter $100; Patron $250; Benefactor $500.

Duxbury

ALDEN HOUSE HISTORIC SITE, 105 Alden St., Duxbury, MA 02332. Mailing Address: P.O. Box 2754, Duxbury, MA 02331-2754. Tel.: 781-934-9092. Fax: 781-934-9149.
E-mail: aldenhouse@comcast.net
Web Site: www.alden.org
Formerly: Alden House Museum
Founded: 1906.
Congressional District: 10
Key Personnel: Pres. (V), Linda Osborne; Sec., Barbara Itz; Cur. & Museum Shop Mgr., James W. Baker.
Personnel Profile: Part-Time Paid 3; Part-Time Volunteers 3.
Governing Authority: nonprofit organization. Owned and operated by Alden Kindred of America, Inc., P.O. Box 2754, Duxbury, MA 02331. Tax-exempt: 501(c)(3).
Historic House Museum: homestead of Pilgrims John Alden and Priscilla Mullins.
Collections: period furnishings; artifacts.
Research Fields: Plymouth Colony history.
Facilities: visitors center.
Activities: guided tours.
Publications: biannual newsletter.

Hours & Admission Prices: June-Sept. Mon.-Sat. 12-4. Adults $5, children 3-17 $3; members no charge. ♿
Attendance: 1,506 (accurate)
Membership: Individual $30; Family $55; Business $100.

ART COMPLEX MUSEUM, (M), 189 Alden St., Duxbury, MA 02332-3801. Mailing Address: P.O. Box 2814, Duxbury, MA 02331-2814. Tel.: 781-934-6634. Fax: 781-934-5117.
E-mail: info@artcomplex.org
Web Site: www.artcomplex.org
Founded: 1967.
Congressional District: 10
Key Personnel: Dir. & C.E.O., Charles A. Weyerhaeuser; Consulting Cur., Alice Hyland; Curatorial Asst. & Registrar, Maureen Wengler; Education Coord., Sally Dean Mello; Special Projects Cur., Craig Bloodgood; Communications Coord., Laura Doherty; Accountant, Steve Polimeno; Asst. to Dir., Mary Curran; Librarian, Cheryl O'Neill; Community Coord., Doris Collins; Staff Asst., Elaine Plakias; Grounds & Maintenance, William Thomas.
Personnel Profile: Full-Time Paid 1; Part-Time Paid 11; Part-Time Volunteers 51.
Governing Authority: nonprofit organization. Parent Institution: Art Complex Inc. Tax-exempt: 501(c)(3).
Art Museum.
Collections: American & European paintings; modern & Old Master prints; Shaker furniture & artifacts; Asian art; Japanese tea house; Native American art.
Facilities: 6,500-vol. library of books on art & artists.
Activities: lectures; gallery talks; concerts; permanent & traveling exhibitions; studio art classes & workshops; contemporary artists education program for all ages; concert series. Museum Sponsors: tea ceremony presentations 4 times per year.
Publications: book, The Lithographs of Ture Bengtz; catalogues, Master Prints 1850-1950, The Shakers, Pure of Spirit Pure of Mind; American Paintings; Rituals of the Land: Native American Art from the Colorado Plateau; Rufus Hathaway, Artist & Physician, Of Matter & Spirit: Dutch Prints of the 17th Century; New Horizons: 19th century American Marine painting; Tribute to Kojiro Tomita; Enduring Nature: Chinese Paintings from the Weyerhaeuser collection; Environmental Arts at the Art Complex Museum; Shaped with a Passion; Japanese Ceramics from the 1970s.
Hours & Admission Prices: Wed.-Sun. 1-4. No charge; donations accepted. Closed legal holidays. ♿
Attendance: 10,000 (estimated)

DUXBURY RURAL AND HISTORICAL SOCIETY, INC., 479 Washington St., Duxbury, MA 02331. Mailing Address: P.O. Box 2865, Duxbury, MA 02331-2865. Tel.: 781-934-6106. Fax: 781-934-5730.
E-mail: aarnold@duxburyhistory.org
Web Site: www.duxburyhistory.org
Founded: 1883.
Congressional District: 10
Key Personnel: Pres. (V), David Jenkins; Exec. Dir., Patrick Browne.
Personnel Profile: Full-Time Paid 1; Part-Time Paid 1; Part-Time Volunteers 75; Interns 1.
Governing Authority: society; executive committee. Tax-exempt.
Historical Society Museum.
Collections: 19th-century decorative arts; textiles; relics of 1869 French-American cable. Historic Houses: 1808-1809, King Caesar Houses; 1808 Captain Gershom Bradford House; 1826 Drew House; Cedarfield on Clark's Island; 1807 Nathaniel Winsor House.
Research Fields: history from Pilgrim times to present; early 19th-century shipbuilding era.
Facilities: library of letters, ships logs & local history available by appointment to the Duxbury Rural & Historical Society.
Activities: guided tours in summer; lectures; permanent & temporary exhibitions.
Publications: books, The Duxbury Book, 1937-1987; Stopping Places Along Duxbury Roads; The Alden Family in the Alden House; Settlement and Growth of Duxbury 1828-1870; booklets, Roundabout Duxbury; A History of the Duxbury Rural & Historical Society; Tall Ships of Duxbury 1815-1850; The French Atlantic Cable 1869; Duxbury, A Guide.
Hours & Admission Prices: King Caesar House: July to Labor Day Wed.-Sun. 1-4. Adults $5; members no charge. Bradford House: July to Labor Day Sun. 1-4. Adults $3; discounts to senior citizens; members no charge. Nathaniel Winsor House Office: Mon.-Fri. 9-4. Closed holidays.
Attendance: 1,852 (accurate)
Membership: Senior Citizen & Student $25; Single $30; Senior Couple $35; Family $45; Contributing $150; Sustaining $250; Life $1,000.

Easthampton

MASSACHUSETTS AUDUBON AT CONNECTICUT RIVER VALLEY SANCTUARIES, 127 Combs Rd., Easthampton, MA 01027-9704. Tel.: 413-584-3009, ext. 12. Fax: 413-584-0250.
E-mail: mshanley@massaudubon.org
Web Site: www.massaudubon.org
Formerly: Massachusetts Audubon at Hampshire Sanctuaries
Founded: 1944.
Congressional District: 1
Key Personnel: Dir., Mary Shanley-Koeber; Chm., Janet Bissel.
Personnel Profile: Full-Time Paid 7; Part-Time Paid 8; Part-Time Volunteers 150.
Governing Authority: society. Parent Institution: Massachusetts Audubon Society, S. Great Rd., Lincoln, MA 01773. Tax-exempt: 501(c)(3) & 170(b)(1)(A).
Nature Center & Wildlife Sanctuary.
Collections: nature center & wildlife sanctuary.
Research Fields: botanical & geological in cooperation with Smith College & University of Massachusetts.
Facilities: 2,000-vol. library on natural science, conservation, ecology & ornithology available for use on premises; botanical garden; nature center; field research station; 80-seat auditorium. Books for sale.
Activities: guided tours; lectures; films; formally organized education programs for adults, children, families & students.
Publications: quarterly newsletter.
Hours & Admission Prices: Office: Mon.-Fri. 8:30-12:30. Grounds: Tues.-Sun. dawn-dusk. Adults $4, children 3-15 & senior citizens $3; members & children under 3 no charge. ♿
Attendance: 20,000 (estimated)
Membership: Student $20; Individual $37; Family $47; Supporting $60; Defender $75; Donor $100; Sponsor $250; Patron $500; Leadership Friend $1,000.

Edgartown

MARTHA'S VINEYARD MUSEUM, (M), 59 School St., Edgartown, MA 02539. Mailing Address: P.O. Box 1310, Edgartown, MA 02539-1310. Tel.: 508-627-4441. Fax: 508-627-4436.
E-mail: info@mvmuseum.org
Web Site: www.mvmuseum.org
Formerly: Martha's Vineyard Historical Society
Founded: 1922.
Congressional District: 12
Key Personnel: C.E.O. & Dir., David Nathans; Pres. (V), Warren Hollinshead; Chief Cur., Dana C. Street; Asst. Cur., Anna Carringer; Genealogist, Catherine M. Mayhew; Dir. Devel., Amy Houghton; Education Dir., Nancy Cole; Devel. Coord., Susan Wilson; Dir. Finance & Museum Shop Mgr., Betsey Mayhew; Admin. Asst., Paige Roth; Cur. Oral History, Linsey Lee.
Personnel Profile: Full-Time Paid 8; Full-Time Volunteers 1; Part-Time Paid 5; Part-Time Volunteers 60; Interns 5.
Governing Authority: nonprofit organization. Parent Institution: Dukes County Historical Society. Tax-exempt: 501(c)(3).
History Museum.
Collections: archaeology; archives; costumes; herbarium; history; Indian artifacts; industry; naval; outdoor museum; whaling industry; period artifacts; glass; china; wooden ware; domestic tools; ship models; Vineyard memorabilia; scrimshaw; Methodist Camp meeting ground; 1856 Gay Head light. Historic Buildings: 1765 Thomas Cooke House; c.1845 Captain Francis Pease House.
Research Fields: genealogy; whaling period; history of Martha's Vineyard; American Indians; glacial period geology; marine history; Island crafts; local oral history.
Facilities: 3,000-vol. library of books on Vineyard history, genealogical records, oral histories, archives including 500 linear feet of material, maritime & whaling history, photographic archives, maps & charts; reading room; garden. Books, postcards & guidebooks for sale.
Activities: guided tours; lectures; permanent & temporary exhibitions; educational programs.
Publications: quarterly journal, Dukes County Intelligencer.
Hours & Admission Prices: Fall & Spring: Mon.-Sat. 10-4; Summer: Mon.-Sat. 10-5. Winter: adults $6, seniors $5, children 6-15 $4; children under 6 & members no charge. Summer: adults $7, seniors $6, children 6-15 $4; children under 6 & members no charge. Closed major holidays. ♿
Attendance: 5,000 (estimated)
Membership: Student $25; Individual $45; Family $60; Sustaining $100; Organization & Business $150; Patron $250; Benefactor $500; President's Circle $1,000; Leadership $2,500; Steward $5,000.

Essex

ESSEX SHIPBUILDING MUSEUM, 66 Main St., Essex, MA 01929-1343. Mailing Address: P.O. Box 277, Essex, MA 01929-0005. Tel.: 978-768-7541. Fax: 978-768-2541.
E-mail: info@essexshipbuildingmuseum.org
Web Site: www.essexshipbuildingmuseum.org
Founded: 1976.
Congressional District: 5
Key Personnel: Pres., Tia Schlaikjer; Treas., Sarah Willwerth-Dyer; Coord. Education, Barbara Jones Low.
Personnel Profile: Part-Time Paid 5; Part-Time Volunteers 15.
Governing Authority: society. Parent Institution: Essex Historical Society & Shipbuilding Museum, Inc. Tax-exempt.
Shipbuilding Museum: housed in 1835 schoolhouse, 1840's hearse house & Maritime History Museum; Historic Site: 1680-1860 burying ground; old Story Yard site where A.D. Story launched 300 fishing schooners.
Collections: old Story yard site, 1813-1985 the Story shipyard used for shipbuilding for 300 years; shipbuilding tools; photographs; shipbuilding memorabilia; archives; local history; half-models; the fishing schooner Evelina M. Goulart, built by A.D. Story in 1927; scale & builders' models from Smithsonian Institution, Washington, DC.
Research Fields: local shipbuilding history; owner-builder correspondence; plans, records, photos of individual vessels; photos of yards; drawings of construction details; builder's models for inboard carpentry.
Facilities: research library of shipbuilding books at 28 Main St.; archives; drydock; Waterline Education Center; meeting room. Books & other museum-related items for sale.
Activities: inter-museum loan; education programs; permanent & temporary exhibitions; lectures at museum & away for special interest groups; annual meeting; trips & tours.
Publications: booklets: Essex, the Shipbuilding Town; Essex Electrics; Dubbing, Hooping & Lofting: Shipbuilding Skills; book, A List of Vessels, Boats & Other Crafts Built in Essex During 1860-1980, 3rd ed., 1992.
Hours & Admission Prices: Call for hours. Adults $7, senior citizens $6, children $5; children under 6 & members no charge.
Attendance: 7,000 (estimated)
Membership: Senior Citizen $20; Individual & Family $35.

HISTORIC NEW ENGLAND/COGSWELLS GRANT, 60 Spring St., Essex, MA 01929-1308. Mailing Address: 141 Cambridge St., Boston, MA 02114-2702. Tel.: 978-768-3632.
Web Site: www.historicnewengland.org
Founded: 1998.
Key Personnel: Pres., Carl Nold; Site Mgr., Kristen Weiss.
Governing Authority: private; nonprofit organization. Parent Institution: Historic New England, Boston, MA. Tax-exempt: 501(c)(3).
Historic House Museum: housed in an 18th century farmhouse used by American folk art collectors Bertram and Nina Fletcher Little as their summer home.
Collections: American folk art including decorative paintings, floor coverings, boxes, & New England pottery; Bertram & Nina Fletcher Little.
Research Fields: decorative arts.
Facilities: Museum-related items for sale.
Activities: guided tours; special events; lectures.
Publications: visitors guide; exhibition catalogues; magazine, Historic New England; monthly newsletter, What's Happening.
Hours & Admission Prices: June to Oct. 15 Wed.-Sun. 11-4. Adults $10; discounts to ICOM, AAA, AAM & WGBH members; members no charge.
Attendance: 5,008 (accurate)
Membership: National $35; Individual $45; Household $55; Garden & Landscape $75; Institutional $85; Contributing $100; Historic Homeowner $200; Supporting $250.

Fall River

FALL RIVER HISTORICAL SOCIETY MUSEUM, 451 Rock St., Fall River, MA 02720-3398. Tel.: 508-679-1071. Fax: 508-675-5754.
E-mail: curator@lizzieborden.org
Web Site: www.lizzieborden.org
Founded: 1921.
Congressional District: 10
Key Personnel: Cur., Michael Martins; Pres. (V), Elizabeth Wells Denning; Asst. Cur., Dennis Binette.
Personnel Profile: Full-Time Paid 4; Part-Time Paid 1; Part-Time Volunteers 25; Interns 1.
Governing Authority: society. Tax-exempt: 501(c)(3).
Historical Society Museum: housed in 1843 Granite House, used as underground railroad station c.1843-1860s.

Collections: glass; china; furniture; costumes; guns; marine; paintings; manuscripts; artifacts relating to the Lizzie Borden murder trial; 19th-century decorative arts; restored mill owners mansion.
Research Fields: local history; genealogy.
Facilities: 3,000-vol. library of general books available on premises; reading room.
Activities: guided tours; lectures; permanent & temporary exhibitions.
Publications: The Fall River Society Quarterly Report-Newsletter.
Hours & Admission Prices: May & Oct. Tues.-Fri. 9-4; June-Sept. Tues.-Fri. 9-4, Sat.-Sun. 1-4:30. Adults $6, children 6-14 $4; discount to groups; children under 6 & members no charge. Closed holidays.
Attendance: 13,265 (accurate)
Membership: Full-Time student up to age 22 $10; Individual $25; Family (two adults & all children under 17 living at the same address) $40; Corporate $100; Life (single) $500, (couple) $800; Sponsor $500; Benefactor $1,000.

GRIMSHAW-GUDEWICZ ART GALLERY, Jackson Art Center, Bristol Community College, 777 Elsbree St., Fall River, MA 02720-7307. Tel.: 508-678-2811, ext. 2439. Fax: 508-730-3285.
E-mail: kathleen.hancock@bristolcc.doc
Web Site: www.bristol.mass.edu/gallery
Key Personnel: Dir., Kathleen Hancock
Art Gallery.
Collections: sculpture; paintings.
Activities: educational programs.
Hours & Admission Prices: Mon., Wed. & Sat. 1-4, Tues. & Thurs-Fri. 10-1. No charge.

THE MARINE MUSEUM AT FALL RIVER, INC., 70 Water St., Fall River, MA 02721-1598. Tel.: 508-674-3533. Fax: 508-674-3534.
Founded: 1968.
Congressional District: 4
Key Personnel: Dir., Paul Simister; Pres., Julian Paul.
Personnel Profile: Full-Time Paid 2; Part-Time Paid 1; Part-Time Volunteers 2; Interns 1.
Governing Authority: nonprofit organization. Tax-exempt: 501(c)(3).
Marine Museum: housed in restored machine shop.
Collections: Fall River Line Steamships (1847-1937) models: The Providence, The Puritan, The Plymouth, The Commonwealth, The Priscilla; artifacts & exhibits of The Titanic including a 28 ft. model & photos taken by Woods Hole Oceanographic Institution; The United Fruit Line Collection pertaining to the company's steam powered banana ships; William King Covell Collection including prints, negatives & glass slides relating to The Fall River Line.
Research Fields: steamships.
Facilities: 2,500-vol. library of maritime history available for use on premises; meeting room. Books & museum-related items for sale.
Activities: guided tours; lectures; slide presentations; formally organized educational programs; permanent & traveling exhibitions; social gatherings.
Publications: quarterly newsletter; brochures.
Hours & Admission Prices: Wed.-Fri. & Sun. 12-4, Sat. 12-5. Adults $5, senior citizens & children 5-12 $4; discounts to groups or 20 or more; members no charge. Closed New Year's Day; Thanksgiving; Christmas. ♿
Attendance: 28,000 (estimated)
Membership: Individual $30; Family $40; Contributing $75; Sustaining $100; Admiral's Club $200-$1,000; Corporate $350; Life $2,500.

OLD COLONY & FALL RIVER RAILROAD MUSEUM, Battleship Cove, Fall River, MA 02720. Mailing Address: P.O. Box 3455, Fall River, MA 02722-3455. Tel.: 508-674-9340.
E-mail: info@ocandfrrailroadmuseum.com
Web Site: www.ocandfrrailroadmuseum.com
Railroad Museum.
Collections: railroad artifacts & memorabilia.
Hours & Admission Prices: Sat.-Sun. 12-4. Adults $3, senior citizens 65 & over $2.50, children 5-12 $1.50; children under 5 no charge.

USS MASSACHUSETTS MEMORIAL COMMITTEE, INC., Battleship Cove, 5 Water St., Fall River, MA 02722-0111. Mailing Address: Battleship Cove, 5 Water St., P.O. Box 111, Fall River, MA 02722-0111. Tel.: 508-678-1100 & 1905; 800-533-3194. Fax: 508-674-5597.
E-mail: battleship@battleshipcove.org
Web Site: battleshipcove.org
Formerly: Battleship Massachusetts
Founded: 1965.
Congressional District: 10
Key Personnel: Exec. Dir., John S. Casey; Pres. (V), Guy A. Archambault; Dir. Finance, David W. Keyes; Cur., Christopher J. Nardi; Museum Shop Mgr., Michelle Cateon.
Personnel Profile: Full-Time Paid 30; Full-Time Volunteers 10; Part-Time Paid 30; Part-Time Volunteers 60; Interns 4.
Governing Authority: federal. Tax-exempt: 501(c)(3).
Historic Ships Museum.
Collections: equipment & memorabilia connected with the operation of the USS Massachusetts, USS Lionfish & USS Joseph P. Kennedy, Jr. during World War II; PT Boat 796 & P.T. Boat 617; World War II Quonset Hut; LCM landing craft; T-28 aircraft; scale model World War II aircraft collection; Japanese, Shinyo, suicide boat; UH-1E Viet Nam era helicopter; Russian Missile Corvette, Hiddensee.
Research Fields: naval history of World War II.
Facilities: 250-vol. library of the history of naval warfare especially during World War II & the history of the development of the battleship as a naval weapon; restaurant; banquet facilities. Flags, ship models, jewelry & sweatshirts for sale.
Activities: self-guided tours; lectures; films; permanent exhibitions.
Publications: quarterly newsletter.
Hours & Admission Prices: Spring daily 9-4:30. Summer daily 9-5. Adults $15, senior citizens & AAA members $13, children 6-12 $9, active military with ID $7; discounts to Historic Naval Ship Association; members, active military in uniform, & children under 6 no charge. Closed New Year's Day; Thanksgiving; Christmas.
Attendance: 95,716 (accurate)
Membership: Individual $35; Family $55; Executive $250; Captain $500; Admiral $1,000.

Falmouth

FALMOUTH HISTORICAL SOCIETY, (M), 55-65 Palmer Ave., Falmouth, MA 02540. Mailing Address: P.O. Box 174, Falmouth, MA 02541-0174. Tel.: 508-548-4857. Fax: 508-540-0968.
E-mail: fhs@cape.com
Web Site: www.FalmouthHistoricalSociety.org
Founded: 1900.
Congressional District: 12
Key Personnel: C.E.O. & Exec. Dir., Carolyn T. Powers; Pres. (V), Margaret Gifford; Cur., Cipperly Good; Archivist, Mary E. Sicchio; Museum Shop Mgr., Caroline Lloyd; Office Asst., Cathleen McDonnell.
Personnel Profile: Full-Time Paid 2; Full-Time Volunteers 35; Part-Time Paid 2; Part-Time Volunteers 85; Interns 5.
Governing Authority: society. Tax-exempt: 501(c)(3).
Historical Society Museum.
Collections: two historic homes, barn, colonial garden; herb garden. Julia Wood House: c.1790 contains 19th century French wallpaper, furnishings, china & paintings from 1790-1932; 1790-1840 doctor's office. Conant House: c.1760; whaling era memorabilia; video theater. Hallett Barn Visitor Center: life of Katharine Lee Bates; early farm implements.
Research Fields: local history; genealogical; maritime.
Facilities: 500-vol. library of 18th- & 19th-century books on genealogy, history & religion available on premises. Conant House: theater. Visitor Center: Museum-related items for sale.
Activities: guided tours; lectures; permanent & temporary exhibitions. Museum Sponsors: Guided Walking Tours June to October; Fridays for Families in July & August; Katharine Lee Bates Poetry Fest in August; Trolley Tours in September & October.
Publications: guides; books, Residential Falmouth; Hotels & Inns of Falmouth; Book of Holdings; quarterly journal, Spiritsail; newsletters & announcements; Falmouth (Images of America Series); Voice of the Tide, Biography of Katharine Lee Bates.
Hours & Admission Prices: June 9-Oct. 10 Tues.-Fri. 10-4, Sat. 10-1; other times by appointment. Adults $5; discounts to AAM, MTA & NEMA members; children 13 & under and members no charge.
Attendance: 4,585 (accurate)
Membership: Individual $30; Family $50; Associate $75; Benefactor $150.

Fitchburg

* **FITCHBURG ART MUSEUM, (M),** Merriam Pkwy., Fitchburg, MA 01420. Mailing Address: 185 Elm St., Fitchburg, MA 01420-7503. Tel.: 978-345-4207. Fax: 978-345-2319.
E-mail: info@fitchburgartmuseum.org
Web Site: www.fitchburgartmuseum.org
Founded: 1925.
Congressional District: 2
Key Personnel: Dir., Peter Timms; Pres. (V), Robert Rossi; Dir. Corp. Member Svcs., Jane Keough; Dir. Membership & Public Rels., Janice Goodrow; Dir. Mktg., Fiona Casey; Dir. Education, Laura Howick; Business Mgr., Sheryl Demers; Cur., Kristina Durocher; Dir. Docents, Ann Descoteaux.
Personnel Profile: Full-Time Paid 7; Part-Time Paid 18; Part-Time Volunteers 20; Interns 6.
Governing Authority: nonprofit organization. Tax-exempt: 501(c)(3).

Art Museum.
Collections: European & American 18th-20th century paintings, photographs, drawings & prints; decorative arts; 15th-20th century illustrated books; pre-Columbian, Asian, Ancient & African art.
Facilities: studio; classroom; sculpture garden; docent & volunteer room.
Activities: guided tours; lectures; gallery talks; formally organized educational programs; inter-museum loan, permanent & temporary exhibitions; annual regional art & craft exhibition; bus excursions; banquet facilities; members' council; volunteer program; corporate art exchange program.
Publications: exhibition catalogs & posters; notices & invitations to members; museum calendar; newsletter.
Hours & Admission Prices: Wed.-Fri. 12-4, Sat.-Sun. 11-5. Adults $7, senior citizens & students $5; discount to AAM members; members no charge. Closed major holidays. ♿
Attendance: 19,000 (accurate)
Membership: Individual $35; Family $50; Supporting $60; Contributor $100; Donor $250; Sponsor $500; Benefactor $1,000. Corporate $250-$1,000.

FITCHBURG HISTORICAL SOCIETY, 50 Grove St., Fitchburg, MA 01420-3116. Mailing Address: P.O. Box 953, Fitchburg, MA 01420-0009. Tel.: 978-345-1157. Fax: 978-345-2229.
E-mail: fitchburghistory@verizon.net
Web Site: fitchburghistory.fsc.edu
Founded: 1892.
Congressional District: 4
Key Personnel: Dir., Susan Roetzer; Chm., C. Deborah Phillips.
Personnel Profile: Full-Time Paid 1; Part-Time Paid 1; Part-Time Volunteers 12.
Governing Authority: society. Tax-exempt: 501(c)(3).
Local History Museum.
Collections: memorabilia of all U.S. wars; local portraits, inventions, maps, artifacts; glass & china; dolls, musical instruments; furniture; archival material of local industries.
Research Fields: genealogy; local history.
Facilities: library; 80-seat auditorium.
Activities: guided tours; permanent & changing exhibits; monthly meetings; lectures.
Publications: quarterly newsletter.
Hours & Admission Prices: Mon.-Tues. 10-4, Wed. 10-6. Historical Society: no charge; donations accepted. Research Library: $10; students & members no charge. Closed holidays.
Attendance: 2,000 (estimated)
Membership: Individual $30; Family $50; Sustaining & Business Member $100; Business Sponsor $250; Business Patron $500; Business Leader $750.

Framingham

DANFORTH MUSEUM OF ART, (M), 123 Union Ave., Framingham, MA 01702-8291. Tel.: 508-620-0050. Fax: 508-872-5542.
Web Site: www.danforthmuseum.org
Founded: 1975.
Congressional District: 5
Key Personnel: Pres. Bd. (V), Michael J. Barry; Dir., Katherine French; Dir. Finance & Operations, Mary Kiely; Museum School Registrar, Jean Maquire; Dir. Education, Pat Walker; Asst. Dir. Devel. & Mktg., Jenn Harris.
Personnel Profile: Full-Time Paid 8; Part-Time Paid 6; Part-Time Volunteers 30; Interns 5.
Governing Authority: nonprofit organization. Supported in part by Framingham State College & local municipal government. Tax-exempt: 501(c)(3).
Art Museum & School.
Collections: paintings; drawings; graphics; sculpture; photographs.
Research Fields: 19th- & 20th-century American art.
Facilities: art library; lecture room. Museum-related items for sale.
Activities: guided tours; lectures; films; gallery talks; concerts; formally organized education programs; docent program; inter-museum loan, permanent, temporary & traveling exhibitions; art on the move activity kits for all grades; family days.
Publications: newsletter; exhibit announcements; exhibition catalogues; Danforth Museum of Art News; school newspaper; course listings and schedule of classes & workshops.
Hours & Admission Prices: Wed.-Thurs. & Sun. 12-5, Fri.-Sat. 10-5. Adults $10, seniors & students $8; discounts to AAM, ICOM & NEMA members; children under 12 & members no charge. ♿
Attendance: 30,000 (estimated)
Membership: Senior Citizens $35; Individual $45; Family $60; Friend $100; Supporter $250; Sponsor $500; Fellow $1,000; Patron $2,500; Benefactor $5,000.

FRAMINGHAM HISTORY CENTER, 16 Vernon St., Framingham, MA 01701-4783. Mailing Address: P.O. Box 2032, Framingham, MA 01703-2032. Tel.: 508-872-3780. Fax: 508-872-3780.
E-mail: office@framinghamhistory.org
Web Site: www.framinghamhistory.org
Formerly: Framingham Historical Society & Museum
Founded: 1888.
Congressional District: 5
Key Personnel: C.E.O. & Dir., Anne Murphy; Pres., Sheryl Martin; Cur., Dana Dauterman Ricciardi, Ph.D.; Research, Frederic A. Wallace; Asst., Vanessa Prescott; Museum Shop Mgr., Grace Shwert; Museum Asst., Jane Whiting.
Personnel Profile: Part-Time Paid 3; Part-Time Volunteers 100.
Governing Authority: society. Tax-exempt: 501(c)(3).
American History Museum.
Collections: 17th-20th centuries American objects of material culture, agricultural, domestic & industrial; archives; photographs; oral history; art & decorative art; books; diaries; manuscripts. Historic Buildings: 1837 Old Framingham Academy; 1873 Edgell Memorial library.
Research Fields: American history from colonial days to the present with focus on Framingham; genealogy.
Facilities: 2,500-vol. library of genealogical records & historical archives available for use by appointment.
Activities: guided tours; lectures; formally organized education programs for children; permanent & temporary exhibitions; special events.
Publications: quarterly, newsletter; book, Framingham: An American Town; exhibition catalogue, Zeal for Healing: A Framingham Trait.
Hours & Admission Prices: Academy & Edgell Memorial Library: Wed.-Sat. 12-4. No charge; donations accepted.
Attendance: 6,140 (accurate)
Membership: Senior & Student $15; Individual $25; Family $40; Friend $100; Supporter $250; Sustaining & Business $500.

* **GARDEN IN THE WOODS OF THE NEW ENGLAND WILD FLOWER SOCIETY,** 180 Hemenway Rd., Framingham, MA 01701-2699. Tel.: 508-877-7630, ext. 0. Fax: 508-877-3658. TTY: 508-877-6553.
E-mail: information@newenglandwild.org
Web Site: www.newenglandwild.org
Founded: 1932.
Congressional District: 4
Key Personnel: Exec. Dir., Debbi Edelstein; Chm. (V), Frances H. Clark; Dir. Education, Bonnie Drexler; Mgr. Mktg. & Public Rels., Steven Ziglar; Dir. Botanic Garden, Scott LaFleur; Dir. Nursery Business, Ron Wik; Dir. Conservation, William Brumback; Dir. Devel. & Membership, Karen Pierce; Sr. Retail Coord. & Merchandiser, Terry Morrow.
Personnel Profile: Full-Time Paid 23; Part-Time Paid 10; Part-Time Volunteers 1,500; Interns 9.
Governing Authority: nonprofit organization. Parent Institution: New England Wild Flower Society. Tax-exempt: 501(c)(3).
Botanical Garden.
Collections: botanical garden & woodland sanctuary with over 1,000 species of native American plants; albinos & other variants; rare & endangered species; over 50,000 slides; books.
Research Fields: propagation; critical habitats; threatened & endangered native plant species; invasive plant management.
Facilities: 3,600-vol. library specializing in botany, gardening & natural history; herbarium; 45 acres; education center; visitor center. Books & plants for sale.
Activities: field trips; lectures; formally organized educational programs; Garden in the Woods tours for adults; nature walks for children; workshops & symposium on native plant conservation, horticulture, & plant identification; nature programs for children & school groups; classes throughout fall & winter; native plant education program.
Publications: magazine, New England Wild Flower; biannual, events catalog; annual, New England Wildflower, Conservation Notes; annual, New England Wild Flower Society Guide to Wild Flowers; Guide to Native Trees, Shrubs & Vines.
Hours & Admission Prices: April 15-July 3 Tues.-Wed., Sat.-Sun. & holiday Mon. 9-5, Thurs.-Fri. 9-7; July 4-Oct. Tues.-Sun. & holiday Mon. 9-5. Guided Tours: Mon.-Fri. 10 am, Sat.-Sun. 2 pm; tours by appointment. Adults $8, children 3-18 $4, senior citizens 65 & over and students with ID $6; members & children under 3 no charge. ♿
Attendance: 25,000 (estimated)
Membership: Student $38; Associate $40; Individual $50; Dual $60; Family & Friends $70; Contributor $100; Supporter $250; Sustainer $500; Patron $1,000; Life $5,000.

Gardner

THE GARDNER MUSEUM, INC., 28 Pearl St., Gardner, MA 01440-2308. Tel.: 978-632-3277.
E-mail: info@thegardnermuseum.com

Web Site: www.thegardnermuseum.com
Founded: 1978.
Congressional District: 4
Key Personnel: Pres., Scott Huntoon; Pres. Elect, Michael Richard; Coord., Sally Sennott; Treas., Robert Venning; Asst. Treas., Thomas Mailloux; Historian, Leonard A. Dorval; Recording Sec., Janet Stankaitis; Corresponding Sec., Doris Forte.
Personnel Profile: Part-Time Paid 1; Part-Time Volunteers 50.
Governing Authority: nonprofit organization. Tax-exempt: 501(c)(3).
Local History Museum: housed in 1888 Richardson Romanesque brick building.
Collections: history & development of Gardner; silver workshop includes equipment, tools & finished pieces by Gardner craftsmen.
Research Fields: local history; local cultural interests.
Activities: guided tours; lectures; films; changing exhibits.
Publications: quarterly newsletter.
Hours & Admission Prices: March-Dec. Wed.-Sun. 1-4. Adults $3; AASLH members & members no charge. Closed occasional holidays. ♿
Attendance: 2,500 (estimated)
Membership: Student $5; Single $15; Family $25; Friend $35; Sponsor $50; Patron $100 & up; Corporate $200; Supporter $250; Contributor $500; Benefactor $1,000.

Georgetown

BROCKLEBANK MUSEUM, 108 E. Main St., Georgetown, MA 01833-2104. Mailing Address: Georgetown Historical Society, P.O. Box 376, Georgetown, MA 01833. Tel.: 978-352-8526.
E-mail: info@georgetownhistoricalsociety.com
Web Site: www.georgetownhistoricalsociety.com
Key Personnel: Pres. (V), Frederic Detwiller; Cur., Stephen Keene
Historic House: built in the late 1600s.
Collections: local history; railroad memorabilia; Baldpate Inn china; shoe industry; period furnishings.
Hours & Admission Prices: July to Columbus Day 2nd & 4th Sun. 2-5; other times by appointment. Adults $3, seniors & students $2.

Gloucester

BEAUPORT, SLEEPER-MCCANN HOUSE, 75 Eastern Point Blvd., Gloucester, MA 01930-4433. Mailing Address: 141 Cambridge St., Boston, MA 02114-2702. Tel.: 978-283-0800; 617-227-3956 (Historic New England). Fax: 978-283-4484.
Web Site: www.historicnewengland.org
Founded: 1942.
Congressional District: 6
Key Personnel: Pres., Carl Nold; Site Mgr., Pilar Garro.
Governing Authority: society; nonprofit organization. Parent Institution: Historic New England, 141 Cambridge St., Boston, MA 02114. Tel.: 617-227-3956. Tax-exempt: 501(c)(3).
Historic House: 1907-34 40-room summer cottage overlooking Gloucester Harbor, built by interior designer Henry Davis Sleeper.
Collections: American, European & Oriental decorative arts.
Activities: guided tours; lectures; special events; evening concerts; teas.
Publications: Beauport, magazine, Historic New England.
Hours & Admission Prices: Tours: June-Oct. 15 Tues.-Sat. 10-4. Adults $10; discounts to seniors, groups, AAM, ICOM, AAA, WGBH members; members & Gloucester residents no charge.
Attendance: 5,290 (accurate)
Membership: National $35; Individual $45; Household $55; Garden & Landscape $75; Institutional $85; Contributing $100; Historic Homeowner $200; Supporting $250.

CAPE ANN HISTORICAL ASSOCIATION DBA CAPE ANN MUSEUM, 27 Pleasant St., Gloucester, MA 01930-5909. Tel.: 978-283-0455. Fax: 978-283-4141.
E-mail: rondafalcon@capeannmuseum.org
Web Site: www.capeannmuseum.org
Founded: 1873.
Congressional District: 6
Key Personnel: Dir., Ronda Faloon; Pres. (V), John Cunningham; Museum Shop Mgr., Jeanette Smith.
Personnel Profile: Full-Time Paid 3; Part-Time Paid 11; Part-Time Volunteers 25.
Governing Authority: society. Tax-exempt: 501(c)(3).
History, Art & Maritime Museum: c.1800 Federal House.
Collections: paintings & drawings by Fitz Henry (Hugh) Lane; paintings & sculpture by other Cape Ann artists; fine period furniture; silver; china; textiles; photographs; fisheries artifacts; 19th-century Gloucester waterfront diorama with schooner models; historic vessels; granite quarrying exhibit. Historic Houses: 1710 house; 1804 house.
Research Fields: 19th century American art; maritime history.
Facilities: 4,000-vol. library of local history, genealogy & the fishing industry available on premises; photo archives; artists' archives; 175-seat auditorium.
Activities: guided tours; lectures; concerts; permanent & temporary exhibitions.
Hours & Admission Prices: March-Jan. Tues.-Sat. 10-5, Sun. 1-4; group tours by appointment only. Adults $8, senior citizens & members $6, students $4.50; children under 6 no charge. Closed major holidays. ♿
Attendance: 17,000 (accurate)
Membership: Individual $30; Family $50; Contributor $100; Sponsor $250; Benefactor $500; Fitz Henry Lane Society $1,000, $2,500, $5,000.

HAMMOND CASTLE MUSEUM, 80 Hesperus Ave., Gloucester, MA 01930-5299. Tel.: 978-283-7673 & 2080. Fax: 978-283-1643.
Web Site: www.hammondcastle.org
Founded: 1930.
Congressional District: 6
Key Personnel: Acting Dir. & Cur. Education, John W. Pettibone; Pres. (V), Craig Lentz.
Governing Authority: nonprofit corporation. Owned by the Hammond Museum, Inc. Tax-exempt.
Historic Building & Museum: castle built in 1928 by inventor John Hays Hammond, Jr., in the style of a combination of Roman, Medieval & Renaissance periods.
Collections: furniture; artifacts; tapestries; stained glass; paintings; icons; early American period furnishings; pipe organ containing over 8,600 pipes.
Facilities: Museum-related items for sale.
Activities: lecture series on Medieval, Gothic & Renaissance art & architecture; early music concert series; organ concert series & other classical concerts; special exhibitions; children workshops; guided tours.
Publications: guide book; gallery catalog; exhibition catalog; Hammond Biography.
Hours & Admission Prices: June-Sept. Tues.-Sun. 10-6; Labor Day to Oct. Sat.-Sun. 10-4; groups by appointment. Adults $10, senior citizens & college students w/ID $8, children 6-12 $6; children under 6 no charge.
Attendance: 69,000
Membership: Individual $20; Family & Dual $30; Contributing $50; Patron $100; Benefactor $250.

NORTH SHORE ARTS ASSOCIATION, 11 Pirate's Lane, Gloucester, MA 01930-3810. Tel.: 978-283-1857.
E-mail: arts@nsarts.org
Web Site: www.nsarts.rog
Founded: 1922.
Key Personnel: Pres. (V), Andrea van Gestel; Dir., Julie Kramer; Treas., John Brennan.
Personnel Profile: Full-Time Paid 3; Part-Time Paid 3; Part-Time Volunteers 50; Interns 1.
Governing Authority: society; nonprofit. Tax-exempt.
Art Gallery: housed in c.1870 barn.
Collections: contemporary regional & U.S. artists.
Research Fields: members since 1922.
Facilities: picnic area.
Activities: lectures; workshops; classes; art activities. Annual Events: 2 art auctions.
Publications: triannual newsletter, Horizon Line.
Hours & Admission Prices: May-Oct. Mon.-Sat. 10-5, Sun. 12-5. No charge; donations accepted. ♿
Attendance: 12,000 (estimated)
Membership: Junior $10; Associate & Patron $40; Artist $75; Corporate Donor $250-$499; Corporate Supporter $500-$999; Corporate Sustainer $1,000-$2,499; Corporate Founder $2,500.

THE SARGENT HOUSE MUSEUM, 49 Middle St., Gloucester, MA 01930-5736. Tel.: 978-281-2432. Fax: 978-281-2432.
E-mail: sargenthouse@verizon.net
Web Site: sargenthouse.org
Founded: 1919.
Key Personnel: Dir., Martha Oaks; Pres. (V), Margaret Flavin; Treas., Amanda Hurd.
Personnel Profile: Part-Time Paid 3; Part-Time Volunteers 20.
Governing Authority: private; nonprofit organization. Tax-exempt: 501(c)(3).
Historic House: 1782 Georgian style house built for early American philosopher, writer & activist Judith Sargent Murray (1751-1820).
Collections: early New England furniture; decorative & fine arts; special collection of works by 20th century artist John Singer Sargent (1856-1925).

Activities: concerts; formal education programs; guided tours; lectures; temporary exhibitions. Annual Events: Year-end holiday party & narrated walking tours.
Publications: biannual newsletter, The Dolphin.
Hours & Admission Prices: Memorial Day to Columbus Day Fri.-Mon. 12-4. Adults $7.50, senior citizens over 65 $5; students, children under 12 & members no charge.
Attendance: 2,500 (accurate)
Membership: Individual $25; Family $40; Donor $150; Life $1500; Corporate $5,000.

Grafton

WILLARD HOUSE AND CLOCK MUSEUM, INC., (M), 11 Willard St., Grafton, MA 01536-2011. Tel.: 508-839-3500.
E-mail: cynthia@willardhouse.org
Web Site: www.willardhouse.org
Founded: 1971.
Congressional District: 3
Key Personnel: Dir., Cynthia Dias-Reid; Chm. Bd., Dr. Roger W. Robinson; Pres., Richard Currier.
Personnel Profile: Full-Time Paid 1; Part-Time Paid 4; Part-Time Volunteers 30.
Governing Authority: society. Tax-exempt: 501(c)(3).
Horological Museum: housed in 1718 Willard Homestead and 1766 Clock Shop.
Collections: over 80 Willard clocks by Benjamin Willard, Simon Willard, Ephraim Willard, Aaron Willard, Benjamin Franklin Willard, Simon Willard Jr., Aaron Willard Jr. & Zabdiel Willard; family portraits, letters, patent rights; tools; 18th century furniture & furnishings; preservation project.
Research Fields: Willard clocks & Willard genealogy.
Activities: guided tours; lectures; formally organized education programs for children; permanent & temporary exhibitions; annual antique show & annual Robinson lecture. Museum Sponsors: Colonial Trades Fair in June.
Publications: member quarterly newsletter; exhibit catalogues.
Hours & Admission Prices: Jan.-March Fri.-Sat. 10-4, Sun. 1-4; April-Dec. Tues.-Sat. 10-4, Sun. 1-4. Adults $7, senior citizens $6, children $3; discounts to AAA members; Willard House members no charge. Closed all major holidays. ♿
Attendance: 2,595 (accurate)
Membership: Individual $25; Family $40; Apprentice $55; Journeyman $100; Ephrain Willard Society $250; Benjamin Willard Society $500; Aaron Willard Society $1,000; Simon Willard Society $5,000; Robinson Society (Life) $10,000.

Greenfield

THE ASSOCIATION FOR GRAVESTONE STUDIES, Greenfield Corporate Center, 101 Munson St., Ste. 108, Greenfield, MA 01301-9675. Tel.: 413-772-0836. Fax: 413-772-0836 (call first).
E-mail: info@gravestonestudies.org
Web Site: www.gravestonestudies.org
Founded: 1977.
Key Personnel: Pres., Ian Brown; Archivist, Marie Ferre; Admin., Patricia Welch.
Personnel Profile: Part-Time Paid 2; Part-Time Volunteers 50.
Governing Authority: private; nonprofit. Tax-exempt.
Preservation Society.
Collections: photographs; personal artifacts.
Research Fields: gravestone studies.
Facilities: library of books, pamphlets, photographs, & files pertaining to gravestone studies.
Activities: annual conference.
Publications: quarterly magazine, AGS Quarterly; annual journal, Markers; monthly e-newsletter.
Hours & Admission Prices: Office: Tues.-Thurs. 9-3. No charge. Closed holidays. ♿
Membership: Student $20; Senior $40; Individual $50; Institutional $60; Supporting $80; Sustaining $150; Contributing $250; Life $1,000.

HISTORICAL SOCIETY OF GREENFIELD, Corner of Church & Union Sts., Greenfield, MA 01302. Mailing Address: P.O. Box 415, Greenfield, MA 01302-0415. Tel.: 413-774-3663 & 5363.
E-mail: hsg1907@yahoo.com
Founded: 1907.
Congressional District: 1
Key Personnel: Pres. (V), Peter S. Miller; Cur., Tim Blagg.
Personnel Profile: Part-Time Volunteers 2.
Governing Authority: society; board of directors. Tax-exempt.
General Museum: housed in 1852 Museum Building.
Collections: photographs; books; local antiques & memorabilia; maps; paintings; artifacts.
Research Fields: local cultural history; genealogies.
Facilities: 600-vol. library of books & pamphlets pertaining to local & county history & genealogies available for research.
Activities: tours & local history lectures for students & other groups. Museum Sponsors: Open Houses & special events in July & August.
Publications: 1926, Historic Greenfield; 1953, Pictorial History of Greenfield; 1975, A New Pictorial History of Greenfield, Massachusetts.
Hours & Admission Prices: Open year-round by appointment; special events & open houses scheduled throughout the year; call for information. No charge.
Attendance: 600 (estimated)
Membership: Senior $12; Individual $15; Couple & Family $20; Sustaining & Business $50; Patron $300.

Groton

GROTON HISTORICAL SOCIETY, 172 Main St., Groton, MA 01450-1238. Mailing Address: P.O. Box 202, Groton, MA 01450-0202. Tel.: 978-448-0092.
E-mail: hostess@grotonhistoricalsociety.org
Web Site: www.grotonhistoricalsociety.org
Founded: 1894.
Congressional District: 5
Key Personnel: Pres., Theodore Roselund; Dir., Bonnie Carter.
Personnel Profile: Full-Time Paid 1; Full-Time Volunteers 10; Part-Time Volunteers 10.
Governing Authority: society; nonprofit organization. Tax-exempt: 501(c)(3).
Historic House: 1851 Governor Boutwell House.
Collections: household furnishings; Revolutionary & Civil War items; local history.
Publications: George S. Boutwell: Human Rights Advocate; Groton Houses.
Hours & Admission Prices: June-Sept. Sun. 2-4. No charge; donations accepted.
Membership: Individual & Corresponding $15; Life $100.

Hadley

HADLEY FARM MUSEUM, 224 River Dr., Hadley, MA 01035-9641. Tel.: 413-584-7459.
Founded: 1930.
Key Personnel: Pres., Thomas West; Sec., Mrs. Glenn Clark.
Governing Authority: association. Tax-exempt: 501(c)(3).
Farm Museum: housed in 1782 barn.
Collections: crafts; farm equipment; plows; winnowing machines; corn shellers; seeders; stage coach; sleighs.
Activities: guided tours.
Hours & Admission Prices: May-Oct. Thurs.-Sat. 11-4:30, Sun. 1:30-4:30; other times by appointment. No charge; donations accepted.
Attendance: 1,000 (estimated)

PORTER-PHELPS-HUNTINGTON FOUNDATION, INC., 130 River Dr., Hadley, MA 01035-9782. Tel.: 413-584-4699.
Web Site: www.pphmuseum.org
Founded: 1948.
Congressional District: 2
Key Personnel: Dir. & C.E.O., Susan J. Lisk; Pres., Tom Harris; Vice Pres. Bd., Dan Huntington Fenn, Jr.; Treas., Sidney Poritz; Clerk, Craig Malone.
Personnel Profile: Part-Time Paid 5; Part-Time Volunteers 15; Interns 1.
Governing Authority: not-for-profit organization. Tax-exempt: 501(c)(3).
Historic House: 1752 Georgian home & grounds.
Collections: furniture; paintings; decorative arts; archives; photographs; clothing; household items belonging to the Porter, Phelps & Huntington families.
Research Fields: women's history; family history; clothing; genealogy.
Facilities: 500-vol. library of reference & history works available to the public; 100 linear ft. Porter-Phelps-Huntington family papers located at Amherst College archives.
Activities: concerts; guided tours; lectures.
Publications: newsletter, Forty Acres.
Hours & Admission Prices: mid-Oct. to mid-May Sat.-Wed. 1-4:30. Adults $5, children $1.
Attendance: 1,870 (accurate)
Membership: Levels: $25; $50; $100; $500; $1,000.

Hampden

LAUGHING BROOK EDUCATION CENTER & WILDLIFE SANCTUARY, 793 Main St., Hampden, MA 01036. Mailing Address: P.O. Box 529, Hampden, MA 01036-0529. Tel.: 413-584-3009, ext. 12. Fax: 413-584-0250.
E-mail: mshanley@massaudubon.org

Web Site: massaudubon.org
Founded: 1968.
Congressional District: 2
Key Personnel: Pres., Laura Johnson; Education Coord., Jane McCarry; Sanctuary Dir., Mary Shanley-Koeber.
Personnel Profile: Full-Time Paid 2; Part-Time Paid 2; Part-Time Volunteers 30.
Governing Authority: society. Parent Institution: Massachusetts Audubon Society, S. Great Rd., Lincoln, MA 01773. Tax-exempt.
Wildlife Sanctuary & Nature Center.
Collections: Historic House: Storyteller's House 1782 in Hampden, home of author Thornton W. Burgess.
Research Fields: natural history.
Facilities: 354-acres of forest, field, stream, pond, wetlands (flora & fauna); classrooms; auditorium; walking trails. Natural history-related items for sale.
Activities: environmental, education & natural history programs for children, adults & families; community outreach programs; college programs.
Publications: quarterly newsletter; program brochure.
Hours & Admission Prices: Trails: Tues.-Sun. dawn to dusk. Buildings: open for scheduled programs only. Adults $3, senior citizens & children under 14 $2; discounts to AAA members; children under 3 & members no charge. Closed New Year's Day; Thanksgiving; Christmas. ♿
Attendance: 15,000 (estimated)
Membership: Individual $37; Family $47.

Hardwick

HARDWICK HISTORICAL SOCIETY, On Hardwick Common, Hardwick, MA 01037. Mailing Address: P.O. Box 492, Hardwick, MA 01037-0492. Tel.: 413-967-4002. Fax: 413-477-0247.
Web Site: townofhardwick.org
Founded: 1959.
Key Personnel: Pres., Randall Noble; Cur., Emily Bancroft; Sec., Sheila MacKinnon.
Governing Authority: society. Tax-exempt.
Local History Museum: housed in 1840 Old Brick School House.
Collections: period furniture and utensils; doll furniture; old books & papers; Indian artifacts; china; costumes; tools; local records; family pictures; memorabilia; historical portraits.
Research Fields: genealogy; history.
Facilities: 150-vol. library of local history books available on premises.
Activities: guided tours; lectures; films; gallery talks; special events; educational programs. Annual Events: Open House; Village Fair.
Publications: annual reports; annual newsletter; Village Tour brochures.
Hours & Admission Prices: By appointment. No charge; donations accepted.
Attendance: 320 (estimated)
Membership: Yearly $10; Life $100.

Harvard

FRUITLANDS MUSEUMS, 102 Prospect Hill Rd., Harvard, MA 01451-1348. Tel.: 978-456-3924. Fax: 978-456-8078.
Web Site: www.fruitlands.org
Founded: 1914.
Congressional District: 2
Key Personnel: Dir., Maud Ayson; Pres. (V), Fay Martin; Chm. (V), Dennis Murphy, III; Museum Shop Mgr., Linda Luosalo.
Personnel Profile: Full-Time Paid 9; Part-Time Paid 5; Part-Time Volunteers 20; Interns 5.
Governing Authority: nonprofit. Tax-exempt: 501(c)(3).
History Museum.
Collections: American paintings (Hudson River School); decorative arts; ethnology; folklore; Indian artifacts; history; memorabilia of Thoreau, Emerson, Margaret Fuller & Lane. Historic Houses: c. 1715 Fruitlands farmhouse used by Bronson Alcott & Transcendentalists; 1794 Shaker House; Shaker furnishings, products & material culture. Historic landscapes: Native American hunting ground, colonial garrison house & farm site.
Research Fields: paintings; history; shakers; transcendentalism; cultural landscape.
Facilities: 10,000-vol. library available by appointment only; luncheon facilities; picnic area; rental facilities; nature trails. Museum-related items for sale.
Activities: films; permanent & temporary exhibitions; concerts; lectures; field trips; nature walks; archaeological sites; natural history interpretation. Museum Sponsors: outdoor music series in summer.
Publications: booklets; quarterly newsletter, Under the Mulberry Tree; A New Eden; History's Daughter.
Hours & Admission Prices: Museums: May 14-Oct. Mon.-Fri. 11-4, Sat.-Sun. & holidays 11-5. Tours: by reservation. Grounds: daily 10-5. Library: by appointment only. Adults $10, seniors 60 and over & students with college ID $8, children 5-17 $4; discounts to AAM, NEMA & AAA members; members no charge. ♿
Attendance: 20,000 (estimated)
Membership: Senior & Student $25; Individual $40; Family $65; Patron $125; Sears Benefactor $350.

Harwich

BROOKS ACADEMY MUSEUM, 80 Parallel St., Harwich, MA 02645-2716. Tel.: 508-432-8089.
E-mail: harwichhistoricalsociety@verizon.net
Web Site: www.harwichhistoricalsociety.org
Founded: 1954.
Congressional District: 10
Key Personnel: Dir., Desiree Mobed; Pres., Jane Neville; Treas., George Lewis; Recording Sec., Jane Michaels; Museum Shop Mgr., Jane Chase.
Personnel Profile: Part-Time Paid 2; Part-Time Volunteers 75.
Governing Authority: society; nonprofit. Parent Institution: Harwich Historical Society. Tax-exempt: 501(c)(3).
Historical Society Museum: housed in c.1844 building that served as a private secondary school.
Collections: Harwich & Cape Cod history; photographs; marine material; glass collection; genealogical material; early cranberry industry equipment; deeds; maps; Indian arrow heads; hand tools; bound copies of 1872-1958, Harwich Independent.
Research Fields: Maritime research; preliminary work on Brooks family papers; Harwich history; Caleb Chase of Chase & Sanborn; Brooks Academy graduates; outerwear & underwear; white textiles & garments, 1860-1920.
Facilities: 100-vol. library; 50-seat auditorium; 5,000 sq. ft. exhibit space. Museum-related items for sale.
Activities: lectures; country auction; temporary exhibitions; docent program; formal education programs for children; guided tours.
Publications: quarterly newsletter, The Powderhouse Quarterly; book, Vital Records of Town of Harwich.
Hours & Admission Prices: late June to mid-Oct. Thurs.-Sat. 1-4. Adults $3; members no charge. Closed Independence Day. ♿
Attendance: 2,000 (accurate)
Membership: Junior $5; Regular $18; Household $25; Life $250.

BROOKS FREE LIBRARY, 739 Main St., Harwich, MA 02645-2752. Tel.: 508-430-7562. Fax: 508-430-7564.
E-mail: bfl_mail@clamsnet.org
Web Site: www.brooksfreelibrary.org
Founded: 1880.
Congressional District: 12
Key Personnel: Dir., Virginia A. Hewitt; Reference Librarian, Jennifer Pickett; Public Svcs. Librarian, Suzanne Martell; Youth Svcs. Librarian, Ann Carpenter; Principal Clerk, Mary Jo Metzger; Sr. Library Technician, Phil Inman; Sr. Library Technician, Pam Paine; Sr. Library Technician, Joanne Clingan.
Personnel Profile: Full-Time Paid 6; Part-Time Paid 5; Part-Time Volunteers 40.
Governing Authority: municipal. Tax-exempt.
Library.
Collections: Rogers' statuary groups.
Facilities: 54,000-vol. library of books available for inter-library loan & for use on the premises; reference department; children's room; public access computers.
Hours & Admission Prices: Tues.-Thurs. 10-7, Fri.-Sat. 10-4. Local History Room: call for hours. No charge. Closed national & state holidays. ♿
Attendance: 82,569 (accurate)

Haverhill

HAVERHILL HISTORICAL SOCIETY, 240 Water St., Haverhill, MA 01830-6433. Tel.: 978-374-4626. Fax: 978-521-9176.
Web Site: haverhillhistory.org
Founded: 1897.
Congressional District: 6
Key Personnel: Pres. (V), Jay Cleary; Cur., Jan Williams; Program Coord., Gwen Sobel; Weekend Supvr., Thomas Spitalere; Bookkeeper, Lisa O'Hearn.
Personnel Profile: Part-Time Paid 3; Part-Time Volunteers 8.
Governing Authority: nonprofit organization. Tax-exempt.
History Museum.
Collections: 17th to 19th-century furniture, paintings & glass; objects relating to the history of the Haverhill area; archeological collections from the lower Merrimack Valley; c.1850 Daniel A. Hunkins Shoe Shop; c.1710 John Ward House; 1814 Duncan House.

Research Fields: Lower Merrimack Valley; archeological collections.
Facilities: historic houses; shoemaker's shop; lecture hall. Museum-related items for sale.
Activities: guided tours; permanent & temporary exhibits; educational programs for children; history camp; lecture series; preschool program; after school programs.
Publications: quarterly newsletter.
Hours & Admission Prices: Summer: Tues.-Sun. 10-5; Winter: Tues.-Sat. 10-5. Adults $5, children $4; discounts to AAM members; members no charge. Closed major holidays. ♿
Attendance: 3,849 (accurate)
Membership: Individual $25; Family $40; Buttonwoods Benefactor $100.

Hingham

BARE COVE FIRE MUSEUM, 45 Bare Cove Park Dr., Hingham, MA 02043. Mailing Address: P.O. Box 262, Hingham, MA 02043-0262. Tel.: 781-749-0028.
E-mail: bcfm.hingham@gmail.com
Web Site: barecovefiremuseum.org
Founded: 1976.
Key Personnel: Pres. & Chief, David Clark; Vice Pres., Jack Crandall; Treas., Lisa Andre; Dir., Joyce Olsen; Dir., Jaclyn Howard; Dir., Russell Clark; Cur., Robert Stella; Clerk & Archivist, Geri Duff.
Personnel Profile: Part-Time Volunteers 90.
Governing Authority: private; nonprofit organization; tax-exempt.
Fire-Fighting Museum.
Collections: hand & horse motored period fire engines; period artifacts; equipment; photos; records; 1920 era maxim fire engines; 1935 Ahrens-Fox pumping engine; restored 1850 era hand operated fire engine.
Facilities: library of records of past fire companies available for public use; 300 sq. ft. exhibit space. Museum-related items for sale.
Activities: films; guided tours; lectures. Museum Sponsors: Open House.
Publications: semiannual newsletter, The Speaking Trumpet.
Hours & Admission Prices: Wed. 7pm-10pm; other times by appointment. No charge; donations accepted. ♿
Attendance: 300 (estimated)
Membership: Family $15 (w/Active); Active $35; Life $500.

HINGHAM HISTORICAL SOCIETY, 34 Main St., Hingham, MA 02043. Mailing Address: P.O. Box 434, Hingham, MA 02043-0434. Tel.: 781-749-7721. Fax: 781-749-0091.
E-mail: director@hinghamhistorical.org
Web Site: www.hinghamhistorical.org
Formerly: Old Ordinary House Museum
Founded: 1914.
Congressional District: 10
Key Personnel: Dir., Suzanne Buchanan; Pres., Michael Studley; Museum Shop Mgr., Susan Achille.
Personnel Profile: Full-Time Paid 1; Part-Time Paid 4; Part-Time Volunteers 50; Interns 1.
Governing Authority: society. Parent Institution: Hingham Historical Society. Tax-exempt: 101(6).
Historical Society.
Collections: architecture; 18th & 19th century furnishings; art; decorative arts; archival collections; photographs; toys.
Major Exhibits: Wrought By My Hand: Schoolgirl Needlework from Society's Collection, 11/09-9/11.
Research Fields: local history & American Decorative Arts.
Facilities: 500-vol. library of history & genealogy books available for use by appointment.
Activities: guided tours; permanent & temporary exhibitions. Annual Event: House Tour in June.
Publications: Hingham Old & New; Two Hundred Years in South Hingham; By the Wayside; Hingham Colonial Industries; Profile of Hingham: News & Notes Out of the Ordinary; cookbook, Out of the Ordinary; Not All Is Changed.
Hours & Admission Prices: mid-June to early Sept. Tues.-Sat. 1:30-4:30; other times by appointment. Adults $5, children under 12 $3; members no charge.
Attendance: 1,000 (estimated)
Membership: Family $40; Sustaining Family $100; Patron Family $250; Sara Derby Society $500; Lincoln Society $1,000.

Holyoke

CHILDREN'S MUSEUM AT HOLYOKE, INC., 444 Dwight St., Holyoke, MA 01040-5842. Tel.: 413-536-7048. Fax: 413-533-2999.
E-mail: kmorneau@childrensmuseumholyoke.org
Web Site: childrensmuseumholyoke.org
Founded: 1981.
Congressional District: 1
Key Personnel: C.E.O. & Pres. (V), Eileen Leahy; Exec. Dir., Mary Paz; Program Coord., Dayna Abrazinski; Mgr. Operations, Amanda Ebel; Museum Shop Mgr., Margaret Boulais; Bookkeeper, Kathleen McCreary; Administrative Asst., Brenda Parent.
Personnel Profile: Part-Time Paid 6; Part-Time Volunteers 6; Interns 2.
Governing Authority: nonprofit organization. Tax-exempt: 501(c)(3).
Children's Museum.
Collections: cultural & natural history artifacts; health & well-being exhibit.
Research Fields: early childhood education.
Facilities: 16,500 sq. ft. exhibit & program space; 100-seat theater; permanent exhibits include: Two story curvy climber, waterworks area, exploration room, paperworks, tot lot, cityscape, Scientific Co., TV studio & workshop room, Family Resource Center. Gift items for sale.
Activities: annual performance series; science & art workshops; preschool & after school programs; junior volunteer program; cultural celebrations; summer & vacation day camps; youth leadership & employment training; summer institutes for teachers, grade level appropriate staff-facilitated science based elementary school group visits.
Hours & Admission Prices: Wed.-Sat. 10-4, Sun. 12-4. Adults & children $6, senior citizens $3; discounts to AAM & AYM members & groups; children under one & members no charge. Closed New Year's Day; Easter; Memorial Day; Independence Day; Labor Day; Thanksgiving; Christmas. ♿
Attendance: 40,000 (accurate)
Membership: You & Me $45; Small Family $65; Family Plus $90; Supporting $140; Sustaining $500; Lifetime $1,000.

HOLYOKE HERITAGE STATE PARK, 221 Appleton St., Holyoke, MA 01040-5714. Tel.: 413-534-1723.
E-mail: mass.parks@state.ma.us
Web Site: www.mass.gov/dcr/parks/central/hhsp.htm
Key Personnel: Supvr., Charlie Lotspeich
Park Museum.
Collections: local history & culture; paper manufacturing; Holyoke's industrial history.
Hours & Admission Prices: Visitor's Center: Tues.-Sun. 12-4. No charge.

VOLLEYBALL HALL OF FAME, 444 Dwight St., Holyoke, MA 01040-5842. Tel.: 413-536-0926. Fax: 413-539-6673.
E-mail: info@volleyhall.org
Web Site: www.volleyhall.org
Key Personnel: Exec. Dir., Jerry Fitzsimons.
Governing Authority: Tax-exempt: 501(c)(3).
Sports Museum.
Collections: volleyball memorabilia.
Hours & Admission Prices: Tues.-Sun. 12-4:30.

WISTARIAHURST MUSEUM, (M), 238 Cabot St., Holyoke, MA 01040-3904. Tel.: 413-322-5660. Fax: 413-534-2344.
E-mail: wistariahurst@ci.holyoke.ma.us
Web Site: www.wistariahurst.org
Founded: 1959.
Congressional District: 1
Key Personnel: Dir., Melissa Boisselle; Chm. (V), Olivia Mausel; Cur., Kate Navarra Thibodeau; Events, Marjorie Latham.
Personnel Profile: Full-Time Paid 2; Part-Time Paid 4; Part-Time Volunteers 100; Interns 5.
Governing Authority: municipal. Parent Institution: city of Holyoke & the Holyoke Historical Commission. Tax-exempt.
Historic House: built in c.1868 26-room mansion & carriage house; former home of local silk manufacturer William Skinner with two additions made in 1914 & 1927.
Collections: furnishings; parquet flooring; leather wall coverings. Historic Structure: c.1874 carriage house; period furniture; costumes; archival materials; distinctive interior architectural detailing.
Major Exhibits: Garden Restoration Exhibition, Spring 2010.
Facilities: 100-seat music room.
Activities: guided tours; concerts; permanent, temporary & traveling exhibitions; school loan & outreach services; volunteer program; group & individual tours by appointment only.
Publications: Wistariahurst Museum Newsletter.
Hours & Admission Prices: Sat.-Mon. 12-4. Adults $5, seniors & students $3; discounts to MA Teachers Association. Closed Christmas. ♿
Attendance: 9,500 (estimated)
Membership: $20-$500.

Hull

HULL LIFESAVING MUSEUM INC., THE MUSEUM OF BOSTON HARBOR HERITAGE, (M), 1117 Nantasket Ave., Hull, MA 02045-1310. Mailing Address: P.O. Box 221, Hull, MA 02045-0221. Tel.: 781-925-5433. Fax: 781-925-0992.
E-mail: info@hulllifesavingmuseum.org
Web Site: hulllifesavingmuseum.org
Founded: 1978.
Congressional District: 10
Key Personnel: C.E.O., Lory Newmyer; Dir. Maritime Program, Edward P. McCabe; Dir. Museum, Corinne Leung; Pres. (V), Robert MacIntyre; Treas., Diana Burns.
Personnel Profile: Full-Time Paid 10; Part-Time Paid 2; Part-Time Volunteers 150; Interns 1.
Governing Authority: private; nonprofit organization. Subsidiary Institutions: HLMI Maritime Program, Hull, MA; HLMI Maritime Program, Seaport District, Boston, MA. Tax-exempt: 501(c)(3).
Maritime Museum: headquarters housed in restored c.1889 Point Allerton United States Life Saving Service Station.
Collections: artifacts; books; prints; clothing; lifesaving vessels & apparatus; photographs; logs; postcards; fleet of traditional small crafts.
Research Fields: history of Massachusetts Humane Society; U.S. lifesaving service; early United States Coast Guard; history & legend of Boston Harbor, it's islands, lighthouses & forts; maritime history of Hull.
Facilities: library. Museum-related items for sale.
Activities: arts festivals; concerts; films; formal education programs; guided tours; hobby workshops; lectures; loan, participatory & temporary exhibitions; training programs for professional museum workers; broadcast programs. Museum Sponsors: Year-round open-water rowing programs in Boston; Head of the Weir Rowing Race; Snow Row; Peddocks Island Row; Northeast Regional Youth Rowing Championship.
Publications: semiannual journal, The Station Log; bimonthly newsletter, The Messenger Line.
Hours & Admission Prices: Wed.-Sun. 10-4. Adults $5, senior citizens $3; AAM & ICOM members, children & members no charge. Closed National holidays. ♿
Attendance: 12,000 (estimated)
Membership: Individual $30; Family $50; Surfman $60; Keeper $100; Superintendent $250; Pt. Allerton Society $500.

Hyannis

THE CAPE COD MARITIME MUSEUM, (M), 135 South St., Hyannis, MA 02601-4014. Mailing Address: P.O. Box 443, Hyannis, MA 02601-0443. Tel.: 508-775-1723. Fax: 508-775-1706.
E-mail: info@capecodmaritimemuseum.org
Web Site: www.capecodmaritimemuseum.org
Founded: 1998.
Key Personnel: Dir., Janet C. Preston; Pres. (V), William Cook; Education & Museum Shop Mgr., Kate Parker; Front Desk, Erin Trainor; Treas., John Damon.
Personnel Profile: Full-Time Paid 2; Part-Time Paid 1; Part-Time Volunteers 4; Interns 2.
Governing Authority: private; nonprofit organization. Tax-exempt: 501(c)(3).
Maritime Museum.
Collections: maritime history & art; books; drawings; models; 3 full-size wooden boats; photographs; Sparrow Hawk.
Research Fields: maritime culture during the 17th-century on Cape Cod.
Facilities: 450-vol. library; educational facilities; 1,200 sq. ft. exhibit space. Museum-related items for sale.
Activities: formal education programs for adults & children; hobby workshops; lectures; loan & participatory exhibitions. Annual Event: Maritime Festival.
Hours & Admission Prices: March-Dec. Tues.-Sat. 10-4, Sun. 12-4. Adults $5, senior citizens & students $4; children under 6 no charge. Closed most holidays. ♿
Attendance: 5,000 (estimated)
Membership: Individual $35; Family $50; Contributor $75; Supporter $100; Associate $250.

JOHN F. KENNEDY HYANNIS MUSEUM, 397 Main St., Hyannis, MA 02601-3914. Mailing Address: P.O. Box 100, Hyannis, MA 02601. Tel.: 508-790-3077.
Web Site: www.hyannis.com
Key Personnel: Dir., Deborah Converse
History Museum.
Collections: over 80 photographs depicting the life of John F. Kennedy on Cape Code from 1934-1963.
Hours & Admission Prices: mid-Feb. to mid-April & Nov.-Dec. Thurs.-Sat. 10-4, Sun. 12-4; April-Memorial Day & day after Columbus Day-Oct. Mon.-Sat. 10-4, Sun. 12-4; May-Columbus Day Mon.-Sat. 9-5, Sun. 12-5. Adults 18 & over $5, children 10-17 $2.50; children under 10 no charge.

ZION UNION HERITAGE MUSEUM, INC., 276 North St., Hyannis, MA 02601-3826. Mailing Address: P.O. Box 2591, Hyannis, MA 02601-7591. Tel.: 508-790-9466.
Web Site: zionunionheritagemuseum.org
History Museum.
Collections: artifacts & memorabilia pertaining to African-Americans & Cape Verdeans on Cape Cod.
Hours & Admission Prices: Feb. to mid-April & Nov.-Dec. Thurs.-Sat. 10-4, Sun. 12-4; mid-April to Oct. Tues.-Sat. 10-4, Sun. 12-4. Adults 18 & over $5, children 10-17 $2; children under 10 no charge.

Indian Orchard

THE TITANIC MUSEUM, 208 Main St., Indian Orchard, MA 01151-1132. Mailing Address: P.O. Box 51053, Indian Orchard, MA 01151-5053. Tel.: 413-543-4770. Fax: 413-583-3633.
E-mail: titanicinfo@titanichistoricalsociety.org
Web Site: www.titanic1.org/museum
Governing Authority: Parent Institution: The Titanic Historical Society.
History Museum.
Collections: artifacts & memorabilia from the Titanic.
Hours & Admission Prices: Mon.-Fri. 10-4, Sat. 10-3. Adults $4, children 6-11 $2; Titanic Historical Society members & children 5 and under no charge.

Ipswich

GREAT HOUSE AT CASTLE HILL ON THE CRANE ESTATE, 290 Argilla Rd., Ipswich, MA 01938. Mailing Address: 572 Essex St., Beverly, MA 01915. Tel.: 978-921-1944, ext. 4009.
E-mail: lcompton@ttor.org
Founded: 1949.
Congressional District: 6
Key Personnel: Education, Lisa Compton; Cur., Susan Hill Dolan.
Personnel Profile: Full-Time Paid 25; Part-Time Paid 50; Part-Time Volunteers 100.
Governing Authority: private; nonprofit organization. Parent Institution: The Trustees of Reservations, Beverly, MA. Tax-exempt: 501(c)(3).
Historic House: housed in an early 20th-century estate; built in 1928.
Collections: furnishings; historic buildings.
Activities: guided tours; lectures; concerts; educational programs; guided house & landscape tours.
Publications: quarterly members magazine, Special Placer.
Hours & Admission Prices: May-Oct. call for hours. Grounds: daily 8am to sunset. Adults $10; discounts to groups of 15 or more; members no charge. ♿
Attendance: 5,000 (accurate)
Membership: Individual $45; Family $65.

IPSWICH HISTORICAL SOCIETY AND MUSEUM, (M), 54 S. Main St., (Rte. 1A), Ipswich, MA 01938-2322. Tel.: 978-356-2811. Fax: 978-356-2817.
E-mail: admin@ipswichmuseum.org
Web Site: www.ipswichmuseum.org
Founded: 1890.
Congressional District: 6
Key Personnel: Dir., Wendy Evans; Pres., Fred Hale; Treas., James Grimes.
Personnel Profile: Full-Time Paid 1; Part-Time Paid 2; Part-Time Volunteers 65; Interns 2.
Governing Authority: private; nonprofit organization. Tax-exempt.
History Museum.
Collections: manuscripts; seafaring artifacts; furniture & arts from China; dolls & toys; costumes & textiles; military memorabilia; Arthur Wesley Dow paintings & prints; carriages; sleighs. Historic Houses: c.1677 John Whipple House with lace displays & artifacts of the 17th, 18th & early 19th century; 1800 John Heard House.
Research Fields: local history.
Facilities: library of local history, genealogy & early religious books; children's galley. Museum-related items for sale.
Activities: guided tours; docent training program; lectures; education programs for students & adults; temporary exhibitions. Annual Events: History Baseball Game; Halloween Party.
Publications: pamphlets of Ipswich history; book, Ipswich Historical Society; quarterly newsletter.
Hours & Admission Prices: Jan.-April Sun. 2-4; May-Oct. Wed.-Sun. 2-4; Oct.-Dec. Wed. 2-4 & 5-8, Thurs.-Sun. 2-4. One House: adults $5; children 6-12 $3; children under 6 & members no charge. Two Houses: adults $7, children 6-12 $3; children under 6 & members no charge.

Attendance: 1,500 (accurate)
Membership: Individual $35; Family $50; Sustaining $75; Sponsor $125; Patron $250; Benefactor $500; Thomas Franklin Waters Circle $1,000.

THE PAINE HOUSE AT GREENWOOD FARM, A PROPERTY OF THE TRUSTEES OF RESERVATIONS, 47 Jeffrey's Neck Rd., Ipswich, MA 01938. Mailing Address: 572 Essex St., Beverly, MA 01915. Tel.: 978-921-1944, ext. 4009.
E-mail: lcompton@ttor.org
Web Site: www.ttor.org
Founded: 1993.
Congressional District: 6
Key Personnel: Education, Lisa Compton; Cur., Susan Hill Dolan.
Personnel Profile: Full-Time Paid 1; Part-Time Paid 1; Part-Time Volunteers 5.
Governing Authority: private; nonprofit organization. Parent Institution: The Trustees of Reservations, Beverly, MA. Tax-exempt: 501(c)(3).
Historic House: housed in the former Paine family farmhouse; built in 1694.
Collections: local history & culture; indoor dairy; early Essex County furniture.
Activities: guided house tour; self-guided walking tours.
Publications: quarterly membership magazine, Special Places.
Hours & Admission Prices: Farm: late May to Columbus Day Sat.-Sun. 1-4; other times by appointment. Grounds: daily 8am to sunset. Tours: House $8; Essex National Heritage Area members & museum members no charge.
Attendance: 200 (estimated)
Membership: Individual $45; Family $65.

Kingston

MAJOR JOHN BRADFORD HOUSE, Maple St. & Landing Rd., Kingston, MA 02364. Mailing Address: P.O. Box 22, Kingston, MA 02364-0022. Tel.: 781-585-6300.
Web Site: www.jrvhs.org
Founded: 1921.
Congressional District: 12
Key Personnel: Pres., Norman P. Tucker.
Governing Authority: nonprofit organization. Administered by Jones River Village Historical Society. P.O. Box 22, Kingston, MA. Tax-exempt: 501(c)(3).
Historic House: 1714 Major John Bradford home.
Collections: child's room with doll collection; furnishings; crewel coverlets; 19th-century halfhulls & other maritime artifacts; period looms; pottery.
Research Fields: textiles; needlework.
Facilities: Museum-related items for sale.
Activities: guided tours; permanent exhibitions.
Publications: quarterly newsletter.
Hours & Admission Prices: Summer: Sun. 9-11:30, tours by appointment. No charge.
Attendance: 2,500 (estimated)
Membership: Senior $10; Single $20; Family $30; Corporate $100.

Lancaster

FIRST CHURCH OF CHRIST UNITARIAN, 725 Main St., Lancaster, MA 01523. Mailing Address: P.O. Box 66, Lancaster, MA 01523-0066. Tel.: 978-365-2427. Fax: 978-368-0194.
E-mail: office@firstchurchlancasterma.org
Web Site: firstchurchlancasterma.org
Formerly: Fifth Meeting House
Founded: 1653.
Congressional District: 3
Key Personnel: Minister, Rev. Dr. Paul Hull; Church Admin., Karen Plaskon.
Governing Authority: church. Affiliated with First Church of Christ, Lancaster, MA. Tax-exempt.
Religious Museum: housed in 1816 The First Church of Christ.
Collections: Historic Buildings: 1st Church of Christ; built 1816.
Publications: monthly bulletin; book, The Founding Mother; The Bulfinch Church in Lancaster; Precious Predecessors; A New England Village Church.
Hours & Admission Prices: Sun. 10:30; other times by appointment. No charge. ♿

Lawrence

LAWRENCE HERITAGE STATE PARK, 1 Jackson St., Lawrence, MA 01840-1613. Tel.: 978-794-1655. Fax: 978-794-9241. TDD: 978-794-1655.
E-mail: lawrence.heritage@state.ma.us
Web Site: www.mass.gov/dcr/parks/northeast/1whp.htm
Founded: 1985.
Congressional District: 5
Key Personnel: Park Supvr., John W. Faro; Chm. (V), Joe Bella; Visitor Svcs. Supvr. & Museum Shop Mgr., Jim Beauchesne; Maintenance, Tom Ceder; Maintenance, Will McDowell.
Personnel Profile: Full-Time Paid 4; Part-Time Paid 4; Part-Time Volunteers 3.
Governing Authority: state. Parent Institution: Commonwealth of Massachusetts. Subsidiary Institutions: Dept. of Conservation and Recreation; Division of State Parks & Recreation. Tax-exempt.
State Park.
Collections: photographs; artifacts; models; c.1847 house.
Research Fields: industrial & labor history.
Facilities: 8-vol. library of Lawrence History Curriculum Project material; fishing; picnic area.
Activities: guided tours; lectures; films; concerts; arts festivals; theater; gallery; organized education programs for children; participatory & temporary exhibitions; school loan service. Museum Sponsors: Bread & Roses Labor Day Festival.
Publications: events calendar.
Hours & Admission Prices: No charge; donations accepted. Closed New Year's Day; Thanksgiving; Christmas. ♿
Attendance: 100,000 (estimated)
Membership: Friends of Lawrence Heritage State Park: Student & Senior Citizen $5; Adult $10.

LAWRENCE HISTORY CENTER: IMMIGRANT CITY ARCHIVES, 6 Essex St., Lawrence, MA 01840-1710. Tel.: 978-686-9230.
E-mail: director@lawrencehistory.org
Web Site: www.lawrencehistory.org
Formerly: Immigrant City Archives, Historical Society of Lawrence and Its People
Founded: 1978.
Congressional District: 5
Key Personnel: Exec. Dir., Barbara Brown; Pres. (V), Pamela Yameen; Asst. to Dir., Amita Kiley.
Personnel Profile: Full-Time Paid 1; Part-Time Paid 4; Part-Time Volunteers 15.
Governing Authority: nonprofit organization. Parent Institution: Immigrant City Archives, Inc. Tax-exempt: 501(c)(3).
Historical Society Museum: housed in 1883 buildings.
Collections: Essex Company business & planning records; immigration; labor; urban planning; social organizations; churches; oral histories; photography; books; archives. Historic Buildings: 4 brick buildings in cobblestone courtyard.
Research Fields: local history; genealogy; ethnic; labor; women; urban planning; 19th-century technology; immigration.
Facilities: 1883 buildings: office, carpenter, forge, stable, warehouse, carpenter, blacksmith, waterpower regulating & testing tools.
Activities: lectures: ethnic, genealogy, labor, local history, workshops for teachers; school groups; tours; lectures; genealogy; cultural events.
Publications: booklet, Lawrence, Massachusetts: The Strike of 1912; Immigrant City Archives Cookbook; walking tour booklets; Lawrence, Massachusetts, Vols. I & II.; newsletter, Lawrence History News.
Hours & Admission Prices: Winter: Tues.-Fri. 9-4, Sat. 9-1 by appointment. Summer: Tues.-Fri. 9-4. Research: members no charge. Closed Independence Day & week; Christmas week. ♿
Attendance: 3,000 (estimated)
Membership: Senior $20; Individual $35; Family $50; Contributor $100; Sponsor $175; Patron $300.

Lenox

BERKSHIRE SCENIC RAILWAY MUSEUM, 10 Willow Creek Rd., Lenox, MA 01240. Mailing Address: P.O. Box 2195, Lenox, MA 01240-5195. Tel.: 413-637-2210. Fax: 413-637-4965.
E-mail: marketing@berkshirescenicrailroad.org
Web Site: www.berkshirescenicrailroad.org
Founded: 1984.
Key Personnel: Pres. (V), Richard Selva; Cur., John Trowill; Mktg., Pieter Lips; Public Rels., Pamela Green; Museum Shop Mgr., Cathleen Chittenden.
Personnel Profile: Part-Time Volunteers 30.
Governing Authority: private; nonprofit organization. Tax-exempt: 501(c)(3).
Train Museum: housed in the restored 1903 Lenox station.
Collections: 1920s-1960s railroad equipment used by the New York, New Haven & Hartford Railroad; turn-of-the-century photographs of Berkshire Hills residences; vintage coaches.
Facilities: 3,000 sq. ft. exhibit space. Museum-related items for sale.
Activities: narrated train ride, Lenox Local. Museum Sponsors: Railroad Operation Lifesaver classes for elementary students; Fire Truck Displays; Antique Engines; Halloween & Santa Specials.
Publications: biannual newsletter, Along the River; annual report.
Hours & Admission Prices: Memorial Day-Oct. Sat.-Sun. & holidays 10-3:30.

Train: Adults $15, seniors $14, children 4-14 $8; children under 4 & members no charge. Museum & Exhibits: no charge. ♿
Attendance: 8,500 (accurate)
Membership: Individual $20; Family $30; Patron $100; Benefactor $250; Lifetime $500.

THE MOUNT ESTATE AND GARDENS, 2 Plunkett St., Lenox, MA 01240-2704. Mailing Address: P.O. Box 974, Lenox, MA 01240-0974. Tel.: 413-551-5111.
E-mail: info@edithwharton.org
Web Site: edithwharton.org
Key Personnel: Exec. Dir., Susan Wissler; Group Sales & Operations Mgr., Elaine Roberts; Publications Dir., David Dashiell; Facilities Mgr., Ross Jolly; Librarian, Molly McFall
House House: former home designed by Pulitzer-Prize winning author Edith Wharton.
Collections: period artifacts & memorabilia.
Hours & Admission Prices: May-Nov 1 daily 10-5; Nov. 7-Dec. 20 Sat.-Sun. 10-4. Adults $16, students $13; children 12 & under no charge.

VENTFORT HALL MANSION AND GILDED AGE MUSEUM, 104 Walker St., Lenox, MA 01240-2725. Tel.: 413-637-3206.
Web Site: gildedage.org
Historic House: former home of Sarah Morgan, sister of J.P. Morgan, built in 1893. Listed on the National Register of Historic Places.
Collections: period artifacts & memorabilia from the 19th century.
Hours & Admission Prices: Daily 10-3. Adults $12, senior citizens 65 & over and college students with ID $10, children 5-17 $5; discount to members; children under 5 no charge. Closed New Year's Day; Easter; Thanksgiving; Christmas.

Leominster

NATIONAL PLASTICS CENTER AND MUSEUM, 210 Lancaster St., Rte. 117, Leominster, MA 01453. Tel.: 978-537-9529.
E-mail: mzephir@plasticindustry.org
Web Site: www.plasticsmuseum.org
Founded: 1982.
Key Personnel: Cur., Marianne Zephir.
Personnel Profile: Full-Time Paid 5; Part-Time Paid 4; Part-Time Volunteers 4; Interns 2.
Governing Authority: Tax-exempt.
Industrial Museum: housed in a school building built in 1888.
Collections: early molding machines; plastics industry history; recycling; hands-on exhibits; toys; plastics in medicine; period furniture; Plastics Hall of Fame.
Facilities: library; 10,000 sq. ft. exhibit space.
Activities: research; meetings; rental facility.
Hours & Admission Prices: Call for hours. Adults $5, children 4-11 & senior 65 & over $3; ASTC members & members no charge. ♿
Attendance: 12,000 (accurate)
Membership: $25; $50; $250; $500; $1,000.

Leverett

LEVERETT HISTORICAL SOCIETY, N. Leverett Rd., Leverett, MA 01054. Mailing Address: P.O. Box 57, Leverett, MA 01054-0057. Tel.: 413-548-9452.
Founded: 1963.
Congressional District: 1
Key Personnel: Dir., Edith Field.
Personnel Profile: Part-Time Volunteers 8.
Governing Authority: nonprofit.
Historic House: 1820s schoolhouse.
Collections: local history items; oral history tapes; textiles; tools; photographs; schoolhouse memorabilia; charcoal kiln model.
Facilities: library of history, genealogy & town records available for research.
Publications: Leverett Massachusetts Historical Center; Historical Architectural Tour - 2004.
Hours & Admission Prices: Schoolhouse: Summer: Sun. 1-3; other times by appointment. Leverett Family Museum: Sat. 10-12; other times by appointment. No charge; donations accepted.
Attendance: 60 (estimated)
Membership: Individual or Family $10.

Lexington

LEXINGTON HISTORICAL SOCIETY, 13 Depot Sq., Lexington, MA 02420. Mailing Address: P.O. Box 514, Lexington, MA 02420-0005. Tel.: 781-862-1703.
E-mail: info@lexingtonhistory.org
Web Site: www.lexingtonhistory.org
Founded: 1886.
Congressional District: 7
Key Personnel: C.E.O., Susan Bennett; Pres. (V), William Mix; Museum Shop Mgr., Carla Fortmann.
Personnel Profile: Full-Time Paid 1; Full-Time Volunteers 1; Part-Time Paid 55; Part-Time Volunteers 100.
Governing Authority: society. Tax-exempt: 501(c)(3).
Historical Society Museum.
Collections: American Revolution period furniture & artifacts; original documents & manuscripts; costumes; photographs; portraits; Lexington history; Battle of Lexington. Historic Houses: c.1700 Munroe Tavern; 1737 Hancock-Clarke House; 1710 Buckman Tavern.
Research Fields: local 18th-century history, Revolutionary War.
Facilities: research archives.
Activities: guided tours; lecture programs.
Publications: society newsletter; booklets; The Story of Buckman Tavern; The Munroe Tavern; The Hancock-Clarke House; The History of the Lexington Historical Society; Lexington Portraits 1734-1884 Lexington: A Century Of Photographs; Lexington: Birthplace of American Liberty.
Hours & Admission Prices: mid-April to Oct. daily. One House: adults $6, children $4. Two Houses: adult $8, children 6-16 $5. Three Houses: adults $10, children 6-16 $6; members & children under 6 no charge.
Attendance: 30,000 (accurate)
Membership: Individual $35; Family $50; Sponsor $ 125; Corporate Patron $500; Life $1,000.

* **NATIONAL HERITAGE MUSEUM, (M),** 33 Marrett Rd., Lexington, MA 02421-5703. Tel.: 781-861-6559. Fax: 781-861-9846. TTY: 781-274-8539.
E-mail: info@monh.org
Web Site: www.nationalheritagemuseum.org
Formerly: Museum of Our National Heritage
Founded: 1971.
Congressional District: 5
Key Personnel: Pres., John William McNaughton; Acting Dir., Richard V. Travis; Dir. Administration & Finance, June Cobb; Dir. Exhibitions & Audience Devel., Hilary Anderson Stelling; Dir. Collections, Aimee Newell; Museum Designer, Michael Rizzo; Registrar, Jill Aszling; Archivist, Catherine Swanson; Public Rels., Linda Patch; Collections Mgr., Maureen Harper; Asst. Cur. Exhibitions, Anne Starr; Museum Shop Mgr., Martha Goodsill; Mgr. Library & Archives, Jeff Croteau.
Personnel Profile: Full-Time Paid 17; Part-Time Paid 8; Part-Time Volunteers 50; Interns 7.
Governing Authority: nonprofit. Parent Institution: Supreme Council Northern Masonic Jurisdiction of U.S.A. Tax-exempt: 501(c)(3).
History Museum.
Collections: American prints; paintings; maps; decorative arts; clocks; furniture; costumes; photographs; memorabilia; Masonic & fraternal.
Major Exhibits: For All Time: Clocks & Watches from the National Heritage Museum, 11/09-2/21/10; The Art of the Movie Theater, 11/09-5/10; Anti-Masonic Collections in the Van Gorden-Williams Library & Archives, 11/09-5/10; The Initiated Eye (T), 12/09-1/11; Jim Henson's Fantastic World (T), 4/3/10-6/27/10.
Research Fields: history of Freemasonry; symbolism of Masonic & fraternal organizations; patriotic iconography.
Facilities: 60,000-vol. library of books, manuscripts & maps; reading room; James F. Farr Conference Center; 400-seat auditorium; cafe. Archival Collection Heritage Shop.
Activities: lectures; concerts; workshops; educational & family programs; school tours; temporary & traveling exhibitions; group tours for adults.
Publications: quarterly calendar & newsletter; exhibit brochures; annual report; catalogs.
Hours & Admission Prices: Tues.-Sat. 10-4:30, Sun. 12-4:30. Library: Tues.-Fri. and 1st & 3rd Sat. 10-4:30. No charge; donations accepted. Closed New Year's Day; Easter; Thanksgiving; Christmas. ♿
Attendance: 58,981 (accurate)
Membership: Student & Senior Citizen $30; Individual $40; Dual $50; Family $60; Contributor $100; Associate $250; Benefactor $500.

Lincoln

CODMAN ESTATE, THE GRANGE, 34 Codman Rd., Lincoln, MA 01773. Mailing Address: 141 Cambridge St., Boston, MA 02114-2702. Tel.: 781-259-8843; 617-227-3956. Fax: 617-227-9204.
Web Site: www.historicnewengland.org
Founded: 1969.
Congressional District: 5
Key Personnel: Pres., Carl Nold; Site Mgr., Wendy Hubbard.
Governing Authority: society; nonprofit organization. Parent Institution: Historic New England, 141 Cambridge St. Boston, MA 02114. Tel.: 617-227-3956. Tax-exempt: 501(c)(3).
Historic House: c.1740 Georgian mansion expanded in 1790s to resemble an English country seat. Home of Codman family through 1968.
Collections: architecture & furnishings of the Georgian, Federal, Victorian & Colonial Revival periods; landscaped grounds including trees & plantings; formal Italian garden; English cutting garden.
Facilities: rental facilities.
Activities: guided tours; lectures; special events & programs; rental facilities.
Publications: Guide to Historic New England.
Hours & Admission Prices: House: June-Oct. 15 1st & 3rd Sat. of month 11-5. Grounds: dawn to dusk. Adults $5; discounts to seniors, AAM, ICOM, AAA & WGBH members; Historic New England members no charge.
Attendance: 9,904 (accurate)
Membership: National $35; Individual $45; Household $55; Garden & Landscape $75; Institutional $85; Contributing $100; Historic Homeowner $200; Supporting $250.

* **DECORDOVA SCULPTURE PARK & MUSEUM, (M),** 51 Sandy Pond Rd., Lincoln, MA 01773-2699. Tel.: 781-259-8355. Fax: 781-259-3650.
E-mail: info@decordova.org
Web Site: www.decordova.org
Founded: 1948.
Congressional District: 4
Key Personnel: Pres. (V), Robert H. Scott; Exec. Dir., Dennis Kois; Dir. External Affairs, Laurie J. LaMothe; Dir. Education, Lynn Thompson; Dir. Institutional Support, Julie Stubbs; Dir. Membership, Karen Crane; Sr. Cur., Nick Capasso; Dir. Bldgs. & Grounds, Douglas Holston; Dir. Retail Operations, David Duddy.
Personnel Profile: Full-Time Paid 25; Part-Time Paid 30; Part-Time Volunteers 200; Interns 10.
Governing Authority: nonprofit organization. Tax-exempt: 501(c)(3).
Arts Center; Sculpture Park.
Collections: American art; 20th-century American painting, graphics, sculpture & photography; emphasis on artists associated with New England.
Research Fields: 20th-century American art with emphasis on contemporary New England artists; large-scale outdoor public sculpture.
Facilities: library; 38,000 sq. ft. exhibit space; 35-acre sculpture park; cafe. Art & Museum-related items for sale.
Activities: changing exhibitions; guided tours; lectures; films; concerts; arts festivals; art classes for children & adults; individual & corporate membership program; outreach programs.
Publications: catalogs, exhibition & school; annual reports; calendar of events.
Hours & Admission Prices: Tues.-Sun. 10-5. Adults $12, children & senior citizens $8; discounts to WGBH, AAA, AAM, ICOM & AAC members; members no charge. Closed major holidays. ♿
Attendance: 100,000 (estimated)
Membership: Individual $60; Household $90; Friend $150; Sponsor $300; Patron $600; Julian Club $1,000.

DRUMLIN FARM EDUCATION CENTER, 208 South Great Rd., Lincoln, MA 01773-4800. Tel.: 781-259-2200 & 2203. Fax: 781-259-7917.
E-mail: drumlinfarm@massaudubon.org
Web Site: www.massaudubon.org
Founded: 1955.
Congressional District: 5
Key Personnel: Pres., Laura Johnson; Dir., Christy Foote-Smith; Program Specialist, Kris Scopinich; Program Specialist, Karen Stein; Farmer Livestock, Caroline Malone; Farmer Crops, Matt Celona; Museum Shop Mgr., Ruth Smith.
Personnel Profile: Full-Time Paid 23; Part-Time Paid 60; Interns 7.
Governing Authority: nonprofit organization. Parent Institution: Massachusetts Audubon Society, Lincoln, MA. Tax-exempt: 501(c)(3).
Living Farm Museum.
Collections: agriculture; aviary; botany; entomology; geology; herpetology.
Research Fields: bird banding; blue bird nesting monitoring; breeding; bird surveys.
Activities: guided tours; lectures; films; rental gallery; formally organized education programs; permanent exhibitions; summer natural history day camps.
Publications: program brochures; electronic newsletters.
Hours & Admission Prices: Tues.-Sun. 9-5; school tours by reservation only. Adults $6, senior citizens & children 2-12 $4; Lincoln residents & children under 2 no charge. Closed New Year's Eve & Day; Thanksgiving; Christmas. ♿
Attendance: 150,000 (estimated)
Membership: Individual $40; Family $50; Supporting $60; Donor $100; Patron $500.

GROPIUS HOUSE, 68 Baker Bridge Rd., Lincoln, MA 01773-3105. Tel.: 781-259-8098. Fax: 781-259-9722.
Web Site: www.historicnewengland.org
Founded: 1985.
Key Personnel: Pres., Carl Nold; Museum Site Mgr., Wendy L. Hubbard.
Personnel Profile: Full-Time Paid 1; Part-Time Paid 6.
Governing Authority: society; nonprofit organization. Parent Institution: Historic New England. Tax-exempt: 501(c)(3).
Historic House: c.1937-38 Walter Gropius, one of the innovators of modern architecture, designed his family residence by combining Bauhaus principles with New England building materials.
Collections: furnishings made in Bauhaus workshops & brought from Germany; American fixtures & materials; industrial grade; decorative art.
Research Fields: decorative arts; modernism.
Facilities: visitor center. Museum-related items for sale.
Activities: guided tours; programs; lecture series; family events.
Hours & Admission Prices: Tours: June-Oct. 15 Wed.-Sun. 11-4 on the hour; Oct. 16-May Sat.-Sun. 11-5 on the hour. Adults $10, seniors $9, children & students $5; discounts to groups, AAA & WGBH members; members, Historic New England members & Lincoln residents no charge.
Attendance: 6,429 (accurate)
Membership: Individual $45; Household $55; Contributing $100; Historic Homeowner $200.

THE THOREAU INSTITUTE AT WALDEN WOODS, 44 Baker Farm, Lincoln, MA 01773-3004. Tel.: 781-259-4730. Fax: 781-259-4730.
E-mail: Jeff.Cramer@walden.org
Web Site: www.walden.org/institute
Founded: 1998.
Congressional District: 5
Key Personnel: Exec. Dir., Kathi Anderson; Cur. Collections, Jeffrey S. Cramer.
Personnel Profile: Full-Time Paid 7; Part-Time Paid 4; Interns 2.
Governing Authority: nonprofit. Parent Institution: Walden Woods Project. Tax-exempt: 501(c)(3).
Historical Society Museum.
Collections: early editions of works by Henry David Thoreau; 19th-century photographs; manuscripts; old maps, including original Thoreau survey maps; Ricketson bust of Thoreau; pencils made by Thoreau family business.
Research Fields: Thoreau and the other 19th-century transcendentalists.
Facilities: 50,000-vol. library of material by & about Thoreau & other New England Transcendentalists, Concord & New England history & 19th-century American literature available for use to serious readers & scholars; reading room; Helen and Scott Nearing papers; Paul Brooks collection.
Activities: lectures; formally organized educational programs.
Hours & Admission Prices: By appointment only. No charge; donations accepted. ♿

Longmeadow

RICHARD SALTER STORRS HOUSE, 697 Longmeadow St., Longmeadow, MA 01106-2215. Tel.: 413-567-3600.
E-mail: LCAsearch@aol.com
Web Site: www.longmeadow.org
Founded: 1899.
Congressional District: 2
Key Personnel: C.E.O. & Pres. (V), Crawford Lincoln; Cur. & Genealogist, Linda C. Abrams.
Personnel Profile: Part-Time Paid 1; Part-Time Volunteers 2.
Governing Authority: society. Administered by the Longmeadow Historical Society. Tax-exempt: 501(c)(3).
Historical Society Museum: housed in 1786 Storrs House.
Collections: early American furnishings; genealogy; local artifacts; decorative arts; history; military; costumes; toys; materials & genealogical memorabilia, 18th- & 19th-century manuscripts; theological & school; written memoirs.
Research Fields: town 18th- to 19th-century archives; genealogy.

Activities: tours & research by appointment. Annual Event: Long Meddowe Days Fair in May.
Publications: The Historic Homes of Longmeadow; assorted booklets of local historical facts, places & people; book, Reflections of Longmeadow; quarterly newsletter, Town Crier.
Hours & Admission Prices: By appointment. Adults $3; discounts to senior citizens, family reunion groups, children 12-18, AAM & ICOM members; members & children under 12 no charge.
Attendance: 800 (estimated)
Membership: Individual $15; Family $25; Life $100.

Lowell

* **AMERICAN TEXTILE HISTORY MUSEUM, (M),** 491 Dutton St., Lowell, MA 01854-4289. Tel.: 978-441-0400. Fax: 978-441-1412.
Web Site: www.athm.org
Formerly: Merrimack Valley Textile Museum
Founded: 1960.
Congressional District: 5
Key Personnel: Chm. & Treas., Kenneth J. McAvoy; Pres & C.E.O., James S. Coleman; Vice Chm., Jan Russell; Vice Chm., Karl Spilhaus; Dir. Advancement, Linda Carpenter; Cur., Karen Herbaugh; Business Mgr., Steven Jackson; Dir. Interpretation, Diane L. Fagan Affleck; Coord. Museum Education Svcs., Sue Bunker; Librarian, Clare Sheridan.
Personnel Profile: Full-Time Paid 15; Part-Time Paid 1; Part-Time Volunteers 45; Interns 2.
Governing Authority: nonprofit organization. Tax-exempt: 501(c)(3).
Textile History Museum.
Collections: textiles; textile samples; costumes; tools; workplace artifacts; books; periodicals; manuscripts; business records; trade literature; ephemera; prints; photography; machinery.
Research Fields: textiles & costume; design; business & labor; technology; community history.
Facilities: study areas; meeting rooms; restaurant. Museum-related items for sale.
Activities: gallery tours; special events; outreach; school programs; speakers bureau.
Publications: newsletter, Textile Times; leaflets; catalogues.
Hours & Admission Prices: Adults $8; members no charge. ♿
Attendance: 47,737 (estimated)
Membership: Individual $50; Dual $65; Family $95; Contributing $125; Supporting $250; Patron $500; Leadership Circle $1,000-$10,000.

LOWELL NATIONAL HISTORICAL PARK, 67 Kirk St., Lowell, MA 01852-1029. Tel.: 978-970-5000. TDD: 978-970-5002.
E-mail: lowe_reservations@nps.gov
Web Site: www.nps.gov/lowe
Founded: 1978.
Congressional District: 5
Key Personnel: Supt., Michael Creasey; Education & Dir. Tsongas Industrial History Center, Patricia Jones; Cur., David Blackburn; Public Information, Sue Andrews; Librarian, Jack Herlihy; Museum Shop Mgr., Joan Gagnon.
Personnel Profile: Full-Time Paid 109; Part-Time Volunteers 50.
Governing Authority: federal; nonprofit organization. Parent Institution: National Park Service. Subsidiary Institution: Boott Cotton Mills Museum, 115 John St., Lowell, MA. Tax-exempt.
History Museum District.
Collections: ethnic & labor items; working textile equipment. Historic Buildings: 37 preserved & restored buildings, construction dates ranging from 1824-1908; mill girl letters & documents; historical engineering drawings & records.
Major Exhibits: Preservation Movement: Then and Now, 5/10-7/10.
Research Fields: labor, social & technology history.
Facilities: 3,500-vol. library of books, including informational folders, photographs & slides available to the public; Boott Cotton Mills Museum; Tsongas Industrial History Center; visitor's center; educational facilities. Books & museum-related items for sale.
Activities: guided tours; special interest tours; lectures; organized programs for children; participatory exhibits; historic canal system & river tours; concerts; folk festivals.
Publications: park brochures; NPS Park Handbook.
Hours & Admission Prices: Visitor Center: call for hours. Boott Cotton Mills Museum: Oct. 11-Nov. 27 daily 9:30-4:30. Adults $6, senior citizens & students $4, youth 6-16 $3; children under 5 no charge. Closed New Year's Day; Thanksgiving Day; Christmas. ♿
Attendance: 350,000 (estimated)

MIDDLESEX CANAL COLLECTION, Center for Lowell History, 40 French St., Lowell, MA 01852-1113. Tel.: 978-934-4997. Fax: 978-934-4995.
E-mail: martha_mayo@uml.edu
Web Site: library.uml.edu/clh
Founded: 1962.
Congressional District: 5
Key Personnel: Dir., Martha Mayo.
Governing Authority: University of Massachusetts Lowell. Affiliated with Middlesex Canal Association.
History Museum/Center.
Collections: Middlesex Canal Assoc. archives; Middlesex Canal County records.
Activities: temporary exhibitions.
Publications: quarterly bulletin, Towpath Topics.
Hours & Admission Prices: Tues. 9-9, Thurs. 9-5, Sat. 10-3. No charge. ♿
Attendance: 15,000 (estimated)
Membership: Associate $4; Proprietor $10.

NEW ENGLAND QUILT MUSEUM, 18 Shattuck St., Lowell, MA 01852-1820. Tel.: 978-452-4207. Fax: 978-452-5405.
E-mail: director@nequiltmuseum.org
Web Site: www.nequiltmuseum.org
Founded: 1987.
Congressional District: 5
Key Personnel: Pres. (V), Marjorie R. Miller; Exec. Dir., Connie Colom Barlow; Museum Shop Mgr., Judith Copeland.
Personnel Profile: Full-Time Paid 1; Part-Time Paid 6; Part-Time Volunteers 60; Interns 2.
Governing Authority: nonprofit organization. Tax-exempt.
Quilt Museum: housed in landmark savings bank building.
Collections: period, contemporary & art quilts.
Major Exhibits: Kinder Komfort: Amish Crib Quilts, 3/4/10-5/9/10; Women's Writes: Signature Quilts & Their Stories, 5/13/10-7/11/10; Contemporary Broderie Perse: An Elegant Revival (T), 7/15/10-10/17/10; Feminism in Contemporary African American Quilts: Motherhood, Sisterhood & the Matriarchs (T), 10/21/10-1/3/11.
Research Fields: American quilts.
Facilities: 1,200-vol. library pertaining to quilting; educational facilities; 6,000 sq. ft. exhibit space; classroom. Gifts & quilts for sale.
Activities: guided tours; lectures; organized educational programs; participatory, loan, temporary & traveling exhibitions; volunteer program; community activities; special events.
Publications: NE Quilt Museum Quilts; CD catalogs of exhibitions; quarterly newsletter, Layers.
Hours & Admission Prices: May-Dec. Tues.-Sat. 10-4, Sun. 12-4; Dec.-April Tues.-Sat. 10-4. Adults $7, senior citizens & students $5; discounts to WGBH & AAM members; members, MTA & AAA members no charge. Closed major holidays. ♿
Attendance: 15,000 (estimated)
Membership: Student & Senior $30; Individual $45; Household $55; Donor $100; Supporter: $250; Patron $500; Benefactor $1,000.

WHISTLER HOUSE MUSEUM OF ART, (M), 243 Worthen St., Lowell, MA 01852-1874. Tel.: 978-452-7641. Fax: 978-454-2421.
E-mail: mlally@whistlerhouse.org
Web Site: www.whistlerhouse.org
Founded: 1878.
Congressional District: 5
Key Personnel: Exec. Dir., Michael H. Lally; Chm. (V), Nancy Donahue; Chm. (V), Richard Donahue; Co Pres. (V), Donald Bedard; Co Pres. (V), Ryan Dunn; Exhibits & Gallery Mgr., James Dyment.
Personnel Profile: Full-Time Paid 1; Part-Time Paid 2; Part-Time Volunteers 2; Interns 3.
Governing Authority: society; nonprofit. Parent Institution: Lowell Art Association. Tax-exempt: 501(c)(3).
Art Gallery: housed in 1823 Whistler House, birthplace of James A. M. Whistler.
Collections: American art including works by Whistler, John Singer Sargent & Arshile Gorky.
Research Fields: James A. M. Whistler; 19th-20th century American art; New England art; art museum education.
Facilities: 400-vol. library on James Whistler & New England artists; 100-seat auditorium; Parker Gallery.
Activities: walking & guided tours; lectures; films; gallery talks; concerts; arts festivals; formally organized education programs; permanent, temporary & traveling exhibitions.
Publications: calendars of events; newsletters; exhibition catalogues.
Hours & Admission Prices: Wed.-Sat. 11-4. Adults $5, senior citizens &

students 6-21 $4; discounts to groups, AAA, AAM & NEMA members; children under 6, museum professionals & members no charge. Closed major holidays.
Attendance: 7,000 (estimated)
Membership: Student $20; Senior $25; Individual $35; Family $45; Donor $100; Sponsor $250; Patron $500.

Lynn

LYNN MUSEUM & HISTORICAL SOCIETY, (M), 590 Washington St., Lynn, MA 01901-1406. Tel.: 781-581-6200. Fax: 781-581-6202.
E-mail: office@lynnmuseum.org
Web Site: www.lynnmuseum.org
Founded: 1897.
Congressional District: 6
Key Personnel: Interim Dir., Sandy Sheckman; Pres., Steven J. Babbitt; Museum Shop Mgr., Kathy Gereck; Museum Shop Mgr., Tom Gereck.
Personnel Profile: Full-Time Volunteers 1; Part-Time Paid 3; Part-Time Volunteers 5.
Governing Authority: society. Lynn Historical Society. Tax-exempt: 501(c)(3).
Local History Museum: housed in old shoe factory building; Lynn Heritage State Park Visitor Center.
Collections: shoes & early shoe making tools; furniture; paintings; costumes; manuscripts; photographs; newspapers.
Research Fields: genealogy; local history; shoe industry.
Facilities: library & reading room for local history & genealogy; 75-seat meeting hall & function room; courtyard. Museum-related items for sale.
Activities: guided tours; lectures; school education program; permanent & temporary exhibitions.
Publications: Records of Ye Towne Meetings of Lynn, Vol. 1-7, 1691-1783; The Lynn Album: A Pictorial History; No Race of Imitators: Lynn & Her People, An Anthology; video, So Hear the Metropolis: The Story of Lynn Woods; A Lasting Impression, The Jan Metzelinger Story; Diners of the North Shore; Portrait of a City: Lynn on Film; The Civil War Diary of Lt. J.E. Hodgkins; J. Sanger Attill and His Craftsman; Lynn Beach Painters: Art Along the North Shore 1880-1920; Lynn Album II: A Pictorial History of the 20th Century; By Candlelight: Samplers in the Lynn Museum; The Brickyard: The Life, Death & Legend an Urban Neighborhood (2005); Arcadia Press: Lynn in the Victorian Era; The Great Fires of Lynn.
Hours & Admission Prices: Museum: Tues.-Wed. & Fri.-Sat. 12-4, Thurs. 12-8. Research & tours by appointment. Adults $5, children $2; discounts to AAA & ICOM members; members & Lynn School children 12 & under no charge. Closed state & national holidays. ♿
Attendance: 12,000 (estimated)
Membership: Student $10; Senior Individual $25; Individual $30; Senior Household $35; Household $45; Heritage Supporter $100; Benefactor $500; Lifetime $750; Dual Lifetime (Couple) $1,000.

Malden

MALDEN PUBLIC LIBRARY, 36 Salem St., Malden, MA 02148-5291. Tel.: 781-324-0218 & 388-0800. Fax: 781-324-4467.
E-mail: dmalgeri@maldenpubliclibrary.org
Web Site: www.maldenpubliclibrary.org
Founded: 1879.
Congressional District: 7
Key Personnel: Librarian, Dina G. Malgeri.
Personnel Profile: Full-Time Paid 23; Part-Time Paid 2.
Governing Authority: board of trustees; nonprofit organization. Tax-exempt.
Public Library with Special Art Collection.
Collections: fine arts objects; oil paintings; sculpture.
Facilities: 201,189-vol. public library.
Activities: permanent & temporary exhibitions; concerts; workshops; lectures.
Publications: booklet, ArtFacts.
Hours & Admission Prices: June-Aug. Mon.-Wed. 9-9, Thurs. 9-1 & 2-6, Fri. 9-6; Sept.-May Mon.-Wed. 9-9, Thurs. 9-1 & 2-9, Fri.-Sat. 9-6. No charge; donations accepted. Closed national holidays. ♿
Attendance: 100,000 (estimated)

Manchester

MANCHESTER HISTORICAL SOCIETY, 10 Union St., Manchester, MA 01944-1553. Tel.: 978-526-7230. Fax: 978-526-0060.
E-mail: manchesterhistorical@verizon.net
Web Site: manchesterhistorical.com
Founded: 1886.
Congressional District: 6
Key Personnel: Pres. (V), Joan McDonald; Vice Pres., Meredith East; Archivist, Esther Proctor.
Governing Authority: nonprofit organization. Tax-exempt: 501(c)(3).
Decorative Arts Museum.
Collections: 18th- & 19th-century Manchester made furniture; photographs.
Research Fields: local history.
Facilities: 200-vol. library of logbooks, diaries & unpublished papers on history of Manchester available for use on premises.
Activities: guided tours; lectures; informally organized education programs for children; temporary exhibitions.
Publications: newsletter.
Hours & Admission Prices: July-Aug. Mon.-Thurs. 9:30-1, Sat. 12-3; Sept.-June Mon.-Thurs. 9:30-1; other times by appointment. No charge; donations accepted. ♿
Membership: Senior $10; Individual $25; Family $40.

Marblehead

MARBLEHEAD ARTS ASSOCIATION - KING HOOPER MANSION, 8 Hooper St., Marblehead, MA 01945-3213. Tel.: 781-631-2608. Fax: 781-639-7890.
E-mail: info@marbleheadarts.org
Web Site: marbleheadarts.org
Founded: 1922.
Congressional District: 6
Key Personnel: Dir., Deborah Greel; Pres. (V), James Regis.
Personnel Profile: Full-Time Paid 1; Part-Time Paid 2; Part-Time Volunteers 40; Interns 1.
Governing Authority: private; nonprofit organization. Tax-exempt: 501(c)(3).
Art Association: housed in c.1728 colonial style mansion of Greenfield Hooper.
Collections: Hooper family furnishings; Marblehead pottery; 1940 prints; Steinway grand piano; wine cellar; historic mansion.
Facilities: educational facilities; Ball Room; garden. Museum-related items for sale.
Activities: arts festivals; concerts; dance recitals; education programs; guided tours by appointment; hobby workshops; lectures; participatory, loan & temporary exhibitions; rentals; theater; special events.
Publications: email newsletter, Marblehead Arts Association; brochure, Hooper Mansion; wedding rental brochure.
Hours & Admission Prices: Tues.-Sat. 10-5, Sun. 1-5. No charge; donations accepted. Large Tours: $3 per person. Closed New Year's Day; Easter; Thanksgiving; Christmas.
Attendance: 5,000 (accurate)
Membership: Student $15; Senior over 65 $30; Associate $35; Artist $50; Family $55.

MARBLEHEAD MUSEUM & HISTORICAL SOCIETY, 170 Washington St., Marblehead, MA 01945-3340. Tel.: 781-631-1768. Fax: 781-631-0917.
E-mail: mmhspeterson@yahoo.com
Web Site: www.marbleheadmuseum.org
Founded: 1898.
Congressional District: 6
Key Personnel: Dir., Pam Peterson; Pres., Richard Carlson; Treas., Richard Settlemeyer; Cur. Jeremiah Lee Mansion, Judy Anderson; Cur. Museum, Karen MacInnis; Registrar, Jean Fallon.
Personnel Profile: Full-Time Paid 2; Part-Time Paid 2; Part-Time Volunteers 100; Interns 2.
Governing Authority: society; nonprofit. Subsidiary Institutions: JOJ Frost Folk Art Gallery; Jeremiah Lee Mansion; G.A.R. and Civil War Museum. Tax-exempt: 170(b)(1)(A).
History & Folk Art Museum.
Collections: 19th- & 20th-century decorative & folk arts; archives & manuscript collection; maritime folk art paintings; historic Marblehead & maritime artifacts; American Colonial decorative arts. Historic Buildings: 1768 Jeremiah Lee Mansion; Grand Army of the Republic-Civil War Museum; J.O.J. Frost Folk Art Gallery.
Research Fields: genealogy; Marblehead history; maritime history; Jeremiah Lee Mansion history; Civil War; G.A.R. history.
Facilities: 500-vol. library of books on history & genealogy available on premises; archives; reading room; garden. Books, postcards, reproductions of J.O.J. Frost paintings for sale.
Activities: walking tours; guided tours; lectures; permanent & temporary exhibitions; docent program; children's enrichment program; study clubs; research. Annual Event: Garden Party; Gingerbread Festival; Wine Tasting Under the Tent.
Publications: brochure; annual report; calendar of events.
Hours & Admission Prices: Society: Tues.-Sat. 10-4. Lee Mansion: June-Oct. Tues.-Sat. 10-4. Mansion: adults $5. Frost Gallery & Civil War Museum: no charge; donations accepted. Closed major holidays.
Attendance: 5,500 (estimated)
Membership: Individual $30; Family & Dual $50; Friend $100; Sponsor $500; Patron $1,000; Benefactor $5,000.

1768 JEREMIAH LEE MANSION, 161 Washington St., Marblehead, MA 01945-3303. Mailing Address: Marblehead Museum & Historical Society, 170 Washington St., Marblehead, MA 01945. Tel.: 781-631-1768. Fax: 781-631-0917.
E-mail: mmhsanderson@yahoo.com
Web Site: www.marbleheadmuseum.org
Founded: 1909.
Congressional District: 6
Key Personnel: Pres. (V), Richard Carlson; Dir., Pam Peterson; Cur. Jeremiah Lee Mansion, Judy Anderson; Research & Collections Cur., Karen MacInnis.
Personnel Profile: Full-Time Paid 2; Part-Time Paid 1; Part-Time Volunteers 100.
Governing Authority: society; nonprofit. Parent Institution: Marblehead Museum & Historical Society. Tax-exempt: 501(c)(3).
Decorative Arts & History Museum.
Collections: 18th- & 19th-century furniture; decorative arts; paintings; maritime & folk art; musical instruments; archives.
Facilities: garden.
Activities: guided tours; lectures; garden events; architecture tours & classes.
Publications: annual report; newsletter; calendar of events.
Hours & Admission Prices: Mansion: June-Oct. Tues.-Sat. 10-4. Adults $5, senior citizens $4.50; discounts to Massachusetts Teachers Assoc.; children, students, & members no charge.
Attendance: 3,000 (estimated)
Membership: Individual $30; Family & Dual $50; Friend $100; Sponsor $500; Patron $1,000; Benefactor $5,000.

Marion

MARION NATURAL HISTORY MUSEUM, 8 Spring St., Marion, MA 02738-1519. Mailing Address: P.O. Box 644, Marion, MA 02738-0011. Tel.: 508-748-2098.
E-mail: lizleid@msn.com
Web Site: www.marionmuseum.org
Key Personnel: Dir., Elizabeth Leidhold
Natural History Museum.
Collections: wildlife including fish, turtles, waterfowl & birds of prey; Native American artifacts.
Hours & Admission Prices: Wed. 12-4, Fri. 12-2, Sat. 10-1.

Marlboro

PETER RICE HOMESTEAD, HOME OF THE MARLBOROUGH HISTORICAL SOCIETY, INC., 377 Elm St., Marlboro, MA 01752-4518. Mailing Address: P.O. Box 513, Marlboro, MA 01752-0513. Tel.: 508-485-4763 & 251-1057.
E-mail: info@historicmarlborough.org
Web Site: www.historicmarlborough.org
Founded: 1962.
Congressional District: 3
Key Personnel: Pres., Janet Licht; Vice Pres., Peggy Ayres.
Governing Authority: society. Tax-exempt: 501(c)(3).
Historic Museum: housed in 1688 Peter Rice homestead.
Collections: 19th-century furniture; industrial collection.
Research Fields: local history; cemeteries; local buildings; genealogy Marlborough families.
Facilities: library of books & manuscripts available for small donation.
Activities: monthly programs; special events; guided tours.
Publications: print & e-mail newsletter; brochure describing Homestead; brochure & map of Homestead indicating points of interest.
Hours & Admission Prices: By appointment and for special events & programs. No charge.
Attendance: 1,200 (estimated)
Membership: Annual $15; Life $150.

Marshfield

HISTORIC 1699 WINSLOW HOUSE, 634 Careswell St., Marshfield, MA 02050-5623. Mailing Address: P.O. Box 531, Marshfield, MA 02050-0531. Tel.: 781-837-5753.
E-mail: mark.schmidt@winslowhouse.org
Web Site: www.winslowhouse.org
Formerly: Isaac Winslow House
Founded: 1920.
Key Personnel: Exec. Dir., Mark A. Schmidt; Pres. (V), Cynthia Hagar Krusell; Cur., Karin J. Goldstein.
Personnel Profile: Full-Time Paid 1; Part-Time Paid 1.
Governing Authority: Parent Institution: Historic Winslow House Association. Tax-exempt.
Historic House Museum: housed in the former home of Hon. Isaac Winslow, Marshfield's founding family; built in 1699.
Collections: period artifacts & furnishings.
Facilities: Museum-related items for sale.
Activities: special events.
Publications: newsletter, Careswell Chronicles.
Hours & Admission Prices: Wed.-Sun. 11-5. Adults $3, children $1; discounts for MA Teachers Association, WGBH, AAM & AAA members; members no charge. Closed Memorial Day; Independence Day; Labor Day.
Membership: Student & Senior $25; Individual (Basic) $40; Individual (Plus) & Family (Basic) $75; Family (Plus) $150; Sustaining $250; Winslow Society $1,000.

Mashpee

CAPE COD CHILDREN'S MUSEUM, 577 Great Neck Rd. S., Mashpee, MA 02649-3708. Tel.: 508-539-8788. Fax: 508-539-3285.
E-mail: info@capecodchildrensmuseum.org
Web Site: www.capecodchildrensmuseum.org
Key Personnel: Exec. Dir., Barbara Cotton; Dir. Exhibits & Operations, Holly Dayton; Controller, Carol Pardee; Program Dir. & Early Childhood Coord., Mary Almeida; Dir. Mktg. & Administration, Conni Baker.
Governing Authority: nonprofit organization.
Children's Museum.
Collections: hands-on exhibits.
Hours & Admission Prices: Summer: Mon.-Sat. 10-5, Sun. 12-5; Winter: Tues.-Thurs. 10-3, Fri.-Sat. 10-5, Sun. 12-5. Adults $6, senior citizens 60 & over $5; discounts to groups; members & children under 1 no charge. Closed New Year's Day; Easter; Independence Day; Labor Day; Thanksgiving; Christmas Eve & Day.

MASHPEE HISTORICAL COMMISSION, 13 Great Neck Rd., N., Mashpee, MA 02649-2521. Mailing Address: 16 Great Neck Rd., N., Mashpee, MA 02649-2528. Tel.: 508-539-1438.
E-mail: historic@ci.mashpee.ma.us
Web Site: www.ci.mashpee.ma.us
Key Personnel: Chm. (V), Lee Gurney; Historian, Rosemary Burns
History Museum.
Collections: local history & culture; memorabilia & artifacts of Mashpee people, places & events.
Hours & Admission Prices: Mon. & Thurs. 10-2 & by appointment

MASHPEE TRIBAL COUNCIL MUSEUM, 483 Great Neck Rd., S., Mashpee, MA 02649-3707. Mailing Address: P.O. Box 1048, Mashpee, MA 02649-1048. Tel.: 508-477-0208. Fax: 508-477-1218.
Web Site: mashpeewampanoagtribe.com
Key Personnel: Chm., Cedric Cromwell; Sec., Marie Stone; Treas., Mark Harding
History Museum. Listed on the National Register of Historic Places.
Collections: period artifacts; tools; baskets; hunting & fishing implements; weapons; domestic utensils.
Hours & Admission Prices: Call for hours.

Mattapoisett

MATTAPOISETT MUSEUM AND CARRIAGE HOUSE, 5 Church St., Mattapoisett, MA 02739-2618. Mailing Address: P.O. Box 535, Mattapoisett, MA 02739-0535. Tel.: 508-758-2844.
E-mail: mattapoisett.museum@verizon.net
Web Site: www.mattapoisetthistoricalsociety.org
Founded: 1959.
Congressional District: 10
Key Personnel: Pres., Seth F. Mendell; Cur., Bette Roberts.
Personnel Profile: Part-Time Paid 1; Part-Time Volunteers 60.
Governing Authority: society; directors. Parent Institution: Mattapoisett Historical Society, Inc. Tax-exempt.
History Museum: housed in 1820 Mattapoisett Christian Meeting House.
Collections: furniture; glass; guns; china; costumes; doll furniture; toys; canes; maritime & whaling items; period farm equipment; carpenters' tools; cobblers' tools; ice-cutting equipment; baskets; kitchen equipment; blacksmith shop; model of saltworks; period horse-drawn vehicles; local, prehistoric stone artifacts; early spinning & weaving equipment. Historic Building: Carriage House.
Research Fields: local cemeteries; whaling paper & photographs; early houses.
Facilities: 100-vol. library of books on local history, genealogy & whaling available for use on premises.
Activities: guided tours; permanent & temporary exhibitions.
Publications: booklets, Historical Summary of Mattapoisett; Shipbuilders of Mattapoisett; Mattapoisett & Old Rochester; postcards, Memories of Mattapoisett.
Hours & Admission Prices: July-Aug. Wed.-Sat. 1-4; Sept.-June by appointment only. Adults $3, children 6 & over $1; discounts to groups; members no charge. ♿

Attendance: 800 (estimated)
Membership: Individual $20; Family $30; Business $100; Life-Individual $150; Life-Couple $200.

Medford

ROYALL HOUSE ASSOCIATION, 15 George St., Medford, MA 02155-4513. Tel.: 781-396-9032.
E-mail: royallhouseevent@aol.com
Web Site: www.royallhouse.org
Founded: 1906.
Congressional District: 7
Key Personnel: Exec. Dir., Tom Lincoln; Vice Pres., John Woods.
Personnel Profile: Part-Time Paid 1; Part-Time Volunteers 20.
Governing Authority: nonprofit organization. Tax-exempt: 501(c)(3).
Colonial History Museum.
Collections: period furniture & furnishings; oil paintings; extant slave quarters.
Activities: guided tours; lectures.
Publications: Royall House Reporter
Hours & Admission Prices: June-Oct. Sat.-Sun. Families $16, adults $7, senior citizens & students $5; discounts to groups; children 17 & under accompanied by an adult & members no charge.
Attendance: 1,837 (accurate)
Membership: Student & Senior Citizen $20; Individual $25; Family $35; Single Life $300; Couple Life $400.

TUFTS UNIVERSITY ART GALLERY, Aidekman Arts Center, 40R Talbot Ave., Medford, MA 02155. Tel.: 617-627-3518. Fax: 617-627-3121.
E-mail: artgallery@tufts.edu
Web Site: www.ase.tufts.edu/gallery
Founded: 1991.
Congressional District: 7 & 8
Key Personnel: Chm. (V), Laura Roberts; Chm. (V), Kenneth Aidekman; Dir. Galleries & Collections, Amy Ingrid Schlegel, Ph.D.; Preparator & Registrar, Doug Bell; Outreach Coord., Jeanne Koles.
Personnel Profile: Full-Time Paid 4; Part-Time Paid 12; Part-Time Volunteers 20; Interns 1.
Governing Authority: private university; nonprofit. Parent Institution: Tufts University. Tax-exempt: 501(c)(3).
University Art Museum.
Collections: contemporary art; 19th- & 20th-century paintings, prints, sculpture, photographs; Greek & Roman antiquities; pre-Columbian art.
Research Fields: 21st-century art.
Facilities: 6,700 sq. ft. exhibit space.
Activities: lectures; loan, temporary & traveling exhibitions; educational outreach program.
Publications: exhibition catalogs, Imagenes e Historias/Images and Histories: Chicana Altar - Inspired Art; Friedel Dzubas: Critical Painting; Pattern Language: Clothing as Communicator; Barbara Zucker: Time Signatures; Ilya and Emilia Kabakov: The Center of Cosmic Energy; Empire and Its Discontents.
Hours & Admission Prices: Tues.-Sun. 11-5, Thurs. 11-8. No charge; donations accepted. Closed major & university holidays. ♿
Attendance: 9,000 (accurate)

Mendon

SOUTHWICK'S ZOO, 2 Southwick St., Mendon, MA 01756-1234. Tel.: 800-258-9182.
Web Site: southwickszoo.com
Zoo.
Collections: over 500 animals representing 100 species from around the world.
Facilities: cafe. Zoo-related items for sale.
Activities: live presentations; shows; field trips.
Hours & Admission Prices: April 11-Oct. 18 daily 10-5. Adults 13 & over $18.75, senior citizens 62 & over and children 3-12 $12.75; children 2 & under no charge.

Middleborough

MIDDLEBOROUGH HISTORICAL ASSOCIATION, INC., 18 Jackson St., Middleborough, MA 02346-2469. Mailing Address: P.O. Box 304, Middleborough, MA 02346-0304. Tel.: 508-947-1969.
Founded: 1960.
Congressional District: 10
Key Personnel: Pres., Nancy Gedraitis; Sec., Cynthia McNair.
Personnel Profile: Part-Time Volunteers 8.
Governing Authority: society; nonprofit. Tax-exempt.
History Museum.
Collections: G.A.R. collection; General & Mrs. Tom Thumb collection; Peirce Academy records; portraits attributed to Cephas Thompson; history; folklore; blacksmith shop; carriage shed including vehicles & early farming implements; manuscripts; ice harvesting; Maxim motor fire vehicle. Historic Houses: 1790 law office; 1700 Outhouse-Sproat Tavern; two 1820 houses.
Facilities: library of Lawrence B. Romaine's personal collection available for use under supervision; research room.
Activities: guided tours; permanent exhibitions.
Hours & Admission Prices: July-Sept. Wed. 12-3; other times by appointment. Adults $5, senior citizens $4, students $2; discounts to groups of 10 or more; children under 6 & Historical Association members no charge. Closed holidays.
Attendance: 400 (estimated)
Membership: Student $5; Single $10; Family $15; Participating $20; Sustaining $50; Benefactor $100; Life $200.

ROBBINS MUSEUM OF ARCHAEOLOGY, 17 Jackson St., Middleborough, MA 02346-2413. Mailing Address: P.O. Box 700, Middleborough, MA 02346-0700. Tel.: 508-947-9005. Fax: 508-947-9005.
E-mail: info@massarchaeology.org
Web Site: www.massarchaeology.org/museum
Founded: 1939.
Congressional District: 4
Key Personnel: Pres. (V), Tonya Largy, M.A.; Vice Pres., Frederica Dimmick; Museum Coord., Eugene Winter; Financial Officer, Ted Ballard.
Personnel Profile: Full-Time Volunteers 2; Part-Time Paid 1; Part-Time Volunteers 25; Interns 2.
Governing Authority: not-for-profit organization. Parent Institution: Massachusetts Archaeological Society, Inc. Tax-exempt.
Archaeology Museum: housed in c.1920 factory building.
Collections: Native American archaeology, Paleo-Indian to present; Society archives; research library; ethnographic collection.
Research Fields: inventory of archaeological sites; collections in the town of Middleborough; native history; artifact from Southeastern Massachusetts.
Facilities: 3,000-vol. library of archaeological & historical books; journals of state society of archaeology, available for use by public; auditorium; educational facilities; 10,000 sq. ft. exhibit space; laboratory & workshop space.
Activities: formal education programs for adults; educational programs & activities for children; loan & temporary exhibitions; semiannual & annual meetings of MAS.
Publications: biannual journal, Bulletin of the Massachusetts Archaeological Society; triannual, Newsletter of the Massachusetts Archaeological Society; occasional publications; quarterly of the Friends of the Robbins Museum, Round Robbins; biannual newsletter; biannual, Round Robbins.
Hours & Admission Prices: Wed. 10-4, Thurs. & Sat. 10-2. Adults $5, children $2. ♿
Attendance: 1,100 (accurate)
Membership: Massachusetts Archaeological Society, Inc.: Family $3 each; Senior Active (65 & over) $10; Student Active $12; Associate $18; Individual Active $25; Foreign Active $30; Sustaining & Institution $35; Foreign Institution $40; Supporting $55; Patron $75; Life $500

Middleton

MIDDLETON HISTORICAL SOCIETY - LURA WOODSIDE WATKINS MUSEUM, 9 Pleasant St., Middleton, MA 01949. Mailing Address: P.O. Box 456, Middleton, MA 01949-0756. Tel.: 978-774-9301.
Founded: 1976.
Congressional District: 6
Key Personnel: Pres., Henry Tragert; Treas., Shirley Raynard; Education, Rita Kelley; Education, Gertrude Dearborn; Cur., Marge Watson.
Governing Authority: society; nonprofit. Parent Institution: Middleton Historical Society. Tax-exempt: 501(c)(3).
Historical Society Museum.
Collections: 18th-century shoe making; early farm implements; 19th-century ladies' fashion; photographs; town government artifacts.
Research Fields: genealogy; historic houses.
Facilities: library available to the public for use on the premises; 50-seat auditorium; 2,000 sq. ft. exhibit space.
Activities: formal education programs for children; guided tours; temporary exhibitions; lectures.
Hours & Admission Prices: Sept.-May by appointment only, meetings 3rd Mon. each month. No charge; donations accepted.
Attendance: 500 (estimated)
Membership: Annual $10.

Milton

BLUE HILLS TRAILSIDE MUSEUM, 1904 Canton Ave., Milton, MA 02186-2335. Tel.: 617-333-0690, ext. 0. Fax: 617-333-0814.
E-mail: bluehills@massaudubon.org

Web Site: www.massaudubon.org
Founded: 1959.
Congressional District: 11
Key Personnel: Dir., Norman Smith; Museum Shop Mgr., Laura Liptak.
Personnel Profile: Full-Time Paid 8; Part-Time Volunteers 92.
Governing Authority: state; society. Operated by Massachusetts Audubon Society for Department of Conservation and Recreation. Tax-exempt.
Natural History Museum & Environmental Education Center.
Collections: herpetology; zoology; geology; aviary; living collection of animals native to Blue Hills; natural history of Northeastern United States; archaeology; history of Blue Hills.
Research Fields: natural & human history of the Blue Hills Reservation; breeding study of Ambystomid salamanders; environmental education; snowy owl telemetry study.
Facilities: 700-vol. resource library; waterfowl pond; live animal displays; auditorium; hiking trails; workshop; residential facility with dormitory; cafeteria; interpretive pond walk. Museum-related items for sale.
Activities: lectures; special events; field trips; teacher training; internships; bird rehabilitation; formally organized education programs; permanent & temporary exhibitions; outreach school & community programs; summer & school vacation camps; weekend public programs; courses & workshops.
Publications: quarterly newsletter.
Hours & Admission Prices: Fri.-Sun. 10-5. Adults $3, senior citizens 65 & over $2, children 3-15 $1.50; members no charge with presentation of MAS membership card. Closed New Year's Day; Thanksgiving; Christmas. ♿
Attendance: 211,000 (estimated)
Membership: Individual $44; Family $58.

CAPTAIN FORBES HOUSE MUSEUM, 215 Adams St., Milton, MA 02186-4215. Tel.: 617-696-1815. Fax: 617-696-1907.
E-mail: info@forbeshousemuseum.org
Web Site: forbeshousemuseum.org
Founded: 1964.
Congressional District: 11
Key Personnel: Dir., Christine M. Sullivan; Chm., Peter Markell; Admin., Nadine A. Leary.
Personnel Profile: Full-Time Paid 1; Part-Time Paid 2; Part-Time Volunteers 90; Interns 2.
Governing Authority: nonprofit. Tax-exempt: 501(c)(3).
Historic House: restored to 1870s-1880s.
Collections: 19th-century Forbes family furnishings & collections; Asian export porcelain, furniture & paintings; Empire & Victorian furniture; American & European paintings, prints, & decorative arts; Abraham Lincoln & Civil War memorabilia.
Research Fields: Forbes family; U.S.-China trade history; U.S. economic development; Civil War & Abraham Lincoln; 19th-century decorative arts; garden of Asian export trees & shrubs; Victorian life.
Facilities: small library of books for use on premises; Lincoln log cabin replica; park-like grounds; education center; publications for sale.
Activities: special exhibitions; education programs; events; docent training; volunteer & internship opportunities; guided & group tours; lecture series.
Publications: quarterly newsletter.
Hours & Admission Prices: Tues.-Thurs. & Sun. 1-4, last tour at 3; other times by appointment. Adults $8, senior citizens & students $5; discounts to teachers and AAM & ICOM members; children under 12 & members no charge.
Attendance: 4,000 (estimated)
Membership: Individual $25; Family $50; Friend $75; Donor $100; Sponsor $250; Benefactor $500; Life $1,000.

SUFFOLK RESOLVES HOUSE, 1370 Canton Ave., Milton, MA 02186-2435. Tel.: 617-333-9700.
E-mail: askmhs@miltonhistoricalsociety.org
Web Site: www.miltonhistoricalsociety.org
Founded: 1904.
Governing Authority: nonprofit organization. Parent Institution: Milton Historical Society, Inc. Tax-exempt.
Historic Society Museum: c.1774.
Collections: archives; furniture.
Activities: programs; workshops.
Publications: Hamilton, History of Milton; Morris-Webster, Story of the Suffolk Resolves; Bodsbinder, Judith, Margaret Sutermeister: Chronicling Seen and Unseen Worlds 1894-1909.
Hours & Admission Prices: By appointment, seasonal open houses. No charge; donations accepted. ♿
Membership: Individual $15; Family $25; Corporate $150; Life $300.

Monterey

THE BIDWELL HOUSE MUSEUM, 100 Art School Rd., Monterey, MA 01245. Mailing Address: P.O. Box 537, Monterey, MA 01245-0537. Tel.: 413-528-6888. Fax: 413-644-9997.
E-mail: bidwellhouse@gmail.com
Web Site: www.bidwellhousemuseum.org
Founded: 1990.
Congressional District: 1
Key Personnel: Pres., Kathryn Roberts; Exec. Dir., Barbara Palmer.
Personnel Profile: Full-Time Paid 1; Part-Time Paid 1; Part-Time Volunteers 20; Interns 2.
Governing Authority: nonprofit organization. Tax-exempt.
Historic House Museum: c.1750.
Collections: 18th-century decorative arts; redware; textiles; furniture; domestic & agricultural tools; lighting devices; quilts; treen.
Research Fields: 18th-century Berkshire life; mid-18th century religion.
Facilities: 1,000-vol. library of books available for use on premises; 200-acre grounds with trails & gardens; picnic area.
Activities: guided tours; lectures; concerts; workshops; trail guides; early winter gatherings; young intern programs. Museum Sponsors: Pumpkin Fest.
Publications: quarterly newsletter, The Bidwell House.
Hours & Admission Prices: Memorial Day to Columbus Day Thurs.-Mon. 11-4. Adults $10, seniors $8, students $5; discounts to AAM & AAA members; children under 6 & members no charge.
Attendance: 600 (accurate)
Membership: Individual $35-$74; Family & Dual $75-$99; Benefactor $100-$149; Patron $150-$249; Old Manse Society $250-$499; Hargis & Brush Circle $500-$1,499; Bidwell Society $1,500 & $5,000.

Nantucket

ARTISTS ASSOCIATION OF NANTUCKET, 19 Washington St., Nantucket, MA 02554-3848. Mailing Address: P.O. Box 1104, Nantucket, MA 02554-1104. Tel.: 508-228-0722 (office) & 0294 (gallery). Fax: 508-228-9700.
Web Site: www.nantucketarts.org
Founded: 1945.
Congressional District: 13
Key Personnel: Mng. Dir., Cecil Barron Jensen; Gallery Dir., Robert Frazier; Gallery Asst., Susan Duane; Special Events & Membership Coord., Alison Cooley; Arts Program, Elizabeth Hunt O'Brien; Office Admin., Lucy Cobb.
Personnel Profile: Full-Time Paid 6; Part-Time Paid 1; Interns 6.
Governing Authority: nonprofit. Affiliated with Artists Association of Nantucket, Inc. Tax-exempt: 101(6).
Art Gallery.
Collections: early 20th-century Nantucket art; contemporary art.
Facilities: Art for sale.
Activities: lectures; films; permanent & temporary exhibitions; arts & crafts workshops; adult & children's art classes. Association Sponsors: annual craft show; annual junior artists show; annual art auction; annual scholarship award.
Publications: brochure; newsletters; seasonal AAN calendar update.
Hours & Admission Prices: Mon.-Fri. 10-3; call for seasonal hours. ♿
Attendance: 5,000
Membership: Patron $75 & up; Nantucket Artist $150.

EGAN MARITIME INSTITUTE, (M), The Coffin School, 4 Winter St., Nantucket, MA 02554-3638. Tel.: 508-228-2505. Fax: 508-228-7069.
E-mail: egan@eganmaritime.org
Web Site: www.eganmaritime.org
Formerly: Egan Maritime Foundation
Founded: 1996.
Key Personnel: Dir., Jean H.M. Grimmer; Pres., Robert A. Egan.
Personnel Profile: Full-Time Paid 2; Full-Time Volunteers 8; Part-Time Paid 10; Part-Time Volunteers 6; Interns 1.
Governing Authority: private; nonprofit organization. Parent Institution: The Albert F. Eagan and Dorothy H. Egan Foundation, Inc. Tax-exempt: 501(c)(3).
Maritime, Art & History Museum.
Collections: Nantucket history from the 18th-20th centuries.
Research Fields: Native Americans on Nantucket; history of the Coffin School; history of Maritime topics relating to Nantucket Island; American art; 19th-century women; Nantucket and Maritime literature; US. Coast Guard; Mass Human Society; Life-Saving & Shipwrecks.
Facilities: 500-vol. library; 150-seat auditorium; classroom. Museum-related items for sale.
Activities: concerts; films; formal educational programs; guided tours; lectures; temporary exhibitions; children's programs.
Publications: books relating to Nantucket; annual report.

Hours & Admission Prices: May-Oct. daily 10-4. Adults $5, student $3; members no charge. ♿
Attendance: 5,000 (estimated)
Membership: Lifesaver $40-$99; Supporter $100-$249; Contributor $250-$999; Patron $1,000-$1,999; Benefactor $2,000 & up.

MARIA MITCHELL ASSOCIATION NATURAL HISTORY MUSEUM, 7 Milk St., Nantucket, MA 02554-2635. Mailing Address: 4 Vestal St., Nantucket, MA 02554-2609. Tel.: 508-228-0898.
Formerly: Hinchman House Natural History Museum
Founded: 1903.
Key Personnel: Exec. Dir., Janet Shulte; Chm. (V), Toni B. McKerrow; Museum Shop Mgr., Cheryl Beaton.
Personnel Profile: Full-Time Paid 1; Part-Time Paid 2.
Governing Authority: Tax-exempt.
Natural History Museum.
Collections: flowers; birds; natural history.
Facilities: Museum-related items for sale.
Activities: nature, bird-watching & marine ecology walks; environmental education.
Hours & Admission Prices: mid-June to early Sept. Mon.-Sat. 10-4; Oct. Fri.-Sat. 10-4. Adults $5, children $4; members no charge. ♿
Attendance: 2,000 (estimated)
Membership: Individual $50; Family $100; $250; $500; $1,000; $2,500; $5,000.

* **NANTUCKET HISTORICAL ASSOCIATION,** 15 Broad St., Nantucket, MA 02554-3502. Mailing Address: Box 1016, Nantucket, MA 02554-1016. Tel.: 508-228-1894, ext. 0. Fax: 508-228-5618.
Web Site: www.nha.org
Founded: 1894.
Congressional District: 10
Key Personnel: Exec. Dir., Dr. William Tramposch; Pres., Janet L. Sherlund; 1st Vice Pres., Kenneth L. Beaugrand; Treas., Thomas J. Anathas; Cur. Library & Archives, Georgen Gilliam Charmes; Chief Cur., Ben Simons; Dir. Interpretation, Kim McCray; Museum Shop Mgr., Georgina Winton.
Personnel Profile: Full-Time Paid 23; Full-Time Volunteers 60; Part-Time Paid 50; Part-Time Volunteers 55; Interns 1.
Governing Authority: trustee; nonprofit. Branch Museums: 1847 Nantucket Whaling Museum; Peter Foulger Museum; 1686 Oldest House; 1805 Old Gaol; 1844 Hadwen House; 1746 Old Mill; 1838 Quaker Meetinghouse; Hose Cart House; Nantucket Historical Association Research Library; Whitney Gallery. Tax-exempt.
History Museum.
Collections: items pertaining to whaling; Nantucket; maritime history; crafts; decorative arts; genealogy; fire fighting; paintings, prints & portraits; tools; furniture; manuscripts; photographs; local memorabilia.
Research Fields: whaling; local & maritime history; Quaker records; genealogy.
Facilities: 5,000-vol. research library of whaleship logbooks, maritime manuscripts, marine books; 45,000 photographs; genealogy & Nantucket history available for use on premises; reading room. Books on Nantucket history & whaling for sale.
Activities: guided tours; films; permanent, temporary & loan exhibitions; manuscript collections.
Publications: quarterly magazine, Historic Nantucket; books; exhibition catalogs; pamphlets.
Hours & Admission Prices: Museum: Memorial Day to Columbus Day daily 10-5, 1st & 3rd Wed. of month 10-8. Historic Sites: Memorial Day to Columbus Day Mon.-Sat. 10-5, Sun. 12-5. Museum: adults $15, seniors $12, children 6-17 $8; discounts to groups; members no charge. Sites: adults $6, children 6-17 $3; discounts to groups; members no charge. Combination tickets available. Walking Tour: adult $10, seniors $8, children 6-17 $4. ♿
Attendance: 102,349 (accurate)
Membership: Individual $40; Supporting $60; Sustaining $100; Contributor $250; Hadwen Circle $500; Thomas Macy Associates $1,000; Mary Gardner Coffin Associates $5,000.

NANTUCKET LIFE-SAVING MUSEUM, 158 Polpis Rd., Nantucket, MA 02554-2320. Mailing Address: 4 Winter St., Nantucket, MA 02554-3638. Tel.: 508-228-1885.
E-mail: info@nantucketshipwreck.org
Web Site: www.nantucketshipwreck.org
Founded: 1967.
Key Personnel: Exec. Dir. Egan Foundation, Jean Grinmer; Pres. (V), Robert W. Read.
Personnel Profile: Full-Time Paid 1.
Governing Authority: nonprofit organization. Parent Institution: Albert F. Egan Jr. & Dorothy H. Egan Foundation. Tax-exempt.
History Museum.
Collections: period surfboats, beach carts & other life-saving apparatus used by the Massachusetts Humane Society, O.S.L.S.S., & U.S. Coast Guard; Fresnel lenses from Brant Point and Great Point Light; photographs.
Facilities: picnic area. Museum-related items for sale.
Activities: interpretive programs; guided tours; hands-on programs for children.
Hours & Admission Prices: Memorial Day to Columbus Day daily 10-4; other times by appointment. Adults $5, students & children $3; discounts to groups, members, AAM & ICOM members; active USCG, CAMM, & museum professionals no charge.
Attendance: 4,121 (estimated)
Membership: Lifesaver $40-$99; Supporter $100-$249; Contributor $250-$999; Patron $1,000-$1,999; Life Benefactor $2,000 & up.

NANTUCKET LIGHTSHIP BASKET MUSEUM, (M), 49 Union St., Nantucket, MA 02554-3869. Mailing Address: P.O. Box 2517, Nantucket, MA 02584-2517. Tel.: 508-228-1177. Fax: 508-228-7092.
E-mail: adminoffice@nantucketlightshipbasketmuseum.org
Web Site: www.nantucketlightshipbasketmuseum.org
Founded: 1997.
Key Personnel: Pres., Daryl Westbrook; Dir., Maryann Wasik; Vice Pres., Kathleen Myers; Vice Pres., Rafael Osona; Clerk, Peggy Kaufman; Treas., Eugene Collatz; Museum Shop Mgr., Beverly Barlow.
Personnel Profile: Full-Time Paid 2; Part-Time Paid 2; Part-Time Volunteers 65.
Governing Authority: private; nonprofit organization. Tax-exempt.
History Museum: housed in c.1821 home.
Collections: lightship baskets from 1850s to present; photographs of early basketmakers; basketmakers workshop.
Research Fields: basketmaking history; the natural progression & evolution.
Facilities: 27-vol. library; 50-seat lecture area; 3,000 sq. ft. exhibit space; outside garden. Museum-related items for sale.
Activities: lectures; demonstrations; docent program; films; formal education programs; guided tours; loan, participatory & temporary exhibitions; broadcast programs. Annual Events: House & Garden Tour; Children's Event.
Publications: newsletter, The Newsletter.
Hours & Admission Prices: Memorial Day to Columbus Day Tues.-Sat. 10-4. Adults $4, senior citizens, students & children over 12 $2; discounts to AAM & ICOM members; members no charge. Closed Independence Day. ♿
Attendance: 3,000 (accurate)
Membership: Individual $25; Family $75;Cross Rip Friend $100; South Shoal Friend $500; Patron $1,000 & up.

NANTUCKET MARIA MITCHELL ASSOCIATION, 4 Vestal St., Nantucket, MA 02554-2609. Tel.: 508-228-9198. Fax: 508-228-1031.
E-mail: info@mmo.org
Web Site: www.mmo.org
Founded: 1902.
Congressional District: 9
Key Personnel: Pres. (V), Toni B. McKerrow; Exec. Dir., Janet Schulte, Ph.D.; Dir. Education, Marjie Thomas; Dir. Astronomy, Vladimir Strelnitski, Ph.D.; Dir. Dept. Natural Science, Robert Kennedy, Ph.D.; Cur. Mitchell House, Jascin Leonardo-Finger.
Personnel Profile: Full-Time Paid 6; Part-Time Paid 20; Part-Time Volunteers 20; Interns 20.
Governing Authority: nonprofit organization. Tax-exempt.
Observatories, Natural Science & Historic House Museum.
Collections: herbarium; botany; zoology. Historic House: 1790 Maria Mitchell birthplace.
Research Fields: astronomy; natural science.
Facilities: 10,000-vol. library of natural science, astronomy & general science books available for loan.
Activities: guided tours; nature & bird walks; lectures; films; formally organized educational programs; aquarium; research training program for college undergraduates; permanent & temporary exhibitions.
Publications: annual report, The Nantucket Maria Mitchell Assn.; specialized publications of research in natural science field & research data in astronomical & astrophysic studies.
Hours & Admission Prices: Historic House & Natural Science Museum: mid-June to Labor Day Mon.-Sat. 10-4. Adults $10, children under 14 $8; library & members no charge. ♿
Attendance: 20,000 (estimated)
Membership: Student & Senior Citizen $25; Individual & Senior Couple $35; Family $50; Contributing $100, $250, $500, $1,000, $2,500.

Natick

MUSEUM OF WORLD WAR II, (M), Natick, MA 01760. Mailing Address: Administrative Office, 46 Eliot St., Natick, MA 01760-6042. Tel.: 508-651-7696. Fax: 508-651-7698.
E-mail: museumofworldwarii@yahoo.com
Web Site: www.museumofworldwarii.com
Founded: 1998.
Key Personnel: Dir. & Pres., Kenneth W. Rendell; Asst., Kathy Foster; Visitation & Veteran Affairs, Michael Chovanes; Speaker, Jon D'Allessandro.
Personnel Profile: Full-Time Paid 1; Full-Time Volunteers 2; Part-Time Volunteers 4.
Governing Authority: Tax-exempt.
Military Museum.
Collections: over 100,000 artifacts relating to WWII including letters & documents, handguns & small spy weapons; photographs;.
Research Fields: World War II.
Facilities: 10,000 sq. ft. exhibition space.
Activities: bi-weekly lectures.
Publications: World War II: Saving the Reality, 2009.
Hours & Admission Prices: By appointment only.

New Bedford

BUTTONWOOD PARK ZOO, 425 Hawthorn St., New Bedford, MA 02740-1418. Tel.: 508-991-6178.
E-mail: info@bpzoo.org
Web Site: bpzoo.org
Zoo.
Collections: over 250 animals including elephants, bison, mountain lions, bears, eagles, seals, otters & farm animals.
Hours & Admission Prices: Daily 10-5. Adults $6, seniors & students $4.50, children 3-12 $3; children under 3 no charge. Closed New Year's; Thanksgiving; Christmas.

MUSEUM OF MADEIRAN HERITAGE, 1 Funchal Pl., New Bedford, MA 02746. Mailing Address: 50 Madeira Ave., New Bedford, MA 02746-2343. Tel.: 508-994-2573. Fax: 508-992-5382.
E-mail: clubesss@gis.net/museum
Web Site: www.portuguesefeast.com
History Museum: dedicated to preserving the art and artifacts of the Portuguese island of Madeira.
Collections: Madeiran art & fine crafts including embroidery, lace, linens, pottery & weaving; traditional costumes.
Facilities: garden.
Hours & Admission Prices: May-Oct. Sun. 1-4. No charge.

NEW BEDFORD ART MUSEUM, 608 Pleasant St., New Bedford, MA 02740-6204. Tel.: 508-961-3072.
E-mail: info@newbedfordartmuseumorg
Web Site: www.newbedfordartmuseum.org
Key Personnel: Interim Dir., Kathryn Dinneen; Pres., Anne Whiting; Treas., Kevin Baptista.
Personnel Profile: Full-Time Volunteers 1; Part-Time Paid 11; Part-Time Volunteers 1.
Governing Authority: Tax-exempt: 501(c)(3).
Art Museum.
Collections: works by local, national & international artists; contemporary & historic art.
Activities: educational programs; lectures. Museum Sponsors: ArtMobile summer program.
Hours & Admission Prices: Memorial Day to Labor Day daily 10-5; Sept.-May Wed.-Sun. 12-5. Adults $3, seniors & students $2; members no charge. Closed holidays. ♿
Attendance: 5,000 (estimated)

NEW BEDFORD FIRE MUSEUM, Old Station No. 4, 51 Bedford St., New Bedford, MA 02740-4815. Tel.: 508-992-2162.
Key Personnel: Dir., Larry Roy.
Governing Authority: nonprofit organization.
Fire Museum: housed in 1867 fire station.
Collections: period fire trucks including 1840 hand-pump engine; uniforms; bells; period fire equipment, records & ledgers; fire fighting history.
Activities: interactive exhibits; historical & educational programs.
Hours & Admission Prices: July-Aug. Mon.-Sat. 12-4. Adults $3, seniors $2, children 6 & over $1; children under 6 no charge.

* **NEW BEDFORD WHALING MUSEUM, (M),** 18 Johnny Cake Hill, New Bedford, MA 02740-6398. Tel.: 508-997-0046. Fax: 508-997-0018.
E-mail: frontdesk@whalingmuseum.org
Web Site: www.whalingmuseum.org
Founded: 1903.
Congressional District: 10
Key Personnel: Chm. Bd., Janet Whitla; Pres., James Russell; Vice Pres. Admin., Kristen Sniezek; Sr. Cur., Stuart W. Frank.
Personnel Profile: Full-Time Paid 20; Part-Time Paid 15; Part-Time Volunteers 137; Interns 4.
Governing Authority: nonprofit organization. Parent Institution: Old Dartmouth Historical Society. Subsidiary Institution: Kendall Institution. Tax-exempt: 501(c)(3) & 170(b)(1)(A).
Whaling Museum.
Collections: history of International whaling; social, political, economic & cultural history of New Bedford area; whaling gear & tools; 89-1/2 foot half-scale model of whaling bark Lagoda which can be boarded; ship models; scrimshaw; paintings of whaling, local area & people; 66-foot complete skeleton of a blue whale; interactive exhibits on whales & conservation.
Research Fields: history of American & Arctic whaling; Arctic and local history.
Facilities: 70,000-vol. library of whaling & local history, including over 2,600 ships' logs of whaling voyages, available for research; reading room; 250-seat auditorium. Books, prints & reproductions for sale.
Activities: guided tours; lectures; films; gallery talks; formally organized education programs for children; docent program or council; inter-museum loan; permanent & temporary exhibitions.
Publications: books; newsletter, Bulletin from Johnny Cake Hill.
Hours & Admission Prices: Jan.-May Mon.-Sat. 9-4, 2nd Thurs. of month 9-9, Sun. 12-4; June-Dec. daily 9-5, 2nd Thurs. of month 9-9. Adults $10, seniors $9, children 6-14 $6; discounts to AAM, ICOM & AAA members; members & 1st Sat. of month no charge. Closed New Year's Day; Thanksgiving; Christmas. ♿
Attendance: 92,000 (accurate)
Membership: Student $20; Individual $40; Dual $60; Family $75.

THE ROTCH-JONES-DUFF HOUSE & GARDEN MUSEUM, INC., (M), 396 County St., New Bedford, MA 02740-4934. Tel.: 508-997-1401. Fax: 508-997-6846.
E-mail: info@rjdmuseum.org
Web Site: www.rjdmuseum.org
Founded: 1984.
Congressional District: 13
Key Personnel: Exec. Dir., Kate Corkum; Pres. (V), Elise Mock; Treas., Nathanel R. Brayton.
Personnel Profile: Full-Time Paid 3; Part-Time Paid 5; Part-Time Volunteers 110; Interns 1.
Governing Authority: nonprofit organization. Tax-exempt: 501(c)(3).
Historic House & Garden: c.1834, Greek Revival house & formal gardens.
Collections: 1800-1980, period furnishings.
Research Fields: historic preservation; horticulture; family genealogy; 19th-20th century decorative arts & furnishings.
Facilities: Museum-related items for sale.
Activities: guided tours; lectures; concerts; organized education programs for adults & children; docent program. Annual Events: Horticultural Symposia and Dinner Dance in June; Christmas Celebration in December.
Publications: newsletter, The Record: Spring, Summer & Fall calendar of events.
Hours & Admission Prices: Mon.-Sat. 10-4, Sun. 12-4. Adults $5, senior citizens & students $4, children under 12 $2; discount to AAA members; members no charge. Closed major holidays. ♿
Attendance: 8,480 (accurate)
Membership: Individual $40; Family $75; Sustainer $100; Sponsor $250; Patron $500; Benefactor $1,000.

UNIVERSITY ART GALLERY, UNIVERSITY OF MASSACHUSETTS DARTMOUTH, College of Visual and Performing Art, 715 Purchase St., New Bedford, MA 02740-6341. Tel.: 508-999-8555. Fax: 508-999-8912.
E-mail: lantonsen@umassd.edu
Web Site: www.umassd.edu/universityartgallery
Founded: 1987.
Congressional District: 3
Key Personnel: Dir., Lasse B. Antonsen.
Personnel Profile: Full-Time Paid 1; Part-Time Paid 7; Interns 2.
Governing Authority: public university; nonprofit. Tax-exempt: 501(c)(3).
Art Gallery.
Collections: paintings; sculpture; photographs.
Facilities: 60-seat auditorium; 2,600 sq. ft. exhibit space; educational facilities.
Activities: arts festivals; concerts; films; formal education programs for

undergraduate & graduate college students; guided tours; lectures; loan & traveling exhibitions; broadcast programs. Annual Event: art auction.
Hours & Admission Prices: June-Aug. Mon.-Sat. 9-6, Sun. 12-5; Sept.-May daily 9-6. No charge. ♿
Attendance: 10,000 (estimated)

New Braintree

NEW BRAINTREE HISTORICAL SOCIETY, 10 Utley Rd., New Braintree, MA 01531-9800. Mailing Address: P.O. Box 112, New Braintree, MA 01531-0112. Tel.: 508-867-8608.
E-mail: NBHS@newbraintreehistoricalsociety.org
Web Site: www.newbraintreehistoricalsociety.org
Key Personnel: Pres., Tom Fiorelli
Historical Society.
Collections: exhibits of town events; artifacts; historical materials; photographs.
Hours & Admission Prices: By appointment only.
Membership: Individual $5; Family $10; Life $100.

Newbury

COFFIN HOUSE, 14 High Rd., Rte. 1A, Newbury, MA 01951. Mailing Address: 141 Cambridge St., Boston, MA 02114-2702. Tel.: 978-462-2634. Fax: 978-462-4022.
Web Site: www.historicnewengland.org
Founded: 1929.
Congressional District: 6
Key Personnel: Pres., Carl Nold; Site Mgr., Bethany Groff.
Governing Authority: society; nonprofit organization. Parent Institution: Historic New England, 141 Cambridge St., Boston, MA 02114. Tel.: 617-227-3956. Tax-exempt: 501(c)(3).
Historic House: c. 1678 Coffin House.
Collections: 17th, 18th & 19-century domestic rooms in rural New England.
Activities: school programs; guided tours & special events.
Publications: Guide to Historic New England.
Hours & Admission Prices: June-Oct. 15 1st & 3rd Sat. of month 11-4. Adults $5; discounts to seniors, AAM, ICOM, AAA, WGBH members. Call Historic New England for further information.
Attendance: 1,234 (accurate)
Membership: National $35; Individual $45; Household $55; Garden & Landscape $75; Institutional $85; Contributing $100; Historic Homeowner $200; Supporting $250.

SPENCER-PEIRCE-LITTLE FARM, 5 Little's Lane, Newbury, MA 01951-1802. Mailing Address: 141 Cambridge St., Boston, MA 02114-2702. Tel.: 978-462-2634. Fax: 978-462-4022.
Web Site: www.historicnewengland.org
Founded: 1971.
Key Personnel: Pres., Carl Nold; Site Mgr., Bethany Groff.
Governing Authority: society; nonprofit organization. Parent Institution: Historic New England, 141 Cambridge St., Boston, MA 02114. Tel. 617-227-3956. Tax-exempt.
Historic House: c.1690 rare stone & brick cruciform-plan house.
Collections: 18th-century glass & ceramic vessels; decorative arts.
Facilities: nature trails.
Activities: guided tours; lectures; school programs; special events; family activities; hiking; Foster Farm program.
Publications: Guide to Historic New England.
Hours & Admission Prices: June-Oct. 15 Thurs.-Sun. 11-5. Adults $5, children $4; discounts to seniors, AAM, ICOM, AAA, WGBH members; Historic New England members no charge. Call for more information.
Attendance: 20,034 (accurate)
Membership: National $35; Individual $45; Household $55; Garden & Landscape $75; Institutional $85; Contributing $100; Historic Homeowner $200; Supporting $250.

Newburyport

THE CUSTOM HOUSE MARITIME MUSEUM, 25 Water St., Newburyport, MA 01950-2754. Mailing Address: Newburyport Maritime Society, 25 Water St., Newburyport, MA 01950. Tel.: 978-462-8681. Fax: 978-462-8740.
E-mail: info@themaritimesociety.org
Web Site: www.customhousemaritimemuseum.org
Founded: 1969.
Congressional District: 6
Key Personnel: Chm., Mark Guay.
Personnel Profile: Part-Time Volunteers 40.
Governing Authority: nonprofit organization. Parent Institution: Newburyport Maritime Society, Inc. Tax-exempt: Chapter #155 Sec. 12A.
Maritime Museum: housed in 1835 Greek Revival style Custom House.
Collections: artifacts relating to the maritime history of Merrimac Valley; objects brought back from the Orient, Europe & the South Seas in the 1800s; ship models; navigational tools & instruments; coast guard artifacts; uniforms.
Research Fields: maritime history of Newburyport & lower Merrimac Valley.
Facilities: 350-vol. library of books on maritime history & related fields, available for use on premises by appointment. Museum-related items for sale.
Activities: permanent & rotating exhibitions; lectures; workshops; education programs.
Publications: quarterly newsletter.
Hours & Admission Prices: May 15-Dec. 15 Tues.-Sat. 10-4, Sun. & Mon. holidays 12-4. Adults $7, senior citizens & students $5; active military, members & children under 12 no charge.
Attendance: 6,600 (accurate)
Membership: Individual $35; Family $50; Sustaining $100.

HISTORICAL SOCIETY OF OLD NEWBURY, CUSHING HOUSE MUSEUM, (M), 98 High St., Newburyport, MA 01950-3053. Tel.: 978-462-2681. Fax: 978-462-0134.
E-mail: info@newburyhist.org
Web Site: www.newburyhist.com
Founded: 1877.
Congressional District: 6
Key Personnel: Co-Pres., Alfred Clifford; Co-Pres., David Mack; Cur., Jay Williamson.
Personnel Profile: Full-Time Paid 1; Part-Time Paid 2; Part-Time Volunteers 12; Interns 1.
Governing Authority: nonprofit organization. Parent Institution: Historical Society of Old Newbury. Subsidiary Institution: Cushing House Museum. Tax-exempt: 501(c)(3).
History Museum: housed in 1808 Cushing House, a Federalist mansion, home of Caleb Cushing, first envoy to China, grounds include a 19th-century barn, garden & summer house.
Collections: paintings; silver; furniture; china; miniatures; dolls; carriages; paperweights; needlework, costumes; glass; toys; clocks; military.
Research Fields: history of Newbury, Newburyport & West Newbury; agrarian & mercantile communities; furniture & decorative arts.
Facilities: 5,000-vol. library of log books, manuscripts, deeds, documents, vital statistics & ledgers available by appointment on premises; carriage house.
Activities: guided tours; lectures; permanent & temporary exhibitions.
Publications: books & pamphlets on local history; catalogs.
Hours & Admission Prices: Museum: May-Oct. Tues.-Fri. 10-4, Sat. 12-4. Library by appointment only. Adults $7, students & children under 12 $2; discounts to groups, AAM & ICOM members; members no charge. Closed holidays.
Attendance: 2,000 (estimated)
Membership: Individual $20; Family $35; Friend $50; Sustaining $100; Benefactor $250; Patron $500.

Newton

* **THE NEWTON HISTORY MUSEUM AT THE JACKSON HOMESTEAD, (M),** 527 Washington St., Newton, MA 02458-1433. Tel.: 617-796-1450. Fax: 617-552-7228.
E-mail: cstone@newtonma.gov
Web Site: historicnewton.org
Formerly: The Jackson Homestead: Newton's Museum & Historical Society
Founded: 1950.
Congressional District: 4
Key Personnel: Dir. & C.E.O., Cynthia Stone; Chm. (V), Harry Lohr, Jr.; Pres. Newton Historical Soc. (V), Anne Larner; Cur., Susan Abele; Public Rels. Mgr., Lynette Aznavourian; Dir. Devel., David Oliver; Cur. Education, Melissa Westlake.
Personnel Profile: Full-Time Paid 2; Part-Time Paid 6; Part-Time Volunteers 60; Interns 3.
Governing Authority: municipal. Parent Institution: City of Newton. Subsidiary Institution: The Newton Historical Society. Tax-exempt: 501(c)(3).
History Museum: 1809 Jackson Homestead.
Collections: 19th-century furnishings; domestic & personal artifacts; costumes; toys; manuscripts, maps & photographs; underground railroad.
Research Fields: Newton architecture; churches; railroads; families; education; 19th to 20th-century suburban development; historic maps of Newton.
Facilities: 500-vol. library & vertical files of Newton historical material available for use by appointment; reading room.
Activities: permanent & changing exhibitions on Newton as an early railroad suburb & the Homestead as a stop on the Underground Railroad; lectures & videos; school programs; neighborhood walking; tours; house tours; research.

Publications: Newton History Museum Newsletter; booklet series, The Older Houses of Newton; Newton Upper Falls; West Newton; Newton Lower Falls & Newton Corner, Newtonville; Newton Centre; Agudas Achim: Newton's Oldest Synagogue; Newton 1699-1988; A Century of Lace; The Jacksons & their Homestead; Newton, Massachusetts; Newton.
Hours & Admission Prices: Tues.-Fri. 11-5, Sat.-Sun. 12-5; research by appointment. Adults $5, senior citizens & children 6-17 $3; discounts to Newton residents, AAM, ICOM & WGBH members; members no charge. ♿
Attendance: 9,000 (estimated)
Membership: Student & Senior $20; Individual $30; Household $45; Supporting $70; Sustaining $125; Leadership $500; 1809 Society $1,000.

North Adams

MASS MOCA, 87 Marshall St., North Adams, MA 01247-2402. Mailing Address: 1040 Mass MoCA Way, North Adams, MA 01247-2499. Tel.: 413-664-4481. Fax: 413-663-8548.
E-mail: info@massmoca.org
Web Site: www.massmoca.org
Founded: 1988.
Congressional District: 1
Key Personnel: C.E.O., Joseph Thompson; Chm. (V), Duncan Brown; Financial Dir., Andrea Hockridge; Cur., Susan Cross; Cur., Denise Markonish; Mktg. & Public Rels., Katherine Myers; Devel., Laurie Werner.
Personnel Profile: Full-Time Paid 65; Part-Time Paid 10; Part-Time Volunteers 2; Interns 4.
Governing Authority: private; nonprofit organization. Tax-exempt: 501(c)(3).
Art Museum.
Collections: post-1960 large-scale installations of sculpture & paintings; Sol Lewitt wall drawing.
Major Exhibits: Gravity Is A Force To Be Reckoned With (The Glass House), 12/09-10/10; Material World, 4/10-3/11.
Research Fields: contemporary art.
Facilities: 650-seat auditorium; 100-seat cafeteria; 175,000 sq. ft. exhibit space. Museum-related items for sale.
Activities: dance recitals; films; formal education programs for children & college students; loan exhibitions; theater.
Hours & Admission Prices: July-Aug. daily 10-6; Sept.-June Wed.-Mon. 11-5. Adults $15, students $10, children $5; discount to groups; members no charge. Closed Thanksgiving; Christmas. ♿
Attendance: 120,000 (estimated)
Membership: Individual $40; Dual & Family $70; Contributor $120; Associate $200; Contemporary Circle $500; Director's Forum $1,000; Angel $2,500; Business $3,000.

NORTH ADAMS MUSEUM OF HISTORY SCIENCE, Western Gateway Heritage State Park, 9 Furnace St. Bypass, North Adams, MA 01247-3820. Tel.: 413-664-4700.
E-mail: nahs@bcn.net
Personnel Profile: Part-Time Volunteers 20.
Historical Society Museum.
Collections: artifacts; photographs.
Hours & Admission Prices: May-Oct. Thurs.-Sat. 10-4, Sun. 1-4; Nov.-April Sat. 10-4, Sun. 1-4. No charge; donations accepted. Closed holidays.
Attendance: 2,301 (accurate)
Membership: Single $10; Family $20.

North Andover

MUSEUM OF PRINTING, 800 Massachusetts Ave., North Andover, MA 01845-4544. Tel.: 978-686-0450.
E-mail: info@museumofprinting.org
Web Site: www.museumofprinting.org
Founded: 1978.
Key Personnel: Exec. Dir., Ted Leigh; Pres. (V), Frank J. Romano.
Personnel Profile: Part-Time Volunteers 11; Interns 2.
Governing Authority: nonprofit organization. Tax-exempt: 501(c)(3).
Printing History Museum.
Collections: printing history, equipment, & technology.
Facilities: library.
Activities: Museum Sponsors: Father's Day Printing Arts Fair.
Publications: newsletter.
Hours & Admission Prices: Fri.-Sat. 10-4; other times by appointment. Adults $5, students & seniors $3; members & children under 6 no charge. Closed national holidays. ♿
Attendance: 1,923 (accurate)
Membership: Individual $40; Sustaining $250; Lifetime $1,000.

NORTH ANDOVER HISTORICAL SOCIETY, (M), 153 Academy Rd., North Andover, MA 01845-4037. Tel.: 978-686-4035. Fax: 978-686-6616.
E-mail: nahistory@juno.com
Web Site: www.northandoverhistoricalsociety.org
Founded: 1913.
Congressional District: 6
Key Personnel: Dir. & C.E.O., Carol Majahad; Pres. (V), Kathy C. Stevens.
Personnel Profile: Full-Time Paid 1; Part-Time Paid 2; Part-Time Volunteers 25; Interns 1.
Governing Authority: society. Branch Museums: Johnson Cottage; 1715 The Parson Barnard House, 179 Osgood St. Tax-exempt: 501(c)(3).
Historical Society.
Collections: genealogical & local history archival collections; Johnson Cottage; period furnishings; cooking utensils; lighting devices; tools; pewter c.1715 Parson Barnard House: preserved & furnished to show living styles of four early owners.
Research Fields: local history including Salem Witch Trials of 1692.
Facilities: 20,000-piece archival collection of local & regional history by appointment; reading room.
Activities: guided tours; lectures; formally organized education programs for children; permanent & temporary exhibitions; Adventures in Time enrichment programs.
Publications: pamphlets, Early Owners of the Parson Barnard House & Their Times; The Parson Barnard House; An Eighteenth Century New England Herbal Sampler; The Glacier Geologic History of North Andover & the Surrounding Area; book, Andover, Symbol of New England; republished book, 1880 Sketches of Andover; A Good Inland Town: 1649-1940.
Hours & Admission Prices: Johnson Cottage: Tues.-Fri. 10-12 & 1-3; other times by appointment. Adults $7, senior citizens 65 & over and children $5; discounts to AAM, ICOM, NEMA, MTA; members no charge. Parson Barnard House: May-Oct. call for hours. Research Library: $15 1st hour, $10 each additional hour; NEMA, AAM & ICOM members no charge. Closed holidays.
Attendance: 3,346 (accurate)
Membership: Senior $15; Individual $20; Family $30; Patron $50; Sponsor $100; Benefactor $250; Donor $500; Life Donor $2,500.

THE STEVENS-COOLIDGE PLACE, A PROPERTY OF THE TRUSTEES OF RESERVATIONS, 137 Andover St., North Andover, MA 01845. Mailing Address: 139 Andover St., North Andover, MA 01845-5111. Tel.: 978-682-3580.
E-mail: cward@ttor.org
Founded: 1962.
Congressional District: 6
Key Personnel: Historic Resources Mgr., Susan Hill Dolan; Supt., Chris Ward; Exec. Dir., Andy Kendall; Historic Resources Educator, Lisa Compton.
Personnel Profile: Full-Time Paid 4; Part-Time Paid 3; Part-Time Volunteers 20; Interns 2.
Governing Authority: The Trustees of Reservations, Long Hill 572 Essex St., Beverly, MA 01915. Tel.: 978-921-1944. Tax-exempt: 501(c)(3).
Historic House: early 19th century restored Colonial Revival style house with period gardens.
Collections: Chinese porcelain; decorative arts; period furnishings.
Research Fields: papers; photographs relating to Stevens & Coolidge families.
Facilities: 91 acres of formal gardens, pastures & woodlands.
Activities: guided tours, programs, lectures. Annual Event: plant sale in May.
Hours & Admission Prices: House: Memorial Day to Labor Day Sat.-Sun. 1-5; groups by appointment. Gardens: daily 8am to sunset. No charge; donations accepted.
Attendance: 1,750
Membership: Trustees of Reservations $20; Individual $45; Family $65; Contributing $100; Supporting $150; Sustaining $300; Sponsor $600; l891 Society $1,000.

North Easton

THE CHILDREN'S MUSEUM IN EASTON, (M), 9 Sullivan Ave., North Easton, MA 02356-1419. Mailing Address: P.O. Box 417, North Easton, MA 02356-0417. Tel.: 508-230-3789. Fax: 508-230-7130.
Web Site: childrensmuseumineaston.org
Founded: 1988.
Congressional District: 9
Key Personnel: C.E.O., Paula J. Peterson; Chm., Maria O'Connell Unda; Museum Shop Mgr., Karen Frick.
Personnel Profile: Full-Time Paid 3; Full-Time Volunteers 10; Part-Time Paid 7; Part-Time Volunteers 200; Interns 3.
Governing Authority: nonprofit. Tax-exempt: 501(c)(3).
Children's Museum: located in fire station in town's historical district.
Collections: hands-on exhibits.
Activities: participatory exhibits; after school workshops & programs; school vacation activities; family performances; parenting workshops.

Publications: seasonal newsletter.
Hours & Admission Prices: Tues.-Fri. 9-5, Sat.-Sun. 12-5; call for holiday & summer hours. Admission $6; discounts to AAM members; children under one & ACM reciprocal members no charge. Closed major holidays.
Attendance: 50,000 (estimated)
Membership: Basic Family (2 people) $60, each additional person $10; ACM Reciprocal $125.

North Oxford

CLARA BARTON BIRTHPLACE MUSEUM, 66 Clara Barton Rd., North Oxford, MA 01537-1301. Mailing Address: P.O. Box 356, North Oxford, MA 01537-0356. Tel.: 508-987-2056, ext. 213. Fax: 508-987-2002.
E-mail: clarabartonbirthplace@bartoncenter.org
Web Site: www.clarabartonbirthplace.org
Founded: 1921.
Congressional District: 2
Key Personnel: Mgr., Emily Thomas.
Personnel Profile: Part-Time Paid 2.
Governing Authority: Owned by the Barton Center for Diabetes Education, Inc. Tax-exempt.
Historic House Museum: c.1818-20 Clara Barton Birthplace.
Collections: Clara Barton & Barton family memorabilia; Civil War relics; American Red Cross history; 19th & early 20th century correspondence.
Research Fields: 19th-century history; American Red Cross; Civil War.
Facilities: library of books & correspondence by Clara Barton available for use by appointment; residential camping facilities available year-round; conference center; meeting facilities available for rent.
Activities: guided tours; workshops; special events; Barton Center for Diabetes Education, Inc. offers year-round programs for children with diabetes & their families.
Publications: Very Sincerely Yours, Clara.
Hours & Admission Prices: June-Aug. Wed.-Sun. 11-5; other times by appointment. Adults $6, children 6-12 $3; discounts to groups, Mass. Teachers Assn., Red Cross volunteers, AAM & ICOM members; members no charge.
Attendance: 1,200 (estimated)
Membership: Individual $20; Family $30; Founding $100; Lifetime $1,000.

North Woburn

RUMFORD HISTORICAL ASSOCIATION, 90 Elm St., North Woburn, MA 01801-1855. Mailing Address: # 11 Lowell St., Woburn, MA 01801-2334.
Founded: 1877.
Congressional District: 7
Key Personnel: Pres., Leonard Harmon.
Governing Authority: nonprofit organization. Tax-exempt: 501(c)(3).
Historic House: 1714 Count Rumford's birthplace.
Collections: history; science.
Facilities: collection of books pertaining to Count Rumford's scientific works available for inter-library loan & for use by trustees' permission.
Activities: permanent & temporary exhibitions.
Hours & Admission Prices: Sat.-Sun. 1-4:30. No charge; donations accepted. Closed New Year's Day; Christmas.

Northampton

THE BOTANIC GARDEN OF SMITH COLLEGE, (M), Lyman Plant House & Conservatory, 16 College Lane, Northampton, MA 01063-6352. Tel.: 413-585-2740 & 2742. Fax: 413-585-2744.
E-mail: garden@smith.edu
Web Site: www.smith.edu/garden
Founded: 1895.
Congressional District: 1
Key Personnel: Dir., Michael Marcotrigiano.
Personnel Profile: Full-Time Paid 11; Part-Time Paid 3; Part-Time Volunteers 35; Interns 6.
Governing Authority: college; nonprofit. Parent Institution: Smith College, Elm St., Northampton, MA 01063. Tax-exempt.
Botanical Garden: housed in 1890s greenhouses built by Lord & Burnham, on site of Smith College campus, a 125 acre arboretum.
Collections: greenhouse, herbaceous gardens; arboretum collections representing the world's flora; herbarium; rock garden.
Research Fields: plant systematics & genetics.
Facilities: botanical garden; classrooms; herbarium; conservatory; arboretum.
Activities: guided tours; formally organized education programs for undergraduate college students; permanent & temporary exhibitions; audio tours.
Publications: Index Seminum; biannual newsletter, Botanic Garden News.
Hours & Admission Prices: Daily 8:30-4. No charge; donations accepted. ♿
Attendance: 100,000

Membership: Student $20; Individual $50; Household $75; Contributor $150; Sustainer $500; Patron $1,000; Champion $2,000.

CALVIN COOLIDGE PRESIDENTIAL LIBRARY & MUSEUM, 20 West St., Northampton, MA 01060-3713. Tel.: 413-587-1014, 1012 or 1011. Fax: 413-587-1015.
E-mail: coolidge@forbeslibrary.org
Web Site: www.forbeslibrary.org
Formerly: Calvin Coolidge Memorial Room, Forbes Library
Founded: 1920.
Congressional District: 1
Key Personnel: Archivist, Julie Bartlett.
Personnel Profile: Part-Time Paid 1; Part-Time Volunteers 5; Interns 1.
Governing Authority: board of trustees, nonprofit. Parent Institution: Forbes Library. Tax-exempt: 501(c)(3).
Presidential Museum.
Collections: manuscripts, books, documents, scrapbooks, personal papers; photographs; portraits; memorabilia associated with Calvin Coolidge, 30th President, Vice President, & Governor of Massachusetts.
Research Fields: manuscripts indexed on computer database.
Facilities: 4,000-vol. library of books associated with Calvin Coolidge available to adult researchers; reading room.
Activities: guided tours; lectures; permanent & temporary exhibitions; manuscript collections.
Publications: folder, Calvin Coolidge: A Chronological Summary; pamphlet, The Coolidges, The Northampton Years.
Hours & Admission Prices: Mon. & Wed. 3-9, Tues. & Thurs. 1-5, Sat. by appointment. No charge. Closed major holidays. ♿

HISTORIC NORTHAMPTON, 46 Bridge St., Northampton, MA 01060-2428. Tel.: 413-584-6011. Fax: 413-584-7956.
E-mail: mailbox@historic-northampton.org
Web Site: www.historic-northampton.org
Founded: 1905.
Congressional District: 1
Key Personnel: Dir., Kerry W. Buckley; Pres., Ronald Story; Museum Asst., Marie Panik.
Personnel Profile: Full-Time Paid 2; Part-Time Paid 2; Part-Time Volunteers 10.
Governing Authority: private; nonprofit organization. Tax-exempt: 501(c)(3).
History Museum.
Collections: furniture; paintings; decorative arts; documents of the upper Connecticut River Valley; collection of regional textiles & costumes; archaeology.
Research Fields: local history; upper Connecticut River Valley; regional costume & textiles.
Facilities: education center. Museum-related items for sale.
Activities: changing & permanent exhibitions; adult public programs; school programs; guided tours; seasonal events; volunteer program.
Publications: brochure, Historical Society, Damon Education Center; Weathervane booklet series: A President in a Two-Family House: Calvin Coolidge of Northampton; books, The Parson's House of the Northampton Historical Society; booklet, Native Peoples & Museums in the Connecticut River Valley: A Guide for Learning; maps; cemetery.
Hours & Admission Prices: Museum: Tues.-Sat. 10-5, Sun. 12-5. Adults $3; members no charge. Research: by appointment. No charge. ♿
Attendance: 2,728 (accurate)
Membership: Student & Senior Citizens $25; Individual $40; Family $60; Supporting $100; Patron $200; Business Membership: Business Member $100; Business Sponsor $250; Business Patron $500.

* **SMITH COLLEGE MUSEUM OF ART, (M),** Elm St. at Bedford Ter., Northampton, MA 01063. Tel.: 413-585-2760. Fax: 413-585-2782.
E-mail: artmuseum@smith.edu
Web Site: www.smith.edu/artmuseum
Founded: 1920.
Congressional District: 1
Key Personnel: Dir., Jessica F. Nicoll; Assoc. Dir. Museum Svcs., David Dempsey; Assoc. Dir. Curatorial Affairs & Cur. Painting & Sculpture, Linda Muehlig; Cur. Prints, Drawings, & Photographs, Aprile Gallant; Collections

Mgr. & Registrar, Louise Laplante; Cur. Education, Ann Musser; Dir. Membership & Mktg., Margi Caplan; Museum Shop Mgr., Nan Fleming.
Personnel Profile: Full-Time Paid 18; Part-Time Paid 77; Part-Time Volunteers 73; Interns 3.
Governing Authority: college. Parent Institution: Smith College. Tax-exempt: 501(c)(3).
Art Museum.
Collections: art from most periods & cultures with special emphasis on 17th to 21st-century European & American paintings & sculpture; drawings & prints from the Renaissance to contemporary; photographs; decorative arts.
Research Fields: 18th- to 20th-century European & American paintings, sculpture, graphics, decorative arts; Asian & African arts.
Facilities: library; cafe. Museum-related items for sale.
Activities: audio guide; guided tours; gallery talks; education programs for undergraduate & graduate college students; inter-museum loan, traveling & temporary exhibitions. Museum Sponsors: Family Days; Second Fridays.
Publications: exhibitions catalogs; members' newsletter & calendar; annual report; SCheMA 2006-2007, The Year in Review; gallery guides; online teacher packets.
Hours & Admission Prices: Tues.-Sat. 10-4, Sun. 12-4, 2nd Fri. of month 10-8. Adults $5, seniors 65 & over $4, students 13 & over $3, youth 6-12 $2; 2nd Fri. of month 4-8 no charge. Closed major holidays. ♿
Attendance: 39,015 (accurate)
Membership: Student & Recent Alumnae $20; Educator $35; Individual $50; Household $75; Contributor $150; Sustainer $500; Patron $1,000; Champion $2,000 & up.

Northborough

NORTHBOROUGH HISTORICAL SOCIETY, INC., 50 Main St., Northborough, MA 01532. Mailing Address: P.O. Box 661, Northborough, MA 01532-0661. Tel.: 508-393-6298 & 2343.
Web Site: www.northboroughhistsoc.org
Founded: 1906.
Congressional District: 3
Key Personnel: Pres., Jim Halpin; Cur., Ellen Racine; Historian, Bob Ellis.
Governing Authority: society. Tax-exempt.
General Museum: housed in 1860 Baptist Church.
Collections: lighting; apothecary supplies; kitchen utensils; clothing; tools; war souvenirs; china; button and comb; manuscripts; genealogy; portraits; school items; toys; books; town history.
Facilities: library; archives; 150-seat auditorium.
Activities: guided tours; permanent & temporary exhibits; guest speakers.
Publications: monthly newsletter.
Hours & Admission Prices: May-June & Sept.-Oct. Sun. 2-4; others times by appointment. No charge; donations accepted.
Attendance: 871 (accurate)
Membership: Student $10; Individual $15; Family $35; Life $250.

Norton

BEARD GALLERY, (M), 26 E. Main St., Norton, MA 02766-2311. Tel.: 508-286-3578 & 3570. Fax: 508-286-3565.
Web Site: www.wheatonma.edu/academic/watson/home.html
Formerly: Watson Gallery, Wheaton College
Founded: 1960.
Congressional District: 4
Key Personnel: Dir., Ann H. Murray; Cur. Collections & Registrar, Leah Niederstadt.
Personnel Profile: Part-Time Paid 2; Interns 2.
Governing Authority: private college; nonprofit. Parent Institution: Wheaton College. Tax-exempt.
College Art Gallery: located within the Norton, MA historic district.
Collections: concentration on American & European paintings, prints & drawings from 15th-21st centuries; period bronzes, coins, jewelry & sculpture; Native American baskets; decorative arts with emphasis on Wedgewood & American glass; contemporary American ceramics.
Research Fields: Native American baskets; drawings; sculpture; artifacts; textiles; decorative arts; prints & paintings.
Facilities: 50-vol. in-house reference library; 1,568 sq. ft. exhibit space.
Publications: biannual exhibition catalogues; collection catalogues.
Hours & Admission Prices: Mon.-Sat. 12:30-4:30. No charge. Closed during college vacations. ♿
Attendance: 2,000 (estimated)
Membership: Wheaton College Friends of Art: Alumnus (within 5 yrs. of graduation) $10; Member $25; Double $40; Sponsor $60-$99; Patron $100-$500.

MASSACHUSETTS GOLF MUSEUM, 300 Arnold Palmer Blvd., Norton, MA 02766-1365. Tel.: 774-430-9100; 800-356-2201. Fax: 774-430-9101.
Web Site: www.mgalinks.org/about_mga/museum.html
Key Personnel: Exec. Dir., Joe Sprague, Jr.
Golf Museum.
Collections: Massachusetts golf history & heritage; golfers; trophies.
Activities: video; interactive exhibits.
Hours & Admission Prices: Mon.-Fri. 10-5. No charge. ♿

Norwell

SOUTH SHORE NATURAL SCIENCE CENTER, INC., (M), 48 Jacobs Lane, Norwell, MA 02061-1149. Mailing Address: P.O. Box 429, Jacobs Lane, Norwell, MA 02061-0429. Tel.: 781-659-2559. Fax: 781-659-5924.
E-mail: ssnsc@comcast.net
Web Site: www.ssnsc.org
Founded: 1962.
Congressional District: 5
Key Personnel: Exec. Dir. & Devel. Officer, Martha B. Twigg; Chm. Bd. (V), Penelope Allen Baltera; Treas., John Bond; Business Mgr., Tracey Cooke; Museum Shop Mgr., Wendy Blomberg; Registrar, Karen Kurkoski.
Personnel Profile: Full-Time Paid 6; Part-Time Paid 20; Part-Time Volunteers 30; Interns 1.
Governing Authority: nonprofit organization. Tax-exempt: 501(c)(3).
Nature Center/Conservation Area.
Collections: wildlife & archaeological exhibits; flora; 16 living habitats; native animal skins & liquids.
Research Fields: bird & salamander counts; acid rain monitoring; mammal & bird road kill research; endangered species.
Facilities: research library; nature center; EcoZone: living habit museum; 100-seat auditorium; educational facilities; educational resource files; outdoor amphitheater; 3 classrooms in main site; separate cabin classroom; kitchen; pond site. Nature related items for sale.
Activities: walking trails; environmental lecture series; study clubs; hobby workshops; organized education programs for children, adults, & families; participatory exhibits; school loan service; teacher workshops; teaching; training; adult field trips; craft programs. Museum Sponsors: Plant Sale; Fall Corn Festival; Nature-theme birthday parties; Travel Teas; Parents 'n Tots; 4's & 5's; Kindergarten; scout programs; nature preschool; summer day camp programs; Summer Garden Tour; after school enrichment.
Publications: quarterly program guide; members newsletter; trail guides; miscellaneous brochures; current elementary science curriculum & materials.
Hours & Admission Prices: Mon.-Sat. 9:30-4:30. Adults $5, seniors $3; discounts to AAM & NEMA members and Massachusetts teachers; members no charge. Closed New Year's; Easter; Memorial Day; Independence Day; Labor Day; Thanksgiving; Christmas. ♿
Attendance: 48,000 (estimated)
Membership: Individual $25; Family $60; Contributing $75; Corporate $130; Sustaining $150; Patron $500; Benefactor $1,000.

Norwood

THE F. HOLLAND DAY HOUSE & NORWOOD HISTORY MUSEUM, 93 Day St., Norwood, MA 02062-2118. Tel.: 781-762-9197.
E-mail: norwoodhistoricalsociety@norwoodhistoricalsociety.org
Web Site: www.norwoodhistoricalsociety.org
Historic House: former home of Fred Holland Day. Listed on the National Register of Historic Places.
Collections: period artifacts; furnishings; paintings; photographs.
Hours & Admission Prices: Tours: June-Aug. Sun. 1-4; group tours & other times by appointment. Adults $4; Norwood Historical Society members no charge.

Onset

PORTER THERMOMETER MUSEUM, 49 Zarahemla Rd., Onset, MA 02558. Mailing Address: P.O. Box 944, Onset, MA 02558. Tel.: 508-295-5504. Fax: 508-295-8323.
E-mail: thermometerman@aol.com
Web Site: members.aol.com/thermometerman/index.html
Founded: 1990.
Congressional District: 5
Key Personnel: Chm. & Cur. (V), Richard T. Porter; Pres. & Museum Shop Mgr. (V), Barbara A. Porter.
Personnel Profile: Full-Time Volunteers 2.
Governing Authority: private individual; nonprofit.
Thermometer Museum.
Collections: over 5,000 thermometer & weather devices.
Research Fields: thermometer companies history.
Facilities: library; 300 sq. ft. exhibit space. Weather devices for sale.
Activities: guided tours; lectures; loan, participatory, temporary & traveling exhibitions; study clubs; broadcast, newspaper & magazine programs. Annual Events: Frigid Festival Open House in January; Salute to Spring; Falling Temps Festival.

Publications: newsletter, Thermometer Collections Club of America; Thermometer chapter in Krause collections book; book, Today's Hottest Collectibles; chapters: Little Museums; A Place Called Peculiar; Maloney's Guide; Ripley's Encyclopedia of the Bizarre; Curious New England; 4 Go Wild in New England; Galileo's Bulb-Past & Present; History of the Thermometer & 25 Years of Collecting Memoirs; Guinness Book of World Records 2005 (50th Anniversary Issue).
Hours & Admission Prices: Daily 24 hours by appointment. No charge; donations accepted.
Attendance: 400 (estimated)

Orleans

FRENCH CABLE STATION MUSEUM IN ORLEANS, 41 S. Orleans Rd., Orleans, MA 02653. Mailing Address: Box 85, Orleans, MA 02653-0085. Tel.: 508-240-1735.
E-mail: info@frenchcablestationmuseum.org
Web Site: www.frenchcablestationmuseum.org
Founded: 1971.
Congressional District: 12
Key Personnel: Pres. (V), Jack Barritt.
Personnel Profile: Full-Time Volunteers 6; Part-Time Volunteers 26.
Governing Authority: nonprofit organization. Tax-exempt: 501(c)(3).
Atlantic Cable Terminal; Communications Museum: housed in 1891 building, built to house cable laid from France to Orleans.
Collections: all the equipment necessary to send and receive submarine cable messages from the United States to Brest, France; Heurtley magnifier; five generations of siphon recorders; artificial cables and circuitry to permit duplex operation.
Activities: guided tours; permanent exhibitions.
Publications: museum tour book.
Hours & Admission Prices: June & Sept. Fri.-Sun. 1-4; July-Aug. Thurs.-Sun. 1-4. No charge; donations accepted.
Attendance: 540 (accurate)
Membership: Junior $1; Individual $10; Contributing $25; Supporting $100; Life $500.

Osterville

OSTERVILLE HISTORICAL MUSEUM, 155 W. Bay Rd., Osterville, MA 02655-2427. Mailing Address: P.O. Box 3, Osterville, MA 02655-0003. Tel.: 508-428-5861. Fax: 508-428-2241.
E-mail: ohs@ostervillemuseum.org
Web Site: www.ostervillemuseum.org
Founded: 1931.
Congressional District: 10
Key Personnel: Exec. Dir., Cynthia D. Hall; Cur., Cathryn Wright; Museum Shop Mgr., Barbara Johann.
Personnel Profile: Part-Time Paid 1; Part-Time Volunteers 50.
Governing Authority: society. Tax-exempt: 501(c)(3).
Historical Society Museum: housed in late 18th-century Jonathan Parker House; 18th-century Cammett House; Wooden Boat Museum; Colonial Garden.
Collections: furniture; textiles; glass; china; paintings; folk art; dolls; toys; old documents & pictures pertaining to the village of Osterville; China trade exhibit; wooden boat building of Crosby catboats; wooden boats; boat building tools.
Research Fields: local history & boat shops.
Facilities: 40-seat conference room.
Activities: lectures; gallery talks; permanent exhibitions.
Publications: brochure, Osterville Historical Society Museum; biannual newsletter.
Hours & Admission Prices: mid-June to Sept. Thurs. & Sat. 1:30-4:30, Fri. 10-4:30; other times by appointment. Admission $5; discounts to ALASH members & Mass Teachers Association; members & children under 12 no charge.
Attendance: 550 (estimated)
Membership: Individual $25; Family $50; First Mate $100; Commodore $250.

Oxford

OXFORD LIBRARY MUSEUM, 339 Main St., Oxford, MA 01540-1729. Tel.: 508-987-6003. Fax: 508-987-3896.
Founded: 1903.
Congressional District: 2
Key Personnel: Head Librarian, Timothy Kelley.
Governing Authority: municipal. Affiliated with Oxford Free Public Library.
Local History Museum.
Collections: Nipmuc prehistoric Indian Exhibit; Colonial New England; Revolutionary & Civil War artifacts; historic relics and displays of Oxford's past & present.
Research Fields: genealogical searches done on request.
Facilities: library of Revolutionary & Civil War records, genealogy records, collection of Elliot P. Joslin, M.D., works of Clara Barton, Huguenot records & turn-of-the-century Oxford newspapers available for use on premises; meeting room.
Activities: guided tours with one week advanced request; formally organized education programs for children; permanent exhibitions; research assistance.
Publications: booklets, Historical Resources; Miss Clara Barton, Founder of the Red Cross; Dr. Elliott P. Joslin, World Renowned Physician in Diabetic Research.
Hours & Admission Prices: By appointment only. No charge; donations accepted. ♿
Attendance: 150 (estimated)

Paxton

FINE ARTS CENTER AT MIRIAM HALL, ANNA MARIA COLLEGE, 50 Sunset Lane, Paxton, MA 01612-1106. Tel.: 508-849-3300, ext. 442. Fax: 508-849-3408.
Web Site: www.annamaria.edu
Formerly: Moll Art Center, Anna Maria College
Founded: 1972.
Key Personnel: Dir. Art Programs, Alice Lambert.
Personnel Profile: Full-Time Paid 1; Part-Time Paid 10.
Governing Authority: private college; nonprofit. Parent Institution: Anna Maria College.
Art Gallery.
Collections: paintings; photographs; sculpture.
Facilities: art classrooms; photo lab.
Activities: formal education programs for students; rental gallery; senior art exhibit; student, faculty, & alumni exhibits; professional exhibits.
Hours & Admission Prices: Call for hours. No charge; donations accepted. Closed major holidays. ♿
Attendance: 600 (estimated)

Peabody

PEABODY HISTORICAL SOCIETY, (M), 35 Washington St., Peabody, MA 01960-5520. Tel.: 978-531-0805. Fax: 978-531-7292.
E-mail: phs_m@juno.com
Web Site: www.peabodyhistorical.org
Key Personnel: Pres., William Power; Vice Pres., Andrew Metropolis; Treas., Thomas Zellen; Cur., Heather Leavell.
Governing Authority: nonprofit organization.
Historical Society Museum: housed in the former home of General Gideon Foster from 1818-1831.
Collections: Peabody's history & heritage; period children's artifacts.
Facilities: Museum-related items for sale.
Activities: Annual Event: Dinner Meeting in May.
Hours & Admission Prices: Wed. 1-4; tours & other times by appointment. No charge.

Pembroke

PEMBROKE HISTORICAL SOCIETY, INC., 116 Center St., Pembroke, MA 02359. Mailing Address: P.O. Box 122, Pembroke, MA 02359-0239. Tel.: 781-293-9083.
E-mail: dtobin@townofpembrokemass.org
Web Site: www.townofpembrokemass.org/historicalsociety
Founded: 1950.
Congressional District: 10
Key Personnel: Pres. (V), Mark DiGiovanni; Vice Pres., Shannon Wilson; Treas., Suzanne Scroggins; Sec. & Co-Cur., Lauren Richmond; Co-Cur., Lynn Neacy; Research Dir., Karen Proctor.
Governing Authority: society.
Historical Society Museums.
Collections: tools; memorabilia & articles of Pembroke. Historic Buildings: 1685 Adah F. Hall Memorial House; School House; Friends Meeting House.
Research Fields: genealogy; local history.
Facilities: archives.
Activities: craft activities. Society Sponsors: annual Herring Fry; annual 5th Grade Children's Day.
Publications: quarterly newsletter.
Hours & Admission Prices: By appointment only. No charge; donations accepted.
Attendance: 200 (estimated)
Membership: Senior $5; Single & Individual $15; Family $20.

Petersham

FISHER MUSEUM OF FORESTRY, 326 N. Main St., Petersham, MA 01366-9504. Mailing Address: 324-326 N. Main St., Petersham, MA 01366. Tel.: 978-724-3302. Fax: 978-724-3595.
E-mail: jokeefe@fas.harvard.edu
Web Site: www.harvardforest.fas.harvard.edu/mus.html
Founded: 1908.
Congressional District: 1
Key Personnel: Dir. Harvard Forest, David R. Foster.
Governing Authority: university. Affiliated with Harvard University. Tax-exempt: 501(c)(3).
Forestry Museum.
Collections: historical & silviculture dioramas & case exhibits; history of land; forest ecology.
Research Fields: ecology; land-use history; effects of disturbances; ecophysiology; soils; paleoecology.
Facilities: 22,000-vol. library of forestry books & journals available for use on premises only; reading room; nature trails.
Activities: permanent & temporary exhibitions; audiovisual presentations; formally organized education programs for graduate & undergraduate students.
Publications: bulletins; papers.
Hours & Admission Prices: May-Oct. Mon.-Fri. 9-4, Sat.-Sun. 12-4; Nov.-April Mon.-Fri. 9-4. No charge; donations accepted. Closed holidays.

PETERSHAM HISTORICAL SOCIETY, INC., 10 N. Main St., Petersham, MA 01366-9500. Mailing Address: P.O. Box 364, Petersham, MA 01366-0364.
Founded: 1912.
Congressional District: 2
Key Personnel: Pres., James Baird.
Personnel Profile: Part-Time Volunteers 32.
Governing Authority: nonprofit organization. Branch Museum: Second East School, East St. Tax-exempt: 501(c)(3).
History Museum.
Collections: local genealogies; town & church records; local historical art by Nathan Negus, George Fuller, Erastus Salisbury Field, C. Frederick Bosworth, Caroline Negus Hildreth; file on Daniel Shays & Shays' Rebellion; local products; manuscript collections.
Research Fields: genealogy & local history.
Facilities: 850-vol. library of local history, genealogy, church & town papers available by appointment on premises.
Activities: guided tours; lectures; occasional informally organized educational programs; permanent & temporary exhibitions.
Publications: book, Song of the Swampland; map of Petersham; 225th anniversary address; Petersham Soldiers in the French & Indian War; semi-annual newsletter.
Hours & Admission Prices: April-Nov. Sun. 1-5, Mon.-Sat. by appointment. No charge; donations accepted.
Attendance: 400 (estimated)
Membership: Single $10; Family $20; Patron $50; Life $150.

Pittsfield

* **BERKSHIRE COUNTY HISTORICAL SOCIETY, INC. - ARROWHEAD, (M),** 780 Holmes Road, Pittsfield, MA 01201-7199. Tel.: 413-442-1793. Fax: 413-443-1449.
E-mail: melville@berkshire.net
Web Site: www.berkshirehistory.org
Founded: 1962.
Congressional District: 1
Key Personnel: C.E.O. & Museum Shop Mgr., Elizabeth Sherma; Pres. (V), Arthur Stein; Office Mgr., Judith Garrett.
Personnel Profile: Full-Time Paid 1; Part-Time Paid 4; Part-Time Volunteers 40.
Governing Authority: bd. of directors. Tax-exempt.
History House Museum: Arrowhead, home of Herman Melville, 1850-1863. A National Historic Landmark.
Collections: period furnishings; costumes; early industries; Berkshire County artifacts; decorative arts; archives; Herman Melville memorabilia; manuscripts.
Research Fields: Berkshire County political, economic, cultural, religious & social history; Herman Melville.
Facilities: 750-vol. library of books; 14,000 photographs; 500 linear feet of manuscripts, postcards, maps & atlases; historic barn with meeting place. Museum-related items for sale.
Activities: guided tours; lectures; field trips; gallery talks; formally organized educational programs; permanent & temporary exhibitions; special events.
Publications: quarterly newsletter.
Hours & Admission Prices: Society: Mon.-Fri. 9:30-4. Library & Archives: by appointment. Arrowhead: Memorial Day-Oct. Fri.-Wed. 10:30-4; other times by appointment. Adults $12, children 6-18 $8; discount to members; AASLH, NEMA, & BSHL members & children under 5 no charge. Closed New Year's Day; Easter; Thanksgiving; Christmas.
Attendance: 4,500 (accurate)
Membership: Individual $35; Family $50; Supporting $75; Sustaining $150; Donor $500; Patron $1,000.

BERKSHIRE MUSEUM, 39 South St., Pittsfield, MA 01201-6169. Tel.: 413-443-7171, ext.10. Fax: 413-443-2135.
E-mail: krawson@berkshiremuseum.org
Web Site: www.berkshiremuseum.org
Founded: 1903.
Congressional District: 1
Key Personnel: Exec. Dir., Stuart A. Chase; Dir. Finance, Jon C. Provost; Chm. (V), Mary Quith; Natural Science Program Mgr., Scott LaGrecha; Natural Science Program Mgr., Scott Gervis; Mgr. Collections, Leanne Hayden; Dir. Education & Programs, Maria Mingalone; Mgr. Advancement & Communications, Chris Hayden; Bldg. & Security Mgr., Brian Warner.
Personnel Profile: Full-Time Paid 21; Part-Time Paid 27; Part-Time Volunteers 191; Interns 5.
Governing Authority: nonprofit organization. Tax-exempt: 501(c)(3).
General Museum.
Collections: American 19th- & 20th-century paintings, sculpture, works on paper; British & European paintings; Greek, Roman, Chinese, Etruscan, Egyptian art; birds; shells; minerals; biological & paleontological specimens; scale model dinosaurs; tenth scale dioramas of animals of the world; fresh & salt water touch tank; vivaria; historical artifacts of Berkshire County; ethnographic collections including Native American & Pacific; global & local history,
Research Fields: American 19th- & 20th-century art; natural science.
Facilities: library; 250-seat auditorium with 35mm projector; classrooms. Museum-related gifts for sale.
Activities: docent tours; lectures; films; gallery talks; performing arts; formally organized education programs; permanent, temporary & traveling exhibitions; special events.
Publications: quarterly calendar; annual report.
Hours & Admission Prices: Mon.-Sat. 10-5, Sun. 12-5; docent tours by appointment. Adults $11, children 3-18 $6; discounts to AAM, ICOM & CNECM members; ASTC members, members & children under 3 no charge. Closed New Year's Day; Memorial Day; Independence Day; Labor Day; Thanksgiving; Christmas. ♿
Attendance: 85,000 (accurate)
Membership: Single $45; Dual $60; Family $75; Special Members $100-$500; Corporate Members $200 & up; Crane Society $1,000 & up.

* **HANCOCK SHAKER VILLAGE, INC., (M),** Rte. 20, W. Housatonic St., Pittsfield, MA 01202. Mailing Address: P.O. Box 927, Pittsfield, MA 01202-0927. Tel.: 413-443-0188. Fax: 413-447-9357.
E-mail: info@hancockshakervillage.org
Web Site: www.hancockshakervillage.org
Founded: 1960.
Congressional District: 1
Key Personnel: C.E.O. & Pres., Ellen Spear; Bd. Trustees Chm., William Vogt; Collections Mgr., Lesley Herzberg; Dir. Interpretation & Education, Todd Burdick.
Personnel Profile: Full-Time Paid 15; Part-Time Paid 30; Part-Time Volunteers 120; Interns 6.
Governing Authority: nonprofit organization. Tax-exempt: 501(c)(3).
Historic Village Museum: 21 buildings with constructions dating back to 1790.
Collections: furniture and artifacts of Shaker communities; agricultural tools & equipment; paintings; crafts; textiles; manuscripts.
Research Fields: Shakers; utopian & communal society studies; American folk art; architecture.
Facilities: 1,000-vol. library of books pertaining to the Shakers; restaurant. Shaker publications & gifts for sale.
Activities: guided tours; lectures; films; docent program; workshops; organized education programs; school for traditional crafts & trades.
Publications: newsletter; calendar of events; flyers; site brochure.
Hours & Admission Prices: Village & Galleries Guided Tours: Nov.-May. Adults $16.50; children no charge. Self-guided Tours: June-Oct. adults $16.50, youth 13-17 $8; discounts to AAM members; children under 12, museum employees & members no charge. Closed New Year's Day; Thanksgiving; Christmas. ♿
Attendance: 70,000 (accurate)
Membership: Individual $50; Family & Joint $75.

LICHTENSTEIN CENTER FOR THE ARTS, 28 Renne Ave., Pittsfield, MA 01201-4720. Tel.: 413-499-9348. Fax: 413-448-9811.
E-mail: berkart@taconic.net
Web Site: www.pittfield-ma.org
Founded: 1975.
Congressional District: 1
Key Personnel: Dir. Cultural Devel., Megan Whilden.
Personnel Profile: Full-Time Paid 2; Full-Time Volunteers 5; Part-Time Paid 12; Part-Time Volunteers 50; Interns 12.
Governing Authority: municipal; nonprofit. Parent Institution: City of Pittsfield. Subsidiary Institution: Friends of Berkshire Artisans, Inc. Tax-exempt: 501(c)(3).
Art Gallery: housed in the former factory building of William Stanley, inventor of alternating current and the birthplace of General Electric.
Collections: 9 photo-realistic public murals by Berkshire Artisans public mural team & Daniel Galvez; glass window by glass sculptor Thomas Patti; sculpture works by Lyn Horton & Brendan Stechenni.
Facilities: 52-vol. library for artists; workshops; darkroom; 37,000 sq. ft. exhibit space; 160-member writers room.
Activities: guided tours; lectures. Annual Event: First Night Pittsfield on New Year's Eve.
Publications: monthly newsletter, Back Street Notes; annual, Berkshire Review.
Hours & Admission Prices: Wed.-Sat. 12-5. No charge; donations accepted. Closed legal holidays. ♿
Attendance: 50,000
Membership: Individual $10; Family $25; Institution $50; Contributing $100; Supporting $200; Sustaining $500; Patron $1,000; Angel $5,000; Trustee $10,000.

Plymouth

HOWLAND HOUSE, 33 Sandwich St., Plymouth, MA 02360-3353. Tel.: 508-746-9590.
E-mail: mcharry@verizon.net
Web Site: www.pilgrimjohnhowlandsociety.org
Founded: 1897.
Congressional District: 10
Key Personnel: Pres. (V), Bradford Gorham; Museum Shop Mgr., Gail Dobbins.
Personnel Profile: Part-Time Paid 8; Part-Time Volunteers 1.
Governing Authority: nonprofit organization. Affiliated with the Pilgrim John Howland Society, Inc., 121 School St., Chelmsford, MA 01824. Tax-exempt: 501(c)(3).
Historic House Museum: 1667 Howland House.
Collections: period household furnishings; textiles; letters by Churchill & US Presidents.
Research Fields: artifacts from archaeological digs.
Facilities: Cards & guidebooks for sale.
Activities: guided tours.
Publications: booklet, The Howland Quarterly; The Pilgrim, John Howland Soc. Centennial Book.
Hours & Admission Prices: Daily 9-5. Tours 10-4:30. Adults $5, students, seniors & AAA members $4, children 6-12 $.75; discounts to AAA, AAM & ICOM members; members & children under 6 no charge.
Attendance: 1,999 (accurate)
Membership: Lineal descendants of Pilgrim John Howland: Annual, Marriage & Parentage $15; Entrance Membership Fee $20; Junior $25; Life $200.

THE JENNEY GRIST MILL, 6 Spring Lane, Plymouth, MA 02360-3400. Tel.: 508-747-4544, Fax: 508-747-5070.
E-mail: info@jenneygristmill.org
Web Site: www.jenneygristmill.org
Historic Site: established in 1636 by Pilgrim, John Jenney.
Collections: local history & culture.
Hours & Admission Prices: April-Nov. Mon., Wed. & Thurs.-Sat. 9:30-5, Sun. 12-5. Adults 13 & over $10, children 5-12 $8; children 4 & under no charge. Closed Easter; Thanksgiving.

MAYFLOWER SOCIETY MUSEUM, 4 Winslow St., Plymouth, MA 02360-3313. Mailing Address: 67 Bay Shore Dr., Plymouth, MA 02360-2085. Tel.: 508-746-2590.
Founded: 1897.
Key Personnel: Cur., Judith A. MacDonald.
Governing Authority: society. Affiliated with General Society of Mayflower Descendants. Tax-exempt: 501(c)(3).
Historic House: 1754 Mayflower Museum.
Collections: archives; history; 18th-century furnishings; manuscripts; quilts; needlepoint; antique fans; Staffordshire plates.
Facilities: genealogical library. Publications & museum-related items for sale.
Activities: guided tours; inter-museum loan & permanent exhibitions.
Publications: booklets, The Mayflower Society Quarterly; school materials.
Hours & Admission Prices: June & Sept. to mid-Oct. Fri.-Sun. 11-4; July-Aug. daily 11-4. Library: Mon.-Fri. 10-3:30. Museum: adults $4, senior citizens $3.50, children $1; discounts for special tours & AARP members; Plymouth residents & members no charge. Library: non-members $5 per day; members no charge. Closed holidays.
Attendance: 2,000 (estimated)

* **PILGRIM HALL MUSEUM, (M),** 75 Court St., Plymouth, MA 02360-3891. Tel.: 508-746-1620. Fax: 508-747-4228.
E-mail: pegbaker@pilgrimhall.org
Web Site: www.pilgrimhall.org
Founded: 1820.
Congressional District: 10
Key Personnel: C.E.O., Peggy M. Baker; Pres. (V), Barrie Young; Assoc. Dir. & Cur., Stephen C. O'Neill; Dir. Devel., Robin Nutter; Museum Shop Mgr., Ann Young.
Personnel Profile: Full-Time Paid 4; Part-Time Paid 7; Part-Time Volunteers 40.
Governing Authority: society. Parent Institution: The Pilgrim Society. Tax-exempt: 501(c)(3).
Historical Society & Museum.
Collections: fine & decorative arts; furniture; manuscripts; books; paintings; archeological artifacts.
Research Fields: Pilgrim history; Plymouth Colony; Town of Plymouth.
Facilities: library.
Activities: tours; lectures; permanent & temporary exhibitions; internships; research.
Publications: books; pamphlets.
Hours & Admission Prices: Feb.-Dec. 30 daily 9:30-4:30. Adults $7, senior citizens $6, children 5-17 $4; members no charge. Closed Christmas Day. ♿
Attendance: 25,000 (accurate)
Membership: Students & Senior Citizen $25; Individual $35; Family & Dual $45; Sustaining $100; Supporting $250; Patron $500; Life $1,000; Dual Life $1,500.

PLIMOTH PLANTATION INC., (M), 137 Warren Ave., Plymouth, MA 02360-2436. Mailing Address: Box 1620, Plymouth, MA 02362-1620. Tel.: 508-746-1622, ext. 8601. Fax: 508-746-3407.
E-mail: jmonac@plimoth.org
Web Site: www.plimoth.org
Founded: 1947.
Congressional District: 12
Key Personnel: Chm. (V), Stephen Brodeur, Jr.; C.E.O. & Exec. Dir., John McDonagh; C.O.O., Ivan Lipton; Dir. Museum Programs, Elizabeth Lodge; C.F.O., Richard Lamontagne; Museum Shop Mgr., Ellie Donovan.
Personnel Profile: Full-Time Paid 125; Part-Time Paid 45; Part-Time Volunteers 100; Interns 9.
Governing Authority: nonprofit organization. Subsidiary Institution: Mayflower II. Tax-exempt: 501(c)(3).
Outdoor Living History Museum.
Collections: archaeology; 17th-century English & Native American artifacts; house furnishings; tools; arms & armor; replica of the Mayflower ship; replica of 1627 Pilgrim Village & Wampanoag Homesite, including various costumes & furnishings; domestic livestock & horticultural practices of the period.
Research Fields: history of Plymouth Colony from 1620-1692; 17th-century English & Native American history & culture.
Facilities: 5,000-vol. library of imprints & manuscripts available for use by appointment; Craft Center; theatre; picnic area; Mayflower II. Books & museum-related items for sale. Period reproductions made for use on site and for sale.
Activities: lectures; films; demonstrations; re-creation, through first & third person interpretation, of daily life in 17th-century Plymouth; formally organized education programs for children, adults & undergraduate college students; temporary exhibits; outdoor period exhibits.
Publications: members newsletter; monographs; magazine, Plimoth Life.
Hours & Admission Prices: Mayflower II: April-Nov. daily 9-5. Adults $8, children 6-12 $6. Other sites: April-Nov. daily 9-5. Combination admission (ship & other sites): adults $25, seniors 62 & over $22; children 6-12 $15. Other sites (HomeSite, Village, Crafts Center & Visitor Center Exhibits: adults $21, seniors $19, children 6-12 $12; discount to groups; members, AAM members, Massachusetts Teacher's Association & children under 5 no charge.
Attendance: 350,000 (estimated)
Membership: Individual $40; One Plus One $55; Family $95; Contributing $135; Supporting $175; Benefactor $500; Life $3,000.

PLYMOUTH ANTIQUARIAN SOCIETY, 126 Water St., Plymouth, MA 02360. Mailing Address: Box 3773, Plymouth, MA 02361-3773. Tel.: 508-746-0012. Fax: 508-746-7908.
E-mail: pasm@verizon.net
Web Site: www.plymouthantiquariansociety.org
Founded: 1919.
Congressional District: 9
Key Personnel: Exec. Dir., Donna D. Curtin; Pres., Marilyn L. Angley.
Personnel Profile: Full-Time Paid 1; Part-Time Paid 4; Part-Time Volunteers 50.
Governing Authority: nonprofit. Tax-exempt: 501(c)(3).
Historic Houses: 1677 Harlow Fort House; 1747 Spooner House; 1809 Hedge House.
Collections: 17th-, 18th- & 19th-century furnishings, dolls, quilts; Chinese export porcelain; fans; toys; costumes, textiles.
Research Fields: 17th-, 18th-, 19th-century family lifestyles; decorative arts, costumes, & textiles; local history after the Pilgrims.
Facilities: 17th-century craft classrooms; garden. Gift items for sale.
Activities: guided tours; changing exhibits; heritage craft demonstrations; education programs; 17th-century household arts program for children; lecture series; special events.
Publications: book, The Plymouth Colony Cook Book; The Peregrinations of Plymouth Rock; brochures; newsletter.
Hours & Admission Prices: 1809 Hedge House: Wed.-Sun. 2-6. 1607 Harlow House: Thurs. 1-4; tour groups by appointment. Adults $5, children $2; discount to AAA members; members & Plymouth residents no charge.
Attendance: 3,000 (estimated)
Membership: Individual $25; Family $40; Life $500.

RICHARD SPARROW HOUSE INC., 42 Summer St., Plymouth, MA 02360-3456. Tel.: 508-747-1240. Fax: 508-746-9521.
E-mail: director@sparrowhouse.com
Web Site: www.sparrowhouse.com
Founded: 1961.
Congressional District: 10
Key Personnel: Dir. & Museum Shop Mgr., Lois Atherton; Pres. (V), Violet Berry.
Personnel Profile: Full-Time Paid 1; Full-Time Volunteers 1; Part-Time Paid 2; Part-Time Volunteers 2.
Governing Authority: nonprofit organization. Tax-exempt.
Historic House Museum: 1640 Richard Sparrow House; a half house with cross-summer beam construction, the house is the oldest in Plymouth. The adjoining 1720 half house, houses a craft shop, supporting local crafts.
Collections: 17th-century decorative arts.
Activities: guided tours. Museum Sponsors: pottery classes.
Publications: brochure.
Hours & Admission Prices: Daily 10-5. Adults $2, children $1.
Attendance: 4,000 (estimated)
Membership: Annual & Individual $10 & $25.

Provincetown

PILGRIM MONUMENT AND PROVINCETOWN MUSEUM, One High Pole Hill Rd., Provincetown, MA 02657. Mailing Address: P.O. Box 1125, Provincetown, MA 02657-1125. Tel.: 508-487-1310. Fax: 508-487-4702.
E-mail: info@pilgrim-monument.org
Web Site: www.pilgrim-monument.org
Formerly: Cape Cod Pilgrim Memorial Association
Founded: 1892.
Congressional District: 13
Key Personnel: Pres., Charles Silva; Exec. Dir., Jim Bakker; Museum Shop Mgr., Bobo Hino.
Personnel Profile: Full-Time Paid 4; Part-Time Paid 10; Part-Time Volunteers 25.
Governing Authority: nonprofit organization. Parent Institution: Cape Cod Pilgrim Memorial Association. Tax-exempt: 501(c)(3).
History Museum: located on the site of the 1907-10, Pilgrim Monument.
Collections: Mayflower pilgrims; whaling; fishing; Arctic Colonial & Victorian home items; theater history; exploration; pirate treasures; marine archaeology & shipwrecks; archives; photographs.
Research Fields: Mayflower family genealogies; Provincetown artists; local history; shipwrecks; civic organizations; Admiral McMillan's papers.
Facilities: 450-vol. library; gardens; conservation lab on exhibit; picnic area. Museum-related items for sale.
Activities: lectures; annual Lighting of the Monument; educational tours; walking tours.
Publications: Provincetown Classics in History, Literature & Art; newsletter; annual report.
Hours & Admission Prices: April-May & mid-Sept to Nov. daily 9-5; June-Sept. 15 daily 9-7. Adults $7, senior citizens 62 & over and students 15 & over with ID $5, youths 4-14 $3.50; discounts to MTA members & groups; children 3 and under no charge. ♿
Attendance: 65,000 (accurate)
Membership: Individual $35; Family $55; Business $100.

* **PROVINCETOWN ART ASSOCIATION AND MUSEUM, (M),** 460 Commercial St., Provincetown, MA 02657-2415. Tel.: 508-487-1750. Fax: 508-487-4372.
E-mail: info@paam.org
Web Site: www.paam.org
Founded: 1914.
Congressional District: 10
Key Personnel: C.E.O., Christine McCarthy; Pres. (V), Richard Wurtman; Asst. Dir. & Registrar, Peter Macara; Archivist, James Zimmerman; Education Coord., Lynn Stanley; Bookkeeper, Steven Roderick; Bldg. & Grounds, Mike Wright.
Personnel Profile: Full-Time Paid 5; Part-Time Paid 7; Part-Time Volunteers 205; Interns 4.
Governing Authority: bd. of trustees. Tax-exempt: 501(c)(3).
Art Museum.
Collections: 3,000 works of art; early Provincetown painters; emphasis on regional, national & international artists related to Provincetown.
Major Exhibits: Robert Fisher, Spring 2010; Anne Peretz, 7/10; Jack Tworkov, 8/10; Edward Hopper Drawings, 9/10.
Research Fields: history of the arts in Provincetown & area.
Facilities: 1,200-vol. library of art books & magazines available for use by membership; studio classrooms. Museum-related items for sale.
Activities: lectures; films; concerts; art classes for children & adults; art festivals; symposiums; formally organized educational programs; inter-museum loan, permanent, temporary & traveling exhibitions; consignment auction; rental facility.
Publications: exhibition catalogs; catalog of the permanent collection; members' newsletters.
Hours & Admission Prices: Memorial Day to Sept. Mon.-Thurs. 11-8, Fri. 11-10, Sat.-Sun. 11-5; Oct.-April Thurs.-Sun. 12-5. Adults $5; discounts to AAM & ICOM members; members & children under 12 no charge. ♿
Attendance: 52,000 (estimated)
Membership: Individual $50; Dual $85; Family $100; Corporate $250; Benefactor $1,000 & up.

Quincy

ADAMS NATIONAL HISTORICAL PARK, 135 Adams St., Quincy, MA 02169-1749. Tel.: 617-773-1177 & 770-1175. Fax: 617-472-7562.
E-mail: adam_visitor_center@nps.gov
Web Site: www.nps.gov/adam
Founded: 1927.
Congressional District: 11
Key Personnel: Supt., Marianne Peak; Cur., Kelly Cobble.
Personnel Profile: Full-Time Paid 15; Part-Time Paid 16; Part-Time Volunteers 18.
Governing Authority: federal. Parent Institution: National Park Service. Branch Museums: John Adams & John Quincy Adams Birthplaces, 133-141 Franklin St., Quincy, MA 02169. Off-Site Visitor Center, 1250 Hancock St., Quincy, MA. Tax-exempt: 501(c)(3).
History Museum: housed in 1731 Adams family home.
Collections: paintings; sculpture; graphics; decorative arts; glass; numismatic. Historic Houses: 1870 stone library; 1873 carriage house.
Research Fields: history.
Facilities: 14,000-vol. library of historic books.
Activities: guided tours; lectures; permanent exhibitions; concerts; symposiums.
Publications: pamphlets, Adams National Historic Site; Grounds & Gardens. booklet, A Family's Legacy to America.
Hours & Admission Prices: April 19-Nov. 10 daily 9-5. Adults $5; children 16 & under no charge when accompanied by an adult; Golden Eagle, Golden Access & Golden Age passports honored. Tours begin at Visitor Center. ♿
Attendance: 185,000 (estimated)
Membership: Park Pass Annual Fee $10.

ADAMS NATIONAL HISTORICAL PARK-JOHN ADAMS AND JOHN QUINCY ADAMS BIRTHPLACES, 133-141 Franklin St., Quincy, MA 02269. Mailing Address: 135 Adams St., Quincy, MA 02169-1749. Tel.: 617-773-1177 & 770-1175. Fax: 617-847-3015.
Web Site: www.nps.gov/adam
Founded: 1897.
Congressional District: 11
Key Personnel: Supt., Marianne Peak; Cur., Kelly Cobble.
Personnel Profile: Full-Time Paid 15; Part-Time Paid 16; Part-Time Volunteers 18.
Governing Authority: federal. National Park Service. Tax-exempt: 501(c)(3).

History Museum: housed in early 18th-century New England saltbox houses.
Collections: reproduction furnishings representing the lifestyles of the Adams family from the periods 1764-1784 & 1805-1807.
Research Fields: history; architecture.
Activities: guided tours.
Publications: pamphlet, John Adams & John Quincy Adams Birthplaces.
Hours & Admission Prices: April 19-Nov. 10 daily 9-5. Adults $5; Golden Eagle, Golden Age, Golden Access & children under 16 no charge. ♿
Attendance: 169,000 (accurate)
Membership: Park Pass Annual Fee $10.

JOSIAH QUINCY HOUSE, 20 Muirhead St., Quincy, MA 02170. Mailing Address: 141 Cambridge St., Boston, MA 02114-2702. Tel.: 617-227-3956. Fax: 617-227-9204.
Web Site: www.historicnewengland.org
Founded: 1937.
Congressional District: 11
Key Personnel: Pres., Carl Nold; Site Mgr., Leah Walczak.
Governing Authority: society; nonprofit organization. Parent Institution: Historic New England, 141 Cambridge St. Boston 02114. Tel.: 617-227-3956. Tax-exempt: 501(c)(3).
Historic House: built in 1770 by Revolutionary War Colonel Josiah Quincy. The family produced three mayors of Boston & president of Harvard University.
Collections: period wall paneling & fireplaces; Quincy family furniture & memorabilia.
Activities: private heritage tours available with reservations; school programs.
Hours & Admission Prices: Call for hours & appointment. Adults $5; members no charge.
Attendance: 673 (accurate)
Membership: National $35; Individual $45; Household $55; Garden & Landscape $75; Institutional $85; Contributing $100; Historic Homeowner $200; Supporting $250.

QUINCY HISTORICAL SOCIETY, Adams Academy Bldg., 8 Adams St., Quincy, MA 02169-2002. Tel.: 617-773-1144. Fax: 617-773-1872.
E-mail: info@quincyhistory.org
Web Site: quincyhistory.org
Founded: 1893.
Congressional District: 10
Key Personnel: Pres. (V), James P. Edwards; Exec. Dir., Edward Fitzgerald, Ph.D.
Governing Authority: society. Tax-exempt: 501(c)(3).
Historical Museum: housed in 1872 Adams Academy building.
Collections: local artifacts & memorabilia; Quincy history from Native Americans to Howard Johnson's ice cream.
Research Fields: regional history; genealogy; shipbuilding; granite industry; Adams family.
Facilities: 10,000-vol. library of regional history books, pamphlets, manuscripts, maps & photographs.
Activities: guided tours; permanent & changing exhibitions; educational & cultural programs; research & publishing; intern program for college students.
Publications: books, Descendants of Edmund Quincy; Calendar of the Papers of General Joseph Palmer 1716-1788; Index to 350 Years of Quincy; The Birthplaces of Presidents John & John Quincy Adams; Wollaston of Mount Wollaston; New Beginnings-Quincy & Norfolk County; The Braintree Iron Works; Quincy's Legacy: Topics from Four Centuries of Massachusetts History; biannual periodical, Quincy History.
Hours & Admission Prices: April 14-Nov. 10 Mon.-Fri. 9-4, Sat. 12-3; mid-Nov. to mid-April Mon.-Fri. 9-4. Adults $3, seniors $1.50; members & children under 14 no charge. ♿
Membership: Student $10; Single $25; Family $35; Friend $50; Patron $100.

UNITED STATES NAVAL SHIPBUILDING MUSEUM, 739 Washington St., Quincy, MA 02169-7330. Tel.: 617-479-7900. Fax: 617-479-8792.
Web Site: www.uss-salem.org
Naval Museum: housed aboard the USS Salem which served a 10 year career as flagship of the US Sixth Fleet in the Mediterranean and the Second Fleet in the Atlantic.
Collections: US history of shipbuilding & naval duty; U.S. Navy Cruiser Sailors Memorial; USS Salem Memorial; USS Newport News Memorial, USS Saint Paul Memorial; U.S. Navy SEALs; photographs; uniforms.
Activities: group tours; birthday parties; special functions; overnight adventure program; reunions; retirements.
Hours & Admission Prices: Sat.-Sun. 10-5; groups of 10 or more by appointment. Adults $5; children 3 & under no charge.

Reading

PARKER TAVERN, 103 Washington St., Reading, MA 01867-3523. Mailing Address: Reading Antiquarian Soc., P.O. Box 842, Reading, MA 01867.
Web Site: parkertavern.org
Founded: 1916.
Congressional District: 7
Key Personnel: Pres. (V), Alan Ulrich.
Personnel Profile: Part-Time Volunteers 6.
Governing Authority: society. Reading Antiquarian Society, P.O. Box 842, Reading, MA 01867. Tax-exempt: 501(c)(3).
History Museum: housed in 1694 Parker Tavern, saltbox style house. Headquarters for Scotch Highlanders prisoners of war during the American Revolution.
Collections: Reading artifacts; Reading history; house furnishings; manuscripts;
Research Fields: local history.
Activities: guided tours; lectures; permanent & temporary exhibitions; school loan service.
Hours & Admission Prices: May-Oct. Sun. 2-5. No charge; donations accepted.
Attendance: 700 (estimated)
Membership: Child $2; Adult $8; Couple $10.

Rehoboth

CARPENTER MUSEUM, 4 Locust St., Rehoboth, MA 02769-2321. Mailing Address: P.O. Box 2, Rehoboth, MA 02769-0002. Tel.: 508-252-3031.
E-mail: carpentermuseum@verizon.net
Web Site: www.carpentermuseum.org
Key Personnel: Dir., Stacey Garretson.
Governing Authority: Parent Institution: Rehoboth Antiquarian Society. Tax-exempt.
History Museum.
Collections: Rehoboth history; portraits; Civil War letters; period artifacts; Peregrine White Clock; Mason Barney Shipyard diorama; personal artifacts.
Activities: internships; lecture series. Museum Sponsors: Historic Treasure Hunt.
Publications: newsletter.
Hours & Admission Prices: March-Nov. Sun. 2-4; other times by appointment. No charge; donations accepted. ♿
Membership: Individual $15; Family $20.

Rockport

ROCKPORT ART ASSOCIATION, (M), 12 Main St., Rockport, MA 01966-1594. Tel.: 978-546-6604. Fax: 978-546-9767.
E-mail: rockportart@verizon.net
Web Site: www.rockportartassn.org
Founded: 1921.
Congressional District: 12
Key Personnel: Exec. Dir., Carol Linsky; Pres. (V), Judi Rotenberg.
Personnel Profile: Full-Time Paid 3; Part-Time Paid 4; Part-Time Volunteers 4.
Governing Authority: nonprofit organization. Tax-exempt: 501(c)(3).
Arts Center.
Collections: Cape Ann, Massachusetts artists; paintings; graphics; sculpture; photographs. Historic Building: 1787 The Old Tavern.
Research Fields: RAA members past & present; Cape Ann artists.
Facilities: 500-vol. library of art books available for use on premises by members only; studio. Cards, reproductions, publications & postcards for sale.
Activities: community events; lectures; gallery talks; concerts; member & invitational exhibits; painting classes for children & adults; sketch groups for adults; adult workshops. Association Sponsors: annual fine arts auction; annual Nativity Pageant.
Publications: quarterly, Newsletter & Calendar of Activities; annual, Catalog of Exhibitions; book, Artists of the Rockport Art Association.
Hours & Admission Prices: Feb.-April Wed.-Fri. 10-4, Sat. 10-5, Sun. 12-5; May Tues.-Fri. 10-4, Sat. 10-5, Sun. 12-5; June to Columbus Day Mon.-Sat. 10-5, Sun. 12-5; Oct.-Dec. Tues.-Sat. 10-4, Sun. 12-5. No charge; donations accepted. Closed New Year's Day; Veterans Day; Thanksgiving; Christmas.
Attendance: 50,000
Membership: Youth $10; Senior Citizens over 65 $30; Associate $40; Family $75; Patron $150; Business $250; Donor $500.

SANDY BAY HISTORICAL SOCIETY & MUSEUMS, INC., 40 King St., Rockport, MA 01966-1460. Mailing Address: P.O. Box 63, Rockport, MA 01966-0063. Tel.: 978-546-9533.
E-mail: info@sandybayhistorical.org
Web Site: www.sandybayhistorical.org

Founded: 1925.
Congressional District: 6
Key Personnel: C.E.O., Ingrid Brown.
Governing Authority: society. Tax-exempt: 501(c)(3).
History Museum.
Collections: local history; glass; Indian artifacts; the Hannah Jumper display; Dogtown relics; dolls; toys; granite quarry artifacts; marine; industrial; archaeology; furniture; glass photographic plates; arts; manuscripts. Historic Buildings: 1832 Sewall-Scripture House & 1711 First Period Salt Box The Old Castle.
Research Fields: Rockport & Cape Ann history.
Facilities: 350-vol. library of books, pamphlets, newspapers & clippings on Cape Ann history available for use by arrangement with the curator; reading room.
Activities: guided tours; lectures; permanent & temporary exhibitions.
Publications: books, Town on Sandy Bay; Planters Plea; Rockport as it Was; Pigeon Cove its early Settlers & Their Farms 1702-1840; A Book of Pictures; booklet, Thacher's Woe & Avery's Fall; Fish, Timber, Granite & Gold; O Rare Harrison Cady.
Hours & Admission Prices: mid-June to mid-Sept. Mon.-Sat. 2-5; other times by appointment. Admission $5; members no charge.
Attendance: 800
Membership: Annual $10; Family $15; Sustaining $25; Life $150.

Rowe

THE KEMP-MCCARTHY MEMORIAL MUSEUM OF THE ROWE HISTORICAL SOCIETY, INC., (M), 288 Zoar Rd., Rowe, MA 01367-9774. Tel.: 413-339-4238.
Founded: 1963.
Congressional District: 1
Key Personnel: Pres., Susan Gleason; Vice Pres., Roger Brown; Sec., Jo-Ann Brown; Treas., Heidi Cousineau; Museum Cur., Alan Bjork.
Governing Authority: society; bd. of trustees. Tax-exempt.
Historical Society Museum.
Collections: Revolutionary era furnishings; town history, its people & their way of life; artifacts; research files; manuscripts. Historic Structures: 1785 one-room schoolhouse; 1835 one-room schoolhouse.
Research Fields: local history & genealogy.
Facilities: meeting room.
Activities: guided tours; permanent & temporary exhibitions.
Publications: quarterly booklet, The Bulletin; books: History of Davis Mine, Story of Myrifield, Geologic History of Rowe.
Hours & Admission Prices: July to 3rd Sun. Oct. 2-5; other times by appointment. No charge. ♿
Attendance: 300 (estimated)
Membership: Junior (18 & under) $2.50; Adult (One Year) $5; Adult (Three Years) $14; Contributing $25; Life $35.

Rowley

ROWLEY HISTORICAL SOCIETY, 233 Main St., Rowley, MA 01969-1503. Mailing Address: P.O. Box 41, Rowley, MA 01969-0041. Tel.: 978-948-7483.
E-mail: info@rowleyhistory.org
Web Site: www.rowleyhistory.org
Founded: 1918.
Congressional District: 6
Key Personnel: Pres., Jack Farrell; Vice Pres., William Cousins; Sec., Kathleen Cousins; Treas., Elizabeth Hicken; Museum Shop Mgr., Shirley G. Todd.
Personnel Profile: Part-Time Volunteers 20.
Governing Authority: society. Tax-exempt.
Historical Building/Site Society Museum.
Collections: old English garden; toys; furniture & furnishings of early America. Historic Houses: 1677 Platt-Bradstreet House; 1830 shoe shop; c.1775 barn contains saws, planes, ice cutting equipment & farm utensils.
Activities: guided tours; social functions.
Publications: member newsletters.
Hours & Admission Prices: By appointment only, call 978-948-2858. Donation $4; children under 12 & members no charge.
Membership: Student & Senior $7.50; Annual $10; Family $20; Life $100.

Roxbury

ROXBURY HERITAGE STATE PARK, 183 Roxbury St., John Eliot Sq., Roxbury, MA 02119-1525. Tel.: 617-445-3399. Fax: 617-445-5883.
E-mail: antonio.menefee@state.ma.us
Web Site: www.mass.gov/dcr/parks/metroboston/rxhp.htm
Founded: 1901.
Congressional District: 9
Key Personnel: Dir., Antonio Menefee.
Personnel Profile: Full-Time Paid 3.
Governing Authority: society; nonprofit organization. Parent Institution: Massachusetts Dept. of Environmental Management. Tax-exempt: 501(c)(3).
History Museum: housed in 1750 Dillaway-Thomas House.
Collections: archives; history; military; photographs of Roxbury. Historic Site: Pulpit Rock.
Research Fields: history.
Facilities: 200-vol. library of books on Roxbury history available for use by appointment.
Activities: lectures; temporary exhibitions; guided tours; consultations.
Publications: newsletter.
Hours & Admission Prices: Pulpit Rock by reservation only. No charge. Dillaway-Thomas House: Tues. & Sat. 10-5; other times by appointment. No charge. Guided walking tours of Roxbury by appointment only. ♿
Attendance: 20,000 (estimated)

Salem

40 WHACKS MUSEUM: THE LIZZIE BORDEN STORY, 203 Essex St., Salem, MA 01970-3727. Tel.: 978-666-4416. Fax: 978-666-4378.
Web Site: www.40whacksmuseum.com
Formerly: The True Story of Lizzie Borden
Key Personnel: Owner, Leonard Pickel; Owner, Jeanne Escher-Pickel; Owner, John Trigg; Owner, Shelia Trigg
History Museum.
Collections: history of the murder of Abby & Andrew Borden on Aug. 4, 1892; trial & acquittal of their daughter, Lizzie Borden; photographs.
Facilities: Museum-related items for sale.
Activities: special events.
Hours & Admission Prices: June-Sept. & Nov. daily 11-6:30; Oct. Mon.-Thurs. 11-6:30, Fri.-Sun. 10-8:30. Adults $10, seniors 65 & over $9, children 8-12 $6; discounts to groups of 10 or more; children under 8 no charge.

THE HOUSE OF THE SEVEN GABLES, 115 Derby St., Salem, MA 01970-5640. Tel.: 978-744-0991. Fax: 978-741-4350. TTY: 978-745-5391.
E-mail: clare@7gables.org
Web Site: www.7gables.org
Founded: 1910.
Congressional District: 6
Key Personnel: Exec. Dir., Anita D. Blackaby; Dir. Settlement, Karen Pelletier; Finance Mgr., Sandra Goren-Fotheringham; Museum Store Dir., Andrea Lombardi.
Personnel Profile: Full-Time Paid 25; Part-Time Paid 20; Part-Time Volunteers 30; Interns 1.
Governing Authority: nonprofit organization. Tax-exempt: 501(c)(3).
Historic Museum Site: located on Salem Harbor, this 2.5 acre area includes five original historic structures representing 17th-, 18th- and 19th-century architecture, Nathaniel Hawthorne and the lives of the people who lived on site.
Collections: furnishings; period artifacts; manuscripts. Historic Houses: 1668 The House of the Seven Gables; 1655 Retire Beckett House; 1682 Hathaway House; c.1750 Nathaniel Hawthorne's birthplace; 1830 Sea Captain's Counting House.
Research Fields: 17th-century architecture; early American decorative arts; Nathaniel Hawthorne; social history.
Facilities: visitor center; colonial gardens; garden cafe. Museum-related items for sale.
Activities: guided tours; teacher preparation kits for school groups. Museum Sponsors: theatrical programs in October and December.
Publications: The House of Seven Gables; Chronicle of Three Old Houses.
Hours & Admission Prices: Jan. 18-June & Nov.-Dec. daily 10-5; July-Oct. daily 10-7. Adults $12, children 5-12 $7.25; discounts to seniors, AAA, NEMA & AAM members; members & children under 6 no charge. Closed New Year's Day; Thanksgiving; Christmas. ♿
Attendance: 125,000 (accurate)
Membership: Senior Citizen & Student $30; Individual $45; Senior Couple $50; Family $65; Patron $150; Benefactor $250; President's Circle $500; Caroline Osgood Emmerton Society $1,000.

NEW ENGLAND PIRATE MUSEUM, 274 Derby St., Salem, MA 01970-3635. Tel.: 978-741-2800. Fax: 978-741-2902.
E-mail: salemwitchpirate@aol.com
Web Site: www.piratemuseum.com
History Museum.
Collections: New England pirate history; pirate treasures; pirate captains including Kidd, Blackbeard, Bellamy & Quelch.
Activities: school programs; walking tours include recreated dockside village, board a pirate ship, & bat cave. Annual Event: Haunted Happenings in October.
Hours & Admission Prices: April & Nov. Sat.-Sun. 10-5; May-Oct. daily 10-5.

Haunted Happenings: extended hours. Adults $8, senior citizens 65 & over $7, children 4-13 $6; discount to groups. ♿

* **PEABODY ESSEX MUSEUM, (M),** E. India Sq., Salem, MA 01970-3783. Mailing Address: 161 Essex St., Salem, MA 01970-3783. Tel.: 978-745-1876 & 9500.
E-mail: pem@pem.org
Web Site: pem.org
Founded: 1799.
Congressional District: 6
Key Personnel: Exec. Dir. & C.E.O., Dan L. Monroe; Chm. (V), Richard C. Carlson; Pres. (V), Robert N. Shapiro; Deputy Dir., Josh Basseches; Chief Cur., Lynda Roscoe Hartigan; Chief Mktg. Officer, Jay Finney; Chief Philanthropy Officer, Chris Reaske; Dir. Education & Interpretation, Peggy Fogelman; Dir. Facilities & Security, Robert Monk; Mgr. Public Rels., April Swieconek; Cur. South Asian & Korean Art, Dr. Susan Bean; H.A. Crosby Forbes Cur. Asian Export Art, Karina Corrigan; Sarah Frasier Robbins Dir. Art & Nature Center and Cur. Natural History, Jane Winchell; Carolyn & Peter Lynch Cur. American Decorative Art, Dean Lahikainen; Russell W. Knight Cur. Maritime Art & History, Dr. Daniel Finamore; Cur. Chinese Art, Dr. Nancy Berliner; Assoc. Cur. Native American Art, Karen Kramer Russell; Dir. Merchandising, Lynne Francis-Lunn; Ann C. Pingree Dir. The Phillips Library, Sidney E. Berger; Dir. Museum Collection Svcs., William Phippen; Dir. Exhibition Design, Fred Johnson; Head Registrar, Claudine Scoville.
Personnel Profile: Full-Time Paid 102; Full-Time Volunteers 1; Part-Time Paid 163; Part-Time Volunteers 120; Interns 30.
Governing Authority: nonprofit organization. Tax-exempt: 501(c)(3) & 170(b)(1)(A).
General Museum.
Collections: American art; Asian export art; African, Chinese, Japanese, Korean, Oceanic, Native American, Indian, & contemporary art; photography; textiles, costumes; natural history; maritime history & art; historic houses.
Major Exhibits: Fiery Pool: Maya and the Mythic Sea (T), 3/10-7/10; Mark Ruwedel: Foot Steps, 9/10-11/10; Treasures of the Qianlong Emperor (T), 9/10-1/11.
Research Fields: maritime art & history; Asian export art; Pacific ethnology; ethnic & folk art; American decorative art, architecture & history 17th century-present; North American archaeology; Chinese art; Indian art; photography.
Facilities: 400,000-vol. research library; reading room; 250-seat auditorium; classrooms; 93,000 sq. ft. exhibit space; gardens.
Activities: guided tours; lectures; gallery talks; educational programs; permanent & temporary exhibitions; outreach programs; special school tours; concerts; family festivals.
Publications: exhibitions & collections catalogues; books; monographic books & pamphlets; monthly members magazine.
Hours & Admission Prices: Daily 10-5. Historic House Tours (Ward, Crowninshield-Bentley, Gardner-Pingree) daily. Adults $15, seniors $13, students $11; discounts to AAM, ICOM & NEMA members; members, youth 16 & under and Salem residents no charge. Chinese House: adults $4. Closed New Year's Day; Thanksgiving; Christmas. ♿
Attendance: 189,000 (accurate)
Membership: Student $40; Senior & Outside New England $50; Individual $60; Dual Senior $85; Dual $90; Family $95; Sponsor $180; Patron $350; Benefactor $600.

PHILLIPS HOUSE, 34 Chestnut St., Salem, MA 01970-3129. Mailing Address: 141 Cambridge St., Boston, MA 02114-2702. Tel.: 978-744-0440. Fax: 978-740-1086.
E-mail: info@phillipsmuseum.org
Web Site: www.historicnewengland.org
Key Personnel: Pres., Carl Nold; Site Mgr., Julie Arrison.
Governing Authority: private; nonprofit organization. Parent Institution: Historic New England, 141 Cambridge St., Boston, MA. Tax-exempt: 501(c)(3).
Historic House Museum: housed in a Federal style mansion, c.1821.
Collections: Federal era furniture; Chinese export porcelain; ship portraits; film archives; artifacts from the Phillips' extensive travels including Fiji throwing clubs, African wood carvings & Native American pottery; oriental carpets; period cars & carriages. Historic Building: brick carriage house.
Facilities: Museum-related items for sale.
Activities: films; guided tours; special events; lectures. Annual Event: Antique Vehicle Meet.
Publications: monthly newsletter, What's Happening; magazine, Historic New England.
Hours & Admission Prices: June-Oct. Tues.-Sun. 11-4; Nov.-May Sat.-Sun. 11-4. Adults $5; members no charge.
Attendance: 4,571 (accurate)

Membership: National $35; Individual $45; Household $55; Garden & Landscape $75; Institutional $85; Contributing $100; Historic Homeowner $200; Supporting $250.

SALEM MARITIME NATIONAL HISTORIC SITE, 160 Derby St., Salem, MA 01970-5643. Tel.: 978-740-1680. Fax: 978-740-1685.
E-mail: sama_orientation_center@nps.gov
Web Site: www.nps.gov/sama
Founded: 1937.
Congressional District: 6
Key Personnel: Supt., Patricia S. Trap; Museum Cur., David Kayser; Chm. (V), Curtis White; Chief of Visitor Svcs., Peter LaChapelle.
Personnel Profile: Full-Time Paid 25; Part-Time Paid 12; Part-Time Volunteers 70; Interns 1.
Governing Authority: federal government. Parent Institution: National Park Service. Tax-exempt.
Maritime, Commerce & World Trade Site: located on 9 acres on Salem Harbor.
Collections: Custom House: mid to late 19th-century office furniture & supplies; 19th-century documents. Public Stores & Scale House: mid to late 19th-century Customs equip. for weighing, measuring & inspecting cargo; trade items. Derby house: late 18th-century furniture; Derby family portraits. Narbonne house: archaeological fragments from the 17th-20th century. Historic Buildings: 1765 Derby wharf; 1790 Central wharf; 1819 Custom house; 1819 Bonded warehouse; 1829 Scale house; c.1800 West India goods store. Historic Houses: 1761 Derby house; 1675 Narbonne house; 1780 Hawkes house.
Research Fields: commercial maritime history, particularly from the Revolutionary War through the War of 1812.
Facilities: 1,200-vol. library on maritime history available on premises. Postcards, maritime history publications & environmental publications for sale.
Activities: guided tours; 17-min. video program; permanent & temporary exhibits; interpretive programs; scheduled programs for school & special interest groups.
Publications: handbook, Maritime Salem in the Age of Sail.
Hours & Admission Prices: Daily 9-5. No charge; donations accepted. Guided tours $5. Closed New Year's Day; Thanksgiving; Christmas. ♿
Attendance: 652,000 (estimated)

SALEM WITCH MUSEUM, 19 1/2 Washington Sq. N., Salem, MA 01970-4096. Tel.: 978-744-1692. Fax: 978-745-4414.
E-mail: faq@salemwitchmuseum.com
Web Site: www.salemwitchmuseum.com
Founded: 1972.
Congressional District: 6
Key Personnel: C.E.O. & Public Rels., Bruce P. Michaud; Dir., Tina Jordan; Education, Alison D'Amario; Dir. Sales., Merry Ward.
Personnel Profile: Full-Time Paid 15; Part-Time Paid 30.
Governing Authority: individual operation; organized for profit.
History Museum.
Collections: history of witches, witchcraft, witch hunts & witch trials.
Facilities: 125-seat theater. Books & gift items for sale.
Activities: broadcast/cable programs; organized education programs for children; training programs for professional museum workers. Museum Sponsors: Haunted Happenings.
Hours & Admission Prices: July-Aug. daily 10-7; Sept.-June daily 10-5. Call for admission prices, discount to AAM members & groups. Closed New Year's Day; Thanksgiving; Christmas. ♿
Attendance: 400,000

Sandwich

* **HERITAGE MUSEUMS & GARDENS,** 67 Grove St., Sandwich, MA 02563-2110. Tel.: 508-888-3300. Fax: 508-888-9535.
E-mail: info@heritagemuseums.org
Web Site: www.heritagemuseumsandgardens.org
Formerly: Heritage Plantation of Sandwich
Founded: 1969.
Congressional District: 10
Key Personnel: Exec. Dir., Dr. Scott T. Swank; Chm. (V) Bd. Trustees, Linda Calmes Jones; Deputy Dir. External Affairs, Wendy Perry; Financial Mgr. & Museum Shop Mgr., Jackie Crosby; Dir. Education, Heather Mead; Dir. Collections, Jennifer Madden; Cur. Living Collections, Jean Gillis; Dir. Mktg., Judith I. Selleck.
Personnel Profile: Full-Time Paid 27; Part-Time Paid 26; Part-Time Volunteers 180; Interns 2.
Governing Authority: nonprofit. Tax-exempt: 501(c)(3).
General Museum.
Collections: American period automobiles; American paintings; sculpture;

American folk art; American toys; working carousel; Currier & Ives prints; Native American artifacts; military miniatures; firearms; scrimshaw.
Major Exhibits: Firefighting on Cape Cod, 6/10-10/10; Frank Vining Smith, south Shore & Cape Cod Art, 7/10-10/10.
Research Fields: American history, industry, art & horticulture.
Facilities: library available by appointment only; theater; cafe. Museum-related items for sale.
Activities: lectures; special events; films; concerts; formally organized education programs for children; temporary exhibitions.
Publications: quarterly newsletter, View From The Cupola; annual report; catalog, The Automobile Collection.
Hours & Admission Prices: April-Oct. daily 10-5; Nov. 23-Dec. Fri.-Sun. 5-9. Adults $12, senior citizens $10, children $6; discounts to school groups, military, teachers, AAM, ICOM & AAA members; members no charge. ♿
Attendance: 80,000 (accurate)
Membership: Individual $42; Family $55; Sustaining $80; Contributing $125; Supporting $250; Patron $500; Benefactor $1,000; Corporate Partner $250, $500, $1,000, $1,500, $2,000.

THE OLD HOXIE HOUSE, Rte. 130, Water St., Sandwich, MA 02563-2280. Mailing Address: Town Hall Annex, 145 Main St., Sandwich, MA 02563-2280. Tel.: 508-888-1173.
Founded: 1960.
Congressional District: 12
Key Personnel: C.E.O., Dir. & Cur., Charlotte Kuzavo.
Personnel Profile: Part-Time Paid 10.
Governing Authority: municipal. Parent Institution: Town of Sandwich Selectmen. Tax-exempt.
Historic House: c.1675 Hoxie House.
Collections: 17th-century furniture & furnishings.
Activities: lectured tours.
Hours & Admission Prices: Memorial Day to mid-June Sat.-Sun. 10-5; mid-June to Columbus Day Mon.-Sat. 10-5, Sun. 1-5. Adults $3, children 6 & over $2. ♿
Attendance: 5,000 (accurate)

SANDWICH GLASS MUSEUM, (M), 129 Main St., Sandwich, MA 02563. Mailing Address: P.O. Box 103, Sandwich, MA 02563-0103. Tel.: 508-888-0251. Fax: 508-888-4941.
E-mail: glass@sandwichglassmuseum.org
Web Site: www.sandwichglassmuseum.org
Founded: 1907.
Congressional District: 12
Key Personnel: C.E.O. & Dir., Bruce A. Courson; Pres. (V), Douglas Reed; Cur., Dorothy Schofield; Museum Shop Mgr., Robert Ward.
Personnel Profile: Full-Time Paid 3; Part-Time Paid 5; Part-Time Volunteers 30.
Governing Authority: bd. of trustees of Sandwich Historical Society. Parent Institution: The Sandwich Historical Society. Tax-exempt: 501(c)(3).
Glass Museum.
Collections: glass collection, mainly Sandwich; local historical items.
Research Fields: history of Sandwich glass; local history.
Facilities: glass reference library; auditorium. Sandwich Glass reproductions & reference books for sale.
Activities: glass & history symposiums during fall; museum docent program; permanent & temporary exhibitions; walking tours; glass & related materials; glassblowing demonstrations. Annual Events: Cape Cod Glass Show & Sale; Annual Fall Symposium. Museum Sponsor: Members' Movie Festivals in February & March.
Publications: quarterly bulletin, The Cullet; annual, The Acorn.
Hours & Admission Prices: Feb.-March Wed.-Sun. 9:30-4; April-Dec. daily 9:30-5. Library by appointment only. Adults $5, children 6-14 $1.25; discounts to groups & AAM members; members no charge. Closed New Year's Day; Thanksgiving; Christmas. ♿
Attendance: 52,345 (accurate)
Membership: Individual $25; Family $35; Sustaining Individual $60; Family Sustaining $75; Sponsor $125; Patron $275.

THORNTON W. BURGESS MUSEUM, 4 Water St., Sandwich, MA 02563. Mailing Address: 6 Discovery Hill Rd., East Sandwich, MA 02537-1316. Tel.: 508-888-6870. Fax: 508-888-1919.
E-mail: info@thorntonburgess.org
Web Site: www.thorntonburgess.org
Founded: 1976.
Congressional District: 12
Key Personnel: Exec. Dir., Gene A. Schott; Pres. (V), Jacqueline Lane; Museum Shop Mgr., John Richmond.
Personnel Profile: Full-Time Paid 5; Part-Time Paid 21; Part-Time Volunteers 205.
Governing Authority: society; nonprofit. Parent Institution: Thornton W. Burgess Society, Inc. Branch: Green Briar Nature Center. Tax-exempt.
History Museum & Nature Center: housed in 1756 Deacon Eldred House.
Collections: published writings of Thornton W. Burgess including many first editions; autographs; original illustrations by Harrison Cady; herb & wild flower garden; taxidermy mounts, moths & butterflies; shells, rocks and minerals; fossils; photographs; historic buildings.
Major Exhibits: 100th Anniversary of Old Mother West Wind, 1/10-12/10.
Research Fields: natural history of southeastern Massachusetts; related environmental issues.
Facilities: gardens; nature trails. Books & museum-related items for sale.
Activities: educational programs; summer story times; live animal programs; loan & temporary exhibitions.
Publications: biennial publication, Briar Patch Observer & program schedule.
Hours & Admission Prices: Jan.-March Tues.-Sat. 10-4; April-Dec. Mon.-Sat. 10-4, Sun. 1-4. No charge; donations accepted. ♿
Attendance: 40,000 (estimated)
Membership: Individual $30; Family $40.

Saugus

SAUGUS IRON WORKS NATIONAL HISTORIC SITE, 244 Central St., Saugus, MA 01906-2188. Tel.: 781-233-0050. Fax: 781-231-7345.
E-mail: sair_iron_works_house@nps.gov
Web Site: www.nps.gov/sair
Founded: 1954.
Congressional District: 6
Key Personnel: Supt., Patricia S. Trap; Museum Cur., Carl Salmons-Perez; Museum Specialist, Janet Regan.
Governing Authority: federal. Administered by the National Park Service, U.S. Dept. of Interior, Washington, DC 20240. Tax-exempt.
Historic Site: 17th century Iron Works House; reconstructed blast furnace, forge & slitting mill.
Collections: 17th-century cast & wrought iron products; tools; hardware; domestic objects; architectural fragments; furnishings; archival holdings; Native American artifacts.
Research Fields: 17th-century iron making technology.
Facilities: 1,000-vol. library of material on iron technology, colonial life, nature & environmental awareness available on premises; nature trail. Books, postcards & museum-related reproductions of colonial items for sale.
Activities: guided & self-guided tours; lectures; films; slide show; formally organized education programs for children; permanent exhibitions.
Hours & Admission Prices: April-Oct. daily 9-5. No charge.
Attendance: 23,000 (estimated)

Scituate

SCITUATE HISTORICAL SOCIETY, Laidlaw Historical Center, 43 Cudworth Rd., Scituate, MA 02066. Mailing Address: P.O. Box 276, Scituate, MA 02066-0276. Tel.: 781-545-1083 & 0942. Fax: 781-544-1249.
E-mail: director@scituatehistoricalsociety.org
Web Site: scituatehistoricalsociety.org
Founded: 1916.
Congressional District: 10
Key Personnel: Chm. (V), Elizabeth Miessner; Pres. (V), David Ball; Sec., Gretchen Mirarchi; Treas., Denise Castro.
Personnel Profile: Full-Time Volunteers 60; Part-Time Volunteers 50.
Governing Authority: bd. of trustees. Subsidiary Institutions: Old Stockbridge Grist Mill; 1810 Old Scituate Lighthouse; Mann Farmhouse & Historical Museum; 1902 Lawson Tower; 1675 Old Oaken Bucket Homestead; 1795 barn; 1636 cattle pound; 1893 The Little Red School House; James house: Marine History & Mossing Museum. Tax-exempt: 501(c)(3).
Historic Building.
Collections: early Colonial; textiles; Indian artifacts; military; Gen. Lafayette's coach; local history; costumes; books & documents; early farming tools; cobbler's tools; sail loft; sail making tools; ship building tools; coaches; historic buildings.
Research Fields: buildings 150 years & older in town; genealogy; pertaining to the collection.
Facilities: 300-vol. library. Museum-related items for sale.
Activities: guided tours; lectures; formally organized education programs for children; field trips to museums by school & adult groups & scout organizations by appointment.
Publications: books, Early Planters of Scituate; Deane's History of Scituate; Old Scituate; Irish Mossers & Scituate Harbor Village; Briggs Shipbuilding on North River; early maps; brochure, Historic Scituate; pamphlet, Scituate 1636-1961. Images of America: Scituate; Scituate Lighthouse Guidebook; bimonthly, The Scituate Historical Society Newsletter.
Hours & Admission Prices: Cudworth House, Mann Farmhouse: Grist Mill, Old Oaken Bucket Homestead, Lawson Tower & Lighthouse: Summer: call

for hours; organizations by appointment. Adults $2; children & New England Museum Assoc. no charge. Little Red Schoolhouse: daily 10-4; organizations by appointment.
Attendance: 7,500 (estimated)
Membership: Basic $25; Silver & Corporate Basic $100; Gold & Corporate Blue $250; Platinum & Corporate Gold $500

SCITUATE MARITIME AND IRISH MOSSING MUSEUM, 301 The Driftway, Scituate, MA 02066-1904. Mailing Address: P.O. Box 276, Scituate, MA 02066-0276. Tel.: 781-545-1083. Fax: 781-544-1249.
E-mail: director@scituatehistoricalsociety.org
Web Site: www.scituatehistoricalsociety.org
Founded: 1997.
Congressional District: 10
Key Personnel: Chm. (V), Elizabeth Miessner; Pres. (V), David Ball.
Personnel Profile: Part-Time Volunteers 20.
Governing Authority: private; nonprofit organization. Parent Institution: Scituate Historical Society, Scituate, MA. Tax-exempt: 501(c)(3).
General Museum.
Collections: maritime history from 17th-century to present; North River shipbuilding; Scituate coast disasters; early U.S. Coast Guard; lighthouse establishment; Irish mossing; lifesaving services. Historic House: 1739 home of Captain Benjamin James.
Research Fields: history of Mossing industry, early lifesaving & shipwrecks in Scituate & along the South Shore.
Facilities: educational facilities. Museum-related items for sale.
Activities: guided tours; lectures; loan & participatory exhibits. Annual Event: Scituate Heritage Days.
Publications: bimonthly newsletter, Scituate Historical Society; books, Images of America: Scituate; Scituate Lighthouse Guidebook.
Hours & Admission Prices: June by appointment; July-Aug. Sat.-Sun. 1-4; Sept.-May Sun. 1-4; call for updated schedule. Adults $4, senior citizens $3; NEMA members, members, children 12 and under no charge.
Attendance: 5,000 (estimated)
Membership: Basic $25; Silver & Corporate Basic $100; Gold & Corporate Blue $250; Platinum & Corporate Gold $500.

Somerville

THE SOMERVILLE MUSEUM, One Westwood Rd., Somerville, MA 02143-1517. Tel.: 617-666-9810.
Founded: 1897.
Congressional District: 8
Key Personnel: Pres. Bd., Regina M. Pisa; Dir., Evelyn M. Battinelli.
Personnel Profile: Full-Time Volunteers 1; Part-Time Volunteers 4.
Governing Authority: society, nonprofit. Parent Institution: Somerville Historical Society. Tax-exempt: 501(c)(3).
General Museum: housed in c.1925 three-story, red brick neo-Federal style building.
Collections: 18th- to 20th-century American history; architectural artifacts; furniture; paintings; prints; photographs; glassware; military & industrial items; scientific & mechanical objects; contemporary art; multi-cultural objects.
Research Fields: material culture; humanities; art.
Facilities: research library pertaining to Somerville history; educational facilities.
Activities: guided tours; lectures; films; concerts; dance recitals; arts festivals; theater; study clubs; hobby workshops; broadcast programs; festivals; participatory, loan, temporary & traveling exhibitions; organized education programs for children, adults & undergraduate or graduate college students; training programs for professional museum workers; special exhibitions & programs.
Publications: brochure; newsletter, Lifting the Veil: The Burning of the Ursuline Convent.
Hours & Admission Prices: Sept.-June Thurs. 2-7, Fri. 2-5, Sat. 12-5. No charge; donations accepted. Closed national holidays.
Membership: Student & Senior $10; Individual $15; Family $25; Contributing $50; Supporting $100; Patron $250; Sustaining $500; Benefactor $1,000.

South Chelmsford

THE CHELMSFORD HISTORICAL SOCIETY, INC., 40 Byam Rd., South Chelmsford, MA 01824-3827. Tel.: 978-256-2311.
E-mail: chelmhist@comcast.net
Web Site: www.chelmhist.org
Founded: 1930.
Congressional District: 5
Key Personnel: Pres. (V), Carol Merriam; Cur., Judy Fichtenbaum; Museum Dir., Donald Patterschal.
Governing Authority: society. Tax-exempt: 501(c)(3) & 170(b)(1)(A).
History Museum: housed in c.1663 Barrett-Byam homestead.
Collections: archives; Indian & war relics; Chelmsford Glass; clothing; model of country store.
Research Fields: genealogy; local history & industry.
Facilities: library of books, newspapers & magazines pertaining to history of Chelmsford, available for use on premises; reading room; authentic gardens & plantings.
Activities: guided tours; lectures; study clubs; formally organized education programs for children; permanent & temporary exhibitions.
Publications: newsletter.
Hours & Admission Prices: By appointment & during special events. No charge; donations accepted. Closed New Year's Day; Memorial Day; Labor Day; Thanksgiving; Christmas. ♿
Attendance: 250 (estimated)
Membership: Senior & Student $6; Individual $10; Family $18; Life $100.

South Deerfield

MAGIC WINGS BUTTERFLY CONSERVATORY & GARDENS, 281 Greenfield Rd., South Deerfield, MA 01373-9790. Tel.: 413-665-2805. Fax: 413-665-4062.
E-mail: info@magicwings.net
Web Site: www.magicwings.com
Conservatory & Garden.
Collections: 3,000 species of butterflies from around the world.
Hours & Admission Prices: Memorial Day-Labor Day daily 9-6; Sept.-May daily 9-5. Adults $12, senior citizens 62 & over $10, children 3-17 $8; children under 3 no charge.

South Hadley

MOUNT HOLYOKE COLLEGE ART MUSEUM, (M), (I), Lower Lake Rd., South Hadley, MA 01075-1499. Tel.: 413-538-2245. Fax: 413-538-2144.
E-mail: artmuseum@mtholyoke.edu
Web Site: www.mtholyoke.edu/go/artmuseum/
Founded: 1875.
Congressional District: 1
Key Personnel: Dir., Marianne Doezema; Chm. (V), Alice DeLana; Cur., Wendy M. Watson; Cur. Asst., Rachel Beaupre; Asst. Cur. Skinner Museum, Meghan Gelardi Holmes; Business & Events Mgr., Debbie Davis; Coord. Education, Jane Gronau; Andrew W. Mellon Coord. Academic Affairs, Ellen Alvord; Mgr. Collections, Linda Delone Best; Publications & Public Rels., Jessica Reynolds Lavallee; Digitization Specialist, Laura Weston; Preparator, Brian Kiernan; Art Advisory Bd. Fellow, Sadie Shillieto.
Personnel Profile: Full-Time Paid 8; Part-Time Paid 4; Part-Time Volunteers 30; Interns 4.
Governing Authority: college; nonprofit. Parent Institution: Mount Holyoke College. Tax-exempt.
Art Museum.
Collections: art of all periods with concentrations in ancient, medieval, Renaissance, Asian & American art; prints; drawings; photographs.
Major Exhibits: Lisette Model and Her Successors (T), 11/09-12/13/09; Dance and Dancers, 11/09-12/13/09; The Art of Devotion: Panel Painting in Early Renaissance Italy, 2/9/10-5/30/10; Wine and the Human Spirit (T), 9/2/10-12/12/10.
Facilities: 20,000-vol. library on art history. Publications & cards for sale.
Activities: guided tours; lectures; films; gallery talks; docent program; formally organized educational programs for students grades 2-9; concerts; inter-museum loan; permanent, temporary & traveling exhibitions.
Publications: exhibition catalogues; Newsletter; semester calendars.
Hours & Admission Prices: Tues.-Fri. 11-5, Sat.-Sun. 1-5. No charge; donations accepted. ♿
Attendance: 11,050 (estimated)
Membership: Individual $25; Family & Dual $50; Patron $100; Sponsor $250; Benefactor $500; Director's Circle $1,000.

THE OLD FIREHOUSE MUSEUM, 4 N. Main St., South Hadley, MA 01075. Mailing Address: P.O. Box 387, South Hadley, MA 01075-0387. Tel.: 413-536-4970.
Fire-Fighting Museum.
Collections: fire-fighting gear; two 19th century hand pumpers; 1926 Dodge Fire Engine; historical documents & artifacts.
Hours & Admission Prices: May-June & Sept. Sun. 1:30-4; July-Aug. Wed. & Sun. 1:30-4. No charge; donations accepted.

THE SKINNER MUSEUM OF MOUNT HOLYOKE COLLEGE, 33 Woodbridge St., South Hadley, MA 01075-1138. Mailing Address: c/o Mount Holyoke College Art Museum, Lower Lake Rd., South Hadley, MA 01075. Tel.: 413-538-2245. Fax: 413-538-2144.
E-mail: artmuseum@mtholyoke.edu

Web Site: www.mtholyoke.edu/go/artmuseum
Founded: 1933.
Congressional District: 1
Key Personnel: Cur., Wendy Watson; Asst. Cur., Meghan Gelardi Holmes.
Personnel Profile: Part-Time Paid 1.
Governing Authority: college. Parent Institution: Mount Holyoke College. Tax-exempt.
History Museum.
Collections: agriculture; archaeology; archives; geology; glass; history; New England home furnishings. Historic Buildings: 1846 Church & School House from Prescott, MA.
Hours & Admission Prices: May-Oct. Wed. & Sun. 2-5. No charge; donations accepted.
Attendance: 350 (estimated)

South Natick

NATICK HISTORICAL SOCIETY, 58 Eliot St., South Natick, MA 01760-5542. Tel.: 508-647-4841.
E-mail: info@natickhistoricalsociety.org
Web Site: www.natickhistoricalsociety.org
Formerly: Historical Natural History & Library Society of Natick dba Natick Historical Society
Founded: 1870.
Congressional District: 10
Key Personnel: C.E.O. & Exec. Dir., Jennifer H. Hance; Pres. (V), Adams K. Shipman, Jr.; Cur., Anne K. Schaller.
Personnel Profile: Full-Time Paid 1; Part-Time Volunteers 18; Interns 4.
Governing Authority: society. Tax-exempt.
Historical Society Museum.
Collections: John Eliot's Algonquin Bible; Native American artifacts; period artifacts; shoe factory; tools; textiles; maps; photographs; Vice Pres. Henry Wilson; Harriet Beecher Stowe; Horatio Alger, Jr.; ornothology.
Major Exhibits: Home of Champions: Sports in Natick, 11/09-2/11.
Research Fields: John Eliot; Praying Indians; genealogy; Henry Wilson.
Facilities: archives.
Activities: tours; permanent exhibitions; programs; special events.
Publications: The Arrow; Images of America-Natick; Natick Air; From Many Backgrounds: The Heritage of the Eliot Church of South Natick.
Hours & Admission Prices: July-Aug. Tues. 2-7, Wed. 2-4:30; Sept.-June Tues. 2-8:30, Wed. 2-4:30, Sat. 10-12:30. No charge; donations accepted. ♿
Attendance: 1,300 (estimated)
Membership: Senior $10; Individual $30; Family $40; Contributing $75; Sponsoring $100; Sustaining $150.

Springfield

HATIKVAH HOLOCAUST EDUCATION CENTER, 1160 Dickinson St., Springfield, MA 01108-3122. Tel.: 413-734-7700. Fax: 413-734-0919.
E-mail: administrator@hatikvah-center.org
Web Site: www.hatikvah-center.org
History Museum.
Collections: Holocaust history; photographs; personal artifacts; documents; audiovisuals.
Major Exhibits: Dr. Seuss Wants You (T), 5/10.
Facilities: Museum-related items for sale.
Activities: special events; educational programs; workshops. Annual Events: Yom HaShoah; Kristallnacht.
Hours & Admission Prices: Mon.-Fri. 9-2, Sun. by appointment. ♿
Attendance: 2,500 (accurate)
Membership: Individual $50; Family $100; Hatikvah Benefactor $500; Hatikvah Patron $1,000.

NAISMITH MEMORIAL BASKETBALL HALL OF FAME, 1000 W. Columbus Ave., Springfield, MA 01105-2518. Tel.: 413-781-6500. Fax: 413-781-1939.
Web Site: www.hoophall.com
Founded: 1959.
Congressional District: 2
Key Personnel: Pres., John Doleva; Vice Pres. Finance & Operations, Don Senecal; Vice Pres. Experience & Programming, Paul Lambert; Dir. Devel., Scott Zuffelato; Dir. Sports Media, Howie Davis; Cur., Michael Brooslin; Archivist & Librarian, Robin Deutsch; Mgr. Events & Group Programs, David Elkins; Sr. Dir. Mktg., Dean O'Keefe; Supvr. Educational Programs, Tom Ashe; Controller, Doug Moss; Dir. Retail Operations, Paula Thompson; Mgr. Facility Operations, James Mullen; Group Sales, Joe Hevey; Dir. Mktg. Partnerships, Steve Sullivan.
Personnel Profile: Full-Time Paid 35; Part-Time Paid 75; Part-Time Volunteers 1; Interns 4.
Governing Authority: nonprofit organization. Tax-exempt: 501(c)(3).
Sports Museum.
Collections: history of basketball, from its beginnings in Springfield, MA in December 1891, to the present; high tech interactive exhibits.
Research Fields: basketball history.
Facilities: 5,000-vol. library pertaining to the history of basketball for research on premises. Gift items for sale.
Activities: films; organized education programs for children; participatory exhibits.
Publications: newsletter; Souvenir Book; annual yearbook.
Hours & Admission Prices: Sun.-Thurs. 10-4, Fri.-Sat. 10-5. Adults $16.99, seniors $13.99, youth 5-15 $11.99; discounts to groups; children 4 & under no charge. Closed New Year's Day; Thanksgiving; Christmas. ♿
Attendance: 300,000 (estimated)
Membership: Call for information.

PAN AFRICAN HISTORICAL MUSEUM, Tower Square, Mezzanine Level, 1500 Main St., Springfield, MA 01115-1001. Tel.: 413-733-1823.
Web Site: visittowersquare.com/entertainment/galleries
History Museum.
Collections: African American artifacts, artwork & sculptures.
Hours & Admission Prices: By appointment.

SPRINGFIELD ARMORY NATIONAL HISTORIC SITE, One Armory Sq., Ste. 2, Springfield, MA 01105-1299. Tel.: 413-734-8551 & 6477. Fax: 413-747-8062.
E-mail: spar_interpretation@nps.gov
Web Site: www.nps.gov/spar/
Founded: 1870.
Congressional District: 2
Key Personnel: Supt., Richard Quijano-West; Cur., James D. Roberts; Visitor Svcs., Joanne M. Gangi; Historian, Richard Colton; Registrar, John R. McCabe; Conservator, David Arnold.
Personnel Profile: Full-Time Paid 12; Part-Time Paid 2; Part-Time Volunteers 3; Interns 3.
Governing Authority: federal. Parent Institution: National Park Service, U.S. Dept. of Interior, Washington, DC. Tax-exempt.
Historic Building & Site Museum: housed in 1850 Arsenal.
Collections: 8,730 military small arms of U.S. & foreign manufacture spanning 3 centuries, available to researchers by appointment under the supervision of a professional staff member; firearms manufactured at Springfield Armory from 1790s to 1968, including experimental & prototypes; Civil War rifle-muskets; Model 1903; M-1 Garand; hand guns; machine guns; edged weapons; manufacturing process; inventions; impact of armory upon the city; 3,000 archaeological artifacts; 7,500 toy soldiers; 21,000 photographs 1930-1968.
Research Fields: 1794-1968, U.S. military firearms development & production; photographs 1930-1968; technical reports; notes; memoranda; contracts; architectural drawings c.1790-1968; S.A. Armorer newsletter; annual reports; historical summaries; manuscripts; post orders; S.A. histories; microfilm correspondence & payroll 1813-1934; N.P.S. & compiled subject files; periodicals & 1,200 books, mainly on production, testing & collection of military arms, U.S. military history & ordinance; oral history interviews.
Facilities: 1,500-vol. library & archives of military firearms books & other research materials; education center; conference space. Armory-related publications for sale.
Activities: programs for school groups; friends group; friends of the Springfield Armory Museum.
Publications: books; fact sheets; site brochure; Springfield Firearms posters; book, Marco Paul at the Springfield Armory; Arms for the Nations; videos.
Hours & Admission Prices: Daily 9-5. No charge; donations accepted. Closed New Year's Day; Thanksgiving; Christmas. ♿
Attendance: 20,000 (estimated)
Membership: Friends of the Springfield Armory $35.

* **SPRINGFIELD MUSEUMS - CONNECTICUT VALLEY HISTORICAL MUSEUM,** 21 Edwards St., Springfield, MA 01103-1548. Tel.: 413-263-6800, ext. 304. Fax: 413-263-6898.
E-mail: info@springfieldmuseums.org
Web Site: www.springfieldmuseums.org
Founded: 1927.
Congressional District: 2
Key Personnel: Pres., Joseph Carvalho, III; Dir., Guy McLain; Chm. (V), Richard B. Collins; C.F.O., Holly Smith-Bove; Asst. Dir. Mktg. & Devel., Sara Orr; Registrar, Diane Barbarisi; Dir. Institutional Advancement & Education, Kathleen Simpson; Head Research Library, Margaret Humberston; Museum Shop Mgr., Lin Jaciow.
Personnel Profile: Full-Time Paid 53; Part-Time Paid 31; Part-Time Volunteers 700; Interns 2.
Governing Authority: nonprofit organization. Parent Institution: Springfield Museums. Tax-exempt: 501(c)(3).
History Museum.

Collections: Springfield, Connecticut Valley, New England history; paintings, furniture, art, manufactured artifacts.
Research Fields: history & material culture of Connecticut Valley from 1600; genealogy of Northeastern U.S., Eastern Canada; immigration to New England.
Activities: age-oriented docent-guided tours; courses for young people & adults; lectures; gallery talks; inter-museum loans; permanent & temporary exhibitions.
Publications: books & videos on local history; exhibit catalogs & gallery guides; quarterly membership publication; annual report.
Hours & Admission Prices: Tues.-Sun. 11-4. Adults $12.50; admission includes entry to 5 museums; discounts to AAM members; children under 3 & members no charge. Closed New Year's Day; Easter; Independence Day; Thanksgiving; Christmas.
Attendance: 74,000 (estimated)
Membership: Basic $35; Dual $45; Household $60; Patron $125; Sustaining $250; Contributing $500; Society of William Rice $1,000 & up.

SPRINGFIELD MUSEUMS - GEORGE WALTER VINCENT SMITH ART MUSEUM, 21 Edwards St., Springfield, MA 01103-1548. Tel.: 413-263-6800, ext. 302. Fax: 413-263-6897.
E-mail: info@springfieldmuseums.org
Web Site: www.springfieldmuseums.org
Founded: 1896.
Congressional District: 2
Key Personnel: Pres. & Exec. Dir., Joseph Carvalho, III; Chm. (V), Richard B. Collins; Dir., Heather Haskell; C.F.O., Holly Smith-Bove; Asst. Dir. Mktg. & Devel., Sara Orr; Registrar, Diane Barbarisi; Dir. Institutional Advancement & Education, Kathleen Simpson; Museum Shop Mgr., Lin Jaciow.
Personnel Profile: Full-Time Paid 53; Part-Time Paid 31; Part-Time Volunteers 700; Interns 6.
Governing Authority: nonprofit organization. Parent Institution: The Springfield Museums, 21 Edwards St., Springfield, MA 01103. Tax-exempt: 501(c)(3).
Decorative Arts Museum: housed in 1895 building designed by Renwick, Aspenwall & Renwick.
Collections: Asian decorative arts of the 17th, 18th & 19th centuries; Middle Eastern rugs; arms & armor; 19th-century American paintings; plaster casts.
Research Fields: Japanese arms & armor; Asian decorative arts.
Facilities: classrooms; art studios; hands-on Art Discovery Center.
Activities: age-oriented docent-guided tours; courses for young people & adults; lectures; gallery talks; inter-museum loans; permanent & temporary exhibitions.
Publications: catalogs & gallery guides; quarterly membership newsletter; annual report.
Hours & Admission Prices: Tues.-Sun. 11-4. Adults $12.50, admission includes entry to 5 museums at same location; discounts to AAM members; children under 3 & members no charge. Closed New Year's Day; Easter; Independence Day; Thanksgiving; Christmas. ♿
Attendance: 79,000 (estimated)
Membership: Basic $35; Dual $45; Household $60; Patron $125-$249; Sustaining $250-$499; Contributing $500-$999; Society of William Rice $1,000 & up.

SPRINGFIELD MUSEUMS - MICHELE & DONALD D'AMOUR MUSEUM OF FINE ARTS, 21 Edwards St., Springfield, MA 01103-1548. Tel.: 413-263-6800, ext. 302. Fax: 413-263-6889.
E-mail: info@springfieldmuseums.org
Web Site: www.springfieldmuseums.org
Founded: 1933.
Congressional District: 2
Key Personnel: Exec. Dir. & Pres., Joseph Carvalho, III; C.F.O., Holly Smith-Bove; Chm. (V), Richard B. Collins; Dir., Heather Haskell; Asst. Dir. Mktg. & Devel., Sara Orr; Registrar, Diane Barbarisi; Dir. Institutional Advancement & Education, Kathleen Simpson; Museum Shop Mgr., Lin Jaciow.
Personnel Profile: Full-Time Paid 53; Part-Time Paid 31; Part-Time Volunteers 700.
Governing Authority: nonprofit organization. Parent Institution: Springfield Museums, 21Edwards St. Tax-exempt: 501(c)(3).
Art Museum.
Collections: European & American paintings; sculpture; graphics; decorative art; Japanese prints.
Facilities: 5,000-vol. library on Asian art & general history of art available for use by appointment; 280-seat auditorium.
Activities: age-oriented docent-guided tours; courses for young people & adults; lectures; gallery talks; inter-museum loans; permanent & temporary exhibitions.
Publications: gallery guides; periodic exhibition catalogues; quarterly membership newsletter; annual report.
Hours & Admission Prices: Tues.-Sun. 11-4. Adults $12.50, includes entry to 5 museums; discounts to AAM members; children under 3 & members no charge. Closed New Year's Day; Easter; Independence Day; Thanksgiving; Christmas. ♿
Attendance: 86,000 (estimated)
Membership: Basic $35; Dual $45; Household $60; Patron $125; Sustaining $250; Contributing $500; Society of William Rice $1,000 & up.

SPRINGFIELD MUSEUMS - MUSEUM OF SPRINGFIELD HISTORY, 21 Edwards St., Springfield, MA 01103-1548. Tel.: 413-263-6800, ext. 304. Fax: 413-263-6898.
E-mail: info@springfieldmuseums.org
Web Site: www.springfieldmuseums.org
Congressional District: 2
Key Personnel: Pres., Joseph Carvalho, III; Dir., Guy McLain; Chm. (V), Richard B. Collins; C.F.O., Holly Smith-Bove; Asst. Dir. Mktg. & Devel., Sara Orr; Registrar, Diane Barbarisi; Dir. Institutional Advancement & Education, Kathleen Simpson; Head Research Library, Margaret Humberston; Museum Shop Mgr., Lin Jaciow.
Personnel Profile: Full-Time Paid 53; Part-Time Paid 31; Part-Time Volunteers 700; Interns 3.
Governing Authority: nonprofit organization. Parent Institution: Springfield Museums. Tax-exempt: 501(c)(3).
History Museum.
Collections: Springfield-built automobiles; Indian motorcycles; local industry & culture during the 19th & 20th centuries; photographs; maps; manuscripts; genealogy.
Research Fields: industrial & commercial history of Springfield and the region in the 19th & 20th centuries.
Facilities: library; archives.
Activities: docent-guided tours; family programs; lectures; children & adult classes; video presentations; permanent & temporary exhibitions.
Publications: books; DVDs; exhibit catalogs; gallery guides; quarterly membership publication.
Hours & Admission Prices: Tues.-Sun. 11-4. Adults $12.50 (admission includes entry to 5 museums); discounts to AAM members; children under 3 & members no charge. Closed New Year's Day; Easter; Independence Day; Thanksgiving; Christmas. ♿
Membership: Basic $35; Dual $45; Household $60; Patron $125; Sustaining $250; Contributing $500; Society of William Rice $1,000 & up.

* **SPRINGFIELD MUSEUMS - SPRINGFIELD SCIENCE MUSEUM, (M),** 21 Edwards St., Springfield, MA 01103-1548. Tel.: 413-263-6800, ext. 325. Fax: 413-263-6884.
E-mail: info@springfieldmuseums.org
Web Site: www.springfieldmuseums.org
Founded: 1859.
Congressional District: 2
Key Personnel: Exec. Dir. & Pres., Joseph Carvalho, III; Chm. (V), Richard B. Collins; Dir., David Stier; C.F.O., Holly Smith-Bove; Registrar, Diane Barbarisi; Dir. Institutional Advancement & Education, Kathleen Simpson; Asst. Dir. Mktg. & Devel., Sara Orr; Museum Shop Mgr., Lin Jaciow.
Personnel Profile: Full-Time Paid 53; Part-Time Paid 31; Part-Time Volunteers 700; Interns 6.
Governing Authority: nonprofit organization. Parent Institution: Springfield Museums. Tax-exempt: 501(c)(3).
Science Museum.
Collections: anthropology; archaeology; astronomy; ecology; ethnology; herpetology; ichthyology; lithology; mammalogy; mineralogy; ornithology; paleontology; physical science; technology; live animals.
Research Fields: ornithology; regional archaeology; Native American; oceanic; ethnographic.
Facilities: 3,000-vol. library of books covering all phases of natural science available for research on premises; planetarium; observatory; aquarium. Museum-related items for sale.
Activities: age-oriented docent-guided tours; courses for young people & adults; lectures; gallery talks; inter-museum loans; permanent & temporary exhibitions; hands-on exhibits.
Publications: brochures; quarterly membership newsletter; annual report.
Hours & Admission Prices: Tues.-Sat. 10-5, Sun. 11-5. Planetarium: hours vary; guided tours available; special events. Museum (includes entry to 5 museums at Quadrangle location). Adults $12.50; discounts to AAM members; children under 3 & members no charge. Planetarium: adults $3, children $2. Closed New Year's Day; Easter; Independence Day; Thanksgiving; Christmas. ♿
Attendance: 228,000 (estimated)
Membership: Basic $35; Dual $45; Household $60; Patron $125-$249; Sustaining Patron $250-$999; Contributing Patron $500-$999; Society of William Rice $1,000 & up.

THE ZOO IN FOREST PARK, 302 Sumner Ave., Springfield, MA 01138. Mailing Address: P.O. Box 80295, Springfield, MA 01138-0295. Tel.: 413-733-2251.
Web Site: forestparkzoo.org
Key Personnel: Dir., John Lewis, Jr.; Dir. Education, Alison Summers
Zoo.
Collections: wildlife.
Hours & Admission Prices: March 29-Oct. 13 daily 10-5; Oct. 14-Nov. Sat.-Sun. 10-3:30. Adults $6, senior citizens & children 5-12 $4, children 2-4 $2; children 1 & under no charge.

Still River

HARVARD HISTORICAL SOCIETY, (M), Still River Baptist Church, 215 Still River Rd., Still River, MA 01467. Mailing Address: P.O. Box 542, Harvard, MA 01451-0542. Tel.: 978-456-8285.
E-mail: curator@harvardhistory.org
Web Site: www.harvardhistory.org
Founded: 1897.
Congressional District: 5
Key Personnel: Pres., Carlene Phillips; Cur., Karen Zaikis.
Personnel Profile: Part-Time Paid 1; Part-Time Volunteers 30.
Governing Authority: bd. of directors. Tax-exempt.
History Museum.
Collections: local history; costumes; furniture; decorative arts; printed materials; photographs; books; cottage. Historic Building: 1832 Still River Baptist Church.
Research Fields: Harvard, Shaker & Transcendentalist history.
Facilities: archives.
Activities: permanent & temporary exhibitions; house tours; musical programs; school education.
Publications: Spring & Fall newsletters. The Harvard Album; Directions of a Town.
Hours & Admission Prices: Mon.-Wed. 2-7; other times by appointment. No charge; donations accepted. ♿
Attendance: 1,000 (estimated)
Membership: Individual $20; Family $30; Friend $50; Patron $100; Benefactor $500.

Stockbridge

BERKSHIRE BOTANICAL GARDEN, Rte. 102 & Rte. 183, Stockbridge, MA 01262. Mailing Address: Box 826, Stockbridge, MA 01262-0826. Tel.: 413-298-3926. Fax: 413-298-4897.
E-mail: jparker@berkshirebotanical.org
Web Site: www.berkshirebotanical.org
Founded: 1934.
Congressional District: 1
Key Personnel: Exec. Dir., John J. Parker; Chm., David Carls; Education Coord., Elisabeth Cary; Gift Shop Mgr., Jill Lipsky.
Personnel Profile: Full-Time Paid 8; Part-Time Paid 4; Part-Time Volunteers 45; Interns 2.
Governing Authority: nonprofit organization. Tax-exempt: 501(c)(3).
Botanic Garden.
Collections: botanic garden; herb & perennial gardens; arboretum; vegetable display garden; lily pond; daylily & rose gardens; rock gardens; conifer garden; woodland preserve; children's garden.
Research Fields: informal research only.
Facilities: 1,000-vol. library of books, catalogs & magazines pertaining to horticulture reference materials; meeting hall. Gift shop with garden-related items including fresh herb products produced by volunteers on the grounds.
Activities: guided tours; lectures; workshops; formally organized education programs; seasonal exhibits. Garden Sponsors: Plant Sale in May; Flower Show in August; Harvest Festival in October; Holiday Marketplace in December.
Publications: newsletter, Cuttings.
Hours & Admission Prices: May to mid-Oct. daily 10-5. Adults $10, senior citizens & students $7; discounts to AAA, AABGA, & MA Teachers Assoc.; American Horticultural Society Reciprocal Admission Program; children 12 & under & members no charge. ♿
Attendance: 24,000 (estimated)
Membership: Student $25; Individual $45; Family $65; Supporter $125; Friend $250; Patron $500; Fence Club $1,000.

CHESTERWOOD, 4 Williamsville Rd., off Rte. 183, Glendale Sect., Stockbridge, MA 01262-0827. Mailing Address: P.O. Box 827, Stockbridge, MA 01262-0827. Tel.: 413-298-3579. Fax: 413-298-3973.
E-mail: chesterwood@nthp.org
Web Site: www.chesterwood.org
Founded: 1955.
Congressional District: 1
Key Personnel: Dir., Donna Hassler; Chm. Advisory Bd., Sarah La Cour; Administrative Asst., Lisa Reynolds; Bldgs. & Grounds Supt., Gerard Blache; Museum Shop Mgr., Patricia Purdy.
Personnel Profile: Full-Time Paid 4; Part-Time Paid 15; Part-Time Volunteers 20; Interns 3.
Governing Authority: nonprofit organization. Parent Institution: National Trust for Historic Preservation, 1785 Massachusetts Ave., N.W., Washington, DC 20036. Tax-exempt: 501(c)(3).
Historic Site: housed in the summer estate of Daniel Chester French (1850-1931).
Collections: works of Daniel Chester French: sculpture; paintings; pastels; sculpture tools & equipment; photographs; blueprints; drawings; papers; books; 18th & 19th-century American & European furniture & decorative arts; manuscripts; art works of DCF contemporaries; sculptures & papers of Margaret French Cresson; literary manuscripts of Mrs. Daniel Chester French; period country place garden; period woodland walk. Historic Buildings: 1898 studio; 1901 house; early 1800s barn.
Research Fields: Daniel Chester French works, life, career & times; Lincoln Memorial Statue; Chesterwood & its collections; museum methodology; Beaux Arts sculpture; The American Renaissance; Gilded Age; landscape architecture; horticulture; Berkshire estates.
Facilities: library of books on Daniel Chester French, art history, sculpture, historic preservation, landscape architecture, decorative arts & museum studies; archives including oral histories, clipping files & microfilms available for use by scholars, graduate students & researchers by appointment; 122 acre site; conference space. Books, reproductions & other museum-related items for sale.
Activities: lectures; formally organized education programs for students K-12; docent program; sculpture demonstrations; gallery & landscape tours; summer & winter intern program for undergraduate & graduate college students; permanent & temporary exhibitions; special events. Museum Sponsors: Contemporary Sculpture Show.
Publications: educational brochures; annual catalogue & brochures; children's guide to Chesterwood; landscape guide; property guidebook.
Hours & Admission Prices: May-Oct. daily 10-5. Adults $15; discounts to AAM members; members no charge. ♿
Attendance: 12,500 (estimated)
Membership: Individual $45; Family $65; Contributing $100; Benefactor $250; Sustaining $500; Daniel Chester French Society $1,000; Abraham Lincoln Laureates Society $2,500.

MERWIN HOUSE, TRANQUILITY, 14 Main St., Stockbridge, MA 01262. Mailing Address: 141 Cambridge St., Boston, MA 02114-2702. Tel.: 617-227-3956. Fax: 617-227-9204.
Web Site: www.historicnewengland.org
Founded: 1966.
Congressional District: 1
Key Personnel: Pres., Carl Nold.
Governing Authority: society; nonprofit organization. Parent Institution: Historic New England, 141 Cambridge St., Boston, MA 02114. Tel.: 617-227-3956. Tax-exempt: 501(c)(3).
Historic House: c.1825 late Federal style period house.
Collections: European & American furniture & decorative arts.
Hours & Admission Prices: By appointment. Adults $4; members no charge.
Attendance: 562 (accurate)
Membership: National $35; Individual $45; Household $55; Garden & Landscape $75; Institutional $85; Contributing $100; Historic Homeowner $200; Supporting $250.

THE MISSION HOUSE, Main St., Stockbridge, MA 01262-9800. Mailing Address: P.O. Box 792, Stockbridge, MA 01262-0792. Tel.: 413-298-3239, ext. 3000. Fax: 413-298-5239.
E-mail: westregion@ttor.org
Web Site: www.thetrustees.org
Founded: 1948.
Congressional District: 1
Key Personnel: Western Rgnl. Dir., Stephen McMahon; Historic Resources Mgr., Will Garrison.
Personnel Profile: Full-Time Paid 1; Part-Time Paid 7.
Governing Authority: nonprofit organization. The Trustees of Reservations, 572 Essex St., Beverly, MA 01915. Tel. 508-921-1944. Tax-exempt.
Historic House: housed in the former home of Rev. John Sergeant, first missionary to the Stockbridge Mohicans; built in 1743.
Collections: period furnishings; Rev. Sergeant cupboard & chairs; Indian exhibit.
Research Fields: early Stockbridge town history; Stockbridge Mohicans.
Activities: guided tours.
Hours & Admission Prices: Memorial Day to Columbus Day daily 10-5. House: guided tours. Gardens: self-guided tours. Adults $6, children 6-12 $2.50; members no charge.

Attendance: 3,550 (accurate)
Membership: Senior & Student $35; Individual $45; Family $65.

NAUMKEAG, 5 Prospect Hill Rd., Stockbridge, MA 01262. Mailing Address: P.O. Box 792, Stockbridge, MA 01262-0792. Tel.: 413-298-3239, ext. 3000. Fax: 413-298-5239.
E-mail: westregion@ttor.org
Web Site: www.thetrustees.org
Founded: 1959.
Congressional District: 1
Key Personnel: Rgnl. Dir., Stephen McMahon; Historic Resources Mgr., Will Garrison; Museum Shop Mgr., Barbara Dowling.
Personnel Profile: Full-Time Paid 5; Part-Time Paid 20; Part-Time Volunteers 1.
Governing Authority: nonprofit organization. The Trustees of Reservations, 572 Essex St., Beverly, MA 01915. Tel. 617-921-1944. Tax-exempt.
Historic House: 1886 shingle style house, designed by architect McKim, Mead, & White, the summer home of Joseph Hodges Choate, U.S. Ambassador to the Court of St. James. Original gardens designed by Fletcher Steele.
Collections: Americana & European decorative arts; Chinese export porcelain.
Research Fields: the Choate family; landscape architecture.
Facilities: 8 acres of formal promenades; gardens.
Activities: guided tours; special events; garden audio tours.
Publications: Naumkeag-History of House & Family.
Hours & Admission Prices: Memorial Day to Columbus Day daily 10-5. House & Garden: adults $12, children 6-12 $3; discounts to AAM members; members no charge.
Attendance: 11,000 (accurate)
Membership: Senior & Student $35; Individual $45; Family $65.

* **NORMAN ROCKWELL MUSEUM, (M),** Rte. 183, 9 Glendale Rd., Stockbridge, MA 01262. Mailing Address: P.O. Box 308, Stockbridge, MA 01262-0308. Tel.: 413-298-4100, ext. 221. Fax: 413-298-4142.
E-mail: inforequest@nrm.org
Web Site: www.nrm.org
Founded: 1967.
Congressional District: 1
Key Personnel: C.E.O. & Dir., Laurie Norton Moffatt; Pres. Bd. Trustees (V) & Chm. (V), Dan Cain; Deputy Dir. & Chief Cur., Stephanie Haboush Plunkett; Assoc. Dir. Visitor Experience, Lise Dube-Scherr; C.O.O., Terry Smith; Cur. Archival Collections, Corry Kanzenberg; Dir. Curatorial Advancement, Mary Ellen Hern; Museum Shop Mgr., Mike Duffy; Mgr. Facilities, Wesley Shufelt; Cur. Rockwell Center for American Visual Studies, Joyce Schiller; Assoc. Registrar, Rob Doane; Information Technology Mgr., Frank Kennedy; Mgr. Collections & Registration, Martin Mahoney; Mgr. Visitors Svcs., Joseph Aubert; Cur. Education, Thomas Daly; Dir. Education, Melinda Georgeson; Mgr. Traveling Exhibitions, Mary Melius; Mgr. Warehouse & Security, Allen Bell; Dir. Human Resources, Holly Coleman.
Personnel Profile: Full-Time Paid 34; Part-Time Paid 38; Part-Time Volunteers 29; Interns 4.
Governing Authority: private educational institution; nonprofit; board of trustees. Tax-exempt: 501(c)(3).
Art Museum: dedicated to education & art appreciation inspired by Norman Rockwell.
Collections: Norman Rockwell original art including paintings, drawings & sketches; artist's studio with working materials & memorabilia; over 100,000 item archive, including photographs, publications, correspondence & papers; sculptures by Peter Rockwell, son of artist Norman Rockwell.
Major Exhibits: Norman Rockwell: Behind the Camera, 11/7/09-5/10; American Chronicles: The Art of Norman Rockwell, 6/5/10-10/24/10; Jerry Pinkney: Stories from the Heart, 11/6/10-5/11.
Research Fields: Norman Rockwell's life, career & art; 20th-century social history interpretation, field of illustration.
Facilities: library, available for use by appointment; archives; 36 acres of grounds; auditorium; classrooms. Museum-related items for sale.
Activities: guided tours; permanent & changing exhibitions; lecture series; image rental program; educational programs; facilities rental; audio tours; hands-on art activities; art classes.
Publications: quarterly newsletter, The Portfolio; books, The Illustrator's Moment, Norman Rockwell: A Definitive Catalogue, Norman Rockwell's Four Freedoms, Norman Rockwell: A Centennial Celebration, Willie Was Different; The Norman Rockwell Museum at Stockbridge - A Guidebook; Pictures for the American People (published with the High Museum of Art, Atlanta, GA, 1999); American Chronicles, The Art of Norman Rockwell; Portfolio: Norman Rockwell Museum, 40 Years of Illustration Art.
Hours & Admission Prices: May-Oct. daily 10-5; Nov.-April Mon.-Fri. 10-4, Sat.-Sun. 10-5. May-Oct. Admission includes studio tour: adults $15, college students $10; discounts to NEMA, AAM, ICOM members & bus tour groups; members, museum staff, Stockbridge residents, children 18 & under accompanied by an adult no charge. Closed New Year's Day; Thanksgiving; Christmas. ♿
Attendance: 130,000 (estimated)
Membership: Individual $50; Family & Dual $75; Illustrator's Roundtable $150; Gallery Guild $250; Artist's Forum $500; Studio Society $1,000; Painter's Council $2,500; Norman Rockwell Circle $5,000 & up. Business Memberships: Business Friends $150-$249: Business Roundtable $250-$499; Business Four Freedoms $500-$999; Business Studio Society $1,000-$2,499; Business Linwood Society $2,500-$4,999; Business Norman Rockwell Circle $5,000 & up.

STOCKBRIDGE LIBRARY HISTORICAL COLLECTION, 46 Main St., Stockbridge, MA 01262. Mailing Address: P.O. Box 119, Stockbridge, MA 01262-0119. Tel.: 413-298-5501.
E-mail: ballen@cwmars.org
Formerly: Historical Room
Founded: 1938.
Congressional District: 1
Key Personnel: Cur., Barbara Allen; C.E.O., Rosemary Schneyer; Pres. (V), Lenore Sundberg; Cur. Asst., Joshua Hall.
Personnel Profile: Full-Time Paid 1; Part-Time Paid 1; Part-Time Volunteers 8; Interns 1.
Governing Authority: nonprofit organization. Parent Institution: Stockbridge Library Association, Main St. Tax-exempt: 501(c)(3).
History Museum.
Collections: inventions by Anson Clark; memorabilia of Cyrus W. Field; 1751 Jonathan Edwards table; local history; archives; Indian artifacts & documents; Rachel Field's doll, Hitty.
Research Fields: local history; Indian artifacts.
Facilities: 1,500-vol. library of local history books & books by local authors available on premises; reading room.
Activities: permanent & temporary exhibitions; research facility.
Hours & Admission Prices: Tues.-Fri. 10-5, Sat. 10-2. No charge; donations accepted. Closed national holidays.
Attendance: 2,500 (estimated)

Stoughton

STOUGHTON HISTORICAL SOCIETY, Lucius Clapp Memorial, 6 Park St., Stoughton, MA 02072. Mailing Address: Box 542, Stoughton, MA 02072-0542. Tel.: 781-344-5456.
E-mail: stoughtonhistoricalsociety@verizon.net
Web Site: www.stoughtonhistory.com
Founded: 1895.
Congressional District: 9
Key Personnel: Chm. (V), Joseph M. Mokrisky; Pres., Dwight Mac Kerron; Historian, Howard Hansen; Cur., Henry J. Herbowy; Archivist, Jack Sidebottom.
Personnel Profile: Part-Time Volunteers 30.
Governing Authority: society; nonprofit. Tax-exempt.
History Museum: housed in Lucius Clapp Memorial.
Collections: artifacts pertaining to civic and cultural aspects of the town; records of Old Stoughton Musical Society & Musical Society in Stoughton; old music books & manuscripts.
Research Fields: Revolutionary War soldiers from the area; old music; history of Stoughton; genealogy of Stoughton families.
Facilities: library of local history documents available for use by appointment; reading room; 60-seat auditorium.
Activities: lectures; musical or historical dramatic programs.
Publications: 100th Anniversary (1995) Historical Booklet; quarterly newsletter; Stoughton - A Pictorial History; History of Old Stoughton Musical Society.
Hours & Admission Prices: Tues. 10-3, Thurs. 6pm-8pm; other times by appointment. No charge; donations accepted.
Attendance: 500 (estimated)
Membership: Individual $10; Family $15.

Stow

RANDALL LIBRARY, 19 Crescent St., Stow, MA 01775-1188. Tel.: 978-897-8572. Fax: 978-897-7379.
E-mail: stow@minlib.net
Founded: 1892.
Congressional District: 3
Key Personnel: Dir., Susan C. Wysk; Chm. (V), Peter Masters.
Governing Authority: municipal.
Historical Society Museum.
Collections: period furnishings; artifacts.
Research Fields: local history.
Facilities: 40,000-vol. library of books, periodicals & A-V materials available for use on premises; reading room.

Activities: permanent exhibitions.
Hours & Admission Prices: July-Aug. Tues.-Thurs. 10-8, Fri. 10-2; Sept.-June Tues.-Thurs. 10-8, Fri. 10-2, Sat. 10-5. No charge. Closed legal holidays. ♿

STOW WEST SCHOOL MUSEUM, Harvard Rd., Stow, MA 01775. Mailing Address: 380 Great Rd., Stow, MA 01775-2127. Tel.: 978-562-6843.
E-mail: kcthreads@earthlink.net
Founded: 1974.
Congressional District: 3
Key Personnel: Chm. (V), Karen C. Gray.
Personnel Profile: Part-Time Volunteers 5.
Governing Authority: private; nonprofit. Parent Institution: Stow Historical Commission. Tax-exempt: 501(c)(3).
Historic House Museum: housed in an 1825 one-room schoolhouse.
Collections: furnishings; maps; old photos; merit awards; school books.
Research Fields: life of early teachers & scholars.
Activities: Museum Sponsors: Open Houses in summer.
Publications: coloring book; brochure.
Hours & Admission Prices: July-Sept. 2nd Sun. of month 3-5:30; other times by appointment. No charge; donations accepted.
Attendance: 150 (estimated)

Sturbridge

OLD STURBRIDGE VILLAGE, (M), 1 Old Sturbridge Village Rd., Sturbridge, MA 01566-1198. Tel.: 508-347-3362. Fax: 508-347-0377. TDD: 508-347-5383.
E-mail: osv@osv.org
Web Site: www.osv.org
Founded: 1946.
Congressional District: 2
Key Personnel: Pres. & C.E.O., Jim Donahue; Chief of Staff, Renee M. Chambers; Trustees Chm., Michael D. Brockelman; Vice Pres. Finance & Info Systems, Paul D. Wykes; Vice Pres. Museum Program, J. Edward Hood; Dir. Facilities & Grounds, Bradley W. King; Dir. Mktg. & Public Rels., Ann Lindblad.
Personnel Profile: Full-Time Paid 57; Part-Time Paid 127; Part-Time Volunteers 135; Interns 13.
Governing Authority: nonprofit organization. Parent Institution: Old Sturbridge, Inc. Tax-exempt: 170(b)(1)(A) & 501(c)(3).
History Museum.
Collections: over 40 historical buildings with historical landscape & gardens; 6 houses; district school; 2 meetinghouses; bank; store; law office; gristmill; carding mill; cider mill; sawmill; tin shop; pottery; working kiln; working farm, livestock & crops; artifacts to 1840; costumes; ceramics; iron; leather goods; farm & craft tools; militia accoutrements; scientific & medical equipment; glass; guns; decorative arts; textiles; clocks; furniture; vehicles; lighting devices; plants & herbs; manuscripts; maps; atlases; photographs.
Research Fields: rural community life; agriculture & horticulture; crafts; technology & industry; historical archaeology; social history; women's history; domestic life; economic history; architectural history; material culture; audience research & evaluation.
Facilities: 33,000-vol. research library of books & bound periodicals; conference center; visitor center; theater. Reproductions of museum originals, books, decorative arts & crafts for sale.
Activities: theme days; workshops; educational programs; children's museum; teacher workshops; demonstrations of working crafts including pottery, coopering, basketmaking, tin work, blacksmithing, shoemaking, bonnet-making, spinning & weaving; membership & volunteer program; History Learning Laboratory online tour; hands-on History Gateway for children & families.
Publications: semi-annual magazine, Old Sturbridge Visitor; thematic leaflets; cookbook; guidebook; booklets & monographs on early New England social & material life, artifacts & customs; educational publications; postcards; brochures; annual report; exhibition catalogs; pictorial calendar; email newsletter; online collections database.
Hours & Admission Prices: Call for hours. Adults $20, senior citizens 65 & over $18, youth 3-17 $6 discount to AAM members; children under 3, members & second visit within 10 days no charge. Closed Christmas. ♿
Attendance: 225,000 (estimated)
Membership: Individual $50 (1 year), $130 (3 years); Individual Plus One $80 (1 year), $195 (3 years); Family $80 (1 year), $195 (3 years); Donor & Corporate: Participating $120; Contributing $150-$249; Pliny & Delia Freeman $250-$499; Emerson & Laura Bixby $500-$999; Federalist $1,000-$2,499; Asa & Susan Knight $2,500-$4,999; Salem & Sally Towne $5,000-$9,999; President's Circle $10,000 and up.

Sudbury

LONGFELLOW'S WAYSIDE INN, Wayside Inn Rd., Sudbury, MA 01776. Mailing Address: 72 Wayside Inn Rd., Sudbury, MA 01776-3224. Tel.: 978-443-1776. Fax: 978-443-8041.
E-mail: history@wayside.org
Web Site: www.wayside.org
Formerly: Howe's Tavern
Founded: 1716.
Congressional District: 5
Key Personnel: Pres. (V), Joseph Vrabel; Innkeeper, John J. Cowden; Museum Svcs. Mgr., Guy R. LeBlanc.
Personnel Profile: Full-Time Paid 2; Part-Time Paid 4; Part-Time Volunteers 2.
Governing Authority: board of trustees; nonprofit organization. Tax-exempt: 501(c)(3).
History Museum.
Collections: period furnishings. Historic Buildings: operative 1716 inn; Redstone School; Martha-Mary Chapel; grist mill; coach house.
Research Fields: tavern keeping; colonial life.
Facilities: 150-vol. library of works by early American authors; archives.
Activities: guided tours; lectures; school groups; recreation historic militia; fife & drum corp; permanent & temporary exhibitions.
Publications: Tales of a Wayside Inn; Wayside Inn Historama.
Hours & Admission Prices: School & Grist Mill: April-Nov. Wed.-Sun. 9-5. No charge, donations accepted. Closed Independence Day; Christmas.
Attendance: 15,000 (estimated)

Swampscott

ATLANTIC NO. 1 VETERANS FIREMEN'S ASSOCIATION, INC., 76 Burrill St., Swampscott, MA 01907-1915. Mailing Address: 41 Lynn Shore Dr., Lynn, MA 01902-4927. Tel.: 781-595-4050.
Founded: 1966.
Congressional District: 6
Key Personnel: Pres., Rowe Austin; Dir., Richard Maitland; Sec., Edna Maitland; Treas., Douglas B. Maitland.
Governing Authority: municipal; nonprofit organization. Tax-exempt.
Fire-Fighting Museum.
Collections: period fire engine; 1845 Hunneman hand tub.
Activities: Museum Sponsors: Muster for Antique Engines during summer.
Hours & Admission Prices: Call for appointment. No charge.
Membership: Individual $5.

SWAMPSCOTT HISTORICAL SOCIETY (SIR JOHN HUMPHREY HOUSE), 99 Paradise Rd., Swampscott, MA 01907-1955. Tel.: 781-599-1297.
Founded: 1921.
Congressional District: 8
Key Personnel: Pres., Mary Cassidy; Acting Treas., Douglas Maitland.
Personnel Profile: Part-Time Volunteers 10.
Governing Authority: nonprofit organization. Tax-exempt: 170(b)(1)(A).
Historic House Museum: 1637 Sir John Humphrey House.
Collections: memorabilia of Swampscott & its residents.
Activities: guided tours; local school tours. Museum Sponsors: special open house events during year; Independence Day celebration.
Publications: newsletter.
Hours & Admission Prices: By appointment. No charge; donations accepted.
Attendance: 500 (estimated)
Membership: Students $10; Individual $20; Family $40; Life $250.

Taunton

OLD COLONY HISTORICAL SOCIETY, (M), 66 Church Green, Taunton, MA 02780-3445. Tel.: 508-822-1622. Fax: 508-880-6317.
E-mail: OldColony@oldcolonyhistoricalsociety.org
Web Site: www.oldcolonyhistoricalsociety.org
Founded: 1853.
Congressional District: 9
Key Personnel: Dir., Jane M. Hennedy; Pres. (V), Cynthia Booth Ricciardi, Ph.D.; Cur., Christie Jackson; Asst. to Dir., Elizabeth Bernier; Archivist, Andrew D. Boisvert.
Personnel Profile: Full-Time Paid 4; Part-Time Paid 2; Part-Time Volunteers 16; Interns 1.
Governing Authority: society; nonprofit. Tax-exempt: 501(c)(3).
Historical Society Museum: housed in 1852 Bristol Academy Building designed by Richard Upjohn.
Collections: decorative arts including furniture, portraits, Rogers Groups, textiles, household utensils; fire fighting equipment; military artifacts; dolls & toys; early fire engine, stoves & tools; local industrial history; silver.
Major Exhibits: Soaring to New Heights: Aviation in Taunton, 1919-2009, 11/09-3/27/10; Taunton, The Inland Port, 4/15/10-8/28/10; Small Things, Big History, 9/18/10-3/11.

Research Fields: genealogy; local history; local decorative arts.
Facilities: 7,000-vol. library; archives.
Activities: guided tours; illustrated talks; internships; children's programs.
Publications: quarterly newsletter; book, A History of Taunton, Massachusetts.
Hours & Admission Prices: Tues.-Sat. 10-4. Adults $4, seniors & children 12-18 $2; discounts to Southeastern Massachusetts Convention & Visitors Center Bureau, AASLH, NEMA, AAM & ICOM members; members no charge. Genealogical Research Admission: $7. Closed Saturdays preceding Monday holidays.
Attendance: 5,892 (accurate)
Membership: Student $20; Individual $35; Dual $55; Family $75; Supporting $100; Sustaining & Corporate $250; Life $500. (Educator's 10% discount)

Templeton

NARRAGANSETT HISTORICAL SOCIETY, 1 Boynton Rd., Templeton, MA 01468. Mailing Address: P.O. Box 354, Templeton, MA 01468-0354. Tel.: 978-939-2303.
E-mail: narragansetthistoricalsociety@yahoo.com
Web Site: www.narragansetthistoricalsociety.org
Founded: 1928.
Key Personnel: Pres. (V), Michael Watt; Historian, Shirley Barnes; Treas., Ralph Henshaw.
Governing Authority: nonprofit organization. Tax-exempt.
Historical Society: housed in 1810 two-story brick house.
Collections: local history.
Facilities: reference library; meeting rooms; garden.
Activities: guided tours; permanent exhibitions.
Publications: quarterly newsletter.
Hours & Admission Prices: July-Aug. Sat. 2-5. No charge; donations accepted.
Membership: Annual $5.50; Lifetime $30.

Topsfield

IPSWICH RIVER WILDLIFE SANCTUARY (MASSACHUSETTS AUDUBON SOCIETY), 87 Perkins Row, Topsfield, MA 01983-1922. Tel.: 978-887-9264. Fax: 978-887-0875.
E-mail: ipswichriver@massaudubon.org
Web Site: www.massaudubon.org
Founded: 1951.
Key Personnel: Dir., Carol J. Decker; Pres., Laura Johnson; Chm. (V), Jon Panek; Adult Program Coord. & Volunteer Coord., Susan Baeslack; Property Mgr., Richard Wolniewicz; Sec., Janet Barnes; Office Mgr., Christina MacDougall; Master Naturalist, Bob Speare; Caretaker & Property Worker, Fred Goodwin; Education Coord., Lois Bairstow; Teacher & Naturalist, Scott Santino; Education Coord., Sally Willard.
Personnel Profile: Full-Time Paid 7; Part-Time Paid 3; Part-Time Volunteers 125.
Governing Authority: society. Parent Institution: Massachusetts Audubon Society, S. Great Rd., Lincoln, MA 01773. Tax-exempt.
Wildlife Refuge and Bird Sanctuary.
Collections: wildlife & their habitats.
Facilities: non-lending library of natural history books; education center; meeting barn; camping. Gift items for sale.
Activities: bird watching; maple sugaring; camping & canoeing for MA Audubon members only; cross-country skiing; river ecology canoe trips; 10 mile hiking trails; natural history programs for adults & children; summer day camp.
Publications: Map of Sanctuary; tri-annual program brochure; day camp brochure; school services brochure; bird list.
Hours & Admission Prices: Sanctuary: Mon. holidays & Tues.-Sun. dawn-dusk. Adults $4, senior citizens & children 2-12 $3; members of MA Audubon no charge. Office: May-Oct. Tues.-Fri. 9-4, Sat.-Sun. 9-5; Nov.-April Tues.-Sun. 9-4.
Attendance: 30,000
Membership: Student $20; Individual $40; Family $50; Supporting $60; Defender $75; Donor $100; Protector $150; Sponsor $250; Patron $500; Leadership Friend $1,250.

TOPSFIELD HISTORICAL SOCIETY, One Howlett St., Topsfield, MA 01983-1409. Mailing Address: P.O. Box 323, Topsfield, MA 01983-0523. Tel.: 978-887-9724.
E-mail: membership@topsfieldhistory.org
Web Site: www.topsfieldhistory.org
Formerly: Parson Capen House and Gould Barn
Founded: 1894.
Congressional District: 6
Key Personnel: Pres. (V) & Museum Shop Mgr., Norman J. Isler; Vice Pres., Anne Barrett; Treas., Richard Carlson.
Personnel Profile: Part-Time Volunteers 20.
Governing Authority: society. Tax-exempt.
Historic Houses: 1683 Parson Capen House & 1710 Gould Barn.
Collections: early American artifacts.
Facilities: library pertaining to historical society's collections & maps of local area.
Activities: tea served Wednesday afternoons.
Publications: catalogue, Houses & Buildings of Topsfield, MA, 1902-1950; brochure: Topsfield and the Witchcraft Tragedy; History of Topsfield 1940.
Hours & Admission Prices: mid-June to early Sept. Wed., Fri. & Sun. 1-4:30. Suggested Donation: $3.
Attendance: 3,500 (estimated)
Membership: Individual $15; Couple $25; Family $35; Contributing $50; Life $350.

Turners Falls

GREAT FALLS DISCOVERY CENTER, 2 Avenue A, Turners Falls, MA 01376-1101. Tel.: 413-863-3221.
Web Site: greatfallsma.org
History Museum.
Collections: exhibits pertaining to Connecticut River Watershed.
Hours & Admission Prices: May-Aug. daily 10-4; Sept.-April Fri.-Sat. 10-4; other times by appointment. No charge. Closed New Year's Day; Thanksgiving; Christmas.

THE HALLMARK MUSEUM OF CONTEMPORARY PHOTOGRAPHY, 85 Avenue A, Turners Falls, MA 01376-1152. Tel.: 413-863-0009.
E-mail: info@hmcp.org
Web Site: hmcp.org
Key Personnel: Founder & Pres., George J. Rosa, III; Exec. Dir., Janice Boudreau; Exhibitions Dir. & Cur., Paul R. Turnbull; Exhibitions Mgr. & Archivist, Kiersten Hanna; Asst. Preparator & Docent, Bill Cleveland; Admin. & Docent, Jeanie Schermesser; Asst. to Dir. & Exhibitions Installer, Stanley Wheeler; Asst. to Dir. & Facilities Mgr., David Descavich; Business Operations Mgr., Ed Martin; Technical Operations Mgr., Thom Burden; Webmaster, Matt Jacobson-Carroll
Photography Museum.
Collections: contemporary photography from national & international artists.
Hours & Admission Prices: Thurs.-Sun. 1-5. No charge. Closed New Year's Day & week; Easter; Thanksgiving; Christmas Day & week.

Wakefield

WAKEFIELD HISTORICAL SOCIETY, Americal Civic Center, 467 Main St., Wakefield, MA 01880. Mailing Address: P.O. Box 1902, Wakefield, MA 01880-5902. Tel.: 781-246-3070.
E-mail: history@wakefieldma.org
Web Site: www.wakefieldma.org
Founded: 1890.
Key Personnel: Pres. (V), Nancy Bertrand; Treas., David Gooch.
Governing Authority: society. Tax-exempt: 501(c)(3).
Local History Museum.
Collections: Wakefield history.
Activities: lectures.
Hours & Admission Prices: Sept.-May second Tues. of month; other times by appointment. No charge.
Membership: Students $5; Individual $15; Family $20; Lifetime $100.

Waltham

CHARLES RIVER MUSEUM OF INDUSTRY & INNOVATION, (M), 154 Moody St., Waltham, MA 02453-5302. Tel.: 781-893-5410. Fax: 781-891-4536.
E-mail: dan@crmi.org
Web Site: www.crmi.org
Founded: 1980.
Congressional District: 8
Key Personnel: Dir. & Exec. Dir., Dan Yaeger; Pres. (V), Arthur Nelson; Treas., Kim Washisuo; Asst. Dir., Kim Kalen.
Personnel Profile: Full-Time Paid 1; Part-Time Paid 4; Part-Time Volunteers 15; Interns 1.
Governing Authority: nonprofit organization. Tax-exempt: 501(c)(3).
Textile and Industrial Museum: museum of innovation.
Collections: textiles; automobile & steam engine; power generation; machine tools.
Research Fields: pertaining to collections; social & cultural history of industrial communities.
Facilities: 4,000-vol. library including trade catalogues, technical manuals & technical drawings; business records; horology collection.
Activities: guided tours; lectures; organized education programs for adults, children & undergraduate or graduate college students; participatory exhibits.

Publications: quarterly newsletter, The Innovator; Canoeing the Charles-Images & Field Notes 1902-1912.
Hours & Admission Prices: Thurs.-Sat. 10-5. Adults $5, seniors & students $3; discounts to WGBH, AAM, AAA & NAWCC members; children under 6 & members no charge. ♿
Attendance: 13,000 (estimated)
Membership: Student & Senior $15; Individual $25; Family $40. Corporate: Member $100; Supporter $250; Patron $500; Guarantor $1,000; Sponsor $2,500; Benefactor $5,000.

* **GORE PLACE, (M),** 52 Gore St., Waltham, MA 02453-6866. Tel.: 781-894-2798. Fax: 781-894-5745.
E-mail: goreplace@goreplace.org
Web Site: goreplace.org
Founded: 1935.
Congressional District: 8
Key Personnel: Pres. (V), Deborah Gates; Exec. Dir., Susan Robertson; Collections Mgr., Lana Lewis; Education Coord., Tamar Agulian; Supt. Grounds, Scott Clarke.
Personnel Profile: Full-Time Paid 4; Full-Time Volunteers 1; Part-Time Paid 9; Part-Time Volunteers 75; Interns 1.
Governing Authority: nonprofit organization. Tax-exempt: 501(c)(3).
Historic House: 1806 22-room Gore Mansion.
Collections: period furniture & Gore pieces; early 19th century American agriculture. Historic Buildings: 1793 carriage house; 1806 mansion built by Christopher & Rebecca Gore; 1835 farmhouse, on a 40 acre historic site.
Research Fields: genealogy; landscape design; architectural history; local history; historic breeds of animals.
Facilities: library; research room.
Activities: guided tours; lectures; special events for members; scholarly research; formally organized education programs for children.
Publications: descriptive brochures; newsletter; books, House Servants Directory; Christopher Gore: Federalist of Massachusetts 1758-1827; educational film, The Gores of Massachusetts; Setting Out to Best Advantage - At Home with Christopher & Rebecca Gore.
Hours & Admission Prices: Tours: April-Nov. Mon.-Fri. 1pm, Sat.-Sun. 12, 1, 2, 3; Dec.-March Mon.-Fri. 1pm. Adults $10, children under 12 $5; members no charge. Closed federal holidays. ♿
Attendance: 16,000 (accurate)
Membership: Waltham-Watertown Resident $25; Individual $30; Dual & Family $50; Sustaining $100-$249; Sponsor (or Corporate) $250-$999; Patron $1,000.

LYMAN ESTATE, THE VALE, 185 Lyman St., Waltham, MA 02452-5645. Mailing Address: 141 Cambridge St., Boston, MA 02114-2702. Tel.: 781-891-4882, ext. 244. Fax: 781-893-7832.
Web Site: www.historicnewengland.org
Founded: 1951.
Congressional District: 8
Key Personnel: Pres., Carl Nold; Functions Dept. Head, Sharron Kenney.
Governing Authority: society; nonprofit organization. Parent Institution: Historic New England, 141 Cambridge St., Boston 02114. Tel.: 617-227-3956. Tax-exempt: 501(c)(3).
Historic House: housed in the country estate of Boston merchant Theodore Lyman; built in 1793
Collections: landscape, grounds & gardens; operating greenhouses containing 100 year-old camellia trees; grapevines; orchids; rare exotic plants.
Facilities: botanical garden; banquet facilities.
Activities: guided tours; lectures & special events; rental facilities.
Publications: Historic New England Guide.
Hours & Admission Prices: Mansion: by appointment. Greenhouse: Wed.-Sun. 9:30-4. Guided Tours: 1st Wed. of month 11-2. Adults $6; members no charge.
Attendance: 8,798 (accurate)
Membership: National $35; Individual $45; Household $55; Garden & Landscape $75; Institutional $85; Contributing $100; Historic Homeowner $200; Supporting $250.

THE ROSE ART MUSEUM OF BRANDEIS UNIVERSITY, (M), 415 South St., MS069, Brandeis Univ., Waltham, MA 02453-2728. Mailing Address: P.O. Box 549110, Waltham, MA 02454-9110. Tel.: 781-736-3434. Fax: 781-736-3439.
E-mail: rosemail@courier.brandeis.edu
Web Site: www.brandeis.edu/rose
Formerly: The Rose Art Museum
Founded: 1961.
Congressional District: 7
Key Personnel: Dir. Museum Operations, Roy Dawes; Collections Mgr., Valerie M. Wright.
Personnel Profile: Full-Time Paid 7; Part-Time Volunteers 11; Interns 7.
Governing Authority: university. Parent Institution: Operated by Brandeis University, Waltham, MA. Tax-exempt.
Art Museum.
Collections: international modern & contemporary art.
Research Fields: modern & contemporary art.
Activities: temporary exhibitions; lectures; tours; members' events; catalog exchange program.
Publications: exhibition catalogs; brochures.
Hours & Admission Prices: Tues.-Sun. 12-5. No charge. Closed major holidays. ♿
Attendance: 13,000 (accurate)
Membership: Individual $50; Couple $75; Friend $125; Associate $250; Patron $500; Benefactor $1,000; Angel $2,500; Director's Circle $5,000; Corporate $5,000 & up; Founder's Circle $10,000.

WALTHAM HISTORICAL SOCIETY, 190 Moody St., Waltham, MA 02453-5384. Tel.: 781-891-5815.
E-mail: waynemccarthy@rcn.com
Web Site: www.walthamhistoricalsociety.org
Founded: 1913.
Congressional District: 7
Key Personnel: Co-Pres., Wayne McCarthy; Co-Pres., Sheila E. FitzPatrick; Treas., Mary Selig; Recording Sec., Leona Lindsay; Corresponding Sec., Joseph Vizard; Cur., Michelle Morello; Communications, Wayne T. McCarthy; Asst. Cur., Winifred W. Kneisel.
Personnel Profile: Part-Time Volunteers 10.
Governing Authority: society. Annex: 760 Main St., Waltham, MA 02453. Tax-exempt: 501(c)3.
Local History Museum: housed in 1813 Francis Cabot Lowell Mill.
Collections: archives; costumes; watch industry; historic objects; agricultural & household tools; photographs.
Facilities: 1,000-vol. library of books, pamphlets, photographs, maps & clippings available for use on premises by appointment.
Activities: lectures; temporary exhibitions.
Publications: Waltham As a Precinct of Watertown & As a Town, 1630-1884; Waltham Industries; The Golden Door: The Story of Waltham's Economic Progress; occasional pamphlets; quarterly newsletter; Driving Tour of North Waltham.
Hours & Admission Prices: By appointment only. Annex: Sun. 1-4. No charge; donations accepted. Closed holidays.
Attendance: 400
Membership: Individual $25; Family $30; Life $150.

THE WALTHAM MUSEUM, 25 Lexington St., Waltham, MA 02452-4415. Tel.: 781-893-9020.
E-mail: aaarena@hotmail.com
Web Site: walthammuseum.com
Founded: 1971.
Congressional District: 8
Key Personnel: Dir., Albert A. Arena, Sr.
Personnel Profile: Part-Time Volunteers 12; Interns 6.
Governing Authority: nonprofit organization. Tax-exempt: 501(c)(3).
Local History Museum.
Collections: local history & culture; period artifacts; watches; clocks; automobiles; bottles; stoves; radios; tools; lanterns; cloth; bicycles; steam engines; period fire engines; cameras; military artifacts; Native American arrowheads & tools; boilers; lathes; local sports exhibits; locally made items.
Research Fields: local history.
Facilities: more than 2,000-vol. library of books on Waltham available by appointment only.
Activities: guided tours; lectures; films; permanent exhibitions; slide shows for organizations; school group tours; cable TV program, This Was Waltham.
Publications: bimonthly newsletter.
Hours & Admission Prices: Tues.-Sat. 1-4:30; other times by appointment. Adults $4, seniors & children $2; members no charge. Closed holidays. ♿
Attendance: 1,000 (estimated)
Membership: Annual $25; Corporations $100.

Watertown

ARMENIAN LIBRARY AND MUSEUM OF AMERICA (ALMA), 65 Main St., Watertown, MA 02472-4400. Tel.: 617-926-2562. Fax: 617-926-0175.
Web Site: www.almainc.org
Founded: 1971.
Congressional District: 8

Key Personnel: Chm. (V), Haig Der Manuelian; Exec. Dir., Mariam Stepanyan; Treas. (V), Jae Erdekian; Cur., Susan Lind-Sinanian; Cur., Gary Lind-Sinanian; Public Rels., Christie Hardiman.
Personnel Profile: Full-Time Paid 3; Part-Time Paid 3; Part-Time Volunteers 50; Interns 1.
Governing Authority: nonprofit organization. Tax-exempt: 501(c)(3).
Cultural Museum.
Collections: Ethnic Armenian historical items; folk art; fine art; textiles; coins; photography; ceramics; religious art.
Major Exhibits: After the Fall: Armenian Traditional Dress, 11/09-10/17/10.
Research Fields: Armenian history; textile arts.
Facilities: 20,000-vol. library; 220-seat auditorium; classroom; 16,000 sq. ft. exhibit space. Museum-related items for sale.
Activities: concerts; docent program; films; formal educational programs; guided tours; lectures; loan & temporary exhibitions; rental gallery; theater.
Publications: bimonthly calendar & in-house news, ALMA Matters; ALMA Newsletter, published 3 times annually.
Hours & Admission Prices: Thurs. 6pm-9pm, Fri.-Sun. 1-5. Adults $5; discounts to MA Teachers Assoc., AAM & ICOM members; members no charge. Closed New Year's Day; Easter; Thanksgiving; Christmas. ♿
Attendance: 7,000 (estimated)
Membership: Student $15; Individual $35; Family $50; Sustaining $100; Supporting $250; Contributing $500 & up.

PERKINS HISTORY MUSEUM, PERKINS SCHOOL FOR THE BLIND, 175 North Beacon St., Watertown, MA 02472-2790. Tel.: 617-924-3434. Fax: 617-926-2027.
E-mail: historymuseum@perkins.org
Web Site: perkins.pvt.k12.ma.us/museum
Formerly: Museum on the History of Blindness, Perkins School for the Blind
Founded: 1829.
Congressional District: 8
Key Personnel: Cur., Betsy L. McGinnity.
Personnel Profile: Part-Time Paid 1.
Governing Authority: private school. Parent Institution: Perkins School for the Blind. Tax-exempt.
History Museum.
Collections: maps; educational aids for blind or deaf students from 19th-century to present; embossed books; period writing & communication devices; Perkins students including Laura Bridgman, Anne Sullivan, & Helen Keller; tactile globe.
Activities: tours by appointment; permanent exhibitions.
Hours & Admission Prices: Tues. & Thurs. 2-4; other times by appointment. No charge. ♿
Attendance: 875 (estimated)

Wayland

WAYLAND HISTORICAL SOCIETY, 12 Cochituate Rd., Wayland, MA 01778. Mailing Address: P.O. Box 56, Wayland, MA 01778-0056. Tel.: 508-358-7959.
E-mail: wayhistsoc@comcast.net
Web Site: www.waylandhistoricalsociety.org
Founded: 1954.
Congressional District: 5
Key Personnel: Pres., Jane Sciacca; Cur., Lois Davis.
Personnel Profile: Part-Time Volunteers 25.
Governing Authority: nonprofit organization. Tax-exempt: 501(c)(3).
General Museum.
Collections: costumes; furniture; local history; local Indian artifacts. Historic House: c.1740 Grout-Heard House.
Research Fields: local genealogy & archaeology; history of old houses.
Facilities: library of history books available for use on premises; reading room.
Activities: guided tours; lectures; formally organized education programs for children.
Publications: bimonthly newsletter.
Hours & Admission Prices: Tues.-Fri. 9:30 to noon. No charge; donations accepted. ♿
Attendance: 2,000 (estimated)
Membership: Junior $2; Single $15; Family $25; Contributing $50; Patron $100; Life $350.

Wellesley

DAVIS MUSEUM AND CULTURAL CENTER, (M), Wellesley College, 106 Central St., Wellesley, MA 02481-8203. Tel.: 781-283-2051. Fax: 781-283-2064.
Web Site: www.davismuseum.wellesley.edu
Founded: 1889.
Congressional District: 10
Key Personnel: Interim Dir., Dennis McFadden; Cur. Paintings, Sculpture & Photography, Dabney Hailey; Asst. Dir. Curatorial & Education and Cur. Prints & Drawings, Elizabeth Wyckoff; Cur. Education, Alexa Miller; Dir. Devel., Nancy Gunn; Security Mgr., David Accorsini.
Personnel Profile: Full-Time Paid 16; Part-Time Paid 5; Part-Time Volunteers 45; Interns 5.
Governing Authority: Wellesley College. Tax-exempt: 501(c)(3).
Art Museum.
Collections: European & American paintings, sculpture, drawings, prints & photographs; period Asiatic, African & pre-conquest Meso-American art.
Facilities: 17,250 sq. ft. gallery space; 167-seat cinema; print, drawing & photo study; study gallery; seminar room.
Activities: permanent & temporary exhibitions; guided tours; lectures; organized education programs for undergraduate students.
Publications: exhibition catalogues; collection handbook.
Hours & Admission Prices: Summer: Tues.-Fri. 12-4, Sept. 9-Dec. 13 Tues. & Thurs.-Sat. 11-5, Wed. 11-8, Sun. 12-4. No charge; donations accepted. Closed holidays; Christmas Eve, Day & week. ♿
Attendance: 30,000 (estimated)
Membership: Recent Alumnae $15; Regular $35; Contributor $50; Sponsor $100; Donor $250; Supporter $500; Benefactor $1,000; Patron $2,500.

WELLESLEY HISTORICAL SOCIETY, INC., 229 Washington St., Wellesley, MA 02481-3105. Tel.: 781-235-6690. Fax: 781-239-0660.
E-mail: info@wellesleyhistoricalsociety.org
Web Site: www.wellesleyhistoricalsociety.org
Founded: 1925.
Congressional District: 4
Key Personnel: Exec. Dir., Elizabeth Krimmel; Pres., Martin Padley.
Personnel Profile: Full-Time Paid 1; Part-Time Volunteers 35.
Governing Authority: society. Tax-exempt: 501(c)(3).
Local History Museum: housed in 1824 Dadmun-McNamara house.
Collections: Archives, artifacts, books, costumes & textiles; fine arts and photographs relating to Wellesley from Native American to present date; Denton butterfly collection; Oldham lace.
Research Fields: Wellesley-people, places, buildings, things.
Facilities: 700-vol. research library pertaining to local history & the Civil War available for use on the premises. Lace reference library; local authors collection.
Activities: changing exhibitions; lecture programs; bus trips; programs for children.
Publications: newsletter; books; exhibit catalogues.
Hours & Admission Prices: Tues.- Wed. 1-4, Thurs. 2-4. No charge; donations accepted. Research by appointment. Research: non-members $10. Closed holidays. ♿
Attendance: 2,000 (estimated)
Membership: Senior 65 & over $20; Individual $35; Family $50; Corporate $150.

Wellfleet

CAPE COD NATIONAL SEASHORE, 99 Marconi Site Rd., Wellfleet, MA 02667. Tel.: 508-255-8925. Fax: 508-240-3291.
E-mail: hope_morrill@nps.gov
Web Site: www.nps.gov/caco
Founded: 1961.
Congressional District: 10
Key Personnel: Chief Interpretation & Cultural Resources, Sue Moynihan; Cur., Hope Morrill.
Governing Authority: federal. Administered by National Park Service, U.S. Dept. of the Interior. Branch Units: Salt Pond Visitor Center, Eastham, MA; Province Lands Visitor Center, near Provincetown. Tax-exempt.
Park Museum & Visitor Center.
Collections: history; natural history; archaeology. Historic Buildings: 18th-century, Atwood-Higgins House; 19th-century Capt. Edward Penniman Home; Old Harbor Life Saving Station; 3 sister Lighthouses.
Research Fields: historic & prehistoric archaeology; natural history.
Facilities: 1,500-vol. library of history & natural history books available for research only on premises. Books for sale at visitor centers.
Activities: guided tours & evening programs; formally organized environmental education program for children during school year; permanent exhibitions; self-guided nature trails open year-round.
Publications: The Archeology of Cape Cod National Seashore; Seashells of Cape Cod National Seashore; Common Trailside Plants of Cape Cod National Seashore; Augusta Penniman Journal of a Whaling Voyage 1864-1868; brochures.
Hours & Admission Prices: Headquarters: Mon.-Fri. 8-4:30. Salt Pond Museum: mid-June to Labor Day daily 9-5; Sept.-May 9-4:30. Salt Pond Visitor Center: Summer 9-5. Province Lands Visitor Center: mid-April to Nov. No charge; donations accepted. Beaches: season pass $45, vehicles $15, pedestrians & bicycles $3. ♿
Attendance: 500,000

Membership: Friends of Cape Cod National Seashore: Individual $20; Family $35; Sustaining $100.

WELLFLEET HISTORICAL SOCIETY MUSEUM, 266 Main St., Wellfleet, MA 02667. Mailing Address: P.O. Box 58, Wellfleet, MA 02667. Tel.: 508-349-9157 & 2216 (Cur.).
Web Site: www.wellfleethistoricalsociety.com
Founded: 1951.
Key Personnel: Cur., Joan Hopkins Coughlin; Staff, David Wright; Staff, Barbara Kennedy.
Personnel Profile: Full-Time Volunteers 1; Part-Time Paid 2.
Governing Authority: nonprofit organization. Parent Institution: Wellfleet Historical Society. Tax-exempt.
Historic Building: c.1800 two-story Victorian building.
Collections: local history; whaling & shell-fishing artifacts; original Thoreau manuscript page from book Cape Cod; scrimshaw; dolls; deeds & manuscripts; maps; genealogy; folk art paintings; needlework; clothing; children's toys & furniture; photographs.
Research Fields: preservation of charcoal painting gift from historian Shebvah Rich; preservation of deeds, documents & town records; preservation of photograph collection onto disc.
Facilities: library & files available for research by public on premises only.
Activities: guided tours; organized education programs for children; loan & temporary exhibitions; historic walking tours.
Publications: pamphlet, Beacon; book, Wellfleet - Famous Beds.
Hours & Admission Prices: June 24-Sept. 6 Tues. & Fri. 10-4, Wed.-Thurs. & Sat. 1-4. No charge; donations accepted.
Attendance: 400 (estimated)
Membership: Annual $5; Family $10; Life $100.

Wenham

* **WENHAM MUSEUM, (M),** 132 Main St., Wenham, MA 01984-1520. Tel.: 978-468-2377. Fax: 978-468-1763.
E-mail: info@wenhammuseum.org
Web Site: www.wenhammuseum.org
Founded: 1921.
Congressional District: 6
Key Personnel: Exec. Dir., Lindsay Diehl; Chm. (V), Charles R. Richey, Jr.; Museum Shop Mgr., Cynthia Novotny.
Personnel Profile: Full-Time Paid 4; Part-Time Paid 9; Part-Time Volunteers 250.
Governing Authority: nonprofit organization. Tax-exempt: 501(c)(3).
History Museum: housed in late 17th-century Claflin-Richards House & modern exhibition building.
Collections: dolls; doll houses; miniatures; toys; toy soldiers; model trains; costumes; textiles; Wenham Lake Ice Industry; fans; embroidery & needlework; quilts; 1890-1921 photographs; early domestic & kitchen utensils; manuscript collections. Historic Buildings: 1840 Merrill shoe shop; c.1690 Claflin-Richards House; 1840 Merrill Shoe Shop.
Research Fields: Wenham history; costumes; dolls; genealogy of local families; ice cutting history.
Facilities: 1,000-vol. library; children's interactive room; reading room; 100-seat hall; classroom. Publications, postcards & gift related items for sale.
Activities: guided tours; lectures; family programs; artisan workshops; formally organized education programs for children; permanent & temporary exhibitions; hands-on exhibits.
Publications: quarterly calendar & newsletter; illustrated annual report; Wenham in Pictures & Prose, The Claflin-Richards House.
Hours & Admission Prices: Tues.-Sun. 10-4. Adults $7, children 1-16 $5; discounts to groups and New England Museum Association, Massachusetts Teachers Assoc. & AAA members; members no charge. Closed Martin Luther King Jr. Day; Presidents' Day; Veterans Day. ♿
Attendance: 35,000 (accurate)
Membership: Senior Citizen $25; Individual $30; Senior Citizen Dual $40; Family $65; Family Plus $90; Contributing $120; Sponsoring $250.

West Barnstable

HIGGINS ART GALLERY - CAPE COD COMMUNITY COLLEGE, 2240 Iyanough Rd., West Barnstable, MA 02668-1599. Tel.: 508-362-2131, ext. 4484. Fax: 508-375-4020.
E-mail: higginsartgalley@capecod.edu
Web Site: www.capecod.mass.edu
Founded: 1989.
Congressional District: 10
Key Personnel: Dir., Betty Carroll Fuller; Pres., Kathleen Schatzberg.
Personnel Profile: Part-Time Paid 2; Interns 4.
Governing Authority: nonprofit; public college. Tax-exempt: 501(c)(3).
Art Museum.
Collections: paintings; prints; drawings; graphics; sculpture; mixed media.
Facilities: 750-seat auditorium; 200-seat cafeteria; classrooms; 600 sq. ft. exhibit space.
Activities: arts festival; workshops; demonstrations; formal education programs for adults (non-credit classes); formal education programs for undergraduate or graduate college students affiliated with Cape Cod Community College; lectures; theater; broadcast programs; live musicians, performers & children's games. Annual Events: Annual Tilden Arts Festival in April & May; Annual Artists in Residence.
Hours & Admission Prices: Sept.-May Mon.-Fri. 10-4; also open prior to events in adjacent college auditorium. No charge. Closed all official national & MA holidays. ♿
Attendance: 2,000 (estimated)

WILLIAM BREWSTER NICKERSON CAPE COD HISTORY ARCHIVES, Cape Cod Community College, 2240 Iyanough Rd., West Barnstable, MA 02668-1532. Tel.: 508-362-2131, ext. 4445. Fax: 508-375-4020.
E-mail: msicchio@capecod.edu
Web Site: www.capecod.mass.edu
Founded: 1971.
Congressional District: 10
Key Personnel: Special Collections Librarian, Mary E. Sicchio.
Personnel Profile: Part-Time Paid 1; Part-Time Volunteers 4.
Governing Authority: public college. Parent Institution: Cape Cod Community College. Tax-exempt: 501(c)(3).
Archives.
Collections: Cape Cod history from Plymouth Colony records to present; Cape Cod Community College & Hyannis Normal School archives; Cape Cod Chamber of Commerce collection; ships' papers.
Facilities: 5,000-vol. library of history books; educational facilities.
Activities: Museum Sponsors: Cape Heritage Week.
Hours & Admission Prices: Mon., Wed. & Fri. 8:30-4:30. No charge. Closed MA state & federal holidays. ♿
Attendance: 500 (accurate)

West Springfield

RAMAPOGUE HISTORICAL SOCIETY, 70 Park St., West Springfield, MA 01089-3318. Mailing Address: P.O. Box 826, West Springfield, MA 01090-0826. Tel.: 413-734-8322 & 732-6187.
Web Site: www.west-springfield.ma.us/
Founded: 1903.
Congressional District: 1
Key Personnel: Pres. (V), Phyllis A. Bertera; Cur., Raymond Wellspeake.
Personnel Profile: Part-Time Volunteers 10.
Governing Authority: society. Tax-exempt: 501(c)(3).
Historic House: 1754 Josiah Day House, original all brick salt box style house.
Collections: 18th-century furniture & accessories with many original Day family possessions.
Research Fields: genealogy of Day family.
Facilities: meeting room.
Activities: guided tours; special events.
Publications: pamphlets; semiannual newsletter.
Hours & Admission Prices: June-Oct. Sat.-Sun. 12-3; other times by appointment. Adults $3; children under 12 & members no charge.
Attendance: 534 (accurate)
Membership: Individual $10; Patron $25; Sponsor $50; Sustaining $100; Individual Life $100; Life Couple $150.

STORROWTON VILLAGE MUSEUM, 1305 Memorial Ave., Eastern States Exposition Grounds, West Springfield, MA 01089-3578. Tel.: 413-205-5051 & 737-2443. Fax: 413-205-5054.
E-mail: storrow@thebige.com
Web Site: thebige.com
Founded: 1929.
Congressional District: 1
Key Personnel: C.E.O., Wayne McCary; Dir., Dennis Picard; Lead Interpreter, Robert Delisle; Admin. Asst., Jacki Sullivan; Museum Shop Mgr., Betsy Goyette.
Personnel Profile: Full-Time Paid 3; Part-Time Paid 3; Part-Time Volunteers 140.
Governing Authority: nonprofit organization. Parent Institution: Eastern States Exposition. Tax-exempt.
Historic Village.
Collections: Historic Buildings: 1767 Phillips House; 1794 Gilbert House; 1810 Schoolhouse; 1810 Eddy law office; 1834 Union Meeting House; late 18th century, Atkinson Tavern; 1822 townhouse; 1776 Potter Mansion; c.1850 blacksmith shop; general store.
Research Fields: herbs & their uses; early New England education & lifestyle.
Facilities: restaurant. Gift items for sale.

Activities: guided tours by costumed interpreters; craft workshops; early American summer day camp; school vacation programs; seasonal special events; formally organized education programs for children; permanent exhibits; classes.
Publications: booklets, Doorways To The Past; Grandmother's Button Box; quarterly newspaper, The Crackerbarrel; cookbook, Aunt Helen's Cookie Recipes; book, Memories of a Door; cookbooks, Out of the Crackerbarrel; Out of the Farmstead Kitchen; Aunt Helen's Cookie Recipes; exhibit guide, Helen Osborn Storrow: The Lady and Her Legacy.
Hours & Admission Prices: Museum: Feb. to 3rd week in June & Sept.-Dec. by appointment only; 3rd week in June to Labor Day Tues.-Sat. 11-3. Admission $5; discounts to NEMA members; AAM members & children under 6 no charge. Administration building, restaurant & gift shops open year round. Closed holidays. ♿
Attendance: 500,000 (estimated)

West Yarmouth

ZOOQUARIUM, 674 Rte. 28, West Yarmouth, MA 02673-5103. Tel.: 508-775-8883.
E-mail: info@zooquariumcapecod.net
Web Site: www.zooquariumcapecod.net
Zoo.
Collections: wildlife.
Hours & Admission Prices: Call for hours. Adults 10 & over $9.75, chidlren 2-9 $6.75; children under 2 no charge.

Westfield

AMELIA PARK CHILDREN'S MUSEUM, 29 S. Broad St., Westfield, MA 01086. Mailing Address: P.O. Box 931, Westfield, MA 01086-0931. Tel.: 413-572-4014. Fax: 413-572-1206.
E-mail: fun@ameliaparkmuseum.org
Web Site: www.ameliaparkmuseum.org
Children's Museum.
Collections: hands-on exhibits.
Activities: special events; birthday parties; play groups.
Hours & Admission Prices: Mon., Wed. & Thurs. 10-4, Fri.-Sat. 10-7, Sun. 10-4. Adults & children $7, seniors $3.50; children under 1 no charge.

JASPER RAND ART MUSEUM, AT WESTFIELD ATHENAEUM, 6 Elm St., Westfield, MA 01085-2904. Tel.: 413-568-7833. Fax: 413-568-0988.
Founded: 1927.
Congressional District: 1
Key Personnel: Dir., Christopher Lindquist; Pres., Bob Brown.
Governing Authority: nonprofit organization. Affiliated with Westfield Athenaeum. Tax-exempt: 101(6).
Art Gallery.
Collections: archives; paintings.
Activities: temporary & traveling exhibitions; permanent collections; art classes for children.
Hours & Admission Prices: July-Aug. Mon.-Thurs. 8:30-8, Fri. 8:30-5; Sept.-June Mon.-Thurs. 8:30-8, Fri.-Sat. 8:30-5. No charge. Closed holidays. ♿

Westford

THE WESTFORD MUSEUM & HISTORICAL SOCIETY, 2 Boston Rd., Westford, MA 01886. Mailing Address: P.O. Box 411, Westford, MA 01886-0411. Tel.: 978-692-5550. Fax: 978-692-5550.
E-mail: museum@westford.com
Web Site: www.westford.com/museum
Founded: 1958.
Key Personnel: Dir., Penny Lacroix
History Museum: housed in the Westford Academy school house, built in 1792.
Collections: local history & culture relating to Westford including yearbooks, photographs & other academic memorabilia.
Research Fields: genealogy; community; genealogy resources; inventory of historic homes; maps; historic newspapers.
Activities: research; genealogy.
Hours & Admission Prices: Sun. 2-4; other times by appointment. No charge; donations accepted. Closed holidays. ♿

Weston

GOLDEN BALL TAVERN MUSEUM, (M), 662 Boston Post Rd., Weston, MA 02493-1511. Mailing Address: P.O. Box 223, Weston, MA 02493-0001. Tel.: 781-894-1751. Fax: 781-861-6218.
E-mail: joanb5@aol.com
Web Site: www.goldenballtavern.org
Founded: 1964.
Congressional District: 5
Key Personnel: Dir., Dr. Joan P. Bines; Chm. (V), William W. Gallagher, III; Pres. (V), William Wiseman.
Personnel Profile: Full-Time Paid 1; Part-Time Paid 1; Part-Time Volunteers 100.
Governing Authority: private; nonprofit organization. Tax-exempt: 501(c)(3).
Historic House: 1768 Georgian house.
Collections: 1768 house; blue & white china; glass; silver; furnishings belonging to the Jones family over 200 years occupation of the house; artifacts found in digs on property; 18th-century tavern and tavern ware; clothing; barn.
Research Fields: archaeology; decorative arts; early taverns; early house construction.
Publications: books, The Grapevine; The Tavern and the Tory; newsletter, Tavern Tidings.
Hours & Admission Prices: Tours: by appointment, call 781-894-1751. Adults $5, senior citizens & students $2; members no charge.
Attendance: 1,350 (estimated)
Membership: Single $15; Family $25; Sustaining $50; Fellow $100; Sponsor $250; Life $1,000; Benefactor $5,000.

SPELLMAN MUSEUM OF STAMPS AND POSTAL HISTORY, (M), 235 Wellesley St., Regis College, Weston, MA 02493-1545. Tel.: 781-768-7331. Fax: 781-768-7332.
E-mail: info@spellman.org
Web Site: www.spellman.org
Founded: 1960.
Congressional District: 5
Key Personnel: Chm. (V), Mark W. Gallagher; Pres. (V), Karen G. Grant; Education & Community Outreach, Henry Lukas; Cur. Philatelic Collections, George Norton; Museum Shop Mgr., Anne O'Keefe.
Personnel Profile: Part-Time Paid 4; Part-Time Volunteers 18.
Governing Authority: nonprofit organization. Tax-exempt: 501(c)(3).
Philatelic Museum.
Collections: over 2,000,000 stamps & covers; general reference philatelic library; particular strengths: United States, European, Vatican, Great Britain, and colonies, Hong Kong, Russia, Central & South America ; air mail stamps and covers.
Research Fields: philatelic & postal history.
Facilities: library of philately & postal history books; meeting rooms; post office. Museum-related items for sale.
Activities: courses; lectures; workshops; guided tours; children's stamp education program; philatelic club meetings.
Publications: newsletter; catalogs; brochure; books, Philatelic Art In America; The Postal History of the Holocaust.
Hours & Admission Prices: July-Aug. Thurs.-Sat. 12-5; Sept.-June Thurs.-Sun. 12-5. Adults $8, seniors & students $5; discounts to AAM, ICOM & NEMA members; children 16 & under and members no charge. Closed Easter; Memorial Day weekend; Labor Day weekend; Thanksgiving & day after; Christmas. ♿
Attendance: 6,395 (accurate)
Membership: Student 16 & under $30; National Associate Living within 50 miles of Weston, MA $35; Individual $40; Household $75; Participating $100; Sustaining $150; Contributing $250; Sponsor $500; Benefactor $1,000.

WESTON HISTORICAL SOCIETY, INC., 358 Boston Post Rd., Weston, MA 02493. Mailing Address: P.O. Box 343, Weston, MA 02493-0002.
Founded: 1963.
Congressional District: 4
Key Personnel: Pres. (V) Weston Historical Society, Pamela W. Fox.
Personnel Profile: Part-Time Volunteers 5.
Governing Authority: society. Parent Institution: Weston Historical Society. Tax-exempt: 501(c)(3).
History Museum.
Collections: photographs; archives; town reports. Historic Building: c.1757 Josiah Smith tavern.
Research Fields: history of Weston.
Facilities: library & archives by appointment; reading room.
Activities: lectures; temporary exhibitions.
Publications: biannual, Bulletin; books, Once Upon a Pung; Random Recollections; One Town in the American Revolution, Weston, Mass.
Hours & Admission Prices: By appointment.
Membership: Family $25; Life $300.

Weymouth

CHILD'S PLAY CHILDREN'S MUSEUM, 293 Libbey Pkwy., Weymouth, MA 02189-3112. Tel.: 781-337-7920.
E-mail: info@childsplaymuseum.com

Web Site: www.childsplaymuseum.com
Children's Museum.
Collections: hands-on exhibits.
Hours & Admission Prices: Mon.-Fri. 9:30-5, Sat. 10-6, Sun. 12-5.

Williamstown

CHAPIN LIBRARY OF RARE BOOKS, 96 School St., Williamstown, MA 01267-2423. Mailing Address: P.O. Box 426, Williamstown, MA 01267-0426. Tel.: 413-597-2462. Fax: 413-597-2929.
E-mail: chapin.library@williams.edu
Web Site: chapin.william.edu
Founded: 1923.
Congressional District: 1
Key Personnel: Asst. Librarian, Wayne G. Hammond; Administrative Asst., Elaine Yanow; Preparation Supvr., Nancy Birkrem; Preparation Asst., Ted Gilley; Custodian, Robert L. Volz.
Personnel Profile: Full-Time Paid 4; Part-Time Paid 1.
Governing Authority: college. Parent Institution: Williams College. Tax-exempt: 501(c)(3).
Library.
Collections: 50,000-vol. collection of rare printed books; 9th to 20th-century manuscripts; bookplates; historical prints; photos; original art work for book illustrations; 15th to 20th-century prints, bibliographical & historical reference books; four founding documents of the United States.
Facilities: library of prints, bibliographical & historical reference books available for use to adults & students.
Activities: permanent & temporary exhibitions; occasional loan exhibitions from other libraries & collectors; lectures; tours by appointment.
Publications: Catalogue of the Collection of Samuel Butler in the Chapin Library; A Short-Title List of the Books in the Chapin Library; The Graphic Art of C.B. Falls; British Book Illustration, 1924-1936; British Ecclesiastical Architecture; Finished by Hand; London: High Life & Low Life.
Hours & Admission Prices: This is our temporary location during renovations until 2011. Mon.-Fri. 10-12 & 1-5. No charge. Closed national holidays except Independence Day.
Attendance: 4,000 (estimated)

* **STERLING AND FRANCINE CLARK ART INSTITUTE, (M), (I),** 225 South St., Williamstown, MA 01267-2891. Mailing Address: P.O. Box 8, Williamstown, MA 01267-0008. Tel.: 413-458-9545. Fax: 413-458-2324.
E-mail: info@clarkart.edu
Web Site: www.clarkart.edu
Founded: 1950.
Congressional District: 1
Key Personnel: Dir., Michael Conforti; Pres. (V), Peter S. Willmott; Deputy Dir., Anthony G. King; Starr Dir. Research & Academic Programs, Michael Ann Holly; Sr. Cur., Richard Rand; Center for Education in the Visual Arts, Michael Cassin; Registrar, Mattie Kelley; Preparator, Paul Dion; Librarian, Susan Roeper; Dir. Communications, Sally Majewski; Museum Shop Mgr., Rachelle Jones.
Personnel Profile: Full-Time Paid 69; Part-Time Paid 34; Interns 10.
Governing Authority: nonprofit organization. Tax-exempt.
Art Museum.
Collections: Italian, Flemish, Dutch & French Old Master paintings from the 14th-18th centuries; French 19th-century paintings, including the Impressionists; selected 19th-century American artists; 19th-century sculpture; Old Master French & American prints & drawings; porcelain; English silver; British art.
Major Exhibits: Giovanni Boldini in Impressionist Paris (T), 2/10-4/10; Picasso/Degas (T), 6/10-9/10.
Research Fields: Visual arts and their role in culture; theory; history and interpretation of works from all periods and genres of art.
Facilities: 250,000-vol. library of art reference books available for inter-library loan & on premises; reading room; 320-seat auditorium. Art books in print; reproductions, postcards & catalogs published by Institute for sale.
Activities: gallery talks; organized educational programs for children; graduate program for MA in art history in collaboration with Williams College; Clark Fellowship; permanent, temporary & traveling exhibitions; social networking art events; film, lecture & concert series.
Publications: catalogs of special exhibitions; guide book; collections catalogues; Clark studies in the visual arts series.
Hours & Admission Prices: July-Aug. daily 10-5; Sept.-June Tues.-Sun. & Mon. holidays 10-5. June-Oct. adults $12.50; discounts to AAM & ICOM members, children under 18 & students; members no charge. Closed New Year's Day; Thanksgiving; Christmas. ♿
Attendance: 191,433 (accurate)
Membership: Individual $50; Family & Dual $75; Sustainer $125; Contributor $250; Sponsor $500; Benefactor $1,000; Scholar's Circle $2,500; Curator's Circle $5,000; Director's Circle $10,000; Sterling Circle $25,000.

* **WILLIAMS COLLEGE MUSEUM OF ART, (M),** 15 Lawrence Hall Dr., Ste. 2, Williamstown, MA 01267-3248. Tel.: 413-597-2429. Fax: 413-458-9017.
E-mail: WCMA@williams.edu
Web Site: www.wcma.org
Founded: 1926.
Congressional District: 1
Key Personnel: Dir., Lisa Corrin; Dir. Asst., Amy Tatro; Mgr. Membership & Special Events, Raymond Torrenti; Dir. Communications & Strategy, Suzanne Silitch; Deputy Dir. & Sr. Cur. Exhibitions, John Stomberg; Sr. Cur. Eugenie Prendergast 19th & 20th Century Art, Nancy Mowll Mathews; Cur. Collections, Vivian Patterson; Interim Assoc. Cur., Kathryn Price; Dir. Museum Donor Rels., Christine Naughton; Public Rels. Asst., Aimee Hirz; Museum Shop Mgr., Michele Migdal; Dir. Museum Registration, Diane Hart; Dir. Education, Cynthia Way; Coord. Education Programs, Joann Harnden; Chief Preparator & Exhibition Designer, Hideyo Okamura; Preparator, Gregory Jay Smith; Preparator, Richard Miller; Budget Admin., Dorothy Lewis; Asst. Registrar, Rachel Tassone; Coord. Mellon Academic Programs, Elizabeth Gallerani; Museum Store Asst., Christine Maher; Security Supvr., Terence White; Museum Security Officer, Jason Wandrei; Museum Security Officer, Michele Alice.
Personnel Profile: Full-Time Paid 20; Part-Time Paid 8; Part-Time Volunteers 50; Interns 21.
Governing Authority: college. Parent Institution: Williams College. Tax-exempt: 501(c)(3).
Art Museum: housed in 1846 Greek Revival rotunda with 1983 & 1986 additions designed by Charles Moore & Robert Harper of Centerbrook Architects & Planners.
Collections: 18th- to 19th-century American art; modern & contemporary American & European art; 9th- to 11th-century South Asian sculpture; 15th- to 19th-century Indian painting & sculpture; African art; Assyrian relief sculptures; 15th- to 18th-century Spanish painting & furniture; medieval art; Italian Renaissance painting & sculpture; European & American prints & drawings; 20th-century American photography; Baroque painting & furniture; holdings of Maurice & Charles Prendergast.
Research Fields: Maurice & Charles Prendergast; modern & contemporary art; American art.
Facilities: auditorium; print study room.
Activities: lectures; gallery talks & tours; concerts; formally organized education programs for undergraduate college students; inter-museum loan, permanent & traveling exhibitions; interpretive programs for children; changing exhibitions of modern & contemporary American, European & non-western art; openings for special exhibitions; sign language interpretation available.
Publications: exhibition catalogues, 2-4 per year.
Hours & Admission Prices: Tues.-Sat. 10-5, Sun. 1-5. No charge; donations accepted. ♿
Attendance: 53,452 (accurate)
Membership: Individual $25; Dual & Family $40; Patron $100; Benefactor $250; Donor $500; WCMA Contemporary $1,000; Prof. Whitney Stoddard 1935 $1,500; Prof. Karl Weston 1896 $2,500; Prof. S. Lane Faison, Jr. 1929 $5,000.

Wilmington

WILMINGTON TOWN MUSEUM, (M), 430 Salem St., Wilmington, MA 01887-1211. Tel.: 978-658-5475.
E-mail: htavern@town.wilmington.ma.us
Web Site: www.town.wilmington.ma.us/tavern1.html
History Museum: housed in the Col. Joshua Harnden Tavern.
Collections: local history & culture relating to the town of Wilmington.
Hours & Admission Prices: July to early Aug. Thurs.-Fri. 10-2; Sept.-June. Tues. & Thurs. 10-2.

Winchendon

WINCHENDON HISTORICAL SOCIETY, INC., 151 Front St., Winchendon, MA 01475-1521. Mailing Address: P.O. Box 279, Winchendon, MA 01475-0279. Tel.: 978-297-2142.
Founded: 1930.
Congressional District: 1
Key Personnel: Pres., Theresa N. Beauvais; Cur., Rita Saveall.
Personnel Profile: Part-Time Volunteers 10.
Governing Authority: nonprofit organization. Parent Institution: Winchendon Historical Society. Tax-exempt.
History Museum.
Collections: archives; manuscripts; toys.
Activities: permanent & temporary exhibitions.
Publications: quarterly newsletter.
Hours & Admission Prices: June 2-Oct. Wed. 10-4, Sun.1-4; other times by appointment. Tours: 1 & 2:30. Adults $5; members no charge.

Attendance: 300 (estimated)
Membership: Student $5; Seniors $15; Individual $20; Family $35.

Winchester

GRIFFIN MUSEUM OF PHOTOGRAPHY, (M), 67 Shore Rd., Winchester, MA 01890-2821. Tel.: 781-729-1158. Fax: 781-721-2765.
E-mail: photos@griffinmuseum.org
Web Site: www.griffinmuseum.org
Formerly: Arthur Griffin Center For Photographic Art
Founded: 1992.
Congressional District: 7
Key Personnel: Pres. (V), Peter Griffin; Exec. Dir., Paula Tognarelli; Vice Pres., John McConnell; Treas., Clarence Kemper; Assoc. Dir., Meredith Mulcahy; Gallery Monitor, Andrea Alberg.
Personnel Profile: Full-Time Paid 2; Part-Time Paid 1; Part-Time Volunteers 20; Interns 4.
Governing Authority: private; nonprofit organization. Tax-exempt: 501(c)(3).
Photography Museum.
Collections: slides & transparencies taken by photographer Arthur Griffin, 1904-present.
Facilities: 1,500 sq. ft. exhibit space; 90-seat theater. Museum-related items for sale.
Activities: formal educational programs; guided tours; photographer workshops; lectures; rental gallery; temporary, loan & traveling exhibitions. Annual Event: Juried Photography Exhibition.
Publications: quarterly newsletter , Focus.
Hours & Admission Prices: Tues.-Thurs. 11-5, Fri. 11-4, Sat.-Sun. 12-4. Adults $5, seniors $2; members, children, students & Thurs. no charge. Closed major holidays. ♿
Attendance: 7,000 (estimated)
Membership: Student $25; Individual $40; Family & Dual $75; Friend $150; Contributor $250; Patron & Corporate $500; Benefactor & Senior Corporate $1,000; Major Benefactor $5,000.

Woods Hole

WOODS HOLE OCEANOGRAPHIC INSTITUTION, OCEAN SCIENCE EXHIBIT CENTER, 15 School St., Woods Hole, MA 02543-1126. Mailing Address: Mail Stop 45, Woods Hole O.I., Woods Hole, MA 02543. Tel.: 508-289-2663. Fax: 508-457-2147.
E-mail: information@whoi.edu
Web Site: www.whoi.edu
Founded: 1930.
Key Personnel: Dir., Susan Avery; Museum Shop Mgr., Kathy Patterson.
Personnel Profile: Full-Time Paid 2; Part-Time Paid 2; Part-Time Volunteers 10.
Governing Authority: Tax-exempt.
Oceanographic Research Institution.
Collections: oceanographic research photographs, data, tools, instruments, vehicles, vessels.
Research Fields: all aspects of oceanography.
Publications: magazines, Woods Hole Currents published quarterly; Oceanus published biannually.
Hours & Admission Prices: April groups by appointment; May-Oct. Mon.-Sat. 10-4:30; Nov.-Dec. Tues.-Fri. 10-4:30. Suggested Donation $2. Closed New Year's Day; Easter; Thanksgiving; Christmas. ♿
Attendance: 30,000

WOODS HOLE SCIENCE AQUARIUM, 166 Water St., Woods Hole, MA 02543-1097. Tel.: 508-495-2001. Fax: 508-495-2382.
Web Site: aquarium.nefsc.noaa.gov
Formerly: Aquarium of the National Marine Fisheries Service
Founded: 1885.
Key Personnel: Aquarium Dir., David Radosh; Cur., George Liles; Dir. Science & Research, Dr. Nancy Thompson.
Personnel Profile: Full-Time Paid 2; Part-Time Volunteers 1; Interns 15.
Governing Authority: federal. Affiliated with U.S. Department of Commerce, National Oceanic & Atmospheric Administration, Northeast Fisheries Center, Water St. & National Marine Fisheries Svc., Washington, DC 20235. Tax-exempt.
Aquarium.
Collections: fish; invertebrate fauna; displays relating to marine environment; problems & methods of fishery research & management; dry exhibits; pictorial displays.
Research Fields: fishery research by Northeast Fisheries Science Center.
Activities: seal feedings: daily 11 & 4.
Hours & Admission Prices: Winter: Mon.-Fri. 11-4; Summer: Tues.-Sat. 11-4. Groups by appointment during school year. No charge; donations accepted. Closed federal holidays. ♿
Attendance: 200,000 (accurate)

Worcester

AMERICAN ANTIQUARIAN SOCIETY, 185 Salisbury St., Worcester, MA 01609-1634. Tel.: 508-755-5221. Fax: 508-753-3311.
E-mail: library@mwa.org
Web Site: www.americanantiquarian.org
Founded: 1812.
Congressional District: 3
Key Personnel: Pres., Ellen S. Dunlap; Vice Pres. Administration, Edward J. Harris; Andrew W. Mellon Cur. Graphic Arts, Georgia Barnhill; Marcus A. McLorison Librarian & Cur. Manuscripts, Thomas Knoles; Dir. Outreach, James David Moran.
Personnel Profile: Full-Time Paid 35; Part-Time Paid 18; Part-Time Volunteers 25; Interns 15.
Governing Authority: society. Tax-exempt.
Research Library.
Collections: Canadian, colonial & early American history up to 1877; graphic arts; newspapers & periodicals; manuscripts & archives; books; pamphlets; music; maps; printed ephemera.
Research Fields: colonial & early American history to 1877; literature; culture.
Facilities: library available for research; reading room.
Activities: guided tours; public programs; lectures; concerts; fellowships offered; K-12 programs, curriculum units & teacher enrichment.
Publications: semi-annual journal, Proceedings of American Antiquarian Society; newsletter; occasional bibliographical & source document books; newsletter, The Book.
Hours & Admission Prices: Mon.-Tues. & Thurs.-Fri. 9-5, Wed. 10-8. No charge; donations accepted. Closed national holidays; New Year's Eve; Thanksgiving weekend; Christmas Eve. ♿
Attendance: 6,993 (accurate)

ECOTARIUM, 222 Harrington Way, Worcester, MA 01604-1899. Tel.: 508-929-2700. Fax: 508-929-2701. TDD: 508-929-2702.
E-mail: info@ecotarium.org
Web Site: www.ecotarium.org
Formerly: New England Science Center
Founded: 1825.
Congressional District: 3
Key Personnel: Pres., Stephen M. Pitcher; Chm. Bd. Trustees, Patty Eppinger; Dir. Mktg. & Devel., Jennifer Glick; Dir. Exhibits & Education, Alexander Goldowsky; Volunteer Coord., Betsy Maloney; Deputy Dir. Administration & Operations, Patricia Crawford.
Personnel Profile: Full-Time Paid 24; Part-Time Paid 22; Part-Time Volunteers 107; Interns 3.
Governing Authority: nonprofit organization. Parent Institution: Worcester Natural History Society. Tax-exempt: 501(c)(3).
Science & Nature Museum.
Collections: mounted birds & mammals; fossils & minerals; physical & natural science; live animal exhibits; shells; historical journals.
Major Exhibits: Cool Moves, 7/09-6/20/10; Bubbles, 7/3/10-9/12/10.
Research Fields: successful breeding of animals in captivity.
Facilities: 55 acres; 20,000 sq. ft. exhibit space; nature trails; 103-seat planetarium; snack bar; classrooms; 225-seat auditorium. Educational toys, books & museum related items for sale.
Activities: lectures; films; formally organized education programs for children; temporary, participatory & permanent exhibitions; narrow gauge passenger railway; tree canopy walkway with zip line; walking trails; summer jazz concerts.
Publications: Siegfried the Dinosaur.
Hours & Admission Prices: Tues.-Sat. 10-5, Sun. 12-5. Adults $10, children 3-18, senior citizens, college students with ID $8; discounts to groups, AAM, AAA, MTA, & NEMA members, and staff members of other museums; members & children under 3 no charge. ASTC Passport Program. Planetarium: $4. Closed New Year's Day; Easter; Thanksgiving; Christmas Eve & Day. ♿
Attendance: 125,376 (accurate)
Membership: Student $25; Individual $45; Dual $60; Family & Grandparent $80; Family Plus & Grandparent Plus $90; Contributor $125; Supporter $250; 1825 Society $500 & up.

* **HIGGINS ARMORY MUSEUM,** 100 Barber Ave., Worcester, MA 01606-2464. Tel.: 508-853-6015 & 6012. Fax: 508-852-7697.
E-mail: higgins@higgins.org
Web Site: www.higgins.org
Founded: 1928.
Congressional District: 3
Key Personnel: Exec. Dir., Nikki Andersen; Pres. (V) & Chm. (V), James C. Donnelly; Paul S. Morgan Cur., Dr. Jeffrey Forgeng; Registrar, Barbara Edsall; Program Dir., Devon Kurtz; Museum Store Mgr., Anne Burke.

Personnel Profile: Full-Time Paid 21; Part-Time Paid 5; Part-Time Volunteers 20; Interns 5.
Governing Authority: nonprofit organization. Tax-exempt: 501(c)(3).
Arms, Armor, History & Art Museum.
Collections: ancient, medieval & Renaissance arms, armor & related material culture.
Major Exhibits: Beyond Relief, 1/10-12/10.
Research Fields: areas pertaining to collections.
Facilities: 2,500-vol. library pertaining to arms & armor available by appointment; 130-seat auditorium; 15,000 sq. ft. exhibit space; classroom. Museum-related items for sale.
Activities: inter-museum loans; changing exhibitions; lectures & demonstrations on arms, armor & related topics; educational programs for groups by reservation; craft activities for children; outreach programs; concerts; guided tours; films; story readings; curatorial evaluations; participatory gallery with try-on armor, costumes, & modern protective devices; games; videos,
Publications: quarterly newsletter for members; teacher materials; gallery study-guide series; annual report.
Hours & Admission Prices: Tues.-Sat. 10-4, Sun. 12-4. Adults $9, children 6-16 $7; discounts to area college students, groups, NEMA & AAM members; members, museum employees & children under 5 no charge. Closed legal holidays. ♿
Attendance: 52,227 (accurate)
Membership: Student & Senior $20; Individual $45; Family & Dual $60; Crusader $100; Squire $250; Knight $500; Corporate $500-$1,000; Renaissance Society $l,000 & up.

IRIS & B. GERALD CANTOR ART GALLERY-COLLEGE OF THE HOLY CROSS, (M), One College St., Worcester, MA 01610-2322. Tel.: 508-793-3356. Fax: 508-793-3030.
E-mail: rhankins@holycross.edu
Web Site: www.holycross.edu/cantorartgallery
Founded: 1983.
Congressional District: 3
Key Personnel: Dir., Roger Hankins.
Personnel Profile: Full-Time Paid 2; Interns 8.
Governing Authority: college. Parent Institution: College of the Holy Cross. Tax-exempt: 501(c)(3).
Art Gallery.
Collections: Rodin & other sculptures; contemporary photographs; contemporary paintings; Indonesian textiles.
Major Exhibits: Pilgrimage & Faith: Christianity, Buddhism, and Islam (T), 1/28/10-4/10; Senior Concentration Seminar, 4/22/10-5/21/10.
Facilities: classrooms; 2,000 sq. ft. exhibit space.
Activities: organized education programs for college students affiliated with Holy Cross College; loan & traveling exhibitions; visiting artists exhibits.
Publications: exhibition catalogs.
Hours & Admission Prices: Mon.-Fri. 10-5, Sat. 2-5. No charge. Closed school holidays. ♿
Attendance: 3,000 (estimated)

* **WORCESTER ART MUSEUM, (M),** 55 Salisbury St., Worcester, MA 01609-3123. Tel.: 508-799-4406. Fax: 508-798-5646.
E-mail: information@worcesterart.org
Web Site: www.worcesterart.org
Founded: 1896.
Congressional District: 3
Key Personnel: Dir., James A. Welu; Pres., J. Christopher Collins; Dir. Devel., Brian Barlow; Cur. Contemporary Art, Susan Stoops; Cur. Asian Art, Louise Virgin; Cur. Prints, Drawings & Photography, David Acton; Cur. American Art, William Rudolph; Chief Preparator & Exhibition Designer, Patrick Brown; Dir. Education, Honee A. Hess; Librarian, Deborah Aframe; Dir. Operations, Francis Pedone; Museum Shop Mgr., Susan Giordano; Cafe Mgr., Laurie Krohn-Andros.
Personnel Profile: Full-Time Paid 72; Part-Time Paid 66; Part-Time Volunteers 162.
Governing Authority: nonprofit organization. Tax-exempt: 501(c)(3).
Art Museum.
Collections: 30,000 objects spanning 5,000 years of art & culture, ranging from Egyptian antiquities & Roman mosaics to Impressionist paintings and pop art.
Research Fields: European & American painting; pertaining to temporary exhibitions; American Portrait Miniatures Gallery.
Facilities: 40,000-vol. library of art reference materials available for interlibrary loan & on the premises; reading room; education wing with studios, classrooms & resource center; cafe. Gift items for sale.
Activities: guided tours; gallery talks; formally organized education programs for children, adults, & undergraduate college students affiliated with Clark University & Worcester Consortium; inter-museum loan, permanent & temporary exhibitions; films; lectures.
Publications: handbook of the Collection; special exhibition catalogues.
Hours & Admission Prices: Wed.-Fri. & Sun. 11-5, third Thurs. of month 11-8, Sat. 10-5. Adults $10, senior citizens & full-time college students with current ID $8; discounts to AAM & ICOM members; members & children 17 & under no charge. Closed holidays. ♿
Attendance: 121,267 (accurate)
Membership: Basic: Individual $55; Family & Household $65. Young Friends: Individual $45; Couple & Household $55. Friend $200-$299; Sponsor $300-$599; Fellow $600-$1,249; Stephen Salisbury $1,250 & up.

WORCESTER CENTER FOR CRAFTS, 25 Sagamore Rd., Worcester, MA 01605-3914. Tel.: 508-753-8183. Fax: 508-797-5626.
E-mail: wcc@worcestercraftcenter.org
Web Site: www.worcestercraftcenter.org
Founded: 1856.
Congressional District: 3
Key Personnel: Exec. Dir., Carol Donnelly; Dir. Finance & Administration, Tammy Nigosian; Head Ceramics Dept., Tom O'Malley; Head Glass Dept., Jacob Vincent; Head Metals Dept., Lauren Beaudoin; Head Fiber Arts, Patti Sims; Head Wood Dept., Tony Gardner; Gallery Dir. & Gallery Shop Mgr., Candace Casey; Mgr. Organization Advancement, Caitlin Barkoskic; Registrar, Bettie Carlson.
Personnel Profile: Full-Time Paid 5; Part-Time Paid 10; Part-Time Volunteers 25; Interns 2.
Governing Authority: bd. of trustees. Tax-exempt.
Arts & Crafts Center.
Collections: 10 exhibitions annually.
Research Fields: clay; glass; metals; enameling; photography; fibers; wood; refinishing.
Facilities: Museum-related items for sale.
Activities: studio craft classes for adults, children & college students; professional craft school for career-oriented students; artists-in-residence program; lectures; films; gallery exhibition program; workshops; summer school; tours; annual craft fairs; craft events & exhibitions. Museum Sponsors: Festival of Crafts in November.
Publications: newsletters; session brochures; event postcards.
Hours & Admission Prices: Mon., Wed. & Fri. 10-5:30, Tues. & Thurs. 10-7:30. No charge; donations accepted. Closed national holidays.
Attendance: 25,000 (estimated)
Membership: Senior, Youth & Student $35; Individual $45; Family $60; Benefactor $1,000; Life $5,000.

WORCESTER HISTORICAL MUSEUM, (M), 30 Elm St., Worcester, MA 01609-2570. Tel.: 508-753-8278. Fax: 508-753-9070.
E-mail: info@worcesterhistory.org
Web Site: www.worcesterhistory.org
Founded: 1875.
Congressional District: 3
Key Personnel: Chm. (V), Scott Reisinger; Exec. Dir., William Wallace.
Personnel Profile: Full-Time Paid 9; Part-Time Paid 7; Part-Time Volunteers 19; Interns 2.
Governing Authority: society. Subsidiary Institution: Salisbury Mansion, 40 Highland St., Worcester, MA 01609. Tel: 508-753-8278. Tax-exempt: 170(b)(1)(A).
History Museum.
Collections: costumes; archives; military; decorative arts; graphics; manuscripts. Historic House: 1772 Salisbury Mansion restored to 1830s.
Research Fields: local history.
Facilities: 6,000-vol. library of local history & general books available.
Activities: guided tours; lectures; permanent & temporary exhibitions.
Publications: books, Proceedings Worcester Society of Antiquity & Proceedings Worcester Historical Society.
Hours & Admission Prices: Tues.-Wed. & Fri.-Sat. 10-4, 4th Thurs. of month 10-8:30. Adults $5; discounts to AAM members; children under 18 & members no charge. Closed major holidays. ♿
Attendance: 22,000 (accurate)
Membership: Individual $40; Family $50; Contributor $50-$99; Sustaining $100-$249; Salisbury Mansion Associate $250-$499; Staples Society $1,000.

Yarmouth Port

HISTORICAL SOCIETY OF OLD YARMOUTH, 11 Strawberry Lane, Yarmouth Port, MA 02675-1726. Mailing Address: Box 11, Yarmouth Port, MA 02675-0011. Tel.: 508-362-3021.
E-mail: hsoy@comcast.net
Web Site: www.hsoy.org
Founded: 1953.

Congressional District: 12
Key Personnel: Pres. (V), Joel Chaison.
Personnel Profile: Full-Time Volunteers 50; Part-Time Paid 2; Part-Time Volunteers 50.
Governing Authority: corporation. Tax-exempt.
Historical & Preservation Society: housed in 1840, Capt. Bangs Hallet House.
Collections: period furniture; ships; models; ships paintings; kitchen equipment.
Research Fields: history; genealogy.
Facilities: library & archives of books on genealogy & ships logs, maps, monographs; reading room; walking trails. Museum-related items for sale.
Activities: guided tours; lectures; walking tours; education programs.
Publications: books: History of Old Yarmouth, All Around the Common; brochures: The Town of Yarmouth: A History 1639-1989; Stories of Yarmouth Shipmasters; Yarmouth's Proud Packets; When South Yarmouth was Quaker Village; The Breeds and the Caretakers of their Englewood Legacy; West Yarmouth, A Village Ignored; Port of the Bay; Images In Time.
Hours & Admission Prices: June-Oct. 15 Thurs.-Sun. 1-3:30; mid-Oct. to Oct. 31 Sun. 1-3:30; other times by appointment. Tours: 1, 2, & 3. Suggested Donation: adults $3, children under 12 $.50; members no charge. Closed holidays.
Attendance: 1,500 (estimated)
Membership: Individual $15; Family $25; Business $30; Patron $50 & up.

WINSLOW CROCKER HOUSE, (Old King's Hwy.) 250 Rte. 6A, Yarmouth Port, MA 02675. Mailing Address: 141 Cambridge St., Boston, MA 02114-2702. Tel.: 617-227-3956, ext. 256. Fax: 617-227-9204.
Web Site: www.historicnewengland.org
Founded: 1935.
Congressional District: 10
Key Personnel: Pres., Carl Nold; Site Mgr., Leah Walczak.
Governing Authority: society; nonprofit organization. Parent Institution: Historic New England, 141 Cambridge St., Boston, MA 02114. Tel.: 617-227-3956. Tax-exempt: 501(c)(3).
Historic House: c.1780 Georgian house.
Collections: 17th to mid-19th century furnishings; Colonial & Federal period furniture; hooked & Oriental rugs; ceramics; pewter.
Activities: guided tours; special events; lectures.
Publications: Guide to Historic New England.
Hours & Admission Prices: June-Oct. 15 2nd & 4th Sat. of month 11-4. Adults $4; discounts to seniors, AAM, ICOM, AAA, WGBH members; Historic New England members no charge.
Attendance: 432 (accurate)
Membership: National $35; Individual $45; Household $55; Garden & Landscape $75; Institutional $85; Contributing $100; Historic Homeowner $200; Supporting $250.

MICHIGAN

(292 listings)

Acme

MUSIC HOUSE MUSEUM, 7377 U.S. 31 N., Acme, MI 49610. Mailing Address: 7377 US 31 N., Box 297, Acme, MI 49610-0297. Tel.: 231-938-9300. Fax: 231-938-3650.
E-mail: info@musichouse.org
Web Site: www.musichouse.org
Founded: 1983.
Congressional District: 11
Key Personnel: Pres. (V), Sally A. Lewis; Museum Shop Mgr., Philip Pelkey.
Personnel Profile: Full-Time Paid 1; Full-Time Volunteers 1; Part-Time Paid 6; Part-Time Volunteers 40.
Governing Authority: nonprofit organization. Tax-exempt: 501(c)(3).
Music/Musical Instrument Museum.
Collections: automatic musical instruments; music boxes; nickelodeons; reproducing pianos; orchestrions; violano; reed organs; band, dance & theater organs; early phonographs, radios & TVs; turn-of-the-century village settings.
Research Fields: music & musical instruments from c.1850-1950.
Facilities: library; 6,000 sq. ft. exhibit space. Music-related items for sale.
Activities: guided tours; lectures; concerts; docent program; silent movies.
Publications: books; brochures; musical recordings.
Hours & Admission Prices: May-Oct. Mon.-Sat. 10-4, Sun. 12-4; Nov.-Dec. Sat.-Sun. Adults $10, children 6-15 $3; discounts to groups; children under 6 no charge. Call for special Christmas schedule. ♿
Attendance: 12,000 (estimated)
Membership: Single $35; Grandparents $45; Family $50; Friend $100; Member $250; Patron $500; Angel $1,000.

Adrian

KLEMM GALLERY, Siena Heights University, 1247 E. Siena Heights Dr., Adrian, MI 49221-1755. Tel.: 517-264-7860 & 7863. Fax: 517-264-7738.
E-mail: pbarr@sienaheights.edu
Web Site: www.studioangelico.com
Founded: 1919.
Key Personnel: Chm. Art Dept., Christine Reising; Dir. Gallery, Peter J. Barr, Ph.D.
Personnel Profile: Part-Time Paid 1.
Governing Authority: college. Affiliated with Siena Heights University. Tax-exempt.
Arts Center and Institute.
Collections: changing monthly exhibits.
Activities: guided tours; lectures; drama; dance recitals; formally organized education programs for adults, undergraduate & graduate college students; temporary exhibitions.
Hours & Admission Prices: Sept.-May Tues.-Fri. 9-4, Sun. 12-4. No charge. Closed Easter; Christmas; semester breaks. ♿

Albion

ALBION COLLEGE DEPARTMENT OF ART AND ART HISTORY, 805 E. Cass St., Albion, MI 49224-1831. Mailing Address: Bobbitt Visual Arts Center, 611 E. Porter St., Albion, MI 49224-1887. Tel.: 517-629-0246 & 0000. Fax: 517-629-0752.
E-mail: bwickre@albion.edu
Web Site: www.albion.edu
Formerly: Albion College Department of Visual Arts
Founded: 1835.
Key Personnel: Prof., Lynne Chytilo; Chm. & Assoc. Prof., Bille Wickre; Prof, Anne McCauley; Asst. Prof., Dr. Kara Morrow; Asst. Prof., Gary Wahl; Asst. Prof., Michael Dixon; Visiting Prof., Anne Barber.
Personnel Profile: Full-Time Paid 1; Part-Time Paid 1.
Governing Authority: college. Affiliated with Albion College. Tax-exempt: 501(c)(3).
Art Museum.
Collections: contemporary art; 15th-century to present prints; folk arts of the world; decorative arts; glass; paintings; sculpture; archaeology.
Facilities: 4,200-vol. library of art books available for inter-library loan.
Activities: guided tours; lectures; gallery talks; arts festivals; formally organized education programs for undergraduate college students; permanent, temporary, traveling & print exhibitions.
Hours & Admission Prices: Sept.-May Mon.-Thurs. 9-9, Fri. 9-5, Sat. 10-2. No charge. Closed school holidays & vacations. ♿
Attendance: 2,000

BRUECKNER MUSEUM OF STARR COMMONWEALTH, 13725 Starr Commonwealth Rd., Albion, MI 49224-9525. Tel.: 517-629-5591; 800-837-5591. Fax: 517-629-2317.
E-mail: info@starr.org
Web Site: www.starr.org
Founded: 1956.
Congressional District: 7
Key Personnel: Pres. & C.E.O., Dr. Martin L. Mitchell.
Governing Authority: nonprofit organization. Parent Institution: Starr Commonwealth; A branch of Starr Commonwealth for Boys. Tax-exempt.
General Museum.
Collections: paintings; sculptures; drawings; prints; period furnishings; ethnic collection; minerals.
Activities: guided tours; permanent, temporary & traveling exhibitions.
Publications: Starr News.
Hours & Admission Prices: Mon.-Fri. 8:30-4:30, Sat.-Sun. by appointment. No charge; donations accepted.
Attendance: 1,000 (estimated)

GARDNER HOUSE MUSEUM, 509 S. Superior St., Albion, MI 49224-2137. Tel.: 517-629-5100.
Web Site: www.forks.org/history
Founded: 1958.
Congressional District: 3
Key Personnel: C.E.O., Marjorie Ulbrich; Chm. & Pres. (V), Andy Zblewski.
Personnel Profile: Part-Time Volunteers 30.
Governing Authority: society. Parent Institution: Albion Historical Society. Tax-exempt: 170(b)(1)(A).
Local History Museum: housed in c.1875 A.P. Gardner House.
Collections: furniture; domestic & commercial artifacts; manuscripts.
Research Fields: local history & genealogy.
Facilities: 1,500-vol. library of local history, family surname & photograph archives available by appointment. Museum-related items for sale.
Activities: guided tours; permanent & temporary exhibition.

Publications: Quarterly Newsletter to members; Albion's Banks & Bankers; A Short History of Albion, Michigan; 1866 Bird's Eye View reprint; Twelfth Night Christmas Cookies; Patchwork Quilts; Gardners House Museum.
Hours & Admission Prices: May-Sept. Sat.-Sun. 2-4. No charge; donations accepted. ♿
Attendance: 2,000 (estimated)
Membership: Junior (15) $2; Senior Citizen $3; Regular $5; Supporting $10; Sustaining $15; Contributing $30; Benefactor $50; Century $100; Endowment $300 & up.

KIDS 'N' STUFF CHILDREN'S MUSEUM, (M), 301 S. Superior, Albion, MI 49224-1752. Mailing Address: P.O. Box 718, Albion, MI 49224-0718. Tel.: 517-629-8023. Fax: 517-629-8024.
E-mail: info@kidsnstuff.org
Web Site: www.kidsnstuff.org
Founded: 2002.
Key Personnel: Dir., Kathy Fischer.
Personnel Profile: Full-Time Paid 1; Part-Time Paid 8.
Governing Authority: Tax-exempt.
Children's Museum.
Collections: hands-on exhibits.
Activities: birthday parties; field trips; girl scout events; Kindermusik; preschool enrichment; after school classes; special events; summer programs.
Hours & Admission Prices: Tues.-Sat. 10-5. Admission 1 & over $4. ♿
Attendance: 23,000
Membership: Family $50; Family Plus One $60.

WHITEHOUSE NATURE CENTER, Albion College, Albion, MI 49224-1887. Tel.: 517-629-0582. Fax: 517-629-0509.
E-mail: tcrupi@albion.edu
Web Site: www.albion.edu/naturecenter
Founded: 1972.
Congressional District: 3
Key Personnel: Dir., Tamara Crupi.
Personnel Profile: Full-Time Paid 1; Part-Time Paid 5; Part-Time Volunteers 5; Interns 1.
Governing Authority: private college; nonprofit. Parent Institution: Albion College. Tax-exempt.
Nature Center & Arboretum.
Collections: wildlife & their habitats; plants; trees; flowers.
Facilities: 500-vol. library of nature & natural science material available to the public; educational facilities; lab.
Activities: guided tours; lectures; films; hobby workshops; organized education programs for children, adults, undergraduate & graduate college students.
Publications: brochure, Whitehouse Nature Center.
Hours & Admission Prices: Mon.-Fri. 9-4:30, Sat.-Sun. 12-5. No charge; donations accepted. Closed national holidays & some Albion College holidays.
Attendance: 12,500 (estimated)

Algonac

ALGONAC/CLAY HISTORICAL SOCIETY, 1240 St. Clair River Dr., Algonac, MI 48001-1472. Mailing Address: P.O. Box 228, Algonac, MI 48001-0228. Tel.: 810-794-9015.
E-mail: achs@algonac-clay-history.com
Web Site: www.algonac-clay-history.com
Governing Authority: nonprofit organization.
Historical Society Museum.
Collections: local history & culture; photographs; personal artifacts; boat building; military.
Activities: special events.
Hours & Admission Prices: June-Aug. Wed. 7pm-9pm, Sat.-Sun. 1-4; Sept.-May Sat.-Sun. 1-4.

Allegan

ALLEGAN COUNTY HISTORICAL SOCIETY AND OLD JAIL MUSEUM, 113 Walnut St., Allegan, MI 49010-1249. Tel.: 269-673-8292.
E-mail: oldjailmuseum@wmwisp.net
Web Site: www.allegancountyhistoricalmuseum.org
Founded: 1962.
Congressional District: 9
Key Personnel: Museum Admin., Debra Post; Pres., Brad Fisher; Treas., Helen Setter.
Personnel Profile: Part-Time Paid 1; Part-Time Volunteers 20.
Governing Authority: society. Parent Institution: Allegan County Historical Society. Tax-exempt.
Regional History Museum: housed in 1906 former county jail & sheriff's home.
Collections: furniture; dolls; historical period rooms; dental, medical & barber equipment; pioneer artifacts; school room; jail cells; Gen. Pritchard Civil War room.
Facilities: library. Books, goat's milk soap & other gift items for sale.
Activities: guided tours; lectures; research.
Publications: books, Early Times in Allegan Township; Allegan & Barry County Biog. History Book-1880; River & Lake, a History of Allegan County; Allegan County Atlases, 1873, 1895, 1913; History of Casco Twp.; Six Months Among the Indians; The Index to River & Lake plus Ghost Towns & Ghost Stories; Ottawa County Atlas & Gazetteer; Allegan County Atlas & Gazetteer; Atlas & Index 1864; Sketches of Early Homes, Churches, Schools and Residents of Allegan, Michigan.
Hours & Admission Prices: Tours: Fri.-Sat. 10-4. Research & Volunteer Day Tues. 10-1. No charge; donations accepted. Closed New Year's Day; Christmas.
Attendance: 1,100 (estimated)
Membership: Individual $10; Family $15.

Allendale

GRAND VALLEY STATE UNIVERSITY ART GALLERY, (M), 1121 Performing Arts Center, Allendale, MI 49401-9403. Tel.: 616-331-2563. Fax: 616-331-8565.
E-mail: bazuinc@gvsu.edu
Web Site: www.gvsu.edu/artgallery
Key Personnel: Dir., Henry Matthews
Art Gallery.
Collections: works by local & regional artists.
Hours & Admission Prices: Winter: Mon.-Wed. & Fri. 10-5, Thurs. 10-7; Summer: Mon.-Fri. 10-4. Closed holidays.

Alpena

* **BESSER MUSEUM FOR NORTHEAST MICHIGAN, (M),** 491 Johnson St., Alpena, MI 49707-1496. Tel.: 989-356-2202. Fax: 989-356-3133.
E-mail: jsmoak@bessermuseum.org
Web Site: www.bessermuseum.org
Formerly: Jesse Besser Museum
Founded: 1962.
Congressional District: 1
Key Personnel: Exec. Dir., Janet Smoak; Pres. (V), David Musch; Cur., Richard Clute, M.A.; Facilities & Exhibits Mgr., Randy Shultz; Museum Shop Mgr., Sharon Anderson.
Personnel Profile: Full-Time Paid 6; Full-Time Volunteers 1; Part-Time Paid 4; Part-Time Volunteers 100.
Governing Authority: nonprofit organization. Tax-exempt: 501(c)(3).
General Museum.
Collections: 19th and 20th-century furnishings & decorative arts; Northern Michigan archaeology; Great Lakes copper culture artifacts; agricultural; lumbering implements; Michigan wildlife; 19th-century shop interiors; Foucault Pendulum; geology & fossils; art, primarily 20th-century graphic art; late 19th & 20th-century historical documents & photographs; manuscripts relating to northern Michigan; 18th- to 20th-century maps of the Great Lakes. Preserved Buildings: 1890 log building; 1872 Maltz Exchange bank; 1860s Homesteader's Line cabin; 1896 Green Township one-room school; 1912 Spratt Church; 1928 fishing tug.
Research Fields: regional history; archaeology; art; zoology.
Facilities: reference library; planetarium; classrooms.
Activities: docent tours; lectures; gallery talks; juried art shows; craft festivals; workshops; education programs; inter-museum loan, permanent, temporary & traveling exhibitions; school loan service; art, science & history classes for adults & children; planetarium shows.
Publications: book, The Town That Wouldn't Die; exhibit brochures; The Limestone Sinkholes of Northeastern Michigan; educational brochures; teacher curriculum guides to the museum.
Hours & Admission Prices: Mon.-Sat. 10-5. Adults $5, children, students & senior citizens $3; discounts to active military, AAA, AAM & ICOM members; members, children under 5, persons with disabilities & Wed. 3-5 no charge. Planetarium Programs: Sat. 2pm. Adults $3, seniors & children $2. Closed major holidays. ♿
Attendance: 23,000 (accurate)
Membership: Senior $20; Individual $25; Senior Couple $35; Family $40; Friend $100; Supporter $250; Patron $500; Leader $1,000.

Ann Arbor

ANN ARBOR ART CENTER, 117 W. Liberty, Ann Arbor, MI 48104-1380. Tel.: 734-994-8004, ext. 101. Fax: 734-994-3610.
E-mail: mchamberlain@annarborartcenter.org
Web Site: annarborartcenter.org

Founded: 1909.
Key Personnel: C.E.O. & Pres. (V), Marsha Chamberlin; Chm. (V), Joseph Fazio; Dir. Operations, James Arkinson; Gallery Dir., Amanda Kragliak; Dir. Education, Lori de Four.
Personnel Profile: Full-Time Paid 12; Part-Time Paid 15; Part-Time Volunteers 200; Interns 12.
Governing Authority: nonprofit organization. Tax-exempt: 501(c)(3).
Art Center.
Collections: multicultural exhibits.
Facilities: 150-vol. library of art history & reference books; classrooms. Original art including oil paintings, watercolors, graphics & ceramics for sale.
Activities: gallery talks; rental gallery; formally organized education programs for children & adults; loan exhibitions; drop-in, hands-on activity studio (Artventures).
Publications: quarterly newsletter.
Hours & Admission Prices: Mon.-Fri. 10-6, Sun. 12-5:30. No charge. Closed legal holidays. ♿
Attendance: 100,000
Membership: Junior $15; Student & Senior $25; Individual $35; Contributing $60; Supporting $100; Patron $250; Sponsor $500; Sustaining $1,000. Corporate: Basic $100; Sponsor $300; Benefactor $2,500 & up.

ANN ARBOR HANDS-ON MUSEUM, 220 E. Ann St., Ann Arbor, MI 48104-1445. Tel.: 734-995-5439. Fax: 734-995-1188.
E-mail: info@aahom.org
Web Site: www.aahom.org
Founded: 1982.
Key Personnel: Dir., Mel Drumm; Museum Shop Mgr., Ari Morris.
Personnel Profile: Full-Time Paid 19; Part-Time Paid 40.
Governing Authority: Tax-exempt.
Science Museum.
Collections: over 250 hands-on exhibits.
Activities: educational programs; field trips; outreach; scouts; camp-in; distance learning; summer classes; demonstrations.
Hours & Admission Prices: Mon.-Sat. 10-5, Sun. 12-5. Admission 2 & over $9; discounts to ASTC members & groups of 20 or more; members & children under 2 no charge. Closed New Year's Day; Memorial Day; Labor Day; Thanksgiving; Christmas. ♿
Attendance: 210,000 (accurate)
Membership: Family $75; Family Plus $100.

ARGUS PLANETARIUM, 601 W. Stadium Blvd., Ann Arbor, MI 48103-5812. Tel.: 734-994-1771. Fax: 734-994-1724.
E-mail: schaffer@aaps.k12.mi.us
Founded: 1956.
Key Personnel: Dir., Stephen A. Schaffer.
Personnel Profile: Part-Time Paid 1.
Governing Authority: public school district. Parent Institution: Ann Arbor Public Schools. Tax-exempt.
Planetarium.
Collections: Digistar 3 SP projector.
Facilities: 59-seat auditorium.
Activities: lectures; formally organized education programs for children & adults.
Hours & Admission Prices: By appointment. School groups outside of district $3 per student, $45 min. ♿
Attendance: 6,000

GERALD R. FORD LIBRARY, 1000 Beal Ave., Ann Arbor, MI 48109-2114. Tel.: 734-205-0555. Fax: 734-205-0571.
Web Site: www.fordlibrarymuseum.gov
Founded: 1977.
Key Personnel: Dir., Elaine K. Didier; Supervisory Archivist, David Horrocks.
Personnel Profile: Full-Time Paid 12; Part-Time Paid 1; Interns 3.
Governing Authority: federal. Parent Institution: National Archives and Records Administration, Washington, D.C. Tax-exempt.
Presidential Library.
Collections: federal government policies & national politics during the Cold War-era; Gerald R. Ford's presidential papers; 300,000 photographs; film, audiotape & videotape.
Facilities: library; 130-seat auditorium; classroom; 1,000 sq. ft. exhibit space.
Activities: lectures; formal education programs for undergraduate or graduate college students; temporary exhibitions; special events.
Publications: semi-annual newsletter, Gerald R. Ford Foundation Newsletter.
Hours & Admission Prices: Mon.-Fri. 8:45-4:45. No charge. Closed New Year's Day; Presidents' Day; Memorial Day; Independence Day; Labor Day; Columbus Day; Veterans Day; Thanksgiving; Christmas. ♿
Attendance: 750 (estimated)

HERBARIUM OF THE UNIVERSITY OF MICHIGAN, 3600 Varsity Dr., Ann Arbor, MI 48108-2228. Tel.: 734-615-6200. Fax: 734-998-0038.
Web Site: herbarium.lsa.umich.edu
Founded: 1921.
Congressional District: 2
Key Personnel: Dir., Paul E. Berry; Cur. Emeritus, Robert L. Shaffer; Cur. Emeritus, Edward Voss; Cur. Emeritus, Rogers McVaugh; Cur. Emeritus, William R. Anderson; Cur. Emeritus, Michael Wynne; Cur., A.A. Reznicek; Cur., Christopher Dick; Cur. Emeritus, Robert Fogel; Asst. Cur., Inigo Granzow-De La Cerda; Research Scientist, Florence S. Wagner; Research Scientist, Christiane Anderson; Asst. Research Scientist, Richard K. Rabeler.
Governing Authority: university. Parent Institution: University of Michigan. Tax-exempt.
Herbarium.
Collections: all groups of plants & fungi.
Research Fields: plant systematics; phytogeography; botanical nomenclature.
Facilities: library of plant systematics & related areas available for use by request.
Activities: research in plant systematics & phytogeography; education programs for college students.
Publications: brochures, Contributions from the University of Michigan Herbarium; Flora Novo-Galiciana; Michigan Flora Pts., I, II, III.
Hours & Admission Prices: Mon.-Fri. 8:30-4. No charge; donations accepted.

* **KELSEY MUSEUM OF ARCHAEOLOGY, (M),** 434 S. State St., Ann Arbor, MI 48109-1390. Tel.: 734-764-9304. Fax: 734-763-8976.
Web Site: www.lsa.umich.edu/kelsey/
Founded: 1928.
Congressional District: 2
Key Personnel: Pres., Mary Sue Coleman; Provost & Exec. Vice Pres. Academic Affairs, Teresa A. Sullivan; Dir. & Cur., Sharon Herbert; Assoc. Dir. & Cur. Academic Outreach, Lauren Talalay; Cur. Conservation, Suzanne Davis; Conservator, Claudia Chemello; Cur. Greece & Near East, Margaret Root; Cur. Hellenistic & Roman Empire, Elaine Gazda; Cur. Dynastic Egypt, Janet Richards; Cur. Graeco-Roman Egypt, Terry Wilfong; Coord. Museums Collections, Michelle Fontenot; Coord. Museum Exhibitions, Scott Meier; Coord. Museum Collections, Sebastian Encina; Editor, Peg Lourie; Coord. Museum Visitor Programs, Todd E. Gerring; Coord. Museum Exhibitions, Barret Roebuck; Gift Mgmt. & Graphic Artist, Lorene Stervier.
Personnel Profile: Full-Time Paid 10; Part-Time Paid 25; Part-Time Volunteers 15; Interns 2.
Governing Authority: state; university. Parent Institution: University of Michigan. Tax-exempt.
Archaeology Museum.
Collections: art & artifacts; classical & Near Eastern archaeology, especially of Roman & early Byzantine Egypt; results of excavations at Roman sites in Egypt & Seleucia on the Tigris, Iraq; Greek & Roman inscriptions; Roman building materials; Byzantine & Islamic textiles; Roman sculpture & glass.
Research Fields: excavation in Tunisia, Italy, Egypt, Israel & Turkey; conservation; Roman & Hellenistic Egypt & the Near East; Greek & Roman sculpture; glass; numismatics; textiles & inscriptions.
Facilities: 5,000-vol. library of materials on archaeology & related subjects available for use by appointment.
Activities: guided tours; lectures; gallery talks; permanent & temporary exhibitions; traveling educational kits for teachers & special interest groups; field research labs; object study areas; classical archaeology graduate program; children's programs.
Publications: Bulletin of the Museums of Art & Archaeology; gallery guide; exhibition catalogs & brochures; associates newsletter; Kelsey Museum Studies Series.
Hours & Admission Prices: Call for hours. No charge; donations accepted. ♿
Attendance: 20,576 (accurate)
Membership: Students $10; Individual $35; Family $50; Contributor $100; Sponsor $250; Patron $500; Benefactor $1,000 & up.

MATTHAEI BOTANICAL GARDENS AND NICHOLS ARBORETUM, 1800 N. Dixboro Rd., Ann Arbor, MI 48105-9741. Tel.: 734-647-7600. Fax: 734-998-6205.
Web Site: www.umich.edu/mbgna
Founded: 1907.
Congressional District: 5
Key Personnel: Dir., Robert E. Grese; Assoc. Dir., Karen Sikkenga.
Personnel Profile: Full-Time Paid 24; Part-Time Paid 4; Part-Time Volunteers 500; Interns 35.
Governing Authority: Parent Institution: University of Michigan. Subsidiary Institution: Nichols Arboretum, 1610 Washington Heights, Ann Arbor, MI. Tax-exempt.
Botanical Garden.

Collections: cacti & succulents; bromeliads; prairie; wildflower garden; tropical & warm temperate species; native flora; roses; perennial garden; orchids; herb garden; garden of new world plants; insectivores display, constructed wetland; rock garden; ornamental grass garden; ethnobotanical trail; exotic & native trees & shrubs of north temperate regions; Appalachian plants; lilacs; peonies; oak-hickory woodland.
Research Fields: prairie, wetland & forest species; landscape & ecology & classification; various disciplines of biology, natural resources, cultural & interpretive arts.
Facilities: horticultural library; conservatory; formal & experimental gardens; herbarium; laboratories; classrooms; nature trails; auditorium.
Activities: docent guided tours of conservatory & trails; adult, youth & family educational activities; university classes; plant sales & lectures; special events; meeting facilities for mission-related organizations & garden clubs; cultural performances.
Publications: quarterly newsletter, Friends.
Hours & Admission Prices: Daily 10-4:30. Conservatory: adults $5, children $2; friends of MBGNA, American Horticultural Society members, UM students & children under 5 no charge. Outdoor Grounds: 8-sunset. No charge. ♿
Attendance: 100,000 (estimated)
Membership: Friends of Matthaei Botanical Gardens & Nichols Arboretum: Student $20; Individual $45; Family $55; Sustaining $100; Sponsor $250; Benefactor $500; Director's Circle $1,000.

SINDECUSE MUSEUM OF DENTISTRY, (M), University of Michigan, 1011 N. University - G565 Dental Bldg., Ann Arbor, MI 48109-1078. Tel.: 734-763-0767. Fax: 734-936-3065.
E-mail: dentalmuseum@umich.edu
Web Site: www.dent.umich.edu/museum
Founded: 1992.
Key Personnel: Cur., Shannon O'Dell.
Personnel Profile: Full-Time Paid 1; Part-Time Paid 3.
Governing Authority: public university. Parent Institution: School of Dentistry, University of Michigan. Tax-exempt.
Dental Museum.
Collections: dental tools & equipment from 18th century to present; dentistry & oral health history; dental advertising; games; toys; photographs.
Research Fields: history of dentistry; University of Michigan Dental School alumni.
Facilities: 500-vol. library; 2,700 sq. ft. exhibit space.
Activities: guided tours by appointment; permanent & temporary exhibitions; university student training programs; lectures; research by appointment. Annual Event: Hall of Honor induction ceremony.
Hours & Admission Prices: Mon.-Fri. 8-6. No charge; donations accepted. Closed New Year's Eve & Day; Memorial Day; Independence Day; Labor Day; Thanksgiving & day after; Christmas Eve, Day & week. ♿
Attendance: 2,000 (estimated)

STEARNS COLLECTION OF MUSICAL INSTRUMENTS, University of Michigan School of Music, 1100 Baits Dr., Ann Arbor, MI 48109-2085. Tel.: 734-936-2891. Fax: 734-647-1897.
E-mail: stearns@umich.edu
Web Site: www.music.umich.edu/research/stearns_collection/index.htm
Founded: 1899.
Congressional District: 2
Key Personnel: Dir., Joseph Lam.
Personnel Profile: Part-Time Paid 2; Part-Time Volunteers 1.
Governing Authority: university. Affiliated with the University of Michigan School of Music. Tax-exempt.
Musical Instrument Museum.
Collections: over 2,000 modern Western, non-Western & period musical instruments.
Research Fields: organological computer cataloguing.
Facilities: research laboratory.
Activities: guided tours; lectures; concerts; permanent & temporary exhibitions; University Sponsors: Lecture series held each semester.
Publications: newsletter.
Hours & Admission Prices: Mon.-Fri. 10-5. No charge; donations accepted. Guided Tours: seniors $1, groups of 25 $30; call 662-7790 for more information. ♿
Attendance: 660
Membership: Student & Senior Citizen $15; Friends $35; Sustaining $100; Patron $500; Benefactor $1000.

UNIVERSITY OF MICHIGAN EXHIBIT MUSEUM OF NATURAL HISTORY, (M), 1109 Geddes Ave., Ann Arbor, MI 48109-1079. Tel.: 734-764-0478 & 763-4190. Fax: 734-647-2767.
E-mail: exmusfeedback@umich.edu
Web Site: www.lsa.umich.edu/exhibitmuseum
Founded: 1881.
Congressional District: 14
Key Personnel: Dir., Amy S. Harris; Exhibit Preparator & Lecturer, John B. Klausmeyer; Exhibit Preparator, Daniel A. Erickson; Exhibit Preparator, Alan R. McWaters; Devel. Officer, Nora Webber; Administrative Assoc., Daniel Madaj; Program Assoc. & Planetarium Dir., Matthew P. Linke; Coord. Visitor Programs, Kira Berman; Exhibit Preparator, Michael Chemey; Museum Shop Mgr., Kelly Sullivan; Administrative Asst., Linda I. Heywood; Program Asst. & Docent Coord., Sarah Thompson.
Personnel Profile: Full-Time Paid 10; Part-Time Paid 2; Part-Time Volunteers 10.
Governing Authority: university. Parent Institution: University of Michigan. Subsidiary Institution: College of Literature, Science & Arts. Tax-exempt: 501(c)(3).
University Natural History Museum.
Collections: Hall of Evolution including exhibits on vertebrate & invertebrate paleontology; paleobotany; Michigan wildlife & ecology; ethnology & anthropology; geology; astronomy.
Research Fields: anthropology; systematics; comparative anatomy; evolution; paleontology.
Facilities: 22,261 sq. ft. exhibit space; classrooms; planetarium. Museum-related items for sale.
Activities: guided tours; planetarium shows; formally organized educational programs for undergraduate & graduate students affiliated with the University of Michigan; museum methods classes; docent program; lectures; temporary & permanent exhibits.
Publications: bimonthly newsletter, The Display Case; brochures.
Hours & Admission Prices: Mon.-Sat. 9-5, Sun. 12-5. Museum: no charge; donations accepted. $10 nonrefundable reservation fee for groups of 10 or more; browse fee for groups of 10 or more. Planetarium shows: $4.75 per person. Closed major holidays. ♿
Attendance: 70,000 (estimated)
Membership: Individual & Couple $35; Grandparents $45; Family $50.

UNIVERSITY OF MICHIGAN MUSEUM OF ANTHROPOLOGY, 4013 Ruthven Museums Bldg., 1109 Geddes, Ann Arbor, MI 48109-1079. Tel.: 734-764-0485. Fax: 734-763-7783.
E-mail: anthro-museum@umich.edu
Web Site: www.lsa.umich.edu/umma/
Founded: 1922.
Congressional District: 2
Key Personnel: Cur. Mediterranean Archaeology, Robert Whallon; Cur. Asian Archaeology, Carla Sinopoli; Cur. North American Archaeology, John D. Speth; Cur. Environmental Archaeology, Kent V. Flannery; Cur. Great Lakes Archaeology, John O'Shea; Cur. Near East Archaeology, Henry T. Wright; Cur. Latin American Archaeology & Ethnohistory, Joyce Marcus.
Personnel Profile: Full-Time Paid 5; Part-Time Paid 8; Part-Time Volunteers 22.
Governing Authority: state. Parent Institution: University of Michigan. Tax-exempt: 501(c)(3).
Anthropology Museum.
Collections: archaeology; ethnology; ethnobotany; zoo archaeology; human osteology; geological.
Research Fields: archaeology; ethnology; human & cultural evolution.
Facilities: ethnobotanical, zoo archaeological, palynological & sedimentological laboratories.
Activities: formally organized education programs for undergraduate & graduate college students; research in anthropology.
Publications: monographs, Occasional Contributions; Anthropological Papers; Memoirs; Technical Reports; electronic publications (CD-Rom).
Hours & Admission Prices: By appointment only. No charge. ♿

* **THE UNIVERSITY OF MICHIGAN MUSEUM OF ART, (M),** 525 S. State St., Ann Arbor, MI 48109-1354. Tel.: 734-764-0395. Fax: 734-764-3731.
E-mail: umma.info@umich.edu
Web Site: www.umich.edu/
Founded: 1946.
Congressional District: 2
Key Personnel: Interim Co-Dir., Ray Silverman; Dir. Education & Interim Co-Dir., Ruth Slavin; Chief Administrative Officer & Interim Co-Dir., Kathryn Huss; Sr. Cur. Western Art, Carole McNamara; Research Cur. Asian Art, Natsu Oyobe; Mgr. Collections & Exhibitions & Chief Registrar, Orian Neumann; Museum Store Mgr., Suzanne Witthoff.
Personnel Profile: Full-Time Paid 44; Part-Time Paid 30; Part-Time Volunteers 100; Interns 6.
Governing Authority: state; university. Parent Institution: The University of Michigan. Affiliated with Regents of The University of Michigan. Tax-exempt: 501(c)(3).
Art Museum. Western painting & sculpture from the 12th century to the

present; Old Master & contemporary prints and drawings; photography; Asian & African art; Islamic ceramics.
Collections: Western art from 6th century to the present prints and drawings; photographs; Asian art; African & Oceanic art; objects from the Islamic World.
Research Fields: permanent art collections & special exhibitions.
Facilities: classrooms; rental facilities.
Activities: guided tours; lectures; gallery talks; formally organized education programs for children & adults; extensive public programs (K-12; adult; university); permanent, temporary & traveling exhibitions; concerts & performance programs.
Publications: exhibition catalogs; Bulletin, Museums of Art and Archaeology; scholarly articles.
Hours & Admission Prices: Gallery: Tues.-Wed. & Sat. 10-5, Thurs.-Fri. 10-10, Sun. 12-5. Suggested donation $5. Closed New Year's Day; Memorial Day; Independence Day; Labor Day; Thanksgiving; Christmas. ♿
Attendance: 200,000 (accurate)
Membership: Student $20; Individual $50; Household $75; Donor $125; Sponsor $250; Curator's Circle $500; Director's Circle Associate $1,000; Director's Circle Patron $2,500; Director's Circle Benefactor $5,000.

WASHTENAW COUNTY HISTORICAL SOCIETY, (M), 500 N. Main St., Ann Arbor, MI 48104-1027. Mailing Address: P.O. Box 3336, Ann Arbor, MI 48106-3336. Tel.: 734-662-9092.
Historical Society Museum.
Collections: county history & cultural heritage; personal artifacts; photographs.
Hours & Admission Prices: Wed. & Sat.-Sun. 12-4; other times by appointment.

Arcadia

ARCADIA AREA HISTORICAL MUSEUM, 3340 Lake St., Arcadia, MI 49613-5157. Mailing Address: P.O. Box 67, Arcadia, MI 49613-0067. Tel.: 231-889-3389.
Web Site: www.arcadiami.com
Formerly: Arcadia Township Historical Commission
Founded: 1992.
Key Personnel: Chm., Edward Howard; Pres. Society (V), Joyce Howard.
Personnel Profile: Part-Time Volunteers 100.
Historical Society & Furniture Museum.
Collections: Lumbertown artifacts; Sawmill furniture factory; mirror works; historical books; shipping; Harriet Quimby.
Publications: newsletter 3 times a year.
Hours & Admission Prices: June 25 to Labor Day Thurs.-Sat. 1-4, Sun. 1-3; other times by appointment. No charge; donations accepted. ♿
Attendance: 800 (estimated)
Membership: Individual $10; Family $15; Business & Organization $25; Silver Patron $50; Gold Patron $100; Benefactor $1,000; Corporate Benefactor $2,500.

Auburn Hills

WALTER P. CHRYSLER MUSEUM, (M), One Chrysler Dr., CIMS 488.00.00, Auburn Hills, MI 48326-2766. Tel.: 888-456-1924. Fax: 248-944-0460.
Web Site: www.wpchryslermuseum.org
Founded: 1998.
Key Personnel: Pres. & C.E.O., Lori Pinter; Exec. Dir. & C.O.O., Jim Worton; Cur., Brandt Rosenbusch; Museum Programs & Admissions Mgr., Doreen Wright.
Personnel Profile: Full-Time Paid 7; Part-Time Paid 4; Part-Time Volunteers 125.
Governing Authority: Parent Institution: Walter P. Chrysler Museum Foundation. Tax-exempt.
Automotive Museum.
Collections: history & contribution of the founder to the automotive industry; 300 historical vehicles.
Facilities: 55,000 sq. ft. exhibit space.
Hours & Admission Prices: Tues.-Sat. 10-5, Sun. 1-5. Adults $8, senior citizens 62 & over $7, juniors 6-12 & groups of 15 and over $4. Closed New Year's Eve & Day; Easter; Independence Day; Thanksgiving & day before; Christmas Eve & Day. ♿
Attendance: 39,000 (accurate)
Membership: Plymouth $45; Dodge $60; Hudson $125; DeSoto $250; LeBaron $500; Imperial $1,000.

Augusta

W.K. KELLOGG BIRD SANCTUARY OF MICHIGAN STATE UNIVERSITY, 12685 East C Ave., Augusta, MI 49012-9707. Tel.: 269-671-2510. Fax: 269-671-2474.
E-mail: scarroll@kbs.msu.edu
Web Site: kbs.msu.edu/birdsanctuary
Founded: 1927.
Key Personnel: Facilities Mgr., Karen Charleston; Environmental Education Coord., Tracey Kast; Office Mgr., Sarah Carroll.
Personnel Profile: Full-Time Paid 3; Part-Time Volunteers 50; Interns 1.
Governing Authority: university. Parent Institution: Michigan State University. Subsidiary Institution: Kellogg Biological Station. Tax-exempt.
Bird Sanctuary.
Collections: avian; mammal; fish; botanical.
Research Fields: Waterfowl ecology.
Facilities: auditorium; educational resource center; trail. Books for sale.
Activities: guided tours; lectures; films; formally organized education programs for children; permanent exhibitions; self-guided trail; spruce lodge available for school, group & small meetings; rental facility.
Hours & Admission Prices: Grounds: May-Oct. daily 9-7; Nov.-April daily 9-5. Adults $4, senior citizens $2, children 2-12 $1; children under 2 no charge. Gift Shop: Mon.-Fri. 9-5, Sat.-Sun. 11-4. Gift Shop: closed major holidays. ♿
Attendance: 12,000 (accurate)
Membership: Student & Senior $15; Individual $20; Household $30; Grandparent $45.

Baraga

BARAGA COUNTY HISTORICAL MUSEUM, US 41, Baraga, MI 49908. Mailing Address: P.O. Box 567, Baraga, MI 49908-0567. Tel.: 906-353-8444 & 6810.
E-mail: jdompier@up.net
Web Site: baragacountyhistoricalmuseum.com
Founded: 1965.
Governing Authority: Parent Institution: Baraga County Historical Society, Inc.
History Museum.
Collections: county history & culture; photographs; personal artifacts; railroad artifacts; logging; household; military; religious artifacts.
Hours & Admission Prices: June-Sept. Tues.-Sat. 11-3; other times by appointment. Adults $2, teens $1; children under 12 no charge.
Membership: Annual $18; Life $100.

Battle Creek

* **ART CENTER OF BATTLE CREEK, (M),** 265 E. Emmett St., Battle Creek, MI 49017-4601. Tel.: 269-962-9511. Fax: 616-969-3838.
E-mail: artcenterofbc@yahoo.com
Web Site: www.artcenterofbattlecreek.com
Founded: 1948.
Congressional District: 3
Key Personnel: Exec. Dir., Linda Holderbaum; Pres. (V), Mark Banghart; Coord. Education, Kay Doyle; Museum Shop Mgr., Jennifer Hepler.
Personnel Profile: Full-Time Paid 3; Part-Time Paid 1; Part-Time Volunteers 50.
Governing Authority: bd. of directors. Tax-exempt.
Art Gallery.
Collections: Michigan art collection.
Major Exhibits: Class Act - Elementary & Secondary Art, 3/7/10-3/26/10; W.K. Kellogg 150th Birthday Exhibit, 4/4/10-4/24/10; Michigan Artist Competition, 6/6/10-6/26/10.
Research Fields: art appreciation programs for grades 1-12; Michigan artists.
Facilities: library; archives. Museum-related items for sale.
Activities: art classes for all ages; workshops; guided tours; kidspace hands-on gallery; outreach art programs for schools, local adult day-care facilities & VA hospital.
Publications: quarterly, newsletter & class schedules.
Hours & Admission Prices: Tues.-Fri. 10-5, Sat. 11-3. Adults $3, seniors & students $2; discounts to AAM & ICOM members; Thurs. & members no charge. Closed national holidays. ♿
Attendance: 35,241 (accurate)
Membership: Student $25; Individual $50; Family $75; Friend $150; Patron $500; Benefactor $1,500; Director's Circle $2,500.

BINDER PARK ZOO, 7400 Division Dr., Battle Creek, MI 49014-9500. Tel.: 269-979-1351. Fax: 269-979-8834.
E-mail: info@binderparkzoo.org
Web Site: www.binderparkzoo.org
Founded: 1975.
Congressional District: 3

Key Personnel: Pres. & C.E.O., Gregory B. Geise; Chm. (V), James Grohalski; C.O.O., Stacey Lawson; Dir. Business & Finance, Amy Riegel; Dir. Wildlife Management, Jenny Barnett; Dir. Animal Health & Research, Thomas W. deMaar, D.V.M.; Dir. Conservation Education, Thomas Funke; Dir. Physical Plant, Eric McNamara; Operations Mgr., Vicki Taft; Mgr. Mktg., Kari Parker; Cur. Collections, Andi Kornak; Cur. Conservation Education, Kathy Fischer.
Personnel Profile: Full-Time Paid 50; Part-Time Paid 150; Part-Time Volunteers 214; Interns 10.
Governing Authority: nonprofit organization. Parent Institution: Binder Park Zoological Society, Inc. Tax-exempt: 501(c)(3).
Zoological Park.
Collections: over 650 animals & 150 species from around the world.
Research Fields: animal management & diseases; education.
Facilities: 1,200-vol. library of natural history & animal management books available for research on premises only; picnic area; 125-seat auditorium; restaurant; amphitheater. Zoo-related items for sale.
Activities: guided tours; lectures; formal organized education programs for children & adults; docent program; permanent & traveling exhibitions; mobile vans; Z.O. & O. railroad rides; Zoomobile Outreach, animal discovery series.
Publications: quarterly newsletter, ZooGoer; newsletter, Zooviews.
Hours & Admission Prices: April-Oct. Mon.-Fri. 9-5, Sat. & holidays 9-6, Sun. 11-6. Adults $11.95, senior citizens 65 & over $10.95, children 2-10 $9.95; discounts to groups by appointment & AAA members; children under 2, AZA, zoo members & reciprocal zoo members no charge. ♿
Attendance: 320,000 (estimated)
Membership: Individual $50; Family & Grandparents $65; Sustaining $125-$249; Contributing $250-$499; Donor $500-$4,999; Life $5,000 & up.

KELLOGG'S CEREAL CITY USA, 171 W. Michigan Ave., Battle Creek, MI 49017-7020. Mailing Address: 77 Michigan Ave. E., Ste. 160, Battle Creek, MI 49017-7020. Tel.: 800-970-7020. Fax: 269-962-3787.
Web Site: www.kelloggscerealcity.com
Industrial Museum.
Collections: history of cereal; simulated cereal production line.
Facilities: restaurant. Museum-related items for sale.
Activities: tour; birthday parties; facilities rental.
Publications: The Tony(R) Times.
Hours & Admission Prices: Tues.-Fri. 10-4, Sat. 10-5, Sun. 12-5. Adults 13-64 $7.95, seniors 65 & over $6.50, children 3-12 $4.95; children 2 & under no charge. Closed Christmas Eve & Day.

KIMBALL HOUSE MUSEUM, 196 Capital Ave., N.E., Battle Creek, MI 49017-3925. Mailing Address: 165 N. Washington, Battle Creek, MI 49037-2929. Tel.: 269-965-2613 & 966-2496. Fax: 269-660-9072.
E-mail: bcarch@net-link.net
Web Site: www.heritagebattlecreek.org/kimball.htm
Founded: 1966.
Congressional District: 3
Key Personnel: Pres., Charlene Lee; Dir. Research, Mary Butler.
Personnel Profile: Full-Time Paid 1; Part-Time Paid 2; Part-Time Volunteers 5.
Governing Authority: society. Parent Institution: Heritage Battle Creek. Tax-exempt: 501(c)(3).
Historic House: 1886 Victorian home.
Collections: Victorian life 1890-1910; household items; furnishings; tools; 1880 medical instruments relating to Battle Creek; Battle Creek historical items; herb garden; Battle Creek Sanitarium; Sojourner Truth.
Research Fields: cereal; industry; health; genealogy; anti-slavery movements; underground railroad.
Facilities: Gifts for sale.
Activities: guided tours; permanent & temporary exhibitions; educational programs.
Publications: bimonthly, Living History; annual, Heritage Battle Creek.
Hours & Admission Prices: April-Dec. Sun. 1-4; tours by appointment. Adults $3, children 12 & under $2; members no charge. ♿
Attendance: 20,000 (estimated)
Membership: Student & Senior $35; Individual $50; Family $60; Annual Contributing $100; Annual Sustaining $500; Annual Benefactor $1,000.

KINGMAN MUSEUM, (M), 175 Limit St., Battle Creek, MI 49037-2176. Tel.: 269-965-5117. Fax: 269-965-3330.
E-mail: sbriggs@kingmanmuseum.org
Web Site: www.kingmanmuseum.org
Founded: 2000.
Key Personnel: C.E.O. & Dir., Sara Ann Briggs; Pres. (V), Annettie Tribbett; Collections, Katie Nelson; Education, Sarah Kelly; Museum Shop Mgr., Kathy Ward.
Personnel Profile: Full-Time Paid 3; Part-Time Paid 2; Part-Time Volunteers 168; Interns 1.
Governing Authority: private; nonprofit organization. Tax-exempt: 501(c)(3).
Natural History Museum.
Collections: fossils; rocks & minerals; Native American artifacts; mounted animals.
Facilities: planetarium. Museum-related items for sale.
Activities: education programs; seasonal day programs; participatory & temporary exhibits; after school programs; outreach programs; discovery kits.
Hours & Admission Prices: Tues.-Thurs. 9-5, Fri. 9-8, Sat. 1-5. Families $15, adults $6, senior citizens $5, children $4; members and children 2 & under no charge. Planetarium: families $5, adults $2, children & members $1. ♿
Attendance: 14,912 (accurate)
Membership: Students, Senior Citizens & Military $20; Individual $30; Military Family $40; Family & Grandparents $50.

Bay City

HISTORICAL MUSEUM OF BAY COUNTY, 321 Washington Ave., Bay City, MI 48708-5837. Tel.: 989-893-5733. Fax: 989-893-5741.
E-mail: director@bchsmuseum.org
Web Site: bchsmuseum.org
Founded: 1919.
Congressional District: 10
Key Personnel: Dir., Ron Bloomfield; Pres. Bd., Judy Jeffers; Vice Pres. Bd., Leon Katzinger; Museum Shop Mgr., Donna Lowe.
Personnel Profile: Full-Time Paid 6; Part-Time Paid 1; Part-Time Volunteers 25.
Governing Authority: society. Parent Institution: Bay County Historical Society. Tax-exempt: 501(c)(3).
County History Museum: housed in 1910 National Guard Armory.
Collections: books; manuscripts; maps; photographs; documents; artifacts relating to the history of Bay County, Michigan & the Great Lakes area.
Research Fields: local, regional & archaeological history; genealogy; sugar beet industry; World War II patrol craft history.
Facilities: 1,000-vol. library of books on Great Lakes & Michigan history for use on premises; reading room. Books & museum-related items for sale.
Activities: guided tours; lectures; museum to the schools program; historic dinner; tour to city hall; craft classes. Museum Sponsors: Tour of Homes Event; Quilt Show; River of Time Living History Encampment.
Publications: newsletter; occasional local history booklets & books; Recipe for a Community: The Historical and Culinary Growth of 19th Century Linwood, Michigan; The Historic Architecture of Bay County, Michigan.
Hours & Admission Prices: Mon.-Fri. 10-5, Sat. 12-4. Research Library: Tues.-Thurs. 1-5 (librarian on duty). No charge; donations accepted. Closed major holidays. ♿
Attendance: 61,000 (estimated)
Membership: Student & Senior Citizen $10; Single $20; Family $35; Supporter $50; Patron $100.

Bay View

BAY VIEW HISTORICAL MUSEUM, Bay View Association Encampment 1715, Bay View, MI 49770. Mailing Address: P.O. Box 583, Petoskey, MI 49770-0583. Tel.: 231-347-6225. Fax: 231-347-4330.
Web Site: bayviewassoc.org
Founded: 1970.
Key Personnel: Pres., Lawrence R. Ternan; Exec. Dir., Rodney J. Slocum; Cur. & Archivist, Anne Lewis; Cur. & Archivist, Sophia McGee.
Personnel Profile: Part-Time Volunteers 13.
Governing Authority: private; nonprofit organization.
Historic Site: a National Historic Landmark consisting of 12 buildings & 430 summer homes.
Collections: historic buildings.
Activities: guided tours; lectures. Annual Event: Chautauqua program in summer.
Publications: book, History of Bay View; reprint from 1894 Bayview Summer, City of Michigan.
Hours & Admission Prices: July 8-Aug. 18 Sun. after church until 1 pm, Wed. 2:30-4:30. No charge; donations accepted.
Attendance: 1,000 (estimated)

Beaver Island

BEAVER ISLAND HISTORICAL SOCIETY, 26275 Main St., Beaver Island, MI 49782-5101. Mailing Address: P.O. Box 263, Saint James, MI 49782-0263. Tel.: 231-448-2254.
E-mail: history@beaverisland.net
Web Site: beaverisland.net/history
Founded: 1957.
Congressional District: 11

Key Personnel: Pres., John Runberg; Dir., Chm. & Museum Shop Mgr., William Cashman; Vice Pres., Alvin LaFreniere.
Personnel Profile: Full-Time Paid 1; Part-Time Volunteers 26.
Governing Authority: private; nonprofit corporation. Subsidiary Institution: Mormon Print Shop & Marine Museum. Tax-exempt: 501(c)(3).
Local History Museum.
Collections: artifacts from 1850-present; maps of island; reprint of early Mormon newspaper; Mormon documents; Irish fishing & lumbering artifacts; logging; boat building; Irish migration to Beaver Island; period furnishings; photographs; 50' gill-net fishing boat; outdoor displays; the Protar home & material. Historic Buildings: 1852 Mormon print shop; marine museum on St. James Harbor.
Research Fields: local history; materials relevant to James J. Strang; Irish Immigration; fishing community; Native Americans; genealogy.
Facilities: archives.
Activities: guided tours; lectures; permanent exhibitions; expeditions to historic sites. Museum Sponsors: annual Museum Week.
Publications: journal, The Journal of Beaver Island History Vols. I, II, III, IV; newsletters; maps; Child of the Sea (1905 Memoir).
Hours & Admission Prices: mid-June to Labor Day Print Shop: Mon.-Sat. 11-5, Sun. 12-3. Maritime Museum: Mon.-Sat. 11-5, Sun. 12-3; other times by appointment. Both Museums: adults $3, children $1; discounts to groups of 15 or more; members no charge. ♿
Attendance: 3,500 (accurate)
Membership: Individual $10; Couple $15; Goodwill & Family $25; Contributing $50; Sustaining $100; Life $200; Patron $500; Honorary Historian $1,000.

Belding

BELDING MUSEUM, (M), 108 Hanover St., Belding, MI 48809-1726. Mailing Address: P.O. Box 45, Belding, MI 48809-0045. Tel.: 616-794-1900 ext. 425.
Founded: 1987.
Key Personnel: Co Dir., Barb Fagerlin; Co Dir., Jill Mason; Treas., Debra Blunt.
Personnel Profile: Part-Time Volunteers 5.
Governing Authority: municipal. Parent Institution: City of Belding, 120 S. Pleasant St., Belding, MI 48809. Tax-exempt: 501(c)(3).
History Museum.
Collections: history of Belding & the silk industry.
Facilities: 80-seat community room. Museum-related items for sale.
Activities: formal education programs; guided tours; temporary exhibitions. Annual Event: Quilt Show.
Publications: quarterly newsletter.
Hours & Admission Prices: 1st Sun. of month 1-4. No charge; donations accepted. Closed New Year's Day; Easter; Independence Day; Thanksgiving; Christmas. ♿
Attendance: 750 (estimated)

Belleville

BELLEVILLE AREA MUSEUM, (M), 405 Main St., Belleville, MI 48111-2617. Tel.: 734-697-1944.
E-mail: dwilson@provide.net
Web Site: www.vanburen-mi.org
Founded: 1989.
Key Personnel: Dir., Diane Wilson; Pres. (V), Fred Hudson
Local History Museum.
Collections: local history & culture; personal artifacts; period furnishings.
Hours & Admission Prices: May to Labor Day Mon.-Fri. 12-4; Sept.-April Tues.-Sat. 12-4; call to confirm hours. Family $3, adults $1, children $.50. Closed holiday weekends. ♿
Membership: Student $5; Individual $15; Dual & Family $25; Sustaining $50; Patron $150; Life $250.

OAKWOODS METROPARK NATURE CENTER, 17845 Savage Rd., Belleville, MI 48111-9668. Tel.: 800-477-3182; 734-697-9181. Fax: 734-782-3956.
E-mail: kevin.arnold@metroparks.com
Web Site: metroparks.com
Founded: 1975.
Congressional District: 15
Key Personnel: Dir., Jim Bresciami; Chief Interpretive Svcs., C. Michael George; Supervising Interpreter, Kevin J. Arnold; Interpreter, Roni Hutchinson.
Personnel Profile: Full-Time Paid 2; Part-Time Paid 2.
Governing Authority: county. Affiliated with Huron-Clinton Metropolitan Authority, 1300 High Ridge Rd., Brighton, MI 48116-8001. Branch Museums: Indian Springs Metropark Nature Center, Clarkston, MI; Kensington Metropark Nature Center, Milford, MI ; Stony Creek Metropark Nature Center, Romeo, MI; Metrobeach Metropark Nature Center, Mt. Clemens, MI; Wolcott Mill Metropark Interpretive Center, Washington, MI; Lake Erie Marshlands Museum, Brownstown, MI. Tax-exempt: 501(c)(3).
Nature Center: located on 1818-1842 Wyandot Indian Reservation.
Collections: botanical; zoological.
Research Fields: local Indian & early white history.
Facilities: nature conservation center; classroom; 100-seat auditorium.
Activities: guided tours; Voyageur canoe tours; lectures; hobby workshops; formally organized education programs for children, adults & graduate students; school visits by interpreters with illustrated programs.
Publications: quarterly events calendar; trail map.
Hours & Admission Prices: June-Aug. daily 10-5; Sept.-May Mon.-Fri. 1-5, Sat.-Sun. 10-5. No charge. Motor vehicle permit required: annual vehicle permit $20, senior citizens $12, daily $4. Closed New Year's Eve & Day; Thanksgiving; Christmas Eve & Day. ♿
Attendance: 100,000 (estimated)

Belmont

HYSER RIVERS MUSEUM, 6440 W. River Rd., N.E., Belmont, MI 49306. Mailing Address: c/o Plainfield Charter Township, 6161 Belmont Ave., N.E., Belmont, MI 49306-9609. Tel.: 616-364-8466; 1182 (museum). Fax: 616-364-6537.
Web Site: www.commoncorners.com
Founded: 1973.
Key Personnel: Pres. (V), Sue Carpenter
Historic House Museum: housed in former home of pioneer surgeon & Civil War Captain William Hyser, built in 1852.
Collections: period artifacts & furnishings.
Hours & Admission Prices: April-Dec. first Sun. of month 2-4:30; other times by appointment. No charge; donations accepted.

Benton Harbor

MORTON HOUSE MUSEUM, 501 Territorial, Benton Harbor, MI 49022. Mailing Address: P.O. Box 173, Benton Harbor, MI 49023-0173. Tel.: 269-925-7011.
E-mail: mortonhousemuseum@yahoo.com
Web Site: www.mortonhousemuseum.com
Founded: 1966.
Congressional District: 44
Key Personnel: Pres., Chuck Jager; Vice Pres., Gloria Kett; Sec. & Treas., Gisela Holtz; House Chm., Denise Reeves; Trustee, Perry Heppler; Trustee, Stuart Boekeloo; Trustee, Gineen Wiley; Trustee, Sinie Bass; Trustee, Kathy Catania; Trustee, Maria Heppler; Trustee, Brenda Layne; Trustee, Miriam Pede.
Personnel Profile: Part-Time Volunteers 15.
Governing Authority: nonprofit. Tax-exempt.
Historic House Museum.
Collections: costumes 1830-1930; foreign small box collection.
Research Fields: shipping lines between Chicago & cities along Lake Michigan.
Facilities: meeting room.
Activities: guided tours; lectures; docent program. Museum Sponsors: Holidays at the Morton House.
Publications: quarterly newsletter.
Hours & Admission Prices: mid-April to Oct. Sun. 1-4. Adults $5; members no charge.
Attendance: 500 (estimated)
Membership: Senior Citizens & Students $15; Individual $25; Friends $100.

SARETT NATURE CENTER, 2300 Benton Center Rd., Benton Harbor, MI 49022-9704. Tel.: 269-927-4832. Fax: 616-927-2742.
E-mail: sarett@sarett.com
Web Site: www.sarett.com
Founded: 1970.
Congressional District: 14
Key Personnel: Dir. & Naturalist, Charles H. Nelson; Pres. (V), Dr. John Sharon.
Personnel Profile: Full-Time Paid 6; Part-Time Paid 4; Part-Time Volunteers 10; Interns 2.
Governing Authority: society. Affiliated with Michigan Audubon Society, 7000 N. Westnedge, Kalamazoo, MI 49001. Tax-exempt: 501(c)(3).
Nature Center & Wildlife Sanctuary.
Collections: wet/dry forest & meadow; bog; prairie; fen.
Facilities: nature trails.
Activities: guided tours; lectures; films; formally organized education programs; temporary exhibitions.
Publications: newsletter.
Hours & Admission Prices: Tues.-Fri. 9-5, Sat. 10-5, Sun. 1-5. Adults $3;

children under 12 no charge. Closed New Year's Day; Easter; Independence Day; Thanksgiving; Christmas. ♿
Attendance: 35,000 (accurate)
Membership: Individual $35; Family $40.

Benzonia

BENZIE AREA HISTORICAL MUSEUM, 6941 Traverse Ave., Benzonia, MI 49616. Mailing Address: P.O. Box 185, Benzonia, MI 49616-0185. Tel.: 231-882-5539. Fax: 231-882-4435.
E-mail: bmuseum@att.net
Web Site: www.bahmuseum.org
Founded: 1969.
Congressional District: 9
Key Personnel: Pres. Bd. Dir. (V), Jerry Slater; Museum Mgr., Dr. Louis Yock.
Personnel Profile: Full-Time Paid 1; Part-Time Volunteers 100.
Governing Authority: society; nonprofit. Parent Institution: Benzie Area Historical Society. Tax-exempt: 501(c)(3).
Historical Museum: housed in 1884-1887 church building.
Collections: Benzie County artifacts from 1850s to present; Bruce Catton & AA car ferries, resorts, 1890 period rooms; logging; agriculture, Gwen Frostic, Civil War.
Research Fields: Benzie area history.
Facilities: library; meeting room. Gift items for sale.
Activities: guided tours; docent program.
Publications: quarterly newsletter.
Hours & Admission Prices: May-Dec. Mon.-Sat. 11-5. No charge; donations accepted. Closed major holidays. ♿
Attendance: 2,000 (estimated)
Membership: Senior Citizen $25; Family $35; Business & Professional $75; Patron $150.

Berrien Springs

BERRIEN COUNTY HISTORICAL ASSOCIATION, History Center at Courthouse Sq., 313W Cass St., Berrien Springs, MI 49103. Mailing Address: P.O. Box 261, Berrien Springs, MI 49103-0261. Tel.: 269-471-1202. Fax: 269-471-7412.
E-mail: bcha@berrienhistory.org
Web Site: www.berrienhistory.org
Founded: 1967.
Congressional District: 4
Key Personnel: Pres. (V), Tom Nelson; Dir., Frances Porter Snyder; Cur., Robert Myers; Museum Shop Mgr., Kristen Patzer.
Personnel Profile: Full-Time Paid 3; Part-Time Paid 1; Part-Time Volunteers 96.
Governing Authority: nonprofit corporation. Affiliated with the County of Berrien. Tax-exempt: 501(c)(3).
Historic Building Museum Complex.
Collections: Berrien County history; repository for county court records & Clark equipment company; genealogical records for Berrien County. Historic Buildings: 1839 Berrien County courthouse; 1830 two-story log house; 1870 sheriff's residence; 1860-1873 county records building; old county jail.
Research Fields: local & regional history; historic preservation.
Facilities: library of Southwest Michigan history; Berrien County court records; Clark equipment company archives; Marx Music Company archives. Books, prints & history-related gift items for sale.
Activities: guided tours; films; formally organized education programs for children; 1860-style baseball team; theatrical performances; permanent & temporary exhibitions; advisory service to local historical organizations; self-guided tour of the 1839 courthouse square.
Publications: books, Historical Sketches of Berrien County; Fort St. Joseph: Berrien County's Colonial Past; stories on local history; historical leaflets from courthouse collections; audio books on county history; books, Adeline & Julia: Growing Up in Michigan and on the Kansas Frontier-Diaries from 19th Century America; Millennial Visions and Earthly Pursuits: The Israelite House of David 1903-Present; Lost on the Lakes: Shipwrecks of Southwest Michigan; Greetings From Berrien Springs; Great Pere Marquette Train Wreck; Story of Buchanan, a history; Greeks of Berrien County; Flight of the Graf Zeppelin; Greetings from Buchanan; Fede, Famiglia e Amici: The Italian Experience in Berrien County 1900-2004.
Hours & Admission Prices: June-Aug. Mon.-Sat. 10-5; Sept.-May Mon.-Fri. 10-5. No charge, donations accepted. Closed holidays. ♿
Attendance: 23,000 (accurate)
Membership: Individual $20; Family $30; Institutional & Contributing $40; Sustaining $50; Patron $100; Benefactor $500.

SIEGFRIED H. HORN ARCHAEOLOGICAL MUSEUM, Andrews University, Institute of Archaeology, Berrien Springs, MI 49104-0990. Tel.: 269-471-3273. Fax: 269-471-3619.
E-mail: hornmuseum@andrews.edu
Web Site: www.andrews.edu/archaeology
Founded: 1970.
Key Personnel: Cur., Constance Gane; Asst. to Cur., L.S. Baker, Jr.
Personnel Profile: Full-Time Paid 3; Part-Time Paid 2.
Governing Authority: church; nonprofit. Parent Institution: Andrews University. Tax-exempt: 501(c)(3).
Archaeological Museum.
Collections: Middle East artifacts: pottery; tools; coins; textiles; papyri; tablets; cuneiform tablets; replicas for teaching purposes.
Research Fields: on-site archaeological excavations in Jordan, Israel.
Facilities: library of books, professional journals, archival pamphlets & clippings of early archaeology of Ancient Near East & slide collection; 1,200 sq. ft. exhibit space; classroom; photo lab; student study areas. Books, pamphlets, replicas, posters & T-shirts for sale.
Activities: guided tours; lectures; temporary, participatory & loan exhibitions.
Publications: quarterly newsletter; occasional monographs; Near East Archaeological Society Bulletin.
Hours & Admission Prices: Museum: temporarily closed for renovations. Temporary exhibit area open to the public Sat. 3-5 by appointment. No charge; donations accepted. Closed holidays. ♿
Attendance: 1,100 (estimated)

Big Rapids

JIM CROW MUSEUM - FERRIS STATE UNIVERSITY, (M), 820 Campus Dr., ASC 2108, Big Rapids, MI 49307-2225. Tel.: 231-591-5873. Fax: 231-591-2541.
E-mail: patricia@ferris.edu
Web Site: www.ferris.edu/jimcrow
Founded: 1996.
Congressional District: 2
Key Personnel: Dir., J. Andy Karafa, Ph.D.; Education, David Pilgrim, Ph.D.
Personnel Profile: Part-Time Paid 3; Part-Time Volunteers 20.
Governing Authority: university.
History Museum.
Collections: early to mid 20th century artifacts; segregation memorabilia including Ku Klux Klan artifacts & pro-segregation signs, tickets, brochures, posters, musical records & magazines; civil rights artifacts; over 3,000 anti-Black caricature artifacts; 200 items related to the leaders & organizations of the civil rights movement.
Research Fields: race relations; prejudice; discrimination.
Facilities: 504 sq. ft. exhibit space.
Activities: formal education programs; guided tours.
Hours & Admission Prices: Mon.-Fri. 8-5 by appointment. No charge. Closed national holidays. ♿
Attendance: 1,500 (estimated)

MECOSTA COUNTY HISTORICAL MUSEUM, 129 S. Stewart St., Big Rapids, MI 49307-1427. Mailing Address: P.O. Box 613, Big Rapids, MI 49307-0613. Tel.: 231-592-5091 & 796-5235.
Founded: 1957.
Congressional District: 10
Key Personnel: Pres. (V), Judy Irvin; Museum Co-Dir., Agnes Tornblom; Museum Co-Dir., Fredda Hankes.
Personnel Profile: Part-Time Volunteers 12.
Governing Authority: state. Parent Institution: Mecosta County Historical Society. Tax-exempt.
General Museum: housed in two-story frame Victorian house.
Collections: agriculture; costumes; folklore; Indian artifacts; numismatic; logging & lumbering exhibits; household items; toys.
Research Fields: agriculture; folklore.
Activities: guided tours; formally organized education programs for children; temporary exhibitions; traveling museum.
Hours & Admission Prices: May-Oct. Sat. 2-4; other times by appointment. No charge; donations accepted.
Attendance: 1,200 (estimated)
Membership: Individual $10; Patron $50; Fitch Phelps Estate $100.

Birmingham

BIRMINGHAM BLOOMFIELD ART CENTER, 1516 S. Cranbrook Rd., Birmingham, MI 48009-1855. Tel.: 248-644-0866. Fax: 248-644-7904.
E-mail: janelinn@bbartcenter.org
Web Site: www.bbartcenter.org
Founded: 1957.
Congressional District: 18
Key Personnel: Pres. & C.E.O., Jane Linn; Chm. Bd., Joshua Sherbin; Vice

Pres. Programs, Cynthia Mills; Dir. Educational Svcs., Deborah Callahan; Gallery Shop & Festival Dir., Peggy Kerr; Vice Pres. Finance, Gwenn Rosseau.
Personnel Profile: Full-Time Paid 10; Part-Time Paid 4; Part-Time Volunteers 250; Interns 2.
Governing Authority: municipal; nonprofit organization. Tax-exempt: 501(c)(3).
Community Art Center.
Collections: Sol Le Witt, Wall Drawing #975 Isometric Outline; Marshall Fredricks, Black Elk Speaks.
Facilities: studios; classrooms. Two and three dimensional work for sale.
Activities: studio art & art history classes; lectures; workshops; holiday shop; auctions & fundraising events; national & international travel programs; competitions. Museum Sponsors: Art Festival in spring.
Publications: exhibition materials; course catalogue; weekly e-blast communications.
Hours & Admission Prices: Mon.-Thurs. 9-6, Fri.-Sat. 9-5, Sun. 1-4. No charge. Closed major holidays. ♿
Attendance: 20,000 (estimated)
Membership: Individual $50; Family & Community $100.

BIRMINGHAM HISTORICAL MUSEUM & PARK, 556 W. Maple, Birmingham, MI 48009-3360. Tel.: 248-530-1928. Fax: 248-530-1681.
E-mail: museum@ci.birmingham.mi.us
Web Site: ci.birmingham.mi.us
Founded: 2001.
Congressional District: 9
Key Personnel: Dir., William K. McElhone.
Personnel Profile: Full-Time Paid 1; Part-Time Paid 2; Part-Time Volunteers 40; Interns 1.
Governing Authority: municipal; nonprofit. Tax-exempt: 501(c)(3).
Historical Society Museum.
Collections: local history from prehistoric to present; personal artifacts; furnishings. Historic Buildings: c.1822 John West Hunter House reflects rural life in the Michigan wilderness in 1840s; c.1928 Allen House is a colonial revival structure built by Birmingham's First Mayor with changing exhibits that reflect the community's historic past.
Research Fields: local history & biographies; early Michigan pioneering history.
Facilities: 500-vol. library of local history books. Museum-related items for sale.
Activities: docent program; formal education programs for children; guided tours; lectures; temporary exhibitions.
Publications: newsletter, Birmingham Heritage
Hours & Admission Prices: Wed.-Sat. 1-4; other times by appointment. Adults $2, members $1. Closed city holidays. ♿
Attendance: 18,000 (estimated)
Membership: $25; $50; $300.

Bloomfield Hills

* **CRANBROOK ART MUSEUM, (M),** 39221 Woodward Ave., Bloomfield Hills, MI 48304-5162. Mailing Address: P.O. Box 801, Bloomfield Hills, MI 48303-0801. Tel.: 248-645-3361. Fax: 248-645-3324.
E-mail: artmuseum@cranbrook.edu
Web Site: www.cranbrookartmuseum.org
Founded: 1927.
Congressional District: 19
Key Personnel: Chm. (V), Maxine Frankel; Dir., Gregory M. Wittkopp; Registrar, Roberta Frey Gilboe; Preparator, Abigail Newbold; Admin. Mgr., Denise Collier; Asst. Cur., Emily Zilber.
Personnel Profile: Full-Time Paid 4; Part-Time Paid 1; Part-Time Volunteers 30.
Governing Authority: nonprofit. Parent Institution: Cranbrook Educational Community. Affiliated with Cranbrook Academy of Art. Tax-exempt: 501(c)(3).
Art Museum.
Collections: 20th-century architectural drawings, ceramics, furniture, metalwork, paintings, sculpture, textiles; study collection of textiles; 19th- & 20th-century prints & ceramics. Historic House: Saarinen House, the 1930 home & studio of Eliel and Loja Saarinen.
Major Exhibits: Cape Farewell: Art and Climate Change (T), 1/31/10-6/13/10.
Research Fields: 20th & 21st century art, crafts, decorative arts, architecture & design.
Facilities: 16,000 sq. ft. exhibition space; 205-seat auditorium. Books & other museum-related items for sale.
Activities: guided tours of exhibitions & architecture; lectures; films; gallery talks; docent program or council; inter-museum loan; permanent, temporary & traveling exhibitions.
Publications: exhibition catalogs, Inigo Manglano-Ovalle; Saarinen House & Garden: A Total Work of Art; Beautiful Scenes: Selections from the Cranbrook Archives; Dream Sites: A Visual Essay; Weird Science: A Conflation of Art & Science; What's Next Newsletter; 100 Treasures of Cranbrook Art Museum; Three Decades of Contemporary Art: The Dr. John & Rose M. Shuey Collection; Richard De Vore.
Hours & Admission Prices: Museum: Fri. 10-10, Sat.-Thurs. 10-5. Adults $9, senior citizens 65 & over and children 2-12 $7; children under 2 & members no charge. Saarinen House: May-Oct. afternoons. Adults $9, senior citizens $8, students $6; discounts to AAM members; members no charge. Closed New Year's Eve & Day; Easter; Independence Day; Labor Day; Thanksgiving; Christmas Eve & Day.
Attendance: 37,000 (estimated)
Membership: Individual General $45; Household General $65; Friends $125; Curators' Circle $250; Saarinen Circle $500; Director's Circle $1,000; Governors' Circle $2,500; Trustees' Circle $5,000.

CRANBROOK HOUSE AND GARDENS AUXILIARY, 380 Lone Pine Rd., Bloomfield Hills, MI 48303-0801. Mailing Address: P.O. Box 801, Bloomfield Hills, MI 48303-0801. Tel.: 248-645-3180. Fax: 248-645-3151.
E-mail: csmith@cranbrook.edu
Web Site: www.cranbrook.edu
Founded: 1971.
Key Personnel: Chm. House & Garden, Juliann Ritter.
Personnel Profile: Part-Time Paid 4.
Governing Authority: nonprofit organization. Affiliated with Cranbrook. Tax-exempt.
Historic House: 1908 home of George Gough & Ellen Scripps Booth.
Collections: art objects; furnishings.
Activities: guided tours; lectures; films; concerts; docent program.
Publications: quarterly newsletter to membership; History of Cranbrook House.
Hours & Admission Prices: Gardens: May-Labor Day Mon.-Sat. 10-5, Sun. 11-5; Sept. daily 11-3; Oct. Sat.-Sun. 11-3. House: June-Sept. Tours: Thurs.-Fri. 11 & 1:15, Sun. 1 & 3; group tours at other times by prior arrangement. Gardens: $6 per person. House Tour & Gardens: $10 per person; discounts to senior citizens; members no charge.
Membership: Senior $30; Friend $40; Group $50; Booster $75; Patron $100; Sustaining $250; Benefactor $500; Life $1,500.

* **CRANBROOK INSTITUTE OF SCIENCE,** 39221 Woodward Ave., Bloomfield Hills, MI 48304-5162. Mailing Address: P.O. Box 801, Bloomfield Hills, MI 48303-0801. Tel.: 248-645-3209. Fax: 248-645-3050.
E-mail: mstafford@cranbrook.edu
Web Site: science.crankbrook.edu
Founded: 1930.
Congressional District: 19
Key Personnel: Chm. Bd. Trustees, James J. Vlasic; Dir., Dr. Michael D. Stafford; Chm. Bd. Governors, Lloyd Reuss; Museum Shop Mgr., Melissa Goldman.
Personnel Profile: Full-Time Paid 46; Part-Time Paid 12; Part-Time Volunteers 300.
Governing Authority: nonprofit organization. Parent Institution: Cranbrook Educational Community. Tax-exempt: 501(c)(3) & 170(b)(1)(A).
Science Museum.
Collections: mineralogy; anthropology; zoology; botany; geology; bats; ethnic & natural history.
Research Fields: botany; anthropology; science education; paleontology; mineralogy.
Facilities: observatory & planetarium; 235-seat auditorium; classrooms; cafe; herbarium; participation physics hall; discovery room. Museum-related items for sale.
Activities: instructional programs for school groups; science education classes for children & adults; workshops; lecture series; permanent & temporary exhibitions; inter-museum loan; field trips; special events on science topics; laser light shows.
Publications: bulletin series focusing on the Institute's areas of specialization, including Michigan Flora, Michigan Lichens, Birds of Southeast Michigan.
Hours & Admission Prices: Fri. 10-10, Sat.-Thurs. 10-5. Adults & children 13 & over $9, senior citizens & children 2-12 $7; discount to AAM members & groups; children under 2, ASTC members & members no charge. Additional fee for Planetarium & Lasera programs. Closed New Year's Day; Independence Day; Thanksgiving; Christmas. ♿
Attendance: 176,000 (accurate)
Membership: Student & Senior $30; Individual $50; Grandparent $60; Family $65; Joint Family & Bat Zone $100; Family Premium $150; Family Ultra Premium $250; Director's Circle $1,000.

Cadillac

WEXFORD COUNTY HISTORICAL SOCIETY & MUSEUM, 127 Beech St., Cadillac, MI 49601-1901. Mailing Address: P.O. Box 124, Cadillac, MI 49601-0124. Tel.: 231-775-1717.
Founded: 1978.
Congressional District: 10
Personnel Profile: Part-Time Paid 1; Part-Time Volunteers 25.
Governing Authority: society; nonprofit. Tax-exempt.
County Historical Society Museum: housed in former Carnegie Library of Cadillac.
Collections: local photographs; paintings of local historical features; logging equipment; county rural one-room school; early fire equipment; railroad memorabilia; general store, post office & barber shop exhibits.
Facilities: 5,000 sq. ft. exhibit space.
Activities: temporary exhibitions; tours; special events; community gatherings.
Publications: newsletter; brochure, A Walking Tour of Cadillac; Rural Schools of Wexford County; Indian Trail of Wexford County; The Shay Locomotive.
Hours & Admission Prices: Memorial Day to Labor Day Wed.-Sat. 12-4. Adults $2; children under 12 & members no charge.
Attendance: 2,800 (accurate)
Membership: Individual $10; Family $25; Friend $100; Lifetime $250; Corporate Patron $500.

Calumet

COPPERTOWN U.S.A., 25815 Red Jacket Rd., Calumet, MI 49913-2904. Mailing Address: 56638 Calumet Ave., Calumet, MI 49913-1965. Tel.: 906-337-4354.
Web Site: www.uppermichigan.com/coppertown
Founded: 1973.
Congressional District: 11
Key Personnel: Pres. (V), Richard Dana.
Personnel Profile: Part-Time Paid 1; Part-Time Volunteers 12.
Governing Authority: nonprofit public corporation.
Restored Mining Co. Complex: situated on the site of the former Calumet & Hecla Mining Co. headquarters complex.
Collections: recreated mineshaft; old railroad equipment; industrial technology & artifacts reflecting the mining of copper & the life of the deep-shaft miner; ethnic displays, reflecting the earlier inhabitants of the area; restored C & H Pattern Shop.
Facilities: visitor orientation center. Gifts & museum-related items for sale.
Hours & Admission Prices: June & Sept. to mid-Oct. Mon.-Sat. 10-5; July-Aug. Mon.-Sat. 10-5, Sun. 12:30-4. Adults $3, National Park Service Pass $2, children $1; children under 12 no charge. ♿
Attendance: 3,000 (estimated)
Membership: Trammer $10; Miner $25; Mine Captain $60; C&H Stockholder $100; Agassiz Society Member $500 & up.

Caspian

IRON COUNTY MUSEUM, Brady at Museum Rd., Caspian, MI 49915. Mailing Address: P.O. Box 272, Caspian, MI 49915. Tel.: 906-265-2617 & 3942. TDD: 906-265-2617.
E-mail: ironcountymuseum@sbcglobal.net
Web Site: www.ironcountymuseum.com
Founded: 1962.
Congressional District: 11
Key Personnel: Pres. (V), John MacPherson; Vice Pres., Allyce Westphal; Chm. (V), M. Bernhardt; Dir., Harold O. Bernhardt; Gallery Dir. & Treas., Shirley Carlson; Cur., Marcia A. Bernhardt; Programs, Audrey Ridolphi; Museum Shop Mgr., Joann Basting.
Personnel Profile: Full-Time Volunteers 3; Part-Time Paid 3; Part-Time Volunteers 60.
Governing Authority: nonprofit organization. Tax-exempt: 501(c)(3).
History Museum.
Collections: 2,000 piece hand-carved miniature logging camp; glass mining dioramas; lumbering & mining tools; farm tools; manuscripts. Historic Buildings: 1890 Stager railroad depot; 1890 Bates Township log barn; 1890 Beechwood log cabin; 1896 one-room schoolhouse; c.1903-1937, Caspian Mine engine house; 1911 Koski log cabin; 1900 Johnson homestead cabin; 1920 Sharrard log lumber cabin; 1890 home of composer Carrie Jacobs-Bond; 1920 Mining Head frame on National Register of Historic Places. Le Blanc Memorial Art Gallery: 140 prints, 50 originals; wildlife art; 12,000 photographs; 8,000 maps (underground & surface). Giovanelli Art Gallery & Studio: Italianate style. Harold & Marcia Bernhardt Art Gallery: contemporary art including presidential artist Simmie Knox.
Research Fields: local communities; mining; lumbering; folklore; agriculture; one room schools; genealogy
Facilities: 200-vol. library of materials on mining, minerals & local lore available for use on premises; archives holding 125 sq. ft. of material primarily on mining. Local publications, books & crafts for sale.
Activities: concerts; hobby workshops; quilt shows; formally organized education programs for children; arts festivals; permanent exhibitions. Museum Sponsors: annual Scandinavian & Italian ethnic festivals; quilt shows; annual Christmas Tree Galleria; St. Lucia Breakfast.
Publications: annual newsletter, Past-Present Prints; ethnic cookbook, The Blend of a Century; books, Iron River History; folklore books, They Came to Iron County, Michigan; The History of Iron County; Black Rock & Roses; The Jewel of Iron Country; Half-Pint Pete; Caspian, A Caring City 1918-1993; Barns, Farms and Yarns, 1999; Men, Mines and Memories 2001; Rural Schools Recollections, 2003; Forty Years of Sports, 2004; Pine to Popple People and Places, 2007; Iron River, A Mining - Logging Town 1885-1925.
Hours & Admission Prices: May-Oct. 1 Mon.-Sat. 10-4, Sun. 1-4. Adults $7, students & children $2.50; discounts for AAM & AAA members. ♿
Attendance: 10,510 (accurate)
Membership: Senior Citizens $5; Contributing $14-$24; Patron $25-$99; Benefactor $100-$999; Life $1,000 & up.

Centreville

NOTTAWA STONE SCHOOL, 204 E. Burr Oak St., Centreville, MI 49032-9620. Tel.: 616-467-5400 & 6155.
Founded: 1968.
Key Personnel: Pres., Richard A. Cripe.
Governing Authority: nonprofit organization. Tax-exempt.
Historic Building: 1870 Stone School.
Collections: school furniture & furnishings.
Publications: Nottawa Stone School Guidelines.
Hours & Admission Prices: Sept.-June Mon.-Fri. No charge.

Charlotte

COURTHOUSE SQUARE ASSOCIATION, (M), 100 W. Lawrence Ave., Charlotte, MI 48813-1494. Mailing Address: P.O. Box 411, Charlotte, MI 48813-0411. Tel.: 517-543-6999. Fax: 517-543-6999.
E-mail: preserve@ia4u.net
Web Site: www.visitcourthouse.square.org
Founded: 1993.
Congressional District: 7
Key Personnel: C.E.O. & Museum Shop Mgr., Jeralyn Bohms; Pres. (V), Carol Ranville.
Personnel Profile: Full-Time Paid 1; Full-Time Volunteers 4; Part-Time Paid 1; Part-Time Volunteers 10.
Governing Authority: private; nonprofit. Tax-exempt: 501(c)(3).
Historic Area: listed on the National Register of Historic Sites.
Collections: emphasis on Eaton County, Michigan & the surrounding mid-Michigan area; military items (Civil War to Vietnam); textiles (quilts & costumes); government records; original documentation for the building including bills of sale, contracts & architectural drawings; political collections; domestic tools; agricultural items; furniture. Historic Buildings: 1873 second empire-style sheriff's residence; 1885 Renaissance revival-style Eaton County courthouse.
Facilities: 2,500-vol. library of Eaton County letters & diaries and government records & documents; genealogical research library; 10,000 sq. ft. exhibit space; 120-seat courtroom.
Activities: guided tours; rental gallery; temporary exhibitions.
Publications: quarterly newsletter, The CSA Ledger.
Hours & Admission Prices: Mon.-Fri. 9-4; other times by appointment. Adults $3; discounts to groups & families; children 12 & under, Wed. and members no charge. Closed major holidays. ♿
Attendance: 2,000 (accurate)
Membership: Individual: Docent $25-$99; Archivist $100-$499; Curator $500-$999; Director $1,000 & up. Business: Scholar $250-$499; Historian $500-$999; Conservator I $1,000-$2,499; Conservator II $2,500 & up.

Chassell

CHASSELL HERITAGE CENTER, 42373 N. Hancock St., Chassell, MI 49916. Mailing Address: P.O. Box 331, Chassell, MI 49916-0331. Tel.: 906-523-1155 & 4612.
Web Site: www.einerlei.com/community/CHO.html
Key Personnel: Pres., Nancy Leonard
Heritage Center.
Collections: local history & culture; period artifacts.
Activities: special events. Museum Sponsors: Strawberry Festival in July; Strawberry Fashion Show in July.
Hours & Admission Prices: July-Aug. Tues. 1-4, Thurs. 4-9.

Cheboygan

CHEBOYGAN COUNTY HISTORICAL MUSEUM COMPLEX, (M), 427 Court Street, Cheboygan, MI 49721-1908. Mailing Address: P.O. Box 5005, Cheboygan, MI 49721-5005. Tel.: 231-627-9597.
E-mail: cheboyganmuseum@straitsarea.com
Web Site: www.cheboyganmuseum.com
Founded: 1971.
Key Personnel: Pres. & Archivist, Lois Ballard; Membership, Ann Gildner; Public Rels., Karen Magee.
Personnel Profile: Part-Time Paid 1; Part-Time Volunteers 40; Interns 1.
Governing Authority: private; nonprofit organization. Tax-exempt: 501(c)(3).
History Museum.
Collections: county history; lumbering; maritime; general store; schoolroom; military artifacts; photographs. Historic Buildings: sheriff residence & jail; log cabin.
Research Fields: history of area culture, fishing, logging & railroads.
Activities: guided tours. Annual Events: Log Cabin Day in June; Yard Sale in August; Autumn Fest in October; Festival of Trees in December.
Publications: quarterly newsletter, The Chronicle.
Hours & Admission Prices: Memorial Day-Sept. Tues.-Sat. 1-4. Adults $5; discounts to groups & AAA members; children & members no charge.
Attendance: 601 (accurate)
Membership: Individual $20; Family under 18 $40; Logger $50-$99; Homesteader $100-$149; Settler $150-$199; Lighthouse Keeper $200-$299; Lumber Baron $300 & up. Business $50; Boss & Gang $100; Chief & Tribe $200; Sheriff & Inmates $300 & up.

Chelsea

GERALD E. EDDY DISCOVERY CENTER, 17030 Bush Rd., Chelsea, MI 48118-9747. Mailing Address: Waterloo Recreation Area, 16345 McClure Rd., Chelsea, MI 48118. Tel.: 734-475-3170. Fax: 734-475-6421.
Web Site: www.michigan.gov/bnr
Founded: 1976.
Key Personnel: Dir., Kathy Kavanagh.
Governing Authority: state; nonprofit. Tax-exempt: 501(c)(3).
Natural history: located on glacial moraine overlooking a kettle lake.
Collections: Precambrian-Carboniferous rocks from Great Lakes region; over 1,000 locally found Indian arrowheads, spear points & stone tools.
Facilities: 77-seat auditorium; 4,000 sq. ft. exhibit space; nature & conservation area; geology interactive room for young people. Geology books, nature reference books, jewelry & other museum-related items for sale.
Activities: guided tours; lectures; videos; slide show; arts festivals; theater; hobby workshops; organized education programs for children & adults. Museum Sponsors: seasonal weekend festivals.
Hours & Admission Prices: Jan.-March Tues.-Sat. 10-5; Summer: daily 10-6; Dec. Tues.-Sun. 10-5. No charge. Parking: daily $6, annual $24. Closed state holidays. ♿
Attendance: 30,859 (accurate)
Membership: Waterloo Natural History Association: Individual $10; Family $20; Patron $30; Sustaining $50; Benefactor $100; Life $500.

Clarkston

CLARKSTON HERITAGE MUSEUM, 6495 Clarkston Rd., Clarkston, MI 48346-1501. Tel.: 248-922-0270.
Web Site: www.clarkstonhistorical.org/museum.htm
Founded: 1999.
Key Personnel: Dir., Toni Smith; Pres. (V), Jennifer Arkwright.
Personnel Profile: Part-Time Paid 1.
Governing Authority: Parent Institution: Clarkston Community Historical Society. Tax-exempt.
Historical Society Museum.
Collections: local history & culture; photographs; documents; photographs; period clothing.
Major Exhibits: 100 Years of Clarkston Schools, 11/09-5/10.
Hours & Admission Prices: Memorial Day to Labor Day Mon.-Thurs. 10-9, Fri. 10-6, Sat. 10-5; Sept.-May Mon.-Thurs. 10-9, Fri. 10-6, Sat. 10-5, Sun. 1-5. No charge.

YESTERYEAR HOUSE-CENTRAL MINE, 7995 Perry Lake Rd., Clarkston, MI 48348-4646. Tel.: 248-625-4296; 906-337-2092.
Founded: 1860.
Congressional District: 110
Key Personnel: C.E.O. & Co-Owner, Nicholas Bell; Co-Owner, Theresa Rekawek.
Governing Authority: individual operation.
Historic House: 1860 house of Central Mine.
Collections: history of the town & family that occupied the house; period furnishings of 1875-1900.
Research Fields: local copper mining history.
Activities: guided tours; lectures; temporary exhibitions.
Hours & Admission Prices: July-Labor Day Mon.-Sat. 10-5. Admission $3.
Attendance: 1,500

Clawson

CLAWSON HISTORICAL MUSEUM, 41 Fisher Ct., Clawson, MI 48017. Mailing Address: 425 N. Main, Clawson, MI 48017-1500. Tel.: 248-588-9169.
E-mail: historicalmuseum@cityofclawson.com
Web Site: cityofclawson.com/museum
Founded: 1973.
Congressional District: 18
Key Personnel: Chm. (V), Joyce McIntyre; Cur., Melodie Nichols.
Personnel Profile: Part-Time Paid 1; Part-Time Volunteers 10.
Governing Authority: municipal. Tax-exempt.
History Museum.
Collections: furniture & household articles from the 1920s; photographs, newspapers & other memorabilia of Clawson.
Research Fields: history of Clawson.
Facilities: 100-vol. library of material on Clawson history, surrounding communities, Oakland County & the State of Michigan available for use on premises with supervision.
Activities: guided tours; lectures; films; docent program or council.
Publications: brochure; newsletter.
Hours & Admission Prices: Wed. & Sun. 1-4. No charge; donations accepted. Closed holidays.
Membership: $5.

Clinton

WINGS OF LOVE, 12803 E. Michigan Ave., Clinton, MI 49236-9420. Tel.: 517-456-8800. Fax: 517-456-8800.
Key Personnel: Exec. Dir., Rev. Dr. Kristina Smith-Speelman
Healing Arts Museum.
Hours & Admission Prices: By appointment. No charge; donations accepted.
Attendance: 10,000 (estimated)

Clinton Township

CLINTON TOWNSHIP HISTORICAL VILLAGE MUSEUM, 40700 Romeo Plank Rd., Clinton Township, MI 48038-2942. Tel.: 586-286-9173.
E-mail: gcthsnewsletter@yahoo.com
Historical Society Museum.
Collections: artifacts & memorabilia pertaining to Clinton Township.
Hours & Admission Prices: Call for hours.

Coloma

NORTH BERRIEN HISTORICAL MUSEUM, (M), 300 Coloma Ave., Coloma, MI 49038-9724. Mailing Address: P.O. Box 207, Coloma, MI 49038-0207. Tel.: 269-468-3330.
Founded: 1966.
Congressional District: 6
Key Personnel: Dir., Alexander Gates; Pres. (V), Scott Young.
Personnel Profile: Full-Time Paid 2; Part-Time Paid 1; Interns 1.
Governing Authority: Tax-exempt.
History Museum.
Collections: Paw Paw Lakes history; fruit farming; cultural heritage.
Major Exhibits: 175 Years Objects & Stories, 11/09-8/10; The Life Atomic (T), 4/10-5/15/10.
Hours & Admission Prices: May-Oct. Wed.-Sat. 10-4; Nov.-April Wed.-Fri. 10-4; other times by appointment. No charge; donations accepted. ♿
Attendance: 2,822 (accurate)
Membership: Student $8; Senior $10; Adult $15; Family $50.

Concord

HISTORIC MANN HOUSE, 205 Hanover St., Concord, MI 49237. Mailing Address: Michigan Historical Museum, 702 W. Kalamazoo, Lansing, MI 48918-0001. Tel.: 517-241-0594.
Web Site: www.michiganhistory.org
Founded: 1970.
Key Personnel: Historian, Dave Bridgens.
Governing Authority: state. Affiliated with the Michigan Historical Museum, 717 W. Allegan St., Lansing, MI 48918. Tax-exempt: 170(b)(A).
Historic House: 1880 Mann House.
Collections: furniture, furnishings & decorative arts from the 1840s to 1920s.
Research Fields: family records.

Activities: guided tours.
Publications: brochure; booklet, The Mann House in Historic Concord.
Hours & Admission Prices: Memorial Day-Labor Day Tues.-Sat. 10-4. No charge.
Attendance: 3,500

Constantine

JOHN S. BARRY HISTORICAL SOCIETY, 300 N. Washington, Constantine, MI 49042. Mailing Address: 485 Centerville Rd., Constantine, MI 49042-0068. Tel.: 269-435-5825.
Founded: 1945.
Congressional District: 4
Key Personnel: Pres. (V), Dr. Vercher; Vice Pres. (V), Robert Ray; Sec. (V), Jane Bickle.
Governing Authority: society; nonprofit. Tax-exempt.
Historical Society Museum: housed in 1835-1847 Governor Barry House, home of Michigan's third elected governor.
Collections: furniture; cookware; needlework; lamps; dolls; clothing; musical instruments; jail cell.
Research Fields: genealogical research into the pioneer families of the community.
Activities: guided tours; lectures; special events. Annual Event: barbeque in September.
Hours & Admission Prices: Open by appointment only. No charge; donations accepted.
Attendance: 550
Membership: Individual $10.

Coopersville

THE COOPERSVILLE AREA HISTORICAL SOCIETY MUSEUM, (M), 363 Main St., Coopersville, MI 49404-1234. Tel.: 616-997-6978.
E-mail: budphoto@j2k.com
Web Site: www.coopersville.com/museum
Key Personnel: Dir., Lillian Budzynski; Cur., Jim Budzynski.
Governing Authority: private; nonprofit organization.
Historical Society Museum.
Collections: railroad memorabilia; gold records & memorabilia belonging to Del Shannon, an early rock-n-roll star; period drugstore re-creation.
Hours & Admission Prices: Aug. to mid-Dec. Sun. 1-4, Tues. 3-8, Wed. 10-1, Sat. 10-4; mid-Dec. to July Tues. 3-8, Wed. 10-1, Sat. 10-4; other times by appointment. Suggested Donation: adults $1. ♿
Attendance: 5,000 (estimated)

Copper Harbor

FORT WILKINS HISTORIC COMPLEX, 15223 US 41, Fort Wilkins State Park, Copper Harbor, MI 49918. Mailing Address: P.O. Box 71, Copper Harbor, MI 49918-0071. Tel.: 906-289-4215. Fax: 906-289-4939.
Web Site: www.michigan.gov/ftwilkins
Founded: 1923.
Congressional District: 11
Key Personnel: Museum Shop Mgr., Barb Wachowski.
Personnel Profile: Full-Time Paid 3; Part-Time Paid 25; Part-Time Volunteers 1.
Governing Authority: state. Parent Institution: Michigan Dept. of History, Arts & Libraries. Subsidiary Institution: Michigan Historical Center. Tax-exempt.
General Museum & Outdoor Museum Complex: including restored Fort Wilkins, the Pittsburgh & Boston Company mine site, Copper Harbor lighthouse.
Collections: military; copper mining; decorative arts c. 1844-1920. Historic Buildings: 1844 soldiers' quarters; mess hall; hospital; bakery; sutler's store; powder magazine; 1849 lightkeeper's dwelling; 1866 lighthouse; 1868 range lighthouse.
Research Fields: mining, marine & early military of the Keweenaw Peninsula.
Facilities: 200-seat auditorium; classrooms. Books for sale.
Activities: permanent exhibits; living history; lectures; audiovisual interpretation.
Publications: booklet, The Fort Wilkins Story; Shipwrecks off Keweenaw; A Keweenaw Guide to Yesterday; Peas Upon a Trencher: A Study of Diet at Fort Wilkins; Lighting the Way: A History of the Copper Harbor Lighthouse; Fort Wilkins Yesterday and Today.
Hours & Admission Prices: mid-May to mid-Oct. daily 8-dusk. Park vehicle permit: daily $6, annual $24; discounts to senior citizens. ♿
Attendance: 150,000 (estimated)

Crystal Falls

HARBOUR HOUSE MUSEUM, 17 N. 4th St., Crystal Falls, MI 49920-1205. Mailing Address: P.O. Box 65, Crystal Falls, MI 49920-0065. Tel.: 906-875-4341.
Key Personnel: Pres. (V), Jackie Rowan; Cur., Ruth Pieper.
Governing Authority: Parent Institution: City of Crystal Falls. Tax-exempt.
History Museum.
Collections: photographs; period clothing & memorabilia; school trophies; personal artifacts; family heirlooms; children's period toys; a miniature carousel; posters; local newspapers dating back to 1887; Ojibwe artifacts; Civil War to Desert Storm.
Research Fields: Diamond Drill; newspapers from 1887.
Activities: guided tours; special events.
Hours & Admission Prices: June-Sept. 4 Tues.-Sat. 10-2. Family $5, adults $2.
Attendance: 350 (estimated)
Membership: Individual $10.

Dearborn

ARAB AMERICAN NATIONAL MUSEUM, (M), 13624 Michigan Ave., Dearborn, MI 48126-3519. Tel.: 313-582-2266. Fax: 313-582-1086.
E-mail: aanm@accesscommunity.org
Web Site: www.arabamericanmuseum.org
Founded: 2005.
Key Personnel: C.E.O. & Dir., Dr. Anan Ameri; Museum Shop Mgr., Janet Elias.
Governing Authority: Parent Institution: ACCESS. Tax-exempt.
History Museum.
Collections: Arab culture; Arab contributions to science, medicine, mathematics & astronomy; Arab architecture & decorative arts; Arab American immigration from 1500 to present; Arab Americans in the U.S.
Activities: school tours; performance series; film festival; cultural competency workshops.
Publications: invisible exhibition catalog; Arab American Encyclopedia.
Hours & Admission Prices: Wed.-Sat. 10-6, Sun. 12-5. Adults $6, students, seniors 62 & over and children 6-12 $3; children 5 & under no charge. Closed New Year's Day; Thanksgiving; Christmas. ♿
Attendance: 50,000
Membership: Student & Senior $25; Individual $35; Family $65.

AUTOMOTIVE HALL OF FAME, INC., 21400 Oakwood Blvd., Dearborn, MI 48124-4078. Tel.: 313-240-4000. Fax: 313-240-8641.
Web Site: www.automotivehalloffame.org
Founded: 1939.
Key Personnel: Pres., Jeffrey K. Leestma; Chm., Jason Vines; Sec., Neil DeKoker; Treas., Ronald J. Martoia.
Personnel Profile: Full-Time Paid 6; Part-Time Paid 6; Part-Time Volunteers 20.
Governing Authority: nonprofit. Tax-exempt: 501(c)(3).
Automotive Museum & Library.
Collections: histories of people, company & corporations.
Research Fields: automotive history.
Facilities: 4,000-vol. library.
Activities: guided tours; films.
Publications: quarterly, The Driving Spirit.
Hours & Admission Prices: Daily 9-5. Adults $6, seniors $5, children 5-18 $3. Closed national holidays. ♿
Attendance: 30,000 (accurate)
Membership: Friend $50; Innovator $100; Driving Spirit $500; Visionary $1,000; Creative Spirit $2,500; Prime Mover $5,000.

DEARBORN HISTORICAL MUSEUM, (M), 915 S. Brady Rd., Dearborn, MI 48124-2322. Tel.: 313-565-3000. Fax: 313-565-4848.
E-mail: kgross@ci.dearborn.mi.us
Web Site: www.cityofdearborn.org
Founded: 1950.
Congressional District: 15
Key Personnel: Chief Cur., Kirt Gross; Archives Specialist, Helen Mamalakis; Registrar, Robin Anderko.
Personnel Profile: Full-Time Paid 2; Part-Time Paid 6.
Governing Authority: municipal. Affiliated with the Dearborn Historical Commission, Div. of the City of Dearborn. Tax-exempt: 501(c)(3).
Local History Museum: housed in 1839 Powder Magazine, now McFadden-Ross House; 1833 Commandant's Quarters; 1831 Gardner House.
Collections: local history artifacts; agriculture; costumes; military; textiles; archives; decorative arts; transportation; industry; manuscripts.
Research Fields: local history; agriculture; costumes; military; archives; Henry Dearborn; Orville L. Hubbard; Alex Pilch; John B. O'Reilly; Lucille McCollough.

Facilities: 2,000-vol. library of local, county, regional & state history; 1942-1978 mayoral papers of Orville L. Hubbard; censuses; 1905-present local newspapers; reading room. Historic reproductions for sale.
Activities: guided tours; lectures; films; study clubs; workshops; formally organized education programs for children & adults; docent program; inter-museum loan, permanent, temporary & traveling exhibitions; school loan service; Museum Guild.
Publications: book, The Bark Covered House; quarterly magazine, The Dearborn Historian; brochures.
Hours & Admission Prices: Commandant's Quarters: Tues.-Fri. 11-4, Sat. 9-1. McFadden-Ross House: Tues.-Fri. 9-5. Archives: Tues.-Fri. 9-4, Sat. by appointment. No charge; donations accepted. Closed holidays.
Attendance: 10,000 (estimated)
Membership: Individual $10; Family $15; Sustaining $20; Student $35; Curator's Circle $50; Commandant's Assembly $125; General Henry Dearborn Club $250; Mayor's Circle $500.

* **THE HENRY FORD, (M),** 20900 Oakwood Blvd., Dearborn, MI 48124-4088. Tel.: 313-982-6100. Fax: 313-982-6250. TDD: 313-271-2455.
E-mail: barbh@thehenryford.org
Web Site: www.thehenryford.org
Formerly: Henry Ford Museum & Greenfield Village
Founded: 1929.
Congressional District: 16
Key Personnel: Pres., Patricia E. Mooradian; Chm. (V), S. Evan Weiner; Vice Pres. Business Operations & C.F.O., Denise Thal; Dir. Information Technology, Michael Butman; Dir. Facilities Mgmt., Robert Hanna; Dir. Human Resources & Security, James Rankine; Dir. Workforce Devel., James Van Bochove; Vice Pres. Museums & Collections, Christian W. Overland; Media & Film Rels., Wendy Metros; Dir. Institutional Advancement, Peg Tallet; Dir. Benson Ford Research Center, Judith Endelman; Dir. External Rels., George Moroz; Dir. Food Service, Susan Schmidt; Dir. Natl. Retail Sales, Terri Anderson; Dir. Visitor Svcs., AmyLouise Bartlett; Dir. Historical Resources & Education, Paula Gangopadhyay; Dir. Greenfield Village & Henry Ford Museum, John Neilson; Chief Mktg. Officer, Carol Kendra.
Personnel Profile: Full-Time Paid 284; Part-Time Paid 1,130; Part-Time Volunteers 642; Interns 24.
Governing Authority: nonprofit organization. Tax-exempt: 501(c)(3).
History Museum.
Collections: 1,000,000 artifacts & collections of artifacts; over 26 million printed & visual materials; 9,000 linear ft. of archival holdings; 80 historic structures.
Research Fields: agriculture; leisure & entertainment; industry; domestic life; transportation; communication.
Facilities: research library; 80 acre village; classrooms; food service; IMAX theater; research center. Museum-related items for sale.
Activities: concerts; study clubs; craft workshops; formally organized education programs; inter-museum loans, permanent, temporary & traveling exhibitions; Ford Rouge factory tours; summer & holiday evening programs. Museum Sponsors: Smart Fun field trips; summer festival.
Publications: on subjects related to museum collections & fields of research interest.
Hours & Admission Prices: Henry Ford Museum: daily 9:30-5. Greenfield Village: April 15-Oct. daily 9:30-5; Nov.-Dec. Fri.-Sun. 9:30-5. Henry Ford Museum: adults $15, children 5-12 $11; discounts to AAM members; members & children under 5 no charge. Greenfield Village: adults $22, children 5-12 $16; discounts to AAM members; members & children under 5 no charge. Closed Thanksgiving; Christmas. ♿
Attendance: 1,500,000 (accurate)
Membership: Student $44; Individual $54; Companion $79; Family $125; Friends $185.

HENRY FORD ESTATE-FAIR LANE, 4901 Evergreen Rd., Dearborn, MI 48128-2406. Tel.: 313-593-5590. Fax: 313-593-5243.
E-mail: grodgers@umd.umich.edu
Web Site: www.henryfordestate.org
Founded: 1957.
Key Personnel: Dir., Gary Rodgers; Group Tour Coord., Bernadette Trisko; Visitor Svcs. & Gen. Tours, Frank Gasiorek.
Personnel Profile: Full-Time Paid 12; Part-Time Paid 5; Part-Time Volunteers 160; Interns 2.
Governing Authority: public university; nonprofit. Parent Institution: University of Michigan. Subsidiary Institution: University of Michigan, Dearborn. Tax-exempt.
Nature Center & Historic House: former home of Henry Ford.
Collections: decorative arts; mechanical equipment; books; landscapes.
Facilities: 1,500-vol. library of books owned by Ford family; cafe. Museum-related items for sale.
Activities: guided tours; lectures; films; organized education program for children. Museum Sponsors: Christmas programs.
Publications: biannual newsletter, The Fair Lane Advisor.
Hours & Admission Prices: Tours: Jan.-March Tues.-Sun. 1:30; April-Dec. Tues.-Sun. 10:30, 11:30, 12:30, 1:30, & 2:30. Adults 13-61 $12, senior citizens 62 & over and students $11, children 6-12 $8; children 5 & under no charge. Closed New Year's Day; Easter; Thanksgiving; Christmas. ♿
Attendance: 150,000 (estimated)

Decatur

HISTORIC NEWTON HOME, 20689 Marcellus Hwy., Decatur, MI 49045-9455. Mailing Address: 24010 Hospital St., #105, Cassopolis, MI 49031-8655. Tel.: 269-445-9016.
Founded: 1974.
Congressional District: 4
Key Personnel: Chm. Cass County Historical Commission, Abigail Schten; Sec., Marjorie Federowski.
Governing Authority: commission. Affiliated with Cass County Historical Commission.
Historic House Museum: 1867 Newton Home.
Collections: Victorian furniture; one room school.
Activities: guided tours.
Hours & Admission Prices: Home: mid-March to mid-Nov. Sun. 1-4:30; tours by appointment all year. School: by appointment. No charge; donations accepted.
Attendance: 110 (estimated)

Deckerville

DECKERVILLE HISTORICAL MUSEUM, 4028 N. Ruth Rd., Deckerville, MI 48427-9355. Tel.: 810-376-6695.
Web Site: www.deckervillelibrary.com/deckerville_historical_museum.htm
History Museum: housed in the Deckerville Train Depot, built in 1883.
Collections: railroad memorabilia; period dishes; portraits of local families; Native American artifacts.
Hours & Admission Prices: May-Sept. by appointment. Adults $2, children 5-12 $1.

Delton

BERNARD HISTORICAL SOCIETY AND MUSEUM, 7135 W. Delton Rd., Delton, MI 49046. Mailing Address: P.O. Box 307, Delton, MI 49046-0307. Tel.: 269-623-3565.
Founded: 1962.
Congressional District: 3
Key Personnel: C.E.O. & Pres. (V), Margery Martin.
Personnel Profile: Part-Time Paid 1; Part-Time Volunteers 35.
Governing Authority: nonprofit organization. Tax-exempt: 501(c)(3).
Local History Museum.
Collections: pioneer family artifacts; farm equipment; manuscripts. Historic Structures: 1873 one-room schoolhouse; 1933 old brick hospital; country store; blacksmith shop; 1865 Seamstress cottage.
Research Fields: history of one-room schools, many local family histories.
Facilities: 800-vol. library of history books, manuscripts & local documents available on premises. Museum-related items & books for sale.
Activities: guided tours; lectures; permanent exhibitions.
Publications: book, 1968, Years Gone By; booklet, The First Twenty Years; quarterly newsletter.
Hours & Admission Prices: June & Sept. Sun. 1-5; July-Aug. Thurs.-Sun. 1-5. No charge; donations accepted. ♿
Attendance: 2,000 (estimated)
Membership: Annual $5; Life $50; Patron $125.

Detroit

ANNA SCRIPPS WHITCOMB CONSERVATORY, Belle Isle Park, Detroit, MI 48207-4345. Tel.: 313-822-2867. Fax: 313-821-5793.
E-mail: thiedep@cadtwr.ci.detroit.mi.us
Web Site: www.bibsociety.org
Founded: 1904.
Congressional District: 13
Key Personnel: Park Mgr., Keith Flournoy; Chm. (V), Janice Ellison; Pres. (V), Joseph Stanton; Floriculture Supvr., Leticia Bertaud.
Personnel Profile: Full-Time Paid 4; Part-Time Volunteers 80.
Governing Authority: municipal. Parent Institution: Floriculture Unit of the Belle Isle Division of the Detroit Department of Recreation, 65 Cadillac Sq., Suite 4000, Detroit, MI 48226. Tax-exempt.
Botanical Garden & Conservatory.
Collections: tropicals; fern; palms, cactus; orchid display.
Facilities: conservation center; gardens.
Activities: guided tours; lectures; permanent exhibitions. Annual Event: Plant Sale in May.

Hours & Admission Prices: Daily 10-5. No charge; donations accepted. ♿
Attendance: 68,700 (estimated)
Membership: Annual: Senior (over 60) & Junior (under 15) $10; Individual $25; Family $35. Club & Individual: Sustaining $50; Donor $100; Benefactor $500. Business & Corporate: Sustaining $250; Donor $1,000; Benefactor $5,000.

BELLE ISLE NATURE ZOO, Belle Isle Park, Detroit, MI 48207. Mailing Address: 8450 W. 10 Mile Rd., Royal Oak, MI 48067-3001. Tel.: 313-852-4056. Fax: 313-852-4074.
Web Site: www.detroitzoo.org
Formerly: Belle Isle Nature Center
Founded: 1976.
Congressional District: 15
Key Personnel: C.E.O., Ron L. Kagan; Mgr., Mike Reed.
Personnel Profile: Full-Time Paid 2; Part-Time Volunteers 21.
Governing Authority: municipal. Parent Institution: Detroit Zoological Society. Tax-exempt.
Nature Zoo.
Collections: natural science artifacts; natural science; native plants; gardens; native animal species.
Research Fields: urban ecology; Great Lakes & unique wetlands studies.
Facilities: woodland trails; outdoor classroom.
Activities: guided tours; films; nature history presentations; formally organized education programs for children; summer day programs; teacher training workshops; outdoor classroom; presentations including bird & bee habitats.
Publications: monthly newsletter, Habitat; seasonal family program guide.
Hours & Admission Prices: Daily 10-5. No charge; donations accepted. Closed New Year's Day; Thanksgiving; Christmas. ♿
Attendance: 56,000 (accurate)
Membership: Individual: $45; Individual Plus: $60; Family & Grandparent $74; Supporter $150.

CENTER GALLERIES, COLLEGE FOR CREATIVE STUDIES, (M), 301 Frederick Douglas Ave., Detroit, MI 48202-4024. Tel.: 313-664-7800. Fax: 313-664-7880.
E-mail: mperron@collegeforcreativestudies.edu
Web Site: www.ccscad.edu
Founded: 1989.
Congressional District: 11
Key Personnel: Dir., Michelle M. Perron.
Personnel Profile: Full-Time Paid 1; Part-Time Paid 1; Interns 3.
Governing Authority: college; nonprofit organization. Parent Institution: College for Creative Studies-College of Art & Design, 201 E. Kirby, Detroit 48202. Tax-exempt: 501(c)(3).
Art Gallery.
Collections: works by CCS student, alumni, & faculty.
Facilities: 3,000 sq. ft. gallery space.
Activities: guided tours; lectures; loan & traveling exhibitions.
Publications: brochures on exhibiting artists.
Hours & Admission Prices: Sept.-July Tues.-Sat. 10-5. No charge. Closed Independence Day; Thanksgiving; Christmas. ♿
Attendance: 12,000 (accurate)
Membership: General $25; Premier $100.

CHARLES H. WRIGHT MUSEUM OF AFRICAN AMERICAN HISTORY, 315 E. Warren Ave., Detroit, MI 48201-1443. Tel.: 313-494-5800. Fax: 313-494-5855.
Web Site: www.maah-detroit.org
Founded: 1965.
Congressional District: 16
Key Personnel: Pres., Juanita Moore; Chm. (V), Elizabeth Brooks; Treas., Edward J. Hannan; Chief Operating Officer, Tyrone Davenport; Chief Financial Officer, Ollette Boyd; Dir. Research & Exhibitions, Robert Smith; Chief Cur., Patrina Chatman; Museum Shop Mgr., Keysha Bell.
Personnel Profile: Full-Time Paid 45; Part-Time Paid 14; Part-Time Volunteers 100.
Governing Authority: nonprofit organization. Tax-exempt: 501(c)(3).
History Museum.
Collections: African & African American art, artifacts, photographs and other items pertaining to African & African American culture.
Research Fields: the provenance of the objects & photographic collections; preservation & conservation of the collections.
Facilities: 1,500-vol. library of monographs, manuscripts, oral histories, periodicals on the African American experience, the Underground Railroad & Civil Rights, with limited public access; 3 classrooms; 2 multi-purpose rooms; orientation amphitheater; 317-seat theater; video room. Museum-related & imported African items for sale.
Activities: African World Festival; variety of performing arts and concerts; docent program; films; workshops and lecture series programs for children, adults affiliated with Wayne State Univ.; guided tours; hobby workshops; lectures; loan, temporary & traveling exhibitions; theatre; training programs for professional museum workers. Museum Sponsors: African World Festival; Juneteenth Celebration; Kwanzaa Celebration and other annual programs.
Publications: quarterly newsletter, African American News; quarterly calendar, MAAH Calendar of Events.
Hours & Admission Prices: Tues.-Sat. 9-5, Sun. 1-5. Adults $8, children $5; discounts to AAM & ICOM members; members no charge. Closed major holidays. ♿
Attendance: 150,000 (estimated)
Membership: Student $5; Senior Citizen $15; Individual $35; Family $65; Contributor $150.

CHILDREN'S MUSEUM/DETROIT PUBLIC SCHOOLS, 6134 Second Ave., Detroit, MI 48202-3404. Tel.: 313-873-8100. Fax: 313-873-3384.
E-mail: dwight.levens@detroitk12.org
Web Site: www.detroitchildrensmuseum.org
Founded: 1917.
Congressional District: 13
Key Personnel: Dir., Dwight R. Levens; Mgr. Collections, Ralph Wittla; Science Teacher, William Zirngibl; Science Teacher, Laura Speegle; Social Studies Teacher, Cetaura Bell Rodgers; Art Teacher, Lana Hardin; Friends Contact, Jonella Mongo; Coord. Community Outreach, Leslie Williams; Coord. Accessioning, Sue Boertmann; Coord. Collections, Marilyn Croff; Multicultural Studies, Janet Barber; Administrative Asst., Nadine Talley.
Personnel Profile: Full-Time Paid 11; Full-Time Volunteers 5; Part-Time Paid 1; Part-Time Volunteers 31.
Governing Authority: public school district. Operated by the Detroit Board of Education, 3031 W. Grand Blvd., Detroit 48202. Tax-exempt: 170(b)(1)(A).
Children's Museum.
Collections: ethnology; natural history; science; folk arts; costumes; textiles; dolls; toys; musical instruments; tools & equipment.
Research Fields: ethnic studies.
Facilities: 2,000-vol. library of reference books available on premises; planetarium; classrooms.
Activities: class lessons; demonstrations; craft & science workshops; clubs; occasional TV programs; formally organized education programs for children & undergraduate college students; permanent & traveling exhibitions; ethnic studies programs; Museum-to-the-Schools program; teacher workshops; loan collections to schools.
Publications: museum services handbook; exhibit brochures; monthly calendar of activities; catalogs of lending collections; workshop resource sheets; African culture portfolios.
Hours & Admission Prices: Office: June-Sept. Mon.-Fri. 8-4; Oct.-May 8-4:45. Museum: Mon.-Fri. 9-4. No charge; donations accepted. Closed national holidays. ♿
Attendance: 43,000 (accurate)
Membership: Senior, Student & Teacher $15; Individual $25; Family $35; Sponsor $100; Patron $250.

CURTIS MUSEUM, 14034 W. McNichols, Detroit, MI 48235. Tel.: 313-341-1512. Fax: 313-341-1571.
E-mail: curtismuseum@sbcglobal.net
Web Site: www.curtismuseum.com
History Museum.
Collections: life & family history of Dr. Austin W. Curtis; historical documents; photographs; personal artifacts.
Hours & Admission Prices: Tues.-Sat. 10-4; tours by appointment. Adults $5, senior citizens & children $3.

DETROIT ARTISTS MARKET, 4719 Woodward Ave., Detroit, MI 48201-1307. Tel.: 313-832-8540. Fax: 313-832-8543.
E-mail: info@detroitartistsmarket.org
Web Site: www.detroitartistsmarket.org
Founded: 1932.
Key Personnel: Chm. Bd. Directors, Katy Locker; Exec. Dir., Nancy Sizer; Gallery Mgr., Sarah Balmer; Gallery Asst., Matthew Hanna.
Personnel Profile: Full-Time Paid 3; Part-Time Volunteers 7; Interns 1.
Governing Authority: nonprofit organization. Tax-exempt: 501(c)(3).
Contemporary Art Museum.
Collections: paintings; photographs; prints; drawings; sculpture; ceramics; glass; wood.
Facilities: 3,500 sq. ft. exhibit space.
Activities: films; formal education programs for adults & children; lectures. Annual Event: Garden Sale.
Publications: catalogue, Journal of Exhibitions; biannual newsletter, Detroit Artists Market Newsletter.
Hours & Admission Prices: Tues.-Sat. 11-6. No charge; donations accepted. ♿

Attendance: 21,000 (estimated)
Membership: Student $20; Artist $30; Individual $40; Household $65; Associate $100; Patron $250; Devotee $500; Collectors' Circle $1,000; Directors' Circle $2,500.

DETROIT HISTORICAL SOCIETY, 5401 Woodward Ave., Detroit, MI 48202-4097. Tel.: 313-833-1805. Fax: 313-833-5342.
Web Site: www.detroithistorical.org
Founded: 1921.
Congressional District: 15
Key Personnel: C.E.O. & Dir., Robert Bury; Chm. (V), Francis W. McMillan, II; Collections Mgr., Marianne Weldon.
Personnel Profile: Full-Time Paid 18; Part-Time Paid 6; Part-Time Volunteers 100; Interns 2.
Governing Authority: Subsidiary Institutions: Dossin Great Lakes Museum; Detroit Historical Museum. Tax-exempt.
History Museum.
Collections: artifacts pertaining to Detroit, Michigan & the Great Lakes; including military & maritime history; costumes; decorative arts; toys; furniture; Woodlands Indian; industrial & automotive history; communications; domestic life; fine arts.
Research Fields: urban, social, industrial, architectural, military & marine history.
Facilities: 1,500-vol. library of fashion reference books available for use by special request; auditorium; classrooms. Museum-related items for sale.
Activities: guided tours of exhibits & local historical sites; lectures; community neighborhood tours; history related workshops; education programs for children; inter-museum loan, permanent, temporary & traveling exhibitions; school tour service. Museum Sponsors: conferences; historic preservation; church & local history; Black Historic Sites committee.
Publications: newsletter; annual report; calendar of events.
Hours & Admission Prices: Wed.-Fri. 9:30-3, Sat. 10-5, Sun. 12-5. Adults $5, senior citizens & students 5-18 $3; discounts to AAM members; members and children 4 & under no charge. Dossin Great Lakes Museum: Sat.-Sun. 11-4. Adults $4, senior citizens & children 5-18 $3; children 4 & under no charge. Closed national holidays. ♿
Attendance: 194,388 (accurate)
Membership: Individual $40; Individual Plus $50; Family $65; Patron $125; Donor $250; Historian $500.

* **DETROIT INSTITUTE OF ARTS, (M),** 5200 Woodward Ave., Detroit, MI 48202-4094. Tel.: 313-833-7900. Fax: 313-833-2357 & 3756. TDD: 313-833-1454.
E-mail: jmetz@dia.org
Web Site: www.dia.org
Founded: 1885.
Congressional District: 13
Key Personnel: Pres. Arts Commission, A. Alfred Taubman; Dir., Graham W.J. Beal; Chm. Bd. Dirs., Eugene A. Gargano, Jr.; C.O.O., Nettie Seabrooks; Cur. European Modern Art, MaryAnn Wilkinson; Cur. Africa, Oceanic, Nii Quarcoopome; Cur. American Art, Kenneth Myers; Cur. European Sculpture & Decorative Arts, Alan P. Darr; Cur. European Paintings & Chief Cur., George S. Keyes; Cur. Prints, Drawings & Photographs, Nancy Sojka; Cur. Film Theatre & Video, Elliot Wilhelm; Native American Art & Vice Pres. Exhibitions & Collection Strategies, David Penney; Cur. Arts of Asia & Islamic World, Heather Ecker; Cur. African-American Art, Valerie Mercer; Head Conservator, Barbara Heller; Head Registrar, Pamela Watson; Vice Pres. & Finance Admin., Loren Lau; Vice Pres. Mktg. & Museum Programs, Annmarie Erickson; Vice Pres. Museum Operations, Sven Gierlinger; Exec. Dir. Exhibitions, Tara Robinson; Dir. Photography, Dirk Bakker; Dir. Publications, Susan Larsen; Operations Mgr., Kurt Vandewiele; Security Chief, Ernie Smith; Museum Shop Mgr., Cathy Sweier.
Personnel Profile: Full-Time Paid 245; Part-Time Paid 106; Part-Time Volunteers 760; Interns 9.
Governing Authority: municipal. Parent Institution: the City of Detroit. Subsidiary Institution: Founders Society-DIA. Tax-exempt: 501(c)(3).
Art Museum.
Collections: European, 20th-century, Ancient, Middle Eastern, Islamic, American, Asian, African, Oceanic, & Native American art; textiles; period rooms; Paul McPharlin Puppetry collection; graphic arts & photography; Diego Rivera Detroit Industry Frescoes; films; film posters.
Research Fields: all objects of art in permanent collection & prospective acquisition.
Facilities: 150,000-vol. non-circulating library of art books & art material available for inter-library loan & on premises; 1,200-seat auditorium; restaurant; cafeteria; 382-seat recital & lecture hall; classrooms; conservation lab. Museum-related items for sale.
Activities: guided tours; student tours; lectures; films; gallery talks; concerts; art & art appreciation classes; professional museum training program; permanent & temporary exhibitions; education programs; outreach programs; workshops; artist demonstrations; drawing in galleries; music. Museum Sponsors: Detroit Film Theatre.
Publications: exhibition & permanent collection catalogues; annual report; periodic bulletin; monthly DIA magazine.
Hours & Admission Prices: Wed.-Thurs. 10-5, Fri. 10-10, with special programming from 6-10, Sat.-Sun. 10-6, with special programming at 2. Suggested Donation: adults $8, children $5; DIA, AAM & ICOM members no charge. Closed holidays. ♿
Attendance: 266,527 (accurate)
Membership: Seniors $50; Individual $55; Family & Friend $80; Family Plus $100; Patron $250; Contributor $500; Conservator $1,000; Associate $1,500; Sustaining Assoc. $2,500; Director's Assoc. $5,000; Chairman's Assoc. $10,000.

DETROIT SCIENCE CENTER, 5020 John R. St., Detroit, MI 48202-4045. Tel.: 313-577-8400. Fax: 313-832-1623.
E-mail: info@sciencedetroit.org
Web Site: www.detroitsciencecenter.org
Founded: 1970.
Congressional District: 13
Key Personnel: Chm. Bd., Francois Castaing; Pres. & C.E.O., Kevin F. Prihod; C.O.O., Ida Tomlin; Dir. Public Rels. & Mktg., Kelly Fulford; C.F.O., Bob Seestadt; Dir. Facilities, Tom Mott; Vice Pres. Science Programs, Todd Slisher; Reservations, Lynell Moore; Dir. Exhibits, Ed Summers; Dir. Exhibits Content, Elizabeth Chilton.
Personnel Profile: Full-Time Paid 35; Part-Time Paid 40; Part-Time Volunteers 90.
Governing Authority: bd. of trustees; nonprofit organization. Tax-exempt: 501(c)(3), 509(a)(1).
Science Museum.
Collections: hands-on exhibits.
Facilities: IMAX dome theater; planetarium; science stage.
Activities: large format films; science demonstrations; formally organized educational programs for children; computer educational programs; permanent & temporary exhibitions.
Publications: quarterly newsletter.
Hours & Admission Prices: Mon.-Fri. 9-3, Sat.-Sun. 10-6. Adults $7.95, senior citizens & children 2-12 $6.95. IMAX & Dassault Systemes Planetarium $5; discounts to ASTC members; members no charge. Closed New Year's Day; Memorial Day; Independence Day; Labor Day; Thanksgiving; Christmas Eve & Day. ♿
Attendance: 250,000 (accurate)
Membership: Student & Senior Citizen $25; Individual Plus $55; Grandparents $65; Family $70; Family Plus $90; Premium $170.

DOSSIN GREAT LAKES MUSEUM, 100 Strand Dr., Belle Isle, Detroit, MI 48207-4372. Tel.: 313-833-5538; 313-821-2661. Fax: 313-833-5342.
Web Site: www.detroithistorical.org
Founded: 1948.
Key Personnel: Public Rels. Dir., Bob Sadler.
Governing Authority: municipal. A branch of the Detroit Historical Museum. Tax-exempt.
Great Lakes History Museum.
Collections: ship models; paintings; period & modern nauticalia; photographs; information files of Great Lakes ships; restored interior from the former lake steamer City of Detroit III; pilothouse from the freighter William Clayford.
Research Fields: Great Lakes commerce.
Facilities: 700-vol. library of government & private records, data files, news clips, photos, negatives of Great Lakes ships & history, available for use on premises. Books, postcards & other museum-related items for sale.
Activities: guided tours; lectures; films; permanent & temporary exhibitions.
Publications: bimonthly magazine, Telescope.
Hours & Admission Prices: Sat.-Sun. 11-4. No charge; donations accepted. Closed major holidays.
Attendance: 70,000
Membership: Libraries/Schools/Associations $20; Regular $40; Benefactor $100; Life $350.

FIRST UNDERGROUND RAILROAD MUSEUM, 33 E. Forest Ave., Detroit, MI 48201-1813. Tel.: 313-831-4080.
Historic Building: housed in the First Congregational Church of Detroit, used to hide slaves en route to freedom.
Collections: underground railroad history; photographs; personal artifacts.
Facilities: restaurant; rental facilities.
Activities: summer camp; electronic arts program.
Hours & Admission Prices: Tues.-Sat. 11-3. Adults $12, children $10; discounts to groups.

FISHER MANSION AND BHAKTIVEDANTA CULTURAL CENTER, 383 Lenox Ave., Detroit, MI 48215-3048. Tel.: 313-331-6740. Fax: 313-822-3748.
Key Personnel: Mgr., Srinandanandan Das
Historic House Museum.
Collections: period furnishings; personal artifacts; photographs; gardens.
Activities: rental facilities; special events.
Hours & Admission Prices: Mansion: daily; other times by appointment. Events on Sun.

INTERNATIONAL GOSPEL MUSIC HALL OF FAME & MUSEUM, 18301 W. McNichols, Detroit, MI 48219-4112. Tel.: 313-592-0017. Fax: 313-592-8762.
E-mail: igmhfm@cs.com
Web Site: www.igmhf.org
Formerly: Gospel Music Hall of Fame & Museum
Founded: 1995.
Key Personnel: C.E.O., Chm. & Pres., David Gough; Vice Chm. & Dir. Devel., Ida Tomlin; Treas., Johnny Stewart; Sec., Carolyn Gough; Archivist & Chief Cur., Sherry Dupree; Program Mgr., Jean Anderson.
Personnel Profile: Full-Time Volunteers 2; Part-Time Volunteers 9.
Governing Authority: private; nonprofit organization. Tax-exempt: 501(c)(3).
Gospel Music Museum.
Collections: archives; photographs; tapes; sound recordings; sheet music; songbooks; magazine clippings; artist biographies; films; musical instruments; clothing & memorabilia associated with the development of gospel music; sight & sound exhibits.
Research Fields: history on each inductee; provenance of the objects & photographic collections; preservation & conservation of the collections.
Facilities: 2,000-vol. library of reference gospel music; 1,200-seat auditorium; multi-purpose room; cafeteria. Museum-related items for sale.
Activities: formal education programs; guided tours; lectures; participatory, temporary & traveling exhibitions; broadcast programs; conferences. Museum Sponsors: Annual Induction Dinner; Black History Program.
Publications: quarterly newsletter, GMHF News Update; brochures; pamphlets.
Hours & Admission Prices: Thurs.-Sat. 10-3. Call for admission fee. Closed all holidays.
Attendance: 250 (estimated)
Membership: Association $50; Gold $100.

MICHIGAN SPORTS HALL OF FAME, Cobo Center, One Washington Blvd., Detroit, MI 48226. Mailing Address: P.O. Box 1073, Farmington, MI 48332-1073. Tel.: 313-877-8777; 248-473-0656. Fax: 248-473-0674.
E-mail: mshof@twmi.rr.com
Web Site: www.michigansportshof.org
Founded: 1955.
Congressional District: 19
Key Personnel: C.E.O. & Pres., William F. McLaughlin; Chm. (V), William Wischman; Treas., Mike Taschner.
Personnel Profile: Full-Time Paid 1.
Governing Authority: state. Tax-exempt: 501(c)(3).
Sports Museum.
Collections: bronze wall plaques & photos of each honoree.
Research Fields: history of each honoree.
Activities: annual induction dinner.
Publications: magazine, Annual Michigan Sports Hall of Fame Yearbook.
Hours & Admission Prices: Daily 8-5. No charge. ♿

MOTOWN HISTORICAL MUSEUM, (M), 2648 W. Grand Blvd., Detroit, MI 48208-1237. Tel.: 313-875-2264. Fax: 313-875-2267.
E-mail: rterry@motownmuseum.com
Web Site: motownmuseum.org
Founded: 1985.
Key Personnel: Founder & Chm., Esther Gordy Edwards; C.E.O. & Exec. Dir., Robin Terry; C.O.O., Audley M. Smith, Jr.; Dir. Facilities & Museum Shop Mgr., Robert Hood.
Governing Authority: private; nonprofit organization. Tax-exempt: 501(c)(3).
History Museum.
Collections: history of Motown Record Corp., recording artists, founder Berry Gordy & his family; archives; sheet music; recordings; photographs; drawings; prints; musical & recording equipment; costumes; personal memorabilia. Historic Buildings: Hitsville, U.S.A., the first headquarters of Motown Records; recording Studio A.
Research Fields: Motown Record Corp.; Berry Gordy & family; development of Motown's sound & its influence on popular culture; the company as it relates to Detroit's history & Motown's artists.
Facilities: 4,000 sq. ft. exhibit space. Museum-related items for sale.
Activities: docent programs; guided tours; participatory exhibits. Annual Event: Gala Fundraiser.

Hours & Admission Prices: Tues.-Sat. 10-6. Adults $10, senior citizens $8, children under 12 $8; discounts to family & group tours of 20 people. Closed New Year's Day; Easter; Memorial Day; Independence Day; Labor Day; Thanksgiving; Christmas Eve & Day. ♿
Attendance: 40,000 (accurate)

MUSEUM OF CONTEMPORARY ART DETROIT, (M), 4454 Woodward Ave., Detroit, MI 48201-1822. Tel.: 313-832-6622. Fax: 313-832-4665.
E-mail: info@mocadetroit.org
Web Site: mocadetroit.org
Founded: 2006.
Key Personnel: Dir., Luis Croquer; Deputy Dir. Operations & Administration, Jeseca Dawson; Exhibition Coord., Zeb Smith; Public Programs Coord., Benjamin Hernandez; Public Rels. Coord. & Exhibitions Asst., Carlie Dennis; Museum Shop Mgr., Brook Campbell; Asst. Admin., Lauren Rossi Harroun; Coord. Special Events, Edward Jackson; Mgr. Cafe, Paul Bancel.
Personnel Profile: Full-Time Paid 5; Part-Time Paid 6; Part-Time Volunteers 50; Interns 8.
Governing Authority: Tax-exempt.
Contemporary Art Museum.
Collections: works by contemporary artists.
Activities: artist talks; lectures; panel discussions; performance-based art; films; readings; music events; children's art workshops.
Publications: special exhibition catalogs; annual arts & literature journal, DETROIT.
Hours & Admission Prices: Wed., Sat.-Sun. 11-5, Thurs.-Fri. 11-8. No charge; donations accepted. ♿
Attendance: 33,000 (estimated)
Membership: Student & Senior $25; Individual $50; Family $100; Friend $250; Supporter $500; Contributor $1,000; $2,500 & up.

PEWABIC POTTERY, 10125 E. Jefferson, Detroit, MI 48214-3138. Tel.: 313-822-0954. Fax: 313-822-6266.
E-mail: pewabic1@pewabic.org
Web Site: www.pewabic.org
Founded: 1903.
Congressional District: 13
Key Personnel: Exec. Dir., Terese Ireland; Pres. (V), Neil Bristol; Dir. Retail, Christina Devlin.
Personnel Profile: Full-Time Paid 35; Part-Time Paid 10; Part-Time Volunteers 6; Interns 7.
Governing Authority: nonprofit organization. Tax-exempt: 501(c)(3).
Arts & Crafts Museum & Pottery Factory: housed in 1907 William Buck Stratton-designed English style structure; built 1906-1907. Pottery founded in 1903 by Mary Chase Perry & Horace J. Caulkins. National Historic Landmark.
Collections: archival material-papers; blueprints; drawings; photographs; ceramics & tile collections of Mary Chase Stratton; art pottery; original arts & crafts furniture; contemporary ceramic art.
Research Fields: historic & contemporary ceramics, architectural tile, arts & crafts movements.
Activities: guided tours; organized education programs for children and adults; participatory, loan, temporary & traveling exhibitions.
Publications: Pewabic Pottery Newsletter.
Hours & Admission Prices: Mon.-Sat. 10-6, Sun. 12-4. Museum: no charge: donations accepted. Tours: adults $5. Workshops: adults $17. Closed New Year's Day; Martin Luther King Jr. Day; Easter; Memorial Day; Independence Day; Labor Day; Thanksgiving; Christmas.
Attendance: 70,000 (estimated)
Membership: Pewabic Society Inc.: Individual $35; Family $50; Supporter $125; Patron $250; Benefactor $500; Associates $1,000; Founder's $2,500; Caulkins $5,000.

WAYNE STATE UNIVERSITY ART GALLERIES, 150 Community Arts Bldg., Dept. of Art, Detroit, MI 48202-3917. Tel.: 313-577-2980. Fax: 313-577-3491.
E-mail: art@wayne.edu
Web Site: www.art.wayne.edu
Founded: 1958.
Congressional District: 13
Key Personnel: Cur. & Dir. Art Exhibitions, Lisa Gonzalez.
Personnel Profile: Full-Time Paid 1; Part-Time Paid 4.
Governing Authority: state; university. Parent Institution: Wayne State University. Subsidiary Institution: Dept. of Art & Art History. Tax-exempt.
Art Gallery.
Collections: paintings; photographs; sculpture.
Facilities: auditorium; conference center.
Activities: monthly exhibitions; concerts; lectures; formally organized education programs for adults, students and the community.

Publications: annual calendar of events.
Hours & Admission Prices: Academic Year: Tues.-Thurs. 10-6, Fri. 10-7; Summer: Tues.-Fri. 12-5. No charge. ♿
Attendance: 15,000 (estimated)
Membership: Senior & Student $15; Gallery Friend $30; Family $40; Contemporary Collector $150; Patron's Circle $500.

WAYNE STATE UNIVERSITY MUSEUM OF ANTHROPOLOGY, 4841 Cass Ave., Detroit, MI 48201-1203. Mailing Address: Dept. of Anthropology, Wayne State University, 3054 Faculty Administration Bldg., 656 W. Kirby, Detroit, MI 48202. Tel.: 313-577-2598. Fax: 313-577-9759.
E-mail: t.bray@wayne.edu
Web Site: www.clas.wayne.edu/anthromuseum
Founded: 1958.
Congressional District: 13
Key Personnel: Dir., Tamara Bray, Ph.D.
Personnel Profile: Full-Time Paid 1; Part-Time Paid 3; Part-Time Volunteers 5.
Governing Authority: university. Affiliated with Wayne State University. Tax-exempt.
Anthropology Museum.
Collections: local archaeology (historic & prehistoric); ethnographic.
Research Fields: archaeology; local anthropology; history
Facilities: 800-vol. library of books available for use by students; archaeology lab; manuscript archives; teaching lab.
Activities: formally organized education programs for undergraduate & graduate college students.
Hours & Admission Prices: Sept.-May Mon.-Fri. call for hours. No charge; donations accepted. ♿
Attendance: 1,200 (accurate)
Membership: Student $15; Senior Citizen $20; Individual $25; Affiliate $50; Patron $100; Benefactor $250.

THE WAYNE STATE UNIVERSITY MUSEUM OF NATURAL HISTORY, Biological Sciences Bldg., Rm. 1155, 5047 Gullen Mall, Detroit, MI 48202-3917. Tel.: 313-577-2872. Fax: 313-577-6891.
E-mail: wmoore@biology.biosci.wayne.edu
Web Site: bio.wayne.edu/outreach/natural_history.html
Founded: 1972.
Congressional District: 13
Key Personnel: Dir., William S. Moore; Cur. Vertebrates, Jesheskel Shoshani; Cur. Insects, Stanley K. Gangwere; Cur. Herbarium, D. Carl Freeman.
Personnel Profile: Part-Time Volunteers 3; Interns 2.
Governing Authority: university. Wayne State University. Parent Institution: State of Michigan. Tax-exempt.
Natural History Museum.
Collections: plants; birds; mammals; insects; vertebrates & invertebrates.
Activities: guided tours; formally organized education programs for elementary & high school students; permanent exhibitions.
Hours & Admission Prices: By appointment. No charge. Closed holidays. ♿

Dexter

DEXTER AREA HISTORICAL SOCIETY & MUSEUM, 3443 Inverness, Dexter, MI 48130-1409. Tel.: 734-426-2519.
E-mail: dexmuseum@aol.com
Web Site: www.hvcn.org/info/dextermuseum
Founded: 1976.
Key Personnel: Pres. Historical Society, Gilbert Campbell; Museum Dir., Nina Doletsky-Rackham; Cur., Mary Kimmel; Genealogist, Nancy Van Blaricum; Museum Shop Mgr., Alice Pastalan.
Personnel Profile: Part-Time Volunteers 28.
Governing Authority: society; nonprofit. Parent Institution: Dexter Area Museum. Subsidiary Institution: Dexter Area Historical Society. Tax-exempt: 501(c)(3).
Historical Museum: housed in 1883 German Lutheran Church.
Collections: local history items; Civil War items; dolls; costumes; photographs; genealogy records; local business, organization & family archives.
Facilities: Museum-related items & folk art for sale.
Activities: guided tours; lectures; loan exhibitions; school tour service.
Publications: bimonthly newsletter.
Hours & Admission Prices: May-Dec. Fri.-Sat. 1-3. No charge; donations accepted.
Attendance: 1,600 (estimated)
Membership: Student $1.50; Individual $10; Family $15; Business $25; Patron $50 & up; Life $150.

Douglas

STEAMSHIP KEEWATIN MARITIME MUSEUM, Harbour Village, Union St. & Blue Star Hwy., Douglas, MI 49406. Mailing Address: P.O. Box 638, Douglas, MI 49406-0638. Tel.: 269-857-2464.
Web Site: www.keewatinmaritimemuseum.com
Founded: 1965.
Key Personnel: Pres., R.J. Peterson; Treas., Sec. & Gift Shop Mgr., Diane Peterson; Museum Shop Mgr., Katherine Murphy.
Personnel Profile: Full-Time Paid 1; Part-Time Paid 8.
Governing Authority: private.
Historic Ship Museum: former 1907 Great Lakes passenger steamship of the Canadian Pacific Railroad, built by the Fairfield Shipbuilding and Engineering Co. Ltd., Govan, Glasgow, Scotland.
Collections: old photos of Saugatuck area; log books; articles & books on ships of the Great Lakes; Tug Reiss, an 88 yr. old retired Great Lakes Steam Tugboat; The S.S. Keewatin, a 350 ft. Great Lakes Passenger Steamship; 1850 steam saw mill replica.
Research Fields: ships built in Saugatuck & other Canadian Pacific Railway steamships.
Facilities: visitors center. Nautical gifts for sale.
Activities: guided tours; separate engine room tours available. Museum Sponsors: high tea.
Publications: brochures.
Hours & Admission Prices: Memorial Day to Labor Day daily 10:30-4. Tours: 10, 1 & 3. Adults $12, children $6; discounts to groups with reservation; preschoolers no charge.
Attendance: 10,000 (estimated)

Dowagiac

HEDDON MUSEUM, 414 West St., Dowagiac, MI 49047-1045. Mailing Address: 204 W. Telegraph St., Dowagiac, MI 49047-1241. Tel.: 269-782-5698.
E-mail: heddonmuseum@lyonsindustries.com
Founded: 1995.
Congressional District: 4
Key Personnel: Dir., Joan Lyons; Dir., Don Lyons.
Personnel Profile: Part-Time Volunteers 1.
Governing Authority: private; nonprofit organization.
History Museum: housed in James Heddon's Sons Fishing Tackle Co.
Collections: over 1,500 Heddon lures; 160 reels; 215 Heddon rods; golf clubs; violin bows; ski poles; box kites; WWII military box kites and antennas, information and models of The Heddon aviation airplane.
Research Fields: James Heddon's Sons Fishing Tackle Co.
Facilities: 50-vol. library available for research; 3,000 sq. ft. exhibit space. Museum-related items for sale.
Activities: guided tours.
Hours & Admission Prices: Tues. 6:30 p.m.-8:30 p.m., last Sun. of month 1:30-4; other times by appointment. No charge; donations accepted. Closed New Year's Eve; Christmas Eve & Day. ♿
Attendance: 500 (estimated)

MUSEUM AT SOUTHWESTERN MICHIGAN COLLEGE, (M), 58900 Cherry Grove Rd., Dowagiac, MI 49047-9726. Tel.: 269-782-1374 & 1000. Fax: 269-782-1460.
E-mail: museum@swmich.edu
Web Site: www.swmich.edu/museum
Formerly: Southwestern Michigan College Museum
Founded: 1982.
Congressional District: 6
Key Personnel: Dir., Steve Arseneau; Chm. (V), Chuck Timmons; Exhibit Designer, Tom J. Caskey; Educator, Dr. Alisea McLeod; Volunteer Coord., Jo Silvia.
Personnel Profile: Full-Time Paid 1; Part-Time Paid 3; Part-Time Volunteers 40.
Governing Authority: nonprofit; public university. Parent Institution: Southwestern Michigan College. Tax-exempt.
History Museum & Science Center.
Collections: local history items; Round Oak Stove Company; Heddon fishing lures; local family items; local industry; Dowagiac Manufacturing Co.; Rudy Furnace Co.
Research Fields: local industry.
Facilities: 250-vol. library of state & local history material available to the public; educational facilities.
Activities: guided tours; organized education programs for children; loan & temporary exhibitions.
Publications: newsletter; Identification & Dating of Round Oak Heating Stoves.
Hours & Admission Prices: Tues.-Fri. 10-5, Sat. 11-3. No charge. Closed college & major holidays. ♿

Attendance: 7,000 (accurate)
Membership: Senior Individual $10; Senior Couple $15; Individual $20; Family $35.

Drummond Island

DRUMMOND ISLAND HISTORICAL MUSEUM, 33492 S. Water St., Drummond Island, MI 49726. Mailing Address: Box 293, Drummond Island, MI 49726-0293. Tel.: 906-493-5245.
E-mail: drhistmuseum@alphacomm.net
Founded: 1961.
Congressional District: 107
Key Personnel: Pres., Gary Cloudman; Township Supvr., Frank Sasso; Sec., Martha Carlin; Dir., Harry Ropp; Dir., Judge Michael McDonald; Cur., Audrey Moser.
Personnel Profile: Full-Time Paid 1.
Governing Authority: society. Parent Institution: Drummond Island Historical Society.
Local History Museum.
Collections: archives; geology; Indian artifacts; manuscripts; articles, books & pictures depicting Island history; specimen glass cases of fossils from prehistoric digs; collection of pre-glacial and other rock formations, including the Pudding Stone; Indian artifacts: basketry, beadwork and prayer books written in Chippewa-Ojibway; restored chimney & fireplace built by British Garrison 1815-1829; swords; pottery & shards; cannon balls; memorabilia of Finnish Colony, 1907: Finnish bibles & other books, costumes, looms, spinning wheels, skis; lumbering tools; sawmill town pictures; mill wheels; farming tools; household items; papier-mache full-size horse & buggy; early medical books; medical & dental instruments; musical instruments; marine corner; ships wheel; old wooden boats; compass; sailors sail-mending kit; sportsmen's gear; guns; fishing rods; decoys; early snowmobile engine; marine engines; snowshoes; home-made utility sleds; Finnish kick sled; antique bicycle; family portrait; period quilts with family names; manuscripts; scrapbooks; family albums; tourist lodge register; town records; toys; oral history tapes; videos; log cabin.
Facilities: library.
Activities: permanent exhibitions. Museum Sponsors: special summer programs for local residents & summer visitors; annual home tours in August.
Hours & Admission Prices: Memorial Day to mid-Oct. daily 1-5. No charge; donations accepted. ♿
Attendance: 3,000
Membership: Individual $1; Life $100.

Dundee

OLD MILL MUSEUM, 242 Toledo St., Dundee, MI 48131-1246. Tel.: 734-529-8596.
E-mail: museum@dundeeoldmill.com
Web Site: www.dundeeoldmill.com
Key Personnel: Dir., Sara Alexin; Pres., Scott Heck; Vice Pres., Mary Schultz; Sec., Meg Heinlen; Treas., Shirley Massingill; Archivist, Randi Kominek; Gift Shop Mgr. & Newsletter Editor, Grace Hudson
History Museum.
Collections: local history & culture; period artifacts; photographs; early furnishings.
Hours & Admission Prices: Fri.-Mon. 12-4. ♿

Eagle Harbor

KEWEENAW COUNTY HISTORICAL SOCIETY, (M), 670 Lighthouse Rd., Eagle Harbor, MI 49950-9683. Tel.: 906-289-4990 & 337-2244.
Web Site: www.keweenawhistory.org
Founded: 1981.
Congressional District: 1
Key Personnel: Pres. (V), Virginia Petermann Jamison.
Personnel Profile: Part-Time Volunteers 45.
Governing Authority: private; society; nonprofit. Tax-exempt: 501(c)(3).
Marine History Museum: housed in Eagle Harbor Lighthouse Complex.
Collections: marine exhibits; copper mining; local photographs; local kitchen artifacts; period furnishings; fire fighting & automotive artifacts; turn-of-the-century school & Knights of Pythias Society Museum at Eagle Harbor. Historic Buildings: 1850 Roman Catholic Church; 1870 copper miner's village of homes; turn-of-the-century blacksmith shop.
Research Fields: Lake Superior; copper mining; Knights of Phythias; general history of Keweenaw County; Roman Catholic Church artifacts from the Keweenaw & Houghton Counties; blacksmithing from the 1890s.
Activities: guided tours; traveling & temporary exhibitions; school loan service.
Publications: quarterly newsletter; annual report.
Hours & Admission Prices: mid-June to mid-Oct. daily 10-5. Adults $4; members and children 13 & under no charge.

Attendance: 10,119 (accurate)
Membership: Historian $20; Copper Miner $35; Lightkeeper $75; Life $500.

East Jordan

EAST JORDAN PORTSIDE ART & HISTORICAL MUSEUM, 01656 S-M66 Hwy., East Jordan, MI 49727. Mailing Address: P.O. Box 1355, East Jordan, MI 49727-1355.
Web Site: www.portsideartsfair.org/histsoc.htm
Founded: 1976.
Congressional District: 11
Key Personnel: C.E.O. & Pres. (V), Paula Vollbach; C.E.O. & Chm. (V), Kim Prebble.
Personnel Profile: Part-Time Volunteers 36.
Governing Authority: nonprofit organization. Parent Institution: East Jordan Historical Museum Society. Tax-exempt: 501(c)(3).
Historical Society Museum.
Collections: pioneer artifacts & photographs; early lumbering & agricultural tools; turn-of-the-century clothing; opera house memorabilia; early railroad items & off-site engine; Purchase Prize collection of contemporary art.
Research Fields: family genealogies; early local businesses.
Activities: guided tours; art fair; student docent program; scavenger hunt in museum.
Publications: annual newsletter; brochure.
Hours & Admission Prices: June & Sept. Sat.-Sun. 1:30-4:30; July-Aug. Tues., Thurs. & Sat.-Sun. 1:30-4:30; other times by appointment. No charge; donations accepted. ♿
Attendance: 3,000 (estimated)
Membership: Family $10; Donor $35; Life $100.

East Lansing

ABRAMS PLANETARIUM, MICHIGAN STATE UNIVERSITY, East Lansing, MI 48824. Tel.: 517-355-4676. Fax: 517-432-3838.
Web Site: www.pa.msu.edu/abrams/
Founded: 1964.
Congressional District: 6
Key Personnel: Dir., D. David Batch; Planetarium Production Coord., John French; Planetarium Education Coord., Shane Horvatin.
Personnel Profile: Full-Time Paid 3; Part-Time Paid 4; Part-Time Volunteers 2.
Governing Authority: university. Parent Institution: Michigan State University. Tax-exempt.
Planetarium.
Collections: historical items pertaining to astronomy & meteorites; manuscripts.
Facilities: sky theater. Books & other items for sale.
Activities: observing sessions; lectures; planetarium programs; formally organized education programs for children & adults; permanent & temporary exhibitions.
Publications: monthly, Sky Calendars.
Hours & Admission Prices: Display Hall: Mon.-Fri. 8:30-12 & 1-4:30. No charge. Programs: Fri.-Sat. 8pm, Sun. 4pm. Adults $3, students & senior citizens $2.50, children 12 & under $2. For public show information call 517-355-4672; for current sky information call 517-332-STAR. Closed national holidays. ♿
Attendance: 32,000 (estimated)
Membership: Student $15; Individual $25; Family $50.

* **KRESGE ART MUSEUM, (M),** Michigan State University, East Lansing, MI 48824-1312. Tel.: 517-353-9834. Fax: 517-355-6577.
E-mail: kamuseum@msu.edu
Web Site: www.artmuseum.msu.edu
Founded: 1959.
Congressional District: 8
Key Personnel: C.E.O., Lou Anna Simon; Pres. (V), Suzanne Brouse; Dir., Dr. Susan J. Bandes; Cur., April Kingsley; Communications, Christine Nichols; Registrar, Rachel Vargas; Educator, Cari Wolfe; Devel., Bridget Paff; Preparator, Norbert J. Freese; Museum Shop Mgr., Angelica Santos.
Personnel Profile: Full-Time Paid 8; Part-Time Paid 12; Part-Time Volunteers 150; Interns 1.
Governing Authority: state; university. Parent Institution: Michigan State University. Tax-exempt: 501(c)(3).
Art Museum.
Collections: European & American painting; sculpture from ancient times to contemporary; 15th to 21st century prints; photographs.
Major Exhibits: The Beginnings of American Abstraction, 1/11/10-3/14/10; Mid-Michigan Collects, 5/1/10-7/30/10; British Textiles, 10/16/10-12/17/10.
Facilities: library available for use on premises.
Activities: lectures; concerts; tours; films; trips; symposia.

Publications: Kresge Art Museum Bulletin; newsletters; occasional catalogues.
Hours & Admission Prices: June-July Tues.-Fri. 11-5, Sat.-Sun. 12-5; Sept.-May Mon.-Wed. & Fri. 10-5, Thurs. 10-8, Sat.-Sun. 12-5. No charge; donations accepted. Closed holiday weekends. ♿
Attendance: 25,000 (estimated)
Membership: Full Time Student $15; Senior Citizen $25; Friend $35; Sponsor $60; Benefactor $100; Patron $250; Grand Patron $500; Honorary Curator $1,000; Honorary Director $2,000.

MICHIGAN STATE UNIVERSITY HERBARIUM, 166 Plant Biology Bldg., East Lansing, MI 48824-1312. Tel.: 517-355-4696. Fax: 517-353-1926.
E-mail: alan@msu.edu
Web Site: herbarium.msu.edu
Founded: 1863.
Congressional District: 6
Key Personnel: Dir. & Cur., Alan Prather; Asst. Cur., Alan Fryday; Sec., John Richardson.
Personnel Profile: Full-Time Paid 3; Part-Time Paid 1; Part-Time Volunteers 1.
Governing Authority: university. Parent Institution: Michigan State University. Tax-exempt: 501(c)(3).
Herbarium.
Collections: vascular plants of all areas with emphasis on Michigan, alpine areas of North America, Mexico, South America, West Indies & Northern Borneo. Lichens & bryophytes of all area with emphasis on Patagonia & southern hemisphere island groups, the West Indies & Canary Islands.
Research Fields: systematic botany & mycology.
Facilities: 1,400-vol. reference library available for use on premises & to visiting investigators.
Activities: formally organized education programs for undergraduate & graduate college students; loan & exchange of specimens.
Hours & Admission Prices: Mon.-Fri. 8-5. No charge. Closed national holidays.

* **THE MICHIGAN STATE UNIVERSITY MUSEUM, (M),** W. Circle Dr., East Lansing, MI 48824-1045. Tel.: 517-355-2370. Fax: 517-432-2846.
E-mail: jilda@msu.edu
Web Site: museum.msu.edu
Founded: 1857.
Congressional District: 6
Key Personnel: Chm. (V), Bill Trevarthan; Chm. (V) & Pres. (V), Denis Maybank; Dir., Gary Morgan; Cur. Folk Art., Dr. C. Kurt Dewhurst; Cur. Mammalogy, Dr. Barbara Lundrigan; Asst. Cur. Ornithology, Dr. Pamela Rasmussen; Specimen Preparator, Paula Hildebrandt; Col. Mgr. Biological Collection, Laura Abraczinskas; Cur. Anthropology, Dr. William Lovis; Cur. Vertebrate Paleontology, Dr. Michael Gottfried; Cur. History, Val Berryman; Extension Specialist & Cur. Education, Dr. Julie Avery; Cur. Exhibits, Juan Alvarez; Collections Mgr., Cultural Collections, Lynne Swanson; Public Rels. Coord., Lora Helou; Education Program Coord., Judy Smyth; Computer Coord., Sunny Wang; Collections Coord., Pearl Wong; Quilt Collections Asst. & Traveling Exhibitions Mgr., Beth Donaldson; Cur. Folk Arts, Dr. Marsha MacDowell; Asst. Cur. Folk Arts, LuAnne Kozma; Asst. Cur. Great Lakes Archaeology, Dr. Jodie O'Gorman; Curatorial Asst., Mary Worrall; Natl. Resources Conservation Specialist & Natl. Science Conservation Info. Specialist, James Harding; Special Projects Coord., Julie Levy-Weston; Museum Shop Mgr., Catherine Huddy; Facilities Mgr. & Volunteer Program Coord., Mike Secord.
Personnel Profile: Full-Time Paid 18; Part-Time Paid 21; Part-Time Volunteers 405; Interns 3.
Governing Authority: university. Parent Institution: Michigan State University. Tax-exempt: 501(c)(3).
Science & Cultural History Museum.
Collections: Great Lakes history; archaeology; anthropology; vertebrate paleontology; folklife; modern vertebrates; agriculture; popular cultures; decorative arts.
Research Fields: vertebrate zoology; vertebrate paleontology; anthropology; folklife; popular culture; history.
Facilities: 100-seat auditorium. Items relating to exhibit programs for sale.
Activities: guided tours; interactive computer stations; TV & radio programs; formally organized education programs for undergraduate college students & graduate students affiliated with Michigan State University; training programs for professional museum workers; inter-museum loan, temporary, permanent & traveling exhibition. Annual Events: Great Lakes Folk Festival; Dinosaur Dash; Chocolate Party; Benefit Wine Tasting Party; reception openings; Darwin Day: Natural History ID Day.
Publications: anthropological, biological, cultural, educational, folklife & paleontological bulletins, catalogues & books published occasionally.
Hours & Admission Prices: Mon.-Fri. 9-5, Sat. 10-5, Sun. 1-5. Suggested Donations: adults $4, children $2; discounts to AAM & ICOM members. Closed New Year's Day; Easter; Memorial Day; Independence Day; Labor Day; Thanksgiving; Christmas. ♿
Attendance: 410,000 (estimated)
Membership: Individual & Family $25; Honorary Assistant Curator $100; Honorary Curator $250; Honorary Director $500; Honorary Trustee $1,000.

W.J. BEAL BOTANICAL GARDEN, 412 Olds Hall, Michigan State University, East Lansing, MI 48824-1047. Tel.: 517-355-9582. Fax: 517-432-1090.
E-mail: telewski@cpa.msu.edu
Web Site: www.cpa.msu.edu/beal/index.htm
Founded: 1873.
Congressional District: 6
Key Personnel: Cur., Dr. Frank W. Telewski; Botanical Garden Technician, Peter Murray; Botanical Garden Technician, Hope Rankin.
Personnel Profile: Full-Time Paid 2; Part-Time Paid 2; Interns 2.
Governing Authority: Michigan State University, Div. of Campus Park & Planning. Tax-exempt.
Botanical Garden.
Collections: 4,500 species & varieties of herbaceous & woody plants arranged in systematic, economic, ecological & landscape groupings; botany; arboretum.
Research Fields: temperate forest ecology; ecology of endangered & threatened plants; culture of woody ornamentals.
Activities: guided tours by appointment.
Publications: annual index seminum; descriptive brochure.
Hours & Admission Prices: Daily sunrise-sunset. No charge. ♿
Attendance: 20,000 (estimated)

East Tawas

IOSCO COUNTY HISTORICAL MUSEUM, 405 W. Bay St., East Tawas, MI 48730-1103. Tel.: 989-362-8911.
Web Site: ioscomuseum.org
Founded: 1976.
Congressional District: 11
Key Personnel: Pres., Janell Reed; Vice Pres., Leonard Wilkuski; Recording Sec., Judy Clark; Treas., Lynne Bigelow.
Personnel Profile: Part-Time Volunteers 20.
Governing Authority: nonprofit. Parent Institution: Iosco County Historical Society. Tax-exempt: 501(c)(3).
Historical Building: built by J.D. Hawks, 1st president of the Detroit & Mackinaw Railway; built in 1903.
Collections: displays of local history; china; clothing; furniture; tools; reference books; funeral records; coins; newspapers from 1800; photographs; fire department equipment; horse drawn hearse; stage coach; Indian birch canoe; carriage house; log mark collection; Detroit & Mackinaw Railroad display; U.S.S. western states artifacts; military room; local school's restored class photos; one room schoolhouse.
Research Fields: genealogy.
Facilities: reference library pertaining to local history. Gift items for sale.
Activities: guided tours; docent program; loan exhibitions.
Publications: quarterly membership newsletter.
Hours & Admission Prices: May-Oct. Fri.-Sat. 1-4; call for tours. Suggested Donation: $2. ♿
Attendance: 1,894 (accurate)
Membership: Senior Citizens over 64 $8; Individual $10; Family $12; Sustaining & Business $25; Patron $50; Benefactor $100 & up.

Edwardsburg

LAW ENFORCEMENT MEMORIAL ASSOCIATION, INC., Edwardsburg, MI 49112-0293. Mailing Address: P.O. Box 293, Edwardsburg, MI 49112-0293. Tel.: 847-409-8691.
E-mail: forgottenheroes@aol.com
Web Site: forgottenheroes-lema.org
Founded: 1989.
Congressional District: 8
Personnel Profile: Full-Time Volunteers 2; Part-Time Volunteers 27.
Governing Authority: private; nonprofit association. Tax-exempt: 501(c)(3).
Law Enforcement Museum.
Collections: documentation information on deaths of law enforcement officers from 1717-present; information, as applicable, on the killers & all information on those who were executed for the crimes; memorabilia relative to the criminal justice system; badges; patches; photographs; uniforms.
Research Fields: crime-law enforcement deaths.
Facilities: library.
Publications: LEMA News.
Hours & Admission Prices: Museum under construction; call for information.
Membership: Regular $25; Supporter $100.

Empire

EMPIRE AREA HERITAGE GROUP, 11544 S. La Core, Empire, MI 49630-9401. Mailing Address: Box 192, Empire, MI 49630-0192. Tel.: 231-326-5568.
Founded: 1972.
Congressional District: 9
Key Personnel: Pres. (V), David Taghon; Vice Pres., Leigh Payment; Sec., Anne Krawczak.
Governing Authority: society; nonprofit. Tax-exempt: 501(c)(3).
History Museum.
Collections: displays depicting logging, lumbering, sailing & the railroad; large barn with horse-drawn vehicles; blacksmith shop; woodworking displays; one-room school with audiovisual center; 1900 saloon; a 1911 Hose House (fire station) with hand pulled fire fighting equipment and related items.
Research Fields: genealogy.
Facilities: Books, CD's & DVD's for sale.
Activities: videos; museum tours. Museum Sponsors: Heritage Day in October.
Publications: annual newsletter, Empire Leader; Remembering Empire Through Pictures; history book, Some Other Day; Empire Museum Cookbook; the Boizard Letters - Civil War letters from 1856 to post war 1900.
Hours & Admission Prices: Memorial Day to June & Labor Day to mid-Oct. Sat.-Sun. 1-4; July-Aug. Thurs.-Tues. 1-4. Suggested Donation: family $5, adults $2. ♿
Attendance: 5,000 (estimated)
Membership: Single $10; Family $25; Business $50; Century Club $100.

SLEEPING BEAR DUNES NATIONAL LAKESHORE, 9922 Front St., (Hwy. M-72), Empire, MI 49630-9797. Tel.: 231-326-5134. Fax: 231-326-5382.
E-mail: slbe_interpretation@nps.gov
Web Site: www.nps.gov/slbe/
Founded: 1972.
Congressional District: 9
Key Personnel: Chief Naturalist, Lisa Myers; Supt., Dusty Shultz.
Personnel Profile: Full-Time Paid 30; Part-Time Paid 30; Part-Time Volunteers 50; Interns 5.
Governing Authority: federal. Parent Institution: National Park Service Department of the Interior, Washington, DC. Tax-exempt.
Park Museum.
Collections: Great Lakes maritime items.
Research Fields: surfboats & rescue equipment used by the U.S. Life Saving Service; U.S Light House Service; Great Lake Maritime History.
Facilities: 150-vol. library of books on general natural history, Great Lakes maritime & geology available on request; 90-seat auditorium. Adult & children's natural & cultural history publications for sale.
Activities: guided tours; lectures; films; formally organized education programs for children, adults, undergraduate & graduate college students; permanent, temporary & traveling exhibitions.
Publications: brochure, Pierce Stocking Scenic Drive; brochure, South Manitou Island.
Hours & Admission Prices: Philip A. Hart Visitor Center: Memorial Day-Labor Day daily 8-6; Sept.-May daily 8:15-4; call for additional hours. Cannery Boat Museum: late-May to early Sept. daily 11-5. Sleeping Bear Point Maritime Museum: mid-May to early Sept. daily 11-5; Sept. to mid-Oct. Sat.-Sun. 12-5. Annual Pass $20; Golden Age Pass (senior citizens) $10; Weekly Pass $10. ♿
Attendance: 1,200,000

Escanaba

DELTA COUNTY HISTORICAL SOCIETY MUSEUM, 16 Waterplant Rd., Escanaba, MI 49829-4052. Tel.: 906-789-6790.
E-mail: deltacountyhistsoc@sbcglobal.net
Web Site: www.deltahistorical.org
Founded: 1947.
Congressional District: 109
Key Personnel: Pres., John Beaumier; Chm., Charles Lindquist; Archives, Clara Mosenfelder.
Personnel Profile: Part-Time Paid 4; Part-Time Volunteers 20.
Governing Authority: society. Parent Institution: Delta County Historical Society. Tax-exempt.
Historical Society Museum & Archives.
Collections: agriculture; archives; Native American artifacts; marine; local historic artifacts; logging; military; railroad; lighthouse & keeper's home; surf boat & boathouse.
Facilities: archives.
Activities: programs; tours.
Publications: newsletter, Delta Historian.
Hours & Admission Prices: Archives: June-Aug. Mon.-Fri. 1-5; Sept. Mon.-Fri. 1-4; Oct.-May Mon. & Thurs. 1-5. Museum: Memorial Day to Labor Day Mon.-Sat. 10:30-5; Sept.-May by appointment. Family $5, adults $3, children $1. Lighthouse: Bus $75, Family $5, Individual $3. Archives: no charge. ♿
Attendance: 7,400 (estimated)
Membership: Basic $25; Family $35; Commercial $100; Individual Life $200.

SANDPOINT LIGHTHOUSE, Sandpoint, Ludington Park, Escanaba, MI 49829. Mailing Address: Delta County Historical Society, 16 Water Plant Rd., Escanaba, MI 49829-4052. Tel.: 906-789-6790.
Web Site: www.deltahistorical.org
Founded: 1990.
Congressional District: 109
Key Personnel: Pres., John Noreus; Bd. of Dir., Peter Strom.
Personnel Profile: Part-Time Paid 6.
Governing Authority: Delta County Historical Society. Tax-exempt.
Historical Society Museum: housed in turn-of-the-century lighthouse.
Collections: maps; charts; pictures; lantern room with 4th order Fresnel lens.
Activities: school & group tours by appointment.
Publications: brochure; grades 1-8, curricular materials; Delta Historian.
Hours & Admission Prices: June-Aug. daily 9-5, Sept. daily 1-4. Adults $1, students under 18 $.50; members & school groups no charge.
Attendance: 8,000 (estimated)
Membership: Basic $20; Family $30; Industrial $50; Commercial $100; Individual Life $200

WILLIAM BONIFAS FINE ARTS CENTER, 700 1st Ave. S., Escanaba, MI 49829-3703. Tel.: 906-786-3833. Fax: 906-786-3840.
E-mail: beth@bonifasarts.org
Web Site: www.bonifasarts.org
Founded: 1974.
Congressional District: 1
Key Personnel: Exec. Dir., Mollie Larsen; Pres. (V), Mrs. Petey Semmens; Information Rels. Asst., Beth Mercier; Visual Arts & Education Dir., Pasqua Warstler; Bookkeeper, Kaymary Rettig; Custodian, Jesse Farkas; Special Events, Beth Cox; Dir. Public Rels., Kathryn Morski.
Personnel Profile: Full-Time Paid 3; Part-Time Paid 3; Part-Time Volunteers 100; Interns 1.
Governing Authority: bd. of directors; nonprofit. Tax-exempt: 501(c)(3).
Arts Center.
Collections: Great Lakes regional art.
Facilities: 240-seat theater; studio; classrooms.
Activities: concerts; arts festivals; musicals; drama; poetry readings; formally organized education programs for children & adults.
Publications: quarterly newsletter, Arts News.
Hours & Admission Prices: Tues.-Fri. 10-5:30, Sat. 10-3. Center: no charge. Classes: discounts to members. Closed major holidays. ♿
Attendance: 4,568 (estimated)
Membership: Annual $30; Family $40; Patron $50; Day Sponsor $100; Art Partner $300; Benefactor $500; Tower Society $1,000; Corporate Friend $1,500.

Farmington

GOVERNOR WARNER MANSION AND MUSEUM, 33805 Grand River Ave., Farmington, MI 48335-3431. Tel.: 248-473-7275.
E-mail: warner_mansion@tds.net
Personnel Profile: Part-Time Volunteers 16.
Historic House Museum: built in 1867.
Collections: family history; period furnishings; photographs; personal artifacts.
Activities: special events. Museum Sponsors: Founder's Festival in July; Heritage Festival in October.
Hours & Admission Prices: April-Dec. Wed. & 1st Sun. of month 1-5. Adults $2.

Farmington Hills

HOLOCAUST MEMORIAL CENTER, 28123 Orchard Lake Rd., Farmington Hills, MI 48334-3738. Tel.: 248-553-2400. Fax: 248-553-2433.
E-mail: info@holocaustcenter.org
Web Site: www.holocaustcenter.org
Key Personnel: Dir. & C.E.O., Rabbi Charles Rosenzveig
History Museum.
Collections: films; artifacts; portraits & biographies; culture of European Jews; internment of Jews on Cyprus; emigration via Spain & Shanghai; efforts to retrieve hidden children & other rescue efforts; postwar pogroms in Poland & the Yedwabne case; migration of survivors to Israel & the United States.
Facilities: library; reading room; 400-seat auditorium; Museum of European Jewish Heritage.

Activities: docent training; reading room; audiovisual presentations; guided tours.
Hours & Admission Prices: Tours: Sun.-Thurs. 1pm. No charge; donations accepted. Closed Jewish holidays; most legal holidays.

MARVIN'S MARVELOUS MECHANICAL MUSEUM, 31005 Orchard Lake Rd., Farmington Hills, MI 48334-1384. Tel.: 248-626-5020.
Web Site: www.marvin3m.com/
Key Personnel: Owner, Marvin Yagoda
Mechanical Machine Museum.
Collections: arcade machines; fortune teller machines; posters; model airplanes; robots; coin operated games; period games; carousels.
Facilities: 5,500 sq. ft. exhibit space.
Activities: birthday parties; children's rides.
Hours & Admission Prices: Mon.-Thurs. 10-9, Fri.-Sat. 10am-11pm, Sun. 12-9. No charge.

Fenton

THE PIONEER MEMORIAL ASSOCIATION OF FENTON AND MUNDY TOWNSHIPS, 2436 N. Long Lake Rd., Fenton, MI 48430. Mailing Address: P.O. Box 154, Fenton, MI 48430-0154. Tel.: 810-955-3336.
E-mail: podunkpioneer@aol.com
Web Site: www.addorio.com/podunk
Founded: 1967.
Congressional District: 82
Key Personnel: Pres., MaryJane Pinkston; Vice Pres., Bill Pinkston; Treas., Ramona Green; Sec., Phyllis Heusted.
Governing Authority: nonprofit organization. Tax-exempt: 501(c)(3).
Historic Society: housed in 1836 Indian Trading Post, now called Pioneer House.
Collections: period furniture & furnishings; old zinc bathtub with water heater attached; hand tools; old pictures & records; fog horn, steam whistle, steering wheel & life saver from the old passenger boat, City of Fenton; family history recordings. Historic Buildings: mid-18th century farm house; 1876 Phelps & Bigelow; 35 ft. windmill.
Research Fields: pioneer life; some genealogies.
Facilities: 20-vol. library of early school books, atlases & books by local authors available for use on premises.
Activities: guided tours; special tours for elementary school history classes. Museum Sponsors: Annual Fall Festival Pioneer Day.
Publications: brochure describing the pioneer house; semiannual newsletter.
Hours & Admission Prices: June-Aug. by appointment only; call Phyllis Yancy, 810-629-8747. Pioneer Day: adults $1, children $.50.
Attendance: 250 (estimated)
Membership: Single $3; Family $5; Contributing $10; Sustaining $25; Life $100.

Flint

* **FLINT INSTITUTE OF ARTS, (M),** 1120 E. Kearsley St., Flint, MI 48503-1915. Tel.: 810-234-1695. Fax: 810-234-1692.
E-mail: info@flintarts.org
Web Site: www.flintarts.org
Founded: 1928.
Congressional District: 7
Key Personnel: Dir., John B. Henry, III; Pres. (V), Elizabeth Murphy; Asst. Dir. Finance & Administration, Michael Mellenbrink; Asst. Dir. Art School, Addie Langford; Coord. Membership, Valarie Shook; Facilities Mgr., Bryan Christie; Cur. Education, Monique Desormeau; Cur. Collections & Exhibitions, Michael Martin; Public Rels., Miles Lam; Registrar, Pete Ott; Museum Shop Mgr., Cory Potter; Asst. Dir. Devel., Kathryn Sharbaugh.
Personnel Profile: Full-Time Paid 23; Part-Time Paid 49; Part-Time Volunteers 150; Interns 2.
Governing Authority: nonprofit organization. Tax-exempt: 501(c)(3).
Art Museum & School.
Collections: 7,500 works of art; 15th to 21st century European paintings, sculpture, graphics & decorative arts; 18th-21st century American paintings, sculpture, graphics & decorative arts; Native American, African & Asian art.
Major Exhibits: The Fine Art of Kansas City Jazz: The Photographs of Dan White (T), 11/21/09-1/10/10; Judy Pfaff: Sculpture, 11/21/09-1/10/10; Mary Lee Bendolph, Gee's Bend Quilts and Beyond (T), 1/23/10-4/18/10; Landscapes From the Age of Impressionism (T), 2/5/10-5/2/10.
Facilities: 6,000-vol. library on art; 9 classrooms; 330-seat auditorium; art sales & rental gallery. Museum-related items for sale.
Activities: inter-museum loan, permanent, temporary & travelling exhibitions; guided tours; lectures; films; concerts; annual art fair; sales & rental gallery; non-credit education programs for children & adults; docent program; Friends of Modern Art & Founders Society.
Publications: exhibition catalogs; annual reports; bimonthly newsletter; collection catalogues, Vanitas; Great Lakes Muse: American Scene Painting in the Upper Midwest, 1910-1960; Thy Brother's Keeper; American Art at the Flint Institute of Arts.
Hours & Admission Prices: Tues.-Wed. 10-5, Thurs.-Sat. 12-9, Sun. 1-5. Collections: no charge. Temporary Exhibits: adult $7, students & seniors $5; discounts to AAM & ICOM members; children under 12 & members no charge. Closed national holidays. ♿
Attendance: 120,901 (accurate)
Membership: Children 6-12 $5, Student $20; Individual $30; Family $40; Contributor $50; Sustainer $100; Sponsor $250; Donor $500; Silver Patron $1,000; Gold Patron $2,500; Benefactor $5,000 & up.

ROBERT T. LONGWAY PLANETARIUM, 1310 E. Kearsley St., Flint, MI 48503-1987. Tel.: 810-237-3400. Fax: 810-237-3417.
E-mail: tshickles@sloanlongway.org
Web Site: www.longway.org
Founded: 1958.
Congressional District: 7
Key Personnel: Dir., Tim Shickles; Office Mgr., Pam Atwell; Lecturer & Instructor, Richard A. Walker; Science Program Presenter, Jennifer Horvatin; Cur. Programs, Laurie Bone; Museum Shop Mgr., Michelle Reed; Receptionist, Cindy Goodall.
Personnel Profile: Full-Time Paid 6; Part-Time Paid 7.
Governing Authority: nonprofit. Parent Institution: Flint Cultural Corp. Tax-exempt.
Planetarium.
Collections: astronomical artifacts; manuscripts.
Facilities: reading room; 285-seat auditorium; theater. Astronomy-related items for sale.
Activities: formally organized education programs for adults, children & undergraduate students.
Publications: Skyguide.
Hours & Admission Prices: Public Astronomy & Laser Shows: Sat.-Sun; Mon.-Fri. by appointment. Adults $4-$6, children $3-$5 depending on program; members no charge. Closed national holidays. ♿
Attendance: 68,267 (accurate)
Membership: Student Pass $20; Share-a-Pass $40; Family Pass $85.

* **SLOAN MUSEUM & LONGWAY PLANETARIUM, (M),** 1221 E. Kearsley St., Flint, MI 48503-1988. Tel.: 810-237-3450. Fax: 810-237-3451.
E-mail: tshickles@sloanlongway.org
Web Site: www.sloanlongway.org
Founded: 1966.
Congressional District: 9
Key Personnel: Dir., Tim Shickles; Assoc. Cur. Collections, Jane McIntosh; Mktg. & Facilities Rental Coord., Cathy Jaruzel; Museum Shop Mgr., David Hutchinson.
Personnel Profile: Full-Time Paid 11; Part-Time Paid 17; Part-Time Volunteers 60; Interns 3.
Governing Authority: private; nonprofit organization. Parent Institution: Flint Cultural Center Corp., 1310 E. Kearsley St., Flint. Tax-exempt: 501(c)(3).
Regional History & Science Museum and Planetarium.
Collections: automotive & horse-drawn carriages; local historical artifacts; natural history artifacts; archaeology; 70 vintage & prototype Buick automobiles & related artifacts.
Research Fields: local & automotive history; carriage industry.
Facilities: library; 40,000 sq. ft. exhibit space; 100-seat auditorium; classroom; cafeteria. Museum-related items for sale.
Activities: guided tours; lectures; docent program; formal education programs for children & University of Michigan students; hobby workshops; rental gallery; loan, participatory, temporary & traveling exhibitions.
Hours & Admission Prices: Mon.-Fri. 10-5, Sat.-Sun. 12-5. Adults $6, senior citizens $5, children 3-11 $4; discounts to groups & AAM members; members & children 2 & under no charge. Closed New Year's Day; Easter; Memorial Day; Independence Day; Labor Day; Thanksgiving; Christmas. ♿
Attendance: 59,246 (accurate)
Membership: Student $20; Share A Pass $40; Family $85.

WHALEY HOUSE MUSEUM, 624 E. Kearsley St., Flint, MI 48503-1909. Tel.: 810-235-6841. Fax: 810-235-6186.
E-mail: 1885@whaleyhouse.com
Web Site: www.whaleyhouse.com
Historic House: former home of Robert and Mary McFarlan Whaley.
Collections: clothing collection; photographs.
Hours & Admission Prices: Mon.-Sat. by appointment, Sun. 1-4. Adults 16 & over $5, youths 6-15 & Time Travelers $3; children 5 & under no charge.

Frankenmuth

*** FRANKENMUTH HISTORICAL MUSEUM, (M),** 613 S. Main, Frankenmuth, MI 48734-1689. Tel.: 989-652-9701. Fax: 989-652-9390.
Web Site: www.frankenmuthmuseum.org
Founded: 1963.
Congressional District: 7
Key Personnel: Dir., Jon Webb; Pres., Mary Anne Ackerman; Cur. Education, Michaela McInerney; Collection Mgr., Mary Nuechterlein; Museum Shop Mgr., Lorraine Eckert; Administrative Asst., Ammiee Kotch.
Personnel Profile: Full-Time Paid 2; Part-Time Paid 5; Part-Time Volunteers 11.
Governing Authority: nonprofit organization. Parent Institution: Frankenmuth Historical Association. Tax-exempt: 501(c)(3).
Regional History Museum.
Collections: regional ethnic artifacts; early pioneer artifacts; primary archival material dating from 1815-1890 manuscripts. Historic Structure: 1890 Fischer Hall theatre.
Research Fields: local history, Bavarian-American immigration.
Facilities: 400-vol. library of German books & periodicals available on premises only. Local craft items, cards & gifts for sale.
Activities: guided tours; performing & cultural arts; educational classes for area schools; inter-museum loan, permanent & temporary exhibitions; historical markers.
Publications: quarterly newsletter, Frankenmuth Historical Assn.; books, Frankenmuth Historical Assn.; Cookbook; Local History.
Hours & Admission Prices: Jan.-March call for hours; April-Dec. Mon.-Thurs. 10:30-5, Fri. 10:30-8, Sat. 10-8, Sun. 11-7. Self Guided Tours: family $5, adults $2, children $1. Guided Tours: adults $2.50, children $1.50; members no charge. Closed New Year's Day; Easter; Thanksgiving; Christmas. ♿
Attendance: 17,000 (accurate)
Membership: Student & Senior Citizen $15; Family & Individual $40; Sustaining $100; Life $500; Founder's Club $1,500.

Franklin

XOCHIPILLI ART GALLERY, 26775 Crestwood Dr., Franklin, MI 48025-1347. Tel.: 248-645-1905.
Key Personnel: Dir., Mary C. Wright
Art Gallery.
Collections: works by local & regional artists.
Hours & Admission Prices: Tues.-Sat. 11-5.

Garden

FAYETTE HISTORIC STATE PARK, 13700 13.25 Lane, Garden, MI 49835-9411. Tel.: 906-644-2603. Fax: 906-644-2666.
Web Site: www.michigan.gov/hal; www.michigan.gov/dnr
Key Personnel: Unit Supvr., Dept. Natural Resources, Randall W. Brown; Dept. of History, Arts & Libraries-Historical Center, Brenda J. Laakso.
Personnel Profile: Full-Time Paid 3.
Governing Authority: Dept. of History, Arts & Libraries-Historical Center in cooperation with the Michigan Department of Natural Resources.
Historic Town Museum: site of iron smelting town 1867-1891, owned & operated by Jackson Iron Co. includes nineteen structures.
Collections: Museum: scale model of the town; hotel; company office; town hall; homes of the company employees; furnace complex & kilns; machine shop; old cemetery; interpretive displays & signs.
Research Fields: charcoal iron industry; economic & cultural development & decline.
Facilities: campgrounds; picnic area.
Activities: self-guided tour; guided tours; permanent exhibitions; overnight boat camping.
Publications: brochures; Fayette Historic Townsite.
Hours & Admission Prices: mid-May to mid-June & Sept. to mid-Oct. daily 9-5; mid-June to Aug. daily 8-9. Motor vehicle permit required; non-Michigan car $8, Michigan car $6. Annual: non-Michigan car $29, Michigan car $24. ♿
Attendance: 85,000 (accurate)

Gaylord

CALL OF THE WILD MUSEUM, 850 S. Wisconsin Ave., Gaylord, MI 49735-1747. Tel.: 989-732-4336. Fax: 989-732-3749.
Web Site: www.gocallofthewild.com
Founded: 1957.
Key Personnel: Bd. Directors, William C. Johnson; Bd. Directors, Judy Fleet; Pres., Janis Vollmer.
Personnel Profile: Full-Time Paid 4; Part-Time Paid 15.
Governing Authority: corporate; bd. of directors. Parent Institution: Call of the Wild, Inc.
Natural History Museum.
Collections: 50 displays of North American wildlife, featuring natural recorded sounds.
Facilities: Collectibles & other museum-related items for sale.
Hours & Admission Prices: mid-June to Labor Day daily 9-9; Sept. to mid-June Mon.-Sat. 9:30-6, Sun. 11-5. Adults $7, seniors 62 & up $6.50, children 5-13 $4.50; discount to AAM members. Closed New Year's Day; Thanksgiving; Christmas. ♿
Attendance: 20,000 (estimated)
Membership: Children $9; Adults $14; Family $40

Gibraltar

GIBRALTAR HISTORICAL MUSEUM, 29450 Munro St., Gibraltar, MI 48197-9720. Tel.: 734-676-3900.
Historical Society Museum.
Collections: artifacts & memorabilia pertaining to the city of Gibraltar.
Hours & Admission Prices: Sun.-Mon. 1-4.

Grand Haven

TRI-CITIES HISTORICAL MUSEUM, (M), 200 Washington Ave., Grand Haven, MI 49417-1357. Tel.: 616-842-0700. Fax: 616-842-3698.
Web Site: www.tri-citiesmuseum.org
Founded: 1962.
Congressional District: 96
Key Personnel: Dir., Dennis W. Swartout; Pres. (V), John Naser; Museum Shop Mgr., Muriel Peterson.
Personnel Profile: Full-Time Paid 5; Part-Time Paid 10; Part-Time Volunteers 75.
Governing Authority: society; nonprofit. Parent Institution: Tri-Cities Historical Society. Tax-exempt: 501(c)(3).
Historical Museum: housed in 1871 Akeley building & 1870 Grand Trunk Railroad Depot.
Collections: archives; medical; farming; photographs; costumes; Native American artifacts; Victorian period rooms; textiles; lumbering; shipping; Coast Guard; railroads; saw mill.
Research Fields: local history; Michigan history.
Facilities: library of newspapers, scrapbooks & memoirs available by special arrangement; audiovisual room.
Activities: guided tours; quarterly programs; permanent & temporary exhibitions.
Publications: quarterly newsletter, The Packet; booklets, History of Grand Haven and Ottawa County; photo history books; In the Path of Destiny.
Hours & Admission Prices: Summer: Tues.-Fri. 9:30-7:30, Sat.-Sun. 12:30-7:30. Winter: Tues.-Fri. 9:30-5, Sat.-Sun. 12:30-5. No charge; donations accepted. ♿
Attendance: 52,000 (accurate)
Membership: Senior: Single $15; Single $20; Couple $25; Family $35; Business & Professional $50.

Grand Rapids

CALVIN COLLEGE CENTER ART GALLERY, (M), 3201 Burton St., S.E., Grand Rapids, MI 49546-4388. Tel.: 616-526-6271. Fax: 616-526-8551.
E-mail: jhz2@calvin.edu
Web Site: www.calvin.edu/centerartgallery
Founded: 1974.
Congressional District: 5
Personnel Profile: Full-Time Paid 1; Part-Time Paid 7.
Governing Authority: college. Parent Institution: Calvin College. Subsidiary Institution: Center Art Gallery. Tax-exempt.
Art Gallery.
Collections: 17th & 19th-century Dutch paintings & drawings; 20th-century prints, drawings, paintings & sculpture.
Research Fields: relating to exhibitions.
Facilities: library; 350-seat auditorium; theater; classrooms.
Activities: guided tours; lectures; films; temporary, permanent, loan & traveling exhibitions.
Publications: catalogs relating to exhibits.
Hours & Admission Prices: Winter: Mon.-Thurs. 9-9, Fri. 9-5, Sat. 12-4. No charge. Closed during school vacations except for special exhibitions. ♿
Attendance: 5,000 (accurate)

FREDERIK MEIJER GARDENS & SCULPTURE PARK, 1000 E. Beltline Ave., N.E., Grand Rapids, MI 49525-5804. Tel.: 888-957-1580 (Toll Free); 616-957-1580.
Web Site: www.meijergardens.org
Key Personnel: Pres. & C.E.O., David S. Hooker
Botanical Garden & Sculpture Park.

Collections: over 100 sculptures; gardens.
Major Exhibits: Spirit and Form: Michele Oka Doner and the Natural World, 1/10-5/10; Butterflies are Blooming, 3/10-4/10; Chihuly at Frederik Meijer Gardens & Sculpture Park: A New Eden, 4/10-9/10; Sculptors Celebrate the Legacy of Fred and Lena Meijer, 6/10-1/11; Color Fall, 9/10-10/10; Christmas and Holiday Traditions Around the World, 11/10-1/11.
Facilities: nature trails; gardens; cafe. Museum-related items for sale.
Activities: tram tours; educational programming.
Publications: quarterly membership newsletter, Seasons.
Hours & Admission Prices: Call for information. ♿
Membership: Call for information.

GERALD R. FORD PRESIDENTIAL MUSEUM, (M), 303 Pearl St., N.W., Grand Rapids, MI 49504-5353. Tel.: 616-254-0400 & 0367. Fax: 616-254-0386.
E-mail: ford.museum@nara.gov
Web Site: www.fordlibrarymuseum.gov
Founded: 1981.
Congressional District: 3
Key Personnel: Dir., Dr. Elaine Didier; Deputy Dir., James R. Kratsas; Cur., Donald Holloway; Exhibits Specialist, Bettina Demetz; Registrar, James Draper; Education, Barbara McGregor; Public Rels., Kristin Mooney; Museum Shop Mgr., Janice Berling.
Personnel Profile: Full-Time Paid 11; Part-Time Paid 4; Part-Time Volunteers 35; Interns 2.
Governing Authority: federal. Affiliated with the National Archives & Records Administration, Washington, DC 20408. Branch Museum: Gerald R. Ford Library, 1000 Beal Ave., Ann Arbor, MI. Tax-exempt: 170(b)(1)(A).
Presidential History Museum.
Collections: personal papers; government records; photographs; motion picture films; audio & video tapes; sound recordings; head of state gifts; gifts from private citizens; political campaign items; personal & family memorabilia; bicentennial folk art.
Research Fields: life, times, career & presidential administration of President Ford.
Facilities: 252-seat auditorium; classrooms. Museum-related items for sale.
Activities: guided tours; lectures; films; permanent, temporary & traveling exhibitions; organized education programs for children, adults, undergraduate or graduate students; docent program. Annual Events: Holiday Open House; Birthday Celebration; Tree Lighting.
Publications: quarterly newsletter; brochure.
Hours & Admission Prices: Daily 9-5. Adults $7, senior citizens & military $6, college students $5, children 6-18 $3; discounts to groups; members and children 5 & under no charge. Closed New Year's Day; Thanksgiving; Christmas. ♿
Attendance: 100,000 (estimated)
Membership: Individual $35; Family $50-$99; Associate $100-$249; Sustaining $250-$499; Patron $500-$999; President's Cabinet $1,000 & up.

* **GRAND RAPIDS ART MUSEUM,** 101 Monroe Center, Grand Rapids, MI 49503-2801. Tel.: 616-831-1000. Fax: 616-831-1001.
E-mail: pr@artmuseumgr.org
Web Site: www.artmuseumgr.org
Founded: 1910.
Congressional District: 5
Key Personnel: C.E.O. & Dir., Celeste M. Adams; Finance Dir., Randy VanAntwerp; Dir. Mktg. & Public Rels. Mgr., Kerri Vanderhoff; Registrar, Kathleen Ferres; Senior Cur., Prints & Photographs, Richard Axson; Asst. Cur., Cindy Buckner; Retail Mgr., Rachel Allen.
Personnel Profile: Full-Time Paid 19; Part-Time Paid 21; Part-Time Volunteers 200; Interns 5.
Governing Authority: nonprofit organization. Tax-exempt: 501(c)(3).
Art Museum.
Collections: European 17th to 20th century paintings; American 19th & 20th-century paintings, prints, drawings, photography; 20th-century design.
Research Fields: curatorial material relevant to the museum's collection; 19th-20th century European & American art.
Facilities: 5,000-vol. library of general art reference; cafe; auditorium. Museum-related items for sale.
Activities: permanent & temporary exhibitions; lectures; gallery talks; concerts; guided tours; education programs for children; docent program.
Publications: members' newsletter; annual report; exhibition catalogues.
Hours & Admission Prices: Tues.-Thurs. & Sat. 10-5, Fri. 10-10, Sun. 12-5. Adults $8, senior citizens 62 & over and college students with ID $7, youth 6-17 $5; discounts to AAM members; members & children under 6 no charge. Closed major holidays. ♿
Attendance: 140,000 (estimated)
Membership: Individual & 1 Guest $50; Family $65; Friend of Art $150; Fine Arts $500; Masters $1,000.

GRAND RAPIDS CHILDREN'S MUSEUM, 11 Sheldon Ave., N.E., Grand Rapids, MI 49503-3218. Mailing Address: 22 Sheldon Ave., N.E., Grand Rapids, MI 49503-3246. Tel.: 616-235-4726, ext. 100. Fax: 616-235-4728.
E-mail: sandersen@grcm.org
Web Site: www.grcm.org
Founded: 1992.
Congressional District: 3
Key Personnel: Exec. Dir., Robert Dean; Dir. Devel., Nancy Brozek; Mktg. & Membership Mgr., Beth Szberowski; Exhibits & Community Rels. Mgr., Jan Stone.
Personnel Profile: Full-Time Paid 10; Part-Time Paid 16; Interns 4.
Governing Authority: private; nonprofit organization. Tax-exempt: 501(c)(3).
Children's Museum.
Collections: hands-on exhibits.
Facilities: 18,000 sq. ft. exhibit space.
Activities: hands-on exhibits; special programs for toddlers; exhibit-based programming.
Publications: newsletter, Play Times; calendar, What's Happening; annual report; brochures; press releases & press kits; flyers; rack cards; guest guides; exhibit poster; exhibit banners; Team Fun cards; Team Fun contracts. Electronic Publications: quarterly teacher newsletter; monthly E-Play update for members.
Hours & Admission Prices: Tues.-Wed. & Fri.-Sat. 9:30-5, Thurs. 9:30-8, Sun. 12-5. Adults $6.50; reciprocal membership & members no charge. ♿
Attendance: 180,166 (accurate)
Membership: Members: $40; $60; $85. Contributing Members: $125.

JOHN BALL ZOOLOGICAL GARDEN, 1300 W. Fulton St., Grand Rapids, MI 49504-6100. Mailing Address: P.O. Box 2506, Grand Rapids, MI 49501-2506. Tel.: 616-336-4301. Fax: 616-336-3907.
E-mail: info@johnballzoosociety.org
Web Site: www.johnballzoosociety.org
Founded: 1949.
Congressional District: 5
Key Personnel: Exec. Dir. Zoological Society, Brenda Stringer; Dir. Zoo, Bert Vescolani; Museum Shop Mgr., Theresa Danneffel.
Personnel Profile: Full-Time Paid 32; Part-Time Paid 15; Part-Time Volunteers 130; Interns 4.
Governing Authority: municipal; society. Parent Institution: County of Kent, MI. Tax-exempt.
Zoological Gardens.
Collections: exotic & native animals including endangered species.
Research Fields: captive animal management.
Facilities: botanical garden; aquarium; 60-seat auditorium; children's zoo; zoological & herpetological laboratories; food concessions; classrooms. Zoo-related gift items for sale.
Activities: guided tours; lectures; films; formally organized education programs for children; on-site school; permanent exhibitions. Museum Sponsors: programs for special education groups; lectures and programs for clubs, churches & charities.
Publications: Zoo News.
Hours & Admission Prices: May 16-Sept. 13 daily 10-6; Sept. 14.-May 19 daily 10-4. Summer: adults $7.50, senior citizens $6.50, children 3-13 $5.50. Winter: adults & senior citizens $3.50, children $3; discount to AAZPA members & other reciprocal zoo members; members and children 2 & under no charge. ♿
Attendance: 300,000 (accurate)
Membership: Senior $25; Individual $30; Family $45.

* **PUBLIC MUSEUM OF WEST MICHIGAN, (M),** 272 Pearl St., N.W., Grand Rapids, MI 49504-5371. Mailing Address: Van Andel Museum Center, 272 Pearl St., N.W., Grand Rapids, MI 49504-5371. Tel.: 616-456-3977. Fax: 616-456-3873. TDD: 616-456-3724.
E-mail: inquiries@grmuseum.org
Web Site: www.grmuseum.org
Formerly: Public Museum of Grand Rapids
Founded: 1854.
Congressional District: 5
Key Personnel: Pres. & C.E.O., Dale A. Robertson; Chm. Foundation (V), Danny R. Gaydou; Dir. Finance & Business Svcs., Karen Wilburn; Dir. Education, Interpretation, & Research, Christian G. Carron; Dir. Collections & Preservation, Marilyn Merdzinski; Planetarium Mgr., Rickey Ainsworth; Dir. Exhibits & Facilities, Tom Bantle; Dir. Mktg., Communications, & Customer Experience, Rebecca Westphal; Membership Svcs. Mgr., Maridell Vander-Baan; Museum Shop Mgr., Wendy Muller.
Personnel Profile: Full-Time Paid 18; Part-Time Paid 165; Part-Time Volunteers 176; Interns 8.
Governing Authority: Parent Institution: Public Museum of Grand Rapids Friends Foundation. Tax-exempt.
General Museum.

Collections: Grand Rapids-made furniture; c.1830-present decorative arts; industrial & agricultural artifacts; costumes; household textiles; ethnographic material; toys; dolls; games; natural history; & paleontology; mammals; birds. Historic Buildings: 1836 Calkins Law Office; 1869 Stilwill Horseshoeing Shop; 1853 Star School; 1866 Robinson-Kuhtic Homestead; 1895 Voigt House; Norton Mounds (Hopewell period).
Research Fields: ethnology; local history; 19th & 20th-century American furniture; domestic material culture; natural history; Native American culture, Great Lakes Woodland.
Facilities: 5,000-vol. library of history & natural history material available for use on premises; archives; research center; planetarium; 260-seat auditorium; classrooms; 87,000 sq. ft. exhibit space; cafe. Museum-related items for sale.
Activities: guided tours; lectures; films; gallery talks; hobby workshops; formally organized education programs; docent program; permanent & temporary exhibitions; facility use program; concerts; planetarium shows.
Publications: membership newsletter; exhibition & collection catalogs.
Hours & Admission Prices: Museum: Mon.-Sat. 9-5, Sun. 12-5. Adults $8, senior citizens $7, children 3-17 $3; discount to AAA & AAM members; museum members no charge. Planetarium: daytime $3 with admission. Closed New Year's Day; Easter; Thanksgiving; Christmas. ♿
Attendance: 247,371 (accurate)
Membership: Student & Senior Citizen $25; Individual $35; Family & Grandparents $60; Whalewatcher $125; Stargazer $250; Corporate $300 & up; 1890 Club $500; Carousel Society $1,000.

URBAN INSTITUTE FOR CONTEMPORARY ARTS, 41 Sheldon Blvd., S.E., Grand Rapids, MI 49503-4227. Tel.: 616-454-7000, ext. 20. Fax: 616-459-9395.
E-mail: info@uica.org
Web Site: www.uica.org
Founded: 1977.
Congressional District: 5
Key Personnel: C.E.O. & Exec. Dir., Jeff Meeuwsen; Film Program Mgr., Ryan Dittmer; Mng. Dir., Janet Teunis; Graphic Designer, Ryan Greaves; Business Mgr., Stacie Carrizzi; Dir. Clay Program, Israel Davis; Mgr. Expressive Arts Program, Elizabeth Goddard; Mgr. Youth Programs, Becca Schaub; Public Rels., Phillip Meade; Dir. Devel., Jill May.
Personnel Profile: Full-Time Paid 8; Part-Time Paid 5; Part-Time Volunteers 200.
Governing Authority: nonprofit organization. Tax-exempt: 501(c)(3).
Civic Art, Cultural Center.
Collections: works by contemporary artists.
Facilities: 170-seat theater; educational center.
Activities: music concerts; dance concerts; performance art events; films; loan & participatory exhibitions; theater; literature readings; interarts.
Publications: monthly, events calendar.
Hours & Admission Prices: Tues.-Sat. noon-10, Sun. noon-7. No charge; donations accepted. ♿
Attendance: 50,000 (accurate)
Membership: Student & Senior $25; Individual $40; Family $75; Reciprocal $150; Off the Wall $500 & up.

Grass Lake

WATERLOO AREA HISTORICAL SOCIETY, 9998 Waterloo-Munith Rd., Grass Lake, MI 49240. Mailing Address: P.O. Box 37, Stockbridge, MI 49285-0037. Tel.: 517-596-2254.
E-mail: info@waterloofarmmuseum.org
Web Site: waterloofarmmuseum.org
Founded: 1962.
Congressional District: 7
Key Personnel: Pres. (V), April Gasbarre; Treas., Arlene R. Kaiser; Museum Shop Mgr., Nancy Wisman.
Personnel Profile: Part-Time Paid 3; Part-Time Volunteers 150.
Governing Authority: society. Parent Institution: Waterloo Area Historical Society. Subsidiary Institution: Waterloo Farm Museum; Dewey School Museum. Tax-exempt.
Agriculture Museum.
Collections: Historic Structures: 1855 Greek Revival farmhouse; 1840s log cabin; 1840s-1880 one-room schoolhouse; 1880s outbuildings.
Research Fields: early Michigan pioneer history.
Facilities: Gift items for sale.
Activities: guided tours; summer & fall classes in pioneer crafts; special events. Museum Sponsors: Living History Program for children in May & September; Eastern Woodland Indian Living History in June; Log Cabin Day in June; Pioneer Day & Dewey School Day in October; Christmas on the Farm and Dewey School in December.
Publications: booklets, Primer for Guides; material for classrooms; newsletters.
Hours & Admission Prices: Fri.-Sun. 1-5. Adults $3, senior citizens over 62 $2.50, Dewey School & children 5-18 $1; discounts to AAA, AAM & Michigan Historical Society members; members & children under 5 no charge.
Attendance: 8,000 (estimated)
Membership: Senior $8; Individual & Senior Couple $10; Couple $12; Family $15; Contributing $35; Business Sponsors $50; Senior Life $125; Individual Life $150.

Greilickville

GREAT LAKES CHILDREN'S MUSEUM, 13240 S. West Bayshore Dr., Greilickville, MI 49684-5570. Mailing Address: P.O. Box 2326, Traverse City, MI 49685-2326. Tel.: 231-932-4526.
Web Site: www.glcm.org
Founded: 1998.
Congressional District: 4
Key Personnel: Exec. Dir., John Noonan; Pres. (V), Andy Robitshek; Museum Educator, Anne Drake; Museum Admin., Martha Belfour; Dir. Devel. & Mktg., Katherine Marciniak-DeGood; Museum Educator, Anne Drake; Museum Shop Mgr., Diane Hubert.
Personnel Profile: Full-Time Paid 3; Part-Time Paid 7; Interns 1.
Governing Authority: Tax-exempt.
Children's Museum.
Collections: hands-on exhibits; water & the Great Lakes.
Activities: birthday parties; member nights; science exploration. Museum Sponsors: Kids Safety Day; Kids Free Fishing Day.
Publications: quarterly newsletter, Wave Review; monthly email bulletin, Info Flash.
Hours & Admission Prices: July-Aug. Mon.-Sat. 10-5, Sun. 1-5; Sept.-June Tues.-Sat. 10-5, Sun. 1-5. Adults $6; members no charge. ♿
Attendance: 25,000 (accurate)
Membership: Individual $50; Grandparents $60; Family $70.

Grosse Ile

GROSSE ILE HISTORICAL SOCIETY, East River and Grosse Ile Pkwy., Grosse Ile, MI 48138. Mailing Address: P.O. Box 131, Grosse Ile, MI 48138-0131. Tel.: 734-675-1250.
Founded: 1959.
Congressional District: 14
Key Personnel: Pres., Marc Lafayette; Mgr., Sarah Lawrence.
Personnel Profile: Part-Time Volunteers 50.
Governing Authority: society. Tax-exempt.
Historical Society Museum.
Collections: documents related to local history; furniture; clothing; artifacts; photos. Historic Buildings: 1906 lighthouse; 1873 customs house; 1904 railroad station.
Research Fields: local history.
Activities: guided tours; permanent & temporary exhibits; membership programs.
Publications: newsletter; local publications.
Hours & Admission Prices: March-Dec. Thurs. 10-12, Sun. 1-4; other times by appointment. No charge; donations accepted. Closed holidays.
Attendance: 1,500 (estimated)
Membership: Individual $10; Family $20; Associate $50; Patron $100; Life $300; Family Life & Corporate $500.

Grosse Pointe Shores

EDSEL & ELEANOR FORD HOUSE, (M), 1100 Lake Shore Rd., Grosse Pointe Shores, MI 48236-4106. Tel.: 313-884-4222. Fax: 313-884-5977.
E-mail: info@fordhouse.org
Web Site: www.fordhouse.org
Founded: 1978.
Congressional District: 14
Key Personnel: Pres., Kathleen Stiso Mullins; Chm. (V), Edsel B. Ford, II; Vice Pres., External Rels., Ann Fitzpatrick; Dir. Education, Christopher Shires; Vice Pres. Internal Operations, David Janssen; Dir. Devel., Bernadette Banke; Cur., Josephine Shea; Treas., Margit Jackson; Dir. Group Tours Sales, Donna Buchanan; Gallery Shop Mgr., Matthew Peplinski.
Personnel Profile: Full-Time Paid 39; Part-Time Paid 51.
Governing Authority: nonprofit organization. Tax-exempt: 501(c)(3).
Historic Building & Site: Family home of Edsel & Eleanor Ford, designed by architect Albert Kahn & built in 1926-29 with interiors from historic English homes & four rooms designed in the modern style by Walter Dorwin Teague. Gardens & grounds designed by Jens Jensen.
Collections: paintings; graphic arts; French & English period furniture; silver; glass; ceramics; historic textiles. Historic Buildings: 60-room Main House; Power House; Play House; Gate Lodge.
Research Fields: history of collection, house & grounds.
Facilities: 87 acres of gardens & grounds with formal Rose garden; tea room; 2,500 sq. ft. exhibition & meeting space. Museum-related items for sale.

Activities: guided tours; lectures; children's programs; traveling fine & decorative art exhibitions. Museum Sponsors: Auto show; art show.
Publications: illustrated history & guide book, Edsel & Eleanor Ford House; Edsel B. Ford, 1893-1943.
Hours & Admission Prices: Jan.-March Tues.-Sun. 12-4; April-Dec. Tues.-Sat. 10-4, Sun. 12-4. Adults $10, senior citizens $9, children 6-12 $6; discounts to AAM members; children 5 & under no charge. Grounds $5. Closed New Year's Day; Thanksgiving; Christmas. ♿
Attendance: 40,000 (estimated)
Membership: Individual $25; Companion $35; Family $45.

Hamtramck

UKRAINIAN-AMERICAN ARCHIVES & MUSEUM, 11756 Charest St., Hamtramck, MI 48212-3059. Tel.: 313-366-9764.
E-mail: ukrainianmuseum@sbcglobal.net
Web Site: www.ukrainianmuseumdetroit.org
Founded: 1958.
Key Personnel: Exec. Dir., Chrystyna Nykorak; Pres., Swetlana Leheta.
Personnel Profile: Full-Time Paid 1; Full-Time Volunteers 1; Part-Time Volunteers 9.
Governing Authority: nonprofit. Tax-exempt: 501(c)(3).
Cultural Center.
Collections: art; culture; costumes; headdresses; ceramics; woodwork; photographs; musical instruments.
Facilities: meeting rooms.
Publications: quarterly newsletter.
Hours & Admission Prices: Daily 9-5; other times by appointment, Sat.-Sun. by appointment or for special events. No charge; donations accepted. Closed holidays.
Attendance: 500 (estimated)
Membership: $10; $25; $35; $100; $1,000 & up.

Hanover

CONKLIN REED ORGAN & HISTORY MUSEUM, 105 Fairview, Hanover, MI 49241-0256. Mailing Address: P.O. Box 256, Hanover, MI 49241-0256. Tel.: 517-563-8927. Fax: 517-563-8927.
E-mail: info@conklinreedorganmuseum.org
Web Site: www.conklinreedorganmuseum.org
Formerly: Lee Conklin Antique Organ Museum
Founded: 1977.
Congressional District: 2
Key Personnel: Pres., Ron McClain; Treas., Richard Tallis; Museum Gift Mgr., Jane Myers.
Personnel Profile: Part-Time Paid 1; Part-Time Volunteers 20.
Governing Authority: nonprofit organization. Parent Institution: Hanover-Horton Area Historical Society Inc. Tax-exempt.
Historical Society & Antique Reed Organ Museum: housed in 1911 Hanover High School.
Collections: reed organs; parlor organs; chapel organs; Melodeons; farm & home equipment; restored early 20th-century classroom; old telephone switchboard; loom; player piano; job press; dog treadmill; local memorabilia; early fire fighting equipment.
Research Fields: local history; Reed organs.
Facilities: 82 acre Heritage Park; nature trails; 100-seat auditorium. Handcrafted items & organ music tapes for sale.
Activities: nature trails; hay wagon rides; guided tours; concerts; organ repair & maintenance workshops. Society Sponsors: Jubilee Musical in spring; Special May Event; Museum Week For Students; 4th of July Celebration; Father's Day Car Show; Rust N Dust Event in August; Fall Festival in September; Corn Maze September-October; Family Fun Night in October; Christmas Open House in December.
Publications: quarterly newsletter, Bulletin of the Hanover-Horton Area Historical Society, Inc.
Hours & Admission Prices: May-Oct. Sun. 1-5; call for additional hours. No charge; donations accepted. Closed Easter. ♿
Attendance: 3,359 (accurate)
Membership: Full-time Student & Senior Citizen $10; Individual $20; Family $25; Business & Senior Citizen Life $100; Life $250.

Harbor Beach

FRANK MURPHY MEMORIAL MUSEUM, 142 S. Huron Ave., Harbor Beach, MI 48441. Mailing Address: P.O. Box 113, Harbor Beach, MI 48441-0113. Tel.: 989-479-6477.
E-mail: pmajeski@harborbeach.com
Web Site: harborbeachchamber.com/murphy.html
Historic House Museum: housed in the home of statesman, Frank Murphy.
Collections: personal artifacts; furniture; photographs.
Activities: tours.
Hours & Admission Prices: Tues.-Fri. 12-4, Sat.-Sun. 10-4. Adults $2, children $1.

THE GRICE HOUSE MUSEUM, 865 N. Huron Ave., Harbor Beach, MI 48441. Mailing Address: Harbor Beach Chamber of Commerce, P.O. Box 113, Harbor Beach, MI 48441-0113. Tel.: 989-479-6477.
Web Site: harborbeachchamber.com/grice.html
Historic House: former home of the Grice family, built in 1875.
Collections: mid-nineteenth century kitchen, parlor, sewing room & bedroom; military artifacts room; history of the Great Lakes room; one-room schoolhouse.
Hours & Admission Prices: Memorial Day-Labor Day Tues.-Fri. 12-4, Sat.-Sun. 10-4.

Harbor Springs

ANDREW J. BLACKBIRD MUSEUM, (M), 368 E. Main St., Harbor Springs, MI 49740-1514. Mailing Address: P.O. Box 678, Harbor Springs, MI 49740-0678. Tel.: 231-526-0612 (museum); 2104 (City of Harbor Springs). Fax: 231-526-6865.
E-mail: cityhs@freeway.net
Founded: 1952.
Congressional District: 11
Key Personnel: Mgr., Joyce Shagonaby; Pres. (V), Robert Shagonaby.
Personnel Profile: Part-Time Paid 1; Part-Time Volunteers 6.
Governing Authority: municipal. Tax-exempt.
Indian Museum: housed in c. 1855 home of Andrew J. Blackbird.
Collections: art; tools; utensils; Odawa Indian clothing.
Major Exhibits: Native American Inventors, 11/09-5/10.
Activities: permanent & traveling exhibitions.
Publications: History of the Ottawa & Chippewa Indians of Michigan; Ottawa Quillwork on Birchbark; Ottawa Quillwork on Birchbark Edition 2007; Beadwork & Textiles of the Ottawa.
Hours & Admission Prices: Mon.-Fri. 10-4. No charge; donations accepted. ♿
Attendance: 600 (estimated)
Membership: $10; $25; $50; $100.

Hastings

HISTORIC CHARLTON PARK VILLAGE AND MUSEUM, 2545 S. Charlton Park Rd., Hastings, MI 49058-8102. Tel.: 269-945-3775. Fax: 269-945-0390.
Web Site: www.charltonpark.org
Founded: 1936.
Congressional District: 3
Key Personnel: Interim Dir., Keith Murphy; Cur., Claire Johnston; Office Mgr., Linda Ferris; Supvr. Operations, Tom Campbell; Special Events Coord., Debbie Smith.
Personnel Profile: Full-Time Paid 5; Part-Time Paid 12; Part-Time Volunteers 100; Interns 2.
Governing Authority: county. Parent Institution: Barry County Parks & Recreation Commission. Tax-exempt.
History Museum.
Collections: rural life in Southern Michigan; agriculture & industrial equipment; crafts; transportation; decorative arts; domestic life; weapons; costumes; gasoline & steam engines; prehistoric settlers & local historical records. Historic Structures: 1852 Bristol Inn; 1885 Church; 1869 Lee School; 1886 Hastings Township Hall; c.1890s Hall House; 1908 Hastings Mutual Insurance Building; 1858 Sixberry House; 1890 Hall House; Blacksmith Shop; Carpenter Shop; Machine Shed; General Store; Hardware Store; Print Shop; Charlton Gas & Steam Building; Barber Shop; Native American Village.
Research Fields: 1827-1940 midwestern rural life.
Facilities: 1,000-vol. library of local history books available for research by request; nature trails.
Activities: guided tours; lectures; organized education programs; living history village; permanent & temporary exhibitions; loan service; annual special events.
Publications: The Villager.
Hours & Admission Prices: Park: Memorial Day to Labor Day daily 8am to dusk. Museum & Village: Memorial Day-Labor Day Mon.-Fri. 8-5; Sept.-May Mon.-Fri. 8-5. Special Events: adults $5, children 5-12 $3; children under 5 no charge. ♿
Attendance: 41,006 (accurate)

Hickory Corners

GILMORE CAR MUSEUM, (M), 6865 Hickory Rd., Hickory Corners, MI 49060-9788. Tel.: 269-671-5089. Fax: 269-671-5843.
E-mail: info@gilmorecarmuseum.org
Web Site: www.gilmorecarmuseum.org

Founded: 1966.
Key Personnel: Dir., Michael J. Spezia.
Personnel Profile: Full-Time Paid 7; Part-Time Paid 5; Part-Time Volunteers 25.
Governing Authority: private; nonprofit organization. Parent Institution: Genevieve & Donald S. Gilmore Foundation. Tax-exempt: 501(c)(3).
Car Museum.
Collections: over 220 automobiles including an 1899 Locomobile, Duesenberg, Tucker '48, the Model T, & muscle cars of the 1960s; replica of 1940s diner; Disney movie set. Historic Buildings: c1890 train depot; barns; 1930s gas station.
Facilities: 90-acrea site; picnic facilities; interpretive center.
Activities: car shows; concourse d'Elegance; swap meets; auctions; auto restoration.
Publications: brochures; newsletter; schedule of events.
Hours & Admission Prices: May-Oct. Mon.-Fri. 9-5, Sat.-Sun. 9-6. Adults $8, senior citizens $7, student 7-15 $6; discounts to AAA members; members & children 6 & under no charge. ♿
Attendance: 27,000 (accurate)
Membership: Individual $35; Family $50; Contributor $100; Supporter $250; Benefactor $500; Life $1,000.

Holland

CAPPON & SETTLERS HOUSE MUSEUMS, 228 W. 9th St., Holland, MI 49423-3116. Mailing Address: 31 W. 10th St., Holland, MI 49423-3101. Tel.: 616-392-6740 & 9084. Fax: 616-394-4756.
E-mail: hollandmuseum@hollandmuseum.org
Web Site: www.hollandmuseum.org
Founded: 1986.
Congressional District: 9
Key Personnel: Chm., Howard Veneklasen; Exec. Dir., Thea Grigsby.
Personnel Profile: Part-Time Paid 3; Part-Time Volunteers 20.
Governing Authority: not-for-profit corporation. Parent Institution: Holland Historical Trust. Tax-exempt: 501(c)(3).
Historic Houses: 1874 Italianate Style home of Holland's first mayor; 1867 cottage of a Great Lakes Ship's Carpenter.
Collections: original furnishings; millwork.
Research Fields: the Cappon family; 19th-century history Holland MI; 19th century immigrant history; 19th century decorative arts.
Activities: guided tours; education programs. Special Events: Ice Cream Social; Tulip Time; lamplight tours; Christmas tours.
Hours & Admission Prices: June-Oct. Wed.-Sat. 1-5; Nov.-May Fri.-Sat. 1-5; special hours during Tulip Time; other times by appointment. Family $14, individual $7, senior $6, student $4; discounts to AAM, ICOM & AAA members; members no charge. ♿
Attendance: 12,626 (accurate)
Membership: Senior Individual (over 64) $20; Individual $25; Senior Couple $30; Family $35; Builder $60; Sponsor $100; Patron $250; Benefactor $500; Wichers Circle $1,000.

DE GRAAF NATURE CENTER, 600 Graafschap Rd., Holland, MI 49423-4549. Tel.: 616-355-1057. Fax: 616-355-1069.
E-mail: degraafnaturecenter@cityofholland.com
Web Site: www.degraaf.org
Founded: 1962.
Congressional District: 2
Key Personnel: Dir. Leisure & Cultural Svcs., Gary Gogolin; Coord. Nature Center, Robert Venner.
Personnel Profile: Full-Time Paid 2; Part-Time Paid 2; Part-Time Volunteers 20; Interns 1.
Governing Authority: municipal; nonprofit. Parent Institution: City of Holland Leisure & Cultural Services. Tax-exempt.
Nature Center.
Collections: Michigan rocks; US rocks; taxidermy including state birds & animals; bird nests; insects; woodland habitat diorama. Historic Building: log cabin c.1847.
Facilities: library of nature related materials available to the public. Books, magnifier boxes, & other gift items for sale.
Activities: guided tours; lectures; films; study clubs; hobby workshops; organized education programs for children; docent program; loan & temporary exhibitions; summer classes for children, grades K-12; regular Sat. programs for children & adults: field trip to natural areas, videos, natural history, tours. Museum Sponsors: Animal Day; Warbler Festival; Pioneer Christmas; Fall Festival.
Publications: quarterly newsletter, Friend News.
Hours & Admission Prices: Brower Interpretive Center: Tues.-Fri. 9-5, Sat. 10-5. No charge. Trails: dawn-dusk. School Programs: students $2.25. Closed holidays. ♿
Attendance: 13,000

Membership: Individual $20; Family $25; Sponsor $50; Sustaining $100; Contributing $250; Benefactor $500.

DEPREE ART CENTER & GALLERY, 160 E. 12th St., Holland, MI 49423-3609. Tel.: 616-395-7500. Fax: 616-395-7499.
E-mail: art@hope.edu
Web Site: hope.edu/academic/art
Founded: 1982.
Congressional District: 4
Personnel Profile: Part-Time Paid 4.
Governing Authority: private college; nonprofit organization. Tax-exempt: 501(c)(3).
Academic Art Center & Gallery.
Collections: paintings; sculptures.
Facilities: 1,300 sq. ft. exhibit space; 100-seat auditorium; 2 classrooms.
Activities: guided tours; lectures; docent program; formal education program for Hope College students; loan, temporary & traveling exhibitions.
Publications: Lamioi Olonade Fakey.
Hours & Admission Prices: May-Aug. Mon.-Fri. 10-5; Sept.-April Mon.-Sat. 10-5, Sun. 1-5; summer hours apply during college breaks. No charge. Closed New Year's Day; Memorial Day; Thanksgiving; Christmas. ♿
Attendance: 20,500 (estimated)
Membership: Patron $50.

HOLLAND AREA ARTS COUNCIL, 150 E. 8th St., Holland, MI 49423-3504. Tel.: 616-396-3278. Fax: 616-396-6298.
Web Site: www.hollandarts.org
Founded: 1967.
Congressional District: 4
Key Personnel: Exec. Dir., Lorma Williams Freestone; Program Dir., Mary Sundstrom; Operations Mgr., Derek Johnson; Asst. to Dir., Tennina Miozza.
Governing Authority: nonprofit organization. Tax-exempt: 501(c)(3).
Arts Council.
Collections: paintings; sculpture; photographs.
Research Fields: West Michigan Arts Registry: registry of artists located in the West Michigan area.
Facilities: 300-vol. library of arts & crafts books; educational facilities; dance studio. Gift items & books for sale.
Activities: arts festivals; concerts; dance recitals; docent program; arts education classes & workshops for children; guided tours; lectures; participatory exhibits; theatre. Annual Events: fundraiser; art competition exhibits; local arts exhibit.
Publications: newsletter, Artupdate.
Hours & Admission Prices: Mon.-Thurs. 10-8, Sat. 10-3. No charge; donations accepted. Closed New Year's Day; Memorial Day; Independence Day; Labor Day; Thanksgiving; Christmas. ♿
Attendance: 50,000
Membership: Individual $35; Family $50; Patron $100; Donor $250; Sponsor $400; Benefactor $1,000 & up.

* **THE HOLLAND MUSEUM, (M),** 31 W. 10th St., Holland, MI 49423-3101. Tel.: 616-394-1362. Fax: 616-394-4756.
E-mail: hollandmuseum@hollandmuseum.org
Web Site: www.hollandmuseum.org
Founded: 1937.
Congressional District: 9
Key Personnel: Chm., Jaron Nyhof; Operations Mgr., Paula Dunlap.
Personnel Profile: Full-Time Paid 6; Part-Time Paid 13.
Governing Authority: nonprofit corporation. Parent Institution: Holland Historical Trust. Tax-exempt: 501(c)(3); 170(b)(1)(A); 509(a)(2).
History Museum: housed in 1914 restored Federal Post Office building.
Collections: Dutch art & culture; early Dutch settlers & local history; the Netherlands collection of Dutch paintings, 17th-20th centuries; decorative arts including delftware; furniture; glassware; traditional Dutch costumes.
Research Fields: local history.
Facilities: research library; archives.
Activities: permanent & temporary exhibits; education programs.
Publications: quarterly newsletter; Review.
Hours & Admission Prices: Mon., Wed.-Sat. 10-5, Sun. 2-5. Families $14, individuals $7, seniors $6, students $4; discounts to AAM, AAA & ICOM members; members no charge. Closed major holidays. ♿
Attendance: 32,411 (accurate)
Membership: Senior 65 & over $20; Individual $25; Senior Couple 65 & over $30; Family $35; Builder $60; Sponsor $100; Patron $250; Benefactor $500; Wichers Circle $1,000.

WINDMILL ISLAND GARDENS, 1 Lincoln Ave., Holland, MI 49423. Tel.: 616-355-1030. Fax: 616-355-1035.
E-mail: windmill@cityofholland.com

Web Site: www.windmillisland.com
Formerly: Windmill Island Municipal Park
Founded: 1965.
Key Personnel: Dir., Ad vanden Akker.
Personnel Profile: Full-Time Paid 2; Part-Time Paid 55.
Governing Authority: municipal. Tax-exempt.
Park Museum: housed in c.1761 restored Dutch windmill, brought to the U.S. from the Netherlands in 1964.
Collections: Little Netherlands Museum, containing panoramic exhibit of town & country in Old Holland.
Facilities: flower garden.
Activities: guided tours; films; permanent exhibitions; wooden shoe dancers; Amsterdam street organ.
Publications: Brochure.
Hours & Admission Prices: late April to early Oct. daily 9:30-5. Tulip Time: daily 9-6. Adults $7.50, children 5-15 $4.50; discounts to groups of 20 or more; children 4 & under no charge. ♿
Attendance: 50,000

Houghton

A. E. SEAMAN MINERAL MUSEUM, 1400 Townsend Dr., Michigan Technological University, Rm. 516, EERC, Houghton, MI 49931-1295. Tel.: 906-487-2572. Fax: 906-487-3027.
E-mail: tjb@mtu.edu
Web Site: www.museum.mtu.edu
Founded: 1902.
Congressional District: 110
Key Personnel: Dir. & Prof., Dr. Theodore J. Bornhorst; Cur. & Prof., Dr. George W. Robinson; Museum Mgr., Darlene M. Comfort; Museum Asst., Karma Maynard.
Personnel Profile: Full-Time Paid 4.
Governing Authority: university. Affiliated with Michigan Technological University, Houghton, MI. Tax-exempt.
Mineralogy Museum.
Collections: midwest & worldwide minerals; native copper; crystals; systematic minerals; research collections.
Research Fields: mineralogy & crystallography. L.S. Copper District geology, mineralogy & mining history.
Facilities: 500-vol. library of books & periodicals pertaining to mineralogy & geology available for use on the premises by mineralogists.
Activities: guided tours & gallery talks by request; traveling & permanent exhibitions.
Hours & Admission Prices: Jan. 4-June & Oct.-Dec. 23 Mon.-Fri. 9-4:30; July-Sept. Mon.-Fri. 9-4:30, Sat.-Sun. 12-4:30. Donations appreciated. Closed national & university holidays. ♿
Attendance: 16,000 (accurate)
Membership: Crystal Society: Single $25, Couple $40; Copper Society $100; Silver Society $500; Gold Society $1,000 & up.

ISLE ROYALE NATIONAL PARK, 800 E. Lakeshore Dr., Houghton, MI 49931-1869. Tel.: 906-482-0984. Fax: 906-482-8753.
E-mail: liz_valencia@nps.gov
Web Site: www.nps.gov/isro
Founded: 1975.
Congressional District: 11
Personnel Profile: Full-Time Paid 1; Part-Time Volunteers 1.
Governing Authority: federal. Parent Institution: National Park Service, Dept. of the Interior, Washington DC. Tax-exempt.
National Park & Historic Site: 1890 Edisen Commercial Fishery complex. Historic Structure: 1855 Rock Harbor Lighthouse. Park Museum: located in Houghton, MI.
Collections: North American Indian baskets; 1928-1931 Isle Royale photographs; archaeological survey collection; manuscripts; shipwreck artifacts; commercial fishery equipment; 19th- & 20th-century summer home resort furnishings; 1840-1895 copper mining tools; geologic artifacts; herbarium. Historic Building: 1855 Rock Harbor Lighthouse on Isle Royale including Great Lakes shipping & maritime history of the area.
Research Fields: copper mining; shipwrecks; Indian baskets; commercial fishing; Isle Royale resorts; lighthouses.
Facilities: 1,000-vol. library pertaining to regional history, shipping, mining & Lake Superior available for research on premises by request June-Sept.; wilderness camping.
Activities: guided tours.
Hours & Admission Prices: Rock Harbor Visitor Center: May-June & Sept. call for hours; July-Aug. daily 8-6. Windigo Visitor Center May-June & Sept. call for hours; July-Aug. daily 8-4:30. Houghton Visitor Center: call for hours. Museum: by appointment. No charge; donations accepted.
Attendance: 2,000 (estimated)

Imlay City

IMLAY CITY HISTORICAL COMMISSION, INC., 77 Main St., Imlay City, MI 48444-1313. Tel.: 810-724-1111.
Web Site: www.hsmichigan.org/imlaycity/
History Museum: housed in the Grand Truck Depot.
Collections: photographs; local artifacts; military artifacts; farm tools; Bob Burman memorabilia; Imlay City High School graduating composites.
Hours & Admission Prices: Wed. 10-2, Sat. 1-4.

Iron Mountain

HOUSE OF YESTERYEAR MUSEUM, W7764 South US-2, Iron Mountain, MI 49801. Mailing Address: P.O. Box 58, Iron Mountain, MI 49801. Tel.: 906-774-0789.
History Museum.
Collections: local history & culture; farm equipment; kitchen utensils; period artifacts & furnishings; photographs.
Hours & Admission Prices: Temporarily closed.

Ironwood

IRONWOOD AREA HISTORICAL MUSEUM, 150 N. Lowell St., Ironwood, MI 49938-2032. Mailing Address: P.O. Box 553, Ironwood, MI 49938-0553. Tel.: 906-932-0287.
Web Site: www.ironwood.org
Founded: 1970.
Congressional District: 11
Key Personnel: Dir., Gary Harrington.
Personnel Profile: Part-Time Volunteers 23.
Governing Authority: city; nonprofit organization. Tax-exempt.
History Museum: housed in former Chicago & Northwestern Depot.
Collections: iron mining memorabilia; local historical photographs; railroad memorabilia; early sports artifacts; household artifacts; Ironwood Chamber of Commerce artifacts.
Research Fields: iron mining maps of Gogebic Range.
Facilities: 100-vol. library of mining material.
Activities: guided tours; lectures; concerts; arts festivals; broadcast programs; participatory & temporary exhibitions. Museum Sponsors: Heritage Day; historical plays.
Publications: periodic newsletter.
Hours & Admission Prices: Memorial Day to Labor Day Mon.-Sat. 12-4; Sept.-May daily 12-4; other times by appointment. No charge; donations accepted. Closed Independence Day. ♿
Attendance: 2,000 (estimated)
Membership: Individual $15; Lifetime $250.

Ishpeming

U.S. SKI & SNOWBOARD HALL OF FAME, 610 Palms, Ishpeming, MI 49849-1035. Mailing Address: P.O. Box 191, Ishpeming, MI 49849-0191. Tel.: 906-485-6323. Fax: 906-486-4570.
Web Site: www.skihall.com
Formerly: U.S. National Ski and Snowboard Hall of Fame & Museum
Founded: 1954.
Congressional District: 11
Key Personnel: C.E.O., J. Thomas West; Chm. (V), Bernard Weichsel; Admin., Ann Schroeder.
Personnel Profile: Full-Time Paid 3; Full-Time Volunteers 2; Part-Time Paid 1; Part-Time Volunteers 6.
Governing Authority: nonprofit organization. Affiliated with the United States Ski Association, P.O. Box 100, Park City, UT 84060. Tax-exempt.
Sports Museum.
Collections: ski-related exhibits.
Research Fields: ski history.
Facilities: 1,000-vol. library of ski-related material, available for research on premises only. Gift items for sale.
Activities: guided tours; formally organized education programs for children; permanent exhibitions.
Publications: quarterly newsletter, National Ski Hall of Fame Newsletter; 75 Years of Skiing; Skiing: Then & Now; Nine Thousand Years of Skis; The Flying Norseman; Midwest Skiing-A Glance Back.
Hours & Admission Prices: Mon.-Sat. 10-5. No charge; donations accepted. Closed New Year's Day; Independence Day; Thanksgiving; Christmas. ♿
Attendance: 10,000 (estimated)
Membership: Regular $40; Family $50; Business $100; Ski Area $250; Contributor $500; Carl Tellefsen Society $1,000.

Jackson

* **ELLA SHARP MUSEUM, (M),** 3225 4th St., Jackson, MI 49203-5094. Tel.: 517-787-2320. Fax: 517-787-2933.
E-mail: info@ellasharp.org
Web Site: www.ellasharp.org
Founded: 1964.
Congressional District: 2
Key Personnel: C.E.O., Charles H. Aymond; Pres., Martha Fuerstenau; Dir. Collections, Judy Horn; Dir. Exhibits, Katie Hill; Museum Shop Mgr., Florence Csage.
Personnel Profile: Full-Time Paid 6; Part-Time Paid 12; Part-Time Volunteers 100; Interns 1.
Governing Authority: nonprofit organization. Tax-exempt: 501(c)(3).
Art & History Museum.
Collections: Jackson County Michigan history; Merriman-Sharp family artifacts. Historic Buildings: farmhouse; woodworking shop; schoolhouse; barns; general store complex; log house.
Research Fields: Victorian restoration, furnishings & decorative arts; leisure & recreation; domestic life; transportation; Jackson County Michigan history.
Facilities: studio classrooms; restaurant. Gift items for sale.
Activities: guided tours; lectures & demonstrations; films; formally organized education programs for children & adults; workshops; permanent & temporary exhibits; gallery talks; docent program; seasonal special events.
Publications: bimonthly newsletter; class bulletins; brochures; illustrated monographs of collections.
Hours & Admission Prices: Tues.-Fri. 10-4, Sat. 11-4, Sun. 12-4. Adults $5, children 5-15 $3; members, children under 5 no charge. Closed major holidays. ♿
Attendance: 100,000 (estimated)
Membership: Individual $35; Dual $45; Grandparents $50; Family $60; Sustainer $100; Investor $200; Benefactor $500; Steward $750; President's Council $1,250.

Kalamazoo

AIR ZOO, (M), 6151 Portage Rd., Kalamazoo, MI 49002-3003. Tel.: 269-382-6555; 866-524-7966 (Toll Free). Fax: 616-382-1813.
Web Site: www.airzoo.org
Formerly: Kalamazoo Aviation History Museum
Founded: 1977.
Congressional District: 6
Key Personnel: Exec. Dir. & C.E.O., Robert E. Ellis; Chm. Bd., Preston S. Parish; Pres., Suzanne D. Parish; Cur. & Registrar, Bill Painter; Cur. Education, Cindy Scheuer; Deputy Dir./Operations, Kim Robinson; Deputy Dir. Mktg., Devel. & Human Resources, Renee Newman; Human Resources & Volunteer Coord., Tamra Stafford; Librarian, Carol Smith; Bldg. Supvr., Jim Ross; Museum Store Mgr., Meredith Martin; Community & Media Rels. Mgr., Jennifer Cunningham; Sr. Cur. Aircraft, Greg Ward.
Personnel Profile: Full-Time Paid 40; Part-Time Paid 20; Part-Time Volunteers 250.
Governing Authority: private; nonprofit organization. Tax-exempt: 501(c)(3).
Aviation Museum.
Collections: Guadalcanal Memorial Museum & Monument; Michigan Aviation Hall of Fame; 70 vintage aircrafts.
Facilities: 3,000-vol. library of aviation-related books; 200,000 sq. ft. exhibit space; restaurant; theatre; banquet facilities. Museum-related items for sale.
Activities: guided tours; education programs; monthly special events; annual events.
Publications: quarterly, Air Zoo Newsletter; Airmail News, monthly volunteer letter.
Hours & Admission Prices: Mon.-Sat. 9-5, Sun. 12-5. Closed Thanksgiving; Christmas Eve & Day. ♿
Attendance: 150,000 (accurate)
Membership: Basic $50; Family $125; Grandparents $150; Supporting $250; Patron $500; P-40 Society $1,000.

ALAMO TOWNSHIP MUSEUM-JOHN E. GRAY MEMORIAL MUSEUM, 8119 N. 6th St., Kalamazoo, MI 49009-8808. Mailing Address: 7180 N. 2nd St., Kalamazoo, MI 49009-8814. Tel.: 269-344-2107.
Founded: 1969.
Congressional District: 47
Key Personnel: Pres. & Chm. (V), Mary Gobel.
Personnel Profile: Part-Time Volunteers 20.
Governing Authority: township. Tax-exempt.
Historic House: built in 1865 as a Presbyterian Church.
Collections: farm implements; church records; tapes of former teachers & pioneers; school records; township records.
Research Fields: genealogy; Alamo Township Pioneers.
Facilities: 50-vol. library of historic records & manuscripts available for use by written request; picnic area.
Activities: guided tours; lectures; films; arts festivals; drama; radio & TV programs; training program for professional museum workers; loan, temporary & permanent exhibitions.
Publications: programs of events, Anvil.
Hours & Admission Prices: May-Oct. Tues. 1-3, Sat.-Sun. 2-4; groups by appointment. No charge; donations accepted. ♿
Attendance: 5,000 (estimated)

KALAMAZOO INSTITUTE OF ARTS, (M), 314 S. Park St., Kalamazoo, MI 49007-5102. Tel.: 269-349-7775, ext. 3001. Fax: 269-349-9313.
E-mail: museum@kiarts.org
Web Site: www.kiarts.org
Founded: 1924.
Congressional District: 6
Key Personnel: Exec. Dir., James A. Bridenstine; Dir. Finance & Personnel, Thomas A. Fox; Registrar, Robin Goodman; Dir. Museum Education, Susan Eckhardt; Dir. Devel., Joe Bower; School Dir., Denise Lisiecki; Dir. Facilities, Ron Boothby; Dir. Mktg., Farrell Howe; Membership Coord., Darlene Pontello; Membership & Devel. Sec., Angelnette Thomas; Librarian, Dennis Kreps; Special Events & Volunteer Coord., Sandy Linabury; Museum Shop Mgr., Karyn Juergens.
Personnel Profile: Full-Time Paid 27; Part-Time Paid 62.
Governing Authority: nonprofit. Tax-exempt: 501(c)(3).
Art Museum/Center & School. Focus: American Art.
Collections: 19th & 20th-century American art; 20th-century European art; 15th to 20th-century graphics; ceramics; small sculpture; photography; works on paper.
Major Exhibits: The Art of Warner Bros. Cartoons (T), 12/12/09-2/21/10; Woodcuts in Modern China (T), 1/23/10-4/18/10; West Michigan Area Show, 4/10/10-5/30/10; On Paper: The Lincoln Center/List Art Collection (T), 6/12/10-8/14/10.
Research Fields: fine arts.
Facilities: 10,000-vol. library of books & periodicals. Works by Michigan artists & museum-related items for sale.
Activities: guided tours; lectures; films; art fair; docent program; formally organized education program for children & adults; school outreach program; bus trips.
Publications: quarterly newsletter; biennial report; exhibition catalogues; program brochures.
Hours & Admission Prices: Tues.-Sat. 10-5, Sun. 12-5. No charge. Closed major holidays. ♿
Attendance: 109,000 (accurate)
Membership: Individual $40; Family $70; Sustaining $100; Donor $150; Patron $250; Benefactor $500; Director's Circle: Founder $1,000-$2,499; Leader $2,500-$4,999; Visionary $5,000 & up.

KALAMAZOO NATURE CENTER, INC., 7000 N. Westnedge Ave., Kalamazoo, MI 49009-6309. Tel.: 269-381-1574. Fax: 269-381-2557.
E-mail: lpanich@naturecenter.org
Web Site: www.naturecenter.org
Founded: 1960.
Congressional District: 3
Key Personnel: C.E.O. & Pres., Willard M. Rose, Ph.D.; Dir. Finance, Sue Sobeck; Dir. Camps, Daniel Keto; Dir. Exhibits & Public Programs, Kara Haas; Dir. School Programs, Sarah Hopkins; Vice Pres. Devel., Michelle Karpinski; Vice Pres. Offsite Programs, Sarah Reding; Museum Shop Mgr., Rose Norwood.
Personnel Profile: Full-Time Paid 27; Part-Time Paid 71; Part-Time Volunteers 250; Interns 3.
Governing Authority: nonprofit organization. Tax-exempt: 501(c)(3).
Nature Center.
Collections: mammal; avian; botanical; rock; insect; farm implements; Indian arrowheads. Historic Buildings: 1858 restored Greek Revival homestead; 1820 log cabin & farmstead; free-flying butterfly house.
Research Fields: ornithology; ecology; human environment.
Facilities: community garden; 160-seat auditorium; self-guiding nature trails. Books, educational materials & gifts for sale.
Activities: guided tours; lectures; films; gallery talks; formally organized education programs for children, adults, undergraduate & graduate students; preschool program; wild animal care & rehabilitation program; avian research; living history programs; simple farm technology program; docent program or council; permanent & temporary exhibitions; ecotour program; wildlife viewing room. Museum Sponsors: classes for handicapped; inner-city programs; summer camp; off-site educational programs that travel to schools and other community organizations, traveling art exhibits; special festivals and events; coordinates program to place interpreters in Michigan State Parks.
Publications: bimonthly periodical, Nature Center News; wild animal rehabilitation manual; The Atlas of Breeding Birds of Michigan; occasional publications, Research Publications, Special Publications, Limited Edition

Prints, The Birds of Michigan, Glimpsing the Whole: The Kalamazoo Nature Center Story; Of Woods and Other Things, Essays; essays, Ramblings, Reflections on Nature.
Hours & Admission Prices: Mon.-Sat. 9-5, Sun. 1-5. Adults $6, senior citizens & students $5, children 4-13 $4; discounts to AAM & AAA members; members & children 3 & under no charge. Closed New Year's Day; Thanksgiving; Christmas Eve & Day. ♿
Attendance: 265,995 (accurate)

* **KALAMAZOO VALLEY MUSEUM, (M),** 230 N. Rose St., Kalamazoo, MI 49007-5803. Mailing Address: P.O. Box 4070, Kalamazoo, MI 49003-4070. Tel.: 269-373-7990. Fax: 269-373-7997.
E-mail: rnorris@kvcc.edu
Web Site: www.kalamazoomuseum.org
Founded: 1927.
Congressional District: 3
Key Personnel: Dir., Dr. Patrick Norris; Operations Mgr., Gina Fischer; Special Events Coord., Jen Austin; Cur. Research, Thomas A. Dietz; Asst. Dir. Program Svcs., Elspeth Inglis; Exhibits Coord., Ron Cleveland; Planetarium Coord., Eric Schreur; Asst. Dir. Collections Svcs., Paula Metzner; Programs Coord., Annette Hoppenworth; Group Reservations Coord., Elizabeth Barker; Flight Dir., Challenger Center, Kathy Godin; Planning Asst., Kari Benjamin; Interpretation Coord., Donna Odom; Design Asst., Megan Burtzloff.
Personnel Profile: Full-Time Paid 13; Part-Time Paid 20; Part-Time Volunteers 150; Interns 4.
Governing Authority: college. Parent Institution: Kalamazoo Valley Community College. Tax-exempt.
Participatory Museum: history, science & technology.
Collections: history; science; technology; decorative arts; ethnology; photography; manuscript collections.
Major Exhibits: Genome: The Secret of How Life Works (T), 11/09-1/10/10; Spirit of the Mask (T), 11/09-2/14/10; Playing With Time (T), 11/09-5/10; Peanuts at Bat (T), 3/10-5/1/10; Storytelling Through the Mail: Tell Tale Postcards (T), 5/14/10-9/26/10; Out of This World: Extraordinary Costumes from Film & TV (T), 6/13/10-9/12/10; Race (T), 10/2/10-1/2/11; Wing Young Huie (T), 10/2/10-1/2/11.
Research Fields: history, science & technology related to collections & south-west Michigan.
Facilities: 60,000 sq. ft. exhibit space; Digistar planetarium; high definition video theater; learning center.
Activities: permanent & temporary exhibitions; interpretive programs for families; Challenger Learning Center space missions; preschool classes; school programs; High Definition Video Programs; Classic Movies & Digistar Planetarium programs.
Publications: seasonal calendar; brochures; quarterly Museography magazine.
Hours & Admission Prices: Mon.-Sat. 9-5, Sun. & holidays 1-5. No charge; donations accepted. Closed Easter; Thanksgiving; Christmas Eve & Day. ♿
Attendance: 130,133 (accurate)

WESTERN MICHIGAN UNIVERSITY RICHMOND CENTER FOR VISUAL ARTS - GWEN FROSTIC SCHOOL OF ART, 1903 W. Michigan Ave., Kalamazoo, MI 49008-5200. Tel.: 269-387-2455. Fax: 269-387-2477.
E-mail: donald.desmett@wmich.edu
Founded: 2007.
Congressional District: 3
Key Personnel: C.E.O. College of Fine Arts, Dean Margaret Merrion; Dir. School of Art, Dr. Joyce Kubiski; Dir. Exhibitions, Don Desmett; Cur. University Art Collection, Milinda Bagnall.
Personnel Profile: Full-Time Paid 32; Part-Time Paid 12; Part-Time Volunteers 25; Interns 2.
Governing Authority: university. Parent Institution: Western Michigan University. Tax-exempt.
Art Galleries.
Collections: prints including intaglio, relief, litho, screenprint, European & American contemporary artists, as well as by younger avant-garde artists; 19th & 20th-century American & European fine & decorative arts.
Facilities: classrooms.
Activities: guided tours; lectures; films; gallery talks; formally organized educational programs for graduate & undergraduate students; temporary, traveling & loan exhibitions; visiting artists program; Sculpture Tour.
Publications: essays, Sculptural Concepts; Charismatic Abstraction; David Henderson; Man O' War.
Hours & Admission Prices: May-July Mon.-Fri. 10-5; Sept.-April Mon.-Thurs. 10-6, Fri. 10-9, Sat. 12-6. No charge; donations accepted. ♿
Attendance: 18,000 (accurate)
Membership: Friends $15-$1,000.

Kaleva

BOTTLE HOUSE MUSEUM, 14551 Wuoksi Ave., Kaleva, MI 49645-9341. Tel.: 231-362-2080.
Founded: 1983.
Governing Authority: Tax-exempt.
Historic House: housed in a home built in 1941 with over 60,000 soft drink bottles.
Collections: local history & culture; lumbering; farming; homemaking; office machines; railroad; period furnishings; photographs; Makinen tackle.
Hours & Admission Prices: Call for hours. Suggested Donation: adults $2.

KALEVA TRAIN DEPOT MUSEUM, Walta St., Kaleva, MI 49645. Mailing Address: P.O. Box 252, Kaleva, MI 49645. Tel.: 231-362-3481 & 2080.
Governing Authority: Parent Institution: Kaleva Historical Society. Tax-exempt.
Historic Building: housed in a former railroad depot; built in 1908.
Collections: local history & culture; railroad artifacts; scale model of depot with train; photographs; restored switch engine on outdoor track.
Hours & Admission Prices: Memorial Day to Oct. Sat. 12-4. No charge; donations accepted.
Membership: Individual $15.

Lake Linden

HOUGHTON COUNTY HISTORICAL MUSEUM SOCIETY, 53102 Hwy. M-26, Lake Linden, MI 49945. Mailing Address: P.O. Box 127, Lake Linden, MI 49945-0127. Tel.: 906-296-4121. Fax: 906-296-8006.
E-mail: president@houghtonhistory.org
Web Site: www.houghtonhistory.org
Founded: 1961.
Congressional District: 1
Key Personnel: Pres. (V), Gerald Perreault; Treas., Tony Oganich.
Personnel Profile: Full-Time Volunteers 1; Part-Time Volunteers 20.
Governing Authority: nonprofit organization. Subsidiary Institution: Copper Country Railroad. Tax-exempt: 170(b)(1)(A).
History Museum: located on Calumet & Hecla Millsite.
Collections: copper country lithographs; local history; steam engine; wagons. Historic Buildings: fire station; church; railroad depot; schoolhouse; mining company garage; log cabin.
Research Fields: local history.
Facilities: 1,000-vol. library of local history available for use under supervision on premises.
Activities: guided tours; lectures; operates John H. Forster press; education programs for adults.
Publications: newsletter; annual report; books on local history.
Hours & Admission Prices: Office: Mon.-Fri. 10-12. Museum: Mon.-Sat. 10-4, Sun. 12-4. Adults $5, seniors & students 6-16 $3. Train Rides: adults $4, students 6-16 & seniors $3. ♿
Attendance: 10,000 (estimated)
Membership: Annual $20; Family $35; Life $300.

Lansing

CARL G. FENNER NATURE CENTER, 2020 E. Mt. Hope Rd., Lansing, MI 48910-1905. Tel.: 517-483-4224. Fax: 517-377-0012. TDD: 517-483-4479.
E-mail: cbratton@ci.lansing.mi.us
Founded: 1959.
Key Personnel: Naturalist, Clara Ann Bratton; Museum Shop Buyer, Leora Laylin.
Personnel Profile: Part-Time Paid 4; Part-Time Volunteers 50.
Governing Authority: municipal. Parent Institution: Lansing Parks & Recreation Dept. Subsidiary Institution: Friends of Fenner Nature Center. Tax-exempt.
Natural History Museum.
Collections: natural history; hands-on exhibits.
Research Fields: birds; native plants; interpretive techniques.
Facilities: 2,400-vol. library of natural history books for adults & children; reading room; classrooms; nature center; picnic site. Museum-related items for sale.
Activities: guided tours; family programs. Museum Sponsors: Fall Apple Butter Festival; Spring Maple Syrup Festival; children's nature camp in summer.
Publications: Friends of Fenner Newsletter.
Hours & Admission Prices: Grounds: daily 8am-dark. Nature Science Building: April-Oct. Tues.-Fri. 10-4, Sat.-Sun. 1-5; Nov.-March Tues.-Fri. 10-4, Sun. 12-4; school groups by appointment. Fees for guided tours & special programs. ♿
Attendance: 40,000 (estimated)
Membership: Individual $15; Family $20.

IMPRESSION 5 SCIENCE CENTER, 200 Museum Dr., Lansing, MI 48933-1914. Tel.: 517-485-8116, ext. 43. Fax: 517-485-8125.
E-mail: larson@impression.org
Web Site: www.impression5.org
Founded: 1972.
Congressional District: 8
Key Personnel: Exec. Dir., Erik D. Larson; Bd. Pres., John LeFevre; Exhibits Officer, Cyrus Miller; Finance Officer, Sandra Dunnebache; Dir. Membership, Marion Contompasis; Dir. Education, Micaela Blazer.
Personnel Profile: Full-Time Paid 8; Part-Time Paid 6; Part-Time Volunteers 105.
Governing Authority: nonprofit organization. Tax-exempt: 501(c)(3) & 170(b)(1)(A).
Interactive Hands-On Learning Center.
Collections: science & technology.
Research Fields: education; exhibit design.
Facilities: energy theatre. Museum-related items for sale.
Activities: formally organized education programs for students and families; permanent & traveling science exhibits; workshops; camp-ins; summer camp; teacher workshops.
Publications: museum newsletter.
Hours & Admission Prices: Mon.-Thurs. 10-5, Fri.-Sat. 10-7, Sun. 12-5. Adults & students $5, seniors 62 & over $4.50; discounts to groups with advance reservation & AAA members; ASTC members, members, children 2 & under no charge. Closed New Year's Day; Easter; Memorial Day; Independence Day; Thanksgiving; Christmas Eve & Day. ♿
Attendance: 75,161 (estimated)
Membership: Individual $40; Grandparent $50; Family $55; Family Plus $125; Supporting $250.

LANSING ART GALLERY, 113 S. Washington Square, Lansing, MI 48933-1703. Tel.: 517-374-6400. Fax: 517-374-6385.
E-mail: lansingartgallery@yahoo.com
Web Site: lansingartgallery.org
Founded: 1965.
Congressional District: 6
Key Personnel: C.E.O. & Exec. Dir., Catherine Babcock; Pres., Daniel Warmels; Gallery Mgr., Barb Whitney.
Personnel Profile: Full-Time Paid 2; Part-Time Paid 4; Part-Time Volunteers 50; Interns 4.
Governing Authority: nonprofit organization. Tax-exempt.
Art Gallery.
Collections: works by Michigan artists.
Facilities: Gift items for sale.
Activities: monthly changing exhibitions & competitions; education outreach; fundraisers & special events; lectures & workshops. Museum Sponsors: Art Scholarship Alert High School Art Competition; Holiday Art Market.
Publications: quarterly newsletter, Image; exhibition announcements.
Hours & Admission Prices: Tues.-Fri. 10-4, Sat. & 1st Sun. of month 1-4. No charge; donations accepted. ♿
Attendance: 25,000 (estimated)
Membership: Youth $25; Artist $35; Individual $50; Family $65; Supporting $100-$249; Picasso Gallery $250-$499; da Vinci Gallery $500-$999; Rembrant Gallery $1,000-$2,499; Masterpiece Gallery $2,500 & up.

* **MICHIGAN HISTORICAL MUSEUM, MICHIGAN HISTORICAL CENTER, (M),** 702 W. Kalamazoo, Lansing, MI 48909-8240. Mailing Address: P.O. Box 30740, Lansing, MI 48909-8240. Tel.: 517-373-3559. Fax: 517-241-4738. TDD: 1-800-827-7007.
E-mail: kwiatkowskip@michigan.gov
Web Site: www.michigan.gov/dnr/0,1607,7-153-54463---,00.html
Founded: 1879.
Congressional District: 6
Key Personnel: C.E.O., Sandra S. Clark; Dir. Museums, Phillip C. Kwiatkowski; Upper Peninsula Mgr., Tom Friggens; Collections & Exhibits Coord., Eve Weipert; Mktg. & Public Rels., Chris Dancisak; Museum Shop Mgr., Mary Toshach; Education Mgr., Tami Averill; Visitor Svcs., Alexandra Raven.
Personnel Profile: Full-Time Paid 29; Part-Time Paid 18; Part-Time Volunteers 200; Interns 21.
Governing Authority: state. Parent Institution: Michigan Historical Center. Branch Museums: 1884 Mann House; Michigan Iron Industry Museum, Negaunee. Historic Sites: Father Marquette Memorial, Straits State Park, St. Ignace; Fayette Townsite & State Park, Fayette; Fort Wilkins Historic Complex & State Park, Copper Harbor; Hartwick Pines Lumbering Museum & State Park, Grayling; Sanilac Petroglyphs, Sanilac Petroglyphs State Park, Cass City; The Walker Tavern, Cambridge Historic Park, Cambridge Junction; Civilian Conservation Corps. Museum, Higgins Lake State Park; Tawas Lighthouse. Tax-exempt: 170(c)(1).
History Museum.
Collections: history of Michigan & Northwest Territory; prehistoric & aboriginal history; Michigan settlement; industry; ethnic influences; technology; transportation; agriculture; domestic life; occupational skills; decorative arts; folklore; ceramics; textiles; 20th-century artifacts.
Activities: guided & self-guided tours; formally organized education programs for children; inter-museum loan, permanent, temporary & traveling exhibitions; seminars; workshops.
Publications: bimonthly magazine, Michigan History; books & pamphlets related to the history of Michigan & the old Northwest Territory.
Hours & Admission Prices: Mon.-Fri. 9-4:30, Sat. 10-4, Sun. 1-5. No charge; donations accepted. Field Museums & Historic Sites: call for information. Closed New Year's Day; Christmas; state holidays. ♿
Attendance: 164,154 (accurate)
Membership: Friends of Michigan History: Basic $40; Contributing $60; Sponsoring $100; Other $101 & up.

MICHIGAN MUSEUM OF SURVEYING, 220 Museum Dr., Lansing, MI 48933-1905. Tel.: 517-484-6605. Fax: 517-484-3711.
E-mail: museumofsurvey@acd.net
Web Site: www.mimuseumofsurveying.org
Founded: 1989.
Congressional District: 8
Key Personnel: C.E.O. & Dir., Lisa D. Jacobs; Pres. (V), Gilbert Bonno.
Personnel Profile: Part-Time Paid 1.
Governing Authority: private; nonprofit organization. Tax-exempt: 501(c)(3).
Surveying History Museum.
Collections: land surveying history & instruments.
Facilities: 340-vol. library available to the public; 2,000 sq. ft. exhibit space.
Activities: temporary exhibitions; reenactment group performs at area festivals & events. Annual Event: Golf Outing.
Publications: semi-annual newsletter; annual magazine.
Hours & Admission Prices: Mon.-Fri. 9-4. No charge; donations accepted. Closed major holidays.
Attendance: 1,781 (accurate)
Membership: Senior & Student $20; Individual $40; Family $75; Deputy Surveyor $150.

MICHIGAN WOMEN'S HISTORICAL CENTER & HALL OF FAME, 213 W. Main St., Lansing, MI 48933-2315. Tel.: 517-484-1880. Fax: 517-372-0170.
E-mail: michiganwomen@sbcglobal.net
Web Site: www.michiganwomenshalloffame.org
Key Personnel: Exec. Dir., Gladys Beckwith, Ph.D.
Women's History Museum & Hall of Fame.
Collections: Michigan women's history; personal artifacts; paintings; portraits; Hall of Fame inductees.
Hours & Admission Prices: Wed.-Fri. 12-5, Sat. 12-4, Sun. 2-4; groups by appointment. Adults $2.50, seniors $2, students 5-18 $1. Closed major holidays.

POTTER PARK ZOO, 1301 S. Pennsylvania Ave., Lansing, MI 48912-1646. Tel.: 517-483-4222. Fax: 517-483-6065.
E-mail: zoocontact@ingham.org
Web Site: www.potterparkzoo.org
Founded: 1917.
Key Personnel: Cur., Gerald Brady; Gift Shop Mgr., Richard Parker.
Personnel Profile: Full-Time Paid 18; Part-Time Paid 10; Part-Time Volunteers 80; Interns 4.
Governing Authority: municipal government. Branch Institution: Potter Park Zoological Society. Tax-exempt: 501(c)(3).
Zoo.
Collections: over 400 animals from around the world.
Research Fields: dietary of certain primate species.
Facilities: 150-vol. library of educational resource materials; zoological park. Gift items for sale.
Activities: arts festivals; docent program; films; formal education programs; guided tours; lectures; participatory & traveling exhibitions; special events. Exploration & Discovery Center available to rent.
Publications: bimonthly newsletter, Potter Park Zoological Society Newsletter.
Hours & Admission Prices: April-Oct. daily 9-6; Nov.-March daily 10-4. Residents: adults $4, senior citizens 60 & over $3, children 3-16 $2; members & children under 3 no charge. Non-Resident: adults $10, senior citizens 60 & up $3, children 3-16 $2; members & children under 3 no charge. ♿
Attendance: 380,000
Membership: Senior $15; Individual $25; Family $40; Director Club $100.

R.E. OLDS TRANSPORTATION MUSEUM, 240 Museum Dr., Lansing, MI 48933-1905. Tel.: 517-372-0529. Fax: 517-372-2901.
E-mail: autos@reoldsmuseum.org

Web Site: reoldsmuseum.org
Founded: 1981.
Congressional District: 6
Key Personnel: Chm. (V), Wayne Burrell; Exec. Dir., Deborah Horstik.
Personnel Profile: Full-Time Paid 1; Part-Time Paid 2; Part-Time Volunteers 40.
Governing Authority: bd. of trustees. Parent Institution: R.E. Olds Museum Association, Inc. Tax-exempt: 501(c)(3).
Transportation Museum.
Collections: REO Speedwagons; wheels; aviation display; photos; 50 vehicles; memorabilia in showcases; 1897 Oldsmobile; two rocket cars; 1901 Curved Dash Olds; license plates.
Research Fields: Lansing-built transportation; R.E. Olds.
Facilities: meeting rooms. Books & gift items for sale.
Activities: guided tours; docent program; films. Participates in: Be A Tourist in Your Own Town; Silver Bells in the City. Museum Sponsors: The Car Capital Celebration in August.
Publications: brochures; pamphlets; quarterly newsletter.
Hours & Admission Prices: April-Oct. Tues.-Sat. 10-5, Sun. 12-5; Nov.-March Tues.-Sat. 10-5. Family of 5 $10, adults $5, senior citizens & students $3; discounts for groups; children under 5 & members no charge. Closed major holidays. ♿
Attendance: 15,000 (estimated)
Membership: Student & Senior Citizen $15; Individual $25; Family $35; Corporate $100; Life $1,000.

WOLDUMAR NATURE CENTER, 5739 Old Lansing Rd., Lansing, MI 48917-8503. Tel.: 517-322-0030. Fax: 517-322-9394.
E-mail: lori@woldumar.org
Web Site: www.woldumar.org
Founded: 1966.
Congressional District: 56
Key Personnel: Exec. Dir., Lori McSweeney; Bd. Chm., Tony Bauer.
Personnel Profile: Full-Time Paid 2; Part-Time Paid 5; Part-Time Volunteers 90; Interns 1.
Governing Authority: nonprofit organization. Parent Institution: Woldumar Nature Association. Tax-exempt: 501(c)(3).
Nature Center Conservation Area & Historic Building.
Collections: bird & mammal live mounts & study skins; early pioneer farm implements & tools. Historic Building: 1860 log house, boyhood home of Darius Moon, architect.
Facilities: 169-seat auditorium; educational facilities; visitors center. Rocks, minerals & other museum-related items for sale.
Activities: guided tours; films; organized education programs for children & adults. Museum Sponsors: Pioneer; American Heritage Festival; Wildflower Weekend; Chili Winter Evening.
Publications: bimonthly newsletter, Woldumar News.
Hours & Admission Prices: Office & Visitors Center: Mon.-Sat. 10-5. Trails: dawn-dark. Donation: $1 per person; discounts to ANCA members & groups; members no charge. Closed New Year's Day; Easter; Memorial Day; Independence Day; Labor Day; Thanksgiving; Christmas. ♿
Attendance: 40,000 (estimated)
Membership: Annual $42.

Leland

LEELANAU HISTORICAL MUSEUM, 203 E. Cedar St., Leland, MI 49654-5015. Mailing Address: P.O. Box 246, Leland, MI 49654-0246. Tel.: 231-256-7475. Fax: 231-256-7650.
E-mail: info@leelanauhistory.org
Web Site: www.leelanauhistory.org
Founded: 1957.
Congressional District: 1
Key Personnel: Dir., M. Egan McGlynn; Pres. (V), Francie Gits; Vice Pres., Bob Brown; Treas., Donna Herman; Sec., Molly Crimmins.
Personnel Profile: Full-Time Paid 1; Full-Time Volunteers 20; Part-Time Paid 2.
Governing Authority: nonprofit organization. Parent Institution: Leelanau Historical Society, Inc. Tax-exempt: 501(c)(3).
Local History Museum.
Collections: traditional handicrafts; photographs; manuscripts; 19th-century period artifacts; local traditional Odawa arts.
Research Fields: history; genealogy; traditional & folk arts; Native American history.
Facilities: 4,000 sq. ft. exhibit space; archives.
Activities: guided tours; school & adult education programs; permanent & temporary exhibits; special activities.
Publications: quarterly newsletter.
Hours & Admission Prices: Wed.-Fri. 10-4, Sat. 10-3. No charge; donations accepted. ♿
Attendance: 5,000 (estimated)
Membership: $50; $100; $250; $500; $1,000.

Lincoln Park

LINCOLN PARK HISTORICAL MUSEUM, 1335 Southfield Rd., Lincoln Park, MI 48146-2370. Tel.: 313-386-3137.
Founded: 1972.
Congressional District: 13
Key Personnel: Dir., Muriel Lobb; Pres. (V), Lucille Stroh; Museum Mgr., Kathy Dunlop; Cur., Jeff Day; Librarian, Mary Cisek.
Personnel Profile: Part-Time Volunteers 25.
Governing Authority: municipal. Parent Institution: City of Lincoln Park. Subsidiary Institution: Lincoln Park Historical Commission. Tax-exempt.
Local & Regional History Museum.
Collections: history of Ecorse Township & City of Lincoln Park.
Major Exhibits: Boy Scout Centennial-Local Emphasis, Winter 2010.
Research Fields: local history from 1700-2010 & story of Lincoln Park People.
Facilities: 2,500-vol. library; 800 newspapers from the time the village was established available for inter-library loan.
Activities: arts & crafts; lecture series. Museum Sponsors: special commemorative events & annual member meeting and dinner.
Publications: quarterly newsletter, Images of America Series: Lincoln Park.
Hours & Admission Prices: Tues.-Thurs. 1-5; other times by appointment. No charge; donations accepted. Closed New Year's Day; Martin Luther King Jr. Day; Easter; Memorial Day; Independence Day; Thanksgiving; Christmas. ♿
Attendance: 6,500 (estimated)
Membership: Student $5; Individual $10; Family $15; Patron $25; Life $200.

Lowell

LOWELL AREA HISTORICAL MUSEUM, (M), 325 W. Main St., Lowell, MI 49331-1609. Mailing Address: P.O. Box 81, Lowell, MI 49331-0081. Tel.: 616-897-7688. Fax: 616-897-7688.
Web Site: lowellmuseum.org
Founded: 1989.
Congressional District: 3
Key Personnel: C.E.O. & Dir., Pat Allchin; Pres., James M. Doyle; Education, Luanne Kaeb; Treas., Cathy Haefner.
Personnel Profile: Part-Time Paid 3; Part-Time Volunteers 40.
Governing Authority: private; nonprofit organization. Tax-exempt: 501(c)(3).
History Museum: listed on the National Register of Historic Places.
Collections: area history from early 1800s to present.
Research Fields: military & oral histories; local residents & obituaries.
Facilities: 750-vol. library; 2,244 sq. ft. exhibit space. Museum-related items for sale.
Activities: docent program; education programs; children's activity workshops; guided tours; lectures; participatory, temporary & traveling exhibitions; military history panels; grade school group tours; oral history panels.
Publications: quarterly newsletter, Lowell Area Historical Museum Newsletter; Where the Rivers Meet-A Pictorial Journey Through Historic Lowell, Michigan.
Hours & Admission Prices: Tues. & Sat.-Sun. 1-4, Thurs. 1-8. Adults $3, students & children $1.50; discounts to groups; members no charge. Closed holidays. ♿
Attendance: 20,000 (accurate)
Membership: Individual $15; Family $25; Business & Donor $50.

Ludington

MASON COUNTY HISTORICAL SOCIETY/HISTORIC WHITE PINE VILLAGE, 1687 S. Lakeshore Dr., Ludington, MI 49431-8316. Tel.: 231-843-4808. Fax: 231-843-7089.
E-mail: info@historicwhitepinevillage.org
Web Site: www.historicwhitepinevillage.org
Founded: 1937.
Congressional District: 9
Key Personnel: Chief Exec. Dir., Ronald M. Wood; Pres. Bd. (V), Jim Newkirk; Museum Shop Mgr., Marie Nelsen.
Personnel Profile: Full-Time Paid 2; Part-Time Paid 4; Part-Time Volunteers 400.
Governing Authority: nonprofit organization. Parent Institution: Mason County Historical Society, Inc., 1687 S. Lakeshore Dr., Ludington 49431. Tax-exempt.
Local History Museum & Reconstructed Historical Village.
Collections: lumber tools; farm tools; Civil War artifacts; textiles; clothing & laces; bibles; hymn books; school textbooks; maps; pattern glass; china; crockery; bottles; silver; marine exhibit; photographs; original paintings in oils; lithographs; prints; model trainferries; sailing vessels; folk art; housewares; dolls; toys. Historic Buildings: over 25 buildings including Rose Hawley Museum, Abe Nelson Lumbering Museum; Scottville Clown

Band's Museum of Music; 1890 one-room school; frame courthouse; post office; farmhouse; hardware store; trapper's cabin; blacksmith shop; chapel; general store; Sugar House; Sports Hall of Fame; Maritime Museum; sawmill.
Research Fields: local history; genealogy; industrial development; Great Lakes shipping; lumbering; agriculture.
Facilities: 4,000-vol. research library of books, archives & genealogy references for research.
Activities: self-guided tours; permanent & temporary exhibits; special events; farm tool skills learning center; lumbering; farmstead. Museum Sponsors: Old Time Baseball matches.
Publications: newsletter, History Happening.
Hours & Admission Prices: mid-April to May & Sept. to mid-Oct. Tues.-Sat. 10-5; Memorial Day to Labor Day Tues.-Sat. 10-5, Sun. 1-5; call for additional hours. Families $25, adults $9, children 6-17 $6; discounts to groups, AAA members, seniors & Great Lakes Co-op cardholders; children 5 & under and MCHS members no charge. Additional charge for special events & food events. ♿
Attendance: 18,000 (accurate)
Membership: Individual $40; Family $60; Supporter $100; Sponsor $250; Patron $500; Benefactor $1,000.

Mackinac Island

MACKINAC STATE HISTORIC PARKS-FORT MACKINAC & MACKINAC ISLAND STATE PARK, 7029 Huron Rd., Mackinac Island, MI 49757. Mailing Address: P.O. Box 873, Mackinaw City, MI 49701-0873. Tel.: 906-847-3328 (Summer); 231-436-4100 (Winter). Fax: 231-436-4210.
E-mail: mackinacparks@michigan.gov
Web Site: www.mackinacparks.com
Founded: 1895.
Congressional District: 1
Key Personnel: Dir., Phil Porter; Chm. (V), Frank Kelley; Park Mgr., Daniel G. Cook; Chief Cur., Steven C. Brisson; Cur. Archaeology, Lynn Evans; Cur. Natural History, Jeffrey A. Dykehouse; Cur. Education, Katherine Cederholm; Public Rels. & Mktg. Officer, Jolene Priest; Registrar, Brian Jaeschke; Conservator, Jennifer Lis; Grant Writer & Membership, Diane A. Dombroski; Chief Devel., Gregory J. Hokans; Group Sales Coord., Scott Witsman; Chief Finance & Accounting, Lana L. Cotton; Exhibit Designer, David A. Kronberg; Museum Shop Mgr., Ronald L. Crandell; Human Resources Coord., Kenneth Fegan.
Personnel Profile: Full-Time Paid 43; Part-Time Paid 101; Part-Time Volunteers 290; Interns 4.
Governing Authority: state; nonprofit. Parent Institution: Mackinac Island State Park Commission. Subsidiary Institution: Mackinac Art Museum. Tax-exempt.
Historic Site: 1780-1895 Fort Mackinac.
Collections: archaeology; 19th-century furnishings; manuscripts; photographs; military items; blacksmithing items; Indian items; carriages; 1814 battlefield; military cemetery. Historic Buildings: 1780 Biddle house; 1838 Indian dormitory; 1869 renovated Benjamin blacksmith shop; 1829 Mission church; 1780 McGulpin house; 1954 renovated Beaumont Memorial; 14 restored original structures.
Facilities: visitor center; theater; restaurant; heritage & research facility; 1,773 acre park includes 70.5 miles of signed roads & trails. Site-related items, publications & reproductions for sale.
Activities: guided tours; lectures; films; interpretive exhibitions; organized education programs; docent program; musket & cannon-firing demonstrations; craft demonstrations; dramatic reenactments of historic events; research.
Publications: 70 publications in print. Catalog available.
Hours & Admission Prices: Mackinac Island State Park: daily. No charge. Fort Mackinac: mid-June to Labor Day daily 9:30-6; Spring & Fall call for reduced hours. Adults $10.50, children 6-17 $6.50; discounts to AAM & ICOM members; members & children 5 & under no charge. ♿
Attendance: 202,071 (accurate)
Membership: Mackinac Heritage $56; Friends $65; Voyageur $85; Sentinel $175; Explorer $400; Commandant's Circle $600; Steward $1,000; Guardian $2,500.

STUART HOUSE CITY MUSEUM, Market St., Mackinac Island, MI 49757-0906. Mailing Address: P.O. Box 906, Mackinac Island, MI 49757-0906. Tel.: 906-847-3553.
Founded: 1930.
Congressional District: 1
Key Personnel: Dir., Armand Horn; Cur. Collections, Daniel Seeley.
Personnel Profile: Part-Time Paid 3; Part-Time Volunteers 3.
Governing Authority: municipal.
Historic House Museum: c.1817 home of American Fur Company resident Mgr. Robert Stuart.
Collections: records of the American Fur Co.'s Fur Post; natural history; Indian artifacts; furs & pelts; furnished rooms typical of the 1800s; trade items; tools; War of 1812 items.
Activities: self-guided tours; permanent exhibitions.
Publications: brochure.
Hours & Admission Prices: Call for hours. No charge; donations accepted.

Mackinaw City

*** MACKINAC ISLAND STATE PARK COMMISSION-MACKINAC STATE HISTORIC PARKS, (M),** 207 W. Sinclair Ave., Mackinaw City, MI 49701-9635. Mailing Address: P.O. Box 873, Mackinaw City, MI 49701-0873. Tel.: 231-436-4100; 906-847-3328. Fax: 231-436-4210; 906-847-3815.
E-mail: mackinacparks@michigan.gov
Web Site: www.mackinacparks.com
Founded: 1895.
Congressional District: 1
Key Personnel: Dir., Phil Porter; Commission Chm. (V), Frank Kelley; Chief Cur., Steven Brisson; Cur. Education, Katherine Cedarholm; Chief Devel. & Mktg., Gregory J. Hokans; Cur. Archaeology, Lynn Evans; Registrar, Brian Jaeschke; Conservator, Jennifer Lis; Michilimackinac Interpretation Supvr., Kate Arbogast; Cur. Natural History, Jeffrey A. Dykehouse; Public Rels. & Mktg. Officer, Jolene Priest; Group Sales Coord., Scott Witsman; Chief Finance & Accounting, Lana L. Cotton; Museum Shop Mgr., Ronald L. Crandell; Grant Writer & Membership, Diane A. Dombroski; Exhibit Designer, David A. Kronberg; Support Svcs. Asst., Sheryl Baxter; Human Resources Coord., Kenneth Fegan.
Personnel Profile: Full-Time Paid 43; Part-Time Paid 101; Part-Time Volunteers 290; Interns 4.
Governing Authority: state. Affiliated with State of Michigan, Department of History, Arts and Libraries, Box 30028, Lansing, MI 48909. Subsidiary Institutions: Mackinac State Historic Parks: Fort Mackinac; Mackinac Island State Park; Colonial Michilimackinac; Historic Mill Creek; Beaumont Museum; Biddle House; Mission Church; Old Mackinac Point Lighthouse; Mackinac Art Museum. Tax-exempt.
Regional History Museum.
Collections: military & social history of the Straits of Mackinac region; archaeological artifacts from site of Fort Mackinac, Colonial Michilimackinac & Mill Creek; Great Lakes maritime materials; Native American artifacts; 110 historic buildings.
Research Fields: 18th-century fur trade in the Great Lakes region; American Indian-White relations; 17th-19th centuries; historical archaeology; British & American military in Great Lakes region, 1760-1895; French Colonial history in Great Lakes region; tourism in Upper Great Lakes, 1890s-present.
Facilities: 3,000-vol. library of books & periodicals including 250 reels of microfilm available for use by appointment; theater; restaurant; nature trails; concessions.
Activities: permanent & temporary exhibits; guided & self-guided tours; school outreach program; lectures; films; TV programs; seminars; craft demonstrations; historic reenactments; interpretive programs for children & adults.
Publications: 70 publications in print. Catalog available.
Hours & Admission Prices: Mackinac Island State Park: daily. Historic Sites: early May to mid-Oct. daily. Park: no charge. Historic Sites: adults $6-$10.50. ♿
Attendance: 366,952 (accurate)
Membership: Mackinac Heritage $56; Friends $65; Voyageur $85; Sentinel $175; Explorer $400; Commandant's Circle $600; Steward $1,000; Guardian $2,500.

MACKINAC STATE HISTORIC PARKS-COLONIAL MICHILIMACKINAC & OLD MACKINAC POINT LIGHTHOUSE, 102 W. Straits Ave., Mackinaw City, MI 49701. Mailing Address: Box 873, Mackinaw City, MI 49701-0873. Tel.: 231-436-4100. Fax: 231-436-4210.
E-mail: mackinacparks@michigan.gov
Web Site: www.mackinacparks.com
Founded: 1909.
Congressional District: 1
Key Personnel: Dir., Phil Porter; Park Supvr., Michael Sutton; Commission Chm. (V), Frank Kelley; Chief Cur., Steven C. Brisson; Cur. Education, Katherine Cederholm; Chief Devel. & Mktg., Gregory J. Hokans; Conservator, Jennifer Lis; Registrar, Brian Jaeschke; Interpretation Supvr., Kate Arbogast; Public Rels. & Mktg. Officer, Jolene Priest; Cur. Archaeology, Lynn Evans; Cur. Natural History, Jeffrey A. Dykehouse; Groups Sales Coord., Scott Witsman; Chief Finance & Accounting, Lana L. Cotton; Grant Writer & Membership, Diane A. Dombroski; Exhibit Designer, David A. Kronberg; Museum Shop Mgr., Ronald L. Crandell; Human Resources Coord., Kenneth Fegan.
Personnel Profile: Full-Time Paid 43; Part-Time Paid 101; Part-Time Volunteers 290; Interns 4.
Governing Authority: state; nonprofit. Parent Institution: Mackinac Island State Park Commission. Tax-exempt.

History Museum: housed in reconstructed French & British military outpost & fur-trading village founded in 1715.
Collections: archaeological; military artifacts; 18th-century furnishings. Historic Structures: 1892 Old Mackinac Point Lighthouse; 1715-1780 Fort Michilimackinac & 16 reconstructed buildings.
Facilities: research library; visitor center; theater; food service; Peterson Archaeology & History Center. Museum-related items for sale.
Activities: guided tours; lectures; films; organized education programs; docent program; black-powder & craft demonstrations; continuing archaeological excavations.
Publications: 70 publications in print. Catalog available.
Hours & Admission Prices: June 15-Labor Day daily 9-6; Fall & Spring: call for reduced hours. Colonial Michilimackinac: adult $10.50, children 6-17 $6.50; discount to AAM & ICOM members; members & children under 5 no charge. Lighthouse: adult $6, children $4. ♿
Attendance: 113,330 (accurate)
Membership: Mackinac Heritage $56; Friends $65; Voyageur $85; Sentinel $175; Explorer $400; Commandant's Circle $600; Steward $1,000; Guardian $2,500.

MACKINAC STATE HISTORIC PARKS-HISTORIC MILL CREEK DISCOVERY PARK, 9001 U.S. 23 S., Mackinaw City, MI 49701. Mailing Address: Box 873, Mackinaw City, MI 49701-0873. Tel.: 231-436-4100. Fax: 231-436-4210.
E-mail: mackinacparks@michigan.gov
Web Site: www.mackinacparks.com
Founded: 1975.
Congressional District: 1
Key Personnel: Commission Chm., Frank Kelley; Dir., Phil Porter; Cur. Education, Katherine Cederholm; Chief Cur., Steven C. Brisson; Registrar, Brian Jaeschke; Conservator, Jennifer Lis; Chief Devel. & Mktg., Gregory J. Hokans; Cur. Natural History, Jeffrey A. Dykehouse; Cur. Archaeology, Lynn Evans; Public Rels. & Mktg. Officer, Jolene Priest; Group Sales Coord., Scott Witsman; Chief Finance & Accounting, Lana L. Cotton; Museum Shop Mgr., Ronald L. Crandell; Park Supvr., Michael Sutton; Human Resources Coord., Kenneth Fegan.
Personnel Profile: Full-Time Paid 43; Part-Time Paid 101; Part-Time Volunteers 290; Interns 4.
Governing Authority: state; nonprofit. Parent Institution: Mackinac Island State Park Commission. Tax-exempt: 501(c)(3).
History Site Museum: reconstructed 18th-century water-powered sawmill and support buildings.
Collections: archaeology; natural science; 18th-century technology; mill dam; 3 reconstructed historic buildings including 1790-1830 sawmill.
Facilities: visitor center; theater; cafeteria; nature center; nature trails; picnic area. Museum & nature related items for sale.
Activities: guided tours; lectures; films; organized education programs; craft demonstrations; forest demonstration areas; multi-media orientation program.
Publications: 70 publications in print. Catalog available.
Hours & Admission Prices: mid-June to Labor Day daily 9-5; Spring & fall: call for hours. Adults $8, children 6-17 $4.75; discounts to AAM & ICOM members; members & children under 6 no charge. ♿
Attendance: 51,551 (accurate)
Membership: Mackinac Heritage $56; Friends $65; Voyageur $85; Sentinel $175; Explorer $400; Commandant's Circle $600; Steward $1,000; Guardian $2,500.

Manistee

MANISTEE COUNTY HISTORICAL MUSEUM, 425 River St., Manistee, MI 49660-1522. Tel.: 231-723-5531.
Founded: 1953.
Key Personnel: Dir., Steve Harold.
Personnel Profile: Full-Time Paid 1; Part-Time Paid 3; Part-Time Volunteers 10.
Governing Authority: society. Tax-exempt: 501(c)(3).
History Museum: housed in 1883 A.H. Lyman Drug Company.
Collections: local history; logging & lumbering; railroads; Great Lakes shipping & passenger boats; costumes; dolls; Civil War artifacts; pioneer days; country store; Victorian period rooms; barber shop; early drug store; historical photos; Indian artifacts; glass; folk material. Historic Building: 1881 Holly Water Works, W. First St.
Research Fields: general local & state history; local genealogy; Lake Michigan Maritime History.
Facilities: 500-vol. library of history books & 10,000 1868-1920 historical photographs. Postcards & booklets for sale.
Activities: guided tours; lectures; education programs; permanent & temporary exhibitions; school visiting services; tours for the handicapped or other special groups.
Publications: Manistee museum log.
Hours & Admission Prices: Tues.-Sat. 10-5. Families $7, adults $3, students $1. Closed national holidays except Independence Day.
Attendance: 10,000 (estimated)
Membership: Single $10; Family $15; Contributing $25; Sustaining $50; Patron $75.

Manistique

SCHOOLCRAFT COUNTY HISTORICAL SOCIETY, Deer St., Pioneer Park, Manistique, MI 49854. Mailing Address: P.O. Box 284, Manistique, MI 49854-0284. Tel.: 906-341-5045.
Formerly: Imogene Herbert Historical Museum
Founded: 1963.
Congressional District: 11
Key Personnel: Dir. & Membership, Janet Hickey; Pres. (V), M. Vonciel Le Duc; Vice Pres., Theresa Neville; Treas., Darlene Furmanek; Cur., Peggy Hoffman.
Personnel Profile: Part-Time Volunteers 12.
Governing Authority: nonprofit. Sponsored by The Schoolcraft County Historical Society. Tax-exempt.
Local History Museum.
Collections: archives; geology; history; history & fiction pertaining to Upper Peninsula of Michigan; plat display; Indian artifacts; period fire engine display. Historic Buildings: 1883 restored log cabin; water tower.
Research Fields: Schoolcraft County history.
Activities: art shows. Museum Sponsors: Pioneer Day, last Saturday in June.
Publications: newsletter.
Hours & Admission Prices: June-Sept. Wed.-Sat. 1-4. Adults $1, children $.50; members no charge.
Attendance: 500 (estimated)
Membership: Annual $10; Life $100.

Marine City

CAPTAIN DAVID LESTER RESIDENCE, 406 S. Main St., Marine City, MI 48039-1628. Tel.: 810-765-5912. Fax: 810-765-5916.
Web Site: www.historicallesterhome.com
Historic House: former home of Captain David Lester.
Collections: period artifacts & memorabilia pertaining to Captain David Lester & his family.
Hours & Admission Prices: Tours: May-Dec. Sat.-Sun. 1 & 3.

MARINE CITY PRIDE & HERITAGE MUSEUM, 405 S. Main St., Marine City, MI 48039-1634. Mailing Address: P.O. Box 184, Marine City, MI 48039-0184. Tel.: 810-765-5446.
Web Site: www.marinecitymuseum.org
Founded: 1983.
Key Personnel: Dir., John Foley; Pres. (V), Gary Beals
History Museum.
Collections: local history, heritage & culture; personal artifacts; period furnishings; business & commercial; blacksmith shop.
Hours & Admission Prices: June-Oct. Sat.-Sun. 1-4; tours by appointment. No charge; donations accepted. ♿
Attendance: 300 (estimated)
Membership: Individual $10.

Marquette

THE DEVOS ART MUSEUM AT NORTHERN MICHIGAN UNIVERSITY, 1401 Presque Isle Ave., Marquette, MI 49855-5305. Tel.: 906-227-1481. Fax: 906-227-2276.
E-mail: mmatusca@nmu.edu
Web Site: art.nmu.edu/devosartmuseum
Key Personnel: Dir. & Cur., Melissa Matuscak.
Personnel Profile: Full-Time Paid 1; Part-Time Volunteers 8; Interns 1.
Governing Authority: Parent Institution: Northern Michigan University. Tax-exempt.
University Art Museum.
Collections: Japanese art & artifacts; Native American art & artifacts; 20th century illustrations; contemporary regional artists.
Activities: workshops; artist lectures; docent tours; film screenings.
Hours & Admission Prices: Mon.-Wed. & Fri. 10-5, Thurs. 12-8, Sat.-Sun. 1-4. No charge; donations accepted. Closed New Year's Eve & Day; Independence Day; Memorial Day; Christmas Eve, Day & week. ♿
Attendance: 10,000 (accurate)
Membership: Student & Retired $15; Friend $30; Family $50; Good Friend $100; Close Friend & Group of Friends $250; Special Friend $500; Best Friend $1,000.

MARQUETTE COUNTY HISTORY MUSEUM, (M), 213 N. Front St., Marquette, MI 49855-4220. Tel.: 906-226-3571. Fax: 906-226-0919.
E-mail: khiebel@sbcglobal.net
Web Site: www.marquettecohistory.org
Founded: 1918.
Congressional District: 11
Key Personnel: Bd. Pres. (V), Susan Hornbogen; Exec. Dir., Kaye Hiebel; Dir. Devel., Cristine Osier; Business Mgr., Jennifer Lammi; Research Librarian, Rosemary Michelin; Cur., Jo DeYoung.
Personnel Profile: Full-Time Paid 3; Part-Time Paid 2; Part-Time Volunteers 4; Interns 2.
Governing Authority: bd. of trustees. Tax-exempt: 501(c)(3).
History Museum: housed in 1891 Fraternity Building.
Collections: archaeology; minerals; logging; shipping; archives; ethnology; folklore; china; glass; silver; toys; costumes; tools; Chippewa Indian culture; geology; marine; technology; transportation; mining, railroad, lumbering history of Marquette County.
Research Fields: history of Central Upper Peninsula & Upper Great Lakes; subjects pertaining to collections.
Facilities: 15,000-vol. library on history of Great Lakes area available by membership or research fee. Historical books & other museum-related items for sale.
Activities: lectures; formally organized education programs for adults; permanent & temporary exhibitions; educational services to schools.
Publications: pamphlets; quarterly magazine, Harlow's Wooden Man; books, The Grand Island Story; North to Lake Superior; Landlooker in the Upper Peninsula; Saga of Iron Mining in Michigan's Upper Peninsula; Dandelion Cottage.
Hours & Admission Prices: June-Aug. Mon.-Fri. 10-5, 3rd Thurs. of month 10-9, Sat. 11-4; Sept.-May Mon.-Fri. 10-5, 3rd Thurs. of month 10-9. Adults $3, students over 12 $1; children & members no charge. Closed legal holidays.
Attendance: 9,100 (accurate)
Membership: Basic Individual $25; Supporting Individual & Basic Family $40; Supporting Family $65; Business $50-$375.

UPPER PENINSULA CHILDREN'S MUSEUM, 123 W. Baraga Ave., Marquette, MI 49855-4744. Tel.: 906-226-3911. Fax: 906-226-7065.
E-mail: nittner@chartermi.net
Web Site: www.upcmkids.org
Key Personnel: Dir., Nheena Weyer Ittner; Dir. 8-18 Media, Dennis Whitley; Mgr. Finance & Operations, Erin Brooks; Explainers Dir. & Gen. Programming Mgr., Jim Edwards; Experience Works Receptionist, Jean Johns; Mgr. Facilities & Exhibits, Aaron Sault.
Personnel Profile: Full-Time Paid 4; Part-Time Paid 5; Part-Time Volunteers 2; Interns 2.
Children's Museum.
Collections: hands-on exhibits.
Facilities: Museum-related items for sale.
Activities: special programs; preschool & elementary school programs; leadership programs for youth 8-18.
Hours & Admission Prices: Mon.-Wed. & Sat. 10-6, Thurs. 10-7:30, Fri. 10-8, Sun. 12-5. Adults & children $5; discounts to Art Serve Michigan, MEA & AAA members. ♿
Attendance: 51,000
Membership: Family $100; Grandparent $125.

Marshall

AMERICAN MUSEUM OF MAGIC & LUND MEMORIAL LIBRARY, INC., 107 E. Michigan, Marshall, MI 49068-1543. Mailing Address: P.O. Box 5, Marshall, MI 49068-0005. Tel.: 269-781-7570.
E-mail: info@americanmuseumofmagic.org
Web Site: americanmuseumofmagic.org
Founded: 1978.
Key Personnel: Pres. Bd. (V), Bradley Taylor; Exec. Dir. & Museum Shop Mgr., Betty Collins; Cur. & Museum Shop Mgr., Jim Klodzen.
Personnel Profile: Part-Time Paid 2; Part-Time Volunteers 6; Interns 1.
Governing Authority: bd. of directors. Subsidiary Institution: Library, 111 E. Mansion St., Marshall, MI 49068. Tax-exempt.
Magic Museum: housed in 1869 building.
Collections: posters; photographs; advertising folders; recordings; coins & tokens; magician apparatus; costumes; scrapbooks; toys; games; figures; magic memorabilia; magic illusions owned by Houdini, Blackstone, Henning, Thurston, & Conklin.
Research Fields: magic; magicians.
Facilities: 25,000-vol. library.
Activities: guided tours; temporary exhibitions. Annual Event: Scarecrow Festival.
Publications: brochure; monthly newsletter.
Hours & Admission Prices: April-Nov. Mon.-Sat. 10-4. Adults $5, seniors & children $3.50; discounts to groups of 10 or more. Closed Memorial Day; Independence Day; Labor Day.
Attendance: 1,200 (estimated)

HONOLULU HOUSE MUSEUM, 107 N. Kalamazoo Ave., Marshall, MI 49068-1526. Tel.: 269-781-8544. Fax: 269-789-0371.
E-mail: mhsdirector@mac.com
Web Site: www.marshallhistoricalsociety.org
Founded: 1962.
Key Personnel: Pres., Mary Jo Byrne; Dir., Jennifer Rupp.
Personnel Profile: Part-Time Paid 4; Part-Time Volunteers 30; Interns 2.
Governing Authority: nonprofit organization. Affiliated with Marshall Historical Society. Branch Museum: Capitol Hill School Children's Museum, Gar Hall. Tax-exempt: 170(b)(1)(A).
History Museum: c.1860 Honolulu House.
Collections: 19th-century Midwest artifacts; decorative arts; folklore; military; letters, diaries, maps & legal documents pertinent to early settlement of Marshall.
Research Fields: 19th-century history of Marshall.
Facilities: 2,000-vol. library of local history available for research by special permission from curator. Books & museum-related items for sale.
Activities: guided tours; lectures; permanent exhibitions.
Publications: book, 19th-Century Homes of Marshall, Michigan; History of Marshall, Michigan.
Hours & Admission Prices: May-Sept. daily 12-5; Oct. Thurs.-Sun. 12-5. Adults $5, senior citizens & students 12-16 $4; members & children under 12 no charge. ♿
Attendance: 8,000 (estimated)
Membership: Individual $20; Family $30.

Marysville

MARYSVILLE HISTORICAL MUSEUM, 887 E. Huron Blvd., Marysville, MI 48040-1573. Tel.: 810-364-6613.
E-mail: mvmuseum@advnet.net
Web Site: www.cityofmarysvillemi.com/museum/index.htm
History Museum.
Collections: local history & culture; photographs.
Hours & Admission Prices: June-Aug. Sun. 1:30-4. Suggested Donation: $1.

THE WILLS STE. CLAIRE AUTO MUSEUM, 2408 Wills St., Marysville, MI 48040-1978. Tel.: 810-987-2854.
E-mail: willsmuseum@sbcglobal.net
Web Site: www.willsautomuseum.org
Key Personnel: Dir., Terry Ernest; Sec., Pete Canjemi; Treas., Laurie Baker
Automobile Museum: former Dow Chemical munitions factory built during WWII.
Collections: period cars.
Hours & Admission Prices: 2nd Sun. of each month 1-5. Adults $5. ♿

Mayville

MAYVILLE AREA MUSEUM OF HISTORY AND GENEALOGY, 2124 Ohmer Rd., Mayville, MI 48744. Mailing Address: P.O. Box 242, Mayville, MI 48744-0242. Tel.: 989-843-7185 & 6249.
Founded: 1972.
Congressional District: 7
Key Personnel: Dir., Pres. & Cur., Frank E. Franzel, Sr.; Vice Pres., Florence Chance; Treas., Marilyn Patterson; Sec., Fran Campbell.
Personnel Profile: Part-Time Volunteers 15.
Governing Authority: nonprofit organization. Tax-exempt.
History & Genealogy Museum.
Collections: artifacts pertaining to the history of Mayville & the surrounding area, dating back to the founding of the village; family records; genealogies; obituary file; local cemetery readings. Historic Buildings: log cabin; one-room rural schoolhouse.
Research Fields: the history of the community; genealogical search.
Facilities: 500-vol. library of books on the history of the area; microfilm of all back issues of Mayville Monitor, the local weekly newspaper; reading room.
Activities: guided tours; early crafts; quilting; flea markets.
Publications: annual progress report; annual newsletter.
Hours & Admission Prices: May-Labor Day Fri.-Sat. 10-4; other times by appointment. No charge; donations accepted. ♿
Attendance: 225 (estimated)
Membership: Annual $5; Family $10; Life $100.

Menominee

MENOMINEE COUNTY HERITAGE MUSEUM, 904 11 Ave., Menominee, MI 49858-3044. Mailing Address: P.O. Box 151, Menominee, MI 49858-0151. Tel.: 906-863-9000.
Founded: 1967.
Congressional District: 1
Key Personnel: Dir., Michael Kaufman; Cur., Barbara Pesola; Pres., Pat Krah; Librarian, Amber Allard.
Personnel Profile: Full-Time Volunteers 1; Part-Time Paid 2; Part-Time Volunteers 52.
Governing Authority: board. Parent Institution: Menominee County Historical Society, Inc. Tax-exempt: 501(c)(3).
General Museum.
Collections: Indian artifacts; oral history tapes; logging; 1900 photographic studio; 1820-1915 Victorian furniture; military room; 1868-1968 probate court records; models; circus display; local history items; commercial fishing. Historic Building: c.1921 brick church with leaded glass windows made in Munich, Germany.
Research Fields: local history.
Facilities: 1,000-vol. library of books, court records, & newspapers.
Activities: guided tours.
Publications: manuscripts; biannual newsletter.
Hours & Admission Prices: Memorial Day-Sept. Mon.-Sat. 10-4. No charge; donations accepted.
Attendance: 5,000 (estimated)
Membership: Friend $15; Supporter $25; Contributor $50; Sustaining $100; Patron $250; Benefactor $500; Heritage $1,000 & up.

Middleville

HISTORIC BOWENS MILLS & PIONEER PARK, 200 Old Mill Rd., Middleville, MI 49333-9194. Mailing Address: 240 Old Mill Rd., Middleville, MI 49333-9194. Tel.: 269-795-7530. Fax: 269-795-7530.
E-mail: carleen@bowensmills.com
Web Site: www.bowensmills.com
Founded: 1978.
Key Personnel: Dir. Operations, Carleen Sabin; Dir. Operations, Owen Sabin.
Governing Authority: nonprofit organization. Tax-exempt.
State Historic Site: 1864 water-powered grist & cider mill.
Collections: Indian artifacts; period tools; farm animals; family histories; firearms; knives; cooper's shop; cobbler's shop; water powered machine shop; blacksmith shop; sewing room; spinning & weaving loft. Historic Buildings: 1830 Plank house & covered bridge; 1850 one room school; 1880 barn; 1860 Victorian house.
Research Fields: area history.
Facilities: library of historic material available to the public on premises only. Antiques, collectibles & reproductions for sale.
Activities: guided tours; lectures; arts festivals; organized education programs for children & adults; temporary exhibitions; horse-drawn hay rides; Civil War & Revolutionary War reenactments; cider pressing demonstrations. Museum Sponsors: 14 Festivals per year; Mountain Man encampments.
Publications: historic booklets; books, Apple Cook Book; Corn Meal Cook Book.
Hours & Admission Prices: May-Dec. by appointment. Mill or Festivals: adults $5, children 5-11 $2; discounts to groups, AAM & ICOM members & groups. Horse-drawn rides with admission to Festivals.
Attendance: 30,000 (estimated)

Midland

ALDEN B. DOW HOME & STUDIO, (M), 315 Post St., Midland, MI 48640-4099. Tel.: 989-839-2744; 866-315-7678 (Toll Free). Fax: 989-839-2611.
E-mail: info@abdow.org
Web Site: www.abdow.org
Key Personnel: House Mgr., Mary Lou Timmons
Historic House Museum: housed in the former home & architectural studio of 20th century architect Alden B. Dow. A National Historic Landmark.
Collections: Dow family history; contemporary architecture; personal artifacts; furnishings.
Activities: educational programs; group tours.
Hours & Admission Prices: Mon.-Fri. 8-5. Tours: Mon.-Thurs. 2pm, Fri.-Sat. 10am. Adults $10, students $5. Children under 8 not admitted. Closed major holidays.

* **ALDEN B. DOW MUSEUM OF SCIENCE AND ART OF THE MIDLAND CENTER FOR THE ARTS, (M),** 1801 W. St. Andrews Rd., Midland, MI 48640-2656. Tel.: 989-631-5930. Fax: 989-631-7890.
E-mail: info@mcfta.org
Web Site: www.mcfta.org
Formerly: Arts Midland: Galleries and School
Founded: 1971.
Congressional District: 4
Key Personnel: C.E.O. & Pres., Bill Henniger; Chm., Melissa Barnard; Dir., Bruce Winslow; Business & Operations Mgr., Eminor Mills; Museum School Mgr., Armin Mersmann; Cur. Science, Debbie Anderson; Administrative Asst., Sarah Brandt.
Personnel Profile: Full-Time Paid 5.
Governing Authority: nonprofit organization. Parent Institution: Midland Center for the Arts. Subsidiary Institution: Science & Technology Museum. Tax-exempt: 501(c)(3).
Science & Art Museum and School.
Collections: science & art exhibits.
Activities: guided tours; lectures; gallery talks; art festivals; education & outreach programs; permanent & traveling exhibitions.
Hours & Admission Prices: Tues.-Sat. 10-5, Sun. 1-5. Adults $8, children 4-14 $3; members & children under 3 no charge. Closed major holidays. ♿
Attendance: 60,000
Membership: Student $25; Single $40; Family $50; Supporter $100.

CHIPPEWA NATURE CENTER, 400 S. Badour Rd., Midland, MI 48640-8661. Tel.: 989-631-0830. Fax: 989-631-7070.
E-mail: dtouvell@chippewanaturecenter.org
Web Site: www.chippewanaturecenter.org
Founded: 1966.
Congressional District: 10
Key Personnel: Exec. Dir., Dick Touvell; Pres., Dr. Marianne McKelvy; Naturalist, Phil Stephens; Naturalist, Janea Little; Business Mgr., Chris Anderson; Office Mgr., Deana Beckham; Naturalist & Facilities Supvr., Tom Lenon; Mgr. Historical Programs, Kyle Bagnall; Dir. Education, Rachel Larimore; Dir. Volunteers & Outreach, Cathy Devendorf; Dir. Interpretation, Dennis Pilaske; Naturalist, Karen Breternitz; Newsletter Editor, Public Rels., Shelley Koop.
Personnel Profile: Full-Time Paid 20; Part-Time Paid 45; Interns 1.
Governing Authority: nonprofit organization. Tax-exempt.
Nature & Historical Center.
Collections: archaeology; tools used by 19th-century settlers; birds; mammals; insects; ecosystem; cultural history. Historic Buildings: 1880 log schoolhouse; 1870 Homestead Farm with maple sugar house & log barn.
Research Fields: archaeology; botany; ornithology; natural resources management; local history.
Facilities: 2,000-vol. library of natural science & archaeology books; 85-seat auditorium; 1200 acres with 14 miles of nature trails; classrooms. Museum-related items for sale.
Activities: guided tours; lectures; films; formally organized education programs for adults, children & undergraduate students affiliated with local colleges; permanent & temporary exhibitions.
Publications: monthly newsletter, CNC News; occasional publications.
Hours & Admission Prices: Mon.-Fri. 8-5, Sat. 9-5, Sun. 1-5. No charge; donations accepted. Closed Thanksgiving; Christmas. ♿
Attendance: 50,000 (accurate)
Membership: College Student $18; Senior $20; Individual $24; Senior Citizen Family $28; Family $42; Meadow Society $100-$249; Woodland Society $250-$499; River Society $500 & up; Life Membership $1,000.

DOW GARDENS, 1809 Eastman Ave., Midland, MI 48640. Mailing Address: 1018 W. Main St., Midland, MI 48640-4292. Tel.: 989-631-2677; 800-362-4874. Fax: 989-631-0675.
E-mail: helmreich@dowgardens.org
Web Site: www.dowgardens.org
Founded: 1899.
Congressional District: 10
Key Personnel: Mng. Dir., Marty McGuire; Vice Pres., Michael L. Dow; Taxonomic Horticulturist, Richard Gillis; Dir. Visitors Center, Michelle Holmes.
Personnel Profile: Full-Time Paid 14; Part-Time Paid 4; Part-Time Volunteers 8; Interns 25.
Governing Authority: nonprofit organization. Parent Institution: Herbert H. & Grace A. Dow Foundation, 1018 W. Main St., Midland, MI 48640-4292. Tax-exempt.
Botanical Garden: located on the Herbert H. Dow Estate.
Collections: tulip; woody plants; crab apple; rhododendron; bedding plants; herb garden; All-American garden; water falls; jungle walk; bridges; mazes; pines; ornamental pool.
Research Fields: propagation of native woody material, including Malus, Acer & Quercus; aquatic plant management; applied forestry management; insect phenology; insect & host interactions.
Facilities: library pertaining to horticulture, pest control, aquatics & herbs available for research on premises; reading room; classroom. Books & other museum-related items for sale.

Activities: guided tours; lectures; concerts; arts festivals; TV programs; radio programs; formally organized education programs for children, adults & undergraduate college students.
Publications: pamphlets & brochures; annual booklets, Bedding Plants Evaluation; Crab Apples & Pruning Booklet.
Hours & Admission Prices: April 15 to Labor Day daily 9-8:30; Sept.-Oct. daily 9-6:30; Nov.-April 14 daily 9-4:15. Adult $5, youth 6-17 $1. Closed New Year's Eve & Day; Thanksgiving; Christmas Eve & Day. ♿
Attendance: 260,500 (accurate)

MIDLAND COUNTY HISTORICAL SOCIETY, (M), 3417 W. Main St., Midland, MI 48640-2055. Tel.: 989-631-5930, ext. 1302. Fax: 989-835-9120.
E-mail: skory@mcfta.org
Web Site: www.mcfta.org/historical_society
Founded: 1952.
Congressional District: 10
Key Personnel: Chm., Floyd Andrick; Dir., Gary F. Skory; Business Mgr., Tammie Swinson; Educational Coord., Trena Winans-Bagnall.
Personnel Profile: Full-Time Paid 2; Part-Time Paid 1; Part-Time Volunteers 250; Interns 4.
Governing Authority: nonprofit organization. Parent Institution: Midland Center for the Arts, Inc. 1801 W. St. Andrews, Midland, MI. Branch Museums: Herbert H. Dow Historical Museum, 3100 Cook Rd., Midland, MI; Bradley Home & Carriage House, 3200 Cook Rd., Midland, MI; The Midland County History Museum, 3417 W. Main St., Midland, MI. Tax-exempt: 501(c)(3).
History Museum.
Collections: Midland & Michigan historical artifacts; silver; glass; textiles; music; photography; lumbering; decorative arts; chemistry; carriages & sleighs; 1890s Dow Chemical Co. reconstruction. Historic Buildings: 1874 vintage house; carriage house with wagon maker's annex.
Major Exhibits: A Scouting We Will Go: A Century of Boy Scouts USA, 3/10-11/10.
Research Fields: lumbering; Victorian life; 19th-20th century Dow Chemical Co. history; early transportation; blacksmithing; genealogy.
Facilities: 500-vol. library of rare books available on premises only; auditorium; classrooms. Museum-related items for sale.
Activities: docent program; guided tours; lectures; gallery talks; formally organized education programs for children; permanent & temporary exhibitions; theater; traveling & local history exhibitions; training programs for professional museum workers.
Publications: book, Building Arts in Midland, Michigan 1800s-1980; Salt of the Earth: A History of Midland County; quarterly newsletter; biannual journal, The Midland Log.
Hours & Admission Prices: Exhibitions: March 15-Nov. 15 Thurs.-Sat. 11-4. Dow Museum, Vintage House & Carriage House: Wed.-Sat. 10-4, Sun. 1-5. Adults $5, children $3; discounts to AAA members; members no charge. Closed New Year's Day; Good Friday; Memorial Day; Thanksgiving; Christmas. ♿
Attendance: 75,000 (estimated)
Membership: Student & Senior $30; Individual $35; Family $45; Collector $100; Researcher $250; Curator $500; Historian $1,000; John Larkin $5,000 & up.

Milan

THE HACK HOUSE MUSEUM, 775 County St., Milan, MI 48160-9701. Mailing Address: Milan Area Historical Society, P.O. Box 245, Milan, MI 48160-0245. Tel.: 734-439-8693.
Web Site: www.historicmilan.com
Founded: 1972.
Historic House.
Collections: period artifacts & memorabilia from the Victorian era.
Hours & Admission Prices: May-Nov. Fri. 1-4.

Milford

KENSINGTON METROPARK NATURE CENTER, 2240 W. Buno Rd., Milford, MI 48380-4410. Tel.: 248-685-0603. Fax: 248-684-5836.
E-mail: bob.hotaling@metroparks.com
Web Site: www.metroparks.com
Founded: 1957.
Congressional District: 19
Key Personnel: Supervising Interpreter, Robert Hotaling; Park Interpreter, Michael Tucker; Park Interpreter, Michael Broughton; Interpreter, Chad Geurts; Interpreter, Andy Swift.
Personnel Profile: Full-Time Paid 3; Part-Time Paid 2; Part-Time Volunteers 20.
Governing Authority: regional park authority. Affiliated with the Huron-Clinton Metropolitan Authority, 13000 High Ridge Dr., P.O. Box 2001, Brighton, MI 48114-9058. Tax-exempt.
Nature Center.
Collections: natural science specimens for study & exhibit.
Facilities: 750-acre nature study area; nature trails.
Activities: guided tours; lectures; temporary exhibitions; school lecture programs.
Publications: Biennial Report.
Hours & Admission Prices: Mon. 1-5, Tues.-Sun. 10-5. Park: $20 annual; $4 per vehicle. Closed Thanksgiving; Christmas. ♿
Attendance: 321,000 (estimated)

MILFORD HISTORICAL MUSEUM, 124 E. Commerce St., Milford, MI 48381-5300. Tel.: 248-685-7308.
E-mail: milfordhistory@hotmail.com
Web Site: www.milfordhistory.org
Founded: 1976.
Congressional District: 18
Key Personnel: Dir., Mary Lou Gharrity; Asst. Dir., Marlene Gomez.
Governing Authority: society; nonprofit. Parent Institution: Milford Historical Society. Tax-exempt: 501(c)(3).
Historical Society Museum: housed in 1853 Greek Revival House.
Collections: local history & memorabilia; photographs; local cemetery records & property tax records.
Facilities: microfilm collection of 1871-present The Milford Times available to the public.
Activities: Museum Sponsors: Granny's Attic Sale in July; Annual Homes Tour in September.
Publications: history book, Ten Minutes Ahead of the Rest of the World; bimonthly newsletter.
Hours & Admission Prices: May to mid-Dec. Wed. & Sat. 1-4. No charge; donations accepted.
Attendance: 450 (estimated)
Membership: Students $5; Seniors $10; Individual $15; Family $25; Small Business $50; Silver & Lifetime $250; Gold $500; Platinum $1,000.

Monroe

MONROE COUNTY HISTORICAL MUSEUM, 126 S. Monroe St., Monroe, MI 48161-2275. Tel.: 734-240-7780. Fax: 734-240-7788.
E-mail: john_gibney@monroemi.org
Web Site: www.co.monroe.mi.us/museum
Founded: 1939.
Congressional District: 16
Key Personnel: Dir., John Gibney; Education Coord., Lynn Reaume; Cur. Collections, James Ryland; Archivist, Christine L. Kull.
Personnel Profile: Full-Time Paid 4; Part-Time Paid 4; Part-Time Volunteers 30.
Governing Authority: county. Branch Museums: Navarre-Anderson Trading Post; Papermill School and Country Store Museum; River Raisin Battlefield Visitor Center. Tax-exempt: 170(b)(1)(A).
History Museum: housed on the site of Gen. George A. Custer home.
Collections: local history artifacts: General George A. Custer; Woodland and Western Indians; tools; costumes; musical instruments; ceramics; medical & dental equipment; domestic appurtenances; manuscripts.
Research Fields: Michigan history, 1785-1940.
Facilities: 2,500-vol. library of printed & manuscript material pertaining to Monroe County & Southeast Michigan available for use by arrangement with archivist. History oriented items for sale.
Activities: guided tours; lectures; gallery talks; permanent & temporary exhibitions.
Publications: books, Legacy of the River Raisin; Brief History of Monroe; Escape to Frenchtown; Women on the Raisin.
Hours & Admission Prices: Jan.-April Wed.-Sat. 10-5; May-Dec. Wed.-Sun.10-5. Adults $2, children 7-17 $1; children under 7 & Sept.-May no charge. Closed New Year's Day; Easter; Thanksgiving; Christmas. ♿
Attendance: 20,000 (accurate)

Montague

MONTAGUE MUSEUM & HISTORICAL ASSOCIATION, Church & Meade Sts., Montague, MI 49437. Mailing Address: 8636 Old Channel Trail, Montague, MI 49437-1365. Tel.: 231-893-3055. Fax: 231-894-9955.
Founded: 1964.
Congressional District: 9
Key Personnel: Pres., Henry E. Roesler, Jr.
Personnel Profile: Part-Time Volunteers 21.
Governing Authority: nonprofit organization. Parent Institution: City of Montague. Tax-exempt.
General Museum: housed in a former United Methodist Church.
Collections: lumbering; Indian; military; farming; musical; religious; rocks;

dolls; toys; local art; clocks; George Washington family artifacts; manikins; bicentennial; telephone exchange; doctors office; barber shop.
Research Fields: local history; 1890-1970 local newspaper.
Facilities: library of books on Michigan history & short story writings by Frank Adams.
Activities: guided tours; lectures; permanent exhibitions.
Hours & Admission Prices: Summer: Sat.-Sun. 1-5; private tours for groups available. No charge; donations accepted.
Attendance: 2,600 (estimated)
Membership: Single $6; Family $10.

Montrose

MONTROSE HISTORICAL & TELEPHONE PIONEER MUSEUM, 144 E. Hickory St., Montrose, MI 48457-9464. Mailing Address: P.O. Box 577, Montrose, MI 48457-0577. Tel.: 810-639-6644.
E-mail: staff@montrosemuseum.com
Web Site: www.montrosemuseum.com
Founded: 1980.
Key Personnel: Pres. (V), Joe Follett.
Personnel Profile: Part-Time Paid 2; Part-Time Volunteers 36.
Governing Authority: Parent Institution: Montrose Area Historical Assoc. Tax-exempt.
History (local) & Telephone Museum.
Collections: period telephone equipment; farming implements; household artifacts; old barber shop; pharmacy, loom.
Activities: genealogy; speakers.
Publications: Memory Lane Gazette.
Hours & Admission Prices: Museum: Jan.-March Sat.-Sun. 1-5; April- Dec. Sun. 1-5. Office: Mon.-Wed. 10-3. Genealogy Room: call for appointment. Tour Groups: adults $2. Closed major holidays. ♿
Attendance: 952 (accurate)
Membership: Student $1; Individual $5; Family $7; Business $10; Individual Life $60; Couple Life $100.

Mount Clemens

CROCKER HOUSE MUSEUM & MACOMB COUNTY HISTORICAL SOCIETY, 15 Union St., Mount Clemens, MI 48043-5502. Tel.: 586-465-2488. Fax: 586-465-2932.
E-mail: crockerdirector@sbcglobal.net
Web Site: www.crockerhousemuseum.com
Founded: 1964.
Congressional District: 14
Key Personnel: Pres., Ross Champion; Dir., Kimberly Parr; Office Mgr., Marcia Swiderski; Museum Shop Mgr., Gladys Stevenson.
Personnel Profile: Full-Time Paid 1; Part-Time Paid 1; Part-Time Volunteers 40; Interns 3.
Governing Authority: society; nonprofit. Parent Institution: Macomb County Historical Society. Tax-exempt: 501(c)(3).
Historical Society Museum: residence built 1869 Crocker House, a Victorian Italianate style house.
Collections: material relating to Macomb County history; mineral bath industry; local industry.
Research Fields: Macomb County history.
Facilities: 500-vol. library of county history & Crocker family genealogy available for use by appointment; reading room. Gift items for sale.
Activities: special projects; temporary exhibits; lectures; teas; historical programs; special events. Annual Events: Cemetery Walk & Funeral Tea; Garden Walk & Tea; Christmas Wassail.
Publications: quarterly newsletter; books, Along the Huron; Crocker House; Beacon Tree; Warner Diary; Christian Clemens; Depression Days in Mount Clemens; Crocker House Museum; Made in Mount Clemens.
Hours & Admission Prices: Tues.-Thurs. 10-4, 1st Sun. of month 1-4. Suggested Donations & Special Events: adults $3, children $1; discounts to members.
Attendance: 2,500 (accurate)
Membership: Individual $20; Family $30; Contributing $50; Century $100; Corporate $200; Benefactor $500; Conservator $1,000 & up.

MICHIGAN TRANSIT MUSEUM, INC., 200 Grand Ave., Mount Clemens, MI 48043-5412. Mailing Address: P.O. Box 12, Mount Clemens, MI 48046-0012. Tel.: 586-463-1863. Fax: 586-463-9814.
E-mail: info@michigantransitmuseum.org
Web Site: www.michigantransitmuseum.org
Founded: 1973.
Congressional District: 10
Key Personnel: Chm. (V) & Pres. (V), Billie H. Henning; Treas., Gary J. Michaels.
Personnel Profile: Part-Time Volunteers 40.
Governing Authority: nonprofit organization. Tax-exempt: 501(c)(3).
Transportation Museum: equipment housed at Selfridge Air National Guard Base & 1859, Grand Trunk Depot Railroad Museum, national historic site.
Collections: 1930, #11 Chicago, South Shore & South Bend Interurban coach; 1924 Chicago Rapid Transit El cars; 1895 Grand Trunk Western Railroad caboose; 1942 Alco Diesel-Electric Locomotive; railroad & transportation items; #4040, ex-USAF diesel electric Switch Locomotive; #268 ex-Detroit PCC streetcar; #4601 ex-Toronto PCC streetcar.
Research Fields: railroads; electric trolleys & interurbans of special interest.
Facilities: Prints, buttons, railroad-related souvenirs & booklets for sale.
Activities: films; temporary exhibitions.
Publications: monthly newsletter, Michigan Transit Museum Gazette.
Hours & Admission Prices: Depot Museum: Sat.-Sun. 1-4. No charge; donations accepted. Train rides: adults $8, children 4-12 $4. ♿
Attendance: 3,500 (estimated)
Membership: Associate $20; Active $30; Life $1,000.

Mount Pleasant

MUSEUM OF CULTURAL & NATURAL HISTORY, 103 Rowe Hall, Corner of Bellows & East Campus Dr., Mount Pleasant, MI 48859-0001. Tel.: 989-774-3829. Fax: 989-774-2612.
E-mail: cmuseum@cmich.edu
Web Site: www.museum.cmich.edu/
Founded: 1970.
Congressional District: 10
Key Personnel: Dir. & Cur., Dr. William S. Pretzer; Science Cur., Dr. Kirsten Nicholson.
Personnel Profile: Full-Time Paid 4; Part-Time Paid 4; Part-Time Volunteers 10.
Governing Authority: university. Affiliated with Central Michigan University. Tax-exempt.
University Museum.
Collections: archaeology; anthropological materials; Michigan Indian artifacts; rocks & minerals; paleontological materials; history materials & zoological collections; contemporary Native American art. Historical Building: 1901 one-room school.
Research Fields: Michigan archaeology & history; herpetology; mammalogy; ornithology.
Activities: guided tours; organized education programs for children, adults, undergraduate & graduate students affiliated with Central Michigan University; permanent & temporary exhibitions; school loan service.
Hours & Admission Prices: Mon.-Fri. 8-5, Sat.-Sun. 1-5. No charge; donations accepted. Closed national & university holidays. ♿
Attendance: 25,000 (estimated)

UNIVERSITY ART GALLERY - CENTRAL MICHIGAN UNIVERSITY, Wightman 132, Mount Pleasant, MI 48859-. Tel.: 989-774-3800.
Web Site: www.uag.cmich.edu
Founded: 1970.
Congressional District: 99
Personnel Profile: Full-Time Paid 1.
Governing Authority: Parent Institution: Department of Art and Design, Central Michigan University.
Art Gallery.
Collections: works by regional & national artists.
Major Exhibits: University Art Gallery 20/40/50 Anniversary Alumni Exhibition, 1/12/10-2/13/10; 2010 Annual Juried CMU Student Art Exhibition, 2/23/10-3/27/10; Central Michigan - University Graphic Design BFA Show, 4/2/10-4/17/10; CMU BFA Candidates, 4/23/10-5/8/10.
Hours & Admission Prices: Sept.-May Tues.-Fri. 11-6, Sat. 11-3; Summer: call for hours. No charge. ♿
Attendance: 6,300 (accurate)

ZIIBIWING CENTER OF ANISHINABE CULTURE & LIFEWAYS, (M), 6650 E. Broadway, Mount Pleasant, MI 48858-8950. Tel.: 989-775-4750. Fax: 989-775-4770.
Web Site: www.sagchip.org/ziibiwing/index.htm
Key Personnel: Dir., Shannon Martin; Asst. Dir., Judy Pamp; Cur., William Johnson.
Governing Authority: Tax-exempt.
General Museum.
Collections: culture & history of the Saginaw Chippewa Indian Tribe of Michigan & other Great Lakes Anishinabek; paintings; government documents.
Facilities: cafe. Museum-related items for sale.
Activities: permanent & temporary exhibits; educational workshops; lectures; special events; rental facilities; films.
Publications: quarterly newsletter, Noodagon; Diba Jimooying, Telling Our Story: A History of the Saginaw Chippewa Indian Tribe of Michigan.
Hours & Admission Prices: Mon.-Sat. 10-6. Adults $6.50, college students $4.50, senior citizens 60 & over, children 5-17 and active military $3.75;

children under 4, members & teachers no charge. Closed New Year's Eve & Day; Thanksgiving; Christmas Eve & Day. ♿

Munising

ALGER COUNTY HISTORICAL SOCIETY, 1496 Washington St., Munising, MI 49862-1492. Tel.: 906-387-4308. Fax: 906-387-4188.
E-mail: algerchs@jamadots.com
Founded: 1966.
Congressional District: 11
Key Personnel: Pres., Mary Jo Cook.
Personnel Profile: Part-Time Paid 1; Part-Time Volunteers 30.
Governing Authority: nonprofit organization. Branch Museum: Grand Island Fur Trader's Cabin. Tax-exempt: 501(c)(3).
Historical Society Museum.
Collections: pioneer artifacts from Alger County homes; portraits; blacksmith shop.
Research Fields: Alger County history.
Facilities: 200-vol. library of books & 1,000 ephemera material library; 100-seat auditorium; research area. Museum-related items for sale.
Activities: guided tours; living history; annual barbeque; workshops; speakers.
Publications: quarterly magazine, Alger Footprints; Alger County Centennial History; Who Were Those People.
Hours & Admission Prices: Tues.-Sat. 12-3. No charge; donations accepted. ♿
Attendance: 1,600 (estimated)
Membership: Individual $10; Family $15; Contributing $25.

Muskegon

GREAT LAKES NAVAL MEMORIAL AND MUSEUM, 1346 Bluff St., Muskegon, MI 49441-1089. Mailing Address: P.O. Box 1692, Muskegon, MI 49443-1692. Tel.: 231-755-1230. Fax: 231-755-5883.
E-mail: SS236sub@aol.com
Web Site: www.glnmm.org
Formerly: USS Silversides & Maritime Museum
Founded: 1987.
Congressional District: 9
Key Personnel: Dir., H. Bryan Hughes; Chm., Mark Fazakerley; Vice Chm., Don Morell; Mgr. Collections, Denise Herzhaft; Asst. Dir., Cathy J. Morin.
Personnel Profile: Full-Time Paid 3; Part-Time Paid 50; Part-Time Volunteers 100.
Governing Authority: nonprofit organization. Parent Institution: Great Lakes Naval Memorial and Museum. Tax-exempt: 501(c)(3).
Historic Ship: World War II navy sub U.S.S. Silversides, served with the Pacific Fleet in waters controlled by the Japanese Empire: East China Sea & through key enemy shipping routes; USCGC McLane (WMEC 146).
Collections: United States World War II submarine; USCGC McLane; 1927 Coast Guard Cutter, enforced prohibition; diving bell; veterans photos & personal artifacts; USS Silversides SS-236; static displays.
Research Fields: U.S. maritime & naval history.
Facilities: Publications & gift items for sale.
Activities: guided tours; overnight camp-ins for groups of 20 to 100.
Publications: UPSCOPE
Hours & Admission Prices: April & Oct. Sat.-Sun. 10-5:30; May & Sept. Mon.-Fri. 1-5:30; June-Aug. daily 10-5:30. Adults $13.50, students 12-18 & senior citizens $11.50, children 5-11 $10.50; discounts to group tours with prior reservations; members & children under 5 no charge. Overnight Program Camping for groups of 20-100 6pm-9:30am Mon.-Thurs. $26 per person, Fri.-Sun. $30, call for reservations. ♿
Attendance: 35,000 (estimated)
Membership: Regular $20; Associate $50; Sustaining $100; Contributing $250; Benefactor $500; Patron $1,000; Life $2,000.

HACKLEY & HUME HISTORIC SITE, W. Webster Ave. & Sixth St., Muskegon, MI 49440. Mailing Address: 430 W. Clay Ave., Muskegon, MI 49440-1002. Tel.: 231-722-7578. Fax: 231-728-4119.
E-mail: dawn@lakeshoremuseum.org
Web Site: www.lakeshoremuseum.org
Founded: 1971.
Congressional District: 96
Key Personnel: Exec. Dir., John H. McGarry, III; Site Mgr., Dawn Willi; Pres. (V), Eric Gielow; Museum Shop Mgr., Peggy Jobe.
Personnel Profile: Full-Time Paid 2; Part-Time Paid 6; Part-Time Volunteers 80.
Governing Authority: nonprofit organization. Parent Institution: The Lakeshore Museum Center. Tax-exempt: 501(c)(3).
Historic Houses: homes of C.H. Hackley & Thomas Hume.
Collections: period furniture & furnishings.
Major Exhibits: Agents of Deterioration, 5/10-12/10.
Research Fields: lumbering; life of Hackley & Hume families; Victorian architecture; decorative arts.
Facilities: visitor information center. Museum-related items for sale.
Activities: guided house tours; school programs; special events. Museum Sponsors: Holiday Tours in November & December.
Publications: brochure; newsletter.
Hours & Admission Prices: May-Oct. Wed.-Sun. 12-4; group tours by appointment; special holiday hours between Thanksgiving & Christmas. Adults $3; children 12 & under no charge. Closed major holidays.
Attendance: 6,776 (accurate)
Membership: Single $20; Family $30; Lumberjack $50; Explorer $100; Timber Cruiser $250; Pathfinder $500; Lumber Baron/Baroness $1,000.

LAKESHORE MUSEUM CENTER, (M), 430 W. Clay, Muskegon, MI 49440-1002. Tel.: 231-722-0278. Fax: 231-728-4119.
E-mail: info@lakeshoremuseum.org
Web Site: www.lakeshoremuseum.org
Formerly: Muskegon County Museum
Founded: 1937.
Congressional District: 96
Key Personnel: Dir., John H. McGarry, III; Pres. (V), Eric Gielow; Mgr. Collections & Technology, Dani LeFleur; Historic Sites Mgr., Dawn Willi; Cur. Exhibits, Melinda Conley; Assoc. Cur. Exhibits, Krista Menacher; Education Cur., Melissa Horton; Assoc. Cur. Education, Jacquelyn Funk; Archivist, Beryl Gabel; Accountant, Cheryl Graves; Maintenance Supvr., George J. Raap; Dir. Communications, Joni Dorsett; Registrar, Sharon McCullar; Museum Shop Mgr., Peggy Jobe.
Personnel Profile: Full-Time Paid 18; Part-Time Paid 7; Part-Time Volunteers 300.
Governing Authority: nonprofit organization. Subsidiary Institution: Hackley & Hume Historic Site. Tax-exempt: 501(c)(3).
Historic Site/Building; Historic Museum; Children's Science Museum.
Collections: Indian, pioneer & lumbering artifacts; archaeology; geology; natural history; maritime history.
Major Exhibits: You Should See This, 1/10-12/10.
Research Fields: lumbering; maritime history; Victorian architecture.
Facilities: library; archives.
Activities: special exhibits & demonstrations; special tours for handicapped.
Publications: bimonthly newsletter; brochure.
Hours & Admission Prices: Mon.-Fri. 9:30-4:30, Sat.-Sun. 12-4. No charge; donations accepted. Closed major holidays. ♿
Attendance: 48,154 (accurate)
Membership: Individual $20; Family $30; Contributing $50; Patron $100; Benefactor $250 & up; Corporate: Business $100; Patron $250; Benefactor $500.

MUSKEGON HERITAGE MUSEUM, (M), 561 W. Western Ave., Muskegon, MI 49440-1042. Tel.: 231-722-1363.
Founded: 1982.
Key Personnel: Chm. (V), Allan Dake.
Personnel Profile: Part-Time Volunteers 4.
Governing Authority: Parent Institution: Muskegon Heritage Association. Tax-exempt.
History Museum.
Collections: local history; Corliss Steam engine; printing presses; woodworking machinery; logging tools; period artifacts; Muskegon Boiler Works records.
Hours & Admission Prices: May to weekend before Christmas Sat. 12-3; other times by appointment. No charge; donations accepted. ♿
Attendance: 1,200 (accurate)
Membership: Individual $10.

* **MUSKEGON MUSEUM OF ART,** 296 W. Webster, Muskegon, MI 49440-1282. Tel.: 231-720-2570 & 2571. Fax: 231-720-2585.
Web Site: www.muskegonartmuseum.org
Founded: 1912.
Congressional District: 9
Key Personnel: Exec. Dir., Judith Hayner; Senior Cur., Dir. Collections & Exhibitions, E. Jane Connell; Public Rels., Marguerite Curran-Gawron; Pres., Larry Hines; Cur. Education, Catherine Mott; Collections Mgr. & Asst. Cur., Art Martin; Preparator, Keith Downie; Museum Store Mgr., Shawnee Larabee.
Personnel Profile: Full-Time Paid 8; Part-Time Paid 9; Part-Time Volunteers 140; Interns 1.
Governing Authority: public school district. Parent Institution: Muskegon Public Schools. Subsidiary Institution: Muskegon Museum of Art Foundation. Tax-exempt: 509(a)(1).
Art Museum.
Collections: American & European paintings & graphic arts; photography; sculpture; Tiffany glass; modern studio glass.
Major Exhibits: Edward Curtis: Selections from The North American Indian,

11/5/09-4/4/10; Birds Art, 12/10/09-2/10/10; Glass 2010: Recent Acquisitions, 2/4/10-4/11/10; Mirror, Mirror (T), 2/18/10-5/2/10; Claire Cliff: In Her Own Time, 4/29/10-8/1/10; 82nd Annual Regional, 5/27/10-8/25/10.
Research Fields: 19th- & early 20th-century American & European art.
Facilities: The Hackley and Walker Wings; 200-seat auditorium; classroom. Museum-related items for sale.
Activities: guided tours; lectures; films; gallery talks; concerts; loan exhibitions; study group; curriculum oriented programs for elementary & secondary students.
Hours & Admission Prices: Winter: Wed. & Fri.-Sat. 10-4:30, Thurs. 10-8, Sun. 12-4:30. Summer: Tues. & Thurs. 10-6, Wed. & Fri.-Sat. 10-4:30, Sun. 12-4:30. Adults $5; members no charge. Closed major holidays. ♿
Attendance: 26,500 (accurate)
Membership: Individual, Educator & Artist $45; Household $55; Friend $150-$499; Patron $500-$749; Walker Assoc. $750-$999; Benefactor $1,000-$1,999; Hackley Circle $2,000 & up.

Newaygo

NEWAYGO COUNTY MUSEUM, 85 Water St., Newaygo, MI 49337. Mailing Address: P.O. Box 68, White Cloud, MI 49349. Tel.: 231-652-9281. Fax: 231-652-2461.
E-mail: newaygocohistory@yahoo.com
Web Site: www.ncshg.org
Founded: 1968.
Congressional District: 2
Key Personnel: Pres. (V), Toni Rumsey.
Personnel Profile: Full-Time Volunteers 1.
Governing Authority: society. Parent Institution: Newaygo County Society of History & Genealogy. Tax-exempt: 501(c)(3).
Regional Museum: housed in the Power House of the Portland Cement Company.
Collections: western Michigan history from prehistory to modern times; military uniforms; logging; Civil War items; costumes.
Research Fields: western Michigan; genealogy.
Facilities: 4,500-vol. library of historical & genealogical material available to the public.
Activities: formal education programs for children; guided tours; school loan service; training programs for student museum workers.
Publications: quarterly, Newaygo County Society of History & Genealogy.
Hours & Admission Prices: Temporarily closed.
Attendance: 8,500 (estimated)
Membership: General $20.

Niles

FERNWOOD BOTANICAL GARDEN & NATURE PRESERVE, 13988 Range Line Rd., Niles, MI 49120-9042. Tel.: 269-695-6491 & 683-8653. Fax: 269-695-6688.
E-mail: visitor@fernwoodbotanical.org
Web Site: www.fernwoodbotanical.org
Founded: 1964.
Congressional District: 4
Key Personnel: C.E.O., Peter J. van der Linden; Pres. (V), Johanna Money; Museum Shop Mgr., Kathy Lawrence.
Personnel Profile: Full-Time Paid 11; Part-Time Paid 8; Part-Time Volunteers 250.
Governing Authority: nonprofit. Tax-exempt.
Garden & Nature Preserve.
Collections: arboretum; botany; geology; herbarium; natural history; paintings; outdoor museum; textiles; zoology.
Research Fields: plant hardiness.
Facilities: library of horticultural & nature books available for use on premises; nature trails; garden; visitor's center; nature center.
Activities: formally organized community education programs; temporary exhibitions; lectures & workshops, nature study, gardening; guided tours by appointment; holiday lights event.
Publications: quarterly newsletter; booklets; annual report.
Hours & Admission Prices: Summer: Tues.-Sat. 10-6, Sun. 12-6; Winter: Tues.-Sat. 10-5, Sun. 12-5. Adults $6, seniors $5, students $4, children 6-12 $3; reciprocal benefits to other gardens & arboretum; members & children 5 & under no charge. Closed New Year's Eve & Day; Easter; Thanksgiving weekend; Christmas Eve, Day & week. ♿
Attendance: 30,000
Membership: Individual $25; Basic $40; Preferred $50; Plym Society $250.

FORT ST. JOSEPH MUSEUM, 508 E. Main St., Niles, MI 49120-2618. Mailing Address: P.O. Box 487, Niles, MI 49120-0487. Tel.: 269-683-4702. Fax: 269-684-3930.
Web Site: fortstjosephmuseum.org
Founded: 1932.
Congressional District: 6
Key Personnel: Dir., Carol Bainbridge.
Personnel Profile: Full-Time Paid 1; Part-Time Paid 2; Part-Time Volunteers 2.
Governing Authority: municipal. City of Niles. Tax-exempt.
History Museum: housed in 1882 Henry A. Chapin Carriage House.
Collections: Ft. St. Joseph artifacts; 1881-83 pictographs by Sitting Bull & Rain-in-the-Face; local history; Plym/Quimby collection of Sioux Indian artifacts; 19th-century furnishings & decorative arts; early American tools & textiles; archives; glass; photographs.
Research Fields: local history; Fort St. Joseph.
Activities: permanent & temporary exhibits; children's activities; history hunts; group programs.
Hours & Admission Prices: Wed.-Fri. 10-4, Sat. 10-3; group tours by appointment. No charge; donations accepted. Closed holidays.
Attendance: 3,138 (accurate)

Northville

MILL RACE HISTORICAL VILLAGE, 215 Griswold St., Northville, MI 48167-1664. Tel.: 248-348-1845. Fax: 248-348-0056.
Web Site: www.millracenorthville.org
Founded: 1964.
Congressional District: 13
Key Personnel: Pres., Larry Last; Vice Pres., Keith Paterson; Office Mgr., Abbie Holden; Archivist, Heidi Nielsen.
Personnel Profile: Part-Time Paid 2; Part-Time Volunteers 75.
Governing Authority: society; nonprofit. Operated by Northville Historical Society, 215 Griswold Ave., Northville, MI. Tax-exempt: 501(c)(3).
Restored Village Museum.
Collections: Victorian furniture & furnishings; clothing; archives; Northville history, 1824-present. Historic Buildings: 1845 New School Church; 1849 Hunter House; 1868 Yerkes House; 1873 Wash Oak School; c.1890 Cottage House; c.1890 Hirsch Blacksmith Shop; c.1831 Cady Inn; c.1895 Interurban Station.
Research Fields: curriculum of one-room school; Northville community & family histories.
Facilities: 200-vol. library of community & surrounding area history; archives; meeting facilities; 400 sq. ft. exhibit space; 100-seat auditorium. Postcards & handcrafts for sale.
Activities: guided tours; lectures; docent program; organized education programs for children & adults; children's Christmas workshop. Museum Sponsors: Independence Day celebration; Victorian Festival in September; Christmas Walk-Village; Cemetery Walk in fall.
Publications: newsletter, Mill Race Quarterly; weekly newspaper column, Mill Race Matters.
Hours & Admission Prices: Grounds: dawn-dusk; Buildings: June to Oct. Sun. 1-4; other times by appointment. Office: Mon.-Fri. 9-1. No charge; donations accepted. Closed New Year's Day; Thanksgiving; Christmas. ♿
Attendance: 2,500 (estimated)
Membership: Senior Citizen $10; Individual $15; Family $20; Business $25; Contributing $50; Sustaining $125; Patron $500; Benefactor $1,000.

Novi

MOTORSPORTS MUSEUM & HALL OF FAME, 43700 Expo Center Dr., Novi, MI 48375-1135. Mailing Address: P.O. Box 194, Novi, MI 48376-0194. Tel.: 800-250-7223. Fax: 248-349-2113.
History Museum.
Collections: over 40 racing & high performance vehicles; photographs; racing manufacturers.
Hours & Admission Prices: Thurs.-Sun. 10-5. Adults $5, seniors over 60 & children under 12 $3.

Ontonagon

ONTONAGON COUNTY HISTORICAL SOCIETY MUSEUM, 422 River St., Ontonagon, MI 49953-1614. Tel.: 906-884-6165. Fax: 906-884-6165.
E-mail: ochsmuse@jamadots.com
Web Site: www.ontonagonmuseum.org
Founded: 1957.
Congressional District: 32
Key Personnel: Pres. (V), Bruce Johanson.
Personnel Profile: Full-Time Paid 2; Full-Time Volunteers 1; Part-Time Paid 1; Part-Time Volunteers 4.
Governing Authority: society; nonprofit organization. Tax-exempt: 501(c)(3).
History Museum.
Collections: period household items & furniture; musical instruments; pictures of the early settlers; early copper mining artifacts; crafts; tools; local archives; railroad display; firemen display.
Research Fields: mining; lumbering; genealogy.

Facilities: library of books, records & correspondence available for research. Gift items for sale.
Activities: guided tours.
Publications: books, Ontonagon Township Schools, 100 Years of History; This Ontonagon Country; This Land, the Ontonagon; In Days of Yore; Victoria, The Gem of Forest Hill; Murder and Mayhem Ontonagon; The River and the Land; The Mining Ventures of this Ontonagon Country; booklets on local industries & villages.
Hours & Admission Prices: Mon.-Fri. 10-5, Sat. 10-4, call for additional hours & to confirm winter hours. Adults $3 (first visit of season, thereafter no charge); discount for large groups; children 15 & under no charge. ♿
Attendance: 2,800 (estimated)
Membership: Junior 15 & under $2; Adult $15; Commercial & Family $25; Life $150.

Orchard Lake

GALERIA, 3535 Indian Trail, Orchard Lake, MI 48324-1623. Tel.: 248-683-0345.
Web Site: orchardlakeschools.org
Founded: 1963.
Congressional District: 18
Key Personnel: Dir. & Artist-in-Residence, Marian Owczarski.
Governing Authority: denominational group; nonprofit.
Art Gallery: housed in former Michigan Military Academy.
Collections: Polish, Polish American & American art; Polish history.
Research Fields: contemporary Polish art.
Facilities: concert hall; lecture hall; reception area.
Activities: guided tours; lectures; concerts; permanent & traveling exhibitions.
Hours & Admission Prices: Mon.-Fri. by appointment, Sat.-Sun. 1-5. No charge; donations accepted. Closed Easter; Thanksgiving; Christmas. ♿
Attendance: 1,250 (estimated)

Ossineke

DINOSAUR GARDENS, LLC, 11160 U.S. 23 S., Ossineke, MI 49766. Mailing Address: 11110 Ossineke Rd., Ossineke, MI 49766-9601. Tel.: 989-471-5477. Fax: 989-471-8032.
Founded: 1934.
Congressional District: 11
Key Personnel: Owner, Frank A. McCourt, II
Governing Authority: individual operation.
Paleontology Museum.
Collections: 25 life-size reproductions of prehistoric animals & birds (hand-sculptured by Paul N. Domke, Sr.) situated in natural outdoor settings; 80 ft., 60,000 lbs. Brontosaurus; flora; fauna; velociraptor sculpture created by artist Joe Donna.
Facilities: 40 acres of nature trails; snack bar; picnic area. Museum-related items for sale.
Activities: tours.
Publications: brochures.
Hours & Admission Prices: May 15 to late May daily 9-4; Memorial Day-Labor Day daily 9-6; Sept. Sat.-Sun 9-4. Adults $5, children 6-11 $4, children under 6 $3. ♿

Owosso

CURWOOD CASTLE, 224 Curwood Castle Dr., Owosso, MI 48867-2723. Mailing Address: 301 W. Main St., Owosso, MI 48867-2915. Tel.: 989-725-0597.
Founded: 1975.
Congressional District: 10
Key Personnel: Chm. (V), Piper Brewer.
Governing Authority: society; municipal; nonprofit organization. Parent Institution: City of Owosso. Subsidiary Institution: Owosso Historical Commission, City Hall, Owosso 48867. Tax-exempt.
Historic Building: 1922 Norman castle, studio of novelist James Oliver Curwood.
Collections: Curwood furniture; furnishings of the early 1900s; books; paintings; manuscripts; documents.
Research Fields: James Oliver Curwood, author & conservationist.
Facilities: Museum-related items for sale.
Activities: guided tours; docent program & council.
Publications: brochures; pamphlets.
Hours & Admission Prices: Feb.-Dec. Tues.-Sun. 1-5, tour groups on off hours by appointment only. Adults $2, children $1. Closed holidays.
Attendance: 4,000

THE MOVIE MUSEUM, 318 E. Oliver St., Owosso, MI 48867-2351. Tel.: 989-725-7621.
E-mail: moviemuseum@aol.com
Founded: 1979.
Congressional District: 10
Key Personnel: C.E.O. (V), Don Schneider; Pres. (V), Kathlyn Wooden; Sec., Lance Lurvey; Advisor, David Wilson; Advisor, Barbara Moore; Advisor, Jason Hale; Advisor, Peter Keay; Advisor, Philip Klusendorf; Advisor, Alan Cook; Advisor, Gerard Guidotti; Advisor, Mike Bruff; Advisor, Roger Snyder; Advisor, Rod Schmidt; Advisor, Kelli Boday.
Personnel Profile: Full-Time Volunteers 1; Part-Time Volunteers 47; Interns 2.
Governing Authority: nonprofit organization. Tax-exempt: 501(c)(3).
Movie Industry Museum.
Collections: machinery; books; costumes; photos; records; music; props; advertising; history; theater.
Research Fields: history of stage, records, radio, movies & TV; humanities history of social conflicts; conflict resolution.
Facilities: library; 100-seat auditorium; archives.
Activities: lectures; demonstrations; films; plays; concerts; tours; parade entry; preparing TV series for PBS-7 researchers compiled books.
Publications: newsletter; fliers; publicity; TV & radio interviews.
Hours & Admission Prices: Daily 9-9. No charge; donations accepted.
Attendance: 400 (estimated)
Membership: Senior & Student $5; Individual $10; Family $12.

STEAM RAILROADING INSTITUTE, 405 S. Washington St., Owosso, MI 48867-3523. Mailing Address: P.O. Box 665, Owosso, MI 48867-0665. Tel.: 989-725-9464. Fax: 989-723-1225.
E-mail: tjgaffney@mstrp.com
Web Site: www.michigansteamtrain.com
Formerly: Michigan State Trust for Railway Preservation, Inc./ MSU Railroad Club
Founded: 1980.
Congressional District: 4
Key Personnel: Pres., Rich Greter; Vice Pres., Bill Watkins; Treas., Richard Duffner; Exec. Dir., T.J. Gaffney; Roundhouse Foreman, Greg Udolph; Museum Shop Mgr. & Business Mgr., Jodi Hak; Membership & Newsletter, Chad Thompson.
Personnel Profile: Full-Time Paid 3; Part-Time Paid 1; Part-Time Volunteers 40; Interns 2.
Governing Authority: private; nonprofit organization. Subsidiary Institution: Steam Railroading Institute. Tax-exempt: 501(c)(3).
Railroad History Museum: housed in the former Ann Arbor Railroad machine shop; built in 1887.
Collections: operational 1941 2-8-4 steam locomotive from the Pere Marquette Railway; steam locomotive shop tools & reference materials; rolling stock and equipment from the era of steam.
Research Fields: railroad history.
Facilities: 150-vol. library of locomotive technical materials; railroad machine shop. Locomotive-related items & art reproductions for sale.
Activities: guided tours; formal education programs; lectures; traveling exhibitions; demonstrations; train & weekend excursions. Annual Events: steam locomotive repair technique seminars; Hand on the Throttle North Pole Express.
Publications: small magazine published three times annually, Project 1225; published three times annually, Members Bulletin.
Hours & Admission Prices: Memorial Day to Labor Day Wed.-Sun. 10-5; Winter: Sat.-Sun. 10-5. Adults $5; discounts to members. Closed major holidays. ♿
Attendance: 20,000 (estimated)
Membership: Subscribing $35; Individual $45; Individual Plus $55; Family $75; Family Plus $95; Donor $175.

Oxford

NORTHEAST OAKLAND HISTORICAL MUSEUM, One N. Washington St., Oxford, MI 48371-4673. Tel.: 248-628-8413 & 391-1367.
E-mail: marengli2@aol.com
Web Site: www.orion.lib.mi.us/nohm
Founded: 1971.
Congressional District: 7
Key Personnel: Pres., Gerald Griffin; Vice Pres., Ron Brock; Cur., Marie English; Treas., Darryl Lambertson.
Personnel Profile: Part-Time Volunteers 10.
Governing Authority: society; nonprofit. Parent Institution: Northeast Oakland Historical Society. Tax-exempt: 501(c)(3).
History Museum.
Collections: clothing; furniture; primitive farm and home items; tin shop from early Oxford hardware store; musical items; Mary Gregory cobalt glass; 2 WPA murals of Oxford size 7'x11'.
Research Fields: local history; genealogy; local cemeteries.
Facilities: library of atlases, history books & family histories available for use on premises. Books on local history & cemeteries & other items for sale.
Activities: guided tours; temporary exhibitions.

Hours & Admission Prices: June-Aug. Wed. & Sat. 1-4; Sept.-May Sat. 1-4. No charge; donations accepted.
Attendance: 1,000 (estimated)
Membership: Student $5; Individual $12; Life $125; Business & Organizations $500.

Paradise

GREAT LAKES SHIPWRECK MUSEUM, 18335 N. Whitefish Point Rd., Paradise, MI 49768-9618. Mailing Address: 400 W. Portage Ave., Sault Ste. Marie, MI 49783-1993. Tel.: 888-492-3747. Fax: 906-492-3383.
Web Site: www.shipwreckmuseum.com
Key Personnel: Dir., Thomas L. Farnquist, Jr.; Museum Shop Mgr., Jenny Oliver; Museum Shop Mgr., Christina Sams.
Personnel Profile: Full-Time Paid 5; Part-Time Paid 20; Part-Time Volunteers 2.
Governing Authority: Tax-exempt.
Maritime Museum.
Collections: maritime history; diving equipment; photographs.
Activities: special events.
Publications: Shipwreck Journal, quarterly; Ghosts of the Shipwreck Coast (The Art and Science of Mapping Lake Superior's Shipwreck Secrets).
Hours & Admission Prices: May-Oct. daily 10-6; other times by appointment. Adults $12, children 6-17 $8; children 5 & under no charge.
Attendance: 65,000 (accurate)
Membership: Individual 1 year $25, 3 years $70; Family 1 year $35, 3 years $100; Business 1 year $100.

Petoskey

CROOKED TREE ARTS CENTER, 461 E. Mitchell St., Petoskey, MI 49770-2623. Tel.: 616-347-4337. Fax: 616-347-5414.
E-mail: liz@crookedtree.org
Web Site: www.crookedtree.org
Founded: 1971.
Congressional District: 1
Key Personnel: Exec. Dir., Liz Gowans Ahrens; Pres. (V), Kurt Wietzke; Cur., Membership & Museum Shop Mgr., Gail Hosner; Business Mgr., Donna McDougall; Cultural Coord., Mary Wiklanski.
Personnel Profile: Full-Time Paid 7; Part-Time Volunteers 200; Interns 4.
Governing Authority: nonprofit organization. Tax-exempt: 501(c)(3).
Arts Center: housed in 1890 Methodist Church.
Collections: paintings; prints; sculpture.
Research Fields: art of Ojibway, Odawa, & Nishnawbe Native American peoples; Great Lakes maritime & history.
Facilities: 3,000 sq. ft. exhibition space; 260-seat theater; dance studio; classrooms. Artwork by Michigan artists for sale.
Activities: guided tours; lectures; films; concerts; dance recitals; arts festivals; theater; rental gallery; organized education programs for children & adults; docent program; participatory & temporary exhibitions. Museum Sponsors: March of the Arts; Art Auction; House Tour.
Publications: bimonthly newsletter, Art News; annual brochure, Native American Nishnawbe Festival.
Hours & Admission Prices: Mon.-Fri. 9-5, Sat. 10-4. Fee charged for concerts & special events. Closed legal holidays. ♿
Attendance: 55,000 (estimated)
Membership: Individual $20; Family & Organization $40; Patron $50; Friend $100; Trustee $500 & up.

LITTLE TRAVERSE REGIONAL HISTORICAL SOCIETY, (M), 100 Depot St., Petoskey, MI 49770-2476. Tel.: 231-347-2620.
Founded: 1971.
Congressional District: 11
Key Personnel: Dir., Michelle Hill; Pres., John Smith.
Personnel Profile: Full-Time Paid 1; Part-Time Volunteers 15; Interns 2.
Governing Authority: state; nonprofit. Tax-exempt: 501(c)(3).
Historical Society Museum.
Collections: local history; archives; Hemingway artifacts.
Research Fields: local history.
Facilities: 4,000-vol. library of local history books & newspapers from 1881 available for use by appointment.
Activities: walking tours; educational programs; school tours & programs; permanent & temporary exhibitions.
Publications: newsletter, The Passenger Pigeon.
Hours & Admission Prices: Memorial Day to mid-Oct. Mon.-Fri. 10-4, Sat. 1-4; mid-Oct. to May Mon.-Fri. 10-4, Sat.-Sun. 1-4. Adults $2, children 5-17 $1; members no charge.
Attendance: 5,000 (estimated)
Membership: Individual $25; Family $40; Business $60; Life $500.

Plymouth

PLYMOUTH HISTORICAL MUSEUM, (M), 155 S. Main St., Plymouth, MI 48170-1635. Tel.: 734-455-8940. Fax: 734-455-7797.
E-mail: director@plymouthhistory.org
Web Site: www.plymouthhistory.org
Founded: 1962.
Congressional District: 13
Key Personnel: Exec. Dir., Elizabeth K. Kerstens; Pres. (V), Bee Friedlander; Museum Shop Mgr., Ruth Jacobs.
Personnel Profile: Part-Time Paid 6; Part-Time Volunteers 150; Interns 2.
Governing Authority: society. Parent Institution: Plymouth Historical Society. Tax-exempt.
History Museum.
Collections: 19th-century historical artifacts; Daisy & Markham air rifles; Alter car; manuscripts; Ford village industries; Petz Abraham Lincoln collection; prints, photographs, statuary, relics, books & research files relating to the life & study of Lincoln; Plymouth, Michigan community history.
Major Exhibits: What We Collect, 2/10-6/10; Bringing Images to Life, 6/10-10/10; Santa Through the Years, 11/10-1/11.
Research Fields: local history; Civil War history; genealogy; archives; Lincoln.
Facilities: 1,500-vol. library of books, pamphlets & records available under staff supervision on premises only. Local history books, pictorial histories & craft items for sale.
Activities: guided tours; permanent, temporary & traveling exhibitions; children's hands-on exhibits; social history classes K-12.
Publications: The Story of Plymouth; Pictures of Plymouth Past & Present; Plymouth's First Century; Postcards of Plymouth.
Hours & Admission Prices: Wed. & Fri.-Sun. 1-4. Family $10, adults $5, students 5-17 $2; discounts to AAA members; members no charge. Closed holidays. ♿
Attendance: 15,000 (estimated)
Membership: Student $10; Individual $25; Family $40; Sustaining $75; Patron & Corporate $150; Lincoln Club $300.

Pontiac

CREATIVE ARTS CENTER, 47 Williams St., Pontiac, MI 48341-1759. Tel.: 248-333-7849. Fax: 248-333-7841.
E-mail: cpaster@aol.com
Web Site: www.pontiac.mi.us/cac
Founded: 1964.
Congressional District: 6
Key Personnel: Dir., Carol Paster.
Personnel Profile: Full-Time Paid 1; Part-Time Paid 2; Part-Time Volunteers 10.
Governing Authority: nonprofit. Tax-exempt: 501(c)(3).
Civic Art & Cultural Center: housed in 1898 Public Library of Oakland County.
Collections: regional, national & international artists.
Research Fields: Michigan artists registry; community artists activities; minority arts programs; arts for the disabled.
Facilities: classrooms.
Activities: formally organized education programs for adults & children; community activities; art classes; summer art camp.
Publications: bimonthly announcements.
Hours & Admission Prices: Wed.-Sat. 10-5; other times by appointment. No charge; donations accepted. Closed holidays. ♿
Attendance: 3,000 (estimated)
Membership: Artist & Seniors $20; Family $50; Organizational $75.

OAKLAND COUNTY PIONEER AND HISTORICAL SOCIETY, 405 Cesar E. Chavez Ave., Pontiac, MI 48342-1068. Tel.: 248-338-6732. Fax: 248-338-6731.
Web Site: www.ocphs.org
Formerly: Pine Grove Historical Museum
Founded: 1874.
Congressional District: 6
Key Personnel: Pres. (V), Michael Willis; Museum Shop Mgr., Judy Hudalla.
Personnel Profile: Full-Time Volunteers 7; Part-Time Volunteers 70.
Governing Authority: Parent Institution: Oakland County Pioneer & Historical Society. Tax-exempt: 501(c)(3).
Historic House Museum: c.1845 Pine Grove, the Governor Moses Wisner Historic House.
Collections: pioneer family furnishings & artifacts; smokehouse. Pine Grove Museum: Wisner Mansion; one-room schoolhouse; summer kitchen; root cellar. The Carriage House: library; pioneer farm museum.
Research Fields: Oakland County history; genealogy; archaeology; architecture; local geography; businesses; industries; commerce; Civil War.

Facilities: research library & archives of print material, manuscripts, photographs, oral histories & maps relating to Oakland County. Gift items for sale.
Activities: guided tours; school groups can rent schoolhouse for field trips. Annual Events: Ice Cream Social; Victorian Christmas open house.
Publications: quarterly newsletter, Oakland Gazette.
Hours & Admission Prices: Library: Tues.-Thurs. 11-4. Museum: group tours by appointment. Guided Tours: by appointment. Adults $5, children $3; members no charge.
Attendance: 1,000 (estimated)
Membership: Individual & Nonprofit Organization $20; Family $35; Patron $100; Benefactor $200; Corporate Sponsor & Friends of OCPHS $500.

Port Austin

HURON CITY MUSEUMS, 7995 Pioneer Rd., Port Austin, MI 48467-9400. Mailing Address: 3169 Robina, Berkley, MI 48072-3816. Tel.: 989-428-4123; 313-640-0123. Fax: 989-428-4473.
E-mail: info@huroncitymuseums.org
Web Site: www.huroncitymuseums.org
Founded: 1950.
Key Personnel: Pres. (V), Kathryn H. Parcells.
Personnel Profile: Full-Time Paid 1; Full-Time Volunteers 1; Part-Time Paid 5.
Governing Authority: nonprofit organization. Parent Institution: William Lyon Phelps Foundation. Tax-exempt.
General Museum.
Collections: local history & culture; photographs; personal artifacts; historic buildings.
Facilities: 12,000-vol. library.
Activities: guided tours.
Hours & Admission Prices: July-Aug. Fri.-Sat. 10-4; groups by appointment. Seven Gables or Village Museum: adults $6, senior citizens $5, youths 10-15 $3. Both Tours: adults $10, senior citizens $8, youths 10-15 $5; discounts to AAM & AAA members; children accompanied by an adult no charge. ♿
Attendance: 1,500 (estimated)

Port Hope

POINTE AUX BARQUES LIGHTHOUSE AND MUSEUM, 7320 Lighthouse Rd., Port Hope, MI 48468-9759. Tel.: 989-428-3035. Fax: 989-856-4505.
E-mail: president@pointeauxbarqueslighthouse.org
History Museum.
Collections: 1857 lighthouse; historical artifacts & memorabilia.
Hours & Admission Prices: Call for hours.

Port Huron

THE KNOWLTON'S ICE MUSEUM, 317 Grand River Ave., Port Huron, MI 48060-3814. Mailing Address: P.O. Box 610234, Port Huron, MI 48061-0234. Tel.: 810-987-5441.
E-mail: antiqueice@juno.com
General Museum.
Collections: tools, tongs, ice boxes, antique ice wagons, milk bottles, license plates, antique cars, dolls & baby buggies.
Hours & Admission Prices: Call for hours.

PORT HURON MUSEUM, 1115 Sixth St., Port Huron, MI 48060-5346. Tel.: 810-982-0891. Fax: 810-982-0053.
E-mail: info@phmuseum.org
Web Site: www.phmuseum.org
Founded: 1967.
Congressional District: 10
Key Personnel: Pres., Dr. Dennis Zembala; Cur. Collections, Suzette Bromley; Coord. Education, Katherine Shaefer; Site Mgr. - U.S. Coast Guard Cutter, Bramble, Michael Popelka; Site Mgr. Huron Lightship, Gerald Rome.
Personnel Profile: Full-Time Paid 7; Part-Time Paid 6; Part-Time Volunteers 85; Interns 1.
Governing Authority: nonprofit organization. Subsidiary Institution: Huron Lightship Museum; Thomas Edison Depot Museum; U.S. Coast Guard Cuter, Bramble. Tax-exempt: 501(c)(3).
General Museum: housed in 1904 Carnegie Library Building. Huron Lightship: National History Landmark. Edison Depot: Historic Train Depot; U.S. Coast Guard Cutter, Bramble.
Collections: marine; history; natural history; surgeon's instruments from Ft. Gratiot, 1814-1879; lumbering pictures & tools; prehistoric Indian artifacts; models of old Great Lakes ships; reconstructed ship's Pilot house; archaeological material from local Indian site, Fort Gratiot site & Thomas Edison boyhood homesite; local & Canadian art; lightship, Huron; U.S. Coast Guard Cutter, Bramble. Historic Building: 1854 pioneer log house.
Research Fields: Michigan & local history; Great Lakes marine history; local archaeological research, prehistoric & historic.
Facilities: 200-vol. library of Michigan & local history available for use on premises. Stationery related to local historical sites & other museum-related items for sale.
Activities: guided tours; lectures; gallery talks; inter-museum loan, permanent, temporary & traveling exhibitions. Museum Sponsors: musical & dramatic productions.
Publications: membership newsletter, Lightship; exhibition catalogs; book, Pictorial History of Port Huron; booklets.
Hours & Admission Prices: Port Huron & Thomas Edison Depot Museums: daily 11-5. Bramble & Huron Lightship Museum: Memorial Day to Labor Day daily 11-5. Adults $7, seniors & students $5; children 5 & under and members no charge. Closed most holidays. ♿
Attendance: 120,000 (estimated)
Membership: Student $15; Senior Citizens 55 & over $25; Individual $30; Family $35.

Port Sanilac

SANILAC COUNTY HISTORICAL VILLAGE AND MUSEUM, 228 S. Ridge St., Port Sanilac, MI 48469-9704. Mailing Address: P.O. Box 158, Port Sanilac, MI 48469-0158. Tel.: 810-622-9946. Fax: 810-622-0374.
E-mail: museum@greatlakes.net
Web Site: www.sanilaccountymuseum.org
Founded: 1964.
Congressional District: 8
Key Personnel: Pres. (V), Art Schlichting; Admin., Lois Schlichting; Museum Shop Mgr., Barbara Logan.
Personnel Profile: Full-Time Paid 1; Part-Time Paid 2.
Governing Authority: society; nonprofit organization. Parent Institution: Sanilac County Historical Society. Tax-exempt.
General Museum.
Collections: marine; medical; military; agriculture; Victorian furnishings; Indian artifacts & period firearms; glassware; artifacts of county dairy industry; reconstructed pioneer barn; artifacts of county farming. Historic Houses: 1872 restored Victorian Loop-Harrison Mansion; 1882 Banner Cabin, restored settlers cabin; restored one room school; restored general store.
Research Fields: recording all cemeteries in county; genealogy-family county histories.
Facilities: library of local history, archives.
Activities: guided tours; permanent & temporary exhibitions; theatre. Museum Sponsors: Log Cabin Day in June; Arts & Crafts Fair in July; Fall Open House; Victorian Christmas open house in December.
Publications: Shingle Shavers & Berry Pickers; Old Forestville & The Saxony Colony; History of Sanilac County 1834-1984; Portrait & Biographical; Sanilac County Plat Book 1906; Sanilac County Plat Book 1894. Biannual; newsletter.
Hours & Admission Prices: June-Labor Day Wed.-Fri. 11-4, Sat.-Sun. 12-4. Adults $5, senior citizens $4, children $2; discounts to AAA & Michigan Historical Society members; Historical Society of Michigan & members no charge.
Attendance: 2,500 (accurate)
Membership: Individual $25; Family $35; Life $150; Family Life $200.

Portage

TRAIN BARN MUSEUM, 10234 E. Shore Dr., Portage, MI 49002-7466. Tel.: 269-327-4016. Fax: 269-327-4012.
Model Railroad Museum.
Collections: O, S, HO, & N gauge model railroading artifacts; O gauge layout; model railroads.
Hours & Admission Prices: Jan. 2 to late Nov. Wed.-Fri. 1-6, Sat. 10-5; late Nov. to Jan. 1 daily.

Rochester

MEADOW BROOK HALL, (M), Oakland University, Rochester, MI 48309-4401. Tel.: 248-364-6200. Fax: 248-364-6201.
E-mail: glaza@oakland.edu
Web Site: www.meadowbrookhall.org
Founded: 1971.
Congressional District: 9
Key Personnel: Interim Exec. Dir., Geoff Upward; Community Rels. Mgr. & Museum Shop Mgr., Kelly Lenda; Coord. Mktg., Shannon O'Berski; Business Mgr., Robin Gardner; Assoc. Dir., Kim Zelinski; Volunteer Coord., Meredith Long; Facility Operations Coord., Nicole Thomas.
Personnel Profile: Full-Time Paid 9; Part-Time Paid 5; Part-Time Volunteers 450; Interns 2.
Governing Authority: public university; nonprofit. Parent Institution: Oakland University, Rochester, MI. Tax-exempt.

Historic House Museum: housed in the tudor-revival style mansion of Matilda Dodge Wilson, widow of automobile pioneer John Dodge & her second husband, Alfred Wilson, a Wisconsin lumber broker.

Collections: paintings; sculpture; prints & drawings; furniture; glass; porcelain & pottery; silver; linen & lace; fashion & costumes; rugs; textiles; archival materials including architectural plans; photographs; films; documents; artifacts; outbuildings.

Research Fields: 20th-century architecture & interior design; 20th-century social history; 20th-century fashion & costume; 19th-20th century Michigan & local history; automotive history.

Facilities: 100-vol. library of art & architecture books available for research only; 55,000 sq. ft. exhibit space; gardens. Museum-related items for sale.

Activities: docent program; formal education program for children & Oakland University students; guided tours; lectures; temporary & traveling exhibitions. Museum Sponsors: Jazz in the Garden; dinner & a movie; holiday walk.

Hours & Admission Prices: Guided Tours: June-Aug. daily 11:30, 12:30, 1:30, 2:30; Sept.-May Mon.-Fri. 1:30, Sat.-Sun. 11:30, 12:30, 1:30, 2:30. Adults $15, senior citizens $10; children 12 & under no charge. Closed Easter; Memorial Day; Independence Day; Labor Day; Thanksgiving; Christmas to New Year's Day.

Attendance: 111,000 (accurate)

OAKLAND UNIVERSITY ART GALLERY, 2200 N. Squirrel Rd., 208 Wilson Hall, Rochester, MI 48309-4401. Tel.: 248-370-3005. Fax: 248-370-3377.

E-mail: goody@oakland.edu

Web Site: www.oakland.edu/ouag

Formerly: Meadow Brook Art Gallery

Founded: 1962.

Congressional District: 9

Key Personnel: Dir., Dick Goody; C.E.O., Ronald Sudol; Asst. to Dir., Jacky Leow.

Personnel Profile: Full-Time Paid 2; Part-Time Paid 6; Part-Time Volunteers 2; Interns 2.

Governing Authority: university. Parent Institution: Oakland University. Subsidiary Institution: College of Art & Science, Dept. of Art & Art History. Tax-exempt.

Art Gallery.

Collections: African, Oceania, Indonesian, pre-Columbian art; contemporary American & European paintings, prints & graphics; outdoor sculptures.

Research Fields: Oriental, primitive, pre-Columbian & contemporary art.

Facilities: theater; concert hall; outdoor music pavillion; outdoor sculpture park.

Activities: lectures; gallery talks; film & slide presentations; music, dance performances in relation to art exhibitions; arts festivals; formally organized education programs for undergraduate college students; inter-museum loan; temporary & traveling exhibitions; school loan service.

Publications: exhibition catalogs.

Hours & Admission Prices: Tues.-Sun. 12-5. Special Events & Meadow Brook Theatre performances: Wed.-Fri. 7pm thru 1st intermission, Sat.-Sun. 5pm thru 1st intermission. No charge; donations accepted. ♿

Attendance: 16,000 (estimated)

Membership: Student $15; Individual $30; Family $50; Friends $100; Artist's Circle $250; Curator's Circle $500; Director's Circle $1,000; Patron's Circle $2,000.

Rochester Hills

ROCHESTER HILLS MUSEUM AT VAN HOOSEN FARM, (M), 1005 Van Hoosen Rd., Rochester Hills, MI 48306-4555. Tel.: 248-656-4663. Fax: 248-608-8198.

E-mail: rhmuseum@rochesterhills.org

Web Site: www.rochesterhills.org

Founded: 1979.

Congressional District: 18

Key Personnel: Mayor, Bryan Barnett; Supvr. Interpretive Services, Patrick J. McKay; Museum Shop Mgr., Sue Thomasson.

Personnel Profile: Full-Time Paid 3; Part-Time Paid 2; Part-Time Volunteers 35; Interns 1.

Governing Authority: municipal; nonprofit. Parent Institution: City of Rochester Hills, MI. Tax-exempt.

History Museum: housed in 1840 Van Hoosen Farmhouse, 1927 Dairy Barn, and 1850 Red House.

Collections: agricultural items; household furnishings; local archaeological artifacts; 20th-century clothing.

Research Fields: Van Doren coverlets; quilts; local history.

Facilities: 800 sq. ft. exhibit space; 60-seat auditorium. Museum-related items for sale.

Activities: guided tours; lectures; concerts; organized education programs; temporary & traveling exhibitions; summer day camps for children-archeology, science, farm. Museum Sponsors: Stonewall Pumpkin Festival; Fun Friday's.

Publications: quarterly, Museum Visitor.

Hours & Admission Prices: Wed.-Sat. 1-4. Adults $5, senior citizen & students $3. Closed major holidays. ♿

Attendance: 20,000 (estimated)

Membership: Individual $30; Individual Plus $40; Family $50; Business $250.

Rogers City

PRESQUE ISLE COUNTY HISTORICAL MUSEUM, 176 W. Michigan Ave., Rogers City, MI 49779-1638. Mailing Address: P.O. Box 175, Rogers City, MI 49779-0175. Tel.: 989-734-4121. Fax: 989-734-4121.

E-mail: bradleymuseum@yahoo.com

Web Site: www.thebradleyhouse.org

Founded: 1973.

Congressional District: 11

Key Personnel: Pres., David Nadolsky; Cur. & Museum Shop Mgr., Rose Buck; Cur., Mark Thompson.

Personnel Profile: Part-Time Paid 1; Part-Time Volunteers 60.

Governing Authority: private; nonprofit organization. Tax-exempt.

General Museum: housed in 1914 home of Carl D. Bradley, owner of Bradley Transportation Line.

Collections: area historical artifacts; maritime exhibit; historical information regarding the Bradley Fleet; original ship model of s/s Carl D. Bradley, which sank in Lake Michigan 11/18/58 taking 33 area residents' lives.

Facilities: 2,000 sq. ft. exhibit space. Museum-related items for sale.

Activities: Annual Event: Mrs. Bradley's Card Party.

Publications: semiannual newsletter.

Hours & Admission Prices: May-Sept. Tues.-Sat. 12-4. No charge; donations accepted.

Attendance: 2,500 (accurate)

Membership: Individual $15; Family $25; Sustaining $100 & up.

Royal Oak

DETROIT ZOOLOGICAL SOCIETY, (M), (I), 8450 W. 10 Mile Rd., Royal Oak, MI 48067-3001. Tel.: 248-541-5717. Fax: 248-398-0504.

Web Site: www.detroitzoo.org

Founded: 1928.

Congressional District: 9

Personnel Profile: Full-Time Paid 167; Part-Time Paid 43; Part-Time Volunteers 1,000.

Governing Authority: Parent Institution: Detroit Zoological Society. Tax-exempt.

Zoo.

Collections: 48 mammal species; 62 bird species; 26 Fish (marine & freshwater) species; 5 invertebrate species; 41 amphibian species; 87 reptile species.

Facilities: 1,500-vol. library pertaining to natural history; aquarium. Natural history books and gift items for sale.

Activities: docent program; guided tours; lectures; mobile vans; Wild Adventure Simulator. Museum Sponsors: summer day camps; special event days.

Publications: monthly newsletter, Habitat.

Hours & Admission Prices: April & Sept.-Oct. daily 10-5; May-Aug. daily 10-8; Nov.-March daily 10-4. Adults 13-61 $11, senior citizens 62 & over and children 2-12 $7; discounts to groups; members & children under 2 no charge. Closed New Year's Day; Thanksgiving; Christmas. ♿

Attendance: 1,090,544 (accurate)

Membership: Individual $45; Individual Plus $60; Family & Grandparents $74; Family Plus $89; Supporter $200; Contributor $500.

Saginaw

CASTLE MUSEUM OF SAGINAW COUNTY HISTORY, 500 Federal Ave., Saginaw, MI 48607-1253. Tel.: 989-752-2861, ext. 301. Fax: 517-752-1533.

E-mail: info@castlemuseum.org

Web Site: www.castlemuseum.org

Founded: 1948.

Congressional District: 8

Key Personnel: Pres., Margaret Clark; Dir., Irene Hensinger; Museum Shop Mgr., Sherri D. Greene.

Personnel Profile: Full-Time Paid 8; Part-Time Paid 5; Part-Time Volunteers 75; Interns 2.

Governing Authority: nonprofit organization. Parent Institution: Historical Society of Saginaw County, Inc. Tax-exempt: 501(c)(3).

History Museum: housed in an 1897 Federal post office building in the style of a French Chateau.

Collections: photographs; costumes; archaeological repository; household furnishings; logging tools; fire equipment; items manufactured by local industries.
Major Exhibits: Community of Hope (T), 2/10; The American Soldier (T), 2/18/10-4/10/10; Fifty Years of Rock & Roll (T), 4/10-5/10; Fighting Fires of Hate (T), 8/20/10-10/4/10; Inside Peanuts (T), 9/10-10/10.
Research Fields: local area history; regional archaeology; Great Lakes fur trade; Michigan lumbering; architectural history; history of postal service; regional Native American history & culture.
Facilities: meeting rooms; 80-seat community room; garden. Museum-related items for sale.
Activities: guided tours; organized education programs; workshops; lectures; films & video; living history programs; participatory archaeology programs; loan & temporary exhibitions; oral history programs.
Publications: newsletter.
Hours & Admission Prices: Tues.-Sat. 10-4:30, Sun. 1-4:30. Adults $1, children $.50; discounts to AAM members; members no charge. Closed major holidays. ♿
Attendance: 13,500 (accurate)
Membership: Individual $25; Contributing $50-$99; Century $100-$499; Museum Patron $500-$999; Museum Benefactor $1,000 & up.

CHILDREN'S ZOO AT CELEBRATION SQUARE, 1730 S. Washington Ave., Saginaw, MI 48601-2876. Tel.: 989-759-1408. Fax: 989-759-1328.
E-mail: info@saginawzoo.com
Web Site: saginawzoo.com
Formerly: Saginaw Valley Zoological Society
Founded: 1929.
Key Personnel: Exec. Dir., Nancy Parker; Mgr. Animal Collection, Rick Ballor.
Personnel Profile: Full-Time Paid 15; Part-Time Paid 20; Part-Time Volunteers 100; Interns 5.
Governing Authority: Parent Institution: Saginaw Valley Zoological Society. Tax-exempt.
Children's Zoo.
Collections: various mammals; reptiles & birds; native & exotic animals; bio diversity & artifacts.
Activities: train rides; pony rides; carousel; awareness amphitheater presentations; hands-on activities; interactive exhibits.
Publications: quarterly newsletter.
Hours & Admission Prices: May-Aug. Mon.-Tues. & Thurs.-Sat. 10-5, Wed. 10-8, Sun. & holidays 11-6; Sept. Mon.-Tues. & Thurs.-Sat. 10-5, Wed. 10-8; Oct. 1st three weekends Sat. 10-5, Sun. 11-6; Nov.-Feb. call for hours. Zoo: admission $7, senior citizens 65 & over on 1st Wed. of month, members & children under one no charge. Carousel or Train Rides: $2. ♿
Attendance: 95,000 (accurate)
Membership: Individual $40; Dual $50; Family & Grandparents $65.

MID-MICHIGAN CHILDREN'S MUSEUM, 315 W. Genesee, Saginaw, MI 48603. Mailing Address: P.O. Box 2283, Saginaw, MI 48605-2283. Tel.: 989-399-6626.
E-mail: info@midmicm.org
Web Site: www.midmicm.org
Key Personnel: Pres., Angela Barris
Children's Museum.
Collections: hands-on exhibits.
Hours & Admission Prices: Mon. & Wed.-Sat. 10-5, Sun. 12-5. Adults $7, seniors 60 & over $6; members & children under 2 no charge.

* **SAGINAW ART MUSEUM,** 1126 N. Michigan Ave., Saginaw, MI 48602-4795. Tel.: 989-754-2491, ext. 201. Fax: 989-754-9387.
E-mail: lreker@saginawartmuseum.org
Web Site: www.saginawartmuseum.org
Founded: 1947.
Congressional District: 8
Key Personnel: Exec. Dir., Les Reker; Pres. (V), Rick Goedert; Cur. Education, Kara Brown; Dir. Mktg. & Devel., Norma Zivich; Dir. Membership, Sheree Shaw; Asst. Cur., Ryan Kaltenbach; Facilities Mgr., Jim Hitchcock; Assoc., Sandy Sawatzi; Assoc., Chelsea Vowell; Bookkeeping, Sue Hagen; Housekeeping, Joan Aguilera.
Personnel Profile: Full-Time Paid 4; Part-Time Paid 5; Part-Time Volunteers 200; Interns 2.
Governing Authority: private; nonprofit organization. Smithsonian Affiliate. Tax-exempt: 501(c)(3).
Art Museum: housed in former residence of Clark L. Ring family, building designed in 1904 by Charles Adams Platt.
Collections: 2,500 BCE to present international fine & applied art; E.I. Couse; Corot; Cropsey; Inness; Blakelock; Minor; Huntington; Demuth; Hassom; African; Etruscan; Chinese; Japanese; European; American; 14th century to present works on paper; archives of Michigan art; interactive Vision Area.
Research Fields: Michigan art & artists.
Facilities: 2,000-vol. art history library; studio & classroom; formal garden. Museum-related items for sale.
Activities: guided tours; lectures; films; gallery talks; workshops; seminars; formally organized education programs; permanent & temporary exhibitions; inter-museum loan; art classes; hands-on children's exhibits.
Publications: quarterly newsletter; catalogs; show announcements.
Hours & Admission Prices: Tues.-Sat. 10-5, Sun. 1-5. Adults $5; Michigan Art Museums reciprocal memberships; discounts to AAM & ICOM members; members no charge. Closed national holidays. ♿
Attendance: 21,411 (accurate)
Membership: Student & Senior Citizen $20; Individual $40; Family $50; Smithsonian $125; Sustaining $200; Contributor $300; Patron $500; Visionary $1,000.

Saint Clair Shores

SELINSKY-GREEN FARMHOUSE MUSEUM, 22500 Eleven Mile Rd., Saint Clair Shores, MI 48081-1312. Tel.: 586-771-9020. Fax: 586-771-8935.
E-mail: stachowm@libcoop.net
Historic House.
Collections: period artifacts & memorabilia about rural life in St. Clair Shores during the late 19th & early 20th centuries.
Hours & Admission Prices: June-Aug. Wed. 1-4; Sept.-May Wed. & Sat. 1-4.

Saint Ignace

FATHER MARQUETTE NATIONAL MEMORIAL, 720 Church St., Saint Ignace, MI 49781-1729. Tel.: 906-643-8620. Fax: 906-643-9329. TDD: 800-827-7007.
Founded: 1980.
Congressional District: 11
Key Personnel: Park Mgr., Wayne Burnett.
Governing Authority: state; nonprofit. Tax-exempt.
National Memorial.
Collections: sculpture.
Hours & Admission Prices: Memorial Day to Labor Day daily 9:30-5. No charge. ♿
Attendance: 14,810 (accurate)

WEIRD MICHIGAN WAX MUSEUM, N895 Martin Lake Rd., Saint Ignace, MI 49781-9864. Mailing Address: P.O. Box 850, Saint Ignace, MI 49781-0850. Tel.: 906-643-8760; 800-331-3530.
Wax Museum.
Collections: life-sized wax figures.
Facilities: Museum-related items for sale.
Hours & Admission Prices: mid-May to Labor Day Mon.-Sat. 9-8, Sun. 10-7; Sept. to mid-Oct. Mon.-Sat. 9-6, Sun. 10-6. Adults 12 & over $7, children 5-11 $5; discounts to groups; children under 5 no charge. ♿

Saint Johns

CLINTON COUNTY HISTORICAL SOCIETY PAINE-GILLAM-SCOTT MUSEUM, 106 Maple Ave., Saint Johns, MI 48879-1838. Mailing Address: P.O. Box 174, Saint Johns, MI 48879-0174. Tel.: 989-224-2894.
E-mail: pgsmuseum@hotmail.com
Web Site: pgsmuseum.com
Founded: 1978.
Congressional District: 8
Key Personnel: Dir., Catherine Rumbaugh.
Personnel Profile: Part-Time Volunteers 10.
Governing Authority: society; nonprofit. Parent Institution: Clinton Co. Historical Society. Tax-exempt: 501(c)(3).
Historic House: Oldest Brick House in St. Johns.
Collections: local history; period furnishings.
Research Fields: county history & genealogy.
Facilities: 90-vol. library of Michigan & Clinton County history material.
Activities: guided tours; organized education programs for children. Museum Sponsors: Mint Festival; Victorian Christmas.
Publications: quarterly genealogist newsletter, Clinton County Trails.
Hours & Admission Prices: April-Dec. Wed. 2-7, Sun. 1-4; other times by appointment. Donations requested. Closed legal holidays.
Attendance: 1,200 (accurate)
Membership: Clinton Historical Society: Single $10; Couple $15.

Saint Joseph

THE CURIOUS KIDS' MUSEUM, 415 Lake Blvd., Saint Joseph, MI 49085-1231. Tel.: 269-983-2543. Fax: 269-983-3317.
E-mail: ckm@curiouskidsmuseum.org
Web Site: www.curiouskidsmuseum.org
Founded: 1988.
Congressional District: 6
Key Personnel: Pres. (V), Tim Passaro; Museum Mgr., Patricia Adams; Program Dir., Gina Mason; Outreach Dir., Sherry Bragg; Facilities Mgr., Phil Rood; Floor Mgr. & Volunteer Coord., Myrna Piehl; Museum Shop Mgr., Becky Spear.
Personnel Profile: Full-Time Paid 2; Part-Time Paid 15; Part-Time Volunteers 52.
Governing Authority: private; nonprofit. Tax-exempt: 501(c)(3).
Children's Museum: located in the former Memorial Hall.
Collections: over 100 hands-on exhibits in science, history & culture; natural (plants); medical; global child; rain forest; volcano; earthquake; space; simple machines; bridge building.
Major Exhibits: Grossology - The Impolite Science of the Human Body (T), 5/25/10-9/5/10.
Research Fields: science, history, & culture technology.
Activities: family programs; day camps; curiosity camps; Girl & Boy Scout badges; outreach traveling exhibits & programs; curious classroom curriculum units; birthday parties.
Publications: newsletter; brochure.
Hours & Admission Prices: June-Labor Day Mon.-Sat. 10-5, Sun. 12-5; Sept.-May Wed.-Sat. 10-5, Sun. 12-5. Adults $6; discounts to groups; children under one, members, ACM reciprocal members no charge. Closed New Year's Day; Easter; Memorial Day; Independence Day; Labor Day; Thanksgiving; Christmas. ♿
Attendance: 65,000 (accurate)
Membership: Individual $25; Family & Grandparents $65; Benefactor $100; Patron $500; Sponsor $1,000.

HERITAGE MUSEUM AND CULTURAL CENTER, 601 Main St., Saint Joseph, MI 49085-3354. Tel.: 269-983-1191.
Formerly: Fort Miami Heritage Society
Key Personnel: Dir., Kenneth R. Pott.
Personnel Profile: Full-Time Paid 1; Part-Time Paid 3; Part-Time Volunteers 25; Interns 1.
Governing Authority: Tax-exempt.
History Museum.
Collections: local history & culture; photographs; period artifacts.
Research Fields: St. Joseph & Benton Harbor; Michigan history.
Facilities: library; archives.
Publications: The Heritage Journal.
Hours & Admission Prices: Tues.-Fri. 10-4. Adults $5; members & children 15 & under no charge. ♿
Membership: Student $20; Senior $30; Individual $40; Family $60; Sponsor $150; Benefactor $500.

* **KRASL ART CENTER, (M),** 707 Lake Blvd., Saint Joseph, MI 49085-1313. Tel.: 269-983-0271. Fax: 269-983-0275.
E-mail: info@krasl.org
Web Site: krasl.org
Founded: 1963.
Congressional District: 4
Key Personnel: Exec. Dir., Donna G. Metz; Pres., Jacquie Johnson; Vice Pres., Jerry Sirk; Administrative Dir. & Museum Shop Mgr., Patrice Rose; Dir. Exhibitions & Collections, Tami Gadbois; Dir. Education, Julia Gourley; Education Asst., Erica Westbrook; Dir. Art Fair, Sara Shambarger; Volunteer Coord., Danielle Shepherd; Office Asst., Caryl Meister.
Personnel Profile: Full-Time Paid 6; Part-Time Paid 4; Part-Time Volunteers 375; Interns 2.
Governing Authority: nonprofit organization. Parent Institution: St. Joseph Art Association, Inc. Tax-exempt: 501(c)(3).
Art Center.
Collections: sculpture.
Major Exhibits: Supporting Artists: Krasl Art Center Members Exhibition, 1/10-2/10; Grand Valley State University Ceramics Exhibition: Instructors, Students & Alumni, 2/10-4/10; Abstract Organic: Ceramic Sculptures by Yumike Goto, 2/10-4/10; Ladislaw Hanka's Marker Trees & Marcia Perry's Abstract Wood Sculptures (T), 4/10-6/10; Intimate Viewing: Fresco & Sculptural Works by Judith Mullen, 4/10-6/10; 2010 Biennial Sculpture Invitational, 6/10-8/10; Ultra-Realistic Sculpture by Marc Sijan (T), 9/10-10/10; Killerkitsch by Three Contemporary Artists, 11/10-12/10; Christmas Kitsch, 11/10-12/10.
Facilities: classrooms. Paintings, sculpture, ceramics, textiles & jewelry for sale.
Activities: guided tours; lectures; films; gallery talks; workshops; formally organized education programs for children & adults.
Publications: bimonthly newsletter; class schedules; exhibition brochures; catalogues.
Hours & Admission Prices: Mon.-Wed. & Fri.-Sat. 10-4, Thurs. 10-9, Sun. 1-4. No charge; donations accepted. Closed holidays. ♿
Attendance: 30,000 (estimated)
Membership: Senior Citizen $28; Youth $30; Individual $35; Family $50; Sponsor $75-$99; Sustainer $100-$249; Benefactor $250-$499; Patron $500-$999; Guarantor $1,000-$2,499; Master $2,500-$4,999; Director's Choice $5,000-$9,999; Director's Circle $10,000 & up.

Sault Ste. Marie

KEMP MINERAL RESOURCES MUSEUM, 650 W. Easterday Ave., Sault Ste. Marie, MI 49783-1656.
E-mail: kmrm@lssu.edu
Web Site: www.lssu.edu
Key Personnel: Cur., Dr. David M. Knowles
Mineral Museum.
Collections: rock & mineral collections.
Hours & Admission Prices: Call for hours.

LE SAULT DE SAINTE MARIE HISTORICAL SITES, INC., 501 E. Water St., Sault Ste. Marie, MI 49783-2038. Tel.: 906-632-3658. Fax: 906-632-9344.
E-mail: admin@saulthistorics.com
Web Site: www.saulthistoricsites.com
Founded: 1967.
Congressional District: 11
Key Personnel: Dir., Rich Brawley; Pres. (V), John P. Wellington; Bookkeeper, Charlotte Hendrickson.
Personnel Profile: Full-Time Paid 1; Part-Time Paid 20.
Governing Authority: nonprofit organization. Tax-exempt: 501(c)(3).
Maritime Museum.
Collections: 1917 550 ft. Great Lakes straight deck bulk carrier; Great Lakes maritime items; mid-19th to early 20th-century items; ethnology; archives.
Facilities: aquarium; 25,000 sq. ft. exhibit space; two 25-seat theaters. Books & gift items for sale.
Activities: guided tours; films.
Publications: Ship's Bell.
Hours & Admission Prices: mid-May to June & Sept. to mid-Oct. Mon.-Sat. 10-4, Sun. 11-4; July to Aug. Mon.-Sat. 10-5, Sun. 11-5 Call for admission prices. ♿
Attendance: 28,100 (accurate)
Membership: Individual $25; Family $50; History Buff $75; Sustaining $100; Benefactor $250; Corporate $500; Lifetime $1,500 & up.

Sebewaing

LUCKHARD MUSEUM - THE INDIAN MISSION, 612 E. Bay St., Sebewaing, MI 48759-1644. Tel.: 989-883-2539 & 3730.
Founded: 1957.
Key Personnel: Dir., Jim Bunke.
Personnel Profile: Part-Time Volunteers 2.
Governing Authority: church; nonprofit. Owned by Michigan District of Missouri Lutheran Church, Ann Arbor, MI. Tax-exempt.
Historic House: 1849 mission home.
Collections: household furnishings; kitchenwares; religious artifacts; period tools & clothing; Native American birch bark canoe, arrowheads, headdress.
Facilities: library of church mission books & diaries.
Activities: guided tours; lectures.
Publications: brochure.
Hours & Admission Prices: June-Sept. 1st Sun. of month 2-4. Sebewaing Sugar Festival: call for hours. No charge; donations accepted.
Attendance: 40 (estimated)

Selfridge ANG Base

SELFRIDGE MILITARY AIR MUSEUM, (M), 127 WG/MU, 27333 C St., Bldg. 1011, Selfridge ANG Base, MI 48045-4901. Tel.: 586-307-5035. Fax: 586-307-6646.
History Museum.
Collections: military history & heritage; aircraft; war memorabilia; photographs.
Hours & Admission Prices: April-Oct. Sat.-Sun. 12-4:30; other times by appointment. Adults $4, children 4-12 $3.

Seney

SENEY NATIONAL WILDLIFE REFUGE VISITOR CENTER, Seney National Wildlife Refuge, Seney, MI 49883. Mailing Address: 1674 Refuge Entrance Rd., Seney, MI 49883-9509. Tel.: 906-586-9851, ext. 15. Fax: 906-586-3800.
E-mail: jennifer_mcdonough@fws.gov
Web Site: www.fws.gov/midwest/seney
Founded: 1963.
Congressional District: 1
Key Personnel: Pres. Seney Natural History Assoc., Dee Phinney; Museum Shop Mgr., Claudia Slater.
Personnel Profile: Part-Time Paid 2; Part-Time Volunteers 50; Interns 3.
Governing Authority: federal. Parent Institution: U.S. Dept. of the Interior, Fish & Wildlife Service. Tax-exempt.
Nature Center.
Collections: wildlife refuge; study skin & full mounted specimens; duck stamp 1934 to present; dioramas of the common loon, eagle & wolf.
Research Fields: yellow rail research project; loon monitoring; swan monitoring; various bird surveys; sharptail grouse research; small mammal research.
Facilities: 75-seat auditorium; nature trails. Nature study books, study aids, wildlife posters & related items for sale.
Activities: educational programs; self-guided auto tour; permanent & temporary exhibitions; summer programs; high definition orientation DVD.
Publications: refuge brochure; hunting brochure; fishing brochure; bird checklist; newsletter.
Hours & Admission Prices: May 15-Oct. 15 daily 9-5. No charge; donations accepted. ♿
Attendance: 60,000 (estimated)
Membership: Seney Natural History Association: Retired & senior $5; Individual $10; Family $15; Contributing $25; Supporting $40; Business $75; Corporate $200; Lifetime $500.

South Haven

MICHIGAN MARITIME MUSEUM, (M), 260 Dyckman Ave., South Haven, MI 49090-1065. Tel.: 269-637-8078; 800-747-3810. Fax: 269-637-1594.
E-mail: info@michiganmaritimemuseum.org
Web Site: michiganmaritimemuseum.org
Founded: 1976.
Congressional District: 4
Key Personnel: Exec. Dir., Ellen Sprouls; Pres. Bd. (V), Steven Holt; Cur., Cobie Ball; Dir. Boat Shed, David Ludwig; Dir. Padnos Boat Shed, Paul D. Ludwig; Registrar, Judy Schlaack; Captain, Tom Kastle; Coord. Programs, Amy Locker; Programs Asst., Amanda Morris; Librarian & Archivist, Kristen Edson; Docent Coord., Mary Stephens; Museum Shop Mgr. & Office Mgr., Mechele Kempski; Asst. Cur., Jed Jaworski.
Personnel Profile: Full-Time Paid 9; Part-Time Paid 13; Part-Time Volunteers 75.
Governing Authority: nonprofit organization. Subsidiary Institution: Great Lakes Center for Maritime Studies. Tax-exempt.
Maritime History Museum.
Collections: historical vessels; archival materials; photos; ship & small craft models; marine art; tools & technological implements; personal artifacts pertaining to Great Lakes regional maritime history; historic replica tall ship; commercial fishing tug; lightkeeper's dwelling. Historic Buildings: 1873 Lightkeeper's Dwelling; 1900 U.S. Life Saving Station crew's quarters including service exhibit.
Research Fields: Great Lakes Maritime History.
Facilities: 4,000-vol. library of materials pertaining to Great Lakes general & maritime history available for research; classrooms; visitor center; Herbert Van Oort Boathouse; Padnos Boat Shed. Gifts & books for sale.
Activities: guided tours; lectures; films; gallery talks; boatbuilding workshops; formally organized education programs for children, adults & undergraduate college students; training programs for professional museum workers; temporary & permanent exhibitions; sail on a tall ship.
Publications: newsletter, Ship's Lamp; collection & monograph books.
Hours & Admission Prices: Mon.-Sat. 10-5, Sun. 12-5. Adults $5, children under 17 $4.50, senior citizens $4; discounts to AAM & ICOM members; members no charge. Closed New Year's Day; Easter; Thanksgiving; Christmas. ♿
Attendance: 30,000 (estimated)
Membership: Senior Citizen $20; Individual $25; Family $40; Ensign $100; Captain $250; Commodore $500; Admiral $1,000.

South Range

COPPER RANGE HISTORICAL MUSEUM, Champion & Trimountain, South Range, MI 49963. Mailing Address: P.O. Box 148, South Range, MI 49963-0148. Tel.: 906-482-6125.
Web Site: www.pasty.com/chrm
Founded: 1988.
Congressional District: 107
Key Personnel: Pres. (V), Jean Pemberton.
Personnel Profile: Part-Time Volunteers 20.
Governing Authority: Tax-exempt.
History Museum.
Collections: area history; furnishings; personal artifacts.
Research Fields: area business; copper mines.
Activities: group tours upon request. Museum Sponsors: Open House in June.
Publications: newsletter 3 times per year.
Hours & Admission Prices: June & Sept.-Oct. Tues.-Sat. 12-3; July-Aug. Mon.-Sat. 12-3. No charge; donations accepted.
Attendance: 865 (accurate)
Membership: Individual $10; Family $15; Supporting $50; Senior Life $75; Life $150; Corporate Sponsor $1,000; Corporate Patron $5,000.

Tecumseh

TECUMSEH AREA HISTORICAL MUSEUM, 302 E. Chicago Blvd., Tecumseh, MI 49286-1551. Mailing Address: P.O. Box 26, Tecumseh, MI 49286-0026. Tel.: 517-423-2374.
Web Site: www.historictecumseh.org
Historical Society Museum: housed in a gothic stone church c.1913.
Collections: local history & culture; photographs.
Hours & Admission Prices: Wed.-Sat. 11-3. No charge.
Membership: Individual $10; Senior $50; Lifetime $100.

Tipton

HIDDEN LAKE GARDENS, 6214 Monroe Rd., (M-50), Tipton, MI 49287-9766. Tel.: 517-431-2060. Fax: 517-431-9148.
E-mail: court33@msu.edu
Web Site: www.hiddenlakegardens.msu.edu
Founded: 1926.
Congressional District: 2
Key Personnel: Mgr., Steven Courtney, N.P.D.; Sec. & Gift Shop Mgr., Cheryl Rittenhouse.
Governing Authority: university. Affiliated with Michigan State University, East Lansing, MI 48823. Tax-exempt.
Arboretum.
Collections: over 2,500 species of woody plants arranged in systematic & use groupings; woodlands; regenerating forest.
Research Fields: plant breeding.
Facilities: 1,800-vol. library on horticulture & allied fields available for use on premises; botanical garden; nature center; nature trails; plant conservatory; 80-seat auditorium; classrooms. Books & prints for sale.
Activities: guided tours; lectures; formally organized education programs for adults; permanent exhibitions.
Hours & Admission Prices: April-Oct. daily 8-dusk; Nov.-March daily 8-4. Admission $3.
Attendance: 48,000 (accurate)
Membership: Single $30; Dual $40; Family & Friends $60.

Traverse City

DENNOS MUSEUM CENTER OF NORTHWESTERN MICHIGAN COLLEGE, (M), 1701 E. Front St., Traverse City, MI 49686-3016. Tel.: 231-995-1055. Fax: 231-995-1597.
E-mail: dmc@nmc.edu
Web Site: www.dennosmuseum.org
Founded: 1991.
Congressional District: 9
Key Personnel: Dir., Eugene A. Jenneman; Registrar, Kim Hanninen; Museum Shop Mgr., Terry Tarnow; Cur. Education, Diana Bolander; Asst. to Dir., Judith Albers.
Personnel Profile: Full-Time Paid 6; Part-Time Paid 5; Part-Time Volunteers 120.
Governing Authority: nonprofit public college. Parent Institution: Northwestern Michigan College. Tax-exempt: 501(c)(3).
College Art Museum.
Collections: contemporary Inuit sculpture & prints; Canadian Indian & Great Lakes Indian art; Japanese prints; 19th- & 20th-century American & European prints; contemporary German prints; outdoor sculpture; photography.
Research Fields: Inuit art.

Facilities: 300-vol. library of Inuit art publications & periodicals; educational facilities; 367-seat theater; 8,000 sq. ft. exhibit space. Museum-related items for sale.
Activities: guided tours; lectures; loan, participatory, temporary & traveling exhibits; concerts; dance recitals; docent program; films; formal education programs; theater.
Publications: quarterly newsletter, Inside.
Hours & Admission Prices: Mon.-Wed. & Fri.-Sat. 10-5, Thurs. 10-8, Sun. 1-5. Adults & senior citizens $6, students & children $4; discounts to groups, AAM & ICOM members; members no charge. Closed New Year's Day; Easter; Memorial Day; Independence Day; Labor Day; Thanksgiving; Christmas. ♿
Attendance: 60,000 (accurate)
Membership: Individual $40; Family $60; Friend $100; Associate $250; Curator's Circle $500; Director's Circle $1,000; Corporate $2,500.

GRAND TRAVERSE HERITAGE CENTER, 322 Sixth St., Traverse City, MI 49684-2414. Tel.: 231-995-0313. Fax: 231-946-6750.
E-mail: gthc@charterinternet.com
Web Site: gtheritagecenter.com
Formerly: Friends of Con Foster Museum, Inc.
Founded: 2000.
Congressional District: 1
Key Personnel: Exec. Dir., Lori Puckett; Pres. (V) & Cur., Steve Harold.
Personnel Profile: Full-Time Paid 1; Part-Time Paid 1; Part-Time Volunteers 40; Interns 1.
Governing Authority: municipal government. Parent Institution: City of Traverse. Subsidiary Institution: Friends of Con Foster Museum. Tax-exempt.
Local History Museum.
Collections: American Indian artifacts; agriculture; local history; transportation; folk art; photographs; railroads; maritime.
Research Fields: local & regional history.
Facilities: temporary & permanent exhibits; classroom & reading room; reference library; archives; meeting rooms.
Activities: guided tours; lectures; special events; educational programs.
Publications: quarterly newsletter to members; occasional special event publications.
Hours & Admission Prices: Heritage Center: Mon.-Fri. 9-5. Museum: Mon.-Sat. 10-4. Adults $3, students $1.50; children 6 & under and members no charge. ♿
Attendance: 15,000 (estimated)
Membership: Student $5; Individual $25; Family $40; Friend $100; Patron $250; Sponsor $500; Life $1,000.

Trenton

TRENTON HISTORICAL MUSEUM, 306 St. Joseph, Trenton, MI 48183-2823. Mailing Address: 2800 Third St., Trenton, MI 48183-2918. Tel.: 734-675-2130.
Web Site: www.trentonhistoricalcommission.org
Founded: 1962.
Congressional District: 16
Key Personnel: Dir., Linda Murdock; Vice Chm. (V), Darlene Schoen.
Personnel Profile: Part-Time Volunteers 17.
Governing Authority: municipal. Tax-exempt.
Historic House Museum: c.1881 Victorian house.
Collections: Victorian era furnishings; Indian arrowheads; horse drawn carriages; Trenton Room. Historic Building & Carriage House.
Research Fields: files, local history information.
Facilities: library of reference books available for use on premises.
Activities: guided tours.
Hours & Admission Prices: Feb.-July & Sept.-Dec. Sat. 1-4. No charge; donations accepted. Closed national holidays.
Attendance: 1,500 (estimated)

Troy

TROY MUSEUM & HISTORIC VILLAGE, (M), 60 W. Wattles Rd., Troy, MI 48098-4699. Tel.: 248-524-3570. Fax: 248-524-3572.
E-mail: museum@troymi.gov
Web Site: www.troymi.gov/museum
Founded: 1968.
Congressional District: 12
Key Personnel: Mgr., Loraine Campbell; Archivist, William Boardman; Museum Asst., Diane Behrendt; Pres. Historical Society, Cheryl Barnard; Historical Interpreter, Gillian Ellis; Historical Interpreter, Nancy Jones; Historical Interpreter, Raymond Lucas; Historical Interpreter, Laura Bunting; Historical Interpreter, Anne Nagrant; Historical Interpreter, Debra Newby; Historical Interpreter, Ginny Czerwinski; Museum Shop Mgr., Vi Smith.
Personnel Profile: Full-Time Paid 2; Part-Time Paid 9; Part-Time Volunteers 75; Interns 4.
Governing Authority: municipal. Parent Institution: City of Troy, MI. Tax-exempt: 501(c)(3).
History Museum.
Collections: local agricultural equipment; early pioneer living collection; local archives & manuscripts; permanent & temporary exhibits. Historic Buildings: 1832 Caswell House; 1877 Poppleton School; c.1918 county store; c.1910 print shop; 1875 Wagon shop; c.1864 Town Hall; 1927 City Hall; 1820 log cabin; 1837 church; 1900 farm house.
Research Fields: local biographical.
Facilities: 500-vol. library. Gift items for sale.
Activities: guided tours; permanent & temporary exhibitions; educational programs. Special Events: Hanging of the Greens; Trick or Treating on the Green; Fall Farm Festival.
Publications: quarterly newsletter, The Troy-Village Press; Troy Museum & Historical Village Activities Book for Children; When Our Country Called: Stories of WWII Veterans from Troy and Troy Township; Troy: A City From the Corners; Troy Twp. Section: 1817-1877 History of Oakland County; The Life of Solomon Caswell.
Hours & Admission Prices: June-Sept. Mon.-Sat. 9-5:30, Sun. 1-5; Oct.-May Mon.-Sat. 9-5:30. Adults $3, children $2. Closed New Year's Eve & Day; Memorial Day; weekend; Independence Day; Labor Day weekend; Thanksgiving weekend; Christmas Eve & Day. ♿
Attendance: 26,025 (accurate)
Membership: Individual $20; Couple & Family $30; Nonprofit Institution $50; Business $100; Life $200.

University Center

MARSHALL M. FREDERICKS SCULPTURE MUSEUM, (M), Arbury Fine Arts Center, Saginaw Valley State University, 7400 Bay Rd., University Center, MI 48710-0001. Tel.: 989-964-7125. Fax: 989-964-7221.
E-mail: mfsm@svsu.edu
Web Site: www.marshallfredericks.org
Founded: 1988.
Congressional District: 8 & 10
Key Personnel: Chm. (V), Sue Vititoe; Dir., Marilyn L. Wheaton; Cur. Education, Andrea Ondish; Sr. Sec., Laurie Allison.
Personnel Profile: Full-Time Paid 5; Part-Time Paid 7; Part-Time Volunteers 1.
Governing Authority: college. Parent Institution: Saginaw Valley State University. Tax-exempt.
Sculpture Museum.
Collections: plaster models; cast & carved sculptures; medals; jewelry; miniatures; drawings; photos; site models; moulds; armatures; tools; machinery; archival materials by Marshall M. Fredericks (1908-1998)
Major Exhibits: Sketches to Sculptures: Rendered Reality Sixty Years with Marshall M. Fredericks, 2/5/10-6/12/10; Regional Biennial Juried Sculpture Exhibition, 7/3/10-9/18/10.
Research Fields: life & work of Marshall M. Fredericks, 1908-1998; American sculpture of the 20th century.
Facilities: 18,000 sq. ft. exhibit space. Museum-related items for sale.
Activities: guided tours; organized education programs for youth; youth summer art camps; docent program; film series.
Publications: exhibition catalogs; Friends of MFSM Newsletter.
Hours & Admission Prices: Mon.-Sat. 12-5. No charge. Closed national & university holidays. ♿
Attendance: 10,000 (estimated)
Membership: Senior & Student $35; Individual $50; Friend $100; Donor $250; Supporter $500; Patron $1,000; Benefactor $2,500.

Vulcan

IRON MOUNTAIN IRON MINE, Hwy. U.S. 2, Vulcan, MI 49892. Mailing Address: P.O. Box 177, Iron Mountain, MI 49801-0177. Tel.: 906-774-7914.
E-mail: ironmine@uplogon.com
Web Site: www.ironmountainironmine.com
Founded: 1956.
Congressional District: 11
Key Personnel: Dir., Eugene R. Carollo; Dir. Public Rels., Dennis Carollo.
Personnel Profile: Full-Time Paid 3; Part-Time Paid 8.
Governing Authority: individual operation.
Mining Museum: located on Menominee Iron Range.
Collections: working mining machinery; diamond drills; stoper drills; water liner drills; underground locomotives.
Facilities: underground lighted cavern. Gift items for sale.
Activities: guided tours; formally organized education programs; permanent exhibitions; underground train rides.
Hours & Admission Prices: Memorial Day to mid-Oct. daily 9-5. Adults $9,

children $7; discount to members, AARP, AAA & school groups; children 5 & under no charge. ♿
Attendance: 16,000 (estimated)

Wayne

CITY OF WAYNE HISTORICAL MUSEUM, 1 Town Square, Wayne, MI 48184-1637. Tel.: 734-722-0113.
Web Site: www.ci.wayne.mi.us/museum/php
Founded: 1964.
Congressional District: 15
Key Personnel: Mgr., Richard L. Story.
Personnel Profile: Part-Time Paid 1.
Governing Authority: municipal. Tax-exempt.
Local History Museum: housed in 1878 Village Hall.
Collections: historical items related to the City of Wayne & vicinity; local area maps; published & unpublished historical articles; reference materials; newspapers; clippings; scrap books; photographs.
Research Fields: local history.
Facilities: over 500-vol. library of material on Wayne, Wayne County & Michigan history available for use on premises.
Activities: guided tours; permanent & temporary exhibits.
Publications: newsletter, Wayne Historical Society.
Hours & Admission Prices: Fri.-Sat. 1-4; groups by appointment. No charge; donations accepted.
Attendance: 1,200 (accurate)
Membership: Year $10; Life $100.

West Bloomfield

SHALOM STREET, 6600 W. Maple Rd., West Bloomfield, MI 48322-3003. Tel.: 877-SHALOM-3. Fax: 248-432-5568.
E-mail: wsadler@shalomstreet.org
Web Site: www.shalomstreet.org
Key Personnel: Dir., Wendy Sadler; Program Coord., Lizzie Doppelt
Children's Museum.
Collections: hands-on exhibits.
Facilities: 4,500 sq. ft. exhibit space.
Activities: special events; educational programs; birthday parties.
Hours & Admission Prices: Sept.-May Sun.-Thurs. 1-5; groups by appointment. Adults $5; discounts to groups.

Wyandotte

WYANDOTTE MUSEUM, 2610 Biddle Ave., Wyandotte, MI 48192-5208. Tel.: 734-324-7284. Fax: 734-324-7283.
E-mail: museum@wyan.org
Web Site: www.wyandotte.net
Founded: 1958.
Congressional District: 16
Key Personnel: Dir. Museums, Jody Chansuolme; Pres. (V), Ken Navarre; Museum Shop Mgr., Sandra Noble.
Personnel Profile: Full-Time Paid 1; Part-Time Paid 2; Part-Time Volunteers 2.
Governing Authority: municipal. Parent Institution: City of Wyandotte. Tax-exempt.
History Museum: housed in 1896 Ford-MacNichol period home.
Collections: Americana; Wyandotte history; Wayne County history; shipbuilding; chemical industry collection. Historic House: 1857 Marx Museum period home; 1896 Ford-MacNichol period home.
Research Fields: local history.
Facilities: 2,000-vol. library of Americana, American history, Michigan history & Native American history available for use on premises.
Activities: guided tours; lectures; temporary exhibitions; school loan service.
Publications: monthly newsletter; pamphlets; brochures; books, Proudly We Record; Our Fame & Fortune in Wyandotte.
Hours & Admission Prices: Tours: Mon.-Fri. 9-5. Adults $2, students $.50; children under 13 & members no charge. Closed Easter; Labor Day; Thanksgiving; Christmas. ♿
Attendance: 999
Membership: Student $1; Adult $15; Contributing $25; Patron $50; Honorary Patron $100 & up.

Ypsilanti

MICHIGAN FIREHOUSE MUSEUM, 110 W. Cross St., Ypsilanti, MI 48197-2445. Tel.: 734-547-0663.
E-mail: firemuseum@msn.com
Web Site: www.michiganfirehousemuseum.org
Fire-Fighting Museum.
Collections: fire-fighting equipment & memorabilia.
Publications: quarterly newsletter, Firehouse News.
Hours & Admission Prices: Tues.-Sat. 10-4, Sun. 12-4. Adults $3, firefighters, senior citizens & students $2, children 6-15 $1.50; children under 6 no charge. ♿
Attendance: 11,000 (accurate)

YANKEE AIR FORCE, INC. (YANKEE AIR MUSEUM), Hangar 2, Willow Run Airport, Ypsilanti, MI 48198. Mailing Address: P.O. Box 590, Belleville, MI 48112-0590. Tel.: 734-483-4030. Fax: 734-483-5076.
E-mail: dick.stewart@yankeeairmuseum.org
Web Site: www.yankeeairmuseum.org
Founded: 1981.
Congressional District: 15
Key Personnel: Pres., Dick Stewart; Vice Pres., Lou Farkas; Treas., Tom Matz; Sec., Speed Gant; Aircraft Appearance Coord., Norman Ellickson; Cur. & Dir. Museum Activities, Gayle Drews; Membership, Jim Race; Public Rels., Bob Hynes; Security, William Tonak; Museum Shop Mgr., Dale Worcester.
Personnel Profile: Full-Time Paid 3; Full-Time Volunteers 12; Part-Time Paid 7; Part-Time Volunteers 450; Interns 6.
Governing Authority: nonprofit organization. Parent Institution: Eastern Michigan University & Michigan State University. Subsidiary Institutions: YAF Northeast Div., East Caldwell, NJ; YAF Saginaw Valley Div., Saginaw, MI; YAF Willow Run Div., Belleville, MI; YAF Wurtsmith Div., Oscoda, MI. Tax-exempt: 501(c)(3).
Aeronautics Museum.
Collections: historic WWII era aircraft including B-17G, B-25D & C-47; costumes; textiles.
Activities: docent program; guided tours; temporary exhibitions; speakers' bureau; flyable historic aircraft participates in air shows & civic events throughout the U.S. & Canada. Museum Sponsors: Open House; Air Show on & off site; weekend event; Historic Flight Experience Rides May to October.
Publications: monthly magazine, Hangar Happenings; newsletter; 4 subsidiary publications.
Hours & Admission Prices: Outdoor Aircraft Display: call for hours. Flight Experience Rides: May-Oct. Museum: temporarily closed. ♿
Attendance: 28,000 (estimated)
Membership: Junior $24; Student $35; General $60; Senior Life (over 59) $500; Life $1,000; Contributor $2,000; Patron $5,000 & up.

YPSILANTI HISTORICAL MUSEUM, 220 N. Huron St., Ypsilanti, MI 48197-2516. Tel.: 734-482-4990.
E-mail: al@rudisill.ws
Web Site: www.ypsilantihistoricalsociety.org
Founded: 1960.
Congressional District: 2
Key Personnel: Pres. (V), Alvin Rudisill; Museum Shop Mgr., Maggie Sell.
Personnel Profile: Part-Time Paid 1; Part-Time Volunteers 30.
Governing Authority: society; municipal. Ypsilanti Historical Society. Affiliated with the City of Ypsilanti. Tax-exempt.
Local History Museum.
Collections: archives; newspapers; Civil War letters; 35,000 cards; genealogical resource from earliest area settlers; city history; township history; photographs; Black history project; manuscripts; obituaries.
Research Fields: local history.
Facilities: archives.
Activities: permanent & temporary exhibitions.
Publications: quarterly newsletter, Gleanings.
Hours & Admission Prices: Museum: Tues.-Sun. 2-5. No charge; donations accepted. ♿
Attendance: 3,000 (estimated)
Membership: Single $10; Family $15; Contributing $25; Life $200.

YPSILANTI'S AUTOMOTIVE HERITAGE MUSEUM & MILLER MOTORS HUDSON, 100 E. Cross, Ypsilanti, MI 48198-2936. Tel.: 734-482-5200.
E-mail: hudsondealer@ypsiautoheritage.org
Web Site: www.ypsiautoheritage.org
Key Personnel: Cur., Jack Miller
Automobile Museum.
Collections: vintage cars & memorabilia.
Hours & Admission Prices: Mon.-Fri. 1:30-5, Sat. 9:30-5, Sun. 12-5. Adults $3; children 13 & under no charge.

Zeeland

THE DEKKER HUIS/ZEELAND HISTORICAL MUSEUM, 37 E. Main St., Zeeland, MI 49464. Mailing Address: P.O. Box 165, Zeeland, MI 49464-0165. Tel.: 616-772-4079.
E-mail: info@zeelandmuseum.org
Web Site: www.zeelandmuseum.org

Founded: 1974.
Congressional District: 2
Key Personnel: Museum Mgr., Anna Van De Venter; Cur., Suzy Frederick.
Personnel Profile: Part-Time Paid 2; Part-Time Volunteers 40.
Governing Authority: Parent Institution: Zeeland Historical Society. Tax-exempt.
Historic House Museum: housed in former home of Dirk Dekker and his wife, built in 1876.
Collections: local history; period artifacts & furnishings.
Publications: member quarterly newsletter, Timeline.
Hours & Admission Prices: Call for hours. No charge; donations accepted.
Attendance: 2,500 (accurate)

MINNESOTA

(225 listings)

Aitkin

AITKIN COUNTY HISTORICAL SOCIETY, 20 Pacific St., S.W., Aitkin, MN 56431-1628. Mailing Address: P.O. Box 215, Aitkin, MN 56431-0215. Tel.: 218-927-3348.
Founded: 1948.
Key Personnel: Dir., Gregory M. Leach; Chm. (V), Donald Niemi; Pres. (V), William Stimac; Museum Shop Mgr., Ruth Carlstrom.
Personnel Profile: Part-Time Paid 1; Part-Time Volunteers 20.
Governing Authority: Branch Museum: Log Museum.
Historical Society Museum: housed in the Northern Pacific Depot, built 1916. Listed on the National Register of Historic Places.
Collections: county history; photographs; documents.
Major Exhibits: Old Time Dentistry, 11/09-3/11; Gone to the Movies, 11/09-3/11; Fashion 1840-2000, 11/09-3/11.
Facilities: Museum-related items for sale.
Activities: educational programs.
Hours & Admission Prices: Wed. & Fri.-Sat. 10-4:30. Adults $2; members no charge. ♿
Membership: Senior $7.50; Individual $15; Family $20; Business $30; Memorial For Deceased $200.

THE JAQUES ART CENTER, 121 Second St., N.W., Aitkin, MN 56431. Tel.: 218-927-2363.
E-mail: info@jaquesart.com
Art Center.
Collections: paintings; sculpture; photographs.
Activities: permanent & temporary exhibits; workshops.
Hours & Admission Prices: Tues.-Sat. 11-4. No charge.

Albert Lea

FREEBORN COUNTY MUSEUM AND HISTORICAL VILLAGE, 1031 Bridge Ave., Albert Lea, MN 56007-2205. Tel.: 507-373-8003. Fax: 507-552-1269.
E-mail: fchm@smig.net
Web Site: www.smig.net/fchm
Formerly: Freeborn County Historical Society
Founded: 1948.
Congressional District: 1
Key Personnel: Exec. Dir., Pat Mulso; Pres. Bd., Bruce Olson; Vice Pres. Bd., Jody Bowron; Museum Shop Mgr., Kathy Freese.
Personnel Profile: Full-Time Paid 2; Part-Time Paid 5; Part-Time Volunteers 150.
Governing Authority: society. Tax-exempt.
History Museum & Historical Village.
Collections: pioneer items; documents; family history; maps; rock 'n roll era singer Eddie Cochran archives & collection; Marion Ross (Mrs. Cunningham); MN Rock & Country Music Hall of Fame. Historic Buildings: 1853 log cabin; 1860 log houses; 1878 Lutheran Church; 1882 county schoolhouse.
Research Fields: genealogy & history of Freeborn County.
Facilities: Museum-related items for sale.
Activities: slide programs & programs for schools, churches, civic groups on home remedies, Native Americans, immigration, genealogy, etc.; guided tours for students of county & adult groups by appointment; special craft demonstrations; special events for elementary & high school students; classes for genealogists.
Publications: Images of America, Freeborn County, Minnesota; quarterly newsletter; Glimpses of Freeborn County, 1930-1980.
Hours & Admission Prices: Museum & Library: Tues.-Fri. 10-5. Village: May-Sept. Tues.-Fri. 10-5. Adults $5, students 12-18 $1; discounts to AAA members; members and children 12 & under no charge. Closed New Year's Day; Independence Day; Thanksgiving; Christmas. ♿
Attendance: 10,000 (accurate)
Membership: Annual $25; Patron $50; Sustaining $100; Col. Albert Lea $250; Leader $500; Heritage Club $1,000.

Alexandria

DOUGLAS COUNTY HISTORICAL SOCIETY, 1219 Nokomis St., Alexandria, MN 56308-3712. Tel.: 320-762-0382. Fax: 320-762-9062.
Key Personnel: Exec. Dir., Rachel Barduson
Historical Society Museum: housed in the former home of Senator Knute Nelson. Listed on the National Register of Historic Places.
Collections: period furnishings; personal artifacts.
Activities: special events.
Hours & Admission Prices: Tours: Mon.-Fri. 9-3, Admission $2. Research: Mon.-Fri. 9-4.

MINNESOTA LAKES MARITIME MUSEUM, 205 3rd Ave., W., Alexandria, MN 56308-1364. Mailing Address: P.O. Box 1216, Alexandria, MN 56308-3216. Tel.: 320-759-1114. Fax: 320-759-1101.
E-mail: boat@mnlakesmaritime.org
Web Site: mnlakesmaritime.org
Maritime Museum.
Collections: history of the Letson House, Blakes Hotel, Geneva Hotel & Dickinson Inn; local resort history including Bedman's Beach resort; Larson boats & memorabilia; wood boats, featuring the Naphtha Launch, Frieda; history of Alexandria Boat Works, builder of wood fishing boats; period tackle & fish mounts; guide stories; fishing memorabilia.
Hours & Admission Prices: May 15-Oct. 15 Tues.-Fri. 10-5, Sat. 10-4, Sun. 12-4; other times by appointment. Family $15, adults $6, seniors $5, students 5-17 $3.

RUNESTONE MUSEUM, 206 N. Broadway, Alexandria, MN 56308-1417. Tel.: 320-763-3160. Fax: 320-763-9705.
E-mail: bigole@rea-alp.com
Web Site: www.runestonemuseum.org
Founded: 1958.
Congressional District: 7
Key Personnel: Museum & Exhibit Mgr., Julie Blank; Gift Shop Mgr., LuWanna Hintermeister.
Personnel Profile: Part-Time Paid 4; Part-Time Volunteers 20.
Governing Authority: nonprofit. Tax-exempt.
History & Youth Museum.
Collections: Discovery Room; Kensington Runestone; wildlife; Fort Alexandria; 1885 schoolhouse, church, cabins & general store; Native Americans; 40 ft. 3/4 scale Viking Ship replica Snorri.
Facilities: theater; outdoor fort. Museum-related items for sale.
Activities: video; outdoor functions.
Publications: Kensington Runestone Brochure; newsletter; A Holy Mission To Minnesota 600 Years Ago.
Hours & Admission Prices: Summer: Mon.-Fri. 9-5, Sat. 9-4, Sun. 11-4; Winter: Mon.-Fri. 10-5, Sat. 10-4. Families $15, adults $6, senior citizens $5, students 5-17 $3; discounts to AAA members; members no charge. ♿
Attendance: 8,000 (accurate)
Membership: Student $10; Individual $25; Family $50; Business $75; Sustaining $100; Patron $500; Corporate $1,000.

Annandale

MINNESOTA PIONEER PARK MUSEUM, 725 Pioneer Park Trail, Annandale, MN 55302-3128. Tel.: 320-274-8489. Fax: 320-274-9612.
E-mail: pioneerp@lakedalelink.net
Web Site: pioneerpark.org
Founded: 1972.
Congressional District: 6
Key Personnel: Pres. (V), Carol Anderson; Treas., Gary Weir; Museum Shop Mgr., Jeanene Anderson.
Personnel Profile: Part-Time Paid 1; Part-Time Volunteers 52.
Governing Authority: nonprofit organization. Tax-exempt.
Historic Site.
Collections: historical buildings & memorabilia from 1850-1940.
Activities: guided tours; school tours; day camps; craft fairs; reunions; weddings; ethnic church services. Museum Sponsors: Pioneer Festival; Halloween Festival; Fiddlers Festival; 1890s Festival; 4th of July Festival.
Publications: newsletter.
Hours & Admission Prices: Memorial Day to Oct. Mon.-Fri. 10-4, Sat. 1-4. Adults $5, senior citizens $4, children 6-16 $3; members and children 5 & under no charge.
Attendance: 8,000 (estimated)
Membership: Single $15; Family $25.

Anoka

ANOKA COUNTY HISTORICAL SOCIETY, 2135 Third Ave. N., Anoka, MN 55303-2258. Tel.: 763-421-0600. Fax: 763-323-0218.
E-mail: achs@ac-hs.org
Web Site: www.ac-hs.org
Founded: 1934.
Congressional District: 5
Key Personnel: Pres. (V), Paul Pierce, III; Exec. Dir., Todd Mahon.
Personnel Profile: Full-Time Paid 1; Part-Time Paid 8; Part-Time Volunteers 140; Interns 2.
Governing Authority: Anoka County Historical Society Board of Directors. Tax-exempt.
County History Museum.
Collections: 1900 period furniture; manuscripts; textiles; period clothing; wedding quilts; dolls; rugs.
Research Fields: Anoka County History; Anoka County genealogical research tools.
Facilities: genealogical reference library; microfilm materials; early settlers reference material.
Activities: guided tours; films; temporary exhibitions; lectures. Museum Sponsors: Home and Garden Tour in July; Barn Dance in September.
Publications: bimonthly newsletter, History Center News.
Hours & Admission Prices: Tues. 10-8, Wed.-Fri. 10-5, Sat. 10-4. Adults $3; discounts to groups of 15 or more; members no charge. Library: no charge. ♿
Attendance: 15,000 (accurate)
Membership: Student and Seniors 62 & over $7; Individual $15; Family $25.

Apple Valley

MINNESOTA ZOO, 13000 Zoo Blvd., Apple Valley, MN 55124-4621. Tel.: 952-431-9200. Fax: 952-431-9336.
Web Site: www.mnzoo.org
Founded: 1978.
Congressional District: 3
Key Personnel: C.E.O., Lee C. Ehmke; Gift Shop Mgr., Laurel Wright.
Personnel Profile: Full-Time Paid 185; Part-Time Paid 74; Part-Time Volunteers 650; Interns 45.
Governing Authority: state. Subsidiary Institution: Minnesota Zoo Foundation. Tax-exempt.
Zoo.
Collections: 2,449 accessioned individual animals representing 445 species; 30,000 tropical rain forest to northern coniferous forest plant specimens.
Research Fields: animal health; physiological norms, providing specimen tissue, sera for outside research projects; animal management; exhibit evaluation; behavior projects with outside researchers; behavioral engineering; curriculum development & evaluation.
Facilities: library of biological & horticultural material available for research on premises only; indoor & outdoor exhibits of animals in nature imitating habitats; monorail; zoological garden; botanical garden; trails; picnic area; theater; classrooms; cafeteria. Zoo-related items for sale.
Activities: guided tours; lectures; films; concerts; arts festivals; hobby workshops; TV programs; bird show; dolphin show; formally organized education programs for children, adults, undergraduate & graduate college students affiliated with Metropolitan University; traveling exhibits; loan & permanent exhibitions; zoomobile; trails; monorail; teacher workshops; grade school curriculum materials; special events & activities throughout the year.
Publications: bimonthly member newsletter, Zoo Tracks.
Hours & Admission Prices: Memorial Day-Labor Day daily 9-6; Sept. & May Mon.-Fri. 9-4, Sat.-Sun. 9-6; Oct.-April daily 9-4. Admission Memorial Day-Labor Day adults 13-64 $16, senior citizens 65 & over and children 3-12 $10; Sept.-May adults 13-64 $13, senior citizens 65 & over and children 3-12 $7; discounts to AZA members; members & children under 2 no charge. Skyrail: $4 per person; discounts to members; children under 2 no charge. Parking: cars $5, buses $10, motor coaches $15; members no charge. Closed Thanksgiving; Christmas. ♿
Attendance: 1,162,696 (accurate)
Membership: Individual $40; Individual Plus $72; Household & Grandparent $95; Household Plus & Grandparent Plus $115; Friends Voyager $250.

Askov

PINE COUNTY HISTORICAL SOCIETY, 3851 Glacier Rd., Askov, MN 55704. Mailing Address: P.O. Box 213, Askov, MN 55704-0213. Tel.: 320-838-3792.
E-mail: lizesp@juno.com
Founded: 1948.
Congressional District: 7
Key Personnel: Pres. (V), Elizabeth Espointour.
Personnel Profile: Part-Time Paid 3; Part-Time Volunteers 12.
Governing Authority: county. Tax-exempt: 501(c)(3).
Historical Society Museum: housed in 1900 Great Northern depot.
Collections: agriculture; manuscripts; archives; folklore. Historic Houses: Old Partbridge Store, Askov; Pine County Rural School, Pine.
Facilities: 1,000-vol. library of English & Finnish culture & literature available for use on premises. Museum-related items for sale.
Activities: guided tours; lectures; films; permanent & temporary exhibitions.
Hours & Admission Prices: Summer: Tues.-Sun. 1-4. No charge, donations accepted. ♿
Attendance: 500 (estimated)
Membership: Individual $7; Family $10.

Austin

THE SPAM MUSEUM, 1937 Spam Blvd., Austin, MN 55912-3690. Tel.: 507-437-5100. Fax: 507-437-6721.
E-mail: jlwhithaus@hormel.com
Web Site: www.spam.com
Founded: 2001.
Key Personnel: Dir. & Cur., Jerry Whithaus; Museum Shop Mgr., Ariana Finholdt.
Personnel Profile: Full-Time Paid 2; Part-Time Paid 23.
Governing Authority: Parent Institution: Hormel Foods Corporation.
General Museum.
Collections: 4,752 cans of SPAM from around the world; photographs; replica signage; recreated vintage products; late 1800s meat counter; letter from President Dwight D. Eisenhower; simulated SPAM production line.
Facilities: 16,500 sq. ft. exhibit space; 42-seat theater. Museum-related items for sale.
Activities: interactive quiz show.
Hours & Admission Prices: May to Labor Day Mon.-Sat. 10-5, Sun. 12-4; Sept.-April Tues.-Sat. 10-5. No charge. Closed New Year's Day; Easter; Thanksgiving; Christmas Eve & Day. ♿
Attendance: 100,000 (accurate)

Baudette

LAKE OF THE WOODS COUNTY MUSEUM, 119 8th Ave., S.E., Baudette, MN 56623. Mailing Address: 206 8th Ave., S.E., Ste. 150, Baudette, MN 56623-2867. Tel.: 218-634-1200.
Founded: 1978.
Congressional District: 7
Key Personnel: C.E.O. & Cur., Marlys Hirst; Chm. (V), Dan Crompton.
Personnel Profile: Full-Time Paid 1; Part-Time Paid 1; Part-Time Volunteers 10.
Governing Authority: county; nonprofit organization. Parent Institution: Lake of the Woods Historical Society. Tax-exempt: 501(c)(3).
County History Museum.
Collections: artifacts; archives; local history.
Research Fields: local history.
Facilities: library & archives.
Activities: permanent exhibitions; oral history.
Publications: newsletter, The LOWdown; books, Lake of the Woods Heritage; Baudette The First 100 Years; Memories of a Rolling Stone; Lake of the Woods County: A History of People, Places and Events.
Hours & Admission Prices: May-Sept. Tues.-Fri. 10-4, Sat. 10-2; other times by appointment. No charge; donations accepted. Closed Labor Day. ♿
Attendance: 3,000 (estimated)
Membership: Single $15; Family $25; Business $30.

Baxter

NORTHLAND ARBORETUM, 14250 Conservation Dr., Baxter, MN 56425-8720. Tel.: 218-829-8770.
Web Site: arb.brainerd.com
Arboretum.
Collections: regional flora & fauna.
Facilities: 500-acres; trails.
Activities: workshops; seminars.
Hours & Admission Prices: Daily dawn to dusk. Adults $3; members no charge. ♿
Membership: Student & Senior $15; Individual $20; Family $30; Contributing $50; Business & Supporting $100 & up.

Becker

SHERBURNE HISTORY CENTER, 10775 27th Ave. S.E., Becker, MN 55308-4656. Tel.: 763-261-4433. Fax: 763-261-4437.
E-mail: schs@izoom.net
Web Site: www.sherburnehistorycenter.org

Formerly: Sherburne County Historical Society
Founded: 1972.
Congressional District: 6
Key Personnel: Exec. Dir., Kurt K. Kragness; Pres., David Graning; Pres. (V), Don Bostrom.
Personnel Profile: Full-Time Paid 3; Part-Time Paid 2; Part-Time Volunteers 70.
Governing Authority: nonprofit organization. Tax-exempt: 501(c)(3).
Historical Society Museum.
Collections: late 19th to early 20th-century costumes, decorative arts, farm machinery; photographs; maps; archival material. Historic Buildings: Herbert M. Fox House, Bailey Gas Station.
Research Fields: Sherburne County History.
Facilities: research library.
Activities: loan, permanent & temporary exhibitions; lectures & outreach programs; internships; traveling exhibit trunks; historic walking trail.
Publications: quarterly newsletter, Historically Speaking.
Hours & Admission Prices: Tues.-Fri. 10-5, Sat. 10-4. No charge; donations accepted. ♿
Attendance: 8,800 (estimated)
Membership: Senior Citizen $15; Individual $30; Family $40; Business Booster $50; Patron $150; Ox Cart $500; Heritage $1,000.

Bemidji

BELTRAMI COUNTY HISTORY CENTER, 130 Minnesota Ave., S.W., Bemidji, MN 56601-4009. Tel.: 218-444-3376. Fax: 218-444-3377.
E-mail: depot@paulbunyan.net
Web Site: www.beltramihistory.org/
Formerly: Beltrami County Historical Society
Founded: 1952.
Congressional District: 7
Key Personnel: Exec. Dir., Wanda Hoyum; Pres., Jean Parkin; Sec., Chyrl McQuaid.
Personnel Profile: Full-Time Paid 1; Part-Time Paid 2; Part-Time Volunteers 7; Interns 2.
Governing Authority: society. Tax-exempt: 501(c)(3).
History Museum.
Collections: Indian artifacts; photographs. Historic Buildings: 1896 log house; 1903 log school with original furnishings; 1912 first consolidated school in northern Minnesota.
Facilities: research library; history center; meeting room. Museum-related items for sale.
Activities: temporary & permanent exhibitions; education program. Museum Sponsors: Downtown History Walk in July; Depot Day in August; Cemetery Walk in September; Lefse Festival in December.
Publications: The Mississippi Headwaters Region: Scenes from the Past; newsletter, Depot Express.
Hours & Admission Prices: History Center: Mon.-Sat. 10-4. Adults $5, seniors & students $4, children 12 & under $1; members no charge. Research fee per half hour: non-members $10; members no charge. Closed New Year's Day; Good Friday; Memorial Day; Independence Day; Labor Day; Thanksgiving; Christmas Eve & Day. ♿
Attendance: 10,000 (accurate)
Membership: Individual $15-$25; Family $26-$49; Sponsor $50-$99; Benefactor $100-$199; Sustaining $200-$999; The Count Beltrami Society $1,000.

HEADWATERS SCIENCE CENTER, 413 Beltrami Ave., Bemidji, MN 56601-3106. Mailing Address: P.O. Box 1176, Bemidji, MN 56619-1176. Tel.: 218-444-4472. Fax: 218-444-4473.
E-mail: contact@hscbemidji.org
Web Site: www.hscbemidji.org/index.htm
Key Personnel: Exec. Dir., Laddie Elwell
Science Center.
Collections: hands-on exhibits; biological & life history processes.
Activities: outreach programs; demonstrations.
Hours & Admission Prices: Mon. & Wed.-Sat. 9:30-5:30, Sun. 1-5. Adults 12 & over $5, children 2-11 $3. Closed New Year's Day; Easter; Thanksgiving; Christmas.

Benson

SWIFT COUNTY HISTORICAL SOCIETY, 2135 Minnesota Ave., Bldg. 2, Benson, MN 56215-2101. Tel.: 320-843-4467.
E-mail: swiftmuseum@embarqmail.com
Founded: 1929.
Key Personnel: Exec. Dir., Marlys Gallagher; Pres. (V), Tom Rice; Archivist, Lowell Moen.
Personnel Profile: Part-Time Paid 2.
Governing Authority: society. Tax-exempt.
History Museum.
Collections: newspapers including Appleton, Benson, Kerkhoven from 1880s, 1876, 1890s to present; period artifacts.
Research Fields: genealogy.
Facilities: library of newspapers available for use on premises.
Activities: outreach programs. Annual Events: Tribute to Veterans & School Week in May; Annual Museum Banquet in July; Christmas Event in December.
Publications: Swift County History Book; pictorial; Swift County Minnesota family histories.
Hours & Admission Prices: Tues.-Fri. 10-4:30, Sat. 10-3. No charge; donations accepted. ♿
Attendance: 1,500 (estimated)
Membership: Senior Citizen & Individual $10; Family $15; Business $30.

Bloomington

BLOOMINGTON ART CENTER, 1800 W. Old Shakopee Rd., Bloomington, MN 55431-3071. Tel.: 952-563-8587. Fax: 952-563-8576. TDD: 952-563-8740.
E-mail: info@bloomingtonartcenter.com
Web Site: www.bloomingtonartcenter.com
Founded: 1976.
Congressional District: 3
Key Personnel: Pres. (V), Lynn James; Interim Exec. Dir., Kathleen Corley; Treas., Karolyn Lee; Vice Pres., Carol Retherford; Sec., Lisa McDaniel; Dir. Exhibitions, Rachel Daly Flentje; Dir. Publicity, Nancy Lamberger; Museum Shop Mgr., Connie Gunderson.
Personnel Profile: Full-Time Paid 4; Part-Time Paid 3.
Governing Authority: nonprofit. Tax-exempt: 501(c)(3).
Art Center.
Collections: paintings.
Facilities: classrooms; theaters; pottery & glass studios. Art works for sale.
Activities: guided tours; lectures; gallery talks; arts festivals; formally organized education programs; theater; visual & performing arts; literature; workshops.
Publications: newsletter; e-newsletter.
Hours & Admission Prices: Mon.-Fri. 8am-10pm, Sat. 9-5, Sun.1-10. No charge; donations accepted. Closed holidays. ♿
Attendance: 36,000 (estimated)
Membership: Individual $30; Household $40.

UNDERWATER ADVENTURES AQUARIUM, Mall of America, 120 E. Broadway, Bloomington, MN 55425-5511. Tel.: 852-883-0202; 888-348-3824. Fax: 952-883-0303.
Web Site: sharky.tv
Aquarium.
Collections: sharks; stingrays; sea turtles.
Hours & Admission Prices: March 13-April 13 Mon.-Thurs. 9:30-8:30, Fri. 9:30-9:30, Sat. 9-9:30, Sun. 10-7; late-April to early March Mon.-Thurs. 10-8, Fri.-Sat. 9:30-8:30, Sun. 10-6:30. Adults 13 & over $18.99, children 3-12 $11.99; children under 2 no charge.

Blue Earth

FARIBAULT COUNTY HISTORICAL SOCIETY, 405 E. Sixth St., Blue Earth, MN 56013-2020. Tel.: 507-526-5421.
Founded: 1948.
Congressional District: 2
Personnel Profile: Part-Time Volunteers 12.
Governing Authority: society. Tax-exempt: 170(b)(1)(A).
Historical Society Museum.
Collections: house furnishings; kitchen artifacts; clothing; farm machinery; tools; military; medical; religious; books; Civil War; Luther Burbank. Historic Buildings: Wakefield House 1868; Good Shepherd Episcopal Church 1871; W.D.L. Church 1886; Krosh log house 1862; woodland school 1870; Guckeen post office 1901; blacksmith shop; period machine shed; general store.
Research Fields: local history.
Facilities: 100-vol. library of books on local history, available for research on premises with supervision.
Activities: guided tours; slide presentations; permanent exhibitions.
Publications: quarterly newsletter.
Hours & Admission Prices: Wakefield Office: Mon.-Fri. 10-4. Buildings: Tues.-Fri. 10-4 & by appointment and during County Fair. Closed holidays. ♿
Attendance: 2,000
Membership: Annual $20; Life $100.

Brainerd

CROW WING COUNTY HISTORICAL SOCIETY, 320 Laurel, Brainerd, MN 56401-3523. Mailing Address: P.O. Box 722, Brainerd, MN 56401-0722. Tel.: 218-829-3268. Fax: 218-828-4434.
E-mail: history@co.crow-wing.mn.us
Web Site: www.crowwinghistory.org/
Founded: 1927.
Congressional District: 8
Key Personnel: Pres. (V), Don Samuelson; Admin., Marilyn Anderson.
Personnel Profile: Part-Time Paid 3; Part-Time Volunteers 25.
Governing Authority: society. Tax-exempt.
Local History Museum.
Collections: Indian artifacts; industrial; paintings; archaeology; costumes; archives.
Research Fields: Crow Wing County history.
Facilities: library of genealogy & history books available for local history research; archives specializing in county & regional history.
Activities: guided tours.
Publications: biannual newsletter.
Hours & Admission Prices: Tues.-Sat. 10-3. Donations: adults $3; children, students & members no charge. Closed holidays. ♿
Attendance: 5,000 (estimated)
Membership: Individual $20; Family $40; Sustaining $50; Booster $100; Benefactor $250; Patron $500 & up.

Breckenridge

WILKIN COUNTY HISTORICAL SOCIETY, 704 Nebraska Ave., Breckenridge, MN 56520-1547. Tel.: 218-643-1303.
Founded: 1965.
Congressional District: 7
Key Personnel: C.E.O. & Pres., Gordon Martinson; Treas., Ruth Poppel; Sec., Sylvia Peterson.
Personnel Profile: Part-Time Paid 2; Part-Time Volunteers 1.
Governing Authority: society. Parent Institution: Minnesota Historical Society. Tax-exempt.
Local History Museum.
Collections: period artifacts; books; maps; school room; manuscripts.
Research Fields: biographies; old newspapers; obituaries.
Activities: tours; open house.
Hours & Admission Prices: Tues.-Thurs. 1:30-4. No charge, donations accepted.
Attendance: 200 (estimated)
Membership: Annual $7.50, Couple $15; Life $100.

Browns Valley

SAM BROWN LOG HOUSE, West Broadway, Browns Valley, MN 56219-0013. Mailing Address: City Hall, Box 334, Browns Valley, MN 56219-0013. Tel.: 320-695-2100.
Founded: 1932.
Congressional District: 2
Key Personnel: Pres. (V), Shirley Ecker; Clerk & Treas., Linda Schwagel.
Personnel Profile: Part-Time Paid 1; Part-Time Volunteers 15.
Governing Authority: Parent Institution: Browns Valley Historical Society & city council.
Historic House: 1863 Joseph & Sam Brown log house.
Collections: guns; clothing; Indian artifacts; furniture; archaeology; arts & crafts.
Research Fields: historical.
Publications: Early History of Browns Valley.
Hours & Admission Prices: Memorial Day weekend to Labor Day Fri.-Sun. 1-6 & holidays; other times by appointment. No charge; donations accepted.
Attendance: 500 (accurate)

Buffalo

WRIGHT COUNTY HISTORICAL SOCIETY, (M), 2001 Hwy. 25 N., Buffalo, MN 55313. Mailing Address: P.O. Box 304, Buffalo, MN 55313-0304. Tel.: 763-682-7323. Fax: 763-682-7324.
Web Site: www.wrighthistory.org
Founded: 1942.
Congressional District: 2 & 3
Key Personnel: Pres., Leander Wetter; Coord. & Cur., Erin Storc; Archivist, Betty Dircks; Business Mgr., Sally Macnab.
Personnel Profile: Full-Time Paid 3; Part-Time Paid 2; Part-Time Volunteers 10.
Governing Authority: society; nonprofit. Tax-exempt: 501(c)(3).
General Museum.
Collections: cultural, social, ethnic & craft themes specific to local history; the Nelsonian, a 32-piece one-man band; Hubert H. Humphrey's 1926 Model T Ford; library; archives; photographs; textiles; agricultural equipment; art; ceramics & metals.
Research Fields: local genealogy; Wright County & Minnesota history.
Facilities: library. Local interest books & museum-related items for sale.
Activities: organized education programs for children; docent program. Museum Sponsors: Children's Days in May.
Publications: books, Women of Wright County; Compendium of Plagues, Politics, Disasters, People, Places & Events; 101 Best Stories of Wright County; D.R. Farnham's History of Wright County; 2-vol. History of Wright County, Minnesota, 1915; 1909 N.W. Magazine; Wright County history reprinted from History of the Upper Mississippi Valley.
Hours & Admission Prices: Mon.-Fri. 8-4:30. No charge; donations accepted. ♿
Attendance: 8,000 (estimated)
Membership: Student $5; Individual & Family $10; Business $25.

Cambridge

ISANTI COUNTY HISTORICAL SOCIETY, 33525 Flanders St., N.E., Cambridge, MN 55008-4157. Tel.: 763-689-4229. Fax: 763-552-0740.
E-mail: ichsdirector@izoom.net
Web Site: www.ichs.ws
Founded: 1965.
Congressional District: 8
Key Personnel: C.E.O. & Dir., Kathleen J. McCully; Chm. (V) & Pres. (V), Roger Anderson.
Personnel Profile: Part-Time Paid 3; Part-Time Volunteers 250.
Governing Authority: county; nonprofit organization. Tax-exempt: 501(c)(3).
Historical Society Museum.
Collections: documents; manuscripts; photographs; oral histories; pioneer artifacts; 1870 to 1930, household & farm equip. Historic Structures: West Riverside school; Spencer Brook school. St. John's German Lutheran Church of Bradford; pioneer log cabin; blacksmith shop.
Research Fields: local history; Swedish immigrants.
Facilities: resource center with newspaper microfilm & oral history on county available for research at the ICHS Heritage Center.
Activities: slide lectures & other programs in county; local history input in county schools; Old Time school session; language & culture day camps for children (Swedish); journaling workshops for all ages; outdoor concerts dealing with folk culture/lore.
Publications: annual newsletter, Isanti Cuttings & monthly updates; Isanti County: Yesterday...Today...Tomorrow.
Hours & Admission Prices: Heritage Center: Mon.-Tues. & Fri. 9-4:30; other times by appointment. Historic Structures: open for special events; other times by appointment. No charge; donations accepted. ♿
Attendance: 2,500 (estimated)
Membership: Student & Senior Citizens over 60 $16; Individual $22; Family $32; Sustaining $43; Supporting $59; Patron $108; Bronze Patron $215; Silver Patron $323; Gold Patron $440; Platinum $540.

Cannon Falls

CANNON FALLS AREA HISTORICAL MUSEUM, 206 W. Mill St., Cannon Falls, MN 55009-2029. Mailing Address: P.O. Box 111, Cannon Falls, MN 55009-0111. Tel.: 507-263-4503.
E-mail: cfmuseum@citlink.net
Web Site: www.citlink.net/~cfmuseum/
Founded: 1979.
Key Personnel: Dir., Heidi Holmes Helgren; Pres. (V), John Otto; Treas., Jean Duden; Sec., Ilene Fox.
Personnel Profile: Part-Time Paid 1.
Governing Authority: society. Tax-exempt.
Historical Society Museum: housed in 1888 town fire hall.
Collections: historical items from the Cannon Falls area.
Research Fields: history of local firms.
Activities: guided tours.
Hours & Admission Prices: Fri. 1-5, Sat. 9-2. No charge; donations accepted. Group tours by appointment.
Attendance: 1,435
Membership: Single $15; Family $25; Sustaining $50; Century Club $100.

Chaska

MINNESOTA LANDSCAPE ARBORETUM, UNIVERSITY OF MINNESOTA, 3675 Arboretum Dr., Chaska, MN 55318-9613. Tel.: 952-443-1413. Fax: 952-443-2521.
E-mail: olinx002@umn.edu
Web Site: www.arboretum.umn.edu
Founded: 1958.
Congressional District: 2

Key Personnel: Dir., Peter J. Olin; Pres. (V), Stephen D. Keating; Head, Dept. Horticultural Science, Dr. Tom Michaels; Dir. Operations, Peter C. Moe; Dir. Devel., Frank Molek; Dir. Education, Tim Kenny; Dir. Research, Stan Hokanson; Librarian, Richard Isaacson; Museum Shop Mgr., Patricia Mirabelli; Tearoom Mgr., Pam Wallace.
Personnel Profile: Full-Time Paid 70; Part-Time Paid 103; Part-Time Volunteers 900.
Governing Authority: university. Parent Institution: University of Minnesota, St. Paul, MN. 55108. Tax-exempt.
Arboretum.
Collections: woody ornamentals; herbaceous ornamentals; fruit; natural landscapes; landscaped gardens; 18,000 books & periodicals in Andersen Horticultural Library.
Research Fields: woody plant breeding; cold hardiness studies; fruit breeding programs; plant stress studies; wetland restoration; ornamental grass breeding.
Facilities: 18,000-vol. non-circulating horticultural library; 1,047 acres of display gardens; natural areas; research lab; Snyder Building with conservatory; Clotilde Irvine Sensory Garden & Therapeutic Horticulture Center. Oswald Visitor Center: restaurant; learning center. Museum-related items for sale.
Activities: guided walking, bus & tram tours; lectures; films; hobby workshops; formally organized education programs for children, adults, families and undergraduate college students; research; excursions; Minnesota Extension Service Outreach.
Publications: bimonthly newsletter; fact sheets; books and videos; The Source List; plant publications.
Hours & Admission Prices: May & Sept.-Oct. Mon.-Sat. 8-6, Sun. 10-6; June-Aug. Mon.-Wed. & Fri.-Sat. 8-6, Thurs. 8-8, Sun. 10-6; Nov.-April Mon.-Sat. 8-4:30, Sun. 10-4:30. Adults $7; children 15 & under and members no charge. ♿
Attendance: 271,000 (accurate)
Membership: Individual $35; Family $55; Family & Friends $75.

Chisholm

MINNESOTA DISCOVERY CENTER, (M), (I), 801 S.W. Hwy. 169, Ste. 1, Chisholm, MN 55719-1846. Tel.: 218-254-7959; 800-372-6437. Fax: 218-254-7971.
E-mail: marketing@ironworld.com
Web Site: www.ironworld.com
Formerly: Ironworld
Founded: 1979.
Congressional District: 8
Key Personnel: Museum Dir., Dr. Melissa Stewart; C.E.O., Mike Andrews; Chm. (V), Richard Puhek; Archivist, Scott Kuzma; Dir. Visitor Svcs., Debra Rowbottom; Cur., Erica Larson; Museum Shop Mgr., Judy Sertich; Librarian, Jessica Oftelie; Coord. Education, Kelly Florence; Exec. Administrative Asst., Amber Goss.
Personnel Profile: Full-Time Paid 20; Part-Time Paid 25.
Governing Authority: state. Parent Institution: Ironworld Development Corp. Tax-exempt.
General Museum.
Collections: iron ore mining company records & artifacts; mine equipment; photographs; government records; personal & business records; social & civic organization records.
Major Exhibits: Thoreau's Walden, 1/16/10-5/2/10; Journey Stories, 5/29/10-7/10/10.
Research Fields: history, genealogy, labor history & immigration to Minnesota's Mesabi, Vermilion & Cuyuna iron ranges.
Facilities: 7,500-vol. library pertaining to Minnesota & mining history; theater; restaurant.
Activities: guided tours; special events; ethnic days; music concerts; educational tours.
Hours & Admission Prices: Research Center: daily. No charge. Park & Museum: Tues.-Wed. & Fri.-Sun. 10-5, Thurs. 10-9. Adults $8, seniors $7, students $6; discounts to AAM & ICOM members; children 6 & under and members no charge. ♿
Attendance: 24,000 (estimated)
Membership: Student $25; Individual $35; Family $50.

MINNESOTA MUSEUM OF MINING, 900 W. Lake St., Chisholm, MN 55719-1736. Mailing Address: P O Box 271, 813 NE 5th Avenue, Chisholm, MN 55719-0271. Tel.: 218-254-5543.
Mining Museum.
Collections: mining history & equipment; underground mine & mining town replicas; trucks; steam shovels; early Mesabi Range lifestyle; simulated underground mine drift; log cabin; steam-driven diamond drill.
Activities: ride mining equipment.
Publications: brochure.
Hours & Admission Prices: Memorial Day to Labor Day Mon.-Sat. 9-5, Sun. 1-5; groups by appointment. Adults $4, seniors $3.50, children 5-17 $3; children under 5 no charge.

Cloquet

CARLTON COUNTY HISTORICAL SOCIETY, 406 Cloquet Ave., Cloquet, MN 55720-1750. Tel.: 218-879-1938. Fax: 218-879-1938.
E-mail: cchs@cpinternet.com
Web Site: www.carltoncountyhs.org
Founded: 1949.
Congressional District: 8
Key Personnel: Dir., Anne Dugan; Pres., Jean Johnson; Vice Pres., Charles Kihiri; Treas., Andy French; Sec., Cynthia Johnson.
Personnel Profile: Part-Time Paid 4; Part-Time Volunteers 35; Interns 2.
Governing Authority: society. Affiliated with Minnesota Historical Society. Subsidiary Institution: Moose Lake Area Historical Society. Tax-exempt: 501(c)(3).
History Museum.
Collections: Indian; agriculture; pioneer; railroad; dairy; business; logging & lumbering; Fires of 1918 memorabilia.
Research Fields: local history.
Activities: tours; permanent & temporary exhibits; narrated slide history interpretive programs.
Publications: newsletter, Society News; Crossroads in Time: A History of Carlton County, Minnesota; Reflections of Our Past: A Pictorial History of Carlton County; Furies of the Flames: A Pictorial History of the Great Forest Fires of 1918; History of the Thomson Farming Area; History of the Pioneers of the Cromwell, MN area; Fire Storm: The Great Fires of 1918; A Hometown Album: Cloquet's Centennial Story; Stories of a Century; Reuben B. Carlton: Frontier Blacksmith and Visionary; A History of Mahtowa Carlton Chronicles.
Hours & Admission Prices: Tues.-Wed. & Fri.-Sat. 9-4, Thurs. 9-8. No charge; donations accepted. ♿
Attendance: 3,000 (estimated)
Membership: Individual $15; Family $25; Supporting, Business & Organization $25; Friend $50; Sponsor $75; Patron $100 & up.

Cokato

COKATO MUSEUM & AKERLUND PHOTOGRAPHY STUDIO, 175 W. 4th St., Cokato, MN 55321-4852. Mailing Address: P.O. Box 686, Cokato, MN 55321-0686. Tel.: 320-286-2427. Fax: 320-286-5876.
E-mail: cokatomuseum@embarqmail.com
Web Site: www.cokato.mn.us/cmhs/
Founded: 1976.
Congressional District: 6
Key Personnel: Dir., Mike Worcester; Pres. (V), Janice Severson; Financial Dir., Shirley Larson-Cole.
Personnel Profile: Full-Time Paid 2; Part-Time Paid 1; Part-Time Volunteers 60.
Governing Authority: municipal. Tax-exempt: 501(c)(3).
History Museum & Historic Site.
Collections: period furnishings; catalogued 2 & 3 dimensional items (thru 1996) numbers 15,235; women's clothing from 1890-1920; Cokato businesses; Finnish culture; agricultural tools & equipment; immigration artifacts; photographs include 4,000 catalogued, plus 14,000 Akerlund photos & negatives; restored 1905 photography studio.
Facilities: library; 3,900 sq. ft. exhibit space.
Activities: concerts; guided tours; lectures; author readings; temporary exhibitions. Annual Events: annual meeting in February; Christmas potluck dinner in December; quarterly programs on local history topics.
Publications: quarterly newsletter, In the Midst Of; books: A Can of Cream: A History of Dairying in Stockholm Township, Wright County, Minnesota; Fire Fighters to the Rescue: A Century of Fires in Cokato, 1896-1996; The Cokato Canneries, 1904-1978; Cokato's First 125 Years, 1878-2003; Why Did They Take The Game Away From Us: The Story of Cokato High School Girls Basketball, 1903 to 1931.
Hours & Admission Prices: Tues.-Fri. 9-4:30, Sat. 9-3, Sun. 12-4. No charge; donations accepted. Tours $2. Closed major holidays. ♿
Attendance: 4,199 (accurate)
Membership: Individual $10; Family $15; Business $25; Supporter $50; Benefactor $100.

Comfrey

JEFFERS PETROGLYPHS HISTORIC SITE, 27160 County Rd. 2, Comfrey, MN 56019-4430. Tel.: 507-628-5591. Fax: 507-628-5593.
E-mail: jefferspetroglyphs@mnhs.org
Web Site: www.jefferspetroglyphs.com
Founded: 1966.
Key Personnel: Site Mgr., Tom Sanders.

Personnel Profile: Full-Time Paid 2; Part-Time Paid 17; Part-Time Volunteers 20.
Governing Authority: state; nonprofit. Parent Institution: Minnesota Historical Society, 345 Kellogg Blvd. W., St. Paul, MN 55102.
History Museum.
Collections: American Indian history & spirituality, 5000 B.C. - 600 A.D.; quartzite stone carvings.
Research Fields: archaeology; geology; prairie grasses & flowers; petroglyphs (carvings) history.
Facilities: library; 1,300 sq. ft. exhibit space; 50-seat theater. Museum-related items for sale.
Activities: formal education programs; guided tours; mobile vans; theater; training programs for professional museum workers.
Publications: book, The Jeffers Petroglyphs.
Hours & Admission Prices: May Fri.-Sat. 10-5, Sun. 12-5; Memorial Day to June Mon.-Fri. 10-5, Sat. 10-8, Sun. 12-5; July-Aug. Thurs.-Sat. 10-5, Sun. 12-5. Sept. call for hours; Oct.-April by appointment. Adults $6, senior citizens $5, children $4; discounts to groups; children under 6 & members no charge.
Attendance: 10,000 (accurate)
Membership: Senior Individual $45; Individual & Senior Household $55; Household $65; Associate $125; Contributing $250; Sustaining $500; North Star Circle $1,000.

Crookston

POLK COUNTY HISTORICAL SOCIETY, 719 E. Robert St., Crookston, MN 56716-2043. Mailing Address: P.O. Box 214, Crookston, MN 56716-0214. Tel.: 218-281-1038.
E-mail: polkcomuseum@rrv.net
Web Site: www.mnhistoricnw.org/Polkchs.htm
Founded: 1930.
Congressional District: 7
Key Personnel: Pres. (V) & Cur., Allen Brolsma; Vice Pres. (V), Ken Hviding; Museum Shop Mgr., Alice Dale.
Personnel Profile: Part-Time Paid 4; Part-Time Volunteers 80.
Governing Authority: county; nonprofit organization. Affiliated with Research Station, University of Minnesota, Technical Institute. Tax-exempt.
History Museum.
Collections: archives; agriculture; anthropology; textiles; Indian artifacts; photographs; industrial; music; medical; military; transportation; archaeology; graphics; costumes; folklore; manuscripts; period automobiles; agriculture equipment; schoolhouse; log cabin & blacksmith shop.
Research Fields: textiles; Indian artifacts; industrial; music; medical; military; transportation; archaeology; local county cemetery.
Facilities: library of books & documents available for use by special permission; 90-seat auditorium; ecumenical chapel; children's museum. Museum-related items for sale.
Activities: guided tours; lectures; gallery talks; country school programs; study clubs; hobby workshops; formally organized education programs for children, adults & undergraduate college students; permanent exhibitions.
Publications: newsletter.
Hours & Admission Prices: 3rd week in May to mid-Sept. Tues.-Sun. 12-5. No charge; donations accepted. ♿
Attendance: 2,900 (estimated)
Membership: Individual $10; Family $20; Patron $25.

Crosby

CUYUNA IRON RANGE NETWORK, 101 First St., N.E., Crosby, MN 56441. Mailing Address: P.O. Box 272, Crosby, MN 56441-0272. Tel.: 218-546-6178 & 545-1166.
E-mail: cchps@crosbyironton.net
Formerly: Cuyuna Range Historical Society & Museum
Founded: 1970.
Congressional District: 7
Key Personnel: Pres. (V), Pete Van Evera.
Personnel Profile: Part-Time Paid 2; Part-Time Volunteers 2.
Governing Authority: board of directors; nonprofit. Parent Institution: Minnesota Historical Society. Tax-exempt.
History Museum: housed in 1910 Soo Line Depot.
Collections: mining & logging memorabilia; tools, furniture, clothing, pictures, store items of settlers & immigrant families.
Research Fields: local history.
Activities: guided tours.
Publications: annual membership letter.
Hours & Admission Prices: June-Aug. Mon.-Sat. 10-4. Adults $1, children $.50. Closed holidays. ♿
Attendance: 1,250 (estimated)
Membership: Annual $10; Sustaining $20 or more; Life $100.

Currie

END-O-LINE RAILROAD PARK & MUSEUM, 440 N. Mill St., Currie, MN 56123-1133. Tel.: 507-763-3708. Fax: 507-763-3996.
E-mail: endoline@co.murray.mn.us
Web Site: www.endoline.com
Founded: 1972.
Congressional District: 7
Key Personnel: Dir., Eugene Short.
Personnel Profile: Part-Time Paid 8; Part-Time Volunteers 4.
Governing Authority: county. Affiliated with the Murray County Parks, Slayton, MN 56172. Tax-exempt.
Railroad Museum.
Collections: historical artifacts; manual-operated turntable; diesel switcher & caboose; engine house; railroad memorabilia; hobo display; restored depot; 1875 Baldwin locomotive; Georgia Northern #102 steam engine; Fairmont motorcars; railroad water tower; section foreman's house; replica coal bunker; Hilfers railroad yard; replica Lake Shetek Mills; general store; rural country school; Murray County Courthouse; 1870s Currie Presbyterian Church; Lakota teepee; American bison.
Research Fields: railroads.
Facilities: picnic facilities; nature trails; 6 mile bike & pedestrian trail. Museum-related items for sale.
Activities: guided tours.
Hours & Admission Prices: Memorial Day-Labor Day Mon.-Sat. 10-5, Sun. 1-5; bus tours & groups by appointment. Suggested Donations: adults $4, senior citizen 60 & over and youth 6-18 $3; youth 5 & under no charge. ♿
Attendance: 5,878 (accurate)

Dassel

THE OLD DEPOT RAILROAD MUSEUM, 651 W. Hwy. 12, Dassel, MN 55325. Mailing Address: P.O. Box 99, Dassel, MN 55325-0099. Tel.: 320-275-3876.
Web Site: www.theolddepot.com/
Founded: 1985.
Key Personnel: C.E.O., Howard K. Page; Museum Shop Mgr., Dana Hesser.
Personnel Profile: Full-Time Paid 1; Part-Time Paid 4.
Railroad Museum: housed in 1913 Great Northern Depot.
Collections: photographs; period trunks & luggage; bells; whistles; signals; telegraph apparatus; conductor uniforms; hats lanterns; wooden caboose; wooden freight cars; China, section cars; posters; calendars.
Hours & Admission Prices: Memorial Day to Oct. 1 daily 10-4:30. Adults $2.50, children under 12 $1; discounts to National Assoc. Railroad historical society members. ♿
Attendance: 2,000 (estimated)

Detroit Lakes

BECKER COUNTY HISTORICAL SOCIETY, 714 Summit Ave., Detroit Lakes, MN 56501-2941. Mailing Address: P.O. Box 622, Detroit Lakes, MN 56502-0622. Tel.: 218-847-2938. Fax: 218-847-5048.
E-mail: mail@beckercountyhistory.org
Web Site: www.beckercountyhistory.org
Founded: 1882.
Congressional District: 7
Key Personnel: Pres. (V), Mike Wommer; Cur. & Mgr., Carrie Johnston.
Personnel Profile: Full-Time Paid 1; Part-Time Paid 2; Part-Time Volunteers 71.
Governing Authority: society. Tax-exempt.
Local History Museum.
Collections: artifacts; relics; articles; implements; tools; materials; pictures; specimens pertaining to area history.
Research Fields: local history; genealogy; White Earth Indian Reservation.
Facilities: 2,200-vol. library of county newspapers, manuscripts, letters, photographs & old books available for use on premises.
Activities: permanent & temporary exhibitions.
Publications: quarterly newsletter; Pioneer History of Becker County.
Hours & Admission Prices: Tues.-Sat. 10-4. No charge; donations accepted. Closed national holidays. ♿
Attendance: 7,500 (estimated)
Membership: Individual $25; Business $35; Family $50.

Duluth

DULUTH ART INSTITUTE, 506 W. Michigan St., Duluth, MN 55802-1517. Tel.: 218-733-7560. Fax: 218-733-7506.
E-mail: getart@duluthartinstitute.org
Web Site: www.duluthartinstitute.org
Founded: 1907.
Congressional District: 68

Key Personnel: Exec. Dir., Samantha Gibb Roff; Pres., Matthew Cartier; Cur., David Hodges; Dir. Education, Shannon Consino; Operations & Devel. Mgr., Christie Culliton; Studio Mgr., Dave Lynas; Studio Mgr., Bruce Ojard.
Personnel Profile: Full-Time Paid 4; Part-Time Paid 3; Part-Time Volunteers 100.
Governing Authority: Tax-exempt.
Art Gallery.
Collections: regional exhibits.
Activities: educational program; artist services.
Publications: news magazine 3 times a year.
Hours & Admission Prices: Adults $12; members no charge. ♿
Attendance: 50,000 (estimated)
Membership: Individual $40; Household $60.

DULUTH CHILDREN'S MUSEUM, 506 W. Michigan St., Duluth, MN 55802-1517. Tel.: 218-733-7543 & 7546. Fax: 218-733-7547.
E-mail: explore@duluthchildrensmuseum.org
Web Site: www.duluthchildrensmuseum.org
Founded: 1930.
Congressional District: 8
Key Personnel: C.E.O., Michael P. Garcia; Cur., Bonnie A. Cusick; Program Dir., Pat A. Castellano.
Personnel Profile: Full-Time Paid 2; Part-Time Paid 2; Part-Time Volunteers 12.
Governing Authority: nonprofit organization. Tax-exempt: 501(c)(3).
Children's & Youth Museum: housed in 1892 French Norman style former railway station, the St. Louis County Heritage & Arts Center including two additional museums, an art institute & five performing arts organizations.
Collections: world cultures; childhood; immigration; two-story walk-through tree.
Research Fields: childhood; immigration.
Activities: formally organized educational programs for children; traveling, permanent & temporary exhibits; family adventure programs; volunteer program; hands-on exhibits; special programs & events; two-story walk-through tree. Museum Sponsors: Whole World Festival.
Publications: Museum Newsletter; books, A Childhood in Minnesota: Exploring the Lives of Ojibwe & Immigrant Families, 1880s-1920s; Growing Up in My Family: A Guide for Recording Information on Family History.
Hours & Admission Prices: Memorial Day to Labor Day daily 9:30-6; Sept.-May Tues.-Sat. 10-5, Sun. 1-5. Adults $10, children 3-13 $5.50; members, Association of Children's Museums, Association of Science & Technology Center reciprocal membership programs; children 2 & under no charge. Closed New Year's Day; Easter; Thanksgiving; Christmas Eve & Day. ♿
Attendance: 54,321 (accurate)
Membership: Discovery $55; Discovery Plus $115; Passport Discovery $130.

GLENSHEEN HISTORIC ESTATE, 3300 London Rd., Duluth, MN 55804-2010. Tel.: 218-726-8910; 888-454-GLEN. Fax: 218-726-8911.
E-mail: info@glensheen.org
Web Site: www.glensheen.org
Founded: 1979.
Congressional District: 8
Key Personnel: Chm. (V), Dennis Lamkin.
Personnel Profile: Full-Time Paid 2; Full-Time Volunteers 40; Part-Time Paid 20; Part-Time Volunteers 40.
Governing Authority: university. Affiliated with the University of Minnesota, Minneapolis, MN 55414. Tax-exempt.
Historic House & Site: 1905-08 Glensheen, 6.7-acre historic estate featuring 39-room Jacobean Revival mansion, built for Chester A. Congdon, along the shore of Lake Superior. Listed on National Register of Historic Places.
Collections: original furnishings; arts & crafts furniture; oriental rugs; stained glass windows; art glass; carriages & sleighs; carriage house, gardener's cottage, boathouse, formal gardens.
Research Fields: arts & crafts movement in the midwest; early 20th-century American painters; regional business & social history.
Facilities: Museum-related items for sale.
Activities: guided tours.
Hours & Admission Prices: mid-May to mid-Oct. daily 9-5:30; mid-Oct. to mid-May Sat.-Sun. 9:30-3:30. Family $40, adults $13, senior citizens $12, children $7; discounts to AAM, ICOM & NTHP members; members & children 5 and under no charge. Closed New Year's Day; Thanksgiving; Christmas. ♿
Attendance: 58,000 (accurate)
Membership: Individual $40.

GREAT LAKES AQUARIUM, 353 Harbor Dr., Duluth, MN 55802-2639. Tel.: 218-740-3474. Fax: 218-740-2020.
E-mail: info@glaquarium.org
Web Site: www.glaquarium.org
Aquarium.
Collections: marine animals; touch tank.
Activities: special events.
Hours & Admission Prices: May-Oct. daily 10-6; Nov.-April daily 10-5. Adults $14.50, seniors 62 & over $11.50, children 3-17 $8.50; children under 3 no charge.

KARPELES MANUSCRIPT LIBRARY MUSEUM, 902 E. First St., Duluth, MN 55805-2142. Tel.: 218-728-0630.
Key Personnel: Dir., Lee R. Fadden; Cur., Karen Fadden
Manuscript Library Museum.
Collections: original documents & manuscripts pertaining to history, music, science, literature & art.
Activities: musical concerts; recitals; school outreach program; lectures; group tours.
Hours & Admission Prices: May-Sept. daily 12-4; Labor Day to Memorial Day Tues.-Sun. 12-4. No charge.

LAKE SUPERIOR MARITIME VISITORS CENTER, 600 Lake Ave., S., Duluth, MN 55802-2322. Mailing Address: P.O. Box 177, Duluth, MN 55801-0177. Tel.: 218-727-2497. Fax: 218-720-5270.
E-mail: info@LSMMA.com
Web Site: www.LSMMA.com
Founded: 1973.
Congressional District: 8
Key Personnel: Dir., Thomas Holden; Public Rels., Beth M. Duncan.
Personnel Profile: Full-Time Paid 4; Part-Time Paid 1; Part-Time Volunteers 8.
Governing Authority: federal. Parent Institution: U.S. Army Corps of Engineers. Tax-exempt.
Marine Museum: located at Duluth Ship Canal.
Collections: Upper Great Lakes commercial navigation history focused on Duluth-Superior harbor, ships, cargoes, shipwrecks, navigation locks, harbor development.
Research Fields: Great Lakes ships; harbor development.
Facilities: 100-seat auditorium; 14,000 sq. ft. exhibit space.
Activities: guided tours; lectures; films; organized education programs for children; participatory, loan & temporary exhibitions; school loan service.
Publications: bimonthly newsletter, The Nor'Easter; factsheets; brochures.
Hours & Admission Prices: Spring & Fall Sun.-Thurs. 10-4:30, Fri.-Sat. 10-6; Summer: daily 10-9; Winter: Fri.-Sun. 10-4:30. No charge; donations accepted. ♿
Attendance: 408,000 (accurate)
Membership: Individual $35; Family $40; Sustaining $75; Patron $100; Donor $150; Sponsor $250; Individual Life $1,000; Corporate $5,000.

LAKE SUPERIOR RAILROAD MUSEUM, (M), 506 W. Michigan St., Duluth, MN 55802-1517. Tel.: 218-733-7590. Fax: 218-733-7596.
E-mail: museum@LSRM.org
Web Site: www.lsrm.org
Founded: 1974.
Congressional District: 8
Key Personnel: Dir., Ken Buehler; Pres. (V), Neal Vanstrom; Dir. Railroad Operations & Museum Shop Mgr., Tim Schandel; Cur., Tom Gannon.
Personnel Profile: Full-Time Paid 5; Part-Time Paid 2; Part-Time Volunteers 35.
Governing Authority: nonprofit organization. Subsidiary Institution: North Shore Scenic Railway. Tax-exempt: 501(c)(3).
Railroad Museum: housed in 1891-92 Duluth Union Depot Building.
Collections: historic railroad equipment; steam locomotives; diesel locomotives; electric locomotives; passenger & freight cars; railway post office car; snowplows; steam wrecking crane; cabooses; china & silver; manuscripts; 8,000 photographs; 300 timetables; advertising; maps; blueprints; company records & scrapbooks. Historic Trains: 1862 William Crooks, locomotive & train; 1941-43 DM&IR Mallet steam locomotive.
Research Fields: regional railroad history.
Facilities: 1,000-vol. library of material primarily related to railroads & railroad equipment serving Minnesota available for research by special arrangement. Railroad books, china & related memorabilia for sale.
Activities: steam & diesel railroad excursions; youth volunteer/mentorship program; outreach programs; guided tours; lectures; films; gallery talks; loan, permanent, temporary & traveling exhibitions.
Publications: quarterly publication, The Junction.
Hours & Admission Prices: Memorial Day-Labor Day Sun.-Tues. 10-5, Wed.-Sat. 10-6. Family $22.50, adults $8, children $5; discounts to AAM

members; members no charge. Closed New Year's Day; Easter; Thanksgiving; Christmas. ♿
Attendance: 100,000 (estimated)
Membership: Retired Railroad & Student $20; Individual $30; Family $45; Contributing $125; Sustaining $250. Call for Corporate Membership Information.

LAKE SUPERIOR ZOOLOGICAL GARDENS, 7210 Fremont St., Duluth, MN 55807-1854. Tel.: 218-730-4500. Fax: 218-723-3750.
E-mail: info@lszoo.org
Web Site: www.lszoo.org
Founded: 1923.
Key Personnel: Pres. Lake Superior Zoological Society, Russ Smith; Assoc. Parks Dir., Jeff Anderson; Museum Shop Mgr., Susan Wolniakowski.
Personnel Profile: Full-Time Paid 19; Full-Time Volunteers 90; Part-Time Paid 15; Part-Time Volunteers 45.
Governing Authority: Tax-exempt: 501(c)(3).
Zoo.
Collections: Polar Shores Northern Territory; Australian Connection; Primate Conservation Center.
Publications: quarterly newsletter, Wild Times.
Hours & Admission Prices: Summer: 10-5; Winter: 10-4. Adults 13 & over $9, children 3-12 $4; discount to AZA members; members & children under 3 no charge. ♿
Attendance: 100,000 (accurate)
Membership: Individual $35; Family & Grandparent $55; Conservationist $80.

THE ST. LOUIS COUNTY HISTORICAL SOCIETY, 506 W. Michigan St., Duluth, MN 55802-1517. Tel.: 218-733-7580. Fax: 218-733-7585.
E-mail: history@thehistorypeople.org
Web Site: www.thehistorypeople.org
Founded: 1922.
Congressional District: 8
Key Personnel: Exec. Dir., JoAnne Coombe; Chm. (V) Veterans' Memorial Hall, Dennis Hughes; Pres. (V), Vernon Zacher; Mgr. Collections, Milissa Brooks Ojibway; Program Asst. Veterans' Memorial Hall, Patra Sevastiades; Veterans' Memorial Hall Program Dir., Daniel Hartman; Administrative Svcs. Mgr., Julie Bolos; Exec. Asst., Susan Schwanekamp.
Personnel Profile: Full-Time Paid 4; Part-Time Paid 3; Part-Time Volunteers 15; Interns 10.
Governing Authority: nonprofit organization. Tax-exempt: 101(6).
History Museum: housed in restored Duluth Union Depot.
Collections: Eastman Johnson paintings of Ojibwe Indians; northern Minnesota history; books, photographs, manuscripts, historical research material related to mining, shipping, lumbering & settlement of northeastern Minnesota history; artifacts & personal stories of area military veterans; 1892 historic building.
Major Exhibits: Fiberwork by the Duluth Fiber Handcrafters' Guild, 11/09-3/31/10.
Research Fields: northeastern Minnesota history.
Facilities: archives located at the Northeast MN Historical Center at University of Minnesota, Duluth, 218-726-8526.
Activities: lectures; programs; workshops; special exhibits; antique appraisals; culture & cuisine series.
Publications: society newspaper; books, Historic Sites & Place Names of the North Shore of Minnesota; We're Standing on Iron; Eastman Johnson's Lake Superior Indians; A County Built on Iron and Invincible: History of the Duluth Boat Club.
Hours & Admission Prices: Summer: daily 9:30-6; Winter: Mon.-Sat. 10-5, Sun. 1-5. Adults $12, children 3-13 $6; discounts to senior citizens, AAA & AARP members; members & children 2 & under no charge. Call 218-727-8025 to confirm holiday closures. ♿
Attendance: 17,577 (estimated)
Membership: Individual $25; Family $45; Supporter $75; Cornerstone $125-$249; Benefactor $250-$499; Patron $500-$999; Directors' Circle $1,000 & up.

TWEED MUSEUM OF ART, (M), Univ. of Minnesota Duluth, 1201 Ordean Ct., Duluth, MN 55812-3041. Tel.: 218-726-8222 & 7823. Fax: 218-726-8503.
E-mail: tma@d.umn.edu
Web Site: www.d.umn.edu/tma
Founded: 1950.
Congressional District: 8
Key Personnel: Dir., Ken Bloom; Cur., Peter Spooner; Registrar, Camille Doran; Museum Education, Susan Hudec; Technician, Eric Dubnicka; Exec. Sec., Kathy Sandstedt; Sec., Sandi Peterson; Museum Shop Mgr., Barbara Boo.
Personnel Profile: Full-Time Paid 7; Part-Time Paid 3; Part-Time Volunteers 60; Interns 8.
Governing Authority: state; university. Parent Institution: University of Minnesota, Duluth, Board of Regents. Tax-exempt: 501(c)(3).
Art Museum.
Collections: modern & contemporary works; paintings; drawings; works on paper; photography; sculpture & ceramics; Glenn C. Nelson international ceramics; 14th to 19th-century European & 19th to 20th-century American paintings, prints & sculpture; Potlatch Royal Canadian Mounted Police illustrations; French Barbizon School; Richard and Dorothy Nelson collection of American Indian art.
Research Fields: 19th to 20th-century American & 17th to 19th-century European paintings, works on paper, ceramics; modern & contemporary paintings, sculpture, photos, works on paper; American Indian art; American modernism.
Facilities: library & archives; lecture room; sculpture conservatory & courtyard. Museum-related items for sale.
Activities: guided tours; lectures; permanent, temporary & traveling exhibitions; gallery talks; artists-in-residence; education programs for children & adults.
Publications: exhibition & collection catalogs.
Hours & Admission Prices: Tues. 9-8, Wed.-Fri. 9-4:30, Sat.-Sun. 1-5. No charge, donations accepted. Closed university holidays. ♿
Attendance: 37,000 (accurate)
Membership: Student & Senior $10; Individual & Senior $35; Household $50; Friend $100; Associate $250; Society of Fellows $500; Leadership Circle $1,000.

Edina

EDINA HISTORICAL SOCIETY, 4711 W. 70th St., Edina, MN 55435-4059. Tel.: 612-928-4577.
Governing Authority: Subsidiary Institution: Edina Historical Center, Frank Tupa Park, 4918 Eden Ave., Edina, MN.
Historical Society Museum.
Collections: Edina history & culture; photographs; early pioneers. Historic Buildings: one-room Cahill School built in 1864; Minnehaha Grange Hall built in 1879.
Hours & Admission Prices: Thurs. 9am-12pm, Sat. 10am-12pm; other times by appointment.

THE WORKS, 5701 Normandale Rd., Edina, MN 55424-2401. Tel.: 952-848-4848.
E-mail: info@theworks.org
Web Site: www.theworks.org
Founded: 1995.
Governing Authority: Tax-exempt: 501(c)(3).
Technology Discovery Center.
Collections: hands-on engineering exhibits for children 5-12.
Activities: hands-on activities for families & school groups.
Hours & Admission Prices: Sat. 10-4. Admission 3 & over $5.
Membership: Family $60.

Elbow Lake

GRANT COUNTY HISTORICAL SOCIETY, 115 2nd St., NE, Hwy. 79E, Elbow Lake, MN 56531. Mailing Address: P.O. Box 1002, Elbow Lake, MN 56531-1002. Tel.: 218-685-4864.
E-mail: gcmnhist@runestone.net
Web Site: www.rootsweb.com/~mngrant/hist.htm
Founded: 1944.
Congressional District: 7
Key Personnel: Dir. & Cur., Patricia Benson; Chm. (V), Christine Spaulding.
Personnel Profile: Part-Time Paid 1; Part-Time Volunteers 12.
Governing Authority: society; nonprofit organization. Tax-exempt.
Historical Society Museum.
Collections: Indian artifacts; agricultural implements; pioneer household wares; prehistoric fossil remains; military artifacts; manuscripts; microfilm of Grant County newspapers; Grant County census & naturalization records; Norwegian Lutheran Church records; Veterans Memorial Hall.
Research Fields: oxcart trails; Indian mounds & camp grounds; sites of prehistoric fossils; genealogy; cemeteries.
Facilities: 2,000-vol. library of bound volumes of Grant County newspapers, local history, military, biographies, school textbooks, township & county records; reading room.
Activities: guided tours; lectures; organized education programs for children & adults; permanent exhibitions.
Publications: Heritage of Grant County, MN (limited edition).
Hours & Admission Prices: Memorial Day weekend to Sept. Mon.-Sat. 10-12 & 1-4; Oct.-May Mon.-Fri. 10-12 & 1-4. No charge; donations accepted.

Closed New Year's Day; Easter; Memorial Day; Independence Day; Labor Day; Thanksgiving; Christmas Day.
Attendance: 800 (estimated)
Membership: Individual $15; Family $25; Life $150.

Elk River

OLIVER KELLEY FARM, 15788 Kelley Farm Rd., Elk River, MN 55330-6234. Tel.: 763-441-6896. Fax: 763-441-6302.
E-mail: kelleyfarm@mnhs.org
Web Site: www.mnhs.org/kelleyfarm
Founded: 1849.
Congressional District: 8
Key Personnel: Site Mgr., Bob M. Quist; C.E.O. & Dir. MHS, Nina M. Archabal.
Personnel Profile: Full-Time Paid 2; Part-Time Paid 16.
Governing Authority: private; not-for-profit organization. Parent Institution: Minnesota Historical Society. Tax-exempt: 501(c)(3).
Living History Farm: 1876 home of Oliver Kelley, founder of the Grange in 1867.
Collections: Minnesota agricultural history, 1850-1876.
Hours & Admission Prices: May & Oct. Sat. 10-5, Sun. 12-5; Memorial Day to Labor Day Tues.-Sat. 10-5, Sun. 12-5; groups of 10 or more by appointment. Adults $8, senior citizens $6, children 6-17 $5; members & children under 6 no charge. Closed New Year's Eve & Day; Christmas. ♿
Attendance: 30,000 (accurate)
Membership: Senior $45; Individual $50; Senior Household $65; Household $75; Household Plus $95; Associate $145; Contributing $250; Sustaining $500; North Star Circle $1,000.

Ely

DOROTHY MOLTER MUSEUM, Hwy. 169, Ely, MN 55731. Mailing Address: P.O. Box 391, Ely, MN 55731-0391. Tel.: 218-365-4451.
Web Site: www.rootbeerlady.com
History Museum: former home of Dorothy Molter.
Collections: local history & culture pertaining to the life of Dorothy Molter.
Hours & Admission Prices: Memorial Day-Labor Day Mon.-Sat. 10-5:30, Sun. 12-5:30. ♿

ELY-WINTON HISTORICAL SOCIETY, 1900 E. Camp St., Ely, MN 55731-1918. Tel.: 218-365-3226. Fax: 218-365-7207.
E-mail: ewhs@vcc.edu
Web Site: www.vcc/edu/ewhs
Formerly: Vermilion Interpretive Center
Personnel Profile: Full-Time Paid 1; Part-Time Paid 1; Part-Time Volunteers 1.
Governing Authority: Tax-exempt.
Historical Society Museum.
Collections: local history & culture; geology; Native American artifacts; logging; mining.
Activities: Museum Sponsors: History Night Programs in July.
Hours & Admission Prices: Summer: Mon.-Fri. 10-4, Sat. 10-1; Winter: Mon.-Fri. 10-4. Adults $3, children 6-16 $2; discounts to AAM & ICOM members; members & children under 6 no charge. Closed New Year's Day; Easter; Labor Day; Thanksgiving; Christmas. ♿
Attendance: 650 (accurate)
Membership: Individual $10; Family $20; Patron $75; Life $100.

INTERNATIONAL WOLF CENTER, 1396 Hwy. 169, Ely, MN 55731-8129. Tel.: 218-365-4695. Fax: 218-365-3318.
E-mail: jedberg@wolf.org
Web Site: www.wolf.org
Founded: 1985.
Key Personnel: Information Svcs. Dir., Jessica Edberg; Operations & Finance Mgr., Linda Frisell; Program Specialist, Tara Johnson; Retail Dir., Nancy Schwartz; Retail Mgr., Rebecca Stouffer; Wolf Cur., Lori Schmidt; Asst. Wolf Cur., Donna Prichard; Administrative Asst., Laurie Feela
Nature Center.
Collections: wolves & their habitats, lives, & survival.
Major Exhibits: Wolves and Moose of Isle Royale (T), 6/10-8/10.
Facilities: Museum-related items for sale.
Activities: workshops; educational programs; wolf watch cams.
Hours & Admission Prices: May 15-June 14 & Aug. 15-Sept. daily 10-5; June 15-Aug. 14 daily 10-7; Oct.-May 14 Fri.-Sat. 10-5. Adults $8.50, children 3-12 $3; children under 3 no charge. Closed major holidays. ♿
Membership: Individual $35; Family $60; International Family $75; Wolf Associate $125; Wolf Sponsor $500.

NORTH AMERICAN BEAR CENTER, 1926 Hwy. 169, Ely, MN 55731-8130. Mailing Address: P.O. Box 161, Ely, MN 55731-0161. Tel.: 218-365-7879; 877-365-7879.
E-mail: info@bear.org
Web Site: www.bear.org
Key Personnel: Mng. Dir. & Bear Cur., Donna Phelan; Assoc. Dir., Sharon Johnson; Membership Dir., Nancy Krause; Program Coord., Sharon Herrell; Group Coord., Glenn Krause
Nature Center.
Collections: live bears & their habitats; black & brown bear mounts; videos; photographs.
Facilities: theater; nature trail. Museum-related items for sale.
Activities: observation areas; educational programs; special events.
Hours & Admission Prices: May 9-Sept. 7 daily 9-7; Sept. 8-Oct. 17 daily 10-4; Dec. 1-May 8 Fri.-Sat. 10-4. Adults $8.50, seniors 60 & over $7, children 3-12 $4.50. Children under 3 & members no charge.

Elysian

LESUEUR COUNTY HISTORICAL MUSEUM-CHAPTER 1, 301 N. 2nd St., Elysian, MN 56028. Mailing Address: P.O. Box 240, Elysian, MN 56028-0240. Tel.: 507-267-4620.
E-mail: director@lchs.mus.mn.us
Web Site: www.lchs.mus.mn.us
Founded: 1966.
Congressional District: 25
Key Personnel: C.E.O. & Genealogist, Shirley Zimprich; Pres., Pat Nusbaum; Financial Dir., Michael LaFrance; Mgr., Nancy Burhop; Staff, Chris Matz; Staff, Ryan Clarke; Staff, Jeremy Zimprich; Staff, Jon Zimprich; Staff, Louise Hager; Security, Louis Hruska.
Personnel Profile: Part-Time Paid 8.
Governing Authority: county; nonprofit. Branch Museums: Ottawa Methodist Church-Chapter 2, Ottawa, MN; Geldner Saw Mill, Cleveland, MN; LeSueur Museum-Chapter 3, LeSueur, MN. All correspondence: Box 240, Elysian. Tax-exempt: 501(c)(3).
General Museum: housed in c.1895 former Elysian School.
Collections: works by local artists; micrometeorite detector of Explorer I; 1900s general store & living quarters; agriculture; original & reproductions of works by Adolf Dehn, Lloyd Herfindahl, Albert Christ-Janer, Roger Preuss & David Maass; American Indian artifacts; LeSueur County history; Little Crow display; Red Wing pottery; Civil War, World War I & World War II artifacts; birth, death, & marriage records; census information; church & cemetery records; microfilmed newspapers; atlases. Historic House: c.1869 log cabin.
Research Fields: local history; genealogy.
Facilities: 100-vol. library of local history books available upon request; field research station; genealogy center. Museum-related items for sale.
Activities: guided tours; lectures. Museum Sponsors: arts festivals; Ice Cream Socials; annual dinner for all members of the society.
Publications: newsletter, History Abounds.
Hours & Admission Prices: May & Sept. Sat.-Sun. 1-5; June-Aug. Wed.-Sun. 1-5. No charge; donations accepted. ♿
Attendance: 3,000 (estimated)
Membership: Individual $15; Couple, Family & Business $25.

Eveleth

UNITED STATES HOCKEY HALL OF FAME MUSEUM, 801 Hat Trick Ave., Eveleth, MN 55734-8640. Mailing Address: P.O. Box 679, Eveleth, MN 55734-0679. Tel.: 218-744-5167. Fax: 218-744-2590.
E-mail: sersha@ushockeyhallmuseum.com
Web Site: www.ushockeyhallmuseum.com
Founded: 1969.
Congressional District: 8
Key Personnel: Exec. Dir. & Cur., Tom Sersha; Chm., David Tomassoni; Pres., Cal Cossalter; Administrative Asst., Michelle Putzel; Museum Shop Mgr., Kerry Rich; Bd. Sec., Mike Lenich.
Personnel Profile: Full-Time Paid 2; Part-Time Paid 9; Part-Time Volunteers 3.
Governing Authority: nonprofit organization. Tax-exempt: 501(c)(3).
Sports Museum.
Collections: Cleve Bennewitz skate collection 1850-1921; 1960 & 1980 Olympics; 1998 women's hockey display; hockey from all cultures; paintings; prints.
Research Fields: American hockey history.
Facilities: library temporarily closed; theater. Hockey-related items for sale.
Activities: temporary exhibits; hands-on exhibits.
Publications: Enshrinement Day Souvenir Edition; Enshrinee Biography booklet; brochures.
Hours & Admission Prices: Memorial Day to Labor Day Mon.-Sat. 9-5, Sun. 10-3; Sept.-May Fri. 12-5, Sat. 9-5, Sun. 10-3. Adults $8, senior citizens & children 13-17 $7, children 6-12 $6; discounts to hocky groups, AAA &

AAM members; members and children 5 & under no charge. Closed New Year's Day; Easter; Memorial Day; Thanksgiving; Christmas. ♿
Attendance: 15,000 (accurate)

Excelsior

EXCELSIOR-LAKE MINNETONKA HISTORICAL SOCIETY, 305 Water St., Excelsior, MN 55331. Mailing Address: P.O. Box 305, Excelsior, MN 55331-0305. Tel.: 952-221-4766.
E-mail: info@elmhs.org
Web Site: www.elmhs.org
Founded: 1972.
Key Personnel: Museum Committee Chm., Randy Lee Julian.
Personnel Profile: Part-Time Volunteers 15.
Governing Authority: society. A branch of the Minnesota State Historical Society & the Hennepin County Historical Society. Tax-exempt.
Local History Museum.
Collections: maps; manuscripts; diaries; scrapbooks; pictures.
Research Fields: local history.
Facilities: 175-vol. library of village records from 1858 state & county reference histories, local church histories & general collection of Minnesota state laws available on premises only.
Activities: guided tours; lectures; gallery talks; formally organized education programs for children & adults; training programs; temporary exhibitions; slides.
Publications: The Excelsior Amusement Park; Eureka, Summer 1939; Happenings Around Excelsior; Happenings Around Wayzata; Historic Excelsior; Lake Minnetonka Historic Hotels; Lydia Ferguson Diary; Movies Come to Excelsior; Picturesque Deephaven; Picturesque Minnetonka; A Record of Old Boats; Sweet Sixteen and Then Some; Tales from Tonka; Walking The Trails of History; Hezekiah Brake, Excelsior Pioneer; Plat Map-Excelsior 1898; Map-Lake Minnetonka, 1896.
Hours & Admission Prices: May-Sept. Thurs. 3-6, Sat. 10-3. No charge.
Membership: Senior $10; Family $20; Silver $50; Gold $100.

Fairmont

PIONEER MUSEUM - MARTIN COUNTY HISTORICAL SOCIETY, 304 E. Blue Earth Ave., Fairmont, MN 56031-2865. Tel.: 507-235-5178. Fax: 507-235-5179.
E-mail: mch@frontiernet.net
Web Site: www.co.martin.mn.us/mchs
Founded: 1929.
Congressional District: 2
Key Personnel: C.E.O., Fred W. Krahmer; Exec. Dir., Lenny Tvedten; Pres. (V), Randy Musser; Cur., James Marushin; Conservator, Sandy Nuss.
Personnel Profile: Part-Time Paid 4; Part-Time Volunteers 50.
Governing Authority: society. Affiliated with Martin County Historical Society. Tax-exempt: 170(b)(1)(A).
County Historical Society Museum.
Collections: early history of Martin County.
Facilities: 600-vol. library of newspaper files available for research on premises.
Activities: permanent & temporary exhibitions.
Publications: newsletter 3 times a year.
Hours & Admission Prices: Mon.-Fri. 8:30-12 & 1-4:30, Sat.-Sun. special tours & by appointment. No charge; donations accepted. ♿
Attendance: 2,500 (estimated)
Membership: Copper $25-$49.99; Bronze $50-$249.99; Gold $500-$999.99; Platinum $1,000 & up.

Falcon Heights

GIBBS MUSEUM OF PIONEER AND DAKOTAH LIFE, 2097 W. Larpenteur Ave., Falcon Heights, MN 55113-5313. Mailing Address: Ramsey County Historical Society, 323 Landmark Center, 75 W. 5th St., Saint Paul, MN 55102. Tel.: 651-646-8629 & 659-0345. Fax: 651-659-0345.
E-mail: gibbs@rchs.com
Web Site: www.rchs.com
Formerly: Gibbs Farm Museum
Founded: 1949.
Congressional District: 4
Key Personnel: C.E.O., Priscilla Farnham; Museum Site Mgr., Ted Lau.
Personnel Profile: Full-Time Paid 8; Part-Time Paid 10; Part-Time Volunteers 40.
Governing Authority: nonprofit organization. Parent Institution: Ramsey County Historical Society, 75 W. Fifth St. No. 323, St. Paul, MN 55102. Tel.: 612-222-0701. Tax-exempt: 501(c)(3).
Turn-of-the-Century Urban Fringe Farming: housed in 1854-1974 Gibbs Farmhouse.
Collections: history of the Gibbs family 1835-1940 & the relationship with the Dakota Native Americans; 19th- & early 20th-century agricultural tools; personal & decorative items; woodworking. Historical Buildings: 1880s Milan, MN one-room schoolhouse; 1910 barn; replica of original soddy; Dakotah tipi & bark lodge.
Research Fields: agricultural techniques & family patterns; interpret urban fringe farming.
Facilities: 125-vol. library of local & Minnesota history books available for research; classrooms. Museum-related & handcraft items for sale.
Activities: guided tours; formally organized education programs for children & adults; docent program or council; loan, permanent, temporary & traveling exhibitions.
Publications: magazine, Ramsey County History; quarterly newsletter, History News & Notes.
Hours & Admission Prices: May-Oct. Tues.-Sun. 12-4; other times by appointment. Adults $7, seniors $6, children 2-16 $4; discounts to AAA members & groups for 15 or more; members no charge. ♿
Attendance: 16,000 (accurate)
Membership: Individual $35; House $40.

Faribault

RICE COUNTY MUSEUM OF HISTORY, (M), 1814 N.W. 2nd Ave., Faribault, MN 55021-3033. Tel.: 507-332-2121. Fax: 507-332-2121.
E-mail: rchs@rchistory.org
Web Site: www.rchistory.org
Founded: 1926.
Congressional District: 1
Key Personnel: Exec. Dir., Susan Garwood; Pres. (V), Jason Reher.
Personnel Profile: Full-Time Paid 1; Part-Time Paid 1; Part-Time Volunteers 86; Interns 1.
Governing Authority: Parent Institution: Rice County Historical Society. Subsidiary Institution: Northfield Historical Society, NFLD; Morristown Grist Mill, Morristown; 3R Landmark School, Lonsdale; Dundas Historical Society. Tax-exempt.
History & Agricultural Museum Complex.
Collections: pioneer & Indian artifacts; turn-of-the-century main street; photographs. Historic Buildings: 1853 Alexander Faribault House; Holy Innocents Church; log house; Pleasant Valley rural schoolhouse; Harvest & Heritage Halls.
Research Fields: genealogy; natural & cultural history of Rice County.
Facilities: library.
Activities: guided tours; slide presentation of history of Rice County; video presentation. Museum Sponsors: semi-annual banquets; USO Dinner and Dance in Spring; Heritage Days in June; Rice County Fair in July.
Publications: newsletter, Rice County Historian.
Hours & Admission Prices: Museum: Mon.-Fri. 9-4. Faribault House: May-Sept. Mon.-Fri. 12-5; other times by appointment. Museum: adults $3, senior citizens 55 & over $2, children 12 & under $1; discounts to AAM members; members no charge. Faribault House: admission $2. ♿
Attendance: 6,000 (estimated)
Membership: Senior Citizen $15; Individual $30; Family $35; Patron $50; Business $200.

Farmington

DAKOTA CITY HERITAGE VILLAGE, Dakota County Fairgrounds, 4008 220th St. W., Farmington, MN 55024. Mailing Address: P.O. Box 73, Farmington, MN 55024-0073. Tel.: 651-460-8050.
Web Site: www.daotacity.org
Founded: 1979.
Key Personnel: Cur. & Collections Mgr., Tracy Behrendt.
Personnel Profile: Full-Time Paid 1; Part-Time Paid 1; Part-Time Volunteers 450; Interns 1.
Governing Authority: Tax-exempt.
Heritage Village.
Collections: 1900-era rural village includes 24 buildings; period furnishings; agricultural equipment.
Facilities: 5 acre site.
Activities: special events; demonstrations; educational programs; celebrations. Annual Events: Bluegrass in the Village; Dakota County Fair; Civil War Weekend; Grand History Days; Village Holidays.
Hours & Admission Prices: May-Sept. Mon.-Sat.; groups of 15 or more by appointment. ♿
Attendance: 30,000 (estimated)
Membership: Individual $35; Family $75.

Fergus Falls

OTTER TAIL COUNTY HISTORICAL SOCIETY, 1110 Lincoln Ave. W., Fergus Falls, MN 56537-1029. Tel.: 218-736-6038. Fax: 218-739-3075.
E-mail: otchs@prtel.com
Web Site: www.otchs.org/
Founded: 1927.
Congressional District: 7
Key Personnel: Exec. Dir., Chris Schuelke; Cur. Collections, Kathy Evavold; Education Coord., Missy Hermes; Office Mgr., LeAnn Neuleib.
Personnel Profile: Full-Time Paid 3; Part-Time Paid 2; Part-Time Volunteers 100; Interns 1.
Governing Authority: private. Tax-exempt: 501(c)(3).
Historical Society Museum.
Collections: 15,000 artifacts including American Indian artifacts; agriculture; Norwegian; Scandinavian; newspapers; photographs; maps; clippings; oral histories.
Research Fields: Otter Tail County and local history; genealogy.
Facilities: library; archives.
Activities: demonstrations; tours; educational services; annual meeting; genealogy & oral history workshops; history conference; rotating & special exhibits; traveling exhibits; research workshops; cemetery records; historic sites and car-tape tour; volunteer program.
Publications: books, The New Deal at the Grass Roots: Programs for the People in Otter Tail County; Homefires & Battlegrounds-A Military History of Otter Tail County; Old Clitherall's Storybook; O.T. Co. History in Brief; History of Fergus Falls; quarterly newsletter, The Otter Tail County Record; A History of the Pelican Lakes; bimonthly newsletter.
Hours & Admission Prices: June-Aug. Mon.-Fri. 9-5, Sat. 1-4; Sept.-May Mon.-Fri. 9-5. Adults $3, children 5-11 $1; members no charge. ♿
Attendance: 9,000 (estimated)
Membership: Basic Individual $20; Supporting Individual or Family $35; Booster $50; Business $50 & up; Sustaining $100; Sponsor $150; Patron $250.

Fountain

FILLMORE COUNTY HISTORICAL CENTER, 202 County Rd. No. 8, Fountain, MN 55935-8805. Tel.: 507-268-4449. Fax: 507-268-4492.
E-mail: fillmorehistory@earthlink.net
Founded: 1934.
Congressional District: 1
Key Personnel: C.E.O., Jerry Henke; Vice Pres., Edwin Wright; Pres. (V), Flora Grabau; Sec., Rita Joerg; Treas., June Hanson.
Personnel Profile: Full-Time Paid 2; Part-Time Volunteers 15.
Governing Authority: corporation. Tax-exempt.
General Museum.
Collections: 45,000 photographic negatives; agriculture; costumes; rural schoolhouse; late 1800-early 1900 home furnishings; obituary files; Civil War artifacts; archives; 1932 SkyScout airplane.
Research Fields: local & county history; genealogy.
Facilities: library of historical books & newspapers on microfilm; reading room.
Activities: guided tours; special programs; demonstrations.
Publications: quarterly newsletter, Rural Roots.
Hours & Admission Prices: Mon.-Fri. 9-4. No charge; donations accepted. Closed major holidays. ♿
Attendance: 8,500 (estimated)
Membership: Student $5; Individual $10; Family $16; Associate $30; Patron $50; Life $150.

Freeport

HEMKER PARK & ZOO, County Rd. 39, Freeport, MN 56331. Mailing Address: Box 262, Freeport, MN 56331-0262. Tel.: 320-836-2426.
Web Site: www.hemkerzoo.com
Zoo.
Collections: wildlife.
Hours & Admission Prices: May-Oct. daily 10-6. Adults $7.25, seniors 60 & over $6.25, children 1-12 $5.25; children under 1 no charge.

Fridley

SPRINGBROOK NATURE CENTER, 100 85th Ave., N.E., Fridley, MN 55432. Mailing Address: 6431 University Ave., N.E., Fridley, MN 55432-4303. Tel.: 763-572-3588.
Web Site: www.springbrooknaturecenter.org
Founded: 1974.
Key Personnel: Dir., Siah L. St. Clair.
Personnel Profile: Full-Time Paid 3; Part-Time Paid 3; Part-Time Volunteers 25.
Governing Authority: municipal government; nonprofit. Parent Institution: City of Fridley.
Nature Center: a 127-acre natural urban park.
Collections: central Minnesota natural history with emphasis on the Anoka County area.
Hours & Admission Prices: Summer: Mon.-Fri. 9-9, Sat. 10-6, Sun. 12-4; Winter: Mon.-Fri. 10-5, Sat. 9-5, Sun. 12-4. No charge. Closed all holidays. ♿
Attendance: 50,000 (accurate)

Glenwood

POPE COUNTY HISTORICAL SOCIETY, 809 S. Lakeshore Dr., Glenwood, MN 56334-9406. Tel.: 320-634-3293.
E-mail: pcmuseum@wisper-wireless.com
Founded: 1931.
Congressional District: 7
Key Personnel: Pres. (V), Nicholas Terhaar; Vice Pres., Carol Cheeseman; Dir., Merlin Peterson; Artifact & Inventory Mgr., Ann Grandy; Admin. Asst. & Research, Jackie Gartner.
Personnel Profile: Part-Time Paid 4; Part-Time Volunteers 20.
Governing Authority: society; board of directors. Tax-exempt.
General Museum.
Collections: county artifacts; county history & genealogy; Helbing collection of Indian artifacts; wildlife; communications; period rooms; trapper's cabin; newspapers dating to 1871; church records; census records; photographs; family histories; 1866 Pope County treasurer & assessors record; 1968, count ledgers, Wolf bounty, country schools; record books of organizations in the county; 44,000 biographical files including business, educational, professional & personal.
Research Fields: county genealogy.
Facilities: library of bound volumes of county newspapers from 1877 to present.
Activities: guided tours; formally organized education programs for children. Museum Sponsors: A Treasure Hunt for Information.
Publications: brochures; newspaper articles; biannual newsletters.
Hours & Admission Prices: Tues.-Sat. 10-5. Adults $3, students 13-18 $1.50, children 6-12 $.50; members no charge. ♿
Attendance: 1,588 (accurate)
Membership: Individual $10; Family $25; Lifetime $100.

Grand Marais

COOK COUNTY HISTORICAL MUSEUM, 5 S. Broadway, Grand Marais, MN 55604-1293. Mailing Address: Cook County Historical Society, Box 1293, Grand Marais, MN 55604-1293. Tel.: 218-387-2883 & 9131.
E-mail: history@boreal.org
Founded: 1966.
Congressional District: 8
Key Personnel: C.E.O., Leonard Sobanja; Dir. Museum, Pat Zankman; Dir. Johnson Heritage Post, Joanne Krause.
Personnel Profile: Part-Time Paid 2; Part-Time Volunteers 20.
Governing Authority: county; society. Administered by Cook County Historical Society. Tax-exempt.
General Museum & Art Museum: housed in 1896 lighthouse keeper's residence.
Collections: photographs; ccc camps; trapping; logging; textiles; folklore; military; agriculture; sports; Indian artifacts; medical; geology; voyageurs; music; commercial fishing; microfilm newspapers; census; 150 manuscripts on pioneer life; history of schools, churches, organizations, communities & industries; video; Johnson Heritage Post: art & artists on the north shore of Lake Superior.
Research Fields: pioneer life history of communities; obituaries; photographs.
Facilities: 4,000 sq. ft. exhibit space. Pamphlets, local books made by local society for sale.
Activities: permanent exhibitions; school loan service; County Fair exhibits.
Publications: historical pamphlets, Grand Marais; History of Gunflint Trail; books, Pioneer Faces & Places, Pioneers in the Wilderness; Law & Order Cook County 100 Years; Faces & Places II; newsletter, Overlook.
Hours & Admission Prices: May 25-Oct. 1 Mon.-Sat. 11-4, Sun. 1-4; Oct.-May Sat. 1-4; other times by appointment. No charge; donations accepted.
Attendance: 15,000 (estimated)
Membership: Annual Single $10; Double $15.

Grand Portage

GRAND PORTAGE NATIONAL MONUMENT, (M), 170 Mile Creek Rd., Grand Portage, MN 55605. Mailing Address: P.O. Box 426, Grand Portage, MN 55605-0426. Tel.: 218-475-0123. TDD: 218-387-2788.
E-mail: grpo_interpretation@nps.gov
Web Site: www.nps.gov/grpo

Founded: 1958.
Congressional District: 8
Key Personnel: Supt., Tim Cochrane; Chief Interpretation, Pam Neil; Chief Resource Management, David Cooper; Park Ranger, Jon Sage.
Personnel Profile: Full-Time Paid 10; Part-Time Paid 10; Part-Time Volunteers 11; Interns 1.
Governing Authority: federal. Parent Institution: U.S. Dept. of Interior. Subsidiary Institution: National Park Service, Washington, DC 20240. Tax-exempt.
Historical Site & Park Museum: housed in 18th-century reconstructed North West Company fur trading depot on its original site.
Collections: archaeological materials from the site; period fur trade artifacts; Chippewa Indian cultural materials.
Research Fields: exploration & fur trading centered on Grand Portage.
Facilities: 900-vol. library dealing with the fur trade including the exploration of the Canadian Northwest & the Chippewa Indians of the region, periodical collection, maps, charts, pamphlets, articles, slide & photograph collection with contemporary & historical information; nature trails; information center.
Activities: guided tours, audiovisual programs; Chippewa craft demonstrations; historical cooking, baking & musket demonstrations. Annual Event: fur trade rendezvous in August.
Publications: brochures; pamphlets.
Hours & Admission Prices: mid-May to mid-Oct. daily 9-5; groups by appointment. Family $6, adults $3; people with Federal National Parks, Golden Access, Golden Age passes and adults 17 & over no charge. ♿
Attendance: 70,000 (estimated)

Grand Rapids

CHILDREN'S DISCOVERY MUSEUM, 2727 U.S. Hwy. 169 S., Grand Rapids, MN 55744. Mailing Address: P.O. Box 724, Grand Rapids, MN 55744-0724. Tel.: 218-326-1900; 866-236-5437 (Toll Free). Fax: 218-326-1934.
E-mail: office@cdmkids.org
Web Site: cdmkids.org
Founded: 1994.
Key Personnel: Dir., John A. Kelsch; Pres. (V), Douglas P. Miner.
Personnel Profile: Full-Time Paid 1; Part-Time Paid 5; Part-Time Volunteers 56.
Governing Authority: Tax-exempt.
Children's Museum.
Collections: hands-on exhibits.
Facilities: Museum-related items for sale.
Activities: school service program.
Hours & Admission Prices: Memorial Day to Sept. daily 10-5; Oct. call for hours. Admission $7; members no charge. Closed New Year's Day; Easter; Thanksgiving; Christmas. ♿
Attendance: 18,951 (accurate)
Membership: Youth $20; Adult $30; Family $40; Grandparent $50; Daycare & Resort $100.

FOREST HISTORY CENTER, 2609 County Rd. 76, Grand Rapids, MN 55744-8646. Tel.: 218-327-4482. Fax: 218-327-4715.
E-mail: foresthistory@mnhs.org
Web Site: mnhs.org/places/sites/fhc
Founded: 1978.
Congressional District: 3
Key Personnel: Site Mgr., Robert Drake; Museum Shop Mgr., Becky Jennings; Asst. Mgr., Ed Nelson.
Personnel Profile: Full-Time Paid 1; Part-Time Paid 18; Part-Time Volunteers 20; Interns 2.
Governing Authority: nonprofit organization. Parent Institution: Minnesota Historical Society. Tax-exempt: 501(c)(3).
Historic Site, Historic Museum, Natural History Museum.
Collections: forestry-related artifacts; logging camp; c.1900 wanigan & batteau used in log drives; cabin; garage; firetower; warehouse.
Research Fields: natural history; human history; agriculture in northern forested areas of the Great Lakes states; Great Lakes environmental history; forest history of Great Lakes states.
Facilities: 750-vol. library; classrooms; 18,000 sq. ft. exhibit space; 90-seat theater; 5 mile nature trail. Forestry & history-related books & gifts for sale.
Activities: guided tours; lectures; films; organized education programs for children, adults & college students affiliated with Bemidji State Univeristy & Itasca Community Collge; docent program; training programs for professional museum workers; participatory & temporary exhibitions; interpretive programs; living history programs.
Hours & Admission Prices: Memorial Day weekend: Wed.-Sat. 10-5, Sun. 12-5; June to Labor Day Mon.-Sat. 10-5, Sun. 12-5. Adults $8, senior citizens $6, children 6-17 $5; discounts to AAA members; members & children under 6 no charge. ♿
Attendance: 20,000 (accurate)
Membership: Senior Citizen $45; Individual $50; Senior Household & Individual Plus $65; Household $75; Household Plus $95.

ITASCA HISTORICAL SOCIETY & ITASCA GENEALOGY, 10-5th St., N.W., Grand Rapids, MN 55744. Mailing Address: P.O. Box 664, Grand Rapids, MN 55744-0664. Tel.: 218-326-6431. Fax: 218-999-7342.
E-mail: ichs@paulbunyan.net
Web Site: itascahistorical.com
Founded: 1948.
Congressional District: 8
Key Personnel: C.E.O., Lilah J. Crowe; Chm. (V), Michelle Rossi; Pres. (V), Esther Hietala; Museum Shop Mgr., Jeremy Anderson.
Personnel Profile: Full-Time Paid 1; Part-Time Paid 4; Part-Time Volunteers 20.
Governing Authority: society; nonprofit. Tax-exempt.
Historical Society Museum: housed in 1895 first consolidated school in county, Central School.
Collections: history of Itasca County; manuscripts; papermaking; early life & career of Judy Garland.
Research Fields: county history.
Facilities: 700-vol. library of books pertaining to area; reading room. Books of local history & museum-related items for sale.
Activities: films; permanent & temporary exhibitions.
Publications: quarterly newsletter.
Hours & Admission Prices: Mon.-Fri. 9:30-5, Sat. 10-4; Summer: Mon.-Fri. 9:30-5, Sat. 10-4, Sun. 11-4. Adults $4, senior 55 & over $3, children 6-12 $2; discounts to school groups, AAA, AAM & ICHS members; members no charge. Closed national holidays. ♿
Attendance: 4,000 (accurate)
Membership: Seniors & Students $15; Individual $20-$100; Household $30-$250; Business $50-$1,000.

JUDY GARLAND MUSEUM, 2727 U.S. Hwy. 169 S., Grand Rapids, MN 55744. Mailing Address: P.O. Box 724, Grand Rapids, MN 55744-0724. Tel.: 800-664-5839.
E-mail: jgarland@uslink.net
Web Site: www.judygarlandmuseum.com/
Founded: 1994.
Key Personnel: Exec. Dir., John Kelsch; Pres. (V), Douglas P. Miner.
Personnel Profile: Full-Time Paid 1; Part-Time Paid 5; Part-Time Volunteers 52.
Governing Authority: Tax-exempt.
Historic House Museum.
Collections: personal artifacts; photographs; furnishings; Emerald City carriage used in the Wizard of Oz; Garland's Tony Award. Historic House: Judy Garland's birthplace.
Research Fields: life & times of Judy Garland.
Activities: weddings. Annual Event: Judy Garland Festival in June.
Hours & Admission Prices: Memorial Day to Sept. daily 10-5; Oct.-May call for hours. Admission $7; members no charge. Closed New Year's Day; Easter; Thanksgiving; Christmas. ♿
Attendance: 18,951 (accurate)
Membership: Youth $20; Adult $30; Family $40; Grandparent $50; Get Happy $100.

Granite Falls

YELLOW MEDICINE COUNTY HISTORICAL SOCIETY AND MUSEUM, Junction of Hwy. 67 & 23, Granite Falls, MN 56241. Mailing Address: Box 145, Granite Falls, MN 56241-0145. Tel.: 320-564-4479. Fax: 320-564-4479.
Founded: 1952.
Congressional District: 7
Key Personnel: Chm., Jan Peterson; Vice Pres., Ernie Streich.
Personnel Profile: Part-Time Paid 1; Part-Time Volunteers 10.
Governing Authority: society. Parent Institution: Yellow Medicine County Agriculture & Machinery Museum, Hanley Falls, MN 56245; Lund-Hoel Home, Canby, MN 56220. Tax-exempt: 170(b)(1)(A).
History Museum.
Collections: geology; archaeology; pioneer artifacts; 8,000 year old bison bones. Historic Buildings: 1870 pioneer log cabin used as a general store; 1877 pioneer home; outside chapel.
Research Fields: genealogy
Facilities: 75-vol. library of history books available for use on premises; reading room. State historical publications, local area history books & other museum-related items for sale.
Activities: lectures; permanent & temporary exhibits. Museum Sponsors: special exhibits & demonstrations Memorial Day to Labor Day.
Publications: quarterly newsletter, Yellow Medicine County Heritage; History of Yellow Medicine County, 1914.

Hours & Admission Prices: Memorial Day to Labor Day Fri.-Sun. 11-5; other times by appointment. No charge; donations accepted. ♿
Attendance: 1,500 (estimated)
Membership: Individual $15; Couple $18; Family $25; Business $50 & up.

Hanley Falls

MINNESOTA'S MACHINERY MUSEUM, 100 N. 1st St., Hanley Falls, MN 56245. Mailing Address: P.O. Box 70, Hanley Falls, MN 56245-0070. Tel.: 507-768-3522 & 3580. Fax: 507-768-3522.
E-mail: agmuseum@frontiernet.net
Founded: 1980.
Congressional District: 20
Key Personnel: Dir., Mavis Gustafson.
Personnel Profile: Full-Time Paid 1; Part-Time Paid 2.
Governing Authority: Parent Institution: Yellow Medicine County. Tax-exempt.
Agriculture & Transportation Museum.
Collections: farm machinery; farm life history; period automobiles; railroad memorabilia; miniature & toy farm machinery; rural art; farm house rooms; quilts; tractors.
Facilities: Museum-related items for sale.
Activities: guided tours; school programs; demonstrations.
Hours & Admission Prices: May-Sept. Mon.-Sat. 10-4, Sun. 1-4:30; other times by appointment. No charge; donations accepted. Closed holidays. ♿
Membership: Individual $10; Sustaining $100; Corporate $250-$500.

Hastings

CARPENTER ST. CROIX VALLEY NATURE CENTER, 12805 St. Croix Trail, Hastings, MN 55033-9499. Tel.: 651-437-4359.
Key Personnel: Exec. Dir., Jim Fitzpatrick
Nature Center
Collections: wildlife habitat.
Facilities: hiking trails.
Activities: birthday parties; educational programs; scout programs.
Hours & Admission Prices: Daily 8-4:30. No charge. Closed New Year's Day; Thanksgiving; Christmas.

Henderson

SIBLEY COUNTY HISTORICAL MUSEUM, 700 Main St. W., Henderson, MN 56044-7711. Mailing Address: P.O. Box 407, Henderson, MN 56044-0407. Tel.: 507-248-3434 & 3818.
Web Site: history.sibley.mn.us
Founded: 1940.
Congressional District: 2
Key Personnel: Chm. (V), Jerome Petersen.
Personnel Profile: Part-Time Volunteers 30.
Governing Authority: society. Tax-exempt.
History Museum: housed in 1884 residence.
Collections: agriculture; period furnishings; industrial; Sibley County, MN family histories. Historic Building: 1860 log cabin.
Research Fields: Joseph R. Brown Cemetery; Sibley County cemeteries; Sibley County family histories; microfilm census; naturalization; Sibley County newspapers & microfilms.
Facilities: library of bibles, maps, county newspapers & photo albums.
Activities: guided tours; formally organized education programs for children.
Publications: quarterly, Sibley County Historical Society Newsletter; books, Henderson to Fort Ridgely Trail: Bits and Pieces, A History of Sibley County; Boys in Blue, 1898-1902; Sibley County flat maps, 1855-1997; Tales of the 10th Regiment Minnesota Volunteers, 1862-1863; Henderson Then & Now, 1852-1994; Joseph R. Brown and His Times; A History of St. Brendans Parish, The Village of Green Isle and First Irish Settlement.
Hours & Admission Prices: June-Oct. Sun. 2-5; other times by appointment. Adults $2, children $1; members no charge. ♿
Attendance: 1,200 (estimated)
Membership: Annual $10; Family $15; Business $25; Corporate $500.

Hendricks

LINCOLN COUNTY PIONEER MUSEUM, 610 W. Elm, Hendricks, MN 56136. Tel.: 507-275-3537.
Founded: 1969.
Congressional District: 3
Key Personnel: Pres., Allen S. Johnson; Vice Pres. & Treas., Dr. Rolland Digre; Sec., Mr. Trygue Trooien.
Governing Authority: county; society. Tax-exempt.
Historical Society Museum: housed in c.1899 train depot & Icelandic church.
Collections: train depot; farm machinery & tools; furniture; period military uniforms; country schoolhouse; an old opera house room; Lincoln County Courthouse artifacts; millinery shop; dolls; fifteen mannequins dressed in clothes from early 1900s; medical instruments; toys; buggies. Historic Buildings: 1918-1919 restored Sears Roebuck house; 1879 Icelandic Church.
Activities: guided tours.
Hours & Admission Prices: Wed.-Fri. 2-5 & 7-9, Sun. 2-5; other times by appointment. No charge; donations accepted. ♿
Attendance: 600 (estimated)

Hibbing

HIBBING HISTORICAL SOCIETY AND MUSEUM, 400 E. 23rd St., Hibbing, MN 55746-1923. Tel.: 218-263-8522.
E-mail: hibbinghistory@mchsi.com
Founded: 1976.
Congressional District: 8
Key Personnel: Pres. (V), Pru Lolich; Vice Pres., Leonard Hirsch; Treas., Howard Marqulus.
Personnel Profile: Part-Time Paid 1.
Governing Authority: society; nonprofit organization. Operated by Hibbing Historical Society. Parent Institution: First Settlers' Association. Affiliated with St. Louis County Historical Society, Duluth, MN 55802. Tax-exempt: 501(c)(3).
History Museum: housed in 1936 Memorial Building.
Collections: children's artifacts; mining; logging; paintings; clothing; research materials on local history; photos; Greyhound Bus history; manuscripts.
Research Fields: local history; genealogy.
Facilities: library of history books available for research on premises. Books, items of the area & postcards for sale.
Activities: guided tours; films; permanent & temporary exhibitions.
Publications: quarterly newsletter, Frank's Place.
Hours & Admission Prices: Memorial Day-Labor Day Mon.-Thurs. 9:30-12:30, Sat. 10-1; other times by appointment. No charge; donations accepted. ♿
Attendance: 389 (accurate)
Membership: Senior Citizen $10; Individual $15; Family $30; Business $50; Life $200.

Hinckley

HINCKLEY FIRE MUSEUM, 106 Old Hwy. 61, Hinckley, MN 55037. Mailing Address: P.O. Box 40, Hinckley, MN 55037-0040. Tel.: 320-384-7338.
Web Site: www.hinckleyfire.com
Founded: 1976.
Congressional District: 8
Key Personnel: Tour Guide & Museum Shop Mgr., Sandy Hinds; Pres. (V), Steve Johnson.
Personnel Profile: Full-Time Paid 1; Part-Time Paid 1; Part-Time Volunteers 5.
Governing Authority: Tax-exempt.
History Museum: housed in 1894, St. Paul & Duluth Railroad Depot.
Collections: artifacts; photographs; maps; newspapers pertinent to fire of Sept. 1894; household furnishings; depot agent's apartment; late 19th-century clothing.
Research Fields: 1837-1894 planning survey of logging operations; Ojibwe Indians in area; state relief effort; fire ecology.
Facilities: 100-seat auditorium; theater. Museum-related items for sale.
Activities: guided tours; lectures; films; concerts; arts festivals; drama; permanent & temporary exhibitions; interactive childrens exhibit.
Publications: newsletter, The Telegraph.
Hours & Admission Prices: May to mid-Oct. Tues.-Sun. 10-5. Adults $5, senior citizens $4, students 13-18 $2, children 6-12 $1; members & children under 6 no charge.
Attendance: 7,000 (estimated)
Membership: Senior Citizen $10; Individual $15; Family $25; Patron & Business $50; Contributor $100 and up; Patron Business $100; Contributing Business $250 and up.

Hutchinson

MCLEOD COUNTY HISTORICAL SOCIETY, (M), 380 School Rd., N.W., Hutchinson, MN 55350-1430. Tel.: 320-587-2109.
E-mail: asa@hutchtel.net
Web Site: www.mcleodhistory.org/index.htm
Founded: 1940.
Congressional District: 2
Key Personnel: Exec. Dir., Lori Pickell-Stangel; Chm. (V) & Pres. (V), Stan Ehrke; Museum Asst., Tami DeKam.
Personnel Profile: Full-Time Paid 1; Full-Time Volunteers 2; Part-Time Paid 1; Part-Time Volunteers 25; Interns 1.
Historical Society Museum.

Collections: county history & culture; photographs; documents; art.
Research Fields: newsletter, McLeod Historical Society; historical booklets.
Facilities: library.
Activities: workshops.
Hours & Admission Prices: Mon. 10-8, Thurs.-Fri. 10-4, Sat. 1-4. Adults $3, seniors $2, students $1. Closed major holidays. ♿
Attendance: 4,000 (estimated)
Membership: Individual $20; Family $35; Lifetime $500.

International Falls

KOOCHICHING COUNTY HISTORICAL MUSEUM, (M), 214 6th Ave., International Falls, MN 56649-2336. Tel.: 218-283-4316. Fax: 218-283-2843.
Founded: 1958.
Congressional District: 8
Key Personnel: C.E.O., Edgar S. Oerichbauer; Pres. (V), Mike Williams.
Personnel Profile: Full-Time Paid 1; Part-Time Paid 5; Part-Time Volunteers 10.
Governing Authority: society. Tax-exempt: 501(c)(3).
History Museum.
Collections: period items; artifacts; paintings; photographs; manuscripts; industry & history of Koochiching County.
Research Fields: logging & lumber; local history; Minnesota & Ontario Pulp and Paper Co.; International Lumber Co.
Facilities: library; 6,600 sq. ft. exhibit space.
Activities: meetings of the society; special events.
Publications: 8 times a year newsletter, Koochiching Chronicles.
Hours & Admission Prices: Mon.-Fri. 9-5. Adults $4, student 5-17 $2; discounts to groups; children under 5 & members no charge. ♿
Attendance: 5,000 (estimated)
Membership: Individual $15; Family $20; Contributing $50, $100, $250, $500.

VOYAGEURS NATIONAL PARK, 3131 Hwy. 53 S., International Falls, MN 56649-8956. Tel.: 218-283-6600 (Park Headquarters).
Web Site: www.nps.gov/voya
Key Personnel: Supt., Michael M. Ward
National Park Visitor Centers.
Collections: local history & culture.
Facilities: nature trails.
Activities: hiking.
Hours & Admission Prices: Park: year-round dawn-dusk. Visitor Centers: call for hours. No charge.

Kellogg

LARK TOYS & CAROUSEL, 171 Lark Lane, Kellogg, MN 55945-9629. Tel.: 507-767-3387. Fax: 507-767-4565.
E-mail: lark@wabasha.net
Web Site: larktoys.com
Key Personnel: Owner, Ron Gray; Owner, Kathy Gray; Owner, Scott Gray-Burlingham; Owner, Miranda Gray-Burlingham
Toy Museum.
Collections: hand-carved carousel; costumes; period toys.
Hours & Admission Prices: Daily 9:30-5:30. Closed New Year's Day; Thanksgiving; Christmas.

Kenyon

GUNDERSON HOUSE, 107 Gunderson Blvd., Kenyon, MN 55946. Mailing Address: 510 4th St., Kenyon, MN 55946-1117. Tel.: 507-789-5936.
Founded: 1895.
Congressional District: 25
Key Personnel: Pres., Lois Easton.
Governing Authority: municipal. Operated by the Kenyon Area Historical Society. Tax-exempt.
Historic House: 1895 Gunderson House. Listed on the National Register of Historic Places.
Collections: Victorian architecture; furnishings.
Research Fields: state & county history.
Activities: guided tours.
Hours & Admission Prices: 3rd Sat. of month. Adults $3, students $1; preschool no charge.
Attendance: 350
Membership: Senior Citizen $3; Individual $5; Family $7.50; Business $25; Life $100.

Lake Bronson

KITTSON COUNTY HISTORY CENTER MUSEUM, 332 E. Main St., Lake Bronson, MN 56734-3448. Tel.: 218-754-4100.
E-mail: history@wiktel.com
Founded: 1973.
Congressional District: 7
Key Personnel: Dir., Cindy Adams; Pres. (V), Robert P. Cameron; Business Officer, Melroe Gunnarson.
Personnel Profile: Full-Time Paid 1; Part-Time Paid 2; Part-Time Volunteers 2.
Governing Authority: society; nonprofit organization. Tax-exempt: 501(c)(3).
Historical Society Museum.
Collections: settlement of county from 1880-present.
Research Fields: local history.
Facilities: 1,000-vol. library of local, county & state information available for research by special permission from director; reading room; microfilm reader-printer with 172 microfilms containing local newspapers.
Activities: films; permanent & traveling exhibits.
Publications: quarterly newsletter.
Hours & Admission Prices: April-May & Sept.-Nov. Mon.-Fri. 9-5; Memorial Day to Labor Day Mon.-Fri. 9-5, Sat.-Sun. & holidays 1-5; Dec.-March Tues.-Fri. 9-5. No charge; donations accepted. ♿
Attendance: 4,000 (estimated)
Membership: Individual $15; Family $25.

Lakefield

JACKSON COUNTY HISTORICAL MUSEUM, 307 N. Hwy. 86, Lakefield, MN 56150-1259. Mailing Address: P.O. Box 238, Lakefield, MN 56150-0238. Tel.: 507-662-5505. Fax: 507-662-5505.
E-mail: jchs@frontiernet.net
Founded: 1931.
Congressional District: 22
Key Personnel: Pres., Mark Titus; Treas., John Hay; Mgr., Mike Kirchmeier.
Personnel Profile: Full-Time Paid 1; Part-Time Paid 2; Part-Time Volunteers 12.
Governing Authority: society. Member of the Minnesota State Historical Society. Parent Institution: Jackson County Historical Society. Tax-exempt.
Local History Museum.
Collections: county newspapers; organizational records; family biographical files; Jackson County history; obituary files; cemetery records; photographs.
Research Fields: genealogy.
Facilities: 150-vol. research library.
Activities: local history tours.
Publications: quarterly newsletter; Jackson County History Vol. I, (1850-1910); Jackson County History Vol. II, (1910-1978).
Hours & Admission Prices: Mon.-Fri. 9:30-4:30, Sat. 8am to noon; other times by appointment. No charge; donations accepted. ♿
Attendance: 400 (estimated)
Membership: Single $20; Family $30; Business $50.

Le Sueur

LE SUEUR MUSEUM, 709 N. 2nd St., Le Sueur, MN 56058-1411. Tel.: 507-665-2050.
Web Site: lesueurcountyhistory.org/
Founded: 1975.
Congressional District: 1
Key Personnel: Pres. (V), Jean Haas.
Personnel Profile: Part-Time Paid 1; Part-Time Volunteers 12.
Governing Authority: county. Parent Institution: LeSueur County Historical Society, Elysian, MN. Tax-exempt: 170(b)(1)(A).
History Museum: housed in first school in LeSueur.
Collections: genealogy; etchings of George T. Plowman; Green Giant Canning Co. records; photographs; canning history; history of veterinary medicine; war memorabilia from 1862 to present; 75 radios; early pharmacy; early hotel furnishings.
Research Fields: genealogy; canning industry; local history; military.
Facilities: library of books on local history & genealogy available for research on premises only; reading room.
Activities: guided tours; lectures; films; loan & permanent exhibitions.
Publications: book, LeSueur, Town on the River; brochure.
Hours & Admission Prices: April-Sept. Tues.-Fri. call for hours; other times by appointment. No charge; donations accepted. Closed holidays.
Attendance: 500 (estimated)
Membership: LeSueur County Historical Society: Individual $15; Family $25.

Lino Lakes

WARGO NATURE CENTER, 7701 Main St., Lino Lakes, MN 55038-8741. Tel.: 651-429-8007. Fax: 651-429-8167.
Web Site: www.anokacountyparks.com/qlinks/wargonc/wargonc.htm
Key Personnel: Mgr., Lisa Gilliland; Program Coord., Deb Gallop; Recreation Specialist, Todd Murawski; Scheduler & Receptionist, Rhonda Lynch
Nature Center.
Collections: native plant & animal life.
Hours & Admission Prices: April-Oct. Tues.-Fri. 8-4:30, Sat. 9-5, Sun. 12-5.

Litchfield

MEEKER COUNTY HISTORICAL SOCIETY MUSEUM & G.A.R. HALL, 308 N. Marshall Ave., Litchfield, MN 55355-2112. Tel.: 320-693-8911.
E-mail: mchsgar@hutchtel.net
Web Site: www.garminnesota.org
Founded: 1885.
Congressional District: 6
Key Personnel: Dir., James Milan; Pres., August Anderson.
Personnel Profile: Part-Time Paid 3; Part-Time Volunteers 3.
Governing Authority: society; nonprofit organization. Parent Institution: Minnesota Historical Society. Tax-exempt: 501(c)(3).
Historic Building: c.1885 G.A.R. Hall.
Collections: firearms; Civil War items; crafts; clothing; photographs; Native American artifacts; clocks; log cabin; newspapers; tools; blacksmith shop; genealogy archives; toys.
Research Fields: Dakota War of 1862; Sioux Uprising; Grand Army of the Republic.
Facilities: library of Civil War files & research books; genealogical research information.
Activities: guided tours; special speakers; social events.
Publications: quarterly newsletter, Meeker County Historical Society.
Hours & Admission Prices: Tues.-Sun. 12-4. Adults $2; children & members no charge. Closed holidays except Memorial Day. ♿
Attendance: 4,000
Membership: General $10; Business & Sustaining $25; Patron $125; Benefactor $500.

Little Falls

CHARLES A. LINDBERGH HISTORIC SITE, 1620 Lindbergh Dr. S., Little Falls, MN 56345. Tel.: 320-616-5421. Fax: 320-616-5423.
E-mail: lindbergh@mnhs.org
Web Site: www.mnhs.org
Key Personnel: Mgr., Charles D. Pautler.
Personnel Profile: Full-Time Paid 1; Part-Time Paid 8; Part-Time Volunteers 4.
Governing Authority: state government. Parent Institution: Minnesota Historical Society, St. Paul, MN. Tax-exempt: 501(c)(3).
Historic House Museum: housed in boyhood home of Charles A. Lindbergh, 1902-1920.
Collections: personal artifacts; furnishings; films.
Research Fields: Lindbergh's aviation, 1924-1927; Lindbergh's involvement in the antiwar effort, 1939-1940; general aviation history 1903-1940; Lindbergh's Pacific war experience, 1944; Lindbergh's environmental work 1960-1974.
Facilities: library; classroom; 2,500 sq. ft. exhibit space; 50-seat theater; visitor's center. Museum-related items for sale.
Activities: guided tours; films; hobby workshops; lectures; participatory & traveling exhibitions; theater; broadcast programs. Special Events: Children's Day; Family Fun Day; Air Show; Film Festivals.
Hours & Admission Prices: Memorial Day to Labor Day Tues.-Sat. 10-5, Sun. 12-5; Sept.-Oct. Sat. 10-4, Sun. 12-4; other times by appointment. Adults $7, senior citizens $6, students & children $5; discounts to groups; members no charge. ♿
Attendance: 14,000 (accurate)

CHARLES A. WEYERHAEUSER MEMORIAL MUSEUM, (M), 2151 S. Lindbergh Dr., Little Falls, MN 56345-0239. Mailing Address: P.O. Box 239, Little Falls, MN 56345-0239. Tel.: 320-632-4007.
E-mail: contactstaff@morrisoncountyhistory.org
Web Site: www.morrisoncountyhistory.org
Founded: 1936.
Congressional District: 7
Key Personnel: Dir., Jan Warner; Pres. (V), A. Arthur Warner; Gen. Mgr., Mary Warner; Collections Mgr., Ann Marie Johnson; Treas., Duane Welle.
Personnel Profile: Part-Time Paid 4.
Governing Authority: society. Parent Institution: Morrison County Historical Society. Tax-exempt: 501(c)(3).
Local History Museum.
Collections: county history artifacts; manuscripts; books; photos; archives.
Research Fields: genealogy; local history.
Facilities: 1,500-vol. library of biographies & early history books of Morrison County, Little Falls, local schools & churches, early pioneers & Indians; 60-seat auditorium; 1,900 sq. ft. exhibit space; nature area. Books & museum-related items for sale.
Activities: guided tours; films; permanent & temporary exhibitions; monthly board of directors meeting; history events; workshops; demonstrations; educational services. Museum Sponsors: Annual Meeting in September or October.
Publications: quarterly newsletter, Morrison County Historical Society Newsletter, "Little Falls on the Big River"; book, A Big Hearted Paleface Man: Nathan Richardson & the History of Morrison County, Minnesota.
Hours & Admission Prices: Tues.-Sat. 10-5; groups by appointment. No charge; donations accepted. Closed holidays. ♿
Attendance: 3,500 (estimated)
Membership: Individual $20; Family $25; Donor $50; Supporting $100; Patron $500; Benefactor $1,000 and up.

MINNESOTA FISHING MUSEUM AND EDUCATION CENTER, 304 W. Broadway, Little Falls, MN 56345-1535. Tel.: 320-616-2011.
E-mail: mnfm@mnfishingmuseum.com
Web Site: www.mnfishingmuseum.com/
Personnel Profile: Part-Time Paid 2.
Fishing Museum.
Collections: over 10,000 fishing artifacts.
Hours & Admission Prices: April 15-Sept. Tues.-Sat. 10-5, Sun. 12-4; Winter: call for hours. Adults $4, seniors 60 & over and students 10-17 $3; discounts to groups & Tues.; children 9 & under no charge. ♿
Attendance: 4,000
Membership: Individual $15; Family $25. Business & Organization: $100-$1,000.

Long Lake

WESTERN HENNEPIN COUNTY PIONEERS ASSOCIATION, 1953 W. Wayzata Blvd., Long Lake, MN 55356-9362. Mailing Address: Box 332, Long Lake, MN 55356-0332. Tel.: 952-473-6557.
E-mail: pioneer_museum@hotmail.com
Web Site: www.whcpa-museum.org
Founded: 1907.
Congressional District: 3
Key Personnel: Pres., Steve Kelley; Sec., Marion Merz; Treas., Denise Williams; Cur., Russ Ferrin.
Governing Authority: private; board of directors. Tax-exempt.
History Museum.
Collections: area transportation, records, tapes, clothing, tools, & pictures; Native American artifacts; farming; local newspaper files; scrap books; family histories; pictures; maps.
Facilities: records of local business & organizations available for research.
Activities: guided tours; lectures; museum programs.
Publications: quarterly newsletter.
Hours & Admission Prices: Museum: Sat. 10-4. Research Center: Sat. 10-1. No charge; donations accepted.
Attendance: 1,400 (estimated)
Membership: Individual $10; Family $20; Business $50.

Long Prairie

THE CHRISTIE HOUSE MUSEUM, 15 1st St., S., Long Prairie, MN 56347-1348. Mailing Address: c/o Chamber of Commerce, 42 N. 3rd St., Long Prairie, MN 56347. Tel.: 320-732-2514.
Historic House: former home of Dr. George R. Christie. Listed on the National Register of Historic Places.
Collections: photographs; personal artifacts; furnishings.
Hours & Admission Prices: Memorial Day-Labor Day Wed.-Sun. 1:30-4:30.

TODD COUNTY HISTORICAL MUSEUM, 333 Central Ave., Long Prairie, MN 56347-1304. Tel.: 320-732-4426.
Key Personnel: Dir. & Pres. (V), Shirley Lunceford; Cur., De Eberle
History Museum.
Collections: local history & culture relating to Todd County.
Publications: quarterly newsletter.
Hours & Admission Prices: Wed. 11:30-6, Thurs.-Fri. 11:30-4. Adults $3; members no charge.
Membership: Senior $7.50; Individual $10; Life $100.

Madison

LAC QUI PARLE COUNTY HISTORICAL SOCIETY, 250 8th Ave., S., Madison, MN 56256-1146. Tel.: 612-598-7678.
Founded: 1948.
Congressional District: 2
Key Personnel: C.E.O. & Pres. (V), Scotty Kuehl; Cur., Janet E. Liebl.
Personnel Profile: Part-Time Paid 2; Part-Time Volunteers 1.
Governing Authority: nonprofit corporation; County Historical Society. Tax-exempt.
General Museum.
Collections: Pioneer & Native American artifacts; manuscripts; military; textiles; Civil War; vehicles; tools; 300 personality dolls; salt & pepper shakers; mounted big game, wildlife and flora & fauna; genealogy; obituary index. Historic Buildings: 1870 log cabin with furnishings; c.1887 rural schoolhouse with equipment; machine shed with early farm machinery; poet Robert Bly studio, used from 1950s-1970s.
Research Fields: county family history.
Facilities: 1,500-vol. library of county & pioneer history books available for use on premises.
Activities: guided tours; lectures; informally organized education programs for children.
Publications: newsletter, Lake Talks.
Hours & Admission Prices: May-Oct. Mon.-Fri. 11-4, Sat. 11-3. Adults $3. Family History Research: $10 per hour. ♿
Attendance: 2,500 (estimated)
Membership: Individual $8; Family $15; Life $100.

Mankato

BLUE EARTH COUNTY HISTORICAL SOCIETY, 415 Cherry St., Mankato, MN 56001-3741. Tel.: 507-345-5566.
E-mail: bechs@hickorytech.net
Web Site: www.bechshistory.com
Founded: 1901.
Congressional District: 1
Key Personnel: C.E.O. & Exec. Dir., Jessica Potter; Pres. (V), Todd Stromswold.
Personnel Profile: Full-Time Paid 3; Part-Time Paid 2; Part-Time Volunteers 50; Interns 5.
Governing Authority: society. Tax-exempt.
History Museum.
Collections: American Indian & settlement artifacts; household items; furniture; clothing & textiles; fine & decorative arts; prints; photographs; transportation & local history artifacts; family history & research paper archives. Historic Houses: 1871 restored mansion & carriage house.
Research Fields: Blue Earth County prehistory & history.
Facilities: archives of cataloged books, letters, pamphlets, documents, memoirs, photographs, atlases, manuscripts, indexed scrapbooks, bound newspapers & vertical file materials of local history available for use on premises; reading room; formal Victorian gardens & herb garden. Historical books for sale.
Activities: guided tours; lectures; formally organized education programs for children; permanent & temporary exhibitions. Museum Sponsors: Ghosts From the Past; Christmas Open House; genealogy workshops; historical social events.
Publications: quarterly research journal, Historian; newsletters; genealogical data & original sources; county history booklet.
Hours & Admission Prices: Tues. 10-8, Wed.-Sat. 10-4. Adult $3; members no charge. Closed legal holidays. ♿
Attendance: 10,000 (estimated)
Membership: Student & Individual Senior $20; Individual $25; Household $35; Contributor $50; Supporter $100; Business $100-$1,000; Booster $250; Advocate $500; Benefactor $1,000.

Mantorville

DODGE COUNTY HISTORICAL SOCIETY, 615 N. Main St., Mantorville, MN 55955-6129. Mailing Address: P.O. Box 456, Mantorville, MN 55955-0456. Tel.: 507-635-5508.
E-mail: dchs@kmtel.com
Web Site: www.dodgecohistorical.addr.com
Founded: 1876.
Congressional District: 32
Key Personnel: Pres. (V), Sue Harwood; Vice Pres. & Acting Treas., Bob Peterson; Sec., Vicki Peterson.
Personnel Profile: Part-Time Paid 1.
Governing Authority: county. Tax-exempt: 170(b)(1)(A).
Historic Buildings & Site: Museum housed in 1869 former Episcopal church.
Collections: Civil War recruiting station; agriculture; paintings; costumes; military; preservation project; Indian artifacts; horse drawn hearse. Historic Houses: c.1860 Civil War recruiting station; 1858 Wasioja village limestone schoolhouse; 1883 country one-room schoolhouse; 1856 frame house.
Facilities: 300-vol. reference library available to the public on-site for educational & historical research; genealogy archives & newspapers.
Activities: guided tours.
Hours & Admission Prices: May 1-Oct. 15 Tues.-Sat. 10-4; Oct. 16-April 26 Thurs.-Sat. 10-4; other times by appointment for tours. Adults 13 & over $4, children 6-12 $2, seniors $1.50; members & children 5 and no charge. Research: hourly fee.
Attendance: 2,500 (estimated)
Membership: One Year $10; 5 Year $35; Lifetime $250.

MANTORVILLE RESTORATION, 407 Main St., Mantorville, MN 55955-6127. Mailing Address: P.O. Box 311, Mantorville, MN 55955-0311. Tel.: 507-269-8704.
E-mail: rruport@kmtel.com
Web Site: www.mantorvilletourism.com
Founded: 1963.
Congressional District: 1
Key Personnel: Historic Pres., Program Mgr. & Treas., Helen Ferry; Chm. (V), Marylyn Schroeder; Museum Shop Mgr., Theresa Hoaglund; Property Chm, Lyle Hoaglund; Devel. Chm., Jane Hardwick.
Personnel Profile: Full-Time Paid 1; Part-Time Paid 17; Part-Time Volunteers 60.
Governing Authority: nonprofit organization. Parent Institution: Mantorville Restoration Assoc. Tax-exempt: 170(b)(1)(A).
Preservation Project: 1856 Temporary Court House & Home.
Collections: mid 19th-century furniture, dishes, utensils, furnishings; historic buildings.
Research Fields: local history & buildings.
Facilities: library of local history books.
Activities: self-guided & guided tours; theater productions; concerts; special events; festivals. Museum Sponsors: Old Tyme Days; Marigold Days; Mulligan Stew.
Publications: tourism & tour guides.
Hours & Admission Prices: May-Oct. Tues.-Sun. 1-5. Requested Donation $2.
Attendance: 25,000 (estimated)
Membership: Single $5; Sustaining $10; Associate $25; Contributing & Institutional $50; Benefactor $500.

Maplewood

MAPLEWOOD NATURE CENTER, 2659 E. 7th St., Maplewood, MN 55119-3815. Tel.: 651-249-2170.
Web Site: www.ci.maplewood.mn.us
Nature Center.
Collections: wildlife.
Facilities: nature trails.
Hours & Admission Prices: Visitor Center: Tues.-Sat. 8:30-4:30.

Marshall

LYON COUNTY HISTORICAL SOCIETY MUSEUM, 356 W. Main St., Marshall, MN 56258. Tel.: 507-537-6580. Fax: 507-537-7699.
Founded: 1934.
Key Personnel: Pres., Nicole DeBoer; Sec., Mary Becker; Treas., Andrea Swenson; Museum Shop Mgr., Ellayne Conyers.
Governing Authority: county. Tax-exempt.
General Museum.
Collections: pioneer relics; Indian artifacts; geology; natural history; clocks; 1950s ice-cream/soda fountain, kitchen & other displays; history of Lyon County.
Research Fields: preservation of township & church records.
Facilities: library.
Activities: guided tours.
Publications: annual, The Lyon Tale; triannual newsletter.
Hours & Admission Prices: Feb.-Dec. Tues.-Fri. 10-5, Sat. 12-4. No charge; donations accepted. Closed national holidays. ♿
Membership: Individual $20; Couple $30; Family $35; Business $100.

MUSEUM OF NATURAL HISTORY, Southwest Minnesota State University, 1501 State St., Marshall, MN 56258-3306. Tel.: 507-537-6178. Fax: 507-537-6218.
E-mail: desy@southwestmsu.edu
Web Site: www.southwestmsu.edu
Founded: 1972.
Key Personnel: Dir., Dr. Elizabeth A. Desy.
Personnel Profile: Part-Time Paid 2; Part-Time Volunteers 5.
Governing Authority: public university; nonprofit. Tax-exempt: state agency.
Natural History Museum.

Collections: concentration on animals & flora of southwest Minnesota.
Facilities: nature & conservation center; planetarium.
Activities: guided tours; participatory, temporary & traveling exhibitions.
Hours & Admission Prices: Academic Year: Mon.-Fri. 8-5; guided tours by appointment. No charge. Closed New Year's Day; Easter; Thanksgiving; Christmas.
Attendance: 800 (estimated)

Mendota

SIBLEY HOUSE HISTORIC SITE, 1357 Sibley Memorial Hwy., Mendota, MN 55150. Mailing Address: P.O. Box 50772, Mendota, MN 55150-0772. Tel.: 651-452-1596. Fax: 651-405-6033.
E-mail: sibleyhouse@mnhs.org
Web Site: www.mnhs.org/places/sites/shs
Founded: 1910.
Congressional District: 4
Key Personnel: Pres. (V), Mrs. Marveen Minish.
Personnel Profile: Full-Time Paid 2; Part-Time Paid 14; Part-Time Volunteers 9.
Governing Authority: nonprofit organization. Parent Institution: Minnesota Historical Society. Subsidiary Institution: Sibley House Association. Tax-exempt: 501(c)(3).
Historic House Museum: 1836 Henry Hastings Sibley house, dwelling & trading house for the American Fur Company factor, later Minnesota's first state governor's house; 1839 residence of trader, Jean Baptiste Faribault, which was a boarding house for visitors to the Fort Snelling area.
Collections: furnishings & material culture of the early to mid-19th century, Euro-American & Dakota; Indian artifacts; textiles & glassware.
Research Fields: history.
Facilities: meeting room in visitor center. Booklets, postcards & other museum-related items for sale.
Activities: guided tours & special weekend events.
Publications: newsletter, A Piece of History.
Hours & Admission Prices: May & Sept.-Oct. Sat. 10-4, Sun. 12:30-4; Memorial Day to Labor Day Sat. & holidays 10-4, Sun. 12:30-4; other times by appointment. Adults $6, senior citizens $5, children 6-17 $4; discounts to AAA, friends of the site & Minnesota Historical Society members; members & children under 6 no charge. ♿
Attendance: 5,000 (accurate)
Membership: Friends of Sibley Historic Site: Senior Citizen & Student $7; Individual $12; Household $18. Minnesota Historical Society: Senior Household $45; Individual $55; Household $65.

Minneapolis

AMERICAN SWEDISH INSTITUTE, 2600 Park Ave., Minneapolis, MN 55407-1090. Tel.: 612-871-4907. Fax: 612-871-8682.
E-mail: info@americanswedishinst.org
Web Site: www.americanswedishinst.org
Formerly: American Institute of Swedish Arts, Literature and Science
Founded: 1929.
Congressional District: 5
Key Personnel: C.E.O. & Pres., Bruce N. Karstadt; Chm. (V), Jan Michaletz; Cur. Collections, Curt Pederson; Publication Editor, Jenn Stromberg; Museum Shop. Mgr., Ann Hildreth; Museum Shop. Mgr., Mary Risso.
Personnel Profile: Full-Time Paid 23; Part-Time Paid 1; Part-Time Volunteers 350.
Governing Authority: society. Tax-exempt: 501(c)(3).
Swedish-American Ethnic Museum.
Collections: Swedish-American & Swedish material culture including household articles; tools; clothing; textiles; furniture; immigrant & pioneer items; Swedish 17th- & 18th-century period artifacts; fine art; folklore; archives. Historic House: 1900 Chateauesque Mansion.
Research Fields: Swedish-American history & material culture; genealogical; Swedish immigration history; conservation of artifacts & archival material.
Activities: guided tours in English & Swedish; lectures; programs; language classes; permanent & temporary exhibitions; scholarships for summer language camp applicants; tours; affiliate organizations in Minnesota & out of state areas.
Publications: newsletter 5 times annually, ASI Posten.
Hours & Admission Prices: Jan.-Oct. Tues. & Thurs.-Sat. 12-4, Wed. 12-8, Sun. 1-5; Nov.-Dec. Tues. & Thurs.-Fri. 12-4, Wed. 12-8, Sat. 10-5, Sun. 1-5. Adults $6, senior citizens $5, children 6-18 $4; children under 6 & members no charge. Closed national holidays. ♿
Attendance: 70,000 (estimated)
Membership: Student $20; Non-Resident & Individual $35; Household $50; Sustaining $100; Patron $150; Turnblad $250; Linnaeus $500; Three Crowns $1,000; Life $3,000.

THE BAKKEN LIBRARY AND MUSEUM, 3537 Zenith Ave. S., Minneapolis, MN 55416-4623. Tel.: 612-926-3878. Fax: 612-927-7265.
E-mail: info@thebakken.org
Web Site: www.thebakken.org
Founded: 1975.
Congressional District: 5
Key Personnel: Exec. Dir., David J. Rhees; Deputy Dir., Cynthia Hartmann; Cur. Instruments, Ellen Kuhfeld; Cur. Exhibits, Paul Maravelas; Dir. Education, Beth Murphy; Dir. Devel., Andrea Nelson; Librarian, Elizabeth Ihrig; Mktg. & Communications Mgr., Jamie Barrie; Business Mgr., Kathy Faust; Property Mgr., Chris Lundeen; Office Mgr., Tamara Andrews; Visitor Svcs. Mgr., Noel Porter; Exec. Asst., Karen Taylor; Media Specialist, Bruce Challgren; Performing Arts Coord., Tim Barrett; Teacher-in-Residence, David Higley; Science Educator, Steve Walrig; Science Educator, Justin Spencer; Science Educator, Alia Mortensen; Housekeeper, Jerome Pilkington.
Personnel Profile: Full-Time Paid 20; Part-Time Paid 16; Part-Time Volunteers 90.
Governing Authority: nonprofit. Tax-exempt.
Science Museum.
Collections: apparatus dating back to 1740, illustrating the use of electricity in medicine and biology; electric fish & other exhibits illustrating electrophysiology; books documenting the history of electricity, magnetism & their applications to medicine, 15th to early 20th centuries.
Research Fields: history & application of electromagnetism in the life sciences; animal magnetism & mesmerism.
Facilities: reading room; education & workshop facilities.
Activities: visiting scholars & researchers; summer and extension courses; workshops for children; Science Sat. for families; development workshops for elementary & high school science teachers.
Publications: historical brochures; newsletter; annual report; program brochures; guides.
Hours & Admission Prices: Tues.-Wed. & Fri.-Sat. 10-5, Thurs. 10-8. Adults $7, seniors & students $5; children under 3 no charge. Closed major holidays. ♿
Attendance: 37,000 (accurate)
Membership: Single $30; Dual $40; Family $60; Family Plus $80.

BELL MUSEUM OF NATURAL HISTORY, (M), Univ. of Minnesota, 10 Church St., S.E., Minneapolis, MN 55455-0145. Tel.: 612-624-4112 & 7083. Fax: 612-626-7704.
E-mail: info@bellmuseum.org
Web Site: www.bellmuseum.org
Founded: 1872.
Congressional District: 5
Key Personnel: Dir., Scott M. Lanyon; Exhibits Coord., Curt Hadland; Editor, Jennifer Amie; Cur. Vascular Plants, Anita Cholewa; Cur. Breckenridge Chm. Ornithology, Bob Zink; Cur. Fungi & Lichens, David McLaughlin; Cur. Ichthyology, Andrew Simons; Cur. Invertebrate Biology, Susan J. Weller; Cur. Frozen Tissues, Kendall W. Corbin; Cur. Education, Gordon R. Murdock; Cur. Education, Kevin Williams; Cur. Exhibits, Donald T. Luce; Devel., Francie Nelson; Head Public Programs, Peggy Korsmo-Kennon.
Personnel Profile: Full-Time Paid 30; Part-Time Paid 35; Part-Time Volunteers 78; Interns 2.
Governing Authority: university. Parent Institution: University of Minnesota. Tax-exempt: 501(c)(3).
Natural History Museum.
Collections: regional & historical collections of birds, fishes, mollusks, mammals, amphibians and reptiles; seeds; frozen tissues; invertebrate & vertebrate fossils; botanical specimens including vascular plants, lichens, bryophytes, fungi & algae; natural history art.
Research Fields: ornithology; mammalogy; ichthyology; paleontology; herpetology; ethology; ecology; intervertebrate zoology; evolution; systematics.
Facilities: Touch & See Room; 385-seat auditorium; bookstore; classrooms; herbarium; research labs. Field guides, nature records & other museum-related gifts for sale.
Activities: guided tours; informal public courses; temporary exhibits; natural history art shows; family programs; phone-in wildlife information & advice; lectures; workshops; loan collection including 120 traveling dioramas; field trips; academic University courses; Bell LIVE! electronic field trip; JASON project; traveling kits for schools.
Publications: occasional papers; booklets; pamphlets; technical reports; newsletter.
Hours & Admission Prices: Tues.-Fri. 9-5, Sat. 10-5, Sun. 12-5. Adults $5, youths 3-16 & senior citizens $3; discounts for AAM & ICOM members; children under 3, Univ. of Minnesota students & members no charge. Closed national holidays. ♿
Attendance: 97,749 (accurate)
Membership: Individual $30; Household $45; Sponsor $100; Patron $300; Benefactor $750.

BLOOMINGTON HISTORICAL SOCIETY, 2215 W. Old Shakopee Rd., Minneapolis, MN 55431-3033. Tel.: 952-948-4327. TDD: 612-887-9677.
Founded: 1964.
Congressional District: 5
Key Personnel: Pres. (V), Vonda Kelly.
Personnel Profile: Part-Time Volunteers 20.
Governing Authority: board of directors. Tax-exempt.
Regional History Museum: housed in 1892 Old Town Hall.
Collections: artifacts pertaining to Bloomington; manuscripts; local history material.
Research Fields: local history.
Facilities: Printed literature for sale.
Activities: guided tours; lectures; meetings; inter-museum loan, permanent, temporary & traveling exhibitions.
Publications: 6 times per year, Bloomington Historical Society Newsletter; book, Bloomington on The Minnesota.
Hours & Admission Prices: Sun. 1-4; call for appointment. No charge.
Attendance: 2,500 (estimated)
Membership: Junior Historian $1; Individual $3; Couple $5; Contributing $10; Sustaining Member $25; Life Member $50; Patron $100; Corporate $200.

ELOISE BUTLER WILDFLOWER GARDEN AND BIRD SANCTUARY, Theodore Wirth Pkwy., Minneapolis, MN 55422. Mailing Address: MPRB Operations Center, 3800 Bryant Ave. S., Minneapolis, MN 55409-1029. Tel.: 612-370-4900 (Nov.-March) & 4903 (April-Oct.). Fax: 612-370-4831.
E-mail: swilkins@minneapolisparks.org
Web Site: www.minneapolisparks.org
Founded: 1907.
Congressional District: 3
Key Personnel: Supt. of Parks, Jon Gurban; Cur. Garden, Susan Wikins; Coord. Environmental Education, MaryLynn Pulscher.
Personnel Profile: Full-Time Paid 1; Part-Time Paid 7; Part-Time Volunteers 60; Interns 2.
Governing Authority: municipal. Parent Institution: Minneapolis Park & Recreation Board.
Wildflower & Bird Sanctuary.
Collections: native wildflowers; trees; shrubs.
Facilities: 300-vol. library available for use on premises; nature center.
Activities: permanent & temporary exhibitions; self-guided brochure & trail.
Publications: guide book.
Hours & Admission Prices: mid-April to mid-Oct. daily 7:30-dusk. No charge; donations accepted.
Attendance: 50,000 (estimated)

FREDERICK R. WEISMAN ART MUSEUM, (M), (I), 333 E. River Rd., Minneapolis, MN 55455-0367. Tel.: 612-625-9494. Fax: 612-625-9630.
E-mail: wamdir@umn.edu
Web Site: www.weisman.umn.edu
Formerly: University Art Museum
Founded: 1934.
Congressional District: 5
Key Personnel: Dir., Lyndel King; Dir. Devel., Matt Nielsen; Dir. Education, Colleen Sheehy; Dir. Public Rels., Christopher James; Accounts & Human Resources Mgr., Carol Stafford; Cur., Diane Mullin; Registrar, Karen Duncan; Assoc. Registrar, Laura Muessig; Museum Shop Mgr., Vanessa Johansson.
Personnel Profile: Full-Time Paid 26; Part-Time Paid 24; Part-Time Volunteers 88; Interns 5.
Governing Authority: university. Parent Institution: University of Minnesota. Tax-exempt.
University Art Museum: housed in a stainless steel & brick building; designed by architect Frank Gehry.
Collections: 20th-century American painting, sculpture & prints; ancient to modern ceramics; Korean furniture.
Research Fields: 20th-century art; 18th-20th century painting, prints & decorative arts; archaeology.
Activities: guided tours; gallery talks; lectures; formally organized education programs for graduate students; inter-museum loan, temporary & traveling exhibitions; art rental program.
Publications: catalog of specific exhibitions.
Hours & Admission Prices: Tues.-Wed. & Fri. 10-5, Thurs. 10-8, Sat.-Sun. 11-5. No charge; donations accepted. Closed university holidays. ♿
Attendance: 130,000 (estimated)
Membership: Student $30; Individual $40; Dual $60; Sustainer $125; Benefactor $350; Founder $500; Patron $1,000; Director's Circle $1,500.

HENNEPIN HISTORY MUSEUM, (M), 2303 3rd Ave. S., Minneapolis, MN 55404-3505. Tel.: 612-870-1329. Fax: 612-870-1320.
E-mail: museum.info@hennepinhistory.org
Web Site: www.hennepinhistory.org
Founded: 1938.
Congressional District: 5
Key Personnel: Exec. Dir., Jada Hansen; Cur., Jack Kabrud.
Personnel Profile: Full-Time Paid 1; Part-Time Paid 6; Part-Time Volunteers 20.
Governing Authority: nonprofit organization. Parent Institution: Hennepin County Historical Society. Tax-exempt: 501(c)(3).
History Museum.
Collections: history of Minneapolis & Hennepin County, Minnesota.
Research Fields: history of Hennepin county.
Facilities: research library.
Activities: permanent & temporary exhibitions; public programs.
Publications: quarterly newsletter; quarterly magazine, Hennepin History.
Hours & Admission Prices: Tues. 10-2, Wed. & Fri.-Sat. 1-5, Thurs. 1-8. Adults $2, students & seniors $.50; members no charge.
Membership: Student & Senior (no magazine) $15; Individual $30; Family $35; Corporate $75; Contributor $100; Patron $500; Donor $1,000.

HENNEPIN MEDICAL HISTORY CENTER, 701 Park Ave., Blue Bldg. Lower Level, Minneapolis, MN 55415-1623. Tel.: 612-873-2512.
Web Site: www.hcmc.org/a_z/serviceleague/museum.htm
Founded: 1976.
Congressional District: 5
Key Personnel: Chm. (V), Rondine Mehling
History Museum.
Collections: photographs & artifacts relating to the medical center.
Hours & Admission Prices: Thurs. 10-2; other times by appointment.

KATHERINE NASH GALLERY, 405 21st Ave. S., Minneapolis, MN 55455-0420. Mailing Address: Regis Center for Art, 405 21st Ave. S., Minneapolis, MN 55455. Tel.: 612-624-6518. Fax: 612-625-0152.
E-mail: nash@tc.umn.edu
Web Site: nash.umn.edu
Founded: 1973.
Congressional District: 5
Key Personnel: C.E.O., Clarence Morgan; Dir., Nicholas B. Shank.
Personnel Profile: Full-Time Paid 1; Part-Time Paid 8; Interns 10.
Governing Authority: public university; nonprofit. Parent Institution: University of Minnesota Dept. of Art. Tax-exempt.
Art Gallery.
Collections: emphasis on local & regional artists and occasionally national artists.
Hours & Admission Prices: Tues.-Sat. 11-7. No charge. Closed University of Minnesota holidays & semester breaks. ♿
Attendance: 18,000 (estimated)

MCAD GALLERY, 2501 Stevens Ave., Minneapolis, MN 55404-4347. Tel.: 612-874-3667. Fax: 612-874-3704. TDD: 612-874-3800.
E-mail: gallery@mcad.edu
Web Site: www.mcad.edu
Formerly: Minneapolis College of Art and Design Gallery
Founded: 1886.
Key Personnel: Dir., Kristin Makholm.
Personnel Profile: Full-Time Paid 1; Part-Time Paid 1; Interns 1.
Governing Authority: college. Parent Institution: Minneapolis College of Art and Design. Tax-exempt: 501(c)(3).
College Art Gallery.
Collections: prints; paintings; sculpture of the 20th century with focus on contemporary American art.
Research Fields: contemporary American art.
Activities: lectures; films; gallery talks; concerts; dance recitals; TV programs; formally organized education programs for undergraduate college students affiliated with Minneapolis College of Art & Design; loan, temporary & traveling exhibitions.
Publications: exhibition catalogues.
Hours & Admission Prices: Mon.-Fri. 9-8, Sat. 9-5, Sun. 12-5. No charge. Closed holidays. ♿

MILL CITY MUSEUM, 704 S. Second St., Minneapolis, MN 55401-2163. Tel.: 612-341-7555.
E-mail: mcm@mnhs.org
Web Site: www.millcitymuseum.org
Governing Authority: Parent Institution: Minnesota Historical Society.
History Museum: former site of the Washburn A Mill.
Collections: artifacts & memorabilia pertaining to the flour milling industry.
Hours & Admission Prices: July-Aug. Mon.-Sat. 10-5, Sun. 12-5; Sept.-June Tues.-Sat. 10-5, Sun. 12-5. Adults $10, seniors & students $8, children 6-17 $5; MHS members no charge.

* **MINNEAPOLIS INSTITUTE OF ARTS, (M),** 2400 Third Ave. S., Minneapolis, MN 55404-3506. Tel.: 612-870-3000 & 3046. Fax: 612-870-3004. TDD: 612-870-3132.
E-mail: miagen@artsMIA.org
Web Site: www.artsMIA.org/MIA
Founded: 1883.
Congressional District: 5
Key Personnel: Pres. & Dir., Kaywin Feldman; Chm. Bd. Trustees, Diane Lilly; Mgr. Bd. Rels., Michele L. Callahan; Deputy Dir., Patricia J. Grazzini; Chm. Education Div., Kate Johnson; Asst. Dir. Curatorial Affairs & Cur. Japanese & Korean Art, Matthew Welch; Cur. Chinese, Indian, & Southeast Asian Art, Robert Jacobsen; Asst. Dir. Exhibitions & Programs and Cur. Contemporary Art, Elizabeth Armstrong; Cur. Paintings, Patrick Noon; Asst. Dir. External Affairs, Leann Standish; Head Registration, Brian Kraft; Dir. Merchandising, Mary Hele.
Personnel Profile: Full-Time Paid 188; Part-Time Paid 67.
Governing Authority: board of trustees. Tax-exempt: 501(c)(3).
Art Museum.
Collections: European & American paintings & sculpture; decorative arts & period rooms; photography; textiles; prints & drawings; Oriental, Native American, African, Oceanic, Islamic & ancient art. Historic Buildings: Purcel-Cutts House; Prairie Schoolhouse.
Research Fields: pertaining to the general collection.
Facilities: 50,000-vol. library of publications pertaining to specialized areas of art history available for inter-library loan & for use on premises; 162,702 sq. ft. exhibit space; reading room; 285-seat auditorium; 50-seat theater; classrooms; restaurant. Books, periodicals, jewelry, posters & replicas of museum pieces for sale.
Activities: guided tours; lectures; films; gallery talks; arts festivals; study clubs; interactive video programs; formally organized education programs for children & adults & the visually impaired; docent program; formally organized education programs for undergraduate & graduate college students affiliated with regional colleges & universities; training programs for professional museum workers; inter-museum loan, permanent, temporary & traveling exhibitions; municipal governmental & school loan service.
Publications: guide, A Guide to the Galleries; exhibition catalogs; monthly magazine, ARTS; education & instructional workbooks.
Hours & Admission Prices: Tues.-Wed. & Fri.-Sat. 10-5, Thurs. 10-9, Sun. 11-5. No charge; donations accepted. Fees for some special exhibitions. Closed Independence Day; Thanksgiving; Christmas. ♿
Attendance: 511,202 (accurate)
Membership: Student, Senior & Non-Resident $30; Individual $45; Dual $60; Family $75; Arts Circle $100-$175; Ambassador $150; Contributor's Circle & Business League $250-$2,000; Patrons' Circle & Corporate Council $2,000.

MINNESOTA PLANETARIUM SOCIETY, 300 Nicollet Mall, Rm. 270, Minneapolis, MN 55401. Mailing Address: 81 S. Ninth St., Ste. 200, Minneapolis, MN 55402-3225. Tel.: 612-630-6150.
E-mail: info@mplanetarium.org
Web Site: www.mplanetarium.org
Formerly: Minnesota Planetarium & Space Discovery Center
Founded: 1961.
Key Personnel: Pres., Angus M. Vaughan; Chm. (V), Margaret Leppick.
Personnel Profile: Full-Time Paid 2; Part-Time Paid 1; Part-Time Volunteers 15.
Governing Authority: Parent Institution: Minnesota Planetarium Society. Tax-exempt: 501(c)(3).
Planetarium.
Collections: astronomy; earth science.
Activities: planetarium star shows.
Hours & Admission Prices: Closed for renovations. ♿
Attendance: 75,000
Membership: Individual $25; Household $35; Patron $50; Sponsor $100; Benefactor $500.

THE MUSEUM OF RUSSIAN ART, (M), 5500 Stevens Ave. S., Minneapolis, MN 55419-1933. Tel.: 612-821-9045.
E-mail: bshinkle@tmora.org
Web Site: www.tmora.org
Founded: 2002.
Congressional District: 3
Key Personnel: Chm. (V), Raymond E. Johnson; Pres., Bradford Shinkle, IV; Pres. & Dir., Judi Dutcher; Special Events Mgr., Lynda Holker; Museum Shop Mgr., Melanie Brooks.
Personnel Profile: Full-Time Paid 2; Full-Time Volunteers 12; Part-Time Paid 5; Part-Time Volunteers 36.
Governing Authority: private; nonprofit organization. Tax-exempt: 501(c)(3).
Art Museum.
Collections: late 19th-century to 1991 Russian art; 20th-century Russian Socialist Realist art from the Soviet era 1934-1975.
Facilities: 500-vol. library; 15,000 sq. ft. exhibit space. Museum-related items for sale.
Activities: lectures; seminars; children's educational events; facility available for corporate & private events.
Publications: semiannual newsletter, View; themed exhibition brochures; English language catalogs & reference books.
Hours & Admission Prices: Jan. 19-Sept. 27 Mon.-Wed. & Fri. 10-5, Thurs. 10-8, Sat. 10-4; Sept. 28-Jan. 18 Mon.-Wed. & Fri. 10-5, Thurs. 10-8, Sat. 10-4, Sun. 1-5. Adults $5, students & seniors 60 & over voluntary donation; discount to AAM members; members no charge. Closed New Year's Day; Memorial Day; Independence Day; Labor Day; Thanksgiving; Christmas Eve & Day. ♿
Attendance: 40,000 (accurate)
Membership: Individual $30; Partner $50; Family $65; Benefactor $125; Patron $250; Leadership $1,000.

* **WALKER ART CENTER, (M),** 1750 Hennepin Ave., Minneapolis, MN 55403-1169. Tel.: 612-375-7675 & 7676. Fax: 612-375-7567. TDD: 612-375-7585.
E-mail: olga.viso@walkerart.org
Web Site: walkerart.org/
Founded: 1879.
Congressional District: 5
Key Personnel: Pres., Deborah Hopp; Dir., Olga Viso; C.O.A., Phillip Bahar; Chief Cur., Darsie Alexander; Registrar, Gwen Bitz; Sr. Cur. Performing Arts, Philip Bither; Cur., Siri Engberg; Design Dir. & Cur., Andrew Blauvelt; Design & Publicatons Dir., Lisa Middag; C.F.O., Mary Polta; Dir. Education & Community Programs, Sarah Schultz; Dir. Mktg. & Public Rels., Ryan French; Chief Finance & Devel., Christopher Stevens; Dir. Merchandising, Nancy Gross; Librarian, Rosemary Furtak.
Personnel Profile: Full-Time Paid 124; Part-Time Paid 43; Part-Time Volunteers 150; Interns 12.
Governing Authority: nonprofit organization. Tax-exempt: 501(c)(3).
Art Museum.
Collections: contemporary art including paintings, sculpture, drawings, prints & films; Minneapolis Sculpture Garden, 11-acre urban garden featuring 40 sculptures & conservatory with horticultural displays.
Major Exhibits: Haegue Yang, 11/09-2/10; Robert Irwin, 11/09-11/10; Event Horizon, 11/09-8/12; Abstract Resistance (T), 2/10-5/10; The Talent Show (T), 2/10-8/10; Everything: Guillermo Kuitca (T), 6/10-9/10; From Here to There: Alec Soth's America (T), 9/10-1/11; Yves Klein (T), 10/10-2/11.
Research Fields: contemporary arts; film & the performing arts.
Facilities: library of 38,000 exhibition catalogues, 1,000 artist books, monographs, clipping files & taped interviews available for graduate student use; 385-seat theater; 344-seat cinema; 150-seat cafe; 85-seat restaurant; lecture room. Books, prints, posters, postcards, note cards, slides, jewelry & designer items for sale.
Activities: guided tours; lectures; films; gallery talks; concerts; dance; theater; music & performance art; formally organized education programs for children, teens, adults & undergraduate students; docent program; film program; inter-museum loan, permanent, temporary & traveling exhibitions.
Publications: monthly Calendar of Events; exhibition catalogs.
Hours & Admission Prices: Tues.-Wed. & Fri.-Sun. 11-5, Thurs. 11-9. Adults $10, seniors 65 & over $8, students & teens $6; discounts to AAM members; members, children under 12, Thurs. 5-9 & 1st Sat. of month no charge. ♿
Attendance: 759,347 (accurate)
Membership: Individual $60; Dual $70; Family $75; Friend $100; Contemporaries $175; Contributing $250-$25,000.

WELLS FARGO HISTORY MUSEUM, 90 S. 7th St., Skyway Level, Minneapolis, MN 55479-1100. Mailing Address: Wells Fargo Historical Services, 420 Montgomery St., MAC-A0101-106, San Francisco, CA 94163-0001. Tel.: 612-667-4210. Fax: 612-316-4361.
Web Site: www.wellsfargohistory.com
Founded: 2000.
Key Personnel: Cur., Megan Schaack; Asst. Cur., Phyllis Thorne.
Governing Authority: Affiliated with Wells Fargo Bank.
Company History Museum.
Collections: Concord stagecoach; Wells Fargo banking & express history; California Gold Rush; gold specimens & coins; working telegraphs; local history.
Facilities: Museum-related items for sale.
Activities: guided tours; imaginary rides on replica stagecoach; audiovisual programs; participatory & temporary exhibitions.
Publications: scholarly pamphlets.

Hours & Admission Prices: Mon.-Fri. 9-5. No charge. Closed bank holidays. ♿
Attendance: 15,447 (accurate)

Montevideo

CHIPPEWA COUNTY HISTORICAL SOCIETY, 151 Arnie Anderson Dr., Montevideo, MN 56265-2127. Mailing Address: P.O. Box 303, Montevideo, MN 56265-0303. Tel.: 320-269-7636.
Founded: 1936.
Congressional District: 6
Key Personnel: Pres. (V), Jeffrey Lopez; Museum Shop Mgr., Carol Westberg.
Personnel Profile: Full-Time Paid 1; Full-Time Volunteers 2; Part-Time Paid 3; Part-Time Volunteers 25.
Governing Authority: county. Parent Institution: Minnesota Historical Society. Tax-exempt.
Historic Village Setting Museum: 23 buildings including 1882 church; rural school; 1870 log cabin.
Collections: Frank Stay collection; Rev. Stephen R. Riggs letters; Sioux Uprising; restored pre-1850s dugout canoe with interpretive material; 1,200 slides on county farmstead, barns & outbuildings; Henry Gippe collection; Civil War photographs. Historic House: 1901-1903 farm house & outbuildings, Swensson farm.
Research Fields: education; farm buildings
Facilities: 400-vol. library of school, religious & local history books. Museum-related gifts for sale.
Activities: guided tours on appointment; lectures; permanent exhibitions.
Publications: monthly newsletter.
Hours & Admission Prices: Chippewa City: Memorial Day to Labor Day Mon.-Fri. 9-5, Sat.-Sun. 1-5; Sept. Mon.-Fri. 9-5. Swensson Farm: Memorial Day to Labor Day Sun. 1-5 & by appointment. Adults $4, youth $2, children 5 & under & members no charge. ♿
Attendance: 5,000 (estimated)
Membership: Individual $15; Family $20; Sustaining $25; Contributing $50; Benefactor $100. Business Memberships: Bronze $50; Silver $75; Gold $100; Platinum $200.

Moorhead

COMSTOCK HISTORIC HOUSE, 506 8th St. S., Moorhead, MN 56560-3504. Tel.: 218-291-4211.
E-mail: comstockhouse@gomoorhead.com
Web Site: www.mnhs.org/places/sites/ch/
Founded: 1975.
Congressional District: 7
Key Personnel: Chm. (V), Kathy Faeth.
Personnel Profile: Part-Time Paid 2; Part-Time Volunteers 4.
Governing Authority: society. Owned & operated by the Minnesota Historical Society. Subsidiary Institution: Comstock Historic House Society. Tax-exempt.
Historical Society: housed in c.1882 Comstock home.
Collections: furnishings; artifacts of Solomon G. Comstock's family.
Research Fields: Ada Louise Comstock.
Facilities: library available to the public; meeting space available.
Activities: guided tours; concerts; organized education programs for children; docent program.
Publications: Comstock Comments.
Hours & Admission Prices: Memorial Day to Labor Day Thurs. 5pm-8pm, Sat.-Sun. 1-4:30. Adults $6, senior citizens $5, students & children 6-17 $4; discounts to AAM members; children under 6 no charge. Closed holidays.
Attendance: 600 (estimated)
Membership: Annual $55.

HISTORICAL AND CULTURAL SOCIETY OF CLAY COUNTY, (M), 202 1st Ave. N., Moorhead, MN 56560-1985. Mailing Address: P.O. Box 157, Moorhead, MN 56561-0157. Tel.: 218-299-5511. Fax: 218-299-5510.
E-mail: maureen.jonason@ci.moorehead.mn.us
Web Site: www.hjemkomst-center.com
Formerly: Heritage-Hjemkomst Interpretive Center
Founded: 1957.
Congressional District: 7
Key Personnel: Interim Exec. Dir., Maureen Kelly Jonason; Archivist, Mark Peihl; Cur., Lisa Vedaa; Coord. Events, Tim Jorgensen; Coord. Visitor Svcs., Markus Krueger; Coord. Communications, Michelle Kittleson.
Personnel Profile: Full-Time Paid 6; Part-Time Paid 1; Part-Time Volunteers 60.
Governing Authority: nonprofit organization. Tax-exempt: 501(c)(3).
History and Cultural Heritage Museum.
Collections: Clay County history & cultural heritage; Viking ship replica; Stave Church replica; 15,000 glass plate negatives from 1872 to late 1930s; clothing; guns; furniture; household items; pioneer artifacts; period files; pioneer cemetery. Historic Buildings: 1895 District 3 rural school house; 1870 Bergquist pioneer cabin.
Major Exhibits: Lincoln in North Dakota (T), 1/10-3/10; WWI & WWII Posters (T), 3/10-6/10; Augustus Frederick Sherman: Ellis Island Portraits 1905-1920 (T), 6/10-9/10; Crime Lab Detectives (T), 9/10-12/10; The Saint John's Bible (T), 10/4/10-1/3/11.
Research Fields: Clay County Red River Valley; Hjemkomst's journey.
Facilities: 300-vol. library & manuscripts available for research on premises; meeting rooms; auditorium. Gift items for sale.
Activities: guided tours; films; permanent, temporary & traveling exhibits; docent program. Museum Sponsors: Viking Village Festival in July; Pangea: Cultivate Our Cultures Festival in November.
Publications: quarterly newsletter, The Hour Glass.
Hours & Admission Prices: Mon. & Wed.-Sat. 9-5, Tues. 9-8, Sun. 12-5. Adults $7, senior citizens & post high school students $6, youth 5-17 $5; discounts to ASTC & AAA members; members & children under 5 no charge. Closed New Year's Eve & Day; Easter; Thanksgiving; Christmas Eve & Day. ♿
Attendance: 30,000 (estimated)
Membership: Individual $30; Household $50; Booster $75; Heritage $125; Patron $250; Benefactor $500; Vanguard $1,000.

Mora

KANABEC HISTORY CENTER, 805 W. Forest Ave., Mora, MN 55051. Mailing Address: P.O. Box 113, Mora, MN 55051-0113. Tel.: 320-679-1665. Fax: 320-679-1673.
E-mail: center@kanabechistory.org
Web Site: www.kanabechistory.org
Founded: 1978.
Congressional District: 14, 18 & 19
Key Personnel: Pres., Marian Rud.
Personnel Profile: Part-Time Paid 4; Part-Time Volunteers 25.
Governing Authority: nonprofit organization. Parent Institution: Kanabec County Historical Society. Tax-exempt: 501(c)(3).
Historical Society Museum.
Collections: Kanabec County artifacts; photographs; manuscripts; newspapers; genealogies; cemetery records.
Research Fields: county history; genealogy; cemetery records; birth, death & marriage records; family histories.
Facilities: library; 37-acre site; fitness course; interpretive nature trail; cross-country ski trails; picnic facilities. Historical & fiction books & gift items for sale.
Activities: lectures; films; special programming; docent program.
Publications: quarterly newsletter.
Hours & Admission Prices: Tues.-Sat. 10-4:30, holidays 12:30-4:30. Adults $3, students K-12 $1; children under 5 & members of KCHS no charge; children under 14 must be accompanied by an adult. Closed New Year's Day; Easter; Independence Day; Thanksgiving; Christmas Eve & Day. ♿
Attendance: 11,656 (accurate)
Membership: Individual $25; Family $40; Family Plus $50; Century $100; Sponsor $150; Corporate $250; Corporate Gold $300.

Morris

STEVENS COUNTY HISTORICAL SOCIETY MUSEUM, 116 W. 6th St., Morris, MN 56267-1922. Tel.: 320-589-1719. Fax: 320-589-1719 call ahead.
Founded: 1920.
Congressional District: 6
Key Personnel: Dir. & Museum Shop Mgr., Randee Hokanson; Historian Researcher, Tami Plank; Pres. (V), Ward B. Voorhees; Collections Registrar, Joan Boleman.
Personnel Profile: Part-Time Paid 5; Part-Time Volunteers 7.
Governing Authority: society; state; county. Tax-exempt.
Local History Museum: housed in 1905 Carnegie Library building.
Collections: clothing; photographs; war material; household furnishings; manuscripts; country church furnishings; farm tools. Historic Buildings: 1900 country school; log cabin.
Research Fields: genealogy & local history.
Facilities: 200-vol. library of old records of the area available for research under supervision; 140 linear ft. archival material; local newspapers 1876-present; 2,000 books & 5,000 photographs in supervised research area.
Activities: guided tours; lectures; films; radio programs; permanent & temporary exhibitions.
Publications: quarterly newsletter; coloring book; books, Syrup Pails & Overshoes: Stories From the Country Schools of Stevens County; An Honest Day's Work; The 40s: A Time for War & A Time for Peace; Celebrating 125 Years of Morris Cookbook.

Hours & Admission Prices: Mon.-Fri. 9-5; other times by appointment. No charge; donations accepted.
Attendance: 2,000 (estimated)
Membership: Annual Individual $15; Annual Family $20; Sustaining $38; Annual Business $50; Annual Benefactor $100.

Morton

BIRCH COULEE BATTLEFIELD, Morton, MN 56270. Mailing Address: Lower Sioux Agency Historic Site, 32469 Redwood County Hwy. 2, Morton, MN 56270. Tel.: 507-697-6321.
E-mail: birchcoulee@mnhs.org
Web Site: www.mnhs.org/places.sites/bc
Historic Site: former site of the Battle of Birch Coulee.
Collections: recreated prairie; guide posts; battle sketches.
Hours & Admission Prices: May-Oct. dawn-dusk. No charge.

Mountain Lake

HERITAGE VILLAGE, County Rd. One, Mountain Lake, MN 56159. Mailing Address: P.O. Box 152, Mountain Lake, MN 56159-0152. Tel.: 507-427-3743.
E-mail: conductorron@swwnet.com
Formerly: Heritage House
Founded: 1972.
Congressional District: 22A
Key Personnel: Chm. Bd, Alvin Dick; Vice Chm., Harvey Buller; Treas., Betty Lou Ritzloff; Sec. & Museum Shop Mgr., Geneva Stoesz.
Personnel Profile: Part-Time Paid 2; Part-Time Volunteers 25; Interns 2.
Governing Authority: private; nonprofit organization. Tax-exempt: 501(c)(3).
Historic House & Village: 20 historic structures representing a late 1800s to early 1900s village.
Collections: immigration of Mennonite people from Russia, as well as Russian-German Lutherans.
Research Fields: history of collection.
Facilities: 21,000 sq. ft. exhibit space; landscape grounds. Museum-related items for sale.
Activities: docent program; guided tours; school loan service. Annual Event: Fall Festival featuring Mennonite food & entertainment in September.
Publications: annual newspaper supplement for the Sept. Heritage Fair.
Hours & Admission Prices: Memorial Day to Labor Day daily 1-5. Adults $5, children over 7 $3; members no charge.
Attendance: 2,000 (estimated)
Membership: Single $25; Family $40.

New Ulm

AUGUST SCHELL BEWERY, 1860 Schell Rd., New Ulm, MN 56073-3834. Tel.: 800-770-5020; 507-354-5528. Fax: 507-359-9119.
E-mail: schells@schellsbrewery.com
Web Site: schellsbrewery.com
Founded: 1860.
Key Personnel: Dir. & Pres., Ted Marti
Company History Museum.
Collections: brewery & founding family history.
Hours & Admission Prices: Museum: Memorial Day-Labor Day daily 12-5; Winter: call for hours. Tours: Memorial Day-Labor Day Mon.-Thurs. 2:30 & 4, Fri. 1, 2:30 & 4, Sat.-Sun. 1, 2, 3 & 4; Sept.-May Fri. 3, Sat. 12, 1, 2, 3 & 4, Sun. 4. Museum: no charge. Tours: adults $3; children 12 & under no charge. ♿
Attendance: 30,000 (estimated)

BROWN COUNTY HISTORICAL SOCIETY, 2 N. Broadway, New Ulm, MN 56073-1714. Tel.: 507-233-2616. Fax: 507-354-1068.
E-mail: bchs@browncountyhistorymnusa.org
Web Site: www.browncountyhistorymnusa.org
Founded: 1930.
Congressional District: 2
Key Personnel: Exec. Dir., Robert Burgess; Research Librarian, Darla Gebhard; Museum Shop Mgr. & Office Mgr., Marilyn Hesse.
Personnel Profile: Full-Time Paid 1; Part-Time Paid 5; Part-Time Volunteers 85.
Governing Authority: society. Supported by Brown County. Tax-exempt: 501(c)(3).
History Museum.
Collections: area history; Dakota & Objiwe Indians; Dakota Conflict of 1862; early biographical & genealogical files; representative collection of regional artists including Wanda & Anton Gag, Chris Heller & Alexander Schwendinger.
Research Fields: Native American-Dakota; Wanda Gag; US-Dakota war 1862; Turner Society; Hermann Monument.
Facilities: 1,000-vol. non-circulating library of books pertaining to Minnesota & local history; research library.
Activities: guided tours; lectures; gallery talks; historical markers; permanent & temporary exhibitions.
Publications: leaflets; brochures; maps; books; news notes.
Hours & Admission Prices: Mon.-Fri. 10-4, Sat. 10-3, call to confirm. Adults $3; students & children no charge. Closed national holidays. ♿
Attendance: 9,812 (accurate)
Membership: Household $25; Nonprofit $35; Business $50; Century Club $100-$499; Benefactor $500.

HARKIN STORE, 66250 County Rd. 21, New Ulm, MN 56073. Mailing Address: P.O. Box 112, New Ulm, MN 56073-0112. Tel.: 507-354-8666 & 934-2160.
E-mail: harkinstore@mnhs.org
Web Site: www.mnhs.org/places/sites/hs
Historic Site: housed in a former general store & post-office; built in 1867.
Collections: local history & culture; original store inventory; period artifacts.
Hours & Admission Prices: May & Sept.-Oct. 15 Sat.-Sun. 10-5; Memorial Day to Labor Day Tues.-Sun. 10-5. Adults 18-64 $3, seniors 65 & over and children 6-17 $2; NSHS & MHS members and children 5 & under no charge.

North Saint Paul

NORTH STAR MUSEUM OF BOY SCOUTING AND GIRL SCOUTING, 2640 Seventh Ave. E., North Saint Paul, MN 55109-3103. Tel.: 651-748-2880. Fax: 651-748-0660.
E-mail: cnicholson@nssm.org
Web Site: www.nssm.org
Formerly: North Star Scouting Memorabilia, Inc.
Founded: 1976.
Congressional District: 4
Key Personnel: Exec. Dir., Claudia J. Nicholson; Chm. (V), Charles W. Opp.
Personnel Profile: Full-Time Paid 1; Part-Time Paid 1; Part-Time Volunteers 60; Interns 4.
Governing Authority: private; nonprofit. Tax-exempt.
Boy Scout & Girl Scout Museum.
Collections: from inception of the Scouting program to the present; 150,000 artifacts; film; photographs; Scouting publications; uniforms; equipment; 5-state upper midwest region especially Minnesota & Western Wisconsin.
Research Fields: Region 10-Boy Scouts of America; boy & girl scouts; girl guiding; councils; camps; history.
Facilities: 3,500-vol. library of Boy's Life & Scouting magazines and merit badge handbooks, Boy Scouting & Girl Scouting books; 8,000 sq. ft. exhibit space; community room.
Activities: films; temporary & traveling exhibitions; special events; lectures; classes & films; service opportunities for Boy Scouts & Girl Scouts. Annual Events: Veteran Scouter Reunion; national conferences; Minnesota State Fair.
Publications: newsletter, North Star Museum News.
Hours & Admission Prices: Visit website for hours. No charge; donations accepted. Closed New Year's Day; Memorial Day; Independence Day; Labor Day; Thanksgiving; Christmas. ♿
Attendance: 3,000 (accurate)
Membership: Individual $35; Family/Unit $50.

Northfield

CARLETON COLLEGE ART GALLERY, (M), One N. College St., Northfield, MN 55057-4001. Tel.: 507-646-4342. Fax: 507-646-7042.
E-mail: lbradley@carleton.edu
Founded: 1971.
Key Personnel: Dir. & Cur., Laurel Bradley.
Personnel Profile: Full-Time Paid 2; Part-Time Paid 16.
Governing Authority: private; college. Tax-exempt: 501(c)(3).
Art Museum.
Collections: 1,400 art related items; 19th & 20th-century printmaking; contemporary photography; American paintings; Asian & ancient artifacts.
Activities: lectures; temporary & traveling exhibitions.
Hours & Admission Prices: Jan. to mid-June & Sept.-Nov. Mon.-Wed. 12-6, Thurs.-Fri. 12-10, Sat.-Sun. 12-4. No charge. Closed New Year's Day; Thanksgiving; spring break.
Attendance: 5,000 (estimated)

FLATEN ART MUSEUM OF ST. OLAF COLLEGE, 1520 St. Olaf Ave., Northfield, MN 55057-1099. Tel.: 507-786-3556 & 3703. Fax: 507-786-3776.
E-mail: ewaldj@stolaf.edu
Web Site: www.stolaf.edu/depts/art/museum

Founded: 1976.
Congressional District: 1
Key Personnel: Dir., Jill Ewald; Registrar, Mona Weselmann.
Personnel Profile: Part-Time Paid 18.
Governing Authority: private college. Parent Institution: St. Olaf College. Tax-exempt.
College Art Museum.
Collections: contemporary & historic prints, paintings, photographs, mixed, sculpture, ceramics; art glass; Yoshida family contemporary Japanese prints; traditional Japanese prints; study collections: African sculpture; post-Romanian paintings, prints, sculpture; Southwest US pottery; Albert Christ-Janer prints; works from around the globe.
Major Exhibits: Judy and Jennifer Onofrio, 2/27/10-4/11/10.
Activities: traveling & temporary exhibitions; lectures; films; concerts; graduating senior exhibits.
Publications: exhibit catalogs.
Hours & Admission Prices: mid-April to mid-May check website; Sept. to mid-April Mon.-Wed. & Fri. 10-5, Thurs. 10-8, Sat.-Sun. 2-5. No charge; donations accepted. Closed during school breaks. ♿
Attendance: 12,000 (accurate)

NORTHFIELD HISTORICAL SOCIETY MUSEUM, 408 Division St., Northfield, MN 55057-2018. Tel.: 507-645-9268; 507-663-6080.
E-mail: nhsmuseum@rconnect.com
Web Site: www.northfieldhistory.org
Founded: 1975.
Congressional District: 1
Key Personnel: Pres., Jodi Lawson; Exec. Dir., Hayes Scriven; Treas., Chuck Sandstrom; Museum Shop Mgr., Dick Waters.
Personnel Profile: Full-Time Paid 1; Part-Time Paid 1; Part-Time Volunteers 80; Interns 12.
Governing Authority: nonprofit organization. Tax-exempt.
Historical Society Museum: housed at the site of the original 1st National Bank of Northfield.
Collections: Northfield area artifacts; items relating to the 1876 attempted bank raid by the James/Younger Gang.
Research Fields: Northfield history; James/Younger Gang; railroad collection.
Facilities: 250-vol. library of books on local history & Jesse James available for research on premises under supervision. Books, notepaper, printed material & other museum-related items for sale.
Activities: guided tours; videotape TV programs; permanent, temporary & traveling exhibitions; adult & children's programming. Annual Events: Defeat of Jesse James Days in September; tour of homes in October.
Publications: quarterly newsletter, Scriver Scribbler.
Hours & Admission Prices: Memorial Day-Labor Day Mon.-Sat. 10-5, Sun. 1-4; Sept.-May Tues.-Sat. 10-4, Sun. 1-4. Guided Tours: Sat.-Sun. Adults & students $4, senior citizens $3, children $1.50; discounts to AAM members; members no charge. Closed New Year's Day; Easter; Independence Day; Thanksgiving; Christmas. ♿
Attendance: 12,000 (accurate)
Membership: Senior $35; Family $50; Building $100; Patron & Business $250; Sustaining $500; Life $1,000.

NORWEGIAN-AMERICAN HISTORICAL ASSOCIATION, St. Olaf College, 1510 St. Olaf Ave., Northfield, MN 55057-1097. Tel.: 507-786-3221. Fax: 507-646-3734.
E-mail: naha@stolaf.edu
Web Site: www.naha.stolaf.edu
Founded: 1925.
Congressional District: 1
Key Personnel: Admin. Dir., Kim Holland; Cur., Jeff Sauve.
Personnel Profile: Part-Time Paid 3; Part-Time Volunteers 1.
Governing Authority: board of directors. Tax-exempt: 501(c)(3).
Archives.
Collections: Norwegian-American history.
Research Fields: Norwegian migration; Norwegian-American history.
Facilities: 7,000-vol. library of books, magazines, pamphlets & newspapers dealing with Norwegian-American history; archives available for research. Books for sale.
Activities: document preservation; scholarly publication program; occasional conferences held in Norway and the U.S.
Publications: Travel & Description series: Norwegian-American Studies; newsletter; Special Publication Series, Authors Series; Topical Studies series; Biographical Series.
Hours & Admission Prices: By appointment only. Admission: $15. ♿
Attendance: 300 (estimated)
Membership: Student $25; Associate $40; Sustaining $75; Patron $125; Life $500 (one payment); Institutional $500 (25 years).

Onamia

MILLE LACS INDIAN MUSEUM, U.S. Hwy. 169, Onamia, MN 56359. Mailing Address: 43411 Oodena Dr., Onamia, MN 56359-2259. Tel.: 320-532-3632.
E-mail: millelacs@mnhs.org
Web Site: www.mnhs.org/places/sites/mlim/index.html
History Museum.
Collections: Mille Lacs Indian culture, language, music & dance.
Activities: workshops; special events; traditional cooking; birch-bark basketry & beadwork.
Hours & Admission Prices: Museum: Memorial Day to Labor Day Wed.-Sat. 10-4; groups by appointment April-May & Sept.-Oct. Adults $7, senior citizens $6, children 6-17 $5; MHS members & children under 6 no charge.

Owatonna

OWATONNA ARTS CENTER, 435 Garden View Lane, West Hills Complex, Owatonna, MN 55060. Mailing Address: P.O. Box 134, Owatonna, MN 55060-0134. Tel.: 507-451-0533. Fax: 507-446-0198.
E-mail: owatonnaartscent@qwest.net
Web Site: www.oacarts.org
Founded: 1974.
Congressional District: 1
Key Personnel: Dir. & Cur., Silvan Durben; Pres., Shari Kropp; Administrative Asst., Sharon Stark; Devel. & Coord., Scott Roberts; Education, Tracy Frederick.
Personnel Profile: Full-Time Paid 2; Part-Time Paid 2; Part-Time Volunteers 35.
Governing Authority: nonprofit organization. Tax-exempt: 501(c)(3).
Art Center.
Collections: Marianne Young 100-piece costume collection from 25 countries; prints & paintings; sculpture by Minnesota artists; 3 sculptures in garden by artists Paul Grandlund, John Rood & Richard Hammel.
Facilities: library of art history primarily for members of arts center; 200-seat performing arts hall; outdoor sculpture garden.
Activities: guided tours; lectures; concerts; vocal & piano recitals; formally organized education programs; loan, permanent, temporary & traveling exhibitions; classes for youth & adults.
Publications: bimonthly newsletter.
Hours & Admission Prices: Tues.-Sun. 1-5. No charge; donations accepted. Closed holidays. ♿
Attendance: 25,000 (estimated)
Membership: Full-Time Student $25; Basic $50; Contributing $100-$249; Sustaining $250-$499; Patron $500-$999; Benefactor $1,000-$2,499; Cultural Advocate $2,500-$4,999; Philanthropist $5,000-$9,999; Leadership $10,000.

Park Rapids

NORTH COUNTRY MUSEUM OF ARTS, 301 Court Ave., Park Rapids, MN 56470-1421. Mailing Address: P.O. Box 328, Park Rapids, MN 56470-0328. Tel.: 218-237-5900.
Founded: 1977.
Congressional District: 8
Key Personnel: Chm., Louie Falk.
Personnel Profile: Full-Time Paid 1; Part-Time Paid 1; Part-Time Volunteers 6.
Governing Authority: nonprofit organization. Tax-exempt: 501(c)(3).
Art Museum: housed in 1900 Hubbard County Courthouse.
Collections: late 15th to 19th-century old-school European paintings; Nigerian arts, crafts & artifacts; works by contemporary artists.
Research Fields: Nigerian arts, crafts, & artifacts (Yoruba, Ibo, Fulani & Hausa); late 15th to 19th-century European paintings.
Facilities: Works by regional artists & craftsmen for sale.
Activities: guided tours; special events; readings; concerts; lectures; classes; workshop; temporary exhibits.
Publications: quarterly newsletter; schedule of events.
Hours & Admission Prices: May-Oct. Tues.-Sun. 11-5. No charge; donations accepted.
Attendance: 4,000 (estimated)
Membership: Individual $15; Family $25.

Perham

IN THEIR OWN WORDS VETERANS MUSEUM, 805 W. Main, Perham, MN 56573-1131. Tel.: 218-346-7678.
E-mail: info@itowmuseum.org
Web Site: www.historymuseumeot.com/itow/index.html
Key Personnel: Project Mgr., Lina Belar
History Museum.
Collections: videos & kiosks relating to veterans of World War I & II, the Korean War & the Vietnam War; personal artifacts; photographs.

Hours & Admission Prices: Mon.-Sat. 10-5, Sun. 1-4. Adults $4; Memorial Day, Veterans Day, Independence Day & veterans no charge.

Pine City

MINNESOTA HISTORICAL SOCIETY'S NORTH WEST COMPANY FUR POST, 12551 Voyager Lane, Pine City, MN 55063. Mailing Address: P.O. Box 51, Pine City, MN 55063-0051. Tel.: 320-629-6356. Fax: 320-629-4667.
Congressional District: 8
Key Personnel: Site Mgr., Patrick Schifferdecker.
Personnel Profile: Full-Time Paid 1; Part-Time Paid 8; Part-Time Volunteers 20.
Governing Authority: private; nonprofit organization. Parent Institution: Minnesota Historical Society, 345 Kellogg Blvd. W., St. Paul, MN 55102-1906.
History Museum: housed in recreated fur trading post & Ojibwe encampment.
Collections: Ojibwe history; fur trade.
Facilities: 2,800 sq. ft. exhibit space; visitor's center. Museum-related items for sale.
Activities: formal education programs for children; guided tours; hobby workshops; hands-on activities.
Hours & Admission Prices: June-Aug. Mon. & Thurs.-Sat. 10-5, Sun. 12-5; Sept.-Oct. Fri.-Sat. 10-5, Sun. 12-5. Adults $8, senior citizens $6, children $5; discounts to groups; members no charge. ♿
Attendance: 13,778 (accurate)
Membership: See Minnesota Historical Society.

Pipestone

PIPESTONE COUNTY HISTORICAL MUSEUM, 113 S. Hiawatha Ave., Pipestone, MN 56164-1664. Tel.: 507-825-2563. Fax: 507-825-2563.
E-mail: pipctymu@iw.net
Web Site: www.pipestoneminnesota.com/museum
Founded: 1880.
Congressional District: 2
Key Personnel: Dir., Susan Hoskins; Pres. (V), Curt Hess.
Personnel Profile: Full-Time Paid 1; Part-Time Paid 3; Part-Time Volunteers 50.
Governing Authority: nonprofit organization. Parent Institution: Pipestone County Historical Society. Tax-exempt: 501(c)(3).
History Museum: housed in 1896 Old Pipestone City Hall.
Collections: pipes; quilled & beaded clothing from the Dakota & Ojibwa tribes; plains Indian saddles; period artifacts; American culture including tools, photographs, quilts, glassware, toys, farming implements, trade items, clothing & furniture; manuscripts.
Major Exhibits: Hear The Whistle Blowing, 11/09-12/10; Eternal Images, 11/09-12/10.
Research Fields: local genealogy; history.
Facilities: 200-vol. library of newspapers, 200-vol. history publications, biographies, land deeds, local history publications & atlas available for research on premises under staff supervision; reading room; microfilm reader-printer with local newspapers; doctors records; Pipestone Indian School records, additional archival resources. Books & local craftwork for sale.
Activities: guided tours; lectures; gallery talks; formally organized education programs; temporary & traveling exhibitions; biannual Civil War Days Festival.
Publications: quarterly newsletter.
Hours & Admission Prices: Memorial Day to Labor Day daily 10-5; Winter: Mon.-Sat. 10-5. Adults $3; children under 12 & members no charge. Tour Bus: Museum Tour or Step-On Tour $50. Closed New Year's Day; Presidents' Day; Easter; Memorial Day; Independence Day; Labor Day; Veterans Day; Thanksgiving; Christmas Eve & Day.
Attendance: 7,377 (accurate)
Membership: Student $5; Senior Citizen $10; Individual $15; Family $25; Life $100; Patron $250; Benefactor $500.

PIPESTONE NATIONAL MONUMENT, 36 Reservation Ave., Pipestone, MN 56164-1269. Tel.: 507-825-5464, ext. 28. Fax: 507-825-2046.
E-mail: gia_wagner@nps.gov
Web Site: www.nps.gov/pipe
Founded: 1937.
Congressional District: 1
Key Personnel: Resource Program Mgr., Gia Wagner.
Personnel Profile: Full-Time Paid 1; Part-Time Paid 1.
Governing Authority: federal. Parent Institution: National Park Service. Tax-exempt: 501(c)(3).
History Museum & Upper Midwest Indian Cultural Center.
Collections: Indian ceremonial pipes & pipestone objects; pipestone quarries; herbarium; insects; archives.
Research Fields: American Indian ceremonial pipes; Indian culture.
Facilities: 500-vol. library of books on Indians, the West, natural history & Bureau of Ethnology reports available for research on premises. Indian-made catlinite pipes & beadwork for sale.
Activities: guided tours; lectures; cultural demonstrations; slide presentations; films; self-guiding trail.
Publications: booklets, Pipestone: A History; Pipes on the Plains.
Hours & Admission Prices: Daily 8-5. Car: $5, Individual $3; Native Americans, children 16 & under & educational groups no charge. Closed New Year's Day; Christmas. ♿
Attendance: 80,000
Membership: Annual $15.

Reads Landing

WABASHA COUNTY MUSEUM, WABASHA COUNTY HISTORICAL SOCIETY AT READS LANDING, 70537 206th Ave., Reads Landing, MN 55968. Mailing Address: P.O. Box 255, Lake City, MN 55041-0255.
E-mail: wabashactyhistoricalsociety@yahoo.com
Founded: 1965.
Congressional District: 1
Key Personnel: Dir., Mary DeRoos; Pres., Helen Myers; Vice Pres., Gail Hill.
Personnel Profile: Part-Time Volunteers 10.
Governing Authority: nonprofit organization. Parent Institution: Wabasha County Historical Society. Tax-exempt: 501(c)(3).
General Museum.
Collections: farm implements; horse drawn farm & home machinery, vehicles; history items; period furniture. Historic Building: 1870 brick and stone school.
Activities: guided tours; permanent exhibitions.
Publications: quarterly newsletter.
Hours & Admission Prices: May-Oct. Sat.-Sun. 1-4; groups by appointment. Adults $5, children 6-12 $3; children 5 & under no charge. ♿
Attendance: 1,450 (accurate)
Membership: Individual $25; Family $40; Patron $50; Corporate $110.

Red Wing

GOODHUE COUNTY HISTORICAL SOCIETY, (M), 1166 Oak St., Red Wing, MN 55066-2447. Tel.: 651-388-6024. Fax: 651-388-3577.
E-mail: goodhuecountyhis@qwestoffice.net
Web Site: www.goodhuehistory.mus.mn.us
Founded: 1869.
Congressional District: 2
Key Personnel: C.E.O., Char Henn; Chm. (V), David Hallstrom; Outreach Coord., Diane Buganski; Collections Mgr., Johanna Grothe; Bldg. Supvr., Barry Dosdall.
Personnel Profile: Full-Time Paid 4; Part-Time Paid 3; Part-Time Volunteers 135; Interns 1.
Governing Authority: nonprofit organization. Tax-exempt.
Historical Museum.
Collections: photographs; manuscripts; biographies; historical books; immigration & early settlement; local government; pioneer artifacts; Dakota Indian artifacts; military history; natural history; industrial history; geology specimens; archaeology; clothing; sports; music; theatrical history; Red Wing stoneware & pottery; Nuremburg trial papers of Judge William Christianson of Red Wing, MN.
Research Fields: folklore; agriculture; archaeology; industrial history; natural history; paleontology; geology; medical history; mineralogy; textiles.
Facilities: approx. 300-vol. library of histories of Goodhue County, atlases, diaries, books on Minnesota, biographies, church publications & Bibles available for use on premises; reading room; historical slide & narrative programs, over 800 oral history tapes & transcripts. Indian-made articles, postcards, publications on geology, archaeology & Minnesota history for sale.
Activities: guided tours; formally organized education programs for children; permanent & temporary exhibitions.
Publications: quarterly, Goodhue County Historical News; The Sea Wing Disaster; 1894 Red Wing Stoneware Company catalog; 1877 plat map of Goodhue County; history of Red Wing Architecture; Goodhue County, Minnesota: A Narrative History; The Ghost Towns & Discontinued Post Offices of Goodhue County; Sky Crashers: A History of the Aurora Ski Club; Uncertain Lives: African-Americans and Their First 150 Years in the Red Wing, Minnesota Area.
Hours & Admission Prices: Call for hours. Adults $5, seniors over 62 $3; discounts to AAM & AASLH members; members no charge. ♿
Attendance: 12,000 (estimated)
Membership: Annual $35-$500; Life $1,000.

Redwood

REDWOOD COUNTY MUSEUM, 915 W. Bridge St., Redwood, MN 56283. Tel.: 507-641-3329.
Founded: 1949.
Congressional District: 2
Key Personnel: Pres. (V), Troy Krause; Chm. (V), Scott Larson; Cur. & Museum Shop Mgr., Patricia Lubeck.
Personnel Profile: Part-Time Paid 2.
Governing Authority: nonprofit organization. Tax-exempt.
General Museum.
Collections: county history; textiles; hand fans; period farm tools; Indian artifacts; natural history; clothing & handwork; doctor's office; one-room rural school; bridal room; military room; music; birds; animals & hides.
Facilities: picnic area.
Activities: guided tours; lectures; permanent exhibitions.
Hours & Admission Prices: May-Sept. Sat.-Sun. & holidays 1-4; groups by appointment. Adults $2, students $1, children under 10 $.50; members no charge. ♿
Attendance: 1,072 (accurate)
Membership: Annual $5; Lifetime $25.

Renville

HISTORIC RENVILLE PRESERVATION COMMISSION, 202 N. Main, Renville, MN 56284. Mailing Address: Box 681, Renville, MN 56284-0681. Tel.: 612-329-3545.
Founded: 1976.
Congressional District: 2
Key Personnel: Pres. (V), Jane Rice; Business Officer, Mildred Zaske.
Governing Authority: nonprofit organization. Tax-exempt.
Historical Society Museum.
Collections: pioneer tools & implements; instruments, journals & books belonging to early day doctors; school artifacts & memorabilia; military uniforms & items; Minnesota River Valley wildlife; Renville's oil & gas station artifacts. Historic Houses: 1904 City Jail.
Research Fields: Indian history; prominent settlers & business people; former riverboat city of Vicksburg.
Facilities: Renville County Genealogy Society research material available.
Activities: lectures; arts festivals; hobby workshops; permanent & temporary exhibitions. Commission Sponsors: Pioneer demonstrations; Renville celebration.
Publications: annual newsletter; monthly article in local paper; paperback, Adrian Looks Back in cooperation with Renville Star Farmer News.
Hours & Admission Prices: June-Sept. Sun. 1-4 & special events. No charge; donations accepted. ♿
Attendance: 700 (accurate)
Membership: Single $2; Family $3.

Richfield

RICHFIELD HISTORICAL SOCIETY, 6901 Lyndale Ave., S., Richfield, MN 55423. Mailing Address: P.O. Box 23304, Richfield, MN 55423-0304. Tel.: 612-798-6140.
E-mail: staff@richfieldhistory.org
Web Site: www.richfieldhistory.org
Key Personnel: Dir., Sarah Hummel.
Personnel Profile: Part-Time Paid 1.
Historic House Museum: listed on the National Register of Historic Places.
Collections: local history & culture; photographs; period artifacts.
Major Exhibits: Richfield's Greatest Generation, 1/10-8/10.
Facilities: History Center: library.
Activities: adult & student education programs; music series.
Publications: book, Richfield: Minnesota's Oldest Suburb.
Hours & Admission Prices: Mon., Wed. & 2nd Sat. of each month 12-4; other times by appointment. House Tour: adults $3; members no charge.

Rochester

MAYO CLINIC HERITAGE HALL, 200 1st St., S.W., Rochester, MN 55905-0002. Tel.: 507-284-8540.
Medical History Museum.
Collections: clinic history; medical instruments; photographs; personal artifacts.
Hours & Admission Prices: Mon.-Fri. 8-5.

OLMSTED COUNTY HISTORICAL SOCIETY DBA HISTORY CENTER OF OLMSTED COUNTY, 1195 W. Circle Dr., S.W., Rochester, MN 55902-6619. Tel.: 507-282-9447. Fax: 507-289-5481.
E-mail: director@olmstedhistory.com
Web Site: www.olmstedhistory.com
Founded: 1926.
Congressional District: 1
Key Personnel: C.E.O., James Lundgren; Pres. (V), Irv Plitzuweit; Archivist, Sherry Sweetman; Accountant, Roxanne Ziecina; Devel. Dir., Jeff Amundson; Museum Shop Mgr., Barbara Dahlin.
Personnel Profile: Full-Time Paid 8; Part-Time Paid 19; Part-Time Volunteers 400; Interns 3.
Governing Authority: society. Tax-exempt: 501(c)(3).
History Museum & Historic Site.
Collections: general local & regional history; farm implements & machinery; manuscripts. Historic Buildings: 1910-1911 Mayowood; 1860 Stoppel Farmstead; 1860 Dee Cabin; 1900 Hadley School.
Research Fields: Olmsted County history.
Facilities: 3,000-vol. library of history, technology, genealogy & local microfilm available for use under supervision; reading room; classrooms. Museum reproductions & books for sale.
Activities: guided tours; lectures; study clubs; formally organized education programs; permanent, temporary & traveling exhibitions; school loan service.
Publications: quarterly newsletter, The Olmsted Historian; every other month newsletter, "The Scribe"; biannual magazine "The Olmsted Historian".
Hours & Admission Prices: Museum: Tues.-Sat. 9-5. Adults $5, children under 15 $2; members no charge. Mayowood Tours: May 7-May 28 & Aug. 13-Oct. 15 Sat. hourly 11-2; June-Aug. 11 Tues.-Thurs. & Sat. hourly 11-2. Adults $12, children $6. Closed national holidays. ♿
Attendance: 25,500 (estimated)
Membership: Seniors 65 & over; Individual $40; Partner & Business Supporter $50 & up; Household (includes children under 17) $65; Business Booster $100 & up; Sponsor $250 & up; Benefactor $500 & up.

ROCHESTER ART CENTER, 40 Civic Center Dr., S.E., Rochester, MN 55904-3773. Tel.: 507-282-8629. Fax: 507-282-7737.
E-mail: dsorom@rochesterartcenter.org
Web Site: www.rochesterartcenter.org
Founded: 1946.
Congressional District: 1
Key Personnel: Exec. Dir., Sarah Stauder; Admininstrative Operations Dir., Joan Lovelace; Chief Cur., Kristopher Douglas; Facility Dir. & Head Preparator, Phillip Ahnen; Mktg. & Public Programs Mgr., Jennifer Buddenhagen; Assoc. Cur. & Cur. Education, Scott Stulen; Devel. Dir., Michele Heidel; Programs Coord., Naura Anderson; Rentals Mgr., Kim Haroldson; Visitor Svcs. Mgr., Marge Elkin.
Personnel Profile: Full-Time Paid 8; Part-Time Paid 18; Part-Time Volunteers 20; Interns 8.
Governing Authority: nonprofit organization. Tax-exempt: 501(c)(3).
Art Center.
Collections: donated artworks.
Facilities: classrooms; sculpture garden; video space.
Activities: tours; lectures; films; concerts; workshops; demonstrations; classes for children & adults; outreach programs in the community.
Publications: newsletter; exhibition catalogs; education department brochures.
Hours & Admission Prices: Tues.-Wed. & Fri.-Sat. 10-5, Thurs. 10-9, Sun. 12-5. Adults $3, seniors $2; discounts to AAM members; members & students no charge. Closed holidays. ♿
Attendance: 25,000 (estimated)
Membership: Senior Citizen, Student & Non-Resident $25; Individual $35; Household & Dual $45; Friend $50-$99; Supporting $100-$249; Sustaining $250-$499; Patron $500-$749; Benefactor $750-$999; Founder $1,000-$2,499; Sponsor $2,500 & up.

Rockford

ROCKFORD AREA HISTORICAL SOCIETY, 8131 Bridge St., Rockford, MN 55373. Mailing Address: P.O. Box 186, Rockford, MN 55373-0186. Tel.: 763-477-5383.
E-mail: storkhouse@cityofrockford.org
Web Site: www.rockfordmnhistory.org
Founded: 1986.
Key Personnel: Dir., Rebecca Mavencamp; Pres. (V), Bonnie Maue.
Governing Authority: Branch Museum: The Ames-Florida-Stork House. Tax-exempt.
Historical Society Museum.
Collections: clothing & textiles; furniture; housewares; library & archival holdings; photographs.
Research Fields: Rockford history & genealogy.
Activities: children's programs; monthly educational classes. Museum Sponsors: Memorial Day Pie and Ice Cream Social; Christmas Tea.
Publications: 6 newsletters per year.
Hours & Admission Prices: May-Sept. Tues. 10-2, Thurs. 11-7. Adults $3; members & children 6 and under no charge.
Attendance: 800 (accurate)

Membership: Individual $10; Family $25; Business $45; Sponsor $100.

Rogers

ELLINGSON CAR MUSEUM, 20950 Rogers Dr., Rogers, MN 55374-9191. Tel.: 763-428-7337. Fax: 763-428-4370.
E-mail: ecmmuseum@mm.com
Web Site: www.ellingsoncarmuseum.com
Founded: 1994.
Key Personnel: Owner, Scott Ellingson.
Personnel Profile: Full-Time Paid 1; Part-Time Paid 6.
Governing Authority: for profit.
Car Museum.
Collections: over 100 cars from early 1900s to 1970.
Facilities: Museum-related items for sale.
Activities: outdoor car shows in summer.
Hours & Admission Prices: Daily 10-5. Adults $5. Closed holidays. ♿
Attendance: 25,000 (estimated)

Rollingstone

ROLLINGSTONE-LUXEMBOURG HERITAGE MUSEUM, 98 Main St., Rollingstone, MN 55969. Mailing Address: P.O. Box 63, Rollingstone, MN 55969-0063. Tel.: 507-689-2307 & 2139.
Founded: 1987.
Key Personnel: Chm. (V) & Museum Shop Mgr., Jean Kalmes; Pres., Diane Bronk.
Personnel Profile: Part-Time Volunteers 8.
Governing Authority: Tax-exempt.
Heritage Museum.
Collections: local history & culture; early immigrants; photographs; period clothing & uniforms; tools; fire equipment; dolls & toys.
Research Fields: local genealogy.
Facilities: library.
Activities: Museum Sponsors: Treipenfest Banquet in January; Fall Fest in September.
Publications: newsletter.
Hours & Admission Prices: Sun. 1-4; other times by appointment. No charge; donations accepted. Closed Easter; Christmas.
Attendance: 1,000 (estimated)
Membership: Individual $5; Family $10.

Roseau

ROSEAU COUNTY HISTORICAL MUSEUM AND INTERPRETIVE CENTER, (M), 121 Center St. E., Ste. 101, Roseau, MN 56751-1127. Tel.: 218-463-1918.
E-mail: rchsroseau@mncable.net
Web Site: www.roseaucohistoricalsociety.org
Founded: 1927.
Congressional District: 1
Key Personnel: Pres. (V), Glenn Holm; Cur. & Dir., Charleen Haugen.
Personnel Profile: Full-Time Paid 1; Part-Time Paid 2; Part-Time Volunteers 45.
Governing Authority: Parent Institution: Roseau County Historical Society. Tax-exempt.
Historical Society Museum & Interpretive Center.
Collections: Historic Building: 1898, restored, Pinecreek church.
Major Exhibits: Women in History 2010 (T), 3/10-9/10; Between Fences (MoMS) (T), 3/27/10-5/8/10.
Research Fields: county & natural history; genealogy.
Facilities: library of short memoirs of early settlers; research center.
Activities: guided tours; annual Minnesota history contest; traveling exhibits; Chautauqua; workshops; research; adult & youth programs.
Publications: Books, Pioneers O Pioneers, History of early settlers in county 1885-1910; Remembrances, An Anthology of Roseau County Minnesota; Pioneers O Pioneers Book II; Roseau County Heritage Book; Roseau County Centennial Book; 75th Anniversary Cookbook.
Hours & Admission Prices: Mon.-Fri. 9:30-5. Museum: no charge; donations accepted. Research Center: adults $5. Closed national holidays. ♿
Attendance: 6,400 (accurate)
Membership: Individual $10; Family $15; Business $25; Sponsor $50; Patron $100; Benefactor $250.

Roseville

HARRIET ALEXANDER NATURE CENTER, 2520 N. Dale St., Roseville, MN 55113-3502. Tel.: 651-765-4262. Fax: 651-792-7160.
E-mail: hanc@ci.roseville.mn.us
Nature Center.
Collections: live animals; anatomy models; furs; botanical.
Facilities: 52 acres.
Hours & Admission Prices: Tues.-Sat. 10-4, Sun. 1-4. No charge.

Saint Cloud

EVELYN PAYNE HATCHER MUSEUM OF ANTHROPOLOGY, Rm. 113, Stewart Hall, St. Cloud State, Saint Cloud, MN 56301. Tel.: 320-308-4790.
Anthropology Museum.
Collections: local history & culture; Native American artifacts; photographs.
Activities: field schools.
Hours & Admission Prices: Mon.-Fri. 9-5.

MINNESOTA AMATEUR BASEBALL HALL OF FAME, St. Cloud Civic Center, 2nd Fl., 10 4th Ave. S., Saint Cloud, MN 56303. Mailing Address: 1325 10th Ave. N., Saint Cloud, MN 56303-1709. Tel.: 320-252-8227. Fax: 320-230-3277.
E-mail: mnbaseballhof@charter.net
Web Site: www.mnamateurbaseballhof.com/
Founded: 1963.
Sports Museum.
Collections: amateur baseball history; uniforms; caps; photographs; bats; balls; gloves; programs.
Activities: Museum Sponsors: Annual Banquet.
Hours & Admission Prices: Call for hours.

MUNSINGER AND CLEMENS GARDENS, 1300 Kilian Blvd., S.E., Saint Cloud, MN 56304-1647. Mailing Address: Friends of the Gardens, 101 S. 7th Ave., Ste. 100, Saint Cloud, MN 56301-4275. Tel.: 320-255-7216.
Web Site: www.munsingerclemens.com
Botanical Gardens.
Collections: plants; trees; flowers.
Facilities: Museum-related items for sale.
Activities: special events; concerts.
Hours & Admission Prices: Spring to Fall daily 7am-10pm. No charge; donations accepted.

* **STEARNS HISTORY MUSEUM, (M),** 235 S. 33rd Ave., Saint Cloud, MN 56301-3752. Tel.: 320-253-8424; 866-253-8424 (toll free). Fax: 320-253-2172. TDD: 320-253-8424.
E-mail: info@stearns.history.museum
Web Site: www.stearns.history.museum
Founded: 1936.
Congressional District: 6
Key Personnel: Interim Exec. Dir., Ann E. Meline; Pres. (V), Donald Kinzer; Asst. Dir. Public Programs, Ann Meline; Cur., Steven Penick; Asst. Dir. Archivist, John Decker; Registrar, Lorie Fischer; Archivist, Sarah LaVine; Business Mgr. & Museum Shop Mgr., Cynthia O'Konek; Administrative Asst., Diane Smith; Archivist, Robert Lommel.
Personnel Profile: Full-Time Paid 7; Part-Time Paid 3; Part-Time Volunteers 100; Interns 2.
Governing Authority: society; nonprofit organization. Tax-exempt: 501(c)(3).
History Museum.
Collections: biographies; research materials; artifacts; large miniature circus & carnival; library of oral history tapes; photographs; local history; dairy farming; resorts & tourism; natural history of central Minnesota; immigration; granite industry; Pan Car & Motor Company; local amateur & professional baseball.
Research Fields: genealogy; history of county & state.
Facilities: research library; archives; museum cultural center.
Activities: educational program; workshops & seminars.
Publications: bimonthly newsletter; annual report; books, topical history series.
Hours & Admission Prices: Mon.-Sat. 10-5, Sun. 12-5. Family $12, adults $5, children $2; discounts to Sept. Days Club, groups, Time Travelers Museum Network, AAA, AAM & ICOM members; children under 5 & members no charge. Closed major holidays. ♿
Attendance: 36,343 (accurate)
Membership: Senior $30; Individual $35; Family Plus $50; Business, Clubs & Organizations $150; Benefactor $250; Corporate $500; Patron's Circle $1,000.

Saint Joseph

BENEDICTA ARTS CENTER OF THE COLLEGE OF SAINT BENEDICTA, College of St. Benedict, 37 S. College Ave., Saint Joseph, MN 56374-2001. Tel.: 320-363-5777. Fax: 320-363-6097.
E-mail: jrule@csbsju.edu
Web Site: www.csbsju.edu/finearts
Founded: 1963.

Congressional District: 6
Key Personnel: Exec. Dir. of Fine Arts, Brian Jose; Permanent Collection Coord., Juliann Rule.
Governing Authority: college. Tax-exempt.
Art Gallery.
Collections: Asian & New Guinea artifacts; contemporary prints, drawings, paintings, sculpture & ceramics.
Major Exhibits: Caitlin Karolczak, Paintings, 12/7/09-2/20/10; Danny Saathoff-Interactive Kinetic Sculpture & Jewelry, 1/11/10-2/20/10; Book Arts, 2/26/10-4/14/10; Mary Hark-Book Arts, 2/26/10-4/14/10; Senior Student Exhibit, 4/19/10-5/8/10.
Facilities: auditorium; theater.
Activities: guided tours; lectures; music, theater & dance presentations; temporary exhibits.
Hours & Admission Prices: Summer: call for hours; Sept.-May daily 10am-9pm. No charge. Closed holidays; school vacations. ♿
Attendance: 5,000 (estimated)

Saint Paul

ALEXANDER RAMSEY HOUSE, MINNESOTA HISTORICAL SOCIETY, 265 S. Exchange St., Saint Paul, MN 55102-2416. Tel.: 651-296-8760. Fax: 651-296-0100.
E-mail: ramseyhouse@mnhs.org
Web Site: www.mnhs.org
Founded: 1964.
Congressional District: 4
Key Personnel: C.E.O., Nina M. Archabal; Dir. & Security, Kevin Maijala; Education, Dana Heimark; Historic Site Admin., Jim Matson.
Personnel Profile: Full-Time Paid 3; Part-Time Paid 15; Part-Time Volunteers 22; Interns 1.
Governing Authority: nonprofit organization; semi-state agency. Parent Institution: Minnesota Historical Society. Tax-exempt.
Historic House: Late 19th-century upper class Victorian mansion.
Collections: original furnishings of the Ramsey family.
Research Fields: Ramsey family history.
Activities: guided tours; lectures; organized education programs for children. Museum Sponsors: Victorian Holiday Program.
Hours & Admission Prices: Jan.-May & Sept.-Nov. 18 Fri.-Sat. & holidays 10-3; June-Aug. Tues.-Sat. & holidays 10-3; Nov. 19-Dec. Wed.-Sat. 10-3. Adults $8, senior citizens $6, children 6-17 $5; discounts for AAM members; children under 5 & members no charge. Closed Thanksgiving; Christmas Eve & Day. ♿
Attendance: 13,500 (accurate)
Membership: Senior Individual $45; Individual & Senior Household $55; Household $65; Associate Member $125.

AMERICAN MUSEUM OF ASMAT ART, 2115 Summit Ave., Mail #57P, Saint Paul, MN 55105-1048. Tel.: 651-962-5512. Fax: 651-962-5861.
E-mail: asmat@stthomas.edu
Web Site: www.asmat.org
Founded: 1995.
Congressional District: 4
Key Personnel: Dir., Julie Risser; Chm. (V), Lori Wiese-Parks; Chm. (V), Phyllis Hischier; Asst. to Dir., Sharon Henrich; Treas., Peter Cote; Museologist, M.J. Czarniecki, III; Bookkeeper, Don Henrich.
Personnel Profile: Full-Time Paid 1; Part-Time Paid 2; Part-Time Volunteers 20; Interns 3.
Governing Authority: private; not-for-profit. Tax-exempt: 501(c)(3).
Ethnological Art Museum.
Collections: art, culture & carvings from the Asmat people of Western Papua & Indonesia.
Research Fields: Asmat art & culture.
Facilities: 220-vol. library on Asmat culture; 600 sq. ft. exhibit space.
Activities: guided tours; lectures; education programs for adults; loan, participatory, temporary & traveling exhibitions; docent program.
Publications: quarterly newsletter, Embodied Spirits; books, Asmat Sketch Book vol. 1-8, Making the Invisible Visible, Asmat Images, The Asmat: Myth & Ritual; The Asmat: Perception of Life in Art.
Hours & Admission Prices: Mon.-Thurs. 8-4, Fri. 8-12, Sat.-Sun. special exhibits. No charge; donations accepted. Closed New Year's Eve & Day; Memorial Day; Independence Day; Labor Day; Thanksgiving; Christmas. ♿
Attendance: 3,720 (accurate)
Membership: Individual $40; Family $60; Institutional $100 & up; Discovery $100-$499; Animating $500-$999; Sustaining $1,000 & up.

ARCHIVES - ARCHDIOCESE OF ST. PAUL AND MINNEAPOLIS, 226 Summit Ave., Saint Paul, MN 55102-2121. Tel.: 651-291-4429. Fax: 651-290-1629.
E-mail: archives@archspm.org
Founded: 1988.
Key Personnel: Chancellor, Andy Eisenzimmer; Archivist, Steven T. Granger, C.A.
Governing Authority: church; nonprofit organization. Tax-exempt: 501(c)(3).
Religious Museum.
Collections: over 1,000 linear ft. of archival materials; archdiocese business records; historic records of Catholic parishes, religious groups & institutions; photographs; maps & plans; religious artifacts.
Facilities: 300-vol. library on Catholic history.
Activities: guided tours; lectures; temporary exhibitions.
Hours & Admission Prices: By appointment.
Attendance: 50 (estimated)

CATHERINE G. MURPHY GALLERY - COLLEGE OF ST. CATHERINE, Visual Arts Bldg., 2004 Randolph Ave., Saint Paul, MN 55105-1789. Tel.: 651-690-6644.
Key Personnel: Dir., Kathleen M. Daniels
Art Gallery.
Collections: Clara Mairs; Adolph Dehn; Corita Kent; Cecilia Lieder.
Hours & Admission Prices: Mon.-Fri. 8-8, Sat.-Sun. 12-6.

COMO PARK ZOO AND CONSERVATORY, 1225 Estabrook. Dr., Saint Paul, MN 55103-1022. Tel.: 651-487-8201. Fax: 651-487-8245.
E-mail: michelle.furrer@ci.stpaul.mn.us
Web Site: www.comozooconservatory.org
Formerly: St. Paul's Como Zoo
Founded: 1897.
Congressional District: 4
Key Personnel: Pres. Como Friends, Dr. Jackie Sticha; Consulting Veterinarian Prof. & Clinician, Univ. of Minn. College of Veterinary Medicine, Dr. Micky Trent; Animal Cur., John Dee; Campus Mgr., Michelle Furrer.
Personnel Profile: Full-Time Paid 84; Part-Time Paid 36; Part-Time Volunteers 1,200; Interns 30.
Governing Authority: Parent Institution: St. Paul Parks & Recreation; affiliated with Univ. of MN. College of Veterinary Medicine for Research & Teaching.
Zoo.
Collections: mammals; birds; reptiles; endangered species; marine mammals.
Research Fields: propagation of large cats & orangutans; animal husbandry with students of veterinary medicine.
Facilities: 800-vol. library of natural history & taxonomic books available for research on premises; zoological park. Postcards, film, booklets & guide books for sale.
Activities: guided tours; lectures; TV & radio programs; docent program; permanent, temporary & traveling exhibitions; school loan service.
Publications: monthly bulletin, newsletter, Como Combo.
Hours & Admission Prices: April-Sept. daily 10-6; Oct.-March daily 10-4. No charge; donations accepted. ♿
Attendance: 1,000,000 (estimated)
Membership: $35-$500

DENLER ART GALLERY AT NORTHWESTERN COLLEGE, Totino Fine Arts Center, 2nd Fl., 3003 Snelling Ave., N., Saint Paul, MN 55113-1501. Tel.: 651-631-5110 (main switchboard).
Web Site: art.nwc.edu/denler
Key Personnel: Dir., Luke Aleckson
Art Gallery.
Collections: artwork by local and national artists.
Hours & Admission Prices: Call for hours.

THE GOLDSTEIN MUSEUM OF DESIGN, 364 McNeal Hall, 1985 Buford Ave., Saint Paul, MN 55108-6134. Tel.: 612-624-7434. Fax: 612-625-5762.
E-mail: gmd@umn.edu
Web Site: goldstein.design.umn.edu
Founded: 1976.
Congressional District: 5
Key Personnel: Dir., Lin Nelson-Mayson; Asst. Cur., Jean McElvain; Registrar, Eunice Haucen; Grants Writer, Kathleen Campbell.
Personnel Profile: Full-Time Paid 4; Part-Time Paid 12; Part-Time Volunteers 40.
Governing Authority: university. University of Minnesota. Tax-exempt.
Design Museum.
Collections: costumes; decorative arts; graphic design; textiles.
Research Fields: costume; textiles; decorative arts; graphic design; architecture; landscape architecture.
Facilities: 1,000-vol. research library.
Activities: guided tours; gallery talks; lectures,
Publications: collections catalogue; catalogues for specific exhibitions.
Hours & Admission Prices: Tues.-Wed. & Fri. 10-4, Thurs. 10-8, Sat.-Sun.

1:30-4:30. No charge; donations accepted. Closed major holidays & university holidays. ♿
Attendance: 5,725 (accurate)
Membership: Student $10; Senior $20; Individual $35; Household $50; Sponsor $150; Patron $250; Benefactor $500; Directors Circle $1,000.

HAMLINE UNIVERSITY, SOEFFKER GALLERY, Hamline University, Drew Fine Arts Center, Saint Paul, MN 55104-1284. Mailing Address: 1536 Hewitt Ave., Saint Paul, MN 55104-1284. Tel.: 651-523-2800, 2386 & 2296. Fax: 651-523-3057.
E-mail: llasansky@hamline.edu
Web Site: www.hamline.edu/art/
Formerly: Hamline University Galleries, Department of Studio Arts & Art History
Founded: 1854.
Key Personnel: Dir., Leonardo Lasansky; Registrar, Becky Harsma; Art Handler, John-Mark Schlink.
Governing Authority: Parent Institution: Hamline University. Tax-exempt: 501(c)(3).
Art Gallery.
Collections: sculpture; paintings; archaeological; decorative arts.
Activities: lectures; films; gallery talks; docent-led exhibition tours; arts festivals; formally organized education programs for undergraduate college students; education programs & hands-on activities for children; inter-museum loan, permanent & temporary exhibitions.
Publications: exhibition catalogs; exhibition posters; Icons of Perfection: Figurative Sculpture from Africa.
Hours & Admission Prices: Mon.-Fri. 10-4. No charge. Closed national holidays.

HISTORIC FORT SNELLING, Ft. Snelling History Center, 200 Tower Ave., Saint Paul, MN 55111-4037. Tel.: 612-726-1171 & 725-2407. Fax: 612-725-2429.
E-mail: ftsnelling@mnhs.org
Web Site: www.mnhs.org/fortsnelling
Founded: 1970.
Key Personnel: Site Mgr., Tom Pfannenstiel; Museum Shop Mgr., Florence Olson.
Personnel Profile: Full-Time Paid 7; Part-Time Paid 55; Part-Time Volunteers 25.
Governing Authority: nonprofit organization. Parent Institution: Minnesota Historical Society. Tax-exempt.
Historic Site.
Collections: 4 original & 14 reconstructed buildings.
Research Fields: Frontier social history & military material culture 1820s-1860s.
Facilities: history center; 3,000 sq. ft. exhibit space; 300-seat theater. Historical reproductions & books for sale.
Activities: guided tours; films; organized education for children; participatory exhibits; living history programs.
Hours & Admission Prices: Fort: May & Sept.-Oct. Sat. 10-5, Sun. 12-5; Memorial Day to Labor Day Mon.-Sat. 10-5, Sun. 12-5. Adults $10, seniors & college students $8, children 6-17 $5; discounts to school group; children 5 & under and members no charge. History Center: May-Oct. daily 9:30-5; Nov.-April Mon.-Fri. 9-4:30. No charge. ♿
Attendance: 100,000 (accurate)
Membership: Through the Minnesota Historical Society.

JAMES J. HILL HOUSE, 240 Summit Ave., Saint Paul, MN 55102-2194. Tel.: 651-297-2555. Fax: 651-297-5655. TDD: 651-282-6073.
E-mail: hillhouse@mnhs.org
Web Site: www.mnhs.org/hillhouse
Founded: 1978.
Key Personnel: Site Mgr., Craig Johnson; Program Supervisor, Sara Scrimshaw.
Personnel Profile: Full-Time Paid 4; Part-Time Paid 16; Part-Time Volunteers 2; Interns 1.
Governing Authority: state agency; nonprofit. Parent Institution: Minnesota Historical Society, 345 Kellogg Blvd. W., St. Paul. Tax-exempt.
Historic House: 1891 family home of James J. Hill, builder of the Great Northern Railway.
Collections: original architecture; decorative elements; technical systems; some original furnishings.
Hours & Admission Prices: Wed.-Sat. 10-3:30. Adults $8, senior citizens 65 & over $6, students & children 6-17 $4; discounts to groups; MHS members and children 5 & under no charge. Closed New Year's Day; Easter; Thanksgiving; Christmas. ♿
Attendance: 44,207 (accurate)
Membership: Senior $45; Individual $50; Individual Plus & Senior Household $65; Household $75; Household Plus $95.

JULIAN H. SLEEPER HOUSE, (M), 66 St. Albans St., S., Saint Paul, MN 55105-3501. Tel.: 651-225-1505.
Web Site: juliansleeperhouse.com
Founded: 1993.
Key Personnel: C.E.O., Dr. Seth C. Hawkins; Chm. Bd. (V), Janet C. Mahoney.
Governing Authority: individual operation; nonprofit.
Historic Site: 1884 Eastlake-Vernacular House, moved to present site in 1911, furnished & decorated in period style.
Collections: Gilded Age furnishings; James A. Garfield memorabilia; Roseville pottery; albums of vintage U.S. & Canadian picture postcards; Slovenian cultural & historical artifacts.
Research Fields: 19th century professional baseball; history of U.S. public speaking.
Activities: guided tours; lectures.
Publications: illustrated catalog of the James A. Garfield collection.
Hours & Admission Prices: Private residence, open by appointment only. Adults $7; discounts to members & AAM members.
Membership: Annual $35.

MACALESTER COLLEGE ART GALLERY, JANET WALLACE FINE ARTS CENTER, 1600 Grand Ave., Saint Paul, MN 55105-1899. Tel.: 651-696-6416. Fax: 651-696-6266.
E-mail: fitz@macalester.edu
Web Site: www.macalester.edu/gallery/index.html
Founded: 1964.
Key Personnel: Cur., Gregory Fitz.
Personnel Profile: Full-Time Paid 1; Interns 10.
Governing Authority: private college; nonprofit.
College Art Gallery.
Collections: British & Asian ceramics; contemporary & historical prints, drawings & paintings; international arts.
Facilities: educational facilities; 2,500 sq. ft. exhibit space.
Hours & Admission Prices: Mon.-Wed. & Fri. 10-4, Thurs. 10-8, Sat.-Sun. 12-4. No charge. Closed college holidays. ♿

MARJORIE MCNEELY CONSERVATORY, 1225 Estabrook Dr., Saint Paul, MN 55103-1022. Tel.: 651-487-8201. Fax: 651-487-8255.
Web Site: www.comozooconservatory.org
Formerly: Como Park Conservatory
Founded: 1915.
Congressional District: 4
Key Personnel: Mgr., Tina Dombrowski; Campus Mgr., Michelle Furrer; Museum Shop Mgr., Terri Scheunemann.
Personnel Profile: Full-Time Paid 9; Part-Time Paid 12; Part-Time Volunteers 540; Interns 4.
Governing Authority: municipal. Parent Institution: City of St. Paul. Subsidiary Institution: Como Park Zoo and Conservatory. Tax-exempt.
Botanical Garden.
Collections: orchids; bonsai; bromeliads; Japanese garden; butterfly garden; palms; tropical plants; ferns.
Activities: limited lectures; permanent exhibitions; plant-related workshops; flower shows.
Publications: newsletter, Views.
Hours & Admission Prices: April-Sept. daily 10-6; Oct.-March daily 10-4. No charge; donations accepted. ♿
Attendance: 1,000,000 (estimated)
Membership: Como Friends: Individual $30; Household $50; Household Advantage $65; Patron $110.

MINNESOTA AIR NATIONAL GUARD HISTORICAL FOUNDATION, INC., (M), 670 General Miller Dr., Saint Paul, MN 55111-0598. Mailing Address: P.O. Box 11598, Saint Paul, MN 55111-0598. Tel.: 612-713-2523. Fax: 612-713-2524.
E-mail: msp04332@isd.net
Web Site: www.mnangmuseum.org
Founded: 1980.
Congressional District: 8
Key Personnel: Chm. (V), John Kahler; Vice Chm., Mark Ness; Museum Shop Mgr., Kathleen Sundby.
Personnel Profile: Full-Time Paid 1; Full-Time Volunteers 50; Part-Time Paid 1; Part-Time Volunteers 50.
Governing Authority: private; nonprofit organization. Tax-exempt: 501(c)(3).
Aviation Museum: located on grounds of the 133rd Airlift Wing, Minnesota Air National Guard.
Collections: aircraft & artifacts flown by the 109th Squadron, Minnesota Air National Guard; history of the Minnesota National Guard; photographs.

Research Fields: construction of reproduction Curtiss Jenny Restoration of 0-2, L-4.
Facilities: 5,000-vol. library; 25,000 sq. ft. exhibit space; classroom. Museum-related items for sale.
Activities: guided tours; formal education programs for children; hobby workshops; participatory & temporary exhibitions. Museum Sponsors: Open Cockpit Days; State Fair Exhibit.
Publications: quarterly newsletter, The Historian.
Hours & Admission Prices: Summer: call for hours. No charge; donations accepted.
Attendance: 1,000 (estimated)
Membership: Basic $10; General $25; Life $100.

MINNESOTA CHILDREN'S MUSEUM, 10 W. 7th St., Saint Paul, MN 55102-2453. Tel.: 651-225-6000. Fax: 651-225-6006.
E-mail: mcm@mcm.org
Web Site: www.mcm.org
Formerly: Minnesota's Aware House
Founded: 1979.
Congressional District: 4
Key Personnel: Pres., Sarah Caruso; Chm. (V), William C. Schmoker.
Personnel Profile: Full-Time Paid 51; Part-Time Paid 39; Part-Time Volunteers 309.
Governing Authority: nonprofit organization. Tax-exempt: 501(c)(3).
Children's Participatory Museum.
Collections: hands-on exhibits of multi-disciplinary nature for children 6 months-10 years; Our World, exploring neighborhoods and appreciating their diversity; Earth World, celebrating stewardship of the Earth; World Works, tools, problem-solving, invention & creativity; Habitot, infant-toddler learning landscape; Rooftop Art Park: art & nature.
Major Exhibits: Dinosaurs: Land of Fire & Ice, 12/19/09-5/10; The Children of Hangzhou (T), 2/6/10-5/16/10; Balancing Act (T), 5/29/10-8/22/10; Wizard of Oz (T), 6/12/10-9/12/10; Living in Space, Fall 2010; Inside Art, Fall 2010.
Research Fields: children's environments; children's behaviors in exhibits; safety in interactive exhibits; customer segments.
Facilities: classrooms; performance area.
Activities: interactive, multidisciplinary exhibits; programs for children, families, teachers & care providers; volunteer program.
Publications: bimonthly newsletter; annual report; case statement.
Hours & Admission Prices: Summer: Fri. 9-8, Sat.-Thurs. 9-5; Winter: Tues.-Thurs. & Sat.-Sun. 9-5, Fri. 9-8. Adults $8.95; discounts to AARP & ACM reciprocal membership program; children under 1 no charge. ♿
Attendance: 404,000 (estimated)
Membership: Nanny $20; Foster Care $50; Passport $89; Passport Deluxe $129; Explorer $250.

* **MINNESOTA HISTORICAL SOCIETY, (M), (I),** 345 Kellogg Blvd. W., Saint Paul, MN 55102-1903. Tel.: 651-259-3000; 800-657-3773. Fax: 651-297-3343. TDD: 651-282-6073.
E-mail: director@mnhs.org
Web Site: www.mnhs.org
Founded: 1849.
Congressional District: 4
Key Personnel: C.E.O. & Dir., Nina M. Archabal; Deputy Dir. External Rels., Andrea Kajer; MHS Pres., Greg Britton; Public Rels., Lory Sutton; Deputy Dir., Michael Fox; Head Exhibits, Dan Spock; Asst. Dir. Historic Sites, William Keyes; Asst. Dir. Finance & Admin., Charles Irrgang; Devel. Officer, Mark Haidet; Museum Shop Mgr., Meta DeVine.
Personnel Profile: Full-Time Paid 360; Part-Time Paid 260; Part-Time Volunteers 1,700; Interns 35.
Governing Authority: society. Branches: Comstock House, Moorhead; Forest History Center, Grand Rapids; Fort Ridgely History Center, Fort Ridgely State Park; Historic Fort Snelling, St. Paul; James J. Hill House, St. Paul; Jeffers Petroglyphs, Bingham Lake; Oliver H. Kelley Farm, Elk River; Lindbergh House History Center, Little Falls; Lower Sioux Agency History Center, Redwood Falls; Mille Lacs Indian Museum, Onamia; Minnesota History Center, St. Paul; Minnesota State Capitol, St. Paul; North West Company Fur Post, Pine City; Alexander Ramsey House, St. Paul; Split Rock Lighthouse History Center, Two Harbors; Historic Forestville, Preston. Historic Sites owned by MHS & operated by other organizations: W.H.C. Folsom House, Taylors Falls; Harkin Store, New Ulm; Lac qui Parle Mission, Montevideo; Minnehaha Depot, Minneapolis; W.W. Mayo House, Le Sueur; Mill City Museum. Tax-exempt: 501(c)(3).
Historic Site & History Center.
Collections: three-dimensional objects, manuscripts; Minnesota state archives; collections of historic & prehistoric archaeological materials to 19th & 20th-century material culture; paintings; maps; photographs; material documenting & describing the history of Minnesota & the Upper Mississippi Valley & Great Lakes Area.
Research Fields: Minnesota; Upper Mississippi River Valley & Great Lakes area; family history; historic preservation; railroads & transportation; business; organizations; politics; wild ricing; Minnesota communities.
Facilities: 550,000-vol. reference library, research center; 44,000 sq. ft. exhibit space; 24 historic sites; auditorium; classrooms; conservation labs; restaurant. Museum-related items for sale.
Activities: permanent, temporary & traveling exhibits; tours; lectures; conferences; public & school programs.
Publications: quarterly journal; membership newsletter & calendar, monthly newsletter for historical organizations; scholarly & general interest books & pamphlets; Minnesota history textbook for grades 5-7.
Hours & Admission Prices: Museum: Tues. 10-8, Wed.-Sat. 10-5, Sun. 12-5. Adults $8; members no charge. Library: Tues. 12-8, Wed.-Sat. 9-5. Historic Sites: $3-$8. Call for hours & admissions pertaining to individual museums & historic sites. Tel: 612-296-6126 or 800-657-3773. ♿
Attendance: 1,100,000 (estimated)
Membership: Senior Individual $45; Individual & Senior Household $55; Household $65; Associate $125.

MINNESOTA MUSEUM OF AMERICAN ART, (M), 50 Kellogg Blvd. W. #341, Saint Paul, MN 55102-1501. Mailing Address: P.O. Box 75782, Saint Paul, MN 55175-0782. Tel.: 651-266-1030. Fax: 651-291-2947.
E-mail: kmakholm@mmaa.org
Web Site: www.mmaa.org
Founded: 1927.
Congressional District: 4
Key Personnel: Chm. Bd. (V), Dave Kelly; Exec. Dir., Kristin Makholm; Mgr. External Rels., Sarah Suemnig; Cur., Theresa Downing; Visitor Svcs. & Member Coord., Ben Gessner.
Personnel Profile: Full-Time Paid 4; Part-Time Paid 3; Part-Time Volunteers 25.
Governing Authority: nonprofit corporation. Museum: 505 Landmark Center, 75 W. 5th St., St. Paul, MN 55102. Tax-exempt: 501(c)(3), 170(b)(1)(A) & 507(b)(1)(A).
Art Museum.
Collections: American, late 19th- to 20th-century fine art & studio craft with emphasis on art of upper midwest.
Research Fields: contemporary American crafts; drawings; Paul Howard Manship; late 19th & early 20th-century American art; art of upper Midwest.
Facilities: 2,000-vol. research library of source material pertaining to the collections; reference room; classroom; two studios.
Activities: community-based partnership programs; lectures; films; gallery talks; education programs; internships for college students; docent program; inter-museum loan, temporary & traveling exhibitions.
Publications: newsletter; educator curriculum materials; brochures; exhibition catalogs; annual report.
Hours & Admission Prices: Tues.-Wed. & Fri.-Sat. 11-4, Thurs. 11-8, Sun. 1-5. Suggested Donation: $2. Special Exhibitions: adults $5; school groups & members no charge. Closed major holidays. ♿
Attendance: 35,000 (estimated)
Membership: Student & Senior $25; Individual $35; Household $50; Patron $75 and up.

MINNESOTA STATE CAPITOL HISTORIC SITE, 75 Rev. Dr. Martin Luther King Jr. Blvd., Saint Paul, MN 55155-1605. Tel.: 651-296-2881. Fax: 651-297-1502.
E-mail: statecapitol@mnhs.org
Web Site: www.mnhs.org/statecapitol
Founded: 1969.
Key Personnel: Mgr., Brian Pease; Site Supvr., Jaymie Korman; Program Administrative Asst., Candice Christensen.
Personnel Profile: Full-Time Paid 3; Part-Time Paid 22.
Governing Authority: private; nonprofit organization. Parent Institution: Minnesota Historical Society, 345 Kellogg Blvd. W., St. Paul, MN 55101. Tax-exempt: 501(c)(3).
Historic Site: designed by 19th-century architect Cass Gilbert.
Collections: 1905 furniture; canvas murals; paintings; plaques; statues & busts; governor's portraits; historic battle flags.
Research Fields: historical figures; capitol construction labor history; political history; Civil War.
Facilities: cafe. Museum-related items for sale.
Activities: view legislature in action; formal education programs; guided tours; temporary exhibitions. Annual Events: Art, Architecture, Minnesota History, & State Government programs.
Publications: quarterly magazine, Minnesota History.
Hours & Admission Prices: Mon.-Sat. 10-3, Sun. 1-4. Tours: hourly. No charge. Special Events: adults $10-$8, senior citizens $7, children 6-17 $5; discounts to members. Closed holidays. ♿
Attendance: 217,232 (accurate)

Membership: Senior $50; Individual Plus & Senior Household $65; Household $75; Household Plus $95; Associate $145; Contributing $250; Sustaining $500; North Star Circle $1,000.

MINNESOTA TRANSPORTATION MUSEUM, INC., (M), 193 Pennsylvania Ave. E., Saint Paul, MN 55130-4319. Tel.: 651-228-0263, ext. 3104. Fax: 651-293-0857.
E-mail: contact@mtmuseum.org
Web Site: www.mtmuseum.org
Founded: 1962.
Congressional District: 2, 4, 5 & 6
Key Personnel: Dir. & Museum Shop Mgr., Pat Kytola; Chm., Nick Modders; Vice Chm., Chris Bwrda; Sec., Aaron Novodvorsky; Treas., Dave Schultz; Gen. Supt. Railroad, Dick Kolter.
Personnel Profile: Full-Time Paid 1; Full-Time Volunteers 1; Part-Time Paid 1; Part-Time Volunteers 400.
Governing Authority: nonprofit organization. Affiliated with the Minnesota Historical Society. Branch Museums: 114 Depot Rd. Osceola, WI 54020; 193 E. Pennsylvania Ave., St. Paul, MN 55103. Tax-exempt: 501(c)(3).
Operating Transportation Museum.
Collections: 1913 MA & CR Locomotive 100; NP Steam Locomotive 328; 1907 NP Steam Engine 2156; various diesel locomotives, coaches built 1900-1960 for various Minnesota railroad companies.
Research Fields: buses; electric steam & diesel railways of Minnesota & adjacent states.
Facilities: material about railroads, electric lines & buses of Minnesota available on premises.
Activities: guided tours; 10- & 20-mile diesel train rides.
Publications: quarterly magazine, Minnegazette.
Hours & Admission Prices: Minnehaha Depot: Memorial Day-Labor Day Sun. & holidays 12:30-4:30. No charge. Osceola & St. Croix Valley Railway: April to late-Oct. Sat.-Sun. & holidays 11, 1, & 2:30. Adults $10-$15, children $5-$8. Jackson Street Roundhouse: Wed. & Sat. 9-5. Admission $5; discounts to AAM members. ♿
Attendance: 70,000 (estimated)
Membership: Individual $35; Family $50; Sponsoring $250; Sustaining $500.

MINNESOTA VETERINARY HISTORICAL MUSEUM, College of Veterinary Medicine, 1365 Gortner Ave., Rm. 143, Animal Science, Saint Paul, MN 55108-1010. Tel.: 612-625-7770.
Web Site: www.mvma.org/historical_museum.asp
Veterinary Museum.
Collections: veterinary history.
Hours & Admission Prices: Wed. 12-3. No charge. Closed holidays.

THE RAPTOR CENTER, College of Veterinary Medicine, University of Minnesota, 1920 Fitch Ave., Saint Paul, MN 55108-6108. Tel.: 612-624-4745.
E-mail: raptor@umn.edu
Web Site: www.raptor.cvm.umn.edu
Founded: 1974.
Key Personnel: Exec. Dir., Dr. Julia Ponder; Education Program Mgr., Gail Buhl; Veterinarian, Dr. Michelle Willette.
Governing Authority: Parent Institution: University of Minnesota Foundation. Tax-exempt.
Conservation Center.
Collections: eagles, hawks, owls & falcons.
Research Fields: Avian clinical medicine & ecosystem health.
Hours & Admission Prices: Tues.-Fri. 10-4, Sat.-Sun. 12-4. No charge; donations accepted. Closed university holidays.
Attendance: 12,000

THE SCHUBERT CLUB MUSEUM OF MUSICAL INSTRUMENTS, (M), 75 W. 5th St., Ste. 302, Saint Paul, MN 55102-1406. Mailing Address: 302 Landmark Center, 75 W. 5th St., Saint Paul, MN 55102. Tel.: 651-292-3267. Fax: 651-292-4317.
E-mail: jkudrna@schubert.org
Web Site: www.schubert.org
Founded: 1972.
Congressional District: 4
Key Personnel: Exec. Dir., Kathleen van Bergen; Museum Mgr., Jason P. Kudrna.
Personnel Profile: Full-Time Paid 3; Part-Time Paid 7; Interns 1.
Governing Authority: private; nonprofit organization. Parent Institution: The Schubert Club. Tax-exempt: 501(c)(3).
Musical Instruments Museum.
Collections: clavichords; harpsichords; pianos; organs; early piano reproductions; Kugler collection includes instruments from India, Javanese gamelan & early phonographs; Gilman Ordway manuscript collection includes musical manuscripts, letters, signed lithographs & photographs of composers & performers.
Facilities: 507-vol. library.
Activities: concerts; guided tours; lectures; temporary exhibitions.
Hours & Admission Prices: Mon.-Fri. 11-3, Sun. 1-5. No charge. Closed New Years Day; Memorial Day; Independence Day; Labor Day; Thanksgiving; Christmas. ♿
Attendance: 7,000 (accurate)

* **THE SCIENCE MUSEUM OF MINNESOTA,** 120 W. Kellogg Blvd., Saint Paul, MN 55102-1202. Tel.: 651-221-9444. Fax: 651-221-4777.
E-mail: info@smm.org
Web Site: www.smm.org
Founded: 1907.
Congressional District: 4
Key Personnel: Chm. Bd. (V), Richard C. Kelly; Pres., Eric Jolly, Ph.D.; Vice Pres. External Rels., Kathleen A. Wilson; Vice Pres. Finance & Admin., Duane J. Kocik; Vice Pres. Education, David Chittenden; Vice Pres. Mktg., Communications & Sales, Jane Eastwood; Senior Vice Pres., Mike Day; Dir. Devel., Leslie Cook; Vice Pres. Exhibits, Paul Martin; Cur. Paleontology, Dr. Kristi Curry Rogers; Div. Head Research & Collections, Ron Lawrenz; Museum Shop Mgr., Steve Fegley.
Personnel Profile: Full-Time Paid 333; Full-Time Volunteers 750; Part-Time Volunteers 796; Interns 21.
Governing Authority: nonprofit organization. Tax-exempt: 501(c)(3).
Science Museum.
Collections: over 1,500,000 catalogued specimens in the fields of biology, anthropology, paleontology, geology.
Research Fields: ethnology; paleontology; biology; zoology; archaeology; geology; geography.
Facilities: Lee & Rose Warner Nature Center; St. Croix Watershed Research Station; William L. McKnight-3M Omnitheater; Explore Store offering science oriented materials.
Activities: lectures; films; hobby workshops; formally organized education programs for children, adults, undergraduate, & graduate college students; volunteer program; permanent, temporary & school loan exhibits; exhibit hall demonstration programs; astronomy programs; outdoor education programs; Omnitheater programs.
Publications: membership newsletter; online newsletter for teachers; magazine, Big Frame; scientific publications, New Series; Monograph Series.
Hours & Admission Prices: Sun.-Wed. 9:30-5, Thurs.-Sat. 9:30-9. Combination Pass: adults $17, senior citizens 60 and over & children 4-12 $14.50. ♿
Attendance: 740,663 (accurate)
Membership: Senior $64; Dual $69; Household $89.

UNIVERSITY SAINT THOMAS ART HISTORY, (M), Mail 57P, 2115 Summit Ave., Saint Paul, MN 55105-1089. Tel.: 651-962-5560. Fax: 651-962-5861.
Web Site: www.stthomas.edu/arthistory
Founded: 1978.
Key Personnel: Chm. Art Historian, Mark Stansbury-O'Donnell; Chief Cur. & Clinical Faculty, Shelly Nordtorp-Madson.
Personnel Profile: Full-Time Paid 2; Interns 4.
Governing Authority: Parent Institution: University of St. Thomas. Tax-exempt.
History & College Graduate Teaching Museum.
Collections: 20th-century American art; videos; oil paintings.
Research Fields: European; African; Colonial; Latin America; Scandinavian textiles; Pacific; textiles.
Facilities: education center.
Activities: graduate program in art history.
Publications: art history newsletter.
Hours & Admission Prices: Mon.-Sat. 9am-10pm, Sun. 12-10. No charge. Closed major holidays. ♿
Attendance: 3,500 (estimated)

WARM (WOMEN'S ART REGISTRY OF MINNESOTA), 550 Rice St., Saint Paul, MN 55103-2116. Tel.: 651-292-1188.
E-mail: info@thewarm.org
Web Site: www.thewarm.org
Founded: 1976.
Congressional District: 5
Key Personnel: Pres. (V), Nicola Dixon.
Personnel Profile: Part-Time Paid 2; Part-Time Volunteers 50.
Governing Authority: nonprofit organization. Tax-exempt: 501(c)(3).
Art Association.
Collections: works by women artists.

Research Fields: women artists of the United States, especially the upper Midwest.
Facilities: on-line members slide registry.
Activities: guided tours; lectures; gallery talks; community based exhibitions; poetry readings; films; performances; slide talks; workshops; mentor program; monthly artist meeting; temporary exhibitions.
Publications: catalogs, Private Collectors & Art by Women; Warm: A Landmark Exhibition; Harmony Hammond: Ten Years, 1970-1980; Structure & Metaphor: Six Contemporary Visions; Women's Sensibilities: A Regional Juried Exhibition.
Hours & Admission Prices: Call for schedule. ♿
Membership: Student & Protegee $30; Individual $60.

Saint Peter

E. ST. JULIEN COX HOUSE, 500 N. Washington Ave., Saint Peter, MN 56082-1979. Mailing Address: 1851 N. Minnesota Ave., Saint Peter, MN 56082-1727. Tel.: 507-934-2160 & 4309. Fax: 507-934-0172.
E-mail: museum@nchsmn.org
Web Site: www.nchsmn.org
Formerly: Nicollet County Historical Society: E. St. Julien Cox House
Founded: 1928.
Congressional District: 2
Key Personnel: C.E.O., Ben Leonard; Pres. (V), Garfield Eckberg.
Personnel Profile: Full-Time Paid 1; Part-Time Volunteers 8; Interns 2.
Governing Authority: society; nonprofit. Parent Institution: Nicollet County Historical Society. Tax-exempt: 501(c)(3).
Historic House: c.1871 Gothic/Italianate style architecture was built by E. St. Julien Cox, a prominent lawyer & judge.
Collections: household goods; 1880s Victorian furniture; Cox family items; glassware; clothing; linens; art.
Research Fields: wallpaper & wood-working of the house; Victorian gardens.
Facilities: 50-vol. library containing Judge Cox's law & family books.
Activities: guided tours. Museum Sponsors: Christmas Teas in December; Christmas at the Cox House features holiday decor & old time traditions in December.
Publications: newsletter, The Crossing.
Hours & Admission Prices: Memorial Day-Labor Day Thurs.-Sat. 10-4; other times by appointment. Adults $3, youth 13-18 $.50; discounts to groups; children 12 & under no charge.
Attendance: 1,000 (accurate)
Membership: Students $10; Individual $30; Family $45; Sustaining $75; Patron $100; Supporting $200; Benefactor $500; Life $1,000.

HILLSTROM MUSEUM OF ART, (M), 800 W. College Ave., Saint Peter, MN 56082-1485. Tel.: 507-933-7171. Fax: 507-933-7205.
E-mail: dmyers@gustavus.edu
Web Site: www.gustavus.edu/oncampus/finearts/hillstrom/index.html
Founded: 2000.
Congressional District: 1
Key Personnel: Dir., Donald Myers.
Personnel Profile: Part-Time Paid 2.
Governing Authority: private college. Tax-exempt: 501(c)(3).
College Art Museum.
Collections: works by regional, national & international artists.
Major Exhibits: Connected with Water (Paintings by Gudrun Westerland), 11/23/09-1/29/10; Swedish-American Works from the Hillstrom Collection, 11/23/09-1/29/10; Focus In/On: Henry Schnackenberg's Dominoes, 11/23/09-1/29/10; Elmyr de Hory, Artist and Faker, 2/15/10-4/18/10; Senior Studio Art Majors Exhibition, 5/1/10-5/30/10.
Facilities: 3,900 sq. ft. exhibit space.
Activities: loan & temporary exhibitions.
Hours & Admission Prices: Mon.-Fri. 9-4, Sat.-Sun. 1-5. No charge. Closed New Year's Day; Easter; Thanksgiving; Christmas; academic breaks.
Attendance: 5,300 (accurate)

NICOLLET COUNTY HISTORICAL SOCIETY, 1851 N. Minnesota Ave., Saint Peter, MN 56082-1727. Tel.: 507-934-2160. Fax: 507-934-0172.
E-mail: museum@nchsmn.org
Web Site: www.nchsmn.org
Formerly: Treaty Site History Center
Founded: 1928.
Congressional District: 2
Key Personnel: C.E.O., Ben Leonard; Pres. (V), Gary Schmidt; Harkin Store Mgr., Ruth Grewe.
Personnel Profile: Full-Time Paid 2; Part-Time Paid 14; Part-Time Volunteers 20; Interns 3.
Governing Authority: society; nonprofit. Parent Institution: Nicollet County Historical Society, Inc. Branch Museum: E. St. Julien Cox House, St. Peter, MN 56082. Tax-exempt: 501(c)(3).
History Museum.
Collections: Nicollet County history; photographs; clothing; tools; household accessories; Civil War & World War II military; Native American & pioneer memorabilia; Native American clothing; Dakota history.
Research Fields: Nicollet County, Minnesota with special focus on the Treaty of 1851 between the Dakota Nation and the US government and how it affected the boundaries and all the people of Minnesota.
Facilities: 1,115-vol. library; archives contain manuscripts, photos & family histories of Nicollet County residents.
Activities: guided tours; organized education programs for children.
Publications: books, Early History of Nicollet County, Nicollet County Bicentennial Historic Markers, Old Traverse des Sioux: A History; quarterly newsletter, The Crossing,
Hours & Admission Prices: Tues.-Sat. 10-4, Sun. 1-4; other times & tours by appointment. Adults $4, children 6-18 $2; discounts to NCHS & AAM members; children 5 and under & members no charge. Combination Pass: E. Julien Cox House and Treaty Site History Center $6. ♿
Attendance: 5,000 (accurate)
Membership: Individual $30; Family $45; Sustaining $75; Patron $100; Business $200; Benefactor $500; Life $1,000.

WILLIAM & JOAN SODERLUND PHARMACY MUSEUM, 201 S. Third St., Saint Peter, MN 56082-2044. Mailing Address: P.O. Box 498, Saint Peter, MN 56082-0498. Tel.: 800-603-8196 (Toll Free); 507-931-4410. Fax: 507-931-5434.
E-mail: bsoderlund@hickorytech.net
Web Site: www.villagedrug.com/index.php
Pharmacy Museum.
Collections: American pharmacy history; period drugs; pharmacy history; drug store furnishings; soda fountain memorabilia; show globes.
Hours & Admission Prices: Mon.-Fri. 8:30-7, Sat. 8:30-2.

Sauk Centre

SINCLAIR LEWIS BOYHOOD HOME & INTERPRETIVE CENTER/MUSEUM, Interpretive Center Museum, 1220 Main St. S., Sauk Centre, MN 56378. Mailing Address: P.O. Box 25, Sauk Centre, MN 56378-0222. Tel.: 320-352-5201. Fax: 320-352-5202.
E-mail: chamber@saukcentrechamber.com
Web Site: www.saukcentrechamber.com
Founded: 1960.
Congressional District: 7
Key Personnel: Pres. (V) & Dir., Colleen Steffes.
Personnel Profile: Part-Time Paid 2; Part-Time Volunteers 10.
Governing Authority: nonprofit organization. Affiliated with the Sinclair Lewis Foundation. Sinclair Lewis House Museum, 810 Sinclair Lewis Ave., Sauk Centre, MN 56378. Tax-exempt: 501(c)(3).
Historic House Museum: 1920 boyhood home of Sinclair Lewis.
Collections: House: books written by Sinclair Lewis; family furnishings & memorabilia; manuscripts. Center: family history; family artifacts; video presentation.
Facilities: library of English & foreign editions of novels by Sinclair Lewis; interpretive center. Museum-related items for sale.
Activities: Interpretive Center: video presentation. Sinclair Lewis House: guided tours; permanent exhibitions.
Hours & Admission Prices: Interpretive Center: Memorial Day-Labor Day Mon.-Fri. 8:30-4:30, Sat.-Sun. 9-5. House: June to Sept. 1 Tues.-Sat. 1-5. Interpretive Center: no charge, donations accepted. House Tours: adults & students $5, children 6-12 $2; discounts for AAA members; children 5 & under no charge. Call to confirm.
Attendance: 4,479 (accurate)
Membership: Senior Citizen $8; Single $12; Couple $14; Business & Organization $25.

Saum

FIRST CONSOLIDATED SCHOOL IN MINNESOTA, Saum Community Club, 41982 Pioneer Rd., N.E., Saum, MN 56650. Mailing Address: 12956 Twin Oaks Rd., N.E., Kelliher, MN 56650-9404. Tel.: 218-647-8531.
Founded: 1962.
Congressional District: 7
Key Personnel: Sec., Eva Stengel; Treas., Ione Smischney.
Personnel Profile: Part-Time Volunteers 10.
Governing Authority: board of directors; society. Saum Community Club. Affiliated with Beltrami Historical Society, P.O. Box 683, 130 Minnesota Ave. S.W., Bemidji, MN 56619. Tax-exempt.
History Museum.
Collections: desks; pictures; fixtures; books & other school furnishings. Historic Buildings: 1903 original log school; 1912 Saum School; 1912 first new Consolidated School in MN.
Facilities: school books available for research on premises.

Activities: guided tours.
Hours & Admission Prices: Open by request only. No charge; donations accepted. ♿
Attendance: 200 (estimated)
Membership: Individual $5.

Shakopee

THE LANDING - MINNESOTA RIVER HERITAGE PARK, 2187 E. Hwy. 101, Shakopee, MN 55379-1750. Tel.: 763-694-7784. Fax: 952-403-9489.
Formerly: Historic Murphy's Landing
Founded: 1969.
Governing Authority: Parent Institution: Three Rivers Park District.
Living History Museum.
Collections: local history & culture; period furnishings; historic buildings.
Facilities: 88-acre park.
Activities: special events; rental facilities; educational programs.
Hours & Admission Prices: May 23-Sept. 7 Mon.-Fri. 10-4, Sat. & holidays 10-5, Sun. 12-5. Adults $8.50, seniors & youth 3-11 $7.

SCOTT COUNTY HISTORICAL SOCIETY, 235 S. Fuller St., Shakopee, MN 55379-1320. Tel.: 952-445-0378; 888-325-2575. Fax: 952-445-4154.
Founded: 1968.
Personnel Profile: Full-Time Paid 2; Part-Time Volunteers 30; Interns 3.
Historical Society Museum.
Collections: Scott County Minnesota history; books; photographs; period artifacts; newspapers; local history; historic house.
Major Exhibits: Read All About It: 1950s Newspaper Headlines in Scott County, 11/09-8/10; Textiles, 11/09-3/10; St. John's Bible Prints, 4/10-5/10; Great Scott: Mysteries of Scott County, 6/10-12/10; Scott County: Greatest Generation, 9/10-8/11.
Facilities: gardens.
Activities: educational programs; special events; permanent exhibitions.
Publications: quarterly newsletter.
Hours & Admission Prices: Tues.-Wed. & Fri. 9-4, Thurs. 9-8, Sat. 10-3. Adults $4, students $2; members & children under 5 no charge. Closed major holidays. ♿
Attendance: 8,217 (accurate)
Membership: Individual $15; Household $25; Sponsor $50; Business $100.

Shevlin

CLEARWATER COUNTY HISTORICAL SOCIETY, 264 1st St. W., Shevlin, MN 56676. Mailing Address: P.O. Box 241, Bagley, MN 56621-0241. Tel.: 218-785-2000. Fax: 218-785-2440.
E-mail: cchshist@gvtel.com
Web Site: mnhistoricnw.org
Founded: 1968.
Congressional District: 7
Key Personnel: C.E.O., James Michel; Museum Shop Mgr., Tamara Edevold.
Personnel Profile: Full-Time Paid 1; Part-Time Paid 2; Part-Time Volunteers 8.
Governing Authority: board of directors; nonprofit organization. Tax-exempt.
Local History Museum.
Collections: agriculture; timber; lumbering; newspapers; military. Historic Buildings: 1895 Gran church; 1890 log school, log house, WPA-built school, Great Northern Depot.
Major Exhibits: MoMS Between Fences (T), 5/10-6/10.
Research Fields: early history; forestry; biology; clarification.
Activities: tours; art shows.
Publications: quarterly newsletter, Clearwater History News.
Hours & Admission Prices: May-Aug. Tues.-Fri. 10-4, Sat. 10-2; Sept.-April Tues.-Fri. 10-4. No charge; donations accepted. Closed Christmas week. ♿
Attendance: 1,300 (estimated)
Membership: Individual $10; Family $15; Patron $25; Sustaining $50 & up; Benefactor $100 & up.

Slayton

MURRAY COUNTY HISTORICAL MUSEUM, 2480 29th St., Slayton, MN 56172. Mailing Address: P.O. Box 61, Slayton, MN 56172-0061. Tel.: 507-836-6533.
Key Personnel: Dir., Diane Clerex
History Museum.
Collections: early radios & phonographs; period farm wagon, tools & machinery; Native American artifacts; family histories; newspapers; census records; military artifacts from Civil War to WWII; naturalization records.
Hours & Admission Prices: Feb.-March Tues.-Thurs. 10-5; April-Dec. Mon.-Fri. 10-5. No charge; donations accepted. Closed holidays. ♿

Sleepy Eye

SLEEPY EYE DEPOT MUSEUM, 100 Oak St., N.W., Sleepy Eye, MN 56085. Mailing Address: P.O. Box 544, Sleepy Eye, MN 56085-0544. Tel.: 507-794-5053.
E-mail: semuseum@sleepyeyetel.net
Web Site: www.sleepyeyeareahistoricalsociety.art.officelive.com
Railroad Depot Museum: listed on the National Register of Historic Places.
Collections: railroad history; Sleepy Eye artifacts; Sleepy Eye Drum & Bugle Corps. memorabilia.
Hours & Admission Prices: May-Nov. 15 Tues.-Sat. 10-4; other times by appointment. No charge; donations accepted. ♿
Membership: Lone Eagle (Single) $15; Band (Family) $25; Trading Post (Business) $30; Buffalo Blanket (Giver of Warmth) $100; Great Teepee Maker (Shelter Giver) $500; The Turtle Mother Earth (Strength of Earth) $1,000.

Soudan

SOUDAN UNDERGROUND MINE STATE PARK, 1379 Stuntz Bay Rd., Soudan, MN 55782. Mailing Address: P.O. Box 335, Soudan, MN 55782-0335. Tel.: 218-753-2245.
E-mail: soudprk.dnr@state.mn.us
Web Site: www.dnr.state.mn.us/state_parks/soudan_underground_mine/index.html
Historic Site & Underground Mine.
Collections: dry house; drill shop; crusher house; engine house; mining equipment & artifacts.
Hours & Admission Prices: Underground Mine Tour & High Energy Physics Lab Tour: call for hours & admission prices. ♿

South Saint Paul

DAKOTA COUNTY HISTORICAL SOCIETY, (M), Lawshe Memorial Museum, 130 3rd Ave., N., South Saint Paul, MN 55075-2002. Tel.: 651-552-7548. Fax: 651-552-7265.
E-mail: dakotahistory@co.dakota.mn.us
Web Site: www.dakotahistory.org
Founded: 1939.
Congressional District: 1, 3 & 4
Key Personnel: Exec. Dir., Chad Roberts; Pres. (V), Bill Wolston; Museum Shop Mgr., Heidi Langenfeld.
Personnel Profile: Full-Time Paid 2; Part-Time Paid 12; Part-Time Volunteers 95; Interns 2.
Governing Authority: board of directors. Subsidiary Institution: LeDuc Historic Estate, 1629 Vermillion St., Hastings, MN 55033. Tax-exempt.
Historical Society Museum.
Collections: Indian artifacts; agriculture; trades & industry items; railroading; Civil War items; World War I & II items; genealogical records; maps; newspapers.
Research Fields: Dakota County history.
Facilities: 1,000-vol. research center containing all county newspapers on microfilm.
Activities: guided tours; traveling exhibits; lectures; living history events; permanent exhibitions; art & craft shows.
Publications: Three-year magazine, Over the Years; Three-year newsletter, Preserving Our History.
Hours & Admission Prices: Wed. & Fri. 9-5, Thurs. 9-8, Sat. 10-3. Lawshe: no charge; donations accepted. LeDuc: mid-June to Oct. Wed.-Sat. 10-5, Sun. 1-5. Tours at 10, 11:30, 1, 2:30 & 4. Adults $6, seniors & military $5, students $3; members no charge. Closed national holidays. ♿
Attendance: 13,000 (accurate)
Membership: Individual $30; Family $50; Sustaining $100; Silver $250; Gold $500; Tower $1,000.

Spring Valley

SPRING VALLEY COMMUNITY HISTORICAL SOCIETY, INC., 220 W. Courtland St., Spring Valley, MN 55975-1232. Tel.: 507-346-7659.
E-mail: wilderinspringvalley@hotmail.com
Web Site: springvalleymnmuseum.org
Founded: 1956.
Congressional District: 1
Key Personnel: Pres. (V), Joseph Bezdicek; Vice Pres., Clarence Klenke.
Personnel Profile: Part-Time Paid 8; Part-Time Volunteers 3.
Governing Authority: society. Tax-exempt.
Pioneer History Museum, A Laura Ingalls Wilder site.
Collections: History Museum: pioneer artifacts. Church Museum: Wilder family photos; religious artifacts, Conley Camera collection. Historic Buildings: 1875-76 Methodist Church Museum; 1860 era Washburn-Zittleman House.

Facilities: Museum-related items for sale.
Activities: guided tours; video tour of church & house museum; formally organized education program for children.
Publications: History of the Methodist Church; History of Village of Washington, Fillmore County; 125-year History of Spring Valley, Minnesota; Spring Valley; The Laura Ingalls Wilder Connection.
Hours & Admission Prices: June-Aug. daily 10-4; Sept.-Oct. Sat.-Sun.; May-Oct. by appointment for groups. Church: adults $4, students $1.50. All Buildings: adults $6, students $2.50; members no charge.
Attendance: 2,500 (accurate)
Membership: Individual $10; Couple & Family $20; Life $100.

St. Louis Park

PAVEK MUSEUM OF BROADCASTING, 3515 Raleigh Ave., St. Louis Park, MN 55416-2625. Tel.: 952-926-8198. Fax: 952-929-6105.
Web Site: www.museumofbroadcasting.org
Founded: 1986.
Congressional District: 5
Key Personnel: Dir. & Chm. (V), Jeffrey T. Bakken.
Personnel Profile: Full-Time Paid 4; Part-Time Paid 2; Part-Time Volunteers 5.
Governing Authority: Tax-exempt.
Technology Museum.
Collections: period radio, television, & broadcast equipment; history of broadcasting.
Facilities: Museum-related items for sale.
Activities: special events.
Publications: newsletter, Pavek Museum of Broadcasting.
Hours & Admission Prices: Tues.-Fri. 10-6, Sat. 9-5; other times by appointment. Adults $6, students & senior citizens $5. Closed holidays.
Attendance: 10,053 (accurate)
Membership: Senior & Student $20; Individual $30; Household $45; Corporate $100.

Stillwater

WASHINGTON COUNTY HISTORICAL SOCIETY WARDEN'S HOUSE MUSEUM, 602 N. Main St., Stillwater, MN 55082-4010. Mailing Address: P.O. Box 167, Stillwater, MN 55082-0167. Tel.: 651-439-5956.
E-mail: brent.peterson@wchsmn.org
Web Site: www.wchsmn.org
Founded: 1941.
Key Personnel: Pres., Monica Fogg; Historic Sites Supvr., Kirsta Benson; Exec. Dir., Brent Peterson.
Personnel Profile: Full-Time Paid 2; Part-Time Paid 1; Part-Time Volunteers 10; Interns 3.
Governing Authority: society; nonprofit organization. Tax-exempt: 501(c)(3).
History Museum: located in 1853 former State Prison Warden's Home.
Collections: lumberjack tools; pictures; costumes; Indian artifacts; military; quilts; furniture; glassware; pottery; children's toys & games; prison artifacts; manuscript collections.
Research Fields: Washington County history, prison history, rural schools, military & lumber company history.
Facilities: 500-vol. library of Minnesota and St. Croix River Valley history books available for use on premises; research department; 15,000 photos of area & residents.
Activities: guided & cemetery tours; vintage baseball club; temporary exhibitions.
Publications: brochure, Washington County Historical Museum, History of the Walden's House Museum; quarterly, Historical Whisperings; book, Washington: A History of the County, Pioneers of the Big Lake Community, Minnesota Beginnings.
Hours & Admission Prices: May-Oct. Thurs.-Sun. 1-5; tours by appointment. Adults $5, children 6-17 $1; discounts to AAA members; members no charge. ♿
Attendance: 5,000 (accurate)
Membership: Seniors $10; Adult $15; Family $25; Patron $50; Sustaining $100; Life $500.

Taylors Falls

THE FOLSOM HOUSE MUSEUM, 272 W. Government Rd., Taylors Falls, MN 55084. Mailing Address: Box 333, Taylors Falls, MN 55084-0333. Tel.: 651-465-3125.
Formerly: The Historic W.H.C. Folsom House
Founded: 1978.
Congressional District: 8
Key Personnel: Site Mgr., William W. Scott; Pres., Sandra Berg.
Personnel Profile: Full-Time Volunteers 1; Part-Time Volunteers 45.
Governing Authority: society; nonprofit organization. Parent Institution: Minnesota Historical Society. Subsidiary Institution: Taylor Falls Historical Society. Branch Museums: 1852 Town House School. Tax-exempt.
Historic House: 1854-55 Historic Folsom House.
Collections: original Folsom family furniture; complete collection of ledgers & day books from Folsom General Store 1851-1876; passenger & cargo journals from Folsom Steamboats.
Research Fields: local history.
Activities: guided tours. Annual Event: Christmas Lighting Festival in November.
Publications: brochure; biannual, Life & Times in Taylor Falls; book, Fifty Years in the Northwest, a sesquicentennial edition of WHC Folsoms book first published in 1888.
Hours & Admission Prices: Memorial Day to mid-Oct. Wed.-Mon. 1-4:30. Adults $4, students 6-12 $1; discounts to groups over 15; members, Minnesota Historical Society & Taylor Falls Historical Society members no charge.
Attendance: 4,000 (estimated)
Membership: Taylors Falls Historical Society: Individual $15; Household $25; Patron $35; Sustaining $100 & up.

Tofte

NORTH SHORE COMMERCIAL FISHING MUSEUM, 7136 Hwy. 61, Junction of Sawbill Trail & Hwy. 61, Tofte, MN 55615. Mailing Address: P.O. Box 2312, Tofte, MN 55615-2312.
Fishing Museum.
Collections: maritime customs & history; commercial fishing industry.
Activities: special events; educational programs.
Hours & Admission Prices: April-Dec. 1 daily 9-5. Adult $3, children 6-16 $1; children under 6 no charge. ♿

Tower

BOIS FORTE HERITAGE CENTER, 1500 Bois Fort Rd., Tower, MN 55790-7800. Tel.: 218-753-6017.
E-mail: rberens@boisforte-NSN.gov
Web Site: boisforte.com/divisions/heritage_center.htm
Key Personnel: Dir. & Historic Preservation Officer, Rose Berens; Cur., William Latady; Gift Shop Supvr., Bev Miller; Interpreter, Rhonda Zuponcic
History Museum.
Collections: Bois Forte Ojibwe Indian history & culture.
Hours & Admission Prices: Call for hours. Adults $5, seniors & children 4-12 $3; children 3 & under and Bois Forte Band members no charge.

Two Harbors

LAKE COUNTY HISTORICAL SOCIETY, 520 South Ave., Depot Bldg., Two Harbors, MN 55616. Mailing Address: P.O. Box 128, Two Harbors, MN 55616-0128. Tel.: 218-834-4898. Fax: 218-834-7198.
E-mail: lakehist@lakenet.com
Web Site: lakecountyhistoricalsociety.org
Founded: 1925.
Congressional District: 8
Key Personnel: C.E.O., Richard Tokarczyk; Pres. (V), Ann Zastera.
Personnel Profile: Full-Time Paid 3; Part-Time Paid 25; Part-Time Volunteers 10.
Governing Authority: self. Tax-exempt: 501(c)(3).
History Museum & Historic Site.
Collections: local manuscripts; photographs on railroading, iron ore, lumbering; mineral collections; shipping & shipwreck artifacts. Depot Museum: general local history museum highlighting 1st shipment of iron ore from Minnesota; veterans room commemorating veterans 1800 on; two steam engines on display outside; 3M/Owan Museum, highlighting creation of Minnesota Mining & Manufacturing and the development & uses of its first successful product, sandpaper; 1892 Lighthouse & Harbor Museum, at Two Harbors Light Station, highlighting historical use & relationship to Lake Superior, commercial fishing, shipping iron ore, development of harbor; Edna G. Tugboat built in 1896, tour one of the last 3 steam powered coal burning tugs left in the U.S.
Research Fields: local oral histories; commercial fishing.
Facilities: 20-vol. library of historical manuscripts available for research on premises.
Activities: guided tours; permanent exhibitions; community education programs.
Publications: quarterly newsletter.
Hours & Admission Prices: May-Sept. daily 10-5; other times by appointment. Lighthouse 9-5 & 6-9. Adults $2.50, youth 9-17 $1; discounts to groups, AAM & ICOM members; children under 8 & members no charge. ♿
Attendance: 38,000 (estimated)
Membership: Individual $15; Family $25.

SPLIT ROCK LIGHTHOUSE HISTORIC SITE, 3713 Split Rock Lighthouse Rd., Two Harbors, MN 55616-2020. Tel.: 218-226-6372. Fax: 218-226-6373.
E-mail: splitrock@mnhs.org
Web Site: www.mnhs.org
Founded: 1976.
Congressional District: 8
Key Personnel: Dir., Lee Radzak; Museum Shop Mgr., Gloria Rosenau.
Personnel Profile: Full-Time Paid 4; Part-Time Paid 30.
Governing Authority: society; nonprofit. Parent Institution: Minnesota Historical Society. Tax-exempt.
Historic Site: located on 25 acres, site of 1910 Split Rock Light Station.
Collections: marine navigation.
Research Fields: U.S. Lighthouse service & marine aids to navigation relating to the Split Rock Lighthouse.
Facilities: library including records of the U.S. Lighthouse; 90-seat theater. Gift items for sale.
Activities: guided tours; films. Annual Events: Open House; interpretation, 1925 light station.
Publications: booklet, Split Rock: Epoch of a Lighthouse.
Hours & Admission Prices: mid-May to mid-Oct. daily 10-6. Visitors Center: Winter Sat.-Sun. 11-4. Adults $8, senior citizens $6, children 6-17 $5; children 5 & under, Minnesota Historical Society members no charge. State Park vehicle permit $7. Closed winter holidays.
Attendance: 101,000 (accurate)
Membership: Minnesota Historical Society: Senior $45; Individual $55; Senior Household $55; Household $65; Associate $125.

Victoria

LOWRY NATURE CENTER, 7025 Victoria Dr., Victoria, MN 55386-9668. Tel.: 763-694-7650.
Web Site: www.threeriversparkdistrict.org/outdoor_ed/center_lowry.cfm
Nature Center.
Collections: native plants & wildlife.
Hours & Admission Prices: Call for hours.

Wabasha

NATIONAL EAGLE CENTER, 50 Pembroke Ave., Wabasha, MN 55981-1241. Mailing Address: P.O. Box 242, Wabasha, MN 55981-0242. Tel.: 651-868-4989; 877-332-4537. Fax: 651-565-5357.
E-mail: marybeth@nationaleaglecenter.org
Web Site: nationaleaglecenter.org
Key Personnel: Dir. Programming & Public Rels., MaryBeth Garrigan; Administrative Mgr., Catherine Cushing
Nature Center.
Collections: Bald Eagles & their habitats; Native American artifacts; preserved wildlife.
Facilities: classrooms. Museum-related items for sale.
Activities: feeding programs; observation decks.
Hours & Admission Prices: March-Nov. Mon.-Thurs. 10-5, Fri.-Sun. 9-6; Dec.-Feb. daily 10-5. Adults $6, seniors 65 & over $5, students 4-17 $4; children under 3 & members no charge.

Wabasso

COUNTY CENTER HISTORICAL SOCIETY, 564 South St., Wabasso, MN 56293. Mailing Address: 1177 Duey St., Wabasso, MN 56293. Tel.: 507-342-5367.
Formerly: Wabasso Center Historical Society
Founded: 1973.
Congressional District: 2
Key Personnel: Pres., Armin Dallman; Treas., Merlln J. Goudy.
Personnel Profile: Part-Time Paid 1; Part-Time Volunteers 1.
Governing Authority: society; nonprofit organization. Tax-exempt.
Historic Society Museum: housed in 1903 Knox Presbyterian Church.
Collections: household items; farm implements; books; pictures; rocks; guns; old newspapers.
Research Fields: sod houses; old artifacts.
Activities: guided tours; arts festivals; formally organized education programs for children; permanent exhibitions.
Hours & Admission Prices: Summer Wed.-Sun. 1-5; other times & tours by appointment. No charge; donations accepted. ♿
Attendance: 75
Membership: Individual $3.

Waconia

CARVER COUNTY HISTORICAL SOCIETY, 555 W. 1st St., Waconia, MN 55387-1221. Tel.: 952-442-4234. Fax: 952-442-2435.
E-mail: historical@co.carver.mn.us
Web Site: www.carvercountyhistoricalsociety.org/index.htm
Founded: 1940.
Congressional District: 3
Key Personnel: Exec. Dir., Wendy Biorn.
Personnel Profile: Full-Time Paid 3; Part-Time Paid 5; Part-Time Volunteers 20; Interns 1.
Governing Authority: society. Tax-exempt.
History Museum.
Collections: pioneer agricultural tools; household tools; county business items; photographs; documents.
Research Fields: Carver county history; biography.
Facilities: microfilm reader/printer; microfilmed county newspapers; newspaper indexes; census records; printed material.
Activities: guided tours; historical research; seminars.
Publications: quarterly newsletter.
Hours & Admission Prices: Mon.-Fri. 10-4:30, Sat. 10-3; groups by appointment. No charge; donations accepted. ♿
Attendance: 4,200 (accurate)
Membership: Senior Citizen $10; Individual $15; Family $25; Sustaining $50.

Walker

CASS COUNTY MUSEUM & RESEARCH CENTER, 205 Minnesota Ave. W., Walker, MN 56484-2189. Mailing Address: P.O. Box 505, Walker, MN 56484-0505. Tel.: 218-547-7251.
Formerly: Cass County Museum & Pioneer School
Founded: 1937.
Key Personnel: Pres., Dan Eikenberry; Dir., Renee Geving; Vice Pres., Lois Orton.
Personnel Profile: Part-Time Paid 2; Part-Time Volunteers 8.
Governing Authority: Cass County Historical Society. Tax-exempt.
History Museum.
Collections: Indian handicraft & artifacts, mainly Ojibway/Chippewa.
Research Fields: Ojibway/Chippewa & Sioux artifacts from late 1800s to early 1900s.
Activities: guided tours.
Hours & Admission Prices: Memorial Day-Labor Day Mon.-Fri. 10-5. Families $9, adults $4, children $1; discounts to groups with reservations. ♿
Attendance: 2,500 (estimated)
Membership: Single $10; Family $15; Benefactor $20; Business $50; Friend $100-$249; Sponsor $250-$999; Patron $1,000.

Walnut Grove

LAURA INGALLS WILDER MUSEUM AND TOURIST CENTER, 330 8th St., Walnut Grove, MN 56180-1114. Tel.: 507-859-2358. Fax: 507-859-2933.
E-mail: lauramuseum@walnutgrove.org
Web Site: www.walnutgrove.org
Founded: 1974.
Congressional District: 2
Key Personnel: Pres., Mary Jo Hendrickson; Dir., Amy Ankrum; Treas., Wilbur Oberg; Collections Mgr., Nicole Elzenga.
Personnel Profile: Full-Time Paid 2; Part-Time Paid 6; Part-Time Volunteers 14.
Governing Authority: nonprofit organization. Tax-exempt.
General Museum: housed in c.1894 railroad station.
Collections: Walnut Grove history; Laura Ingalls Wilder memorabilia; quilts; furniture; toys; complete printing press; 250 dolls from 1860-1980s; native Minnesota grass & flowers. Historic House: 1890 house with three pre-1920s furnished rooms & doll museum with over 250 exhibits.
Research Fields: Walnut Grove history.
Facilities: Museum-related items for sale.
Activities: self guided tours.
Publications: brochures; fan club newsletter; book, Walnut Grove Story.
Hours & Admission Prices: April & Oct. Mon.-Sat. 10-4, Sun. 12-4; May & Sept. Mon.-Sat. 10-5, Sun. 12-5; June-Aug. daily 10-6. Adults $5, children 6-12 $2; members & children 5 and under no charge. ♿
Attendance: 17,500 (accurate)
Membership: Individual $10; Couple Annual $15; Family $20; Lifetime $100 & up.

Warren

MARSHALL COUNTY HISTORICAL SOCIETY MUSEUM, 808 E. Johnson Ave., Warren, MN 56762. Mailing Address: P.O. Box 103, Warren, MN 56762-0103. Tel.: 218-745-4803.
E-mail: mchs@wiktel.com
Founded: 1933.
Congressional District: 7
Key Personnel: C.E.O. & Pres. (V), Delvin Potucek; Dir., Cur. & Museum Shop Mgr., Ethel Thorlacius.
Personnel Profile: Part-Time Paid 2; Part-Time Volunteers 9.
Governing Authority: county; nonprofit organization. Tax-exempt.
Historical Society Museum.
Collections: period farm machinery; business & household artifacts. Historic Buildings: 1886 log cabin; c.1880s schoolhouse; 1893 church; 1905 Soo line depot.
Research Fields: local history; agriculture.
Activities: Museum Sponsors: annual County Fair in July; Old Time School Days tour for 5th graders in September; monthly programs on historical topics.
Publications: self Portrait of Marshall County. book: Do you believe in UFO's History of the Old Mill State Park.
Hours & Admission Prices: May-Sept. Wed.-Fri. 9-5, Sat.-Sun. by appointment. No charge; donations accepted. Closed major holidays. ♿
Attendance: 2,100 (estimated)
Membership: Singles $10; Family $15.

Waseca

FARMAMERICA, THE MINNESOTA AGRICULTURAL INTERPRETIVE CENTER, 7367 360th Ave., Waseca, MN 56093-4414. Tel.: 507-835-2052. Fax: 507-835-2053.
E-mail: farmamer@hickorytech.net
Web Site: farmamerica.org
Founded: 1978.
Congressional District: 26
Key Personnel: Chm. Bd. (V), Ed Frederick; Exec. Dir., Harlan Holmquist; Office Mgr., Crystal Paulson.
Personnel Profile: Full-Time Paid 2; Part-Time Paid 5; Part-Time Volunteers 450.
Governing Authority: nonprofit organization. Tax-exempt: 501(c)(3).
Farm Equipment Museum.
Collections: farm machines; tools; crops; photo archives; decorative arts; c.1850 settlement farm; 1870-1880 settlement farm town hall, one room schoolhouse; feed mill; period gardens; blacksmith shop; c.1920 dairy farm; 1920s & 1930s farm; country church; grain mill.
Research Fields: Minnesota agriculture; local history.
Facilities: interpretive center; mini-museum; conference center; 10-acre native prairie.
Activities: festivals; self-guided tours; lectures.
Publications: quarterly newsletter, Over the Fence Post.
Hours & Admission Prices: June -Aug. Tues.-Fri. 9-2. Adults $5, children $3. ♿
Attendance: 15,000 (estimated)
Membership: Individual $25; Family $50; Sustaining $100; Contributing $250; Patron $500; Visionary $1,000.

WASECA COUNTY HISTORICAL SOCIETY, MUSEUM AND RESEARCH LIBRARY, 315 2nd Ave., N.E., Waseca, MN 56093-2936. Mailing Address: P.O. Box 314, Waseca, MN 56093-0314. Tel.: 507-835-7700. Fax: 507-835-7811.
E-mail: director@historical.waseca.mn.us
Web Site: www.historical.waseca.mn.us
Founded: 1938.
Congressional District: 1
Key Personnel: Co Dir., Joan Mooney; Co Dir., Sheila Mooris; Pres. (V), Donald Wynnemer; Museum Shop Mgr., Joan Mooney.
Personnel Profile: Part-Time Paid 5; Part-Time Volunteers 10.
Governing Authority: nonprofit organization; board of directors. Branch Museums: Hodgson Hall. Tax-exempt.
Local History Museum.
Collections: agriculture; archives; costumes; decorative arts.
Research Fields: local history.
Facilities: library of history books & local newspapers; reading room; gardens.
Activities: permanent exhibitions; educational programs; annual & special events; research.
Publications: quarterly newsletter, History Notes.
Hours & Admission Prices: May-Nov. Mon.-Fri. 8-12 & 1-5, Sat. 1-5; Dec.-April Mon.-Fri. 8-12 & 1-5; other times by appointment. Hodgson Hall: by appointment only. No charge; donations accepted. ♿
Membership: Individual $25; Family $35; Business & Organization $200; Benefactor $1,000.

West Saint Paul

DODGE NATURE CENTER, 365 Marie Ave., W., West Saint Paul, MN 55118-3848. Tel.: 651-455-4531. Fax: 651-455-2575.
Web Site: www.dodgenaturecenter.org
Founded: 1967.
Key Personnel: Exec. Dir., Ben Van Gundy.
Personnel Profile: Full-Time Paid 18; Part-Time Paid 18; Part-Time Volunteers 130; Interns 12.
Governing Authority: private; not-for-profit organization. Tax-exempt: 501(c)(3).
Nature Center.
Collections: arboretum; collections of pressed, mounted & identified plants & stuffed animals; live reptiles & amphibians; film & photos of history of nature center; heirloom plant garden.
Activities: restoration ecology; environment education; interpretive farm; heirloom garden; preschool.
Hours & Admission Prices: Mon.-Fri. 8-4:30 pre-registered school & other groups only, Sat. 10-4; occasional evening. Special Programs: adults & senior citizens $2-$5, students & children $2-$4; no charge for entrance. ♿
Attendance: 42,000 (estimated)
Membership: Individual $30; Family $40; Supporting $60; Sustaining $100; Patron $500; Benefactor $1,000.

Wheaton

TRAVERSE COUNTY HISTORICAL SOCIETY, 1201 Broadway, Wheaton, MN 56296. Mailing Address: 601 1st Ave. S., Wheaton, MN 56296-1712. Tel.: 320-563-8520.
E-mail: cjuelich@frontiernet.net
Web Site: www.cityofwheaton.com
Founded: 1977.
Congressional District: 2
Key Personnel: Pres., Clarence Juelich; Sec., Vivian Krumwiede.
Governing Authority: nonprofit organization. Tax-exempt: 501(c)(3).
Historical Society Museum: housed in c.1906 railroad depot.
Collections: refurbished caboose; one-man band; theme rooms; kitchen; dental office; meat market; produce buying station; one room schoolhouse; farm machinery; church exhibit; furniture; toys; mounted animals; c.1882 organ; bicycle with wood rims & handlebars; 1907 surrey; 1924 gas truck; 1912 hand drawn fire & hose cart; 1926 Graham Page fire truck; photographs; newspaper printing equipment; printing press; rural schoolhouse; physician's office equipment; bank; post office; jewelry.
Facilities: depot.
Hours & Admission Prices: Memorial Day-Labor Day Wed.-Sun. 1-5. ♿
Attendance: 486
Membership: Annual Individual $3; Life $25.

White Bear Township

TAMARACK NATURE CENTER, 5287 Otter Lake Rd., White Bear Township, MN 55110-5851. Tel.: 651-407-5350. Fax: 651-407-5354.
E-mail: tamarack@co.ramsey.mn.us
Web Site: www.co.ramsey.mn.us/parks/tamarack/index.htm
Nature Center.
Collections: wildlife.
Facilities: nature trails; dock.
Hours & Admission Prices: Visitor Center: Mon.-Fri. 8-4:30, Sat. 9-5, Sun. 12-5.

Willmar

KANDIYOHI COUNTY HISTORICAL SOCIETY, (M), 610 Hwy. 71, N.E., Willmar, MN 56201-2650. Tel.: 320-235-1881. Fax: 320-235-1881.
E-mail: kandhist@msn.com
Web Site: kandimuseum.com
Founded: 1898.
Congressional District: 6
Key Personnel: C.E.O. & Dir., Andria Carlson; Pres. (V), Lois Linn.
Personnel Profile: Full-Time Paid 1; Part-Time Paid 2; Part-Time Volunteers 20; Interns 1.
Governing Authority: nonprofit organization. Tax-exempt: 501(c)(3).
History Museum.
Collections: transportation; preservation project; history, archives; manuscripts; books; newspapers; photo; Indian artifacts.
Research Fields: local history.
Facilities: 1,500-vol. library of state and local history books; research center; 450 linear ft. archives.
Activities: guided tours; lectures; gallery talks; concerts; arts festivals; inter-museum loan, permanent, temporary & traveling exhibitions; historic sites tours; informal education programs for adults & children; program speakers bureau.

Publications: quarterly, Kandi Express.
Hours & Admission Prices: Memorial Day-Labor Day Mon.-Fri. 9-5, Sat.-Sun. 1-5; Sept.-May Mon.-Fri. 9-5. Suggested Donation $2. ♿
Attendance: 7,500 (accurate)
Membership: Individual $15; Family $25; Friend $50; Supporter $100; Patron $250; Benefactor $500.

Windom

COTTONWOOD COUNTY HISTORICAL SOCIETY, 812 Fourth Ave., Windom, MN 56101-1657. Tel.: 507-831-1134. Fax: 507-831-2665.
E-mail: cchs@windomnet.com
Founded: 1901.
Congressional District: 5
Key Personnel: Pres., Thomas Wickie; Dir., Linda Fransen; Treas., Margaret McDonald; Sec., Marilyn F. Erickson.
Personnel Profile: Part-Time Paid 5; Part-Time Volunteers 25.
Governing Authority: society; nonprofit organization. Tax-exempt.
History Museum.
Collections: artifacts pertaining to the history of Cottonwood County including late 19th century immigrant items; Victorian era artifacts; military memorabilia; medical artifacts; photographs of local events and places; newspapers from 1871-present; farm-related items; general store items; post office; REA kitchen items; church items; books; paintings & prints and Indian stone tools.
Major Exhibits: Wild About Art by Alex Yonker, 1/10-3/10; Cottonwood County Student Art Show, 4/10; From Forest and Studio, 5/10-8/10; Midwestern Heart by Aaron Horkey, 9/12/10-11/20/10; Festival of Trees, 12/1/10-12/23/10.
Research Fields: local history; genealogical research, including county, state & federal census obits, plat books & many family histories; cemetery records.
Facilities: library of material on local history including census and tax records, country school records, plat maps & complete set of Civil War books available for use on premises; meeting room; copy machine; reader printer for microfilm & computer lab.
Activities: guided tours; lectures; bus tours; art receptions and an educational program entitled Tour Through County History for all third grade students. Host the Festival of Trees each December.
Publications: quarterly newsletter; book, Cottonwood County Courthouse, 1804-2004.
Hours & Admission Prices: Mon.-Fri. 8-4, Sat. 10-4. No charge; donations accepted. Research library: $2; members no charge. ♿
Attendance: 8,000 (estimated)
Membership: Individual $15-$45; Family (Couple) $25-$80; Business $40-$100. Life: Individual $200; Family (Couple) $150; Business $400.

Winnebago

WINNEBAGO AREA MUSEUM, 16 Main St. S., Winnebago, MN 56098. Mailing Address: P.O. Box 595, 16 Main St. S., Winnebogo, MN 56098-0595. Tel.: 507-893-4660.
E-mail: wmuseum@bevcomm.net
Founded: 1977.
Congressional District: 2
Key Personnel: Chm. (V), Pete Haight; Treas., Lola Baxter; Sec., Millicent Hanson.
Personnel Profile: Part-Time Paid 1; Part-Time Volunteers 15.
Governing Authority: nonprofit organization. Tax-exempt: 501(c)(3).
Historical Society & Archaeology Museum.
Collections: 900-1500 AD Oneota artifacts; 8000 BC-1000 BC Woodland artifacts; 1000 BC-1700 AD Archaic artifacts; paintings; pictures; pottery exhibit; bead work of the Chippewa & Sioux; 1890 bedroom; 1842-1854 gun exhibit; 1858-1876 military display; cemetery records for area; early kitchen & farm tools; papers; ledgers; land grant papers; clothing; costumes; genealogies; U.S. Census records from 1872-1874, 1897-1898 & 1903; index of local papers 1864-present; 1865-1900 handcraft display; papers on microfilm 1870-1947; period clothing 1860-1950; photographs of barns & houses in the local area; military display, 1858 civil war & Spanish-American World War I & II; photo & story of canning factory 1924-1967 now closed; all cemetery records from 4 townships since 1858; family histories.
Research Fields: genealogy; Oneota history & 100-year farms in the area; early industry in area: tile plants, carriage manufacturing company, cigar companies, shingle factory, well drilling, steam powered saw mill.
Facilities: library of brochures & Indian cultures available for inter-library loan; classrooms.
Activities: guided tours; films; organized education programs for children; exhibits arranged for special events. Museum Sponsors: Ex. Quilt show for 125th anniversary; Early toys for Moto-Fest celebration; barn photo exhibit; early homes photo exhibit.
Publications: book, Reflections from Winnebago, Minnesota; cookbook, Are We Dunn Yet?
Hours & Admission Prices: Call for hours & admission prices. ♿
Attendance: 930 (accurate)
Membership: Pioneer $25-$49.99; Partner $50-$99.99; Sustainer $100-$249.99; Heritage $250-$499.99; Legacy $500 & up.

Winona

ARCHES MUSEUM OF PIONEER LIFE, Hwy. 14, 9 mi. west of Winona, Winona, MN 55987-3434. Mailing Address: Winona County Historical Society, 160 Johnson St., Winona, MN 55987-3434. Tel.: 507-454-2723 & 523-2111. Fax: 507-454-0006.
E-mail: info@winonahistory.org
Web Site: winonahistory.org
Founded: 1964.
Congressional District: 1
Key Personnel: Exec. Dir., Mark F. Peterson; Chm. (V), Laurie Lucas; Cur., Jodi Brom; Asst. Dir., Jennifer Weaver.
Personnel Profile: Full-Time Paid 2; Part-Time Paid 4; Part-Time Volunteers 150.
Governing Authority: society. Parent Institution: Winona County Historical Society, 160 Johnson St., Winona, MN 55987. Tax-exempt.
History Museum.
Collections: windmill; one-room schoolhouse; period farm & household articles; natural history. Historic Buildings: 1845-50 Log House; c.1900 Log Barn.
Activities: guided tours; permanent & temporary exhibitions.
Publications: bimonthly newsletter, The Argus.
Hours & Admission Prices: June-Aug. Wed.-Sun. 1-5. Adults $5, students $3; members no charge. ♿
Attendance: 600 (estimated)
Membership: Senior Citizen $25; Individual $30; Family $45.

MINNESOTA MARINE ART MUSEUM, (M), 800 Riverview Dr., Winona, MN 55987-2272. Tel.: 866-940-6626 (Toll Free); 507-474-6626. Fax: 507-474-6625.
E-mail: info@minnesotamarineart.org
Web Site: www.minnesotamarineart.org
Key Personnel: Exec. Dir., Betsy Midthun.
Governing Authority: Tax-exempt.
Art Museum.
Collections: works by regional & national artists.
Hours & Admission Prices: Tues.-Sat. 10-5, Sun. 11-5. Adults $6, students $3; members and children 4 & under no charge. Closed major holidays. ♿
Membership: Annual $25-$70.

WINONA COUNTY HISTORICAL MUSEUM, 160 Johnson St., Winona, MN 55987-3461. Tel.: 507-454-2723. Fax: 507-454-0006.
E-mail: info@winonahistory.org
Web Site: www.winonahistory.org
Founded: 1935.
Congressional District: 34B
Key Personnel: Exec. Dir., Mark F. Peterson; Asst. Dir., Jennifer Weaver; Pres. (V), Laurie Lucas; Archivist, Walt Bennick; Archivist, Marianne Masterbrook; Cur. Collections, Jodi Brom.
Personnel Profile: Full-Time Paid 2; Part-Time Paid 5; Part-Time Volunteers 150.
Governing Authority: private; nonprofit society. Branch Museums: Historic Bunnell House; Arches Museum of Pioneer Living. Tax-exempt: 501(c)(3).
Local History Museum.
Collections: artifacts from prehistoric to present times.
Research Fields: county and area history; Upper Mississippi River lore.
Facilities: Laird Lucas Memorial Library containing materials on state, local and Mississippi River history. Local crafts for sale.
Activities: guided tours; lectures; formally organized youth & adult education programs; permanent & temporary exhibitions; special shows; early craft programs.
Publications: bimonthly newsletter, The Augus; Scenes & Sites: Views from Winona County; books, Uses of History; Free Enterprise; Pioneers Forever; A History of St. Charles; 1874 Andreas Atlas of Minn.; I Grew Up in West Burns Valley; Timber Roots; Rivertown Winona.
Hours & Admission Prices: Historical Society Museum: Jan.-Feb. Mon.-Fri. 9-5; March-Dec. Mon.-Fri. 9-5, Sat.-Sun. 12-4. Bunnell House: June-Aug. Wed.-Sat. 10-5, Sun. 1-5. Adults $5, students $3; members no charge. Arches Museum: June-Aug. Wed.-Sun. 1-5. Closed New Year's Day; Easter; Thanksgiving; Christmas. ♿
Attendance: 25,000 (estimated)
Membership: Senior Citizens $20; Regular $25; Senior Household $30; Family $40; Sustaining $50 & up; Business $100-$175.

Worthington

NOBLES COUNTY HISTORICAL SOCIETY & PIONEER VILLAGE, 407 12th St., Ste. 2, Worthington, MN 56187-2471. Tel.: 507-376-4431. Fax: 507-376-3005.
E-mail: nchs@frontiernet.net
Web Site: www.noblespioneervillage.com
Founded: 1933.
Congressional District: 2
Key Personnel: Co Pres., LeAnne Meyer; Co Pres., Jacoba Nagel; Dir. Pioneer Village, Roy Reimer; Office Mgr., Carolyn Soper.
Personnel Profile: Full-Time Paid 1; Part-Time Paid 3; Part-Time Volunteers 150; Interns 1.
Governing Authority: county; nonprofit organization. Tax-exempt: 501(c)(3).
Historical Society Museum.
Collections: Nobles County Pioneer Village, 45 buildings on 6 acres; horse-drawn machinery; furniture; toys; books; tools; household items; clothing; arrowheads; harness; early power machinery; general store; medical; mortuary; gardens.
Facilities: 100-vol. general library available for research on premises.
Activities: Village: self-guided tours. Museum: guided tours.
Publications: Nobles County Historical Society, Pioneer Village News; quarterly newsletter.
Hours & Admission Prices: Memorial Museum: Mon.-Fri. 12-4; other times by appointment. No charge; donations accepted. Nobles County Pioneer Village: May-Sept. Mon.-Sat. 10-5, Sun. 1-5. Adults $6; discounts to groups; senior citizens 90 & over, children under 6 and members no charge. ♿
Attendance: 9,000 (estimated)
Membership: Settler $15; Sod-Buster $30; Homesteader $50; Prairie Builder & Business $100.

MISSISSIPPI

(131 listings)

Amory

AMORY REGIONAL MUSEUM, (M), 801 Third St., S., Amory, MS 38821-5233. Tel.: 662-256-2761.
E-mail: suebrown@midsouth.com
Web Site: www.amoryms.us
Founded: 1976.
Congressional District: 1
Key Personnel: Dir., Bo Miller; Computer Operator, Sue Brown; Tour Guides, Betty Benedict.
Personnel Profile: Full-Time Paid 1; Part-Time Paid 4; Part-Time Volunteers 24; Interns 1.
Governing Authority: municipal; nonprofit organization. Parent Institution: City of Armory. Tax-exempt.
History Museum: housed in 2-story Greek Revival brick hospital building.
Collections: archaeological artifacts; Chickasaw Indian artifacts exhibit; Lawrence E. (Rabbit) Kennedy memorabilia; historical pictures; photographs; office furniture; medical instruments & equipment; railroad coach; hospital & sterilization rooms; Frisco Railroad memorabilia; 1838-1840 regulator log cabin.
Research Fields: genealogy; history of Monroe County, Amory, Chickasaw Indians, Cotton Gin Port, railroads.
Facilities: 60-vol. library of research material, available for use on premises only; meeting rooms.
Activities: guided tours; slides; tapes; TV programs; permanent, temporary & traveling exhibitions. Museum Sponsors: Pioneer Day in April; children's month in July; Autumn Festival in October; Christmas Open House in November.
Publications: brochure.
Hours & Admission Prices: Tues.-Fri. 9-5, Sat.-Sun. 1-5. No charge; donations accepted. Closed New Year's Day; Thanksgiving; Christmas. ♿
Attendance: 3,500 (estimated)

Baldwyn

BRICE'S CROSSROADS, 607 Grisham St., Baldwyn, MS 38824-8541. Tel.: 662-365-3969.
E-mail: bcr@dixie-net.com
Web Site: www.bricecrossroads.com
Key Personnel: Cur., Edwina Carpenter
History Museum.
Collections: local history & culture; Civil War artifacts from the Brice's Crossroads battlefield; photographs.
Hours & Admission Prices: Visitor Center: Tues.-Sat. 9-5. Adults $3, children $1; discounts to groups.

Bay Saint Louis

ALICE MOSELEY FOLK ART AND ANTIQUE MUSEUM, 214 Bookter St., Bay Saint Louis, MS 39520. Mailing Address: 509 Dunton Rd., Clinton, MS 39056-4301. Tel.: 228-467-9223 & 216-1678.
E-mail: alicemoseley@gmail.com
Web Site: www.alicemoseley.com
Governing Authority: nonprofit. Tax-exempt: 501(c)(3).
Folk Art Museum.
Collections: Alice Moseley's paintings; period furniture; pottery; prints; collectible glass; video.
Activities: guided tour.
Hours & Admission Prices: Tues.-Sat. 10-4, Sun. 1-4; other times by appointment. No charge; donations accepted. ♿

Belzoni

CATFISH MUSEUM AND VISITOR CENTER, 111 Magnolia St., Belzoni, MS 39038. Mailing Address: P.O. Box 385, Belzoni, MS 39038-0385. Tel.: 800-408-4838; 662-247-4838. Fax: 662-247-4805.
E-mail: catfish@belzonicable.com
Web Site: www.belzonims.com
Formerly: Catfish Capital Visitors Center and Museum
History Museum.
Collections: local history & culture; photographs; paintings; personal artifacts; sculpture.
Facilities: Museum-related items for sale.
Hours & Admission Prices: Mon.-Fri. 9-5. No charge. ♿

THE ETHEL WRIGHT MOHAMED STITCHERY MUSEUM, 307 Central, Belzoni, MS 39038-3603. Mailing Address: P.O. Box 254, Belzoni, MS 39038. Tel.: 662-247-3633. Fax: 662-247-1433.
E-mail: hwilson493@aol.com
Web Site: www.mamasdreamworld.com
Key Personnel: Cur., Carol Mohamed Ivy
Stitchery Museum: housed in the former home of Ethel Wright Mohamed, often called Mississippi's Grandma Moses of stitchery.
Collections: embroidered pictures.
Activities: guided tours.
Hours & Admission Prices: By appointment only. Admission $2; children under 12 no charge.

JAKE TOWN MUSEUM, 116 W. Jackson St., Belzoni, MS 39038-3514. Mailing Address: P.O. Box 145, Belzoni, MS 39038-0145. Tel.: 662-247-2151. Fax: 662-247-4805.
History Museum.
Collections: local history & culture; period furnishings; personal artifacts; photographs.
Hours & Admission Prices: Daily 10-4. No charge. ♿

Biloxi

BEAUVOIR, THE JEFFERSON DAVIS HOME AND PRESIDENTIAL LIBRARY, 2244 Beach Blvd., Biloxi, MS 39531-5002. Tel.: 228-388-4400. Fax: 228-388-7800.
Web Site: www.beauvoir.org
Founded: 1902.
Congressional District: 5
Key Personnel: Chm. (V), Richard V. Forte, Sr.; Cur., Richard Flowers; Business Mgr., George G. (Rusty) Trowbridge; Facilities Mgr., Quentin Kersten; Museum Shop Mgr., Rosemary Potter; Security Chief, Jay Peterson.
Personnel Profile: Full-Time Paid 6; Full-Time Volunteers 1; Part-Time Paid 17; Part-Time Volunteers 2.
Governing Authority: nonprofit. Mississippi Division, United Sons of Confederate Veterans, 2244 Beach Blvd., Biloxi, MS 39531. Tax-exempt: 501(c)(3).
Historic Site: housed in the post-war home of Confederate President Jefferson Davis; built in 1853.
Collections: 19th-century period furnishings & decorative; Jefferson Davis family effects & papers; Civil War militaria; Confederate Veterans Cemetery.
Research Fields: Jefferson Davis; Jefferson Davis Soldiers' Home; Confederate military history; 19th-century Southern History.
Facilities: 6,000-vol. Jefferson Davis Presidential Library; 51 acre complex; gardens. Museum-related items for sale.
Activities: self-guided tours; guided tours by appointment; educational outreach program; special events.
Publications: books, The Uncivil War; Adapt or Perish: The Life of Roger A. Pryor; Historic Beauvoir; booklets, Beauvoir, A Walk Through History; The Conspiracy Against Jefferson Davis; Jefferson Davis: The Unforgiven;

Jefferson Davis: A Judicial Estimate; Jefferson Davis: The Making of a President; The Life of Jefferson Davis; The Autobiography of Jefferson Davis; The Chronicles of Beauvoir.
Hours & Admission Prices: Daily 9-5. Adults $9. Closed Thanksgiving; Christmas. ♿
Attendance: 31,000 (estimated)
Membership: Individual $25; Family $50; Patron $100-$249; Sustaining $250-$499; Corporate $500 & up; Benefactor $500-$999; Sponsor $1,000-$4,999; President's Cabinet $5,000 & up.

MARITIME & SEAFOOD INDUSTRY MUSEUM, (M), 115 First St., Biloxi, MS 39530. Mailing Address: P.O. Box 1907, Biloxi, MS 39533-1907. Tel.: 228-435-6320. Fax: 228-435-6309.
E-mail: schooner@maritimemuseum.org
Web Site: www.maritimemuseum.org
Founded: 1986.
Congressional District: 5
Key Personnel: Exec. Dir., Robin Krohn-David; Schooner Captain, Brandon Boudreaux; Office Mgr., Megan Seymour; Museum Shop Mgr., Robert Sweeting.
Personnel Profile: Full-Time Paid 5; Part-Time Paid 20; Part-Time Volunteers 40.
Governing Authority: board of directors.
Seafood Industry Museum: housed in Coast Guard station.
Collections: maritime crafts, fishing & boatbuilding implements, early photographs of industry & watercraft; local history of city & seafood industry; hurricane history.
Research Fields: local history.
Facilities: 18,000 sq. ft. exhibit space. Museum-related items for sale.
Activities: annual museum festival; live demonstration of maritime crafts; trips available on replicated Biloxi oyster schooner.
Publications: member newsletter, Seafood Industry Museum.
Hours & Admission Prices: Mon.-Fri. 9-5. Adults $5, seniors $4, children $3; discounts to groups; children under 5 & members no charge. ♿
Attendance: 150,000
Membership: Senior $10; Individual $25; Family $50; Patron $250; Lifetime $1,000.

OHR-O'KEEFE MUSEUM OF ART, (M), 1596 Glenn Swetman Dr., Biloxi, MS 39530-3353. Tel.: 228-374-5547. Fax: 228-436-3641.
E-mail: director@georgeohr.org
Web Site: www.georgeohr.org
Formerly: George E. Ohr Arts & Culture Center
Founded: 1989.
Congressional District: 5
Key Personnel: Dir., Denny Mecham; Pres. (V), Larry Clark.
Personnel Profile: Full-Time Paid 9; Full-Time Volunteers 20; Part-Time Paid 6; Part-Time Volunteers 75; Interns 1.
Governing Authority: nonprofit organization. Tax-exempt: 501(c)(3).
Art Museum.
Collections: George Ohr pottery; ceramics & pottery from around the world
Activities: guided tours; lectures; films; concerts; dance recitals; study clubs; organized education programs for children, adults, undergraduate & graduate students; docent program.
Publications: bimonthly newsletter, The Crack'd Pot; exhibition catalogs.
Hours & Admission Prices: Mon.-Fri. 9-4:30. No charge; donations accepted. ♿
Attendance: 35,000 (estimated)
Membership: Student $35; Adult $50; Family $75; Patron $100; Benefactor $500; Sustaining $1,000. Corporate Membership: Bronze $100; Silver $500; Gold $1,000; Platinum $5,000.

WEST END HOSE CO. NO. 3 MUSEUM AND FIRE EDUCATIONAL CENTER, 1046 Howard Ave., Biloxi, MS 39530. Tel.: 228-435-6119.
E-mail: jboney@biloxi.ms.us
Web Site: biloxi.ms.us/museums/firemuseum
Founded: 1990.
Key Personnel: Pres. (V), Larry Smith; Museum Shop Mgr., Joe Boney
Fire Museum.
Collections: period fire-fighting tools, apparatus & photographs; 1880's hose cart; 1908 American LaFrance steam fire engine; 1923 American LaFrance chain-driven fire engine; memorabilia.
Hours & Admission Prices: Sat. 9-3; other times by appointment. No charge; donations accepted. ♿
Attendance: 1,000 (estimated)

Booneville

RAILS & TRAILS MUSEUM, 100 W. Church St., Booneville, MS 38829-3406. Tel.: 662-728-4130; 800-300-9302.
Historic Building: housed in the Gulf, Mobile & Ohio Depot; built in 1913.
Collections: depot & railroad history; photographs; fossils; Native American artifacts; Civil War; documents; agriculture.
Hours & Admission Prices: Thurs.-Sat. 10-4; other times by appointment. No charge.

Brandon

RANKIN COUNTY HISTORICAL MUSEUM, 1415 Government St., Brandon, MS 39043. Mailing Address: P.O. Box 841, Brandon, MS 39043-0841. Tel.: 601-825-4668.
Web Site: therankincountyhistoricalsociety.org
History Museum.
Collections: county history & culture; photographs.
Hours & Admission Prices: 1st Sat. of month 9-4, 1st Sun. of month 2-4. No charge; donations accepted.

Camp Shelby

MISSISSIPPI ARMED FORCES MUSEUM, (M), Bldg. 850, Camp Shelby Training Site, Camp Shelby, MS 39407-0001. Tel.: 601-558-2757 & 2347. Fax: 601-558-2377.
E-mail: chad.e.daniels@us.army.mil
Web Site: www.armedforcesmuseum.us
Founded: 2001.
Congressional District: 4
Key Personnel: Dir., Chad E. Daniels, M.A., M.S.; Pres. (V), MG Richard S. Poole, MSARNG (Ret.); Mgr. Collections, Col. (Ret.) James T. Darrah, Jr.; Arms & Military Vehicle Conservator, MSG (Ret.) Glenn L. Husted, III, MSARNG; Archivist, Christy A. Jones; Registrar, Lisa Foster; Cur. Education, Wendy Stockton; Administrative Asst., Brenda Crowley.
Personnel Profile: Full-Time Paid 8; Part-Time Paid 5; Part-Time Volunteers 2.
Governing Authority: Parent Institution: Mississippi Military Department. Tax-exempt 501(c)(3).
Military Museum.
Collections: monuments; military vehicles; weapons; history of Mississippi's veterans & training facilities; War of 1812; Mexican War; American Civil War; Spanish-American War; WWI & WWII; Korean War; Vietnam War; Gulf War; Global War on Terrorism.
Research Fields: military history.
Facilities: 4,500-vol. library; 16,000 sq. ft. exhibit space; theater. Museum-related items for sale.
Activities: simulations of real battlefield sights, sounds & smells.
Publications: newsletter, Mississippi Armed Forces Museum.
Hours & Admission Prices: Tues.-Sat. 9-4:30; groups by appointment. Current auto insurance & photo ID required to enter post. No charge; donations accepted. Closed holidays. ♿
Attendance: 43,097 (accurate)
Membership: Annual $25; Sponsor $50; Benefactor $100; Gold Star $250; Minutemen $500; Patriot $1,000; Governor Shelby $2,500 & up.

Canton

CANTON MOVIE MUSEUMS, 147 N. Union St., Canton, MS 39046-3740. Mailing Address: P.O. Box 53, Canton, MS 39046. Tel.: 800-844-3369; 601-859-1307. Fax: 601-859-0346.
E-mail: canton@cantontourism.com
Key Personnel: Exec. Dir., Jo Ann Gordon
Movie History Museum.
Collections: movie history & memorabilia; photographs; movie props; films; equipment; posters.
Hours & Admission Prices: Welcome Center: Mon.-Fri. 10-5, Sat. 10-2. One Movie Museum: adults $4, senior citizens $3, children & students $2. Two Movie Museums: adults $6, senior citizens $5, children & students $3. Multi-Cultural Museum: adults $3, students 12 & over $2, children 5-12 $1. All Museums: adults $7, senior citizens $6, children 5-12 $4.

CANTON MULTICULTURAL CENTER & MUSEUM, 147 N. Union St., Canton, MS 39046-3740. Mailing Address: P.O. Box 53, Canton, MS 39046-0053. Tel.: 601-859-1307. Fax: 601-859-0346.
History Museum.
Collections: slavery; civil rights; early African American businesses; education; family; music.
Hours & Admission Prices: Mon.-Fri. 9-5, Sat. 10-2. Adults $3, students 12 & over $2, children K-11 $1.

Centreville

CAMP VAN DORN WORLD WAR II MUSEUM, 138 E. Main, Centreville, MS 39631. Mailing Address: P.O. Box 1113, Centreville, MS 39631-1113. Tel.: 601-645-9000.
E-mail: info@vandorn.org
Military Museum.
Collections: local & World War II history; photographs; personal artifacts.
Hours & Admission Prices: Mon.-Fri. and 1st & 3rd Sat. of the month 10-4. No charge; donations accepted. ♿

Choctaw

CHOCTAW MUSEUM OF THE SOUTHERN INDIAN, Hwy. 16 W., Choctaw, MS 39350. Mailing Address: Mississippi Band of Choctaw Indians, P.O. Box 6010, Choctaw, MS 39350-6010. Tel.: 601-656-5251. Fax: 601-650-3684.
E-mail: info@choctaw.org
Web Site: www.choctaw.org
Native American History Museum.
Collections: exhibits & archives on the culture of Southeastern Indian tribes; photographs; personal artifacts.
Hours & Admission Prices: Call for hours.

Clarksdale

DELTA BLUES MUSEUM, #1 Blues Alley, Clarksdale, MS 38614-4336. Mailing Address: P.O. Box 459, Clarksdale, MS 38614-0459. Tel.: 662-627-6820. Fax: 662-627-7263.
E-mail: shelley@deltabluesmuseum.org
Web Site: www.deltabluesmuseum.org
Founded: 1979.
Congressional District: 2
Key Personnel: C.E.O. & Dir., Shelley Ritter; Chm. (V), Bill Gresham; Museum Shop Mgr., Christopher Coleman.
Personnel Profile: Full-Time Paid 5; Part-Time Paid 4; Part-Time Volunteers 35; Interns 2.
Governing Authority: nonprofit organization. Parent Institution: City of Clarksdale. Tax-exempt.
Music Museum: housed in renovated freight depot.
Collections: books & periodicals on Blues music, artists; recordings of Blues artists; videotape, slide & sound programs on the Blues; art work; musical instruments; musicians personal artifacts.
Research Fields: American music & Black history.
Facilities: 90,000-vol. library of books, monographs, art reports, recordings & videotapes, reading room; 5,000 sq. ft. gallery space; classroom; outdoor stage.
Activities: lectures; permanent & temporary exhibitions; performances. Museum Co-Sponsors: Sunflower River Blues & Gospel Festival in August.
Publications: brochure; electronic newsletter.
Hours & Admission Prices: March-Oct. Mon.-Sat. 9-5; Nov.-Feb. Mon.-Sat. 10-5. Adults $7, children $5; discounts to groups, AAM, ICOM & Blues Society members; members & children under 6 no charge. Closed major holidays. ♿
Attendance: 26,500 (estimated)
Membership: Student & Senior $20; Individual $30; Family $40; Supporter $50-$149; Patron $150-$499; Benefactor $500-$999.

ROCK 'N ROLL & BLUES HERITAGE MUSEUM, 113 E. Second St., Clarksdale, MS 38614-4205. Tel.: 901-605-8662.
History Museum.
Collections: blues and rock & roll history; memorabilia from the 1920s to 1960s; period furnishings; movie posters.
Facilities: Museum-related items for sale.
Activities: special events.
Hours & Admission Prices: April-Oct. Thurs.-Sat. 11-5; Sun. by appointment. Admission $5.

Cleveland

FIELDING L. WRIGHT ART CENTER, Delta State University, Cleveland, MS 38733. Mailing Address: Box D 2, Delta State University, Cleveland, MS 38733. Tel.: 662-846-4720. Fax: 662-846-4726.
E-mail: artinfo@deltastate.edu
Web Site: www.deltastate.edu/academics/artsci/artdept.com
Founded: 1924.
Congressional District: 2
Key Personnel: Chm., Ron Koelher; Art Gallery Dir., Patricia Brown.
Governing Authority: university. Affiliated with Delta State University. Tax-exempt.
Art Center.
Collections: prints by Kathe Kollwitz, Salvadore Dali, G. B. Piranesi; works of Walter Anderson; Marie Hull; Andrew Bucci; Japanese prints, woodblocks; sculptured Greek heads from Crete c.500 B.C.; medals struck in Paris Mint; works of Southern artists; works of Mississippi artists.
Research Fields: Southern art; Southern Folk art.
Facilities: library; reading room; classrooms.
Activities: lectures; films; gallery talks; formally organized education programs for children, undergraduate & graduate college students; temporary & traveling exhibitions.
Publications: announcements & publications for special exhibitions.
Hours & Admission Prices: during University Sessions: Mon.-Thurs. 8-8:30, Fri. 8-3:30. No charge. ♿
Attendance: 10,000

Clinton

MISSISSIPPI BAPTIST HISTORICAL COMMISSION, Mississippi College Library-College St., Clinton, MS 39058-0001. Mailing Address: P.O. Box 4024, Clinton, MS 39058-0001. Tel.: 601-925-3434. Fax: 601-925-3435.
E-mail: mbhc@mc.edu
Web Site: www.mc.edu
Founded: 1887.
Congressional District: 4
Key Personnel: C.E.O. (V), Edward McMillan, Ph.D.; Pres. (V), Dr. Talmadge Smith.
Personnel Profile: Full-Time Paid 1; Part-Time Paid 2.
Governing Authority: church. Parent Institution: Mississippi Baptist Convention.
Religious Museum.
Collections: Baptist history; old church minute books; documents; manuscripts.
Research Fields: Baptist history.
Facilities: 570-vol. library of books, periodicals, church & associational minutes & vertical files, on Baptist history available for use on premises; reading room; microfilm reader.
Publications: books, A History of Mississippi Baptists, 1780-1970; Mississippi Baptist Convention ministers: current biographies; Highlights of Mississippi Baptist history.
Hours & Admission Prices: Mon.-Fri. 8-12 & 1:4:30. No charge. Closed some college vacations. ♿
Attendance: 150 (estimated)

Columbus

AMERICAN-INDIAN ARTIFACTS MUSEUM, 179 State Line Rd., Columbus, MS 39702-7134. Tel.: 662-251-1125; 800-327-2686.
Native American History Museum.
Collections: Native American artifacts; personal artifacts.
Hours & Admission Prices: Call for hours. No charge; donations accepted.

THE FLORENCE MCLEOD HAZARD MUSEUM, 316 7th St. N., Columbus, MS 39701-4680. Mailing Address: P.O. Box 789, Columbus, MS 39703-0789. Tel.: 662-329-3533. Fax: 662-329-1027.
Web Site: historic-columbus.org
Founded: 1959.
Congressional District: 2
Key Personnel: Dir., Heather Roland; Pres. (V), Libba Johnson.
Personnel Profile: Full-Time Paid 1; Part-Time Paid 30.
Governing Authority: society; nonprofit. Parent Institution: The Columbus & Lowndes County Historical Society.
Historical Society Museum: housed in c.1847 Blewett-Harrison-Lee Home.
Collections: c.1833-1908 clothing; portraits; silver; furniture; china; glass; guns; documents; diaries; pictures; books; medical instruments.
Facilities: library of old newspapers, books, letters, documents, wills, scrapbooks, available for use on premises. Books & other museum-related items for sale.
Activities: guided tours; docent program; formally organized education programs for undergraduate college students affiliated with the Mississippi University for Women; permanent exhibitions.
Publications: book, I Remember When.
Hours & Admission Prices: Fri. 10-4; other times by appointment. Adults $5; students & children no charge. Closed Thanksgiving; Christmas.
Membership: Individual $10.

MISSISSIPPI UNIVERSITY FOR WOMEN, ARCHIVES AND MUSEUM, 1100 College St., W-1625, Columbus, MS 39701-5831. Tel.: 662-329-7332. Fax: 662-329-7348.
Web Site: www.muw.edu
Founded: 1978.

Congressional District: 5
Governing Authority: university. Affiliated with the Mississippi University For Women, College St., Columbus, MS. 39701. Tax-exempt.
College Museum: housed in 1885 Orr Building.
Collections: University documents; photographs; memorabilia donated by alumni; rare books; china; artifacts; history of dance; early science & domestic science implements; dolls; manuscripts & documents. Historic Structure: university chapel with restored stained glass windows.
Research Fields: University history; history of women; business & government research in Tennessee Tombigbee Waterways, barges & old ports.
Publications: Finding Aid, 1979; Introductory Guide to the Tennessee Tombigbee Waterway Development Authority; printed guide to early photographs of students, faculty & buildings.
Hours & Admission Prices: Sun.-Thurs. 2-10, Fri. 7:30-5, Sat. 9-5. No charge.

STEPHEN D. LEE HOME MUSEUM, 316 Seventh St., N., Columbus, MS 39701-4680. Tel.: 662-327-8888; 800-920-3533.
Web Site: www.columbus-ms.org
Historic House Museum: housed in the former home of Confederate Gen. Stephen D. Lee; built in 1847. Listed on the National Register of Historic Places.
Collections: local history; Civil War artifacts; period furnishings; photographs.
Activities: rental facilities.
Hours & Admission Prices: Fri. 10-4; other times by appointment. Adults $7.50.

Corinth

CORINTH COCA-COLA MUSEUM, 305 E. Waldron St., Corinth, MS 38834-4756. Tel.: 662-284-4848.
Company Museum.
Collections: Coca-Cola company history; memorabilia; period drink machines; photographs.
Hours & Admission Prices: Tues.-Fri. 10-4, Sat. 10-2. Adults $3, children 6-16 $1; children 5 & under no charge.

CROSSROADS MUSEUM, 221 N. Fillmore St., Corinth, MS 38834-5635. Tel.: 662-287-3120. Fax: 662-287-3120.
E-mail: northeastmiss115@bellsouth.net
Web Site: www.crossroadsmuseum.com
Formerly: Northeast Mississippi Museum
Founded: 1980.
Congressional District: 1
Key Personnel: Dir., Ed Lucas; Pres. (V), Sandy Walker; Treas., Becky Williams.
Personnel Profile: Full-Time Paid 2; Part-Time Paid 1; Part-Time Volunteers 3; Interns 1.
Governing Authority: private; nonprofit organization. Tax-exempt: 501(c)(3).
History Museum.
Collections: fossils; American Indian; Civil War; railroad; photographs; local arts & crafts gallery; history of Northeast Mississippi with emphasis on the history of the city of Corinth & Alcorn County.
Major Exhibits: Inspiring the Next Generation, 12/09-1/10; Corinth Food Exhibit, 4/10-4/11.
Facilities: 475-vol. library; 2,500 sq. ft. exhibit space. Museum-related items for sale.
Activities: guided & school tours; temporary exhibitions; summer children's camps. Museum Sponsors: Annual meeting of Museum membership; bimonthly education luncheons.
Publications: quarterly newsletter, NE MS Museum News.
Hours & Admission Prices: Tues.-Sat. 10-4, Sun. 1-4. Adults $5, senior citizens, military students $3; discounts to groups; children 16 & under and members no charge. Closed Thanksgiving; Christmas. ♿
Attendance: 6,500 (estimated)
Membership: Senior, Student & Educator $25; Friend $50; Supporter $100; Contributor $250; Sponsor $500; Patron $1,000.

JACINTO FOUNDATION, INC., Jacinto Courthouse, 3568 County Rd. 367, Corinth, MS 38382. Mailing Address: P.O. Box 1174, Corinth, MS 38835-1174. Tel.: 662-286-8662. Fax: 662-286-6500.
Founded: 1966.
Congressional District: 1
Key Personnel: C.E.O., Beth Whitehurst; Pres. (V), John C. Ross.
Personnel Profile: Part-Time Paid 4.
Governing Authority: nonprofit organization. Tax-exempt.
Historic Foundation: housed in 1854 Jacinto Courthouse. Listed on the National Register of Historic Places.
Collections: local history & culture; period artifacts.
Facilities: nature & conservation center. Museum-related items for sale.
Activities: guided tours; drama. Foundation Sponsors: July 4th Festival.
Hours & Admission Prices: Tues.-Sat. 10-5, Sun. 1-5. No charge; donations accepted.

VERANDAH HOUSE, (M), 705 Jackson St., Corinth, MS 38834. Mailing Address: Corinth Visitor's Bureau, 215 N. Tillmore, Corinth, MS 38834. Tel.: 800-748-9048.
E-mail: tourism@corinth.net
Historic House Museum: housed in the headquarters for Confederate Generals Braxton Bragg, John Bell Hood, Earl Van Dorn & Union Generals Henry W. Halleck & Granville Dodge; built in 1857. A National Historic Landmark.
Collections: Civil War history; period furnishings; personal artifacts.
Hours & Admission Prices: Tours by appointment only.

Crystal Springs

ROBERT JOHNSON HERITAGE & BLUES MUSEUM, 218 E. Marion Dr., Crystal Springs, MS 39059. Mailing Address: P.O. Box 1005, Crystal Springs, MS 39059-1005. Tel.: 601-892-7883. Fax: 601-892-7884.
E-mail: robertjohnsonblu@bellsouth.net
Web Site: www.robertjohnsonbluesfoundation.org/museum.html
History Museum.
Collections: Robert Johnson & Delta Blues history; murals; guitars.
Facilities: Museum-related items for sale.
Hours & Admission Prices: Mon.-Fri. 10-5, Sat. 10-2; other times by appointment. Suggested Donation: adults $2, children $1.

Ellisville

DEASON HOME, Deason St., Ellisville, MS 39437. Tel.: 601-477-3314.
Historic House Museum: built in 1845.
Collections: Deason family history; period furnishings; personal artifacts; photographs.
Hours & Admission Prices: By appointment only. $5 per person.

Fayette

HARRISON HOUSE, 414 River Rd., Fayette, MS 39069. Mailing Address: P.O. Box 310, Fayette, MS 39069. Tel.: 601-786-6448. Fax: 601-786-6448.
Key Personnel: Dir., M. Louise Coleman
Historic House Museum: built in 1900.
Collections: local history & culture; memorabilia; documents; manuscripts; photographs.
Facilities: Museum-related items for sale.
Hours & Admission Prices: Daily by appointment. Adults $5, children under 12 $3.

Flora

MISSISSIPPI PETRIFIED FOREST, 124 Forest Park Rd., Flora, MS 39071. Mailing Address: P.O. Box 37, Flora, MS 39071-0037. Tel.: 601-879-8189. Fax: 601-879-8165.
E-mail: info@mspetrifiedforest.com
Web Site: www.mspetrifiedforest.com
Founded: 1963.
Congressional District: 3
Key Personnel: Dir. & Owner, C. J. McNamara; Museum Shop Mgr., Deborah Shoemaker; Park Mgr.-Outdoor Museum, Doug Shoemaker.
Personnel Profile: Part-Time Paid 3.
Governing Authority: individual operation.
Geology Museum.
Collections: petrified wood; mineral collections; vertebrate & invertebrate fossil collections; lapidary art; native wildlife.
Research Fields: identification of petrified wood.
Facilities: nature & conservation center; black light display; picnic area; campground. Lapidary equipment & supplies, books & gift items for sale.
Activities: permanent & temporary exhibitions; nature trail through Natural Petrified Forest; gemstone flume.
Publications: Mississippi Petrified Forest: A Place of Fascination; All In A Nutshell, history of vegetable ivory-tagua; Out of the Past, a scrapbook of Time.
Hours & Admission Prices: April to Labor Day daily 9-6; Sept.-May daily 9-5. Adults $7, seniors $6, students grades 1-12 $6; discounts to AAA members & groups of 15 or more; pre-school children no charge. Closed Thanksgiving; Christmas. ♿
Attendance: 15,000 (estimated)

Friars Point

NORTH DELTA MUSEUM, 748 2nd St., Friars Point, MS 38631. Tel.: 662-645-5063. Fax: 662-383-0057.
E-mail: flolarson@bellsouth.net
Key Personnel: Dir., Flo Larson
History Museum.
Collections: Civil War; Native American artifacts; personal artifacts; photographs.
Hours & Admission Prices: Tues.-Sat. 9-3; other times by appointment. Adults $4, children under 7 $2.

Greenville

GREENVILLE HISTORY MUSEUM, 409 Washington Ave., Greenville, MS 38701-3617. Tel.: 662-335-5802.
Key Personnel: Dir., Ben Nelken
History Museum: housed in the restored Miller Building.
Collections: memorabilia, photographs & newspapers relating to Greenville.
Hours & Admission Prices: Mon.-Fri. 9-5; other times by appointment. Adults $5, children $3.

OLD FIREHOUSE MUSEUM, 230 Main St., Greenville, MS 38701. Mailing Address: P.O. Box 897, Greenville, MS 38702-0897. Tel.: 662-378-1554. Fax: 662-378-1612.
Web Site: www.greenville.ms.us
Founded: 1994.
Congressional District: 2
Key Personnel: C.E.O., Mayor Heather Hudson; Treas., Tommy Jefcoat; Security, Chief Lester Carter.
Personnel Profile: Full-Time Paid 1; Full-Time Volunteers 1.
Governing Authority: municipal; nonprofit. Tax-exempt.
General Museum.
Collections: photographs; firefighting equipment.
Facilities: 50-vol. library of manuals & directories; 500 sq. ft. exhibit space; interactive play area.
Activities: formal educational programs for children; guided tours; participatory exhibits.
Publications: semiannual newsletter, Firehouse News.
Hours & Admission Prices: By appointment. No charge. Closed New Year's Day; Martin Luther King Jr. Day; Memorial Day; Independence Day; Labor Day; Thanksgiving; Christmas. ♿
Attendance: 2,340 (accurate)

WINTERVILLE MOUNDS, 2415 Hwy. 1 N., Greenville, MS 38703-9476. Tel.: 662-334-4684. Fax: 662-378-5559.
E-mail: wmounds@mdah.state.ms.us
Web Site: mdah.state.ms.us/hprop/winterville.html
Governing Authority: Parent Institution: Mississippi Department of Archives & History.
Historic Site.
Collections: Native American artifacts.
Hours & Admission Prices: Grounds: daily dawn to dusk. Museum: Mon.-Sat. 9-5, Sun. 1:30-5. No charge; donations accepted.
Attendance: 15,000 (accurate)

Greenwood

BACK IN THE DAY MUSEUM, 200 Young St., Greenwood, MS 38930-4637. Tel.: 662-453-2742.
E-mail: deltablueslegendtours@yahoo.com
Web Site: deltablueslegendtours.com
Founded: 2006.
Key Personnel: Museum Shop Mgr., Mary Ann Hoover.
Personnel Profile: Full-Time Volunteers 1.
History Museum.
Collections: local history, heritage & culture; personal artifacts; period furnishings; photographs.
Hours & Admission Prices: Call for hours. No charge; donations accepted.

COTTONLANDIA MUSEUM, (M), 1608 Highway 82 W., Greenwood, MS 38930-2725. Tel.: 662-453-0925. Fax: 662-455-7556.
E-mail: cottonlandia@bellsouth.net
Web Site: www.cottonlandia.org
Founded: 1969.
Congressional District: 2
Key Personnel: Interim Dir., David Freeman; Pres., Hugh Warren, III; Vice Pres., Gary McDonald; Museum Shop Mgr., Jeanett Loftin; Education & Art Coord., Jennifer Whites.
Personnel Profile: Full-Time Paid 3; Part-Time Paid 1; Part-Time Volunteers 70.
Governing Authority: Parent Institution: Cottonlandia Educational & Recreational Foundation, Inc. Tax-exempt: 501(c)(3).
General Museum.
Collections: Avent & Jones collection of polychrome ceramics from Humber-McWilliams site; Mississippian period Indians; historical regional agricultural implements & household furnishings; hands-on natural science room; contemporary Mississippi art; military history; artifacts from Lower-Yazoo Basin region; bone, bead, lithic & ceramic analysis of pre- & proto-historic Indian relics; European trade bead collection; wildflower garden; diorama of Mississippi Wetlands.
Research Fields: Mississippi archaeology: history, authors; regional archaeology: both pre- & proto-historic.
Facilities: banquet & lecture hall; meeting room.
Activities: guided tours; gallery talks; hobby workshops; docent program; permanent & temporary exhibitions; premises available for after-hour events; children's educational summer programs; scout programs.
Publications: research papers, The Southeastern Ceremonial Complex: Artifacts & Analysis; Early 16th-Century Glass Beads in the Spanish Colonial Trade.
Hours & Admission Prices: Mon.-Fri. 9-5, Sat.-Sun. 2-5; other times by appointment. Adults $5, seniors $3.50, students $2; discounts to AAM members, Mississippi Museums Association, Southeast Museums Conference, Civil War Trust; members no charge. ♿
Attendance: 7,000 (estimated)
Membership: Individual $25; Family $35; Patron $75; Sponsor $150; Corporate $250; Benefactor $500 & up.

FLOREWOOD STATE PARK, 1999 County Rd. 145, Greenwood, MS 38930. Mailing Address: 1505 Eastover Dr., Jackson, MS 39211-6322. Tel.: 662-455-3904.
E-mail: florewood@mdwfp.ms.state.us
Web Site: www.mdwfp.com
Formerly: Florewood River Plantation
Founded: 1976.
Congressional District: 2
Personnel Profile: Full-Time Paid 10; Part-Time Paid 6.
Governing Authority: state. Affiliated with Mississippi Dept. of Wildlife, Fisheries & Parks. Tax-exempt: 170(b)(1)(A).
History Museum & Living History Plantation: located on 1860 plantation.
Collections: 1800-1865 furniture including Empire, Victorian & primitive pieces; household accessories including bottles, books, crockery, lighting devices; food preparation utensils; collection of 19th-century blacksmith & carpentry tools; farm implements; steam engines; sorghum mill; grist mill; wagons.
Research Fields: life in mid 19th-century America; life on an Old South cotton plantation.
Facilities: 20-vol. library of books on slavery, period furnishings, interpretation of historic sites, museum administration, arts & crafts, available for use by permission of the park director; 100-seat auditorium; snack area. Craft & museum-related items for sale.
Activities: self-guided tours; arts festivals; loan, permanent & traveling exhibitions.
Hours & Admission Prices: Temporarily closed.
Attendance: 37,500 (estimated)

GREENWOOD BLUES HERITAGE MUSEUM & GALLERY, 222 Howard St., Greenwood, MS 38930-4334. Tel.: 662-451-7800. Fax: 662-451-7800.
E-mail: 3deuces@bellsouth.net
Web Site: threedeuces.net
Founded: 2001.
Key Personnel: Dir. & Museum Shop Mgr., Stephen C. Lavere; Pres., George E. Vasquez.
Personnel Profile: Full-Time Paid 2.
Governing Authority: Parent Institution: Greenwood Blues, LLC. Subsidiary Institution: Greenwood Heritage Tours.
History Museum.
Collections: life, music & career of Robert Johnson; blues history & artists; photographs; personal artifacts; recordings; books; films; local history & culture; steamboat & railroad memorabilia.
Activities: tours.
Hours & Admission Prices: Mon.-Sat. 10-5; other times by appointment.
Attendance: 3,500 (estimated)

Gulfport

LYNN MEADOWS DISCOVERY CENTER, 246 Dolan Ave., Gulfport, MS 39507-1310. Tel.: 228-897-6039. Fax: 228-248-0071.
E-mail: lmdc@lmdc.org
Founded: 1998.

Key Personnel: Exec. Dir., Cynthia Minton
Children's Museum.
Collections: hands-on exhibits.
Activities: educational programs.
Hours & Admission Prices: Tues.-Sat. 10-5. Admission $7, active military & seniors $5; children under one no charge. Closed New Year's Day; Thanksgiving; Christmas.

Harriston

THE FROG FARM STUDIO, 186 Old Hwy. 61, Harriston, MS 39081. Mailing Address: P.O. Box 310, Fayette, MS 39069-0310. Tel.: 601-786-6448.
Web Site: www.artmarketing.com/gallery/frogfarm
Founded: 1998.
Folk Art Museum.
Collections: frogs, other amphibians, birds, & reptile sculptures.
Hours & Admission Prices: By appointment. No charge; donations requested.

Hattiesburg

AFRICAN AMERICAN MILITARY HISTORY MUSEUM, (M), 305 E. Sixth St., Hattiesburg, MS 39401-2029. Tel.: 601-268-3220.
E-mail: museums@hattiesburg.org
Military History Museum.
Collections: African American military men & women history; photographs; personal artifacts; paintings; murals; military uniforms; military medals & equipment.
Hours & Admission Prices: Call for hours.

HATTIESBURG AREA HISTORICAL SOCIETY AND HAHS MUSEUM, 723 Main Street, Hattiesburg, MS 39401-3431. Mailing Address: P.O. Box 1573, Hattiesburg, MS 39403-1573. Tel.: 601-582-5460; 268-0234.
Founded: 1970.
Congressional District: 5
Key Personnel: Pres. (V), Paula Harvey; Dir., Ursula Jones.
Personnel Profile: Part-Time Volunteers 35.
Governing Authority: private; nonprofit organization. Tax-exempt: 501(c)(3).
History Museum.
Collections: area history; education; patriotism.
Research Fields: local building preservation.
Facilities: 183-vol. library; 3,800 sq. ft. exhibit space.
Activities: formal education programs for children; guided tours; temporary exhibitions. Museum Sponsors: programs.
Publications: newsletters; book, The History of Forrest County, MS.
Hours & Admission Prices: Mon., Tues. & Thurs. 2-5 & by appointment. No charge. ♿
Attendance: 500 (estimated)
Membership: Single $10; Couple $15; Life $100.

HATTIESBURG ARTS COUNCIL GALLERY, 723 Main St., Hattiesburg, MS 39401-3431. Mailing Address: P.O. Box 693, Hattiesburg, MS 39403-0693. Tel.: 601-583-6005.
Art Gallery.
Collections: works by Mississippi artists.
Hours & Admission Prices: Mon.-Fri. 10-3. No charge. ♿

MUSEUM OF ART, Department of Art and Design-The University of Southern Mississippi, 118 College Dr., #5033, Hattiesburg, MS 39406-0001. Tel.: 601-266-5200.
E-mail: artmuseum@usm.edu
Web Site: www.usm.edu/visualarts/museum.php
Founded: 1978.
Key Personnel: Dir., Jan L. Siesling; Asst. Dir., Mark Rigsby.
Personnel Profile: Full-Time Paid 2.
Governing Authority: Parent Institution: University of Southern Mississippi.
Art Museum.
Collections: regional, international, historical & contemporary artwork.
Hours & Admission Prices: Jan.-May & Sept.-Dec. Tues.-Fri. 10-5, Sat. 10-4; June-Aug. Tues.-Fri. 12-5. No charge.

TURNER HOUSE MUSEUM, 500 Bay, Hattiesburg, MS 39401-3933. Tel.: 601-582-4249.
Founded: 1970.
Congressional District: 6
Key Personnel: Dir., Cur. & Chm., David Sheley.
Governing Authority: private; nonprofit foundation.
Historic House: 1905 Turner House, Edwardian Mansion of cypress & pine construction.
Collections: 18th-century French, English & American furniture, with emphasis on the Edwardian period of decoration; silver; crystal chandelier; English, American & French art from the Impressionist & post-Impressionist periods; old masters; tapestries; 18th- to 20th-century Persian Rug collection.
Facilities: 10,000-vol. library of English writers, including some signed first editions.
Activities: tours.
Hours & Admission Prices: By appointment only. No charge; donations accepted. Closed major holidays.

Hazlehurst

HAZLEHURST DEPOT MUSEUM, 138 N. Ragsdale Ave., Hazlehurst, MS 39083-3019. Mailing Address: P.O. Box 446, Hazlehurst, MS 39083-0446. Tel.: 601-894-3752. Fax: 601-894-3752.
History Museum.
Collections: local history; railroad artifacts; Robert Johnson's personal artifacts.
Facilities: Museum-related items for sale.
Hours & Admission Prices: Daily. No charge. ♿

ROBERT JOHNSON HERITAGE HOUSE, 201 Downing St., Hazlehurst, MS 39083-3003. Tel.: 601-894-5777.
E-mail: robertjohnsonblu@bellsouth.net
Web Site: www.robertjohnsonbluesfoundation.org
Historic House Museum: housed in the home of blues guitarist & singer, Robert Johnson; c.1900.
Collections: personal artifacts; period furnishings; photographs.
Facilities: Museum-related items for sale.
Hours & Admission Prices: Call for hours. No charge. ♿

Hernando

DESOTO COUNTY MUSEUM, 111 E. Commerce St., Hernando, MS 38632-2376. Tel.: 662-429-8852. Fax: 662-429-8852.
E-mail: info@desotomuseum.org
Web Site: www.desotomuseum.org
Founded: 2003.
Congressional District: 1
Key Personnel: Dir., Brian Hicks; Chm., Dr. Roma Thorn.
Personnel Profile: Full-Time Paid 1; Part-Time Paid 1; Part-Time Volunteers 35.
Governing Authority: private; nonprofit organization. Tax-exempt: 501(c)(3).
History Museum.
Collections: DeSoto County history from 1541 to present; Native American artifacts; Civil War; personal artifacts.
Research Fields: local archaeology.
Facilities: 7,000 sq. ft. exhibit space; classroom. Museum-related items for sale.
Activities: school tours. Annual Event: DeSoto County Museum Anniversary & BBQ.
Hours & Admission Prices: Tues.-Sat. 10-5. Adults $3, senior citizens & children $2; members no charge. Closed federal holidays. ♿
Attendance: 6,000 (estimated)
Membership: Basic: Student $5; Senior Citizen $10; Individual $15; Family $25; Corporate $100. Golden Circle: Friend $25-$99; Contributor $100-$199; Donor $200-$399; Sponsor $400-$999; Patron $1,000-$2,499; Major Benefactor $5,000 & up.

Holly Springs

IDA B. WELLS BARNETT MUSEUM, 220 N. Randolph St., Holly Springs, MS 38635-2412. Tel.: 662-252-3232. Fax: 662-252-3232.
Web Site: www.idabwells.org
Art Museum: housed in the birthplace of journalist & women's activist, Ida B. Wells.
Collections: works by African & African American artists; personal artifacts; documents.
Facilities: Museum-related items for sale.
Hours & Admission Prices: Mon.-Fri. 10-5, Sat. 12-5. Adults $3, children 12 & under $2. Closed New Year's Day; Easter; Thanksgiving; Christmas. ♿

MARSHALL COUNTY HISTORICAL MUSEUM, 220 E. College Ave., Holly Springs, MS 38635-3122. Mailing Address: P.O. Box 806, Holly Springs, MS 38635-0806. Tel.: 662-252-3669. Fax: 662-252-3669.
E-mail: marshallcomuseum@bellsouth.net
Founded: 1970.
Congressional District: 1

Key Personnel: Pres. (V) & Chm. (V), Bobby Mitchell; Dir., Lois Swanee Shipp; Chm. (V) & Treas., Nancy Hutchins; Museum Shop Mgr., Jennifer Bone.
Personnel Profile: Full-Time Paid 1; Full-Time Volunteers 1; Part-Time Paid 3; Part-Time Volunteers 2.
Governing Authority: society. Tax-exempt.
Historical Society Museum: housed in 1903 former Mississippi Synodical College Building.
Collections: Marshall County period artifacts; farm tools; period costumes & textiles; relics from the Civil War, the War of 1812, the Spanish-American War & World Wars I & II; Chickasaw Indian artifacts; physician office examining room equipment; wildlife room; toys of yesteryear; schools of the past; library; genealogy files.
Research Fields: genealogical.
Facilities: 3,000-vol. library of books gathered from family libraries, dating from 1715 to the present, available for use on premises; reading room. Museum-related items for sale.
Activities: guided tours; films; lectures & slide lectures on local architecture; permanent & temporary exhibitions. Annual Event: Holiday House Tour in December.
Publications: quarterly newsletter, Marshall County Historical Society Newsletter; cookbook, A Taste in Time; books, It Happened Here; Holly Springs, Mississippi to the Year 1878; History of Holly Springs; History of Southeast Marshall County; Architectural Treasures of Holly Springs; Growing Up in Holly Springs; History of Southwest Marshall County & Byhalia; History of North Marshall County & Red Banks.
Hours & Admission Prices: Mon.-Fri. 10-5. $5 per person. Closed Thanksgiving; Christmas Eve, Day & weekend after. ♿
Attendance: 7,000
Membership: Individual $30.

Indianola

B.B. KING MUSEUM AND DELTA INTERPRETIVE CENTER, (M), 400 Second St., Indianola, MS 38751-2851. Tel.: 662-887-9539.
E-mail: info@bbkingmuseum.org
Web Site: www.bbkingmuseum.org
Key Personnel: Exec. Dir., Connie S. Gibbons; Dir. Operations, Mary L. Shepherd
History Museum.
Collections: artifacts relating to B.B. King.
Hours & Admission Prices: Mon.-Sat. 10-6. Adults $10, seniors & children $5.

Iuka

TISHOMINGO COUNTY ARCHIVES & HISTORY MUSEUM (TCAHM), 203 E. Quitman St., Iuka, MS 38852-1938. Mailing Address: PO Box 273, Iuka, MS 38852-0273. Tel.: 662-423-3500.
E-mail: tishomingocountymuseum@yahoo.com
Web Site: www.tishomingohistory.com
Formerly: Tishomingo County Mississippi Archives & History Museum
Founded: 2004.
Congressional District: 1
Key Personnel: Dir., Jan Anglin; Chm. (V), Cindy W. Nelson; Pres. (V), RaNae S. Vaughn.
Governing Authority: Parent Institution: Tishomingo County Historical & Genealogical Society. Tax-exempt.
History Museum: housed in historic courthouse; built in 1889.
Collections: Indian artifacts; Civil War & other military memorabilia from the Battle of Iuka; local industry; period furnishings; photographs; local history; genealogy; medical office artifacts.
Activities: Annual Events: Family History Fair in May; Camp Courthouse in June; Camp Courthouse in July; Christmas at the Courthouse in December.
Publications: quarterly, Chronicles & Epitaphs from the Courthouse.
Hours & Admission Prices: Tues.-Fri. 10-4. Suggested Donation: $2. Closed federal holidays. ♿
Membership: Senior $20; Regular $25; I Care $50; Lifetime $1,000.

Jackson

EUDORA WELTY HOUSE, (M), 1119 Pinehurst St., Jackson, MS 39202-1812. Mailing Address: 1109 Pinehurst St., Jackson, MS 39202. Tel.: 601-353-7762.
Web Site: www.eudoraweltyhouse.com
Historic House Museum: a National Historic Landmark.
Collections: Welty's life; books; period furniture; art.
Activities: Museum Sponsors: Welty's Birthday in April.
Hours & Admission Prices: Wed.-Fri. 9-11 & 1-3. Adults $5, students $3; discounts to groups; children under 6 no charge.

FIRE MUSEUM & PUBLIC FIRE SAFETY EDUCATION CENTER, 355 Woodrow Wilson, Jackson, MS 39213. Tel.: 601-960-2433. Fax: 601-960-2432.
Key Personnel: Cur., Sherri Gibson
Fire Museum.
Collections: fire fighting history & equipment; photographs; helmets & uniforms; 1904 horse-drawn steamer; 1917 chain-driven American LaFrance; 1936 Seagrave.
Hours & Admission Prices: Mon.-Fri. 9-5. No charge.

INTERNATIONAL MUSEUM OF MUSLIM CULTURES, 201 E. Pascagoula St., Jackson, MS 39201-4114. Tel.: 601-960-0440.
Islamic History & Culture Museum.
Collections: Islamic history & culture; photographs; period artifacts.
Facilities: Museum-related items for sale.
Hours & Admission Prices: Tues.-Sat. 10-5, Sun. 12-5.

JACKSON ZOOLOGICAL PARK, INC., 2918 W. Capitol St., Jackson, MS 39209-4293. Tel.: 601-352-2581. Fax: 601-352-2594.
E-mail: jzpdir@aol.com
Web Site: www.jacksonzoo.org
Founded: 1919.
Key Personnel: Dir., Beth Poff; Chm. & Pres. (V), Milton Cash; Animal Cur., David Wetzel; Museum Shop Mgr., Kathy Byrd.
Personnel Profile: Full-Time Paid 35; Part-Time Paid 6; Part-Time Volunteers 18.
Governing Authority: private; nonprofit corporation. Parent Institution: Friends of the Jackson Zoo. Tax-exempt.
Zoo.
Collections: endangered species.
Facilities: children's zoo; snack shop. Museum-related items for sale.
Activities: temporary & permanent exhibitions.
Publications: brochure, Jackson Zoological Park Zoo; bimonthly, Wild Things.
Hours & Admission Prices: Fall & Winter: daily 9-5; Spring & Summer: daily 9-6. Adults $8, senior citizens 65 & over $7.20, military $7, children 12 & under $5; members & children under 2 no charge. ♿
Attendance: 185,180 (accurate)
Membership: Individual $15; Companion $25; Family $35; Zoo Buff $60; Sponsor $120; Patron $1,000.

* **MANSHIP HOUSE MUSEUM, (M),** 420 E. Fortification St., Jackson, MS 39202-2340. Tel.: 601-961-4724. Fax: 601-354-6043.
E-mail: manship@mdah.state.ms.us
Web Site: www.mdah.state.ms.us/museum/manship
Founded: 1980.
Congressional District: 4
Key Personnel: C.E.O., Hank T. Holmes; Pres. Bd. Trustees, Kane Ditto; Dir., Marilynn Jones; Education Coord., Michael Busbin; Collections Mgr., Tyler Nowell; Historian, Hewitt Jones.
Personnel Profile: Full-Time Paid 4; Part-Time Paid 1; Part-Time Volunteers 2.
Governing Authority: state. Parent Institution: Mississippi Dept. of Archives & History. Tax-exempt.
Historic House Museum: 1857 restored Gothic Revival cottage of C.H. Manship.
Collections: 19th-century Mississippi furnishings & decorative arts.
Research Fields: 19th-century Mississippi architecture & decorative arts; local history; lifestyle of Charles Henry Manship & family, c.1888.
Facilities: 200-vol. library of books pertaining to architecture & decorative arts in the 19th century available for research in adjacent visitor center.
Activities: guided tours; concerts; formally organized education programs for children; docent program; summer workshops for children; video loan program; lectures. Annual Events: Christmas at the Manship House; Summer Dress.
Publications: brochure; guide book.
Hours & Admission Prices: Tues.-Fri. 9-4, Sat. 10-4. No charge; donations accepted. Closed major holidays. ♿
Attendance: 8,000 (accurate)

MEDGAR EVERS HOME MUSEUM, 2332 Margaret Walker Alexander Dr., Jackson, MS 39213-6411. Tel.: 601-977-7710.
Historic House Museum: housed in the former home of civil rights leader, Medgar Evers' & the site of his assassination in 1963.
Collections: Medgar Evers' life & career; period furnishings; personal artifacts; photographs.
Hours & Admission Prices: Call for hours.

MISSISSIPPI AGRICULTURE & FORESTRY/NATIONAL AGRICULTURAL AVIATION MUSEUM, 1150 Lakeland Dr., Jackson, MS 39216-4728. Tel.: 601-713-3365. Fax: 601-982-4292.
E-mail: sandy@mdac.state.ms.us

Web Site: www.mdac.state.ms.us
Founded: 1983.
Congressional District: 4
Key Personnel: Dir., Charlie Dixon; Pres., Lester Spell, Jr., D.V.M.; Sales, Deborah Barlow; Education & Tourist Info, Sandy Havard; Museum Shop Mgr., Judy McClure.
Personnel Profile: Full-Time Paid 9; Part-Time Paid 2; Part-Time Volunteers 4; Interns 2.
Governing Authority: state; nonprofit organization. Tax-exempt: 501(c)(3).
General Museum.
Collections: history of agriculture, forestry & agricultural aviation in Mississippi; period artifacts; furnishings.
Facilities: 35,000 sq. ft. exhibit space; nature trail; 150-seat large screen theater; rental facilities. Museum-related items for sale.
Activities: arts festivals; concerts; docent program; guided tours; formal education programs; theater. Annual Events: Harvest Festival; Celtic Festivals.
Hours & Admission Prices: Mon.-Sat. 9-5. Adults $5, senior citizens $4, children 5-18 $3, children 3-4 $1; discounts to groups & AAA members. Closed New Year's Day; Thanksgiving; Christmas Eve & Day. ♿
Attendance: 100,000 (accurate)
Membership: Individual $15; Family $35.

MISSISSIPPI GOVERNOR'S MANSION, 300 E. Capitol, Jackson, MS 39201-3403. Tel.: 601-359-3175. Fax: 601-359-6473.
Web Site: www.mdah.state.ms.us
Founded: 1842.
Congressional District: 4
Key Personnel: Dir. Dept. Archives & History, H.T. Holmes; Cur., Mary Lohrenz.
Personnel Profile: Full-Time Paid 1; Part-Time Volunteers 50.
Governing Authority: state; nonprofit. Parent Institution: Mississippi Department of Archives & History. Tax-exempt: 170(b)(1)(A).
Historic Building: 1842 Governor's Mansion, constructed 1839-1841.
Collections: 19th-century furniture & furnishings.
Research Fields: 19th-century furniture & furnishings.
Activities: guided tours; docent program.
Publications: brochure, Illustrated Guide to the Mississippi Governor's Mansion.
Hours & Admission Prices: Tues.-Fri. 9:30-11; tours given on the half-hour. No charge; donations accepted. ♿
Attendance: 15,224 (accurate)

MISSISSIPPI MUSEUM OF ART, (M), 380 S. Lamar St., Jackson, MS 39201-4007. Tel.: 601-960-1515. Fax: 601-960-1505.
Web Site: www.msmuseumart.org
Founded: 1911.
Congressional District: 4
Key Personnel: Dir., Betsy Bradley; Chm., Peder R. Johnson; Dir. Finance, Stephanie Palmertree; Dir. Mktg. & Devel., Emmie King; Dir. Communications, Nina Moss; Dir. Membership & Annual Giving, Ann Harkins; Cur. Education, Lianne K. Takemori; Deputy Dir. Programs, Daniel Piersol; Chief Preparator, L.C. Tucker, Jr.; Asst. Preparator, Melvin Johnson; Chief Security, James A. Steverson; Cur. Education, Ivy Alley; Cur. Exhibitions, Robin Dietrick; Dir. Administration, Mindy Kunz; Museum Store Mgr., Elizabeth Blanks; Visitor Information Coord., Annette French; Graphic Design, Maggie Lacey; Preparator, Tom Jones; Public Rels. Assoc., Jana Brady; Registrar, Joanna Biglane; Cur. Collection, Beth Batton.
Personnel Profile: Full-Time Paid 22; Part-Time Paid 10; Part-Time Volunteers 400.
Governing Authority: nonprofit organization. Tax-exempt: 501(c)(3).
Art Museum.
Collections: 19th- & 20th-century American & Mississippi art; mid 18th- to early 19th-century English painting; Native American basket collection; 19th- & 20th-century European & American prints; Southeastern folk art & photography; Oriental & ethnographic art; pre-Columbian art.
Major Exhibits: Jim Henson's Fantastic World (T), 12/09-3/10; Scholastic Art & Writing Awards MS Regional Competition, 2/10-4/10; The Dorothy and Herbert Vogel Collection: Fifty Works for Fifty States (T), 4/10-7/10; The Luxury of Exercise: Drawings and Small Sculpture By Claudia DeMonte, 4/10-7/10; On the Wall/Off The Wall: Modern American Masterpieces from the Permanent Collection, 4/10-7/10.
Research Fields: 19th- & 20th-century American, Southern & Mississippi art; 18th- & 19th-century British painting; photography.
Facilities: 4,500-vol. library of art books available for research on premises only; restaurant; art instruction studios; garden. Museum-related items for sale.
Activities: guided tours; visitor services; lecture series; inter-museum loan; formally organized education programs; docent program; monthly jazz series; monthly classical music series; new collector's club.
Publications: newsletter; exhibition catalogs.
Hours & Admission Prices: Mon.-Sat. 10-5, Sun. 12-5; call to confirm. Adults $5, seniors 60 & over $4, students $3; children 5 & under no charge. Closed New Year's Day; Easter; Thanksgiving; Christmas. ♿
Attendance: 40,000 (estimated)
Membership: Senior $35; Individual $45; Senior Family & Dual $50; Family Dual $60; Supporting $100; Partner $250; Curator $500; Junior Rembrandt $600; Rembrandt $1,000; Director's Rembrandt $2,500; Chairman's Rembrandt $5,000.

* **MISSISSIPPI MUSEUM OF NATURAL SCIENCE, (M),** 2148 Riverside Dr., Jackson, MS 39202-1353. Tel.: 601-354-7303. Fax: 601-354-7227.
E-mail: libby.hartfield@mmns.state.ms.us
Web Site: www.mdwfp.com/museum
Founded: 1932.
Congressional District: 4
Key Personnel: Dir., Libby Hartfield; Exhibits Supvr., Ray Terry; Exhibits Supvr., Norton McKeigney; Asst. Dir., Charles Knight; Research Coord., Lisa Yager; Natural Heritage Data Base Coord., Sherry Surrette; Education Coord. & Project WILD Coord., Angel Rohnke; Plant Community Ecologist, Heather Sullivan; Volunteer Coord., Ann Peden; Zoologist, Dr. Robert Jones; Librarian, Mary Stevens.
Personnel Profile: Full-Time Paid 45; Part-Time Paid 9; Part-Time Volunteers 75.
Governing Authority: state. Parent Institution: Mississippi Dept. of Wildlife, Fisheries & Parks. Tax-exempt.
Natural Science Museum.
Collections: herpetology; ichthyology; mammalogy; ornithology; invertebrate; paleontology & botany with emphasis on Mississippi material; dioramas & aquaria depicting Mississippi habitats.
Research Fields: herpetology; ichthyology; mammalogy; paleontology; ornithology; invertebrate biology, botany; National Heritage Data.
Facilities: 15,000-vol. reference library of natural history material available for use on the premises; aquariums; 200-seat theater; 300 acre natural area; diorama; interactive gallery; 30,000 sq. ft. exhibit hall; nature trails; preschool room.
Activities: guided tours; lectures; films; formally organized education programs for children, adults, undergraduate & graduate college students; permanent & temporary educational exhibitions. Museum Sponsors: special exhibits and kits on loan to Mississippi schools; Mississippi Natural Area Registry.
Publications: leaflets; newsletter; publications on Mississippi.
Hours & Admission Prices: Mon.-Fri. 8-5, Sat. 9-5, Sun. 1-5. Adults $5, seniors 60 & over $4, children 3-18 $3; members no charge. Closed Memorial Day; Easter; Independence Day; Labor Day; Thanksgiving; Christmas. ♿
Attendance: 150,000 (accurate)
Membership: Individual $35; Family $60; Friend $100; Donor $250; Patron $500; Benefactor $750; Sustaining $1,000.

MISSISSIPPI SPORTS HALL OF FAME & MUSEUM, 1152 Lakeland Dr., Jackson, MS 39216-4701. Tel.: 601-982-8264; 800-280-FAME. Fax: 601-982-4702.
E-mail: generalinfo@msfame.com
Web Site: www.msfame.com
Founded: 1996.
Congressional District: 3
Key Personnel: Dir., Michael Rubenstein; Chm. & Pres., Nick Crutcher.
Personnel Profile: Full-Time Paid 4; Part-Time Paid 6; Part-Time Volunteers 33.
Governing Authority: Tax-exempt.
Sports Museum.
Collections: sports history; hands-on exhibits.
Facilities: Museum-related items for sale.
Activities: rental facility; conference center; group tours; birthday parties; special events.
Hours & Admission Prices: Mon.-Sat. 10-4. Adults $5, seniors 60 & over and students 6-17 $3.50; discounts to groups of 12 or more; members and children 5 & under no charge. ♿
Attendance: 35,000 (estimated)
Membership: Individual $25; Family $100; Life $1,000; Corporate $5,000.

MUSEUM OF MISSISSIPPI HISTORY/MUSEUM DIVISION, (M), 929 High St., Jackson, MS 39202-3508. Mailing Address: Box 571, Jackson, MS 39205-0571. Tel.: 601-576-6800. Fax: 601-576-6815.
E-mail: mmh@mdah.state.ms.us
Web Site: www.mdah.state.ms.us
Formerly: Old Capitol Museum of Mississippi History

Congressional District: 3
Key Personnel: C.E.O., H.T. Holmes; Dir., Lucy J. Allen; Pres. (V), Kane Ditto; Cur. Exhibits, John Gardner; Cur. Collections, Cindy Gardner; Registrar, Nan Prince; Dir. Education & Programs, Stacey Everett.
Personnel Profile: Full-Time Paid 11; Part-Time Paid 2; Part-Time Volunteers 107.
Governing Authority: state. Parent Institution: Mississippi Dept. of Archives & History; 200 North St., Jackson, MS 39201. Tax-exempt.
History Museum.
Collections: Civil War flags; quilts.
Research Fields: Mississippi history including textiles, armament and personal artifacts.
Facilities: Books, pottery, baskets, handcrafts for sale in the Winter Archives and History building.
Activities: temporary, loan & traveling exhibitions; outreach educational programs; traveling trunk program for schools; docent program; research & production of original educational films.
Publications: exhibit catalogs; brochures; Made by Hand: Mississippi Folk Art; Welty; Strangers in Their Own Land: A Choctaw Portfolio; Eudora; Walter Anderson Posters; Walter Anderson Birthday Book; Mississippi Homespun: Nineteenth Century Textiles & the Women Who Made Them; Persistence of Pattern in Mississippi Choctaw Culture; All Shook Up: Mississippi Roots of American Popular Music; Eudora Welty: Other Places; Pride of the Fleet: The USS Mississippi; Mississippi: The Bulwark of New Spain; Two Rivers Unleashed.
Hours & Admission Prices: Temporarily closed. Temporary exhibits are on display in the William F. Winter Archives and History building.

MUSEUM OF THE SOUTHERN JEWISH EXPERIENCE, (M), 4915 I-55 N., Ste. 204B, Jackson, MS 39206. Mailing Address: P.O. Box 16528, Jackson, MS 39236-6528. Tel.: 601-362-6357. Fax: 601-366-6293.
E-mail: information@msje.org
Web Site: www.msje.org
Founded: 1989.
Congressional District: 3
Key Personnel: C.E.O. & Pres., Macy B. Hart; Chm. (V), Rayman L. Solomon; Dir. History Dept. & Museum Projects Dir., Dr. Stuart Rockoff; Administrator, Kate Lubarsky.
Personnel Profile: Full-Time Paid 28; Part-Time Paid 3; Part-Time Volunteers 10; Interns 4.
Governing Authority: private; nonprofit organization. Parent Institution: Institute of Southern Jewish Life. Tax-exempt: 501(c)(3).
Religious History Museum.
Collections: silver ritual Judaica & ceremonial items; Alsatian artifacts; furniture & architectural elements from Southern synagogues; historic photos; family & congregational papers; Bill Aron contemporary photos of Jewish life in the deep South; Southern Jewish artifacts & memorabilia.
Research Fields: Southern Jewish history, including family, institutions, congregations, communities & architecture; oral history of Southern Jews; Southern Jewish folklore & foodways.
Facilities: library of Judaica & general resource materials on Jewish experiences, history, museum education & Judaic texts; theater; auditorium. Museum-related items for sale.
Activities: formal education programs; guided tours; lectures; loan, temporary & traveling exhibitions.
Publications: newsletter, Circa; videos, Natchez Jewish Experience, May the Light Shine Forever.
Hours & Admission Prices: Daily by appointment. Adults $5; discounts to ICOM members & groups; members no charge. ♿
Attendance: 4,950 (estimated)
Membership: Friend $100; Patron $250; Sponsor $500; Benefactor $1,000; Humanitarium $5,000 & up.

MYNELLE GARDENS, 4736 Clinton Blvd., Jackson, MS 39209-2400. Tel.: 601-960-1894.
Garden.
Collections: plants ranging from amaryllises, daylilies, gardenias, pinks & camellias; roses; Asiatic magnolias. Historic Houses: Westbrook House c.1917 & Greenbrook House c.1920.
Facilities: Museum-related items for sale.
Hours & Admission Prices: March-Oct. Mon.-Sat. 12-5:15, Sun. 12-4:15; Nov.-Feb. daily 8-4:15. Family pass $30, student pass $5, adults $4, children 4-12 $1. Closed New Year's; Martin Luther King Jr. Day; Independence Day; Thanksgiving & day after; Christmas. ♿

THE OAKS HOUSE MUSEUM, 823 N. Jefferson St., Jackson, MS 39202-4140. Tel.: 601-353-9339.
E-mail: oakshousemuseum@jam.rr.com
Web Site: theoakshousemuseum.org
Founded: 1960.
Congressional District: 4
Key Personnel: Dir. & Chm. (V), Linda Robertson.
Personnel Profile: Full-Time Volunteers 26; Part-Time Paid 4; Part-Time Volunteers 24.
Governing Authority: society. Parent Institution: National Society of the Colonial Dames in the State of Mississippi. Subsidiary Institution: The Oaks House Museum Corporation. Tax-exempt.
Local History Museum: housed in c.1850 historic building site, The Oaks.
Collections: family life in Jackson, Mississippi from 1846-1860s; furniture & furnishings of the period; old fashioned garden.
Activities: tours; holiday events; dramatic presentations; archaeology camps; seminars.
Publications: brochure.
Hours & Admission Prices: Tues.-Sat. 10-3; other times by appointment. Adults $4.50, senior citizens 65 & over $4, children $3.50; discount to groups of 10 or more & AAA members. Closed major holidays.
Attendance: 1,200 (estimated)

OLD CAPITOL MUSEUM, 100 S. State St., Jackson, MS 39201-4400. Mailing Address: P.O. Box 571, Jackson, MS 39205-0571. Tel.: 601-576-6920. Fax: 601-576-6981.
Web Site: www.oldcapitolmuseum.com
Founded: 2009.
Congressional District: 3
Key Personnel: Dir., Clay Williams; Education, Maura Callaway; Exhibits/Collections, Lauren Miller.
Personnel Profile: Full-Time Paid 5; Part-Time Paid 2; Part-Time Volunteers 15.
Governing Authority: state; nonprofit. Tax-exempt: 501(c)(3).
Historic Building: building served as Mississippi's statehouse from 1839-1903.
Collections: building history; state government; period artifacts; photographs; furnishings; House Chamber auditorium.
Facilities: 5,000 sq. ft. exhibit space; classroom. Museum-related items for sale.
Activities: docent program; formal education programs; guided tours; lectures.
Hours & Admission Prices: Tues.-Sat. 9-5, Sun. 1-5. No charge; donations accepted. Closed New Year's Day; Easter; Memorial Day; Labor Day; Thanksgiving; Christmas. ♿

RUSSELL C. DAVIS PLANETARIUM, 201 E. Pascagoula St., Jackson, MS 39201-4101. Mailing Address: P.O. Box 17, Jackson, MS 39201. Tel.: 601-960-1552. Fax: 601-960-1555.
E-mail: lhfeatherstone@city.jackson.ms.us
Web Site: www.thedavisplanetarium.com
Founded: 1978.
Congressional District: 4
Key Personnel: Asst. Mgr., LaNeysa Harris-Featherstone.
Personnel Profile: Full-Time Paid 6; Part-Time Paid 1; Interns 1.
Governing Authority: municipal. Parent Institution: City of Jackson. Tax-exempt: 170(b)(1)(A).
Planetarium.
Collections: hemisphere projection technology; hemisphere cinematography.
Research Fields: projection technology.
Facilities: 190-seat planetarium and hemispheric film theatre. Gift items for sale.
Activities: planetarium programs; hemispheric large-format films; laser light shows; formally organized education programs for children and adults; special school programs for students preschool-college.
Publications: annual program guide for teachers & group leaders.
Hours & Admission Prices: Call 601-960-1552 for current program, show, and ticket information. Large-format Films & Laser Light Shows: adults $6.50, children $4, school groups $3. Sky Shows: adults $5.50, seniors $4.50, children $3, school groups $2; discount to ASTC members. Closed New Year's Day; Martin Luther King Jr. Day; Presidents' Day; Easter; Memorial Day; Labor Day; Independence Day; Thanksgiving; Christmas Eve & Day. ♿
Attendance: 45,000 (accurate)

SMITH ROBERTSON MUSEUM & CULTURAL CENTER, 528 Bloom St., Jackson, MS 39202-4005. Tel.: 601-960-1457. Fax: 601-960-2070.
Founded: 1984.
Congressional District: 4
Key Personnel: Mgr. & Museum Shop Mgr., Pamela D. Junior; Sec., Euerla Christian Bester; Gift Shop Attendant, Mary Funches.
Personnel Profile: Full-Time Paid 3; Part-Time Volunteers 25; Interns 2.
Governing Authority: municipal. Tax-exempt: 501(c)(3).
History Museum: housed in first school built with public funds for Blacks in Jackson, MS.

Collections: life, history & culture of Black Mississippians from territorial to the present day.
Research Fields: Black church in Mississippi.
Facilities: Museum-related items for sale.
Activities: guided tours; lectures; films; concerts; dance recitals; arts festivals; theater; study clubs; rental gallery; organized education programs for children; docent program; loan exhibitions; school loan service.
Publications: quarterly newsletter, Smith Robertson Museum News.
Hours & Admission Prices: Mon.-Fri. 9-5, Sat. 10-1. Adults $4.50, seniors $3, children under 18 $1.50. Closed New Year's Day; Martin Luther King Jr. Day; Memorial Day; Independence Day; Labor Day; Thanksgiving; Christmas. ♿
Attendance: 15,000 (estimated)
Membership: Individual $10; Family $25; Contributing $50; Corporate $250; Sustaining Corporate $500; Supporting Corporate $1,000.

WAR MEMORIAL BUILDING, 120 N. State St., Jackson, MS 39201-2810. Tel.: 601-354-7207.
Military History Museum.
Collections: military artifacts; personal artifacts; photographs; replica of the Tomb of the Unknown Soldier.
Hours & Admission Prices: Daily. No charge.

Kosciusko

KOSCIUSKO MUSEUM AND VISITORS CENTER, Natchez Trace Pkwy., Kosciusko, MS 39090. Mailing Address: 124 N. Jackson St., Kosciusko, MS 39090-3730. Tel.: 662-289-2981. Fax: 662-289-2986.
Key Personnel: Vice Pres., Tonya Threet
History Museum.
Collections: local history & culture; photographs; personal artifacts.
Hours & Admission Prices: Daily 9-4. No charge. ♿

Laurel

* **LAUREN ROGERS MUSEUM OF ART, (M),** 565 N. 5th Ave., Laurel, MS 39440. Mailing Address: P.O. Box 1108, Laurel, MS 39441-1108. Tel.: 601-649-6374. Fax: 601-649-6379.
Web Site: www.lrma.org
Founded: 1923.
Congressional District: 4
Key Personnel: Dir., George Bassi; Chm. (V), Pat McLean; Pres. (V), Mary Anne Sumrall; Bldg. Supt., Todd Sullivan; Dir. Mktg., Holly Green; Registrar, Tommie Rodgers; Cur., Jill Chancey, Ph.D.; Cur. Education, Mandy Buchanan; Head Librarian, Donnelle Conklin; Librarian, Donna Smith; Business Mgr., JoLynn Helton; Dir. Devel., Allyn C. Boone; Visitor Svcs. Coord., Pam Ward.
Personnel Profile: Full-Time Paid 11; Part-Time Paid 4; Part-Time Volunteers 107; Interns 4.
Governing Authority: nonprofit organization. Parent Institution: Eastman Memorial Foundation. Tax-exempt: 509(a).
Art Museum.
Collections: 19th-20th-century American & European paintings; drawings; 18th-century Japanese Ukiyo-e woodblock prints; Native American Indian baskets; 18th-century English Georgian silver.
Research Fields: visual arts; history.
Facilities: 20,000-vol. library with emphasis on art, local history, Mississippiana available for use by public on premises; reading room.
Activities: guided tours; lectures; films; gallery talks; concerts; docent program; permanent, temporary & traveling exhibitions; classes; workshops. Annual Events: Blues Bash; Fall Festival.
Publications: brochure; quarterly members newsletter; LRMA Handbook of the Collections; exhibition catalogs, By Native Hands: Woven Treasures from the Lauren Rogers Museum of Art.
Hours & Admission Prices: Tues.-Sat. 10-4:45, Sun. 1-4. Suggested Donation: $3. Closed major holidays. ♿
Attendance: 37,000 (estimated)
Membership: Student $15; Associate $25; Friend $50; Sponsor $100; Patron $150; Donor $250; Benefactor $500; Grand Benefactor $1,000; Sustaining Benefactor $1,500; Laureate $2,500.

VETERANS MEMORIAL MUSEUM, 920 Hillcrest Dr., Laurel, MS 39440-4726. Tel.: 601-428-4008.
Military Museum.
Collections: military history; movies & documentaries; Honor Wall etched with names of veterans from Southeast Mississippi.
Facilities: library.
Hours & Admission Prices: Tues.-Fri. 10-4. No charge. ♿

Leakesville

GREENE COUNTY MUSEUM & HISTORICAL SOCIETY, Greene County House, 400 Main St., 4th Fl., Leakesville, MS 39451. Mailing Address: P.O. Box 841, Leakesville, MS 39451-0841. Tel.: 601-394-4343.
E-mail: museum@tds.net
Web Site: greenmuseum.org
Historical Society Museum.
Collections: local history & culture relating to Greene County.
Hours & Admission Prices: Mon.-Tues. & Thurs. 9-4, Wed., Fri. and first Sat. of each month 9-12. No charge; donations accepted.

Leland

HIGHWAY 61 BLUES MUSEUM, 307 N. Broad St., Leland, MS 38756-2744. Tel.: 662-686-2063.
Blues Museum.
Collections: local history; Delta bluesmen & their music; photographs; personal artifacts.
Hours & Admission Prices: Mon.-Sat. 10-5; other times by appointment.

Louisville

THE AMERICAN HERITAGE "BIG RED" FIRE MUSEUM, 332 N. Church Ave., Louisville, MS 39339-2302. Mailing Address: 650 N. Church Ave., Louisville, MS 39339-2033. Tel.: 662-773-3421. Fax: 662-773-9183.
Web Site: www.taylorbigred.com
Founded: 1989.
Congressional District: 3
Key Personnel: C.E.O., W.A. "Lex" Taylor, III; Restoration Specialist, Vick Reed; Registrar, Kay Reynolds.
Governing Authority: private.
Fire-Fighting Museum.
Collections: early fire equipment; late 1700 hand pumpers; hose reels; horse drawn ladder trucks; Cole Brother and Silsby steam pumpers; hand pulled reel & wagons; ALF pumpers; 1921 ladder trucks; 1924 Ahrens Fox; 1957 Seagrave ladder truck; taxidermic wildlife; Indian artifacts; model planes & ships; art.
Hours & Admission Prices: Mon.-Fri. by appointment only. No charge. Closed holidays.

McComb

MCCOMB CITY RAILROAD DEPOT MUSEUM, 108 N. Railroad Blvd., McComb, MS 39649-7220. Mailing Address: P.O. Box 7220, McComb, MS 39649-7220. Tel.: 601-684-2291.
E-mail: trainmaster@mcrrmuseum.com
Web Site: www.mcrrmuseum.com
Key Personnel: C.E.O., Winnie Len Howell; Museum Shop Mgr., Bob Bellipanni.
Personnel Profile: Part-Time Paid 1; Part-Time Volunteers 50.
Governing Authority: city of McComb. Tax-exempt.
Railroad Museum.
Collections: railroad memorabilia.
Hours & Admission Prices: Mon.-Fri. 12-4.
Attendance: 5,000 (estimated)

Meridian

JIMMIE RODGERS MUSEUM, 1725 Highland Park Dr., Meridian, MS 39307. Mailing Address: P.O. Box 4555, Meridian, MS 39304-4555. Tel.: 601-485-1808.
E-mail: jimmie_rodgers@hotmail.com
Founded: 1976.
Congressional District: 3
Key Personnel: C.E.O., Betty Lou Jones; Chm. (V), Greg Hatcher.
Personnel Profile: Part-Time Paid 3.
Governing Authority: municipal; nonprofit organization. Parent Institution: Jimmie Rodgers Foundation. Tax-exempt: 170(b)(1)(A).
Folk Art Museum.
Collections: items belonging to the late Jimmie Rodgers, father of country music.
Activities: guided tours.
Hours & Admission Prices: Tues.-Thurs. 10-4; other times by appointment. Adults $5; discounts for school tours; children under 10 no charge. Closed legal holidays. ♿
Attendance: 7,000 (estimated)

MERIDIAN MUSEUM OF ART, 628 25th Ave., Meridian, MS 39301. Mailing Address: P.O. Box 5773, Meridian, MS 39302-5773. Tel.: 601-693-1501. Fax: 601-485-3175.
E-mail: meridianmuseum@bellsouth.net
Web Site: meridianmuseum.org
Founded: 1969.
Congressional District: 3
Key Personnel: Dir., Kate Cherry; Pres., Dr. Judith Miller.
Personnel Profile: Full-Time Paid 1; Part-Time Paid 3; Part-Time Volunteers 40.
Governing Authority: municipal; nonprofit. Affiliated with Meridian Art Association. Tax-exempt: 501(c)(3).
Art Museum Gallery.
Collections: Caroline Durieux lithographs; works by Will Barnet, Alexander Van Laer, Marie Hull, Nell Blaine, George Ault, Mary Frank, Alice Neel; collection of 18th-century British portraits; continental landscapes; Boehm porcelain.
Research Fields: museum outreach.
Facilities: classrooms; lecture room.
Activities: art classes for children & adults; artists group; lecture series; workshops; school outreach program.
Publications: biannual brochure; monthly newsletter.
Hours & Admission Prices: Wed.-Sat. 11-5. No charge; donations accepted. Closed holidays.
Attendance: 10,098 (accurate)
Membership: Individual $30; Dual Family $50; Patron $150; Sponsor $300; Benefactor $500; Grand Benefactor $1,000; Silver Circle $2,500; Gold Circle $5,000; Platinum Circle $10,000.

Mississippi State University

COBB INSTITUTE OF ARCHAEOLOGY, College of Arts & Sciences, Mississippi State University, MS 39762-5542. Mailing Address: P.O. Box AR, Mississippi State University, MS 39762-5542. Tel.: 662-325-3826. Fax: 662-325-8690.
E-mail: jds1@ra.msstate.edu
Web Site: www.cobb.msstate.edu
Founded: 1972.
Congressional District: 2
Key Personnel: Dir., Joe Seger; Administrative Sec., Kathleen Elliott; Cur. Artifacts, John O'Hear.
Personnel Profile: Part-Time Paid 4.
Governing Authority: university. Parent Institution: Mississippi State University. Tax-exempt.
Archaeology Museum.
Collections: Middle Eastern archaeological remains; southeastern U.S. archaeological materials.
Research Fields: Middle East & southeastern U.S. archaeology.
Facilities: 10,000-vol. library; research laboratories.
Activities: museum tours; lectures.
Publications: reports; occasional papers; biannual newsletter, Cobb Institute of Archaeology.
Hours & Admission Prices: Call for hours. No charge; donations accepted. Closed school holidays. ♿
Attendance: 3,000 (estimated)

DUNN-SEILER MUSEUM, Dept. of Geosciences, Mississippi State University, MS 39762. Mailing Address: P.O. Box 5448, Mississippi State Univ., MS 39762-5448. Tel.: 662-325-3915. Fax: 662-325-9423.
E-mail: rclary@geosci.msstate.edu
Web Site: www.msstate.edu/dept/geosciences/museum.htm
Founded: 1947.
Key Personnel: Dir., Dr. Renee M. Clary; Cur., Dr. Chris Dawey; Mgr. Collections, Amy Moe Hoffman.
Governing Authority: university. Parent Institution: Mississippi State University. Tax-exempt.
Natural History Museum.
Collections: Mesozoic & Cenozoic paleontology; Upper Cretaceous lepadomorph barnacles; mineralogy; geology.
Research Fields: geology.
Activities: guided tours; lectures; formally organized education programs for children, adults & undergraduate college students; permanent & temporary exhibitions.
Hours & Admission Prices: Mon.-Fri. 8-5. No charge; donations accepted. Closed school holidays & vacations. ♿
Attendance: 1,000 (estimated)

MISSISSIPPI ENTOMOLOGICAL MUSEUM, Dept. of Entomology and Plant Pathology, Mississippi State University, MS 39762. Mailing Address: P.O. Box 9775, Mississippi State University, MS 39762-9775. Tel.: 662-325-2990. Fax: 662-325-8837.
Web Site: www.mississippientomologicalmuseum.org.msstate.edu
Key Personnel: Professor Entomology & Dir. Museum, Dr. Richard Brown; Cur., Terence L. Schiefer; Asst. Cur. & Scientific Illustrator, Joe A. MacGown.
Governing Authority: university. Parent Institution: Mississippi State University.
Entomology Museum.
Collections: over 1,000,000 pinned specimens; H. E. Weed; Henry Dietrich, J. M. Langston, R. W. Harned, Gladys Hoke-Lobdell, E. W. Stafford, M. R. Smith, William H. Cross, Leon W. Hepner, and Charles Bryson; taxa from Central and South America, the Seychelles, New Caledonia, and Fiji Islands; the MacDonald collection, emphasizing Lepidoptera of Panama; Ross E. Hutchins collection of photographs.
Research Fields: taxa in Araneae, Acarina, Plecoptera, Homoptera, Coleoptera, Lepidoptera, and Diptera.
Hours & Admission Prices: Call for hours.

Natchez

* **GRAND VILLAGE OF THE NATCHEZ INDIANS, (M),** 400 Jefferson Davis Blvd., Natchez, MS 39120-5110. Tel.: 601-446-6502. Fax: 601-446-6503.
E-mail: gvni@cableone.net
Web Site: mdah.state.ms.us
Founded: 1976.
Congressional District: 3
Key Personnel: Dir., James F. Barnett, Jr.; C.E.O., H.T. Holmes; Pres. (V), Kane Ditto; Sec., Sharon Ogden; Sales Shop Mgr., Janice Sago; Historian, Rebecca Anderson.
Governing Authority: state. Affiliated with the State of Mississippi Department of Archives and History, Div. of Historic Properties, Old Capitol Green, P.O. Box 571, Jackson, MS 38205. Tax-exempt: 170(b)(1)(A).
Anthropology Museum: 1700-1730, Natchez Indian ceremonial mound center.
Collections: artifacts collected from the site; Indian ceramics; stone implements; early 18th-century French trade items.
Research Fields: culture of the Natchez Indians; archaeological survey of prehistoric & historic sites within Mississippi.
Facilities: 50-vol. library of ethnographic & archaeological reports available for research on premises only; field research station; separate laboratory operation; 60-seat auditorium. Southeastern Indian crafts & books for sale.
Activities: guided tours; lectures; films; hobby workshops; school & group tours; permanent exhibitions; craft demonstration program.
Publications: The Natchez Indians.
Hours & Admission Prices: Mon.-Sat. 9-5, Sun. 1:30-5. No charge; donations accepted. Closed New Year's Day; Labor Day; Thanksgiving; Christmas.
Attendance: 35,000 (accurate)

MISSISSIPPI SOCIETY DAUGHTERS OF THE AMERICAN REVOLUTION ROSALIE HOUSE MUSEUM, 100 Orleans St., Natchez, MS 39120-3452. Tel.: 601-445-4555 & 446-5676. Fax: 601-304-1376.
E-mail: rosaliemansion@yahoo.com
Web Site: www.rosaliemansion.com
Founded: 1898.
Key Personnel: Chm. (V), Cindy Phillips; Museum Shop Mgr., Karlyn Ritchie.
Personnel Profile: Full-Time Paid 1; Part-Time Paid 20; Part-Time Volunteers 30.
Governing Authority: Parent Institution: Mississippi State Society D.A.R. Tax-exempt.
Historic Site Museum: housed in c.1820 house & gardens located on Old Fort Rosalie grounds.
Collections: original period furnishings including Belter and C. Lee furniture; decorative arts; historic structures.
Research Fields: genealogy library.
Facilities: library of genealogy and history books relating to Mississippi & Natchez; gardens.
Activities: guided tours; formally organized education programs for children. Annual Events: USS Mississippi on Memorial Day, Independence Day & Veterans Day.
Publications: Miss DAR Magazine.
Hours & Admission Prices: Daily 9-5; group tours available upon request. Adults $10, children $8; Mississippi DAR members & children under 6 no charge. Closed Easter; Thanksgiving; Christmas. ♿
Attendance: 25,000 (accurate)

NATCHEZ COSTUME & DOLL MUSEUM, 215 S. Pearl St., Natchez, MS 39120. Tel.: 601-442-6672; 800-647-6742. Fax: 601-446-8687.
General Museum.

Collections: period dolls; costume gowns worn by queens of past pageants during Spring Pilgrimage.
Hours & Admission Prices: Mon.-Fri. 9-4, Sat. 10-4. Admission $6.

NATCHEZ MUSEUM OF AFRICAN-AMERICAN HISTORY AND CULTURE, 301 Main St., Natchez, MS 39120-3461. Mailing Address: P.O. Box 1844, Natchez, MS 39121-1844. Tel.: 601-445-0728.
History Museum.
Collections: local history & culture depicting African-American life in Mississippi; photographs; artifacts.
Hours & Admission Prices: Tues.-Sat. 1-4:30. Adults $5, children $1.

New Albany

UNION COUNTY HERITAGE MUSEUM, (M), 114 Cleveland St., New Albany, MS 38652-4050. Mailing Address: P.O. Box 657, New Albany, MS 38652-0657. Tel.: 662-538-0014. Fax: 662-538-6019.
E-mail: uchm@ucheritagemuseum.com
Web Site: www.ucheritagemuseum.com
Founded: 1991.
Congressional District: 1
Key Personnel: Dir., Jill Smith; Pres. (V) & Museum Shop Mgr., Betsey Hamilton.
Personnel Profile: Full-Time Paid 2; Full-Time Volunteers 1; Part-Time Paid 1; Part-Time Volunteers 25.
Governing Authority: nonprofit. Parent Institution: Union County Historical Society.
History Museum.
Collections: scale model of William Faulkner's birthplace; Faulkner memorabilia & local history; Faulkner Literary Garden.
Research Fields: William C. Faulkner.
Facilities: archives.
Publications: cookbook, Worth Savoring.
Hours & Admission Prices: Mon.-Fri. 9-4, Sat. 10-3. No charge; donations accepted. ♿
Attendance: 10,000 (estimated)
Membership: Single $15; Associate $25; Supporter $50; Sponsor $100; Patron $250; Donor $500; Contributor $1,000.

Ocean Springs

G.I. MUSEUM, 5796 Ritcher Rd., Ocean Springs, MS 39564-2291. Tel.: 228-872-1943.
Web Site: www.gimuseum.com
Founded: 2005.
Key Personnel: Dir., Doug Mansfield.
Personnel Profile: Full-Time Volunteers 3; Part-Time Volunteers 3.
Governing Authority: Tax-exempt.
Military Museum.
Collections: military artifacts & memorabilia.
Activities: Museum Sponsors: Living History Events in March & November.
Publications: 30 min. weekly television show, "Local Heros".
Hours & Admission Prices: 1st & 3rd Sun. of month & Wed. 10-5; other times by appointment. No charge; donations accepted. ♿

J.L. SCOTT MARINE EDUCATION CENTER AND AQUARIUM, GULF COAST RESEARCH LABORATORY COLLEGE OF MARINE SCIENCES, THE U. OF SOUTHERN MISSISSIPPI, 703 E. Beach Dr., Ocean Springs, MS 39564-5326. Tel.: 228-818-8890. Fax: 228-818-8894.
E-mail: marine.education@usm.edu
Web Site: www.aquarium.usm.edu
Founded: 1972.
Congressional District: 5
Key Personnel: Admin., Sharon H. Walker, Ph.D.; Coord. Education Programs, Susan Culipher-Ross; Administrative Asst., Johnette Bosarge; Aquarium Supvr. & Facilities Coord., Alex (Buck) Schesny; Museum Shop Mgr., Sylvia Covacevich.
Personnel Profile: Full-Time Paid 21; Part-Time Paid 3; Part-Time Volunteers 80; Interns 25.
Governing Authority: state. Parent Institution: Gulf Coast Research Laboratory, University of Southern Mississippi. Tax-exempt: 501(c)(3).
Aquarium, Marine Museum & Education Center.
Collections: 71 aquariums; snake enclosures; vivarium with reptiles & amphibians; touch tank; displays of marine artifacts, including a whale skeleton; mounted fish specimens; crabs of the Gulf of Mexico; various interactive exhibits.
Research Fields: breeding habits of North American native fishes; development & implementation of pre-college & informal educational programs.
Facilities: teacher resource programs library; nature & conservation center; aquarium; 313-seat auditorium.
Activities: aquarium tour & habitat interpretation; family membership program; formally organized education programs for children, adults, undergraduate college students & graduate students during the academic year; overnight scouting programs; advisory series; numerous static exhibits.
Publications: various leaflets; monthly newsletter, Marine Briefs.
Hours & Admission Prices: Mon.-Sat. 9-4. Adults $4, senior citizens $3.50, children 3-17 $2.50; discounts to groups & AAA members; children under 3 & members no charge. ♿
Attendance: 75,000 (estimated)
Membership: Student & Senior Citizen $15; Individual $25; Family $50; Family Plus $60; Sponsor $75; Patron $100; Corporate $1,000.

* **WALTER ANDERSON MUSEUM OF ART, (M),** 510 Washington Ave., Ocean Springs, MS 39564-4632. Tel.: 228-872-3164. Fax: 228-875-4494.
E-mail: wama@walterandersonmuseum.org
Web Site: www.walterandersonmuseum.org
Founded: 1991.
Congressional District: 4
Key Personnel: Exec. Dir., Gayle Petty-Johnson; Pres. Bd., Nicholas Van Wiser; Cur., Douglas Walker; Dir. Devel., Makalah Brown; Museum Shop Mgr., Betsy Myers.
Personnel Profile: Full-Time Paid 8; Part-Time Paid 2; Part-Time Volunteers 46.
Governing Authority: nonprofit. Tax-exempt: 501(c)(3).
Art Museum: located in Historic District of Ocean Springs.
Collections: concentration on the works of Mississippi artist Walter Inglis Anderson; murals; paintings; sculpture; linoleum block prints; ceramics; decorative arts; changing exhibits feature other artists whose works are related to Anderson's.
Research Fields: art & life of Walter Anderson.
Facilities: 3,000 sq. ft. exhibit space. Posters & illustrated books featuring works of Walter Anderson, children's books, art books, art & science-related merchandise, jewelry, T-shirts, educational toys & museum-related items for sale.
Activities: guided tours; lectures; arts festivals; concerts; dance recitals; films; docent program; formal education programs for adults & children; temporary & loan exhibits. Annual Events: Art Blooms at WAMA in May; Monthly Art Activities for Children; summer art camp.
Publications: quarterly newsletter, Motif.
Hours & Admission Prices: Mon.-Sat. 9:30-5, Sun. 12-5. Adults $7, seniors, students 16-24 with ID, AAA members & military $6, children 5-17 $5; discounts to groups with advance reservation, AAM, AFA, SEMC & MMA members; children under 5 & members no charge. Closed New Year's Day; Mardi Gras; Easter; Independence Day; Thanksgiving; Christmas Eve & Day. ♿
Attendance: 30,000 (accurate)
Membership: Student $20; Seniors $30; Individual $40; Family Senior $50; Family $60; Sustainer $100; Patron $250; Benefactor $500; President's Club $1,000.

WILLIAM M. COLMER VISITOR CENTER, 3500 Park Rd., Davis Bayou Area, Ocean Springs, MS 39564-9709. Tel.: 228-875-9057 & 0074 ext. 100. Fax: 228-872-2954 & 875-2358.
Web Site: www.nps.gov/guis/
Founded: 1971.
Congressional District: 5
Key Personnel: District Interpreter, Susan Blair.
Personnel Profile: Full-Time Paid 3; Part-Time Paid 1; Part-Time Volunteers 20; Interns 3.
Governing Authority: federal. U.S. Dept. of the Interior, National Park Service, Washington, DC (See separate listings for Fort Pickens Area-Gulf Islands National Seashore, Santa Rosa Island, FL & Gulf Islands National Seashore, Gulf Breeze, FL for more complete information.)
National Park & Natural & Cultural History Museum: located on & part of Gulf Islands National Seashore.
Collections: items & artifacts pertaining to gulf ecosystem coastal fortifications & orientation to Gulf Islands; history of Ship Island.
Research Fields: natural history; history; archaeology.
Activities: permanent exhibitions.
Publications: pamphlets; newspaper.
Hours & Admission Prices: Daily 8:30-4:30. No charge; donations accepted. ♿

Attendance: 50,000 (estimated)

Oxford

ROWAN OAK, HOME OF WILLIAM FAULKNER, 916 Old Taylor Ave., Oxford, MS 38655. Mailing Address: Univ. of Mississippi Museum, P.O. Box 1848, University, MS 38677-1848. Tel.: 662-234-3284. Fax: 662-915-7035.
E-mail: wgriffit@olemiss.edu
Web Site: www.olemiss.edu
Founded: 1972.
Congressional District: 1
Key Personnel: Dir., Albert Sperath; Cur., William D. Griffith.
Personnel Profile: Full-Time Paid 6; Full-Time Volunteers 9; Part-Time Paid 4; Part-Time Volunteers 4; Interns 1.
Governing Authority: public university; nonprofit. Parent Institution: University of Mississippi. Tax-exempt: 501(c)(3).
Historic House Museum: home of William Faulkner, 1930-1962. A National Historic Landmark & National Literary Landmark.
Collections: furniture; personal artifacts.
Hours & Admission Prices: Tues.-Sat. 10-4, Sun. 1-4. Adults $5; children no charge. Closed New Year's Eve & Day; Independence Day; Thanksgiving; Christmas Eve & Day. ♿
Attendance: 27,000 (accurate)

UNIVERSITY MUSEUM & HISTORIC HOUSES, THE UNIVERSITY OF MISSISSIPPI, (M), 5th St. & University Ave., Oxford, MS 38655. Mailing Address: P.O. Box 1848, University, MS 38677-1848. Tel.: 662-915-7073. Fax: 662-915-7035.
E-mail: museums@olemiss.edu
Web Site: www.olemiss.edu/depts/u_museum
Founded: 1939.
Congressional District: 1
Key Personnel: Dir., William Andrews; Chancellor, Dan Jones; Collections Mgr., William Griffith; Consultant in Classics, Dr. Aileen Ajootian; Preparator, Bob Pekala.
Personnel Profile: Full-Time Paid 5; Part-Time Paid 10; Part-Time Volunteers 10; Interns 2.
Governing Authority: university; state; nonprofit organization. Parent Institution: University of Mississippi. Subsidiary Institutions: Walton-Young Historic House; Rowan Oak, William Faulkner's Home. Tax-exempt.
General Museum.
Collections: David M. Robinson collection of ancient Greek & Roman pottery; coins; sculpture; surgical instruments; architectural fragments; inscriptions; Sumerian clay tablets; Roman glass; Egyptian antiquities; John Millington & F.A.P. Barnard collection of 19th-century scientific instruments; Theora Hamblett paintings; antique dolls; Victorian memorabilia; West African art; folk art of the American South; technology.
Research Fields: ancient Greece; 19th-century physics & astronomy instruments; anthropology, technology, folk art.
Facilities: 1,500-vol. library available for use on premises; classroom; meeting room.
Activities: guided tours; lectures; organized programs; permanent, temporary & traveling exhibitions; traveling trunk shows; picture files & videotapes for schools.
Publications: newsletters 3 times a year; brochures; catalogs.
Hours & Admission Prices: Museum: Tues.-Sat. 9:30-4:30, Sun. 1-4:30. Walton-Young House: Fri. 10-12, 2-4. Rowan Oak: Tues.-Sat. 10-4, Sun. 1-4. Museum & Walton-Young House: no charge. Rowan Oak: adults $5; members no charge. Closed national & university holidays. ♿
Attendance: 19,000 (accurate)
Membership: Student $10; Individual $25; Family $40; Patron $100; Supporting & Corporate Member $250; Director's Circle & Corporate Supporting $500; Sponsor & Corporate Sponsor $1,000; Sustaining & Corporate Sustaining $5,000.

Pascagoula

SCRANTON NATURE CENTER, 3928 Nathan Hale Dr., Pascagoula, MS 39581-4727. Mailing Address: P.O. Drawer 908, Pascagoula, MS 39568-0908. Tel.: 228-938-6612.
Nature Center.
Collections: owls; fossils; sea life; plants; rocks; minerals.
Facilities: nature trails.
Activities: educational programs.
Hours & Admission Prices: Tues.-Sat. 10-5.

SCRANTON SHRIMP BOAT MUSEUM, River Park, Pascagoula, MS 39568. Mailing Address: P.O. Drawer 908, Pascagoula, MS 39568-0908. Tel.: 228-938-6612.
History Museum: housed on a 70 ft. commercial shrimp boat.
Collections: period furnishings; bunk room; wheelhouse; boat history; fishing industry.
Hours & Admission Prices: Tues.-Sat. 10-4, Sun. 1-4. No charge.

Philadelphia

NESHOBA COUNTY-PHILADELPHIA HISTORICAL MUSEUM, 303 Water Ave., Philadelphia, MS 39350-2621. Tel.: 601-656-1000. Fax: 601-656-1066.
History Museum: housed in the home of George Pegram Woodward, c.1860.
Collections: county history; period furnishings.
Hours & Admission Prices: Mon.-Thurs. 10-3, Sat. 9-12. No charge.

Picayune

THE CROSBY ARBORETUM, MISSISSIPPI STATE UNIVERSITY, 370 Ridge Rd., Picayune, MS 39466-8151. Mailing Address: P.O. Box 1639, Picayune, MS 39466-1639. Tel.: 601-799-2311, ext. 21. Fax: 601-799-2372.
E-mail: drackett@ext.msstate.edu
Web Site: www.crosbyarboretum.msstate.edu
Founded: 1980.
Congressional District: 5
Key Personnel: Dir., Dr. Janine Conklin; Sr. Cur., Pat Drackett.
Personnel Profile: Full-Time Paid 4; Part-Time Paid 1; Part-Time Volunteers 20.
Governing Authority: nonprofit organization. Parent Institution: Mississippi State University. Subsidiary Institution: Coastal Research & Extension Center. Tax-exempt: 501(c)(3).
Arboretum.
Collections: woody & herbaceous plants of the Pearl River Drainage Basin of Mississippi and Louisiana; photo archives; herbarium.
Research Fields: botany; ecology; landscape architecture; horticulture.
Facilities: Pinecote: 104-acres native plant center; aquatic, savannah & woodland succession exhibits; nature paths; visitors center.
Activities: guided tours; field trips to natural areas; lectures; films; formally organized education programs; special events for members; seminars; native plant sales.
Publications: quarterly, News Journal; books, Native Woody Plant Species of the Pearl River Basin, Guide to the Natural Areas of the Crosby Arboretum; Checklist of the Native Woody Plants of the Pearl River Basin.
Hours & Admission Prices: Wed.-Sun. 9-5. Adults $4, senior citizens $3, children $2; discounts to AAM, ICOM members, arboretum members & American Horticultural Society Reciprocal Garden members; members no charge. Closed New Years Eve & Day; Thanksgiving; Christmas Eve & Day. ♿
Attendance: 5,500 (estimated)
Membership: Student $10; Individual $25; Family $35; Donor & Business $100; Patron $250-$999; Benefactor $1,000.

Piney Woods

LAURENCE C. JONES MUSEUM, Piney Woods School, Hwy. 49 S., Piney Woods, MS 39148. Mailing Address: P.O. Box 99, Piney Woods, MS 39148-0037. Tel.: 601-845-2214. Fax: 601-845-2604.
Web Site: www.pineywoods.org
Founded: 1909.
Congressional District: 4
Key Personnel: C.E.O., Reginald T.W. Nichols, Ed.D.; Chm., Gen. Wallace Arnold; Dir. Operations, John May.
Personnel Profile: Full-Time Paid 1; Part-Time Paid 1.
Governing Authority: private school; nonprofit. Parent Institution: The Piney Woods School. Tax-exempt: 501(c)(3).
History Museum: housed in c.1922 Community House, The Piney Woods Country Life School.
Collections: Piney Woods Country Life School history; the life of its founder, Laurence C. Jones; school archives; African American artifacts.
Research Fields: oral history interviews of former students & employees.
Facilities: 245-vol. library of Piney Woods history; archives; 4,139 sq. ft. exhibit space.
Activities: guided tours; temporary exhibitions; videos.
Publications: quarterly newsletter, The Pine Torch.
Hours & Admission Prices: Mon.-Fri. 8-5. No charge; donations accepted. Closed major holidays. ♿
Attendance: 15,000 (estimated)

Pontotoc

TOWN SQUARE POST OFFICE & MUSEUM, 59 S. Main St., Pontotoc, MS 38863-2824. Mailing Address: P.O. Box 141, Pontotoc, MS 38863-0141. Tel.: 662-488-0388. Fax: 662-488-0398.
Founded: 1998.
Key Personnel: Dir., Martha Coleman; Pres. (V) Pontotoc County Historical Society, James L. Roberts, Jr.
Personnel Profile: Part-Time Paid 1; Part-Time Volunteers 10.
Governing Authority: Parent Institution: Pontotoc County Historical Society. Tax-exempt.
History Museum.
Collections: paintings by local artists; Chickasaw Indian artifacts; tools; period artifacts.
Facilities: Museum-related items for sale.
Hours & Admission Prices: Mon.-Fri. 10-4:30; other times by appointment. No charge; donations accepted.

Poplarville

PEARL RIVER COMMUNITY COLLEGE MUSEUM, (M), 101 Hwy. 11 N., Poplarville, MS 39470-2201. Tel.: 601-403-1000; 877-772-2338 (Toll Free).
Web Site: www.prcc.edu/museum
Key Personnel: Dir., Ronn Hague
History Museum.
Collections: college & Pearl River history; documents; photographs.
Hours & Admission Prices: Mon.-Fri. 8-11 & 1-4; other times by appointment.

Port Gibson

GRAND GULF MILITARY PARK, 12006 Grand Gulf Rd., Port Gibson, MS 39150-4549. Tel.: 601-437-5911. Fax: 601-437-2929.
E-mail: grandgulfpark@aol.com
Web Site: www.grandgulfpark.state.ms.us
Founded: 1958.
Congressional District: 4
Key Personnel: Chm., Robert St. John; Admin. Asst., Cathi Dodgen.
Personnel Profile: Full-Time Paid 7; Part-Time Paid 2; Part-Time Volunteers 6.
Governing Authority: state. Parent Institution: State of Mississippi. Tax-exempt.
Military Museum & Historic Site.
Collections: archaeology; Civil War relics; Indian arrowheads; period buggies & coaches; rifle pits; gun emplacements; waterwheel; 42 RV camper pads; cemetery. Historic Houses: 1790 Spanish House; 1815 Dog Trot House; 1820 Wheeless House; 1830 cottage in park; 1868 Sacred Heart Catholic Church; carriage house; jailhouse; firehouse; 2 Civil War forts.
Research Fields: Civil War battlefields.
Facilities: library; reading room; picnic pavilion; observation tower; road to Mississippi River; full hook up camper pads; bath house; laundry room, tent camping.
Activities: lectures; tours; Civil War reenactments; living histories.
Publications: archaeological reports, The Confederate Upper Battery Site, Grand Gulf MS., Excavations, 1982; The Confederate Magazine at Fort Wade Grand Gulf, MS. Excavations, 1980-81.
Hours & Admission Prices: Daily 8-5. Museum & Grounds: adults $3, senior citizens $2, students K-12 $1; discount to groups with reservations; pre-schoolers no charge. Closed major holidays. ♿
Attendance: 80,000 (estimated)

Ridgeland

CRAFTSMEN'S GUILD OF MISSISSIPPI & MISSISSIPPI CRAFT CENTER, 950 Rice Rd., Ridgeland, MS 39157-3040. Tel.: 601-856-7546. Fax: 601-856-7531.
E-mail: info@mscrafts.org
Web Site: www.mscrafts.org
Founded: 1973.
Congressional District: 4
Key Personnel: Exec. Dir., Julia Daily; Bd. Pres., Barbara Dearman; Chm. (V), Judy Barnett; Museum Shop Mgr., Michelle Escude.
Personnel Profile: Full-Time Paid 4; Part-Time Paid 8; Part-Time Volunteers 100.
Governing Authority: nonprofit. Parent Institution: The Craftsmen's Guild of Mississippi, Inc. Subsidiary Institution: The Mississippi Crafts Center. Tax-exempt: 501(c)(3).
Fine Crafts Gallery & Guild.
Collections: pottery; hand-woven items; quilts; baskets; jewelry; hand blown glass; woodcarvings; willow furniture; Indian basketry; metal sculpture; hand crafted toys.
Research Fields: Choctaw Indian culture.
Facilities: Craft items for sale.
Activities: lectures; arts festivals; organized education programs for children & adults; craft demonstrations on weekends. Museum Sponsors: Indian and Pioneer Heritage Festival; Chimneyville Crafts Festival.
Publications: books, The Language of Mississippi Choctaw Crafts, The Guild at Twenty-Five, A Portrait of the Craftmen's Guild of Mississippi.
Hours & Admission Prices: Mon.-Sat. 9-5. No charge; donations accepted. ♿
Attendance: 150,000 (estimated)
Membership: Friend & Student $50; Apprentice $100-$199; Journeyman $200-$499; Journeyman II $500-$999; Master Craftsmen $1,000-$2,499; Patron $2,500-$4,999; Benefactor $5,000-$9,999; Partner $10,000 & up.

Ripley

TIPPAH COUNTY HISTORICAL MUSEUM, 106 N. Siddell St., Ripley, MS 38663-2036. Tel.: 662-512-0099.
History Museum.
Collections: local history & culture; weapons; clothing; tools; Indian artifacts.
Hours & Admission Prices: Tues.-Sat. 10-2. No charge; donations accepted.

Senatobia

HERITAGE MUSEUM FOUNDATION OF TATE COUNTY, INC., 135 N. Front St., Senatobia, MS 38668-0375. Mailing Address: P.O. Box 375, Senatobia, MS 38668-0375. Tel.: 662-562-8715.
Founded: 1977.
Congressional District: 2
Key Personnel: Pres., Deborah Perkins; Sec., Janie Mortimer; Treas., Sara S. Henley.
Personnel Profile: Part-Time Volunteers 2.
Governing Authority: nonprofit organization. Tax-exempt: 170(b)(1)(A) & 509(a)(1).
Historic Foundation Museum: housed in historic Tate County Courthouse.
Collections: general artifacts of the history of Tate County, MS.
Research Fields: Tate County local history.
Activities: self-guided tours.
Publications: brochure.
Hours & Admission Prices: Mon.-Fri. 8-5, except on Courthouse holidays. No charge; donations accepted. ♿
Attendance: 150 (estimated)
Membership: Student $3; Individual $5; Couple $10; Life $1,000.

Starkville

OKTIBBEHA COUNTY HERITAGE MUSEUM, 206 Fellowship St., Starkville, MS 39759-3378. Tel.: 662-323-0211 & 6511.
Founded: 1979.
Congressional District: 4
Key Personnel: Pres. (V), Joan Wilson; Chm. (V), Mary Bell.
Personnel Profile: Part-Time Volunteers 20.
Governing Authority: board of trustees. Parent Institution: City of Starkville/Oktibbeha County. Tax-exempt.
History Museum: housed in 1800s The G M & O Depot.
Collections: local history; artifacts from the county's past such as maps, books, pictures, farm equipment, old dairy equipment, wedding dresses, military service uniforms, quilts, cradles, Indian arrowheads; train exhibit including dated nails found in old cross ties, railroad stock, old tickets, time tables, telegraph system & 1800 & 1875 models of passenger trains; early radios; doctor's instruments case; period dolls and doll furniture.
Facilities: meeting room.
Activities: guided tours.
Publications: brochure.
Hours & Admission Prices: Tues.-Thurs. 1-4, Sat. call for hours. No charge; donations accepted. ♿
Attendance: 1,500 (accurate)

Taylorsville

WATKINS MUSEUM, Eureka St., Taylorsville, MS 39168. Mailing Address: P.O. Box 617, Taylorsville, MS 39168-0617. Tel.: 601-785-6531. Fax: 601-785-9816.
E-mail: jrglenn@magamate.com
Founded: 1968.
Congressional District: 3
Key Personnel: Cur., Rosalyn Glenn.
Governing Authority: municipal.
General Museum: housed in c.1900 Taylorsville Signal & General Store.
Collections: c.1837 hand printing press; early medical & farm equipment; manuscripts; period bottles; clothing; country store equipment; typewriter; catalogs; early 1900s house plans.
Facilities: 150-vol. library of books; magazines; newspapers available for use on premises only.

Activities: guided tours; permanent & temporary exhibitions.
Hours & Admission Prices: Temporarily closed for renovation.
Attendance: 100

Tougaloo

TOUGALOO COLLEGE, Tougaloo College Art Collection, 500 W. County Line Rd., Tougaloo, MS 39174-0578. Mailing Address: P.O. Box 578, Tougaloo, MS 39174-9799. Tel.: 601-977-7743. Fax: 601-977-7714.
E-mail: art@tougaloo.edu
Web Site: www.tougaloo.edu/artcolony
Founded: 1869.
Congressional District: 3
Key Personnel: Pres., Beverly Wade Hogan; Assoc. Professor Art, Bruce O'Hara; Professor & Dept. Chair Collections, Johnnie M. Maberry-Gilbert; Head Librarian, Orthello Moman; Archives Mgr., Minnie Watson.
Personnel Profile: Part-Time Volunteers 1.
Governing Authority: board of trustees; college. Affiliated with United Church Board for Homeland Ministries & The American Missionary Association, 132 W. 31st St., New York, NY 10001. Tel.: 212-239-8700. Tax-exempt.
Historic Site/Building: located on historic Tougaloo College Campus. Housed in the Bennie Thompson Building.
Collections: European & African American & African art from 17th-21st century.
Facilities: 3,000-vol. library of books available for research with patron's card; reading room; auditorium; theater; classrooms; cafeteria.
Activities: guided tours; lectures; films; gallery talks; concerts; drama; rental gallery; formally organized education programs for undergraduate college students; cooperative with Mississippi Museum of Art; loan, permanent, temporary & traveling exhibitions.
Publications: 1968-1978 The Tougaloo College Art Collections; Silver Jubilee, 1963-1988 (a history); catalog, The Turbulent Years.
Hours & Admission Prices: Temporarily closed for renovation. ♿
Attendance: 1,000 (estimated)

Tunica

TUNICA MUSEUM, One Museum Blvd., Tunica, MS 38676. Mailing Address: P.O. Box 1914, Tunica, MS 38676-1914. Tel.: 662-363-6631. Fax: 662-363-6651.
E-mail: drdick@tunicamuseum.com
Web Site: www.tunicamuseum.com
Founded: 1997.
Key Personnel: Dir., Richard Taylor; Pres. (V), Lynn Arnold; Museum Shop Mgr., Darlene Griffith.
Personnel Profile: Full-Time Paid 4; Part-Time Paid 2; Part-Time Volunteers 1.
History Museum.
Collections: area history; Native American artifacts; railroad memorabilia.
Facilities: library. Museum-related items for sale.
Publications: newsletter.
Hours & Admission Prices: Mon.-Sat. 10-5, Sun. 1-5. No charge; donations accepted. ♿
Attendance: 30,000

Tupelo

ELVIS PRESLEY BIRTHPLACE AND MUSEUM, 306 Elvis Presley Dr., Tupelo, MS 38804-2812. Tel.: 662-841-1245. Fax: 662-690-6623.
E-mail: info@elvispresleybirthplace.com
Web Site: www.elvispresleybirthplace.com
Key Personnel: Exec. Dir., Dick Guyton
History Museum: housed in the birthplace of Elvis Presley, born in 1935.
Collections: furnishings.
Facilities: picnic area; Memorial Chapel. Museum-related items for sale.
Activities: Museum Sponsors: Annual Fan Appreciation Day in August.
Hours & Admission Prices: May-Sept. Mon.-Sat. 9-5:30, Sun. 1-5; Oct.-April Mon.-Sat. 9-5, Sun. 1-5. House: adult $4, child $2. Museum: adult $8, child $4. Combined: adult $12, child $6; discounts to groups of 15 or more. Closed Thanksgiving; Christmas.

GUMTREE MUSEUM OF ART, 211 W. Main St., Tupelo, MS 38804-3917. Mailing Address: P.O. Box 786, Tupelo, MS 38802-0786. Tel.: 662-844-2787. Fax: 662-844-9751.
E-mail: tina@gumtreemuseum.com
Web Site: www.gumtreemuseum.com
Formerly: Tupelo Artist Guild Gallery
Founded: 1985.
Congressional District: 5
Key Personnel: Exec. Dir. & Public Rels., Tina Lutz; Chm. (V), Nancy Diffee; Asst., DeLane Patrick.
Personnel Profile: Full-Time Paid 1; Part-Time Paid 1; Part-Time Volunteers 15.
Governing Authority: nonprofit organization; local board. Tax-exempt: 501(c)(3).
Art Museum.
Collections: paintings; photographs.
Activities: guided tours; lectures; study clubs; education programs for youth & adults.
Hours & Admission Prices: Tues.-Sat. 10-4. No charge; donations accepted. Closed New Year's Day; Independence Day; Thanksgiving; Christmas. ♿
Attendance: 13,200 (estimated)
Membership: Student & Senior Citizen $15; Individual $35; Family $65; Donor $100; Patron $250; Benefactor $500; Guild Sponsor $1,000.

NATCHEZ TRACE PARKWAY, 2680 Natchez Trace Pkwy., Tupelo, MS 38804-9715. Tel.: 662-680-4025. Fax: 662-680-4036.
E-mail: christina_smith@nps.gov
Web Site: www.nps.gov/natr
Founded: 1938.
Congressional District: 1
Key Personnel: Supt., Cameron H. Sholly; Interpretive Specialist, Ernie Price.
Governing Authority: federal. Parent Institution: National Park Service. Tax-exempt.
Visitor Center & Archival Study Collection.
Collections: Indian trails; 18th-century trade route; 1800 post road; archaeology; ethnology; geology; parkway construction 1930s-present. Historic Site: 1785 Mount Locust.
Research Fields: parkway construction.
Facilities: 1,400-vol. library of historical reference material; herbarium; picnic areas; trails.
Activities: orientation film; unscheduled talks.
Publications: folders, Parkway, Tupelo/Brices Crossroads; assorted informational handouts.
Hours & Admission Prices: Daily 8-4:30. No charge. Closed Christmas. ♿
Attendance: 51,991 (accurate)

OREN DUNN CITY MUSEUM, (M), 689 Rutherford Rd., Tupelo, MS 38803. Mailing Address: P.O. Box 2674, Tupelo, MS 38803-2674. Tel.: 662-841-6438. Fax: 662-841-6458.
E-mail: museum@ci.tupelo.ms.us
Web Site: www.orendunnmuseum.org
Formerly: Tupelo City Museum
Founded: 1984.
Key Personnel: Advisory Bd., Dr. Mike Currie; Chm. Friends of the Museum, Dr. Harold Hudson; Dir., Cur. & Museum Shop Mgr., Kenneth McGehee; Outreach Coord., Rae Mathis; Museum Educator, Janice Anthony; Facility Mgr., Jerry Duckett.
Governing Authority: city. Tax-exempt: 501(c)(3).
History Museum.
Collections: local history & culture from 1870s to present; period Tupelo fire trucks; 1948 Lee County Book Mobile; Memphis trolley car turned diner; one room chapel; one room school; veterans' artifacts. Historic Building: 1870s Dog-Trot Cabin.
Major Exhibits: African American Inventors (T), 1/10-2/10; Rhythm & Roots (T), 4/10-6/10; Tupelo Quilt Connection, 10/10-11/10; Holiday Exhibit, 12/10.
Activities: rental facilities; summer camp. Museum Sponsors: Dudie Burger Festival in May; Fall Festival in October; Scarecrows! Community Fair in October.
Hours & Admission Prices: Tues.-Fri. 9-4, Sat. 10-3. Adults $3, seniors 60 & over $1; children under 3 no charge. Closed City of Tupelo holidays. ♿
Attendance: 9,000 (estimated)

TUPELO AUTOMOBILE MUSEUM, 1 Otis Blvd., Tupelo, MS 38804-4015. Tel.: 662-842-4242.
E-mail: chale@tupeloauto.com
Web Site: www.tupeloauto.com
Founded: 2002.
Key Personnel: Cur., Allen McDaniel; Business Mgr., Mary Thompson; Dir. Mktg., Cindy Hale; Visitor Coord., Dot Lamb
Automobile Museum.
Collections: over 100 cars from 1880s to 1990s including movie & celebrity-owned vehicles; neon signs; period artifacts; Elvis memorabilia.
Major Exhibits: Salute to Sunshine, 1/9/10-9/23/10; Chevelles, 2/6/10-2/27/10; Horses in the House, 3/6/10-3/27/10; Farming, 4/10/10-4/24/10; Tupelo Blue Suede Cruise, 4/29/10-5/2/10; Corvette Summer, 6/5/10-6/19/10; Hidden Treasures, 7/10-8/10; Late Great Chevys, 11/6/10-11/27/10; Blue Christmas, 12/4/10-12/18/10.
Facilities: 120,000 sq. ft. exhibit space.

Activities: tours; rental facilities; special events. Annual Events: Blue Suede Cruise in May; Our Rags to Riches Tour.
Publications: quarterly newsletter, The Rear View Mirror.
Hours & Admission Prices: March-Oct. Tues.-Sat. 10-6, Sun. 12-5; Nov.-Feb. Tues.-Sat. 10-5, Sun. 12-5. Adult $10, seniors $8, children 5-12 $5; discounts to groups of 10 or more & AAA members; children 4 & under no charge. Closed New Year's; Easter; Thanksgiving; Christmas. ♿
Membership: Individual $35; Family $50; Contributor $100; Sustainer $250; Patron $500; Benefactor $1,000.

Union

BOLER STAGECOACH INN MUSEUM, 205 E. Jackson Rd., Hwy. 492, Union, MS 39365. Mailing Address: 1130 Stamper Pond Rd., Union, MS 39365. Tel.: 601-635-3160.
Historic Building: c. 1856.
Collections: period furnishings & artifacts from 1830-1920; photographs; personal artifacts.
Hours & Admission Prices: By appointment. Adults $5, children $1.

Vicksburg

BIEDENHARN COCA-COLA MUSEUM, 1107 Washington St., Vicksburg, MS 39183-2959. Tel.: 601-638-6514. Fax: 601-636-5010.
E-mail: vburgfoundation@aol.com
Web Site: biedenharncoca-colamuseum.com
Founded: 1979.
Key Personnel: Exec. Dir., Nancy H. Bell; Chm. (V), Charlie Gholson; Treas., Denny Allman.
Personnel Profile: Full-Time Paid 1; Part-Time Paid 3; Part-Time Volunteers 4.
Governing Authority: private; nonprofit organization. Parent Institution: Vicksburg Foundation for Historic Preservation. Tax-exempt: 501(c)(3).
History Museum: housed in the first Coca-Cola bottling company in the world, 1894.
Collections: history of Coca-Cola; the Biedenharn family; bottling works; Coca-Cola memorabilia; soda fountain; period bottles; advertising; signs; ice chests.
Facilities: 20-vol. library; 5,000 sq. ft. exhibit space; soda fountain. Museum-related items for sale.
Hours & Admission Prices: Mon.-Sat. 9-5, Sun. 1:30-4:30. Adults $3, students & children $2; discounts to groups, families, AAM & ICOM members; members no charge. Closed New Year's Day; Easter; Thanksgiving; Christmas.
Attendance: 25,000 (accurate)
Membership: Individual $25; Family $35; Contributing $50; Sustaining $75; Patron $100-$499; Gold Patron $500 & up.

CEDAR GROVE MANSION INN, 2200 Oak St., Vicksburg, MS 39180-4008. Tel.: 601-636-1000. Fax: 601-634-6126.
E-mail: info@cedargroveinn.com
Web Site: cedargroveinn.com
Founded: 1959.
Congressional District: 2
Key Personnel: C.E.O., Owner & Innkeeper, Colleen Small.
Governing Authority: privately owned.
Historic Site & Building: 1840-1858 Southern mansion located at the site of the Siege of Vicksburg.
Collections: original furnishings; Civil War cannonball embedded in parlor wall; Regina music box; Bohemian glass; original works of art; 15 Italian marble mantelpieces; Aubusson rugs; terra cotta statues; urns; pre-Civil War magazines.
Facilities: old volumes on law, medicine, history and botany available on premises; iron gazebo; formal gardens; restaurant; Antebellum Inn offers overnight accommodations.
Activities: guided tours.
Hours & Admission Prices: Tours daily 9:30-11 & 1-4. Adults $6, children 6-12 $4; discounts to groups; children under 6 no charge. ♿

THE JACQUELINE HOUSE AFRICAN AMERICAN MUSEUM, 1325 Main St., Vicksburg, MS 39183-2647. Tel.: 601-636-0941.
History Museum.
Collections: African American history & culture; photographs; books; manuscripts; music; posters; newspapers.
Activities: lectures; special events; rental facilities; film festivals.
Hours & Admission Prices: Sat. 10-5; other times by appointment.

NATIONAL PARK SERVICE VICKSBURG NATIONAL MILITARY PARK-CAIRO MUSEUM, 3201 Clay St., Vicksburg, MS 39183-3495. Tel.: 601-636-2199 (Museum) & 0583 (Park). Fax: 601-638-7329.
Web Site: www.nps.gov/vick
Founded: 1980.
Congressional District: 2
Key Personnel: Museum Cur., Elizabeth Joyner; Park Historian, Terry Winschel; Chief Operations, Rick Martin; Park Supt., Monika Mayr.
Personnel Profile: Full-Time Paid 3.
Governing Authority: federal. Affiliated with National Park Service. Tax-exempt.
History Museum & Visitors Center: located on the site of the 1863 Union siege of the city of Vicksburg, MS.
Collections: official records of the Union and Confederate Armies & Navies; Historic House: 1800s Shirley House. Historic Restored Gunboat: U.S.S. Cairo Museum, containing artifacts from ironclad gunboat.
Research Fields: pertaining to those who fought in the Vicksburg campaign.
Facilities: 150-vol. library on Civil War naval history & artifacts available for use on premises; U.S.S. Cairo Museum. Civil War Naval literature for sale.
Activities: self-guided tours; lectures; films; audiovisual program; formally organized education programs for children & adults on and off premises; living history demonstration in summer.
Publications: book, Hardluck Ironclad; park folder; site bulletins on various topics pertaining to Civil War naval history & Vicksburg campaign.
Hours & Admission Prices: Cairo Museum: April 6-Oct. 30 9:30-6; Oct. 31-April 5 8:30-5. Park: $8 per car. Museum located inside park. Closed New Year's Day; Thanksgiving; Christmas. ♿
Attendance: 500,000 (estimated)

OLD COURT HOUSE MUSEUM-EVA WHITAKER DAVIS MEMORIAL, 1008 Cherry St., Court Square, Vicksburg, MS 39183-2540. Tel.: 601-636-0741.
E-mail: societyhistorica@bellsouth.net
Web Site: www.oldcourthouse.org
Founded: 1947.
Congressional District: 1
Key Personnel: C.E.O. & Pres. Historical Society, Randy McCollum; Dir. & Cur., George C. Bolm; Pres. (V), Charles D. Mitchell.
Personnel Profile: Full-Time Paid 3; Part-Time Paid 3; Part-Time Volunteers 2.
Governing Authority: sponsored by the Vicksburg & Warren County Historical Society.
Historic Building: housed in the 1858 Old Warren County Courthouse. A National Historic Landmark.
Collections: Civil War & Indian artifacts; antebellum South; photographic glass negatives & prints of steamboats by Mack Moore; clothing; art; furniture.
Research Fields: genealogy; history pertaining to our local area.
Facilities: 1,400-vol. library of general material available for use by individuals paying a research fee. Postcards & museum-related items for sale.
Activities: Museum Sponsors: Old Court House Flea Market; Confederate Christmas Ball; Sacred Harp Singing; Sporting Clay.
Publications: annual newsletter; weekly newspaper column on local history.
Hours & Admission Prices: Mon.-Sat. 8:30-5, Sun. 1:30-5. Adults $5, senior citizens $4.50, students grades 1-12 $3. Closed New Year's; Thanksgiving; Christmas Eve & Day. ♿
Attendance: 32,763 (accurate)
Membership: Individual $25; Friend $50; Contributing $100; Supporting $500; Patron of History $1,000.

VICKSBURG BATTLEFIELD MUSEUM, 4139 I-20 Frontage Rd., Vicksburg, MS 39183-3427. Tel.: 601-638-6500. Fax: 601-638-8746.
E-mail: thegunboat@bellsouth.net
Web Site: vicksburgbattlefieldmuseum.net
Founded: 1993.
Congressional District: 2
Key Personnel: C.E.O., Lamar Roberts; Museum Shop Mgr., Sue Roberts.
Personnel Profile: Full-Time Paid 2; Part-Time Paid 2; Part-Time Volunteers 2.
History Museum.
Collections: Civil War diorama recreating the battles of the Siege of Vicksburg including 2500 miniature soldiers; Civil War gunboat models; film documentary; models of U.S. Navy vessels named for Mississippians; paintings by Herb Mott; sculptures by Dan Rickardson; maps; clothing; photos.
Facilities: theater.
Activities: film presentation.
Hours & Admission Prices: Mon.-Sat. 9-5. Adults $5.50. Closed Easter; Thanksgiving; Christmas. ♿
Attendance: 19,000 (accurate)

YESTERDAY'S CHILDREN ANTIQUE DOLL & TOY MUSEUM, 1104 Washington St., Vicksburg, MS 39183-2960. Tel.: 601-638-0650.
E-mail: mbakarich@aol.com
Web Site: www.yesterdayschildrenmuseum.com
Founded: 1986.
Key Personnel: Dir., Michael N. Bakarich; Cur., Carolyn C. Bakarich.

Personnel Profile: Full-Time Volunteers 2; Part-Time Volunteers 3.
Toy and Doll Museum.
Collections: over 1,000 dolls including mid-1800 China heads to late 1800 French & German bisques, 1900 compositions, Madame Alexanders, Shirley Temples, Barbies, barefoot children, ventriloquist dolls, contemporary dolls from 1940 to present, & artist dolls. Boys' toys include pedal cars, trucks, trains, guns, soldiers, cars, planes, construction & farm equipment, G.I. Joes.
Facilities: 2,688 sq. ft. exhibit space. Museum-related items for sale.
Publications: brochure, Yesterday's Children Antique Doll & Toy Museum.
Hours & Admission Prices: Mon.-Sat. 10-4; other times by appointment. Adults $3, children $2; discounts to groups of 10 or more. Closed Thanksgiving; Christmas. ♿
Attendance: 12,000 (estimated)

Washington

HISTORIC JEFFERSON COLLEGE, 16 Old North St., Washington, MS 39190. Mailing Address: P.O. Box 700, Washington, MS 39190-0700. Tel.: 601-442-2901. Fax: 601-442-2902.
E-mail: hjc@mdah.state.ms.us
Web Site: mdah.state.ms.us
Founded: 1971.
Congressional District: 4
Key Personnel: C.E.O., Hank Holmes; Dir., Robin Seage Person; Historian, Clark Burkett; Sec. & Sales Shop Mgr., Maxine Clay; Historian, Kay McNeil.
Personnel Profile: Full-Time Paid 4; Part-Time Volunteers 15.
Governing Authority: state; nonprofit organization. Parent Institution: the Mississippi Dept. of Archives & History, P.O. Box 571, State St., Jackson 39205. Tel.: 601-354-6218. Branch Museums: Windsor Ruins Historic Site, Claiborne County. Tax-exempt: 501(c)(3).
Historic Site: Campus chartered in 1802 by Mississippi Territorial Legislature.
Collections: college related artifacts such as uniforms; books; weapons; cemetery. Historical Houses: 1817 East Wing; 1839 West Wing; 1836 West Kitchen; 1839 East Kitchen; c.1828 President's House; 1915 Raymond Hall; 1931 Prospere Hall; 1937 Carpenter Hall.
Research Fields: historical; preservation; restoration.
Facilities: 5,000-vol. library; picnic area; 40 acre nature trail. Books for sale.
Activities: self-guided tours daily; special programs; summer camps; lunchtime lecture series; educational program for students; Civil War reenactments. Museum Sponsors: Nature Fest.
Publications: alumni newsletter, Jefferson Military College.
Hours & Admission Prices: Mon.-Sat. 9-5, Sun. 1-5. No charge; donations accepted. Closed New Year's Day; Labor Day; Thanksgiving; Christmas.
Attendance: 15,000 (estimated)
Membership: Jefferson Military College Alumni Foundation $50.

Water Valley

THE WALTER VALLEY CASEY JONES RAILROAD MUSEUM, 105 Railroad Ave., Water Valley, MS 38965-3312. Tel.: 601-473-1154.
E-mail: gurnerjk@watervalley.net
Web Site: www.watervalley.net/users/caseyjones/home.htm
Key Personnel: Cur., J. K. Gurner
Railroad Museum.
Collections: railroad memorabilia.
Hours & Admission Prices: Thurs.-Sat. 2-4; other times by appointment.

West Point

SAM WILHITE TRANSPORTATION MUSEUM, 210 Depot Dr., West Point, MS 39773. Tel.: 662-494-6385.
Transportation Museum.
Collections: early West Point transportation; 1927 Model T Ford car; model railroad; replica railroad ticket office; railroad clocks; telegraph; period telephones.
Hours & Admission Prices: Thurs.-Sat. 10-4. No charge; donations accepted.

Woodville

ROSEMONT PLANTATION, Rosemont Plantation, Hwy. 24 E., Woodville, MS 39669. Mailing Address: P.O. Box 814, Woodville, MS 39669-0814. Tel.: 601-888-6809. Fax: 601-888-3327.
E-mail: pbeacroft@aol.com
Web Site: www.rosemontplantation.com
Founded: 1971.
Key Personnel: Owner, Percival T. Beacroft; Publicity & Tours, Jenny Angeline.
Personnel Profile: Full-Time Paid 2; Full-Time Volunteers 1; Part-Time Paid 1; Part-Time Volunteers 1.
Governing Authority: individual operation.
Historic House Museum: 1810, originally named Poplar Grove, family home of Jefferson Davis; family cemetery located on grounds.
Collections: Davis furniture, artifacts & portraits; furnishings; original house & reconstructed outbuildings.
Research Fields: genealogy of all descendants of Davis family compiled by Ernesto Caldeira.
Activities: guided tours; permanent exhibitions; Davis family reunion every two years.
Publications: brochure; newsletter, Davis Family.
Hours & Admission Prices: March to mid-Dec. Tues.-Fri. 10-4; groups by appointment; additional hours during Natchez Spring & Fall Pilgrimages. Suggested Donations: adults $8, seniors 55 & over $7, students $4.

WILKINSON COUNTY MUSEUM, Courthouse Square, Woodville, MS 39669. Mailing Address: P.O. Box 1055, Woodville, MS 39669-1055. Tel.: 601-888-7151. Fax: 601-888-3327.
E-mail: wilkmuseum@aol.com
Web Site: www.historicwoodville.org
Founded: 1971.
Congressional District: 4
Key Personnel: C.E.O., Ernesto Caldeira; Pres. (V), David Wilkerson; Dir., David Abner Smith.
Personnel Profile: Full-Time Volunteers 2; Part-Time Volunteers 38.
Governing Authority: nonprofit organization. Parent Institution: Woodville Civic Club, Inc. Branch Museum: The African American Museum, Bank St., Woodville, MS.
History Museum: housed in a Greek Revival Temple style office & banking house of the West Feliciana Railroad; built in 1834.
Collections: decorative arts from county plantations & homes; photographs; archives; genealogical files; general area history.
Research Fields: Wilkinson County history.
Activities: lectures; loan, temporary & traveling exhibitions.
Publications: annual, The Journal of Wilkinson County History; reprints of 1899 cookbook.
Hours & Admission Prices: Mon.-Fri. 10-12 & 2-4, Sat. 10-12.
Attendance: 4,900 (accurate)
Membership: Individual Adult $1; Friend $15; Donor $100; Supporter $101-$499; Patron $500-$999; Benefactor & Founders Plaque $1,000 & up.

Yazoo City

SAM OLDEN HISTORICAL SOCIETY MUSEUM, 332 N. Main St., Yazoo City, MS 39194-3958. Mailing Address: P.O. Box 186, Yazoo City, MS 39194. Tel.: 662-746-1815; 800-381-0662.
E-mail: yazoo@yazoo.org
Formerly: Yazoo Historical Museum
Governing Authority: city.
History Museum.
Collections: exhibits relating to the pre-historic, pioneer, ante-bellum, Victorian & modern time periods.
Hours & Admission Prices: Mon.-Fri. 8:30-4:30, Sat. 12-4. No charge; donations accepted.

MISSOURI

(242 listings)

Agency

AGENCY FORD MUSEUM, 11351 Rte. FF, Agency, MO 64401. Tel.: 816-253-9301.
E-mail: sharonrumpf@yahoo.com
Personnel Profile: Part-Time Volunteers 2.
History Museum.
Collections: agency history from 1836 to present.
Hours & Admission Prices: By appointment only. No charge.

Altenburg

LUTHERAN HERITAGE CENTER & MUSEUM OF THE PERRY COUNTY LUTHERAN HISTORICAL SOCIETY, 75 Church St., Altenburg, MO 63732. Mailing Address: P.O. Box 53, Altenburg, MO 63732-0053. Tel.: 573-824-6070.
Formerly: The Perry County Lutheran Historical Society of Altenburg, Missouri, Inc.
Founded: 1910.
Congressional District: 8
Key Personnel: Pres. (V), Robert Schmidt; Dir., Carla L. Jordan; Museum Shop Mgr., Evelyn Meyr.

Personnel Profile: Part-Time Paid 1; Part-Time Volunteers 40; Interns 1.
Governing Authority: denominational group. Parent Institution: Perry County Lutheran Historical Society. Branch Museums: 1839 Concordia Log Cabin College; 1845 Big School. Tax-exempt.
Religious Museum: located on the site of the principal settlement of Saxon immigrants in 1839; the nucleus for the Lutheran Church, Missouri Synod; regional history.
Collections: religious books; bibles; sermon books; pictures; records; early history of Saxon immigration, 1839; First By-laws, Trinity Lutheran Church; Lutheran history; regional cultural German-American history; period artifacts from 1838-1839.
Research Fields: Mo-synod Lutheran Church history; Saxon immigration to East Perry County, MO; genealogical research of synodical history & the founding families of the 1938-39 immigration.
Facilities: library of religious books available for use on premises by appointment.
Activities: lectures; self-guided & guided tours; presentations.
Publications: History of Trinity Lutheran Church; By-Laws of the Trinity Church, Altenburg, MO; History of Trinity Church, Altenburg, MO; Except the Corn Die, Koestering; DVD, From Faith to Faith.
Hours & Admission Prices: Daily 10-4. No charge; donations accepted. Closed New Year's Eve & Day; Christmas Eve & Day. ♿
Attendance: 4,000 (accurate)

Arcadia

IRON COUNTY HISTORICAL SOCIETY MUSEUM, 630 Hwy. 21, Arcadia, MO 63621. Mailing Address: P.O. Box 183, Ironton, MO 63650-0183. Tel.: 573-546-3513.
E-mail: ironcohissoc@hotmail.com
Web Site: www.rootsweb.ancestry.com/~moichs
Key Personnel: Pres., Wilma Cofer
Historical Society Museum.
Collections: local history & culture; photographs.
Hours & Admission Prices: April-Nov. Mon.-Sat. 10-4, Sun. 1-4; Dec.-March Fri.-Sat. 10-4, Sun. 1-4.

Arrow Rock

ARROW ROCK STATE HISTORIC SITE, 4th & Van Buren, Arrow Rock, MO 65320. Mailing Address: P.O. Box 1, Arrow Rock, MO 65320-0001. Tel.: 660-837-3330. Fax: 660-837-3300.
Web Site: www.mostateparks.com
Founded: 1923.
Congressional District: 6
Key Personnel: Dir., Michael Dickey; Museum Shop Mgr., Cindy Imhoff.
Personnel Profile: Full-Time Paid 6; Part-Time Paid 4.
Governing Authority: state. Parent Institution: Div. of State Parks, Missouri Dept. of Natural Resources, P.O. Box 176, Jefferson City, MO 65102. Tax-exempt.
Village Museum Complex: c.1830-1870, town located near eastern end of Santa Fe Trail.
Collections: period furnishings; paintings; manuscripts; textiles; artifacts; exhibits interpreting the Boone's Lick region in the early 19th century. Historic Houses: c.1840 general store; 1846 Dr. Matthew Hall house; 1837 George Caleb Bingham house; 1835 court house; 1830 Academy boarding house; 1834 Arrow Rock tavern; 1870 jail house.
Research Fields: Missouri history; Santa Fe Trail; westward movement; 19th-century agriculture; 19th-century architecture; Missouri River trade; historic preservation; African-American, Osage & Missouri Indian culture & history.
Facilities: restaurant; recreation & camping areas. Gift items & supplies for sale.
Activities: guided tours; seminars; crafts festivals; camping.
Publications: brochures; George Caleb Bingham House, Arrow Rock Site.
Hours & Admission Prices: Walking Tour: April-May & Sept.-Oct. Sat.-Sun. 1-4:30; June-Aug. daily 10-4. Museum & Interpretive Center: March-May & Sept.-Nov. daily 10-4; June-Aug. daily 10-5; Dec.-Feb. Fri.-Sun. 10-4. No charge. Walking tour of village: adults $5, children 6-12 $1.50; discounts to groups of 8 or more; children under 6 no charge. Campground: April-Oct. $8 & $14; Nov.-March $7 & $12. ♿
Attendance: 156,000 (accurate)

FRIENDS OF ARROW ROCK, INC., (M), 310 Main St., Arrow Rock, MO 65320. Mailing Address: Box 124, Arrow Rock, MO 65320-0124. Tel.: 660-837-3231. Fax: 660-837-3230.
E-mail: kborgman@iland.net
Web Site: www.friendsar.org
Founded: 1959.
Congressional District: 6
Key Personnel: Pres. (V), Dr. Thomas B. Hall, III; Admin., Kathy Borgman.
Personnel Profile: Full-Time Paid 2; Part-Time Paid 2.
Governing Authority: nonprofit corporation. Tax-exempt: 501(c)(3).
Historic Buildings.
Collections: antiques; crafts. Historic Houses & Buildings: 1844 John P. Sites gun shop; 1875 John P. Sites house; 1868 I.O.O.F. Hall; Dr. John Sappington Museum; 1872 Christian Chapel; 1880 African American properties: Brown's Chapel, Baptist Church; Black Masonic Lodge.
Facilities: theater; state park camping; restaurants; information center; craft shop. Museum-related items for sale.
Activities: guided tours; children's hands-on tours; lectures; arts festival; permanent exhibitions; demonstrations. Museum Sponsors: Craft Festival in October; summer professional theater.
Publications: books, Arrow Rock Cook Book; Arrow Rock: Crossroads of the Missouri Frontier; Dr. John Sappington of Saline County; Along the Old Trail; Medicine on the Santa Fe Trail; Over the Santa Fe Trail in 1857.
Hours & Admission Prices: Tours: April-May & Sept.-Oct. Sat.-Sun. & by appointment; Memorial Day to Labor Day daily 10, 11:30, 1:30 & 3; groups by appointment. Adults $5, children $1.50; discounts to groups. ♿
Attendance: 4,000 (estimated)
Membership: Supporting $30; Sustaining $50; Sponsor $100; Patron $250; Benefactor $500; Life $1,000.

Bellefontaine Neighbors

GENERAL DANIEL BISSELL HOUSE, 10225 Bellefontaine Road, Bellefontaine Neighbors, MO 63137-2307. Tel.: 636-532-7298; 314-554-6224. TTY: 314-615-7840.
E-mail: jfoley@stlouisco.com
Web Site: www.co.st-louis.mo.us/parks/bissel.html
Founded: 1960.
Key Personnel: Dir. & Site Supvr., Jim Foley.
Governing Authority: county; nonprofit. Parent Institution: St. Louis County Dept. of Parks & Recreation, 41 S. Central Ave., St. Louis, MO 63105.
Historic House: Federal Style home of Gen. Daniel Bissell, Commander of the Upper Louisiana Territory, Revolutionary War soldier, gen. in the War of 1812.
Collections: Bissell family artifacts; 1812-1850 decorative arts & furnishings.
Research Fields: slavery in St. Louis; history of Fort Belle Fontaine & Bissell family.
Activities: guided tours.
Hours & Admission Prices: Tours by appointment only.

Belton

BELTON GRANDVIEW AND KANSAS CITY RAILROAD CO., 502 E. Walnut St., Belton, MO 64012-2516. Tel.: 816-331-0630.
E-mail: info@beltonrailroad.org
Web Site: www.beltonrailroad.org
Railroad Museum.
Collections: display equipment; freight cars; Club Car; instruction car; two static display steam locomotives.
Hours & Admission Prices: Train departures: May Sat.-Sun. at 2; June-Aug. Sat. at 11 & 2, Sun. at 2; Sept.-Oct. Sat.-Sun. 2. Adults $8.50; children 2 & under no charge.

BELTON MUSEUM OF HISTORY, 512 Main St., Belton, MO 64012-2583. Tel.: 816-331-8044 & 2255.
History Museum.
Collections: local history & culture; photographs; Dale Carnegie; Carry Nation; Harry Truman.
Hours & Admission Prices: March-Dec. Tues. & Thurs. 1-4, Sat. 10-1. No charge; donations accepted.
Membership: Annual $15; Business $25; Lifetime $150.

Bloomfield

STARS AND STRIPES MUSEUM/LIBRARY, 17377 Stars and Stripes Way, Bloomfield, MO 63825-8487. Mailing Address: P.O. Box 1861, Bloomfield, MO 63825-0463. Tel.: 573-568-2055.
E-mail: stripes@newwavecomm.net
Web Site: starsandstripesmuseumlibrary.org
Key Personnel: Pres., Dr. Joe Baker
Military Museum.
Collections: U.S. Armed Forces military newspapers from the Civil War to present; personal artifacts.
Facilities: Museum-related items for sale.
Hours & Admission Prices: Mon. & Wed.-Fri. 10-4, Sat. 10-2, Sun. 1-4; other times by appointment. Closed New Year's Day; Easter; Thanksgiving; Christmas. ♿

STODDARD COUNTY MUSEUM, 501 Center St., Bloomfield, MO 63825. Mailing Address: 15248 Palo Verde Lane, Dexter, MO 63841. Tel.: 573-568-2163.
Key Personnel: Pres., Anita Peters
History Museum.
Collections: early farm machinery; 1875 period parlor & kitchen display.
Hours & Admission Prices: May-Oct. fourth Sun. of each month 2-4. No charge; donations accepted.

Blue Springs

THE DILLINGHAM-LEWIS MUSEUM, 101 S. 15th St., Blue Springs, MO 64015-3511. Mailing Address: Blue Springs Historical Society, P.O. Box 762, Blue Springs, MO 64013. Tel.: 816-224-8979.
Governing Authority: Parent Institution: Blue Springs Historical Society.
Historical Society Museum.
Collections: local history & culture; furnishings; photographs.
Hours & Admission Prices: By appointment only.

Bolivar

THE ELLA CAROTHERS DUNNEGAN GALLERY OF ART, 511 N. Pike, Bolivar, MO 65613-1568. Mailing Address: P.O. Box 468, Bolival, MO 65613-0468. Tel.: 417-326-3438.
E-mail: dunnegan@windstream.net
Web Site: www.dunnegangallery.com
Key Personnel: Dir., Jo Roberts
Fine Arts Museum.
Collections: paintings.
Major Exhibits: Art & The Animal (T), 3/14/10-4/16/10; National Oil & Acrylic Painters' Society Best of America (NOAPS) (T), 9/10-10/10.
Hours & Admission Prices: Mon., Wed. & Fri. 1-4, Sun. call for hours. No charge; donations accepted. Closed bank holidays. ♿

Boonesboro

BOONE'S LICK STATE HISTORIC SITE, State Rd. 187, Boonesboro, MO 65233. Mailing Address: Arrow Rock State Historic Site, P.O. Box 1, Arrow Rock, MO 65320-0001. Tel.: 660-837-3330. Fax: 660-837-3300.
Web Site: www.mostateparks.com/booneslick.htm
Founded: 1960.
Congressional District: 6
Key Personnel: Dir., Michael Dickey.
Personnel Profile: Full-Time Paid 7; Part-Time Paid 1.
Governing Authority: state. Owned & operated by Div. of State Parks, Missouri Dept. of Natural Resources, P.O. Box 176, Jefferson City, MO 65102. Tax-exempt.
Historic Site: c.1805 early salt manufacturing site.
Collections: housed at Arrow Rock State Historic Site: salt kettles, tools, wooden buckets, water wheel drive shaft excavated on site; outdoor interpretive exhibits.
Research Fields: pioneer salt industry.
Facilities: interpretive pavilion; 1/4 mile trail; picnic area; salt springs.
Hours & Admission Prices: Sunrise-sunset. Closed during periods of snow or ice. ♿
Attendance: 10,000 (estimated)

Branson

AMERICA'S PRESIDENCY MUSEUM AND GALLERY OF AMERICAN HISTORY, 2849 Gretna Rd., Ste. 300, Branson, MO 65616-3387. Tel.: 417-334-8683. Fax: 417-334-4927.
E-mail: amerpresidency@aol.com
Web Site: www.americanpresidentialmuseum.com
Founded: 2005.
Key Personnel: Dir., Stormy Lynn Snow; Chm. (V), James A. Levander; Museum Shop Mgr., Michele Shanan.
Personnel Profile: Full-Time Volunteers 2; Part-Time Paid 2; Part-Time Volunteers 4.
Governing Authority: Parent Institution: National Center for Presidential Studies. Tax-exempt.
American History Museum.
Collections: America's Presidential history; photographs; personal artifacts.
Research Fields: American presidents; American history.
Activities: public programs; outreach; special events.
Publications: quarterly newsletter.
Hours & Admission Prices: Tues.-Sat. 9-5. Adults $10, seniors 55 & over $9; discounts to AAM & ICOM members; children 16 & under no charge. Closed Thanksgiving; Christmas. ♿
Attendance: 50,000 (estimated)
Membership: $10; $35; $50; $100.

HOLLYWOOD WAX MUSEUM, 3030 W. Hwy. 76, Branson, MO 65616-8312. Tel.: 417-337-8277.
E-mail: branson@hollywoodwax.com
Web Site: www.hollywoodwax.com/
Key Personnel: General Mgr., Chuck O'Day
Wax Museum.
Collections: wax figures & scenes; television & movie history.
Activities: birthday parties; school tours.
Hours & Admission Prices: Daily 8am-12pm. Adults $14.95; seniors 65+ $13.95; children 4-11 $7.95. ♿
Attendance: 100,000

THE ROY ROGERS-DALE EVANS MUSEUM AND THEATER, 3950 Green Mountain Dr., Branson, MO 65616-8555. Tel.: 417-339-1900.
E-mail: administrator@royrogers.com
Web Site: www.royrogers.com
Founded: 1967.
Congressional District: 40
Key Personnel: C.E.O. & Pres., Roy Dusty Rogers, Jr.; Museum Shop Mgr., Dustin Rogers.
Personnel Profile: Full-Time Paid 8; Part-Time Paid 5.
Governing Authority: privately owned. Tax-exempt: 501(c)(3).
Specialized Museum: pertaining to the lives & careers of Western entertainers Roy Rogers & Dale Evans.
Collections: costumes; cowboy & western memorabilia; displays of awards & honors; scale model western vehicles; Rose Parade saddle; gun collection; religious heritage display; mounted figures of Trigger, Trigger Jr., Buttermilk & Bullet; dioramas containing trophies from Africa; patriotic room.
Facilities: Books, cassettes, souvenirs & museum-related items for sale.
Activities: two theaters, one showing documentaries, one for live music.
Publications: brochure; quarterly newsletter.
Hours & Admission Prices: Jan. 4-Jan. 13 Thurs.-Sat. 9-5:30; Jan. 16-March Tues.-Sat. 9-5:30; April-Sept., Nov.-Dec. 15 & Dec. 26-Dec. 29 Mon.-Sat. 9-5:30; Oct. daily 9-5:30; call for extended hours. Museum: adults $13, senior citizens 65 & over, veterans and AAA members $11, children 13-17 $6.50; children 12 & under and members no charge. Additional fee for theater performances. ♿
Attendance: 100,000 (estimated)
Membership: Single $50; Family & Grandparents $100; Single Life $500; Family Life $1,000.

TITANIC MUSEUM, 3235 76 Country Blvd., (& Hwy. 165), Branson, MO 65616-3551. Tel.: 417-334-9500; 800-381-7670 (Toll Free).
History Museum.
Collections: Titanic history; photographs; lifeboat; period artifacts; clothing.
Hours & Admission Prices: Jan.-Feb. & Dec. 17-Dec. 26 daily 9-5; March-May 17 & Dec. 27-Dec. 31 daily 9-7; May 18-Dec. 16 daily 9-9. Adults $18.82, children 5-12 $9.99; children 4 & under no charge. Closed Christmas. ♿

VETERANS MEMORIAL MUSEUM, 1250 W. 76 Country Music Blvd., Branson, MO 65616-2211. Tel.: 417-336-2300. Fax: 417-336-2301.
Web Site: www.veteransmemorialbranson.com
History Museum.
Collections: American war veterans; personal artifacts; sculptures; memorabilia; photographs.
Hours & Admission Prices: Summer: daily 8am-9pm; Winter: daily 8-5. Adults $13.50, veterans $12.50, students 13-17 $10, children 5-12 $5; children 4 & under no charge.

WORLD'S LARGEST TOY MUSEUM AND HAROLD BELL WRIGHT, 3609 W. Hwy. 76, Branson, MO 65616. Tel.: 417-332-1499. Fax: 417-332-0017.
E-mail: torwbeck@inter-linc.net
Web Site: www.worldslargesttoymuseum.com
Founded: 2001.
Toy & Harold Bell Wright Historical Museum.
Collections: Toy Museum: toys from 1800s to present including planes; trains; boats; carriages; bears; fishing; toy soldiers; bicycles; lunch boxes; dolls; cast iron & tin wind-ups; pedal cars; cap guns; trucks; motorcycles; automobiles; Charles Dickens' A Christmas Carol window display. Harold Bell Wright Museum: paintings & handwritten copies of Harold Bell Wright's books; Civil War memorabilia; period guns; biography video.
Facilities: Museum-related items for sale.
Hours & Admission Prices: Call for hours & admission prices.

Bridgeton

PAYNE-GENTRY HOUSE, 4211 Fee Fee Rd., Bridgeton, MO 63044-2217. Tel.: 314-739-5599.
Historic House: former home of Elbridge and Mary Elizabeth Payne, built in 1870.
Collections: photographs; furnishings; personal artifacts
Hours & Admission Prices: Feb.-Dec. first & third Sun. of the month 1-4; other times by appointment. Adults $1; children under 14 no charge.

Burfordville

BOLLINGER MILL STATE HISTORIC SITE, 113 Bollinger Mill Rd., Burfordville, MO 63739-9051. Tel.: 573-243-4591. Fax: 573-243-5385.
E-mail: bollinger.mill.state.historic.site@dnr.mo.gov
Web Site: www.mostateparks.com
Founded: 1967.
Congressional District: 10
Key Personnel: Site Admin., Lesley McDaniel; Park Maintenance Worker, Lee Haines.
Personnel Profile: Full-Time Paid 3; Part-Time Paid 3.
Governing Authority: state. Parent Institution: Missouri Dept. of Natural Resources, Div. of State Parks, Box 176, Jefferson City, MO 65102. Tax-exempt.
Historic Site.
Collections: mill machinery. Historic Buildings: 1867 Bollinger Mill; c.1868 Burfordville covered bridge.
Research Fields: 19th-century milling; George Frederick Bollinger; covered bridges; Southeast Missouri history; Solomon Richard Burford; Sarah Daugherty; Cape County Milling Company.
Facilities: 19th-century mill & covered bridge.
Activities: self-guided & guided tours.
Publications: site brochures.
Hours & Admission Prices: April-Nov. Mon.-Sat. 10-4, Sun. 12-4; Dec.-March Tues.-Sat. 10-4. Guided Tours: adults $2.50, children $1.50; discount to groups of 15 or more with advanced reservations; children under 6 no charge. Closed New Year's Day; Easter; Thanksgiving; Christmas. ♿
Attendance: 9,984 (accurate)

Bynum

TWO MEDICINE DINOSAUR CENTER, 120 2nd Ave. S., Bynum, MO 59419. Mailing Address: P.O. Box 786, Bynum, MO 59419-0786. Tel.: 800-238-6873; 406-469-2211.
E-mail: dinoinfo@tmdinosaur.org
Paleontology Center.
Collections: fossils; dinosaur skeleton models; dinosaur bones.
Activities: education programs; seminars.
Hours & Admission Prices: Call for hours. Adults $4, seniors 55 & over, children 12 & under and military $3.

Cameron

CAMERON RAILROAD DEPOT MUSEUM, 210 N. Walnut, Cameron, MO 64429. Mailing Address: 11510 N.E. Hwy. 69, Cameron, MO 64429-2093. Tel.: 816-632-7414.
History Museum.
Collections: local history & culture; railroad memorabilia.
Hours & Admission Prices: Call for hours.

Canton

LEWIS COUNTY HISTORICAL SOCIETY MUSEUM, 102 N. 4th St., Canton, MO 63435-1317. Tel.: 573-288-5713.
Key Personnel: Pres. (V), Cynthia S. Barker.
Governing Authority: Tax-exempt.
Historical Society Museum.
Collections: local history, culture & memorabilia; personal artifacts; period furnishings; photographs; local family genealogy.
Hours & Admission Prices: Tues. & Thurs. 8-3; other times by appointment. ♿

REMEMBER WHEN TOY MUSEUM, 19481 Rte. B, Canton, MO 63435. Tel.: 573-288-3995.
Toy Museum.
Collections: vintage Marx toys.
Hours & Admission Prices: By appointment. Adults $5, children $3.

Cape Girardeau

CAPE RIVER HERITAGE MUSEUM, 538 Independence St., Cape Girardeau, MO 63703-6227. Tel.: 573-334-0405.
E-mail: info@caperiverheritagemuseum.com
Web Site: www.caperiverheritagemuseum.com
History Museum.
Collections: river-related artifacts; steamboats; period fire engine.
Hours & Admission Prices: March to mid-May & Sept.-Dec. Thurs.-Sat. 1-5; late May to Aug. Tues.-Sat. 10-4, Sun. 1-5.

GLENN HOUSE/HISTORICAL ASSOCIATION OF GREATER CAPE GIRARDEAU, 325 S. Spanish, Cape Girardeau, MO 63703-7442. Mailing Address: P.O. Box 1982, Cape Girardeau, MO 63702-1982.
Founded: 1972.
Congressional District: 10
Key Personnel: Pres. (V), Tom Grantham.
Personnel Profile: Part-Time Volunteers 30.
Governing Authority: private; nonprofit organization. Tax-exempt.
Historic House Museum: housed in c.1883 Victorian home.
Collections: structures; furnishings.
Activities: guided tours.
Publications: newsletter, Heritage Review.
Hours & Admission Prices: April-Oct. Tues.-Sat. 10-4, Sun. 1-4. Adults $5, children $2; discounts to groups; members no charge.
Attendance: 1,077 (accurate)
Membership: Annual $15; Family $25; Corporate $100; Lifetime $1,000.

ROSEMARY BERKEL AND HARRY L. CRISP II MUSEUM, (M), One University Plaza, Southeast Missouri State University, MS 7875, Cape Girardeau, MO 63701-4710. Tel.: 573-651-2260.
E-mail: museum@semo.edu
Web Site: www5.semo.edu/museum
Formerly: Southeast Missouri Regional Museum
Founded: 1976.
Key Personnel: Dir., Peter Nguyen; Asst. Dir., Peggy Haney; Cur. Collections, James Phillips; Cur. Education, Ellen Hahs.
Personnel Profile: Full-Time Paid 6; Part-Time Paid 4; Part-Time Volunteers 10; Interns 1.
Governing Authority: public university; nonprofit. Parent Institution: Southeast Missouri State University.
University Museum.
Collections: fine art; American military history; regional history; university history; archaeology.
Activities: lectures related to exhibitions.
Publications: exhibition brochures.
Hours & Admission Prices: Jan., April & July Tues.-Fri. 10-5, Sat.-Sun. 1-4; Feb.-March, May-June. & Aug.-Dec. Tues.-Fri. 10-5, 1st Fri. of month 10-8, Sat.-Sun. 1-4. ♿
Attendance: 6,232 (accurate)
Membership: Associate $25; Family $50; Patron $100; Benefactor $500; Beckwith Associate $1,000.

Carthage

PHELPS HOUSE, 1146 Grand Ave., Carthage, MO 64836-2832. Tel.: 417-358-1776.
Web Site: www.phelpshouse.org
Governing Authority: Parent Institution: Carthage Historic Preservation, Inc.
Historic House.
Collections: period furnishings; photographs.
Hours & Admission Prices: Tours: April-Nov. Wed. 10-4.

POWERS MUSEUM, (M), 1617 Oak St., Carthage, MO 64836. Mailing Address: P.O. Box 593, Carthage, MO 64836-0593. Tel.: 417-358-2667. Fax: 417-359-9627.
E-mail: infonow@powersmuseum.com
Web Site: www.powersmuseum.com
Founded: 1982.
Congressional District: 7
Key Personnel: Dir., Michele Hansford; Pres. (V), George Boyd.
Personnel Profile: Full-Time Paid 1; Part-Time Paid 2; Part-Time Volunteers 1; Interns 2.
Governing Authority: municipal; nonprofit. Parent Institution: City of Carthage. Tax-exempt.
History Museum.
Collections: Carthage history; late 19th- to 20th-century decorative arts; 1870-1960 textiles & costumes; late 19th- to early 20th-century music; photographs; archives; medical equipment & books; family letters, 1880-1981.

Major Exhibits: "Lee & Grant" from NEH (T), 9/1/10-10/20/10.
Research Fields: role of women in Carthage & related women's history; early highways; late 19th- to early 20th- century musical history; local history; limestone & lead/zinc mining of tri-state district; WWII to contemporary military action oral histories.
Facilities: 2,000-vol. library; educational facilities; 2,000 sq. ft. exhibit space; archives. Museum-related items for sale.
Activities: lectures; films; organized educational programs for children & adults; loan, temporary & traveling exhibitions; school loan service; digital exhibits.
Hours & Admission Prices: mid-March to Oct. Tues.-Sat. 11-4. No charge; donations accepted. ♿
Attendance: 7,500 (accurate)

Charleston

MISSISSIPPI COUNTY HISTORICAL SOCIETY, 403 N. Main, Charleston, MO 63834-1028. Mailing Address: P.O. Box 312, Charleston, MO 63834-0312. Tel.: 314-683-4348.
Founded: 1966.
Congressional District: 8
Key Personnel: Pres. (V), Tom Graham.
Personnel Profile: Part-Time Volunteers 20.
Governing Authority: society. Tax-exempt.
General Museum.
Collections: archaeology; archives; costumes; military; Indian artifacts; agricultural techniques & tools; documents related to the Jadwin Plan.
Facilities: turn-of-the-century home. Gift items for sale.
Activities: temporary art exhibitions; rental of home for receptions & parties.
Hours & Admission Prices: Tues. 1:30-3:30; other times by appointment only. Adults $3; members no charge.
Attendance: 1,600 (estimated)
Membership: Individual $10; Family $20; Life $100.

Chesterfield

FAUST PARK FOUNDATION, 15189 Olive Blvd., Chesterfield, MO 63017-1805. Tel.: 314-615-8383 & 7373. Fax: 636-519-7050. TDD: 314-615-7840.
E-mail: dwhite@stlouisco.com
Web Site: www.stlouisco.com/parks
Formerly: Faust Cultural Heritage Foundation-The St. Louis Carousel
Founded: 1985.
Key Personnel: Chm. (V), Patrick Donelan; Museum Shop Mgr., Phyllis Goldberg.
Personnel Profile: Part-Time Paid 8.
Governing Authority: county. Parent Institution: St. Louis County Dept. of Parks & Recreation. Tax-exempt.
General Museum.
Collections: carousel building for operating 1920s Dentzel carousel.
Research Fields: carousels; Dentzel Co. of Philadelphia.
Facilities: 200-seat gallery; 3,500 sq. ft. exhibit space. Museum-related items for sale.
Activities: arts festivals; rental gallery; festivals; park programs.
Hours & Admission Prices: Exhibits: Tues.-Sun. 10-4. Carousel Ride: $1; children 3 & under accompanied by an adult & members no charge. ♿
Attendance: 150,000
Membership: Senior $60; Family $70; Contributing $125; Sponsor $275; Patron $500.

FAUST PARK-THORNHILL HISTORIC SITE & FAUST HISTORIC VILLAGE, 15185 Olive Blvd., Chesterfield, MO 63017-1805. Tel.: 314-615-4328; 636-532-7298. Fax: 636-532-0604.
E-mail: jfoley@stlouisco.com
Web Site: www.stlouisco.com/parks
Founded: 1968.
Key Personnel: Dir. Cultural Site, Jim Foley; Dir. Parks, Lindsey Swanick; Cur. Park, Jesse Francis; Office Coord., Rhonda Swagman.
Personnel Profile: Full-Time Paid 10; Part-Time Paid 5; Part-Time Volunteers 40; Interns 1.
Governing Authority: county. Parent Institution: St. Louis County Parks & Recreation. Tax-exempt.
Historic House & Preservation Project.
Collections: Frederick Bates' personal artifacts, 1777-1825; Bates family library; 19th century period furniture; agricultural & archaeology artifacts; 19th century heritage gardens. Historic Buildings: c.1820 estate of Frederick Bates, second Governor of Missouri; historic structures.
Research Fields: Frederick Bates; early St. Louis and Missouri history; cultural heritage of St. Louis area.
Activities: guided tours; lectures; historic craft festivals; history hayrides; education programs for children & adults; carousel rides; summer concert series. Museum Sponsors: Craft Fair; holiday events.
Publications: calendar of events; self guided tour pamphlets.
Hours & Admission Prices: Thronhill Tours: Thurs.-Fri. by appointment. Adults $4; discounts to groups; Mother's Day weekend no charge. Historic Village: May-July 3rd & 4th Sat.-Sun. of the month 1-5. No charge. Carousel: $1 per person. ♿
Attendance: 425,000 (accurate)

Chillicothe

THE GRAND RIVER HISTORICAL SOCIETY & MUSEUM, 1401 Forest Dr., Chillicothe, MO 64601. Mailing Address: P.O. Box 154, Chillicothe, MO 64601-0154. Tel.: 660-646-3430 & 4323.
E-mail: drfstark@cmuonline.net
Founded: 1959.
Congressional District: 6
Key Personnel: Pres., Dr. Frank Stark; Treas., John Cook; Cur., Dr. John R. Neal; Sec., Barbra Cook.
Governing Authority: society. Tax-exempt 501(c)(3).
Local History Museum.
Collections: period artifacts; local artifacts.
Research Fields: history & development of rural schools in county & areas of national backgrounds.
Activities: guided tours; lectures; demonstrations; school program.
Publications: quarterly, Harold.
Hours & Admission Prices: April-Oct. Sat.-Sun. 1-4; other times by appointment. No charge; donations accepted. ♿
Attendance: 1,500 (estimated)
Membership: Single $10; Family $15; Life $30.

Clayton

HISTORIC HANLEY HOUSE, 7600 Westmoreland Ave., Clayton, MO 63105-3807. Mailing Address: The Center of Clayton, Parks Dept., 50 Gay Ave., Clayton, MO 63105. Tel.: 314-226-9893. Fax: 314-226-9326.
E-mail: sumlauf@ci.clayton.mo.us
Web Site: www.hanleyhouse.org
Key Personnel: Community Resource Coord., Sarah Umlauf.
Personnel Profile: Full-Time Paid 1; Part-Time Volunteers 10.
Governing Authority: municipal; not-for-profit. Tax-exempt: 501(c)(3).
Historic House.
Collections: furnishings; family photographs & letters.
Activities: docent programs.
Hours & Admission Prices: Sat.-Sun. 12-4; other times by appointment. Adults $3; children under 12 no charge. Closed New Year's Day; Memorial Day; Independence Day; Christmas.
Attendance: 1,000 (estimated)

ST. LOUIS ARTISTS' GUILD, 2 Oak Knoll Park, Clayton, MO 63105-3008. Tel.: 314-727-6266 (gallery); 9599 (office). Fax: 314-727-9190.
E-mail: askus@stlouisartguild.org
Web Site: www.stlouisartistsguild.org
Founded: 1886.
Congressional District: 3
Key Personnel: Gallery Dir., Davide Weaver; Pres. (V), Brad Wastler; Museum Shop Mgr., Karen Roodman.
Personnel Profile: Full-Time Paid 3; Part-Time Paid 3; Part-Time Volunteers 200; Interns 1.
Governing Authority: nonprofit organization. Tax-exempt.
Arts Center.
Collections: paintings; sculpture; graphics; photography; fine crafts.
Activities: lectures; films; gallery talks; concerts; arts festivals; temporary & traveling exhibitions; open competitive & invitational exhibits; classes; workshops.
Publications: quarterly newsletter; annual membership directory.
Hours & Admission Prices: Tues.-Sun. 12-4. No charge; donations accepted. Closed holidays. ♿
Attendance: 30,000 (estimated)
Membership: Junior $25; Individual $55; Family $75; Supporting $100.

Clinton

HENRY COUNTY MUSEUM AND CULTURAL ARTS CENTER, (M), 203 W. Franklin St., Clinton, MO 64735-2008. Tel.: 660-885-8414. Fax: 660-890-2228.
E-mail: hcmus@midameric.net
Web Site: henrycountymomuseum.org
Founded: 1974.
Congressional District: 4
Key Personnel: Dir. & Chm. (V), Alta Dulaban; Pres. (V), Neil Crayden; Museum Shop Mgr., Mary Smarr; Genealogy Library, Pat Waugh.
Personnel Profile: Full-Time Paid 1; Part-Time Paid 1; Part-Time Volunteers 100.

Governing Authority: society. Parent Institution: Henry County Historical Society. Tax-exempt: 501(c)(3).
Historical Museum: housed in 1886 restored Anheuser-Busch Building; 1850s Dog Trot Log House; 1887 bldg. on adjoining property.
Collections: historic artifacts & furnishings; Louis Freund paintings; genealogical research room; period rooms; Courtney Thomas Collection; late 1800s to early 1900s village (7 stores under one roof).
Research Fields: genealogical records.
Facilities: kitchen; 150-seat hospitality room.
Activities: permanent exhibitions.
Publications: brochures; quarterly newsletter.
Hours & Admission Prices: April-Dec. Mon.-Sat. & special occasions 10-4. Adults $3, children 12 & under, members and Tues. no charge. Closed New Year's Day; Memorial Day; Labor Day; Thanksgiving; Christmas. ♿
Attendance: 4,093 (accurate)
Membership: Individual $15; Family $25; Sustaining $100; Life $300.

Columbia

DAVIS ART GALLERY, Stephens College, Columbia, MO 65215-0001. Mailing Address: P.O. Box 2012, Stephens College, Columbia, MO 65215-0001. Tel.: 573-876-7175. Fax: 573-876-7248.
E-mail: mudboy@stephens.edu
Founded: 1962.
Congressional District: 8
Key Personnel: Cur., Robert Friedman.
Personnel Profile: Full-Time Paid 1; Part-Time Volunteers 1.
Governing Authority: college. Parent Institution: Stephens College. Tax-exempt.
Art Gallery.
Collections: modern paintings & graphics; Melanesian sculpture.
Activities: formally organized education programs for undergraduate college students; temporary & traveling exhibitions.
Hours & Admission Prices: Mon.-Fri. 10-3. No charge; donations accepted. Closed school holidays. ♿
Attendance: 500 (estimated)

MASONIC LIBRARY AND MUSEUM, 6033 Masonic Dr., Ste. A, Columbia, MO 65202-6568. Tel.: 800-434-9804; 573-814-4663. Fax: 573-814-4660.
Key Personnel: Chm. (V), Elmer E. Revelle
History Museum.
Collections: Masonic history; photographs; personal artifacts.
Hours & Admission Prices: Mon.-Fri. 9-4:30. No charge; donations accepted. ♿

MUSEUM OF ANTHROPOLOGY, UNIVERSITY OF MISSOURI, 104 Swallow Hall, University of Missouri, Columbia, MO 65211-0001. Tel.: 573-882-3573 & 3764. Fax: 573-884-3627.
E-mail: anthromuseum@missouri.edu
Web Site: anthromuseum.missouri.edu
Founded: 1939.
Congressional District: 9
Key Personnel: Dir., Michael J. O'Brien; Assoc. Cur., Candace A. Sall; Asst. Cur., Jessica Boldt; Asst. Cur., Brandy Tunmire; Administrative Asst., Christine Hudson.
Personnel Profile: Full-Time Paid 5; Part-Time Paid 10; Part-Time Volunteers 2; Interns 2.
Governing Authority: university. Parent Institution: University of Missouri. Tax-exempt: 501(c)(3).
Anthropology Museum.
Collections: prehistoric Missouri archaeological artifacts; ethnographic material from native North American cultures in the Arctic, the Northwest coast, the Southwest, the Basin & the Great Plains; the Grayson Collection of archery & archery-related material from around the world.
Research Fields: archaeology; ethnography; ethnohistory.
Facilities: library; 22,000 sq. ft. curation center; work room.
Activities: guided tours; lectures; outreach programs; permanent & temporary exhibits.
Publications: Museum Briefs; Monograph Series.
Hours & Admission Prices: Mon.-Fri. 9-4. Scheduled tours available. No charge; donations accepted. Closed university holidays. ♿
Attendance: 5,500 (accurate)

* **MUSEUM OF ART AND ARCHAEOLOGY, UNIVERSITY OF MISSOURI, (M),** University Ave. & Ninth St., 1 Pickard Hall, Columbia, MO 65211-0001. Tel.: 573-882-3591. Fax: 573-884-4039.
E-mail: museumuser@missouri.edu
Web Site: maa.missouri.edu
Founded: 1957.
Congressional District: 8
Key Personnel: Dir., Alex W. Barker, Ph.D.; Asst. Dir., Coord. Membership, Mktg. & Museum Shop Mgr., Bruce Cox; Assoc. Cur. European & American Art, Mary Pixley; Assoc. Cur. Ancient Art, J. Benton Kidd; Registrar, Jeff Wilcox; Preparator, Larry Stebbing; Dir. Missouri Folk Arts Program, Lisa Higgins; Specialist, Deborah Bailey; Assoc. Educator, Cathy Callaway; Security Officer, Larry Lepper; Collections Specialist, Kenyon Reed.
Personnel Profile: Full-Time Paid 7; Part-Time Paid 7; Part-Time Volunteers 37; Interns 1.
Governing Authority: university. Parent Institution: University of Missouri-Columbia. Tax-exempt: 170(b)(1)(A).
University Art Museum.
Collections: ancient art & archaeology including Egypt, Palestine, Iran, Cyprus, Greece, Etruria, Rome, early Christian & Byzantine art; paintings; Kress study collection; 15th- to 20th-century European & American sculpture, drawings, prints & paintings; African, pre-Columbian, Chinese, Japanese, South & Southeast Asian art & artifacts.
Major Exhibits: Connecting With Contemporary Sculpture, 1/10-5/10; The Voyage of a Contemporary Italian Goldsmith in the Classical World, 6/10-9/10; Ancient Bronzes from the Asian Grasslands from the Arthur M. Sackler Foundation (T), 10/10-12/10.
Research Fields: old world archaeology; European & American paintings; sculpture graphics; South & Southeast Asia; Pre-Columbian & African art.
Facilities: 6,000-vol. library of sales & exhibition catalogs, museum bulletins & reference books available for use on premises & upon special request; 116-seat lecture hall. Museum-related items for sale.
Activities: guided tours; gallery talks; formally organized education programs for undergraduate & graduate students affiliated with University of Missouri, Columbia; educational outreach programs; permanent & temporary exhibitions.
Publications: Muse, Annual of the Museum of Art & Archaeology; magazine; Handbook of The Collections; Catalogue of Gandharan Art; British Comic Art, 1730-1830; The Art of the July Monarchy: France 1830 to 1848; Pasture to Polis: Art in the Age of Homer; Commitment: Fatherhood in Black America; The Samuel H. Kress Study Collection at the University of Missouri; New Light on a Dark Age; Corpus Vasorum Antiquorum; The Art of the Book; Testament of Time; Feeling, Thought and Spirit: The Ceramic Work of Glen Lukens.
Hours & Admission Prices: Tues.-Fri. 9-4, Sat.-Sun. 12-4. No charge; donations accepted. Closed national & university holidays; Christmas through New Year's Day. ♿
Attendance: 33,745 (accurate)
Membership: Student $20; Senior $35; Individual $40; Household $60; Friend $100; Founder $250; Sponsor $500; Fellow $1,000; Patron $5,000.

STATE HISTORICAL SOCIETY OF MISSOURI, (M), 1020 Lowry St., Columbia, MO 65201-7298. Tel.: 573-882-7083. Fax: 573-884-4950.
E-mail: shsofmo@umsystem.edu
Web Site: shs.umsystem.edu
Founded: 1898.
Congressional District: 9
Key Personnel: Exec. Dir., Gary R. Kremer; Pres. (V), Doug Crews.
Personnel Profile: Full-Time Paid 24; Part-Time Paid 2; Part-Time Volunteers 10.
Governing Authority: state. Tax-exempt.
Art Museum.
Collections: paintings; sculpture; drawings; prints; photographs; maps; cartoons; manuscripts; Missouri newspapers, 1808-present.
Major Exhibits: Missouri Portraits: Famous and Familiar, 1/10-3/10; The Golden Age of the Comic Strip 1930-1960, 1/10-5/10; Mark Twain and Tom Benton: Picture, Prose and Song, 4/10-8/10.
Research Fields: Missouri, Trans-Alleghenian & Far Western history; American Indians.
Facilities: library of books, pamphlets & periodicals available for use in reading room.
Activities: guided tours; rotating exhibitions; lectures; speakers' bureau; theatrical presentations.
Publications: quarterly magazine, Missouri Historical Review; books & booklets on Missouri history; Thomas Hart Benton: Artist, Writer, Intellectual; A Centennial History of the State Historical Society of Missouri, 1898-1998; Marking Missouri History; quarterly newsletter, Missouri Times; The Civil War in Missouri: Essays from the Missouri Historical Review, 1906-2006; Kansas City America's Crossroads & Essays from the Missouri Historical Review, 1906-2006; Filling Leisure Hours: Essays from the Missouri Historical Review, 1906-2006.
Hours & Admission Prices: Society: Mon.-Fri. 8-4:45, Sat. 8-3:30. Art Gallery: Tues.-Fri. 8-4:45, Sat. 8-3:30. No charge; donations accepted. Closed national holidays; holiday weekends. ♿
Attendance: 10,860 (estimated)

Membership: Individual $20; Family $30; Contributing $50; Supporting $100; Sustaining $200-$499; Patron $500 & up; Life $1,500.

WALTERS-BOONE COUNTY HISTORICAL MUSEUM AND VISITORS CENTER, 3801 Ponderosa St., Columbia, MO 65201-5460. Tel.: 573-443-8936. Fax: 573-875-5268.
History Museum.
Collections: county heritage & history; early pioneers; photographs.
Research Fields: genealogy; local history.
Facilities: genealogy library. Museum-related items for sale.
Activities: speaker's series. Museum Sponsors: Boone Piano Concerts; Holiday House Tour; Heritage Festival.
Publications: County Lines.
Hours & Admission Prices: April-Oct. Wed.-Sun. 12:30-4:30; Nov.-March Wed. & Fri.-Sun. 12:30-4:30. Boone Junction: June-Sept. Thurs.-Sun. 12:30-4:30. Adults $4, children $2. ♿
Attendance: 24,000 (estimated)
Membership: Individual $25; Family $30; Supporting $60; Patron $100; Life $300; Life Family $500.

Concordia

CONCORDIA MUSEUM, 802 S. Gordon St., Concordia, MO 64020-9363. Tel.: 660-463-2105.
E-mail: concordiamuseum@yahoo.com
History Museum.
Collections: local history & culture; period artifacts.
Hours & Admission Prices: Call for hours.

Crestwood

SAPPINGTON HOUSE MUSEUM, 1015 S. Sappington Rd., Crestwood, MO 63126-1004. Tel.: 314-822-8171 (museum) & 9469 (library). Fax: 314-729-4794.
Founded: 1967.
Congressional District: 3
Key Personnel: Library Chm., Ruth B. Jones.
Personnel Profile: Full-Time Volunteers 1; Part-Time Paid 6; Part-Time Volunteers 100.
Governing Authority: municipal; not-for-profit. Affiliated with City of Crestwood, 1 Detjen Dr., Crestwood, MO. Tax-exempt: 501(c)(3).
Historic House: Thomas Sappington House, 1808 Federal architecture.
Collections: decorative arts; Federal period furnishings.
Research Fields: decorative arts; American history; Missouri & local history.
Facilities: 2,000-vol. library of books on Americana history & decorative arts available for research; American historical house; restaurant. Museum-related items for sale.
Activities: guided tours; speakers' bureau. Museum Sponsors: spring & fall exhibits; Christmas in 1808.
Publications: quarterly newsletter, Sappinton House Volunteer Newsletter.
Hours & Admission Prices: Feb.-Dec. Wed.-Fri. 11-2, Sat. by appointment; last tour at 2:30. Adults $3, children 6-12 $.50; discounts to seniors; school groups & scouts with prior reservations no charge. Closed New Year's Eve & Day; Good Friday & day after; Memorial Day weekend; Independence Day; Labor Day weekend; Thanksgiving Eve & Day; Christmas Eve & Day; Sat. preceding holidays. ♿
Attendance: 1,250 (estimated)
Membership: Basic $10; Sponsoring $25; Patron $50.

Davisville

DILLARD MILL STATE HISTORIC SITE, 142 Dillard Mill Rd., Davisville, MO 65456-4014. Tel.: 573-244-3120.
E-mail: moparks@dnr.mo.gov
Web Site: www.mostateparks.com/dillardmill.htm
Historic Site.
Collections: local history & culture; photographs; water-powered gristmill.
Facilities: picnic sites; nature trail.
Hours & Admission Prices: March-Nov. Mon.-Sat. 10-4, Sun. 12-5; Dec.-Feb. Thurs.-Sat. 10-4, Sun. 12-4.

Defiance

DANIEL BOONE HOME AND BOONESFIELD VILLAGE, LINDENWOOD UNIVERSITY, 1868 Highway F, Defiance, MO 63341-1908. Tel.: 636-798-2005 & 2903. Fax: 636-798-2914.
E-mail: boonehome@lindenwood.edu
Web Site: www.lindenwood.edu/boone
Founded: 1803.
Congressional District: 9
Key Personnel: Dir. Operations, Pam Jensen.
Personnel Profile: Full-Time Paid 7; Full-Time Volunteers 4; Part-Time Paid 4; Part-Time Volunteers 200; Interns 2.
Governing Authority: Parent Institution: Lindenwood University.
Historic House: 1803-1810 designed & built by Daniel Boone and patterned after his father's home in Pennsylvania. Historic village era 1801-1850; guided tour.
Collections: authentic documents, furniture and artifacts of the Boone family.
Facilities: Museum-related items for sale.
Activities: guided tours; permanent exhibitions; chapel weddings & christenings.
Publications: brochure, True Brief History of Daniel Boone; newspaper, Boonesfield Gazette.
Hours & Admission Prices: mid-April to Oct. daily 9-6; Nov. to mid-April daily 9-5. Tours: 9:30-4. Museum Shop: 9-5. Boone Home: adults $7, senior citizens $6, children $4; discounts to AAM members. Boone Home & Boonesfield Village: adults $12, senior citizens $10, children $6; discounts to AAM members. Closed New Year's Day; Easter; Thanksgiving; Christmas Eve & Day. ♿
Attendance: 50,000 (accurate)
Membership: Friend $15; Good Friend $30; Best Friend $45; Special Friend $55.

Diamond

GEORGE WASHINGTON CARVER NATIONAL MONUMENT, 5646 Carver Rd., Diamond, MO 64840-8314. Tel.: 417-325-4151. Fax: 417-325-4231.
E-mail: gwca_superintendent@nps.gov
Web Site: www.nps.gov/gwca
Founded: 1943.
Congressional District: 7
Key Personnel: Pres. (V), Rev. Harry Givens; Supt., Reginald Tiller; Museum Shop Mgr., Pauline Charles.
Governing Authority: federal. Parent Institution: National Park Service. Subsidiary: George W. Carver Birthplace Assn. Tax-exempt: 501(c)(3).
National Monument.
Collections: historic materials relating to George Washington Carver; manuscript collections; herbarium. Historic House: c.1881 Moses Carver house.
Research Fields: history.
Facilities: 300-vol. library of biographies of George Washington Carver & local history books available for use by special arrangement; 3/4-mile nature trail; science discovery center. Books & postcards for sale.
Activities: guided tours; permanent & temporary exhibitions; film on the life of George Washington Carver; summer programs; Carver Science Discovery Center: living history programs; guided tours.
Publications: bulletin, Carver of Tuskegee.
Hours & Admission Prices: Museum, Center & House: daily 9-5. No charge; donations accepted. Closed New Year's Day; Thanksgiving; Christmas. ♿
Attendance: 50,000
Membership: Nonprofit Association: Student & Senior Citizen $10; Individual $15; Family $25; Club & Organization $100; Life & Corporate $250; Benefactor $500.

Eagle Rock

PROMISED LAND ZOO, 32297 Hwy. 86, Eagle Rock, MO 65641-7108. Tel.: 417-271-3324.
Web Site: www.plzoo.com
Founded: 1999.
Zoo.
Collections: zebras; dromedary camels; red kangaroos; ring-tailed lemurs; aoudad; miniature donkeys; pot-bellied pigs; Reeves Muntjac; American bison; Scimitar-horned Oryx; Nilgai antelope; Eland antelope; Fallow deer; American elk; emu.
Hours & Admission Prices: Daily 10-7. Adults $12, children 2-12 and seniors 65 & over $8; foster parents with ID no charge. ♿

East Prairie

TOWOSAHGY STATE HISTORIC SITE, East Prairie, MO 63845. Mailing Address: c/o Hunter-Dawson State Historic Site, P.O. Box 308, New Madrid, MO 63869-0308. Tel.: 573-748-5340.
E-mail: moparks@dnr.mo.gov
Web Site: www.mostateparks.com/towosahgy.htm
Archaeological Site.
Collections: local history & culture; ceremonial mounds.
Facilities: kiosk; trails.
Hours & Admission Prices: Call for hours.

Edina

KNOX COUNTY HISTORICAL SOCIETY MUSEUM, Court House, 107 N. 4th St., Edina, MO 63537. Mailing Address: 309 E. Marion, P.O. Box 75, Edina, MO 63537-1248. Tel.: 660-397-2349. Fax: 660-397-3331.
Founded: 1967.
Congressional District: 9
Key Personnel: Pres., Brent Karhoff.
Governing Authority: society. Tax-exempt.
Local History Museum.
Collections: local history & culture; period artifacts; photographs.
Research Fields: genealogy.
Facilities: 100-vol. library of newspapers and books available for use on premises.
Activities: guided tours.
Hours & Admission Prices: By appointment. No charge; donations accepted. Closed legal holidays. ♿
Membership: Individual $2.

Ellsinore

ELLSINORE PIONEER MUSEUM, 11 S. Herren Ave., Ellsinore, MO 63937. Tel.: 573-322-5297.
History Museum.
Collections: local history & culture; photographs.
Facilities: Museum-related items for sale.
Hours & Admission Prices: May-Aug. Wed. & Sat. 10-5.

Excelsior Springs

EXCELSIOR SPRINGS MUSEUM & ARCHIVES, 101 E. Broadway, Excelsior Springs, MO 64024-2513. Mailing Address: P.O. Box 144, Excelsior Springs, MO 64024-0144. Tel.: 816-630-0101.
Web Site: www.exsmo.com/museum
History Museum.
Collections: Excelsior Springs history; personal artifacts; period furnishings; genealogy; newspapers, 1890s to present.
Facilities: archives; theater.
Activities: children's films.
Publications: quarterly newsletter, Phunn.
Hours & Admission Prices: Tues.-Sat. 11-5; other times by appointment. No charge; donations accepted. Closed New Year's Day; Memorial Day; Independence Day; Thanksgiving; Christmas. ♿
Attendance: 6,500 (accurate)
Membership: Regular $10; Family $25; Business $50; Patron $100; Lifetime $200.

Fayette

THE ASHBY-HODGE GALLERY OF AMERICAN ART, CENTRAL METHODIST UNIVERSITY, 411 Central Methodist Square, Fayette, MO 65248-0009. Tel.: 660-248-6324 & 6304 (office). Fax: 660-248-2622.
E-mail: jegeist@centralmethodist.edu
Web Site: www.centralmethodist.edu
Founded: 1993.
Congressional District: 6
Key Personnel: Chm. Bd. & Cur., Joseph E. Geist, Ph.D.; Chief Docent, Virginia Monroe.
Personnel Profile: Full-Time Paid 1; Part-Time Paid 1; Part-Time Volunteers 35.
Governing Authority: private college; nonprofit. Parent Institution: Central Methodist University. Tax-exempt: 501(c)(3).
Art Museum.
Collections: midwestern regionalist artists including Thomas Hart Benton, Fred Shane, Grant Wood, Charles Banks Wilson, Robert MacDonald Graham, Jr., Emile Gruppe, Aaron Bohrod & Birger Sandzen; lithographs; oils; acrylic; drawings; watercolors & bronzes.
Facilities: 500-vol. library of art books & periodicals available to the public; 3,300 sq. ft. exhibit space; 52 acre campus designated a National Historic District.
Activities: docent program; guided tours; loan, temporary & traveling exhibitions. Annual Events: GALA celebration of opening of Gallery in October.
Hours & Admission Prices: Tues.-Thurs. 1:30-4:30; Special Exhibits: Sun. 1:30-4:30; groups by special arrangement. No charge; donations accepted. ♿
Attendance: 5,000 (accurate)
Membership: Angels $50; Archangels $100; Cherubim $150; Principalities $200; Seraphim $300.

THE STEPHENS MUSEUM, Central Methodist University, T. Berry Smith Hall, Fayette, MO 65248. Tel.: 660-248-3391 & 6370. Fax: 660-248-2622.
E-mail: delliott@centralmethodist.edu
Web Site: cmu.edu
Founded: 1879.
Congressional District: 6
Key Personnel: C.E.O., Dana R. Elliott, Ph.D.
Personnel Profile: Full-Time Paid 1; Part-Time Paid 3.
Governing Authority: college. Parent Institution: Central Methodist University. Tax-exempt.
College Museum: housed in 1896 Romanesque educational building, T. Berry Smith Hall.
Collections: natural history; history & art; bird collection of 274 mounted specimens, 423 skins & 163 eggs; shells; mammals; geological displays; history of Boonslick Region; articles of the Methodist Church in Missouri; folk art; original tombstones of Daniel & Rebecca Boone; five original paint brushes of George Caleb Bingham; Lithograph John Wesley; artifacts commemorating the coronation of Czar Nicholas II, Russia, 1896; bird specimen now in extinction-passenger pigeon, Carolina parakeet; American Indian artifacts (arrowheads etc.).
Facilities: classrooms.
Activities: guided tours; lectures; temporary exhibitions.
Hours & Admission Prices: Academic Year: Tues.-Thurs. 2-4:30; other times by appointment. Closed college vacations. No charge; donations accepted.
Attendance: 1,000 (estimated)

Florida

MARK TWAIN BIRTHPLACE STATE HISTORIC SITE, 37352 Shrine Rd., Florida, MO 65283-2127. Tel.: 573-565-3449. Fax: 573-565-3718.
E-mail: mark.twain.birthplace.state.historic.site@dnr.mo.gov
Web Site: www.mostateparks.gov
Founded: 1960.
Congressional District: 9
Key Personnel: Site Admin., Connie Ritter, IRS II
Personnel Profile: Full-Time Paid 1; Part-Time Paid 2.
Governing Authority: state. Owned & operated by Div. of State Parks, Missouri Dept. of Natural Resources, P.O. Box 176, Jefferson City, MO 65102. Tax-exempt.
Historic House: 1835 Samuel L. Clemens birthplace.
Collections: period furnishings; paintings; manuscripts; Samuel Clemens memorabilia.
Research Fields: local history; Mark Twain.
Facilities: 800-vol. library of books, pamphlets, letters & other material relating to life & writings of Mark Twain available on premises; reading room.
Activities: guided tours; lectures; films; gallery talks; formally organized education programs for children & adults.
Publications: brochure; quarterly newsletter, Mark Twain Research Foundation Twainian.
Hours & Admission Prices: April-Oct. daily 10-5; Nov.-March Wed.-Sun. 10-4:30. Adults & children over 12 $2.50, children 6-12 $1.50; discount to groups; children under 6 no charge. Closed New Year's Day; Thanksgiving; Christmas. ♿
Attendance: 17,277 (accurate)

Florissant

FLORISSANT VALLEY HISTORICAL SOCIETY, 1896 S. Florissant Rd., Florissant, MO 63031. Mailing Address: P.O. Box 298, Florissant, MO 63032-0298. Tel.: 314-524-1100, 839-3626 & 921-5563.
E-mail: fredmary2@aol.com
Founded: 1958.
Congressional District: 9
Key Personnel: Pres., Joseph McDavid; Sec., Mary Kay Gladbach.
Governing Authority: board of directors; society; nonprofit organization. Tax-exempt: 501(c)(3).
Historic House: 1790 Taille de Noyer log cabin.
Collections: furnishings; personal artifacts; recreational artifacts.
Facilities: 100-vol. library books on local history. Gift items for sale.
Activities: guided tours.
Publications: magazine, Florissant Valley Quarterly.
Hours & Admission Prices: March.-Dec. Sun. 1-4; group tours by appointment. Adults $2, children $1. Closed New Year's Day; Thanksgiving; Christmas.
Attendance: 2,500 (estimated)
Membership: Individual $10; Life $100.

OLD ST. FERDINAND'S SHRINE, Friends of Old St. Ferdinand, Inc., One Rue St. Francois, Florissant, MO 63031. Mailing Address: P.O. Box 222, Florissant, MO 63032-0222. Tel.: 314-837-2110. Fax: 314-839-3829.
E-mail: oldstferdinandshrine@gmail.com
Web Site: www.oldstferdinandshrine.com
Founded: 1958.
Congressional District: 2
Key Personnel: Chm. & Pres. (V), Bill Bray; Sec. & Membership Chm., Geri Debo; Museum Shop Mgr., Lucille Cortese.
Personnel Profile: Full-Time Volunteers 4; Part-Time Paid 1; Part-Time Volunteers 20.
Governing Authority: nonprofit corporation. Tax-exempt: 501(c)(3).
History Museum: housed in historic site of church complex & community center from 1789-1957.
Collections: nun dolls in pre-Vatican II habits; church paraphernalia; early vestments; statues; pews; altars; 1789 tabernacle of St. Ferdinand Church; funeral cape worn by Father DeSmet; paintings; foot pump organ; 1855-1860 nun & student letters; ice skates; rings for hanging lamps; 1825 newspaper clippings; 1600-1955 multicultural artifacts; survival instruments & tools from 1700s to 1955; 1690 paintings from the House of Rueben; 1500s sanctuary lamp; wax figure of St. Valentine from 270 AD; artifacts from an ongoing archaeological dig; Mastadon bone found in Coldwater Creek 25-35,000 BC
Facilities: archival items. Books, maps & other museum-related items for sale.
Activities: self-guided & group tours by appointment.
Publications: newsletter, brochures.
Hours & Admission Prices: Sun. 1-4; other times by appointment. Tours: $2. Closed New Year's Day; Easter; Independence Day; Thanksgiving; Christmas. ♿
Attendance: 15,000 (estimated)
Membership: Individual $25; Patron $50; Business $100; Lifetime $250.

Fort Leonard Wood

U.S. ARMY CHEMICAL CORPS MUSEUM, 495 S. Dakota Ave., Bldg. 1607, Fort Leonard Wood, MO 65473-8851. Tel.: 573-596-0240.
E-mail: leon.usacbrnsmuseum@conus.army.mil
Web Site: www.wood.army.mil/ccmuseum/ccmuseum/main.htm
Military Museum.
Collections: military history; photographs; documents.
Activities: educational programs.
Hours & Admission Prices: Mon.-Fri. 8-4, Sat. 10-4. Closed Federal holidays.

U.S. ARMY ENGINEER MUSEUM, 495 S. Dakota Ave., Fort Leonard Wood, MO 65473-5165. Tel.: 573-596-0780.
Web Site: www.wood.army.mil/museum
Founded: 1972.
Congressional District: 4
Key Personnel: Dir., Frank McGrane; Museum Shop Mgr., Glenn A. Stines.
Personnel Profile: Full-Time Paid 5; Full-Time Volunteers 2; Part-Time Volunteers 4; Interns 1.
Governing Authority: federal. Parent Institution: U.S. Army, Fort Leonard Wood. Tax-exempt.
Military History & Engineer Museum: including a restored WWII company compound consisting of 14 buildings on 50-acre site.
Collections: life & career of Gen. Leonard Wood; Fort Leonard Wood history; Army engineer training; firearms; uniforms; insignia; engineer vehicles; library archives; photographs.
Research Fields: military engineering history & evaluation of military training from 1940-present; POW's in the United States; minority military experiences.
Facilities: library pertaining to military history reference works; auditorium; educational facilities.
Activities: guided tours; lectures; films; broadcast & cable programs; organized education programs for children, adults & college students; docent program; loan & temporary exhibitions.
Publications: brochure, History of Fort Leonard Wood.
Hours & Admission Prices: Mon.-Sat. 8-4. No charge. Closed federal holidays. ♿
Attendance: 150,000 (estimated)

U.S. ARMY MILITARY POLICE CORPS MUSEUM, 495 S. Dakota Ave., Bldg. 1607, Fort Leonard Wood, MO 65473-8851. Tel.: 573-596-0604. Fax: 573-596-0603.
E-mail: leon.usampsmuseum@conus.army.mil
Web Site: www.wood.army.mil/usamps/museum/default.htm
Formerly: Military Police Corps Regimental Museum
Founded: 1960.
Congressional District: 3
Key Personnel: Dir. & Cur., Scott L. Norton; Museum Tech, Jeanni Wilson.
Personnel Profile: Full-Time Paid 3.
Governing Authority: nonprofit organization. Parent Institution: U.S. Army MP School. Tax-exempt.
Military Museum.
Collections: items pertaining to the history of the Military Police Corps; uniforms; weapons; flags; insignia; badges; military artifacts from allied countries.
Research Fields: military police history.
Facilities: 10,000 sq. ft. exhibit space. Museum-related items for sale.
Activities: guided tours; lectures; permanent exhibitions.
Publications: Military Police Corps History; various historical vignettes.
Hours & Admission Prices: Mon.-Fri. 8-4, Sat. 10-4. Closed holidays. ♿
Attendance: 20,000 (accurate)

Fulton

WINSTON CHURCHILL MUSEUM, Westminster College, 501 Westminster Ave., Fulton, MO 65251-1230. Tel.: 573-592-5234. Fax: 573-592-5222.
E-mail: sara.winingear@westminster-mo.edu
Web Site: www.churchillmemorial.org
Formerly: Winston Churchill Memorial and Library
Founded: 1962.
Congressional District: 9
Key Personnel: Exec. Dir., Dr. Rob Havers; Chm. (V), Suzanne Richardson; Asst. Dir., Sara Winingear.
Personnel Profile: Full-Time Paid 3; Part-Time Paid 6; Part-Time Volunteers 6; Interns 3.
Governing Authority: college. Affiliated with Westminster College, Westminster Ave. Tax-exempt.
Historic Building: relocated & reconstructed Church of St. Mary the Virgin, Aldermanbury designed by Christopher Wren (original site: London, England). Historic Site: site on which Sir Winston Churchill delivered the Sinews of Peace Speech March 5, 1946.
Collections: Churchill memorabilia; Wren architecture; rare map collection; paintings; graphics; sculpture; numismatic; manuscripts; philatelic; motion pictures; photographs; sound recordings.
Research Fields: life of Sir Winston Churchill; World War II; Anglo-American relations; life & works of Sir Christopher Wren.
Facilities: research & microfilm libraries; theater. Museum-related items for sale.
Activities: guided tours; concerts; lectures; permanent & temporary exhibitions; religious services; festivals; self-guided tours; interactive exhibits.
Publications: periodic newsletter; visitor guide, The Words and the Man; John Findley Green Lecture Series; Crosby Kemper Lectures.
Hours & Admission Prices: Daily 10-4:30. Adults $6, senior citizens $5, youth 12-18 & college students $4, children 6-11 $3; discounts to AAM & AAA members; children 5 & under no charge. Closed New Year's Day; Thanksgiving; Christmas. ♿
Attendance: 25,000
Membership: Subaltern $50; Member of Parliament $100; First Lord of the Admiralty $250; Chancellor of the Exchequer Prime Minister $1,000.

Glasgow

GLASGOW MUSEUM, 381 County Rd. 220, Glasgow, MO 65254-9755. Tel.: 660-338-9949.
Key Personnel: Dir., Marion Weber; Chm. (V), Sonny Shive
History Museum: housed in a Presbyterian Church.
Collections: church & local history; Civil War artifacts; photographs.
Activities: tours; church service.
Hours & Admission Prices: April-Oct. 1 daily 9-3; other times by appointment. No charge.
Attendance: 300 (estimated)

Glencoe

WABASH FRISCO AND PACIFIC ASSOCIATION, INC. "THE UNCOMMON CARRIER", 199 Grand Ave., Glencoe, MO 63038. Mailing Address: 1569 Ville Angela Lane, Hazelwood, MO 63042-1630. Tel.: 636-587-3538; 314-351-9385.
E-mail: it1569djn@earthlink.net
Web Site: www.wfprr.com
Founded: 1939.
Congressional District: 2
Key Personnel: Pres., Stephen F. Marx; Treas., Gregory Wapelhorst; Sec., Robert Hardt.
Personnel Profile: Part-Time Volunteers 150.
Governing Authority: nonprofit organization. Tax-exempt: 501(c)(3).
Mini-Steam Tourist Railway Museum: located on the site of the original mainline right of way of the Pacific Railroad; building began westward from St. Louis, MO in 1852.

Collections: ten 12-inch gauge steam locomotives, 1907-2005; 31 riding cars including flat & gondola cars; 1925 Canadian Pacific (Treasure Island Railway) locomotives used in the Sesquicentennial in Philadelphia, PA; 5 diesel outline locomotives, 1945-2001; 2 cabooses; track maintenance cars; two 40 ft. highway trailers to pull equipment out of Meramec River flooding; lathes; milling machines; Bridgeport Mill; round house with turntable & eight tracks for storage of locomotives; car barn to store cars with 11 tracks; photographs.
Research Fields: maintaining steam locomotives & riding cars; utilizing scientific evaluations to keep locomotives operational.
Activities: 2 1/2 mile roundtrip train ride.
Publications: triennial newsletter, Whiffenpoof.
Hours & Admission Prices: May-Oct. Sun. 11-4:15. Trains depart every 20 minutes. $3 per person; discount to groups; members & children under 3 no charge.
Attendance: 14,000
Membership: Student $10; Individual $25; Family $35.

Goldman

SANDY CREEK COVERED BRIDGE STATE HISTORIC SITE, Old Lemay Ferry Rd., Goldman, MO Mailing Address: 1050 Charles J. Becker Dr., Imperial, MO 63052-3524. Tel.: 636-464-2976. Fax: 636-464-3768.
Web Site: www.mostateparks.com
Founded: 1967.
Congressional District: 3
Key Personnel: DNR Dir., Mark Templeton; District Supvr., Delecia Huitt.
Governing Authority: state. Parent Institution: Missouri Dept. of Natural Resources, P.O. Box 176, Jefferson City, MO 65102. Subsidiary Institution: Div. of State Parks. Tax-exempt.
Historic Site: 1872 covered bridge.
Collections: bridge.
Research Fields: covered bridges.
Facilities: picnic area; interpretive shelter.
Publications: brochure.
Hours & Admission Prices: Daily 8-5. No charge. ♿
Attendance: 71,023 (estimated)

Grandview

HARRY S TRUMAN NATIONAL HISTORIC SITE - TRUMAN FARM HOME, 12301 Blue Ridge Blvd., Grandview, MO 64030-1159. Mailing Address: 223 North Main St., Independence, MO 64050-2804. Tel.: 816-254-2720 & 9929. Fax: 816-254-4491.
E-mail: larry_villalva@nps.gov
Web Site: www.nps.gov/hstr/
Founded: 1994.
Congressional District: 5
Personnel Profile: Full-Time Paid 17; Part-Time Paid 6; Part-Time Volunteers 14.
Governing Authority: federal. Parent Institution: U.S. Dept. of the Interior. Subsidiary Institution: National Park Service. Tax-exempt.
Historic Site Museum: 1906-1917 home of former President Harry S Truman; family farm which he operated with his father.
Collections: period furniture & furnishings.
Research Fields: life of Harry S Truman emphasizing pre-1917; local agriculture & rural life.
Facilities: Farm home, outbuildings and 5+ acres.
Activities: tours of farm home during summer months.
Publications: bulletin; tour brochure.
Hours & Admission Prices: Farm: daily. Home: Memorial Day to Sept. Fri.-Sun. 9:30-4. Adults 16 & over $4. Closed New Year's Day; Thanksgiving; Christmas. ♿
Attendance: 4,992 (accurate)

Hamilton

J.C. PENNEY MUSEUM AND BOYHOOD HOME, 312 N. Davis St., Hamilton, MO 64644-1145. Tel.: 816-583-2168.
Historic House and Museum: former boyhood home of the entrepreneur J.C. Penney.
Collections: artifacts & memorabilia pertaining to J.C. Penney's life.
Hours & Admission Prices: Call for hours. No charge; donations accepted.

Hannibal

MARK TWAIN BOYHOOD HOME & MUSEUM, 120 N. Main St., Hannibal, MO 63401-3537. Tel.: 573-221-9010. Fax: 573-221-7975.
E-mail: noan.conrad@marktwainmuseum.org
Web Site: marktwainmuseum.org
Founded: 1936.
Congressional District: 9
Key Personnel: Exec. Dir., Dr. Cindy Lovell; Pres. (V), David Mobley; Cur., Henry Sweets; Office & Gift Shop Mgr., Dena Ellis; Mgr. Mktg. & Community Rels., Ryan Murray.
Personnel Profile: Full-Time Paid 5; Part-Time Paid 17; Part-Time Volunteers 35; Interns 5.
Governing Authority: nonprofit. Mark Twain Home Foundation. Tax-exempt.
Historic House: 1844 Mark Twain's boyhood home.
Collections: Mark Twain letters, photographs, foreign language editions, 1st editions; Mark Twain popular culture; historic restorations; American history & literature. Historic Buildings: 1839 Pilaster House; 1839 Grant's Drugstore; 1840 John Marshall Clemens' Justice of the Peace Office; pre-1853 Becky Thatcher House.
Research Fields: Mark Twain; Hannibal.
Facilities: 2,700-vol. library of books & numerous publications pertaining to Mark Twain.
Activities: art exhibitions; lectures; educational programs; performing arts; teachers workshop. Museum Sponsors: Mark Twain Birthday Celebration.
Publications: bimonthly, The Fence Painter.
Hours & Admission Prices: April-May & Sept.-Oct. daily 9-5; June-Aug. daily 9-7; Nov.-March Mon.-Sat. 10-5, Sun. 12-5. Adults $9, seniors $7.50, children 6-12 $4; discounts to AAM & ICOM members; members & Hannibal residents no charge. Closed New Year's Day; Easter; Thanksgiving; Christmas. ♿
Attendance: 65,000
Membership: Newsletter $15; Student $25; Individual $50; Couple $75; Family $100.

ROCKCLIFFE MANSION, 1000 Bird St., Hannibal, MO 63401-3436. Tel.: 573-221-4140; 877-423-4140 (Toll Free).
Web Site: www.rockcliffemansion.com
Historic House.
Collections: period furnishings; photographs; personal artifacts.
Activities: Annual Event: Candlelight Evening Tours in November & December.
Hours & Admission Prices: Daily 9-4. Closed New Year's Eve & Day; Easter; Thanksgiving; Christmas Eve & Day.

Hermann

DEUTSCHHEIM STATE HISTORIC SITE, 107 W. Second St., Hermann, MO 65041-1045. Tel.: 573-486-2200. Fax: 573-486-2249.
E-mail: deutschheim.state.historic.site@dnr.mo.gov
Web Site: www.mostateparks.com/deutschheim.htm
Founded: 1979.
Congressional District: 8
Key Personnel: Site Admin. & Museum Shop Mgr., Bruce Ketchum.
Personnel Profile: Full-Time Paid 3; Part-Time Paid 1; Part-Time Volunteers 15.
Governing Authority: state. Affiliated with Div. of State Parks, Missouri Dept. of Natural Resources, P.O. Box 176, Jefferson City, MO 65102. Tax-exempt.
German Heritage Museum.
Collections: period furnishings & decorative arts; furniture; books; household items & agricultural tools of 19th-century German immigrants in Missouri. Historic Houses: 1840 Pommer Gentner House; 1842 Strehly House; 1857 Winery; 1883 Barn.
Research Fields: German American daily life & folk ways; German immigration & settlement; decorative arts; Missouri in focus; German architecture; German gardens & culture.
Facilities: four historic buildings; gardens; museum galleries. Museum-related items for sale.
Activities: guided tours; historic preservation activities; changing exhibits; shows; special events.
Publications: Missouri Germans & Slavery; A Midwest German Christmas (Cookbook); journal, Der Maibaum.
Hours & Admission Prices: Tours: 10-3. Adults $2.50, children 6-12 $1.50. Closed New Year's Day; Easter; Thanksgiving; Christmas.
Attendance: 6,000 (estimated)
Membership: Journal, Student & Senior Citizen $15; Friend $25; Family $35; Curator's Club $50; Director's Club $100.

HISTORIC HERMANN MUSEUM, 312 Schiller St., Hermann, MO 65041-1154. Mailing Address: P.O. Box 105, Hermann, MO 65041-0105. Tel.: 573-486-2017.
Web Site: www.historichermann.com
Founded: 1956.
Congressional District: 110
Key Personnel: Pres. (V), Joy Kallmeyer; Sec., Carol Kallmeyer; Treas. & Museum Shop Mgr., Donna Layman.

Personnel Profile: Part-Time Paid 1; Part-Time Volunteers 18.
Governing Authority: society; nonprofit organization. Parent Institution: Historic Hermann, Inc. Tax-exempt.
Historic Museum: housed in 1871 German school building.
Collections: wine making & history of wineries; textiles; marine; Indian artifacts; restored loom; photographs river room; children's room; farm tools; kitchen utensils, spinning wheels; guns; old Bibles; books; restored 1886 pump organ; 6-piece bedroom set early 1800s; immigrant's trunk; steamboat models & equipment; early dolls & doll houses; heritage room; river room.
Research Fields: German-American history.
Facilities: 200-vol. library of German history & religion books; children's museum.
Activities: guided tours; guest lectures.
Publications: The German Settlement.
Hours & Admission Prices: April-Oct. Tues.-Sat. 10-4, Sun. 12-4. Adults $3, children ages 6-12 $1; discount to groups; children under 6 no charge.
Attendance: 5,000 (accurate)
Membership: Individual $10; Couple $15; Business or Organization $20.

Higginsville

CONFEDERATE MEMORIAL STATE HISTORIC SITE, 211 W. First St., Higginsville, MO 64037-8158. Tel.: 660-584-2853. Fax: 660-584-5134.
E-mail: confederate.memorial.state.historic.site@dnr.mo.gov
Web Site: www.mostateparks.com
Founded: 1925.
Congressional District: 4
Key Personnel: Site Admin., Greta Marshall.
Personnel Profile: Full-Time Paid 3; Part-Time Paid 1; Part-Time Volunteers 1.
Governing Authority: state. Parent Institution: Missouri Dept. of Natural Resources, P.O. Box 176, Jefferson City, MO 65102. Subsidiary Institution: Div. of State Parks. Tax-exempt.
Historic Site: Chapel, cemetery, family cottage & park are remnants of the Confederate Home of Missouri opened in 1892.
Collections: documents; photographs; confederate home archives.
Research Fields: confederate homes; confederate cause in Missouri.
Activities: Museum Sponsors: special events.
Hours & Admission Prices: Site: daily dawn to dusk. Chapel: Summer: Sun. 12-5, Mon.-Sat. 9-4. Winter: Thurs.-Sat. 9-4. No charge; donations accepted. ♿
Attendance: 90,000 (estimated)

Imperial

MASTODON STATE HISTORIC SITE, 1050 Charles J. Becker Dr., Imperial, MO 63052-3524. Tel.: 636-464-2976.
Web Site: www.mostateparks.com
Founded: 1976.
Congressional District: 3
Personnel Profile: Full-Time Paid 5; Part-Time Paid 4; Part-Time Volunteers 10; Interns 3.
Governing Authority: Parent Institution: Missouri Department of Natural Resources. Subsidiary Institution: Missouri Division of State Parks. Tax-exempt.
History Museum & Historic Site: listed on the National Register of Historic Places.
Collections: natural & cultural history; archaeology; paleontology; Mastodon bones.
Facilities: 431-acres; picnic area; trails; youth campground.
Hours & Admission Prices: Site: daily 8 to sunset. Museum: March-Nov. Mon.-Sat. 9-4:30, Sun. 12-4:30; Dec.-Feb. Mon. & Thurs.-Sat. 11-4, Sun. 12-4. Closed New Year's Day; Easter; Thanksgiving; Christmas.

Independence

THE BINGHAM-WAGGONER ESTATE, 313 W. Pacific, Independence, MO 64051. Mailing Address: P.O. Box 1163, Independence, MO 64051-0663. Tel.: 816-461-3491. Fax: 816-461-1540.
E-mail: binghamwaggoner@juno.com
Web Site: www.bwestate.org
Historic House: former home of Missouri Civil War artist George Caleb Bingham.
Collections: furnishings; paintings.
Hours & Admission Prices: April-Oct. Mon.-Sat. 10-4, Sun. 1-4. Adults $5, senior citizens $4.50, children & students $2.

CHILDREN'S PEACE PAVILION, 1001 W. Walnut, Independence, MO 64050-3562. Tel.: 816-521-3033.
Founded: 1995.
Key Personnel: Interim Dir., Chm. (V) & Museum Shop Mgr., Phyllis Moore.
Personnel Profile: Full-Time Paid 1; Part-Time Volunteers 25.
Governing Authority: Tax-exempt.
Children's Museum.
Collections: hands-on exhibits.
Facilities: Museum-related items for sale.
Activities: special events; Girl Scout programs.
Hours & Admission Prices: Tues.-Sat. 9:30-4. No charge; donations accepted. Closed New Year's Day; Memorial Day; Independence Day; Thanksgiving; Christmas. ♿
Attendance: 8,028 (accurate)

COMMUNITY OF CHRIST, The Temple, 1001 W. Walnut, Independence, MO 64050-3562. Tel.: 816-833-1000, ext. 2333. Fax: 816-521-3089.
E-mail: cloving@cofchrist.org
Web Site: www.cofchrist.org
Formerly: Reorganized Church of Jesus Christ of Latter Day Saints
Founded: 1830.
Congressional District: 5
Key Personnel: Admin. Asst., Joy Goodwin.
Personnel Profile: Part-Time Paid 1; Part-Time Volunteers 17.
Governing Authority: church. Supported by historic sites at Independence, MO; Kirtland, OH; Nauvoo, IL; Lamoni, IA; Beloit, WI; Far West, MO. Tax-exempt: 501(c)(3).
Religious History Museum.
Collections: artifacts; manuscript & pictorial collections; archival materials related to the history of the church.
Research Fields: Latter Day Saint (Mormon) history.
Facilities: library; archives; reading room.
Activities: guided tours; films; permanent & temporary exhibitions.
Publications: Herald; The Restoration Witness.
Hours & Admission Prices: Mon.-Sat. 9-5, Sun. 1-5. Prayer for Peace daily 1-1:15. No charge. ♿
Attendance: 12,000 (accurate)

1859 JAIL, MARSHAL'S HOME & MUSEUM, 217 N. Main St., Independence, MO 64050-2804. Tel.: 816-252-1892.
Web Site: www.jchs.org
Founded: 1959.
Congressional District: 5
Key Personnel: Exec. Dir., Steve Noll; C.E.O., Brad Pace; Pres. (V), Ben Mann.
Personnel Profile: Full-Time Paid 1; Part-Time Paid 1; Part-Time Volunteers 33; Interns 1.
Governing Authority: nonprofit. Parent Institution: Jackson County Historical Society. Tax-exempt: 501(c)(3).
History Museum: adjoining 1859 restored Jackson County Jail and federal style Marshal's House & office.
Collections: period furnishings; local history items; 12-cell county jail and dwelling for jailor; weapons & law enforcement tools; furnishings & household accessories; Civil War & Reconstruction period artifacts; Border War & Jesse James Brothers memorabilia. Historic Building: c.1870 one-room schoolhouse.
Research Fields: local history.
Activities: self-guided tours; permanent & changing exhibitions. Museum Sponsors: week of living history in one-room schoolhouse in spring.
Publications: magazine, Jackson County Historical Society Journal.
Hours & Admission Prices: April-Oct. Mon.-Sat. 10-4, Sun. 1-4. Adults $5, senior citizens 62 & over $4.50, children 5-15 $2; children under 5 & members no charge. Closed New Year's Day; Thanksgiving; Christmas.
Attendance: 11,000 (estimated)
Membership: Individual $35; Family $50; Donor $50; Patron $100; Sponsor $250-$500; Life $1,000.

HARRY S. TRUMAN LIBRARY & MUSEUM, 500 West U.S. Hwy. 24, Independence, MO 64050-1798. Tel.: 816-268-8200; 800-833-1225. Fax: 816-268-8295.
E-mail: truman.library@nara.gov
Web Site: www.trumanlibrary.org
Founded: 1957.
Congressional District: 5
Key Personnel: Dir., Michael J. Devine; Deputy Dir., Amy Williams.
Personnel Profile: Full-Time Paid 40; Part-Time Paid 7; Part-Time Volunteers 90; Interns 15.
Governing Authority: federal. Parent Institution: National Archives & Records Administration, Washington, DC 20408. Subsidiary Institution: Office of Presidential Libraries. Tax-exempt: 170(b)(1)(A).
Presidential Library.
Collections: personal papers; government records; still photographs; motion picture films; audio & video tapes; sound recordings; head of state gifts;

gifts from private citizens; political campaign items; personal & family memorabilia; Truman Oval Office Replica & the White House Gallery.
Major Exhibits: Capture the Moment (T), 11/09-1/10; Korean War Revisited: 60th Anniversary Exhibition, 4/10-1/11.
Research Fields: life, times, career & presidential administration of President Truman.
Facilities: 240-seat auditorium; meeting rooms. Museum-related items for sale.
Activities: guided tours; lectures; films; permanent, temporary & traveling exhibitions; organized education programs for children, adults, undergraduate & graduate students.
Publications: general information brochure; booklet.
Hours & Admission Prices: May-Sept. Mon.-Wed. & Fri.-Sat. 9-5, Thurs. 9-9, Sun. 12-5. Adults $8, senior citizens 65 & up $7, children 6-15 $3, bus groups of 15 or more with reservation $5.75; Honorary Fellows, members & children 5 & under no charge. Closed New Year's Day; Thanksgiving; Christmas. ♿
Attendance: 100,000 (accurate)
Membership: Basic $35; Family $50; Associate $120; Diplomat $250; Ambassador $500; Benefactor $750; Presidential $1000.

HARRY S TRUMAN NATIONAL HISTORIC SITE - TRUMAN HOME, 223 N. Main St., Independence, MO 64050-2804. Tel.: 816-254-2720 & 9929. Fax: 816-254-4491.
E-mail: larry_villalva@nps.gov
Web Site: www.nps.gov/hstr/
Founded: 1983.
Congressional District: 5
Key Personnel: Supt., Larry Villalva; Cur. Museum, Carol J. Dage.
Personnel Profile: Full-Time Paid 17; Part-Time Paid 6; Part-Time Volunteers 14.
Governing Authority: federal; nonprofit. Parent Institution: Dept. of Interior. Subsidiary Institution: National Park Service. Tax-exempt.
National Historic Site & Building: former home of President Harry S Truman.
Collections: furnishings; clothing; personal possessions of Pres. Harry S Truman & Bess Wallace Truman; furnishings also reflect occupation of Bess Wallace Truman's grandparents, the Gates family, and Bess's mother and siblings, the Wallaces; four generations of furnishings & personal possessions from 1867-1982. Visitor Center: audio visual program on Pres. & Mrs. Truman.
Research Fields: personal possessions & lives of Pres. Harry S Truman & Bess Wallace Truman.
Facilities: Truman home. Visitor Center: bookstore.
Activities: ranger guided tours; site orientation films; summer walking tours of Truman neighborhood.
Publications: folder; bulletin.
Hours & Admission Prices: Visitor Center: daily 8:30-5. Truman House Tours: June-Aug. daily 9-4:45; Labor Day to Memorial Day Tues.-Sun. 9-4:45. Adults 16 & over $4. Closed New Year's Day; Thanksgiving; Christmas Day. ♿
Attendance: 36,953 (accurate)

HARRY S. TRUMAN OFFICE & COURTROOM, Jackson County Courthouse, 114 S. Main St., Independence, MO 64050-3703. Mailing Address: Jackson County Historical Society, 114 S. Main St., #103, Independence, MO 64050-3703. Tel.: 816-252-7454.
Founded: 1973.
Congressional District: 4
Key Personnel: Dir. Parks & Recreation, Gary Salva; Supt. Heritage Programs & Museums, Gordon Julich.
Personnel Profile: Full-Time Paid 1; Part-Time Paid 2; Part-Time Volunteers 50.
Governing Authority: county. Affiliated Jackson County Historical Society, Tel.: 816-252-7454. Tax-exempt: 170(c)(1).
Historic Site Museum: Harry S. Truman's office, 1933-1934; courtroom used by Truman during 2nd term as Presiding Judge of County Court.
Collections: Judge Truman's office & courtroom; memorabilia of Truman era.
Research Fields: life of Harry S. Truman, with emphasis on pre-Senatorial years.
Facilities: Museum-related items for sale.
Activities: guided tours; permanent & temporary exhibitions; audiovisual program.
Hours & Admission Prices: Fri.-Sat. 9-4:30. Adults $2, senior citizens & children $1; discount to groups with advance reservation; members & children under 5 no charge. Closed New Year's Day; Thanksgiving; Christmas. ♿
Attendance: 886 (accurate)
Membership: Individual $20; Family $30.

LEILA'S HAIR MUSEUM, 1333 S. Noland Rd., Independence, MO 64055-1303. Tel.: 816-833-2955.
E-mail: lcohoon@aol.com
Web Site: www.hairwork.com/leila
Founded: 1995.
Congressional District: 5
Key Personnel: Owner, Leila Cohoon.
Personnel Profile: Full-Time Paid 2.
Art Museum.
Collections: 400 wreaths & over 2,000 pieces containing human hair including watch fobs, bracelets, necklaces, earrings, chains, brooches, hat pins, postcards & photographs.
Hours & Admission Prices: Tues.-Sat. 8:30-4. Adults $5, senior citizens over 65 & children under 12 $2.50. ♿
Attendance: 1,000

MORMON VISITORS CENTER, 937 W. Walnut St., Independence, MO 64050-3646. Tel.: 816-836-3466. Fax: 816-252-6256.
E-mail: vcindepend@ldschurch.org
Web Site: www.ldschurch.org
Formerly: Independence Visitors Center
Founded: 1971.
Key Personnel: Dir., Gerald W. Tedrow.
Personnel Profile: Full-Time Volunteers 20; Part-Time Volunteers 8.
Governing Authority: church. Parent Institution: The Church of Jesus Christ of Latter-Day Saints, 50 E. North Temple, Salt Lake City, UT 84150. Tax-exempt.
Religious History Museum.
Collections: art & period artifacts representing Mormon life in Missouri from 1831 to 1839.
Facilities: visitors center.
Activities: guided tours; lectures; films.
Hours & Admission Prices: Daily 9-9. No charge. ♿
Attendance: 57,000 (accurate)

NATIONAL FRONTIER TRAILS MUSEUM, 318 W. Pacific, Independence, MO 64050-4372. Tel.: 816-325-7575 & 7576. Fax: 816-325-7579.
Web Site: frontiertrailsmuseum.org
Founded: 1990.
Congressional District: 5
Key Personnel: Dir. & Archivist, John Mark Lambertson; Pres., Kathy Vest; Finance Dir. City of Independence, James Harlow; Cur., David Aamodt; Museum Shop Mgr., Debbie Stewart.
Personnel Profile: Full-Time Paid 5; Part-Time Paid 5; Part-Time Volunteers 12; Interns 2.
Governing Authority: municipal government; nonprofit. Parent Institution: State of Missouri; City of Independence.
History Museum: housed in 19th-century mill warehouses. Site is the location of an 1840s grist mill and public spring. The wagon caravans leaving from Independence used water from the spring before starting out for Oregon, California or Santa Fe. Designated a Santa Fe National Historic Trail Category I interpretive site.
Collections: trails history 1800-1870; early Independence western trails, archives & library; trades & craft tools; decorative arts; costumes; photographs.
Research Fields: inventory of trails diaries and journals from our archives; information will be used by a national project, Census of Overland Emigrant Diaries sponsored by the Oregon & California Trail Association.
Facilities: 3,000 vol. library; 3,500 sq. ft. exhibit space; 120-seat auditorium. Books, 19th-century craft kits, handmade baskets, games, wood carvings, maps, metalware, reproductions, videos, museum-related items for sale.
Activities: guided tours; formal education programs.
Publications: The Trail Scout.
Hours & Admission Prices: Mon.-Sat. 9-4:30, Sun. 12:30-4:30. Adults $5, senior citizens $4, students 6-17 $3; discounts to groups & tours; Friends of the National Frontier Trails Museum, Oregon-California Trails Assoc., Santa Fe Trail Assoc. members, children under 5 & members no charge. Closed New Year's Day; Thanksgiving; Christmas. ♿
Attendance: 17,000 (accurate)
Membership: Adult $15; Family $25; Benefactor $50; Sponsor $250; Corporate $500.

VAILE MANSION-DEWITT MUSEUM, 1500 N. Liberty, Independence, MO 64050-1821. Mailing Address: Tourism Dept., 111 E. Maple, Independence, MO 64050. Tel.: 816-325-7111. Fax: 816-325-7932.
Web Site: www.visitindependence.com
Founded: 1983.
Congressional District: 5

Key Personnel: C.E.O. & Pres. (V), Jean Kimball; Chm. (V) & Coord., Cathy Offutt.
Personnel Profile: Part-Time Volunteers 50.
Governing Authority: city government. Subsidiary Institution: Vaile Victorian Society. Tax-exempt.
Historic House: c.1881 30-room Victorian Mansion.
Collections: 1880s furnishings.
Facilities: library. Gift items for sale.
Activities: guided tours; arts festivals; participatory, loan & temporary exhibitions. Annual Events: Opening Tea in March; Strawberry Festival in June; Spirit of Christmas Past.
Publications: quarterly mailer, Vaile Victorian Society.
Hours & Admission Prices: April-Oct.& late Nov.-Dec. Mon.-Sat. 10-4, Sun. 1-4. Adults $5, senior citizens 62 & over $4.50, children 6-16 $2; discount to groups; members no charge. Closed Easter; Mother's Day; Thanksgiving; Christmas.
Attendance: 10,000 (accurate)
Membership: Individual $15; Vaile Squire & Damsel $50; Vaile Lady or Colonel $100; Vaile Colonel & Lady $150; Life $500.

Jefferson City

COLE COUNTY HISTORICAL MUSEUM, 109 Madison, Jefferson City, MO 65101-3015. Tel.: 573-635-1850.
E-mail: cchs@socket.net
Web Site: www.colecohistsoc.org
Founded: 1941.
Key Personnel: Pres., Kathy Wilbers; Treas., Steve Gurwell; Sec., Jane Oliver; Dir., Alicia Pigg.
Personnel Profile: Full-Time Paid 1; Part-Time Volunteers 45.
Governing Authority: society. Tax-exempt.
Historic House Museum: housed in 1871 Federal style row house (3 units), built by Gov. B. Gratz Brown, 20th governor of Missouri.
Collections: inaugural ball gowns of governors' wives; archives; wine glasses; historical 19th-century furniture; war relics.
Research Fields: history; genealogy.
Facilities: 900-vol. library of books on history & genealogy available only on premises. Limited section of local history books & postcards for sale.
Activities: guided tours; school tours; permanent & temporary exhibitions. Museum Sponsors: annual dinner meeting; Historic Suitcase-to-Go lectures.
Publications: membership newsletter.
Hours & Admission Prices: Feb. to mid-Dec. Tues.-Sat. 1-3. Adults $3, grades K-12 $1; members & children under 5 no charge. Special tours at other times if arranged in advance. Office: Mon.-Thurs. 8:30-2:30. Closed national holidays except Independence Day. ♿
Attendance: 2,898 (accurate)
Membership: Docent $5; Senior Citizen $10; Individual $15; Family $25; Business $50; Life & Endowment $500; Patron $1,000.

JEFFERSON LANDING STATE HISTORIC SITE, 100 Jefferson St., Jefferson City, MO 65101. Mailing Address: Capitol Bldg., Rm. B-2, Jefferson City, MO 65101. Tel.: 573-751-2854. Fax: 573-526-2927.
E-mail: missouri.capitol.tours@dnr.mo.gov
Web Site: www.mocapitoltours.com
Founded: 1976.
Congressional District: 9
Key Personnel: Dir., Kurt Senn; Site Admin., Linda Endersby; Cur. Exhibits, Julie Kemper; Tours, Chris Sterman; Cur. Collections, Kate Keil.
Personnel Profile: Full-Time Paid 10; Part-Time Paid 10; Interns 2.
Governing Authority: state. Parent Institution: Missouri State Museum, Capitol Bldg., Rm. B-2, Jefferson City, MO 65101. Subsidiary Institution: Division of State Parks. Tax-exempt.
Historic Site: Two buildings that were part of original steamboat landing on the Missouri River.
Collections: artifacts and documents dealing with Missouri State Capitol and the settlement of Jefferson City. Historic Buildings: c.1839 Lohman Building; c.1855 Union Hotel.
Research Fields: travel & life on the Missouri River; Jefferson City; development of river landing.
Facilities: theatre; conservation lab.
Activities: videos; special events; traveling & temporary exhibits; guided tours; exhibit workshops.
Publications: book, Jefferson Landing: Commercial Center of the Steamboat Era.
Hours & Admission Prices: Tues.-Sat. 10-4. No charge. Closed New Year's Day; Easter; Thanksgiving; Christmas. ♿
Attendance: 20,801 (accurate)

MISSOURI STATE MUSEUM, (M), 201 W. Capitol Ave., Jefferson City, MO 65101-1556. Mailing Address: Capitol Bldg., Rm. B-2, Jefferson City, MO 65101. Tel.: 573-751-2854. Fax: 573-526-2927.
E-mail: dsp.state.museum@dnr.mo.gov
Web Site: www.mocapitoltours.com
Founded: 1919.
Congressional District: 9
Key Personnel: Dir., Kurt Senn; Asst. Dir., Linda Endersby; Cur. Exhibits, Julie Kemper; Cur. Collections, Katherine Keil; Tour & Museum Shop Mgr., Chris Sterman.
Personnel Profile: Full-Time Paid 10; Part-Time Paid 15; Interns 2.
Governing Authority: state. Parent Institution: Missouri Dept. of Natural Resources, P.O. Box 176, Jefferson City, MO 65102. Subsidiary Institution: Div. of State Parks. Tax-exempt.
General Museum.
Collections: Missouriana; artifacts; documents; specimens dealing with history & resources of Missouri.
Research Fields: cultural & natural history of Missouri.
Facilities: conservation laboratory.
Activities: guided tours; special events; permanent, temporary & traveling exhibits; exhibits workshop.
Publications: pamphlets; Souvenir Guide to Missouri's Capitol; The Thomas Hart Benton Mural in the Missouri State Capitol; book, Jefferson Landing: Commercial Center of the Steamboat Era.
Hours & Admission Prices: Daily 8-5. No charge; donations accepted. Closed New Year's Day; Easter; Thanksgiving; Christmas. ♿
Attendance: 277,664 (accurate)

Joplin

DOROTHEA B. HOOVER HISTORICAL MUSEUM, 504 Schifferdecker, Joplin, MO 64801-3321. Mailing Address: P.O. Box 555, Joplin, MO 64802-0555. Tel.: 417-623-1180. Fax: 417-623-2341.
E-mail: jopmusm@ipa.net
Web Site: www.joplinmuseum.org
Founded: 1973.
Congressional District: 7
Key Personnel: Bd. Pres., John Jones; Exec. Dir., Brad Belk; Dir. Education, Dr. Jacqueline O'Dell; Resident Geologist, Dr. John Knapp; Administrative Asst., Dina Taylor; Coord. Devel., Yvonne Weeks; Cur., Christopher Wiseman.
Personnel Profile: Full-Time Paid 5; Part-Time Volunteers 50; Interns 4.
Governing Authority: society; nonprofit organization. Parent Institution: Joplin Historical & Mineral Museums Inc. Tax-exempt: 501(c)(3).
Local History Museum.
Collections: Joplin's early history; Victorian era room settings; textiles; dolls; miniature circus; 1902 child's playhouse; 1927 LeFrance fire engine; Joplin Sports Hall of Fame; cookie cutters.
Research Fields: area history; area architecture.
Facilities: 300-seat auditorium; classroom; 9,564 sq. ft. exhibit space. Books & gift items for sale.
Activities: guided tours; lectures; docent program; internship program; temporary & traveling exhibitions; special events. Museum Sponsors: biannual toy train shows in March & November; Easter Egg Hunt; Open House with Linda Lindquist Baldwin; Breakfast with Santa.
Publications: quarterly newsletter; brochure, Joplin Museum Complex.
Hours & Admission Prices: Tues. 10-7, Wed.-Sat. 10-5, Sun 2-5; call for holiday hours & group tour information. Families $5, adults $2; discounts to groups of 3 or more, AAM & ICOM members; Tues., Fri. & members no charge. Closed New Year's; Thanksgiving; Christmas.
Attendance: 135,211 (accurate)
Membership: Student $20; Single $35; Family $50; Patron $100.

GEORGE A. SPIVA CENTER FOR THE ARTS, (M), 222 West 3rd St., Joplin, MO 64801-2513. Tel.: 417-623-0183. Fax: 417-623-3805.
E-mail: jmueller@spivaarts.org
Web Site: www.spivaarts.org
Founded: 1947.
Congressional District: 7
Key Personnel: Dir., Jo Mueller; Pres. (V), Cleo Copeland.
Personnel Profile: Full-Time Paid 2; Part-Time Paid 5; Part-Time Volunteers 100; Interns 2.
Governing Authority: nonprofit. Tax-exempt: 501(c)(3).
Art Museum & Center.
Collections: paintings; sculpture; drawings.
Major Exhibits: Works From Perception (T), 1/9/10-2/21/10; Out of the Woods, 1/9/10-2/26/10; PhotoSpiva 2010, 3/6/10-4/25/10; New Directions: Nick Kyle, 3/6/10-4/30/10; At the Center: Robert Higgs, 5/8/10-7/2/10; Jim Bray 10/55, 5/8/10-7/9/10; Louviere & Vanessa, 7/17/10-9/3/10; Small Works, 9/11/10-10/29/10; Bill Rainey, 9/11/10-11/5/10; 63rd Membership Show, 11/13/10-12/26/10.

Facilities: 250-vol. research art library; classroom. Museum-related items for sale.
Activities: temporary & traveling exhibitions; lectures; gallery talks; formally organized education programs; docent program; children's classes; studio workshops for adults.
Publications: quarterly newsletter; exhibition catalog, PhotoSpiva.
Hours & Admission Prices: Tues.-Sat. 10-5, Sun. 1-5. No charge; donations accepted. Closed major holidays. ♿
Attendance: 10,000 (estimated)
Membership: Student $20; Educator, Working Artist and Senior 60 & over $30; Individual $35; Senior Couple $40; Family & Dual $50; Friend of the Arts $100; Spiva Circle $300 & up; Business Partner $300-$10,000.

TRI-STATE MINERAL MUSEUM, 400 Schifferdecker Ave., Joplin, MO 64801. Mailing Address: P.O. Box 555, Joplin, MO 64802-0555. Tel.: 417-623-1180. Fax: 417-623-2341.
E-mail: jopmusum@ipa.net
Web Site: www.joplinmuseum.org
Founded: 1931.
Congressional District: 7
Key Personnel: Bd. Pres., John Jones; Exec. Dir., Brad Belk; Devel. Officer, Yvonne Weeks; Cur., Christopher Wiseman; Dir. Education, Dr. Jacqueline O'Dell; Resident Geologist, Dr. John Knapp; Administrative Asst., Dina Taylor.
Personnel Profile: Full-Time Paid 5; Part-Time Volunteers 50; Interns 4.
Governing Authority: society; nonprofit organization. Parent Institution: Joplin Historical & Mineral Museums Inc. Tax-exempt: 501(c)(3).
Mineralogical Museum.
Collections: lead & zinc ore dating back to Joplin's mining days; mining tools & equipment; mining models.
Research Fields: area minerals.
Facilities: Museum-related items for sale.
Activities: guided group tours; lectures; docent program; internship program; temporary & traveling exhibitions. Museum Sponsors: Tri-State Gem & Mineral Show.
Publications: semiannual newsletter; quarterly newsletter; brochure, Joplin Museum Complex.
Hours & Admission Prices: Tues. 10-7, Wed.-Sat. 10-5, Sun. 2-5; call for holiday hours & group tour information. Adults $2; discounts to groups of 3 or more, AAM & ICOM members; members no charge. Closed major holidays.
Attendance: 135,211 (accurate)
Membership: Student $20; Single $35; Family $50; Patron $100.

Kansas City

ADVERTISING ICON MUSEUM, (M), 4600 Madison Ave., Ste. 1500, Kansas City, MO 64112-3016. Tel.: 816-960-5254. Fax: 816-399-6254.
E-mail: howardboasberg@bradu.com
Web Site: www.advertisingiconmuseum.com
Founded: 2005.
Key Personnel: Exec. Dir., Howard Boasberg.
Governing Authority: Tax-exempt.
Advertising Icon Museum
Collections: over 4,000 early 1900s advertising icons.
Hours & Admission Prices: Closed until 2010. ♿

AIRLINE HISTORY MUSEUM, Kansas City Downtown Airport, Hangar 9, 201 N.W. Lou Holland Dr., Kansas City, MO 64116-4223. Tel.: 816-421-3401; 800-513-9484. Fax: 816-421-3421.
Founded: 1985.
Key Personnel: Exec. Dir., Larry A. Brown; Exec. Asst., Gwyneth Bowen.
Personnel Profile: Full-Time Paid 1; Full-Time Volunteers 7; Part-Time Paid 1; Part-Time Volunteers 500.
Governing Authority: Tax-exempt.
Airline History Museum.
Collections: Lockheed L1049 Super G Constellation; Martin 404; Douglas DC-3; propeller airline aircraft & artifacts 1920-1965; photographs; audio-visual displays; printed materials; uniforms; personal artifacts.
Research Fields: Airline Histories.
Facilities: Museum-related items for sale.
Activities: tours; special events. Museum Sponsors: summer dance & dinners; Hangar dances.
Publications: bi-monthly newsletter.
Hours & Admission Prices: Mon.-Sat. 10-4, Sun. 12-4. Adults 14 & over $7, senior citizens 65 & over $6, children 6-13 $3; US Military with ID & children under 6 no charge. ♿
Attendance: 15,000 (estimated)
Membership: Annual $110.

ALEXANDER MAJORS HISTORIC HOUSE & MUSEUM, 8201 State Line Rd., Kansas City, MO 64114-2002. Tel.: 816-333-5556.
Historic House: former home of Alexander Majors, co-founder of the Pony Express.
Collections: local history & culture; photographs; personal artifacts.
Hours & Admission Prices: Mid-April to early Dec. Sat.-Sun. 1-4. Adults $3, children $1.50.

AMERICAN JAZZ MUSEUM, (M), 1616 E. 18th St., Kansas City, MO 64108-1610. Tel.: 816-474-8463, ext. 207. Fax: 816-474-0074.
E-mail: info@kcjazz.org
Web Site: www.americanjazzmuseum.org
Founded: 1997.
Congressional District: 5
Key Personnel: Exec. Dir., Juanita Moore; C.E.O., Greg Carroll; Chm. (V), Nikki Newton; Museum Shop Mgr., Barbara Thomas.
Personnel Profile: Full-Time Paid 17; Part-Time Paid 12.
Governing Authority: bd. of directors. Tax-exempt.
Jazz Museum.
Collections: jazz masters including Louis Armstrong, Duke Ellington, Ella Fitzgerald & Charlie Parker; artifacts from legendary jazz performers; Charlie Parker's saxophone.
Hours & Admission Prices: Tues.-Sat. 9-6, Sun.12-6. AJM: Adults $8, children $3; discounts to AAM members & groups. AJM & NLBM: adults $10, children $5; discounts to groups & AAM members. ♿
Attendance: 300,000 (estimated)
Membership: Student $15; Senior $35; Jazz Solo $50; Jazz Duo $100; Jazz Trio $250; Jazz Quartet $500; Bebop $1,000; Kansas City Jazz $2,500.

AMERICAN ROYAL MUSEUM & VISITORS CENTER, 1701 American Royal Court, Kansas City, MO 64102-1097. Tel.: 816-569-4043. Fax: 816-221-8189.
E-mail: ald@americanroyal.com
Web Site: www.americanroyal.com
Founded: 1992.
Key Personnel: C.E.O. & Pres., Jim McNair; Education Mgr., Al Davis.
Personnel Profile: Full-Time Paid 2; Part-Time Volunteers 10.
Governing Authority: nonprofit organization. Parent Institution: American Royal Association. Tax-exempt: 501(c)(3).
Agriculture Museum and Visitors Center.
Collections: collections from American Royal Livestock, Rodeo & Horse Shows; Kansas City stockyards; history of Kansas City & the West; cowboys.
Activities: guided tours; educational programs; agricultural displays.
Hours & Admission Prices: Tues.-Fri. 10-4; call for weekend hours. Adults $3, senior citizens $2.50, students & children 3-12 $2; discounts to AAM members. Closed holidays. ♿
Attendance: 15,341 (estimated)

AMERICAN TRUCK HISTORICAL SOCIETY, 10380 N. Ambassador Dr., Kansas City, MO 64153-1378. Mailing Address: P.O. Box 901611, Kansas City, MO 64190-1611. Tel.: 816-891-9900. Fax: 816-891-9903.
E-mail: info@aths.org
Web Site: www.aths.org
Founded: 1971.
Congressional District: 6
Key Personnel: Mng. Dir., Shelley Ruhlman; Exec. Dir., Bill Johnson; Pres., Thomas Amaducci; Treas., Michael C. Colton.
Personnel Profile: Full-Time Paid 7.
Governing Authority: nonprofit society. Tax-exempt: 501(c)(3).
Truck Library.
Collections: Ernie Sternberg (Sterling Truck) Collection; PIE (Pacific Intermountain Express) Collection; White Motor Company (of Cleveland) Archives including nine other truck names under the White umbrella at one time; over 28,000 truck transport magazine titles from around the world; sales literature on all truck makes from turn-of-the-century forward; 5,000 owner, repair, parts & sales manuals for trucks; 110,000 photos of trucks dating from the early 1900s.
Facilities: 1,200-vol. library of truck-related books; 28,000 magazines; 120 videos available for use on premises.
Activities: Annual Events: Convention; Antique Truck Show.
Publications: bimonthly magazine, Wheels of Time; ATHS Antique Truck Registry; ATHS Show Time Collector's Special Issue.
Hours & Admission Prices: Mon.-Fri. 8-4:30. No charge. Closed national holidays. ♿
Attendance: 300 (estimated)
Membership: Youth $20; General $42; Family $52; Endowing $200 per year for 5 years; Company $225; Associate $500; Life $1,000.

ARABIA STEAMBOAT MUSEUM, 400 Grand Blvd., Kansas City, MO 64106-1111. Tel.: 816-471-1856. Fax: 816-471-1616.
Web Site: www.1856.com
Founded: 1991.
Congressional District: 5
Key Personnel: Pres. & Treas., Bob Hawley; Cur., Public Rels. & Archivist, David Hawley; Museum Shop Mgr., Florence Hawley.
Personnel Profile: Full-Time Paid 10; Part-Time Paid 15.
Governing Authority: private organization.
General Museum.
Collections: hardware; personal artifacts; tools; textiles; leather; glassware; china; tin; international goods; parts & equipment from the steamboat itself.
Facilities: 85-seat large screen theater; 70-seat restaurant. Museum-related items for sale.
Activities: guided tours; theater; traveling exhibitions.
Publications: books, Treasure in a Cornfield; Treasures of the Steamboat Arabia, A Big Adventure for a Small Seed; Don't Let the Bedbugs Bite.
Hours & Admission Prices: Mon.-Sat. 10-5:30 (tours every half-hour, last one 4), Sun. 12-5 (tours every half-hour, last one 3:30). Adults $12.50, senior citizens $11.50, children 4-12 $4.75, groups of 25 or more $10.50; children 3 & under no charge. Closed New Year's Day; Easter; Thanksgiving; Christmas Eve & Day. ♿
Attendance: 85,000 (accurate)

BRUCE R. WATKINS CULTURAL HERITAGE CENTER AND MUSEUM, 3700 Blue Pkwy., Kansas City, MO 64130-2800. Tel.: 816-513-0700.
Web Site: www.kcmo.org/parks.nsf/web/watkins
History Museum.
Collections: local history & culture; photographs.
Facilities: resource library; auditorium; children's workspace.
Hours & Admission Prices: Tues.-Sat. 10-6. No charge.

THE HARRIS KEARNEY HOUSE, 4000 Baltimore, Kansas City, MO 64111-7403. Tel.: 816-561-1821.
E-mail: info@westporthistorical.org
Governing Authority: Parent Institution: The Westport Historical Society.
Historic House: former home of Col. John Harris.
Collections: local history & culture; photographs; furnishings; personal artifacts.
Hours & Admission Prices: Call for hours.

THE JOHN WORNALL HOUSE MUSEUM, 6115 Wornall Rd., Kansas City, MO 64113-1417. Tel.: 816-444-1858. Fax: 816-361-8165.
E-mail: kandice@wornallhouse.org
Web Site: www.wornallhouse.org
Founded: 1972.
Congressional District: 5
Key Personnel: Dir., Kandice Walker; Chm. & Pres. Bd. (V), Marianne Noll; Museum Shop Mgr., Margueritte Milliken.
Personnel Profile: Full-Time Paid 1; Part-Time Paid 1; Part-Time Volunteers 75; Interns 1.
Governing Authority: nonprofit organization. Parent Institution: John Wornall House Museum, Inc. Tax-exempt: 501(c)(3).
Historic House: c.1858 Greek Revival home used as a hospital during the Civil War.
Collections: Civil War era; furniture; textiles; ceramics; glass; silver; ironware; period herb garden.
Research Fields: social history of western Missouri in mid-19th century.
Facilities: Books, kitchen items, toys & craft items for sale.
Activities: guided tours; lectures; organized education programs; docent program; school loan service.
Publications: membership newsletter.
Hours & Admission Prices: Tues.-Sat. 10-4, Sun. 1-4. Adult $4, children 5-12 $3; discounts to AAM members & military personnel; children under 4 & members no charge. Closed holidays. ♿
Attendance: 6,286 (accurate)
Membership: Friends: Student & Senior $25; Individual $35; Family $50. Society of 1858: Contributing $100; Sponsoring $250; Sustaining $500; Benefactor $1,000 & up.

KALEIDOSCOPE, 2500 Grand, Kansas City, MO 64108. Mailing Address: P.O. Box 419580, Kansas City, MO 64141-6580. Tel.: 816-274-8301 & 8934. Fax: 816-274-3148.
E-mail: lavery1@hallmark.com
Web Site: www.hallmarkkaleidoscope.com
Founded: 1969.
Congressional District: 5
Key Personnel: Admin., Regi Ahrens; Exhibit Mgr., Linda Avery; Volunteer Coord., Jeanine Ellis.
Personnel Profile: Full-Time Paid 8; Part-Time Paid 11; Part-Time Volunteers 150.
Governing Authority: company. Parent Institution: Hallmark Cards, Inc.
Children's Participatory Art Exhibit.
Collections: hands-on exhibits.
Facilities: 8,000 sq. ft. exhibit space; art studio.
Activities: guided tours; participatory art experience for children & their families.
Hours & Admission Prices: Call for hours. No charge. Closed New Year's Day; Memorial Day; Independence Day; Labor Day; Thanksgiving; Christmas Eve & Day. ♿
Attendance: 140,500 (accurate)

KANSAS CITY MUSEUM, 3218 Gladstone Blvd., Kansas City, MO 64123-1199. Tel.: 816-483-8300. Fax: 816-483-6050.
Web Site: kcmuseum.com
Founded: 1940.
Key Personnel: Dir., George Guastello; Chm. (V), Michael Haverty.
Personnel Profile: Full-Time Paid 14; Part-Time Paid 1; Part-Time Volunteers 48; Interns 6.
Governing Authority: Parent Institution: Union Station Kansas City, Inc. Tax-exempt.
History Museum: housed in an urban estate built in 1910.
Collections: local & regional history; early costumes.
Facilities: 50-seat auditorium; visitor center.
Activities: special events.
Publications: community curator series, Natural History on the Head; past exhibitions information; Loula Long Combs: Fashion Paper Doll Collection; What We Did for Love: AIDS Walk T-shirt Collection; Restoration of a Window; Pocket Museum.
Hours & Admission Prices: Visitor Center: Tues.-Sat. 9:30-4:30, Sun. 12-4:30. StoryTarium Programs: Tues.-Sat. 11, 1, & 3, Sun. 12:30, 1:30, 3:30. No charge; donations accepted. ♿
Attendance: 25,000
Membership: Individual $25; Family $35; Corporate $50; R.A. Long Society $500.

KANSAS CITY ZOO, 6800 Zoo Dr., Kansas City, MO 64132-1711. Tel.: 816-513-5800. Fax: 816-513-5850.
E-mail: randywisthoff@fotzkc.org
Web Site: www.kansascityzoo.org
Formerly: Kansas City Zoological Gardens
Founded: 1909.
Congressional District: 5
Key Personnel: C.E.O. & Dir., Randy Wisthoff; Chm., Carol Hallquist; Dir. Finance, Gene Howe; Dir. Devel., Laura Berger; Dir. Facilities, Mike Stuckey; Dir. Mktg. & Membership, Julie Neemeyer; Gen. Cur., Liz Harmon; Dir. Education, Debra Ryder; Museum Shop Mgr., Donna Shackford; Veterinarian, W. Kirk Suedmeyer, D.V.M.
Personnel Profile: Full-Time Paid 130; Part-Time Paid 250; Part-Time Volunteers 225; Interns 10.
Governing Authority: municipal. Parent Institution: Friends of the Zoo, Inc., Kansas City, MO. Tax-exempt.
Zoological Park.
Collections: 215 species; 900 specimens including endangered or threatened species; domesticated animals; African Elephant exhibit, waterfowl exhibit; Australian exhibit; African Forest & African Plains exhibits.
Research Fields: animal behavioral studies & accumulation of physiological data from routine medical treatment.
Facilities: 300-vol. library of books on animal sciences, natural history, ethology, exotic animal management & medicine available for research by permission of the director; outdoor refreshment stands. Guidebooks & other zoo-related items for sale.
Activities: lectures; films; formally organized education programs for children & adults; docent program; permanent exhibitions; zoomobile; outreach program.
Publications: quarterly newsletter, Friends of the Zoo Newsletter.
Hours & Admission Prices: March-Oct. daily 9:30-5; Nov.-Feb. daily 10-4. Adults $10.50, seniors $9.50, children 3-11 $7. Tues: adults $8, seniors $7, children 3-11 $6; discounts to groups & reciprocal Zoos Friends members; members & children under 3 no charge. Closed New Year's; Thanksgiving; Christmas. ♿
Attendance: 460,000 (accurate)
Membership: Individual $45; Individual Plus $55; Family $75; Sustaining $110; Associate $135; Patron $250; Benefactor $500.

KEMPER MUSEUM OF CONTEMPORARY ART, 4420 Warwick Blvd., Kansas City, MO 64111-1821. Tel.: 816-753-5784. Fax: 816-753-5806.
E-mail: info@kemperart.org

Web Site: www.kemperart.org
Founded: 1994.
Congressional District: 5
Key Personnel: Chm. (V), R. Crosby Kemper, Jr.; Dir., Rachael Blackburn Cozad; Cur., Christopher Cook; Cur. Education, Beth Harris; Curatorial Asst., Angela Lewis; Devel. Officer, Dawn Taylor Biegelsen; Mktg. & Communications, Margaret A. Keough; Mktg. & Communications Assoc., Becca Ramspott; Registrar, Amy Duke; Coord. Membership, Steve Crays; Accounting & Human Resources Mgr., Teresa Metz; Museum Shop Mgr., Megan England; Preparator, Christopher Bell; Security Supvr., Ted Wilson; Administrative Asst., Angela Dennis; Special Events Coord., Julie Collingwood Blumenthal; Visitor Svcs. & Volunteer Coord., Jennifer Lapka Pfeifer; Exec. Chef, Jennifer Maloney; Gen. Mgr., Cafe Sebastienne, Pam Tibbs.
Personnel Profile: Full-Time Paid 25; Part-Time Paid 48; Part-Time Volunteers 40; Interns 2.
Governing Authority: nonprofit organization. Parent Institution: Kemper Museum Operating Foundation. Tax-exempt: 501(c)(3).
Contemporary Art Museum.
Collections: Bebe & Crosby Kemper Collection; contemporary art in all media.
Research Fields: contemporary art, design & architecture in all media.
Facilities: meeting room; cafe; 20,039 sq. ft. exhibition space.
Activities: films; formal education programs; guided tours; lectures; loan, temporary & traveling exhibitions.
Publications: quarterly newsletter; exhibition catalogues; exhibition-related materials.
Hours & Admission Prices: Tues.-Thurs. 10-4, Fri.-Sat. 10-9, Sun. 11-5. Cafe: Tues.-Sun. 11-2:30, Fri.-Sat. 5:30-9:30. No charge; donations accepted. Closed New Year's Day; Independence Day; Thanksgiving Day; Christmas. ♿
Attendance: 130,000 (estimated)
Membership: Individual $35; Family $50; Friend $100; Director's Circle $250; Benefactor $500; Special Benefactor $750; Contributing $1,000; Special Contributing $2,500; Sustaining Individual $5,000. Corporate membership: Small Business Partner $500-$1,000; Business Partner $2,500; Corporate Partner $5,000; Corporate Fellow $10,000; Executive Partner $25,000; Executive Fellow $50,000.

THE MONEY MUSEUM-FEDERAL RESERVE BANK OF KANSAS CITY, One Memorial Dr., Kansas City, MO 64198-0002. Tel.: 816-881-2683 & 2000. Fax: 816-881-2569.
Web Site: www.kc.frb.org
Formerly: The Roger Guffey Gallery-Federal Reserve Bank of Kansas City
Founded: 2001.
Key Personnel: C.E.O., Thomas M. Hoenig; Vice Pres., Diane M. Raley.
Governing Authority: federal reserve system. Tax-exempt.
Money Gallery: housed in the lobby of the Federal Reserve Bank of Kansas City; focuses on how money has evolved throughout banking history to present day.
Collections: The Harry S. Truman coin collection (453 coins dating back to George Washington's presidency through Jimmy Carter's term in office).
Facilities: 50-seat meeting room.
Activities: guided tours; lectures; films; participatory exhibits.
Publications: brochures.
Hours & Admission Prices: Mon.-Fri. 8:30-4:30. No charge. Closed banking holidays. ♿

NATIONAL WORLD WAR I MUSEUM AT LIBERTY MEMORIAL, (M), 100 W. 26th St., Kansas City, MO 64108-4616. Tel.: 816-784-1918. Fax: 816-784-1929.
E-mail: info@theworldwar.org
Web Site: www.theworldwar.org
Founded: 1926.
Congressional District: 5
Key Personnel: Pres. & C.E.O., Brian Alexander; Vice Pres. Museum Programs, Eli Paul; Chm. Bd. Governors, Tim Kristl; C.F.O., Jeffrey Walker; Cur., Doran Cart; Dir. Devel., Tim Dykes; Vice Pres. Communications, Denise Rendina; Archivist, Jonathan Casey; Education Coord., James Barkley; Dir. Business Operations, Kathy Jarboe.
Personnel Profile: Full-Time Paid 29; Part-Time Paid 1; Part-Time Volunteers 170; Interns 7.
Governing Authority: bd. of trustees. Tax-exempt: 501(c)(3).
Military History Museum.
Collections: World War I history, veterans, documents & artifacts, 1914-1918; Pantheon de la Guerre mural conceived by French artists, Pierre-Carrier-Belleuse & Auguste Gorguet, 1914-1918; murals by Daniel MacMorris; artillery; weapons; uniforms; equipment; posters; photographs; letters; maps.
Research Fields: weapons, uniforms & posters, insignia of World War I; American involvement in the war.
Facilities: archives & library of maps, photographs, military unit histories & over 1,200 posters of World War I available for research.
Activities: permanent, temporary & traveling exhibitions.
Publications: information brochure; newsletter.
Hours & Admission Prices: Tues.-Sun. 10-5. Admission 12-64 $10, seniors 65 & over $8, children 6-11 $5; discounts to AAM members; members no charge. Closed major holidays. ♿
Attendance: 147,950 (accurate)
Membership: Individual $30; Family $55; Sustaining $75; Associate $125; Patron $250.

NEGRO LEAGUES BASEBALL MUSEUM, (M), 1616 E. 18th St., Kansas City, MO 64108-1610. Tel.: 816-221-1920.
Key Personnel: Dir., Gregory D. Bahn; Chm. (V), Dewey Alexander; Museum Shop Mgr., Johnnie Lee.
Personnel Profile: Full-Time Paid 10.
Governing Authority: Tax-exempt.
African-American Baseball History Museum.
Collections: African-American baseball history; photographs; bronze sculptures; baseball artifacts.
Facilities: Museum-related items for sale.
Activities: education programs; traveling exhibits; rental facility.
Hours & Admission Prices: Tues.-Sat. 9-6, Sun. 12-6. Adults $8, children under 12 $3; discounts to groups; children under 5 no charge. ♿
Membership: Major Leaguer $25-$49; All Star $50-$99; MVP $100-$499; Hall of Fame $500-$999; Legacy $1,000 & up.

* **THE NELSON-ATKINS MUSEUM OF ART, (M),** 4525 Oak St., Kansas City, MO 64111-1873. Tel.: 816-751-1278. Fax: 816-561-4011.
Web Site: www.nelson-atkins.org
Founded: 1933.
Congressional District: 5
Key Personnel: Dir. & C.E.O., Marc F. Wilson; C.O.O., Karen L. Christiansen; Chm. Bd. Trustees, Harry McCray; Cur. Art of Ancient World, Dr. Robert Cohon; Dir. Conservation & Collections Mgmt., Elisabeth Batchelor; Mgr. Mktg. & Communications, Toni Wood; Sr. Conservator Paintings, Scott Heffley; Sr. Conservator Objects, Kathleen Garland; Investment & Compliance, William W. Markey, CPA; Finance & Accounting, Harland Hunt; Chief Registrar, Ann Erbacher; Visual Resources Librarian, Noriko Ebersole; Samuel Sosland Sr. Cur. American Art, Dr. Margaret C. Conrads; Helen Jane & R. Hugh "Pat" Uhlmann Cur. Decorative Arts, Dr. Catherine L. Futter; Louis C. & Adelaide C. Ward Cur. European Painting & Sculpture, Ian Kennedy; Fred & Virginia Merrill Sr. Cur. American Indian Art, Gaylord Torrence; Museum Store Mgr., Elly Miles; Coord. Mail Svcs., Mike Welch; Sanders Sosland Cur. Modern & Contemporary Art, Dr. Jan Schall; Mgr. Volunteer Svcs., Mary Beth Sloan; Cur. Exhibitions Management, Cindy Cart; Dir. Presentation, Steve Waterman; Consultative Cur. Medieval Art, Dr. Marilyn Stokstad; Mgr. Individual Giving, Nicolle Ratliff; Mgr. Donor & Information Svcs., Kerry Peak; Design Project Specialist, Rebecca Young; Mgr. Graphic Design, Michele Boeckholt; Mgr. Fabrications, Bruce Smith; Mgr. Major Gifts, Barb Head; Mgr. Grants & Foundations, Ann Friedman; Chief Preparator, Mark Milani; Head, Imaging Svcs., Louis Meluso; Mgr. Event Planning, DeSaix Adams; Lead Engineer, Paul Watts; Mgr. Engineering, Brad Masuen; Mgr. Maintenance, Angela Graham; Purchasing Coord., Kelly Heaton; Mgr. Facilities, Security & Visitor Svcs., Michael Cross; Dir. Human Resources, Kelly Summers; Dir. Public Programs & Interpretation, Christine Minkler.
Personnel Profile: Full-Time Paid 193; Part-Time Paid 34; Part-Time Volunteers 500; Interns 12.
Governing Authority: nonprofit organization. Parent Institutions: The Nelson Gallery Foundation and The William Rockhill Nelson Trust. Tax-exempt: 501(c)(3).
Art Museum.
Collections: European, American & ancient painting, sculpture, drawing, prints & decorative arts; Kansas City Sculpture Park including the Henry Moore Sculpture Garden; Asiatic, Native American, Oceanic & pre-Columbian art.
Major Exhibits: Edward Steichen: In High Fashion (T), 5/09-7/10; 75th Anniversary Collecting Initiative, 2/10-3/10; Exploring Egypt: 19th Century Expeditionary Photography, 2/10-7/10; Venice: Three Artists - Three Visions (T), 2/10-8/10; KCAI 125th Anniversary, 7/10-10/10; Through African Eyes: The European in African Art, 1500 to Present (T), 9/10-1/11; Alfred Jacob Miller: Watercolors from the Bank of America Collection, 9/10-1/11.
Research Fields: European & American art; Asiatic art, emphasis on China.
Facilities: 145,000-vol. library of art reference books, monographs & catalogs available on premises; museum archives; reading room; 66 galleries; 9 period rooms; conservation laboratory; 510-seat auditorium; restaurant; Ford Learning Center. Art books, reproductions & other museum related-items for sale.

Activities: guided tours; lectures; films; gallery talks; concerts; formally organized education programs for children & adults; docent programs; permanent & temporary exhibitions.
Publications: biannual members magazine; bimonthly calendar, Explore Art.
Hours & Admission Prices: Wed. 10-4, Thurs.-Fri. 10-9, Sat. 10-5, Sun. 12-5. No charge; donations accepted. Closed New Year's Day; Memorial Day; Independence Day; Thanksgiving; Christmas Eve & Day. ♿
Attendance: 350,000 (estimated)
Membership: Print Society: Individual $25; Couple $35; Sustaining $100; Patron $250. Friends of Art: Individual $60; Dual $90; Family $100; Associate $250; Sponsor $350. National 100 miles outside of Kansas City $45. Society of Fellows: Patron $850; Sustaining Patron $1,750; Nelson Society $2,750; Benefactor $5,000; Ambassador $10,000. Annual Business Council: Corporate Associate $3,000-$4,999; Corporate Contributor $5,000-$9,999; Corporate Director $10,000-$24,999; Corporate Sponsor $25,000-$49,000; Corporate Bronze Circle Sponsor $50,000-$99,999; Corporate Silver Circle Sponsor $100,000-$249,999; Corporate Gold Circle Sponsor $250,000 & up.

PIPER MEMORIAL MEDICAL MUSEUM, (M), 1000 Carondelet Dr., Kansas City, MO 64114-4673. Tel.: 816-943-2183. Fax: 816-943-2786.
Founded: 1971.
Key Personnel: Cur., Joan Hilger-Mullen.
Personnel Profile: Part-Time Paid 1; Part-Time Volunteers 3.
Governing Authority: Parent Institution: St. Joseph Medical Center. Tax-exempt.
Medical Museum.
Collections: St. Joseph Medical Center history from 1874 to present.
Hours & Admission Prices: Daily 8-8. No charge; donations accepted. ♿

SHOAL CREEK LIVING HISTORY MUSEUM, 7000 N.E. Barry Rd., Kansas City, MO 64156-1278. Tel.: 816-792-2655.
E-mail: parks@kcmo.org
Web Site: www.kcmo.org
Founded: 1976.
Congressional District: 6
Key Personnel: C.E.O., Pres. (V) & Museum Shop Mgr., Sharon Sumner; Chm. (V), Cindy Udris.
Personnel Profile: Full-Time Volunteers 30; Part-Time Volunteers 92.
Governing Authority: municipal; nonprofit. Parent Institution: City of Kansas City, Missouri Dept. of Parks, Recreation and Boulevards. Subsidiary Institution: Shoal Creek Association. Tax-exempt.
History Museum: comprised of 20 buildings dating from 1807-1890.
Collections: concentration on 19th-century daily Missouri life.
Research Fields: 19th century women's lives; history of Freemasonry & Masonic architecture.
Facilities: Period reproductions including clothes, millinery & other items related to daily life for sale.
Activities: docent program; formal education programs; guided tours. Annual Events: Civil War Battles; A Visit with St. Nicholas; Harvest Festival.
Publications: quarterly newsletter, The Mouse in the Attic.
Hours & Admission Prices: March-Dec. Mon.-Sat. 9-3. Tours, school programs & reenactments by appointment. Adults $3; additional fees for programs & events; discounts to AAM and ICOM members. Closed government holidays. ♿
Attendance: 10,000 (estimated)
Membership: Individual $15; Family $50; Corporate $500.

THOMAS HART BENTON HOME AND STUDIO STATE HISTORIC SITE, 3616 Belleview, Kansas City, MO 64111-3808. Tel.: 816-931-5722. Fax: 816-931-5722.
E-mail: benton.home.state.historic.site@dnr.mo.gov
Web Site: www.mostateparks.com/benton.htm
Founded: 1977.
Congressional District: 5
Personnel Profile: Full-Time Paid 3; Part-Time Paid 1.
Governing Authority: state. Parent Institution: Div. State Parks, Missouri Dept. of Natural Resources, P.O. Box 176, Jefferson City, MO 65102. Tax-exempt.
Historic House: home & studio of Thomas Hart Benton.
Collections: original furnishings relating to the life of Thomas Hart Benton.
Activities: guided tours; off-site presentations.
Publications: brochure, Thomas Hart Benton Home.
Hours & Admission Prices: Winter: Mon.-Sat. 10-4, Sun. 11-4; Summer: Mon.-Sat. 10-4, Sun. 12-5. Groups of 15 or more by appointment. Adults $2.50, children 6-12 $1.50; discount to groups; children under 6 no charge. Closed New Year's Day; Thanksgiving; Christmas. ♿
Attendance: 5,706 (accurate)
Membership: Individual $35; Founder $50.

THORNHILL GALLERY AT AVILA UNIVERSITY, Dallavis Center, 11901 Wornall Rd., Kansas City, MO 64145-1007. Tel.: 816-501-3659. Fax: 816-846-4726.
E-mail: aylwardme@avila.edu
Web Site: www.avila.edu
Founded: 1978.
Congressional District: 5
Key Personnel: C.E.O., Susan Lawlor; Cur., Marci Aylward.
Personnel Profile: Part-Time Paid 3.
Governing Authority: college; nonprofit organization. Parent Institution: Avila University.
Art Gallery.
Collections: works by national & international artists.
Facilities: 850 sq. ft. exhibit space.
Activities: traveling exhibits. Annual Event: High School Invitational Visual Arts Day.
Publications: annual calendar.
Hours & Admission Prices: Tues.-Fri. 12-3; other times by appointment. No charge; donations accepted. Closed New Year's Day; Easter; Memorial Day; Independence Day; Labor Day; Christmas; spring & fall breaks. ♿
Attendance: 2,400 (estimated)

TOY & MINIATURE MUSEUM OF KANSAS CITY, (M), 5235 Oak St., Kansas City, MO 64112-2824. Tel.: 816-333-9328. Fax: 816-333-2055.
E-mail: berryja@umkc.edu
Web Site: www.toyandminiaturemuseum.org
Founded: 1981.
Congressional District: 5
Key Personnel: Exec. Dir., Jamie A. Berry; Operations Mgr., Sandi Russell; Museum Asst., Rita Papini; Admin. Asst., Tony Julo; Registrar, Calleen Carver; Collections Coord., Mary Wheeler; Cur., Kristi Dobbins; Museum Educator, Laura Taylor.
Personnel Profile: Full-Time Paid 8; Full-Time Volunteers 2; Part-Time Paid 1; Part-Time Volunteers 60; Interns 2.
Governing Authority: nonprofit organization. Tax-exempt: 501(c)(3).
Toy & Miniature Museum: housed in 1911 Truman Mansion.
Collections: antique dolls; dollhouses; toys; contemporary scale miniatures.
Research Fields: antique toys & doll houses of German origin.
Facilities: 900-vol. library pertaining to toys & doll houses; 21,500 sq. ft. exhibit space. Reproduction paper dolls, collectors reference book & scaled miniature items for sale.
Activities: guided tours; lectures & slides; temporary exhibitions; classes.
Publications: quarterly newsletter; museum catalog; children's book.
Hours & Admission Prices: Jan.-Aug. & Oct.-Dec. Wed.-Sat. 10-4, Sun. 1-4. Adults $6, students & senior citizens $5, children $4; discount to groups; members & children under 5 no charge. Closed New Year's Day; Easter; Independence Day; Thanksgiving; Christmas. ♿
Attendance: 14,665 (accurate)
Membership: Individual $30; Family & Grandparent $40; Patron $100; Donor $250; Founder's Circle $1,000.

TRAILSIDE CENTER, 9901 Holmes Rd., Kansas City, MO 64131-4205. Tel.: 816-942-3581.
E-mail: info@trailsidecenter.org
Founded: 2004.
History Museum.
Collections: local history & culture; photographs; interactive exhibits.
Hours & Admission Prices: Tues.-Sat. 10-3, Sun. 3:30-5. ♿

UNION STATION KANSAS CITY, INC., (M), 30 W. Pershing Rd., Kansas City, MO 64108-2410. Tel.: 816-460-2000. Fax: 816-460-2260.
E-mail: info@unionstation.org
Web Site: www.unionstation.org
Formerly: Science City at Union Station/Kansas City Museum
Founded: 1939.
Congressional District: 5
Key Personnel: Pres. & C.E.O., Andi Udris; Exec. Vice Pres. & C.F.O., Art Chaudry; Chm. Bd., Michael R. Haverty; Vice Pres. Human Resources & Security, Tim Spellman; Dir. Science City, Raymond Shubinski; Dir. Education, Linda Segebrecht; Dir. Mktg., Pat D'Amico; Dir. Historic Site, Jay Smith; Dir. Guest Svcs. & Sales, Lori Glazer; Dir. Collections, Denise Morrison; Museum Shop Mgr., Kay Hyde.
Personnel Profile: Full-Time Paid 145; Part-Time Paid 58; Part-Time Volunteers 100.
Governing Authority: nonprofit organization. Tax-exempt: 501(c)(3).
Science & History Museum.
Collections: archaeology; costumes & textiles; general history; historic & prehistoric Indians; archives; geology; paleontology; technology; carriages

& tack; Native American artifacts; railroad artifacts; period rail cars; hands-on railroad exhibits.
Research Fields: Kansas City history & natural history.
Facilities: 2,500-vol. library & archives available for research; indoor city with 50 interactive settings; 440-seat 15/70-3D theater; 200-seat stage theater; 150-seat dome planetarium; discovery area; Challenger Center. Educational items for sale.
Activities: Interactors; temporary exhibitions; theater shows; educational programs; special programs & events.
Publications: newsletter; pamphlets; brochures; annual report; school group programs.
Hours & Admission Prices: Memorial Day to Labor Day Wed.-Sat. 10-6, Sun. 12-6; Sept.-May Wed.-Fri. 9:30-5, Sat. 10-5, Sun. 12-5. All Venues: adults $13.95. Science City, Planetarium & Traveling Exhibit: adults $7.95. Theater, Planetarium or Rail: adults $4.95. Discounts to AAM & ICOM members and reserved groups of 15 & over; children 3 & under, ASTC members and members no charge. Closed Thanksgiving; Christmas. ♿
Attendance: 436,378 (accurate)
Membership: Couple $49.95, $19.95 additional person.

UNIVERSITY OF MISSOURI-KANSAS CITY GALLERY OF ART, 203 Fine Arts Bldg., 5100 Rockhill Rd., Kansas City, MO 64110-2499. Tel.: 816-235-1501. Fax: 816-235-5507.
E-mail: art@umkc.edu
Web Site: cas.umkc.edu/art/gallery.cfm
Founded: 1975.
Congressional District: 5
Key Personnel: Dir., Craig A. Subler; Dir. & Chm., Burton L. Dunbar; Devel., Bill French.
Personnel Profile: Full-Time Paid 5; Part-Time Paid 2; Part-Time Volunteers 18; Interns 2.
Governing Authority: university; nonprofit organization. Tax-exempt: 501(c)(3).
Art Gallery.
Collections: paintings; sculpture; photographs.
Research Fields: contemporary.
Facilities: educational facilities.
Activities: lectures; formal education programs for undergraduate & graduate college students; guided tours; loan & traveling exhibitions. Museum Sponsors: workshop symposium.
Publications: catalogues.
Hours & Admission Prices: Mon., Wed. & Fri.-Sat. 11-4. No charge; donations accepted. Closed holidays. ♿
Attendance: 10,000 (estimated)
Membership: Director $50; Associate $100; Host $250; Sponsor $500; Patron $1,000.

Kearney

JESSE JAMES FARM & MUSEUM, (M), 21216 Jesse James Farm Rd., Kearney, MO 64060-9343. Tel.: 816-628-6065. Fax: 816-628-6676.
E-mail: jessejames@claycogov.com
Web Site: home.co.clay.mo.us
Founded: 1978.
Congressional District: 6
Key Personnel: Historic Sites Admin., Elizabeth Gilliam-Beckett; Asst. Dir., Rebecca Prestwood.
Personnel Profile: Full-Time Paid 2; Part-Time Paid 20; Part-Time Volunteers 10.
Governing Authority: county. Parent Institution: Clay County Parks, Recreation & Historic Site. Tax-exempt.
Historic Buildings & Site.
Collections: 1845 James farm; restored birthplace of Jesse James; 1858 Claybrook Plantation & restored house; Mt. Gilead Church & School; Jesse James Bank Museum.
Research Fields: life & career of Jesse W. James; Claybrook Plantation history; history of Mt. Gilead Church and School.
Activities: guided tours; laser disc show; simulated 19th-century school classes.
Hours & Admission Prices: May-Sept. daily 9-4; Oct.-April Mon.-Fri. 9-4, Sat.-Sun. 12-4. Adults $7.50, seniors $6.50, children $4; discounts to seniors & Clay County citizens. ♿
Attendance: 12,000 (estimated)

Kennett

DUNKLIN COUNTY MUSEUM, INC., 122 College, Kennett, MO 63857-2007. Mailing Address: 604 College, Kennett, MO 63857-2015. Tel.: 573-888-6620.
E-mail: cbrown@sheltonbbs.com
Founded: 1976.
Congressional District: 10
Key Personnel: Chm. Bd. Dirs., Mrs. Charles B. Brown; Chm. (V), Sandra Brown.
Personnel Profile: Part-Time Volunteers 10.
Governing Authority: nonprofit. Tax-exempt: 509(a)(1).
History Museum: housed in 1904 City Hall & Masonic Temple.
Collections: historical items; general store items; World War I & II uniforms & memorabilia; 1879 General Electric generator; manuscripts; primitive tools; pictures; nature display; 40 model engines showing power from wind, water, gas, steam, electricity; photographs of 1900 Bootheel area; Miles family personal artifacts; Mississippian culture of Dunklin County; stone & pottery artifacts.
Major Exhibits: Star Pattern Quilt of the Century, 11/09-5/10.
Activities: guided tours; docent program; permanent & temporary exhibitions.
Hours & Admission Prices: March-Dec. Wed. 12-5, Sat. by appointment; tours by appointment. No charge; donations accepted.
Attendance: 1,500 (estimated)
Membership: Contributing $100; Patron $100-$1,000; Founder $1,000 & up.

Keytesville

GENERAL STERLING PRICE MUSEUM, 412 Bridge St., Keytesville, MO 65261-1016. Mailing Address: P.O. Box 40, Keytesville, MO 65261-0040. Tel.: 660-288-3204.
Founded: 1964.
Congressional District: 6
Key Personnel: Pres., Janet Weaver; Treas., Kessie Friesz; Sec., Jan Canyon.
Personnel Profile: Part-Time Paid 2.
Governing Authority: nonprofit. Parent Institution: Friends of Keytesville, Inc. Tax-exempt.
General Museum.
Collections: china; glass; silver; geology; fossilized insects; furniture; arrowheads; items belonging to Gen. Price; manuscript collections.
Facilities: library pertaining to the era of Gen. Price available on premises.
Activities: guided tours; permanent & temporary exhibitions. Annual Event: Sterling Price Day Celebration in September.
Publications: brochures, Gen. Sterling Price; book, Keytesville-150 Years, John Price Emigrant (Jamestown Colony) 1620 with some of his descendents; 1996 Keytesville Cookbook; 1976 Keytesville Cookbook; Hill House Letters, letters between William & Bettie Hill, 1864-1865.
Hours & Admission Prices: May 15-Oct. 15 Mon. & Thurs.-Fri. 2-5. No charge; donations accepted. Closed holidays.
Attendance: 300 (accurate)
Membership: Individual $10; Couple $15.

Kirksville

ADAIR COUNTY HISTORICAL SOCIETY, INC., 211 S. Elson St., Kirksville, MO 63501-3466. Tel.: 660-665-6502.
E-mail: peeve@cableone.net
Web Site: www.aarcohs.org
Founded: 1976.
Congressional District: 9
Key Personnel: C.E.O., Pres. & Devel., Mr. Pat Ellebracht; Treas., Mrs. Denise Treasure; Cur., Archivist & Security, Mr. Walter Davison.
Personnel Profile: Full-Time Volunteers 2; Part-Time Volunteers 4.
Governing Authority: private; nonprofit organization. Tax-exempt: 501(c)(3).
Historical Society Museum.
Collections: history of Adair county from prehistoric to modern times; Indian artifacts; artifacts from early settlers to modern times.
Research Fields: genealogy.
Facilities: 200-vol. library available for use on premises; 2,000 sq. ft. exhibit space. Books for sale.
Activities: guided tours; traveling exhibitions. Museum Sponsors: dinners.
Publications: quarterly newsletter, The Adair Historian; booklet, A Pocket Book History of Adair County; booklets, Sgt. John Shaver's The Last Roll Call; And There Arose A Mighty Wind.
Hours & Admission Prices: Wed.-Fri. 1-4. No charge; donations accepted. Closed New Year's Eve & Day; Memorial Day; Independence Day; Labor Day; Thanksgiving; Christmas Eve, Day & week.
Attendance: 25 (estimated)
Membership: Individual $15-$60; Family $25-$100; Sustaining $50-$200; Life $200-$600.

E.M. VIOLETTE MUSEUM, Truman State University, John R. Kirk Memorial, Kirksville, MO 63501-4221. Tel.: 660-785-4532. Fax: 660-785-7415.
E-mail: emdoak@truman.edu
Web Site: library.truman.edu/weblinks/violette_museum/mainpage.htm
Founded: 1913.
Congressional District: 9

Key Personnel: Dir. Div. Libraries & Museums, Richard J. Coughlin; Head Special Collections & Archives (Acting Cur.), Elaine M. Doak.
Governing Authority: university. Parent Institution: Truman State University.
History Museum.
Collections: northeast Missouri history; military & Indian artifacts; university history.
Activities: guided tours.
Hours & Admission Prices: Temporarily closed. ♿
Attendance: 1,400 (estimated)

STILL NATIONAL OSTEOPATHIC MUSEUM, (M), 800 W. Jefferson St., Kirksville, MO 63501-1443. Tel.: 660-626-2359. Fax: 660-626-2984.
E-mail: museum@atsu.edu
Web Site: www.atsu.edu/museum
Founded: 1978.
Congressional District: 9
Key Personnel: Dir., Jason Haxton; Education Coord., Lisa Perkins; Cur., Debra Loguda-Summers; Exhibit Preparator, Robert Clement.
Personnel Profile: Full-Time Paid 4; Full-Time Volunteers 1; Part-Time Paid 1; Part-Time Volunteers 10; Interns 1.
Governing Authority: nonprofit organization. Parent Institution: Kirksville College of Osteopathic Medicine. Tax-exempt: 501(c)(3).
Medical Museum Complex: housed in the education building on the campus of Kirksville College of Osteopathic Medicine.
Collections: artifacts, literature, memorabilia & material illustrative of the development of the osteopathic profession. Historic Houses: log cabin birthplace of A.T. Still, founder of osteopathy; c.1892 first classroom building.
Research Fields: 19th-century medicine; local history; osteopathic/medical history.
Facilities: 1,500-vol. library pertaining to osteopathic & related medical subjects available to the public. Books, pictures & gift items for sale.
Activities: guided tours; school discovery programs; health & wellness programs; loan, temporary, & traveling exhibitions.
Publications: brochure; semiannual newsletter; exhibition catalogues.
Hours & Admission Prices: Mon.-Wed. & Fri. 10-4, Thurs. 10-7, Sat. 12-4; other times by appointment. No charge; donations accepted. ♿
Attendance: 8,910 (accurate)
Membership: Student $5; Intern $15; Associate $25; Organization & Friend of the Museum $50; Patron $100; Life $1,000; Director's Circle $5,000.

Laclede

GENERAL JOHN J. PERSHING BOYHOOD HOME STATE HISTORIC SITE, 1100 Pershing Dr., Laclede, MO 64651. Mailing Address: P.O. Box 141, Laclede, MO 64651-0141. Tel.: 660-963-2525. Fax: 660-963-2520.
Web Site: www.mostateparks.com/pershingsite
Founded: 1960.
Congressional District: 11
Key Personnel: Admin., Denzil R. Heaney; Interpretation, Jana Keune; Interpretation, Jean Peacher; Maintenance, Wayne Murrell.
Personnel Profile: Full-Time Paid 3; Part-Time Paid 2.
Governing Authority: state. Parent Institution: Dept. of Natural Resources. Subsidiary Institution: Div. of State Parks. Tax-exempt.
State Historic Site.
Collections: life & military career of Gen. John J. Pershing from early childhood to his death in 1948; personal artifacts; period furnishings; bronze statue of Gen. Pershing; Wall of Honor. Historic Building: c.1870 one room schoolhouse.
Research Fields: First World War; Punitive Expedition; Philippine Insurrection; Spanish American War; Russo-Japanese War; Buffalo soldiers of 9th & 10th cavalry; Indian Wars; Civil War in northern Missouri; military leaders of northern Missouri relating to the life & career of General John J. Pershing.
Facilities: library of books, pamphlets, clippings & documents available for use on premises; war memorial.
Activities: guided tours. Museum Sponsors: Pershing Days; Victorian Christmas Open House.
Publications: brochure, Gen. John J. Pershing Boyhood Home.
Hours & Admission Prices: April 15-Oct. 15 Mon.-Sat. 10-4, Sun. 12-6; Oct. 16-April 14 Mon.-Sat. 10-4, Sun. 12-5. Adults $2.50, children 6-12 $1.25; discount to groups; children under 6 no charge. Closed New Year's Day; Easter; Thanksgiving; Christmas. ♿
Attendance: 8,500 (estimated)

LOCUST CREEK COVERED BRIDGE STATE HISTORIC SITE, US 36, Dart Rd., Laclede, MO 64651. Mailing Address: P.O. Box 141, Laclede, MO 64651-0141. Tel.: 660-963-2525 & 2520.
E-mail: moparks@dnr.mo.gov
Web Site: www.missouristateparks.com
Founded: 1968.
Congressional District: 11
Key Personnel: C.E.O., Dr. Douglas Eiken; Site Admin., Denzil R. Heaney; Interpretation, Jana Keune; Interpretation, Jean Peacher; Maintenance, Wayne Murrell.
Personnel Profile: Full-Time Paid 3; Part-Time Paid 1.
Governing Authority: state. Parent Institution: Missouri Dept. of Natural Resources, Div. of State Parks, P.O. Box 176, Jefferson City, MO 65102. Tax-exempt.
Historic Site: 1868 151-foot covered bridge.
Collections: covered bridges; Pike's Peak ocean to ocean highway across Northern Missouri; Pershing transportation route.
Research Fields: history of covered bridges in America; local history; Pike's Peak ocean to ocean highway; Pershing transportation route.
Facilities: quarter mile foot trail to bridge.
Activities: guided tours as requested.
Publications: pamphlet on 4 covered bridges in Missouri.
Hours & Admission Prices: Daily dawn-dusk. No charge; donations accepted.
Attendance: 18,400 (accurate)

Lamar

HARRY S TRUMAN BIRTHPLACE STATE HISTORIC SITE, 1009 Truman Ave., Lamar, MO 64759-1543. Tel.: 417-682-2279. Fax: 417-682-6304.
E-mail: moparks@dnr.mo.gov
Web Site: mostateparks.com/trumansite.htm
Founded: 1959.
Congressional District: 4
Key Personnel: Site Admin., Pam Myers.
Personnel Profile: Full-Time Paid 3; Full-Time Volunteers 3; Part-Time Paid 2; Part-Time Volunteers 2.
Governing Authority: state. Parent Institution: Div. of Parks, Recreation & Historic Preservation, Missouri Dept. of Natural Resources, P.O. Box 176, Jefferson City, MO 65102. Tax-exempt.
Historic House & Museum: housed in c.1880 Harry S. Truman birthplace.
Collections: period furnishings.
Activities: guided tours.
Publications: brochure, Harry S Truman Birthplace.
Hours & Admission Prices: Mon.-Sat. 10-4, Sun. 12-4. No charge; donations accepted. ♿
Attendance: 26,649 (accurate)

OSAGE VILLAGE STATE HISTORIC SITE, 1009 Truman Ave. & 11th St., Lamar, MO 64759-1543. Tel.: 417-682-2279. Fax: 417-682-6304.
Web Site: mostateparks.com/osagevillage.htm
Founded: 1984.
Congressional District: 4
Key Personnel: C.E.O., Pam Myers.
Personnel Profile: Full-Time Paid 3; Part-Time Paid 3; Part-Time Volunteers 2.
Governing Authority: state. Parent Institution: Div. of State Parks, Recreation & Historic Preservation, Missouri Dept. of Natural Resources, P.O. Box 176, Jefferson City, MO 65102. Maintained by: Harry S. Truman Birthplace State Historic Site, 417-682-2279. Tax-exempt.
Archaeological Site.
Collections: local history & culture; Native American artifacts.
Facilities: interpretive kiosk; interpretive trail.
Activities: self-guided tours; text & illustrations in a kiosk display.
Publications: brochure, Walking Trail Guide.
Hours & Admission Prices: Mon.-Sat. 10-4, Sun. 12-4. No charge; donations accepted.
Attendance: 6,000 (estimated)

Lawson

WATKINS WOOLEN MILL STATE HISTORIC SITE & PARK, 26600 Park Rd., N., Lawson, MO 64062-8939. Tel.: 816-580-3387 & 3782. Fax: 816-580-3784.
E-mail: watkins.woolen.mill.state.historic.site@dnr.mo.gov
Web Site: www.mostateparks.com
Founded: 1964.
Congressional District: 6
Key Personnel: Facility Mgr., Mike Beckett; Historic Site Admin., Matt Carletti; Part Supt., Ron Sutton; Coord. Education, Melissa Hall; Coord. Period Clothing, Terri Gardner; Volunteer Coord., Amanda Coonce; Park Maintenance II, Russell Teague; Park Maintenance II, Farriel O'Dell; Park Maintenance II, Joe Green; Park Maintenance III, Tim Clifford; Clerk Typist, Linda Zink.
Personnel Profile: Full-Time Paid 11; Part-Time Paid 9; Part-Time Volunteers 60.

Governing Authority: state. Parent Institution: Div. of State Parks, Missouri Dept. of Natural Resources, P.O. Box 176, Jefferson City, MO 65102. Tax-exempt.
Industrial & Agricultural Museum: 1839 Bethany, 19th-century plantation.
Collections: 60 textile production machines including carding engines, spinning jacks, looms, plyers & finishing machines; complete textile factory; over 30 archaeological sites of farm & factory support buildings & workers houses. Historic Buildings: 1860 Watkins woolen mill; 1850 W.L. Watkins family home; 1856 Franklin school (Octagonal); 1871 Mt. Vernon church; 1850-1880 miscellaneous outbuildings.
Research Fields: industrialization; agricultural history, 1820-1920; mid-1800s, textile industry.
Facilities: 600-vol. library of books, pamphlets, catalogs, manuscripts & photographs available on premises. Books for sale.
Activities: guided tours; lectures; exhibitions; special events.
Publications: brochure, Watkins Woolen Mill; walking tour guide; guidebook; video tape.
Hours & Admission Prices: Summer: Mon.-Sat. 9:30-5, Sun. 10:30-5; Winter: Mon.-Sat. 10-4:30, Sun. 11-4:30. Adults $2.50, children 6-12 $1.50; discounts to pre-scheduled groups of 15 or more; children under 6 no charge. Closed New Year's Day; Thanksgiving; Christmas. ♿
Attendance: 15,500 (accurate)

Lebanon

NATURE INTERPRETIVE CENTER, Bennett Spring State Park, Lebanon, MO 65536-6797. Mailing Address: Bennett Spring State Park, 26250 Hwy. 64A, Lebanon, MO 65536-6797. Tel.: 417-532-3925 & 4338. Fax: 417-532-7006.
Web Site: www.mostateparks.com/bennett.htm
Founded: 1969.
Congressional District: 7
Key Personnel: Dir., Diane Tucker.
Personnel Profile: Full-Time Paid 2; Part-Time Paid 3; Part-Time Volunteers 1.
Governing Authority: state. Div. of Parks & Historic Preservation, Missouri Dept. of Natural Resources, P.O. Box 176, Jefferson City, MO 65102. Tax-exempt.
Natural History Museum.
Collections: botany; zoology; geology.
Research Fields: botany; zoology; geology; ecology; area history.
Facilities: nature center with displays; indoor classrooms; work areas; amphitheater; trails.
Activities: nature hikes; lectures; film & slide programs; formally organized education programs; permanent exhibitions; adult programs; demonstrations; outdoor education programs.
Publications: booklet, Self Guiding Trail; bird checklist.
Hours & Admission Prices: Daily 9-5. No charge; donations accepted. Closed Thanksgiving; Christmas. ♿
Attendance: 35,000 (estimated)

Lecoma

UNIVERSITY OF MISSOURI-ROLLA MINERALS MUSEUM, 125 McNutt Hall, Lecoma, MO 65401. Tel.: 573-341-4616. Fax: 573-341-6935.
E-mail: rocks@umr.edu
Founded: 1870.
Congressional District: 8
Personnel Profile: Part-Time Volunteers 1.
Governing Authority: university.
Mineralogy Museum.
Collections: mineralogy; paleontology; geology.
Research Fields: economic geology.
Activities: guided tours; permanent exhibitions.
Hours & Admission Prices: Mon.-Fri. 8-5. No charge. Closed holidays. ♿
Attendance: 200 (estimated)

Lee's Summit

LEE'S SUMMIT HISTORICAL SOCIETY & DEPOT MUSEUM, 220 S.E. Main, Lee's Summit, MO 64063-2332. Tel.: 816-525-9440.
E-mail: contact@leessummithistory.net
Web Site: www.leessummithistory.net
Historical Society Museum: housed in the 1905 train depot.
Collections: maps, photographs & artifacts pertaining to Lee's Summit.
Hours & Admission Prices: Sat. 10-4; other times by appointment. No charge.

MISSOURI TOWN 1855, 8010 E. Park Rd., Lee's Summit, MO 64015. Mailing Address: 22807 Woods Chapel Rd., Blue Springs, MO 64015-9799. Tel.: 816-503-4860. Fax: 816-795-7938. TDD: 800-735-2966.
E-mail: gjulich@jacksongov.org
Web Site: www.jacksongov.org
Founded: 1963.
Congressional District: 5
Key Personnel: Dir. Parks & Recreation, Michele Newman; Program Specialist, Cindy Henley; Supt. Heritage Museums & Programs, Gordon Julich; Museum Admin., Gary Sutton; Museum Shop Mgr., Debbie Smith.
Personnel Profile: Full-Time Paid 4; Full-Time Volunteers 6; Part-Time Paid 2; Part-Time Volunteers 150; Interns 1.
Governing Authority: county. Affiliated with Jackson County Parks & Recreation, 22807 Woods Chapel Rd., Blue Springs, MO 64050. Tax-exempt: 170(c)(3).
Village Museum: over 25 structures c.1821-1860 from western Missouri.
Collections: agriculture; costumes; decorative arts; folklore; general; history; technology; textiles; furnishings; period gardens. Historic Buildings: 1855 mercantile, blacksmith shop & surrey; church; law office; livery stable; school & stagecoach stop tavern.
Research Fields: 1850-1860 pioneer lifestyles.
Facilities: wedding chapel; nature trails; surrounding park offers boating, fishing, camping & picnic facilities.
Activities: living history demonstrations; workshops; seminars; special events; volunteer program; weddings; corporate picnics; educational programs; youth activities; outreach educational programs. Museum Sponsors: annual Arts & Crafts Festival; Living History Week; Independence Day; Children's Day; Tradesmen Day Spirits From the Past; Christmas Open House; Christmas Candlelight Tour; Special Interpretive weekends.
Publications: Guidebook: Missouri Town 1855, A Program in Architectural Preservation; brochures; quarterly newsletter.
Hours & Admission Prices: March-Nov. 15 Tues.-Sun. 9-4:30; Nov. 16-Feb. Sat.-Sun. 9-4:30. Adults $5, senior citizens & youths $3; discounts to groups with advance reservation; members & children under 5 no charge. Closed New Year's Day; Thanksgiving; Christmas. ♿
Attendance: 12,672 (accurate)
Membership: Individual $35; Family $45.

Lexington

BATTLE OF LEXINGTON STATE HISTORIC SITE, 1101 Delaware St., Lexington, MO 64067. Mailing Address: P.O. Box 6, Lexington, MO 64067-0006. Tel.: 660-259-4654. Fax: 660-259-2378.
E-mail: battle.of.lexington.state.historic.site@dnr.mo.gov
Web Site: www.mostateparks
Founded: 1959.
Congressional District: 4
Key Personnel: C.E.O. & Site Admin., Janae Fuller.
Personnel Profile: Full-Time Paid 4; Part-Time Paid 6; Part-Time Volunteers 6.
Governing Authority: state. Parent Institution: State of Missouri, Dept. of Natural Resources, P.O. Box 176, Jefferson City, MO 65102. Tax-exempt.
Historic House & Battlefield: 1853 Col. Oliver Anderson & Tilton Davis Home, located at site of Battle of the Hemp Bales.
Collections: Civil War artifacts; manuscripts; period furnishings; original Union trenches.
Research Fields: Civil War history; hemp cultivation; Missouri River Valley lifestyle; Lexington; the Anderson & Davis families; soldiers & units that fought at the battle.
Facilities: Gift items for sale.
Activities: guided tours; Civil War encampments & reenactments; living history events.
Publications: brochure, Battle of Lexington Walking Tour.
Hours & Admission Prices: Call for hours & admission. Closed New Year's Day; Easter; Thanksgiving; Christmas. ♿
Attendance: 25,000 (estimated)

LEXINGTON HISTORICAL MUSEUM, 112 S. 13th St., Lexington, MO 64067-1402. Tel.: 660-259-6313 & 2900.
Web Site: www.lexingtonmuseum.org
History Museum: housed in the 1846 Cumberland Presbyterian Church.
Collections: Osage Indians; the Pony Express; steamboats; Civil War; coal mining.
Hours & Admission Prices: Call 660-259-2900 for hours. Adults $2, students $1; members no charge.
Attendance: 500 (estimated)
Membership: Individual $15.

Liberty

CLAY COUNTY HISTORICAL MUSEUM, 14 N. Main, Liberty, MO 64068-1638. Tel.: 816-792-1849.
E-mail: info@claycountymuseum.org
Web Site: www.claycountymuseum.org
Founded: 1965.
Congressional District: 6
Key Personnel: Pres., John Ricker; Cur., Jay Thorne; Sec., Ann Cole.

Personnel Profile: Part-Time Paid 1; Part-Time Volunteers 1.
Governing Authority: nonprofit organization. Parent Institution: Clay County Museum & Historical Society, Inc., 14 N. Main. Tax exempt: 501(c)(3).
Local History Museum: housed in 1855 old drug store building.
Collections: medical & druggist equipment; furniture dating from 1800-1930s; clothing & personal belongings; items relating to Civil War, Mexican War and World War I & World War II; Indian artifacts; history of local colleges.
Research Fields: local & regional history.
Facilities: archives.
Activities: guided tours; quarterly meetings; special projects.
Publications: bimonthly newsletter, Our Clay Heritage.
Hours & Admission Prices: Mon.-Sat. 1-4. No charge; donations accepted. Closed national holidays.
Attendance: 4,200 (estimated)
Membership: Single & Sustaining $25; Family $35; Patron $250; Life $1,000.

JESSE JAMES BANK MUSEUM, 103 N. Water, Liberty, MO 64068-1736. Tel.: 816-781-4458 & 628-6065. Fax: 816-628-6676.
Web Site: www.claycogov.com
Founded: 1966.
Congressional District: 5
Key Personnel: Admin., Elizabeth Gilliam Beckett; Asst. Dir., Rebecca Prestwood.
Personnel Profile: Full-Time Paid 2; Part-Time Paid 20; Part-Time Volunteers 1; Interns 1.
Governing Authority: county. Parent Institution: Clay County Dept. of Parks, Recreation & Historic Sites. Tax-exempt.
Banking Museum: housed in 1858 old Liberty Bank building, site of James Gang bank robbery, Feb. 13, 1866.
Collections: Civil War banking; pictures & documents pertaining to the James Gang.
Research Fields: James; Younger; Quantrell; banking history.
Facilities: Gifts & books for sale.
Activities: guided tours; permanent exhibitions.
Publications: books, Good Bye, Jesse James; The Ancestry of Jesse James.
Hours & Admission Prices: Mon.-Sat. 10-4. Adults $5.50, senior citizens over 55 $5, children 8-15 $3.50; discounts to groups; children under 8 no charge. ♿
Attendance: 4,420 (accurate)

LIBERTY JAIL HISTORIC SITE, 216 N. Main, Liberty, MO 64068-1629. Tel.: 816-781-3188. Fax: 816-781-7311.
Formerly: Historic Liberty Jail Visitors Center Historic Site
Founded: 1963.
Key Personnel: C.E.O., Gerald Tedrow.
Personnel Profile: Full-Time Volunteers 13; Part-Time Volunteers 4.
Governing Authority: church group. Parent Institution: Church of Jesus Christ of Latter-Day Saints, 50 E. N. Temple., Salt Lake City, UT 84150. Tax-exempt.
Religious History Museum.
Collections: religious history items. Historic Building: 1859 jail.
Research Fields: history.
Facilities: 2 film rooms; visitors center.
Activities: guided tours; lectures; films; interactive video.
Publications: brochure, Liberty Jail.
Hours & Admission Prices: Daily 9-9. No charge. ♿
Attendance: 48,000 (accurate)

Linn Creek

CAMDEN COUNTY HISTORICAL SOCIETY & MUSEUM, 206 S. Locust St., Linn Creek, MO 65052. Mailing Address: P.O. Box 19, Linn Creek, MO 65052-0019. Tel.: 573-346-7191.
Web Site: camdencountymuseum.com
Founded: 1962.
Congressional District: 9
Key Personnel: Chm. (V), Patricia Kitterman; Pres. (V), Daphne Jeffries; Museum Shop Mgr., Shirley Childers.
Personnel Profile: Full-Time Volunteers 2; Part-Time Volunteers 17.
Governing Authority: Parent Institution: Camden County Historical Society.
History Museum.
Collections: local history & culture; photographs.
Publications: Camden County Historian; books, Before the Dam Waters; Camden County History; Early History of Camden County; The Meteorite in Decaturville; 2000 Glimpses of History.
Hours & Admission Prices: March-Oct. 10-4; Nov.-Feb. by appointment. No charge; donations accepted. ♿
Membership: Individual $12; Family $15

Lone Jack

CIVIL WAR MUSEUM OF LONE JACK, JACKSON COUNTY, 301 S. Bynum Rd., Lone Jack, MO 64070-8508. Mailing Address: Jackson County Parks & Recreation, County Courthouse, 308 W. Kansas, Independence, MO 64050. Tel.: 816-697-8833.
Web Site: www.historiclonejack.org
Founded: 1964.
Congressional District: 4
Key Personnel: Chm. & Pres. (V), Alinder Miller.
Governing Authority: county. Affiliated with Jackson County Parks & Recreation, County Courthouse, Independence, MO 64050. Tax-exempt: 170(c)(1).
Civil War Museum: housed in modern museum building on site of the Battle of Lone Jack, Aug. 16, 1862.
Collections: military; local history; Civil War; artifacts; dioramas; electric map.
Research Fields: Jackson County Civil War activity; local history; biography of soldiers at Lone Jack.
Facilities: picnic area.
Activities: guided tours; permanent & temporary exhibitions; living history interpretation. Annual Event: Commemoration in August.
Publications: pamphlet.
Hours & Admission Prices: April-Oct. Wed.-Sat. 10-4, Sun. 1-4; Nov.-March Sat. 10-4, Sun. 1-4. Adult $3, children $1. Closed New Year's Day; Easter; Thanksgiving; Christmas.
Attendance: 3,357 (accurate)

Malden

BOOTHEEL YOUTH MUSEUM, 700A N. Douglas, Malden, MO 63863-1510. Mailing Address: P.O. Box 182, Malden, MO 63863-0182. Tel.: 573-276-3600.
E-mail: info@bootheelyouthmuseum.org
Web Site: www.bootheelyouthmuseum.org
Founded: 1994.
Congressional District: 8
Key Personnel: Exec. Dir., Patsy Reublin.
Personnel Profile: Full-Time Paid 2; Part-Time Paid 6.
Children's Museum.
Collections: hands-on exhibits.
Facilities: 22,000 sq. ft. exhibit space; 180-seat theater. Museum-related items for sale.
Activities: educational programs; birthday parties; rental facilities.
Hours & Admission Prices: Tues.-Sat. 10-4, Sun. 1-4, Mon. by appointment. Children 3-17 $5, adults $3; discounts to Assoc. of Childrens Museums & groups of 8 or more. ♿
Attendance: 27,440 (accurate)
Membership: $50-$100.

Mansfield

LAURA INGALLS WILDER-ROSE WILDER LANE HISTORIC HOME & MUSEUM, (M), 3068 Hwy. A, Mansfield, MO 65704-8104. Tel.: 417-924-3626. Fax: 417-924-8580.
E-mail: liwhome@getgoin.net
Web Site: www.lauraingallswilderhome.com
Founded: 1957.
Congressional District: 146
Key Personnel: Dir., Jean C. Coday; Treas., Jane K. Coday; Museum Shop Mgr., Judy Cantrell.
Personnel Profile: Full-Time Paid 4; Full-Time Volunteers 4; Part-Time Paid 20.
Governing Authority: private; nonprofit organization. Parent Institution: Laura Ingalls Wilder Home Association. Tax-exempt: 501(c)(3).
History Museum: next to the home of author Laura Ingalls Wilder.
Collections: five of the original nine Little House books handwritten manuscripts; family photographs; Pa's fiddle; historic artifacts; organ; translations of Little House books; handwritten manuscripts; clothing.
Research Fields: history of Laura and Almanzo Wilder & Rose Wilder Lane.
Activities: guided tours.
Publications: brochures; biannual newsletter for association members, Rocky Ridge Review; mail order catalog.
Hours & Admission Prices: March-Nov. 15 Mon.-Sat. 9-5, Sun. 12:30-5; Nov. 16 to mid-Dec. by appointment only. Adults $8, senior citizens 65 & over $6, children 6-18 $4; children under 6 no charge. Closed Easter. ♿
Attendance: 55,000 (estimated)
Membership: Student $25; Individual $50; Supporter $100; Life: Sponsor $500; Patron $1,000; Benefactor $5,000.

Marceline

WALT DISNEY HOMETOWN MUSEUM, 120 E. Santa Fe Ave., Marceline, MO 64658-1144. Tel.: 660-376-3343.
Web Site: www.waltdisneymuseum.org
History Museum.
Collections: personal letters from the early 1900s to the late 1960s; photographs of Roy & Walt Disney; Mickey Mouse dolls; Midget Autopia car.
Hours & Admission Prices: April-Oct. Tues.-Sat. 10-4, Sun. 1-4. Adults $5, children 6-10 $2.50; children under 6 & members no charge.

Marshall

SALINE COUNTY HISTORICAL SOCIETY MUSEUM, 101 N. Lafayette St., Marshall, MO 65340-1747. Tel.: 660-886-7546.
Historical Society Museum.
Collections: artifacts & memorabilia pertaining to Saline County's history.
Hours & Admission Prices: April-Dec. Tues.-Fri. 9:30-12 & 1-4, Sat.-Sun. by appointment.

Maryland Heights

HISTORIC AIRCRAFT RESTORATION MUSEUM, 3127 Creve Coeur Mill Rd., Maryland Heights, MO 63146. Tel.: 314-434-3368. Fax: 314-878-6453.
Key Personnel: Dir., Al Stix
Aircraft Museum.
Collections: classic, sport, & period aircraft.
Facilities: Museum-related items for sale.
Activities: airplane rides.
Hours & Admission Prices: Guided Tours: Sat.-Sun. 10-4; other times by appointment. Adults $10, children 5-12 $5; discounts to groups; children under 5 no charge. Airplane Rides $80-$110 per person.

Maryville

WARREN STUCKI MUSEUM OF BROADCASTING, Northwest Missouri State University, 800 University Dr., Maryville, MO 64468-6015. Tel.: 660-562-1163.
Web Site: www.nwmissouri.edu
Broadcasting Museum.
Collections: 30 vintage radio sets; Edison phonograph with cylinder records; vintage television gear & recording equipment.
Hours & Admission Prices: Mon.-Fri. 8-5; other times by appointment.

Memphis

DOWNING HOUSE/BOYER HOUSE & MEMPHIS DEPOT MUSEUM COMPLEX, S. Main St., Memphis, MO 63555. Tel.: 660-465-2275.
Founded: 1978.
Key Personnel: Chm. (V) & Cur., Wilma June Kapfer.
Governing Authority: Parent Institution: Scotland County Historical Society.
History Museum: 14 room brick mansion built in 1858.
Collections: period furnishings; Ella Ewing; Scotland County's history; Civil War; aviation history; personal artifacts; Tom Horn history.
Publications: annual newsletter.
Hours & Admission Prices: April to Labor Day. Adults $5; children under 10 no charge.
Attendance: 750

Mexico

AMERICAN SADDLEBRED HORSE MUSEUM, 501 S. Muldrow, Mexico, MO 65265-2082. Mailing Address: P.O. Box 398, Mexico, MO 65265-0398. Tel.: 573-581-7155 & 3910.
E-mail: info@swbell.net
Web Site: www.audrain.org
Founded: 1970.
Congressional District: 9
Key Personnel: Exec. Dir., Dana Keller; Pres. (V), John Dial; Vice Pres., Ron Hopkins.
Governing Authority: society; nonprofit organization. The Audrain County Historical Society. Branch Museum: Audrain Historical Museum. Tax-exempt.
General History Museum: located on the grounds of the Audrain Historical Museum (see separate listing).
Collections: ribbons; bits; bridles; saddles; paintings; photographs; miscellaneous items connected with trainer Tom Bass; memorabilia from the Lee Brothers Stables, Cunningham Stables & Art Simmons Stables; George Ford Morris drawings.
Research Fields: American saddle horse.
Facilities: library of books magazines & photographs pertaining to the history of saddle horses; American Saddle Horse Register available.
Hours & Admission Prices: Feb.-Dec. Tues.-Sat. 10-4, Sun. 1-4. Adults $3, children under 12 $1; members no charge. Closed national holidays. ♿
Attendance: 1,600 (accurate)
Membership: Individual $15; Family $30; Life (single) $300; Life (couple) $500.

AUDRAIN HISTORICAL MUSEUM, GRACELAND, 501 S. Muldrow, Mexico, MO 65265-2082. Mailing Address: P.O. Box 398, Mexico, MO 65265-0398. Tel.: 573-581-3910. Fax: 573-581-7155.
E-mail: info@audrain.org
Web Site: www.audrain.org
Founded: 1952.
Congressional District: 9
Key Personnel: Exec. Dir., Dana Keller; Pres. (V), John Dial.
Governing Authority: society. Parent Institution: Audrain County Historical Society; nonprofit organization. Branch Museum: American Saddle Horse Museum. Tax-exempt.
History Museum: housed in 1857 John P. Clark home, later lived in by Judge James E. Ross & his descendants, restored 1958.
Collections: furniture; paintings; piano; dolls; toys; antique glass; agriculture; costumes; history; Indian artifacts; industrial; medical; military; naval; 4,000 photographs, county related from 1837. Historic Building: Audrain country school, an original rural one-room schoolhouse.
Research Fields: genealogy; local history.
Facilities: 400-vol. library of local history books, pamphlets, genealogical & cemetery records.
Activities: guided tours; permanent & temporary exhibitions.
Publications: quarterly newsletter.
Hours & Admission Prices: Feb.-Dec. Tues.-Sat. 10-4, Sun. 1-4. Adults $3, children 12 & under $1; members no charge. Closed holidays. ♿
Attendance: 1,600 (accurate)
Membership: Individual $15; Couple $25; Family $30; Life (single) $300; Life (couple) $500.

Miami

VAN METER STATE PARK, 32146 N. Hwy. 122, Miami, MO 65344. Mailing Address: P.O. Box 47, Miami, MO 65344. Tel.: 660-886-7537. Fax: 660-886-7512.
E-mail: moparks@dnr.mo.gov
Web Site: www.mostateparks.com/vanmeter.htm
Founded: 1932.
Key Personnel: Interpretive Resource Technician, Cynthia Stevens; Historic Site Admin., Connie Winfrey; Park Maintenance Worker II, Randall Forbes.
Personnel Profile: Full-Time Paid 3; Part-Time Paid 4; Part-Time Volunteers 2.
Governing Authority: state. Parent Institution: State of Missouri Dept. of Natural Resources & Div. of State Parks. Tax-exempt.
Park Museum & Visitor Center: located on Missouri Indian village archaeological site.
Collections: Missouri, Oneota, Woodland & Archaic Indian archaeological discoveries; early pioneer artifacts of Van Meter family.
Research Fields: archaeology of Missouri Indians.
Facilities: 40-seat auditorium. Books & gift items for sale.
Activities: guided tours; lectures; films; study clubs; organized education programs for children & adults; docent program; participatory exhibits.
Hours & Admission Prices: Park: daily 8-sunset. American Indian Cultural Center: May-Sept. Mon.-Sat. 10-4, Sun. 1-5; Oct.-April holiday Mon. & Thurs.-Sat. 10-4, Sun. 1-5. No charge; donations accepted. Closed New Year's Day; Thanksgiving; Christmas. ♿
Attendance: 50,000 (accurate)

Milan

SULLIVAN COUNTY HISTORICAL SOCIETY MUSEUM, 117 N. Water St., Milan, MO 63556-1341. Mailing Address: 900 S. Main St., Milan, MO 63556. Tel.: 660-445-2034.
E-mail: webmaster@sullivanhistory.org
Web Site: sullivanhistory.org
Historical Society Museum.
Collections: local history & culture; photographs
Hours & Admission Prices: Call for hours.

Montgomery City

GRAHAM CAVE STATE PARK, 217 Hwy T.T., Montgomery City, MO 63361-5509. Tel.: 573-564-3476. Fax: 573-564-2534.
E-mail: moparks@dnr.mo.gov
Founded: 1964.
Congressional District: 9

Key Personnel: Supt., Debra Ray.
Governing Authority: state. Parent Institution: Div. of Parks & Historic Preservation, Missouri Dept. of Natural Resources, Box 176, Jefferson City, MO 65102. Tax-exempt.
State Park.
Collections: archaeology; anthropology; Indian artifacts.
Research Fields: archaeology; anthropology; Indian artifacts.
Facilities: interpretive center; campsites; hiking trails.
Activities: tours in summer.
Hours & Admission Prices: Park: daily 7am to sunset. Visitor Center: April-Oct. daily 9-11 & 12:30-4; Nov.-March Mon.-Fri. 9-11 & 12:30-4. No charge. ♿
Attendance: 55,000

Nelson

SAPPINGTON CEMETERY STATE HISTORIC SITE, Junction Hwy. AA & TT, Nelson, MO 65347. Mailing Address: Arrow Rock State Historic Site, P.O. Box 1, Arrow Rock, MO 65320-0001. Tel.: 660-837-3330. Fax: 660-837-3300.
E-mail: moparks@dnr.mo.gov
Web Site: www.mostateparks.com/sappingtoncem.htm
Founded: 1969.
Congressional District: 6
Key Personnel: Site Admin., Michael Dickey.
Governing Authority: state. Operated by Division of Parks & Historic Preservation. Parent Institution: Missouri Department of Natural Resources, P.O. Box 176, Jefferson City, MO 65102. Subsidiary Institution: Division of State Parks. Tax-exempt.
Historic Site: resting places of prominent Missourians, including Claiborne Fox Jackson, Dr. John Sappington & Gov. M.M. Marmaduke.
Collections: 2 acre cemetery.
Facilities: 2 acre cemetery.
Hours & Admission Prices: Daily. No charge.
Attendance: 5,000

Neosho

CROWDER COLLEGE-LONGWELL MUSEUM & CAMP CROWDER COLLECTION, 601 La Clede, Neosho, MO 64850-9165. Tel.: 417-451-3223. Fax: 417-455-5539.
Web Site: www.crowder.edu
Founded: 1970.
Congressional District: 39
Governing Authority: college. Tax-exempt.
Art Museum/Center & History Museum.
Collections: oil paintings by Ozark artist Daisy Cook; original prints by Birger Sandzen, Grant Wood, John Steuart Curry, Peter Hurd & Thomas Hart Benton; Japanese wood block prints; Chinese paper cuts; Camp Crowder, Army Signal Corp. collection.
Research Fields: family papers from Warren Cook, c.1850; archive letters.
Activities: lectures; films; study clubs; hobby workshops; broadcast programs; loan & temporary exhibitions; school loan service.
Publications: catalogues.
Hours & Admission Prices: Mon.-Fri. 10-4. No charge; donations accepted. Closed college holidays. ♿
Attendance: 800 (estimated)

Nevada

BUSHWHACKER MUSEUM, 212 W. Walnut St., Nevada, MO 64772-2341. Tel.: 417-667-9602.
E-mail: bushwhackerjail@sbcglobal.net
Web Site: www.bushwhacker.org
Founded: 1964.
Congressional District: 4
Key Personnel: C.E.O. & Chm., Joe C. Kraft; Pres. (V), Stafford Agee; Museum Shop Mgr., Terry Ramsey.
Personnel Profile: Full-Time Paid 1; Part-Time Paid 2.
Governing Authority: nonprofit organization. Parent Institution: Vernon County Historical Society. Branch Museum: 212 W. Walnut, Nevada, MO 64772. Tax-exempt: 501(c)(3).
History Museum.
Collections: archaeology; Indian artifacts; medicine; local history; Civil War & outlaw period; Victorian clothing; primitive tools; military history. Historic Buildings: 1860s Vernon County jail; 1871 jailer's home; 1920 Ford Agency Bldg.; Dr. Hornback's 1930s home & medical offices.
Major Exhibits: New Harmonies - American Roots Music (T), 10/10-11/12/10.
Research Fields: local & regional history.
Facilities: archives.
Activities: guided tours; temporary & permanent exhibitions.
Publications: quarterly newsletter, Bushwhacker Musings.
Hours & Admission Prices: May-Oct. Tues.-Sat. 10-4. Adults $3, children 12-18 $2, children under 12 $1; discounts to AAA members; AASLH & members no charge. Closed Memorial Day; Independence Day; Labor Day. ♿
Attendance: 3,055 (accurate)
Membership: Individual $15; Family $25; Business & Benefactor $50.

New Madrid

HUNTER-DAWSON STATE HISTORIC SITE, (M), Dawson Rd., Hwy. U, New Madrid, MO 63869. Mailing Address: P.O. Box 308, New Madrid, MO 63869-0308. Tel.: 573-748-5340. Fax: 573-748-7228.
E-mail: hunter-dawson.state.historic.site@dnr.mo.gov.
Web Site: www.mostateparks.com
Founded: 1967.
Congressional District: 10
Key Personnel: Historic Site Specialist III, Michael Comer; Interpretive Resource Specialist, Delois Ellis; Interpretive Resource Specialist, Vicki Jackson; Park Maintenance Worker I, Chadd Thomas; Park Maintenance Worker III, Lee Haines.
Personnel Profile: Full-Time Paid 5; Part-Time Paid 3; Part-Time Volunteers 1.
Governing Authority: state. Div. of Parks & Historic Preservation, Missouri Dept. of Natural Resources, P.O. Box 176, Jefferson City, MO 65102. Tax-exempt.
Historic House: c.1859 Hunter-Dawson House, a yellow cyprus frame house in the Greek Revival & Italianate style.
Collections: Period furnishings; 1860 collection of Mitchell & Rammelsburg furniture; three state champion trees, one over 300 years old. Historic building; 80% of original furnishings displayed.
Research Fields: historic restoration; 1860s southern culture and lifestyles; William W. Hunter papers.
Activities: guided tours; Civil War boot camp for children; Civil War outreach program; Victorian mourning customs. Museum Sponsors: Christmas Tour; Easter Egg Hunt.
Hours & Admission Prices: March-Nov. Mon.-Sat. 10-4, Sun. 12-4; Dec.-Feb. Tues.-Sat. 10-4. Adults $2.50, children 6-12 $1.50; children under 6 no charge. Closed New Year's Day; Easter; Thanksgiving; Christmas Day. ♿
Attendance: 8,098 (accurate)

NEW MADRID HISTORICAL MUSEUM, (M), 1 Main St., New Madrid, MO 63869. Tel.: 573-748-5944.
History Museum.
Collections: local history & culture; photographs; period furnishings; personal artifacts; quilts.
Facilities: Museum-related items for sale.
Hours & Admission Prices: Call for hours.

Ozark

CHRISTIAN COUNTY HISTORICAL SOCIETY AND MUSEUM, 202 E. Church St., Ozark, MO 65721. Mailing Address: P.O. Box 442, Ozark, MO 65721-0442. Tel.: 417-988-7191.
E-mail: christiancohistorical@gmail.com
Web Site: www.christiancohistory.com
Key Personnel: Pres. & Webmaster, Shirley Scott; Vice Pres. & Volunteer Coord., Linda Myers; Sec., Culah Nixon; Treas., Avaline Harris; Property Mgmt. & Cur., John Nixon
Historical Society Museum.
Collections: local history & culture; personal artifacts.
Hours & Admission Prices: April-Oct. Sun. 2-4; other times by appointment.

Paris

UNION COVERED BRIDGE STATE HISTORIC SITE, County Rd. C, Paris, MO 65275. Mailing Address: Mark Twain Birthplace, 37352 Shrine Rd., Florida, MO 65283-2127. Tel.: 573-565-3449. Fax: 573-565-3718.
E-mail: mark.twain.birthplace.state.historic.site@dnr.mo.gov
Web Site: www.mostateparks.com/unionbridge.htm
Founded: 1968.
Congressional District: 9
Key Personnel: Site Admin., Connie Ritter.
Personnel Profile: Full-Time Paid 1; Part-Time Paid 2.
Governing Authority: state. Owned & operated by Div. of State Parks, Missouri Dept. of Natural Resources, P.O. Box 176, Jefferson City, MO 65102. Tax-exempt.
Historic Site: 1871 Union covered bridge.
Collections: newspaper clippings.
Research Fields: Monroe County Missouri, covered bridges.
Publications: brochure.
Hours & Admission Prices: Daily 8-5. No charge.

Attendance: 175,000

Pilot Knob

FORT DAVIDSON STATE HISTORIC SITE, 118 E. Maple St., Pilot Knob, MO 63663-0509. Mailing Address: P.O. Box 509, Pilot Knob, MO 63663-0509. Tel.: 573-546-3454. Fax: 573-546-2713.
E-mail: fort.davidson.state.historic.site@dnr.mo.gov
Web Site: www.mostateparks.com/ftdavidson.htm
Founded: 1969.
Congressional District: 8
Key Personnel: Pres. (V), Terry Cadenbach; Rgnl. Supvr., Delecia Huitt; Site Admin., Walter Busch; Cur., Brick Autry.
Personnel Profile: Full-Time Paid 4; Part-Time Paid 6; Part-Time Volunteers 1.
Governing Authority: state. Div. of State Parks, Missouri Dept. of Natural Resources, P.O. Box 176, Jefferson City, MO 65102. Tax-exempt.
Historic Site: 1864 Battle of Pilot Knob; Civil War battlefield.
Collections: Civil War Artifacts; S.E. Missouri Civil War history.
Research Fields: primary focus on eastern Missouri Civil War history & Arcadian Valley local Civil War lore.
Facilities: walking tour; interpretive center.
Activities: periodic battle reenactments; living history.
Publications: brochures.
Hours & Admission Prices: April 16-Nov. daily 10-4; Dec.-April 15 Tues.-Sun. 10-4. No charge. Closed New Year's Day; Thanksgiving; Christmas. ♿
Attendance: 63,147 (accurate)

Platte City

BEN FERREL 1882 MINI MANSION MUSEUM, 220 Ferrel St., Platte City, MO 64079-9511. Tel.: 816-431-5121.
Historic House: built in 1882.
Collections: period furnishings & memorabilia.
Hours & Admission Prices: April-Oct. Thurs.-Sat. 12-4; Nov.-March by appointment. Adults $5.

Point Lookout

THE RALPH FOSTER MUSEUM, (M), College of the Ozarks, One Cultural Ct., Point Lookout, MO 65726. Tel.: 417-690-3407. Fax: 417-690-2606.
E-mail: museum@cofo.edu
Web Site: www.rfostermuseum.com
Founded: 1930.
Congressional District: 7
Key Personnel: Dir. & Museum Shop Mgr., Annette J. Sain; C.E.O. & Pres., Dr. Jerry Davis; Cur., Jeanelle Ash; Cur., Thomas A. Debo; Cur., Gary Ponder.
Personnel Profile: Full-Time Paid 4; Part-Time Paid 28.
Governing Authority: college. Parent Institution: College of the Ozarks. Tax-exempt: 501(c)(3).
General Museum.
Collections: late 19th- & early 20th-century Ozarkiana; prehistory of the Ozark region; history of the Ozark Plateau; fire arm collections; Rose O'Neill memorabilia; natural history; Si Siman music room dedicated to country, western & Ozark music; history of College of the Ozarks; military display, Conflicts of the 20th century.
Research Fields: history of the Ozark Plateau 1200 A.D.-present; weapons; dolls; glassware; textiles; late 19th- & early 20th-century tools.
Facilities: Lois Brownell Research library available for research with Director's permission.
Activities: Outreach program to pre-school, elementary & high schools.
Hours & Admission Prices: Feb. to mid-Dec. Mon.-Sat. 9-4:30. Adults $6, seniors 62 & over and groups 20 or more $5; discounts to AAM & ICOM members; students no charge; special arrangements for tour groups. Closed Thanksgiving week ♿
Attendance: 60,000 (estimated)

Poplar Bluff

MARGARET HARWELL ART MUSEUM, 421 N. Main St., Poplar Bluff, MO 63901-5107. Tel.: 573-686-8002. Fax: 573-686-8017.
E-mail: ethel@mham.org
Web Site: www.mham.org
Founded: 1981.
Congressional District: 8
Key Personnel: Dir., Tina M. Magill; Pres. (V), Nancy Buttry; Museum Shop Mgr., Gerry Vandervort.
Personnel Profile: Full-Time Paid 1; Part-Time Paid 1; Part-Time Volunteers 50.
Governing Authority: municipal government. Parent Institution: City of Poplar Bluff. Tax-exempt: 170(b)(1)(A).
Art Museum: housed in 1883 mansion.
Collections: various forms of contemporary art media; mid 19th-century clothing and textiles; temporary exhibits change monthly & feature regional and nationally known artists.
Major Exhibits: Warm Wool, Delicate Silk, 1/10; Painting Missouri - The Art of Billy O'Donnell (T), 2/6/10-2/28/10; Tierra Suave: The Art of Sean Shrum, 3/6/10-3/28/10; 10th Annual High School Juried Regional Art Exhibit, 4/6/10-4/25/10; 25th Annual Harwell Mail-In Art Show, 5/1/10-5/30/10; The Enchanted Colors of St. Lucia's Island - Talitha Horn, 6/5/10-6/27/10; The 23rd Annual Pictures By The People, 7/3/10-7/25/10.
Facilities: classrooms.
Activities: guided tours; lectures; organized educational programs; docent program.
Publications: quarterly newsletters.
Hours & Admission Prices: Tues.-Fri. 12-4, Sat.-Sun. 1-4. No charge; donations accepted. Closed national holidays. ♿
Attendance: 18,000 (estimated)
Membership: Student $5; Patron $25; Business $50; Contributing $100; Supporting $250; Life $2,000.

Princeton

CASTEEL-LINN HOUSE AND MUSEUM, 902 E. Oak St., Princeton, MO 64673-1255. Mailing Address: P.O. Box 1583, Palm Springs, CA 92263-1583. Tel.: 660-748-3905.
Founded: 1982.
Congressional District: 6
Key Personnel: C.E.O. & Dir. (V), Joe Dale Linn; Pres., Cur. & Public Rels. (V), Nancy Paige Linn; Archivist, Pamela Elizabeth Kidd; Security, Cy Linn.
Personnel Profile: Full-Time Volunteers 3; Part-Time Volunteers 2.
Governing Authority: private; not-for-profit organization.
Historic House: built on a historic site where Civil War reunions were held.
Collections: library with concentration on world history, Missouri & Mercer County history; art and art history; china & glass; railroad china & antiques; antique toys; portraits; bronzes; period furniture.
Research Fields: Western art history; Missouri & Mercer County history; sociology.
Facilities: 6,500-vol. library available to scholars & researchers.
Activities: guided tours.
Publications: monthly newsletter, Great American West: Art & Books; books, Linn's Mercer County History Series (8 vols.).
Hours & Admission Prices: April-Dec. by appointment only. No charge. ♿
Attendance: 200 (estimated)

MERCER COUNTY GENEALOGICAL AND HISTORICAL SOCIETY, 601 Grant St., Princeton, MO 64673-1023. Mailing Address: P.O. Box 97, Princeton, MO 64673-0097. Tel.: 660-748-3725 & 4755. Fax: 660-748-3723.
Web Site: www.rootsweb.ancestry.com/~momercer/mcghs.html
Founded: 1965.
Congressional District: 6
Key Personnel: Mgr., Randi Ferguson.
Governing Authority: nonprofit. Tax-exempt: 501(c)(3).
Local History Museum: housed in Mercer County Library.
Collections: history; period artifacts; costumes; furniture; china; geology.
Publications: reprint, 1888 History of Harrison & Mercer Counties, Mo.; The Pioneer Press; Linn's History of Mercer County, Mo.; 1911 Roger's History of Mercer County; The Mercer County History of 1883.
Hours & Admission Prices: By appointment only. No charge. Closed national holidays.
Membership: Individual $3.

Republic

GENERAL SWEENY'S MUSEUM, 5242 S. State Hwy. ZZ, Republic, MO 65738-9255. Mailing Address: 6424 W. Farm Rd. 182, Republic, MO 65738. Tel.: 417-732-1224. Fax: 417-732-1224.
Web Site: www.civilwarmuseum.com
Key Personnel: Dir., Dr. Tom Sweeney
History Museum.
Collections: Civil War history; military artifacts; photographs.
Hours & Admission Prices: March-Oct. Wed.-Sun. 10-5. Adults $4.50, seniors over 55 $4, children 5-11 $3.50.

WILSON'S CREEK NATIONAL BATTLEFIELD, 6424 W. Farm Rd. 182, Republic, MO 65738-9492. Tel.: 417-732-2662. Fax: 417-732-1167.
E-mail: Connie_Langum@nps.gov
Web Site: www.nps.gov/wicr
Founded: 1960.

Congressional District: 7
Key Personnel: Supt., T. John Hillmer; Chief Resource Mgmt., Gary Sullivan; Historian, Connie Langum.
Personnel Profile: Part-Time Volunteers 1.
Governing Authority: federal. Parent Institution: U.S. Dept. of the Interior, National Park Service, Washington, DC. Tax-exempt.
Military Museum: located on the battlefield on which the August 10, 1861 engagement of Wilson's Creek occurred.
Collections: Battle of Wilson's Creek & the Civil War artifacts; documents, diaries, letters, discharge papers; mid-19th century cultural artifacts; flags; weapons; medical instruments; photographs. Historic House: 1852 The Ray House.
Research Fields: Battle of Wilson's Creek; the Civil War in Missouri & the Trans-Mississippi.
Facilities: visitor's center.
Activities: formally organized education programs for children & undergraduate college students.
Hours & Admission Prices: Park: seasonal hours. Museum: Nov.-March daily 9-12 & 1-4. Park & Museum: adults 16 & over $5, maximum $10 per vehicle; school groups no charge. Closed New Year's Day; Thanksgiving; Christmas. ♿
Attendance: 200,000 (estimated)

Rolla

MISSOURI DEPARTMENT OF NATURAL RESOURCES, DIVISION OF GEOLOGY AND LAND SURVEY, 111 Fairgrounds Rd., Rolla, MO 65401-2909. Mailing Address: P.O. Box 250, Rolla, MO 65402-0250. Tel.: 573-368-2100 & 2118. Fax: 573-368-2111.
Web Site: www.dnv.mo.gov/geology
Formerly: Ed Clark Museum of Missouri Geology
Founded: 1963.
Congressional District: 8
Key Personnel: Dir. & State Geologist, Joseph A. Gillman; Public Rels., Hylan Beydler.
Governing Authority: State of Missouri. A branch of Div. of Geology & Land Survey, Missouri Dept. of Natural Resources. Tax-exempt.
Geology Museum.
Collections: geology; mineralogy; paleontology; fossils; mastodon tusk; geologic maps; map making tools.
Research Fields: geology.
Facilities: labs & library of the Geological Survey Div.
Activities: permanent, temporary & traveling exhibitions.
Publications: pamphlets; reports; information circulars; books; brochures; geologic maps; posters.
Hours & Admission Prices: Mon.-Fri. 8-5. No charge. Closed national & Missouri holidays. ♿
Attendance: 3,000

Saint Charles

FIRST MISSOURI STATE CAPITOL-STATE HISTORIC SITE, 200-216 S. Main St., Saint Charles, MO 63301-2855. Tel.: 636-940-3322. Fax: 636-940-3324.
E-mail: first.state.capitol.state.historic.site@dnr.mo.gov
Web Site: www.dnr.state.mo.us
Founded: 1971.
Congressional District: 2
Key Personnel: Site Admin., Victoria Love; Asst. Site Admin., Robert Adams; Interpretive Resource Tech., Dale Hallett; Interpretive Resource Tech., Sue Love.
Personnel Profile: Full-Time Paid 5; Part-Time Paid 5; Part-Time Volunteers 12.
Governing Authority: state. Parent Institution: Div. of Parks & Historic Preservation, Missouri Dept. of Natural Resources, P.O. Box 176, Jefferson City, MO 65102. Tax-exempt.
Historic Buildings: c.1818 first Missouri State Capitol; temporary seat of government 1821-1826.
Collections: period furnishings; 11 restored rooms.
Research Fields: pre-1830 Missouri history.
Activities: guided tours.
Publications: brochures.
Hours & Admission Prices: Mon.-Sat. 9-4, Sun. 11-5. Family $12, adults $2.50, children 6-11 $1.50; group rates available on a reservation basis, families $12 maximum; children under 6 no charge. Closed New Year's Day; Easter; Thanksgiving; Christmas. ♿
Attendance: 52,000 (accurate)

LEWIS & CLARK BOAT HOUSE AND NATURE CENTER, 1050 Riverside Dr., Saint Charles, MO 63301-3481. Tel.: 636-947-3199. Fax: 636-916-0240.
E-mail: lewisandclarkmuseum@yahoo.com
Web Site: www.lewisandclarkcenter.org
Founded: 1985.
Congressional District: 2
Key Personnel: Dir., Bill Brecht; Pres., Larry Kluesner; Museum Shop Mgr., Bob Learned.
Personnel Profile: Part-Time Paid 5; Part-Time Volunteers 200.
Governing Authority: private; nonprofit organization. Tax-exempt: 501(c)(3).
History Museum.
Collections: dioramas; Missouri River history; replica of expedition boats; Lewis & Clark campsite; St. Charles history.
Facilities: 1,200 sq. ft. exhibit space. Museum-related items for sale.
Activities: formal education programs; guided tours; lectures; participatory exhibits; scout programs.
Hours & Admission Prices: Mon.-Sat. 10-5, Sun. 12-5. Adults $2.50, children under 17 $1.50; discounts to groups. Closed New Year's Day; Easter; Thanksgiving; Christmas. ♿
Attendance: 40,675 (accurate)

ST. CHARLES COUNTY HISTORICAL SOCIETY, INC., 101 S. Main St., Saint Charles, MO 63301-2802. Tel.: 636-946-9828.
E-mail: scchs@mail.win.org
Web Site: www.scchs.org
Founded: 1956.
Congressional District: 2
Key Personnel: Archivist, William Popp.
Personnel Profile: Part-Time Paid 3; Part-Time Volunteers 20.
Governing Authority: nonprofit organization. Tax-exempt: 501(c)(3).
Local History Museum.
Collections: archives; American Indian artifacts; St. Charles County Circuit & Probate Court records; indexes to St. Charles County Church records; tax records; naturalization; city directories & census.
Research Fields: archive.
Facilities: archives.
Activities: Society quarterly lunch meetings with guest speaker.
Publications: quarterly, Heritage; monthly, SCCHS Archives Newsletter.
Hours & Admission Prices: Library & Archives: Mon., Wed. & Fri. 10-3; 2nd & 4th Sat. 10-3. Adults $3; members no charge.
Attendance: 550 (accurate)
Membership: Student $10; Individual $25; Family $35.

Saint James

MARAMEC MUSEUM, THE JAMES FOUNDATION, Maramec Spring Park, 21880 Maramec Spring Dr., Saint James, MO 65559. Mailing Address: 320 S. Bourbeuse St., Saint James, MO 65559-1498. Tel.: 573-265-7124. Fax: 573-265-8770.
E-mail: jamesfoundation@centurytel.net
Web Site: maramecspringpark.com
Founded: 1971.
Key Personnel: Rgnl. Mgr., Danny Marshall; Dir. Interpretive Svcs., Lloyd Callies.
Personnel Profile: Full-Time Paid 1; Part-Time Paid 6.
Governing Authority: foundation. Parent Institution: The New York Community Trust. The James Foundation. Tax-exempt.
History Museum.
Collections: model of Maramec Village, 1860; scale models of Old Maramec Iron Works 1826-1876; dioramas of iron works, grist mill, iron ore bank, charcoal pits & early Indian village; geology of springs, sinkholes, caves in Ozarks; archaeology related to Maramec & Indian culture; Indian artifacts; modes of transportation, trails & roads 1820-1860; life at the Iron Works; two aquaria of fish of Maramec Spring Branch; working rain/recharge model; wildlife display.
Research Fields: local history.
Activities: guided tours; group tours for students; illustrated talks to groups; permanent & temporary exhibits.
Publications: Frontier Iron, The Maramec Iron Works 1826-1876; Lucy Wortham James 1880-1938; brochures, Maramec Museum; Maramec Iron Works; Maramec Spring Park; The Rise & Fall of Maramec Iron Works.
Hours & Admission Prices: April & Oct. Sat.-Sun. 12-4; May Mon.-Fri. 10-3, Sat.-Sun. 12-4; June-Aug. Mon.-Sun. 11-5; Sept. Wed.-Sun. 12-4. No charge. ♿
Attendance: 30,496 (accurate)

Saint Joseph

* **THE ALBRECHT-KEMPER MUSEUM OF ART, (M),** 2818 Frederick Ave., Saint Joseph, MO 64506-2903. Tel.: 816-233-7003; 888-254-2787. Fax: 816-233-3413.
E-mail: frontdesk@albrecht-kemper.org
Web Site: www.albrecht-kemper.org
Founded: 1914.
Congressional District: 6
Key Personnel: Dir., Mr. Terry L. Oldham; Pres. (V), John Wilson; Cur. Education, Jennifer Zeller; Registrar, Ann Tootle; Catering Mgr., Robyn Enright; Dir. Mktg. & Special Events, Christina Lund; Coord. Membership & Museum Shop Mgr., Chelsea Howlett-Weideman.
Personnel Profile: Full-Time Paid 3; Part-Time Paid 5; Part-Time Volunteers 200; Interns 2.
Governing Authority: nonprofit organization. Tax-exempt: 501(c)(3).
Art Museum.
Collections: 18th to 21st century paintings, drawings, photographs & prints.
Facilities: 1,500-vol. noncirculating Bradley Art Library; reading room; classrooms; meeting rooms; 147-seat theatre/lecture hall; restaurant; formal rose garden. Museum-related items for sale.
Activities: guided tours; lectures; gallery talks; formally organized education programs; docent program; permanent & temporary exhibitions; space available for rent.
Publications: Catlin's Indians: The Kemper Portfolio; quarterly newsletter, Art Matters; exhibition catalog, Under The Influence: The Students of Thomas Hart Benton; William Christenberry: Retrospective; Native American Basketry: The Hartman Collection; The Art of Thomas King Baker; The Albrecht-Kemper Museum of Art, A History and Guide to the Collection.
Hours & Admission Prices: Tues.-Fri. 10-4, Sat.-Sun. 1-4. Adults $5, seniors 60 & over $2, students $1; members, AAM & ICOM members & children under 6 no charge. Closed major holidays. ♿
Attendance: 22,504 (accurate)
Membership: Student $15; Teacher $20; Nonresident $25; Individual $35; Family & Dual $55; Associate $100; Sustaining $300; Supporting $500; Business Sponsor $600; Sponsoring $1,000; Patron & Business Patron $1,500; Corporate Sponsor $2,500; Corporate Patron $5,000.

HEATON-BOWMAN-SMITH FUNERAL HOME MUSEUM, 3609 Frederick Ave., Saint Joseph, MO 64506-3033. Tel.: 816-232-3355.
General Museum.
Collections: artifacts & memorabilia including wicker body basket used for Jesse James.
Hours & Admission Prices: Call for hours.

JESSE JAMES HOME MUSEUM, 12th & Penn Sts., Saint Joseph, MO 64502. Mailing Address: P.O. Box 1022, Saint Joseph, MO 64502-1022. Tel.: 816-232-8206. Fax: 816-232-3717.
Web Site: www.st.joseph.net/ponyexpress
Founded: 1939.
Congressional District: 6
Key Personnel: Museum Dir., Gary Chilcote; Pres. (V), John Rotterman; Cur. Collections, Doug Chilcote; Business Mgr., Amy Neely.
Personnel Profile: Full-Time Paid 3; Full-Time Volunteers 1; Part-Time Paid 3; Part-Time Volunteers 10.
Governing Authority: association. Parent Institution: Pony Express Historical Association. Subsidiary Institution: Jesse James Home. Tax-exempt: 501(c)(3).
Historic Building: 1879 house where Jesse James was killed in 1882.
Collections: Jesse James furnishings; the 1995 exhumation of Jesse James for DNA tests, including artifacts from the grave.
Research Fields: Jesse James & the James-Younger Gang.
Facilities: Gifts & museum-related items for sale.
Activities: permanent exhibitions. Annual Event: Jesse James Bus Tour.
Publications: monthly newsletter, Pony Express Mail.
Hours & Admission Prices: April-Oct. Mon.-Sat. 10-5, Sun. 1-5; Nov.-March Sat.-Sun. Adults $3, seniors 60 & over $2, students $1.50; discounts to groups; members no charge. Closed New Year's Day; Easter; Thanksgiving; Christmas. ♿
Attendance: 17,483 (accurate)
Membership: Individual $15; Sustaining $25; Corporate $30; Associate $50; Sponsor $100; Life $500.

NATIONAL MILITARY HERITAGE MUSEUM, 701 Messanie St., Saint Joseph, MO 64501-2219. Tel.: 816-233-4321. Fax: 816-279-9667.
E-mail: info@nationalmilitaryheritagemuseum.com
Web Site: www.nationalmilitaryheritagemuseum.com
Key Personnel: Exec. Dir., Franklin A. Flesher
Military History Museum.
Collections: military artifacts from 1800s to present; photographs.
Hours & Admission Prices: Mon.-Fri. 9-5, Sat. 9-1. Adults $2, students $.50.

PATEE HOUSE MUSEUM, 1202 Penn St., Saint Joseph, MO 64503-2560. Mailing Address: P.O. Box 1022, Saint Joseph, MO 64502-1022. Tel.: 816-232-8206. Fax: 816-232-3717.
Web Site: www.stjoseph.net/ponyexpress
Founded: 1963.
Congressional District: 6
Key Personnel: Museum Dir., Gary Chilcote; Pres. (V), John Rotterman; Office Mgr., Amy Neely; Cur. Collections, Doug Chilcote; Library & Archives, Carolyn Chilcote.
Personnel Profile: Full-Time Paid 4; Full-Time Volunteers 1; Part-Time Paid 4; Part-Time Volunteers 25.
Governing Authority: nonprofit organization. Parent Institution: Pony Express Historical Association. Subsidiary Institution: Jesse James Home. Tax-exempt: 501(c)(3).
Western Museum: housed in 1856-1858, Patee hotel, used as headquarters for the Pony Express in 1860. National Historic Landmark.
Collections: 1860, Hannibal & St. Joseph steam locomotive; first railroad mail car; cars; trucks; buggies; wagons; fire trucks; restored Pony Express office; railroad office; general store; printing shop; hotel lobby; apothecary shop; dental office; Gay Nineties house; ice cream parlor; 1917 Japanese Tea House; 1854 Buffalo saloon; The Toy Carousel Shop; 1882 jail contains exhibit of local crimes & murders; 1903-1950 St. Joseph News-Press & Gazette; bound volumes; H-O gauge model railroad surrounded by 24 large vaudeville & silent movie posters from the turn-of-the-century belonging to the Great Renos acrobats & magicians; 4ft. bronze Pony Express statue by sculptor Avard Fairbanks; 1941 Allan-Herschel Hand-Carved Carousel; George Warfel art; "Westerners on Wood" 43 life-sized paintings of Jesse James & other westerners.
Research Fields: local history; Pony Express; Jesse James.
Facilities: 4,500-vol. library of old texts on history, religion, available by application to the board. Museum-related items for sale.
Activities: guided tours; lectures; gallery talks; TV programs; carousel rides. Annual Events: Pony Express rerun in June; Jesse James Bus Tour.
Publications: monthly newsletter, Pony Express Mail.
Hours & Admission Prices: Feb.-March & Nov. Sat. 10-5, Sun. 1-5; April-Oct. Mon.-Sat. 10-5, Sun. 1-5. Adults $5, seniors 60 & over $4, students under 18 $3; discount to groups; members & preschool children no charge. Closed New Year's Day; Easter; Thanksgiving; Christmas. ♿
Attendance: 18,417 (accurate)
Membership: Regular $15; Sustaining $25; Corporate $30; Associate $50; Sponsor $100; Life $500.

PONY EXPRESS MUSEUM, 914 Penn St., Saint Joseph, MO 64503-2544. Tel.: 816-279-5059 & 800-530-5930. Fax: 816-233-9370.
E-mail: pcdirector@ponyexpress.net
Web Site: www.ponyexpress.org
Founded: 1959.
Congressional District: 6
Key Personnel: Dir. Devel., Cindy Daffron; Pres. (V), Richard N. DeShon; Museum Shop Mgr., Stephanie Mazey.
Personnel Profile: Full-Time Paid 2; Part-Time Paid 3; Part-Time Volunteers 3.
Governing Authority: nonprofit corporation. Tax-exempt: 501(c)(3).
Historic Building Museum: 1858 original stables of the Pony Express, formally known as the Pike's Peak Stables, located on the site from which the first Pony Express rider left St. Joseph heading west to Sacramento.
Collections: exhibits relating to the Pony Express; manuscripts.
Research Fields: Pony Express; Westward Expansion.
Facilities: Pony Express & 19th-century western items for sale.
Activities: guided tours; lectures; films; permanent, temporary & traveling exhibitions; special events.
Publications: quarterly newsletter, Pony Trails.
Hours & Admission Prices: Mon.-Sat. 9-5, Sun. 1-5. Adults $4, seniors & group adults $3, students & children 7-18 $2, group students $1; children 6 & under and members no charge. Closed New Year's Eve & Day; Easter; Thanksgiving; Christmas Eve & Day. ♿
Attendance: 27,000 (accurate)
Membership: Individual $30; Family $50; Founder $5,000.

ROBIDOUX ROW MUSEUM, 3rd & Poulin, Saint Joseph, MO 64501. Tel.: 816-232-5861.
Founded: 1981.
Key Personnel: Dir. & Museum Shop Mgr., Clyde Weeks.
Personnel Profile: Full-Time Paid 1; Part-Time Paid 1; Part-Time Volunteers 6.
Governing Authority: Parent Institution: Saint Joseph Historical Society. Tax-exempt.
History Museum: housed in the city founded by Joseph Robidoux in 1843. Listed on the National Register of Historic Places.

Collections: local history; period artifacts; structures.
Publications: Saint Joseph Historical Society Journal.
Hours & Admission Prices: Feb.-Dec. call for hours. Adults $2.50, seniors 62 & over $2, students 6-18 $1; members and children 5 & under no charge.
Attendance: 5,730 (accurate)
Membership: Individual $15; Family $20; Friend $25; Sustaining $50; Patron $100; Benefactor $500; Life $750.

ST. JOSEPH DOLL MUSEUM, 1115 S. 12th St., Saint Joseph, MO 64503-2515. Tel.: 816-233-1420.
Web Site: www.stjosephdollmuseum.com
Doll Museum.
Collections: over 1,000 period dolls, toys & doll furniture.
Hours & Admission Prices: May & Oct. Fri.-Sat. 11:30-4:30; June-Sept. Wed.-Sat. 11:30-4:30. Adults $2.50, senior citizens 65 & over $2, children 6-16 $1; children 5 & under no charge.

* **ST. JOSEPH MUSEUM INC., (M),** 3406 Frederick, Saint Joseph, MO 64506-2913. Mailing Address: P.O. Box 8096, Saint Joseph, MO 64508-8096. Tel.: 816-232-8471. Fax: 816-232-8482.
E-mail: sjm@stjosephmuseum.org
Web Site: www.stjosephmuseum.org
Founded: 1927.
Congressional District: 6
Key Personnel: Exec. Dir., Jacqueline A. Lewin; Pres. & Chm. (V), Merry Burtner; Cur. Collections, Sarah M. Elder; Head Security & Maintenance, Andy Meyer; Asst. Dir. Admin. & Retail Operations Mgr., Susan Noland; Head of Public Rels., Kathy Reno; Education Dir., Amy Grier.
Personnel Profile: Full-Time Paid 6; Part-Time Paid 4; Part-Time Volunteers 10.
Governing Authority: municipal; nonprofit corporation. Subsidiary Institutions: The Wyeth-Tootle Mansion; The Black Archives of St. Joseph; Mount Mora Cemetery; Round the Town Tours; Platte Purchase Publishers; The Glore Psychiatric Museum. Tax-exempt: 501(c)(3).
Ethnology, Local, Natural, Ethnic & Medical History.
Collections: ethnology of North American Indians, Mezo-Americans & Philippines; vertebrate animals; geology; invertebrates; St. Joseph history; western expansion; Pony Express; Civil War; Jesse James; post Civil War & Victorian; manuscripts; psychiatric history.
Research Fields: Pony Express; archaeology; Jesse James; St. Joseph history; western ethnography; psychiatry; local black history.
Facilities: 7,000-vol. library of anthropology, ethnology, St. Joseph history, Western expansion, Pony Express, Civil War, Jesse James & natural history available by staff approval for use on the premises; reading room. Books, postcards & gift items relating to North American Indians, natural history & the Pony Express for sale.
Activities: guided tours; lectures; films; special events; formally organized education programs for children; inter-museum loan, permanent, temporary & traveling exhibitions; school loan service.
Publications: quarterly newsletter, The Happenings; books, On the Winds of Destiny: A Biographical Look at Pony Express Riders; Old St. Jo: Gateway to the West 1799-1932; A Darkness Ablaze; St. Joe Road; Fishing on Deep River; As the Mockingbird Sang; history book by local authors.
Hours & Admission Prices: Mon.-Sat. 10-5, Sun. 1-5. Adults $5, children 7-15 $1; discount to AAM members; members no charge. Closed New Year's Eve & Day; Martin Luther King Jr. Day; President's Day; Memorial Day; Independence Day; Labor Day; Thanksgiving; Christmas Eve & Day. ♿
Attendance: 17,000 (estimated)
Membership: Student $20; Individual $50; Family $75; Contributor $100; Sponsor $250; Benefactor $500; Patron $1,000; Director's Circle $2,500; President's Circle $5,000; Trustee's Circle $10,000.

Saint Louis

A.K.C. MUSEUM OF THE DOG, 1721 S. Mason Rd., Saint Louis, MO 63131-1518. Tel.: 314-821-3647. Fax: 314-821-7381.
E-mail: dogarts@aol.com
Web Site: www.museumofthedog.org
Founded: 1982.
Key Personnel: Exec. Dir., Barbara Jedda McNab; Chm. (V), Gilbert S. Kahn; Pres. (V), Dorothy Welsh.
Personnel Profile: Full-Time Paid 3; Part-Time Paid 4.
Governing Authority: nonprofit. Tax-exempt: 501(c)(3).
Fine Arts Museum: housed in c.1853 Jarville Estate.
Collections: dog related artwork; paintings; sculpture; decorative arts; works on paper; books; medals; historic dog collars.
Research Fields: pure bred dogs.
Facilities: 1,500-vol. library available to the public; 14,000 sq. ft. exhibit space. Museum-related items for sale.
Activities: guided tours; lectures; organized education programs for children & adults; docent program; loan, temporary & traveling exhibitions.
Publications: triannual newsletter, Sirius.
Hours & Admission Prices: Tues.-Sat. 10-4, Sun. 1-5. Adults $5, senior citizens $2.50, children 5-14 $1; members & children under 5 no charge. Closed holidays. ♿
Attendance: 12,000
Membership: Student & Senior $25; Annual $35; Family $65; Participating $100; Supporting $500; Patron $1,000.

ANHEUSER-BUSCH BREWERY, 12th & Lynch Sts., Saint Louis, MO 63101. Mailing Address: One Busch Place, Saint Louis, MO 63118-1852. Tel.: 314-577-2626.
Web Site: www.budweisertours.com
Company History Museum.
Collections: company history; Clydesdale horses; brewing process.
Facilities: Museum-related items for sale.
Activities: special events. Annual Event: Clydesdale Camera Days.
Hours & Admission Prices: March-May & Sept.-Oct. Mon.-Sat. 9-4, Sun. 11:30-4; June-Aug. Mon.-Sat. 9-5, Sun. 11:30-5; Nov.-Feb. Mon.-Sat. 10-4, Sun. 11:30-4. No charge. ♿

ARCHIVES & MUSEUM OF OPTOMETRY, (M), 243 N. Lindbergh Blvd., Saint Louis, MO 63141-7851. Tel.: 800-365-2219. Fax: 314-991-4101.
E-mail: ljdraper@aoa.org
Founded: 1966.
Governing Authority: Parent Institution: American Optometric Association Foundation.
Optometry History Museum.
Collections: eyeglasses; contact lenses; cases; instruments; eyewear history; optical industry; vision testing methods; photographs.
Hours & Admission Prices: Call for hours. No charge.

ATRIUM GALLERY LTD., 4728 McPherson Ave., Saint Louis, MO 63108-1918. Tel.: 314-367-1076. Fax: 314-367-7676.
E-mail: atrium@earthlink.net
Web Site: www.atriumgallery.net
Founded: 1986.
Key Personnel: C.E.O. & Dir., Carolyn P. Miles.
Personnel Profile: Full-Time Paid 2; Part-Time Paid 2.
Governing Authority: company; profit.
Art Gallery.
Collections: exhibitions of contemporary art: paintings, drawings & sculpture by living artists.
Activities: formal education programs for adults; lectures.
Hours & Admission Prices: Tues.-Sat. 10-6, Sun. 12-4; other times by appointment. No charge. Closed New Year's Day; Memorial Day; Independence Day; Labor Day; Thanksgiving; Christmas. ♿
Attendance: 2,300 (estimated)

CAMPBELL HOUSE MUSEUM, 1508 Locust St., Saint Louis, MO 63103-1816. Tel.: 314-421-0325. Fax: 314-421-0113.
E-mail: ahahn@stlouis.missouri.org
Web Site: www.campbellhousemuseum.org
Founded: 1943.
Congressional District: 1
Key Personnel: C.E.O., Andrew Hahn; Pres. (V), Janice K. Broderick; Museum Shop Mgr., Mrs. Earl C. Lindburg.
Personnel Profile: Full-Time Paid 1; Full-Time Volunteers 1; Part-Time Volunteers 45; Interns 5.
Governing Authority: nonprofit organization. Tax-exempt.
Historic House: 1851 Campbell House.
Collections: decorative arts; 1840-1900 home furnishings (original); family photo albums; letters; Lucas Place archives.
Research Fields: Robert Campbell & family; fur trade, westward expansion; St. Louis history.
Activities: guided tours; lectures; school programs.
Publications: quarterly newsletter, Campbell House Courier.
Hours & Admission Prices: Wed.-Sat. 10-4, Sun. 12-4. Adults $6; discounts to groups; children & members no charge. Closed national holidays.
Attendance: 6,000 (estimated)
Membership: Active $50; Century $100; Campbell Associate $300; 1851 Society $750; Lucas Place Partner $1,000; Museum Benefactor $2,500.

CARONDELET HISTORIC CENTER, 6303 Michigan Ave., Saint Louis, MO 63111-2504. Tel.: 314-481-6303.
E-mail: carondlt@stlouis.missouri.org
Founded: 1967.

Key Personnel: Ron Bolte
History Museum.
Collections: Carondelet history & culture; photographs; military artifacts; furniture; personal artifacts.
Activities: special events.
Hours & Admission Prices: Tues.-Wed. & Fri. 9:30 to noon, Sat. 10:30-2. Adults $2, children 12 & under $1; school groups no charge. ♿

CHATILLON-DEMENIL MANSION, 3352 DeMenil Place, Saint Louis, MO 63118-3211. Tel.: 314-771-5828. Fax: 314-771-3475.
Web Site: www.demenil.org
Founded: 1965.
Congressional District: 3
Key Personnel: Pres. (V), Ted Atwood; Dir., Kevin O'Neill.
Personnel Profile: Full-Time Paid 1; Part-Time Paid 1; Part-Time Volunteers 12.
Governing Authority: nonprofit corporation. Affiliated with Chatillon-Demenil House Foundation. Tax-exempt: 501(c)(3).
History Museum: housed in 1848 brick farm house of Henri Chatillon, 1863 Greek Revival addition by Dr. Nicolas N. DeMenil.
Collections: mid-Victorian furnishings; furniture; paintings; decorative arts; 1904 World's Fair artifacts.
Facilities: restaurant; garden area. Museum-related items for sale.
Activities: guided tours; weddings; meeting space; special events; private parties.
Publications: quarterly newsletter; brochures.
Hours & Admission Prices: Tues.-Sat. 10-4, last tour 3:00. Adults $5, children $2; discounts to members, groups, AAA, AAM & ICOM members. Closed national holidays.
Attendance: 3,000 (estimated)
Membership: Educator $25; Associate $40; Family $75; Madame Chouteau Associate $100; Henri Chatillon Associate $500; Nicolas DeMenil Society $1,000.

CITY MUSEUM, 701 N. 15th St., Saint Louis, MO 63103-1925. Mailing Address: P.O. Box 66972, Saint Louis, MO 63166-6972. Tel.: 314-231-2489. Fax: 314-231-1009.
E-mail: info@citymuseum.org
Web Site: www.citymuseum.org
Founded: 1997.
Key Personnel: Creative Dir., Bob Cassilly; Museum Dir., Rick Erwin; everydaycircus, Jessica Hentoff; Archivist, Bruce Gerrie; Mirth, Mystery & Mayhem, Bill Christman; Museum Shop Mgr., Stephanie Von Drasek; World Aquarium, Leonard Sonnenschein; Store 4, Giovanna Cassilly.
Personnel Profile: Full-Time Paid 27; Part-Time Paid 40; Interns 2.
Governing Authority: private.
General Museum.
Collections: historical artifacts; salvaged architectural relics; miniature train; circus artifacts.
Facilities: aquarium; 100-seat restaurant; classroom; rental space available. Museum-related items for sale.
Activities: guided tours; hobby workshops; artist demonstrations; 5-story outdoor climbing structure; maze of indoor caves; Roof Atop the City; everydaycircus; Shoelace Factory; Museum of Mystery; Mirth and Mayhem; Architecture Museum; Skateless Park.
Hours & Admission Prices: Memorial Day to Labor Day Mon.-Thurs. 9-5, Fri.-Sat. 9-1, Sun. 11-5; Sept. to mid-March Wed.-Thurs. 9-5, Fri.-Sat. 9-1, Sun. 11-5. Museum: admission 3 & over $12. Roof Atop the City: $5. World Aquarium: $6; discounts to groups & Fri.-Sat. after 5pm. Closed New Year's Day; Easter; Thanksgiving; Christmas. ♿
Attendance: 680,714 (accurate)
Membership: Level 1 $200; Level 2 $375; Gold Card $500.

CONCORDIA HISTORICAL INSTITUTE, 804 Seminary Place, Saint Louis, MO 63105-3014. Tel.: 314-505-7900. Fax: 314-505-7901.
E-mail: chi@chi.lcms.org
Web Site: chi.lcms.org
Founded: 1927.
Congressional District: 1
Key Personnel: Interim Dir. & Assoc. Dir. Archives Library, Rev. Marvin Huggins; Pres. (V), Larry Lumpe; Business Mgr., David Rutledge.
Personnel Profile: Full-Time Paid 5; Part-Time Paid 6; Part-Time Volunteers 15.
Governing Authority: church. Affiliated with The Lutheran Church, Missouri Synod, 1333 S. Kirkwood Rd., St. Louis, MO 63122. Tax-exempt: 501(c)(3).
Religious History Museum.
Collections: Reformation & Lutheran medals and coins; costumes & crafts; works by Lutheran artists; materials pertaining to the Lutheran Church; archives; manuscripts; historical library; audiovisual material; 43 original Albrecht Durer woodcuts. Historic Building: Saxon Lutheran Memorial at Frohna, MO; Hill of Peace, Friedenberg at Perryville, MO.
Research Fields: Lutheranism in America; German-Americana; immigration & family history.
Facilities: 58,000-vol. library of books, pamphlets & periodicals relating to Lutheranism in America available for inter-library loan & upon application; reading room. New & used books for sale.
Activities: guided tours; lectures; inter-museum loan, temporary & traveling exhibitions.
Publications: quarterly magazine, Concordia Historical Institute Quarterly; Historical Footnotes.
Hours & Admission Prices: Mon.-Fri. 8:30-4. No charge; donations accepted. Closed national holidays. ♿
Attendance: 5,000 (estimated)
Membership: Subscription $28; Active $35; Congregations, Organizations & Patron $50; Friend $100; Sponsor $500; Pacesetter $1,000; Life $5,000.

CONTEMPORARY ART MUSEUM ST. LOUIS, 3750 Washington Blvd., Saint Louis, MO 63108-3612. Tel.: 314-535-4660. Fax: 314-535-1226.
E-mail: info@camstl.org
Web Site: www.camstl.org
Formerly: Forum for Contemporary Art
Founded: 1981.
Congressional District: 1
Key Personnel: Dir., Paul Ha; Chm., David Hoffmann; Exhibitions Mgr., Cole Root; Deputy Dir. & Dir. Devel., Lisa Grove; Mgr. Institutional Giving, Shannon Bailey; Dir. Public Rels. & Mktg., Jennifer Gaby; Asst. Cur., Laura Fried; Chief Cur., Anthony Huberman; Visitor Svcs. & Retail Operations Coord., Kiersten Torrez; Membership & Communications Mgr., Maria Quinlan; Dir. Finance & Administration, Mary Walters; Graphic Designer, Bruce Burton.
Personnel Profile: Full-Time Paid 11; Part-Time Paid 17; Part-Time Volunteers 19; Interns 20.
Governing Authority: nonprofit organization. Tax-exempt: 501(c)(3).
Art Museum.
Collections: contemporary art from around the world.
Major Exhibits: For the Blind Man in the Dark Room Looking for the Black Cat That Isn't There (T), 11/09-1/3/10; The Front Room, 11/09-12/10; Sean Landers, 1/22/10-4/4/10; Stephen Prima, 1/22/10-4/4/10; Great Rivers Biennial 2010, 4/23/10-8/1/10.
Facilities: 27,000 sq. ft. space.
Activities: guided tours; lectures; films; concerts; organized educational programs for children; loan & traveling exhibitions.
Publications: exhibition catalogs; brochures; gallery guides; semi-annual magazine, MESH; artist books.
Hours & Admission Prices: Wed.-Sat. 10-5, Sun. 11-4. Adults $5; discounts to AAM members & seniors; members, students, Wed. & Sat. no charge. Closed national holidays. ♿
Attendance: 30,811 (accurate)
Membership: Individual $45; Artlink $65; Family & Dual $80; Contributor $150; Fellow $250; Benefactor $500; Patron $1,000; Curator Circle $2,500; Director Circle $5,000; Chairman Circle $10,000.

CRAFT ALLIANCE, 6640 Delmar Blvd., Saint Louis, MO 63130-4503. Tel.: 314-725-1177. Fax: 314-725-2068.
E-mail: gallery@craftalliance.org
Web Site: www.craftalliance.org
Founded: 1964.
Congressional District: 1
Key Personnel: Exec. Dir., Boo McLoughlin; Sr. Dir. Education & Exhibition Prog., Luanne Rimel; Opers. Dir., Lexi Glynias; Finance Mgr., Bob Lewis; Community Outreach Mgr., Robert Longyear; Studios Mgr., Dan Barnett; Museum Shop Mgr., Kris Richards.
Personnel Profile: Full-Time Paid 8; Part-Time Paid 40; Part-Time Volunteers 5.
Governing Authority: nonprofit organization. Tax-exempt: 501(c)(3).
Arts & Crafts Museum.
Collections: craft arts; study collection.
Facilities: 100-vol. library of books & catalogues; studio classes and workshops; 1,500 sq. ft. exhibit space. Art & craft items for sale.
Activities: guided tours; lectures; traveling & loan exhibitions; formally organized education programs for children & adults; docent program. Annual Events: fundraising projects; annual Holiday Show.
Publications: 3 times annually, Newsletter/Class Brochure.
Hours & Admission Prices: Tues.-Thurs. 10-5, Fri.-Sat. 10-6, Sun. 11-5. Classes: daily. Exhibits: no charge; donations accepted. Closed national holidays. ♿
Attendance: 12,000 (estimated)
Membership: National Associate $45; Senior Citizen $50; Basic Household

$55; Family Sponsor $100; Supporter $250; Benefactor $500; Craft Partners Council $1,000.

EUGENE FIELD HOUSE AND ST. LOUIS TOY MUSEUM, (M), 634 S. Broadway, Saint Louis, MO 63102-1613. Tel.: 314-421-4689. Fax: 314-588-9328.
E-mail: info@eugenefieldhouse.org
Web Site: eugenefieldhouse.org
Founded: 1936.
Congressional District: 3
Key Personnel: Chm. & Pres. (V), William Piper.
Personnel Profile: Full-Time Paid 2; Part-Time Paid 2; Part-Time Volunteers 10; Interns 2.
Governing Authority: Eugene Field House Foundation, Inc., 634 S. Broadway, St. Louis, MO. 63102. Tax-exempt: 501(c)(3).
Historic House: built 1845, birthplace of poet & toy collector, Eugene Field; home of Roswell Field, lawyer for Dred Scott & family during 1857 U.S. Supreme Court Decision.
Collections: manuscripts; 19th century furnishings & housewares; period toys & dolls.
Facilities: 200-vol. library on the works of Eugene Field; reference books on toys & dolls. Reproductions of period toys & dolls for sale.
Activities: guided tours; permanent & temporary exhibitions.
Publications: quarterly newsletter for members, Field Notes.
Hours & Admission Prices: March-Dec. Wed.-Sat. 10-4, Sun. 12-4; other times by appointment. Adults $5, children under 12 $1; discounts to groups, AAM, ICOM & AAA members; E.F. Foundation members no charge. Closed New Year's Day; Easter; Independence Day; Thanksgiving; Christmas.
Attendance: 7,000 (estimated)
Membership: Field Friend $50; Columnist Corner $75; Roswell Partner $150; Poet's Patron $250; 1845 Benefactor $1,000.

GRIOT MUSEUM OF BLACK HISTORY, 2505 St. Louis Ave., Saint Louis, MO 63106-2324. Tel.: 314-241-7057. Fax: 314-241-7058.
E-mail: blkwaxmusm1@aol.com
Formerly: Blackworld History Museum
Founded: 1992.
Congressional District: 1
Key Personnel: Dir., Lois D. Conley.
Personnel Profile: Full-Time Paid 2; Part-Time Volunteers 10.
Governing Authority: bd. Parent Institution: Diaspora Connections Unlimited. Tax-exempt.
Black History Museum.
Collections: Missouri's African-American history from slavery to present; photographs; wax sculptures; documents.
Major Exhibits: Color in Freedom (T), 2/10-3/10; Grass Roots: African Origins of and American Art, 6/10-8/10.
Facilities: Museum-related items for sale.
Activities: heritage preservation youth training program.
Hours & Admission Prices: Jan. 16-Dec. 14 Tues.-Sat. 10-5; other times by appointment. Adults $5, youth 13-17 $4, seniors 60 & over $3.50, children 12 & under $2.50; discounts to AAM & ICOM members. ♿
Attendance: 7,530 (estimated)
Membership: Youth $15; Elder $25; Basic $35.

HISTORIC SAMUEL CUPPLES HOUSE, 3673 W. Pine Mall, Saint Louis, MO 63108-3303. Mailing Address: 221 N. Grand Blvd., Saint Louis, MO 63103. Tel.: 314-977-2666. Fax: 314-977-3581.
E-mail: sluma@slu.edu
Web Site: cupples.slu.edu
Founded: 1977.
Congressional District: 1
Key Personnel: Dir., Petruta Lipan; Education, Neil Metzger; Public Rels. Affairs, Mary Marshall; Registrar, Claire Frandsen; Cur., David Suwalsky; Dir. Facilities, Barth Breneman; Museum Shop Mgr., Nathanael Mooningham; Security, Dennis Thompson.
Personnel Profile: Full-Time Paid 6; Part-Time Paid 9; Part-Time Volunteers 2; Interns 2.
Governing Authority: private university. Parent Institution: Saint Louis University, St. Louis, MO. Subsidiary Institution: Saint Louis University Museum of Art, 3663 Linden Blvd., St. Louis, MO 63108. Tel.: 314-977-3399. Tax-exempt: 501(c)(3).
Art & Decorative Art Museum: housed in a Richardsonian-Romanesque style mansion; built in 1888.
Collections: American & European glass, furniture & costumes; 16th-19th century European & American art.
Research Fields: decorative arts; American & European glass 1880-1940; American furniture; northern Renaissance art.
Facilities: 500-vol. library; educational facilities; 2,000 sq. ft. exhibit space. Museum-related items for sale.
Activities: formal education programs; guided tours; lectures; internships.
Publications: brochure, House History.
Hours & Admission Prices: Tues.-Sat. 11-4. Adults $5; members, students & children no charge. Closed national holidays.
Attendance: 7,136 (accurate)
Membership: Regular $50; Family $75; Contributing $100; Sustaining $150; Supporting $250; Associate $500; Sponsor $1,000; Patron $1,500; Fellow $2,500; Benefactor $5,000; Director's Circle $10,000.

HOLOCAUST MUSEUM & LEARNING CENTER, 12 Millstone Campus Dr., Saint Louis, MO 63146-5776. Tel.: 314-432-0020, ext. 3711.
Web Site: www.hmlc.org
History Museum.
Collections: pre-Holocaust life; the Holocaust; post-Holocaust; photographs; Jewish history & life; audio presentations.
Facilities: Museum-related items for sale.
Activities: special events.
Hours & Admission Prices: Mon.-Thurs. 9:30-4:30, Fri. 9:30-4, Sun. 10-4:30; other times by appointment. School Tours: sixth grade & up; not recommended for young children. No charge. ♿
Attendance: 40,000

JEFFERSON BARRACKS HISTORIC SITE, 533 Grant Rd., Saint Louis, MO 63125-4121. Tel.: 314-638-2100. Fax: 314-638-5009. TDD: 314-615-7840.
E-mail: mkollbaum@stlouisco.com
Web Site: www.stlouisco.com/parks/j-b.html
Founded: 1826.
Key Personnel: Dir., Jim Foley; Dir. St. Louis County Parks & Recreation, Genie Zakrzewski; Chm. (V), Sue Kuhnert; Pres. & Museum Shop Mgr. (V), Glenda Stockton; Cur., Marc Kollbaum; Exhibition & Maintenance, Mike Kladky.
Personnel Profile: Full-Time Paid 3; Full-Time Volunteers 1; Part-Time Paid 4; Part-Time Volunteers 75; Interns 1.
Governing Authority: county government. Parent Institution: St. Louis County Dept. of Parks & Recreation. Tax-exempt.
Historic Preservation Project: military post/museum.
Collections: artifacts related to history of Jefferson Barracks Military Post 1826-1946.
Research Fields: Westward Expansion; military history; Missouri military; U.S. Troop movement/expansion, St. Louis history.
Facilities: classrooms; 2,000 sq. ft. exhibit space. Museum-related items for sale.
Activities: guided tours; lectures; films; arts festivals; organized education programs for children & adults; docent program; traveling exhibition. Museum Sponsors: Story-telling Festival; Concerts.
Publications: JB Newsletter; Powder Magazine & Laborers House.
Hours & Admission Prices: Permanent Exhibits & Historic House: Wed.-Sun. 12-4. Jefferson Barracks Visitor Center: Wed.-Sun. 8:30-4:30. Adults $2, children $1. ♿
Attendance: 250,000 (accurate)
Membership: Friends of Jefferson Barracks: Individual $5; Family $10; Sustaining $25.

* **JEFFERSON NATIONAL EXPANSION MEMORIAL, (M),** 11 N. 4th St., Saint Louis, MO 63102-1810. Tel.: 314-655-1700 & 1600. Fax: 314-655-1639. TDD: 1-800-735-2466.
E-mail: jeff_superintendent@nps.gov
Web Site: www.nps.gov/jeff
Founded: 1935.
Congressional District: 1
Key Personnel: Supt., Tom Bradley; Facility Mgr., David Bubac; Exec. Dir. JNPA, David Grove; Chief Museum Svcs. & Interpretation, Ann Honious; Cur. Cultural Resources, Kathryn Thomas.
Governing Authority: federal. Parent Institution: National Park Service, U.S. Dept. of Interior, 18th St. & Virginia, N.W., Washington, DC 20240. Subsidiary Institution: Jefferson National Parks Association. Tax-exempt.
History Museum: Museum of Westward Expansion located beneath the Gateway Arch. Historic Building: Old Courthouse.
Collections: 19th-century Western American artifacts; American-Indian artifacts; local history; horse-drawn transportation; architectural; archives. Historic Buildings: 1839-1862 Old Courthouse with exhibit galleries & furnished courtrooms.
Research Fields: 19th-century westward expansion; St. Louis history; park administrative history.
Facilities: 4,900-vol. library on westward expansion & St. Louis history;

70mm Odyssey Theater; two 16mm/video theaters. History books, postcards & other museum-related items for sale.
Activities: permanent & temporary exhibitions; interpretive & educational programs; group tours; films; concerts; tram to top of Arch.
Publications: books on 19th-century westward expansion history & other park-related themes; park newspaper; site bulletins.
Hours & Admission Prices: Old Courthouse: daily 8-4:30. Museum of Westward Expansion: Memorial Day to Labor Day daily 8am-10pm; Sept.-May daily 9-6. Family $6, adults $3; additional fees for films & tram ride. Closed New Year's Day; Thanksgiving; Christmas. ♿
Attendance: 3,705,447 (estimated)

* **LAUMEIER SCULPTURE PARK & MUSEUM, (M),** 12580 Rott Rd., Saint Louis, MO 63127-1212. Tel.: 314-821-1209, ext. 10. Fax: 314-821-1248.
E-mail: info@laumeier.org
Web Site: www.laumeier.org
Founded: 1976.
Congressional District: 3
Key Personnel: Interim Dir., Marie Oberkirsch; Chm. Bd., John Wuest; Dir. Exhibitions & Collections, Kim Humphries; Dir. Communications & Public Rels., Mike Venso; Dir. Accounting, Mary Ruskin; Cur. Education, Karen Mullen; Cur. Educational Interpretation, Clara Collins Coleman; Mgr. Membership & Museum Svcs., Jennie Swanson; Site Mgr., J. D. Magurany; Mgr. Operations, Bill Briggs; Devel. Assoc., Marie Oberkirsch; Exhibits Preparator, Robert Goetz; Administrative Asst., Julia Norton; Librarian & Archivist, Joy Wright.
Personnel Profile: Full-Time Paid 9; Part-Time Paid 7; Part-Time Volunteers 566; Interns 2.
Governing Authority: nonprofit. St. Louis County Parks. Tax-exempt: 503 (c)(3).
Art Museum & Sculpture Park.
Collections: contemporary art; monumental and site-specific sculpture and related works; representative examples of Vito Acconci, Mark di Suvero, Jackie Ferrara, Charles Ginnever, Michael Heizer, Alexander Liberman, Beverly Pepper, and Ursula Von Rydingsvard; Ernest Trova sculptures.
Facilities: library; 105-acre open-air museum and park; educational center; amphitheater; trails.
Activities: temporary indoor & outdoor art exhibitions; permanent installations; educational programs and workshops for children and adults; guided tours; concert series; lecture; docent program; art fair; special events.
Publications: site map; exhibition brochures & catalogues; special event guides; quarterly newsletter.
Hours & Admission Prices: Sculpture Park: 8am to half hour past sunset. Indoor Galleries: Tues.-Fri. 10-5, Sat.-Sun. 12-5. No charge; donations accepted. Closed legal holidays. ♿
Attendance: 300,000 (estimated)
Membership: Art Link E $20; Friends $45; Family $65; Casting Circle $125; Sculptor's Forum $250; Director's Circle $500; Collector's Circle $1,000-$2,499; Laumeier Society $2,500 & up; Visionary $5,000 & up.

THE MAGIC HOUSE, ST. LOUIS CHILDREN'S MUSEUM, 516 S. Kirkwood Rd., Saint Louis, MO 63122-5926. Tel.: 314-822-8900, ext. 24. Fax: 314-822-8930.
E-mail: info@magichouse.org
Web Site: www.magichouse.org
Founded: 1979.
Congressional District: 2
Key Personnel: Pres., Elizabeth Fitzgerald; Chm., William Canfield; C.F.O., Cheryl Darr; Dir. Community Education, Julie Tubbs; Dir. Design, Beth Hasek; Grant Mgr., Hedy Ehrlich; Mktg. & Devel. Coord., Vicki Muhs; Dir. Human Resources, Elizabeth Hartman; Vice Pres., Carolyn Daniel; Asst. Dir. Education, Carla Krahoviak; Business Mgr., Anne Spinner; Dir. Mktg. & Devel., Kim Geminn; Dir. Visitor Svcs., Paula Burdge; Special Events & Membership Mgr., Whitney Fraier; Museum Shop Mgr., Bethany Altis.
Personnel Profile: Full-Time Paid 15; Part-Time Paid 80; Part-Time Volunteers 40.
Governing Authority: nonprofit organization. Tax-exempt: 501(c)(3).
Children's Museum: housed in 1901 home of George Lane Edwards.
Collections: hands-on, participatory exhibits.
Activities: organized education programs for children; docent program; participatory exhibits; teacher workshops; outreach programs; field trips.
Publications: brochure; books: A Guide to The Magic House; A Taste of Science; Wonder House; Wonder Boat.
Hours & Admission Prices: Memorial Day to Labor Day Mon.-Tues., Thurs. & Sat. 9:30-5:30, Wed. & Fri. 9:30-9, Sun. 11-5:30; Sept.-May Tues.-Thurs. 12-5:30, Fri. 12-9, Sat. 9:30-5:30, Sun. 11-5:30. Admission one & over $7.50; discounts to AAM members & groups. Closed New Year's Day; Easter; Thanksgiving; Christmas. ♿
Attendance: 407,930 (accurate)
Membership: Family $60; Magical $120; Mega Magical $500; Best Friends Circle $1,000 & up.

MARYVILLE UNIVERSITY - MORTON J. MAY FOUNDATION GALLERY, 650 Maryville University Dr., Saint Louis, MO 63141-7299. Tel.: 314-529-9381. Fax: 314-529-9940.
E-mail: jbaltrushunas@maryville.edu
Congressional District: 2
Key Personnel: Exec. Dir., Dr. Mark Lombardi, Ph.D.; Dir., Roxanne Phillips, M.F.A.; Treas., Larry Hays, Ph.D.
Personnel Profile: Full-Time Paid 1; Part-Time Paid 1.
Governing Authority: nonprofit organization. Parent Institution: Maryville University. Tax-exempt.
Art and Design Gallery.
Collections: paintings; prints; sculpture; photographs.
Activities: formal education programs for university students; lectures; guided tours; participatory & student exhibits.
Publications: Maryville Student Art Journal.
Hours & Admission Prices: Mon.-Thurs. 8am-10pm, Fri.-Sat. 8-6, Sun. 2-10. No charge. ♿
Attendance: 30,000 (estimated)

* **MILDRED LANE KEMPER ART MUSEUM, (M),** One Brookings Dr., Saint Louis, MO 63130-4862. Mailing Address: Campus Box 1214, One Brookings Dr., Saint Louis, MO 63130-4862. Tel.: 314-935-5423. Fax: 314-935-7282.
E-mail: kemperartmuseum@wustl.edu
Web Site: www.kemperartmuseum.wustl.edu
Formerly: Washington University Gallery of Art
Founded: 1881.
Congressional District: 1
Key Personnel: Dir. & Chief Cur., Dr. Sabine Eckmann; Coord Education & Public Programs, Mike Murawski; Communications & Events Coord., Kimberly Singer; Exhibition Preparator, Ron Weaver; Registrar, Rachel Keith; Administrative Coord., Jason Chew; Mng. Editor Publications, Jane Neidhardt; Facilities Mgr. & Preparator, Janet Hessel; Security Supvr., John Launius; Asst. Cur., Meredith Malone.
Personnel Profile: Full-Time Paid 11; Part-Time Paid 55; Part-Time Volunteers 8; Interns 4.
Governing Authority: university. Parent Institution: Washington University. Tax-exempt: 501(c)(3).
Art Museum.
Collections: 16th- to 20th-century European painting & sculpture; old master & modern prints; 19th- to 20th-century American painting & sculpture; antiquities; drawings; numismatics; contemporary art.
Research Fields: 19th, 20th & 21st-century European and American art.
Facilities: 50,000-vol. library of art history, fine arts, fashion design & architecture periodicals and catalogs available for inter-library loan & use by public for research; 300-seat auditorium.
Activities: guided tours; gallery talks; lectures; films; workshops; concerts.
Publications: semiannual, Calendar of Events; bulletin; exhibition catalogues.
Hours & Admission Prices: Wed.-Thurs. & Sat.-Mon. 11-6, Fri. 11-8. No charge. Closed university holidays. ♿
Attendance: 47,982 (accurate)
Membership: Student $20; Faculty & Staff $40; Individual $50; Family $80; Century Club $100-$249; Fellows $250-$499; Dean's Committee $500-$999; William Greenleaf Eliot Society $1,000.

MINIATURE MUSEUM OF GREATER ST. LOUIS, 4746 Gravois, Saint Louis, MO 63116-2437. Tel.: 314-832-7790.
E-mail: FZerb@aol.com
Web Site: www.miniaturemuseum.org
Founded: 1989.
Key Personnel: Pres. (V) & Museum Shop Mgr., Joanne Martin.
Governing Authority: Tax-exempt.
Miniature Museum.
Collections: miniature dollhouses & rooms.
Major Exhibits: Spring Scenes & Spring Holidays, 1/13/10-4/11/10; Summer Holidays & Summer Fun, 4/13/10-8/29/10; School Days & Fall Scenes in Miniature, 9/10-11/14/10; Winter Scenes & Winter Holidays, 11/17/10-1/9/11.
Activities: workshops; miniature shows.
Publications: quarterly newsletter.
Hours & Admission Prices: Wed.-Sat. 11-4, Sun. 1-4. Adults $5, seniors & youth 13-18 $4, children 12 & under $2; members & children under 2 no charge. Closed New Year's Eve & Day; Easter; Independence Day; Thanksgiving; Christmas Eve & Day. ♿
Attendance: 3,750 (estimated)
Membership: Club $13; Individual $15; Family $25; Supporting $50; Sustaining $100; Benefactor $500.

* **MISSOURI BOTANICAL GARDEN,** 4344 Shaw Blvd., Saint Louis, MO 63110-2291. Mailing Address: P.O. Box 299, Saint Louis, MO 63166-0299. Tel.: 314-577-5111. Fax: 314-577-9595.
Web Site: www.mobot.org
Founded: 1859.
Congressional District: 3
Key Personnel: Pres., Peter H. Raven, Ph.D.; Exec. Vice Pres., Robert Herleth; Chm. Bd. Trustees, Nicholas L. Reding; Pres. Members Bd., Janet Lange; Sr. Vice Pres. Institutional Advancement, Sharon Mertzlufft; Sr. Vice Pres. Research, Robert Magill, Ph.D.; Vice Pres. Information Technology & Chief Information Officer, Chuck Miller; Vice Pres. Education, Deborah Frank; Vice Pres. Horticulture, Jim Cocos; Sr. Vice Pres. Human Resources Management, Rebecca Ingram Kutey; Sr. Vice Pres. Gen. Svcs., Paul Brockmann; Sr. Vice Pres. Communications, Peggy Lents; Vice Pres. Financial Svcs. & Controller, Michael Olson; Vice Pres. Center for Conservation & Sustainable Devel., Olga Martha Montiel; Volunteer Coord., Jackie Juras; Vice Pres. Retail Operations & Museum Shop Mgr., Jan Simons; Dir. Shaw Nature Reserve, John Behrer; Dir. Butterfly House, Joe Norton; Dir. Earthways Center, Glenda Abney.
Personnel Profile: Full-Time Paid 416; Part-Time Paid 96; Part-Time Volunteers 1,788; Interns 19.
Governing Authority: nonprofit organization. Tax-exempt.
Botanical Garden: located on the site of the garden of Henry Shaw, developed in 1850s; national historic landmark.
Collections: herbarium including over 6 million plant specimens; manuscripts; Boehm porcelain; butterfly house; children's garden; archives. Historic Houses: 1849 Tower Grove House; 1850 Town House; 1859 Museum Building; 1882 Linnean House; 1858 Flora Gate (now Spink Pavilion); 1883 Mausoleum; 1960 Climatron (R).
Research Fields: botany; horticulture.
Facilities: 178,500 vol. library of systematic botany & gardening available for inter-library loan & by permission of librarian; 79 acres of gardens & conservatories; field research stations; reading room; 400-seat auditorium; classrooms; restaurant; nature trails. Items related to gardening & botany, including books & plants, for sale.
Activities: guided tours; lectures; study clubs; public events; flower shows; formally organized education programs for adults, children, & graduate students affiliated with Washington University, St. Louis University, Southern Illinois University in Edwardsville & University of Missouri in St. Louis; docent program or council; inter-museum loan; tram tours; plant society show & sales.
Publications: quarterly: Annuals of the Missouri Botanical Garden, Novon; quarterly: Missouri Botanical Garden Bulletin; irregular: Monographs in Systematic Botany from The Missouri Botanical Garden.
Hours & Admission Prices: Memorial Day to Labor Day Wed.-Thurs. 9-9, Fri.-Tues. 9-5; Sept.-May daily 9-5. Grounds: Sun.-Tues. & Thurs.-Fri. 9-5, Wed. & Sat. 7-5. Adults 13-64 $8; discounts to St. Louis County residents; members & children under 12 no charge. Shaw Nature Reserve: call for information, 636-451-3512. Butterfly House: call for information 636-530-0076. Children's Garden: children $3, adults no charge; some special events may require additional charge. Closed Christmas. ♿
Attendance: 961,409 (accurate)
Membership: Senior $55; Regular $60; Family $150; Sustaining $225; Sponsoring $300; Dir. Assoc. $600; Henry Shaw Assoc. $1,200; Garden Fellows $2,500; Garden Ambassador $5,000; Peter H. Raven Society $10,000.

* **MISSOURI HISTORICAL SOCIETY, (M),** Lindell & De Baliviere, 5700 Lindell Blvd., Saint Louis, MO 63112. Mailing Address: P.O. Box 11940, Saint Louis, MO 63112-0040. Tel.: 314-454-3150. Fax: 314-746-4548.
E-mail: info@mohistory.org
Web Site: www.mohistory.org
Founded: 1866.
Congressional District: 1
Key Personnel: C.E.O. & Pres., Dr. Robert R. Archibald; Mng. Dir. Operations, Karen M. Goering; Mng. Dir. Institutional Advancement, Vicki Kaffenberger; C.F.O., Harry Rich; Dir. Exhibitions & Research, Margaret Koch; Conservator, Linda Landry; Museum Shop Mgr., Susan Ponciroli; Mng. Dir. Community Education & Events, Melanie Adams; Cur. Special Projects, Carolyn Gilman; Sr. Cur., Shannon Berry; Mng. Dir. Museum Svcs., Katie Van Allen.
Personnel Profile: Full-Time Paid 121; Part-Time Paid 40; Part-Time Volunteers 208; Interns 28.
Governing Authority: nonprofit organization. Parent Institution: St. Louis Zoo-Museum Tax District; Library & Research Center, 225 S. Skinker Blvd. Tax-exempt: 501(c)(3).
History Museum.
Collections: St. Louis, Missouri & Urban history; exploration of the West, Lewis and Clark; artifacts; broadsides & maps; costumes; manuscripts; photographs; painting; sculpture; Charles A. Lindbergh collection; Richard Gephardt Congressional papers.
Major Exhibits: Treasure! (T), 11/09-1/3/10; Race: Are We So Different? (T), 1/17/10-5/2/10; Treasures of Napoleon (T), 11/21/10-2/13/11.
Research Fields: history of St. Louis, Missouri, Mississippi Valley & western expansion.
Facilities: 70,000-vol. library & Research Center; Missouri Historical Society Press; Jefferson Memorial Building and Emerson Center house exhibits; community programs department. Museum-related items for sale.
Activities: guided tours; lectures; formally organized community programs for adults & children; permanent, temporary & traveling exhibitions.
Publications: online magazine, Voices; magazine, Gateway; newsletter, Members' News; monographs; books.
Hours & Admission Prices: Museum: Tues. 10-8, Wed.-Mon. 10-5. No charge. Closed Thanksgiving; Christmas. Library & Research Center: Tues.-Fri. 12-5, Sat. 10-5. No charge. Closed major holidays; Sat. holidays. ♿
Attendance: 306,356 (accurate)
Membership: Senior $55; Regular $60; Family Plus $85; Contributing $150; Sustaining $250; Sponsoring $500; Thomas Jefferson Society $1,000-$25,000.

MUSEUM OF CONTEMPORARY RELIGIOUS ART (MOCRA)-ST. LOUIS UNIVERSITY, (M), 3700 W. Pine Mall Blvd., Saint Louis, MO 63108-3306. Mailing Address: 221 N. Grand Blvd., Saint Louis, MO 63103-2006. Tel.: 314-977-7170. Fax: 314-977-2999.
E-mail: mocra@slu.edu
Web Site: mocra.slu.edu
Founded: 1993.
Congressional District: 1
Key Personnel: C.E.O. & Cur., Rev. Terrence E. Dempsey, S.J.; Chm. (V), Jane Daggett Dillenberger; Devel. & Education, David Brinker; Registrar, Michelle Hake.
Personnel Profile: Full-Time Paid 3; Part-Time Paid 7.
Governing Authority: private university. Tax-exempt: 501(c)(3).
Interfaith Religious Contemporary Art Museum: housed in former Jesuit seminarian chapel.
Collections: contemporary art from all religious traditions which engages in a serious manner the religious and spiritual dimensions.
Research Fields: the intersection of the spiritual & religious dimensions in contemporary art.
Activities: guided tours; films; lectures; loan & traveling exhibitions.
Publications: exhibition catalogue, Bernard Maisner: Entrance to the Scriptorium.
Hours & Admission Prices: Tues.-Sun. 11-4. No charge; donations accepted. Closed New Year's Day; Martin Luther King Jr. Day; Easter; Memorial Day; Independence Day; Labor Day; Thanksgiving; Christmas. Closed between exhibitions; call for more information. ♿
Attendance: 4,200 (accurate)

MUSEUM OF TRANSPORTATION, 3015 Barrett Station Rd., Saint Louis, MO 63122-3398. Tel.: 314-615-8668. Fax: 314-965-0242.
E-mail: mbutterworth@stlouisco.com
Web Site: www.museumoftransport.org
Founded: 1944.
Congressional District: 2
Key Personnel: Cultural Site Mgr., Molly Butterworth; Pres. (V), Don Musick; Association Dir., Terri McEachern; Museum Shop Mgr., Sandra Williams.
Personnel Profile: Full-Time Paid 9; Part-Time Paid 3; Part-Time Volunteers 125.
Governing Authority: nonprofit organization; bd. of dirs. Parent Institution: St. Louis County Dept. of Parks & Recreation. Subsidiary Institution: Transport Museum Association. Tax-exempt: 509(c)(3) & 501(c)(3).
Transportation Museum.
Collections: locomotives; railway cars; automobiles; streetcars; buses; trucks; horse drawn vehicles; aircraft; pipeline & communication devices; history of the technology & design of transportation and communication. Historic Site: roadbed of first railroad west of Mississippi River.
Research Fields: transportation history.
Facilities: 10,000-vol. library on transportation & communication available for research on premises; meeting rooms. Educational & museum related items for sale.
Activities: guided tours; education programs for adults & children; docent program.
Publications: newsletter, News & Views; papers; news releases.
Hours & Admission Prices: Summer: Mon.-Sat. 9-5, Sun. 11-5; Winter: Tues.-Sat. 9-4, Sun. 11-4. Adults $6, senior citizens & children 5-12 $4; members no charge. Closed New Year's Day; Thanksgiving; Christmas. ♿
Attendance: 107,423 (accurate)
Membership: Active $35; Associate $50; Sustainer $100; Contributor $250; Sponsor $500; Patron $1,000; Life $5,000.

OLD CATHEDRAL MUSEUM, 209 Walnut, Saint Louis, MO 63102-2499. Tel.: 314-231-3250. Fax: 314-231-4280.
Web Site: www.catholic-forum.com/stlouisking
Founded: 1970.
Key Personnel: C.E.O., Rev. Msgr. Jerome Billing; Museum Shop, Mrs. Mary Dieterman.
Personnel Profile: Full-Time Paid 3; Part-Time Volunteers 6.
Governing Authority: church. Parent Institution: The Archdiocese of St. Louis. Subsidiary Institution: The Basilica of St. Louis, The King. Tax-exempt: 501(c)(3).
Religious Museum: housed in 1834 Cathedral.
Collections: religious history items.
Facilities: Religious articles & other museum-related items for sale.
Activities: permanent exhibitions.
Publications: History of the Old Cathedral.
Hours & Admission Prices: Mon.-Fri. 9:30-2:30. No charge; donations accepted. Closed New Year's Day; Easter; Independence Day; Christmas. ♿
Attendance: 22,000 (estimated)

THE PRINCIPIA SCHOOL OF NATIONS MUSEUM, (M), 13201 Clayton Rd., Saint Louis, MO 63131-1099. Tel.: 314-514-3073.
Founded: 1930.
Key Personnel: Dir., Nancy Boyer-Rechlin.
Personnel Profile: Full-Time Paid 1; Part-Time Paid 1; Part-Time Volunteers 2.
Governing Authority: college. Parent Institution: The Principia Corp. Affiliated with Principia College, Elsan, IL and The Principia School, St. Louis, MO. Tax-exempt: 501(c)(3).
General Museum & Arts and Crafts Museum.
Collections: American Indian & Pre-Columbian artifacts; objects of Asian art; decorative arts; textiles; costumes; dolls; pottery.
Activities: guided tours; formally organized education programs for undergraduate college students affiliated with Principia College & pre-K through high school students affiliated with the Principia School; permanent & temporary exhibitions; children's hands-on exhibits; visual aids program.
Publications: e-newsletter, The Principia School of Nations News.
Hours & Admission Prices: Sept.-June by appointment only. No charge. Closed school vacations.

*** SAINT LOUIS ART MUSEUM, (M),** One Fine Arts Dr., Forest Park, Saint Louis, MO 63110-1380. Tel.: 314-721-0072. Fax: 314-721-6172. TDD: 314-721-4807.
E-mail: publicrelations@slam.org
Web Site: www.slam.org
Founded: 1879.
Congressional District: 1
Key Personnel: Dir., Brent Benjamin; Pres. Bd. Commissioners, John D. Weil; Chm. Bd. Trustees, Barbara W. Roberts; Asst. Dir. Public Programs & Education, William Appleton; Assoc. Cur. Decorative Arts & Design, David Conradsen; Cur. Modern & Contemporary Art, Charlotte Eyerman; Cur. Ancient & Islamic Art, Sid Goldstein; Dir. Retail Sales, Cliff Harrison; Assoc. Cur. Asian Art, Philip Hu; Asst. Cur. Prints, Drawings & Photographs, Eric Lutz; Dir. Devel. & Campaign, Sheila Manion; Cur. European Art to 1800, Judith Mann; Controller & Asst. Dir. Finance, Carolyn Schmidt; Dir. External Affairs, Jennifer Stoffel; Asst. Dir. Exhibitions & Collections, Linda Thomas; Asst. Dir. Curatorial Affairs & Cur. American Art, Andrew Walker.
Personnel Profile: Full-Time Paid 179; Part-Time Paid 76; Part-Time Volunteers 245; Interns 14.
Governing Authority: municipal. Special Zoo Museum District. Managed by Museum Commission. Tax-exempt.
Art Museum: housed in 1904 World's Fair building.
Collections: more than 30,000 works of art; Oceanic art; pre-Columbian art; ancient Chinese bronzes; European & American art of the late 19th & 20th centuries; 20th-century German painting; Max Beckman prints; Henri Matisse's "Bathers with a Turtle"; George Caleb Bingham's "Election Series"; Hans Holbein the Younger's "Mary Lady Guilford"; Vincent van Gogh's "Stairway at Auvers"; Bartolomeo Manfredi's "Apollo and Maryas".
Major Exhibits: Joe Jones: Painter of the American Scene, Fall 2010.
Research Fields: pertaining to the collections; featured exhibitions material; archaeology; textiles.
Facilities: 110,000-vol. library on art history, decorative arts, auction & museum catalogs, available for limited inter-library loan & on premises; teachers' resource center; reading room; study room for prints, drawings & photographs; 480-seat auditorium; classrooms; restaurant; conservation center. Art books, prints & other museum-related items for sale in Museum Shop.
Activities: guided tours; lectures; films; gallery talks; performances; formally organized education programs for children & adults; docent program; inter-museum loan. Museum Sponsors: featured exhibitions.
Publications: biennial report; quarterly magazine; quarterly programs & events guide; exhibition catalogues; collection/exhibition brochures; visitor guides.
Hours & Admission Prices: Tues.-Thurs. & Sat.-Sun. 10-5, Fri. 10-9. No charge. Closed New Year's Day; Thanksgiving; Christmas. ♿
Attendance: 376,360 (accurate)
Membership: Regular $55; Family $75; Contributing $100; Sustaining $150; Supporting $250; Associate $500; Sponsor $1,000; Beaux Arts Council $1,500; Patron $2,500; Benefactor $5,000; Director's Circle $10,000; President's Circle $25,000; Chairman's Circle $50,000.

ST. LOUIS CARDINALS HALL OF FAME MUSEUM, 700 Clark St., Saint Louis, MO 63102-1727. Tel.: 314-345-6340.
Founded: 1968.
Personnel Profile: Full-Time Paid 3; Part-Time Paid 18.
Governing Authority: Parent Institution: St. Louis Cardinals, LLC.
Sports Museum.
Collections: over 100 years of baseball history; photographs; memorabilia; uniforms; Hall of Fame inductees; sports equipment; trophies; awards.
Hours & Admission Prices: Closed until 2010. ♿
Attendance: 30,000 (estimated)

*** ST. LOUIS SCIENCE CENTER, (M),** 5050 Oakland Ave., Saint Louis, MO 63110-1460. Tel.: 314-289-4400. Fax: 314-289-4420.
Web Site: www.slsc.org
Founded: 1959.
Congressional District: 1
Key Personnel: C.E.O. & Pres., Douglas R. King; Chm. Bd. of Commissioners, Theodore W. Hellman; Chm. Bd. of Trustees, Jerry E. Ritter; Senior Vice Pres. & Assoc. Dir., Carol J. Valenta; Senior Vice Pres. Business Division, Brad Nuccio; C.F.O. & Vice Pres. Finance & Information, Thomas Jaskiewicz; Vice Pres. Strategic Initiatives & Facilities, John G. Wharton; Senior Dir. Design & Galleries, Joe Seidler; Assoc. Dir. Volunteers & Intern, Halcyone Brown; Vice Pres. Human Resources & Volunteers, Deborah Washington; Senior Vice Pres. Community, Diane Miller; Vice Pres. Devel., Pat Williams; Vice Pres. Aerospace Science, Gregg Maryniak; Vice Pres. Public Understanding of Science, Al Wiman; Senior Vice Pres. Visitor Experience, Marti Cortez; Membership Mgr., Jim Schallom; Explorastore Gen. Mgr., Karen Headley.
Personnel Profile: Full-Time Paid 232; Part-Time Paid 56; Part-Time Volunteers 285; Interns 5.
Governing Authority: metropolitan district. Parent Institutions: St. Louis Science Center subdistrict of the Metropolitan Zoological Park and Museum District; St. Louis Science Center Foundation. Tax-exempt: 501(c)(3).
Science/Technology Museum.
Collections: pre-Columbian North American Indian artifacts emphasizing Missouri; technology including aeronautics communications, lighting equipment, period radios, cameras, medical equipment; space artifacts; ethnology; geology; minerals; natural history including mammalogy, ornithology, entomology, herpetology & malacology.
Major Exhibits: Dinosaurs Unearthed (T), 11/09-3/28/10; Pirates (T), 3/5/10-8/30/10; Darwin (T), 4/10/10-7/31/10.
Facilities: 64,759 sq. ft. exhibit space; Exploradome; collections & resource center; 315-seat OMNIMAX(R)Theater; James S. McDonnell Planetarium Building/Space Station; 8 meeting rooms. Museum-related items for sale.
Activities: boy & girl scout badge programs; formally organized education programs for children & adults; permanent, temporary & traveling exhibitions; gallery demonstrations; lecture programs; school loan service; field trips; speakers bureau; portable planetarium; astronomy & outreach programs.
Publications: New Science; EE & P report; annual report.
Hours & Admission Prices: Memorial Day-Labor Day daily 9:30-5:30; Sept.-May daily 9:30-4:30. Museum: no charge. OMNIMAX(R)Theater: adults $8, children $7. Closed Thanksgiving; Christmas. ♿
Attendance: 1,071,690 (accurate)
Membership: Science Supporter $50; Individual & Guest $60; Family & Friends $85; Family & Friends Plus $120; Family & Friends Max $175; Galileo Society $250; Newton Society $500; Albert Einstein Society $1,000; Albert Einstein Society Patron $2,500; Albert Einstein Society Fellow $5,000; Albert Einstein Society Presidents Council $10,000. Corporate Partners Associates $1,000; Corporate Partners Patron $2,500; Corporate Partners Fellow $5,000; Corporate Partners Presidents Council $10,000; Corporate Partners Leadership Council $25,000. Senior (60 and over) $5 discount on all member levels.

SAINT LOUIS UNIVERSITY MUSEUM OF ART, 3663 Lindell Blvd., Saint Louis, MO 63108. Mailing Address: 221 N. Grand Blvd., Saint Louis, MO 63103. Tel.: 314-977-2666. Fax: 314-977-3581.
E-mail: sluma@slu.edu
Web Site: www.slu.edu/sluma.xml
Founded: 2002.
Congressional District: 1
Key Personnel: Dir., Petruta Lipan; Education, Neil Metzger; Public Rels. Affairs, Mary Marshall; Registrar, Claire Frandsen; Cur., David Suwalsky; Dir. Facilities, Barth Breneman; Security, Dennis Thompson.
Personnel Profile: Full-Time Paid 6; Part-Time Paid 12; Part-Time Volunteers 2; Interns 6.
Governing Authority: private university. Tax-exempt: 501(c)(3).
Art Museum.
Collections: 16th-21st century European & American art; Japanese art; midwest Jesuit Mission; southeast Asian art.
Research Fields: collections; special exhibitions material.
Facilities: 7,500-vol. library; 20,000 sq. ft. exhibit space; educational facilities.
Activities: formal education programs; guided tours; lectures; loan, traveling & temporary exhibitions; internships.
Publications: exhibition catalogs & brochures.
Hours & Admission Prices: Wed.-Sun. 11-4. No charge; donations accepted. Closed New Year's Day; Easter; Thanksgiving; Christmas. ♿
Attendance: 5,948 (accurate)
Membership: Regular $50; Family $75; Contributing $100; Sustaining $150; Supporting $250; Associate $500; Sponsor $1,000; Patron $1,500; Fellow $2,500; Benefactor $5,000; Director's Circle $10,000; President's Circle $25,000.

SAINT LOUIS ZOO, (M), Forest Park, Saint Louis, MO 63110-1395. Mailing Address: 1 Government Dr., St. Louis, MO 63110-1395. Tel.: 314-781-0900. Fax: 314-647-7969.
E-mail: bonner@stlzoo.org
Web Site: www.stlzoo.org
Founded: 1910.
Congressional District: 1
Key Personnel: Chm. Zoological Park Commission, Mark J. Schnuck; Pres. & C.E.O., Jeffrey P. Bonner, Ph.D.; Exec. Asst., Kelly Fesler; Sr. Vice Pres. & Dir. Zoological Operations and the Wildcare Institute, R. Eric Miller, D.V.M.; Dir. Animal Health, Randy Junge, D.V.M.; Dir. Research, Cheryl Asa, Ph.D.; Dir. Education, Louise Bradshaw; Vice Pres. Animal Collection, Jack Grisham; Asst. Gen. Cur., Bill Houston; Cur. Aquatics & Herps, Jeff Ettling; Cur. Mammals & Carnivores, Steve Bircher; Cur. Mammals & Primates, Ingrid Porton; Cur. Birds, Michael Macek; Cur. Mammals & Ungulates, Martha Fischer; Cur. Invertebrates, Ed Spevak; Cur. Children's Zoo, Alice Seyfried; Supvr. Life Support Systems, David Jarvis; Animal Registrar, Rae Lynn Haliday; Vice Pres. Business Operations & C.F.O., Steve Barth; Controller, Cassandra Ray; Dir. Facilities Management, Dan Snyder; Dir. Food Svc., Ken Stover; Dir. Housekeeping & Grounds, Ernest Frost; Dir. Purchasing & Distribution, Patrick Williamson; Dir. Guest Svcs., Joan Sisco; Mgr. Business Operations, Jim Madison; Dir. Information Systems, Jerry French; Vice Pres. External Rels., Cynthia S. Holter, CFRE; Dir. Devel., Jeffrey C. Huntington, CFRE; Dir. Planned Gifts, Steve Rosenblum; Dir. Mktg., Ginnie Westmoreland; Dir. Public Rels., Janet Powell; Dir. Sales, Kathy Lunders; Dir. Corp. & Foundation Gifts, Diane Bauhof; Vice Pres. Internal Rels., Wyndel Hill; Mgr. Safety & Risk Management, Philip Sonderman; Mgr. Comp & Benefits, Tim Rakers; Mgr. Training & Staff Devel., Lucy Bailey; Dir. Security, Michael Siemers; Mgr. Volunteer Svcs., Elaine Gill; Human Resources Specialist, Debbie Lammering; Payroll Specialist, Martha Michael; Dir. Human Resources, Dustin Deschamp; Vice Pres. Architecture & Planning, David McGuire.
Personnel Profile: Full-Time Paid 300; Part-Time Paid 140; Part-Time Volunteers 1,343; Interns 84.
Governing Authority: municipal by special Zoo Museum District. Managed by Zoological Commission. Tax-exempt.
Zoo.
Collections: 17,955 specimens, 719 species of mammals, birds, reptiles, amphibians, fish & invertebrates.
Research Fields: zoo animal reproduction & conservation.
Facilities: 5,000-vol. library on zoology, conservation & related topics available for use by professional staff, area teachers & others by appointment; classrooms; auditorium; Endangered Species Research Center & Veterinary Hospital. Zoo-related items for sale.
Activities: guided tours; lectures; films; formally organized education programs for children, adults & undergraduate college students; training programs; permanent & temporary exhibitions.
Publications: bimonthly magazine, stlzoo.
Hours & Admission Prices: Summer: Mon.-Thurs. 8-5, Fri.-Sun. & holidays 8-7; Sept.-May 9-5. No charge; donations accepted. Closed New Year's Day; Christmas. ♿
Attendance: 2,956,741 (accurate)
Membership: Conservation Advocate, Student & Senior $50; Young Zoo Friends & Regular $60; Family, Grandparents $80; Naturalist $120; Keeper $175; Zoologist $250; Curator $500; Director $750; Marlin Perkins Society, Animal Kingdom Club $1,000; Safari Circle $1,500; Wildlife Circle $2,500; Steward's Circle $5,000; Conservationist Circle $10,000; President's Circle $25,000.

SCOTT JOPLIN HOUSE - STATE HISTORIC SITE, 2658 Delmar Blvd., Saint Louis, MO 63103-1404. Tel.: 314-340-5790. Fax: 314-340-5793.
Web Site: www.mostateparks§cottjoplin.html
Founded: 1982.
Congressional District: 1
Personnel Profile: Full-Time Paid 3; Part-Time Paid 3; Part-Time Volunteers 9; Interns 1.
Governing Authority: state. Tax-exempt.
Historic House Museum: c.1860. Listed on the National Register of Historic Places.
Collections: Joplin family history; African American cultural history; Ragtime history.
Research Fields: ragtime.
Facilities: rental facilities.
Activities: rental facilities; tours; educational & private events. Museum Sponsors: Live Ragtime Events.
Hours & Admission Prices: March-Oct. Mon.-Sat. 10-4, Sun. 12-4; Nov.-Feb. Tues.-Sat. 10-4. Adults $2.50, children 6-12 $1.50; discounts to groups; children 5 & under no charge. Closed New Year's Day; Easter; Thanksgiving; Christmas. ♿
Attendance: 12,500

SOLDIERS MEMORIAL MILITARY MUSEUM, 1315 Chestnut St., Saint Louis, MO 63103-2317. Tel.: 314-622-4550. Fax: 314-622-4237.
Founded: 1938.
Congressional District: 1
Key Personnel: Museum & Collections Exec., Lynnea Magnuson, Ph.D.
Governing Authority: municipal. Tax-exempt.
Military Museum.
Collections: uniforms; weapons; war mementos; photographs of St. Louis soldiers; local military history.
Facilities: auditorium; rental rooms.
Activities: programs; special memorial services on national holidays; veterans programs & events.
Hours & Admission Prices: Mon.-Fri. 9-4:30, Sat.-Sun. 10-3. No charge; donations accepted. Closed New Year's Day; Thanksgiving; Christmas. ♿

Sainte Genevieve

BOLDUC HOUSE MUSEUM, 123 S. Main St., Sainte Genevieve, MO 63670. Tel.: 573-883-3105. Fax: 573-883-3415.
E-mail: bolduchouse@sbcglobal.net
Web Site: www.bolduchouse.com
Founded: 1770.
Congressional District: 3
Personnel Profile: Part-Time Volunteers 3.
Governing Authority: society; nonprofit. Parent Institution: The National Society of the Colonial Dames of America in the State of Missouri. Tax-exempt: 501(c)(3).
Historic Houses Museum: 1770 Bolduc House, a National Historic Landmark; 1820 Bolduc LeMeilleur House; Herb Cottage; Gemien Beauwais House.
Collections: Bolduc House: period French furnishings. Bolduc LeMeilleur House: French & American architecture & construction styles; Federal style furnishings. Gemien Beauwais House: Anglo-American structure; 19th-century furnishings; society headquarters & offices. Herb Cottage: detached kitchen reproduction.
Research Fields: French Colonial history, period furnishings & gardens.
Facilities: French Colonial garden. Gifts, books, homemade herbal jellies from the Bolduc garden and plants & seeds from gardens for sale.
Activities: guided tours; permanent exhibitions. Gardens: special events; tours; educational events; book signings. Herb Cottage: educational talks & hands-on participation in herbal creations. Museum Sponsors: Linden House Christmas event. Annual Events: Jour de Fete in August; Christmas walk in December.
Publications: Story of Old Ste. Genevieve; cookbook; Louis Bolduc, His Family and His House.
Hours & Admission Prices: April-Oct. Mon.-Sat. 10-4, Sun. 11-5, extended hours during Jour de Fete. Bolduc House: adults $5, children K-12 $2; discounts to groups of 15 or more; Colonial Dames no charge. Closed Easter.
Attendance: 15,200

FELIX VALLE STATE HISTORIC SITE, 198 Merchant St., Sainte Genevieve, MO 63670-1682. Mailing Address: P.O. Box 89, Ste. Genevieve, MO 63670-0089. Tel.: 573-883-7102. Fax: 573-883-9630. TDD: 800-379-2419.
E-mail: felix.valle.state.historic.site@dnr.mo.gov
Web Site: www.mostateparks.com
Founded: 1970.
Congressional District: 10
Key Personnel: Site Admin., James Baker.
Personnel Profile: Full-Time Paid 3; Part-Time Paid 3; Interns 1.
Governing Authority: state. Parent Institution: Div. of State Parks, Missouri Dept. of Natural Resources, P.O. Box 176, Jefferson City, MO 65102. Tax-exempt.
History Museum.
Collections: American Empire furniture; French colonial vertical-log buildings. Amoureux House: 9' x 11' diorama depicting village of Ste. Genevieve in 1832. Historic House: 1792 St. Gemme/Amoureux House; 1793 Delassus-Kern structure; 1818 Felix Valle House; 1819 Dr. Benjamin Shaw house.
Research Fields: early Ste. Genevieve & French-American period in Mississippi River Valley.
Facilities: restored & furnished home.
Activities: special events during summer. Museum Sponsors: French Christmas Open House.
Publications: brochure.
Hours & Admission Prices: April-Oct. Mon.-Sat. 10-4, Sun. 12-5; Nov.-March Thurs.-Sat. 10-4, Sun. 12-5. Adults $2.50, children 6-12 $1.50; discount to groups; children under 6 no charge. Closed New Year's Day; Easter; Thanksgiving; Christmas.
Attendance: 13,000 (estimated)

STE. GENEVIEVE MUSEUM, Merchant & DuBourg St., Sainte Genevieve, MO 63670. Tel.: 573-883-3461.
Founded: 1935.
Congressional District: 8
Key Personnel: Dir., Dr. Deborah Woelich; Pres., James Baker; Treas., Dolores Koetting.
Personnel Profile: Part-Time Paid 2.
Governing Authority: Parent Institution: Museum Bd. Tax-exempt.
History Museum.
Collections: folk art; Indian artifacts; historical relics from Ste. Genevieve; historical books; sketches; weapons; documents.
Facilities: Museum-related items for sale.
Hours & Admission Prices: April-Oct. Mon.-Sat. 10-4, Sun. 12-4; Nov.-March daily 12-4. Adults $2, students K-12 $.50; members no charge. Closed New Year's Eve & Day; Easter; Thanksgiving; Christmas Eve & Day. ♿
Attendance: 5,750 (estimated)
Membership: Single $10; Family $20; Business $50.

Savannah

ANDREW COUNTY MUSEUM & HISTORICAL SOCIETY, (M), 202 E. Duncan Dr., Savannah, MO 64485-1264. Mailing Address: P.O. Box 12, Savannah, MO 64485-0012. Tel.: 816-324-4720. Fax: 816-324-5271.
E-mail: acmuseum@stjoelive.com
Web Site: www.andrewcountymuseum.org
Founded: 1972.
Congressional District: 5
Key Personnel: Pres. (V), Harold Johnson; Museum Admin., Shirley Brown; Office Asst., Christy Sipes.
Personnel Profile: Full-Time Paid 2; Part-Time Paid 1; Part-Time Volunteers 100.
Governing Authority: bd. of dirs. Parent Institution: Andrew County Historical Society. Tax-exempt.
History Museum.
Collections: local history & culture from 1841 to present; farming; agriculture; local businesses; early 19th-century French & German dolls; old Hummel figurines; Gatling gun; period cars; Victorian material; cultural items; Rose O'Neill art; personal items; kewpie dolls; Navajo textiles; western folk art.
Research Fields: local history; genealogy.
Facilities: agricultural interpretive building.
Activities: guided tours; docent program; loan & temporary exhibitions.
Publications: quarterly newsletter, Diggin History; seven cemetery inscription volumes; census information; marriage records; birth & death records.
Hours & Admission Prices: Tues.-Sat. 10-4. No charge; donations accepted. ♿
Attendance: 3,102 (accurate)
Membership: Student & Senior Citizen $8; Individual $12; Joint $20; Family $25; Patron $50; Benefactor $100.

Sedalia

DAUM MUSEUM OF CONTEMPORARY ART, (M), State Fair Community College, 3201 W. 16th St., Sedalia, MO 65301-2188. Tel.: 660-530-5888. Fax: 660-530-5890.
E-mail: info@daummuseum.org
Web Site: www.daummuseum.org
Formerly: Goddard Gallery
Founded: 2001.
Congressional District: 4
Key Personnel: Dir., Thomas Piche, Jr.; Pres., Dr. Marsha Drennon; Museum Specialist, Renee Weller; Museum Coord., Victoria Weaver.
Personnel Profile: Full-Time Paid 3; Part-Time Paid 6; Part-Time Volunteers 40.
Governing Authority: Parent Institution: State Fair Community College.
Contemporary Art Museum.
Collections: works from the last third of the 20th century to present.
Research Fields: contemporary art.
Activities: art & lecture series; workshops; symposium; children's busing program.
Publications: catalogs, Betty Woodman; Sculptural Clay Invitational; Awakenings; Jun Kaneko; Bay Area Ceramic Sculptures: Second Generation; Michiko Itatani; Vera Klement; Joyce Jablonski; Judy Onofrio; Jim Shrosbree; Jim Sajovic; Steven Montgomery; Ruth Borgenight; Jeffrey Mongrain; Peter Callas; Ron Ehrlich; Albert Pfarr; Richard Deon.
Hours & Admission Prices: Tues.-Fri. 11-5, Sat.-Sun. 1-5. No charge; donations accepted. ♿
Attendance: 26,000 (accurate)
Membership: Student $35; Individual $50; Family $60; Associate $250; Benefactor $500; Sponsor $1,000; Underwriter $2,500; Season $5,000.

PETTIS COUNTY HISTORICAL SOCIETY, 228 Dundee, Sedalia, MO 65301-2339.
Founded: 1943.
Congressional District: 4
Key Personnel: Pres., Charles W. Wise; Vice Pres., Rhonda Chalfant; Sec. & Treas., Clell Furnell.
Personnel Profile: Part-Time Volunteers 4.
Governing Authority: nonprofit organization.
Historical Society Museum.
Collections: military; war; agriculture; farm life; costumes; science nature; Indian artifacts; history. Historic House: 1883 McVey School #3, known as the Little Red Schoolhouse, State Hwy. 50 East, Sedalia.
Activities: guided tours & lectures at McVey School; by appointment spring & summer.
Publications: bimonthly newsletter.
Hours & Admission Prices: Call for hours & admission prices. ♿
Membership: Individual $5; Family $8; Business $10.

Sibley

FORT OSAGE NATIONAL HISTORIC LANDMARK, 107 Osage St., Sibley, MO 64088. Mailing Address: 22807 Woods Chapel Rd., Blue Springs, MO 64015-9799. Tel.: 816-503-4860. Fax: 816-795-7938. TDD: 800-735-2966.
E-mail: gjulich@jacksongov.org
Web Site: www.jacksongov.org
Founded: 1948.
Congressional District: 6
Key Personnel: Dir. Parks & Recreation, Michele Newman; Interpretive Specialist, Steve Wilson; Supt. Heritage Museums & Programs, Gordon Julich; Museum Shop Mgr., Laura King.
Personnel Profile: Full-Time Paid 5; Part-Time Paid 1; Part-Time Volunteers 30.
Governing Authority: county. Parent Institution: Jackson County Parks & Recreation, 22807 Woods Chapel Rd., Blue Springs, MO 64015. Tax-exempt: 170(c)(3).
Historic Site: 1808-1827 Fort Osage.
Collections: history; military; Indians; archaeology; westward expansion fur trade; Osage Indians; fur trade. Historic Buildings: restored trade house; military compound including soldiers quarters; private civilian quarters; trade room; blacksmith's shop.
Research Fields: history of Fort Osage; U.S. factory system; early fur trade; Osage Indian life; 1812 military.
Facilities: education center; park complex featuring picnic grounds and boat ramp.
Activities: tours; permanent & temporary exhibitions; living history interpretation; youth program; craft and skills demonstrations; volunteer program; other special events. Museum Sponsors: annual celebration of fur trade era third weekend in June.
Publications: Fort Osage, Mother of the West.

Hours & Admission Prices: Tues.-Sun. 9-4:30. Adults $7, youth $4, senior citizens $3. Closed Martin Luther King Jr. Day; Thanksgiving; Christmas. ♿
Attendance: 11,800 (accurate)
Membership: Individual $35; Family $45.

Springfield

AIR AND MILITARY MUSEUM OF THE OZARKS, (M), 2305 E. Kearney, Springfield, MO 65803-4970. Tel.: 417-864-7997. Fax: 417-866-2448.
Military Museum.
Collections: military history & memorabilia; military equipment; photographs.
Activities: aircraft shows; educational programs.
Hours & Admission Prices: Tues.-Sat. 12-4; other times by appointment. Adults $5, children 6-12 $3; children 5 & under no charge.
Attendance: 6,000 (accurate)
Membership: Single $25; Couple $36.

DICKERSON PARK ZOO, 1401 W. Norton Rd., Springfield, MO 65803-1023. Mailing Address: 3043 N. Fort Ave., Springfield, MO 65803-1079. Tel.: 417-833-1570. Fax: 417-833-4459.
E-mail: info@dickersonparkzoo.org
Web Site: www.dickersonparkzoo.org
Founded: 1923.
Congressional District: 7
Key Personnel: Dir., Michael Crocker; Pres. (V), Todd Brierly; Zoological & Gen. Cur., John Collette; Museum Shop Mgr., Joni Baurichter.
Personnel Profile: Full-Time Paid 39; Part-Time Paid 24; Part-Time Volunteers 81; Interns 10.
Governing Authority: municipal. Branch of Springfield/Greene County Park Bd., 1923 N. Weller, Springfield, MO 65803. Tel.: 417-864-1049. Tax-exempt: 501(c)(3).
Zoological Park.
Collections: gen. zoological collection of indigenous & exotic species.
Research Fields: elephant breeding biology & mgmt.
Facilities: 600-vol. library of biological & zoological text and reference material, available for use on certified research projects or school papers; reading room; classrooms.
Activities: lectures; films; concerts; broadcast programs; formally organized education programs; docent program or council; training programs for professional museum workers; special events.
Publications: bimonthly magazine, Wildtimes.
Hours & Admission Prices: April-Sept. daily 9-5; Oct.-March daily 10-4. Adults $7, children 3-12 $5; discounts to groups of 15 or more paying individuals & members of reciprocal zoos, AZA; members & children under 3 no charge. Closed New Year's Day; Thanksgiving; Christmas. ♿
Attendance: 201,757 (accurate)
Membership: Family, Plus One & Grandparents $65; Wildlife Club $75; Safari Club $100; Keepers Club $250; Curator's Club $500; Director's Club $1,000.

DISCOVERY CENTER OF SPRINGFIELD, 438 E. St. Louis St., Springfield, MO 65806-2312. Tel.: 417-862-9910, ext. 0 or ext. 700. Fax: 417-862-6898.
E-mail: efox@discoverycenter.org
Web Site: www.discoverycenter.org/
Founded: 1991.
Key Personnel: Bd. Pres. (V), Julie Brown; C.E.O., Emily Fox; Museum Shop Mgr., Steven Duillio.
Personnel Profile: Full-Time Paid 14; Part-Time Paid 3; Part-Time Volunteers 50; Interns 5.
Governing Authority: nonprofit organization. Tax-exempt: 501(c)(3).
Science Center.
Collections: hands-on exhibits.
Facilities: Immersion Cinema.
Activities: lectures; arts festivals; organized education programs; participatory & temporary exhibits. Annual Events: Festival of Trees; Einstein on Ice.
Hours & Admission Prices: Tues.-Thurs. 9-5, Fri. 9-8, Sat. 10-5, Sun. 1-5. Adults $9, seniors over 60 $8, children 3-15 $7; discounts to ASTC museum member; member no charge. ♿
Attendance: 100,000 (estimated)
Membership: Basic (1 or 2 people) $50; Family (up to 4) $75; Family plus (up to 6) $95; Corporate (50 single entry passes) $1,000.

HISTORY MUSEUM FOR SPRINGFIELD-GREENE COUNTY, (M), 830 Boonville, Springfield, MO 65802-3832. Tel.: 417-864-1976. Fax: 417-864-2019.
E-mail: info@springfieldhistorymuseum.org
Web Site: www.springfieldhistorymuseum.org
Founded: 1975.
Congressional District: 7
Key Personnel: Exec. Dir., John E. Sellars; Cur., Joan Hampton-Porter; Educator, Beth Jones; Museum Shop Mgr., Maxine Whittaker.
Personnel Profile: Full-Time Paid 3; Part-Time Paid 1; Part-Time Volunteers 12; Interns 2.
Governing Authority: nonprofit. Tax-exempt: 501(c)(3).
History Museum: housed in 1894 City Hall.
Collections: furnishings; tools & equipment; costumes; textiles; decorative arts; archives; photographs; dolls; toys; Civil War, World War I & World War II items; railroad & business collections; office equipment; household items.
Research Fields: local history; costumes; needlework; historic photographs.
Facilities: 6,075-vol. library pertaining to local history available to the public; 2,500 sq. ft. exhibit space; 35,000 item archival collection available to scholars. Historic gift items for sale.
Activities: guided tours; lectures; films; docent programs; loan, temporary & traveling exhibitions; organized education programs for undergraduate or graduate college students.
Publications: bimonthly newsletter, History Museum Bulletin; book, Crossroads at the Spring: A Pictorial History of Springfield, Missouri.
Hours & Admission Prices: Museum: Tues.-Sat. 10:30-4:30. Office: Mon.-Fri. 9-5. Suggested Donation: adults $3, senior citizens $2.50, children $1; discounts to groups; members no charge. Closed major holidays. ♿
Attendance: 10,000 (estimated)
Membership: Postmaster $15; Pioneer $25; Archivist $50; Historian $75; Founder $100.

SPRINGFIELD ART MUSEUM, (M), 1111 E. Brookside Dr., Springfield, MO 65807-1899. Tel.: 417-837-5700. Fax: 417-837-5704.
E-mail: ArtMuseum@ci.springfield.mo.us
Web Site: www.springfieldmogov.org/egov/art/
Founded: 1928.
Congressional District: 7
Key Personnel: Dir., Jerry A. Berger; Chm. (V), Earl Holmer; Cur. Collections, Chalen Phillips; Cur. Exhibitions, Sarah Buhr; Museum Educator, Dan Carver; Preparator, Cindy Quayle-Hauck; Librarian, Susan Potter; Exec. Sec., Tyra Knox.
Personnel Profile: Full-Time Paid 13; Part-Time Paid 1; Part-Time Volunteers 40; Interns 2.
Governing Authority: municipal. Parent Institution: City of Springfield, MO. Tax-exempt: 501(c)(3).
Art Museum.
Collections: 18th, 19th & 20th-century American and European painting, sculpture, drawing, photography, prints & decorative arts.
Research Fields: related to collections & special exhibitions.
Facilities: 6,600-vol. library on art history, architecture & contemporary art; auction & museum catalogues available for inter-library loan & use on premises; reading room; 400-seat auditorium; classrooms.
Activities: guided tours; lectures; films; concerts; dance recitals; formally organized art school offering classes for children & adults; inter-museum loan, permanent, temporary & circulating exhibitions.
Publications: bimonthly bulletin; Studio School of Art bulletins; temporary exhibition catalogues.
Hours & Admission Prices: Tues.-Wed. & Fri.-Sat. 9-5, Thurs. 9-8, Sun. 1-5. No charge; donations accepted. Closed City of Springfield Day; national holidays. ♿
Attendance: 50,000 (estimated)
Membership: Student & Senior over 55 $15; Member $25; Contributor $50; Sponsor $100; Corporate Member $250; Patron & Corporate Contributor $500; Benefactor & Corporate Sponsor $1,000; Corporate Patron $2,500; Corporate Benefactor $5,000.

Tarkio

TARKIO COLLEGE ALUMNI MUSEUM, 314 N. Main, Tarkio, MO 64491-1543. Mailing Address: P.O. Box 111, Tarkio, MO 64491-0111. Tel.: 660-736-47208.
E-mail: tcaa@asde.net
Web Site: www.tarkioalumni.org/museum.html
Alumni Museum.
Collections: photographs; memorabilia.
Hours & Admission Prices: Call for hours.

Trenton

GRUNDY COUNTY MUSEUM, 1100 Mabel St., Trenton, MO 64683. Tel.: 660-359-2411.
Web Site: www.grundycountymuseum.org
Founded: 1976.
Key Personnel: Pres., Bob Chenoweth; Recording Sec., Phil Schlarb.

Governing Authority: Tax-exempt: 501(c)(3).
History Museum: built in 1895 by William McVay.
Collections: Grundy County history, culture & artifacts; 18th century dugout canoe; weaving loom; farm machinery; stationary vertical steam engine & boiler; lanterns, signals, uniforms, keys & photos; drawings of Trenton's past & classic buildings; letter written by Felix Grundy; old maps of Missouri; early wall cabinets; Civil War souvenirs; period costumes & furniture; Rock Island caboose; windmill; restored one-room schoolhouse & desks; military uniforms, weapons, & medals; Civil War, WWI, & WWII artifacts.
Hours & Admission Prices: May-Oct. Sat.-Sun. & holidays 2-5; other times by appointment. Suggested Donation: adults $2; Life members no charge. ♿

Tuscumbia

MILLER COUNTY HISTORICAL SOCIETY & MUSEUM, 2005 Highway 52, Tuscumbia, MO 65082. Mailing Address: P.O. Box 57, Tuscumbia, MO 65082-0057. Tel.: 573-369-3500.
E-mail: millercountymuseum@hughes.net
Web Site: www.millercountymuseum.org
Founded: 1980.
Key Personnel: Pres. (V), Joe Pryor; Dir., Nancy Thompson.
Personnel Profile: Full-Time Volunteers 1; Part-Time Volunteers 30.
Governing Authority: bd. of directors.
Historical Society Museum.
Collections: local history & culture; photographs; period artifacts; memorabilia.
Research Fields: steamboat; genealogy.
Facilities: library.
Publications: quarterly newsletter.
Hours & Admission Prices: mid-May to mid-Oct. Mon., Wed. & Fri.-Sat. 10-4. No charge; donations accepted. Closed holidays. ♿
Attendance: 3,000
Membership: Individual $15; Lifetime $50.

Van Buren

OZARK NATIONAL SCENIC RIVERWAYS, 404 Watercress Dr., Van Buren, MO 63965-9100. Mailing Address: P.O. Box 490, Van Buren, MO 63965-0490. Tel.: 573-323-8822. Fax: 573-323-4140 & 8823. TDD: 573-323-4270.
Web Site: www.nps.gov/ozar
Founded: 1972.
Congressional District: 8
Key Personnel: Supt., Reed Detring.
Personnel Profile: Full-Time Paid 1; Part-Time Paid 1.
Governing Authority: federal. Midwest Region, National Park Service, Washington DC. Subsidiary Institution: Alley Mill. Tax-exempt.
Park Museum.
Collections: Ozark culture & milling equipment; herbarium; oral history tapes; photographs; insects; fish; civilian conservation Corps. Historic Building: mill.
Research Fields: CCC development of the area; current river region history & uses; civilian conservation corps programs; folk life; material culture; Ozarks; regional natural history.
Facilities: 1,000-vol. library of books pertaining to natural history, regional histories & geology; visitor center; visitor contact station. Adult & children's cultural & natural history publications for sale.
Activities: evening programs; guided walks; cave tours in summer; cultural demonstrations of milling, quilting, johnboat making; folk music presentations.
Publications: brochures, Ozark Riverways; maps; pamphlets; site bulletins.
Hours & Admission Prices: Park: daily. Visitor Contact Station & Center: call for hours & information. Demonstrations April-Oct. Sat.-Sun.; other times by appointment. No charge. ♿
Attendance: 22,000 (estimated)

Versailles

MORGAN COUNTY HISTORICAL SOCIETY, 120 N. Monroe St., Versailles, MO 65084-1288. Tel.: 573-378-5530.
Web Site: morgancohistory.org
Founded: 1965.
Personnel Profile: Part-Time Volunteers 3.
Governing Authority: bd. Tax-exempt.
County Historical Society: housed in the former Martin Hotel, built in 1877 & 1884.
Collections: local history & culture; photographs; period artifacts; military artifacts; tools; family & county histories; Martin family artifacts; hotel registers.
Hours & Admission Prices: mid-March to mid-Dec. Tues.-Thurs. 10-3; other times by appointment. Adults $3; handicapped no charge.
Attendance: 1,200
Membership: Individual $10; Business $100.

Warrensburg

ARTHUR F. MCCLURE II ARCHIVES AND UNIVERSITY MUSEUM, (M), JCK Library 1470, 601 S. Missouri, Warrensburg, MO 64093-5040. Tel.: 660-543-4649 & 4404.
E-mail: vrichardson@ucmo.edu
Formerly: Central Missouri State University Archives and Museum
Founded: 1968.
Congressional District: 114
Key Personnel: Asst. Dir., Vivian Richardson.
Personnel Profile: Full-Time Paid 1; Part-Time Paid 1.
Governing Authority: university. Parent Institution: Central Missouri State University. Tax-exempt: 170(b)(1)(A).
General Museum.
Collections: archaeology; ethnology; history; biology; Rohmiller shell collection; Haymaker Hispanic-American collection; Schmidt Meso-American; Nance Middle East collection; university history.
Research Fields: archaeology; cultural resource mgmt.; university history.
Facilities: 250-vol. gen. library available for use by permission of dir.
Activities: guided tours; temporary & traveling exhibitions; school loan service; lectures.
Publications: Museum Research Series, Archaeology.
Hours & Admission Prices: During University Sessions: Mon.-Fri. 9-12 & 1-4; other times by appointment. No charge. Closed holidays. ♿

JOHNSON COUNTY HISTORICAL SOCIETY MUSEUM, 302 N. Main St., Warrensburg, MO 64093-1554. Tel.: 660-747-6480.
E-mail: curator_jchs@embarqmail.com
Web Site: jchs64093.org
Founded: 1920.
Congressional District: 4
Key Personnel: Cur., Lisa Irle.
Personnel Profile: Part-Time Paid 1; Part-Time Volunteers 30.
Governing Authority: nonprofit. Parent Institution: Johnson County Historical Society. Tax-exempt: 501(c)(3).
Regional History Museum: 1838 federal style courthouse; Mary Miller Smiser Heritage Library; one room schoolhouse.
Collections: archives; folklore; lawn mowers; general historical & cultural items.
Research Fields: local history; 19th-century cultural artifacts.
Facilities: 500-vol. library of local and regional history books; photographs; clippings, available for use in library only; reading room. Museum-related items for sale.
Activities: guided tours; lectures; permanent & temporary exhibitions; work-day activities for college students.
Publications: The Bulletin, Johnson County Historical Society.
Hours & Admission Prices: Mon.-Fri. 1-4. Tours: Adults $3; students & members no charge. Closed New Year's; Independence Day; Thanksgiving; Christmas. ♿
Attendance: 3,000 (estimated)
Membership: Individual $15; Family $20; Corporate $25; Lifetime $125.

Waynesville

THE OLD STAGECOACH STOP, 105 Lynn St., Waynesville, MO 65583. Mailing Address: P.O. Box 585, Waynesville, MO 65583-0585. Tel.: 573-762-9683.
Web Site: www.oldstagecoachstop.org
Founded: 1983.
Key Personnel: Pres. (V), Stephanie Nutt; Museum Shop Mgr., Jan Primas.
Personnel Profile: Part-Time Volunteers 15.
Governing Authority: Parent institution: Old Stagecoach Stop Foundation. Tax exempt.
House Museum: listed on the National Register of Historic Places.
Collections: local history & culture; period rooms; 19th - 20th century furnishings collection; archeological collection; photographs.
Major Exhibits: Smithsonian Museum on Main Street Journey Stories Exhibit, fall/winter 2010 (T).
Research Fields: Pulaski County history.
Publications: annual, Old Settlers Gazette; seasonal newsletter, OSS News.
Hours & Admission Prices: April-Sept. Sat. 10-4. No charge.
Attendance: 1,652 (accurate)
Membership: Individual $10; Family $15; Patron $25; Life $250.

PULASKI COUNTY COURTHOUSE MUSEUM, 301 A Historic Rte. 66, Waynesville, MO 65583. Tel.: 573-774-5368.
E-mail: mscott1108@cablemo.net

Key Personnel: Cur., Marge Scott.
Personnel Profile: Part-Time Paid 4.
Governing Authority: Parent Institution: Pulaski County Historical Society. Tax-exempt.
History Museum.
Collections: historical information on WWI, WWII & desert storm, Korean War, Civil War, Trail of Tears; toys; antique irons; arrowhead collection; farm equipment; art gallery; domestic room; medical room; original courtroom.
Publications: historical society newsletter, three times per year.
Hours & Admission Prices: April-Oct. Sat. 10-4, other times by appointment. No charge; donations accepted.
Attendance: 1,200 (estimated)
Membership: Annual $10; Lifetime $50.

Webster Groves

MAY GALLERY AT WEBSTER UNIVERSITY, (M), 8300 Big Bend Blvd., Webster Groves, MO 63119-3114. Mailing Address: 470 E. Lockwood Ave., St. Louis, MO 63119-3194. Tel.: 314-246-7673.
E-mail: mgallery@webster.edu
Web Site: www.webster.edu/maygallery
Founded: 1988.
Congressional District: 3
Key Personnel: Dir., Bill Barrett.
Governing Authority: Parent Institution: Webster University. Tax-exempt.
Art Gallery.
Collections: photographs.
Activities: special events.
Publications: mini show catalogs.
Hours & Admission Prices: Mon.-Fri. 9-9, Sat.-Sun. 12-5. No charge. ♿
Attendance: 4,500 (estimated)

Weston

HERBERT BONNELL MUSEUM, 20755 Lamar Rd., Weston, MO 64098-9173. Mailing Address: P.O. Box 238, Weston, MO 64098-0238. Tel.: 816-386-5587.
Web Site: www.westonmo.com/history/museums_hist.html
Founded: 1987.
Key Personnel: Trust, Frank Green; Co Trust, Belinda Farris
History Museum.
Collections: personal artifacts & memorabilia; farm equipment.
Hours & Admission Prices: May-Oct. Sat.-Sun. 1-5; other times by appointment.

NATIONAL SILK ART MUSEUM, The Saint George Hotel, 500 Main St., Weston, MO 64098-1249. Tel.: 816-640-9902.
Web Site: www.nationalsilkartmuseum.com
Key Personnel: Cur., John Pottie; Asst. Cur., Adrienne Haake; Librarian, Venessa Pottie
Art Museum.
Collections: over 200 French silk tapestries by artists from the 19th & 20th century.
Hours & Admission Prices: Call for hours.

WESTON HISTORICAL MUSEUM, 601 Main St., Weston, MO 64098-1207. Mailing Address: P.O. Box 266, Weston, MO 64098-0266. Tel.: 816-386-2977.
Web Site: www.westonhistoricalmuseum.org
Founded: 1960.
Congressional District: 6
History Museum.
Collections: Native American moccasins; early physician instruments; period clothing; Civil War artifacts; newspaper office; household items; tools; glassware; china; furniture; historical documents.
Hours & Admission Prices: late March to early Dec. Tues.-Sat. 1-4, Sun. 1:30-4:30. No charge. Closed holidays.

Wildwood

RIVER HILLS VISITOR CENTER, Dr. Edmund A. Babler Memorial State Park, 800 Guy Park Dr., Wildwood, MO 63005. Mailing Address: P.O. Box 176, Jefferson City, MO 65102-0176. Tel.: 636-458-3813. Fax: 636-458-9105.
E-mail: moparks@dnr.mo.gov
Web Site: www.mostateparks.com/babler.htm
Founded: 1972.
Congressional District: 91
Key Personnel: Sr. Naturalist, Andrea Putnam; Supt., Jeff Robinson.
Personnel Profile: Full-Time Paid 13; Part-Time Paid 15; Part-Time Volunteers 12.
Governing Authority: state. Parent Institution: Div. of State Parks, MO Dept. of Natural Resources, P.O. Box 176, Jefferson City, MO 65102. Tax-exempt.
Park Museum & Visitor Center.
Collections: geology; habitats, fauna, flora; exhibits on the Missouri River Hills; slide show about the park.
Research Fields: natural history; ecology; environmental education.
Facilities: visitor orientation & observation area; auditorium; classroom; picnic facilities; hiking trails; primitive scout camping area, available by advance reservation by calling 314-458-3813; park headquarters.
Activities: nature walks; environmental education program for schools, grades K-12 & adults; swimming; camping; Jacob L. Babler Outdoor Education Center for campers with special handicaps, call 314-458-3048 for reservations; daily naturalist programs Memorial Day through Labor Day.
Hours & Admission Prices: Daily 8:30-4. No charge. ♿
Attendance: 393,000

ROCKWOODS RESERVATION, 2751 Glencoe Rd., Wildwood, MO 63038-1919. Tel.: 636-458-2236. Fax: 636-458-6726.
Founded: 1938.
Key Personnel: Naturalist, Anna Lisa Tucker; Naturalist, Shanna Raeker.
Personnel Profile: Full-Time Paid 3; Part-Time Paid 1; Part-Time Volunteers 25.
Governing Authority: state. Affiliated with the Missouri Dept. of Conservation, North Ten Mile Drive, Jefferson City, MO 65101. Tax-exempt.
Conservation Education Center.
Collections: native animals exhibit; old limestone mine; conservation exhibits.
Facilities: interpretive hiking trails; nature & conservation center; 65-seat classroom.
Activities: lectures; nature programs; films; permanent, temporary & traveling exhibitions.
Publications: monthly newsletter, Conservation Connections.
Hours & Admission Prices: Visitor Center daily 8-5; Area open daily sunrise to 1/2 hour after sunset. No charge. Closed all state holidays. ♿
Attendance: 150,000 (estimated)

Willow Springs

FIRE MUSEUM OF MISSOURI, 908 E. Business Rte. 60-63, Willow Springs, MO 65793. Tel.: 417-469-4589.
E-mail: jlows@socket.net
Web Site: www.usfirehouse.com
Fire-Fighting Museums.
Collections: 23 period fire engines; hose cart; photographs; fire extinguishers; Fire, Police, & Emergency Medical Service uniform patches; period cars from 1929 to 1972; over 3,000 soda pop bottles; soda pop & beer cans; period signs; vending machines from late 30s to early 60s.
Activities: patch trading.
Hours & Admission Prices: Adults $5, children 10-17 $3; children under 10 no charge.

MONTANA

(140 listings)

Anaconda

COPPER VILLAGE MUSEUM & ARTS CENTER OF DEER LODGE COUNTY, 401 E. Commercial, Anaconda, MT 59711-2360. Tel.: 406-563-2422 & 2220.
Founded: 1971.
Congressional District: 1
Key Personnel: Chief Exec. Dir. & Dir. Community Affairs, Carol Jette; Pres. (V), Marylynn McKenna; Co-Pres., Sally Ralston; Dir. Education, Kristie Brothers.
Personnel Profile: Full-Time Paid 2; Part-Time Paid 1.
Governing Authority: county. Subsidiary Institution: Anaconda/Deer Lodge County Historical Society. Tax-exempt: 501(c)(3); 170(b)(1)(A).
Contemporary & Historic Art Gallery and Museum.
Collections: local history artifacts; house furnishings of 1900; ghost town mining artifacts; chronological development of area Indians, trappers, ranchers, miners; industry; bottles & artifacts from Anaconda's first drug store; antique doctor's furniture & books; barbed wire collection; renovated antique Victorian dollhouse; Marcus Daley Copper Empire Display: copper smelter, smelting process, workers.
Facilities: Museum-related items for sale.
Activities: guided tours; lectures; films; gallery talks; drama; monthly art exhibits; workshops; art classes; community theatre group; special festivals;

summer recreational arts program for students ages 7-13. Museum Sponsors: annual champagne dinner & auction at Fairmont Hot Springs Resort; Art in Washoe Park in July.
Publications: quarterly newsletter.
Hours & Admission Prices: Tues.-Sat. 10-5. No charge; donations accepted. Closed legal holidays.
Membership: Senior Citizen & Student $10; Individual $15; Family $25; Sponsor $35; Patron & Associate $50; Benefactor $100 & up.

Bainville

PIONEER'S PRIDE MUSEUM, 6013 Rd. 1011, Bainville, MT 59212-9625. Tel.: 406-769-2596.
History Museum.
Collections: pioneer bedroom, kitchen & music room; old jail from Mon-Dak; 1929 fire truck.
Hours & Admission Prices: Memorial Day-Labor Day Tues.-Sun. 1:30-4:30. No charge.

Baker

O'FALLON HISTORICAL MUSEUM, 723 S. Main St., Baker, MT 59313. Mailing Address: P.O. Box 285, Baker, MT 59313-0285. Tel.: 406-778-3265. Fax: 406-778-3967.
E-mail: ofmuseum@midrivers.com
Web Site: www.falloncounty.net
Founded: 1968.
Key Personnel: C.E.O., Harold Jensen; Dir., Lora Heyen.
Personnel Profile: Full-Time Paid 2.
Governing Authority: nonprofit organization. Tax-exempt.
History Museum.
Collections: local homestead articles from 1908; Indian artifacts.
Activities: permanent exhibitions.
Publications: newsletter, O'Fallon Flashbacks; O'Fallon Flashbacks I & II - Homestead Recipe Book.
Hours & Admission Prices: June-Sept. daily 9-12 & 1-5; Oct.-May Mon.-Fri. & Sun 9-12 & 1-5. No charge; donations accepted. Closed legal holidays. ♿
Attendance: 1,300 (estimated)
Membership: Individual $15; Couples $20; Life $100.

Belt

BELT MUSEUM, 37 Castner St., Belt, MT 59412-8029. Mailing Address: P.O. Box 442, Belt, MT 59412-0442. Tel.: 406-277-3574.
History Museum: housed in the old jail building, built in 1895.
Collections: historic jail cell; coal mine; records & photographs.
Hours & Admission Prices: Memorial Day-Labor Day daily 12-4.

Big Timber

CRAZY MOUNTAIN MUSEUM, Exit 367 Cemetery Rd., Hwy. I-90, Big Timber, MT 59011. Mailing Address: P.O. Box 83, Big Timber, MT 59011-0083. Tel.: 406-932-5126.
Founded: 1990.
Key Personnel: Chm. & Pres. (V), John Esp; Dir., Fran Elgen; Treas., Joan Van Daveer; Cur., Rita Esp; Cur., Elli Hawks; Sec., Judy Cosgriff.
Personnel Profile: Part-Time Paid 4; Part-Time Volunteers 70.
Governing Authority: private; nonprofit organization. Tax-exempt: 501(c)(3).
History Museum.
Collections: history of Sweet Grass County & surrounding area.
Research Fields: people & subjects of county.
Facilities: library; 4,000 sq. ft. exhibit space. Museum-related items for sale.
Activities: docent program; guided tours; hobby workshops; temporary exhibitions. Annual Events: Memorial Day Festival. Permanent Exhibits: 1 Room School; 1907 Model Big Timber; Norwegian Stabbur.
Publications: newsletter, The New Breeze.
Hours & Admission Prices: Memorial Day to Sept. Mon.-Sat. 10-4:30, Sun. 1-4:30. No charge; donations accepted. ♿
Attendance: 5,000 (estimated)
Membership: General $10; Donor $25; Founder $100.

Billings

BILLINGS CURATION CENTER, (M), 5001 Southgate Dr., Billings, MT 59101-4669. Tel.: 406-896-5213. Fax: 406-896-5317.
Web Site: www.mt.blm.gov/BCC
Founded: 1994.
Key Personnel: BLM State Archaeologist, Gary Smith; Cur., David K. Wade.
Personnel Profile: Full-Time Paid 2; Part-Time Volunteers 4; Interns 4.
Governing Authority: Parent Institution: Bureau of Land Mgmt. Subsidiary Institution: Montana State Office.
Federal Agency Repository & Archaeology Site.
Collections: federal land artifacts; maps; fossils & artifacts; homesteading; mining; ghost towns; early northwest exploration.
Research Fields: history and pre-history of the Northern Plains.
Facilities: library; lab; archives.
Hours & Admission Prices: Mon.-Fri. 9-4:30. No charge. ♿

MOSS MANSION HISTORIC HOUSE MUSEUM, 914 Division St., Billings, MT 59101-1921. Tel.: 406-256-5100. Fax: 406-252-0091.
E-mail: mossmansion@mossmansion.com
Web Site: www.mossmansion.com
Founded: 1986.
Congressional District: 1
Key Personnel: House & Collections Dir., Rebecca Peterson; Pres., Ashley Borleson; 1st Vice Pres., Mike Mathew; Sec., Katherine Bermes; Treas., Steve Cranston; Volunteer & Tour Coord., Joedi Johnson; Bd. Member, Lou Ponich; Education, Mandie Asay; Public Rels., Melanie Schwarz; Registrar, Karen Wegner; Museum Shop Mgr., Denise Larson.
Personnel Profile: Full-Time Paid 2; Part-Time Paid 3; Part-Time Volunteers 200; Interns 2.
Governing Authority: nonprofit organization. Parent Institution: Billings Preservation Society, Inc. Tax-exempt: 501(c)(3).
Historic House Museum: housed in the Moss Mansion built in 1901-1903.
Collections: period furnishings; clothing & personal effects; city directories 1949-1998.
Research Fields: family history.
Facilities: classroom. Museum-related items for sale.
Activities: guided tours; hobby workshops. Museum Sponsors: Country Fair; Murder Mysteries; Christmas at The Moss.
Publications: quarterly newsletter, Billings Preservation Society Newsletter; quarterly volunteer newsletter, MMVIP Newsletter.
Hours & Admission Prices: Summer: Mon.-Sat. 9-5, Sun. 1-4; Winter, Fall & Spring: daily 1-4. Adults $7, senior citizens & students $5, children $3; members no charge. Closed New Year's Day; Thanksgiving; Christmas. ♿
Attendance: 18,535 (accurate)
Membership: Student, Teacher & Senior 62 and over $30; Individual $40; Family $60; Preservationist $125; Patron $250; Benefactor $500; Founder $1,000.

MUSEUM OF WOMEN'S HISTORY, 2824 3rd Ave. N., Billings, MT 59101-1932. Mailing Address: 2822 3rd Ave. N., B-3, Billings, MT 59101-1934. Tel.: 406-248-2015.
E-mail: founder45@aol.com
Founded: 1995.
Key Personnel: Dir. & Devel., Dorothy McLaughlin; Cur. & Archivist, George F. Sherman.
Personnel Profile: Full-Time Volunteers 2; Part-Time Volunteers 10.
Governing Authority: private; nonprofit organization. Tax-exempt: 501(c)(3).
History Museum.
Collections: women's history.
Research Fields: women in WWII.
Facilities: library; 1,500 sq. ft. exhibit space.
Activities: guided tours; lectures; broadcast programs.
Publications: quarterly newsletter, The Mirror.
Hours & Admission Prices: Mon.-Tues. & Thurs. 1-4; other times by appointment. No charge; donations accepted. Closed legal holidays.
Attendance: 1,500 (estimated)
Membership: Individual $40; Sustaining $300; Business $500.

* **WESTERN HERITAGE CENTER, (M),** 2822 Montana Ave., Billings, MT 59101-2305. Tel.: 406-256-6809. Fax: 406-256-6850.
E-mail: julie@ywhc.org
Web Site: www.ywhc.org
Founded: 1971.
Congressional District: 2
Key Personnel: Exec. Dir., Julie Dial; Community Historian, Kevin Kooistra-Manning; Fundraising & Mktg., Lisa Olinsted; Bldg. Supt., Albert Gehring.
Personnel Profile: Full-Time Paid 4; Part-Time Paid 2; Part-Time Volunteers 20.
Governing Authority: county. Tax-exempt: 501(c)(3).
Regional History Museum: housed in 1901 Parmly Billings Memorial Library Building.
Collections: material culture of the Yellowstone Valley; photographs & manuscripts.
Research Fields: history & contemporary characteristics of settlers in Eastern Montana & the Yellowstone River Valley.
Facilities: theater. Museum-related items for sale.

Activities: lectures; films; workshops; organized education programs for children & adults; docent program; changing exhibitions; oral history program; rental facilities; teachers professional development.
Publications: quarterly newsletter, Reflections; books, Images of Billings: A Photographic History, Pieces & Places of Billings: Local Monuments & Markers, Stories from An Open Country: Essays about The Yellowstone River Valley.
Hours & Admission Prices: Tues.-Sat. 10-5. Adults $5, seniors $3, children $1; members no charge. Closed major holidays. ♿
Attendance: 17,800 (estimated)
Membership: Individual $35; Family $75; Homesteader $125; Rancher $250; Partner $500; Heritage $1,000; Legacy $2,000.

YELLOWSTONE ART MUSEUM, 401 N. 27th St., Billings, MT 59101-1290. Tel.: 406-256-6804. Fax: 406-256-6817.
E-mail: artinfo@artmuseum.org
Web Site: yellowstone.artmuseum.org
Founded: 1964.
Congressional District: 2
Key Personnel: Exec. Dir., Robyn G. Peterson; Pres., Val Jeffries; Cur., Robert C. Manchester; Registrar, Nancy Clark; Dir. Devel., Kim Sapone; Dir. Education, Linda Ewert; Admin. & Finance Dir., Lisa Berke.
Personnel Profile: Full-Time Paid 13; Part-Time Paid 11; Part-Time Volunteers 300; Interns 2.
Governing Authority: private; nonprofit organization. Tax-exempt: 501(c)(3).
Regional Art Museum
Collections: contemporary regional collection: paintings; sculpture; ceramics; photography; L.A. Huffman photographs; Poindexter Collection of New York abstract expressionists; Snook collections of Will James; western historic art.
Major Exhibits: Post Secret (T), 11/09-1/10; Speaking Volumes: Transforming Hate (T), 3/10-6/10; Polly Apfelbaum: Mini Hollywood (T), 4/10-9/10; John Buck: Iconography (T), 7/10-10/10.
Research Fields: contemporary art of the northern Rockies.
Facilities: 300-vol. library of visual arts available by appointment; reading room; 100-seat auditorium; education studio. Museum-related items for sale.
Activities: guided tours; lectures; films; gallery talks; concerts; arts festivals; formally organized education programs for children & adults; docent program or council; inter-museum loan, temporary & traveling exhibitions; outreach education.
Publications: newsletter; exhibition catalogs & brochures.
Hours & Admission Prices: Memorial Day-Labor Day Mon.-Wed. & Fri.-Sat. 10-5, Thurs. 10-8, Sun. 12-5. Sept.-May Tues.-Wed. & Fri.-Sat. 10-5, Thurs. 10-8, Sun. 12-5. Adults $5; discounts to AAM, ICOM & AAA members; museum members no charge. Closed major holidays. ♿
Attendance: 42,000 (estimated)
Membership: Student & Senior Citizen $30; Individual $40; Family & VIP Individual $65; VIP Family $90; Aficionado $125; Education Circle $300; Collection Circle $500; Exhibition Circle $1,000; Patron Circle $2,500.

YELLOWSTONE COUNTY MUSEUM, 1950 Airport Terminal Circle, Billings, MT 59105-1988. Tel.: 406-256-6811. Fax: 406-254-6031.
E-mail: ycm@tctwest.net
Web Site: yellowstonecountymuseum.org
Formerly: Peter Yegen Jr. Yellowstone County Museum
Founded: 1956.
Congressional District: 2
Key Personnel: Chm. (V), Charlie Yegen; Exec. Dir., Suzanne Warner; Sec., Brenna Yegen; Treas., Bob Everson.
Personnel Profile: Full-Time Paid 1; Part-Time Paid 1; Part-Time Volunteers 2.
Governing Authority: Yellowstone County. Tax-exempt.
Montana & Western History Museum: portion of which is housed in an 1890s log structure belonging to Montana pioneer Paul McCormick.
Collections: Native American collection representing 27 tribes-includes bead-work, quillwork, clothing, toys, games, utilitarian items; artifacts relating to the ranching industry-both sheep & cattle; cowboy memorabilia; natural history exhibits; art work by world renown western artists, J.K. Ralston & LeRoy Greene; transportation artifacts, railroad, wagons; military artifacts, weaponry, uniforms, personal artifacts dating from the War of 1812 to the Korean War; extensive textiles collection, afghans, quilts, handiwork, clothing 1840s-1950s; women's personal items; everyday household goods; various occupational artifacts, medical & dental tools; prehistoric tools; art gallery.
Research Fields: photo archives; internships; mentoring programs.
Facilities: 6,000 sq. ft. exhibit space.
Activities: guided tours; educational programs; monthly programs & lectures. Foundation Sponsors: Hot Irons-Barbeque & Barndance, annual fundraiser in July.
Publications: quarterly newsletter, Cabin Chat.
Hours & Admission Prices: Mon.-Fri. 10:30-5, Sat. 10:30-3. Suggested Donation $1. Closed New Year's Day; Christmas.
Attendance: 20,119 (accurate)
Membership: Senior $15; Individual $20; Family $25; Corporate $100; Lifetime $1,000.

ZOO MONTANA, 2100 S. Shiloh Rd., Billings, MT 59106-3908. Tel.: 406-652-8100. Fax: 406-652-9281.
E-mail: zoomt@zoomontana.org
Founded: 1993.
Key Personnel: Dir., Jackie Worstell; Chm. (V) & Public Rels., Sean O'Donnell; Education & Museum Shop Mgr., Lindi O'Brien; Cur., Kim Frank.
Personnel Profile: Full-Time Paid 11; Part-Time Paid 4; Part-Time Volunteers 20; Interns 5.
Governing Authority: private; nonprofit organization. Tax-exempt: 501(c)(3).
Zoo.
Collections: native & exotic animals from the northern regions of the world; medicinal, exotic & native Montana plants.
Research Fields: restoration of wetlands and PZP vaccine.
Facilities: classroom; nature center; Botanical Garden; zoological park; nature trails; Science and Conservation Center. Museum-related items for sale.
Activities: concerts; docent program; formal education programs for children; children's interactive barn & pizza garden; internships; guided tours; lectures; participatory & traveling exhibitions. Annual Events: Zooper Bowl in January; Woo at the Zoo in February; Highland Games in June; Margazooville in August; Zoofari in September; Pumpkin Panda-monium & Boo At The Zoo in October; Fantasy of Lights in December.
Publications: quarterly newsletter, Zoo Montana.
Hours & Admission Prices: March to mid-May & Sept. to early Oct. daily 10-4; mid-May to Aug. daily 10-5; mid-Oct. to late Oct. Wed.-Sun. 10-5; Nov.-March Sat.-Sun. 10-4. Adults $6, senior citizens $4, children $3; discounts to AZA members; members no charge. Closed New Year's; Thanksgiving; Christmas. ♿
Attendance: 77,000 (estimated)
Membership: Individual $40; Household & Grandparent $50; Supporting $100; Contributing $250.

Bozeman

AMERICAN COMPUTER MUSEUM, 2304 N. 7th Ave., Ste. B, Bozeman, MT 59715-2571. Mailing Address: P.O. Box 7190, Bozeman, MT 59771-7190. Tel.: 406-582-1288. Fax: 406-587-9620.
E-mail: director@compustory.com
Web Site: www.compustory.com
Computer Museum.
Collections: history of the information age; period office equipment including typewriters, Arithmometers, adding machines, furniture, electric fans; mainframe computers.
Facilities: theater.
Activities: tours; video presentation.
Hours & Admission Prices: June-Aug. Thurs. 10-7, Fri.-Wed. 10-4; Sept.-May Tues.-Sat. 11-4. Adults $5, children 6-12 $3; discounts to groups; children under 6 no charge. Closed New Year's Day; Thanksgiving; Christmas.

CHILDREN'S MUSEUM OF BOZEMAN, 202 S. Willson Ave., Bozeman, MT 59715-4631. Tel.: 406-522-9087.
E-mail: info@cmbozeman.org
Web Site: www.cmbozeman.org
Founded: 2001.
Key Personnel: Exec. Dir., Susan Denson-Guy; Pres. (V), Tim Dwyer.
Personnel Profile: Full-Time Paid 4; Part-Time Paid 6; Part-Time Volunteers 100; Interns 1.
Children's Museum.
Collections: hands-on exhibits.
Major Exhibits: Great Places 2 See Around Bozeman, 11/09-6/10.
Activities: special events; educational programs; parties.
Hours & Admission Prices: June-Aug. Mon.-Thurs. & Sat. 10-5, Fri. 10-8; Sept.-May Mon.-Thurs. & Sat. 10-5, Fri. 10-8, Sun. 12-5; groups of 12 or more by appointment. Admission $5; discounts to group; Fri. 5-8pm no charge.
Attendance: 21,187 (accurate)
Membership: Family $60; Family Plus $80; ACM $110.

GALLATIN HISTORICAL SOCIETY, (M), 317 W. Main St., Bozeman, MT 59715-4576. Tel.: 406-522-8122. Fax: 406-522-0367.
Web Site: www.pioneermuseum.org
Key Personnel: Exec. Dir., John C. Russell; Asst. Dir., Ann Butterfield.
Personnel Profile: Full-Time Paid 2; Part-Time Paid 1; Part-Time Volunteers 50.

Historical Society Museum.
Collections: Gallatin Valley history & culture; Native American artifacts; farm & ranch tools; period automobiles; household items.
Activities: educational programs.
Publications: quarterly, Pioneer Museum.
Hours & Admission Prices: Memorial Day to Labor Day Mon.-Sat. 10-5; Winter: Tues.-Sat. 11-4. Adults $5; school groups, children 12 & under and members no charge. ♿
Membership: $40 & up.

HELEN E. COPELAND GALLERY, MSU School of Art, 242 Haynes Hall, Bozeman, MT 59717-3700. Tel.: 406-994-2562. Fax: 406-994-3680.
E-mail: ewanderson@montana.edu
Web Site: www.montana.edu/art
Founded: 1974.
Key Personnel: Dir., Erin W. Anderson.
Governing Authority: university. Parent Institution: Montana State University. Tax-exempt.
Art Gallery.
Collections: print collections; international craft items; ceramics.
Activities: lectures; gallery talks; arts festivals; symposiums visiting artists; loan, temporary & traveling exhibitions.
Publications: brochures; catalogues.
Hours & Admission Prices: Mon.-Fri. 8-5. No charge. Closed state & federal holidays. ♿
Attendance: 5,000

* **MUSEUM OF THE ROCKIES, (M),** 600 W. Kagy Blvd., Bozeman, MT 59717-2730. Tel.: 406-994-6342. Fax: 406-994-2682.
E-mail: susan@montana.edu
Web Site: museumoftherockies.org
Founded: 1956.
Congressional District: 1
Key Personnel: Dean & Dir., Sheldon McKamey; Pres. Bd., Joanne Pieper; Cur. Paleontology, John R. Horner; Asst. Dir. & Assoc. Cur. Art & Photography, Steven B. Jackson; Cur. Textiles, Margaret M. Woods; Cur. History, Michael Fox; Administrative Dir. Exhibits, Patrick Leiggi; Mgr. Planetarium, David Binnewies; Registrar, Pat Roath; Dir. Finance, Jeff Krauss; Dir. Public Rels. & Public Outreach, Jamie Cornish; Museum Shop Mgr., Christine Fuller.
Personnel Profile: Full-Time Paid 26; Part-Time Paid 26; Part-Time Volunteers 201.
Governing Authority: university. Parent Institution: Montana State University-Bozeman. Tax-exempt: 501(c)(3).
General Regional Museum.
Collections: geology; astronomy; paleontology; history; Western art; living history; textiles; archaeology.
Research Fields: paleontology.
Facilities: photo archives; planetarium; auditorium; classrooms; laboratories; nature area; 22-acre site owned by university. Museum-related items for sale.
Activities: guided tours; classes; field schools; field trips; lectures. Museum Sponsors: Gallery Openings.
Publications: Maia-A Dinosaur Grows Up; occasional paper #1, Lifeways of Intermountain & Plains Montana Indians; occasional paper #2, Cranial Morphology of Prosaurolophus; quarterly members newsletter, MOR News.
Hours & Admission Prices: Memorial Day-Labor Day daily 8-8; Sept.-May Mon.-Sat. 9-5, Sun. 12:30-5. Museum: adults $10, MSU student $7; discounts to AAA members; children 4 & under, members & ASTC members no charge. Laser Shows $5. Planetarium $3; children 4 & under and ASTC members no charge. Closed New Year's Day; Thanksgiving; Christmas. ♿
Attendance: 143,318 (accurate)
Membership: Students $25; Individual $30; Family & Grand Family $75; Contributing $150; Sustaining $250; Director's Circle $500; Director's Guild $1,000.

Broadus

POWDER RIVER HISTORICAL MUSEUM AND MAC'S MUSEUM, 102 W. Wilson, Broadus, MT 59317. Mailing Address: P.O. Box 573, Broadus, MT 59317-0573. Tel.: 406-436-2977.
Founded: 1988.
Governing Authority: Tax-exempt.
Local History Museum.
Collections: Powder River: photographs; books; Native American artifacts; guns & ammunition; period automobiles; tractors & farm implements; military. Mac's Museum: arrowheads; birds' eggs; butterflies; geologic specimens; sea shells; vintage clothing.
Hours & Admission Prices: Memorial Day to Sept. Mon.-Fri. 9-5, Sat. 11-4; other times by appointment. No charge; donations accepted. ♿
Membership: Annual $5; Lifetime $50.

Browning

MUSEUM OF THE PLAINS INDIAN, Junction of Hwy. 2 & 89 W., Browning, MT 59417. Mailing Address: P.O. Box 410, Browning, MT 59417-0410. Tel.: 406-338-2230. Fax: 406-338-7404.
E-mail: mpi@3rivers.net
Web Site: www.iacb.doi.gov
Founded: 1941.
Congressional District: 14
Key Personnel: Cur., David Dragonfly; Museum Shop Mgr., Darnell Rides at the Door.
Personnel Profile: Full-Time Paid 2.
Governing Authority: federal. Administered & operated by Indian Arts & Crafts Board, U.S. Dept. of Interior, Room 4004, Washington, DC 20240. Tax-exempt.
Indian Art Museum.
Collections: historic, contemporary, social & ceremonial arts of the Northern Plains Indians; traditional costumes; painted tepees; murals; monument dedicated to a 1930 sign language conference.
Research Fields: historic & contemporary Native American arts of the United States.
Activities: guided tours by appointment; lectures; gallery talks; permanent, temporary & changing exhibitions.
Publications: exhibition brochures.
Hours & Admission Prices: June-Sept. daily 9-4:45; Oct.-May Mon.-Fri. 10-4:30. Adults $4, seniors $3, children $1; discounts to groups of 10 or more; children under 6 no charge. Closed New Year's Day; Thanksgiving; Christmas.
Attendance: 25,000 (estimated)

Butte

BUTTE-SILVER BOW ARTS CHATEAU, 321 W. Broadway, Butte, MT 59701-9126. Tel.: 406-723-7600.
Web Site: www.artschateau.org
Founded: 1977.
Key Personnel: C.E.O., Glenn Bodish; Pres., Erik Nelson; Museum Shop Mgr., Jana Faught.
Personnel Profile: Full-Time Paid 1; Part-Time Paid 5; Part-Time Volunteers 5.
Governing Authority: nonprofit organization. Parent Institution: Butte-Silver Bow Arts Foundation. Subsidiary Institution: Arts Chateau. Tax-exempt: 501(c)(3).
Period Museum & Arts Center: housed in 1898 The Charles Clark Mansion.
Collections: contemporary regional art; Western art by Elizabeth Lochrie; dolls; vintage clothing; over 600 bells; period furniture collection.
Research Fields: local folklore.
Facilities: period museum; multi-purpose room. Museum-related items & original works by Montana artists for sale.
Activities: gallery talks; guided tours; lectures; slide program; workshops; art events; permanent & temporary art exhibits; history course; performing arts events. Museum Sponsors: Textile medium, Contemporary Quilt Exhibition & Competition; Satellite for Very Special Arts, Montana.
Publications: cookbook, Butte's Heritage Cookbook (ninth printing); newsletter; schedule of events.
Hours & Admission Prices: June-Aug. Tues.-Sun. 12-5; Sept.-May Tues.-Sat. 11-4, Sun. 12-5. Family $10, adults $3, AAA, & CAA members $2.50, senior citizens 50 & up $2, children 16 & under $1; discounts to AAM members & groups of 10 or more; members no charge. Closed major holidays.
Attendance: 4,900 (accurate)
Membership: Seniors & Students $10; Individual $15; Family $25; Contributing $50; Sustaining $100; Patron $500; Benefactor $1,000. Business: Contributing $100; Sustaining $500; Patron $750; Benefactor $1,000.

COPPER KING MANSION, 219 W. Granite St., Butte, MT 59701-9235. Tel.: 406-782-7580.
E-mail: esigl@in-tch.com
Web Site: www.thecopperkingmansion.com
Founded: 1966.
Congressional District: 2
Key Personnel: Gen. Mgr., John Thompson.
Personnel Profile: Full-Time Paid 1; Full-Time Volunteers 1; Part-Time Paid 10; Part-Time Volunteers 1.
Governing Authority: partnership.
Historic House: 1884-1888, mansion built by William Andrews Clark including period furnishings.
Collections: Victorian furniture; crystal; cut glass; silver; porcelains; art.

Research Fields: local history.
Facilities: library of old literature, novels, encyclopedias available on premises only; catered parties, dinners & weddings. Arts & craft items for sale. Bed & Breakfast year round.
Activities: guided tours; lectures; gallery talks.
Hours & Admission Prices: May-Sept. daily 9-4; Oct.-April by appointment. Adults $7, students 6-18 $3.50; children under 6 no charge.
Attendance: 10,000 (estimated)

MAI WAH SOCIETY, 17 W. Mercury St., Butte, MT 59701-2019. Mailing Address: P.O. Box 404, Butte, MT 59703-0404. Tel.: 406-723-3231.
E-mail: info@maiwah.org
Web Site: www.maiwah.org
Governing Authority: nonprofit organization.
Asian Heritage Museum.
Collections: history & culture of Asian people in the Rocky Mountain West; photographs.
Facilities: Museum-related items for sale.
Activities: lectures; workshops; movies. Museum Sponsors: Chinese New Year Parade in February.
Hours & Admission Prices: late May to Sept. Tues.-Sat. 11-5.

MINERAL MUSEUM, Montana Tech. of the University of Montana, 1300 W. Park St., Butte, MT 59701-8932. Tel.: 406-496-4414 & 4152. Fax: 406-496-4451.
E-mail: dberg@mtech.edu
Web Site: www.mbmg.mtech.edu/museum.htm
Founded: 1900.
Congressional District: 1
Key Personnel: Cur., Dr. Richard B. Berg; Program Dir., Ginette Abdo.
Personnel Profile: Part-Time Paid 3.
Governing Authority: state. Parent Institution: Montana Tech. of the University of Montana. Subsidiary Institution: Montana Bureau of Mines & Geology. Tax-exempt: 501(c)(3).
Mineralogy Museum.
Collections: 1,300 mineral specimens from around the world on display; fossils; relief map of Montana.
Research Fields: mineralogy.
Facilities: display & storage areas. Museum-related items for sale.
Activities: guided tours; workshops.
Hours & Admission Prices: June 15-Sept. 15 daily 9-5; Winter: Mon.-Fri. 9-4. No charge; donations accepted. ♿
Attendance: 11,000 (estimated)

PICCADILLY TRANSPORTATION MEMORABILIA MUSEUM, 20 W. Broadway, Butte, MT 59701-9222. Tel.: 406-723-3034. Fax: 406-723-7425.
E-mail: info@piccadillymuseum.com
Web Site: www.piccadillymuseum.com
Transportation & Advertising Art Museum.
Collections: transportation memorabilia from over 100 countries including highway & subway markers, license plates, vintage cars, advertising art.
Activities: special events.
Hours & Admission Prices: Memorial Day to Oct. 1 Mon.-Sat. 10-5; Fall & Winter: by appointment only. No charge; donations accepted.

WORLD MUSEUM OF MINING, 155 Museum Way, Butte, MT 59703-0033. Mailing Address: P.O. Box 33, Butte, MT 59703-0033. Tel.: 406-723-7211. Fax: 406-723-7211(call first).
E-mail: info@miningmuseum.org
Web Site: www.miningmuseum.org
Founded: 1963.
Congressional District: 1
Key Personnel: Dir., Tina Green; Pres. (V), Jerry Jordan; Sec., Judy Kruzich.
Personnel Profile: Full-Time Paid 2; Part-Time Paid 9; Part-Time Volunteers 25.
Governing Authority: nonprofit corporation. Tax-exempt: 501(c)(3).
Mining Museum: located on the site of the Orphan Girl Mine, an early day zinc & silver mine, once owned by Butte Copper King Marcus Daly.
Collections: mining & ethic history of Butte and the surrounding region.
Research Fields: mining history, social & cultural history of Butte.
Facilities: 33 acres of grounds; 50 buildings with exhibits; picnic area; extensive photo archives available for research & purchase. Museum-related items for sale.
Activities: gold panning; scavenger hunt; underground mine tour.
Publications: book, The Orphan Girl Mine; Remembering Butte, Montana's Richest City (photobook about Butte's history).
Hours & Admission Prices: April-Oct. daily 9-5:30, last ticket sold at 4:30, grounds close at 5:30. Adults 19 & over $7, seniors $ 6, children 13-18 $5, children 5-12 $2; children 4 & younger no charge, school tours (advanced notice required) adults $3, students $2. Underground Tours: Adults $10, students & seniors $8, members $7, children $5. Tour guides available.
Attendance: 25,000 (accurate)
Membership: Golden Age $15; Individual $25; Family $40; Nipper $60. Corporate: Copper $150-$499; Silver $500-$999; Gold $1,000-$4,999; Platinum $5,000-$9,999; Palladium $10,000.

Bynum

TWO MEDICINE DINOSAUR CENTER, 120 2nd Ave. S., Bynum, MT 59419. Mailing Address: P.O. Box 786, Bynum, MT 59419-0786. Tel.: 406-469-2211; 800-238-6873.
E-mail: dinoinfo@tmdinosaur.org
Web Site: www.tmdinosaur.org
Research and Education Institution.
Collections: dinosaur exhibits; fossils.
Hours & Admission Prices: Call for hours.

Charlo

NINEPIPES MUSEUM OF EARLY MONTANA, 69316 Hwy. 93, Charlo, MT 59824-9789. Tel.: 406-644-3435. Fax: 406-644-2928.
Founded: 1997.
Key Personnel: Dir., Vern Cheff, Jr.; Chm. & Pres. (V), Rod Wamsley; Admin., Laurel Cheff.
Personnel Profile: Full-Time Volunteers 4; Part-Time Paid 1; Part-Time Volunteers 16.
Governing Authority: bd. of directors. Tax-exempt.
History Museum: named after Chief Joseph Ninepipes, a Bitterroot Salish Chief.
Collections: Montana history; Native American artifacts; photographs; paintings; documents; mounted wildlife; Indian camp replica.
Publications: quarterly newsletter.
Hours & Admission Prices: May-Oct. 29 daily 9:30-5:30. Adults $4, students $3, children 6-12 $2; discounts to groups of 20 or more; members & children under 6 no charge. Closed Thanksgiving; Christmas. ♿
Attendance: 5,500 (estimated)
Membership: Student $15; Individual $20; Family $35; Sustaining $100; Donor $500; Lifetime $1,000.

Chester

LIBERTY COUNTY MUSEUM, 230 Second St. E., Chester, MT 59522. Mailing Address: P.O. Box 417, Chester, MT 59522-0417. Tel.: 406-759-5256.
Founded: 1969.
Key Personnel: Pres. (V), Betty L. Marshall.
Personnel Profile: Part-Time Paid 4; Part-Time Volunteers 7.
Governing Authority: nonprofit. Tax-exempt.
General Museum.
Collections: agriculture; archaeology; costumes; Indian artifacts; outdoor museum; one-room schoolhouse; old machinery; military & medical display; mock-trading company store; Great Northern R.R. display; working Blacksmith Shop.
Publications: book, Our Heritage.
Hours & Admission Prices: May to Labor Day daily 1-5 & 7-9. No charge; donations accepted.
Attendance: 500 (estimated)

LIBERTY VILLAGE ARTS CENTER & GALLERY, 410 W. Main St., Chester, MT 59522-0269. Mailing Address: P.O. Box 269, Chester, MT 59522-0269. Tel.: 406-759-5652. Fax: 406-759-5652.
E-mail: lvac@mtintouch.net
Web Site: libertyvillagearts.org
Founded: 1976.
Congressional District: 2
Key Personnel: Dir., Mary Ann Zorn; Pres. Bd. (V), Ginger Green; Museum Shop Mgr., Marla McKinley Forbes.
Personnel Profile: Part-Time Paid 2; Part-Time Volunteers 11; Interns 1.
Governing Authority: state; nonprofit. Tax-exempt: 501(c)(3); 170(b)(1)(A).
Folk Arts Center: housed in 1910 church building.
Collections: multi-media; sculpture & paintings.
Facilities: classrooms. Paintings, prints, pottery & jewelry for sale.
Activities: lectures; films; gallery talks; arts festivals; rental gallery; temporary & traveling exhibitions.
Hours & Admission Prices: mid-Jan. to Dec. Tues.-Wed. & Fri. 12:30-4:30, Thurs. 12:30-8. No charge; donations accepted. Closed New Year's Day; Easter; Independence Day; Thanksgiving; Christmas. ♿
Attendance: 3,500 (estimated)
Membership: Individual $25; Family $30; Friend of the Arts $50; Patron of the Arts $100; Benefactor $250 & up.

Chinook

BLAINE COUNTY MUSEUM, 501 Indiana, Chinook, MT 59523. Mailing Address: P.O. Box 927, Chinook, MT 59523-0927. Tel.: 406-357-2590. Fax: 406-357-2199.
E-mail: blmuseum@mtintouch.net
Web Site: www.chinookmontana.com
Founded: 1977.
Congressional District: 2
Key Personnel: C.E.O., Stuart C. MacKenzie; Cur., Jude Sheppard.
Personnel Profile: Full-Time Paid 1; Part-Time Paid 1; Part-Time Volunteers 3.
Governing Authority: county. Tax-exempt.
History Museum: housed in 1915 former recreation center.
Collections: local history; multi-media presentation on the Nez Perce Indians & the Battle of the Bear's Paw; paleontology; old west artifacts; Indian culture; one room school; doctor's & dentist's office; Tar paper Homestead Shack; photographs.
Activities: guided tours.
Hours & Admission Prices: May & Sept. Mon.-Fri. 8-5; June-Aug. Mon.-Sat. 8-5, Sun. 12-5; Oct.-April Mon.-Fri. 1-5. No charge; donations accepted. ♿
Attendance: 3,640 (accurate)

Choteau

OLD TRAIL MUSEUM, 823 N. Main St., Choteau, MT 59422-9272. Tel.: 406-466-5332.
E-mail: otm@3rivers.net
Web Site: theoldtrailmuseum.org
Founded: 1985.
Congressional District: 11
Key Personnel: Chm. & Pres. (V), Gina Dalrymple; Treas., Mary Christiaens; Operations, Dave Wedum; Museum Shop Mgr., Julie Dalrymple.
Personnel Profile: Full-Time Paid 1; Part-Time Paid 3; Part-Time Volunteers 2.
Governing Authority: individual operation. Parent Institution: Chicago Field Museum. Subsidiary Institution: Project Exploration. Tax-exempt.
Village Museum: housed in 1920 six building cleaning plant.
Collections: period artifacts; Indian artifacts; fossils; dinosaur exhibit; Metis cabin exhibit; schoolhouse; grizzly cabin; paleontology antechamber. Historic Structures: two 1890 log cabins; stagecoach stop.
Research Fields: fossils; Native American heritage.
Facilities: Victorian ice-cream parlor; art studio.
Activities: guided & self-guided tours; study clubs for children; loan, permanent & temporary exhibitions.
Publications: brochures; pamphlets; newsletter.
Hours & Admission Prices: Memorial Day to Labor Day daily 9-5. Adults $4, children over 6 $2; discount to groups; members no charge. ♿
Attendance: 6,000 (estimated)
Membership: Senior Citizen $15; Individual $20; Family $30; Business $50.

Circle

MCCONE COUNTY MUSEUM, 1507 Ave. B, Circle, MT 59215-0127. Mailing Address: P.O. Box 127, Circle, MT 59215-0127. Tel.: 406-485-2414.
Founded: 1953.
Congressional District: 2
Key Personnel: Pres. & Cur., Wendell Pawlowski.
Personnel Profile: Full-Time Paid 1.
Governing Authority: nonprofit organization. Tax-exempt: 501(c)(3).
History Museum.
Collections: history; county newspapers, 1914-present; animal husbandry; geology; Indians; wildlife exhibit; dinosaurs.
Research Fields: local history.
Facilities: reading room.
Activities: permanent exhibitions. Museum Sponsors: Open House.
Publications: books, Pioneers & Progress on the Prairie; The Depression Years: 1930-1939; Circle-Then & Now.
Hours & Admission Prices: May-Oct. 1 Mon.-Fri. 10-5, Sat.-Sun. call for hours. Adults $5. ♿
Membership: Adults $5.

Clancy

JEFFERSON COUNTY MUSEUM, 9 N. Main, Clancy, MT 59634-9547. Mailing Address: P.O. Box 50, Clancy, MT 59634-0050. Tel.: 406-933-5463. Fax: 406-933-5439.
History Museum: housed in the 1898 Clancy Schoolhouse.
Collections: items pertaining to Jefferson County; exhibits on mining, ranching & railroading.
Hours & Admission Prices: Call for hours.

Colstrip

SCHOOLHOUSE HISTORY & ART CENTER, 400 Woodrose St., Colstrip, MT 59323. Mailing Address: P.O. Box 430, Colstrip, MT 59323-0430. Tel.: 406-748-4822.
E-mail: shac@tctwest.net
Web Site: www.schoolhouseartcenter.com
Key Personnel: Exec. Dir., Lu Shomate
History & Art Center: housed in former schoolhouse built in 1924.
Collections: period artifacts; furnishings; photographs.
Facilities: Museum-related items for sale.
Activities: children's activities; educational programs; art classes.
Hours & Admission Prices: Mon.-Fri. 11-5. No charge; donations accepted. ♿

Conrad

CONRAD TRANSPORTATION AND HISTORICAL MUSEUM, 402 S. Virginia St., Conrad, MT 59425. Mailing Address: P.O. Box 675, Conrad, MT 59425-2211. Tel.: 406-278-0178.
E-mail: hbolson@3rivers.net
Founded: 1963.
Key Personnel: Dir. & Pres. (V), Harold Olson; Museum Shop Mgr., Charlotte Hovde.
Personnel Profile: Part-Time Paid 1; Part-Time Volunteers 30.
Governing Authority: Parent Institution: Pondera History Assoc. Tax-exempt.
Transportation & Historical Museum.
Collections: local history & culture; early cash register; period autos & steering wheels; license plates; petroleum products; gas pumps; oil dispensers; oil cans; auto accessories; petro memorabilia; drug store; blacksmith shop; homestead; business artifacts.
Activities: Museum Sponsors: October-Fest; Christmas Stroll.
Publications: biannual, Transportation Times.
Hours & Admission Prices: May-Oct. Mon.-Fri. 10-4, Sat. 1-4; Nov.-April by appointment. Adults $3; discounts to seniors & school groups; members no charge. Closed Independence Day. ♿
Attendance: 619 (accurate)
Membership: Individual $20; Family $25.

Crow Agency

LITTLE BIGHORN BATTLEFIELD NATIONAL MONUMENT, Interstate 90 & Hwy. 212, Crow Agency, MT 59022. Mailing Address: P.O. Box 39, Crow Agency, MT 59022-0039. Tel.: 406-638-3204. Fax: 406-638-2623.
E-mail: darrell_cook@nps.gov
Web Site: www.nps.gov/libi
Founded: 1940.
Congressional District: 2
Key Personnel: Chief Historian, John A. Doerner; Supt., Darrell J. Cook; Business Mgr., Loreen Walks Over Ice.
Personnel Profile: Full-Time Paid 1; Part-Time Paid 2; Part-Time Volunteers 2; Interns 2.
Governing Authority: federal. Administered by National Park Service, Washington, DC. Tax-exempt.
History Museum.
Collections: Indian & military items, manuscripts, photographs & documents associated with Gen. George A. Custer, the Battle of Little Big Horn & the Sioux War, 1876-90; Northern Plains Indians, Crow, Arikara, Lakota Sioux, Cheyenne, & Arapaho; Seventh U.S. Cavalry.
Research Fields: Battle of Little Big Horn; George A. Custer; Plains Indian Wars.
Facilities: library & archives; battlefield grounds; visitor center. Publications related to the battle of the Little Big Horn & the Indian Wars for sale.
Activities: permanent & temporary exhibitions; interpretive services, including historical talks, walks, demonstrations, self-guiding trail, park tour road & tape recorded audio stations; guided bus tours.
Publications: books.
Hours & Admission Prices: April-May & Sept.-Oct. daily 8-6; Memorial Day to July daily 8am-9pm; Aug. to Labor Day daily 8-8; Nov.-March daily 8-4:30. Vehicle $10, Individual $5; discounts to Golden Age & Annual pass holders. Closed New Year's Day; Thanksgiving; Christmas. ♿
Attendance: 400,000 (estimated)

Culbertson

CULBERTSON MUSEUM, Hwy. 2 E., Culbertson, MT 59218. Mailing Address: P.O. Box 95, Culbertson, MT 59218-0095. Tel.: 406-787-6320 & 5337.
Founded: 1990.
Key Personnel: Pres., Lois Raaum; Treas., Ruth Mattelin; Dir. Volunteers, Sue Houle.

Personnel Profile: Part-Time Paid 6; Part-Time Volunteers 30.
Governing Authority: private; nonprofit organization. Tax-exempt: 501(c)(3).
History Museum.
Collections: pioneer & homesteader history in northeastern Montana & the Culbertson area, from the 1880s to the depression era & WWII; artifacts; photographs; cowboy, pioneer & homesteader artifacts; chuckwagon; one horse sleigh; buggy charcoal; Sadd; gas domestic irons; period dishes; medical equipment; wildflower garden.
Research Fields: family histories.
Facilities: 50-vol. library of pictorial Montana area books, county & community history books; 6,000 sq. ft. exhibit space; garden.
Activities: guided tours; special events. Museum Sponsors: school tours in May & September; Birthday Bash; Chuckwagon Meal; County Fair Educational booth; Frontier Days parade float; Pie Social for Annual Threshing Bee.
Publications: annual newsletter; brochure.
Hours & Admission Prices: May & Sept. 8-6; June-Aug. 8-8. No charge; donations accepted. ♿
Attendance: 4,800 (estimated)
Membership: Individual $5; Family $15; Business $35.

NORTHEASTERN MONTANA THRESHERS AND ANTIQUE ASSOCIATION, Culbertson, MT 59218-0012. Mailing Address: P.O. Box 12, Culbertson, MT 59218-0012. Tel.: 406-787-5265.
Founded: 1964.
Congressional District: 2
Key Personnel: Pres. (V), David Krogedal; Vice Pres. (V), Robert Bahls; Sec., Allison Krogedal; Treas., Maurice Gonitzke.
Personnel Profile: Part-Time Volunteers 50.
Governing Authority: nonprofit organization. Tax-exempt: 501(c)(3).
Local Agriculture Antiques Museum.
Collections: agriculture; pioneer house; steam & gasoline tractors; small engines; pioneer artifacts.
Facilities: free camper space during show; food concession.
Activities: self-guided tours; temporary exhibitions. Museum Sponsors: Threshing Bee & Antique Show in September.
Publications: 1981 book, Spirit of Yesteryear.
Hours & Admission Prices: Call for information. Adults $6.
Attendance: 2,000 (estimated)
Membership: Individual $20.

Cut Bank

GLACIER COUNTY HISTORICAL SOCIETY & MUSEUM, 107 Old Kevin Hwy., Cut Bank, MT 59427. Mailing Address: P.O. Box 576, Cut Bank, MT 59427-0576. Tel.: 406-873-4904.
E-mail: gcmuseum@sofast.net
Web Site: www.glaciercountymt.org/museum
Founded: 1980.
Key Personnel: Pres. (V), Ken Finstad; Dir., Dennis Seglem.
Governing Authority: Tax-exempt.
Historical Society Museum.
Collections: Glacier County history & cultural heritage.
Hours & Admission Prices: Memorial Day to Labor Day Tues.-Sun. 10-5; other times by appointment. No charge; donations accepted. ♿
Membership: $25 & up.

Darby

DARBY PIONEER MEMORIAL MUSEUM, 101 E. Tanner, Darby, MT 59829. Mailing Address: P.O. Box 37, Darby, MT 59829-0037. Tel.: 406-821-3753 & 3748. Fax: 406-821-3244.
Web Site: darbymontana.usa.net
History Museum.
Collections: local history & culture; photographs & memorabilia of Darby and it's people; home & business artifacts.
Hours & Admission Prices: June-Sept. daily 1-5. ♿
Attendance: 556 (accurate)

Deer Lodge

GRANT-KOHRS RANCH NATIONAL HISTORIC SITE, 266 Warren Lane, Deer Lodge, MT 59722-1002. Tel.: 406-846-2070, ext. 224. Fax: 406-846-3962.
E-mail: laura_rotegard@nps.gov
Web Site: www.nps.gov/grko/home.htm
Founded: 1972.
Congressional District: 1
Key Personnel: Chm. (V), Julie Croglio; Facility Mgr., Alan Stewart; Sales Shop Mgr., Lyndel Meikle; Admin. Officer, Anita Dore; Chief Interpretation, David Wyrick; Cur., Chris Ford; Museum Tech., Peggy Gow; Supt., Laura Rotegard.
Personnel Profile: Full-Time Paid 11; Full-Time Volunteers 2; Part-Time Paid 8; Part-Time Volunteers 6; Interns 6.
Governing Authority: federal. U.S. Dept. of the Interior, National Park Service, Washington, DC 20240. Tax-exempt.
National Historic Site: 1862-1890 23-room ranch house & 1861-1960 bunkhouse, barns & outbuildings.
Collections: 19th & 20th-century ranch equipment; horse drawn vehicles; blacksmith equipment; tack; bunkhouse furnishings; Victorian household furnishings; textiles; archives.
Research Fields: frontier cattle ranching.
Facilities: library on cattle ranching & household arts, primarily of the 19th century, available for use on premises. Postcards & books for sale.
Activities: guided tours; cattle ranching; draft horses; formally organized education programs for children.
Hours & Admission Prices: Memorial Day-Labor Day daily 9-5:30; Sept.-May daily 9-4:30. No charge; donations accepted. ♿
Attendance: 37,000 (accurate)

OLD PRISON MUSEUMS, 1106 Main St., Deer Lodge, MT 59722-1426. Tel.: 406-846-3111. Fax: 406-846-3156.
E-mail: info@pcmaf.org
Web Site: pcmaf.org
Formerly: Old Montana Prison
Founded: 1980.
Congressional District: 1
Key Personnel: Dir., John O'Donnell; Pres., Dick Bauman; Treas., Betty Hoffman; Sec., Ed Gill; Mgr. Collection, K.C. Sackman; Business Mgr., Julia Smith.
Personnel Profile: Full-Time Paid 6; Full-Time Volunteers 20; Part-Time Paid 22; Part-Time Volunteers 20; Interns 2.
Governing Authority: nonprofit organization. Parent Institution: Powell County Museum & Arts Foundation. Tax-exempt: 501(c)(3).
Historic Monument & Complex: 1867 site, comprised of 12 structures surrounded by 1893 sandstone wall, serving as a territorial & state prison from 1871-1979.
Collections: contraband exhibits & display areas; photographs; archives; 1900-1980s vintage cars. Historic Building: 1912 cell house; original Montana territorial prison.
Research Fields: prison history.
Facilities: administrative building; prison yard; prison-related structures.
Activities: guided & self-guided tours; permanent & temporary exhibitions.
Publications: brochures; pamphlets; books.
Hours & Admission Prices: Daily 9-6. Adults $8, children 10-15 $4; discounts to groups, senior citizens, AAA & Good Sam members; members & children under 9 no charge. ♿
Attendance: 52,600 (accurate)
Membership: Senior Citizen $15; Individual $20; Family $30; Commercial $75; Museum Patron $130.

POWELL COUNTY MUSEUM, 1106 Main St., Deer Lodge, MT 59722-1489. Tel.: 406-846-3111. Fax: 406-846-3156.
E-mail: info@pcmaf.org
Web Site: www.pcmaf.org
Founded: 1964.
Congressional District: 1
Key Personnel: Pres., Dick Bauman; Dir., John O'Donnell; Business Mgr., Julia Smith; Sec., Ed Gill.
Personnel Profile: Full-Time Volunteers 1; Part-Time Volunteers 5.
Governing Authority: nonprofit organization. Parent Institution: Powell County Museum & Arts Foundation. Branch Museums. Old Montana Territorial Prison; Yesterday's Playthings; Montana Auto Museum. Tax-exempt: 501(c)(3).
Local History Museum.
Collections: area artifacts; mastodon fossils; trapping & mining tools; ranching artifacts; 26,000 photographs; railroad exhibit.
Research Fields: local history.
Facilities: visitor center. Museum-related items for sale.
Activities: guided tours available for groups. Museum Sponsors: local arts presentations; local theater group; professional summer theater.
Publications: newsletter, Museum Post; local history books; brochures.
Hours & Admission Prices: Memorial Day-Labor Day 12-5. No charge; donations accepted. ♿
Attendance: 5,000 (estimated)
Membership: Senior Citizen $15; Individual $20; Family $30.

Dillon

BANNACK STATE PARK & TOWN SITE, 4200 Bannack Rd., Dillon, MT 59725-9685. Tel.: 406-834-3413. Fax: 406-834-3548.
Park & History Museum.

Collections: Bannack history; mining; cultural heritage; geology.
Activities: school programs; special events; camping; gold panning.
Hours & Admission Prices: Park: May-Oct. daily 8am-9pm; Nov.-April daily 8-5. Town Site: May & Sept.-Oct. daily 8am to dusk; Memorial Day to Labor Day daily 8am-9pm; Nov.-April daily 8-5. Visitor Center: May-Aug. daily 10-6; Sept.-Oct. Sat.-Sun. 11-5. Out-of-State Residents: vehicle $5, bus & walk-ins $3; Montana residents no charge. Closed Christmas Eve & Day.

BEAVERHEAD COUNTY MUSEUM, 15 S. Montana, Dillon, MT 59725-2433. Tel.: 406-683-5027.
E-mail: bvhdmuseum@bmt.net
Founded: 1947.
Congressional District: 1
Key Personnel: C.E.O. & Dir., Lyle Dechant; Chm. (V) & Pres. (V), Lynn Westad; Sec., Ruth Little; Museum Shop Mgr., Joan McDougall.
Personnel Profile: Full-Time Paid 1; Part-Time Volunteers 30.
Governing Authority: nonprofit organization. Subsidiary Institution: County Mill. Tax-exempt: 501(c)(3).
History Museum.
Collections: Indian artifacts, relics of mining & displays of business and household articles brought to the area by early settlers; branded boardwalk; rare photos of local pioneers; livestock & agriculture; natural history; Lewis & Clark exhibit. Historic Buildings: 1885 Homesteader Cabin; one room schoolhouse; 1908 Train Depot.
Research Fields: Montana history; Beaverhead County History.
Facilities: 100-vol. library of county history books available for research on premises; 4,500 photographic reprints indexed & identified; outdoor interpretive area; theater.
Activities: tours. Museum Sponsors: Traveling Trunk Program.
Publications: quarterly newsletter.
Hours & Admission Prices: May 30-Sept. 5 Mon.-Fri. 8-5, Sat. 9-5; Sept. 6-May 29 Mon.-Fri. 8-5. Adults $2, senior citizens & children 13-18 $1; discounts to AAM & ICOM members; members, school tours & children 12 & under no charge. ♿
Attendance: 14,000 (accurate)
Membership: Individual $17.50; Family $25; Business $45.

THE UNIVERSITY OF MONTANA WESTERN ART GALLERY & MUSEUM, 710 S. Atlantic, Dillon, MT 59725-3511. Tel.: 406-683-7232. Fax: 406-683-7493.
E-mail: R_Horst@umwestern.edu
Web Site: www.umwestern.edu
Formerly: Western Montana College Gallery Museum
Founded: 1986.
Key Personnel: Dir., Randy Horst; Campus Security, Bob Campbell.
Personnel Profile: Part-Time Paid 3; Interns 1.
Governing Authority: university; nonprofit. Parent Institution: The University of Montana Western.
Art Gallery & Museum: housed in 1893 main building.
Collections: wildlife trophies from Africa, Asia & North America (Seidensticker Collection); northwest regional artists.
Activities: temporary art exhibits.
Hours & Admission Prices: Mon.-Fri. 9-4. No charge. Closed holidays. ♿
Attendance: 2,000 (estimated)

Drummond

OHRMANN MUSEUM AND GALLERY, 6155 Hwy. 1, Drummond, MT 59832. Tel.: 406-288-3319.
E-mail: ohrmann@blackfoot.net
Web Site: www.ohrmannmuseum.com
Art Museum.
Collections: paintings, woodcarvings, bronzes & sculptures of Bill Ohrmann.
Hours & Admission Prices: Daily 10-5.

East Glacier Park

JOHN L. CLARKE WESTERN ART GALLERY & MEMORIAL MUSEUM, 900 Montana Hwy. 49, East Glacier Park, MT 59434. Mailing Address: P.O. Box 141, East Glacier Park, MT 59434-0141. Tel.: 406-226-9238.
Founded: 1977.
Art Gallery and Museum.
Collections: wood carvings & paintings by John L. Clarke.
Hours & Admission Prices: May-Sept. Mon.-Sat. 10-8, Sun. 10-5.

East Helena

KLEFFNER RANCH, 305 Hwy. 518, East Helena, MT 59635-9602. Tel.: 406-495-9090; 406-227-3521.
E-mail: kleffner@mt.net
Web Site: www.kleffnerranch.com
Historic Site: former estate of William Child, an early Montana entrepreneur. Listed on the National Historic Register.
Collections: local history & culture; photographs.
Hours & Admission Prices: By appointment.

Ekalaka

CARTER COUNTY MUSEUM, 306 N. Main St., Ekalaka, MT 59324. Mailing Address: P.O. Box 445, Ekalaka, MT 59324-0445. Tel.: 406-775-6886.
E-mail: ccmuseum@midrivers.com
Web Site: cartercountymuseum-ekalaka.org
Founded: 1936.
Congressional District: 2
Key Personnel: Dir., Warren O. White; Receptionist, Gwen Schultz; Sec. & Museum Shop Mgr., Shirley White.
Personnel Profile: Full-Time Paid 1; Full-Time Volunteers 1; Part-Time Paid 1.
Governing Authority: county. Tax-exempt: 170(b)(1)(A).
Natural History Museum.
Collections: mounted dinosaur skeletons; anatosaurus, triceratops & pachycephalosaurus skulls; nanotyrannus skull; ichthyosaur skeleton; local historical material; pictures; Indian artifacts; fluorescent mineral exhibit; Fossil Bison skull, Bison crassicornis; Civil War to Desert Storm artifacts.
Research Fields: vertebrate paleontology; archeology.
Facilities: 800-vol. library available on request.
Activities: permanent & temporary exhibitions; guided tours.
Hours & Admission Prices: Tues.-Fri. 9-12 & 1-5, Sat.-Sun. 1-5. No charge; donations accepted. Closed legal holidays. ♿
Attendance: 5,500 (accurate)
Membership: Individual $5.

Forsyth

ROSEBUD COUNTY PIONEER MUSEUM, 1335 Main St., Forsyth, MT 59327. Mailing Address: P.O. Box 88, Forsyth, MT 59327-0088. Tel.: 406-346-7457.
Founded: 1966.
Key Personnel: Pres. (V), Cal MacConnel.
Governing Authority: county. Tax-exempt.
Pioneer History Museum.
Collections: pioneer memorabilia.
Facilities: 100-vol. library of books & newspapers.
Hours & Admission Prices: May to mid-Sept. Mon.-Sat. 9-6, Sun. 1-6. No charge; donations accepted. ♿
Attendance: 2,000 (accurate)

Fort Benton

FORT BENTON MUSEUM OF THE UPPER MISSOURI, 1810 Front St., Fort Benton, MT 59442. Mailing Address: P.O. Box 262, Fort Benton, MT 59442-0262. Tel.: 406-622-5316. Fax: 406-622-3725.
E-mail: fbmuseums@mtintouch.net
Web Site: www.fortbenton.com
Founded: 1957.
Key Personnel: Chm. (V) & Pres. (V), John G. Lepley; Museum Shop Mgr., Diane Vielleux; Museum Shop Mgr., Pam Schoonover.
Personnel Profile: Full-Time Volunteers 6; Part-Time Volunteers 10.
Governing Authority: nonprofit organization. Parent Institution: River & Plains Society. Tax-exempt.
History Museum: located in park near ruins of Fort Benton, fur trading post of 1846 American Fur Co.
Collections: artifacts; maps; models; pictures & dioramas of early trade routes; Lewis & Clark expedition; founding of Fort Benton; Indian artifacts. Historic House: 1866-67 I.G. Baker House.
Research Fields: history of upper Missouri.
Facilities: library; archives. Museum-related items for sale.
Activities: guided tours; permanent exhibitions.
Publications: High Plains Chronicles.
Hours & Admission Prices: May-Sept. Mon.-Sat. 10-4, Sun. 12-4. Adults $10, children $1 (admission includes admittance to Museum of the Northern Great Plains, Museum of the Upper Missouri River, Upper Missouri River Breaks Interpretive Center & Old Fort Benton); discounts to AAM members. ♿
Attendance: 19,000 (accurate)

MUSEUM OF THE NORTHERN GREAT PLAINS, 1205 20th St., Fort Benton, MT 59442. Mailing Address: P.O. Box 262, Fort Benton, MT 59442-0262. Tel.: 406-622-5316. Fax: 406-622-3725.
E-mail: fbmuseums@mtintouch.net
Web Site: www.fortbenton.com
Founded: 1989.
Key Personnel: Dir. & Pres. (V), John G. Lepley; Museum Shop Mgr., Pam Schoonover; Museum Shop Mgr., Diane Vielleux.
Personnel Profile: Part-Time Paid 6; Part-Time Volunteers 40.
Governing Authority: nonprofit organization. Parent Institution: River & Plains Society, Inc. Subsidiary Institution: Museum Northern County Plains. Tax-exempt.
History Museum.
Collections: concentration on the homesteading era on the Northern Great Plains, 1910-present.
Research Fields: Overholser Historical Research Center-history on people & places; research lab.
Facilities: library; archives. Museum-related items for sale.
Activities: guided tours; permanent exhibitions.
Publications: High Plains Chronicles; histories of Fort Benton.
Hours & Admission Prices: May-Sept. Mon.-Sat. 10-4, Sun. 12-4. Adults $10, children $1 (admission includes admittance to Museum of the Upper Missouri, Old Fort Benton, & the Upper Missouri River Breaks Interpretive Center). ♿
Attendance: 10,000 (accurate)

Fort Peck

FORT PECK INTERPRETIVE CENTER, Yellowstone Rd., Fort Peck, MT 59223. Mailing Address: P.O. Box 208, Fort Peck, MT 59223-0208. Tel.: 406-526-3493. Fax: 406-526-3593.
E-mail: dll-cenwo-fphistory@usace.army.mil
Web Site: www.nwo.usace.army.mil/html/Lake_Proj/fortpeck/museum.html
Key Personnel: Project Engineer, John E. Daggett.
Governing Authority: federal. Affiliated with the Corps of Engineers, Omaha District, 6014 USPO & Courthouse, Omaha, NE 68102. Tel.: 402-221-1221. Tax-exempt.
Paleontology Museum.
Collections: paleontology from Cretaceous hellcreek & bearpaw formations; Fort Peck Dam construction history; area wildlife; aquariums.
Activities: guided tours; permanent exhibitions; guided tours; self-guided tours; film.
Hours & Admission Prices: May-Sept. daily 9-5; Oct.-April Tues.-Fri. 10-4; groups of 10 or more by appointment. No charge; donations accepted. ♿
Attendance: 30,000 (accurate)

Fromberg

CLARK'S FORK VALLEY MUSEUM, 101 East River St., Fromberg, MT 59029. Mailing Address: 679 Joliet Fromberg Rd., Fromberg, MT 59029-9502. Tel.: 406-668-7650.
History Museum.
Collections: area artists & artisans; watercolors; drawings; photographs.
Facilities: Museum-related items for sale.
Activities: Museum Sponsors: Open House Reception.
Hours & Admission Prices: Late June to Sept. Wed.-Sun. 11-3; groups by appointment. No charge; donations accepted.

THE LITTLE COWBOY BAR & MUSEUM, 105 W. River, Fromberg, MT 59029. Mailing Address: P.O. Box 183, Fromberg, MT 59029-0183. Tel.: 406-668-9502.
Founded: 1990.
Key Personnel: Dir., Shirley Smith.
Governing Authority: nonprofit.
General Museum.
Collections: local history, region & culture; western history.
Facilities: library of historical books.
Hours & Admission Prices: No charge; donations accepted.
Attendance: 5,000 (estimated)

Gardiner

YELLOWSTONE NATIONAL PARK, 200 Old Yellowstone Trail, Gardiner, MT 59030. Mailing Address: P.O. Box 168, Yellowstone Park, WY 82190-0168. Tel.: 307-344-2664. Fax: 406-848-9958. TDD: 307-344-2386.
Web Site: www.nps.gov/yell/
Founded: 1872.
Key Personnel: Supt., Suzanne Lewis; Cur., Colleen E. Curry; Botanist, Jennifer Whipple; Registrar, Bridgette Guild; Museum Technician, Carolyn Krippene; Historian, Lee Whittlesey; Museum Technician, Alicia Murphy; Archives Technician, Mariah Robertson.
Personnel Profile: Full-Time Paid 7; Interns 6.
Governing Authority: federal. Parent Institution: National Park Service. Tax-exempt: 101(6).
National Park Museums & Visitor Centers.
Collections: anthropology; archives; paintings; archaeology; botany; entomology; ethnology; geology; herbarium; history; Indian artifacts; mineralogy; biology; zoology; Thomas Moran watercolors & oil painting. Grant Village Visitor Center: wilderness exhibits; slide program. Fishing Bridge Visitor Center: lake ecology; wildlife & geology. Canyon Visitor Center: bison; geology; slide program. Norris Museum: geothermal exhibits and Albright Visitor Center. Mammoth Hot Springs: park history; paintings; photographs; natural & human history; wildlife exhibits; film on Yellowstone. Old Faithful Visitor Center: movie. Museum of the National Park Ranger: history of the ranger profession. Historic Sites: 1891-1913, 23 structures of Fort Yellowstone. Old Faithful Inn: Shaw & Powell Camping Company exhibit. Historic Structures: 1891-1923, Lake Hotel; 1936-1937, Mammoth Hot Springs Hotel; 1920 Roosevelt Lodge; 1917-1930, Old Faithful Lodge; 1919-1926, Lake Lodge; 1,000 historic structures.
Research Fields: management-oriented studies of wildlife, vegetation, geology; human history of park.
Facilities: 20,000-vol. library of history and natural history books available for inter-library loan and for use on premises; ranger stations; general stores; 90,000 item photo archive. Publications for sale.
Activities: permanent exhibitions; slide programs; guided walks & talks throughout the park in winter & summer; films.
Publications: publications by Yellowstone Association; interpretive leaflets.
Hours & Admission Prices: Horace M. Albright Visitor Center in Mammoth Hot Springs: early Oct. to late May 9-5, late May to Labor Day 8-7. Museum of the National Park Ranger (Norris): late May to Labor Day 9-6. Grant Village, Fishing Bridge, Canyon Visitor Centers: late May to Labor Day 8-7. Norris Geyser Basin Museum: late May to early Oct. 10-5. Old Faithful: late May to Labor Day 8-7, winter while road is open 9-5. Heritage & Research Center: Mon.-Fri. 8-5. Yellowstone Research Library Tues.-Fri. 9-4. Park's Archives & Museum Collections: by appointment to researchers. Call to confirm hours & dates, 307-344-2251. Park: $25 per car; Museums no charge. Closed Christmas. ♿
Attendance: 4,123,667 (estimated)
Membership: Golden Access Passport (for permanently disabled) no charge; U.S. Senior Citizen Golden Age Passport $10; Annual Area Pass (Yellowstone & Grand Teton National Parks) $40; National Parks Pass (free entrance to all national parks) $50; Golden Eagle Passport (free entrance to all national parks and other selected federal areas) $65.

Garryowen

CUSTER BATTLEFIELD MUSEUM, (M), Town Hall, Garryowen, MT 59031-0200. Mailing Address: P.O. Box 200, Garryowen, MT 59031-0200. Tel.: 406-638-1876. Fax: 406-638-2019.
E-mail: chris@custermuseum.org
Web Site: www.custermuseum.org
Founded: 1994.
Congressional District: 1
Key Personnel: C.E.O., Christopher Kortlander.
Personnel Profile: Full-Time Paid 2; Full-Time Volunteers 2; Interns 2.
Governing Authority: private; nonprofit organization. Tax-exempt: 501(c)(3).
Historic Site: the site of Sitting Bull's camp, where Major Reno's division of Lt. Col. George A. Custer's Seventh Cavalry attacked on June 25, 1876.
Collections: original artifacts; photographs; paintings; rare books; manuscripts related to Custer, the Battle of the Little Bighorn and other frontier subjects.
Research Fields: onsite research.
Facilities: 400-vol. library of books on western America; 1,800 sq. ft. exhibit space.
Activities: films; guided tours; lectures; temporary exhibitions; broadcast programs. Annual Events: Anniversary ceremonies in June.
Hours & Admission Prices: Memorial Day-Labor Day daily 8-8; Sept.-May daily 9-5. Adults $5, senior citizens $4; children under 12 no charge. ♿
Attendance: 50,000 (estimated)
Membership: Individual Plus Guest $30; Family & Dual $40; Contributing $100-$249; Sustaining $250-$499; Patron $500-$999; Eagle Society $1,000-$2,499; Golden Eagle Society $2,500-$4,999; President's Society $5,000 & up.

Glasgow

VALLEY COUNTY PIONEER MUSEUM, Hwy. #2 W., Glasgow, MT 59230. Mailing Address: P.O. Box 44, Glasgow, MT 59230-0044. Tel.: 406-228-8692.
E-mail: vcmuseum@nemontel.net
Web Site: valleycountymuseum.com
Founded: 1964.
Congressional District: 1

Key Personnel: Pres. (V) & Museum Shop Mgr., Mary Helland; Chm. (V), Virgil Nelson; Cur., Carol Cotton.
Personnel Profile: Part-Time Paid 5; Part-Time Volunteers 15.
Governing Authority: county; appointed board of directors. Parent Institution: Valley County Historical Society. Subsidiary Institution: Friends of the Pioneer Museum. Tax-exempt: 501(c)(3).
History Museum.
Collections: pioneer memorabilia from northeast Montana; Indian artifacts & dioramas; wildlife exhibit; farm machinery; From Dinosaur Bones to Moonwalk; Progressive time history to the right: Fossils, Indians & Buffalo, Historic Dinosaurs, The Cattle & Sheep; The Railroad Irrigation, Wildlife, Veterans, Fort Peck Dam, Woodcarving, Flight & Technology with artifacts to fill in; Collection of Assiniboine Indian artifacts, including hand-crafted buckskin & beaded clothing, sacred medicine, warbonnet, hide tepee & dried foods.
Research Fields: history of local area & families.
Facilities: library of tapes; archive; tourist information center; county newspaper dating back over 100 years through 1936 acquired from State Historical Society after microfilmed; audio & transcribed family history to match family pictures.
Activities: guided tours; art shows.
Publications: brochures; summer newsletters; Valley County collectively published a three volume history in 1991 which includes 1200 family histories.
Hours & Admission Prices: May-Sept. Mon.-Sat. 8:30-5:30. Adults $3, children $2; discounts to Life members. ♿
Attendance: 4,000 (estimated)
Membership: Student $15; Family $25; Sustaining $30; Life $250.

Glendive

FRONTIER GATEWAY MUSEUM, 201 State St., Glendive, MT 59330. Mailing Address: P.O. Box 1181, Glendive, MT 59330-1181. Tel.: 406-377-8168 & 365-2769.
Web Site: www.frontiergatewaymuseum.org
Founded: 1963.
Congressional District: 2
Key Personnel: Treas., Noreen Turnquist; Cur., Louise Cross.
Personnel Profile: Full-Time Volunteers 1; Part-Time Paid 2.
Governing Authority: county; nonprofit; board of trustees. Tax-exempt: 501(c)(3).
History Museum.
Collections: fossils; mammoth; mastodon; buffalo; Indian; cattlemen; homesteaders; fashions; photographs.
Facilities: library; 10,080 sq. ft. exhibit space. Museum-related items for sale.
Activities: tours; demonstrations; workshops; lectures. Annual Events: Open House.
Publications: annual members newsletter.
Hours & Admission Prices: mid-May to mid-Sept. Mon.-Sat. 9-12 & 1-5, Sun. & holidays 1-5. No charge; donations accepted. ♿
Attendance: 1,721 (accurate)
Membership: Individual $5; Life $50.

MAKOSHIKA DINOSAUR MUSEUM, 111 W. Bell St., Glendive, MT 59330-1614. Tel.: 406-377-1637.
Founded: 2004.
Personnel Profile: Part-Time Volunteers 12.
Governing Authority: Tax-exempt.
Paleontology Museum.
Collections: dinosaur history; fossil sculptures & casts.
Activities: educational programs; dinosaur exploration.
Hours & Admission Prices: Tues.-Sat. 10-5; other times by appointment.

MAKOSHIKA STATE PARK VISITOR CENTER, 1301 Snyder Ave., Glendive, MT 59330. Tel.: 406-377-6256.
Park Visitor Center.
Collections: local history & geology; fossils; photographs; video.
Facilities: Museum-related items for sale.
Activities: video; hands-on exhibits.
Hours & Admission Prices: Memorial Day to Labor Day daily 10-6; Sept.-May daily 9-5. Park: $5 per vehicle, $1 per person.

Great Falls

* **C.M. RUSSELL MUSEUM, (M),** 400 13th St. N., Great Falls, MT 59401-1498. Tel.: 406-727-8787. Fax: 406-727-2402.
Web Site: www.cmrussell.org
Founded: 1953.
Congressional District: 1
Key Personnel: Exec. Dir., Dr. Darrell Beauchamp; Pres. Bd Dirs., David Solberg; Collections Mgr., Brenda Kornick; Membership Coord., Public Rels. & Mktg. Dir., Kate Swartz; Museum Shop Admin., Donna Camp; Education & Public Programs, Kim Kapalka; Museum Operations Mgr., Chuck Keen.
Personnel Profile: Full-Time Paid 17; Part-Time Paid 17; Part-Time Volunteers 220; Interns 2.
Governing Authority: nonprofit organization. Parent Institution: Trigg-C. M. Russell Foundation, Inc. Tax-exempt: 501(c)(3).
Art Museum: located adjacent to the Russell home & log studio.
Collections: art of the American West with emphasis on C.M. Russell art: paintings & bronzes; contemporary western art; Plains Indian art & artifacts.
Major Exhibits: The Bison: American Icon, Heart of Plains Indian Culture, 12/09-11/19.
Research Fields: C.M. Russell; Western American art & history; Northern Plains Indians.
Facilities: 5,000-vol. library of publications on Western art, artists, history & Native Americans. Museum-related items for sale.
Activities: guided tours; docent program; lectures; library research; inter-museum loan, permanent, temporary & traveling exhibitions; hands-on gallery; junior visitor program; western history tour.
Publications: quarterly members' magazine.
Hours & Admission Prices: May-Sept. daily 9-6; Labor Day-Memorial Day Tues.-Sat. 10-5; tours by appointment. Adults $9, senior citizens & groups $7, students & children $4; discounts to AAM & ICOM members; children 5 & under and members no charge. Closed New Year's Day; Easter; Thanksgiving; Christmas. ♿
Attendance: 60,000 (accurate)
Membership: Individual $40; Family $60; Sustaining $125; Patron $300; Director's Circle $500; Missouri Society $1,000; Bitterroot Society $1,500; Russell Society $2,500; Brush and Palette Society $5,000; Western Masters Society $10,000. Charlie's Friends: Individual $15; Family $25.

CHILDREN'S MUSEUM OF MONTANA, 22 Railroad Sq., Great Falls, MT 59401-4003. Tel.: 406-452-6661. Fax: 406-452-4462.
E-mail: info@childrensmuseumofmt.org
Web Site: www.childrensmuseumofmt.org
Key Personnel: Exec. Dir., Sandie Wright
Children's Museum.
Collections: hands-on exhibits.
Activities: special events; summer camps.
Hours & Admission Prices: Mon.-Sat. 9:30-5. Adults $3, seniors $2; children under 2 & members no charge. Closed New Year's Day; Independence Day; Thanksgiving; Christmas.

GALERIE TRINITAS, 1301 20th St., S., Great Falls, MT 59405-4934. Tel.: 406-791-5367.
E-mail: mdriskell@ugf.edu
Web Site: www.ugf.edu/aboutus/galarie.htm
Founded: 1994.
Key Personnel: Chm., Marcia Driskell; Chm. (V), Virginia Wieck.
Personnel Profile: Part-Time Paid 1; Part-Time Volunteers 20.
Governing Authority: Parent Institution: University of Great Falls. Tax-exempt.
Art Museum.
Collections: religious art; paintings; weaving; ceramics; religious artifacts.
Hours & Admission Prices: Tues. & Thurs. 12-3. No charge; donations accepted.

THE HISTORY MUSEUM, 422 2nd St. S., Great Falls, MT 59405-1816. Tel.: 406-452-3462. Fax: 406-761-3805.
E-mail: info@thehistorymuseum.org
Formerly: Cascade County Historical Society Museum
Founded: 1976.
Congressional District: 2
Key Personnel: Interim Exec. Dir., Marcia Clary; Chm. (V), Jeanne Pugh; Archivist, Judy Ellinghausen; Bookkeeper, Sarah Schumacher; Coord. Membership, Kristen Bokovoy; Museum Shop Mgr., Jane Boxengard.
Personnel Profile: Full-Time Paid 2; Part-Time Paid 4; Part-Time Volunteers 100.
Governing Authority: nonprofit organization. Tax-exempt.
Historical Museum: housed in c.1929 International Harvester building.
Collections: north central Montana history.
Major Exhibits: Ft. Shaw Indian School Girl's Basketball Team, 11/09-12/10.
Research Fields: MT-local & state history.
Facilities: archives; banquet facilities. Gift-related items for sale.
Activities: museum tours; exhibit programs; archival research; rental facilities.
Publications: newsletter; occasional local histories.
Hours & Admission Prices: Tues.-Fri. 10-5, Sat.-Sun. tours by appointment.

Adults $5; members no charge. Closed New Year's Day; Easter; Memorial Day; Independence Day; Labor Day; Thanksgiving; Christmas. ♿
Attendance: 52,000 (accurate)
Membership: Individual $25; Family $40; Sustainer $75; Sponsor $125; Patron $250; Benefactor $500; Corporate $1,000.

LEWIS AND CLARK NATIONAL HISTORIC TRAIL INTERPRETIVE CENTER, 4201 Giant Springs Rd., Great Falls, MT 59405-0900. Mailing Address: P.O. Box 1806, Great Falls, MT 59403-1806. Tel.: 406-727-8733. Fax: 406-453-6157.
Web Site: www.fs.fed.us/r1/lewisclark/lcic
Founded: 1998.
Key Personnel: Dir., Jane Weber; Museum Shop Mgr., Sally Murphy.
Personnel Profile: Full-Time Paid 5; Part-Time Paid 4; Part-Time Volunteers 97; Interns 3.
Governing Authority: Parent Institution: USDA, Forest Service. Tax-exempt.
History Museum.
Collections: Lewis & Clark history; photographs; period artifacts & reproductions.
Major Exhibits: On the Brink of Change, 1/10-12/10.
Facilities: 158-seat theater; education room; nature trails. Museum-related items for sale.
Activities: school group programmings; summer day camps. Museum Sponsors: Winter Warmups January to March; Winter Film Festival January to March; 11th Anniversary Celebration in May; Indian Voices in summer; Lawnchair Programs in summer; Lewis and Clark Festival in June; Voices in the Shadows in October; Drop & Shop in December.
Hours & Admission Prices: Memorial Day to Sept. daily 9-6; Oct.-May Tues.-Sat. 9-5, Sun. 12-5; groups by appointment. Adults 16 & over $8; children 15 & under no charge. Closed New Year's Day; Thanksgiving; Christmas. ♿
Attendance: 70,000

PARIS GIBSON SQUARE MUSEUM OF ART, 1400 1st Ave. N., Great Falls, MT 59401-3299. Tel.: 406-727-8255. Fax: 406-727-8256.
E-mail: info@the-square.org
Web Site: www.the-square.org
Founded: 1976.
Congressional District: 2
Key Personnel: Exec. Dir., Kathy Lear; Cur. Art, Bob Durden.
Personnel Profile: Full-Time Paid 6; Part-Time Paid 6; Part-Time Volunteers 250.
Governing Authority: nonprofit organization. Tax-exempt: 501(c)(3).
Art Museum: housed in c.1895 stone building built as the first High School in Great Falls.
Collections: modern & contemporary art of the American Northwest including native American contemporary art; 20th-century American outsider art; special collections.
Research Fields: contemporary art; native & folk art; modernism.
Facilities: classrooms; meeting rooms. Works by Montana artists for sale.
Activities: guided tours; lectures; formally organized education programs for children & adults; docent program; temporary & traveling exhibitions; catered events.
Publications: educational publication & calendar; quarterly newsletter; posters; catalogues.
Hours & Admission Prices: Mon. & Wed.-Fri. 10-5, Tues. 10-5 & 7-9, Sat. 12-5. No charge; donations accepted. Closed national holidays. ♿
Attendance: 25,653 (accurate)
Membership: Student $20; Individual $30; Dual $35; Family $45; Sustainer $60; Sponsor $100; Benefactor $250; Patron $500; Director's Circle $1,000 & up.

Hamilton

DALY MUSEUM, Hwy. 269, at mile marker 2, Hamilton, MT 59840. Mailing Address: P.O. Box 223, Hamilton, MT 59840-0223. Tel.: 406-363-6004. Fax: 406-375-0048.
Founded: 1987.
Congressional District: 88
Key Personnel: Dir., Kim Morris; Pres. (V), Howard Recht.
Personnel Profile: Full-Time Paid 1; Part-Time Paid 1; Interns 2.
Governing Authority: Parent Institution: Daly Mansion Preservation Trust. Tax-exempt.
History Museum.
Collections: local history & culture.
Activities: Museum Sponsors: Kentucky Derby; Community Band Concert; Kids in the Garden; Cross Country Meet; Drum Brothers; Shakespeare in the Park.
Publications: quarterly members' newsletter.
Hours & Admission Prices: April-Oct. call for hours. Adults $8, seniors $7, youth 6-17 $5; discounts to AAA members; children under 6 no charge. ♿
Attendance: 10,000 (estimated)
Membership: Annual $35-$5,000.

RAVALLI COUNTY MUSEUM/BITTER ROOT VALLEY HISTORICAL SOCIETY, 205 Bedford, Hamilton, MT 59840-2853. Tel.: 406-363-3338. Fax: 406-363-6588.
E-mail: rcmuseum@qwestoffice.net
Founded: 1955.
Key Personnel: Exec. Dir., Tamar Stanley; Dir. Devel., John Recore; Archivist, Beverly Adams; Museum Shop Mgr., Dona Fisher.
Personnel Profile: Full-Time Paid 1; Part-Time Paid 3; Part-Time Volunteers 60.
Governing Authority: private; nonprofit organization. Parent Institution: Bitter Root Valley Historical Society. Tax-exempt: 501(c)(3).
History Museum.
Collections: Discovery Room-Native American and Lewis & Clark collection; Bitter Root Valley history; pioneer rooms; a trapper miner cabin, school room & kitchen; Bertie Lord & Ernst Peterson photographic collections; Ricketts room develops the history of the Rocky Mountain Laboratory & the discovery of a serum for Rocky Mountain Spotted fever; Veteran's room; archives of newspapers from the valley, catalogued, historic books, historic photo collection, vertical file & periodicals.
Facilities: 900-vol. library on Montana & Native Americans; educational facilities; 150-seat theater. Museum-related items for sale.
Activities: concerts; films; guided tours; weekly lectures; temporary exhibitions; court room theater. Annual Events: Bitter Root Day; Veterans Day Observance; Christmas Exhibit; Treasurer State Fine Art Show; poetry, music & art event; Sunday Series Program; McIntosh Apple Day; Farmer's Market May to October.
Publications: newsletter, The Newsletter; Bitter Root Trails I, II, and The Bitter Root Trails III; Bitter Root Pioneer Families of the South End of the Valley.
Hours & Admission Prices: Mon. & Thurs.-Fri. 10-4, Sat. 9-1, Sun. 1-4. Couple $5, adult $3, students 6-18 $1; members no charge. Closed major holidays. ♿
Attendance: 10,000 (estimated)
Membership: Individual $15; Family $25; Sponsor $50; Copper & Business $100; Gold $500; Platinum $1,000.

Hardin

BIG HORN COUNTY HISTORICAL MUSEUM, R.R. 1, Hardin, MT 59034-9720. Mailing Address: Box 1206A, Hardin, MT 59034-9720. Tel.: 406-665-1671. Fax: 406-665-3068.
E-mail: di@bhwi.net
Web Site: www.bighorncountymuseum.org
Founded: 1979.
Congressional District: 2
Key Personnel: Dir., Diana Scheidt; Pres. (V), Beth Mehling; Treas., Margaret Koebbe; Museum Asst., Bonnie Stark; Museum Shop Mgr., Joan Miller.
Personnel Profile: Full-Time Paid 3; Part-Time Paid 7; Part-Time Volunteers 35.
Governing Authority: private; nonprofit organization. Tax-exempt: 501(c)(3).
History Museum.
Collections: horse drawn equipment; restored tractor & farm equipment; cultures that settled in this area including Crow Indians, the Northern Cheyenne Indians, Japanese, German, Russian, Korean & Norwegian. Historic Buildings: farmhouse; barn; 18 historic structures moved to site from around the county.
Facilities: library; 23 acre farm. Museum-related items for sale.
Activities: guided tours. Annual Events: Tractor Show; Auction.
Publications: quarterly newsletter, On the Big Horn.
Hours & Admission Prices: May-Sept. daily 8-6; Oct.-April Mon.-Fri. 9-5. No charge; donations accepted. Closed New Year's Day; Thanksgiving; Christmas. ♿
Attendance: 25,000 (accurate)
Membership: Individual $15; Family $25; Business $50; Lifetime $500.

Harlowton

UPPER MUSSELSHELL HISTORICAL SOCIETY, 11 S. Central, Harlowton, MT 59036. Mailing Address: P.O. Box 364, Harlowton, MT 59036-0364. Tel.: 406-632-5519.
E-mail: museum@mtintouch.net
Web Site: harlowtonmuseum.com
Founded: 1985.
Congressional District: 14
Key Personnel: Chm. (V), R.C. Brown; Treas., Don Amundson; Cur., Judy Blaquier.
Personnel Profile: Part-Time Paid 2; Part-Time Volunteers 6.
Governing Authority: private; nonprofit organization. Tax-exempt: 501(c)(3).

General Museum.
Collections: local area items dating back to the dinosaur age.
Facilities: library; 10,000 sq. ft. exhibit space. Museum-related items for sale.
Activities: guided tours; loan exhibitions. Museum Sponsors: pot luck dinner.
Publications: annual newsletter.
Hours & Admission Prices: May-Aug. Tues.-Sat. 10-5, Sun. 1-5; Sept. call for hours. Adults $2.
Attendance: 1,500 (estimated)
Membership: Annual $12; Life $100.

Havre

H. EARL CLACK MUSEUM, (M), 1753 US Hwy. 2 N.W. #30, Havre, MT 59501-3464. Mailing Address: Holiday Village Mall, 1753 Hwy. 2 N.W. #30, Havre, MT 59501. Tel.: 406-265-4000. Fax: 406-265-4000.
E-mail: clackmuseum@co.hill.mt.us
Founded: 1964.
Key Personnel: Mgr., John Gilbert.
Personnel Profile: Part-Time Paid 5.
Governing Authority: county. Parent Institution: Hill County. Tax-exempt.
Local History Museum.
Collections: dinosaur fossils; history of Hill Country; Fort Assinniboine; homestead era; development of communities in Hill Co.; Indian artifacts & history of Chippewa-Cree, Wahkpa Chu'gn buffalo jump site; excavations & artifacts; military.
Research Fields: local history; Indians; archaeology studies.
Facilities: Western items & other museum-related items for sale.
Activities: guided tours; museum & buffalo jump.
Hours & Admission Prices: Memorial Day to Labor Day Mon.-Sat. 10-5, Sun. 12-5; Sept.-May daily 1-5. No charge; donations accepted. Closed major holidays. ♿
Attendance: 6,550 (accurate)

Helena

HOLTER MUSEUM OF ART, (M), 12 E. Lawrence St., Helena, MT 59601-4019. Tel.: 406-442-6400. Fax: 406-442-2404.
E-mail: info@holtermuseum.org
Web Site: www.holtermuseum.org
Founded: 1987.
Congressional District: 1
Key Personnel: Exec. Dir., Liz Gans; Deputy Dir., Patty White; Pres. (V), Jeff Miller; Cur. Education, Katie Knight; Cur. Education, Sondra Hines; Business Mgr., Janet Seymour; Publications Designer, Jan Novy; Collection Specialist & Asst. Registrar, Phoebe Toland; Membership & Outreach Mgr., Kim Patterson; Visitor Svcs., David Spencer; Asst. Cur. & Registrar, Cherl Thornton.
Personnel Profile: Full-Time Paid 4; Part-Time Paid 7; Part-Time Volunteers 8; Interns 1.
Governing Authority: nonprofit. Tax-exempt.
Art Museum.
Collections: regional works of art.
Research Fields: contemporary art & crafts of Northwest region.
Facilities: library; 17,000 sq. ft. exhibit space; 2 classrooms
Activities: gallery talks; lectures; docent program; tours; classes; permanent, temporary & traveling exhibitions.
Publications: exhibition catalogues; Rudy Autio: The Infinite Figure; Robert Deweese, A Look Forward; Curatorial Choice: A Northwest Survey; semi-annual newsletter; educational schedule; Elizabeth Lochrie: Portraits of A People; Telling Compelling Tales: Narration in Contemporary Glass; Old Paint New: The Image of the Horse in Contemporary Art; Brad Rude: Original Nature; A Ceramic Continuum: Fifty Years of the Archie Bray Influence; Nick Cave: Soundsuits; Michael Haykin: Intimate Terrain; Peter Koch: Nature/Morte; Frances Senska: A Life in Art.
Hours & Admission Prices: Tues. & Thurs.-Fri. 10-5:30, Wed. 12-8, Sat. 10-4:30, Sun. 11:30-4:30. No charge; donations accepted. Closed major holidays. ♿
Attendance: 32,000 (accurate)
Membership: Individual $40; Family $60; General Business & Contributor $100; Patron $250; Benefactor $500; Guardian $1,000; Guardian Fellow $2,500.

* **MONTANA HISTORICAL SOCIETY, (M),** 225 N. Roberts, Helena, MT 59601-4514. Mailing Address: P.O. Box 201201, Helena, MT 59620-1201. Tel.: 406-444-2694. Fax: 406-444-2696.
E-mail: dking@mt.gov
Web Site: www.montanahistoricalsociety.org
Founded: 1865.
Congressional District: 1
Key Personnel: Dir., Richard Sims; Museum Program Mgr, Bill Mercer; Cur. Collections, Jennifer Bottomly-O'Looney; Archivist, Jodie Foley; Public Rels., Tom Cook; Security, John Ashmore; Museum Store Mgr., Sherry Jonckeere; Preservation Office, Mark Baumler.
Personnel Profile: Full-Time Paid 50; Part-Time Paid 14; Part-Time Volunteers 110; Interns 2.
Governing Authority: state. Parent Institution: Montana Historical Society. Subsidiary Institution: Montana's Museum Original Governor's Mansion. Tax-exempt: 170(c)(1).
Historical Society Museum.
Collections: human history of Montana & the region; archaeology; Native American material culture; costumes & textiles; decorative arts & furnishings; ranching, mining, transportation, agricultural & veterinary artifacts; weapons; American Western art including Mackay collection of C.M. Russell art; over 200,000 photographs of Montana & Western subjects; diaries, manuscripts, oral histories & documents; Montana newspapers from 1865; historical library of Montana & the West.
Research Fields: history, art & culture of Montana.
Facilities: 112,000-vol. library of Western & Montana history with public reading room; 20,000 sq. ft. exhibit space; photograph archives reference room; meeting room. Books & museum-related items for sale.
Activities: guided tours; lectures; gallery talks; docent program; formal education programs for adults & children; inter-library loan; curriculum resources for schools; web-based activities; permanent, temporary & traveling exhibits; tours of State Capitol & Original Governor's Mansion; museum services. Annual Events: Montana History Conference; Western Rendezvous of Art; Original Governor's Mansion Holiday Tours; Original Governor's Mansion Secret Garden Tour; Summer Under the Tent Activities Days.
Publications: quarterly scholarly journal, Montana The Magazine of Western History; quarterly newsletter, The Montana Post; books by the Montana Historical Society Press.
Hours & Admission Prices: Mon.-Wed. & Fri.-Sat. 9-5, Thurs. 9-8. Adults $5; discounts to National Trust Time Travelers, AAM & AAA members; members no charge. Closed holidays. ♿
Attendance: 40,256 (accurate)
Membership: Individual $45; Family $60; Explorer $100; Prospector $200; Homesteader $400; Patron $800; Benefactor $1,000.

MONTANA MASONIC MUSEUM, 425 N. Park Ave., Helena, MT 59601-5020. Mailing Address: P.O. Box 1158, Helena, MT 59624-1158. Tel.: 406-442-7774. Fax: 406-442-1321.
E-mail: mtglsec@grandlodgemontana.org
Web Site: www.grandlodgemontana.org
History Museum.
Collections: Masonry in Montana; early Montana history; manuscripts; books.
Hours & Admission Prices: Mon.-Fri. 9-4.

Huntley

HUNTLEY PROJECT MUSEUM OF IRRIGATED AGRICULTURE, 770 Railroad Hwy., Huntley, MT 59037. Mailing Address: P.O. Box 353, Huntley, MT 59037-0353. Tel.: 406-348-2533.
E-mail: hpmia@huntleyprojectmuseum.org
Web Site: www.huntleyprojectmuseum.org
Key Personnel: Dir., Tracey L. Livingston
Agriculture Museum.
Collections: everyday items of homesteader families; records & photographs of the communities; quilts; dresses; dishes & cookbooks; hand tools; saddles; farm machinery; handmade toys.
Hours & Admission Prices: May-Sept. Tues.-Sat. 10-4; Oct.-April Mon.-Tues. 10-4. Suggested Donations: Families $5, adults $2, children & seniors $1.

Hysham

TREASURE COUNTY 89'ERS MUSEUM, 325 Elliott Ave., Hysham, MT 59038. Mailing Address: P.O. Box 489, Hysham, MT 59038-0489. Tel.: 406-342-5252.
History Museum.
Collections: local history; American heritage; period artifacts; Lewis and Clark.
Hours & Admission Prices: Memorial Day to Labor Day Mon.-Sat. 1-5; other times by appointment. ♿

Jordan

GARFIELD COUNTY MUSEUM, , Montana Hwy. 200, Jordan, MT 59337. Mailing Address: P.O. Box 36, Brusett, MT 59318. Tel.: 406-557-2517.
Dinosaur Museum.
Collections: Cretaceous fossils; T-rex skull; Triceratops replica; Pachycephalosaur domed skull.
Hours & Admission Prices: June-Sept. daily 1-5. No charge; donations accepted.

Kalispell

CONRAD MANSION NATIONAL HISTORIC SITE MUSEUM, (M), Btwn. Third & Fourth Sts. on Woodland Ave., Kalispell, MT 59901. Mailing Address: P.O. Box 1041, Kalispell, MT 59903-1041. Tel.: 406-755-2166. Fax: 406-755-2176.
E-mail: conradmansion@centurytel.net
Web Site: www.conradmansion.com
Founded: 1975.
Congressional District: 1
Key Personnel: Exec. Dir., Kate Daniels; Pres. (V), Mark Norley; Vice Pres., Tia Robbin; Museum Shop Mgr., Sylvie Wood.
Personnel Profile: Full-Time Paid 1; Part-Time Paid 11; Part-Time Volunteers 12.
Governing Authority: nonprofit organization. Tax-exempt: 170(b)(1)(A).
Historic House: Conrad Mansion is a Victorian style home completed in 1895 where 90% of furnishings are original to the Conrad family.
Collections: 1895 & earlier period furniture, clothing, toys, pictures & documents.
Facilities: 23-room Norman structure; 12,000 sq. ft. exhibit space. Gift items for sale.
Activities: guided tours; special events. Annual Event: Holiday Tours Thanksgiving to New Year's Eve by appointment.
Publications: brochures; book of family history; guide book.
Hours & Admission Prices: May 15-Oct. 15 Tues.-Sun. 10-5. Adults $8, senior citizens $7, children 12 & under $3; discounts to groups, Montana PBS, AAM & AAA members; members no charge.
Attendance: 10,000 (estimated)
Membership: Student $25; Senior $35; Individual $40; Family $60; Business $150; Associate $125-$400; Corporate $250 & up; Mansion Patron $500-$999; Bronze $1,000-$4,999; Silver $5,000-$9,999; Gold $10,000 & up.

HOCKADAY MUSEUM OF ART, 302 Second Ave. E., Kalispell, MT 59901-4942. Tel.: 406-755-5268. Fax: 406-755-2023.
Web Site: www.hockadaymuseum.org
Founded: 1968.
Congressional District: 1
Key Personnel: Pres. (V), Tabby Ivy; Exec. Dir., Lucy Smith.
Personnel Profile: Full-Time Paid 1; Part-Time Paid 5; Part-Time Volunteers 65.
Governing Authority: private; nonprofit organization. Tax-exempt.
Art Museum.
Collections: contemporary & historic art and culture of Montana; portraits, paintings, prints, sculpture & pottery of Glacier National Park.
Facilities: art library available for use on premises; sales gallery; six exhibition galleries; classroom.
Activities: guided tours; lectures; films; gallery talks; formally organized education programs for children & adults; permanent, temporary & traveling exhibitions; art auction; summer arts festival. Museum-related items for sale.
Publications: newsletter; flyers; exhibition catalog.
Hours & Admission Prices: Tues.-Sat. 10-5, Sat. 10-5. Adults $5, seniors $4, college students $2; children K-12 & members no charge. Closed major holidays. ♿
Attendance: 10,000 (estimated)
Membership: Senior $35; Individual $40; Family $60; Associate $75; Friend of the Hockaday $125; Cultural Member $250; Heritage Member $500; Patron of the Arts $1,000 and up.

THE MUSEUM AT CENTRAL SCHOOL, Northwest Montana Historical Society, 124 Second Ave., E., Kalispell, MT 59901-4569. Tel.: 406-756-8381. Fax: 406-257-5719.
E-mail: history@yourmuseum.org
Web Site: www.yourmuseum.org
Founded: 1999.
Key Personnel: Exec. Dir., Gil Jordan; Exec. Asst., Nancy Glarun Arestad; Accounting, Doreen Harper; Office Mgr. & Membership, Cathy Peterson; Museum Shop Mgr., Doreen Harper.
Personnel Profile: Full-Time Paid 1; Part-Time Paid 3; Part-Time Volunteers 75.
Governing Authority: Tax-exempt.
History Museum: housed in the historic Central School building, which opened in 1894.
Collections: Native American artifacts; Northwest Montana records & documents; paintings; sculptures; photographs.
Publications: quarterly newsletter.
Hours & Admission Prices: Mon.-Fri. 10-5. Adults $5, seniors $4; children & members no charge. Closed New Year's; Independence Day; Thanksgiving; Christmas. ♿
Attendance: 12,000 (accurate)
Membership: Senior $20; Regular $30; Lifetime $750.

Lewistown

CENTRAL MONTANA HISTORICAL ASSOCIATION, INC. MUSEUM, 408 N.E. Main St., Lewistown, MT 59457-2019. Tel.: 406-535-3642.
Founded: 1955.
Congressional District: 2
Key Personnel: Pres. (V), Frank Hruska; Chm. (V), Doris Moore.
Personnel Profile: Part-Time Volunteers 30.
Governing Authority: society. Affiliated with Central Montana Historical Association. Tax-exempt.
History Museum.
Collections: geology; Native American artifacts; history.
Activities: permanent & temporary exhibitions.
Publications: book, Guarding the Carroll Trail.
Hours & Admission Prices: Memorial Day to Oct. daily 10-4; Nov.-May Mon.-Fri. 8-5; other times by appointment. No charge; donations accepted. ♿
Attendance: 4,000 (estimated)
Membership: Student $2; Senior Citizen $7.50; Single $10; Family $25; Organization $25; Contributing $50-$149; Sustaining $150-$499; Patron $500; Benefactor $1,000 & up.

LEWISTOWN ART CENTER, 801 W. Broadway, Lewistown, MT 59457-2450. Tel.: 406-535-8278. Fax: 406-535-8278.
E-mail: lac@midrivers.com
Founded: 1971.
Key Personnel: Exec. Dir., Karen Kuhlmann; Chm. (V), Vickey Cowen
Art Center.
Collections: works by local & state artists.
Facilities: Museum-related items for sale.
Hours & Admission Prices: Tues.-Sat. 11:30-5:30. No charge.

Libby

THE HERITAGE MUSEUM, 34067 US Hwy. 2 S., Libby, MT 59923. Mailing Address: P.O. Box 628, Libby, MT 59923-0628. Tel.: 406-293-7521.
E-mail: heritagemuseum@frontier.com
Web Site: www.libbyheritagemuseum.org
History Museum.
Collections: local history & culture; exhibits on the Shay Locomotive, historic Jennings, Kootenai Indians & early mining; photographs.
Hours & Admission Prices: June-Aug. Mon.-Sat. 10-5, Sun. 1-5; other times by appointment. No charge; donations accepted.

Livingston

LIVINGSTON DEPOT CENTER, 200 W. Park, Livingston, MT 59047-2629. Mailing Address: P.O. Box 1319, Livingston, MT 59047-1319. Tel.: 406-222-2300. Fax: 406-222-2401.
Web Site: www.livingstondepot.org
Founded: 1985.
Congressional District: 1
Key Personnel: C.E.O. & Pres. (V), John Sullivan; Dir., Diana L. Seider.
Personnel Profile: Full-Time Paid 1; Part-Time Paid 2; Part-Time Volunteers 60.
Governing Authority: nonprofit organization. Tax-exempt: 501(c)(3).
Historic Building: 1902 Northern Pacific railroad station.
Collections: objects related to the history of railroads in the Pacific Northwest.
Research Fields: railroad history; local history.
Facilities: 4,000 sq. ft. exhibit space. Western culture books & other gift items for sale.
Activities: railroad exhibition; temporary & traveling exhibitions; museum tours; lectures; special events & programs; annual railroad memorabilia show; outdoor Festival of the Arts & Holiday activities.
Publications: annual newsletter, Depot Center.
Hours & Admission Prices: May-Sept. Mon.-Sat. 9-5, Sun. 1-5; winter by event. Adults $3, senior citizens, students & children $2; school & group tours available (call in advance); members no charge. Closed New Year's Day; Thanksgiving; Christmas. ♿
Attendance: 25,000 (accurate)
Membership: Individual $30; Family $50; Centennial $100; Sponsor $250; Benefactor $500; Patron $1,000.

YELLOWSTONE GATEWAY MUSEUM OF PARK COUNTY, (M), 118 W. Chinook, Livingston, MT 59047-2011. Tel.: 406-222-4184. Fax: 406-222-4146.
Web Site: livingstonmuseums.org
Formerly: Park County Museum, House of Memories
Founded: 1976.
Congressional District: 1
Key Personnel: Dir., Brian K. Sparks; Pres. & Museum Shop Mgr., Susan Kraft; Chm. (V), Donna Armentano.
Personnel Profile: Full-Time Paid 1; Full-Time Volunteers 32; Part-Time Paid 1; Part-Time Volunteers 37.
Governing Authority: county. Tax-exempt.
Historical Society Museum: housed in 1906 North Side School.
Collections: tools used by early ranchers, miners, professionals; 1871-1950 Northern Pacific Railroad artifacts & photographs; 1869-1950 Yellowstone Park memorabilia; archaeological artifacts; clothing; household furniture; Wild West displays including Lewis & Clark, Calamity Jane & Buffalo Bill Cody; pioneer living artifacts & buildings; military artifacts from 1864 to WWII; 1868 Ft. Parker; mining & 10 stamp gold mill.
Research Fields: archaeology; local history; railroad history; genealogy.
Facilities: 350-vol. library of bound & unbound material, consisting of history books & newspapers, available for use on premises; theater; educational facilities. Local handcrafts & historical books for sale.
Activities: guided tours; radio programs; formally organized education programs; lectures; loan exhibitions.
Publications: biannual newsletter, News From the Red Caboose.
Hours & Admission Prices: Memorial Day weekend to Labor Day daily 10-5; Sept. Tues.-Sat. 10-4; other times by appointment. Adults $4, senior citizens $3.50, children 6-12 $2; discounts to AAM members; members & children under 6 no charge.
Attendance: 2,800 (accurate)
Membership: Individual $15; Family $25; Business $50; Lifetime $150; Gold $500; Platinum $1,000.

Lolo

HOLT HERITAGE MUSEUM, 6800 Lewis & Clark Tr., Lolo, MT 59847. Mailing Address: P.O. Box 129, Lolo, MT 59847-0129. Tel.: 406-273-6743. Fax: 406-273-6378.
E-mail: info@holtheritagemuseum.com
Web Site: www.holtheritagemuseum.com
Key Personnel: Owner, Bill Holt; Owner, Ramona Holt
History Museum.
Collections: celebrity & collector western boots; saddles & tack; original artwork; wagon; Indian ceremonial display.
Hours & Admission Prices: By appointment.

Loma

EARTH SCIENCE MUSEUM, 208 Broadway Ave., Loma, MT 59460. Mailing Address: P.O. Box 207, Loma, MT 59460-0207. Tel.: 406-739-4282.
Science Museum.
Collections: gems; minerals; fossils; Native American artifacts; train memorabilia.
Facilities: Museum-related items for sale.
Hours & Admission Prices: Memorial Day to Labor Day daily 10-5. ♿

HOUSE OF A THOUSAND DOLLS, 106 First St., Loma, MT 59460. Mailing Address: P.O. Box 136, Loma, MT 59460-0136. Tel.: 406-739-4338.
Founded: 1979.
Key Personnel: C.E.O., Marion Britton.
Personnel Profile: Full-Time Volunteers 1.
Governing Authority: individual operation.
Toy & Doll Museum.
Collections: dolls & toys from 1830 to present.
Hours & Admission Prices: By appointment only. Adults $1, children $.50.
Attendance: 600 (estimated)

Malta

GREAT PLAINS DINOSAUR MUSEUM AND FIELD STATION, 405 N. 1st St. E., Malta, MT 59538. Mailing Address: P.O. Box 170, Malta, MT 59538. Tel.: 406-654-5300.
Founded: 2001.
Key Personnel: Pres. (V), Carolyn Schmoeckel; Museum Shop Mgr., Sue Frary.
Personnel Profile: Full-Time Paid 1; Part-Time Paid 2.
Governing Authority: Parent Institution: Judith River Foundation, Inc.
History Museum.
Collections: dinosaur history; photographs.
Major Exhibits: Eichorn Sea Life, 1/10-12/10; Eichorn Fossils, 1/10-12/10.
Research Fields: dinosaur fossils.
Facilities: Museum-related items for sale.
Activities: educational programs; lectures.
Hours & Admission Prices: Mon.-Sat. 10-5, Sun. 12:30-5. Adults $5; discounts to school groups; members no charge. ♿
Attendance: 8,740 (accurate)
Membership: $25; $100; $250; $500.

PHILLIPS COUNTY MUSEUM, 431 U.S. Hwy. 2 E., Malta, MT 59538. Mailing Address: P.O. Box 518, Malta, MT 59538. Tel.: 406-654-1037.
History Museum.
Collections: local history & culture; period furnishings; personal artifacts; photographs; Native American art; period clothing.
Hours & Admission Prices: Mon.-Sat. 10-5, Sun. 12:30-5. Adults $5, children over 5 $3; discounts to groups.

Miles City

CUSTER COUNTY ART & HERITAGE CENTER, Waterplant Rd., Miles City, MT 59301. Mailing Address: P.O. Box 1284, Miles City, MT 59301-1284. Tel.: 406-234-0635. Fax: 406-234-0637.
E-mail: ccartc@midrivers.com
Web Site: www.ccac.milescity.org
Founded: 1975.
Congressional District: 1
Key Personnel: C.E.O. & Exec. Dir., Mark Browning; Dir. Education, Keely Perkins; Resident Artist, Jim Bailey; Exec. Asst., Jaime Burkhalter.
Personnel Profile: Full-Time Paid 3; Part-Time Paid 1; Part-Time Volunteers 35.
Governing Authority: nonprofit organization. Tax-exempt: 501(c)(3).
Visual Arts Center & Museum: housed in 1910 waterworks building.
Collections: 20th-century Western art with emphasis on contemporary work by Montana artists; photographs of L.A. Huffman, Edward S. Curtis, Evelyn Cameron; underground museum; former water holding tanks of Old Miles City water works.
Facilities: pottery studio. Gift shop with works by Montana & regional artists.
Activities: temporary & traveling exhibitions; gallery talks; lectures; performing arts programs; workshops. Museum Sponsors: Quick Draw in park in May; fall art auction.
Publications: quarterly newsletter; exhibit brochures.
Hours & Admission Prices: May-Sept. Tues.-Sun. 9-5; Oct.-March Tues.-Sun. 1-5. No charge; donations accepted. Closed New Year's Day; Easter; Thanksgiving; Christmas. ♿
Attendance: 10,000 (accurate)
Membership: Student & Senior Citizen $15; Individual $25; Family $40; Business $60; Contributing $50; Sustaining $75; Sponsor $100; Patron $300; Benefactor $500.

RANGE RIDERS MUSEUM, 435 LP Anderson Rd., Miles City, MT 59301-4753. Tel.: 406-232-6146 & 4483.
Key Personnel: C.E.O. & Dir., Bob Barthelmess
History Museum: housed on the site of the 1876 Fort Keogh cantonment.
Collections: pioneer history; period furnishings & artifacts; photographs.
Hours & Admission Prices: April-Oct. daily 8-6.

Missoula

CHILDREN'S MUSEUM MISSOULA, 225 W. Front St., Missoula, MT 59802-4301. Tel.: 406-541-7529.
E-mail: info@learnplayimagine.org
Web Site: www.learnplayimagine.org
Founded: 2000.
Key Personnel: Dir., Coco Ballew.
Personnel Profile: Full-Time Paid 1; Part-Time Paid 10; Part-Time Volunteers 10; Interns 1.
Governing Authority: Parent Institution: Families First. Tax-exempt.
Children's Museum.
Collections: hands-on exhibits.
Facilities: Museum-related items for sale.
Activities: special events; educational programs; interactive exhibits.
Hours & Admission Prices: Tues.-Sat. 10-5, Sun. 12-5. Admission $4.25; children under one no charge. ACM members reciprocal program. ♿
Attendance: 29,000 (estimated)
Membership: Grandparentship $45; Familyship $65; Friendship $100; Starship $250; Leadership $500.

ELK COUNTRY VISITOR CENTER, 5705 Grant Creek Rd., Missoula, MT 59808-9394. Tel.: 406-523-4545.
Visitor Center.
Collections: North American elk history; ecology; biology; game management; hunting; antlers.
Hours & Admission Prices: Jan.-May Mon.-Fri. 8-5, Sat. 10-5; June-Dec. Mon.-Fri. 8-6, Sat.-Sun. 9-6. No charge.

* **HISTORICAL MUSEUM AT FORT MISSOULA, (M),** Bldg. 322, Fort Missoula, Missoula, MT 59804. Tel.: 406-728-3476. Fax: 406-543-6277.
E-mail: ftmslamuseum@montana.com
Web Site: www.fortmissoulamuseum.org
Founded: 1975.
Congressional District: 1
Key Personnel: Chm. (V), Gary Glynn; Pres. (V), Pat Turnage; Exec. Dir., Robert M. Brown; Dir. Devel., Diane Sands; Cur., Jason Bain; Dir. Education, Dorene Might-Dyer; Museum Shop Mgr., Brenda Steward; Museum Asst., Rachel Bartlett; Museum Aide, Sharon Garner; Education Asst., Carolyn Thompson.
Personnel Profile: Full-Time Paid 3; Part-Time Paid 4; Part-Time Volunteers 40; Interns 2.
Governing Authority: county. Parent Institution: Missoula County. Tax-exempt.
Historical Museum Complex & Site: housed in 1911 brick quartermaster's warehouse, located on 32-acres (Historic District) at the core of what was Fort Missoula (1877-1947).
Collections: 19th & 20th-century furnishings, textiles, clothing, tools; USFS artifacts; logging tools; U.S. army uniforms, weapons & vehicles; alien detention records. Historical Buildings: 1878 Log NCO quarters; 1910 railroad depot; 1863 log church; 1933 USFS Lookout; 1907 Grant Creek school; 1910 USFS guard cabin; 1908 quartermaster's root house (cellar); 1940 U.S. Army warehouse; 1911 quartermaster's warehouse; 1941 internment camp barracks building; 1941 Alien Detention Camp headquarters building.
Major Exhibits: 1910: The Days the Mountains Roared, 3/10-1/11.
Research Fields: Missoula County & Fort Missoula history; history of forest management & timber production in western Montana; World War II Alien Detention Center.
Facilities: 500-vol. library of museum administration, western history & historical school books available for research by bona fide researchers; meeting room; Iris Test Gardens. Books related to Montana & western history for sale.
Activities: guided tours; gallery talks; formally organized education programs for children & adults; training programs for professional museum workers; loan, long term, changing & traveling exhibitions; lecture series. Museum Sponsors: Forest Day in April; Independence Day celebration.
Publications: booklet, The Military History of Fort Missoula; postcard series; Missoula, The Way It Was; Purple & Gold, A 60 Year History of Missoula County High School.
Hours & Admission Prices: Memorial Day-Labor Day Mon.-Sat. 10-5, Sun. 12-5; Sept.-May Tues.-Sun. 12-5. Adults $3, seniors $2, students $1; discounts to AAA, AAM, ICOM members & museum professionals; children under 6 & members no charge. ♿
Attendance: 40,000 (estimated)
Membership: Friend $25; Family $50; Patron $100; Contributor $500; Sustainer $1,000; Historian $2,000; Partner $5,000.

* **MISSOULA ART MUSEUM, (M),** 335 N. Pattee St., Missoula, MT 59802-4520. Tel.: 406-728-0447. Fax: 406-543-8691.
E-mail: museum@missoulaartmuseum.org
Web Site: www.missoulaartmuseum.org
Founded: 1975.
Congressional District: 1
Key Personnel: Exec. Dir., Laura J. Millin; Pres. (V), Sharon Shavely; Cur. Education, Renee Taaffe; Dir. Visitor Svcs., Linden How; Cur. Exhibitions, Stephen Glueckert; Registrar, Theodore Hughes; Office Mgr., Pam Adams; Asst. Cur. & Preparator, John Calsbeek; Devel. & Membership Dir., Nici Holt; Visitor Svcs. Assoc., Alicia Jones; Dir. Mktg. & Communications, Katie Stanton.
Personnel Profile: Full-Time Paid 9; Part-Time Paid 1; Part-Time Volunteers 75; Interns 2.
Governing Authority: nonprofit organization. Tax-exempt: 501 (c)(3).
Contemporary Art Museum: housed in 1903 Carnegie Library.
Collections: Art by artists who lived or worked in the Western US with an emphasis on contemporary Montana artists; contemporary American Indian art collection.
Major Exhibits: Roger Shimomura: Minidoka on My Mind, 11/09-1/6/10; Scott Fife: Big Trouble The Idaho Project, 11/09-2/10/10; Image of Sacajawea, 12/09-2/22/10; 38th Benefit Art Auction Exhibition, 1/8/10-2/4/10; Kevin Red Star, 4/13/10-8/30/10.
Research Fields: contemporary art of the western United States; Montana artists; contemporary American Indian art; contemporary artists of the region.
Facilities: library; classrooms. Museum-related items for sale.
Activities: summer art school; interactive tours; lectures; performances; gallery talks; concerts; formally organized education programs for children & adults; loan & traveling exhibitions; resource library.
Publications: books, Hmong Voices in Montana; Ernie Pepion: Dreams on Wheels; catalogs, Gennie Deweese Retrospective; Lynne Hull, Dreaming Missoula; Hamish Fulton; Cathy Weber's Grief Series; Corwin Clairmont; Halfway Between Here and There; Anne Appleby & Wes Mills; James Todd Retrospective 1941-2002; catalogue, Lela Autio; Stan Healty: Artist's Eye; Nancy Erickson: Recent Works; Native Perspectives on the Trail: A Contemporary American Indian Portfolio; John Armstrong: Engaged Abstractions; M.A. Papanek-Miller: A Snowman Cares for Our Memory of Water; Missoula Art Museum's 2009 Montana Triennial.
Hours & Admission Prices: Wed.-Fri. 10-5, Sat.-Sun. 10-3. No charge; donations accepted.
Attendance: 40,000 (accurate)
Membership: Artist, Student, Senior & Non-Resident of Missoula County $30; Individual $40; Family & Dual $60; Friend $100; Patron $250; Benefactor $500 & up. Small Business $250; Business Friend $500; Business Patron $1,000; Business Benefactor $5,000 & up.

MONTANA MUSEUM OF ART & CULTURE, (M), Main Hall 006, University of Montana, 32 Campus Dr., Missoula, MT 59812-0001. Tel.: 406-243-2019. Fax: 406-243-2797.
E-mail: museum@umontana.edu
Web Site: www.umt.edu/montanamuseum
Founded: 1956.
Congressional District: 1
Key Personnel: Dir., Barbara Koostra; Cur., Manuela Well-Off-Man; Registrar, Lucy Capehart; Asst. to Cur., Bill Queen; Coord. Programs & Publications, Rebecca Garner; Dir. Devel., Sara Portzel; Collections Assoc., Kay Grissom Kiely; Administrative Assoc., Jennifer Malagrida.
Personnel Profile: Full-Time Paid 1; Part-Time Paid 7; Part-Time Volunteers 2; Interns 2.
Governing Authority: Parent Institution: The University of Montana. Tax-exempt.
Art Museum.
Collections: Western & European Painters: Sharp, Paxson, Mauer, Chase, Fra Dana; American Painters: Krasner & Motherwell contemporary prints; Autio, Voulkos ceramic sculpture; Montana area artifacts; Chinese & Japanese art; Native American art with Montana emphasis.
Research Fields: art history; museology; historical & contemporary Montana artists; Native American artists; Asian art.
Activities: guided tours; lectures; films; arts festivals; organized educational programs for children & University of Montana students; participatory, temporary, traveling & loan exhibitions; school loan service.
Hours & Admission Prices: June-Aug. Wed.-Sat. 11-3; Sept.-May Tues.-Thurs. 11-3, Fri.-Sat. 4-8:30. No charge; donations accepted. Closed Montana state holidays. ♿
Attendance: 9,000 (estimated)

MONTANA NATURAL HISTORY CENTER, 120 Hickory St., Missoula, MT 59801-1820. Tel.: 406-327-0405.
E-mail: office@montananaturalist.org
Web Site: www.montananaturalist.org
Key Personnel: Exec. Dir., Arnold Olsen, Ph.D.; Youth Programs Coord., Lisa Bickell; Community Programs Coord., Jessie Sherburne; Field Notes Coord. & Montana Naturalist Editor, Caroline Kurtz; Naturalist, Brian William; Volunteer Coord. & Database Mgr., Kathryn Socie; Administrative Asst., Jenny Gray.
Governing Authority: Tax-exempt: 501(c)(3).
Natural History Center.
Collections: birds; reptiles; plants.
Facilities: library.
Hours & Admission Prices: Tues.-Fri. 12-5, Sat. 12-4. Adults $1, children 3-12 & under $.50; children under 3 & MNHC members no charge.

MUSEUM OF MOUNTAIN FLYING, Missoula International Airport, Missoula, MT 59801. Mailing Address: 713 S. Third St., Missoula, MT 59801-2513. Tel.: 406-721-3644. Fax: 406-728-9280.
Founded: 1993.
Key Personnel: Stan Cohen Rick Nash.
Personnel Profile: Part-Time Volunteers 12.
Governing Authority: bd.

Aviation History Museum.
Collections: area mountain flying history; aircraft; hands-on exhibits.
Hours & Admission Prices: April-Oct. 10-4. Family $10, adult $3, children, seniors & military $2; members no charge. ♿
Attendance: 3,000 (estimated)
Membership: Single $25; Couple $35; Family $50; Life $1,000.

PHILIP L. WRIGHT ZOOLOGICAL MUSEUM AND UNIVERSITY OF MONTANA HERBARIUM, Division of Biological Sciences, University of Montana, 32 Campus Dr. #4824, Missoula, MT 59812-0001. Tel.: 406-243-5222. Fax: 406-243-4184.
E-mail: dave.dyer@mso.umt.edu
Web Site: www.zoologicalmuseum.dbs.umt.edu
Founded: 1909.
Key Personnel: Assoc. Dean College Arts & Sciences, Dr. Charles Janson; Cur. Ornithology, Dr. Richard Hutto; Cur. Mammalogy, Dr. Kerry Foresman; Cur. Collections, David Dyer.
Personnel Profile: Full-Time Paid 1; Part-Time Paid 4; Part-Time Volunteers 3; Interns 2.
Governing Authority: public university; nonprofit. Parent Institution: University of Montana. Tax-exempt: 501(c)(3).
Zoological Museum & Herbarium: the herbarium is housed in the Natural Sciences Building, which is a contributive structure within the University of Montana Historical District.
Collections: Museum: over 23,500 specimens of fish, birds & mammals from the Northern Rockies, particularly Montana; Chinese & Russian specimens. Herbarium: over 130,000 specimens of plants from the Northern Rocky Mountains, particularly Montana & to a lesser extent North America & the world.
Research Fields: small mammal population & systematic studies, particularly species of bats & shrews; neotropical bird studies.
Facilities: university library facilities; classrooms; laboratories; field research station.
Activities: formal education programs for undergraduate & graduate students affiliated with the University of Montana; programs are conducted in conjunction with the Montana Natural History Center & includes field trips, seminars, workshops, traveling natural history trunks & a weekly radio program.
Publications: biannual newsletter.
Hours & Admission Prices: research & teaching collections not open to general public. ♿

ROCKY MOUNTAIN MUSEUM OF MILITARY HISTORY, Bldgs. T-310 & T-316 at Fort Missoula, Missoula, MT 59807. Mailing Address: P.O. Box 7263, Missoula, MT 59807-7263. Tel.: 406-549-5346.
E-mail: info@fortmissoula.org
Web Site: www.fortmissoula.org
Key Personnel: Exec. Dir., Tate Jones.
Governing Authority: Tax-exempt: 501(c)(3).
Military History Museum.
Collections: documents & artifacts from Civil War artillery to Vietnam-Era anti-tank missiles.
Hours & Admission Prices: June-Labor Day daily 12-5; mid-Sept.-May Sat.-Sun. 12-5.

Pablo

THE PEOPLE'S CENTER, 53253 Hwy. 93 W., Pablo, MT 59855. Mailing Address: P.O. Box 278, Pablo, MT 59855-0278. Tel.: 406-675-0160. Fax: 406-675-0160.
E-mail: peoplescenter@cskt.org
Web Site: www.peoplescenter.net
Native American History Museum.
Collections: photographs & negatives, artifacts, beaded bags, stone tools & dance outfits pertaining to the Salish, Kootenai & Pend d'Oreille tribes.
Hours & Admission Prices: June-Aug. Mon.-Sat. 9-5; Sept.-May Mon.-Fri. 9-5.

Philipsburg

GRANITE COUNTY MUSEUM & CULTURAL CENTER, 135 S. Sansome, Philipsburg, MT 59858. Mailing Address: P.O. Box 502, Philipsburg, MT 59858-0502. Tel.: 406-859-3020.
History Museum.
Collections: American heritage; period artifacts; local history.
Facilities: Museum-related items for sale.
Hours & Admission Prices: May-Oct. 15 daily 10-4. ♿

Plentywood

SHERIDAN COUNTY MUSEUM, 4262 Hwy. 16 S., Plentywood, MT 59254. Mailing Address: 115 Broadmore St., Plentywood, MT 59254-1910. Tel.: 406-765-1733.
History Museum.
Collections: local history & culture; paintings; photographs; furnishings.
Hours & Admission Prices: Memorial Day-Labor Day daily 1-5; other times by appointment.

Polson

MIRACLE OF AMERICA MUSEUM INC., 36094 Memory Lane, Polson, MT 59860-8446. Tel.: 406-883-6804.
E-mail: info@miracleofamericamuseum.org
Web Site: miracleofamericamuseum.org
Founded: 1985.
Key Personnel: Dir., Mel Adams; Dir., Cathleen Wilde; C.E.O., W. Gilbert Mangels; Treas. & Museum Shop Mgr., Joanne Mangels.
Personnel Profile: Full-Time Volunteers 2; Part-Time Paid 0; Part-Time Volunteers 12.
Governing Authority: nonprofit organization. Tax-exempt: 501(c)(3).
General Museum.
Collections: Native Americans; woodworking; cowboys; musical instruments; blacksmithing; agriculture; engines; tractors; toys & dolls; Civil War-present, guns & militaria; motorcycles; snow vehicles; pioneer village; timber industry; wildlife; schools; clothing; wooden boats; vintage autos & trucks.
Facilities: 2,000-vol. library; sheet music; 41,000 sq. ft. exhibit space. Gift items & books for sale.
Activities: docent program; formal education programs for children; guided tours; lectures; loan & temporary & participatory exhibitions. Annual Event: Living History Days in July.
Publications: quarterly newsletter; souvenir booklet; brochure.
Hours & Admission Prices: June-Aug. daily 8-dusk; Sept.-May daily 8-5. Adults $4, children 3-12 $1; discounts to AAA, seniors & students; members & children under 3 no charge. Closed Christmas. ♿
Attendance: 14,000 (estimated)
Membership: Family $25; Sustaining $100; Life $1,000.

POLSON-FLATHEAD HISTORICAL MUSEUM, 708 Main St., Polson, MT 59860-3225. Mailing Address: P.O. Box 206, Polson, MT 59860-0206. Tel.: 406-883-3049.
Web Site: www.polsonflatheadmuseum.org
Founded: 1964.
Key Personnel: Pres. (V), Lois Hart.
Personnel Profile: Part-Time Paid 2.
Governing Authority: board. Tax-exempt.
History Museum.
Collections: Salish Cootenia tribal history; homesteading; stagecoach; chuck-wagon; buggies; 1884 trading post; guns; boat; weld animal display; farm equipment.
Hours & Admission Prices: Memorial Day-Labor Day Mon.-Sat. 10-5, Sun. 12-3. No charge; donations accepted. ♿
Attendance: 2,500 (estimated)
Membership: Individual $15; Family $25; Lifetime $200.

Poplar

POPLAR MUSEUM, 210 US Hwy. 2 E., Poplar, MT 59255. Mailing Address: P.O. Box 157, Poplar, MT 59255-0157. Tel.: 406-768-5223.
Personnel Profile: Part-Time Paid 1; Part-Time Volunteers 2.
Governing Authority: bd.
History Museum: housed in old Tribal Jail, built around 1920.
Collections: Frontier & Indian collections; photographs; personal artifacts.
Hours & Admission Prices: June - Labor Day Mon.-Sat. 11-5. No charge; donations accepted.

Pryor

CHIEF PLENTY COUPS MUSEUM, Egdar Rd., Pryor, MT 59066. Mailing Address: P.O. Box 100, Pryor, MT 59066-0100. Tel.: 406-252-1289. Fax: 406-252-6668.
E-mail: plentycoups@plentycoups.org
Web Site: www.plentycoups.org
Founded: 1972.
Congressional District: 2
Key Personnel: State Parks Mgr. Region 5, Doug Habermann; Chief Plenty Coups Museum Park Mgr., Susan Stewart.
Personnel Profile: Full-Time Paid 1; Part-Time Paid 2; Part-Time Volunteers 2; Interns 1.

Governing Authority: state. Parent Institution: Montana Fish, Wildlife & Parks.
Crow Indian Museum.
Collections: ethnographic materials of the Crow people; paintings; drawings; prehistoric artifacts. Historic Structure: c.1909 building.
Research Fields: prehistory & history of the Crow people.
Facilities: Books, prints, Crow beadwork & handicrafts for sale.
Activities: guided tours. Annual Event: Chief Plenty Coups Day of Honor.
Publications: annual newsletter, Friends of Chief Plenty Coups Association.
Hours & Admission Prices: Park: daily 8-8. Museum: May-Sept. daily 10-5. Admission: $2 per person; state residents no charge. ♿
Attendance: 12,000 (estimated)
Membership: Friends of Chief Plenty Coups Association $5; $25; $50; $100; $200 & up.

Red Lodge

CARBON COUNTY HISTORICAL SOCIETY AND MUSEUM, 224 N. Broadway, Red Lodge, MT 59068. Tel.: 406-446-3667. Fax: 406-446-1920.
Web Site: www.carboncountyhistory.com
Key Personnel: Dir., Donna Madson; Pres. (V), Paul Henry; Preservation Officer, Deb Hronek; Collections, Dana Wahlquist; Museum Store Mgr., Cathy Wiltgen.
Personnel Profile: Full-Time Paid 2; Part-Time Paid 2; Part-Time Volunteers 10.
Governing Authority: Tax-exempt.
History Museum.
Collections: local history & culture; photographs; personal artifacts.
Hours & Admission Prices: Summer: Mon.-Sat. 10-6, Sun. 11-3; Winter: Tues.-Fri. 10-5, Sat. 11-3; groups by appointment. Adults $3, students $2; discounts to AAA members; school groups and children 5 & under no charge.
Membership: Annual $15-$10,000.

Richey

RICHEY HISTORICAL SOCIETY, 122 S. Main St., Richey, MT 59259. Mailing Address: Box 264, Richey, MT 59259-0264. Tel.: 406-773-5615.
Founded: 1973.
Key Personnel: Pres., Janice Hrubes; C.E.O., Jeff Brost; Sec., Treas. & Chief Cur., Kristen Strohm.
Personnel Profile: Part-Time Paid 1.
Governing Authority: nonprofit organization. Tax-exempt: 501(c)(3).
Historical Society Museum.
Collections: farm tools; ranch items; books & photographs; post office items; homestead shack; old time store; clocks; piano; reed organs; typewriters; musical instruments; kitchen & living room furniture; kitchen utensils; clothing; machinery; newspaper files; church & school items; local histories. Historic Buildings: 1913 Lisk Creek School #92; 1916 Old Richey Jail; 1916-1928 Richey National Bank.
Facilities: library of newspapers, school textbooks, U.S. Post Office record books from Richey, Axtell, Sullivan & Paxton and other books, available for use on premises.
Activities: guided tours; permanent exhibitions.
Publications: Honyocker's Heritage; Richey School Memories: A History of Richey Schools 1916-1991; Richey 1916-1966; History of Community United Methodist Church of Richey 1914-1989.
Hours & Admission Prices: Mon. 2-5; other times by appointment. No charge; donations accepted.
Attendance: 200 (estimated)
Membership: Individual $5; Couple $8; Life $100.

Ronan

GARDEN OF THE ROCKIES MUSEUM, 45356 Hwy. 93 S., Ronan, MT 59864-9649. Tel.: 406-676-3390 & 0977.
History Museum: housed in a church, built in the early 1900s.
Collections: one-room schoolhouse; tool shed; farm machinery building.
Hours & Admission Prices: Memorial Day-Labor Day Mon.-Fri. 11-4.

Roundup

MUSSELSHELL VALLEY HISTORICAL MUSEUM, 524 First W., Roundup, MT 59072-2437. Tel.: 406-323-1403 & 1662.
E-mail: dparrott@midrivers.com
Web Site: www.mvhm.us
Founded: 1972.
Congressional District: 2
Key Personnel: Pres., Jeri Webber; Vice Pres., Bonnie DeMaio; Asst. Dir. & Treas., Shirley Parrott; Sec., Nancy Kemler.
Personnel Profile: Part-Time Volunteers 15.
Governing Authority: nonprofit organization. Tax-exempt: 501(c)(3).
History Museum.
Collections: schoolhouse, post office and country store displays; Indian artifacts; fossils; crystals; coal mine; blacksmith shop; local wildlife; cowboys; newspapers from 1908 to present. Historic Structures: 1884 cabin; 1932 Peitenpol airplane; 1920 brick school building.
Research Fields: fossils; artifacts.
Facilities: 7,000 sq. ft. exhibit space. Russell prints, postcards & books of local origin for sale.
Activities: guided tours; arts festivals; formally organized education programs; permanent & temporary exhibitions.
Publications: book, Roundup on Musselshell; settlers' ethnic cookbook, Old Time Chuck; Horizons or the Musselshell.
Hours & Admission Prices: May-Sept. daily 1-5. No charge; donations accepted.
Attendance: 2,000 (accurate)
Membership: Annual $5; Initial Membership $10; Life $100.

Scobey

DANIELS COUNTY MUSEUM AND PIONEER TOWN, (M), 7 W County Rd., Scobey, MT 59263. Mailing Address: P.O. Box 133, Scobey, MT 59263-0133. Tel.: 406-487-5965 & 2061.
E-mail: dcmuseum@nemont.net
Web Site: scobey.org
Founded: 1965.
Congressional District: 1
Key Personnel: Pres., Mike Thierin; Vice Pres., Edgar Richardson; Exec. Dir. & Museum Shop Mgr., Mary Richardson; Dir., Jacki Oic; Dir., Gordy Blomquist; Dir., Kristi Shipstead; Dir., Justin Hanson; Dir., Frank Edwards; Dir. & Sec., Gorden Crandell.
Personnel Profile: Full-Time Volunteers 2; Part-Time Paid 1; Part-Time Volunteers 80.
Governing Authority: individual operation. Tax-exempt: 501(c)(3).
Village Museum & Pioneer Town.
Collections: Daniels County history; cultural & heritage artifacts; house; bank; blacksmith shop; service station; general store; saloon; ladies' shop; shack; fire hall; doctor's & dentist's office; post office; implement building; funeral home; school; watch repair shop; tractors & cars; 3 churches; hotel; visitors center; theatre; period cars; City Hall.
Research Fields: Daniel County.
Facilities: community rooms.
Activities: guided tours; rental facilities. Museum Sponsors: threshing bee & antique show.
Hours & Admission Prices: Memorial Day to Labor Day daily 12:30-4:30; Sept.-May Tues.10-2, Fri. 1-4; other times by appointment. Tours: adults $7, children 6-11 $4; discounts to AAM members; members & children under 5 no charge. ♿
Attendance: 1,500 (estimated)
Membership: Individual $15; Family $40.

Seeley Lake

SEELEY LAKE HISTORICAL MUSEUM AND VISITOR CENTER, 2920 Hwy. 83, Seeley Lake, MT 59868. Mailing Address: P.O. Box 1261, Seeley Lake, MT 59868-1261. Tel.: 406-677-2990.
Founded: 2004.
Personnel Profile: Part-Time Volunteers 7.
Governing Authority: Parent Institution: Seeley Lake Historical Society. Tax-exempt.
History Museum.
Collections: local history & culture; school artifacts; logging; Native American; photographs; documents.
Publications: Cabin Fever.
Hours & Admission Prices: Memorial Day to Labor Day daily 11-4; Winter: Tues.-Sat. 11-4. No charge; donations accepted. ♿
Attendance: 2,000 (estimated)
Membership: $30; $50; $100; $200.

Shelby

MARIAS MUSEUM OF HISTORY AND ART, 206 12th Ave. N., Shelby, MT 59474-1708. Tel.: 406-424-2551. Fax: 406-424-5422.
Founded: 1963.
Congressional District: 2
Key Personnel: C.E.O., Chm. (V) & Pres. (V), Larry Munson; Bd. Member & Vice Pres., Dean Hellinger; Bd. Member, Meredith Beckedahl; Bd. Member & Treas., Yvonne McAlpine; Bd. Member, Mary Mielke; Bd. Member & Sec., Carol Mundt; Bd. Member, Charlotte Hanson; Bd. Member, Ray Tomsheck; Bd. Member, Barbara Mercer; Bd. Member, Warren Iverson; Bd. Member, April Carr; Bd. Member, Marian Hinds; Bd. Member, Albert Lunda; Bd. Member, Mike Mellinger; Bd. Member, Merle Raph; Bd. Member, George Rankin; Bd. Member, Peggy Taylor.

Personnel Profile: Part-Time Paid 3; Part-Time Volunteers 5.
Governing Authority: county; nonprofit. Tax-exempt.
History Museum.
Collections: rocks; fossils; American Indian artifacts; military guns; bottles; toys; clothing; glassware; silver; musical instruments; cameras; phones; office furniture; rooms depicting early-day scenes; 1923 world champion boxing match memorabilia.
Research Fields: local history of school, churches, communities.
Facilities: library of early newspapers, books, magazines & maps.
Activities: temporary exhibits; hands-on exhibits for children.
Publications: Toole County History Calendar: Toole County School Treasures.
Hours & Admission Prices: June-Aug. Mon.-Fri. 1-5 & 7-9, Sat. 1-5; Sept.-May Tues. 1-4; other times by appointment. No charge; donations accepted. ♿
Attendance: 1,327 (accurate)
Membership: Annual $1; Life $25.

Sidney

MONDAK HERITAGE CENTER, 120 Third Ave., S.E., Sidney, MT 59270-4324. Tel.: 406-433-3500. Fax: 406-433-3503.
E-mail: mdhc@richland.org
Web Site: www.mondakheritagecenter.org
Founded: 1971.
Congressional District: 2
Personnel Profile: Full-Time Paid 3; Part-Time Paid 1; Part-Time Volunteers 35.
Governing Authority: individual operation. Parent Institution: MonDak Historical & Art Society. Tax-exempt.
Historical Museum & Art Gallery.
Collections: historical artifacts; original art of the western U.S.; street scene composed of over 12 displays, including a school, church, sheriff's office & homesteader town.
Research Fields: local history.
Facilities: 250-vol. art library & 1,200-vol. history library. Museum-related items for sale.
Activities: gallery talks; arts festivals; hobby workshops; formally organized education programs; permanent & temporary exhibitions.
Publications: book of family histories, Courage Enough, Courage Enough II, Focus on Our Roots; newsletter.
Hours & Admission Prices: Tues.-Wed. & Fri. 10-4, Thurs. 10-7, Sat. 1-4. No charge; donations accepted. ♿
Attendance: 7,500 (accurate)
Membership: Senior Citizen $15; Family $35; Business & Professional $50; Other $50-$1,000.

Stanford

JUDITH BASIN COUNTY MUSEUM, 93 S. 3rd St., Stanford, MT 59479. Mailing Address: P.O. Box 38, Stanford, MT 59479-0038. Tel.: 406-566-2277 (Sept.-June 1); 566-2277, ext. 130 (June-Aug.); 566-2305.
Founded: 1966.
Congressional District: 2
Key Personnel: Pres. (V) & Dir., Florence E. Harris; Dir., Oliver Olson; Cur., Virginia Hayes; Dir., Gene Ernst; Dir., Tess Brady; Dir., Lorraine Boeck.
Personnel Profile: Full-Time Paid 1; Part-Time Paid 1.
Governing Authority: Judith Basin County. Tax-exempt.
General Museum.
Collections: American Indian artifacts; period furnishings; 2,500-piece salt & pepper shaker collection; 50,000 piece button collection; Russell prints; period toys; clothes; canes; war items.
Hours & Admission Prices: June-Aug. Mon.-Fri. & Sun. 9-12 & 1-5. No charge; donations accepted. Closed major holidays. ♿
Attendance: 150 (estimated)

Stevensville

HISTORIC ST. MARY'S MISSION, West End of 4th St., Stevensville, MT 59870. Mailing Address: P.O. Box 211, Stevensville, MT 59870-0211. Tel.: 406-777-5734.
E-mail: stmary@cybernet1.com
Web Site: www.saintmarysmission.org
History Museum: founded in 1841 by Jesuit priests.
Collections: original hand-carved furnishings; Salish artifacts; historic documents; photographs.
Hours & Admission Prices: April 17-Oct. 15 Tues.-Sat. 10-4.

STEVENSVILLE MUSEUM, 517 Main St., Stevensville, MT 59870-2838. Mailing Address: P.O. Box 750, Stevensville, MT 59870-0750. Tel.: 406-777-1007 & 3546.
History Museum.
Collections: local history & culture; photographs; Native American; period furnishings.
Hours & Admission Prices: Memorial Day to Labor Day Thurs.-Sat. 11-4, Sun. 1-4; groups by appointment. No charge, donations accepted. ♿

Superior

MINERAL COUNTY MUSEUM & HISTORICAL SOCIETY, 2nd Ave. E., Superior, MT 59872-0301. Mailing Address: P.O. Box 533, Superior, MT 59872-0533. Tel.: 406-822-3543.
E-mail: mchs1976@blackfoot.net
Web Site: mineral-museum.tripod.com
Founded: 1975.
Congressional District: 1
Key Personnel: Pres. Historical Society, Dennis Kimzey; Vice Pres., Peggy Temple; Cur. & Sec., Cathryn Strombo.
Personnel Profile: Part-Time Volunteers 2.
Governing Authority: county. Tax-exempt.
Mineralogy Museum: housed in old hospital building; John Mullan & Mullan Trail Information Center.
Collections: history of Gold Rush; minerals; history of Milwaukee & Northern Pacific Railroad; Native American artifacts; tree nursery; mineral collection; manuscript collection; Captain John Mullan Papers, materials related to Mullan Military Road.
Research Fields: Western Montana Pioneers; Lewis & Clark Trail; collection of folklore; Captain John Mullan, U.S. Army engineer.
Facilities: library.
Activities: guided tours; films; formally organized education programs for children; loan, permanent & temporary exhibitions; costume loan.
Publications: quarterly, Mullan Chronicles.
Hours & Admission Prices: By appointment. No charge; donations accepted. ♿
Attendance: 1,000
Membership: Individual $5; Family $10.

Terry

PRAIRIE COUNTY MUSEUM AND CAMERON GALLERY, 101 S. Logan, Terry, MT 59349. Mailing Address: P.O. Box 426, Terry, MT 59349-0426. Tel.: 406-635-4040 & 2108.
Founded: 1974.
Key Personnel: Dir. & Pres. (V), Wynona Breen.
Personnel Profile: Full-Time Volunteers 19.
Governing Authority: Parent Institution: Prairie County. Tax-exempt.
Historic Building: housed in the 1916 State Bank of Terry.
Collections: local history & culture; early pioneer life; photographs; Terry Tribune Newspapers 1907-2007; obituary file 1907-2007; manuscripts 1880-2007.
Research Fields: genealogy; local history.
Facilities: library.
Hours & Admission Prices: Memorial Day to Labor Day Mon. & Wed.-Fri. 9-3, Sat.-Sun. 1-4; other times by appointment. No charge; donations accepted.
Attendance: 1,000 (estimated)

Thompson Falls

OLD JAIL MUSEUM, 109 S. Madison St., Thompson Falls, MT 59783. Mailing Address: P.O. Box 774, Thompson Falls, MT 59873-0774. Tel.: 406-827-4002.
History Museum: former jail, sheriff's office & residence.
Collections: historical artifacts; photographs; maps.
Hours & Admission Prices: Mother's Day-Labor Day daily 12-4.

Three Forks

HEADWATERS HERITAGE MUSEUM, 202 S. Main, Three Forks, MT 59752. Mailing Address: P.O. Box 116, Three Forks, MT 59752-0116. Tel.: 406-285-4778.
E-mail: museumthreeforks@aol.com
Founded: 1979.
Key Personnel: Dir., Cur. & Museum Shop Mgr., Robin Cadby-Sorensen; Pres. (V), Pat O'Brien Townsend; Treas., Patrick Finnegan.
Personnel Profile: Full-Time Volunteers 1; Part-Time Volunteers 49.
Governing Authority: private; nonprofit organization. Tax-exempt: 501(c)(3).
History Museum.
Collections: local history artifacts & memorabilia; anvil from a fur trappers trading post, 1810; barbed wire; fossils; rocks; arrowheads; maps; agricultural tools; photographs; papers; canoe; 29 1/2 lb brown trout; quilts; railroad memorabilia.
Facilities: Museum-related items for sale.

Activities: guided tours; lectures; loan, temporary & traveling exhibitions; docent program. Annual Events: Horse Drive; Christmas Stroll.
Publications: annual newsletter.
Hours & Admission Prices: June-Sept. Mon.-Sat. 9-5, Sun. 11-3; other times by appointment. No charge; donations accepted.
Attendance: 2,800 (estimated)
Membership: Individual $5; Family $8; Sustaining $25; Life $125; Patron $250; Benefactor $500; Contributor $1,000; Sponsor $5,000; Founder $10,000.

Townsend

BROADWATER COUNTY MUSEUM, 133 N. Walnut, Townsend, MT 59644-2324. Tel.: 406-266-5252.
Founded: 1976.
Key Personnel: Pres. (V), Sharley Ragen; Cur., Mike Castleberry.
Personnel Profile: Full-Time Paid 1; Part-Time Paid 1.
Governing Authority: Tax-exempt.
History Museum.
Collections: local history; mining; dental; homestead cabin; general store; blacksmith shop; early photographic equipment; fossils; Lewis and Clark; military; artifacts; genealogy.
Hours & Admission Prices: May 15-Sept. 15 daily 1-5. No charge; donations accepted. ♿
Attendance: 600 (estimated)
Membership: Individual $3; Family $5; Commercial $20.

Utica

UTICA MUSEUM, 20 Southfork Rd., Utica, MT 59452. Mailing Address: 43 Antelope Creek Rd., Hobson, MT 59452-8623. Tel.: 406-423-5531 & 5208.
Founded: 1965.
Congressional District: 2
Key Personnel: Pres., Floyd Forbes; Treas., Barbara Twiford; Sec., Kathy Hodge.
Personnel Profile: Full-Time Volunteers 15; Part-Time Volunteers 10.
Governing Authority: nonprofit. Affiliated with the Utica Historical Society. Tax-exempt: 170(b)(1)(A).
Historical Society Museum.
Collections: artifacts pertaining to early homesteaders & ranchers.
Research Fields: local history.
Facilities: reading room. Charles Russel prints, agate & yogo sapphire jewelry for sale.
Activities: permanent exhibitions.
Publications: book, Utica I & II.
Hours & Admission Prices: Memorial Day-Labor Day Sat.-Sun 10-5; other times by appointment. No charge; donations accepted. ♿
Attendance: 300 (estimated)
Membership: Individual $5; Life $100.

Victor

VICTOR HERITAGE MUSEUM, Blake & Main St., Victor, MT 59875. Mailing Address: P.O. Box 610, Victor, MT 59875-0610. Tel.: 406-642-3997.
E-mail: victormuseum@cybernet1.com
Founded: 1989.
Key Personnel: Pres. (V), Joann Hosko.
Personnel Profile: Part-Time Volunteers 10.
Governing Authority: private; nonprofit organization. Tax-exempt: 501(c)(3).
History & Heritage Museum: housed in the former NP Railroad Depot Building.
Collections: Victor's history from early 1900s; personal artifacts; folk culture.
Research Fields: Victor area residents before the 1930s.
Activities: Annual Events: Chocolate Tasting Party & Auction in December.
Hours & Admission Prices: Memorial Day to Labor Day Tues.-Sat. 1-4. No charge; donations accepted. ♿
Attendance: 275 (estimated)
Membership: Individual $10.

Virginia City

VIRGINIA CITY J. SPENCER WATKINS MEMORIAL MUSEUM, 219 W. Wallace St., Virginia City, MT 59755. Mailing Address: P.O. Box 215, Virginia City, MT 59755-0215. Tel.: 406-843-5500 (Summer) & 5484. Fax: 406-843-5303.
E-mail: madsnian@3rivers.net
Formerly: Virginia City Madison County Historical Museum
Founded: 1958.
Key Personnel: C.E.O. & Dir., Daryl L. Tichenor.
Personnel Profile: Full-Time Paid 1; Part-Time Paid 1.
Governing Authority: municipal. Tax-exempt: 501(c)(3).
History Museum.
Collections: mounted animals; historical western items; furniture, mining & other things dating back to the 1800's.
Facilities: Books, gifts & Western paintings for sale.
Publications: book, Foot-Steps thru History
Hours & Admission Prices: mid-June to mid-Sept. daily 10-6. No charge; donations accepted.
Attendance: 14,000 (estimated)
Membership: Individual, Family & Business $25.

West Glacier

GLACIER NATIONAL PARK MUSEUM, Glacier National Park, West Glacier, MT 59936. Mailing Address: P.O. Box 128, West Glacier, MT 59936. Tel.: 406-888-7936. Fax: 406-888-7937.
E-mail: deirdre_shaw@nps.gov
Founded: 1930.
Congressional District: 2
Key Personnel: Cur., Deirdre Shaw.
Personnel Profile: Full-Time Paid 1; Part-Time Paid 2; Part-Time Volunteers 1.
Governing Authority: federal government agency.
Park Museum.
Collections: geologic, bird, insect & animal specimens collected within the park; photographs, negatives, lantern slides, prints, film & oral histories of the park, Blackfeet Indians, visitors, residents & park personnel; clothing & furnishings documenting park history; herbarium.
Facilities: 14,000-vol. library of history & scientific material, available for use by the public.
Activities: tours & research by appointment only.
Hours & Admission Prices: Research: Mon.-Fri. 8-4:30. No charge. Closed federal holidays.

West Yellowstone

GRIZZLY & WOLF DISCOVERY CENTER, 201 S. Canyon, West Yellowstone, MT 59758. Mailing Address: P.O. Box 996, West Yellowstone, MT 59758-0996. Tel.: 800-257-2570; 406-646-7001. Fax: 406-646-7004.
E-mail: info@grizzlydiscoveryctr.com
Web Site: grizzlydiscoveryctr.org
Founded: 1993.
Governing Authority: nonprofit organization.
Wildlife Preserve.
Collections: bears; wolves; taxidermic bear mounts; photographs.
Facilities: Museum-related items for sale.
Hours & Admission Prices: Daily 8am to dusk; call to confirm. Adults 13 & over $10.50, seniors 62 & over $9, children 5-12 $5; discounts to groups; children under 5 no charge. ♿
Attendance: 120,000 (estimated)

MADISON CANYON EARTHQUAKE LAKE VISITOR CENTER, U.S. Hwy. 287, West Yellowstone, MT 59758. Mailing Address: P.O. Box 520, West Yellowstone, MT 59758-0520. Tel.: 406-682-7620. Fax: 406-823-6990.
History Museum.
Collections: 1959 earthquake history; geology; seismograph.
Activities: educational programs.
Hours & Admission Prices: Call for hours.

YELLOWSTONE HISTORIC CENTER MUSEUM, 104 Yellowstone Ave., West Yellowstone, MT 59758. Tel.: 406-646-1100.
E-mail: info@yellowstonehistoriccenter.org
Web Site: www.yellowstonehistoriccenter.org
Key Personnel: Cur., Paul Shea
History Museum: housed in the historic Union Pacific Depot.
Collections: memorabilia collected by early visitors; historic transportation pieces; photographs; personal diaries & journals.
Hours & Admission Prices: Call for hours.

White Sulphur Springs

MEAGHER COUNTY HISTORICAL ASSOCIATION CASTLE MUSEUM, 310 1/2 2nd Ave., N.E., White Sulphur Springs, MT 59645. Mailing Address: P.O. Box 716, White Sulphur Springs, MT 59645-0389. Tel.: 406-547-2324.
Founded: 1967.
Congressional District: 1
Key Personnel: Pres., James Reed; Vice Pres., Vonnie Pederson; Sec., Marga Johnson; Treas., Polly Hanson.

Personnel Profile: Full-Time Paid 1; Part-Time Paid 1; Part-Time Volunteers 6.
Governing Authority: nonprofit organization. Tax-exempt.
Historical Society Museum: housed in 1890 restored Victorian Mansion.
Collections: furniture & furnishings; Indian artifacts; carriages in new buildings.
Activities: guided tours.
Publications: The Man Who Built The Castle; Born To Be.
Hours & Admission Prices: Mid-May to mid-Sept. daily 10-6. Adults $5, children & senior citizens $2; discount to groups of 10 or more; members no charge. ♿
Attendance: 4,012 (estimated)
Membership: Individual $10.

Whitefish

STUMPTOWN HISTORICAL SOCIETY MUSEUM, 500 Depot St., Ste. 101, Whitefish, MT 59937-2567. Tel.: 406-862-0067.
Web Site: www.stumptownhistoricalsociety.org
Key Personnel: Exec. Dir., Jill Evans
Historical Society Museum.
Collections: railroad & community artifacts; photographs.
Hours & Admission Prices: Mon.-Sat. 10-4.

Whitehall

JEFFERSON VALLEY MUSEUM, 303 S. Division, Whitehall, MT 59759. Mailing Address: P.O. Box 902, Whitehall, MT 59759-0902. Tel.: 406-287-7813. Fax: 406-287-7813.
E-mail: jvmuseum@in-tch.com
Web Site: gallery.in-tch.com/~jvmmuseum
Founded: 1990.
Key Personnel: Sec., Roy Millegan
History Museum: housed in a restored 1914 barn.
Collections: area history & heritage; genealogy; railroad memorabilia; personal artifacts; photographs.
Activities: research.
Hours & Admission Prices: Memorial Day to Labor Day Tues.-Sun. 12-4; other times by appointment. No charge; donations accepted. ♿
Attendance: 900
Membership: Active $10; Family $20; Sustaining $25; Commercial $100; Life $250; Patron $500; Benefactor $1,000.

Wibaux

WIBAUX MUSEUM, 112 E. Orgain Ave., Wibaux, MT Mailing Address: P.O. Box 72, Wibaux, MT 59353-0072. Tel.: 406-796-9969 & 2594. Fax: 406-796-2625.
E-mail: wpmuseum@midrivers.com
History Museum.
Collections: local history; personal artifacts; early settlers; period barber shop; livery stable; Montana Centennial Train Car; gardens.
Facilities: gardens. Museum-related items for sale.
Activities: children's activities; tours.
Hours & Admission Prices: May-Sept. Mon.-Sat. 9-5, Sun. 1-5. ♿

Winifred

WINIFRED MUSEUM, 210 Main St., Winifred, MT 59489. Mailing Address: P.O. Box 181, Winifred, MT 59489-0181. Tel.: 406-462-5425. Fax: 406-462-5425.
E-mail: winimuse@mtintouch.net
Founded: 2005.
History Museum.
Collections: over 3,000 Tonka toys; archaeological, homestead & military displays.
Hours & Admission Prices: Memorial Day weekend-Labor Day weekend Wed.-Sun. 12:30-5:30. No charge; donations accepted.

Wisdom

BIG HOLE NATIONAL BATTLEFIELD, 16425 Hwy. 43 W., Wisdom, MT 59761. Mailing Address: P.O. Box 237, Wisdom, MT 59761-0237. Tel.: 406-689-3155. Fax: 406-689-3151.
E-mail: biho_visitor_information@nps.gov
Web Site: www.nps.gov/biho
Founded: 1910.
Congressional District: 1
Key Personnel: Unit Mgr., Tami DeGrosky.
Personnel Profile: Full-Time Paid 8; Part-Time Volunteers 4; Interns 1.
Governing Authority: federal. Parent Institution: National Park Service, U.S. Dept. of Interior. Tax-exempt.
Visitor Center Exhibit Hall: located on land which includes all major sites relating to the 1877 Battle of the Big Hole between the Nez Perce Indians & the 7th U.S. Infantry. Plus a small number of citizen volunteers.
Collections: historical & ethnological specimens of Nez Perce Indian culture; archaeology; 1870s army accoutrements, equipment, uniforms & firearms; manuscript collection.
Research Fields: Indian wars; Nez Perce War.
Facilities: 300-vol. library of books & microfilms available on premises; 35-seat auditorium. Publications for sale.
Activities: self-guided tours; lectures; films; gallery talks; permanent exhibitions; interpretive programs.
Publications: pamphlet, Big Hole National Battlefield, Montana; annual visitor guide.
Hours & Admission Prices: Winter & Spring: 10-5; Summer: 9-6; Fall: 9-5. No Charge; donations accepted. Closed New Year's Day; Thanksgiving; Christmas. ♿
Attendance: 50,000 (accurate)

Wolf Point

WOLF POINT AREA HISTORICAL SOCIETY, INC., 220 2nd Ave. S, Wolf Point, MT 59201-1507. Mailing Address: 209 E. Indian St., Wolf Point, MT 59201-1920. Tel.: 406-653-1912 & 1958.
Founded: 1972.
Congressional District: 2
Key Personnel: Chm. (V) & Pres. (V), Diane MacDonald; Museum Shop Mgr., Herman Shumway.
Governing Authority: nonprofit organization. Tax-exempt: 170(b)(1)(I).
Historical Society Museum.
Collections: Western artifacts & pictures; Native American artifacts; ranching; homesteading; bead work; star quilt making; wood carving; free-hand paintings.
Activities: narrated video tape of museum exhibits at senior citizens center.
Hours & Admission Prices: June-Aug. Mon.-Fri. 10-5. No charge; donations accepted.
Attendance: 610 (estimated)

NEBRASKA

(189 listings)

Ainsworth

THE COLEMAN HOUSE MUSEUM AND BROWN COUNTY HISTORICAL SOCIETY, 456 Old Highway #7, Ainsworth, NE 69210. Mailing Address: 339 North Ash St., Ainsworth, NE 69210-1612.
Founded: 1973.
Congressional District: 3
Key Personnel: Pres., Les Nickel; Financial Dir., Shirley Crone.
Personnel Profile: Part-Time Volunteers 22.
Governing Authority: private; nonprofit organization. Parent Institution: The Brown County Historical Society, Ainsworth, NE. Tax-exempt: 170(b)(1)(A).
History Museum: housed in 1918 home.
Collections: history of Brown County, NE & Nebraska; books on local history.
Research Fields: local history; genealogy.
Activities: guided tours; quilting.
Publications: newsletter; Pioneer Doctors of Brown County; Tales of Brown County, Nebraska; Early History of Brown County, Nebraska; Postal History of Brown County, NE; reprinted pioneer stories of Brown, Keya Paha & Rock Counties, NE.
Hours & Admission Prices: Mon.-Thurs. 11-4; other times by appointment. No charge; donations accepted. Closed Memorial Day; Independence Day; Thanksgiving; Christmas. ♿
Attendance: 231 (accurate)
Membership: Individual $10; Sustaining $12; Business $25; Lifetime $100.

SELLORS BARTON MUSEUM AKA LOG CABIN MUSEUM, 606 E. 4th St., Ainsworth, NE 69210-1213. Mailing Address: HC 65, Ainsworth, NE 69210. Tel.: 402-387-2740 (City Office).
Key Personnel: Dir., Carol Larson.
Governing Authority: city.
History Museum: housed in log cabin built in 1936.
Collections: local history; furnishings; household artifacts; clothing; photographs.
Hours & Admission Prices: late May to early Sept. Mon.-Fri. 10:30-4:30, Sat.-Sun. 1-5. No charge; donations accepted. ♿
Attendance: 500 (estimated)

Allen

DIXON COUNTY MUSEUM & HISTORICAL SOCIETY, 225 S. Clark St., Allen, NE 68710. Mailing Address: Box 95, Allen, NE 68710-0095. Tel.: 402-635-2582.
Web Site: www.ci.allen.ne.us
History Museum.
Collections: county history; household & farming artifacts.
Hours & Admission Prices: June-Aug. Sun. 2-4; other times by appointment. No charge. ♿

Alliance

CARNEGIE ARTS CENTER, 204 W. 4th St., Alliance, NE 69301-3332. Tel.: 308-762-4571. Fax: 308-762-4571.
E-mail: carnegieartscenter@bbc.net
Web Site: www.carnegieartscenter.com
Personnel Profile: Full-Time Paid 1; Part-Time Paid 2; Part-Time Volunteers 8.
Governing Authority: nonprofit organization. Tax-exempt.
Art Gallery.
Collections: art exhibits.
Publications: quarterly activities newsletter.
Hours & Admission Prices: Tues.-Sat. 10-4, Sun. 1-4. No charge. Closed major holidays. ♿
Attendance: 3,500 (accurate)
Membership: Individual $25; Family $45.

KNIGHT MUSEUM, (M), 908 Yellowstone, Alliance, NE 69301. Mailing Address: P.O. Box D, Alliance, NE 69301-0770. Tel.: 308-762-2384. Fax: 308-762-2384.
E-mail: museum@cityofalliance.net
Web Site: www.cityofalliance.net
Formerly: Knight Museum of High Plains Heritage
Founded: 1965.
Congressional District: 49
Key Personnel: C.E.O., Richard Cayer; Chm. (V), Ellen Christensen; Dir., Becci Thomas.
Personnel Profile: Full-Time Paid 1; Part-Time Paid 2; Part-Time Volunteers 10.
Governing Authority: municipal. Parent Institution: City of Alliance. Tax-exempt: 170(b)(1)(A).
General Museum.
Collections: local history & railroad items; Indian artifacts; sod house; one room school; genealogy.
Research Fields: Burlington Railroad; western Nebraska history; genealogy; World War II Alliance Air Base.
Facilities: historical & genealogical library; replica sod house in pioneer setting.
Activities: guided tours; lectures; programs. Museum Sponsors: monthly ethnic display June-August.
Publications: brochure.
Hours & Admission Prices: May to Labor Day Mon.-Sat. 10-6, Sun.1-5; Sept. to April Tues.-Sat. 12-5. No charge; donations accepted. ♿
Attendance: 15,250 (accurate)

SALLOWS MILITARY MUSEUM, 1109 Niobrara St., Alliance, NE 69301. Mailing Address: P.O. Box D, Alliance, NE 69301-0770. Tel.: 308-762-2384 & 2385.
Military Museum.
Collections: military history from WWI to present; Alliance Airbase artifacts; personal artifacts; photographs.
Hours & Admission Prices: Tues.-Sat. 1-5; other times by appointment.

Arapahoe

FURNAS-GOSPER HISTORICAL SOCIETY & MUSEUM, 401 Nebraska Ave., Arapahoe, NE 68922. Mailing Address: P.O. Box 202, Arapahoe, NE 68922-0202. Tel.: 308-962-5236.
Web Site: www.visitnebraska.org
Founded: 1966.
Congressional District: 3
Key Personnel: C.E.O. & Pres., Robert Trosper; Treas. & Sec., Connie Graning.
Personnel Profile: Part-Time Volunteers 11.
Governing Authority: county. Parent Institution: Furnas & Gosper Counties Historical Society. Tax-exempt.
General Museum.
Collections: clothing; books; glassware; piano; sewing machines; crockery; roll top desk; flags; pictures.
Research Fields: 1874 Justice of Peace court records of Furnas Co.; 1900s records of Furnas Co.
Facilities: 100-vol. set of encyclopedias & medical books of pioneer doctors available for research on premises.
Activities: guided tours; permanent & temporary exhibitions.
Hours & Admission Prices: Sat.-Sun. 1-5; 1st Wed. of the month 7-9, other times by appointment 308-268-2208. No charge; donations accepted. ♿
Attendance: 1,200 (estimated)
Membership: Individual $10; Family $20; Corporate $75; Life $150.

Ashland

STRATEGIC AIR & SPACE MUSEUM, 28210 West Park Hwy., Ashland, NE 68003-3525. Tel.: 800-358-5029; 402-827-3100, ext. 214. Fax: 402-944-3160.
E-mail: news@strategicairandspace.com
Web Site: www.strategicairandspace.com
Formerly: Strategic Air Command Museum
Founded: 1959.
Congressional District: 2
Key Personnel: Exec. Dir., Mac McLean; Cur., Brian York; Deputy Dir., Evonne Williams; Chief Structural Specialist, Mark Hamilton; Dir. Operations, Tom York.
Personnel Profile: Full-Time Paid 22; Part-Time Paid 18; Part-Time Volunteers 52; Interns 12.
Governing Authority: private; nonprofit organization. Parent Institution: Strategic Air Command & Museum Memorial Society, Inc. Tax-exempt.
Aviation & Space History Museum.
Collections: aircraft; missiles; aviation artifacts.
Research Fields: aerospace history; SAC history; formation of the USAF; WWII; Cold War.
Facilities: research library; cafeteria; gallery; aircraft restoration area; theater; children's interactive educational programs. Museum-related items for sale.
Activities: symposia; films; permanent & temporary exhibitions; education programs; group tours.
Publications: newsletters; quarterly educator newsletter, Wings; e-newsletter.
Hours & Admission Prices: Daily 9-5. Adults $7, children 5-12 $6; discounts to groups, AAA members, senior citizens & military; children under 5 & members no charge. Closed New Year's Day; Easter; Thanksgiving; Christmas. ♿
Attendance: 225,000 (estimated)
Membership: Senior & Military $30; Individual $35; Family $50; Contributing $75-$199; Patron $200-$499; Benefactor $500 & up.

Ashton

POLISH HERITAGE CENTER, INC., 226 Carlton Ave., Ashton, NE 68817. Mailing Address: P.O. Box 3, Ashton, NE 68817-0003. Tel.: 308-738-2249 & 2260.
E-mail: pp1335@nctc.net
Founded: 1997.
Key Personnel: Mgr. & Museum Shop Mgr., Phyllis Piechota; Pres. (V), John Maschka; Sec., Peggy Knapp; Treas., Virginia Pokorski
Polish Heritage Center.
Collections: Polish culture & traditions; books; music; local genealogical records; photographs; art.
Facilities: library. Museum-related items for sale.
Activities: dance performances; special events; educational events. Annual Event: Polish Fest in September; Wigilia Christmas Dinner in December.
Publications: newsletter, Polish Heritage Center, Inc.
Hours & Admission Prices: Sun. 2-4; other times by appointment. Admission $3; members no charge. ♿
Attendance: 750 (estimated)
Membership: Yearly $10; Lifetime $100.

Atkinson

STURDEVANT-MCKEE MUSEUM & FOUNDATION, 308 S. Main St., Atkinson, NE 68713-4982. Mailing Address: P.O. Box 225, Atkinson, NE 68713-0225. Tel.: 402-925-2726.
E-mail: sturdevantmckeemuseum@hotmail.com
Key Personnel: Dir., Diane Alden
History Museum.
Collections: local history; architecture; furnishings; household artifacts.
Hours & Admission Prices: By appointment. No charge; donations accepted.

Auburn

NEMAHA VALLEY MUSEUM, 1423 19th St., Auburn, NE 68305-2350. Tel.: 402-274-3203.
History Museum.
Collections: Nemaha Valley history & industry; quilts; artwork; family histories; school records; historic buildings.

Activities: permanent & temporary exhibits; research.
Hours & Admission Prices: April-Dec. Tues.-Sun. 1-4:30; other times by appointment. No charge; donations accepted.

Aurora

EDGERTON EXPLORIT CENTER, 208 16th St., Aurora, NE 68818-3009. Tel.: 402-694-4032. Fax: 402-694-4035.
E-mail: explorit@edgerton.org
Web Site: www.edgerton.org
Founded: 1995.
Congressional District: 3
Key Personnel: Exec. Dir., Ken Schroeder.
Personnel Profile: Full-Time Paid 3; Part-Time Paid 6; Part-Time Volunteers 120; Interns 5.
Governing Authority: private; nonprofit organization. Tax-exempt: 501(c)(3).
Science Museum.
Collections: hands-on science exhibits for all ages; personal & work related materials of Dr. Harold E. Edgerton, an inventor, educator & explorer.
Facilities: educational facilities; 10,000 sq. ft. exhibit space; 75-seat large screen theater. Museum-related items for sale.
Activities: guided tours; hobby workshops; lectures; mobile vans; school loan service; participatory & traveling exhibitions.
Publications: quarterly newsletter, Explorit News; quarterly teachers program guide, The Science Edge.
Hours & Admission Prices: Mon.-Sat. 9-5. Adults $5, students $3.50, senior citizens $4; discounts to groups, AAM, ASTC members; children under 3 & members no charge. Closed New Year's Day; Thanksgiving; Christmas. ♿
Attendance: 16,722 (accurate)
Membership: Individual $25; Family $40; Associate $250; Supporting $500; Sustaining $1,000; Benefactor $5,000; Edgerton Society $10,000 & up.

PLAINSMAN MUSEUM, (M), 210 16th St., Aurora, NE 68818-3009. Tel.: 402-694-6531. Fax: 402-694-6531.
E-mail: plainsman@hamilton.net
Web Site: www.plainsmanmuseum.org
Founded: 1935.
Congressional District: 3
Key Personnel: Dir. & Cur., Megan Sharp; Asst. Dir. & Museum Shop Mgr., Gary Gustafson.
Personnel Profile: Full-Time Paid 2; Part-Time Volunteers 60.
Governing Authority: society. Parent Institution: Hamilton County Historical Society. Tax-exempt: 501(c)(3).
Historical Society Museum.
Collections: murals & mosaics tracing the local & regional history from prehistoric times to the 1860s; photographs of Hamilton County; E.A. Carlson Collection; 1,200 dolls including the Doris Lord collection; iron toys; period rooms including prairie chapel, Main Street, Pioneer Hamilton county; farmstead including cow barn, windmill, blacksmith shop surrounded with vintage implements & vehicles; schoolhouse. Historic Buildings: 1859 log cabin; sod house; 1881 homestead house; 1876 home of General Delevan Bates, Civil War Medal of Honor winner.
Research Fields: genealogies; ethnic groups in Hamilton County, Nebraska.
Facilities: 600-vol. library of books & publications available by appointment for research on premises; microfilm of 1890-1947 Hamilton Co. newspapers; microfilm reader/printer available for general use; reading room.
Activities: guided tours; lectures; local oral histories; permanent & temporary exhibitions; hands-on activities; musicals.
Publications: brochures; quarterly newsletter.
Hours & Admission Prices: April-Oct. Mon.-Sat. 9-5, Sun. 1-5; Nov.-March daily 1-5. Adults $6, senior citizens over 62 $4, youth 5-16 $2; discounts to groups of 30 or more; children under 5 & members no charge. Closed New Year's Day; Easter; Thanksgiving; Christmas. ♿
Attendance: 4,000 (estimated)
Membership: Individual $15; Family $25; Life $1,000.

Bancroft

JOHN G. NEIHARDT STATE HISTORIC SITE, 306 W. Elm, Bancroft, NE 68004-4127. Mailing Address: P.O. Box 344, Bancroft, NE 68004-0344. Tel.: 402-648-3388. Fax: 402-648-3388.
E-mail: neihardt@gpcom.net
Web Site: www.neihardtcenter.org
Formerly: John G. Neihardt Center
Founded: 1976.
Congressional District: 1
Key Personnel: Dir. & Museum Cur., Nancy S. Gillis.
Personnel Profile: Part-Time Paid 3; Part-Time Volunteers 10.
Governing Authority: state; nonprofit organization. Parent Institution: Nebraska State Historical Society. Tax-exempt: 501(c)(3).
Preservation Project.
Collections: memorabilia of John G. Neihardt, poet laureate of Nebraska, author of Black Elk Speaks & A Cycle of the West.
Research Fields: literature; history on Native Americans; mountain men; western history.
Facilities: Neihardt Study building; Neihardt Center Museum; Sacred Hoop Prayer Garden.
Activities: school tours; research, literary programs; lectures.
Publications: brochures, Nebraska Historical Society; quarterly newsletter.
Hours & Admission Prices: March-Nov. Mon.-Sat. 9-5, Sun. 1:30-5; Dec.-Feb. Mon.-Fri. 9-5. No charge; donations accepted. Closed New Year's Day; Memorial Day; Independence Day; Labor Day; Thanksgiving; Christmas. ♿
Attendance: 3,439 (accurate)
Membership: Individual $25; Family & Sustaining $30.

Bartlett

WHEELER COUNTY HISTORICAL SOCIETY AND COURTHOUSE MUSEUM, Maine St. between 2nd & 3rd Sts., Bartlett, NE 68622. Mailing Address: P.O. Box 194, Bartlett, NE 68622-0194. Tel.: 308-654-3424.
History Museum.
Collections: local history; pioneer artifacts.
Hours & Admission Prices: By appointment. No charge.

Bayard

BAYARD DEPOT MUSEUM, 103 S. Main St., Bayard, NE 69334. Tel.: 308-586-1496.
E-mail: barker@actcom.net
Web Site: bayardmuseum.tripod.com/home
Founded: 1993.
Congressional District: 3
Personnel Profile: Part-Time Volunteers 10.
Governing Authority: Tax-exempt.
History Museum.
Collections: Bayard history; pioneer machinery; tools; quilts; schoolroom; kitchen & bedroom artifacts.
Hours & Admission Prices: Memorial Day to Labor Day Mon.-Sat. 9-4, Sun. 1-4; other times by appointment. No charge. ♿
Attendance: 900 (estimated)
Membership: Annual $10; Lifetime $100.

CHIMNEY ROCK NATIONAL HISTORIC SITE AND VISITORS CENTER, Chimney Rock Rd., Bayard, NE 69334. Mailing Address: P.O. Box F, Bayard, NE 69334. Tel.: 308-586-2581.
Historic Site & Visitors Center.
Collections: local history & culture; early 19th century westward migration; photographs; period artifacts.
Hours & Admission Prices: Daily 9-5. Adults $3. Closed major holidays.

Beatrice

GAGE COUNTY HISTORICAL SOCIETY AND MUSEUM, 101 N. 2nd, Beatrice, NE 68310. Mailing Address: P.O. Box 793, Beatrice, NE 68310-0793. Tel.: 402-228-1679.
E-mail: gagecountymuseum@beatricene.com
Web Site: gagecountymuseum.org
Founded: 1971.
Congressional District: 1
Key Personnel: Pres., Stan Wirth; Vice Pres., Ken Pinkerton; Dir., Lesa Arterburn; Treas., Doug Horracks; Cur. & Museum Shop Mgr., Rita Clawson.
Personnel Profile: Full-Time Paid 2; Part-Time Paid 1; Part-Time Volunteers 100.
Governing Authority: board of directors. Parent Institution: Gage County Historical Society. Branch Museum: Elijah Filley Stone Barn, 13282 E. Scott Rd., Filley, NE 68357. Tax-exempt.
County History Museum: housed in 1906 Burlington Passenger Station.
Collections: railroad artifacts; agricultural implements; materials on the industrial development; medical equipment; artifacts of the communities & the people of Gage County. Historic Building: 1874 Elijah Filley Stone Barn.
Research Fields: local history.
Facilities: local history research materials available for use on premises only.
Activities: guided tours; annual meeting; programs of historical nature; lectures; special events. Annual Events at the Elijah Filley Stone Barn: Living History Program; Harvest Festival in October.
Publications: quarterly newsletter; books, Queen City of the Blue, Beatrice, NE; Gage County History; 1888 Beatrice Illustrated; Kansas City, Wyandotte & Northwestern Railroad Co. - Beatrice, NE.
Hours & Admission Prices: June-Sept. Tues.-Sat. 9-12 & 1-5, Sun. 1:30-5;

Oct.-May Tues.-Fri. 9-12 & 1-5, Sun. 1:30-5. No charge; donations accepted. Closed New Year's Day; Presidents Day; Memorial Day; Independence Day; Labor Day; Thanksgiving; Christmas Eve & Day. ♿
Attendance: 6,000 (accurate)
Membership: Individual $15; Family $25; Trailblazer $50; Sodbuster $100; Homesteader $250.

HOMESTEAD NATIONAL MONUMENT OF AMERICA, 8523 W. State Hwy., Beatrice, NE 68310-6743. Tel.: 402-223-3514. Fax: 402-228-4231.
E-mail: home_interpretation@nps.gov
Web Site: www.nps.gov
Founded: 1936.
Congressional District: 1
Personnel Profile: Full-Time Paid 14; Full-Time Volunteers 8; Part-Time Paid 2; Part-Time Volunteers 400; Interns 3.
Governing Authority: federal. Parent Institution: National Park Service. Tax-exempt.
Agriculture Museum: homestead era history.
Collections: artifacts pertaining to homesteading during the late 19th century. Historic Buildings: 1867 Palmer-Epard Cabin; 1872 Brick School House.
Research Fields: U.S. land laws history; agricultural history; settlement & emigration patterns; prairie restoration.
Facilities: 400-vol. library of general history on Westward expansion & land reform, available for use on the premises; historic cabin & school; auditorium; 5,200 objects research collection. Books, postcards and slides for sale.
Activities: interpretive exhibits & programs; orientation film; education programs (by reservation) & teacher workshops; 3-mile self-guided trail through prairie & woodlands.
Publications: Homestead National Monument of America Handbook.
Hours & Admission Prices: Mon.-Fri. 8:30-5, Sat.-Sun. 9-5. No charge, donations accepted. Closed New Year's Day; Thanksgiving; Christmas. ♿
Attendance: 70,000 (accurate)

Bellevue

FONTENELLE NATURE ASSOCIATION, 1111 Bellevue Blvd. N., Bellevue, NE 68005-4008. Tel.: 402-731-3140. Fax: 402-731-2403.
E-mail: info@fontenelleforest.org
Web Site: www.fontenelleforest.org
Founded: 1913.
Congressional District: 2
Key Personnel: Exec. Dir., Tom Arndorfer; Pres. (V), Rick Sanders; Dir. Science & Stewardship, Gary Garabrandt; Dir. Education, Marty Pagel; Dir. Devel., Laura Shiffermiller; Museum Shop Mgr., Pat Millard.
Personnel Profile: Full-Time Paid 16; Part-Time Paid 6; Part-Time Volunteers 100.
Governing Authority: nonprofit organization. Parent Institution: Fontenelle Nature Association Board of Directors. Subsidiary Institutions: Fontenelle Forest Nature Center & Neale Woods Nature Center. Tax-exempt: 501(c)(3).
Nature Center: Fontenelle Forest Nature Center located on 1,400-acre natural forest; Neale Woods Nature Center located on 550 acre wooded & prairie reserve.
Collections: indigenous flora & fauna of the Missouri River Valley forest and adjacent Loess Hills; deciduous forest; wetlands; prairie; live animals.
Research Fields: urban deer population, movements & control.
Facilities: Fontenelle Forest Nature Center: 1,400 acres of woods & wetlands; 17 miles of trails; boardwalks. Buffett Forest Learning Center: classrooms. Museum-related items for sale. Hitchcock Wetlands Learning Center: classrooms; offices; exhibits. Neale Woods Nature Center: 550 acres of woods & prairies; 9 miles of trails. Jonas Interpretive Center: exhibits; classroom; offices. Millard Observatory: telescopes; star watch deck.
Activities: environmental educational programs for children through adults; teacher training workshops; children & family campouts; summer day camp; children's nature clubs; astronomy programs; guided hikes; field trips; canoe trips; nature photography; permanent & temporary exhibitions. Annual Events: Earthday, Native American Music Festival; Halloween & Christmas special events.
Publications: quarterly newsletter; Self-Guided Trail Guide; Mammals of Eastern Nebraska; Checklist of Nebraska Birds; Annual Report; School Programs Guide.
Hours & Admission Prices: Fontenelle Forest: daily 8-5. Adults $7, seniors $6, children 3-11 $5; variable fees for school groups & public programs; members no charge. Neale Woods Nature Center: Sat. 8-5, Sun. 12-5. Adults $5, senior $4, children $3. Closed New Year's Day; Thanksgiving; Christmas. ♿
Attendance: 90,000 (estimated)
Membership: Individual $35; Family $50.

SARPY COUNTY HISTORICAL MUSEUM, 2402 Clay St., Bellevue, NE 68005-3932. Tel.: 402-292-1880. Fax: 402-292-6045.
E-mail: sarpymuseum@netexpress.net
Founded: 1970.
Congressional District: 2
Key Personnel: Dir., Gary Iske; Pres. (V), Rosemary Lucky.
Personnel Profile: Full-Time Paid 1; Part-Time Volunteers 50.
Governing Authority: historical society; nonprofit. Tax-exempt: 501(c)(3).
Historical Society Museum.
Collections: Sarpy County history & geographical area from 1800 to present; prehistoric Indian artifacts. Historic House: 1840 The Log Cabin. Historic Site: 1835 Moses Merrill mission; 1869 first Nebraska depot.
Research Fields: local history; county architecture; oral history; genealogy.
Facilities: library & archives on Nebraska & Sarpy County history.
Activities: guided tours; lectures; outreach program; permanent, temporary & special exhibitions.
Publications: monthly newsletter.
Hours & Admission Prices: Tues.-Sun. 9-4. Adults $2, senior citizen $1, student 5-18 $.50; school groups no charge. ♿
Attendance: 3,400 (accurate)
Membership: Individual $10; Family $18; Sustaining $25; Patron $50; Century $100.

Benkelman

DUNDY COUNTY HISTORICAL SOCIETY, 522 Araphahoe, Benkelman, NE 69021. Mailing Address: P.O. Box 634, Benkelman, NE 69021-0634. Tel.: 308-423-2750.
Founded: 1970.
Congressional District: 4
Key Personnel: Co-Pres., Betty Deyle; Co-Pres., Dee Fries; Vice Pres., Lanita Anderson; Sec. & Treas., Shirley Mullanix.
Personnel Profile: Part-Time Volunteers 7.
Governing Authority: society; board of directors. Tax-exempt.
General Museum.
Collections: rural school mementos; homestead days; Indian artifacts; relics of open range era; replicas of brands; railroad depot; doll collection; bank & post office artifacts; drug store.
Research Fields: tapes & information on pioneer life research library.
Facilities: collection of rural school textbooks & historical books available for research by appointment; reading room.
Activities: guided tours; lectures; hobby display specials, twice during summer.
Publications: biannual newsletter.
Hours & Admission Prices: June-Sept. Thurs. 2-5; other times by appointment. No charge; donations accepted.
Attendance: 573 (accurate)

Boys Town

BOYS TOWN HALL OF HISTORY & FATHER FLANAGAN HOUSE, 14057 Flanagan Blvd., Boys Town, NE 68010. Tel.: 402-498-1185. Fax: 402-498-1159.
E-mail: lyncht@boystown.org
Web Site: www.boystown.org
Founded: 1986.
Congressional District: 2
Key Personnel: C.E.O. & Mgr., Thomas J. Lynch; Collections Assoc., Mark Daniels.
Personnel Profile: Full-Time Paid 2; Part-Time Paid 3; Part-Time Volunteers 40; Interns 2.
Governing Authority: nonprofit organization. Parent Institution: Father Flanagan's Boys' Town. Tax-exempt: 501(c)(3).
History Museum: located in Boys Town.
Collections: public & administrative archives; film, tape & video archives; 500,000 photograph collection.
Research Fields: history of Father Edward J. Flanagan & Boys Town; The Boys Town Journal.
Facilities: 200-vol. library, including yearbooks & newsletters from 1918 to present; 8,500 sq. ft. exhibit space; 20-seat theater.
Activities: guided tours; docent program; organized educational programs for children & undergraduate and graduate college students affiliated with University of Nebraska at Omaha and Creighton University; temporary & traveling exhibitions; biannual alumni convention; elderhostel program.
Hours & Admission Prices: Daily 10-4:30. No charge; donations suggested. Closed New Year's Day; Easter morning; Thanksgiving; Christmas. ♿
Attendance: 60,000 (estimated)

Broken Bow

CUSTER COUNTY HISTORICAL SOCIETY, INC., 445 S. 9th St., Broken Bow, NE 68822-2015. Mailing Address: P.O. Box 334, Broken Bow, NE 68822-0334. Tel.: 308-872-2203.
E-mail: cchs@inebraska.com
Web Site: www.rootsweb.com/~necuster
Founded: 1962.
Congressional District: 3
Key Personnel: Pres., Dee Adams; Researcher, Mary Landkamer; Sec., Don Davis; Museum Shop Mgr., Chard Hirsch.
Personnel Profile: Part-Time Paid 1; Part-Time Volunteers 24.
Governing Authority: society. Affiliated with Custer County Historical Society. Tax-exempt: 501(c)(3).
General Museum.
Collections: history of Custer County; items used in sod houses; store items from Wescott, Gibbins & Bragg store, Comstock; microfilm reader; 230 rolls of microfilm; S.D. Butcher photographs.
Research Fields: County history.
Facilities: library of local & state history; genealogical books available on premises; reading room.
Activities: guided tours; lectures.
Publications: biannual newsletter, Custer County Times.
Hours & Admission Prices: Mon.-Fri. 1-5. No charge; donations accepted. Closed national holidays.
Attendance: 3,000 (estimated)
Membership: Individual $20; Sustaining $25; Patron $50; Benefactor $100.

Brownville

BROWNVILLE HISTORICAL SOCIETY MUSEUM, 213 Main St., Brownville, NE 68521. Mailing Address: Box 1, Brownville, NE 68321-0001. Tel.: 402-825-6001.
E-mail: rpchitwood@alltel.net
Web Site: brownville-ne.com
Founded: 1956.
Congressional District: 1
Key Personnel: Pres. Brownville Historical Society, Dr. Robert P. Chitwood.
Personnel Profile: Part-Time Paid 1; Part-Time Volunteers 24.
Governing Authority: nonprofit organization. U.S. Army Corps of Engineer's Dredge Meriwether Lewis Museum. Subsidiary Institution: Brownville Fine Arts Association; Brownville Village Theatre. Tax-exempt: 501(c)(3).
General Museum: 1958 Captain Bailey House; 1868 Gov. Furnas House.
Collections: history; costumes; glass; agriculture; Indian artifacts; children's furniture; tools. Wheel Museum: depot; land office; dental office. Historic Houses: 1860-1880 John Carson House; 1868 Gov. Furnas House.
Facilities: library.
Activities: guided tours; art & music festivals; drama; workshops; craft seminars.
Publications: triannual, The Bulletin; book, The Brownville Story; annual newspaper, The Brownville Banner.
Hours & Admission Prices: mid-May to mid-Oct. Fri.-Sun. 1-5. Adults $2, children $1; members no charge.
Attendance: 3,200 (estimated)

MERIWETHER LEWIS DREDGE MUSEUM, Brownville State Recreation Area, Brownville, NE 68321. Mailing Address: 73088 646th Ave., Brownville, NE 68321-6025. Tel.: 402-825-3341.
Founded: 1977.
Congressional District: 1
Key Personnel: Pres. (V), Harold Davis; Museum Shop Mgr., Clay W. Kennedy.
Personnel Profile: Full-Time Volunteers 1; Part-Time Paid 1; Part-Time Volunteers 10.
Governing Authority: foundation. Meriwether Lewis Foundation in connection with Peru State College. Tax-exempt: 501(c)(3).
History Museum: housed in The Captain Meriwether Lewis, a former Corps of Engineers steam powered dredge.
Collections: river-related material.
Research Fields: Missouri River Steam Boats 1817 to present.
Activities: Museum Sponsors: River Rats Reunion.
Publications: brochure.
Hours & Admission Prices: May & mid-Sept. to mid-Oct. Sat.-Sun. 1-5, open on weekdays for prearranged groups; June to mid-Sept. daily 1-5. Adults $3, children 6-12 $1; discount to members; children under 5 no charge.
Attendance: 5,000 (estimated)
Membership: First Mate $15, Chief $25; Ensign $50; Captain $100; Commodore $500; Admiral $1,000.

Burwell

FORT HARTSUFF STATE HISTORICAL PARK, 46067 Sioux Creek Loop, Burwell, NE 68823-6122. Tel.: 308-346-4715. Fax: 308-346-4715.
Web Site: www.ngpc.state.ne.us
Founded: 1874.
Congressional District: 3
Key Personnel: Park Supt., Jim Domeier; Museum Shop Mgr., Mary Hughes.
Personnel Profile: Full-Time Paid 2; Part-Time Paid 6; Part-Time Volunteers 15.
Governing Authority: state. Parent Institution: Nebraska Game & Parks Commission. Nebraska State Historical Parks Bureau, 2200 N. 33rd, Lincoln, NE 68503. Tel. 402-464-0641. Tax-exempt.
Military Museum: housed in 1874-1881 Fort Hartsuff.
Collections: period furniture; archaeological collections; military uniforms and equipment; tools; firearms collection. Historic Structures: nine restored 1870s military structures.
Research Fields: Great Plains military history.
Facilities: picnic area.
Activities: orientations by pre-arrangement; lectures; permanent exhibitions; firearms demonstration. Museum Sponsors: living history demonstrations May to September.
Publications: brochure.
Hours & Admission Prices: Memorial Day-Labor Day daily 9-8; other times by appointment. State park vehicle entry permit required: annual $20, daily $4. ♿
Attendance: 20,000 (estimated)

Butte

COMMUNITY HISTORICAL CENTER AND MUSEUM, 721 First St., Butte, NE 68722. Mailing Address: 39355 W. Hwy. 46, Wagner, SD 57380-7128. Tel.: 605-384-3509. Fax: 605-384-5460.
E-mail: frenchine@neb.rr.com
Founded: 1990.
Key Personnel: Co Founder, Chm. (V) & Museum Shop Mgr., Mardell E. Schroeder; Co Founder & Pres. (V), Margaret Houke.
Governing Authority: city. Tax-exempt.
History Museum.
Collections: area history & culture; geological artifacts.
Activities: Museum Sponsors: Annual Open House.
Hours & Admission Prices: By appointment. No charge; donations accepted. ♿
Attendance: 7,500 (estimated)

Cambridge

CAMBRIDGE MUSEUM, 612 Penn St., Cambridge, NE 69022. Mailing Address: P.O. Box 129, Cambridge, NE 69022-0129. Tel.: 308-697-4385.
Founded: 1938.
Key Personnel: Pres. (V), Marilyn Kester; Cur., Marjorie Ridpath.
Personnel Profile: Full-Time Paid 1; Part-Time Paid 1; Part-Time Volunteers 1.
Governing Authority: public college; nonprofit. Tax-exempt.
Local History Museum.
Collections: mounted birds; mounted animals; firearms; fossils; Indian artifacts; art pieces; photographs; dental room.
Facilities: library of school books, newspapers & magazines available to the public.
Activities: traveling exhibitions & art shows.
Hours & Admission Prices: April-Oct. Tues.-Sun. 1-5; Nov.-March Sat.-Sun. 1-5. No charge; donations accepted. ♿
Attendance: 950 (estimated)

Central City

MERRICK COUNTY HISTORICAL MUSEUM, 211 E. St., Central City, NE 68826-1326. Tel.: 308-946-3489 & 2757.
History Museum.
Collections: county history & culture; local artifacts.
Hours & Admission Prices: May-Oct. Sun. 2-4; other times by appointment. No charge; donations accepted.

Chadron

DAWES COUNTY HISTORICAL SOCIETY MUSEUM, 341 Country Club Rd., Chadron, NE 69337-7329. Mailing Address: P.O. Box 1319, Chadron, NE 69337-1319. Tel.: 308-432-4999 & 2309.
E-mail: tajbright@aol.com
Web Site: www.chadron.com/dchm
Founded: 1964.
Congressional District: 3

Key Personnel: C.E.O. & Pres. (V), Rollin Curd; Chm. (V) & Museum Shop Mgr., Belvadine Lecher.
Personnel Profile: Full-Time Volunteers 1; Part-Time Volunteers 50; Interns 1.
Governing Authority: public; society; nonprofit. Parent Institution: Dawes County Historical Society, Inc. Tax-exempt: 501(c)(3).
Local History Museum.
Collections: exhibits emphasizing Dawes County history from prehistoric to modern times; Dawes County Cemetery records; World War I & World War II items; Spanish-American War items; fossils; marine biology; quilts; farm machinery; tools; player organ; fence maker; 1895 bicycle; harmonium; egg case maker; guns; hub caps; pens; archives; blacksmith shop; railroad room; general store; hospital room; log house; log barn; C & NW Railroad caboose; antique car collection; Crawford & Chadron local newspapers 1886 to present. Historic Buildings: c.1890 schoolhouse; rural church c.1890.
Research Fields: Dawes County history; family history.
Facilities: 3,400-vol. library of family, local, county & Nebraska history for research; original Dawes County marriage records 1884 through 1961; delayed birth registrations; obituaries from c.1920; postal appointment books 1940-1970 for all Nebraska counties & site locations; Dawes County civil & criminal record books from 1885; manuscripts; letters & diaries.
Activities: guided tours; films; temporary exhibitions; monthly historical programs open to the public. Annual Event: History In Action in September.
Publications: quarterly newsletter; monthly newspaper, Golden Age Courier.
Hours & Admission Prices: Mon.-Sat 10-4, Sun. & holidays 1-5. No charge; donations accepted. ♿
Attendance: 2,086 (estimated)
Membership: Students $1; Adult $6; Life $100; Life Homestead $500; Heritage $1,000 & up.

ELEANOR BARBOUR COOK MUSEUM OF GEOLOGY, Math & Science Building, Chadron State College, 1000 Main St., Chadron, NE 69337-2667. Tel.: 308-432-6377. Fax: 308-432-6434.
E-mail: mleite@csc.edu
Web Site: www.csc.edu
Founded: 1939.
Congressional District: 3
Key Personnel: Cur. & Professor Geoscience, Michael Leite.
Governing Authority: college. Affiliated with Chadron State College.
Science Museum.
Collections: paleontology; archaeology; geology.
Research Fields: paleontology; geology.
Facilities: area available for display; preparation lab.
Activities: guided tours; permanent & temporary exhibitions.
Hours & Admission Prices: Sept. to early May Mon.-Fri. 8-4:30; other times by appointment. No charge. Closed spring break; major holidays. ♿
Attendance: 400 (estimated)

HIGH PLAINS HERBARIUM, 1000 Main St., Chadron, NE 69337-2667. Tel.: 308-432-6385.
Herbarium.
Collections: ethnobotanical, medicinal plants; historic pharmaceutical specimens.
Hours & Admission Prices: Daily 8-5; tours by appointment. ♿

MARI SANDOZ HIGH PLAINS HERITAGE CENTER, 1000 Main, Chadron, NE 69337-2667. Tel.: 308-432-6401. Fax: 308-432-6464.
Web Site: www.csc.edu/sandoz
Formerly: Mari Sandoz Room Museum
Founded: 2002.
Congressional District: 3
Key Personnel: Dir., Sarah Polak.
Personnel Profile: Full-Time Paid 3; Part-Time Paid 4; Part-Time Volunteers 1; Interns 2.
Governing Authority: Parent Institution: Chadron State College. Tax-exempt.
History Museum.
Collections: books by Sandoz & local authors; manuscripts; photographs; tour maps; manuscripts; oral histories; Northern High Plains cattle ranching; local & regional authors.
Facilities: library.
Activities: guided tours; permanent & temporary exhibitions; museum studies program; in-school outreach. Museum Sponsors: History Day District Contest.
Publications: newsletter.
Hours & Admission Prices: Mon.-Fri. 8-12 & 1-4, Sat. 9-12 & 1-4. No charge; donations accepted. Closed college holidays. ♿
Attendance: 8,000 (estimated)

MUSEUM OF THE FUR TRADE, (M), 6321 E. Hwy. 20, Chadron, NE 69337-5325. Tel.: 308-432-3843. Fax: 308-432-5943.
E-mail: museum@furtrade.org
Web Site: www.furtrade.org
Founded: 1955.
Congressional District: 3
Key Personnel: C.E.O. & Dir., Gail DeBuse Potter; Pres., Dr. George D. Watson; Museum Shop Mgr., Ann M. Hanson; Editor, Dr. James A. Hanson.
Personnel Profile: Full-Time Paid 1; Full-Time Volunteers 2; Part-Time Paid 1; Part-Time Volunteers 63.
Governing Authority: nonprofit organization. Parent Institution: Museum Association of the American Frontier. Tax-exempt: 501(c)(3).
History Museum.
Collections: trade goods; weapons & equipment; American Indian & Alaskan objects; native cultural materials of the North American fur trade, 1500-1900; Plains Indian garden. Historic Building: c.1837 James Bourdeaux Trading Post.
Major Exhibits: The Voyageurs, 2010-2011.
Research Fields: methods of the North American fur trade, 1500-1900; commercial interchange between Native Americans & European settlers.
Facilities: 10,000-vol. library of books, periodicals, microfilm; botanical garden; 5,000 sq. ft. exhibit space; Plains Indian garden. Books, American Indian beadwork & fur trade reproductions for sale.
Activities: lectures; films; study clubs; hobby workshops; permanent exhibitions
Publications: quarterly journal, Museum of the Fur Trade Quarterly; newsletter.
Hours & Admission Prices: May-Oct. daily 8-5; other times by appointment. Adults $5; discount to groups of 20 or more, AAA & AAM members; members & children with parents no charge. Audio tours available. ♿
Attendance: 40,736 (accurate)
Membership: Annual $15; Benefactor $1,000.

Champion

CHAMPION MILL STATE HISTORICAL PARK, US 6 W. to Spur 15A, Champion, NE 69023-0117. Mailing Address: 73122 338 Ave., Enders, NE 69027-2718. Tel.: 308-882-5860 & 394-5118.
E-mail: enders@ngpc.ne.gov
Web Site: www.ngpc.state.ne.us
Founded: 1969.
Congressional District: 3
Key Personnel: Supt., Bill Christensen.
Personnel Profile: Full-Time Paid 2; Part-Time Paid 3; Part-Time Volunteers 2.
Governing Authority: state. Parent Institution: Historical Parks Section, Nebraska Game & Parks Commission, Box 30370, Lincoln, NE 68503. Tax-exempt.
Historical Park: Nebraska's last functioning water-powered mill.
Collections: milling machinery; tools.
Research Fields: flour & feed milling; water-powered milling.
Facilities: working mill.
Activities: guided tours; organized education programs for children.
Hours & Admission Prices: Grounds: open year-round. Mill: Memorial Day-Labor Day Sat. 8-5, Sun. 1-4. Park permit required. Primitive camping fee $6. ♿
Attendance: 10,500 (estimated)

CHASE COUNTY HISTORICAL MUSEUM, Jct. of Chase & Broadway Sts., Champion, NE 69023. Mailing Address: P.O. Box 237, Imperial, NE 69033-0237. Tel.: 308-882-4056 & 4519.
E-mail: osler@chase3000.com
Founded: 1963.
Key Personnel: Dir., John Osler.
Governing Authority: Tax-exempt.
History Museum.
Collections: county artifacts; period clothing; WWI & II uniforms; farm machinery; Indian artifacts; cameras; native grasses; guns & ammunition; woodworking tools.
Hours & Admission Prices: Mother's Day to Labor Day Sun. 1:30-4:30. No charge; donations accepted.
Attendance: 850 (accurate)
Membership: Individual $5; Life $100.

Chappell

CHAPPELL MUSEUM ASSOCIATION AND SUDMAN-NEUMANN HERITAGE HOUSE, 701 5th St., Chappell, NE 69129. Tel.: 308-874-2865.
Key Personnel: Dir., Lester L. Becker
History Museum.
Collections: period furniture; household artifacts.

Hours & Admission Prices: May to Labor Day Sun. 2-4; other times by appointment. No charge.

Clarkson

CLARKSON HISTORICAL MUSEUM, 221 Pine St., Clarkson, NE 68629-4093. Mailing Address: P.O. Box 121, 221 Pine St., Clarkson, NE 68629-0121. Tel.: 402-892-3863. Fax: 402-892-3059.
Founded: 1967.
Congressional District: 23
Key Personnel: Chm. (V), Nancy Doernemann; Pres. (V), Ruth D. Waters.
Personnel Profile: Part-Time Volunteers 8.
Governing Authority: nonprofit organization. Tax-exempt: 501(c)(3).
General Museum.
Collections: period artifacts; musical instruments; horsedrawn farm implements; early household artifacts; photographs; clothing; Czech heritage artifacts; military; over 300 farm toys.
Research Fields: photographs; family histories; town & county histories.
Activities: guided tours; lectures; films; permanent & temporary exhibitions. Museum Sponsors: Czech Day Celebration in June.
Hours & Admission Prices: April & Aug.-Sept. 1st Sun. of month 11:30-3; Memorial Day weekend Sun. 11:30-3; June 20-21 9:30-7; other times by appointment. No charge; donations accepted. ♿
Attendance: 550 (estimated)
Membership: Annual $5; Lifetime $50.

Clay Center

CLAY COUNTY MUSEUM & HISTORICAL SOCIETY, 320 W. Glenville St., Clay Center, NE 68933-1153. Mailing Address: P.O. Box 191, Clay Center, NE 68933-0191. Tel.: 402-762-3563.
Web Site: www.oldtrusty.org/history.html
History Museum.
Collections: county history; one-room schoolhouse; railroad caboose; period tractors; steam & stationary engines; buggies; cars; trucks; fire equipment; blacksmith shop equipment; agricultural equipment.
Hours & Admission Prices: Mon.-Thurs. 10-4; other times by appointment. No charge.

Columbus

PLATTE COUNTY MUSEUM, 2916 16th St., Columbus, NE 68601-4200. Mailing Address: P.O. Box 31, Columbus, NE 68602-0031. Tel.: 402-564-1856.
Web Site: www.megavision.net/museum
History Museum.
Collections: county history & artifacts. Historic Structures: 1857 lob cabin; 1912 Challenger windmill.
Hours & Admission Prices: mid-May to Sept. Fri.-Sun. 1-4; Oct.-April 1st Sun. each month 1-4. Adults $3; children under 14 no charge.

Cozad

THE 100TH MERIDIAN MUSEUM, 206 E. 8th, Cozad, NE 69130-1834. Mailing Address: P.O. Box 325, Cozad, NE 69130-0325. Tel.: 308-784-1100.
Founded: 1994.
Congressional District: 3
Key Personnel: Pres. (V), Patrick Leahy; Vice Pres., Curtis Sargent; Treas., Mike Erickson; Recording Sec., Glenda France; Corresponding Sec., Marilyn Peterson.
Personnel Profile: Part-Time Volunteers 150.
Governing Authority: private; nonprofit organization. Parent Institution: Cozad Historical Society. Tax-exempt: 501(c)(3).
Antiques Museum.
Collections: local history & archives; antique touring coach used by President Taft in Yellowstone in 1907; china & silver; farm equipment; telephone equipment; historical photographs; piano; 1927 Chevrolet truck.
Research Fields: dinosaurs; archaeology.
Facilities: music center. Museum-related items for sale.
Activities: workshops; loan & temporary exhibitions.
Publications: The 100th Meridian Museum; brochures; newsletters.
Hours & Admission Prices: Memorial Day weekend to Labor Day Mon.-Fri. 10-5, Sat. 1-5, Sun. by appointment. Suggested Donation: $2. ♿
Attendance: 1,500 (estimated)
Membership: General $15; Life $250.

ROBERT HENRI MUSEUM & HISTORICAL WALKWAY, 218 E. 8th St., Cozad, NE 69130-1834. Mailing Address: P.O. Box 355, Cozad, NE 69130-0355. Tel.: 308-784-4154.
E-mail: rhenri@cozadtel.net
Web Site: roberthenrimuseum.org
History Museum.
Collections: pioneer schoolhouse; Pony Express station; local arts & crafts; historic walkway.
Hours & Admission Prices: May-Sept. Tues.-Sat. 10-5, Sun. & holidays by appointment. Adults $3, children 14 & under $1.

Crawford

CRAWFORD HISTORICAL MUSEUM, 337 2nd St., Crawford, NE 69339. Mailing Address: P.O. Box 165, Crawford, NE 69339. Tel.: 308-665-1732.
History Museum.
Collections: local history; Native American artifacts; rocks; business ledgers; beaded handbags; photographs; local newspapers; pamphlets; posters; postcards.
Hours & Admission Prices: Memorial Day to Labor Day Mon.-Sat. 10-12 & 1-5. No charge; donations accepted.

HUDSON-MENG MUSEUM & ARCHAEOLOGY RESEARCH CENTER, 1811 Meng Dr., Crawford, NE 69339. Mailing Address: Mammoth Site of Hot Springs, P.O. Box 692, Hot Springs, SD 57747-0692. Tel.: 308-665-3900; 3907; 3090. Fax: 308-665-3908.
E-mail: news@mammothsite.org
Archaeology Museum.
Collections: local history & culture; photographs.
Hours & Admission Prices: May 17-Labor Day daily 9-5. Adults $5, seniors 60 & over $4.50, children 5-12 $3; children 4 & under no charge.

NEBRASKA STATE HISTORICAL SOCIETY'S FORT ROBINSON MUSEUM, 3200 U.S. Hwy. 20, Crawford, NE 69339. Mailing Address: P.O. Box 304, Crawford, NE 69339-0304. Tel.: 308-665-2919. Fax: 308-665-2917.
E-mail: fortrob@bbc.net
Web Site: www.nebraskahistory.org
Formerly: Fort Robinson Museum
Founded: 1956.
Congressional District: 3
Key Personnel: C.E.O. & Exec. Dir., Michael J. Smith; Assoc. Dir., Ann Billesbach; Cur., Thomas R. Buecker; Chief Education & Research Officer, Lynne Ireland.
Personnel Profile: Full-Time Paid 2; Part-Time Paid 2; Part-Time Volunteers 1.
Governing Authority: state; society. Parent Institution: Nebraska State Historical Society. Tax-exempt: 501(c)(3).
Military Museum: Fort Robinson history.
Collections: Indian artifacts; military items; archaeology. Historic Buildings: 1875 reconstructed log guardhouse; 1875 post adjutant's office; wheelwright shop; 1904-1906 blacksmith shop, harness repair shop; 1887 adobe officer's quarters; 1905 Post Headquarters, items related to Fort Robinson 1874-1948, Red Cloud Agency 1873-1877; 1908 veterinary hospital.
Research Fields: archaeology; anthropology; military; horses; history of the West.
Facilities: 400-vol. library of books on history of Nebraska & Western Americana, microfilm records available for use on premises by appointment. Publications & postcards for sale.
Activities: guided tours; lectures; permanent exhibitions; fifteen minute video on the history of Fort Robinson.
Publications: Nebraska History Magazine; Fort Robinson and the American West: 1874-1899; Fort Robinson and the American Century: 1900-1948; 1887 Adobe Barracks, Fort Robinson; The Cheyenne Outbreak Barracks, Fort Robinson; Self-Guided Tour of Fort Robinson.
Hours & Admission Prices: Memorial Day-Labor Day Mon.-Sat. 8-5, Sun. 9-5; Sept.-May Mon.-Fri. 8-5. Adults $2; discount to Time Travelers; members & children with adult no charge. ♿
Attendance: 11,000 (accurate)
Membership: Individual $40; Household $55; Contributing $100; Supporting $250; Sustaining $500; Founder $1,000.

TRAILSIDE MUSEUM OF NATURAL HISTORY, 3200 W. U.S. Hwy. 20, Crawford, NE 69339-3112. Tel.: 308-665-2929.
Web Site: www.trailside.unl.edu
Art & History Museum.
Collections: local history & culture; fossils; geology; paintings.
Hours & Admission Prices: April-May & Sept.-Oct. Mon.-Fri. 10-5; Memorial Day to Labor Day daily 9-6; other times by appointment. Adults 19 & over $3, children 5-18 $1; children 4 & under no charge.

Crete

THE MAPLES HERITAGE COMPLEX AND BENNE MEMORIAL MUSEUM, 800 W. 13th St., Crete, NE 68333-2006. Tel.: 402-826-4656 & 5270.
Web Site: www.creteheritage.org
Founded: 1976.
Personnel Profile: Part-Time Volunteers 10; Interns 2.
Governing Authority: bd. of directors. Parent Institution: Crete Heritage Society. Tax-exempt.
History Museum.
Collections: exhibits that interpret Crete area history.
Major Exhibits: Vintage Musical Instruments, 1/10-6/10.
Hours & Admission Prices: Sun. 1-4; other times by appointment.

Crofton

LEWIS AND CLARK VISITOR CENTER, 55245 N.E. Hwy. 121, Crofton, NE 68730. Mailing Address: P.O. Box 710, Yankton, SD 57078-0710. Tel.: 402-667-2546. Fax: 402-667-2547.
E-mail: karla.j.zeutenhorst@usace.army.mil
Founded: 1976.
Personnel Profile: Full-Time Paid 3; Part-Time Paid 6; Part-Time Volunteers 6.
Governing Authority: federal; nonprofit. Parent Institution: U.S. Army Corps of Engineers. Tax-exempt.
Visitor Center.
Collections: birds & fish of the Missouri River region; scientific instruments used to build the dam. History of the Missouri River, including geological, paleontological, cultural & natural history.
Facilities: 150-vol. library; 2,700 sq. ft. exhibit space; 50-seat theater. Museum-related items for sale.
Activities: formal education programs for children; guided tours; participatory exhibit.
Publications: brochure, Rack Card.
Hours & Admission Prices: Memorial Day to Labor Day Sun.-Thurs. 8-6, Fri.-Sat. 8-7. Sept.-May Mon.-Fri. 8-4:30. No charge; donations accepted. ♿
Attendance: 29,650 (accurate)

Dakota City

DAKOTA COUNTY HISTORICAL SOCIETY & O'CONNOR HOUSE, Rural Rte. 1, Dakota City, NE 68731. Mailing Address: P.O. Box 971, Dakota City, NE 68731-0971. Tel.: 402-698-2288 & 2538.
Web Site: www.dakotacountyhistoricalsociety.com
History Museum.
Collections: local artifacts; household items; furnishings; tractors; American Indian clothing. Historic House: O'Connor House, Homer, NE.
Hours & Admission Prices: Memorial Day to Labor Day Sat. 10-5, Sun. 12-5; other times by appointment. No charge; donations accepted.

Dalton

DALTON PRAIRIE SCHOONER MUSEUM, 109 U.S. Hwy. 385, Dalton, NE 69131. Tel.: 308-377-2637.
History Museum.
Collections: community history; model railroad engines.
Hours & Admission Prices: Memorial Day to Labor Day Sat.-Sun. 1-4; other times by appointment. No charge.

David City

BONE CREEK MUSEUM OF AGRARIAN ART, (M), 575 "E" St., David City, NE 68632-1638. Tel.: 402-367-4488.
E-mail: info@bonecreek.org
Web Site: www.bonecreek.org
Art Museum: housed in the boyhood home of agrarian artist Dale Nichols.
Collections: agrarian art; Nichols notes, drawings, & letters; works by Robert Bateman, Gary Ernest Smith, John Stewart Curry, Robert Gwathmey, Birger Sandzen, Winslow Homer & Thomas Hart Benton.
Major Exhibits: John Roush, Meditations from Missouri, 12/09-2/10; Jim Hamil Retrospective: Farmland USA, 3/10-5/10; Nancy Bass, My Virginia Farm, 5/10-8/10; Leonard Steinaver, 9/10-11/10.
Research Fields: Agrarian art; regional art.
Activities: lectures; workshops by artists exhibiting at the museum; permanent & temporary exhibitions.
Hours & Admission Prices: Wed.-Sat. 10-4, Sun. 1-4. No charge; donations accepted. Closed major holidays.

Dorchester

SALINE COUNTY HISTORICAL SOCIETY, INC., 1145 State Hwy. 33, Dorchester, NE 68343. Mailing Address: 561 County Rd. S., Tobias, NE 68453-2007. Tel.: 402-946-2129 & 243-2356.
E-mail: rjrada@diodecom.net
Founded: 1956.
Congressional District: 1
Key Personnel: C.E.O. & Pres. (V), Judith K. Rada; Sec., Mary Ann Placek.
Personnel Profile: Part-Time Volunteers 20.
Governing Authority: society. Tax-exempt: 501(c)(3).
Agriculture Museum.
Collections: agriculture; machinery; household items; books; paintings by local artists; glass; clothing. Historic Houses and Buildings: 1873 rural school; 1888 Center Hall; 1896 rural post office; 1868 home; 1868 log cabin; 1871 train depot; In Loving Memory, burial customs & items c.1890-1910.
Research Fields: special exhibit, Saline County settler's funeral customs.
Activities: guided tours.
Publications: articles in all 4 County newspapers.
Hours & Admission Prices: Sun. 2-5; other times by appointment. No charge; donations accepted. ♿
Attendance: 478 (estimated)
Membership: Individual $5.

Ellsworth

CRESCENT LAKE NATIONAL WILDLIFE REFUGE, 10630 Rd. 181, Ellsworth, NE 69340. Tel.: 308-635-7851.
Wildlife Refuge.
Collections: nesting & migratory birds.
Facilities: nature trails.
Activities: hiking.
Hours & Admission Prices: Call for hours.

Elmwood

BESS STREETER ALDRICH HOUSE & MUSEUM, 204 East F St., Elmwood, NE 68349. Mailing Address: P.O. Box 167, Elmwood, NE 68349-0167. Tel.: 402-994-3855.
Web Site: www.bessstreeteraldrich.org
Founded: 1978.
Personnel Profile: Part-Time Paid 1; Part-Time Volunteers 20.
Governing Authority: Parent Institution: Bess Streeter Aldrich Foundation. Museum: 124 West D St., Elmwood, NE.
Historic House Museum: housed in the former home of author, Bess Streeter Aldrich, 1881-1954.
Collections: House: life of Bess Aldrich; period furnishings; personal artifacts; writings; history of the home; memorabilia; Elmwood's history. Museum: personal letters; movie memorabilia; family history; manuscript; childhood doll; video.
Facilities: House: museum-related items for sale.
Activities: Museum: video.
Hours & Admission Prices: House: May-Oct. Wed.-Thurs. & Sat.-Sun. 2-5; Nov.-April Sat.-Sun. 2-5; groups by appointment. Museum: by appointment only. House: adults $5, children 6-12 $3; discount to AAM members; children under 6 no charge. Museum: no charge with paid house admission.
Attendance: 1,000 (estimated)
Membership: Spring Came on Forever $20; The Rim of the Prairie $50; A Lantern in Her Hand $100.

Fairbury

FAIRBURY CITY MUSEUM, 1128 Elm St., Fairbury, NE 68352-1427. Tel.: 402-729-5126.
E-mail: info@fairburynebraska.net
History Museum.
Collections: period artifacts & memorabilia relating Fairbury's history.
Hours & Admission Prices: Thurs., Sat. & Sun. 1-4; other times by appointment.

ROCK CREEK STATION STATE HISTORIC PARK, 57426 710th Rd., Fairbury, NE 68352. Tel.: 402-729-5777.
E-mail: ngpc.rock.creek.station@nebraska.gov
Web Site: www.outdoornebraska.org
Founded: 1980.
Congressional District: 3
Key Personnel: Supt., Wayne Brandt; Asst. Supt., Jeff Bargar.
Personnel Profile: Full-Time Paid 2; Part-Time Paid 6.
Governing Authority: state. Affiliated with the Nebraska Game & Parks Commission, 2200 N. 33rd St., Lincoln, NE 68503. Tel. 402-464-0641. Tax-exempt.

Historic Site: Pony Express Station, stage & freight station, road ranches along trail & toll bridge along the Oregon Trail.
Collections: blacksmith; wagons & stock; historical & interpretive displays.
Facilities: park; picnic area; nature trail; visitor's center; information theater; campgrounds.
Activities: park tours; interpretive programs; slide programs; blacksmith demonstrations.
Hours & Admission Prices: May 1 to mid-Sept. daily 10-5; mid-Sept. to Oct. 24 Sat.-Sun. 1-5. State park entry permit required; annual $20, daily $4 per vehicle. ♿
Attendance: 48,000 (estimated)

Fort Calhoun

FORT ATKINSON STATE HISTORICAL PARK, 7th & Madison, Fort Calhoun, NE 68023. Mailing Address: Box 240, Fort Calhoun, NE 68023-0240. Tel.: 402-468-5611. Fax: 402-468-5066.
E-mail: fort.atkinson@ngpc.ne.gov
Web Site: ngpc.state.ne.us
Founded: 1963.
Congressional District: 1
Key Personnel: Supt., John Slader; Asst. Supt., Jerry Farber.
Personnel Profile: Full-Time Paid 2; Part-Time Paid 6; Part-Time Volunteers 30.
Governing Authority: state. Div. of Nebraska Game & Parks Commission, Lincoln, NE 68503. Parent Institution: State of Nebraska. Tax-exempt.
Historical Park: site of 1804 Lewis & Clark's Council on the Bluff & 1819-1827 U.S. Army's Ft. Atkinson.
Collections: artifacts from Fort period.
Research Fields: early log construction techniques; 1820's military history.
Facilities: interpretative center; records & reports of Fort period.
Activities: guided tours; reconstruction projects; changing exhibits. Museum Sponsors: events associated with early fur trade.
Publications: brochure.
Hours & Admission Prices: Park: Spring & Summer: daily 8-7; Fall & Winter: 8-sunset. Interpretative Center: May & Sept.-Oct. 21 Sat.-Sun. 10-5; Memorial Day to Labor Day daily 10-5. Park Entry Permit: annual $14, daily $2.50. ♿
Attendance: 47,500 (estimated)

WASHINGTON COUNTY HISTORICAL ASSOCIATION, 102 N. 14th St., Fort Calhoun, NE 68023-3532. Mailing Address: P.O. Box 25, Fort Calhoun, NE 68023-0025. Tel.: 402-468-5740. Fax: 402-468-5741.
E-mail: info@newashcohist.org
Web Site: www.newashcohist.org
Founded: 1938.
Congressional District: 1
Key Personnel: Chm. (V), Diane Jensen; C.E.O. & Dir., Mark Schulze.
Personnel Profile: Part-Time Paid 3; Part-Time Volunteers 20.
Governing Authority: society. Subsidiary Institutions: Frahm House, Fontanelle Town Hall, Fontanelle, NE. Tax-exempt: 501(c)(3).
General Museum.
Collections: Fort Atkinson relics & records; pioneer farm implements; weapons associated with exploration & settlement of area; historic & pre-historic Indian artifacts; furniture; glass; toys; hand crafts; needle works; clothing; musical instruments; manuscript collection. Historic Homes: 1905 Fred Frahm home, late 19th-century & turn-of-the-century furniture; 1855-1865 Fontanelle Town Hall; documents, letters; county records; genealogical records; Lewis & Clark diorama; photographic material; maps; genealogical material.
Research Fields: Fort Atkinson history & pioneer history in Washington County; fur-trading era and Lewis & Clark Expedition on the Missouri and its tributaries.
Facilities: 1,200-vol. library of history books of the county; early textbooks; local biographical material; magazine files available for research on premises; three galleries; reading room; many records & information relative to Fort Atkinson 1819-1827. Books & booklets for sale.
Activities: guided tours; programs incorporating museum material; guided tours of Frahm House & Fontanelle Town Hall by appointment only.
Publications: booklet, Fort on the Prairie, Portal to the Plains; 1985 reprint with name index of History of Washington Co. Nebraska, 1875.
Hours & Admission Prices: Wed.-Fri. 9-4, Sat.-Sun. 1-4; other times by appointment. Adults $3; members no charge. ♿
Attendance: 3,000 (estimated)
Membership: Friend $1-$299; Bronze $300; Silver $500; Gold $750; Platinum $1,000.

Franklin

FRANKLIN COUNTY MUSEUM, 1309 H Rd., Franklin, NE 68939-5168. Tel.: 308-425-3030. Fax: 530-425-3033.
E-mail: welovehistory@gtmc.net
Web Site: www.rootsweb.ancestry.com/~nefrankl/museum/fcmuseum
Founded: 1932.
Congressional District: 3
Key Personnel: Dir., Connie Osterbuhr; Chm. & Pres. (V), Jim Gorman.
Personnel Profile: Part-Time Volunteers 2.
Governing Authority: Parent Institution: Franklin County Historical Society, Inc. Tax-exempt.
County History.
Collections: county history; pioneer & Native American artifacts; military; agriculture; one-room schoolhouse; Franklin Academy; Ol' Towne Main St.; Pierce Lyden; Frank Cyr; Clarence Mitchell.
Research Fields: Franklin County genealogy.
Activities: monthly board meetings; educational programs. Museum Sponsors: Memorial Day Weekend Events; Harvest Fest in October; Christmas Open House.
Publications: Franklin, Nebraska 1879-2002, The Best of the Good Life; These Good Old Golden Rural Days.
Hours & Admission Prices: April-May & Sept.-Dec. Sat.-Sun. 1-4; June-Aug. 1-5; other times by appointment. No charge; donations accepted. Closed major holidays.
Attendance: 1,400 (estimated)
Membership: Individual $5; Family $7.50.

Fremont

LOUIS E. MAY MUSEUM, 1643 N. Nye, Fremont, NE 68025-3327. Mailing Address: P.O. Box 766, Fremont, NE 68026-0766. Tel.: 402-721-4515. Fax: 402-721-8354.
E-mail: maymuseum@juno.com
Web Site: www.connectfremont.org
Founded: 1969.
Congressional District: 1
Key Personnel: Pres., Lori Dahl; Cur. & Museum Shop Mgr., Patty Manhart.
Personnel Profile: Part-Time Paid 3; Part-Time Volunteers 75.
Governing Authority: county; society. Affiliated with Dodge County Historical Society. Tax-exempt.
History Museum.
Collections: furniture; photographs; farm implements; rural school; general store; dolls. Historic House: 1874 Theron Nye residence.
Major Exhibits: The Prairie My Garden, 12/09-12/10.
Research Fields: historic sites; oral history; local history.
Facilities: library; 2 gardens.
Activities: guided tours; permanent & temporary exhibitions; art exhibits. Museum Sponsors: Homesteaders Fair.
Publications: newsletter.
Hours & Admission Prices: April & Sept.-Nov. Wed.-Sat. 1:30-4:30; May-Aug. Wed.-Sun. 1:30-4:30. Adults $4, children $.50; members no charge. ♿
Attendance: 5,000 (accurate)
Membership: Student $5; Individual $10; Family $20; Contributing $50; Business $100; Life $250; Corporate Life $1,000.

Genoa

GENOA HISTORICAL SOCIETY & MUSEUM, 402 Willard Ave., Genoa, NE 68640. Mailing Address: P.O. Box 279, Genoa, NE 68640-0279. Tel.: 402-993-2875 & 2330.
Historical Society Museum.
Collections: Pawnee weapons, tools, & personal artifacts; Mormon Trail; U.S. Indian School; Pawnee Indian agency.
Hours & Admission Prices: Memorial Day to Labor Day Fri.-Sun. 1-5; other times by appointment. Requested Donations: adults $2, children $1.

Gering

FARM AND RANCH MUSEUM, 2930 Old Oregon Trail, Gering, NE 69341. Tel.: 308-436-1989.
Web Site: www.farmandranchmuseum.com
Founded: 1988.
Congressional District: 3
Key Personnel: Pres., Leo Heinemann; Vice Pres., Jack Preston; Sec., Charlie Fenster; Treas., Dennis Wiedeman.
Personnel Profile: Part-Time Paid 1; Part-Time Volunteers 100.
Farm Museum.
Collections: farm tractors & machinery; agricultural history.
Research Fields: agriculture.
Facilities: library; archives.

Activities: annual business meeting; special events. Museum Sponsors: Harvest Festival.
Publications: quarterly newsletter.
Hours & Admission Prices: May-Sept. Mon.-Sat. 10-5, Sun. 1-5; Oct.-April Mon.-Fri. 10-5, Sat.-Sun. by appointment. Donations: adults $3; discounts to members. ♿
Attendance: 7,000
Membership: Annual $20.

NORTH PLATTE VALLEY MUSEUM, 11th & J Streets, near Hwy. 92 & 71, Gering, NE 69341. Mailing Address: P.O. Box 435, Gering, NE 69341-0435. Tel.: 308-436-5411.
E-mail: npvm@earthlink.net
Web Site: www.npvm.org
Founded: 1969.
Congressional District: 3
Key Personnel: C.E.O. & Museum Shop Mgr., Barbara Netherland; Pres. (V), Kent Harvey.
Personnel Profile: Full-Time Paid 1; Part-Time Volunteers 50.
Governing Authority: nonprofit organization. Parent Institution: North Platte Valley Historical Assoc., Inc. Tax-exempt: 501(c)(3).
Local History Museum: located on the Oregon Trail.
Collections: 1889 Sod House; 1890 log house; tools; furnishings; photographs; horse drawn vehicles; military; cattlemen; Indian artifacts; Oregon trail history.
Research Fields: local history; Oregon Trail.
Facilities: access to campground, playground. Books on Western lore & locally handcrafted gifts for sale.
Activities: guided tours; lectures; public meetings; living history exhibits.
Publications: quarterly newsletter.
Hours & Admission Prices: Memorial Day to Labor Day Mon.-Fri. 9-4, Sat.-Sun.1-4; Sept.-April Mon.-Fri. 8:30-4; other times by appointment. Adults $3, children under 12 $1; discount to AAM members; members no charge. ♿
Attendance: 7,000 (estimated)
Membership: Individual $20; Participating Couple $30; Family $35; Contributing & Business $50; Supporting $100; Life & Sustaining $200; Patron $500.

OREGON TRAIL MUSEUM, Scotts Bluff National Monument, 190276 Old Oregon Trail, Gering, NE 69341. Mailing Address: Scotts Bluff National Monument, P.O. Box 27, Gering, NE 69341-0027. Tel.: 308-436-4340 (National Park Office) & 2975 (Oregon Trail Museum Assoc.). Fax: 308-436-7611.
Web Site: www.nps.gov/scbl
Founded: 1919.
Congressional District: 3
Key Personnel: Supt., Ken Maybery; Park Ranger, Eric Haugland; Administrative Officer, Kelly Mansfield; Business Mgr. & Museum Shop Mgr., Jolene Kaufman.
Governing Authority: federal. National Park Service, Dept. of Interior, Washington, DC 20240. Tax-exempt.
National Monument: dominant natural feature of the North Platte Valley which has been a human migration corridor for centuries.
Collections: historical artifacts; paintings; vegetation; natural wildlife; geology; paleontology.
Research Fields: prairie restoration.
Facilities: 1,200-vol. library of historical material available for use on premises.
Activities: living history exhibits; conducted hikes; slide presentations.
Publications: book, Scotts Bluff Handbook.
Hours & Admission Prices: Summer: daily 8-7; Winter: daily 8-5. $5 per vehicle. Annual park pass $15. ♿
Attendance: 150,000 (estimated)
Membership: See separate listing for Oregon Trail Museum Assoc.

SCOTTS BLUFF NATIONAL MONUMENT, 190276 Old Oregon Trail, Gering, NE 69341. Mailing Address: P.O. Box 27, Gering, NE 69341-0027. Tel.: 308-436-9700. Fax: 308-436-7611.
Web Site: www.nps.gov/scbl
Founded: 1919.
Congressional District: 3rd
Key Personnel: Supt., Ken Mabery; Gift Shop Mgr., Jolene Kaufmann.
Personnel Profile: Full-Time Paid 9; Part-Time Paid 5; Part-Time Volunteers 2.
Governing Authority: federal. Parent Institution: U.S. National Park Service.
History Museum.
Collections: Oregon Trail history 1830-1880; prehistoric & historic objects; sketches & watercolors by pioneer photographer William Henry Jackson; historic & prehistoric Plains Indian pieces.
Research Fields: Oregon Trail history; William H. Jackson, pioneer photographer; fire management; prairie restoration; flora & fauna surveys; collections internship projects.
Facilities: reference library available to the public; 30-seat auditorium. Books, posters, postcards & stationery for sale.
Activities: lectures; films; hiking; Summit Road; temporary exhibitions.
Publications: informational brochures; handbook, Overland Migrations.
Hours & Admission Prices: Winter: daily 8-5; Summer: 8-7. Seven-day Pass: $5 per vehicle; Annual Pass: $15 per vehicle; senior pass & federal recreation lands pass no charge. ♿
Attendance: 111,000 (accurate)
Membership: Family & Tri-Park Pass $15.

WILDCAT HILLS NATURE CENTER, N.E. Hwy. 71, Gering, NE 69341. Mailing Address: P.O. Box 65, Gering, NE 69341. Tel.: 308-436-3777.
Nature Center.
Collections: local history; local flora & fauna; fossils; paintings.
Activities: simulated fossil dig.
Hours & Admission Prices: Call for hours.

WILDLIFE WORLD WYOBRASKA NATURAL HISTORY MUSEUM, 950 U St., Gering, NE 69341-2246. Mailing Address: P.O. Box 623, Gering, NE 69341-0623. Tel.: 308-436-7104. Fax: 308-436-7104.
Web Site: www.wyobraskawildlifemuseum.com
Natural History Museum.
Collections: over 500 wild animals from seven continents.
Hours & Admission Prices: Summer: Mon.-Fri. 9-5, Sat. 10-4. Winter: Tues.-Sat. 10-4. Adults $3.50, seniors $3, children $1.

Gibbon

GIBBON HERITAGE CENTER, 2nd & Court St., Gibbon, NE 68840. Mailing Address: 411 Lawn Ave., Gibbon, NE 68840-6016. Tel.: 308-468-6109 & 5608.
Founded: 1975.
Congressional District: 36
Personnel Profile: Part-Time Volunteers 6.
History Museum.
Collections: history of area schools & businesses; religious memorabilia; church.
Hours & Admission Prices: 1st Sun. of month 2-4; other times by appointment. No charge; donations accepted.
Attendance: 125 (estimated)

Goehner

SEWARD COUNTY HISTORICAL SOCIETY MUSEUM, 364th Rd., I-80 Exit 373, Goehner, NE Mailing Address: 1500 Main St., Seward, NE 68434-1643. Tel.: 402-643-4935 & 523-4055 (museum).
E-mail: info@sewardcountymuseum.org
Web Site: sewardcountymuseum.org
Founded: 1978.
Congressional District: 1
Key Personnel: Pres., Larry Hansen; Vice Pres., Larry Ray; Chm., Dave Gies; Treas., Dick Miers; Sec., Mary Lou Eberspacher; Chm. Exhibits, Alta Krasser; Membership & Exhibits, Della Miers; Miniature Train Owner & Operator, Jim Culver.
Personnel Profile: Full-Time Volunteers 10; Part-Time Volunteers 10.
Governing Authority: society; nonprofit organization. Tax-exempt: 501(c)(3).
Historical Society Museum.
Collections: toys; 1910-1930 kitchen & dining room; 1900 bedroom; food preservation; furnishings; miniature farm; dolls; 2 dining rooms; butchering equipment; sewing room; locally-made single-engine plane; furnished one-room schoolhouse; 1908 Seward County two story furnished farm home; farm machinery; Civil & World Wars memorabilia; doctor's office; dentist's office; country store; bootery; beauty shop; furnished log cabin; miniature railroad system; steam engine.
Facilities: approx. 100-vol. library of books on Seward County, available for use by public on premises; 14,400 sq. ft. exhibit space; youth room. Books for sale.
Activities: train ride on miniature train 2nd & 4th Sun. Museum Sponsors: Antique Car Show.
Publications: Seward County Historical Society Newsletter.
Hours & Admission Prices: May-Oct. Thurs. 10-4, Sun. 1:30-5. No charge; donations accepted. ♿
Attendance: 1,200 (estimated)
Membership: Annual $10; Sustaining $25; Life $150.

Gordon

SCAMAHORN CHURCH MUSEUM, 200 Block of W. 5th St. in Wayland Park, Gordon, NE 69360. Mailing Address: 516 N. Elm St., Gordon, NE 69360. Tel.: 308-282-2915.
Key Personnel: Pres., Harlen Wheeler
History Museum.
Collections: local history; quilts; obituaries; period medical equipment; office furnishings; furniture; Native American beadwork; photographs; period clothing; military artifacts from WWI & WWII; dollhouse.
Hours & Admission Prices: Memorial Day to mid-Sept. Mon.-Fri. 1-5. No charge.

SHERIDAN GALLERY, 117 N. Main St., Gordon, NE 69343. Mailing Address: P.O. Box 237, Gordon, NE 69343. Tel.: 308-282-9972.
Art Gallery.
Collections: works by local artists including Jean Ann Curry-Hess; photographs; paintings.
Activities: workshops; classes.
Hours & Admission Prices: Call for hours.

THE TRI-STATE OLD TIME COWBOYS MEMORIAL MUSEUM, Gordon, NE 69343. Mailing Address: P.O. Box 202, Gordon, NE 69343-0202. Tel.: 308-282-0749.
History Museum.
Collections: early chuck wagon; old saddles; chaps; spurs; tools & gear used from early ranches of the late 1880s to modern-day; artifacts & relics pertaining to ranching & cowboys.
Hours & Admission Prices: June-Sept. 15 daily 1-5; other times by appointment. No charge; donations accepted. ♿

Gothenburg

GOTHENBURG HISTORICAL MUSEUM, 1420 Ave. F., Gothenburg, NE 69138. Mailing Address: P.O. Box 263, Gothenburg, NE 69138. Tel.: 308-537-4293.
E-mail: annea@gothenburgdelivers.com
Web Site: www.gothenburgdelivers.com
History Museum.
Collections: local history & culture; personal artifacts; period furnishings; photographs.
Hours & Admission Prices: Call for hours. No charge.

PONY EXPRESS STATION MUSEUM, 1500 Lake Ave., Gothenburg, NE 69138. Mailing Address: P.O. Box 263, Gothenburg, NE 69138. Tel.: 308-537-3505.
Web Site: www.gothenburgdelivers.com
Historic Building: housed in the Sam Macchette station used by the Pony Express between 1860-1861.
Collections: local history & culture; Pony Express memorabilia; early pioneer artifacts; photographs.
Facilities: Museum-related items for sale.
Hours & Admission Prices: Call for hours. No charge.

SOD HOUSE MUSEUM, I-80 & Hwy. 47, Gothenburg, NE 69138. Tel.: 308-537-2680.
E-mail: sodlady2001@hotmail.com
Founded: 1988.
Congressional District: 39
Key Personnel: Dir., Merle Block; Museum Shop Mgr. & Mgr., Linda Block.
Personnel Profile: Full-Time Volunteers 2; Part-Time Paid 2.
Governing Authority: private.
Historic Site & Historic House: c.1800 Farmstead & Sod House.
Collections: homesteader memorabilia; photographs of sod house era; barbed wire buffalo sculpture (life size) containing 4-l/2 miles of wire; Indian & Pony barbed wire sculpture; Pony Express history; Indian artifacts.
Facilities: barn housing museum; wooden windmill. Gift items for sale.
Activities: guided tours.
Publications: annual brochure, Pony Express Times.
Hours & Admission Prices: May & Sept. daily 9-6; June-Aug. daily 8-8. Family $5, adult $1. ♿
Attendance: 20,000 (estimated)

Grand Island

* **STUHR MUSEUM OF THE PRAIRIE PIONEER, (M),** 3133 W. Hwy. 34, Grand Island, NE 68801-7485. Tel.: 308-385-5316. Fax: 308-385-5028.
E-mail: info@stuhrmuseum.org
Web Site: www.stuhrmuseum.org
Founded: 1961.
Congressional District: 3
Key Personnel: Exec. Dir., Joe Black; Chm. (V), Renee Goble; Dir. Education, Ann Atkins; Dir. Mktg., Mike Bockoven; Finance & Human Resources Mgr., Steve Stump; Visitor Svcs. Coord. & Museum Shop Mgr., Martha Grigsby; Historian & Research Center Mgr., Karen Keehr; Collections Mgr., Leslie Vollnogle; Historical Interpretation Mgr., Kay Cynova.
Personnel Profile: Full-Time Paid 21; Full-Time Volunteers 10; Part-Time Paid 90; Part-Time Volunteers 200; Interns 3.
Governing Authority: county. Hall County Museum Board. Tax-exempt: 501(c)(3).
History Museum: Stuhr Building designed by Edward Durell Stone.
Collections: 60 restored & furnished houses & businesses; farm; clothing; household wares; pioneer crafts; 20 period railroad cars & engines; farm machinery; period autos & farm machinery; Indian & Old West artifacts; restored 19th-century Railroad Town; Gus Fonner Memorial Rotunda. Historic Buildings: 1860s Road Ranch; 1890s rural settlement & farm; Pawnee Indian Earth Lodge.
Research Fields: mid 19th to early 20th-century prairie town building; homes; business; lifestyle; material culture; agriculture; Plains Indians; steam railroading.
Facilities: 200-acres 3 modern exhibit buildings; research center; over 60 historic homes & shops arranged in 5 different 19th-century prairie communities; 100-seat auditorium; activity center; arboretum. Museum-related items for sale.
Activities: structured educational programs; seasonal interpretive programs; period trades on site; interpretive history exhibits; special events; guided tours; lectures; films; concerts; workshops for children & adults; volunteer program; permanent, temporary & traveling exhibitions; hands-on activities.
Publications: semi-monthly newsletter.
Hours & Admission Prices: Mon.-Sat. 9-5, Sun. 12-5. May-Sept. 30: adults $8, senior citizens $7, youth 7-12 $6; members no charge. Oct.-April: adults $6, senior citizens $5, youth 7-12 $4; members no charge. Closed New Year's; Thanksgiving; Christmas. ♿
Attendance: 68,000 (accurate)
Membership: Individual $30; Companion $35; Family & Grandparents $40.

Grant

PERKINS COUNTY HISTORICAL SOCIETY, Central Ave. & 6th, Grant, NE 69140. Mailing Address: P.O. Box 562, Grant, NE 69140-0562. Tel.: 308-352-4977 & 4698. Fax: 308-352-2346.
Founded: 1964.
Congressional District: 44
Key Personnel: Pres. (V), Brenda Styskal.
Personnel Profile: Part-Time Volunteers 7.
Governing Authority: nonprofit organization. Tax-exempt.
General Museum: housed in 1910 two-story frame home with wrap around porch.
Collections: archives; agriculture; costumes. Historic Buildings: 1900 Brandon Rural School; 1975 Metal Building housing farm equipment.
Facilities: 300-vol. library of school books; religious books; fiction; history available on premises.
Activities: permanent exhibitions.
Publications: book, Plainscape, A Portrait of Perkins County.
Hours & Admission Prices: Temporarily closed.
Attendance: 112 (accurate)

Greeley

GREELEY COUNTY HISTORICAL SOCIETY COURTHOUSE MUSEUM, Courthouse Square, Greeley, NE 68842. Mailing Address: P.O. Box 6, Greeley, NE 68842-0006. Tel.: 308-428-3115.
Key Personnel: Dir., Jim Dutcher
History Museum.
Collections: military artifacts; jewelry; photographs; American Indian utensils; tools; clothing; books; Veterans' Wall & Memorial.
Hours & Admission Prices: Mon.-Fri. 9-4. No charge. ♿

Greenwood

GREENWOOD HISTORICAL SOCIETY DEPOT MUSEUM, 440 Broad St., Greenwood, NE 68366. Mailing Address: P.O. Box 83, Greenwood, NE 68366-0083. Tel.: 402-430-0238.
Railroad Museum.
Collections: depot & railroad history; photographs.
Hours & Admission Prices: Spring to Fall Mon.-Wed. 10-5; other times by appointment. No charge.

Gretna

AK-SAR-BEN AQUARIUM OUTDOOR EDUCATION CENTER, 21502 W. Hwy. 31, Gretna, NE 68028-7264. Tel.: 402-332-3901. Fax: 402-332-5853.
Web Site: www.ngpc.state.ne.us/fishing/programs/aquaticEd/aquarium.asp
Founded: 1979.
Congressional District: 2
Key Personnel: Dir., Tony Korth.
Personnel Profile: Full-Time Paid 4; Part-Time Paid 3.
Governing Authority: state; Parent Institution: Nebraska Game & Parks Commission, 2200 N. 33rd, Lincoln, NE 68504. Tel.: 402-471-0641. Tax-exempt.
Aquarium: located on site of 1882, Hatch House, first fish hatchery & public picnic area in Nebraska.
Collections: fish, turtles & frogs native to Nebraska.
Facilities: aquarium; 103-seat auditorium; classrooms.
Activities: guided tours; lectures; films, hobby workshops.
Publications: informational pamphlets on facility.
Hours & Admission Prices: Memorial Day weekend-Labor Day Mon.-Fri. 10-4:30, Sat.-Sun. & holidays 10-5; Sept.-May Wed.-Mon. 10-4:30. Adults $1, children 6-15 $.50; children under 6 no charge. Closed New Year's Day; Thanksgiving; Christmas. ♿
Attendance: 65,000 (estimated)
Membership: Annual $15.

Harrisburg

BANNER COUNTY HISTORICAL SOCIETY, 200 N. Pennsylvania Ave., Harrisburg, NE 69345. Mailing Address: P.O. Box 74, Harrisburg, NE 69345-0074. Tel.: 308-436-7228.
E-mail: bannercountyhistoricalsociety@yahoo.com
Web Site: bannercountyhistoricalsociety.com
Founded: 1969.
Congressional District: 3
Key Personnel: C.E.O. & Cur., Judy Leafdale; Pres., George Jerred; Vice Pres., Vicki Stone; Treas., Reta Pahl; Sec., Sherry Gifford.
Personnel Profile: Part-Time Volunteers 15.
Governing Authority: society. Tax-exempt: 501(c)(3).
Historical Society Museum.
Collections: 1800-1940 farm & household artifacts of western Nebraska; transportation; arrowhead collection; steam engine; period vehicles. Historic Buildings: sod house; log house; frame church; one-room log schoolhouse; 1900 drug store; c.1920 horse barn; c.1930 filling station; c.1920 bank.
Facilities: library of area history books, available for use by public; 10,800 sq. ft. exhibit space.
Activities: guided tours; lectures; program on late-1800s pioneer lifestyle for fourth grade students. Annual Event: Open House in June.
Publications: Banner County Historical Newsletter, 3 times per year.
Hours & Admission Prices: June to mid-Sept. Sun. 1-5; other times by appointment. No charge; donations accepted. ♿
Attendance: 3,000 (estimated)
Membership: Junior $1; Adult $5.

Harrison

AGATE FOSSIL BEDS NATIONAL MONUMENT, 301 River Rd., 22 miles south of Harrison & 3 miles east of Hwy. 29, Harrison, NE 69346-2734. Tel.: 308-668-2211. Fax: 308-668-2318.
Web Site: www.nps.gov/agfo/
Founded: 1965.
Congressional District: 3
Key Personnel: Supt., James Hill; Cur., Mark Hertig; Museum Shop Mgr., Jolene S. Kaufmann.
Personnel Profile: Full-Time Paid 6; Part-Time Paid 6; Part-Time Volunteers 1; Interns 2.
Governing Authority: federal. Parent Institution: National Park Service, Washington, DC. Tax-exempt.
Park Museum/Visitor Center: located near the site of 19-22 million year old mammal fossil remains & historic Agate Springs Ranch on the Niobrara River.
Collections: Miocene fossils; Plains Indian artifacts, 1880-1930; James H. Cook & Harold J. Cook historical papers collection; articles of 19th-century western America.
Research Fields: paleontology; prairie & fire; river water quality; Cook Indian collection; early ranching
Facilities: visitor center; life-size fossil diorama; interactive exhibits; Plains Indian exhibits; movie theater. Books & postcards for sale.
Activities: self-guided tour to fossil beds; self-guided tour to Daemonelix area; guided tours for schools; slide & video programs; permanent & temporary exhibitions.
Publications: book, Agate Fossil Beds Handbook 107.
Hours & Admission Prices: Memorial Day-Labor Day daily 8-6; Sept.-May daily 8-4. Adults $3, $5 per car; Golden Eagle, Golden Age, Golden Access card no charge. Closed New Year's Day; Thanksgiving; Christmas. ♿
Attendance: 17,500 (estimated)

Hastings

CHILDREN'S MUSEUM OF CENTRAL NEBRASKA, Imperial Mall, 12th & Marian Rd., Hastings, NE 68901. Mailing Address: P.O. Box 1502, Hastings, NE 68902-1502. Tel.: 402-463-3300.
E-mail: info@cmocn.org
Web Site: www.cmocn.org
Key Personnel: Pres. Bd., David Bosle; Exec. Dir. & Vice Pres., Patrick Cecil; Sec., Julie Nash; Treas., DeWayne Boesen.
Governing Authority: nonprofit. Tax-exempt: 501(c)(3).
Children's Museum.
Collections: hands-on exhibits.
Facilities: 10,000 sq. ft. exhibit space. Museum-related items for sale.
Activities: summer science & nature programs; birthday parties; facility rental; field trips.
Publications: newsletter, Hands on Learning.
Hours & Admission Prices: Tues.-Sat. 10-6, Sun. 1-5. Admission $5; discounts to groups of 10 or more; members & children under 2 no charge. ♿

HASTINGS MUSEUM, (M), 1330 N. Burlington, Hastings, NE 68901-3099. Mailing Address: P.O. Box 1286, Hastings, NE 68902-1286. Tel.: 402-461-2399. Fax: 402-461-2379.
E-mail: hastingsmuseum@windstream.net
Web Site: www.hastingsmuseum.org
Founded: 1926.
Congressional District: 3
Key Personnel: C.E.O. & Dir., Rebecca Matticks; Pres. (V), Jack Steiner; Dir. Mktg. & Devel., Drew Ceperley; Dir. Planetarium, Dan Glomski; Dir. Education, Russanne Erickson; Cur., Teresa Kreutzer-Hodson; Museum Shop Mgr., Virginia Long.
Personnel Profile: Full-Time Paid 10; Part-Time Paid 16; Part-Time Volunteers 200; Interns 1.
Governing Authority: municipal. Tax-exempt: 170(b)(1)(A) & 501(c)(3).
Natural Science & History Museum.
Collections: North American mammals & birds; fossils; rocks; minerals; firearms; clothing; glassware; pioneer items; clocks; china; regional history items; period rooms; Kool Aid.
Major Exhibits: "I Spy", 11/09-10/10.
Facilities: 1,000-vol. library of natural science & historical books and pamphlets available on premises; planetarium; discovery center: large-format theater. Educational items, gifts & books for sale.
Activities: guided tours, lectures & films for schools; study clubs; films; planetarium programs; permanent, temporary & traveling exhibitions; historic demonstrations; summer education program for children; hoilday activities for families.
Publications: periodical, Highlights.
Hours & Admission Prices: Museum: Summer: Sun. 12-6, Mon.-Thurs. 9-5, Fri.-Sat. 9-8; Winter: Sun. 12-6, Tues.-Thurs. 9-5, Fri.-Sat. 9-8. Adults $7, senior citizens $6, children 3-12 $5. Theatre: Adults $7.50, senior citizens $6.50, children $5.50. Combo Ticket: Adults $12.50, senior citizens $10.50, children 3-12 $8.50; discounts to schools, groups, Hastings Museum members & AAM members; children under 2 no charge. Closed Thanksgiving; Christmas Day. ♿
Attendance: 70,000 (accurate)
Membership: VIP Add-on Program $20; Individual $35; Companion $40; Family & Grandparent $45; Bronze $100; Silver Premiere $125; Gold Premiere $275; Platinum Premiere $525.

Hay Springs

HERITAGE CENTER MUSEUM, 230 N. Baker St., Hay Springs, NE 69347. Mailing Address: P.O. Box 291, Hay Springs, NE 69347-0291. Tel.: 308-638-7643.
History Museum.
Collections: local history & culture; period artifacts; photographs. Historic Buildings: 1887 Methodist Church; 1910 school house; log cabin.
Hours & Admission Prices: Memorial Day to Labor Day Mon.-Fri. 1-4; other times by appointment. No charge.

HERITAGE CENTER MUSEUM II, 133 N. Main St., Hay Springs, NE 69347. Mailing Address: P.O. Box 291, Hay Springs, NE 69347-0291. Tel.: 308-638-7643.
Historic Building: housed in the former hardware store.
Collections: local history & culture; period furnishings; personal artifacts; photographs.
Hours & Admission Prices: Memorial Day to Labor Day Mon.-Fri. 1-4; other times by appointment. No charge.

Hershey

STONES AND BONES GALLERY AND EMPORIUM, 105 E. 2nd St., Hershey, NE 69143. Mailing Address: P.O. Box 85, Hershey, NE 69143. Tel.: 308-368-7400.
Art Gallery.
Collections: western & wildlife art; period artifacts; photographs
Activities: demonstrations.
Hours & Admission Prices: Call for hours.

Holdrege

NEBRASKA PRAIRIE MUSEUM OF THE PHELPS COUNTY HISTORICAL SOCIETY, 2701 Burlington St., Holdrege, NE 68949-1347. Mailing Address: P.O. Box 164, Holdrege, NE 68949-0164. Tel.: 308-995-5015. Fax: 308-995-2241.
Web Site: www.nebraskaprairie.org
Formerly: Phelps County Historical Museum
Founded: 1966.
Congressional District: 3
Key Personnel: Vice Pres., Eileen Schrock; Chm. (V), Dr. Bob Butz; Sec., Joan Burbach.
Personnel Profile: Full-Time Paid 1; Part-Time Paid 2; Part-Time Volunteers 50.
Governing Authority: nonprofit organization. Parent Institution: Phelps County Historical Society. Tax-exempt: 170(b)(1)(A).
General Museum.
Collections: agriculture; antiques; religious; art; anthropology; ethnology; Indians; World War II German prisoner of war exhibit.
Research Fields: county & state history.
Facilities: 5,000-vol. library.
Activities: guided tours; lectures; permanent & temporary exhibitions; genealogy research.
Publications: book, History of Phelps County; quarterly newsletter, Stereoscope; Prisoners on the Plains.
Hours & Admission Prices: Summer: Mon.-Fri. 9-5, Sat.-Sun. 1-5; Winter: call for hours. Adults $5, children 6-12 $2. Closed holidays. ♿
Attendance: 15,000 (estimated)
Membership: Annual $20; Life $1000.

Hyannis

GRANT COUNTY MUSEUM & HISTORIC SOCIETY, Grant County Courthouse, 105 E. Harrison, Hyannis, NE 69350-9706. Mailing Address: P.O. Box 82, Hyannis, NE 69350-0082. Tel.: 308-458-2371. Fax: 308-458-2485.
Founded: 1963.
Congressional District: 3
Key Personnel: C.E.O., Harry Merrihew.
Personnel Profile: Part-Time Paid 1; Part-Time Volunteers 2.
Governing Authority: nonprofit organization. Parent Institution: Grant County Historic Society. Tax-exempt.
General Museum: housed in the Grant County Court House.
Collections: Grant County history; cowboy artifacts & pictures; Western culture; Indian artifacts; barbed wire; John Wayne; saddles; stuntman, Chuck Hayward; genealogy.
Research Fields: Genealogy; history; local.
Activities: guided tours; permanent exhibitions; special school tours for town & country schools. Special Events: Windmill Days; Quilt Show; Arrowhead and Artifact Show; Alumni Grant Co. Fair, County Government Day.
Publications: book, History of Grant County; Nebraska, Our Towns; Grant County - It's Friends & Neighbors.
Hours & Admission Prices: Tues.-Wed. 1-4; other times by appointment. No charge; donations accepted. ♿
Attendance: 238 (accurate)
Membership: Annual $10; Life $50.

Kearney

FORT KEARNEY MUSEUM, 131 S. Central Ave., Kearney, NE 68847-7908. Tel.: 308-234-5200.
Founded: 1950.
Key Personnel: Dir., Marlo L. Johnson.
Personnel Profile: Full-Time Paid 2; Part-Time Paid 3.
Governing Authority: individual operation.
General Museum.
Collections: Indian and pioneer relics, tools & arms; European and Oriental material; Egyptian & African objects; history; natural history; glass; anthropology; archaeology; mineralogy; music; geology; costumes; numismatics; paintings; sculpture; graphics; circus.
Research Fields: natural history; glass; anthropology; archaeology; mineralogy; music; geology; costumes; numismatic; history.
Facilities: Gift items for sale.
Activities: permanent exhibitions; glass bottom boat rides.
Publications: brochure, Fort Kearney Museum.
Hours & Admission Prices: Memorial Day-Labor Day Thurs.-Sat. 10:30-5, Sun. 1-5. Museum: Adults $2.50; discount to groups; children under 12 no charge. Boat Rides: Adults $3, children under 12 $2.50. ♿

FORT KEARNY STATE HISTORICAL PARK, 1020 V Rd., Kearney, NE 68847-8043. Tel.: 308-865-5305. Fax: 308-865-5306.
E-mail: ngpc.fort.kearny@nebraska.gov
Web Site: www.outdoornebraska.org
Founded: 1929.
Congressional District: 3
Key Personnel: Supt., Eugene A. Hunt; Asst. Supt., Joe Blazek.
Personnel Profile: Full-Time Paid 2; Part-Time Paid 8; Interns 2.
Governing Authority: state. Affiliated with Nebraska Game and Parks Commission, Statehouse, Box 30370, 2200 N. 33rd St., Lincoln, NE. 68503. 402-471-0641. Tax-exempt.
Historic Building & Site.
Collections: 1848-1871 military records; letters; dispatches; military orders; Oregon Trail history.
Facilities: 66-seat auditorium; microfilm. Books pertaining to Western history & other museum-related items for sale.
Activities: self-guided tours; lectures; films; broadcast programs; permanent & temporary exhibitions.
Publications: pamphlet.
Hours & Admission Prices: Memorial Day-Labor Day daily 9-5. Grounds: sunrise-sunset; other times by appointment; game & parks sticker required. ♿
Attendance: 61,000 (estimated)

THE FRANK HOUSE AT THE UNIVERSITY OF NEBRASKA-KEARNEY, 2010 University Dr., Kearney, NE 68849-0001. Tel.: 308-865-8284.
E-mail: sullivandw@unk.edu
Web Site: www.frankhouse.org
Key Personnel: Dir., KrisAnn Sulivan.
Personnel Profile: Full-Time Paid 1; Part-Time Paid 1; Part-Time Volunteers 10; Interns 1.
Governing Authority: Parent Institution: University of Nebraska. Tax-exempt.
Historic House Museum: housed in the former home of G.W. Frank & his family; built in 1889. Listed on the National Register of Historic Places.
Collections: household artifacts; furnishings; Tiffany windows.
Research Fields: early Kearney; Frank family; hospital for tuberculosis.
Activities: Museum Sponsors: Holiday Open House; Edible Flower Tea; Titanic Diner.
Hours & Admission Prices: Mon.-Fri. 2-5; Sat. 12-5. No charge; donations accepted. Closed university holidays & breaks.
Attendance: 4,160 (accurate)

KEARNEY AREA CHILDREN'S MUSEUM, 2005 1st Ave., Kearney, NE 68847-5305. Tel.: 308-698-2228. Fax: 308-698-2229.
E-mail: kearneychildrensmuseum@windstream.net
Web Site: www.kearneykidzone.com
Founded: 1989.
Congressional District: 3
Key Personnel: Exec. Dir., Julie Bray; Chm., Sara O'Neill; Vice Chm., Erin Becker; Treas., Mike Sandstedt; Sec., Sarah Focke.
Personnel Profile: Full-Time Paid 1; Part-Time Paid 2; Part-Time Volunteers 40.
Governing Authority: nonprofit organization. Tax-exempt: 501(c)(3).
Children's Museum.
Collections: science; hands on exhibits; music.
Facilities: theatre.
Activities: educational programs for children & families; crafts; workshops; music; shadow room.
Publications: quarterly newsletter, KACM.
Hours & Admission Prices: Wed.-Sat. 10-5, Sun. 1-5, 1st Thurs. of month 10-8. Admission $3; Association of Children's Museums, reciprocal members, KACM & children 2 & under no charge. Closed all major holidays. ♿

Attendance: 12,000 (estimated)
Membership: Family & Grandparents $50; Family & Grandparents Plus 2 $60; Patron $100; Sharing & Caring $75 & $125.

MUSEUM OF NEBRASKA ART, (M), 2401 Central Ave., Kearney, NE 68847-4501. Tel.: 308-865-8559. Fax: 308-865-8104.
E-mail: monet@unk.edu
Web Site: monet.unk.edu/mona
Founded: 1976.
Congressional District: 3
Key Personnel: Bd. Pres., Steve Chatelain; Dir., Audrey S. Kauders; Cur., Teliza Rodriguez; Collections Supvr., Jean Jacobson; Dir. Devel., Mark Foradori; Museum Shop Mgr., Merilyn Anderson; Museum Shop Mgr., Janet Fox; Museum Shop Mgr., Kay Horner.
Personnel Profile: Full-Time Paid 4; Part-Time Paid 8; Part-Time Volunteers 120; Interns 1.
Governing Authority: Parent Institution: University of Nebraska Kearney. Tax-exempt: 501(c)(3).
Art Museum: housed in Renaissance revival building listed on the National Register of Historic Places.
Collections: Nebraska art & artists from early 19th century to present; sculpture garden.
Research Fields: historic & contemporary Nebraska artists.
Facilities: archival library containing records & documents related to Nebraska art & artists for public use; sculpture garden.
Activities: guided tours; lectures; organized education programs for children & adults; docent program; organized education programs for undergraduate or graduate college students affiliated with University of Nebraska at Kearney; traveling, temporary & loan exhibitions; school loan service.
Publications: exhibition catalogues; collection catalogues; quarterly newsletter.
Hours & Admission Prices: Tues.-Sat. 11-5, Sun. 1-5. No charge; donations accepted. Closed major holidays. ♿
Attendance: 21,974 (accurate)
Membership: Student & Senior $15; Individual $25; Dual Senior $30; Family $40; Patron $50; Sustainer $100; Benefactor $250; Bronze $500; Silver $1,000; Gold $2,500; Platinum $5,000.

TRAILS & RAILS MUSEUM, (M), 710 W. 11th St., Kearney, NE 68845-7340. Mailing Address: BCHS, P.O. Box 523, Kearney, NE 68848. Tel.: 308-234-3041.
E-mail: bchs@bchs.us
Congressional District: 3
Key Personnel: Dir., Jennifer Murrish; Pres. (V), Dan Speirs; Education Coord., Lyn Hoffman.
Personnel Profile: Full-Time Paid 2; Part-Time Paid 8; Part-Time Volunteers 20; Interns 3.
Governing Authority: Parent Institution: Buffalo County Historical Society.
History Museum.
Collections: area history; locomotive; photographs; personal artifacts; livery barn. Historic Buildings: Union Pacific Depot; 1898 church; school house; log cabin; Freighters Hotel; Boyd Ranch house.
Facilities: archives. Museum-related items for sale.
Activities: groups tours; special events. Annual Events: Wagons West Day in June; 1/2 Marathon; Trivia Contest; Fiddle Contest; Christmas Tree Walk in December.
Publications: Buffalo Tales.
Hours & Admission Prices: Memorial Day to Labor Day Mon.-Sat. 10-6, Sun. 1-5; Sept.-May Mon.-Fri. 1-5; groups by appointment. Adults $5, children $2; members and children 12 & under no charge.
Attendance: 4,463 (accurate)
Membership: Individual $35; Family $40; Institutional $50; Supporting $75.

Lewellen

ASH HOLLOW STATE HISTORICAL PARK, Hwy. 26, Lewellen, NE 69147. Mailing Address: P.O. Box 70, Lewellen, NE 69147-0070. Tel.: 308-778-5651.
Web Site: www.ngpc.state.ne.us
Founded: 1967.
Congressional District: 3
Key Personnel: Supt., Jeffery Uhrich.
Personnel Profile: Full-Time Paid 1; Part-Time Paid 8.
Governing Authority: state. Parent Institution: State of Nebraska. Subsidiary Institution: Nebraska Game and Parks Commission, P.O. Box 30370, Lincoln, NE 68503. Tax-exempt.
Historic Site: camp site along the Oregon Trail.
Collections: archaeology; Indian artifacts; pioneer trail history.
Facilities: visitors center; historic sites.
Hours & Admission Prices: Memorial Day to Labor Day Tues.-Sun. 10-4. Park permit required. Daily $4; annual $20. ♿
Attendance: 20,562 (accurate)

Lexington

DAWSON COUNTY HISTORICAL MUSEUM, (M), 805 N. Taft St., Lexington, NE 68850-2029. Mailing Address: P.O. Box 369, Lexington, NE 68850-0369. Tel.: 308-324-5340.
E-mail: dcmuseum@atcjet.net
Web Site: www.dchmuseum.com
Founded: 1958.
Congressional District: 3
Key Personnel: Pres., Gail Hall; Dir., Barbara Vondras; Research Asst., Eileen Lauby; Admin. Asst., Carol Nelson.
Personnel Profile: Full-Time Paid 1; Part-Time Paid 2; Part-Time Volunteers 75.
Governing Authority: nonprofit organization. Parent Institution: Dawson County Historical Society. Tax-exempt: 501(c)(3).
Local History Museum.
Collections: local history items; pioneer household artifacts; photographs & archives; quilts; clothing; glassware; period rooms & offices; 15,000 year-old remains of a Columbian mammoth discovered in Dawson County in 1993; educational exhibits concerning the early history of Central Nebraska including Wheels of Progress: The Automobile in Dawson County; 1917 McCabe Baby Biplane; 1903 Baldwin steam locomotive. Historic Buildings: 1888 rural schoolhouse; 1885 Union Pacific Depot; 1865 loghouse; farm history building.
Research Fields: local history; genealogy; historical preservation; agricultural history.
Facilities: 80-seat meeting room; art gallery. Gift items for sale.
Activities: guided tours; inter-museum loan, temporary & permanent exhibitions; craft & hobby showings; special speakers on state & local history; monthly art shows.
Publications: brochures; quarterly newsletter; books.
Hours & Admission Prices: Mon.-Sat. 9-5. No charge; donations accepted. Closed New Year's Eve & Day; Easter; Memorial Day; Thanksgiving; Christmas. ♿
Attendance: 8,000 (accurate)
Membership: Individual $12.50; Family $20; Sustaining $25; Business $50; Life $150; Joint Life (husband/wife) $200. Corporate Life (3 levels) $250; $500; $1,000.

HEARTLAND MUSEUM OF MILITARY VEHICLES, 606 Heartland Rd., Lexington, NE 68850-5666. Tel.: 308-324-6329.
E-mail: heartlandmuseum@cozadtel.net
Web Site: www.heartlandmuseum.com
Military Museum.
Collections: period military vehicles.
Facilities: library.
Hours & Admission Prices: Mon.-Sat. 10-5, Sun. 1-5.

Lincoln

AMERICAN HISTORICAL SOCIETY OF GERMANS FROM RUSSIA, 631 D. St., Lincoln, NE 68502-1149. Tel.: 402-474-3363. Fax: 402-474-7229.
E-mail: ahsgr@ahsgr.org
Web Site: www.ahsgr.org
Founded: 1968.
Congressional District: 1
Personnel Profile: Full-Time Paid 2; Part-Time Paid 4.
Governing Authority: society members.
Historical Society Museum.
Collections: memorabilia brought from Russia by the Germans; summer kitchen, chapel, country store.
Facilities: research library.
Activities: annual convention.
Publications: four journals; four newsletters.
Hours & Admission Prices: Mon.-Fri. 9-4, Sat. by appointment. Tours: Mon.-Fri. 2 or by appointment. No charge; donations accepted. Closed major holidays & annual convention week. ♿
Attendance: 1,800 (accurate)
Membership: Youth $8; Student $15; Individual & Family $50; Contributing $75; Sustaining $100; Life $750, $900, $1,050.

ELDER ART GALLERY, NEBRASKA WESLEYAN UNIVERSITY, Rogers Center for Fine Arts, 50th St. & Huntington Ave., Lincoln, NE 68504-2230. Mailing Address: Art Depart., Nebraska Wesleyan University, 5000 St. Paul Ave., Lincoln, NE 68504-2760. Tel.: 402-466-2371 & 465-2273. Fax: 402-465-2179.
E-mail: dp@nebrwesleyan.edu
Founded: 1965.
Congressional District: 2
Key Personnel: Pres., Fred Ohles; Dir., Donald Paoletta; Gallery Asst., Regina O'Rear.
Governing Authority: university. Parent Institution: Nebraska Wesleyan University. Tax-exempt: 501(c)(3).
Art Museum.
Collections: graphics; paintings; sculpture; ethnic & contemporary crafts.
Activities: guided tours; lectures; gallery talks; concerts; permanent, temporary & traveling exhibitions.
Hours & Admission Prices: Tues.-Fri. 10-4, Sat.-Sun. 1-4. No charge; donations accepted. Closed school holidays & between shows. ♿
Attendance: 1,500 (estimated)

FRANK H. WOODS TELEPHONE MUSEUM, 2047 M St., Lincoln, NE 68510-1029. Mailing Address: P.O. Box 81309, Lincoln, NE 68501-1309. Tel.: 402-436-4640. Fax: 402-436-4914.
Web Site: www.woodstelephonepioneers.org/museum
Founded: 1996.
History Museum: named for the founder of the Lincoln Telephone Company, 1903.
Collections: history of the telephone industry; independent telephony; The Lincoln Telephone and Telegraph company and it's founder, Frank H. Woods.
Activities: tours.
Hours & Admission Prices: Sun. 1-4; other times by appointment. No charge; donations accepted. Closed major holidays.

GREAT PLAINS ART MUSEUM, (M), University of Nebraska-Lincoln, 1155 Q Street, Lincoln, NE 68588-0250. Tel.: 402-472-6220.
E-mail: amohr2@unl.edu
Web Site: www.unl.edu/plains
Formerly: Great Plains Art Collection
Founded: 1980.
Congressional District: 1
Key Personnel: Dir., James Stubbendieck; Cur., Amber Mohr.
Personnel Profile: Full-Time Paid 2; Part-Time Paid 7; Part-Time Volunteers 12; Interns 4.
Governing Authority: nonprofit organization. Parent Institution: University of Nebraska-Lincoln. Subsidiary Institution: Center for Great Plains Studies, University of Nebraska. Tax-exempt: 170(b)(1)(a).
Art Museum.
Collections: Western art with emphasis on Great Plains; sculpture; paintings; graphics; photographs.
Research Fields: history, literature & art of the American West.
Facilities: 4,000-vol. library relating to the history of the American West available for research on premises only.
Activities: guided tours; gallery talks; changing exhibitions.
Publications: exhibition catalogs; brochures.
Hours & Admission Prices: Tues.-Sat. 10-5, Sun. 1:30-5. No charge; donations accepted. Closed holidays; between exhibitions. ♿
Attendance: 17,150 (accurate)
Membership: Family $35; Donor $50; Sustaining $100; Sponsor $250.

INTERNATIONAL QUILT STUDY CENTER & MUSEUM - UNIVERSITY OF NEBRASKA-LINCOLN, (M), 1523 N. 33rd St., Lincoln, NE 68583-0838. Tel.: 402-472-6549. Fax: 402-472-2008.
Web Site: www.quiltstudy.org
Founded: 1997.
Congressional District: 1
Key Personnel: Dir., Patricia Cox Crews.
Personnel Profile: Full-Time Paid 8; Part-Time Paid 8; Part-Time Volunteers 140.
Governing Authority: Parent Institution: University of Nebraska. Tax-exempt.
History Museum.
Collections: quilts & related textiles.
Major Exhibits: Four Part Harmony (T), 11/09-3/10; Perspectives: Art, Craft, Design & the Studio Quilt (T), 11/21/09-5/9/10; A Closer Look (T), 4/10-8/10; South Asian Seams: Quilts from India, Pakistan & Bangladesh (T), 5/15/10-11/7/10; Mass Quilts, 9/10-11/10; Marseilles (T), 11/13/10-6/8/11.
Research Fields: quiltmaking traditions worldwide; textiles & material culture.
Facilities: classroom; reception hall.
Activities: educational programs; classes; special events.
Publications: quarterly e-newsletter for members; annual report; exhibition catalogs.
Hours & Admission Prices: Tues.-Sat. 10-4:30, Sun. 1-4:30. Adults $5; UNL faculty, staff & students and members no charge. Closed major holidays; university winter break. ♿
Attendance: 21,499 (accurate)
Membership: Individual $40; Family $60; Contributing $100-$249; Sustaining $250 & up.

LARSEN TRACTOR MUSEUM, (M), University of Nebraska, 35th & Fair Sts., Lincoln, NE 68583. Mailing Address: P.O. Box 830833, Lincoln, NE 68583-0833. Tel.: 402-472-8389. Fax: 402-472-8367.
E-mail: jsteele4@unl.edu
Web Site: tractormuseum.unl.edu
Formerly: Lester F. Larsen Tractor Test & Power Museum
Key Personnel: Dir., Dr. Bill Splinter; Cur., Lou Leviticus; Museum Devel. Assoc., Jeremy Steele.
Personnel Profile: Full-Time Paid 1; Full-Time Volunteers 1; Part-Time Volunteers 6.
Governing Authority: Parent Institution: University of Nebraska. Subsidiary Institution: Department of Biological Systems Engineering. Tax-exempt.
Agriculture Museum: housed in the original Nebraska Tractor Test facility built in 1919. A Historic Landmark.
Collections: 30 historic tactors including a 1915 Ford B Tractor, Waterloo Boy, Heider, 1918 Moline Universal D, Allis Chalmers WC & Fordson; period hand tools; planters; cultivators; horse-drawn plows; sod cutter; haying tools; household implements.
Hours & Admission Prices: Mon.-Fri. 8:30-12 & 1:30-4:30; other times by appointment. ♿

LENTZ CENTER FOR ASIAN CULTURE, (M), Hewit Place Bldg., Lower Level, 1155 Q St., Lincoln, NE 68588-0252. Mailing Address: P.O. Box 880252, Lincoln, NE 68588-0252. Tel.: 402-472-5841. Fax: 402-472-0463.
E-mail: bbanks1@unl.edu
Web Site: www.unl.edu/lentz
Founded: 1986.
Congressional District: 1
Key Personnel: Dir. & Cur., Dr. Barbara Banks, Ph.D.; Project Asst., Kristina Tucker; Gallery Monitor, Nancy Hong.
Personnel Profile: Full-Time Paid 2; Part-Time Paid 2.
Governing Authority: public university; nonprofit. Parent Institution: University of Nebraska - Lincoln. Tax-exempt: 501(c)(3).
Art Museum & Center.
Collections: artifacts; Asian art collection: ceramic, ivory, jade, metal, textiles, lacquer, prints; musical instruments; Tibetan & Bhutanese ritual & secular art.
Research Fields: 18th century Chinese painter, Chin Tingbiao; horse in ancient China, Sumida Ware.
Facilities: 2,000-vol. library of art books.
Activities: concerts; guided tours; lectures; loan, traveling & temporary exhibitions.
Publications: exhibition notes.
Hours & Admission Prices: Tues.-Fri. 10-5, Sat. 11-5, Sun. 1:30-4; groups by appointment. No charge; donations accepted. Closed Easter; Independence Day; Christmas to New Year's Day; university holidays; between exhibitions. ♿
Attendance: 2,324 (accurate)
Membership: Suggested Donation $2.

LINCOLN CHILDREN'S MUSEUM, 1420 P St., Lincoln, NE 68508-1635. Tel.: 402-477-4000. Fax: 402-477-2004.
E-mail: info@lincolnchildrensmuseum.org
Web Site: www.lincolnchildrensmuseum.org
Founded: 1989.
Key Personnel: Exec. Dir., Darren Macfee; Pres. Bd., Steve Schmidt; Dir. Mktg., Kevin Sheen; Dir. Education, Sarah DeWald; Dir. Philanthropy, Jessica Greenwald; Dir. Operations, Evan Killeen; Museum Shop Mgr., Marilyn Geier.
Personnel Profile: Full-Time Paid 10; Part-Time Paid 20; Part-Time Volunteers 900; Interns 4.
Governing Authority: private; nonprofit organization. Tax-exempt.
Children's Museum.
Collections: interactive hands-on exhibits & activities.
Activities: participatory & traveling exhibits. Annual Events: Wonderful Wednesdays; Creation Station; New Year's Eve Family Celebration; Stuff a Scarecrow workshop; Candyhouse Funshop; Adult Night; Music & Mozzarella.
Publications: quarterly newsletter, Fingerprints.
Hours & Admission Prices: Tues.-Sat. 9:30-5, Sun. 1-5. Admission $6, seniors

62 & over $5.50; discounts to groups, AAM & AYM members; children under 2 & members no charge. Closed major holidays. ♿
Attendance: 150,000 (estimated)
Membership: Family & Grandparent $60; Care Giver $75; Patron $125.

LINCOLN CHILDREN'S ZOO, 1222 S. 27th St., Lincoln, NE 68502-1832. Tel.: 402-475-6741. Fax: 402-475-6742.
E-mail: jchapo@lincolnzoo.org
Web Site: www.lincolnzoo.org
Formerly: Folsom Children's Zoo and Botanical Garden
Founded: 1959.
Key Personnel: C.E.O. & Pres., John P. Chapo; Dir. Business Operations & Museum Shop Mgr., Michelle Cartwright; Gen. Cur., Randy Scheer; Dir. Education, Mimi Wickless; Dir. Institutional Advancement, Rachelle Humiston.
Personnel Profile: Full-Time Paid 17; Part-Time Paid 20; Part-Time Volunteers 400.
Governing Authority: nonprofit organization. Affiliated with A.R. Folsom Zoological Society. Tax-exempt: 501(c)(3).
Children's Zoo.
Collections: zoology; horticulture; aviary; herpetology; animal sculpture; environmental education.
Facilities: theater; classrooms; concessions. Museum-related items for sale.
Activities: self-guided tour maps; education programs for children; volunteer opportunities; amphitheater presentations; critter encounter area.
Publications: four publications yearly, Zoo Tracks.
Hours & Admission Prices: April 15-May & Sept.-Oct. 15 daily 10-5; June-Aug. Wed. 10-8, Thurs.-Tues. 10-5. Adults $6.50, seniors 60 & over and children 2-11 $5.50; members & children under 2 no charge. ♿
Attendance: 155,000 (accurate)
Membership: Individual & One $55; Grandparents & Family $65.

LINCOLN FIRE & RESCUE DEPARTMENT MUSEUM, 1801 "Q" St., Lincoln, NE 68508-1774. Tel.: 402-441-8360.
Fire Fighting Museum.
Collections: uniforms & helmets; fire fighting equipment; fire trumpet; 1911 motorized fire engine; photographs.
Activities: group tours.
Hours & Admission Prices: Daily 9-8.

LUX CENTER FOR THE ARTS, 2601 N. 48th St., Lincoln, NE 68504-3632. Tel.: 402-466-8692. Fax: 402-466-3786.
E-mail: info@luxcenter.org
Web Site: www.luxcenter.org
Formerly: University Place Art Center
Founded: 1978.
Congressional District: 2
Key Personnel: Exec. Dir., JoAnn Emerson; Chm. (V), Carl Eskridge; Dir. Education & Gallery, Stephanie Leach; Business Mgr., Lettie Vanhemert; Cur., Susan Soriente.
Personnel Profile: Full-Time Paid 3; Part-Time Paid 2; Part-Time Volunteers 100; Interns 4.
Governing Authority: private; nonprofit organization. Tax-exempt: 501(c)(3).
General Museum.
Collections: over 1,700 historical & collectible dolls; paperweights; 450 19th & 20th-century master prints from the United States, Europe & Asia; contemporary art.
Facilities: 225-vol. library of art & collectible books; 4,800 sq. ft. exhibit space; educational facilities.
Activities: studio art classes; lectures; tours; temporary exhibitions. Museum Sponsors: Art of Fine Craft Conference.
Publications: newsletter; class brochure; monthly, exhibition announcements.
Hours & Admission Prices: Tues.-Fri. 11-5, Sat. 10-5. No charge; donations accepted. Closed New Year's Day; Memorial Day; Independence Day; Labor Day; Thanksgiving; Christmas. ♿
Attendance: 8,500 (estimated)
Membership: Individual $40; Household $70; Charter $100; Benefactor $250; Philanthropist $500; Founder $1,000.

MUSEUM OF AMERICAN SPEED - SMITH COLLECTION, Speedway Motors Corp. Campus, 340 Victory Lane, Lincoln, NE 68501. Mailing Address: P.O. Box 81906, Lincoln, NE 68501-1906. Tel.: 402-416-4110.
Web Site: www.speedwaymotors.com
History Museum.
Collections: cars & car engines; pedal cars; gas & oil art; license plates; air pumps; pennants; radiator caps; monkey wrenches; toys; lunch boxes.
Activities: guided tours; rental facilities.
Hours & Admission Prices: Tours: May-Sept. Mon.-Fri. 2pm; Oct.-April Fri. 2pm. Admission. $10.

NATIONAL MUSEUM OF ROLLER SKATING, (M), 4730 South St., Lincoln, NE 68506-1256. Tel.: 402-483-7551, ext. 16. Fax: 402-483-1465.
E-mail: directorcurator@rollerskatingmuseum.com
Web Site: www.rollerskatingmuseum.com
Founded: 1980.
Congressional District: 1
Key Personnel: C.E.O. & Pres. (V), Annelle Anderson; Dir., James Vannurden.
Personnel Profile: Full-Time Paid 1.
Governing Authority: nonprofit organization. Tax-exempt.
Sports & Technology Museum.
Collections: roller skates, 1819-present; patents; trophies & medals; costumes; posters; photos, films & videotape; books; periodicals manuscripts.
Research Fields: all aspects of roller skating history; sports; technology; industries; roller rinks; personalities involved in the sport.
Facilities: library of books, periodicals & manuscripts. Museum-related items for sale.
Activities: films; temporary, permanent & traveling exhibitions.
Publications: quarterly, newsletter; brochures; booklets; catalogues; books, The History of Roller Skating; The Evolution of the Roller Skate; The Allure of the Rink.
Hours & Admission Prices: Mon.-Fri. 9-5. No charge; donations accepted. Closed holidays. ♿
Attendance: 2,200 (estimated)
Membership: Individual & Family $35; Donor $50; Associate Patron $100; Patron $250; Benefactor $500.

NEBRASKA CONFERENCE UNITED METHODIST HISTORICAL CENTER, Nebraska Wesleyan Univ., 5000 St. Paul Ave., Lincoln, NE 68504-2796. Mailing Address: 3333 Landmark Circle, Lincoln, NE 68504-0553. Tel.: 402-464-5994 & 465-2175. Fax: 402-464-6203.
E-mail: traburn@umcneb.org
Web Site: www.gcah.org
Founded: 1968.
Congressional District: 1
Key Personnel: Dir., Terri Raburn.
Personnel Profile: Part-Time Paid 1; Part-Time Volunteers 4; Interns 1.
Governing Authority: church. Parent Institution: United Methodist Conference Offices. Subsidiary Institution: Commission on Archives & History, Nebraska Conference, United Methodist Church. Tax-exempt.
Religious Archives.
Collections: artifacts related to the United Methodist Church & its predecessor denominations in Nebraska; documents & legal papers; bibles; hymnals; memorabilia from United Methodist Churches & institutions of Nebraska.
Research Fields: United Methodist persons, local churches, Conference agencies & institutions.
Facilities: 11,000-vol. library of historical material of the United Methodist Church & its predecessor denominations available on premises; archives; reading room.
Activities: permanent & temporary exhibitions; research services.
Publications: Methodist History.
Hours & Admission Prices: Tues. 10:30-4, Wed.-Thurs. 8-4 by appointment. Research Fee: $30 an hour. Closed holidays. ♿
Attendance: 200 (estimated)

* **NEBRASKA HISTORY MUSEUM, (M),** 131 Centennial Mall N., Lincoln, NE 68508-3805. Mailing Address: P.O Box 82554, Lincoln, NE 68501-2554. Tel.: 402-471-4754. Fax: 402-471-3314.
E-mail: ann.billesbach@nebraska.gov
Web Site: www.nebraskahistory.org
Formerly: Nebraska State Historical Society's Museum of Nebraska History
Founded: 1878.
Congressional District: 1
Key Personnel: C.E.O. & Exec. Dir., Michael J. Smith; Deputy Dir., Lynne Ireland; Museum Dir. & Assoc. Dir. Museums Historic Sites, Ann Billesbach; Senior Museum Cur., Deborah Arenz; Exhibits Dept. Mgr., Charles McWilliams; Museum Shop Mgr., Deb McWilliams; Assoc. Dir. Conservation, Julie Reilly; Museum Educator, Judy Keetle; Education Assoc., John Lindahl; Senior Research Folklorist, John E. Carter.
Personnel Profile: Full-Time Paid 69; Part-Time Paid 11; Part-Time Volunteers 250.
Governing Authority: state. Parent Institution: Nebraska State Historical Society. Historic Sites: Fort Robinson Museum, Crawford; George W. Norris State Historic Site; McCook; Neligh Mill State Historic Site; Neligh; John G. Neihardt State Historic Site; Bancroft; Kennard House, Lincoln; Willa Cather State Historic Site, Red Cloud; Gerald R. Ford Conservation Center, Omaha; Chimney Rock National Historic Site; Bayard. Tax-exempt: 501(c)(3).
History Museum.
Collections: items relating to Nebraska & the Central Plains; art; manuscript

collections; anthropology; archaeology; archives; costumes; ethnology; military items; photographs.
Research Fields: anthropology; archaeology; ethnology; western history.
Facilities: auditorium. Museum-related items for sale.
Activities: guided tours; gallery talks; inter-museum loan, permanent & temporary exhibitions; films; monthly lecture series; Investigation Station, an experiential learning environment for all ages.
Publications: educational leaflets; exhibit catalogs & checklists; anthropology publications; quarterly, Nebraska History; Nebraska History newspaper for kids, Nebraska Trailblazer.
Hours & Admission Prices: Tues.-Fri. 9-4:30, Sat.-Sun. 1-4:30. Suggested Donation $2. Closed federal holidays. ♿
Attendance: 88,000 (estimated)
Membership: Individual $40; Household $55; Contributing $100; Supporting $250; Sustaining $500; Founder $1,000.

NEBRASKA STATE CAPITOL, 1445 K St., Lincoln, NE 68508-2731. Mailing Address: Office of the Capitol Commission, P.O. Box 94696, Lincoln, NE 68509-4696. Tel.: 402-471-0448. Fax: 402-471-6952.
Web Site: www.capitol.org
Founded: 1932.
Congressional District: 1
Key Personnel: Capitol Admin., Robert C. Ripley.
Personnel Profile: Full-Time Paid 34; Part-Time Volunteers 6; Interns 1.
Governing Authority: state. Parent Institution: State of Nebraska. Subsidiary Institution: Nebraska Capitol Commission. Tax-exempt.
Historic Building & Site: 1922-1932, state capitol.
Collections: 5,000 drawings & blueprints, 30 ft. of specifications & correspondence; decorative arts; sculpture; murals.
Facilities: 280,500-vol. law library & public library, available for inter-library loan. Brochures, booklets & other museum-related items for sale.
Activities: guided tours; inter-museum loan & permanent exhibitions.
Publications: books, Architectural Wonder of The World; Building Landmark; A Harmony of The Arts-The Nebraska State Capitol.
Hours & Admission Prices: Mon.-Fri. 8-5, Sat. & holidays 10-4, Sun. 1-5. No charge; donations accepted. Closed New Year's Day; Thanksgiving & day after; Christmas. ♿
Attendance: 100,000 (estimated)

NEBRASKA STATE HISTORICAL SOCIETY'S THOMAS P. KENNARD HOUSE, 1627 H St., Lincoln, NE 68508. Mailing Address: Box 82554, Lincoln, NE 68501-2554. Tel.: 402-471-4764.
E-mail: john.lindahl@nebraska.gov
Web Site: www.nebraskahistory.org
Formerly: Thomas P. Kennard House Nebraska Statehood Memorial
Founded: 1968.
Congressional District: 1
Key Personnel: C.E.O. & Dir., Michael J. Smith; Assoc. Dir., Ann Billesbach; Site Supvr., John Lindahl; Deputy Dir., Lynne Ireland.
Personnel Profile: Part-Time Paid 1; Part-Time Volunteers 3.
Governing Authority: state. Parent Institution: Nebraska State Historical Society. Tax-exempt: 501(c)(3).
Historic House: 1869 The Kennard House.
Collections: period furnishings; 1870s period furniture.
Research Fields: 1870s Nebraska life.
Activities: guided tours; special exhibits. Annual Event: Victorian Holidays Past in December.
Publications: Nebraska History magazine; educational leaflets.
Hours & Admission Prices: Mon.-Fri. by appointment. Adults $3; discounts to groups of 20 or more; children under 18 accompanied by adults, Time Travelers & members no charge. Closed state holidays.
Attendance: 1,391 (accurate)
Membership: Individual $40; Household $55; Contributing $100; Supporting $250; Sustaining $500; Founder $1,000.

PIONEERS PARK NATURE CENTER, 3201 S. Coddington, Lincoln, NE 68522-9212. Mailing Address: 2740 A St., Lincoln, NE 68502-3113. Tel.: 402-441-7895. Fax: 402-441-6468.
E-mail: nfurman@lincoln.ne.gov
Web Site: parks.lincoln.ne.gov
Founded: 1963.
Congressional District: 1
Key Personnel: Natural Resources Mgr., Terry Genrich; Nature Center Coord., Nancy Furman; Naturalist, Becky Seth.
Personnel Profile: Full-Time Paid 5; Part-Time Paid 50; Part-Time Volunteers 200; Interns 2.
Governing Authority: municipal government. Parent Institution: City of Lincoln. Subsidiary Institution: Parks & Recreation. Tax-exempt.
Nature Center.
Collections: indoor & outdoor exhibits emphasizing Nebraska native fauna & flora; prairie grass.
Research Fields: prairie restoration, interpretative techniques, ecological studies.
Facilities: 668 acres of prairie, woodlands, marsh, stream & pond habitats; over 8.5 miles of trails; 3,200 sq. ft. of indoor exhibits; herb garden; interpretive facilities. Museum-related items for sale.
Activities: interpretive school programs; hikes; special interest classes; special events; teacher & parent workshops; wilderness nature camps; Young Naturalist Club; outreach programs & field trips; overnights; adult retreats; hayrack rides; pre-school program.
Publications: quarterly newsletter, From The Trails.
Hours & Admission Prices: Mon.-Sat. 8:30-5, Sun. 12-5. No charge, donations accepted. Closed New Year's Day; Thanksgiving; Christmas. ♿
Attendance: 68,000 (accurate)

ROBERT HILLESTAD TEXTILE GALLERY - UNIVERISTY OF NEBRASKA-LINCOLN, 234 Home Economics Bldg., Lincoln, NE 68588-0338. Tel.: 402-472-2911.
Governing Authority: nonprofit organization. Tax-exempt: 501(c)(3).
Textile Museum.
Collections: works of art from regional, national & international artists.
Activities: educational programs.
Publications: brochures.
Hours & Admission Prices: Mon.-Fri. 8:30-4; other times by appointment. Closed university holidays; between shows.

*** SHELDON MUSEUM OF ART AND SCULPTURE GARDEN/UNIVERSITY OF NEBRASKA-LINCOLN, (M),** 12th and R Sts., Lincoln, NE 68588-0300. Mailing Address: P.O. Box 880300, Lincoln, NE 68588-0300. Tel.: 402-472-2461. Fax: 402-472-4258.
E-mail: sheldon@unl.edu
Web Site: www.sheldonartgallery.org
Founded: 1963.
Congressional District: 1
Key Personnel: Pres. (V), Kathy LeBaron; Dir., Jorge Daniel Veneciano; Dir. Education, Karen Janovy; Collections Mgr., Stacey Walsh; Mktg. Mgr., Tom White; Office Mgr., Monica Babock; Museum Shop Mgr., Vonni Sparks.
Personnel Profile: Full-Time Paid 12; Part-Time Paid 6; Part-Time Volunteers 100; Interns 6.
Governing Authority: university. Parent Institution: University of Nebraska-Lincoln. Tax-exempt: 170(b)(1)(A).
American Art Museum.
Collections: 19th to 21st-century American art with emphasis on 20th century; American modernism & sculpture from Rodin to Roxy Paine.
Major Exhibits: Dan Christensen: Forty Years of Painting (T), 11/09-1/10; Migrations: New Directions in Native American Art, 1/10-4/10; Esphyr Slobodkina: Rediscovering & Pioneer of American Abstraction, 1/10-4/10.
Research Fields: 19th- & 20th-century American art.
Facilities: 25,000 vol. research library; campus-wide sculpture garden; 300-seat auditorium. Art & gift items for sale.
Activities: guided tours; lectures; films; gallery talks; concerts; annual statewide touring exhibition; inter-museum loans; formally organized education programs for children; docent program; permanent, temporary & traveling exhibitions.
Publications: exhibition catalogues, Sculpture Collection; The American Painting Collection of the Sheldon Memorial Art Gallery; quarterly newsletter.
Hours & Admission Prices: Tues. 10-8, Wed.-Sat. 10-5, Sun. 12-5. No charge, donations accepted. Closed New Year's Eve & Day; Memorial Day; Independence Day; Labor Day; Thanksgiving; Christmas. ♿
Attendance: 50,000 (accurate)
Membership: Student $15; Senior & Out of Town $25; Senior Dual, Out of Town Dual & Individual $45; Dual & Family $60; Contributor $150; Patron $250; Benefactor $500; Curator's Circle $1,000; Director's Circle $2,500; Trustee Circle $5,000; Sheldon Circle $10,000.

THE BRYAN MUSEUM, 49th St., (and Sumner St.), Lincoln, NE 68506-1299. Tel.: 402-481-8303.
Web Site: www.bryanlgh.org
Historic House: former home of William Jennings Bryan.
Collections: displays & recordings; photographs
Hours & Admission Prices: Mon.-Fri. 10-4. Tours: by appointment. No charge. Closed New Year's; Thanksgiving; Christmas.

UNIVERSITY OF NEBRASKA-LINCOLN BOTANICAL GARDEN & ARBORETUM, 1340 N. 17th St, Lincoln, NE 68588-0609. Tel.: 402-472-2679. Fax: 402-472-9615.
Botanical Garden.

Collections: native plants & trees; perennials.
Activities: educational programs; special events; tours.
Hours & Admission Prices: Call for hours. No charge.

* **UNIVERSITY OF NEBRASKA STATE MUSEUM, (M),** 307 Morrill Hall, South of 14th and VIne Sts., Lincoln, NE 68588-0338. Tel.: 402-472-3779 & 2642 (Research Collections). Fax: 402-472-8899.
E-mail: pgrewl@unl.edu
Web Site: www.museum.unl.edu
Founded: 1871.
Congressional District: 1
Key Personnel: Chancellor, Harvey Perlman; Dir., Dr. Priscilla C. Grew; Assoc. Dir., Mark W. Harris; Cur., Professor & Informal Science Education, Dr. Judy Diamond; Cur. Zoology, Dr. Patricia Freeman; Cur. Anthropology, Dr. Alan Osborn; Cur. Entomology, Dr. Brett C. Ratcliffe; Cur. Geology & Mineralogy, Dr. Samuel B. Treves; Cur. Invertebrate Paleontology, Roger K. Pabian; Cur. Invertebrate Paleontology, Dr. David K. Watkins; Cur. Vertebrate Paleontology, Dr. Robert M. Hunt; Cur. Parasitology, Scott L. Gardner; Collection Mgr. Entomology, Matt Paulsen; Exhibits Specialist, Ron Pike; Collection Mgr. Vertebrate Paleontology, R. George Corner; Graphics Specialist Exhibits, Joel Nielsen; Collection Mgr. Zoology & Botany, Thomas E. Labedz; Collection Mgr. Parasitology, Gabor Racz; Highway Salvage Paleontologist, Shane Tucker; Coord. Planetarium Programs, Jack A. Dunn; Education Coord., Kathleen A. French; Scientific Illustrator, Angie Fox; Preparator Vertebrate Paleontology, Gregory W. Brown; Preparator Vertebrate Paleontology, Robert I. Skolnick; Preparator Vertebrate Paleontology, Ellen Stepleton; Supt. Ashfall Fossil Beds State Historical Park, Rick Otto; Head Security & Public Service Assoc., Linda Thompson; Museum Educator, Ann E. Cusick; Friends Liaison, Dana Ludvik; Sec. Research & Publications, Gail A. Littrell; Ashfall Fossil Beds State Historical Park Asst., Sandy S. Mosel; Trailside Natural History Museum Staff Asst., Susan K. Veskerna; Accounting Clerk, Judy Ray; Museum Asst., Public Service, Brandon Earnest; Museum Educator, Cindy Loope; Museum Educator, Reservations, Ina van der Veen; Museum Educator, Carrie Ford; Museum Educator, Saundra Frerichs; Collections Asst. Anthropology & NAGPRA Asst., Susan Curtis; Cur. Vertebrate Paleontology, Ross Secord; Collections Asst. Botany, Linda Rader; Preparator Hwy. Salvage Paleontology, Nicholas Famoso.
Personnel Profile: Full-Time Paid 29; Part-Time Paid 9; Part-Time Volunteers 4.
Governing Authority: state; university. Parent Institution: University of Nebraska-Lincoln. Branch Museums: Trailside Natural History Museum, Ft. Robinson, Crawford, NE; Ashfall Fossil Beds State Historical Park, Royal, NE. Tax-exempt.
Natural History Museum.
Collections: 15,000,000 specimens, primarily from the Central Plains; anthropology; archives; archaeology; botany; entomology; geology; mineralogy; invertebrate & vertebrate paleontology; parasitology; paleobotany; numismatic; philatelic; zoology.
Major Exhibits: Weapons Throughout Time, 11/09-10/10.
Research Fields: anthropology; archaeology; botany; entomology; geology; mineralogy; invertebrate & vertebrate paleontology; mammalogy; parasitology; zoology.
Facilities: 60,000 sq. ft. natural science exhibit area; planetarium; 150-seat auditorium; science teacher resource center.
Activities: hands-on natural science discovery room; inquiry-based gallery programs; science outreach kits; planetarium; professional development for teachers.
Publications: scientific bulletin, Bulletin of the University of Nebraska State Museum; Mammoth; scientific reports & guidebooks.
Hours & Admission Prices: Museum: Mon.-Wed. & Fri.-Sat. 9:30-4:30, Thurs. 9:30-8, Sun. 1:30-4:30. Planetarium: Tues.-Sat. 9:30-4:30, Sun. 1:30-4:30. Show times vary. Museum (Lincoln, NE): adults $5, children 5-18 $3. Planetarium: adults $8, children $5.50. Trailside Museum of Natural History (Crawford, NE): adults $3, children 5-18 $1. Ashfall Fossil Beds State Historical Park (Royal, NE): adults $5, children 6-18 $3; friends members, ASTC & AAM members no charge. Closed New Year's Day; Easter; Independence Day; Thanksgiving; Christmas Eve & Day. ♿
Attendance: 86,419 (accurate)
Membership: Individual $30; Family $45; Tusker Club $60-$99; Fossil Funder $100-$249; Nautilus Club $250-$499; Scarab Society $500-$999; Mammoth Circle $1,000-$2,499; Morrill Hall Star $2,500 & up; Ashfall additional $10.

Lodgepole

LODGEPOLE DEPOT MUSEUM, 722 McCall St., Lodgepole, NE 69149. Tel.: 308-483-5620.
E-mail: museum@lodgepole.us
History Museum: housed in the former Union Pacific Railroad Depot.
Collections: horse buggies; antique furniture; historical clothing; antique clothes irons & bells; antique machinery.
Hours & Admission Prices: By appointment. No charge; donations accepted. ♿

Long Pine

LONG PINE HERITAGE SOCIETY AND HERITAGE HOUSE MUSEUM, 199 W. 3rd St., Long Pine, NE 69217-0337. Tel.: 402-273-4453.
E-mail: wardene@nntc.net
History Museum.
Collections: local history & genealogy.
Hours & Admission Prices: Memorial Day weekend-Labor Day weekend Sat. 1-4; other times by appointment.

Madison

MADISON COUNTY HISTORICAL SOCIETY, 210 W. 3rd St., Madison, NE 68748. Tel.: 402-454-2827.
History Museum.
Collections: local history & culture; period furnishings; personal artifacts; photographs; quilts; glassware; military equipment & uniforms; Native American artifacts. Historic Buildings: 1856 Bevington-Kaser mansion; 1872 Winterset train depot; 1881 Zion Church; c.1920 field mercantile store; 1856 stone barn.
Hours & Admission Prices: Mon.-Fri. 2-5; other times by appointment.

McCook

MUSEUM OF THE HIGH PLAINS, 421 Norris Ave., McCook, NE 69001-2003. Tel.: 308-345-3661.
Founded: 1969.
Congressional District: 3
Key Personnel: Chm. Bd. & Pres. (V), Russell Dowling; Vice Pres., Del Harsh; Dir. & Sec., Marilyn Hawkins; Treas., Korey Burkert.
Personnel Profile: Part-Time Paid 3; Part-Time Volunteers 40.
Governing Authority: society. Parent Institution: High Plains Historical Society.
History Museum.
Collections: German bibles; diaries; manuscripts; fashion from 1779-present; 1800 kitchen; 1800 pharmacy; farm tools; musical instruments; piano organ; sheet music; records; doll collection; railroad memorabilia; medical equip.; pioneer memorabilia; military uniforms dating from Spanish-American War-Vietnam War; paintings done by World War II German prisoners-of-war; memorabilia from World War II's McCook Air Base; flour mill; oil industry exhibit; B.N. caboose, semaphole, way car; Hendley shop where Kool-Aid was developed; general store.
Research Fields: history of the area.
Facilities: 500-vol. library available for use on premises; reading room. Books for sale.
Activities: guided tours; lectures; permanent & temporary exhibitions.
Publications: book, McCook's First 100 Years.
Hours & Admission Prices: Tues.-Sat. 1-5, Sun. 2-4. No charge; donations accepted. Closed major holidays. ♿
Attendance: 10,000 (estimated)
Membership: Voting $5; Life $200.

NEBRASKA STATE HISTORICAL SOCIETY'S GEORGE NORRIS STATE HISTORIC SITE, 706 Norris Ave., McCook, NE 69001-3142. Tel.: 308-345-8484. Fax: 308-345-8484.
E-mail: norris@mccooknet.com
Web Site: www.nebraskahistory.org
Formerly: Senator George Norris State Historic Site
Founded: 1969.
Congressional District: 3
Key Personnel: C.E.O. & Exec. Dir., Michael J. Smith; Assoc. Dir., Ann Billesbach; Site Supvr., Don Hall; Chief Education & Research Officer, Lynne Ireland.
Personnel Profile: Part-Time Paid 1; Part-Time Volunteers 4.
Governing Authority: state. Parent Institution: Nebraska State Historical Society. Tax-exempt: 501(c)(3).
Historic House Museum: 1886 home of Senator George W. Norris (1899-1944).
Collections: period furnishings.
Research Fields: George W. Norris; Nebraska history.
Activities: guided tours; fifteen minute video on George Norris.
Publications: pamphlets.
Hours & Admission Prices: Tues.-Sat. 1-5. Adults $3; members, children with adults & Time Travelers no charge. Closed state holidays.
Attendance: 821 (accurate)
Membership: Individual $40; Household $55; Contributing $100; Supporting $250; Sustaining $500; Founder $1,000.

Minden

HAROLD WARP PIONEER VILLAGE FOUNDATION, 138 E. Hwy. 6, Minden, NE 68959-2500. Tel.: 308-832-1181 & 800-445-4447. Fax: 308-832-1181.
E-mail: manager@pioneervillage.com
Web Site: www.pioneervillage.org
Founded: 1953.
Congressional District: 37
Key Personnel: Pres., Harold G. Warp; Gen. Mgr., Marshall S. Nelson.
Personnel Profile: Full-Time Paid 20; Part-Time Paid 45; Part-Time Volunteers 15.
Governing Authority: board of directors. Tax-exempt.
General Museum.
Collections: transportation; 350 cars; period rooms from 1830-present; farm machinery; musical instruments; household appliances; china; cut glass; hobbies; toys; art; general store; 50,000 historical items displayed in 26 buildings; John Rogers statuary; Jackson paintings; statuettes. Historic Buildings: 1860 Pony Express station; 1869 Elm Creek Stockade.
Research Fields: 1830 to present day on all items of development.
Facilities: restaurant; campground; motel.
Activities: crafts demonstrations.
Publications: History of Man's Progress; Over the Hill & Past Our Place; 500 Fascinating Facts; Sister Clara's Letters.
Hours & Admission Prices: Daily 8am. Adults & children over 12 $10.95, children 6-12 $6; discount to groups; second day admission & children under 6 no charge. ♿
Attendance: 60,000 (accurate)

KEARNEY COUNTY HISTORICAL MUSEUM, 530 N. Nebraska Ave., Minden, NE 68959. Mailing Address: 713 S. Minden Ave., Minden, NE 68959-2319. Tel.: 308-832-1765.
Founded: 1925.
Congressional District: 3
Key Personnel: Dir. (V), Mary Bergsten.
Personnel Profile: Part-Time Volunteers 30.
Governing Authority: society. Tax-exempt: 501(c)(3).
Historical Society Museum: housed in 1881 first schoolhouse in Minden.
Collections: items used by Kearney County residents dating back to early 1880; family genealogy; early business, school & church records; scrapbooks. Historic Buildings: depot; grocery store & post office; rural schoolhouse.
Facilities: 25-vol. library of historical books available on premises.
Activities: guided tours; cub scouts; cemetery tours; 4th grade school tours.
Hours & Admission Prices: June-Aug. daily 2-4. No charge; donations accepted. ♿
Attendance: 300 (estimated)
Membership: Individual & One Year $5; Five Year $25; Life $100.

Nebraska City

ARBOR LODGE STATE HISTORICAL PARK, 2600 Arbor Ave., Nebraska City, NE 68410-1072. Mailing Address: P.O. Box 15, Nebraska City, NE 68410-0015. Tel.: 402-873-7222. Fax: 402-874-9885.
E-mail: ngpc.arbor.lodge@nebraska.gov
Founded: 1923.
Congressional District: 1
Key Personnel: Dir., Rex Amack; Supt., Randall J. Fox; Asst. Supt., Mark Kemper; Asst. Dir., Jim Swenson.
Personnel Profile: Full-Time Paid 2; Part-Time Paid 17.
Governing Authority: state. Affiliated with the Nebraska Game & Parks Commission, Box 30370, 2200 N. 33rd St., Lincoln, NE 68503. Tax-exempt: 501(c)(3).
Historic House Museum: 1855 home of J. Sterling Morton with addition made by eldest son Joy Morton in 1903-1905.
Collections: personal property & correspondence of J. Sterling Morton including carriages; furniture; Tiffany glassware; silverware; paintings & other art items. Historic Houses: 1890 log cabin; 1901 greenhouse; 1903 carriage house.
Facilities: 72-acre arboretum; formal gardens; monument square; nature trails. Museum-related items for sale.
Activities: tours; permanent & traveling exhibitions. Museum Sponsors: Living History Demonstrations in October.
Publications: brochures; pamphlets.
Hours & Admission Prices: mid-April to mid-Oct. daily 11-5. Adults $4, children 3-12 $1; children under 3 no charge. Closed Thanksgiving; Christmas.
Attendance: 75,000 (estimated)

OLD FREIGHTERS MUSEUM, 407 N. 14th St., Nebraska City, NE 68410-1947. Mailing Address: P.O. Box 175, Nebraska City, NE 68410-0175. Tel.: 402-873-9360.
History Museum: former home of the Russell-Majors-Waddell Freighting Company in 1858.
Collections: transportation artifacts.
Hours & Admission Prices: By appointment. Adults $3, children $1.

TAYLOR-WESSEL-BICKEL (NELSON) HOUSE, 711 3rd Corso, Nebraska City, NE 68410-2817. Mailing Address: Nelson House, 806 1st Ave., Nebraska City, NE 68410-0075. Tel.: 402-873-9360.
Governing Authority: Parent Institution: Nebraska City Historical Society.
Historic House. Built in 1857.
Collections: period furnishings; artifacts; interpretive materials; art; photographs.
Hours & Admission Prices: By appointment. Adults $2, children $1.

WILDWOOD HISTORIC CENTER, 420 S. Steinhart Park Rd., Nebraska City, NE 68410-3300. Tel.: 402-873-6340.
E-mail: wildwoodbarn@windstream.net
Founded: 1967.
Congressional District: 2
Key Personnel: Pres. (V), Brad Kaufman; Acting Chm., Pat Friedle; Museum Shop Mgr., Gail Wurtele.
Personnel Profile: Full-Time Paid 1; Part-Time Paid 8.
Governing Authority: municipal. Tax-exempt: 501(c)(3).
Historic House Museum: c.1869 restored two-story Victorian frame home.
Collections: Victorian furnishings.
Facilities: Original art & craft items for sale.
Activities: guided tours. Center Sponsors: Arts & craft show.
Hours & Admission Prices: Mon.-Sat. 10-5, Sun. 1-5. Adults $3, children 12 & under $1; discounts to AAM members. Barn no charge. ♿
Attendance: 8,000 (estimated)

Neligh

JAIL MUSEUM, 509 L St., Neligh, NE 68756-1419. Tel.: 402-887-5046.
E-mail: jailmuseum@jailmuseum.net
Web Site: www.jailmuseum.net
Formerly: Antelope County Historical Museum
Founded: 1965.
Congressional District: 3
Key Personnel: Pres., Ruth Strassler; Vice Pres., Levern Hauptmann; Treas., Harlen Frasier.
Personnel Profile: Part-Time Paid 2; Part-Time Volunteers 6.
Governing Authority: society. Administered by the Antelope County Historical Society, Neligh, NE. Parent Institution: Antelope County Historical Society. Subsidiary Institution: Antelope County Museum. Tax-exempt.
Local History Museum: housed in 1892, Gates College gymnasium; later used as county jail.
Collections: Indian artifacts of the area; pioneer-present day memorabilia; 1887 Episcopal Church; log cabin.
Research Fields: county cemetery records; genealogy research by mail.
Facilities: library of books from Gates College which was closed in 1899; newspapers of the area; books on Nebraska & Antelope County; Indian Room; furnished log cabin.
Activities: guided tours; reading room aiding genealogical research.
Publications: History of Antelope County 1868-1883; Neligh Centennial 1873-1973; Early Day Stories; Antelope County - The War Years (World War II); articles of special events; maps of county; Antelope County Pioneers; Early Pioneer Stories.
Hours & Admission Prices: Fri.-Sun. 1:30-4:30. Adults $3; children 12 & under and members no charge; call for fees on memorial plaques and genealogy research.
Attendance: 600 (estimated)
Membership: Single $10; Family $15; Sustaining $100.

NEBRASKA STATE HISTORICAL SOCIETY'S NELIGH MILL STATE HISTORIC SITE, N St. & Wylie Dr., Neligh, NE 68756. Mailing Address: P.O. Box 271, Neligh, NE 68756-0271. Tel.: 402-887-4303. Fax: 402-887-4303.
E-mail: mill@gpcom.net
Web Site: www.nebraskahistory.org
Formerly: Neligh Mills
Founded: 1971.
Congressional District: 3
Key Personnel: C.E.O. & Exec. Dir., Michael J. Smith; Assoc. Dir., Ann Billesbach; Site Supvr., Don Ofe; Chief Education & Research Officer, Lynne Ireland.
Personnel Profile: Full-Time Paid 1; Part-Time Volunteers 4.

Governing Authority: state. Parent Institution: Nebraska State Historical Society. Tax-exempt: 501(c)(3).
Historic Building Museum: 1873 Neligh Mills.
Collections: 500-barrel a day flour mill with seven stands of rollers, two extra mills, thirty six elevators, two plan sifters, four purifiers, three reel sifters, four sackers, water powered turbine. Historic Building: 1883 Mill Office.
Research Fields: flour milling; water power; wheat agriculture.
Facilities: Society publications & postcards for sale.
Activities: 15 min. video on the history of the Neligh Mill & flour milling; guided tours; permanent exhibits.
Publications: Neligh Mills Cookbook; Nebraska History Magazine; Self-Guided Tour of Neligh Mill; Flour Milling in Nebraska; Water Powered Flour Mills in Nebraska.
Hours & Admission Prices: Memorial Day-Labor Day Tues.-Sat. 10-5, Sun. 1-5; Sept.-May Mon.-Fri. 10-5. Adults $3, groups of 20 $2, children $1; discount to Time Travelers; children accompanied by an adult, youth groups, Nebraska State Historical Society members & families no charge. Closed most federal holidays.
Attendance: 2,003 (accurate)
Membership: Individual $40; Household $55; Contributing $100; Supporting $250; Sustaining $500; Founder $1,000.

Niobrara

NIOBRARA HISTORICAL SOCIETY MUSEUM, 89054 519 Ave., Niobrara, NE 68760-6013. Tel.: 402-857-3794.
Founded: 1977.
Governing Authority: Tax-exempt.
History Museum.
Collections: local history & culture; photographs; personal artifacts; hood ornaments.
Hours & Admission Prices: Memorial Day to Labor Day Wed. & Sun. 1-3, Sat. 10-3; other times by appointment. ♿
Attendance: 1,300 (estimated)
Membership: Individual $5.

Norfolk

ELKHORN VALLEY MUSEUM & RESEARCH CENTER, 515 Queen City Blvd., Norfolk, NE 68701-4060. Tel.: 402-371-3886. Fax: 402-371-3886.
Web Site: www.elkhornvalleymuseum.org
Founded: 1957.
Personnel Profile: Full-Time Paid 1; Part-Time Paid 2; Part-Time Volunteers 30; Interns 2.
Governing Authority: Board of Directors.
General Museum.
Collections: history of Norfolk & Elkhorn Valley; genealogy; documents; Johnny Carson Gallery; historical exhibits; Square Turn Tractor.
Facilities: bird library. Museum-related items for sale.
Activities: special events. Museum Sponsors: Pioneer Day in the Park in August.
Publications: bimonthly newsletter.
Hours & Admission Prices: Mon.-Sat. 10-5, Sun. 1-5. Adults $4, students & seniors $3, children 5-12 $2; members no charge. Closed New Year's; Easter; Thanksgiving; Christmas. ♿
Attendance: 3,500 (accurate)
Membership: Individual $30; Family $60; Friend $125; Patron $250; Benefactor $500; Distinguished Benefactor $1,000; Pacesetter $2,500; Visioneer $5,000.

North Platte

BUFFALO BILL RANCH STATE HISTORICAL PARK, 2921 Scouts Rest Ranch Rd., North Platte, NE 69101-8444. Tel.: 308-535-8035. Fax: 308-535-8070.
E-mail: buffalo.bill@ngpc.ne.gov
Founded: 1964.
Congressional District: 3
Key Personnel: Supt., Steve Kemper; Asst. Supt., Aric Riggins.
Personnel Profile: Full-Time Paid 2; Part-Time Paid 8; Part-Time Volunteers 2.
Governing Authority: state. Affiliated with the Nebraska Game and Parks Commission, Box 30370, 2200 N. 33rd St., Lincoln, NE 68503. Tax-exempt: 501(c)(3).
History Museum: housed in 1886 home of William (Buffalo Bill) Cody.
Collections: personal property and correspondence of Buffalo Bill; showbills; photographs; film clips. Historic Structure: 1886 home of William Cody; 1887 barn.
Research Fields: Wild West Show; life & activities of Cody.
Facilities: theater. Books relating to the history of the West & Buffalo Bill & other museum-related items for sale.
Activities: guided tours; films; permanent & temporary exhibitions.
Hours & Admission Prices: April-May & Sept.-Oct. Mon.-Fri. 10-4; Memorial Day-Labor Day daily 9-5. State park permit required: daily $4 per vehicle.
Attendance: 20,030 (accurate)

CODY PARK RAILROAD MUSEUM, 1400 N. Jeffers, North Platte, NE 69101. Tel.: 308-535-6700.
Web Site: www.ci.north-platte.ne/us/publicservices
Railroad Museum.
Collections: Union Pacific memorabilia; railroad history; photographs; telephone & telegraph equipment; Union Pacific's steam locomotive, Challenger 3977; Union Pacific DD40AX; baggage car; mail car; caboose; depot.
Hours & Admission Prices: May-Sept. daily 10-6. No charge.

LINCOLN COUNTY HISTORICAL MUSEUM, (M), 2403 N. Buffalo Bill Ave., North Platte, NE 69101-9702. Tel.: 308-534-5640.
E-mail: lincomuseum@hamilton.net
Web Site: www.lincolncountymuseum.org
Founded: 1976.
Congressional District: 3
Key Personnel: Chm. (V), Kaycee Dye; Pres. (V), Lloyd Speicher; Dir., Cur. & Museum Shop Mgr., James Griffin.
Personnel Profile: Full-Time Paid 1; Part-Time Paid 1; Part-Time Volunteers 140.
Governing Authority: private nonprofit. Tax-exempt.
General Museum.
Collections: Lincoln County Nebraska history; WWII Canteen exhibit; village of 15 outbuildings: two-story log house, a log pony express station building, log military fort building, log cabin, church, one-room schoolhouse, large barn, railroad depot, general store, two-story frame house.
Facilities: Gift-related items for sale.
Activities: guided tours. Annual Event: Heritage Festival in June.
Publications: quarterly newsletter.
Hours & Admission Prices: May-Sept. Mon.-Sat. 9-5, Sun. 1-5. Adults 13 & over $3; discount to groups of 10 & over ♿
Attendance: 12,000 (accurate)
Membership: Individual $20; Couple & Family $40; Lifetime $200.

NORTH PLATTE CHILDREN'S MUSEUM, 314 N. Jeffers St., North Platte, NE 69101. Mailing Address: P.O. Box 2088, North Platte, NE 69101. Tel.: 308-532-3512.
Children's Museum.
Collections: hands-on exhibits.
Activities: rental facilities.
Hours & Admission Prices: Wed. & Fri. 9-3, Thurs. 9-7, Sat. 9-5, Sun. 12:30-5. Admission $4; discounts to seniors over 60; children 2 & under no charge.

O'Neill

HOLD COUNTY HISTORICAL SOCIETY MUSEUM, 402 E. Douglas, O'Neill, NE 68763. Tel.: 402-336-2344.
E-mail: holtcounty@telebeep.com
Historical Society Museum.
Collections: local history & culture; genealogy; photographs; personal artifacts.
Activities: book signings; lectures; monthly meetings Feb.-Nov. Annual Events: St. Patrick's Day Celebration; Summerfest Celebration.
Publications: biannual newsletter.
Hours & Admission Prices: Mon.-Thurs. 10-12 & 1-4; other times by appointment. No charge; donations accepted. Closed major holidays.
Membership: Annual & Contributing $10; Supporting, Business, Professional, & Institutional $25; Life $100; Joint Life $150.

Ogallala

FRONT STREET, 519 E. First, Ogallala, NE 69153-2620. Tel.: 308-284-6000. Fax: 308-284-0865.
E-mail: frontstreet@charterinternet.com
Web Site: www.megavision.net/frontstreet
Founded: 1964.
Congressional District: 3
Key Personnel: Mgr., Darlan Rezac.
Governing Authority: nonprofit organization. Tax-exempt: 501(c)(3).
History Museum.
Collections: cowboy items; saddles; farm tools; 1890s clothing; schoolhouse artifacts; Sam Bass history; medicine items; barber shop; funeral parlor; jail.
Facilities: library of books. Gift items for sale.
Publications: newspapers.

Hours & Admission Prices: Mon.-Sat. 9-9. No charge; donations accepted. Closed New Year's Day; Thanksgiving; Christmas. ♿
Attendance: 10,000

LAKE MCCONAUGHY VISITOR/WATER INTERPRETIVE CENTER, 1450 Hwy. 61 N., Ogallala, NE 69153. Tel.: 308-284-8800.
Web Site: www.outdoornebraska.org
History Museum.
Collections: water significance to Nebraska's past, present & future.
Facilities: aquarium; 50-seat theater.
Hours & Admission Prices: Summer: daily 8-5; Winter Mon.-Fri. 8-5.

MANSION ON THE HILL, 100 N. Spruce St., Ogallala, NE 69153. Mailing Address: Keith County Historical Society, P.O. Box 5, Ogallala, NE 69153. Tel.: 308-284-4066; 800-658-4390.
Governing Authority: nonprofit organization. Parent Institution: Keith County Historical Society.
Historic House: built in 1887. Listed on the National Register of Historic Places.
Collections: local history; period furnishings; personal artifacts; photographs.
Hours & Admission Prices: Memorial Day to mid-Sept. Tues.-Sat. 9-12 & 1-4, Sun. 1-4. Adults $2, children 5-12 $1; children under 5 no charge.

PETRIFIED WOOD GALLERY, 525 E. 1st St., Ogallala, NE 69153-2620. Tel.: 308-284-9996.
Natural History Museum.
Collections: woods & fossils from around the world; Native American artifacts; arrowheads.
Facilities: Museum-related items for sale.
Hours & Admission Prices: Call for hours.

Omaha

CATHEDRAL CULTURAL CENTER, 3900 Webster St., Omaha, NE 68131-1810. Tel.: 402-551-4888.
Web Site: www.cathedralartsproject.org
Founded: 2003.
Key Personnel: C.E.O., Bro. William Woeger, F.S.C.; Assoc. Dir., Dorothy Begley; Chm., Lucy Franks; Treas., Charles Schultz; Public Rels., John Wees; Museum Shop Mgr., Kathy White.
Personnel Profile: Part-Time Paid 3; Part-Time Volunteers 20.
Governing Authority: church group.
Religious Museum.
Collections: heritage of Saint Cecilia Cathedral & it's architect, Thomas Rogers Kimball; videos & CDs.
Research Fields: cultural history of Saint Cecilia Cathedral & interfaith heritage.
Facilities: 75-seat lecture room; 1,000 sq. ft. exhibit space. Museum-related items for sale.
Activities: concerts; docent program; films; formal education programs for children; guided tours; lectures; loan exhibitions; rental gallery. Annual Events: art shows.
Publications: book, Beauty of Thy House.
Hours & Admission Prices: Tues.-Fri. 11-4, third Sun. of each month 10:30-4:30. Suggested Donation: $2 per person. Closed religious holidays. ♿
Attendance: 5,000 (estimated)
Membership: Cornerstone $35; Pillar $50; Keystone $100; Pier $250; Rose Window $500; Arch $1,000; Portal $2,500; Capstone $5,000.

THE DURHAM MUSEUM, (M), 801 S. 10th St., Omaha, NE 68108-3205. Tel.: 402-444-5071. Fax: 402-444-5397.
E-mail: info@durhammuseum.org
Web Site: www.durhammuseum.org
Formerly: Durham Western Heritage Museum
Founded: 1975.
Congressional District: 2
Key Personnel: Chm., Richard Bell; Exec. Dir., Christi Janssen; Deputy Dir. & Dir. Finance, Scott Wallace; Dir. Community Rels., Shawna Forsberg; Exhibition Design Svcs., Tim Hantula; Tour Coord. & Educational Programs, Mick Hale; Cur., Carrie Wieners; Bldg. Supvr., Ron Lund; Administrative Asst., Andrea Boschult; Museum Shop Mgr., Diane Hileman.
Personnel Profile: Full-Time Paid 32; Part-Time Paid 10; Part-Time Volunteers 200.
Governing Authority: nonprofit organization. Tax-exempt.
History Museum: housed in c.1930, former Union Pacific Railroad Station.
Collections: railroad memorabilia; furniture; 1930s soda fountain; clothing; decorative arts; pioneering tools; archival photography collection of 500,000 negatives & prints; Byron Reed coins, paper money & manuscripts; six restored train cars; model train layout measuring 85 feet in length with 40 train cars; Union Pacific Railroad artifacts & memorabilia.
Research Fields: Omaha, Nebraska History; Great Plains Regional History; railroad history; photographs; numismatics.
Facilities: conference rooms; catered dinners with seating for up to 1,000; 4 historic classrooms. Museum-related items for sale.
Activities: guided tours; special events; education programs for children & adults; docent programs; permanent, temporary & traveling exhibitions; offers exhibit design services to other institutions.
Publications: quarterly newsletter, Timelines.
Hours & Admission Prices: Tues. 10-8, Wed.-Sat. 10-5, Sun. 1-5. Adults $7, senior citizens $6, children 3-12 $5; children under 3 & members no charge. Closed New Year's Day, Memorial Day, Independence Day, Labor Day, Thanksgiving, Christmas. ♿
Attendance: 118,464 (accurate)
Membership: Student, Educator, Senior & Military $25; Individual $30; Educator Family $40; Family $50; Community Group $80; Bronze $100; Silver $250; Gold $500.

EL MUSEO LATINO, 4701 S. 25th St., Omaha, NE 68107-2728. Tel.: 402-731-1137. Fax: 402-733-7012.
E-mail: mgarcia@elmuseolatino.org
Web Site: elmuseolatino.org
Founded: 1993.
Congressional District: 2
Key Personnel: Exec. Dir., Magdalena A. Garcia; Pres. (V), Jim Mammel; Vice Pres., Jeffrey Keating; Treas., Maria Arbelaez; Sec., Rita Melgares.
Personnel Profile: Full-Time Paid 2; Part-Time Paid 4; Part-Time Volunteers 25; Interns 3.
Governing Authority: nonprofit organization. Tax-exempt: 501(c)(3).
Latino Art & History Museum.
Collections: concentration of art, history, artifacts & archival material of the Latino people of the Americas.
Research Fields: art & history of Latin America; Latino & Hispanic presence in Nebraska; Latina women.
Facilities: 500-vol. bilingual reference & resource library; reading room; video & slide library.
Activities: permanent & traveling exhibits; lectures; guided tours; gallery talks; workshops; art festivals; docent program; teen, youth & bilingual docent programs; bilingual programming including films, videos, slide presentations, art & art history classes. Museum Sponsors Hispanic & Latino celebrations: Cinco de Mayo, May; Hispanic Heritage Month, mid-Sept. to mid-Oct.
Publications: exhibition catalogue, Augustin Victor Casasola: The Mexican Revolution.
Hours & Admission Prices: Mon., Wed. & Fri. 10-5, Tues. & Thurs. 1-5, Sat. 10-2. Adults $5, college students $4, senior citizens & students K-12 $3.50; discounts to AAM & ICOM members; children under 5 & members no charge. Closed New Year's Eve & Day; Independence Day; Thanksgiving; Christmas. ♿
Attendance: 50,000 (accurate)
Membership: Senior & Student $25; Individual $30; Family $50; Individual Patron & Business Associate $100; Corporate Sponsor $250.

FREEDOM PARK NAVY MUSEUM, 2497 Freedom Park Rd., Omaha, NE 68110-2745. Mailing Address: 1523 S. 24th St., Omaha, NE 68108. Tel.: 402-444-5955.
Governing Authority: Parent Institution: City of Omaha Parks, Recreation & Public Property Dept.
Military Museum.
Collections: military displays including the USS Hazard, World War II minesweeper, the USS Marlin, a training submarine & the USS LSM-45, a landing ship.
Hours & Admission Prices: May 15-Sept. 15 daily 8-8; Sept. 16-May 14 daily 8-3. No charge.

GENERAL CROOK HOUSE MUSEUM AND LIBRARY/ARCHIVES CENTER, 5730 N. 30th St., 11B, Omaha, NE 68111-1658. Tel.: 402-455-9990. Fax: 402-453-9448.
E-mail: house@omahahistory.org
Web Site: www.omahahistory.org
Founded: 1956.
Congressional District: 1
Key Personnel: Exec. Dir. Historical Society, Betty J. Davis; Pres. Bd. Dirs., Mary Maxwell; Cur. General Crook House, Patricia Pixley; Chm. (V) & Museum Shop Mgr., Virgie Ward; Dir. Education & Public Programs, Liz Rea; Dir. Library Archives Center, Travis Sing; Archivist & Librarian, Don Snoddy; Research Specialist, Gary Rosenberg; Registrar, Elizabeth Krecek.
Personnel Profile: Full-Time Paid 4; Part-Time Paid 7; Part-Time Volunteers 50; Interns 1.

Governing Authority: nonprofit organization. Parent Institution: Historical Society of Douglas County. Subsidiary Institution: Crook House Guild. Tax-exempt: 501(c)(3).
Library & Historical House Museum: 1878 General Crook House & archives center located at Historic Fort Omaha now the campus of Metropolitan Community College.
Collections: artifacts interpreting life style of a commanding officer on a major frontier fort; fort life; pieces interpreting the history of Douglas County; authentic Victorian heirloom garden; 30,000 photographs & documents dating back to the mid 1800s.
Research Fields: military history surrounding Fort Omaha & the westward movement; history & development of Omaha & Douglas County, NE; wallpaper in the Midwest; genealogy.
Facilities: 2,000-vol. library pertaining to county history available for research on premise; 6,000,000-piece archive; reading room; 30-seat auditorium; classrooms.
Activities: guided tours; lectures; study clubs; formally organized education programs for children & adults; docent program; traveling, permanent & temporary exhibitions; step-on guides for motorcoach requests.
Publications: newsletter, Banner; books, Omaha & Douglas County: A Panoramic View; Sautter House Five: Wallpapers of a German-American Homestead; A.V. Sorensen & the New Omaha; reprint of History of Omaha; oral history interviews.
Hours & Admission Prices: Museum: Mon.-Fri. 10-4, Sat.-Sun. 1-4; other times by appointment. Library: Tues.-Fri. 10-4. Adults $5, students $4, children 6-12 $3; members & library no charge. Closed holidays. ♿
Attendance: 18,000 (estimated)
Membership: Student $20; Senior $25; Individual $30; Family $40; Historian $60; Century $100; Patron $250; Lieutenant's Council $500; General's Council & Corporate $1,000.

GERALD R. FORD CONSERVATION CENTER, 1326 S. 32nd St., Omaha, NE 68105-2044. Tel.: 402-595-1180. Fax: 402-595-1178.
Founded: 1995.
Governing Authority: Parent Institution: Nebraska State Historical Society. Tax-exempt.
Conservation Center.
Collections: life & career of President Gerald R. Ford; photographs; personal artifacts.
Hours & Admission Prices: By appointment only. ♿

HENRY DOORLY ZOO, 3701 S. 10th St., Omaha, NE 68107-2200. Tel.: 402-733-8401. Fax: 402-733-7868.
Web Site: www.omahazoo.com
Founded: 1965.
Congressional District: 2
Key Personnel: Dir., Dr. Lee G. Simmons, D.V.M.; Pres. (V), John Boyer.
Personnel Profile: Full-Time Paid 225; Full-Time Volunteers 2,353; Part-Time Paid 210; Part-Time Volunteers 1,648; Interns 7.
Governing Authority: society; nonprofit organization.
Zoo.
Collections: approx. 16,500 live zoological specimens.
Research Fields: preventive medicine; nutrition; reproductive physiology; primate behavior.
Facilities: 200-vol. library for use on the premises; zoological park.
Activities: guided tours; lectures; films; formally organized education programs for children; docent program; tours for blind, disabled & underprivileged.
Publications: quarterly, Zoo Newsletter; guidebook.
Hours & Admission Prices: Daily 9:30-5. Adults 12 & over $11, senior citizens $9.50, children 3-11 $7.25; discounts to AAZPA members; members & children under 3 no charge. Closed New Year's; Thanksgiving; Christmas. ♿
Attendance: 1,535,662 (accurate)
Membership: Family $78; Patron $200.

* **JOSLYN ART MUSEUM, (M),** 2200 Dodge St., Omaha, NE 68102-1292. Tel.: 402-342-3300. Fax: 402-342-2376.
E-mail: info@joslyn.org
Web Site: www.joslyn.org
Founded: 1931.
Congressional District: 2
Key Personnel: Dir., J. Brooks Joyner; Chm. (V), James Young; Deputy Dir. Collections & Programs, Anne El-Omami; C.F.O., Miranda Templeman; Dir. Mktg., Denise Hallquist; Dir. Devel., Sabrina Weiss; Assoc. Cur. Education, Adult & Special Programs, Susie Severson; Assoc. Cur. Education, Youth, Family & Community, Nancy Round; Asst. to Dir., Frances Osugi; Curatorial Coord., Ruby Hagerbaumer; Dir. Membership, Wendy Hamilton; Dir. Museum Shop, Jane Precella; Facility Dir., Steven J. Tlsty; Holland Cur. American Western Art & Cur. American Art, Sarah L. Burt.
Personnel Profile: Full-Time Paid 60; Part-Time Paid 12; Part-Time Volunteers 153; Interns 2.
Governing Authority: nonprofit organization. Tax-exempt: 501(c)(3).
Art Museum.
Collections: ancient through contemporary art, including European & American paintings, sculpture, graphics; art of the Western frontier; Native American art.
Major Exhibits: The Human Touch: RBC Collection (T), 1/9/10-4/18/10; Michael Forsburg: Great Plains America's Lingering Wilds (T), 2/6/10-5/16/10; Landscapes from the Age of Impressionism (T), 6/4/10-8/29/10; Space Silent Spirit: Maynard Dixon (T), 6/19/10-10/14/10; Kent Bellows, 9/6/10-1/2/11.
Research Fields: interdisciplinary study of the American West; 19th & 20th-century European & American Art.
Facilities: 25,600-vol. non-circulating research library; 1,000-seat concert hall, 140-seat lecture hall; classrooms; restaurant. Museum-related items for sale.
Activities: guided tours; lectures; films; gallery talks; concerts; formally organized education programs for children & adults; special training programs for educators; cooperative curriculum oriented school programs; inter-museum loan, permanent, temporary & traveling exhibitions.
Publications: members magazine; catalogs; brochures.
Hours & Admission Prices: Tues.-Sat. 10-4, Sun. 12-4. Adults $7, senior citizens & college students $5, youth $4; discounts to AAA, AAM & ICOM members; members & children 4 & under no charge. Closed national holidays. ♿
Attendance: 200,000 (estimated)
Membership: Student & Senior $30; Educator Family & Military Family $35; Individual $45; Dual Senior Citizens 62 & over $55; Family & Dual $60; Contributor $100 & up; Patron $500 & up.

MORMON TRAIL VISITORS CENTER, 3215 State St., Omaha, NE 68112. Tel.: 402-453-9372.
Visitors Center.
Collections: local history & culture; Mormon migration from Illinois to Utah; early pioneer life; period log cabin; ox drawn covered wagon; hand-carts; personal artifacts.
Hours & Admission Prices: Daily 9-9. Closed Christmas. ♿

NEBRASKA JEWISH HISTORICAL SOCIETY AND RIEKES MUSEUM, 333 S. 132nd St., Omaha, NE 68154-2106. Tel.: 402-334-6442.
E-mail: njhs@jewishomaha.org
History Museum.
Collections: artifacts & images pertaining to Jewish life and culture since the 1880s; photographs.
Hours & Admission Prices: Mon.-Thurs. 10-4. Tours by appointment. No charge. ♿

OMAHA CHILDREN'S MUSEUM, 500 S. 20th St., Omaha, NE 68102-2505. Tel.: 402-342-6164 & 930-2340. Fax: 402-342-6165.
E-mail: discover@ocm.org
Web Site: www.ocm.org
Founded: 1977.
Congressional District: 2
Key Personnel: Exec. Dir., Lindy Hoyer; Pres., Sue Seline; Dir. Devel., Kathy Aultz; Dir. Mktg., Christina Kahler; Dir. Education, Tom Simons; Dir. Finance & Human Resources, Gayla Houck; Museum Shop Mgr. & Dir. Guest Svcs., Jennie Mathisen.
Personnel Profile: Full-Time Paid 18; Part-Time Paid 14; Part-Time Volunteers 150; Interns 3.
Governing Authority: nonprofit organization. bd. of dirs. Tax-exempt: 501(c)(3).
Children's Museum.
Collections: participatory exhibits in the arts, sciences & humanities.
Research Fields: science & technology; visual & performing arts; cultural & ethnic heritage; summer camps; outreach programs.
Facilities: 60,000 sq. ft. building.
Activities: art, science & humanities; special interest exhibits; theme-related workshops.
Publications: bimonthly newsletter, Fun Times; quarterly donor, Building Blocks; annual, Field Notes Program Guide.
Hours & Admission Prices: Tues.-Wed. & Fri.-Sat. 10-5, Thurs. 10-8, Sun. 1-5. Admission $6.50, seniors & group tours $5.50 per person; discounts to reciprocal program, ASTC & ACM members; children under 2 & members no charge. Closed New Year's Day; Easter; Memorial Day; Independence Day; Labor Day; Thanksgiving; Christmas Eve & Day. ♿
Attendance: 206,164 (accurate)
Membership: Family & Grandparent $65; Family Plus $80; Patron $125.

SOKOL SOUTH OMAHA CZECHOSLOVAK MUSEUM, 2021 U St., Omaha, NE 68107. Tel.: 402-291-2893.
Czech & Slovak Cultural History.
Collections: Czech & Slovak life, culture & history; hand-cut lead crystal; costumes; photographs.
Facilities: library. Museum-related items for sale.
Hours & Admission Prices: By appointment. ♿

WINTER QUARTERS MILL MUSEUM, 9102 N. 30th St., Omaha, NE 68112-1816. Tel.: 402-551-1233.
Founded: 1999.
Key Personnel: Pres. (V), Linda Meigs
History Museum: founded in 1846 as the Mormon Winter Quarters gristmill. Listed on the National Register of Historic Places.
Collections: historic photographs; newspaper clippings; objects from the pioneer era.
Hours & Admission Prices: May-Sept. 1 Tues.-Sun. 1-5; other times by appointment. No charge; donations accepted.
Membership: Friends of the Mill $20; Business Friend of the Mill $100.

Oshkosh

HISTORICAL SOCIETY OF GARDEN COUNTY, West 1st & Avenue E, Oshkosh, NE 69154. Mailing Address: P.O. Box 193, Oshkosh, NE 69154-0193. Tel.: 308-772-3848.
Founded: 1969.
Congressional District: 3
Key Personnel: Pres., Verna Bairn; Vice Pres., Betty Kechely.
Personnel Profile: Full-Time Volunteers 9; Part-Time Paid 1; Part-Time Volunteers 29.
Governing Authority: nonprofit organization. Branch Museum: Rock School, W. 2nd & Avenue G, Oshkosh, NE. Tax-exempt.
General Museum: housed in 1906-1907 Silver Hill Museum.
Collections: mounted birds; Indian artifacts; pioneer household furnishings, machinery & apparel, fossils; local history of schools; old photographs; barbed wire; other memorabilia.
Research Fields: archaeological specimens.
Facilities: 100-vol. library of textbooks, fiction & history.
Activities: guided tours; period equipment demonstrations.
Publications: brochures; annual newsletter.
Hours & Admission Prices: Memorial Day-Labor Day Mon.-Sat. 9-4, Sun. 2-6. No charge; donations accepted. Call for special tours during the year; the Garden County Fair. ♿
Attendance: 345 (accurate)
Membership: Annual $10.

Pawnee City

PAWNEE CITY HISTORICAL SOCIETY & MUSEUM, Hwy. 50/8 East, Pawnee City, NE 68420. Mailing Address: P.O. Box 33, Pawnee City, NE 68420-0033. Tel.: 402-852-3131.
Web Site: www.rootsweb.com/~nepawnee/county/resources/pchsm.html
Founded: 1968.
Congressional District: 1
Key Personnel: Chm., Roy Mullin; Vice Pres., Burt DeKoning; Treas., Yvonne Dalluge.
Personnel Profile: Part-Time Paid 1; Part-Time Volunteers 10.
Governing Authority: society; bd. of dirs. Tax-exempt.
Regional History Museum.
Collections: period dishes; photographs; papers; furniture; farm machinery; wire; 1,600 pairs of salt & pepper shakers; tailwind airplane; barbed wire. Historic Houses: 1868 first schoolhouse in Pawnee City; 1862 home of first governor of Nebraska; 1857 Smithery Log Cabin; country store; library; church; dentist office.
Facilities: 20 buildings.
Activities: guided tours; arts & crafts display; motorcoach tours; Living Village. Annual Events: children's workshops in June; Civil War workshop in September; Civil War Reenactments in September.
Publications: biannual newsletter.
Hours & Admission Prices: Summer: Tues.-Fri. 9-2, Sat. 9-12 & 1-4, Sun. 1-4; other times by appointment. Winter: Tues.-Thurs. 9-4. Adults $5; members no charge. ♿
Attendance: 2,500 (estimated)
Membership: Household $15; Lifetime $150.

Pierce

PIERCE HISTORICAL SOCIETY, 200 Mill St., Pierce, NE 68767. Mailing Address: P.O. Box 122, Pierce, NE 68767. Tel.: 402-329-4265.
Congressional District: 3
Personnel Profile: Part-Time Volunteers 50.
Governing Authority: Tax-exempt.
Historical Society Museum.
Collections: local history & culture; period furnishings; personal artifacts; movie projection equipment; printing equipment; military uniforms; farm equipment. Historic Buildings 1880 depot; school house; blacksmith shop.
Activities: special events.
Hours & Admission Prices: Memorial Day to Labor Day Sun. 1-4; other times by appointment. No charge; donations accepted.
Attendance: 550
Membership: Individual $5; Family $10; Business $25.

Pilger

HISTORICAL SOCIETY OF STANTON COUNTY MUSEUMS AT STANTON AND PILGER, 345 N. Main St., Pilger, NE 68768. Mailing Address: P.O. Box 213, Pilger, NE 68768-0213. Tel.: 402-396-3422.
E-mail: rjensen98@cableone.net
Web Site: www.stantoncountyhistoricalsociety.org
Founded: 1965.
Congressional District: 3
Key Personnel: Pres. (V), James Duncan; Vice Pres., Rebecca Frerichs; Treas., Virgine Jensen; Sec., Gloria Koch.
Governing Authority: society. Parent Institution: Historical Society of Stanton County. Branch Museum: Stanton Heritage Museum, 1106 Ivy St., P.O. Box 234, Stanton, NE 68779. Tel. 402-439-2208; EUB Historic Church, 706 Kingwood, Stanton, NE 68779; Restored Rural School, 1108 Ivy St., Stanton, NE 68779. Tax-exempt.
Historical Society Museum.
Collections: Indian artifacts; antiques. Historic Buildings: rural schoolhouse & c.1880 restored church in Stanton & Pilger.
Research Fields: Pioneer records; biographies of country Pioneers; old cemeteries.
Activities: permanent & temporary exhibitions; cataloging of county cemeteries; taped interviews with county residents.
Publications: biannual newsletter, Historical Times.
Hours & Admission Prices: Pilger Museum: Memorial Day, Pilger Days & Labor Day; other times by appointment. Stanton Heritage Museum: May-Oct. Sat. 2-4; other times by appointment. No charge; donations accepted.
Attendance: 450 (estimated)
Membership: Student $.50; Active $5; Institutional $15; Lifetime $100.

Plainview

PLAINVIEW HISTORICAL SOCIETY, 304 S. Main St., Plainview, NE 68769. Mailing Address: P.O. Box 495, Plainview, NE 68769. Tel.: 402-582-4730.
Historic Building: housed in a former railroad depot; built in 1880.
Collections: local history & culture; railroad history & memorabilia; photographs; period furnishings; clothing; cooking utensils & appliances; personal artifacts.
Hours & Admission Prices: May to Labor Day Tues.-Sun. 1-5; other times by appointment.

PLAINVIEW KLOWN DOLL MUSEUM, Hwy. 20, Plainview, NE 68769. Mailing Address: P.O. Box 813, Plainview, NE 68769-0813. Tel.: 402-582-4433.
E-mail: clowndollmuseum@yahoo.com
Web Site: www.plvwtelco.net/clowndollmuseum
Founded: 1980.
Congressional District: 3
Key Personnel: Chm. (V), Lee Warneke; Museum Shop Mgr., Mary Hamilton.
Governing Authority: Parent Institution: Plainview Chamber of Commerce. Tax-exempt.
Clown Doll Museum.
Collections: over 4,500 clown dolls.
Hours & Admission Prices: Memorial Day-Labor Day Mon.-Sat. 10-5; Sept.-May Mon.-Fri. 1-5; other times by appointment. No charge; donations accepted. ♿
Attendance: 1,500 (accurate)

Plattsmouth

CASS COUNTY HISTORICAL SOCIETY MUSEUM, 646 Main St., Plattsmouth, NE 68048-1852. Tel.: 402-296-4770.
E-mail: ccohsm@windstream.net
Web Site: www.nebraskamuseums.org/casscountymuseum.htm
Founded: 1936.
Congressional District: 2
Key Personnel: Pres., George Miller; Vice Pres., Susan Rice; Treas., Diane Berlett; Sec., Pat Meisinger; Cur., Margo Prentiss.

Personnel Profile: Full-Time Paid 1; Part-Time Paid 1; Part-Time Volunteers 58.
Governing Authority: society; nonprofit organization. Parent Institution: Cass County Historical Society. Branch Museums: Rock Bluffs One Room School House; Joseph Cook Log House; Burlington Northern Caboose. Tax-exempt: 501(c)(3).
Historical Society Museum.
Collections: minerals & fossils; tools & equipment; household belongings; clothing & textiles; decorative arts; works of art; manuscripts & archives; photographs.
Research Fields: County History; Genealogical.
Facilities: 600-vol. library of history material; Searl S. & Leila C. Davis Conference Room. Gift-related items for sale.
Activities: guided tours; lectures; workshops; slide programs; permanent & temporary exhibitions; open houses.
Publications: quarterly newsletter.
Hours & Admission Prices: April-Oct. Tues.-Sun. 12-4; Nov.-March Tues.-Sat. 12-4. Adults $2.50; AAM, ICOM members & members no charge. Closed holidays.
Attendance: 3,000 (estimated)
Membership: Friend $15; Booster $30; Promoter $50; Century $100; Investor $250; Benefactor $500 & up; Patron $1,000 & up.

Red Cloud

WEBSTER COUNTY HISTORICAL MUSEUM, 721 W. 4th Ave., Red Cloud, NE 68970-2221. Mailing Address: P.O. Box 464, Red Cloud, NE 68970-0464. Tel.: 402-746-2444.
E-mail: wchmdirector@gpcom.net
Founded: 1965.
Congressional District: 35
Key Personnel: Pres. (V), Ron Gestring; Dir., Joyce Terhune.
Personnel Profile: Part-Time Paid 3; Part-Time Volunteers 2.
Governing Authority: county. Tax-exempt.
General Museum.
Collections: agriculture; period artifacts; natural history; history; medical; military; mill levey.
Facilities: library of local history available for use on the premises; nature center; reading room.
Activities: guided tours; permanent exhibitions.
Hours & Admission Prices: April-Nov. daily 1-5. Adults $4, high school students $1.50, elementary school students $1; members no charge. Closed Easter; Mother's Day; Independence Day.
Attendance: 1,700
Membership: Individual $15; Family $25; Sustaining $50.

WILLA CATHER PIONEER MEMORIAL AND EDUCATIONAL FOUNDATION, 413 N. Webster, Red Cloud, NE 68970-2466. Tel.: 402-746-2653. Fax: 402-746-2652.
E-mail: wcpm@gpcom.net
Web Site: www.willacather.org
Founded: 1955.
Congressional District: 3
Key Personnel: Exec. Dir., Dennis M. Norris; Chm. (V), Jay Yost; Museum Shop Mgr., Stephany Thompson.
Personnel Profile: Full-Time Paid 6; Part-Time Paid 4; Part-Time Volunteers 10; Interns 3.
Governing Authority: nonprofit organization. Subsidiary Institution: Nebraska State Historical Society. Tax-exempt.
Art Gallery & Historic Museum.
Collections: various forms of art; letters; photographs.
Research Fields: archives.
Facilities: Literature, slides, books, stationery & prints of some original oils for sale.
Activities: guided tours; lectures.
Publications: newsletter & literary review.
Hours & Admission Prices: Extensive town & country tours, call in advance. Adults $10, children 12 & under $4; members no charge. Closed major holidays. ♿
Attendance: 10,000 (estimated)
Membership: Student $20; General $50; Sustaining $125; Friend $250; Patron $500; Benefactor $1,000; Cather Circle $2,500.

Schuyler

SCHUYLER/COLFAX COUNTY MUSEUM, 309 E. 11th St., Schuyler, NE 68661. Tel.: 402-352-5145.
History Museum.
Collections: county history & culture; photographs; personal artifacts.
Hours & Admission Prices: April-Dec. Sun. 2-4; tours by appointment.

Scottsbluff

RIVERSIDE ZOO, 1600 S. Beltline Hwy. West, Scottsbluff, NE 69361-1331. Tel.: 308-630-6236. Fax: 308-632-2953.
E-mail: tfrench@city.scottsbluff.org
Web Site: riversidezoo.org
Founded: 1950.
Congressional District: 3
Key Personnel: Dir., Tim French; Coord. Visitor Svcs., Rene Owens.
Personnel Profile: Full-Time Paid 14; Part-Time Paid 2; Part-Time Volunteers 200.
Governing Authority: municipal. A branch of the City of Scottsbluff. Tax-exempt.
Zoo.
Collections: domestic & wild animals; Chimpanzee Conservation Center; Moose Woods; tiger facility; red pandas; rainforest discovery center.
Facilities: Chimpanzee Conservation Center; Moose Woods; tiger facility; discovery center; vending area; walk-through aviary. Zoo-related gift items for sale.
Activities: guided tours; feed waterfowl on the zoo's lake; call for information on special events.
Publications: newsletter, Zoo Tales.
Hours & Admission Prices: April-Oct. daily 9:30-4; Nov.-March daily 10-4. Adults $2.50, senior citizens $2, children 5-12 $1; discounts to AZA members, groups & reciprocating zoos; children 4 & under and members no charge. ♿
Attendance: 34,000 (estimated)
Membership: Individual $25; Family $35; Extended Family $55; Supporting $100; Booster $250; Sustaining $500; Trail Blazer $1,000.

Seward

MARXHAUSEN ART GALLERY, Concordia University, 800 N. Columbia Ave., Seward, NE 68434-1500. Tel.: 402-643-3651 & 7490. Fax: 402-643-4073.
E-mail: james.bockelman@cune.edu
Web Site: www.cune.edu/finearts/art/5878/
Founded: 1951.
Congressional District: 1
Key Personnel: Dir., James E. Bockelman.
Personnel Profile: Part-Time Paid 1.
Governing Authority: denominational group. Parent Institution: Concordia College. Tax-exempt: 501(c)(3).
Art Gallery.
Collections: over 300 works of art by national & international artists; screenprints; etchings; lithographs; prints.
Activities: gallery talks; rental gallery; temporary & traveling exhibitions.
Hours & Admission Prices: Sept.-May Mon.-Fri. 11-4, Sat.-Sun. 1-4. No charge; donations accepted. Closed Easter weekend; week of Thanksgiving; weeks before & after Christmas; school recesses including summer break.

Sidney

FORT SIDNEY MUSEUM & POST COMMANDER'S HOME, 6th Ave. & Jackson St., Sidney, NE 69162. Mailing Address: P.O. Box 596, Sidney, NE 69162-0596. Tel.: 308-254-2150.
Founded: 1954.
Congressional District: 3
Key Personnel: Pres., Glenn Johnson; Vice Pres., Roger Jorgensen; Treas., Charlotte Steffens; Bd. Member, Tammara Beyer; Bd. Member, Cheryl Nelson; Bd. Member, Don Nightingale; Bd. Member, Esther Henke; Bd. Member, Joan Olsen; Sec., Becky Wyatt; Guide, Sharon Flessner.
Personnel Profile: Full-Time Paid 1; Part-Time Paid 3; Part-Time Volunteers 12.
Governing Authority: nonprofit organization. Parent Institution: Cheyenne Co. Historical Assoc. Tax-exempt.
General Museum on a Historic Building & site: 1871 Commanding Officer's Quarters; 1872 Powder House or Magazine; 1884 Officers' Quarters; Carriage House.
Collections: 1894 furnishings; artifacts; 1900 carriage; military collection; railroad room; Ladies Dressmaking and Millinery Shop; Sioux Army Depot Room; Pioneer Room; library of old & valuable books, maps & stereographs.
Research Fields: history of Fort Sidney; Cheyenne County history; Sioux army depot history.
Facilities: library.
Activities: guided tours; organized education programs for children & adults; 4th of July celebration, continuous entertainment 1-4; Old Fashion Christmas, decorations & entertainment.
Publications: pamphlet, History of Ft. Sidney; Walking Tour of Sidney Historic Downtown District.

Hours & Admission Prices: Museum: Memorial Day to Labor Day daily 9-11 & 1-3. Commander's Home: June-Aug. & Old Fashioned Christmas. No charge; donations accepted. ♿
Attendance: 2,808 (accurate)
Membership: Annual $5.

St. Paul

MUSEUM OF NEBRASKA MAJOR LEAGUE BASEBALL, 619 Howard Ave., St. Paul, NE 68873-2022. Tel.: 308-754-5558.
Web Site: www.nebraskabaseballmuseum.com
Baseball Museum.
Collections: trading cards; photographs; artifacts.
Hours & Admission Prices: Memorial Day-Labor Day Mon.-Fri. 10-4, Sat. 10-2; other times by appointment.

Stuart

WHITE HORSE MUSEUM, 46376 879th Rd., Stuart, NE 68780-5847. Tel.: 402-924-3168.
E-mail: visitorinfo@stuartwhitehorsemuseum.com
Web Site: www.stuartwhitehorsemuseum.com
History Museum.
Collections: White Horse Ranch memorabilia; period artifacts; furnishings; photographs.
Hours & Admission Prices: Call for hours.

Syracuse

OTOE COUNTY MUSEUM OF MEMORIES, 1621 Thorne St., Syracuse, NE 68446-9730. Tel.: 402-269-2355.
Founded: 1972.
Congressional District: 1
Key Personnel: Pres., Phyllis Witte; Cur. & Treas., Rose Garey.
Personnel Profile: Full-Time Volunteers 6; Part-Time Volunteers 9.
Governing Authority: society.
History Museum.
Collections: parlor, kitchen & bedroom from the turn-of-the-century; local Indian artifacts; loom & sewing room; Thomas A. Edison exhibit; U.S. flag display; tent show exhibit; Kramer collection of big game trophies, small animals & birds; butcher shop; 1890 general store; doctor's office; carriage house & cutter; original church altar & furnishings; old fashioned herb garden; county room exhibit; tools & small farm equipment.
Research Fields: Chick Boyes tent show; financial records; play scripts; costumes & props; genealogy.
Facilities: library of history & personal memories of residents of Otoe County; meeting rooms.
Activities: tours; school tours; art exhibits; permanent exhibits. Museum Sponsors: local artists show; quilt show; crotchet show; apron show.
Hours & Admission Prices: May-Sept. Sun. 1:30-4. No charge; donations accepted. ♿
Attendance: 1,500 (estimated)
Membership: Individual $10; Family $15.

Table Rock

TABLE ROCK HISTORICAL SOCIETY AND MUSEUMS, 414-16 Houston St., Table Rock, NE 68447. Mailing Address: P.O. Box 194, Table Rock, NE 68447-0194. Tel.: 402-839-4135. Fax: 402-839-4135.
Founded: 1965.
Congressional District: 1
Key Personnel: Pres. (V), Floyd Vrtiska.
Personnel Profile: Part-Time Paid 1; Part-Time Volunteers 10.
Governing Authority: society.
General Museum.
Collections: furnishings; antiques; paintings; tools and equipment; Indian artifacts; school items; automobiles; religious exhibits; military exhibits, WWI & WWII; Table Rock Argus Print Shop. Historic Houses: 1854 Turner Log Cabin; 1877 St. John's Catholic Church; 1893 Old Opera House.
Activities: guided tours; Living History Day.
Publications: brochures.
Hours & Admission Prices: May-Sept. Sun. 1-4; other times by appointment. No charge; donations accepted. ♿
Attendance: 800 (accurate)
Membership: Individual $2; Sustaining $5; Life $100.

Tecumseh

JOHNSON COUNTY HISTORICAL SOCIETY, INC., 231 Lincoln St., Tecumseh, NE 68450-2116. Tel.: 402-335-5900.
Founded: 1962.
Congressional District: 1
Key Personnel: Pres. & Cur., Boyd Maddox.
Governing Authority: county. Branch Museum: 1872 Johnson County Historic Jail, Fourth Jackson Sts., Tecumesh, NE. Tax-exempt: 170(b)(1)(a).
History Museum: housed in 1889 Christian Church Building.
Collections: Indian artifacts; tools; 3,000 wooden household articles; clothing; linens; silver; china; glass; toys; World War I objects; memorabilia; pictures; scrapbooks; newspapers; books. Historic House: 1870, one-room schoolhouse.
Research Fields: genealogy.
Facilities: 75-vol. library of old atlases; records; bibles; newspapers; songs; books written by Johnson County residents; available for use on premises. Museum-related items for sale.
Activities: arts festivals; guided tours; study clubs; formally organized education programs for children & adults; docent program or council; temporary exhibitions.
Hours & Admission Prices: May-Oct. Tues.-Fri. 1-4; other times by appointment. No charge; donations accepted.
Attendance: 100 (estimated)
Membership: Individual $10; Family $20.

Tekamah

BURT COUNTY MUSEUM, 319 N. 13th St., Tekamah, NE 68061-1503. Mailing Address: P.O. Box 125, Tekamah, NE 68061-0125. Tel.: 402-374-1505.
E-mail: burtcomuseum@huntel.net
Founded: 1967.
Congressional District: 16
Key Personnel: Co-Pres., Rick Nelsen; Co-Pres., Marlene Kaeding; Chm. (V), Arlene Weatherly; Treas., Dee Bottger.
Personnel Profile: Part-Time Paid 4; Part-Time Volunteers 12.
Governing Authority: board of directors. Tax-exempt.
General Museum: housed in c.1904 home of E.C. Houston, listed on National Register of Historic Places.
Collections: agriculture; clothing; furniture; photos; manuscript collection.
Research Fields: genealogy.
Facilities: meeting rooms. Museum-related items for sale.
Activities: guided tours; permanent & temporary exhibitions; one-act performances; tour of homes; candle light tours at Christmas; coffee on the porch (alumni/Memorial weekend); Independence Day Celebration.
Publications: Tekamah Cemetery Book; quarterly newsletters; brochures; flyers; book, Decatur & Tekamah.
Hours & Admission Prices: Tues., Thurs. & Sat. 1-5. No charge; donations accepted. Closed major holidays.
Attendance: 2,560 (estimated)
Membership: Annual $5; Five Years $10; Life $20.

Tobias

TOBIAS COMMUNITY HISTORICAL SOCIETY, Main St., Tobias, NE 68453-2073. Mailing Address: 561 County Rd. 5, Tobias, NE 68453-2073. Tel.: 402-243-2356.
E-mail: rjrada@diodecom.net
Founded: 1968.
Congressional District: 1
Key Personnel: Pres. (V), Judith K. Rada; Sec. & Cataloging, Mary Kronhofman.
Personnel Profile: Part-Time Volunteers 1.
Governing Authority: municipal. Tax-exempt.
General Museum: housed in original bank & Tobias Print Shop, saved in the 1891 fire which burned most of the business district.
Collections: period bottles; kitchen wares; household appliances; photographs; tools; philatelic; medical; military; Tobias High School trophies & pictures; newspapers.
Research Fields: local history.
Activities: permanent & temporary exhibitions.
Hours & Admission Prices: By appointment only. No charge; donations accepted. ♿
Attendance: 100 (estimated)
Membership: Individual $1; Individual Life $15; Couple Life $25.

Valentine

CHERRY COUNTY HISTORICAL SOCIETY, Main St. & Hwy. 20, Valentine, NE 69201. Mailing Address: P.O. Box 284, Valentine, NE 69201-0284. Tel.: 402-376-2015.
Founded: 1928.
Congressional District: 3
Key Personnel: C.E.O. & Pres. (V), Joyce Muirhead; Cur. & Museum Shop Mgr., Jan Howell.
Personnel Profile: Full-Time Volunteers 4; Part-Time Paid 2; Part-Time Volunteers 3.
Governing Authority: county. Tax-exempt.
History Museum.
Collections: newspapers from 1883; county records from 1884; pictures; buttons; clothing from 1885-present; home furnishings; musical instruments; Indian artifacts.
Research Fields: history; family tree data.
Facilities: 250-vol. genealogy library of history, western stories, old school books, Nebraska & Indian history.
Activities: guided tours; microfilms; films; study clubs.
Publications: A Sandhills Century; Murder on the Plains.
Hours & Admission Prices: Memorial Day to Sept. 15 Thurs.-Sat. 1-5; other times by appointment. Special openings $5 per hour, adults $2, children under 12 $.50; members no charge. ♿
Attendance: 450 (estimated)
Membership: Individual $5; Ten Year $25; Lifetime $100.

FORT NIOBRARA NATIONAL WILDLIFE REFUGE, Hidden Timber Rte., HC 14, Valentine, NE 69201. Mailing Address: HC 14-Box 67, Valentine, NE 69201-9706. Tel.: 402-376-3789. Fax: 402-376-3217.
E-mail: fortniobrara@fws.gov
Web Site: fortniobrara.fws.gov
Founded: 1912.
Congressional District: 3
Key Personnel: Refuge Mgr., Steven Hicks.
Personnel Profile: Full-Time Paid 10; Part-Time Paid 1.
Governing Authority: federal. Branch of Dept. of the Interior, Fish & Wildlife Service, Washington, D.C. Tax-exempt.
Wildlife Refuge.
Collections: birds; small mammals; local historical photographs; photographs of military reservation 1879-1906; aviary.
Facilities: visitor center.
Activities: permanent exhibitions.
Publications: Fort Niobrara 1880-1906.
Hours & Admission Prices: Daily sunrise-sunset. No charge. Visitor Center: Memorial Day-Labor Day daily 8-4:30; Sept.-May Mon.-Fri. 8-4:30. No charge. ♿
Attendance: 130,000 (estimated)
Membership: Single $5; Family $8.

SAWYER'S SANDHILLS MUSEUM, 440 Valentine St., Valentine, NE 69201-1942. Tel.: 402-376-3293.
Founded: 1958.
Key Personnel: Owner, Dorothy Sawyer.
Governing Authority: private; nonprofit organization.
General Museum.
Collections: period autos; guns; Indian artifacts; musical instruments; lamps; dishes; a moonshine still.
Hours & Admission Prices: Memorial Day-Labor Day by appointment only. Adults $5, children 5-13 $1.

Valley

VALLEY COMMUNITY HISTORICAL SOCIETY, INC., 218 W. Alexander St., Valley, NE 68064. Mailing Address: P.O. Box 685, Valley, NE 68064-0685. Tel.: 402-359-5544 & 5323.
Web Site: www.valleyne.org
Founded: 1966.
Congressional District: 2
Key Personnel: Pres. (V), Helen Soll; Vice Pres. (V), Max Johnson; Treas. & Sec., Julia A. Allen.
Governing Authority: society; nonprofit. Tax-exempt: 501(c)(3).
Local History Museum: housed in 1872 schoolhouse, then served as a Baptist Church & later a Catholic Church.
Collections: personal artifacts; manuscripts; Indian artifacts; fossils.
Activities: lectures; films; permanent exhibitions.
Publications: annual pamphlet, Yearly Report.
Hours & Admission Prices: May-Sept. Sun. 2-4; other times by appointment. No charge; donations accepted.
Attendance: 195 (accurate)
Membership: Individual $5; Life $100.

Wahoo

SAUNDERS COUNTY HISTORICAL COMPLEX, 240 N. Walnut, Wahoo, NE 68066-1858. Tel.: 402-443-3090. Fax: 402-443-3090 (call first).
E-mail: saunderscomuseum@hotmail.com
Web Site: www.visitsaunderscounty.org
Founded: 1963.
Congressional District: 23
Key Personnel: Pres. (V), Dorothy M. Meduna; Dir. & Cur., Erin Hauser; Museum Shop Mgr., Lila Zech.
Personnel Profile: Full-Time Paid 1; Part-Time Paid 2; Part-Time Volunteers 75.
Governing Authority: nonprofit organization. Saunders County Historical Society. Tax-exempt: 501(c)(3).
Historical Society Museum Complex.
Collections: agricultural equipment; business machines; furniture; household equipment; costumes; decorative arts; photographs; memorabilia relating to Saunders County; materials pertaining to Czech, German & Swedish ethnic groups. Historic Houses: c.1890 Rural School; 1886 Burlington-Northern Railroad Depot; 1889 Weston Presbyterian Church; 1893 Hanson Historical House; 1873 Log House; 1950 Post Office.
Research Fields: county history; genealogy.
Facilities: 400-vol. library pertaining to state & county histories available for research on premises only.
Activities: guided tours; permanent, temporary & traveling exhibitions; educational programs. Annual Event: Christmas program.
Publications: brochure; newsletter.
Hours & Admission Prices: April-Sept. Tues.-Sat. 10-4, Sun. 1:30-4:30; Oct.-March Tues.-Fri. 10-4. No charge; donations accepted. Closed major holidays. ♿
Attendance: 5,700 (estimated)
Membership: Individual $15; Family $20; Business $30; Lifetime $150.

Walthill

SUSAN LA FLESCHE PICOTTE CENTER, 505 Matthewson St., Walthill, NE 68067. Tel.: 402-406-5966.
Historic Building: housed in the former hospital built in 1910 by Dr. Susan La Flesche Picotte, the first Native American woman physician in the U.S.
Collections: Dr. Susan La Flesche Picotte's life; photographs; personal artifacts.
Hours & Admission Prices: By appointment.

Weeping Water

WEEPING WATER VALLEY HISTORICAL SOCIETY, 215 W. Eldora Ave., Weeping Water, NE 68463. Mailing Address: P.O. Box 43, Weeping Water, NE 68463-0043. Tel.: 402-267-4925.
E-mail: wd85407@navix.net
Founded: 1969.
Congressional District: 2
Key Personnel: Chm. & Pres. (V), Doris Duff; Treas., Dale Nielsen.
Personnel Profile: Part-Time Volunteers 30.
Governing Authority: society; nonprofit. Parent Institution: Weeping Water Valley Historical Society. Tax-exempt: 501(c)(3).
History & Medical Museum: located on the site of the oldest First Congregational Parsonage in state.
Collections: Dr. Lloyd N. Kunkels prehistoric Indian artifacts from 20,000 years ago to Plains Indians; fossils, period furniture, pioneer artifacts, guns & tools. Historic Buildings: 1870 chapel, 1880 original office of Dr. Jesse Fate; 1867 residence, originally the Congregational parsonage, detailing businesses housed in Weeping Water from the 1860's to the present, original soda fountain, general store, barber shop; Kevin Brack's celebrity collection.
Research Fields: archeology; excavation of prehistoric Indian houses in vicinity.
Facilities: 50-vol. library of old medical books; Nebraska history available for inter-library loan & on premises. Fossils for sale.
Activities: guided tours; lectures; permanent & temporary exhibitions.
Publications: brochure.
Hours & Admission Prices: May-Oct. Sun. 1-4; other times by appointment, call 402-267-4925. Memory Lane Mon.-Fri. 10-2. No charge; donations accepted. ♿
Attendance: 2,200 (estimated)
Membership: Annual $1; Life $25.

Wilber

WILBER CZECH MUSEUM, 102 W. 3rd, Wilber, NE 68465. Mailing Address: P.O. Box 7, Wilber, NE 68465-0007. Tel.: 402-821-2183.
Founded: 1965.
Congressional District: 32
Key Personnel: Gift Shop Mgr., Lillian Wanek.
Personnel Profile: Part-Time Volunteers 12; Interns 1.
Governing Authority: nonprofit organization. Parent Institution: Nebraska Czechs of Wilber. Tax-exempt: 170(b)(1)(A).
General Museum.
Collections: textiles; glass; Czech doll collection; Czech dishes; quilt collection; replicas of early immigrant homes & early Wilber businesses; agriculture; paintings; specialized laces & Czech costumes; decorative arts; medical; guns; antiques.
Research Fields: local history; history of Czechoslovakia.
Facilities: Crafts, quilted pillows, quilts, hand loomed rugs & other museum-related items for sale.
Activities: guided tours; permanent & temporary exhibitions; quilting; rug making; Czech Festival reflecting origins of the past.
Publications: brochure; book, Poetic History of Wilber.
Hours & Admission Prices: Daily 1-4; other times by appointment. No charge; donations accepted. Closed national holidays. ♿
Attendance: 1,244 (estimated)

Wisner

WISNER HERITAGE MUSEUM, 920 Ave. "E", Wisner, NE 68791. Mailing Address: P.O. Box 842, Wisner, NE 68791-0842. Tel.: 402-529-3226.
Founded: 1995.
Key Personnel: Pres. (V), Gregg Moeller
History Museum.
Collections: local history & culture relating to the city of Wisner.
Hours & Admission Prices: Sat.-Sun. 1-4; other times by appointment. No charge; donations accepted. ♿
Attendance: 200 (estimated)
Membership: Individual $10; Family $20; Lifetime $150.

York

ANNA BEMIS PALMER MUSEUM, 211 E. 7th St., York, NE 68467-3022. Tel.: 402-363-2630. Fax: 402-362-0347.
Founded: 1967.
Congressional District: 3
Key Personnel: Dir., Paula Christensen.
Personnel Profile: Part-Time Volunteers 4.
Governing Authority: municipal. Tax-exempt: 170(b)(1)(A).
General Museum.
Collections: York County History 1870-1960; agricultural implements; covered wagon; living room & bedroom; military artifacts.
Facilities: 500-vol. library of histories of York County; atlases; newspaper artifacts; old bibles; school books available for use on premises; 200-seat auditorium.
Activities: guided tours; arts festivals; permanent & temporary exhibitions.
Hours & Admission Prices: Daily 8-5. No charge; donations accepted. Closed national holidays. ♿
Attendance: 1,387 (estimated)

NEVADA

(102 listings)

Amargosa Valley

ASH MEADOWS NATIONAL WILDLIFE REFUGE, HCR 70, Amargosa Valley, NV 89020. Tel.: 775-372-5435. Fax: 775-372-5436.
E-mail: sharon_mckelvey@fws.gov
Web Site: www.fws.gov/desertcomplex/ashmeadows
Wildlife Refuge.
Collections: fish; plants; native wildlife.
Hours & Admission Prices: Sunrise to sunset. No charge.

Austin

AUSTIN HISTORICAL SOCIETY, 180 Main St., Austin, NV 89310. Mailing Address: P.O. Box 25, Austin, NV 89310-0025. Tel.: 775-964-1202. Fax: 775-964-2306.
Web Site: www.ausnvhistsoc.com
Key Personnel: Pres., Nancy Gordon
Historical Society Museum.
Collections: local history & culture; photographs; personal artifacts.
Hours & Admission Prices: Call for hours.
Membership: Individual $10.

BERLIN-ICHTHYOSAUR STATE PARK, HC 61, Austin, NV 89310. Mailing Address: HC 61, Box 61200, Austin, NV 89310. Tel.: 775-964-2440. Fax: 775-964-2012.
Park Museum.
Collections: plants; native wildlife; fossils; geological; 20th century mining camp.
Hours & Admission Prices: Daylight hours. Park: $3 per vehicle. Fossil House Tour: $2 per person.

Baker

GREAT BASIN NATIONAL PARK, 100 Great Basin Natl. Park, Baker, NV 89311-9701. Tel.: 775-234-7331. Fax: 775-234-7269.
Web Site: www.nps.gov/grba
Founded: 1986.
Congressional District: 2
Key Personnel: Supt., Andy Ferguson; Chief Resources, Tod Williams; Cultural Resource Mgr., Eva A. Jensen.
Governing Authority: federal. Parent Institution: National Park Service. Tax-exempt.
Park Museum.
Collections: speleothems; historical objects found in cave; botanical specimens; photographs; archaeology.
Facilities: 750-vol. library of natural history & geology books available for use on premises; 30-seat restaurant; nature center; 35-seat theater. Books & museum-related items for sale.
Activities: guided tours; self-guiding nature trail; evening programs; films; exhibit room; formal interpretation programs for adults & children.
Hours & Admission Prices: Winter: daily 8:30-4:30; Summer: daily 7:30-6. Visitors Center: Cave Tours: 90-minute tours: Adults 12 & over $8, youth 5-11 $4; children 4 & under not allowed. 60-minute Tours: Adults $6, youth $3. 30-minute Tours: Adults $2; children 11 & under no charge. Closed New Year's Day; Thanksgiving; Christmas. ♿
Attendance: 86,457 (estimated)

Beatty

BEATTY MUSEUM AND HISTORICAL SOCIETY, 417 Main St., Beatty, NV 89003. Mailing Address: P.O. Box 244, Beatty, NV 89003-0244. Tel.: 775-553-2967.
Founded: 1995.
Key Personnel: Pres., Mary Revert; Vice Pres., Riley McCoy; Sec., Kay Parsons; Treas., Suzy McCoy.
Personnel Profile: Full-Time Paid 1; Part-Time Paid 1; Part-Time Volunteers 4.
Governing Authority: private; nonprofit organization. Tax-exempt: 501(c)(3).
Historical Society Museum.
Collections: Bullfrog Mining District & Southern Nye County history; photographs; books; personal artifacts.
Activities: meetings.
Hours & Admission Prices: Daily 10-4. No charge; donations accepted. ♿
Attendance: 10,245 (estimated)

Blue Diamond

SPRING MOUNTAIN RANCH STATE PARK, State Rte. 159, Blue Diamond, NV 89004. Mailing Address: P.O. Box 124, Blue Diamond, NV 89004-0124. Tel.: 702-875-4141.
E-mail: smrrangers@parks.nv.gov
Web Site: www.parks.nv.gov/smr.htm
Park Museum.
Collections: local history; period furnishings; photographs; historic ranch.
Activities: living history programs; guided tours; rental facilities.
Hours & Admission Prices: Daily 10-4.

Boulder City

BOULDER CITY/HOOVER DAM MUSEUM, 1305 Arizona St., Boulder City, NV 89005-2613. Mailing Address: P.O. Box 60516, Boulder City, NV 89006-0516. Tel.: 702-294-1988. Fax: 702-294-4380.
E-mail: info@bcmha.org
Web Site: www.bcmha.org
Formerly: Boulder City Museum/Hoover Dam Museum
Founded: 1981.
Congressional District: 1
Key Personnel: Vice Pres., Darryl Martin; Treas., Mike Penuelas; Gen. Mgr., Roger Shoaff; Mgr., Roseanne Shoaff.

Personnel Profile: Full-Time Paid 1; Part-Time Paid 5; Part-Time Volunteers 20.
Governing Authority: nonprofit organization. Parent Institution: Boulder City Museum & Historical Association. Tax-exempt: 501(c)(3).
History & Industrial Museum.
Collections: historical & industrial items related to the building of Hoover (Boulder) Dam & Boulder City and lower Colorado River development.
Research Fields: oral research; audio & video memories of period when Hoover (Boulder) Dam was being built; photographs; manuscripts; personal papers; three-dimensional artifacts; serials; monographs.
Facilities: 4,719 sq. ft. exhibit space. Books, videos & souvenirs regarding the construction of Hoover (Boulder) Dam & Boulder City for sale.
Activities: films; guided tours; lectures; temporary & loan exhibitions; Chatauqua cultural affair. Annual Events: Luncheon for Thirty-Oners; Fundraiser.
Publications: quarterly newsletter, BCMHA Newsletter.
Hours & Admission Prices: Mon.-Sat. 10-5, Sun. 12-5. Adults $2, seniors & children $1; members no charge. Closed New Year's Day; Easter; Mother's Day; Thanksgiving Day; Christmas. ♿
Attendance: 16,000 (accurate)
Membership: Student $10; Individual $20; Organization $60; Lifetime $400.

LAKE MEAD NATIONAL RECREATION AREA, 601 Nevada Hwy., Boulder City, NV 89005-2426. Tel.: 702-293-8906. Fax: 702-293-8936.
Web Site: www.nps.gov/lame/index.htm
Founded: 1968.
Congressional District: 3
Key Personnel: Cultural Resource Mgr., Rosie Pepito; Park Archeologist, Steve Daron; Book Shop Mgr., MaryLou Seely.
Governing Authority: federal. Parent Institution: National Park Service, Dept. of the Interior. Subsidiary Institution: Western National Parks Association. Tax-exempt.
National Park & Visitor Center.
Collections: mammals; birds; archaeology; mining; geology; herbarium; entomology.
Research Fields: history; archaeology; bighorn sheep; fish; endangered plants, mammals, birds, amphibians & reptiles.
Facilities: 1,400-vol. library pertaining to the Lake Mead area, available for inter-library loan & general circulation; botanic garden; 120-seat auditorium; visitor center with exhibits; theater. Books & maps for sale.
Activities: guided walks; lectures; films; environmental education programs; permanent & temporary exhibits.
Publications: Auto Tour guide of Lake Mead; Flowering Plants of Lake Mead Region; Guide to Desert Geology of the Lake Mead Region.
Hours & Admission Prices: Visitor's Center: daily 8:30-4:30. No charge. Closed New Year's Day; Thanksgiving; Christmas. ♿
Attendance: 200,000 (estimated)

Caliente

CALIENTE RAILROAD DEPOT & BOXCAR MUSEUM, 100 Depot, Caliente, NV 89008. Mailing Address: P.O. Box 1006, Caliente, NV 89008-1006. Tel.: 775-726-3129.
Historic Building: built in 1923.
Collections: railroad history; railway station; photographs; period artifacts.
Hours & Admission Prices: Mon.-Fri. 10-2. No charge; donations accepted.

Carson City

BREWERY ARTS CENTER, 449 W. King St., Carson City, NV 89703-4205. Tel.: 775-883-1976. Fax: 775-883-1922.
Web Site: www.breweryarts.org
Key Personnel: Dir., John Procaccini
Arts Center.
Collections: fine arts; paintings.
Facilities: theater; classrooms. Museum-related items for sale.
Activities: performances; special events.
Hours & Admission Prices: Call for hours.

CHILDREN'S MUSEUM OF NORTHERN NEVADA, 813 N. Carson St., Carson City, NV 89701-4009. Tel.: 775-884-2226. Fax: 775-884-2179.
E-mail: info@cmnn.org
Web Site: www.cmnn.org/
Key Personnel: Exec. Dir., Jim Peckham.
Personnel Profile: Full-Time Paid 2; Part-Time Paid 1; Part-Time Volunteers 20.
Governing Authority: private; nonprofit organization.
Children's Museum.
Collections: hands-on, virtual reality & interactive exhibits.
Facilities: Museum-related items for sale.
Activities: birthday parties; special events.
Hours & Admission Prices: Daily 10-4:30. Adults $5, seniors 55 & over $4, children $3; discount to groups, AAM & ICOM members; children 1 & under no charge. Closed New Year's Day; Easter; Thanksgiving; Christmas. ♿
Attendance: 30,000 (accurate)

HISTORIC BOWERS MANSION, 4005 U.S. Hwy. 396 N., Carson City, NV 89704. Tel.: 702-849-0201.
Historic House Museum.
Collections: local history & culture; Bowers family; photographs; period furnishings.
Hours & Admission Prices: May & Sept. 4-Oct. Sat.-Sun. 11-4:30; June-Sept. 3 daily 11-4:30. Closed Thanksgiving; Christmas.

NEVADA STATE LIBRARY AND ARCHIVES, 100 N. Stewart St., Carson City, NV 89701-4285. Tel.: 775-684-3360. Fax: 775-684-3330.
Library and Archives.
Collections: books; pamphlets; manuscripts.
Facilities: library.
Hours & Admission Prices: Mon.-Fri. 8-5. No charge.

* **NEVADA STATE MUSEUM, (M),** 600 N. Carson Street, Carson City, NV 89701-4004. Tel.: 775-687-4810. Fax: 775-687-4168.
Web Site: www.nevadaculture.org
Founded: 1939.
Congressional District: 2
Key Personnel: Chm., Robert Stoldal; Dir., Jim Barmore; Exhibits Mgr., Ray Geiser; Accountant, Carol Edling; Cur. Natural History, George Baumgardner; Cur. Anthropology, Gene Hattori; Cur. History, Bob Nylen; Cur. Clothing & Textiles, Jan Loverin; Registrar, Sue Ann Monteleone; Facility Supvr., Scott Klette; Cur. Education, Deborah Stevenson; Coord. Membership, Holly Payson; Museum Shop Mgr., Leslie Phillips.
Personnel Profile: Full-Time Paid 18; Part-Time Paid 4; Part-Time Volunteers 70; Interns 3.
Governing Authority: state. Parent Institution: Nevada Department of Cultural Affairs, Division of Museums & History. Tax-exempt.
General Museum: located at the former U.S. Mint in Carson City; 1869.
Collections: history; natural history; anthropology.
Major Exhibits: Selections from the Collections, 1/10-12/10; Interwoven (T), 3/10-7/10.
Research Fields: Nevada natural and cultural history.
Facilities: 19,500-vol. library of historical, biological, geological & anthropological books & periodicals available on premises; classrooms; research center. Museum-related items for sale.
Activities: long term, temporary, & traveling exhibits; lectures; guided tours; activities for children; coin press demonstrations; special events; outreach educational trunks; research service; internships; Friends organization.
Publications: newsletter, Mint Edition; books, Anthropological Papers; Popular Series.
Hours & Admission Prices: Wed.-Sat. 8:30-4:30. Adults $6, seniors $4; discounts to AAM & ICOM members; children under 18 & members no charge. Closed New Year's Day; Thanksgiving; Christmas. ♿
Attendance: 52,010 (accurate)
Membership: Senior Citizens $20; Individual $35; Family $50; Sustaining $100; Contributing $250; Patron $500; Benefactor $1,000; Corporate $2,500; Corporate Silver $5,000; Corporate Gold $10,000.

NEVADA STATE RAILROAD MUSEUM, 2180 S. Carson St., Carson City, NV 89701-5552. Tel.: 775-687-6953. Fax: 775-687-8294.
E-mail: pbarton@nevadaculture.org
Web Site: www.nevadaculture.org
Founded: 1980.
Congressional District: 2
Key Personnel: Cur. History, Wendell Huffman; Restoration Supvr., Chris DeWitt; Museum Store Mgr., John Walker; Facility Supvr., Brian Sheldon.
Personnel Profile: Part-Time Paid 12; Part-Time Volunteers 125.
Governing Authority: state. Parent Institution: State of Nevada Department of Cultural Affairs. Tax-exempt: 501(c)(3).
Railroad Museum.
Collections: history; Virginia & Truckee Railway Collection of cars & locomotives; 70 pieces of railroad equipment.
Research Fields: Nevada history; history of Virginia & Truckee Railway and other Nevada railroads; restoration program.
Facilities: library of historical books available on premises; conference room; 13-acre site; 40,000 sq. ft. space. Books, postcards, notepapers, arts & crafts for sale.
Activities: temporary exhibitions; annual history symposium; operation of railroad equipment; school outreach program.

Publications: quarterly newsletters, The Sagebrush Headlight.
Hours & Admission Prices: Fri.-Mon. 8:30-4:30; live steamups on holiday weekends; motor car ride on weekends. Adults $4; discounts to AAM & ICOM members; members & children under 18 no charge. Closed New Year's Day; Thanksgiving; Christmas. ♿
Attendance: 27,973 (accurate)
Membership: Students & Senior Citizens $20; Regular $35; Family $50; Sustaining $100; Contributing $250; Corporate Engineer Roster $500; Corporate Conductor's Roster $1,000.

ROBERT'S HOUSE MUSEUM, 1207 N. Carson St., Carson City, NV 89701-1203. Tel.: 775-887-2174.
Governing Authority: Parent Institution: Carson City Historical Society.
Historic House Museum.
Collections: local history & culture; photographs; period furnishings.
Activities: special events.
Hours & Admission Prices: Fri.-Sun. 1-3.

STEWART INDIAN SCHOOL MUSEUM, 5366 Snyder Ave., Carson City, NV 89701-6743. Tel.: 775-882-6929 & 687-8333. Fax: 775-882-1061.
History Museum.
Collections: American Indian history; arrowheads; baskets; grinding rocks; Great Basin artifacts; pottery; photographs.
Facilities: Museum-related items for sale.
Hours & Admission Prices: Temporarily closed.

WARREN ENGINE COMPANY #1 MUSEUM, 777 S. Stewart St., Carson City, NV 89701-5218. Tel.: 775-887-2210. Fax: 775-887-2209.
Fire-Fighting Museum.
Collections: Carson Fire Department history; fire equipment; lithographs; photographs; period artifacts.
Hours & Admission Prices: Mon.-Fri. 8-5.

Dayton

DAYTON HISTORICAL SOCIETY MUSEUM, 485 Shady Lane, at Logan Alley, Dayton, NV 89403. Mailing Address: P.O. Box 485, Dayton, NV 89403-0485. Tel.: 775-246-6316.
E-mail: clements@775.net
Web Site: daytonnvhistory.org
Founded: 1991.
Key Personnel: Museum Shop Mgr., Ruby MacFarland.
Governing Authority: Parent Institution: Historical Society of Dayton Valley. Tax-exempt.
Historical Society Museum.
Collections: Dayton history; photographs; personal artifacts; mining & milling artifacts; railroad artifacts; Native American; gold discovery.
Activities: local school group tours. Museum Sponsors: Railroad Jamboree in April; Historic Preservation Month in May; Dayton Valley Days in September; Ghostly Pioneers of Old Town Dayton Return in October.
Hours & Admission Prices: March-April & June-Nov. Sat. 10-4, Sun. 1-4; May Mon.-Fri. 11-3, Sat. 10-4, Sun. 1-4. No charge; donations accepted.
Attendance: 1,500
Membership: Single $12; Family $25; Lifetime $250.

Elko

NORTHEASTERN NEVADA MUSEUM, (M), 1515 Idaho St., Elko, NV 89801-4021. Tel.: 775-738-3418. Fax: 775-778-9318.
E-mail: info@museum-elko.us
Web Site: www.museum-elko.us
Founded: 1968.
Key Personnel: C.E.O., Kim Steninger; Dir., Claudia Wines; Registrar, Jacki Alexander; Archivist, Toni Mendive; Exhibit Coord., Catherine Wines; Maintenance Supvr., Jim Burns; Museum Shop Mgr., Tracy Beatty; Bookkeeper, Elaine Parry.
Personnel Profile: Full-Time Paid 5; Part-Time Paid 9; Part-Time Volunteers 8; Interns 1.
Governing Authority: nonprofit organization. Parent Institution: Northeastern Nevada Historical Society. Tax-exempt: 501(c)(3).
General Museum.
Collections: historical; Indian artifacts; natural history; prehistory; art; manuscript collections; photographs; newspapers. Historic Building: 1860 Ruby Valley Pony Express Station.
Research Fields: Northeastern Nevada history.
Facilities: 3,750-vol. library of Northeastern Nevada newspapers & census records on microfilm, & bound books publications, cataloged & cross-referenced photograph and negative file, books & manuscripts available for research on premises; reading room; 30,000 photos with negatives cataloged. Area subject publications, art, Indian-made items, stationery & postcards for sale.
Activities: lectures; films; arts festivals; formally organized education programs for children and adults; permanent & temporary exhibitions; audio & visual history productions.
Publications: Northeastern Nevada Historical Society Quarterly.
Hours & Admission Prices: Tues.-Sat. 9-5, Sun. 1-5. Adults $5, senior & students $3, children 3-12 $1; discount to groups, AAM & AASLH members; members, children under 2 & the last Sunday of every month no charge. Closed New Year's Day; Thanksgiving; Christmas. ♿
Attendance: 30,000 (estimated)
Membership: Individual $20; Family $35; Contributing & Business $50; Sustaining $100; Pioneer Life $500; Life $1,000.

WESTERN FOLKLIFE CENTER, 501 Railroad St., Elko, NV 89801-3752. Tel.: 775-738-7508. Fax: 775-738-2900.
E-mail: wfc@westernfolklife.org
Web Site: www.westernfolklife.org
Key Personnel: Exec. Dir., Charlie Seemann; Artistic Dir., Meg Glasser.
Governing Authority: nonprofit organization.
Cultural Center.
Collections: American West culture.
Activities: special events; rental facility.
Hours & Admission Prices: Mon.-Sat. 10-5. Adults $5, students & seniors 60 & over $3, children 6-12 $1; 1st Sat. of month, members and children 5 & under no charge.

Ely

EAST ELY RAILROAD DEPOT MUSEUM, 1100 Avenue A, Ely, NV 89301-2486. Tel.: 775-289-1663. Fax: 775-289-1664.
E-mail: esm@mwpower.net
Founded: 1992.
Key Personnel: Cur., Sean Pitts; Program Asst., Keith Stone.
Personnel Profile: Full-Time Paid 2; Part-Time Volunteers 1.
Governing Authority: state.
Railroad Depot Museum.
Collections: mining & transportation heritage; Nevada's industrial development; payroll ledgers; right of way maps.
Facilities: library.
Hours & Admission Prices: Mon.-Fri. 8-4. No charge; donations accepted.
Attendance: 15,800 (accurate)

NEVADA NORTHERN RAILWAY MUSEUM, 1100 Avenue A, Ely, NV 89301-2486. Mailing Address: P.O. Box 150040, Ely, NV 89315-0040. Tel.: 775-289-2085. Fax: 775-289-6284.
Web Site: www.nnry.com
Founded: 1985.
Key Personnel: Exec. Dir., Mark S. Bassett; Museum Shop Mgr., Gwyneth Palmer.
Personnel Profile: Full-Time Paid 12; Part-Time Paid 4; Part-Time Volunteers 100.
Governing Authority: private; nonprofit organization. Tax-exempt: 501(c)(3).
History & Transportation Museum.
Collections: railroad equipment; 3 steam locomotives; 8 diesel locomotives; Nevada Northern Railroad artifacts; White Pine County mining rail equipment.
Facilities: railroad yard. Museum-related items for sale.
Activities: guided tours; docent program; formal education programs; temporary exhibitions; steam & diesel train rides. Annual Events: Teen Rail Camp; Adult Rail Camp; Locomotive Rental Program; Polar Express.
Publications: quarterly newsletter, Ghost Tracks.
Hours & Admission Prices: June-Aug. Wed.-Mon. 8-7; Sept.-May Wed.-Mon. 8-5. Adults $4; discounts to National Trust for Historic Preservation members; members no charge. Closed New Year's Eve & Day; Thanksgiving; Christmas Eve & Day. ♿
Attendance: 32,000 (estimated)
Membership: Basic $15; Active $30; Family $50; Tie $75; Centennial $100; Sustaining $250; Patron $500; Life $1,000.

WHITE PINE PUBLIC MUSEUM, 2000 Aultman St., Ely, NV 89301-1824. Tel.: 775-289-4710. Fax: 775-289-4710.
E-mail: wpmuseum@sbcglobal.net
Web Site: wpmuseum.org
Founded: 1959.
Congressional District: 2
Key Personnel: Chm. & C.E.O., Daniel L. Braddock; Dir., Nancy Davis.
Governing Authority: nonprofit. Branch Museum: The McGill Historical Drug Company, #11 Fourth St., Hwy. 93, McGill, NV. Tax-exempt.

General Museum.
Collections: Indian artifacts; geology; mining items; dolls; antiques; historic costumes; natural history items; trains; railroad depot; 50,000 year old short-faced prehistoric cave bear; Shellengerger Cabin; Cherry Creek Depot. McGill Historical Drug Company: 1930 Drug Store with working soda fountains; 1950s-1970s store artifacts; business records, invoices & prescriptions dating back to 1915.
Research Fields: eastern Nevada history.
Facilities: 2,500 sq. ft. exhibit space. Books and other museum related items for sale.
Activities: school exhibitions.
Publications: book, Saving Our Heritage (Ethnic Heritage of Ely, Nevada).
Hours & Admission Prices: Daily 10-4. Adults $4, seniors $3, children 4-12 $2. Closed New Year's; Memorial Day; Thanksgiving; Christmas. ♿
Attendance: 11,000 (estimated)
Membership: Senior Citizen & Student $5; Regular $10; Business $25; Contributing $50; Sustaining $100; Life $500.

Eureka

EUREKA COUNTY COURTHOUSE, 10 S. Main St., Eureka, NV 89316. Tel.: 775-237-5270.
Historic Building: built in 1879.
Collections: local history; period furnishings; paintings; courtroom; walk-in vaults.
Hours & Admission Prices: Call for hours.

EUREKA OPERA HOUSE, 31 S. Main St., Eureka, NV 89316. Mailing Address: Convention & Cultural Arts Center, P.O. Box 284, Eureka, NV 89316-0289. Tel.: 775-237-6006. Fax: 775-237-6040.
Key Personnel: Dir., Wally Cuchine
Historic Building: built in 1880.
Collections: theater history; period furnishings; fine arts.
Facilities: 300-seat auditorium; rental facilities.
Activities: rental facilities; permanent & traveling exhibits.
Hours & Admission Prices: Call for hours.

EUREKA SENTINEL MUSEUM, (M), 10 N. Monroe St., Eureka, NV 89316. Mailing Address: P.O. Box 82, Eureka, NV 89316-0082. Tel.: 775-237-5010. Fax: 775-237-6040.
E-mail: esm@eurekanv.org
Web Site: www.co.eureka.nv.us
Founded: 1982.
Key Personnel: Dir., Ree Taylor.
Personnel Profile: Full-Time Paid 1; Part-Time Paid 1; Part-Time Volunteers 1.
Historic Building: housed in the 1879 Eureka Sentinel Newspaper Building.
Collections: 1860's press equipment; mining; ranching; kitchen; parlor; Fraternal organizations; barbershop.
Facilities: research library.
Hours & Admission Prices: May-Oct. daily 10-6; Nov.-April Tues.-Sat. 10-6. No charge; donations accepted.
Attendance: 5,000 (estimated)

Fallon

CHURCHILL COUNTY MUSEUM AND ARCHIVES, (M), 1050 S. Maine St., Fallon, NV 89406-8815. Tel.: 775-423-3677. Fax: 775-423-3662.
E-mail: ccmuseum@phonewave.net
Web Site: ccmuseum.org
Founded: 1967.
Congressional District: 2
Key Personnel: Pres. (V), Kelly Helton; Dir. & Cur., Jane Pieplow.
Personnel Profile: Full-Time Paid 1; Part-Time Paid 9; Part-Time Volunteers 10.
Governing Authority: county. Parent Institution: Churchill County Museum Association. Tax-exempt: 501(c)(3).
Local History Museum.
Collections: anthropology; archaeology; Churchill County & City of Fallon archives; museum archives; costumes; geology; glass; Indian artifacts; quilts; mineralogy; natural history; 1904 restored store; buggies & wagons; 1909 steam road roller; steam traction engine; horse-drawn transportation; fire fighting; telephone system.
Research Fields: Nevada and Churchill County history & prehistory.
Facilities: Books & museum-related items for sale.
Activities: guided tours; lectures; permanent & temporary exhibitions.
Publications: quarterly newsletter, Musenews; annual journal, Churchill County Museum Association, Churchill County In Focus.
Hours & Admission Prices: March-Nov. Mon.-Sat. 10-5, Sun. 12-5; Dec.-Feb. Mon.-Sat. 10-4, Sun. 12-4. Hidden Cave Tours: 2nd & 4th Sat. of each month, 9:30 am, weather permitting. No charge; donations accepted. Closed Easter; Thanksgiving; Christmas. ♿
Attendance: 12,000 (estimated)
Membership: Junior $15; Senior 60 & over $20; Individual $25; Family $30; Wagonmaster $50; Pioneer & Business $75 & up; Homesteader $100 & up.

Fernley

WIGWAM NATIVE AMERICAN MUSEUM, 225 W. Main St., Fernley, NV 89408. Mailing Address: P.O. Box 97, Fernley, NV 89408-0097. Tel.: 775-575-2573. Fax: 775-575-5280.
History Museum.
Collections: Native American artifacts; arrowheads; stone tools; woven baskets; art; Kachina dolls.
Hours & Admission Prices: Daily.

Gardnerville

DOUGLAS COUNTY HISTORICAL SOCIETY - CARSON VALLEY MUSEUM & CULTURAL CENTER, 1477 Hwy. 395 N., Ste. B, Gardnerville, NV 89410-5214. Tel.: 775-782-2555. Fax: 775-783-8802.
E-mail: dchs@wpti.net
Web Site: historicnevada.org
Founded: 1995.
Congressional District: 2
Key Personnel: Pres. (V), Grace Bower; Museum Shop Mgr., Ellen Martin; Office Mgr., Cindy Rogers.
Personnel Profile: Full-Time Paid 1; Part-Time Paid 1; Part-Time Volunteers 100.
Governing Authority: private; nonprofit organization. Branch Museum: Courthouse Museum Genoa, 2304 Main St., Genoa, NV 89411. Tax-exempt: 501(c)(3).
History Museum: housed in restored 1915 high school.
Collections: Washoe Indian history; Carson Valley history 1850 to present; early settlements; ranching; farming; Main Street businesses; women in history.
Major Exhibits: Gambling, 1/10-12/10.
Research Fields: agriculture; commerce; local towns; newspapers; Washo culture; Basque culture; wild mustangs; local history.
Facilities: library of local history books; educational facilities; 12,000 sq. ft. exhibit space; rental room; classrooms; research library. Museum-related items for sale.
Activities: cultural activities; guided tours; lectures; film & video series; rental room; temporary exhibitions; formal education programs. Annual Events: woman's history program; Young Chautauqua; cemetery tour; Holiday Open House.
Publications: quarterly newsletter; booklets, Keepsake series; Town of Gardnerville: Then & Now.
Hours & Admission Prices: Mon.-Sat. 10-4. Adults $3, children over 6 $2; discounts to AASLH & groups; members no charge. Closed New Year's Day; Carson Valley Day; Independence Day; Nevada Day; Thanksgiving; Christmas Eve & Day. ♿
Attendance: 6,000 (estimated)
Membership: Senior Individual $20; Individual & Senior Couple $30; Family $40; Business Bronze $50; Business Silver $100; Business Gold $500; Business Platinum $1,000.

Genoa

DOUGLAS COUNTY HISTORICAL SOCIETY - GENOA COURTHOUSE MUSEUM, 2304 Main St., Genoa, NV 89411. Mailing Address: 1477 Hwy. 395 N, Suite B, Gardnerville, NV 89410-5570. Tel.: 775-782-4325. Fax: 775-783-8802.
E-mail: dchs@wpti.net
Web Site: historicnevada.org
Founded: 1961.
Congressional District: 2
Key Personnel: Chm. (V) & Museum Shop Mgr., Dee Hart; Pres. (V), Grace Bower; Museum Shop Mgr., Lois Ihran.
Personnel Profile: Part-Time Paid 2; Part-Time Volunteers 100.
Governing Authority: private; nonprofit organization. Parent Institution: Douglas County Historical Society, 1477 Hwy. 395 N, Gardnerville, NV 89410-5214. Tax-exempt: 501(c)(3).
History Museum: housed in 19th-century courthouse.
Collections: original courthouse & jail; registry of early residents in Carson Valley; artifacts 1850-1900.
Research Fields: local history; Snowshoe Thompson; Pony Express; Indian culture.
Facilities: 6,000 sq. ft. exhibit space. Museum-related items for sale.
Activities: guided tours; temporary exhibitions.
Publications: quarterly newsletter.

Hours & Admission Prices: May 5-Oct. 15 daily 10-4:30. Adults $3, children over 6 $2; discounts to groups; members no charge.
Attendance: 4,200 (estimated)
Membership: Senior 65 & over $20; Individual & Senior Couple 65 & over $30; Family $40; Lifetime $500.

MORMON STATION STATE HISTORIC PARK, 2295 Main St., Genoa, NV 89411. Mailing Address: P.O. Box 302, Genoa, NV 89411-0302. Tel.: 775-782-2590 & 687-4379. Fax: 775-687-8972.
E-mail: mormonstation@parks.nv.gov
Web Site: www.parks.nv.gov/ms.htm
Founded: 1947.
Congressional District: 1
Key Personnel: Rgnl. Mgr., Brad Kosch; Park Supvr., Suzanne Sturtevant.
Personnel Profile: Full-Time Paid 1; Part-Time Paid 2; Part-Time Volunteers 8.
Governing Authority: state. Nevada Div. of State Parks, 1300 S. Curry St. Carson City, NV 89703-5202. Tax-exempt: 501(c)(3).
Park, Museum & Visitor Center: site of first building in the state.
Collections: artifacts. Historic Building: 1851 Mormon Station, reconstructed in 1947.
Facilities: picnic area.
Activities: permanent exhibits.
Publications: descriptive brochure.
Hours & Admission Prices: Museum: May to mid-Oct. daily 9-4:30. Admission $2; children 12 & under no charge. ♿
Attendance: 95,000 (estimated)

Hawthorne

MINERAL COUNTY MUSEUM, 400 Tenth St., Hawthorne, NV 89415. Mailing Address: P.O. Box 1584, Hawthorne, NV 89415-1584. Tel.: 775-945-5142.
E-mail: gm@mcmuseum.hawthorne.nv.us
Web Site: www.web0.greatbasin.net/~mcmuseum/
Governing Authority: nonprofit.
History Museum.
Collections: local history; early 1800s Mission Bells; mining, fire & railroad equipment; horse drawn vehicles; turn of the century pharmacy; wildlife & fossils; rocks & minerals; Victorian furniture; cameras; vintage clothing, shoes & hats.
Facilities: Museum-related items for sale.
Hours & Admission Prices: April-Oct. Tues.-Sat. 11-5; Nov.-March Tues.-Sat. 12-4; other times by appointment. No charge.

Henderson

CLARK COUNTY MUSEUM, 1830 S. Boulder Hwy., Henderson, NV 89002-8502. Tel.: 702-455-7955. Fax: 702-455-7948.
E-mail: ryz@co.clark.nv.us
Web Site: www.co.clark.nv.us
Formerly: Clark County Heritage Museum
Founded: 1968.
Congressional District: 1
Key Personnel: Museum Admin., Mark Hall-Patton; Cur. Exhibits., Dawna Jolliff; Cur. Education, Christie Leavitt; Registrar, Suzanne Turgeon; Museum Senior Financial Office Specialist, Jeanette Spittell; Museum Guild Pres. (V), Carolyn Boes; Museum Program Specialist, Malcom Vuksich; Asst. Cur. Education, Kitty Heckendorf.
Personnel Profile: Full-Time Paid 6; Part-Time Paid 21; Part-Time Volunteers 115.
Governing Authority: county government. Parent Institution: Clark County Parks & Recreation Dept. Subsidiary Institutions: Searchlight Historical Museum, Searchlight, NV; Howard W. Cannon Aviation Museum at McCarran International Airport. Tax-exempt: 170(B)A.1.
History Museum.
Collections: prehistoric; southwest Indians; miners; 1880 ghost town; ranchers; gambling exhibits; cultural history; aviation history collection. Historic Buildings: 1912 Beckley House; 1930s P.S. Goumond House; 1931 Historic Boulder City Depot; 1890s Donald W. Reynolds printshop replica; 1940s Henderson Townsite house; 1900s Barcus-Giles house; 1935 Boulder City/Dam house; 1966 candlelight wedding chapel; 1911 railroad cottage; 1935 Grand Canyon Airlines ticket office; 1950 Esslinger barn; 1966 Candelight Wedding Chapel.
Major Exhibits: Urbanizing the Desert (T), 4/10-7/10.
Research Fields: Southwestern history; southern Nevada history & aviation.
Facilities: searchlight Nevada museum exhibit center; cactus garden; nature trail; outdoor exhibits; Heritage St. project area; Mojave outdoor classroom with 2 acres of botanical specimens. Museum-related items for sale.
Activities: permanent, temporary & traveling exhibits; special programs; historic preservation projects; video. Museum Sponsors: Native American Festival in April; Ghosts and Goblins of Nevada's Past Clark County Museum Guild Community Program in October.
Publications: Desert Airways; A Short History of Clark County Aviation: 1920-1948; Asphalt Memories, Origins of Some of the Street Names in Clark County.
Hours & Admission Prices: Daily 9-4:30; call for information on holiday hours; bus tours by appointment. Adults $1.50, children under 16 & senior citizens $1; members no charge. Closed New Year's Day; Thanksgiving; Christmas. ♿
Attendance: 43,214 (accurate)
Membership: Senior & Student $15; Individual $25; Family $35; Contributor $50; Sponsor $100-$149; Business Sponsor $150-$249; Donor $250-$249; Benefactor & Business Patron $500-$999; Silver Patron $1,000 & up.

HENDERSON BIRD VIEWING PRESERVE, 2400 Moser Dr., Henderson, NV 89011-4490. Tel.: 702-267-4180.
Bird Preserve.
Collections: 200 species of birds.
Facilities: 147 acre preserve; nature trails. Museum-related items for sale.
Activities: educational programs.
Hours & Admission Prices: Daily 6am-3pm; groups by appointment. ♿

Incline Village

THUNDERBIRD LODGE PRESERVATION SOCIETY, 5000 Hwy. 28, Incline Village, NV 89451. Mailing Address: P.O. Box 6812, Incline Village, NV 89450-6812. Tel.: 775-832-8750. Fax: 775-832-8798.
E-mail: askus@thunderbirdlodge.org
Web Site: www.thunderbirdlodge.org
Preservation Society: listed on the National Register of Historic Places.
Collections: local history; period furnishings; personal artifacts. Historic Buildings: main house; card house; caretaker's cottage; cook/butler's house; elephant garage; admiral's house; boathouse; gatehouse.
Activities: guided tours.
Hours & Admission Prices: June-Sept.

Las Vegas

ATOMIC TESTING MUSEUM, (M), 755 E. Flamingo Rd., Las Vegas, NV 89119-7363. Tel.: 702-794-5161. Fax: 702-794-5155.
Web Site: atomictestingmuseum.org
Key Personnel: Dir., William G. Johnson, Ph.D.; Office Mgr., Jennifer Ervin; Devel. & Community Outreach, Peggy Hallterberg; Registrar, Vanya Scott; Museum Store & Operations Mgr., Karen Green; Cur. Education & Exhibits, Ellen Leigh; Office Asst., Rachel Warrick; Mktg. & Events Dir., Maggie Smith.
Governing Authority: nonprofit organization. Parent Institution: Nevada Test Site Historical Foundation. Tax-exempt: 501(c)(3).
Science & Technology Museum.
Collections: Nevada Test Site history; narratives; environmental re-creations; theatrical devices; iconic artifacts.
Facilities: 8,000 sq. ft. exhibit space. Museum-related items for sale.
Activities: multimedia presentations; environmental re-creations; narratives.
Hours & Admission Prices: Mon.-Sat. 9-5, Sun. 1-5. Adults $12, seniors, military & students $9; members and children 6 & under no charge. Closed New Year's Day; Thanksgiving; Christmas.

THE AUTO COLLECTIONS AT THE IMPERIAL PALACE, 3535 Las Vegas Blvd., S., Las Vegas, NV 89109-8921. Tel.: 702-794-3174. Fax: 702-369-7430.
Car Museum.
Collections: over 250 automobiles including period cars, classic cars, muscle cars, custom hot rods, movie cars, celebrity cars, restored cars, race cars, Indy 500 race & pace cars, & concept cars.
Facilities: Cars for sale.
Activities: buy, sell or trade vehicles.
Hours & Admission Prices: Daily 10-6:30.

BELLAGIO CONSERVATORY & BOTANICAL GARDENS, 3600 S. Las Vegas Blvd., Las Vegas, NV 89109-4303. Tel.: 702-693-7111.
Botanical Gardens.
Collections: over 7,500 plants including orchids, ferns, lilies, & tropical flowers.
Facilities: 14,000 sq. ft. conservatory.
Activities: Seasonal Themes: Chinese New Year; Spring Celebration; Summer Garden Party; Harvest Show; Holiday Show.
Hours & Admission Prices: Daily. No charge.

BELLAGIO GALLERY OF FINE ARTS, 3600 Las Vegas Blvd. S., Las Vegas, NV 89109-4339. Tel.: 702-693-7871. Fax: 702-693-7872.
E-mail: fineartgallery@bellagioresort.com
Web Site: www.bellagio.com/amenities/gallery-of-fine-art.aspx
Founded: 1998.
Art Museum.
Collections: works by national & international artists.
Facilities: 2,576 sq. ft. exhibit space. Museum-related items for sale.
Activities: intern program; school group tours; school & library outreach.
Hours & Admission Prices: Sun.-Thurs. 10-6, Fri.-Sat. 10-7. Adults $15, NV residents & seniors 65 and over $12, students, teachers, & military $10; children under 12 no charge. ♿
Membership: Student, Teacher, & Senior $35; Individual $50; Dual $75; Family $100.

CENTAUR ART GALLERIES, Fashion Show Mall, 3200 S. Las Vegas Blvd., Ste. 1040, Las Vegas, NV 89109-0728. Tel.: 702-737-1234.
Art Gallery.
Collections: works of art from the 16th century to modern times; paintings; sculpture.
Activities: permanent & temporary exhibits.
Hours & Admission Prices: Mon.-Sat. 10-9, Sun. 11-7. No charge.

DONNA BEAM FINE ART GALLERY, UNLV, 4505 Maryland Pkwy., Las Vegas, NV 89154-9900. Mailing Address: 4505 Maryland Pkwy., Box 5002, Las Vegas, NV 89154-9900. Tel.: 702-895-3893. Fax: 702-895-3751.
E-mail: jerry.schefcik@unlv.edu
Web Site: donnabeamgallery.unlv.edu/
Founded: 1960.
Congressional District: 1
Key Personnel: Dir., Jerry A. Schefcik.
Personnel Profile: Full-Time Paid 1; Interns 3.
Governing Authority: university. Parent Institution: University of Nevada Las Vegas. Tax-exempt: 170(b)(1)(A).
Art Museum & Center.
Collections: contemporary American art; Dorothy and Herbert Vogel collection: Fifty Works for Fifty States.
Research Fields: contemporary art.
Activities: gallery talks; lectures; formally organized education programs for undergraduate college students; temporary & traveling exhibitions.
Publications: exhibition catalogues; brochures.
Hours & Admission Prices: Mon.-Fri. 9-5, Sat. 10-2. No charge. Closed major holidays. ♿
Attendance: 8,000 (estimated)

HOWARD W. CANNON AVIATION MUSEUM, McCarran International Airport, 5757 Wayne Newton Blvd., Las Vegas, NV 89119. Mailing Address: 1830 S. Boulder Hwy., Henderson, NV 89002-8502. Tel.: 702-455-7968. Fax: 702-455-7948.
E-mail: mhp@co.clark.nv.us
Web Site: www.co.clark.nv.us/Parks/Clark_County_Museum.htm
Formerly: McCarran Aviation Heritage Museum
Founded: 1993.
Key Personnel: Admin., Mark P. Hall-Patton; Registrar, Suzanne Turgeon.
Personnel Profile: Full-Time Paid 2; Part-Time Paid 3; Part-Time Volunteers 3.
Governing Authority: county/regional government. Tax-exempt: 170(b)(1)(A).
Aviation Museum.
Collections: history of aviation of southern Nevada; commercial, general & military; uniforms; insignia; desk models; instruments; souvenirs; documents; aircraft, a Cessna 172 which holds the world endurance aloft record; automobile, 1956 Ford Thunderbird outfitted as a crashwagon used at the airport in the late 1950s; two aircraft engines an R-4360 & R-670; 38 five-minute history videos.
Research Fields: commercial & general aviation in Southern Nevada; world endurance flight 1958-1959.
Facilities: 3,500-vol. library of commercial & military aviation history and aviation history magazines available to the public; 3,000 sq. ft. exhibit space in McCarran International Airport.
Publications: monographs, Desert Airways; Barnstorming the Desert, The Life of Randall Henderson; videos, History of Aviation in Southern Nevada; They Flew On and On: The 1958-59 World Endurance Flight & A View from the Top: A History of McCarran International Airport.
Hours & Admission Prices: Airport Exhibits: 24 hours daily. Office: Mon.-Fri. 8-5. No charge. ♿
Attendance: 440,000 (estimated)

LAS VEGAS ART MUSEUM, 9600 W. Sahara Ave., Las Vegas, NV 89117-5959. Tel.: 702-360-8000. Fax: 702-360-8080.
E-mail: info@lasvegasartmuseum.org
Web Site: www.lasvegasartmuseum.org
Founded: 1950.
Congressional District: 1
Key Personnel: Bd. Pres., Gerald Facciani; Exec. Dir., Libby Lumpkin; Cur., Dr. James Mann; Museum Shop Mgr., Don Jones.
Personnel Profile: Full-Time Paid 6; Full-Time Volunteers 1; Part-Time Paid 3; Part-Time Volunteers 220; Interns 1.
Governing Authority: nonprofit organization. Tax-exempt: 501(c)(3).
Art Museum.
Collections: contemporary international art.
Activities: classes; lectures; art in schools.
Publications: quarterly newsletter; exhibition catalogues.
Hours & Admission Prices: Tues.-Sat. 10-5, Sun. 1-5. Adults $6, senior citizens $5, students $3; children 12 & under and members no charge. ♿
Attendance: 50,000 (estimated)
Membership: Student $25; Senior $35; Family $50; Supporting $100; Sustaining $250; Sponsor $500; Benefactor $1,000; Patron $2,500; Pacesetter $5,000; Leadership Contributor $10,000.

LAS VEGAS CLUB SPORTS HALL OF FAME, 18 E. Fremont St., Las Vegas, NV 89101-5678. Tel.: 702-385-1664.
Sports Museum.
Collections: sports memorabilia; photographs; World Series bat; autographed baseballs; gloves; jerseys; Hall of Fame inductees.
Hours & Admission Prices: Daily. No charge.

LAS VEGAS INTERNATIONAL SCOUTING MUSEUM, 2915 W. Charleston Blvd., Ste. 2, Las Vegas, NV 89102-1903. Tel.: 702-878-7268. Fax: 702-822-2020.
E-mail: lvismpresident@aol.com
Web Site: www.worldscoutingmuseum.org
Founded: 1996.
Key Personnel: Exec. Dir., Robert Lynn Horne, M.D.; Cur., James Arriola.
Personnel Profile: Part-Time Volunteers 5.
Governing Authority: private; nonprofit organization.
Scouting Museum.
Collections: memorabilia.
Hours & Admission Prices: By appointment only. No charge; donations accepted.
Membership: Friend $25; Associate $50; Contributing $100; Sustaining $250; Patron $500; Benefactor $1,000; Life $2,500.

LAS VEGAS NATURAL HISTORY MUSEUM, (M), 900 Las Vegas Blvd., N., Las Vegas, NV 89101-1112. Tel.: 702-384-3466. Fax: 702-384-5343.
E-mail: dino@lvnhm.org
Web Site: www.lvnhm.org
Founded: 1989.
Congressional District: 1
Key Personnel: Dir., Marilyn Gillespie; Chm. (V), Denny Weddle; Museum Shop Mgr., Bobbi Gillespie.
Personnel Profile: Full-Time Paid 6; Part-Time Paid 14; Part-Time Volunteers 31.
Governing Authority: nonprofit organization. Tax-exempt: 501(c)(3).
Natural History Museum.
Collections: sharks; prehistoric dinosaurs & animals; world wildlife; Nevada wildlife habitat; marine life; live sharks.
Facilities: 27,000 sq. ft. exhibit space; educational & group meeting space; activity area for children. Prints, books, toys & other gift items for sale.
Activities: guided tours; lectures; organized education programs for children; participatory, loan, traveling & temporary exhibitions; museum extension academy.
Publications: quarterly newsletter.
Hours & Admission Prices: Daily 9-4. Adults $8, senior citizens, students & military $7, children 3-11 $4; discounts to groups, AAA & AAM members; children 2 & under and members no charge. ♿
Attendance: 87,473 (accurate)
Membership: Individual $30; Grandparent $35; Family $45; Honor Roll $100; Friends $250.

LAS VEGAS SPRINGS PRESERVE, 333 S. Valley View Blvd., Las Vegas, NV 89107. Mailing Address: P.O. Box 98947, Las Vegas, NV 89193-8947. Tel.: 702-822-7700. Fax: 702-822-8700.
E-mail: springs.preserve@springspreserve.org
Web Site: www.springspreserve.org
Founded: 2007.
Congressional District: 1
Key Personnel: Mng. Dir., Elizabeth Herridge; Gen. Cur., Jay Nichols; Education & Volunteerism Mgr., Marcel Parent; Mgr. Guest Svcs., Mike Dagenais; Museum Shop Mgr., Christie Brown.

Personnel Profile: Full-Time Paid 69; Part-Time Paid 23.
Governing Authority: Parent Institution: Las Vegas Valley Water District. Tax-exempt.
Historical & Cultural Complex.
Collections: local history; gardens; historic buildings.
Major Exhibits: Robert Beckman: Elemental Landscape, 11/09-1/7/10; S A Schimmel Gold: Junk Mail Art, 11/14/09-3/14/10; ACT Responsible-Advertising Sustainability, 11/14/09-3/14/10; Don Simon-Unnaturalism, 3/26/10-5/31/10; Nevada Watercolor Society Spring Show 2010, 5/7/10-7/11/10; Springs Preserve Photo Contest 2010, 7/16/10-9/12/10; Periphery, 9/18/10-1/16/11.
Research Fields: restoration ecology; wildlife biology; Las Vegas history; archaeology.
Facilities: 10,000-vol. library; 180 acres; gardens; nature trails; 2,000-seat amphitheater; movie theater; cafe; meeting area. Museum-related items for sale.
Activities: school outreach programs; special events; permanent & temporary exhibits; intern program; research; tours; lectures.
Publications: quarterly educational program guide; member newsletter.
Hours & Admission Prices: Call for hours. Adults $18.95. Annual: individual $25, family $60. Closed Thanksgiving; Christmas. ♿
Attendance: 200,000 (accurate)
Membership: Individual $40; Premier Individual $70; Family $75; Premier Family $125.

LIBERACE MUSEUM & FOUNDATION, 1775 E. Tropicana Ave. (at Spencer), Las Vegas, NV 89119-6529. Tel.: 702-798-5595. Fax: 702-798-7386.
E-mail: info@liberace.org
Web Site: www.liberace.org
Founded: 1979.
Congressional District: 1
Key Personnel: Exec. Dir., R. Darin Hollingsworth; Chm. (V), Jeff Koep; Pres. (V) & Mgr. Museum Operations, Tanya Combs; Mgr. Groups & Events, Carole Fishman; Museum Shop Mgr., Connie Spaan.
Personnel Profile: Full-Time Paid 14; Part-Time Paid 12; Part-Time Volunteers 15.
Governing Authority: board of trustees; nonprofit organization. Parent Institution: Liberace Foundation for the Performing & Creative Arts. Tax-exempt: 501(c)(3).
Specialized Museum: pertaining to entertainer-pianist, Liberace.
Collections: pianos; jewelry; cars; photographs; awards; performing & creative arts; costumes; paper, audio & video archives; furnishings.
Research Fields: personal & professional history of Liberace; recipients of Liberace Foundation Scholarships; Las Vegas entertainment history; costumes; pianos; cars; jewelry.
Facilities: 15,000 sq. ft. exhibit space; cafe. Museum-related items for sale.
Activities: daily guided tours; Liberace scholars performances; self-guided tours; rental facility.
Publications: brochure; newsletter.
Hours & Admission Prices: Museum: Tues.-Sat. 10-5, Sun. 12-4. Requested Donation: adults $15, senior citizens 65 & over and students $10; discounts to tour groups; members & children under 6 no charge. Cabaret Show: Tues.-Wed. & Sat. 1pm. Admission $17.50. Closed New Year's Day; Easter; Thanksgiving; Christmas. ♿
Attendance: 50,414 (accurate)
Membership: Student & Senior $25; Individual $35; Family & Dual $50; Silver Candelabra $100; Gold Candelabra $500; Platinum Candelabra $1,000.

LIED DISCOVERY CHILDREN'S MUSEUM, 833 Las Vegas Blvd. N., Las Vegas, NV 89101-2059. Tel.: 702-382-3445. Fax: 702-382-0592.
E-mail: info@ldcm.org
Web Site: www.ldcm.org
Founded: 1984.
Congressional District: 1
Key Personnel: Exec. Dir., Linda Quinn; Pres., Judy Cebulko.
Personnel Profile: Full-Time Paid 15; Part-Time Paid 25; Part-Time Volunteers 50.
Governing Authority: nonprofit organization. Tax-exempt: 501(c)(3).
Children's Museum.
Collections: hands-on exhibits.
Major Exhibits: Little Builders (T), 1/10-5/10; Torn From Home (T), 9/10-1/11.
Facilities: library.
Activities: guided tours; organized education programs for children; docent program; participatory exhibits. Museum Sponsors: Artist Residencies, Cultural Celebrations; Science Demonstrations; Early Childhood Pavilion & Programs; Youth Explainer Program.
Publications: quarterly newsletter, Discovery News; teacher materials; family guides.
Hours & Admission Prices: Tues.-Fri. 9-4, Sat. 10-5, Sun. 12-5. Adults $8, children 1-17 $7; discounts to ASTC & AYM members; members no charge. ♿
Attendance: 100,000 (estimated)
Membership: Basic (4 people) $60; Discovery Club $125; Science Tower Club $275; Director's Club $500; President's Club $1,000; Museum Associates $2,500; Building Block Council $5,000; Kid's Corner $10,000; Stars for Children $25,000.

MADAME-TUSSAUD'S WAX MUSEUM, LAS VEGAS, 3377 Las Vegas Blvd. S., Ste. 2001, Las Vegas, NV 89109-8910. Tel.: 702-862-7800. Fax: 702-862-7851.
E-mail: info@madametussaudslv.com
Web Site: www.mtvegas.com
Key Personnel: Head Mktg., Rosita Chapman
Wax Museum.
Collections: over 100 wax figures of celebrities, politicians, athletes & legends.
Activities: parties; special events.
Hours & Admission Prices: Call for hours & admission prices.

THE NEON MUSEUM, 821 Las Vegas Blvd. N., Las Vegas, NV 89101-2030. Tel.: 702-387-6366. Fax: 702-477-7751.
E-mail: info@neonmuseum.org
Web Site: www.neonmuseum.org
General Museum.
Collections: neon signs from 1940 to present.
Hours & Admission Prices: By appointment. Office: Tues.-Sat. 11-5. Tours: adults $15.

*** NEVADA STATE MUSEUM, LAS VEGAS, (M),** 700 Twin Lakes Dr., Las Vegas, NV 89107-2104. Tel.: 702-486-5205. Fax: 702-486-5172.
Web Site: www.nevadaculture.org
Formerly: Nevada State Museum & Historical Society
Founded: 1982.
Congressional District: 1
Key Personnel: Exec. Dir., David Millman; Chm. (V), Robert Stohldal; Cur. History, Dennis McBride; Cur. Education, Barbara Slivac; Cur. Natural History, Barbara Adams; Dir. Exhibits, Thomas Dyer; Museum Shop Mgr., Harvey Foutz.
Personnel Profile: Full-Time Paid 15; Part-Time Paid 1; Part-Time Volunteers 25; Interns 2.
Governing Authority: state. Nevada Department of Cultural Affairs. Tax-exempt: 501(c)(3).
General Museum.
Collections: southern Nevada history, natural history & anthropology; paleontology; photographs; manuscripts; newspapers; Las Vegas history.
Research Fields: Nevada history; Las Vegas newspapers; Las Vegas neon signs; butterflies; historic preservation.
Facilities: 3,000-vol. Cahlan library available to the public; 100-seat auditorium; 13,000 sq. ft. exhibit space.
Activities: guided tours; lectures; films; organized education programs for adults & children; docent program; participatory, loan, temporary & traveling exhibitions.
Publications: quarterly scholarly publication; exhibit catalogs.
Hours & Admission Prices: Daily 9-5. Adults $4, senior citizens $3; discounts to AAM, Nevada Museums Assoc. & Western Museums Assoc. members; children & members no charge. Closed New Year's Day; Thanksgiving; Christmas. ♿
Attendance: 65,000 (accurate)
Membership: Student & Senior Citizen $15; Regular $25; Family $35; Sustaining $50; Contributing $100; Departmental Fellow $250; Benefactor $500; Patron $1,000. Business Support Program for Corporate & Commercial members.

OLD LAS VEGAS MORMON FORT STATE HISTORIC PARK, 500 E. Washington Ave., Las Vegas, NV 89101-1000. Tel.: 702-486-3511. Fax: 702-486-3734.
E-mail: oldfort@parks.nv.gov
Web Site: www.parks.nv.gov/olvmf.htm
Key Personnel: Park Supvr., Scott Egy
History Museum.
Collections: pioneer settlers; personal artifacts; period furnishings; historic building.
Activities: educational programs; guided tours.
Hours & Admission Prices: Tues.-Sat. 8-4:30. Adults 12 & over $1.

OUT OF THIS WORLD MUSEUM, 3019 McLeod Dr., Las Vegas, NV 89121-2239. Tel.: 702-457-1377.
E-mail: thirdeyemike@cox.net
Web Site: www.relationshipfever.com
Formerly: Museum of Ancient Artifacts
Founded: 1990.
Congressional District: 8
Key Personnel: C.E.O. (V), Treas. & Cur., Michael J. Kurban; Chm. (V), Archivist, Education & Museum Shop Mgr., Lynn McCormick; Public Rels., Grace De La Riva; Security, Rick Enrique.
Personnel Profile: Full-Time Volunteers 2; Part-Time Volunteers 3.
Governing Authority: private; nonprofit organization. Tax-exempt: 501(c)(3).
Ancient Artifacts Museum.
Collections: rare photographs & gems; tapestries; artwork; books & artifacts from 500 AD to present; botanical & geological collections.
Research Fields: psychic phenomena; Art: oils, statues, history.
Facilities: 200-vol. library of books on occult, religion, health areas available to the public; botanical garden; educational facilities; 1,500 sq. ft. exhibit space. Museum-related items for sale.
Activities: films; formal education programs for adults; guided tours; lectures; school loan service; broadcast programs. Annual Events: workshops on specialty photography in January; Unusual art in May; lectures on psychic phenomena in November.
Publications: monthly newsletter, News and Views.
Hours & Admission Prices: Wed. & Sun. 11-7. Adults $5, senior citizens, students & children 12 & under $3; discounts on tour groups 15 or more & family of 6 or more; member adults no charge. Closed New Year's Eve; Easter; Independence Day; Christmas.
Attendance: 1,000 (estimated)
Membership: Adult $20; Family $30.

RED ROCK CANYON VISITOR CENTER AND NATIONAL CONSERVATION AREA, 1000 Scenic Loop Dr., HCR 33, Las Vegas, NV 89124. Mailing Address: Box 5500, Las Vegas, NV 89124. Tel.: 702-515-5350.
Web Site: www.redrockcanyonlv.org
National Park.
Collections: geology; botanical; zoological.
Facilities: hiking trails; picnic areas. Books for sale.
Activities: hiking.
Hours & Admission Prices: Daily 8-4:30. Adults $5.

SHELBY AUTOMOBILES, 6755 Speedway Blvd., Las Vegas, NV 89115-1761. Tel.: 702-942-7325. Fax: 702-932-6272.
Automobile Museum.
Collections: sports cars.
Facilities: cafe.
Hours & Admission Prices: Call for hours.

SOUTHERN NEVADA ZOOLOGICAL-BOTANICAL PARK, 1775 N. Rancho Dr., Las Vegas, NV 89106-1020. Tel.: 702-647-4685. Fax: 702-648-5955.
Zoo.
Collections: over 150 species of plants & animals; endangered cats; chimpanzee; eagles; ostriches; emus; parrots; wallabies; flamingos; reptiles; cycads; bamboos.
Facilities: 3 acre park.
Hours & Admission Prices: Daily 9-5. Adults $8, children 2-12 and seniors 62 & over $6; children under 2 no charge.

UNLV MARJORIE BARRICK MUSEUM, (M), 4505 Maryland Pkwy., Las Vegas, NV 89154-9900. Mailing Address: P.O. Box 454012, Las Vegas, NV 89154-4012. Tel.: 702-895-3381. Fax: 702-895-5737.
E-mail: unlvarboretum@unlv.edu
Web Site: hrc.nevada.edu/museum/
Founded: 1967.
Congressional District: 1
Key Personnel: Dir., Dr. Klaus Stetzenbach; Cur. Exhibits, Aurore Giguet; Cur. Invertebrates, Dr. William Pratt; Cur. Herpetology, Alex Heindl; Cur. Ornithology, Dr. John Klicka; Registrar, Melissa Batterson.
Personnel Profile: Full-Time Paid 8; Part-Time Paid 4.
Governing Authority: university. Parent Institution: University of Nevada System, Las Vegas & Reno, NE. Tax-exempt: 501(c)(3).
Cultural & Natural History Museum.
Collections: archaeology, ethnology & anthropology with emphasis on cultures of the Southwest United States and Mesoamerica; ornithology; entomology; invertebrate & vertebrate zoology.
Research Fields: archaeology; ornithology; vertebrate & invertebrate zoology; entomology & environmental sciences.
Facilities: archaeological, ornithological & environmental research centers; banquet facilities.
Activities: permanent & traveling exhibitions; permanent & traveling exhibits. Annual Events: Braunstein Symposium of Pre-Columbian Art.
Publications: notes from the Braunstein Symposium.
Hours & Admission Prices: Mon.-Fri. 8-4:45, Sat. 10-2. No charge; donations accepted. Closed national & state holidays. ♿
Attendance: 30,000 (estimated)

THE WALKER AFRICAN AMERICAN MUSEUM & RESEARCH CENTER, 705 W. Van Buren Ave., Las Vegas, NV 89106-3042. Tel.: 702-647-2242; 399-8016; 649-2238.
E-mail: walkeraamuseum@aol.com
Web Site: www.churchesinlasvegas.com/walkermuseum
Founded: 1993.
Key Personnel: Pres. (V), Dir. & Cur., Gwendolyn Walker; Devel., Cynthia Lemley; Education, Margaret Crawford; Public Rels., Lillian McMorris; Treas., Juanita Walker; Security, Jimmie Nunley, Jr.; Museum Shop Mgr., Vivian Cook.
Personnel Profile: Full-Time Volunteers 8; Part-Time Volunteers 4.
Governing Authority: nonprofit. Tax-exempt: 501(c)(3).
History Museum.
Collections: books; publications; documents; artifacts; articles on African Americans in Nevada from 1800s to present.
Research Fields: early business owned by African Americans in Nevada.
Facilities: library; 800 sq. ft. exhibit space. Museum-related items for sale.
Activities: guided tours; arts festival; films. Annual Event: African American Cultural Arts Festival.
Publications: annual booklet, Black Pioneers of Nevada; book, From the Kitchen to the Boarder, Nevada's Black Women; Courage, Strength & Faith, Nevada's Black Men.
Hours & Admission Prices: Tues.-Sat. 10-6. Adults $2, children $1. Closed Christmas.
Attendance: 750 (estimated)
Membership: Members $25; Supporting $100.

Laughlin

DON LAUGHLIN'S CLASSIC CAR COLLECTION, Riverside Resort Hotel & Casino, 1650 S. Casino Dr., Laughlin, NV 89029-1512. Tel.: 800-227-3849; 702-298-2535.
Key Personnel: Cur., Mark Osborn
Classic Car Collection.
Collections: over 80 automobiles, trucks & motocycles.
Hours & Admission Prices: First Floor Show Room: daily 10-10. Third Floor Show Room: Sun.-Thurs. 9am-10pm, Fri.-Sat. 9am-11pm. No charge. ♿
Attendance: 300,000 (estimated)

Logandale

OLD LOGANDALE SCHOOL HISTORICAL AND CULTURAL SOCIETY, 3011 N. Moapa Valley Blvd., Logandale, NV 89021-0065. Mailing Address: P.O. Box 65, Logandale, NV 89021. Tel.: 702-398-7272 & 7273.
Historic Building: housed in the former Logandale School; built in 1899.
Collections: local history & culture; period furnishings; personal artifacts; photographs.
Hours & Admission Prices: Call for hours.

Lovelock

PERSHING COUNTY COURTHOUSE, 400 Main St., Lovelock, NV 89419. Mailing Address: P.O. Box 986, Lovelock, NV 89419-0986. Tel.: 702-273-7144. Fax: 702-273-7647.
Historic Building: built in 1919. Listed on the National Register of Historic Places.
Collections: local history & culture; photographs; period furnishings; personal artifacts.
Hours & Admission Prices: Mon.-Fri. 10-4. No charge.

PERSHING COUNTY MARZEN HOUSE MUSEUM, 25 Marzen Lane, Lovelock, NV 89419. Mailing Address: P.O. Box 861, Lovelock, NV 89419-0861. Tel.: 775-273-7213.
Historic House Museum: built in 1874.
Collections: mining equipment; furnishings; Native American artifacts.
Hours & Admission Prices: May-Oct. daily 9-4; Nov.-April Mon.-Fri. 9-1:30. No charge; donations accepted.

McGill

HISTORIC MCGILL DRUG COMPANY, U.S. 93 E., McGill, NV 89318. Mailing Address: P.O. Box 757, McGill, NV 89318-0757. Tel.: 775-235-7082. Fax: 775-235-7802.
E-mail: bhaven1@sbcglobal.net
Web Site: www.mcgilldrugstoremuseum.org
Key Personnel: Dir., Evie Pinneo
Historic Building: built in 1909.
Collections: drugstore history & memorabilia; period furnishings.
Hours & Admission Prices: By appointment.

Mesquite

SPIRIT WIND GALLERY, 742 Pioneer Blvd., Mesquite, NV 89027-8835. Tel.: 702-346-5136; 877-793-4968.
Art Gallery.
Collections: Native American art; paintings; sculpture; masks; jewelry.
Hours & Admission Prices: Call for hours.

VIRGIN VALLEY HERITAGE MUSEUM, 35 W. Mesquite Blvd., Mesquite, NV 89027-4707. Tel.: 702-346-5705.
Web Site: www.mesquitenv.gov/parkfacility/virginvalleymuseum
Founded: 1985.
Key Personnel: C.E.O. & Dir., Don Montegomery
Heritage Museum.
Collections: local history; pioneer artifacts from late 1800s to early 1900s; Skookum dolls; sewing machine; photographs; movie projector; furnishings; slot machine; quilts; wedding dresses.
Hours & Admission Prices: Tues.-Sat. 10-4. No charge; donations accepted. Closed most holidays.

Nixon

PYRAMID LAKE PAIUTE CULTURAL CENTER, 709 State St., Nixon, NV 89424. Mailing Address: P.O. Box 256, Nixon, NV 89424-0256. Tel.: 775-574-1088. Fax: 775-574-1090.
Cultural Center.
Collections: tribal history & culture; photographs; personal artifacts.
Hours & Admission Prices: Summer: Mon.-Sat. 8-4:30; Winter: Mon.-Fri. 8-4:30.

North Las Vegas

LEFT OF CENTER ART GALLERY & STUDIO, 2207 W. Gowan, North Las Vegas, NV 89032-7961. Tel.: 702-647-7378. Fax: 702-647-7340.
Key Personnel: Dir., Vicki Richardson.
Governing Authority: nonprofit organization. Tax-exempt: 501(c)(3).
Art Gallery.
Collections: works by national & local artists.
Activities: workshops; lectures; classes.
Hours & Admission Prices: Call for hours.

THE PLANETARIUM - COLLEGE OF SOUTHERN NEVADA, 3200 E. Cheyenne Ave., North Las Vegas, NV 89030-4296. Mailing Address: Sort Code S1A, 3200 E. Cheyenne Ave., North Las Vegas, NV 89030-4296. Tel.: 702-651-4759 & 4138.
Founded: 1977.
Congressional District: 1
Planetarium.
Collections: Evans & Sutherland Digistar 3 projects images of the hemisphere onto the theater dome.
Facilities: theater. Museum-related items for sale.
Activities: educational programs.
Hours & Admission Prices: Call for hours. ♿
Attendance: 17,890 (accurate)

Overton

LOST CITY MUSEUM, (M), 721 S. Moapa Blvd., Overton, NV 89040. Mailing Address: P.O. Box 807, Overton, NV 89040-0807. Tel.: 702-397-2193. Fax: 702-397-8987.
E-mail: lostcity@nevadaculture.org
Web Site: www.nevadaculture.org
Founded: 1935.
Congressional District: 1
Key Personnel: Dir., Kathryne Olson; Admin. Asst., Janie Shakespear.
Personnel Profile: Full-Time Paid 6; Part-Time Paid 2; Part-Time Volunteers 15.
Governing Authority: state. Tax-exempt.
Archaeology Museum.
Collections: Puebloan artifacts excavated from Pueblo Grande de Nevada, Lost City; Paiute Indian artifacts; historic baskets; Southwestern Indian crafts; minerals; fossils; historic Mormon & mining artifacts.
Research Fields: Puebloan archaeology; historic archaeology; historic architecture; Paiute ethnology; Mormon history.
Facilities: 400-vol. library pertaining to archaeology, history, museum techniques & natural history available to the public. Books, Native American crafts, rocks, minerals & other museum-related items for sale.
Activities: guided tours; lectures; docent program; loan, temporary & traveling exhibitions; school loan service.
Publications: brochure, Nevada's Lost City Museum; booklet, Nevada's Lost City: A Treasure Trove of Mystery.
Hours & Admission Prices: Thurs.-Sun. 8:30-4:30. Adults over 18 $4, seniors 65 & over $3; discounts to AAM members; members & children under 18 no charge. Closed New Year's Day; Thanksgiving; Christmas. ♿
Attendance: 20,933 (accurate)
Membership: Senior Citizen $20; Individual $35; Family $50; Sustaining $100; Contributing $250; Patron $500; Benefactor $1,000.

Pahrump

PAHRUMP VALLEY MUSEUM, 401 E. Basin Ave., Pahrump, NV 89048. Mailing Address: P.O. Box 1510, Pahrump, NV 89041-1510. Tel.: 775-751-1970.
E-mail: pahrumpmuseum@att.net
Key Personnel: Pres., Gordon Scott; Cur., Rob Mobley
History Museum.
Collections: local history & culture; President Lincoln memorabilia; photographs; personal artifacts.
Hours & Admission Prices: Tues.-Sat. 10-4. No charge.

Pioche

LINCOLN COUNTY HISTORICAL MUSEUM, 69 Main St., Pioche, NV 89043. Mailing Address: P.O. Box 515, Pioche, NV 89043-0515. Tel.: 775-962-5207.
History Museum.
Collections: local history & culture; Chinese & Native American artifacts; mining tools; furniture; musical instruments; minerals.
Hours & Admission Prices: Daily 10-1 & 2-4. No charge; donations accepted. Closed Thanksgiving; Christmas.

Reno

FLEISCHMANN PLANETARIUM, (M), 1650 N. Virginia St., Reno, NV 89503-0703. Mailing Address: Univ. of Nevada, Reno/272, Reno, NV 89557-0001. Tel.: 775-784-4812. Fax: 775-784-4822.
Web Site: planetarium.unr.edu
Founded: 1963.
Congressional District: 1
Key Personnel: Dir., Dr. Dee W. Henderson; Management Asst., JoAnne Robb-Black; Assoc. Dir., Dan Ruby; Exhibit Coord. & Museum Shop Mgr., Johanna Bell.
Personnel Profile: Full-Time Paid 5; Part-Time Paid 7; Part-Time Volunteers 3.
Governing Authority: state. Affiliated with University of Nevada. Reno, NV. Tax-exempt.
Planetarium.
Collections: collection of meteorites.
Major Exhibits: Visual Perception, 11/09-12/10.
Research Fields: audio-visual techniques in planetarium.
Facilities: planetarium; theater; classroom.
Activities: lectures; films; hobby workshops; permanent, temporary & traveling exhibitions; telescope viewing; planetarium programs for school & public; rental facilities; children's birthday parties; toddler morning activities; rocket building classes.
Hours & Admission Prices: Daily call for hours. Exhibits no charge. Planetarium Show: adults (13-59) $6, children under 13 & seniors over 59 $4; discount to groups, AAM, ASTC, IPS & planetarium members. Closed New Year's Day; Thanksgiving; Christmas. ♿
Attendance: 48,953 (accurate)
Membership: Student & Senior $30; Individuals $40; Family $100; one-time Patron of the Planetarium (life) $2,500.

NATIONAL AUTOMOBILE MUSEUM (THE HARRAH COLLECTION), (M), 10 South Lake St., Reno, NV 89501-1558. Tel.: 775-333-9300. Fax: 775-333-9309.
E-mail: info@automuseum.org
Web Site: www.automuseum.org
Founded: 1989.
Congressional District: 2

Key Personnel: Exec. Dir. & C.E.O., Jackie L. Frady; Chm. (V), Ranson Webster; Assoc. Dir. Operations, Randy Edwards; Mgr. Business & Membership, Lisa Panko; Sales & Mktg. Mgr., Esther Isaac; Support Svcs. Mgr., Barbara Clark; Mgr. Automotive Collections, Jay Hubbard; Museum Store Mgr., Barbara Bolenbaker; Events Mgr., Jeff Giles.
Personnel Profile: Full-Time Paid 7; Part-Time Paid 4; Part-Time Volunteers 90.
Governing Authority: private; nonprofit organization. Tax-exempt: 501(c)(3).
Automobile Museum.
Collections: horseless carriage; antique, vintage, classic & special interest vehicles.
Major Exhibits: Movie Cars: Cinematic Stars on Wheels, 11/09-4/14/10; On the Road with Alice Ramsey: 100 Years Ago, 11/09-4/14/10; NY to Paris Automobile Race of 1908, 11/09-12/10; Even in Africa, 1/19/10-1/11/10; Roadside Attractions, 1/19/10-1/11/10.
Research Fields: automotive.
Facilities: library with 322,000 items pertaining to automotive history; audiovisual theater. Automotive-related gifts for sale.
Activities: rotating & permanent exhibitions.
Publications: magazine, Precious Metal.
Hours & Admission Prices: Mon.-Sat. 9:30-5:30, Sun. 10-4. Adults $10, senior citizens $8, students 6-18 $4; discounts to AAM & AMG members; staff, museum members & children under 5 no charge. Closed Thanksgiving; Christmas. ♿
Attendance: 65,000 (accurate)
Membership: Individual $45; Companion $60; Family $70; Contributing $150; Patron $500; Corporate $700; Driving Force $1,000.

* **NEVADA HISTORICAL SOCIETY, (M),** 1650 N. Virginia St., Reno, NV 89503-1799. Tel.: 775-688-1190. Fax: 775-688-2917.
Web Site: www.nevadaculture.org
Founded: 1904.
Congressional District: 2
Key Personnel: Cur. Photography, Lee Brumbaugh; Research Librarian, Michael Maher; Registrar & Cur. Museum Artifacts, Sheryln Hayes-Zorn; Museum Shop Mgr., Judy Dandini.
Personnel Profile: Full-Time Paid 8; Part-Time Volunteers 60; Interns 5.
Governing Authority: state. Parent Institution: Dept. of Cultural Affairs, Division of Museums & History. Tax-exempt.
History Museum.
Collections: items relating to Nevada history, from earliest cultures to 21st century; manuscript collections; photography.
Research Fields: all aspects of Nevada history.
Facilities: 20,000-vol. library of books, 3,000 manuscripts, 3,500 MSS collections, 450,000 photographs & periodicals, 55,000 maps, bound newspapers and government publications on Nevada & Western America available on premises.
Activities: guided tours; lectures; docent program or council; inter-museum loan exhibitions; historic preservation studies; field trips.
Publications: magazine, Nevada Historical Society Quarterly; occasional series & monographs.
Hours & Admission Prices: Museum: Wed.-Sat. 10-5. Library: Wed.-Sat. 12-4. Adults $3, seniors $2; discounts to AAM, ICOM, AAA & Nevada Div. of Museum/History members; children 17 & under no charge. Closed New Year's Day; Martin Luther King Jr. Day; Memorial Day; Independence Day; Labor Day; Veterans Day; Admissions Day; Thanksgiving; Christmas; state holidays. ♿
Attendance: 40,000 (accurate)
Membership: Senior $20; Individual $35; Family $50; Sustaining $100; Contributing $250; Patron $500; Benefactor $1,000.

* **NEVADA MUSEUM OF ART, (M),** 160 W. Liberty, Reno, NV 89501-1916. Tel.: 775-329-3333. Fax: 775-329-1541.
E-mail: art@nevadaart.org
Web Site: www.nevadaart.org
Founded: 1931.
Congressional District: 2
Key Personnel: Pres., Michael Hillerby; Exec. Dir., David B. Walker; Deputy Dir., Amy Oppio; Cur., Ann Wolfe; Dir. Operations, Vic Hopner; Registrar, Sara McRay; Volunteer Coord., Rosalind Bedell; Cur. Education, Colin Robertson; Dir. Communications & Mktg., Alexia Bratiotis; Museum Shop Mgr., Jackie Clay.
Personnel Profile: Full-Time Paid 20; Part-Time Paid 20; Part-Time Volunteers 125.
Governing Authority: nonprofit organization. Tax-exempt.
Art Museum.
Collections: five focus areas centered on the aesthetic articulation of our land and environment.
Major Exhibits: Quilts of Lee's Bend (T), 2/6/10-4/11/10; The Baroque World of Fernando Botero (T), 5/10-7/25/10; Other Realities, Contemporary Chinese Art, 11/6/10-2/13/11.
Research Fields: permanent collection; natural built & virtual environments.
Facilities: library; museum school; sculpture galleries; education gallery; classrooms; discovery center; cafe; theater. Museum-related items for sale.
Activities: docent programs; guided tours; lectures; education programs for children & adults; loan, temporary & traveling exhibitions; museum school classes.
Publications: exhibition catalogues; quarterly newsletter; exhibition notes.
Hours & Admission Prices: Wed. & Fri.-Sun. 11-6, Thurs. 11-8. Adults $10, senior citizens & students $8, children $1; discount to AAM & ICOM members; members no charge. Closed national holidays. ♿
Attendance: 90,000 (accurate)
Membership: Student $25; Individual $35; Dual $50; Family $75; Associate $150; Supporting $250; Contributing $500; Benefactor $750; Sierra Circle $1,000.

SHEPPARD FINE ARTS GALLERY, CFA 162, University of Nevada, Reno, NV 89557-0001. Mailing Address: Dept Art-224, University of Nevada, Reno, NV 89557-0001. Tel.: 775-784-6658. Fax: 775-784-6655.
E-mail: mvecchio@unr.edu
Web Site: www.unr.edu/art/site/galleriesevents/sheppard_gallery.html
Founded: 1960.
Key Personnel: Dir., Marjorie Vecchio; Mgr., Amy Winberg.
Personnel Profile: Full-Time Paid 1; Part-Time Paid 1; Part-Time Volunteers 10; Interns 4.
Governing Authority: university. Parent Institution: University of Nevada, Reno. Tax-exempt.
Fine Arts Gallery.
Collections: print collection; drawings; sculpture; photographs; paintings.
Major Exhibits: EunKang Koh Printmaking and Book Arts Show (T), 1/18/10-1/29/10; Love Lost and Found: 10th Biennial Valentine Auction, 2/1/10-2/12/10; Iraqi Memorial, 2/15/10-3/12/10; MFA Thesis Exhibition - Katy Govan, 4/19/10-4/30/10; MFA Thesis Exhibition - Pete Whittenberger, 5/3/10-5/14/10.
Research Fields: modern Nevada art.
Activities: guided tours; lectures; films; gallery talks; arts festivals; TV & radio programs; loan, temporary & traveling exhibitions.
Publications: exhibitions catalogs.
Hours & Admission Prices: Mon.-Thurs. 11-5, Fri. 11-2. No charge. Closed state holidays. ♿
Attendance: 30,000 (estimated)

SIERRA SAFARI ZOO, 10200 N. Virginia St., Reno, NV 89506-9203. Tel.: 775-677-1101. Fax: 775-677-7874.
E-mail: lori@sierrasafarizoo.org
Web Site: www.sierrasafarizoo.org
Key Personnel: Gen. Mgr., Lori Acordagoitia
Zoo.
Collections: over 150 animals of 40 species.
Facilities: Museum-related items for sale.
Hours & Admission Prices: April-Oct. daily 10-5. Adults $7, children 3-12 and seniors 55 & over $6; children 2 & under no charge.

STREMMEL GALLERY, 1400 S. Virginia St., Reno, NV 89502-2806. Tel.: 775-786-0558. Fax: 775-786-0311.
E-mail: info@stremmelgallery.com
Key Personnel: Mgr., Sara Gray
Art Gallery.
Collections: works by contemporary artists.
Hours & Admission Prices: Mon.-Fri. 9-5:30, Sat. 10-3. Closed holidays.

W.M. KECK MUSEUM, Mail Stop 168, Mackay School of Mines, University of Nevada, Reno, NV 89557-0001. Tel.: 775-784-4528. Fax: 775-784-1766.
E-mail: rdolbier@unr.edu
Web Site: mines.unr.edu/museum/
Founded: 1908.
Congressional District: 2
Key Personnel: Admin., Rachel A. Dolbier.
Governing Authority: university. Affiliated with Mackay School of Mines, University of Nevada. Tax-exempt: 501(c)(3).
Geology, Paleontology & Mineralogy Museum.
Collections: metallurgical; paleontological; geological; fossils; mineralogical; history of mining.
Activities: guided tours; permanent exhibitions.
Hours & Admission Prices: Mon.-Fri. 9-4. No charge. Closed university holidays. ♿

WILBUR D. MAY MUSEUM, 1595 N. Sierra St., Reno, NV 89503-2862.89503-1716. Tel.: 775-785-5961. Fax: 775-325-6891.
E-mail: lynda@maycenter.com
Web Site: www.maycenter.com
Founded: 1985.
Congressional District: 2
Key Personnel: Dir. Washoe County Regl. Parks, Doug Doolittle; Cur., Kristy Lide.
Personnel Profile: Full-Time Paid 1; Part-Time Paid 1; Part-Time Volunteers 50; Interns 1.
Governing Authority: county; nonprofit organization. Parent Institution: Washoe County Parks Dept. Subsidiary Institution: Rancho San Rafael Park. Tax-exempt.
General Museum.
Collections: western art; big game trophies; silver & pewter; guns & swords; photographs; art & music material; ceramics & glass; ethnology & archaeology items.
Facilities: garden; 2 auditoriums; full kitchen; banquet facilities. Museum-related items for sale.
Activities: hands-on traveling exhibits; guided tours; lectures; gift fair; docent program; rental facilities. Special Event: Balloon Art Show.
Publications: brochures.
Hours & Admission Prices: Call for hours. ♿
Attendance: 55,000 (estimated)

WILDFLOWER VILLAGE, 4395 W. Fourth St., Reno, NV 89523-8830. Tel.: 775-827-5250 & 787-3769.
Art Gallery.
Collections: art glass; photography; painting; ceramics.
Facilities: cafe.
Activities: art events; classes; retreats; rental facilities.
Hours & Admission Prices: By appointment.

Searchlight

SEARCHLIGHT HISTORIC MUSEUM & MINING PARK, 200 Michael Wendell Way, Searchlight, NV 89046. Mailing Address: P.O. Box 36, Searchlight, NV 89046-0036. Tel.: 702-297-1642.
Founded: 1989.
Congressional District: 3
Key Personnel: Founder, Jane Bunker Overy.
Personnel Profile: Part-Time Volunteers 1.
Governing Authority: county government; nonprofit. Parent Institution: Clark County Museum, Henderson, NV. Tax-exempt: 501(c)(3).
History Museum.
Collections: photographs; early mining days of Searchlight; personal artifacts; furnishings; geological.
Research Fields: early Searchlight through photographs.
Facilities: 500 sq. ft. exhibit space.
Activities: rental facility for private group events. Biennial Event: Searchlight Town Founding Birthday Celebration in October.
Hours & Admission Prices: Mon.-Fri. 9-5, Sat. 9-1. No charge; donations accepted. Closed holidays. ♿
Attendance: 5,000 (estimated)
Membership: Founder $5; Promoter $15; Prospector $25; Surveyor $50; Miner $75; Grubstaker $100; Recorder $1,000 & up; Assessor $5,000 & up.

Silver Springs

FORT CHURCHILL STATE HISTORIC PARK, 1000 Hwy. 95A, Silver Springs, NV 89429. Tel.: 775-577-2345.
Historic Site: former U.S. Army fort; built in 1861.
Collections: fort's history; building ruins.
Facilities: nature trails; visitor center.
Activities: camping; picnicking; hiking; educational programs; canoeing.
Hours & Admission Prices: Call for hours.

Sparks

ANIMAL ARK, 1250 Disc Dr., Sparks, NV 89436. Tel.: 775-626-9922.
E-mail: info@vistagrille.com
Web Site: www.vistagrille.com
Wildlife Sanctuary & Nature Center.
Collections: wildlife & their habitats.
Facilities: 38 acre site.
Activities: educational programs.
Hours & Admission Prices: April-Nov. Tues.-Sun. 10-4:30. Adults $8, seniors & children 3-12 $6; children 2 & under no charge.

SPARKS HERITAGE FOUNDATION & MUSEUM, (M), 820 Victorian Ave., Sparks, NV 89431-5077. Tel.: 775-355-1144. Fax: 775-355-6788.
Web Site: www.sparksmuseum.org
History Museum.
Collections: local history; Native American artifacts; mining; prospecting; farming; ranching; railroad history; photographs.
Facilities: Museum-related items for sale.
Publications: quarterly newsletter.
Hours & Admission Prices: Tues.-Fri. 11-4, Sat. 1-4. Adults $5; members no charge. Closed holidays. ♿
Attendance: 2,500 (accurate)
Membership: Single $30; Contributing $150.

Tonopah

CENTRAL NEVADA MUSEUM, 1900 Logan Field Rd., Tonopah, NV 89049. Mailing Address: P.O. Box 326, Tonopah, NV 89049-0326. Tel.: 775-482-9676. Fax: 775-482-5423.
E-mail: cnmuseum@citlink.net
Web Site: www.tonopahnevada.com
Founded: 1977.
Key Personnel: Asst. Cur., Eva La Rue; Researcher, Angela Haag.
Personnel Profile: Full-Time Paid 1; Full-Time Volunteers 1; Part-Time Paid 1; Part-Time Volunteers 1.
Governing Authority: county. Parent Institution: Central Nevada Historical Society. Subsidiary Institution: Nye County, NV. Tax-exempt.
Historical Society Museum.
Collections: central Nevada history from prehistoric times to present; including Nye & Esmeralda Counties.
Research Fields: Tonopah Army Air Field (WWII B24-P39 training base); Central Nevada history; self-guided tours.
Facilities: 4,000-vol. research library; 6,000 sq. ft. exhibit space. Museum-related items for sale.
Activities: films; school loan service; temporary exhibitions; special events.
Publications: annual, Central Nevada's Glorious Past.
Hours & Admission Prices: Tues.-Sat. 9-5. No charge; donations accepted. Closed state & federal holidays. ♿
Membership: Individual $15; Family $20; Business $25; Life $200; Family & Business Life $350.

TONOPAH HISTORIC MINING PARK, 520 McCulloch Ave., Tonopah, NV 89049. Mailing Address: P.O. Box 151, Tonopah, NV 89049-0151. Tel.: 775-482-9274. Fax: 775-482-9327.
E-mail: tonopahminingpark@gmail.com
Web Site: http://www.tonopahhistoricminingpark.com
Founded: 1992.
Congressional District: 2
Governing Authority: Parent Institution: Town of Tonopah. Tax-exempt.
Mining History Museum.
Collections: mining history & artifacts; mining equipment; mineral specimens; historic buildings.
Research Fields: mining; geology; early 1900 history in relation to Tonopah mining.
Facilities: Visitor Center. Museum-related items for sale.
Activities: underground tours; video; walking tour; walking bridge; Polaris tour.
Publications: member newsletter, Tailings.
Hours & Admission Prices: April-Sept. daily 9-5; Oct.-March Wed.-Sun. 10-4. Walking tour: adults $5, children 7-12 $3; seniors, veterans, active military & children under 6 no charge.
Attendance: 5,000 (estimated)
Membership: Individual $20; Family $25; Business $50; Individual Life $250; Business/Family Life $350; Indivdual/Family Life Benefactor $1,000; Business Life Benefactor $1,500.

Virginia City

COMSTOCK GOLD MILL, F St., Virginia City, NV 89440. Mailing Address: P.O. Box 1074, Virginia City, NV 89440-1074. Tel.: 775-742-9694.
Mining History Museum.
Collections: local mining history; stamp mills; mining equipment.
Activities: working mine tour; stagecoach rides.
Hours & Admission Prices: April-Oct. Wed.-Mon. 10-5. Adults $8, children 5-12 $4; children 4 & under no charge. Stagecoach Rides: Wed.-Mon. 11-5. Adults $10; children 4 & under no charge.

FOURTH WARD SCHOOL MUSEUM, 537 S. C St., Virginia City, NV 89440. Mailing Address: P.O. Box 4, Virginia City, NV 89440-0004. Tel.: 775-847-0875. Fax: 775-847-1011.
Web Site: www.fourthwardschool.org
Founded: 1986.
Key Personnel: Dir., Barbara Mackey; Pres. (V), Ron Gallagher; Museum Shop Mgr., Erlene Flanagan.
Personnel Profile: Full-Time Paid 1; Part-Time Paid 6.
Governing Authority: Parent Institution: Historic Fourth Ward School Museum Foundation. Tax-exempt.
History Museum.
Collections: Comstock history; mining; Mark Twain; personal artifacts.
Research Fields: Comstock history & genealogy.
Facilities: archives; research center.
Activities: workshops; rental facilities.
Publications: newsletter, History of the Fourth Ward School.
Hours & Admission Prices: May-Oct. daily 10-5. Adults $5, children 6-16 $3; discounts to AAM & National Trust members; members & children under 6 no charge. ♿
Attendance: 23,700 (accurate)
Membership: $30; $50; $75; $100; $250; $500; $1,000.

MACKAY MANSION, 129 S. D St., Virginia City, NV 89440. Mailing Address: P.O. Box 971, Virginia City, NV 89440-0971. Tel.: 775-847-0173.
Historic House: built in 1859. Listed on the National Register of Historic Places.
Collections: family history; period furnishings; photographs.
Activities: rental facilities.
Hours & Admission Prices: Call for hours.

MARK TWAIN HISTORICAL BOOKSTORE, 111 S. C St., Virginia City, NV 89440. Mailing Address: P.O. Box 449, Virginia City, NV 89440-0449. Tel.: 775-847-0454. Fax: 775-847-9010.
Web Site: www.marktwainbooks.com
History Museum & Bookstore.
Collections: local history & culture; books; personal artifacts; photographs; Native American; mining; geology; early railroads.
Hours & Admission Prices: Call for hours.

MARSHALL MINT MUSEUM, 96 N. C St., Virginia City, NV 89440. Mailing Address: P.O. Box 447, Virginia City, NV 89440-0447. Tel.: 775-847-0777; 800-321-6374. Fax: 775-847-9543.
Mint Museum: housed in the Assay Office building; built in 1861.
Collections: minerals & gems; jewelry; coins.
Facilities: Museum-related items for sale.
Activities: view coins being minted and jewelry produced in the press & assembly rooms.
Hours & Admission Prices: Daily 10-5. Closed Thanksgiving; Christmas.

NEVADA GAMBLING MUSEUM, 50 S. C St., Virginia City, NV 89440. Mailing Address: 86 S. C St., P.O. Box 920, Virginia City, NV 89440-0920. Tel.: 775-847-9022.
Gambling Museum.
Collections: gaming memorabilia; slot machines; cheating devices; photographs; gambling saloon & poker room replicas; period U.S. money.
Hours & Admission Prices: April-Sept. daily 10-6; Oct.-March daily 10-5. Admission $1; children under 11 no charge.

NEVADA STATE FIRE MUSEUM & COMSTOCK FIREMEN'S MUSEUM, 125 S. C St., Virginia City, NV 89440. Mailing Address: P.O. Box 466, Virginia City, NV 89440-0466. Tel.: 775-847-0717. Fax: 775-847-9010.
Web Site: comstockfiremuseum.com
Founded: 1979.
Key Personnel: Chm. (V), Michael E. Nevin; Sec. & Treas., Joseph L. Curtis; Museum Shop Mgr., Eleanor Curtis.
Personnel Profile: Full-Time Paid 1; Full-Time Volunteers 1; Part-Time Volunteers 6.
Governing Authority: Parent Institution: Storey County Volunteer Fire Department. Subsidiary Institution: Virginia City District. Tax-exempt: 501(c)(3).
Fire-Fighting Museum: housed in c.1870 structure.
Collections: uniforms; leather helmets; belts; trumpets; photographs; manuscripts; tools; 1860 & 1856 hand-pumped fire engines; Virginia City & Comstock Lode area history; magazines; brochures; 1839, 1860 & 1879 hand-drawn hose carriages; 1877 horse-drawn hose carriage; motorized apparatus; 1874 hand-drawn ladder truck; operational 1879 fire steamer-horse drawn.
Research Fields: history of firefighting in Nevada; background and genealogy of members of the Virginia City and Gold Hill fire departments.
Facilities: Museum-related items for sale.
Activities: guided tours; lectures; study clubs; media programs; participatory, loan & temporary exhibitions.
Publications: brochures; annual newsletter.
Hours & Admission Prices: late April & Nov.-Dec. Sat.-Sun. 10-5 weather permitting; May-Oct. daily 10-5. No charge; donations accepted. ♿
Attendance: 43,917 (accurate)
Membership: Student & Senior Citizen $5; General $10-$50; Corporate $200; Life $500-$1,000.

THE WAY IT WAS MUSEUM, 113 N. C St., Virginia City, NV 89440. Mailing Address: P.O. Box 158, Virginia City, NV 89440-0158. Tel.: 775-847-0766. Fax: 775-847-9613.
History Museum.
Collections: local history & culture; Comstock mining artifacts; photographs; lithographs; maps.
Hours & Admission Prices: Daily 10-6. Adults $2.50; children 11 & under no charge. Closed Christmas.

WESTERN HISTORIC RADIO MUSEUM, 109 S. F St., Virginia City, NV 89440. Mailing Address: P.O. Box 73, Virginia City, NV 89440-0073. Tel.: 775-847-9047.
E-mail: radiomuseum@msn.com
Web Site: www.radioblvd.com
Key Personnel: Owner & Operator, Henry Rogers; Owner & Operator, Sharon Rogers
Radio History Museum.
Collections: period radios; radio history; horn speakers; cone speakers; early radio accessories; broadcast microphones; early electrical instruments; photographs of famous radio personalities; period ham gear.
Hours & Admission Prices: May-Oct. daily 10-5, call to confirm; Nov.-April by appointment. Adults $4, Children under 15 $2.

Washoe Valley

BOWERS MANSION, Franktown Rd., Washoe Valley, NV 89704-9518. Tel.: 775-849-0201. Fax: 775-849-9568.
Founded: 1946.
Key Personnel: Cur., Mrs. Betty Hood.
Personnel Profile: Full-Time Paid 1; Part-Time Paid 2.
Governing Authority: county; nonprofit. Affiliated with Washoe County Dept. of Parks & Recreation & Bowers Mansion Restoration Committee, 2601 Plumas St., Reno, NV 89510.
Historic House: c.1864 restored & refurbished Mansion built by L.S. Bowers.
Collections: furnishings.
Activities: guided tours; formally organized education programs for children; permanent exhibitions.
Hours & Admission Prices: May & Sept.-Oct. Sat.-Sun. 11-4:30; Memorial Day-Labor Day daily 11-4:30. Adults 17-61 $5, seniors $4.
Attendance: 7,000 (accurate)

Winnemucca

BUCKAROO HALL OF FAME, 30 W. Winnemucca Blvd., Winnemucca, NV 89445-3129. Mailing Address: 30774 Culp Lane, Burns, OR 97720. Tel.: 775-623-2225. Fax: 800-962-2638.
Key Personnel: Cur., Carl Hammond
Art Museum.
Collections: paintings; sculpture; drawings.
Hours & Admission Prices: Daily 8-12 & 1-5. No charge; donations accepted.

HUMBOLDT COUNTY HISTORICAL MUSEUM, 175 W. Jungo Rd. & Maple Ave., Winnemucca, NV 89446. Mailing Address: P.O. Box 819, Winnemucca, NV 89446-0819. Tel.: 775-623-2912. Fax: 775-623-5640.
E-mail: museum@winnemucca.net
Key Personnel: Dir., Nancy Larson
History Museum.
Collections: Native American artifacts; pioneer household items; tools; utensils; local history; period automobiles; historic buildings.
Hours & Admission Prices: Mon.-Fri. 9-4, Sat. 1-4. No charge; donations accepted.

Yerington

LYON COUNTY MUSEUM, 215 S. Main St., Yerington, NV 89447-2536. Tel.: 775-463-6576.
Personnel Profile: Part-Time Volunteers 13.
History Museum.
Collections: local history; natural history; blacksmith shop; general store; schoolhouse.
Hours & Admission Prices: April-Oct. Thurs.-Fri. & Sun. 1-4, Sat. 10-1; Nov.-March Thurs.-Sun. 1-4; other times by appointment. No charge.

NEW HAMPSHIRE

(136 listings)

Allenstown

MUSEUM OF FAMILY CAMPING, Bear Brook State Park, 157 Deerfield Rd., Allenstown, NH 03275-2503. Mailing Address: 100 Athol Rd., Richmond, NH 03470-4200. Tel.: 603-239-4768.
Web Site: www.ucampnh.com/museum/welcome.html
Governing Authority: Tax-exempt.
Camping History Museum.
Collections: family camping history; camp stove; 1935 campsite; 1895 sleeping bag; Native American artifacts; cooking equipment; camping gear; period campers; Hall of Fame inductees.
Hours & Admission Prices: Memorial Day to Sept. daily 10-4. No charge; donations accepted.

THE NEW HAMPSHIRE SNOWMOBILE MUSEUM, Bear Brook State Park, Rte. 28, Allenstown, NH 03275. Mailing Address: P.O. Box 10112, Concord, NH 03301-0112. Tel.: 603-648-2304.
E-mail: stephenburdick@nhsnowmobilemuseum.com
Web Site: www.nhsnowmobilemuseum.com
Founded: 1985.
Key Personnel: Dir., Stephen Burdick; Pres., Dan Lewis; Vice Pres., George Burdick.
Governing Authority: nonprofit organization.
Snowmobile Museum.
Collections: history of snowmobiling; snowmobiles
Activities: special events. Annual Events: NHSMA 24th Annual Winter Event in February; 5th Annual Vintage Round-Up in March.
Hours & Admission Prices: Jan.-March Sat. 1-3; Memorial Day to Columbus Day by appointment. No charge; donations accepted.

Alton

THE HAROLD S. GILMAN MUSEUM, Alton, NH 03809. Mailing Address: 1 Monument Square, P.O. Box 637, Alton, NH 03809-0637. Tel.: 603-875-2161.
Web Site: www.alton.nh.gov/museum.asp
History Museum.
Collections: guns; furniture; dolls; buttons; toys; family papers & photographs.
Hours & Admission Prices: Call for hours.

Amherst

THE CHAPEL MUSEUM, Corner of Middle and Church Sts., Amherst, NH 03031. Mailing Address: Historical Society of Amherst, P.O. Box 717, Amherst, NH 03031-0717. Tel.: 603-673-8029; 9831.
Web Site: www.hsanh.org
Key Personnel: Cur., Susan Fischer; Dir. Museums, Bonnie Struss.
Governing Authority: Parent Institution: Historical Society of Amherst.
History Museum: built in 1858.
Collections: memorabilia relating to Amherst; maps; photographs; scrapbooks; clothing; furniture.
Hours & Admission Prices: Call for hours. No charge; donations accepted.

THE WIGWAM MUSEUM, Corner of Middle and Cross Sts., Amherst, NH 03031. Mailing Address: Historical Society of Amherst, P.O. Box 717, Amherst, NH 03031-0717. Tel.: 603-672-9831; 8029.
Web Site: www.hsanh.org
Key Personnel: Genealogy Chair, Jackie Marshall; Dir. Museums, Bonnie Struss; Cur., Chris Marshall.
Governing Authority: Parent Institution: Historical Society of Amherst.
History Museum: former Methodist chapel built in 1839.
Collections: artifacts relating to Amherst; Concord Coach; old jailhouse door.
Hours & Admission Prices: Call for hours. No charge; donations accepted.

Ashland

ASHLAND RAILROAD STATION MUSEUM, 69 Depot St., Ashland, NH 03217. Mailing Address: P.O. Box 175, Ashland, NH 03217-0175.
Founded: 1999.
Congressional District: 2
Key Personnel: Pres. Historical Society, David Ruell; Treas., Philip Preston.
Personnel Profile: Part-Time Volunteers 7.
Governing Authority: private; nonprofit organization. Parent Institution: Ashland Historical Society, P.O. Box 175, Ashland, NH 03217. Tax-exempt: 501(c)(3).
Transportation Museum: housed in c.1869 Victorian railroad station.
Collections: railroad related items & documents.
Activities: lectures; occasional train rides.
Hours & Admission Prices: July-Aug. Sat. 1-4. Suggested Donation: Adults $2; members, school groups & children no charge. ♿
Attendance: 750 (estimated)
Membership: Individual $10; Family $15; Supporter $25; Patron $50; Benefactor $100.

PAULINE E. GLIDDEN TOY MUSEUM, 49 Main St., Ashland, NH 03217. Mailing Address: P.O. Box 14, Ashland, NH 03217-0014. Tel.: 603-968-7289.
Founded: 1991.
Congressional District: 2
Key Personnel: Pres. Historical Society, David Ruell; Dir. Toy Museum, Shirley Splaine.
Personnel Profile: Part-Time Volunteers 29.
Governing Authority: nonprofit. Parent Institution: Ashland Historical Society. Tax-exempt: 501(c)(3).
Early Toy Museum.
Collections: period toys; children's books; games; dolls; schoolroom; doll houses; penny toys.
Facilities: Museum-related items for sale.
Activities: Annual Events: Young Ladies Tea; Appraisal Day.
Publications: newsletter.
Hours & Admission Prices: July-Aug. Thurs.-Fri. 1-4. Adults $2; children 12 & under no charge.
Attendance: 275 (accurate)
Membership: Individual $10; Family $20; Sponsor $50; Patron $100.

WHIPPLE HOUSE MUSEUM, ASHLAND HISTORICAL SOCIETY, 14 Pleasant St., Ashland, NH 03217. Mailing Address: P.O. Box 175, Ashland, NH 03217-0175. Tel.: 603-968-7716. Fax: 603-968-7716.
Web Site: www.oldashlandnh.org
Founded: 1970.
Congressional District: 2
Key Personnel: Pres., David Ruell; Vice Pres., Jane Sawyer; Cur., Sandra Ray; Treas., Philip Preston.
Personnel Profile: Part-Time Volunteers 20.
Governing Authority: nonprofit organization. Parent Institution: Ashland Historical Society. Subsidiary Institution: Pauline E. Glidden Toy Museum, Pleasant St., Ashland, NH 03217; Ashland Railroad Station Museum. Tax-exempt: 501(c)(3).
Local History Museum: 1837 brick house, birthplace & childhood home of George Hoyt Whipple, winner of the Nobel Prize for medicine.
Collections: local historical items; furniture; household items; tools; agricultural items.
Facilities: library of material available to the public for use on premises only.
Activities: guided tours; lectures; temporary exhibitions.
Hours & Admission Prices: July-Aug. Wed. & Fri. 1-4. Suggested Donation: adults $2; children, school groups & members no charge.
Attendance: 400 (estimated)
Membership: Annual $10; Family $15; Supporter $25; Patron $50; Benefactor $100.

Auburn

MASSABESIC AUDUBON CENTER, 26 Audubon Way, Auburn, NH 03032-3109. Tel.: 603-668-2045.
Web Site: www.nhaudubon.org
Nature Center.
Collections: wildlife & their habitats.
Facilities: nature trails.
Activities: educational programs; workshops.
Hours & Admission Prices: Call for hours.

Bath

HARRIMANS FALLS EDUCATIONAL CENTRE AND MUSEUM, 11 Rum Hill Rd., Bath, NH 03740. Mailing Address: 7 W. Bath Rd., Bath, NH 03740. Tel.: 603-747-2200. Fax: 603-747-2203.
E-mail: fsi@together.net
Founded: 2004.
Key Personnel: Exec. Dir. & Pres., Charles M. Diamond; Vice Pres. & Dir., Kevin M. O'Brien; Dir., Thomas A. Rappa, Jr.; Dir., Fayez Azeez; Treas., Richard L. Weinburg, Jr.
Governing Authority: private; nonprofit organization. Tax-exempt: 501(c)(3).
Village Museum.
Collections: period furnishings & artifacts. Historic Building: Payson Mansion.
Hours & Admission Prices: Closed for renovation.

Bedford

BEDFORD HISTORICAL SOCIETY, 24 N. Amherst Rd., Bedford, NH 03110-5404. Tel.: 603-471-6336.
History Museum.
Collections: local history & culture; photographs; period furnishings.
Hours & Admission Prices: By appointment.

Berlin

THE MOFFETT HOUSE MUSEUM & GENEALOGY CENTER, 119 High St., Berlin, NH 03570-2062. Mailing Address: P.O. Box 52, Berlin, NH 03570-0052. Tel.: 603-752-7928.
Web Site: www.aannh.org/heritage/coos/moffett.php
Founded: 1997.
Key Personnel: Pres. (V), Renney Morneau; Museum Shop Mgr., Odette Leclerc; Recording Sec., Jacklyn Nadeau.
Personnel Profile: Part-Time Volunteers 7.
Governing Authority: Parent Institution: Berlin & Coos County Historical Society. Tax-exempt.
Historic House: former home and office of Dr. and Mrs. Irving Moffett.
Collections: military memorabilia; photographs; Brown Company bulletins; souvenir china.
Publications: semi-annual newsletter, News From The House.
Hours & Admission Prices: Tues.-Sat. 12-4; other times by appointment. No charge. Closed major holidays.
Attendance: 500 (estimated)
Membership: Annual $10.

NORTHERN FOREST HERITAGE PARK & BROWN HOUSE MUSEUM, 961 Main St., Berlin, NH 03570-3031. Tel.: 603-752-7202. Fax: 603-752-7222.
E-mail: heritage@ncia.net
Web Site: www.northernforestheritage.org
Park & Historic House.
Collections: logging history; river artifacts; works of art; period furnishings.
Facilities: outdoor amphitheater. Museum-related items for sale.
Activities: 3 acre site; lectures; seminars; concerts; cultural festivals; lumberjack competitions; blacksmith demonstrations; special events.
Hours & Admission Prices: Park: late May to early Oct. Tues.-Sat. 11-6. House: mid-June to mid-Oct. daily 10-7; mid-Oct. to mid-June Mon.-Fri. 10-7. Boat Tours: June-Oct. Wed.-Sun. Tours: adult $15, children 5-11 $8; children under 5 no charge.

Bethlehem

CROSSROADS OF AMERICA, 6 Trudeau Rd., Bethlehem, NH 03574-5106. Tel.: 603-869-3919.
E-mail: cofa@together.net
Founded: 1981.
Key Personnel: C.E.O. & Owner, Roger Hinds.
Governing Authority: for-profit company.
Model Railroad & Toy Museum: housed in c.1890 Trudeau Estate.
Collections: model railroads in operation; over 40 antique outboard motors; old toys; period cameras; collectibles; 40 classic guitars; ferroequinology; diecast & model cars; miniature flags; beer cans.
Research Fields: model railroad construction techniques; model construction; antique out board motor repair.
Facilities: 100-vol. library of train books; 1,550 sq. ft. exhibit space.
Activities: guided tours.
Hours & Admission Prices: Temporarily closed.

Canaan

CANAAN HISTORICAL SOCIETY AND MUSEUM, Canaan St., Canaan, NH 03741. Tel.: 603-523-7364.
E-mail: fleethamdaniel@netzero.com
Key Personnel: Pres. (V), Daniel W. Fleetham, Sr.
History Museum.
Collections: local history; photographs; period furniture; school desks; science equipment.
Hours & Admission Prices: June-Oct. Sat. 1-4. No charge.

Candia

FITTS MUSEUM, 185 High St., Candia, NH 03034. Mailing Address: c/o Town Office, 74 High St., Candia, NH 03034-2751. Tel.: 603-483-8881.
E-mail: fittsmuseum@comcast.net
Web Site: www.fittsmuseum.org
Personnel Profile: Part-Time Volunteers 3.
Historic House Museum.
Collections: local history & culture; photographs; period furnishings; personal artifacts.
Activities: research.
Hours & Admission Prices: July-Aug. Sat. 1-4; other times by appointment. No charge; donations accepted.

Canterbury

CANTERBURY SHAKER VILLAGE, INC., 288 Shaker Rd., Canterbury, NH 03224-2728. Tel.: 603-783-9511, ext. 200. Fax: 603-783-9362.
Web Site: www.shakers.org
Founded: 1969.
Congressional District: 2
Key Personnel: Exec. Dir., Funi Burdick; Chm. (V), Deane Morrison; Archivist, Renee Fox; Museum Store Mgr., Dawn Demers.
Personnel Profile: Full-Time Paid 10; Part-Time Paid 40; Part-Time Volunteers 159; Interns 1.
Governing Authority: nonprofit organization. Tax-exempt: 501(c)(3).
Historic Site & Village: 1792 preserved Shaker community consisting of 25 buildings on 694 acres.
Collections: artifacts, manuscripts & photographs related to Shaker history.
Facilities: visitor center; 140-seat restaurant; gardens; education center. Museum-related items for sale.
Activities: guided tours; lectures; craft demonstrations & workshops; organized education programs for children; special events; self-guided nature trails.
Publications: members newsletter; A Shaker Sister's Drawings; Heaven on Earth: The Art and Architecture of the Canterbury Shakers; Annual Workshops and Events brochure; cookbook; Historic Structure Reports; collection catalogs; annual report.
Hours & Admission Prices: May 16-Oct. daily 10-5. Adults $17, children 6-17 $8; discounts to groups & families; members & children under 6 no charge. ♿
Attendance: 30,000 (estimated)
Membership: Dual $55; Grandparent $65; Family $75; Steward $100; Shaker $250.

Center Sandwich

SANDWICH HISTORICAL SOCIETY, 4 Maple St., Center Sandwich, NH 03227. Mailing Address: P.O. Box 244, Center Sandwich, NH 03227-0244. Tel.: 603-284-6269. Fax: 603-284-6278.
E-mail: sandwichhistory@earthlink.net
Web Site: www.sandwichhistorical.org
Founded: 1917.
Congressional District: 1
Key Personnel: Dir., Matthew Powers; Pres. (V), Tom Shevenell.
Personnel Profile: Part-Time Paid 4; Part-Time Volunteers 50.
Governing Authority: society; bd. of directors. Tax-exempt.
Local History Museum: housed in c.1850 Elisha Marston House.
Collections: vehicles; housewares; furniture; art; crafts; farm implements & tools; trade & textile tools; archives; spinning & weaving tools.
Major Exhibits: Highlights from the Archives, 6/10-10/10.
Research Fields: town, church, family & commercial records.
Facilities: local history library; genealogical research.
Activities: permanent & temporary exhibitions; lectures; tours; member receptions. Society Sponsors: annual picnic.
Publications: bulletin, Annual Excursion of the Sandwich Historical Society; Sandwich New Hampshire 1763-1900; Seven Wonders of Sandwich; Schoolhouses of Sandwich; newsletters.
Hours & Admission Prices: June-Oct. Tues.-Sat. 10-4; other times by appointment. No charge; donations accepted.
Attendance: 2,000 (estimated)
Membership: Single $20; Family & Institutional $35; Sustaining $75; Patron $125; Life $500.

Charlestown

THE FORT AT NO. 4 LIVING HISTORY MUSEUM, 267 Springfield Rd., Rte. 11, Charlestown, NH 03603. Mailing Address: P.O. Box 1336, Charlestown, NH 03603-1336. Tel.: 603-826-5700. Fax: 603-826-3368.
E-mail: info@fortat4.com
Web Site: www.fortat4.org
Formerly: Old Fort Number 4 Associates
Founded: 1947.
Congressional District: 2
Key Personnel: C.E.O., Cheryl Cavanaugh; Chm. (V), Charles Aiken; Pres. (V), Wells Chandler.
Personnel Profile: Full-Time Paid 3; Part-Time Paid 12; Part-Time Volunteers 65; Interns 2.
Governing Authority: nonprofit organization. Tax-exempt: 501(c)(3).

Historic Site Museum: granted in 1735 by Crown Province of Massachusetts, completed as a fortified village in 1744.
Collections: Native American artifacts; colonial furnishings & tools; weapons; canoes; 14 reconstructed buildings; two original barns; French-Indian War.
Research Fields: New England life & history, 1743-1760; King George's War; frontier fortification; families of Fort at No. 4 during 1740s-1750s.
Facilities: 18th-century reproductions of period pieces, books & handcrafts for sale.
Activities: lectures; films; demonstrations; recreation of daily life at the fortified village of No. 4; formally organized educational programs; online educational resource.
Publications: newsletter, The Advocate.
Hours & Admission Prices: School Tours: April-Oct. Wed.-Fri.; Public Tours: June-Oct. Wed.-Sun. 10-4:30. Adults $8, senior citizens $6, children 6-12 $5; discounts to AAM & AAA members; members & children under 6 no charge. ♿
Attendance: 14,000 (estimated)
Membership: Student & Senior $20; Individual $30; Family $50; Contributor $100-$499; Supporter $500-$999; Benefactor $1,000.

Claremont

THE CLAREMONT, NEW HAMPSHIRE HISTORICAL SOCIETY, INC., 26 Mulberry St., Claremont, NH 03743-2538. Tel.: 603-543-1400.
E-mail: claremont_historical@yahoo.com
Web Site: www.claremonthistoricalsociety.org
Founded: 1966.
Key Personnel: Pres. & Chm. Bd. Trustees, Colin J. Sanborn.
Governing Authority: society. Tax-exempt.
Local History Museum.
Collections: paintings, furnishings, tools, books & manuscripts pertaining to the early history of Claremont.
Research Fields: genealogy.
Facilities: 950-vol. historical library available for use on premises by appointment.
Activities: guided tours; lectures; formally organized education programs for children; permanent & temporary exhibitions.
Publications: The Historical Papers of George Baxter Upham.
Hours & Admission Prices: mid-June to mid-Sept. Sun. 2-5. Admission $1.
Membership: Student $5; Individual $10; Family $15; Business & Professional $50; Corporate $200; Life $300.

Colebrook

COLEBROOK AREA HISTORICAL MUSEUM, Colebrook Town Hall, 2nd Fl., 10 Bridge St., Colebrook, NH 03576. Mailing Address: P.O. Box 32, Colebrook, NH 03576-0032. Tel.: 603-237-4470.
E-mail: agoodrum@ncia.net
Web Site: www.aannh.org/heritage/coos/colebrookhs.php
Key Personnel: Pres., Arnold Goodrum; Sec., David Collins.
Personnel Profile: Part-Time Volunteers 5.
History Museum.
Collections: 15,000 artifacts including fine arts; folk arts; costumes & textiles; household items; maps; photographs; manuscripts; court records; local history items.
Hours & Admission Prices: July & Aug. Sat. 10-2. ♿
Membership: Individual $5.

Concord

ART CENTER IN HARGATE, ST. PAUL'S SCHOOL, 325 Pleasant St., Concord, NH 03301-2552. Tel.: 603-229-4643. Fax: 603-229-5696.
E-mail: ccallahan@sps.edu
Web Site: www.sps.edu
Founded: 1967.
Congressional District: 2
Key Personnel: Dir., Colin J. Callahan.
Personnel Profile: Full-Time Paid 1; Part-Time Paid 1.
Governing Authority: nonprofit. Tax-exempt: 501(c)(3).
Art Gallery.
Collections: variety of works by well-known & up-and-coming artists; permanent collection concentrates on art donated by the school's alumni & includes original pieces by Alexander Calder, Henry Moore, Daniel Chester French, Rembrandt Peale, George Inness, Hans Hofmann, George Braque, Frederic Remington, Augustus St. Gaudens & others.
Facilities: 2,500-vol. library; 97-seat auditorium; classrooms, labs & studios; 1,600 sq. ft. exhibit space.
Activities: guided tours; lectures; loan, temporary & traveling exhibitions.
Hours & Admission Prices: Sept.-May Tues.-Sat. 9:30-4. No charge. Closed spring break (three weeks in March); Thanksgiving break; Christmas vacation. ♿
Attendance: 3,700 (estimated)

AUDUBON SOCIETY OF NEW HAMPSHIRE, 84 Silk Farm Rd., Concord, NH 03301-8311. Tel.: 603-224-9909. Fax: 603-226-0902.
E-mail: nha@nhaudubon.org
Web Site: www.nhaudubon.org
Founded: 1914.
Congressional District: 2
Key Personnel: C.E.O. & Pres., Michael Bartlett; Chm. (V), David Reis; Dir. Organizational Devel., Patricia Casey; Museum Shop Mgr., Sarah Wall.
Personnel Profile: Full-Time Paid 44; Part-Time Paid 26; Part-Time Volunteers 1,500.
Governing Authority: nonprofit organization. Subsidiary Institutions: Loon Preservation committee; Amoskeag Fishways Learning Center; Massabesic Audubon Center; McLane Center; Newfound Audubon Center; Prescott Farm Audubon Center. Tax-exempt: 501(c)(3).
Nature Center & Conservation Area.
Collections: stuffed birds; live wild animals.
Research Fields: endangered species & wildlife habitat.
Facilities: 2,500-vol. library on natural history available to the public; meeting room auditorium; educational facilities; field research station; nature conservation center. Museum-related items for sale.
Activities: guided tours; lectures; films; concerts; temporary exhibitions; hobby workshops; rental gallery; organized education programs; teacher workshops. Annual Events: holiday fair; library book sale; Loon Festival; backyard winter bird survey; Birdathon.
Publications: books; booklets; leaflets; bimonthly newsletter, Afield; quarterly newsletter, New Hampshire Bird Records.
Hours & Admission Prices: Mon.-Fri. 9-5, Sat. 10-5. No charge; donations accepted. Closed legal holidays. ♿
Attendance: 100,000 (estimated)
Membership: Senior & Introductory $24; Individual $39; Family $55; Donor $75; Contributor $100; Supporter $250; Environmentalist $500; Conservation Partner $1,000.

KALEIDOSCOPE CHILDREN'S MUSEUM, LLC, 250 Commercial St., Waumbec Mill, Ste. 1004, Concord, NH 03101-1142. Tel.: 603-606-3381.
E-mail: kaleid01@conversent.net
Web Site: www.kaleidoscopechildrensmuseum.net
Children's Museum.
Collections: hands-on interactive exhibits.
Hours & Admission Prices: Mon. & Wed.-Thurs. 9-4, Fri.-Sat. 9-6, Sun. 12-5. Children $9.99; adults, children under 1 & adults no charge.

KIMBALL JENKINS ESTATE, 266 N. Main St., Concord, NH 03301-5053. Tel.: 603-225-3932.
Web Site: www.kimballjenkins.com
Art Gallery.
Collections: paintings; sculpture; photographs.
Hours & Admission Prices: Mon.-Thurs. 10-4; other times by appointment.

MARY BAKER EDDY HISTORIC HOME, 62 N. State St., Concord, NH 03301-4330. Tel.: 603-225-3444.
Historic House: built c.1850.
Collections: local history & culture; personal artifacts; period furnishings; photographs.
Hours & Admission Prices: May-Oct. Thurs. & Sat. 11-2; other times by appointment.

MCAULIFFE-SHEPARD DISCOVERY CENTER, 2 Institute Dr., Concord, NH 03301-7422. Tel.: 603-271-7827. Fax: 603-271-7832.
Web Site: www.starhop.com
Formerly: Christa McAuliffe Planetarium
Founded: 1990.
Congressional District: 2
Key Personnel: C.E.O., Jeanne T. Gerulskis; Chm. (V), Richard Ashooh; Producer, Sandt Michener; Dir. Special Events & Visitor Svcs., Gina Bowler; Visitor Svcs. Asst., Jane Ann Fuller; Visitor Svcs. Asst., Cheryl Stinson; Dir. Education, David McDonald, M.Ed.; Education Specialist, Mal Cameron; Astronomer, Kathryn Michener; Astronomy Educator, Tiffany Picard; Coord. Mktg., Jennifer Jones; Coord. Membership, Dinah Martell; Dir. Devel., Kathleen Regan; Devel. Asst., Debra Andrews; Educator, R.P. Hale; Producer, Sandt Michener; Maintenance Engineer, Mike LaRochelle; Science Store Mgr., Susan Jacques; Engineer, Jeff Hill; Accountant, Martha Laurie.
Personnel Profile: Full-Time Paid 14; Part-Time Paid 27; Part-Time Volunteers 6; Interns 1.
Governing Authority: state; planetarium commission. Parent Institution: State

of New Hampshire. Subsidiary Institution: New Hampshire NASA Educator Resource Center. Tax-exempt: 170(d)(1)(A).
Planetarium & Space Science Center.
Collections: U.S. Space Program memorabilia; Christa McAuliffe memorabilia; interactive exhibits; indoor & outdoor astronomy exhibits & space science; Alan Shepard memorabilia.
Research Fields: astronomy; space science; aviation; earth science.
Facilities: 103-seat planetarium; NASA Educator Resource Center; 45,000 sq. ft. exhibit space; garden. Museum-related items for sale.
Activities: docent program; formal education programs; guided tours; lectures; participatory & temporary exhibitions; indoor & outdoor exhibits on astronomy & space science; planetarium shows; monthly skywatch; lecture series; monthly Teen Night; NASA Educator Resource Center teacher workshops & training; birthday parties; rental facilities. Museum Sponsors: Astronomy Day first Sat. in May; Astronomy Fair in conjunction with NH Astronomical Society, rides, activities, & telescope workshops.
Publications: e-newsletter.
Hours & Admission Prices: Mon.-Thurs. 10-5, Fri. 10-9, Sat.-Sun. 10-5. Center: adults $9, seniors & students $8, children $6; members, ASTC members, and children 2 & under no charge. Planetarium: additional fee charged. Closed New Year's Day; Easter; Memorial Day; Independence Day; Labor Day; Thanksgiving; Christmas. ♿
Attendance: 54,387 (accurate)
Membership: Student $25; Individual $40; 2 Person $60; Family $80; Family & Friends $150; Gold $250. Plus level memberships available (include unlimited admission to planetarium).

* **NEW HAMPSHIRE HISTORICAL SOCIETY, (M),** 6 Eagle Sq., Concord, NH 03301-4956. Mailing Address: 30 Park St., Concord, NH 03301-6384. Tel.: 603-228-6688. Fax: 603-228-6308.
E-mail: jdesmarais@nhhistory.org
Web Site: www.nhhistory.org
Founded: 1823.
Congressional District: 2
Key Personnel: C.E.O. & Exec. Dir., William P. Veillette; Pres. (V), John R. Robinson; Asst. Exec. Dir., Joan Desmarais; Dir. Collections & Exhibitions, Wesley Balla; Dir. Publications, Donna-Belle Garvin; Dir. Devel., Anne M. Hamilton; Registrar, Douglas Copeley; Reference Librarian, William N. Copeley; Library Dir., Peter A. Wallner.
Personnel Profile: Full-Time Paid 13; Part-Time Paid 28; Part-Time Volunteers 80.
Governing Authority: society. Parent Institution: New Hampshire Historical Society. Tax-exempt: 501(c)(3).
History Museum.
Collections: decorative & fine arts; New Hampshire artifacts; furniture; silver; paintings; manuscripts; ceramics; costumes & textiles; photos; books; manuscripts; ephemera; newspapers; maps.
Research Fields: history; fine & decorative arts of New Hampshire.
Facilities: 1911 library; 125-seat auditorium; classroom. Museum-related items for sale.
Activities: lectures; workshops; school programs; concerts; permanent, temporary & traveling exhibitions.
Publications: semi-annual, Historical New Hampshire; quarterly newsletter; New Hampshire Architecture, An Illustrated Guide; Plain and Elegant, Rich & Common: Documented N. H. Furniture; New Hampshire Scenery: A Dictionary of 19th-Century Artists of New Hampshire Mountain Landscapes; Instruments of Change: New Hampshire Hand Tools & Their Makers; On the Road North of Boston: New Hampshire Taverns and Turnpikes, 1700-1900; Abbot-Dowing & the Concord Coach; At What Cost? Shaping the Land We Call New Hampshire; Capital Views, A Photographic History of Concord, N.H. 1850-1930; Beauty Caught and Kept: Benjamin Champney in the White Mountains; Soldiers, Sailors. Slaves and Ships: The Civil War Photographs of Henry P. Moore; The Years of the Life of Samuel Lane: A New Hampshire Man and His World; Consuming Views: Art and Tourism in The White Mountains, 1850-1900.
Hours & Admission Prices: Jan.-June & Oct. 16-Nov. Tues.-Sat. 9:30-5, Sun. 12-5; July-Oct. 15 & Dec. Mon.-Sat. 9:30-5, Sun. 12-5. Adults $5.50, seniors 55 & up $4.50, children 6-18 $3; discounts to AAM members; children under 6 & society members no charge. Closed some holidays. ♿
Attendance: 42,154 (accurate)
Membership: Individual, Library & Non-profit Organization $40; Couple $50; Family & Library with museum pass $60; Business $250-$5,000.

THE PIERCE MANSE/NEW HAMPSHIRE POLITICAL LIBRARY, 14 Horseshoe Pond Lane, Concord, NH 03301-5028. Mailing Address: P.O. Box 2512, Concord, NH 03302-0425. Tel.: 603-225-4555. Fax: 603-225-0540.
E-mail: camport@politicallibrary.org
Web Site: www.politicallibrary.org
Founded: 1966.
Congressional District: 1
Key Personnel: C.E.O., Michael P. Chaney; Dir. Programs, Caroline Amport; Dir. External Affairs, Celina Hurley.
Personnel Profile: Full-Time Paid 3; Full-Time Volunteers 4; Part-Time Paid 2; Part-Time Volunteers 20; Interns 1.
Governing Authority: nonprofit organization. Operated by The Pierce Brigade Inc., Concord, NH 03301. Tax-exempt: 501(c)(3).
Historic House Museum: 1842-1848 home of President Franklin Pierce.
Collections: furniture & memorabilia of President Pierce & his family; NH Presidential Primary history.
Research Fields: Franklin Pierce; NH Presidential Primary; NH politics; national politics.
Facilities: 50-vol. library of historical material; research reading room; 50-seat auditorium. Souvenir items for sale.
Activities: guided tours.
Hours & Admission Prices: Pierce Manse: June 17-Sept. 1 Tues.-Sat. 11-3; other times by appointment; groups of 10 or more by appointment. Family $15, adults $7, senior citizens $6, children & students $3. Closed holidays.
Attendance: 1,100 (accurate)
Membership: Student $10; Individual $20; Family $35.

Contoocook

THE LITTLE NATURE MUSEUM, 656 Gould Hill Rd., Contoocook, NH 03229. Mailing Address: 216 Tucker Dr., Hopkinton, NH 03229-2426. Tel.: 603-746-6121.
E-mail: info@littlenaturemuseum.org
Web Site: www.littlenaturemuseum.org
Founded: 1955.
Key Personnel: Dir., Pres. & Founder, Sandra W. Martin.
Personnel Profile: Part-Time Volunteers 12.
Natural History Museum.
Collections: fossils; rocks; minerals; mounted birds & mammals; seashells & corals; insects; fungi & galls; lichens; cones; nests.
Activities: Museum Sponsors: Nature Fest in September.
Publications: quarterly newsletter; annual report.
Hours & Admission Prices: June 27-July 26 Mon.-Fri. by appointment, Sat.-Sun. & holidays 1-4; Aug. 1-Nov. 1 Mon.-Fri. by appointment, Sat.-Sun. 11-4. Tours: $1.
Attendance: 2,600 (accurate)
Membership: Individual $10; Family $25; Friend $30; Supporter $50; Sponsor $100; Benefactor $250; Naturalist $500 & up.

Conway

EASTMAN LORD HOUSE, 100 Main St., Conway, NH 03818. Mailing Address: Conway Historical Society, P.O. Box 1949, Conway, NH 03818-1949. Tel.: 603-447-5551. Fax: 603-447-1991.
E-mail: conwayhistory@myfairpoint.net
Web Site: www.conwayhistory.org/eastman_lord_museum.html
Key Personnel: Acting Cur., Jim Arnold
Historic House Museum: housed in the home of Conway mill owner, William Kimball Eastman, c.1818. Listed on the National Register of Historic Places
Collections: personal artifacts; period furnishings.
Facilities: Museum-related items for sale.
Hours & Admission Prices: Memorial Day to Labor Day Wed. 2-4, Sat. 1-4; groups & other times by appointment. Family $6, adults $3; members no charge.

Cornish

* **SAINT-GAUDENS NATIONAL HISTORIC SITE, (M),** 139 Saint Gaudens Rd., Cornish, NH 03745-4232. Tel.: 603-675-2175, ext. 100. Fax: 603-675-2701.
E-mail: bj_dunn@nps.gov
Web Site: www.nps.gov/saga
Founded: 1926.
Congressional District: 2
Key Personnel: Supt., BJ Dunn; Administrative Officer, April May Preston; Supvr. Interpretation, Chief Ranger, Volunteer Coord. & Museum Shop Mgr., Gregory C. Schwarz; Cur. & Chief of Cultural Resources, Henry Duffy, Ph.D.; Facility Mgr., Mike Healy; Chief of Natural Resources, Stevem Walasewicz.
Personnel Profile: Full-Time Paid 12; Part-Time Paid 5; Part-Time Volunteers 14; Interns 2.
Governing Authority: federal. Parent Institution: U.S. Dept. of the Interior, National Park Service. Affiliated Institution: Saint-Gaudens Memorial, Inc. Affiliated Association: Trustees of the Saint-Gaudens Memorial, 17 E. 47th St., New York, NY 10017. Tax-exempt.
Art Museum: home & studio of Augustus Saint-Gaudens, American sculptor (1848-1907), situated on over 150 acres.

Collections: works of American sculptor Augustus Saint-Gaudens including bronze, sculpture, marble, plaster, molds & historic furnishings; works of Cornish Colony artists.
Research Fields: sculpture, life & works of Augustus Saint-Gaudens, 1848-1907; American art & sculpture; Cornish art colony (1885-1966).
Facilities: 2,000-vol. library on American art & sculpture; temporary exhibitions; historic gardens.
Activities: guided tours; gallery talks; education programs; inter-museum loans for temporary exhibitions; concerts.
Publications: catalogues, Catalog of Saint-Gaudens' works; 1907 U.S. Gold Coinage; The Shaw Memorial: A Celebration of an American Masterpiece; Augustus Saint-Gaudens 1848-1907: A Master of American Sculpture. Augustus Saint Gaudens American Sculptor of the Gildedage; Paul St. Gaudens Ceramic Artist.
Hours & Admission Prices: late May to Oct. daily 9-4:30. Adults $5; discounts to US fee area, National Park Pass, Golden Age, Golden Eagle & annual pass; children under 17 & educational groups no charge.
Attendance: 40,000

Derry

ROBERT FROST FARM, 122 Rockingham Rd., Rte. 28, Derry, NH 03038. Mailing Address: P.O. Box 1075, Derry, NH 03038-1075. Tel.: 603-432-3091.
E-mail: info@robertfrostfarm.org
Web Site: www.robertfrostfarm.org
Founded: 1968.
Congressional District: 1
Key Personnel: Chm., Clair Ternam; Sec., Laura Burnham; Historic Site Specialist, Ben Wilson; Museum Shop Mgr., William Gleed.
Personnel Profile: Part-Time Paid 2; Part-Time Volunteers 1; Interns 1.
Governing Authority: state. Parent Institution: State of New Hampshire. Tax-exempt.
Historic Site: 1900-1909 home of Robert Frost & setting for 43 of his poems.
Collections: early 1900s furniture; some family belongings.
Facilities: 30-vol. library about Robert Frost; nature-poetry walk. Robert Frost books of poetry for sale.
Activities: guided tours; summer lecture series; films; youth poet program for NH 4th graders; poetry readings.
Publications: newsletter, Friends of the Robert Frost Farm.
Hours & Admission Prices: May-June 22 & Sept. 3-Columbus Day Wed.-Sun. 10-5; June 23-Sept. 1 daily 10-5; groups by appointment. Adults $7, children 6-17 $3; NH residents and children 5 & under no charge.
Attendance: 6,500 (estimated)
Membership: Robert Frost Farm Trustees: Student $10; Individual $20; Family $35; Sponsor $50; Supporting $250; Corporate $500.

Dover

ANNIE E. WOODMAN INSTITUTE MUSEUM, 182 Central Ave., Dover, NH 03821-0146. Mailing Address: P.O. Box 146, Dover, NH 03821-0146. Tel.: 603-742-1038.
Founded: 1916.
Congressional District: 1
Governing Authority: nonprofit organization. Tax-exempt.
History Museum.
Collections: Indian artifacts; mineralogy; archaeology; insects; geology; herpetology; period furnishings; fire-fighting equipment; guns; toys; dolls; whaling; clothing; farm tools; local history; furniture; war memorial floor; paintings; Lincoln room. Historic Houses: c.1813 U.S. Senator John P. Hale Home; c.1818 Woodman House; c.1827 Keefe House; c.1675 Colonial Garrison House.
Research Fields: local area history.
Activities: gallery talks; permanent & temporary exhibitions.
Publications: newsletter.
Hours & Admission Prices: April-Nov. Wed.-Sun. 12:30-4:30. Adults $5, seniors 65 & over and students $4, children 14-16 $2; children under 12 when accompanied by an adult & members no charge. Closed holidays.
Membership: Individual $15; Family $25; Business $100.

THE CHILDREN'S MUSEUM OF NEW HAMPSHIRE, 6 Washington St., Dover, NH 03820-3814. Tel.: 603-742-2002. Fax: 603-742-2044.
E-mail: questions@childrens-museum.org
Web Site: www.childrens-museum.org
Formerly: The Children's Museum of Portsmouth
Founded: 1983.
Key Personnel: Exec. Dir., Denise K. Doleac; Chm. Bd., Michael Kenison; Exhibit Dir., Sue Kaufmann; Dir. Education, Jane Bard; Educator & Museum Shop Mgr., Carol Chambers; Dir. Visitor Svcs., Doug Tilton; Business Mgr., Sarah Osgood; Dir. Mktg., Heidi Duncanson; Volunteer Coord., Gabe Doleac; Membership & Special Programs, Katie West; Dir. Devel., Stephanie Ancona; Devel. Asst., Liz Bright; Exhibits Developer, Eric Yuan; Exhibits Developer, Xanthi Gray.
Personnel Profile: Full-Time Paid 11; Part-Time Paid 5; Part-Time Volunteers 115; Interns 3.
Governing Authority: nonprofit organization. Tax-exempt: 501(c)(3).
Children's Museum.
Collections: custom-created hands-on exhibits emphasizing world cultures; natural science; engineering; marine research; music; art; brainwaves & paleontology.
Facilities: Books, educational & museum-related items for sale.
Activities: performances; classes; education outreach programs; curriculum themed school visits; special events; daily art projects; after school & summer programs; community outreach.
Publications: quarterly newsletter; annual report; brochure.
Hours & Admission Prices: Summer Mon.-Sat. 10-5, Sun. 12-5; Spring, Fall & Winter: Tues.-Sat. 10-5, Sun. 12-5. Adults & children over one $8, seniors 65 & over $7; discounts to groups of 10 or more; ACM & ASTC members, museum members & children under one no charge. Closed New Year's Day; Easter; Labor Day; Thanksgiving; Christmas Eve & Day. ♿
Attendance: 97,829 (estimated)
Membership: Grandparent $44; individual $55, $5 each additional family member; Family of 2 $70, each additional family member $10; ACM & ASTC $120; contributing membership $250.

Durham

DURHAM HISTORIC ASSOCIATION MUSEUM, Rte. 108 & Main St., Durham, NH 03824-2815. Mailing Address: 15 Newmarket Rd., Durham, NH 03824-2815. Tel.: 603-868-5436.
E-mail: durhamhistoricassn@comcast.net
Web Site: www.ci.durham.nh.us/community/historic/dha.html
Founded: 1851.
Congressional District: 1
Key Personnel: Pres., Richard Lord.
Personnel Profile: Part-Time Paid 1; Part-Time Volunteers 5.
Governing Authority: society. Tax-exempt: 501(c)(3).
Local History Museum: housed in c.1825 Town Hall.
Collections: history pertaining to Durham; railroad benches; costumes; doctors' equipment; American Indian artifacts; lighting fixtures; handiwork of town's women; school equipment; maps; manuscripts; account books; church pewter; pew; cupola; 1835 lap organ; 1855 melodeon; 1757 Thomas Wille clock.
Research Fields: genealogy; church history; construction & history of Gundalow in the Piscataqua Basin; Durham Town History.
Facilities: approx. 300-vol. library of books on New Hampshire & local history available by special arrangement.
Activities: lectures; formally organized education programs for children; permanent & temporary exhibitions; walking tour of Durham's historic district.
Publications: quarterly newsletter, Walking Tour - Historic District; books, Landmarks in Ancient Dover, 1892; If Only Uncle Ben, 1971; History of Durham, New Hampshire in an Oystershell: 1600-1976; Durham, New Hampshire: A History 1900-1985; History of Durham, New Hampshire, 1913; Stackpole, reprinted 2 vols. in 1, 1994.
Hours & Admission Prices: June-Aug. Wed. 1-3; other times by appointment. No charge; donations accepted.
Attendance: 100 (estimated)
Membership: Regular & Contributing $10; Life $50.

JESSE HEPLER LILAC ARBORETUM, UNIVERSITY OF NEW HAMPSHIRE, 38 College Rd., Plant Biology Dept., Durham, NH 03824-3597. Tel.: 603-862-3222 & 3205. Fax: 603-862-4757.
Founded: 1941.
Congressional District: 1
Key Personnel: Head Arboretum, Dr. Owen M. Rogers; Sec. Plant Biology Dept., Charlotte Cooper.
Governing Authority: college. Affiliated with the University of New Hampshire. Tax-exempt.
Arboretum.
Collections: lilac species; cultivars.
Research Fields: breeding of late blooming lilacs.
Facilities: botanical garden; field research station.
Activities: guided tours.
Hours & Admission Prices: Mon.-Fri. 9-4:30; guided tours by appointment. No charge. Closed state & national holidays.

MUSEUM OF ART, UNH, (M), Paul Creative Arts Center, 30 Academic Way, Durham, NH 03824-2617. Tel.: 603-862-3712. Fax: 603-862-2191.
E-mail: museum.of.art@unh.edu
Web Site: www.unh.edu/moa
Founded: 1960.

Congressional District: 1
Key Personnel: Interim Dir., Weston LaFountain; Asst. Dir., Astrida Schaeffer; Education & Publicity Coord., Catherine A. Mazur; Administrative Asst., Cynthia Farrell.
Personnel Profile: Full-Time Paid 4; Part-Time Paid 11; Part-Time Volunteers 10; Interns 3.
Governing Authority: university. Affiliated with Univ. of New Hampshire. Tax-exempt.
Art Museum.
Collections: 20th-century works on paper; 19th-century American landscape paintings; 19th-century Japanese woodblock prints.
Major Exhibits: Guernica and Other Tales of War and Remembrance, 1/30/10-4/8/10; Langdon Quin, 1/30/10-4/8/10; 2010 Senior B.A. and B.F.A. Exhibition, 4/17/10-5/21/10; 2010 M.F.A. Thesis Exhibition, 4/17/10-5/21/10.
Facilities: 5,350 sq. ft. exhibition space.
Activities: inter-museum loan; temporary exhibitions & permanent collection; lectures; educational programs.
Publications: booklets; exhibition catalogues, A Stern & Lovely Scene: A Visual History of the Isles of Shoals, Circle of Friends: Art Colonies of Cornish & Dublin, The White Mountains: Place & Perceptions, By Good Hands: New Hampshire Folk Art, Hyman Bloom: Paintings & Drawings; Realism & Invention in the Prints of Albrecht Durer; Deeply Rooted: New Hampshire Traditions in Wood; On Great Bay: Paintings by Christopher Cook and Arthur Di Mambro; The Simple Art: Printed Images in an Age of Magnificence; Gabriel Laderman: Unconventional Realist.
Hours & Admission Prices: Sept.-May Mon.-Wed. 10-4, Thurs. 10-8, Sat.-Sun. 1-5. No charge; donations accepted. Closed university holidays. ♿
Attendance: 6,238 (accurate)
Membership: Contributor $25; Partner $50; Donor $100; Patron $500; Benefactor $1,000.

Enfield

ENFIELD SHAKER MUSEUM, 447 NH Rte. 4A, Enfield, NH 03748-3503. Tel.: 603-632-4346.
E-mail: info@shakermuseum.org
Web Site: www.shakermuseum.org
Formerly: Museum at Lower Shaker Village
Founded: 1987.
Congressional District: 2
Key Personnel: Dir., Mary Rose Boswell; Chm., Mardy High; Treas., Carolyn Maloney; Property Mgr., Tom Boswell; Interpreter, Arthur Gagnon; Herbalist, Happy Griffiths; Museum Shop Mgr. & Office Coord., Patricia Loven.
Personnel Profile: Full-Time Paid 5; Part-Time Paid 12; Part-Time Volunteers 95; Interns 2.
Governing Authority: private; nonprofit organization. Tax-exempt: 501(c)(3).
Historic Village: 1793 Shaker community.
Collections: Enfield Shaker Village history from 1790s to present; agricultural equipment; furniture; photographs; clothing; display herb, vegetable, & flower gardens.
Research Fields: Shaker herb gardening; Enfield Shaker history.
Facilities: limited library of Shaker history & garden resource material available to the public by appointment; botanical garden; classrooms; 1,500 sq. ft. exhibit space; 28 acres of land. Museum-related items for sale.
Activities: guided tours; lectures; films; concerts; workshops; formal education programs for adults; docent program; loan exhibitions. Overnight programs: Shaker Forum. Museum Sponsors: Taste of the Upper Valley; Festival of Shaker Crafts & Herbs; Harvest Festival; Christmas Cookie Fair.
Publications: brochure; newsletter, The Friends' Quarterly.
Hours & Admission Prices: Jan.-Memorial Day Mon.-Sat. 10-4, Sun. 12-4; late-May to Dec. Mon.-Sat. 10-5, Sun. 12-5. Adults $7.50, senior citizens $6.50, college students $5, children $3; discounts to AAM & ICOM members, bicycle tour groups & NICHE members; members no charge. Closed Easter; Thanksgiving; Christmas. ♿
Attendance: 8,000 (estimated)
Membership: Individual $30; Family & Dual $40.

LOCKEHAVEN SCHOOLHOUSE MUSEUM, Lockehaven Rd., Enfield, NH 03748. Mailing Address: P.O. Box 612, Enfield, NH 03748-0612. Tel.: 603-632-7740.
Founded: 1947.
Congressional District: 2
Key Personnel: C.E.O., John Goodwin; Vice Pres., Helen Goodwin; Treas., John P. Carr; Historian, Marjorie A. Carr.
Governing Authority: Affiliated with Enfield Historical Society. Tax-exempt.
Historic Building: 1864 Lockehaven Schoolhouse.
Collections: school textbooks & registers; town reports; scrapbooks; seats & desks; photos of former teachers back to 1854; early photos of Lockehaven & schools of surrounding districts.
Hours & Admission Prices: mid-June to Sept. Sun. 2-4. No charge; donations accepted.
Attendance: 150 (estimated)
Membership: Individual $10; Family $15; Contributing $25; Sustaining $50; Donor $100.

Enfield Center

ENFIELD HISTORICAL SOCIETY MUSEUM, Rte. 4A, Enfield Center, NH 03749. Mailing Address: P.O. Box 612, Enfield, NH 03748-0612. Tel.: 603-632-7740.
Founded: 1991.
Congressional District: 2
Key Personnel: Pres., John Goodwin; Vice Pres., Helen Goodwin; Treas., John P. Carr; Historian, Marjorie A. Carr.
Governing Authority: Affiliated with Enfield Historical Society. Tax-exempt.
Historical Society Museum: housed in an 1851 structure that was used as a schoolhouse for 95 years.
Collections: items emphasizing the history & manner of living in Enfield.
Facilities: 500-vol. library of newspaper clippings, private writings & photographs; 30-seat auditorium; 650 sq. ft. exhibit space.
Activities: permanent exhibitions.
Publications: newsletter.
Hours & Admission Prices: mid-June to Labor Day 2nd & 4th Sat. 2-4. No charge; donations accepted.
Attendance: 150 (estimated)
Membership: Individual $10; Family $15; Contributing $25; Sustaining $50; Patron $100.

Epping

EPPING HISTORICAL SOCIETY, 2 Water St., Epping, NH 03802. Mailing Address: P.O. Box 348, Epping, NH 03042-0348. Tel.: 603-679-2944.
Historical Society Museum.
Collections: local history & culture; photographs; geneaology; period furnishings; personal artifacts.
Hours & Admission Prices: Mon. 6pm-9pm, Wed. 10-2.

Exeter

AMERICAN INDEPENDENCE MUSEUM, One Governors Lane, Exeter, NH 03833-2420. Tel.: 603-772-2622. Fax: 603-772-0861.
E-mail: info@independencemuseum.org
Web Site: www.independencemuseum.org
Founded: 1991.
Congressional District: 1
Key Personnel: Dir., Gail Nessell Colglazier; Pres. (V), Eric MacDonald.
Personnel Profile: Full-Time Paid 1; Part-Time Paid 3; Part-Time Volunteers 40; Interns 4.
Governing Authority: nonprofit organization. Parent Institution: American Independence Center. Tax-exempt: 501(c)(3).
Historic House Museum: c.1721 Ladd-Gilman House & c.1775 Folsom Tavern.
Collections: historic documents; Revolutionary War era artifacts; Society of the Cincinnati in NH archives; 18th-19th centuries decorative arts.
Research Fields: New Hampshire & national history pertaining to the Revolutionary War & the founding of the government; Ladd, Folsom & Gilman families; Society of the Cincinnati in NH.
Facilities: library. Museum-related items for sale.
Activities: guided & self-guided tours; school & adult group programs; special programs for families, children & adults; rental facilities; research. Annual Event: American Independence Festival in July.
Publications: quarterly newsletter.
Hours & Admission Prices: May-Oct. Wed.-Sat. 10-4. Adults $5, students $3; discounts to AAA & AAM members; children under 6 & members no charge.
Attendance: 6,340 (accurate)
Membership: Individual $25; Family & Dual $40; Partner $100; Patron $250; Steward $500; Benefactor $1,000.

EXETER HISTORICAL SOCIETY, 47 Front St., Exeter, NH 03833-2707. Tel.: 603-778-2335.
Historical Society Museum.
Collections: local history & culture; photographs; documents; maps; period artifacts; china; dolls.
Activities: educational programs.
Hours & Admission Prices: Tues. & Thurs. 2-4:30, Sat. 9:30 to noon.

GILMAN GARRISON HOUSE, 12 Water St., Exeter, NH 03833. Mailing Address: 141 Cambridge St., Boston, MA 02114-2702. Tel.: 603-436-3205; 617-227-3956 (Historic New England). Fax: 617-227-9204.
Web Site: www.historicnewengland.org
Founded: 1965.
Congressional District: 1
Key Personnel: Pres., Carl Nold; Site Mgr., Elizabeth Farish.
Governing Authority: society; nonprofit organization. Parent Institution: Historic New England, 141 Cambridge St. Boston, MA 02114. Tax-exempt: 501 (c)(3).
Historic House: 1709 Gilman Garrison House.
Collections: furnishings; period artifacts.
Hours & Admission Prices: June-Oct. 15 by appointment. Adults $5.
Attendance: 433 (accurate)
Membership: National $35; Individual $45; Household $55; Garden & Landscape $75; Institutional $85; Contributing $100; Historic Homeowner $200; Supporting $250.

THE LAMONT GALLERY, (M), Phillips Exeter Academy, 11 Tan Lane, Exeter, NH 03833. Mailing Address: 20 Main St., Exeter, NH 03383. Tel.: 603-777-3461. Fax: 603-777-4371.
E-mail: gallery@exeter.edu
Web Site: www.exeter.edu/arts/8160.aspx
Founded: 1953.
Congressional District: 1
Key Personnel: Dir., Karen Burgess Smith; Gallery Mgr., Sara Zela.
Personnel Profile: Full-Time Paid 2; Part-Time Paid 3.
Governing Authority: preparatory school. Affiliated with The Phillips Exeter Academy, Exeter, NH. Tax-exempt.
Art Gallery.
Collections: paintings; photographs.
Major Exhibits: Emma Amos: Heroes & Folk, 11/16/09-1/23/10; Environments: Works by Evan Anderman '83, Liz Musick & Winslow Myers '58, 2/3/10-3/3/10; Apartheid: Angola and Beyond - Photographs by Jo Ractliffe, 3/29/10-5/1/10.
Facilities: 85-seat auditorium.
Activities: lectures; films; gallery talks; formally organized education program for students affiliated with The Phillips Exeter Academy; temporary & traveling exhibitions.
Hours & Admission Prices: Academic Year: Mon. 1-5, Tues.-Sat. 9-5; July Tues.-Fri. 9-4. No charge. Closed school holidays. ♿
Attendance: 5,000 (estimated)

Farmington

E3 CHILDREN'S MUSEUM & SCIENCE CENTER, 302 N. Orchard Ave., Farmington, NH 87401-6227. Tel.: 505-599-1425.
Key Personnel: Museum Coord., Crystal Williams
Children's Museum and Science Center.
Collections: science exhibits pertaining to dinosaurs, sound, light, magnetism & shadows art.
Hours & Admission Prices: Tues.-Sat. 12-5.

Fitzwilliam

FITZWILLIAM HISTORICAL SOCIETY & AMOS J. BLAKE HOUSE MUSEUM, 66 Rte. 119 - Village Green, Fitzwilliam, NH 03447. Mailing Address: P.O. Box 87, Fitzwilliam, NH 03447-0087. Tel.: 603-585-7742.
E-mail: fitzhs@peoplepc.com
Web Site: www.fitzhistoricalsociety.org/
Founded: 1966.
Key Personnel: Pres., Theresa Sillapaa.
Personnel Profile: Part-Time Volunteers 2.
Governing Authority: Parent Institution: Fitzwilliam Historical Society. Tax-exempt.
History Museum.
Collections: local history; furnishings; period artifacts; household items.
Facilities: library.
Activities: special events.
Publications: biannual newsletter.
Hours & Admission Prices: Museum: Memorial Day to Labor Day Sat. 1-4; other times by appointment. Research: Thurs. 9-11. No charge; donations accepted. ♿
Attendance: 35 (estimated)

Franconia

FRANCONIA HERITAGE MUSEUM, 553 Main St., Franconia, NH 03580. Mailing Address: P.O. Box 169, Franconia, NH 03580-0169.
E-mail: museum@franconiaheritage.org
Web Site: www.franconiah.org
Founded: 1998.
Congressional District: 2
Key Personnel: Pres., Philip Krill; Vice Pres., Ernest Hansberger.
Personnel Profile: Part-Time Paid 1; Part-Time Volunteers 10.
Governing Authority: Parent Institution: Franconia Area Heritage Council. Tax-exempt: 501(c)(3).
Historic House Museum.
Collections: personal artifacts; furnishings; Brooks; Parker; Dow Academy; Franconia College; Old Man of the Mountain.
Publications: semiannual newsletter.
Hours & Admission Prices: May-Oct. Thurs. & Sat. 1-4; other times by appointment. No charge; donations accepted. ♿
Attendance: 640 (accurate)
Membership: Individual $10; Family $25; Contributing $50; Supporting $75; Sustaining $150; Plus Major Donor $250; Lifetime $1,000.

THE FROST PLACE, Ridge Rd., Franconia, NH 03580. Mailing Address: P.O. Box 74, Franconia, NH 03580-0074. Tel.: 603-823-5510.
E-mail: rfrost@ncia.net
Web Site: www.frostplace.org
Founded: 1976.
Key Personnel: Admin., Therese Reger; Chm. Bd. (V), Deming P. Holleran
History Museum.
Collections: first editions of Robert Frost's works; memorabilia; poems; personal artifacts.
Activities: nature trail; summer conferences; school programs. Annual Events: Frost Day Celebration in July; Festival Conference in July & August.
Hours & Admission Prices: Memorial Day to July 1 Sat.-Sun. 1-5; July-Oct. 12 Wed.-Mon. 1-5. Suggested Donations: adults $5, seniors $4, children $3.

NEW ENGLAND SKI MUSEUM, Franconia Notch State Park, Pkwy. Exit 34B, Franconia, NH 03580. Mailing Address: P.O. Box 267, Franconia, NH 03580-0267. Tel.: 603-823-7177. Fax: 603-823-9505.
E-mail: staff@skimuseum.org
Web Site: www.skimuseum.org
Founded: 1977.
Congressional District: 2
Key Personnel: Exec. Dir., Jeffrey R. Leich; Pres. (V), Bo Adams; Museum Shop Mgr. & Front Desk Staffer, Linda Bradshaw; Front Desk Staffer, Kay Kerr.
Personnel Profile: Full-Time Paid 2; Part-Time Paid 3; Part-Time Volunteers 12.
Governing Authority: nonprofit. Tax-exempt: 501(c)(3).
Ski Museum.
Collections: ski artifacts; clothing; posters; photographs; films dating to the early 1930s; trophies & awards; oral history tapes; artwork.
Major Exhibits: Nordic Skiing from Stone Age to Skating, 11/09-5/10.
Research Fields: origins & development of skiing; ski technique; ski equipment.
Facilities: 1,500-vol. library pertaining to skiing, including scrapbooks, photo albums, organizational records & competition records; 35-seat auditorium; videos. Ski-related items for sale.
Activities: guided tours; lectures; loan & temporary exhibitions; film screenings on video. Annual Events: Hannes Schneider Meister Cup Race in March; Bretton Woods Nordic Marathon in March; Annual Meeting & Spirit of Skiing Award Presentation in Fall.
Publications: quarterly journal; books, Tales of the 10th, Over the Headwall; DVDs, Thrill and Spills, Ski Sentinels; reproduction vintage ski posters & photographs; postcards.
Hours & Admission Prices: Memorial Day-March daily 10-5. No charge; donations accepted. Closed Christmas. ♿
Attendance: 15,000 (accurate)
Membership: Individual $35; Family $50; Ski Clubs & Supporting $75; Sustaining $125; Life $1,000; Corporate $100, $250, $500, $1,000.

Franklin

DANIEL WEBSTER BIRTHPLACE, North Rd., off Rte. 127, Franklin, NH 03235. Mailing Address: P.O. Box 1856, Concord, NH 03302-1856. Tel.: 603-271-3556.
Web Site: www.nhstateparks.com/danielwebster.html
Key Personnel: Dir., Ben Wilson
Historic Site.
Collections: local history & culture relating to Daniel Webster.
Hours & Admission Prices: June 21-Sept 1. Sat.-Sun. 9-5. Adults $7, children 6-11 $3; New Hampshire residents & children 5 and under no charge.

Gilford

THOMPSON-AMES HISTORICAL SOCIETY, Gilford, NH 03247. Mailing Address: P.O. Box 7404, Gilford, NH 03247-7404. Tel.: 603-293-2877.
E-mail: thomames@metrocast.net
Web Site: www.gilfordhistoricalsociety.org
Key Personnel: Pres. (V), Karin Landry; Vice Pres., Donna Shinlever; Sec., Mary Jane Kwist; Treas., Rick Moses
Historical Society Museum.
Collections: Historic Houses: The Mt. Belknap Grange/John J. Morrill Store c.1857; The Union Meetinghouse c.1834; The Benjamin Rowe House c.1838.
Hours & Admission Prices: By appointment.

Gorham

GORHAM HISTORICAL SOCIETY AND RAIL MUSEUM, 25 Railroad St., Gorham, NH 03581-1638. Mailing Address: P.O. Box 351, Gorham, NH 03581-0351. Tel.: 603-466-5338.
E-mail: gorhamhistoricalsociety@gmail.com
Web Site: www.gorhamnewhampshire.com/railroadmuseum.html
Founded: 1973.
Key Personnel: Pres., Reuben Rajala
History Museum.
Collections: Gorham history; steam engine; box cars; period artifacts; clothing; photographs.
Hours & Admission Prices: Memorial Day weekend-Columbus Day daily 10-2 other times by appointment. No charge.

Hampton

TUCK MUSEUM, 40 Park Ave., Hampton, NH 03843-1601. Mailing Address: P.O. Box 1601, Hampton, NH 03843-1601. Tel.: 603-926-2543.
E-mail: info@hamptonhistoricalsociety.org
Web Site: www.hamptonhistoricalsociety.org
Founded: 1925.
Congressional District: 1
Key Personnel: Pres. (V), Bennett Moore; Dir., Betty Moore.
Personnel Profile: Full-Time Volunteers 1; Part-Time Volunteers 25.
Governing Authority: nonprofit organization. Parent Institution: Hampton Historical Society. Tax-exempt: 501(c)(3).
Local History Museum: Tuck Memorial Museum, located on the site of the original settlement of Hampton in 1638.
Collections: period artifacts & documents pertaining to colonial Hampton; trolley exhibit of E. H. & A. St. Ry. Co.; one-room district schoolhouse; fire museum; farm museum.
Research Fields: historical research of colonial Hampton.
Facilities: 500-vol. library of old books available on premises. Historical booklets, note paper, postcards & historical maps for sale.
Activities: guided tours; permanent exhibitions.
Publications: brochure; newsletter, Gatherings
Hours & Admission Prices: Wed., Fri. & Sun. 1-4; other times by appointment. No charge; donations accepted. ♿
Attendance: 1,200 (estimated)
Membership: Student & Senior Citizen $10; Individual $15; Family $25; Business $100.

Hancock

HANCOCK HISTORICAL SOCIETY, 7 Main St., Hancock, NH 03449-6008. Mailing Address: P.O. Box 138, Hancock, NH 03449-0138. Tel.: 603-525-9379.
E-mail: history@hancocknh.org
Web Site: www.hancocknh.org/hhs
Founded: 1903.
Congressional District: 2
Key Personnel: C.E.O. & Pres. (V), Ken Chester; Vice Pres., Maribeth Sullivan; Museum Dir., Cindy Amiden.
Personnel Profile: Part-Time Volunteers 25.
Governing Authority: private; nonprofit organization. Tax-exempt: 501(c)(3).
General Museum: housed in c.1809 Federal-style brick building which was possibly a tavern when built.
Collections: 18th to 20th-century archives & artifacts related to Hancock.
Research Fields: collection-related research.
Facilities: archive library of photographs & unpublished papers from Hancock natives available for public viewing. Museum-related items for sale.
Activities: docent program; guided tours; lectures; loan & temporary exhibitions.
Publications: quarterly newsletter, Hancock Historical Society News.
Hours & Admission Prices: Call for hours. No charge; donations accepted.
Attendance: 150 (estimated)
Membership: Individual $10; Life $250.

Hanover

* **HOOD MUSEUM OF ART, (M),** Wheelock St., Dartmouth College, Hanover, NH 03755. Mailing Address: Dartmouth College, HB 6034, Hanover, NH 03755. Tel.: 603-646-2808. Fax: 603-646-1400.
E-mail: hood.museum@dartmouth.edu
Web Site: www.hoodmuseum.dartmouth.edu
Founded: 1772.
Congressional District: 2
Key Personnel: Dir., Brian P. Kennedy; Assoc. Dir. & Cur. Academic Programming, Katherine Hart; Asst. Dir., Juliette Bianco; Security & Bldg. Mgr., Gary Alafat; Cur. European Art, T. Barton Thurber; Cur. Education, Lesley Wellman; Cur. American Art, Barbara J. MacAdam; Registrar & Collections Mgr., Katherine Hart; Assoc. Registrar, Kathleen O'Malley; Asst. Registrar, Cynthia Gilliland; Adjunct Cur. Costumes, Margaret E. Spicer; Lead Preparator, John Reynolds; Business Mgr., Nancy A. McLain; Gift Shop Mgr., Mary Ellen Rigby; Business Asst., Christine Macdonald; Exec. Asst., Roberta Shin; Data Mgr., Deborah Haynes; Coord. Public Rels., Rachel Tardelli Vermeal; Publications & Web Mgr., Nils Nadeau; Exhibitions Designer, Patrick Dunfey; School & Family Programs Coord., Neely McNulty; Preparator, Matthew Zayatz; Exhibitions & Events Coord., Karen Miller; Asst. Cur. Education, Amy Driscoll; Tour Coord., Adrienne Kermond; Coord. Membership, Sharon Reed.
Personnel Profile: Full-Time Paid 25; Full-Time Volunteers 4; Part-Time Paid 8; Part-Time Volunteers 35; Interns 7.
Governing Authority: college. Parent Institution: Dartmouth College. Tax-exempt: 501(c)(3).
Art Museum.
Collections: The Hood preserves approximately 65,000 works of art representing a broad range of cultural areas and historical periods. Selections that are always on view encompass ancient, Asian, Native American, Oceanic and African collections, European old master prints and nineteenth-century paintings, American colonial silver, portraiture, drawings, watercolors and paintings, as well as major works of modern and contemporary art.
Research Fields: art; ethnography; history.
Facilities: auditorium; seminar room; collections study. Museum-related items for sale.
Activities: permanent & traveling exhibitions; inter-museum loans; gallery talks; lectures; symposia; family and school programs; tours; receptions; summer music series.
Publications: exhibition catalogues; special publications; handbook, Treasures of the Hood Museum of Art; Hood Quarterly; gallery brochures; general brochures.
Hours & Admission Prices: Tues. & Thurs.-Sat. 10-5, Wed. 10-9, Sun. 12-5. No charge; donations accepted. Closed Independence Day; Thanksgiving. ♿
Attendance: 45,000 (accurate)

Haverhill

MUSEUM OF AMERICAN WEATHER, S. Common, Haverhill, NH 03765. Tel.: 603-989-3167.
History Museum.
Collections: New England weather history including the Blizzard of 1888, the 1938 hurricane, the 1927 Vermont flood, & a Worcester, MA tornado.
Hours & Admission Prices: Call for hours. No charge.

Hebron

PARADISE POINT NATURE CENTER, North Shore Rd., Hebron, NH 03241. Mailing Address: P.O. Box 142, Hebron, NH 03241-0142. Tel.: 603-744-3516 (July-Sept); 224-9909 (Sept.-July). Fax: 603-744-3516.
E-mail: nha@nhaudubon.org
Web Site: www.nhaudubon.org
Founded: 1969.
Governing Authority: nonprofit organization. Parent Institution: Audubon Society of New Hampshire. Branch Facility: Hebron Marsh Wildlife Sanctuary. Tax-exempt: 501(c)(3).
Nature Center & Wildlife Sanctuary.
Collections: live wildlife exhibits; taxidermal bird & mammal species; wildlife artifacts; natural history materials & specimens. Historic House: late 1800's, Ash Cottage.
Facilities: resource library; educational facilities; 400 sq. ft. exhibit space; nature trails; 43 acres of grounds. Natural history related books & gifts for sale.
Activities: lectures; organized educational programs; participatory exhibits; summer festival; summer day camp.
Hours & Admission Prices: July-Sept. Mon.-Sat. 10-4; other times by appointment. No charge; donations accepted.

Membership: Individual $25; Family $35.

Henniker

NEW ENGLAND COLLEGE GALLERY, 7 Main St., Henniker, NH 03242-6225. Tel.: 603-428-2329. Fax: 603-428-2266.
E-mail: dfurtkamp@nec.edu
Web Site: www.nec.edu
Founded: 1988.
Congressional District: 2
Key Personnel: Dir., Darryl Furtkamp.
Personnel Profile: Full-Time Paid 1; Part-Time Paid 1; Interns 2.
Governing Authority: private college; nonprofit. Parent Institution: New England College. Tax-exempt.
College Art Gallery.
Collections: concentration on contemporary art; paintings; photographs; works on paper.
Research Fields: computer imaging; children's book illustration; politically sensitive art; contemporary and post-modern art; photography.
Facilities: 1,300 sq. ft. exhibit space.
Activities: lectures; loan, participatory, temporary & traveling exhibits; training programs for professional museum workers.
Hours & Admission Prices: Tues.-Thurs. 11-6, Fri. 11-3. No charge. Closed Thanksgiving week; Christmas break. ♿
Attendance: 1,500 (estimated)

Hillsborough

THE FRANKLIN PIERCE HOMESTEAD, Rte. 31 & Rte. 9, Hillsborough, NH 03244. Mailing Address: P.O. Box 896, Hillsborough, NH 03244-0896. Tel.: 603-478-3165. Fax: 603-478-5500.
E-mail: c_chadwick@conknet.com
Web Site: www.franklinpierce.ws/homestead/homestead.html
Founded: 1804.
Congressional District: 2
Key Personnel: Chm. (V), Christina Chadwick; Pres. (V), Jane H. Waters; Architectural Historian, James Garvin, III; Museum Shop Mgr., Pat Bradley.
Personnel Profile: Part-Time Paid 2; Part-Time Volunteers 42.
Governing Authority: municipal; state; society. Parent Institution: Hillsborough Historical Society. Tax-exempt: 501(c)(3).
Historic House Museum: 1804 Mansion, built by Benjamin Pierce; childhood home of Franklin Pierce, 14th U.S. President.
Collections: period furniture; farm & household equipment; Pierce furniture, clothing, pictures & campaign posters.
Research Fields: economic & political lives of Benjamin & Franklin Pierce; early 19th century rural life.
Facilities: 70-seat auditorium; 5,000 sq. ft. exhibit space.
Activities: guided & walking tours; lectures; organized education programs for children; loan exhibitions.
Hours & Admission Prices: June & Sept. Sat. 10-4, Sun. 1-4; July-Aug. Mon.-Sat. 10-4, Sun. 1-4; other times by appointment. Adults $5, children 6-17 $1; NH residents over 65, Hillsboro residents, members & children under 6 no charge. ♿
Attendance: 4,750 (estimated)
Membership: Individual $5; Family $10; Corporate $25; Patron $100.

Holderness

SQUAM LAKES NATURAL SCIENCE CENTER, 23 Science Center Rd., Holderness, NH 03245. Mailing Address: P.O. Box 173, Holderness, NH 03245-0173. Tel.: 603-968-7194. Fax: 603-968-2229.
E-mail: info@nhnature.org
Web Site: www.nhnature.org
Formerly: Science Center of New Hampshire
Founded: 1966.
Congressional District: 2
Key Personnel: Chm. (V), Peter Wood; Exec. Dir., Iain MacLeod; Dir. Operations, Elizabeth Rowe; Museum Shop Mgr., Mary Ellen Downing.
Personnel Profile: Full-Time Paid 16; Part-Time Paid 18; Part-Time Volunteers 250; Interns 3.
Governing Authority: nonprofit organization. Tax-exempt: 501(c)(3).
Natural Science Museum.
Collections: 700 birds & mammals; Charles Goodhue collection.
Research Fields: environmental education.
Facilities: nature trails; indoor classrooms.
Activities: outdoor discovery hikes; lecture-demonstrations for school groups during school year; natural history cruises; special member programs.
Publications: quarterly newsletter; annual report.
Hours & Admission Prices: May-Nov. daily 9:30-4:30. Adults $13; discounts to ANCA members; AZA reciprocal admission; members no charge. ♿
Attendance: 78,505 (accurate)
Membership: Individual $40; Family $60; Family & Friends $80; Family & More Friends $100; Wetlands $125; Field $250; Forest $500; Mt. Fayal $1,000.

Hollis

HOLLIS HISTORICAL SOCIETY, 20 Main St., Hollis, NH 03049. Mailing Address: P.O. Box 754, Hollis, NH 03049-0754. Tel.: 603-465-3935.
Web Site: www.hollis-history.org
Historical Society Museum: housed in the Wheeler House.
Collections: local history & culture; permanent exhibits on the history of Hollis, NH; photographs. Historic House: The Always Ready Engine House.
Hours & Admission Prices: April-Oct. 1st & 3rd Sun. 1-4.

Hopkinton

NEW HAMPSHIRE ANTIQUARIAN SOCIETY, 300 Main St., Hopkinton, NH 03229-2627. Tel.: 603-746-3825.
E-mail: nhas@tds.net
Web Site: www.nhantiquarian.org
Founded: 1859.
Congressional District: 2
Key Personnel: Dir., Heather Mitchell; Pres. (V), Dr. Robert Wilson.
Personnel Profile: Part-Time Paid 2; Part-Time Volunteers 7; Interns 1.
Governing Authority: society. Tax-exempt: 501(c)(3) & 170(b).
Local History Museum.
Collections: Hopkinton genealogies from 1737 to present; town histories; early music books; NH imprints; costumes; local Indian artifacts; local household & agricultural equipment; early textbooks; almanacs; family Bibles; portraits.
Research Fields: local history; genealogy.
Facilities: 2,000-vol. library of local history & genealogy books available for use by appointment on premises.
Activities: programs for the public.
Publications: newsletter; books; calendar; poster.
Hours & Admission Prices: Thurs.-Fri. 9-4, Sat. 9-1. Admission charge for special events & exhibits only. Closed holidays. ♿
Attendance: 1,500 (estimated)
Membership: Individual $25; Family & Couple $40; Patron $100; Benefactor $250; Life Member $500.

Intervale

HARTMANN MODEL R.R. & TOY MUSEUM, Rte. 16, 15 Town Hall Rd., Intervale, NH 03845. Mailing Address: P.O. Box 165, Intervale, NH 03845-0165. Tel.: 603-356-9922. Fax: 603-356-9958.
E-mail: info@hartmannrr.com
Web Site: www.hartmannrr.com
Key Personnel: Dir., Roger Hartmann
Model Railroad Museum.
Collections: operating model train layouts from G to Z scales.
Facilities: cafe. Museum-related items for sale.
Hours & Admission Prices: June & Sept.-Oct. Wed.-Mon. 10-5; July-Aug. daily 10-5; Nov.-May Fri.-Mon. 10-5: Closed Easter; Mother's Day; Thanksgiving; Christmas.

Jaffrey

JAFFREY CIVIC CENTER, 40 Main St., Jaffrey, NH 03452-6144. Tel.: 603-532-6527. Fax: 603-532-6527.
E-mail: jaffreycntr@aol.com
Web Site: www.jaffreyciviccneter.com
Founded: 1966.
Key Personnel: Exec. Dir., Dion Owens.
Personnel Profile: Part-Time Paid 2; Part-Time Volunteers 33.
Governing Authority: nonprofit organization. Affiliated with Jaffrey Gilmore Foundation. Tax-exempt.
Art Foundation & Historical Society.
Collections: paintings; photographs; sculptures; drawings.
Facilities: research library specializing in nature, art, Americana; meeting room, classroom; auditorium & art gallery.
Activities: meeting space for cultural & civic organizations; art exhibitions, classes & workshops, outreach art & history program with the schools.
Hours & Admission Prices: Tues. 10-6, Wed.-Fri. 1-5, Sat. 10-2. No charge. Closed national holidays.
Attendance: 12,000 (estimated)

MELVILLE ACADEMY MUSEUM, Thorndike Pond Rd., Jaffrey, NH 03452. Mailing Address: P.O. Box 722, Jaffrey, NH 03452-0722. Tel.: 603-532-7455.
Founded: 1920.
History Museum.
Collections: area history; period furnishings; Hannah Davis bandboxes; scrapbooks; 19th century kitchen; agricultural tools.
Hours & Admission Prices: July-Aug. Sat.-Sun. 2-4; other times by appointment. No charge; donations accepted.
Attendance: 240 (estimated)

Jefferson

JEFFERSON HISTORICAL MUSEUM, Rte. 2 900 Presidential Hwy., Jefferson, NH 03583. Mailing Address: P.O. Box 143, Jefferson, NH 03583-0143. Tel.: 603-586-7021.
Key Personnel: Pres., Joe Marshall
Historic Building: housed in an 1868 church.
Collections: Jefferson history; period artifacts.
Hours & Admission Prices: June to Columbus Day Tues., Thurs, & Sat. 11-2. No charge.

Keene

HISTORICAL SOCIETY OF CHESHIRE COUNTY, 246 Main St., Keene, NH 03431-4143. Mailing Address: P.O. Box 803, Keene, NH 03431-0803. Tel.: 603-352-1895. Fax: 603-352-9226.
E-mail: hscc@hsccnh.org
Web Site: www.hsccnh.org
Founded: 1927.
Congressional District: 2
Key Personnel: Dir. & C.E.O., Alan F. Rumrill; Pres. (V), Carl Jacobs.
Personnel Profile: Full-Time Paid 2; Part-Time Paid 2; Part-Time Volunteers 100; Interns 1.
Governing Authority: society. Branch Museums: Wyman Tavern Museum. Tax-exempt: 501(c)(3).
Historical Society: housed in c.1870 Italianate Mansion.
Collections: period furnishings; glass; pottery; silver; toys; photographs; archives.
Research Fields: local history.
Facilities: 3,000-vol. library pertaining to local history & genealogy available to the public; 3,500 sq. ft. exhibit space.
Activities: lectures; films; radio programs; organized education programs for children & undergraduate & graduate college students affiliated with Keene State College; temporary exhibitions.
Publications: bimonthly newsletter.
Hours & Admission Prices: Tues. & Thurs.-Fri. 9-4, Wed. 9-9, Sat. 9-12. No charge; donations accepted. ♿
Attendance: 24,000 (estimated)
Membership: Senior $25; Individual $30; Family $40; Sponsor $50; Contributing $100.

HORATIO COLONY HOUSE MUSEUM & NATURE PRESERVE, 199 Main St., Keene, NH 03431-3780. Tel.: 603-352-0460.
E-mail: colonymuseum@webryders.com
Web Site: horatiocolonymuseum.org
Founded: 1977.
Key Personnel: C.E.O., Anita Carroll-Weldon; Pres. (V), Frank Coolidge; Financial Dir., Stedman Buttrick.
Personnel Profile: Full-Time Paid 1; Part-Time Volunteers 8; Interns 1.
Governing Authority: private; nonprofit organization. Tax-exempt.
Historic Houses & Historic Buildings: c.1806 family home of antique collector & author Horatio Colony, grandson of Keene's first mayor & owner of the city's woolen mill.
Collections: 19th - early 20th century furniture; furnishings; decorative arts; portraits; photos; diaries; personal artifacts; cribbage boards; ink wells; door stops; porcelain figures; pitchers; engravings; napkin rings; glass paper weights; bottles & decanters; transferware platters; Middle Eastern brass artifacts; oriental rugs; period books; Buddhist & Hindu images.
Major Exhibits: Civil War Engravings & Letters, 5/10-10/15/10.
Research Fields: oriental rug collection.
Facilities: 400 sq. ft. exhibit space; garden; 615 acre nature preserve at a non-contiguous site.
Activities: concerts; docent program; guided tours; lectures; rental gallery; temporary exhibitions.
Hours & Admission Prices: May to mid-Oct. Tues.-Sat. 11-4; mid-Oct. to April by appointment. No charge.
Attendance: 2,000 (accurate)

THORNE-SAGENDORPH ART GALLERY, (M), Wyman Way, Keene, NH 03435-0001. Mailing Address: 229 Main St., Keene State College, Keene, NH 03435-3501. Tel.: 603-358-2720. Fax: 603-358-2238.
E-mail: thorne@keene.edu
Web Site: www.keene.edu/tsag
Founded: 1965.
Congressional District: 2
Key Personnel: Dir., Maureen Ahern.
Personnel Profile: Part-Time Paid 4; Part-Time Volunteers 40; Interns 1.
Governing Authority: Keene State College. Tax-exempt.
Art Gallery.
Collections: paintings; prints; drawings; sculpture; crafts; regional & national artists; slide collections of all exhibits.
Major Exhibits: Biennial KSC Art Faculty Exhibit, 1/23/10-2/10; Emerging Art, KSC Art Student Exhibit, 4/10-5/8/10.
Activities: guided tours; lectures; films; gallery talks; concerts; formally organized education programs for children; loan, temporary & traveling exhibitions.
Publications: catalogs & brochures of exhibitions.
Hours & Admission Prices: June-Aug. Wed.-Sun. 12-4; Sept.-May Thurs.-Fri. 12-7, Sat.-Wed. 12-4; other times by appointment. No charge; donations accepted. Closed academic holidays; semester breaks. ♿
Attendance: 6,000 (estimated)
Membership: Senior Citizens & Students $15; Individual $20; Family $30; Donor $50-$99; Sponsor $100-$249; Associate $250-$499; Benefactor $500 & up.

THE WYMAN TAVERN, 339 Main St., Keene, NH 03431. Mailing Address: P.O. Box 803, Keene, NH 03431-0803. Tel.: 603-352-1895. Fax: 603-352-9226.
Web Site: www.hsccnh.org
Founded: 1968.
Congressional District: 2
Key Personnel: C.E.O., Alan F. Rumrill; Chm. & Pres. (V), Carl B. Jacobs.
Personnel Profile: Full-Time Paid 2; Part-Time Paid 2; Part-Time Volunteers 20; Interns 1.
Governing Authority: society. Parent Institution: Historical Society of Cheshire County, Inc. Tax-exempt: 501(c)(3).
Historic House: 1762 Wyman Tavern.
Collections: early 19th-century furnishings; portraits; objects made or owned locally.
Research Fields: local history.
Facilities: Postcards & note paper for sale.
Activities: guided tours; permanent & temporary exhibitions; craft demonstrations; school tours; special group tours; lecture series; music programs; living history.
Publications: newsletter.
Hours & Admission Prices: June to Labor Day Thurs.-Sat. 11-4. Adults $3; children under 12 & members no charge.
Attendance: 1,500 (estimated)
Membership: Senior $25; Individual $30; Family $40; Contributing $100.

Laconia

THE BELKNAP MILL SOCIETY, 25 Beacon St. East, The Mill Plaza, Laconia, NH 03246-3445. Tel.: 603-524-8813. Fax: 603-528-1228.
E-mail: director@belknapmill.org
Web Site: www.belknapmill.org
Founded: 1970.
Congressional District: 1
Key Personnel: Acting Dir. & C.O.O., John Moriarty; Pres., Chris Guilmett; Cur., Roger Gibbs; Curatorial Asst., Ted Shastany; Curatorial Asst., John Pounds; Curatorial Asst., Stewart Ramsay; Curatorial Asst., Allan Richardson; Visitor Svcs. Specialist, Nancy Paquette; Business Svcs. Specialist, Patricia Guevin; Facilities Specialist, Todd Frazier; Archivist, Inge Hilberg; Gift Shop Mgr., Tour Guide & Administrative Asst., Barbara Waite.
Personnel Profile: Full-Time Paid 2; Part-Time Paid 12; Part-Time Volunteers 115; Interns 2.
Governing Authority: nonprofit organization. Tax-exempt: 501(c)(3).
Art & History Museum: housed in 1823 brick textile building.
Collections: mill architecture; textile machinery and knitted products; industrial knitting; photographs; documents.
Research Fields: industrial knitting.
Facilities: library; 16,000 sq. ft. exhibit space; 260-seat theatre; art gallery; permanent exhibit. Art, crafts & mill-related items for sale.
Activities: guided tours; lectures; concerts; arts festivals; theatre; participatory, loan, temporary & traveling exhibits; outdoor concerts & walking tours by the river. Society Sponsors: Book Sale; Mill Anniversary.
Publications: program booklet; quarterly newsletter; teacher packet.
Hours & Admission Prices: Mon.-Fri. 9-5, Sat. 9-3, Sun. 10-2, call to confirm; other days & evenings during special events. Fees for special events;

discounts to AAM & ICOM members; no charge; donations accepted. Closed New Year's Day; Memorial Day; Independence Day; Labor Day; Christmas. ♿
Attendance: 50,000 (accurate)
Membership: Children $10; Individual $25; Family $40; Contributing & Associate $50; Patron $100; Donor $250; Benefactor $500; Friend $1,000; Bell Ringer $5,000.

LAKE WINNIPESAUKEE MUSEUM & HISTORICAL SOCIETY, 503 Endicott St. N., Rte. 3, Laconia, NH 03246-1725. Mailing Address: P.O. Box 5386, Weirs, NH 03247-5386. Tel.: 603-366-5950; 603-366-7301.
E-mail: info@lwhs.us
Web Site: www.lwhs.us
Founded: 1985.
Key Personnel: Chm. (V), Robert Lawton; Pres. (V), Brian Vincent; Museum Shop Mgr., Vynnie Hale.
Governing Authority: Tax-exempt.
Historic House Museum.
Collections: local history; boats; beaches; photographs; models.
Hours & Admission Prices: May-Oct. Tues.-Sat. 10-2. No charge; donations accepted. ♿
Attendance: 1,000 (accurate)
Membership: 1 year $10; 5 years $25; Lifetime $100.

Lancaster

THE LANCASTER HISTORICAL SOCIETY, 226 Main St., Lancaster, NH 03584-3038. Mailing Address: P.O. Box 473, Lancaster, NH 03584-0473. Tel.: 603-788-3004.
Founded: 1964.
Congressional District: 1
Key Personnel: Pres. (V), Lawrence Powell.
Governing Authority: nonprofit organization. Tax-exempt: 501(c)(3).
Local History Museum: housed in 1780 Wilder-Holton House, first two-story house built in the county.
Collections: history; archives pertaining to people of Lancaster; manuscript collections.
Research Fields: local manufacturing; architecture; local artists; local history.
Facilities: 50-vol. library of local history; books by local authors available for use on premises. Second-hand books. Postcards & bicentennial items for sale.
Activities: guided tours; films; permanent & temporary exhibitions.
Publications: quarterly newsletter.
Hours & Admission Prices: Open by appointment only; tours during summer months. No charge; donations accepted. ♿
Membership: Single $10.

Lebanon

AVA GALLERY AND ART CENTER, 11 Bank St., Lebanon, NH 03766-1749. Tel.: 603-448-3117. Fax: 603-448-4827.
E-mail: constance@avagallery.org
Web Site: www.avagallery.org
Key Personnel: Exec. Dir., Bente Torjusen; Dir. Education, Adam Blue; Office Mgr., Constance Creed; Publications & Web, Barbara Jones; Coord. Exhibition, Kiku Langford; Studio Mgr., Murray Ngoima; Bookkeeper, Abagail Murphy.
Governing Authority: Tax-exempt: 501(c)(3)
Art Gallery.
Collections: paintings; photographs; sculpture.
Hours & Admission Prices: Tues.-Sat. 11-5; other times by appointment. No charge. ♿

Manchester

ALVA DEMARS MEGAN CHAPEL ART CENTER, (M), 100 Saint Anselm Dr. #1718, Saint Anselm College, Manchester, NH 03102-1308. Tel.: 603-641-7470 & 7000. Fax: 603-641-7116.
E-mail: chapelartcenter@anselm.edu
Web Site: www.anselm.edu/chapelart
Founded: 1967.
Congressional District: 1
Key Personnel: Dir., Iain MacLellan, O.S.B.; Asst. Cur., Jessica Pappathan; Administrative Asst., Lorraine Kulik.
Personnel Profile: Full-Time Paid 2; Part-Time Paid 1.
Governing Authority: college. Parent Institution: Saint Anselm College. Tax-exempt: 501(c)(3).
College Art Museum & Center.
Collections: works by area craftsmen; sculpture; paintings; graphics.
Research Fields: 19th- & 20th-century art.
Facilities: 1923 former college chapel, decorated with wall & ceiling frescoes & stained glass, 1923-31.
Activities: lectures; gallery talks; loan, temporary & traveling exhibitions.
Hours & Admission Prices: Tues.-Wed. & Fri.-Sat. 10-4, Thurs. 10-8. No charge. Closed holidays; college breaks; between exhibitions. ♿
Attendance: 5,000 (accurate)

AMERICA'S CREDIT UNION MUSEUM, 418-420 Notre Dame Ave., Manchester, NH 03102. Mailing Address: P.O. Box 603, Manchester, NH 03105-0603. Tel.: 603-629-1553. Fax: 603-629-1595.
Key Personnel: Exec. Dir., Peggy Powell
History Museum.
Collections: credit union history; photographs; personal artifacts.
Hours & Admission Prices: Mon., Wed. & Fri. 10-12 & 1-4; other times by appointment.

* **CURRIER MUSEUM OF ART, (M),** 150 Ash St., Manchester, NH 03104-4347. Tel.: 603-669-6144, ext. 108. Fax: 603-669-7194.
E-mail: visitor@currier.org
Web Site: www.currier.org
Founded: 1929.
Congressional District: 1
Key Personnel: C.E.O. & Dir., Susan E. Strickler; Pres. (V), David Jensen; Deputy Dir., Susan Leidy; Dir. Finance, Sherry Collins; Chief Cur., P. Andrew Spahr; Assoc. Cur., Kurt Sundstrom; Head Public Programs, Leah Fox; Art Center Dir., Bruce Mc Coll; Public Rels., Karen Tebbenhoff; Museum Shop Mgr., Heidi Norton.
Personnel Profile: Full-Time Paid 29; Part-Time Paid 50; Part-Time Volunteers 150.
Governing Authority: nonprofit organization. Tax-exempt: 501(c)(3).
Art Museum.
Collections: European and American painting & sculpture; American 17th, 18th & early 19th-century furniture, silver, glass, pewter and textiles; graphics; 15th-century Tournai tapestry. Historic House: 1950 Zimmerman House, a Usonian home designed by Frank Lloyd Wright.
Research Fields: pertaining to collections.
Facilities: 7,000-vol. library of art books; periodicals; 180-seat auditorium; classrooms. Paperback books, postcards, reproductions & gallery publications for sale.
Activities: guided group tours of museum & Zimmerman house; lectures; gallery talks; concerts; formally organized educational programs; children's studio art classes; docent program or council; inter-museum loan, permanent & temporary exhibitions.
Publications: annual report; exhibition catalogs; calendar; membership & exhibition brochures.
Hours & Admission Prices: Sun.-Mon. & Wed.-Fri. 11-5, Sat. 10-5, 1st Thurs. of month 11-8. Adults $10, seniors $9, students $8; members & children under 18 no charge. ♿
Attendance: 50,407 (accurate)

FRANCO-AMERICAN CENTRE, 52 Concord St., Manchester, NH 03101-1806. Tel.: 603-669-4045. Fax: 603-669-0644.
Founded: 1990.
Congressional District: 1
Key Personnel: Pres. (V), Thomas DeBlois.
Personnel Profile: Part-Time Paid 1; Part-Time Volunteers 12.
Governing Authority: Tax-exempt.
French Heritage Museum.
Collections: French heritage & culture; paintings; photographs; personal artifacts; period furnishings; sculpture.
Facilities: library.
Activities: cultural programs; musical performances; temporary exhibitions; special events; film series.
Hours & Admission Prices: Mon.-Fri. 10-4. No charge; donations accepted. Closed holidays. ♿
Membership: Student & Senior $35; Single $40; Dual & Family $60; Contributor $100; Cartier $250; Frontenac $500; Lafayette $1,000 & up.

LAWRENCE L. LEE SCOUTING MUSEUM, 40 Blondin Rd., Manchester, NH 03109-5907. Mailing Address: 571 Holt Ave., Manchester, NH 03109-5213. Tel.: 603-669-8919; 603-625-6431. Fax: 603-625-2467.
E-mail: administrator@scoutingmuseum.org
Web Site: www.scoutingmuseum.org
Founded: 1969.
Congressional District: 1
Key Personnel: Scout Exec., Michael Kaufman.
Personnel Profile: Full-Time Paid 1; Part-Time Volunteers 12.
Governing Authority: nonprofit. Daniel Webster Council, Boy Scouts of America, Manchester. Tax-exempt: 501(c)(3).

Scouting Museum.
Collections: Boy Scouts of America memorabilia; uniforms; equipment; badges & patches; books; manuals; manuscripts; periodicals; items from world Scouting; Scouts on stamps.
Research Fields: pertaining to Scouting.
Facilities: 2,800 plus-vol. library of official handbooks; training manuals; yearbooks; diaries; pamphlets; fiction; Boys' Life & Scouting magazines; manuscripts & photographs, available for use on-site by the public; 3,000 sq. ft. exhibit space. Scouting items for sale.
Activities: guided tours; scavenger hunt; Jamboree-on-the-Air.
Publications: quarterly Scouting historical journal, Scout Memorabilia.
Hours & Admission Prices: July-Aug. Mon.-Sat. 10-4; Sept.-June Sat. 10-4. No charge; donations accepted. Closed Independence Day; Christmas. ♿
Attendance: 3,037 (accurate)
Membership: Friend $25; Associate $50; Advocate $100; Patron $250; Benefactor $500; Golden Eagle $1,000.

MILLYARD MUSEUM, (M), 200 Bedford St., Manchester, NH 03101. Mailing Address: 200 Bedford St., 1st Fl., Manchester, NH 03101-1132. Tel.: 603-622-7531. Fax: 603-641-8191.
E-mail: history@manchesterhistoric.org
Web Site: www.manchesterhistoric.org
Founded: 1896.
Congressional District: 2
Key Personnel: Exec. Dir., Aurore Eaton; Pres., Elizabeth L. La Rocca; Cur. Museum Collection, Marylou Ashooh Lazos; Cur. Library Collection, Eileen O'Brien.
Personnel Profile: Full-Time Paid 4; Part-Time Paid 4; Part-Time Volunteers 10; Interns 4.
Governing Authority: society. Parent Institution: Manchester Historic Association. Tax-exempt: 501(c)(3).
Local History Museum.
Collections: history of greater Manchester area from prehistory to present; decorative arts; architectural illustrations & fragments; fire-fighting equipment; tools; costumes; paintings; prints; guns; toys; photographs; business records & maps; manuscripts; textile manufacturing records.
Major Exhibits: Abraham Lincoln: Manchester Remember, 11/09-6/10.
Research Fields: history of the Manchester area; early textile industry; labor history; Native Americans; immigration.
Facilities: research center.
Activities: guided tours; lectures; inter-museum loan; permanent & temporary exhibitions; special events; historic preservation workshops; concerts; walking tours; programs for children & families.
Publications: MHA News; calendar of events; Picturing Manchester; Photos from the MHA Collection; reprint of 1948 Manchester on the Merrimack; Manchester Streetcars; Valley Cemetery Walking Tour; Video: Preserving Manchester; Lake Massabesic; Images Then & Now; Remembering the Valley Cemetery; Manchester Stories.
Hours & Admission Prices: Museum: Wed.-Sat. 10-4. Research Center: Wed. & Sat. 10-4. Adults $6, seniors & college students $5, children 6-18 $2; discounts to AASLH & NEMA members; children under 6, members & library no charge. Closed New Year's Day; Independence Day; Veterans Day; Thanksgiving; Christmas Eve & Day. ♿
Attendance: 6,000 (estimated)
Membership: Student & Senior $25; Individual $30; Senior Family $50; Family & Dual $60; Patron $125; Benefactor $250; Sponsor $500; F.P. Carpenter Circle $1,000; Corporate $250-$10,000.

NEW HAMPSHIRE INSTITUTE OF ART, 148 Concord St., Manchester, NH 03104-4858. Tel.: 603-623-0313. Fax: 603-641-1832.
Founded: 1898.
Congressional District: 1
Key Personnel: Pres., Roger Williams; Academic Dean, Patrick McCay; Dir. Devel., Jessica Kinsey; Dir. Admissions, Liam Sullivan; Vice Pres. Finance & Administration, Erik Gross; Shop Mgr., Joe Vivilecchia; Dir. Gallery, Alison Williams.
Personnel Profile: Full-Time Paid 48; Part-Time Paid 17.
Governing Authority: school; nonprofit educational. Tax-exempt: 501(c)(3).
Art Institute.
Collections: contemporary regional fine arts & traditional crafts.
Research Fields: fine arts; institute; contemporary arts.
Facilities: rental facilities; 450-seat auditorium.
Activities: academic & public programs; educational services for schools & teachers; visual arts exhibitions; concerts; programs for young people.
Publications: admissions viewbook; quarterly newsletter; CE course catalogs; annual report; exhibition postings.
Hours & Admission Prices: Mon.-Fri. 9-5, Sat. 9-12. No charge. Closed legal holidays. ♿
Attendance: 27,500 (estimated)

SEE SCIENCE CENTER, 200 Bedford St., Manchester, NH 03101-1132. Tel.: 603-669-0400. Fax: 603-669-0400.
E-mail: info@see-sciencecenter.org
Web Site: www.see-sciencecenter.org
Founded: 1986.
Congressional District: 1
Key Personnel: Dir., Douglas Heuser; Education & Membership, Rebecca Mayhew; Operations & Design, Adele Maurier; Devel. Coord., Peter Gustafson.
Personnel Profile: Full-Time Paid 5; Part-Time Paid 6; Part-Time Volunteers 20.
Governing Authority: private; nonprofit organization. Tax-exempt: 501(c)(3).
Science Museum.
Collections: hands-on exhibitions; Lego reproduction of Millyard.
Facilities: educational facilities. Museum-related items for sale.
Activities: formal education programs; moon walk; Van de Graaf generator; chem lab; momentum chair; guided tours; traveling exhibitions.
Publications: quarterly newsletter, SEE News.
Hours & Admission Prices: Mon.-Fri. 10-4, Sat.-Sun. 10-5. Admission $6; children under 1 & members no charge. Closed New Year's Day; Easter; Memorial Day; Independence Day; Labor Day; Thanksgiving; Christmas. ♿
Attendance: 75,000 (estimated)
Membership: Family $70.

Melvin Village

TUFTONBORO HISTORICAL SOCIETY & MUSEUM, Rte. 109, Melvin Village, NH 03850. Mailing Address: P.O. Box 372, Melvin Village, NH 03850-0372. Tel.: 603-544-7225.
Key Personnel: Dir., Margaret Bashe
History Museum.
Collections: local Tuftonboro history.
Hours & Admission Prices: July & Aug. Mon.-Fri. 2-4. No charge.

Meredith

MEREDITH CHILDREN'S MUSEUM, 28 Lang St., Meredith, NH 03253-5824. Tel.: 603-279-6307.
Children's Museum.
Collections: hands-on exhibits.
Activities: hands-on exhibits.
Hours & Admission Prices: Mon.-Fri. 10-4, Sat.-Sun. 12-4. Admission $6. Closed Easter; Thanksgiving; Christmas.
Membership: Family $125.

Meriden

AIDRON DUCKWORTH ART MUSEUM, 21 Bean Rd., Meriden, NH 03770. Mailing Address: P.O. Box 61, Meriden, NH 03770-0061. Tel.: 603-469-3444.
E-mail: info@aidronduckworthmuseum.org
Web Site: www.aidronduckworthmuseum.org
Personnel Profile: Full-Time Volunteers 1.
Governing Authority: Parent Institution: Aidron Duckworth Art Preservation Trust. Tax-exempt.
Art Museum.
Collections: artwork by Aidron Duckworth & local artists.
Major Exhibits: Exhibition XV - The Phoenix Paintings, 5/10-7/25/10; Exhibition XVI - Interior Imaging, 7/31/10-10/24/10.
Research Fields: Aidron Duckworth's art & writings on teaching art.
Facilities: archives.
Activities: temporary exhibitions.
Publications: booklet, The Paintings and Drawings by Aidron Duckworth.
Hours & Admission Prices: Fri.-Sun. 10-5; other times by appointment. No charge; donations accepted. ♿
Attendance: 375 (estimated)

Milton

NEW HAMPSHIRE FARM MUSEUM, INC., (M), 1305 White Mountain Hwy., Milton, NH 03851. Mailing Address: P.O. Box 644, Rte. 125, Milton, NH 03851-0644. Tel.: 603-652-7840. Fax: 603-652-7840 (call first).
E-mail: info@farmmuseum.org
Web Site: www.farmmuseum.org
Founded: 1970.
Congressional District: 1
Key Personnel: Exec. Dir., Kathleen Shea; Pres. (V), Victor Becker.
Personnel Profile: Full-Time Paid 1; Part-Time Paid 4; Part-Time Volunteers 6; Interns 2.
Governing Authority: board of trustees; nonprofit organization. Tax-exempt: 501(c)(3).

Agriculture & Rural Life Museum: former Jones Farm with buildings dating from 1780s-1900s; the Plummer Homestead.
Collections: farm tools; machinery; implements; oral histories; photographs; books; artifacts from late 1800s to early 1900s; farm buildings; shoe shop; blacksmith shop; family farm life of the 1890's; tractors; carriages.
Research Fields: agriculture; New England farming.
Facilities: library.
Activities: house tours; country store; special events; workshops; demonstrations; displays. Annual Events: Farm Day; Children's Day.
Publications: quarterly newsletter; special events brochure & calendar.
Hours & Admission Prices: Memorial Day to mid-Oct. Wed.-Sun. 10-4. Adults $6, children 3-17 $3; discount to groups of 20 or more; members no charge. ♿
Attendance: 4,000 (estimated)
Membership: Individual $20; Couple $30; Family $45; Contributing $50; Supporting $100; Sustaining $300; Patron $500.

Moultonborough

CASTLE IN THE CLOUDS, 455 Old Mountain Rd., Moultonborough, NH 03254. Mailing Address: P.O. Box 687, Moultonborough, NH 03254-0687. Tel.: 603-476-5900. Fax: 603-476-2512.
Key Personnel: Gen. Mgr., Jim Cande
Historic House: housed in the former estate of Tom & Olive Plant; built in 1914.
Collections: family history; personal artifacts; period furnishings; photographs.
Facilities: cafe.
Hours & Admission Prices: Call for hours. Adults $12, seniors 65 & over $9, youth 7-14 $5; children under 6 no charge.

Nashua

ABBOT-SPALDING HOUSE MUSEUM, 5 Abbot St., Nashua, NH 03064-2119. Tel.: 603-883-0015. Fax: 603-889-8515.
E-mail: nashuahistorical@comcast.net
Web Site: www.nashuahistoricalsociety.org
Founded: 1870.
Personnel Profile: Full-Time Paid 1; Full-Time Volunteers 2; Part-Time Paid 3; Part-Time Volunteers 62.
Governing Authority: Parent Institution: Nashua Historical Society. Tax-exempt.
House Museum.
Collections: Nashua history & genealogy; period furnishings; fine glass & china; paintings.
Research Fields: Nashua history & genealogy.
Facilities: library.
Publications: newsletter.
Hours & Admission Prices: Abbot-Spalding Museum: by appointment. Florence H. Speare Memorial Museum: March-Thanksgiving weekend Tues.-Thurs. 10-4; other times by appointment. No charge; donations accepted.
Membership: Student $5; Adult $25; Family $40; Lifetime $250.

HUNT MEMORIAL BUILDING, 6 Main St., Nashua, NH 03064-2712. Tel.: 603-594-3661.
Historic Building: housed in the former Nashua Public Library. Listed on the National Register of Historic Buildings.
Collections: local history; photographs; period furnishings.
Activities: rental facilities.
Hours & Admission Prices: Tours: by appointment.

New Ipswich

BARRETT HOUSE, FOREST HALL, 79 Main St., New Ipswich, NH 03071-3716. Mailing Address: 141 Cambridge St., Boston, MA 02114-2702. Tel.: 860-928-4074; 617-227-3956. Fax: 617-227-9204.
Web Site: www.historicnewengland.org
Founded: 1948.
Congressional District: 2
Key Personnel: Pres., Carl Nold; Site Mgr., Lisa Centola.
Governing Authority: society; nonprofit organization. Parent Institution: Historic New England, 141 Cambridge St., Boston, MA 02114. Tax-exempt: 501 (c)(3).
Historic House: c.1800 Barrett House, Forest Hall, Federal residence.
Collections: 18th- & 19th-century furniture; period musical instruments; Gothic Revival summer house.
Activities: guided tours; lectures; outdoor events.
Publications: visitors guide.
Hours & Admission Prices: June-Oct. 15 2nd & 4th Sat. of month 11-4. Grounds: dawn to dusk. Adults $5; discounts to seniors, AAM, AAA, ICOM, WGBH members Historic New England members no charge.
Attendance: 760 (accurate)
Membership: Individual $35; Household $45; Contributing $65; Sustaining $100; Supporting $250; Appleton Circle $1,500 and up; Appleton Circle Patron $3,000 & up. National Level: $25 (limited benefits for those living outside New England).

New London

NEW LONDON HISTORICAL SOCIETY, 179 Little Sunapee Rd., New London, NH 03257. Mailing Address: P.O. Box 965, New London, NH 03257-0965. Tel.: 603-526-6564.
E-mail: info@newlondonhistoricalsociety.org
Web Site: www.nlhs.net
Founded: 1954.
Congressional District: 2
Key Personnel: Pres. (V), J.L. Tonner.
Personnel Profile: Part-Time Volunteers 50.
Governing Authority: society. Tax-exempt.
General Museum.
Collections: folklore; outdoor museum; agriculture; archives; costumes; manuscript collection; military; horse drawn vehicles; firefighting equipment. Historic Buildings: 1800 Griffin barn; 1820 Scytheville house; 1820 blacksmith shop; 1830 country store; 1830 Pleasant St. schoolhouse; 1830 carriage house; 1830 corn crib; violin & carriage painting shop; meeting house; acquisitions building; Hearse house; Concord coach; transportation building.
Facilities: 40-vol. collection of handwritten town records, school records, store ledgers, manuscripts available for inter-library use.
Activities: guided tours; lectures; films; formally organized education programs for children; permanent & temporary exhibitions; special programs.
Publications: biannual, Newsletter; Cemetery Census; irregular local history articles.
Hours & Admission Prices: Memorial Day to June & Sept.-Columbus Day Sun. & Tues. 12:30-3:30; July-Aug. Tues. 12:30-3:30; other times by appointment. No charge; donations accepted for tours. ♿
Attendance: 2,500 (estimated)
Membership: Regular $30; Contributing $50; Supporting $100; Sustaining $150; Life $1,000.

Newbury

THE FELLS, 456 Rte. 103A, Newbury, NH 03255. Mailing Address: P.O. Box 276, Newbury, NH 03255-0276. Tel.: 603-763-4789. Fax: 603-763-2452.
E-mail: info@thefells.org
Web Site: www.thefells.org
Key Personnel: Exec. Dir., Karen Zurheide
Historic House: former estate of American writer and diplomat John M. Hay. Listed on the National Register of Historic Places.
Collections: local history & culture.
Research Fields: New Hampshire history; John Milton Hay.
Facilities: formal gardens; nature trails; meeting facilities.
Activities: guided tours; hiking; classes; programs; temporary & permanent exhibits; children's camps, programs, & nature explorer backpacks.
Publications: biannual newsletter.
Hours & Admission Prices: Gardens & Trails: dawn to dusk. Main House: Memorial Day-Columbus Day Sat.-Sun. & Mon. holidays 10-4; June 17 to Labor Day Wed.-Sun. 10-4. Adults $8, seniors 65 & over and students with ID $7, children 6-17 $3; discounts to families & during the off season; members and children 5 & under no charge. ♿
Attendance: 10,000 (accurate)
Membership: Individual $35; Household $50; Sponsor $125; Fellow $250; Patron $500; Benefactor $1,000; Sustainer $2,500.

North Conway

CONWAY SCENIC RAILROAD, INC., 38 Norcross Circle, North Conway, NH 03860. Mailing Address: P.O. Box 1947, North Conway, NH 03860-1947. Tel.: 603-356-5251; 800-232-5251. Fax: 603-356-7606.
E-mail: info@conwayscenic.com
Web Site: www.conwayscenic.com
Founded: 1974.
Congressional District: 1
Key Personnel: Pres., Russell G. Seybold; Operations Mgr., Paul Hallett.
Personnel Profile: Full-Time Paid 8; Part-Time Paid 36; Part-Time Volunteers 6.
Governing Authority: for profit corporation.
Railroad Museum: housed in 1874 Victorian, wood-framed railroad station. A National Historic Landmark.
Collections: railroad artifacts & memorabilia; northern New England railroad

items; period locomotives & railroad cars; 1897 Pullman sleeper-parlor-observation car; roundhouse; operating turntable; restored, operating dining car, old photographs.
Research Fields: New England railroad history.
Facilities: 250-vol. library of railroad materials; 47-seat railroad dining car. Museum-related items for sale.
Activities: organized guided tours for groups by reservation; self-guided walking tour; participatory exhibits. Museum Sponsors: Railfan's Day in October.
Hours & Admission Prices: Train rides of varying duration: Valley Train: mid-April to mid-May & Nov. to mid-Dec. Sat.-Sun.; mid-May to late Oct. daily. Notch Train, scenic train rides through Crawford Notch: late-June to early-Sept Tues.-Sat.; early-Sept. to mid-Oct. daily. Adults $13 & up; discounts to groups & AAA members; museum & grounds no charge. ♿
Attendance: 100,000 (accurate)

MOUNT WASHINGTON MUSEUM AND THE WEATHER DISCOVERY CENTER, 2779 White Mountain Hwy., North Conway, NH 03860-5194. Mailing Address: P.O. Box 2310, North Conway, NH 03860-2310. Tel.: 603-356-2137, ext. 203. Fax: 603-356-0307.
E-mail: email@mountwashing.org
Web Site: www.mountwashington.org
Founded: 1932.
Congressional District: 2
Key Personnel: C.E.O., John Hammer; Pres., Drew Landry; Exec. Dir., Scot Henley; Dir. Museum Operations & Museum Shop Mgr., Bill Grenfell; Dir. Education, Michelle Cruz.
Personnel Profile: Full-Time Paid 15; Part-Time Paid 5; Part-Time Volunteers 15; Interns 4.
Governing Authority: nonprofit corporation. Parent Institution: Mount Washington Observatory. Tax-exempt: 501(c)(3).
Park & Weather Museum: located on summit of Mount Washington.
Collections: over 100 specimens of local flora; White Mountains literature; artifacts; historical photos.
Research Fields: cloud physics; icing; cosmic rays.
Facilities: 2,600-vol. library of books on the White Mountains available for research on site; field research station. Educational material, books, pamphlets, weather instruments, photographs, slides & posters for sale.
Activities: occasional topical workshops; annual symposia.
Publications: quarterly, News Bulletin, Windswept.
Hours & Admission Prices: Mount Washington Museum: late May to mid-Oct. daily 9-6. Weather Discovery Center: Jan. to late May Sat.-Sun. 10-5; late May to Dec. daily 10-5. Adults $3; discounts to ASTC members; members no charge. ♿
Attendance: 40,000 (estimated)
Membership: Student $30; Senior $35; Individual $45; Family $70.

North Hampton

FULLER GARDENS, 10 Willow Ave., North Hampton, NH 03862-2228. Tel.: 603-964-5414. Fax: 603-964-8901.
E-mail: fullergrdn@aol.com
Web Site: www.fullergardens.org
Founded: 1927.
Key Personnel: C.E.O. & Dir., Jamie Colen; Pres. (V), Beverly Lord; Museum Shop Mgr., Cathy Cryans.
Personnel Profile: Full-Time Paid 3; Part-Time Paid 6; Part-Time Volunteers 20.
Governing Authority: nonprofit organization. Parent Institution: Fuller Foundations. Tax-exempt: 501(c)(3).
Botanical Garden.
Collections: horticultural display gardens; 1,500 rose bushes; English perennial gardens, Japanese garden; Hosta garden; tropical & desert conservatory.
Facilities: gardens.
Activities: self-guided tour of estate & formal gardens; summer calendar of social events & seminars. Gift items for sale.
Hours & Admission Prices: mid-May to Oct. daily 10-5:30. Adults $7, senior citizens $6, students $5, children under 12 $3; discounts to groups of 10 or more.
Attendance: 11,000 (estimated)
Membership: Annual $35; Perennial $45; Rose $60.

North Salem

AMERICA'S STONEHENGE, 105 Haverhill Rd., North Salem, NH 03073. Mailing Address: P.O. Box 84, North Salem, NH 03073-0084. Tel.: 603-893-8300.
E-mail: info@stonehengeusa.com
Web Site: www.stonehengeusa.com
Founded: 1958.
Key Personnel: C.E.O. & Pres., Robert E. Stone; Gen. Mgr. & Public Rels., Dennis W. Stone; Operations Mgr., Patricia Stone.
Personnel Profile: Full-Time Paid 5; Part-Time Paid 1.
Governing Authority: for-profit organization; private operation.
Archaeological Site: located on Mystery Hill, site of 4,000 year old archaeo-astronomical site.
Collections: late 18th- & early 19th-century rural household items; late Archaic, early & late Woodland tools & pottery; stone tools; carved petroglyphs; archives.
Research Fields: Mystery Hill site origins & attribution of controversial elements; archival research; preservation.
Facilities: library of research files & photographs; site related books & clippings; food service; picnic area; educational facilities; 300 sq. ft. exhibit space; 50-seat theatre; snack bar. Books & museum-related items for sale.
Activities: self-guided tours with guide maps; guided tours for groups of 20 or more.
Publications: annual bibliography of material; newsletter, Horizon; booklets, Quarry Techniques; Myth & Mythology in the Land of Academe.
Hours & Admission Prices: Jan.-June 21 & Labor Day to Nov. 15 daily 9-5; June 22 to Sept. daily 9-6; Nov. 16-Dec. daily 9-4. Adults $9, seniors $7, children 13-18 $6, children 6-12 $5. Closed Thanksgiving; Christmas. ♿
Attendance: 35,000 (estimated)
Membership: Single $30; Family $60.

Peterborough

MARIPOSA MUSEUM & WORLD CULTURE CENTER, 26 Main St., Peterborough, NH 03458-2420. Tel.: 603-924-4555. Fax: 603-924-7893.
E-mail: info@mariposamuseum.org
Web Site: www.mariposamuseum.org
Founded: 2002.
Key Personnel: Dir., David Blair; Pres. (V), Francoise Bourdon; Admin., Mose Olenik; Museum Mgr., Nadiya Weidman.
Personnel Profile: Full-Time Paid 1; Part-Time Paid 5; Part-Time Volunteers 50.
Governing Authority: board of directors. Parent Institution: Journeys in Education, Inc. Tax-exempt.
Art Museum.
Collections: cultural arts from around the world; costumes; toys; musical instruments; puppets; paintings.
Facilities: library. Museum-related items for sale.
Activities: workshops; hands-on exhibits; special events & programs; temporary exhibitions.
Hours & Admission Prices: Summer: daily 11-5; Winter: Wed.-Sun. 11-5; groups by appointment. Adults $5, children $3; first Fri. of month 5-9 & members no charge. Closed Federal holidays. ♿
Attendance: 5,000 (estimated)
Membership: Teacher $25; Adult & one Child $40; Family $60; Crescent $100; Admiral $150; Viceroy $250; Queen $500; Monarch $1,000.

PETERBOROUGH HISTORICAL SOCIETY, 19 Grove St., Peterborough, NH 03458-1422. Mailing Address: P.O. Box 58, Peterborough, NH 03458-0058. Tel.: 603-924-3235. Fax: 603-924-3200.
E-mail: director@peterboroughhistory.org
Web Site: www.peterboroughhistory.org
Founded: 1902.
Congressional District: 2
Key Personnel: Exec. Dir., Michelle M. Stahl.
Personnel Profile: Full-Time Paid 1; Part-Time Paid 3; Part-Time Volunteers 60; Interns 4.
Governing Authority: society. Tax-exempt: 501(c)(3).
Historical Society Museum.
Collections: town & state history artifacts; 19th-century manuscripts pertaining to textile mills & village life.
Research Fields: small town life; 19th-century New England; 19th-century mills.
Facilities: Morison Library & Archives containing books, ephemera and primary source documents. Research by appointment.
Activities: guided tours; permanent & temporary exhibitions.
Hours & Admission Prices: Tues.-Sat. 10-4. Adults $3; members no charge. ♿
Attendance: 7,500 (estimated)
Membership: Children $4-$9; Educator $20; Individual $25; Family $40; Sustaining $50; Benefactor $100; Patron $500.

Plymouth

KARL DRERUP ART GALLERY, (M), Plymouth State College, 17 High St., MSC 21B, Plymouth, NH 03264-1595. Tel.: 603-535-2614. Fax: 603-535-2938. TDD: 603-535-2679.
E-mail: camidon@plymouth.edu
Web Site: www.plymouth.edu/psc/gallery/

Founded: 1969.
Congressional District: 2
Key Personnel: Gallery Dir., Catherine Amidon.
Personnel Profile: Full-Time Paid 1; Part-Time Paid 9; Interns 1.
Governing Authority: public university; nonprofit. Tax-exempt: 501(c)(3).
University Art Gallery.
Collections: paintings; drawings.
Activities: lectures; formal programs for undergraduate & graduate students in conjunction with certain exhibitions; traveling exhibits; poetry readings; films; discussions.
Hours & Admission Prices: Sept.-May Mon.-Tues. & Thurs.-Sat. 10-4, Wed. 10-8. No charge. Closed spring break; college holidays; Thanksgiving; Christmas. ♿
Attendance: 6,000 (accurate)
Membership: Associate $10; Member $25; Supporter $50; Art Appreciator $100; Art Friend $500; Art Connoisseur $1,000 & up.

Portsmouth

ALBACORE PARK SUBMARINE MUSEUM, 600 Market St., Portsmouth, NH 03801-7313. Tel.: 603-436-3680.
E-mail: info@ussalbacore.org
Web Site: www.ussalbacore.org
Submarine Museum.
Collections: Albacore history; photographs; submarine artifacts; crew member history.
Facilities: visitor center; garden. Museum-related items for sale.
Hours & Admission Prices: Memorial Day to Columbus Day daily 9:30-5; Oct.-May Thurs.-Mon. 9:30-4; groups by appointment. Family $10, adults $5, military $4, children 7-17 $3; children under 7 no charge.

CONGRESS STREET GALLERY, 75 Congress St., Portsmouth, NH 03801-4006. Tel.: 603-436-9590.
Art Gallery.
Collections: paintings; photographs; sculpture.
Hours & Admission Prices: Mon.-Sat. 10-6, Sun. 11-5.

ELLO GALLERY, 110 State St., Portsmouth, NH 03801-3826. Mailing Address: 11 Naves Rd., Hampton, NH 03842-2062. Tel.: 603-433-9110.
Art Gallery.
Collections: works by young & emerging contemporary artists including paintings & drawings.
Facilities: Museum-related items for sale.
Activities: temporary exhibitions.
Hours & Admission Prices: Thurs.-Mon. 12-5; other times by appointment.

GOVERNOR JOHN LANGDON HOUSE, 143 Pleasant St., Portsmouth, NH 03801-4506. Mailing Address: 141 Cambridge St., Boston, MA 02114-2702. Tel.: 603-436-3205; 617-227-3956. Fax: 617-227-9204.
Web Site: www.historicnewengland.org
Founded: 1947.
Key Personnel: Pres., Carl Nold; Site Mgr., Elizabeth Farish.
Governing Authority: society; nonprofit organization. Parent Institution: Historic New England, 141 Cambridge St., Boston, MA 02114. Tel.: 617-227-3956. Tax-exempt: 501(c)(3).
Historic House: 1784 home of Governor John Langdon.
Collections: carvings; furniture & other artifacts from the 18th & 19th century.
Facilities: rental facilities.
Activities: guided tours; lectures; special events.
Publications: Historic New England Guide
Hours & Admission Prices: June-Oct. 15 Fri.-Sun. 11-4. Adults $6; discounts to seniors, AAM, ICOM, AAA, WGBH members; Historic New England members no charge.
Attendance: 6,214 (accurate)
Membership: National $35; Individual $45; Household $55; Garden & Landscape $75; Institutional $85; Contributing $100; Historic Homeowner $200; Supporting $250.

HARBOR ARTS MUSEUM, 75 Albany St., Portsmouth, NH 03801-4976. Tel.: 603-436-8596.
History Museum.
Collections: period instruments & musical memorabilia; playbills; posters; photographs.
Hours & Admission Prices: Call for hours.

JACKSON HOUSE, 76 Northwest St., Portsmouth, NH 03801-3556. Mailing Address: 141 Cambridge St., Boston, MA 02114-2702. Tel.: 603-436-3205.
Web Site: www.historicnewengland.org
Key Personnel: Pres., Carl Nold.
Governing Authority: private; nonprofit organization. Parent Institution: Historic New England, 141 Cambridge St., Boston, MA. Tax-exempt: 501(c)(3).
Historic House: built by Richard Jackson.
Collections: local history.
Publications: monthly newsletter, What's Happening; magazine, Historic New England.
Hours & Admission Prices: June-Oct. 15 1st & 3rd Sat. of month 11-4. Adults $6; members no charge.
Attendance: 692 (accurate)
Membership: National $35; Individual $45; Household $55; Garden & Landscape $75; Institutional $85; Contributing $100; Historic Homeowner $200; Supporting $250.

JOHN PAUL JONES HOUSE MUSEUM, 43 Middle St., Portsmouth, NH 03801-4302. Mailing Address: P.O. Box 728, Portsmouth, NH 03802-0728. Tel.: 603-436-8420.
E-mail: info@portsmouthhistory.org
Web Site: www.portsmouthhistory.org
Founded: 1920.
Congressional District: 1
Key Personnel: Pres., Joshua Scott; Sec., M. Marguerite Mathews; Dir., Sandra Rux.
Personnel Profile: Full-Time Paid 1; Part-Time Paid 6; Part-Time Volunteers 20; Interns 1.
Governing Authority: society. Parent Institution: Portsmouth Historical Society. Tax-exempt: 501(c)(3).
History Museum: housed in 1758 John Paul Jones House.
Collections: costumes; glass; canes; documents; paintings; furniture; oriental rugs; ship models including Ranger; John Paul Jones artifacts; colonial through Victorian artifacts; 18th & 19th-century ceramics.
Facilities: welcome center; gardens.
Activities: guided tours by house guides.
Publications: booklet, Touring John Paul Jones House Museum; newsletter.
Hours & Admission Prices: Memorial Day to Oct. daily 11-5. Adults $6, Portsmouth residents & AAA members $5; discounts to groups; children 12 and under & members no charge.
Attendance: 3,000 (estimated)
Membership: Friend $25; Dual $50; Contributing $100; Patron $150; Benefactor $250; Exemplar $1,000.

MOFFATT-LADD HOUSE AND GARDEN, 154 Market St., Portsmouth, NH 03801-7708. Tel.: 603-436-8221. Fax: 603-431-9063.
E-mail: moffatt-ladd@juno.com
Web Site: moffattladd.org
Founded: 1911.
Congressional District: 1
Key Personnel: Dir. & Cur., Dr. Barbara McLean Ward; Pres., Patricia S. Meyers; Museum Shop Mgr., Mrs. Peter Webster.
Personnel Profile: Full-Time Paid 1; Part-Time Paid 12; Part-Time Volunteers 50; Interns 1.
Governing Authority: organization. Parent Institution: The National Society of The Colonial Dames of America in the State of New Hampshire. Tax-exempt: 501(c)(3).
Historic House Museum: c.1763 house built by Captain John Moffatt.
Collections: ancestral portraits; Portsmouth furniture & other period furnishings, early wallpaper, textiles & clothing; Georgian architecture; colonial revival garden. Historic Buildings: coach house; counting house.
Research Fields: Portsmouth history; American decorative arts, furniture, paintings & textiles; women's history.
Facilities: 100-vol. library of genealogical material available to members only; historical colonial revival garden. Museum-related items for sale.
Activities: guided tours of house & garden; permanent exhibitions; rental facility; garden lectures.
Publications: The Moffatt-Ladd House Cookbook II; Alexander H. Ladd's Garden Book, 1888-1895; A 19th century view of Portsmouth; The Moffatt-Ladd House and its Garden; The Moffatt-Ladd House.
Hours & Admission Prices: mid-June to mid-Oct. Mon.-Sat. 11-5, Sun. 1-5. Adults $6, children 7-12 $2.50. Garden: $2; discounts for groups with appointment and NEMA & AAA members; children under 7, members & NSCDA no charge.
Attendance: 2,100 (accurate)
Membership: Friends of the Moffatt Ladd House: Friendly Neighbor $35 & up; Friend $50 & up; Family Friend $100 & up; Business Friend $250 & up; Very Good Friend $500 & up; Best Friend $1,000 & up.

PISCATAQUA FINE ARTS, 23 Ceres St., Portsmouth, NH 03801-3727. Tel.: 603-431-4110.
Web Site: www.dongorvettgallery.com

Art Gallery.
Collections: paintings; drawings; prints.
Activities: workshops; classes.
Hours & Admission Prices: Call for hours.

PORTSMOUTH ATHENAEUM, 9 Market Square, Portsmouth, NH 03801. Mailing Address: Box 848, Portsmouth, NH 03802-0848. Tel.: 603-431-2538. Fax: 603-431-7180.
E-mail: info@portsmouthathenaeum.org
Web Site: www.portsmouthathenaeum.org
Founded: 1817.
Congressional District: 1
Key Personnel: Keeper, Tom Hardiman; Pres., Carvel Tefft; Librarian, Robin Silva; Archives, Courtney Maclachlan.
Personnel Profile: Part-Time Paid 6; Part-Time Volunteers 30.
Governing Authority: corporation. Subsidiary Institution: Athenaeum Condominium Assoc. Tax-exempt.
Library Museum: housed in 1805 Portsmouth Athenaeum building.
Collections: research library: books on local history, literature, architecture & genealogy; early New Hampshire newspapers; historic photographs & maps; library: books on art, history, theology, science, geography, and voyages & travels; over 70 large manuscript collections; ephemera; postcards; Isles of Shoals material; records of many local churches & institutions; family & business papers; portraits; ship models & objects related to regional history and maritime traditions.
Research Fields: Portsmouth & Piscataqua - region history overall emphasis on 19th century; maritime & military history; architectural history.
Facilities: 40,000-vol. library; reference & research library available for use on the premises under supervision.
Activities: permanent exhibitions; temporary exhibits on historic regional culture; lectures; concerts.
Publications: newsletter.
Hours & Admission Prices: Museum: Thurs. 1-4. Reference Library: Tues & Thurs. 1-4, Sat. 10-4; other times by appointment. Exhibition Gallery: Tues., Thurs. & Sat. 1-4. No charge; donations accepted. Call for holiday closings. ♿
Attendance: 2,500 (estimated)
Membership: Annual Assessment $200; Proprietors $500 (one-time charge).

PORTSMOUTH MUSEUM OF FINE ART, 1 Harbour Place, Ste. 275, Portsmouth, NH 03801-3873. Tel.: 603-436-0332.
Art Museum.
Collections: paintings; photographs; sculpture.
Activities: studio workshops; lectures; literary readings; fine arts programming; classes; films.
Hours & Admission Prices: Mon.-Fri. 11-5, Sat.-Sun. 12-6; other times by appointment.

ROBERT LINCOLN LEVY GALLERY, 136 State St., Portsmouth, NH 03801-3826. Tel.: 603-431-4230.
Art Gallery.
Collections: paintings; photographs; sculpture; drawings; graphic arts.
Hours & Admission Prices: Wed.-Sat. 10-5, Sun. 12-4.

RUNDLET-MAY HOUSE, 364 Middle St., Portsmouth, NH 03801-5016. Mailing Address: 141 Cambridge St., Boston, MA 02114-2702. Tel.: 603-436-3205; 617-227-3956. Fax: 617-227-9204.
Web Site: www.historicnewengland.org
Founded: 1971.
Key Personnel: Pres., Carl Nold; Site Mgr., Elizabeth Farish.
Governing Authority: society; nonprofit organization. Parent Institution: Historic New England, 141 Cambridge St., Boston, MA 02114. Tax-exempt: 501(c)(3).
Historic House: 1807 three-story Federal mansion with original outbuildings, courtyard & formal gardens.
Collections: furnishings; Rumford roaster & range; kettle set.
Activities: guided tours.
Publications: Historic New England Guide.
Hours & Admission Prices: June-Oct. 15 1st & 3rd Sat. of month 11-4. Adults $6; discounts to seniors, AAM, ICOM, AAA, WGBH members; Historic New England members no charge. Call for further information.
Attendance: 697 (accurate)
Membership: National $35; Individual $45; Household $55; Garden & Landscape $75; Institutional $85; Contributing $100; Historic Homeowner $200; Supporting $250.

STRAWBERY BANKE MUSEUM, (M), Marcy St., Portsmouth, NH 03801. Mailing Address: P.O. Box 300, Portsmouth, NH 03802-0300. Tel.: 603-433-1100. Fax: 603-433-1129.
E-mail: info@strawberybanke.org
Web Site: www.strawberybanke.org
Founded: 1958.
Congressional District: 1
Key Personnel: Pres., Lawrence Yerdon; Chm. Overseers Committee (V), William Wiseman; Chm. Bd. Trustees (V), Jeffery Gilbert; Vice Pres. Institutional Advancement, Joanna Brode; Vice Pres. Collections & Interpretation, Elizabeth Garrett; Registrar, Tara Webber; Cur., Carolyn Roy; Cur., Kimberly Alexander, Ph.D.; Collections Mgr., Rodney Rowland; Mgr. Education, Michelle Moon; Education Coord., Beth Ann Schmitt; Education Coord., Bekki Coppola; Devel. Officer, Nancy Lowenberg; Dir. Mktg. & Communication, Stacey Brooks; Events & Facilities Rental Mgr., Amy Sherwood; Archaeology, Martha Pinello; Finance Mgr., Johanna Thomas; Visitor Svcs. Coord., Jonathan Brown; Volunteer Coord., Randa Charland; Dir. Merchandising, Nancy Gulley; Restoration, John Schnitzler; Cur. Historic Landscapes, John Forti; Human Resources Mgr., Nancy Grannan; Dir. Corporate Rels., Billie Tooley; Historic Costume Design, Dot Fisher; Merchandising Asst., Ramona Fraser; Properties Coord., Michelle Gore; Mktg. Assoc., Heather Pitts McLellan.
Personnel Profile: Full-Time Paid 35; Part-Time Paid 12; Part-Time Volunteers 400; Interns 4.
Governing Authority: nonprofit organization. Tax-exempt: 501(c)(3).
Historic Site: 17th-20th century Portsmouth & New England Seacoast.
Collections: decorative arts; tools; architectural specimens; archaeological; maritime; period gardens. Historic Buildings & Gardens: 42 historic buildings dating from 1695-1955.
Research Fields: material culture including decorative arts; architectural restoration; small boatbuilding; crafts; archaeological studies; historic landscaping; social and cultural history of the Piscataqua Region; ceramics; Portsmouth furniture; ceramics; Portsmouth furniture.
Facilities: 7,000-vol. library available for use by appointment only; restaurant; working craft shops; water vessel; period gardens. Museum-related items for sale.
Activities: guided & self-guided tours; lectures; concerts; organized education programs; permanent & temporary exhibitions; craft & teacher workshops; education programs in local & maritime history; undergraduate & graduate internships; special events; field schools in archaeology; historic landscapes preservation & restoration. Museum Sponsors: Candlelight Stroll; Brewers Festival; Bluesfest.
Publications: quarterly newsletter; booklets; Official Guide Book; Portsmouth and the Piscataqua; Social History & Material Culture; Portsmouth Historic & Picturesque; reprint, The Story of A Bad Bay.
Hours & Admission Prices: May-Oct. daily 10-5; Nov.-April Thurs.-Sat. 10-2, Sun. 12-2. Family $40, adults $15, youth 5-17 $10; discounts to groups of 10 or more; AAM, AAA, members, employees of other museums, and children 4 & under no charge. ♿
Attendance: 66,056 (estimated)
Membership: Student $25; Individual $35; Double $55; Family $65; Sponsor $125; Donor $250; Patron $500; Benefactor $1,000. Business Memberships: Associate $125; Sponsor $250; Donor $500; Patron $1,000; Benefactor $1,500; Leader $2,500; Joshua Drisco Club $5,000.

THREE GRACES GALLERY, 105 Market St., Portsmouth, NH 03801-3703. Tel.: 603-436-1988.
Art Gallery.
Collections: paintings; sculpture; pottery; mixed-media.
Hours & Admission Prices: Sun. 12-5, Mon.-Tues. & Thurs.-Sat. 10-6, Wed. by appointment.

WARNER HOUSE, 150 Daniel St., Portsmouth, NH 03801-3831. Mailing Address: Box 895, Portsmouth, NH 03802-0895. Tel.: 603-436-5909.
E-mail: housemanager@warnerhouse.org
Web Site: www.warnerhouse.org
Formerly: MacPheadris/Warner House
Founded: 1931.
Congressional District: 1
Key Personnel: Co Chm., Deborah Richards; Co Chm., Ronan Donohoe; Treas., Lorn Buxton; Sec., Peter Michaud; Cur., Carolyn Roy; Cur., Louise Richardson.
Personnel Profile: Part-Time Paid 5; Part-Time Volunteers 10.
Governing Authority: nonprofit organization. Tax-exempt: 509(A).
Historic House Museum: c.1716 Macpheadris-Warner House.
Collections: period furniture & decorated accessories; five Blackburn portraits; restored c.1720 murals; early 1700s books; original & other Portsmouth furnishings illustrating six generations from 1716-1930 who lived in the Macpheadris-Warner House; 18th century copper plate bed hangings.

Facilities: Plates, needlecrafts, pewterware, books & other museum-related items for sale.
Activities: guided tours; formally organized educational programs.
Publications: newsletter.
Hours & Admission Prices: mid-June to mid-Oct. Tues. & Thurs.-Sat. 12-4. Adults $5, senior citizens $4, children under 7-12 $.75; discounts to groups, AAA members & Time Travelers; children under 7 & members no charge.
Attendance: 2,000 (estimated)
Membership: Macpheadris $25; Penhallow $50; Wentworth $100; Wendell $250; Sherburne $500; Warner $1,000.

WENTWORTH-COOLIDGE MANSION, 375 Little Harbor Rd., Portsmouth, NH 03801-5527. Tel.: 603-436-6607. Fax: 603-436-9889.
E-mail: wcmansion@gwi.net
Web Site: www.wentworthcoolidge.org
Founded: 1954.
Congressional District: 1
Key Personnel: Dir., Mark J. Sammons; Chm. (V), Mary Griffin; Rgnl. Supvr. Parks & Recreation, Johanna Lyons; State Cur., Russell Bastedo.
Personnel Profile: Part-Time Paid 6; Part-Time Volunteers 6.
Governing Authority: commission; state. Wentworth-Coolidge Commission & New Hampshire Div. of Parks & Recreation. Tax-exempt.
Historic House: c.1750 home of first Royal Governor of New Hampshire.
Collections: 18th-20th century furniture; Wentworth & Coolidge family belongings; late 19th-century photographs; 18th-century wallpaper; lilac plantings of 18th-century origin.
Research Fields: mid-18th century wallpaper; lilac history, cultivation & preservation.
Facilities: gardens & grounds. Postcards for sale.
Activities: guided tours; lectures; art classes.
Publications: leaflet.
Hours & Admission Prices: Tours: late June to early Sept. Wed.-Sun. 10-4; early Sept. to mid-Oct. Sat.-Sun. 10-4; other times by appointment. Adults $7, children 6-11 $3; NH residents & children 5 & under no charge.
Attendance: 7,763 (accurate)
Membership: Student $15; Individual $25; Family & Household $40; Caretaker $100; Steward $250; Overseer $500; Benefactor $1,000; Founder $2,500; Councillor $5,000.

WENTWORTH GARDNER & TOBIAS LEAR HOUSES ASSOCIATION, 50 Mechanic St., Portsmouth, NH 03801. Mailing Address: P.O. Box 563, Portsmouth, NH 03802-0563. Tel.: 603-436-4406.
E-mail: info@wentworthgardnerandlear.org
Web Site: www.wentworthgardnerandlear.org
Founded: 1941.
Key Personnel: Pres., Judy Capobianco; Treas., Catherine Anderson; Sec., Haden Gerrish.
Personnel Profile: Full-Time Paid 1; Part-Time Paid 1; Part-Time Volunteers 10.
Governing Authority: nonprofit organization. Tax-exempt: 501(c)(3).
Historic House: 1760 Wentworth Gardner House, Georgian mansion.
Collections: Colonial furniture & furnishings. Historic House: 1740 Tobias Lear House.
Activities: guided tours; lectures; temporary exhibitions. Annual Events: Flag Day opening; Dorothy Vaughan lecture.
Publications: biannual, WGTL Newsletter.
Hours & Admission Prices: June 14-Oct. 15 Thurs.-Sun. 12-4. Adults $5, children $2; discount to groups; members no charge.
Membership: Individual $15; Family & Dual $25; Associate $50; Contributor $125; Sponsor $250; Patron $500; Benefactor $1,000.

Raymond

RAYMOND HISTORICAL SOCIETY, 1 Depot Rd., Raymond, NH 03077. Mailing Address: P.O. Box 94, Raymond, NH 03077-0094. Tel.: 603-895-2866.
Web Site: raymondhistoricalsociety.home.comcast.net/~raymondhistorical society
Historical Society Museum: housed in the Old Raymond Train Depot.
Collections: local history & culture; photographs; archives.
Hours & Admission Prices: Call for hours.

Rye

SEACOAST SCIENCE CENTER, 570 Ocean Blvd., Rye, NH 03870-2131. Tel.: 603-436-8043. Fax: 603-433-2235.
E-mail: w.lull@seacentr.org
Web Site: seacoastsciencecenter.org
Founded: 1992.
Congressional District: 1
Key Personnel: Pres., Wendy W. Lull; Chm. (V), Pamela Hall; Vice Pres., James E. Chase; Dir. Education, Perrin Chick; Dir. Devel., Nichole Rutherford; Museum Shop Mgr., Donna Johnson.
Personnel Profile: Full-Time Paid 12; Part-Time Paid 42; Part-Time Volunteers 100; Interns 4.
Governing Authority: nonprofit organization. Tax-exempt.
Aquarium.
Collections: seatanks & habitat exhibits; New Hampshire cultural & natural environmental history; humpback whale skeleton.
Facilities: 10,000 sq. ft. exhibit areas; distance learning studio. Museum-related items for sale.
Activities: school & teacher programs; day camps; youth & adult group programs; nature walks; lecture series; distance learning programs.
Publications: newsletter; Teacher's Guide to Rocky Shore; Teachers Guide to Salt Marsh; Footprints in Time, A Walk Where New Hampshire Began.
Hours & Admission Prices: April-Oct. daily 10-5; Nov.-March Sat.-Mon. 10-5. Park: adults $5, children 3-12 $2. Center: $1 per person; discounts to New England Museum Assoc. members; members no charge. ♿
Attendance: 60,000 (accurate)
Membership: Individual $40; Family $65; Family Plus $100. Annual Giving Societies: Merrimack $300-$749; Piscataqua $750-$1,999; Gulf of Maine $2,000-$4,999; World Oceans $5,000 & up.

Salisbury

SALISBURY HISTORICAL SOCIETY, (M), Salisbury Heights, Rte. 4, Salisbury, NH 03268. Mailing Address: 67 Warner Rd., Salisbury, NH 03268-5200. Tel.: 603-648-2774.
Founded: 1966.
Congressional District: 1
Key Personnel: Cur., Wendy Barrett; Pres., Patrick Walsh.
Governing Authority: Salisbury Historical Society. Tax-exempt: 501(c)(3).
History Museum: housed in 1791 Old Baptist Church.
Collections: clothing; tools; silver; books; manuscripts; furniture.
Research Fields: genealogy; town history.
Facilities: 225-vol. library of local & state history available on premises by appointment; reading room; 200-seat auditorium. Local maps, historical books & museum-related items for sale.
Activities: guided tours; lectures; permanent & temporary exhibitions.
Publications: Salisbury Historical Newsletter.
Hours & Admission Prices: April-Oct. Sat. 1-4. No charge; donations accepted.
Attendance: 250 (estimated)
Membership: Active $5; Family $8; Life $100.

Sandown

SANDOWN HISTORICAL SOCIETY AND MUSEUM, 1 Depot Rd., Sandown, NH 03873. Mailing Address: P.O. Box 300, Sandown, NH 03873-0373. Tel.: 603-887-6688 & 6100 (Depot Museum).
E-mail: history@sandownnh.com
Web Site: www.sandownnh.com/history
Founded: 1977.
Congressional District: 1
Key Personnel: C.E.O. & Pres. Historical Society, Douglas Martin; Cur. & Museum Shop Mgr., Bertha Deveau.
Personnel Profile: Part-Time Volunteers 6.
Governing Authority: society; nonprofit. Tax-exempt.
Railroad & Local History Museum: housed in 1873 railroad station.
Collections: World War I uniform; World War II items; ration books; military buttons; handmade shoes; wagon jack; sleds; tools; 1860-1900 period adult & children clothes; telegraph key; hand-cranked telephone; lanterns; mailbag; railroad artifacts & equipment; two Flanger cars; velocipede; books; pictures; magazines; posters; victrola; graphaphone; wooden tubs; foot pedal jigsaw; foot pedal sewing machine; bicycle lamp; hand carved wooden wash board; hoops for skirts; put-put gas-powered 4-wheel rail car used to bring materials to repair track; 1910 double-runner sled; 1895 Torrington Conn. Sweeper with vacuum; 1744 powder horn Jonathan Lund; Scrimshaw including ships, mermaid, animals, maze, wine glass, birds, woman; two Maine Central Flanger cars; 2-man hand car; signal light; velocipede.
Research Fields: Indian research regarding King Philip of Rhode Island; genealogy; American Indian graves; arrowheads; scraper; trail map; local history books.
Facilities: library of railroad & children's books available to the public; picnic area. Railroad items & other museum-related items for sale.
Activities: guided tours; lectures; temporary exhibitions; hands-on exhibits. Museum Sponsors: Trip By Train; Old Home Day; Hobo Day in October.
Publications: brochure; The View from Meeting House Hill; 1921 Cookbook, Sandown, NH.
Hours & Admission Prices: May-Oct. Sat.-Sun. & holidays 1-5; other times by appointment, call 727-808-0443. No charge; donations accepted. ♿

Attendance: 230 (estimated)
Membership: Student $5; Individual $10; Couple $15; Family $25.

Sharon

THE SHARON ARTS CENTER, INC., 457 NH Rte. 123, Sharon, NH 03458-7116. Tel.: 603-924-7256 & 2787. Fax: 603-924-6074.
E-mail: register@sharonarts.org
Web Site: www.sharonarts.org
Founded: 1947.
Congressional District: 2
Key Personnel: Pres., Elizabeth Smith; Chm. (V), David Howe; Cur., Randall Hoel.
Personnel Profile: Full-Time Paid 7; Part-Time Paid 11; Part-Time Volunteers 10; Interns 2.
Governing Authority: nonprofit corporation. Tax-exempt: 501(c)(3).
Art Gallery.
Collections: Nora S. Unwin wood engravings; Warfield collection.
Research Fields: wood engraving.
Facilities: library of art magazines, craft magazines, art history & craft books; classrooms; handcraft shop; school of arts & crafts. Handcrafted items by New England craftsmen for sale.
Activities: guided tours; gallery talks; monthly exhibits; formally organized education programs.
Publications: 25 Wood Engravings.
Hours & Admission Prices: Summer: Mon.-Thurs. & Sat. 10-6, Fri. 10-7, Sun. 11-4; Winter: Mon.-Thurs. 11-6, Fri. 11-7, Sat. 10-6, Sun. 12-5; Fall: Wed.-Thurs. 10-6, Fri. 10-7, Sat. 10-6, Sun. 12-5. No charge; donations accepted. ♿
Attendance: 36,000 (estimated)
Membership: Individual $35; Family $50.

South Sutton

SOUTH SUTTON OLD STORE MUSEUM, 12 Meeting House Hill Rd., South Sutton, NH 03273. Mailing Address: P.O. Box 555, South Sutton, NH 03273-0555. Tel.: 603-927-4416.
Founded: 1954.
Congressional District: 2
Governing Authority: municipal. Parent Institution: Town of Sutton.
Historic Building: c.1850 general store.
Collections: tools; dolls; bottles; patent medicines; books; linens; toys; wallpaper; photographs; costumes; store artifacts.
Activities: guided tours.
Hours & Admission Prices: Call for hours. No charge; donations accepted.
Attendance: 100 (estimated)

Sugar Hill

SUGAR HILL HISTORICAL MUSEUM, Main St. (Rte. 117), Sugar Hill, NH 03586. Mailing Address: P.O. Box 591, Sugar Hill, NH 03586-0591. Tel.: 603-823-5336.
E-mail: kittyh@roadrunner.com
Web Site: www.sugarhillnh.org
Founded: 1976.
Key Personnel: Chm. (V), Maxine Aldrich.
Personnel Profile: Part-Time Volunteers 10.
Governing Authority: bd. of trustees.
History Museum.
Collections: Sugar Hill history from 1780 to present; carriage barn; blacksmith shop; sleigh shed.
Facilities: photographic library.
Hours & Admission Prices: June 5-Oct.17 Fri.-Sat. 11-3. No charge; donations accepted. ♿
Attendance: 1,000 (accurate)
Membership: $25-$200.

Sunapee

SUNAPEE HISTORICAL SOCIETY MUSEUM, 74 Main St., Sunapee Harbor, Sunapee, NH 03782. Mailing Address: P.O. Box 501, Sunapee, NH 03782-0501. Tel.: 603-763-9872.
History Museum.
Collections: local history; steamboats; boating.
Hours & Admission Prices: Summer: Tues. & Thurs.-Sun. 1-4, Wed. 7pm-9pm; Sept.-Oct. Sat.-Sun. 1-4. No charge; donations accepted.

Suncook

4-H NATURE CENTER, Bear Brook State Park & Campground, off Rte. 28, Allenstown, Suncook, NH 03275. Mailing Address: 157 Deerfield Rd., Allenstown, NH 03275-2503. Tel.: 603-485-9874. Fax: 603-485-4358.
Web Site: www.nhstateparks.com/bearbrook.html
Formerly: Bear Brook Nature Center
Founded: 1961.
Congressional District: 2
Key Personnel: Park Mgr., David Evans.
Governing Authority: state. Parent Institution: New Hampshire 4-H Clubs.
Natural History Museum.
Collections: live & mounted specimens of New Hampshire plants & animals; New Hampshire rocks & minerals.
Facilities: 200-vol. library of natural history books; three self-guiding nature trails; special trail for the blind.
Activities: guided field trips; demonstrations; slide shows; school program.
Hours & Admission Prices: Memorial Day-Labor Day Fri.-Tues. 10-5. Museum: call for hours. Park Entrance Fee: adults $4, children 6-11 $2; children under 5 and NH residents 65 & over no charge. ♿
Attendance: 1,500

Tamworth

REMICK COUNTRY DOCTOR MUSEUM AND FARM, 58 Cleveland Hill Rd., Tamworth, NH 03886. Mailing Address: P.O. Box 250, Tamworth, NH 03886-0250. Tel.: 603-323-7591; 800-686-6117. Fax: 603-323-8382.
E-mail: info@remickmuseum.org
Web Site: www.remickmuseum.org
Founded: 1993.
Congressional District: 1
Key Personnel: Exec. Dir., Robert Cottrell; Chm. (V), Mona Perrault.
Personnel Profile: Full-Time Paid 11; Part-Time Paid 2; Part-Time Volunteers 12; Interns 1.
Governing Authority: private; nonprofit. Tax-exempt: 501(c)(3).
Medical Museum: one of the three building complexes the museum is housed in is the Capt. Enoch Remick House.
Collections: three complexes of historic houses, barns & outbuildings; agricultural tools and equipment; 99 years of medical history, 1894-1993; livestock including dairy cattle, horse, pigs, sheep & chickens; historic farm house, home & barns.
Research Fields: medical history, 1894-1993; agricultural history, 1750-1993; architecture, 1750-1993; harness racing, 1900-1993.
Facilities: 7,650 sq. ft. exhibit space; visitor's center; hiking trails.
Activities: guided tours; K-12 historic workshops; Foodways workshops; summer tours. Special Events: Winter Carnival & Ice Harvesting; Maple Sugaring; Fishing Derby; Capt. Enoch Remick House - Open House; Historic Thanksgiving; Victorian Christmas; Traditional Tea; Harvest Festival; Ox & Rocks; Hearthside Dinners.
Publications: newsletter, The Remick Farm Journal.
Hours & Admission Prices: early July to Oct. Mon.-Sat. 10-4; Nov. to Independece Day Mon.-Fri. 10-4. Farm Tours: 11 & 2:30. Milking Activity: 10:30am. Daily Educational Activity: 12:30-1pm. Enoch Remick Tour: 1pm. Adults $3; discounts to AAM & ICOM members; members no charge. Closed major holidays. ♿
Attendance: 9,040 (accurate)
Membership: Student & Senior $15; Individual $25; Grandparent Family $45; Family $50; Patron $100; Supporting $250; Steward $500; Corporate & Benefactor $1,000.

Warner

MT. KEARSARGE INDIAN MUSEUM, 18 Highlawn Rd., Warner, NH 03278. Mailing Address: P.O. Box 142, Warner, NH 03278-0142. Tel.: 603-456-2600 & 3244.
Founded: 1990.
Key Personnel: Dir., Shawn Olson; Chm. (V), Elizabeth Janeway; C.F.O. & Museum Shop Mgr., Carolyn Bullock; Visitor Svcs., Volunteer Coord. & Membership Dir., Edie Daigle; Museum Educator, Steve Daigle; Museum Educator, Suzanne Tellford.
Personnel Profile: Full-Time Paid 1; Part-Time Paid 4; Part-Time Volunteers 180; Interns 1.
Governing Authority: nonprofit organization. Tax-exempt.
Native American History Museum.
Collections: Native American heritage & art; Native American dwellings; garden; The Medicine Woods; archaeology.
Major Exhibits: Crooked Knives of the Woodlands, 5/10-11/10; Basket Making in New Hampshire (T), 5/10-11/10.
Facilities: nature trail. Museum-related items for sale.
Activities: lectures; hands-on activities; films; teacher workshops; school programs. Annual Event: festival.

Hours & Admission Prices: May-Oct. Mon.-Sat. 10-5, Sun. 12-5, Nov.-Dec. Sat. 10-5, Sun. 12-5 by appointment; other times by appointment. Adults $8.50, senior citizens, students & children 6-12 $6.50; discounts to AAM, AAA & AARP members; members & children under 6 no charge. ♿
Attendance: 12,000 (estimated)
Membership: Senior/Student $25; Individual $33; Couple $44; Family $55; Library/Nonprofit $75; Business Basic $100; Business Plus $101-$149; Benefactor $150-$249; Friendship Circle $250-$499; Sage Council $500-$999; Visionary $1,000 & up.

NEW HAMPSHIRE TELEPHONE MUSEUM, 22 E. Main St., Warner, NH 03278-4421. Mailing Address: P.O. Box 444, Warner, NH 03278-0444. Tel.: 603-456-2234.
E-mail: info@nhtelephonemuseum.com
Web Site: www.nhtelephonemuseum.com
Key Personnel: Chm. (V), Alderico "Dick" Violette; Pres. (V), Paul E. Violette; Museum Shop Mgr., Laura French
History Museum.
Collections: history relating to the telephone.
Hours & Admission Prices: May-Oct. Tues., Thurs. & Sat. 10-4; Nov.-April Wed. & Sat. 10-4. Adults $5, seniors 60 & over $4, students $3; members no charge. ♿
Membership: Student & Senior $20; Individual $25; Family $40; Benefactor $100; Corporate $250.

Wilton

FRYE'S MEASURE MILL, 12 Frye Mill Rd., Wilton, NH 03086. Tel.: 603-654-6581 & 5345.
Web Site: www.fryesmeasuremill.com
Founded: 1858.
Congressional District: 2
Key Personnel: C.E.O., Archivist & Public Rels., Harland Savage, Jr.; Pres. (V) & Gift Shop Mgr., Pamela Savage.
Governing Authority: company organized for profit.
Industrial Museum: housed in 1858 measure mill, the last surviving in the United States.
Collections: water-powered measure mill with associated machinery; 1850-1860, hand card machines; 19th & 20th-century colonial containers: measures, piggins, boxes.
Research Fields: colonial wooden ware; textile: hand card facing machines.
Facilities: 250-vol. library of industrial machinery & town history material. Museum-related items for sale.
Activities: guided tours; temporary exhibitions.
Publications: brochure.
Hours & Admission Prices: Jan.-March Wed.-Sat. 10-4; April to mid-Dec. Tues.-Sat. 10-5, Sun. 12-5. Tours: Jan.-March call for hours; June-Oct. Sat. at 2. Adults $5.75; discount to groups; children under 12 no charge. Closed national holidays.

Wolfeboro

LIBBY MUSEUM, 755 N. Main St., Wolfeboro, NH 03894. Mailing Address: P.O. Box 629, Wolfeboro, NH 03894-0629. Tel.: 603-569-1035. Fax: 603-569-2246.
E-mail: libbymus@metrocast.net
Web Site: www.wolfeboroonline.com/libby
Founded: 1912.
Congressional District: 1
Key Personnel: Dir., Patricia F. Smith.
Personnel Profile: Full-Time Paid 1; Part-Time Paid 7; Part-Time Volunteers 2.
Governing Authority: municipal; nonprofit organization. Parent Institution: Town of Wolfeboro. Tax-exempt.
History & Natural History Museum.
Collections: mounted specimens of local birds, fish, animals; skeletal exhibits; Indian relics; local history; maps.
Research Fields: history of the area.
Facilities: picnic area.
Activities: special events; childrens wildlife classes; Native American classes; films; winter traveling museum; evening lectures; family adventure programs.
Publications: maps, Indian Trails of the Lakes Region of New Hampshire.
Hours & Admission Prices: Memorial Day to late Sept. Tues.-Sat. 10-4, Sun. 12-4. Adults $2; members no charge. ♿
Attendance: 3,000 (estimated)
Membership: Friends of the Libby Museum: Student & Senior Citizen $10; Individual $15; Family $25; Associate $100; Sponsor $250; Patron $500.

WOLFEBORO HISTORICAL SOCIETY, S. Main St., Wolfeboro, NH 03894. Mailing Address: P.O. Box 1066, Wolfeboro, NH 03894-1066. Tel.: 603-569-1683 (Sept.-Nov.); 912-961-6562 (Nov.-June).
E-mail: protopipnit@comcast.net
Web Site: www.wolfeborohistoricalsociety.org
Founded: 1925.
Key Personnel: Pres., James Rogers.
Personnel Profile: Part-Time Paid 1; Part-Time Volunteers 25.
Governing Authority: nonprofit organization; board of directors. Tax-exempt.
Historical Society Museum.
Collections: history; pewter; china; furniture; five 1800 fire fighting equipment. Historic Houses: 1778 Clark house; c.1820 Pleasant Valley School; c.1862 Monitor Engine Co. Firehouse.
Research Fields: local genealogy.
Facilities: 1,200-vol. library of local history books.
Activities: guided tours; monthly speakers. Museum Sponsors: Pot Luck Dinner; Flea Market; 3rd Graders Day; 1820 Barn Restoration.
Publications: pamphlets; 3 volumes, History of Wolfeboro 1770-1994; annual, Clark House Crier; History of Wolfeboro Historical Society; Parker's History of Wolfeboro.
Hours & Admission Prices: July-Labor Day Wed.-Fri. 10-4, Sat. 10-2; other times by appointment. Adults $4, students $2; children under 12 & members no charge. ♿
Attendance: 900 (accurate)
Membership: Individual $10; Donor $25; Sponsor $50; Patron $100; Benefactor $100 & up.

WRIGHT MUSEUM OF HISTORY, 77 Center St., Rte. 28, Wolfeboro, NH 03894-4368. Mailing Address: P.O. Box 1212, Wolfeboro, NH 03894-1212. Tel.: 603-569-1212. Fax: 603-569-6326.
E-mail: info@wrightmuseum.org
Web Site: wrightmuseum.org
Founded: 1982.
Congressional District: 1
Key Personnel: Chm. (V), Roy Ballentine; Dir., Mark Foynes; Volunteer Coord., Diane Wright.
Personnel Profile: Full-Time Paid 2; Part-Time Paid 4; Part-Time Volunteers 45.
Governing Authority: nonprofit organization. Tax-exempt: 501(c)(3).
History Museum.
Collections: World War II American military & home front including artifacts, memorabilia, film, written materials, costumes & vehicles.
Activities: educational & family events; school outreach programs; speakers bureau.
Publications: quarterly newsletter; annual report.
Hours & Admission Prices: Feb.-April Sun. 12-4; May-June & Sept.-Oct. Mon.-Sat. 10-4, Sun. 12-4; July-Aug. Mon. & Wed.-Sat. 10-4, Tues. 10-4 & 6:30-9, Sun. 12-4; other times by appointment. Adults $6, senior citizens & veterans $5, students $3; discounts to AAM & NICHE members; children under 8 & members no charge. ♿
Attendance: 14,000 (accurate)
Membership: Individual $50; Family & Household $75; Contributing $100; Sponsor $500; Patron $1,000.

Wolfeboro Falls

NEW HAMPSHIRE BOAT MUSEUM, 397 Center St., Wolfeboro Falls, NH 03896. Mailing Address: P.O. Box 1195, Wolfeboro Falls, NH 03896-1195. Tel.: 603-569-4554. Fax: 603-569-5931.
E-mail: museum@nhbm.org
Web Site: www.nhbm.org
Founded: 1992.
Key Personnel: Museum Shop Mgr., Dodie Houle.
Personnel Profile: Part-Time Volunteers 2.
Governing Authority: bd. of trustees. Tax-exempt.
Boat Museum.
Collections: period boats; canoes; guide boats; sail boats; photographs; trophies.
Activities: youth & family boat building; youth sailing; lecture series. Annual Events: Boat Auction; Boathouse Tour; Biannual Vintage Raceboat Regatta.
Publications: quarterly journal, Boathouse News.
Hours & Admission Prices: Memorial Day to Columbus Day Mon.-Sat. 10-4, Sun. 12-4. Adults $5, seniors 65 & over $4, students $3; members and children 12 & under no charge. ♿
Attendance: 3,000 (accurate)
Membership: Single $30; Couple $40; Family 75; Donor $100; Friend $1,000.

NEW JERSEY

(253 listings)

Allentown

HISTORIC WALNFORD, 78 Walnford Rd., Allentown, NJ 08501. Mailing Address: Monmouth County Park System, Newmann Springs Rd., Lincroft, NJ 07738. Tel.: 609-259-6275; 732-842-4000. Fax: 609-259-0384. TDD: 732-219-9484.
E-mail: info@monmouthcountyparks.com
Web Site: www.monmouthcountyparks.com
Founded: 1985.
Congressional District: 3
Key Personnel: Park Mgr., William O'Shaughnessy; Historic Site Supvr., Sarah Bent; Cur., Cheryl Stoeber-Goff.
Personnel Profile: Full-Time Paid 3; Part-Time Paid 2; Part-Time Volunteers 5.
Governing Authority: county. Parent Institution: Monmouth County Park System, Newman Springs Rd., Lincroft, NJ 07738. Tax-exempt.
Historic Site: 20th-century colonial revival interpretation of 19th-century milling technology; 18th-century industrial village.
Collections: tools & equipment of an operating 1873 grist mill. Historical Buildings: 1773 Georgian Plantation Home; 1873 Grist Mill; 1872 Carriage House; barns; sheds & out buildings restored to early 20th-century colonial revival period.
Research Fields: grist & sawmills; colonial revival landscapes & architecture; 18th-19th century Quakers in west NJ; 18th-19th century merchant mills & shipping.
Facilities: 11 structures.
Activities: interpretive site tours; environmental tours, changing landscapes, wetland, flora & fauna; demonstration of operating grist mill; special seasonal events; educational programs.
Publications: interpretive flyers; brochures; activity directory.
Hours & Admission Prices: Gristmill: April 15-Nov. 15 daily 8-4 & by appointment. Park: daily 8-4. No charge; donations accepted. ♿
Attendance: 20,000 (accurate)

Asbury Park

CRANE HOUSE, 508 4th Ave., Asbury Park, NJ 07712-6010. Tel.: 732-775-5682.
Historic House Museum: housed in the former home of author, Stephen Crane; c.1877.
Collections: Stephen Crane's personal artifacts; photographs; period furnishings.
Activities: special events.
Hours & Admission Prices: Call for hours.

Atlantic City

ABSECON LIGHTHOUSE AND KEEPER'S HOUSE MUSEUM, 31 S. Rhode Island Ave., Atlantic City, NJ 08401-7760. Tel.: 609-449-1360. Fax: 609-449-1919.
History Museum & Historic Lighthouse: built in 1857.
Collections: local history; photographs; maritime artifacts; lighthouse memorabilia.
Facilities: Museum-related items for sale.
Activities: lighthouse tours.
Hours & Admission Prices: July-Aug. daily 10-5; Sept.-June Thurs.-Mon. 11-4. Adults $7, seniors 60 & over $5, children 4-12 $4; children 3 & under and active military no charge. Closed major holidays.

ATLANTIC CITY HISTORICAL MUSEUM, Garden Pier, Atlantic City, NJ 08401. Mailing Address: 204 S. Vermont Ave., Atlantic City, NJ 08401-7820. Tel.: 609-347-5839 & 344-1943. Fax: 609-347-5284.
Web Site: www.acmuseum.org
Founded: 1982.
Congressional District: 2
Key Personnel: Chm., Robert E. Ruffolo, Jr.; Vice Chm., Herbert B. Stern; Treas., Linda Tiso; Exhibit Dir., Vicki Gold Levi; Sec., Joan Sless.
Personnel Profile: Part-Time Volunteers 20.
Governing Authority: private; nonprofit. Tax-exempt.
History Museum: situated on the Atlantic City Boardwalk on Garden Pier, built in 1912.
Collections: furnishings; personal artifacts; prints, drawings; graphic arts; costumes; textiles; photographs.
Activities: guided tours; participatory exhibits. Annual Event: ACHM Benefit Auction, Dinner & Historical Show.
Publications: quarterly newsletter, Message From The Chairman; annual photo calendar of old Atlantic City.
Hours & Admission Prices: Daily 10-4. No charge; donations accepted. ♿
Attendance: 3,000 (estimated)
Membership: Individual $10; Family $20; Life $100; Benefactor $500; Corporate Sponsor $1,000.

HISTORIC GARDNER'S BASIN, 800 N. New Hampshire Ave., Atlantic City, NJ 08401-2900. Tel.: 609-348-2880. Fax: 609-345-4238.
Web Site: www.oceanlifecenter.com
Founded: 1976.
Congressional District: 1
Key Personnel: Chm. Bd., James L. Cooper; Vice Chm., Murray Raphel; Exec. Dir., Jack Keith.
Governing Authority: nonprofit organization. Tax-exempt: 501(c)(3).
Maritime Village & Ocean Life Center: housed in pre-1900 waterfront homes, located on site where Atlantic City was founded.
Collections: water craft; maritime artifacts; seafaring memorabilia; working & living exhibits on lobstermen & clammers; paintings; sculpture.
Research Fields: maritime history, particularly of South Jersey; oceanographic interests; marine mammal ecological interests; documentations of the family histories of early occupants of the houses in the Basin area.
Facilities: aquarium; field research station; laboratory; 400-seat amphitheater; classrooms; 100-seat restaurant. Nautical items, shells, carvings, models & other museum-related items for sale.
Activities: guided tours; lectures; films; gallery talks; concerts; arts festivals; formally organized education programs; permanent, temporary & loan exhibitions; 3-hour sails on the square rigger Young America.
Hours & Admission Prices: Daily 10-5. Adults $7, seniors $5, children $4; children under 3 no charge. Closed New Year's Day; Thanksgiving; Christmas.
Membership: Seaman $10; Chief Petty Officer $25; Lieutenant $50; Commander $100; Captain $500; Admiral $1,000.

RIPLEY'S BELIEVE IT OR NOT! MUSEUM, 1441 Boardwalk, Atlantic City, NJ 08401-7144. Tel.: 609-347-2001.
E-mail: info@ripleysatlanticcity.com
Web Site: www.ripleys.com
Key Personnel: Gen. Mgr., Chris Connelly
General Museum.
Collections: personal artifacts & oddities from 198 countries; lock of George Washington's hair; 27 room miniature wood carved castle; videos; photographs.
Facilities: Museum-related items for sale.
Activities: tours; private parties; groups; birthdays.
Hours & Admission Prices: May-Aug. daily 10-10; Sept.-April Sun.-Fri. 10-6, Sat. 10-8. Adults 13 & over $14.99, students $12.99, senior citizen $11.99, children 5-12 $9.99; discounts to AAA members. ♿

Avalon

AVALON HISTORICAL SOCIETY, (M), 215 39th St., Avalon, NJ 08202-1648. Tel.: 609-967-0090.
Web Site: www.avalonmuseum.org
Key Personnel: Pres. (V), Ms. Barbara Juzaitis.
Governing Authority: nonprofit.
History Museum.
Collections: Avalon history & culture; photographs.
Hours & Admission Prices: Mon.-Sat. 11-3. No charge; donations accepted. ♿

Basking Ridge

ENVIRONMENTAL EDUCATION CENTER, SOMERSET COUNTY PARK COMMISSION, 190 Lord Stirling Rd., Basking Ridge, NJ 07920-1329. Tel.: 908-766-2489, ext. 0. Fax: 908-766-2687. Relay Service 711.
E-mail: cschrein@scparks.org
Web Site: www.somersetcountyparks.org
Founded: 1970.
Congressional District: 5
Key Personnel: Mgr., Catherine Schrein; Environmental Science Supvr., Kurt Bender; Administrative Asst., Jane Bodnar; Naturalist, Maria Rossi; Naturalist, Monica Juhasz; Naturalist, Daryl Anne Villard; Naturalist, Christa Wood; Naturalist, Rich Hoffman; Naturalist, Mary Bozenmayer; Naturalist, Carrie Gazal; Foreman, Jim Bodnar; Maintenance Worker, Vlad Levitski; Museum Shop Mgr., Jean Stamey.
Personnel Profile: Full-Time Paid 14; Part-Time Paid 11; Part-Time Volunteers 50.
Governing Authority: county. Affiliated with Somerset County Park Commission, P.O. Box 5327, North Branch, NJ 08876. Tel. 908-722-1200. Tax-exempt.
Environmental Education Center: located on site of Lord Stirling's Estate.
Collections: herbarium collection of vascular plants of Great Swamp; fungi of

northern New Jersey; natural history photographic slides; bird nests, vertebrate & aquatic invertebrate of Great Swamp Basin.
Research Fields: field succession; management techniques relevant to county park lands; archaeological field project at c.1763 Lord Stirling Manor Site and at paleo-Indian site.
Facilities: 6,000-vol. library of natural history, environmental education, New Jersey & local history available for research on premises; trails, boardwalk; observation blinds; field research station; classrooms. Museum, natural history science theme items for sale.
Activities: guided tours by appointment; lectures; films; concerts; rental gallery; formally organized education programs; docent program or council; training programs; loan & permanent exhibitions.
Publications: newsletter, Parks, Programs & People; environmental information sheets.
Hours & Admission Prices: Daily 9-5. Trails: daily sunrise to sunset. No charge; donations accepted. Closed major holidays. ♿
Attendance: 10,000 (estimated)
Membership: Program Guide: $5 annual.

Bayville

BERKELEY TOWNSHIP HISTORICAL MUSEUM, 630 Rte. 9, Bayville, NJ 08721. Mailing Address: P.O. Box 303, Bayville, NJ 08721-0303. Tel.: 732-269-0643.
History Museum.
Collections: local history & culture; personal artifacts; photographs.
Hours & Admission Prices: June 18 to mid-Sept. Wed. 6pm-8pm, Sun. 2-4; other times by appointment.

Beach Haven

LONG BEACH ISLAND HISTORICAL ASSOCIATION, 129 Engleside Ave., Beach Haven, NJ 08008-1762. Tel.: 609-492-0700.
History Museum: housed in the former Holy Innocents' Episcopal Church built in 1882.
Collections: local history & culture; photographs; personal artifacts; period furnishings.
Activities: walking tours; lectures; craft shows; flea markets. Museum Sponsors: Annual Porch Party; Island Singers Concerts.
Hours & Admission Prices: Spring & Fall Sat.-Sun. 2-4; Summer: Tues. & Fri. 10-4, Wed.-Thurs. & Sat.-Mon. 2-4 & 7-9. Suggested Donation: $3.

MUSEUM OF NEW JERSEY MARITIME HISTORY, 528 Dock Rd., Beach Haven, NJ 08008-1833. Tel.: 609-492-0202. Fax: 609-492-7575.
Key Personnel: Cur., Deb Whitcraft; Cur., Jim Vogel
Maritime History Museum.
Collections: maritime history; photographs; historic documents; newspapers; artifacts recovered from New Jersey wreck sites.
Facilities: library. Museum-related items for sale.
Activities: research.
Hours & Admission Prices: June daily 10-4; July-Aug. daily 10-6; Sept.-May Fri.-Sun. 10-4; other times by appointment. No charge; donations accepted. ♿
Membership: Student & Senior $25; Surfman $50; Surfman Family $100; Keeper $250; Superintendent $500; Lifetime Individual $1,000; Lifetime Family $2,500; Lifetime Corporate $5,000 & up; Lifetime Benefactor $10,000 & up.

Bedminster

JACOBUS VANDERVEER HOUSE, (M), Rte. 206 S., Bedminster, NJ 07921. Mailing Address: P.O. Box 723, Bedminster, NJ 07921-0723. Tel.: 908-212-7000, ext. 611.
E-mail: info@jvanderveerhouse.com
Web Site: www.jvanderveerhouse.com
Key Personnel: Pres., Jay Petrillo.
Governing Authority: Parent Institution: The Friends of the Jacobus Vanderveer House. Tax-exempt: 501(c)(3).
Historic House Museum.
Collections: period artifacts & furnishings.
Hours & Admission Prices: Call for hours.

Bloomfield

HISTORICAL SOCIETY OF BLOOMFIELD NEW JERSEY, 90 Broad St., Bloomfield, NJ 07003-2585. Tel.: 973-566-6220 & 743-8844.
E-mail: bloomfhist@aol.com
Founded: 1966.
Congressional District: 8
Key Personnel: C.E.O. & Pres. (V), Ina Campbell.
Personnel Profile: Part-Time Volunteers 6.
Governing Authority: society. Tax-exempt: 501(c)(3).
Local History Museum: housed in Bloomfield Public Library.
Collections: furniture; clothing & accessories; tools; household articles; paintings; toys; posters; memorabilia; dioramas; early maps & newspapers; postcards; letters; documents; books.
Research Fields: local history; genealogy.
Activities: guided tours; lectures; permanent exhibitions.
Publications: quarterly newsletter.
Hours & Admission Prices: June-Aug. Wed. 2-5; Sept.-May Wed. 2-4, Sat. 10-12:30; other times by appointment. No charge; donations accepted. ♿
Attendance: 380 (estimated)
Membership: Student $5; Individual & Nonprofit Organization $10; Couple $15; Commercial Organization $25.

Bridgeton

NAIL HOUSE MUSEUM, 1 Mayor Aitken Dr., Bridgeton, NJ 08302-1347. Tel.: 856-455-4100.
History Museum: housed in the former Cumberland Nail and Iron Company.
Collections: local history; period furnishings; photographs; personal artifacts.
Activities: special events.
Hours & Admission Prices: Temporarily closed.

WOODRUFF MUSEUM OF INDIAN ARTIFACTS, 150 E. Commerce St., Bridgeton, NJ 08302-2613. Tel.: 856-451-2620.
Founded: 1976.
Congressional District: 2
Key Personnel: Library Dir., Gail Robinson.
Personnel Profile: Part-Time Volunteers 4.
Governing Authority: municipal. Parent Institution: Bridgeton Public Library. Tax-exempt: 501(c)(3).
Native American History Museum.
Collections: Native American artifacts; photographs.
Facilities: 300-vol. library.
Activities: guided tours.
Hours & Admission Prices: Mon.-Fri. 1-4, Sat. 11-2; other hours by appointment. No charge; donations accepted. Closed New Year's Day; Martin Luther King Jr. Day; Presidents' Day; Good Friday; Memorial Day; Independence Day; Labor Day; Veterans Day; Columbus Day; Election Day; Thanksgiving & day after; Christmas.
Attendance: 500 (estimated)

Bringantine

BRIGANTINE BEACH HISTORICAL MUSEUM & SOCIETY, 3607 Brigantine Blvd., Bringantine, NJ 08203-1001. Tel.: 609-266-9339.
Historical Society Museum.
Collections: local history & culture; photographs; personal artifacts.
Hours & Admission Prices: Spring-Fall Sat. 11-2, Sun. 1-4; Summer Mon.-Sat. 11-2, Sun. 1-4.

Burlington

BURLINGTON COUNTY HISTORICAL SOCIETY, (M), 451 High St., Burlington, NJ 08016-4521. Tel.: 609-386-4773. Fax: 609-386-4828.
E-mail: burlcohistsoc@verizon.net
Web Site: www.burlingtoncountyhistoricalsociety.org
Founded: 1915.
Congressional District: 4
Key Personnel: Exec. Dir., Lisa Fox-Pfeiffer; Pres. (V), Bernadette Boyle; Dir. Education, Jeffrey J. Macechak; Librarian, Annie Brogan.
Personnel Profile: Full-Time Paid 4; Part-Time Paid 1; Part-Time Volunteers 15.
Governing Authority: society. Branch Museums: c.1740 Capt. James Lawrence Birthplace; c.1743 Bard-How House; c.1782 James Fenimore Cooper Birthplace; Delia Biddle Pugh Library; Museum Galleries. Tax-exempt.
Historical Society: historic house museums & local history museum.
Collections: lighting equipment; clocks; quilts; samplers; tools & equipment; decoys; costumes; period furnishings; paintings.
Research Fields: genealogical & local history research.
Facilities: local history books deeds, manuscripts & genealogical material available for research on premises.
Activities: tours; trips; educational programs.
Publications: reprint of Scott's 1876 Atlas; 1883 History of Burlington Co., Freedom Papers: 1776-1781; After Freedom; Burlington County Remembered: Landmarks; Delaware River Decoys of Burlington County; Ingenuity & Craftmanship: The Culture of Production in Burlington County.
Hours & Admission Prices: Tours: Tues.-Sat. 1-5, groups by appointment. Library: Tues.-Sat. 1-5. Adults $5, children under 12 $2.50; discounts to AAM members; members no charge. ♿

Attendance: 7,000 (accurate)
Membership: Individual $20; Household $45; Patron $60; Patron Household $75; Benefactor $120; Benefactor Household $150.

CITY OF BURLINGTON HISTORICAL SOCIETY, c/o Philip Augustyn, Philip's Furniture & Antiques, 307 High St., Burlington, NJ 08016-4411. Tel.: 609-386-0200, ext. 135. Fax: 609-386-0214.
Web Site: www.tourburlington.org
Founded: 1975.
Congressional District: 4
Key Personnel: Pres., Ray Lowdon; Financial Dir., Dolores Troxell; Devel. & Membership, Sam Ballinger; Museum Shop Mgr., JoAnn Viconto.
Personnel Profile: Part-Time Volunteers 50.
Governing Authority: municipal. Subsidiary Institution: The Carriage House.
Historical Society Museum: housed in c.1797 Hoskins House.
Collections: period artifacts; artifacts from the Burlington area. Historic Houses: c.1797 Hoskins House; c.1876 Carriage House; c.1792 Friend School House.
Activities: guided tours; concerts. Society Sponsors: Art Show in September; Christmas Parade & Tree Lighting in December; Christmas House Tour.
Publications: newsletter.
Hours & Admission Prices: By appointment only. Adults $4, senior citizens & children $3; members no charge.
Attendance: 3,000
Membership: Member $5.

COLONIAL BURLINGTON FOUNDATION, INC., 213 Wood St., Burlington, NJ 08016. Mailing Address: P.O. Box 1552, Burlington, NJ 08016-7152. Tel.: 609-386-6686. Fax: 609-386-3415.
Founded: 1939.
Congressional District: 4
Key Personnel: Pres., Matt Penisi.
Governing Authority: nonprofit organization. Tax-exempt.
Historic House Museum: 1685 Thomas Revell House.
Collections: furnishings; herb garden; boxwood garden.
Facilities: meeting room.
Activities: open house tours; private tours. Museum Sponsors: Annual Craft Fair.
Publications: biannual history newssheet, The Burlington Story.
Hours & Admission Prices: first Sat. after Labor Day; other times by appointment. No charge; donations accepted.
Attendance: 10,000

Butler

BUTLER MUSEUM, Main St., Butler, NJ 07405. Mailing Address: One Ace Rd., Butler, NJ 07405-1348. Tel.: 973-838-7222. Fax: 973-283-9895.
E-mail: butlermuseumj@optonline.net
Web Site: www.butlermuseumnj.org
Key Personnel: Cur., Alan Bird
Military History Museum.
Collections: military history from Civil War to Desert Storm; period artifacts; tools.
Hours & Admission Prices: Sat. 10-2. No charge. Closed holidays.

Caldwell

GROVER CLEVELAND BIRTHPLACE, 207 Bloomfield Ave., Caldwell, NJ 07006-5115. Tel.: 973-226-0001. Fax: 973-226-1810.
E-mail: gcmuseum@gmail.com
Web Site: www.westessexguide.com
Founded: 1913.
Key Personnel: Dir. & Cur., Sharon Farrell.
Personnel Profile: Full-Time Paid 1; Part-Time Paid 1.
Governing Authority: state. Parent Institution: New Jersey Dept. of Environmental Protection, Div. of Parks & Forestry, Trenton, NJ 08625. Tax-exempt.
Historic House Museum: 1832 Old Manse of the Caldwell First Presbyterian Church; birthplace of President Grover Cleveland, 22nd & 24th President of the United States.
Collections: furnishings & mementos of Grover Cleveland & of the period.
Activities: guided tours.
Publications: brochure.
Hours & Admission Prices: Wed.-Sun. 10-12 & 1-4. No charge. Closed state & federal holidays.
Attendance: 1,800 (accurate)
Membership: $10 yearly.

Camden

ADVENTURE AQUARIUM, 1 Riverside Dr., Camden, NJ 08103-1060. Tel.: 856-365-3300, ext. 309; 800-616-JAWS (advance tickets). Fax: 856-365-3311. TDD: 856-541-8863.
E-mail: info@njaquarium.org
Web Site: www.adventureaquarium.com
Formerly: New Jersey State Aquarium
Founded: 1992.
Congressional District: 5
Key Personnel: Pres. & C.E.O., Brian DuVall; Exec. Dir., Greg Charbeneau; Husbandry Dir., Denise Aster; Vice Pres. Education, Angie Wenger.
Personnel Profile: Full-Time Paid 110; Part-Time Paid 53; Part-Time Volunteers 263.
Governing Authority: nonprofit organization. Tax-exempt: 501(c)(3).
Aquarium.
Collections: 4,000+ fish & aquatic animals; 36 sharks; 760,000 gallon open ocean tank; outdoor seal pool.
Research Fields: biology, zoology.
Facilities: 150-seat indoor & 300-seat outdoor restaurant; 120,000 sq. ft. exhibit space. Museum-related items for sale.
Activities: seal shows; docent program; films; formal education programs for children; lectures; mobile vans; participatory exhibits; volunteer programs in many areas including SCUBA diving demonstrations in Open Ocean Tank; Drama Gills performances.
Publications: quarterly members publication, AQ.
Hours & Admission Prices: Daily 9:30-5. Adults $19.95, senior citizens & children 2-12 $15.95; children under 2 no charge. ♿
Attendance: 510,000 (accurate)
Membership: General Membership: Individual Plus $55; Family $75; Family Plus $95. Sea Adventure Society: Friend $150; Supporter $300; Patron $600; Benefactor $1,250.

BATTLESHIP NEW JERSEY MUSEUM & MEMORIAL, (M), 62 Battleship Place, Camden, NJ 08103-3302. Tel.: 856-966-1652, ext. 126. Fax: 856-966-8228.
E-mail: j.schuck@battleshipnewjersey.org
Web Site: www.battleshipnewjersey.org
Founded: 2001.
Congressional District: 1
Key Personnel: Chm., Patricia Egan Jones; Immediate Past Chm., John Mattheusen; Museum Shop Mgr., Edwin Bishop.
Personnel Profile: Full-Time Paid 11; Part-Time Paid 8; Part-Time Volunteers 1,200; Interns 6.
Governing Authority: Parent Institution: Home Port Alliance for the USS New Jersey, Inc. Tax-exempt.
Naval Museum: one of the largest battleships ever built, the Iowa-class ship is our Nation's most decorated.
Collections: 16-inch gun turrets; the Combat Engagement Center; Crew's quarters; BB 62's weapon's systems.
Facilities: Museum-related items for sale.
Activities: self-guided, guided & multimedia tours; special events; educational programs for students; overnight encampment; flight simulator; adult & children's audio tour.
Publications: member & donor newsletter, Scuttlebutt.
Hours & Admission Prices: Feb. 5-March 11 Fri.-Sun. 10-3; March 12-April & Sept. 7-Jan. 3 daily 9:30-3; May-Sept. 6 daily 9:30-5. General Quarters: adults $18.50, seniors, veterans, & children 6-11 $14. Fire Power: adults $19.95, seniors, veterans, & children 6-11 $15. City at Sea: adults $19.95, seniors, veterans, & children 6-11 $15. 4D Flight Simulator: $6.50. Closed New Year's Day; Thanksgiving; Christmas. ♿
Attendance: 175,000 (estimated)
Membership: Individual $40; Family $80; Contributing $125; Sustaining $300; Benefactor $500-$999.

CAMDEN COUNTY HISTORICAL SOCIETY, 1900 Park Blvd., Camden, NJ 08103-3697. Mailing Address: P.O. Box 378, Collingswood, NJ 08108-0378. Tel.: 856-964-3333. Fax: 856-964-0378.
E-mail: cchsnj@verizon.net
Web Site: www.cchsnj.com
Founded: 1899.
Congressional District: 1
Key Personnel: Bd. Pres., Richard Pillatt; Chm. (V), Dale Chimel; Exec. Dir., Linda R. Gentry; Dir. Museum, Sarah Hagarty; Dir. Library, Rachel Pekar; Coord. Education, Charla Lewis; Administrative Asst., Joseph Sperlunto.
Personnel Profile: Full-Time Paid 1; Part-Time Paid 4; Part-Time Volunteers 35.
Governing Authority: board of trustees; society. Tax-exempt: 501(c)(3).
History Museum.
Collections: Pomona Hall: 18th & 19th-century furnishings displayed in the

18th-century restored Georgian style residence. Museum: exhibits focus on history of Camden County & Southern New Jersey, 1600 to present. Exhibits include tools of early handcrafts displayed in craft shops (blacksmith, cooper, candle-maker, spinning & weaving, carpenter, cobbler); early firefighting equip.; early American glass; Victor Talking Machine Co.; lighting devices; military, American Revolution-Civil War; toys; one room school; ethnic exhibits; regional industry exhibits, including Victor Talking Machine Co.; textiles; costumes.
Research Fields: social, cultural & economic history of Southern New Jersey; genealogy; historic preservation.
Facilities: 21,000-vol. library of the history of Camden County & Southern NJ; maps; 1800-1959 manuscripts, newspapers of area; photographs; slides. Postcards, pamphlets, books & museum-related items for sale.
Activities: guided tours; colonial open-hearth cooking; lectures; formally organized education programs for children; permanent & temporary exhibitions; spinning demonstrations; seminars. Museum Sponsors: programs pertaining to history of Southern New Jersey and region; occasional symposia; bus trips.
Publications: bulletins; newsletters; books; pamphlets; monographs.
Hours & Admission Prices: Wed.-Fri. 12:30-4:30, Sun. 12-5. Pomona Hall Tours: Thurs. & Sun.; other times by appointment. Library or Museum: adults $5, seniors & students $4; members no charge. Pomona Hall: adults $5, seniors & students, $4; members no charge. Pomona Hall & Museum: adults $8, senior citizens & students $6; members no charge. Closed New Year's Eve & New Year's Day; Easter; Christmas; national holidays.
Attendance: 3,800 (accurate)
Membership: Seniors & Students $15; Individual $25; Family $35.

STEDMAN GALLERY, Rutgers-Camden Center for the Arts, 314 Linden St., Camden, NJ 08102-1403. Tel.: 856-225-6245 & 6350. Fax: 856-225-6597.
E-mail: arts@camden.rutgers.edu
Web Site: www.rutgerscamdenarts.org
Founded: 1975.
Congressional District: 1
Key Personnel: Dir., Virginia Oberlin Steel; Deputy Dir. & Gallery Cur., Nancy Maguire; Cur. Arts Education & Outreach, Noreen Scott Garrity; Mktg. & Public Rels. Mgr., Simone Jones; Dir. Devel., Jennifer Jordan; Dir. Theater Programs, Stefan Arnarson; Asst. Cur. Arts Education, Lynda Hitchman; Multimedia Production Specialist, Steve McMaster; Mgr. Community & Artist Programs, Carmen Pendleton.
Personnel Profile: Full-Time Paid 9; Part-Time Paid 2; Part-Time Volunteers 4; Interns 4.
Governing Authority: university; nonprofit. Parent Institution: Rutgers, The State University of New Jersey. Subsidiary Dept.: Rutgers-Camden Center for the Arts. Tax-exempt: 170 (b)(1)(A).
Art Museum.
Collections: contemporary American works on paper; paintings; sculpture; 20th-century European works on paper.
Facilities: theater; black box.
Activities: temporary exhibitions; children's education program; lectures; films; concerts; museum studies program.
Publications: exhibition catalogs.
Hours & Admission Prices: Jan. 3-Dec. 23 Mon.-Sat. 10-4; call for additional hours. No charge; donations accepted. Closed New Year's Eve & Day; Memorial Day; Independence Day; Labor Day; Thanksgiving; Christmas Eve & Day; between exhibitions. ♿
Attendance: 18,300 (accurate)

WALT WHITMAN HOUSE MUSEUM AND LIBRARY, 330 Mickle Blvd., Camden, NJ 08103-1126. Tel.: 856-964-5383. Fax: 856-964-1088.
Founded: 1946.
Congressional District: 1
Key Personnel: Cur., Richard Ryan.
Personnel Profile: Full-Time Paid 1; Part-Time Paid 5; Interns 2.
Governing Authority: nonprofit organization. Parent Institution: New Jersey State Park Service. Tax-exempt: 501(c)(3).
Historic Home Museum: 1884-1892 Walt Whitman home.
Collections: furniture; photographs; memorabilia; rare books; manuscripts; archival material.
Research Fields: literary work of Walt Whitman.
Facilities: 1,500-vol. library containing rare books, manuscripts & works of Whitman; educational facilities.
Activities: symposia, seminars & other public lectures & dialogues; educational programs & teacher workshops; poetry readings, contests, exhibitions; guided tours of Whitman's home.
Publications: biannual brochure, The Walt Whitman Assoc. Newsletter.
Hours & Admission Prices: June 15 to Labor Day Mon.-Fri. 11-4, Sat.-Sun. 12-5; Winter: Wed.-Fri. 1-4, Sat.-Sun. 11-4. Adults $4, seniors $3; members and children 18 & under no charge. Closed New Year's Day; Thanksgiving; Christmas.
Attendance: 3,000 (accurate)
Membership: Student $10; Senior $15; Individual $20; International (outside U.S) $25; Sponsor $50; Patron $100; Corporate & Benefactor $250.

Cape May

HISTORIC COLD SPRING VILLAGE, (M), 720 Rte. 9 S., Cape May, NJ 08204-4636. Tel.: 609-898-2300. Fax: 609-884-5926.
E-mail: 4info@hcsv.org
Web Site: www.hcsv.org
Founded: 1981.
Key Personnel: Dir., Anne Salvatore; Dir. Mktg., Sydney Perkins; Museum Shop Mgr., Clare Juechter
History Museum.
Collections: early American history; 26 restored period buildings.
Activities: demonstrations.
Hours & Admission Prices: June to Labor Day call for hours. Adults $8, seniors 62 & over $7, children 3-12 $6; children under 3 no charge.
Attendance: 30,000

MID-ATLANTIC CENTER FOR THE ARTS/EMLEN PHYSICK ESTATE/CAPE MAY LIGHTHOUSE/FIRE CONTROL TOWER NO. 23, (M), 1048 Washington St., Cape May, NJ 08204-1737. Mailing Address: P.O. Box 340, Cape May, NJ 08204-0340. Tel.: 609-884-5404; 800-275-4278. Fax: 609-884-2006.
E-mail: mac4arts@capemaymac.org
Web Site: www.capemaymac.org
Founded: 1970.
Congressional District: 2
Key Personnel: Dir. & C.E.O., B. Michael Zuckerman; Pres. (V), Diane Hutchinson; C.O.O., William Ten Eyck; Cur., Elan Zingman-Leith; Chief Outreach Officer, Mary Stewart; Mktg. & Communications Dir., Jean Barraclough; Dir. Visitor Svcs., Janice Coyle; C.F.O., Charles Kealy; Museum Education Coord., Robert Heinly; Tearoom Mgr., Roh Guldin; Publications Assoc., Doree Bardes; Tour Dir., Nanci Coughlin; Museum Shop Mgr., James Horner.
Personnel Profile: Full-Time Paid 30; Part-Time Paid 120; Part-Time Volunteers 300.
Governing Authority: nonprofit organization. Tax-exempt.
Historic Building.
Collections: Victoriana, including costumes; books; ephemera; tools; furniture. Historic Buildings: 1879 Physick house, attributed to Frank Furness; Carriage House Gallery at the Physick Estate; 1859 Cape May lighthouse; 1942 Fire Control Tower No. 23.
Research Fields: 1878-1916 Victorian & Edwardian periods; maritime/lighthouse history; World War II history.
Facilities: reference library of Victoriana. Physick Estate: Carriage House Tearoom & Cafe. Museum-related items for sale.
Activities: tours. Museum Sponsors: Cape May's Spring Festival April-May; Cape May Music Festival May-June; Victorian Week in October; Christmas in Cape May November-December.
Publications: quarterly newsletter; This Week in Cape May, 14 issues per year; Emlen Physick Estate (illustrated booklet); Sentinel of the Jersey Cape.
Hours & Admission Prices: Physick Estate Guided Tours: daily. Lighthouse Self-guided Tours: Feb-Dec. Architectural Trolley Tours: daily. Guided Walking Tours: daily. Self-guided Historic House Tours: April-May & Oct.-Dec. audio walking tour of Cape May's historic district. Around Cape Island Boat Tours: April-Oct.; World War II Trolley Tour: April-Oct.; Delaware Bay Lighthouse Adventures (boat cruises) May-Sept. Tours: Jan.-March Sat.-Sun.; April-Dec. daily. House Museum Tours: adults $10, children $5. Lighthouse: adults $7, children $3. Trolley Tours: adults $10, children $5; discounts to AAM; museum members, writers, journalists & tour guides from other historic sites with ID no charge. ♿
Attendance: 300,000 (accurate)
Membership: Student $10; Individual $30; Joint $40; Grandparent & Family $50; Sponsor $100; Business $150; Benefactor $500.

Cape May Airport

NAVAL AIR STATION WILDWOOD AVIATION MUSEUM, 500 Forrestal Rd., Cape May Airport, NJ 08242-2203. Tel.: 609-886-8787.
Military Aviation Museum.
Collections: Navy airmen commemoration; 26 aircraft; military artifacts; photographs.
Facilities: library.
Activities: aviation festivals; concerts; veterans' ceremonies; lectures; school field trips; senior tours.

Hours & Admission Prices: April-Sept. daily 9-5; Oct.-Nov. daily 9-4; Dec.-March Mon.-Fri. 9-4. Adults $7, children 3-12 $5; children under 3 no charge.
Membership: Individual $25; Family $40; Friend $75; Patron $100; Benefactor $500; Visionary $1,000.

Cape May Court House

CAPE MAY COUNTY HISTORICAL MUSEUM AND GENEALOGICAL SOCIETY, 504 Rte. 9 N., Cape May Court House, NJ 08210-1953. Tel.: 609-465-3535. Fax: 609-465-4274.
E-mail: museum@co.cape-may.nj.us
Web Site: www.cmcmuseum.org
Founded: 1927.
Congressional District: 1
Key Personnel: Pres. Historical Society, James Waltz; Dir. & Cur., Pary Woehlcke; Administrative Asst., Judi Davis; Museum Shop Mgr., Ruth Ann Nelson; Library Coord., Sonia L. Forry.
Personnel Profile: Full-Time Paid 2; Part-Time Paid 2; Part-Time Volunteers 25; Interns 4.
Governing Authority: board of trustees. Parent Institution: Cape May County & the Cape May County Historical & Genealogical Society. Tax-exempt.
History Museum: housed in the Cresse-Holmes House, 1704.
Collections: Native American artifacts; 18th-century kitchen & bedroom; Victorian artifacts; China, glass, & furniture; whaling; decoys; military & maritime; Cape May Lighthouse lens; toys; medical instruments & tools; carriages. Historic Buildings: 11 room historic house; 5 room historic barn.
Research Fields: historical; genealogical.
Facilities: library of Cape May County genealogy & local history. Gift items for sale.
Activities: guided tours; programs; fund raising activities; civic presentations; slide/tape programs; in-school presentations; lectures; museum kids club; assistance to teachers.
Publications: annual magazine, The Cape May County Magazine of History and Genealogy; quarterly newsletter, Reflections.
Hours & Admission Prices: Library: by appointment, call for hours & admission prices. Research fees. Museum: June-Sept. Tues.-Sat. 10-3; Oct.-May Fri. 10-2, Sat. 10-3. Adults $5, seniors & students $4, children 4-12 $2; under 4 no charge. ♿
Attendance: 3,000 (estimated)
Membership: Student $20; Individual $25; Family $35; Family Plus $55; Conservator $200; Archivist $500; Curator $1,000.

CAPE MAY COUNTY PARK AND ZOO, 707 Rte. 9 N., Cape May Court House, NJ 08210. Mailing Address: 4 Moore Rd., DN 801, Cape May Court House, NJ 08210-1645. Tel.: 609-465-5271. Fax: 609-465-5421.
Web Site: www.capemaycountygov.net
Founded: 1963.
Congressional District: 2
Key Personnel: Parks Dir., Michael Laffey; Zoo Dir., Dr. Hubert Paluch.
Personnel Profile: Full-Time Paid 41; Part-Time Paid 6; Part-Time Volunteers 10; Interns 3.
Governing Authority: county; nonprofit. Parent Institution: Cape May County Park Dept. Subsidiary Institution: Cape May County Zoological Society. Tax-exempt.
Zoo.
Collections: over 180 animal species & endangered species.
Facilities: botanical garden; zoological park. Museum-related items for sale.
Hours & Admission Prices: Zoo: Fall & Winter: daily 10-3:45; Spring & Summer: daily 10-4:45. Park: 9-dusk. No charge; donations accepted. Closed Christmas.
Attendance: 700,000 (estimated)

Cape May Courthouse

LEAMING'S RUN GARDEN & COLONIAL FARM, 1845 Rt. 9 N., Cape May Courthouse, NJ 08210-1436. Tel.: 609-465-5871.
E-mail: info@leamingsrun.com
Web Site: leamingsrungardens.com
Founded: 1978.
Congressional District: 3
Key Personnel: C.E.O., Jack Aprill; Pres. (V), Emily Aprill; Dir., Gregg Aprill.
Governing Authority: individual operation; organized for profit.
Agricultural Museum: housed in last remaining whaler's house in New Jersey.
Collections: vegetables; farm animals; historic chicken breeds.
Facilities: botanical garden; nature & conservation center. Dried flowers & gift items for sale.
Activities: guided tours.
Hours & Admission Prices: May 15-Oct.10 daily 9:30-5. Adults $8, children 7-14 $4, children 6 & under no charge; discount to groups. ♿
Attendance: 40,000
Membership: Annual $20.

Cedar Grove

CEDAR GROVE HISTORICAL SOCIETY, 903 Pompton Ave., Cedar Grove, NJ 07009-1225. Mailing Address: P.O. Box 461, Cedar Grove, NJ 07009-0461. Tel.: 973-239-5414.
Founded: 1968.
Congressional District: 8
Key Personnel: Pres., Barbara Young; Treas. & Office Mgr., Ren Chandler.
Personnel Profile: Part-Time Volunteers 25.
Governing Authority: private; nonprofit organization. Tax-exempt: 501(c)(3).
Historical Society Museum: housed in mid 19th-century early Victorian vernacular Morgan family farmhouse.
Collections: letters, receipts & plans related to the farming operations on the site from 1908-1985; agricultural magazines; books; tools & equipment; sports equipment; furnishings; textiles; late 18th- to early 20th-century cemetery; barn; civic park.
Research Fields: history of agriculture in Essex County.
Facilities: 700-vol. library of books & magazines, as well as letters & receipts; 1,200 sq. ft. exhibit space; nature trails.
Activities: guided tours; lectures. Museum Sponsors: pumpkin & apple sale in Fall.
Publications: monthly Cedar Grove Historical Society Newsletter.
Hours & Admission Prices: Wed. morning; other times by appointment. Volunteer work sessions: Wed. 10-1. No charge; donations accepted. ♿
Attendance: 500 (estimated)
Membership: Single $15; Family $20.

Cherry Hill

BARCLAY FARMSTEAD, 209 Barclay Lane, Cherry Hill, NJ 08034-2832. Tel.: 856-795-6225.
Web Site: www.barclayfarmstead.org
Historic House: built in 1816.
Collections: local history; period furnishings; personal artifacts; tool shed; corn crib; springhouse; barn; gardens.
Activities: special events; group tours; picnic area.
Hours & Admission Prices: Tues.-Fri. 12-4, 1st Sun. of month 1-4 by appointment. Adults $2, seniors & children 3-18 $1.

GARDEN STATE DISCOVERY MUSEUM, 2040 Springdale Rd., Ste. 100, Cherry Hill, NJ 08003-2082. Tel.: 856-424-1233. Fax: 856-424-6516.
E-mail: roree@discoverymuseum.com
Web Site: www.discoverymuseum.com
Founded: 1994.
Key Personnel: Exec. Dir., Roree Iris-Williams
Children's Museum.
Collections: hands-on activities.
Facilities: Museum-related items for sale.
Activities: educational workshops & performances; rental facilities; activity rooms; birthday parties; classes.
Publications: newsletter.
Hours & Admission Prices: May-Sept. 9:30-5:30; Oct.-April Mon.-Fri. & Sun. 9:30-5:30, Sat. 9:30-8:30. Adults $9.95, senior citizens $8.95; children under one no charge. Closed Thanksgiving; Christmas. ♿
Attendance: 150,000 (estimated)
Membership: Family $99; Family & Friends $149.

Clark

DR. WILLIAM ROBINSON PLANTATION & MUSEUM, 593 Madison Hill Rd., Clark, NJ 07066-3103. Mailing Address: Clark Historical Society, Municipal Bldg., 430 Westfield Ave., Clark, NJ 07066. Tel.: 732-340-1571.
E-mail: dr.robinsonplantation@hotmail.com
Web Site: www.clarkhistoricalsociety.org
Founded: 1974.
Congressional District: 7
Key Personnel: Dir., Scott McCabe; Asst., Trish Plummer; Asst., Lisa Jo Jennings.
Personnel Profile: Part-Time Volunteers 10.
Governing Authority: nonprofit organization. Parent Institution: Clark Historical Society. Tax-exempt: 501(c)(3).
Historic Society Museum; Historic House: c.1690, farmhouse with features of the Tudor period.
Collections: medical items; medicinal herb garden; farm equipment: milk wagon, saws, harvesting equipment, butter churns, spinning wheels, open hearth fireplace with oven.
Facilities: herb garden. Gift items for sale.
Activities: guided tours; organized education programs for children.

Publications: brochure; Historical Society booklet; directory of members & friends.
Hours & Admission Prices: 3rd Sun. of month 1-4; other times by appointment. No charge; donations accepted.
Attendance: 1,000 (estimated)
Membership: Annual $25.

Clifton

HAMILTON VAN WAGONER MUSEUM, 971 Valley Rd., Clifton, NJ 07013-4028. Tel.: 973-744-5707.
E-mail: normaleeclf@aol.com
Formerly: Hamilton House Museum-van Wagoner Museum
Founded: 1974.
Congressional District: 8
Key Personnel: Pres. Bd. Trustees, Marlene Walcott; Cur. & Museum Shop Mgr., Norma Lee Smith.
Personnel Profile: Part-Time Paid 1; Part-Time Volunteers 20.
Governing Authority: municipal council. Tax-exempt: 170(b)(1)(A).
Historic House Museum: 1815 Hamilton Van Wagoner House.
Collections: period furnishings of the 19th century.
Research Fields: local history.
Activities: guided tours; early craft workshops; formally organized education programs for children; cooking 1st Sun.
Publications: quarterly, Newsletter.
Hours & Admission Prices: Sun. 2-4; call for private tours. Adults $3. Closed major holidays.
Attendance: 500 (estimated)
Membership: Student $2; Individual $5; Family $10; Sustaining $25.

Clinton

HUNTERDON MUSEUM OF ART, 7 Lower Center St., Clinton, NJ 08809-1384. Tel.: 908-735-8415. Fax: 908-735-8416.
E-mail: info@hunterdonartmuseum.org
Web Site: www.hunterdonartmuseum.org
Founded: 1952.
Congressional District: 13
Key Personnel: Exec. Dir., Marjorie Frankel Nathanson; Pres. Bd. Trustees (V), Jim McDevitt; Dir. Exhibitions, Mary Birmingham; Dir. Education, Jennifer Brazel; Dir. Devel., Caryn Tomljanovich.
Personnel Profile: Full-Time Paid 7; Part-Time Paid 20; Part-Time Volunteers 80; Interns 1.
Governing Authority: nonprofit organization. Tax-exempt: 501(c)(3).
Contemporary Art Museum: housed in 1836 restored stone grist mill.
Collections: contemporary works on paper.
Facilities: Museum-related items for sale.
Activities: tours; lectures; special events; gallery talks; formally organized education programs; loan, temporary, & traveling exhibitions; juried & non-juried exhibitions; art classes; docent tours; gallery talks; special events.
Publications: newsletter, Hunterdon Museum of Art; exhibition catalogues; general brochure.
Hours & Admission Prices: Tues.-Sun. 11-5. Suggested Donation: adults $5. ♿
Attendance: 33,000 (estimated)
Membership: Senior $30; Individual $40; Family $50; Contributor $100; Sponsor $250; Patron $500; Benefactor $1,000.

RED MILL MUSEUM VILLAGE, 56 Main St., Clinton, NJ 08809-1328. Tel.: 908-735-4101. Fax: 908-735-0914.
E-mail: chuck@theredmill.org
Web Site: theredmill.org
Formerly: Hunterdon Historical Museum
Founded: 1960.
Congressional District: 13
Key Personnel: Pres., Richard Miller; Exec. Dir., Dr. Charles Speierl; Collections Mgr., Jean Daly; Office Sec., Wanda Piersen; Museum Shop Mgr., Janet Dunsby.
Personnel Profile: Full-Time Paid 2; Full-Time Volunteers 2; Part-Time Paid 3; Part-Time Volunteers 70.
Governing Authority: private; nonprofit organization. Tax-exempt: 501(c)(3).
Historic Site & History Museum.
Collections: 18th-, 19th- & early 20th-century rural American life; industrial; agricultural; domestic. Historic Buildings: 1810 Hunt's Mill; 1860 Bunker Hill schoolhouse; log cabin; blacksmith; general store; lime kilns; quarry & stone crusher.
Research Fields: 18th-, 19th- & early 20th-century social, industrial & agricultural history.
Facilities: herb garden; outdoor concert stage. Handcrafted & other gift items for sale.
Activities: group tours; concert series; children's workshops; lecture series. Museum Sponsors: car shows.
Publications: newsletter; The Old Mill Wheel.
Hours & Admission Prices: April-Oct. Tues.-Sat. 10-4, Sun. 12-5; admission gate closes at 4. Adults $8, senior citizens $7, children 6-16 $6; discounts to AAM members; members & children under 6 no charge. Closed Memorial Day; Independence Day; Labor Day.
Attendance: 18,000 (accurate)
Membership: Individual $30; Family $45; Patron $500; Sustaining $1,000.

Closter

BELSKIE MUSEUM OF ART & SCIENCE, 280 High St., Closter, NJ 07624-1812. Tel.: 201-768-0286. Fax: 201-768-4220.
E-mail: belskiemuseum@hotmail.com
Web Site: www.belskiemuseum.com
Founded: 1994.
Personnel Profile: Part-Time Volunteers 25.
Art Museum.
Collections: works of Abram Belskie, 1907-1988 including drawings, sculpture, medical models, metallic molds; local & international artists.
Activities: student & instructor exhibits.
Hours & Admission Prices: Sat.-Sun. 1-5; other times by appointment. No charge. ♿
Attendance: 3,000 (estimated)
Membership: $25-$100.

Columbus

MANSFIELD TOWNSHIP HISTORICAL SOCIETY (1849 GEORGETOWN SCHOOL/MUSEUM), 4 Fitzgerald Lane, Columbus, NJ 08022-2383. Tel.: 609-298-4174.
Founded: 1973.
Congressional District: 8
Key Personnel: Pres. (V), Pearl J. Tusim.
Personnel Profile: Part-Time Volunteers 4.
Governing Authority: society; nonprofit. Tax-exempt: 501(c)(3).
Historical Society Museum: housed in a rebuilt one-room school.
Collections: township history.
Facilities: 50-vol. library of 1800's school books available to the public; educational facilities.
Activities: guided tours; lectures. Annual Event: Field Day in June.
Hours & Admission Prices: by reservation call 609-298-4174. No charge; donations accepted.
Attendance: 100 (estimated)
Membership: Mansfield Twp. Historical Soc. $5 per year.

Cranbury

CRANBURY HISTORICAL & PRESERVATION SOCIETY, 4 Park Place E., Cranbury, NJ 08512-3208. Mailing Address: P.O. Box 77, Cranbury, NJ 08512-0077. Tel.: 609-860-1889.
Founded: 1967.
Congressional District: 12
Key Personnel: Pres., Audrey Smith; Vice Pres., Mia Lindberg; Vice Pres., Michelle Newman-Dickey; Dir. History Center, Roi Taylor; Cur., Lisa Beach; Cur., Karen Kelley; Cur., Jerry Pevahouse; Treas., Barbara Wahlers.
Personnel Profile: Part-Time Volunteers 53.
Governing Authority: society; nonprofit organization. Tax-exempt.
Historical Society Museum: housed in restored 1834 Dr. Garrett Voorhees house. Cranbury History Center: housed in restored gristmiller's house c.1860, 6 S. Main St.
Collections: oral history tapes; Cranbury local history; photographs, slides & maps; genealogical data; church records; vital statistics; Revolutionary & Civil War service records; census & cemetery records; historic house museum furnishings.
Research Fields: Cranbury history; data on families, houses.
Facilities: library of books, maps, photographs, newspapers, oral history tapes, genealogical records of Cranbury, New Jersey, and Revolutionary & Civil War records for use on premises by appointment only.
Activities: guided tours of museum & village; house & garden tours; lectures & cultural programming; loan & temporary exhibitions; municipal preservation initiatives.
Publications: quarterly newsletter; pamphlets: Sara's Garden; Historic Cranbury; Books: Cranbury Past & Present; Cook's Tour of Cranbury; pamphlets, Walking Tour Historic Cranbury.
Hours & Admission Prices: Museum: Sun. 1-4. History Center: 10:30-1:30; other times by appointment. No charge; donations suggested.
Attendance: 1,000 (estimated)
Membership: Individual $15; Family $25; Sponsor $35; Patron $50; Corporate $150 & up.

Cranford

CRANFORD HISTORICAL SOCIETY, The Hanson House, 38 Springfield Ave., Cranford, NJ 07016-2144. Tel.: 908-276-0082.
E-mail: cranfordhistoricalsociety@verizon.net
Web Site: cranfordhistoricalsociety.org/
Key Personnel: Pres., Patrick Paulak; Trustee, Robert Fridlington.
Governing Authority: Branch Museum: Crane Phillips Living Museum, North Union Ave., Cranford, NJ.
Historical Society Museum.
Collections: photographs; scrapbooks; glass negatives; furniture; tools; kitchen & farm implements; Indian artifacts; costumes & textiles; books; letters; personal artifacts.
Research Fields: genealogy.
Activities: tours.
Hours & Admission Prices: Mon.-Thurs. 9-12; other times by appointment.

Demarest

THE ART SCHOOL AT OLD CHURCH, 561 Piermont Rd., Demarest, NJ 07627-1615. Tel.: 201-767-7160. Fax: 201-767-0497.
E-mail: gallery@tasoc.org
Web Site: tasoc.org
Formerly: Old Church Cultural Center
Founded: 1974.
Congressional District: 39
Key Personnel: Exec. Dir., Maria Danziger; Pres. (V), Mikhail Zakin; Gallery Dir., Rachael Faillace.
Personnel Profile: Full-Time Paid 4; Part-Time Paid 45; Part-Time Volunteers 10.
Governing Authority: private; nonprofit organization. Tax-exempt: 501(c)(3).
Art & Cultural Center.
Collections: paintings; photographs; sculpture.
Facilities: 950 sq. ft. exhibit space; 4 classrooms.
Activities: education programs. Annual Events: Small Works Show in March; Student Exhibition in April; Faculty Show in September; Pottery Show & Sale in December.
Publications: quarterly course catalog, Semester; biannual newsletter, Centerline; annual catalog, Pottery Show.
Hours & Admission Prices: Gallery & Office: Mon.-Fri. 9:30-5, Sat. 9:30-3. Please call for extended hours. No charge for exhibitions. Closed federal holidays; most Jewish holidays. ♿
Attendance: 2,200 (estimated)
Membership: Youth $20; Adult $40; Family $50.

Dover

COMMUNITY CHILDREN'S MUSEUM, 77 E. Blackwell St., Dover, NJ 07801-4037. Tel.: 973-366-9060.
E-mail: ccmuseum@gmail.com
Web Site: www.communitychildrensmuseum.org
Key Personnel: Exec. Dir., Jody Marcus
Children's Museum.
Collections: hands-on exhibits.
Facilities: Museum-related items for sale.
Activities: birthday parties; special events.
Hours & Admission Prices: Winter: Thurs.-Sat. 10-5; Summer: call for hours. Admission 6 months & over $5, seniors $4.

East Brunswick

EAST BRUNSWICK MUSEUM CORPORATION, 16 Maple St., East Brunswick, NJ 08816-4450. Mailing Address: P.O. Box 875, East Brunswick, NJ 08816-0875. Tel.: 732-257-1508. Fax: 732-257-1508.
Founded: 1978.
Congressional District: 12
Key Personnel: Pres., Karen Scott; Vice Pres., Martha Hess.
Governing Authority: nonprofit organization. Subsidiary Institution: Alice Appleby Devoe Library/Harold Hoffman Memorial Archive. Tax-exempt: 501(c)(3).
Local & Regional History Museum: housed in 1860 Simpson Methodist Church & 1850 Appleby/Devoe House.
Collections: local & regional history objects.
Major Exhibits: Textiles, 2/10; Holiday Wear, 12/10.
Facilities: 300-vol. library of reference materials; archives.
Activities: guided tours; historic cemetery tours; lectures; docent program; participatory & loan exhibitions; workshops; book sale. Museum Sponsors: Village Street Fair; haunted house tour; holiday exhibit.
Publications: periodic newsletter; exhibition catalogues.
Hours & Admission Prices: Sat.-Sun. 1:30-4; groups at other times by appointment. No charge; donations accepted. Closed New Year's Day; Easter; Mother's Day; Memorial Day; Father's Day; Independence Day; Labor Day; Thanksgiving; Christmas. ♿
Attendance: 8,000
Membership: Student & Senior Citizen $10; Individual $15; Corporate $100; Life $300; Corporate Life $500.

Edison

THOMAS ALVA EDISON MEMORIAL TOWER AND MENLO PARK MUSEUM, 37 Christie St., Edison, NJ 08820-3860. Mailing Address: Edison Memorial Tower Corporation, P.O. Box 656, Edison, NJ 08818. Tel.: 732-494-4194.
Web Site: www.menloparkmuseum.com
History Museum.
Collections: Edison's life & history; innovations including wireless transmission, the carbon button transmitter, & the Edison Effect (the foundation for the field of electronics); photographs; personal artifacts; company artifacts.
Hours & Admission Prices: Thurs.-Sat. 10-4; call to confirm. Suggested Donation: $2.

Elizabeth

BELCHER OGDEN MANSION, 1046 E. Jersey St., Elizabeth, NJ 07201-2504. Mailing Address: 1045 E. Jersey St., Ste. 101, Elizabeth, NJ 07201-2503. Tel.: 908-581-7555.
Historic House Museum.
Collections: local history & culture; period furnishings; photographs.
Hours & Admission Prices: By appointment.

Englishtown

BATTLEGROUND HISTORICAL SOCIETY, Village Inn, 2 Water St., Englishtown, NJ 07726. Mailing Address: P.O. Box 61, Tennent, NJ 07763-0061. Tel.: 732-462-4947.
E-mail: thevillageinnenglishtown@verizon.net
Web Site: www.thevillageinn.org
Founded: 1969.
Congressional District: 12
Key Personnel: Pres., Hans Kernast; Treas., Kathy Doherty.
Personnel Profile: Part-Time Volunteers 15.
Governing Authority: private; nonprofit organization. Tax-exempt: 501(c)(3).
Historic Building.
Collections: Englishtown Village Inn is a restored 18th-century tavern which was used by American forces at the time of the Battle of Monmouth on June 28, 1778.
Facilities: Museum-related items for sale.
Activities: guided tours. Annual Events: monthly meetings of Battleground Historical Society January-May & September-October at Inn; spring luncheon.
Publications: newsletter, Matchaponix Journal.
Hours & Admission Prices: By appointment only. No charge; donations accepted.
Attendance: 200 (estimated)
Membership: Individual $12; Family $20; Individual Life $100.

Ewing

THE COLLEGE ART GALLERY, (M), The College of New Jersey, Holman Hall, 2000 Pennington Rd., Ewing, NJ 08628. Mailing Address: P.O. Box 7718, Ewing, NJ 08628-0718. Tel.: 609-771-2198. Fax: 609-637-5193.
E-mail: tcag@tcnj.edu
Web Site: www.tcnj.edu/~tcag
Founded: 1855.
Key Personnel: Dir., Sarah Cunningham.
Governing Authority: public college. Parent Institution: The College of New Jersey. Tax-exempt.
Art Gallery.
Collections: photography; printmaking; paintings; drawings; sculpture.
Hours & Admission Prices: Tues.-Thurs. 12-7, Sun. 1-3. No charge. ♿
Attendance: 5,000 (estimated)

Far Hills

UNITED STATES GOLF ASSOCIATION MUSEUM, (M), 77 Liberty Corner Rd., Far Hills, NJ 07931-2570. Mailing Address: P.O. Box 708, Far Hills, NJ 07931-0708. Tel.: 908-234-2300. Fax: 908-470-5013.
E-mail: museum@usga.org
Web Site: www.usgamuseum.com
Formerly: Golf House, Museum & Library

Founded: 1935.
Congressional District: 7
Key Personnel: Dir., Rand Jerris, Ph.D.; Asst. Dir., David Normoyle; Cur. Education & Outreach, Beth Morrison; Film & Video Archivist, Shannon Doody; Chm. (V), C. Jay Rains; Librarian, Nancy Stulack; Asst. Mgr. Photograph Archives, Ellie Kaiser; Security, James Rau; Museum Shop Mgr., Kim Gianetti.
Personnel Profile: Full-Time Paid 10; Part-Time Paid 3; Part-Time Volunteers 20; Interns 3.
Governing Authority: nonprofit organization. Parent Institution: United States Golf Association. Tax-exempt: 501(c)(3).
Golf Museum & Library: housed in 1919 Georgian style home, designed by John Russell Pope.
Collections: clubs; balls; tees; costumes; ceramics; glass; silver; gold; stamps; bags; tins; archives; photographs; books; paintings.
Research Fields: golf.
Facilities: 30,000-vol. library of golf-related material, including books, magazines & pamphlets available to the public; 16,000 sq. ft. exhibit space; research & test center; 16,000 sq. ft. putting green. Gift items for sale.
Activities: guided tours by appointment; traveling & special exhibitions.
Hours & Admission Prices: Tues.-Sun. 10-5. Adults $7, children 13-17 $3.50; discounts to AAM, ICOM, & museum members; children under 12 no charge. Closed major holidays. ♿
Attendance: 20,000 (estimated)

Farmingdale

ALLAIRE VILLAGE INC., 4265 Atlantic Ave., Farmingdale, NJ 07727-3715. Mailing Address: P.O. Box 220, Farmingdale, NJ 07727-0220. Tel.: 732-919-3500 & 938-2253. Fax: 732-938-3302.
E-mail: allairevillage@bytheshore.com
Web Site: www.allairevillage.org
Formerly: Historic Allaire Village Inc.
Founded: 1957.
Congressional District: 11
Key Personnel: Exec. Dir., John Curtis; Asst. Exec. Dir., Diana Ioanid; Chm. (V), William Gerhanser, Ph.D.; Vice Chm. (V), Hance Sitkus, CPA; Mgr. Group Devel., Mary C. Halasz.
Personnel Profile: Full-Time Paid 5; Part-Time Paid 18; Part-Time Volunteers 160; Interns 3.
Governing Authority: nonprofit organization. Subsidiary Institution: Allaire Village Auxiliary. Tax-exempt: 501(c)(3).
Preservation Project & Museum Complex: 1830s Howell iron works.
Collections: natural science; farm tools; textiles; decorative arts; furniture; trade artifacts; letters to & from James P. & Hal Allaire; blacksmithing tax records. 12 Historic Structures: carriage house; enameling furnace; blast furnace; general store; bakery; blacksmith shop; managers house; Allaire residence; church; workers' row houses; foreman's cottage; carpenter's shop.
Research Fields: 1821-1858 cast iron manufactory business records; business & personal correspondence of James P. Allaire; genealogical information on inhabitants of the village during the 1830s decade.
Facilities: 300-vol. library of books on Allaire; snack bar. Museum-related items for sale.
Activities: educational & interpretive living history events; school & self-guided tours; workshops; lectures; antique & art shows; demonstrations; saw mill & cast iron manufactory available on premises by appointment.
Publications: book, Historic Allaire Village souvenir booklet; periodical, Calendar of Events; map, Self-Guided Tour; bimonthly volunteer newsletter, The Village Star.
Hours & Admission Prices: Historic Village: Memorial Day-Labor Day Wed.-Sun. 12-4; Sept.-Nov. & May Sat.-Sun. 12-4 Parking: $5 per car. State Park: Spring & Fall daily 8-6; Memorial Day-Labor Day daily 8-8; Winter daily 8-4:30. Adults $3, children $2. Members no charge; donations accepted. Group tours by appointment. ♿
Attendance: 185,000 (estimated)
Membership: Senior Citizen, Student & Volunteer $20; Individual $25; Family $40; Sponsor $100; Contributor $150; Distinguished Donor $300; Chairman's Circle $800 & up; Chairman Circle $1,000.

Flemington

DORIC HOUSE, 114 Main St., Flemington, NJ 08822-1415. Tel.: 908-782-1091.
Founded: 1885.
Congressional District: 5
Key Personnel: Pres. (V), Richard H. Stothoff; Librarian & Corresponding Sec., Roxanne K. Carkhuff.
Personnel Profile: Part-Time Paid 2; Part-Time Volunteers 20.
Governing Authority: society. Affiliated with Hunterdon County Historical Society. Tax-exempt: 501(c)(3).
General Museum: housed in the home of architect & builder, Mahlon Fisher; built in 1846.
Collections: period domestic & agricultural furnishings; Indian artifacts; manuscripts; paintings.
Research Fields: Hunterdon County local history & genealogy.
Facilities: 4,500-vol. library of state & local history; genealogy available for use on premises during regular hours or by appointment; reading room. Publications, reprints & current books of interest for sale.
Activities: guided tours; lectures.
Publications: triannual, Hunterdon Historical Newsletter.
Hours & Admission Prices: House: by appointment. Library: Thurs. 1-3 & 7-9 pm; other times by appointment. No charge; donations accepted. Closed national holidays.
Attendance: 600 (estimated)
Membership: Student 18 & under $3; Annual $15; Family $18; Contributing $25; Sustaining $50; Institutional $50 & up; Century Club $100 & up; Life $200.

FLEMING CASTLE MUSEUM, 5 Bonnell St., Flemington, NJ 08822-1311. Mailing Address: 38 Park Ave., Flemington, NJ 08822-1321. Tel.: 908-782-4607.
E-mail: flemingcastle@yahoo.com
Web Site: www.flemingcastle.com
Key Personnel: Pres. Bd. Trustees (V), Carmen Grimes; Vice Pres., William Wachter
Historic House Museum.
Collections: Flemington history; period furnishings.
Activities: group tours.
Hours & Admission Prices: 2nd Sun. of month 1-4. No charge; donations accepted.

Florham Park

IMAGINE THAT, A NEW JERSEY CHILDREN'S MUSEUM, 4 Vreeland Rd., Florham Park, NJ 07932-1555. Tel.: 973-966-8000.
E-mail: itmuseum@aol.com
Web Site: www.imaginethatmuseum.com
Formerly: Imagine That Children's Museum
Founded: 1992.
Interactive Children's Museum.
Collections: over 50 hands-on exhibits including dance, science, art, & computers.
Facilities: cafe.
Activities: birthday parties; drop-off service.
Hours & Admission Prices: Daily 10-5:30; groups by appointment. Children $9.95, adults $7.95; discounts to groups & AAA members; children under one no charge. Closed Christmas & Thanksgiving. ♿

Forked River

LACEY HISTORICAL SOCIETY, 126 S. Main St., Rte. 9, Forked River, NJ 08731. Mailing Address: Box 412, Forked River, NJ 08731-0412. Tel.: 609-971-0467.
Formerly: Old Schoolhouse Museum
Founded: 1962.
Congressional District: 3
Key Personnel: C.E.O. & Pres. (V), Eleanor F. Ditton; Museum Shop Mgr., Mary Jensen.
Personnel Profile: Part-Time Volunteers 40.
Governing Authority: society. Parent Institution: Lacey Historical Society. Tax-exempt.
General Museum: housed in 1860 old schoolhouse.
Collections: local artifacts.
Activities: permanent & temporary exhibitions.
Publications: West Jersey: Under Four Flags; Lacy Township: People and Progress.
Hours & Admission Prices: June 15-Aug. Mon., Wed. & Fri. 1-3, Sat. 10-12; other times by appointment. No charge; donations accepted. ♿
Attendance: 1,000 (estimated)
Membership: General $3; Lifetime $50.

Fort Dix

FORT DIX MUSEUM, 6501 Pennsylvania Ave., Fort Dix, NJ 08640-5300. Tel.: 609-562-6983. Fax: 609-562-2164.
E-mail: daniel.zimmerman@dix.army.mil
Founded: 1984.
Congressional District: 13
Key Personnel: Pres. & Chm. (V), Joseph DeFazio; Dir., Daniel W. Zimmerman; Vice Pres., John Warrick.
Personnel Profile: Full-Time Paid 2; Part-Time Paid 1; Interns 1.

Governing Authority: federal. Tax-exempt: 501(c)(3).
Military Museum.
Collections: firearms; uniforms; military equipment; personal equipment; decorative arts; lithographs; archives; photographs.
Research Fields: military history.
Facilities: reference library pertaining to military history; archives.
Activities: guided tours; lectures.
Hours & Admission Prices: Mon.-Fri. 8-4. No charge. ♿
Attendance: 7,650 (accurate)

Fort Hancock

SANDY HOOK NATIONAL SEASHORE, 58 Magruder Rd., Fort Hancock, NJ 07732-4054. Mailing Address: P.O. Box 530, Fort Hancock, NJ 07732. Tel.: 732-872-5970.
Web Site: www.nps.gov/gate
Formerly: Gateway NRA, Sandy Hook Unit
Founded: 1974.
Congressional District: 6
Key Personnel: Historian, Thomas Hoffman; Museum Cur., Mary Rasa.
Personnel Profile: Full-Time Paid 7; Part-Time Volunteers 70; Interns 1.
Governing Authority: federal. U.S. Dept. of the Interior, National Park Service, Gateway National Recreation Area.
National Park Museum: housed in the 1899 Fort Hancock Guard House or Post Stockade. Museum is part of Sandy Hook Historic Landmark.
Collections: 8,000 historical photographs & papers; 4,000 blueprints & maps; books & Army manuals; military uniforms, weapons, accoutrements & insignia; models & dioramas; artifacts relating to U.S. Lifesaving & Lighthouse Services; personal & societal items; herbarium, insect & vertebrate collections.
Research Fields: natural, military, maritime & social history.
Facilities: reference library; photographs, maps & other archival materials available for research by appointment.
Activities: guided tours; permanent & temporary exhibitions.
Publications: pamphlets on Ft. Hancock, Sandy Hook Lighthouse; volunteer newsletter, Sandpiper.
Hours & Admission Prices: Visitor's Center: daily 10-5. Museum: Winter: Sat.-Sun. 1-5; Summer: daily 1-5. Historic House: Sat.-Sun. 1-5. Sandy Hook Lighthouse & Light Keepers Quarters: April-Oct. Mon.-Fri. 1-5, Sat.-Sun. 12-4:30; Nov. Sat.-Sun. 12-5. Parking: buses $25, cars $10; after Labor Day no charge. ♿
Attendance: 50,000

Fort Lee

FORT LEE HISTORIC PARK & MUSEUM, Hudson Terrace, Fort Lee, NJ 07024. Tel.: 201-461-1776. Fax: 201-461-7275.
E-mail: flhp@njpalisades.org
Web Site: www.njpalisades.org
Founded: 1976.
Key Personnel: Dir., John Muller; Pres., Jim Hall; Museum Shop Mgr., J. Muller.
Personnel Profile: Full-Time Paid 5; Part-Time Paid 1; Part-Time Volunteers 3.
Governing Authority: municipal; nonprofit. Parent Institution: Palisades Interstate Park Commission. Tax-exempt.
History Museum: located in Historic Park.
Collections: reproductions.
Research Fields: Revolutionary War military history; life & times of Revolutionary War soldier.
Facilities: library; 204-seat theater; 1,200 sq. ft. exhibit space.
Activities: guided tours; lectures; concerts; organized education programs; training programs for professional museum workers; loan exhibitions. Museum Sponsors: encampments; musters.
Hours & Admission Prices: March-Dec. Wed.-Sun. 10-5. No charge. Parking: $4. ♿
Attendance: 25,998 (accurate)

Fort Monmouth

U.S. ARMY COMMUNICATIONS-ELECTRONICS MUSEUM, Kaplan Hall, Bldg. 275, Fort Monmouth, NJ 07703. Tel.: 732-532-1682.
Founded: 1976.
Congressional District: 3
Key Personnel: Dir., Mindy Rosewitz.
Personnel Profile: Full-Time Paid 1.
Governing Authority: federal. Tax-exempt.
Military Communications Museum: located on the site of 1917 Camp Alfred Vail, the main training camp for the Signal Corps during World War I; 1925 redesignated Fort Monmouth to commemorate 1778 Battle of Monmouth.
Collections: heliographs; early radio & telegraph equipment; large collection of vacuum tubes; international communications equipment; state of the art communication equipment.
Facilities: 1,000-vol. library of technical manuals.
Activities: guided tours; lectures; films; inter-museum loan, permanent & temporary exhibitions.
Publications: pamphlet.
Hours & Admission Prices: By appointment. No charge. Closed national holidays. ♿
Attendance: 5,000 (estimated)

Franklin

FRANKLIN MINERAL MUSEUM, 32 Evans St., Franklin, NJ 07416-1419. Mailing Address: P.O. Box 54, Franklin, NJ 07416-0054. Tel.: 973-827-3481. Fax: 973-827-0149.
E-mail: fmm1954@earthlink.net
Web Site: franklinmineralmuseum.com
Founded: 1965.
Congressional District: 24
Key Personnel: Pres. (V), Steven Phillips; Treas., A. Lee Lowell; Mgr., Doreen Longo.
Personnel Profile: Full-Time Paid 4; Full-Time Volunteers 2; Part-Time Paid 4; Part-Time Volunteers 15.
Governing Authority: private; nonprofit organization. Tax-exempt: Form 990.
Geology & Mining Museum: adjacent to zinc mines, located in old mine engine house, built in late 19th century.
Collections: rocks & minerals from local zinc mines and from around the world; local mining artifacts; fossils; Native American relics.
Research Fields: museum research & education fund dedicated to the science & history of the Franklin & Ogdensburg, N.J. zinc mining district.
Facilities: 2,000-vol. library relating to geology, mineralogy, mining history & crystallography; educational facilities. Museum-related items for sale.
Activities: rock collecting on mine dump; guided tours; study clubs; temporary exhibitions. Annual Events: Miner's Day; mineral shows.
Publications: newsletter, Franklin Mineral Museum.
Hours & Admission Prices: April-Nov. Mon.-Fri. 10-4, Sat.-Sun. 10-5. Adults $7, seniors $5, children $4; members no charge. Closed Easter; Thanksgiving. ♿
Attendance: 20,000 (accurate)
Membership: Individual $15; Family $25; Patron $50; Life $500; Benefactor $1,000; Sustaining $5,000.

Franklin Lakes

THE GALLERY AT THE PRESBYTERIAN CHURCH AT FRANKLIN LAKES, 730 Franklin Lake Rd., Franklin Lakes, NJ 07417. Tel.: 201-891-0511.
Art Museum.
Collections: paintings; photographs; sculpture.
Hours & Admission Prices: Call for hours.

Freehold

MONMOUTH COUNTY HISTORICAL ASSOCIATION, 70 Court St., Freehold, NJ 07728-1710. Tel.: 732-462-1466. Fax: 732-462-8346.
Web Site: www.monmouthhistory.org
Founded: 1898.
Congressional District: 12
Key Personnel: Dir., Lee Ellen Griffith, Ph.D; Pres., Judith Stanley Coleman; Dir. Devel., James P. McMahon; Cur., Bernadette Sigler Rogoff; Office Mgr., Patricia Glasser; Librarian, Laura M. Poll.
Personnel Profile: Full-Time Paid 5; Part-Time Paid 5; Part-Time Volunteers 30.
Governing Authority: nonprofit organization. Branch Museums: Marlpit Hall, Middletown, NJ; Holmes-Hendrickson House, Holmdel, NJ; Covenhoven House, Freehold, NJ; Allen House, Shrewsbury, NJ. Tax-exempt: 501(c)(3).
Historical Society Museums.
Collections: 20,000 artifacts, 17th-20th century relating to the history of Monmouth County, N.J.; strong in decorative arts; folk art; paintings; silver; furniture; glass; ceramics; toys & household artifacts.
Research Fields: history & architecture of houses maintained; collections; county history; architecture; genealogy; New Jersey material culture.
Facilities: 5,000-vol. library manuscript materials, maps, ephemera, postcards, all relating to Monmouth County, N.J. & surrounding area; museum & four 18th century historic house museums.
Activities: guided tours; lectures; films; formally organized education programs; permanent & temporary exhibitions.
Publications: newsletter; The Diary of Sarah Tabita Reid 1868-1873; Steamboats in Monmouth County: A Gazetteer.
Hours & Admission Prices: Library: Wed.-Sat. 10-4. Museum: Tues.-Sat. 10-4. Adults $5, senior citizens & children 6-18 $2.50; discounts to AAM members; members and children under 6 no charge, groups by reservation. Historic Houses: call for information. Closed New Year's Day; Independence Day; Thanksgiving; Christmas Eve & Day. ♿

Attendance: 13,046 (accurate)
Membership: Student & Senior Citizens $25; Individual $35; Family $50; Supporting $100; Patron $250; Benefactor $500.

Frenchtown

DECOYS & WILDLIFE GALLERY, 55 Bridge St., Frenchtown, NJ 08825-1229. Tel.: 908-996-6501; 888-996-6501 (Toll Free). Fax: 908-996-0807.
E-mail: decoys@decoyswildlife.com
Art Gallery.
Collections: wildlife art; duck decoys; paintings; sculpture.
Activities: workshops; special events. Museum Sponsors: Open House in February; Original Miniature in the Fall.
Hours & Admission Prices: Daily 10-6; other times by appointment. Closed Christmas.

Glassboro

GLASSBORO HERITAGE GLASS MUSEUM, 25 E. High St., Glassboro, NJ 08028-2519. Tel.: 856-881-7468.
Founded: 1979.
Key Personnel: Vol. (V), Carol Schoepske; Museum Shop Mgr., Doris Ratzell.
Personnel Profile: Full-Time Volunteers 10; Part-Time Volunteers 10.
Governing Authority: Tax-exempt.
Glass Museum.
Collections: bottles & jars from Whitney, Clevenger, Wheaton, & Stanger Glass Works.
Activities: educational & historical talks.
Publications: newsletter.
Hours & Admission Prices: Wed. 12-3, Sat. 11-2, 4th Sun. 1-4. No charge; donations accepted.
Attendance: 1,000 (accurate)
Membership: Single $15; Family $25; Business $75; Life $250.

Greenwich

CUMBERLAND COUNTY HISTORICAL SOCIETY, 960 YeGreate St., Greenwich, NJ 08323. Mailing Address: P.O. Box 16, Greenwich, NJ 08323-0016. Tel.: 856-455-4055 & 8580. Fax: 856-455-8580.
E-mail: cchistsoc@verizon.net
Web Site: www.cchistsoc.org
Founded: 1905.
Congressional District: 2
Key Personnel: C.E.O., Joan McAllister; Pres., Charles Griffiths; Vice Pres., Jonathan E. Wood; Sec., Ruth Ann Fox; Treas., Judith Uber; Clerk & Cur., Robert H. Francois; Dir. Library, Warren Q. Adams; Museum Shop Mgr., Kenneth Miller.
Personnel Profile: Part-Time Paid 4; Part-Time Volunteers 50.
Governing Authority: nonprofit organization. Tax-exempt.
General Museum: housed in furnished 1730 Gibbon house.
Collections: agriculture; archives; costumes; Civil War artifacts; furnishings. Historic Building: Prehistorical Museum (fossil & Indian artifacts); Barn Museum; 1650 Swedish Log Granary; maritime museum; manuscripts.
Research Fields: genealogical and historical research.
Facilities: Warren Lummis Library: 500-vol. library of N.J. history & family histories available on premises. Postcards, pamphlets & note paper for sale.
Activities: guided tours; lectures; films; concerts; hobby workshops; formally organized education programs for children; docent program; permanent exhibitions. Annual Events: craft fair; antique show; Farm Day; annual private home tour.
Publications: historic pamphlets; biannual newsletter, Cumberland Patriot; books.
Hours & Admission Prices: Gibbon House: April-Dec. Tues.-Sat. 1-4. Adults $2; society members no charge. Warren Lummis Gen. & Hist. Library: Wed. 10-4, Sat.-Sun. 1-4. John Dubois Maritime Museum, Matthew Potter's Tavern & Old Stone Church: by appointment only. Prehistorical Museum: Wed. & Sat.-Sun. 12-4. No charge; donations accepted.
Attendance: 5,000 (estimated)
Membership: Single $20; Couple $30; Life $200.

Hackensack

NEW JERSEY NAVAL MUSEUM, 78 River St., Hackensack, NJ 07601-7110. Tel.: 201-342-3268. Fax: 201-342-3268.
E-mail: njnavalmuseum@yahoo.com
Web Site: www.njnm.com
Founded: 1974.
Key Personnel: C.E.O., Chris Buermeyer.
Personnel Profile: Part-Time Paid 1; Part-Time Volunteers 18.
Governing Authority: private; nonprofit organization. Parent Institution: Submarine Memorial Association. Tax-exempt: 501(c)(3).
Naval Military Museum: located at World War II submarine USS Ling SS-297 in Hackensack River.
Collections: World War II submarine; pictures; ship models; battle flags; missiles, Vietnam river patrol boat; naval equipment; personal mementos; torpedoes; cannons; Japanese Kaiten suicide submarine; German Seehund 2 man submarine.
Facilities: library of original boat plans, prints, letters & scrapbook; 1,300 sq. ft. exhibit space. Museum-related items for sale.
Activities: guided tours; hobby workshops; loan & temporary exhibitions; children's birthday parties. Annual Events: Pearl Harbor Day, Memorial Day & Veterans Day Services.
Publications: newsletter published three times annually, Patrol Report.
Hours & Admission Prices: Sat.-Sun. 10-4 . Tours: adults $8, senior citizens $5; children under 12 $3. Museum & Grounds: no charge. Closed New Year's Day; Easter; Thanksgiving; Christmas.
Attendance: 15,000 (accurate)
Membership: Junior Supporting $5; Supporting $20; Commanders Club $50; Captains Club $250; Admiral Club $500.

Hackettstown

HACKETTSTOWN HISTORICAL SOCIETY MUSEUM & LIBRARY, 106 Church St., Hackettstown, NJ 07840-2206. Tel.: 908-852-8797.
Web Site: www.hackettstownhistory.com
Founded: 1975.
Congressional District: 24
Key Personnel: Archivist, Ray Lemasters.
Personnel Profile: Part-Time Volunteers 20.
Governing Authority: society; nonprofit organization. Tax-exempt.
Local History & Genealogy Museum: housed in 1915 Theodore G. Plate House.
Collections: Hackettstown history; regional history; archives; 500 photographs; Warren County cemetery records.
Research Fields: genealogy; history of Hackettstown & surrounding area & buildings.
Facilities: library of local history & genealogy.
Activities: guided tours; temporary exhibitions; historical society meetings. Society Sponsors: Open House; House Tours.
Hours & Admission Prices: Mon.-Tues. 9-2, Wed. & Fri. 9-4, Sun. 2-4; other times & groups by appointment. No charge; donations accepted. Closed major holidays.
Attendance: 250 (estimated)
Membership: Student under 21 $2; Individual $10; Contributing Member $20; Institution & Group $50; Life $200.

Haddonfield

HISTORICAL SOCIETY OF HADDONFIELD, 343 Kings Hwy. E., Haddonfield, NJ 08033-1214. Tel.: 856-429-7375.
E-mail: info@historicalsocietyofhaddonfield.org
Web Site: www.historicalsocietyofhaddonfield.org
Founded: 1914.
Congressional District: 3
Key Personnel: Pres. & Cur., Dianne H. Snodgrass; Financial Dir., Thomas Mervine, Jr.; Archivist & Librarian, Katherine Tassini.
Personnel Profile: Part-Time Paid 1; Part-Time Volunteers 20.
Governing Authority: private; nonprofit. Tax-exempt: 501(c)(3).
Historical Society Museum: administers two state & nationally certified historic houses. The Samuel Mickle House, the oldest extant dwelling in Haddonfield, was moved to its current property in the 1960s & houses the Society's library. Greenfield Hall, built in 1841 with an earlier wing from the mid-18th century, is a two and a half story Georgian style brick house with Classic Revival features.
Collections: history of Haddonfield & its environs; furnishings including four tall case clocks, a table & mirror which was owned by Elizabeth Haddon Estaugh, founder of Haddonfield; library's manuscripts on local & southern New Jersey history; ledgers & minute books of 300 local organizations, businesses & individuals; 3,000 photographs.
Research Fields: history of the Indian King Tavern & the local Black community.
Facilities: 5,000-vol. library relating to the history of New Jersey, Haddonfield & genealogy; Greenfield Hall available for rental. Museum-related items for sale.
Activities: guided tours; lectures; temporary exhibitions. Annual Events: Candlelight Dinner in March; Holly Festival in December.
Publications: quarterly newsletter, Bulletin.
Hours & Admission Prices: Museum: Sept.-July Wed.-Fri. 1-4. Adults $5. Library: June-July Mon.-Tues. 9:30-11:30; 1st Sun. of month 1-3; Sept.-May Tues. & Thurs. 9:30-11:30, 1st Sun. of month 1-3. Closed major holidays.
Attendance: 350 (estimated)

Membership: Senior Citizen $25; Contributing $35; Household $55; Patron $150; Patron Household $250; Life $1,000; Life Household $1,500.

INDIAN KING TAVERN MUSEUM, 233 Kings Hwy., E., Haddonfield, NJ 08033-1909. Tel.: 856-429-6792.
Web Site: www.levins.com/tavern.html
Founded: 1903.
Congressional District: 13
Key Personnel: Museum Mgr., William J. Mason.
Personnel Profile: Full-Time Paid 1; Part-Time Volunteers 23.
Governing Authority: state. Parent Institution: Div. of Parks & Forestry, New Jersey, Dept. of Environmental Protection, Trenton, NJ 08625. Tax-exempt.
Historic Tavern House Museum: 1750 formerly the Creighton House.
Collections: period & tavern/house furnishings; historical items.
Research Fields: 18th-century taverns; Revolutionary War.
Activities: guided tours; special programs.
Publications: quarterly newsletter, Committee of Cabinetmakers, Docents, etc.
Hours & Admission Prices: Wed.-Sat. 10-12 & 1-4, Sun. 1-4; groups of 7 or more by appointment. Call to confirm hours. No charge; donations accepted. Closed New Year's Day; Thanksgiving; Christmas; Wed. following a national holiday.
Attendance: 4,277 (accurate)

Haledon

AMERICAN LABOR MUSEUM, BOTTO HOUSE NATIONAL LANDMARK, (M), 83 Norwood St., Haledon, NJ 07508-1363. Tel.: 973-595-7953. Fax: 973-595-7291.
E-mail: labormuseum@aol.com
Web Site: www.labormuseum.org
Founded: 1982.
Congressional District: 8
Key Personnel: Pres. (V), Michael Goodwin; Project Mgr., Amy Hofer; Dir., Angelica M. Santomauro; Financial Dir., Thomas Maselli; Dir. Education, Evelyn M. Hershey.
Personnel Profile: Full-Time Paid 2; Part-Time Paid 1; Part-Time Volunteers 16; Interns 2.
Governing Authority: nonprofit organization. Tax-exempt: 501(c)(3).
History Museum: housed in 1908 Botto House, a national landmark.
Collections: photographs illustrating turn-of-the-century working class Italian immigrants (the Bottos); textile artifacts dating from 1890s to present day; labor union memorabilia; restored period rooms; history & contemporary issues of immigrants.
Major Exhibits: What Work Is by Juan Giraldo, 1/10-4/10.
Research Fields: labor & immigrant studies.
Facilities: 950-vol. library of books on labor, labor history & ethnicity; educational facilities; gardens. Books & materials on union/labor & immigration/ethnicity for sale.
Activities: guided tours; lectures; films; school loan service; formally organized education programs; docent program; participatory, loan, temporary & traveling exhibitions; arts festivals; classes. Annual Event: Labor Day parade/picnic.
Publications: quarterly newsletter; annual report.
Hours & Admission Prices: Wed.-Sat. 1-4; other times by appointment. Suggested Donation: adults $3; discounts to AAM & ICOM members; AAA members, children under 12 & members no charge. Closed major holidays except Labor Day.
Attendance: 16,578 (estimated)
Membership: Senior Citizen & Student $10; Individual $20; Supporting Couples $25; Family $30; Benefactor $50.

Hamilton

GROUNDS FOR SCULPTURE, (M), 18 Fairgrounds Rd., Hamilton, NJ 08619-3447. Tel.: 609-586-0616. Fax: 609-586-7303.
E-mail: info@groundsforsculpture.org
Web Site: www.groundsforsculpture.org
Founded: 1992.
Key Personnel: Cur., Ellen Landis; Mgr. Education & Grants, Christina Ely; Registrar, Faith McClellan; Community & Patron Rels. Mgr., Bonnie Brown; Education Mgr., Christina Ely; Event Planner, Rena Perrone; Facility Rental Mgr., Christopher Carrell; C.F.O., Robert Gross; Supvr. Admissions, Yvonne Exedaktilos; Museum Shop Mgr., Jenifer Micikas.
Personnel Profile: Full-Time Paid 70; Part-Time Paid 15; Part-Time Volunteers 100.
Governing Authority: public; nonprofit. Tax-exempt: 501(c)(3).
Sculpture Park.
Collections: contemporary sculpture.
Major Exhibits: Jacobo De Serna Reflections On Tradition, 11/09-4/10; International Sculpture Center Student Awards (T), 11/09-1/10; Albert Paley, 11/09-4/10; Flo Perkins, 1/10-4/10.
Facilities: 20-seat seasonal outdoor cafe; 40-seat indoor/50-seat outdoor cafe; restaurant; 20,000 sq. ft. exhibit space; 35 acre sculpture park.
Activities: permanent & temporary exhibitions; educational programs; special events.
Publications: exhibition catalogues; event guides; family guide.
Hours & Admission Prices: Tues.-Sun. 10-6. Adults $10, student & seniors $8, children 6-12 $6; members and children 5 & under no charge. Closed New Year's Day; Thanksgiving; Christmas. ♿
Attendance: 100,000 (estimated)
Membership: Seniors & Students $45; Individual $55; Dual & Family $90; Contributor $150.

HISTORICAL SOCIETY OF HAMILTON TOWNSHIP JOHN ABBOTT II HOUSE, 2200 Kuser Rd., Hamilton, NJ 08690. Mailing Address: P.O. Box 1776, Yardville, NJ 08620. Tel.: 609-585-1686.
Founded: 1976.
Congressional District: 4
Key Personnel: Pres. (V), James A. Federici; Vice Pres., Gordon Kontrath; Treas., Robert Boldt; Sec., Ruth Applegate.
Personnel Profile: Part-Time Volunteers 12.
Governing Authority: society; nonprofit. Parent Institution: Historical Society of Hamilton Township. Tax-exempt: 501(c)(3).
Historical House: c.1730 farm house & 1840 addition.
Collections: Colonial & Victorian furnishings; textiles.
Facilities: 200-vol. library pertaining to local history. Museum-related items for sale.
Activities: guided tours; organized education programs for children. Special Events: Septemberfest; Christmas Wassail Party.
Publications: booklets, John Abbott II House; Old Nottingham; pamphlet, John Abbott II House; Narrative History of Hamilton Township.
Hours & Admission Prices: March-Dec. Sat.-Sun. 12-4:30 by appointment only. No charge; donations accepted. Closed Christmas.
Attendance: 4,000 (estimated)
Membership: Individual $10; Family $15.

KUSER FARM MANSION, 390 Newkirk Ave., Hamilton, NJ 08610-4845. Mailing Address: 2090 Greenwood Ave., P.O. 00150, Hamilton, NJ 08609-2312. Tel.: 609-890-3630. Fax: 609-890-3632.
Web Site: www.hamiltonnj.com
Founded: 1979.
Congressional District: 4
Key Personnel: Mayor, John F. Bencivengo.
Personnel Profile: Full-Time Paid 1; Part-Time Paid 8.
Governing Authority: municipal; nonprofit. Parent Institution: Township of Hamilton. Tax-exempt.
Historic House: c.1892 Queen Anne style mansion & outbuildings, former summer home of Fred Kuser & his family.
Collections: early motion picture projection room; Mercer motor car memorabilia; carved fireplaces; 45-foot dining room. Historic Structures: coach house; 1907 clay tennis court & tennis house; windmill; barn; chicken building; pavilion; laundry house; corn crib.
Research Fields: local history related to Kuser family & their business connections.
Facilities: 60-vol. library pertaining to turn-of-the-century period, restoration sources & ideas available for inter-library loan; 22-acre park; projection room; tourism center.
Activities: guided tours; concerts; organized education programs; self-guided walking tours of the grounds; special lectures & demonstrations; weddings. Special Events: Summer Concerts in the Park; Winter Wonderland; Jersey Valley Model Railroad Club Open House; Christmas Holiday Open House.
Publications: brochures, Kuser Farm Mansion & Park; booklet, The Kuser Story, Paperdolls (3 versions), Coloring Sheet; General Rack Card; bookmark; Self-Guided Walking Tour map.
Hours & Admission Prices: Call for information. No charge; donations accepted.

Hammonton

BATSTO VILLAGE, 31 Batsto Rd., Hammonton, NJ 08037-5502. Tel.: 609-561-0024. Fax: 609-567-8116.
E-mail: info@bastovillage.org
Web Site: www.batstovillage.org
Formerly: Historic Batsto Village
Founded: 1954.
Key Personnel: Supt., Rob Auermuller; Museum Shop Mgr., Terry Schmidt.
Personnel Profile: Full-Time Paid 15; Part-Time Paid 5; Part-Time Volunteers 12; Interns 1.
Governing Authority: state. Parent Institution: N.J. Div. of Parks & Forestry, Dept. of Environmental Protection, Trenton, NJ 08625. Tax-exempt.
Historic Site Museum: Batsto Village, 33 historic buildings built in the 1800s.
Collections: 19th century life in South Jersey; archives & manuscripts;

bog-iron & glass making industries; agricultural equipment & implements; transportation; decorative arts; archaeology; postal history; nature center; furnishings.

Research Fields: bog iron; glass making; agriculture; Pine Barrens; lumbering & forestry; postal history; company town; commerce; genealogy.

Facilities: 100-seat auditorium; visitor center.

Activities: guided & self-guided tours.

Publications: Batsto Village newsletter.

Hours & Admission Prices: Batsto Mansion: call for schedule. Visitor Center: daily 9-4:30. Grounds: daily dawn to dusk.; groups by appointment only. Tours: adults $2, children 6-12 $1; children under 6 no charge. Parking Fee: Sat.-Sun., holidays & Memorial Day weekend to Labor Day. Closed New Year's Day; Thanksgiving; Christmas. ♿

Attendance: 100,000 (estimated)

Hancock's Bridge

HANCOCK HOUSE, 3 Front St., Hancock's Bridge, NJ 08038. Mailing Address: P.O. Box 139, Hancocks Bridge, NJ 08038-0139. Tel.: 856-935-4373. Fax: 856-935-2079.

E-mail: hancockhousenj@comcast.net

Web Site: www.nj.us/dep/forestry/histsite.htm

Founded: 1932.

Congressional District: 2

Key Personnel: Supt., Vince Bonica; Resource Interpretive Specialist, Alicia Bjornson.

Personnel Profile: Full-Time Paid 1; Part-Time Volunteers 15.

Governing Authority: state. Administered by the Division of Parks & Forestry, New Jersey Dept. of Environmental Protection, Trenton, NJ 08625. Tax-exempt.

Historic House Museum: 1734 Hancock House, built by Judge William Hancock & scene of Revolutionary War's British Massacre March 21, 1778.

Collections: 18th & 19th-century regional furnishings.

Activities: guided tours; concerts; craft shows; reenactments; public programs; school programs on-site & off-site.

Hours & Admission Prices: Wed.-Sat. 10-4, Sun. 1-4. No charge; donations accepted. Call prior to your visit. Closed New Year's Day; Thanksgiving; Christmas.

Attendance: 4,000 (estimated)

Membership: Individual $10; Household $18; Silver $25.

Highlands

TWIN LIGHTS HISTORIC SITE, Lighthouse Rd., Highlands, NJ 07732. Tel.: 732-872-1814.

Governing Authority: Parent Institution: NJ Division of Parks and Forestry.

Lighthouse: built in 1828. Listed on the National Register of Historic Places.

Collections: 9 ft. bivalve lens; lighthouse & maritime history.

Hours & Admission Prices: Memorial Day to Labor Day daily 10-4:30; Sept.-May Wed.-Sun. 10-4:30. No charge; donations accepted. Closed New Year's Day; Thanksgiving; Christmas. ♿

Attendance: 80,000 (accurate)

Membership: Basic: Friends & Family $25.

Hillside

WOODRUFF HOUSE/EATON STORE MUSEUM/PHIL RIZZUTO SPORTS EXHIBIT, 111 Conant St., Hillside, NJ 07205-2801. Tel.: 908-353-8828.

Web Site: www.woodruffhouse.org

Founded: 1978.

Key Personnel: Dir., Chm. & Pres. (V), Alan D. Zimmerman; Devel., Ann Pettigrew; Treas., Helen Witting.

Personnel Profile: Part-Time Volunteers 10.

Governing Authority: private; nonprofit organization. Operated by the Hillside Historical Society.

Historical Society Museum.

Collections: local history & culture; photographs; period artifacts; water pump; well; farm equipment; Phil Rizzuto sports memorabilia & Baseball Hall of Fame. Historic Buildings: 1735 farm house; 1900s general store.

Research Fields: township of Hillside history.

Facilities: archives.

Activities: guided tours.

Hours & Admission Prices: 3rd Sun. of month 2-4; other times by appointment. No charge.

Attendance: 850 (estimated)

Membership: Single $7.50; Family $15; Sustaining $25.

Ho-Ho-Kus

THE HERMITAGE, Friends of the Hermitage, Inc., 335 N. Franklin Turnpike, Ho-Ho-Kus, NJ 07423-1035. Tel.: 201-445-8311. Fax: 201-445-0437.

E-mail: info@thehermitage.org

Web Site: www.thehermitage.org

Formerly: Friends of the Hermitage, Inc.

Founded: 1972.

Congressional District: 5

Key Personnel: Exec. Dir., Richard A. Sgritta; Pres. (V), Carol W. Greene; 1st Vice Pres., Thomas R. Brome; 2nd Vice Pres., Patricia A. Ricci; Treas., Thomas Burgin; Sec., Roberta Svarre.

Personnel Profile: Full-Time Paid 2; Part-Time Paid 4; Part-Time Volunteers 40; Interns 2.

Governing Authority: state. Division of Parks & Forestry, P.O. Box CN 404, Trenton, NJ 08625; & Friends of the Hermitage, Inc. Tax-exempt: 501(c)(3).

National Historic Landmark Gothic Revival Historic House 1847designed by William Ranlett. Incorporates 18th century stone house that was Washington headquarters in July 1778. Estate of Rosencrantz family 1807-1970.

Collections: 19th century furnishing; decorative arts; recreational & everyday artifacts; costumes & textiles; Rosencrantz family archives (1807-1970); smokehouse; summer kitchen.

Research Fields: 19th century cultural, social, and industrial history; Gothic Revival domestic architecture; 18th & 19th century; costumes and textiles.

Facilities: 4.9 acre property; archives of family, estate, and mill records and oral history tapes available for use by appointment; education & conference center with classroom, meeting room, catering kitchen. Museum-related items for sale.

Activities: guided tours; permanent & temporary exhibitions; school & scout programs; children & family programs; summer children's history camp; senior & educational outreach programs; reenactments; 19th century theater; history roundtable; lectures; docent programs. Special Events: antique and craft fairs.

Publications: newsletter.

Hours & Admission Prices: Wed.-Sun. 1-4; clubs & groups by special appointment. Adults $5, children 6-12 $2; discounts to AASCH, AAM & AAA members; children under 6 & members no charge. ♿

Attendance: 15,000 (estimated)

Membership: Student & Senior $20; Individual $35; Family & Business $75; Mary Elizabeth Circle $125; Aaron Burr Guild $250; Theodosia Society $500; Benefactor's Club $1,000.

Hoboken

HOBOKEN HISTORICAL MUSEUM, 1301 Hudson St., Hoboken, NJ 07030-7427. Mailing Address: P.O. Box 3296, Hoboken, NJ 07030-1603. Tel.: 201-656-2240.

E-mail: info@hobokenmuseum.org

Web Site: www.hobokenmuseum.org

Key Personnel: Dir., Bob Foster

History Museum.

Collections: Hoboken history; photographs.

Hours & Admission Prices: Tues.-Thurs. 2-7, Fri. 1-5, Sat.-Sun. 12-5.

Holmdel

LONGSTREET FARM, Holmdel Park, 44 Longstreet Rd., Holmdel, NJ 07733. Mailing Address: Monmouth County Park System, 805 Newmann Springs Rd., Lincroft, NJ 07738-1628. Tel.: 732-946-3758 & 842-4000. Fax: 732-946-0750. TDD: 732-219-9484.

E-mail: info@monmouthcountyparks.com

Web Site: www.monmouthcountyparks.com

Founded: 1967.

Congressional District: 3

Key Personnel: Site Mgr., Sandra Byard; Supvr., Sean O'Herron.

Personnel Profile: Full-Time Paid 7; Part-Time Paid 10; Part-Time Volunteers 15; Interns 1.

Governing Authority: county. Parent Institution: Monmouth County Park System, Newman Springs Rd., Lincroft, NJ 07738. Tax-exempt.

Historic Farm: 1890 Longstreet Farm.

Collections: living history: an operating farm, including the farm animals, equipment & tools necessary for its operation; 19th-century agricultural items; 19th-century household artifacts. Historic Buildings: 19 structures including 18th-century Dutch barn; 1880 carriage house; farmhouse; barns; sheds; outbuildings.

Research Fields: agriculture & rural life in central New Jersey.

Activities: interpretive farm walks; demonstration of farm practices, including sheep-shearing, making apple cider, leather work, horseshoeing, cornhusking & threshing of grain, depending on the season of the year.

Publications: interpretive flyers.
Hours & Admission Prices: June-Labor Day daily 9-5; Sept.-May daily 10-4. No charge; donations accepted. ♿
Attendance: 88,000 (accurate)

VIETNAM ERA EDUCATIONAL CENTER, (M), 1 Memorial Lane, Garden State Pkwy. Exit 116, Holmdel, NJ 07733. Mailing Address: P.O. Box 648, Holmdel, NJ 07733-0648. Tel.: 732-335-0033. Fax: 732-335-1107.
E-mail: kwitzig@njvvmf.org
Web Site: www.njvvmf.org
Founded: 1998.
Congressional District: 12
Key Personnel: Project & Collections Mgr., Katie Witzig; Deputy Dir. Education & Operations, Ken Gurbisz; Administrative Asst., Lynn Duane.
Personnel Profile: Full-Time Paid 4; Part-Time Paid 1; Part-Time Volunteers 80; Interns 4.
Governing Authority: NJ Vietnam Veterans' Memorial Foundation. Tax-exempt.
Historical & Military Museum.
Collections: photos, letters, personal items, documents, objects related to the Vietnam era.
Research Fields: Vietnam War; Vietnam era; military service; political protest; 1960's & 1970's.
Facilities: library; resource room.
Activities: tours; classes; seminars; ceremonies.
Hours & Admission Prices: Tues.-Sat. 10-4. Adults $4, seniors & students $2; veterans, active military & children under 10 no charge. ♿
Attendance: 20,000 (estimated)
Membership: Student $25; Individual $30; Enhanced Individual $45; Family $75; Enhanced Family $100; Silver Sustaining $250; Gold Partner $500; Platinum Benefactor $1,000.

Hope

HOPE HISTORICAL SOCIETY, 323 High St., Hope, NJ 07844. Mailing Address: P.O. Box 52, Hope, NJ 07844-0052. Tel.: 908-637-4120 & 459-4268.
Founded: 1950.
Congressional District: 5
Key Personnel: Pres., Joy Fernbacher; Vice Pres., Alice Lee.
Personnel Profile: Part-Time Volunteers 14.
Governing Authority: society. Tax-exempt: 170(b)(1)(A).
General Museum: housed in early 1800s private home.
Collections: local area furniture; old photographs; store ledgers; maps.
Activities: permanent exhibitions.
Publications: booklet, The Moravian Contribution to the Town of Hope, N.J.; walking tour brochure.
Hours & Admission Prices: Sun. 1-3; groups by appointment. No charge; donations accepted.
Attendance: 200 (estimated)
Membership: Individual $10; Family $15; Patron $25; Benefactor $50.

Hopewell

HOPEWELL MUSEUM, 28 E. Broad St., Hopewell, NJ 08525-1828. Tel.: 609-466-0103.
Founded: 1924.
Key Personnel: Pres., David M. Mackey; Cur., Beverly Weidl.
Governing Authority: nonprofit. Tax-exempt: 501(c).
General Museum.
Collections: history of area from Colonial period to 1900; costumes; furnishings; equipment; weapons; art; agricultural implements; documents; pictures; Native American artifacts; natural history; glass; manuscripts.
Facilities: 100-vol. library of local history & genealogy books.
Activities: guided tours; permanent & temporary exhibitions.
Publications: book, reprint of 1963 Pioneers of Old Hopewell; map, reprint of 1875 Map of Hopewell Township; book, Hopewell Valley Heritage.
Hours & Admission Prices: Mon., Wed. & Sat. 2-5. Research: Mon. & Wed. No charge; donations accepted. Closed national holidays.
Attendance: 960

Howell

HOWELL HISTORICAL SOCIETY & COMMITTEE MUSEUM, 427 Lakewood-Farmingdale Rd., Howell, NJ 07731-8723. Mailing Address: P.O. Box 694, Farmingdale, NJ 07727-0694. Tel.: 732-938-2212.
E-mail: howellhist@aol.com
Web Site: www.howellnj.com/historic/
Founded: 1971.
Congressional District: 3
Key Personnel: Pres. (V), Steve Meyer; Corresponding Sec., Kay Coakley; Sec., Sandra Solly; Treas., Doris Howard; Museum Shop Mgr., Virginia Krzyzanowski.
Personnel Profile: Part-Time Volunteers 25.
Governing Authority: society. Tax-exempt: 501(c)(3).
Historical Society Museum.
Collections: primary & secondary source material; decorative arts; manuscripts; ceramics; glass; furniture; paintings; costumes; photographs. Historic Houses: c.1855 one room schoolhouse; c.1807-1855 Grist Miller's home; c.1870 Horse Shed.
Research Fields: local history.
Facilities: 200-vol. library of books, photographs, newspapers, postcards & maps available for research by special request. Museum-related items for sale.
Activities: guided tours; lectures; films; art festivals; reading room; docent program; permanent & temporary exhibitions.
Publications: pamphlet; calendar of events; book, History of Howell; monthly newsletter, Howell Heritage.
Hours & Admission Prices: Grist Miller's home: Sat. 9-12:30. Schoolhouse: last Sun. of month 1-4; other times by appointment. No charge; donations accepted.
Attendance: 1,000 (estimated)
Membership: Individual $10; Family $15; Sponsor $30; Patron $50.

Jersey City

AFRO-AMERICAN HISTORICAL SOCIETY MUSEUM, 1841 Kennedy Blvd., Jersey City, NJ 07305-2106. Tel.: 201-547-5262. Fax: 201-547-5392.
Web Site: www.cityofjerseycity.org/docs/afroam.shtml
Founded: 1977.
Congressional District: 13
Key Personnel: Dir. & Pres. (V), Neal E. Brunson; Consultant, Theodore Brunson.
Governing Authority: nonprofit organization. Tax-exempt: 501(c)(3).
History Museum.
Collections: 1800-present, New Jersey African American history; civil rights posters; musical instruments from Africa and African American communities; black dolls; black police & firemen; artifact; quilts; coverlets; Pullman porters.
Research Fields: Jersey City black history.
Facilities: 3,500-vol. library.
Activities: guided tours; lectures; films; organized education programs for children; temporary exhibitions.
Publications: Newsletter.
Hours & Admission Prices: mid-June to Aug. Mon.-Fri. 12-5; Sept. to mid-June Mon.-Sat. 10-5. No charge; donations accepted. Closed all legal holidays; election days.
Attendance: 7,500 (estimated)

JERSEY CITY MUSEUM, 350 Montgomery St., Jersey City, NJ 07302-4041. Mailing Address: P.O. Box 428, Jersey City, NJ 07303-0428. Tel.: 201-413-0303. Fax: 201-413-9922. TTY: 201-413-6339.
E-mail: info@jerseycitymuseum.org
Web Site: www.jerseycitymuseum.org
Founded: 1901.
Congressional District: 13
Key Personnel: Exec. Dir., Laurene Buckley; Chm. Bd. Trustees, Nathan J. Sambul; Dir. Devel. & Mktg., Nancy Shannon; Registrar, Motrja Fedorko; Museum Shop Mgr., Lady-Grace Cervantes.
Personnel Profile: Full-Time Paid 15; Part-Time Paid 8; Part-Time Volunteers 20; Interns 6.
Governing Authority: private; nonprofit organization. Tax-exempt: 501(c)(3).
Art Museum.
Collections: 19th- & 20th-century paintings, sculptures, & works on paper; Jersey City & New Jersey related artifacts; documents & objects; emphasis on art of social content from the 1930s to present; contemporary art which reflects U.S. cultural diversity.
Research Fields: 20th-century American art with a focus on socially engaged & multiculturalism; Jersey City industrial history.
Facilities: 152-seat auditorium; 2 classrooms; video gallery. Museum-related items for sale.
Activities: lectures; guided tours; symposia; programs for teens; workshops for school children; intern programs; traveling exhibitions; family programs.
Publications: exhibition catalogs; posters; reproductions of art work on cards; quarterly newsletter.
Hours & Admission Prices: Wed.-Fri. 11-5, Sat. 12-5. Adults $5, students with ID and seniors 62 & over $3; members & children under 12 no charge. Closed legal holidays. ♿
Attendance: 21,000 (accurate)
Membership: Student, Senior Citizens & Artists $35; Friend $50; Friends &

Family $80; Patron $125; Contemporary $250; Benefactor $500; August Will Circle $1,000.

LIBERTY SCIENCE CENTER, (M), Liberty State Park, 222 Jersey City Blvd., Jersey City, NJ 07305-4636. Tel.: 201-253-1201. Fax: 201-451-6949. TDD: 201-200-1993.
E-mail: ekoster@lsc.org
Web Site: www.lsc.org
Founded: 1980.
Congressional District: 31
Key Personnel: Pres. & C.E.O., Emlyn H. Koster, Ph.D.; Vice Pres. Learning & Teaching, Deborah Cook; Vice Pres. Mktg. & Communications, Mark Mattia; Vice Pres. Experience Integration, Jeff Sasson; Vice Pres. Resource Administration, Connie Claman; Vice Pres. Devel., Jonathan Sandville; Vice Pres. Exhibitions & Featured Experiences, Wayne LaBar.
Personnel Profile: Full-Time Paid 95; Part-Time Paid 151; Part-Time Volunteers 313.
Governing Authority: nonprofit organization. Tax-exempt: 501(c)(3).
Science Center.
Collections: health, invention & environmental hands-on exhibits; photographs; geological; botanical; zoological; films.
Major Exhibits: A T-Rex Named Sue, 1/10-4/10.
Research Fields: entomology.
Facilities: educational facilities; 60,000 sq. ft. exhibit space; 400-seat IMAX Dome theater; 300-seat auditorium & 3D theater; 100-seat teleconferencing theater; cafe. Museum-related items for sale.
Activities: education programs for children & families; teacher professional development; theatre; participatory & traveling exhibitions; videoconferencing; camp-ins; facility rental.
Publications: E-newsletter; newsletter, Insiders Club.
Hours & Admission Prices: April-June daily 9-5; July-Aug. Mon.-Fri. 9-4, Sat.-Sun. 9-5; Sept.-March Tues.-Fri. 9-4, Sat.-Sun. 9-5. Adults $15.75, senior citizens & children $11.50; members no charge. ♿
Attendance: 700,000 (accurate)
Membership: Senior Citizen $45; Individual $55; Duo (two adults) $100; Basic Family (2 adults & up to 4 children) $140; Large Family (up to 10 individuals) $240. Corporate: Scholar $2,500-$4,999; Inventor $5,000-$9,999; Pioneer $10,000-$24,999; Explorer $25,000-$49,999; Innovator $50,000 & up.

NEW JERSEY ASSOCIATION OF MUSEUMS, c/o Liberty Science Center, 222 Jersey City Blvd., Jersey City, NJ 07305-4636. Tel.: 201-451-0006, ext. 201.
E-mail: eromanaux@lsc.org
Web Site: www.njmuseums.org/index.cfm
Founded: 1973.
Key Personnel: Pres., Elizabeth Romanaux.
Governing Authority: nonprofit organization. Tax-exempt: 501(c)(3).
Museum Service Organization: represents 124 museums in the state.
Activities: training programs for professional museum workers; annual meeting.
Publications: museum directory, Guide to New Jersey Museums; newsletter, NJAM Briefs.
Hours & Admission Prices: Mon.-Fri. 9-5.
Membership: Affiliate $20; Individual $30; Corporate $500; Institutional based on budget size.

Kearny

KEARNY MUSEUM, (M), Kearny Public Library, 318 Kearny Ave., Kearny, NJ 07032-2505. Tel.: 201-998-2666.
Web Site: www.kearnylibrary.org/museum.htm
History Museum.
Collections: photographs; articles of clothing; war memorabilia; Kearny High School yearbooks.
Hours & Admission Prices: Winter: Wed. 6:30pm-7:30pm, Sat. 10-12.

Keyport

KEYPORT HISTORICAL SOCIETY-STEAMBOAT DOCK MUSEUM, American Legion Dr., Keyport, NJ 07735-0312. Mailing Address: P.O. Box 312, Keyport, NJ 07735-0312. Tel.: 732-264-6119.
Founded: 1976.
Congressional District: 4
Key Personnel: Pres., William Longo; Treas., Catherine Moore; Cur., Angela Jeandron; Historian, Jack Jeandron; Museum Shop Mgr., Nola Waterman.
Personnel Profile: Part-Time Volunteers 25.
Governing Authority: private; nonprofit. Tax-exempt.
Historical Society Museum: housed in the former steamboat ticket office & repair shop.
Collections: Keyport artifacts & documents, including business ledgers and photographs of commercial, industrial & domestic life.
Research Fields: genealogical data.
Facilities: 100-vol. library of children's books; auditorium. Museum-related items for sale.
Activities: guided tours; hobby workshops; temporary exhibitions; school group visits.
Publications: quarterly newsletter.
Hours & Admission Prices: May-Sept. Sun. 1-4, Mon. 10-12; Oct.-April by appointment. No charge; donations accepted. ♿
Attendance: 450 (estimated)
Membership: Youth & Senior $3; General $5; Family $10; Contributing $25; Life $250.

Kingston

ROCKINGHAM, 84 Laurel Ave., Kingston, NJ 08528. Mailing Address: P.O. Box 496, Kingston, NJ 08528-0496. Tel.: 609-683-7132.
E-mail: rockingham1783@yahoo.com
Web Site: www.rockingham.net
Founded: 1896.
Key Personnel: Dir., Lisa A. Flick.
Personnel Profile: Full-Time Paid 1; Part-Time Paid 1; Part-Time Volunteers 40; Interns 2.
Governing Authority: state. Parent Institution: Division of Parks & Forestry, Department of Environmental Protection, Trenton, NJ 08625. Tax-exempt.
Historic House: 1710 Berrien Mansion, Washington's final wartime headquarters while Continental Congress was in session in Princeton.
Collections: period furnishings; paintings; sewing samplers; prints; reverse prints on glass; 100 pieces of textiles; Washington's military reproductions; colonial kitchen garden; life-size Washington mannequin; children's hands-on exhibits; military equipment.
Facilities: 18th century kitchen garden.
Activities: guided tours; special event days; local travel baskets; lectures.
Publications: The Rockingham Story; Colonial Herbs at Rockingham; newsletter, The Sundial.
Hours & Admission Prices: Call for hours. No charge; donations accepted. ♿
Attendance: 4,000 (accurate)
Membership: $35.

Lakewood

LAKEWOOD HERITAGE MUSEUM, 655 Princeton Ave., Lakewood, NJ 08701-2882. Mailing Address: 245 Martine Way, Lakewood, NJ 08701-7332. Tel.: 732-276-7944.
E-mail: lakewoodmuseum@optonline.net
Web Site: www.twp.lakewood.nj.us/parkrec_cultur.htm
History Museum.
Collections: Lakewood history & culture; paintings; postcards; photographs; sports trophies; military artifacts.
Facilities: Museum-related items for sale.
Hours & Admission Prices: July-Aug. Tues. & Thurs. 2-5; Sept.-June Tues. & Thurs. 2-5, Sun. 2-4.

Lambertville

HOLCOMBE-JIMISON FARMSTEAD MUSEUM, 1605 Daniel Bray Hwy. (Rte. 29), Lambertville, NJ 08530-2402. Tel.: 609-397-2752.
Historic Building.
Collections: agricultural history; farm tools & equipment; period artifacts & furnishings; household implements & appliances; outbuildings.
Activities: demonstrations; guided tours; educational programs.
Hours & Admission Prices: May-Oct. Sun. 1-4, Wed. 9 am-12 pm; groups by appointment. Suggested Donation: adults $5, students $3.
Membership: Annual $25.

HOWELL LIVING HISTORY FARM, 70 Woodens Lane, Lambertville, NJ 08530. Mailing Address: 101 Hunter Rd., Titusville, NJ 08560-1902. Tel.: 609-737-3299. Fax: 609-737-6524.
E-mail: pwatson@howellfarm.com
Web Site: www.howellfarm.org
Founded: 1974.
Congressional District: 12
Key Personnel: Admin., Pete Watson; Farm Mgr., Gary Houghton; Pres. (V) Friends of Howell Farm, Charles Hunter; Education, Susan DeVore; Program Coord., Kathy Brilla; Cur., Margaret Newman.
Personnel Profile: Full-Time Paid 9; Part-Time Paid 10; Part-Time Volunteers 100; Interns 9.
Governing Authority: county government. Parent Institution: Mercer County Park Commission. Tax-exempt: 501(c)(3).

Agricultural History Museum: living history farm where farm life & farming of 1900-1910 have been recreated.
Collections: 1900-1910 farm implements; period household items.
Research Fields: oral histories of local neighbors.
Facilities: 700-vol. library. Museum-related items for sale.
Activities: formal education programs; guided tours; hands-on farming activities. Annual Events: plowing match; heirloom tomato contest; ice harvest; maple sugaring.
Publications: quarterly newsletter, The Furrow; weekly press releases.
Hours & Admission Prices: Feb.-Nov. Tues.-Sat. 10-4, Sun. 12-4. No charge; donations accepted. Closed legal holidays.
Attendance: 50,000 (estimated)
Membership: Basic $40; Supporting & Business $100; Benefactor $500; Patron $1,000.

Landing

LAKE HOPATCONG HISTORICAL MUSEUM, (M), Hopatcong State Park, Landing, NJ 07850. Mailing Address: P.O. Box 668, Landing, NJ 07850-0668. Tel.: 973-398-2616.
E-mail: lhhistory@att.net
Web Site: www.hopatcong.org/museum
Founded: 1955.
Congressional District: 11
Key Personnel: Pres., Martin Kane; C.E.O., Robert Kays; Museum Shop Mgr., Laurie Martin.
Personnel Profile: Full-Time Volunteers 3; Part-Time Volunteers 15.
Governing Authority: Tax-exempt.
Local History Museum: housed in 18th century Morris Canal Lock Tender's house.
Collections: Native American; Morris Canal; Lake Hopatcong, NJ history; former residents including Lotta Crabtree, Hudson Maxim, & Joe Cook.
Facilities: 200-vol. library of books; pamphlets; maps pertaining to history of New Jersey, available for research by approval of the Trustees.
Activities: guided tours; lectures; permanent exhibitions.
Publications: quarterly newsletter.
Hours & Admission Prices: March-May & Oct.-Dec. Sun. 12-4; Summer: call for hours. No charge; donations accepted. ♿
Attendance: 2,500 (accurate)
Membership: Annual $20.

Lawrenceville

NATIONAL GUARD MILITIA MUSEUM OF NEW JERSEY - LAWRENCEVILLE, Artillery Armory, 151 Eggert Crossing Rd., Lawrenceville, NJ 08648. Tel.: 609-530-6802.
Military Heritage Museum.
Collections: military history & heritage; weapons; uniforms; military equipment & vehicles; tanks; cannon; photographs.
Activities: group tours.
Publications: newsletter.
Hours & Admission Prices: Call for hours.

Lincroft

* **THE MONMOUTH MUSEUM, (M),** Newman Springs Rd., Brookdale C.C. Campus, 765 Newman Springs Rd., Lincroft, NJ 07738. Mailing Address: P.O. Box 359, Lincroft, NJ 07738-0359. Tel.: 732-747-2266. Fax: 732-747-8592.
Web Site: www.monmouthmuseum.org
Formerly: Monmouth Museum & Cultural Center
Founded: 1963.
Congressional District: 12
Key Personnel: Exec. Dir., Avis H. Anderson; Chm. (V), Marion P. Becker; Public Rels., Julia Fiorino; Coord. Special Events, Mary Suszkowski; Cur. Education, Marian Kanaga; Coord. Membership, Maureen Starace; Museum Shop Mgr., Helen Brown.
Personnel Profile: Full-Time Paid 5; Part-Time Paid 17; Part-Time Volunteers 65; Interns 2.
Governing Authority: nonprofit. Tax-exempt: 501(c)(3).
General Museum.
Collections: sewing birds.
Major Exhibits: Dr. Maxlin's Astro Photographs, 11/29/09-1/10/10; Monmouth County Arts Council Juried Exhibition, 1/16/10-2/21/10; George Segal Exhibition, 2/28/10-4/11/10; David Locuta's Photographs of George Segal, 2/21/10-3/21/10; New Jersey Emerging Artist Series Jill Baker Gower: Metal Sculpture, 3/26/10-4/25/10; Art From Found Objects, 4/23/10-6/20/10; New Jersey Emerging Artists Series Riccardo Berlinger: Paper Sculpture, 4/30/10-5/30/10; New Jersey Emerging Artists Series Michael Hynes: Photography, 6/4/10-7/3/10; Annual Holiday Exhibition, 11/23/10-1/3/11.
Facilities: Museum-related items for sale.
Activities: guided tours; lectures; gallery talks; formally organized education programs; day trips; travel trunks.
Publications: quarterly newsletter; brochures; teacher education packets.
Hours & Admission Prices: Tues.-Sat. 10-4:30, Sun. 1-5. Admission $7; discounts to AAM & PBS members; members no charge. Closed New Year's Day; Easter; Memorial Day; Independence Day; Labor Day; Thanksgiving; Christmas. ♿
Attendance: 55,000 (accurate)
Membership: Student & Senior Citizen $25; Individual $35; Household $75; Contributing $100; Associate $150; Supporting $250; Patron $500; Benefactor $1,000.

Little Falls

YOGI BERRA MUSEUM AND LEARNING CENTER, Montclair State Univ., 8 Quarry Rd., Little Falls, NJ 07424-2161. Tel.: 973-655-2378. Fax: 973-655-6894.
Web Site: www.yogiberramuseum.org
Founded: 1998.
Key Personnel: Dir., Dave Kaplan; Pres. (V), Kevin Carral; Treas., Julie Jackson; C.O.O., Art Berke; Dir. Special Events, Joni Bronander; Business Mgr., Bettylou O'Dell.
Personnel Profile: Full-Time Paid 3; Part-Time Paid 3; Part-Time Volunteers 50; Interns 3.
Governing Authority: private; nonprofit organization. Tax-exempt: 501(c)(3).
Sports Museum.
Collections: concentration on Yankees history with special interest on Yogi Berra's career; baseball history.
Facilities: 110-seat theater; 4,500 sq. ft. exhibit space. Museum-related items for sale.
Activities: arts festivals; films; formal educational programs for children; guided tours; lectures; rental gallery; loan, temporary & traveling exhibitions; broadcast programs. Annual Events: book festival; film series; symposia.
Publications: quarterly newsletter, The Yogi Berra Museum Newsletter.
Hours & Admission Prices: Wed.-Sun. 12-5. Adults $6, senior citizens $5, students & children $4; discounts to AAA, ICOM & AAM members; members no charge. Closed New Year's Eve & Day; Easter; Mother's Day; Memorial Day; Independence Day; Labor Day; Columbus Day; Christmas Eve & Day. ♿
Membership: Rookie $20; Individual $35; Family $65; Business $5,000.

Long Branch

800 GALLERY & ROTARY ICE HOUSE GALLERY, Dept. Art & Design, Monmouth University, 600 Bldg., Rm. AW-6, Long Branch, NJ 07764-1804. Tel.: 732-571-3428.
Web Site: www.monmouth.edu/academics/art/faculty/default.asp
Key Personnel: Dir. Galleries & Collections, Scott Knauer
Art Museum.
Collections: paintings; photographs; sculpture; drawing; ceramics.
Activities: special events; receptions; temporary exhibits.
Hours & Admission Prices: Call for hours.

LONG BRANCH HISTORICAL MUSEUM, 1260 Ocean Ave., Long Branch, NJ 07740-4550. Mailing Address: P.O. Box 2204, Elberon, NJ 07740-2204. Tel.: 732-223-0874.
Web Site: www.churchofthepresidents.org
Founded: 1953.
Congressional District: 10
Key Personnel: C.E.O. & Pres. (V), Karen Van Hise; 1st. Vice Pres., James Foley.
Governing Authority: society. Tax-exempt.
History Museum: housed in 1879 Saint James Episcopal Chapel, Church of the Presidents. Worshippers included: Presidents James A. Garfield, Ulysses S. Grant, Rutherford B. Hayes, Chester A. Arthur, Woodrow Wilson, Benjamin Harrison, William McKinley.
Collections: post Civil War bronze presidential plaques; historic flags; furniture; pictures; fire engine. Historic Building: Garfield Hut.
Activities: guided tours; permanent exhibitions.
Hours & Admission Prices: Closed for restoration.
Membership: Individual $25; Family $50; Organization $100; Lifetime $250; Patron $1,000; Donor $2,500; Benefactor $5,000.

Loveladies

LONG BEACH ISLAND FOUNDATION OF THE ARTS & SCIENCES, 120 Long Beach Blvd., Loveladies, NJ 08008-6131. Tel.: 609-494-1241. Fax: 609-494-0662.
Key Personnel: Exec. Dir., Christopher Seiz

Art, Craft, & Science Museum.
Collections: works by local & national artists.
Activities: special events; performances; lectures; adult classes & workshops; youth programs; films.
Hours & Admission Prices: Thurs.-Sun. 9-4.

Lumberton

AIR VICTORY MUSEUM, INC., 68 Stacy Haines Rd., Lumberton, NJ 08048-4106. Tel.: 609-267-4488. Fax: 609-702-1852.
Web Site: airvictorymuseum.com
Founded: 1989.
Key Personnel: Chm. & Pres. (V) & Cur., Fred Koch.
Personnel Profile: Full-Time Volunteers 1; Part-Time Volunteers 1.
Governing Authority: nonprofit organization. Tax-exempt: 501(c)(3).
Aeronautics Museum.
Collections: aircraft from Korea to present conflicts; military artifacts; uniforms; Norden bomb sight; navigation instruments; engines; equipment.
Facilities: research library.
Activities: educational tours with study guides; teacher educational programs. Annual Event: living history encampment WWII-Vietnam.
Publications: biannual newsletter.
Hours & Admission Prices: Wed.-Sat. 10-4, Sun. 11-4. Museum Aircraft: tours available. Adults $4, group rate $3; discounts to military w/ID & AAA members; members and children 3 & under no charge. ♿
Attendance: 12,000 (accurate)
Membership: Student $10; Senior Citizen $20; Adult $25; Family $50; Sustaining $60; Patron $100; Corporate $250. Building Fund: call for further information.

Lyndhurst

NEW JERSEY MEADOWLANDS ENVIRONMENT CENTER, 2 DeKorte Park Plaza, Lyndhurst, NJ 07071. Tel.: 201-460-8300. Fax: 201-842-0630.
Web Site: www.meadowlands.state.nj.us
Formerly: Hackensack Meadowlands Development Commission Environment Center & Museum
Founded: 1969.
Key Personnel: Exec. Dir., Joseph V. Doria, Jr.; Treas., James A. Anzevno; Environmental Education, Linda Mercurio; Operations Mgr. & Museum Shop Mgr., Donna McKnight.
Personnel Profile: Full-Time Paid 10; Part-Time Paid 1; Part-Time Volunteers 3.
Governing Authority: state. Parent Institution: New Jersey Meadowlands Commission. Tax-exempt.
Nature Center.
Collections: native natural history species with emphasis on birds; aquarium for live fish; wetlands diorama; living natural areas to demonstrate salt marsh wetlands & native upland habitats; interactive exhibits on past, present and future of the Hackensack Meadowlands.
Facilities: library on environmental education, wetlands & solid waste; 280-seat auditorium; educational facilities; 8,031 sq. ft. exhibit space. Gift items for sale.
Activities: guided tours; hobby workshops; formal education programs for children; teacher training in environmental education; nature tours; boating; canoeing. Annual Event: Children's Halloween Celebration.
Publications: biannual, Schedule of Events.
Hours & Admission Prices: Center: Mon.-Fri. 9-5, Sat.-Sun. 10-3. Store: daily 10-3. Trails: daily 8 to dusk. Adults $2; discount program fees for members; children under 12 & discovery trails no charge ♿
Attendance: 50,000 (accurate)
Membership: Individual $25; Family $50; Contributor $100; Patron $200; Corporate $500.

Madison

MUSEUM OF EARLY TRADES & CRAFTS, (M), 9 Main St., Madison, NJ 07940-1819. Tel.: 973-377-2982, ext. 10. Fax: 973-377-7358.
E-mail: info@metc.org
Web Site: www.metc.org
Founded: 1969.
Congressional District: 25
Key Personnel: Chm., Allen Black; Vice Chm., Michele Faas; Dir., Vivian C.R. James; Cur., Peter Rothenberg; Business Mgr., Patrice Servidea.
Personnel Profile: Full-Time Paid 4; Part-Time Volunteers 25; Interns 2.
Governing Authority: nonprofit organization. Tax-exempt.
Trades & Crafts Museum: housed in 1900 Richardsonian Romanesque style building, the former town library.
Collections: tools & products of 18th to 19th-century New Jersey home, farm & shop crafts; woodworking & metalworking tools.
Research Fields: regional trades history; craftsmanship.
Facilities: classrooms. Museum-related items for sale.
Activities: guided tours; demonstrations; craft workshops; family, school, scout & group programs; special & rotating exhibits; lectures; gallery talks; summer camp for children; receptions.
Publications: quarterly newsletter.
Hours & Admission Prices: Summer: Tues.-Sat. 10-4; Winter: Tues.-Sat. 10-4, Sun. 12-5. Adults $5, seniors, students, & children $3; AAM members & museum members no charge. Closed major holidays. ♿
Attendance: 17,500 (estimated)
Membership: Individual $30; Family $50; Patron $100.

Matawan

BURROWES MANSION MUSEUM, 94 Main St., Matawan, NJ 07747-2630. Mailing Address: 24 Monroe St., Matawan, NJ 07747-3218. Tel.: 732-566-3817 & 5605.
Founded: 1976.
Congressional District: 6
Key Personnel: Museum Shop Mgr. & Head Docent, Sarah Ellison; Historic Site Mgr., Howard Henderson.
Personnel Profile: Part-Time Volunteers 15.
Governing Authority: commission. Parent Institution: Historic Sites Commission. Subsidiary Institution: Historical Society. Tax-exempt: 501(c)(3).
Historic House: 1723 Georgian half-house with gambrel roof, located on a Revolutionary War skirmish site.
Collections: 18th- & 19th-century furniture; postcards; costumes; photographs; archives; local history.
Research Fields: local history; cultural survey; furnishings.
Facilities: 175-vol. research library; 1,750 sq. ft. exhibit space; Mt. Pleasant Cemetery; Philip Freneau grave site; index to Mt. Pleasant Cemetery.
Activities: guided tours; lectures; concerts; organized educational programs for children; Christmas Musical.
Publications: biannual newsletter, Matawan Historical Society Newsletter.
Hours & Admission Prices: March-Dec. 1st & 3rd Sun. of each month 2-4; other times by appointment. No charge; donations accepted. Closed Easter.
Attendance: 900 (accurate)
Membership: Student $1; Adult $7.50; Family $12; Patron $25; Benefactor $100.

Mays Landing

WARREN E. FOX NATURE CENTER, 109 Boulevard Rte. 50, Mays Landing, NJ 08330-4323. Tel.: 609-645-5960.
Key Personnel: Dir., Jerry Barbiero
Nature Center.
Collections: local history; plants; ecology; live animals.
Facilities: 50-seat auditorium.
Activities: public programs; lectures; school groups tours; field studies; teacher workshops.
Hours & Admission Prices: Mon.-Fri. 8-4:30, Sat.-Sun. & holidays 8-4. No charge.

Medford

MEDFORD HISTORICAL SOCIETY, 275 Church Rd., Medford, NJ 08055. Tel.: 609-654-7767.
Historical Society Museum: built in 1785.
Collections: local history & culture; photographs; period furnishings; personal artifacts.
Activities: special events.
Hours & Admission Prices: Call for hours.

Mendham

RALSTON HISTORICAL ASSOCIATION, JOHN RALSTON MUSEUM, 313 Mendham Rd., W., Mendham, NJ 07945-1000. Tel.: 973-543-6878. Fax: 973-543-1149.
E-mail: pfr14@aol.com
Web Site: www.ralstonmuseum.org
Founded: 1964.
Congressional District: 11
Key Personnel: Pres. (V), R. Jeffrey Purcell; Vice Pres., Tracy Kinsell.
Personnel Profile: Part-Time Paid 1; Part-Time Volunteers 15.
Governing Authority: nonprofit organization. Tax-exempt: 501(c)(3).
Historical Society Museum: housed in the oldest building used as a post office in the United States, 1780s.
Collections: local artifacts; agricultural tools before 1814; hand-blown glass; industry; local papers & documents; herbarium; manuscripts. Historic Site: 1732 Wills Family cemetery.
Activities: guided tours; temporary & permanent exhibitions; lectures.

Publications: annual newsletter; book, The Mendhams; The Rock-A-Bye Baby Railroad.
Hours & Admission Prices: June-Oct. Sun. 2-5. No charge; donations accepted.
Attendance: 250 (estimated)
Membership: Senior Citizen $15; Individual $25; Family & Institution $40; Sustaining $100; Life $250; John Ralston Society $1,000.

Middletown

PORICY PARK CONSERVANCY, 345 Oak Hill Rd., Middletown, NJ 07748. Mailing Address: Box 36, Middletown, NJ 07748-0036. Tel.: 732-842-5966. Fax: 732-842-6833.
Web Site: www.poricypark.org
Founded: 1978.
Congressional District: 3
Key Personnel: Exec. Dir., Joyce Ferejohn; Treas., Lee Beaumont.
Personnel Profile: Full-Time Paid 3; Part-Time Paid 12; Part-Time Volunteers 100.
Governing Authority: nonprofit organization. Poricy Park Citizen's Committee. Tax-exempt: 501(c)(3).
Nature Center: located on 250-acre nature preserve; restored colonial farmhouse & barn located on original site.
Collections: mounted animals; fossils; 18th-century clothing, cooking utensils, furnishings. Historic House: 18th-century farmhouse & barn.
Facilities: 150-vol. library pertaining to natural history, 18th-century life, Murray's; educational facilities; nature center. Museum-related items for sale.
Activities: guided tours; lectures; hobby workshops; organized education programs; docent program; participatory & temporary exhibitions.
Publications: newsletter & program schedule; program brochures for groups, scouts & special events.
Hours & Admission Prices: Park: daily dawn to 10pm. Nature Center: Mon.-Fri. 9-4. No charge; donations accepted. Fees for special programs. Closed national holidays. ♿
Attendance: 22,000 (estimated)
Membership: Senior $25; Individual $35; Family $50; Patron $100; Supporter $150; Champion $250; Guardian $350; Benefactor $500.

Milford

VOLENDAM WINDMILL MUSEUM INC., 231 Adamic Hill Rd., Holland Twsp., Milford, NJ 08848-1736. Tel.: 908-995-4365.
Web Site: CharlieBrowns-TreeFarm.com
Founded: 1965.
Congressional District: 5
Key Personnel: C.E.O., Charles T. Brown, III
Personnel Profile: Part-Time Volunteers 3.
Governing Authority: nonprofit organization. Tax-exempt: 501(c)(3).
Windmill History Museum.
Collections: c.1700-1800, milling implements, antique mill machinery; old farm tools; wooden shoes.
Research Fields: windmill design & operation in Holland & Denmark.
Facilities: Delft Ware, wooden shoes & other Dutch memorabilia for sale.
Activities: guided tours; lectures; formally organized education programs for adults, children & graduate students; permanent exhibitions.
Hours & Admission Prices: Closed for repairs.

Milltown

EUREKA FIRE MUSEUM, 39 Washington Ave., Milltown, NJ 08850-1219. Tel.: 732-828-7207 & 7400.
E-mail: webmaster@milltownfire.org
Web Site: www.milltownfire.org/museum.htm
Founded: 1981.
Key Personnel: Chm. (V), Brian E. Harto; Treas., Mark Steeber.
Personnel Profile: Part-Time Volunteers 2.
Governing Authority: private; nonprofit organization.
Fire-Fighting Museum.
Collections: 200 years worth of fire fighting equipment; fire patches, badges & insignia from around the world; uniforms; helmets; fire extinguishers; hand-drawn fire apparatus; 1921 & 1947 American LaFrance pumpers; local history; photographs.
Facilities: 200-vol. library.
Hours & Admission Prices: By appointment only. No charge; donations accepted.
Attendance: 150 (estimated)

Millville

MILLVILLE ARMY AIR FIELD MUSEUM, 1 Leddon St., Millville Airport, Millville, NJ 08332-4822. Tel.: 856-327-2347. Fax: 856-327-5737.
E-mail: museum@p47millville.org
Web Site: www.millvilleairshow.com
Founded: 1983.
Congressional District: 2
Governing Authority: federal; nonprofit organization.
Military Museum.
Collections: military aviation history; photographs; military artifacts; airfield's history; WWII.
Facilities: library; education center.
Activities: tours; programs. Annual Event: Air Show.
Publications: newsletter, Thunderbolt.
Hours & Admission Prices: Mon. by appointment only, Tues.-Sun. 10-4; guided tours by appointment. No charge; donations accepted. ♿
Attendance: 2,000
Membership: Individual $25; Family $40; Booster $100; Patron $250; Guardian Angel $500.

* **MUSEUM OF AMERICAN GLASS AT WHEATON ARTS AND CULTURAL CENTER, (M),** 1501 Glasstown Rd., Millville, NJ 08332-1566. Tel.: 856-825-6800. Fax: 856-825-2410.
E-mail: museum@wheatonarts.org
Web Site: www.wheatonarts.org
Formerly: Museum of American Glass at Wheaton Village
Founded: 1968.
Congressional District: 2
Key Personnel: Chm., Rita Moonsammy; Registrar, Elizabeth G. Wilk; Museum Shop Mgr., Catharine Nolan.
Personnel Profile: Full-Time Paid 2; Part-Time Paid 3; Part-Time Volunteers 33.
Governing Authority: nonprofit organization. Parent Institution: Wheaton Arts and Cultural Center. Tax-exempt: 501(c)(3).
American Glass Museum.
Collections: United States glass; operating reproduction of 19th century glass factory; glass decorating.
Research Fields: U.S. glass; U.S. & N.J. glasshouses; individual artists.
Facilities: 3,200-vol. library of material on glass, southern N.J. history, original documents & ephemera, available for use on premises; classroom; restaurant; Country Inn hotel; 16 restored & recreated buildings. Museum-related items & crafts for sale.
Activities: guided tours; lectures; workshops; loan, permanent & traveling exhibitions; seminars; glass artists fellowship; study clubs; concerts; performances.
Publications: catalogs, Out of The Mold; Clevenger Brothers: The Persistence of Tradition; Maximizing the Minimum: Small Glass Sculpture; Distinctively Durand: The Art Glass of Vineland, N.J.; The Wistars & Their Glass, 1739-1777; Colorful Cutting; Thousands of Flowers: American Millefiori Glass; book, Under Sail: The Dredgeboats of Delaware Bay; Gillinder Glass: Story of a Company; It Figures: American Sculptural Bottles; Flights of Fancy: The Quezal Art Glass & Decorating Company; Slivers of Light: Rich Cut Oil Lamps; Contemporary Flameworked Glass; Vanity Vessels: The Story of the American Perfume Bottle; For Show, Not Play: Glass Chess Sets; 20/20 Vision; Glass Threads: Tiffany, Quezal, Imperial, Durand; The Fires Burn On: 200 Years of Glassmaking in Millville, New Jersey.
Hours & Admission Prices: Jan.-March call for hours; April-Dec. Tues.-Sun. 10-5. Adults $10, senior citizens $9, students $7; discounts to groups, AAM, ICOM & AAA members; members no charge. Closed New Year's Day; Easter; Thanksgiving; Christmas. ♿
Attendance: 70,000 (estimated)
Membership: Students & Seniors $25; Individual $35; Dual $45; Family $55.

Monroe Township

THE STONE MUSEUM, 608 Spotswood-Englishtown Rd., Monroe Township, NJ 08831-3222. Tel.: 732-521-2232. Fax: 732-521-3388.
E-mail: displayworld@erols.com
Web Site: www.thestonemuseum.com
Key Personnel: Museum Shop Mgr., Pat Ciecko.
Personnel Profile: Full-Time Volunteers 2.
Governing Authority: private; nonprofit organization. Parent Institution: Greeks Playland.
Geology Museum.
Collections: minerals & fossils from over 80 countries; fluorescent rock; seashells; dinosaurs & dinosaur egg from China; whale vertebra; hands-on exhibits; M60 tank; Cola hellicopter.
Hours & Admission Prices: Call for hours. No charge. Closed New Year's Day; Memorial Day; Independence Day; Labor Day; Christmas. ♿
Attendance: 20,000 (estimated)

Montclair

* **MONTCLAIR ART MUSEUM, (M),** 3 S. Mountain Ave., Montclair, NJ 07042. Tel.: 973-746-5555. Fax: 973-746-9118 & 0920.
Web Site: www.montclairartmuseum.org
Founded: 1914.
Congressional District: 11
Key Personnel: Pres., Reginald Hollinger; Dir., Lora Urbanelli; Chief Cur., Gail Stavitsky, Ph.D.; Dir. Finance, Megan Fennessey; Dir. Education, Gary Schneider; Dir. Operations, Crlos Galvez; Cur. Native American Art, Twig Johnson; Dir. Mktg. & Communications, Michael Gillespie; Museum Shop Mgr., Lana Stollman.
Personnel Profile: Full-Time Paid 30; Part-Time Paid 25; Part-Time Volunteers 250; Interns 23.
Governing Authority: nonprofit organization. Tax-exempt: 501(c)(3); 170(b).
Art Museum: housed in Neo-classic brick & stone building.
Collections: American art; prints; drawings; sculpture; The Rand Collection of Native American art; Morgan Russell Archive & Collection.
Major Exhibits: Citanne and American Modernism (T), 11/09-1/3/10; Out of the Vault: 95 Years of Collecting At MAM, 11/09-12/10.
Research Fields: American paintings; Morgan Russell Archives.
Facilities: art school; reading room; auditorium. Museum-related items for sale.
Activities: guided tours; lectures; films; gallery talks; art classes for adults & children; concerts; permanent & temporary exhibitions.
Hours & Admission Prices: Tues.-Wed. & Fri.-Sun. 12-5, Thurs. 12-9. Adults $12, seniors & students $10; discounts to AAM & ICOM members; members & children under 12 no charge. Closed major holidays. ♿
Attendance: 60,000 (estimated)
Membership: College Student $35; Individual $50; Dual & Family $70; Friend $165; Patron $325; Sponsor $750; Benefactor $1,500; Director's Circle $3,000; Inness $5,500.

MONTCLAIR HISTORICAL SOCIETY, 108 Orange Rd., Montclair, NJ 07042-2133. Tel.: 973-744-1796. Fax: 973-783-9419.
E-mail: mail@montclairhistorical.org
Web Site: www.montclairhistorical.org
Founded: 1965.
Congressional District: 8
Key Personnel: Exec. Dir., Carlos Pomares; Pres. (V), John Weisel.
Personnel Profile: Full-Time Paid 2; Part-Time Paid 1; Part-Time Volunteers 100; Interns 2.
Governing Authority: society. Subsidiary Institution: Israel Crane Museum and Evergreens; The Charles S. Shultz House. Tax-exempt: 501(c)(3).
Historic House Museum: Israel Crane House and 1896 Evergreens House Museum.
Collections: period rooms; 18th-century gardens; period costumes; period tools; history of Montclair, NJ from 1600s to present. Nathaniel Crane House c.1818 houses country store including store fixtures & contents; The Clark House c.1894 houses offices, classrooms containing schoolhouse contents & reference library.
Research Fields: family life of 19th-century to early 20th-century in Montclair, NJ; 18th-century open hearth cooking; 18th & early 19th-century arts & skills; genealogy materials of area families.
Facilities: 1,000-vol. library of New Jersey & Montclair history & genealogy; early American crafts; period tools.
Activities: education programs.
Publications: History of Montclair Township; Fanny Pierson Crane, Her Receipts, 1796; The Thirteen Colonies Cookbook; monthly newsletter.
Hours & Admission Prices: Crane House Tours: March-Dec. Sun. 1 & 2; other times by appointment. Adults $5, children 11-17 $3; members and children 10 & under no charge. Evergreen Tours: March-Dec. Sun. 3pm. Adult $5, children 11-17 $3; members and children 10 & under no charge. Clark House Tours: March-Dec. 1st Sun. of month 12pm. Adults $5, children 11-17 $3; member and children 10 & under no charge. ♿
Attendance: 4,800 (accurate)
Membership: Individual $25; Family $35; Sustaining & Business $60; Patron $100; Friend $250; Benefactor $500; Society Circle $1,000; Life $2,500.

Montville

MONTVILLE TOWNSHIP HISTORICAL MUSEUM, 6 Taylortown Rd., Montville, NJ 07045. Mailing Address: P.O. Box 519, Montville, NJ 07045. Tel.: 973-334-3665.
Web Site: www.montvillenj.org
Founded: 1963.
Congressional District: 11
Key Personnel: Pres., Kathleen Fisher.
Personnel Profile: Full-Time Volunteers 6; Part-Time Volunteers 6; Interns 1.
Governing Authority: society; municipal. Parent Institution: Montville Historical Society. Tax-exempt: 501(c)(3).
General Museum: housed in c. 1867 School House.
Collections: agriculture; children's museum; costumes; decorative arts; general; geology; history; Indian artifacts; manuscripts; photographs.
Research Fields: houses, genealogies, town records, church records.
Facilities: library containing books, tapes, letters, deeds, medical, church and account records available for use on premises.
Activities: lectures; formally organized education programs; permanent exhibitions.
Publications: book, reprints of historical maps of Montville 1853 & 1868; pamphlets, Tours of Montville.
Hours & Admission Prices: Sept.-June Sun. 1-4. No charge; donations accepted. Closed national holidays.
Attendance: 1,200 (accurate)
Membership: Student $5; Individual $15; Family $20; Corporate $100; Life $200.

Moorestown

PERKINS CENTER FOR THE ARTS, 395 Kings Hwy., Moorestown, NJ 08057-2725. Tel.: 856-235-6488; 800-387-5226. Fax: 856-235-6624.
E-mail: create@perkinscenter.org
Web Site: www.perkinscenter.org
Founded: 1977.
Key Personnel: Dir., Alan Willoughby; Pres. (V), Edward DeMarco.
Governing Authority: nonprofit organization. Satellite: 30 Irvin Ave., Collingswood, NJ 08108. Tax-exempt: 501(c)(3).
Art Center: housed in 1910 Tudor Revival House, designed by Herbert C. Wise, first editor of House & Garden magazine.
Collections: paintings; sculpture; photographs.
Facilities: visual arts studios; pottery studio; dance studio, music rooms.
Activities: guided tours; lectures; concerts; dance recitals; organized education programs; performing arts; pottery co-op; participatory & temporary exhibitions.
Publications: newsletter/catalogue published quarterly per year.
Hours & Admission Prices: Thurs.-Fri. 10-4, Sat.-Sun. noon to 4. No charge; donations accepted. ♿
Membership: Student & Senior $30; Individual $35; Senior Family $50; Family $55; Family Plus $95.

SMITH-CADBURY MANSION, 12 High St., Moorestown, NJ 08057-3504. Tel.: 856-235-0353.
E-mail: moorestownhistory@verizon.net
Governing Authority: Parent Institution: Historical Society of Moorestown.
Historic House Museum.
Collections: local history & culture; photographs; period furnishings.
Facilities: Museum-related items for sale.
Hours & Admission Prices: Tues. 1-4, 2nd Sat. 1-4.

Morganville

NEW JERSEY SCOUT MUSEUM, 705 Ginesi Dr., Morganville, NJ 07751-1235. Tel.: 732-536-2347.
E-mail: pacfam4@aol.com
Web Site: www.njscoutmuseum.org
Founded: 2004.
Key Personnel: Chm. (V), Fred Pachman.
Personnel Profile: Part-Time Paid 1; Part-Time Volunteers 10.
History Museum.
Collections: girl & boy scout history & memorabilia with concentration on New Jersey; personal artifacts; photographs.
Hours & Admission Prices: Sept.-June Wed. 6pm-8pm; other times by appointment. No charge; donations accepted. ♿
Membership: Youth $10; Family $25; Century $100; Patron $250; Life $1,000.

Morris Plains

THE STICKLEY MUSEUM AT CRAFTSMAN FARMS, (M), 2352 Rt. 10 W., Manor Lane, Morris Plains, NJ 07950. Tel.: 973-540-0311 & 1165. Fax: 973-540-1167.
E-mail: craftsmanfarms@att.net
Web Site: www.stickleymuseum.org
Formerly: Craftsman Farms Foundation
Founded: 1989.
Congressional District: 26
Key Personnel: C.E.O. & Exec. Dir., Heather E. Stivison, CFRE; Pres. (V), Davey Willans; Visitor Svcs. Coord., Betty Wyka; Dir. Education, Vonda Givens; Dir. Devel., Shunzyu Haigler; Registrar, Jennifer De Maio.
Personnel Profile: Full-Time Paid 3; Part-Time Paid 3; Part-Time Volunteers 70; Interns 2.
Governing Authority: private; nonprofit organization. Tax-exempt: 501(c)(3).

Historic House & Site: former Craftsman log house of Gustav Stickley, one of America's leading proponents of the Arts & Crafts movement in the early 1900s.
Collections: furniture & decorative arts from the American Arts & Crafts movement of 1890-1920; emphasis on Stickley's interiors.
Research Fields: life of Gustav Stickley & his family; the history of Craftsman Farms; the American Arts & Crafts movement.
Facilities: library of original Craftsman Magazines; log house; original Stickley structures on 30 acres. Museum-related contemporary items for sale.
Activities: guided tours; school tours; girl scout badge workshops; lectures; temporary exhibitions; volunteer programs; workshops; craft fair; outdoor family days. Museum Sponsors: annual exhibition at Grove Park Inn, Asheville, NC; holiday program in December.
Publications: quarterly newsletter; exhibit catalogs; guidebook; books on the arts & crafts movement.
Hours & Admission Prices: Wed.-Thurs. 12-3, Sat.-Sun. 11-4. Adults $7, seniors $5, children $3; discounts to AAM & ICOM members and North American Reciprocal members; members & children under 6 no charge. Closed major holidays. ♿
Attendance: 8,800 (accurate)
Membership: Individual $30; Dual & Family $50; Friend $100; Patron $150.

STICKLEY MUSEUM AT CRAFTSMAN FARMS, 2352 Rt. 10 W., #5, Morris Plains, NJ 07950-3443. Tel.: 973-540-1165. Fax: 973-540-1167.
E-mail: info@stickleymuseum.org
Web Site: www.stickleymuseum.org
Governing Authority: nonprofit organization. Parent Institution: The Township of Parsippany. Tax-exempt: 501(c)(3).
Historic House Museum: housed in the former home of designer Gustav Stickley.
Collections: local history & culture; period furnishings; personal artifacts; photographs.
Facilities: Museum-related items for sale.
Hours & Admission Prices: April-Nov. 16 Wed.-Fri. 12-3, Sat.-Sun. 11-4; Nov. 17-March Sat.-Sun. 11-4. Closed major holidays.

Morris Township

THE GEORGE G. FRELINGHUYSEN ARBORETUM, 53 E. Hanover Ave., Morris Township, NJ 07960-3161. Mailing Address: P.O. Box 1295, Morristown, NJ 07962-1295. Tel.: 973-326-7600. Fax: 973-644-2726. TDD: 1-800-852-7899.
E-mail: info@parks.morris.nj.us
Web Site: www.arboretumfriends.org
Founded: 1970.
Congressional District: 11
Key Personnel: C.E.O., David Helmer; Pres. (V), Judith Schliecher; Treas., Glenn Roe; Dir. Park Maintenance, Ed Vath; Pres. Friends of Arboretum, Sue Acheson; Supt. Education, Lesley Parness; Mgr. Horticulture, John Morse; Dir. Visitors Svcs., Denise Lanza.
Personnel Profile: Full-Time Paid 12; Part-Time Paid 12; Part-Time Volunteers 200; Interns 1.
Governing Authority: county; nonprofit organization. Parent Institution: Morris County Park Commission. Branch Museums: Willowwood Arboretum, Bamboo Brook Outdoor Education Center, P.O. Box 1295, Morristown, NJ 07962-1295. Tax-exempt.
Arboretum: located on 1891 Whippany Farm Residence, summer home of George Griswold Frelinghuysen.
Collections: labeled collections of trees & shrubs. Historic Building: c.1891 Colonial Revival House.
Research Fields: hardy ornamentals recommended for the home landscapes of Northern New Jersey.
Facilities: 2,500-vol. library of botanical & horticultural literature available for research on premises by appointment; botanical garden; education center: 180-seat auditorium; two classrooms.
Activities: guided tours; lectures; films; concerts; docent program; arts festivals; study clubs; hobby workshops; formally organized education programs for children, adults & undergraduate college students; docent program or council; permanent, temporary & traveling exhibitions. Annual Events: plant sale; Gingerbread Wonderland.
Publications: quarterly newsletter, Arboretum Leaves.
Hours & Admission Prices: Grounds: daily 8am-dusk. Education Center: daily 9-4:30. No charge; donations accepted. Closed New Year's Day; Thanksgiving; Christmas. ♿
Attendance: 400,000 (estimated)
Membership: Friends of Frelinghuysen Arboretum: Individual $25; Family $35; Associate $50; Organizational $75; Affiliate & Supporting $100; Contributing $250; Patron $500; Benefactor $1,000.

Morristown

FOSTERFIELDS LIVING HISTORICAL FARM, 73 Kahdena Rd., Morristown, NJ 07960-3524. Tel.: 973-326-7645. Fax: 973-631-5023.
Web Site: www.morrisparks.net
Founded: 1978.
Congressional District: 12
Key Personnel: C.E.O., Dave Helmer; Dir. Historic Sites, Mark Texel; Pres. Park Comm., Judith Scheicher; Pres. Friends of Fosterfields, Charlie Spencer; Cur. Collections & Exhibits, Lynn Laffey; Farm Supvr., Rob Kibbe.
Personnel Profile: Full-Time Paid 12; Part-Time Paid 21; Part-Time Volunteers 100.
Governing Authority: county; nonprofit. Parent Institution: Morris County Park Commission, Tel.: 973-326-7600. Tax-exempt: 501(c)(3).
Living Historical Farm; Agricultural Museum: located on a 230-acre farm site.
Collections: turn-of-the-century farm buildings, machinery & tools; furniture & decorative arts; photographs; farm records; diary. Historic House: 1854 Gothic Revival House; 1920s farmhouse.
Research Fields: turn-of-the-century agricultural practices; period clothing.
Facilities: 500-vol. library pertaining to agriculture; 70-seat auditorium; classrooms; farm site.
Activities: guided tours; lectures; films; hobby workshops; audiovisual presentations; organized education programs; living history programs; docent program; training programs for professional museum workers; participatory & temporary exhibitions. Museum Sponsors: Harvest Activities; Holiday House Tour.
Publications: quarterly newsletter, The Farm & Mill Gazette.
Hours & Admission Prices: Farm: April-Oct. Wed.-Sat. 10-5, Sun. 12-5. Adults $6, seniors $5, children 4-16 $4; discounts to AAM & AAA members; children under 3 no charge. ♿
Attendance: 24,000 (accurate)
Membership: Individual $35; Family $45; Patron $100; Contributor $250.

HISTORIC SPEEDWELL, 333 Speedwell Ave., Morristown, NJ 07960-9384. Tel.: 973-285-6550. Fax: 973-285-6541.
E-mail: msutherland@morrisparks.net
Web Site: www.morrisparks.net
Formerly: Historic Speedwell - Birthplace of the Telegraph
Founded: 1966.
Congressional District: 5
Key Personnel: Pres. (V), Joseph Kane; Site Supt., Mark Sutherland; Administrative Asst., Abagail Eckert; Collections Specialist, Melanie Holster; Program Specialist, Maressa McFarlane; Program Specialist, Joshua Kandebo.
Personnel Profile: Full-Time Paid 5; Part-Time Paid 2; Part-Time Volunteers 65; Interns 2.
Governing Authority: county. nonprofit organization. Parent Institution: Morris County. Subsidiary Institution: Morris County Park Commission. Tax-exempt.
Historic site: 19th century homestead estate.
Collections: wooden patterns from the Speedwell Iron Works; manuscripts; decorative objects; portraits by Samuel F. B. Morse; telegraph instruments; furniture. Historic Buildings: 1844 Vail house; homestead carriage house; 1849 carriage house; Granary Factory where telegraph was first demonstrated; L'Hommedieu house; Estey house; Ford cottage.
Research Fields: genealogy; architecture; decorative arts; industry; transportation; telegraph communication; iron industry.
Activities: guided tours; docent programs; permanent & temporary exhibitions; special events; educational programs.
Publications: books, At Speedwell In the 19th Century; The Speedwell Ironworks: A History of Workers & Work; student activity book.
Hours & Admission Prices: April-June Tues.-Sat. 10-5; July-Oct. Wed.-Sat. 10-5, Sun. 12-5. Adults $4, seniors $3, students & children 4-16 $2; discounts to groups & AAM members; children under 4 no charge. ♿
Attendance: 6,000 (accurate)
Membership: Student & Senior 65 & over $15; Individual $20; Family $50; Journeyman $100; Molder $250; Founder $500; Ironmaster $1,000.

MACCULLOCH HALL HISTORICAL MUSEUM & GARDENS, (M), 45 Macculloch Ave., Morristown, NJ 07960-9374. Tel.: 973-538-2404. Fax: 973-538-9428.
E-mail: acutler@maccullochhall.org
Web Site: www.maccullochhall.org
Founded: 1950.
Congressional District: 11
Key Personnel: Interim Dir., Alice D. Cutler; Pres. (V), JoAnn Burk; Treas., Sharon Cross; F.M. Kirby Cur. Collections, Ryan Hyman; Admin., Jane E. Morgan.
Personnel Profile: Full-Time Paid 3; Part-Time Paid 1; Part-Time Volunteers 45; Interns 1.

Governing Authority: nonprofit organization. Affiliated with W. Parsons Todd Foundation, New York, NY. Tax-exempt: 501(c)(3).
Historic House: 1810 George Macculloch Home.
Collections: 18 & 19th century English & American decorative arts; oriental rugs & china; Macculloch family & Todd family archives; Thomas Nast collection; Morris Canal; archives & library.
Research Fields: Thomas Nast, Miller & Macculloch families.
Facilities: archives; garden.
Activities: guided tours; lectures; permanent & temporary exhibitions; concerts; children's programs.
Publications: brochure; catalog, newsletter.
Hours & Admission Prices: Wed.-Thurs. & Sun. 1-4; groups by appointment. Adults $6, senior citizens & students $5; discounts to AAM members; members no charge. Closed New Year's Eve & Day; Memorial Day; Independence Day; Labor Day; Thanksgiving & Day after; Christmas Eve, Day & week.
Attendance: 4,000 (accurate)
Membership: Individual $30; Family $50; Sponsor $75, Loyalist $100; Federalist $250; Whig $500; Neoclassicist $1,000.

MORRIS COUNTY HISTORICAL SOCIETY (ACORN HALL HOUSE MUSEUM), (M), 68 Morris Ave., Morristown, NJ 07960-4315. Tel.: 973-267-3465. Fax: 973-267-8773.
E-mail: acornhall@juno.com
Web Site: www.acornhall.org
Founded: 1945.
Congressional District: 11
Key Personnel: Dir., Bonnie-Lynn Nadzeika; Pres., David G. Holdsworth; Vice Pres., Diane Kafel; Cur., Debra Westmoreland; Museum Shop Mgr., Diane Freedman; Outreach Coord., Karen Ann Kurlander; Education Coord., Carie Levin.
Personnel Profile: Full-Time Paid 2; Part-Time Paid 2; Part-Time Volunteers 100; Interns 3.
Governing Authority: society. Tax-exempt: 501(c)(3).
Historical Society Museum: housed in c.1853 Acorn Hall.
Collections: Crane-Hone collection of Victorian furniture; 1853 original furnishings.
Research Fields: 19th-century & mid-Victorian period; Morris County history.
Facilities: 2,500-vol. research library of books on Victorian era; garden. Historic books, maps, postcards & Victorian items for sale.
Activities: guided tours; adult & children's workshops; vintage dancing; lecture series; oral history; trip program. Museum Sponsors: Victorian Weekend.
Publications: quarterly newsletter, Munsell's History of Morris County, 1739-1882; New Jersey's Revolutionary War Powder Mill; Tours in Historic Morris County; One Hundred Years, One Hundred Miles: The Morris Canal; DVD docudrama, Hard Winter.
Hours & Admission Prices: Mon.-Thurs. 10-4, Sun. 1-4, group tours by appointment. Adults $6, senior citizens $5, students $3; discount to AAM members; children under 12 & members no charge. Closed New Year's Eve & Day; Christmas Eve, Day & week.
Attendance: 3,500 (estimated)
Membership: Student $15; Senior Citizen $20; Individual $30; Family & Institution $50; Contributor $100; Sustaining $250; Sponsor $500; Patron $1,000; Life $2,500.

* **THE MORRIS MUSEUM, (M),** 6 Normandy Heights Rd., Morristown, NJ 07960-4627. Tel.: 973-971-3700. Fax: 973-538-0154.
Web Site: www.morrismuseum.org
Founded: 1913.
Congressional District: 12
Key Personnel: Pres., C.E.O. & Chief Cur., Steven H. Miller; Chm. (V), Mary Chandor; Vice Pres., Deborah Farrar Starker; Vice Pres., Jean Aspen; Mgr. Collections, Molly Gibbons; Artistic Dir. Bickford Theatre, Eric Hafen; Cur. Exhibitions, Ann Aptaker; Cur. Guinness Collection, Ellen Snyder-Grenier; Museum Shop Mgr., Bridget Meyer.
Personnel Profile: Full-Time Paid 24; Part-Time Paid 34; Part-Time Volunteers 450; Interns 12.
Governing Authority: nonprofit organization. Subsidiary Institution: The Morris Museum Foundation. Tax-exempt: 501(c)(3).
General Museum.
Collections: anthropology; archaeology; zoology; geology; paleontology; natural history; cultural history; fine & decorative art; folk art; automata; Murtogh D. Guinness mechanical musical instruments.
Facilities: 312-seat theater; classrooms. Museum-related items for sale.
Activities: lectures; films; gallery talks; concerts; dance recitals; arts festivals; drama; extension talks to schools & hospitals; mineral astronomy & archaeology clubs; formally organized education programs for children, adults & undergraduate college students; docent program; permanent, traveling & temporary exhibitions; school loan service; inter-museum loan; rentals.
Publications: 3-month newsletters; exhibition catalogs; flyers.
Hours & Admission Prices: Tues.-Wed. & Fri.-Sat. 10-5, Thurs. 10-8, Sun. 1-5. Adults $10, senior citizens, children & students $3; discounts to AAM & ICOM members; Thurs. 5-8, children under 3 & members no charge. Closed major holidays. ♿
Attendance: 220,000 (accurate)
Membership: Students & Senior Citizens $40; Individual $45; Couple & Family & Nonprofit Organizational $60; Patron $120; Benefactor $300; Sponsor $600; Director's Circle $1,200.

MORRISTOWN NATIONAL HISTORICAL PARK, 30 Washington Place, Morristown, NJ 07960-4299. Tel.: 973-539-2016. Fax: 973-539-8361. TDD: 973-539-5072.
E-mail: jude_pfister@nps.gov
Web Site: nps.gov/morr
Founded: 1933.
Congressional District: 12
Key Personnel: Supt., Randy Turner; Chief Interpretation, Anne DeGraaf; Museum Specialist, Joni Rowe; Chief Cultural Resources, Dr. Jude M. Pfister.
Personnel Profile: Full-Time Paid 30; Part-Time Volunteers 10; Interns 6.
Governing Authority: federal. Parent Institution: National Park Service, U.S. Dept. of the Interior, Washington, DC 20240. Branch Units: Washington's Headquarters; Jockey Hollow; Fort Nonsense; New Jersey Brigade. Tax-exempt.
Historic Site: 1777, 1779-1782 winter encampment sites of the Continental Army; 1779-1780 Washington's Headquarters.
Collections: preserved archaeological sites; 18th-century military weapons & equipment; decorative arts; paintings; furnishings; archaeology; rare books & manuscripts; reconstructed soldier huts; Revolutionary War. Historic Houses: 1772 Ford Mansion (Washington's Headquarters); 1750 Wick Farm; c.1770 Guerin House.
Research Fields: 18th-century military and domestic life, especially that relating to Morristown & the Revolutionary War in New Jersey; George Washington & the Continental Army; archaeology; early American decorative arts & 18th-century imprints; cultural & political aspects of western European history, 1550-1900.
Facilities: 50,000-vol. research library; 250-seat auditorium; visitor center; 24 miles of hiking trails & historic traces with interpretive waysides covering 1,700 acres of park land. Books for sale.
Activities: guided tours; lectures; organized educational programs for groups; audiovisual programs; living history demonstrations; nature & history walks; special events.
Publications: handbook, Morristown NHP; books, A Certain Splendid House; Morristown: The War Years, 1777-1780; booklets; special event bulletins; research monographs; guide to manuscript collections.
Hours & Admission Prices: Daily 9-5. Adults $4, annual family pass $15; children under 16 no charge. Closed New Year's Day; Thanksgiving; Christmas. ♿
Attendance: 200,000 (estimated)

SCHUYLER-HAMILTON HOUSE, 5 Olyphant Place, Morristown, NJ 07960-4231. Tel.: 973-267-4039. Fax: 973-539-7502.
E-mail: abren8527@aol.com
Web Site: www.co.morris.nj.us/mchc/directory-museums.html#schuyler
Founded: 1923.
Congressional District: 11
Key Personnel: Co-1st Vice Regent & Museum Shop Mgr., Patricia Sanftner; Co-2nd Vice Regent, Mariane Browne.
Personnel Profile: Part-Time Volunteers 22.
Governing Authority: society. Parent Institution: National Society Daughters of the American Revolution. Subsidiary Institution: Morristown Chapter. Tax-exempt: 501(c)(3) & 216-018-192.
Historic House Museum: 1760 home of Dr. Jabez Campfield, Revolutionary War army doctor.
Collections: 1720-1850 period furnishings; engravings.
Research Fields: herb garden.
Facilities: 30-vol. library of Revolutionary period books & patriot's index available for use on premises; kitchenette; small garden. Dolls, toy cannons, postcards & notecards for sale.
Activities: guided tours; lectures; permanent exhibitions; society meetings open to the public.
Publications: pamphlet on house history & garden.
Hours & Admission Prices: Sun. 2-4 & by appointment. Adults $4, children 12 to high school $.50; children under 12 no charge.
Attendance: 1,000 (estimated)
Membership: Associate $18; D.A.R. Members $40.

Mount Holly

HISTORIC BURLINGTON COUNTY PRISON MUSEUM, 128 High St., Mount Holly, NJ 08060-1402. Mailing Address: Burlington County Division of Parks, 49 Rancocas Rd., Mount Holly, NJ 08060. Tel.: 609-265-5858 & 5476 (museum). Fax: 609-265-5797.
E-mail: parks@co.burlington.nj.us
Web Site: www.prisonmuseum.net
Founded: 1966.
Congressional District: 3
Key Personnel: Pres. (V) Historic Burlington County Prison Museum Assn., Janet L. Sozio; Supt. Burlington County Division of Parks, Jeffrey F. Kerchner; Historic Preservation Specialist, Eric Baratta; Site Attendant, Marisa Sassaman.
Personnel Profile: Full-Time Paid 12; Part-Time Paid 1; Part-Time Volunteers 7.
Governing Authority: county. A body politic & corporate of the State of New Jersey. Tax-exempt: 501(c)(3).
Historic Building: 1810 Burlington County Prison declared National Historic Landmark 1986.
Collections: items related to penology, prisons & Robert Mills, architect.
Facilities: library of penology books available for inter-library loan & on premises.
Activities: guided tours; lectures; permanent & temporary exhibitions.
Publications: pamphlets.
Hours & Admission Prices: Thurs.-Sat. 10-4, Sun. noon-4. Adults $4, seniors & students $2; children under 5 no charge. ♿
Attendance: 5,000 (accurate)
Membership: Individual $10.

JOHN WOOLMAN MEMORIAL, 99 Branch St., Mount Holly, NJ 08060-1866. Mailing Address: P.O. Box 427, Mount Holly, NJ 08060-0427. Tel.: 609-267-3226.
Web Site: www.woolmancentral.com
Founded: 1915.
Congressional District: 6
Key Personnel: Dir., Jack Walz; Dir., Carol Walz.
Governing Authority: denominational group. Tax-exempt: 501(c)(3).
Historic Building & Site: 1783 John Woolman Memorial.
Collections: artifacts.
Activities: guided tours.
Publications: annual report.
Hours & Admission Prices: Call for hours. No charge, donations requested. ♿
Attendance: 2,500 (estimated)

Mountainside

DEACON ANDREW HETFIELD HOUSE, Constitution Plaza, Mountainside, NJ 07092. Mailing Address: Mountainside Historical Preservation Committee, 1385 Rte. 22 E., Mountainside, NJ 07092-2605. Tel.: 908-687-3636.
E-mail: info@mountainsidehistory.org
Historic House Museum: built in 1760. Listed on the National Register of Historic Places.
Collections: local history & culture; photographs; period artifacts.
Hours & Admission Prices: March-May & Sept.-Oct. 3rd Sun. of month 1-3.

TRAILSIDE NATURE AND SCIENCE CENTER, 452 New Providence Rd., Mountainside, NJ 07092-1409. Tel.: 908-789-3670. Fax: 908-789-3270.
E-mail: pbertsch@ucnj.org
Web Site: www.ucnj.org/trailside
Founded: 1941.
Congressional District: 7
Key Personnel: Dir., Patricia Bertsch; Asst. Dir., Karen Inzillo; Museum Shop Mgr., Lenore Mangan.
Personnel Profile: Full-Time Paid 7; Part-Time Paid 15; Part-Time Volunteers 5.
Governing Authority: county. Parent Institution: Union County Department of Parks & Community Renewal. Tax-exempt: 170(b)(1)(A).
Natural Science Museum.
Collections: snakes; turtles; frogs; aquatic life; minerals; fluorescent minerals; Watchung Reservation geology; taxidermy birds & mammals; Native American artifacts; hands-on exhibits.
Facilities: library; classrooms; 4,500 sq. ft. exhibit space; 13 miles of hiking trails; theater; children's discovery room.
Activities: guided tours; lectures; children, family & adults workshops; teacher training workshops; school & community programs; boy & girl scout programs; birthday parties.
Hours & Admission Prices: Visitor Center: daily 12-5. No charge; donations accepted. Closed New Year's Day; Easter; Independence Day; Thanksgiving & following day; Christmas Eve & Day. ♿
Attendance: 50,000 (estimated)

New Brunswick

AMERICAN HUNGARIAN FOUNDATION/MUSEUM OF THE AMERICAN HUNGARIAN FOUNDATION, (M), 300 Somerset St., New Brunswick, NJ 08901-2248. Mailing Address: P.O. Box 1084, New Brunswick, NJ 08903-1084. Tel.: 732-846-5777. Fax: 732-249-7033.
E-mail: info@ahfoundation.org
Web Site: www.ahfoundation.org
Formerly: American Hungarian Foundation/Hungarian Heritage Center Museum
Founded: 1954.
Congressional District: 6
Key Personnel: Pres. & Acting Dir., August J. Molnar; Chm. (V), Zsolt Harsanyi; Treas., Scott B. Lukacs; Librarian, Margaret Papai; Cur., Patricia L. Fazekas.
Governing Authority: nonprofit organization. Tax-exempt: 501(c)(3).
Cultural Heritage Center.
Collections: art & artists born in Hungary who later worked in the United States; history of Hungarian immigration to the United States from colonial to modern times; Hungarian contributions to American life; art; coins; weapons; decorative arts; glass; photographs; archives; Hungarian folk art, furniture, textiles, & ceramics.
Research Fields: history of Hungarian immigration; history of Hungarian contributions to American life; Hungarian art.
Facilities: 60,000-vol. library of books dealing with Hungarian history, art & culture, available for inter-library loan & use by public. Museum-related items for sale.
Activities: guided tours; lectures; films; concerts; hobby workshops; organized education programs; loan, traveling & temporary exhibitions; school loan service.
Hours & Admission Prices: Tues.-Sat. 11-4, Sun. 1-4. Suggested Donation: $5. Closed New Year's Day; Easter; Memorial Day; Independence Day; Labor Day; Thanksgiving; Christmas Day. ♿
Attendance: 4,000 (estimated)
Membership: Associate $25; Sustaining $40; Participating $65; Friend $100; Donor $500; Sponsor $1,000; Patron $2,500; Benefactor $5,000.

BUCCLEUCH MANSION, 200 College Ave., Buccleuch Park, New Brunswick, NJ 08901. Mailing Address: Jersey Blue Chapter NSDAR, P.O. Box 27, New Brunswick, NJ 08903. Tel.: 732-745-5094.
E-mail: jkgennaro@aol.com
Founded: 1915.
Congressional District: 6
Key Personnel: Cur., Judy Gennaro.
Governing Authority: municipal; society. Mansion & park owned by city of New Brunswick, NJ; Affiliated with Jersey Blue Chapter, Daughters of the American Revolution, New Brunswick NJ. Tax-exempt.
Historic House: 1739 three-story Colonial house, located on the site of 1776 Revolutionary War fortifications.
Collections: 18th-century to late Victorian period rooms; c.1815 Du Four wallpaper; furniture of N.J. cabinetmakers; crafts items, including spinning wheels, carders, metal dress patterns; toys; costumes; textiles.
Research Fields: research related to house and its previous occupants.
Facilities: 80-acre park.
Activities: guided tours; permanent & temporary exhibitions.
Publications: brochure.
Hours & Admission Prices: June-Oct. last of month Sun. 1-4; groups by appointment year round. No charge; donations accepted. ♿
Attendance: 1,500 (estimated)

CENTER FOR LATINO ARTS & CULTURE, 122 College Ave., New Brunswick, NJ 08901-1165. Tel.: 732-932-1263. Fax: 732-932-1589.
Web Site: clac.rutgers.edu
Key Personnel: Dir., Carlos Fernandez; Program Coord., Silismar Suriel
Latino Arts & Culture.
Collections: Latino, Hispanic, Caribbean, & Latin American arts & culture.
Hours & Admission Prices: Mon.-Fri. 9-5; other times by appointment.

HENRY GUEST HOUSE, 58 Livingston Ave., New Brunswick, NJ 08901-2521. Mailing Address: 60 Livingston Ave., New Brunswick, NJ 08901-2520. Tel.: 732-745-5108. Fax: 732-846-0226.
E-mail: nbfpl@lmxac.org
Founded: 1760.
Congressional District: 17
Key Personnel: Dir., Robert Belvin.

Governing Authority: municipal. Parent Institution: New Brunswick Public Library, New Brunswick. Tax-exempt.
Historic House: 1760 Henry Guest House. Listed on the National Register of Historic Places.
Collections: local history & culture; period furnishings; personal artifacts.
Activities: guided tours; permanent exhibitions.
Hours & Admission Prices: By appointment. No charge.

JANE VOORHEES ZIMMERLI ART MUSEUM, (M), Rutgers, The State University of New Jersey, 71 Hamilton St., New Brunswick, NJ 08901-1248. Tel.: 732-932-7237. Fax: 732-932-8201. TDD: 732-232-2444.
E-mail: brenowit@rci.rutgers.edu
Web Site: www.zimmerlimuseum.rutgers.edu
Founded: 1966.
Congressional District: 17
Key Personnel: Dir., Susan Delehanty; Chm. (V), Jane V. Blitz; Mgr. Membership & Publications, Stacy Smith; Coord. Public Rels. & Volunteers, Rebecca Brenowitz; Accountant, Bernadette Clapsis; Senior Cur., Jeffrey Wechsler; Cur. Education, Alfredo Franco; Mgr. Operations, Edward Schwab; Research Cur., Dodge Collection, Jane Sharp; Cur. & Dir. Morse Center for Graphic Arts, Marilyn Symmes; Registrar, Leslie Kriff; Museum Shop Mgr., Andrea Cunnell.
Personnel Profile: Full-Time Paid 17; Part-Time Paid 64; Part-Time Volunteers 60; Interns 4.
Governing Authority: state. Parent Institution: Rutgers, The State University of New Jersey. Tax-exempt: 501(c)(3) & 170(b)(1)(A).
Art Museum.
Collections: paintings; graphics; sculpture; turn-of-the-century French graphic art; Russian & Soviet nonconformist art; American & European art; Japonisme archives for printmaking studios; original illustrations for children's literature.
Research Fields: 19th-century French graphics & sculpture; 20th-century American art; paintings; Japonisme; Russian art; Soviet nonconformist art; graphic arts.
Facilities: 500-vol. library of art catalogs; 4,000-vol. of French fin de siecle illustrated books & periodicals.
Activities: guided tours; weekly cultural series; children's programs; high school workshops; inter-museum loan & temporary exhibitions.
Publications: triannual newsletter; yearly collections journal; exhibition catalogs.
Hours & Admission Prices: July Wed.-Fri. 10-4:30, Sat.-Sun. 12-5; Sept.-June Tues.-Fri. 10-4:30, Sat.-Sun. 12-5. Adults $3; discounts to AAM & ICOM members; Rutgers faculty, staff & students and members no charge. Closed New Year's Day; Memorial Day; Independence Day; Labor Day; Thanksgiving & day after; Christmas. ♿
Attendance: 32,000 (accurate)
Membership: Student $15; Individual & Educator $45; Dual Household $65; Associate $100; Patron $150; Sponsor $300; Curator's Circle $500; Director's Gallery $1,000.

THE RUTGERS GARDENS, 112 Ryders Ln., New Brunswick, NJ 08901-8519. Tel.: 732-932-8451. Fax: 732-932-7060.
E-mail: rugardens@aesop.rutgers.edu
Web Site: rutgersgardens.rutgers.edu
Founded: 1927.
Congressional District: 6
Key Personnel: Dir., Dr. Bruce Crawford; Volunteer Coord., Mary Ann McMillan; Supt., Matthew Jamicky.
Personnel Profile: Full-Time Paid 4; Part-Time Paid 1; Part-Time Volunteers 70; Interns 4.
Governing Authority: university. Parent Institution: Rutgers-The State University of NJ., New Brunswick, NJ 08903. Tel.: 908-932-9325. Subsidiary Institution: Cook College. Tax-exempt.
Research Arboretum.
Collections: cultivars of Ilex opaca & Cornus Florida; shade tree & small tree collection; rhododendron & azalea garden; garden for sun & shade; Donald B. Lacey Display garden; Ella Quimby water conservation garden; evergreen & shrub garden; bamboo forest.
Research Fields: plant breeding; ornamental trees & shrubs.
Facilities: botanical garden; field research station.
Activities: guided tours; formally organized education programs for undergraduate college students; professional students; elementary, secondary & pre-school students; youth at risk; general public.
Publications: newsletter.
Hours & Admission Prices: Daily 8:30 am-dusk. No charge; donations accepted.
Attendance: 50,000 (estimated)

New Providence

SALTBOX MUSEUM, 1350 Springfield Ave., New Providence, NJ 07974. Mailing Address: Mason Rm., 377 Elkwood Ave., New Providence, NJ 07974-1837. Tel.: 908-665-1065.
Founded: 1966.
Key Personnel: Pres. (V), John Bale.
Personnel Profile: Part-Time Paid 27.
Governing Authority: Parent Institution: New Providence Historical Society. Tax-exempt.
Historic House Museum.
Collections: period artifacts & furnishings.
Publications: Turkey Tracks.
Hours & Admission Prices: March-Nov. 1st & 3rd Sun. 1-3. No charge; donations accepted.
Membership: Individual $15; Family $20; Contribution $30; Sustaining $50; Life $100.

New Vernon

TUNIS-ELLICKS HISTORIC HOUSE AND MUSEUM, 16 Village Rd., New Vernon, NJ 07976. Mailing Address: P.O. Box 1777, New Vernon, NJ 07976. Tel.: 973-292-3661.
E-mail: hardinghist@comcast.net
Founded: 1977.
Historic House Museum.
Collections: local history & culture; photographs; aerial maps.
Hours & Admission Prices: Call for hours. No charge.

Newark

ALJIRA, A CENTER FOR CONTEMPORARY ART, 591 Broad St., Newark, NJ 07102-4403. Tel.: 973-622-1600. Fax: 973-622-6526.
E-mail: info@aljira.org
Web Site: www.aljira.org
Key Personnel: Exec. Dir., Victor L. Davson; Art Dir. Aljira Design, Cicely Cottingham; Dir. Exhibitions & Programs, Edwin Ramoran; Deputy Dir., Nathea Lee
Art Center.
Collections: works of emerging & under-represented artists.
Hours & Admission Prices: Wed.-Fri. 12-6, Sat. 11-4.

THE NEW JERSEY HISTORICAL SOCIETY, 52 Park Place, Newark, NJ 07102-4302. Tel.: 973-596-8500. Fax: 973-596-6957.
E-mail: contactnjhs@jerseyhistory.org
Web Site: www.jerseyhistory.org
Founded: 1845.
Congressional District: 10
Key Personnel: Chm. (V), John G. Zinn; Pres. & C.E.O., Linda Epps; Collections Mgr., Timothy Decker; Dir. Finance & Admin, Steve Tettamanti; Cur. Manuscripts & Acting Dir. Library, Julia Telonidis; Cur. Education & Programs, Margaret Renn.
Personnel Profile: Full-Time Paid 21; Part-Time Paid 2; Part-Time Volunteers 40; Interns 9.
Governing Authority: society. Tax-exempt: 501(c)(3).
History Museum & Library.
Collections: N.J. & American history; transportation; industry; costumes; paintings; prints; drawings; furniture; glass; ceramics; silver; textiles; household utensils; jewelry; coins; sculpture; Indian artifacts; photographs; N.J. maritime material; c.1790-1815.
Research Fields: history; art history; graphics; decorative & fine arts; architecture; genealogy.
Facilities: 65,000-vol. library of books; 1,600 manuscript groups; maps; rare books; pamphlets; broadsides & newspapers pertaining to New Jersey history & genealogy available for use on premises; reading room; 3 museum galleries; 73-seat auditorium. Books, periodicals & museum-related items for sale.
Activities: guided tours; lectures; films; gallery talks; education programs; docent program; inter-museum loan, temporary exhibitions; seminars; community programs.
Publications: biannual journal, New Jersey History; newsletter, New Jersey Historical Society News; occasional books & catalogs.
Hours & Admission Prices: Museum: Tues.-Sat. 10-5. Library: Wed.-Thurs. & Sat. 12-5; school & group tours by appointment. Suggested Donation: $4. Closed major holidays. ♿
Attendance: 20,000 (estimated)
Membership: Individual Educator $25; Individual $30; Library & Nonprofit $45; Household $60; Supporter $100; Friend $250; Patron $500; Benefactor $750; President's Circle $1,500.

* **THE NEWARK MUSEUM, (M),** 49 Washington St., Newark, NJ 07102-3176. Tel.: 973-596-6550. Fax: 973-642-0459. TDD: 973-596-6355.
Web Site: www.newarkmuseum.org
Founded: 1909.
Congressional District: 10
Key Personnel: Chm. Bd. (V), Arlene Lieberman; Pres., Andrew Richards; Pres. of Volunteers, Joyce Hamlin; Dir., Mary Sue Sweeney Price; Deputy Dir. Finance & Administration, Meme Omoqbai; Deputy Dir. Mktg., Mark Albin; Deputy Dir. Devel., Peggy Dougherty; Cur. Asian Collections, Dr. Katherine Anne Paul; Cur. Decorative Arts, Ulysses G. Dietz; Cur. Africa, the Americas, & the Pacific, Dr. Christa Clarke; Assoc. Cur. American Art, Dr. Holly Pyne Connor; Dir. Science Dept., Dr. Ismael Calderon; Cur. Natural Sciences, Dr. Sule Oygur; Astronomer, Kevin Conod; Cur. Living Collections, Kristen Schmid; Deputy Dir. Collections, Rebecca A. Buck; Deputy Dir. Education, Ted Lind; Asst. Dir. Education, Kevin Heller; Asst. Dir. Education, Linda Nettleton; Dir. Special Projects & Exhibit Planning, Alison Edwards; Dir. Exhibits, Tim Wintemberg; Dir. Operations, Rick Stomber; Mgr. Visitor Svcs., David May; Mgr. Arts Workshop, Stephen J. McKenzie; Mgr. Educational Loan Collections, Helene Peters; Archivist, Jeffrey Moy; Librarian, Dr. William A. Peniston; Museum Shop Mgr., Lorelei Rowars; Public Rels., Allison McCartney; Dir. Special Events, Carol Blunda; Sr. Cur. American Art, Beth Venn; Asst. Cur. American Art, Mary Kate O'Hare.
Personnel Profile: Full-Time Paid 115; Part-Time Paid 250; Part-Time Volunteers 190; Interns 15.
Governing Authority: nonprofit organization. Parent Institution: The Newark Museum Association. Tax-exempt: 501(c)(3).
Art & Science Museum.
Collections: American painting & sculpture18th- to 20th-century; 19th & 20th century decorative arts; Asian art, esp. Tibet; ancient art: Egyptian, Greek, Coptic & Roman; numismatics; arts of Africa, Oceania and Americas, (pre-Columbian to present); natural sciences; live animal collection; planetarium. Historic Houses: 1784 schoolhouse, Ward Carriage House with Newark Fire Museum; 1885 Ballantine House (National Historic Landmark).
Major Exhibits: 100 Masterpieces of Art & Pottery, 11/09-1/10; Skies Alive: Bird Migration in Garden State, 11/09-12/10; Constructive Spirit: Abstract Art in South & North America, 2/10-5/10; Gustav Stickley & North American Arts & Crafts Movement, 9/10-1/11.
Research Fields: art; history & ethnology; natural sciences; numismatics.
Facilities: 40,000-vol. library of art & science reference; local & New Jersey material available for inter-library loan & on premises; planetarium; garden; auditorium; cafe. Books, postcards, children's items for sale.
Activities: guided tours; lectures; films; gallery talks; concerts; dance recitals; organized education programs; docent program; adult art school; inter-museum loan, permanent, temporary exhibitions; lending department; volunteer organization.
Publications: quarterly magazine, Access: The Newark Museum; exhibitions catalogues.
Hours & Admission Prices: Wed.-Fri. 12-5, Sat.-Sun. 10-5. Suggested Donation: adults $7; discounts to AAM members; members no charge. Public planetarium performances: adults $4, children under 12 $2. Closed New Year's Eve & Day; Independence Day; Thanksgiving; Christmas. ♿
Attendance: 948,663 (accurate)
Membership: Individual $50; Family $60; Sustaining $150; Benefactor $350; Sponsor $750; Director's Circle $1,500.

PAUL ROBESON GALLERIES-RUTGERS UNIVERSITY, Rutgers University - Newark, 350 Dr. Martin Luther King, Jr. Blvd., Paul Robeson Campus Center, Newark, NJ 07102. Tel.: 973-353-1610. Fax: 973-353-5912.
E-mail: galleryr@andromeda.rutgers.edu
Web Site: www.andromeda.rutgers.edu/artgallery
Founded: 1979.
Key Personnel: Interim Dir. & Assoc. Cur., Anonda Bell
Art Gallery.
Collections: photography; paintings & drawings.
Hours & Admission Prices: Mon.-Wed. 10-5, Thurs. 12-7. No charge. ♿
Attendance: 5,000 (accurate)

Newfield

MATCHBOX ROAD MUSEUM, 17 Pearl St., Newfield, NJ 08344-2603. Tel.: 856-697-6900. Fax: 856-697-6909.
E-mail: mbroad@aol.com
Web Site: mbroad.com
Founded: 1992.
Key Personnel: Everett Marshall, III
Toy Museum.
Collections: 35,000 miniature Matchbox vehicles including cars, tractors, double-decker buses, milk wagons, garbage trucks, moving vans, horse carriers, taxis & oil trucks.
Facilities: Museum-related items for sale.
Hours & Admission Prices: Call for appointment. No charge; donations accepted.

Newton

NEWTON FIRE DEPARTMENT, Fire Museum, 150 Spring St., Newton, NJ 07860-2009. Tel.: 973-383-0396.
E-mail: director@newtonfiremuseum.org
Web Site: www.newtonfiremuseum.org
Key Personnel: Dir., Daniel Finkle.
Governing Authority: nonprofit organization. Tax-exempt: 501(c)(3).
Fire-Fighting Museum: housed in an historic firehouse built in 1891.
Collections: firefighting equipment from the late 1800s to present.
Hours & Admission Prices: May-Oct. Thurs. 5pm-8pm, Sat. 11-3; groups by appointment.

SUSSEX COUNTY HISTORICAL SOCIETY, 82 Main St., Newton, NJ 07860-2046. Mailing Address: P.O. Box 913, Newton, NJ 07860-0913. Tel.: 973-383-6010. Fax: 973-383-4911.
E-mail: schs@tellurian.net
Web Site: sussexcountyhistory.org
Founded: 1904.
Congressional District: 12
Key Personnel: Pres., Alex Everitt, Jr.; Vice Pres., Nellie Stires-Howell; Sec., Kathy Esposito; Treas., Ruth Ann Whitesell; Corresponding Sec., June J. Dobson.
Personnel Profile: Full-Time Volunteers 4; Part-Time Paid 1; Part-Time Volunteers 3.
Governing Authority: society. Tax-exempt.
History Museum.
Collections: local history; American Indian artifacts; archaeology; mastodon; genealogy.
Facilities: 1,000-vol. library of genealogical & local history books available on premises.
Publications: Society Newsletter; books & pamphlets written by members; quarterly, Old Sussex Almanack.
Hours & Admission Prices: Fri. 9-1, Sat. 9-12. Museum: No charge; donations accepted. Library $15 daily.
Attendance: 400 (estimated)
Membership: Junior (under 18) $5; Individual $15; Husband & Wife $25; Business $100; Life $200; Contributing $500; Benefactor $1,000.

North Brunswick

THE NEW JERSEY MUSEUM OF AGRICULTURE, College Farm Rd. & Rte. 1, North Brunswick, NJ 08902. Mailing Address: P.O. Box 7788, North Brunswick, NJ 08902-7788. Tel.: 732-249-2077. Fax: 732-247-1035.
E-mail: info@agriculturemuseum.org
Web Site: www.agriculturemuseum.org
Founded: 1984.
Congressional District: 6
Key Personnel: Mgr., Dana S. Vallely; Cur., Cooper Morris; Cur. Collections, Coles Roberts; Program Coord. & Admin., Kelleen Madden; Cur. Archives, George Coyne; Coord. Education, Usha Luna; Facility Coord., Nelson Seda.
Personnel Profile: Full-Time Paid 2; Part-Time Paid 5; Part-Time Volunteers 40; Interns 5.
Governing Authority: independent, nonprofit corporation; board of trustees. Tax-exempt.
Agriculture, Educational & History Museum.
Collections: agricultural; machinery; equipment; tools; housewares; photographs; glass plate negatives; lantern slides; negatives & prints; archival documents.
Research Fields: agricultural history; household technology; scientific photography; environmental science; social change; economics.
Facilities: library of books, pamphlets, catalogs, & reports relating to agriculture & household application available for inter-library loan & by request; 130-seat meeting room.
Activities: guided tours; educational programs; seminars; field trips.
Publications: quarterly newsletter; brochures.
Hours & Admission Prices: Tues.-Sat. 10-3; Sun. for special events. Adults $4, senior citizens $3, children 4-12 $2; discounts to AAM & ICOM members; children under 4 & members no charge. Closed major holidays. ♿
Attendance: 40,000 (accurate)
Membership: Student $10; Seniors & Teachers $15; Individual $25; Family $35; Supporting $100; Sustaining $250; Benefactor $500; Patron $1,000.

North Plainfield

THE FLEETWOOD MUSEUM, 614 Greenbrook Rd., North Plainfield, NJ 07063-1621. Mailing Address: 135 Sandford Ave., North Plainfield, NJ 07060. Tel.: 908-756-7810.
Founded: 1985.
Congressional District: 7
Key Personnel: Dir. & Chm. (V), Nicholas A. Ciampa.
Personnel Profile: Part-Time Paid 4; Part-Time Volunteers 2.
Governing Authority: borough. Tax-exempt.
Art Museum: housed in the Vermeule Mansion. Listed on the National Register of Historic Places.
Collections: cameras; oil paintings; 900-vol. photo library; music boxes; musical instruments.
Hours & Admission Prices: Sat. 10-4. No charge; donations accepted. Closed major holidays. ♿
Attendance: 1,100 (estimated)

North Wildwood

HEREFORD INLET LIGHTHOUSE, 111 N. Central Ave., North Wildwood, NJ 08260-5955. Mailing Address: P.O. Box 784, Rio Grande, NJ 08242-0784. Tel.: 609-522-4520. Fax: 609-522-8590.
Web Site: www.herefordlighthouse.org
Founded: 1982.
Congressional District: 1
Key Personnel: Mayor, Aldo Palombo; Chm. (V), Historical Grants, Paul DiFilippo; Vice Chm., Grounds & Exterior Bldg., Steve Murray; Mgr. & Educator, Betty Mugnier; Public Rels., Peter Harp.
Personnel Profile: Full-Time Paid 1; Full-Time Volunteers 7; Part-Time Paid 6; Part-Time Volunteers 25.
Governing Authority: municipal; nonprofit. Tax-exempt: 501(c)(3).
Historic Site & Maritime Museum: listed in the National Directory of Historic Places.
Collections: local maritime artifacts; photographs of local history.
Research Fields: maritime history & local architecture; development of historical commission with emphasis on historic buildings.
Facilities: library; botanical garden; nature/conservation center. Museum-related items for sale.
Activities: arts festivals; craft shows; concerts; guided tours; lectures; rental gallery; study clubs; temporary & traveling exhibitions.
Publications: semiannual newsletter; annual brochure.
Hours & Admission Prices: mid-May to mid-Oct. daily 9-5; mid-Oct. to mid-May Wed.-Sun. 10-4. Adults $4, students 12-17 $1.50, children under 12 $1; Tours: $1 per person; active Coast Guard & NJ Lighthouse Society members no charge.
Attendance: 30,000 (accurate)
Membership: Associate $15; Family $25.

Northfield

THE CASTO HOUSE AND NORTHFIELD MUSEUM, Birch Grove Park, Burton Ave., Northfield, NJ 08225. Mailing Address: 1600 Shore Rd., Northfield, NJ 08225-2251. Tel.: 609-383-1505.
Formerly: Northfield Bicentennial Museum
Founded: 1976.
Key Personnel: Chm. (V), Carol A. Patrick; Cur., Roy W. Clark.
Personnel Profile: Part-Time Volunteers 5.
Governing Authority: city. Subsidiary Institution: Northfield Historical Society. Tax-exempt.
Local History Museum.
Collections: Northfield history; period artifacts & furnishings; area history; Evelyn C. Ryon obituary; quilts; period clothing; Mill Road school photographs; military artifacts.
Publications: Northfield.
Hours & Admission Prices: Sun. & Wed. 1-3; other times by appointment. No charge; donations accepted. Closed some holidays. ♿

Ocean City

DISCOVERY SEASHELL MUSEUM, 2721 Asbury Ave., Ocean City, NJ 08226-2329. Mailing Address: P.O. Box 121, Ocean City, NJ 08226-0121. Tel.: 609-398-2316.
Seashell Museum.
Collections: over 10,000 varieties of seashells from around the world; coral; carved shells; air plants.
Facilities: Museum-related items for sale.
Activities: tours.
Hours & Admission Prices: Memorial Day to Dec. Mon.-Sat. 10-8, Sun. 12-6. No charge. ♿

OCEAN CITY HISTORICAL MUSEUM, INC., Cultural Community Center, 1735 Simpson Ave., Ocean City, NJ 08226-3070. Tel.: 609-399-1801. Fax: 609-399-0544.
E-mail: info@ocnjmuseum.org
Web Site: ocnjmuseum.org
Formerly: Friends of the Ocean City Historical Museum, Inc.
Founded: 1964.
Congressional District: 1
Personnel Profile: Part-Time Paid 2; Part-Time Volunteers 50; Interns 2.
Governing Authority: municipal.
Local History Museum.
Collections: local history & heritage; shipwreck & maritime artifacts; costumes; paintings.
Facilities: 300-vol. library of material on New Jersey & Ocean City history; deeds; documents; maps available for use on premises. Period glassware, china & museum-related items for sale.
Activities: guided tours; lectures; summer weekly lecture series; educational programs; outreach.
Publications: History of Ocean City; Ocean City Memories; videotape, The Sindia: Her Final Resting Place; The Saga of the Sindia.
Hours & Admission Prices: Call for hours. No charge; donations accepted. Closed major holidays. ♿
Attendance: 4,000 (estimated)
Membership: Call or visit website for information.

Ocean Grove

HISTORICAL SOCIETY OF OCEAN GROVE, NEW JERSEY, 50 Pitman Ave., Ocean Grove, NJ 07756-1557. Mailing Address: P.O. Box 446, Ocean Grove, NJ 07756-0446. Tel.: 732-774-1869. Fax: 732-774-1684.
E-mail: info@oceangrovehistory.org
Web Site: oceangrovehistory.org
Founded: 1969.
Congressional District: 3
Key Personnel: C.E.O. & Pres. (V), Raymond Russomano; Librarian & Archivist, Rhoda Newman; Museum Shop Mgr., Martha Rakita; Museum Shop Mgr., Elizabeth Ogden.
Personnel Profile: Full-Time Paid 1; Part-Time Paid 1.
Governing Authority: society; nonprofit. Subsidiary Institution: Centennial Cottage. Tax-exempt: 501(c)(3).
Historical Society Museum: located in Ocean Grove Historic District; emphasizing history of Ocean Grove & the history of the camp meeting.
Collections: local history; Victoriana; original Stokes (founder of Ocean Grove) painting, pastel, chair & desk; original trustees' desks from Ocean Grove Camp Meeting Association; pictures; postcards; religious items & costumes. Historic Building: 1870 Centennial Cottage & gardens.
Facilities: 250-vol. library of Ocean Grove history & Victoriana material, including 100 manuscripts available to the public; 500 sq. ft. exhibit space. Notepads, calendars, & postcards for sale.
Activities: guided tours; lectures; temporary exhibitions. Annual Event: house tours.
Publications: quarterly newsletter.
Hours & Admission Prices: May 29-June 19 Fri.-Sat. 10-4; June 21-Sept. Mon. & Wed.-Thurs. 10-4, Fri.-Sat. 10-5; Oct.-Dec. Sat. 10-4. No charge; donations accepted.
Attendance: 6,000 (accurate)
Membership: Student and Senior 62 & over $10; Individual $20; Family $35; Patron & Corporate $250; Life Individual $250.

Oceanville

THE NOYES MUSEUM OF ART, 733 Lily Lake Rd., Oceanville, NJ 08231. Tel.: 609-652-8848. Fax: 609-652-6166.
E-mail: info@noyesmuseum.org
Web Site: www.noyesmuseum.org
Founded: 1983.
Congressional District: 2
Key Personnel: Exec. Dir., Michael Cagno; Dir. Education & Community Programs, Saskia Schmidt; Mgr. Exhibitions, Dorrie Papademetriou.
Personnel Profile: Full-Time Paid 5; Part-Time Paid 8; Part-Time Volunteers 5; Interns 3.
Governing Authority: nonprofit organization. Parent Institution: Fred Winslow Noyes Foundation. Tax-exempt: 501(c)(3).
Art Museum.
Collections: 20th-century American paintings & sculpture, folk art from the mid-Atlantic region including decoys, contemporary American arts & crafts
Activities: guided tours; gallery talks; Meet the Artist; environmental talks; Educators' Symposia; concerts; rotating & traveling exhibitions; Artist-in-Residence at local schools; hands-on art activities for children; trips to other institutions; craft shows & sale; facility rental.

Publications: New Jersey Arts Annual; crafts & fine arts catalogs; brochures; exhibition catalogues; quarterly newsletter.
Hours & Admission Prices: Tues.-Sat. 10-4:30, Sun. 12-5. Adults $4, seniors & students over 12 $3; discounts to AAM, & N.J. Association of Museums members; children under 6 & members no charge. Closed national holidays. ♿
Attendance: 17,000 (estimated)
Membership: Student & Teacher $30; Senior 60 & over $35; Individual $45; Household & Family $65; Supporting $125; Sustaining $250; Benefactor $500; Leadership $1,000.

Ogdensburg

STERLING HILL MINING MUSEUM, INC., 30 Plant St., Ogdensburg, NJ 07439-1126. Tel.: 973-209-7212. Fax: 973-209-8505.
Web Site: www.sterlinghill.org
Founded: 1990.
Congressional District: 5
Key Personnel: Pres. (V), Richard Hauck; Museum Shop Mgr., Rhea Cianfichi.
Personnel Profile: Full-Time Paid 5; Part-Time Paid 14; Part-Time Volunteers 10.
Governing Authority: private; nonprofit organization. Tax-exempt: 501(c)(3).
Mining Museum: former New Jersey zinc company mine; national historic site.
Collections: geology & mineralogy of the Sterling Hill zinc ore deposit; mining technology; equipment; mining artifacts; rare minerals; mining equipment.
Publications: newsletter twice a year.
Hours & Admission Prices: April-Nov. daily 10-3; March by appointment; Dec. Sat.-Sun. weather permitting; Christmas week to New Year's Eve. Adults $10, senior citizens $9, children under 12 $7.50; discount to groups of 10 or more with reservations & AAA members. Closed New Year's Day; Easter; Thanksgiving; Christmas. ♿
Attendance: 34,000 (accurate)
Membership: Calcite-Individual $15; Calcite-Family $25; Willemite $50; Zincite $100; Lifetime & Club $500.

Old Bridge

THOMAS WARNE HISTORICAL MUSEUM & LIBRARY, 4216 Rte. 516, Old Bridge, NJ 08857. Mailing Address: Madison Twp. Historical Society, 4216 Rte. 516, Matawan, NJ 07747-7032. Tel.: 732-566-0348 & 2108. Fax: 732-566-6943.
E-mail: info@thomas-warne-museum.com
Web Site: www.thomas-warne-museum.com
Founded: 1964.
Congressional District: 6
Key Personnel: Pres., Nancy Parr Giamerese; Treas. (V), Richard Kujawinski; Cur., David E. Johns.
Personnel Profile: Full-Time Volunteers 4; Part-Time Volunteers 4.
Governing Authority: private; nonprofit organization. Parent Institution: Madison Township Historical Society, Inc., Old Bridge Township, NJ. Tax-exempt.
History Museum: housed in an 1885 one room school house.
Collections: photographs; post cards; Edison phonograph & records sheet music; pottery; carpenter tools; clothing; Indian artifacts; textiles; local & NJ research files; old school books; research books of genealogy; concentration on local history, Middlesex & Monmouth Counties from fossils to World War II; agricultural tools.
Research Fields: local history & genealogy.
Facilities: library of genealogy & NJ history. Gift items for sale.
Activities: guided tours; lectures; participatory, loan & temporary exhibitions; study clubs; resource information. Annual Event: Apple Festival.
Publications: biannual, Timepiece; local history book, At the Headwaters of Cheesequake Creek; cookbook, From Groaning Board Cooks; Arcadia book, Images of America, Old Bridge.
Hours & Admission Prices: Fri. 12-4, Sat.-Sun. 12-6; other times by appointment. No charge; donations accepted. Closed New Year's Day; Christmas. ♿
Attendance: 560 (estimated)
Membership: Individual $10.

Oradell

HIRAM BLAUVELT ART MUSEUM, (M), 705 Kinderkamack Rd., Oradell, NJ 07649-1504. Mailing Address: 24 Maple Hill Dr., Woodcliff Lake, NJ 07677-7851. Tel.: 201-261-0012. Fax: 201-391-6418.
E-mail: maja218@verizon.net
Web Site: www.blauveltartmuseum.com
Founded: 1940.
Congressional District: 5
Key Personnel: Dir., Marijane Singer, Ph.D.; Pres. & Treas. (V), James Bellis, Jr.; Education Coord. & Registrar, Rosa Lara; Museum Asst., Diane Rivera; Artist-in-Residence, Guy Combes.
Personnel Profile: Full-Time Paid 4; Full-Time Volunteers 1; Part-Time Paid 3; Part-Time Volunteers 6; Interns 2.
Governing Authority: not-for-profit organization. Parent Institution: Blauvalt-Demarest Foundation. Subsidiary Institutions: 1678 Demarest House, River Edge, NJ; Old French Cemetery, New Milford, NJ. Tax-exempt: 501(c)(3).
Art Museum: located in an 1893 shingle & turret-style carriage house.
Collections: period furnishings & artifacts; Audubon folio, extinct birds & an ivory collection; North American mammals, big game, birds & a dioramic recreation of the African Water Hole Group by Louis Paul Jonas; artists: Douglas Allen, Dennis Anderson, John James Audubon, Richard Bishop Braithman, Paul Branson, Charles Livingston Bull, John Etti, Arthur B. Frost, Dwayne Harty, Lynn Bogue Hunt, Robert Kuhn, George Edward Lodge, Richard Loffler, Roy W. Mason, Walter Matia, Carl Milles, Dino Paravano, Alexander Proctor, Frederic Remington, John Schoenherr, W.J. Schaldach, Sir Peter Scott, David Shepherd, Arthur Tait, Archibald Thorburn, Eustracz Ziegler, Geordie Millar, Robert Guelich, Rene Headings, Wayne Trimm, Lanford Monroe, John Pitcher, Pati Stajcar, John Banovich, Kent Ullberg, Charles Allmond, Nancy Glazier & Terry Miller; Matthew Hillier; Judy Chapman; Julie Chapman; Daniel Smith; Peter Zaluzec; Dale Weiler; Alan Hunt; Robert Bateman; James Coe; Guy Combes. Historic House: 1678 Demarest House.
Major Exhibits: The Art of Conservation II, 11/09-1/14/10; The World of Guy Coheleach, 1/10-6/10.
Research Fields: wildlife artists.
Facilities: library.
Activities: arts festivals; guided tours; temporary exhibitions; educational programs for schools; demonstrations in wildlife/landscape painting; lectures; artist in residence program; artist roundtables.
Publications: Charles Livingston Bull; Douglas Allen; John Schoenherr catalogs; Art and the Animal - Society of Animal Artists 2003; catalogs; Art and the Animal - Society of Animal Artists 2004; Africa and Beyond, 2006.
Hours & Admission Prices: Wed.-Fri. 10-4, Sat.-Sun. 2-5. No charge; donations accepted. Closed holidays. ♿
Attendance: 13,986 (accurate)

Oxford

SHIPPEN MANOR, 8 Belvidere Ave., Oxford, NJ 07863-3014. Tel.: 908-453-4381. Fax: 908-453-4981.
E-mail: wcchc@nac.net
Web Site: www.wcchc.org
Key Personnel: Cur. & Music Program Dir., Susan Morgan
Historic House: listed on the National Register of Historic Places.
Collections: period furnishings; personal artifacts.
Activities: classes.
Hours & Admission Prices: Call for hours. Suggested Donation: adults $3; students & young children no charge. Closed holidays.

Paramus

BERGEN COUNTY ZOOLOGICAL PARK, 216 Forest Ave., Paramus, NJ 07652-5349. Tel.: 201-262-3771. Fax: 201-986-1788.
E-mail: zoofc@bergen.org
Web Site: www.co.bergen.nj.us/parks/zoo.htm
Founded: 1960.
Key Personnel: Dir., Timothy Gunther; Cur. Education, Liz Carletta; Gen. Cur., Cindy Norton.
Personnel Profile: Full-Time Paid 13; Part-Time Paid 1; Part-Time Volunteers 40.
Governing Authority: county. Parent Institution: Bergen County Dept. of Parks, 21 Main St., Court Plaza S., Hackensack, NJ 07601. Tax-exempt: 501(c)(3).
Zoo.
Collections: zoological specimens comprised of 71 mammals, 111 birds & 44 reptiles; antique farm equipment; 1860, Hackensack River Valley farm yard.
Research Fields: breeding endangered species.
Facilities: classrooms.
Activities: guided tours; lectures; hobby workshops; TV programs; formally organized education programs for children, adults & undergraduate college students affiliated with Ramapo College; permanent & temporary exhibitions.
Publications: newsletter, Bergen County Zoo.
Hours & Admission Prices: Daily 10-4:30. Adults $6, children 3-12 $3, seniors $2; discounts to residents; children under 3 & members no charge. ♿
Attendance: 450,000 (accurate)
Membership: Individual $20; Family $30.

BUEHLER CHALLENGER & SCIENCE CENTER, 400 Paramus Rd., Parking Lot G, Paramus, NJ 07652-1508. Mailing Address: P.O. Box 647, Paramus, NJ 07653-0647. Tel.: 201-251-8589. Fax: 201-251-9049.
E-mail: missionservices@bcsc.org
Web Site: www.bcsc.org
Founded: 1994.
Key Personnel: Mission Coord., Peggy Silverman
Science Museum.
Collections: space mission simulations; science exhibits; hands-on exhibits.
Activities: space mission simulations; public programs; space camps; tours; camp-in; teacher workshops. Museum Sponsors: Family Science Morning.
Hours & Admission Prices: Call for further information. ♿

THE NEW JERSEY CHILDREN'S MUSEUM, 599 Valley Health Plaza, Paramus, NJ 07652-3616. Tel.: 201-262-2638. Fax: 201-262-0560.
E-mail: nycminfo@aol.com
Web Site: www.njcm.com
Founded: 1992.
Key Personnel: Exec. Dir., Anne R. Sumers, MD; Chm., Elliott H. Sumers, MD
Personnel Profile: Full-Time Paid 12; Part-Time Paid 20.
Governing Authority: self-governing; profit.
Children's Museum.
Collections: hands-on exhibits; 100 sq. ft. interactive train set.
Facilities: 14,000 sq. ft. exhibit space. Museum-related items for sale.
Activities: films; lectures; participatory exhibits; broadcast programs; puppet shows; story telling; skits; craft project.
Publications: quarterly newsletter.
Hours & Admission Prices: May-Sept. Tues.-Thurs. 10-5, Fri.-Sun. 10-7; Oct.-April daily 10-6. Admission $10; discount to groups; children under one no charge. Closed Thanksgiving; Christmas. ♿
Attendance: 150,000 (estimated)

Park Ridge

PASCACK HISTORICAL SOCIETY, (M), 19 Ridge Ave., Park Ridge, NJ 07656-1138. Mailing Address: P.O. Box 85, Park Ridge, NJ 07656-0285. Tel.: 201-573-0307.
E-mail: phs@verizon.net
Web Site: www.pascackhistoricalsociety.com
Founded: 1942.
Congressional District: 9
Key Personnel: Pres., Carol Riccardo; Museum Shop Mgr., John Farina; Museum Shop Mgr., Barbara Farina.
Personnel Profile: Full-Time Volunteers 20; Part-Time Volunteers 40; Interns 5.
Governing Authority: nonprofit. Tax-exempt.
General Museum: local history, housed in 1873 former Congregational Church.
Collections: history; archives; costumes; glass paperweights; kitchen, farm & country store displays; Baylor Massacre; wampum & wampum making tools; wampum drilling machine; quilts & coverlets; Lenape artifacts; Tice wedding dress quilt c.1781.
Major Exhibits: Working in the Past-Interactive Exhibits, 1/15/10-12/10.
Research Fields: quilts; Dutch buildings; Pascack Valley History; Third Continental Dragoons; Lenape Indians; Jersey Dutch language.
Facilities: research library. Publications, reproduction wampum & local history articles for sale.
Activities: films; permanent exhibits; special meeting programs; children's activities.
Publications: quarterly, Relics; book, Pascack Valley tales.
Hours & Admission Prices: Wed. 10 to noon, Sun. 1-4; other times by appointment. No charge; donations accepted. ♿
Attendance: 4,000 (estimated)
Membership: Active $25; Dual $35; Contributing $50; Patron $100; Corporate $150; Life $400.

Paterson

PASSAIC COUNTY COMMUNITY COLLEGE, One College Blvd., Paterson, NJ 07505-1179. Tel.: 973-684-6555. Fax: 973-523-6085.
E-mail: jhaw@pcc.edu
Web Site: www.pccc.edu/art/gallery
Founded: 1968.
Congressional District: 35
Key Personnel: Exec. Dir. Cultural Affairs, Maria Mazziotti Gillan; Gallery Cur., Jane Haw; Asst. Dir., Aline Papazian.
Personnel Profile: Full-Time Paid 4; Part-Time Paid 3.
Governing Authority: county & state government; public college; nonprofit. Tax-exempt.
College Museum.
Collections: contemporary, 19th & early 20th century paintings & sculpture collections.
Activities: drawing & art history courses. Annual Events: community celebrations of various ethnic groups, such as African American & Hispanic Heritage month.
Publications: Passaic County Arts News.
Hours & Admission Prices: June-Aug. Mon.-Thurs. 9-9; Sept.-May Mon.-Fri. 9-9, Sat. 9-5. No charge. ♿
Attendance: 54,000 (estimated)

PASSAIC COUNTY HISTORICAL SOCIETY & LAMBERT CASTLE MUSEUM, 3 Valley Rd., Paterson, NJ 07503-2932. Tel.: 973-247-0085. Fax: 973-881-9434.
E-mail: lambercastle@verizon.net
Web Site: lambertcastle.org
Founded: 1926.
Congressional District: 7
Key Personnel: Dir., Alison Krawiec Faubert; Pres., Lorraine Yurchak.
Personnel Profile: Full-Time Paid 2; Part-Time Paid 5; Part-Time Volunteers 50.
Governing Authority: society; nonprofit organization. Tax-exempt: 501(c)(3).
Historical Society Museum: housed in 1893, Lambert Castle.
Collections: Passaic County & New Jersey; 18th to 19th-century decorative arts; furniture; paintings; sculpture; textiles; costumes; photographs; industrial history; genealogy; archives.
Research Fields: Passaic County history; silk industry; Victorian & Edwardian Era.
Facilities: library of books, archives, manuscripts, documents & maps on the history of Passaic County & northern N.J.; genealogy library.
Activities: guided tours; lectures; permanent, temporary & traveling exhibitions; educational programs for students; genealogy club.
Publications: newsletters, The Historic County, Castle Genie; catalogue, Gaetano Federici-The Artist as Historian; Silk & Sandstone: The Story of Catholina Lambert & His Castle; At The Sign Of The Brass Dog: Passaic County Folk Art.
Hours & Admission Prices: Museum: July-Aug. Wed.-Fri. 1-4, Sat.-Sun. 12-4; Sept.-June Wed.-Sun. 1-4. Adults $5, seniors $4, children 5-17 $3; discounts to AAM members; children under 5 & members no charge. ♿
Attendance: 27,500 (estimated)
Membership: Student $10; Senior $20; Individual & Regular $25; Family $35; Sustaining $50; Benefactor $100; Corporate $150.

THE PATERSON MUSEUM, 2 Market St., Paterson, NJ 07501-1726. Tel.: 973-321-1260. Fax: 973-881-3435.
Founded: 1925.
Congressional District: 8
Key Personnel: Dir., Giacomo R. DeStefano; Pres. (V), Florence Bottler; Cur. History, Bruce Balistrieri; Exhibit Artist Designer, Joseph Ruffilo; Photo Archivist, Joseph Costa; Museum Attendant, Mohamed Khalil.
Personnel Profile: Full-Time Paid 4; Interns 3.
Governing Authority: municipal. Tax-exempt.
History, Natural History & Science Museum: housed in 1871, Thomas Rogers Building, locomotive erecting shop.
Collections: mineralogy; New Jersey Indian artifacts; local history; entomological specimens; zoological specimens; John P. Holland's first & second successful submarine; Colt Paterson revolver collection 1837-1841; Silk City: textile machinery; model train layout; industrial history.
Research Fields: city atlas & local history library.
Facilities: library.
Activities: guided tours; lectures; films; gallery talks; formally organized education programs for children; permanent & temporary exhibitions.
Publications: booklets, Great Falls/S.U.M.; Historic District Walking Tour; The Colt Family; Lenni Lenape, New Jersey's Native Americans.
Hours & Admission Prices: Tues.-Fri. 10-4, Sat.-Sun. 12:30-4:30. Suggested Donation: adults $2; discount to AAM & ICOM members; children no charge. Closed major holidays. ♿
Attendance: 17,500 (estimated)

Pemberton

NORTH PEMBERTON RAILROAD STATION MUSEUM AND RAIL TRAIL, 3 Fort Dix Rd., Pemberton, NJ 08068-1439. Tel.: 609-894-0546. Fax: 609-894-0568.
E-mail: pthtrust@yahoo.com
Governing Authority: nonprofit organization. Tax-exempt: 501(c)(3).
Historic Building: housed in a former railroad station; built in 1892. Listed on the National Register of Historic Sites.
Collections: local & railroad history; period artifacts; cranberry & blueberry industry; photographs; personal artifacts.
Facilities: 2.5 mile rail trail. Museum-related items for sale.
Activities: research; walking trail; special events. Annual Events: MS Walk and

Volunteer Picnic; Day at the Station & Lantern Show in June; Train, Toy & Collectible Show in November; Holiday Hayride in December.
Hours & Admission Prices: Museum: Wed. & Fri.-Sun. 10-4; other times by appointment. Rail Trail: dawn to dusk. ♿

Pennsville

CHURCH LANDING FARMHOUSE, 86 Church Landing Rd., Pennsville, NJ 08070-1203. Tel.: 856-678-4453.
E-mail: wmasten@pennsvillenb.com
Web Site: www.pvhistorical.njcool.net
Governing Authority: Parent Institution: Pennsville Historical Society.
History Museum.
Collections: period furnishings; personal artifacts; flower & herb gardens.
Facilities: gardens.
Activities: guided tours; school group programs. Annual Event: Day at the Farm.
Hours & Admission Prices: Wed. & Sun. 1-3; groups by appointment. Adults $2, seniors $1; members no charge.

Perth Amboy

THE KEARNY COTTAGE, 63 Catalpa Ave., Perth Amboy, NJ 08861-4617. Tel.: 732-826-1826.
E-mail: writer@ptd.net
Founded: 1928.
Congressional District: 15
Key Personnel: C.E.O., Anne Rothlein.
Personnel Profile: Part-Time Paid 1; Part-Time Volunteers 25.
Governing Authority: municipal. Parent Institution: Kearny Cottage Historical Association, Inc. Tax-exempt: 501(c)(3).
Local History Museum.
Collections: Roger Statuettes furniture; documents; works by local artists. Historic Houses: Kearny cottage; home of Captain (Commodore) Lawrence Kearny.
Research Fields: local history of Perth Amboy & New Jersey; local citizens.
Activities: public meetings; open house tours; demonstrations of colonial crafts.
Hours & Admission Prices: Mon., Thurs. & last Sun. of month 2-4. Admission by appointment. No charge; donations accepted.
Attendance: 260 (estimated)
Membership: Membership $12.

PROPRIETARY HOUSE, THE ROYAL GOVERNOR'S MANSION, 149 Kearny Ave., Perth Amboy, NJ 08861-4700. Tel.: 732-826-5527. Fax: 732-826-8889.
E-mail: info@proprietaryhouse.org
Web Site: www.proprietaryhouse.org
Founded: 1967.
Congressional District: 13
Key Personnel: C.E.O. & Pres. (V), Tom Ward.
Personnel Profile: Part-Time Paid 1; Part-Time Volunteers 30.
Governing Authority: private; nonprofit association. Tax-exempt.
Historic Building.
Collections: 1764 Royal Governor's original mansion; paintings; architectural fragments; 18th- & 19th-century furnishings; ephemera.
Activities: general audience tours, school programs, special events, outreach programs.
Publications: newsletter, booklet on history of site.
Hours & Admission Prices: Mon. & Wed.-Fri. 10-4 by appointment. Closed New Year's Day; Easter; Mother's Day; Father's Day; Thanksgiving; Christmas Eve & Day. ♿
Attendance: 1,000 (estimated)
Membership: Student & Senior $15; Individual & Family $25-$49; Sustaining $50-$99; Supporting $100-$499; Benefactor $500-$999; Patron $1,000 & up.

Piscataway

CORNELIUS LOW HOUSE/MIDDLESEX COUNTY MUSEUM, 1225 River Rd., Piscataway, NJ Mailing Address: 703 Jersey Ave., New Brunswick, NJ 08901-3651. Tel.: 732-745-4177 & 4489. Fax: 732-745-4507. TDD: 732-745-3888.
E-mail: info@cultureheritage.org
Web Site: co.middlesex.nj.us/culturalheritage
Founded: 1979.
Congressional District: 6
Key Personnel: Exec. Dir., Anna M. Aschkenes; Cur. Exhibitions, Katie Zavoski; Asst. Cur. Facilities & Educator, Kenneth M. Helsby.
Personnel Profile: Full-Time Paid 2.
Governing Authority: county; nonprofit. Parent Institution: Middlesex County Cultural & Heritage Commission, 703 Jersey Ave., New Brunswick. Tax-exempt.
History Museum & Historic House: housed in a c.1741 Georgian style home featuring a wainscoted central hall, original floors & staircase & Delft-tiled fireplaces.
Collections: state & local history.
Major Exhibits: New Jersey Medicine 1800-1960, 4/10-6/11.
Research Fields: New Jersey history.
Activities: student workshops; public programs.
Hours & Admission Prices: Tues.-Fri. & Sun. 1-4; groups by appointment. No charge; donations accepted. Closed federal holidays. ♿

EAST JERSEY OLDE TOWNE, 1050 River Rd. & Old Hoes Lane, Piscataway, NJ 08855. Mailing Address: 703 Jersey Ave., New Brunswick, NJ 08901-3651. Tel.: 732-745-3030 & 4489. Fax: 732-463-1086. 732-745-3888 (TTY).
E-mail: culturalandheritage@co.middlesex.nj.us
Web Site: co.middlesex.nj.us/culturalheritage
Founded: 1971.
Key Personnel: Exec. Dir., Anna M. Aschkenes.
Personnel Profile: Full-Time Paid 3; Part-Time Volunteers 25.
Governing Authority: county; Parent Institution: Middlesex County Cultural & Heritage Commission. Tax-exempt.
Historic Building District: 18th-century village.
Collections: 18th-century furnishings & farm equipment. Historic Buildings: 17 18th-century buildings.
Research Fields: Piscataway historic village genealogy.
Facilities: library; botanical garden.
Activities: guided tours; lectures; workshops; programs; storytelling; demonstrations.
Publications: monthly newsletter; cultural calendar; event notification; exhibit guides, large print & Braille (on request).
Hours & Admission Prices: Tues.-Fri. 8:30-4:15, Sun. 1-4. Tours: Tues.-Fri. 1:30, Sun. rotating schedule; groups by appointment. Call for holiday hours & seasonal schedule. No charge. ♿
Attendance: 6,000 (estimated)

Plainfield

THE DRAKE HOUSE MUSEUM, 602 W. Front St., Plainfield, NJ 07060-1004. Tel.: 908-755-5831. Fax: 908-755-0132.
E-mail: thedrakehousemuseum@verizon.net
Web Site: drakehousemuseum.tripod.com
Founded: 1921.
Congressional District: 7
Key Personnel: Pres. (V), Eloise Bryant Tinley; 1st Vice Pres., Nancy Piwowar; 2nd Vice Pres., John Eklund; Corresponding Sec., Sandy Gursh-man; Office Mgr., Danielle Franklin.
Personnel Profile: Part-Time Paid 2.
Governing Authority: municipal. Tax-exempt: 501(c)(3).
History Museum: housed in 1746 Drake house.
Collections: collection of Americana; period furnishings.
Research Fields: Drake family genealogy; local history.
Facilities: Slides, postcards, stationery, books & museum-related items for sale.
Activities: guided tours; lectures; films; formally organized education programs; docent program; temporary & traveling exhibitions; luncheons.
Publications: newsletter, Communique.
Hours & Admission Prices: Mon.-Fri. 9-3, Sat. 11-1; other times by appointment. Suggested Donation $3; members no charge. Closed holiday weekends.
Attendance: 1,800
Membership: Student & Senior Citizen $7; Active $10; Contributing $25; Corporate & Sustaining $50 and up.

Point Pleasant

NEW JERSEY MUSEUM OF BOATING, Johnson Bros. Boat Works, Bldg. #12, 1800 Bay Ave., Point Pleasant, NJ 08742-4584. Tel.: 732-295-2072.
Governing Authority: nonprofit organization. Tax-exempt: 501(c)(3).
Boating Museum.
Collections: boating history; photographs; boatbuilding woods; maritime arts.
Activities: book signings; maritime art & photo shows; youth sailing classes. Annual Events: Spring Fling; Antique & Classic Boat Show in Sept.; Holiday Party.
Hours & Admission Prices: Daily 10-4. No charge.

Port Norris

BAYSHORE DISCOVERY PROJECT - DELAWARE BAY MUSEUM & SCHOONER A.J. MEERWALD, 2800 High St., Port Norris, NJ 08349-3126.
Port Norris, NJ 08349-3126. Tel.: 856-785-2060 (Museum); 800-485-3072 (Schooner Day Camp). Fax: 856-785-2893.
E-mail: info@bayshorediscoveryproject.org
Web Site: www.ajmeerwald.org
Governing Authority: Schooner Location: High St., Port Norris.
Maritime Museum.
Collections: maritime artifacts; shipbuilding; oystering; commercial fishing; photographs; 115 ft. schooner.
Activities: Schooner: education sail for school & youth groups; charter events; public sails; special events.
Hours & Admission Prices: Closed for renovation.

Princeton

HISTORICAL SOCIETY OF PRINCETON, (M), Bainbridge House, 158 Nassau St., Princeton, NJ 08542-7006. Tel.: 609-921-6748. Fax: 609-921-6939.
E-mail: information@princetonhistory.org
Web Site: www.princetonhistory.org
Founded: 1938.
Congressional District: 12
Key Personnel: Exec. Dir., Erin Dougherty; Pres., John Dumont; Cur. Collections, Eileen Morales; Dir. Devel., Barbara Webb; Museum Shop Mgr., Julie Janokowicz.
Personnel Profile: Full-Time Paid 4; Part-Time Paid 4; Part-Time Volunteers 100; Interns 1.
Governing Authority: society; nonprofit organization. Tax-exempt: 501(c)(3).
History Museum: housed in 1766 Bainbridge House.
Collections: arts; artifacts; documents; photographs; glass-plate negatives; historical archives; architectural research materials.
Research Fields: history of Princeton & New Jersey.
Facilities: library of Princeton and New Jersey books & documents available on premises.
Activities: exhibitions; tours; lectures; publications; educational programs for adults & school groups.
Publications: journal, Princeton History, Nos. 1-16; exhibit catalogues; guide to manuscript collections.
Hours & Admission Prices: Tues.-Sun. 12-4. No charge; donations accepted. Library: Tues. & Sat. 1-4. Adults $5; discounts to AAM members; library members no charge. Closed New Year's Day; Independence Day; Thanksgiving; Christmas. ♿
Attendance: 18,500 (accurate)
Membership: Senior $40; Individual $45; Family & Household $60; Contributor $85; Bainbridge Club Member $175; Bainbridge Club Patron $250; Bainbridge Club Benefactor $500; Bainbridge Club Sponsor $1,000.

MORVEN MUSEUM & GARDEN, (M), 55 Stockton St., Princeton, NJ 08540-6812. Tel.: 609-924-8144. Fax: 609-924-8331.
E-mail: info@morven.org
Web Site: www.historicmorven.org
Formerly: Historic Morven
Founded: 1987.
Congressional District: 12
Key Personnel: Mng. Dir., Clare Michel Smith; Pres. (V), Georgia T. Schley; Cur. Exhibitions, Anne Gossen.
Personnel Profile: Full-Time Paid 1; Part-Time Paid 9; Part-Time Volunteers 25; Interns 1.
Governing Authority: state; nonprofit organization. Parent Institution: New Jersey State Museum, Trenton, NJ. Tax-exempt: 501(c)(3).
Historic House Museum: former home of five New Jersey governors and a signer of the Declaration of Independence.
Collections: history of the site and its occupants with special emphasis on New Jersey history; New Jersey decorative & fine arts; cultural heritage of New Jersey.
Research Fields: site & its inhabitants; garden history; central New Jersey history; New Jersey fine and decorative arts.
Facilities: guided tours; lectures; school programs; temporary exhibitions.
Publications: biannual newsletter, For the Eye of a Friend.
Hours & Admission Prices: Wed.-Fri. 11-3, Sat.-Sun. 12-4. Adults $5, seniors 60 & older and students $4; discounts to members. Closed New Year's Day; Independence Day; Thanksgiving; Christmas. ♿
Attendance: 5,000 (estimated)
Membership: Student & Senior $25; Individual $40; Dual & Family $50; Patron $100; Sustainer $250; Sponsor $500; Benefactor $1,000 & up.

* **PRINCETON UNIVERSITY ART MUSEUM, (M),** Princeton, NJ 08544-1018. Tel.: 609-258-3788 & 1860. Fax: 609-258-3610.
E-mail: artmuseum@princeton.edu
Web Site: artmuseum.princeton.edu
Formerly: The Art Museum, Princeton University
Founded: 1882.
Congressional District: 5
Key Personnel: Dir., James C. Steward; Docent Chm. (V), Kathy Oechler; Friends Pres. (V), Alice St. Claire-Long; Cur. Ancient Art, J. Michael Padgett; Research Cur. Later Western Art, Betsy Rosasco; Peter J. Sharp Cur. & Lecturer, Art of Ancient America, Bryan Just; Museum Shop Mgr., Christine Hacker; Cur. Asian Art, Cary Y. Liu; Assoc. Cur. American Art, Karl Kusserow; Mgr. Mktg. & Public Rels., Christine Liggio; Mng. Editor, Jill Guthrie; Conservator, Norman Muller; Chief Registrar, Maureen McCormick; Cur. Prints & Drawings, Laura M. Giles; Cur. Education, Caroline Harris; Business Mgr., Michael Brew; Curatorial Fellow, Contemporary Art, Kelly Baum; Asst. Cur. Prints & Drawings, Calvin Brown; Cur. Photography, Joel Smith; Asst. Cur. Prints & Drawings - Italian, Lia Markey; Asst. Cur. Asian Art, Xiaojin Wu.
Personnel Profile: Full-Time Paid 53; Part-Time Paid 9; Part-Time Volunteers 120; Interns 13.
Governing Authority: university. Parent Institution: Princeton University. Tax-exempt: 501(c)(3).
Art Museum.
Collections: ranging from ancient to modern art; Classical; Far Eastern Art especially Chinese; pre-Columbian, African, European & American paintings, sculpture, prints & drawings; European, American & Japanese photographs.
Major Exhibits: Emmet Gowin: A Collective Portrait, 11/09-2/10; Architecture as Icon: Perception and Representation in Byzantine Art (T), 3/10-6/10; Inner Sanctum: Memory and Meaning in Princeton's Faculty Room at Nassau Hall, 4/10-7/10; Gaugin's Paradise Remembered: The Noa Noa Prints, 9/10-1/11; Land, Space, Territory, 10/10-1/11.
Research Fields: related to collections.
Facilities: Art & museum-related items for sale.
Activities: permanent & temporary exhibitions; gallery and children's talks; guided tours for groups by appointment; viewing of print, drawing and photograph collections by appointment; Sat. & Sun. Highlights Tours.
Publications: quarterly newsletter, Record of the Princeton University Art Museum; catalogs of special exhibitions; notecards; postcards; posters; reproductions.
Hours & Admission Prices: Tues.-Sat. 10-5, Sun. 1-5. No charge; donations accepted. Closed national holidays. ♿
Attendance: 104,082 (accurate)
Membership: University $40; Friend $75; Associate $100; Contributor $200; Patron $350; Benefactor $500; Sponsor $1,000.

PRINCETON UNIVERSITY MUSEUM OF NATURAL HISTORY, Princeton University, Guyot Hall, Princeton, NJ 08544-0001. Mailing Address: 110 W. College Box 430, Princeton, NJ 08544-0430. Tel.: 609-258-4102 & 3832. Fax: 609-258-1334.
E-mail: ehorn@princeton.edu
Founded: 1805.
Congressional District: 7
Key Personnel: Cur. Biological Collections, Elizabeth Horn.
Personnel Profile: Part-Time Paid 1.
Governing Authority: university. Affiliated with Princeton University. Tax-exempt.
Natural History Museum.
Collections: invertebrate paleontology; geology & mineralogy; ornithology; ethnology; archaeology; osteology.
Research Fields: ecology & ornithology.
Activities: formally organized education programs for undergraduate college & graduate students affiliated with Princeton University; inter-museum loan, permanent & temporary exhibitions.
Publications: books & monographs published by Princeton University press.
Hours & Admission Prices: Call for hours. No charge. Closed holidays. ♿

THOMAS CLARKE HOUSE/PRINCETON BATTLEFIELD STATE PARK, 500 Mercer Rd., Princeton, NJ 08540-4810. Tel.: 609-921-0074. Fax: 609-921-0074.
E-mail: pbsp@aol.com
Founded: 1976.
Congressional District: 12
Key Personnel: Cur., John K. Mills.
Personnel Profile: Full-Time Paid 1; Part-Time Paid 1; Part-Time Volunteers 25.
Governing Authority: state. Parent Institution: N.J. Department of Environmental Protection, Division of Parks & Forestry, Trenton, NJ 08625. Tax-exempt.

Historic House: c.1772 Quaker Farm, field hospital after Battle of Princeton.
Collections: Delaware Valley furniture; Revolutionary War displays; Quaker culture; 18th-century farming & domestic items; weapons.
Research Fields: Quaker culture; Battle of Princeton; Princeton & Delaware Valley history; 18th-century farming.
Facilities: 85-acre park.
Activities: guided tours; lectures; films; hobby workshops; organized education programs; docent program; participatory exhibits; demonstrations of historic skills; special events.
Hours & Admission Prices: Wed.-Sat. 10-12 & 1-4, Sun. 1-4. No charge; donations accepted. Closed New Year's Day; Thanksgiving; Christmas. ♿
Attendance: 90,000 (estimated)

Rahway

MERCHANT AND DROVERS TAVERN MUSEUM, 1632 St. Georges Ave., Rahway, NJ 07065-2006. Mailing Address: P.O. Box 1842, Rahway, NJ 07065-7842. Tel.: 732-381-0441.
E-mail: mdtavernmuseum@gmail.com
Web Site: www.merchantanddrovers.org
Key Personnel: Pres., Annette Satkowski; Vice Pres., Ted Nevins; Dir. Museum Operations, Alex Shipley; Progrma Mgr., David Walker; Museum Shop Mgr., Genea Johnson
Historic Building: built in c.1795 . Listed on the National Register of Historic Places.
Collections: early tavern life; local history & culture; photographs; period furnishings.
Facilities: Museum-related items for sale.
Activities: special events; educational programs.
Hours & Admission Prices: Thurs.-Fri., and 1st & 3rd Sat. of month 10-4, 2nd & 4th Sun. of month 1-4; other times by appointment.

Rancocas

INDIAN HERITAGE MUSEUM, 730 Rancocas Rd., Rancocas, NJ 08073. Mailing Address: P.O. Box 225, Rancocas, NJ 08073-0225. Tel.: 609-261-4747.
E-mail: powhatan@powhatan.org
Web Site: www.powhatan.org/museum.html
Governing Authority: Parent Institution: Powhatan Renape Nation.
American Indian History Museum.
Collections: American Indian history & culture; outdoor recreated woodland village; personal artifacts; crafts; art.
Facilities: nature trails.
Activities: tours.
Hours & Admission Prices: Sept.-June Tues. & Thurs. by appointment, 1st & 3rd Sat. 10-3. Adults $7, senior & children $5.

Randolph

HISTORICAL SOCIETY OF OLD RANDOLPH, 630 Millbrook Ave., Randolph, NJ 07869-3730. Mailing Address: P.O. Box 1776, Ironia, NJ 07845-1776. Tel.: 973-989-7095.
E-mail: hsor@juno.com
Web Site: www.randolphnj.org/get_to_know_us/historical_society
Founded: 1979.
Congressional District: 25
Key Personnel: Museum Shop Mgr., Joan Brembs.
Governing Authority: Tax-exempt.
Historical Society Museum: housed in an 1860 farmhouse.
Collections: Randolph's history including industrial, agricultural, resort & suburbia eras; oral histories; school room.
Activities: colonial clothing dress-up for children.
Hours & Admission Prices: Sun. 1-4; tours & other hours by appointment. Adults $2; discounts to AAM & ICOM members; members no charge.
Attendance: 1,500 (estimated)
Membership: Senior 65 & up $10; Individual $15; Family $25; Sustaining $100.

Readington

COLD BROOK SCHOOL, Potterstown Rd., Readington, NJ 08870. Mailing Address: P.O. Box 216, Stanton, NJ 08885-0216. Tel.: 908-236-2327.
Historic Building: housed in a one-room school house, built in 1828.
Collections: period furnishings; personal artifacts.
Activities: tours; demonstrations; 4th grade Partners in History Program. Museum Sponsors: Open House.
Hours & Admission Prices: Call for hours.

Ridgewood

SCHOOLHOUSE MUSEUM OF THE RIDGEWOOD HISTORICAL SOCIETY, INC., 650 E. Glen Ave., Ridgewood, NJ 07450-1905. Tel.: 201-447-3242.
Web Site: www.ridgewoodhistoricalsociety.org
Founded: 1949.
Congressional District: 5
Key Personnel: Pres., Sheila Brogan.
Personnel Profile: Part-Time Volunteers 20.
Governing Authority: nonprofit. Parent Institution: Ridgewood Historical Society. Subsidiary Institution: Schoolhouse Museum. Tax-exempt.
General Museum.
Collections: Bergen County & New Jersey heirlooms from the 17th, 18th & 19th centuries; local Indian artifacts; blacksmith tools; farm tools before the machine age; military; quilts, coverlets. Historic House: 1875 one-room schoolhouse; depicts life in early America in Bergen County from Dutch Era to Victorian Age.
Major Exhibits: Road to Revolution: 18th Century Paramus Valley, 11/09-7/10.
Research Fields: local, community & New Jersey history.
Facilities: reference library of local history, maps & genealogy.
Activities: guided tours; for school children, scouts & adult groups; program meetings; field trips; special exhibits.
Publications: pamphlets, Local History.
Hours & Admission Prices: Thurs. & Sat. 1-3, Sun. 2-4. Adults $5.
Attendance: 400 (estimated)
Membership: Single $25; Family $50; Patron $100; Life $500.

Ringwood

NEW JERSEY BOTANICAL GARDEN AT SKYLANDS (NJBG), Morris Rd., Ringwood, NJ 07456. Mailing Address: P.O. Box 302, Ringwood, NJ 07456-0302. Tel.: 973-962-9534 & 7527. Fax: 973-962-1553.
E-mail: info@njbg.org
Web Site: www.njbg.org
Founded: 1966.
Congressional District: 5
Key Personnel: Pres. (V), Tom Grissom; Treas., Andy Noll; Vice Pres., John Gall; Sec., Frank Dyer; Archivist, John Bristow; Landscape Designer, Rich Flynn; Park Supvr., Rebecca Fitzgerald; Museum Shop Mgr., Sonja Vieth.
Personnel Profile: Part-Time Paid 2; Part-Time Volunteers 205.
Governing Authority: private; nonprofit organization. Parent Institution: Skylands Association. Tax-exempt: 501(c)(3).
Historic House & Site: 44-room Tudor-style manor house & 96-acre botanical garden.
Collections: 16th-century paneling; 42 stained glass medallions dating to Middle Ages.
Facilities: 600-vol. library on gardening & horticulture; 1,200 sq. ft. exhibit space apart from museum. Museum-related items for sale.
Activities: guided house & garden tours; botanical craft workshops; lectures. Annual Events: plant sale; Champagne and Candle-Light Evenings; Harvest Festival; Holiday Open House in December.
Publications: quarterly newsletter, The Skylands Journal; self-guiding brochures, Self-Guiding Tour-Skylands, A Guide to Skylands Manor; A Guide to Garden Ornamentation at Skylands; Solar System; Birding; Lilac; Wildflower.
Hours & Admission Prices: Gardens: daily 8-8. No charge. Manor House Tours: selected Sun. Adults $5, senior citizens $3, children 6-18 $1; children under 6 no charge.
Attendance: 98,000 (estimated)
Membership: Student & Senior $20; Individual $30; Family & Dual $55; Organization & Sponsor $100; Friend $250.

RINGWOOD MANOR, Ringwood State Park, 1304 Sloatsburg Rd., Ringwood, NJ 07456-1706. Tel.: 973-962-2240. Fax: 973-962-2247.
E-mail: rspris@verizon.net
Web Site: www.ringwoodmanor.com
Formerly: The Forges and Manor of Ringwood
Founded: 1936.
Congressional District: 5
Key Personnel: Supt., Rebecca Fitzgerald; Historic Preservationist, Sue Shutte; Cur., Elbertus Prol; Museum Shop Mgr., Ralph Colfax; Asst. Supt., Eric Pain.
Personnel Profile: Full-Time Paid 1; Part-Time Paid 4; Part-Time Volunteers 5; Interns 3.
Governing Authority: state. Parent Institution: New Jersey Dept. of Environmental Protection. Subsidiary Institution: Division of Parks & Forestry. Tax-exempt.
Historic House Museum.
Collections: furniture; archives; paintings; graphics; decorative arts.
Research Fields: New Jersey iron industry 1740-1940.

Facilities: Books & other museum-related items for sale.
Activities: guided tours; permanent exhibitions. Museum Sponsors: Declaration of Independence read in July; Victorian Christmas in December.
Hours & Admission Prices: Wed.-Sun. 10-4. Memorial Day-Labor Day Sat.-Sun. $5; Sept.-May no charge; donations accepted. Closed New Year's Day; Good Friday; Thanksgiving; Christmas. ♿
Attendance: 15,000 (accurate)
Membership: Associate $10; Active $12; Patron $25, $50, $100 & up.

River Edge

BERGEN COUNTY HISTORICAL SOCIETY, (M), 1201-1209 Main St., River Edge, NJ 07661-2026. Mailing Address: P.O. Box 55, River Edge, NJ 07661-9998. Tel.: 201-343-9492.
E-mail: contactbchs@bergencountyhistory.org
Web Site: www.bergencountyhistory.org
Founded: 1902.
Congressional District: 9
Key Personnel: Pres., Deborah Powell; 1st Vice Pres., Michael Trepicchio; Sec., Rosann Pelligrino.
Governing Authority: private; nonprofit organization. Tax-exempt.
Local History Museum: housed in c.1713, 1752 Steuben House.
Collections: furniture; furnishings; china; glass; farm & household tools; paintings; sculptures; books; maps; manuscripts; photographs; toys; quilts & coverlets; folk art; Wolfkiel pottery; clothing.
Research Fields: history of Bergen County; genealogy; architecture.
Facilities: 1,000-vol. library of New Jersey history located at Felician College, Lodi, NJ, available for research by anyone over 18.
Activities: lectures; formally organized programs for adults; inter-museum loan, permanent & temporary exhibitions; outreach program to 4th & 5th grade school children; black studies committee; marker program for historic bldgs.
Publications: softcover, Bergen County history; hardcover, The United Churches of Hackensack & Schraalenburgh; newsletter, In Bergen's Attic.
Hours & Admission Prices: Call for hours. No charge; donations accepted. Closed New Year's; Thanksgiving; Christmas. ♿
Attendance: 15,000
Membership: Student $5; Individual, Historic Organizations & Libraries $15; Family $25; Contributing $30; Corporate $200; Benefactor $1,000.

Roselle Park

ROSELLE PARK MUSEUM, 9 W. Grant Ave., Roselle Park, NJ 07204-1915. Mailing Address: Roselle Park Historical Society, P.O. Box 135, Roselle Park, NJ 07204. Tel.: 908-245-1776.
Web Site: www.rosellepark.org/history/museuminfo.html
Key Personnel: Historian, Pat Pagnetti
History Museum.
Collections: local history; photographs; personal artifacts.
Hours & Admission Prices: Mon. 7pm-9pm, Wed. 10-2.

Rutherford

MEADOWLANDS MUSEUM, 91 Crane Ave., Rutherford, NJ 07070-2539. Tel.: 201-935-1175. Fax: 201-935-9791.
E-mail: meadowlandsmuseum@verizon.net
Web Site: www.meadowlandsmuseum.org
Founded: 1961.
Congressional District: 9
Key Personnel: Dir., Jackie Bunker-Lohrenz; Museum Shop Mgr., Jean Weaver.
Personnel Profile: Part-Time Paid 1; Part-Time Volunteers 16.
Governing Authority: nonprofit organization. Tax-exempt: 501(c)(3).
Local History Museum: housed in Dutch Colonial farm house.
Collections: children's toys & games; local & fluorescent rocks & minerals; textiles; household & kitchenware; local history photographs; local history archives.
Research Fields: local history.
Facilities: 300-vol. library of local history & reference books related to exhibitions available for use on premises by appointment. Museum-related items for sale.
Activities: guided tours; lectures; gallery talks; craft workshops; circulating exhibits; educational work with schools; programs for Girl & Boy scouts.
Publications: e-newsletter.
Hours & Admission Prices: July-Aug. Mon.-Thurs. 1-4, Sun. 2-4; Sept.-June Mon., Wed. & Sat. 1-4, Sun. 2-4; groups by appointment. No charge; donations accepted. Closed New Year's Day; Memorial Day; Independence Day; Labor Day; Thanksgiving; Christmas.
Attendance: 2,500 (estimated)
Membership: Senior & Student $15; Individual $25; Family & Contributor $40; Donor $100; Sponsor $150; Patron $250; Benefactor $500.

Salem

SALEM COUNTY HISTORICAL SOCIETY, (M), 79-83 Market St., Salem, NJ 08079-1910. Tel.: 856-935-5004. Fax: 856-935-0728.
E-mail: info@salemcountyhistoricalsociety.com
Web Site: www.salemcountyhistoricalsociety.com
Founded: 1884.
Congressional District: 2
Key Personnel: Exec. Dir., Tamara C. Barnes; Pres., Phillip G. Correll; Library Staff, Beverly Stanley.
Personnel Profile: Part-Time Paid 6; Part-Time Volunteers 50.
Governing Authority: society; board of trustees. Tax-exempt.
Historic Building, Site & History Museum.
Collections: archaeology; archives; costumes; glass; furniture; art; Indian artifacts; military; textiles; china; silver; glass; early agricultural, manufacturing & fishing equipment. Historic Buildings: 1721 headquarters, Grant Building; 1735 brick law office; 1840s log cabin.
Research Fields: local genealogy research; local history and culture.
Facilities: 1,000-vol. library of historic deeds & records; education center.
Activities: guided tours; lectures; student programs. Society Sponsors: Salem County House & Garden Tour in May.
Publications: quarterly newsletter.
Hours & Admission Prices: Tues.-Sat. 12-4. Adults $3; discounts to WHYY and AAA members; members no charge.
Attendance: 16,000 (estimated)
Membership: Student $10; Individual $25; Family & Household $40; Partner $100; Oak Tree Associate $100-$249; Benefactor $250; Pedersen Provider $250-$499; Life $500; Goodwin Provider $500-$999; Fenwick Benefactor $1,000 & up.

Scotch Plains

OSBORN CANNONBALL HOUSE, 1840 Front St., Scotch Plains, NJ 07076-1103. Tel.: 908-322-6700.
Key Personnel: Cur., Ginger Bishop
Historic House: housed in the former home of John & Abigail Osborn; built c.1760.
Collections: local history; period furnishings & farming equipment; photographs.
Hours & Admission Prices: March-Dec. 1st Sun. of month 2-4.

Sea Girt

NATIONAL GUARD MILITIA MUSEUM OF NEW JERSEY - SEA GIRT, National Guard Training Center, Rte. 71 & Sea Girt Ave., Sea Girt, NJ 08750. Mailing Address: P.O. Box 277, Sea Girt, NJ 08750-0277. Tel.: 732-974-5966.
Governing Authority: nonprofit organization.
Military Heritage Museum.
Collections: New Jersey military heritage; Army National Guard; Air National Guard; Naval Militia of New Jersey; photographs; uniforms; weapons; military vehicles; art; personal artifacts.
Activities: groups tours.
Publications: newsletter.
Hours & Admission Prices: Tues. & Thurs. 10-3; other times by appointment.
Membership: Individual $10; Life $250.

Sea Isle City

SEA ISLE CITY HISTORICAL MUSEUM, 4208 Landis Ave., Sea Isle City, NJ 08243. Mailing Address: P.O. Box 443, Sea Isle City, NJ 08243-0743. Tel.: 609-263-2992.
Founded: 1983.
Key Personnel: Pres. (V), Michael Stafford.
Personnel Profile: Part-Time Volunteers 30.
Historical Museum.
Collections: local history; period furnishings; clothing; photographs.
Facilities: Museum-related items for sale.
Publications: newsletter, Excursion.
Hours & Admission Prices: Summer: Mon.-Sat. 10-1; Winter: by appointment. No charge.
Membership: Annual $10.

Short Hills

CORA HARTSHORN ARBORETUM AND BIRD SANCTUARY, 324 Forest Dr. S., Short Hills, NJ 07078-2308. Tel.: 973-376-3587. Fax: 973-379-5059.
E-mail: info@hartshornarboretum.com
Web Site: www.hartshornarboretum.com
Founded: 1960.

Congressional District: 1
Key Personnel: Exec. Dir., James Peck; Pres., Steve Kany; Bus. Mgr., Ann Brandeis.
Personnel Profile: Full-Time Paid 2; Part-Time Paid 5; Interns 4.
Governing Authority: nonprofit. Tax-exempt.
Nature Center.
Collections: fossils; birds; insects.
Facilities: nature conservation center; classrooms. Museum-related items for sale.
Activities: guided tours; lectures; hobby workshops; formally organized education programs; docent program or council.
Hours & Admission Prices: Gardens & Grounds: dawn to dusk. Stone House: Mon.-Fri. 9-5, Sat. 10-3. Closed New Year's Eve & Day; Christmas Eve, Day & week.
Membership: Individual $20; Family $30; Sponsor & Group $50; Patron $100; Benefactor $500; Life $1,000.

Somers Point

ATLANTIC HERITAGE CENTER, (M), 907 Shore Rd., Somers Point, NJ 08244-2335. Mailing Address: P.O. Box 301, Somers Point, NJ 08244-0301. Tel.: 609-927-5218.
E-mail: ahcinfo@comcast.net
Web Site: www.atlanticheritagecenternj.org
Formerly: Atlantic County Historical Society
Founded: 1913.
Congressional District: 2
Key Personnel: Pres., Richard Squires; Cur., Ruth C. Gold; Asst. Cur., Allen Pergament; Librarian, Dale Lonkart.
Personnel Profile: Full-Time Volunteers 2; Part-Time Paid 1; Part-Time Volunteers 30; Interns 2.
Governing Authority: executive board. Subsidiary Institution: Risley Homestead Committee. Tax-exempt.
History Museum.
Collections: Victorian & 20th-century decorative, useful & fine arts; costumes; textiles; maritime including ship models & half-hulls; instruments; paintings; American Indian; images 1860-1960; military including weapons & uniforms; manuscripts from 1695; collectibles. Historic Houses: 1714 Somers Mansion: house is state owned but furnished (on loan) from our 18th & early 19th-century collections; c.1790 Risley Homestead: Oysterman's farmhouse, 19th & 20th-century furnishings.
Research Fields: genealogy; local & U.S. history.
Facilities: research library; lecture hall.
Activities: guided tours; lectures; permanent & temporary exhibitions.
Publications: yearbook; newsletter, Atlantic Heritage; books, Absegami Yesteryear; Railroading in Atlantic County; Early History of Atlantic County; Glory At Last; Our Stories.
Hours & Admission Prices: Museum: Wed.-Sat. 10-3:30. No charge; donations accepted. Library: Wed.-Sat. 10-3:30. Research: $5; members no charge. Closed New Year's Day; Good Friday & day after; Independence Day; Thanksgiving; Christmas.
Attendance: 2,500
Membership: Junior $10; Summer $15; Individual $25; Family $35; Nonprofit Organization $50; Corporate Partner $250; Life $250-$500; Corporate Patron $500; Corporate Benefactor $1,000.

SOMERS MANSION, 1000 Shore Rd., Somers Point, NJ 08244-2360. Tel.: 609-927-2212. Fax: 609-927-1827.
Founded: 1941.
Congressional District: 2
Key Personnel: Resource Interpretive Specialist-Historic Research, John Morsa.
Personnel Profile: Full-Time Paid 1.
Governing Authority: state. Parent Institution: NJ Division of Parks & Forestry 08625. Tax-exempt.
Historic House: 1720 Richard Somers House.
Collections: period furnishings.
Activities: guided tours.
Hours & Admission Prices: Wed.-Sun. 10-12 & 1-4. No charge. Closed New Year's Day; Thanksgiving; Christmas.
Attendance: 3,500 (accurate)

Somerset

UKRAINIAN MUSEUM OF NEW JERSEY, INC., 135 Davidson Ave., Somerset, NJ 08873-1358. Tel.: 732-356-0090.
Formerly: Museum of the Ukrainian Orthodox Memorial Church
Key Personnel: Dir., Archbishop Antony
Religious Museum.
Collections: Ukrainian history; religious artifacts; photographs; Ukrainian famine memorial.
Hours & Admission Prices: Call for hours.

Somerville

OLD DUTCH PARSONAGE, 71 Somerset St., Somerville, NJ 08876-2812. Tel.: 908-725-1015.
Founded: 1947.
Key Personnel: Cur., Jim Kurzenberger.
Governing Authority: state. Administered by the Division of Parks & Forestry, New Jersey, Dept. of Environmental Protection, Trenton, NJ 08625.
Historic House: 1751 old Dutch parsonage, home of Jacob Hardenbergh, founder of Rutgers University and its first president.
Collections: Dutch furnishings; replica of period pieces.
Activities: guided tours; hands on workshops for adults & children; lectures; concerts.
Hours & Admission Prices: Wed.-Sat. 10-12 & 1-4, Sun. 1-4; groups by appointment. No charge. Closed federal & state holidays.
Attendance: 5,000

WALLACE HOUSE, 71 Somerset St., Somerville, NJ 08876-2812. Tel.: 908-725-1015.
Founded: 1947.
Key Personnel: Cur., Jim Kurzenberger.
Governing Authority: state. Administered by the Division of Parks & Forestry, New Jersey, Department of Environmental Protection, Trenton, NJ 08625.
Historic House: 1778 Wallace House, Washington's headquarters during winter of 1778-79.
Collections: original architectural features; kitchen and slave quarters; furnishings; glass.
Research Fields: Revolutionary War; local history.
Activities: guided tours; interpretation programs.
Publications: newsletter, Washington Place Dispatch.
Hours & Admission Prices: Wed.-Sat. 10-12 & 1-4, Sun. 1-4. Groups of 10 or more by appointment only; school groups limited to 30 students at a time. Closed federal & state holidays.
Attendance: 5,000
Membership: Individual $7; Family $10

South Orange

WALSH GALLERY, SETON HALL UNIVERSITY, 400 S. Orange Ave., South Orange, NJ 07079-2697. Tel.: 973-275-2033. Fax: 973-761-9550.
E-mail: jeanne.brasile@shu.edu
Web Site: library.shu.edu/gallery
Key Personnel: Dir., Jeanne Brasile
Art Gallery.
Collections: paintings; photographs; sculpture.
Hours & Admission Prices: Mon.-Thurs. 10:30-4:30; call to confirm.

Springfield

SPRINGFIELD HISTORICAL SOCIETY, 126 Morris Ave., Springfield, NJ 07081. Mailing Address: 166 Milltown Rd., Springfield, NJ 07081-2313. Tel.: 973-376-4784 & 912-4464.
Web Site: www.springfield-nj.us/index.php?page=history
Founded: 1954.
Congressional District: 7
Key Personnel: Pres., Margaret Bandrowski
Local History Museum.
Collections: local history items; drawings; prints; decorative arts; costumes; textiles. Historic House: c.1741 The Cannon Ball House.
Facilities: 500-vol. library of local history books available for use by appointment.
Activities: guided tours.
Publications: book, Battle of Springfield.
Hours & Admission Prices: By appointment. Donation Requested $1. Closed holidays.
Attendance: 50 (estimated)
Membership: Annual $7.50; Institutional $25; Life $100.

Stanton

BOUMAN-STICKNEY FARMSTEAD, (M), 114 Dreahook Rd., Stanton, NJ 08885. Mailing Address: P.O. Box 216, Stanton, NJ 08885-0216. Tel.: 908-236-2327.
Key Personnel: Museum Admin., Amy Hollander.
Governing Authority: Parent Institution: Readington Museums.
Historic Buildings.
Collections: period furnishings. Historic Buildings: 1741 Dutch stone bank house; 19th century double corn crib; 1820 Dutch barn.

Activities: demonstrations; tours; educational programs. Museum Sponsors: Open House.
Hours & Admission Prices: Call for hours.

Stone Harbor

THE WETLANDS INSTITUTE, 1075 Stone Harbor Blvd., Stone Harbor, NJ 08247-1424. Tel.: 609-368-1211. Fax: 609-368-3871.
E-mail: coc@wetlandsinstitute.org
Web Site: www.wetlandsinstitute.org
Founded: 1969.
Congressional District: 1
Key Personnel: C.E.O. & Dir., Cindy O'Connor; Chm. (V), Wayne Renniesen; Education, Phil Broder; Museum Shop Mgr., Barbara Whitiker.
Personnel Profile: Full-Time Paid 9; Full-Time Volunteers 20; Part-Time Paid 7; Part-Time Volunteers 40; Interns 19.
Governing Authority: private; nonprofit. Tax-exempt.
Nature Center.
Collections: aquarium, turtles; duck stamp; 6,000 acres of salt marsh; decorative carved decoy collection.
Research Fields: coastal environment.
Facilities: library of coastal wildlife & plants material; aquarium; educational facilities; nature & conservation center; birdwatching trails; viewing decks. Gift items for sale.
Activities: guided tours; lectures; films; study clubs; hobby workshops; organized education programs for children, adults, undergraduate & graduate students; docent program; annual events.
Publications: quarterly newsletter; annual report.
Hours & Admission Prices: mid-May to mid-Oct. Mon.-Sat. 9:30-4:30, Sun. 10-4; mid-Oct. to mid-May Tues.-Sat. 9:30-4:30. Adults $7, children under 12 $5; discounts to AAM members; members no charge. Closed national holidays & two weeks at Christmas. ♿
Attendance: 50,000 (estimated)
Membership: Individual $25; Family $40; Friend $75; Supporting $150; Osprey Club $500; Patron $1,000.

Summit

THE CARTER HOUSE, 90 Butler Pkwy., Summit, NJ 07901-1617. Tel.: 908-277-1747.
E-mail: president@summitnjhistory.org
Web Site: www.summitnjhistory.org/carter.php
Key Personnel: Pres., Lynn Forsell.
Governing Authority: Parent Institution: The Summit Historical Society.
Historic House: former home of Benjamin Carter; built in 1741.
Collections: local history; period furnishings; books; photographs.
Hours & Admission Prices: Call for hours. No charge.

REEVES-REED ARBORETUM, 165 Hobart Ave., Summit, NJ 07901-2908. Tel.: 908-273-8787. Fax: 908-273-6869.
E-mail: reevesreedarboretum@juno.com
Web Site: www.reeves-reedarboretum.org
Founded: 1974.
Congressional District: 12
Key Personnel: Exec. Dir., Gayle Petty-Johnson; Pres., Patty Olsen.
Personnel Profile: Full-Time Paid 7; Part-Time Paid 3; Interns 1.
Governing Authority: nonprofit organization.
Arboretum & Botanical Garden.
Collections: specimen trees; herbs; rose garden; daffodils; perennials; wildflowers; daylilies; wildlife habitat with pond and aquatic life; azaleas; rhododendrons; historical formal gardens. Historic Building: 1889 house.
Research Fields: environmental education; preservation; conservation; horticulture; gardening & garden design.
Facilities: 700-vol. library of botanical & horticultural books available for research to the public & members during office hours, members may check out books; woodlands; formal, historical gardens; classrooms; education center. Museum-related items for sale.
Activities: guided tours; lectures; docent program; adult garden tours; gardening; workshops; field trips; guided trail walks for groups; special environmental education classes outdoors for Scouts or Brownies; children's summer nature camp; poetry readings & concerts; rental facilities. Arboretum Sponsors: Networks to Nature; Elephant Tree nature camp; family events; fund-raisers; collaborative education classes outdoors for inner-city children.
Publications: newsletters; trail guides; brochures: adult education & membership information; herb garden brochure.
Hours & Admission Prices: Grounds: daily dawn-dusk. Office: Mon.-Fri. 9-5. No charge; donations accepted. ♿
Attendance: 25,000 (estimated)
Membership: Senior Citizen $35; Individual $50; Family & Club $75; Friend $100; Patron & Corporate $250; Benefactor $500; Sponsor $1,000. Tuition reductions for members.

* **VISUAL ARTS CENTER OF NEW JERSEY, (M),** 68 Elm St., Summit, NJ 07901-3472. Tel.: 908-273-9121. Fax: 908-273-1457.
E-mail: info@artcenternj.org
Web Site: www.artcenternj.org
Founded: 1933.
Congressional District: 7
Key Personnel: Exec. Dir., Marion Grzesiak; Chm. Bd. Trustees, Rachel Weinberger.
Personnel Profile: Full-Time Paid 10; Part-Time Paid 6; Part-Time Volunteers 300; Interns 2.
Governing Authority: nonprofit. Tax-exempt: 501(c)(3).
Visual Arts Center.
Collections: works by contemporary artists.
Research Fields: artists with disabilities.
Facilities: educational facilities. Art work for sale.
Activities: lectures; concerts; temporary & permanent exhibitions; workshops; classes; demonstrations; education programs; docent tours.
Publications: newsletter; exhibition catalogues; quarterly class brochure.
Hours & Admission Prices: Mon.-Thurs. 9:30-8, Fri. 9:30-4:30; tours by appointment. Suggested Donation: adults $5, seniors & children $3; discounts to AAM & ICOM members; seniors & children under 12 no charge. Closed New Year's Eve & Day; Martin Luther King Jr. Day; Easter; Memorial Day; Independence Day; Labor Day; Columbus Day; Thanksgiving & day after; Christmas Eve & Day. ♿
Attendance: 50,000 (estimated)
Membership: Senior, Students 18 & over, & Art Educator $35; Individual $50; Dual & Family $75; Contributor $250; Friend $125; Supporter $500; Benefactor $1,000; Art Patron $5,000.

Sussex

DAR VAN BUNSCHOOTEN MUSEUM, 1097 Rte. 23, Sussex, NJ 07461-3732. Tel.: 973-875-5335 & 4058.
E-mail: bjsauve@ptd.net
Historic House Museum: housed in the former home of Rev. Elias Van Bunschooten; built in 1787. Listed on the National Register of Historic Places.
Collections: personal artifacts; furnishings; clothing; quilts; china & cookware; Revolutionary War weapons; paintings; dolls; farm implements. Historic Buildings: barn; ice house; wagon house.
Facilities: library.
Activities: docent-led tours; research. Annual Event: Christmas in July.
Hours & Admission Prices: May 15 to Oct. 15 Thurs. & Sat. 1-4; groups by appointment. Adults $4, children $1.

SPACE FARMS ZOO AND MUSEUM, 218 Rt. 519, Sussex, NJ 07461-2800. Tel.: 973-875-3223. Fax: 973-875-9397.
E-mail: info@spacefarms.com
Web Site: www.spacefarms.com
Founded: 1927.
Congressional District: 5
Key Personnel: C.E.O., Parker Space; Museum Shop Mgr., Jill Space.
Personnel Profile: Full-Time Paid 5; Part-Time Paid 10; Part-Time Volunteers 2.
Governing Authority: individual operation.
General Museum and Zoo.
Collections: early American tools; household equipment; clocks; phonographs; dolls; guns; autos; wagons; sleighs; farm machinery; Indian artifacts; antiques; mounted wildlife specimens; musical instruments; live wild animals.
Facilities: restaurant; picnic area. Books & gifts for sale.
Activities: formally organized education programs for children.
Hours & Admission Prices: April-Oct. daily 9-5. Adults 13-64 $13.50, seniors 65 & over $12.50, children 3-12 $9; discounts to groups.
Attendance: 80,000

Tenafly

AFRICAN ART MUSEUM OF THE S.M.A. FATHERS, 23 Bliss Ave., Tenafly, NJ 07670-3001. Tel.: 201-894-8611. Fax: 201-541-1280.
E-mail: museum@smafathers.org
Web Site: www.smafathers.org
Founded: 1963.
Congressional District: 9
Key Personnel: Pres., Rev. Michael Moran, S.M.A.; Dir., Robert J. Koenig; Registrar & Collections Mgr., Peter H. Cade.
Personnel Profile: Full-Time Paid 1; Full-Time Volunteers 1; Part-Time Paid 4; Part-Time Volunteers 1.

Governing Authority: board of trustees. Parent Institution: Society of African Missions, Inc. (American Province), 23 Bliss Ave., Tenafly 07670. Tax-exempt: 170(b)(1)(A).
African Art Museum: located at the Society of African Missions, American Provincialate.
Collections: traditional arts of sub-Saharan Africa; masks; sculpture; ritual objects; weapons; musical instruments; architectural elements; tools; household implements; furniture; textiles; costumes & jewelry from Liberia, Ivory Coast, Ghana, Mali, Sierra Leone, Benin, Nigeria, Cameroon, Congo, Gabon, Zaire, Kenya, Tanzania, Ethiopia & South Africa.
Research Fields: traditional visual arts of sub-Saharan Africa.
Facilities: 500-vol. library pertaining to African art, by appointment only; changing collection and special loan exhibitions; 1,300 sq. ft. exhibition space; adjacent cloister garden & chapel; extensive documentary catalogs, brochures & educational materials.
Activities: lectures; concerts; special childrens programs. Museum Sponsors: Annual African Film Festival.
Publications: brochures & catalogs.
Hours & Admission Prices: Daily 10-5; group tours by appointment. No charge; donations accepted. Closed national & religious holidays. ♿
Attendance: 3,000 (estimated)
Membership: Student & Senior Citizen $6; Individual $10; Family $20; Patron $100-$500; Benefactor $600-$2,500.

Teterboro

AVIATION HALL OF FAME AND MUSEUM OF NEW JERSEY, 400 Fred Wehran Dr., Teterboro, NJ 07608-1114. Tel.: 201-288-6344. Fax: 201-288-5666.
E-mail: njahof@verizon.net
Web Site: www.njahof.org
Founded: 1972.
Key Personnel: Dir., Shea Oakley; Pres. (V), W. Timothy McSwain.
Governing Authority: Tax-exempt.
Aviation Museum.
Collections: NJ aviation heritage; military vehicles, aircraft & artifacts; Bell 47C helicopter; 1950s surgical suite replica; Hall of Fame room; Korean War; Curtiss Wright J-5 Whirlwind engine used by Charles Lindbergh; space travel; lighter-than-air flight; photographs; Martin 202 Airliner; AH-1 Cobra helicopter; Lockheed Bushmaster; OV-1A Mohawk; Convair 880 cockpit.
Facilities: research library; theater. Museum-related items for sale.
Activities: lectures; conferences; group meetings; special events.
Hours & Admission Prices: Tues.-Sun. 10-4. Adults $7, senior citizens & children 2 & over $5; discounts to groups of 10 or more; members no charge. Closed New Year's Eve & Day; Easter; Independence Day; Thanksgiving; Christmas Eve & Day.
Attendance: 5,000 (accurate)
Membership: Junior $5; Senior $20; Individual $25; Family $35; Supporting $50; Sustaining $100; Patron $250; Corporate $500.

Titusville

JOHNSON FERRY HOUSE MUSEUM, Washington Crossing State Park, 355 Washington Crossing Penn Rd., Titusville, NJ 08560-1517. Tel.: 609-737-2515. Fax: 609-818-9017. TDD: 609-737-0623.
E-mail: jfhwashxing@fast.net
Founded: 1912.
Congressional District: 5
Key Personnel: JFH - Resource Interpretive Specialist, Nancy Carter Ceperley; VC - Resource Interpretive Specialist, Clay Craighead.
Personnel Profile: Full-Time Paid 1; Part-Time Paid 1; Part-Time Volunteers 7.
Governing Authority: state. Parent Institution: New Jersey Dept. of Environmental Protection, Trenton, NJ. Tax-exempt.
Historic Building Museum & Visitor Center: housed in a c.1740, ferry house in which George Washington & his officers met after crossing the Delaware River & before the march to Trenton.
Collections: Ferry House Museum: houses colonial furniture, domestic & decorative items; recreation of 18th-century kitchen garden. Visitors Center: houses 900 American Revolutionary War artifacts.
Research Fields: domestic life on an 18th-century ferry plantation before & during the Revolution; early American spiritual heritage.
Facilities: picnic areas; playgrounds; foot paths.
Activities: guided tours of house & garden by request; living history activities & demonstrations; special musical & military events; historic cooking & food preparation; walking & outreach tours; Great Awakening Outreach Tours; lectures; discussions.
Publications: brochure, Johnson Ferry House.
Hours & Admission Prices: Ferry House: Wed.-Sat. 10-4, Sun. 1-4; groups by appointment only. No charge; donations accepted. Parking Fee: Memorial Day-Labor Day Sat.-Sun. $5 per car. Closed New Year's Day; Thanksgiving; Christmas. ♿
Attendance: 10,000 (accurate)
Membership: Friends of the Ferry House: Annual $5.

Toms River

COLONEL CHARLES WATERHOUSE MUSEUM, 17 Washington St., 2nd Fl., Toms River, NJ 08753-7630. Tel.: 732-818-9040. Fax: 732-818-9811.
E-mail: waterhousemuseum@aol.com
Web Site: www.waterhousemuseum.org
Key Personnel: Exec. Dir., Edward C. Sere.
Governing Authority: nonprofit organization.
Art Museum.
Collections: paintings; illustrations; sculpture.
Hours & Admission Prices: Thurs.-Sat. 12-4.

INSECTROPOLIS, 1761 Rte. 9, Toms River, NJ 08755-1296. Tel.: 732-349-7090.
E-mail: info@insectropolis.com
Web Site: www.insectropolis.com
Key Personnel: Pres., Thomas Koerner
Bug Museum.
Collections: hands-on exhibits; insects.
Hours & Admission Prices: July & Aug. Mon.-Sat. 10-3; Sept.-June Tues.-Sat. 10-3. Admission $7; discounts to groups of 15 or more; children under 3 no charge. Closed holidays.

OCEAN COUNTY HISTORICAL SOCIETY, (M), 26 Hadley Ave., Toms River, NJ 08753-7540. Tel.: 732-341-1880. Fax: 732-341-4372.
E-mail: oceancounty.history@verizon.net
Web Site: www.oceancountyhistory.org
Founded: 1950.
Congressional District: 3
Key Personnel: Pres., Hal Unger; Museum Clerk, Kathleen Parente; Clerk Typist, Donna Malfitano.
Personnel Profile: Full-Time Paid 3; Part-Time Volunteers 50.
Governing Authority: society. Affiliated with Ocean County Historical Society. Tax-exempt.
Victorian House Museum; History Museum.
Collections: Indian artifacts; one room schoolhouse interior; LTA history of the dirigible & Naval Air Station at Lakehurst; Revolutionary War salt works; early Ocean County industry; Victorian furniture & costumes; cranberry & blueberry industry.
Research Fields: local genealogy.
Facilities: research library.
Activities: lectures; films; guided school tours.
Publications: picture albums; The New Jersey Coast & Pines, originally published in 1889; History of Monmouth & Ocean Counties New Jersey, originally published in 1890; Tides of Time, originally published in 1940; The Woolman & Rose Atlas of the Jersey Coast, originally published in 1878; Place Names of Ocean County New Jersey 1609-1849; Three Centuries on Island Beach; Chickaree In The Wall: a history of the one-room schools of Ocean County; Along the Toms River; Moored to the Mast: A history of lighter than air at Naval Air Station, Lakewood, NJ; From Manahawkin To New Gretna published 1997; F. Slade Dale: The Life of His Choice published 1998; Living With the Pine Barrens, by Jack Cervetto.
Hours & Admission Prices: Museum: Tues. & Thurs. 1-3, 1st Sat. of month 1-4. Research Facilities: Tues.-Wed & 1st Sat. of month. 1-4, 1st Sat of month. No charge; donations accepted. ♿
Attendance: 10,000 (estimated)
Membership: Individual $30; Family $45; Patron $60; Sponsor $100; Benefactor $250.

TOMS RIVER SEAPORT SOCIETY & MARITIME MUSEUM, 78 E. Water St., Toms River, NJ 08753-7554. Mailing Address: P.O. Box 1111, Toms River, NJ 08754-1111. Tel.: 732-349-9209. Fax: 732-349-2498.
Key Personnel: Pres., Dan Crabbe; Museum Shop Mgr., Crickett Kersens.
Governing Authority: nonprofit organization.
Maritime Museum.
Collections: local maritime heritage & history; watercraft; ship models.
Activities: Annual Event: Wooden Boat Show.
Publications: biannual, Seafarer.
Hours & Admission Prices: Tues., Thurs. & Sat. 10-2. No charge.
Attendance: 2,000 (estimated)
Membership: Individual $15; Family $20; Business $25.

Trenton

MEREDITH HAVENS FIRE MUSEUM OF TRENTON, Trenton Fire Dept. Headquarters, 244 Perry St., 1st Fl., Trenton, NJ 08618-3926. Tel.: 609-989-4038. Fax: 609-989-4280.
E-mail: firemuseum@trentonnj.org
Web Site: trentonfiremuseum.org
Key Personnel: Dir., Richard Laird
Fire Museum.
Collections: fire-fighting history & equipment; photographs; personal artifacts.
Hours & Admission Prices: Mon.-Fri. 9-5, Sat. 10-4; groups of 10 or more by appointment.

MUSEUM OF CONTEMPORARY SCIENCE, (M), 675 S. Clinton Ave., Trenton, NJ 08611-1811. Tel.: 609-396-2002. Fax: 609-396-0676.
E-mail: info@mocsnj.org
Web Site: www.mocsnj.org
Formerly: The New Jersey Center for Life Science
Founded: 1995.
Key Personnel: C.E.O., Daine L. Carroll; Chm. (V), Michael O'Hara.
Personnel Profile: Full-Time Paid 14; Full-Time Volunteers 15; Part-Time Paid 1; Part-Time Volunteers 45; Interns 1.
Governing Authority: Tax-exempt.
Science Museum.
Collections: themes include science, technology & industrial history.
Hours & Admission Prices: Call for hours.

NEW JERSEY OFFICE OF HISTORIC SITES, (M), 501 E. State St., Trenton, NJ 08609-1101. Mailing Address: NJ Div. of Parks & Forestry, P.O. Box 404, Trenton, NJ 08625-0404. Tel.: 609-777-0238. Fax: 609-984-0503.
E-mail: beverly.weaver@dep.state.nj.us
Web Site: www.njparksandforests.org/historic
Founded: 1903.
Key Personnel: Admin., Beverly A. Weaver.
Personnel Profile: Full-Time Paid 1; Interns 1.
Governing Authority: state. Parent Institution: State of New Jersey Dept. of Environmental Protection, Div. of Parks & Forestry. Branch Museums: Allaire Village, Farmingdale; Batsto Village, Hammonton; Boxwood Hall, Elizabeth; Clarke House, Princeton; Craig House, Freehold; Delaware & Raritan Canal State Park, Somerset; Liberty State Park, CRRNJ Terminal, Jersey City; Grover Cleveland Birthplace, Caldwell; Hancock House, Hancock's Bridge; Indian King Tavern, Haddonfield; Johnson Ferry House, Titusville; Old Dutch Parsonage, Somerville; Ringwood Manor, Ringwood; Rockingham, Kingston; Somers Mansion, Somers Point; Steuben House, River Edge; Twin Lights, Highlands; Wallace House, Somerville; Walt Whitman House, Camden; Monmouth Battlefield, Freehold; Princeton Battlefield, Princeton; Fort Mott, Pennsville; Washington Crossing State Park, Titusville; Double Trouble State Park, Bayville. Tax-exempt.
Historic Sites & Villages.
Collections: period furnishings, decorative art; tools; fire engines; manuscripts; transportation vehicles.
Research Fields: 18th- to 20th-century American, New Jersey & maritime history.
Facilities: library; meeting rooms. Museum-related items for sale.
Activities: guided & self-guided tours; permanent & changing exhibits; school programs; special events; craft demonstrations; lecture series; films; reenactments. Annual Event: State History Fair.
Publications: brochures; posters; guidebooks.
Hours & Admission Prices: Wed.-Sat. 10-12 & 1-4, Sun. 1-4. No charge; donations accepted. Closed New Year's Day; Thanksgiving; Christmas; Wed. after a Mon. holiday. ♿
Attendance: 970,000 (estimated)

NEW JERSEY STATE HOUSE, 125 W. State St., Trenton, NJ 08608-1101. Mailing Address: State House Tour Office, State House Annex, P.O. Box 068, Trenton, NJ 08625-0068. Tel.: 609-633-2709. Fax: 609-292-1498.
E-mail: dapril@njleg.org
Web Site: www.njleg.state.nj.us
Founded: 1792.
Congressional District: 4
Key Personnel: Tour Program Coord., David April; Tour Program Educator, Sarah Schmidt.
Personnel Profile: Full-Time Paid 4; Part-Time Paid 2; Part-Time Volunteers 50.
Governing Authority: state; nonprofit. Parent Institution: State of New Jersey. Subsidiary Institution: Office of Legislative Services. Tax-exempt.
Historic Building: The New Jersey State House constructed in 1792.
Collections: period furnishings & equipment associated with New Jersey history and the operations of state government from the early federal period to present day, with special emphasis on portraits of former Governors and legislative figures.
Facilities: multi-purpose space. Museum-related items for sale.
Activities: docent program, guided tours. Museum Sponsors: Heritage Days; Holiday Open House.
Publications: monthly newsletter, Volunteer News.
Hours & Admission Prices: Mon.-Fri. 10-3, Sat. 12-3. No charge. Closed state holidays. ♿
Attendance: 39,277 (accurate)

* **NEW JERSEY STATE MUSEUM, (M),** 205 W. State St., Trenton, NJ 08608-1001. Mailing Address: P.O. Box 530, Trenton, NJ 08625-0530. Tel.: 609-292-6300 & 6301. Fax: 609-599-4098.
E-mail: feedback@sos.state.nj.us
Web Site: www.newjerseystatemuseum.org
Founded: 1895.
Congressional District: 4
Key Personnel: Exec. Dir., Eric Pryor; Pres. Bd. Trustees, Adam Kaufman; Pres. Friends, Mary Flamer; Asst. Cur. Archaeology & Ethnology, Karen Flinn; Business Mgr., Barbara Bower; Supvr. Exhibits, Elizabeth Beitel; Cur. Natural History, David Parris; Asst. Cur. Planetarium, Jay Schwartz; Cur. Fine Art, Margaret M. O'Reilly; Asst. Cur. Natural History Interpretation, Anthony Miskowski; Registrar, Archaeology & Ethnology, Gregory Lattanzi; Asst. Cur. Natural History, Jason Schein; Natural History Registrar, Rodrigo Pellegrini; Cur. Cultural History, Nicholas Ciotola; Museum Shop Mgr., Gini Scataloni; Friends of the State Museum Exec. Dir., Nicole Jannotte; Registrar Fine Art & Cultural History, Jenny Martin-Wicoff.
Personnel Profile: Full-Time Paid 26; Part-Time Paid 10; Part-Time Volunteers 198; Interns 9.
Governing Authority: state. Parent Institution: New Jersey Dept. of State, P.O. Box 300, Trenton, NJ 08625. Tax-exempt.
General Museum.
Collections: fine arts; decorative arts; cultural history; archaeology; ethnology; natural history.
Research Fields: art, science, history, decorative arts, archaeology & ethnology of New Jersey.
Facilities: staff library; planetarium; auditorium; meeting rooms. Museum-related items for sale.
Activities: guided tours; lectures; films; gallery talks; concerts; arts festivals; formally organized education programs; inter-museum loan, permanent, temporary & traveling exhibitions; specimen loans to schools.
Publications: newsletter/calendar; exhibition catalogs; scholarly publications.
Hours & Admission Prices: Tues.-Sat. 9-4:45, Sun. 12-5. No charge; donations accepted. Closed state holidays. ♿
Attendance: 300,000 (estimated)
Membership: Student & Senior $20; Individual $40; Family $60; Contributor $100; Sponsor $250; Patron $500; Founder $1,000; Director's Associate $2,500; Chairman's Circle $5,000.

* **OLD BARRACKS MUSEUM, (M),** 101 Barrack St., Trenton, NJ 08608-2007. Tel.: 609-396-1776. Fax: 609-777-4000.
E-mail: barracks@voicenet.com
Web Site: www.barracks.org
Founded: 1902.
Congressional District: 15
Key Personnel: Exec. Dir., Richard Patterson; Pres. (V), Robert A. Rusciano; Office Mgr., Carolyn M. Cudnik; Museum Shop Mgr., Noelle Voorhees; Chief Historical Interpreter, Gloria Bell; Tour Coord., Linda Mathies.
Personnel Profile: Full-Time Paid 12; Part-Time Paid 7; Part-Time Volunteers 371.
Governing Authority: nonprofit organization. Tax-exempt: 501(c)(3).
History Museum: housed in British military barracks built in 1758 during the French & Indian War.
Collections: Revolutionary War; period rooms; American furniture; ceramics; Chinese porcelain; American silver, firearms & accoutrements; portraits; books & manuscripts; reconstructed barracks interior; exhibits on the Battle of Trenton; 18th century beehive bake oven.
Major Exhibits: A Pawn in the Great Conflict for Empire: NJ's Role in the French & Indian War, 11/09-12/10.
Research Fields: 18th-century American military & social history; decorative arts; Delaware Valley culture.
Facilities: Museum-related items for sale.
Activities: tours; permanent & temporary exhibitions; educational programming; first-person historical interpretation; summer history day camp; Fife & Drum camp.
Publications: brochures & pamphlets; quarterly newsletter, The Parade; various publications on the barracks building, collections & the War for Independence in New Jersey.
Hours & Admission Prices: Daily 10-5. Adults $8, senior citizens & students

$6; discounts to adult groups & AAM members; active military, children under 6 & members no charge. Call ahead for handicap assistance. Closed New Year's Day; Easter; Thanksgiving; Christmas Eve & Day. ♿
Attendance: 27,000 (estimated)
Membership: Cadet (Student w/ID) $30; Ensign $40; Lieutenant $60; Captain $125; Major $200. Seniors may deduct 20% off membership levels.

THE 1719 WILLIAM TRENT HOUSE MUSEUM, 15 Market St., Trenton, NJ 08611-2147. Tel.: 609-989-3027. Fax: 609-278-7890.
Web Site: www.williamtrenthouse.org
Formerly: William Trent House
Founded: 1939.
Congressional District: 4
Key Personnel: Dir., M.M. Pernot.
Personnel Profile: Full-Time Paid 4; Part-Time Paid 3; Part-Time Volunteers 18; Interns 3.
Governing Authority: nonprofit organization; municipal. Parent Institution: City of Trenton. Subsidiary Institution: Trent House Association. Tax-exempt: 501(c)(3).
Historic House: 1719 William Trent House.
Collections: early baroque furniture & decorative arts; ceramics; glass.
Research Fields: local history of the Colonial period; biographies of residents; foundation & development of Trenton.
Facilities: 100-vol. library of local history books; classroom; picnic area. Museum-related items & Colonial reproductions for sale.
Activities: guided tours; lectures; programs; events.
Publications: periodic newsletter; brochures; booklet, The 1719 William Trent House Museum.
Hours & Admission Prices: Daily 12:30-4; groups by appointment. Adults $4, senior citizens, students & children 12 and under $2; discounts to AAA & AAM members; members no charge. Closed holidays. ♿
Attendance: 22,000 (estimated)
Membership: Association: Individual $25; Family $45; Sustaining $100; Patron $250; Sponsor $500 & up; Benefactor $1,000 & up.

TRENTON CITY MUSEUM, Ellarslie, in Cadwalader Park, Trenton, NJ 08608. Mailing Address: 319 E. State St., Trenton, NJ 08608-1809. Tel.: 609-989-3632. Fax: 609-989-3624.
E-mail: brianohill@ellarslie.org
Web Site: www.ellarslie.org
Founded: 1971.
Congressional District: 12
Key Personnel: C.E.O. & Dir., Mr. Brian O. Hill; Pres. (V), Brian Murphy; Museum Shop Mgr., Mary Kay Girmsheid.
Personnel Profile: Full-Time Paid 1; Part-Time Paid 2; Part-Time Volunteers 33; Interns 2.
Governing Authority: municipal; nonprofit. Parent Institution: City of Trenton, NJ. Subsidiary Institution: The Trenton Museum Society. Tax-exempt.
General Museum: housed in c.1850 Ellarslie 34-room Tuscan Villa, designed by John Notman.
Collections: Trentoniana; Trenton-made pottery; porcelain; paintings; furniture.
Research Fields: Trenton ceramics; Trenton history; Trenton industry.
Facilities: specialized reference library. Museum-related items for sale.
Activities: guided tours; lectures; films; gallery talks; concerts; docent program; inter-museum loan; permanent, temporary & traveling exhibitions.
Publications: annual, Museum Society Newsletter.
Hours & Admission Prices: Tues.-Sat. 11-3, Sun. 1-4. Suggested Donation: adults $2. Closed national holidays. ♿
Attendance: 13,500 (estimated)
Membership: Student & Senior Citizen $20; Individual $45; Family $65; Patron $125; Donor $250; Sponsor $500; Benefactor & Corporate $1,000.

Tuckerton

GIFFORDTOWN SCHOOLHOUSE MUSEUM, 35 Leitz Blvd., Tuckerton, NJ 08087. Mailing Address: P.O. Box 43, Tuckerton, NJ 08087. Tel.: 609-294-1547.
Governing Authority: Parent Institution: Tuckerton Historical Society.
Historic Building: housed in the former Giffordtown one-room schoolhouse.
Collections: local history & culture; photographs; documents; clothing; newspapers; Native American artifacts; period furnishings; genealogy.
Hours & Admission Prices: June-Sept. Wed. 10-4, Sat. 2-4; Oct.-May Wed. 10-4.

TUCKERTON SEAPORT MUSEUM, (M), 120 W. Main St., Tuckerton, NJ 08087-2237. Mailing Address: P.O. Box 52, Tuckerton, NJ 08087-0052. Tel.: 609-296-8868. Fax: 609-296-5810.
E-mail: info@tuckertonseaport.org
Web Site: www.tuckertonseaport.org
Formerly: Tuckerton Seaport A Project of Barnegat Bay Decoy & Baymen's Museum, Inc.
Founded: 1989.
Congressional District: 3
Key Personnel: Exec. Dir., Paul Hart; Pres. (V), Joseph Martin, Esq.; Dir. Jersey Shore Folklife Center, Jaclyn Stewart; Museum Shop, Charlene Ackerman; Administrative Asst., Dot Dow.
Personnel Profile: Full-Time Paid 4; Part-Time Paid 18; Part-Time Volunteers 400; Interns 2.
Governing Authority: private; nonprofit. Parent Institution: Barnegat Bay Decoy and Baymen's Museum.Tax-exempt: 501(c)(3).
Maritime Museum.
Collections: baymen's tools: oyster tongs, clamming rakes, decoys, eel & clam pots, shrimp nets, snapper poles, fyke nets, bird calls, boat & sail-making tools; charterboats, sneakboxes, garveys, sloops; photographs; life car.
Research Fields: Folk life; folk art.
Activities: lectures; loan exhibitions; workshops; classes; children & adult programs; tours; boat rides (summer). Annual Events: ecotours.
Publications: quarterly newsletter.
Hours & Admission Prices: Daily 10-5. Adults $8, senior citizens 62 & over $6, children 6-12 $3; discounts to AAM members; members, children 5 & under no charge. Closed New Year's Eve & Day; Easter; Thanksgiving; Christmas. ♿
Attendance: 30,000 (accurate)
Membership: Individual $25; Family $35.

Union

CALDWELL PARSONAGE, 909 Caldwell Ave., Union, NJ 07083-6754. Tel.: 908-964-9047.
Founded: 1957.
Congressional District: 7
Key Personnel: Dir., Michael Yesenko; Chm. (V), Thomas Beisler; Pres. (V), Barbara Grillo; Vice Pres. & Museum Shop Mgr., David Arminio; Sec., Nancy Segale; Treas., Anita Centeno.
Personnel Profile: Full-Time Volunteers 1; Part-Time Volunteers 1.
Governing Authority: Parent Institution: Union Township Historical Society. Tax-exempt.
History & Culture Museum: housed in the former home of Presbyterian minister, Rev. James Caldwell; built in 1782. Listed on the National Register of Historic Places.
Collections: local history & culture; clothing, furniture, & paintings of Rev. James & Hannah Caldwell; Revolutionary War history & military artifacts including muskets, swords, cannon balls, & maps; household artifacts; photographs; period artifacts; tools.
Major Exhibits: Farm Tools, 2/10-11/10.
Research Fields: local history.
Publications: Township of Union: A Bicentennial History; Reverend James & Hannah Caldwell.
Hours & Admission Prices: 3rd Sun. of month 1-5; other times by appointment. No charge; donations accepted. ♿
Attendance: 1,000
Membership: Individual $20; Lifetime $100.

CAS GALLERY, Kean University, 1000 Morris Ave., Union, NJ 07083-7133. Tel.: 908-737-4452 & 0392. Fax: 908-737-4416.
E-mail: ntetkows@kean.edu
Web Site: www.kean.edu/~gallery/cas-gallery.html
Formerly: James Howe Gallery
Founded: 1971.
Congressional District: 12
Key Personnel: Dir. University Galleries, Neil Tetkowski.
Governing Authority: state. Parent Institution: Kean University. Tax-exempt.
College Art Gallery.
Collections: 19th & 20th century artists: Audubon, Walter Darby Bannard, Werner Drewes, Homer, Nordfeldt, Rauschenberg, Rosenquest, Max Ernst, Tony Smith, Joseph Stella; art by alumni, faculty & undergraduates.
Research Fields: original exhibitions; historical & contemporary; visual communications; interior design & crafts.
Facilities: library of liberal arts & education, college archives, New Jersey history, rare books & rare art books, maps, prints; 1,000 seat auditorium; faculty dining room. Books and crafts for sale in book store.
Activities: gallery talks to community; programs for museum training, theory, practice, internship; gallery openings.
Publications: George Segal Portraits: Drawings & Sculpture.
Hours & Admission Prices: Sept.-May Mon.-Thurs. 11-5; other times by appointment. No charge. Closed college holidays. ♿

LIBERTY HALL MUSEUM AT KEAN UNIVERSITY, 1003 Morris Ave., Union, NJ 07083-7120. Tel.: 908-527-0400. Fax: 908-352-8915.
E-mail: libertyhall@kean.edu
Web Site: kean.edu/libertyhall
Founded: 1968.
Congressional District: 7
Key Personnel: C.E.O., John Kean, Sr.; Pres. (V), Joel D. Siegel, Esq.; Exec. Dir., Richard J. O'Neill; Dir. Operations, William P. Schroh, Jr.; School & Family Programs, Lorraine Bartone; Collections & Historic Bldgs., Susan Garino.
Personnel Profile: Full-Time Paid 4; Interns 10.
Governing Authority: private; nonprofit organization. Tax-exempt: 501(c)(3).
Historic Building: c.1772 home of Gov. William Livingston, the first elected governor of New Jersey.
Collections: Livingston & Kean family history from 1770s-1990s. Historic Buildings: carriage house; wagon shed; ice house; fire house.
Facilities: formal gardens. Museum-related items for sale.
Activities: docent program; formal education programs for children; guided tours; seasonal special events.
Hours & Admission Prices: Wed.-Sat. 10-4, Sun. 12-4. Adults $10, seniors & students $6; discounts AAM & ICOM members; children under 3 & members no charge. ♿
Attendance: 12,000 (accurate)
Membership: Senior & College Student $20; Individual $25; Grandparent & Single Parent $35; Family $45; Military $75; Colonist $150; Rebel $250; Patriot $500.

Upper Montclair

MONTCLAIR STATE UNIVERSITY ART GALLERIES, (M), Valley Rd. & Normal Ave., Upper Montclair, NJ 07043. Tel.: 973-655-3382. Fax: 973-655-7665.
E-mail: artgalleries@mail.montclair.edu
Web Site: www.montclair.edu/arts/galleries
Founded: 1972.
Congressional District: 8
Key Personnel: Dir., Teresa Rodriguez.
Personnel Profile: Full-Time Paid 2; Part-Time Paid 3; Interns 2.
Governing Authority: public college; nonprofit. Tax-exempt.
University Art Gallery.
Collections: sculpture; drawings; photos; fine art; paintings; posters; prints.
Facilities: 1,800 sq. ft. exhibit space.
Activities: temporary exhibitions.
Publications: catalogs; brochures.
Hours & Admission Prices: Sept.-July Tues.-Wed. & Fri.-Sat. 10-5, Thurs. 12:30-7:30. No charge; donations accepted. Closed New Year's Day; Good Friday; Easter; Labor Day; Thanksgiving; Christmas. ♿
Attendance: 5,000 (estimated)

THE PRESBY MEMORIAL IRIS GARDENS, 474 Upper Mountain Ave., Upper Montclair, NJ 07043-1523. Tel.: 973-783-5974. Fax: 973-783-3833.
E-mail: presbyiris@comcast.net
Web Site: presbyirisgardens.org
Founded: 1927.
Key Personnel: Pres. (V), Fran Pelzman Liscio; Dir., Linda Sercus.
Governing Authority: Tax-exempt.
Display Garden.
Collections: 6 species & over 2,000 varieties of irises.
Activities: children's outreach programs; children's iris art exhibit; group tours; iris identification classes; composting classes. Museum Sponsors: Memorial Weekend Lawn Party.
Hours & Admission Prices: mid-May to early June 10-8. No charge; donations accepted. ♿
Attendance: 6,000 (estimated)
Membership: Annual $35.

Upper Saddle River

UPPER SADDLE RIVER HISTORICAL SOCIETY, 245 Lake St., Upper Saddle River, NJ 07458-1699. Tel.: 201-327-8644.
Web Site: usrhistoricalsociety.org
Historical Society Museum: housed in the Hopper-Goetschius House.
Collections: area history & culture; photographs; personal artifacts.
Activities: special events; meetings. Museum Sponsors: Spring Concert; Harvest Fair in Fall; Old Time Holiday Open House in December.
Hours & Admission Prices: June-July Sun. 2-4; other times by appointment.

Wayne

BEN SHAHN GALLERIES AT WILLIAM PATERSON UNIVERSITY OF NEW JERSEY, 300 Pompton Rd., Wayne, NJ 07470-2152. Tel.: 973-720-2654. Fax: 973-720-3290.
E-mail: einreinhofern@wpunj.edu
Web Site: www.wpunj.edu
Founded: 1969.
Key Personnel: Dir. & Cur., Nancy Einreinhofer, Ph.D.; Public Rels., Mary Beth Zeman; Gallery Asst., Margaret Culmone.
Personnel Profile: Full-Time Paid 2; Part-Time Paid 6; Part-Time Volunteers 10; Interns 3.
Governing Authority: state government & public college. Parent Institution: The William Paterson University of New Jersey. Tax-exempt: 501(c)(3).
College Art Gallery.
Collections: 19th-century landscape paintings; sculptures; 1950s-present; African & Oceanic; artists' book; outdoor sculpture.
Facilities: 5,000 sq. ft. exhibit space.
Activities: guided tours; lectures; traveling exhibitions. Museum Sponsors: Art at Lunch, seven slide & lectures by faculty & docents on Thursdays during each semester - fee required.
Publications: exhibition catalogs.
Hours & Admission Prices: Mon.-Fri. 10-5, Sat.-Sun. by appointment. No charge. Closed holidays. ♿
Attendance: 10,000 (estimated)
Membership: Student & Senior $10; General $20.

DEY MANSION MUSEUM, 199 Totowa Rd., Wayne, NJ 07470-3108. Tel.: 973-696-1776. Fax: 973-696-1365; 973-523-8712 (parks).
Formerly: Dey Mansion/Washington's Headquarters
Founded: 1934.
Congressional District: 8
Key Personnel: Dir. & Cur., Raymond J. Wright; Coord., Arlene R. Potenzone.
Governing Authority: county. Maintained & operated by The Passaic County Dept. of Parks.
Historic House Museum: headquarters of the Continental Army during July, October-November, 1780.
Collections: period furniture restored & furnished in 18th-century style; early American artifacts; gardens.
Research Fields: history.
Facilities: picnic area.
Activities: guided tours. Annual Events: Military Group Day; Craft Days.
Publications: quarterly newsletter.
Hours & Admission Prices: Wed.-Fri. 1-4, Sat.-Sun. 10-12 & 1-4; group tours by appointment, last tour begins at 3:30. Adults $1; children under 10 no charge. Closed major holidays.
Attendance: 3,500 (accurate)

VAN RIPER-HOPPER HOUSE MUSEUM AND MEAD-VAN DUYNE HOUSE MUSEUM, 533 Berdan Ave., Wayne, NJ 07470-2026. Tel.: 973-694-7192 & 1800, ext. 3258. Fax: 973-694-9100.
Web Site: www.waynetownship.com/
Founded: 1964.
Congressional District: 8
Key Personnel: Chm., Wayne Histcom; Pres., Bob Monacelli.
Governing Authority: municipal. Affiliated with Township of Wayne. Tax-exempt.
Historic House: 1786 Dutch Colonial Farmhouse restored.
Collections: furnishings from Colonial period to 1860; Indian artifacts; clothing; artifact display; A.P. Terhune, Sunnybank & Collie artifacts and books. Historic House: 18th century, Mead-Van Duyne House Museum.
Research Fields: early Township homes; brick making; local archaeology.
Facilities: 100-vol. library available by appointment for higher education research & local genealogy; archaeology lab. Postcards, pamphlets & local history books for sale.
Activities: guided tours; lectures; formally organized education programs; slides; films; concerts; school loan service; lectures; historic skills workshops.
Publications: book, Under The Sign of the Eagle; The Van Riper Hopper House; Artist Coloring Book of Historical Wayne N.J; A Wondrously Beautiful Valley & Commemorative History of Wayne, NJ; The Singack and Mead's Basin Brickyards in Wayne Township; The Archaeology of Wayne; Max Schrabisch Rockshelter Archaeologist; pictorial history of Wayne.
Hours & Admission Prices: Sept.-June 1st Sat. 10-2; other times by appointment. Guided House Tour: adult $5, child $3. Closed New Year's Day; Christmas.
Attendance: 1,200 (accurate)
Membership: Individual $15; Family $25; Lifetime $100; Corporate & Business $250.

West Milford

WEST MILFORD MUSEUM, 1480 Union Valley Rd., West Milford, NJ 07480-1338. Tel.: 973-728-1823.
E-mail: museum@westmilford.org
Web Site: www.westmilfordmuseum.org
Key Personnel: Chairperson, Tonya Cubby; Vice Chairperson, Mary Kochka; Treas., Adrian Birdsall
History Museum: built in 1860s, originally a Methodist Episcopal Church, later became West Milford's Town Hall 1912-1958.
Collections: town history; 19th century life; art; music; political memorabilia; weaponry; farming tools; toys; Native American artifacts.
Activities: lectures; demonstrations; special events.
Hours & Admission Prices: Sat. 1-4, group visits by appointment.

West Orange

EDISON NATIONAL HISTORIC SITE, 221 Main St., West Orange, NJ 07052-5612. Tel.: 973-324-9973. Fax: 973-736-8496. TDD: 973-243-9122.
E-mail: edis_superintendent@nps.gov
Web Site: www.nps.gov/edis
Founded: 1956.
Congressional District: 8
Key Personnel: Supt., Maryanne Gerbauckas; Asst. Supt., Theresa Flynn Jung; Assoc. Historian, Tom Jeffrey.
Personnel Profile: Full-Time Paid 20.
Governing Authority: federal. Administered by National Park Service, U.S. Dept. of Interior. Tax-exempt.
Historic Site: 20 historic structures from 1880-1887 including Glenmont home & laboratory of Thomas A. Edison.
Collections: Edison archives; photographs; sound recordings; industrial & scientific machinery & equipment; late 19th-century decorative arts.
Research Fields: 19th to 20th-century American history; history of technology & science; Edison related technologies including electricity, motion picture & sound recording.
Facilities: archives of 4.5 million documents for use by appointment only. Books, postcards, & museum-related items for sale.
Activities: guided tours; films; permanent exhibitions; education programs; special events.
Publications: The Papers of Thomas A. Edison.
Hours & Admission Prices: Estate: Fri.-Sun. 12-4. Grounds: 11:30-5. Laboratory: Wed.-Sun. 9-5; groups by appointment. Adults $7 (seven day pass); youth under 16 no charge. Annual Park Pass: $30. ♿
Attendance: 60,000 (estimated)
Membership: Friends of Edison National Historic Site: Individual $15; Family $25; Patron $100.

ESSEX COUNTY'S TURTLE BACK ZOO, 560 Northfield Ave., West Orange, NJ 07052-2431. Tel.: 973-731-5800. Fax: 973-731-1059.
Web Site: www.turtlebackzoo.com
Founded: 1963.
Congressional District: 13
Key Personnel: C.E.O., Jeremy Goodman, D.V.M.; Zoological Society Pres. (V), John Doefinger.
Personnel Profile: Full-Time Paid 22; Part-Time Paid 100; Part-Time Volunteers 80; Interns 5.
Governing Authority: county. Parent Institution: Essex County Park System. Tax-exempt.
Zoo.
Collections: Wolf Woods; tortoises; farm animals; specimens of live wild animals; bobcats; llamas; bison; elk; penguins; otters; cougars; reptiles; wallabies; bears; monkeys.
Facilities: food service available. Museum-related items for sale.
Activities: lectures; formally organized & informal education programs for children; permanent & traveling exhibitions; rental facilities; catering.
Publications: zoo newsletter, Turtle Talk.
Hours & Admission Prices: Mon.-Sat. 10-4:30, Sun. 11-5:30. Adults $9, children $5; children under 2 & members no charge. Closed New Year's Day; Thanksgiving; Christmas. ♿
Attendance: 420,000 (accurate)
Membership: Individual $30; Individual Plus One $45; Family $75; Family Plus One $90; Supporting $125; Patron $500; Benefactor $1,000; Director's Circle $5,000.

West Trenton

NEW JERSEY STATE POLICE MUSEUM, River Rd., West Trenton, NJ 08628-0068. Mailing Address: P.O. Box 7068, West Trenton, NJ 08628-0068. Tel.: 609-882-2000, ext. 6401. Fax: 609-882-0321.
Web Site: www.njspmuseum.org
Founded: 1982.
State Police History Museum.
Collections: N.J. State Police history; Trooper training; photographs; videos; Lindbergh kidnapping artifacts; early police facilities, transportation, & weaponry; criminal investigation equipment; surveillance equipment; forensic lab gear; fingerprint-lifting tools; interactive microscopes; seized firearms; police vehicles.
Activities: guided tours.
Hours & Admission Prices: Mon.-Fri. 10-4, Sat. & groups by appointment. No charge. Closed state holidays. ♿

West Windsor

THE GALLERY, MERCER COUNTY COMMUNITY COLLEGE, Communications Center, 1200 Old Trenton Rd., West Windsor, NJ 08550-3407. Tel.: 609-586-4800, ext. 3589.
E-mail: gallery@mccc.edu
Web Site: www.mccc.edu/community-gallery.shtml
Art Museum.
Collections: paintings; photographs; sculpture.
Facilities: 1,300 sq. ft. exhibit space.
Activities: presentations; special events; receptions.
Hours & Admission Prices: Tues. 9-4, Wed. 9-3 & 6-8, Thurs. 11-3. No charge.

Westfield

MILLER-CORY HOUSE MUSEUM, 614 Mountain Ave., Westfield, NJ 07090-3044. Mailing Address: P.O. Box 455, Westfield, NJ 07091-0455. Tel.: 908-232-1776. Fax: 908-232-1740.
Web Site: www.millercoryhouse.org
Founded: 1972.
Key Personnel: C.E.O. & Chm. Bd. Governors, Richard Weiss; Pres. (V), Patricia D'Angelo; Acquisitions, Eileen O'Shea; Museum Shop Mgr., Debbie Bailey.
Personnel Profile: Part-Time Paid 2; Part-Time Volunteers 85.
Governing Authority: nonprofit organization. Parent Institution: Westfield Historical Society, P.O. Box 613, Westfield, NJ 07091. Tel. 908-654-1794. Tax-exempt.
Living Museum & Historic House: 1740 Miller-Cory House, two-story farmhouse.
Collections: period furniture; farm implements; cooking & craft utensils; 18th-century farmhouse & gardens.
Research Fields: 18th-century living, crafts, cooking, history & gardens; relationship of family to town & general area; New Jersey history.
Facilities: library; education center; working open-hearth kitchen; gardens. 18th-century craft items for sale.
Activities: guided tours; lecture & slide shows; open-hearth cooking & craft demonstrations during museum hours; showcase program of 18th-century skills at schools or on premises.
Publications: quarterly bulletin, The Bee Line; in-house bulletin, The Broadside; how-to sheets on 18th-century crafts & skills; study guide; cookbooks, The Groaning Board & Pleasures of 18th-Century Cooking in conjunction with New Jersey Historical Society; children's coloring book on 18th-Century Family Life.
Hours & Admission Prices: mid-Sept. to mid-June Sun. 2-4; Mon.-Fri. group tours by appointment. Adults $2.50, children $1; members no charge. Closed holiday weekends.
Attendance: 2,300 (estimated)
Membership: Volunteer Membership: Junior $5; Active Individual $15; Inactive Individual $25. Friends of Miller-Cory: Supporter $30; Benefactor $50; Patron $100; Life $1,000.

Whippany

WHIPPANY RAILWAY MUSEUM, 1 Railroad Plaza, Rte. 10 W. & Whippany Rd., Whippany, NJ 07981-1505. Mailing Address: P.O. Box 16, Whippany, NJ 07981-0016. Tel.: 973-887-8177.
E-mail: wrym-web@comcast.net
Web Site: www.whippanyrailwaymuseum.net
Founded: 1973.
Congressional District: 11
Key Personnel: Pres. (V), Steven P. Hepler.
Governing Authority: Tax-exempt.
Railway Museum.
Collections: New Jersey's railroad history & transportation heritage; railroad equipment & artifacts; Rahway Valley Locomotive #16; M&E Section Gang Car No. TC-1; delivery truck; PRR Cabin Car 477823; M&E Caboose #1; Railbus No. 10; handcars; Whitcomb switcher; 1907 steam locomotive No. 385; 1942 steam locomotive No. 4039.
Facilities: picnic area.
Activities: train excursions; carry-in picnics.
Hours & Admission Prices: April-Oct. Sun. 12-4. Adults $1, children under 12 $.50.

Whitehouse

EVERSOLE-HALL HOUSE, 511 Rte. 523 S., Whitehouse, NJ 08888. Mailing Address: P.O. Box 216, Stanton, NJ 08885-0216. Tel.: 908-236-2327.
Web Site: www.readingtontwp.org/museum_eversole-hall.html
Key Personnel: Museum Admin., Amy Hollander
Historic Buildings.
Collections: period furnishings; personal artifacts. Historic Buildings: 1830s farmhouse; shoemaker's show; outbuildings.
Activities: tours; demonstrations; 5th grade Partners in History Program; summer camp. Annual Events: Open House; Fall Frolic Family Day.
Hours & Admission Prices: Call for hours.

Wildwood

WILDWOOD HISTORICAL SOCIETY, INC., 3907 Pacific Ave., Wildwood, NJ 08260-4722. Tel.: 609-523-0277.
Formerly: George F. Boyer Museum
Founded: 1963.
Congressional District: 1
Key Personnel: Pres. (V) & Dir., Anna M. Vinci; Cur., Robert J. Scully; Mgr. & Historian, Robert E. Bright.
Personnel Profile: Part-Time Paid 1; Part-Time Volunteers 8.
Governing Authority: municipal. Tax-exempt.
Historical Society Museum.
Collections: 1898-present local newspapers; 120 picture books.
Research Fields: local, county & state history.
Facilities: 1,200-vol. library of New Jersey history available for public use; reading room.
Publications: biannual newsletter.
Hours & Admission Prices: June 16-Sept. Mon.-Sat. 9-2; Oct.-June 15 Thurs.-Sat. 9-2. No charge; donations accepted. Closed national holidays. ♿
Attendance: 5,150 (accurate)
Membership: Student $5; Individual $10; Family $15; Business $50; Life $200.

Wildwood Crest

WILDWOOD CREST HISTORICAL SOCIETY, 116 E. Heather Rd., Wildwood Crest, NJ 08260-4253. Tel.: 609-729-4515.
Web Site: cresthistory.org
Key Personnel: Pres., Kirk Hastings; Sec., Theresa Williams
Historical Society Museum.
Collections: local history & culture; photographs; period furnishings; personal artifacts.
Hours & Admission Prices: Call for hours.

Woodbine

THE SAM AZEEZ MUSEUM OF WOODBINE HERITAGE, 610 Washington Ave., Woodbine, NJ 08270. Mailing Address: P.O. Box 517, Woodbine, NJ 08270-0517. Tel.: 609-861-5355.
Web Site: www.thesam.org
Key Personnel: Exec. Dir., Jane Stark
History Museum.
Collections: local history & culture; photographs; personal artifacts.
Hours & Admission Prices: Wed.-Fri. & Sun. 10-4. Closed New Year's Day; Christmas Day.

Woodbridge

BARRON ARTS CENTER & MUSEUM, 582 Rahway Ave., Woodbridge, NJ 07095-3419. Tel.: 732-634-0413. Fax: 732-634-8633.
E-mail: barronarts@twp.woodbridge.nj.us
Web Site: www.twp.woodbridge.nj.us/barronarts/
Key Personnel: Dir. Cultural Arts, Cynthia Knight.
Personnel Profile: Full-Time Paid 3.
Governing Authority: municipal. Tax-exempt.
Art Museum.
Collections: Woodbridge history.
Hours & Admission Prices: Mon.-Fri. 11-4, Sat.-Sun. 2-4; call to confirm. No charge. Closed holidays. ♿
Attendance: 25,000 (estimated)

Woodbury

FRIENDSHIP FIRE COMPANY MUSEUM, 29 Delaware St., Woodbury, NJ 08096-5925. Tel.: 856-845-0066.
Fire Fighting Museum.
Collections: photographs; badges & awards; wooden water main; leather, tin & high tech plastic helmets; alarm boxes; leather buckets; parade belts & hats from 1843 to present; alarm box list; 1911 Ahrens-Fox steamer; 1799 Philip Mason hand pumper.
Activities: tours.
Hours & Admission Prices: Mon.-Fri. 7:30-4.

GLOUCESTER COUNTY HISTORICAL SOCIETY, 58 N. Broad St., Woodbury, NJ 08096-4629. Mailing Address: 17 Hunter St., Woodbury, NJ 08096-4605. Tel.: 856-848-8531 (museum); 845-7881 (business office); 845-4771 (library). Fax: 856-845-0131.
E-mail: gchs@net-gate.com
Web Site: www.rootsweb.com/~njgchs
Founded: 1903.
Congressional District: 3
Key Personnel: Pres., Barbara L. Turner; Museum Coord., Kathleen Fleming; Library Coord., Barbara Price; Coord. Museum Collections, Patricia A. Hrynenko.
Personnel Profile: Part-Time Paid 4; Part-Time Volunteers 50.
Governing Authority: nonprofit organization. Tax-exempt: 501(c)(3).
General Museum.
Collections: Colonial & Victorian furniture; archives; history; textile collection including quilts, samplers & wedding gowns; glass; children's museum; costumes; militaria; Native American artifacts; newspapers 1824-2008; deeds; maps; census; vital statistics; church records; cemetery inscriptions; court records; wills. Historic Houses: 1765 Hunter-Lawrence-Jessup House; 1786 Moravian Church.
Facilities: 10,000-vol. library of genealogical and historical books & manuscripts.
Activities: genealogy programs & lectures.
Publications: books & pamphlets on the history & genealogy of South Jersey; quarterly bulletin.
Hours & Admission Prices: Museum: Mon., Wed. & Fri. 1-4, last Sun. of month 2-5; other times by appointment. Library: Oct.-May Mon. & Wed.-Fri. 1-4, Tues. 1-4 & 6-9:30, first Sat. of month 10-4, last Sun. of month 2-5; June-Sept. Mon. & Wed.-Fri. 1-4, Tues. 1-4 & 6-9:30, last Sun. of month 2-5. Museum: adults $5, children 6-18 $1; children under 5 & members no charge. Closed national holidays. ♿
Attendance: 3,000 (estimated)
Membership: Student $10; Individual $30; Family $40; Business $100; Life $500.

Wyckoff

JAMES A. MCFAUL ENVIRONMENTAL CENTER OF BERGEN COUNTY, 150 Crescent Ave., Wyckoff, NJ 07481-2751. Tel.: 201-891-5571. Fax: 201-891-5583. TDD: 201-343-7249.
Web Site: www.co.bergen.nj.us/parks
Founded: 1967.
Congressional District: 7
Key Personnel: C.E.O. & Dir., Raymond Dressler; Mgr., Peter Both.
Personnel Profile: Full-Time Paid 7; Part-Time Paid 2; Part-Time Volunteers 6.
Governing Authority: county. Parent Institution: Bergen County Dept. of Parks. Tax-exempt.
Nature Center; Park Museum.
Collections: native wild animals, including birds of prey; plant material of horticultural interest; specialized gardens.
Facilities: 1,000-vol. library of environmental subjects, available for research on premises during regular hours; nature conservation center; 175-seat auditorium; classrooms; 81-acre park; nature trail; herb gardens; ornamental grass garden; observation deck; gazebo; informal gardens featuring rhododendrons, azaleas, large daffodil collection & numerous ground covers; exhibit hall; observatory overlooking small pond.
Activities: guided tours; lectures; films; formally organized education programs for children; permanent & temporary exhibitions; monthly nature art display; study workshops; various recreational activities; wildlife programs.
Publications: Calendar of Events; Nature Trail Guide; Herb Garden Guide.
Hours & Admission Prices: Building: Mon.-Fri. 8:30-4:45, Sat.-Sun. 1-4:45. Park Grounds: Mon.-Fri. 8-sunset, Sat.-Sun. & holidays 8:30-sunset. No charge. ♿
Attendance: 50,000 (estimated)

NEW MEXICO

(167 listings)

Abiquiu

GHOST RANCH PIEDRA LOMBRE EDUCATION & VISITOR'S CENTER, U.S. Hwy. 84, Abiquiu, NM 87510. Mailing Address: HCR 77, Box 15, Abiquiu, NM 87510-9601. Tel.: 505-685-4312.
E-mail: info@ghostranch.org
Web Site: www.ghostranch.org
Formerly: Florence Hawley Ellis Museum of Anthropology and Ruth Hall Museum of Paleontology
Founded: 2005.
Congressional District: 42
Key Personnel: Dir., Cheryl L. Muceus; Cur. Paleontology, Alex Downs; Museum Shop Mgr., Lorraine Velasquez.
Personnel Profile: Full-Time Paid 2; Part-Time Paid 1; Part-Time Volunteers 4.
Governing Authority: nonprofit. Parent Institution: Ghost Ranch in Abiquiu and in Santa Fe. Tax-exempt.
Anthropology Museum.
Collections: prehistoric Gallina & ancestral Tewa cultures; modern ethnographic material of Navajo, Apache, Ute & Spanish; Triassic period reptiles & crelophysis.
Research Fields: archaeological field school at Ghost Ranch.
Facilities: library; conference center; Ruth Hall Museum of Paleontology. Museum-related items for sale.
Activities: loan exhibitions; elderhostel programs. Annual Events: archaeology seminar in summer; fossil collecting seminar in summer; intergenerational dinosaur in summer.
Publications: From Drought to Drought, Gallina Culture Patterns; San Gabriel del Yungue as seen by an Archeologist; Archaeological Remote Sensing Survey of Two Jicarilla Apache Sites.
Hours & Admission Prices: Jan.-Nov. Tues.-Sat. 9-12 & 1-5. Suggested Donation: adults $2, seniors & children $1. Closed Easter; Thanksgiving. ♿
Attendance: 15,496 (accurate)

Acoma Pueblo

ACOMA PUEBLO MUSEUM, NM 23 (12 miles SW of I-40), Acoma Pueblo, NM 87034. Mailing Address: P.O. Box 309, Acoma Pueblo, NM 87034-0309. Tel.: 505-252-1139.
History Museum.
Collections: Indian pottery from the 15th century to the present; photographs & documents relating to the history of Acoma.
Hours & Admission Prices: Winter: 8-4:30. Summer: 8am-7pm.

Alamogordo

ALAMEDA PARK ZOO, 1321 N. White Sands Blvd., Alamogordo, NM 88310. Mailing Address: 1376 E. Ninth St., Alamogordo, NM 88310-5855. Tel.: 505-439-4290. Fax: 505-439-4103.
E-mail: sdiehl@ci.alamogordo.nm.us
Web Site: ci.alamogordo.nm.us/coa/communityservices/zoo.htm
Founded: 1898.
Congressional District: 2
Key Personnel: Dir., Steve Diehl; Support Asst. & Gift Shop Mgr., Kathy Chase.
Personnel Profile: Full-Time Paid 4; Part-Time Paid 4; Part-Time Volunteers 20.
Governing Authority: municipal. Parent Institution: City of Alamogordo. Subsidiary Institution: Alamogordo Friends of the Zoo. Tax-exempt.
Zoo: located in 1898 park.
Collections: 250 animals, 90 indigenous & exotic species.
Research Fields: raptor rehabilitation; Mexican gray wolf captive management program; ring-tailed lemur species survival program.
Facilities: zoological park. Museum-related items for sale.
Activities: guided tours; formally organized education programs for children; temporary exhibitions.
Publications: AFOTZ Thoughts.
Hours & Admission Prices: Daily 9-5. Adults $2.50, senior citizens & children 3-11 $1.50; discounts to groups, AZA & AAZK members. Closed New Year's Day; Christmas. ♿
Attendance: 50,941 (accurate)
Membership: Alamogordo Friends of the Zoo: Junior & Senior Citizen $7.50; Individual $15; Family (inside Otero County) $25; Family (outside Otero County) & Patron $35; Benefactor $75.

* **NEW MEXICO MUSEUM OF SPACE HISTORY, (M),** Top of New Mexico, Hwy. 2001, Alamogordo, NM 88310. Mailing Address: P.O. Box 5430, Alamogordo, NM 88311-5430. Tel.: 575-437-2840; 877-333-6589 (Toll Free). Fax: 575-437-7722.
E-mail: randall.hayes@state.nm.us
Web Site: www.nmspacemuseum.org
Formerly: The Space Center
Founded: 1976.
Congressional District: 2
Key Personnel: C.E.O., Randall Hayes; Chm. & Pres., Rick Berry; Cur., George M. House; Public Affairs, Cathy Harper; Museum Shop Mgr., Val Cory.
Personnel Profile: Full-Time Paid 28; Part-Time Paid 2; Part-Time Volunteers 35.
Governing Authority: state; nonprofit organization. Parent Institution: New Mexico Department of Cultural Affairs, State of New Mexico. Tax-exempt: 501(c)(3).
Space Museum: located near White Sands, home of America's early space program.
Collections: objects documenting the histories of astronautics, astronomy, & space exploration; astronaut memorial garden; International Space Hall of Fame.
Research Fields: scholarly & collection-oriented historical research, astronomy materials for planetarium programs; oral history programs.
Facilities: research library & archives; IMAX dome theatre & planetarium; air & space park. Museum-related items for sale.
Activities: guided tours; lectures; shuttle camp; educational outreach; workshops. Annual Events: Astronomy Day; International Space Day; Independence Day fireworks; Star Party.
Publications: assorted brochures; schedule cards; museum guide book; New Mexico Space Journal; scholarly journals.
Hours & Admission Prices: Daily 9-5. Museum: adults $6, senior citizens & military $5, children 4-12 $4; members & children under 4 no charge. Theatre: adults $6, senior citizens & military $5.50, children 4-12 $4.50. Closed New Year's Day; Christmas. ♿
Attendance: 115,674 (accurate)
Membership: Student $15; Individual $20; Family/Corporate $45, $100 & $250.

TOY TRAIN DEPOT MUSEUM AND TRAIN RIDE, 1991 N. White Sands Blvd., Alamogordo, NM 88310-6200. Tel.: 888-207-3564.
E-mail: railfanewmexico@hotmail.com
Web Site: www.toytraindepot.homestead.com
Key Personnel: Chm., Richard Haskell
History Museum.
Collections: railroad history of New Mexico & Alamogordo; railroad of all scales & gauges.
Hours & Admission Prices: Museum: Wed.-Sun. 12-4. Train: Wed.-Sun. 12:30-4:30. Museum: adults $4. Train: adults $4. Closed Thanksgiving; Christmas.

TULAROSA BASIN HISTORICAL SOCIETY MUSEUM, (M), 1301 N. White Sands Blvd., Alamogordo, NM 88310-6659. Tel.: 505-434-4438. Fax: 505-437-6334.
E-mail: tbhs@zianet.com
Founded: 1964.
Congressional District: 2
Key Personnel: Pres. (V), Dr. Rick Miller; Cur., Dawn T. Santiago; Museum Shop Mgr., M.J. Callaway.
Personnel Profile: Part-Time Paid 1; Part-Time Volunteers 30.
Governing Authority: nonprofit. Parent Institution: Tularosa Historical Society. Tax-exempt.
Historical Society Museum.
Collections: Indian artifacts; fossils; displays dating from early man to the atomic age, centering around the Tularosa Basin; early photographs of the Tularosa Basin & Sacramento mountains; oral histories.
Research Fields: local (Tularosa Basin, Sacramento Mountains, Otero County) history.
Facilities: research library, by appointment for large projects.
Activities: guided tours; lectures; temporary exhibitions.
Publications: quarterly newsletter; semiannual monograph; calendar.
Hours & Admission Prices: Mon.-Fri. 10-4, Sat. 10-3, Sun. 12-3. No charge; donations accepted. Closed federal holidays.
Attendance: 5,500 (accurate)
Membership: Student $5; Individual $15; Family $20; Subscriber $30; Contributing & Life $100. Corporate: Regular $50; Sustaining $500; Benefactor $1,000.

WHITE SANDS NATIONAL MONUMENT, 19955 U.S. Hwy. 70, Alamogordo, NM 88310. Mailing Address: P.O. Box 1086, Holloman A.F.B., NM 88330-1086. Tel.: 505-679-2599. Fax: 505-479-4333.
E-mail: whsa_administration@nps.gov
Web Site: www.nps.gov/whsa
Founded: 1933.
Congressional District: 2
Key Personnel: Supt., Cliff Spencer; Chief Ranger, Rusty Jensen.
Governing Authority: federal, National Park Service. Parent Institution: U.S. National Park Service. Tax-exempt.
Park Museum.
Collections: insects; herbs; birds; mammals; reptiles; amphibians; cultural artifacts; selenite crystals.
Research Fields: local natural history; bird observations.
Facilities: 500-vol. library of material on natural history and geology available on premises & on loan by special written permission of superintendent; native plant display area. General natural history items for sale.
Activities: guided tours; lectures; sound & light geology program; permanent exhibitions.
Publications: brochures; booklets.
Hours & Admission Prices: Winter: daily 8-5; Summer: daily 8-6. Adults $3; children 16 & under no charge. Closed Christmas. ♿
Attendance: 449,471 (accurate)

Albuquerque

ALBUQUERQUE BIOLOGICAL PARK, 903 Tenth St., S.W., Albuquerque, NM 87102-4029. Tel.: 505-768-2000. Fax: 505-764-6281. TDD: 505-764-6297.
E-mail: biopark@cabq.gov
Web Site: www.cabq.gov/biopark
Founded: 1927.
Congressional District: 1
Key Personnel: Dir., Rick Janser; Dir. Dept., Ray D. Darnell.
Personnel Profile: Full-Time Paid 160; Part-Time Paid 20; Part-Time Volunteers 430.
Governing Authority: municipal. Tax-exempt.
Zoo, Aquarium & Botanical Garden.
Collections: mammals; birds; reptiles; fish; plants
Facilities: 250-vol. library of medical & zoological reference material available for use by request.
Activities: guided tours; volunteer programs; education & outreach programs.
Publications: Zooscape.
Hours & Admission Prices: Summer: Mon.-Fri. 9-5, Sat.-Sun. 9-6; Winter: daily 9-5. Aquarium or Zoo: adults 13-64 $7, senior citizens over 64 & children 3-12 $3; discount to AZA members; members & children under 3 no charge. Closed New Year's Day; Thanksgiving; Christmas. ♿
Attendance: 975,000 (accurate)
Membership: Family $50.

*** ALBUQUERQUE MUSEUM OF ART & HISTORY, (M), (I),** 2000 Mountain Rd., N.W., Albuquerque, NM 87104-1459. Tel.: 505-243-7255. Fax: 505-764-6546.
E-mail: clwright@cabq.gov
Web Site: www.cabq.gov/museum
Founded: 1967.
Congressional District: 1
Key Personnel: Chm. (V) Bd., David Smoak; Dir., Cathy L. Wright; Asst. Dir., Thomas C. O'Laughlin; Cur. History, Deb Slaney; Cur. Art, Andrew Connors; Cur. Education, Elizabeth Becker; Museum Shop Mgr., Leah Persons.
Personnel Profile: Full-Time Paid 30; Part-Time Paid 2; Part-Time Volunteers 200.
Governing Authority: municipal. Parent Institution: City of Albuquerque, Albuquerque Museum Foundation. Tax-exempt: 501(c)(3).
Art & History Museum; Sculpture Garden.
Collections: general; decorative arts; regional fine arts & crafts; costumes; photography; objects & artifacts from the Middle Rio Grande Valley from 1500-present.
Major Exhibits: Albuquerque Now, 11/09-4/18/10; Ships on the Line: Albuquerque & The Golden Age of Aviation (T), 11/09-7/10; New Town Albuquerque, 11/22/09-7/10; Turner to Cezanne: Selections from the Davies Collection/National Gallery of Wales (T), 5/16/10-8/8/10; Once More with Feeling: Revisiting Synesthesia in American Art (T), 8/29/10-1/2/11.
Research Fields: Southwestern history & art.
Facilities: 85-seat auditorium; studio classroom; special events room; amphitheater. Books, contemporary fine art, jewelry & crafts for sale.
Activities: guided tours; lectures; films; gallery talks; inter-museum loan, permanent & temporary exhibitions.
Publications: foundation newsletter; exhibition catalogs; local history publications; gallery guides.
Hours & Admission Prices: Tues.-Sun. 9-5. Adults $4, in-state residents $3; discounts to AAM & ICOM members; members no charge. Closed holidays. ♿
Attendance: 111,500 (accurate)
Membership: Senior Individual $40; Senior Couple $45; Individual $50; Family & Dual $60; ArtEdge (25-49) $75; Friend $100; Supporter $250; Benefactor $500; Patrons' Circle Bronze $1,000-$2,499; Patrons' Circle Silver $2,500-$4,999; Patrons' Circle Gold $5,000 & up.

ANDERSON/ABRUZZO ALBUQUERQUE INTERNATIONAL BALLOON MUSEUM, 9201 Balloon Museum Dr., N.E., Albuquerque, NM 87113-2425. Tel.: 505-768-6020. Fax: 505-768-6021.
Web Site: www.cabq.gov/balloon; www.balloonmuseum.com
Founded: 2000.
Congressional District: 1
Key Personnel: Dir., Jeffrey P. Cooper-Smith; Chm. Bd. Trustees (V), Donald Bragg; Foundation Pres. (V), Gerald Landgraf; Foundation Dir., Tom Levine; Cur. Collections, Dr. Marilee Schmit Nason; Devel. Coord., Toni Fleisher; Museum Shop Mgr., Jennifer Taylor.
Personnel Profile: Full-Time Paid 8; Part-Time Paid 8; Part-Time Volunteers 45.
Governing Authority: nonprofit. Parent Institution: City of Albuquerque, Cultural Services Department, Museum Division.
International Balloon Museum: named after Albuquerque balloon pilots Maxie Anderson and Ben Abruzzo, the first individuals to fly a balloon across the Atlantic.
Collections: art, culture, history, science & sport of ballooning and other lighter-than-air craft; balloons, airships & their artifacts; letters dated 1783 from the Montgolfier brothers, founders of ballooning; 6,000 objects from 1783 to present; personal artifacts; technological information; films; music; literature; stamps; coins.
Major Exhibits: A Fiesta Patchwork: Images Through Time, 11/09-3/10; Children of War, Voices for Peace: Japanese and American Perspectives, 11/09-6/10; The Clouds of La Palma: Clouds, Weather and Ballooning, 11/09-9/10; Fun and Games in Ballooning, 11/09-12/10.
Research Fields: art, culture, history, science, & sport of ballooning, airships & other lighter-than-air craft from 1783 to present.
Facilities: library; 25,000 sq. ft. exhibit space; classrooms; meeting rooms. Museum-related items for sale.
Activities: interactive exhibits; guided tours; formal education programs; community outreach; balloon demonstrations; arts and crafts; school field trips; community open houses; Balloon Summer Camp; facility rental programs. Annual Event: participation in the Albuquerque International Balloon Fiesta in October.
Publications: membership newsletter, Double Eagle; volunteer newsletter, Above And Beyond.
Hours & Admission Prices: Tues.-Sun. 9-5. Adults $4, seniors 65 & over $2, children 4-12 $1; discount to New Mexico residents with ID; 1st Fri. each month, Sun. 9-1, AAM & ICOM members and children 3 & under no charge. Closed New Year's Day; Thanksgiving; Christmas. ♿
Attendance: 64,329 (accurate)
Membership: Student & Senior $20; Individual & Senior Couple $35; Family $60; Associate $100; Patron $250; Benefactor $500.

EXPLORA, 1701 Mountain Rd., N.W., Albuquerque, NM 87104-1396. Tel.: 505-224-8300. Fax: 505-224-8323.
E-mail: explora@explora.us
Web Site: www.explora.us
Formerly: Explora Science Center & Children's Museum of Albuquerque
Founded: 1996.
Congressional District: 1
Key Personnel: Exec. Dir., Patrick Lopez; Pres. (V), Tim Hendry; Assoc. Dir., Paul Tatter; Dir. Exhibits, Betsy Adamson; External Rels., Ellen Welker; Dir. Visitor Svcs., Armelle Casau; Dir. Educational Svcs., Kristen Leigh; Dir. Operations, Alfonso Romero.
Personnel Profile: Full-Time Paid 65; Part-Time Paid 16; Part-Time Volunteers 215; Interns 30.
Governing Authority: private; nonprofit organization. Tax-exempt: 501(c)(3).
Science Center & Children's Museum.
Collections: transactive hands-on exhibits.
Activities: after-school programs; camp-in programs; classes & demonstrations; curriculum materials; field trips; school outreach; science kits; science camps; youth employment programs; workshops & institutes for teachers; homeschoolers programs; senior citizens programs.
Publications: quarterly newsletter; calendar; annual report.
Hours & Admission Prices: Mon.-Sat. 10-6, Sun. 12-6. Adults $7, senior citizens 65 & over $5, children 1-11 $3; ASTC reciprocal membership

program; children under 1 & members no charge. Closed New Year's Day; week after Labor Day; Independence Day; Thanksgiving; Christmas. ♿
Attendance: 204,678 (accurate)
Membership: Student $25; Senior (Individual) $30; Individual $40; Senior (Couple) $50; Family, Helping Hand & Grandparents $75; Family Plus $100; Helping Hand $150.

HOLOCAUST & INTOLERANCE MUSEUM OF NEW MEXICO, 616 Central Ave., S.W., Albuquerque, NM 87102. Mailing Address: P.O. Box 1762, Albuquerque, NM 87103-1762. Tel.: 505-247-0606. Fax: 505-247-0606 (call first).
E-mail: info@nmholocaustmuseum.org
Founded: 2001.
History Museum.
Collections: Holocaust history; photographs; personal artifacts.
Major Exhibits: Varian Fry, Assignment: Rescue, 1940-41 (T), 3/10-5/10.
Hours & Admission Prices: Tues.-Sat. 11-3:30. No charge; donations accepted. Closed major holidays. ♿
Attendance: 5,617 (accurate)

INDIAN PUEBLO CULTURAL CENTER, 2401 12th St., N.W., Albuquerque, NM 87104-2397. Tel.: 505-843-7270. Fax: 505-842-6959.
Web Site: www.indianpueblo.org
Founded: 1976.
Congressional District: 1
Key Personnel: Interim Museum Dir., Marth B. Becktell; C.E.O., Ronald J. Solimon; C.O.O., Dwayne Virgint; Collections Management Specialist, Amy Johnson; Gift Shop Mgr., Ira Wilson; Education, Antonita Trancosa; Volunteer & Membership Coord., Jennifer Pretzeus; Coord. Outreach Education, Felipe Estudillo-Colon.
Personnel Profile: Full-Time Paid 5; Part-Time Paid 2; Part-Time Volunteers 100; Interns 1.
Governing Authority: nonprofit organization. Tax-exempt: 501(c)(3).
Pueblo Indian Museum.
Collections: anthropology; ethnology; contemporary arts & crafts; pueblo culture, history, & architecture; archaeology.
Major Exhibits: Saints of the Pueblos, 11/09-1/12.
Research Fields: Pueblo Indian culture & history.
Facilities: archival library; restaurant; conference & meeting rooms. Museum-related items for sale.
Activities: guided tours; lectures; films; arts festivals; theater; organized education programs for children & adults; docent program; special event planning; temporary & permanent exhibits; artist demonstration. Museum Sponsors: Arts & Crafts Fair; American Indian Week; Indian Children Art Contest; Indian Traditional Dances.
Publications: Pueblo Horizons.
Hours & Admission Prices: Daily 9-5. Adults $6, senior citizens $5.50, military $4.75, NM residents $4, students $3; discounts to groups of 10 or more; members and children 4 & under no charge. Closed New Year's Day; Memorial Day; Independence Day; Labor Day; Thanksgiving; Christmas. ♿
Attendance: 100,000 (estimated)
Membership: Student $20; Senior $25; Individual & Senior Plus One $40; Family $60; Coral $100; Turquoise $250.

INSTITUTE OF METEORITICS METEORITE MUSEUM, 200 Yale Blvd., N.E., Albuquerque, NM 87131-0001. Mailing Address: MSCO3 2050, 1 University of New Mexico, Albuquerque, NM 87131-0001. Tel.: 505-277-2747. Fax: 505-277-3577.
Web Site: epswww.unm.edu/iom/
Founded: 1944.
Key Personnel: Dir. & Cur., Dr. Carl Agee.
Governing Authority: university. Affiliated with the University of New Mexico. Tax-exempt.
Meteorite Museum.
Collections: meteorites; tektite, impact glasses & other shocked rock from terrestrial impact craters.
Research Fields: mineralogy & petrology of meteorites, lunar rocks & terrestrial basalts.
Activities: self-guided tours; lectures; temporary & loan exhibitions.
Publications: Catalog of the Meteorite Collection of the Institute of Meteoritics, University of New Mexico, Special Publications.
Hours & Admission Prices: Mon.-Fri. 9-4. No charge; donations accepted. Closed university holidays. ♿
Attendance: 2,500 (estimated)

JONSON GALLERY OF THE UNIVERSITY OF NEW MEXICO ART MUSEUM, Central Ave. & Cornell Dr., Albuquerque, NM 87131-0001. Mailing Address: MSC04 2570, 1 University of New Mexico, Albuquerque, NM 87131-0001. Tel.: 505-277-8927. Fax: 505-277-7315.
E-mail: cware@unm.edu
Web Site: www.unm.edu/~jonsong
Founded: 1950.
Congressional District: 1
Key Personnel: Cur., Robert Ware; Cur. Asst., Shelley Simms.
Personnel Profile: Full-Time Paid 1; Part-Time Volunteers 2.
Governing Authority: university. Parent Institution: University of New Mexico. Branch Museum: University of New Mexico Art Museum, Fine Arts Center, Albuquerque, NM 87131. 505-277-4001. Tax-exempt: 501(c)(3).
Art Museum.
Collections: Jonson Permanent & Estate collections, works by 20th-century & contemporary artists.
Major Exhibits: Raymond Jonson: 1920-1940s, 9/10-12/10.
Research Fields: paintings; graphics; modernist.
Facilities: 400-vol. library of art books, catalogs & brochures; archives.
Activities: revolving exhibitions of works by Jonson; exhibitions by contemporary artists; permanent & temporary exhibition areas.
Publications: catalogues, William Lumpkins Works Paper 1930-1986; The Developing Image: Continuity & Change in a Chicago Artistic Tradition; Mullican & Mullican; Raymond Jonson: CityScapes; The Art of Raymond Jonson; Transcendental Painting Group, NM, 1938-1941; Ray Jonson Geometric Form; Ray Jonson Centennial Year; Ed Garman Ideal-Modern; Charles Ross-Star Axis; Raymond Jonson Symbolizing New Mexico; Paula Hocks Media/Contra/Media; Mutton Man Discovers Columbus; Jonson's Chicago Little Theatre Years 1913-1917; Raymond Jonson 1945; Arsuna: The Culmination of an Ideal, 1937-1942; University of New Mexico Art Museum Highlights of the Collections; Illustrious Alumni; Albuquerque 50s; A Life in Balance: The Art of Conrad House.
Hours & Admission Prices: Tues. 10-8, Wed.-Fri. 10-4, Sat.-Sun. 1-4. No charge; donations accepted. Closed holidays. ♿
Attendance: 2,502 (accurate)
Membership: Friends of Art membership: Student & Senior $10; Individual $15; Contributing $50; Supporting $100.

* **MAXWELL MUSEUM OF ANTHROPOLOGY, (M),** University of New Mexico, Albuquerque, NM 87131-0001. Mailing Address: MSCO1 1050, 1 University of New Mexico, Albuquerque, NM 87131-0001. Tel.: 505-277-4405. Fax: 505-277-1547.
E-mail: maxwell@unm.edu
Web Site: www.unm.edu/~maxwell
Founded: 1932.
Congressional District: 1
Key Personnel: Dir., E. James Dixon; Sr. Research Coord., Bruce B. Huckell; Dir. Education, Amy Grochowski; Dir. Exhibits, Ian Wagoner; Cur. Osteology, Heather Edgar; Photo Archives, Catherine Baudoin; Admin., Catherine Joy; Data Mgr., Dorothy Larson; Cur. Archaeology, David Phillips; Cur. Ethnology, Kathryn Klein.
Personnel Profile: Full-Time Paid 14; Part-Time Paid 2; Part-Time Volunteers 42.
Governing Authority: university. Parent Institution: University of New Mexico. Tax-exempt: 501(c)(3).
Science & Anthropology Museum.
Collections: archaeology; ethnology; osteology; archives; library; specialized Southwestern collections; Navajo & other Southwestern weaving; silver; Mimbres & Pueblo pottery; American Indian basketry; musical instruments; Pakistani textiles & jewelry; worldwide ethnology; anthropology library; Pakistani & South American textiles; Native American easel art.
Research Fields: archaeology; osteology; ethnology.
Facilities: 12,500-vol. general library with North American specialization available on premises; photo archive emphasizing the Southwest; laboratory of physical anthropology; archaeology laboratory; reading room. Ethnic art, books, Navajo & Pueblo silver jewelry & textiles for sale.
Activities: guided tours; lectures; formally organized education programs for children, adults, undergraduate & graduate students; docent program; permanent & temporary exhibitions; school loan service; funding of public service programs.
Publications: exhibition catalogs; newsletters; brochures; occasional papers; Weaving of the Southwest; Anthropological Papers Series; General Publications including: The Fetish Carvers of Zuni; Across the Colorado Plateau: Anthropological Studies for the Transwestern Pipeline Expansion Project, Vol. VII-XX Vol. XII: Before the Sky Fell: The Pre-Eruptive Sinagua of the Flagstaff Area; Vol XIII: Excavation of Cohonina & Cerbat Sites in the Western Arizona Uplands; Vol XIV: Excavation & Interpretation of Aceramic & Archaic Sites; Vol. XV: Subsistence & Environment; Vol. XVI: Interpretation of Ceramic Artifacts; Vol. XVII: Architectural Studies, Lithic Analysis & Ancillary Studies; Vol XVIII: Human Remains & Burial Goods;

Vol. XIX: Hot Nights, San Francisco Whiskey, Baking Powder & a View of the River: Life on the Southwestern Frontier; Vol. XX: Conclusions & Synthesis-Communities, Boundaries & Cultural variation; Zuni: A Village of Silversmiths; Cuando Hablan Los Santos: Contemporary Santero Traditions from Northern New Mexico; Before Pecos; Environmental Disaster & the Archaeology of Human Response; Anasazi Regional Organization.
Hours & Admission Prices: Tues.-Fri. 9-4, Sat. 10-4. No charge; donations accepted. Closed holidays. ♿
Attendance: 60,000 (estimated)
Membership: Student & Senior Citizen $15; Individual & Senior Couple $25; Family $35; Friend $50-$199; Sponsor $200-$499; Sustaining $500-$2,499; Life Benefactor $2,500 & up.

MUSEUM OF SOUTHWESTERN BIOLOGY, (M), MSC03 2020, 1 University of New Mexico, Albuquerque, NM 87131-0001. Tel.: 505-277-1360. Fax: 505-277-1351.
E-mail: cosborn@unm.edu
Web Site: msb.unm.edu
Founded: 1930.
Congressional District: 1
Key Personnel: C.E.O. & Dir., Dr. Thomas F. Turner; Cur. Mammals & Interim Cur. Genomic Resources, Dr. Joseph C. Cook; Collections Mgr. Mammals (0.4) & (0.6), Jon Dunnum; Cur. Birds, Dr. Christopher Witt; Collection Mgr. Birds, Andrew B. Johnson; Cur. Amphibians & Reptiles, Dr. Howard L. Snell; Collection Mgr., Tom Giermakowski; Cur. Anthropods, Dr. Kelly Miller; Collection Mgr. Arthropods (0.5), Dr. Sandra Brantley; Collection Mgr. Anthropods (0.5), Dr. David Lightfoot; Collection Mgr. Fishes, Alexandra M. Snyder; Cur. Herbarium, Dr. Timothy K. Lowrey; Collection Mgr. Herbarium, Jane Mygatt; USGS Cur., Dr. Michael A. Bogan; USGS Collection Mgr., Cindy A. Ramotnik; Collection Mgr. Genomic Resources, Cheryl Parmenter; Collection Mgr. NHNM, Rayo McCullough; Dir. Natural Heritage New Mexico, Dr. Esteban Muldavin.
Personnel Profile: Full-Time Paid 17.
Governing Authority: university. Parent Institution: University of New Mexico. Tax-exempt.
Research Museum.
Collections: plants; mammals; birds; reptiles; amphibians; fish; anthropods; manuscripts; slide library; frozen tissue collection.
Research Fields: systematics; biogeography; ecology; evolution; biodiversity; conservation; behavior; bioacoustics; museum science; bioinformatics & education to government & business leaders, natural resource managers; parasitology.
Facilities: 26,000 sq. ft. of space for offices, wet and dry storage areas & data management.
Activities: formally organized education programs for undergraduate & graduate students.
Publications: occasional papers and special publications of the Museum of Southwestern biology.
Hours & Admission Prices: Tours by appointment. No charge; donations accepted. ♿
Attendance: 1,500 (accurate)

NATIONAL HISPANIC CULTURAL CENTER, ART MUSEUM, 1701 4th St., S.W., Albuquerque, NM 87102-4508. Tel.: 505-246-2261. Fax: 505-724-4760.
Web Site: www.nhccnm.org
Founded: 1993.
Congressional District: 1
Key Personnel: Exec. Dir., Dr. Estevan Rael-Galvez; Dir. Visual Arts, Tey Marianna Nunn; Dir. Education, Shelle Sanchez; Dir. Performing Arts, Reeve Love; Dir. History & Literary Arts, Carlos Vasquez; Dir. Technology, Ruby Williams; Exec. Admin., Rosemary Garcia.
Personnel Profile: Full-Time Paid 28; Part-Time Paid 5; Part-Time Volunteers 136; Interns 5.
Governing Authority: state; nonprofit. Parent Institution: Department of Cultural Affairs, Santa Fe, New Mexico. Tax-exempt: 501(c)(3).
Art Museum.
Collections: contemporary & historic art from New Mexico, United States, western hemisphere, Spain & the Spanish diaspora; books; historic photographs; archival materials.
Research Fields: Latino & Hispanic visual, culinary & performing arts, history, literature & Spanish language learning resources.
Facilities: 11,000-vol. library; 11,000 sq. ft. exhibition space; 600-seat theater; 300-seat film house; lecture hall; classrooms; meeting rooms; 125-seat restaurant. Museum-related items for sale.
Activities: arts festivals; concerts; dance recitals; docent program; films; formal education programs for children & University of New Mexico students; guided tours; lectures; loan, traveling & temporary exhibitions; theater; training programs. Annual Events: Dia del Nino (Day of the Child); Dia de Muertos (Day of the Dead).
Publications: quarterly newsletter, Que Pasa.
Hours & Admission Prices: Tues.-Sun. 10-5. Adults $3, senior citizens $2; school groups, children under 16, members & Sun. no charge. Closed New Year's Day; Easter; Thanksgiving; Christmas. ♿
Attendance: 233,034 (accurate)

NATIONAL MUSEUM OF NUCLEAR SCIENCE AND HISTORY, (M), 601 Eubank Blvd., S.E., Albuquerque, NM 87123. Tel.: 505-245-2137. Fax: 505-242-4537.
E-mail: info@nuclearmuseum.org
Web Site: www.nuclearmuseum.org
Formerly: National Atomic Museum
Founded: 1969.
Congressional District: 1
Key Personnel: Dir., Jim Walther; Deputy Dir. & Exhibits Coord., Greg Shuman; Pres. (V), Richard Peebles; Cur., David Hoover; Registrar, Sandra Fye; Dir. Mktg. & Public Rels., Jeanette Miller; Dir. Education, Malva Knoll; Museum Store Mgr., Sally Jackson; Volunteer Coord., Dennis Verstynen; Special Events & Facility Rental Coord., Marina Colon; Devel. Assoc., Nadine Scala.
Personnel Profile: Full-Time Paid 14; Part-Time Paid 6; Part-Time Volunteers 129.
Governing Authority: federal. Parent Institution: Department of Energy; Sandia National Laboratories. Subsidiary Institution: Lockheed Martin Corp. Tax-exempt: 501(c)(3).
Nuclear Science & History Museum.
Collections: nuclear weapon cases & related materials; nuclear medicine; weapons; history of the atom; aircraft including B-29, B-52B, A7; cruise missiles; weapon systems.
Research Fields: nuclear weapons history; nuclear medicine; special exhibits that portray the events & personalities of the atomic age.
Facilities: library of books & photographs on the history of nuclear weapons & various energy programs available on premises; exhibits relating to nuclear weapons history; current & future nuclear energy programs; theater. Museum-related items for sale.
Activities: guided tours; films; temporary & permanent exhibitions.
Publications: newsletter, Nuclear Times.
Hours & Admission Prices: Daily 9-5. Adults $8, senior citizens 60 & over and youth 6-17 $7; discounts to groups & active military; members and children 5 & under no charge. Closed New Year's Day; Easter; Thanksgiving; Christmas. ♿
Attendance: 80,000 (accurate)
Membership: Senior Citizen & Student $25; Individual $35; Family $75; Seaborg $150-$299; Fermi $300-$499; Oppenheimer $500-$999; Curie $1,000-$4,999; Einstein $5,000 & up; Corporate $10,000 & up.

*** NEW MEXICO MUSEUM OF NATURAL HISTORY & SCIENCE, (M),** 1801 Mountain Rd., N.W., Albuquerque, NM 87104-1375. Tel.: 505-841-2846. Fax: 505-841-2844. TDD: 505-841-2878.
E-mail: denise.hidalgo@state.nm.us
Web Site: www.NMnaturalhistory.org
Founded: 1986.
Congressional District: 1
Key Personnel: Pres. (V) Bd. Trustees, Gary Friedman; Pres. Volunteers' Assoc., Linda Walton; Exec. Dir., Hollis J. Gillespie; Foundation Exec. Dir., Jotina Trussell; Deputy Dir., Alicia Borrego Pierce; Mgr. Capital Projects, Robert Ungnade; Finance Mgr., Sherice Padilla; Collections Mgr., Justin Spielmann; Public Information Officer, Roxanne Witt-Celeskey; Dir. Education, Jessica Sapunar-Jursich; Museum Shop Mgr., Beth Ricker; Exec. Asst. to Dir., Denise Hidalgo.
Personnel Profile: Full-Time Paid 85; Part-Time Paid 4; Part-Time Volunteers 374; Interns 2.
Governing Authority: state government. Department of Cultural Affairs, Santa Fe, NM. Tax-exempt. 501(c)(3).
Natural History & Science Museum.
Collections: natural history materials representative of New Mexico & southwest; botany, geology, paleontology & zoology specimens; microcomputer memorabilia.
Major Exhibits: Nature Journals, 6/10-8/10; Nikon Small World (T), 6/10-8/10; All That Glitters, 8/10-10/10; 2010 Naturescapes Photo Salon, 9/10-12/10.
Research Fields: paleontology; botany; zoology; geology.
Facilities: 440-book & 5,000 journal library pertaining to natural history; 50,000 sq. ft. exhibit space; Extreme Screen DynaTheater; 280-seat IWERKS; 20,000 sq. ft. Education & Research Complex; naturalist center; class rooms; educational facilities. Museum-related items for sale.
Activities: guided tours; lectures; concerts; organized education programs for children, adults, undergraduate & graduate students; docent program; training programs for professional museum workers; participatory, temporary & traveling exhibitions.

Publications: quarterly newsletter, Timetracks; brochures; exhibit catalog; posters; biennial report; science bulletin.
Hours & Admission Prices: Jan. & Sept. Tues.-Sun. & holiday Mon. 9-5; Feb.-Aug. & Oct.-Dec. daily 9-5. Museum: adults $7, seniors 60 & up $6, children 3-12 $4. Extreme Screen DynaTheater: adults $7, seniors 60 & up $6, children 3-12 $4. Planetarium: adults $7, seniors 60 & up $6, children 3-12 $4; discounts to AAM, ICOM & ASTC members; members & children under 3 no charge. Combination packages available. Closed New Year's Day; Thanksgiving; Christmas. ♿
Attendance: 237,267 (accurate)
Membership: Student $25; Senior $30; Individual $45; Senior Couple $50; Family & Grandparent $75; Family Plus $100.

NEW MEXICO STATE FAIR FINE ARTS GALLERY, 300 San Pedro, N.E., Albuquerque, NM 87108-2812. Mailing Address: P.O. Box 8546, Albuquerque, NM 87198-8546. Tel.: 505-222-9700. Fax: 505-222-9756.
Key Personnel: Interim Dir. Art, Sundi Tyler
Art Gallery.
Collections: Hispanic & Indian art; fine art; African American art.
Hours & Admission Prices: Call for hours. No charge; donations accepted. Closed holidays.

PETROGLYPH NATIONAL MONUMENT, 6001 Unser Blvd., N.W., Albuquerque, NM 87120-2069. Tel.: 505-899-0205, ext. 331. Fax: 505-899-0207.
Web Site: www.nps.gov/petr
Founded: 1990.
Personnel Profile: Full-Time Paid 23; Part-Time Paid 4; Part-Time Volunteers 10.
Governing Authority: Parent Institution: National Park Service.
National Park & Landmark.
Collections: petroglyph etchings by local Native Americans.
Facilities: hiking trails.
Hours & Admission Prices: Daily 8-5. Sat.-Sun. $2, Mon.-Fri. $1. Closed holidays.

RATTLESNAKE MUSEUM (AMERICAN INTERNATIONAL), 202 San Felipe, N.W., Albuquerque, NM 87104-1442. Tel.: 505-242-6569. Fax: 505-242-6569 (call first).
E-mail: snakemuseum@aol.com
Web Site: www.rattlesnakes.com
Founded: 1990.
Key Personnel: Dir., Bob Myers.
Personnel Profile: Full-Time Paid 2; Part-Time Volunteers 34.
Governing Authority: private; profit.
Herpetology & Animal Conservation Museum.
Collections: American history; Native American culture & art; fine art; photography; medical artifacts; textiles; music; toys & games; anatomical; symbolism; folk art; advertising.
Activities: field trips; training programs & school field trips.
Hours & Admission Prices: Summer: Mon.-Sat. 10-6, Sun. 1-5; Sept.-May Mon.-Fri. 11:30-5:30, Sat. 10-6, Sun. 1-5. Adults $3.50, seniors, military & students $3. Closed New Year's Day; Easter; Thanksgiving; Christmas. ♿
Attendance: 50,000 (accurate)
Membership: Children $5; Adults $10.

RIO GRANDE NATURE CENTER STATE PARK, 2901 Candelaria Rd., N.W., Albuquerque, NM 87107-2965. Tel.: 505-344-7240. Fax: 505-344-4505.
E-mail: friends@rgnc.org
Web Site: www.rgnc.org
Founded: 1982.
Congressional District: 2
Key Personnel: Pres., Jo Fairbanks; Office Mgr., Paula Dwall; Museum Shop Mgr., Marilyn Cimalore; Park Supt., Beth Dillingham.
Personnel Profile: Full-Time Paid 8; Part-Time Paid 3; Part-Time Volunteers 150; Interns 2.
Governing Authority: state government; nonprofit. Parent Institution: New Mexico State Parks Division, Santa Fe, NM 87504-1147. Tax-exempt.
Nature Center: preservation & protection of wetland and riverine resources in the Rio Grande Valley & the surrounding Bosque (woods); to educate visitors on the importance of wetlands and river resources in the arid Southwest.
Collections: botanical; zoological.
Facilities: visitor center; gardens; trails. Museum-related items for sale.
Activities: classes; guided tours; special events.
Publications: quarterly member newsletter; park brochure; trail guides.
Hours & Admission Prices: Park: daily 8-5. Visitor Center: daily 10-5. Parking Fee: car $3, van & buses $15. Closed New Year's Day; Thanksgiving; Christmas. ♿
Attendance: 50,000 (accurate)
Membership: Student & Senior (62 & up) $15; Individual & Family $30; Donor $50; Sponsor $100; Sustaining $250; Benefactor $500; Life $1,000.

SAN FELIPE DE NERI CHURCH MUSEUM, San Felipe de Neri Parish, 2005 North Plaza N.W., Albuquerque, NM 87104. Mailing Address: P.O. Box 7007, Albuquerque, NM 87194-7007. Tel.: 505-243-4628 & 224-9495.
E-mail: webmaster@sanfelipedeneri.org
Web Site: www.sanfelipedeneri.org/museum.html
Historic Church.
Collections: period furnishings; religious art.
Hours & Admission Prices: Call for hours. No charge.

TELEPHONE MUSEUM OF NEW MEXICO, 110 Fourth St., N.W., Albuquerque, NM 87102-3268. Mailing Address: P.O. Box 1892, Albuquerque, NM 87103-1892. Tel.: 505-842-2937.
E-mail: telmuseum@hotmail.net
Web Site: www.nmculture.org
Formerly: Telephone Pioneer Museum
Founded: 1961.
Key Personnel: C.E.O. & Chm. (V), Gigi Galassini; Dir., Sue Turner.
Personnel Profile: Full-Time Volunteers 8; Part-Time Volunteers 69.
Governing Authority: Tax-exempt.
Telephone & Communication Museum.
Collections: telephones; switchboards; insulators; directories; hand tools; photographs.
Major Exhibits: Alexander G. Bell Experiments, 3/10; Olympic Telephones, 6/10; Authentic Working Coin Phone Display, 8/10; N.M. Telephone Personnel thru Decades, 10/10.
Research Fields: Growth & development of wire communications in Southwest.
Facilities: reading room.
Activities: permanent & temporary exhibitions.
Publications: books, 50 Little Known Facts About Alexander G. Bell; Theodore Vail.
Hours & Admission Prices: Mon., Wed. & Fri. 10-2; large tours by appointment. Adults $2, children under 12 $1. Tours on off-hours: $4 per person. Closed holidays. ♿
Attendance: 1,200 (estimated)

TURQUOISE MUSEUM, 2107 Central N.W., Albuquerque, NM 87104-1605. Mailing Address: P.O. Box 7598, Albuquerque, NM 87194-7598. Tel.: 505-247-8650. Fax: 505-247-8765.
E-mail: turquoisemuseum@yahoo.com
Web Site: turquoisemuseum.com
Founded: 1993.
Congressional District: 1
Key Personnel: Pres. & Cur., Joe Dan Lowry; Museum Shop Mgr., Katy Lowry.
Personnel Profile: Full-Time Paid 4; Part-Time Paid 2.
Governing Authority: private; for profit.
General Museum.
Collections: J.C. Zachary, Jr. largest natural turquoise collection; educational information: history, mining, geology, cutting, marketing.
Facilities: 60-seat auditorium. Museum-related items for sale.
Activities: lapidary demonstrations.
Publications: Turquoise Unearthed.
Hours & Admission Prices: Mon.-Fri. 9:30-5, Sat. 9:30-4. Adults $4, senior citizens & children $3. Closed Independence Day; Thanksgiving; Christmas. ♿
Attendance: 9,375 (accurate)

UNIVERSITY ART MUSEUM, THE UNIVERSITY OF NEW MEXICO, (M), UNM Center for the Arts, Cornell & Central N.E., Albuquerque, NM 87131-0001. Mailing Address: UNM Art Museum, MSC04 2570, 1 University of New Mexico, Albuquerque, NM 87131-0001. Tel.: 505-277-4001. Fax: 505-277-7315.
E-mail: artmuse@unm.edu
Web Site: unmartmuseum.unm.edu
Founded: 1963.
Congressional District: 1
Key Personnel: Dir., E. Luanne McKinnon; Cur. Photographs & Prints, Michele Penhall; Cur. Raymond Jonson Gallery, Robert Ware; Cur. Academic Initiatives, Sara Otto-Diniz; Mgr. Collections, Bonnie Verardo; Mgr. Exhibitions, Lee Savary; Office Mgr., Angela Berkson; Asst. Cur. Photographs & Prints, Sherri Sorensen; Curatorial Asst., Steven Hurley.

Personnel Profile: Full-Time Paid 9; Part-Time Paid 3; Part-Time Volunteers 10.
Governing Authority: university. Parent Institution: University of New Mexico. Tax-exempt: 501(c)(3).
Art Museum.
Collections: photographs; Beaumont Newhall collection; prints; Harold Edgerton collection; Tamarind Lithography archive; 19th- to 20th-century art; Old Master paintings & sculpture; Albert A. Anella collection; Spanish colonial art; Field collection.
Major Exhibits: Man Ray, African Art & The Modernist Lens (T), 2/10-5/10; Tamarind Touchstone, 9/10-12/10; Patrick Nagatani: Desire For Magic, 9/10-12/10; Raymond Jonson: 1920-1940s, 9/10-12/10.
Research Fields: photography; graphics, with emphasis on lithography; 20th-century American painting & sculpture; Spanish colonial art, with emphasis on domestic silver.
Facilities: print & photography study room.
Activities: guided tours by appointment; lectures; gallery talks; formally organized education programs for graduate students; training programs for professional museum workers; inter-museum loan, temporary & traveling exhibitions.
Publications: calendar; catalogues; gallery guides; 19th Century Photographs at the University of New Mexico Art Museum; Tamarind Lithography Workshop, Inc. 1960-1970 Catalogue Raisonne; For My Best Beloved Sister Mia, An Album of Photographs; The Potters of Mata Ortiz; Nineteenth Century Lithography in Europe.
Hours & Admission Prices: Tues. 10-8, Wed.-Fri. 10-4, Sat.-Sun. 1-4. No charge; donations accepted. Closed holidays. ♿
Attendance: 44,374 (accurate)
Membership: Student & Senior Citizen $15; Individual $25; Family $35; Contributing $50; Supporting $100; Benefactor $500; Corporate $1,000.

THE UNSER RACING MUSEUM, 1776 Montano N.W., Albuquerque, NM 87107-3245. Tel.: 505-341-1776.
E-mail: cathy@unserracingmuseum.com
Web Site: www.unserracingmuseum.com
Racing Museum.
Collections: four generations of race cars; uniforms; period cars; trophies; pace cars; artwork.
Facilities: Museum-related items for sale.
Activities: rental facilities.
Hours & Admission Prices: Daily 10-7. Adults $7, seniors $4, children $3.

WHEELS TRANSPORTATION MUSEUM, 1501 1st St., N.W., Albuquerque, NM 87102-1535. Mailing Address: P.O. Box 747, Albuquerque, NM 87103-0747. Tel.: 505-243-6269.
E-mail: info@wheelsmuseum.org
Web Site: www.wheelsmuseum.org
Key Personnel: Pres., Leba Freed.
Governing Authority: Tax-exempt: 501(c)(3).
Transportation Museum.
Collections: historic industrial plant history; 18 structures.
Hours & Admission Prices: Call for hours. No charge.

Artesia

ARTESIA HISTORICAL MUSEUM & ART CENTER, (M), 505 Richardson Ave., Artesia, NM 88210-2062. Tel.: 575-748-2390. Fax: 575-748-7345 (attn: Museum).
E-mail: artesiamuseum@pvtn.net
Web Site: artesiamuseum.org
Founded: 1970.
Congressional District: 2
Key Personnel: Mgr., Nancy Dunn; Registrar, Naomi Florez.
Personnel Profile: Full-Time Paid 2; Part-Time Paid 1.
Governing Authority: municipal; museum commission. Parent Institution: City of Artesia. Tax-exempt.
History Museum: located in 1904-05 Moore-Ward House.
Collections: agriculture; ranching; archaeology; geology; oil fields; oral histories; newspapers; local artists; photographs; clothing & objects of early residents; Native American artifacts; printing press; windmill; phonograph records.
Research Fields: local & area history; local film history; Seven Rivers settlement; genealogy.
Facilities: library of books, newspapers, manuscripts; oral history tapes available for research on premises by arrangement.
Activities: guided tours; permanent, temporary, loan & participatory exhibits; educational outreach classroom programs available. Annual Events: Quilt Show; Art & Photography Show; Living Treasures Awards Ceremony.
Hours & Admission Prices: Tues.-Fri. 9-12 & 1-5, Sat. 1-5. No charge; donations accepted. Closed New Year's Day; Memorial Day; Independence Day; Labor Day; Thanksgiving & day after; Christmas Eve & Day. ♿
Attendance: 2,000

Aztec

AZTEC MUSEUM AND PIONEER VILLAGE, 125 N. Main Ave., Aztec, NM 87410-1923. Tel.: 505-334-9829. Fax: 505-334-9829.
Web Site: www.aztecmuseum.org
Founded: 1963.
Congressional District: 2
Personnel Profile: Full-Time Paid 2.
Governing Authority: private association. Parent Institution: Aztec Museum Association, Inc. Tax-exempt.
General Museum: housed in 1940 City Hall building; Pioneer Village.
Collections: Lobato collection of rocks, minerals, fossils, artifacts; Abrams collection of prehistoric Anasazi pottery; 1900 barber shop; early fashions; furnished living room, bedroom & kitchen; antique farm & ranch equipment; pioneer hand tools & household items; historic oil & gas equipment including a 1920 spudder; frontier village; sheriff's office; jail; lawyer's office; doctor's office; 1880 log cabin; 1905 replica of bank; D&RG narrow gauge caboose replica; general store; post office; print shop; tin shop; replica of early 1900s farm house.
Research Fields: pioneer living & working c.1880s; oil & gas from 1920s to present.
Activities: self-guided tours; permanent & loan exhibitions.
Publications: monthly newsletter; walking tour; brochure.
Hours & Admission Prices: Winter: Mon.-Sat. 10-4; Summer: Mon.-Sat. 9-5. Adults $3, students 11-17 $1; discounts to members; children 10 & under no charge. Closed New Year's Day; Good Friday; Memorial Day; Labor Day; Veterans Day; Independence Day; Thanksgiving; Christmas. ♿
Attendance: 4,000 (estimated)
Membership: Regular $25; Patron $250; Lifetime $500.

AZTEC RUINS NATIONAL MONUMENT, 84 County Rd. 2900, Aztec, NM 87410-9715. Tel.: 505-334-6174. Fax: 505-334-6372. TDD: 505-334-6174.
E-mail: azru_curatorial@nps.gov
Web Site: www.nps.gov/azru
Founded: 1923.
Congressional District: 3
Key Personnel: Supt., Dennis Carruth; Acting Cur., Chief Visitor Svcs. & Resources Management, Theresa Nichols.
Governing Authority: federal. Parent Institution: Dept. of the Interior. Affiliated with National Park Service. Tax-exempt.
Archaeology Museum.
Collections: archaeological materials of ancestral Puebloan people, late 1000s-1200 A.D.
Research Fields: Chaco archaeology.
Facilities: 280-vol. library on ethnology & archaeology of Southwest Indians & prehistoric Pueblo Indians. Publications, postcards, slides & guidebooks for sale.
Activities: lectures; self-guiding trail; 25 min. video.
Publications: orientation brochure; trail guide; leaflet.
Hours & Admission Prices: Memorial Day to Labor Day daily 8-6; Sept.-May daily 8-5. Adults $5; discounts for Golden Eagle, Golden Age & Golden Access passport holders; children under 15 no charge. Closed New Year's Day; Thanksgiving; Christmas. ♿
Attendance: 50,000 (estimated)

Belen

VALENCIA COUNTY HISTORICAL SOCIETY'S HARVEY HOUSE MUSEUM, 104 N. 1st St., Belen, NM 87002-4302. Mailing Address: P.O. Box 166, Belen, NM 87002-0166. Tel.: 505-861-0581.
Key Personnel: C.E.O. & Dir., Maurine McMillan
History Museum.
Collections: period furnishings; Santa Fe railroad artifacts.
Hours & Admission Prices: Tues.-Sat. 12:30-3:30. No charge.

Bernalillo

CORONADO STATE MONUMENT, 485 Kuava Rd., Rte. 44, Bernalillo, NM 87004-7099. Mailing Address: Box 95, Bernalillo, NM 87004-0095. Tel.: 505-867-5351; 800-419-3738. Fax: 505-867-1733.
E-mail: Kuaua@lobo.net
Web Site: www.nmmonuments.org
Founded: 1940.
Key Personnel: Mgr., Angie Manning.
Personnel Profile: Full-Time Paid 3; Part-Time Paid 1; Part-Time Volunteers 5.
Governing Authority: state. Parent Institution: Museum of New Mexico. Tax-exempt: 170(c)(3).

Historic Site: Site of Tiwa Pueblo named Kuaua dating from AD 1300.
Collections: local history & culture; Native American & Spanish artifacts; murals.
Activities: guided tours; lectures; Indian storytelling. Museum Sponsors: Preservation Month in May; Christmas event in December.
Hours & Admission Prices: Wed.-Mon. 8:30-5. Adults $3; discount to senior groups of 10 or more; seniors on Wed. with N.M.I.D., children 16 & under, AAM members, school groups by appointment & New Mexico residents on Sun. no charge. Coronado State Monument & Jemez State Monument: two day pass $5 each site. Annual Site Pass: $10. Closed New Year's Day; Easter; Thanksgiving; Christmas Day. ♿
Attendance: 18,260 (accurate)
Membership: Student & Teacher $15; Senior Individual (65 & up) $25; Individual $30; Senior Couple $35; Family/Dual $40; Benefactor Business $300 & up.

SANDOVAL COUNTY HISTORICAL SOCIETY MUSEUM, 161 Edmond Rd., Bernalillo, NM 87004. Mailing Address: P.O. Box 692, Bernalillo, NM 87004-0692. Tel.: 505-867-2755. Fax: 505-867-5872.
Web Site: www.sandovalhistory.com/
Founded: 1977.
Congressional District: 3
Personnel Profile: Part-Time Volunteers 6.
Governing Authority: private; nonprofit organization. Tax-exempt: 501(c)(3).
Historical Society Museum: housed in the former home of oil painter, Edmond DeLavy.
Collections: local history & culture; photographs; local genealogical records; personal artifacts; paintings; local geology.
Facilities: 150-vol. library; 100-seat auditorium; 2,700 sq. ft. exhibit space.
Activities: society meetings; art shows; concerts; lectures; loan, participatory, temporary & traveling exhibitions.
Publications: quarterly newsletter, El Cronicon.
Hours & Admission Prices: Sept.-June Wed. 10-12, Sun. 2-4. Adults $5; members no charge. ♿
Attendance: 1,000 (accurate)
Membership: Single $15; Couple $25.

Bloomfield

SAN JUAN COUNTY ARCHAEOLOGICAL RESEARCH CENTER AND LIBRARY AT THE SALMON RUIN/SAN JUAN COUNTY MUSEUM ASSOCIATION, (M), 6131 U.S. Hwy. 64, Bloomfield, NM 87413. Mailing Address: P.O. Box 125, Bloomfield, NM 87413-0125. Tel.: 505-632-2013. Fax: 505-632-8633.
E-mail: sreducation@sisna.com
Web Site: www.salmonruins.com
Founded: 1973.
Congressional District: 2
Key Personnel: Pres., David Casey; Exec. Dir., Larry L. Baker; Dir. Education, Nancy Sweet Espinosa; Acting Librarian & Museum Shop Mgr., Diane Hayden.
Personnel Profile: Full-Time Paid 4; Full-Time Volunteers 1; Part-Time Paid 1; Part-Time Volunteers 17; Interns 1.
Governing Authority: nonprofit. Parent Institution: San Juan County Museum Association. Tax-exempt: 501(c)(3).
Archaeological and Cultural Museum, Library and Research Center.
Collections: historical; archaeological; anthropological. Heritage Park: cultural habitations of the Four Corners region. Salmon Homestead Complex: 1898 adobe house & outbuilding;
Research Fields: four corners archaeology; ruins stabilization & historic structure rehabilitation; rock art; petroglyphs; local history, living cultures of the Four Corners area (Navajo, Ute, Jicarilla Apache, Hispanic).
Facilities: 7,000-vol. research library of books on archaeology, anthropology & Southwestern history; picnic area; amphitheatre; nature trails. Books, native arts & crafts and museum-related items for sale.
Activities: lectures; workshops; arts & crafts fair; permanent & temporary exhibitions; outdoor theater; Journey into the Past guided tours.
Publications: Survey & mitigation reports of sites; historic series; report, Thirty Five Years of Archaeological Research at Salmon Ruins, Volumes I, II, & III.
Hours & Admission Prices: May-Oct. daily 8-5; Nov.-April Mon.-Sat. 8-5, Sun. 12-5. Adults 16 & over $3, senior citizens $2, children 6-15 $1; discounts to AAM Members; children under 6, members & student groups no charge. Closed New Year's Day; Easter; Thanksgiving; Christmas. ♿
Attendance: 7,339 (accurate)
Membership: Student & Single Senior $10; Individual & Senior Couple $15; Family $25; Institution $50; Patron $100; Lifetime $500.

Capitan

SMOKEY BEAR MUSEUM, 118 W. Smokey Bear Blvd., Capitan, NM 88316. Mailing Address: P.O. Box 591, Capitan, NM 88316-0891. Tel.: 575-354-2748. Fax: 575-354-6012.
Web Site: smokeybearpark.com/
General Museum.
Collections: over 500 Smokey artifacts & memorabilia from around the world from early 1940's to present; baby bottle that fed Smokey the Bear cub when he was first rescued from the fire in the Capitan Mountains; Golden Bear, a 1944 stuffed Teddy Bear photographed with President Eisenhower.
Hours & Admission Prices: Daily 9-5. Adults 13 & over $2, children 7-12 $1; children 6 & under no charge. Closed New Year's Day; Thanksgiving; Christmas.

WILDLAND FIREFIGHTERS MUSEUM, 111 W. Smokey Bear Blvd., Capitan, NM 88316. Mailing Address: P.O. Box 1304, Capitan, NM 88316-1304. Tel.: 505-354-4251.
Firefighters Museum.
Collections: fire prevention; fire-fighting equipment; photographs; clothing; personal artifacts.
Facilities: Museum-related items for sale.
Hours & Admission Prices: Call for hours. No charge; donations accepted.

Capulin

CAPULIN VOLCANO NATIONAL MONUMENT, 46 Volcano Rd., Capulin, NM 88414. Mailing Address: P.O. Box 40, Capulin, NM 88414-0040. Tel.: 505-278-2201. Fax: 505-278-2211.
E-mail: christopher_moos@nps.gov
Web Site: www.nps.gov/cavo/
Founded: 1916.
Congressional District: 3
Key Personnel: Dir., Christopher R. Moos; Park Ranger Interpretation, Joyce Umbach.
Governing Authority: federal. Parent Institution: U.S. Dept. of the Interior. Subsidiary Institution: Natl. Park Svc. Tax-exempt.
Natural Science Museum.
Collections: herbarium; geological & zoological specimens; entomology collection; lepidopteran collection.
Research Fields: volcanism.
Facilities: 500-vol. library of natural history books & reference material available on premises; nature center; self-guided trails.
Activities: 10-min. movie of natural history of the area; permanent exhibits.
Publications: orientation brochures.
Hours & Admission Prices: Winter daily 8-4; Summer daily 7:30-6:30. Entrance fee: $10 per vehicle. All federal passes accepted. ♿
Attendance: 48,994 (accurate)

Carlsbad

CARLSBAD CAVERNS NATIONAL PARK, 3225 National Parks Hwy., Carlsbad, NM 88220-5254. Tel.: 575-785-3116. Fax: 575-785-2317. TDD: 575-885-8884.
E-mail: david_kayser@nps.gov
Web Site: www.nps.gov
Founded: 1923.
Congressional District: 2
Key Personnel: Collections Mgr., David W. Kayser.
Personnel Profile: Full-Time Paid 1; Part-Time Paid 2; Part-Time Volunteers 2.
Governing Authority: federal. Parent Institution: the U.S. Dept. of Interior, National Park Service. Tax-exempt.
Natural History & Archaeology Museum.
Collections: history of the caverns; botany; entomology; geology; paleontology; archaeology; herpetology; archives.
Major Exhibits: The Cavern Through Artists Eyes, 11/09-12/10; Carlsbad Caverns National Park, 11/09-12/10; Annual Art Show, 11/09-12/10; Historic Photographs, 11/09-12/10.
Research Fields: geology; paleontology; history; archeology.
Facilities: 4,000-vol. library; restaurant. Gift items for sale.
Activities: cavern tours; permanent exhibitions; backcountry day & overnight hiking; bird watching; nature & plant trail.
Publications: Carlsbad Caverns National Park, Silent Chambers; Timeless Beauty; What About Bats; Bats of Carlsbad Caverns National Park.
Hours & Admission Prices: Visitor Center: daily 8-5. Cave: Labor Day-Memorial Day call for hours. Adults $6, senior citizens $3; discounts to National Parks pass holders, Golden Eagle Passport holders & Golden Age pass holders; children under 15 no charge. Ranger-guided Tours: $7-$20. Closed Christmas. ♿
Attendance: 250,000 (accurate)

Membership: Carlsbad Caverns-Golden Age (62 & over) $20; Guadalupe Association: Annual $25; Golden Eagle $75.

CARLSBAD MUSEUM & ART CENTER, (M), 418 W. Fox St., Carlsbad, NM 88220-5743. Tel.: 505-887-0276. Fax: 505-885-8809.
E-mail: carlsbad_museum@msn.com
Founded: 1931.
Congressional District: 2
Key Personnel: Pres., Carolyn Olson; Dir., Virginia Dodier.
Personnel Profile: Full-Time Paid 1; Part-Time Paid 3; Part-Time Volunteers 2; Interns 1.
Governing Authority: municipal. Parent Institution: City of Carlsbad. Tax-exempt.
General Museum and Art Center.
Collections: archaeology; regional history; New Mexico art; Pueblo pottery; Peruvian antiquities.
Facilities: art classroom; lecture hall.
Activities: permanent & temporary exhibits.
Publications: newsletter, Amigos; exhibition brochures.
Hours & Admission Prices: Summer: Mon.-Sat. 10-6; Winter: Mon.-Sat. 10-5. No charge; donations accepted. Closed New Year's Day; Martin Luther King, Jr. Day; Memorial Day; Independence Day; Labor Day; Veterans Day; Thanksgiving & day after; Christmas Eve & Day. ♿
Attendance: 8,489 (accurate)
Membership: Single $15; Family $25; Patron $100; Corporate $250.

LIVING DESERT ZOO AND GARDENS STATE PARK, 1504 Miehls Dr., Carlsbad, NM 88220-3057. Mailing Address: P.O. Box 100, Carlsbad, NM 88221-0100. Tel.: 505-887-5516. Fax: 505-885-4478.
Web Site: www.nmparks.com
Founded: 1971.
Congressional District: 2
Key Personnel: C.E.O. New Mexico State Parks, David Simon; Chm. (V), Linda Frank; Park Supt., Ken Britt; Cur. Botanical, Chris Dawson; Museum Shop Mgr., Tina Brummett.
Personnel Profile: Full-Time Paid 14; Part-Time Paid 3; Part-Time Volunteers 70; Interns 1.
Governing Authority: state. Parent Institution: New Mexico State Parks Div., P.O. Box 1147, Santa Fe, NM 87504 (Not affiliated or associated with The Living Desert in Palm Desert, CA). Tax-exempt.
Zoological & Botanical State Park.
Collections: birds, mammals & reptiles of the Chihuahuan Desert; cacti & succulents, featuring native Southwestern plants & exotics; mineral collection; exhibits of plants & animals representing different habitats found within the northern Chihuahuan Desert; nocturnal exhibit.
Facilities: 500-vol. library of botanical & zoological material available for use in park only; botanical garden; zoological garden; nature & conservation center; 1.3-miles of trails. Natural history publications, curios, gifts, postcards, plants & cacti for sale.
Activities: tours; lectures; concerts; study clubs; radio & TV programs; education programs; docent environmental education programs; plant sale; Annual Events: Mescal Roast.
Publications: booklet, A Guide to Living Desert Zoological and Botanical State Park, 1989.
Hours & Admission Prices: Memorial Day-Labor Day daily 8-5 (last entrance 3:30); Sept.-May daily 9-5 (last entrance 3:30). Adults $5, children 7-12 $3, organized youth groups $.50 per person; discounts to groups & AZA members; children 6 & under no charge. ♿
Attendance: 50,750 (accurate)
Membership: Horticultural Society Individual & Friends of the Park Family Individual $20; Family $40; Supporting $50; Life $500; Corporate (variable).

Cedar Crest

MUSEUM OF ARCHAEOLOGY & MATERIAL CULTURE, 22 Calvary Rd., Cedar Crest, NM 87008-9314. Mailing Address: P.O. Box 582, Cedar Crest, NM 87008-0582. Tel.: 505-281-2005.
E-mail: info@museumarch.org
Web Site: www.turquoisetrail.org
Key Personnel: Dir., Bradley Bowman
Archaeology Museum.
Collections: science of archaeology & history; Native American; Sandia Cave & turquoise mining.
Hours & Admission Prices: May-Nov. 1 daily 12-7. Adults $3, children 6-12 $1.50; children under 6 no charge.

Chimayo

CHIMAYO MUSEUM, Plaza del Cerro, Chimayo, NM 87522. Mailing Address: P.O. Box 727, Chimayo, NM 87522-0727. Tel.: 505-351-0945.
Web Site: www.chimayomuseum.org
History Museum: former home of Jose Ramon & Petra Mestas Ortega.
Collections: local history & culture relating to Chimayo.
Hours & Admission Prices: Tues.-Sat. 11-3.

Church Rock

RED ROCK MUSEUM, Red Rock Park, Church Rock, NM 87311. Mailing Address: P.O. Box 10, Church Rock, NM 87311-0010. Tel.: 505-722-3839. Fax: 505-905-1277.
E-mail: redrockpark@ci.gallup.nm.us
Web Site: www.ci.gallup.nm.us
Founded: 1951.
Congressional District: 3
Key Personnel: Parks Exec. Dir., Ben Welch; Parks Specialist, Beverly Lovett.
Personnel Profile: Full-Time Paid 5; Part-Time Paid 5.
Governing Authority: municipal. Parent Institution: City of Gallup, NM 87301. Subsidiary Institution: Red Rock Park. Tax-exempt: 501(c)(3).
Anthropology & Natural History.
Collections: fine arts, crafts & artifacts of the prehistoric Anasazi & historic Navajo, Hopi, Zuni, Rio Grande Pueblos, Apache; geological & botanical artifacts.
Research Fields: community history; human & natural history of Gallup area.
Facilities: 500-seat auditorium; ethnobotanical garden.
Activities: Annual Event: Gallup Inter-Tribal Indian Ceremonial in August.
Hours & Admission Prices: Mon.-Fri. 8-5. No charge; donations accepted. Closed national holidays. ♿
Attendance: 20,500 (estimated)

Cimarron

PHILMONT MUSEUMS, Philmont Scout Ranch, 17 Deer Run Rd., Cimarron, NM 87714-9638. Tel.: 575-376-2281, ext. 1256. Fax: 575-376-2602.
E-mail: smcfarla@netbsa.org
Web Site: www.scouting.org/philmont/
Founded: 1967.
Congressional District: 3
Key Personnel: Dir., Seth McFarland; Librarian, Robin Taylor.
Personnel Profile: Full-Time Paid 4; Part-Time Paid 14.
Governing Authority: nonprofit organization. Parent Institution: Boy Scouts of America. Tax-exempt: 170(b)(1)(A).
History & Art Museums: housed in Philmont Museum - Seton Memorial Library & Kit Carson Museum, located on the Philmont Scout Ranch.
Collections: art; archaeology; archives; ethnology; history of the Southwest; 1910-present day artifacts of the Boy Scouts of America.
Research Fields: Ernest Thompson Seton; Boy Scouts of America; History & Art of the Southwest.
Facilities: 3,000-vol. library pertaining to art, history, & anthropology available for research on premise only.
Activities: guided tours; lectures; study clubs; inter-museum loan, permanent & temporary exhibitions.
Hours & Admission Prices: June-Aug. daily 8-5; Sept.-May Mon.-Sat. 8-12 & 1-5. Kit Carson Museum: Summer: daily 8-5. No charge; donations accepted. ♿
Attendance: 35,000 (estimated)

Clayton

HERZSTEIN MEMORIAL MUSEUM, S. Second & Walnut, Clayton, NM 88415. Mailing Address: P.O. Box 75, Clayton, NM 88415-0075. Tel.: 505-374-2977.
Congressional District: 3
Key Personnel: Dir., Kristen Christy; Pres. (V), Ron Seaman; Museum Shop Mgr., Mary Ann Mannes.
Personnel Profile: Full-Time Paid 1; Part-Time Paid 2; Part-Time Volunteers 12.
Governing Authority: nonprofit organization. Parent Institution: Union County Historical Society. Tax-exempt.
Regional Historical Museum.
Collections: history of Union County & Northeastern New Mexico; photographs.
Facilities: archives.
Activities: monthly programs including family history, music, & Santa Fe Trail; genealogy club; research.
Publications: quarterly newsletter, Union County Historical Society Review.
Hours & Admission Prices: Tues.-Sat. 10-4; other times by appointment. No charge; donations accepted. Closed major holidays. ♿

Attendance: 700 (estimated)
Membership: Individual $25; Family $40; Supporting $100; Business $250; Lifetime $750; President's Council $1,000.

Cleveland

CLEVELAND ROLLER MILL MUSEUM, Rte. 518, Cleveland, NM 87715. Mailing Address: P.O. Box 287, Cleveland, NM 87715-0287. Tel.: 505-387-2645.
Web Site: www.angelfire.com/folk/roller_mill
Key Personnel: Dir., Dan Cassidy
Historic Building.
Collections: mill history; photographs; log mill.
Activities: demonstrations. Museum Sponsors: Millfest in September.
Hours & Admission Prices: Memorial Day to Labor Day Sat.-Sun. 10-3. Adults $2, children 12-17 $1; children under 12 no charge.

Cloudcroft

SACRAMENTO MOUNTAINS HISTORICAL MUSEUM, 1000 U.S. Hwy. 82, Cloudcroft, NM 88317. Mailing Address: P.O. Box 435, Cloudcroft, NM 88317-0435. Tel.: 575-682-2932. Fax: 575-682-3638.
E-mail: smhsmuseumoffice@yahoo.com
Web Site: cloudcroftmuseum.com
Founded: 1977.
Congressional District: 2
Key Personnel: Pres., Dr. Bill Boverie; Dir., Windy Jenkins.
Personnel Profile: Full-Time Paid 1; Part-Time Volunteers 10.
Governing Authority: nonprofit organization. Parent Institution: Sacramento Mountains Historical Society. Tax-exempt: 501(c)(3).
History Museum: housed in 1943 log cabin.
Collections: micro-filmed newspapers; photographs; maps; books. Historic Buildings: 1887 house; 1899 J. Arthur Eddy summer cottage.
Research Fields: oral history; local cemeteries.
Facilities: Books & museum-related items for sale.
Activities: lectures; guided tours. Museum Sponsors: Living History Events.
Publications: brochure, History of the Sacramento Mountains; Railroad to Cloudcroft; Logging Railroads of the Lincoln National Forest; Saga of the Sierra Blanca; Harrowing Adventures of an Old-Time Cowboy & Sheriff; book, In Pursuit of a Railroad.
Hours & Admission Prices: Summer: Mon.-Tues. & Fri.-Sat. 10-4, Sun. 1-4; Winter: Fri.-Sat. 10-4. Adults $5, children 6-12 $3; discounts to military; members & children under 6 no charge. Closed holidays. ♿
Attendance: 3,000 (estimated)
Membership: Adult $15; Couple $30; Family $40; Extended Family & Corporate $50.

Clovis

CLOVIS DEPOT MODEL TRAIN MUSEUM, 221 W. First St., Clovis, NM 88101-7409. Tel.: 575-762-0066; 888-762-0064. Fax: 575-762-0066 (call first).
E-mail: philipw@3lefties.com
Web Site: www.clovisdepot.com/
Founded: 1995.
Key Personnel: Dir, Cur, Phil Williams.
Personnel Profile: Full-Time Volunteers 2.
Model Train Museum.
Collections: area railroad history; period documents & photographs; model trains; operating telegraph station.
Facilities: library. Museum-related items for sale.
Hours & Admission Prices: March-Aug. & Oct.-Jan. Wed.-Sun. 12-5.

EULA MAE MUSEUM & ART GALLERY, Clovis Community College, 417 Schepps Blvd., Clovis, NM 88101-8345. Tel.: 505-769-4115.
Art Gallery and Museum.
Collections: artwork from local artists.
Hours & Admission Prices: Mon.-Thurs. 8:30-5, Fri. 9-1.

NORMAN & VI PETTY ROCK & ROLL MUSEUM, 105 E. Grand Ave., Clovis, NM 88101-7509. Tel.: 575-763-3435.
Web Site: www.pettymuseum.com
History Museum.
Collections: artifacts & memorabilia on Norman & Vi Petty.
Hours & Admission Prices: Mon.-Fri. 8-12 & 1-5, Sat. & group tours by appointment. Adults $5.

Columbus

COLUMBUS HISTORICAL SOCIETY MUSEUM, Hwy. 9 & 11, Columbus, NM 88029. Mailing Address: P.O. Box 562, Columbus, NM 88029-0562. Tel.: 505-531-2620.
Key Personnel: Acting Cur., Betty Dean; Pres. (V), Richard Dean.
Governing Authority: Tax-exempt.
Historical Society Museum.
Collections: local history & culture; American & Indian collection; military & weapons collection; Pancho Villa's Raid; photographs.
Facilities: Museum-related items for sale.
Hours & Admission Prices: Daily 10-4. No charge; donations accepted. Closed Christmas.
Membership: $45-$100.

PANCHO VILLA STATE PARK, Hwy. 9 & 11, Columbus, NM 88029. Mailing Address: P.O. Box 450, Columbus, NM 88029-0450. Tel.: 505-531-2711. Fax: 505-531-2115.
E-mail: victor.trujillo@state.nm.us
Key Personnel: Park Mgr., Victor Trujillo
State Park: located on the grounds of the former Camp Furlong.
Collections: replica of Curtiss JN-3 "Jenny" airplane; 1916 Dodge touring car; historic artifacts; military weapons & ribbons. Historic Sites: 1902 former U.S. Customs House; two adobe structures from the Camp Furlong-era; Camp Furlong Recreation Hall.
Hours & Admission Prices: Daily 8-5.

Deming

DEMING LUNA MIMBRES MUSEUM, 301 S. Silver St., Deming, NM 88030-3761. Tel.: 505-546-2382. Fax: 505-544-0121.
E-mail: director@deminglunamimbresmuseum.com
Web Site: www.deminglunamimbresmuseum.com
Founded: 1957.
Congressional District: 2
Key Personnel: Museum Shop Mgr., Joyce Peterson.
Personnel Profile: Full-Time Volunteers 1; Part-Time Volunteers 80.
Governing Authority: society; non-profit. Parent Institution: Luna County Historical Society. Tax-exempt: 501(c)(3).
Historical Society Museum & Historic House: housed in 1916 Deming National Armory; it once housed the unit that marched against Pancho Villa after his raid on Columbus NM & in 1941 housed men who were in the Bataan Death march; The Custom House, belonged to Seaman Field, an early custom agent.
Collections: Louise Southerland Toys & Doll Collection; Gem & Mineral Society Collection; Bessie C. May Collection of Clothing from 1880; Southwestern New Mexico early photography; military artifacts from frontier period-present; Mimbres Indian artifacts; Diamond A. Chuck-wagon; quilt room; 1863 concert grand piano; Indian Basket Collection; antique lace display; medical & dental room; art gallery; transportation annex; four-rooms depicting 1930s living; Indian Kiva; Old Deming Street scenes; blacksmith & forge exhibit; 1909 RH drive Ford Roadster; 1907 Red, 1912 Allison La France Fire Truck etc.; Ruth Anderson Bell Collection; A.J. Fabian Whiskey Bottle Collection; John & Mary Alice King Indian pottery exhibit; archives for research on SW New Mexico; Geode Kid collection of thunder eggs.
Research Fields: Mimbres Indian pottery; Luna County & Southwestern United States histories.
Facilities: research library on Mimbres Indian Art & Culture; archives southwestern corner of New Mexico. Handcrafted items, Indian crafts, sand paintings, turquoise and silver jewelry, books & notepaper for sale.
Activities: guided tours; formally organized education programs; permanent exhibitions; continuous art show of local artists.
Publications: book & supplement one, The History of Luna County.
Hours & Admission Prices: Mon.-Sat. 9-4, Sun. 1:30-4; groups by appointment. Adults $2; members no charge. Closed New Year's Day; Easter; Thanksgiving; Christmas. ♿
Attendance: 21,000 (accurate)
Membership: Individual $3; Life $100; Endowment Fund $1,000 & up.

Edgewood

WILDLIFE WEST NATURE PARK, 87 N. Frontage Rd., Edgewood, NM 87015. Mailing Address: P.O. Box 1359, Edgewood, NM 87015-1359. Tel.: 505-281-7655; 877-981-9453. Fax: 505-281-7170.
E-mail: info@wildlifewest.org
Web Site: www.wildlifewest.org
Wildlife Nature Park.
Collections: wildlife.
Hours & Admission Prices: Summer: daily 10-6; Winter: daily 12-4. Adults $7, seniors $6, students $4; children under 5 no charge.

Espanola

BOND HOUSE MUSEUM, 706 Bond St., Espanola, NM 87532-2727. Mailing Address: 405 N. Paseo De Onate, Espanola, NM 87532-2619. Tel.: 505-747-8535.
E-mail: mail@plazadeespanola.com
Historic House: former home of Frank Bond & his family. Listed on the National Register of Historic Places.
Collections: historical artifacts & photographs; personal artifacts; furnishings.
Hours & Admission Prices: Mon.-Fri. 12-4, Sat. 11-3. No charge.

Farmington

BOLACK ELECTROMECHANICAL MUSEUM, B Square Ranch, 3901 Bloomfield Hwy., Farmington, NM 87401-2831. Tel.: 505-325-4275.
Founded: 1990.
Key Personnel: Dir., Tommy Bolack
Electromechanical Museum.
Collections: artifacts representing electric power, broadcasting, medical, agriculture, oil & gas; display of slate & marble switchboard; small power distribution objects.
Hours & Admission Prices: Mon.-Sat. 9-3. No charge. Closed holidays.
Attendance: 3,500

BOLACK MUSEUM OF FISH AND WILDLIFE, B Square Ranch, 3901 Bloomfield Hwy., Farmington, NM 87401-2831. Tel.: 505-325-4275.
Founded: 1975.
Key Personnel: Dir., Tommy Bolack.
Governing Authority: Tax-exempt.
Fish and Wildlife Museum.
Collections: over 2,500 specimens
Hours & Admission Prices: Mon.-Sat. 9-3. No charge. Closed holidays. ♿
Attendance: 18,000

FARMINGTON MUSEUM, (M), 3041 E. Main St., Farmington, NM 87402-7621. Tel.: 505-599-1174. Fax: 505-326-7572.
E-mail: bwilsey@fmtn.org
Web Site: www.farmingtonmuseum.org
Founded: 1980.
Congressional District: 3
Key Personnel: Dir., Bart Wilsey; Collections Mgr., Debbie Doggett; Education Coord., David Meyers; Children's Museum Coord., Crystal Williams; Cur., Don Snoddy; Education Specialist, Donna Thatcher; Exhibit Coord., Mitchell McAlexander; Volunteer Coord., Kandy LeMoine; Office Mgr., Andrea Logan; Hospitality Supvr., Amy Homer.
Personnel Profile: Full-Time Paid 9; Part-Time Paid 7; Part-Time Volunteers 20.
Governing Authority: municipal; nonprofit organization. Parent Institution: City of Farmington, Office of Cultural Affairs. Tax-exempt.
General Museum.
Collections: artifacts from the history of the San Juan Basin & Four Corners area; archives; photographs; manuscripts; costumes; oil & gas industry; trading post; oral histories, oil & gas boom, trading post families; nature center; living history farm & orchards.
Research Fields: local & regional history.
Facilities: library of material on pioneer families of Farmington & records of several oil & gas booms available for research by appointment; reading room. Museum-related items for sale.
Activities: guided tours; lectures; permanent & traveling exhibitions; video & slide presentations.
Publications: bimonthly newsletter, The Confluence.
Hours & Admission Prices: Mon.-Sat. 8-5. No charge; donations accepted. Closed New Year's Day; Thanksgiving; Christmas. ♿
Attendance: 75,000 (accurate)
Membership: Senior Individual $15; Individual $20; Senior Couple $25; Family $35; School, Organization, Friend & Business $75; Patron $100 & up; Sponsor $250; Benefactor $1,000 & up.

HARVEST GROVE FARM & ORCHARDS EXHIBIT BARN, Animas Park off Browning Pkwy., Farmington, NM 87402. Mailing Address: 3041 E. Main St., Farmington, NM 87402-7621. Tel.: 505-599-1423.
Web Site: www.farmingtonmuseum.org
Historic House.
Collections: period tractors; early agricultural equipment.
Activities: special events; temporary exhibits.
Hours & Admission Prices: By appointment.

RIVERSIDE NATURE CENTER, Animas Park off Browning Pkwy., Farmington, NM 87401. Mailing Address: 3041 E. Main St., Farmington, NM 87402-7621. Tel.: 505-599-1422.
Web Site: www.farmingtonmuseum.org
Nature Center.
Collections: wildlife & their habitats.
Facilities: Museum-related items for sale.
Activities: educational programs; special events.
Hours & Admission Prices: Tues.-Sat. 1-6, Sun. 1-5; other times by appointment.

Folsom

FOLSOM MUSEUM, INC., Main Street, Folsom, NM 88419. Mailing Address: P.O. Box 454, Folsom, NM 88419-0454. Tel.: 505-278-3616 (Sept.-May) & 2122 (June-Aug. & Sat.-Sun. in May & Sept.).
E-mail: bkthompson@bacavalley.com
Web Site: www.folsommuseum.org
Founded: 1967.
Congressional District: 2
Key Personnel: Pres., Abbie Reaves; Sec., MariJo Balmer; Treas., Kay Thompson.
Personnel Profile: Part-Time Paid 2; Part-Time Volunteers 1.
Governing Authority: nonprofit organization. Parent Institution: Folsom Museum. Tax-exempt.
Archaeology Museum: housed in the 1896 Doherty Mercantile Store Building.
Collections: Folsom Man discovery; local artifacts; historic items used in the settling of the area.
Major Exhibits: Smithsonian Music Exhibit (T), 8/10-9/10.
Facilities: Books & museum-related items for sale.
Publications: books, The Folsom, New Mexico Story and a Pictorial Review; The Folsom Hotel Story; pamphlet, Folsom Man; books, Arrowheads & Stone Artifacts; From Martyrs to Murders; The Story of Folsom; Folsom 1888-1988, Then & Now.
Hours & Admission Prices: May & Sept. Sat.-Sun. 10-5; June-Aug. Mon.-Fri. 10-5; other times by appointment. Adults $1.50; members no charge. ♿
Attendance: 1,700 (estimated)
Membership: Individual $10; Family $20; Lifetime $200; Homesteaders $250; Storekeeper $500; Banker $1,000.

Fort Sumner

BILLY THE KID MUSEUM, 1435 E. Sumner Ave., Fort Sumner, NM 88119-9606. Tel.: 575-355-2380. Fax: 575-355-1380.
E-mail: btkmuseum@plateautel.net
Web Site: billythekidmuseumfortsumner.com
Founded: 1953.
Key Personnel: Owner, Donald E. Sweet; Museum Shop Mgr., Tim Sweet; Museum Shop Mgr., Lula Sweet.
Governing Authority: individual operation.
Local History Museum.
Collections: Old West, local & Billy the Kid memorabilia.
Facilities: Museum-related items for sale.
Activities: tours.
Publications: brochures.
Hours & Admission Prices: Jan. 16-May 14 & Oct. 2-Dec. Mon.-Sat. 8:30-5; May 15-Oct. 1 daily 8:30-5. Adults $5, senior citizens 62 & over $4, children ages 7-15 $3; children under 7 no charge. Closed Easter; Thanksgiving; Christmas. ♿
Attendance: 20,000 (accurate)

BOSQUE REDONDO MEMORIAL FORT SUMNER STATE MONUMENT, 3647 Billy the Kid Rd., Fort Sumner, NM 88119-0356. Mailing Address: Box 356, Fort Sumner, NM 88119-0356. Tel.: 505-355-2573. Fax: 505-355-2575.
E-mail: hweeldi@plateautel.net
Web Site: www.nmmonuments.org
Formerly: Fort Sumner State Monument
Founded: 1968.
Key Personnel: Monument Mgr., Angie Manning; Pres. (V) & Museum Shop Mgr., MaryAnn Cortese.
Personnel Profile: Full-Time Paid 3.
Governing Authority: state. Parent Institution: Museum of New Mexico. Subsidiary Institution: New Mexico State Monuments. Tax-exempt: 170(c)(1).
Historic Site: 1862-1869 frontier fort; control & supply station for Bosque Redondo Indian Reservation; relocation site of the Mescalero, Apache & Navajo peoples in the early 1860s; destination of The Long Walk.
Collections: local history & culture; Native American artifacts; photographs; personal artifacts.
Facilities: 700 sq. ft. exhibit space.

Activities: guided tours; lectures; living history demos; film.
Publications: El Palacio.
Hours & Admission Prices: Daily 8:30-5. Adults $5; AAM members, school groups & children 17 & under no charge. Closed New Year's Day; Easter; Thanksgiving; Christmas.
Attendance: 10,126 (accurate)
Membership: Individual $10; Partner $25; Corporate $100 & up; Negotiated Sponsor: Please call 505-355-2573.

Gallup

STORYTELLER MUSEUM, 201 E. Hwy. 66, Gallup, NM 87301-6126. Tel.: 505-863-4131.
E-mail: jeremy@cia-g.com
Web Site: gallupculturalcenter.org
Key Personnel: Dir., Jeremy Boucher.
Governing Authority: Parent Institution: Southwest Indian Foundation. Tax-exempt.
Native American History.
Collections: pottery; basketry; rug weaving; Kachina dolls; model trains; exhibits on silversmithing & traditional sandpaintings.
Facilities: Museum-related items for sale.
Hours & Admission Prices: Memorial Day to Labor Day Mon.-Sat. 9-4; Winter: Mon.-Fri. 8-5. No charge.

Grants

NEW MEXICO MINING MUSEUM, 100 N. Iron Ave., Grants, NM 87020-3657. Mailing Address: P.O. Box 297, Grants, NM 87020-0297. Tel.: 505-287-4802; 800-748-2142. Fax: 505-287-8224.
E-mail: discover@grants.org
Web Site: www.grants.org
Key Personnel: Exec. Dir., Star Gonzales
Mining Museum.
Collections: mining history; Native American artifacts; minerals; mining machinery; drilling & blasting equipment.
Hours & Admission Prices: Mon.-Sat. 9-4. Adults 19-59 $3, seniors 60 & over and youth 7-18 $2; children 6 & under no charge. Closed holidays.

Hillsboro

BLACK RANGE MUSEUM, Hwy. NM 152, Hillsboro, NM 88042. Mailing Address: P.O. Box 454, Hillsboro, NM 88042-0454. Tel.: 505-895-5685.
Founded: 1961.
Key Personnel: Dir., June Anders
History Museum.
Collections: local history; mining artifacts.
Hours & Admission Prices: Thurs.-Sat. 11-4, Sun. 1-5. No charge; donations accepted. Closed Easter; Thanksgiving; Christmas.
Attendance: 800 (estimated)

Hobbs

LINAM RANCH MUSEUM, West of Lea County Airport on U.S. 180, Hobbs, NM 88240. Mailing Address: P.O. Box 743, Hobbs, NM 88241-0743. Tel.: 505-393-4784.
History Museum.
Collections: Indian artifacts & pioneer mementos; photographs.
Hours & Admission Prices: By appointment.

NEW MEXICO WING-CONFEDERATE AIR FORCE MUSEUM, Hobbs/Lea County Airport, Hwy. 62-180, Hobbs, NM 88240. Mailing Address: 1318 N. Dal Peso, Hobbs, NM 88240-4528. Tel.: 505-391-2934.
Military Museum.
Collections: airworthy aircraft; land vehicles; aircraft engines; artifacts from WWII.
Hours & Admission Prices: Daily 8-sunset. No charge.

WESTERN HERITAGE MUSEUM COMPLEX & LEA COUNTY COWBOY HALL OF FAME, 5317 Lovington Hwy., NMJC Campus, Hobbs, NM 88240-9121. Tel.: 575-392-6730. Fax: 575-492-2680.
E-mail: themuseum@nmjc.edu
Web Site: www.westernheritagemuseumcomplex.org
Founded: 1978.
Congressional District: 2
Key Personnel: Chm. Bd. (V), Ray Battaglini; Exec. Dir. Western Heritage Museum Complex, Calvin Smith; Cur., Erin Anderson.
Personnel Profile: Full-Time Paid 5; Part-Time Paid 2; Interns 3.
Governing Authority: college; nonprofit organization. Parent Institution: New Mexico Junior College. Tax-exempt: 501(c)(3).
History & Archaeology Museum.
Collections: historical & archaeological artifacts from southeastern New Mexico; ranching; rodeo; archaeological & petroleum-related artifacts & archives related to Lea County, NM.
Research Fields: archaeology of southeastern NM.
Facilities: 5,000 sq. ft. exhibit space.
Activities: guided tours; lectures; slide programs; temporary exhibitions; movies; performances; special events. Museum Sponsors: Ranch Rodeo; Special Family Nights.
Publications: quarterly newsletter.
Hours & Admission Prices: Tues.-Sat. 10-5, Sun. 1-5; tours by appointment. Adults $3, seniors & students 6-18 $2; children 5 & under, NMJC students & members no charge. Closed major holidays; college holidays; Spring & Christmas break.
Attendance: 8,000 (accurate)
Membership: Student $5; LCCNOF $20; Individual $25; Family $50; Associate, Civic & Nonprofit Organization $100; Provider $250; Investor $500; Endorser $1,000; Corporate Organization $1,000; Life $1,500.

Jemez Springs

JEMEZ STATE MONUMENT, One mile North of Jemez Springs, State Hwy. 4, Jemez Springs, NM 87025. Mailing Address: P.O. Box 143, Jemez Springs, NM 87025-0143. Tel.: 505-829-3530; 800-495-1279. Fax: 505-829-3530.
E-mail: giusewa@valornet.com
Web Site: www.nmmonuments.org
Founded: 1935.
Congressional District: 65
Key Personnel: Monuments Dir., Jose Cisneros; Monument Mgr., Richard Reycraft; Ranger, Jennifer Miksula; Ranger, Joshua Madalena; Receptionist, Brenda Tafoya.
Personnel Profile: Full-Time Paid 4; Part-Time Volunteers 1.
Governing Authority: state. Parent Institution: Department of Cultural Affairs. Tax-exempt: 170(c)(1).
Historic Site: ruins of Towa Pueblo, Giusewa, occupied 1280-1680; ruins of Spanish mission, San Jose de los Jemez.
Collections: local history & culture; Indian village ruins; Native American artifacts.
Activities: guided tours; lectures; films. Annual Events: Arts Festival; Indian Dances.
Hours & Admission Prices: Nov.-April 1 Wed.-Mon. 8:30-5, April 2-Oct. daily 8:30-4:30. Adults $3, senior residents Wed. $1; discount to AAM & ICOM members; MNM Foundation member, New Mexico seniors with I.D. on Sun. and children 16 & under no charge. Coronado & Jemez 2 Day Pass $5. Annual Site Pass $10. Annual Museum & Monument Pass $25. Closed New Year's Day; Easter; Thanksgiving; Christmas.
Attendance: 18,000 (estimated)
Membership: Student $20; Senior Individual $35; Individual $40; Senior Couple $45; Family $50; Sponsor $75; higher levels of membership with related benefits are available.

Kingston

HISTORIC PERCHA BANK MUSEUM, HC66 Main St., Kingston, NM 88042. Mailing Address: HC66, Box 119A, Kingston, NM 88042-9701. Tel.: 505-895-5032.
Web Site: www.perchabank.com
Historic Bank Museum.
Collections: bank history; period furnishings; photographs; mining artifacts; newspapers.
Hours & Admission Prices: Summer: Fri.-Sun. 10-4; other times by appointment. No charge; donations accepted.

Las Cruces

THE BRANIGAN CULTURAL CENTER, (M), 501 N. Main St., Las Cruces, NM 88001-1207. Tel.: 575-541-2154. Fax: 575-541-2152.
E-mail: gcourts@las-cruces.org
Web Site: www.museums.las-cruces.org
Formerly: Las Cruces Historical Museum & Cultural Center
Founded: 1981.
Congressional District: 2
Key Personnel: Dir., Garland Courts; Cur. Education, Mary Kay Shannon; Cur. Exhibits, J. Carey Crane.
Personnel Profile: Full-Time Paid 3; Part-Time Paid 2.
Governing Authority: municipal; nonprofit organization. Subsidiary Institutions: Las Cruces Museum of Natural History, Las Cruces, NM; Las Cruces Museum of Art; Las Cruces Railroad Museum. Tax-exempt: 501(c)(3).
Art & History Museum: housed in the former city library built in 1934. Listed on the National Register of Historic Places.

Collections: Las Cruces history
Research Fields: Mexican cultural exchange.
Facilities: 100-seat auditorium; educational facilities; 2,000 sq. ft. exhibit space; 100-seat theater.
Activities: arts festivals; concerts; dance recitals; docent program; films; formal education programs for adults, children, & college students; lectures; school loan service; temporary & traveling exhibitions; theater.
Publications: quarterly e-newsletter; annual report.
Hours & Admission Prices: Mon.-Fri. 10-4, Sat. 9-1. No charge; donations accepted. Closed Federal holidays. ♿
Attendance: 53,191 (accurate)

CITY OF LAS CRUCES MUSEUM SYSTEM, 151 N. Church St., Las Cruces, NM 88001. Mailing Address: Museums Administration, City of Las Cruces, P.O. Box 20000, Las Cruces, NM 88004-9002. Tel.: 575-541-2296. Fax: 575-525-8587.
E-mail: wticknor@las-cruces.org
Web Site: museums.las-cruces.org
Founded: 1982.
Congressional District: 2
Key Personnel: Dir., Will Ticknor; Volunteer Coord. & Cur. Education, Julia Hansen; Sr. Cur. Exhibits, J. Carey Crane; Sr. Cur. Collections, Stephanie Long.
Personnel Profile: Full-Time Paid 6; Part-Time Volunteers 125.
Governing Authority: municipal; nonprofit organization. Branch Museums: Branigan Cultural Center, 500 N. Water St., Las Cruces, NM; Las Cruces Museum of Art, 490 N. Water St., Las Cruces, NM; Las Cruces Railroad Museum, 351 N. Mesilla St., Las Cruces, NM; Las Cruces Museum of Natural History, 700 Telshor Blvd., Las Cruces, NM; The Rio Grande Theatre; Las Cruces, NM. Tax-exempt.
Art & History Museums: Branigan Cultural Center is listed on the National & State Register of Historic Places. Railroad Museum: housed in the Santa Fe Depot; listed on the National Register of Historic Places. Rio Grande Theatre, built 1926, listed on the National Register of Historic Places.
Collections: Branigan Cultural Center: local history; paintings. Las Cruces Museum of Art (MoA): contemporary art. Museum of Natural History: natural history, science, & the Chihuahuan Desert. Railroad Museum: railroad history.
Facilities: library; auditorium; educational facilities; 4,700 sq. ft. exhibit space; observation platform.
Activities: dance recitals; docent program; formal education programs for adults & children; guided tours; lectures; temporary & traveling exhibitions; theater.
Publications: quarterly e-newsletter; annual report.
Hours & Admission Prices: Mon.-Fri. 8-5. No charge; donations accepted. Closed Federal holidays. ♿
Attendance: 292,603 (accurate)
Membership: Foundation $25.

LAS CRUCES MUSEUM OF ART, 491 N. Main St., Las Cruces, NM 88001. Mailing Address: P.O. Box 20000, Las Cruces, NM 88004. Tel.: 575-541-2137. Fax: 575-541-2371.
E-mail: lpugh@las-cruces.org
Web Site: museums.las-cruces.org
Founded: 1999.
Key Personnel: Dir., Lisa Pugh; Cur. Education, Greg Phillipy; Cur. Exhibits, Joy Miller.
Personnel Profile: Full-Time Paid 3; Part-Time Paid 3; Part-Time Volunteers 10.
Governing Authority: municipal; nonprofit organization.
Art Museum.
Collections: works of contemporary art; paintings; prints; sculpture; ceramics; photographs.
Major Exhibits: Margi Weir: Three Decades, 11/09-1/10; Swarm: Julia Barello, 11/09-1/10; Mirage: Rachelle Thiewes, 11/09-1/10; Images of the 20th Century, 2/10-4/10; NMSU - BFA Exhibition, 5/10; Looking Ahead - Mott-Warsh Collection (T), 12/10-1/11.
Facilities: educational facilities; 3,500 sq. ft. exhibit space. Museum-related items for sale.
Activities: arts festivals; concerts; docent program; formal education programs for adults & children; temporary exhibitions; studio program school; guided tours; lectures; loan, temporary & traveling exhibitions; study clubs.
Hours & Admission Prices: Mon.-Fri. 10-4, Sat. 9-1. No charge; donations accepted. Closed Federal holidays. ♿
Attendance: 75,000 (accurate)

LAS CRUCES MUSEUM OF NATURAL HISTORY, 700 S. Telshor in the Mesilla Valley Mall, Las Cruces, NM 88011. Tel.: 575-522-3122. Fax: 575-532-3370.
E-mail: mwalczak@las-cruces.org
Web Site: www.museums.las-cruces.org
Founded: 1984.
Congressional District: 2
Key Personnel: Dir., Michael Walczak; Cur. Education, Kimberly Hanson; Cur. Exhibits, Carey Crane.
Personnel Profile: Full-Time Paid 3; Part-Time Paid 4.
Governing Authority: municipal; nonprofit organization. Parent Institution: City of Las Cruces Museum System.
Science & Nature Museum.
Collections: nature & science focused on the Chihuahuan Desert including reptiles, insects, amphibians & fish.
Facilities: 3,900 sq. ft. exhibit space.
Activities: docent program; formal education programs for adults & children; guided tours; lectures; temporary & traveling exhibitions.
Publications: quarterly e-newsletter; annual report.
Hours & Admission Prices: Closing in April 2010 for relocation until Spring 2012. Mon.-Thurs. & Sat. 10-5, Fri. 10-8, Sun. 1-5. No charge; donations accepted. Closed Federal holidays. ♿
Attendance: 158,097 (accurate)

LAS CRUCES RAILROAD MUSEUM, 351 N. Mesilla St., Las Cruces, NM 88001. Tel.: 575-647-4480.
Founded: 2004.
Congressional District: 2
Key Personnel: Dir., Rebecca Slaughter; Cur. Education, Joanne Beer; Cur. Exhibits, Carey Crane.
Personnel Profile: Full-Time Paid 1; Part-Time Paid 1.
Governing Authority: municipal; nonprofit organization. Parent Institution: City of Las Cruces Museum System. Operated by the Branigan Cultural Center.
Railroad History Museum: housed in an Atchison, Topeka & Santa Fe, Pueblo Revival style depot; built in 1910. Listed on the National Register of Historic Places.
Collections: local railroad history; railroad memorabilia; photographs; period artifacts; historic buildings.
Facilities: library; 3,000 sq. ft. exhibit space.
Activities: docent program; formal education programs for adults & children; guided tours; lectures; temporary exhibits. Annual Events: Railroad Days in April & May; Annual Holiday Lighting & Celebration in December.
Publications: quarterly e-newsletter; annual report.
Hours & Admission Prices: Thurs.-Sat. 10-4. No charge; donations accepted. Closed Federal holidays. ♿
Attendance: 10,871 (accurate)

NEW MEXICO FARM & RANCH HERITAGE MUSEUM, 4100 Dripping Springs Rd., Las Cruces, NM 88011-5067. Tel.: 505-522-4100. Fax: 505-522-3085.
E-mail: cmassey@frh.state.nm.us
Web Site: www.nmfarmandranchmuseum.org
Founded: 1991.
Congressional District: 2
Key Personnel: Dir., Mark Santiago; Foundation Pres. (V), Tommy Perez; Collections Mgr., Holly Radke; Exec. Dir. Foundation, Shawnna Brown; Education, Scott Green; Public Rels., Craig Massey; Museum Shop Mgr., Maria Vessel.
Personnel Profile: Full-Time Paid 28; Part-Time Paid 3; Part-Time Volunteers 150; Interns 2.
Governing Authority: state; nonprofit. Parent Institution: New Mexico Office of Cultural Affairs, 228 E. Palace Ave., Santa Fe 87503. Subsidiary Institution: New Mexico Farm & Ranch Heritage Foundation. Tax-exempt: 501(c)(3).
Agriculture, History & Science Museum.
Collections: concentration on history of agriculture in New Mexico from prehistoric to modern times. Historic Buildings: blacksmith shop; barn.
Research Fields: oral history-institutional beginnings & rural life.
Facilities: 2,000-vol. library of books on agricultural history; 144-seat auditorium; botanical garden; 140-seat restaurant; 2 classrooms; 25,000 sq. ft. exhibit space; 47 acres consisting of crops.
Activities: arts festivals; concerts; dance recitals; docent program; formal education programs for adults, children & college students (internships, New Mexico State University); guided tours; hobby workshops; lectures; loan, participatory, temporary & traveling exhibitions; theater; training programs for professional museum workers; broadcast programs; desert gardening. Annual Events: San Isidro Day, Patron Saint of Agriculture, in May; Cowboy Days, music and poetry festival in March.

Publications: quarterly newsletter, New Mexico Farm & Ranch Heritage.
Hours & Admission Prices: Mon.-Sat. 9-5, Sun. 12-5. Adults $5, children 5-17 $2; discount to seniors 60 & over; members no charge. Closed Thanksgiving; Christmas. ♿
Attendance: 35,000 (estimated)
Membership: Individual $35.

UNIVERSITY ART GALLERY, NEW MEXICO STATE UNIVERSITY, (M), University Ave., E. of Solano, Las Cruces, NM 88003-8001. Mailing Address: Box 30001, Dept. Box 3572, Las Cruces, NM 88003-8001. Tel.: 505-646-2545. Fax: 505-646-8036.
E-mail: artglry@nmsu.edu
Web Site: www.nmsu.edu/~artgal
Founded: 1973.
Congressional District: 2
Key Personnel: C.E.O., Preston Thayer; Head Art Dept., Spencer Fidler.
Personnel Profile: Full-Time Paid 2; Part-Time Paid 8; Part-Time Volunteers 10; Interns 1.
Governing Authority: university; nonprofit. Parent Institution: New Mexico State University. Tax-exempt: 501(c)(3).
University Art Gallery.
Collections: 19th-century Mexican retablos; contemporary prints; photographs; painting & works on paper.
Research Fields: contemporary art; retablos.
Facilities: 4,600 sq. ft. exhibition gallery; lecture hall.
Activities: guided tours; lectures; gallery talks; workshops; symposia; temporary, loan & traveling exhibits.
Publications: biannual newsletter, Visiones.
Hours & Admission Prices: Summer: Tues.-Fri. 11-4; Winter: Tues.-Fri. 10-5, Sat. 12-4. No charge; donations accepted. Closed university holidays. ♿
Attendance: 21,000 (accurate)
Membership: Students & Senior Citizens $25; Individual & Family $50; Patron $150; Benefactor $400.

UNIVERSITY MUSEUM, NEW MEXICO STATE UNIVERSITY, (M), Univ. Ave. at Solano Dr., Kent Hall, Las Cruces, NM 88003. Mailing Address: P.O. Box 30001, MSC 3564, Las Cruces, NM 88003-8001. Tel.: 575-646-5161. Fax: 575-646-1419. TDD: 505-646-3739.
E-mail: museum@nmsu.edu
Web Site: www.nmsu.edu/~museum/
Founded: 1959.
Congressional District: 2
Key Personnel: Dir., Dr. Monte McCrossin; Cur. Collections & Exhibitions, Dr. Jennifer Robles; Public Program Coord., Katherine Brooks.
Personnel Profile: Full-Time Paid 2; Part-Time Paid 3; Interns 2.
Governing Authority: university. Parent Institution: New Mexico State University. Tax-exempt: 301(b).
University Anthropology Museum.
Collections: Southwestern U.S. & Northwestern Mexico archaeology; ethnology; history; science.
Major Exhibits: Communicating with the Spirits: Hopi Katsina Dolls, 2/10-6/10; Trails of the Southwest, 2/10-6/10; Behind the Mask: Exploring the Origins of Pascua Yaqui Chapayekam Rituals, 2/10-6/10.
Research Fields: Southwestern U.S. archaeology; ethnology; history.
Facilities: research library; archaeology labs.
Activities: guided tours; field trips; lectures; workshops; temporary exhibitions.
Publications: newsletter; Taylor, Mary Daniels (2004) A Place as Wild as the West Ever Was: Mesilla, New Mexico, 1848-1872; New Mexico State University Museum, Las Cruces.
Hours & Admission Prices: Tues.-Sat. 10-4. No charge; donations accepted. Closed major and university holidays. ♿
Attendance: 21,000 (estimated)
Membership: Student $10; Individual & Family $25; Contributing $50; Sustaining $100; Patron $250.

Las Vegas

CITY OF LAS VEGAS MUSEUM AND ROUGH RIDER MEMORIAL COLLECTION, (M), 727 Grand Ave., Las Vegas, NM 87701. Mailing Address: 1700 N. Grand Ave., Las Vegas, NM 87701-4731. Tel.: 505-454-1401, ext. 283. Fax: 505-425-7335.
E-mail: museum@desertgate.com
Web Site: lasvegasmuseum.org
Founded: 1960.
Congressional District: 3
Key Personnel: Admin., Linda Gegick.
Personnel Profile: Full-Time Paid 1; Part-Time Paid 3; Part-Time Volunteers 5.
Governing Authority: municipal. Tax-exempt: 170(b).
History Museum: Santa Fe Trail interpretive site.
Collections: military artifacts; photographs; Rough Riders' Cuban campaign of the Spanish-American War; Rough Riders' reunion; 19th-20th century Las Vegas history; agriculture; ranching; industry; post 1880 Santa Fe Trail artifacts.
Facilities: Museum-related items for sale.
Activities: community involvement; volunteer program; cultural programs.
Publications: brochures.
Hours & Admission Prices: Tues.-Sat. 10-4. No charge; donations accepted. Closed most holidays. ♿
Attendance: 3,500 (accurate)
Membership: Student & Senior $10; Individual $15; Family $25; Supporting $30-$59; Sustaining $60-$99; Sponsor $100-$499; Patron $500 & up.

THE RAY DREW GALLERY-NEW MEXICO HIGHLANDS UNIVERSITY, National Ave., Las Vegas, NM 87701. Tel.: 505-454-3338 & 3332. Fax: 505-454-0026.
E-mail: gallery@nmhu.edu
Formerly: The Fine Arts Gallery-New Mexico Highlands University
Founded: 1982.
Key Personnel: C.E.O., Dr. Jim Fries; Dir., Bob Read.
Personnel Profile: Full-Time Paid 1.
Governing Authority: university; nonprofit. Tax-exempt: 501(c)(3).
Art Museum.
Collections: fine art prints from 1500 to present.
Facilities: classrooms; 800 sq. ft. exhibit space.
Activities: fine art exhibitions.
Hours & Admission Prices: Mon.-Fri. 8-5. No charge. Closed major holidays.
Attendance: 9,000 (estimated)

Lincoln

HISTORIC LINCOLN, Hwy. 380, Lincoln, NM 88338. Mailing Address; P.O. Box 36, Lincoln, NM 88338-0036. Tel.: 505-653-4025. Fax: 505-653-4668.
E-mail: moth@zianet.com
Founded: 1968.
Congressional District: 2
Key Personnel: Dir., Jean Stoddard; Site Mgr., Dee Kessler.
Personnel Profile: Full-Time Paid 1; Part-Time Paid 7; Part-Time Volunteers 10.
Governing Authority: nonprofit organization. Subsidiary Institution: The Hubbard Museum of the American West, 841 Hwy. 70, W., Ruidoso Downs, NM.
History Museum.
Collections: local Hispanic & Native American cultural artifacts; Lincoln, County War & Billy the Kid collections; historic photographs; furniture; medical instruments; Buffalo Soldiers military artifacts; historic buildings.
Research Fields: Lincoln County War; Buffalo Soldiers; Billy the Kid
Facilities: 1,000-vol. library; 4 historic buildings. Museum-related items for sale.
Activities: outdoor campfire circle programs; permanent & temporary exhibitions; educational programs; summer arts workshops for children; guided tours; lectures.
Publications: book, Heroes and Villains of the Lincoln County War.
Hours & Admission Prices: Daily 8:30-4:30. Adults $6; discounts to senior citizens & New Mexico residents on Wed. & Sun.; members, museum employees and children 16 & under no charge. Closed New Year's Day; Easter; Thanksgiving; Christmas.
Attendance: 28,602 (accurate)
Membership: Supporting $60; Associate $100; Sponsor $250; Sustaining $500; Friends Circle $1,000; Patron Circle $2,500; Directors Circle $5,000.

LINCOLN STATE MONUMENT, Hwy. 380, Lincoln, NM 88338. Mailing Address: P.O. Box 36, Lincoln, NM 88338-0036. Tel.: 575-653-4372. Fax: 575-653-4372.
Founded: 1940.
Key Personnel: Monument Mgr., DeAnn Kessler; Ranger, Bennie Long; Ranger, Ira Rabke; Receptionist, Sandra Smith.
Governing Authority: state. Parent Institution: Museum of New Mexico. Tax-exempt: 170(c)(1).
Historic Site: location of Lincoln County War where Billy the Kid fought.
Collections: Courthouse Museum; Tunstall Store Museum; San Juan Mission; Torreon & Montano Store.
Facilities: exhibit space.
Activities: guided tours; lectures; films. Museum Sponsor: Old Lincoln Days.
Hours & Admission Prices: Daily 8:30-4:30. Adults $6; youth 16 & under no charge. Closed New Year's Day; Easter; Thanksgiving; Christmas. ♿
Attendance: 41,000 (estimated)

OLD LINCOLN COUNTY COURTHOUSE MUSEUM, Lincoln State Monument, Hwy. 380, Lincoln, NM 88338. Mailing Address: P.O. Box 36, Lincoln, NM 88338-0036. Tel.: 575-653-4372; 800-434-6320 (NM only). Fax: 575-653-4372.
E-mail: deannkessler@state.nm.us
Web Site: www.nmmonuments.org
Founded: 1937.
Key Personnel: Monument Mgr., DeAnn Kessler.
Personnel Profile: Full-Time Paid 3.
Governing Authority: state. New Mexico State Monuments: 1880 Brent House; 1860 Convento; 1850 Torreon; 1874 Tunstall Store Museum; 1890 Fresquez House & Watson House; 1874 Wortley Hotel; 1887 San Jaun Mission; 1874 Courthouse Museum. Tax-exempt.
History Museum.
Collections: Indian artifacts; papers; furniture; clothing; tools; art objects.
Research Fields: history of southeast New Mexico, Lincoln County.
Facilities: library of research files on history of area; reading room; restaurant.
Activities: permanent & temporary exhibitions; films; interpretive tours.
Hours & Admission Prices: Daily 8:30-4:30; groups by appointment. Adults $6; children under 16 no charge. Closed New Year's Day; Easter; Thanksgiving; Christmas. ♿
Attendance: 40,000 (accurate)

Lordsburg

LORDSBURG-HIDALGO COUNTY MUSEUM, 710 E. 2nd St., Lordsburg, NM 88045. Tel.: 575-542-9086.
Web Site: www.lordsburghidalgocounty.net/museum/museumhome.htm
History Museum.
Collections: Prisoner of War memorabilia; Johnson photographs; Dr. Baxter's personal artifacts; mining; military; period tools; arrowheads; minerals & rocks.
Hours & Admission Prices: Mon.-Fri. 1-5.

SHAKESPEARE GHOST TOWN, 2 1/2 Miles South of Main St., Lordsburg, NM 88045. Mailing Address: P.O. Box 253, Lordsburg, NM 88045-0253. Tel.: 505-542-9034.
Web Site: www.shakespeareghostown.com
Founded: 1970.
Key Personnel: Pres. & Dir., Emanuel D. Hough; Treas., Linda Erikson.
Personnel Profile: Full-Time Volunteers 4; Part-Time Volunteers 20.
Governing Authority: nonprofit organization. Tax-exempt: 501(c)(3).
History Museum.
Collections: southwest history 1856-1935; furniture; period guns; custom made holsters, saddles & tack.
Facilities: 300-vol. library of southwest history books; 8,900 sq. ft. exhibit space. Books & handmade blacksmith items for sale.
Activities: guided tours; lectures. Annual Events: Living History Events in April, June, August & October.
Publications: quarterly newsletter, Shakespeare Quarterly.
Hours & Admission Prices: Tours: 2nd weekend of month 10-12 & 2-4. Adults $4, children 6-12 $3. Living History Events: 4th weekend in April, June, Aug. & Oct. 10-12 & 2-4. Adults $5, children 6-12 $4. ♿
Attendance: 3,000 (accurate)
Membership: Individual $10; Family $25; Business $50; Patron $100; Lifetime $500.

Los Alamos

THE ART CENTER AT FULLER LODGE, 2132 Central Ave., Los Alamos, NM 87544-4041. Tel.: 505-662-9331. Fax: 505-662-9334.
E-mail: director@artful.org
Web Site: artfulnm.org
Founded: 1977.
Congressional District: 3
Key Personnel: Chm. (V), Carole Rinald; Exec. Dir., John Werenko; Dir., Gloria Gilmore-House; Asst. Dir., Craig Carmer; Office Mgr., Betty Hettich; Museum Shop Mgr., Maria Theye.
Personnel Profile: Part-Time Paid 4; Part-Time Volunteers 40; Interns 1.
Governing Authority: nonprofit organization. Tax-exempt: 501(c)(3).
Art Center & Gallery.
Collections: various forms of art media.
Activities: guided tours; lectures; films; gallery talks; traveling & invitational exhibitions; rental & sales gallery; juried exhibits; docent training programs. Annual Events: summer & autumn arts & crafts fairs; Affordable Art Benefit Sale in December.
Publications: quarterly bulletin, The Memberletter.
Hours & Admission Prices: Mon.-Sat. 10-4. No charge; donations accepted. Closed New Year's; Thanksgiving; Christmas. ♿
Attendance: 18,000 (accurate)
Membership: Senior $20; Individual & General $25; Family $35; Contributing Donor $100; Patron $250.

BANDELIER NATIONAL MONUMENT, 15 Entrance Rd., Los Alamos, NM 87544-9508. Tel.: 505-672-3861 & 0343. Fax: 505-672-9607.
E-mail: band-administration@nps.gov
Web Site: www.nps.gov/band
Founded: 1916.
Congressional District: 3
Key Personnel: Park Supt., Brad Traver; Chief Protection, Fred Patton; Chief Interpretation, Lynne Dominy; Chief Facility Management, Liza Ermelling; Park Archeologist, Rory Gauthier; Museum Technician, Gary Roybal.
Governing Authority: federal. Parent Institution: National Park Service, Dept. of Interior, Washington, DC. Tax-exempt.
National Park & Archaeological Site Museum.
Collections: archaeological & ethnological items of Pueblo Indians of the Pajarito Plateau; plant & animal specimens of the Jemez Mountains & the Pajarito Plateau; research reports; environmental documents; maps; drawings; plans; photographs; entomology; historic structures.
Research Fields: history, archaeology, ethnographical & natural science of the site.
Facilities: campsites; visitor center. Interpretive materials for sale.
Activities: lectures; films; interpretive slide programs; campfire programs; summer night walks; culture/arts demonstrations; guided tours & self-guided tours & backcountry hiking.
Publications: quarterly guide book & trail booklet, The Tuff times.
Hours & Admission Prices: Winter: daily 8-4:30; Spring & Fall 9-5:30; Summer: 8-6. Admission $12 per car; call park for commercial vehicle fees. Annual Pass: seniors 62 & over $10; Bandelier pass $30; inter-agency pass $80. Closed New Year's Day; Christmas Day. ♿
Attendance: 300,000 (accurate)

BRADBURY SCIENCE MUSEUM, 15th & Central, Los Alamos, NM 87544. Mailing Address: MSC330, Los Alamos Natl. Lab., Los Alamos, NM 87545-0001. Tel.: 505-667-4444. Fax: 505-665-6932.
E-mail: web-bsm@lanl.gov
Web Site: bsm.lanl.gov
Founded: 1963.
Congressional District: 3
Key Personnel: Dir., Linda Deck; Community Programs Coord., Mary Ellen Ortiz; Facilities Mgr., Mike Kolb; Exhibits Designer, Omar Juveland.
Personnel Profile: Full-Time Paid 8; Part-Time Paid 13.
Governing Authority: federal. University of California, on contract to the Dept. of Energy. Parent Institution: Los Alamos National Laboratory.
Science Museum.
Collections: scientific exhibits; historical events of Manhattan Project.
Research Fields: weapons; energy; biomedical; environmental; nature of matter; current laboratory research.
Facilities: introductory area; history wall; research hall; theatre.
Activities: lectures; films; traveling exhibits; classroom programs; science drama; summer camp; science demonstrations.
Publications: brochure.
Hours & Admission Prices: Sun.-Mon. 1-5, Tues.-Sat. 10-5. No charge. Closed New Year's Day; Thanksgiving; Christmas. ♿
Attendance: 86,732 (accurate)

LOS ALAMOS HISTORICAL MUSEUM, Fuller Lodge Cultural Center, 1921 Juniper St., Los Alamos, NM 87544. Mailing Address: P.O. Box 43, Los Alamos, NM 87544-0043. Tel.: 505-662-6272 (weekdays 10-4) & 4493. Fax: 505-662-6312.
E-mail: historicalsociety@losalamoshistory.org
Web Site: www.losalamoshistory.org
Founded: 1968.
Congressional District: 1
Key Personnel: C.E.O. & Dir., Hedy Dunn; Pres. & Chm. (V), Dennis Erickson; 1st. Vice Pres., Beth Plassmann; Archivist, Rebecca Collinsworth; Website Admin., Heather McClenahan; Museum Shop Mgr., Kathy Ankeny.
Personnel Profile: Part-Time Paid 7; Part-Time Volunteers 35; Interns 1.
Governing Authority: county; historical society. Tax-exempt: 501(c)(3).
Local History Museum.
Collections: outdoor exhibit includes ruins of prehistoric Indian pueblo; archaeology; geology; paleontology; homesteading, history of 1918-1943 Los Alamos Ranch school; wartime atomic bomb memorabilia; slides; photos; tape recordings; manuscripts; photographs; prehistoric Pueblo Indian artifacts; documents. Historic House: 1920 guest cottage of Los Alamos Ranch school; Homesteader's cabin.
Research Fields: archaeology; land grants; wartime history; Los Alamos Ranch School history; Los Alamos Manhattan Project history.

Facilities: library; archives.
Activities: self-guided tours; lectures; audiovisual history programs; formally organized education programs for students; inter-museum loan; permanent & temporary exhibitions; school loan service; periodic arts & crafts shows; demonstrations; slide & film shows; field trips; docent training sessions.
Publications: books include Los Alamos: The First 50 Years; Inside Box 1663; Los Alamos Outdoors; newsletter, Los Alamos Historical Society Newsletter; A Hiker's Guide to Bandelier; Manhattan District History: Nonscientific Aspects of Los Alamos Project Y 1942-1946; Los Alamos: Beginning of an Era. Standing By Making Do: Women of Wartime Los Alamos; Non-Technical History of Project Y; Sentinels On Stone (area petroglyphs); Los Alamos Place Names. Quads, Shoeboxes and Sunken Living Rooms: A History of Los Alamos Housing, A Boy on the Hill; Savoring the Past-Recipes from 3 Cultures; Secrets! of a Los Alamos Kid 1946-1953; A Guide to the Nuclear Arms Control Treaties; Life Within Limits; Robert Oppenheimer 1904-1967; Plutonium Metallurgy at Los Alamos 1943-1945; Twilight Time - A Soldiers Role in the Manhattan Project at Los Alamos; The Secret Project Notebook, Gatekeeper to Los Alamos; Just Crazy to Ski: A 50-Year History of Skiing in Los Alamos; The Forest and the Fire; The Secret Project Notebook; Tales of Los Alamos; The Forgotten Physicist; Historic Roads of Los Alamos (2009).
Hours & Admission Prices: Exhibit Hall: Summer Mon.-Sat. 9:30-4:30, Sun. 1-4; Winter Mon.-Sat. 10-4, Sun. 1-4. Archives: Mon.-Fri. 10-4. Tour: $1 donation. Museum shop discounts to members. Closed New Year's Day; Easter; Thanksgiving; Christmas. ♿
Attendance: 34,700 (accurate)
Membership: Student & Senior $35; Individual & Senior Couple $40; Family $50; Heritage Friend $100-$499; Heritage Contributor $500-$999; Heritage Supporter $1,000-$2,499; Heritage Benefactor $2,500 & up.

Lovington

LEA COUNTY MUSEUM, 103 S. Love, Lovington, NM 88260-4218. Tel.: 505-396-4805. Fax: 505-396-4805.
E-mail: leacomuseum@leaco.net
Web Site: www.leacountymuseum.org
Key Personnel: Dir., Jim Harris.
Governing Authority: nonprofit organization. Tax-exempt: 501(c)(3).
History Museum.
Collections: local history; Native Americans; ranchers; farmers; homesteaders; town builders; oil men; residents of Southeast New Mexico; wagons; buggies. Historic Buildings: Commercial Hotel; 1908 Love House; 1914 Baker School; 1913 Store and Post Office; 1908 Dugout; 1913 Caprock Store; 1950 Reed House.
Hours & Admission Prices: Tues.-Fri. 1-5, Sat. 9-5; other times by appointment. No charge. Closed New Year's Day; Independence Day; Thanksgiving; Christmas.

Madrid

OLD COAL MINE MUSEUM, 2846 State Hwy. 14, (on the Turquoise Trail), Madrid, NM 87010. Tel.: 505-438-3780; 505-473-0743 (schedule tour).
E-mail: ocm@themineshafttavern.com
Web Site: www.themineshafttavern.com
Founded: 1982.
Mine Museum.
Collections: mine history; 1900 locomotive; period autos & trucks; firefighting equipment; medical & office equipment; farm, homemaking & carpentry equipment; early silent & sound movie projectors; blacksmith shop.
Activities: rental facilities.
Hours & Admission Prices: Fri.-Mon. 10-5; other times by appointment weather permitting. Adults $5. Closed Thanksgiving; Christmas.
Attendance: 3,575 (estimated)

Magdalena

BOX CAR MUSEUM, 108 N. Main St., Magdalena, NM 87825. Tel.: 575-854-2261. Fax: 575-854-2273.
Key Personnel: Dir., Lucy Pino
History Museum.
Collections: local history & culture; photographs; railroad history.
Hours & Admission Prices: Mon.-Fri. 11-4. No charge; donations accepted.

Mesilla

GADSDEN MUSEUM, 1875 Boutz Rd., Mesilla, NM 88046. Mailing Address: Box 147, Mesilla, NM 88046-0147. Tel.: 505-526-6293.
Web Site: www.nmohwy.com/g/gadsdemeu.htm
Founded: 1931.
Key Personnel: Cur. & Co-Owner, Mary F. Bird; Co-Owner, R. Eileen Betzen.
Personnel Profile: Full-Time Volunteers 1; Part-Time Volunteers 1; Interns 1.
Governing Authority: individual operation.
History Museum.
Collections: Indian artifacts from the Southwest; pottery; baskets; Apache, Navajo, Jemez, arrowheads, peace medals, beaded leather goods; pictures painted on deerskin; artifacts representing Penitente lifestyle; Colonel Albert Jennings Fountain; Santo collection.
Activities: permanent exhibitions; tours for school students; formally organized education programs for children & college students.
Publications: pamphlet.
Hours & Admission Prices: Mon.-Sat. 9-11am & 1-5; groups & Sun. by appointment. Adults $5, children 6-12 $3. Closed New Year's Day; Easter; Independence Day; Thanksgiving; Christmas. ♿
Attendance: 100 (estimated)

Moriarty

MORIARTY HISTORICAL SOCIETY & MUSEUM, 202 Broadway St., Moriarty, NM 87035. Mailing Address: P.O. Box 1366, Moriarty, NM 87035-1366. Tel.: 505-832-0839. Fax: 505-832-9286.
E-mail: momuseum@yahoo.com
Web Site: www.moriartymuseum.org
Founded: 1981.
Key Personnel: Pres., Sammie Pachta; Vice Pres., Tina Ortega; Past Pres. & Historian, Joseph H. "Choppo" McComb; Cur. & Archivist, Barbara Takiguchi.
Personnel Profile: Full-Time Paid 7; Full-Time Volunteers 5; Part-Time Paid 3; Part-Time Volunteers 9.
Governing Authority: municipal; private; nonprofit organization. Branch Museum: Moriarty Historical Society, Moriarty, NM. Tax-exempt: 501(c)(3).
General Museum.
Collections: 19th to mid-20th century homesteading/ranching area history.
Research Fields: Route 66 from 1930-1960; Estancia Valley papers 1893-1950.
Facilities: 100-vol. library of state & local history books.
Activities: guided tours; lectures; school loan service; Moriarty History presentations.
Publications: book, My Life in New Mexico; Torrance County History (reprint).
Hours & Admission Prices: Tues.-Fri. 10-5, Sat. 10-2; other times by appointment. No charge; donations accepted. Closed New Year's Day; Memorial Day; Independence Day; Thanksgiving; Christmas. ♿
Attendance: 11,000 (accurate)
Membership: Single $7; Family $10.

U.S. SOUTHWEST SOARING MUSEUM, 918 E. Old Hwy. 66, Moriarty, NM 87035. Mailing Address: P.O. Box 3626, Moriarty, NM 87035-3626. Tel.: 505-832-0755.
E-mail: usssm1@yahoo.com
Web Site: www.swsoaringmuseum.org
Key Personnel: Pres., George Applebay.
Governing Authority: Tax-exempt: 501 (c)(3).
History Museum.
Collections: western U.S. history; glider models; mural.
Hours & Admission Prices: Mon.-Fri. 9-4; other times by appointment. No charge; donations accepted.

Mountainair

SALINAS PUEBLO MISSIONS NATIONAL MONUMENT, 102 S. Ripley Ave., Mountainair, NM 87036. Mailing Address: P.O. Box 517, Mountainair, NM 87036-0517. Tel.: 505-847-2585. Fax: 505-847-2441.
E-mail: derektoms@nps.gov
Web Site: www.nps.gov
Founded: 1909.
Congressional District: 1 & 3
Key Personnel: Supt., Glenn Fulfer; Chief Park Ranger & Interpretive Specialist, Norma Pineda.
Personnel Profile: Full-Time Paid 18; Part-Time Paid 4; Part-Time Volunteers 2.
Governing Authority: federal. Parent Institution: U.S. National Park Service, Interior Bldg., Washington, DC 20240. Tax-exempt.
Archaeology Museum: located near the site of prehistoric pithouses c.800 A.D.; prehistoric Indian ruins c.1100-1670 A.D.; four Spanish mission ruins c.1622-1672.
Collections: archaeological artifacts from historic and prehistoric ruins; manuscript collection; photograph collection of approx. 5,000 prints, negatives and slides. Historic Buildings: 1627 San Isidro Mission; 1659 San Buenaventure Mission; 1300-1670 Pueblo de Las Humanas; 1630-1672 San Gregorio de Abo; 1100-1672 Pueblo de Abo; 1630-1672 Nuestra Senora de la Purisina Concepcion Mission; 1300-1672 Pueblo de Quarai.
Research Fields: archaeological; historical; botanical; environment.

Facilities: 1,000-vol. library of archaeology, history, natural science, ethnology books available for use on premises by approval of superintendent; picnic area. Books, slides & postcards for sale.
Activities: guided tours for organized groups; lectures; permanent & temporary exhibitions; 17 minute audiovisual program; 45 minute video; self-guiding trail.
Publications: orientation brochures; trail guides; excavation reports; historic structures report.
Hours & Admission Prices: Memorial Day to Labor Day daily 9-6; Sept.-May daily 9-5. No charge; donations accepted. ♿
Attendance: 48,215 (accurate)

Nageezi

CHACO CULTURE NATIONAL HISTORICAL PARK, 1808 Rd. 7950, Nageezi, NM 87037. Mailing Address: P.O. Box 280, Nageezi, NM 87037-0280. Tel.: 505-786-7014. Fax: 505-786-7061.
Web Site: www.nps.gov/chcu
Founded: 1907.
Congressional District: 3
Key Personnel: Supt, Barbara West; Park Archeologist, Dabney Ford; Park Cur., Wendy Bustard.
Personnel Profile: Full-Time Paid 3; Part-Time Paid 4; Part-Time Volunteers 1.
Governing Authority: federal. Parent Institution: National Park Service. Subsidiary Institution: Southwest Region. Tax-exempt.
Archaeology Museum.
Collections: archaeology; ethnology; prehistoric & historic sites.
Research Fields: archaeology of the Chaco Anasazi & the San Juan Basin.
Facilities: 1,300-vol. library of archaeology, ethnology, natural history, available for use by special permission; visitor center; campground. Publications for sale.
Activities: guided & self-guiding tours; lectures; films; permanent exhibitions.
Publications: orientation brochures; booklets; guide leaflets; technical reports.
Hours & Admission Prices: Park: daily sunrise-sunset. Visitor Center: 8-5. Weekly Pass: Vehicle $8, Individual $4. Closed New Year's Day; Thanksgiving; Christmas. ♿
Attendance: 100,000 (estimated)

Organ

THE SPACE MURALS MUSEUM, 12450 Hwy. 70 E., Organ, NM 88052. Mailing Address: P.O. Box 243, Organ, NM 88052-0243. Tel.: 505-382-0977.
E-mail: klin@zianet.com
Web Site: www.zianet.com
Space Museum.
Collections: over 2,500 air & space photographs; model airplanes; replica of Space Station Freedom; astronaut gallery; air & space artifacts; 1/8 scale replica of space shuttle Challenger memorial; Nike Hercules Missle; V-2 nose cone & tail piece.
Hours & Admission Prices: Mon.-Sat. 9-6, Sun. 10-6. No charge.

Pecos

PECOS NATIONAL HISTORICAL PARK, State Rd. 63, 2 mi. south of Pecos, Pecos, NM 87552. Mailing Address: P.O. Box 418, Pecos, NM 87552-0418. Tel.: 505-757-6414, ext. 1. Fax: 505-757-8460.
E-mail: peco_visitor_information@nps.gov
Web Site: www.nps.gov/peco
Founded: 1965.
Congressional District: 3
Key Personnel: Supt., Kathy Billings; Chief Education & Visitor Svcs., Christine Beekman; Cur., Heather Young; Chief Cultural Resources, Jeff Brown.
Personnel Profile: Full-Time Paid 1.
Governing Authority: federal. Parent Institution: National Park Service. Tax-exempt.
Cultural & Natural Historic Site.
Collections: Pecos area archaeology; 17,000 artifacts of A.V. Kidder collection 1915-1929; artifacts from Mission Churches; Kiva excavations. Historic Building: 17th & 18th-century Nuestra Senora de Los Angeles de Porciuncula missions & associated buildings. Spanish mission; Spanish homestead; Santa Fe trail; Civic War battlefield; Route 66, & 20th Century Ranching.
Research Fields: archaeology; anthropology; history.
Facilities: 300-vol. library of books on archaeology, anthropology, history, & Kidder archaeological volumes available for research on premises; visitor center including exhibit room. Books for sale.
Activities: guided tours by arrangements; permanent exhibitions; introductory film.
Publications: orientation brochures; trail guide; book, Pecos: Gateway to Pueblos and Plains, The Anthology. From Folsom to Fogelson: A Cultural Resources Inventory Survey of Pecos National Historical Park.
Hours & Admission Prices: Memorial Day-Labor Day: daily 8-6; Sept.-May daily 8-5. Adult $5; Golden Age Passport (62 & over), Golden Eagles Card, National Park Pass & children under 16 no charge. Closed Christmas. ♿
Attendance: 40,000 (accurate)
Membership: Senior 62 & over $10; Annual $80.

Pinos Altos

PINOS ALTOS HISTORICAL MUSEUM, Main St., Pinos Altos, NM 88053. Mailing Address: P.O. Box 88053, Pinos Altos, NM 88053. Tel.: 505-388-1882.
E-mail: info@pinosaltoscabins.com
Web Site: www.pinosaltos.org/museum/schaferlogcabin.html
History Museum: housed in the Schafer Log Cabin c.1860.
Collections: 19th century Americana, including old maps & photographs; period furniture & artifacts; mining tools; weathered wood relics of the old west.
Facilities: Museum-related items for sale.
Hours & Admission Prices: Daily 10-5.

Portales

BLACKWATER DRAW MUSEUM, 42987 Hwy. 70, Portales, NM 88130. Mailing Address: Eastern NM Univ., Station 3, Portales, NM 88130. Tel.: 505-562-2202 & 1011. Fax: 505-562-2291.
E-mail: matthew.hillsman@enmu.edu
Web Site: www.enmu.edu
Founded: 1969.
Congressional District: 3
Key Personnel: Dir., Dr. John Montgomery; Archaeologist, George Crawford; Cur., Matthew Hillsman.
Personnel Profile: Full-Time Paid 2; Part-Time Paid 2; Interns 3.
Governing Authority: university. Parent Institution: Eastern New Mexico University & State of New Mexico. Tax-exempt.
Archaeological Site: 1932 America's first multi-cultural, paleoindian archaeological site.
Collections: paleoindian archaeology & geology; paleontology; anthropology.
Research Fields: Paleoindian archaeology.
Facilities: Publications & t-shirts on early man for sale.
Activities: guided tours; lectures; formally organized education programs for children, adults, undergraduate & graduate college students; permanent & temporary exhibitions; films on anthropology, archaeology & ecology.
Publications: Eastern New Mexico University Contributions in Anthropology.
Hours & Admission Prices: Museum: Memorial Day -Labor Day Mon.-Sat. 10-5, Sun. 12-5; Sept.-May Tues.-Sat. 10-5, Sun. 12-5. Adults $3, seniors 60 & up $2, students $1; discount to school groups; children under 6 no charge. ♿
Attendance: 7,000 (estimated)

MILES MINERAL MUSEUM, Eastern New Mexico University Campus, Roosevelt Hall, Portales, NM 88130. Mailing Address: Station 33, Eastern New Mexico University, Portales, NM 88130. Tel.: 505-562-2651 & 2174. Fax: 505-562-2192.
E-mail: jim.constantopoulos@enmu.edu
Web Site: w3a.enmu.edu/services/museums/miles-mineral
Founded: 1969.
Congressional District: 3
Key Personnel: Dir., Dr. Jim Constantopoulos.
Governing Authority: university. Affiliated with Eastern New Mexico University. Branch Museums: Blackwater Draw Museum & the Paleo-Indian Institute; Roosevelt Count Museum; Natural History Museum. Tax-exempt.
Geology Museum.
Collections: minerals; rocks; fossils.
Research Fields: mineralogy.
Facilities: x-ray diffraction & x-ray fluorescence.
Activities: guided tours; lectures; formally organized education programs for children, adults, undergraduate & graduate college students; permanent & temporary exhibitions.
Hours & Admission Prices: Mon., Wed. & Fri. 8-5. No charge; donations accepted. ♿
Attendance: 3,600 (accurate)

NATURAL HISTORY MUSEUM, Station 33, Eastern New Mexico University, Portales, NM 88130. Tel.: 575-562-2862 & 2706. Fax: 575-562-2192.
E-mail: marv.lutnesky@enmu.edu
Web Site: www.enmu.edu/academics
Founded: 1968.
Congressional District: 66
Key Personnel: Dir. & Cur., Marvin Lutnesky; Cur. Plants, Dr. Dann Brown; Cur. Invertebrates, Dr. Gary Pfaffenberger.

Governing Authority: university. Parent Institution: Eastern New Mexico University. A unit of the Llano Estacado Center for Advanced Professional Studies & Research. Tax-exempt.
Natural History Museum: housed in Roosevelt Hall, originally used as a men's dormitory.
Collections: 10,500 specimens of mammals; 5,000 specimens of reptiles & amphibians; 600 specimens of birds; 10,000 specimens of fish; invertebrates.
Research Fields: aquatic, & terrestrial ecology & conservation.
Activities: guided tours; permanent & temporary collections; research.
Publications: book, Studies in Natural Sciences.
Hours & Admission Prices: Mon.-Fri. 8-5. No charge. ♿

ROOSEVELT COUNTY MUSEUM, Eastern New Mexico Univ., Station 9, Portales, NM 88130. Mailing Address: 1200 W. University, Portales, NM 88130. Tel.: 575-562-2592. Fax: 575-562-2362.
E-mail: mark.romero@enmu.edu
Web Site: enmu.edu
Founded: 1940.
Congressional District: 3
Key Personnel: C.E.O., Dr. Steven Gamble; Coord. Research Svcs., Dr. Gerald Gies; Cur., Mark Romero.
Personnel Profile: Full-Time Paid 1; Part-Time Paid 3.
Governing Authority: university; nonprofit. Parent Institution: Eastern New Mexico University. Tax-exempt.
History Museum.
Collections: technology; early settlers & Native American artifacts; ethnology; folklore; archives; costumes; numismatic; ranching artifacts; Roosevelt County historical artifacts.
Activities: lectures; seminars; art shows; outreach program; video & slide shows; permanent & temporary exhibitions. Museum Sponsors: musical permanent & temporary exhibitions.
Hours & Admission Prices: July-Aug. Mon.-Fri. 8-12 & 1-5; Sept.-June Mon.-Fri. 8-12 & 1-5, Sat.-Sun. call for hours. No charge; donations accepted. Closed university Christmas break; national holidays.
Attendance: 2,000 (estimated)

Pueblo of Acoma

SKY CITY CULTURAL CENTER, I-40 West, Exit 102, SPA 30 @ 32, Pueblo of Acoma, NM 87034. Mailing Address: P.O. Box 310, Pueblo of Acoma, NM 87034-0310. Tel.: 800-747-0181; 505-469-1052. Fax: 505-552-7204.
Web Site: www.acomaskycity.org
Formerly: Acoma Tourist & Visitation Center
Founded: 1978.
Congressional District: 3
Key Personnel: Gen. Mgr., Connie Garcia; C.E.O., Marvis Aragor; Chm., Fred S. Vallo, Sr.; Museum Shop Mgr., Marva Toya.
Personnel Profile: Full-Time Paid 23; Part-Time Paid 9.
Governing Authority: Parent Institution: Acoma Tribal Government. Subsidiary Institution: Acoma Business Enterprises, Inc. Tax-exempt.
Indian Historical & Cultural Museum.
Collections: photo archives & documents related to the history of Acoma; historic pottery. Historic Building: 16th century church, Old Pueblo.
Research Fields: Acoma Culture.
Facilities: library; archives.
Activities: guided tour of Old Acoma & Sky City.
Publications: catalog, One Thousand Years of Clay.
Hours & Admission Prices: Due to construction please call to confirm hours. May-Oct. 8-6; Nov.-April 8-5; last tour one hour before closing. Adults $10, senior citizens $9, children 6-17 $7; discounts to AAM members & groups. ♿
Attendance: 71,880 (accurate)

Quemado

DIA CENTER FOR THE ARTS, Quemado, NM 87829. Mailing Address: P.O. Box 2993, Corrales, NM 87048-2993. Tel.: 505-898-3335. Fax: 505-898-3336.
E-mail: info@lightningfield.org
Web Site: www.diacenter.org
Key Personnel: Admin., Kathleen Shields
Art Museum
Collections: 400 stainless steel poles; work of land art by Walter De Maria, The Lightning Field.
Hours & Admission Prices: May-June & Sept.-Oct. $150 per person; July-Aug. $250 per person. Call for reservations & information.

Radium Springs

FORT SELDEN STATE MONUMENT, 1280 Ft. Selden Rd., Radium Springs, NM 88054. Mailing Address: P.O. Box 2087, Radium Springs, NM 88054. Tel.: 505-476-1150. Fax: 505-476-1220.
Founded: 1973.
Key Personnel: Dir. State Monuments, Ernesto Ortega; Ranger, Elva Melendrez; Ranger, Jeff Wooten; Ranger, Dave Harkness; Ranger, Robert Pierson.
Personnel Profile: Full-Time Paid 5.
Governing Authority: state. Parent Institution Museum of New Mexico, Box 2087, Santa Fe, NM 87504. Tax-exempt: 170(c)(1).
Military Museum: located on site of 1865-1891 army fort; 1884-1886 home of Douglas McArthur.
Collections: artifacts found on the site; military artifacts, including uniforms, saddles & an 1864 Springfield rifle.
Research Fields: military history pertaining to the Indian Wars period.
Facilities: 100-vol. library of books on the Indian Wars available for research on premises; botanical garden.
Activities: guided tours; TV programs; formally organized education programs for children & adults; living history programs in summer or on special request; traveling & loan exhibitions; living history demos; annual Old Fort Days.
Publications: book, Fort Selden.
Hours & Admission Prices: Wed.-Mon. 8:30-5. Adults $3, NM residents $ 1 on Sun.; members & children 16 and under no charge. Closed New Year's Day; Easter; Thanksgiving; Christmas. ♿

Ramah

EL MORRO NATIONAL MONUMENT, Hwy. 53-42 mi. S.W. of Grants, Ramah, NM 87321. Mailing Address: HC 61 Box 43, Ramah, NM 87321-9603. Tel.: 505-783-4226. Fax: 505-783-4689.
Web Site: www.nps.gov/elmo
Founded: 1906.
Congressional District: 3
Key Personnel: Supt., Kayci Cook Collins.
Governing Authority: federal. National Park Service.
National Monument, Historical & Archaeological Site Museum: located at site of Inscription Rock, bearing inscriptions dating from 1605-1906; prehistoric Pueblo Ruins.
Collections: archaeological finds, pots, implements, handcrafts, weapons, religious items, dating from 17th-19th centuries; prehistoric pottery; Spanish exploration artifacts; Southwest historic artifacts, inscriptions & petroglyphs.
Research Fields: archaeology, Spanish-Colonial & American-Exploratory history; southwest biology, botany & geology.
Facilities: 400-vol. library of archaeology, history, zoology & botany, available for research by personnel.
Activities: Interpretive talks and guided walks in the summer.
Publications: brochures; pamphlets.
Hours & Admission Prices: Winter: daily 9-5; Summer: daily 8-7; Spring & Fall: daily 9-6. Adults $3; under 16 no charge. NPS, Golden Eagle & Golden Age/Golden Access passes issued & honored. Closed New Year's Day; Christmas. ♿
Attendance: 80,000 (accurate)

WILD SPIRIT WOLF SANCTUARY, 378 Candy Kitchen Rd., Ramah, NM 87321. Mailing Address: HC 61, P.O. Box 28, Ramah, NM 87321-9601. Tel.: 505-775-3304. Fax: 505-775-3824.
E-mail: leyton@wildspiritwolfsanctuary.org
Web Site: www.wildspiritwolfsanctuary.org
Key Personnel: Exec. Dir., Leyton Cougar; Memberships, Education & Admin., Angel Bennet; Newsletter, Advertising, Publications, Georgia Cougar
Wildlife Sanctuary.
Collections: wolves.
Hours & Admission Prices: Tours: Tues.-Sun. 11, 12:30, 2 & 3:30. Adults $5, senior citizens $4, children $3.

Raton

BOY SCOUT MUSEUM, 400 S. 1st St., Raton, NM 87740-4063. Tel.: 505-445-1413.
Web Site: www.santafetrailnm.org/site558.html
Key Personnel: Owner & Cur., Dennis Downing; Owner & Cur., Sue Downing
History Museum.
Collections: boy scout history; personal artifacts.
Hours & Admission Prices: Daily 10-5; other times by appointment.

COLFAX COUNTY SOCIETY OF ART, HISTORY AND ARCHAEOLOGY, 108 S. 2nd St., Raton, NM 87740-3906.
Founded: 1938.
Congressional District: 3
Key Personnel: Pres., Kathy McQueary; Archivist, Roger Sanchez.
Personnel Profile: Full-Time Paid 1; Part-Time Volunteers 20.
Governing Authority: private; nonprofit organization.
General Museum.
Collections: displays, artifacts & photographs of the railroad, 7 coal mining camps & ranching from 1880 to 1950; history of Raton & its early settlers.
Activities: docent program; guided tours; lectures; traveling exhibitions.
Hours & Admission Prices: Summer: May-Sept. Tues.-Sat. 9-5; Winter: Oct.-April Wed.-Sat. 10-4. No charge; donations accepted. ♿
Attendance: 6,000 (accurate)
Membership: Individual $25.

RATON MUSEUM, 108 S. 2nd St., Raton, NM 87740-3906. Tel.: 505-445-8979.
Founded: 1939.
Congressional District: 3
Key Personnel: C.E.O., Roger Sanchez; Pres. (V), Kathy McQueary.
Personnel Profile: Full-Time Paid 1; Part-Time Volunteers 20.
Governing Authority: board of directors/trustees; nonprofit organization. Parent Institution: Colfax County Society of Art History & Archaeology. Tax-exempt: 170(b)(1)(A).
Historical Society Museum.
Collections: railroading; coal mining; ranching; the history of Raton & its early settlers. Historic Buildings: 1890 & 1906 buildings.
Research Fields: railroading; mining; ranching; the development of Raton & surrounding area.
Activities: lectures; docent program; traveling exhibitions; outreach program.
Publications: newsletter.
Hours & Admission Prices: May-Aug. Tues.-Sat. 9-5; Sept.-April Wed.-Sat. 10-4; will open for special groups. No charge; donations accepted. Closed New Year's Day; Memorial Day; Independence Day; Thanksgiving; Christmas. ♿
Attendance: 6,000 (accurate)
Membership: Individual $25.

Rio Rancho

J&R VINTAGE AUTO MUSEUM, 3650 NM Hwy. 528, Rio Rancho, NM 87144-7524. Tel.: 505-867-2881.
E-mail: info@jrvintageautos.com
Web Site: www.jrvintageautos.com
Auto Museum.
Collections: 70 automobiles; die cast toys.
Facilities: Museum-related items for sale.
Hours & Admission Prices: May-Oct. Mon.-Sat. 10-5, Sun. 1-5; Nov.-April Mon.-Sat. 10-5. Adults $6, senior citizens $5, children 6-12 $3; discounts to groups; children under 6 no charge.

Roswell

ANDERSON MUSEUM OF CONTEMPORARY ART, 409 E. College Blvd., Roswell, NM 88201-7524. Mailing Address: P.O. Box 1, Roswell, NM 88202-0001. Tel.: 575-623-5600. Fax: 575-623-5603.
E-mail: email@roswellamoca.org
Web Site: www.roswellamoca.org
Founded: 1994.
Congressional District: 2
Key Personnel: C.E.O. & Pres., Donald B. Anderson; Exec. Dir., Sally M. Anderson; Education, Cymantha Liakos; Public Rels., Nancy Fleming; Treas., Lanice White.
Personnel Profile: Full-Time Paid 1; Full-Time Volunteers 2; Part-Time Paid 2; Part-Time Volunteers 21.
Governing Authority: private; nonprofit organization. Tax-exempt: 501(c)(3).
Contemporary Art Museum.
Collections: works by Roswell Artist-in-Residence program students; paintings; prints; drawings; photographs; sculpture; digital media.
Facilities: research library; 22,000 sq. ft. exhibit space. Museum-related items for sale.
Activities: guided tours by request.
Publications: brochure; newsletter.
Hours & Admission Prices: Mon.-Fri. 9-4, Sat.-Sun. 1-5. Closed New Year's Day; Independence Day; Thanksgiving; Christmas. ♿
Attendance: 10,000 (estimated)

THE GENERAL DOUGLAS L. MCBRIDE MUSEUM, NEW MEXICO MILITARY INSTITUTE, 101 West College Blvd., Roswell, NM 88201-5100. Tel.: 505-624-8220. Fax: 505-624-8258.
E-mail: klopfer@nmmi.edu
Web Site: www.nmmi.cc.nm.us/museum
Founded: 1983.
Congressional District: 2
Key Personnel: Dir., Col. Jerry Klopfer; Administrative Asst., Liz Bolin.
Personnel Profile: Full-Time Paid 1; Part-Time Volunteers 1.
Governing Authority: public college. New Mexico Military Institute. Tax-exempt.
Military Museum: housed in c.1912 Luna Natatorium.
Collections: military & NMMI history; Civil War-present, small weapons; New Mexico Military Institute memorabilia; artifacts from 20th-century conflicts; Hall of Fame; Valor Rooms.
Research Fields: achievements of New Mexico Military Institute alumni; 20th-century general military history.
Facilities: 300-vol. library of books on weapons; uniforms; military history; 100-vols. New Mexico Military Institute yearbooks available for use by the public.
Activities: self-guided tours.
Hours & Admission Prices: Mon.-Fri. 8-4; other times by appointment. No charge; donations accepted. Closed national holidays. ♿
Attendance: 4,000
Membership: Annual $100.

HISTORICAL CENTER FOR SOUTHEAST NEW MEXICO, (M), 200 N. Lea Ave., Roswell, NM 88201-4655. Tel.: 575-622-8333. Fax: 575-623-8746.
E-mail: history@dfn.com
Web Site: www.hssnm.net
Founded: 1976.
Congressional District: 2
Key Personnel: Pres., Ron Higginbotham; Administrative Dir. & Museum Dir., Roger K. Burnett; Museum Shop Mgr., Alice Wagoner; Cur. Exhibitions, Collections & Registrar, Jean Rockhold; Librarian & Archivist, Elvis E. Fleming; Administrative Asst., Tina Williams.
Personnel Profile: Part-Time Paid 2; Part-Time Volunteers 38.
Governing Authority: nonprofit organization. Tax-exempt: 501(c)(3).
Historical Museum & Archives Center: housed in 1910-12 J.P. White, Sr. House.
Collections: 1875-1936 period furniture & furnishings; 12,000 collection of Southeastern New Mexico, Pecos Valley & Chaves County photographs; books; audio tapes; manuscripts; periodicals.
Research Fields: Southeastern New Mexico; Pecos Valley; Chaves County & local history.
Facilities: library of photographs, manuscripts, papers, maps and books on Southeastern, New Mexico and local history, available for use with approval of archivist. Books on Southeastern Americana, photographs and other museum-related items for sale.
Activities: guided tours; lectures; docent program; permanent exhibitions.
Publications: quarterly newsletter, Facts and Traditions; books, Roundup on the Pecos; Treasures of History: Historic Buildings in Chaves County, 1870-1935; A Brief Historical Survey of the Middle Pecos River Basin; Treasures of History II: Chaves County Vignettes; The Bitter River; Treasures of History III: Southeastern New Mexico, People, Places and Events; Chaves County Schools 1881-1968; Captain Joseph C. Lea, From Confederate Guerrilla to New Mexico Patriarch; Treasures of History IV; Roundup on the Pecos II; Brief History of Rosewell from Stoneage to All American City.
Hours & Admission Prices: Daily 1-4. No charge; donations accepted.
Attendance: 4,000 (accurate)
Membership: Volunteer & Bronze $25; Silver $35; Gold $50; Business $125; Donor $500; Benefactor $1,000.

INTERNATIONAL UFO MUSEUM AND RESEARCH CENTER, 114 N. Main St., Roswell, NM 88203-4706. Tel.: 505-625-9495. Fax: 505-625-1907.
Web Site: roswellufomuseum.com
Founded: 1991.
Governing Authority: nonprofit organization. Tax-exempt: 501(c)(3).
General Museum.
Collections: the Roswell Incident, 1947; history, science & research of UFO events worldwide.
Activities: special events. Museum Sponsors: International UFO Festival. Annual Event: Roswalien Experience UFO Festival.
Hours & Admission Prices: Daily 9-5. Adults $5; discounts to seniors & military; members no charge. ♿
Attendance: 160,000 (accurate)
Membership: Annual $20.

* **ROSWELL MUSEUM AND ART CENTER, (M),** 100 West 11th, Roswell, NM 88201-4998. Tel.: 505-624-6744. Fax: 505-624-6765.
E-mail: rmac@roswellmuseum.org
Web Site: www.roswellmuseum.org
Founded: 1937.
Congressional District: 2
Key Personnel: Dir., Laurie Rufe; Asst. Dir., Caroline Brooks; Pres. (V), Bob Phillips; Cur. Education, Ellen K. Moore; Cur., Andrew John Cecil; Registrar, Stacie Petersen; Museum Shop Mgr., Charles Bentley; Membership Coord., Dee Nallie.
Personnel Profile: Full-Time Paid 14; Part-Time Paid 5; Part-Time Volunteers 145; Interns 2.
Governing Authority: municipal government. Parent Institution: City of Roswell. Tax-exempt: 501(c)(3).
General & Art Museum.
Collections: 20th-century American paintings & sculpture; European & American prints; Southwestern painting; paintings & prints by Peter Hurd & Henriette Wyeth; ethnological & archaeological collection of Southwestern Native American art; Rogers Aston collection of the American West; Robert H. Goddard experimental liquid-propellant rocket collection.
Major Exhibits: New Mexico: 20th Century Visions, 1/10-12/10; Ray Wielgus: Firearms As Art, 6/5/10-1/2/11; Landscapes, 11/19/10-9/14/11.
Research Fields: Southwestern art; Federal Arts Project in New Mexico, early liquid-fueled rocketry.
Facilities: 8,000-vol. library of art, archeology & crafts, available for research by museum students, area teachers, college students; planetarium; auditorium; classrooms; exhibition galleries. Books, reproductions, pottery & museum-related items for sale.
Activities: guided tours; lectures; films; gallery talks; formally organized education programs; inter-museum loan, permanent, temporary & traveling exhibitions.
Publications: quarterly, Roswell Museum Bulletin; monthly, catalogs of exhibitions.
Hours & Admission Prices: Mon.-Sat. 9-5, Sun. & holidays 1-5. No charge; donations accepted. Closed New Year's Day; Thanksgiving; Christmas. ♿
Attendance: 39,000 (accurate)
Membership: Senior Citizen $15; Educator $20; Individual $25; Family $35; Donor $100; Patron $250; Benefactor $500; Fellow $1,000; Corporate: I $250; II $500; III $1000.

SPRING RIVER PARK & ZOO, College & Atkinson Sts., Roswell, NM 88201-9506. Mailing Address: P.O. Drawer 1838, Roswell, NM 88202-1838. Tel.: 505-624-6760. Fax: 505-624-6941.
E-mail: roswellzoo@dfn.com
Web Site: www.roswellmysteries.com
Founded: 1966.
Congressional District: 5
Key Personnel: Dir. Parks & Recreation, Kim Elliott; Dir. Zoo, Elaine Mayfield.
Personnel Profile: Full-Time Paid 9; Part-Time Paid 1.
Governing Authority: municipal.
Zoo.
Collections: aviary; zoo exhibits; birds & animals; Prairie Dog Town; early wooden horse carousel; miniature train; longhorn ranch exhibit; early carousel; miniature train.
Facilities: picnic area.
Activities: group meetings; youth & family recreation.
Hours & Admission Prices: Summer: 10-8; Winter: 10-5:30, weather permitting. No charge; donations accepted. ♿
Attendance: 90,000 (estimated)
Membership: Friends of the Roswell Zoo Support Group $15.

Ruidoso Downs

THE HUBBARD MUSEUM OF THE AMERICAN WEST, (M), 841 Hwy. 70, W., Ruidoso Downs, NM 88346. Mailing Address: P.O. Box 40, Ruidoso Downs, NM 88346-0040. Tel.: 505-378-4142. Fax: 505-378-4166.
Web Site: www.hubbardmuseum.org
Formerly: Museum of the Horse
Founded: 1989.
Congressional District: 2
Key Personnel: Chm. (V), Mayor Tom Armstrong; Museum Dir., Jay Smith; Cur. Exhibits, David Mandel; Cur. Collections, Gwen McCausland; Cur. Education, Patsy Jackson; Devel., Jim Kofakis; Mktg. & Graphics, Janis Rowe; Gift Shop Mgr., Donna Franklin; Outreach, Adele Karolik; Administrative Sec., Anne Spotts; Facilities, Wayne Anzak; Custodial, Patricia Valdez.
Personnel Profile: Full-Time Paid 10; Part-Time Paid 4; Part-Time Volunteers 20; Interns 1.
Governing Authority: city; nonprofit organization. Tax-exempt: 501(c)(3).
History Museum.
Collections: wagons; stagecoach; sleighs; saddles & other horse-related items; fine art; furniture; Indian artifacts; children's interactive area; equine monument; historic buildings.
Facilities: 2,500-vol. library relating to horses, the American West & the Lincoln County War; 12 acre site.
Activities: changing exhibits; special event programs; school programs; lectures; performing arts.
Publications: brochures; newsletter; exhibition catalogs.
Hours & Admission Prices: Daily 9-5. Adults $6, senior citizens over 65 & military $5, children 6-16 $2, Ruidoso Downs residents 6 & over $1; members and children 6 & under no charge. Closed Thanksgiving; Christmas. ♿
Attendance: 30,000 (accurate)
Membership: The Scout $50; The Explorer $100; The Wagon Master $150; The Wrangler $250; The Trail Boss $500; The Rancher $1,000; The Stradling Patron $1,500; The Hubbard Patron $3,000; The Free Spirits Patron $5,000.

San Antonio

EL CAMINO REAL INTERNATIONAL HERITAGE CENTER, 300 E. County Rd., San Antonio, NM 87832. Mailing Address: P.O. Box 175, Socorro, NM 87801-0175. Tel.: 505-854-3600. Fax: 505-854-3609.
Web Site: www.elcaminoreal.org
History Museum.
Collections: oldest U.S. trail history; local cultural heritage; NM history; history of the first European & Spanish settlements.
Facilities: outdoor amphitheater; gardens; nature trails. Museum-related items for sale.
Activities: performances; special events.
Hours & Admission Prices: Wed.-Mon. 8:30-5. Adults $5; discounts to AAM & ICOM members; children under 16 no charge. Closed New Year's Day; Easter; Thanksgiving; Christmas. ♿
Membership: Regular $30; Family $40; Senior $60; Nonprofit Educational Institution $200; Government & Corporate Entity $500; Charter $1,000.

San Ildefonso Pueblo

SAN ILDEFONSO PUEBLO MUSEUM, Rte. 5, San Ildefonso Pueblo, NM 87506. Mailing Address: Box 315 A, San Ildefonso Pueblo, NM 87506. Tel.: 505-455-3549.
History Museum.
Collections: contemporary & traditional pottery; paintings; San Ildefonso artifacts; historic items.
Hours & Admission Prices: Mon.-Fri. 8-4:30. Vehicles $7.

Sandia Park

TINKERTOWN MUSEUM, 121 Sandia Crest Rd., Sandia Park, NM 87047. Mailing Address: P.O. Box 303, Sandia Park, NM 87047-0303. Tel.: 505-281-5233. Fax: 505-286-9335 (call first).
E-mail: tinker4u@tinkertown.com
Web Site: www.tinkertown.com
Founded: 1983.
Congressional District: 1
Key Personnel: Dir., Carla Ward.
Personnel Profile: Part-Time Paid 3.
Governing Authority: private.
Folk Art Museum.
Collections: wood carvings; miniature animated western town & three ring circus; hand made dolls & toys; 140 wedding cake couples; swords; circus banners & memorabilia; side show giant shoes & pants; period mechanical coin operated arcade machines; western livery & mining memorabilia.
Facilities: Museum-related items for sale.
Activities: Annual Event: Festival of Tinkering.
Publications: The Tinkertown Story; Emily Finds a Dog - A Tinkertown Tale.
Hours & Admission Prices: April to Nov. 1 daily 9-6. Adults $3, senior citizens $2.50, children $1; discounts to groups, AAM & ICOM members. ♿
Attendance: 21,075 (accurate)

Santa Fe

BATAAN MEMORIAL MILITARY MUSEUM & LIBRARY, 1050 Old Pecos Tr., Santa Fe, NM 87505-2688. Tel.: 505-474-1670.
Military Museum.
Collections: military artifacts & memorabilia.
Hours & Admission Prices: Tues., Wed. & Fri. 9-4, Sat. 9-1. No charge; donations accepted.

EL RANCHO DE LAS GOLONDRINAS MUSEUM, 334 Los Pinos Rd., Santa Fe, NM 87507-4363. Tel.: 505-471-2261. Fax: 505-471-5623.
E-mail: mail@golondrinas.org
Web Site: www.golondrinas.org
Founded: 1970.
Congressional District: 3
Key Personnel: Dir., George B. Paloheimo; Cur. Education & Interpretation, Mike King; Cur. Collection, Dr. Donna Pierce; Dir. Devel., John A. Berkenfield; Cur. Textiles, Beatrice Maestas; Cur. Agriculture, Julie Anna Lopez; Cur. Programs, Amanda Crocker; Site Rental Mgr., Carol Hilgers; Museum Shop Mgr., Lolly Martin.
Personnel Profile: Full-Time Paid 18; Part-Time Paid 6; Part-Time Volunteers 180.
Governing Authority: Parent Institution: El Rancho de las Golondrinas, Inc. Tax-exempt.
Living Historical Farm & Village: housed on 1700-1885 Las Golondrinas Ranch on pre-colonial Indian location.
Collections: Spanish colonial; religious. Historic Houses: Leger Gristmill; Talpa Water Mill, Padilla Water Mill, Barela Water Mill; Apodaca Blacksmith Shop; Casias Wheelwright shop; Gallegos Winery; Raton Schoolhouse; Las Trampas country store; hacienda-type dwellings of various periods & styles representing northern New Mexico of the Spanish colonial period; Morada & Oratorio Chapels.
Research Fields: Spanish colonial lifestyle; agriculture & textiles; backbreeding sheep.
Facilities: lecture & film hall; food service pavilion & kitchen.
Activities: guided tours; lectures; films; formally organized education programs for children; craft workshops; permanent & temporary exhibitions. Museum Sponsors: demonstrations, workshops & hands on activities June to August; Spring Festival in June; Wine Festival in July; Summer Festival in August; Harvest Festival in October.
Publications: official guidebook, El Rancho De Las Golondrinas; photo book, Through The Seasons at El Rancho De Las Golondrinas; coloring book; The Exposition on the Province of New Mexico, 1812; El Rancho de las Golondrinas; The Ranch of the Swallows.
Hours & Admission Prices: June-Sept. Wed.-Sun. 10-4. Tours: April-Oct. by appointment. Adults $5, military, children 13-18 and senior citizens 62 & over $4, children 5-12 $2. Festivals/Civil War: June-Aug. first Sat.-Sun. 10-4; Oct. Sat.-Sun. 10-4. Adults $7, military, children 13-18 and senior citizens 62 & over $5, children 5-12 $3. Wine Festival: adults 21 & over $7, youth 13-20 $4; discounts for members of Association for Living Historical Farms & Agricultural Museums; Los Amigos del Museo no charge to most events; members no charge. Closed Independence Day; Labor Day. ♿
Attendance: 49,000 (accurate)
Membership: Single $30; Family $50; Sustaining $75; Supporting $100; Patron $150; Benefactor $500; Life $1,000.

*** GEORGIA O'KEEFFE MUSEUM,** 217 Johnson St., Santa Fe, NM 87501-1826. Tel.: 505-946-1000. Fax: 505-946-1091.
E-mail: info@okeeffemuseum.org
Web Site: www.okeeffemuseum.org
Founded: 1995.
Congressional District: 3
Key Personnel: Dir., George G. King; Pres. (V), Saul Cohen; Exec. Asst., Debra Liggett; Dir. Devel., Jackie Hall; Dir. Finance, Carl Brown; Cur. & Research Center Dir., Barbara Buhler Lynes; Dir. Education, Jackie M.; Education Coord., Sarah Zurick; Registrar & Collections Mgr., Judith C. Smith; Librarian, Archivist & Asst. Dir. Research Ctr., Eumie Imm Stroukoff; Grant Writer & Researcher, Kaaren Boulosa; Human Resources Mgr., Sylvie S. Ward; Chief Security, Gary Smith; Operations Mgr., Amy Green; Public Rels. & Mktg. Mgr., Erin Newbrand; Museum Shop Mgr., Janice Wrhel.
Personnel Profile: Full-Time Paid 60; Part-Time Paid 9; Part-Time Volunteers 98; Interns 7.
Governing Authority: Tax-exempt.
Art Museum.
Collections: over 3,000 works of art including 1,700 by Georgia O'Keeffe.
Major Exhibits: Susan Rothenberg: Moving in Place (T), 1/22/10-5/16/10; 2010 Georgia O'Keeffe: Abstraction (T), 5/28/10-9/12/10; O'Keeffiana, 9/24/10-4/20/11.
Facilities: 5,000-vol. non-circulating research library; research center; education facility; video orientation rooms. Museum-related items for sale.
Activities: permanent, traveling & temporary exhibitions; guided & audio tours; captioned orientation video; lectures; concert series; docent program; workshops; field trips; training programs for educators; school tours; onsite symposiums.
Publications: monographs; collection & exhibition catalogues; critical studies & theory; educational brochures; members newsletters; teachers resources.
Hours & Admission Prices: Daily 10-5. Adults $10, seniors $8; students under 18, Fri. 5pm-8pm & members no charge. Closed Thanksgiving; Christmas. ♿
Attendance: 172,877 (accurate)
Membership: Individual $55; Contributor $75; Supporter $150; Friend $250; Sustainer $500; Benefactor $1,000; President's Council $5,000; O'Keeffe Circle $10,000.

GERALD PETERS GALLERY, 1011 Paseo de Peralta, Santa Fe, NM 87501-2735. Tel.: 505-954-5700. Fax: 505-954-5754.
E-mail: info@gpgallery.com
Web Site: www.gpgallery.com
Key Personnel: Dir., Elizabeth Hubbard
Art Gallery.
Collections: paintings; sculpture.
Hours & Admission Prices: Mon.-Sat. 10-5. ♿

THE GOVERNOR'S GALLERY, State Capitol, Rm. 400, 491 Old Santa Fe Trail, Santa Fe, NM 87501-2753. Tel.: 505-476-5072. Fax: 505-476-5076.
E-mail: merry.scully@state.nm.us
Web Site: www.mfasantafe.org
Founded: 1975.
Congressional District: 1
Key Personnel: Cur., Merry Scully; Museum Shop Mgr., Anna Burgess.
Personnel Profile: Full-Time Paid 2; Part-Time Volunteers 5.
Governing Authority: state. Parent Institution: New Mexico Office of Cultural Affairs. Subsidiary Institution: Museum of Fine Arts. Tax-exempt: 170(b)(1)(A).
Art Gallery: housed in State Capitol on Old Santa Fe Trail.
Collections: paintings; photographs; sculpture.
Activities: promotion of New Mexico artists & regional art forms.
Hours & Admission Prices: Mon.-Fri. 8-5. No charge. ♿
Attendance: 30,000 (accurate)

MUSEUM OF CONTEMPORARY NATIVE ARTS, (M), A Center of the Institute of American Indian Arts, 108 Cathedral Place, Santa Fe, NM 87501-2027. Tel.: 505-983-8900. Fax: 505-983-1222.
E-mail: museum@iaia.edu
Web Site: www.iaia.edu/museum
Founded: 1972.
Congressional District: 1
Key Personnel: Dir., Patsy Phillips; Interim Pres., Rich Tobin; Chm. (V), Jeanne Givens; Registrar, Paula Rivera; Administrative & Finance Officer, Jary Earl; Special Projects & Community Rels. Officer, Larry Phillips; Museum Shop Mgr., Maggie Ohnesorgen; Security Supvr., Thomas Atencio; Art Design Asst., Sallie Wesaw; Cur., Joseph Sanchez; Assoc. Cur., Tatiana Lomahaftewa Slock; Membership Officer, Heather Doherty; Educational Program Asst., Loni Manning.
Personnel Profile: Full-Time Paid 18; Part-Time Paid 3; Interns 2.
Governing Authority: college. Parent Institution: Institute of American Indian & Alaska Native Culture and Arts Development. Tax-exempt.
Culturally Specific.
Collections: over 7,000 items contemporary American Indian art; American Indian artists archive.
Research Fields: contemporary American Indian art.
Facilities: 400-vol. library of books related to American Indian art & general art history; classrooms; national Native American videotape archives; BIA Bicentennial Videotape Archives available by written request to museums & researchers. North American Indian arts & books for sale.
Activities: guided tours; lectures; films; gallery talks; arts festivals; workshops; undergraduate college students; training programs for professional museum workers; inter-museum loan; permanent, temporary & traveling exhibitions.
Publications: anthologies of student written works; exhibit catalogues & brochures; books: Creativity is Our Tradition; Gallery handouts; members newsletter, Artwinds.
Hours & Admission Prices: June-Oct. Mon.-Sat. 10-5, Sun. 12-5; Nov.-May Mon. & Wed.-Sat. 10-5, Sun. 12-5. Adults $4, students & senior citizens with ID $2.50; children under 16, members, & Native Americans no charge. Closed major holidays. ♿
Attendance: 39,761 (accurate)
Membership: Individual $40; Family $50; Sponsor $100; Patron $500; Benefactor $1,000.

MUSEUM OF INDIAN ARTS & CULTURE/LABORATORY OF ANTHROPOLOGY, 710 Camino Lejo, Santa Fe, NM 87505-7511. Mailing Address: P.O. Box 2087, Santa Fe, NM 87504-2087. Tel.: 505-476-1250 & 1247. Fax: 505-476-1330.
E-mail: info@miaclab.org
Web Site: www.indianartsandculture
Founded: 1909.

Congressional District: 3
Key Personnel: Dir., Dr. Shelby J. Tisdale; Finance, Monica Vigil; Cur. Archaeological Research Collections, Julia Clifton; Cur. Ethnology, Antonio Chavarria; Cur. Archaeology, Dr. Melissa Powell; Asst. Cur. Archaeological Research Collections, Dody Fugate; Cur. Individually Cataloged Collections, Valerie Verzuh; Rights & Reproductions, David McNeece; Collections Mgr. Archaeological Research Collections, Tony Thibodeau; Archaeological Collection Specialist, Rachel Johnson; Archivist, Diane Bird; Librarian, Allison Colborne; Dir. Living Traditions Center, Joyce Begay-Foss; Educator, Dawn Kaufmann; Exhibitions Preparator, Dennis Culver; Museum Shop Mgr., John Stafford.
Personnel Profile: Full-Time Paid 31; Part-Time Paid 4; Part-Time Volunteers 90.
Governing Authority: state; nonprofit. Parent Institution: Department of Cultural Affairs. Tax-exempt: 170(c)(1).
Native American Arts & Culture Museum: Laboratory of Anthropology is housed in 1931 Spanish-Pueblo revival architecture designed by John Gaw Meem.
Collections: American Indian Art material culture & ethnology of the native peoples of the Southwest; prehistoric & historic jewelry, pottery, baskets, textiles, accessories; Kachinas; sculpture; paintings.
Major Exhibits: A River Apart: The Pottery of Santo Domingo & Cochiti Pueblos, 11/09-10/1/11; Huichol Art & Culture: Balancing the World, 4/11/10-3/6/11.
Research Fields: archaeology of the Southwest; anthropology of native peoples of Southwest; contemporary arts & aesthetics.
Facilities: 45,000-vol. library on anthropology of the Southwest available to the public; educational classrooms; resource center; 30,000 sq. ft. exhibit space; field research section; amphitheater.
Activities: guided tours; lectures; films; concerts; training programs; organized education programs for children, adults, undergraduate & graduate students; internships. Annual Event: Native Treasures Indian Arts Festival in May.
Publications: popular articles in Museum of New Mexico magazine El Palacio; Secrets of Casas Grandes; A River Apart: The Pottery of Cochiti & Santo Domingo Pueblo; Huichol Art & Culture: Balancing the World; Painting the Native World: Life, Land and Animals.
Hours & Admission Prices: Memorial Day to Labor Day daily 10-5; Sept.-May Tues.-Sun. 10-5. Four-day pass to all five Museums $20, a single Museum $9; discounts to students, and AAM & ICOM members; NM residents with ID Sun. & members no charge. Closed New Year's Day; Easter; Thanksgiving; Christmas. ♿
Attendance: 56,722 (accurate)
Membership: Student & Teacher $30; Senior $50; Senior Couple $60; Individual $65; Family & Dual $75-$124; Sponsor $125-$249; Patron $250-$499; Benefactor $500-$1,499; Regent's Circle $1,500-$2,499; Governor's Circle $2,500-$4,999; National Council $5,000-$9,999; Chairman's Council $10,000 & up.

MUSEUM OF INTERNATIONAL FOLK ART, Museum Hill at Camino Lejo, Santa Fe, NM 87505. Mailing Address: P.O. Box 2087, Santa Fe, NM 87504-2087. Tel.: 505-476-1200 & 1204. Fax: 505-476-1300.
E-mail: info@moifa.org
Web Site: www.moifa.org
Founded: 1953.
Congressional District: 1
Key Personnel: Dir., Dr. Marsha C. Bol; Asst. Dir., Jacqueline Duke; Collections Mgr., Paul Smutko; Cur. Latin American Folk Art, Dr. Barbara Mauldin; Cur. U.S. Latino, Hispano, & Spanish Colonial Collections, Nicolasa Chavez; Cur. Textiles & Costumes, Dr. Bobbie Sumberg; Dir. Education, Aurelia Gomez; Librarian, Archivist & Image Rights Coord., Ree Mobley; Special Events Coord., Laura Lovejoy-May; Administrative Sec., Christine Vitagliano; Cur. Asian & Middle Eastern Folk Art, Felicia Katz Harris; Museum Educator, Patricia Sigala; Security, Andy Perea.
Personnel Profile: Full-Time Paid 28; Part-Time Paid 2; Part-Time Volunteers 115; Interns 1.
Governing Authority: state. Parent Institution: Cultural Affairs Dept. Subsidiary Institute: Museum of New Mexico. Tax-exempt.
International Folk Art Museum.
Collections: international collection of folk art including textiles, costumes, ceramics, dolls & toys; Spanish colonial religious art; Southwest Hispanic folk art & furniture; jewelry; amulets; religious, ceremonial & ritual objects.
Research Fields: Spanish colonial arts, textiles, costumes; folk art.
Facilities: 16,000-vol. library of books & journals pertaining to folk art; 180-seat auditorium; 25,000 sq. ft. exhibit space; outdoor plaza & restaurant; labyrinth; gardens. Museum-related items for sale.
Activities: guided tours; lectures; films; concerts; arts festivals; organized education programs for children & adults; docent program.
Publications: magazine, El Palacio.
Hours & Admission Prices: Memorial Day to Labor Day daily 10-5; Sept.-May Tues.-Sun. 10-5. Four-day pass to five museum facilities in Santa Fe $18. Single Museum: in-state $6, out of state $9; discounts to AAM & ICOM members; children 16 & under, school groups, NM seniors 60 & over on Wed., museum foundation members & NM residents on Sun. no charge. Closed New Year's Day; Easter; Thanksgiving; Christmas. ♿
Attendance: 85,000 (accurate)
Membership: Student with ID $25; Senior Individual over 62 $40; Individual & Senior Couple over 62 $50; Family $60-$99; Sponsor $100-$249; Patron $250-$499; Benefactor $500-$999; Regent's Circle $1,000-$2,499; Governor's Circle $2,500-$4,999; National Council $5,000 and up.

* **MUSEUM OF NEW MEXICO, (M),** 725 Camino Lejo, Santa Fe, NM 87505-7516. Mailing Address: P.O. Box 2087, Santa Fe, NM 87504-2087. Tel.: 505-476-1125. Fax: 505-476-1127.
E-mail: info@moifa.org
Web Site: www.museumofnewmexico.org
Founded: 1909.
Congressional District: 1,2 & 3
Key Personnel: Deputy Dir. Museum Resources Division & Mktg. & Outreach Dir., Shelley Thompson; Dir. Museum of International Folk Art, Dr. Joyce Ice; Dir. Museum of Indian Arts & Culture/Laboratory of Anthropology, Dr. Shelby Tisdale; Dir. Museum of Fine Arts, Dr. Marsha C. Bol; Dir. NM State Monuments, Ernesto Ortega; Dir. Palace of the Governors, Dr. Frances Levine; Deputy Dir. NM History Museum, John McCarthy; Chief Conservator, Claire Munzenrider; Senior Conservator, Maureen Russell; Chief Publications, Anna Gallegos; Cur. Contemporary Photography, Dr. Steve Yates; Cur. Contemporary Art, Museum of Fine Arts, Laura Addison; Cur. 20th-Century Art, Joseph Traugott; Chief Librarian History Library, Tomas Jaehn; Educator, Palace of the Governors, Erica Garcia; Cur. Historic Photography, Cary McStay; Cur. ARC, Julia Clifton; Asst. Cur. ARC, Dody Fugate; Archivist, Diane Bird; Cur. Archaeological Collections, Dr. Melissa Powell; Cur. Ethnology, Anthony Chavarria; Cur. Asian & Middle Eastern, Felicia Katz Harris; Cur. Latin American Art, Barbara Mauldin; Collections Mgr., Paul Smutko; Cur. Hispanic & Latino, Dr. Tey Marianna Nunn; Cur. European & American, Annie Carlano; Cur. Textiles, Bobbie Sumberg; Registrar, Deborah Garcia; Office Archaeological Studies Dir., Dr. Tim Maxwell; Exhibitions Dept. Chief Fabricator, Marvin Valdez; Exhibitions Designer, John Tinker; Graphic Designer, Susan Hyde-Holmes; Video Production, Tom McCarthy; Educator Museum of Indian Arts & Culture, Lisa Sheppard; Educator Museum of Indian Arts & Culture, Joyce Begay; Educator Museum of Fine Arts, Ellen Zieselman; Educator Museum of International Folk Art, Aurelia Gomez; Education, Sharon Berman; Librarian Laboratory of Anthropology, Mara Yarbrough; Museum Shop Mgr., John Stafford.
Personnel Profile: Full-Time Paid 285; Part-Time Paid 28; Part-Time Volunteers 510; Interns 6.
Governing Authority: state. Parent Institution: Dept. of Cultural Affairs. Branch Museums: Palace of the Governors, Santa Fe; New Mexico Museum of Arts, Santa Fe; Museum of International Folk Art, Santa Fe; Museum of Indian Arts & Culture/Laboratory of Anthropology, Santa Fe; Fort Sumner State Monument, Fort Sumner; Coronado State Monument, Bernalillo; Jemez State Monument, Jemez Springs; Fort Selden State Monument, Radium Springs; Lincoln State Monument, Lincoln; El Camino Real Heritage Center, Socorro. Tax-exempt: 170(b)(1)(A).
History, Art, Folk Art & Anthropology Museums.
Collections: anthropology, archaeology & ethnology of the Southwest; fine arts with emphasis on southwestern painters; international folk art; Spanish colonial history; history of New Mexico; photographic archives; American Indian art & cultures; six historic site state monuments at Lincoln, Fort Sumner, Jemez Springs, Fort Selden, Bernalillo & Socorro.
Research Fields: anthropology; folk art; history of New Mexico; Spanish Colonial history; art; archaeomagnetic dating; non-destructive trace elements dating.
Activities: guided tours; lectures; films; concerts; art competitions; docent program; inter-museum loan, permanent, temporary & traveling exhibitions; school loan service; educational aid kits for schools.
Publications: magazine, El Palacio; 80 titles covering southwestern art, history, archaeology, ethnology & crafts; monthly newsletter.
Hours & Admission Prices: Memorial Day to Labor Day daily 10-5; Sept.-May Tues.-Sun. 10-5. Four-day pass to five Santa Fe museums $18, single visit NM residents $6, nonresidents $8; discounts to students, groups of 10 or more, AAM & ICOM members; school groups, NM residents on Sun., NM seniors on Wed., children 16 & under no charge. Closed New Year's Day; Easter; Thanksgiving; Christmas. ♿
Attendance: 642,100 (accurate)
Membership: Individual $50; Family/Dual $60-$99; Sponsor $100-$249; Patron $250-$499; Benefactor $500-$1,499.

MUSEUM OF SPANISH COLONIAL ART - MOSCA, 750 Camino Lejo, Santa Fe, NM 87505-7511. Mailing Address: P.O. Box 5378, Santa Fe, NM 87502-5378. Tel.: 505-982-2226. Fax: 505-982-4585.
E-mail: museum@spanishcolonial.org
Web Site: www.spanishcolonial.org
Formerly: Spanish Colonial Arts Society
Founded: 1925.
Congressional District: 3
Key Personnel: C.E.O., William Field; Pres., Larry Lujan; Museum Shop Mgr., Sarah Rinehart.
Personnel Profile: Full-Time Paid 6; Part-Time Paid 3; Part-Time Volunteers 54; Interns 2.
Governing Authority: private; nonprofit organization. Parent Institution: Spanish Colonial Arts Society, Inc. Tax-exempt.
Spanish Colonial Arts Museum.
Collections: Spanish colonial art; furniture; bultos; retablos; straw applique; textiles; tinwork; jewelry; developments in Hispanic art forms.
Facilities: 3,600 sq. ft. exhibit space.
Activities: Annual Events: Spanish market in July; Winter market in December.
Publications: newsletter, Que Pasa?
Hours & Admission Prices: Tues.-Sun. 10-5. Adults $6, New Mexico residents $3; discounts to AAM & ICOM members; N.M. residents on Sun. & members no charge. ♿
Attendance: 50,000 (accurate)
Membership: Spanish Market Artist $35; Individual $40; Family & Dual $60; Supporter $100; Sponsor $300; Sustainer $500; Patron $1,000 & up; Benefactor $2,500 & up; Chairman's Council $5,000 & up.

NEW MEXICO MUSEUM OF ART, 107 W. Palace Ave., Santa Fe, NM 87501-2014. Mailing Address: P.O. Box 2087, 107 W. Palace Ave., Santa Fe, NM 87504-2087. Tel.: 505-476-5072. Fax: 505-476-5076.
E-mail: mary.jebsen@state.nm.us
Web Site: nmartmuseum.org
Formerly: Museum of Fine Arts
Founded: 1917.
Congressional District: 1
Key Personnel: Acting Dir., Mary Jebsen; Cur. 20th Century Art, Dr. Joe Traugott; Librarian, Devon Skeele; Cur. Education, Ellen Zieselman; Mgr. Special Events, Martha Landry; Cur. Contemporary Art, Laura Addison; Admin., Theresa Garcia; Registrar, Daniel Goodman; Chief Registrar, Michelle Roberts; Cur. Collections, Christine Mather; Cur. Photography, Katherine Ware; Preparator, Tim Jag; Chief Cur., Tim Rodgers; Museum Shop Mgr., John Stafford; Administrative Asst., Laura Kohl.
Personnel Profile: Full-Time Paid 27; Part-Time Paid 1; Part-Time Volunteers 8.
Governing Authority: state; nonprofit. Parent Institution: Museum of New Mexico. Tax-exempt: 170(c)(1).
Art Museum: housed in an architectural structure patterned after New Mexico mission churches.
Collections: over 23,000 fine art pieces emphasizing the Southwest; paintings; prints; drawings; photographs; sculpture; exhibitions on 20th-century American art.
Major Exhibits: Manmade: Notions of Landscapes from the Lannan Collection, 11/09-1/10/10; Play It Louder: Alexander Girard, 12/18/09-2/21/10; Museums in the 21st Century (T), 1/29/10-4/18/10; New Architecture in New Mexico, 3/5/10-5/2/10; Art on the Edge: FOCA Biennial Juried Exhibition, 4/16/10-8/1/10; Sole Mates: Cowboy Boots and Art, 5/14/10-9/12/10; Finish/Fetish: Ross and Tinker, 8/13/10-1/30/11; Photography and Environmental Activism, 10/1/10-5/8/11.
Research Fields: American art, specializing in New Mexico.
Facilities: 10,000-vol. library relating to art in the Southwest available to the public; St. Francis Auditorium; three sculpture courtyards. Museum-related items for sale.
Activities: guided tours; lectures; films; concerts; dance recitals; organized education programs for children; traveling exhibitions; triennial fine arts competition.
Publications: quarterly journal, El Palacio; exhibition catalogues.
Hours & Admission Prices: Winter: Tues.-Sun. 10-5; Summer: daily 10-5. Four-day pass to 4 Santa Fe museums $20, single non-resident $9, single NM residents $6; discounts to AAM & ICOM members; school groups, NM residents on Sun., seniors 60 & over on Wed., Fri. 5-8 & museum members no charge. Closed New Year's Day; Easter; Thanksgiving; Christmas. ♿
Attendance: 125,000 (accurate)

PALACE OF THE GOVERNORS/NEW MEXICO HISTORY MUSEUM, On the Plaza, Santa Fe, NM 87501. Mailing Address: P.O. Box 2087, Santa Fe, NM 87504-2087. Tel.: 505-476-5100 (Palace) & 5200 (NMHM). Fax: 505-476-5104.
E-mail: carla.ortiz@state.nm.us
Web Site: www.palaceofthegovernors.org
Founded: 1909.
Congressional District: 3
Key Personnel: Dir., Frances Levine, Ph.D.; Deputy Dir., John J. McCarthy; Asst. Dir., Rene Harris; Finance Officer, Judy Morse; Cur., Josef Diaz; Cur. Historical Photography, Mary Anne Redding; Mgr. Collections, Wanda Edwards; Asst. Collections Mgr., Pennie McBride; Imaging Specialist, Nicholas Chiarella; Palace Press, Thomas Leech; Palace Press, James Bourland; Photo Archivist, Daniel Kosharek; Chief Librarian, Tomas Jaehn; Sr. Cataloger, Patricia Hewitt; Archivist, Lou Jaureguiberry; Coord. Public Programs, Carlotta Boettcher; Security Captain, Steve Baca; Education, Erica Garcia; Education, Emily Fijol; Exhibit Designer, Caroline Lajoie; Public Rels. & Mktg., Kate Nelson; Coord. Special Events, Inessa Williams; Graphic Design, Natalie Beca.
Personnel Profile: Full-Time Paid 38; Part-Time Paid 1; Part-Time Volunteers 70.
Governing Authority: state; nonprofit. New Mexico History Museum, 113 Lincoln, Santa Fe, NM 87501.
History Museum: housed in c.1610 Spanish-style government building.
Collections: New Mexico & Southwest history from European contact, colonial period to the present; firearms; religious art; decorative arts; photos; archives; pottery; silver; furniture.
Major Exhibits: Fashioning New Mexico, 11/09-4/11/10; Archaeology of an Ancient City, 11/29/09-12/10; Ernest Thompson Seton, 5/23/10-5/15/11.
Research Fields: New Mexico, Southwestern, Latin American & borderlands history.
Facilities: 12,000-vol. library relating to the history of the Southwest; manuscripts; 380,000 photographs; 15,000 artifact collection.
Activities: guided walking tours of Santa Fe; foreign tours to Spain, Mexico's Central & South America; lectures; films; concerts. Museum Sponsors: Mountain Trade Fair; Christmas at the Palace; Las Posadas; Native American Dances; Portal Native American Venders Program.
Publications: Friends of the Palace Press; historical novels.
Hours & Admission Prices: Labor Day to Memorial Day Tues.-Sun. 10-5. Adults $9 nonresident, $6 residents; New Mexico residents on Sun., NM seniors on Wed., Fri. 5-8, children 16 and under, AAM & ICOM members no charge. Closed New Year's Day; Easter; Thanksgiving; Christmas. ♿
Attendance: 100,000

PUEBLO OF POJOAQUE, POEH MUSEUM, (M), 78 Cities of Gold Rd., Santa Fe, NM 87506-0918. Tel.: 505-455-3334. Fax: 505-455-0174.
Web Site: poehmuseum.com
Founded: 1987.
Congressional District: 3
Key Personnel: Dir., Vernon G. Lujan; Asst. Dir., Francine Maestas; Exec. Dir., George Rivera; Cur., Melissa Talachy; Museum Shop Mgr., Andrea Tse-Pe'.
Personnel Profile: Full-Time Paid 5; Part-Time Paid 2; Interns 1.
Governing Authority: Parent Institution: Poeh Cultural Center and Museum. Tax-exempt.
Tribal Museum.
Collections: archaeological to contemporary art from Pueblos of New Mexico; Tewa Pueblo communities; photographs; Native American; NAGPRA repository.
Research Fields: language & cultural preservation.
Facilities: classroom. Museum-related items for sale.
Activities: guided tours; temporary exhibitions.
Hours & Admission Prices: Mon.-Fri. 8-5, Sat. 9-4. No charge; donations accepted. Closed Thanksgiving; Feast Day; Christmas. ♿
Attendance: 750 (estimated)

SITE SANTA FE, (M), 1606 Paseo de Peralta, Santa Fe, NM 87501-3724. Tel.: 505-989-1199. Fax: 505-989-1188.
E-mail: info@sitesantafe.org
Web Site: www.sitesantafe.org
Founded: 1995.
Congressional District: 3
Key Personnel: Exec. Dir., Laura Steward Heon; Deputy Dir., Catherine Putnam; Honorary Chm., Joann Phillips; Honorary Chm., Bobbie Foshay; Chm. Bd., Marlene Nathan Meyerson; Bd. Pres., Cornelia Bryer; Pres. Emeritus, John L. Marion; Dir. Devel., Marc Dorfman; Dir. Education, Juliet Myers; Dir. External Affairs, Anne Wrinkle; Exhibitions Admin., Tyler Auwarter; Membership, Jo-Anne Skinner.
Personnel Profile: Full-Time Paid 11; Part-Time Paid 18; Part-Time Volunteers 19; Interns 4.
Governing Authority: private; nonprofit organization. Tax-exempt: 501(c)(3).
Contemporary Art Museum.
Collections: contemporary art.
Facilities: 15,000 sq. ft. exhibit space. Books & catalogues for sale.
Activities: concerts; films; formal education programs for adults & children; guided tours; lectures; traveling exhibitions; artists' commissions.
Publications: exhibition catalogs: Looking for a Place; Roni Horn; Robert

Therrien; Allan Graham; Jose Bedia; Sarah Charlesworth; Truce; Longing & Belonging; Thomas Ashcraft; Jim Hodges; Conceal/Reveal; Tom Sachs; Alan Rath; Postmark; Beau Monde: Toward a Redeemed Cosmopolitanism; Gary Simmons: Ghost House; Dara Friedman; Ernesto Neto; Teresita Fernandez; Mona Hatoum: Domestic Disturbance; Erika Wanenmacher: Grimoire; Monica Bonvicini; Doris Salcedo; Roxy Paine: Second Nature; Uta Barth: White Blind (Bright Red); Disparities and Deformations: Our Grotesque; Jim Campbell: Quantizing Effects; Paul Sarkisian; Still Points of the Turning World; Stephen Bush: Gelderland; Barry X Ball; Steina: 1970-2000 (2008); Lucky Number Seven; catalogue, SITE's 7th International Biennial.
Hours & Admission Prices: Exhibition: Wed.-Thurs & Sat. 10-5, Fri. 10-7, Sun. 12-5. Adults $10, seniors, students & children $5; discounts to AAM & ICOM members; members & Fri. 10-7 no charge. Closed national holidays. ♿
Attendance: 40,000 (estimated)
Membership: Student, Senior & Educator $35; Friend $50; Family $75; Supporter $125; Patron $250; Contemporary Circle $500; Director's Circle $1,000.

SAN MIGUEL MISSION CHURCH, 401 Old Santa Fe Trail, Santa Fe, NM 87501-2746. Tel.: 505-983-3974.
E-mail: sanmiguelsantafe@yahoo.com
Founded: 1610.
Congressional District: 3
Key Personnel: C.E.O., Saundra Johnson Austin.
Personnel Profile: Full-Time Paid 1.
Governing Authority: church; nonprofit organization. Parent Institution: St. Michael's H.S. Tax-exempt.
Historic Building: built in 1610.
Collections: Indian art; religious artifacts; pottery; oldest bell in U.S.; Spanish colonial art.
Facilities: archives; church. Religious articles for sale.
Activities: guided tours; lectures; masses.
Publications: book, Story of San Miguel.
Hours & Admission Prices: Summer: Mon.-Sat. 9-5, Sun. 10-4. Latin Mass: Sun. 2pm. Mass: Sun. 5pm. Tours: $1 per person; children under 6 no charge. ♿
Attendance: 65,000 (accurate)

SANTA FE CHILDREN'S MUSEUM, 1050 Old Pecos Trail, Santa Fe, NM 87505-2688. Tel.: 505-989-8359. Fax: 505-989-7506.
E-mail: children@santafechildrensmuseum.org
Web Site: www.santafechildrensmuseum.org
Founded: 1985.
Congressional District: 3
Key Personnel: Exec. Dir., David Tesseo; Pres. (V) & Chm. Bd. (V), Fidel Gutierrez; Public Rels., Jennifer Padilla; Volunteer Coord., Gail Wittenberg; Earthworks Educator, Griet Laga; Floor Mgr., Liz Crosman; Floor Mgr., Sunny Zamora; Museum Shop Mgr., Veronica Roybal; Bookkeeper, Josephine Valencia; Administrative Asst., Martha Lee Romero; Assoc. Dir., Jason Scott; Dir. Devel., Ginger Roherty; Education Programs Dir., Elisabeth Keller.
Personnel Profile: Full-Time Paid 11; Part-Time Paid 6; Part-Time Volunteers 100; Interns 9.
Governing Authority: not-for-profit organization. Tax-exempt: 501(c)(3).
Children's Museum: located in Santa Fe's historic district.
Collections: interactive exhibits pertaining to the arts, humanities & science.
Research Fields: informal learning.
Facilities: 500-vol. library on education & life studies, available to the public; 5,000 sq. ft. exhibit space; 1 acre horticultural garden. Museum-related items for sale.
Activities: concerts; formal education programs for adults; environmental education; workshops; demonstrations; art & science education programs; interactive exhibits. Annual Events: auction; concert; holiday programming; ice cream Sunday.
Publications: quarterly newsletter; annual ad brochure, annual report; Voices of Violence, Visions of Peace; Families: Celebrating the Journey.
Hours & Admission Prices: June-Aug. Tues.-Sat. 10-5, Sun. 12-5; mid-Sept. to May Wed.-Sat. 10-5, Sun. 12-5. Adults $8, NM residents with ID $4; school groups no charge. Closed New Year's Day; Easter; Independence Day; Thanksgiving; Christmas. ♿
Attendance: 68,818 (accurate)
Membership: Individual $35; Family $60; Grandparent $75; Family Plus $120; Gold Family $250; Sponsor $500; Patron $1,000; Silver Patron $2,500; Gold Patron $5,000.

SANTUARIO DE NUESTRA SENORA DE GUADALUPE, 100 S. Guadalupe St., Santa Fe, NM 87501-5503. Tel.: 505-983-8868, ext. 21.
Founded: 1975.
Congressional District: 1
Personnel Profile: Full-Time Paid 1; Part-Time Volunteers 9.
Governing Authority: nonprofit organization. Tax-exempt: 501(c)(3).
Religious Museum & Historic Site: housed in c.1780 church built by the Franciscans.
Collections: Spanish colonial mural; New Mexican Santero art.
Research Fields: living Indo-Hispanic artists & their works; adobe structures.
Facilities: plants of the Holy Land garden.
Activities: guided tours; lectures; gallery talks; concerts; arts festivals; drama.
Publications: quarterly newsletter, Noticias.
Hours & Admission Prices: Mon.-Fri. 9-12 & 1-4. No charge; donations accepted. ♿
Attendance: 21,000
Membership: Individual $15; Family & Business $25; Sponsor $50; Patron $100; Business Patron $200; Benefactor $500; Life $1,000 & up.

SCHOOL FOR ADVANCED RESEARCH, INDIAN ARTS RESEARCH CENTER, 660 Garcia St., Santa Fe, NM 87505-2858. Mailing Address: P.O. Box 2188, Santa Fe, NM 87504-2188. Tel.: 505-954-7205 & 7200. Fax: 505-954-7207.
E-mail: iarc@sarsf.org
Web Site: www.sarweb.org
Formerly: School of American Research
Founded: 1907.
Congressional District: 1
Key Personnel: Pres., James Brooks; Vice Pres. Business Administration, Sharon Tison; Co Dir. Publications, Lynn Baca; Vice Pres. Academic & Institutional Advancement, John Kantner; Dir. Indian Arts Research Center, Dr. Cynthia Chavez Lamar.
Personnel Profile: Full-Time Paid 28; Part-Time Paid 6; Part-Time Volunteers 23.
Governing Authority: nonprofit organization. Parent Institution: School for Advanced Research. Subsidiary Institution: Indian Arts Research Center. Tax-exempt: 501(c)(3).
Indian Arts Research Center.
Collections: representative historic & contemporary Southwestern Pueblo Indian pottery; Navajo & Pueblo Indian textiles & jewelry collection; Native American easel paintings; Southwest Indian basketry; Katsinam & other ethnographic objects pertaining to historic & contemporary Southwest American Indian art.
Research Fields: anthropology; archaeology; Southwest Indian arts.
Facilities: library; 8 acre historic estate.
Activities: resident scholar program; advanced seminars; Southwest Indian arts research; archaeology; publications; public education.
Publications: books on Southwest Indian art, archaeology & anthropology.
Hours & Admission Prices: Mon.-Fri. 9-5 by appointment only; public tours Fri. 2 pm, call for reservations. Adults $15; discounts to AAM members; members no charge. ♿
Attendance: 1,145 (accurate)
Membership: Arroyo Hondo $40; Pecos $70; Mesa Verde $150; Chaco $500; Bandelier $1,000.

∗ **THE WHEELWRIGHT MUSEUM OF THE AMERICAN INDIAN, (M),** 704 Camino Lejo, Santa Fe, NM 87505-7511. Mailing Address: P.O. Box 5153, Santa Fe, NM 87502-5153. Tel.: 505-982-4636 & 1-800-607-4636. Fax: 505-989-7386.
E-mail: info@wheelwright.org
Web Site: www.wheelwright.org
Founded: 1937.
Congressional District: 3
Key Personnel: Dir. & C.E.O., Jonathan Batkin; Cur., Cheri Falkenstien-Doyle; Collections Mgr., Mary Katherine Logan; Business Mgr., Patricia Martinez; Preparator, Arthur Esquibel; Mgr. Case Trading Post, Robb Lucas; Public Rels., Diana M. Ceres.
Personnel Profile: Full-Time Paid 11; Part-Time Paid 7; Part-Time Volunteers 130.
Governing Authority: nonprofit organization. Subsidiary Institution: Wheelwright Foundation: Tax-exempt: 501(c)(3).
Anthropology & Art Museum.
Collections: traditional & contemporary Native American Art including Navajo, Pueblo & other Native Americans of New Mexico ethnography; art history.
Major Exhibits: Through Their Eyes: Paintings from the Santa Fe Indian School, 11/09-4/10.
Research Fields: Native American art & culture.
Facilities: 6,000-vol. library of books on Navajo studies & Native American Art. Museum-related items for sale.

Activities: guided tours; lectures; films; gallery talks; temporary exhibitions; fieldtrips; craft demonstrations; children's activities; book signings.
Hours & Admission Prices: Mon.-Sat. 10-5, Sun. 1-5. No charge; donations accepted. Closed New Year's Day; Thanksgiving; Christmas. ♿
Attendance: 33,000 (accurate)
Membership: Individual $30; Family $50; Behind the Scenes $100; Supporter & Business $250; Benefactor $500; Corporate $1,000.

Santa Rosa

ROUTE 66 AUTO MUSEUM, 2866 Will Rogers Ave., (Historic Rte. 66), Santa Rosa, NM 88435. Tel.: 505-472-1966.
E-mail: info@route66automuseum.com
Web Site: www.route66automuseum.com
Key Personnel: Owner, Bozo Cordova
Car Museum.
Collections: over 30 vehicles on display.
Hours & Admission Prices: April-Oct. Mon.-Sat. 7:30am-6pm, Sun. 10-5; Nov.-March Mon.-Sat. 8-5, Sun. 10-5. Adults $5; discount to family & groups.

Santa Teresa

WAR EAGLES AIR MUSEUM, Dona Ana County Airport, Santa Teresa, NM 88008. Mailing Address: 8012 Airport Rd., Santa Teresa, NM 88008-9719. Tel.: 575-589-2000.
E-mail: mail@war-eagles-air-museum.com
Web Site: www.war-eagles-air-museum.com/
Founded: 1989.
Personnel Profile: Full-Time Paid 6; Full-Time Volunteers 6; Part-Time Paid 3; Part-Time Volunteers 12.
Governing Authority: nonprofit organization.
Military Aviation History.
Collections: aircraft from World War II & the Korean Conflict era including P-51 Mustang, P-38 Lightning, P-40 Warhawk, F-4U-4 Corsair; twin-engine Invader bomber, DC-3 transport; German observation aircraft, the Fiesler-Storch.
Facilities: Museum-related items for sale.
Activities: rental facilities; educational programs; special events.
Hours & Admission Prices: Tues.-Sun. 10-4. ♿

Silver City

FRANCIS MCCRAY GALLERY, Western NM Univ., 1000 College Ave., Silver City, NM 88062. Mailing Address: Western NM Univ., P.O. Box 680, Silver City, NM 88062-0680. Tel.: 575-538-6517 & 6616. Fax: 575-538-6619.
Web Site: www.wnmu.edu
Founded: 1960.
Key Personnel: C.E.O. & Assoc. Professor, Michael Metcalf; Professor, Claude Smith, III; Gallery Dir. & Assoc. Professor, Gloria Maya.
Personnel Profile: Full-Time Paid 1; Part-Time Paid 3.
Governing Authority: university. Parent Institution: Western New Mexico University. Tax-exempt.
University Art Gallery
Collections: contemporary American art: paintings, prints, sculpture, pottery.
Facilities: classrooms; 1,600 sq. ft. exhibit space; 990-seat theater.
Activities: lectures; films; concerts; dance recitals; arts festivals; rental gallery; education programs for college students affiliated with Western New Mexico University; loan, temporary & traveling exhibitions. Museum Sponsors: Scholarship Art Sale.
Publications: monthly, flyer.
Hours & Admission Prices: Sept.-May Mon.-Fri. 10-4:30; other times by appointment. No charge; donations accepted. Closed university holidays. ♿
Attendance: 2,400 (estimated)

* **SILVER CITY MUSEUM, (M),** 312 W. Broadway, Silver City, NM 88061-4921. Tel.: 505-538-5921. Fax: 505-388-1096.
E-mail: info@silvercitymuseum.org
Web Site: www.silvercitymuseum.org
Founded: 1967.
Key Personnel: Dir., Susan Berry; Chm. Bd., Sandra Hicks; Pres. Silver City Museum Society, Thomas E. Hines, Ph.D.; Cur. Collections, Jackie Becker; Coord., Barbara Nance; Museum Coord., Jessica Tumposky; Museum Shop Mgr., Charmeine Wait.
Personnel Profile: Full-Time Paid 3; Part-Time Paid 4; Part-Time Volunteers 50.
Governing Authority: municipal; nonprofit. Parent Institution: Town of Silver City. Tax-exempt.
History Museum: housed in the former home of H. B. Ailman; 1881.
Collections: frontier Victorian objects & artifacts; Native American artifacts; items from early 20th-century model mining town; collection of photographs & documents relating to the history of southwest New Mexico.
Research Fields: southwest New Mexico history; architecture.
Facilities: library of microfilms & printed matter covering material from 1875-1943; modern publications available for use on premises; biographical files; photo archive; indexes to local records; files on area historic buildings; microfilmed local records; U.S. census microfilms for southwest New Mexico.
Activities: guided tours; lecture series; permanent & temporary exhibitions; outreach program; special events.
Publications: newsletter, The Mansardian.
Hours & Admission Prices: Tues.-Fri. 9-4:30, Sat.-Sun. 10-4. Suggested donation $3. Closed New Year's Day; Presidents' Day; Easter; Thanksgiving; Christmas Eve & Day. ♿
Attendance: 14,104 (accurate)
Membership: Active Volunteer $15; Student $20; Seniors $25; Individual $30; Family $40; Contributor $60; Business & Sponsor $100; Patron $250-$499; Benefactor $500 & up.

WESTERN NEW MEXICO UNIVERSITY MUSEUM, (M), Fleming Hall at 10th St., 1000 W. College St., Silver City, NM 88062. Mailing Address: P.O. Box 680, Silver City, NM 88062-0680. Tel.: 575-538-6386. Fax: 575-538-6385.
Web Site: www.wnmu.edu/univ/museum.htm
Founded: 1974.
Congressional District: 2
Key Personnel: Chm. (V), Dr. Dale F. Giese; Dir., Dr . Cynthia Ann Bettison; Museum Shop Mgr., Phillip Cave.
Personnel Profile: Full-Time Paid 2; Part-Time Paid 7; Part-Time Volunteers 14.
Governing Authority: University. Parent Institution: Western New Mexico University. Tax-exempt.
Anthropology Museum.
Collections: Eisele Collection of Southwest Native American artifacts including Mimbres painted pottery, Casas Grandes pottery, Anasazi pottery, chipped & groundstone; stone tools; basketry; The Hunter Collection containing mining implements; D.C. Hinman Photographs; archives & artwork of Editha Watson; Alvan N. White Memorial archives & memorabilia; Miller collection of baskets; c.1850 Scott Nichols single horse doctor buggies; Margaret Kelly collection of historic Navajo rugs & saddle blankets.
Research Fields: history & anthropology.
Facilities: alumni lounge; 1923 classroom; special exhibit room; shop & workroom. Gift items for sale.
Activities: museum internships for high school juniors & seniors and Western New Mexico University undergraduates & graduates; oral history; permanent, temporary & traveling exhibits; school loan service; instruction in both archaeology & museology.
Publications: quarterly newsletter, WNMU Museum.
Hours & Admission Prices: Mon.-Fri. 9-4:30, Sat.-Sun. 10-4. No charge: donations accepted. Research: Mon.-Fri. 9-4. Closed university holidays. ♿
Attendance: 14,500 (estimated)
Membership: Volunteer $7; Individual & Senior $10; Family $15; Supporter & Business Patron $50; Sponsor $100; Patron $500; Benefactor $1,000.

Socorro

HAMMEL MUSEUM, 500 Sixth St., Socorro, NM 87801-4227. Mailing Address: P.O. Box 923, Socorro, NM 87801-0923. Tel.: 575-835-8927.
Key Personnel: Dir., Debra Dean
History Museum: housed in the former Hammel Brewery & later operated as an ice house and soft drink bottling plant until the 1950s.
Collections: brewery history; period furnishings; equipment & machinery; industrial & commercial history.
Activities: tours.
Hours & Admission Prices: Sat. 9-12. No charge.

NEW MEXICO BUREAU OF GEOLOGY MINERAL MUSEUM, New Mexico Tech, 801 Leroy Place, Socorro, NM 87801-4681. Tel.: 505-835-5140 & 5420. Fax: 505-835-6333.
E-mail: vwlueth@nmt.edu
Web Site: geoinfo.nmt.edu
Formerly: New Mexico Bureau of Mines Mineral Museum
Founded: 1889.
Congressional District: 3
Key Personnel: Cur., Virgil W. Lueth, Ph.D.; Asst. Cur., Christopher McKee.
Personnel Profile: Full-Time Paid 1; Part-Time Paid 1; Interns 5.
Governing Authority: state. Parent Institution: New Mexico Institute of Mining & Technology. Subsidiary Institution: New Mexico Bureau of Mines & Mineral Resources, Campus Station, Socorro, NM 87801. Tax-exempt.

Mineral Museum.
Collections: minerals & fossils.
Research Fields: mineralogy; petrology; economic geology; mining history; paleontology.
Facilities: X-ray diffraction & X-ray fluorescence equipment; electron microprobe.
Activities: guided tours; lectures; permanent, temporary & loan exhibitions.
Publications: bulletins, memoirs, circulars, maps & other documents relative to New Mexico's geology & mineral resources.
Hours & Admission Prices: Mon.-Fri. 8-5, Sat.-Sun. 10-3; other times by appointment. No charge; donations accepted. Closed state holidays. ♿
Attendance: 13,136 (accurate)

Springer

SANTA FE TRAIL MUSEUM, 516 Maxwell Ave., Springer, NM 87747. Tel.: 505-483-5554.
Web Site: www.santafetrail.nm.org/site58.html
History Museum: housed in the former Colfax County Court House, built in 1881.
Collections: local history & culture; art; early pioneering life.
Hours & Admission Prices: Memorial Day-Labor Day daily 9-4.

Taos

GOVERNOR BENT MUSEUM, 117 Bent St., Taos, NM 87571-6075. Mailing Address: P.O. Box 153, Taos, NM 87571-0153. Tel.: 505-758-2376. Fax: 505-758-2376.
E-mail: gnideon@laplaza.org
Founded: 1958.
Congressional District: 3
Key Personnel: C.E.O. & Museum Shop Mgr., Tom Noeding.
Personnel Profile: Full-Time Paid 1.
Governing Authority: individual operation.
History Museum: housed in c.1825 home belonging to Charles Bent, first American Governor of New Mexico territory, site of his death in 1847 during an uprising.
Collections: Indian artifacts; Bent family possessions; old Americana antiques; Eskimo collection; guns; spinning wheels; paintings; photographs; anthropology; mineralogy; archaeology; graphics.
Facilities: paintings; prints; books; rocks. Indian artifacts, jewelry & pottery for sale.
Activities: gallery talks; permanent exhibitions.
Hours & Admission Prices: Daily 10-5. Adults $3, children 8-15 $1; discount to groups; children under 8 with parents no charge.
Attendance: 7,000 (estimated)

THE HARWOOD MUSEUM OF ART OF THE UNIVERSITY OF NEW MEXICO, (M), 238 Ledoux St., Taos, NM 87571-7009. Tel.: 505-758-9826. Fax: 505-758-1475.
E-mail: info@hartwoodmuseum.com
Web Site: www.harwoodmuseum.org
Formerly: The Harwood Foundation of the University of New Mexico
Founded: 1923.
Congressional District: 3
Key Personnel: Dir., Charles M. Lovell; Pres., Deborah McLean; Vice Pres., Gus Foster; Devel. Officer, L. Rupert Chambers; Cur., Margaret E. Bullock; Cur. Education, Lucy Perera Adams; Museum Shop Mgr., Joan McGrane; Coord. Special Events, Lyn Bleiler; Finance, Sherry Carlton.
Personnel Profile: Full-Time Paid 8; Part-Time Paid 10; Part-Time Volunteers 12; Interns 1.
Governing Authority: university. Parent Institution: University of New Mexico. Tax-exempt.
Art Museum.
Collections: Taos artists in all media from early 20th century to the present; 19th- & 20th-century Santos & Spanish colonial furniture of Hispanic culture; paintings; Agnes Martin Gallery.
Research Fields: history of Taos art colony.
Facilities: seven galleries.
Activities: permanent & changing exhibitions; childrens & adults education programs; artist in residence & lecture programs.
Publications: biannual newsletter; museum collection handbook; selected exhibition catalogues; catalogs, Clemente in Taos; The Triumph of Beatrice Mandelman; Contemporary Art/Taos; Taos Pueblo Painters; Wayne Thiebaud: Country City; Jack Smith: Taos Portraits; Lilly Fenichel: Just You/Just Me; In Praise of Mountains, Images of Breast Cancer; Christine Taylor Patten; Stitched Marks; John Suazo 30 Year Retrospective; Sabra Moore: Out of the Woods; Dieberkorn in New Mexico.
Hours & Admission Prices: Tues.-Sat. 10-5, Sun. 12-5. Adults $8; discounts to members, groups, AAM & ICOM members; children under 12 no charge. Closed major holidays. ♿
Attendance: 20,276 (accurate)
Membership: Student & Senior $25; Individual $35; Dual Family $55; Business $75; Contributor $125; Associate $250; Benefactor $500; Patron $1,000 & up.

KIT CARSON HOME & MUSEUM, INC., 113 Kit Carson Rd., Taos, NM 87571-5949. Tel.: 505-758-4945.
E-mail: director@kitcarsonhome.com
Founded: 1918.
Congressional District: 3
Key Personnel: Dir., Mark Drummond; Chm. (V), John D. Farr.
Personnel Profile: Full-Time Paid 5; Part-Time Volunteers 6.
Governing Authority: private; nonprofit organization. Tax-exempt: 501(c)(3).
Historic House Museum: home of Kit & Josefa Carson, 1843-1865.
Collections: life & culture of Kit Carson & his family; structures.
Hours & Admission Prices: Daily 9-6. Adults $5, senior citizens $4, students $3, children $2; discounts to groups; members no charge. Closed New Year's Day; Easter; Christmas.
Attendance: 23,500 (accurate)

*** MILLICENT ROGERS MUSEUM OF NORTHERN NEW MEXICO, (M),** 1504 Museum Rd., 4 miles north of Taos, Taos, NM 87571. Mailing Address: P.O. Box 1210, Taos, NM 87571-1210. Tel.: 505-758-2462. Fax: 505-758-5751.
E-mail: mrm@newmex.com
Web Site: www.millicentrogers.org
Founded: 1956.
Congressional District: 3
Key Personnel: Exec. Dir., Jill Hoffman, Ph.D.; Bd. Pres., Beth Rosenbloom; Museum Shop Mgr., Joy Jensen.
Personnel Profile: Full-Time Paid 7; Part-Time Paid 3; Part-Time Volunteers 26; Interns 2.
Governing Authority: private; nonprofit organization. Tax-exempt: 501(c)(3).
Ethnology & Art Museum.
Collections: Southwestern Native American (Pueblo and Athabascan) jewelry, textiles, pottery, baskets, Kachinas, paintings, & works of art on paper; Maria Martinez family pottery collection; Southwestern Hispanic textiles, paintings, santos, tinwork, woodwork, Colcha embroidery, & domestic articles of the Colonial Period; historic & contemporary photography of the Southwest; jewelry of Millicent Rogers; contemporary jewelry design.
Research Fields: art; material culture & design of Northern New Mexico; southwestern jewelry; registry of Hispanic & Native American New Mexican artists.
Facilities: permanent & temporary galleries; reference library. Museum-related items for sale.
Activities: guided tours; permanent & temporary exhibits; lectures; workshops; field trips; collections available for research or exhibit loans.
Publications: newsletter, Las Palabras; museum rack card & brochure; catalogues: Hebras De Vision/Threads of Vision; Retratos Nuevomexicanos, Collection of Hispanic New Mexican Photography; Oremos, Oremos; New Mexican Midwinter Masquerades; book, Padre Martinez: New Perspectives from Taos; catalogue, The Art of the Book in the Southwest.
Hours & Admission Prices: April-Oct. daily 10-5; Nov.-March Tues.-Sun. 10-5. Family $12, adults $10, seniors $8, students $6, New Mexican residents $5, children under 16 $2; discounts to AAM & ICOM members; members no charge. Tours 10 & over $4 with 24 hr. notice. Closed New Year's Day; Easter; San Geronimo Day (Sept. 30, Taos Pueblo feast day); Thanksgiving; Christmas. ♿
Attendance: 24,392 (accurate)
Membership: Personal Memberships: Individual $35; Dual Family $50; Contributing $125; Sustaining $250; Directors Circle $500; Millicent Club 1,000 & up. Commercial Memberships: Regular $100; Supporting $250; Sustaining $500; Benefactor $1,000 & up.

TAOS ART MUSEUM, 227 Paseo del Pueblo Norte, Taos, NM 87571-7316. Mailing Address: P.O. Box 1848, Taos, NM 87571-1848. Tel.: 575-758-2690. Fax: 575-758-7320.
E-mail: museum@taosartmuseum.org
Web Site: www.taosartmuseum.org
Key Personnel: Exec. Dir., Erion Simpson
Art Museum: housed in the former studio & home of Nicolai Fechin; built 1927-1933.
Collections: early 20th century Taos art; paintings by the Taos Society of Artists.
Hours & Admission Prices: Tues.-Sun. 10-5. Adults $8; Taos County residents on Sun. no charge.

TAOS COUNTY HISTORICAL SOCIETY, INC., 121 N. Plaza, Taos, NM 87571-4110. Mailing Address: P.O. Box 2447, Taos, NM 87571-2447.
E-mail: tylerh@newmex.com

Web Site: www.taos-history.org
Founded: 1952.
Congressional District: 3
Key Personnel: Pres. (V), L.A. Lindquist.
Personnel Profile: Part-Time Volunteers 12.
Governing Authority: private; nonprofit organization. Tax-exempt: 501(c)(3).
Historical Society.
Collections: audio & video tapes of lecture speakers sponsored by our society.
Research Fields: history of Taos area; identifying historic sites.
Facilities: 500-vol. library of news clippings & magazine articles; 150 sq. ft. exhibit space apart from museum.
Activities: guided tours; lectures. Annual Events: luncheon to honor historic preservation work.
Publications: semi-annual publication, Ayer y hoy en Taos; quarterly newsletter.
Hours & Admission Prices: Mon., Wed. & Fri. 1-3. No charge.
Attendance: 264 (estimated)
Membership: Individual $15; Family $20; Sustaining $30.

TAOS HISTORIC MUSEUMS, 222 Ledoux St., Taos, NM 87571-5944. Mailing Address: P.O. Box 3409, Taos, NM 87571-3409. Tel.: 575-758-0505. Fax: 575-758-0330.
E-mail: director@taoshistoricmuseums.org
Web Site: www.taoshistoricmuseums.org
Formerly: Kit Carson Historic Museums
Founded: 1949.
Congressional District: 3
Key Personnel: Dir., Morris Witten; Collections, Anita McDaniel.
Personnel Profile: Full-Time Paid 3; Part-Time Paid 5; Part-Time Volunteers 20.
Governing Authority: nonprofit organization. Parent Institution: Kit Carson Historic Museums. Tax-exempt: 501(c)(3).
History & Art Museum: 1797 Ernest L. Blumenschein Home; 1800-1827 Martinez Hacienda.
Collections: manuscript collections; Spanish colonial Taos; early fur trade period; archives; photographs; art by early Taos & Indian artists; antique furniture; furnishings of Ernest L. Blumenschein home. Historic Houses: 1797 Ernest L. Blumenschein home; 1804 La Hacienda de los Martinez; 1830 La Morada de Don Fernando de Taos.
Research Fields: Western history; fur trade; Spanish colonial period; Taos artists.
Facilities: 5,500-vol. library on fur trade, archaeology, military, Southwestern history available for use on premises; historical & anthropological research center. Books, slides, postcards, prints for sale.
Activities: guided tours; lectures; permanent & temporary exhibitions; museum of Spanish colonial & contemporary Hispanic folk arts; demonstrations.
Publications: booklets, Kit Carson, He Led the Way; Kit Carson, Patriot; The Real Kit Carson; book, Kit Carson's Own Story of his Life; A Brief History of Taos; The Short Truth About Kit Carson and the Indians.
Hours & Admission Prices: Blumenschein Home & Martinez Hacienda: May-Sept. daily 9-5; Winter: call for hours. Adults $8; reduced rate combination tickets for all sites available; discounts to AAM members, groups & families; members no charge. Closed New Year's Day; Easter; Thanksgiving; Christmas. ♿
Attendance: 31,957 (accurate)
Membership: Individual $35; Partners $60; Supporting $100; Sustaining $150; Benefactor $250; Sponsor $500; Patron $1,000.

Tome

TOME PARISH MUSEUM, 7 Church Loop, Tome, NM 87060-6001. Mailing Address: P.O. Box 100, Tome, NM 87060-0100. Tel.: 505-865-7497. Fax: 505-865-7622 (call first).
E-mail: mabaca@icchurchtome.org
Web Site: www.icchurchtome.org
Founded: 1966.
Congressional District: 2
Key Personnel: Dir., Fr. Carl Feil, O.S.M.; Museum Coord., Elena Calles.
Governing Authority: church group. Parent Institution: Immaculate Conception Parish. Tax-exempt.
Religious Museum.
Collections: religion; paintings; santos statues.
Activities: permanent exhibitions.
Hours & Admission Prices: Tues.-Sat. 9-1. No charge; donations accepted. ♿

Truth or Consequences

GERONIMO SPRINGS MUSEUM, (M), 211 Main St., Truth or Consequences, NM 87901-2838. Tel.: 575-894-6600. Fax: 575-894-2888.
Founded: 1972.
Congressional District: 2
Key Personnel: Dir. & Museum Shop Mgr., LaRena Miller; Pres., Ed Irwin.
Personnel Profile: Full-Time Paid 1; Part-Time Paid 2; Part-Time Volunteers 10.
Governing Authority: nonprofit organization. Affiliated with the Sierra County Historical Society. Tax-exempt: 501(c)(3).
History Museum.
Collections: local history Indian artifacts; art; Mimbres & area pottery; rocks & minerals; Ralph Edwards Room; area fossils and mastodon skulls display; authentic log cabin moved log by log to museum; military history.
Major Exhibits: Smithsonian New Harmonies Music Series (T), 3/10-4/10.
Facilities: library of magazine & newspaper items & books on local & New Mexico history. Jewelry, pottery & handcrafted items for sale.
Activities: films; art festivals; permanent collections; Armendaris Ranch tours. Museum Sponsors: Fiesta Art Exhibit; annual membership dinner; open houses for special or traveling displays or special community events.
Publications: museum guide booklet.
Hours & Admission Prices: Mon.-Sat. 9-5, Sun. 11-4. Adults $5, students under 18 $2.50; discounts to families; members & pre-school children no charge. Closed New Year's Day; Easter; Independence Day; Thanksgiving; Christmas. ♿
Attendance: 9,011 (accurate)
Membership: Annual $15; Couple $20; Business & Professions $30; Lifetime $500 & up; Lifetime Major Contributor $5,000 & up.

Tucumcari

MESALANDS COMMUNITY COLLEGE'S DINOSAUR MUSEUM, (M), 222 E. Laughlin, Tucumcari, NM 88401-2730. Mailing Address: 911 S. Tenth St., Tucumcari, NM 88401-3390. Tel.: 575-461-3466. Fax: 575-461-1901.
Web Site: www.mesalands.edu
Founded: 2000.
Key Personnel: Dir., Craig T. Currell; Education & Cur., Axel Hungerbeuhler, Ph.D.; Museum Shop Mgr., Mary Quintana.
Personnel Profile: Full-Time Paid 1; Part-Time Paid 3; Part-Time Volunteers 5; Interns 2.
Governing Authority: public college; nonprofit. Tax-exempt.
Paleontology Museum.
Collections: life-sized bronze prehistoric skeletons; paintings; sculptures; geological; paleontological.
Research Fields: Mesozoic vertebrate paleontology.
Facilities: 259-vol. library; laboratory; classrooms; 9,000 sq. ft. exhibit space; 360-acre dig site. Museum-related items for sale.
Activities: formal educational programs.
Publications: quarterly, Bare Bones.
Hours & Admission Prices: March to Labor Day Tues.-Sat. 10-6; Sept.-Feb. Tues.-Sat. 12-5. Adults $6, senior citizens $5, college students & educators $4, children $3.50; discounts to members, active military & groups. Closed New Year's Day; Thanksgiving; Christmas. ♿
Attendance: 15,486 (accurate)
Membership: Individual $7.50; Family $15; Business $30.

TUCUMCARI HISTORICAL RESEARCH INSTITUTE, 416 S. Adams, Tucumcari, NM 88401-2718. Tel.: 505-461-4201. Fax: 505-461-2049.
E-mail: citymus@shipleysystems.com
Web Site: www.cityoftucumcari.com
Founded: 1958.
Congressional District: 2
Key Personnel: Pres., Duane Moore; Vice Pres., Danny Wallace; Sec., Lucy Nials; Treas., Joy Young.
Personnel Profile: Full-Time Paid 1; Part-Time Paid 2.
Governing Authority: municipal; nonprofit. Tax-exempt: 501(c)(3).
History & Folk Art Museum: housed in 1903 school.
Collections: agriculture; anthropology; archaeology; archives; art association with permanent Western collections; botany; costumes; folklore; geology; glass; herbarium; Indian artifacts; industrial; junior museum; mineralogy; military; music; natural history; paleontology; preservation project; transportation; restored 1926 fire truck; newspapers 1905 to present; Southwest Indian tipi.
Research Fields: archaeology; history; folklore; anthropology.
Facilities: 50-vol. library of books on geology, anthropology & history available on premises.
Activities: guided tours; permanent exhibitions.
Hours & Admission Prices: May-Aug. Mon.-Sat. 8-5; Sept.-April Mon.-Fri. 8-5. Closed holidays. ♿
Attendance: 3,000 (estimated)
Membership: Individual $10; Family $20.

Watrous

FORT UNION NATIONAL MONUMENT, I 25 Exit 366, 8 mi on Hwy. 161, Watrous, NM 87753. Mailing Address: P.O. Box 127, Watrous, NM 87753-0127. Tel.: 505-425-8025. Fax: 505-454-1155.
E-mail: foun_administration@nps.gov
Web Site: www.nps.gov/foun/
Founded: 1954.
Congressional District: 3
Key Personnel: Supt., Marie Sauter; Museum Shop Mgr., Jessica Gonzales.
Personnel Profile: Full-Time Paid 1.
Governing Authority: federal. Parent Institution: National Park Service. Tax-exempt: 501(c)(3).
Historic Site & Building.
Collections: exhibits & objects pertaining to 1851-1891, the three Fort Unions & their significance in the development of the Santa Fe trail, the Civil War & the settling of the West; historic buildings; 1860s Fort Union.
Research Fields: military history.
Facilities: 1,300-vol. library on the history of the West. Publications for sale.
Activities: guided tours; self-guided trail with audio stations. Museum Sponsors: living history interpretive activities June-Sept.
Publications: brochures; handbook.
Hours & Admission Prices: Summer: daily 8-6; Winter: daily 8-5; tours by appointment. Adults $3; senior citizens with Golden Age Passport & children under 17 no charge. Closed New Year's Day; Thanksgiving; Christmas. ♿
Attendance: 15,782 (accurate)

Zuni

A:SHIWI A:WAN MUSEUM AND HERITAGE CENTER, 02E Ojo Caliente Rd., Zuni, NM 87327. Mailing Address: P.O. Box 1009, Zuni, NM 87327-1009. Tel.: 505-782-4403. Fax: 505-782-4503.
Founded: 1992.
Congressional District: 6
Key Personnel: Chm. & Pres. (V), Norman Cooeyate; Exec. Dir., Jim Enote; Museum Technician, Curtis Quam; Financial Administrative Officer, Valerie Epaloose.
Personnel Profile: Full-Time Paid 3.
Governing Authority: nonprofit individual operation. Tax-exempt: 501(c)(3).
Native American Museum.
Collections: Zuni photographs from 1880s to present; Zuni Tribe art & artifacts.
Research Fields: Zuni folk life.
Facilities: 625 sq. ft. exhibit space. Books & publications for sale.
Activities: arts festivals; guided tours; temporary exhibitions of local collections.
Publications: book, A Zuni Artist Looks at Frank H. Cushing: Cartoons by Phil Hughtie; Dialogues with Zuni Potters; Zuni: A Village of Silversmiths; Idonapshe: Zuni Cookbook; Journeys Home.
Hours & Admission Prices: Mon.-Fri. 9-5. No charge; donations accepted. Closed major holidays. ♿
Attendance: 7,000 (estimated)

NEW YORK

(723 listings)

Albany

ALBANY HERITAGE AREA VISITORS CENTER, 25 Quackenbush Square, Albany, NY 12207-2311. Tel.: 518-434-0405. Fax: 518-434-0887.
E-mail: info@albany.org
Web Site: albany.org
History Museum.
Collections: Albany's history; photographs; local & regional arts and science.
Facilities: Museum-related items for sale.
Activities: lectures; demonstrations; educational programs; special events.
Hours & Admission Prices: Mon.-Fri. 9-4, Sat. 10-3, Sun. 11-3. No charge; donations accepted. ♿
Attendance: 30,000 (accurate)

* **ALBANY INSTITUTE OF HISTORY & ART, (M),** 125 Washington Ave., Albany, NY 12210-2296. Tel.: 518-463-4478. Fax: 518-462-1522.
E-mail: information@albanyinstitute.org
Web Site: www.albanyinstitute.org
Founded: 1791.
Congressional District: 21
Key Personnel: Dir. & C.E.O., Christine M. Miles; Bd. Chm. (V), George R. Hearst, III; Deputy Dir. Collections & Exhibitions, Tammis K. Groft; Public Rels. & Mktg. Mgr., Steve Ricci; Dir. Business & Finance, Lori Veshia; Dir. Education, Erika Sanger; Dir. Facilities, Robert Nilson; Museum Shop Mgr., Elizabeth Bechand.
Personnel Profile: Full-Time Paid 20; Part-Time Paid 5; Part-Time Volunteers 360; Interns 35.
Governing Authority: nonprofit organization. Tax-exempt: 501(c)(3).
History & Art Museum.
Collections: fine arts, decorative arts, historical artifacts, photographs, manuscripts, documents, sketchbooks relating to the history, art & culture of Albany & the upper Hudson Valley, New York State & America from the 17th-century to present; 18th-century Hudson Valley portraits & scripture paintings; Hudson River School landscapes; regional folk art; 18th- to 20th-century portraits; paintings & documentary materials on Thomas Cole, Erastus Dow Palmer & Walter Launt Palmer; cast-iron stoves; 17th- to 19th-century Albany-made silver; New York State furniture; New York Central Railroad collections.
Major Exhibits: Hudson River Panorama: 400 Years of History Art & Culture, 11/09-1/3/10; Life Along the Hudson: Photographs by Joseph Squillante (T), 11/09-1/3/10; The Eternal Light of Egypt: Photographs by Sarile Sanders (T), 1/23/10-4/10.
Research Fields: American, regional, New York art, history & culture.
Facilities: 13,000-vol. library, 85,000 photographs, maps & broadsides, all pertaining to the city of Albany & the Upper Hudson area, available for public reference; reading room; 150-seat multi-purpose auditorium. Gifts & books for sale.
Activities: temporary, thematic & traveling exhibitions; education programs for children & adults; lecture series; family programs; teachers' workshops; volunteer tour guide program; art & history education classes; public programs including lectures, films, gallery talks; special domestic tours. Museum Sponsors: Festival of Trees; annual Book & Ephemera Fair.
Publications: exhibit & collection catalogs; newsletter; calendars; books; annual report.
Hours & Admission Prices: Wed.-Sat. 10-5, Sun. 12-5. Adults $10, senior citizens & students $8, children 6-12 $6; discounts to AAM, ICOM, NARM, AAA, Empire State reciprocal & North American reciprocal members; children 5 & under and members no charge. Closed major holidays. ♿
Attendance: 90,000 (estimated)
Membership: Teacher & Student $25; Individual $50; Dual $70; Family $80; Supporter $125; Sponsor $250; Sustainer $500; Patron of the arts $1,000 & up. Seniors receive 10% discount off individual, dual or family rates.

ALBANY PINE BUSH DISCOVERY CENTER, 195 New Karner Rd., Albany, NY 12205-4605. Tel.: 518-456-0655.
E-mail: info@albanypinebush.org
Web Site: www.albanypinebush.org
Key Personnel: Dir., Michael Venuti.
Governing Authority: Parent Institution: Albany Pine Bush Commission.
Nature Center.
Collections: hands-on exhibits; ecology; cultural history.
Facilities: Museum-related items for sale.
Activities: audio tours; educational programs; special events.
Hours & Admission Prices: Tues.-Fri. 9-4, Sat.-Sun. 10-4. No charge. Closed New Year's Day; Thanksgiving; Christmas.

ESTHER MASSRY GALLERY, 1002 Madison Ave., Albany, NY 12203. Tel.: 518-485-3902 & 337-2390. Fax: 518-337-4967.
E-mail: flanagaj@strose.edu
Web Site: www.strose.edu/gallery
Formerly: The College of Saint Rose Massry Center for the Arts
Founded: 1972.
Key Personnel: Dir. & Cur., Jeanne Flanagan.
Personnel Profile: Full-Time Paid 1.
College Art Gallery.
Collections: works by regional, national & international artists.
Major Exhibits: Recent Paintings By Larry Poons, 1/31/10-3/21/10.
Facilities: recital hall; classrooms; 400-seat theater.
Activities: musical performances; art gallery receptions; lectures.
Hours & Admission Prices: Sept. 21-May 8 Mon.-Thurs. 10-8, Fri. 10-4:30, Sun. 12-4. No charge. Closed school holidays; winter & spring break. ♿
Attendance: 5,000 (accurate)

* **HISTORIC CHERRY HILL, (M),** 523 1/2 S. Pearl St., Albany, NY 12202-1111. Tel.: 518-434-4791. Fax: 518-434-4806.
E-mail: info@historiccherryhill.org
Web Site: www.historiccherryhill.org
Founded: 1964.
Congressional District: 21
Key Personnel: C.E.O. & Dir., Liselle LaFrance; Pres., Michael R. Beiter; Dir.

Education, Rebecca Watrous; Cur., Deborah Emmons-Andarawis; Business Mgr., Lauren Mastin.
Personnel Profile: Full-Time Paid 3; Part-Time Paid 6; Part-Time Volunteers 50; Interns 2.
Governing Authority: nonprofit organization. Tax-exempt.
Historic House: 1787 Cherry Hill.
Collections: furnishings; textiles; ceramics; paintings; silver, personal papers & belongings of the Van Rensselaer-Rankin family from the 18th-20th centuries. Historic Building: 1787 Georgian Style house.
Research Fields: Van Rensselaer family history; Hudson Valley decorative arts; New York State; branded furniture; Colonial Revivalism.
Facilities: over 5,000-vol. library of books available for research by appointment on premises only. Books on Cherry Hill & other museum-related items for sale.
Activities: guided tours; volunteer program; lectures; workshops; special events; student intern program; NYS curriculum-related education programs.
Publications: books, Cherry Hill, The History & Collections of a Van Rensselaer Family; Murder at Cherry Hill; Different Voices, Different Truths: The 1827 Murder at Cherry Hill; Creating a Dignified Past: Museums and the Colonial Revival; Kittie Putman and the Cherry Hill Household: 1860-1884; bibliography, Selections from a Van Renesselaer Family Library, 1536-1799; On the Score of Hospitality: selected receipts of a Van Rensselaer Family, 1785-1835; The Confession of Jesse Strang.
Hours & Admission Prices: Temporarily closed for renovations.
Attendance: 10,400 (accurate)
Membership: Basic $35; Family/Household $50; Copper $100; Brass $250; Silver $500; Gold $1,000.

IRISH AMERICAN HERITAGE MUSEUM, (M), 991 Broadway, Ste. 101, Albany, NY 12204-2586. Tel.: 518-432-6598. Fax: 518-449-2540.
E-mail: irishamermuseum@cs.com
Web Site: irishamericanheritagemuseum.org
Founded: 1986.
Congressional District: 29
Key Personnel: C.E.O. & Chm. (V), Edward Collins; Financial Dir., David Stack.
Personnel Profile: Full-Time Paid 3; Full-Time Volunteers 1; Part-Time Volunteers 14.
Governing Authority: not-for-profit organization. Branch Museum: 2267 Rt. 145, East Durham, NY 12423. Tax-exempt: 501(c)(3).
Ethnic Museum: housed in c.1850 Italianate building.
Collections: objects representing the history of the Irish in America; archives.
Major Exhibits: Soldiers Are We: The Irish in Military Service, 5/10-9/10.
Research Fields: Irish immigration experience; the history of the 69th NY Regiment; great hunger; Irish American women; Irish in religion; Irish in Labor; Ancient Order of Hibernians; corporate Irish.
Facilities: 2,000-vol. library of books on the history of Ireland & the Irish in America. Museum-related items for sale.
Activities: concerts; lectures; loan & traveling exhibitions; storytelling.
Publications: Irish American Heritage Museum Newsletter.
Hours & Admission Prices: Museum: Memorial Day to Labor Day Wed.-Sun. 12-4. Library: Mon.-Fri. 8:30-4; groups by appointment. No charge; donations accepted. East Durham Museum: Memorial Day to Labor Day Wed.-Sun. 12-4; groups by appointment. Families $9, adults $3.50, seniors & students $2. ♿
Attendance: 230,000 (estimated)
Membership: Senior Citizen & Student $15; Individual $25; Family $45; Associate $100; Sustaining $500; Patron $1,000.

THE LITTLE GALLERY, SAGE COLLEGE OF ALBANY, 140 New Scotland Ave., Rathbone Hall, Albany, NY 12208-3491. Tel.: 518-292-8625.
Key Personnel: Coord., Crystal Martin
Art Gallery.
Collections: works by faculty & student artists.
Hours & Admission Prices: Mon.-Fri. 12-4, Sun. 12-4.

THE MUSEUM OF PRINTS AND PRINTMAKING, Albany, NY 12206-0578. Mailing Address: P.O. Box 6578, Albany, NY 12206-0578. Tel.: 518-449-4756.
E-mail: pcaprint@nycap.rr.com
Web Site: pcaprint.org
Founded: 1990.
Congressional District: 23
Key Personnel: Pres. (V), Thomas Andress; Sec., Pam Williams; Cur., Charles Semowich.
Personnel Profile: Part-Time Volunteers 20.
Governing Authority: nonprofit. Chartered by New York State Board of Regents, Print Club of Albany. Tax-exempt.
Print Museum.
Collections: prints from the collections of the Print Club of Albany; archives of print makers including Dorothy Lathrop & Alice P. Schaefer.
Research Fields: prints; print making; print makers.
Facilities: 400-vol. library of art & print making books available to the public; 300 sq. ft. exhibit space. Prints & other museum-related items for sale.
Activities: guided tours; lectures; traveling, temporary & loan exhibitions; participatory exhibits in association with the Print Club of Albany.
Publications: 5 times annually, shares newsletter with the Print Club of Albany.
Hours & Admission Prices: By appointment only. No charge. ♿
Membership: Print Club of Albany.

NEW YORK STATE - EMPIRE STATE PLAZA ART COLLECTION, 2978 Corning Tower, 1 Empire State Plaza, Albany, NY 12242-0001. Tel.: 518-473-7521. Fax: 518-474-0984.
E-mail: curatorial.services@ogs.state.ny.us
Art Collection.
Collections: paintings; sculptures; tapestries.
Hours & Admission Prices: Concourse & Plaza: daily 6-6. Corning Tower: Mon.-Fri. 6-6. By appointment. No charge.

NEW YORK STATE MUSEUM, (M), Rm. 3023, Cultural Education Center, Empire State Plaza, Albany, NY 12230-0001. Tel.: 518-474-5877 & 5812. Fax: 518-486-3696.
E-mail: cryan@mail.nysed.gov
Web Site: www.nysm.nysed.gov
Founded: 1858.
Congressional District: 29
Key Personnel: Dir., Clifford A. Siegfried; Chief Geological Survey, William Kelly; Head Education, Jeanine Grinage; Dir. Research & Collections, John Hart; Dir. Communications, Joanne Guilmette; Dir. Exhibits, Mark Schaming.
Personnel Profile: Full-Time Paid 152; Full-Time Volunteers 3; Part-Time Paid 29; Part-Time Volunteers 346; Interns 27.
Governing Authority: state. Parent Institution: New York State Education Dept., Albany, NY 12224. Tax-exempt: 170(b)(1)(A).
General Museum.
Collections: entomology; geology; mineralogy; archaeology; New York Indian ethnology; zoology; New York historical artifacts including architecture; African American history; costume; decorative art; fire engines; militaria; musical instruments; Shakeriana; toys; transportation; agricultural, industrial & domestic technology; gas and oil; art works by New York artists; botany; tissue samples; World Trade Center.
Research Fields: entomology; geology; paleontology; mineralogy; zoology; ecology; botany; mycology; Indians of New York; history of New York, archaeology; gas and oil resources.
Facilities: 9,000-vol. library; field research station; 425,112 sq. ft. of exhibitions; lab, office, & collection storage space. Museum-related items for sale.
Activities: lectures; films; formal & informal education programs; school loan service; permanent & temporary exhibits; musical performances.
Publications: various annual bulletins; map & chart series; handbooks; memoirs; circulars; educational leaflet series; exhibit catalogs; special publications.
Hours & Admission Prices: Daily 9:30-5. No charge; donations accepted. Closed New Year's Day; Thanksgiving; Christmas. ♿
Attendance: 774,432 (accurate)
Membership: Senior Citizen $30; Individual $35; Contributing $40; Family $50; Supporting $60; Smithsonian Affiliate $75; Sustaining $100; Discovery Club $150; Curator's Circle $250.

NEW YORK STATE OFFICE OF PARKS, RECREATION & HISTORIC PRESERVATION, Agency Bldg., #1, Rockefeller Empire State Plaza, Albany, NY 12238-0001. Mailing Address: P.O. Box 219, Waterford, NY 12188-0219. Tel.: 518-237-8643. Fax: 518-235-4248.
E-mail: kjk@niagara.edu
Web Site: www.nysparks.state.ny.us
Founded: 1972.
Congressional District: 28
Key Personnel: Commissioner Parks, Recreation & Historic Preservation, Carol Ash; Asst. Dir. Bureau Historic Sites, John Lovell; Chm. New York State Board Historic Preservation, Dr. Robert Mackay; Dir. Field Service Bureau, Ruth L. Pierpont.
Governing Authority: state. New York State Executive Dept., State Capitol, Albany, NY. The Bureau of Historic Sites, together with park regions administers following state historic sites: Fort Ontario, Oswego; Sackets Harbor Battlefield, Sackets Harbor; Lorenzo, Cazenovia; Oriskany Battlefield, Oriskany; Steuben Memorial, Remsen; Herkimer Home, Little Falls;

Johnson Hall, Johnstown; Guy Park, Amsterdam; John Brown Farm, Lake Placid; Crown Point, Crown Point; Bennington Battlefield, Walloomsac; Crailo, Rensselaer; Schuyler Mansion, Albany; John Burroughs Memorial, Roxbury; Olana, Hudson; Clermont, Germantown; Senate House, Kingston; Mills Mansion, Staatsburg; New Windsor Cantonment, Vails Gate; Knox Headquarters, Vails Gate; Washington's Headquarters, Newburgh; Stony Point Battlefield, Stony Point; John Jay Homestead, Katonah; Philipse Manor Hall, Yonkers; Walt Whitman House, Huntington Station; Ganondagan, Victor; Grant Cottage, Wilton; Hyde Hall, East Springfield; Rexford Aqueduct, Rexford; Schoharie Crossing, Fort Hunter; Clinton House, Poughkeepsie; Old Fort Niagara, Youngstown; Planting Fields Arboretum, Oyster Bay; Old Erie Canal, Kirkville; Old Croton Aqueduct, Dobbs Ferry; Caumsett, Huntington; Sonnenberg Gardens & Mansion, Canandaigua. Refer to individual listings for further information. Tax-exempt: 501(c)(3).
Historic Preservation Agency.
Collections: see individual listings.
Research Fields: preservation of historic sites & structures; state history; archeology military & social history; conservation of collections.
Activities: maintains two bureaus for the administration of New York's historic sites & preservation programs. The Bureau of Field Services administers the State & National Registers of Historic places; reviews projects affecting properties; eligibility for listing on the registers; provides services to developers seeking to use preservation provisions of the Economic Recovery Tax; offers technical services to owners of historic properties. See Bureau of Historic Sites listed under Waterford, N.Y.
Publications: books; pamphlets; newsletters; technical reports.
Hours & Admission Prices: Office: Mon.-Fri. 8-5. See individual site listings for hours & admissions. ♿

OPALKA GALLERY, SAGE COLLEGE OF ALBANY, 140 New Scotland Ave., Albany, NY 12208-3491. Tel.: 518-292-7742.
Key Personnel: Dir., Jim Richard Wilson
Art Gallery.
Collections: paintings; photographs; sculpture.
Facilities: 75-seat lecture hall.
Activities: poetry readings; recitals; symposia.
Hours & Admission Prices: Winter: Mon.-Thurs. 10-4:30 & 6pm-8pm, Fri. 10-4:30, Sun. 12-4; Summer: Mon.-Fri. 10-4; other times by appointment.

SCHUYLER MANSION STATE HISTORIC SITE, 32 Catherine St., Albany, NY 12202-1605. Tel.: 518-434-0834. Fax: 518-434-3821.
E-mail: heidi.hill@oprhp.state.ny.us
Web Site: www.nysparks.com/hist
Founded: 1911.
Congressional District: 28
Key Personnel: Historic Site Mgr., Heidi Hill; Interpretive Programs Asst., Darlene Rogers; Interpreter, Michelle Mavigliano.
Personnel Profile: Full-Time Paid 5; Part-Time Paid 7; Part-Time Volunteers 20; Interns 1.
Governing Authority: state. Parent Institution: New York State Office of Parks, Recreation & Historic Preservation, Saratoga & Capital District Region. Tax-exempt: 501(c)(3).
Historic Building & Site: 1761 home of American Revolution Gen. Philip Schuyler and his family.
Collections: 18th-century furnishings & decorative arts; Schuyler family possessions; books; glass; silver.
Research Fields: Gen. Philip Schuyler; Schuyler family; 18th-century Dutch in New York; colonial Albany; American Revolution in New York State; post Revolution.
Facilities: visitor center.
Activities: guided tours; lectures; gallery talks; school program; special programs & demonstrations; reenactments; museum theater productions. Museum Sponsors: Independence Day Celebration; Twelfth Night.
Publications: Schuyler Mansion: Historic Structure Report; Schuyler Genealogy: A Compendium of Sources Pertaining to the Schuyler Families in America prior to 1900.
Hours & Admission Prices: mid-May to Oct. Wed.-Sun. 11-5; Nov. to mid-May by appointment; groups by appointment. Adults $4, senior & students $3; children under 12 & members no charge. Closed New Year's Day; Thanksgiving; Christmas. ♿
Attendance: 10,000 (estimated)

SHAKER HERITAGE SOCIETY, Heritage Lane, Albany, NY 12211-1051. Mailing Address: 875 Watervliet Shaker Rd., Ste. 2, Albany, NY 12211-1051. Tel.: 518-456-7890. Fax: 518-452-7348.
E-mail: shakerwv@crisny.org
Web Site: www.shakerheritage.org
Founded: 1977.
Congressional District: 21
Key Personnel: Exec. Dir., Starlyn D'Angelo; Pres., Phoebe Bender; Coord. Education, Anne Clothier; Museum Shop Mgr., Patricia Williams.
Personnel Profile: Full-Time Paid 2; Part-Time Paid 2; Part-Time Volunteers 150; Interns 4.
Governing Authority: nonprofit. Tax-exempt: 501(c)(3).
Historical Society Museum: housed in c.1848 meeting house.
Collections: Shaker artifacts & history 1776-1938; cemetery. Historic Buildings: 1830 Trustees House; 1822 Brethrens Shop & Workshop; 1916 barn; 1856 Herb Storage & Milk House; 1820 Ministry; 1920 garage; 1848 meeting house.
Research Fields: Shaker history; oral history; religious history.
Facilities: Shaker herb garden. Books, Shaker items & other related items for sale.
Activities: guided tours; K-12 education programs; outreach programs; programs for nursing home residents; heritage breed farm animal & herb garden program. Museum Sponsors: Outdoor craft fairs in July & September; Shaker Christmas shop in November & December.
Publications: quarterly newsletter, Watervliet Shaker Journal.
Hours & Admission Prices: Feb.-Dec. Tues.-Sat. 10-4. No charge; donations accepted. Closed major holidays. ♿
Attendance: 18,000 (estimated)
Membership: Individual $25; Household $35; Supporting $50-$99; Sustaining $100-$499; Benefactor $500 & up.

TEN BROECK MANSION - ALBANY COUNTY HISTORICAL ASSOCIATION, 9 Ten Broeck Place, Albany, NY 12210-2524. Tel.: 518-436-9826. Fax: 518-436-1489.
E-mail: achadirector@onecommail.com
Web Site: www.tenbroeckmansion.org
Founded: 1942.
Congressional District: 23
Key Personnel: Exec. Dir., Wendy Burch; Pres., Matthew Kirk; First Vice Pres., Keith Bennett; Second Vice Pres., Lois Conklin; Treas., Thomas A. Devane, Jr.; Sec., Angela Markessinis.
Personnel Profile: Part-Time Paid 2; Part-Time Volunteers 20.
Governing Authority: Parent Institution: University of the State of New York Boad of Regents. Tax-exempt: 501(c)(3).
Historic House Museum: 1798 Arbor Hill, Federal style mansion, home of General Abraham Ten Broeck & later the Olcott family.
Collections: Federal & Empire furniture; herb garden; decorative arts; 19th-century wine cellar; Victorian gardens.
Research Fields: local & regional history; industrial; social; military.
Facilities: meeting rooms; gardens.
Activities: guided tours; lectures; permanent & temporary exhibitions; educational programs; concerts; bus trips; auction; wine tastings; rental space available. Annual Events: House & Garden Tour; Haunted Mansion; Holiday House.
Publications: quarterly newsletter, Prospect.
Hours & Admission Prices: May-Dec. Thurs.-Fri. 10-4, Sat.-Sun. 1-4. Adults $5, students & seniors $4, children $3; children under 5 & members no charge. Closed all major holidays.
Attendance: 5,925 (accurate)
Membership: Student & Senior Citizen $20; Individual $35; Family $50; Supporting $75; Patron $100; Sustaining $200; Corporate $500.

UNIVERSITY ART MUSEUM, UNIVERSITY AT ALBANY, (M), State University of New York, 1400 Washington Ave., Albany, NY 12222-0001. Tel.: 518-442-4035. Fax: 518-442-5075.
E-mail: museum@albany.edu
Web Site: www.albany.edu/museum
Founded: 1967.
Congressional District: 23
Key Personnel: Dir., Janet Riker; Assoc. Dir., Corinna Ripps Schaming; Exhibit Designer, Zheng Hu; Preparator, Jeffrey Wright-Sedam; Collections Mgr., Wren Panzella; Exhibition & Outreach Coord., Naomi Lewis; Admin. Asst., Joanne Lue; Admin. Asst., Patricia VanAlstyne.
Personnel Profile: Full-Time Paid 4; Part-Time Paid 6.
Governing Authority: state. Parent Institution: University at Albany. Affiliated with State University of New York. Tax-exempt.
Contemporary Art.
Collections: over 2,500 late modern & contemporary works including paintings, photographs & drawings.
Research Fields: Western & non-Western contemporary art.
Activities: temporary exhibitions, lectures, gallery talks, films, inter-museum loans.
Publications: exhibition catalogs.
Hours & Admission Prices: Summer: Tues.-Sat. 11-4; Sept.-June Tues.-Fri. 10-5, Sat.-Sun. 12-4. No charge. Closed major holidays & during installations. ♿

Attendance: 37,500 (estimated)

Albertson

CLARK BOTANIC GARDEN, 193 I.U. Willets Rd., Albertson, NY 11507-2298. Tel.: 516-484-8600 & 2208. Fax: 516-625-3718.
E-mail: darcyj@northhempstead.com
Web Site: www.clarkbotanic.org
Founded: 1966.
Congressional District: 6
Key Personnel: Bd. Chm. (V), Jerilyn Dreitlein; Commissioner, Gerard Olsen; Office Mgr., Carol Murphy.
Personnel Profile: Full-Time Paid 5; Part-Time Paid 3; Part-Time Volunteers 10; Interns 3.
Governing Authority: nonprofit. Parent Institution: Fanny Dwight Clark Memorial Garden Inc. Tax-exempt.
Botanical Garden.
Collections: roses, wildflowers, ferns, herbs, annuals, perennials, rock garden, flowering shrubs & dwarf trees; ponds; honey bee hives; maze & children's garden; rhododendrons, azaleas, magnolias; spring bulbs.
Facilities: botanical garden; library; classrooms. Museum-related items for sale.
Activities: guided tours; lectures; concerts; formally organized education programs; special events.
Publications: biannual, Clark Garden Newsletter; Horticultural Bulletin.
Hours & Admission Prices: Summer: daily 10-4; Winter: Mon.-Fri. 10-4. No charge; donations accepted. ♿
Attendance: 20,000 (estimated)
Membership: Individual $20; Family $35; Group & Associate $50; Sponsor $100; Benefactor $250; Patron $500; Donor $1,000.

Alden

ALDEN HISTORICAL SOCIETY, INC., 13213 Broadway, Alden, NY 14004-1312. Mailing Address: 1594 Westcott Ave., Alden, NY 14004-1122. Tel.: 716-937-7606.
E-mail: aldenhist@gmail.com
Web Site: www.alden.erie.gov
Founded: 1965.
Congressional District: 38
Key Personnel: Pres., Roberta Vincent; Vice Pres., Sal Sardella; Cur., Karen Muchow; Treas., Ralph Davis, Jr.; Asst. Cur., Laura Airey; Sec., Janet Koelbl.
Governing Authority: nonprofit organization.
History Museum: housed in 1859 Alden Historical Society House.
Collections: farm tools; kitchen utensils; town memorabilia; Early American bedroom; Victorian living room.
Research Fields: history of town of Alden & surrounding area.
Facilities: 125-vol. library of old books available on premises by appointment with curator.
Activities: guided tours; lectures; permanent & temporary exhibitions.
Publications: booklet, A History of Town of Alden: 125 Years & Growing; The Village of Alden; video, A Complete History of Alden, New York.
Hours & Admission Prices: Sat. 10-2; other times by appointment. No charge; donations accepted. ♿
Attendance: 500 (estimated)
Membership: Individual $5; Lifetime $50.

Alfred

THE SCHEIN-JOSEPH INTERNATIONAL MUSEUM OF CERAMIC ART, (M), Binns-Merrill Hall, Room 259, Alfred University Campus, Alfred, NY 14802. Mailing Address: 2 Pine St., Alfred, NY 14802-1214. Tel.: 607-871-2421. Fax: 607-871-2615.
E-mail: ceramicsmuseum@alfred.edu
Web Site: ceramicsmuseum.alfred.edu
Founded: 1900.
Key Personnel: Collections Mgr., Susan Kowalczyk.
Personnel Profile: Part-Time Paid 1.
Governing Authority: university. Parent Institution: New York State College of Ceramics at Alfred University. Tax-exempt: 501(c)(3).
Ceramic Museum.
Collections: Korean ceramics; Charles Fergus Binns ceramics; pottery of the Ancient Americas; Corsaw ceramics; Cybis collection; ceramic of Alfred-trained ceramists; early pottery; European porcelain; American studio ceramics from 1900-present; ceramics from around the world; technical ceramics; advanced ceramics.
Research Fields: ceramic history.
Facilities: 1,500 sq. ft. temporary location in Binns-Merrill Hall on the Alfred University campus.
Activities: lectures; organized education programs for undergraduate or graduate college students; permanent & loan exhibitions.
Publications: biannual newsletter, Ceramophile; exhibition catalogues.
Hours & Admission Prices: Wed.-Fri. 10-4. Call for exhibition information. No charge; donations accepted. Closed school holidays. ♿
Attendance: 2,613 (accurate)
Membership: Student & Senior Citizen $15; Individual $25; Family $35; Sustaining $50-$99; Contributing & Business $100-$249; Patron $250-$499; Benefactor $500 & up.

Almond

ALMOND HISTORICAL SOCIETY/HAGADORN HOUSE MUSEUM, 7 N. Main St., Almond, NY 14804. Mailing Address: 1 Park St., Box 234, Almond, NY 14804-0234. Tel.: 607-276-6781.
Web Site: www.rootsweb.com/-nyahs/almondhs.html
Founded: 1965.
Congressional District: 34
Key Personnel: Pres., Lee A. Ryan; Vice Pres., Helen Spencer; Sec., Donna Ryan; Treas., Teresa Johnson.
Personnel Profile: Part-Time Volunteers 25.
Governing Authority: society; nonprofit organization. Tax-exempt: 501(c)(3).
Historical Society Museum: housed in 1830 Hagadorn House.
Collections: genealogical files of 1500 local families beginning in 1794 with the Esterbrooks; 1800-1991 local artifacts; photographs; costumes; diaries; scrap books; amateur oil paintings; 1830-1940 furniture, glass, pottery & china; locally made tools; 1837 Jesse/Angel; 1800 cooking fireplace; 1837 6 room & stairway addition; 1794 Count Rumford Plan; the Littly Gallery.
Research Fields: monograph & maps; forgotten cemeteries.
Facilities: 700-vol. library of books, magazines, 1840's records & ledgers available for research by appointment only on premises; reading room. Postcards, note paper, monographs & area maps for sale.
Activities: guided tours; lectures; films; permanent exhibitions. Museum Sponsors: Strawberry Festivals; Christmas Open House music program; Trash and Treasures Sale.
Publications: quarterly newsletter, Almond Historical Society; books, School Days Recollections of Horace Stillman 1854-1951; Forgotten Cemeteries of Almond 1975; 175th Anniversary Souvenir Program; The Cooking Fireplace; My Father's Old Fashioned Drugstore; When Grandfather Ran a General Store, 1937 reprint by permission of Christian Science Monitor; 1991 Monograph of Autographs 1885-1932.
Hours & Admission Prices: Fri. 2-4; other times by appointment. No charge. ♿
Attendance: 1,500 (estimated)
Membership: Single $8; Couple $12; Family $15; Business $20; Single Life $125; Couple Life $200.

Amagansett

EAST HAMPTON TOWN MARINE MUSEUM, 301 Bluff Rd., Amagansett, NY 11930. Mailing Address: 101 Main St., East Hampton, NY 11937-2714. Tel.: 631-324-6850. Fax: 631-324-9885.
E-mail: info@easthamptonhistory.org
Web Site: www.easthamptonhistory.org
Founded: 1966.
Congressional District: 2
Key Personnel: Pres. (V), Arthur Graham; Exec. Dir., Richard Barons.
Personnel Profile: Full-Time Paid 2; Part-Time Paid 3; Part-Time Volunteers 18.
Governing Authority: Affiliated with East Hampton Historical Society, Main St., East Hampton, NY. Associated Museums: Clinton Academy; Mulford Farm; Jackson-Osborne House. Tax-exempt: 170(b)(1)(A); 501(c)(3).
Marine Museum.
Collections: marine; history & technology of eastern Long Island, NY.; whaling & commercial fishing; small water craft; folklore; archaeology.
Research Fields: folklife & technology of eastern Long Island fishermen.
Facilities: photography collections; children's discovery rooms.
Activities: guided tours; permanent exhibitions; classes in wooden boat building; classes in nautical subject matter & skills.
Hours & Admission Prices: Memorial Day to Columbus Day Sat.-Sun. 10-5. Adults $4, senior citizens $3, students $1; discounts to AAM & AAA members; members & preschoolers no charge.
Attendance: 8,000 (estimated)
Membership: Individual $35; Family & Couple $60; Business $100.

Amenia

WETHERSFIELD ESTATE AND GARDENS, (M), 214 Pugsley Hill Rd., Amenia, NY 12501-5032. Tel.: 845-373-8037.
Key Personnel: Mgr., Kevin Malloy
Historic House Museum.
Collections: sculptures; carriages; gardens.
Facilities: gardens.

Hours & Admission Prices: June-Sept. Wed. & Fri.-Sat. 12-5 by appointment.

Amherst

AMHERST MUSEUM, 3755 Tonawanda Creek Rd., Amherst, NY 14228-1599. Tel.: 716-689-1440. Fax: 716-689-1409.
E-mail: amherstmuseum@gmail.com
Web Site: www.amherstmuseum.org
Founded: 1970.
Congressional District: 27
Key Personnel: Exec. Dir., Joseph G. Weickart; Pres. (V), Patrick Lucey; Senior Cur., Jessica A. Johnson; Education Cur., Jean W. Neff; Cur. Library & Archives, Toniann Scime; Museum Shop Mgr., Maria Greco.
Personnel Profile: Full-Time Paid 9; Part-Time Volunteers 250.
Governing Authority: nonprofit; chartered by NYS Board of Regents; joint governing with Town of Amherst. Parent Institution: Town of Amherst. Tax-exempt: 501(c)(3).
Historical Museum: includes 13 historic houses & buildings; Shaw Administration Building houses exhibits on local history, costume gallery, children's museum & Gallery of the Senses for visually impaired; emphasis on Amherst within the Niagara Frontier region of Western NY.
Collections: 19th-& 20th century material culture; technology; American art; photographs; archives; research material relating to the history of the Niagara Frontier & Town of Amherst, New York.
Research Fields: 19th-20th century material & technological culture of Town of Amherst & Niagara Frontier.
Facilities: 5,500-vol. research library; 35-acre site; herb period gardens; wildflower gardens.
Activities: organized school & group tour programs; permanent & temporary exhibitions; living history reenactments; guided tours; folk art classes; local history lectures. Special Events: Scottish Festival & Highland Games; Harvest Festival; Halloween Celebration; Holiday Celebration & Candlelight Tours; annual Quilt & Lace seminars; Biennial International Quilt Show; Biennial Herb Festival.
Publications: quarterly newsletter, Ephemera.
Hours & Admission Prices: April-Sept. Tues.-Fri. 9:30-4:30, Sat.-Sun. 12:30-4:30; Oct.-March Tues.-Fri. 9:30-4:30. Family $12, adults $5; discounts to museum & AAM members; members no charge. Closed municipal holiday weekends. ♿
Attendance: 42,000 (estimated)
Membership: Individual $20; Family $35; Patron $50; Supporter $75; Contributor $100; Business I $250; Business II $500.

Amityville

LAUDER MUSEUM - AMITYVILLE HISTORICAL SOCIETY, 170 Broadway, Amityville, NY 11701-2704. Mailing Address: P.O. Box 764, Amityville, NY 11701-0764. Tel.: 631-598-1486; 631-598-7399. Fax: 631-598-7399.
Web Site: www.amityvillehistoricalsociety.com
Founded: 1973.
Congressional District: 2
Key Personnel: C.E.O., William T. Lauder; Pres., Ellen Ricciuti; Treas., Susan Martinson; Cur., Seth Purdy; Devel., Caroline D'Antonio.
Personnel Profile: Part-Time Paid 1; Part-Time Volunteers 50.
Governing Authority: private; nonprofit organization.
Historical Museum: 1909 brick edifice formally used for a bank.
Collections: history of Amityville, NY.
Facilities: 1,000-vol. library. Museum-related items for sale.
Activities: docent program; guided tours; lectures; temporary exhibitions. Annual Events: Heritage Fair, craft vendors, historic tours & exhibits.
Publications: quarterly newsletter, The Dispatch.
Hours & Admission Prices: Tues. & Fri.-Sun. 2-4. No charge; donations accepted. Closed New Year's Day; Easter; Independence Day; Christmas. ♿
Attendance: 3,500 (estimated)
Membership: Senior $10; Adult $15; Family $20; Business & Patron $50; Friend $75; Fellow $100; Lifetime & Benefactor $1,000.

Amsterdam

WALTER ELWOOD MUSEUM, 366 W. Main St., Amsterdam, NY 12010-2228. Tel.: 518-843-5151. Fax: 518-843-6098.
E-mail: info@walterelwoodmuseum.org
Web Site: www.walterelwoodmuseum.org
Founded: 1933.
Congressional District: 28
Key Personnel: Exec. Dir., Ann Peconie; Bd. of Trustees, Lionel Fallows; Pres., Jacki Meola.
Personnel Profile: Part-Time Paid 2; Part-Time Volunteers 15.
Governing Authority: bd of trustees. Tax-exempt: 501(c)(3).
General Museum.
Collections: early American & Indian material; history; natural history; ethnology; costumes; prints & paintings; local & area historical displays; artifacts; antiques; Civil War artifacts; early lighting; fans; dolls from around the world; Victorian era.
Research Fields: local history.
Facilities: 1,500-vol. research library of books pertaining to 19th-century American children, school & literature available for research by arrangement with curator & for inter-library loan; reading room; galleries; classrooms; children's museum; junior museum. Children's books, minerals & other museum-related & gift items for sale.
Activities: guided tours; lectures; formally organized education programs for children; inter-museum loan, permanent, temporary & traveling exhibitions; adult oil-painting classes; films; gallery talks; school loan service.
Publications: brochures; membership newsletters.
Hours & Admission Prices: Mon.-Fri. 9-4; groups by appointment. Adults $4; discounts to members and AAM & ICOM members. Closed most major & school holidays ♿
Attendance: 5,000
Membership: Senior Citizen & Student $15; Individual $20; Family $30; Professional $50.

Annandale-on-Hudson

CENTER FOR CURATORIAL STUDIES AND THE HESSEL MUSEUM OF ART, Bard College, 33 Garden Rd., Annandale-on-Hudson, NY 12504. Mailing Address: Bard College, P.O. Box 5000, Annandale-on-Hudson, NY 12504-5000. Tel.: 845-758-7598. Fax: 845-758-2442.
E-mail: ccs@bard.edu
Web Site: www.bard.edu/ccs
Founded: 1990.
Congressional District: 26
Key Personnel: Exec. Dir., Tom Eccles; Dir. Graduate Program, Maria Lind; Admin. Graduate Program, Letitia Smith; Asst. Dir. Administration & Devel., Jaime Henderson; Asst. Dir. Museum, Marcia Acita; Administrative & Devel. Coord., Noelle Deola; Dir. Library & Archives, Ann Butler; Registrar, Rachel von Wettberg; Preparator, Mark DeLura; Mgr. Security, Peter Amentas.
Personnel Profile: Full-Time Paid 11.
Governing Authority: private college; nonprofit. Parent Institution: Bard College. Tax-exempt: 501(c)(3).
Art Museum.
Collections: contemporary visual art primarily from the United States, Western Europe, Latin America & Asia, focusing on the period from the mid-1960s to present including paintings, drawings, sculpture, photographs, video, installation art & artists' books.
Research Fields: contemporary visual arts; international exhibition practice & history; curatorial pedagogy & museum education.
Facilities: 21,000-vol. library of books & catalogs on contemporary art; 26,300 sq. ft. exhibit space.
Activities: two-year MA degree program in curatorial studies; lectures; temporary exhibitions.
Publications: exhibition catalogues.
Hours & Admission Prices: Center: call for hours. Museum: Wed.-Sun. 1-5. Administration: Mon.-Fri. 9-5. Library: Sept.-June: Mon.-Wed. 10-7, Thurs.-Fri. 10-5, Sat. 1-5, Sun. 1-7. Summer: Mon.-Fri. 1-5. No charge. Closed New Year's Day; Independence Day; Thanksgiving; Christmas. ♿
Attendance: 12,000 (accurate)

Arcade

ARCADE HISTORICAL SOCIETY, 331 W. Main St., Arcade, NY 14009-1110. Mailing Address: P.O. Box 236, Arcade, NY 14009-0236. Tel.: 585-492-4466.
Founded: 1956.
Congressional District: 29
Key Personnel: Pres. (V), Julianne Braun.
Personnel Profile: Part-Time Paid 1; Part-Time Volunteers 12.
Governing Authority: society. Tax-exempt: 501(c)(3).
Historical Society Museum: housed in 1903 Queen Anne-style house.
Collections: crafts; local history, 1865-present; photographs; 1903-1933 household items; toys; archives.
Research Fields: history & development of the Arcade area.
Facilities: 100-vol. library of local history & fiction books; magazines available to the public; 500 sq. ft. exhibit space. Museum-related items for sale.
Activities: guided tours; lectures; organized education programs for children; temporary exhibitions; annual meeting. Special Events: exhibit openings.
Publications: quarterly newsletter, The Arcade Historical Society News.
Hours & Admission Prices: Tues.-Wed. 10-4; other times by appointment. No charge; donations accepted. Closed New Year's Day; Christmas.

Attendance: 714 (accurate)
Membership: Student $2; Basic $5; Family $10; Business $25; Patron $50; Sustaining $100; Life $1,000.

Arden

ORANGE COUNTY HISTORICAL SOCIETY, 21 Clove Furnace Dr., Arden, NY 10910. Mailing Address: P.O. Box 55, Arden, NY 10910-0055. Tel.: 845-351-4696.
Founded: 1971.
Historical Society Museum.
Collections: local history & culture; photographs; historic buildings.
Hours & Admission Prices: Mon.-Fri. 8-4:30.

Armonk

THE NORTH CASTLE HISTORICAL SOCIETY, 440 Bedford Rd., Armonk, NY 10504-2502. Tel.: 914-273-4510.
Founded: 1971.
Congressional District: 24
Key Personnel: Pres. (V), Joan Krantz; Town Historian, Doris Finch Watson; Public Rels. & Publications Dir., Sharon Tomback; Museum Shop Mgr., Jodie Burns.
Personnel Profile: Part-Time Volunteers 75.
Governing Authority: board of trustees. Tax-exempt: 501(c)(3).
Historical Society Museum: housed in c.1776 Smith's Tavern; Brundage Blacksmith Shop; East Middle Patent One Room Schoolhouse; c.1798 Quaker Meeting House.
Collections: various eras depicting home styles, fashions, tools, farm implements; blacksmith shop & forge; East Middle Patent one-room schoolhouse.
Research Fields: history of North Castle.
Facilities: library of local history, slides, photographs, movies, diaries, newspapers and manuscripts, available for use by special permission. Museum-related items for sale.
Activities: guided tours; dinners; antique shows; lectures; films; formally organized education programs for children; docent program; permanent & temporary exhibitions.
Publications: annual booklet, North Castle History; quarterly newsletter.
Hours & Admission Prices: April-Dec. Sun. 2-5, Wed. 2-4; other times by appointment. Suggested Donations: adults $5, member adults $3, children $1. ♿
Attendance: 750 (estimated)
Membership: Individual $20; Family $30; Sustaining $50; Corporate & Business $100; Life $300.

Astoria

* **MUSEUM OF THE MOVING IMAGE, (M),** 35 Ave. at 37th St., Astoria, NY 11106. Tel.: 718-784-4520. Fax: 718-784-0077.
E-mail: info@movingimage.us
Web Site: www.movingimage.us
Founded: 1977.
Congressional District: 9
Key Personnel: C.E.O. & Dir., Rochelle Slovin; Chm. (V), Herbert S. Schlosser; Deputy Dir. Collections, Exhibitions & Operations, Wendell Walker; Deputy Dir. & Dir. Digital Media, Carl Goodman; Chief Cur. Film, David Schwartz; Museum Shop Mgr., Chris Gioia.
Personnel Profile: Full-Time Paid 38; Part-Time Paid 18; Part-Time Volunteers 15; Interns 11.
Governing Authority: nonprofit organization. Tax-exempt: 501(c)(3).
Art, History & Technology Museum of Film, Television & Digital Media.
Collections: 125,000 artifacts & materials related to the art, production, technology, craft, business & history of motion pictures, television & digital media; technical apparatus & installations, production design, licensed merchandise & other ancillary materials, photographs, promotional materials.
Research Fields: cinema; television; video studies; digital media.
Facilities: 190-seat theater; two 50-seat screening rooms; 16,000 sq. ft. exhibition space; cafe. Museum-related items for sale.
Activities: film & video screenings; lectures; seminars; permanent & changing exhibits; education programs in conjunction with New York City public schools; 13 computer-based interactive exhibits.
Publications: program notes; education guides; bimonthly calendar of exhibitions & programs.
Hours & Admission Prices: Tues.-Thurs. 10-4, Fri. 10-6:30. Admission $7; members, children under 5, and AAM & ICOM members no charge. ♿
Attendance: 80,323 (accurate)
Membership: Individual $50; Dual $75; Contributor $125; Sponsor $250; Patron $500; Benefactor $1,000; Director's Council $2,500; Producer's Council $5,000.

THE PEOPLE'S MUSEUM, 22-27 Crescent St., Astoria, NY 11105-3105. Tel.: 718-204-7941 & 0031.
E-mail: thepeoplesmuseum@hotmail.com
Web Site: thepeoplesmuseum.org
Founded: 2000.
Congressional District: 14
Key Personnel: Dir., Chm. & Pres., Mark Allen Sepanski; Devel., Education & Public Rels., April D. Sepanski; Treas., Howard S. Rose; Sec., Dr. Pamela Estelle Ransom; Registrar, Brandon Ballengee; Cur., Paul L. Sieswerda; Archivist, Fred Douglas Wilson; Trustee, Henry Galiano; Trustee, Jeffrey R. Myers; Accounting CPA Partner, Martin Berkowitz.
Personnel Profile: Full-Time Volunteers 5; Part-Time Volunteers 60.
Governing Authority: private; nonprofit organization. Charter by the Board of Regents of the Education Dept. of the State of New York. Tax-exempt: 501(c)(3) and 170(b)(1)(a)
General Museum.
Collections: African; Amazonian; Americana; Native American; fossils; oceanic; Oriental; pre-Columbian; Egyptian; military including guns, swords, period arms & armor from Renaissance Europe, American Revolutionary War, Civil War, Sudan War, 1879 Zulu War, Boer War, WWI & WWII; bones; coins; stamps; toys; contemporary & modern art; photographs; rare books; decorative art; fire & police department; musical instruments; archaeology; geology; zoology; New York artists art work; astronomy.
Research Fields: archaeology.
Facilities: 16,300-vol. library.
Activities: arts festivals; docent program; films; lectures; school loan service; temporary & traveling exhibitions; broadcast programs.
Publications: newsletters, The People's Museum; The People's Museum on Art & Archaeology; The People's Museum on General History; The People's Museum on Military History; membership brochure; annual report.
Hours & Admission Prices: By appointment. No charge; donations accepted. ♿
Membership: Individual $25; Family $30; Contributing $75; Corporate $100; Supporting $250; Patron $500.

Auburn

CAYUGA MUSEUM & CASE RESEARCH LAB MUSEUM, (M), 203 Genesee St., Auburn, NY 13021-3304. Tel.: 315-253-8051. Fax: 315-253-9829.
E-mail: cayugamuseum@roadrunner.com
Web Site: www.cayuganet.org/cayugamuseum
Founded: 1936.
Congressional District: 33
Key Personnel: Dir., Eileen McHugh; Pres. (V), Peter Maciulewicz; Cur., Lauren Chyle; Business Mgr., Lynn Palmieri.
Personnel Profile: Full-Time Paid 3; Part-Time Paid 3; Part-Time Volunteers 20.
Governing Authority: nonprofit organization. Tax-exempt: 501(c)(3).
Local History Museum.
Collections: Bundy Thousand-Year Clock, inventor of the time clock; Case Research Lab; invention of sound-on-film; John Clark Collection: Civil War & Native American documents.
Research Fields: commercialization of sound film.
Facilities: 2,000-vol. library of books on history & archaeology. Books, prints & other museum-related items for sale.
Activities: guided tours; lectures; films; concerts; formally organized education programs; permanent, temporary & traveling exhibitions.
Publications: quarterly newsletter.
Hours & Admission Prices: Tues.-Sun. 12-5. No charge; donations accepted. Closed holidays. ♿
Attendance: 9,300 (accurate)
Membership: Individual $25; Family & Household $35; Sponsor $50; Patron $100; Benefactor $250.

THE HARRIET TUBMAN HOME, 180 South St., Auburn, NY 13021-5636. Tel.: 315-252-2081.
E-mail: khill@harriethouse.org
Web Site: www.harriethouse.org
Key Personnel: Exec. Dir., Karen V. Hill
History Museum.
Collections: life & history of Harriet Tubman; period furniture; personal artifacts.
Activities: Museum Sponsors: special events in May.
Hours & Admission Prices: Tues.-Fri. 10-4, Sat. 10-3.

SCHWEINFURTH MEMORIAL ART CENTER, 205 Genesee St., Auburn, NY 13021-3304. Tel.: 315-255-1553. Fax: 315-255-0871.
E-mail: mail@schweinfurthartcenter.org

Web Site: www.myartcenter.org
Founded: 1975.
Congressional District: 33
Key Personnel: Exec. Dir., Donna Lamb; Pres. (V), Nancy Kramer; Asst. Dir., Stephanie Schuster.
Personnel Profile: Full-Time Paid 4; Part-Time Paid 3; Part-Time Volunteers 25.
Governing Authority: nonprofit organization. Tax-exempt: 501(c)(3).
Cultural Art Center.
Collections: Julius A. Schweinfurth architectural drawings & renderings.
Facilities: cultural center. Museum-related items for sale.
Activities: tours; lectures; concerts; temporary exhibitions; special events.
Publications: monthly calendar; exhibition catalogs.
Hours & Admission Prices: Tues.-Sat. 10-5, Sun. 1-5. Suggested admission $5; children under 12 & members no charge. Closed holidays. ♿
Attendance: 20,000 (accurate)
Membership: Student $15; Senior $25; Individual $35; Family $50; Benefactor $100; Patron $250; Corporate $2,000.

SEWARD HOUSE MUSEUM, (M), 33 South St., Auburn, NY 13021-3929. Tel.: 315-252-1283. Fax: 315-253-3351.
E-mail: director@sewardhouse.org
Web Site: sewardhouse.org
Founded: 1951.
Congressional District: 24
Key Personnel: Pres. (V), Daniel Fessenden; Exec. Dir., Peter A. Wisbey; Collections Mgr., Paul McDonald; Cur. Education & Outreach, Jennifer Haines.
Personnel Profile: Full-Time Paid 4; Part-Time Paid 2; Part-Time Volunteers 72.
Governing Authority: nonprofit organization. Tax-exempt: 501(c)(3).
Historic House: 1816 home of William H. Seward.
Collections: articles of Seward's career; original furnishings; Civil War material; paintings; uniforms; china; original costumes; Alaskan memorabilia & artifacts.
Research Fields: furniture; decorations; clothing 1816-1900; Civil War; politics, Alaska.
Facilities: 10,000-vol. library of books on Civil War & Abraham Lincoln available by appointment.
Activities: guided tours; permanent exhibitions; lectures; special topic tours
Publications: booklet; members quarterly newsletter, Diplomatic Pouch.
Hours & Admission Prices: July to mid-Oct. Tues.-Sat. 10-4, Sun. 1-4; mid-Oct. to June Tues.-Sat. 10-4. Adults $7, senior citizens $6, students $2; discounts to AAM & ICOM members; members no charge. Closed major holidays. ♿
Attendance: 12,981 (accurate)
Membership: Student $15; Individual $25; Family $40; Supporting $90; Sustaining $125.

WARD W. O'HARA AGRICULTURAL MUSEUM, 6880 E. Lake Rd., Auburn, NY 13021. Tel.: 315-252-7644 & 5009. Fax: 315-253-5199.
Web Site: www.cayuganet.org/agmuseum
Founded: 1975.
Congressional District: 33
Key Personnel: C.E.O., Chm. (V) & Pres. (V), Norman Riley; Dir. & Museum Shop Mgr., Timothy J. Quill; Asst., Mike Walsh; Asst., Car Brier.
Personnel Profile: Part-Time Paid 3; Part-Time Volunteers 10.
Governing Authority: county. Tax-exempt.
Agricultural Museum.
Collections: agriculture machinery & implements; country kitchen; blacksmith shop; wheelwright shop; country store; photos of rural Cayuga County; dairy processing; sleighs; buggies; milking equipment; cooper's bench; early woodworking shop, tillage & planting equipment, tractors & power engines, veterinarians office & equipment; live bee colony; early 1900 Birdsal saw mill; Osburn equipment; over 500 historical photos.
Research Fields: Cayuga County businesses & farms relating to agricultural field.
Activities: guided tours; lectures; slide shows; hobby workshops; formally organized educational programs; loan, permanent, temporary & traveling exhibitions; school loan service; weaving.
Hours & Admission Prices: mid-May to mid-Sept. daily 11-4; other times by appointment. No charge; donations accepted. ♿
Attendance: 3,000 (estimated)

Auriesville

KATERI GALLERIES, SHRINE OF OUR LADY OF MARTYRS AKA THE NATIONAL SHRINE OF THE NORTH AMERICAN MARTYRS, 136 Shrine Rd., Auriesville, NY 12016. Tel.: 518-853-3033. Fax: 518-853-3051.
E-mail: office@martyrshrine.org
Web Site: www.martyrshrine.org
Founded: 1885.
Congressional District: 31
Key Personnel: Dir., Rev. Peter J. Murray, S.J.; Dir. Operations, Mr. Thomas F. Ralph; Dir. Mktg. & Devel., Fran Ralph; Maintenance Supvr., Donald R. Wagoner; Museum Shop Mgr., Dorothea Smith.
Personnel Profile: Full-Time Paid 11; Part-Time Paid 7; Part-Time Volunteers 6.
Governing Authority: nonprofit organization; church. National Shrine of the North American Martyrs. Tax-exempt: 501(c)(3).
Museum Complex & Historic Site: housed in c.1900 frame structure, located on the site of the 1646 martyrdom of Father Isaac Jogues, French Jesuit priest & 1656 birthplace of Kateri Tekakwitha.
Collections: local American Indian artifacts; paintings & charts; geology; anthropology; contemporary nationwide American Indian handicrafts; American Indian log house; dioramas.
Facilities: 300-vol. library pertaining to early history of New York & 1897, set of Jesuit Relations available for research by appointment on premises; reading room; 6,500-seat Coliseum Church; 50-seat media room. Museum-related items for sale.
Activities: guided tours; lectures; films; drama; permanent exhibitions.
Publications: weekly newsletter, Pilgrim; brochures.
Hours & Admission Prices: May-Oct. Visitor Center: Sun.-Fri. 10-5, Sat. 10-5:30. Mass Schedule: Mon.-Sat. 11:30 & 4, Sun. 9, 10:30, & 4. No charge; donations accepted. ♿
Attendance: 60,000 (estimated)

Baldwin

BALDWIN HISTORICAL SOCIETY AND MUSEUM, 1980 Grand Ave., Baldwin, NY 11510-2836. Mailing Address: P.O. Box 762, Baldwin, NY 11510-0586. Tel.: 516-536-7015.
Founded: 1971.
Congressional District: 5
Key Personnel: C.E.O., Pres. (V) & Public Rels. Dir., Constance Grando; C.E.O. & Pres. (V), Jack Bryck; Museum Shop Mgr., Geri Griffin.
Personnel Profile: Part-Time Volunteers 25.
Governing Authority: society; nonprofit organization.
Historical Society Museum.
Collections: history of Baldwin; Baldwin photographic collection; Baldwin related artifacts & archives.
Research Fields: local history.
Facilities: library of books on local & Long Island history available by appointment only. Stock of 1910-30s Baldwin postcards & other museum-related items for sale.
Activities: guided tours; lectures; formally organized education programs.
Publications: newsletter.
Hours & Admission Prices: Mon. & Fri. 9-11:30, Wed. & Sun. 1-4. No charge. Closed New Year's Day; Easter; Christmas. ♿
Attendance: 200 (estimated)
Membership: Student $1; Individual $5; Family $10; Organizations $25; Life $150; Patron $250; Benefactor $500; Friend of the Museum $1,000.

Ballston Spa

NATIONAL BOTTLE MUSEUM, 76 Milton Ave., Ballston Spa, NY 12020-1405. Tel.: 518-885-7589. Fax: 518-885-0317.
E-mail: nbm@crisny.org
Web Site: www.nationalbottlemuseum.org
Founded: 1996.
Key Personnel: Dir., Jan Rutland.
Governing Authority: Tax-exempt: 501(c)(3).
History Museum.
Collections: early bottle making methods; hand tools; 1800s glass furnace model; handmade bottles; stoneware.
Facilities: library.
Activities: research; classes; flameworking lessons.
Publications: newsletter, The Bottle Muse.
Hours & Admission Prices: June-Sept. daily 10-4; Oct.-May Mon.-Fri. 10-4. No charge; donations accepted. Closed New Year's Day; Christmas.
Attendance: 3,750 (estimated)
Membership: Friends $10-$49; Supporters $50-$149; Benefactors $150 & up; Corporate Donors $500 & up.

SARATOGA COUNTY HISTORICAL SOCIETY, BROOKSIDE MUSEUM, 6 Charlton St., Ballston Spa, NY 12020-1707. Tel.: 518-885-4000. Fax: 518-885-4055.
E-mail: info@brooksidemuseum.org
Web Site: www.brooksidemuseum.org
Formerly: Brookside, Saratoga County Historical Society
Founded: 1962.

Congressional District: 24
Key Personnel: Exec. Dir., Joy Houle; Pres. (V), Meg O'Leary; Dir. Education, Linda Gorham; Cur., Kathleen Coleman; Mgr. Public Programs, Rebecca Codner.
Personnel Profile: Full-Time Paid 1; Full-Time Volunteers 2; Part-Time Paid 3; Part-Time Volunteers 20; Interns 1.
Governing Authority: society. Operated by Saratoga County Historical Society. Tax-exempt: 501(c)(3).
General Museum: housed in 1792 Aldridge House & Resort Hotel.
Collections: Saratoga County history; items relating to area residents; art; costumes; toys & sports; agriculture; lumbering; resort life; manuscripts; Saratoga County surname files.
Research Fields: county history.
Facilities: 1,000-vol. library of local history materials; photographic collection; program space; 1,500 sq. ft. exhibit space. Museum-related items for sale.
Activities: group tours; traveling education programs; living history events; craft classes; hobby workshops; concerts; docent program; formal education programs; participatory & temporary exhibitions; lectures; school loan service.
Publications: yearly journal, The Grist Mill; bimonthly newsletter, Columns.
Hours & Admission Prices: Tues.-Fri. 10-4, Sat. 10-2. Family $5, adults $2, senior citizens $1.50, students & children $1; museum, AASLH & MANY members no charge. Closed New Year's Day; Easter; Thanksgiving; Christmas. ♿
Attendance: 11,000 (accurate)
Membership: Senior & Student $15; Individual $25; Family $35; Contributor $50; Supporter $75; Patron $100

Batavia

THE HOLLAND LAND OFFICE MUSEUM, 131 W. Main St., Batavia, NY 14020-2021. Tel.: 585-343-4727.
E-mail: info@hollandlandoffice.com
Web Site: www.hollandlandoffice.com
Founded: 1894.
Congressional District: 26
Key Personnel: Dir., Patrick Weissend; Museum Shop Mgr., Corinne Iwanicki.
Personnel Profile: Full-Time Paid 1; Part-Time Paid 1; Part-Time Volunteers 15.
Governing Authority: county. Parent Institution: Holland Purchase Historical Society. Tax-exempt: 501(c)(3).
General Museum: housed in 1815 cut-stone structure erected for use as the office of Holland Land Co. where land was offered for sale in 1800s.
Collections: medical; military; glass & china; early furniture; musical instruments; guns; toys; costumes; early hand tools; fireplace tools; cooking utensils; woodenware; Indian artifacts.
Research Fields: pertaining to museum collections; 19th-century rural & town life; western New York in early 1800s.
Activities: guided tours; permanent exhibitions; museum quilt guild; children's programs.
Publications: booklets, Music in Genesee County; The Sesquicentennial 1802-1952; History of Genesee County New York, 1890-1982.
Hours & Admission Prices: Jan.-May & Sept.-Nov. Tues.-Sat. 10-4; Memorial Day to Labor Day Mon.-Sat. 10-4; late-Nov. to Dec. Tues.-Sat. 10-4, Sun. 12:30-4:30. No charge; donations accepted. Closed legal holidays. ♿
Attendance: 6,500 (accurate)
Membership: Individual $20; Family $35; Patron $50; Sponsor $100; Benefactor $250; Life $500.

Bayside

QCC ART GALLERY/CUNY, 222-05 56th Ave., Bayside, NY 11364-1497. Tel.: 718-631-6396. Fax: 718-631-6620.
E-mail: qccartgallery@qcc.cuny.edu
Web Site: www.qccartgallery.org
Founded: 1966.
Congressional District: 8
Key Personnel: Dir., Mr. Faustino Quintanilla; Asst. Dir., Deanne DeNyse.
Governing Authority: nonprofit organization.
College Art Gallery.
Collections: ethnic diversity of the College, community & the role art plays in the cultural history of people; primarily based on American artists after 1950 & women artists.
Research Fields: Trans-expressionism & spiritual behavior in art; African art; Pre-Columbian art.
Facilities: library at Queensborough Community College Art Gallery; small library of exhibition catalogues, Queens Artists Registry, & African art books available to students & community members.
Activities: guided tours; lectures; temporary, traveling & loan exhibitions; training programs for professional museum workers; formally organized education programs for adults, undergraduates & graduates affiliated with Queensborough Community College.
Publications: exhibit catalogues.
Hours & Admission Prices: Tues. & Fri. 10-5, Wed.-Thurs. 10-7, Sat.-Sun. 12-5. No charge; donations accepted. Closed major holidays. ♿
Attendance: 35,000 (estimated)
Membership: Senior Citizen & Student $25; Associate $50; Sustaining $100; Patron $250; Benefactor $500; President's Circle $1,000 & up.

Beacon

BEACON HISTORICAL SOCIETY, 477 Main St., Beacon, NY 12508-3819. Mailing Address: P.O. Box 89, Beacon, NY 12508-0089. Tel.: 845-831-0514.
Web Site: www.beaconhistoricalsociety.org
Founded: 1976.
Key Personnel: Pres. (V), Robert Murphy.
Personnel Profile: Part-Time Volunteers 5.
Governing Authority: private; nonprofit organization.
Historical Museum.
Collections: paper archives; photographs; personal & Beacon government historical records; maps; pictures; news & personal items; memorabilia.
Facilities: 300-vol. library pertaining to Hudson River area; field research station.
Activities: slide collections; temporary exhibitions.
Publications: monthly newsletter.
Hours & Admission Prices: Thurs. 10-12, Sat. 1-3. Archival Research: 4th Tues. of each month. Open Meetings 7:30pm. No charge.
Attendance: 500 (estimated)
Membership: Individual $10.

DIA: BEACON, 3 Beekman St., Beacon, NY 12508. Mailing Address: 535 W. 22 St., New York, NY 10011-1119. Tel.: 212-989-5566 & 293-5518. Fax: 212-989-4055.
E-mail: info@diaart.org
Web Site: www.diaart.org
Formerly: Dia: Chelsea
Founded: 1974.
Congressional District: 17
Key Personnel: Exec. Dir., Philippe Vergne; Chm. Bd. (V), Nathalie de Gunzburg; Cur., Lynne Cooke; Dir. Operations, James P. Schaeufele; Dir. Digital Media, Sara Tucker; Publications, Karen Kelly; Asst. Dir., Steven Evans; Museum Shop Mgr., Jill Petrush Rogers.
Governing Authority: nonprofit organization. Subsidiary Institutions: The Earth Room by Walter De Maria, New York, NY; The Broken Kilometer by Walter De Maria, New York, NY; Dan Flavin Institute/Dia Center for the Arts, Bridgehampton, NY; The Lightning Field by Walter De Maria, Quemado, NM. Tax-exempt: 501(c)(3).
Art Center.
Collections: contemporary American & European art.
Facilities: 2,800-vol. library of art books; catalogs; periodicals; 100-vols. videotapes & books on poetry; 45,000 sq. ft. exhibit space. Artists' books & exhibition catalogs for sale.
Activities: lectures; loan, temporary & traveling exhibitions; year long exhibitions of new works by individual artists; worldwide website commissions, artists web projects; Readings in Contemporary Poetry; education program; symposia; Robert Lehman Lectures on Contemporary Art.
Publications: semiannual calendar; exhibition catalogues & brochures; symposia publications; world wide web pages.
Hours & Admission Prices: Winter: Fri.-Mon. 11-4. Fall: Thurs.-Mon. 11-4. Adults $10, students & seniors $7; children under 12 no charge. ♿
Attendance: 84,000 (estimated)
Membership: General $50; Family $100; Friend $500; Art Circle $5,000.

DIA:BEACON, RIGGIO GALLERIES, 3 Beekman St., Beacon, NY 12508-2521. Mailing Address: c/o Dia Art Foundation, 535 W. 22nd St., 4th Fl., New York, NY 10011. Tel.: 845-440-0100. Fax: 845-440-0092.
E-mail: info@diaart.org
Web Site: www.diaart.org
Founded: 2003.
Key Personnel: Chm. (V), Nathalie de Gonzburg; Dir., Philippe Vergne; Deputy Dir., Laura Raicovich; Financial Dir., Carolyn Kay Carson; Cur., Lynne Cooke; Museum Shop Mgr., Jill Petrush.
Governing Authority: private; nonprofit organization. Parent Institution: Dia Art Foundation, New York, NY. Tax-exempt: 501(c)(3).
Art Museum.
Collections: art from 1960s to present.
Facilities: classroom; 50-seat cafeteria; 240,000 sq. ft. exhibit space. Museum-related items for sale.
Activities: guided tours; formal education programs for children.

Publications: semiannual, program calendar; exhibition publications.
Hours & Admission Prices: mid-April to mid-Oct. Thurs.-Mon. 11-6; Oct.-April Fri.-Mon. 11-4. Adults $10, senior citizens & students $7; discounts to AAM members; children under 12 no charge. Closed New Year's Eve & Day; Thanksgiving; Christmas Eve & Day. ♿
Attendance: 80,000 (accurate)
Membership: Senior, Artist & Student $30; Individual $50; Family $100; Friend $500; Art Council $5,000.

THE MADAM BRETT HOMESTEAD, 50 Van Nydeck Ave., Beacon, NY 12508-3326. Tel.: 845-831-6533.
Founded: 1954.
Congressional District: 19
Key Personnel: Regent, Kathie Halvey; Cur. & Museum Shop Mgr., Evelyn Mark; Dir. Tours, Anne Thomas.
Personnel Profile: Part-Time Volunteers 20.
Governing Authority: society. Operated by the Melzingah Chapter of the Daughters of the American Revolution, 1776 D St. N.W., Washington, D.C., Melzingah Chapter, NSDAR, 50 Van Nydeck Ave. Beacon, NY 12508. Tax-exempt.
Historic Site: c.1709 & c.1740 Madam Brett Homestead.
Collections: furnishings of seven generations of the Brett family; costumes; doll room; local history room.
Facilities: colonial garden. Museum-related items for sale.
Activities: guided tours.
Publications: brochure; booklet, Points of Historical Interest in Southern Dutchess.
Hours & Admission Prices: April-Dec. 2nd Sat. of month. Adults $5, students $2.
Attendance: 600 (estimated)

MOUNT GULIAN HISTORIC SITE, (M), 145 Sterling St., Beacon, NY 12508-1483. Tel.: 845-831-8172.
E-mail: info@mountgulian.org
Web Site: www.mountgulian.org
Key Personnel: Exec. Dir., Elaine Hayes
Historic House Museum: housed in an 18th century Dutch Colonial Homestead.
Collections: local history; period furnishings.
Activities: weddings; rental facilities; special events; guided tours; school & group programs.
Hours & Admission Prices: Wed.-Fri. & Sun. 1-5; tours by appointment. Adults $8, seniors $6, youth 6-18 $4; member no charge.

Bear Mountain

BEAR MOUNTAIN TRAILSIDE MUSEUMS AND ZOO, Bear Mountain State Park, Bear Mountain, NY 10911. Mailing Address: Palisades Interstate Park Commission, Bear Mountain, NY 10911-0427. Tel.: 845-786-2701, ext. 263. Fax: 845-786-7157.
Web Site: www.palisadesparksconservancy.org/parks/5/
Founded: 1927.
Key Personnel: Exec. Dir., James Hall.
Governing Authority: state. Palisades Interstate Park Commission.
Natural History Museum.
Collections: local collections of animals, plants, minerals & rocks; Indian artifacts; history.
Research Fields: local history.
Facilities: approx. 3,000-vol. library of natural & local history available for use by appointment; botanical garden; zoological park; aquarium.
Activities: permanent exhibitions.
Hours & Admission Prices: Daily 10-4:30. Adults & children 13 and over $1, children 6-12 $.50; children under 5 no charge. Parking in state park $6.

Bedford

MUSEUM OF THE BEDFORD HISTORICAL SOCIETY, 612 Old Post Rd., Bedford, NY 10506. Mailing Address: P.O. Box 491, Bedford, NY 10506-0491. Tel.: 914-234-9751. Fax: 914-234-5461.
E-mail: bedhist@bestweb.net
Web Site: www.bedfordhistoricalsociety.org
Founded: 1916.
Congressional District: 21
Key Personnel: Exec. Dir., Evelyne H. Ryan; Chm. (V), Jeffrey C. Tweedy; Pres. (V), Peter T. Michaelis; Cur., Emily Zucker.
Personnel Profile: Full-Time Paid 1; Part-Time Paid 2; Part-Time Volunteers 30.
Governing Authority: society. Tax-exempt: 501(c)(3).
Local History Museum.
Collections: archives; costumes; general; history; manuscript collections; Native American artifacts. Historic Buildings: 1806 Historical Hall; 1838 general store; 1787 Court House; 1829 schoolhouse; 1838 Post Office.
Research Fields: costumes; archives; genealogy.
Facilities: library of manuscripts, periodicals & old books available for use by appointment.
Activities: guided tours; permanent & temporary exhibitions.
Publications: books, Pilgrim's Progress Bedford Version; Historical Tour of Bedford; The Burning of Bedford - July 1779.
Hours & Admission Prices: Museum: Thurs.-Sat. 12-3; other times by appointment. Suggested Donation: $5; educational institutions, local children's organizations & all educational tours no charge. ♿
Attendance: 200 (estimated)
Membership: Student $15; Member $35; Family $100; Sponsor $250; Patron $500; Benefactor $1,000.

Bedford Corners

WESTMORELAND SANCTUARY, INC., 260 Chestnut Ridge Rd., Bedford Corners, NY 10549-4812. Tel.: 914-666-8448. Fax: 914-242-1175.
E-mail: westsanc@optonline.net
Web Site: westmorelandsanctuary.org
Founded: 1957.
Congressional District: 21
Key Personnel: Dir. & Naturalist, Stephen Ricker.
Personnel Profile: Full-Time Paid 2; Part-Time Paid 1; Part-Time Volunteers 30.
Governing Authority: nonprofit organization. Tax-exempt.
Nature Sanctuary.
Collections: rocks; minerals; mammal skulls; furs; turtle shells; colonial tools; mounted fish, mammals & birds; seasonal displays; live animals. Historic Building: 1783 church.
Research Fields: wildlife; botanical.
Facilities: 300-vol. library of natural science books available for research upon special request; nature center; 625-acre area; maple sugar house; auditorium; classroom; bird observation window.
Activities: guided tours; maple sugaring; outdoor lectures on wildlife management, ornithology, pond ecology & general ecology; evening lecture series; annual fall festival; nature programs for school groups, families & adults; workshops.
Publications: seasonal activity calendar; book, Ferris Family Cemetery in Westmoreland.
Hours & Admission Prices: Trails: daily dawn-dusk. Museum: Mon.-Sat. 9-5, Sun. 10:30-5. No charge; donations accepted.
Attendance: 40,000 (estimated)
Membership: Student $20; Individual $25; Family $50; Sponsor $100; Patron $150; Benefactor $300 & up.

Bellport

BELLPORT-BROOKHAVEN HISTORICAL SOCIETY AND MUSEUM, (M), 31 Bellport Lane, Bellport, NY 11713-2739. Tel.: 631-286-0888; 631-776-7640.
E-mail: president@bbhsmuseum.org
Web Site: www.bbhsmuseum.org
Founded: 1963.
Congressional District: 3
Key Personnel: Pres. (V), Jan Harting-McChesney; Museum Shop Mgr., Robert Duckworth.
Personnel Profile: Part-Time Volunteers 30.
Governing Authority: society. Tax-exempt: 501(c)(3).
Local History Museum: housed in 1833 buildings.
Collections: wild fowl & shore bird decoys; memorabilia of Great South Bay & Fire Island Beach; dolls; toys; tools; guns; batteries; whaling artifacts; original scooter; textiles; Sperry gyroscope instruments; 19th-century household artifacts & costumes; tinware; early American decoration; genealogical information. Historic Buildings: c.1800's, Barn Museum; Brown Building; Post-Crowell House; Blacksmith Shop; Milk House.
Research Fields: local history.
Facilities: Museum-related items for sale.
Activities: guided tours; quarterly meetings. Museum Sponsors: Antiques Fair.
Publications: book, History of Bellport-Brookhaven; quarterly newsletter.
Hours & Admission Prices: Memorial Day to Labor Day Thurs.-Sat. 1-4; other times by appointment. Adults $5, seniors citizens 65 & over and children 13-17 $4; discounts to AAM & ICOM members; children 12 & under and members no charge. Gift Shop: May-Dec. Thurs.-Sat. 11-5. ♿
Attendance: 400 (estimated)
Membership: Student $15; Senior $20; Individual & Family $35; Sponsor $50; Patron $100; Benefactor $250; Individual Life $500; Couple Life $650.

Belmont

ALLEGANY COUNTY MUSEUM, 11 Wells St., Belmont, NY 14813-1052. Mailing Address: Court House Court St., Belmont, NY 14813. Tel.: 585-268-9293. Fax: 716-268-9446.
E-mail: historian@alleganyco.com
Founded: 1970.
Congressional District: 29
Key Personnel: Dir., Craig R. Braack.
Personnel Profile: Full-Time Paid 1; Part-Time Paid 1.
Governing Authority: county. Affiliated with the County Board of Legislators, Belmont, NY 14813. Tax-exempt.
History Museum: housed in 1842 Greek Revival Church.
Collections: local land office records, maps & preservation records; impact statements; 19th century tools & furnishings.
Research Fields: genealogy; industry.
Facilities: 1,000-vol. library of books & government reports on genealogy & general history available for research on premises; 30-seat auditorium.
Activities: guided tours; lectures; formally organized education programs for children; permanent & traveling exhibitions.
Hours & Admission Prices: Mon.-Fri. 9-4:30; other times by appointment. No charge. Closed holidays. ♿

Bergen

BERGEN MUSEUM OF LOCAL HISTORY, 7547 Lake Rd., Bergen, NY 14416. Mailing Address: 13 S. Lake Ave., Bergen, NY 14416-9420. Tel.: 585-494-0080 & 704-4119 (cell). Fax: 585-494-1488.
Founded: 1964.
Congressional District: 35
Key Personnel: Mgr. & Museum Shop Mgr., Peggy Denton; Pres., Myrna List; Vice Pres., Theresa Alexander; Sec., Nancy Charcolla; Sec., Jean Stewart; Treas., Lisa Teremy.
Governing Authority: municipal. Affiliated with Bergen Historical Society. Tax-exempt.
Local History Museum: housed in 1843 schoolhouse.
Collections: photographs & documents of town residents; decorative arts; folklore; pottery; early implements & tools; farm, trade & home articles; livery.
Research Fields: history of town and people.
Activities: lecture tours for schools and organizations; formally organized education programs for children; permanent & temporary exhibitions.
Publications: Bergen Historical Newsletter; 175th History Bergen.
Hours & Admission Prices: June-Oct by appointment. No charge; donations accepted. Closed legal holidays. ♿
Attendance: 175 (estimated)
Membership: Single $10; Family $15; Sustaining $25.

HARFORD BARN MUSEUM, 13 S. Lake Ave., Bergen, NY 14416. Tel.: 585-494-1121. Fax: 585-494-1488.
E-mail: vdenton@rochester.rr.com
Founded: 2003.
Historic Building: housed in a restored barn; built in the 1800s.
Collections: local history & culture; pioneer life from 1800-1900s; folk culture; sculpture; personal artifacts.
Activities: temporary & permanent exhibits.
Hours & Admission Prices: June-Oct. by appointment. No charge; donations accepted. ♿
Attendance: 325 (estimated)

Bethel

THE MUSEUM AT BETHEL WOODS, (M), 200 Hurd Rd., Bethel, NY 12720. Mailing Address: P.O. Box 222, Liberty, NY 12754-0222. Tel.: 845-583-2075. Fax: 845-583-4242.
E-mail: wlawrence@bethelwoodscenter.org
Web Site: www.bethelwoodscenter.org
Founded: 2008.
Congressional District: 22
Key Personnel: Dir., Wade Lawrence; Museum Shop Mgr., Carole Couture.
Personnel Profile: Full-Time Paid 4; Part-Time Paid 8; Part-Time Volunteers 92; Interns 2.
Governing Authority: Parent Institution: The Bethel Performing Arts Center, LLC. Tax-exempt.
History Museum & Historic Site: housed on the site of the 1969 Woodstock Music and Art Fair.
Collections: graphic arts; photography; video; sound recordings; clothing; manuscripts; period artifacts; ephemera.
Research Fields: 1960s popular culture; Woodstock Music & Art Fair.
Facilities: permanent exhibit gallery; special exhibit gallery; rental facilities; classrooms; cafe; 1,000-seat amphitheater; outdoor concert pavilion; administrative office. Museum-related items for sale.
Activities: film; interactive exhibits; educational programs & events; concerts; performances.
Hours & Admission Prices: April-Dec. call for hours. Adults $13; discounts to AAM & ICOM members. Closed New Year's Day; Thanksgiving; Christmas Eve & Day. ♿
Membership: Individual $50; Couple $80; Family $125; Supporter $225.

Binghamton

BINGHAMTON ZOO AT ROSS PARK, 60 Morgan Rd., Binghamton, NY 13903-3667. Mailing Address: 185 Park Ave., Binghamton, NY 13903-3643. Tel.: 607-724-5461. Fax: 607-724-5454 & 5453.
E-mail: info@rosspark.com
Web Site: www.rossparkzoo.com
Formerly: Ross Park Zoo
Key Personnel: Exec. Dir., Mike Janis; Business Mgr., Amanda Padwa.
Personnel Profile: Full-Time Paid 17; Full-Time Volunteers 40.
Zoo.
Collections: native & exotic animals including the American bison, Siberian lynx, Arctic fox & Coati Mundi; timber wolves; barred owl; African clawless otter; endangered species.
Facilities: picnic facilities; cafe. Gift items for sale.
Activities: carousel; educational programs.
Hours & Admission Prices: April-Nov. daily 10-5. Adults $7, seniors 55 & over and military with ID $6, children 3-11 $4.50; discount to groups; children under 2 & members no charge. ♿
Attendance: 90,000 (estimated)

THE BROOME COUNTY HISTORICAL SOCIETY, 185 Court St., Binghamton, NY 13901-3503. Tel.: 607-778-3572. Fax: 607-778-6429.
E-mail: localhistory@bclibrary.info
Web Site: www.bclibrary.info/history.htm
Founded: 1919.
Congressional District: 27
Key Personnel: Pres. (V), David J. Dixon.
Personnel Profile: Part-Time Paid 1; Part-Time Volunteers 20; Interns 1.
Governing Authority: Tax-exempt.
History Museum: housed in Roberson Museum.
Collections: historic 1907 Renaissance Revival Residence; artifacts; manuscripts; decorative arts; regional history library maintained in Broome County Public Library.
Research Fields: local & New York state history; art; archaeology.
Facilities: 5,000-vol. library & photo archives on regional New York history available on premises.
Activities: guided tours; lectures; permanent, temporary & traveling exhibitions.
Publications: Broome County History Bulletin; exhibition catalogs.
Hours & Admission Prices: Mon.-Thurs. 10-8, Fri.-Sat. 10-4. No charge; donations accepted. ♿
Attendance: 42,000 (estimated)
Membership: Individual $20; Family $30.

THE BUNDY ARTS & VICTORIAN MUSEUM, 129 Main St., Binghamton, NY 13905-2742. Tel.: 607-772-9179. Fax: 607-221-6872.
History Museum.
Collections: Bundy Time Recording Clocks; African artifacts; broadcasting pioneers & artifacts; period barbershop; Asian art; personal artifacts.
Facilities: Museum-related items for sale.
Activities: permanent & temporary exhibitions; special events; educational programs; lectures.
Hours & Admission Prices: Tues.-Sat. 11-5.

CUTLER BOTANIC GARDEN, 840 Upper Front St., Binghamton, NY 13905-1542. Tel.: 607-772-8953. Fax: 607-723-5951.
E-mail: broome@cornell.edu
Web Site: www.cce.cornell.edu/broome
Founded: 1979.
Congressional District: 28
Key Personnel: C.E.O., David A. Bradstreet; Program Assoc., Renee Schloupt.
Personnel Profile: Full-Time Paid 1; Part-Time Paid 2; Part-Time Volunteers 64; Interns 24.
Governing Authority: nonprofit. Parent Institution: Cornell Cooperative Extension of Broome County. Tax-exempt.
Botanical Garden.
Collections: individual beds of annuals, perennials, herbs, vegetables; rock garden; heath & heather garden; antique rose border; Heritage fruit & vegetable garden; All-America display garden; seasonal theme gardens; demonstration composting site.

Research Fields: testing of hardiness & ornamental or economic value of plants.
Facilities: botanical garden.
Activities: guided tours; lectures; training programs for professional museum workers; master gardener program.
Publications: garden brochure.
Hours & Admission Prices: June-Oct. daily during daylight hours. No charge; donations accepted. ♿
Attendance: 15,000 (estimated)
Membership: Friend $10; Family $25; Benefactor $50.

THE DISCOVERY CENTER OF THE SOUTHERN TIER, (M), 60 Morgan Rd., Binghamton, NY 13903-3667. Tel.: 607-773-8750 & 8661, ext. 201. Fax: 607-773-8019.
E-mail: pr@thediscoverycenter.org
Web Site: www.thediscoverycenter.org
Founded: 1983.
Congressional District: 28
Key Personnel: C.E.O., Margaret S. Crocker; Pres., Wendy Graham; Financial Dir., Catherine Fiacco; Asst. Dir., Donna J. Flamik; Dir. Mktg., Martha J. Steed; Museum Shop Mgr., Jennifer Fiala.
Personnel Profile: Full-Time Paid 5; Part-Time Paid 29; Part-Time Volunteers 200; Interns 3.
Governing Authority: organization; nonprofit. Tax-exempt: 501(c)(3).
Children's Museum: located in historic Ross Park. Discovery Center chartered in 1984.
Collections: fossils; minerals; natural science specimens, shells, African artifacts; textiles; contemporary & historical objects for standard exhibit or use in context; children's material culture objects of childhood.
Major Exhibits: Pedal Power, 11/09-12/10; Ecokids: Woodland Wonders, 11/09-1/14.
Facilities: two classrooms; 4,800 sq. ft. exhibit space; 175-seat theater; cafe; zoological park. Educational toys, books & other museum-related items for sale.
Activities: concerts; docent program; hobby workshops; lectures; participatory & temporary exhibits; theater; formal education programs for children & college undergraduate & graduate students; after school program, Discovery Kids; performing arts; environmental studies; paleontology; family workshops; pre-school. Annual Events: Truck Day; Super Hero Day; Martin Luther King Day; Afro-American History Month; Business Day; Parlor City Boys Chorus. Museum Sponsors: early childhood programs weekly; Center Kids monthly.
Publications: quarterly newsletter, Discoverings.
Hours & Admission Prices: July-Aug. Mon.-Fri. 10-4, Sat. 10-5, Sun. 12-5; Sept.-June Tues.-Fri. 10-4, Sat. 10-5, Sun. 12-5. Children 2 & over $6, adults $5; discounts to groups, ACM & AAM members; children 1 & under and members no charge. ♿
Attendance: 52,130 (accurate)
Membership: Individual $45; Family $65; Family Plus $75; Contributing & ACM $125; Supporting $175; Patron $300.

* **ROBERSON MUSEUM AND SCIENCE CENTER, (M),** 30 Front St., Binghamton, NY 13905-4779. Tel.: 607-772-0660. Fax: 607-771-8905.
E-mail: blake@roberson.org
Web Site: www.roberson.org
Founded: 1954.
Congressional District: 28
Key Personnel: C.E.O., Terry McDonald; Pres. (V), Diana Bendz; Exhibition Devel., Peter Klosky; Cur., Eve Daniels.
Personnel Profile: Full-Time Paid 8; Part-Time Paid 9.
Governing Authority: nonprofit. Parent Institution: Roberson Memorial, Inc. & Roberson Museum & Science Center. Tax-exempt: 501(c)(3).
General Museum.
Collections: decorative arts; American art; mounted specimens of birds & mammals; local & regional history; ethnological & archaeological collections. Historic House: Roberson Mansion (c.1904).
Research Fields: regional; cultural; ethnic & social history.
Facilities: local history research library; 60-seat planetarium; 10-acre nature site. Museum-related items for sale.
Activities: guided tours; lectures; concerts; family activities; classes; special events; school programs.
Publications: exhibit catalogues; local history monographs; newsletter.
Hours & Admission Prices: Wed.-Thurs. & Sat.-Sun. 12-5, Fri. 12-9. Adults $8, seniors & students $6, $20 family maximum (6 people maximum), reciprocal agreement with ASTC, Arnot Art Museum & 19 other New York State museums; discount to AAM & ICOM members; members no charge. Closed major holidays. ♿
Attendance: 35,000 (estimated)
Membership: Individual $40; Family $65.

UNIVERSITY ART MUSEUM, Binghamton University, Binghamton, NY 13902-6000. Mailing Address: P.O. Box 6000, Binghamton, NY 13902-6000. Tel.: 607-777-2634. Fax: 607-777-2613.
E-mail: hogan@binghamton.edu
Web Site: artmuseum.binghamton.edu
Founded: 1967.
Congressional District: 27
Key Personnel: Dir. Asst., Jacqueline Hogan; Registrar, Silvia Ivanova.
Personnel Profile: Full-Time Paid 4; Part-Time Paid 2; Interns 2.
Governing Authority: university. Parent Institution: State University of New York at Binghamton & Foundation, Binghamton, NY. Tax-exempt.
Art Museum.
Collections: paintings; sculpture; graphics; decorative arts; Wedgwood ceramics; Asian art; ancient pottery; African Art.
Facilities: 50,000-vol. fine arts library of catalogs; journals & books available for inter-library loan.
Activities: lectures; internships; inter-museum loan; temporary exhibits; faculty & student shows; educational class (Curatorial Practice) for graduate students; education outreach to public schools.
Publications: exhibition catalogs; newsletter, calendar of events.
Hours & Admission Prices: Summer: Tues.-Fri. 12-4; Sept.-June Tues.-Wed. & Fri.-Sat. 12-4, Thurs. 12-7; other times by appointment. No charge. Closed holidays. ♿

Bloomfield

A.W.A. ELECTRONIC-COMMUNICATION MUSEUM, 2 South Ave., Bloomfield, NY 14469. Tel.: 585-657-6260.
E-mail: tpflab@aol.com
Web Site: www.antiquewireless.org
Founded: 1952.
Congressional District: 29
Key Personnel: Dir., Thomas Peterson; Deputy Dir., Allan Pellnat; Registrar, Edward Gable; Treas., Stan Avery.
Personnel Profile: Full-Time Volunteers 1; Part-Time Volunteers 30.
Governing Authority: Tax-exempt: 501(c)(3).
Radio Museum: housed in c.1840 restored East Bloomfield Academy building.
Collections: radio & communications; electricity & electronics.
Research Fields: radio & communications.
Facilities: 2,000-vol. library of books, magazines, & catalogs on radios & electrical material available for research for members of association; photographic library; historical magnetic tape library; motion picture collection available for research by request & approval of Board.
Activities: guided tours; lectures; films; temporary exhibitions; film shows. Museum Sponsors: Annual Historical Radio Conference.
Publications: annual review; quarterly journal, Old Timers Bulletin.
Hours & Admission Prices: May-Sept. Sat. 2-4, Sun. 2-5; other times by appointment. No charge; donations accepted. Closed Independence Day.
Attendance: 1,000 (estimated)
Membership: Annual: U.S. $20; Canada & Overseas $25.

Blue Mountain Lake

* **THE ADIRONDACK MUSEUM, (M),** Rt. 28 N. & 30, Blue Mountain Lake, NY 12812-0099. Mailing Address: P.O. Box 99, Blue Mountain Lake, NY 12812-0099. Tel.: 518-352-7311, ext. 114. Fax: 518-352-7021.
E-mail: cwelsh@adkmuseum.org
Web Site: www.adirondackmuseum.org
Founded: 1952.
Congressional District: 24
Key Personnel: Dir., Caroline M. Welsh; Chm., Kevin J. Arquit; Chief Cur., Laura S. Rice; Cur., Hallie Bond; Dir. Library, Jerold L. Pepper; Collections Mgr., Doreen Alessi; Dir. Finance, Mitchel Smith; Dir. Mktg., Susan Dineen; Dir. Institutional Advancement, Sarah Lewin; Membership Coord., Michelle Bashaw; Museum Shop Mgr., Victoria Sandiford; Human Resources Mgr., Colleen Bush Sage.
Personnel Profile: Full-Time Paid 30; Part-Time Paid 6; Part-Time Volunteers 21; Interns 5.
Governing Authority: nonprofit organization. Parent Institution: The Adirondack Historical Association. Tax-exempt: 501(c)(3).
Regional History & Art Museum.
Collections: regional lumbering & mining industries; transportation; boats; animal husbandry; agriculture; period furniture; fine art; period photographs; manuscripts; maps; films; oral histories; newspapers; tourism; decorative arts.
Major Exhibits: A Wild Unsettled Country - Early Reflections of the Adirondacks, 11/09-10/10; Common Threads: 150 Years of Adirondack Quilts and Comforters (T), 11/09-10/10; Let's Eat: Adirondack Food and Foodways, 5/10-10/11.
Research Fields: regional history; life & culture in Adirondacks; historical ecology; art history in the Adirondacks.

Facilities: research library consisting of books, pamphlets, maps, microfilms of newspapers, & photographs; cafe. Museum-related items for sale.
Activities: permanent & temporary exhibitions; research collections; school programs; continuing education programs; daily programs for children & families.
Publications: books; catalogues; monographs.
Hours & Admission Prices: Museum: Memorial Day to mid-Oct. daily 10-5. Adults $16, children 6-12 $8; discounts to groups of 15 or more, AAM & MANY members; children 5 & under no charge. Library: Mon.-Fri. 9-5 by appointment. ♿
Attendance: 69,080 (accurate)
Membership: Individual $35; Companion $65; Family $80.

Bolton Landing

BOLTON HISTORICAL MUSEUM, 4924 Main St., Bolton Landing, NY 12814. Mailing Address: P.O. Box 441, Bolton Landing, NY 12814-0441. Tel.: 518-644-9960.
Web Site: www.boltonhistorical.org
Personnel Profile: Part-Time Paid 2; Part-Time Volunteers 25.
Governing Authority: Parent Institution: The Historical Society of the Town of Bolton.
History Museum: housed in a former church; built in 1890.
Collections: local history & culture; photographs; harvesting & farm equipment; clothing; personal artifacts.
Hours & Admission Prices: Call for hours.

MARCELLA SEMBRICH OPERA MUSEUM, 4800 Lake Shore Dr. (Rte. 9N), Bolton Landing, NY 12814. Mailing Address: P.O. Box 417, Bolton Landing, NY 12814-0417. Tel.: 518-644-2431. Fax: 518-644-9831.
E-mail: sembrich@verizon.net
Web Site: www.operamuseum.org
Founded: 1937.
Congressional District: 20
Key Personnel: Pres., William Hubert; Vice Pres., Lisa Hall; Sec., Jane Caldwell; Admin., Faith Bouchard; Artistic Dir., Richard Wargo.
Personnel Profile: Full-Time Paid 3; Part-Time Paid 2; Part-Time Volunteers 30.
Governing Authority: nonprofit organization. Parent Institution: Marcella Sembrich Memorial Association, Inc., P.O. Box 417, Bolton Landing, NY 12814, 518-644-2431. Tax-exempt: 501(c)(3).
Opera Museum & Historic Building: 1923 The Sembrich Studio, former teaching studio of Madame Marcella Sembrich, opera singer, teacher & director of the vocal departments at the Curtis Institute & the Juilliard School.
Collections: art objects, furniture, books, paintings, scores, costumes, photographs representative of the Golden Age of Opera, c.1877-1935; awards, trophies & plaques given to Madame Sembrich; opera history during the life & career period of Marcella Sembrich's lifetime.
Research Fields: opera; singing.
Facilities: 1,000-vol. library of operatic history, collection of material such as contracts, letters, reviews, available for study by scholars upon request. Biography, cassette, musical scores & CD recordings of Madame Sembrich, and postcards & books for sale.
Activities: guided tours; concerts in museum & the Lake George area; musical programs; permanent exhibitions; lectures.
Publications: biannual newsletter; book, A Recollection of Marcella Sembrich.
Hours & Admission Prices: June 15-Sept. 15 daily 10-12:30 & 2-5:30; May & Oct. by appointment. No charge; donations accepted. ♿
Attendance: 2,000 (accurate)
Membership: Individual $35; Sustaining $50; Patron $100; Benefactor $500.

Brewster

SOUTHEAST MUSEUM ASSOCIATION, INC., 67 Main St., Brewster, NY 10509-1416. Tel.: 845-279-7500. Fax: 845-279-1992.
E-mail: sem@bestweb.net
Web Site: www.southeastmuseum.org
Founded: 1963.
Congressional District: 19
Key Personnel: Exec. Dir., Amy Campanaro; Pres. (V), Elizabeth Ryder; Cur., Joan Crawford; Museum Shop Mgr., Eleanor Keefe.
Personnel Profile: Full-Time Paid 2; Part-Time Paid 4; Part-Time Volunteers 30.
Governing Authority: nonprofit organization. Tax-exempt: 501(c)(3).
Historical Museum.
Collections: McLane Railroad Exhibit of the History of the Harlem Line; Trainer collection of minerals; Borden Condensed Milk Factory collection; costume & quilt collection; local historical memorabilia illustrating economic & social history from 19th-century to the present; early circus items; large 19th-century barn implement & tool collection.
Research Fields: Croton water system; Tilly Foster Mines; local circus history; Harlem Railroad; local Borden's Milk Condensary.
Facilities: photographs, document slides available to researchers by appointment.
Activities: guided tours; permanent & changing exhibits; lectures; family programs & workshops; films.
Publications: newsletter, Southeast Sentinel; booklet accompanying permanent & temporary exhibits.
Hours & Admission Prices: April-Dec. Tues.-Sat. 10-4. No charge; donations accepted.
Attendance: 4,500 (estimated)
Membership: Senior Citizen $15; Individual $25; Family $35; Friend $50; Contributing $100; Sponsor $250; Supporter $500; Patron $1,000; Sustainer $3,000; Benefactor $5,000.

Bridgehampton

BRIDGEHAMPTON HISTORICAL SOCIETY, 2368 Main St. & Corwith Ave., Bridgehampton, NY 11932-0977. Mailing Address: P.O. Box 977, Bridgehampton, NY 11932-0977. Tel.: 631-537-1088. Fax: 631-537-4225.
E-mail: bhhs@optonline.net
Web Site: www.bridgehamptonhistoricalsociety.org
Founded: 1956.
Congressional District: 1
Key Personnel: Exec. Dir., John Eilertsen; Pres., Gerrit Vreeland.
Personnel Profile: Full-Time Paid 1; Full-Time Volunteers 1; Part-Time Paid 1; Part-Time Volunteers 12.
Governing Authority: private; nonprofit organization. Tax-exempt: 501(c)(3) & 170(b).
General Museum.
Collections: period furniture; agriculture; costumes; tools; archival material; Hildreth Machine Shop with antique engines & early farm machines. Historic Houses: Corwith House c.1840; wheelwright shop c.1872; jail c.1902.
Research Fields: local history.
Facilities: library of local history books and records available for research in reading room.
Activities: guided tours; permanent exhibitions; annual fair; special changing exhibits each summer; Road Rallye, Engine Run.
Publications: annual magazine, The Bridge; newsletter.
Hours & Admission Prices: March-May & mid-Sept. to Dec. Mon.-Fri. 9-3; June to mid-Sept. Mon.-Fri. 10-3; other times by appointment. Admission $1. ♿
Attendance: 5,000 (accurate)
Membership: Contributing $25; Sustaining $50; Patron $100-$499; Benefactor $500 & up.

CHILDREN'S MUSEUM OF THE EAST END, 376 Bridgehampton/Sag Harbor Turnpike, Bridgehampton, NY 11932. Mailing Address: P.O. Box 316, Bridgehampton, NY 11932-0316. Tel.: 631-537-8250. Fax: 631-537-2413.
E-mail: steve@cmee.org
Web Site: www.cmee.org
Founded: 1997.
Key Personnel: Dir., Steve Long.
Personnel Profile: Full-Time Paid 6; Part-Time Paid 4; Part-Time Volunteers 5.
Governing Authority: Tax-exempt: 501(c)(3).
Children's Museum.
Collections: hands-on exhibits.
Activities: summer programs; classes; workshops; birthday parties.
Hours & Admission Prices: Mon. & Wed.-Sat. 9-5, Sun. 10-5; groups by appointment. Admission $7; children under one no charge. ♿
Membership: CMEE Be Happy 1 $60; CMEE Be Happy 2 $75; CMEE Be Grand $95; CMEE Be Delighted $125; CMEE Jump for Joy $250; CMEE Sponsor $750; CMEE Visionary $2.500; CMEE Corporate Circle $10,000.

Brockport

TOWER FINE ARTS GALLERY (SUNY BROCKPORT), (M), Tower Fine Arts Bldg., 180 Holley St., Brockport, NY 14420-2985. Mailing Address: 350 New Campus Dr., Brockport, NY 14420-2985. Tel.: 585-395-2805. Fax: 585-395-2588.
E-mail: tmassey@brockport.edu
Web Site: www.brockport.edu/finearts/
Founded: 1964.
Congressional District: 32
Key Personnel: Chm., Phyllis Kloda; Dir., Timothy Massey.
Personnel Profile: Part-Time Paid 4.
Governing Authority: university; nonprofit organization. Parent Institution: SUNY College at Brockport. Tax-exempt.
Art Museum.

Collections: works of E.E. Cummings.
Facilities: 1,900 sq. ft. exhibit space.
Activities: arts festivals; lectures; training programs for professional museum workers.
Publications: exhibit catalogs.
Hours & Admission Prices: Academic Year: Mon.-Fri. 10-5, Sun. 1-4. No charge. ♿
Attendance: 6,000 (estimated)

Bronx

BARTOW-PELL MANSION MUSEUM, CARRIAGE HOUSE & GARDENS, 895 Shore Rd., Pelham Bay Park, Bronx, NY 10464-1030. Tel.: 718-885-1461. Fax: 718-885-9164.
E-mail: info@bpmm.org
Web Site: www.bartowpellmansionmuseum.org
Founded: 1914.
Congressional District: 19
Key Personnel: Pres., Regina Gallagher; Exec. Dir., Ellen Bruzelius; Site Mgr., Mary Ellen Williamson; Mgr. Education, Jennifer Pollick; Dir. Garden, Frazier Holloway.
Personnel Profile: Full-Time Paid 1; Part-Time Paid 6; Part-Time Volunteers 100; Interns 2.
Governing Authority: trustees of Bartow-Pell Landmark Fund. Parent Institution: International Garden Club, Inc. Tax-exempt: 501(c)(3).
Historic House Museum: 1842-1888 Bartow-Pell Mansion, Greek-Revival mansion.
Collections: c. 1842 Greek revival house; Empire period furnishings; paintings; c.1915 formal garden designed by Delano & Aldrich; carriage house & gardens.
Research Fields: Empire period furniture; accessories; preservation; gardens; Greek revival architecture; colonial history of Pelham Manor; development of Pelham Bay Park area of Bronx.
Facilities: 500-vol. library of books on architecture, gardening & herbs.
Activities: luncheon & tea tours; lectures; permanent exhibitions; concerts; demonstrations; public programs for adults & families; summer tunes for kids. Annual Events: Candlelight Tour; Harvest Festival.
Publications: quarterly newsletter.
Hours & Admission Prices: Wed. & Sat.-Sun. 12-4. Adults $5, seniors & students $3; discounts for AAM & ICOM members & groups; children under 6 & members no charge. Closed New Year's Eve & Day; Easter; Thanksgiving weekend; Christmas.
Attendance: 15,000 (estimated)
Membership: Friend $40; Associate $80; Family Friend $100; Heritage Individual $180; Heritage Family $300; Bartow Pell Society $500; Conservation Society $1,000; Leadership Circle $3,500.

THE BRONX COUNTY HISTORICAL SOCIETY, 3309 Bainbridge Ave., Bronx, NY 10467-2850. Tel.: 718-881-8900. Fax: 718-881-4827.
E-mail: agreene@bronxhistoricalsociety.org
Web Site: www.bronxhistoricalsociety.org
Founded: 1897.
Congressional District: 7, 8, 16 & 17
Key Personnel: Exec. Dir., Dr. Gary D. Hermalyn; Pres. (V), Jacqueline Kutner; Cur. & Mgr. Edgar Allan Poe Cottage, Kathleen A. McAuley; Assoc. Librarian, Laura Tosi; Archivist, Dr. Peter Derrick; Valentine-Varian House Mgr., Marcus Hickman; Dir. Education, Anthony Greene; Education Outreach, Daniel Richards; Historian, Prof. Lloyd Ultan; Researcher, Dr. Stephen Stertz; Journal Editor, Dr. Elizabeth Beirne; Bronx African American Project, Dr. Brian Purnell.
Personnel Profile: Full-Time Paid 12; Full-Time Volunteers 5; Part-Time Paid 10; Part-Time Volunteers 7; Interns 2.
Governing Authority: nonprofit organization. Branch Museum: Edgar Allan Poe Cottage; Museum of Bronx History. Tax-exempt: 501(c)(3).
Historical Society.
Collections: items pertaining to the Bronx, New York City & Westchester from 1639-present.
Research Fields: social, colonial & urban history & geography.
Facilities: library pertaining to history for inter-library & public use; The Bronx County Archives. Books for sale.
Activities: guided tours; lectures; films; concerts; dance recitals; arts festivals; theater; expeditions, commemorations & conferences; study clubs; broadcast programs; organized education programs for children & adults; docent program; organized education programs for undergraduate or graduate college students; training programs for professional museum workers; participatory, loan & traveling exhibitions; temporary exhibitions of your own collections.
Publications: books, Geography: The Earth, The Poles & NYC; The Bronx Cookbook; The Hudson River; NYC at the Turn of the Century; biannual journal; books, History In Asphalt: The Origin of Bronx Street & Place Names Encyclopedia: The Study and Writing of History; The Beautiful Bronx, The Bronx in the Innocent Years; McNamara's Old Bronx; Elected Public Officials of the Bronx since 1898; Signers of the U.S. Constitution; Signers of The Declaration of Independence; Presidents of the U.S.; Chief Justices of the Supreme Court; Historic Landmarks & Districts; The First Public High Schools of NYC; The Bronx: It Was Only Yesterday; Morris High School and the Creation of the New York City Public High School System; 1st Senate of the U.S.; 1st House of Representatives and the Bill of Rights; The Centennial of Greater New York; Poems & Tales of Edgar Allan Poe at Fordham; Time & the Calendar; Bronx Views: Postcards of the Bronx; Documents of the Bronx; The Student Writing of History; Yankee Stadium, The Bronx Then & Now.
Hours & Admission Prices: Mon.-Fri. 9-5, Sat. 10-4, Sun. 1-5. Adults $5, senior citizens, children & students $3; discounts to AAM members; members no charge. ♿
Attendance: 85,000 (estimated)
Membership: Student & Senior Citizen $20; Individual, Nonprofit & Libraries $25; Family $35; Sustaining $100; Business & Fellow $250; Benefactor $2,500; Patron $5,000.

THE BRONX MUSEUM OF THE ARTS, 1040 Grand Concourse, Bronx, NY 10456-3901. Tel.: 718-681-6000. Fax: 718-681-6181.
E-mail: info@bronxmuseum.org
Web Site: www.bronxmuseum.org
Founded: 1971.
Congressional District: 21
Key Personnel: Chm., R. Douglas Rice; Exec. Dir., Holly Block; Acting Dir. Programs, Sergio Bessa; Dir. Finance, Gregory M. Castro, III; Dir. Devel., Yvonne Garcia.
Personnel Profile: Full-Time Paid 20; Part-Time Paid 6; Part-Time Volunteers 2; Interns 2.
Governing Authority: nonprofit organization. Tax-exempt.
Art Museum.
Collections: modern & contemporary works by artists of African, Latin American & Asian descent.
Research Fields: Bronx history; contemporary art; local artists; Latino & Latin American artists; African-American art; Asian American art.
Activities: formally organized education programs; internship program; film programs; curatorial & administrative apprenticeships; temporary & traveling exhibitions; demonstrations; gallery talks; live concert series; art festivals; special events.
Publications: catalogs of exhibitions; educational workbooks; brochures; gallery guides.
Hours & Admission Prices: Thurs.-Sun. 11-6. Adults $5, students & seniors $3; members & children under 12 no charge. Closed New Year's Day; Thanksgiving; Christmas. ♿
Attendance: 14,971 (accurate)
Membership: Student & Senior Citizen $25; Individual $35; Family & Joint $50; Sustaining $100; Associate $250; Patron $500; Benefactor $1,000; Major Donor $2,500.

BRONX ZOO, 2300 Southern Blvd., Bronx, NY 10460-1090. Tel.: 718-220-5100. Fax: 718-220-2685.
E-mail: PR@wcs.org
Web Site: www.wcs.org
Founded: 1895.
Congressional District: 10
Key Personnel: Pres. & C.E.O., Steven Sanderson; Dir. Operations, Ken Hutchinson; Vice Pres. Business Svcs., Robert Moskovitz; Sr. Vice Pres. & Gen. Dir. Living Institutions, Wildlife Conservation Society, Dr. Robert Cook; Exec. Vice Pres. & C.F.O., Patricia Calabrese.
Personnel Profile: Full-Time Paid 700; Part-Time Paid 675; Part-Time Volunteers 275; Interns 20.
Governing Authority: society. Parent Institution: The Wildlife Conservation Society. Tax exempt: 501(c)(3).
Zoo.
Collections: birds; mammals; reptiles; amphibians; invertebrates.
Research Fields: ornithology; herpetology; mammalogy; natural history; animal behavior; reproductive biology.
Facilities: library by appointment or interlibrary loan. Museum-related items for sale.
Activities: guided tours; lectures; films; formally organized education programs; permanent & occasional temporary exhibitions.
Publications: bimonthly magazine, Wildlife Conservation; book; annual report; map.
Hours & Admission Prices: Zoo: April-Oct. Mon.-Fri. 10-5, Sat.-Sun. & holidays 10-5:30; Nov.-March 10-4:30. Call for rates; discounts to AAA members; members, children under 2, & Wed. no charge. Additional fees for some exhibits & rides. ♿
Attendance: 1,932,638 (accurate)
Membership: Wildlife Conservation Society: Senior $60; Senior Individual

Premium $72; Individual $75; Individual Premium $90; Senior Family $96; Family $120; Family Premium $150; Conservation Supporter $250; Conservation Fellow $500; Conservation Partner $750; Annual Patron $1,500.

CITY ISLAND NAUTICAL MUSEUM, City Island, 190 Fordham St., Bronx, NY 10464. Mailing Address: P.O. Box 82, Bronx, NY 10464-0082. Tel.: 718-885-0008 & 0507. Fax: 718-885-0507.
E-mail: cihs@cityislandmuseum.org
Web Site: www.cityislandmuseum.org
Founded: 1964.
Congressional District: 10
Key Personnel: Pres., Edward Sadler; Vice Pres. & Cur., Tom Nye; Chm. (V), Dr. Fred Hess; Treas., Carol Stewart; Vice Pres., Barbara Dolensek; Sec., Russell Schaller; Museum Shop Mgr., Barbara Hoffman; Docent, Christopher McGowan.
Personnel Profile: Part-Time Volunteers 12.
Governing Authority: nonprofit organization. Parent Institution: City Island Historical Society Inc., City Island, P.O. Box 82, The Bronx, NY 10464. Tax-exempt.
Nautical Historical Museum: housed in 1897-98, P.S. 17, one of the first school buildings built in the Bronx.
Collections: paintings, photographs, artifacts, documents and memorabilia from Indian times to the present, with special emphasis on the part played by City Island in the yachting industry and the America's Cup Races and the Hell Gate Pilots, archaeological collections.
Research Fields: local history both land and nautical.
Facilities: 700-vol. library on local history available for use on premises.
Activities: guided tours; lectures; films; formally organized education programs; permanent & temporary exhibitions.
Publications: newsletter; informative brochure.
Hours & Admission Prices: Sat. & Sun. 1-5 or by special appointment. No charge; donations accepted. ♿
Attendance: 1,500 (estimated)
Membership: Senior Citizen $10; Individual $20; Family $25.

EDGAR ALLAN POE COTTAGE, Poe Park, Grand Concourse at E. Kingsbridge Rd., Bronx, NY 10458. Mailing Address: Bronx County Historical Society, 3309 Bainbridge Ave., Bronx, NY 10467-2840. Tel.: 718-881-8900. Fax: 718-881-4827.
E-mail: kmcauley@bronxhistoricalsociety.org
Web Site: www.bronxhistoricalsociety.org
Founded: 1955.
Key Personnel: C.E.O., Dr. Gary Hermalyn; Pres. (V), Jacqueline Kutner; Cur., Kathleen A. McAuley.
Personnel Profile: Full-Time Paid 4; Part-Time Paid 7; Part-Time Volunteers 10.
Governing Authority: nonprofit historical & preservation society. Parent Institutions: Bronx County Historical Society; The Historic House Trust of New York City, The Arsenal, Room 203, Central Park, New York, NY 10465; New York City Dept. of Parks & Recreation. Tax-exempt.
Historic House: housed in the former residence of poet Edgar Allen Poe; built in 1812.
Collections: 19th-century furnishings; paintings & sculptured portraits of Poe; photographs; drawings.
Research Fields: Edgar Allan Poe's life, particularly his final years, 1846-1849.
Activities: film presentation; guided tours.
Publications: semiannual journal, Bronx County Historical Society; annual books & booklets.
Hours & Admission Prices: Mon.-Fri. 9-5, Sat. 10-4, Sun. 1-5; group tours by appointment. Adults $5, seniors, students & children $3; members & Historic House Trust of NYC members no charge.
Attendance: 30,350 (estimated)
Membership: Student & Senior $20; Individual $25; Family $35; Sustaining $100; Fellow $250.

THE HALL OF FAME FOR GREAT AMERICANS, Bronx Community College, 2155 University Ave., Bronx, NY 10453-2804. Tel.: 718-289-5161. Fax: 718-289-6496.
Web Site: www.bcc.cuny.edu/halloffame
Founded: 1900.
Congressional District: 22
Key Personnel: Co Dir., Susan Zuckerman; Co Dir., Art Zuckerman.
Governing Authority: Trustees of The Hall of Fame for Great Americans; affiliated with Bronx Community College of the City University of NY. Tax-exempt.
Art & History Museum.
Collections: 98 original bronzes of notable Americans in the arts, sciences, humanities, government, business & labor, elected by a College of Electors.
Research Fields: American history; biography; sculpture; American architecture designed by Stanford White.
Facilities: outdoor columned arcade for display of sculptures.
Activities: guided tours plus video introduction.
Publications: brochure; tour guide.
Hours & Admission Prices: Daily 10-5. No charge; donations accepted.
Attendance: 25,000

LEHMAN COLLEGE ART GALLERY, (M), 250 Bedford Park Blvd. W., Bronx, NY 10468-1589. Tel.: 718-960-8731. Fax: 718-960-6991.
E-mail: susan@lehman.cuny.edu
Web Site: www.lehman.edu/gallery
Founded: 1984.
Congressional District: 19
Key Personnel: Dir., Susan Hoeltzel; Chm., Elisabeth Lorin; Devel. Assoc., Mary Ann Siano.
Personnel Profile: Full-Time Paid 3; Part-Time Paid 3; Part-Time Volunteers 10; Interns 5.
Governing Authority: nonprofit organization. Tax-exempt: 501(c)(3).
College Art Museum.
Collections: works by contemporary artists.
Major Exhibits: After Nature: Flora & Fauna, 2/10-5/10; State of Ku Dao, 2/10-5/10; Chance Predictions, 9/10-12/10.
Facilities: educational facilities.
Activities: guided tours; lectures; films; organized education programs for children; docent program; participatory & loan exhibitions.
Publications: exhibition notes; catalogues; teacher guides.
Hours & Admission Prices: June-Aug. open by appointment; Sept.-June Tues.-Sat. 10-4. No charge. ♿
Attendance: 22,000 (estimated)
Membership: Senior & Student $20; Individual $30; Dual Family $50; Supporting $100; Sustaining $250; Sponsor $500; Benefactor $1,000.

MARITIME INDUSTRY MUSEUM AT FORT SCHUYLER, (M), 6 Pennyfield Ave., Bronx, NY 10465-4127. Tel.: 718-409-7218. Fax: 718-409-6130.
E-mail: maritimeindustry@sunymaritime.edu
Web Site: sunymaritime.edu/maritime museum
Founded: 1986.
Key Personnel: Dir., Capt. Eric J. Johansson; Chm., Capt. James J. McNamara; Treas., Harold A. Parnham; Cur., William Sokol, Jr.
Personnel Profile: Full-Time Paid 1; Part-Time Paid 2; Part-Time Volunteers 10.
Governing Authority: nonprofit.
Maritime Museum.
Collections: over 250 ship models; Tufnell watercolor; Frank Cronican models; Maritime College history; Works Project Act (WPA) art; Ocean Liner; Victory & Liberty Ship; Robert G. Herbert ship models; Louis Weickum art; SS United States; Morro Castle; navigation instruments; underwater sea; Brooklyn Navy Yard diorama; evolution of seafaring.
Facilities: library; 7,000 sq. ft. exhibit space. Museum-related items for sale.
Activities: formal education programs for Maritime College students; guided tours; lectures; loan & participatory exhibits.
Publications: newsletter, Voyage Abstract.
Hours & Admission Prices: Mon.-Sat. 9-4. No charge; donations accepted. ♿
Attendance: 10,000 (estimated)
Membership: Senior $20; Regular $30; Chief Mate's Club $100; Captain's Club $200; Admiral Life $1,000.

* **THE NEW YORK BOTANICAL GARDEN, (M),** Bronx River Pkwy. & Fordham Rd., Bronx, NY 10458. Mailing Address: 2900 Southern Blvd., Bronx, NY 10458-5153. Tel.: 718-817-8700. Fax: 718-220-6504.
E-mail: pubrel@nybg.org
Web Site: www.nybg.org
Founded: 1891.
Congressional District: 18
Key Personnel: Chm. Bd. (V), Wilson Nolen; C.E.O. & Pres., Gregory R. Long; C.O.O., J.V. Cossaboom; Dean & Vice Pres. Science, Dr. James Miller; Vice Pres. Laboratory Science, Dr. Dennis W. Stevenson; Vice Pres. Institute of Economic Botany, Dr. Michael J. Balick; Vice Pres. Garden Retail & Business Devel., Catherine Hipp; Assoc. Vice Pres. Mktg., Marisa Biehl; Vice Pres. Corporate & Foundation Rels., Mercia Weyand; Dir. Herbarium, Dr. Barbara M. Thiers; Vice Pres. Mktg., Business Devel. & Visitor Experience, Claudia Keenan Hough; Cur., Dr. Scott A. Mori; Cur., Dr. Christine Padoch; Cur., Dr. William R. Buck; Vice Pres. Communications, Karl F. Lauby; Dir. Retail Operations, Richard M. Pickett; Dir. Museum Shop, Margaret Csala.
Personnel Profile: Full-Time Paid 422; Part-Time Paid 65; Part-Time Volunteers 1,090; Interns 64.

Governing Authority: nonprofit corporation. Educational affiliation with Lehman College of City University of New York, New York University, Cornell University, Columbia University & Yale University. Tax-exempt: 501(c)(3).
Botanical Garden & Nature Center.
Collections: 250 acres including comprehensive tree & shrub collections, specialized garden & conservatory collections of tropical & subtropical plants; manuscripts & photo collection; 7.2 million specimens in herbarium; 1,000,000 items in the LuEsther T. Mertz Library; stock culture collection of micro-organisms, principally basidiomycetes; native woodland; horticultural exhibits; 50 gardens; plant collections. Historical Landmarks: 250-acre site (national landmark); Enid A. Haupt Conservatory (NYC landmark); 1840 Shuff Mill.
Research Fields: floras & monographs, including flowering plants, ferns, fungi, mosses, plant ecology; plant geography, plant nutrition, physiology & pathology of fungi; plant-insect relationships; plant evolution; problems concerned with diseases & pests of ornamental plants; economic botany; ecosystem studies; urban horticulture; molecular systematics studies & plant genomics.
Facilities: 375,000-vol. library plus over one million non-book items on botanical art, photos, manuscripts, archives, Lord & Burnham architectural plans, seed & nursery catalogs available for public reference; research laboratories; reading room. Books & publications relating to botany & gardening and botanical & plant-related items for sale.
Activities: guided tours; lectures; concerts; workshops; formal education programs for adults & school children; permanent & temporary exhibitions; horticultural therapy training; School of Professional Horticulture two-year New York state licensed program; post-secondary work-study program; symposia for plant professionals.
Publications: field notes; Garden News; serials, Botanical Review; Brittonia; Economic Botany; monographs, Memoirs of New York Botanical Garden; North American Flora; Advances in Economic Botany; Flora Neotropica; reprint series & books.
Hours & Admission Prices: Grounds: April-Oct. Tues.-Sun. 10-6; Nov.-March Tues.-Sun. 10-5. Garden: adults $6, senior citizens & students $3, children 2-12 $1; discounts to AAM members; members no charge. Combo: adults $20, seniors $18, children 2-12 $8. Parking: $12 per vehicle. ♿
Attendance: 800,000 (accurate)
Membership: Individual $75; Dual $100; Family $120; Supporting $250; Contributing $600; Sustaining $1,000; discounts to seniors.

NEW YORK YANKEES MUSEUM, One E. 161st St., Bronx, NY 10451-2100. Tel.: 646-9778687.
Key Personnel: Cur., Brian Richards
Baseball Museum.
Collections: baseball & franchise history; personal artifacts; photographs; baseball memorabilia; monuments.
Facilities: Museum-related items for sale.
Hours & Admission Prices: Museum: Game Day - from the time the gates open until the end of the 8th inning. No charge. Non-Game Days: museum access is part of the Yankee Stadium tour. Yankee Stadium Tours: May-Sept. call for hours. Tours: adults $20, children 14 & under and seniors 60 & over $15.

VALENTINE-VARIAN HOUSE/MUSEUM OF BRONX HISTORY, Varian House Park, 3266 Bainbridge Ave. at E. 208th St., Bronx, NY 10467. Mailing Address: Bronx County Historical Society, 3309 Bainbridge Ave., Bronx, NY 10467-2850. Tel.: 718-881-8900. Fax: 718-881-4827.
E-mail: kmcauley@bronxhistoricalsociety.org
Web Site: www.bronxhistoricalsociety.org
Founded: 1955.
Congressional District: 16 & 17
Key Personnel: Exec. Dir., Dr. Gary D. Hermalyn; Pres. (V), Jacqueline Kutner; Cur., Kathleen McAuley; Education Coord., Anthony Greene.
Personnel Profile: Full-Time Paid 4; Part-Time Paid 7; Part-Time Volunteers 10.
Governing Authority: nonprofit historical & preservation society. Parent Institution: Bronx County Historical Society. Tax-exempt.
Historical House: second oldest house in the Bronx built by Isaac Valentine in 1758; sold to Isaac Varian in 1792; residence of former New York City mayor Isaac Varian, Jr., 1839-1841.
Collections: 18th-19th century furnishings; domestic artifacts; herb garden; monument.
Research Fields: New York City history, colonial period through 20th-century.
Facilities: herb garden.
Activities: guided tours.
Publications: semi-annual journal, Bronx County Historical Society; annual books & booklets; maps.
Hours & Admission Prices: Sat. 10-4, Sun. 1-5, Mon.-Fri. tours by appointment. Adults $3, seniors, students & children $2; members & Historic House Trust of NYC no charge.
Attendance: 50,228 (estimated)
Membership: Student & Senior $20; Individual $25; Non-profile & Libraries $30; Family $35; Sustaining $100; Fellow & Corporate $250; Benefactor $2,500; Patron $5,000.

VAN CORTLANDT HOUSE MUSEUM, Van Cortlandt Park, Broadway at 246th St., Bronx, NY 10471. Mailing Address: 6393 Broadway, Bronx, NY 10471-2798. Tel.: 718-543-3344. Fax: 718-543-3315. TDD: 800-281-5722.
E-mail: info@vancortlandhouse.org
Web Site: www.vancortlandhouse.org
Founded: 1896.
Congressional District: 15
Key Personnel: Dir., Laura Carpenter; Pres., Ann Crawford; Museum Shop Mgr., Juana Vasquez.
Personnel Profile: Full-Time Paid 2; Part-Time Paid 2; Part-Time Volunteers 50.
Governing Authority: society. Parent Institution: National Society of Colonial Dames in the State of New York. Tax-exempt: 501(c)(3).
Historic House: c.1748 house built by Frederick Van Cortlandt.
Collections: 17th- & 18th-century decorative & useful arts.
Research Fields: 18th-century social history; decorative arts; the American Colonial Revival.
Facilities: assembly room; Colonial Revival herb garden. Gift items for sale.
Activities: formal education programs for children; guided tours; lectures; living history demonstrations. Annual Event: Candlelight tours.
Publications: newsletter, To Absent Friends.
Hours & Admission Prices: Tues.-Fri. 10-3, Sat.-Sun. 11-4; groups by appointment. Adults $5, senior citizens & students $3; discounts to AAM members; children under 12, Wed. & members of Colonial Dames no charge. Closed major holidays.
Attendance: 8,600 (accurate)
Membership: Student & Senior $20; Friend $25; Family $35; Sustaining Friend $100; Sponsoring Friend $500.

WAVE HILL, W 249th St. & Independence Ave., Bronx, NY 10471-2899. Mailing Address: 675 W. 252nd St., Bronx, NY 10471-2899. Tel.: 718-549-3200. Fax: 718-884-8952.
E-mail: information@wavehill.org
Web Site: www.wavehill.org
Founded: 1965.
Congressional District: 17
Key Personnel: Exec. Dir. & Pres., Claudia Bonn; Chm. (V), Cathy Marks Weinroth; Deputy Dir., Michele Rossetti; Dir. Horticulture, Scott Canning; Dir. Education, Courtney White; Dir Visitor Svcs. & Museum Shop Mgr., Suzy Brown; Dir. Devel. & Public Rels., Kathryn Heinz; Cur. Visual Arts Program, Jennifer McGregor.
Personnel Profile: Full-Time Paid 40; Part-Time Paid 10; Part-Time Volunteers 100; Interns 50.
Governing Authority: nonprofit organization. Tax-exempt.
Nature Center.
Collections: cactus & succulents; tropical plants; herbs; aquatic garden; flower garden; arboretum; historic house.
Research Fields: horticulture; land management; inquiry-based education.
Facilities: gardens; greenhouse; conference room; 28-acre estate; 150-seat conference performing hall.
Activities: lectures; concerts; guided tours; school education programs in science & art; classes; workshops; visual & performing arts programs.
Publications: quarterly newsletter; trail & garden guides; exhibition catalogues.
Hours & Admission Prices: April 15-May & Aug.-Oct. 14 Tues.-Sun. 9-5:30; June-July Tues. & Thurs.-Sun. 9-5:30, Wed. 9-9; Oct. 15-April 14 Tues.-Sun. 9-4:30. Adults $6, seniors 65 & over and students $3; members, children under 6, Sat. 9-12 & Tues. no charge. Closed New Year's Day; Thanksgiving; Christmas.
Attendance: 110,000 (estimated)
Membership: Seniors 65 & over $35; Individual $40; Family & Dual $60; Supporting $125; Sponsor $250; Patron $500; Wave Hill Partners $1,000.

Bronxville

EASTCHESTER HISTORICAL SOCIETY - 1835 MARBLE SCHOOLHOUSE, 390 California Rd., Bronxville, NY 10708. Mailing Address: P.O. Box 37, Eastchester, NY 10709-0037. Tel.: 914-793-1900.
E-mail: marbleschoolhouse@yahoo.com
Founded: 1959.
Congressional District: 23
Key Personnel: Pres. (V), Sheila Marcotte.
Personnel Profile: Part-Time Volunteers 15.
Governing Authority: nonprofit. Tax-exempt: 501(c)(3).
Historical Society Museum: housed in c.1835 Marble School House & separate library building.

Collections: toys; 19th-century costumes; archives; photographs; furniture; manuscripts; 19th-century juvenile literature; costumes & textiles; school artifacts. Historic Building: restored c.1835 one-room school.
Research Fields: local history; St. Paul's National Historic Site; Eastchester history; genealogy.
Facilities: 6,000-vol. research library of general history of New York State, New York City, Westchester County & Eastchester; Mt. Vernon; Tuckahoe; Bronxville; juvenile literature of 19th century.
Activities: guided tours; lectures; films; formally organized education programs for children; inter-museum loan, temporary & traveling exhibitions; school loan service; 1881-1913 birth records.
Publications: books, Records of the Town of Eastchester, New York; Minutes of the Town of Eastchester; The Book of Strays & the Alteration of Roads; Overseers of the Poor; Minutes of the Trustees of Public Lands, Eastchester, New York; Town Property; Register of the Proceedings of St. Paul's Church at Eastchester; Burial Records of St. Paul's Church; military records of the town of Eastchester; Book of Births, Eastchester, New York 1881-1913.
Hours & Admission Prices: By appointment. Schoolhouse: adults $3; members no charge.
Attendance: 300 (estimated)
Membership: Regular $20; Sustaining $40; Business $50; Life $200.

Brooklyn

BRIC CONTEMPORARY ART, 33 Clinton St., Brooklyn, NY 11201-2706. Mailing Address: 647 Fulton St., Brooklyn, NY 11217-1139. Tel.: 718-875-4047, ext. 10. Fax: 718-488-0609.
E-mail: rotunda@briconline.org
Web Site: www.briconline.org/rotunda
Formerly: The Rotunda Gallery
Founded: 1981.
Congressional District: 13
Key Personnel: Dir., Elizabeth Ferrer; Chm. (V), Lizanne Fontaine.
Personnel Profile: Full-Time Paid 4; Part-Time Paid 2; Interns 2.
Governing Authority: not-for-profit organization. Parent Institution: BRIC Arts/Media/Brooklyn (formerly BRIC/Brooklyn Information & Culture). Tax-exempt.
Art Museum.
Collections: exhibits of work in all media focusing on emerging and mid-career Brooklyn-affiliated artists.
Major Exhibits: Artists from the Registry II, 11/09-12/09.
Research Fields: contemporary Brooklyn-affiliated artists.
Facilities: computerized slide registry of Brooklyn-affiliated artists; educational facilities.
Activities: educational school programs; Lori Ledis Emerging Curator program; training programs for Brooklyn-based visual artists.
Publications: exhibition catalogs.
Hours & Admission Prices: Tues.-Fri. 12-6, Sat. 12-5. No charge; donations accepted. ♿
Attendance: 12,000 (estimated)

BROOKLYN BOTANIC GARDEN, 1000 Washington Ave., Brooklyn, NY 11225-1099. Tel.: 718-623-7200. Fax: 718-857-2430.
E-mail: presidentsoffice@bbg.org
Web Site: www.bbg.org
Founded: 1910.
Congressional District: 13
Key Personnel: Chm. Bd., Frederick Bland; C.E.O. & Pres., Scott Medbury; Vice Pres. Mktg., Noreen Bradley; Dir. Emeritus, Elizabeth Scholtz; Vice Pres. Finance & C.F.O., Keith L. Stubblefield; Vice Pres. Science, Steven Clemants; Dir. Individual Giving & Corporate Sponsorship, Elizabeth Fallon Culp; Vice Pres. Devel., Leslie Findlen; Vice Pres. Education, Sharon Myrie; Dir. Library Svcs., Patricia Jonas; Dir. Children & Family Programs, Marilyn Smith; Dir. Security, Anthony Quarless; Dir. Capital Projects, Ralph Morgan; Dir. Continuing Education, Julie Warsowe; Dir. Government & Community Affairs, Bahia Ramos; Dir. Public Affairs, Leeann Lavin; Dir. Science, Gerry Moore; Dir. Program, BGCI (US), Dan Shepard; Dir. Computer Technology, Paul Turcotte; Dir. Institutional Funding, Kirsten Munro; Dir. Human Resources, Rochelle Cabiness; Dir. Horticulture, Jacqueline Fazio; Dir. Mktg., Marie Leahy; Dir. Facilities, Gerard Rudloff; Dir. Brooklyn Greenbridge, Ellen Kirby; Dir. Publishing, Janet Marinelli; Dir. Visitor Svcs. & Volunteers, Louis Cesario; Dir. Public Programs, Anita Jacobs; Dir. Major Gifts, Sarah Young.
Personnel Profile: Full-Time Paid 154; Part-Time Paid 96; Part-Time Volunteers 646; Interns 23.
Governing Authority: nonprofit organization. Tax-exempt.
Arboretum & Botanical Garden.
Collections: 14,000 different Taxa; Japanese Hill & Pond Garden; rock garden; herb garden; fragrance garden; local flora section; rose garden; Shakespeare garden; children's garden; dwarf conifer collection; special collections of rhododendrons, lilacs, cherries, magnolias, conifers, water lilies; conservatories containing tropical plants, cacti & succulents, bromeliads, ferns, bonsai, orchids; insectivorous plants; house plants; aquatic plants; trail of evolution.
Research Fields: plant taxonomy.
Facilities: 55,000-vol. library of botany; horticulture; science available for inter-library loan & for use on premises; separate laboratory operation; reading room; classrooms; herbarium; four classrooms & three teaching greenhouses; discovery center for children; Palm House for special events; exhibition gallery; house museum; 44,000 sq. ft. conservatory, children's garden; garden-produced documentary films on horticultural subject & slide shows available for purchase or rent. Plants, books, horticultural supplies & other museum-related items for sale.
Activities: guided tours; lectures; films; formally organized education programs; docent program; permanent & temporary exhibitions; plant information service; plant & disease identification service.
Publications: quarterly handbook, 21st Century Gardening Series; quarterly newsletter, P & G News; monograph, Brooklyn Botanic Garden Contributions, educational booklets for parents & teachers; gardening booklet & video for children & parents.
Hours & Admission Prices: Garden: Tues.-Fri. 8-4:30, Sat.-Sun. 10-4:30. Adults $8, seniors 65 & over and students 12 & over $4; children under 12, members, school groups, & Tues. no charge. ♿
Attendance: 685,000 (estimated)
Membership: Subscriber & Senior Citizen Individual $35; Individual $40; International Subscriber $45; Senior Citizen Family Dual $70; Family Dual $75; Family Dual Plus $95; Signature $150; Sponsor $300; Patron $500; Gager Society $1,500.

* **BROOKLYN CHILDREN'S MUSEUM, (M),** 145 Brooklyn Ave., Brooklyn, NY 11213-1900. Tel.: 718-735-4400. Fax: 718-604-7442. TDD: 718-735-4402.
Web Site: www.brooklynkids.org
Founded: 1899.
Congressional District: 12
Key Personnel: Pres., Carol Enseki; Chm., William Rifkin; Dir. Collections, Beth Alberty; Vice Pres. Programs, Paul Pearson.
Personnel Profile: Full-Time Paid 56; Full-Time Volunteers 1; Part-Time Paid 34; Interns 26.
Governing Authority: nonprofit organization. The Brooklyn Children's Museum Corp., 145 Brooklyn Ave., Brooklyn 11213. Tax-exempt: 170(b)(1)(A), 501(c)(3) & 509(a)(1).
General Children's Museum.
Collections: ethnology & natural history; folk crafts worldwide.
Major Exhibits: Top Secret: Mission Toy (T), 11/09-1/10; Tales from the Land of Gullah (T), 2/10-5/10; Children of Hangzhou (T), 6/10-9/10; Out on a Lamb (T), 10/10-1/11.
Facilities: children's library; outdoor theater; indoor theater; garden; cafe; party room; classrooms. Museum-related items for sale.
Activities: art, science & cultural interactions; inter-museum loan, permanent & temporary exhibitions; classes; public programs; school loan program of cultural history, natural history & science items.
Publications: educational materials; quarterly newsletter, annual report.
Hours & Admission Prices: July-Aug. Tues.-Sun. 10-5; Sept.-June Wed.-Fri. 12-5, Sat.-Sun. 10-5; holidays & school vacations 10-6. Adults $7.50; discounts to AAM, ASTC & ACM members; members no charge. ♿
Attendance: 250,000 (accurate)
Membership: Family Passport $75; City Traveler $125; World Explorer $275, add a grandparent/caregiver $15.

THE BROOKLYN HISTORICAL SOCIETY, 128 Pierrepont St., Brooklyn, NY 11201-2711. Tel.: 718-222-4111. Fax: 718-222-3794.
Web Site: www.brooklynhistory.org
Formerly: Long Island Historical Society
Founded: 1863.
Congressional District: 13
Key Personnel: Pres., Deborah Schwartz; Chm. (V), James Rossman; Vice Pres. Exhibits & Education, Kate Fermoile; Dir. Education, Andrea Del Valle; Dir. Finance & Operations, Jason Pietrangeli; Reference Librarian, Elizabeth Call; Museum Shop Mgr., Janice Monger.
Personnel Profile: Full-Time Paid 14; Part-Time Paid 5; Part-Time Volunteers 4; Interns 6.
Governing Authority: bd. trustees. Tax-exempt: 501(c)(3).
History Museum: housed in building designed by architect, George B. Post.
Collections: paintings, graphics, sculpture, photographs, costumes; books; manuscripts; ephemera. Historic 1881 Building: houses museum & library.
Major Exhibits: Pages of the Past: The Breukelen Adventures of Jasper Danckarts, 11/09-1/3/10.
Research Fields: Brooklyn history 16th-century to present.
Facilities: library of local history books.

Activities: lectures; walking & bus tours; family activities; genealogy workshops; school, after-school & summer programs; performances; readings; rental facilities.
Publications: newsletter; exhibition catalogs; Neighborhood History Guides.
Hours & Admission Prices: Wed.-Fri. & Sun. 12-5, Sat. 10-5. Adults $6, students & seniors $4; discounts to AAM members; members no charge. Closed New Year's Day; Independence Day; Thanksgiving; Christmas. ♿
Attendance: 15,000 (estimated)
Membership: Student, Senior Citizen & Teacher $35; Friend $50; Family & Partner $70; Advocate $125; Champion $275; Community Leader $550; President's Circle $1,500 & up.

* **BROOKLYN MUSEUM, (M),** 200 Eastern Pkwy., Brooklyn, NY 11238-6099. Tel.: 718-638-5000. Fax: 718-501-6300. TDD: 718-783-6501.
E-mail: information@brooklynmuseum.org
Web Site: www.brooklynmuseum.org
Formerly: Brooklyn Museum of Art
Founded: 1823.
Congressional District: 2
Key Personnel: Chm., Norman M. Feinberg; Dir., Arnold L. Lehman; Deputy Dir. Institutional Advancement, Cynthia Mayeda; Deputy Dir. Administration, Judith Frankfurt; Vice Chm., Norman M. Feinberg; Vice Chm., Barbara Manfrey Vogelstein; Vice Chm., Barbara Knowles Debs; Cur. American Painting & Sculpture, Teresa Carbone; Vice Dir. Devel., Judith Paska; Vice Dir. Operations, Frantz Vincent; Vice Dir. Planning & Architecture, Joan Darragh; Vice Dir. Merchandising, Sallie Stutz; Vice Dir. Finance & Administration, David Kleiser; Vice Dir. Education & Program, Radiah Harper; Chief Conservator & Vice Dir. Collections, Kenneth Moser; Government & Community Rels. Officer, Lavita McMath; Public Information Officer, Sally Williams; Publications & Editorial Svcs., James Leggio; Cur. Prints & Drawings, Marilyn Kushner; Cur. Contemporary Art, Charlotta Kotik; Cur. Arts of the Americas, Nancy Rosoff; Cur. Decorative Arts, Kevin Stayton; Chm. Egyptian, Classical & Ancient Middle Eastern Art, Richard Fazzini; Cur. Asian Art, Amy Poster; Cur. European Paintings & Sculpture, Elizabeth Easton; Cur. African & Oceanic Art, William Siegmann; Cur. Islamic Art, Aimee Froom; Chief Registrar, Liz Reynolds; Museum Shop Mgr., Kati Moran; Community Involvement Mgr., Schawannah Wright; Information Systems Mgr., Mathew Morgan; Community Committee Chair, Lynn Schiller; Head Librarian, Deirdre Lawrence; Volunteer Coord., Belle Tanenhaus.
Personnel Profile: Full-Time Paid 302; Part-Time Paid 52; Part-Time Volunteers 285; Interns 29.
Governing Authority: nonprofit corporation. Parent Institute: The Brooklyn Institute of Arts & Sciences. Subsidiary Institution: Brooklyn Museum Fund, Inc. Tax-exempt: 501(c)(3).
Art Museum.
Collections: ancient Egyptian art, predynastic through Coptic; Greek & Roman art; Islamic & pre-Islamic Middle Eastern art; Asian art; pre-Columbian Central & South American collections; American Indian collections; art of Africa & of the Pacific; European & American prints, drawings & photographs; 27 American period rooms 1675-1930; American & European decorative arts; costumes & textiles; American paintings & sculpture, colonial to contemporary; European paintings & sculpture medieval to 20th century; contemporary paintings & sculpture; outdoor sculpture garden.
Research Fields: collection-related research; archaeological expeditions to Egypt.
Facilities: 125,000-vol. library of art reference, featuring art history books; periodicals and the Wilbour Library of Egyptology; reading room; newly renovated Schapiro Wing provides an additional 30,000 sq. ft. of gallery space; museum cafe; 460-seat Iris & B. Gerald Cantor Auditorium. Books, international folk art & exclusive items based on designs from the museum's collection for sale.
Activities: guided tours; lectures; films; gallery talks; concerts; dance recitals; arts festivals; formally organized education programs; curatorial & technician apprenticeships; Wilbour fellowships in Egyptology; permanent & temporary exhibitions.
Publications: handbooks; guides to various collections; Wilbour monographs on ancient art; catalogs of major exhibitions.
Hours & Admission Prices: Wed.-Fri. 10-5, Sat.-Sun. 11-6, first Sat. every month 11-11. Suggested Donations: adults $10, students & senior citizens $6; discounts to AAM & ICOM members; members no charge. Closed New Year's Day; Thanksgiving; Christmas. ♿
Attendance: 325,501 (accurate)
Membership: Artist & Student $45; Individual $55; Family & Household $85; Contributor $150; Patron $350; Donor $600; Fellow $1,000; Director's Circle $2,500; Benefactor's Circle $5,000.

CONEY ISLAND MUSEUM, 1208 Surf Ave., Brooklyn, NY 11224-2816. Tel.: 718-372-5159. Fax: 718-372-5101.
E-mail: info@coneyisland.com
Web Site: www.coneyisland.com/museum.shtml
Key Personnel: Museum Dir., Aaron Beebe; Mng. Dir., David Gratt
History Museum.
Collections: history of Coney Island; the Steeplechase horse; boardwalk rolling chair; Funhouse distortion mirrors; period souvenirs & bumping cars.
Facilities: Museum-related items for sale.
Activities: lectures; films; walking tours; private parties; rental facilities; research; weddings.
Hours & Admission Prices: Sat.-Sun. 12-5. Admission $.99.

FRANKLIN FURNACE ARCHIVE, INC., 80 Arts-The James E. Davis Arts Building, 80 Hanson Pl., #301, Brooklyn, NY 11217-1506. Tel.: 718-398-7255. Fax: 718-398-7256.
E-mail: mail@franklinfurnace.org
Web Site: www.franklinfurnace.org
Founded: 1976.
Congressional District: 10
Key Personnel: C.E.O. & Dir., Martha Wilson; Admin., Harley Spiller; Program Coord., Angel Nevarez; Archivist, Michael Katchen.
Personnel Profile: Full-Time Paid 2; Part-Time Paid 2; Interns 50.
Governing Authority: nonprofit organization. Tax-exempt.
Art Museum.
Collections: installation & performance art documentation.
Research Fields: artists' publishing from 1900 to present; performance art.
Activities: multimedia performance art presentations; showing time based arts.
Publications: biannual calendar; CD-ROMs.
Hours & Admission Prices: Mon.-Fri. 10-6. No charge.
Membership: By and By $33 & under; Bright Tomorrow $66 & up; In The Offing $99 & up; Happily Ever After $333 & up; For All Posterity $999 & up; Eternity & Beyond $33,000.

HARBOR DEFENSE MUSEUM, Harbor Defense Museum of Fort Hamilton, 230 Sheridan Loop, Brooklyn, NY 11252-9523. Tel.: 718-630-4349. Fax: 718-630-4888.
E-mail: info@harbordefensemuseum
Web Site: www.harbordefensemuseum.com
Founded: 1980.
Congressional District: 14
Key Personnel: Dir., Paul Morando.
Personnel Profile: Full-Time Paid 2; Part-Time Volunteers 23.
Governing Authority: federal. Parent Institution: Department of Defense. Subsidiary Institution: United States Army. Tax-exempt.
Military Museum: housed in 1825-1831 Fort Hamilton.
Collections: 17th-century to present U.S. military; coast defense 1800-1950; artifacts reflecting Lt. Col. Rodman's career; artifacts, models, images & dioramas detailing New York's harbor defenses including an original Pattern 1844, 24-pounder flank howitzer & projectiles; operating mutoscope; NY National Guard uniforms; M1883 Gatling gun; French M1763 Charleville musket; World War II U.S. infantry weapons.
Research Fields: coast defense; fortification; New York military history.
Facilities: reference library & archives.
Activities: guided tours; temporary exhibits; lectures & presentations; classroom.
Hours & Admission Prices: Mon.-Fri. 10-4, Sat. 10-2. No charge; donations accepted. Closed national holidays. ♿
Attendance: 24,000 (estimated)

JEWISH CHILDREN'S MUSEUM, 792 Eastern Pkwy., Brooklyn, NY 11213-3502. Tel.: 718-467-0600. Fax: 718-467-1300.
E-mail: info@jcm.museum
Web Site: www.jcmonline.org
Children's Museum.
Collections: Jewish cultural heritage & history; hands-on exhibits; photographs.
Facilities: library; restaurant. Museum-related items for sale.
Activities: facilities rental; special events; shows.
Hours & Admission Prices: Mon.-Thurs. 10-4, Sun. 10-6; school & youth groups by appointment. Admission $10; children under 2 no charge.

THE KURDISH MUSEUM, 144 Underhill Ave., Brooklyn, NY 11238-3907. Tel.: 718-783-7930. Fax: 718-398-4365.
E-mail: kurdishlib@aol.com
Web Site: kurdishlibrarymuseum.com
Founded: 1988.
Key Personnel: Dir., Dr. Vera Beaudin Saeedpour.
Governing Authority: state government. Supported by Kurdish Heritage Foundation of America. Tax-exempt: 501(c)(3).
Ethnic Museum.

Collections: focuses on costumes, costume accessories & jewelry, weavings, rugs, photographs & art artifacts.
Research Fields: Kurds; Middle East; all branches of social sciences & humanities.
Facilities: audiovisual & reading rooms.
Activities: lectures; exhibits.
Publications: sponsors Kurdish Heritage series; The International Journal of Kurdish Studies (1986); Kurdish Life (1991).
Hours & Admission Prices: Sun.-Thurs. 1-5; other times by appointment. Special Exhibits: $5.
Attendance: 500 (estimated)

LEFFERTS HISTORIC HOUSE, Flatbush Ave., Prospect Park, Brooklyn, NY 11215-3709. Mailing Address: Prospect Park Alliance, 95 Prospect Park W., Brooklyn, NY 11215-3709. Tel.: 718-789-2822. Fax: 718-789-4724.
E-mail: lefferts@prospectpart.org
Web Site: www.prospectpark.org
Formerly: Lefferts Homestead
Founded: 1918.
Congressional District: 10 & 12
Key Personnel: Prospect Park Admin., Tupper Thomas; Dir., B.H. Holliday.
Personnel Profile: Full-Time Paid 3; Part-Time Paid 6; Part-Time Volunteers 3.
Governing Authority: Parent Institution: New York City Dept. of Parks & Recreation, Prospect Park Alliance, Inc. Tax-exempt.
Historic House: built c.1783 Dutch-American architecture.
Collections: period furniture; historic documents; household items.
Research Fields: everyday lives of the people living in western Long Island in the early 19th-century, including European, African or Native American ancestry.
Facilities: demonstration garden.
Activities: school tours; research games; craft demonstrations; concerts; family programs; storytelling; crafts for kids; special events; games.
Publications: brochures; seasonal calendar; newsletter.
Hours & Admission Prices: April-June & Sept.-Nov. Thurs.-Sun. & holidays 12-5; July-Aug. Thurs.-Sun. 12-6; Dec.-March Sat.-Sun. & school holidays 12-4. No charge; donations accepted. Closed New Year's Day; Thanksgiving; Christmas Eve & Day. ♿
Attendance: 25,000 (estimated)

LESBIAN HERSTORY EDUCATIONAL FOUNDATION, INC. AKA LESBIAN HERSTORY ARCHIVES, 484 14th St., Brooklyn, NY 11215-5702. Mailing Address: P.O. Box 1258, New York, NY 10116-1258. Tel.: 718-768-3953. Fax: 718-768-4663.
Web Site: www.lesbianherstoryarchives.org
Founded: 1974.
Key Personnel: Treas., Deborah Edel.
Personnel Profile: Part-Time Volunteers 25; Interns 10.
Governing Authority: private; nonprofit organization. Tax-exempt: 501(c)(3).
Lesbian History & Culture Museum.
Collections: photographs; books; videos.
Major Exhibits: Fierce Pussy Retrospective, 11/09-1/10.
Research Fields: preservation of lesbian history & culture.
Facilities: 15,000-vol. library available to the public.
Activities: guided tours; loan, traveling & temporary exhibitions; slide show. Annual Event: At Home Series.
Publications: newsletter, Lesbian Herstory Archives News.
Hours & Admission Prices: By appointment only. No charge; donations accepted. ♿
Attendance: 2,000 (estimated)

MOCADA - THE MUSEUM OF CONTEMPORARY AFRICAN DIASPORAN ARTS, (M), James E. Davis Art Bldg., 80 Hanson Place, Brooklyn, NY 11217-1506. Tel.: 718-230-0492. Fax: 718-230-0246.
E-mail: lc@mocada.org
Web Site: www.mocada.org
Key Personnel: Exec. Dir., Laurie Cumbo; Dir. Exhibitions, Kimberli Grant; Dir. Education, Regine Romain; Museum Shop Mgr., Paul Bispo
Art Museum.
Collections: African American history & culture; paintings; sculpture; photographs.
Facilities: Museum-related items for sale.
Activities: educational programs; special events; internships.
Hours & Admission Prices: Wed.-Sun. 11-6. Adults $4, students $3; children 12 & under no charge.

NEW YORK AQUARIUM, Surf Ave. & W. 8th St., Brooklyn, NY 11224-3495. Tel.: 718-265-3400 & 3405. Fax: 718-265-3482.
E-mail: fhackett@wcs.org
Web Site: www.nyaquarium.com
Founded: 1896.
Congressional District: 13
Key Personnel: C.E.O., Ward Woods; Pres., Steve Sanderson; Dir., Jon F. Dohlin; Dir. Operations, Dennis Ethier; Cur., Dave DeNardo; Public Rels. Mgr., Fran Hackett; Cur. Animal Hospital, Kate McClave.
Personnel Profile: Full-Time Paid 95; Full-Time Volunteers 20; Part-Time Paid 30; Part-Time Volunteers 150; Interns 5.
Governing Authority: nonprofit organization. Parent Institution: The Wildlife Conservation Society, Bronx Park, Bronx, NY 10460. Tax-exempt: 170(b)(1)(A).
Aquarium.
Collections: living aquatic animals.
Research Fields: all aspects of aquatic animal biology; fish genetics.
Facilities: 2,000-vol. library of books & periodicals pertaining to aquatic environment available for use on premises; separate laboratory operation; 200-seat auditorium; 1,800-seat sea lion arena; restaurant. Aquatic & other museum-related items for sale.
Activities: lectures; films; gallery talks; formally organized education programs; permanent & temporary exhibitions; docent program; private events; public events.
Hours & Admission Prices: Memorial Day-Labor Day Mon.-Fri. 10-5, Sat.-Sun. & holidays 10-7; Sept.-May daily 10-4:30. Adults $13, senior citizens $10, children $9; discount to student groups; Fri. after 3, children under 3 & members no charge. ♿
Attendance: 746,526 (accurate)
Membership: Individual $75; Family $120.

PROSPECT PARK ZOO, 450 Flatbush Ave., Brooklyn, NY 11225-3707. Tel.: 718-399-7339. Fax: 718-399-7337.
Web Site: www.prospectparkzoo.com
Formerly: Prospect Park Wildlife Center
Founded: 1993.
Congressional District: 11
Key Personnel: Chm. (V), Ward Wood; Pres., Dr. Steven Sanderson; Sr. Vice Pres. & Gen. Dir., Robert Cook; Sr. Vice Pres. & C.F.O., Patti Calabrese; Supervising Librarian & Archivist, Steve Johnson; Dir., Dr. Donald Moore; Asst. Dir. & Cur. Animals, Dr. Patricia Cole; Cur. Education, Karen Tingley; Public Rels., Barbara Russo.
Personnel Profile: Full-Time Paid 67; Part-Time Volunteers 48.
Governing Authority: private; nonprofit organization. Parent Institution: Wildlife Conservation Society, 185th St. & Southern Blvd., Bronx, NY 10460. Tax-exempt: 501(c)(3).
Zoo.
Collections: wildlife from around the world.
Research Fields: Wyoming toads; intake & digestion in hyrax; animal cognition & behavior.
Facilities: 6,183-vol. library; 2 classrooms; 34,000 sq. ft. exhibit space; zoological park; discovery center.
Activities: docent program; formal education programs; participatory exhibits. Annual Events: Fleece Festival in April; Keeping up with Keepers in September; Boo at the Zoo in October; Presents to the Animals in December.
Publications: bimonthly magazine, Wildlife Conservation; biannual newsletter, Wildlife; quarterly newsletter, Membership News.
Hours & Admission Prices: Winter: daily 10-4:30; Summer: Mon.-Fri. 10-5, Sat.-Sun. 10-5:30. Adults $7, senior citizens $4, children 3-12 $3; members and children under 3 no charge. ♿
Attendance: 232,426 (accurate)
Membership: Senior $33; Individual $75; Family $120; Conservation Supporter $250; Conservation Partner $750; Patron $1,500.

THE RUBELLE & NORMAN SCHAFLER GALLERY, Pratt Institute, 200 Willoughby Ave., Brooklyn, NY 11205-3802. Tel.: 718-636-3517. Fax: 718-399-4230.
E-mail: exhibits@pratt.edu
Web Site: www.pratt.edu/exhibitions
Founded: 1984.
Congressional District: 11
Key Personnel: Dir., Nick Battis; Asst. Dir., Jen Osborne; Exhibit Designer, Katherine Davis.
Personnel Profile: Full-Time Paid 2; Part-Time Paid 1.
Governing Authority: nonprofit. Parent Institution: Pratt Institute. Subsidiary Institution: Pratt Manhattan Gallery, 144 W. 14th St., 2nd Fl., New York, NY 10011. Tel.: 212-647-7778. Tax-exempt: 501(c)(3).
Art & University Museum.
Collections: 19th-21st century paintings, sculptures, prints, photography, & graphic arts by European & American artists.
Research Fields: contemporary fine arts, design & architecture.
Facilities: 185,000-vol. library of books; 135,000 pictures, 50,000 slides, 22,000 microforms, & 130,000 government documents pertaining to art &

architecture; 2,300 sq. ft. exhibit space; classrooms; multi-media center; 300-seat restaurant.
Activities: lectures; performances; panel discussions & receptions; organized education programs for undergraduate or graduate students affiliated with Pratt Institute.
Publications: exhibition announcements; biannual exhibitions & events calendars.
Hours & Admission Prices: Schafler Gallery: Mon.-Fri. 9-5. Pratt Manhattan Gallery: Sept.-July Tues.-Sat. 11-6. No charge. Closed major holidays.
Attendance: 10,000 (estimated)

WATERFRONT MUSEUM, 290 Conover St., Pier 44, Brooklyn, NY 11231-1020. Tel.: 718-624-4719.
E-mail: dsharps@waterfrontmuseum.org
Web Site: www.waterfrontmuseum.org
Founded: 1986.
Congressional District: 8
Key Personnel: Pres. & C.E.O., David Sharps; Chm. (V), Alison Tocci.
Personnel Profile: Full-Time Paid 1; Part-Time Paid 4; Part-Time Volunteers 35.
Governing Authority: private; nonprofit organization. Tax-exempt: 501(c)(3).
Maritime Museum: housed aboard the 1914 Lehigh Valley Railroad Barge #79 used during the Lighterage Era 1860-1960, when goods were transferred from port docks to railhead terminals by tug & barge. Listed on the National Register of Historic Places.
Collections: maritime artifacts.
Research Fields: creating docking for historic vessels in NYC.
Facilities: library containing all issues of Transfer Magazine; floating classroom; 149-seat showboat. Museum-related items for sale.
Activities: maritime & environmental education; cultural programs; community meetings; special events; knot-tying; concerts; formal education programs; guided tours; theater. Museum Sponsors: CIRCUSundays.
Hours & Admission Prices: Thurs. 4-8, Sat. 1-5; groups by appointment. Suggested Donation: $5.
Attendance: 11,000 (estimated)

THE WYCKOFF FARMHOUSE MUSEUM, 5816 Clarendon Rd., Brooklyn, NY 11203-5444. Tel.: 718-629-5400. Fax: 718-629-3125.
E-mail: info@wyckoffassociation.org
Web Site: wyckoffassociation.org
Formerly: The Pieter Claesen Wyckoff House Museum
Founded: 1982.
Congressional District: 12
Key Personnel: Chm. (V), E. Lisk Wyckoff, Jr.; Pres., Naj Wikoff; Exec. Dir., Byron C. Saunders; Dir. Education, Shirley Brown Alleyne; Gardener & Caretaker, Walter Howell; Devel. Project Mgr., Yvette Windley.
Personnel Profile: Full-Time Paid 4; Part-Time Paid 4; Part-Time Volunteers 10.
Governing Authority: nonprofit organization. Parent Institution: Wyckoff House & Association, Inc. Tax-exempt: 501(c)(3).
Historic House: c.1652 Dutch Colonial farmhouse.
Collections: colonial & early American furnishings; documents dating from 1670-1866.
Research Fields: Dutch-Colonial; New York history; labor & immigration history.
Facilities: colonial kitchen garden; picnic area. Museum-related items for sale.
Activities: education programs for children; guided tours; lectures; children's colonial crafts workshops. Annual Events: St. Nicholas Day Celebration; Pinkster Celebration; African Lives: From Wyckoff to Weeksville; Apple Festival.
Publications: annual bulletin; annual, Calendar of Events; quarterly newsletter.
Hours & Admission Prices: April-Oct. Tues.-Sun. 10-4; Nov.-March Tues.-Sat. 10-4. Adults $5, senior citizens & children $3; discounts to AAM & ICOM members; Wyckoff Assoc. & members no charge. Closed New Year's Day; Thanksgiving; Christmas. ♿
Attendance: 6,000 (estimated)
Membership: Basic $40; Family $60; Supporter $70-$80; Benefactor $115-$175; Patron $550-$1,100.

Brooklyn Heights

NEW YORK TRANSIT MUSEUM, (M), Corner of Boerum Pl. & Schermerhorn St., Brooklyn Heights, NY 11201. Mailing Address: 130 Livingston St., 10th Fl., Brooklyn, NY 11201-5106. Tel.: 718-694-1600 & 1873. Fax: 718-694-1791.
E-mail: gabrielle.shubert@nyct.com
Web Site: www.mta.info/museum
Founded: 1976.
Congressional District: 13
Key Personnel: Dir., Gabrielle Shubert; Chm. (V), Susan Gilbert; Deputy Dir., Carlos Gutierrez-Solana; Tour Coord., Luz Montano; Asst. Dir. & Devel. Officer, Marcia Ely; Admin. Mgr., Angela Agard Solomon; Operations Mgr., Timothy Keiley; Sr. Cur., Charles L. Sachs; Sr. Mgr. Exhibits, Robert Del Bagno; Mgr. Education, Laura Joseph; Cur., Carissa Amash; Assoc. Cur., Chandra Buie; Coord. Education, Virgil Talaid; Archivist, Carey Stumm; Mgr. Retail & MTA Products Devel., Gail Goldberg; Registrar, Kathryn Kearns; Museum Educator, Lynette Morse; Museum Preparator, Sara Deane; Asst. Mgr. Retail Operations, Yuri McKenna.
Personnel Profile: Full-Time Paid 26; Part-Time Paid 26; Part-Time Volunteers 2; Interns 6.
Governing Authority: municipal; nonprofit. Parent Institution: Metropolitan Transportation Authority. Subsidiary Institution: Friends of NY Transit Museum. Gallery Annex: Grand Central Terminal. Tax-exempt.
Urban Transportation Museum: located in a decommissioned subway station c.1936.
Collections: N.Y. transportation artifacts; history of public transportation in New York including subways, buses, bridges, tunnels & commuter railroads; 1904-1968 subway cars & elevated cars; signs; signals; 250,000 photographs; architectural & engineering drawings; uniforms; mosaics; tools & equipment.
Major Exhibits: Last Day of the Myrtle Avenue El: Photographs by Teresa King, 11/09-2/10; Where New York Began: South Ferry Archaeology, 2/10-7/10; Arts for Transit: 25 Years Along the Way, 7/10-10/10; 9th Annual Holiday Train Show, 11/10-1/11.
Research Fields: New York Metropolitan region transportation history and the effects these have on the development of the region.
Facilities: 3,500-vol. archive pertaining to NYC Transit history; 18,000 sq. ft. exhibit space; 75-seat theater. Museum-related items for sale.
Activities: guided tours; lectures; films; organized education programs; docent program; participatory & temporary exhibitions; readings.
Publications: exhibition catalogues; oral history book; educational materials; tri-annual Calendar of Events; Court Street Shuttle Newsletter.
Hours & Admission Prices: Tues.-Fri. 10-4, Sat.-Sun. 12-5. Adults $5, senior citizens & children under 17 $3; discounts to AAM, ICOM & ASTC members; members no charge. GCT Annex: Mon.-Fri. 8-8, Sat.-Sun. 10-6. No charge. Closed New Year's Eve & Day; Memorial Day; Independence Day; Labor Day Weekend; Thanksgiving; Christmas. ♿
Attendance: 458,656 (accurate)
Membership: Senior Citizen, Student & MTA Employee $30; Friend $40; Family $55; Contributing $80; Sustaining $150; Patron $250.

Brookville

HILLWOOD ART MUSEUM, (M), C. W. Post Campus, Long Island University, 720 Northern Blvd., Brookville, NY 11548-1319. Tel.: 516-299-4073. Fax: 516-299-2787.
E-mail: museum@cwpost.liu.edu
Web Site: www.liu.edu/museum
Founded: 1973.
Congressional District: 4
Key Personnel: Dir., Barbara Applegate; Pres., Dr. David Steinberg.
Personnel Profile: Full-Time Paid 2; Part-Time Paid 8; Part-Time Volunteers 2; Interns 3.
Governing Authority: university. Parent Institution: C. W. Post, Long Island University. Tax-exempt.
Art Museum & Public Art Program.
Collections: paintings; prints; photography; sculpture; ethnographic.
Research Fields: pre-Columbian; Chinese; African; photography; European & American prints; textiles.
Facilities: located in student union complex: restaurant; lecture hall; cinema; concert theater.
Activities: tours; lectures; performances; public art program; exhibitions for academic & surrounding community; 6 major shows per year.
Publications: catalogues for each exhibition & public art program; newsletter, MuseumNews; exhibition catalogues; exhibition guides; study guides.
Hours & Admission Prices: June-July Mon.-Fri. 9-4:30; Sept.-May Mon.-Wed. & Fri. 9:30-4:30, Thurs. 9:30-8, Sat. 11-3. No charge; donations accepted. ♿
Attendance: 15,000 (accurate)
Membership: Call for information.

Brownville

GENERAL JACOB BROWN HISTORICAL SOCIETY, 116 E. Main St., Brownville, NY 13615. Tel.: 315-782-4508. Fax: 315-786-1178.
Founded: 1978.
Congressional District: 30
Key Personnel: Pres. (V) & Corresponding Sec., Constance G. Hoard; Vice Pres., Randy L. McIntyre.
Governing Authority: municipal; nonprofit. Tax-exempt.
Historical Society Museum: housed in 1811-1815 General Brown Mansion.

Collections: Brown furnishings; period pieces; dishes & cooking utensils; tools; weapons; paintings.
Research Fields: Brown Family memorabilia; local history of Brownville; War of 1812.
Facilities: Village library of books on local Jefferson County History; research materials.
Activities: guided tours upon request; lectures; films; concerts; permanent & temporary exhibitions.
Publications: pamphlet describing mansion & General Brown's achievements are available with no charge upon request.
Hours & Admission Prices: By appointment only. No charge; donations accepted.
Membership: Individual $2; Family $5.

Buffalo

* **ALBRIGHT-KNOX ART GALLERY, (M),** 1285 Elmwood Ave., Buffalo, NY 14222-1096. Tel.: 716-882-8700. Fax: 716-882-8773.
E-mail: mmorreale@albrightknox.org
Web Site: www.albrightknox.org
Founded: 1862.
Congressional District: 38
Key Personnel: Dir., Louis Grachos; Deputy Dir., Karen Spaulding; Pres. (V), Charles Banta; Sr. Cur., Douglas Dreishpoon, Ph.D.; Assoc. Cur., Holly Hughes; Cur. Education, Mariann Smith; Registrar, Laura Fleischmann; Librarian, Susana Tejada; Dir. External Affairs, Maria Morreale; Dir. Advancement, Elaine Pyne; Museum Shop Mgr., Tracey Levy.
Personnel Profile: Full-Time Paid 65; Part-Time Paid 20; Part-Time Volunteers 195; Interns 21.
Governing Authority: nonprofit organization. Parent Institution: Buffalo Fine Arts Academy. Tax-exempt: 501(c)(3).
Art Museum.
Collections: 18th-century English paintings; 19th-century French & American paintings; 20th-21st century painting & sculpture; 3000 B.C.-present, sculpture; drawings; graphics; photography.
Facilities: 30,000-vol. art reference library by appointment; print & drawing study room; 345-seat auditorium; classrooms; restaurant. Art books, catalogues, reproductions & other museum-related items for sale.
Activities: guided tours; lectures; films; concerts; rental sales gallery; organized education programs; docent program or council; inter-museum loan, permanent, temporary & traveling exhibitions; speakers' bureau; educational exhibitions; handicap programs; artists' workshop; school resource service; special programs for high school students; participatory tours.
Publications: Annual report; exhibition catalogs; quarterly newsletter.
Hours & Admission Prices: Wed.-Thurs. & Sat.-Sun. 10-5, Fri. 10-10. Adults $12; discounts to AAM members; members & Fri. 3-10 no charge. Closed New Year's Day; Independence Day; Thanksgiving; Christmas. ♿
Attendance: 143,653 (accurate)
Membership: Students $25; Senior Citizens $30; Individual $50; Family $75; Reciprocal $150; Contributing $300; Sustaining $500; Clyfford Still Circle $1,000; Andy Warhol Circle $2,500; Jackson Pollock Circle $5,000; Georgia O'Keeffe Circle $10,000; Henri Matisse Circle $25,000.

THE BENJAMIN & DR. EDGAR R. COFELD JUDAIC MUSEUM OF TEMPLE BETH ZION, (M), 805 Delaware Ave., Buffalo, NY 14209-2005. Mailing Address: 700 Sweet Home Rd., Buffalo, NY 14226-1444. Tel.: 716-836-6565. Fax: 716-831-1126.
Web Site: www.tbz.org
Founded: 1981.
Congressional District: 33
Personnel Profile: Part-Time Volunteers 12; Interns 6.
Governing Authority: Parent Institution: Temple Beth Zion. Tax-exempt.
Judaic Museum.
Collections: Judaic artifacts from the 10th century to present including coins, medallions, books, holocaust remembrances, historical memorabilia, folk art and textiles; Jewish ceremonial artifacts.
Research Fields: Judaic artifacts.
Facilities: 12,000-vol. library pertaining to the Jewish faith available to the public; 500-seat auditorium.
Activities: guided tours; films; organized education programs; temporary & traveling exhibitions; mobile mini museum.
Publications: catalog; pamphlets; brochure, Contributions of Jews to America.
Hours & Admission Prices: Mon.-Fri. 9-4, Sat. 11-12; tours by appointment. No charge; donations accepted. ♿
Attendance: 16,000

BUFFALO AND ERIE COUNTY BOTANICAL GARDENS, (M), 2655 South Park Ave., Buffalo, NY 14218-1526. Tel.: 716-827-1584, ext. 200. Fax: 716-828-0091.
Web Site: www.buffalogardens.com
Founded: 1898.
Congressional District: 30
Key Personnel: Dir. Administration, Julie DeCarolis.
Personnel Profile: Full-Time Paid 11; Part-Time Paid 4; Part-Time Volunteers 280.
Governing Authority: municipal government. A branch of the County of Erie Dept. of Parks, Recreation & Forestry. Tax-exempt.
Botanical Garden.
Collections: tropical & exotic plants; hardy trees, shrubs, & flowers; orchids; ivy; herbs; palms; begonias; cacti; succulents; bromeliads; koi.
Research Fields: plant taxonomy; horticulture; botany.
Facilities: greenhouse.
Activities: guided tours; special flower & plant shows; special events; fashion show; farmers market; concerts; pet events; art show; gala; harvest festival; holiday events; educational offerings; summer camp; school tours; private events; weddings.
Publications: newsletter, Under the Dome; the complete garden guide; monthly updated maps for visitors; volunteer newsletter; seasonal flyers.
Hours & Admission Prices: Daily 10-5. Adults & students $6, seniors $5, children 6-13 $3; children under 6 & members no charge. Closed Thanksgiving; Christmas. ♿
Attendance: 40,000 (estimated)
Membership: Senior & Student with ID $30; Individual Gardener $40; Family & Grandparent $60; Gardener $75; Gardener Plus $100; Garden Club & Plant Society $150; Master Gardener $250; Bronze $500; Silver $1,000; Gold $2,500.

* **BUFFALO AND ERIE COUNTY HISTORICAL SOCIETY, (M),** 25 Nottingham Court, Buffalo, NY 14216-3119. Tel.: 716-873-9644. Fax: 716-873-8754.
E-mail: bechs@bechs.org
Web Site: www.bechs.org
Founded: 1862.
Congressional District: 41
Key Personnel: Exec. Dir., Cynthia Conides, Ph. D.; Pres. (V), Richard A. Wiesen; Dir. Museum Collections, Walter Mayer; Dir. Library & Archives, Cynthia Van Ness; Sr. Dir. Admin. & Operations, Sarah E. Treanor.
Personnel Profile: Full-Time Paid 15; Part-Time Paid 12; Part-Time Volunteers 200; Interns 2.
Governing Authority: society. Tax-exempt: 501(c)3.
Local/Regional History Museum: housed in the only permanent building constructed for the 1901 Pan American Exposition. National Historic Landmark.
Collections: archaeology; ethnology; costumes; crafts; industry; military; stamps; coins; transportation; agriculture; marine; household china, glass, furnishings; jewelry; toys; medical items; ephemera; manuscripts; photographs; communication artifacts; tools & equipment for communication, materials, science & technology; Pan-American artifacts.
Research Fields: history of the Niagara frontier; military; Great Lake maritime; genealogy.
Facilities: 20,000-vol. library of historical books of western New York & the Niagara frontier available for inter-library loan with restrictions; reading room; 250-seat auditorium.
Activities: guided tours by appointment; lectures; formally organized education programs for children; inter-museum loan, permanent, temporary & traveling exhibitions; loan service.
Publications: quarterly newsletter; books, Buffalo & Erie County Town Histories; Superior in Design & Execution: Pressed Glass catalogue; Coming of Age in Buffalo; Second Looks-A Pictorial History of Buffalo & Erie County; Patterns in Time: Quilts of Western New York.
Hours & Admission Prices: Museum: Tues.-Sat. 10-5, Sun. 12-5. Adults $6, senior citizens & students 13-21 $4, children 7-12 $2.50; discounts for groups, AAM & ICOM members; children under 7 & members no charge. Reference Library: Wed.-Sat. 1-5. Non-members $6. Closed New Year's Day; Thanksgiving; Christmas. ♿
Attendance: 65,000 (estimated)
Membership: Individuals: Basic $30; Teacher & Grandparent & Senior $35; Family & Household $45; Sustaining $60; Supporting $100; Collector $150; Pan-American $500.

BUFFALO AND ERIE COUNTY NAVAL & MILITARY PARK, One Naval Park Cove, Buffalo, NY 14202-4114. Tel.: 716-847-1773. Fax: 716-847-6405.
E-mail: info@buffalonavalpark.org
Web Site: www.buffalonavalpark.org
Founded: 1979.
Congressional District: 33
Key Personnel: Chm. (V), Donald Alessi; Exec. Dir., Patrick J. Cunningham; Ship's Supt. & Staff Duty Officer, Richard Smith; Office Mgr., Anita Baril; Ship's Store Mgr., Dolores Kwiatkowski.

Personnel Profile: Full-Time Paid 14; Part-Time Paid 26; Part-Time Volunteers 67.
Governing Authority: nonprofit organization. Tax-exempt: 501(c)(3).
Historical Ships & Military Museum.
Collections: military history & the five armed forces; photographs; archives; uniforms; 8 ship models; naval artifacts; U.S.S. The Sullivans-DD 537; M41 tank; U.S.S. Little Rock-CLG 4; U.S.S. Croaker - SS-246; P-39 Bell Airacobra; M-84 Armored Personnel Carrier; F-101 Voodoo Air Force Jet; FJ4B Navy Fury Jet; PTF-17.
Research Fields: exhibit & interpretational development.
Facilities: 4,500 sq. ft. exhibit space.
Activities: guided & self-guided tours; films; docent program; overnight encampment of scout groups.
Publications: quarterly newsletter, Ship 'N Shore.
Hours & Admission Prices: April-Oct. daily 10-5; Nov. Sat.-Sun. 10-4. Adults $9, senior citizens & children 6-16 $6; discounts to groups, active military personnel, AAM & ICOM members; children 5 & under and members no charge. ♿
Attendance: 55,000 (estimated)
Membership: Individual $15; Family $25; Life & Corporate $250.

* **BUFFALO MUSEUM OF SCIENCE, (M),** 1020 Humboldt Pkwy., Buffalo, NY 14211-1293. Tel.: 716-896-5200; 866-291-6660. Fax: 716-897-6723.
E-mail: mmortenson@sciencebuff.org
Web Site: www.buffalomuseumofscience.org
Founded: 1861.
Congressional District: 37
Key Personnel: Pres. & C.E.O., Mark Mortenson; Chm. (V), Randall Burkard; Business Office Mgr., Lynn Metzger; Dir. Center for Science Learning, Karen Wallace; Dir. Operations & Exhibits, Thom Furtado; Dir. Science & Research, Dr. John Grehan; Dir. Devel. & External Rels., Michelle Rudnicki; Cur. Collections, Kathy Leacock; Museum Shop Mgr., Collin Gehl.
Personnel Profile: Full-Time Paid 32; Part-Time Paid 17; Part-Time Volunteers 200; Interns 8.
Governing Authority: Buffalo Society of Natural Sciences. Subsidiary Institution: Tifft Nature Preserve. Tax-exempt: 501(c)(3).
Natural History Museum.
Collections: anthropology; botany; eteology; zoology; mycology.
Research Fields: botany; geology; mycology; anthropology; vertebrate & invertebrate zoology.
Facilities: 42,000-vol. library available for research & inter-library loan; Kellogg Observatory; solar observatory; field research station; 260-acre nature preserve.
Activities: guided tours; lectures; field trip; study trips; formally organized education programs; inter-museum loan; permanent & temporary exhibitions; hands-on discovery room for children.
Hours & Admission Prices: Summer: Mon.-Sat. 10-5; Winter: Wed.-Sat. 10-5, Sun. 12-5. Adults $7, senior citizens $6, children & students $5; discounts to AAM, ICOM & ASTC members; members & children under 3 no charge. ♿
Attendance: 125,554 (accurate)
Membership: Student $20; Senior $30; Senior Couple $40; Family & Grandparent $50; Contributing $75; Sustaining $150.

BUFFALO TRANSPORTATION PIERCE-ARROW MUSEUM, 263 Michigan Ave., Buffalo, NY 14203-2900. Mailing Address: 24 Myrtle Ave., Buffalo, NY 14204-2048. Tel.: 716-853-0084.
Founded: 1997.
Transportation Museum.
Collections: period automobiles; transportation history; photographs.
Major Exhibits: Women and the Automobile, 1/10-1/11.
Activities: rental facilities; special events; meetings; dinners.
Hours & Admission Prices: Call for hours. ♿
Attendance: 10,000 (estimated)

BUFFALO ZOOLOGICAL GARDENS, 300 Parkside Ave., Buffalo, NY 14214-1999. Tel.: 716-837-3900, ext. 100. Fax: 716-837-0738.
Web Site: www.buffalozoo.org
Founded: 1875.
Congressional District: 37
Key Personnel: Pres., Donna M. Fernandes, Ph.D.; Chm. (V), Hal D. Payne; Dir. Admin. & Finance, Mrs. Denise Maloney; Gen. Cur., Gerald D. Aquilina; Museum Shop Mgr., David Dinardo.
Personnel Profile: Full-Time Paid 66; Part-Time Paid 80; Part-Time Volunteers 744.
Governing Authority: society. Tax-exempt: 501(c)(3).
Zoological Gardens & Children's Zoo.
Collections: aviary; mammals; herpetology; botanical gardens; South American rainforest.
Research Fields: rare & endangered animal exhibition, propagation & management.
Facilities: 23.5 acre park; gardens; children's resource center; concession stand. Museum-related items for sale.
Activities: guided tours; lectures; permanent, temporary & traveling exhibitions; interactive & educational activities; hands-on children's zoo; animal presentation area; train rides; carousel; playground.
Publications: quarterly zoo magazine, ZOOLOG.
Hours & Admission Prices: Winter: Gates daily 10-4; Buildings 10-4.30; Grounds 10-5. Summer: Gates daily 10-5; Buildings 10-5.30; Grounds 10-6. Adults 15-62 $9.50, senior citizens 63 & over and student 22 & under $7, youth 2-14 $6; discounts to AZA members & groups; children under 2 & zoo members no charge. Closed Thanksgiving; Christmas. ♿
Attendance: 414,794 (accurate)
Membership: Individual $40; Grandparents $50; Individual Plus $55; Grandparent Plus $60; Family $65; Family Plus $80; Supporting $125; Sponsor $250; Patron $500; Benefactor $1,000.

* **BURCHFIELD-PENNEY ART CENTER, (M),** Buffalo State College, 1300 Elmwood Ave., Buffalo, NY 14222-1004. Tel.: 716-878-6012. Fax: 716-878-6003.
E-mail: burchfld@buffalostate.edu
Web Site: www.burchfieldpenney.org
Founded: 1966.
Congressional District: 140
Key Personnel: Dir. & Pres., Ted Pietrzak; C.O.O., David M. Tanner; Mktg. & Public Rels., Kathleen Heyworth; Dir. Devel., Becky Power; Head Collections, Nancy Weekly; Cur. Education, Kathy Gaye Shiroki; Head Programs, Don Metz; Facilities Mgr., William Menshon.
Personnel Profile: Full-Time Paid 14; Part-Time Paid 2; Part-Time Volunteers 65; Interns 3.
Governing Authority: nonprofit. Tax-exempt: 501(c)(3).
Art Museum: housed on the State University College at Buffalo Campus.
Collections: paintings, drawings, sketches, wallpapers, prints, by Charles Burchfield; works by contemporary Western New York artists; works by historical Western New York artists; works by Charles E. Burchfield's contemporaries; archival materials relating to Charles Burchfield & Western New York artists; manuscripts; Penney collections of work by Charles Burchfield; Roycroft artists; craft artists.
Major Exhibits: Lecture on Weather: John Cage, 1/23/10-2/14/10; Heatwaves in a Swamp: Charles E. Burchfield, 3/10-5/10; Steina, 6/10-8/10; Celia Rumsey: Craving, 1/10-5/10; John McQueen, 1/10-7/10.
Research Fields: American art; Western New York art; Charles Burchfield's art & life.
Facilities: 2,500-vol. library; archives; cafe. Museum-related items for sale.
Activities: guided tours; lectures; gallery talks; concerts; poetry reading; education programs for children, adults, undergraduate & graduate college students affiliated with State University College at Buffalo; loan, temporary & traveling exhibitions; school loan service; workshops; special events.
Publications: Burchfield Penney Art Center newsletter; exhibition catalogues; books on Charles Burchfield.
Hours & Admission Prices: Tues.-Wed. & Fri.-Sat. 10-5, Thurs. 10-9, Sun. 1-5. Adults & seniors $7, students 6-18 $4; discounts to AAM & NARM members; members & children under 6 no charge. Empire State Reciprocal membership. Closed legal holidays. ♿
Attendance: 70,000 (accurate)
Membership: Individual $45; Family & Dual $60; Friend $100; Curator's Circle $250; Director's Circle $500; Burchfield Circle $1,000.

CENTER FOR EXPLORATORY AND PERCEPTUAL ART, 617 Main St., #201, Buffalo, NY 14203-1400. Tel.: 716-856-2717. Fax: 716-270-0184.
E-mail: info@cepagallery.com
Web Site: www.cepagallery.org
Founded: 1974.
Congressional District: 37
Key Personnel: C.E.O., Exec. Dir. & Cur., Lawrence Brose; Chm. (V), Jim Rolls; Artistic Dir., Sean Donaher; Education, Lauren Tent; Administrative Asst., Lynda Kaszubski.
Personnel Profile: Full-Time Paid 3; Part-Time Paid 1; Part-Time Volunteers 12; Interns 12.
Governing Authority: nonprofit. Tax-exempt.
Art Gallery.
Collections: photographs; audiovisual.
Facilities: library; 7,500 sq. ft. exhibit space.
Activities: films; dark room & computer workshops; public art. Annual Event: photography art auction.
Publications: CEPA Journal; CEPA newsletter.

Hours & Admission Prices: Mon.-Fri. 10-5, Sat. 12-4. No charge; donations accepted. ♿
Attendance: 1,000,000 (estimated)
Membership: Artist, Senior & Student with ID $25; Individual $35; Household & Institution $60; Patron $100; Collectors Program: Supporter $200; Sustainer $500.

DARWIN D. MARTIN HOUSE, 125 Jewett Pkwy., Buffalo, NY 14214-2301. Tel.: 716-856-3858. Fax: 716-856-4009.
E-mail: info@darwinmartinhouse.org
Web Site: www.darwinmartinhouse.org
Key Personnel: Exec. Dir., Mary F. Roberts
Historic House: housed in the former home of Darwin & Isabelle Martin; designed by Frank Lloyd Wright; built in 1904. Listed on the National Register of Historic Places.
Collections: family history; period furnishings; photographs.
Hours & Admission Prices: Call for hours.

IRA G. ROSS AEROSPACE MUSEUM, 1 Seymour H. Knox III Plaza, (at Perry St. in HSBC Arena), Buffalo, NY 14203-3007. Tel.: 716-858-4340. Fax: 716-278-0257.
E-mail: info@wnyaerospace.org
Web Site: www.wnyaerospace.org
Formerly: Niagara Aerospace Museum
Key Personnel: Exec. Dir., Jack Wysocki
Aviation History Museum.
Collections: Western New York aviation history; aerospace innovations.
Facilities: 140-seat theater.
Activities: group tours.
Hours & Admission Prices: Sat.-Sun. 11-4. Adults $6, senior citizens 62 & over and students $5, children 12 & under $2; discount to groups; members no charge. Closed New Year's Eve & Day; Thanksgiving; Christmas Eve & Day.

MUSEUM OF DISABILITY HISTORY, (M), 1291 N. Forest Rd., Buffalo, NY 14221-3230. Mailing Address: P.O. Box 9033, Buffalo, NY 14231-9033. Tel.: 716-817-7261. Fax: 716-817-7234.
Web Site: www.museumofdisability.org
Founded: 2003.
Congressional District: 26
Key Personnel: Dir., Theresa Fraser; Educator, Elizabeth Marotta; Cur., Douglas A. Platt; Research Specialist, Reid Dunlavey.
Personnel Profile: Full-Time Paid 5; Full-Time Volunteers 1; Part-Time Paid 3; Interns 1.
Governing Authority: private; nonprofit organization. Parent Institution: People, Inc., Williamsville, NY. Tax-exempt: 501(c)(3).
Disability History Museum.
Collections: medical & social disability history, care & treatment; photographs; books; film.
Research Fields: history of developmental disabilities; western New York institutions; self-advocacy movement.
Facilities: 500-vol. reference library; 800 sq. ft. exhibit space.
Activities: guided tours; films; formal educational programs for adults & children; lectures; temporary & traveling exhibitions. Museum Sponsors: Kids on the Block (R) Disability Awareness Puppet Troup; Disability Awareness Scout Merit Badge Program. Annual Event: Disability Film Festival.
Hours & Admission Prices: Mon.-Fri. 10-4; other times by appointment. No charge; donations accepted. Closed municipal holidays. ♿
Attendance: 400

THEODORE ROOSEVELT INAUGURAL NATIONAL HISTORIC SITE, 641 Delaware Ave., Buffalo, NY 14202-1079. Tel.: 716-884-0095. Fax: 716-884-0330.
E-mail: thri_administration@nps.gov
Web Site: www.nps.gov/thri/
Founded: 1971.
Congressional District: 28
Key Personnel: Exec. Dir. & Site Supt., Molly Quackenbush; Pres. (V), Lawrence Seymour; Vice Pres. (V), Karen Gaughan Scott; Admin. Officer, Sally Goris; Cur., Lenora Henson; Education Dir., Mark Lozo; Administrative Asst., Wendy Phelps; Asst. Dir., Janice Kuzan; Maintenance Chief, Albert LaBruna; Interpreter, Mark Comito.
Personnel Profile: Full-Time Paid 6; Part-Time Paid 7; Part-Time Volunteers 273; Interns 6.
Governing Authority: nonprofit organization. Parent Institution: Theodore Roosevelt Inaugural Site Foundation & National Park Service, U.S. Dept. of Interior. Tax-exempt: 501(c)(3).
Historic Building & Site: housed in c.1838 Buffalo Barracks, the site of the inauguration of Pres. Theodore Roosevelt in 1901.
Collections: artifacts relating to Theodore Roosevelt's inauguration in 1901, the Ansley Wilcox house in 1901, Theodore Roosevelt's life, Wilcox house 1838-1933 & 1937-1960, William McKinley's death, Pan-American exposition & turn-of-the-20th century furnishings.
Research Fields: Theodore Roosevelt's Presidency; Buffalo history; Wilcox family history; restoration; Pan-American Exposition.
Facilities: carriage house visitor center with multi-purpose gallery; meeting rooms; classroom. Museum-related items for sale.
Activities: guided tours; volunteer program; school programs; permanent & changing exhibitions; architectural walking tours; lecture series; naturalization ceremonies; Inaugural reenactment. Museum Sponsors: Victorian Christmas program during month of December; children's summer programs; Victorian Teas; Teddy Bear Picnics.
Publications: books, Theodore Roosevelt, An American Hero in Caricature: essays explaining Puck magazine covers (1898-1909); newsletter, The Columns; Guidebook to the Theodore Roosevelt Inaugural National Historic Site.
Hours & Admission Prices: Closed for renovation. Closed New Year's Eve & Day; Easter; Memorial Day; Independence Day; Labor Day; Thanksgiving; Christmas Eve & Day. ♿
Membership: Individual $30; Family $45; Rough Rider $75; Governor $100; Vice President $250; President $500.

UNIVERSITY AT BUFFALO ART GALLERIES, (M), 201 Center for the Arts, Buffalo, NY 14260-6000. Tel.: 716-645-6912. Fax: 716-645-6753.
E-mail: sholsen@buffalo.edu
Web Site: www.ubartgalleries.org
Founded: 1994.
Key Personnel: Dir., UB Art Galleries, Sandra H. Olsen, Ph.D; Cur., UB Art Gallery, Sandra Firmin; Finance & Gen. Operations Mgr., Jennifer Markee; Cur. Education, UB Anderson Gallery, Ginny Lohr; Sec., UB Art Gallery, Kitty Marmion; Asst. Dir., UB Anderson Gallery, Mary Moran; Registrar & Collections Mgr., Bob Scalise; Staff Asst., Jim Snider; Head Preparator, Ken Short; Asst. Preparator, UB Art Gallery, Tim Roby; Maintenance Supvr., Paul Wilcox.
Personnel Profile: Full-Time Paid 11; Full-Time Volunteers 11; Part-Time Paid 10; Part-Time Volunteers 12; Interns 12.
Governing Authority: public university; nonprofit. Parent Institution: State University of New York system. Subsidiary Institutions: UB Art Gallery; UB Anderson Gallery. Tax-exempt.
University Art Gallery & Museum.
Collections: over 1,200 works of art including modern & contemporary paintings, prints, drawings, sculpture, & early 19th-century works; cultural art from the Annette Cravens collection; Martha Jackson & David Anderson Gallery collections.
Major Exhibits: Carlos Estevez, 11/09-2/10; Best of Senior Thesis, 11/09-2/10; Dinh Q. Le (T), 3/10-5/10; Alberto Rey, 3/10-5/10; Artpark 1974-1984, 9/10-12/10.
Research Fields: .
Facilities: educational facilities; 10,000 sq. ft. exhibit space.
Activities: formal education programs for adults & college students; participatory & traveling exhibits. Annual Events: temporary exhibits followed by lectures, panel discussions & receptions for artists.
Publications: exhibition brochures & catalogs.
Hours & Admission Prices: Tues.-Wed. & Fri.-Sat. 11-5, Thurs. 11-7. No charge; donations accepted. Closed New Year's Day; Independence Day; Labor Day; Thanksgiving; Christmas. ♿
Attendance: 10,000 (estimated)

Byron

BYRON HISTORICAL MUSEUM, 6407 Town Line Rd., Byron, NY 14422. Mailing Address: 6451 Mill Pond Rd., Byron, NY 14422-9758. Tel.: 585-548-9008.
E-mail: byron-historian@juno.com
Founded: 1967.
Congressional District: 137
Key Personnel: Pres. (V), Alvin Shaw; Historian, Beth Wilson; Historian, Bob Wilson.
Personnel Profile: Part-Time Paid 2; Part-Time Volunteers 30.
Governing Authority: society. Affiliated with Byron Historical Society. Tax-exempt.
General Museum.
Collections: history; pulpit, organ & altar of former church; general; home & farm displays of the area.
Activities: permanent & temporary exhibitions.
Hours & Admission Prices: June-Sept. Sun. 2-4; other times by appointment. No charge.
Attendance: 235
Membership: Annual $2.

Caledonia

BIG SPRINGS MUSEUM, (M), 3095 Main St., Caledonia, NY 14423-1237. Mailing Address: Box 41, Caledonia, NY 14423-0041. Tel.: 585-538-9880.
Founded: 1936.
Key Personnel: Pres. (V), Sue Deragon; Cur., Patty Garrett; Docent, Lois Waldron.
Personnel Profile: Part-Time Paid 2; Part-Time Volunteers 40.
Governing Authority: society. Affiliated with Big Springs Historical Society. Tax-exempt.
General Museum.
Collections: early farm implements; Native American collection; early pictures; documents; letters; Civil War, World War I & II collections; household objects; toys; games; dolls; costumes; weaving equipment; school room articles; china; glass; medical.
Facilities: library of bound copies of local newspaper dating back to the 1900s; material on local & county histories, available for research on premises. Local historic plates, tiles, history booklets, notepaper for sale.
Activities: guided tours; lectures; formally organized education programs for children; permanent & temporary exhibitions.
Hours & Admission Prices: Sun. 1-4, Mon. 9-12; call for additional hours. No charge; donations accepted. Closed Easter; Memorial Day; Independence Day; Christmas. ♿
Attendance: 1,800 (estimated)
Membership: Senior $10; Individual $15; Family $20; Silver Patron $35; Gold Patron $50; Platinum Patron $100.

Calverton

GRUMMAN MEMORIAL PARK, Rte. 25 & 25A, Calverton, NY 11933. Mailing Address: P.O. Box 147, Calverton, NY 11933-0147. Tel.: 631-369-1826.
E-mail: gmpark@optonline.net
Web Site: www.grummanpark.org
Formerly: East End Aircraft L.I. Corp.
Founded: 1998.
Congressional District: 1
Key Personnel: Chm. (V), Joe Van de Wetering.
Personnel Profile: Part-Time Volunteers 7.
Governing Authority: private; nonprofit organization. Parent Institution: East End Aircraft L.I. Corp. Tax-exempt: 501(c)(3).
Military Museum.
Collections: military aircraft; F14; A6E.
Hours & Admission Prices: Daily 9-5. No charge. ♿
Attendance: 15,000 (estimated)
Membership: One Year $10; Five Years $40; Ten Years $75.

Camden

QV HISTORICAL SOCIETY AT CARRIAGE HOUSE MUSEUM, 2 N. Park St., Camden, NY 13316-1306. Mailing Address: P.O. Box 38, Camden, NY 13316-0038. Tel.: 315-245-4652.
E-mail: historycamden@verizon.net
Founded: 1975.
Congressional District: 31
Key Personnel: Pres. (V), J.C. Kuttruff.
Personnel Profile: Part-Time Volunteers 9.
Governing Authority: society; nonprofit. Tax-exempt.
Historical Society Museum.
Collections: tools; bottles; books; photographs; local history; china; town hall bell; maps; soil samples; barb wire; surveying instruments; jewelry; dolls; paintings; furniture; clothing; manuscripts; genealogy information; Camden's postcards; history of Camden's churches, schools, homes & Main Street stores; one room schoolhouse.
Research Fields: local history; family searches.
Facilities: library.
Activities: permanent exhibitions; research.
Publications: Camden postcard booklet; brochures.
Hours & Admission Prices: May-Oct. Wed. & Fri.-Sat. 1-4; call to confirm; other times by appointment. No charge; donations accepted. Closed holidays.
Attendance: 500 (estimated)
Membership: Student $2; Individual $10; Family $20.

Canaan

CANAAN HISTORICAL SOCIETY, INC., 13 Warner Crossing Rd., Canaan, NY 12029. Mailing Address: 84 Old Hudson Turnpike, Canaan, NY 12029-2801. Tel.: 518-781-4228 & 4605.
E-mail: nyvetcounsil@yahoo.com
Founded: 1963.
Congressional District: 29
Key Personnel: Pres. (V), Gary Flaherty; Cur., Tammy Flaherty; Historian, Anna Mary Dunton.
Personnel Profile: Part-Time Volunteers 8.
Governing Authority: society. Affiliated with University of the State of New York. Tax-exempt.
Historic Building: 1829 former Meeting House, Presbyterian Society.
Collections: glassware; china; silver; artifacts from the Shakers; furniture; Civil War items; Canaan militia Civil War artifacts; quilts; military artifacts of Captain William Henry Warner; books by Susan & Anna Warner.
Facilities: genealogy library available for research on premise by appointment; meeting room. Museum-related items for sale.
Activities: guided tours; temporary exhibitions. Museum Sponsors: various special programs in July & August.
Publications: semi-annual newsletter, Canaan Eagle; book, Reflections: Canaan, NY 1776-1976.
Hours & Admission Prices: July-Aug. Sat. 1-4; other times by appointment. No charge; donations accepted. ♿
Attendance: 200 (estimated)
Membership: Junior $1; Regular $10; Family $15; Business $25; Benefactor $50; Memorial $100; Life $200.

Canajoharie

CANAJOHARIE LIBRARY AND ART GALLERY, (M), 2 Erie Blvd., Canajoharie, NY 13317-1198. Tel.: 518-673-2314. Fax: 518-673-5243.
E-mail: etrahan@sals.edu
Web Site: www.clag.org
Founded: 1929.
Congressional District: 31
Key Personnel: Dir., Eric Trahan; Pres. (V), Oliver Simonsen.
Personnel Profile: Full-Time Paid 3; Part-Time Paid 5.
Governing Authority: nonprofit organization. Tax-exempt: 509(a).
Library & Art Gallery.
Collections: American art including works by Winslow Homer, The American Impressionists, the Ash Can Artists, the Hudson River School, and American Watercolorists.
Facilities: library of books of general interest & special collection of art of America available for inter-library loan on short term.
Activities: guided tours; gallery talks.
Publications: quarterly newsletter; booklet, A Walking Tour of the Village of Canajoharie; catalog of the art collection.
Hours & Admission Prices: Mon.-Thurs. 10-7, Fri. 10-5, Sat. 12:30-5. No charge; donations accepted. Closed holidays. ♿
Attendance: 55,000 (accurate)
Membership: Student $15; Individual $25; Family $35; Organization $50.

Canandaigua

THE GRANGER HOMESTEAD SOCIETY, INC., 295 N. Main St., Canandaigua, NY 14424-1228. Tel.: 585-394-1472. Fax: 585-394-6958.
E-mail: info@grangerhomestead.org
Web Site: www.grangerhomestead.org
Founded: 1946.
Congressional District: 33
Key Personnel: Exec. Dir., Tricia Reddick Carey; Pres. (V), Jack Schuppenhauer; Business Mgr., Jo-el Hibbard; Administrative Asst., Libby Campbell; Dir. Mktg., Jane Clark; Museum Shop Mgr., Susan Pevear; Maintenance, Thomas Hilarski.
Personnel Profile: Full-Time Paid 2; Part-Time Paid 4; Part-Time Volunteers 200; Interns 1.
Governing Authority: society; nonprofit. Branch Museum: The Granger Homestead Carriage Museum. Tax-exempt: 501(c)(3).
Historic House Museum: 1816 Gideon Granger Mansion.
Collections: decorative arts; furniture; silver; china; glass & textiles; 1820-1930 horse-drawn vehicles; over 70 antique carriages; progress of light, oil lamps & brass fixtures.
Research Fields: architecture; 19th-century decorative arts & interiors; horse-drawn vehicles.
Facilities: research library; archives. Museum-related items for sale.
Activities: guided tours; lectures; concerts; workshops; classes; educational programs; docent program; special events; private rentals; society business. Museum Sponsors: carriage rides in summer; Festival of Trees; Craft Fair Fundraiser; lawn sale; art lecture; art show; historical recitals & concerts.
Publications: bimonthly newsletter, Gideon's Trumpet.
Hours & Admission Prices: June-Oct. Tues.-Wed. & Sat.-Sun. 1-5, Thurs.-Fri. 11-5. Adults $6, senior citizens $5, children $2; discounts to groups, AAA and AAM members & Sonnenberg Gardens visitors; members no charge. Additional charge for special events. Closed New Year's Eve & Day; Presidents' Day; Memorial Day; Independence Day; Labor Day; Columbus Day; Thanksgiving; Christmas Eve, Day & week. ♿

Attendance: 16,000 (accurate)
Membership: Individual $35; Family $50; Friend $75; Benefactor $125; Gold $175; Platinum $250; Diamond $500; Gideon's Circle $1,000.

ONTARIO COUNTY HISTORICAL SOCIETY, (M), 55 N. Main St., Canandaigua, NY 14424-1438. Tel.: 585-394-4975. Fax: 716-394-9351.
E-mail: director@ochs.org
Web Site: www.ochs.org
Founded: 1902.
Congressional District: 31
Key Personnel: Exec. Dir. & Museum Shop Mgr., Edward Varno; Pres. (V), Thomas Walter; Bookkeeper, Ernest Mor; Cur., Wilma T. Townsend; Educator, Nancy Parsons; Library Mgr., Linda Alexander; Computer Admin., Bruce Stewart; Museum Shop Mgr., Maureen O'Connell Baker.
Personnel Profile: Full-Time Paid 3; Full-Time Volunteers 1; Part-Time Paid 2; Part-Time Volunteers 62.
Governing Authority: society. Tax-exempt: 501(c)(3).
Historical Society Museum.
Collections: 15,000 objects & 60,000 manuscripts & photographs relating to history of Ontario County; genealogy of the region.
Major Exhibits: Lincoln, Self-Made in America (T), 2/10.
Research Fields: history of western New York state; genealogy.
Facilities: 2,000-vol. library of books pertaining to western NY state, local history & genealogies available for research on premises; 2 galleries.
Activities: tours; lectures; school programs; permanent & temporary exhibitions.
Publications: newsletter, books & pamphlets on local history; photographic histories; quarterly newsletter, Chronicles; Roseland, Playground of The Finger Lakes, 1935-1985.
Hours & Admission Prices: Tues. & Thurs.-Sat. 10-5, Wed. daily 10-9. Adults $3; discounts to AAA members & Time Travelers; members no charge. Research Room: by appointment. Research: $7.50. Research by Mail: $30 an hour. Closed national holidays. ♿
Attendance: 7,500 (accurate)
Membership: Senior $30; Individual $35; Family $50; Friend $75; Centennial $100; Benefactor $150; Heritage Circle $250; Real Good Friend $1,000 & up.

SONNENBERG GARDENS & MANSION STATE HISTORIC PARK, 151 Charlotte St., Canandaigua, NY 14424-1363. Tel.: 585-394-4922. Fax: 585-394-2192.
E-mail: director@sonnenberg.org
Web Site: www.sonnenberg.org
Founded: 1970.
Congressional District: 31
Key Personnel: Chm., Robert Lowenthal; Dir., David Hutchings; Pres. (V), Jim Ingalls; Museum Shop Mgr., Natalie Saxton.
Personnel Profile: Full-Time Paid 6; Part-Time Paid 14; Part-Time Volunteers 305; Interns 5.
Governing Authority: nonprofit organization. Tax-exempt: 501(c)(3).
Historic House & Botanical Garden: 1887 Sonnenberg Mansion & Gardens.
Collections: period furniture & furnishings; Victorian estate garden.
Research Fields: history of mansion & original owners; historical landscape practices-early 20th century.
Facilities: 50 acres of Victorian gardens; Finger Lake Wine Center. Museum-related items for sale.
Activities: guided tours; lectures; concerts; workshops; formally organized education programs; docent program or council; loan, permanent & temporary exhibitions.
Publications: brochure.
Hours & Admission Prices: May 13-Oct. 8. Adults $10, seniors $9; discounts to AAA & American Horticultural Society members; children under 12 & members (excluding special events) no charge. ♿
Attendance: 32,000 (accurate)
Membership: Single $35; Dual $55; Family $65; Patron $200; Rose Society $500; Orchid Society $1,000.

Canton

PIERREPONT MUSEUM, 864 State Hwy. 68, Canton, NY 13617-3468. Mailing Address: 872 State Hwy. 68, Canton, NY 13617-3468. Tel.: 315-386-8311 & 379-0804. Fax: 315-379-0415.
E-mail: barbara@northnet.org
Founded: 1977.
Congressional District: 26
Key Personnel: Historian, Barbara J. Daniels.
Governing Authority: society. Parent Institution: Pierrepont Historical Society. Tax-exempt.
Antiques Museum: housed in early 1800 district school house.
Collections: rural school setting; farm tools of the pre-machine era; veterans exhibit; antique text books; kitchen artifacts; clothing dating from 1800-1875; paintings & biographies of local artists; minerals from local mines.
Facilities: 100-vol. library of text books, scrap books, documentaries available for research on premises by appointment by phoning town historian.
Activities: tours.
Publications: booklet, Pierrepont Memories-People, Places & Things.
Hours & Admission Prices: Memorial Day-Labor Day Sat. 10-1; other times by appointment. No charge; donations accepted.
Attendance: 150
Membership: Annual $2; Family $6; Life $50.

* **ST. LAWRENCE COUNTY HISTORICAL ASSOCIATION - SILAS WRIGHT HOUSE, (M),** 3 E. Main, Canton, NY 13617-1416. Mailing Address: P.O. Box 8, Canton, NY 13617-0008. Tel.: 315-386-8133. Fax: 315-386-8134.
E-mail: info@slcha.org
Web Site: www.slcha.org
Founded: 1947.
Congressional District: 23
Key Personnel: C.E.O., Trent Trulock; Pres., Carlton Stickney.
Personnel Profile: Full-Time Paid 2; Part-Time Paid 2; Part-Time Volunteers 111; Interns 3.
Governing Authority: nonprofit organization. Parent Institution: St. Lawrence County Historical Association. Tax-exempt: 501(c)(3).
Preservation Project: housed in 1834 home of Governor Silas Wright.
Collections: early 19th-century furniture; costumes; household utensils; local history artifacts & archives.
Research Fields: St. Lawrence County history & folklore.
Facilities: 1,500-vol. library of local history material; genealogical information; Wright family papers.
Activities: guided tours; lectures; temporary & permanent exhibits; special events; programs for school children.
Publications: magazine, The Quarterly; bimonthly newsletter; books: Old Hollywood; 1878 History of St. Lawrence County; The County Chronicler; Silas Wright, The Farmer Statesman; The Wright House Paper Model Book.
Hours & Admission Prices: Museum & Archives: Tues.-Thurs. & Sat. 12-4, Fri. 12-8. Museum: no charge. Archives: adults $5, college students $2.50; discounts to AAM & ICOM members; members & children no charge. Closed New Year's Eve & Day; Martin Luther King, Jr. Day; Presidents' Day; Memorial Day; Independence Day; Labor Day; Columbus Day; Thanksgiving & day after; Christmas Eve, Day and week. ♿
Attendance: 8,739 (accurate)
Membership: Senior Citizen & Student $25; Individual $30; Family $40; Contributing $55; Supporting $100; Patron $250 & up.

ST. LAWRENCE UNIVERSITY - RICHARD F. BRUSH ART GALLERY AND PERMANENT COLLECTION, (M), 23 Romoda Dr., Canton, NY 13617-1501. Tel.: 315-229-5174. Fax: 315-229-7445.
E-mail: ctedford@stlawu.edu
Web Site: www.stlawu.edu/gallery
Founded: 1967.
Congressional District: 30
Key Personnel: Dir., Catherine L. Tedford; Asst. Dir., Carole Mathey; Arts Programming Coord., Juli Pomainville.
Personnel Profile: Full-Time Paid 2; Part-Time Paid 1; Interns 25.
Governing Authority: college. Parent Institution: St. Lawrence University. Tax-exempt: 501(c)(3).
University Art Gallery.
Collections: 20th-century European & American works of art on paper including prints, photographs, drawings, and artists' books and portfolios, with emphasis on American photography; 19th- & 20th-century American & European painting, sculpture, and ceramics.
Research Fields: pertaining to collections.
Facilities: three exhibition galleries; 75-seat auditorium; classrooms.
Activities: lectures; films; gallery talks; arts festivals; training programs; loan, permanent, temporary & traveling exhibitions.
Publications: exhibition brochures; book, Photographs at St. Lawrence University.
Hours & Admission Prices: Mon.-Thurs. 10-8, Fri. 10-5, Sat. 12-5. No charge. Closed college recesses. ♿
Attendance: 20,000 (estimated)

Cape Vincent

CAPE VINCENT HISTORICAL MUSEUM, James St., Cape Vincent, NY 13618. Mailing Address: P.O. Box 376, Cape Vincent, NY 13618-0376. Tel.: 315-654-4400.
Founded: 1968.
Congressional District: 26
Key Personnel: Pres. (V), Jeanne Thompson; Dir., Mary Hamilton; Dir. & Town Historian, Peter Margrey.

Governing Authority: municipal. Affiliated with the Cape Vincent Town Board. Tax-exempt.
General Museum: housed in a stone building used as barracks in the War of 1812.
Collections: archives; history.
Research Fields: growth of Cape Vincent; family histories.
Facilities: library of scrapbooks, history books on early French settlers, family histories, historic buildings & activities available for use by appointment; reading room.
Activities: guided tours; permanent & temporary exhibitions.
Publications: pamphlet, History of Cape Vincent.
Hours & Admission Prices: July-Aug. Mon.-Sat. 10-4, Sun. 1-3. Historical research & family histories by appointment. No charge; donations accepted. ♿
Attendance: 3,000 (estimated)

Castile

WILLIAM PRYOR LETCHWORTH MUSEUM, One Letchworth State Park, Castile, NY 14427-9714. Tel.: 585-493-3600. Fax: 716-493-5272. TDD: 716-493-3070.
E-mail: brian.scriven@oprhp.state.ny.us
Web Site: www.nysparks.state.ny.us
Founded: 1913.
Key Personnel: Park Mgr., Roland Beck; Museum Dir. & Historic Site Mgr., Brian Scriven.
Personnel Profile: Full-Time Paid 1; Part-Time Paid 5; Part-Time Volunteers 2.
Governing Authority: state. Parent Institution: Genesee State Park & Recreation Region Executive Dept. Tax-exempt.
State Park Museum.
Collections: history; ethnology; Indian artifacts; Civilian Conservation Corps. History; pioneer artifacts. Historic Houses: pre-Revolution Council House; c.1800 Nancy Jemison cabin; William Pryor Letchworth papers.
Research Fields: Genesee Valley history; Western New York history.
Facilities: 500-vol. library of W.P. Letchworth's personal collection & his reference library of penal & epileptic institutions & Genesee Valley historical material available for research under supervision.
Activities: permanent exhibitions; interpretive historical video.
Publications: museum brochure; historical booklet.
Hours & Admission Prices: May-Oct. daily 10-5. No charge; donations accepted. ♿
Attendance: 25,000 (accurate)

Cattaraugus

CATTARAUGUS AREA HISTORICAL CENTER, 23 Main St., Cattaraugus, NY 14719-1032. Mailing Address: 26 S. Franklin St., Cattaraugus, NY 14719-1130. Tel.: 716-257-9500.
Founded: 1955.
Congressional District: 34
Key Personnel: Pres. (V), Robert B. Waite; Sec., Dawn D. Waite.
Governing Authority: Executive Council of Cattaraugus Area Historical Society. Subsidiary Institution: Medora Ball Historical Museum, Otto, NY 14766. Tax-exempt.
Historical Society Museum: housed in historic building owned by Village of Cattaraugus.
Collections: agriculture; archives; costumes; general; Indian artifacts; manuscripts; industry; military; eight-foot, hand-carved Statue of Liberty; over 200 photos, yearbooks & historical documents of the schools of the town of New Albion, from 1800s & up. Historic Building: 1862 Otto Congregational Church.
Research Fields: local history of the Cattaraugus area: villages of Cattaraugus, Otto, East Otto and immediate rural area.
Activities: permanent & temporary exhibitions; bimonthly public programs.
Hours & Admission Prices: By appointment only. No charge; donations accepted.
Attendance: 200 (estimated)
Membership: Annual $5; Life $25.

Cazenovia

CAZENOVIA COLLEGE - ART GALLERY AT REISMAN HALL ART & DESIGN CENTER, Cazenovia College, 22 Sullivan St., Cazenovia, NY 13035-1085. Tel.: 315-655-7138. Fax: 315-655-2190.
E-mail: jpepper@cazenovia.edu
Web Site: www.cazenovia.edu
Formerly: Cazenovia College - Art & Design Gallery
Founded: 1978.
Key Personnel: Dir., Jen Pepper.
Personnel Profile: Full-Time Paid 1.
Governing Authority: private college; nonprofit. Tax-exempt.
Art Gallery.
Collections: works by international, national & regional artists including paintings; sculpture; prints; photographs; video; digital
Facilities: 1,000 sq. ft. exhibit space.
Hours & Admission Prices: Spring, Fall & Winter: Mon.-Thurs. 1-4 & 7-9, Fri. 1-4, Sat.-Sun. 2-6. Summer hours vary. No charge; donations accepted. Closed when college is not in session. ♿
Attendance: 1,000 (estimated)

LORENZO STATE HISTORIC SITE, 17 Rippleton Rd., Cazenovia, NY 13035-9601. Tel.: 315-655-3200. Fax: 315-655-4304.
E-mail: Barbara.Bartlett@oprhp.state.ny.us
Web Site: www.lorenzony.org
Founded: 1968.
Congressional District: 32
Key Personnel: Dir., Barbara Bartlett; Interpretive Programs Asst., Sharon M. Cooney; Cur. Asst., Jackie Vivirito.
Personnel Profile: Full-Time Paid 6; Part-Time Paid 6; Part-Time Volunteers 60.
Governing Authority: state. New York State Office of Parks, Recreation and Historic Preservation, Central Region.
Historic House Museum: 1807 Federal-style mansion built for John Lincklaen, land agent for the Holland Land Co.
Collections: Lincklaen/Ledyard family furnishings; 19th-century decorative arts; fine arts; carriages; regional archive of family documents; furniture. Historic Buildings: c.1892 Carriage House & Barn; tool building; garage; playhouse; smokehouse; c.1814 schoolhouse.
Research Fields: Lincklaen/Ledyard family; local history; early land development & transportation.
Facilities: 4,000-vol. library of family manuscripts & 100,000 papers available for use by advance request; formal gardens; picnic area; visitor center.
Activities: guided tours; lectures; gallery talks; special events; annual horse & carriage pleasure driving competition; cross-country skiing.
Publications: newsletter; Lorenzo Guidebook.
Hours & Admission Prices: May-Oct. Wed.-Sun. 10-4:30; other times by appointment. Adults $5, tour groups & NY state senior citizens $4; Friends of Lorenzo & members no charge. ♿
Attendance: 45,000 (estimated)
Membership: Friends of Lorenzo: Regular Single $25; Regular Family $35; Benefactor $100; Patron $150; Sponsor $250 & up.

ROTHSCHILD PETERSEN PATENT MODEL MUSEUM, 4796 W. Lake Rd., Cazenovia, NY 13035-9670.
E-mail: museum@patentmodel.org
Web Site: www.patentmodel.org
Key Personnel: Owner, Alan Rothschild
General Museum.
Collections: patent models.
Hours & Admission Prices: By appointment only.

STONE QUARRY HILL ART PARK, INC., 3883 Stone Quarry Rd., Cazenovia, NY 13035-8447. Mailing Address: P.O. Box 251, Cazenovia, NY 13035-0251. Tel.: 315-655-3196. Fax: 315-655-5742.
E-mail: office@stonequarryhillartpark.org
Web Site: www.stonequarryhillartpark.org
Founded: 1991.
Key Personnel: Exec. Dir., Joseph A. Scala; Pres. (V), Dick Tuttle; Site Mgr., Dylan Otts; Arts Admin., Amber Blanding.
Personnel Profile: Full-Time Paid 3; Part-Time Paid 1; Part-Time Volunteers 10.
Governing Authority: private; nonprofit organization. Tax-exempt: 501(c)(3)
Sculpture Art Park.
Collections: outdoor sculpture consisting of site-specific installations and a permanent collection mounted in a natural setting consisting of woodlands, meadows & wetlands.
Major Exhibits: Juried - Town of Cazenovia Artists, 6/13/10-7/11/10; The Contemporary Portrait, 7/25/10-8/15/10; Juried - National Landscape Exhibition (T), 9/12/10-10/10.
Facilities: 3,000-vol. library of art books available to members by appointment; 2,400 sq. ft. exhibit space; 80-seat classroom; 104 acre park; nature trails.
Activities: arts festivals; concerts; informal education programs; guided tours; lecture; workshops. Annual Events: Syracuse Ceramic Guild Sale; Society for New Music; Art in the Sky, kite fest; Talons: Birds of Prey.
Publications: biannual newsletter, Newsletter; exhibition catalogs; e-newsletters.
Hours & Admission Prices: Park: daily dawn to dusk. Gallery: daily 10-5. Suggested Donation: $5 per car; members no charge. ♿
Attendance: 30,000 (estimated)

Membership: Student $10; Seniors 65 & over $25; Individual $35; Senior Couple $45; Couple $50; Family $70.

Centerport

* **SUFFOLK COUNTY VANDERBILT MUSEUM, (M),** 180 Little Neck Rd., Centerport, NY 11721-1145. Mailing Address: P.O. Box 0605, Centerport, NY 11721-0605. Tel.: 631-854-5555. Fax: 631-854-5594.
E-mail: info@vanderbiltmuseum.org
Web Site: www.vanderbiltmuseum.org
Founded: 1950.
Congressional District: 3
Key Personnel: Exec. Dir., Carl Ghiorsi Hart; Pres. Bd. Trustees (V), Noel Gish; Dir. Public Programming, Lorraine Vernola; Education, Beth Laxer-Limmer; Museum Shop Mgr., Betty McQueeny; Museum Shop & Business Office, Barbara Oster.
Personnel Profile: Full-Time Paid 17; Part-Time Paid 69; Part-Time Volunteers 54; Interns 1.
Governing Authority: county. Chartered by Education Dept. of University of the State of New York. Tax-exempt: 501(c)(3).
Historical Site: Marine & Natural History Museum & Planetarium. 1910-36, Spanish Revival mansion located on 43-acre landscaped estate of William K. Vanderbilt, II.
Collections: Marine Biology & Wildlife; European, 19th-century & Late Gothic Fine Arts; medieval-19th-century decorative arts including Far & Near East, European & American furniture, metal work, ceramics & carpets; Oriental, Muslim & European firearms & swords; South Pacific, Asian, African & Persian anthropology and ethnology; original Vanderbilt natural history exhibits; marine biology, butterfly, bird & shell collections; ship models and chandlery; maritime books & paintings; documents of the Vanderbilt family; library containing the private collection of Mr. Vanderbilt including the nine books he wrote; antique & classic automobiles; Aeolian player organ.
Research Fields: Vanderbilt history & collections; astronomy & space science.
Facilities: science library available to institutions of higher learning through exchange; planetarium; specimen trees including 12 lindens, statuary & garden ornaments. Museum-related items & educational material for sale.
Activities: guided tours; lectures; workshops; concerts; classes; sky shows.
Publications: pamphlet; guide book; newsletter, The Eagle's Nest; brochures; posters.
Hours & Admission Prices: Grounds & Mansion: Tues.-Fri. 12-5, Sat. 11-5, Sun. 12-5. Planetarium Sky Shows: Fri. 8, 9, & 10pm, Sat. 11, 12, 1, 2, 3, 4, 7pm, 8pm, 9pm, 10pm, Sun. 12, 1, 2, 3, 4. Daytime General Admission: adults $7, seniors & students $6, children under 12 $3. Mansion Tour: additional $5 per person. Planetarium Show: additional $5 per person. Evening Planetarium: adults $7, seniors & students $6, children under 12 $3.50.
Attendance: 200,000 (estimated)
Membership: Student & Senior Citizen $20; Individual $40; Family $50; Donor $75; Patron $150; Benefactor $300; Corporate $250-$2,500.

Chappaqua

NEW CASTLE HISTORICAL SOCIETY - HORACE GREELEY HOUSE, (M), 100 King St., Chappaqua, NY 10514-3433. Mailing Address: P.O. Box 55, Chappaqua, NY 10514-0055. Tel.: 914-238-4666. Fax: 914-238-1296.
E-mail: newcastlehs@aol.com
Web Site: www.newcastlehistoricalsociety.org
Founded: 1966.
Congressional District: 24
Key Personnel: Pres., Frances Osborne; Exec. Dir., Betsy Towl; Museum Shop Mgr., Toni Hutin.
Personnel Profile: Part-Time Paid 4; Part-Time Volunteers 85; Interns 1.
Governing Authority: nonprofit organization; society. Parent Institution: New Castle Historical Society. Tax-exempt.
History Museum: housed in the Horace Greeley family country home, 1864-1872 .
Collections: New Castle history; Quakers; Horace Greeley memorabilia; costumes; photographs; postcards.
Major Exhibits: Readers' Digest in Chappaqua, 1/10-1/11.
Research Fields: genealogy & local history with emphasis on Horace Greeley & the Quakers.
Facilities: 100-vol. library of books on Horace Greeley, Westchester history & Quakers; period herb garden. Notepapers, maps of community, pamphlets for sale.
Activities: guided tours; lectures; permanent & temporary exhibitions; oral history workshops; school programs & workshops. Special Event: annual indoor antiques show.
Publications: books, The Early Quaker Hamlet of Old Chappaqua; The Chappaqua Life of Horace Greeley; Deeds & Misdeeds, 1657-1763; A Bicentennial History of the Town of New Castle: 1791-1991; The Battle of White Plains; The 1872 Nomination & Presidential Campaign of Horace Greeley; Rare Architectural Heritage - Old Houses of Chappaqua & Millwood; Annandale Farm; video, Our Quaker Heritage; newsletter; annual report; exhibition catalogues; postcards; note paper; maps; Images of America - Newcastle: Chappaqua and Millwood.
Hours & Admission Prices: Aug. Tues.-Thurs. 1-4; Sept.-July Tues.-Thurs. & Sat. 1-4. No charge; donations accepted. Closed New Year's Day; Christmas. ♿
Attendance: 4,309 (accurate)
Membership: Members $35; Contributor $50; Patron $100; Supporter $250; Benefactor $500; Pacesetter $1,000.

Chazy

THE ALICE T. MINER COLONIAL COLLECTION, (M), 9618 Main St., Chazy, NY 12921. Mailing Address: P.O. Box 628, Chazy, NY 12921-0628. Tel.: 518-846-7336.
E-mail: minermuseum@westelcom.com
Web Site: www.minermuseum.org
Founded: 1924.
Congressional District: 31
Key Personnel: C.E.O., Pres. (V) & Chm. (V), Mrs. Joan T. Burke; Dir. & Cur., Amanda A. Palmer.
Personnel Profile: Full-Time Paid 1; Part-Time Paid 2; Part-Time Volunteers 10.
Governing Authority: nonprofit organization. Tax-exempt: 501(c)(3).
Colonial Revival Museum: housed in 1824 limestone building.
Collections: paintings; decorative arts; furnishings; glass; Indian; military; manuscripts.
Facilities: 900-vol. library of books of the 18th,19th & 20th centuries available on premises.
Activities: guided tours; permanent exhibitions; educational programs; entertainment events.
Hours & Admission Prices: Tues.-Sat. 10-4. Guided Tours: 10am, 12 & 2pm. Adults $3, seniors $2, students $1; student groups no charge.
Attendance: 2,500 (estimated)

Cherry Valley

CHERRY VALLEY MUSEUM, 49 Main St., Cherry Valley, NY 13320. Mailing Address: P.O. Box 115, Cherry Valley, NY 13320-0115. Tel.: 607-264-3303 & 3098. Fax: 607-264-9320.
E-mail: museum@celticart.com
Web Site: cherryvalleymuseum.com
Founded: 1958.
Congressional District: 31
Key Personnel: Chm. (V) & Museum Shop Mgr., Barbara Bell; Pres. (V), James Johnson.
Personnel Profile: Part-Time Paid 2; Part-Time Volunteers 30.
Governing Authority: society. Affiliated with the Cherry Valley Historical Association. Tax-exempt: 501(c)(3).
History Museum: housed in 1832 home.
Collections: 15 rooms of exhibits pertaining to farm & village life in Cherry Valley since late 18th century.
Research Fields: genealogy.
Facilities: 100-vol. library of books & genealogies available for use on premises; reading room. Books on Cherry Valley history for sale.
Activities: guided tours; permanent exhibitions.
Publications: book, The History of Cherry Valley from 1740 to 1898; DVD & video tape, The Border Warfare of N.Y. During the Revolution; The Annals of Tryon County.
Hours & Admission Prices: Memorial Day to mid-Oct. daily 10-5. Adults $5, senior citizens 60 & over $4.50; discounts to groups of 10 or more & AAA members; children under 11 & members no charge. Closed Independence Day. ♿
Attendance: 1,450 (estimated)
Membership: Youth 18 & under $2; Annual $5; Joint $9; Sustaining $15; Life $150.

Chittenango

CHITTENANGO LANDING CANAL BOAT MUSEUM, 7010 Lakeport Rd., Chittenango, NY 13037-9594. Tel.: 315-687-3801 & 7759. Fax: 315-687-3801.
E-mail: clcbm@centralny.twcbc.com
Web Site: www.chittenangolandingcanalboatmuseum.com
Founded: 1986.
Key Personnel: Exec. Dir., Joan DiChristina; Cur. & Archivist, Barbara Richardson; Devel., Lynn DeOrio.
Personnel Profile: Full-Time Volunteers 5; Part-Time Paid 4; Part-Time Volunteers 60.

Governing Authority: private; nonprofit. Tax-exempt: 501(c)(3).
Transportation Museum: housed in a 19th century structure.
Collections: artifacts & structural features recovered from the site & used for interpretation; artifacts relating to the canal boat repair building & social aspects of the canal; original canal boat drawings.
Research Fields: archaeological investigation of site to identify & delineate historic features; investigation of canal boat building practices of the 19th century; area residents related to those workers of the original & enlarged Erie Canal and to the dry docks at Chittenango Landing.
Facilities: 700-vol. library related to boat building & canal history; 1,625 sq. ft. exhibit space; 5-acre archaeological site; visitors center. Museum-related items for sale.
Activities: formal education programs; guided tours; lectures; participatory exhibits; 4 elderhostel programs yearly. Annual Events: July 4th Community Celebration; Winter Fun Day.
Publications: quarterly newsletter, From the Boatyard.
Hours & Admission Prices: May-June Sat.-Sun. 1-4; July-Aug. daily 10-4; Sept.-Oct. Sat.-Sun. 1-4. Adults $5, senior citizens $3; children 12 & under no charge. Closed New Year's Day; Easter; Thanksgiving; Christmas. ♿
Attendance: 12,000 (estimated)
Membership: Hoggee under 18 & Canaller 55 & over $7; Drydocker $12; Towpath Traveler $20; Bronze Anchor $30; Silver Anchor $50; Gold Anchor $100; Boat Builder $250; Steersman $500; Captain $1,000; Lockmaster $2,500.

Clarence

HISTORICAL SOCIETY OF THE TOWN OF CLARENCE, 10465 Main St., Clarence, NY 14031-1617. Mailing Address: P.O. Box 86, Clarence, NY 14031-0086. Tel.: 716-759-8575.
Founded: 1954.
Congressional District: 38
Key Personnel: Pres., Elaine Dinola; Cur., Mrs. Alicia L. Braaten.
Personnel Profile: Part-Time Paid 1; Part-Time Volunteers 19.
Governing Authority: society; nonprofit organization. Tax-exempt.
Historical Society & Genealogy Museum.
Collections: archaeology; genealogy of Clarence & Western New York families; Indian artifacts; the garage & workshop where Wilson Greatbatch invented the implantable pacemaker. Historic Structure: lob cabin c.1825.
Research Fields: archaeology; Clarence history; Indian artifacts.
Facilities: collection of local & Western New York history available on premises; reading room.
Activities: guided tours; lectures; formally organized education programs for children; permanent & temporary exhibitions.
Publications: newsletter, A Ransom Note; Clarence bicentennial historical books; local history books.
Hours & Admission Prices: March-Oct. Sun. 1-4, Wed 10-2; Nov.-April Wed. 10-2; other times by appointment. No charge; donations accepted. Closed holidays. ♿
Attendance: 2,300 (accurate)
Membership: Single $8; Individual $15; Couple $25; Family $30; Life $150.

Clayton

THE ANTIQUE BOAT MUSEUM, (M), 750 Mary St., Clayton, NY 13624-1119. Tel.: 315-686-4104. Fax: 315-686-2775.
E-mail: info@abm.org
Web Site: www.abm.org
Founded: 1964.
Congressional District: 30
Key Personnel: Exec. Dir., John MacLean; Cur., Daniel Miller; Dir. Devel., Barbara Maddocks; Dir. Events, Charlotte Brooks; Business Mgr., Dale Cursa; Cur. Education, Lora A. Nadolski; Museum Shop Mgr., Alan Hutchinson; Collections Asst., Ryan Mahoney; Devel. Asst., Christine Brown; Supvr. Facilities, Bud Gray; Coord. Membership, Robyn Lewis; Facility Asst., Jim Mellowship; Accountant Clerk, Norma Zimmer.
Personnel Profile: Full-Time Paid 13; Part-Time Paid 15; Part-Time Volunteers 125.
Governing Authority: board of trustees; nonprofit organization. Tax-exempt: 501(c)(3).
Antique Boat Museum.
Collections: St. Lawrence sailing & rowing skiffs; power skiffs; canoes; duckboats; outboards; outboard & inboard engines; launches; runabouts; utilities; ice boats; racing boats; photography collection; boat building molds & tools; nautical artifacts; St. Lawrence River culture.
Research Fields: freshwater recreational boating, St. Lawrence regional history.
Facilities: 700-vol. library of books pertaining to nautical & history of the Thousand Islands region available for research upon request; educational facilities. Museum-related items for sale.
Activities: guided tours; lectures; hobby workshops; loan, permanent & traveling exhibitions; charters & cruises; boat building & restoration classes; children's classes; boat rides every hour on the hour. Museum Sponsors: antique boat show, auction, small craft festival, regatta.
Publications: triannual newsletter, Gazette; brochures; pamphlets; exhibition catalogues.
Hours & Admission Prices: mid-May to mid-Oct. daily 9-5; other times by appointment. Adults $12, students 13 & over $10, children 7-12 $6; discounts to AAM, ICOM & AAA members, senior citizens, military personnel & groups; children under 6 & members no charge. ♿
Attendance: 33,295 (accurate)
Membership: Individual $50; Family $65; Supporting $125; Contributing $250; Patron $500; Friends of the Museum $1,000 & up.

THE HANDWEAVING MUSEUM & THOUSAND ISLANDS ARTS CENTER, 314 John St., Clayton, NY 13624-1017. Tel.: 315-686-4123. Fax: 315-686-3459.
E-mail: rebecca@tiartscenter.org
Web Site: www.tiartcenter.org
Formerly: American Handweaving Museum and Thousand Islands Craft School
Founded: 1966.
Congressional District: 26
Key Personnel: Exec. Dir., Rebecca Hopfinger; Chm. (V), Barbara Vars; Education Coord., Meghan Caddick.
Personnel Profile: Full-Time Paid 4; Part-Time Paid 2; Part-Time Volunteers 21; Interns 1.
Governing Authority: nonprofit organization. Tax-exempt: 501(c)(3).
Textile Museum: housed in late 19th-century two-story frame home.
Collections: over 1,400 textiles from ancient Egyptian to present including 20th century handwovens; archives including books, photographs & correspondence; 1,600 textile-oriented books.
Research Fields: 20th-century American handweaving.
Facilities: library; archives; pottery studio; weaving studio; garden. Museum-related items for sale.
Activities: guided tours; arts festivals; hobby workshops; organized education programs; temporary exhibitions. Museum Sponsors: fiber arts workshops; annual art & antique show & sale; annual juried crafts show & sale; Annual Weaving History Conference.
Publications: quarterly newsletter, Hand-Crafted; Introduction to the Collection.
Hours & Admission Prices: Mon.-Fri. 9-5, Sat. 10-5. No charge; donations requested. Closed New Year's Day; Martin Lulther King Jr. Day; Presidents' Day; Memorial Day; Independence Day; Labor Day; Veterans Day; Columbus Day; Thanksgiving & day after; Christmas. ♿
Attendance: 12,000 (estimated)
Membership: Member $25; Family & Household $50; Sponsor $100; Benefactor $250; Patron $500.

THOUSAND ISLANDS MUSEUM, (M), 312 James St., Clayton, NY 13624-1012. Mailing Address: P.O. Box 27, Clayton, NY 13624-0027. Tel.: 315-686-5794. Fax: 315-686-4867.
E-mail: info@timuseum.org
Web Site: www.timuseum.org
Founded: 1964.
Congressional District: 30
Key Personnel: C.E.O., Linda Schleher; Pres. (V), Michael Strouse; Museum Shop Mgr., Sheila Thomson Honeywell.
Personnel Profile: Full-Time Paid 1; Full-Time Volunteers 2; Part-Time Volunteers 10.
Governing Authority: nonprofit corporation. Parent Institution: Thousand Islands Museum. Tax-exempt: 501(c)(3).
Local & Regional History Museum.
Collections: decoy carving; muskie fishing; pictorial history of Clayton & 1000 Islands; home of the St. Lawrence Tartan; St. Lawrence River Heritage.
Major Exhibits: Made in Clayton, 1/10-12/10.
Research Fields: history of St. Lawrence River & Thousand Islands region.
Facilities: library. Museum-related items for sale.
Activities: permanent & rotating exhibits. Museum Sponsors: fund-raiser, Decoy & Wildlife Art Show; Model Boat Show; Quilt Show; History At Noon Program in July & August.
Publications: brochure; newsletter.
Hours & Admission Prices: mid-May to mid-Oct. 10-5. No charge; donations accepted. ♿
Attendance: 15,000 (accurate)
Membership: Individual $25; Family $35; Supporting $50; Patron $100; Benefactor (5 yrs) $250; Contributing $1,251-$4,999; Architect $5,000.

Clinton

THE EMERSON GALLERY, (M), Hamilton College, 198 College Hill Rd., Clinton, NY 13323-1218. Tel.: 315-859-4396; 866-556-5116 (toll free). Fax: 315-859-4060.
E-mail: emerson@hamilton.edu
Web Site: hamilton.edu/college/emerson_gallery
Founded: 1982.
Congressional District: 32
Key Personnel: Consulting Dir., Ian Berry; Assoc. Dir. & Cur., Susanna White; Cur. Hamilton Collects, Bill Salzillo; Registrar, Dana Krueger; Gallery Office Asst., Megan Austin.
Personnel Profile: Full-Time Paid 3; Part-Time Paid 12; Part-Time Volunteers 4.
Governing Authority: Hamilton College. Tax-exempt.
Art Gallery
Collections: works on paper 15th-20th century with emphasis on 19th-20th century British & American; 19th-& 20th century paintings; Native American objects; Greek vases; Roman glass; Asian painting, sculpture & ceramics; Beinecke collection of 16th-to 19th century prints, drawings & maps of West Indies.
Activities: 6-10 art exhibitions per year; lectures; films; tours; gallery talks; concerts; performances.
Publications: The Art of Music: American Paintings & Musical Instruments, 1770-1910; Wonderful Heroes, Fearsome Creatures: Art of the Northwest Coast; Marsden Hartley in Bavaria; A Neat Plain Modern Stile: Philip Hooker & His Contemporaries, 1790-1840.
Hours & Admission Prices: Mon.-Fri. 10-5, Sat.-Sun. 1-5. No charge; donations accepted. Closed New Year's Day; Memorial Day; Independence Day; Christmas Day. ♿
Attendance: 8,000 (estimated)
Membership: $25 for all levels.

Cold Spring

PUTNAM COUNTY HISTORICAL SOCIETY & FOUNDRY SCHOOL MUSEUM, (M), 63 Chestnut St., Cold Spring, NY 10516-2613. Tel.: 845-265-4010. Fax: 845-265-2884.
E-mail: office@pchs-fsm.org
Web Site: www.pchs-fsm.org
Founded: 1906.
Congressional District: 21
Key Personnel: Exec. Dir., Mindy Krazmien; Cur., Trudie Alexis Grace; Historical Records, Charlotte B. Eaton.
Personnel Profile: Full-Time Paid 3; Part-Time Paid 3; Part-Time Volunteers 6.
Governing Authority: society. Parent Institution: Putnam County Historical Society. Subsidiary Institution: Foundry School Museum. Tax-exempt: 501(C)(3).
Local History Museum: housed in 1828 Foundry Schoolhouse.
Collections: 19th-century paintings; items from the West Point Foundry including manufactured articles; photos; documents; records; letters; local genealogical records; manuscripts.
Research Fields: local history; genealogy; West Point Foundry.
Facilities: 1,500-vol. library of history books available for use by appointment on premises; reading room. Museum-related items for sale.
Activities: guided tours; lectures; gallery talks; historical research; inter-museum loan exhibitions; school loan service; school program.
Publications: book, A Brief Story of the American Revolution in the Hudson Highlands; occasional pamphlets.
Hours & Admission Prices: March-Dec. Wed.-Sun. 11-5. Adults $5; members no charge. ♿
Attendance: 1,800 (estimated)
Membership: Student & Senior $25; Individual $40; Family $70; Friend $150; Supporting $300; Sustaining $500; Patron $750; Benefactor $1,000.

Cold Spring Harbor

* **COLD SPRING HARBOR WHALING MUSEUM, (M),** 301 Main St., Cold Spring Harbor, NY 11724. Mailing Address: P.O. Box 25, Cold Spring Harbor, NY 11724-0025. Tel.: 631-367-3418. Fax: 631-692-7037.
E-mail: cshwm@optonline.net
Web Site: www.cshwhalingmuseum.org
Founded: 1936.
Congressional District: 5
Key Personnel: Exec. Dir., Paul B. DeOrsay; Pres. (V), Douglas Arthur; Dir. Education, Nomi Dayan; Museum Shop Mgr., Willa Davis.
Personnel Profile: Full-Time Paid 5; Part-Time Paid 6; Part-Time Volunteers 65.
Governing Authority: society. Tax-exempt: 501(c)(3).
Whaling Museum.
Collections: scrimshaw collection; ship models; maritime paintings; manuscript collection; 19th-century whaleboat; whaling implements; permanent exhibit on Long Island Whaling industry; marine mammal conservation display.
Major Exhibits: Tales & Treasures from Attic to Archive, 11/09-9/10.
Research Fields: whales & whaling with emphasis on conservation.
Facilities: 2,000-vol. library on whales & whaling, film library and manuscripts by appointment. Nautical items for sale.
Activities: guided tours; lectures; films; gallery talks; formally organized education programs; permanent, rotating & changing exhibitions; maritime workshops for children & adults; walking tours; special weekend programs.
Publications: triannual newsletter, A Whaling Account; books; booklets; collection catalogues; In Their Hours of Ocean Leisure.
Hours & Admission Prices: Memorial Day-Labor Day daily 11-5; Sept.-May Tues.-Sun. 11-5; tours by appointment. Family $19, adults $6, senior citizens & students 5-18 $5; discounts to CAMM, ICOM & AAM members, & other museum professionals; active military, members & children under 5 no charge. Sun. special programs 11-1 & 3 pm. ♿
Attendance: 22,000 (accurate)
Membership: Individual $35; Family $50; Patron $100; Associate $250; Sponsor $500; Benefactor $750.

SOCIETY FOR THE PRESERVATION OF LONG ISLAND ANTIQUITIES, 161 Main St., Cold Spring Harbor, NY 11724-0148. Mailing Address: P.O. Box 148, Cold Spring Harbor, NY 11724-0148. Tel.: 631-692-4664. Fax: 631-692-5265.
E-mail: info@splia.org
Web Site: splia.org
Founded: 1948.
Congressional District: 1
Key Personnel: Pres., Paul Vermylen; Dir., Robert B. MacKay; Dir. Education, Patricia Hildebrandt; Property Mgr., Alan Tewksbury; Operations Mgr., Rosemary DeSensi; Museum Shop Mgr., Mildred Luckett.
Personnel Profile: Full-Time Paid 6; Part-Time Paid 14; Part-Time Volunteers 25.
Governing Authority: nonprofit organization. Tax-exempt: 501(c)(3).
Preservation Society.
Collections: decorative arts, textiles, ceramics, glass, photographs, paintings, prints, manuscripts, pertaining to house museums. Historic Houses: 1767 Joseph Lloyd manor, village of Lloyd Neck, Long Island; c.1700 Thompson house, Setauket, Long Island; 1730-1780 Sherwood-Jayne house, E. Setauket, Long Island; c.1800 Custom house, Sag Harbor, Long Island; The Gallery, Main St., Cold Spring Harbor, Long Island.
Research Fields: Long Island history & material culture.
Activities: education programs; publications; preservation services; special projects.
Publications: periodical, Preservation Notes; books, A History of the Joseph Lloyd Manor House; Long Island Domestic Architecture of the Colonial & Federal Periods; Long Island is My Nation: The Decorative Arts & Craftsmen 1640-1830; Windmills of Long Island; Between Ocean & Empire: An Illustrated History of Long Island; Useful Art: Long Island Pottery; A Forgotten People: Discovering the Black Experience in Suffolk County; Long Island Country Houses & their Architects, 1860-1940; Saving Large Estates; Edward Lange's Long Island; Woven History: The Technology & Innovation of Long Island Coverlets, 1800-1860; AIA Guide to Nassau & Suffolk Counties, Long Island.
Hours & Admission Prices: Thompson House: closed for renovation. Custom House: June & Sept. Sat.-Sun. 10-5; July-Aug. daily 10-5; groups by appointment. Joseph Lloyd Manor: Memorial Day to Columbus Day Sat.-Sun. 1-5; groups by appointment. Sherwood-Jayne House: April-Nov. by appointment only. Adults $3, seniors & children 7-14 $1.50. SPLIA Gallery: Jan.-April Sat.-Sun. 11-5; May-Oct. Tues.-Sun. 11-5; Nov.-Dec. 11-5. No charge; donations accepted. ♿
Attendance: 16,221 (accurate)
Membership: Student & Senior Citizen $15; General $25; Family $35; Sustaining $100; Corporation & Contributing $250; Life $1,000 Patron $2,500; Founder $5,000.

Commack

LONG ISLAND CULTURE HISTORY LAB & MUSEUM, Hoyt Farm Park, New Hwy., Commack, NY 11725. Mailing Address: P.O. Box 1542, Stony Brook, NY 11790-0910. Tel.: 631-929-8725. Fax: 631-929-6967.
E-mail: gaystone@optonline.net
Web Site: www.scaa-ny.org
Founded: 1975.
Congressional District: 1
Key Personnel: Pres. (V), Douglas DeRenzo; Dir., Gaynell Stone, Ph.D.
Personnel Profile: Full-Time Paid 1; Part-Time Paid 20; Part-Time Volunteers 5.

Governing Authority: society. Parent Institution: Suffolk County Archaeological Assn. Subsidiary Institution: Blydenburgh County Park, New Mile Rd., Smithtown, NY 11787. Tax-exempt: 501(c)(3).
Historical Site: prehistoric park with an 18th-century house & 20th-century outbuildings. Site 1: Native American complex. Site 2: 18th- & 19th-century house & outbuildings; Dutch architecture.
Collections: prehistoric & historic artifacts; photographs.
Research Fields: Long Island archaeology; ethnohistory; technology; material culture; historic photographs.
Facilities: 300-vol. library; classrooms; culture history center & interactive museum.
Activities: guided tours; lectures; organized education programs; workshops.
Publications: triannual newsletter; biannual reference series, Readings in Long Island Archaeology & Ethnohistory; biannual student series, Prehistoric Natives of Long Island; posters, Native Technology & Native Long Island; workbook, Native Life & Archaeology; Native Forts of the Long Island Sound Area.
Hours & Admission Prices: Sept.-June Mon.-Fri. 10-2 by appointment. Admission fee for programs. ♿
Attendance: 10,000 (accurate)
Membership: Student $10; Individual $20; Family $30; Institution $50; Contributing $100; Patron $200; Life $400.

Cooperstown

* **THE FARMERS' MUSEUM, INC., (M),** 5775 State Hwy. 80, Cooperstown, NY 13326. Mailing Address: P.O. Box 30, Cooperstown, NY 13326-0030. Tel.: 607-547-1450. Fax: 607-547-1404.
E-mail: info@nysha.org
Web Site: www.farmersmuseum.org
Founded: 1943.
Congressional District: 31
Key Personnel: Pres. & C.E.O., D. Stephen Elliott; Chm. Bd., Jane Forbes Clark; Vice Pres. Education, Garet Livermore; Dir. Finance, Marnie Auld; Vice Pres., Chief Cur. & Acting Dir. Library, Paul D'Ambrosio; Sr. Dir. Operations, Joseph Siracusa; Sr. Dir. Human Resources, Barbara Fischer; Cur. Collections, Douglas Kendall; Registrar, Christine Olsen; Museum Shop Mgr., Amy Blechman.
Personnel Profile: Full-Time Paid 90; Part-Time Paid 68; Part-Time Volunteers 225; Interns 4.
Governing Authority: Tax-exempt.
Village Museum: housed in early 19th-century Village including 29 buildings.
Collections: crafts; farm implements & technology; agriculture; transportation; textiles; 19th-century rural & village life.
Major Exhibits: Wild Times: A New York Animal Road Trip, 11/09-10/10.
Research Fields: farm implements; New York rural life history; agriculture; textiles; village architecture.
Facilities: 80,000-vol. library shared with the New York State Historical Association.
Activities: Museum Sponsors: conferences, seminars & graduate level courses of study with New York State Historical Association.
Publications: early 19th-century book reprints series; conference papers.
Hours & Admission Prices: April to mid-May & early Oct. Tues.-Sun. 10-4; mid-May to Columbus Day daily 10-5. Adults $11, seniors 65 & over $9.50, children $5; discounts to AAM & ICOM members; children under 7 & New York State Historical Association members no charge. ♿
Attendance: 70,000 (accurate)

HYDE HALL, INC., (M), 267 Glimmerglass State Park Rd., Cooperstown, NY 13326. Mailing Address: P.O. Box 721, Cooperstown, NY 13326-0721. Tel.: 607-547-5098 & 6129. Fax: 607-547-8462.
E-mail: dianeelliott@hydehall.org
Web Site: www.hydehall.org
Formerly: Friends of Hyde Hall, Inc.
Founded: 1964.
Congressional District: 23
Key Personnel: Dir. Operations, Linda VanCleef; Bd. Chm. (V), Andrew M. Blum; Museum Shop Mgr., Anne Clarke Logan.
Personnel Profile: Full-Time Paid 2; Full-Time Volunteers 1; Part-Time Paid 15; Part-Time Volunteers 2.
Governing Authority: Tax-exempt.
Historic House Museum.
Collections: family artifacts dating from 1820.
Research Fields: family archives & collections.
Facilities: rooms for meetings; grounds available for rental.
Activities: special events.
Hours & Admission Prices: Tours: mid-May to Oct. Thurs.-Tues. 10-4. Adults $10, seniors $8, children 5-14 $5; discounts to groups & State Park visitors; members & children under 5 no charge. ♿
Attendance: 4,000 (estimated)
Membership: Friend $35-$49; Dual Family $50-$99; Century Club $100-$499; Wellington Club $500-$999; Halcyon Circle $1,000-$4,999; Founders Circle $5,000 and up.

NATIONAL BASEBALL HALL OF FAME AND MUSEUM, INC., (M), 25 Main Street, Cooperstown, NY 13326-1300. Tel.: 607-547-7200. Fax: 607-547-2044.
E-mail: pclark@baseballhalloffame.org
Web Site: www.baseballhalloffame.org
Founded: 1936.
Congressional District: 31
Key Personnel: Pres., Jeffrey Idelson; Sr. Vice Pres., William Haase; Vice Pres. Mktg., Sean Gahagan; Sr. Dir. Communications & Education, Brad Horn; Controller, Fran Althiser; Cur. Collections, Peter P. Clark; Sr. Dir. Exhibits & Collections, Erik Strohl; Librarian, Jim Gates; Sec., William T. Burdick; Museum Shop Mgr., Diane Adams.
Personnel Profile: Full-Time Paid 73; Part-Time Paid 107; Part-Time Volunteers 2; Interns 30.
Governing Authority: nonprofit organization. Tax-exempt: 501(c)(3).
Sports Museum.
Collections: plaques of members of Baseball Hall of Fame; autographed baseballs; bats; trophies; books; pictures; paintings; cigarette & gum cards; uniforms; cartoons; history time line; video tapes of World Series & All-Star Games; research library.
Major Exhibits: Olympic Baseball, 4/15/10-12/10; Hank Aaron, 5/15/10-12/10; Olympic Baseball, 5/30/10-12/10.
Research Fields: baseball statistics; history.
Facilities: 1,200-vol. library of scrapbooks, complete sets of Guides & record books, clippings, newspapers, magazines, photographs, microfilm, motion pictures, phonograph records, tapes, August Herrmann & A. G. Mills correspondence pertaining to baseball available by appointment on premises; reading room; 200-seat Baseball Experience theater; 60-seat bullpen-style theater in library. Books, baseballs & other museum-related items for sale.
Activities: films; loan & temporary exhibits; audio & visual displays; special educational programs for children grades 4-6, Nov.-April; distance learning capability. Annual Events: Baseball Symposium in June; special Sandlot Series in summer; Artifact Spotlights in summer; Hall of Fame Classic Game & Induction Ceremony.
Publications: annual yearbook, National Baseball Hall of Fame and Museum; brochure, descriptive folder of Museum; six times per year newsletter; membership magazine, Memories & Dreams; Donor brochure; membership brochure.
Hours & Admission Prices: Memorial Day to Labor Day daily 9-9; Sept.-May daily 9-5. Adults $16.50, senior citizens $11, children 7-12 $6; discount to AAM members & groups with advance reservations; members, military no charge. Closed New Year's Day; Thanksgiving; Christmas. ♿
Attendance: 301,755 (accurate)
Membership: Junior 12 & under $20; Individual $40; Family $70; Sustaining $100; Patron $175; President's Circle $500; Benefactor $1,000 & up.

* **NEW YORK STATE HISTORICAL ASSOCIATION/FENIMORE ART MUSEUM, (M),** 5798 St. Hwy. 80, Cooperstown, NY 13326. Mailing Address: P.O. Box 800, Cooperstown, NY 13326-0800. Tel.: 607-547-1400. Fax: 607-547-1404.
E-mail: info@nysha.org
Web Site: www.nysha.org
Founded: 1899.
Congressional District: 31
Key Personnel: Chm. Bd., Dr. Douglas E. Evelyn; Pres. & C.E.O., D. Stephen Elliott; Vice Pres., Chief Cur. & Acting Dir. Library, Paul D'Ambrosio; Vice Pres. Education, Garet Livermore; Dir. Finance, Marnie Auld; Sr. Dir. Operations, Joseph Siracusa; Sr. Dir. Human Resources, Barbara Fischer; Dir. Cooperstown Graduate Program, Gretchen Sorin; Cur. Collections, Douglas Kendall; Registrar, Christine Olsen; Museum Shop Mgr., Amy Blechman.
Personnel Profile: Full-Time Paid 82; Part-Time Paid 36; Part-Time Volunteers 157; Interns 9.
Governing Authority: Subsidiary Institution: Fenimore Art Museum. Tax-exempt: 501(c)(3).
Historical Association & Art Museum.
Collections: Fenimore Art Museum: academic & folk art; costumes; sculpture; graphics; history; decorative arts; manuscripts and American Indian Art.
Major Exhibits: Connecting Threads: 19th Century Upstate Fashion, 4/10-12/10; John Singer Sargent: Painting the Feminine Ideal, 5/21/10-12/10.
Research Fields: decorative arts; U.S. & New York State history; museum studies; art history.
Facilities: 80,000-vol. library of books; reading room. Books for sale.
Activities: formally organized education programs for children, adults & graduate students; graduate program in History Museum Studies in conjunction with State University College of New York at Oneonta; technical advisory services to museums.

Publications: quarterly journal, New York History; annual magazine, Heritage; monographs; various books; collections catalogs.
Hours & Admission Prices: April to mid-May & Oct.-Dec. Tues.-Sun. 10-4; mid-May to Columbus Day daily 10-4. Adults $11, seniors 65 & over $9.50, children 7-12 $5; discounts to AAM members; members & children under 7 no charge. Closed Thanksgiving; Christmas. ♿
Attendance: 41,700 (accurate)
Membership: Student & Educator $25; Individual $50; Far-Away Friends $50; Family & Household $80; Culture Club 21-41 $80-$100; Sustaining $115; Contributing $250; Benefactor $500; Fenimore Society $1,000.

Corning

* **THE CORNING MUSEUM OF GLASS, (M), (I),** One Museum Way, Corning, NY 14830-2253. Tel.: 607-937-5371. Fax: 607-974-8470.
Web Site: www.cmog.org
Founded: 1951.
Congressional District: 39
Key Personnel: Chm. (V), James B. Flaws; Exec. Dir., David B. Whitehouse; Pres. (V), E. Marie McKee; Cur., Jane S. Spillman; Cur., Tina Oldknow; Cur., Florian Knothe; Sr. Dir. Creative Svcs. & Mktg., Robert K. Cassetti; Research Scientist, Dr. Robert Brill; Dir. Finance, David Togni; Head of Publication Dept., Richard Price; Conservator, Stephen Koob; Photographer, Nicholas L. Williams; Librarian, Diane Dolbashian; Dir. Finance & Administration, Nancy J. Earley; Mgr. Hot Glass Programs, Steve Gibbs; Dir. Devel., Education & The Studio, Amy Schwartz; Operations Mgr., Fred Bierline; Glass Market & Guest Svcs. Mgr., Victor Nemard; Dir. Human Resources, Ellen Corradini; Registrar, Warren Bunn; Communications Mgr., Yvette Sterbenk.
Personnel Profile: Full-Time Paid 123; Part-Time Paid 4; Part-Time Volunteers 265.
Governing Authority: nonprofit educational institution. Tax-exempt: 501(c)(3).
Glass Art & History Museum.
Collections: comprehensive collection of glass vessels; objects; archaeological remains from every period & area of glass history.
Research Fields: glass history; early technology; archaeology; conservation; chemical analysis & examination; isotope studies; physical property measurements.
Facilities: 50,000-vol. research library on art, history, technology & archaeology of glass; periodicals, trade catalogs, microfilm, microfiche, films, videotapes, slides for use on premises; cafe & snack bar; 6,000 sq. ft. studio, offering instruction & practical experience in the art & craft of glassmaking; glassworking studio. Museum publications for sale.
Activities: self-guided tours; lectures; films; gallery talks; formally organized education programs for children; paid guided tour service; inter-museum loan, permanent & temporary exhibitions; seminars on glass history; live glassmaking demonstrations; try-it-yourself glassmaking.
Publications: annuals, Journal of Glass Studies; New Glass Review; recent books: The Corning Museum of Glass, A Decade of Glass Collecting; Chemical Analysis of Early Glass, Vol. 1 & 2; Innovations in Glass; The Glass Skin; The American Cut Glass Industry: T.G. Hawkes and His Competitors; Designs in Miniature: The Story of Mosaic Glass (CD-ROM), produced by the Victoria and Albert Museum (London); The Corning Museum of Glass & Art of Memory; Roman Glass in The Corning Museum of Glass Vol. 1, 2 & 3; Beyond Venice: Glass in Venetian Style 1500-1750; 25 Years of New Glass Review; European Glass Furnishings for Eastern Palaces; Glass of the Alchemists: Lead Crystal - Gold Ruby 1650-1750; Contemporary Glass Sculptures and Panels: Selections from the Corning Museum of Glass; DVD, Glass Masters at Work: Lino Tagliapietra.
Hours & Admission Prices: June-Aug. daily 9-8; Sept.-May daily 9-5. Adults $12.50; discounts to senior citizens, college students, AAA, AAM & ICOM; members & children 19 and under no charge. Free to Rediscover: sign-up pay admission once & no charge to end of year. Closed New Year's Day; Thanksgiving; Christmas Eve & Day. ♿
Attendance: 316,000 (accurate)
Membership: Student $20; Senior & Long-Distance $30; Individual $35; Senior Couple $40; Family & Household $60; Donor $100; Supporting $250; Patron $500; Benefactor $1,000.

PATTERSON INN MUSEUM/CORNING - PAINTED POST HISTORICAL SOCIETY, 59 W. Pulteney St., Corning, NY 14830-2212. Tel.: 607-937-5281.
E-mail: pattersoninnmuseum@verizon.net
Web Site: www.pattersonmuseum.org
Formerly: The Benjamin Patterson Inn Museum
Founded: 1976.
Congressional District: 39
Key Personnel: C.E.O. & Dir., Jessica Cunningham; Pres. (V), Sheri Golder.
Personnel Profile: Full-Time Paid 1; Part-Time Paid 2; Part-Time Volunteers 50; Interns 6.
Governing Authority: board of trustees. Parent Institution: Corning-Painted Post Historical Society. Tax-exempt: 501(c)(3).
Historic Building: 1796 Benjamin Patterson Inn.
Collections: furnishings & artifacts appropriate to the Inn & the years 1800-1850; local history items; extensive costume collection. Historic Buildings: c.1850 log cabin; c.1878 one-room schoolhouse; c.1860s four bay barn; blacksmith shop; c.1881 Delaware, Lackawana & Western Railroad Station.
Research Fields: local history.
Facilities: 300-vol. library of local & area history books available for research on premises only. Books, stationery, traditional toys & other gift items for sale.
Activities: guided tours; lectures; school programs.
Publications: bimonthly newsletter.
Hours & Admission Prices: Mon.-Fri. 10-4; other times by appointment. Adults $4, senior citizens 60 & over $3.50, students $2; discounts to groups over 10 & AAA members; preschool children & members no charge. Closed major holidays.
Attendance: 10,000 (estimated)
Membership: Student $10; Senior Citizen $20; Individual $25; Family $40; Donor $50; Patron $100; Corporate $250; Benefactor $500 & up.

* **ROCKWELL MUSEUM OF WESTERN ART, (M),** 111 Cedar St., Corning, NY 14830-2632. Tel.: 607-937-5386. Fax: 607-974-4536.
E-mail: info@rockwellmuseum.org
Web Site: www.rockwellmuseum.org
Founded: 1976.
Congressional District: 31
Key Personnel: Exec. Dir., Kristin Swain; C.E.O. & Chm. (V), A. John Peck, Jr.; Dir. Education, Gigi Alvare; Dir. Public Programs, Visitor Svcs. & Museum Shop Mgr., Cindy Weakland; Cur. Collections, Sheila Hoffman; Mktg. Specialist, Beth Manwaring; Controller, Andrew Braman.
Personnel Profile: Full-Time Paid 13; Part-Time Paid 1; Part-Time Volunteers 30; Interns 1.
Governing Authority: nonprofit education institution. Tax-exempt: 501(c)(3).
American Western & Native American Art Museum.
Collections: 19th- & 20th-century art of the North American West and Native American Art, including paintings, sculpture, works of art on paper & related materials; firearms.
Major Exhibits: Las Artes de Mexico (T), 11/09-1/30/10; The Photographs of Edward S. Curtis, 1/15/10-5/9/10; Human Nature: Artists as Explorers in the Early American West, 1/15/10-5/9/10; 21st Century Regionalists: Art of the Next West, 5/20/10-1/11.
Research Fields: American Western Art; Native American Art.
Facilities: 2,500-vol. library. Southwestern crafts & jewelry; books on Western American art & other museum-related items for sale.
Activities: guided tours; formally organized education programs for children; docent training program; temporary & permanent exhibitions; lectures; symposiums.
Publications: exhibition catalogues; annual report; brochures; postcards; slides; prints; posters; catalog of western art collection.
Hours & Admission Prices: Memorial Day to Labor Day daily 9-8; Sept.-May daily 9-5. Family $20, adults $6.50, senior citizens $5.50; discounts to groups, AAA, ICOM, AAM, Upstate New York Art Museum Consortium members & Museums West Consortium members; members and youth under 19 no charge. Closed New Year's Day; Thanksgiving; Christmas Eve & Day. ♿
Attendance: 30,200 (accurate)
Membership: Individual $40; Family $70; Turquoise $125-$249; Copper $250-$499; Nickel $500-$999; Silver $1,000-$2,499; Gold $2,500 & up.

Cornwall-on-Hudson

HUDSON HIGHLANDS NATURE MUSEUM, 25 Boulevard, Cornwall-on-Hudson, NY 12520. Mailing Address: P.O. Box 337, Cornwall-on-Hudson, NY 12520-0337. Tel.: 845-534-5506. Fax: 845-534-4581.
E-mail: mgoldin@hhnaturemuseum.org
Web Site: www.museumhudsonhighlands.org
Formerly: Museum of the Hudson Highlands
Founded: 1962.
Congressional District: 97
Key Personnel: Exec. Dir., Jacqueline Grant; Chm. (V), David N. Redden; Vice Pres., Susan W. Christensen; Coord. Education, Judy Onnfer; Business Mgr. & Museum Shop Mgr., Candace Rivera; Mktg. Assoc., Marian Goldin; Cur. Living Exhibits, Pam Golben; Young Naturalist & Head Teacher, Sandy Dixon.
Personnel Profile: Full-Time Paid 6; Part-Time Paid 10; Part-Time Volunteers 25; Interns 1.
Governing Authority: private. Subsidiary Institution: Outdoor Discovery Center, 20 Kenridge Farm Dr., Cornwall, NY; Kenridge Farm, Rte. 9W, Cornwall. Tax-exempt: 501 (c)(3).

Nature & Environmental Museum.
Collections: preserved fishes, reptiles, amphibians, live animals, Indian artifacts and geological specimens indigenous to the Hudson Valley; ichthyology collection from Hudson River tributaries.
Research Fields: exhibiting live animals; regional phenological data; field surveys; restoration of the Bald Eagle, Peregrine Falcon & Osprey populations along the Hudson River; restoration of Hudson River tidal freshwater marshes.
Facilities: library; classrooms. Boulevard: hiking trails. Kenridge Farm: nature trails. Gifts items for sale.
Activities: evening film/lecture series; volunteer program for high school students, in-museum and in-school educational programs; creative art courses; community special events; creative art courses for children and adults; summer environmental workshops for elementary students. Kenridge Farms: bird watching, cross-country skiing; maple sugaring; seasonal events.
Publications: quarterly, Member's Bulletin; biannual, Teachers Bulletin.
Hours & Admission Prices: Boulevard Museum: Fri.-Sat. 10-5, Sun. 1-5. Wildlife Education Center: Fri.-Sun. 12-4. Outdoor Discovery Center: Sat.-Sun. 10-4. Museum on the Hudson Highlands Kenridge Farm: daily dawn to dusk. Wildlife Education Center: $3; members no charge. Outdoor Discovery Center: $3; members no charge. ♿
Attendance: 40,000 (estimated)
Membership: Highlander $35; Partner $60; Pathfinder $100; Explorer $250; Naturalists Club $500; Curator's Club $1,000; President's Circle $5,000.

Corona

LOUIS ARMSTRONG HOUSE & ARCHIVES, (M), 34-56 107th St., Corona, NY 11368-1226. Tel.: 718-997-3670 & 478-8274.
Web Site: www.louisarmstronghouse.org
Key Personnel: Dir., Michael Cogswell
Historic House Museum.
Collections: Armstrong history & cultural legacy; personal artifacts; photographs.
Hours & Admission Prices: Tues.-Fri. 10-5, Sat.-Sun. 12-5; groups by appointment. Adults $8, seniors, students & children $6; discounts to groups; members no charge.

Cortland

BOWERS SCIENCE MUSEUM, State Univ. of New York, Cortland Bowers Hall, Cortland, NY 13045. Tel.: 607-753-2900. Fax: 607-753-2927.
Founded: 1964.
Key Personnel: Dir. & Cur., Dr. Peter K. Ducey.
Personnel Profile: Interns 2.
Governing Authority: state; university. Parent Institution: State University College at Cortland & State University of New York, 8 Thurlow Terrace, Albany, 12201. Tax-exempt.
Science Museum.
Collections: anatomy; local plants; gems & industrial collection; local birds & mammals; teaching skins; mounted fish & heads of game animals; local fossils; mollusks; human biology; ecology; ethology; geology & fungi.
Research Fields: conservation biology; plant, animal & fungal systematics; vertebrate evolution; ornithology; herpetology; many facets of ecology.
Facilities: nature/conservation center; field research station; planetarium; reading room; 300 seat auditorium; classrooms; nature trail; teaching units.
Activities: guided tours; lectures; films; formally organized education programs for children, undergraduate & graduate college students; permanent & temporary exhibitions; training classes for biology teachers graduate course in techniques & methods of collecting, culturing & preserving specimens.
Hours & Admission Prices: Summer: Mon.-Fri. 8-4; Sept.-June Mon.-Fri. 9-6; special group tours by appointment with Biology Dept. or Science Bldg. Coord. No charge. Closed holidays. ♿
Attendance: 4,000

CORTLAND COUNTY HISTORICAL SOCIETY, 25 Homer Ave., Cortland, NY 13045-2056. Tel.: 607-756-6071.
E-mail: cortlandcountyhistoricalsociety@centralny.twcbc.com
Web Site: www.cortlandhistory.com
Founded: 1925.
Congressional District: 24
Key Personnel: Pres., Diane Ames; Dir., Mindy Leisenring; Mgr. Collections, Anita Wright.
Personnel Profile: Full-Time Paid 2; Full-Time Volunteers 1; Part-Time Paid 1; Part-Time Volunteers 50; Interns 1.
Governing Authority: nonprofit organization; board of directors. Tax-exempt: 501(c)(3).
Historical Society Museum: housed in 1882 Suggett House built by James Suggett, holder of patents on the driven well.
Collections: clothing; military items from Revolutionary War to Desert Storm; furniture; textiles; paintings; photographs; tools; utensils; pottery; items relating to local industries; lighting devices; glass; silver; china; hair wreaths & jewelry; manuscripts; archival materials; collections related to the 200-year history of the county.
Research Fields: local history & genealogy.
Facilities: over 3,000-vol. library of books; letters, manuscripts, maps, tapes, documents & microfilms relating to Cortland County; 14,000 negatives of Brockway Motor Truck Co.; catalogs, broadsides & genealogical materials available for use in library wing. Publications of the Historical Society & other museum-related items for sale.
Activities: guided tours; walking tours; bus tours; lectures; craft classes & demonstrations; permanent & temporary exhibitions; school loan service; outreach services to clubs, organizations & schools.
Publications: newsletter, News Notes; pamphlet, Bulletin; books, Chronicles Vols. II, III, IV & V; Paris Lived in Homer; Residents of Cortland County 1800-1810; Growing up in Cortland; Index to Personal & Place Names, French's Gazetteer of NYS 1860; Rails Through Cortland; booklet, Historical Markers of Cortland County; annual pictorial calendar; A Regiment Remembered: The 157th NYV.
Hours & Admission Prices: Gift Shop: Tues.-Sat. 9:30-5. Museum: Tues.-Sat. 1-5. Library: Tues.-Sat. 1-5. Museum Tours: adults $3. Research Library $8 & $5; members no charge. Closed New Year's Day; Independence Day; Thanksgiving; Christmas. ♿
Attendance: 3,200 (accurate)
Membership: Senior Citizen $18; Individual $25; Family & Nonprofit $35; Supporting $60; Sustaining $125; Sponsor $300; Patron $600; Benefactor $1,200.

DOWD FINE ARTS GALLERY, STATE UNIVERSITY OF NEW YORK COLLEGE AT CORTLAND, SUNY Cortland, Dowd Fine Arts Center, Rm. 162, Cortland, NY 13045. Mailing Address: SUNY Cortland, P.O. Box 2000, Cortland, NY 13045-0900. Tel.: 607-753-4216. Fax: 607-753-5728.
E-mail: mounta@cortland.edu
Web Site: www.cortland.edu/art/html/gallery.html
Founded: 1967.
Congressional District: 25
Key Personnel: Dir., Andrew Mount.
Personnel Profile: Full-Time Paid 1; Interns 5.
Governing Authority: State University of New York College at Cortland. Tax-exempt.
University Art Gallery.
Collections: 19th- to 20th-century European & American paintings, prints, drawings, sculpture.
Research Fields: contemporary & modern art.
Facilities: 2,500 sq. ft. exhibit space.
Activities: docent program; films; guided tours; lectures; loan & temporary exhibitions; gallery talks.
Publications: exhibition catalogs in conjunction with temporary exhibits.
Hours & Admission Prices: Tues.-Sat. 10-4; other times by appointment. No charge; donations accepted. Closed major & university holidays. ♿
Attendance: 6,201 (accurate)

THE 1890 HOUSE-MUSEUM & CENTER FOR ARTS, 37 Tompkins St., Cortland, NY 13045-2555. Tel.: 607-756-7551. Fax: 607-756-7551 (call first).
E-mail: the 1890house@verizon.net
Web Site: www.1890house.org
Founded: 1976.
Congressional District: 32
Key Personnel: C.E.O., Dr. Laura Gathagan; Dir., Deanna L. Pace.
Personnel Profile: Part-Time Volunteers 30.
Governing Authority: nonprofit organization. Tax-exempt: 501(c)(3).
Historic House: 1890 Victorian chateauesque style mansion.
Collections: architectural & decorative features of the mansion, including parquet floors, hand carved oak & cherry woodwork, stained glass windows & skylights; 19th to early 20th century furniture; decorative arts; photographs; china; silver; glassware; textiles; clothing; paintings; wall stenciling; Victorian art.
Research Fields: family & site history.
Facilities: 500-vol. library of books on architecture & Victorian decorative arts; reading room. Museum-related items for sale.
Activities: guided tours; lectures; films; concerts; formally organized education programs; docent program; loan, permanent, temporary & traveling exhibitions; lectures; educational programs; school programs.
Publications: newsletter, Whispers Near the Inglenook.
Hours & Admission Prices: Thurs.-Sat. Adults $5, students & senior citizens $3; discounts to groups; children under 12 no charge. Closed major holidays. ♿
Attendance: 5,000 (estimated)

Membership: Senior & Student $15; General $25; Contributing $26-$249; Sustaining $250-$999; Benefactor $1,000 & up.

Coxsackie

BRONCK MUSEUM, Rte. 9W, Coxsackie, NY 12051-3022. Mailing Address: P.O. Box 44, Coxsackie, NY 12051-0044. Tel.: 518-731-6490. Fax: 518-731-7672.
E-mail: gchsbm@mhcable.com
Web Site: www.gchistory.org/
Founded: 1929.
Congressional District: 29
Key Personnel: Site Mgr., Shelby Mattice; C.E.O., Pres. (V) & Museum Shop Mgr., Robert Hallock; Chm. (V), Raymond Beecher.
Personnel Profile: Full-Time Paid 1; Part-Time Paid 2; Part-Time Volunteers 40.
Governing Authority: society. Parent Institution: The Greene County Historical Society. Tax-exempt: 501(c)(3).
Historic House Museum: 1663 home of Pieter Bronck, cousin of the first settler north of the Harlem River for whom Bronx Borough of New York was named.
Collections: art; silver; furniture; painting; pottery; textiles; carriages; early tools; weaving paraphernalia; manuscripts; 1663 Dutch dwelling; Dutch domestic & agricultural architecture. Vedder Memorial Library; manuscripts.
Research Fields: local history; genealogy.
Facilities: 5,000-vol. library of books; newspapers; manuscripts; photographs of Greene County & the Catskill Region. Museum-related items for sale.
Activities: guided tours; lectures; permanent & temporary exhibitions.
Publications: quarterly journal; books, Out to Greenville & Beyond; Historical Sketches of Greene County; Letters from a Revolution; book, Under Three Flags: A History of the Coxsackie, Earlton & Climax Settlements.
Hours & Admission Prices: Memorial Day to Oct. 15 Wed.-Fri. 12-4, Sat. 10-4, Sun. 1-4. Adults $5, youth 12-15 $3, children 5-11 $2; children under 5 & members no charge.
Attendance: 2,284 (accurate)
Membership: Individual $10-$19; Family $15-$24; Supporting, Sustaining & Business $25.

Croghan

AMERICAN MAPLE MUSEUM, 9756 Main St., Croghan, NY 13327. Mailing Address: P.O. Box 81, Croghan, NY 13327-0081. Tel.: 315-346-1107.
E-mail: maplehalloffame@westelcom.com
Web Site: www.lcida.org/maplemuseum.html
Founded: 1977.
Congressional District: 30
Key Personnel: Pres., Dale Moser; Treas., Jane Yancey; Sec., Eleanor Allen; Cur., Constance Yousey.
Personnel Profile: Part-Time Paid 1; Part-Time Volunteers 22.
Governing Authority: nonprofit organization. Tax-exempt.
Agricultural Museum.
Collections: historic & modern materials from the maple products industry.
Research Fields: history of maple products & production systems.
Facilities: 100-vol. library of periodicals of the maple products industry available for research by appointment only; 150-seat auditorium. Maple syrup, maple products, hand-crafted items for sale.
Activities: guided tours; lectures; permanent exhibitions. Annual Events: Maple Festival in May; Concert & Ice Cream Social in July; Fall Foliage Run in October.
Hours & Admission Prices: June Mon. & Fri.-Sat. 11-4; July-Labor Day Mon.-Sat. 11-4; off season visits by appointment. Adults $4, children 5-12 $1; discounts to AAA & CAA members. Group Tours: appointment requested.
Attendance: 1,710 (estimated)

Cross River

TRAILSIDE NATURE MUSEUM, Ward Pound Ridge, Rte. 35 & Rte. 121, Cross River, NY 10518. Mailing Address: P.O. Box 236, Cross River, NY 10518-0236. Tel.: 914-864-7322. Fax: 914-864-7323.
Web Site: www.trailsidemuseum.org
Founded: 1937.
Key Personnel: Cur., Michael Gambino.
Personnel Profile: Full-Time Paid 2; Part-Time Paid 1; Part-Time Volunteers 8.
Governing Authority: county. Parent Institution: County of Westchester Dept. of Parks, Recreation & Conservation, County Office Building, White Plains, 10601. Subsidiary Institution: Friends of Trailside Nature Museum. Tax-exempt.
Natural History Museum.
Collections: native American library; mounted birds of prey; songbirds; mammals; insects; geology; local history.
Research Fields: natural & local history.
Facilities: 1,500-vol. library of reference books, Delaware Indian Resource Center collection of rare books, tapes, & photographs devoted to the study of the coastal Algonkian tribes available for research on premises.
Activities: lectures; arts festivals; organized educational programs; permanent & temporary exhibitions.
Publications: quarterly calendar of events; educational leaflets; members newsletter.
Hours & Admission Prices: Winter: Tues.-Sun. 9-4; Summer: Mon.-Fri. 9-4. No charge. Parking Fee: $4 with resident permit, $8 without permit. ♿
Attendance: 20,000 (estimated)
Membership: Individual $10; Husband & Wife $15; Family $25; Sustaining $50; Supporting $100; Sponsor $250; Patron $500-$1,000.

Crown Point

CROWN POINT STATE HISTORIC SITE, 739 Bridge Rd., Crown Point, NY 12928-2817. Tel.: 518-597-4666. Fax: 518-597-4668.
Founded: 1910.
Congressional District: 30
Key Personnel: Historic Site Mgr., Tom Hughes; Site Interpreter, Thomas Nesbitt.
Personnel Profile: Full-Time Paid 1; Part-Time Paid 2.
Governing Authority: state. New York State Office of Parks, Recreation and Historic Preservation, and Saratoga Capital District Region. Tax-exempt: 501(c)(3).
Historic Site: 1734 remains of French fort, 1759 British Fort Crown Point & Outwork fortifications controlling Lake Champlain.
Collections: military materials; archaeological artifacts; 18th-century domestic materials.
Research Fields: French & Indian Wars; American Revolution; regional history.
Facilities: 60-seat auditorium; interpretive center; picnic area.
Activities: guided tours; lectures; audiovisual program; gallery talks; permanent exhibitions; special programs & demonstrations.
Hours & Admission Prices: Museum: May-Oct. Wed.-Mon. 9-5; other times by appointment. Adults $3, senior citizens $2, children $1. Grounds: Summer dawn to dusk.

Cuddebackville

NEVERSINK VALLEY AREA MUSEUM, 26 Hoag Rd., Cuddebackville, NY 12729. Mailing Address: P.O. Box 263, Cuddebackville, NY 12729-0263. Tel.: 845-754-8870. Fax: 845-754-8870.
E-mail: nvam@frontiernet.net
Web Site: neversinkmuseum.org
Founded: 1967.
Congressional District: 19
Key Personnel: C.E.O. & Pres. (V), Stephen Skye; Exec. Dir., Seth Goldman; Educational Dir., Susan Clayton.
Personnel Profile: Full-Time Paid 1; Part-Time Paid 1; Part-Time Volunteers 35.
Governing Authority: nonprofit organization. Tax-exempt: 501(c)(3).
Preservation Project & History Museum: housed in 2 buildings including a 1790, salt box-type house, part of the Delaware & Hudson Canal Park Historic Landmark.
Collections: local history of the Delaware & Hudson Canal; 19th century lifestyles in the Neversink River Valley area; early motion picture history.
Research Fields: 19th-century history; early motion pictures.
Facilities: 400-vol. library of historical material & periodicals; herb garden. Museum-related items for sale.
Activities: canal tours; school & group tours; craft demonstrations; lecture series; special canal boat activity center for children; permanent & changing exhibits.
Publications: quarterly newsletter.
Hours & Admission Prices: Thurs.-Sun. 12-4. Adults $3, children $1.50; children under 6 & members no charge. ♿
Attendance: 7,000 (accurate)
Membership: Individual $15; Family $25; Donor $50; Business $100; Contributor $125; Sponsor $250; Sustainer $500; Founder $1,000.

Derby

GRAYCLIFF CONSERVANCY, (M), 6472 Old Lake Shore Rd., Derby, NY 14047-9731. Mailing Address: P.O. Box 823, Derby, NY 14047-0823. Tel.: 716-947-9217. Fax: 716-947-2086.
E-mail: Graycliff@verizon.net
Web Site: graycliff.bfn.org
Founded: 1997.

Congressional District: 27
Key Personnel: Exec. Dir., Reine Hauser; Pres. (V), Diane Chrisman; Museum Shop Mgr., Katie Henneberg; Group Tour Coord., Shannon Lyons.
Personnel Profile: Full-Time Paid 1; Part-Time Paid 6; Part-Time Volunteers 300.
Governing Authority: private; nonprofit organization. Tax-exempt: 501(c)(3).
Historic House Museum: housed in the summer home of Isabelle and Darwin Martin; estate designed by Frank Lloyd Wright, 1926-1929.
Collections: furnishings, documents & personal artifacts of Frank Lloyd Wright, the Martin Family & the Larkin Soap Company.
Research Fields: gardens & grounds of Graycliff; historic furnishings of Graycliff.
Facilities: 100-vol. library; botanical garden. Museum-related items for sale.
Activities: docent program; formal education programs for adults; guided tours; lectures; participatory exhibits; special events. Annual Events: American Scholar Day.
Publications: biannual newsletter, Graycliff.
Hours & Admission Prices: early April to late May & Sept.-Nov. Thurs.-Tues.; Memorial Day to Labor Day daily; Winter: call for hours. Tours: call for hours. Adults $15, students 10-21 $10; discounts to groups of 20 or more; members no charge. Closed New Year's Day; Thanksgiving; Christmas. ♿
Attendance: 8,300 (accurate)
Membership: Student $20; Individual $35; Family $60; Benefactor $100; Gold $250; Platinum $500; Jewel $1,000.

Douglaston

ALLEY POND ENVIRONMENTAL CENTER, INC., 228-06 Northern Blvd., Douglaston, NY 11362-1096. Tel.: 718-229-4000, ext. 200. Fax: 718-229-0376.
E-mail: info@alleypond.com
Web Site: www.alleypond.com
Founded: 1976.
Congressional District: 6
Key Personnel: Exec. Dir., Irene V. Scheid; Pres. (V), Rita Sherman; Dir. Education, Aline Euler, Ph.D.; Museum Shop Mgr., Barbara Friedman.
Personnel Profile: Full-Time Paid 8; Part-Time Paid 5; Part-Time Volunteers 30; Interns 5.
Governing Authority: nonprofit organization. Tax-exempt: 501(c)(3).
Nature & Environmental Center.
Collections: historical maps; period artifacts; indigenous animals & marine life.
Research Fields: local flora & fauna; impact statements on construction & development.
Facilities: auditorium; classrooms; interpretive trails. Museum-related items for sale.
Activities: guided tours; lectures; films; hobby workshops; formally organized education programs; conservation.
Publications: bimonthly program guide & newsletter; APEC field guides; Secrets of the Marsh; Our Wild Friends Coloring Book.
Hours & Admission Prices: Mon.-Sat. 9-4:30, Sun. 9-3:30. Nominal fee for special programs. Closed New Year's Eve & Day; Martin Luther King Jr. Day; Presidents' Day; Easter; Mother's Day; Independence Day; Labor Day; Columbus Day; Thanksgiving & day after; Christmas Eve & Day. ♿
Attendance: 55,000 (accurate)
Membership: Senior Citizen $20; Individual $30; Family $40; School $50; Sponsor $100; Organization $200; Corporate $250; Life $500.

East Aurora

AURORA HISTORICAL SOCIETY, INC., 363 Oakwood Ave., East Aurora, NY 14052-2319. Mailing Address: P.O. Box 472, East Aurora, NY 14052-0472. Tel.: 716-652-4735.
Founded: 1951.
Congressional District: 38
Key Personnel: Pres., Rebecca Suttell; Cur. Elbert Hubbard Museum, Mary Ann Meyers; Cur. Elbert Hubbard Museum, Genevieve Steffen; Cur. Millard Fillmore House, Lyn Chemera; Cur. Millard Fillmore House, Marie Schnurr; Town Historian, Donald Dayer; Museum Shop Mgr., Grace Demme.
Governing Authority: society. Branch Museums: Elbert Hubbard Museum; Millard Fillmore House; Town Hall Museum. Tax-exempt.
Museum Complex & Historic District: national landmark known as Roycroft Campus, originated c.1896 by Elbert Hubbard as a haven to promote all types of arts & crafts; still in operation.
Collections: Historic Houses: c.1825 The President Millard Fillmore House-Museum, a national historic landmark; period furnishings; rose garden; herb garden, barn with collections. The Aurora Historical Museum: located in 1899 Town Hall; paintings; Indian artifacts; memorabilia; Kuster collection of Indian arrowheads; maps; atlases; photographs; genealogy files; books. Scheidemantel House, home of Elbert Hubbard Museum, a craftsman period home, housing artifacts and books of Elbert Hubbard and his Roycroft organization.
Facilities: library of history books and iconography; 115 years of East Aurora Advertiser newspapers on microfilm, available in the Town's Historian's office by request.
Activities: guided tours; self-guided tours of the campus.
Publications: books; pamphlets; brochures.
Hours & Admission Prices: June-Oct. Wed. & Sat.-Sun. 1-4. Fillmore & Hubbard museums $3 each location; Town Museum no charge.
Attendance: 3,200 (estimated)
Membership: Individual $10; Life $100.

COPPER SHOP GALLERY, 31 S. Grove St., East Aurora, NY 14052-2325. Tel.: 716-655-0261. Fax: 716-655-8498.
E-mail: info@roycroftcampuscorp.com
Web Site: www.roycroftcampuscorporation.com
Key Personnel: Pres., Douglas Swift; Exec. Dir., Christine Peters.
Governing Authority: Parent Institution: Roycroft Campus Corp.
History Museum.
Collections: local history; photographs; Roycroft artifacts; Dard Hunter window pane; early letter press; period furnishings.
Hours & Admission Prices: Daily 10-5.

ELBERT HUBBARD-ROYCROFT MUSEUM, 363 Oakwood Ave., East Aurora, NY 14052-2319. Mailing Address: P.O. Box 472, East Aurora, NY 14052-0472. Tel.: 716-652-4735 & 655-1321.
Web Site: www.roycrofter.com/museum.htm
Founded: 1962.
Congressional District: 30
Key Personnel: Co-Cur., Marion Fisher; Co-Cur., Genevieve Steffen; Co-Cur., Bruce F. Bland; Co-Cur., Mary Ann Myers; Chm. (V), Rita Hubbard.
Personnel Profile: Part-Time Volunteers 25.
Governing Authority: municipal. society; Parent Institution: The Aurora Historical Society, Inc. (see separate listing for branch museums). Tax-exempt: 501(c)(3).
Library and History Museum: housed in 1910 Scheide Mantel Home.
Collections: history & culture of Roycroft community & Elbert Hubbard; books, furniture & craft items of Roycroft Shops.
Facilities: 1,100-vol. library of books, magazines & pamphlets printed at Roycroft Shops from 1895-1936 available for inter-library loan & for use on premises; reading room.
Activities: lectures; gallery talks; permanent, temporary & traveling exhibitions.
Publications: pamphlet, Elbert Hubbard & the Roycrofters; pamphlet, A Message to Garcia.
Hours & Admission Prices: June-Oct. Wed. & Sat.-Sun. 1-4. Adults $3, school children $1; Aurora Historical Society Members no charge.
Attendance: 2,000 (estimated)
Membership: Individual $10; Life $200.

EXPLORE & MORE...A CHILDREN'S MUSEUM, 300 Gleed Ave., East Aurora, NY 14052-2983. Tel.: 716-655-5131. Fax: 716-655-5466.
E-mail: mail@exploreandmore.org
Web Site: www.exploreandmore.org
Founded: 1994.
Key Personnel: C.E.O. & Dir., Barbara Park Leggett; Chm., Thomas Hayes; Vice Pres., Pete Anderson; Education, Claudia Newton; Exhibits, Ann Frank; Treas., Barb Kolich; Museum Shop Mgr., Elizabeth Brown.
Personnel Profile: Full-Time Paid 1; Part-Time Paid 13; Part-Time Volunteers 40.
Governing Authority: private; nonprofit organization. Tax-exempt.
Children's Museum.
Collections: hands-on children's exhibits including building & architecture, food & nutrition, brain teasers, world cultures and infant & toddler play.
Activities: formal education programs for children; participatory exhibits; school loan service.
Publications: bimonthly newsletter, Explorations.
Hours & Admission Prices: Wed.-Sat. 10-5, Sun. 12-5, first Fri. of month 10-8, Mon.-Tues. large groups by appointment. Admission $5; ACM reciprocal; members no charge. Closed New Year's Day; Easter; Independence Day; Thanksgiving; Christmas. ♿
Attendance: 38,840 (accurate)
Membership: Creativity $45; Discovery & Discovery Grandparent $60; Imagination $100.

MILLARD FILLMORE HOUSE, 24 Shearer Ave., East Aurora, NY 14052. Mailing Address: Box 472, East Aurora, NY 14052-0472. Tel.: 716-652-8875 & 2432.
Founded: 1951.

Congressional District: 31
Key Personnel: Pres., Diane Meade; Cur., Marie Schnurr; Cur., Lyn Chemera; Cur., Rachelle Francis; Cur., Vivian Pikett.
Personnel Profile: Part-Time Volunteers 45.
Governing Authority: society. Parent Institution: The Aurora Historical Society, Inc. Tax-exempt.
Historical Society Museum: housed in 1826 home of the 13th U.S. President, Millard Fillmore.
Collections: period Fillmore furnishings; stenciled walls; barn; tools & farm implements; formal rose garden; herb garden.
Activities: tours.
Publications: brochures & postcards; books: local history.
Hours & Admission Prices: June-Oct. 15 Wed. & Sat.-Sun. 1-4; other times & tours by appointment. Adults $5; children under 12 no charge.
Attendance: 1,500 (estimated)
Membership: Annual $10; Life $100.

East Bloomfield

BLOOMFIELD ACADEMY MUSEUM, 8 South Ave., East Bloomfield, NY 14443. Mailing Address: P.O. Box 212, E. Bloomfield, NY 14443-0212. Tel.: 585-657-7244. Fax: 585-657-7244.
E-mail: director@ebhs1838.org
Web Site: www.ebhs1838.org
Founded: 1967.
Congressional District: 35
Key Personnel: C.E.O., William Burlingame; Cur., Stephen Beaulieu; Museum Shop Mgr., Richard Delong.
Personnel Profile: Part-Time Paid 1; Part-Time Volunteers 50.
Governing Authority: nonprofit organization. Parent Institution: Historical Society of the Town of East Bloomfield. Tax-exempt.
Historic Agency: housed in 1838 Bloomfield Academy Building.
Collections: local artifacts; clothing; furniture; household furnishings; dolls; tools; shells; inkwells; agricultural tools; genealogical research materials; period textbooks; agricultural artifacts; local authors' publications; reference materials; ledgers; diaries.
Research Fields: genealogical & historical research materials & personnel.
Facilities: library of early books on town of East Bloomfield & Ontario County available for research on premises & by special request. Locally handmade crafts & museum publications for sale.
Activities: guided tours; lectures; films; arts festivals; drama; docent program; permanent & temporary exhibitions; school loan service; genealogical programs; children's programs in summer; summer concerts. Museum Sponsors: Antique Car Show in July.
Publications: monthly newsletter, Academy Chronicles; quarterly magazine; books, Bloomfield Bicentennial Historical Sketchbook; Bloomfield Schools Revisited; Bloomfield Village Walking Tour; The War Years in Bloomfield 1941-1945; 1874 town & village maps.
Hours & Admission Prices: April-Dec. Wed.-Fri. 9-2, Sat. 9-12. No charge; donations accepted. Closed major holidays.
Attendance: 1,000 (estimated)
Membership: Senior Citizen $10; Individual $12; Senior Family $15; Family $20; Friend $35; Sustaining $35-$99. Corporate: Patron $100-$499; Benefactor $500-$1,000.

East Durham

DURHAM CENTER MUSEUM/RESEARCH LIBRARY, State Rte. 145, East Durham, NY 12423. Mailing Address: P.O. Box 192, East Durham, NY 12423-0192. Tel.: 518-239-8461 & 4081. Fax: 518-239-4081.
E-mail: durhamcentermu@aol.com
Founded: 1960.
Congressional District: 102
Key Personnel: C.E.O. & Pres. (V), Bruce Hamm; Exec. Dir., Asst. Cur. & Museum Shop Mgr., Sancie Thomsen; Cur., Douglas Thomsen.
Personnel Profile: Part-Time Volunteers 4.
Governing Authority: nonprofit organization. Tax-exempt.
General Museum.
Collections: folk art; local & Greene County artifacts; Civil War; genealogical.
Major Exhibits: Doctor, Doctor (Medical Exhibition), 6/10-7/10; Emily Weeks Exhibit, 8/10-9/10; The 19th Century Home, 10/10.
Research Fields: Susquehanna Turnpike; Catskill Canajoharie Railroad.
Facilities: library of historical books & genealogy records available for research on premises; reading room.
Activities: permanent exhibitions; special exhibits of local ephemera & photography; arts & crafts workshops. Museum Sponsors: Musical Program.
Publications: Catskill-Canojaharie RR; Lyman Tremaine, Rebels at Rest; James Barker Patroon-Yesteryear Fireside Recollections.
Hours & Admission Prices: Museum: 3rd week of May to Columbus Day Thurs.-Sun. 1-4. Adults $2.50, children under 12 $1.50; discount to AAM & ICOM members; children under 5 accompanied by adult no charge. ♿
Attendance: 500 (estimated)
Membership: $10-$2,000.

East Hampton

CLINTON ACADEMY MUSEUM, 151 Main St., East Hampton, NY 11937-2716. Mailing Address: 101 Main St., East Hampton, NY 11937-2714. Tel.: 631-324-6850. Fax: 631-324-9885.
E-mail: info@easthamptonhistory.org
Web Site: www.easthamptonhistory.org
Founded: 1921.
Congressional District: 2
Key Personnel: Pres. (V), Arthur Graham; Exec. Dir., Richard Barons.
Personnel Profile: Full-Time Paid 2; Full-Time Volunteers 5; Part-Time Paid 6; Part-Time Volunteers 35; Interns 1.
Governing Authority: nonprofit. Parent Institution: The East Hampton Historical Society. Branch Museums: Osborn-Jackson House; Mulford Farm Complex; Town House; Marine Museum. Tax-exempt: 501(c)(3).
History Museum: housed in a former school; built in 1784. Listed on the National Register of Historic Places.
Collections: decorative & fine arts; textiles; tools & equipment.
Major Exhibits: Pots & Pans: 300 Years of Hampton's Dining, 7/10-9/10.
Research Fields: eastern Long Island history; decorative & fine arts.
Activities: temporary exhibitions; lectures.
Publications: brochures; exhibition catalogues.
Hours & Admission Prices: Memorial Day to June & Sept. to Columbus Day Sat. 10-5, Sun. 12-5; July-Aug. Fri.-Sat. 10-5, Sun. 12-5. No charge; donations accepted. ♿
Attendance: 1,800 (estimated)
Membership: Individual $35; Family & Couple $60; Friend $75; Business $100.

EAST HAMPTON HISTORICAL SOCIETY, INC., (M), 101 Main St., East Hampton, NY 11937-2714. Tel.: 631-324-6850. Fax: 631-324-9885.
E-mail: info@easthamptonhistory.org
Web Site: www.easthamptonhistory.org
Founded: 1921.
Congressional District: 2
Key Personnel: Exec. Dir., Richard Barons; Pres. (V), Arthur Graham.
Personnel Profile: Full-Time Paid 2; Part-Time Paid 7; Part-Time Volunteers 50; Interns 1.
Governing Authority: nonprofit organization. Branch Museums: Clinton Academy; Mulford Farm; Osborn-Jackson House; Town House; Marine Museum. Tax-exempt: 501(c)(3).
Historical Society Museum.
Collections: decorative & fine arts; textiles; tools & equipment; historic structures & landscapes; maritime artifacts.
Research Fields: Eastern Long Island history.
Facilities: East Hampton Town Marine Museum; Clinton Academy; Town House; Mulford House & Barn; Osborn-Jackson House.
Activities: lectures; walking tours; children's programs; exhibitions; special events; school programs; historic preservation; summer camp; summer theater.
Publications: walking tour booklet; exhibition guides.
Hours & Admission Prices: Office: Tues.-Sat. 10-5. No charge; donations accepted. ♿
Attendance: 10,000 (estimated)
Membership: Individual $35; Family & Couple $60; Friend $75; Business $100.

* **GUILD HALL MUSEUM,** 158 Main St., East Hampton, NY 11937-2795. Tel.: 631-324-0806. Fax: 631-324-2722.
E-mail: museum@guildhall.org
Web Site: www.guildhall.org
Founded: 1931.
Congressional District: 1
Key Personnel: Exec. Dir., Ruth Stevens Appelhof, Ph.D.; Chm. Bd. (V), Melville Straus; Museum Dir. & Chief Cur., Christina Mossaides Strassfield; Museum Shop Mgr., Michelle Vertucci.
Personnel Profile: Full-Time Paid 12; Part-Time Paid 16; Part-Time Volunteers 200; Interns 4.
Governing Authority: board of trustees. Tax-exempt.
Art Museum.
Collections: 1,900 works by 19th-20th century regional artists, including Lynda Benglis, Ross Bleckner, James Brooks, Chuck Close, Audrey Flack, Willem de Kooning, Childe Hassam, Lee Krasner, Roy Lichtenstein, Thomas Moran, Robert Motherwell, Jackson Pollock, Larry Rivers; Miriam Schapiro.

Research Fields: late 19th & 20th-century art; artists of the region.
Facilities: art library & archives; theater; classroom; meeting space. Museum-related items for sale.
Activities: temporary, permanent & traveling exhibitions; lectures; films; gallery talks; concerts; dance recitals; arts festivals; drama & poetry readings; arts & crafts workshops; educational programs; inter-museum loan. Museum Sponsors: Clothesline Art Sale in August.
Publications: exhibition catalogues: seasonal calendars.
Hours & Admission Prices: June-Labor Day daily 11-5; Sept.-May Wed.-Sat. 11-5, Sun. 12-5. Suggested Donation: $7 per person; discounts to AAM & ICOM members; members no charge. Closed New Year's Day; Thanksgiving; Christmas. ♿
Attendance: 50,000 (accurate)
Membership: Student & Senior Citizen $30; Individual $45; Supporting $70; Family $80; Donor $100; Sustaining $250; Gold Card $500; Sponsor $1,000; Patron $2,500; Benefactor $5,000; Chairman's Circle $10,000.

HOME SWEET HOME MUSEUM, 14 James Lane, East Hampton, NY 11937-2710. Tel.: 631-324-0713 & 4150. Fax: 631-324-0713 & 4189.
Web Site: www.easthampton.com/homesweethome
Founded: 1928.
Congressional District: 1
Key Personnel: Historic Site Mgr., Hugh King.
Personnel Profile: Full-Time Paid 1; Part-Time Paid 4.
Governing Authority: nonprofit. Parent Institution: Inc. Village of East Hampton, 86 Main St., East Hampton, NY 11937. Tax-exempt.
Historic House: mid-18th century saltbox dedicated to the memory of John Howard Payne, 19th-century actor, playwright & author of Home Sweet Home.
Collections: Lustreware, Staffordshire & English ceramics of late 18th & early 19th centuries; 17th-19th century American furniture including 1640 Mulliner chest; needlework & textiles.
Research Fields: 18th & early 19th-century English ceramics & textiles; Life & Times of John Howard Payne, 1791-1852.
Activities: guided tours; educational programs; temporary & permanent exhibitions.
Hours & Admission Prices: May-Sept. Mon.-Sat. 10-4, Sun. 2-4; Oct.-Nov. Fri.-Sun.; other times by appointment. Adults $4, children $2. Closed New Year's Day; Thanksgiving; Christmas. ♿
Attendance: 500 (accurate)

LONGHOUSE RESERVE, (M), 133 Hands Creek Rd., East Hampton, NY 11937-3808. Tel.: 631-329-3568. Fax: 631-329-4299.
Web Site: www.longhouse.org
Founded: 1991.
Congressional District: 1
Key Personnel: Exec. Dir., Matko Tomicic; Founder, Jack Lenor Larsen; Co Pres., Dianne Benson; Co Pres., Angela Mariana Frye; Treas., Mark Levine; Cur., Wendy Van Deusen.
Personnel Profile: Full-Time Paid 4; Full-Time Volunteers 2; Part-Time Paid 1; Part-Time Volunteers 30.
Governing Authority: private; nonprofit organization. Tax-exempt: 501(c)(3).
General Museum.
Collections: decorative arts; arboretum; sculpture garden.
Activities: arts festivals; concerts; dance recitals; guided tours; lectures; loan & temporary exhibitions.
Publications: quarterly newsletter, LongHouse.
Hours & Admission Prices: April-June & Sept.-Oct. 6 Wed. & Sat. 2-5; July-Aug. Wed-Sat. 2-5. Adults $10, senior citizens $8; children & members no charge.
Attendance: 7,000 (accurate)
Membership: Student $35; Friend $75; Friends Duo $150; Founder $300; Patron $500; Fellow $1,000; Benefactors $5,000; President's Circle $10,000; Corporate $2,500.

MULFORD FARM MUSEUM, 10 James Lane, East Hampton, NY 11937-2714. Mailing Address: East Hampton Historical Society, 101 Main St., East Hampton, NY 11937-2714. Tel.: 631-324-6850. Fax: 631-324-9885.
E-mail: info@easthamptonhistory.org
Web Site: www.easthamptonhistory.org
Founded: 1948.
Congressional District: 2
Key Personnel: Exec. Dir., Richard Barons; Pres. (V), Arthur Graham.
Personnel Profile: Full-Time Paid 2; Part-Time Paid 6; Part-Time Volunteers 35; Interns 1.
Governing Authority: nonprofit. The East Hampton Historical Society. Branch Museums: Osborn-Jackson House; Clinton Academy; Town House; Marine Museum. Tax-exempt: 501(c)(3).
Historic Farm Complex: c.1680 frame salt box farm house and c.1720 barn with several outbuildings, continuously belonging to eight generations of the Mulford family 1710-1948 located on 3 acres.
Collections: farm implements; 17th-18th century decorative arts; crafts & domestic equipment; period of restoration 1770-1780.
Research Fields: social & economic history; agricultural; architecture; East Hampton town history.
Activities: guided tours; lectures; classes in local history & crafts; fairs; traditional skills demonstrations; living history demonstrations.
Publications: garden guide.
Hours & Admission Prices: Memorial Day-June & Sept.-Columbus Day Sat. 10-5, Sun. 12-5; July-Aug. Fri.-Sat. 10-5, Sun. 12-5. Adults $4, seniors $3, students $2; discounts to AAM & AAA members; members no charge.
Membership: Student $10; Individual $35; Family & Couple $60; Friend $75; Business $100; Corporate & Foundation $150.

OSBORN-JACKSON HOUSE, 101 Main St., East Hampton, NY 11937-2714. Mailing Address: East Hampton Historical Society, 101 Main St., East Hampton, NY 11937. Tel.: 631-324-6850. Fax: 631-324-9885.
E-mail: info@easthamptonhistory.org
Web Site: www.easthamptonhistory.org
Founded: 1979.
Congressional District: 2
Key Personnel: Exec. Dir., Richard Barons; Pres. (V), Arthur Graham.
Personnel Profile: Full-Time Paid 2; Part-Time Paid 6; Part-Time Volunteers 35; Interns 1.
Governing Authority: nonprofit organization. The East Hampton Historical Society. Branch Museums: Clinton Academy; Mulford Farm Complex; Town House; Marine Museum. Tax-exempt: 501(c)(3).
History Museum: housed in 1740 two-story frame salt box house.
Collections: 18th-century decorative & fine arts; 3 furnished period rooms; East End history.
Research Fields: Long Island decorative arts; East Hampton town history; colonial & Revolutionary War history; domestic life.
Activities: lectures; guided tours; changing exhibitions; craft demonstrations; antique shows; walking tours; special events.
Publications: walking tour brochures; gallery guides.
Hours & Admission Prices: Tues.-Sat. 10-5. Adults $4, seniors $3, students $2; discounts to AAM members.
Membership: Student $10; Individual $35; Family/Couple $60; Friend $75; Business $100; Corporate & Foundation $150.

East Islip

ISLIP ART MUSEUM, 50 Irish Lane, East Islip, NY 11730-2003. Tel.: 631-224-5402. Fax: 631-224-5417.
E-mail: info@islipartmuseum.org
Web Site: islipartmuseum.org
Founded: 1973.
Congressional District: 2
Key Personnel: Exec. Dir., Mary Lou Cohalan; Financial Dir., Membership & Public Rels., Susan Simmons; Cur., Karen Shaw; Cur. Permanent Collection, Janet Goleas; Public Rels., Elizabeth Tonis; Carriage House Mgr., William Smith; Museum Shop Mgr., Sharyn Lanza.
Personnel Profile: Full-Time Paid 2; Part-Time Paid 10; Interns 3.
Governing Authority: municipal government. Tax-exempt.
Art Museum.
Collections: contemporary & avant-garde art.
Major Exhibits: Glass Art Now, 11/25/09-1/24/10.
Research Fields: contemporary art.
Facilities: educational facilities; 3,500 sq. ft. exhibit space. Museum-related items for sale.
Activities: arts festivals; concerts; formal education programs; guided tours; lectures; loan, traveling & participatory exhibitions.
Publications: bimonthly exhibition brochures.
Hours & Admission Prices: Wed.-Sat. 10-4, Sun. 12-4. No charge; donations accepted. Closed New Year's Day; Easter; Memorial Day; Independence Day; Labor Day; Thanksgiving & day after; Christmas. ♿
Attendance: 12,000 (accurate)
Membership: Member $25; Patron $75; Sponsor $125; Benefactor $250; Special Benefactor $500; Founder $1,000.

East Meadow

NASSAU COUNTY, DIVISION OF MUSEUM SERVICES, DEPARTMENT OF RECREATION, PARKS & MUSEUMS, Eisenhower Park, East Meadow, NY 11554. Tel.: 516-572-0200. Fax: 516-572-0260.
Web Site: nassaucountyny.gov/parks
Founded: 1956.
Congressional District: 4
Key Personnel: Commissioner, Jose Lopez; Dir. Museum Svcs. Div., Herbert Mills; Sands Pt. Preserve Supvr., Gary Haglich; Old Bethpage Village

Restoration Supvr., Jim McKenna; Historic Sites Cur., Harrison Hunt; Life Science Cur. & Tackapausha Museum Supvr., Lois Lindbergh; African/American Cur., David Byer-Tyre; Muttontown Preserve Supvr., Al Lindberg; Garvies Point Museum Supvr., Kathryne Natale.
Personnel Profile: Full-Time Paid 35; Part-Time Paid 54; Part-Time Volunteers 500.
Governing Authority: county; nonprofit organization, Affiliated with Friends for Long Island Heritage. Branch Museums: 1700s Saddle Rock Grist Mill, Saddle Rock; 1934 Christopher Morley Knothole, North Hills; Old Bethpage Village Restoration, Round Swamp Rd., Old Bethpage (includes: c.1760 Schenck house; early 1840s Hewlett Farm; 1815 Cooper House; c.1850 Conklin House; c.1840 Luyster Store; 1860 Williams House & Carpentry Shop; late 1820s, Lawrence House; c.1850 Noon Inn; c.1840 Kirby House; c.1830 Ritch House & Hat Shop; 1829 Benjamin House; c.1850 Powell House; c.1857 Manetto Hill Church; c.1860 Prime Storage Building; c.1865 Layton Store-House; c.1870 Bach Blacksmith Shop; c.1845 District School #6; c.1835 Bedell House; Garvies Point Museum, Barry Drive, Glen Cove; Tackapausha Museum, Washington Ave., Seaford; Sands Point Preserve (includes: c.1923 Falaise; c.1912 Hempstead House; c.1902 Castle Gould); Muttontown Preserve (included Chelsea Cultural Art Center); African American Museum, Hempstead; Welwyn Preserve, Glen Cove; Roslyn Grist Mill, Roslyn; Cedarmere (William Cullen Bryant's Homestead), Roslyn Harbor; Cradle of Aviation Museum, Mitchel Field; Long Island Studies Institute in cooperation with Hofstra University, Hempstead. Tax-exempt.
Preservation Project: Old Bethpage Village, farm community of pre-Civil War era, 45 historic structures; Jericho historic preserve, six structures from early 1800s, Sands Point Preserve, four early 1900s Gold Coast estate structures.
Collections: American history material before 1870; archaeological, geological & natural history specimens of local area; L.I. made aircraft & aviation artifacts.
Research Fields: history & natural history pertaining to Long Island region.
Activities: permanent & traveling exhibits: guided tours: films; formally organized education programs; inter-museum loan.
Publications: history booklet series.
Hours & Admission Prices: Call for information.
Attendance: 767,019 (accurate)

East Meredith

HANFORD MILLS MUSEUM, 73 County Hwy. 12, Corner of County Hwys. 10 & 12, East Meredith, NY 13757. Mailing Address: P.O. Box 99, East Meredith, NY 13757-0099. Tel.: 607-278-5744. Fax: 607-278-6299.
E-mail: info@hanfordmills.org
Web Site: www.hanfordmills.org
Founded: 1973.
Congressional District: 27
Key Personnel: Dir., Elizabeth Callahan; Chm. (V), Katie Boardman; Asst. Dir., Caroline de Marrais; Cur., Suzanne Soden; Mill Operations Foreman, Dawn Raudibaugh; Museum Shop Mgr., Louise Storey.
Personnel Profile: Full-Time Paid 5; Part-Time Paid 9; Part-Time Volunteers 50.
Governing Authority: nonprofit organization. Tax-exempt.
Historic Site & Industrial Museum: housed in water powered mill & 16 historic structures.
Collections: historic structures from c.1840-1920; sawmilling, woodworking, gristmilling equipment; historical archives of Hanford Mill from 1860-1960; historic documents.
Research Fields: history of water milling in upper watershed of Delaware, Susquehanna & Schoharie River systems; vernacular engineering of mill dams & structures; social history of mill villages; history of site & village of East Meredith; power transmission technology; historic woodworking practices & production techniques; local social & cultural history.
Facilities: 250-vol. library of period catalogs of manufacturers of water, turbines, gas engines, saw mills, wagons, available for research by appointment on premises.
Activities: guided tours; formally organized education programs; permanent, temporary & traveling exhibitions; working machinery demonstrations; orientation film.
Publications: newsletter; collection catalogs, Made By Machine; The Hanford Photographs; East Meredith Memories; The Butter Business.
Hours & Admission Prices: mid-May to mid-Oct. Tues.-Sun. 10-5; other times by appointment. Adults $8.50, seniors $5; discounts to AAA & AAM members; members & children 12 and under no charge. Buses welcome. ♿
Attendance: 8,200 (estimated)
Membership: Individual $15; Joint $20; Family $25.

Elizabethtown

ADIRONDACK HISTORY CENTER, (M), 7590 Court St., Elizabethtown, NY 12932. Mailing Address: P.O. Box 428, Elizabethtown, NY 12932-0428. Tel.: 518-873-6466.
E-mail: echs@adkhistorycenter.org
Web Site: adkhistorycenter.org
Founded: 1954.
Congressional District: 22
Key Personnel: Pres. (V), Elizabeth H.W. Lawrence; Dir., Margaret Gibbs.
Personnel Profile: Full-Time Paid 1; Part-Time Paid 6; Part-Time Volunteers 4.
Governing Authority: nonprofit. Parent Institution: Essex County Historical Society. Tax-exempt: 501(c)(3).
History Museum.
Collections: horse-drawn vehicles, farm implements; tools; household items; dolls; mining equipment; surveying equipment; military artifacts; costumes; artifacts relating to camping, hiking & hunting; Adirondack mountain fire tower; sugar house.
Research Fields: History of Essex County.
Facilities: library; garden.
Activities: permanent, temporary & traveling exhibitions; lecture series; summer performance tour; ghost tour. Annual Events: Maple Sugar Festival; Fall Festival.
Publications: On The Trail of John Brown; A Basic Guide to Genealogical and Family History Resources for Essex County, New York.
Hours & Admission Prices: Memorial Day to Columbus Day daily 10-5. Adults $5, seniors $4, students $2; discounts to AAM members; members, school groups & children under 6 no charge. ♿
Attendance: 10,000 (estimated)
Membership: Individual $15; Family $30; Contributing $50; Sustaining $100; Sponsor $250; Patron $500; Benefactor $1,000.

Elmira

* **ARNOT ART MUSEUM, (M),** 235 Lake St., Elmira, NY 14901-3191. Tel.: 607-734-3697. Fax: 607-734-5687.
E-mail: rick@arnotartmuseum.org
Web Site: arnotartmuseum.org
Founded: 1913.
Congressional District: 39
Key Personnel: Consultant Dir., Rick Pirozzolo; Business Mgr., Lynda Williams; Dir. Tour Svcs., Wendy Taylor; Facilities Caretaker, Gregg Leavenworth.
Personnel Profile: Full-Time Paid 6; Part-Time Paid 2; Part-Time Volunteers 75; Interns 3.
Governing Authority: nonprofit organization. Tax-exempt: 509(a)(1).
Art Museum: housed in 1833 Greek Revival style home of Matthias H. Arnot with 1985 Graham Gund Addition, and Carriage House Education Center.
Collections: restored 1890s picture gallery containing 17th-, 18th- & 19th-century European paintings; 19th- to 20th-century American Paintings; graphics; sculpture; decorative arts, emphasis on contemporary representational art.
Research Fields: 17th- & 19th-century European Salon paintings; 19th- & 20th-century American art; contemporary representation.
Activities: guided tours; lectures; films; gallery talks; concerts; formally organized education programs for children; docent program; inter-museum loan, permanent & temporary exhibitions.
Publications: catalogue, A Collector's Vision: The Bequest of Matthias H. Arnot; bimonthly members, The Column; special exhibition catalogues.
Hours & Admission Prices: Tues.-Sat. 10-5, Sun. 1-5. Adults $5; discounts to AAM & ICOM members; weekends & members no charge; reciprocal membership with 15 New York State museums. Closed national holidays. ♿
Attendance: 12,701 (accurate)
Membership: Single $35; Dual & Family $50; Friend $100; Patron $250; Sustaining $500; Arnot Associate $1,000; Benefactor $5,000. Seniors may deduct 10% from single, dual or family categories.

* **CHEMUNG VALLEY HISTORY MUSEUM, (M),** 415 E. Water St., Elmira, NY 14901-3410. Tel.: 607-734-4167 & 4168. Fax: 607-734-1565.
E-mail: cchs@chemungvalleymuseum.org
Web Site: www.chemungvalleymuseum.org
Founded: 1923.
Congressional District: 29
Key Personnel: Pres., Bryan Reddic; Dir., Amy H. Wilson; Cur., Casey Lewis; Coord. Education, Kerry Lippincott; Archivist, Rachel Dworkin; Administrative Asst., Peggy Malorzo; Journal Editor, Michele Neurauter.
Personnel Profile: Full-Time Paid 4; Part-Time Paid 1; Part-Time Volunteers 25; Interns 6.
Governing Authority: society. Parent Institution: Chemung County Historical Society. Tax-exempt: 501(c)(3).
Historical Society Museum.

Collections: Civil War & Indian artifacts; Mark Twain collection; local history; archives; costumes; military; industry; agriculture; archaeology; textiles; transportation; 30,000 manuscript items; 11,500 maps & architectural records.
Research Fields: local history; archaeology. Historic Building: 1833 bank.
Facilities: 4,500-vol. library of local history books. Publications, reproductions, Mark Twain postcards & other museum-related items for sale.
Activities: guided tours; lectures; TV programs; formally organized education programs for students; permanent exhibitions; school loan service; historical excursions; veterans history project partner.
Publications: quarterly magazine, The Chemung Historical Journal; books, Chemung County, Its History; A Link in the Great Chain, A History of the Chemung Canal; booklet, Mark Twain in Elmira; newsletter, Banknotes.
Hours & Admission Prices: Museum: Mon.-Sat. 10-5. Office: Mon.-Fri. 9-5. Library & Research: Mon.-Fri. 1-5. Tours: adults $3; discounts to AAM & museum members. Closed holidays. ♿
Attendance: 10,000 (estimated)
Membership: Senior Citizen $25; Senior Household & Individual $35; Household $50; Research Sponsor $100; Society Patron $250; History Patron $500.

NATIONAL SOARING MUSEUM, (M), Harris Hill, 51 Soaring Hill Dr., Elmira, NY 14903-9204. Tel.: 607-734-3128. Fax: 607-732-6745.
E-mail: nsm@soaringmuseum.org
Web Site: www.soaringmuseum.org
Founded: 1969.
Congressional District: 34
Key Personnel: Dir., Peter W. Smith; Pres., Moses Acee; Dir. Museum Svcs., Mary D. Flasphaler; NSM Journal Editor & Cur. Education, Bill Gallagher; Museum Shop Mgr., Lisa C. Bartlett; Dir. Education & Mktg., Norman C. Smith; Exec. Asst., Sue Schneck.
Personnel Profile: Full-Time Paid 5; Part-Time Paid 3; Part-Time Volunteers 23; Interns 2.
Governing Authority: nonprofit organization. Tax-exempt: 501(c)(3).
Aeronautics Museum: located on the site of the earliest recognized center for soaring flight in the United States.
Collections: motorless aircraft (gliders & sailplanes); archives including Soaring Society of America; film library; manuscripts; displays relating to motorless flight.
Research Fields: aerodynamics of low speed flight; motorless flight.
Facilities: library; archives; theater; community & special events room; classroom; 25,000 sq. ft. exhibit space. Museum-related items for sale.
Activities: guided group tours; lectures; films; special events; classes; permanent & temporary exhibitions; aviation summer camp; science & aviation programs; encampments.
Publications: NSM Journal; NSM News.
Hours & Admission Prices: Daily 10-5. Adults $6.50, senior citizens $5.50, youth 7-17 $4; discounts to groups, members & AAA members; children under 6 no charge. ♿
Attendance: 22,000 (accurate)
Membership: Individual $35; Family $50

REGIONAL SCIENCE & DISCOVERY CENTER, 425 Pennsylvania Ave., Elmira, NY 14904-1762. Mailing Address: 114 Pine St., Ste. 201, Corning, NY 14830-2654. Tel.: 607-734-4453 (educator); 962-4693 (business). Fax: 607-734-7740.
E-mail: educators@sdcsciencecenter.org
Web Site: www.sdcsciencecenter.org
Founded: 1996.
Congressional District: 52
Key Personnel: C.E.O. & Chm. (V), Dale Wexell; Exec. Dir. & Devel., Patricia T. Dann; Treas., Kenneth Sofio; Museum Site Mgr., Lisa Gibson; Museum Site Mgr., Herbert Wolf; Education Programs, Terry Burke; Education Programs, Marylyn Davis; Public Rels., Alan Donnelly.
Personnel Profile: Full-Time Paid 3; Part-Time Paid 6; Part-Time Volunteers 75; Interns 1.
Governing Authority: private; nonprofit organization. Tax-exempt: 501(c)(3).
Children's Museum.
Collections: hands-on exhibits; physical & biological sciences.
Facilities: 7,500 sq. ft. exhibit space; discovery room for toddlers; fiber optics lab. Museum-related items for sale.
Activities: formal education programs for children; guided tours.
Publications: quarterly newsletter, Discover.
Hours & Admission Prices: Mon.-Wed. 10-6, Thurs.-Sat. 10-9:30, Sun. 11-6. Children $3, senior citizens $1.50; discounts to groups; members & adult with child & ASTC members no charge. Closed Easter; Thanksgiving; Christmas Day.
Attendance: 20,329 (accurate)
Membership: Junior Scientist 6-21 $15; Adult $20; Family $35; Supporting $100-$499; Patron $500 & up.

TANGLEWOOD NATURE CENTER AND MUSEUM, 443 Coleman Ave., Elmira, NY 14903-9311. Tel.: 607-732-6060. Fax: 607-732-6210.
E-mail: elainems@stny.rr.com
Web Site: www.tanglewoodnaturecenter.com
Founded: 1973.
Congressional District: 31
Key Personnel: Office Mgr., Cathy Morroni; Pres. Bd., Merrill Lynn; Exec. Dir., Elaine Farwell; Volunteer Coord., Emily Hofelich-Jack; Cur., Valerie Heywood; Grounds & Bldg., Rich Gridley; Museum Shop Mgr., Lydia Lynn.
Personnel Profile: Full-Time Paid 3; Full-Time Volunteers 2; Part-Time Paid 3; Interns 2.
Governing Authority: private; nonprofit organization. Tax-exempt.
Nature Center.
Collections: live animals; walk through immersion habitat.
Facilities: 300-vol. nature library; walk though museum; 200-seat auditorium; 400 acres of nature trails. Museum-related items for sale.
Activities: concerts; formal education programs for adults, children & interns; lectures; theatre; special events.
Publications: quarterly newsletter, Tanglewood Talk.
Hours & Admission Prices: Call for hours. No charge; donations accepted. ♿
Attendance: 30,000 (estimated)
Membership: Individual $30; Senior Family $35; Family $40; Supporting $50-100.

Elmsford

GREATER HUDSON HERITAGE NETWORK, (M), 2199 Saw Mill River Rd., Elmsford, NY 10523-3812. Tel.: 914-592-6726. Fax: 914-592-6946.
E-mail: info@greaterhudson.org
Web Site: www.greaterhudson.org
Formerly: Lower Hudson Conference of Historical Agencies and Museums
Founded: 1979.
Congressional District: 22
Key Personnel: C.E.O. & Exec. Dir., Tema Harnik; Pres. (V), Jacquetta Haley; Project Mgr., Dianne Macpherson.
Personnel Profile: Full-Time Paid 1; Part-Time Paid 2; Part-Time Volunteers 3; Interns 1.
Governing Authority: nonprofit organization. Tax-exempt: 501(c)(3).
Museum Service Organization
Collections: museum, history and archival resource library for technical assistance and collections care.
Research Fields: management of museums & historical societies; collections care & management; programming; interpretation.
Facilities: library of museum-related technical publications.
Activities: workshops; lectures; training programs for professional & volunteer museum workers; technical assistance; conferences; museum tours; meetings. Annual Event: awards program in October.
Publications: biannual newsletter; on-line newsletter; History Keepers' Companion: Guide; Emergency Preparedness & Recovery Handbook.
Hours & Admission Prices: Mon.-Fri. 9-4. No charge; fees for training programs. Workshop & seminar fee discount to GHHN member organizations & individuals. Closed Westchester County & New York state holidays. ♿
Membership: Student with valid ID $15; Individuals $40; Professional & Consultant $75; Sustaining $100. Organizations: Budget under $25,000 $50; Budget $25,000-$99,000 $75; Budget $100,000-$249,000 $100; Budget $250,000-$499,000 $125; Budget $500,000-$999,000 $175; Budget $1,000,000 & up $200; Business Member $500.

WESTCHESTER COUNTY HISTORICAL SOCIETY, 2199 Saw Mill River Rd., Elmsford, NY 10523-3812. Tel.: 914-592-4323. Fax: 914-231-1515.
E-mail: info@westchesterhistory.com
Web Site: www.westchesterhistory.com
Founded: 1874.
Congressional District: 23
Key Personnel: Exec. Dir., Katherine Hite; Chm. (V), Allen Elliott; Librarian, Diana Deichert; Asst. Librarian & Office Mgr., Patrick Raftery.
Personnel Profile: Full-Time Paid 3; Part-Time Volunteers 10.
Governing Authority: Tax-exempt.
Historical Society Library & Research Center.
Collections: manuscripts; photographs; maps; books; pamphlets; diaries; periodicals; newspapers on Westchester County.
Research Fields: genealogy & local history.
Facilities: genealogy library; county history library.
Activities: programs featuring local history; education program; trips to historic areas in & out of the county.
Publications: quarterly, The Westchester Historian; books.
Hours & Admission Prices: Research Library: Tues.-Wed. 9-4. No charge. ♿
Attendance: 2,500 (estimated)

Membership: Member $35; Contributor $60; Friend $100; Sponsor $150; Benefactor $250; Patron $500; Sustainer $1,000.

Esperance

GEORGE LANDIS ARBORETUM, 174 Lape Rd., Esperance, NY 12066. Mailing Address: P.O. Box 186, Esperance, NY 12066-0186. Tel.: 518-875-6935. Fax: 518-875-6394.
E-mail: info@landisarboretum.org
Web Site: www.landisarboretum.org
Founded: 1951.
Congressional District: 21
Key Personnel: Exec. Dir., Thom O'Connor; Pres. (V), Ann Donnelly; Science Educator, George Steele; Dir. Horticulture & Operations, Fred Breglia.
Personnel Profile: Part-Time Volunteers 178; Interns 1.
Governing Authority: nonprofit educational organization, chartered by Regents of New York State. Tax-exempt: 501(c)(3).
Arboretum & Botanical Garden.
Collections: native & exotic trees & shrubs; perennial & spring bulb gardens; herbarium.
Research Fields: hardiness & performance testing of species of European & Asian origin.
Facilities: 548 acres including 40 acres planted to formal collections and over 20 acre native woodland with nature trail; visitor center; classroom; greenhouse.
Activities: guided tours; lectures; education programs for adults; horticulture & natural history programs for youth & adults; self-guided tours & trails; guided tours for groups.
Publications: quarterly newsletter; annual calendar of events.
Hours & Admission Prices: Daily dawn to dusk. No charge; donations accepted.
Attendance: 8,000 (estimated)
Membership: Student $20; Basic $50; Garden Club $100; Business $200; Patron $250; Benefactor $500; Founders Circle $1,000; Lifetime $2,500.

Fairport

FAIRPORT HISTORICAL MUSEUM, Perinton Historical Society, 18 Perrin St., Fairport, NY 14450-2122. Tel.: 585-223-3989.
E-mail: info@perintonhistoricalsociety.org
Web Site: www.angelfire.com/ny5/fairporthistmuseum
Founded: 1935.
Congressional District: 28
Key Personnel: Dir., William Keeler.
Personnel Profile: Full-Time Volunteers 40; Part-Time Paid 1; Part-Time Volunteers 30.
Governing Authority: society. Parent Institution: Perinton Historical Society. Tax-exempt.
Local History Museum.
Collections: local history & culture; Native American artifacts; 19th-century industry; farm, home & village items.
Research Fields: local history.
Facilities: 385-vol. library of local history, historical fictions of local setting, state institution reports, genealogical reports, & books on local families available for use on premises; herb garden. Museum-related items for sale.
Activities: tours; support of school programs. Museum Sponsors: monthly meetings with speakers Sept.-April.
Publications: monthly newsletter, The Historigram.
Hours & Admission Prices: Sept.-May Sun. & Tues. 2-4, Thurs. 7-9; June-Aug. Sun. & Tues. 2-4, Thurs. 2-4 & 7-9. No charge; donations accepted. Closed major holidays. ♿
Attendance: 1,223 (estimated)
Membership: Seniors $5; Individual $10; Family $15.

Fayetteville

THE STICKLEY MUSEUM, 300 Orchard St., Fayetteville, NY 13066-2120. Mailing Address: P.O. Box 480, Manlius, NY 13104-0480. Tel.: 315-682-5500. Fax: 315-682-6306.
Web Site: www.stickleymuseum.com
Founded: 2007.
Key Personnel: Dir., Gregory Vadney.
Governing Authority: Parent Institution: L. & J.G. Stickley, Inc.
Furniture Museum.
Collections: family furniture-making history; Stickley furniture & accessories.
Hours & Admission Prices: Tues. 11:30-5, Sat. 10-5; other times by appointment. No charge. ♿

Fineview

THE MINNA ANTHONY COMMON NATURE CENTER AT WELLESLEY STATE PARK, 44927 Cross Island Rd., Fineview, NY 13640-3105. Tel.: 315-482-2479. Fax: 315-482-2785.
Web Site: nysparks.com
Founded: 1969.
Key Personnel: Educator, Kimbrie Cullen; Pres. (V), Kerry Roberge.
Personnel Profile: Full-Time Paid 2; Part-Time Paid 7; Part-Time Volunteers 100; Interns 5.
Governing Authority: Parent Institution: New York State Office of Parks, Recreation and Historic Preservation. Subsidiary Institution: Wellesley Island State Park.
Nature Center.
Collections: 3-dimensional displays; taxidermy; river art work; environmental exhibits.
Facilities: 8-mile hiking trail; 8-mile cross country ski trail; Butterfly House.
Activities: nature hikes; environmental education programs. Annual Events: Autumn Festival; Earth Day Activities.
Publications: newsletter, Friends of Nature Center; Geology of Wellesley Island Guide; Northfield Loop Self Guiding Booklet; bird checklist.
Hours & Admission Prices: Museum: daily call for hours. Trails: sunrise to sunset. Summer $7; Winter no charge. Closed Thanksgiving; Christmas. ♿
Attendance: 50,000 (estimated)
Membership: Individual $10; Family $15; Sponsor $25; Patron $50; Bluebird $100; Benefactor $250; Eagle $500; Life $1,000.

Fishkill

VAN WYCK HOMESTEAD MUSEUM, 504 Rte. 9, Fishkill, NY 12524. Mailing Address: P.O. Box 133, Fishkill, NY 12524-0133. Tel.: 845-896-9560.
E-mail: vanwyckhomestead@aol.com
Web Site: www.pojonews.com
Founded: 1962.
Congressional District: 25
Key Personnel: Pres., Roy Jorgenson; Second Vice Pres., Steve Lynch; Museum Shop Mgr., Helga Mackenzie.
Personnel Profile: Part-Time Volunteers 20.
Governing Authority: society; nonprofit organization. Parent Institution: Fishkill Historical Society. Tax-exempt: 501(c)(3).
Historic House Museum: 1732 Dutch Colonial Homestead, site headquarters during the Revolutionary War for northern supply depot 1776-83.
Collections: early Dutch settler artifacts; Revolutionary War items; archaeology; archives; agriculture; technology; manuscripts; local genealogy; Ammi Phillips' art.
Research Fields: local history; archaeology.
Facilities: approx. 800-vol. library of history; reading room. Gift items for sale.
Activities: guided tours; lectures; formally organized educational programs; permanent exhibitions; extensive craft program; summer archeological research project. Annual Events: craft fair & sale; Dutch Legacy Weekend; Revolutionary War Weekend; Historic Bike Tour of Fishkill; Hudson River Valley Ramble; Christmas Open House.
Publications: monthly newsletter, Van Wyck Dispatch; Around Fishkill, Picture History of Fishkill.
Hours & Admission Prices: By appointment. No charge; donations accepted.
Attendance: 3,500 (estimated)
Membership: Individual $15; Family $20; Contributing $25; Sustaining $100; Life $500.

Flanders

THE BIG DUCK, 1012 Flanders Rd., Flanders, NY 11901. Mailing Address: P.O. Box 144, West Sayville, NY 11796. Tel.: 631-852-3377.
Governing Authority: Parent Institution: Suffolk County Parks Dept.
Historic Building: listed on the National Register of Historic Places.
Collections: duck souvenirs; Long Island specialties; tourism information.
Facilities: tourism center. Museum-related items for sale.
Activities: special events. Annual Event: Holiday Lighting of the Big Duck.
Hours & Admission Prices: Tues.-Sat. 10-5, Sun. 2-5, call to confirm.

Floral Park

QUEENS COUNTY FARM MUSEUM, 73-50 Little Neck Pkwy., Floral Park, NY 11004-1129. Tel.: 718-347-3276, ext. 10. Fax: 718-347-3243. TDD: 800-281-5722.
E-mail: amy@queensfarm.org
Web Site: www.queensfarm.org
Founded: 1975.
Congressional District: 6

Key Personnel: Exec. Dir. & Events Coord., Amy Fischetti; Pres. (V), James A. Trent; Chm. (V), Samuel Shapiro; Cur., Renee Tone; Dir. Education, Interpreter & Museum Shop Mgr., Diane Miller; Dir. Agriculture, Gary Mitchell; Dir. Horticultural, Iris Ganpant; Administrative Asst., Fran Erato; Interpreter, Linda Grasso; Museum Shop Mgr., Diane Squillari.
Personnel Profile: Full-Time Paid 6; Part-Time Paid 181; Part-Time Volunteers 60; Interns 2.
Governing Authority: nonprofit organization. Parent Institution: Colonial Farmhouse Restoration Society of Bellerose, Inc. Tax-exempt: 501(c)(3).
Historic House: c.1772 Adriance Farmhouse.
Collections: farm animals; historic orchard; 19th-20th century farm tools & household artifacts.
Research Fields: restored farmhouse & grounds of a 20th-century urban truck farm; farming history of Queens 1772-1927; social history of farm families of Queens; truck farming in the 20th-century.
Facilities: Books, colonial reproductions & other museum-related items for sale.
Activities: guided, self-guided & school tours; concerts; fairs; festivals; docent program; quilting classes; workshops.
Publications: bimonthly newsletter, Broadside.
Hours & Admission Prices: Outdoors: daily 10-5. House Tours: Sat.-Sun. 10-5; discounts to museums council of New York City members. School tours $4-$8 per person. School Workshops $5-$8 per person. Special Events $4-$9 per person. ♿
Attendance: 500,000 (accurate)
Membership: Student $20; Senior $30; Individual $40; Family $70; Sustaining Life $300; Sustaining Life Family Plus $500.

Flushing

THE BOWNE HOUSE HISTORICAL SOCIETY, 37-01 Bowne St., Flushing, NY 11354-5628. Tel.: 718-359-0528. Fax: 718-359-0873.
E-mail: office@bownehouse.org
Web Site: www.bownehouse.org
Founded: 1945.
Congressional District: 8
Key Personnel: Exec. Dir., Franklin Vagnone; Pres., Rosemary Vietor.
Personnel Profile: Full-Time Paid 1; Part-Time Paid 2; Part-Time Volunteers 1; Interns 2.
Governing Authority: Tax-exempt: 501(c)(3).
Historic House Museum: 1661 home of John Bowne, religious freedom advocate.
Collections: 17th-19th century furnishings; artifacts; paintings & documents; period herb garden.
Research Fields: Bowne, Parsons & related families including the signers of the Flushing Remonstrance; early American history including religions, social, architecture & decorative arts.
Activities: school & off-site programs.
Publications: Bowne Family of Flushing Long Island.
Hours & Admission Prices: Museum is under restoration. Please call for appointment. ♿
Membership: Individual $25; Family $50; Sustaining $100; Corporate $500; Life $1,000.

THE GODWIN-TERNBACH MUSEUM, (M), Queens College, 405 Klapper Hall, 65-30 Kissena Blvd., Flushing, NY 11367-1575. Tel.: 718-997-4747. Fax: 718-997-4734.
E-mail: gtmuseum@qc.cuny.edu
Web Site: www.qc.cuny.edu/godwin_ternbach
Formerly: Frances Godwin & Joseph Ternbach Museum
Founded: 1957.
Congressional District: 7
Key Personnel: Dir. & Cur., Dr. Amy Winter.
Personnel Profile: Full-Time Paid 2; Part-Time Paid 2.
Governing Authority: Board of Trustees. Parent Institution: Queens College, CUNY. Tax-exempt.
Art Museum.
Collections: ancient Near-Eastern, Asian, Western & contemporary art; graphics; paintings; glass; sculpture; prints.
Major Exhibits: Scholars, Explorers & Priests: How the Renaissance Gave Us the Modern World, 2/10-3/10; Dali Today: Dance & Beyond, 4/10-6/10.
Activities: permanent & temporary exhibitions; formally organized education programs for undergraduate & graduate students; lecture series; special events.
Publications: exhibition catalogs; Queens College Art Collection; brochure.
Hours & Admission Prices: Mon.-Thurs. 11-7, Sat. 11-5. No charge; donations accepted. ♿
Attendance: 5,000 (estimated)
Membership: Students & Seniors $10; Individual $25; Donor $100-$499; Sponsor $500-$999; Patron $l,000 & up.

QUEENS BOTANICAL GARDEN, 43-50 Main St., Flushing, NY 11355-4758. Tel.: 718-886-3800. Fax: 718-463-0263.
E-mail: info@queensbotanical.org
Web Site: www.queensbotanical.org
Founded: 1946.
Congressional District: 8
Key Personnel: Chm., Frank Mirovsky; Exec. Dir., Susan Lacerte; Dir. Capital Projects, Jennifer Ward Souder; Dir. Mktg. & Devel., Tim Heimerle; Dir. Finance & Admin., Karen Simonson; Dir. Education Visitor Svcs., Patrice Kleinberg; Maintenance Supvr., Peter Sansone; Supvr. Gardeners, Marianne Kristoff; Sr. Attendant Guard, James Adams.
Personnel Profile: Full-Time Paid 29; Part-Time Paid 17; Interns 24.
Governing Authority: society. Tax-exempt: 501(c)(3).
Botanical Garden and Arboretum.
Collections: 39 acres including an herb garden; perennial garden tulip & annual displays; bee garden; rose garden; wedding garden; demonstration backyard gardens; 21-acre arboretum; compost home demonstration site. Fragrance walk; wetlands exhibit.
Research Fields: ethnobotanical.
Facilities: auditorium; classrooms; facilities available for weddings, receptions & banquets. Plants & plant accessories for sale.
Activities: guided tours; lectures; concerts; workshops; formally organized education programs; senior & children's gardening programs.
Publications: biannual newsletter, Lecture & Workshop Schedules; map & brochure printed in English, Spanish, Korean, & Chinese.
Hours & Admission Prices: April-Oct. Tues.-Fri. 8-6, Mon. holiday & Sat.-Sun. 8-7; Nov.-March Tues.-Sun. & Mon. holiday 8-4:30. No charge; donations accepted. ♿
Attendance: 350,000 (estimated)
Membership: Individual Senior $30; Individual $35; Dual Senior $45; Dual $50; Family $60; Supporting $100; Associations & Horticultural Organizations $150; Friend $250; Patron $500.

QUEENS HISTORICAL SOCIETY, (M), 143-35 37th Ave., Flushing, NY 11354-5729. Tel.: 718-939-0647, ext. 17. Fax: 718-539-9885.
E-mail: queenshistoricalsociety@verizon.net
Web Site: www.queenshistoricalsociety.org
Founded: 1968.
Congressional District: 5
Key Personnel: Pres. (V), James Driscoll; Exec. Dir., Marisa Berman; Treas., Linda Mandell; Recording Sec., Peter Byrne; Education & Programs, Katrina Raben; Mgr. Collections, Richard Hourahan; Museum Assoc., Danielle Hilkin; Membership Sec., Catherine Williams; Museum Shop Mgr., Connie DeMartino; Administrative Asst., Anne Owens.
Personnel Profile: Full-Time Paid 1; Full-Time Volunteers 1; Part-Time Paid 4; Part-Time Volunteers 50; Interns 5.
Governing Authority: nonprofit organization. Subsidiary Institution: Kingsland Homestead; Moore-Jackson Cemetery. Tax-exempt: 501(c)(3).
Historic Site: c.1785 Kingsland Homestead, located in Weeping Beech Park.
Collections: borough of Queens & Long Island history, 1600s-present; maps; memorabilia; textiles; photos; furniture; ephemera; documents; papers; decorative arts.
Research Fields: Queens; New York City, Long Island.
Facilities: library of Queens related material; archives; multimedia & lecture room. Weeping Beech Park. Publications for sale.
Activities: docent program; guided tours; lectures; temporary & traveling exhibitions; workshops; outreach programs; preservation advocacy; panel discussions.
Publications: quarterly newsletter, Queens Historical Society; Angels of Deliverance: The Struggle Against Slavery in Queens and Long Island; The Road to Freedom: The Underground Railroad, New York and Beyond; 300 Years of Long Island City, 1630-1930; History of Flushing, NY; Teaching With Documents, Slavery in New York; Everything You Ever Wanted to Know About Queens - A Book of Trivia; Friends of Freedom: The Underground Railroad in Queens and on Long Island.
Hours & Admission Prices: Office: Mon.-Fri. 9:30-5. Museum: Tues. & Sat.-Sun. 2:30-4:30. Adults $3, senior citizens, students & children $2; discounts to AAM & ICOM members; members no charge. Closed major holidays. ♿
Attendance: 6,000 (estimated)
Membership: Senior & Student $10; Individual $15; Family $40; Business Patron $100; Corporate $250; Life Sponsor $500; Corporate Benefactor $750; Corporate Leader $1,000.

WILDLIFE CONSERVATION SOCIETY, QUEENS ZOO, 53-51 111th St., Flushing, NY 11368-3301. Tel.: 718-271-1500, ext 126. Fax: 718-271-4441.
E-mail: ssilver@wcs.org
Web Site: www.queenszoo.org
Key Personnel: Dir. & Cur. Animals, Dr. Scott Silver; Asst. Cur. Animals,

Craig Gibbs; Mgr. Operations, Jeffrey Blatz; Mgr. Security & Admissions, Vincent Capobianco; Cur. Education, Tom Hurtubise.
Personnel Profile: Full-Time Paid 60; Part-Time Paid 10; Part-Time Volunteers 30.
Governing Authority: Parent Institution: Wildlife Conservation Society.
Zoo.
Collections: animals from the Americas.
Hours & Admission Prices: April-Oct. Mon.-Fri. 10-5, Sat.-Sun. & holidays 10-5:30; Nov.-March daily 10-4:30. Adults $6, senior citizens $2.25, children 3-12 $2; children under 3 no charge. ♿
Attendance: 208,389 (accurate)

Fonda

NATIVE AMERICAN EXHIBIT, NATIONAL KATERI SHRINE, Rte. 5, 1/2 mi. West of Fonda, Fonda, NY 12068. Mailing Address: Box 627 RD1, Fonda, NY 12068-0627. Tel.: 518-853-3646. Fax: 518-853-3371.
E-mail: kkenny@nycap.rr.com
Web Site: www.katerishrine.com
Founded: 1949.
Congressional District: 103
Key Personnel: Dir., Rev. Kevin Kenny, O.F.M.Conv.; Assoc. Dir. & Museum Shop Mgr., Rev. James Amrhein, O.F.M.Conv.
Personnel Profile: Full-Time Volunteers 2; Part-Time Paid 1; Part-Time Volunteers 3.
Governing Authority: church. Parent Institution: Order Minor Conventuals. Subsidiary Institution: National Kateri Shrine. Tax-exempt.
Religious Shrine & Historic Archaeological Site: 1666-1693 staked out Mohawk Indian castle & 1666-1676 residence of Kateri Tekakwitha.
Collections: Native Americans & the shrine; Dutch Farmhouse & barn c.1782.
Facilities: library; chapel; 3 mile nature trail; picnic pavilion & grounds; Way of the Cross in wooded area. Religious & museum-related items for sale.
Activities: school tours.
Publications: brochures & triannual newsletter.
Hours & Admission Prices: May-Oct. daily 9-6; other times by appointment. No charge; donations accepted. Mass schedule: Sat. 4:30, Sun. 10:30. ♿
Attendance: 50,000 (estimated)
Membership: $7.

Fort Edward

OLD FORT HOUSE MUSEUM, 29 Lower Broadway, Fort Edward, NY 12828. Mailing Address: P.O. Box 106, Fort Edward, NY 12828-0106. Tel.: 518-747-9600. Fax: 518-747-9700 (call first).
E-mail: oldfort@localnet.com
Web Site: www.ftedward.com
Founded: 1925.
Congressional District: 24
Key Personnel: C.E.O. & Historian, R. Paul McCarty; Pres. (V), Mary R. Smith; Dir. Education & Sec., Elizabeth O'Leary.
Personnel Profile: Part-Time Paid 3; Part-Time Volunteers 52.
Governing Authority: society. Parent Institution: Fort Edward Historical Association. Tax-exempt: 501(c)(3).
Local History Museum: housed in 1772-73 Old Fort House.
Collections: archaeology; glass; history; colonial-Victorian period furniture; Indian & colonial war artifacts; local pottery; 19th century dolls & toys; clothing; photographs; medicinal herb garden. Historic Site: Wait law office & toll house; one room schoolhouse; Cronkhite Pavilion.
Research Fields: local history; genealogy.
Facilities: research center.
Activities: guided walking tours; lectures; films; permanent & temporary exhibitions.
Hours & Admission Prices: June-Aug. daily 1-5; Sept. to Columbus Day Tues.-Sun. 1-5. Adults $5; members no charge. Closed national holidays. ♿
Attendance: 9,300 (accurate)
Membership: Senior Citizen $10; Individual $15; Family $25; Patron $50; Contributing $100; Supporting $250; Sustaining $500; Life $1,000. Corporation & Organization: Member $100; Contributing $150; Supporting $300; Sustaining $500; Benefactor $750; Angel - pacesetter $1,000.

Fort Hunter

SCHOHARIE CROSSING STATE HISTORIC SITE, 129 Schoharie St., Fort Hunter, NY 12069-0140. Mailing Address: P.O. Box 140, Fort Hunter, NY 12069-0140. Tel.: 518-829-7516. Fax: 518-829-7491.
Founded: 1966.
Congressional District: 28
Key Personnel: Historic Site Mgr., Janice M. Fontanella; Historic Site Asst., David Sweeney; Supvr. Maintenance, Don Drew; Coord. Education, Tricia Shaw; Equipment Mgr., Vincent Choffo.
Personnel Profile: Full-Time Paid 6; Part-Time Paid 7.
Governing Authority: state. Parent Institution: New York State Office of Parks, Recreation & Historic Preservation, & Saratoga/Capital District State Park, Recreation & Historic Preservation Commission. Tax-exempt: 501(c)(3).
Historic Site.
Collections: Erie Canal history; remains of first ditch; parts of original locks of the Erie Canal; Schoharie Aqueduct, 1841.
Research Fields: Erie Canal; history of transportation in the Mohawk Valley.
Facilities: boat landings & launching; hiking trails; bike paths; cross-country ski trails; picnic area; visitor center with exhibits on Erie Canal; restored 1850s canal store building.
Activities: guided walking tours; self guided tours.
Publications: book, Erie Canal coloring book.
Hours & Admission Prices: Daily during daylight hours, weather permitting. Visitor Center: May & Oct. Wed.-Sat. 10-5, Sun. 1-5; Memorial Day to Labor Day Wed.-Mon. 10-5. No charge. ♿
Attendance: 80,000 (estimated)

Fort Johnson

OLD FORT JOHNSON, Rte. 5, Fort Johnson, NY 12070. Mailing Address: Fort Johnson, P.O. Box 196, Fort Johnson, NY 12070-0196. Tel.: 518-843-0300.
E-mail: museum@oldfortjohnson.org
Web Site: www.oldfortjohnson.org
Founded: 1904.
Congressional District: 30
Key Personnel: Pres. (V), Dennis Drenzek.
Personnel Profile: Part-Time Paid 2; Part-Time Volunteers 15.
Governing Authority: Montgomery County Historical Society. Tax-exempt: 501(c)(3).
General Museum: housed in 1749 Fort Johnson, home of Sir William Johnson, Supt. of Indian affairs & general of the Royal Militia & scene of Indian councils, military assemblies & Indian administration for British colonies.
Collections: 18th-19th century furnishings of the Johnson family & the Mohawk Valley; Mohawk Valley Indian artifacts; 19th-century textiles & costumes; Civil War & Montgomery County artifacts; manuscripts. Historic Structure: 1749 Fort Johnson.
Major Exhibits: Around the World With Richmond and Frey, 5/10-11/10.
Research Fields: Fort Johnson; William Johnson; c.1740-1850 decorative arts of Montgomery County.
Facilities: 500-vol. library on Mohawk Valley & New York Colonial, Revolutionary War & later history available by appointment for use at the museum.
Activities: guided tours; lectures; inter-museum loan, permanent, temporary & traveling exhibitions.
Publications: Quilts From Montgomery County, NY; Rufus A. Grider: Artist & Historian.
Hours & Admission Prices: May 15-Oct. 15 Wed.-Sat 10-4, Sun. 1-5. Adults $4; members & children under 12 no charge.
Attendance: 3,500 (estimated)
Membership: Regular $15; Family $20; Sustaining $25; Corporate $100; Life $200.

Fort Plain

FORT PLAIN MUSEUM, 389 Canal St., Fort Plain, NY 13339-1160. Mailing Address: P.O. Box 324, Fort Plain, NY 13339-0324. Tel.: 518-993-2527.
E-mail: fortplainmuseum@yahoo.com
Web Site: www.fortplainmuseum.com
Founded: 1963.
Congressional District: 31
Key Personnel: Chm., Norm Bollen; Vice Chm., Robert Perry; Museum Shop Mgr., Patricia Perry.
Personnel Profile: Part-Time Volunteers 28.
Governing Authority: nonprofit corporation. State Education Dept. Tax-exempt: 501(c)(3).
History Museum: housed in restored 19th-century farmhouse.
Collections: Native Americans; Revolutionary War; Erie Canal; history; anthropology; archaeology.
Research Fields: American Revolutionary period; Mohawk Valley development.
Facilities: Museum-related items for sale.
Activities: temporary exhibitions; films; junior museum; tours; seminars.
Publications: Revolutionary War Fort Plain: A Closer Look.
Hours & Admission Prices: June-Aug. daily 1-5; Sept.-May by appointment. Donations accepted. ♿
Attendance: 2,500 (estimated)
Membership: Sponsor $50; Patron $100; Sustainer $500.

Franklinville

ISCHUA VALLEY HISTORICAL SOCIETY, INC., 9 Pine St., Franklinville, NY 14737-1111. Mailing Address: P.O. Box 166, Franklinville, NY 14737. Tel.: 716-676-2590 & 2325.
E-mail: fvillenyhist@aol.com
Founded: 1966.
Congressional District: 34
Key Personnel: Pres., Bruce D. Fredrickson; Treas., Carol Merkle; Sec., Ida Gardner.
Personnel Profile: Part-Time Volunteers 50.
Governing Authority: nonprofit organization. Tax-exempt: 501(c)(3).
Historical Society Museum: listed on State & National Historic Registers.
Collections: local artifacts & documents. Historic Houses: 1814 Howe-Prescott - Salt Box; 1895 Miner's Cabin - Victorian.
Research Fields: local history; genealogy.
Facilities: library of newspapers, written local histories, scrapbooks & assorted documents available for research by appointment on site; reading room; photographs.
Activities: tours; pie socials; monthly programs.
Publications: quarterly newsletter.
Hours & Admission Prices: Miner's Cabin: Memorial Day-Labor Day Sun. 2-5. Howe-Prescott House: by appointment only. No charge; donations accepted.
Attendance: 700 (estimated)
Membership: General $5; Contributing $10; Business $25; Life $100.

Fredonia

D.R. BARKER HISTORICAL MUSEUM, 20 E. Main St., Fredonia, NY 14063. Mailing Address: 7 Day St., Fredonia, NY 14063-1813. Tel.: 716-672-2114.
E-mail: barkermu@netsync.net
Web Site: www.barkermuseum.net
Formerly: Historical Museum of the D.R. Barker Library
Founded: 1884.
Congressional District: 39
Key Personnel: Pres. (V), Peter Clark; Vice Pres., Keith Sullivan; Cur., Nancy Brown.
Personnel Profile: Full-Time Paid 1; Part-Time Paid 3; Part-Time Volunteers 10; Interns 3.
Governing Authority: nonprofit organization. Parent Institution: Darwin R. Barker Library Association. Tax-exempt: 501(c)(3).
Genealogy Library & History Museum: housed in 1821 Leverett Barker Home.
Collections: portraits; photographs; period costumes and accessories; military uniforms and records; documents and letters, including the records of the Fredonia Academy from 1821-1867; newspapers; genealogical reference works; period furniture and furnishings, tools and equipment.
Research Fields: local history; genealogy.
Facilities: 4,572-vol. genealogy & history library with material relating to the history of Western New York, the Village of Fredonia, the Town of Pomfret and Chautauqua County, and other genealogical materials available for use on premises; 1,968 sq. ft. exhibit space; meeting room.
Activities: concerts; films; hands-on activities; lectures related to exhibitions; guided tours of current exhibits on request; variety of school programs; children's programs; public programming relating to collections; permanent & temporary exhibitions.
Publications: quarterly newsletter, Barker Historical Newsletter; pamphlets, Fredonia by Gaslight, A Diary Year: 1866, The Barker Library & Museum: A History; The Dunkirk & Fredonia Telephone Company 1898-1999-A History; Photographers of Fredonia.
Hours & Admission Prices: Tues. & Thurs. 1-5 & 7-9, Wed. & Fri.-Sat. 1-5. Children's Museum: Sat. 1-5. No charge; donations accepted. Closed national holidays. ♿
Attendance: 3,958 (accurate)
Membership: Senior Citizens & Students $7; Individual $10; Family $15; Contributing $25; Donor $50; Sponsor $100; Patron $100 & up.

MICHAEL C. ROCKEFELLER ARTS CENTER GALLERY, State University College, Fredonia, NY 12070-1127. Tel.: 716-673-4897. Fax: 716-673-4990.
Web Site: www.fredonia.edu/rac
Founded: 1826.
Congressional District: 34
Key Personnel: Dir., Jefferson Westwood.
Personnel Profile: Part-Time Paid 1; Interns 3.
Governing Authority: university. Affiliated with the State University of New York, Fredonia. Tax-exempt: 170(b)(1)(A).
Art Gallery.
Collections: contemporary sculpture, prints & drawings.
Activities: inter-museum loan; permanent, temporary & traveling exhibitions.
Hours & Admission Prices: Academic School Year: Tues.-Thurs. & Sun. 2-6, Fri.-Sat. 2-8. No charge; donations accepted. Closed legal holidays. ♿
Attendance: 2,800 (accurate)
Membership: Annual $25.

Garden City

CRADLE OF AVIATION MUSEUM, Charles Lindbergh Blvd., Garden City, NY 11530. Mailing Address: One Davis Ave., Garden City, NY 11530-6743. Tel.: 516-572-4111. Fax: 516-572-4065.
Web Site: www.cradleofaviation.org
Founded: 1979.
Congressional District: 4
Key Personnel: Exec. Dir., Andrew Parton; Vice Pres. Programs, Tom Gwynne; Chm. Bd. (V), Todd Richman; Dir. Education, Jennifer Baxmeyer; Financial Dir., Dan Boehm; Cur., Joshua Stoff; Visitor Svcs., Gary Monti.
Personnel Profile: Full-Time Paid 20; Part-Time Paid 23; Part-Time Volunteers 250.
Governing Authority: private; nonprofit organization. Tax-exempt: 501(c)(3).
Aviation Museum.
Collections: 73 aircraft & spacecraft significant to the aerospace heritage of Long Island.
Research Fields: history of Long Island airports.
Facilities: 6,300-vol. library; 250-seat cafeteria; classroom; 44,000 sq. ft. exhibit space; 300-seat IMAX theater. Museum-related items for sale.
Activities: concerts; docent program; formal education programs for teachers; educational programs for children; school tour programs; club meetings; lectures.
Hours & Admission Prices: Daily 9:30-5. Museum: adult $9, seniors 62 & over and children 4-12 $8; additional fees for other attractions. Closed Thanksgiving; Christmas. ♿
Attendance: 225,000 (accurate)
Membership: Seniors & Veterans $40; Individual $50; Family $85; Supporter $250; Sponsor $500; IMAX Seat Sponsor $1000.

FIREHOUSE ART GALLERY, NASSAU COMMUNITY COLLEGE, One Education Dr., Garden City, NY 11530-6793. Tel.: 516-572-0619. Fax: 516-572-9673.
E-mail: gallery@ncc.edu
Web Site: firehouse.ncc.edu
Founded: 1965.
Key Personnel: Dir., Lynn Rozzi; Cur., Meg Oliveri.
Personnel Profile: Full-Time Paid 1; Part-Time Paid 4; Part-Time Volunteers 2; Interns 2.
Governing Authority: public college; nonprofit. Tax-exempt: 501(c)(3).
College Art Gallery.
Collections: over 450 works of fine art including paintings, prints, & sculpture, 16th-century to present.
Activities: guided tours; lectures; temporary exhibitions. Annual Events: Highlights of Contemporary American Art; student & faculty shows; regional competition.
Publications: monthly mailer; events calendar.
Hours & Admission Prices: Mon., Wed.-Thurs. & Sat. 11-4, Tues. 11-7. No charge. Closed college holidays. ♿
Attendance: 12,000 (estimated)

LONG ISLAND CHILDREN'S MUSEUM, (M), Charles Limburgh Blvd., Garden City, NY 11530. Mailing Address: 11 Davis Ave., Garden City, NY 11530-6745. Tel.: 516-224-5800 & 5814. Fax: 516-302-8188.
E-mail: development@licm.org
Web Site: www.licm.org
Founded: 1993.
Congressional District: 4
Key Personnel: Exec. Dir., Suzanne LeBlanc; Co Chm. (V), Robert S. Lemle; Co Chm. (V), Scott Rechler; Museum Shop Mgr., Audrey Fichtenbaum.
Personnel Profile: Full-Time Paid 36; Part-Time Paid 70; Part-Time Volunteers 131.
Governing Authority: nonprofit. Tax-exempt.
Children's Museum.
Collections: Interactive; interdisciplinary.
Major Exhibits: Wizard of Oz (T), 2/10-4/10; Games (T), 6/10-8/10; Jump to Japan (T), 10/10-12/10.
Facilities: 40,000 sq. ft. exhibit space.
Activities: hands-on fun experiences; weekend multicultural workshops & performances.
Publications: newsletter; monthly calendars.
Hours & Admission Prices: July-Aug. daily 10-5; Sept.-June Tues.-Sun. 10-5. Admission $10, seniors 65 & over $9; members & children under one no charge. ♿
Attendance: 275,375 (accurate)

Membership: Inventor $60; Discoverer $120; Grandparent $150; Adventurer $170; Explorer $325.

Gardiner

LOCUST LAWN AND TERWILLIGER HOUSE, 400 Rte. 32 S., Gardiner, NY 12525. Mailing Address: Huguenot Historical Society, 18 Broadhead Ave., New Paltz, NY 12561-1403. Tel.: 845-255-1660. Fax: 845-255-0376.
E-mail: info@huguenotstreet.org
Web Site: www.locustlawn.org
Founded: 1894.
Congressional District: 27
Key Personnel: Exec. Dir., Eric J. Roth; Pres. (V), Eileen Crispell Ford; Coord. Patron Svcs., Laura Lucas; Cur. Education, Victoria Hughes; Cur., Leslie LeFevre Stratton; Cur. Historic Properties, Linda Pate; Museum Shop Mgr., Julianna de Grandis.
Personnel Profile: Full-Time Paid 5; Part-Time Paid 15; Part-Time Volunteers 30; Interns 2.
Governing Authority: Society. Parent Institution: The Huguenot Historical Society, 18 Brodhead Ave., New Paltz. Tax-exempt: 501(c)(3).
Historic House & Estate: 1814 Locust Lawn house; 1738 Terwilliger house.
Collections: period furnishings from Queen Anne-Early Victorian; china; fabrics; laces; textiles; toys; paintings; coaches; tools & farm implements; paintings by Ammi Phillips. Historic Buildings: 1738 Terwilliger House; 1814 Locust Lawn house; slaughter-house; smoke house; carriage house.
Research Fields: furniture; paintings; decorative arts.
Activities: tours; children's programs; family events.
Publications: brochures.
Hours & Admission Prices: June-Oct. Sat.-Sun. 11-4; tours by appointment. Adults $7, seniors & AAA members $6, students $3; discounts to groups; members and children 5 & under no charge.
Membership: Individual $35; Household $50; Business & Contributor $100; Donor $250; Patron $500; Benefactor $1,000.

MOHONK PRESERVE, INC., 3197 Rte. 44/55, Gardiner, NY 12525. Mailing Address: P.O. Box 715, New Paltz, NY 12561-0715. Tel.: 845-255-0919. Fax: 845-255-5646.
E-mail: info@mohonkpreserve.org
Web Site: mohonkpreserve.org
Founded: 1963.
Congressional District: 26
Key Personnel: Pres. Bd. Dir. (V), Ronald G. Knapp; Exec. Dir., Glenn D. Hoagland; Dir. Finance & Administration, Scott Brown; Dir. Communications, Nadia Steinzor; Dir. Research, Paul C. Huth; Dir. Stewardship, Hank Alicandri; Dir. Devel., Joe Alfano; Dir. Education, Kathy Ambrosini; Dir. Land Protection, Jennifer Garofalini.
Personnel Profile: Full-Time Paid 22; Part-Time Paid 28; Part-Time Volunteers 380; Interns 4.
Governing Authority: nonprofit organization. Tax-exempt: 501(c)(3).
Historic Site & Nature Center: located on 6,500 acres in the Shawangunk Mountains.
Collections: natural history records; Northern Shawanqunk Ridge history.
Research Fields: all aspects of ecosystem research; weather recording.
Facilities: 6,500 acres of land, visitor center; research center; teaching pavilion; 65 miles of carriage roads & trails; 4 trailheads.
Activities: public program series; K-12 education program.
Publications: newsletter; book, Time & the Mountain: A Guide to the Geology of the Northern Shawangunks; articles; monographs.
Hours & Admission Prices: Preserve: daily sunrise-sunset. Visitor Center: Mon.-Fri. 9-5. Adults: climbers $15, bikers & hikers $10; discount to ANCA members & groups; members & children under 13 no charge. Closed New Year's Day; Thanksgiving; Christmas Eve & Day. ♿
Attendance: 150,000 (estimated)
Membership: Individual $55; Supporting $300; Sustaining $500; Sentinel $1,000; Life Endowment $3,000. Business memberships available.

Garrison

BOSCOBEL HOUSE & GARDENS, 1601 Rte. 9D, Garrison, NY 10524-4406. Tel.: 845-265-3638. Fax: 845-265-4405.
E-mail: info@boscobel.org
Web Site: www.boscobel.org
Founded: 1955.
Congressional District: 25
Key Personnel: Exec. Dir., Geoffrey Platt, Jr.; Pres. (V), Barnabas McHenry; Deputy Exec. Dir., Carolin C. Serino; Coord. Events & Mktg., Donna Blaney; Coord. Tours, Linda Moore; Museum Shop Mgr., Renate Smoller; Collections Mgr., Judith Pavelock; Maintenance Supvr., Richard Soedler.
Personnel Profile: Full-Time Paid 8; Part-Time Paid 28; Part-Time Volunteers 50.
Governing Authority: nonprofit organization. Tax-exempt: 501(c)(3).
Historic House Museum: c.1808 New York Federal style home built by States Morris Dyckman.
Collections: 1800-1820 neo-classical furniture by cabinetmakers Duncan Phyfe & Michael Allison; federal period decorative arts; china, glass & silver purchased by Dyckman in London; Federal period paintings & decorative arts.
Research Fields: Dyckman Family & property history; Decorative Arts & Architecture; everyday life in America during the Federal Period.
Facilities: visitor center; gardens; one mile woodland trail. Books and museum-related items for sale.
Activities: guided tours; school tours; workshops; lectures; study kits on life in Federal Period & the Decorative Arts available to schools; changing & permanent exhibitions. Annual Events: Hudson Valley Shakespeare Festival June-August; Big Band Concert in September; Horse and Carriage Day in October.
Publications: brochure; booklet, History of Boscobel; catalogue, Federal Furniture and Decorative Arts at Boscobel; summer art exhibition catalogue.
Hours & Admission Prices: April-Oct. Wed.-Mon. 9:30-5; Nov.-Dec. Wed.-Mon. 9:30-4. House & Grounds: Family of 4 $40; adults $16, senior citizens 62 & over $12; children 6-14 $7. Grounds: Family of 4 $25, adults $8, children 6-14 $5; discounts to groups of 12 or more & AAM members; museum employees of local museums in Hudson Valley with proper ID & members no charge. Closed Thanksgiving; Christmas. ♿
Attendance: 52,211 (accurate)
Membership: Senior Citizens 62 & over $30; Individual $40; Family $60; Loyalists $150; Federalists $300; Patriots $500; Neoclassicists $1,000.

GARRISON ART CENTER, 23 Garrison's Landing, Garrison, NY 10524-3648. Mailing Address: P.O. Box 4, Garrison, NY 10524-0004. Tel.: 845-424-3960.
E-mail: dir@garrisonartcenter.org
Web Site: www.garrisonartcenter.org
Key Personnel: Pres., Bill Burback; Vice Pres., Meg Staley; Exec. Dir., Carinda Swann
Art Center.
Collections: works by local artists.
Hours & Admission Prices: Tues.-Sun. 12-5.

MANITOGA/THE RUSSEL WRIGHT DESIGN CENTER, (M), 584 Rte. 9D, Garrison, NY 10524. Mailing Address: P.O. Box 249, Garrison, NY 10524-0249. Tel.: 845-424-3812. Fax: 845-424-4043.
E-mail: info@russelwrightcenter.org
Founded: 1984.
Congressional District: 9
Key Personnel: Dir., Kathryn McCullough; Pres. (V), David McAlpin; Asst. Dir. & Museum Shop Mgr., Lori Moss.
Personnel Profile: Full-Time Paid 3; Part-Time Paid 1; Part-Time Volunteers 12; Interns 2.
Governing Authority: Tax-exempt.
Historic House Museum: housed in the former home & studio of designer Russel Wright. A National Historic Landmark.
Collections: Wright's life & family history; personal artifacts; period furnishings; photographs.
Facilities: nature trails.
Activities: guided tours; special educational programs & events.
Hours & Admission Prices: Tours: May-Oct. Mon.-Fri. call for hours, Sat.-Sun. 11 & 1:30; groups by appointment. Adults $15; discounts to American Horticultural Society, Long House Preserve members; members no charge.
Attendance: 3,500 (estimated)
Membership: Student $25; Individual $40; Family & Dual $70; Moss Circle $150-$300; Fern Circle $250-$500; Laurel Circle $1,000; Manitoga Circle $2,500; Dragon Rock Circle $5,000 & up.

Geneseo

BERTHA V.B. LEDERER GALLERY, SUNY Geneseo, Brodie Hall, 1 College Circle, Geneseo, NY 14454-1401. Tel.: 585-245-5814.
Founded: 1966.
Congressional District: 26
Key Personnel: Dir., Cynthia Hawkins.
Personnel Profile: Full-Time Paid 1; Part-Time Paid 12; Interns 2.
Art Gallery.
Collections: works on paper; paintings; sculpture; photographs; prints; ceramics.
Major Exhibits: Drawing Invitational, 1/10-3/10; 2010 Annual Student Juried Show, 3/10; Senior Thesis Show, 4/10-5/8/10.
Facilities: 2,000 sq. ft. exhibit space.
Activities: temporary exhibitions.

Publications: catalogs.
Hours & Admission Prices: Mon.-Thurs. 12-4, Fri.-Sat. 12-6. No charge; donations accepted. Closed Thanksgiving; Christmas, fall & spring breaks. ♿
Membership: Student $10; Basic $40; Patron $100; Benefactor $250; Bertha Lederer Society $500; President's Club $1,000.

LIVINGSTON COUNTY HISTORICAL SOCIETY MUSEUM, 30 Center St., Geneseo, NY 14454-1204. Tel.: 716-243-2281 & 9147.
E-mail: lchistory@frontier.com
Web Site: www.livingstoncountyhistoricalsociety.org
Formerly: Cobblestone Museum
Founded: 1876.
Congressional District: 30
Key Personnel: Pres., Scott Canaan.
Personnel Profile: Part-Time Paid 1; Part-Time Volunteers 20; Interns 1.
Governing Authority: society. Tax-exempt: 501(c)(3).
Historical Society Museum: housed in 1838 cobblestone building.
Collections: agriculture; transportation; military; archaeology; archives; clothing; household items; toys; Indian artifacts; china; education; silver; period fire apparatus; 1,100 books; documents; Concord Coach; Shaker prayer stone replica. Historic Buildings: cobblestone schoolhouse; 1890 Hose Cart Firehouse.
Major Exhibits: Croquet Exhibit, 11/09-12/10.
Facilities: 1,100-vol. library.
Activities: guided tours; formally organized education programs for children; monthly programs for adults.
Publications: Historical Coloring Book of Livingston County; historic newsletter, History of Cobblestone Museum.
Hours & Admission Prices: May-June & Sept.-Oct. Thurs. & Sun. 2-5; July-Aug. Thurs. & Sun. 2-5. Call for other information or appointments. No charge; donations accepted. ♿
Attendance: 1,250
Membership: Children $5; Single $10; Corporate $50; Life $100.

Geneva

GENEVA HISTORICAL SOCIETY & ROSE HILL MANSION, Rte. 96A, Geneva, NY 14456. Mailing Address: 543 South Main St., Geneva, NY 14456-3106. Tel.: 315-789-5151 & 3848. Fax: 315-789-0314.
E-mail: info@genevahistoricalsociety.com
Web Site: www.genevahistoricalsociety.com
Founded: 1968.
Congressional District: 24
Key Personnel: C.E.O., Kenneth Shefsiek; Dir. Education, Anne Dealy; Museum Shop Mgr., Frankie Allen.
Personnel Profile: Full-Time Paid 6; Part-Time Paid 11; Part-Time Volunteers 25.
Governing Authority: nonprofit organization. Parent Institution: Geneva Historical Society. Subsidiary Institution: Weaver Tile Museum. Branch Museums: Prouty-Chew House; Balmanno Cottage. Tax-exempt: 501(c)(3).
Historic House: 1839 Greek Revival twenty-four-room mansion that was built by Gen. William K. Strong in 1839 and belonged to the Robert J. Swan family.
Collections: Empire-style period furniture: eight bedrooms; kitchen; front & rear parlors; banquet hall; library; music room.
Activities: guided tours.
Publications: brochure; Rose Hill Book.
Hours & Admission Prices: May-Oct. Tues.-Sat. 10-4, Sun. 1-5. Adults $7, senior citizens $6, children 10-18 $4; discount to Time Travelers, AASLH & AAM members & groups; children under 10 & Geneva Historical Society members no charge. ♿
Attendance: 4,356 (accurate)
Membership: Single $25; Family $35; Friend $50; Patron $100; Sustaining $150; Sponsor $250; Benefactor $500; Life $1,000.

GENEVA HISTORY MUSEUM, (M), 543 S. Main St., Geneva, NY 14456-3194. Tel.: 315-789-5151. Fax: 315-789-0314.
E-mail: info@genevahistoricalsociety.com
Web Site: genevahistoricalsociety.com
Founded: 1883.
Congressional District: 24
Key Personnel: C.E.O., Kenneth Shefsiek; Pres. (V), Karen Fouracre; Historic Properties Mgr., Adam Chase; Cur. Collections, John C. Marks; Archivist, Karen D. Osburn; Cur. Education & Public Info, Anne F. Dealy; Business Mgr., Frankie Allen; Asst. Educator, Kathryn White.
Personnel Profile: Full-Time Paid 7; Part-Time Paid 10; Part-Time Volunteers 60.
Governing Authority: nonprofit educational organization. Parent Institution: Geneva Historical Society. Branch Museums: 1839 Rose Hill Mansion; Johnston House; Balmanno Cottage. Tax-exempt: 501(c)(3).
Local History Museum & Historic Houses.
Collections: Federal, Empire & Victorian furnishings & accessories; material of local historical interest; archival material; agricultural; military; industrial; costumes; toys; manuscripts; paintings & graphics by local artists; extensive photograph collection.
Research Fields: local history, historic architecture; decorative arts; local artists.
Facilities: 1,600-vol. library & research archive of local history & genealogy available on premises; exhibit space; reading room; 75-seat auditorium.
Activities: guided tours; lectures; school programs; summer camp; permanent & temporary exhibits.
Publications: newsletter, published 6 times per year; annual report; local history publications: A Walking Tour-South Main Street, Geneva, NY; A Driving Tour-Architectural Landmarks; 19th-century Architecture in Geneva; Gentle Enthusiasts in Art: Geneva's Landscape Painting Families; Treasures of American Architecture; Make a Way Somehow: African-Americans in Geneva, NY 1790-1965; To Dress & Keep the Earth: The Nurseries & Nursery Men of Geneva, NY; Close to the Heart of the War: Geneva & World War II; Images of America: Geneva, 1790-1945; Images of America: Geneva, 1945-1980.
Hours & Admission Prices: July-Aug. Mon.-Fri. 9:30-4:30, Sat.-Sun. 1:30-4:30; Sept.-June Tues.-Fri. 9:30-4:30, Sat. 1:30-4:30. No charge; donations accepted.
Attendance: 18,535 (accurate)
Membership: Single $35; Family $50; Friend $75; Patron $100; Sustaining $150; Sponsor $250; Benefactor $500; Investor $1,000.

Germantown

CLERMONT STATE HISTORIC SITE, One Clermont Ave., Germantown, NY 12526-5632. Tel.: 518-537-4240 & 8687. Fax: 518-537-6240.
E-mail: fofc@valstar.net
Web Site: www.friendsofclermont.org
Founded: 1962.
Congressional District: 29
Key Personnel: Dir., Susan Boudreau; Pres. (V), Carl Brandt; Education Dir., Kjirsten Gustavson; Administrative Asst., Roberta Nolan; Board Coordr., Audrey Reifler; Historic Horticulturist, Jane Lehmuller.
Personnel Profile: Full-Time Paid 8; Part-Time Paid 16; Part-Time Volunteers 70; Interns 1.
Governing Authority: state. Parent Institution: NYS Office of Parks, Recreation & Historic Preservation. Tax-exempt: 501(c)(3).
Historic House Museum & Estate Grounds: located on 500-acre Hudson Valley estate, with c.1730 home belonging to seven generations of the Livingston family.
Collections: 16th- through 20th-century library volumes; 18th- through 20th-century furnishings & decorative arts; Livingston family possessions; photographic & manuscripts.
Research Fields: Livingston family history; Livingston-Fulton manuscripts; American Revolution & early Federal period; landowning in the Hudson Valley.
Facilities: 3,500-vol. family library available for use by advance request; 1,100-vol. reference library; visitor center; four formal gardens; picnic area; former carriage drives for hiking; horseback riding; cross-country skiing.
Activities: guided tours; lectures; gallery talks; concerts; school programs; workshops; temporary exhibits; bird walks; Sunday garden strolls; special events & craft demonstrations; children's summer camp.
Publications: newsletters three times per year, Views from Clermont; Friends of Clermont, Inc.
Hours & Admission Prices: House: April-Oct. Tues.-Fri. 11-5 (last tour 4:30); Nov.-March Sat.-Sun. 11-4. Adults $5, seniors over 62 $4; children under 12 no charge. Visitor Center: Jan. 2-April 1 Sat.-Sun. Grounds: daily 8:30-sunset. Visitor Center & Grounds no charge. Closed holidays. ♿
Attendance: 100,000 (estimated)
Membership: Individual $30; Dual & Family $50; Contributor $100; Benefactor $200; Patron $500; Chancellor's Court $1,000.

Glen Cove

GARVIES POINT MUSEUM & PRESERVE, 50 Barry Dr., Glen Cove, NY 11542-1765. Tel.: 516-571-8010.
Web Site: www.garviespointmuseum.com
Key Personnel: Dir., Lealana Loiodice
History Museum.
Collections: county history & heritage; Native American artifacts; archaeology; geology; photographs.
Facilities: Museum-related items for sale.
Activities: research; educational programs.

Hours & Admission Prices: Tues.-Sun. 10-4. Adults $3, children 5-12 $2. Closed winter holidays.

Glens Falls

THE CHAPMAN HISTORICAL MUSEUM, 348 Glen St., Glens Falls, NY 12801-3520. Tel.: 518-793-2826. Fax: 518-793-2831.
E-mail: director@chapmanmuseum.org
Web Site: chapmanmuseum.org
Founded: 1967.
Congressional District: 22
Key Personnel: Exec. Dir., Timothy Weidner; Cur., Jilian Mulder; Educator, Andrea Kinderman.
Personnel Profile: Full-Time Paid 3; Part-Time Paid 3; Part-Time Volunteers 50.
Governing Authority: nonprofit organization. Affiliated with the Glen Falls-Queensbury Historical Association, Inc. Tax-exempt.
Regional History Museum: housed in c.1868 Zopher Isaac DeLong House & attached Carriage House Gallery.
Collections: social & industrial history of the Upper Hudson-Southeastern Adirondack area including the City of Glen Falls & the Town of Queensbury; Stoddard collection of photographs, paintings, published works & memorabilia; The Glens Falls YMCA & Glen Falls Insurance Company collections; Glen Falls City School System records; diaries & archival materials; costumes; textiles; household articles; decorative arts.
Research Fields: local social & industrial history; photography of the Greater Glens Falls-Southeastern Adirondack Area.
Facilities: 600-vol. library of primary & secondary materials on local, regional & state history available for use on premises or loan by special permission; 20,000 piece photographic library for on-site use by arrangement.
Activities: guided tours; lectures; formally organized educational programs; docent program; permanent, temporary & traveling exhibitions; school loan service; oral history projects; architectural surveys; school kits.
Publications: book, Bridging the Years; The Adirondacks Illustrated; newsletter, The Echo; 19th-century map reprints.
Hours & Admission Prices: Tues.-Sat. 10-4, Sun. 12-4. No charge. Closed major holidays. ♿
Attendance: 15,000 (accurate)
Membership: Senior $22; Individual $40; Family $50; Contributing $75; Supporting $100; Sponsor $250; Patron $500; Benefactor $1,000.

* **THE HYDE COLLECTION, (M),** 161 Warren St., Glens Falls, NY 12801-4562. Tel.: 518-792-1761. Fax: 518-792-9197.
E-mail: info@hydecollection.org
Web Site: www.hydecollection.org
Founded: 1952.
Congressional District: 29
Key Personnel: Exec. Dir., David F. Setford; Chm., Beth S. Saunders; Financial Officer, Lynne Mason; Registrar & Collections Mgr., Barbara Rathburn; Cur., Erin M. Coe; Dir. Devel., Christine Dawson; Membership Mgr., Dede Potter; Asst. to Dir., Kathy Reed; Curatorial Asst., Susan Bishop; Dir. Education, Sara Hallberg.
Personnel Profile: Full-Time Paid 14; Part-Time Paid 18; Part-Time Volunteers 200; Interns 4.
Governing Authority: bd. of trustees. Tax-exempt.
Art Museum.
Collections: European & American paintings, drawings and sculpture 14th-20th centuries including works by Botticelli, Chase, Courbet, Davies, Degas, Eakins, El Greco, Hassam, Homer, Matisse, Picasso, Raphael, Rembrandt, Renoir, Rubens, Ryder, Seurat and Whistler; Italian Renaissance, Baroque & 18th-century French furnishings; incunabula & rare first editions; Bigelow & Wadsworth designed 1912 founders' residence.
Major Exhibits: An Enduring Legacy: American Impressionist Landscape Paintings from the Thomas Clark Collection, 11/14/09-3/28/10; Andrew Wyeth: An American Legend, 6/12/10-9/5/10; Exhibition by Artists of the Mohawk-Hudson Region, 10/10-12/12/10.
Research Fields: European & American paintings, drawings & sculpture.
Facilities: 144-seat auditorium. Museum-related items for sale.
Activities: guided tours; lectures; concerts; school & community outreach programs; special & traveling exhibitions; family activities; gallery talks; facility rentals; adult & children's art studios.
Publications: quarterly members newsletter, The Hyde Collection Catalogue; exhibition catalogues & brochures including: Arthur B. Davies: Dweller on the Threshold; Family Matters: American Impressionism & Realism; FORM(ATION): Modern & Contemporary Works from the Feibes and Schmitt Collection; Painting Lake George, 1774-1900, Adolph Gottlieb: 1956; Degas & Music.
Hours & Admission Prices: Tues.-Sat. 10-5, Sun. 12-5. Small fee for group tours. No charge; donations accepted. Closed major holidays. ♿
Attendance: 28,000 (estimated)
Membership: Student $35; Senior $40; Educator & Artist $40; Individual $60; Dual $75; Family $85; Participating $125; Donor $250; Sustaining $500; Steward $750; Patron $1,000; Conservator $1,500; Benefactor $2,500; Philanthropist $5,000.

WORLD AWARENESS CHILDREN'S MUSEUM, 89 Warren St., Glens Falls, NY 12801-4509. Tel.: 518-793-2773.
E-mail: admin@worldchildrensmuseum.org
Web Site: www.worldchildrensmuseum.org
Founded: 1995.
Key Personnel: Exec. Dir., Jacquiline Touba, Ph.D.; Chm., Paul Pontiff, Esq.; Chm. (V), Anthony Taverni.
Personnel Profile: Full-Time Paid 2; Part-Time Paid 5; Part-Time Volunteers 5.
Governing Authority: Tax-exempt.
Children's Museum.
Collections: hands-on exhibits; international children's art; clothing & educational artifacts from around the world; international artifacts.
Activities: traveling exhibitions.
Hours & Admission Prices: Closed for renovations.
Membership: Senior & Student $10; Individual $25; Family $35; Business $50; Traveler $100; Explorer $250.

Glenville

EMPIRE STATE AEROSCIENCES MUSEUM, 250 Rudy Chase Dr., Glenville, NY 12302-7104. Tel.: 518-377-2191, ext. 10. Fax: 518-377-1959.
E-mail: esam@esam.org
Web Site: www.esam.org
Founded: 1984.
Congressional District: 21
Key Personnel: Pres. (V), Kevin Millington; Museum Shop Mgr., Joyce Newkirk.
Personnel Profile: Full-Time Volunteers 3; Part-Time Paid 3; Part-Time Volunteers 110.
Governing Authority: nonprofit organization. Tax-exempt 501(c)(3).
Aerosciences & Airplane Museum.
Collections: concentration on New York State aviation items with emphasis on hands-on items for children.
Research Fields: aviation.
Facilities: research library; outdoor air park.
Publications: monthly newsletter: Aeronotes.
Hours & Admission Prices: Wed. & Sun. 12-4, Thurs.-Sat. 10-4. Adults $8, seniors & military $6, youth 6-16 $2, students $1; discounts to AAA members; members & children under 6 no charge. Closed New Year's Day; Thanksgiving; Christmas. ♿
Attendance: 15,000 (estimated)
Membership: Senior Citizen & Student $30; Individual $35; Family $50; School & Not-for-Profit Organization $50; Small Business $100; Business (over 10 employees) $250.

Gloversville

FULTON COUNTY MUSEUM, 237 N. Kingsboro Ave., Gloversville, NY 12078-1428. Mailing Address: P.O. Box 711, Gloversville, NY 12078-0711. Tel.: 518-725-2203.
Web Site: www.fultoncountymuseum.com
Founded: 1891.
Congressional District: 26
Key Personnel: Pres. (V), Joan Loveday; Suprv., Donna Terranova.
Personnel Profile: Part-Time Paid 1; Part-Time Volunteers 10; Interns 1.
Governing Authority: society. Parent Institution: Fulton County Historical Society, 237 N. Kingsboro Ave., Gloversville, NY 12078. Tax-exempt.
Historical Society & Industrial Craft Museum: housed in Old Kingsborough School, located on the site of the original Kingsborough Academy built in 1831.
Collections: local history, with emphasis on the glove and leather industry; 18th & 19th-century weavings; 1800-present day glove machinery; leather tanning room; 18th & 19th-century muskets, pistols, swords & daggers; early school room; blacksmith shop; Indian longhouse; railroad artifacts; dioramas, photographs & documents of the Sacandaga valley from mid-1800 before the flood; Indian artifacts.
Research Fields: local city & county history; glove & leather industry, early man in Fulton county, railroads.
Facilities: 500-vol. library of material on local, regional & state history, natural history, available for use on premises; reading room; classroom; 40-seat auditorium.
Activities: guided tours; lectures; permanent & temporary exhibitions; weaving demonstrations.
Publications: brochures; newsletters; program flyers.

Hours & Admission Prices: May-June & Sept.-Oct. Tues.-Sat. 12-4; July-Aug. Tues.-Sat. 10-4. No charge; donations accepted. Closed Independence Day. ♿
Attendance: 1,470 (accurate)
Membership: Annual Single $8; Family $15; Life $125.

Goshen

THE HARNESS RACING MUSEUM AND HALL OF FAME, (M), 240 Main St., Goshen, NY 10924-2157. Tel.: 845-294-6330. Fax: 845-294-3463.
E-mail: hrm@frontiernet.net
Web Site: www.harnessmuseum.com
Formerly: Trotting Horse Museum/Hall of Fame of the Trotter
Founded: 1951.
Congressional District: 22
Key Personnel: Dir., Gail C. Cunard; Pres., Elbridge T. Gerry, Jr.; Museum Shop Mgr., Betty Anne Sosinski.
Personnel Profile: Full-Time Paid 10; Part-Time Paid 10; Part-Time Volunteers 4.
Governing Authority: nonprofit organization. Tax-exempt: 501(c)(3).
Sports Museum: housed in 1913 Tudor-styled stable located next to Historic Track.
Collections: Currier & Ives lithographs; photographs; original wood carvings; dioramas; books; bronzes; statuettes; oil paintings & wash drawings of the American trotting horse; equipment used in trotting; American Standard-bred Horse history.
Research Fields: history of trotting races; breeding of the American Standard-bred; artists of the sport; genealogy of people in the sport.
Facilities: 1,000-vol. library of bound magazines, manuscripts, videos & books on the history of harness racing available on the premises; 200-seat auditorium. Books & other museum-related items for sale.
Activities: guided tours; lectures; films; gallery talks; formally organized education programs for children; permanent, temporary & traveling exhibitions; concerts; art festivals.
Publications: quarterly newsletter; gift shop catalog; souvenir journal.
Hours & Admission Prices: General Admission: no charge. Docent Guided Group Tours: $4. ♿
Attendance: 27,000 (accurate)
Membership: Active $35; Sustaining $50; Contributing $100; Fellow $150; Patron $500-$999; Benefactor $1,000 & up.

Gouverneur

GOUVERNEUR HISTORICAL ASSOCIATION, 30 Church St., Gouverneur, NY 13642-1416. Tel.: 315-287-0570.
Founded: 1974.
Key Personnel: Pres. (V) & Cur. History, Joseph Laurenza; Vice Pres., John Phillips; Treas., R. Joseph Weekes; Cur. Acquisitions, Joseph Laurenza.
Personnel Profile: Part-Time Volunteers 40.
Governing Authority: nonprofit organization. Tax-exempt: 501(c)(3).
Historical Society Museum: housed in 1890 Presbyterian Manse.
Collections: furnishings of a Victorian house; military; rock & minerals collection; farm tools; fire fighting wagon; women's Victorian clothing; children's clothing & toys; Western Indians collection: clothes, pottery, paintings, dolls, sculpture.
Research Fields: local history; genealogy.
Facilities: 100-vol. library of local history; classrooms. Museum-related items for sale.
Activities: guided tours; lectures; concerts; hobby workshops; formally organized education programs for adults; school loan service; temporary & permanent exhibitions.
Hours & Admission Prices: Wed. & Sat. 1-3; other times by appointment. No charge; donations accepted. Closed New Year's Day; Christmas.
Attendance: 461 (accurate)
Membership: Annual $5.

Granville

PEMBER MUSEUM OF NATURAL HISTORY, 33 W. Main St., Granville, NY 12832-1320. Tel.: 518-642-1515.
E-mail: info@pembermuseum.com
Web Site: www.pembermuseum.com
Founded: 1909.
Congressional District: 24
Key Personnel: Dir., Patricia Bailey; Pres. (V), Dan Wilson.
Personnel Profile: Full-Time Paid 1; Part-Time Paid 3; Part-Time Volunteers 30; Interns 1.
Governing Authority: Parent Institution: Pember Library & Museum. Subsidiary Institution: Pember Nature Preserve. Affiliated with the Hebron Pember Nature Preserve. Tax-exempt: chartered under state education law.
Natural History Museum, Nature Center & Conservation Area.
Collections: 1862-1924 private collection of Franklin Pember; 2,000 birds; 500 mammals; 860 egg sets & nests; 2,000 insects; 1,500 herbarium mounts; rocks; minerals; fossils; mollusk shells.
Facilities: 200-vol. library available on premises only; nature center; 125-acre nature preserve with trails & schoolhouse. Museum-related items for sale.
Activities: guided tours; lectures; organized educational programs; interpretive museum activities for families, adults, children, school groups & other scheduled groups; outreach & loan kits; field trips & charters; school loan service. Museum Sponsors: field trips.
Publications: book, The Pember Museum of Natural History; quarterly newsletter.
Hours & Admission Prices: Tues.-Fri. 1-5, Sat. 10-3. No charge. Closed holidays.
Attendance: 17,518 (accurate)
Membership: Individual $15; Family $25; Small Business $30; Friend $50; Supporter & Corporate $100; Sustainer $250; Patron $500; Lifetime $1,000.

SLATE VALLEY MUSEUM, 17 Water St., Granville, NY 12832-1316. Tel.: 518-642-1417. Fax: 518-642-1417.
E-mail: mail@slatevalleymuseum.org
Web Site: www.slatevalleymuseum.org
Founded: 1995.
Congressional District: 22
Key Personnel: Exec. Dir., Mary Lou Willits; Bd. Pres. (V), David P. Bridges; Treas., Gladys Frustaci; Asst. Dir. & Educator, Sarah Benway.
Personnel Profile: Full-Time Paid 2; Part-Time Paid 1; Part-Time Volunteers 20.
Governing Authority: private; nonprofit organization. Tax-exempt: 501(c)(3).
History Museum.
Collections: the history of slate quarrying & the slate industry; geological specimens; photographs; prints; paintings; artifacts; ceramics; furniture; costumes; maps; paper materials & books.
Research Fields: history of individual slate businesses in the slate valley of NY & VT 1839-present; WPA Federal Art Project mural: Men Working in Slate Quarry, Martha Levy 1939; immigration of Welsh, Irish, Eastern Europeans & Italians to the Slate regions of the U.S.
Facilities: 100-vol. library; classroom; 4,000 sq. ft. exhibit space. Museum-related items for sale.
Activities: concerts; docent program; films; formal educational programs; guided tours; lectures; loan & temporary exhibitions; school loan service. Annual Event: Holiday Open House.
Publications: newsletter 3 times a year, Slate Valley Museum Newsletter; ethnic cookbook, Cooking in the Slate Valley.
Hours & Admission Prices: Memorial Day to Columbus Day Tues.-Sat. 10-5, Sun. 1-4; mid-Oct.-May Tues.-Fri. 1-5, Sat. 10-4. Adults $5; discounts to ICOM & AAM members; members, children 12 & under and Slate company employees no charge. Closed New Year's Day; Independence Day; Thanksgiving; Christmas. ♿
Attendance: 7,000 (accurate)
Membership: Individual $30; Family $55; Business Patron $70; Corporate Partner $105; Benefactor $130; Guardian $500.

Great River

BAYARD CUTTING ARBORETUM, 440 Montauk Hwy., Great River, NY 11739. Mailing Address: P.O. Box 466, Oakdale, NY 11769-0466. Tel.: 631-581-1002. Fax: 631-581-1031.
E-mail: grace.wagner@oprhp.state.ny.us
Web Site: www.bayardcuttingarboretum.com
Founded: 1952.
Congressional District: 2
Key Personnel: Dir., Joy Kaminsky; Dir. Grounds, Lillian Wykert; Bd. Chm., Prof. Barbara Schaedler.
Personnel Profile: Full-Time Paid 8; Part-Time Paid 12; Part-Time Volunteers 20; Interns 1.
Governing Authority: state; board of trustees. Parent Institution: New York State Parks. Subsidiary Institution: Office of Parks, Recreation & Historic Preservation. Tax-exempt.
Arboretum: located on 1886 National Register Historic Site.
Collections: conifers; rhododendrons; oaks; dwarf evergreens; hollies; mounted birds; local Indian artifacts; Tiffany glass; antique woodwork.
Facilities: botanical garden; nature conservation center; 130-seat auditorium; classrooms; cafeteria.
Activities: guided tours; lectures; concerts; arts festivals; formally organized education programs; guided historic house tours; holiday decorations in December. Museum Sponsors: flower show.
Publications: book, Bayard Cutting Arboretum A History.
Hours & Admission Prices: April-Oct. daily 10-5; Nov.-March daily 10-4.

Buses: $35-$75, Limos: $12, Car: $6; discounts to senior citizens & handicapped persons with New York State park passes. ♿
Attendance: 150,000 (estimated)

Greenport

EAST END SEAPORT MUSEUM AND MARINE FOUNDATION, 3rd St. at Ferry Dock, Greenport, NY 11944. Mailing Address: P.O. Box 624, Greenport, NY 11944-0624. Tel.: 631-477-2100. Fax: 631-477-0004.
E-mail: eseaport@verizon.net
Web Site: www.eastendseaport.org
Founded: 1990.
Congressional District: 1
Key Personnel: Chm. & Pres., George Peter; Museum Shop Mgr., Kelly Logsdon.
Personnel Profile: Part-Time Paid 3.
Governing Authority: private; nonprofit organization. Tax-exempt: 501(c)(3).
Maritime Museum: housed in c.1894 historic Long Island Railroad Station depicting maritime heritage & seaport history of Eastern Long Island.
Collections: text; shipbuilding in Greenport during World War II photographs; tools; models; lighthouse artifacts; saltwater aquarium; yacht racing & maritime women highlights; Picket Patrol, story of sailboat warriors in WWII; J-Boats racing yachts of the 1930s; 1800s to 1900 maritime events of Eastern Long Island.
Facilities: aquarium. Museum-related items for sale.
Activities: lectures; guided tours; oral history of East End Maritime history. Museum Sponsors: Maritime Festival; Opening Reception.
Hours & Admission Prices: May 17-June Sat.-Sun. 11-5; July-Sept. Wed.-Mon. 11-5. Gate $2. ♿
Attendance: 9,500 (accurate)
Membership: Regular $25; Family $40; First Mate $100; Captain $250; Commodore $500; Admiral (life) $1,000.

Greenwich

WASHINGTON COUNTY FAIR FARM MUSEUM, 392 Old Schuylerville Rd., Greenwich, NY 12834-4615. Tel.: 518-692-2464. Fax: 518-692-1021.
E-mail: markwashfair@aol.com
Web Site: washingtoncountyfair.com
Founded: 1971.
Key Personnel: Fair Mgr., Mark St. Jaques; Education, Joan Prouty.
Personnel Profile: Full-Time Volunteers 20; Part-Time Paid 2; Part-Time Volunteers 30.
Governing Authority: private; nonprofit organization. Parent Institution: Washington County Fair, Inc., Greenwich, NY. Tax-exempt: 501(c)(3).
History Museum.
Collections: agricultural equipment; farm-related artifacts. Historic Buildings: 1850s schoolhouse, corn crib, milkhouse, summer kitchen.
Facilities: library. Museum-related items for sale.
Activities: guided tours. Annual Events: Planting Activities; Youth Art Show & Competition; Harvesting Activities.
Hours & Admission Prices: May-Oct. call for schedule; other times by appointment. No charge; donations accepted. ♿
Attendance: 25,000 (estimated)

Hamilton

* **THE PICKER ART GALLERY, (M),** Colgate University, 13 Oak Dr., Hamilton, NY 13346-1398. Tel.: 315-228-7634. Fax: 315-228-7932.
E-mail: pickerart@mail.colgate.edu
Web Site: www.pickerartgallery.org
Founded: 1966.
Congressional District: 23
Key Personnel: Dir., Scott Habes; Cur., Joachim Homann; Coord. Education, Melissa Davies; Registrar, Michael Sample; Administrative Asst., Tammy Larson; Technology Coord., Michelle VanAuken.
Personnel Profile: Full-Time Paid 4; Part-Time Paid 2; Part-Time Volunteers 14; Interns 12.
Governing Authority: Parent Institution: Colgate University. Tax-exempt: 101(6).
Art Gallery.
Collections: Luther W. Brady DFA, 88 20th century works on paper; Herman Collection of modern Chinese woodcuts; Gary M. Hoffer '74 Memorial Photography Collection; Louis de Hoyos '43 pre-Columbian Art; Soviet photographer Evgeny Khaldei collection; Herbert Mayer '29 paintings & sculpture.
Research Fields: various forms of art media.
Facilities: graphic arts studyroom; classrooms.
Activities: lectures; films; gallery talks; inter-museum loan, temporary & traveling exhibitions.
Publications: newsletter; annual report; exhibition catalogues.
Hours & Admission Prices: Tues.-Sat. 10-5, Sun. 1-5. No charge. Closed major holidays & Mon.-Thurs. during academic breaks. ♿
Attendance: 5,705 (accurate)
Membership: Student $10; Contributing $25; Sponsoring $50; Supporting $100; Sustaining $500; Patron $1,000; Life $5,000; Benefactors $200,000 in cash or works of art.

Hammondsport

GLENN H. CURTISS MUSEUM, (M), 8419 State Rte. 54, Hammondsport, NY 14840-9795. Tel.: 607-569-2160. Fax: 607-569-2040.
E-mail: info@glennhcurtissmuseum.org
Web Site: www.glennhcurtissmuseum.org
Founded: 1961.
Congressional District: 39
Key Personnel: C.E.O. & Dir., Trafford Doherty; Pres. (V), Marcia Coon; Cur., Rick Leisenring; Museum Shop Mgr., Lynne Mason.
Personnel Profile: Full-Time Paid 3; Part-Time Paid 5; Part-Time Volunteers 160.
Governing Authority: local. Tax-exempt.
Aviation & Local History Museum.
Collections: history of Glenn Curtiss aircraft & engines; local history; aviation; Curtiss Aeroplane & Motor Co.; Curtiss motorcycles; Curtiss-Wright Corp. Wine-making.
Research Fields: Glenn H. Curtiss, father of American Naval Aviation, founder of the American aircraft industry, early aviation.
Facilities: 2,600-vol. library of books & 750 periodicals devoted to Curtiss Aviation & the history of aviation.
Activities: guided tours; school tours.
Publications: quarterly, The Aerogram.
Hours & Admission Prices: June-Oct. Mon.-Sat. 9-5, Sun. 10-5; Nov.-May daily 10-4. Adults $7.50, senior citizens $6, students $4; discounts to groups of 10 or more & AAA members; children 7 & under and members no charge. Closed New Year's Day; Easter; Thanksgiving; Christmas Eve & Day. ♿
Attendance: 25,000 (estimated)
Membership: Basic $35; Contributing $50; Supporting $125; Donor $250; Patron $500; Benefactor $1000.

THE WINE MUSEUM OF GREYTON H. TAYLOR, 8843 Greyton H. Taylor Memorial Dr., Hammondsport, NY 14840-9635. Mailing Address: P.O. Box 458, Hammondsport, NY 14840-0458. Tel.: 607-868-4814 & 3610. Fax: 607-868-3205.
E-mail: bullyhil@ptd.net
Web Site: www.bullyhill.com
Founded: 1967.
Key Personnel: Pres., Lillian Taylor; Museum Shop Mgr., Paul Sprague.
Personnel Profile: Full-Time Paid 1.
Governing Authority: nonprofit. Tax-exempt: 501(c)(3).
Technology Museum: housed in 1880 Taylor Wine Company building.
Collections: old winemaking equipment; cooperage; wine bottles & labels; presidential glass.
Research Fields: viticulture; archives; paintings.
Facilities: 1,500-vol. library of books on winemaking, viticulture & wine cookery available for use on premises; reading room.
Activities: guided & self guided tours; temporary exhibitions.
Hours & Admission Prices: Mon.-Sat. 10-5, Sun. 12-5. No charge; donations requested. ♿
Attendance: 6,500 (estimated)

Harpursville

COLESVILLE & WINDSOR MUSEUM AT ST. LUKE'S CHURCH, Maple St. & Monroe St., Harpursville, NY 13787. Mailing Address: P.O. Box 318, Harpursville, NY 13787-0318. Tel.: 607-693-1222.
Founded: 1971.
Congressional District: 27
Key Personnel: Pres., Ronald Henry; Cur., Marjory Hinman; Historian-Colesville, Val La Clair.
Personnel Profile: Part-Time Volunteers 10.
Governing Authority: nonprofit organization. Parent Institution: Old Onaquaga Historical Society. Tax-exempt.
History Museum: housed in 1823 Episcopal Church.
Collections: American Indian artifacts; period furnishings; early agricultural tools & industries; period American utensils; architecture; craft tools; maps; life in the towns of Windsor & Colesville in Broome County, New York.
Research Fields: American Indian history; genealogy; public records of town & county.
Facilities: library of public records & history books available on premises by request; 100-seat sanctuary.

Activities: guided tours; lectures; formally organized education programs; permanent & temporary exhibitions.
Hours & Admission Prices: June-Oct. 2nd Sun. 2-5; other times by appointment. No charge; donations accepted.
Attendance: 450 (estimated)
Membership: Family $10.

Hempstead

* **HOFSTRA UNIVERSITY MUSEUM, (M),** 112 Hofstra University, Hempstead, NY 11549-1120. Tel.: 516-463-5672. Fax: 516-463-4743.
E-mail: beth.e.levinthal@hofstra.edu
Web Site: www.hofstra.edu/museum
Founded: 1963.
Congressional District: 5
Key Personnel: Exec. Dir., Beth E. Levinthal; Dir. Museum Education, Nancy Richner; Cur. Collections, Eleanor Rait; Asst. Dir. Exhibitions & Collections, Karen Albert; Public Rels., Lindsey Calabrese; Coord. Devel. & Membership, Eileen Matte.
Personnel Profile: Full-Time Paid 6; Part-Time Paid 8; Part-Time Volunteers 17; Interns 2.
Governing Authority: university. Parent Institution: Hofstra University. Tax-exempt: 170(b)(1)(A).
Art Museum.
Collections: 19th- to 20th-century paintings, sculpture, prints, drawings & photographs; Asian paintings & sculpture; African, Oceanic & pre-Columbian sculpture; outdoor sculpture; permanently installed blue stone 11-circuit labyrinth.
Major Exhibits: Something's Afoot, 1/4/10-5/28/10; Children's Pleasures: American Celebrations of Childhood, 2/2/10-4/18/10; Settling Into Nature: Photography of Mikael Levin, 5/4/10-6/10; 75 Years of Collecting Treasures from the Hofstra University Museum, 9/14/10-12/17/10; A Hofstra History: The 1st 75 Years, 9/27/10-2/4/11.
Research Fields: 20th-century & contemporary American painting & sculpture; modern European, Asian, African & Dutch art.
Facilities: 1,500-vol. library of art books, catalogues & periodicals available for use by appointment; Emily Lowe Gallery; Filderman Gallery; outdoor sculpture area; Lowenfeld Exhibition Hall; arboretum.
Activities: guided tours; school programs K-12; lectures; symposia; inter-museum & temporary exhibitions; sculpture garden tours; gallery talks. Museum Sponsors: Family Festivals.
Publications: catalogs, The America of Currier & Ives; British Watercolors; Cobra; Paris: Nature in the City; Androgyny in Art; Harlem Renaissance: The Blossoming of New Promises; 1935: Jung & the Abstract Expressionists; Mother & Child: The Art of Henry Moore; People at Work: Seventeenth Century Dutch Art; The Transparent Thread: Asian Philosophy in American Art; Appeasing the Spirits: Sui & Early Tang Tomb Sculpture from the Schloss Collection; The Butcher, the Baker, the Candlestick Maker: Jan Luyken's Mirrors of 17th-Century Dutch Daily Life; Endless is the Way Leading Home: The Art of Stephen Csoka; 4 + 1 + 5 Artists in Korea: Contemporary Painting and Sculpture from Seoul, Korea; Beyond the Frame: Animation Art and Paintings; Paul Jenkins 1954-1960 The Early Years in New York and Paris; British Prints from the Hofstra Museum Collection; Fine Art and Paper Money in Jacksonian America 1820-1860; Abstract Expressionism: Then and Now; Artists After Moby Dick; Swiss Poster: The Art of Ten Masters; The Hofstra Museum at 40; Tabletop; Breaking the Walls of Bias: Survivors' Art; Places Made Sacred; Where the Island Begins; New, New Media: Recent Trends in Web Design; Bailey Musica: Preserving Hispanic Culture on Long Island; Robert Rauschenberg: Artist/Citizen; Views of Old New York City: D.T. Valentine's Manuals 1841-1870; The Photography of Ruth Orkin; Sally Gall: Selected Landscapes; Euclid to ebooks: Ideal Images, Moving Ideas; Twardowicz-Dodson: Artists in Parallel; Voiceless In The Presence of Realities: 9/11/01 Remembrances from the Long Island Studies Institute; On Location: Women Photographers from the Hofstra University Museum Collection; Stan Brodsky, The Figure: 1951-2006; Ancient Echoes in Contemporary Printmaking; Tranquil Power: The Art of Perle Fine.
Hours & Admission Prices: Tues.-Fri. 10-5, Sat.-Sun. 1-5. No charge; donations accepted. Closed Independence Day; Thanksgiving & weekend after; Christmas; university recesses. ♿
Attendance: 14,040 (estimated)
Membership: Student $15; Senior Citizen $25; Hofstra Alumni Individual $30; Individual $35; Hofstra Alumni Family & Senior Citizen Family $40; Family & Dual $60; Supporter $150; Supporter Alumni Hofstra $125; Sustainer $300; Hofstra Alumni Sustainer $250; Friend $500; Hofstra Alumni Friend $450; Fellow $1,000-$4,999; Director's Circle $5,000 & up.

Herkimer

HERKIMER COUNTY HISTORICAL SOCIETY, 400 N. Main St., Herkimer, NY 13350-1955. Tel.: 315-866-6413.
E-mail: herkimerhistory@yahoo.com
Web Site: www.rootsweb.com/~nyhchs
Founded: 1896.
Congressional District: 31
Key Personnel: Pres. (V), Jeff Steele; Exec. Dir., Susan R. Perkins; Administrative Asst., Caryl Hopson.
Personnel Profile: Full-Time Paid 2; Part-Time Volunteers 20.
Governing Authority: society. Tax-exempt: 637.
Local History Museum.
Collections: items of Herkimer County; German Palatine Settlement artifacts; memorabilia of major wars; tools & items related to industries; Herkimer County typewriter; doll house miniature collection; exhibition on Criminal Justice.
Research Fields: history of Herkimer County; genealogy.
Facilities: 2,000-vol. library of books on genealogy and history available for use on premises.
Activities: summer & fall monthly programs.
Publications: books, Genealogy of Mohawk Valley Bellingers and Allied Families; Genealogy of Mohawk Valley Caslers and Allied Families; The Petries of the Mohawk Valley; Mohawk Valley Rasbachs & Allied Families; Mohawk Valley Herkimers & Allied Families; Cookbook, Victuals & Vignettes; Prayer & Praise: Churches in County; Mohawk Valley Herkimers & Allied Families; Mohawk Valley Harters and Allied Families; A New History of Herkimer County; Herkimer County at 200; Mohawk Valley Starings and Allied Families.
Hours & Admission Prices: Mon.-Fri. 10-4. No charge; donations accepted. Closed national holidays. ♿
Attendance: 4,000 (estimated)
Membership: Student $15; Individual $40; Family $75; Sustaining $100; Friend $300.

Hicksville

THE HICKSVILLE GREGORY MUSEUM, (M), 1 Heitz Place, Hicksville, NY 11801-3101. Tel.: 516-822-7505. Fax: 516-822-3227.
E-mail: mail@gregorymuseum.org
Web Site: gregorymuseum.org
Founded: 1963.
Congressional District: 4
Key Personnel: Pres., Richard Althaus; Cur. & Museum Shop Mgr., Donald Curran; Historian, Richard Evers.
Personnel Profile: Full-Time Paid 1; Part-Time Paid 4; Part-Time Volunteers 12; Interns 4.
Governing Authority: nonprofit organization. Tax-exempt: 501(c)(3).
Science & Technology Museum: housed in 1895 Heitz Place Court House-Jail.
Collections: minerals; fossils; Indian artifacts; sea shells; butterflies; moths; natural jewelry; nature photography; fluorescent mineral pictures; Long Island local historical artifacts.
Major Exhibits: 100 Years of Scouting, 2/10-12/10.
Research Fields: local history; rocks; minerals; wild flowers; entomology; birds.
Facilities: 400-vol. library of science & nature books available on premises; field research station; lecture hall. Museum-related items for sale.
Activities: guided tours; lectures; films; slide programs; arts festivals; temporary & traveling exhibitions; formally organized educational programs; classes.
Publications: booklet, Faceting; Making A Cabochon; Maps on Mineral Locations; Hicksville-Yesterday & Today 1648-1981; annual bulletins.
Hours & Admission Prices: Tues.-Fri. 9:30-4:30, Sat.-Sun. 1-5. Adults $5, students & senior citizens $3; members no charge. Closed major holidays. ♿
Attendance: 10,000 (estimated)
Membership: Family $20; Sponsor $50; Patron $100; Benefactor $250.

High Falls

DELAWARE AND HUDSON CANAL HISTORICAL SOCIETY AND MUSEUM, 23 Mohonk Rd., High Falls, NY 12440. Mailing Address: P.O. Box 23, High Falls, NY 12440-0023. Tel.: 845-687-9311. Fax: 845-687-9311.
E-mail: info@canalmuseum.org
Web Site: www.canalmuseum.org
Founded: 1966.
Congressional District: 26
Key Personnel: Pres., E. Camasso.
Personnel Profile: Part-Time Paid 1; Part-Time Volunteers 18.
Governing Authority: society. Tax-exempt.

Transportation Museum: housed in 1885 Episcopal Church.
Collections: canal-related documents; maps; photographs; dioramas; scale models; artifacts on canal; canal operation & related industries.
Research Fields: historical development of 19th-century canals; transportation; related industries & their impact on the communities.
Facilities: 20-vol. library of books of D&H canal-related material available for research on premises only; 50-seat meeting hall. Canal & museum-related items for sale.
Activities: guided tours; lectures; temporary exhibitions; Exploring the D&H Canal & Environs. Museum Sponsors: Five Locks Walk.
Publications: newsletter.
Hours & Admission Prices: May-Oct. Sat.-Sun. 11-5. Adults $4, children under 12 $2; members no charge. ♿
Attendance: 6,000 (estimated)
Membership: Canawler $25; Barge Crew $40; Lock Tender $60; Tavern Keeper $100; Boat Captain $200; Paymaster $500; Financier $1,000; Tycoon $1,500.

Hogansburg

AKWESASNE MUSEUM, 321 State Rte. 37, Hogansburg, NY 13655-3114. Tel.: 518-358-2240 & 2461. Fax: 518-358-2649.
E-mail: akwmuse@northnet.org
Web Site: www.akwesasneculturalcenter.org
Founded: 1972.
Congressional District: 30
Key Personnel: C.E.O., Glory Cole; Pres. (V), William Herne; Museum Shop Mgr., Sue Ellen Herne.
Personnel Profile: Full-Time Paid 2; Part-Time Paid 1; Interns 1.
Governing Authority: nonprofit organization. Parent Institution: Akwesasne Cultural Center, Inc. Subsidiary Institution: Museum & Library. Tax-exempt: 170(b)(1)(A).
Cultural Center.
Collections: Mohawk traditional artifacts & basketry; Akwesasne Mohawk culture; contemporary Iroquoian artifacts & ethnological exhibitions.
Research Fields: local history & folklife; Mohawk Indian, Iroquois history; Kanien'kehaka (Mohawk); Haudenosaunee (Iroquois).
Facilities: library of books relating to Native Americans; reading room; classrooms. Gift items for sale.
Activities: guided tours by appointment; lectures; educational programs; training programs; loan, permanent, temporary & traveling exhibitions.
Publications: leaflets pertaining to exhibitions; films Onenhakenhra; White Seed, Music & Dance of the Mohawk; Teionkwahontasen: Basketmakers of Akwesasne; gallery guides on history, culture & traditional arts; DVD, Akwesasne Mohawk Basketry Traditions.
Hours & Admission Prices: Mon.-Thurs. 8:30-4, Fri. 8:30-3:30, Sat. by appointment; guided tours by appointment only. Adults $2, children $1; Native Americans & children 5 & under no charge. Closed all major holidays. ♿
Attendance: 1,822 (accurate)

Hoosick Falls

BENNINGTON BATTLEFIELD STATE HISTORIC SITE AND BARNETT HOMESTEAD VISITORS' CENTER, 30 Caretaker's Rd., Hoosick Falls, NY 12090-4801. Tel.: 518-686-8266.
Web Site: www.nysparks.state.ny.us
Congressional District: 29
Key Personnel: Park Mgr., Tom Conklin; Site Coord., Phyllis Chapman.
Personnel Profile: Part-Time Paid 4; Part-Time Volunteers 4; Interns 1.
Governing Authority: state. Parent Institution: New York State Parks & Recreation.
Historic Site: 1777 Revolutionary War battle site includes monuments to participating states, map of actual battle & panorama display of the battle site.
Collections: prints; sculpture; historic reproductions; 19th century artifacts.
Research Fields: New York State, 1777 campaign; early 19th century agricultural life.
Facilities: picnic area.
Activities: interpretive signs; picnicking; hiking; game fields; self guided tours & display; costumed tour guides; demonstrations; hands-on programs.
Publications: brochure.
Hours & Admission Prices: May to Labor Day daily 10-7; Sept.-Nov. 1 Sat.-Sun. 10-7. Visitors' Center: Thurs.-Sat. 1-4. Adults $5, children & seniors $3.
Attendance: 19,066 (accurate)
Membership: Individual $10.

Hornby

HORNBY MUSEUM, Co. Rte. 41, Hornby, NY Mailing Address: 185 South Place, Corning, NY 14830-2219. Tel.: 607-962-4471.
E-mail: sjmoore@stny.rr.com
Web Site: homepages.rootsweb.com/~hornby/hornby.html
Founded: 1958.
Key Personnel: Pres., Susan J. Moore.
Personnel Profile: Part-Time Volunteers 10.
Governing Authority: society. Tax-exempt.
Local History Museum: housed in a small country schoolhouse.
Collections: 19th-century household & farm items; journals; books; one-room schoolhouse artifacts.
Activities: permanent exhibitions; tours; scouts; school classes.
Publications: quarterly newsletter.
Hours & Admission Prices: July-Aug. Sun. 1-3; other days by appointment. No charge; donations accepted.
Attendance: 74 (accurate)
Membership: Individual $4; Family $6.

Horseheads

WINGS OF EAGLES DISCOVERY CENTER, 17 Aviation Dr., Horseheads, NY 14845-1102. Tel.: 607-739-8200. Fax: 607-739-8374.
E-mail: bbenza@wingsofeagles.com
Web Site: www.wingsofeagles.com
Formerly: National Warplane Museum
Founded: 1983.
Congressional District: 31
Key Personnel: C.E.O. & Pres., Michael S. Hall; Pres. (V), Clyde Robins; Dir. Restoration, Ed Knitter; Cur., Edward Flesch.
Personnel Profile: Full-Time Paid 3; Full-Time Volunteers 1; Part-Time Paid 3; Part-Time Volunteers 200; Interns 1.
Governing Authority: nonprofit. Chartered by The NY State Board of Regents. Tax-exempt: 501(c)(3).
Aviation Museum.
Collections: WWII-era flying aircraft: C-47/R4D Skytrain; liaison; training & cargo; foreign & domestic; non-flying jet & propeller driven aircraft; engines; instruments; uniforms; insignia; flight gear & clothing from WWII, Korea & Vietnam.
Research Fields: military aviation history & air power.
Facilities: 7,000-vol. library containing books, manuals, periodicals, reference files & a/v materials; theater; snack bar. Museum-related items for sale.
Activities: guided tours; organized education programs for high school groups, college students & adults; volunteer & docent programs; temporary & permanent exhibits; community events; speaker programs. Museum Sponsors: Airfest.
Publications: airfest program, Wings of Eagles.
Hours & Admission Prices: Wed.-Sat. 10-4, Sun. 12-4. Adults $7, senior citizens $5.50, children 6-17 $4; discounts to families, AAM, ICOM, ASTC & AAA members; children under 6 & members no charge. Closed New Year's Day; Thanksgiving; Christmas. ♿
Attendance: 80,000 (estimated)
Membership: Regular $35; Twin $55; Supporting $100; Donor $250; Patron $500.

Howes Cave

IROQUOIS INDIAN MUSEUM, 324 Caverns Rd., Howes Cave, NY 12092. Mailing Address: P.O. Box 7, Howes Cave, NY 12092-0007. Tel.: 518-296-8949. Fax: 518-296-8955.
E-mail: info@iroquoismuseum.org
Web Site: www.iroquoismuseum.org
Founded: 1980.
Congressional District: 23
Key Personnel: C.E.O. & Dir., Erynne Ansel; Chm. & Pres., Larry Joyce; Educator, Mike Tarbell; Museum Shop Mgr., Steph Shultes.
Personnel Profile: Full-Time Paid 1; Part-Time Paid 7; Part-Time Volunteers 40.
Governing Authority: nonprofit.
Anthropology Museum & Site: focus on Iroquois art and culture.
Collections: contemporary art & craft work of the Iroquois Indians; prehistoric materials of the Iroquois & their immediate antecedents relating to Schoharie County; color slides; black & white prints; photographic collection of Iroquois arts; living plants & their native use.
Research Fields: contemporary Iroquois arts; archaeology of Schoharie County; relationship between early settlers & the Iroquois in the county; ethnobotany of the Iroquois.
Facilities: 1,100-vol. library of books on the Iroquois & other Native American groups available for research on request for use on premises; nature trail. Art work & craftwork made by Iroquois & books for sale.

Activities: guided tours; docents; loan, permanent & temporary exhibitions; Archaeology Dept. & school programs; lectures; arts & craft demonstrations. Museum Sponsors: Iroquois Indian Festival.
Publications: quarterly newsletter, Museum Notes; exhibition catalogs.
Hours & Admission Prices: April-June & Labor Day to Dec. Tues.-Sat. 10-5, Sun. 12-5; July-Aug. Mon.-Sat. 10-5, Sun. 12-5. Adults $8, seniors & youths 13-17 $6.50, children 5-12 $5; discounts to groups, AAM & ICOM members; children under 5 members no charge. Closed Easter; Thanksgiving; Christmas Eve & Day. ♿
Attendance: 24,300 (accurate)
Membership: Students (full-time) & Single Seniors $20; Individuals & Senior Couples $25; Family $35; Friend $50; Donor $100; Sponsor $250; Patron $500; Benefactor $1,000.

Hudson

FASNY MUSEUM OF FIRE FIGHTING, (M), 117 Harry Howard Ave., Hudson, NY 12534-1601. Tel.: 518-822-1875, ext. 10. Fax: 518-822-8520.
E-mail: wendy@fasnyfiremuseum.com
Web Site: www.fasnyfiremuseum.org
Formerly: American Museum of Fire Fighting
Founded: 1925.
Congressional District: 24
Key Personnel: Pres. Bd. Dirs., Jamie Smith; Vice Pres., John Montrose; Cur., Wendy McDavis; Museum Shop Mgr., Paul Roemer.
Personnel Profile: Full-Time Paid 4; Part-Time Paid 1; Part-Time Volunteers 4.
Governing Authority: nonprofit organization. Parent Institution: Firemen's Association of the State of New York, 107 Washington Ave., Albany, NY 12210. Tax-exempt.
Fire-Fighting Antiques Museum.
Collections: period fire-fighting apparatus; art gallery; tools & equipment of the trade; photographs; prints.
Research Fields: history of the Volunteer Fire Service.
Facilities: 1,700-vol. library of books, magazines & minutes available by appointment with curator. Museum-related items for sale.
Activities: guided tours.
Hours & Admission Prices: Daily 10-5. Adults $5, children 5 & over $2; FASNY & museum members and children 4 & under no charge. Closed major holidays. ♿
Attendance: 10,000 (accurate)
Membership: Firefighter $25; Lieutenant $50; Captain $100.

OLANA STATE HISTORIC SITE, (M), 5720 Rte. 9-G, Hudson, NY 12534. Tel.: 518-828-0135. Fax: 518-828-6742.
E-mail: linda.mclean@oprhp.state.ny.us
Web Site: www.olana.org; www.nysparks.com
Founded: 1966.
Congressional District: 29
Key Personnel: Dir. Olana State Historic Site, Linda E. McLean; Dir. Education, Carri L. Manchester; Cur., Evelyn Trebilcock; Assoc. Cur., Valerie Balint; Archivist & Librarian, Ida Brier; Historic Site Asst., Jason Allen; Maintenance Chief, Timothy Dodge; Pres. Olana Partnership, Sara Griffen; Chm. (V) The Olana Partnership, Washburn Oberwarger; Vice Pres. Devel. of The Olana Partnership, Bob Burns; Public Rels. & Admin. Olana Partnership, Nelson Sterner; Museum Shop Mgr., Rachel Patton.
Personnel Profile: Full-Time Paid 6; Part-Time Paid 15; Part-Time Volunteers 87; Interns 2.
Governing Authority: state. Parent Institution: New York State Office of Parks, Recreation & Historic Preservation. Tax-exempt: 501(c)(3).
Historic House: 1870 Persian style villa residence of 19th-century landscape artist, Frederic E. Church.
Collections: 19th-century decorative arts, furnishings; 19th-century American art featuring Frederic E. Church; Old Masters; 19th-century photographs; church family library; archives; sketches, papers & correspondence; 19th-century landscape.
Major Exhibits: Frederic Church & Jamaica, 6/10-10/10.
Research Fields: art of the Hudson River School; Frederic E. Church; Fritz Melbye; Camille Pissarro; art, decoration & furnishings; Romantic style landscape; 19th-century art culture & American art.
Facilities: research library including family & photo archives available for research with advance written notice; visitor center; 49-seat theater; garden; 5 mile walking trail; picnic facilities. Museum-related items for sale.
Activities: guided & self-guided tours on the landscape; guided tour of furnished 19th-century home & studio; video history; concerts; children's summer arts camp; docent program; formal education programs. Annual Events: May Symposium; August Arts Weekend; holiday reception.
Publications: biannual newsletter, The Crayon.
Hours & Admission Prices: Grounds: daily 8 to sunset. House Tours: April to late Nov. Tues.-Sun. & Mon. holidays 10-5; late Nov. to March Fri.-Sun. 11-4. Group tours with advance reservation. Standard House Tour: adults $9, seniors & students $8; children under 12 no charge; Second Floor & Gallery: adults $6, seniors & students $5, children under 12 no charge. Combined House & Second Floor: adults $12, seniors & students $10. Members of the Olana Partnership no charge. Vehicle Fee: May-Oct. Sat.-Sun. $5. Closed New Year's Day; Easter; Thanksgiving; Christmas. ♿
Attendance: 38,917 (accurate)
Membership: Individual $30; Family $60; Business $50-$150; Contributing $75; Artist's Circle $150; Sponsor $500; Patron $1,000; Corporate Patron $1,500; Benefactor $5,000.

PARKER-O'MALLEY AIR MUSEUM, 435 Old Rte. 20, Hudson, NY 12075. Mailing Address: P.O. Box 216, Ghent, NY 12075-0216. Tel.: 518-392-7200. Fax: 518-392-2227.
Founded: 1991.
Key Personnel: C.E.O., James E. McMahon.
Personnel Profile: Part-Time Volunteers 2.
Governing Authority: private. Tax-exempt: 501(c)(3).
Aeronautics Museum.
Collections: aircraft from the 1920s-1940s; paintings of historical aviation achievements.
Facilities: 13,000 sq. ft. hangar.
Hours & Admission Prices: By appointment only. Adults $5, children $3. ♿

Huntington

DAVID CONKLIN FARMHOUSE, 2 High St., Huntington, NY 11743-3416. Mailing Address: 209 Main St., Huntington, NY 11743-6907. Tel.: 631-427-7045. Fax: 631-427-7056.
E-mail: rkissam@huntingtonhistoricalsociety.org
Web Site: www.huntingtonhistoricalsociety.org
Founded: 1903.
Congressional District: 3
Key Personnel: Exec. Coord., Robert "Toby" Kissam; Pres. (V), Carl Lawrence.
Personnel Profile: Full-Time Paid 1; Part-Time Paid 7; Part-Time Volunteers 110.
Governing Authority: society; nonprofit. Parent Institution: Huntington Historical Society, 209 Main St., Huntington, NY 11743. Branch Museums: Huntington Trade School; Dr. Daniel W. Kissam House; Soldiers & Sailors Memorial Building. Tax-exempt: 501(c)(3).
Historic Site.
Collections: period rooms furnished in Colonial, Empire, & Victorian styles; coverlets; quilts; textile preparation equipment; dolls; toys; kitchen items; pottery. Historic Buildings: c.1750 shingled house with added c.1820 2 1/2 story three-quarter house & c.1900 Victorian bay window; restored 18th-century barn.
Research Fields: decorative arts; genealogy; history of Huntington & central Long Island.
Facilities: 50-capacity auditorium; classroom.
Activities: guided tours; lectures; study clubs; hobby workshops; organized education programs; docent program; loan & permanent exhibitions; school loan service.
Publications: newsletters, The New Portico; Family History Newsletter; books on regional history.
Hours & Admission Prices: Thurs.-Fri. & Sun. 1-4. Adults $5, students & seniors $3; discounts to AAM members; children under 5 & museum members no charge. Closed New Year's Day; Easter; Thanksgiving; Christmas. ♿
Attendance: 10,500 (estimated)
Membership: Student & Senior Citizens $25; Individual $35; Family $55; Friend $100; Supporting $200; Heritage Friend $300.

DR. DANIEL W. KISSAM HOUSE, 434 Park Ave., Huntington, NY 11743. Mailing Address: 209 Main St., Huntington, NY 11743-6907. Tel.: 631-427-7045. Fax: 631-427-7056.
E-mail: rkissam@huntingtonhistoricalsociety.org
Web Site: www.huntingtonhistoricalsociety.org
Formerly: Kissam House
Founded: 1903.
Congressional District: 3
Key Personnel: Exec. Coord., Robert "Toby" Kissam; Pres. (V), Carl Lawrence.
Personnel Profile: Full-Time Paid 1; Part-Time Paid 7; Part-Time Volunteers 110.
Governing Authority: society; nonprofit. Parent Institution: Huntington Historical Society, 209 Main St., Huntington, NY 11743. Branch Museums: David Conklin Farmhouse; Huntington Trade School; Soldiers & Sailors Memorial Building. Tax-exempt: 501(c)(3).
Historic House: c.1795 Federal shingled house with added c.1830 kitchen wing.

Collections: home of early Huntington physicians. Historic Structures: c.1787 three-bay English style barn; sheepshed; 2 smokehouses.
Research Fields: decorative arts; genealogy; local & central Long Island history.
Facilities: Museum-related items for sale.
Activities: guided tours; organized education programs; docent program; loan & permanent exhibitions; school loan service.
Publications: monthly newsletter, The New Portico; books on regional history.
Hours & Admission Prices: Sun. 1-4. Adults $5, children under 12 $3; discounts to AAM members; members no charge. Closed New Year's Day; Easter; Thanksgiving; Christmas. ♿
Attendance: 10,500 (estimated)
Membership: Student & Senior Citizens $25; Individual $35; Family $55; Friend $100; Supporting $200; Heritage Friend $300.

* **HECKSCHER MUSEUM OF ART, (M),** 2 Prime Ave., Huntington, NY 11743-7702. Tel.: 631-351-3250. Fax: 631-423-2145.
E-mail: info@heckscher.org
Web Site: www.heckscher.org
Founded: 1920.
Congressional District: 5
Key Personnel: Chm. (V), Margaret Hargraves; Interim Exec. Dir., H.E. "Skip" Show, Jr.; Chief Cur. Collections & Exhibitions, Kenneth Wayne; Registrar, William Titus; Dir. Education, Joy Weiner; Office Mgr., Nancy O'Brien.
Personnel Profile: Full-Time Paid 13; Part-Time Paid 15; Part-Time Volunteers 204; Interns 13.
Governing Authority: nonprofit educational corporation. Parent Institution: Town of Huntington. Tax-exempt: 501(c)(3).
Art Museum.
Collections: 16th-century to present European & American paintings, sculpture & works on paper, with emphasis on American artists of the 19th-20th centuries; works by Lucas Cranach, Inness, Durand, Moran family, Arthur Dove, Asher B. Durand, George Inness, & Helen Torr; paintings & works on paper by George Grosz including Eclipse of the Sun; works by artists associated with Long Island, including Fairfield Porter, Elaine Dekooning, Ray Johnson, & the Tile Club; photography including works by Eadweard Muybridge, Berenice Abbott, Man Ray, Garry Winogrand, Leon Levinstein, & Larry Fink.
Major Exhibits: Arcadia/Suburbia: Domestic Architecture on Long Island, 1/16/10-4/11/10; Long Island's Best: Young Artists at the Heckscher, 4/17/10-5/2/10; Recent Acquisitions, 5/8/10-7/25/10; Long Island Biennial, 7/31/10-9/26/10; The Resplendent Glass of Louis Comfort Tiffany, 10/2/10-1/9/11.
Research Fields: 19th- to 20th-century American & European artists; Long Island artists.
Activities: guided tours; lectures; gallery talks; formally organized education programs for children; inter-museum loan exhibitions; permanent & traveling exhibitions.
Publications: semi-annual newsletter; quarterly programming guides; catalogue of the collection; exhibition catalogues; educational brochures; educational videotapes.
Hours & Admission Prices: Tues.-Fri. & holiday Mon. 10-5, 1st Fri. each month 10-8:30, Sat.-Sun. 1-5. Adults $8, seniors 60 & over $6, students 10 & over $5; discount to AAM members & Huntington residents; children under 10 & members no charge. Closed Thanksgiving; Christmas. ♿
Attendance: 22,836 (accurate)
Membership: Student & Senior Citizen $35; Individual (Supporter) $40; Dual $65; Family $75; Fellow $175; Patron $500; Benefactor $1,000-$2,499; Director's Circle $2,500-$4,999; Chairman's Club $5,000 & up.

HUNTINGTON SEWING & TRADE SCHOOL, 209 Main St., Huntington, NY 11743-6907. Tel.: 631-427-7045. Fax: 516-427-7056.
E-mail: cmaguire@huntingtonhistoricalsociety.org
Web Site: www.huntingtonhistoricalsociety.org
Founded: 1903.
Congressional District: 3
Key Personnel: Exec. Dir., Carol A. Maguire; Pres. (V), Kevin Arloff.
Personnel Profile: Full-Time Paid 1; Part-Time Paid 7; Part-Time Volunteers 110.
Governing Authority: society; nonprofit. Parent Institution: Huntington Historical Society, 209 Main St., Huntington, NY 11743. Branch Museums: David Conklin Farmhouse; Dr. Daniel W. Kissam House; Soldiers & Sailors Memorial Building. Tax-exempt: 501(c)(3).
Historical Building: c.1905, 2 1/2 story Jacobean Revival Trade School designed by Cady, Berg & See.
Collections: maps; diaries; family & business records & papers; genealogies; local census & newspaper microfilm manuscripts; regional photographs.
Research Fields: genealogy; Huntington history & central Long Island; photography.
Facilities: 3,500-vol. library pertaining to genealogy, local & Long Island history; reading room; classrooms. Museum-related items for sale.
Activities: guided tours; lectures; concerts; study clubs; organized education programs; docent program; loan & permanent exhibitions; school loan service.
Publications: The New Portico; Family History Newsletter.
Hours & Admission Prices: Office: Mon.-Fri. 9:30-5. Archives & Library: Wed.-Thurs. 1-4. Adult $4; discounts to AAM members; members no charge. Call for special exhibit fees. Closed New Year's Day; Easter; Thanksgiving; Christmas. ♿
Attendance: 10,500 (estimated)
Membership: Student & Senior Citizens $25; Individual $35; Family $55; Friend $100; Supporting $200; Heritage Friend $300.

SOLDIERS & SAILORS MEMORIAL BUILDING, 228 Main St., Huntington, NY 11743-6915. Tel.: 631-427-7045. Fax: 631-427-7056.
E-mail: rkissam@huntingtonhistoricalsociety.org
Web Site: www.huntingtonhistoricalsociety.org
Formerly: Huntington Historical Society
Founded: 1903.
Congressional District: 3
Key Personnel: Exec. Coord., Robert "Toby" Kissam; Pres. (V), Carl Lawrence.
Personnel Profile: Full-Time Paid 1; Part-Time Paid 7; Part-Time Volunteers 40.
Governing Authority: nonprofit organization. Parent Institution: Huntington Historical Society. Branch Museums: Huntington Trade School; David Conklin Farmhouse; Dr. Daniel Kissam House. Tax-exempt: 501(c)(3).
History Museum: housed in 1892 Civil War Memorial building & 1st community library.
Collections: costumes; textiles; decorative arts; paintings; prints.
Research Fields: local history; genealogy & decorative arts.
Facilities: 3,500-vol. library & 25,000 photographs available in the Huntington Trade School.
Activities: guided tours; lectures; formally organized education programs; docent program; intermuseum, permanent & temporary exhibitions.
Publications: The New Portico Newsletter, Huntington/Babylon Town History, Index to the Long Islander & others.
Attendance: 12,000 (estimated)
Membership: Student $15; Senior Citizens $25; Individual $30; Family $50; Small Business $60; Sustaining $90; Contributing $120; Corporate $150; Sponsoring $250.

Huntington Station

WALT WHITMAN BIRTHPLACE STATE HISTORIC SITE AND INTERPRETIVE CENTER, 246 Old Walt Whitman Rd., Huntington Station, NY 11746-4148. Tel.: 631-427-5240. Fax: 631-427-5247.
E-mail: director@waltwhitman.org
Web Site: www.waltwhitman.org
Founded: 1949.
Congressional District: 5
Key Personnel: Exec. Dir. & Public Rels., Cynthia Shor; Pres. (V), Thomas F. Casey; Museum Shop Mgr., Sue Anne Dennehy; Archivist, Richard A. Ryan.
Personnel Profile: Full-Time Paid 1; Part-Time Paid 12; Part-Time Volunteers 50; Interns 2.
Governing Authority: state. New York State Office of Parks, Recreation & Historic Preservation, & Long Island State Park, Recreation & Historic Preservation Commission. Subsidiary Institution: Walt Whitman Birthplace Assoc. Tax-exempt: 501(c)(3).
Historic House: c.1819 birthplace & early home of Walt Whitman.
Collections: period furnishings; literary materials; Whitman memorabilia; 130 portraits of Walt Whitman; original letters, manuscripts & artifacts; writing desk used by Whitman; first editions of the books Leaves of Grass & Specimen Days; Whitman's voice on tape.
Research Fields: Walt Whitman; his life & works.
Facilities: 500-vol. library; visitor center; 1,500 sq. ft. exhibit space; classroom; performance space; bookstore. Museum-related items for sale.
Activities: guided tours; permanent & changing exhibits; poetry readings; poet-in-residence; education programs; lectures; audiovisual presentation. Annual Events: Walt Whitman Walk and Poetryfest; Marathon Reading of Leaves of Grass; Annual Walt Whitman Birthday Celebration.
Publications: newsletter, Starting from Paumanok; Tour to Whitmanland.
Hours & Admission Prices: June 15 to Labor Day Mon.-Fri. 11-4, Sat.-Sun. 11-5; Winter: Wed.-Fri. 1-4, Sat.-Sun. 11-4. Adults $5, senior citizens & students $4; discounts to AAM & ICOM members; children under 18, members and children 6 & under no charge. Closed major holidays. ♿
Attendance: 16,500 (accurate)
Membership: Student & Senior over 65 $20; Individual $30; Family $40;

Friend $50; Patron $100; Sponsor $250; Donor $500; Benefactor $1,000-$4,999; Guardian $5,000-$10,000.

Hurleyville

SULLIVAN COUNTY HISTORICAL SOCIETY, INC., (M), 265 Main St., Hurleyville, NY 12747-0247. Mailing Address: P.O. Box 247, Hurleyville, NY 12747-0247. Tel.: 845-434-8044. Fax: 845-434-8044.
E-mail: schs@sullivancountyhistory.org
Web Site: www.sullivancountyhistory.org
Founded: 1929.
Congressional District: 27
Key Personnel: Pres., Robert Decker; Finance Officer, Allan Dampman; Genealogy, Barbara Viele; Cur. & Archivist, Arthur Hessigner; Museum Shop Mgr., W.F. Burns.
Personnel Profile: Part-Time Paid 1; Part-Time Volunteers 22.
Governing Authority: society; nonprofit organization. Tax-exempt: 501(c)(3).
Historical Society Museum.
Collections: O & W Railroad; ledgers; Anti-Rent War artifacts; Sullivan County maps; manuscripts; Stephen Crane collection; historical Sullivan County postcards; Judge Lawrence Cooke Room; Dr. Frederick A. Cook Room-polar explorer; tanneries; personal diaries, euphemeria, papers & documents; all federal & state census records & abstracts; microfilm records of all county newspapers from 1838-present.
Research Fields: genealogy.
Facilities: 300-vol. library of material pertaining to the development of Sullivan County, available for research by written request; 200-seat auditorium.
Activities: guided tours; docent program; permanent & temporary exhibitions; genealogy research.
Publications: quarterly newsletter, Observer; History of Sullivan County.
Hours & Admission Prices: Museum: Tues.-Sat. 10-4:30, Sun. 1-4:30. Archives: Wed. 10-4:30. No charge; donations accepted. Closed New Year's Day; Thanksgiving; Christmas. ♿
Attendance: 8,500 (accurate)
Membership: Single $20; Couple $30; Corporate $100.

Hyde Park

ELEANOR ROOSEVELT NATIONAL HISTORIC SITE, 4097 Albany Post Rd., Hyde Park, NY 12538-1917. Tel.: 845-229-9115 & 9116. Fax: 845-229-0739.
Web Site: www.nps.gov/elro/
Founded: 1977.
Congressional District: 24
Key Personnel: Museum Shop Mgr., Anne Meisner.
Personnel Profile: Full-Time Paid 18; Part-Time Paid 2; Interns 1.
Governing Authority: federal. National Park Service, Dept. of the Interior, Washington, DC 20240. Tax-exempt.
Historic House: Val-Kill, home of Eleanor Roosevelt from 1945-1962.
Collections: Eleanor Roosevelt's original & replacement furnishings.
Activities: guided tours; introductory movie. Museum Sponsors: Special Christmas exhibit in December.
Publications: site brochure.
Hours & Admission Prices: May-Oct. daily 9-5; Nov.-April Thurs.-Mon. 9-5. Adults $8; children under 15 no charge. Reservation for tours call 800-967-2283. Closed New Year's Eve & Day; Thanksgiving; Christmas. ♿
Attendance: 58,000 (accurate)

FRANKLIN D. ROOSEVELT PRESIDENTIAL LIBRARY-MUSEUM, (M), 4079 Albany Post Rd., Hyde Park, NY 12538-1999. Tel.: 800-337-8474; 845-486-7770. Fax: 845-486-1147.
E-mail: roosevelt.library@nara.gov
Web Site: www.fdrlibrary.marist.edu
Founded: 1940.
Congressional District: 24
Key Personnel: Dir., Cynthia M. Koch; Deputy Dir., Lynn Bassanese; Supervisory Archivist, Robert Clark; Supervisory Museum Cur., Herman Eberhardt; Education Specialist, Jeff Urbin; Public Affairs Specialist, Cliff Laube; Museum Store Mgr., Amy Northup.
Personnel Profile: Full-Time Paid 21; Part-Time Paid 7; Part-Time Volunteers 19; Interns 8.
Governing Authority: federal. Parent Institution: National Archives & Records Administration. Tax-exempt: 170(b)(1)(A).
Presidential Library.
Collections: life and times of Franklin & Eleanor Roosevelt, specifically FDR's first fifty years, the Presidential Years, WWII, & life and accomplishments of Eleanor Roosevelt; President Roosevelt's White House Oval Office desk; FDR's Library Study; FDR's 1936 Ford Phaeton; personal papers; government records; photographs; motion picture films; audio & video tapes; sound recordings; head of state gifts; gifts from private citizens; political campaign items; personal & family memorabilia; President Roosevelt's collection on U.S. naval history.
Research Fields: life, career & presidential administration of President Franklin D. Roosevelt; life & career of Mrs. Roosevelt; Great Depression and New Deal; World War II; Historic Hudson Valley, New York.
Facilities: research library; visitors center; education & conference areas; theater; cafe. Museum-related items for sale.
Activities: organized educational programs for elementary, secondary school & undergraduate students; permanent, temporary & interactive exhibitions; lectures; film series; special events; elder hostels.
Publications: general information brochures; books, Franklin D. Roosevelt & Conservation; Franklin D. Roosevelt & Foreign Affairs; bibliography, The Era of Franklin D. Roosevelt, 1945-1971; bibliography, Historical Materials in the Franklin D. Roosevelt Library, 1997; microfilm, Press Conferences of Franklin D. Roosevelt; microfilm, Roosevelt-Churchill Messages, microfilm Diary of Adolf A. Berle; microfilm, Henry A. Wallace Papers, 1941-1945.
Hours & Admission Prices: April-Oct. daily 9-6; Nov.-March daily 9-5. Combination Museum & Roosevelt Home: adults $14; discounts to Golden Age & Golden Eagle passports and AAM & ICOM members; AASLH members with advance reservation, children 16 & under and school groups no charge. Closed New Year's Day; Thanksgiving; Christmas. ♿
Attendance: 110,000 (accurate)

HOME OF FRANKLIN D. ROOSEVELT NATIONAL HISTORIC SITE, Rte. 9, Hyde Park, NY 12538. Mailing Address: 4097 Albany Post Rd., Hyde Park, NY 12538-1997. Tel.: 845-229-9115 & 9116. Fax: 845-229-0739.
Web Site: www.nps.gov/hofr
Founded: 1946.
Congressional District: 24
Key Personnel: Supt., Sarah Olson; Museum Shop Mgr., Anne Meisner.
Personnel Profile: Full-Time Paid 18; Part-Time Paid 3; Part-Time Volunteers 4.
Governing Authority: federal. Unit of the National Park Service, Dept. of the Interior, Washington, DC 20240. Branch Museum: Vanderbilt Mansion. Tax-exempt.
Historic House: Hudson River home of F.D.R.
Collections: original furnishings including ancestral portraits; naval prints; memorabilia.
Facilities: library; Rose Garden and Gravesite; The Henry A. Wallace Visitor & Education Center; cafe; auditorium. Museum-related items for sale.
Publications: pamphlets, F.D. Roosevelt and Hyde Park; Art in the Home of Franklin D. Roosevelt; Springwood: The Grounds of the Home of Franklin Delano Roosevelt National Historic Site.
Hours & Admission Prices: Daily 9-5. Adults $14; discounts to Golden Age Passport & National Park Pass holders; children under 15 & school groups no charge. Reservation required for motorcoach tours & school groups, call 800-967-2283. Closed New Year's Day; Thanksgiving; Christmas. ♿
Attendance: 105,000 (accurate)

VANDERBILT MANSION NATIONAL HISTORIC SITE, Rte. 9, Hyde Park, NY 12538. Mailing Address: 4097 Albany Post Rd., Hyde Park, NY 12538-1917. Tel.: 800-337-8474. Fax: 845-229-0739.
Web Site: www.nps.gov/vama
Founded: 1940.
Congressional District: 24
Key Personnel: Supt., Sarah Olson; Museum Shop Mgr., Anne Meisner.
Personnel Profile: Full-Time Paid 18; Part-Time Paid 3; Part-Time Volunteers 18.
Governing Authority: federal. National Parks Service, Dept. of the Interior, Washington, DC 20240. Branch Museum: Home of Franklin D. Roosevelt. Tax-exempt.
Historic House Museum: 1896-1899 Beaux-Arts style Mansion, designed by McKim, Mead, & White.
Collections: Beaux-Arts interiors by turn-of-the-century decorators include furniture; tapestries; rugs; porcelains.
Facilities: coachhouse; formal garden restoration; view of Hudson River. Slides, books & postcards for sale.
Activities: guided tours; slide video.
Publications: Vanderbilt Mansion handbook; Vanderbilt Photo Essay Book; The Grounds at the Vanderbilt Mansion; brochure, Vanderbilt Mansion NHS Site.
Hours & Admission Prices: Daily 7am to sunset. Adults $8; discounts to National Park Golden Age & Access card holders; children 15 & under &school groups no charge. Closed New Year's Day; Thanksgiving; Christmas. ♿
Attendance: 359,000 (accurate)

Ilion

REMINGTON FIREARMS MUSEUM AND COUNTRY STORE, 14 Hoefler Ave., Ilion, NY 13357-1888. Tel.: 315-895-3200 & 3301. Fax: 315-895-3543.
E-mail: john.balio@remington.com
Web Site: www.remington.com
Founded: 1959.
Congressional District: 23
Key Personnel: Cur. & Archives Coord., Fred Supry; Museum Shop Mgr., John Balio.
Personnel Profile: Full-Time Paid 1; Part-Time Paid 2.
Governing Authority: profit-making organization. Parent Institution: Remington Arms Co. Inc.
Firearms Museum.
Collections: Remington firearms & artifacts from 1820s to the present; wildlife & related art.
Research Fields: early & current firearms manufactured by the Remington Arms Company, Inc.; factory tour of custom gun shop.
Facilities: Custom gun shop.
Activities: custom gun shop tour.
Publications: brochure.
Hours & Admission Prices: May-Oct. Mon.-Fri. 8-5; Nov.-April Mon.-Fri. 8-4. Tours: May-Oct. 10 & 1. No charge. Closed major holidays. ♿
Attendance: 50,000 (estimated)

Interlaken

INTERLAKEN HISTORICAL SOCIETY, Main St., Interlaken, NY 14847. Mailing Address: P.O. Box 270, Interlaken, NY 14847-0270. Tel.: 607-532-4213.
E-mail: Orchardland@Zoom-dsl.com
Web Site: www.interlakenhistory.org
Founded: 1960.
Congressional District: 27
Key Personnel: Pres. (V), Diane Bassette Nelson; Vice Pres., Bill Schaffner; Sec., Ann Buddle; Treas., Karen King.
Personnel Profile: Full-Time Volunteers 9; Part-Time Volunteers 36.
Governing Authority: society. Tax-exempt: 170(b)(1)(A).
Historical Society & Farmers Museum: housed in 1826 Lockwood Hinman House and relocated grain cradle factory.
Collections: tools; pictures of local scenes & people; manuscripts & genealogy.
Research Fields: local history, genealogy.
Facilities: 200-vol. library of local history books available for research on premises.
Activities: guided tours; permanent & temporary exhibitions.
Publications: quarterly newsletter.
Hours & Admission Prices: July-Aug. Sun. 1-3, Sat. 10-1; other times by appointment. No charge; donations accepted. ♿
Attendance: 400 (estimated)
Membership: Adult/Family $10; Life $100.

Ithaca

THE CORNELL PLANTATIONS, One Plantations Rd., Ithaca, NY 14850-2799. Tel.: 607-255-2400. Fax: 607-255-2404.
E-mail: plantations@cornell.edu
Web Site: www.cornellplantations.org
Founded: 1935.
Congressional District: 27
Key Personnel: Dir., Donald A. Rakow; Dir. Education, Sonja Skelly; Dir. Devel., Beth Anderson.
Personnel Profile: Full-Time Paid 30; Part-Time Paid 21; Part-Time Volunteers 85; Interns 7.
Governing Authority: university. Cornell University, Roberts Hall. Tax-exempt: 501(c)(3).
Arboretum.
Collections: arboretum; botanical; horticultural; outdoor laboratory; natural area; interpretive trail, Plantations Path.
Research Fields: horticulture; natural sciences; education; conservation.
Facilities: Books & museum-related items for sale.
Activities: guided tours; lectures; seminars; publications; short courses; education festival; concerts.
Publications: magazine, The Cornell Plantations; informative & interpretive materials; newsletter; Path Handbook; Path video.
Hours & Admission Prices: Daily sunrise-sunset. Fee for guided tours; by appointment.
Attendance: 200,000 (estimated)
Membership: Basic Membership $50.

HANDWERKER GALLERY, (M), 1170 Gannett Center, Ithaca College, Ithaca, NY 14850-7276. Tel.: 607-274-3018. Fax: 607-274-1774.
E-mail: handwerker@ithaca.edu
Web Site: www.ithaca.edu/handwerker
Founded: 1977.
Key Personnel: Dir. & Asst. Prof., Cheryl Kramer.
Governing Authority: Parent Institution: Ithaca College. Tax-exempt.
Art Gallery & College Museum.
Collections: contemporary work of faculty, students & local artists; historical shows.
Research Fields: new museology.
Activities: critical forum; video screenings; movies.
Publications: catalogues & newsletter.
Hours & Admission Prices: Sept.-May Mon.-Wed. & Fri. 10-6, Thurs. 10-9, Sat.-Sun. 12-5. No charge. Closed vacation breaks. ♿
Attendance: 8,900 (estimated)

* **HERBERT F. JOHNSON MUSEUM OF ART, (M),** Cornell University, Ithaca, NY 14853-0001. Tel.: 607-255-6464. Fax: 607-255-9940.
E-mail: museum@cornell.edu
Web Site: www.museum.cornell.edu
Founded: 1973.
Congressional District: 27
Key Personnel: Dir., Franklin W. Robinson; Chm. (V), Ira Drukier; Assoc. Dir. Finance Admin., Peter Gould; Chief Cur. & Cur. Asian Art, Ellen Avril; Senior Cur., Nancy Green; Cur. Modern & Contemporary Art, Andrea Inselmann; Ames Assoc. Dir. & Cur. Education, Cathy Klimaszewski; Coord. School & Children's Programs, Carol Hockett; Coord. Adult & Community Programs, Hannah Dunn Ryan; Registrar, Matthew Conway; Chief of Security, Alvin Miller; Chief Preparator, Wil Millard; Dir. Devel., Marrie Neumer; Publications Coord., Andrea Potochniak; Assoc. Cur. & Master Teacher, Andrew Weislogel; Mellon Asst. Coord. of Univ. Outreach, Mariel Gabet.
Personnel Profile: Full-Time Paid 19; Part-Time Paid 15; Part-Time Volunteers 35; Interns 19.
Governing Authority: university. Affiliated with Cornell University. Tax-exempt: 701(b)(1)(A).
Art Museum.
Collections: Asian art; European and American painting; sculpture; prints; drawings; photographs; art from Africa, Oceania & the Americas.
Facilities: 4,000-vol. library of art books and exhibitions catalogs; 80-seat auditorium; reading room.
Activities: permanent, temporary & traveling exhibitions, educational programs; lectures; guided tours; film series.
Publications: newsletters; annual report; exhibition brochures & catalogs; educational publications; collection research.
Hours & Admission Prices: Tues.-Sun. 10-5. No charge; donations accepted. Closed Memorial Day; Independence Day; Labor Day; Thanksgiving; Christmas to New Year's Day. ♿
Membership: Individual $20-$44; Family $45-$99; Supporting $100-$249; Sustaining $250-$499; Charter $500-$999; Quadrangle $1,000-$4,999; Tower $5,000 & up.

THE HISTORY CENTER IN TOMPKINS COUNTY, 401 E. State St., Ste. 100, Ithaca, NY 14850-4400. Tel.: 607-273-8284. Fax: 607-273-6107.
E-mail: welcome@thehistorycenter.net
Web Site: www.thehistorycenter.net
Formerly: DeWitt Historical Society of Tompkins County & Tompkins County Museum
Founded: 1935.
Congressional District: 26
Key Personnel: Dir., Jean Currie; Pres. Bd. (V), Elizabeth Bixler; Photographer, Carl Koski; Community Liaison, Wylie Schwartz; Archivist, Donna Eschenbrenner; Elementary Education, Carole West; Adult & Secondary Education, Paul Miller.
Personnel Profile: Full-Time Paid 1; Part-Time Paid 7; Part-Time Volunteers 30; Interns 5.
Governing Authority: society. Subsidiary Institution: Tompkins County Museum. Tax-exempt: 501(c)(3).
Historical Society Museum.
Collections: 19th-20th century Tompkins County history; photographs including Verne Morton collection of 11,000 rural life images, 1897-1945; costumes; quilts; coverlets; books, documents; maps; tools; toys; sports memorabilia; art; Native American artifacts. Historic Building: 1827 octagonal school building.
Research Fields: local history; genealogy.
Facilities: 4,000-vol. research library; archives. Museum-related items for sale.

Activities: guided tours; lectures; films; formally organized education programs; inter-museum loan; permanent & temporary exhibitions; school loan service; living history program.
Publications: quarterly newsletter; books & monographs relating to area.
Hours & Admission Prices: Tues., Thurs. & Sat. 11-5. Museum: no charge; donations accepted. Research Library: call for fees. Closed New Year's Day; Thanksgiving; Christmas. ♿
Attendance: 6,000 (estimated)
Membership: Donors up to $99; Friends $100-$249; Researchers $250-$499; Historians $500-$999; Leadership Circle $1,000-$4,999; Director's Circle $5,000-$9,999; Chairman's Circle $10,000 & up.

L.H. BAILEY HORTORIUM, 412 Mann Library, Cornell University, Ithaca, NY 14853-4301. Tel.: 607-255-2131. Fax: 607-255-5407.
Web Site: www.plantbio.cornell.edu
Founded: 1935.
Congressional District: 27
Key Personnel: Chm. & Professor, William Crepet; Assoc. Professor, Melissa Luckow; Professor, David M. Bates; Professor, Eloy Rodriguez; Assoc. Professor & Cur., Kevin C. Nixon; Assoc. Professor, Jerrold I. Davis; Professor, Jeffrey J. Doyle; Research Aide, Sherry Vance; Librarian, Peter Fraissinet.
Personnel Profile: Full-Time Paid 20; Part-Time Volunteers 2.
Governing Authority: university. Affiliated with Cornell University. Tax-exempt.
Horticulture & Botanical Museum.
Collections: vascular plants; 860,000 sheet herbarium; 132,000 nursery & seed catalogue collection; natural history; botany.
Research Fields: taxonomy of cultivated & economic plants; systematic botany.
Facilities: 12,000-vol. library of botanical books available for inter-library loan & for research.
Activities: guided tours; lectures; formally organized education programs for undergraduate & graduate college students; plant identification & information; plant locating service.
Hours & Admission Prices: Mon.-Fri. 9-5. No charge. Closed national holidays. ♿
Attendance: 1,000 (estimated)

MCGRAW HALL MUSEUM, 150 McGraw Hall, Cornell University, Ithaca, NY 14853-4601. Tel.: 607-255-5137.
Web Site: falcon.arts.cornell.edu/anthro/collections.html
Founded: 1872.
Anthropology Museum.
Collections: 20,000 ethnographic & archaeological objects including pre-Columbian textiles & pottery from Peru; Native American baskets; prehistoric Mississippian pottery; Ndembu ritual masks & costumes from Africa; Yir Yoront tools & weapons from Australia; Egyptian mummy cases.
Major Exhibits: Anthropology at Cornell, 1870-1970, 11/09-2/10; People and Their Staff, 11/09-12/10.
Hours & Admission Prices: Call for hours.

PALEONTOLOGICAL RESEARCH INSTITUTION, 1259 Trumansburg Rd., Ithaca, NY 14850-1398. Tel.: 607-273-6623, ext. 10. Fax: 607-273-6620.
Web Site: www.museumoftheearth.org
Founded: 1932.
Congressional District: 26
Key Personnel: Dir., Dr. Warren D. Allmon; Pres., Patricia Kelley; Dir. Exhibits, Sarah Chicone; Devel. Operations Mgr. & Membership Coord., Sarah Degen; Dir. Collections, Greg Dietl; Dir. Mktg. & Communications, Billy Kepner.
Personnel Profile: Full-Time Paid 14; Full-Time Volunteers 1; Part-Time Volunteers 157.
Governing Authority: nonprofit organization. Tax-exempt: 501(c)(3).
Paleontology Museum.
Collections: paleontology.
Research Fields: paleontology; conchology; geology.
Facilities: 50,000-vol. library of science material available for use on premises by special permission.
Activities: lectures; educational programs; permanent & temporary exhibitions.
Publications: Bulletins of American Paleontology; Palaeontographica Americana; American Paleontologist; special publications.
Hours & Admission Prices: Summer: Mon.-Sat. 10-5, Sun. 11-5; Winter: Mon. & Thurs.-Sat. 10-5, Sun. 11-5. Adults $8, seniors & college students $5, children 4-17 $3; children under 3 & under no charge. Closed New Year's Day; Thanksgiving; Christmas. ♿
Attendance: 3,537 (accurate)
Membership: Cecil Kids Club children 10 & under $10; Student $20; Regular $30; Family $50; Life $600.

* **SCIENCENTER, (M),** 601 First St., Ithaca, NY 14850-3507. Tel.: 607-272-0600. Fax: 607-277-7469.
E-mail: info@sciencenter.org
Web Site: www.sciencenter.org
Founded: 1983.
Congressional District: 26
Key Personnel: Exec. Dir., Charles H. Trautmann; Chm. Bd., G. Walton Cottrell; Assoc. Dir., Lara Kimber; Dir. Visitor Svcs. & Operations, Kerry Flannery; Dir. Education, Rae Ostman; Exhibits Mgr., Robin Burlingham; Business Mgr., Brian Gold; Gift Shop Mgr. & Front Desk Coord., Susan Trask.
Personnel Profile: Full-Time Paid 17; Full-Time Volunteers 3; Part-Time Paid 4; Part-Time Volunteers 350; Interns 3.
Governing Authority: private; not-for-profit organization. Tax-exempt: 501(c)(3).
Science & Technology Museum.
Collections: over 250 hands-on science & technology exhibits; outdoor science park.
Facilities: 9,000 sq. ft. outdoor science playground.
Activities: school classes; demonstrations; birthday parties; facility rentals; seasonal mini science golf course; 1,200-meter outdoor walking model of Solar System; school outreach; amphitheater presentation.
Publications: Passport to the Solar System $2.
Hours & Admission Prices: July-Aug. Mon.-Sat. 10-5, Sun. 12-5; Sept.-June Tues.-Sat. 10-5, Sun. 12-5. Adults $7, senior citizens $6, children 3-17 $5; discount to AAM members; members, reciprocal ASTC & ACM members, children under 3 & members no charge. Closed New Year's Day; Thanksgiving; Christmas. ♿
Attendance: 94,000 (accurate)
Membership: Senior $25; Individual $45; Family $60; Family Plus & Grandparents $75; Voyager Society $125.

Jamaica

JAMAICA CENTER FOR ARTS & LEARNING (JCAL), 161-04 Jamaica Ave., Jamaica, NY 11432-6112. Tel.: 718-658-7400, ext. 123. Fax: 718-658-7922.
E-mail: info@jcal.org
Web Site: www.jcal.org
Founded: 1972.
Congressional District: 6
Key Personnel: Acting Exec. Dir., Anita Romero-Segarra; Bd. Chm., Leilani M. Brown; Dir. Finance & Admin., Jennifer Chiang; Cur. Visual Arts, Heng-Gil Han.
Personnel Profile: Full-Time Paid 13; Part-Time Paid 4; Part-Time Volunteers 5; Interns 4.
Governing Authority: nonprofit organization. Tax-exempt: 501(c)(3).
Multidisciplinary Art Center.
Collections: works by international artists.
Major Exhibits: John L. Moore, Paintings and Drawings, 11/09-1/16/10; AHL Foundation/Conundrum Express, 2/10-3/10; Jamaica Flux 2010 - Workspace and Windows, 4/10-6/10; Priscila de Carvalho, 7/10-8/10.
Facilities: 99-seat theatre; performance studios.
Activities: arts workshops; after school performing & visual arts program; concerts; films; commissioned art work for public spaces; guided tours; temporary exhibitions.
Publications: spring & fall newsletter; exhibit announcements; catalogs; posters; brochures; rack cards.
Hours & Admission Prices: Galleries: Mon.-Sat. 10-6. Fees vary. Closed major national holidays. ♿
Attendance: 25,000 (estimated)

KING MANOR MUSEUM, (M), 150-03 Jamaica Ave., King Park, Jamaica, NY 11432. Mailing Address: 90-04 161st St., Ste. 704, Jamaica, NY 11432-6103. Tel.: 718-206-0545. Fax: 718-206-0541.
E-mail: kingmanor1@earthlink.net
Web Site: www.kingmanor.org
Founded: 1900.
Congressional District: 6
Key Personnel: C.E.O., Mary Anne Mrozinski; Pres. (V), Richard Yeretzian.
Personnel Profile: Full-Time Paid 3; Part-Time Volunteers 25; Interns 2.
Governing Authority: board of directors, King Manor Association. Building owned by city of NY; administered by department of parks. Tax-exempt: 501(c)(3).
Historic Building/Site; History Museum: Now the centerpiece of an 11-acre historic park, King Manor was the home of Rufus King from 1805-1827. King was a signer of the U.S. Constitution, senator from NY State and

ambassador to Great Britain under four presidents, and outspoken opponent of slavery. 1819 & 1820, King led the Senate debate against admission of Missouri as a slave state.
Collections: 18th & 19th-century furniture, decorative arts, memorabilia including some related to the King family, local community of Jamaica.
Research Fields: local & national roles of Rufus King & his son John Alsop King in the early anti-slavery movement; life & work at King Manor; archaeology of slavery & freedom; Jamaica in early 19th century.
Facilities: education center.
Activities: guided tours; formally organized education programs; permanent & temporary exhibits; special events.
Publications: seasonal newsletter; calendar of events.
Hours & Admission Prices: Thurs.-Fri. 12-2, Sat.-Sun. 1-5; groups of 10 or more by appointment. Suggested Admission: adults $5, seniors & students $3; discounts to groups, AAM, ICOM and NYC Historic House Trust members; children 16 & under and members no charge.
Attendance: 6,155 (accurate)
Membership: Friend $25; Family $45; Delegate $100; Senator $250; Ambassador $500.

Jamestown

THE CCC WEEKS GALLERY, 525 Falconer St., Jamestown, NY 14701-1920. Mailing Address: P.O. Box 20, Jamestown, NY 14702-0020. Tel.: 716-665-9188. Fax: 716-338-1451.
E-mail: jimcolby@mail.sunyjcc.edu
Web Site: www.sunyjcc.edu/gallery
Formerly: The Weeks Gallery
Founded: 1969.
Congressional District: 34
Key Personnel: Dir., James Colby; Advisory Bd. Dir., Roz Newton; Arts Admin., Collin Shaffer.
Personnel Profile: Full-Time Paid 1; Interns 1.
Governing Authority: nonprofit. Parent Institution: Jamestown Community College, Jamestown. Tax-exempt: 501(c)(3).
Art Gallery.
Collections: paintings; sculpture; photographs.
Research Fields: contemporary art.
Facilities: auditorium; classroom; 1,000 sq. ft. exhibit space.
Activities: formal education programs for adults, undergraduate & graduate college students; lectures.
Publications: catalogs for selected exhibitions.
Hours & Admission Prices: Mon.-Wed. 11-5, Thurs. 11-7, Fri. 11-3. No charge. Closed school holidays; spring break; winter break. ♿
Attendance: 8,500 (estimated)

FENTON HISTORY CENTER-MUSEUM & RESEARCH CENTER, 67 Washington St., Jamestown, NY 14701-6697. Tel.: 716-664-6256. Fax: 716-483-7524.
E-mail: information@fentonhistorycenter.org
Web Site: www.fentonhistorycenter.org
Founded: 1964.
Congressional District: 39
Key Personnel: Pres. (V), Michael T. Rohlin; Dir., Joni Blackman; Dir. Education, Frances Fair; Collections Mgr., Normon P. Carlson; Registrar, Photograph Archivist & Volunteer Mgr., Sylvia Lobb; Librarian & Archivist, Karen E. Livsey; Membership, Office & Gift Shop Mgr., Paula Bechmann.
Personnel Profile: Full-Time Paid 2; Part-Time Paid 5; Part-Time Volunteers 1; Interns 1.
Governing Authority: nonprofit organization. Tax-exempt: 501(c)(3).
History Museum: housed in 1863 Italian villa style mansion of Reuben E. Fenton, U.S. Congressman, Senator, NY. State Governor & founder of NYS Republican Party.
Collections: local history.
Research Fields: genealogy; local history.
Facilities: 7,000-vol. library of local history & genealogy available on premises.
Activities: guided tours; educational programs; genealogy support group; Jr. historians (grades 1-3); history club (grades 4-6); adult history club (grades 7 & up); long-term & temporary exhibits; self-guided tours of museum & community walking tours.
Publications: book, Chautauqua Lake Steamboats; book, Trolleys & Railroads of Chautauqua County; quarterly newsletter; book, Saga from the Hills: A History of the Swedes in Jamestown; book, Electricity & Politics; book, Chautauqua Lake Hotels; book, The Civil War letters of Wm. Depledge; book, Camp James M. Brown: Jamestown's Civil War Rendezvous; A History of Chautauqua County, NY.
Hours & Admission Prices: Museum & Research Center: Jan. 18 to Nov. Mon.-Sat. 10-4; Thanksgiving to Jan. 17 Mon.-Sat. 10-4, Sun. 1-4. Family $20, adults $5, children 4-12 $4; discounts to AAA, AAM & ICOM members; children under 4 & members no charge. Closed major holidays.
Attendance: 17,500 (accurate)
Membership: Student $15; Senior $30; Individual $40; Family $60; Supporting $100; Friend $200; Sustaining $500; Benefactor $1,000.

JAMES PRENDERGAST LIBRARY ASSOCIATION, ART GALLERY, 509 Cherry St., Jamestown, NY 14701-5098. Tel.: 716-484-7135. Fax: 716-487-1148.
E-mail: reference@cclslib.org
Web Site: www.prendergastlibrary.org
Founded: 1880.
Congressional District: 39
Key Personnel: Dir., Catherine A. Way; Gallery Coord., Anne Plyler.
Governing Authority: municipal. Tax-exempt: 501(c)(3).
Art Museum & Gallery.
Collections: art books; art reproductions; 19th-century American & European paintings.
Facilities: circulating collection of art books.
Activities: films; permanent, temporary & traveling exhibitions; recitals.
Publications: catalogue, The Mirror Up to Nature.
Hours & Admission Prices: Mon.-Tues. & Thurs.-Fri. 10-8, Wed. 10-4:30, Sat. 10-3:30. No charge; donations accepted. ♿
Attendance: 5,599 (accurate)

LUCILLE BALL-DESI ARNAZ CENTER, 300 N. Main St., Jamestown, NY 14701-5109. Tel.: 716-484-0800. Fax: 716-484-1018.
E-mail: info@lucy-desi.com
Web Site: www.lucy-desi.com
Key Personnel: Dir., Rick Wyman; Pres. (V), Lucie Arnaz; Museum Shop Mgr., Raina Montroy.
Governing Authority: Tax-exempt.
General Museum.
Collections: photographs; wardrobe; personal artifacts; family portraits; Wildcat memorabilia, the 1961 musical that was Lucille Ball's only Broadway Show.
Facilities: Museum-related items for sale.
Activities: special events. Museum Sponsors: Annual Festivals in May & August; Legacy of Laughter Seminars.
Publications: quarterly members newsletter, Lucy-Desi News.
Hours & Admission Prices: Mon.-Sat. 10-5:30, Sun. 1-5. Adults $10, senior $9, youth $7; members no charge. Closed New Year's Eve & Day; Easter; Thanksgiving; Christmas Eve & Day. ♿
Membership: Cast $50; Director $125; Producer $250; Executive Producer $500.

ROGER TORY PETERSON INSTITUTE OF NATURAL HISTORY, 311 Curtis St., Jamestown, NY 14701-9620. Tel.: 716-665-2473; 800-758-6841. Fax: 716-665-3794.
E-mail: information@rtpi.org
Web Site: www.rtpi.org
Founded: 1984.
Congressional District: 34
Key Personnel: Pres., James M. Berry; Chm., John Rappole; Treas., Bruce Rowan; Museum Shop Mgr., Linda Pierce.
Personnel Profile: Full-Time Paid 6; Part-Time Paid 6; Part-Time Volunteers 142; Interns 2.
Governing Authority: private; nonprofit organization. Tax-exempt.
Natural History Museum & Art Gallery: building was designed by Robert A.M. Stern.
Collections: concentrate on environmental education & environmental issues; wildlife art & photography; artifacts of naturalists; the life's work of Roger Tory Peterson.
Research Fields: environmental education; nature art.
Facilities: 4,000-vol. library of natural history & environmental education; 27 acre site; nature trails. Museum-related items for sale.
Activities: lectures; artists receptions; formal educational programs; loan exhibitions. Annual Events: Birding Festival; Banff Mountain Film Festival World Tour event; forum topics related to environmental education.
Publications: bi-monthly newsletter, The Peterson Journal; The Peterson Journal for Teaching Nature Education.
Hours & Admission Prices: Tues.-Sat. 10-4, Sun. 1-5. Family $12, adults $5, children $3; members no charge. Closed national holidays. ♿
Attendance: 12,747 (accurate)
Membership: Friend $35 & up.

Johnstown

JOHNSON HALL STATE HISTORIC SITE, 139 Hall Ave., Johnstown, NY 12095-1615. Tel.: 518-762-8712. Fax: 518-762-2330.
E-mail: wanda.burch@oprhp.state.ny.us
Web Site: www.nysparks.com
Founded: 1763.
Congressional District: 31
Key Personnel: Historic Site Mgr., Wanda Burch.
Personnel Profile: Full-Time Paid 2; Part-Time Paid 3; Part-Time Volunteers 15.
Governing Authority: New York State Office of Parks, Recreation & Historic Preservation, Saratoga Capital District. Tax-exempt: 501(c)(3).
Historic site; Historic House Museum: 1763 home of Sir William Johnson, superintendent of Indian Affairs of the Six Nations Confederacy.
Collections: period furnishings; Johnson family possessions. Historic Structure: stone outbuilding.
Research Fields: Sir William Johnson; Mohawk Valley history & settlement; Loyalists in the American Revolution.
Facilities: orientation center; herb garden; picnic area.
Activities: guided tours; lectures; gallery talks; school programs; special programs & demonstrations. Annual Event: 18th-century Market Fair in June.
Publications: brochures.
Hours & Admission Prices: Call for hours. Adults $4; members no charge. Closed most holidays. ♿
Attendance: 13,000
Membership: Friends of Johnson Hall: call for information.

JOHNSTOWN HISTORICAL SOCIETY, 17 N. William St., Johnstown, NY 12095-2115. Tel.: 518-762-7076.
Founded: 1892.
Congressional District: 31
Key Personnel: Pres. (V), Catherine Levee; Cur., James F. Morrison.
Personnel Profile: Full-Time Volunteers 2; Interns 5.
Governing Authority: society; nonprofit organization. Tax-exempt: 501(c)(3); 101-6.
Historical Society Museum.
Collections: local history & historical notables associated with Johnstown: Sir William Johnson; Molly Brant; Fife-Major Nicholas Stoner; Capt. Silas Talbot; Lafayette; Washington Irving; Governor Enos Throop; E.L. Henry; Aaron Burr; Brigadier-Gen. Edgar S. Dudley; Grace Livingston Hill; Rose M. Knox; Elizabeth Cady Stanton; Keck Zouaves; Knox gelatin; glove industry equipment; Cooper's barrel making equipment. Historic House: 1763 restored schoolmaster's house.
Research Fields: local history; historic notables associated with Johnstown; genealogy.
Facilities: 1,600-vol. library of old books, newspaper clippings, genealogical material; 2,300 photographs, 43 maps, 105 scrapbooks & 1,350 documents for researching early information about Johnstown & vicinity, available for research on premises or can be loaned under special circumstances; reading room.
Activities: guided tours; lectures; permanent & temporary exhibitions.
Publications: quarterly, newsletter; The Johnstown Historical Society; book, Now I am Ninety.
Hours & Admission Prices: Wed. & Sat.-Sun. 1:30-4:30, Thurs.-Fri. by appointment. No charge; donations accepted. Closed New Year's Day; Memorial Day; Independence Day; Labor Day; Thanksgiving; Christmas.
Attendance: 794 (accurate)
Membership: Students & Senior Citizens $5; Individual $7.50; Family $15; Patron $25; Life $100; Benefactor $1,000.

Katonah

CARAMOOR CENTER FOR MUSIC & THE ARTS, INC., (M), 149 Girdle Ridge Rd., Katonah, NY 10536-3815. Mailing Address: Box 816, Katonah, NY 10536-0816. Tel.: 914-232-5035, ext. 221. Fax: 914-232-5521.
E-mail: museum@caramoor.org
Web Site: www.caramoor.org
Founded: 1946.
Congressional District: 21
Key Personnel: Chm. Bd. (V), Judy Evnin; Exec. Dir. & C.E.O., Michael Barrett; Managing Dir., Paul Rosenblum; Interim Dir. Devel., Gary Himes; Museum Mgr. & Dir. Programs, Merceds Santos-Miller; Archivist, Hilton Bailey; Admin., Tammy Belanger-Turner; Dir. Education, Marilyn Reynolds; Exec. Asst. & Bd. Liaison, Ameila Wierzbicki; Mgr. & Opera Liaison, Robin Valovich; Mgr. Annual Giving, Alithia Dutschke; Dir. Special Events & Rentals, Christine Bosco; Mktg. Mgr., Sal Vaccard; Education Asst., Scott Ellison; Museum Shop Mgr., Angie Pippenger.
Personnel Profile: Full-Time Paid 22; Part-Time Paid 14; Part-Time Volunteers 220; Interns 2.
Governing Authority: nonprofit. Subsidiary Institution: Caramoor House-Museum. Tax-exempt: 501(c)(3).
House Museum: housed in 54 room Mediterranean style villa.
Collections: Renaissance & 17th-19th century furniture; sculpture; painting; decorative arts; Chinese jade & porcelains; cloisonne works; Chinese hand painted wallpapers; Oriental carpets; period textiles; chinoiserie; 16th century Maiolica; Calwell collection; Theremin instruments & music scores.
Research Fields: decorative arts; 20th-century American social history, painting & sculpture; Renaissance art & furnishings; Theremin.
Facilities: theater; gardens; landscaped grounds. Museum-related items for sale.
Activities: guided tours; lectures; concerts; arts festivals; docent program; temporary & permanent exhibitions; education programs for school children; afternoon teas.
Publications: biannual newsletter; brochures; pamphlets; books, A Guide to the Collections of Caramoor; Caramoor.
Hours & Admission Prices: May-Oct. Wed.-Sun. 1-4, last tour at 3 except during festival on Sat. 1-5, last tour at 4; Nov.-April Tues.-Fri. by appointment only. Adults $10; discounts to AAM members; members, children 16 & under no charge. ♿
Attendance: 60,000 (estimated)
Membership: Individual $60-$249; Participant $250-$399; Donor $400-$999; Patron $1,000-$2,499; Conductor Society $2,500-$4,999; Composer Society $5,000-$9,999; Festival Society $10,000 & up.

JOHN JAY HOMESTEAD STATE HISTORIC SITE, 400 Rte. 22, Katonah, NY 10536. Mailing Address: P.O. Box 832, Katonah, NY 10536-0832. Tel.: 914-232-5651. Fax: 914-232-8085. TDD: 845-889-4100.
E-mail: heather.iannucci@oprhp.state.ny.us
Web Site: www.nysparks.com
Founded: 1958.
Congressional District: 25
Key Personnel: C.E.O. & Historic Site Mgr., Heather Iannucci; Interpretive Programs Asst., Allan Weinreb.
Personnel Profile: Full-Time Paid 8; Part-Time Paid 3; Part-Time Volunteers 34.
Governing Authority: state. Parent Institution: New York State Office of Parks, Recreation and Historic Preservation. Tax-exempt: 501(c)(3).
Historic House Museum: federal style country home reflects the residence of U.S. Chief Justice & New York state Governor John Jay & family living here in the first third of the 19th century.
Collections: portraits; Jay family personal artifacts including c.1800-1833 American Art, furniture & decorative arts; archives & library; 12 structures & archaeological sites; grounds & outbuildings are interpreted through the 1930's; home, parts of original farmstead, restored gardens & 62 acres of the original 750 accessible to visitors.
Research Fields: American history; art history; Jay family; Revolutionary & Civil War history; slavery & abolition; period farms; 19th-century social history; New York State history; coaching.
Facilities: 4,000-vol. historic family library, personal papers & manuscripts available for use by advance request; formal gardens & grounds with trails; picnic area; lecture facility.
Activities: self-guided walking tour of the site & gardens; guided tours; lectures; concerts; permanent exhibitions; lecture series; educational programs; group tours; public events & programs.
Publications: John Jay; The Jays of Bedford; The Jay Genealogy; newsletter, Friends of John Jay Newsletter; The Herb Garden, A Walking Tour; The Farm of Mr. Jay, A Walking Tour.
Hours & Admission Prices: April-Nov. Tues.-Sat. 10-4, Sun. 11-4. Grounds: daily 8-dusk. Adults $7, senior citizens $5; Friends and children 12 & under no charge. ♿
Attendance: 60,721 (accurate)
Membership: Friends of John Jay Homestead: Student $25; Individual $35; Family $70; Contributing $100; Sponsor $250; Patron $500; Benefactor $1,000; Statesman $2,500; Founder $5,000.

* **KATONAH MUSEUM OF ART, (M),** 134 Jay St., Katonah, NY 10536-3737. Tel.: 914-232-9555, ext. 0. Fax: 914-232-3128.
E-mail: info@katonahmuseum.org
Web Site: www.katonahmuseum.org
Founded: 1953.
Congressional District: 25
Key Personnel: Pres. (V) Bd. Trustees, Yvonne S. Pollack; Exec. Dir., Neil Watson; Dir. Education, Karen Stein; Registrar, Nancy Hitchcock; Dir. Special Events, Kristina Leamy; Coord. Learning Center, Naomi Leiseroff.
Personnel Profile: Full-Time Paid 10; Part-Time Paid 21; Part-Time Volunteers 217; Interns 12.

Governing Authority: nonprofit organization. Tax-exempt.
Art Museum.
Collections: paintings; photographs; sculptures.
Research Fields: pertaining to varied exhibition schedule.
Facilities: sculpture garden; children's learning center.
Activities: guided tours; lectures; films; formally organized education programs for schools; school loan service; docent training; teacher workshops; art trips for members; children's workshops; summer jazz concerts.
Publications: catalogues, The American Eagle: Spirit & Symbol, 1782-1882; American Painting, 1900-1976; Utopia: The Art of William Morris & His Circle; Dreams in Motion: The Art of Windsor McCay; Le Fantastique Reel: Graphic Works by Odilon Redon; Forever Wild: The Adirondack Experience; George Rickey: The Art & Movement; The Intimate Eye of Edouard Vuillard; Sticks & Stones: Ten Artists Work with Nature; The Technological Muse; Tradewinds: The Lure of the China Trade; Watercolors from the Abstract Expressionism Era; Asobi: Play in the Arts of Japan; Dorothy Dehner: Sixty Years of Art; Friends & Family: Portraiture in the World of Florine Stettheimer; Block/Plate/Stone: What a Print Is; Shelter & Dreams: Playhouses by Architects & Artists; Against the Stream: Milton Avery, Adolph Gottlieb & Mark Rothko in the 1930's; Vladimir Tytla: Master Animator; Medieval Monsters: Dragons & Fantastic Creatures; The Reconstructed Figure: The Human Image in Contemporary Art; At Home with Art: Paintings in American Interiors, 1780-1920; Object as Insight: Japanese Buddhist Art & Ritual; Toying with Architecture; Revisiting American Art: Works from the Collections of Historically Black Colleges and Universities; Polish Posters: Combat on Paper, 1960-1990; Pavel Tchelitchew: The Landscape of the Body; Latin America Still Life in the Twentieth Century; Horse Tales: American Images and Icons 1800-2000; The Innocent Eye: American Folk Art from Colonial Williamsburg; The Human Comedy; Edward Giobbi: Paintings; Food Matters: Explorations in Contemporary Art; The Birth of the Banjo; Sol LeWitt: Recent Work; catalogues, I Love The Burbs; Eternal Presence: Handprints and Footprints in Buddhist Art; Richard Diebenkorn Prints 1948-1993.
Hours & Admission Prices: Tues.-Sat. 10-5, Sun. 12-5. Adults $5, students & seniors $3; discounts to AAM & WNET Channel 13 members; members, children under 12 & 10am to noon no charge. ♿
Attendance: 40,000 (estimated)
Membership: Individual $50; Dual & Family $85; Museum Supporter $150; Curator's Circle $375; Friend's Circle $500; Director's Circle $1,000; President's Circle $2,500; Exhibition Patron $5,000.

STEPPING STONES, (M), 62 Oak Rd., Katonah, NY 10536-1810. Tel.: 914-232-4822. Fax: 914-232-2580.
E-mail: tara@steppingstones.org
Web Site: www.steppingstones.org
Founded: 1979.
Congressional District: 89
Key Personnel: Dir., Annah Perch; Pres. (V), Michael Kelly.
Personnel Profile: Full-Time Paid 1; Part-Time Paid 1; Part-Time Volunteers 8.
Governing Authority: private; nonprofit organization. Tax-exempt.
Historic House Museum: housed in the former home of Bill & Lois Wilson, co-founders of Alcoholics Anonymous and Al-Anon.
Collections: Bill & Lois Wilson's personal artifacts; AA & Al-Anon archives.
Facilities: 200-vol. library. Museum-related items for sale.
Activities: guided tours. Annual Event: picnic.
Publications: annual newsletter, Stepping Stones News.
Hours & Admission Prices: Daily by appointment. No charge; donations accepted. Closed Easter; Thanksgiving; Christmas.
Attendance: 1,800 (accurate)

Kinderhook

COLUMBIA COUNTY HISTORICAL SOCIETY, INC., 5 Albany Ave., Kinderhook, NY 12106-0311. Mailing Address: P.O. Box 311, Kinderhook, NY 12106-0311. Tel.: 518-758-9265. Fax: 518-758-2499.
E-mail: cchs@cchsny.org
Web Site: www.cchsny.org
Founded: 1916.
Congressional District: 16
Key Personnel: Exec. Dir., Ann-Eliza Lewis; Pres., Russell Pomeranz; Cur., Diane Shewchuk.
Personnel Profile: Full-Time Paid 2; Part-Time Paid 6; Part-Time Volunteers 50.
Governing Authority: society. Tax-exempt: 501(c)(3).
Historic House Museums: c.1820 James Vanderpoel House; 1737 Luykas Van Alen House; c.1850 Ichabod Crane School House (interpretation date: c.1925). History Museum: Columbia County Museum.
Collections: New York Federal furnishings, decorative & fine arts; New York Dutch furnishings, decorative & fine arts; Columbia County documents & historical artifacts; genealogical; costumes & textiles.
Research Fields: county & regional art; decorative arts; folk art; architecture; local & regional history; county architecture; genealogy.
Facilities: 3,000-vol. library of county & state historical reference & collections; manuscripts, documents & photographs.
Activities: guided tours; lectures; inter-museum loan, permanent & temporary exhibits; concerts; educational program; docent program; workshops; school programs.
Publications: magazine, Columbia County History & Heritage; books; exhibit catalogs.
Hours & Admission Prices: Museum: Mon. & Thurs.-Sat. 10-4, Sun. 12-4. No charge. Historic Properties: Memorial Day to Labor Day Fri.-Sat. 10-4, Sun. 12-4. Adults $5, students & senior citizens 55 & over $3; children under 12 & members no charge. Group tours May-Oct. by appointment.
Attendance: 24,500 (accurate)
Membership: Senior Citizen $30; Senior (dual) $40; Individual $50; Family $60; Patron $100; Sponsor $250; Benefactor $500; Second Century Circle $1,000.

MARTIN VAN BUREN NATIONAL HISTORIC SITE, Rt. 9H, Kinderhook, NY 12106. Mailing Address: 1013 Old Post Rd., Kinderhook, NY 12106-3605. Tel.: 518-758-9689. Fax: 518-758-6986.
Web Site: www.nps.gov/mava
Founded: 1974.
Congressional District: 20
Key Personnel: C.E.O., Dan Dattilio; Cur., Dr. Patricia West; Chief Interpretation, James A. McKay.
Personnel Profile: Full-Time Paid 11; Part-Time Paid 5; Part-Time Volunteers 1; Interns 1.
Governing Authority: federal. Parent Institution: National Park Service. Tax-exempt.
Historic House: home of President Martin Van Buren.
Collections: home furnishings; personal effects of President Martin Van Buren.
Research Fields: political history; Pres. Van Buren; Van Buren Home.
Facilities: 2,000-vol. research library; microfilm material.
Activities: mansion tours & special events during summer months.
Publications: brochure.
Hours & Admission Prices: mid-May to Oct. daily 9-4. Family $12, adults $5; children under 16 & members no charge. ♿
Attendance: 21,000 (accurate)

Kings Point

AMERICAN MERCHANT MARINE MUSEUM, United States Merchant Marine Academy, Kings Point, NY 11024-1699. Mailing Address: US Merchant Marine Academy, 300 Steamboat Road, Kings Point, NY 11024-1699. Tel.: 516-773-5515. Fax: 516-482-5340.
E-mail: smithj@usmma.edu
Web Site: www.usmma.edu/about/museum/default.htm
Founded: 1978.
Key Personnel: Chm. (V), Capt. Warren Leback; Interim Coord., Joshua M. Smith.
Personnel Profile: Full-Time Paid 1; Part-Time Paid 1; Part-Time Volunteers 8; Interns 1.
Governing Authority: federal.
Maritime Museum: American Merchant Marine.
Collections: ship models, paintings & artifacts relating to American Merchant Marine; National Maritime Hall of Fame; period nautical instrument collection; Sperry navigation wing; restored emery rice steam engine; re-creation of the 1945 victory ship Radio Room; Japanese sword from WWII; ship passenger lists; immigration records.
Research Fields: American Merchant Marine WWII to present; history of the American shipping companies.
Facilities: library.
Activities: guided tours; organized education programs for children; temporary exhibitions; lectures. Museum Sponsors: Annual Bowditch Award; induction ceremonies for National Maritime Hall of Fame; annual reunion of American merchant marine veterans; reunions for former employees of U.S. shipping companies.
Hours & Admission Prices: Aug. to mid-June Tues.-Fri. 10-3, Sat.-Sun. 1-4:30; groups by appointment. No charge; donations accepted. Closed federal holidays. ♿
Attendance: 4,000 (estimated)
Membership: Basic $30; $40; $50; $100; $500; Patron $1,000; Corporate $1,000 & up.

Kingston

FRIENDS OF HISTORIC KINGSTON, FRED J. JOHNSTON HOUSE MUSEUM, 63 Main St., Kingston, NY 12401-3801. Mailing Address: P.O. Box 3763, Kingston, NY 12402-3763. Tel.: 845-339-0720.
E-mail: fohk@verizon.net

Web Site: www.fohk.org
Founded: 1965.
Congressional District: 26
Key Personnel: Dir., Jane Kellar; Pres. (V), Patricia Murphy.
Personnel Profile: Full-Time Paid 1; Part-Time Paid 1; Part-Time Volunteers 40.
Governing Authority: private; nonprofit organization. Tax-exempt: 501(c)(3).
History Museum.
Collections: local history; period rooms.
Research Fields: architectural history of local buildings.
Facilities: 200-vol. library; 500 sq. ft. exhibit space. Museum-related items for sale.
Activities: docent program; formal education programs for children; gallery talks; guided tours; lectures; temporary exhibitions.
Publications: newsletter, Friends of Historic Kingston; walking tour brochures.
Hours & Admission Prices: May-Oct. Sat.-Sun. 1-4; other times by appointment. Adults $5, children $2; members no charge. ♿
Attendance: 4,100 (estimated)
Membership: Student & Senior $15; Household $45; Patron $500.

HUDSON RIVER MARITIME MUSEUM, (M), 50 Rondout Landing, Kingston, NY 12401-6092. Tel.: 845-338-0071, ext. 10. Fax: 845-338-0583.
E-mail: hrmm@hvc.rr.com
Web Site: www.hrmm.org
Founded: 1980.
Congressional District: 28
Key Personnel: Pres., Steven Digilio; Exec. Dir., Russell Lange; Cur., Allynne Lange; Museum Shop Mgr., Bob Van Etten.
Personnel Profile: Part-Time Paid 4; Part-Time Volunteers 30.
Governing Authority: nonprofit organization. Tax-exempt: 501(c)(3).
Maritime Museum.
Collections: Hudson River steamboats & towing industry history; Hudson River lighthouses; Ruge ice boats; photographs; brickmaking & ice-cutting artifacts & documents; ship & boatbuilding industries; Anton Otto Fischer maritime paintings; boat models.
Research Fields: Hudson River maritime history; commerce; industries; commercial & recreational vessels; Hudson River lighthouses.
Facilities: 450-vol. library on Hudson River steam & sail vessels; archives of regional river industries. Books, prints & other related items for sale.
Activities: permanent & temporary exhibits; group tours; research; educational programs for children; college intern program; waterfront events; ecology workshops; annual lecture series.
Publications: newsletter, Focs'le News; calendar of events; brochure; annual, Pilot Club Log; book, Focs'le Days; Thomas Cornell & The Cornell Steamboat Company.
Hours & Admission Prices: May-Oct. daily 11-4; other times by appointment. Museum: adults $5, seniors & children $4; discounts to CAMM members; members no charge. ♿
Attendance: 25,000 (estimated)
Membership: Individual $25; Household $40; Friend $50; Sustaining $100-$249; Patron $250-$499; Fellow $500-$999; Pilot $1,000.

SENATE HOUSE STATE HISTORIC SITE, 296 Fair St., Kingston, NY 12401-3836. Tel.: 845-338-2786. Fax: 845-334-8173.
E-mail: pam.malcolm@oprhp.state.ny.us
Web Site: www.nysparks.com
Founded: 1887.
Congressional District: 25
Key Personnel: Rgnl. Historical Preservation Supvr., Rich Goring.
Personnel Profile: Full-Time Paid 6; Part-Time Paid 5; Part-Time Volunteers 25; Interns 1.
Governing Authority: state. Parent Institution: New York State Office of Parks, Recreation and Historic Preservation, & Palisades Interstate Park Commission. Subsidiary Institution: Friends of Senate House, Inc. Tax-exempt: 501(c)(3).
Historic Site.
Collections: period furnishings; paintings by John Vanderlyn, Ammi Phillips, James Bard & other regional artists; archives; genealogy. Historic Houses: c.1676 Senate (Van Gaasbeek) House; 1873 Louhgran House.
Research Fields: state government; John Vanderlyn; Dutch culture; regional history.
Facilities: 1,000-vol. library of historical and genealogical material 40,000 item manuscript collection available for research on premises.
Activities: guided tours; lectures; films; gallery talks; concerts; special programs; permanent, traveling & temporary exhibitions.
Publications: brochures.
Hours & Admission Prices: April 15-Oct. Wed.-Sat. 10-5, Sun. 1-5; other times by appointment. Adults $4, seniors & groups $3; children under 12 no charge. Closed most holidays. ♿
Attendance: 25,000 (estimated)
Membership: Individual $20; Joint $30; Family $40; Supporting $50-$99; Contributor $100-$499; Patron $500-$999; Benefactor $1,000 & up.

TROLLEY MUSEUM OF NEW YORK, (M), 89 E. Strand, Kingston, NY 12401-6001. Mailing Address: P.O. Box 2291, Kingston, NY 12402-2291. Tel.: 845-331-3399.
E-mail: admin@tmny.org
Web Site: tmny.org
Founded: 1955.
Congressional District: 26
Key Personnel: Pres. (V), Jon McGrew; Archivist, Evan Jennings; Treas., William Brandt; Admin., Steve Ladin; Museum Shop Mgr., Glendon Moffett.
Personnel Profile: Part-Time Paid 1; Part-Time Volunteers 20.
Governing Authority: private; nonprofit organization. Tax-exempt: 501(c)(3).
Transportation Museum.
Collections: trolley; subway cars; artifacts; photographs.
Facilities: 10,000 sq. ft. exhibit space; 30-seat theater. Museum-related items for sale.
Activities: Annual Events: Trolley 5K Run; National Trails Day Clean-up; Halloween Fright Train; Trolley rides with Santa in December.
Publications: bimonthly email newsletter; volunteer bulletin.
Hours & Admission Prices: 1st weekend May, Memorial Day to Columbus Day, Mother's Day & 1st weekend Dec. Sat.-Sun. & holidays 12-5. Also open for special events. Trolley: call for hours. Ride Fare: adults $5, senior citizens & children $3; discounts to AAM members; members & Association of Railway Museum members no charge. Visitor's Center: no charge; donations accepted.
Attendance: 5,000 (estimated)
Membership: Individual $20; Family $30; Friend $60; Patron $120; Corporate $150; Fellow $250; Motorman's Club $500; President's Club $1,000.

VOLUNTEER FIREMEN'S MALL AND MUSEUM OF KINGSTON, 265 Fair St., Kingston, NY 12401-3807. Mailing Address: P.O. Box 1501, Kingston, NY 12402-1501. Tel.: 845-331-0866 & 338-1247.
Founded: 1980.
Key Personnel: Pres. (V) & Treas., Ronald Matthews.
Personnel Profile: Part-Time Volunteers 15.
Governing Authority: private; nonprofit organization. Tax-exempt: 501(c)(3).
Fire-Fighting Museum.
Collections: personal artifacts; furnishings; firemanic artifacts; fire engines; hose carriages.
Hours & Admission Prices: April-May & Sept.-Oct. Fri. 11-3, Sat. 10-4; June-Aug. Wed.-Fri. 11-3, Sat. 10-4. No charge; donations accepted.
Attendance: 2,500 (estimated)

LaFargeville

NORTHERN NEW YORK AGRICULTURAL HISTORICAL SOCIETY, AGRICULTURAL MUSEUM AT STONE MILLS, (M), 30950 NYS Rte. 180, LaFargeville, NY 13656. Mailing Address: P.O. Box 108, LaFargeville, NY 13656-0108. Tel.: 315-658-2353.
E-mail: agstonemills@westelcom.com
Web Site: www.stonemillsmuseum.org
Founded: 1968.
Congressional District: 30
Key Personnel: Pres., Leon Hunter; Dir., Marguerite Raineri.
Personnel Profile: Full-Time Paid 1; Part-Time Paid 1.
Governing Authority: society. Tax-exempt: 501(c)(3).
Agricultural History Museum Complex.
Collections: early farm & home equipment; old maps, books, records & slates; early milk handling equipment; Home Arts Exhibit Hall; Carriage House for large agriculture equipment; authentic Ice House. Historic Buildings: 1836 Stone Meeting House; Cheese Factory; 1838 one-room schoolhouse; 1800s active blacksmith shop and wood shop; 1865 Saw Mill; restored granary working wind mill.
Research Fields: restoration of property; history of local agriculture.
Facilities: food service available on weekends.
Activities: permanent & temporary exhibitions. Museum Sponsors: annual three-day Craft Show with over 200 craftsmen demonstrating skills; Draft Horse Show & Horse Pull; barbecues; Old Time Gas Engines; Tractor pulls; Sheep & Wool Festival; Quilt Show; Old Time Music; Blue Grass Festival; Horse Shows; Harvest Fest in September; Family Farmer Boy Day.
Publications: brochures.
Hours & Admission Prices: May by appointment; June-Sept. Wed.-Mon. 9-3. Adult $5; discounts to AAM members; children 16 & under and life members no charge. ♿
Attendance: 17,500 (estimated)
Membership: Individual $10; Family $15; Business $25; Life $100.

Lake George

FORT WILLIAM HENRY MUSEUM, 48 Canada St., Lake George, NY 12845-1600. Tel.: 518-668-5471 & 964-6647. Fax: 518-668-4926.
Web Site: www.fwhmuseum.com
Founded: 1952.
Key Personnel: C.E.O. & Pres., Robert Flacke; C.F.O., Kathy Uncil; Cur., Gerald Bradfield; Museum Shop Mgr., Dawn Littrell.
Personnel Profile: Full-Time Paid 3; Part-Time Paid 1.
Governing Authority: profit-making organization. Affiliated with The Fort William Henry Corp.
Historic Site Museum: restored c.1750 Fort William Henry.
Collections: artifacts from site, c.1750-1760; Colonial documents, 1750-1790; weapons; manuscripts.
Research Fields: colonial wars of Lake George region.
Facilities: 1,500-vol. library of maps; documents; books; newspapers pertaining to Colonial period available for research by approval of director; reading room; cafeteria. Museum-related items for sale.
Activities: guided tours; lectures; films; gallery talks; formally organized education programs; permanent, temporary & traveling exhibitions; school loan service.
Hours & Admission Prices: May-Oct. 28 daily 9-6. Adults $14.95, senior citizens $12.95, children 3-11 $7.95; discount to groups; children under 3 no charge.
Attendance: 43,150 (accurate)

HOUSE OF FRANKENSTEIN WAX MUSEUM, 213 Canada St., Lake George, NY 12845-1401. Tel.: 518-668-3377.
Web Site: frankensteinwaxmuseum.com
Wax Museum.
Collections: wax figures.
Hours & Admission Prices: April to mid-May Fri. 12-9, Sat. 10-10, Sun. 10-6; mid-May to June 19 Sun.-Thurs. 10-6, Fri. 12-9, Sat. 10-10; June 20-Sept. 1 daily 9am-11pm; Sept. 5 to Nov. 2 Fri.-Sat. 11-9, Sun. 10-6. Adults $9, students 13-17 $8, children 6-12 $4.50.

LAKE GEORGE HISTORICAL ASSOCIATION MUSEUM, Old Warren County Courthouse, Canada & Amherst St., Lake George, NY 12845. Mailing Address: P.O. Box 472, Lake George, NY 12845-0472. Tel.: 518-668-5044.
E-mail: lgha@verizon.net
Web Site: lakegeorgehistorical.org
Founded: 1964.
Key Personnel: Pres. Bd. Trustees (V), Alex Parrott; Dir., Maggie McClure.
Personnel Profile: Part-Time Paid 2.
Governing Authority: Lake George Historical Association. Tax-exempt: 501(c)(3).
Historical Society Museum: housed in 1845 Warren County Courthouse, located in the region of famous battles of the French & Indian War and American Revolution.
Collections: paintings; history; natural history; photographs; Indian artifacts; tramp art; boats; local history.
Research Fields: local history.
Facilities: 150-vol. library of Adirondack history; reading room; 1845 courthouse & courtroom for presentations; bookstore.
Activities: guided tours; lectures; films; permanent & temporary exhibitions; family activities; mid-1800s jail cells.
Publications: 1889 Seneca Ray Stoddard Map of Lake George.
Hours & Admission Prices: May 19-June & Oct. 1-Oct. 16 Sat.-Sun. 11-4, July-Aug. Tues. & Fri.-Sat. 11-4, Wed.-Thurs. 3-8; Sept. Fri.-Sun. 11-4. No charge.
Attendance: 3,500
Membership: Senior Citizen $5; Individual $15; Family $25; Business & Contributing $50; Patron $1,000.

Lake Placid

THE HISTORY MUSEUM, LAKE PLACID-NORTH ELBA HISTORICAL SOCIETY, 242 Station St., Lake Placid, NY 12946-1949. Mailing Address: P.O. Box 189, 242 Station St., Lake Placid, NY 12946-0189. Tel.: 518-523-1608.
Founded: 1967.
Key Personnel: Dir. Administration, Patricia Kelly; Pres., Chuck Damp; Treas., John B. Huttlinger, Jr.
Personnel Profile: Full-Time Paid 1; Part-Time Volunteers 20.
Governing Authority: society. Tax-exempt: 501(c)(3).
Historic House: 1904 D&H train station.
Collections: general store replica; Adirondack Mountains & Lake Placid memorabilia; Victor Herbert & Kate Smith collections; railroad memorabilia; Dewey decimal system collection; rustic furniture; Adirondack Guideboat.
Facilities: library of brochures, newspapers, maps, pamphlets & photographs available for research on premises only.
Activities: guided tours; permanent & temporary exhibitions.
Publications: semiannual newsletter.
Hours & Admission Prices: Memorial Day to mid-June & Labor Day to mid-Sept. Sat.-Sun. 10-4; mid-June to Sept. & mid-Sept. to Columbus Day Wed.-Sun. 10-4. Suggested Donation: adults $2; members no charge.
Attendance: 1,685 (accurate)
Membership: Individual $20; Family $30; Sustaining Patron $50; Business $100.

JOHN BROWN FARM STATE HISTORIC SITE, 115 John Brown Rd., Lake Placid, NY 12946-3248. Tel.: 518-523-3900. Fax: 518-523-3951.
E-mail: brendan.mills@oprhp.state.ny.us
Web Site: nysparks.state.ny.us/sites/info.asp?siteid=14
Founded: 1895.
Congressional District: 30
Key Personnel: Historic Site Asst., Brendan Mills.
Governing Authority: state. New York State Office of Parks, Recreation & Historic Preservation, Thousand Islands State Park, Recreation & Historic Preservation Commission & New York State Dept. of Environmental Conservation. Tax-exempt: 501(c)(3).
Historic House Museum: 1855 frame house occupied by John Brown & his family while he carried on his anti-slavery campaigns; the burial place of John Brown.
Collections: period furnishings; personal possessions of John Brown & his family.
Research Fields: John Brown & his family; regional history.
Facilities: farm trail.
Activities: special programs.
Hours & Admission Prices: May-Oct. Wed.-Mon. 10-5. Adults $2, seniors & children $1; children under 12 no charge. ♿
Attendance: 37,000 (accurate)

1932 & 1980 LAKE PLACID WINTER OLYMPICS MUSEUM, 216 Main St., Lake Placid, NY 12946-3648. Mailing Address: NYS Olympic Rgnl. Devel. Authority, Olympic Center, P.O. Box 2002, Lake Placid, NY 12946-3648. Tel.: 518-523-1655, ext. 226. Fax: 518-523-9275.
Key Personnel: Dir., Liz DeFazio
Sports Museum.
Collections: Olympic history; athletes; uniforms; equipment; videos.
Hours & Admission Prices: Daily 10-5. Adults $5, seniors & children $3. Closed Thanksgiving; Christmas.

LeRoy

LEROY HOUSE & JELL-O GALLERY, (M), 23 E. Main St., LeRoy, NY 14482-1209. Tel.: 585-768-7433. Fax: 585-768-7579.
E-mail: info@jellogallery.org
Web Site: www.jellomuseum.com
Founded: 1940.
Congressional District: 137
Key Personnel: Exec. Dir. & Cur., Lynne J. Belluscio; Pres. (V), Jim Newkirk; Museum Shop Mgr., Carolyn Bolin.
Personnel Profile: Full-Time Paid 1; Part-Time Paid 10; Interns 1.
Governing Authority: society. Parent Institution: LeRoy Historical Society. Tax-exempt: 501(c)(3).
Historical Society Museum.
Collections: archives; paintings; decorative arts; textiles; agriculture; graphics; children's museum; costumes; glass; history; genealogy of local families; Jell-O memorabilia.
Research Fields: archives; history.
Facilities: 1,000-vol. library of books & genealogy manuscripts available by appointment.
Activities: guided tours; lectures; study clubs; formally organized education programs.
Publications: booklets; monthly newsletters; annual report; review of pertinent historical events & year's activities; genealogical booklets; quarterly newsletter.
Hours & Admission Prices: Leroy House: call for hours. Jell-O Gallery: Jan.-March Mon.-Fri. 10-4; April-Dec. Mon.-Sat. 10-4, Sun. 1-4. Adults $4, children 6-11$1.50; discounts to groups, tours, AAM & AAA members; children 5 & under and members no charge. Closed New Year's Day; Thanksgiving; Christmas.
Attendance: 11,000 (estimated)
Membership: Individual $20; Family $30; Sustaining $50; Supporting $100; Life $350.

Lewiston

NEW YORK POWER AUTHORITY-NIAGARA POWER PROJECT VISITORS' CENTER, 5777 Lewiston Rd., Lewiston, NY 14092-2152. Tel.: 716-286-6661. Fax: 716-286-6654.
Web Site: www.nypa.gov/vc/niagara.htm
Key Personnel: Mgr. Community Rels., Lou Paonessa.
Governing Authority: private; nonprofit organization.
Electricity & Technology Museum.
Collections: over 50 hands-on exhibits; hydroelectricity & local history.
Facilities: classroom; 40-seat theater; community room.
Activities: age specific educational programs by reservation; special events.
Hours & Admission Prices: Daily 9-5. No charge. Closed New Year's Eve & Day; Thanksgiving; Christmas Eve & Day. ♿
Attendance: 80,000 (accurate)

Lindenhurst

OLD VILLAGE HALL MUSEUM, 215 S. Wellwood Ave., Lindenhurst, NY 11757-4904. Mailing Address: P.O. Box 296, Lindenhurst, NY 11757-0296. Tel.: 631-957-4385.
Founded: 1958.
Congressional District: 13
Key Personnel: Chm. (V) & Dir., Johanna Sandy.
Personnel Profile: Part-Time Paid 3.
Governing Authority: municipal. Parent Institution: Lindenhurst Historical Society and maintained by the Village of Lindenhurst, Inc. Tax-exempt.
Local History Museum.
Collections: period artifacts; photographs; archives; industrial; costumes; architectural plans & blueprints of local buildings; music. Historic Buildings: 1901 restored railroad depot & freight house.
Research Fields: local history, architecture & music; salt hay.
Facilities: 30-vol. library of microfilms of old local newspapers available for use at Lindenhurst Memorial Library.
Activities: guided tours; lectures; concerts; formally organized education programs for children; permanent, temporary & traveling exhibitions.
Hours & Admission Prices: Wed. & Fri.-Sat. 2-4. No charge; donations accepted. Closed holidays.
Attendance: 1,129 (accurate)
Membership: Individual $5; Life $30.

Little Falls

HERKIMER HOME STATE HISTORIC SITE, 200 State Rte. 169, Little Falls, NY 13365-5818. Tel.: 315-823-0398. Fax: 315-823-0587.
E-mail: thomas.kernan@oprhp.state.ny.us
Web Site: www.nysparks.com
Founded: 1913.
Congressional District: 31
Key Personnel: Historic Site Mgr., Thomas J. Kernan.
Personnel Profile: Full-Time Paid 5; Part-Time Paid 6; Part-Time Volunteers 60.
Governing Authority: state. Parent Institution: New York State Office of Parks, Recreation & Historic Preservation. Subsidiary Institution: The Friends of Herkimer Home, Inc. Tax-exempt: 501(c)(3).
Historic House: c.1760 home & gravesite of Gen. Nicholas Herkimer.
Collections: period furnishings; items belonging to the Herkimer family, representative of early German culture in the Mohawk Valley.
Research Fields: Mohawk Valley history; Palatine German settlement in the Mohawk Valley; American Revolution.
Facilities: visitor center; picnic area; bike trail.
Activities: guided tours; lectures; gallery talks; permanent exhibitions; school programs; seasonal farm life & craft demonstrations.
Hours & Admission Prices: mid-May to mid-Oct. Wed.-Sat. 10-5, Sun. & Mon. holidays 1-5. Adults $4, seniors & students $3; children 12 & under no charge. ♿
Attendance: 29,316 (accurate)
Membership: Student & Senior $5; Adult $10.

LITTLE FALLS HISTORICAL SOCIETY MUSEUM, 319 S. Ann St., Little Falls, NY 13365-1362. Tel.: 315-823-0643; 4852.
E-mail: lfhistor@ntcnet.com
Web Site: www.littlefallsny.com/museum
Founded: 1962.
Congressional District: 30
Personnel Profile: Part-Time Volunteers 10; Interns 1.
Governing Authority: society; nonprofit organization. Tax-exempt: 170(b)(1)(A).
Local History Museum: housed in 1833 Greek Revival bank building.
Collections: books; scrapbooks; genealogical records; pictures; artifacts.
Research Fields: local history.
Activities: guided tours; lectures; films; permanent & temporary exhibitions.
Publications: Historic Preservation in Little Falls.
Hours & Admission Prices: June-Sept. Tues.-Fri. 1-4, Sat. 12-4. No charge, donations accepted. Closed holidays. ♿
Attendance: 466 (accurate)
Membership: $10.

Liverpool

SAINTE MARIE AMONG THE IROQUOIS, 6680 Onondaga Lake Pkwy., Liverpool, NY 13088-5061. Mailing Address: 106 Lake Dr., Liverpool, NY 13088-5118. Tel.: 315-453-6768. Fax: 315-453-6772.
E-mail: stemarie1657@yahoo.com
Web Site: onondagacountyparks.com
Key Personnel: Park Supt., Dale Grinolds
History Museum: housed in re-created 1657 French Mission which stood on the shores of Onondaga Lake.
Collections: 17th-century Haudenosaunee (Iroquois) culture; daily life in the 1650s.
Hours & Admission Prices: mid-May to mid-Oct. Mon.-Fri. 9-3, Sat.-Sun. 12-5; mid-Oct. to mid-May Mon.-Fri. 9-3. Mid-May to mid-Oct. adults $3, senior citizens 62 & over $2.50, children 6-17 $2; children 5 & under no charge. Mid-Oct. to mid-May no charge; donations accepted.

SALT MUSEUM, Onondaga Lake Park, Liverpool, NY 13088. Mailing Address: 106 Lake Dr., Liverpool, NY 13088-5118. Tel.: 315-453-6715; 6712. Fax: 315-453-6764.
E-mail: olp@ongov.net
Web Site: www.onondagacountyparks.com/parks/olp/salt-museum.php
Founded: 1934.
Congressional District: 27
Key Personnel: Park Supt., Dale Grinolds; Museum Shop Mgr., Rhoda Sikes.
Personnel Profile: Part-Time Paid 2; Part-Time Volunteers 1.
Governing Authority: county. Dept. of Parks & Recreation. Tax-exempt.
Historic Site: salt block; reconstruction & exhibit gallery.
Collections: paintings; photographs; manuscripts; documents; tools; vehicles; technical & social history of Onondaga; central New York's 19th & 20th-century salt industry.
Research Fields: salt manufacturing industry of Central New York in the 19th & early 20th centuries.
Facilities: library. Museum-related items for sale.
Activities: guided tours; permanent exhibits; craft demonstrations; lectures.
Publications: book, Salt: A History of Salt Manufacturing in Onondaga County; teacher resource packets.
Hours & Admission Prices: mid-May to mid-Oct. daily 1-6. No charge; donations accepted. ♿
Attendance: 20,000 (accurate)
Membership: Individual $15; Family $25; Patron $50; Corporate $100.

Livingston Manor

CATSKILL FLY FISHING CENTER & MUSEUM, (M), 1031 Old Rte. 17, Livingston Manor, NY 12758. Mailing Address: P.O. Box 1295, Livingston Manor, NY 12758-1295. Tel.: 845-439-4810. Fax: 845-439-3387.
E-mail: flyfish@catskill.net
Web Site: www.cffcm.net
Founded: 1981.
Congressional District: 28
Key Personnel: Exec. Dir., Jim Krul; Pres. (V), Miriam Stone; Vice Pres., Jorie Andrews; Vice Pres., Luke Edwards; Treas., Frederick Eck; Office Mgr. & Museum Shop Mgr., Susan C. Krupp.
Personnel Profile: Full-Time Paid 1; Full-Time Volunteers 2; Part-Time Paid 5; Part-Time Volunteers 5.
Governing Authority: nonprofit organization. Tax-exempt: 501(c)(3).
Fly Fishing Museum.
Collections: memorabilia & history of fly fishing.
Major Exhibits: Hall of Fame, Fly Fishing, 1/10-10/10/10; Fly Fishing in Non Fishing Advertising, 3/28/10-12/30/10; Dead Fish, 3/28/10-12/30/10; Fishing Postcards, 3/28/10-12/30/10; Flies from Sweden, 3/28/10-3/20/11.
Research Fields: preserving the history of fly fishing.
Facilities: visitors center; education building; outdoor pavilion; nature trail; picnic tables; trout stream.
Activities: traveling exhibitions; on-site exhibitions; formal education programs for children, adults & handicapped persons; fly casting & rod-building demonstrations. Museum Sponsors: Fisherman's Flea Market; Casting Tournament; Annual Fund Raising Auction.
Publications: monthly newsletter, Castabout.
Hours & Admission Prices: April-Oct. daily 10-4; Nov.-March Tues.-Fri. 10-1, Sat. 10-4. Adults $3; members no charge. Closed New Year's Day; Thanksgiving; Christmas. ♿

Attendance: 9,000 (accurate)
Membership: Student $15; Individual $35; Family $60; Sustaining Member $100; Patron $250; Benefactor $1,000.

Lockport

NIAGARA COUNTY HISTORICAL SOCIETY DBA THE HISTORY CENTER OF NIAGARA, 215 Niagara St., Lockport, NY 14094-2605. Tel.: 716-434-7433. Fax: 716-434-3309.
Web Site: niagarahistory.org
Founded: 1921.
Congressional District: 38
Key Personnel: C.E.O. & Cur., Melissa L. Dunlap; Registrar, Linda B. Covell; Dir. Erie Canal Discovery Center, Dir. Devel. Niagara County Historical Society, Douglas V. Farley; Education Coord. & Asst. Dir., Ann Marie Linnabery.
Personnel Profile: Full-Time Paid 3; Part-Time Volunteers 45; Interns 3.
Governing Authority: nonprofit organization. Parent Institution: Niagara County Historical Society, Inc. Branch Museums: Erie Canal Discovery Center, 24 Church St., Lockport, NY; Col. William Bond/Jesse Hawley House, 143 Ontario St., Lockport, NY. Tel.: 716-439-0431. Tax-exempt: 501(c)(3).
History Museum.
Collections: Niagara area artifacts; Civil War artifacts; Iroquois Indian culture; medical room; toys; dolls; military; pioneer kitchen; paintings; law office; fire fighting equipment; barn; furniture; glassware; Erie Canal artifacts. Historic House: 1824 Col. Bond/Jesse Hawley house furnished with Empire period furnishings.
Research Fields: local history of Niagara County; genealogy; business history.
Facilities: 600-vol. library of historical & genealogical material, vertical files, directories, history publications available for use on premises; reading room; auditorium; Erie Canal Discovery Center.
Activities: guided tours; monthly program meetings; permanent & temporary exhibitions; educational programs in conjunction with area schools; summer youth programs; Erie Canal programming; Erie Canal movie; local history DVDs.
Publications: bimonthly newsletter; DVDs.
Hours & Admission Prices: Niagara County Historical Society: Mon.-Sat. 9-5. Closed holidays. Erie Canal Discovery Center: May-Oct. daily 9-5. Col. Bond/Jessee Hawley House: July-Dec. Mon.-Wed. by appointment. Fee varies per site.
Attendance: 21,600 (accurate)
Membership: Individual $15; Family $20; Business $35; Life $250.

Long Island City

DORSKY GALLERY, 11-03 45th Ave., at corner of 11th St., Long Island City, NY 11101-5109. Tel.: 718-937-6317.
Art Gallery.
Collections: works by contemporary artists.
Facilities: 1,200 sq. ft. exhibit space.
Hours & Admission Prices: Thurs.-Mon. 11-6; other times by appointment.

FISHER LANDAU CENTER FOR ART, 38-27 30th St., Long Island City, NY 11101-2716. Tel.: 718-937-0727.
Art Center.
Collections: works of contemporary art.
Hours & Admission Prices: Thurs.-Mon. 12-5. No charge.

ISAMU NOGUCHI GARDEN MUSEUM, (M), 9-01 33rd Rd., (@ Vernon Blvd.), Long Island City, NY 11106. Mailing Address: 32-37 Vernon Blvd., Long Island City, NY 11106-4926. Tel.: 718-204-7088. Fax: 718-278-2348.
E-mail: museum@noguchi.org
Web Site: www.noguchi.org
Founded: 1985.
Congressional District: 9
Key Personnel: Chm., Samuel Sachs, II; Dir., Jenny Dixon; Dir. Devel., Jennifer Burlenski; Head Education, Heather Brady; Finance Mgr., Zehava Fishman; Admin. Dir., Amy Hau; Registrar, Larry Giacoletti; Dir. Collections Cur., Bonnie Rychlak; Museum Shop Mgr., Peter Scibetta.
Personnel Profile: Full-Time Paid 21; Part-Time Paid 21; Interns 2.
Governing Authority: nonprofit organization. Parent Institution: Isamu Noguchi Foundation and Garden Museum. Tax-exempt: 501(c)(3).
Art Museum: housed in former studio of Isamu Noguchi.
Collections: sculpture; models; writings; drawings; photographic video & audio documentation of works by Noguchi.
Major Exhibits: Noguchi Reinstalled, 11/09-10/24/10; On Becoming an Artist, 11/17/10-4/11.
Research Fields: life & works of Isamu Noguchi.
Facilities: outdoor sculpture garden.
Activities: education programs; public programs; tours in Japanese.
Publications: catalogue of collection, exhibition brochures & catalogues; seasonal calendar.
Hours & Admission Prices: Wed.-Fri. 10-5, Sat.-Sun. 11-6. Adults $10, students & seniors $5; discounts to AAM & ICOM members and employees of NYC Museum Council Institutions. Pay what you wish 1st Fri. of month. ♿
Attendance: 26,000 (estimated)
Membership: Single $75; Dual $150.

LAGUARDIA AND WAGNER ARCHIVES, LaGuardia Community College, 31-10 Thomson Ave., Rm. E-238, Long Island City, NY 11101-3007. Tel.: 718-482-5065. Fax: 718-482-5069.
E-mail: richardli@lagcc.cuny.edu
Web Site: www.laguardiawagnerarchive.lagcc.cuny.edu
Founded: 1981.
Congressional District: 9
Key Personnel: Dir., Richard K. Lieberman; Archivist, Douglas DiCarlo.
Personnel Profile: Full-Time Paid 9; Part-Time Paid 5.
Governing Authority: Parent Institution: City University of New York. Tax-exempt.
History Museum.
Collections: 20th-century New York City; papers of Mayors Fiorello H. LaGuardia, Robert F. Wagner, Abraham D. Beame & Edward I. Koch, records of New York City Housing Authority & the piano maker Steinway & Sons; Queens local history; NY City Council.
Research Fields: 20th-century New York City political & social history.
Facilities: library relating to New York City history & social history available to the public; 18 exhibit museum on the history of New York City; archives.
Activities: group tours available.
Publications: brochure; annual calendar; fourth grade curriculum; Finding Aids for the Fiorello H. LaGuardia, Robert F. Wagner & New York City Housing Authority collections, Abraham D. Beame & Steinway & Sons; museum guide.
Hours & Admission Prices: Exhibits: Mon.-Fri. 7am-10pm, Sat.-Sun. 7-5. Research & Archives: Summer: Mon.-Thurs. 9:30-4:30; Fall, Winter & Spring: Mon.-Fri. 9:30-4:30. No charge. Closed major holidays. ♿

THE MUSEUM FOR AFRICAN ART, 36-01 43rd Ave., Long Island City, NY 11101-1736. Tel.: 718-784-7700. Fax: 718-784-7718.
Web Site: www.africanart.org
Founded: 1984.
Congressional District: 17
Key Personnel: Pres., Elsie McCabe Thompson; Bd. Co-Chm. (V), Jonathan Green; Bd. Co-Chm. (V), Onuoha Odim; Sr. Advisor to Pres., Jerome Vogel; Deputy Dir., Kenita Lloyd; Chief Cur., Enid Schildkrout; Devel. Assoc., Erika Woods; Devel. Assoc., Claire Hoffman; Curatorial Assoc., Donna Ghelerter; Asst. Cur., Lisa Binder; Assoc. Dir. Education, Nathaniel Johnson, Jr.; Traveling Exhibition Coord., Brendan Wattenberg; Registrar, Katherine Caiazza; Education Coord. & Security, Lawrence Ekechi; Controller, Michelle Pinedo; Publications Mgr., Carol Braide; Accountant, Idalia Caijas; Sr. Devel. Officer, Margo Donaldson; Sr. Devel. Assoc., Nicolet Gatewood; Mgr. Operations & Administration, Bridget Foley; Education Assoc., Dana Elmquist.
Personnel Profile: Full-Time Paid 19; Full-Time Volunteers 45; Part-Time Paid 2; Part-Time Volunteers 15; Interns 3.
Governing Authority: nonprofit organization. Tax-exempt: 501(c)(3).
Museum for African Art.
Collections: paintings; photographs; sculpture.
Research Fields: traditional & contemporary African art.
Facilities: Publications for sale.
Activities: guided tours; lectures; organized educational programs; docent program; loan & traveling exhibitions.
Publications: brochures; exhibition catalogues: African Masterpieces from the Musee de l'Homme; Yoruba: Nine Centuries of African Art & Thought; Sets, Series & Ensembles in African Art; Likeness & Beyond: Portraits from Africa & the World; Closeup: Lessons in the Art of Seeing African Sculpture; Aesthetics of African Art: Perspectives, Angles of African Art; African Masterpieces from Munich; Art/Artifact: Art of Collecting African Art; Africa & the Renaissance; Wild Spirits Strong Medicine; Africa Explores: 20th-Century African Art; Faces of the Gods: Art & Altars of Africa and the African Americans; Exhibitionism: Museums and African Art; Animals in African Art: From the Familiar to the Marvelous; Secrecy: African Art that Conceals and Reveals; Western Artists/African Art; Fusion: West African Artists at the Venice Biennale; Home & the World: Architectural Sculpture by Two Contemporary African Artists; Exhibition-ism: Museums & African Art; Animals in African Art: From the Familiar to the Marvelous; Memory: Luba Art & the Making of History; Art of the Baga: A Drama of Cultural Reinvention; Art that Heals: The Image as Medicine in Ethiopia; African Faces, African Figures: The Arman Collection; Hair in

African Art and Culture; Liberated Voices: Contemporary from South Africa; A Congo Chronicle: Patrice Lumumba in Urban Art; In the Presence of Spirits: Selections from the National Museum of Ethnology, Lisbon; African Forms: Addendum; Bamana: The Art of Existence in Mali; Facing the Mask; Material Differences: Art and Identity in Africa; Looking Both Ways: Art of the Contemporary African Diaspora; Where Gods and Mortals Meet: Continuity and Renewal in Urhobo Art; Personal Affects: Power and Poetics in Contemporary South African Art; Resonance from the Past: African Sculpture from the New Orleans Museum of Art; Grass Roots: African Origins of an American Art; Desert Jewels: North African Jewelry and Photography from the Xavier Guerrand-Hermes Collection.
Hours & Admission Prices: Office: Mon.-Fri. 10-6. See Web site for exhibition hours & locations. ♿
Attendance: 80,000
Membership: Student & Senior $35; Individual $50; Family & Dual $75; Associate $125; Supporter $250; Contributor $500; Friend $1,000; Benefactor Benefits $2,500; President's Circle Benefits $5,000.

P.S. 1 CONTEMPORARY ART CENTER, 22-25 Jackson Ave., Long Island City, NY 11101-4309. Tel.: 718-784-2084. Fax: 718-482-9454.
E-mail: mail@ps1.org
Web Site: www.ps1.org
Founded: 1971.
Congressional District: 9
Key Personnel: Dir. Devel., Todd Bishop.
Personnel Profile: Full-Time Paid 14; Part-Time Paid 40; Interns 11.
Governing Authority: nonprofit. Parent Institution: The Museum of Modern Art, NY. Tax-exempt: 501(c)(3).
Contemporary Art Museum: housed in 19th-century Romanesque Revival schoolhouse.
Collections: site-specific installation pieces by James Turrell, Richard Serra and Alan Saret, Pipilotti Rist & Julian Schabel.
Facilities: 125,000 sq. ft. exhibit space.
Activities: guided tours; lectures; films; concerts; dance; organized educational programs; traveling exhibitions; National & International Studio Programs.
Publications: exhibition catalogues; artist publications.
Hours & Admission Prices: P.S. 1: Wed.-Mon. 12-6. Suggested Donation: adults $5, students & senior citizens $2; members no charge. Closed New Year's Day; Memorial Day; Independence Day; Thanksgiving; Christmas. ♿
Attendance: 150,000
Membership: Student & Artist $25-$49; Regular $50-$99; Sustaining $100-$499; Contributing $500-$999; Patron $1,000-$2,499; Benefactor $2,500-$4,999; Leader $5,000-$9,999; President $10,000 & up.

SCULPTURE CENTER, (M), 44-19 Purves St., Long Island City, NY 11101-2907. Tel.: 718-361-1750. Fax: 718-786-9336.
E-mail: mceruti@sculpture-center.org
Web Site: www.sculpture-center.org
Key Personnel: Exec. Dir., Mary Ceruti; Mgr. Operations, Katie Bode; Asst. Dir. Devel. & Admin., Alexandra Lane; Cur., Fionn Meade
Art Gallery.
Collections: contemporary sculpture.
Activities: educational programs.
Hours & Admission Prices: Thurs.-Mon. 12-6. Suggested Donation: $5.

SOCRATES SCULPTURE PARK, 32-01 Vernon Blvd. (at Broadway), Long Island City, NY 11106. Mailing Address: P.O. Box 6259, Long Island City, NY 11106-0259. Tel.: 718-956-1819. Fax: 718-626-1533.
E-mail: info@socratessculpturepark.org
Web Site: socratessculpturepark.org
Founded: 1986.
Congressional District: 14
Key Personnel: Dir., Alyson Baker; Pres. (V), Mark diSuvero; Dir. Public Programs & Community Rels., Tara Sansone; Dir. Devel. & Communications, Ellen Staller; Mgr. Exhibition Programs, Marychris Ty; Mgr. Education Programs, Katherine Novick.
Personnel Profile: Full-Time Paid 4; Part-Time Paid 6; Part-Time Volunteers 20; Interns 2.
Governing Authority: Tax-exempt.
Sculpture Park.
Collections: sculpture garden; contemporary art.
Facilities: working artist studio.
Activities: classes, film screenings & special events.
Publications: exhibition catalogues.
Hours & Admission Prices: Daily 10 to sunset. No charge. ♿
Attendance: 85,000 (estimated)

Lowville

LEWIS COUNTY HISTORICAL SOCIETY MUSEUM, 7552 S. State St., Lowville, NY 13367-1529. Mailing Address: 7552 S. State St., P.O. Box 446, Lowville, NY 13367-0446. Tel.: 315-376-8957.
E-mail: lewiscountyhistoricalsociety@hotmail.com
Web Site: www.frontiernet.net/~lehs/
Founded: 1926.
Congressional District: 26
Key Personnel: Exec. Dir. & County Historian, Lisa Becker; Pres., Helen McHale; Vice Pres., Christopher Miller; Treas., David Allen; Gift Shop Chm., Helen McHale.
Personnel Profile: Part-Time Paid 2; Part-Time Volunteers 1; Interns 2.
Governing Authority: nonprofit organization. Tax-exempt: 501(c)(3).
History Museum.
Collections: archaeology; costumes; documents; family heirlooms; geology; history; military; photographs; technology; local history; manuscripts.
Research Fields: local history.
Facilities: 500-vol. library of diaries, journals, local and general history books, historical periodicals, museum maintenance publications, antique books available for research on premises; photocopies of original documents; Lewis County Historian's Room is housed at this facility: open for general research.
Activities: guided tours; lectures; films; inter-museum loan; permanent & temporary exhibitions.
Publications: Journal of the Lewis County Historical Society; newsletter, Artifacts.
Hours & Admission Prices: Historical Society: Tues.-Sat. 10-4. Historian's Office: June to mid-Oct. Tues.-Thurs. 10-3; mid-Oct. to early June Wed. 10-3. No charge; donations accepted. Closed federal holidays. ♿
Attendance: 1,900 (estimated)
Membership: Individual $25; Family $35; Sustaining $70; Life $500.

Lyons

WAYNE COUNTY HISTORICAL SOCIETY'S MUSEUM OF WAYNE COUNTY HISTORY, (M), 21 Butternut St., Lyons, NY 14489-1124. Tel.: 315-946-4943. Fax: 315-946-0069.
E-mail: info@waynehistory.org
Web Site: www.waynehistory.org
Formerly: Wayne County Historical Society
Founded: 1946.
Congressional District: 29
Key Personnel: Exec. Dir., Larry Ann Evans; Museum Mgr., Mary Erle; Educator, Erin Gardner.
Personnel Profile: Full-Time Paid 2; Part-Time Paid 1; Part-Time Volunteers 10.
Governing Authority: Wayne County Historical Society. Tax-exempt: 501(c)(3).
Historical Society Museum.
Collections: glass & ceramics; local history artifacts; early criminology; agriculture. Historic Houses: 1854 sheriff's residence; 1854 county jail; 1913 sheriff's barn.
Research Fields: local history.
Facilities: 1,500-vol. general library available on premises; reading room. Museum-related items for sale.
Activities: permanent, temporary & traveling exhibitions; school loan service; lecture programs. Museum Sponsors: holiday boutique; annual dinner; dramatic reading.
Publications: quarterly, Wayne County Historical Society Newsletter; Index to History of Pioneer Settlement of Phelps & Gorham's Purchase; Wayne County Game-The Battle of Sodus Point - War of 1812; Seth Cole Exhibit Catalog. Wayne County: The Aesthetic Heritage of a Rural Area; The Fruit Industry in Wayne County, New York 1823-1984; Wayne County: Looking Back, 1988; Annals of Arcadia; The Sodus Shaker Community; Wayne County Turning the Century; exhibit catalog; Pre-History of the Savannah, New York Area; The History of the Wayne Co. Jail, 1856-1960; Pen Pals from the Past subscription letters from 1800s on Erie Canal, Letters from the Wayne County Jail, Underground Railroad & Early Wayne County; Remembering Wayne: A Pictorial View of the People, Places & Pastimes of Wayne County, NY; ABC Book of Wayne County; Wayne County Activity Book.
Hours & Admission Prices: April-Oct. Tues.-Sat. 10-4; Nov.-March Tues.-Fri. 10-4, Sat. 10-1. Adults $4, children $2; members no charge. Closed legal holidays.
Attendance: 8,000 (accurate)
Membership: Drumlin $25; Cobblestone $30; Old Jail $35; Clyde Glass & Lyons Pottery $50 & up; Peppermint $75; Chimney Bluffs $100; Erie Canal $500 & up. Business: Bronze $100; Silver $250; Gold $500; Platinum $1,000.

Macedon

MACEDON HISTORICAL SOCIETY, INC., 1185 Macedon Center Rd., Macedon, NY 14502. Mailing Address: P.O. Box 303, Macedon, NY 14502-0303. Tel.: 385-388-0629.
Web Site: www.macedonhistoricalsociety.org
Founded: 1962.
Congressional District: 29
Key Personnel: Pres. (V), David Taber; Vice Pres., Charles Packard; Cur., Sally Millick.
Governing Authority: society. Tax-exempt.
Historical Society Museum.
Collections: Quaker schoolhouse artifacts; personal artifacts; scrapbooks. Historic Buildings: 1853 Macedon Academy; 1868 Orthodox Quaker Church, meeting house.
Activities: temporary exhibitions.
Publications: Pioneers of Macedon, Bicentennial Edition 1975-1976; Pioneers of Macedon, 1912.
Hours & Admission Prices: Summer: call for hours; other times by appointment. No charge; donations accepted. ♿
Membership: Individual $2; Couple $3.

Mahopac

THE PUTNAM CHILDREN'S DISCOVERY CENTER, 854 Rte. 6, Mahopac, NY 10541-1721. Mailing Address: P.O. Box 222, Carmel, NY 10512-0222. Tel.: 845-621-1260. Fax: 845-276-2078.
E-mail: info@discoveryctr.org
Web Site: www.discoveryctr.org
Key Personnel: Exec. Dir., Janice Newman
Children's Museum.
Collections: hands-on exhibits.
Activities: outreach programs; scout month; educational programs; birthday parties; workshops.
Hours & Admission Prices: Call for hours.

Malone

FRANKLIN COUNTY HISTORICAL & MUSEUM SOCIETY, 51 Milwaukee St., Malone, NY 12953-1916. Mailing Address: P.O. Box 388, Malone, NY 12953-0388. Tel.: 518-483-2750.
E-mail: fchms@franklinhistory.org
Web Site: www.franklinhistory.org
Founded: 1903.
Congressional District: 23
Key Personnel: Pres. (V), Timothy Hullquist; Exec. Dir., Anne Werley Smallman; Treas., Margaret McCarthy.
Personnel Profile: Part-Time Paid 1; Part-Time Volunteers 34.
Governing Authority: society. Parent Institution: Franklin County Historical & Museum Society. Subsidiary Institutions: Schryer Center for Historical & Genealogical Research; House of History. Tax-exempt: 501(c)(3).
County History Museum.
Collections: headquarter papers of the 16th Civil War Regiment of New York State Volunteers; history; agriculture; period rooms: memorial room, 1877-1881 V.P. William Almon Wheeler Room; 1,000 items of clothing from 1830-present; copy of first County newspaper; reproduction of old documents; early pictures of the area; local history books.
Research Fields: Franklin County.
Facilities: 500-vol. library of general & local history; maps available for research on premises. Farmer Boy (Almanzo Wilder) books & booklets & other museum-related items for sale.
Activities: guided tours; lectures; temporary exhibitions; genealogical services; formally organized education programs for children; summer concert series. Museum Sponsors: Museum Day craft demonstrations for 4th grade students of Franklin County; craft demonstrations for groups by appointment & at Museum Open Houses.
Publications: annual periodical, Franklin Historical Review; Architecture from the Adirondack Foothills; Franklin County Family Album.
Hours & Admission Prices: Research: June-Aug. Tues.-Fri. 1-4; Winter: by appointment. Museum Tours: by appointment. Tours: adults $5; discounts to AASLH members; members no charge. Research: adults $10; members no charge. Closed holidays. ♿
Attendance: 1,200 (estimated)
Membership: Individual $20; Family $25; Patron $50; Business $100; Benefactor $500.

Mamaroneck

LARCHMONT HISTORICAL SOCIETY, 740 W. Boston Post Rd., Ste. 301, Mamaroneck, NY 10543-3345. Mailing Address: P.O. Box 742, Larchmont, NY 10538-0742. Tel.: 914-381-2239 & 834-5136.
E-mail: lhs@larchmonthistory.org
Web Site: www.larchmonthistory.org
Founded: 1980.
Congressional District: 18
Key Personnel: Pres. (V), Colette Rodbell; Treas., Jim Sweeney; Archivist, Lynne Crowley; Membership Coord., Lauren Gottfried.
Personnel Profile: Part-Time Paid 1; Part-Time Volunteers 10; Interns 2.
Governing Authority: private; nonprofit organization. Tax-exempt: 501(c)(3).
Historical Society Museum.
Collections: history of village & postal district of Larchmont, NY.
Research Fields: architectural sites survey; June Freeman Allen costume collection (1865-1930); Flint family papers.
Facilities: 400-vol. library; 28 sq. ft. exhibit space; archives.
Activities: guided tours; lectures; temporary exhibitions; special events. Annual Event: Spring House Tour.
Publications: monthly newsletter, Gazebo Gazette; books & booklets on Larchmont subjects.
Hours & Admission Prices: Tues. & Thurs. 9-2; other times by appointment. No charge. ♿
Attendance: 300 (estimated)
Membership: Senior & Student $5; Individual $15; Family $25; Institutional $25; Sustaining $50; Life $150.

Manhasset

HISTORICAL SOCIETY OF THE TOWN OF NORTH HEMPSTEAD, 200 Plandome Rd., Manhasset, NY 11030-2326. Mailing Address: P.O. Box 3000, Manhasset, NY 11030-3000. Tel.: 516-869-7646.
Web Site: www.northhempstead.com
Founded: 1963.
Congressional District: 6
Key Personnel: Pres., Hon. Dolores Sedacca.
Governing Authority: society.
Historical Society Museum.
Collections: agriculture; history; arboretum; aviary; botany; herbarium; Indian artifacts; transportation; manuscripts.
Facilities: library of books, maps, photographs & clippings available for use by appointment.
Activities: guided tours; lectures; formally organized education programs for children; inter-museum loan; permanent, temporary & traveling exhibitions.
Hours & Admission Prices: by appointment. No charge.
Membership: Student $3; Individual $5; Contributing $10; Sustaining $25; Corporate $50; Life $100; Life Corporate $1,000.

SCIENCE MUSEUM OF LONG ISLAND, Leeds Pond Preserve, 1526 N. Plandome Rd., Manhasset, NY 11030. Mailing Address: P.O. Box 908, Plandome, NY 11030-0908. Tel.: 516-627-9400, ext. 11. Fax: 516-365-8927.
E-mail: info@smli.org
Web Site: smli.org
Founded: 1963.
Congressional District: 3
Key Personnel: Dir., John Loret, Ph.D.; C.E.O., Ronni Graf; Pres. (V), Eugene Petracca, Jr.
Personnel Profile: Full-Time Paid 3; Part-Time Paid 15; Part-Time Volunteers 18.
Governing Authority: nonprofit organization. Tax-exempt: 501(c)(3).
Science Center.
Collections: natural history artifacts; live animal exhibits; physics & technology exhibits.
Research Fields: technology; alternative energy; aquaculture, hydroponics.
Facilities: laboratories; classrooms; wildlife preserve; pond. Museum-related items for sale.
Activities: school science programs; adult education & lecture series; lecture demonstrations; workshops for pre-kindergarten-junior high school students; advanced study & research programs for high school students; barrier-free nature trails; experimental garden with greenhouse; films; summer science studies program; after-school workshops; weekend family workshops.
Publications: quarterly newsletter, workshop brochures.
Hours & Admission Prices: Office: Mon.-Fri. 9-3:30. Call for information on charges & activities; discount to museum members. ♿
Attendance: 15,000 (estimated)
Membership: Senior Citizen $25; Individual $40; Family $65; Sponsor $70; Patron $125; Corporate $250; Life $500.

Manlius

MANLIUS HISTORICAL SOCIETY AND MUSEUM, 101 Scoville Ave., Manlius, NY 13104. Mailing Address: P.O. Box 28, Manlius, NY 13104-0028. Tel.: 315-682-6660. Fax: 315-682-6660.
E-mail: mhsdirector@aol.com
Web Site: www.manliushistory.org
Founded: 1976.
Congressional District: 33
Key Personnel: Dir., Elizabeth A. Smith; Pres., Bonny Moser; Business Officer, Ruth Wood.
Personnel Profile: Part-Time Paid 1; Part-Time Volunteers 8.
Governing Authority: society; nonprofit organization. Tax-exempt.
Historical Society Museum.
Collections: farm & carpentry tools; wheelwright implements & tools; operating blacksmith shop; colonial ironware; herb garden; late 19th-century medical tools & doctor's pharmacy; early 20th-century toys; locally-made products; 3 locally made antique violins made between 1870 & 1900; documents related to school, church & personal histories.
Research Fields: town history.
Facilities: 600-vol. library of books & documents on local history available for research by appointment on premises; reading room.
Activities: guided tours; lectures; hobby workshops; docent program or council; loan, permanent & temporary exhibitions.
Publications: quarterly newsletter, The Seraph; People & Places: Fayetteville, Manlius, Minoa & Neighbors, Vol. I, II & III.
Hours & Admission Prices: Museum: Sat. 11-3; groups & other times by appointment. Research Center: Mon.-Thurs. 9-2. No charge; donations accepted. Closed Easter; Thanksgiving; Christmas.
Attendance: 2,200 (estimated)
Membership: Senior Citizen $20; Individual $25; Family $45; Sustaining $75; Partner $125; Benefactor $250; Patron $500.

Marbletown

ULSTER COUNTY HISTORICAL SOCIETY, 2682 Rte. 209, Marbletown, NY Mailing Address: P.O. Box 279, Stone Ridge, NY 12484-0279. Tel.: 845-338-5614.
E-mail: director@bevierhousemuseum.org
Web Site: www.ulstercountyhistoricalsociety.org
Founded: 1939.
Congressional District: 96
Key Personnel: Dir., Jessica Phinney; Pres., Suzanne Hauspurg.
Personnel Profile: Part-Time Paid 2; Part-Time Volunteers 5.
Governing Authority: nonprofit organization. Tax-exempt.
Bevier House: stone farm house owned by the Bevier family from 1715-1938; registered county historic landmark & National Historic Register.
Collections: furniture; paintings; ceramics; decorative arts; Civil War items; tools.
Facilities: 250-vol. library of monographs, periodicals (on local history) & Ulster County manuscripts from 1670 to c.1880 available by appointment.
Activities: guided tours; lectures; occasional loan exhibitions.
Publications: newsletter published three times annually, Ulster County Gazette.
Hours & Admission Prices: May-Oct. Thurs.-Sun. 12-5. Adults $5, seniors $4, children $3; AAM & ICOM members no charge.
Attendance: 500 (estimated)
Membership: Student & Senior $15; Individual $25; Household $40; Patron $50.

Marcellus

MARCELLUS HISTORICAL SOCIETY, 18 North St., Marcellus, NY 13108. Mailing Address: P.O. Box 165, Marcellus, NY 13108-0165.
Founded: 1960.
Congressional District: 33
Key Personnel: Pres., Peg Nolan; Vice Pres., Douglas Nightingale; Treas., Hollis Abbott; Sec., Carrie Beth Pottinger.
Personnel Profile: Part-Time Volunteers 6.
Governing Authority: society. Tax-exempt.
History Museum: housed in early 1830s house.
Collections: household & farm utensils; treadmill; guns; china; agricultural implements; furniture; microfilm of Marcellus Observer Newspaper 1879-present day; historic documents, photographs, business items, genealogies.
Research Fields: local history.
Facilities: meeting room.
Activities: guided tours; permanent exhibitions; monthly meetings with guest speakers.
Publications: advertising flyer with brief history; quarterly newsletter.
Hours & Admission Prices: Sun.-Mon. 1-3, Tues. 7-9, Thurs. 1-4; other times by appointment. No charge; donations accepted. Closed holidays. ♿
Attendance: 300 (estimated)
Membership: Senior & Student $4; Individual $5; Family $12; Senior & Student Sustaining $20; Individual Sustaining $25; Family Sustaining $60.

Marilla

MARILLA HISTORICAL SOCIETY MUSEUM, 1810 Two Rod Rd., Marilla, NY 14102. Mailing Address: P.O. Box 36, Marilla, NY 14102-0036. Tel.: 716-652-1827 & 7608.
Founded: 1960.
Congressional District: 38
Key Personnel: Pres., Mary Beth Serafin; Vice Pres., Cindy Petrinec; Treas., John Foss; Sec., Judy Mees.
Governing Authority: society. Tax-exempt.
Local History Museum.
Collections: local history; period artifacts.
Facilities: library of books on local history available for use on premises.
Activities: informal programs for children; permanent exhibitions.
Hours & Admission Prices: Sept.-June Tues. 7pm-9pm, 3rd Sun. of month 2-4. No charge; donations accepted. ♿
Attendance: 200 (estimated)
Membership: Children & Senior Citizens $5; Regular $7.

Marlboro

GOMEZ MILL HOUSE MUSEUM AND HISTORIC SITE, (M), 11 Mill House Rd., Marlboro, NY 12542-6514. Mailing Address: 15 W. 16th St., New York City, NY 10011-6301. Tel.: 845-236-3126.
E-mail: gomezmillhouse@juno.com
Web Site: www.gomez.org
Founded: 1979.
Congressional District: 28
Key Personnel: Exec. Dir., Ruth K. Abrahams; Pres. (V), Robert Jacobs, Jr.; Museum Site Mgr., Ellen Healy.
Personnel Profile: Full-Time Paid 2; Part-Time Paid 2; Part-Time Volunteers 5.
Governing Authority: private; nonprofit organization. Foundation Executive Offices, 15 W. 16th St., 6th Fl., New York City, NY 10011. Tel.: 212-294-8329. Tax-exempt: ST-119-1.
Historic House & Living History Museum.
Collections: decorative arts; furniture; artifacts; paintings; documents.
Research Fields: American history; paper history; Jewish American history.
Facilities: Dard Hunter Paper Mill.
Activities: public programs; tours; papermaking demonstrations.
Hours & Admission Prices: mid-April to Oct. Wed.-Sun. 10-4. Adults $10, seniors $5, students $2; discount to groups, WNET, AAM, ICOM & Channel 13 members; members & children under 6 no charge. Closed Easter; Thanksgiving; Jewish holidays; Christmas; national holidays.
Attendance: 5,000 (estimated)
Membership: Student & Senior $35; General $50; Gift Memberships: Associate $250; Sponsor $500; Patron $1,000; Benefactor $2,500; Guardian $5,000; Champion $10,000 & up.

Mastic Beach

FIRE ISLAND NATIONAL SEASHORE, William Floyd Estate, 245 Park Dr., Mastic Beach, NY 11951. Mailing Address: 120 Laurel St., Patchogue, NY 11772-3596. Tel.: 631-399-2030. Fax: 631-399-0017.
Web Site: www.nps.gov/fiis
Founded: 1964.
Congressional District: 1 & 2
Key Personnel: Cur., Steven Czarniecki.
Governing Authority: federal. Administered by the National Park Service United States Dept. of the Interior.
National Park.
Collections: fauna & flora. Historic House: located at Mastic Beach on mainland, furnished c.1700s estate of William Floyd.
Research Fields: beach environment.
Facilities: Visitor Center: 1,000-vol. library of natural history available for research by appointment; nature trails; picnic area; campsites; wildlife refuge & bird sanctuary; boardwalk trail for handicapped. Natural history-related publications for sale.
Activities: guided tours; lectures; films; gallery talks; demonstrations; wilderness hiking; fishing.
Publications: pamphlets; brochures.
Hours & Admission Prices: Grounds: Memorial Day to Oct. Fri.-Sun. 9-6. William Floyd Estate: Memorial Day to Oct. 8 Fri.-Sun. 10-4. No charge. Closed holidays.
Attendance: 8,000

Medina

MEDINA RAILROAD MUSEUM, 530 West Ave., Medina, NY 14103-1554. Mailing Address: P.O. Box 136, Medina, NY 14103-0136. Tel.: 585-798-6106. Fax: 585-798-1086.
E-mail: office@railroadmuseum.net
Web Site: www.railroadmuseum.net
Founded: 1997.
Congressional District: 26
Key Personnel: Dir., Martin C. Phelps; Pres. (V), James L. Dickinson; Public Rels. & Museum Shop Mgr., Linda Klein; Treas., Hugh F. James.
Personnel Profile: Full-Time Paid 1; Full-Time Volunteers 4; Part-Time Paid 2; Part-Time Volunteers 35.
Governing Authority: private; nonprofit organization. Tax-exempt: 501(c)(3).
Railroad Museum.
Collections: railroad artifacts, memorabilia, photographs, models & toys; firefighting artifacts, memorabilia & toys.
Facilities: 9,300 sq. ft. exhibit space. Museum-related items for sale.
Activities: guided tours; loan exhibitions; broadcast programs. Annual Events: Excursion Train Rides; Day Out With Thomas.
Hours & Admission Prices: Tues.-Sun. 11-5. Adults $6.50, senior citizens $5, students $4, children 2-12 $3; discounts to AAM members; members no charge. Closed Christmas. ♿
Attendance: 33,000 (estimated)
Membership: Individual $20; Family $35; Business $50; Corporate $100.

Middletown

HISTORICAL SOCIETY OF MIDDLETOWN AND THE WALLKILL PRECINCT, INC., 25 East Ave., Middletown, NY 10940-5818. Mailing Address: P.O. Box 34, Middletown, NY 10940-0034. Tel.: 845-342-0941.
E-mail: enjine@aol.com
Founded: 1923.
Congressional District: 26
Key Personnel: Pres. (V), C.E.O. & Cur., Marvin H. Cohen; Sec., Francis Cleary; Treas., Joanne Norbury.
Personnel Profile: Part-Time Volunteers 6.
Governing Authority: society. Tax-exempt: 501(c)(3).
Local History Museum: housed in 1886 building.
Collections: photographs; Indian artifacts; clothing; china; mixed exhibits of historical objects; local genealogy.
Research Fields: city of Middletown, New York & town of Wallkill.
Facilities: 500-vol. library of genealogy & history books available for use on premises by appointment; reading room.
Activities: guided tours; lectures; permanent exhibitions; slides; pictures.
Publications: quarterly newsletter; booklets, The History of Our Society, Music in Middletown 100 Years Ago, The Clemson Story, Sally Sunflower & the Bloomer, History of Orange County Telephone Co., Clemson Park, Memoirs of Dr. Moses Ashby Stivers, Wallkill Academy, Middletown Hotels & Inn Keepers, Churches & Synagogues of Middletown and Nearby Communities, Middletown Theatres, Early Man in Orange County, New York.
Hours & Admission Prices: Wed. 1-5; other times call 845-343-4219 for appointment. No charge.
Attendance: 300 (estimated)
Membership: Regular $12; Couples $17; Institutional $25; Life $100.

THE INTERACTIVE MUSEUM, (M), 23 Center St., Middletown, NY 10940. Mailing Address: P.O. Box 453, Middletown, NY 10940-0453. Tel.: 845-344-3131.
Children's Museum.
Collections: hands-on exhibits.
Activities: permanent & temporary exhibits; educational programs; classes; performances; summer camp; special events.
Hours & Admission Prices: Thurs.-Sat. 1-4, Sun. 2-4.

Millbrook

MILLBROOK SCHOOL, TREVOR ZOO, 131 Millbrook School Rd., Millbrook, NY 12545-4932. Tel.: 845-677-3704. Fax: 845-677-3774.
E-mail: trevorzoo@millbrook.org
Web Site: www.trevorzoo.org
Founded: 1936.
Congressional District: 22
Key Personnel: Dir., Jonathan Meigs; Assoc. Dir., Alan Tousignant; Education, Jane H. Meigs; Animal Care Coord., Jessica Bennett.
Personnel Profile: Full-Time Paid 5; Part-Time Paid 1; Part-Time Volunteers 60; Interns 2.
Governing Authority: secondary school; nonprofit. Parent Institution: Millbrook School. Tax-exempt.
Zoo.
Collections: 160 animals from around the world.
Facilities: over 6 acres.
Activities: Millbrook School students (grades 9-12) are involved with the care of the animals.
Hours & Admission Prices: Daily 8-5. Adults $5, children $3; discounts to groups. Summer Family Pass $40. ♿
Attendance: 22,000 (estimated)

Monroe

MUSEUM VILLAGE, (M), 1010 Rte. 17 M, Monroe, NY 10950-1625. Tel.: 845-782-8248. Fax: 845-782-6432.
E-mail: info@museumvillage.org
Web Site: www.museumvillage.org
Founded: 1950.
Congressional District: 96
Key Personnel: Exec. Dir., Kate Mitchell; Chm. (V), Paul Campanella; Collections Mgr., Chris Cantrell; Education Coord., Lori Siccardi; Museum Shop Mgr., Virginia Mina.
Personnel Profile: Full-Time Paid 4; Part-Time Paid 30; Part-Time Volunteers 25.
Governing Authority: nonprofit organization.
Living History Museum.
Collections: life & work of 19th-century Hudson Valley; recreation of 19th-century village with over 25 buildings; drug store, log cabin, broom shop, natural history museum, firehouse, printshop, farm tools, schoolhouse, candleshop, livery stable, museum, wagon maker, blacksmith, dress exhibit, weave shop, pottery, store exhibit, barber shop, shoemaker, cooperage, energy exhibit.
Research Fields: mid-19th century material culture.
Facilities: 500-vol. library of research books available for use on premises; snack bar; picnic area. Books, crafts & other museum-related items for sale.
Activities: formally organized education program for children; permanent & temporary exhibitions; craft demonstrations; living history re-enactments; special events throughout season.
Publications: newsletter; calendar of special events; exhibit guide; education brochure.
Hours & Admission Prices: April-June Mon.-Fri. 10-2; Sept.-Nov. Mon.-Fri. 10-2, Sat.-Sun. 11-5; July-Aug. Tues.-Sun. 11-5. Adults $10, senior citizens $6, children 3-15 $5; discounts to AASLH partner institutions; members no charge.
Attendance: 30,757 (accurate)
Membership: Individual $40; Dual $55; Family $75; Donor $125; Sponsor $250; Patron $500; Corporate $1,000.

Montauk

MONTAUK POINT LIGHTHOUSE MUSEUM, 2000 Montauk Hwy., Montauk, NY 11954-5600. Tel.: 631-668-2544. Fax: 631-668-2546.
E-mail: keeper@montauklighthouse.com
Web Site: www.montauklighthouse.com
Founded: 1987.
Congressional District: 2
Key Personnel: Dir. Site Management, Tricia Wood; Chm., Treas. & Museum Shop Mgr., Elizabeth L. White.
Personnel Profile: Full-Time Paid 3; Part-Time Paid 27.
Governing Authority: private; nonprofit organization. Parent Institution: Montauk Historical Society, P.O. Box 943, Montauk, NY 11954. Tax-exempt: 501(c)(3).
Lighthouse Museum.
Collections: Fresnel lens; paintings; photographs; maritime artifacts; documents; 19th-20th century lanterns; original document signed by Thomas Jefferson commissioning the Montauk Point Lighthouse under the 2nd Congress; documents by founder, Ezra L'Honmidieu.
Research Fields: erosion control; building maintenance & preservation.
Facilities: library; 1,350 sq. ft. exhibit space; 30-seat theater.
Activities: guided tours; permanent exhibitions; films; formal education programs for adults & children; lectures. Annual Events: Montauk Point Lighthouse Sprint Triathlon & Relay; Lighthouse weekend.
Publications: newspaper, The Beacon; newsletter, Daymark.
Hours & Admission Prices: Call for hours. Adults $8.50, senior citizens $7, children $4; discounts to groups. Children must meet a minimum height requirement of 41 inches. ♿
Attendance: 80,000 (estimated)

Montgomery

BRICK HOUSE, 850 Rte. 17K, Montgomery, NY 12549. Mailing Address: 211 Rte. 416, Montgomery, NY 12549. Tel.: 845-457-4921 & 4905. Fax: 845-457-4906.
E-mail: stucker@co.orange.ny.us

Founded: 1979.
Key Personnel: Park Commissioner, Richard Rose; Dir., Susan Tucker.
Personnel Profile: Full-Time Paid 1; Part-Time Paid 1; Part-Time Volunteers 30.
Governing Authority: county. Orange County Dept. of Parks, Recreation & Conservation, 550 Rte. 416, Montgomery, NY. Tel. 914-294-5151, ext. 1870. Branch Museum: Hill-Hold, Campbell Hall, NY. Tax-exempt.
Historic House: 1768 Georgian style house, built by Nathaniel Hill.
Collections: family homestead furnishings, late 17th-century to present; family papers.
Activities: guided tours.
Publications: brochures; newsletter.
Hours & Admission Prices: mid-May to early Oct. Sat.-Sun. 10-4:30. Family $7, adults $3, children $2; discounts to groups. Closed Memorial Day; Independence Day; Labor Day. ♿
Attendance: 4,000 (accurate)
Membership: Single $15; Family $25; Patron $50.

HILL-HOLD MUSEUM, 128 Rte. 416, Montgomery, NY 12549. Mailing Address: 211 Rte. 416, Montgomery, NY 12549. Tel.: 845-291-2404.
E-mail: stucker@co.orange.ny.us
Founded: 1976.
Key Personnel: Parks Commissioner, Richard Rose; Dir., Susan Tucker.
Governing Authority: county. Affiliated with Orange County Dept. of Parks, Recreation and Conservation, RD 3, Montgomery, NY. Branch: Brick House, Montgomery, NY. Tax-exempt.
Historic House: 1769 Georgian style stone house.
Collections: Hudson Valley furnishings from 17th-century to 1830s.
Research Fields: 19th-century farm life & customs.
Facilities: Museum-related items for sale.
Activities: guided tours. Museum Sponsors: Candlelight Tour in December.
Publications: An Educational Guide to Hill-Hold.
Hours & Admission Prices: mid-May to mid-Oct. Wed.-Sun. 10-4:30. Family $7, adults $3, children $2; groups by appointment. Closed Memorial Day; Independence Day; Labor Day. ♿
Attendance: 8,000
Membership: Individual $15; Family $25; Patron $50 & up.

Montour Falls

SCHUYLER COUNTY HISTORICAL SOCIETY, INC., 108 N. Catharine, Montour Falls, NY 14865. Mailing Address: P.O. Box 651, Montour Falls, NY 14865-0651. Tel.: 607-535-9741.
E-mail: info@schuylerhistory.org
Web Site: www.schuylerhistory.org
Founded: 1960.
Congressional District: 51
Key Personnel: Dir., Andrew E. Tompkins; Pres., Nancy Whipple; Vice Pres., Jerome Smyder; Journal Editor, Glenda Gephart.
Personnel Profile: Part-Time Paid 2; Part-Time Volunteers 12.
Governing Authority: society; nonprofit organization. Tax-exempt.
Local History Museum.
Collections: local history; agriculture; artifacts; costumes; art; archives; toys; Indians; local sanitarium; quilts; music; period clothing; paintings; artifacts from the 1900s: pioneer kitchen; old tools; one-room school; research aides in library.
Research Fields: local history.
Facilities: 1,000-vol. library of local history reference books, pamphlets, scrapbooks & files; available on premises; reading room.
Activities: lectures; formally organized educational programs; temporary exhibits; 7 general meetings with historical programs; permanent exhibits.
Publications: quarterly, Schuyler County Historical Society Journal; pamphlet, Historical Sites of Schuyler County; quarterly Journal.
Hours & Admission Prices: May 2 to mid-Oct. Tues.-Fri. 10-4, Sat. 9-1; mid-Oct to May 1 Tues.-Fri. 10-4; other times by appointment. No charge; donations accepted. Research room: $5 per hour. Closed holidays. ♿
Attendance: 2,000 (accurate)
Membership: Individual $20; Couple $25; Patron $50; Benefactor $100.

Moravia

CAYUGA-OWASCO LAKES HISTORICAL SOCIETY, 14 W. Cayuga, Moravia, NY 13118. Mailing Address: P.O. Box 247, Moravia, NY 13118-0247. Tel.: 315-497-3906.
E-mail: colhs@localnet.com
Web Site: www.colhs.org
Founded: 1966.
Congressional District: 33
Key Personnel: Pres., Roger Phillips; Sec., Sandy Morehouse.
Governing Authority: N.Y. State Charter; nonprofit. Tax-exempt: 501(c)(3).
Local History & Genealogy Museum: housed in pre-1850 History House.
Collections: photos; clothing, household & farm artifacts; family files; manuscripts; cemetery & census microfilm & reader; vital records; newspaper abstracts; Millard Fillmore articles; scrapbooks; maps; genealogies; post cards; early era fossils.
Research Fields: local historic sites; genealogy & local history.
Facilities: library of historical, church & vital records; 800 family data files; microfilm of Moravia newspaper, cemetery & census records, available for research on premises.
Activities: guided tours; lectures; films; genealogical workshops; field trips; permanent & temporary exhibitions.
Publications: newsletter.
Hours & Admission Prices: June-Aug. Mon. 9-12, Sat. 10-2; Sept.-May Mon. 9-12; other times by appointment. No charge; donations accepted. Closed holidays. ♿
Attendance: 400 (estimated)
Membership: Individual $10; Family $15.

Mount Kisco

COUNTY OF WESTCHESTER, DEPARTMENT OF PARKS, RECREATION AND CONSERVATION, 25 Moore Ave., Mount Kisco, NY 10549-3112. Tel.: 914-864-7000 & 366-5109 (Lighthouse). Fax: 914-864-7053.
Web Site: www.westchestergov.com/parks
Founded: 1961.
Key Personnel: County Exec., Andrew J. Spano; Commissioner, Joseph Stout; Naturalist, Beth Herr.
Governing Authority: county. Branch Facilities: Bridge Gallery, 2nd Fl., County Office Building; Muscoot Park Interpretive Farm Tel. 914-864-7282; Trailside Nature Museum Tel. 914-864-7322; Marshlands Conservancy Tel. 914-835-4466; Kingsland Point Lighthouse Tel. 914-366-5109; Kingsland Point Park Tel. 914-366-5109; Washington Headquarters, Virginia Rd., North White Plains Tel. 914-864-PARK; Cranberry Lake Preserve Tel. 914-428-1005; Lenoir Preserve Tel. 914-968-5851; Silver Lake Preserve Tel. 914-864-7000; Mildred D. Lasdon Bird Sanctuary Tel. 914-864-7000; Edith G. Read Natural Park & Wildlife Sanctuary Tel. 914-967-8720; Croton Point Nature Center Tel. 914-862-5297. Tax-exempt.
Nature Centers, Sanctuaries & Historic Sites.
Collections: colonial artifacts & furnishings; farm animals; natural science. Historic House: 1732 George Washington's headquarters, Virginia Rd., North White Plains; Historic Farm: Muscoot Park, turn-of-the-century 777-acre working farm with Manor House.
Activities: guided tours; lectures; permanent & temporary exhibitions; demonstration of colonial tools & machines.
Publications: quarterly calendar.
Hours & Admission Prices: Washington's Headquarters by appointment only. Trailside Museum & Marshlands Conservancy: call for hours. No charge. Cranberry Lake Preserve: Tues.-Sun. 9-5. Lenoir Preserve: Tues.-Sun. 9-5. Silver Lake Preserve: daily 9-4. Lasdon Bird Sanctuary: daily dawn-dusk. Read Natural Park & Wildlife Sanctuary: Tues.-Sun. 9-5. Tarrytown Lighthouse: by appointment only.

Mountainville

STORM KING ART CENTER, (M), Old Pleasant Hill Rd., Mountainville, NY 10953-0280. Mailing Address: P.O. Box 280, Mountainville, NY 10953-0280. Tel.: 845-534-3115. Fax: 845-534-4457.
E-mail: dr.collens@stormkingartcenter.org
Web Site: www.stormkingartcenter.org
Founded: 1960.
Congressional District: 19
Key Personnel: Pres., John P. Stern; Chm., H. Peter Stern; Dir. & Cur., David R. Collens; Admin., Georgene Zlock; Comptroller, Rose Wood; Mgr. Visitor Center, Colleen Zlock.
Personnel Profile: Full-Time Paid 10; Full-Time Volunteers 2; Part-Time Paid 17; Part-Time Volunteers 36.
Governing Authority: nonprofit organization. Tax-exempt: 501(c)(3).
Art Museum & Sculpture Park.
Collections: 20th-century American & International sculpture including: Noguchi, Serra, di Suvero, Nevelson, David Smith, Armajani, Calder, Goldsworthy; Abakanowicz; von Rydingsvard.
Research Fields: 20th-century American & International sculpture.
Facilities: 2,000-vol. art library; 500-acre sculpture park. Museum-related items for sale.
Activities: permanent & temporary exhibitions; site-specific sculpture; docent guided tours; handicap accessible tram tours; Acoustiguide rental; meet the artist events; lectures; music in the park; school programs; family events; hikes; docent education; outreach to community; free admission days.
Publications: exhibition catalogues; newsletter; self-guides to outdoor sculpture collection & tram tours.
Hours & Admission Prices: April 2-Nov. 1 Wed.-Sun. 11-5:30; Nov. 2-Nov. 15

Wed.-Sun. 11-5. Adults $10, senior citizens & college students with valid ID $9, elementary & high school students $7; discounts to AAM & ICOM members and bus groups of 15 or more with 2-week advance reservations; children 5 and under & members no charge. ♿
Attendance: 55,000 (estimated)
Membership: Individual $35; Household $50; Contributor $100; Donor $250; Sponsor $500; Patron $1,000.

Mumford

GENESEE COUNTRY VILLAGE & MUSEUM, 1410 Flint Hill Rd., Mumford, NY 14511-0310. Mailing Address: P.O. Box 310, Mumford, NY 14511-0310. Tel.: 585-538-6822. Fax: 585-538-2887 & 6927.
E-mail: email@gcv.org
Web Site: www.gcv.org
Founded: 1966.
Congressional District: 35
Key Personnel: Pres. & C.E.O., Peter S. Arnold; Chm., A. Thomas Hildebrandt; C.F.O., Robert C. Titus; Dir. Retail & Visitor Svcs., Robin Lott; Sr. Dir. Programs & Collections, Charles A. LeCourt; Sr. Dir. Devel., Jeffrey L. Bagel; Dir. Education Svcs., Maria Neale; Dir. Interpretation, Brian Nagel; Sr. Dir. Human Resources & Volunteer Svcs., Cheryl Barney; Sr. Dir. Facilities & Operations, Edward Coons; Museum Shop Mgr., Cheryl Maier.
Personnel Profile: Full-Time Paid 40; Part-Time Paid 180; Part-Time Volunteers 550; Interns 2.
Governing Authority: nonprofit organization. Tax-exempt.
Art Gallery, Nature Center, Recreated Village & Living History Museum.
Collections: 68 19th-century buildings including residences, shops, offices, churches, taverns, schools, stores, brewery, barn & outbuildings; manuscripts; documents; photographs; maps; furnishings & period artifacts; Gallery of Wildlife & Sporting Art, containing 18th-, 19th- & 20th-century paintings, sculptures & graphics; Carriage Museum, containing 50 19th- & 20th-century horse-drawn vehicles.
Research Fields: the settlement & 19th-century development of Genesee Country including its traditions, customs, occupations & professions; histories of the component buildings of Genesee Country Museum's Country Village.
Facilities: 6,800-vol. library of reference books & periodicals; gardens; cafeteria & restaurant. Handcrafted objects, related reproductions & other museum-related items for sale.
Activities: 19th-century crafts; organized programs for elementary & secondary school students; internship programs with area colleges & universities; intermuseum loan & permanent exhibitions. Museum Events: Vintage Baseball; Highland Gathering; Independence Day Celebration; Civil War Battle Reenactment; Old Time Fiddler's Fair; Agriculture Society Fair, Halloween Celebration; Annual Christmas Sale & Yuletide in the Country.
Publications: Genesee Country Museum: Scenes of Town & Country in the 19th Century; Four Centuries of Sporting Art; brochures; biannual magazine, Eagle.
Hours & Admission Prices: May 16-Oct. 18 Tues.-Fri. 10-4, Sat.-Sun. 10-5. Adults $15, senior citizens over 62 & students $12, youth 4-16 $9; members and children 3 & under no charge. ♿
Attendance: 76,418 (estimated)
Membership: Friend $60; Friend & one $80; Family $90.

Munnsville

FRYER MEMORIAL MUSEUM, William St., Munnsville, NY 13409.
E-mail: davidsadler_13043@yahoo.com
Founded: 1976.
Congressional District: 32
Key Personnel: Town Historian, David Sadler.
Personnel Profile: Full-Time Volunteers 1; Part-Time Volunteers 1.
Governing Authority: municipal; nonprofit. Parent Institution: Town of Stockbridge. Tax-exempt: 170(b)(1)(A).
Local History Museum: housed in 1886 Munnsville Post Office. Specialize in genealogical & local history research.
Collections: genealogical materials; artifacts; manuscripts; maps; photographs; published local history books; Munnsville Plow Co. tools & manufactured items.
Research Fields: genealogy; local Indians; cemetery records; local industry.
Activities: lectures; permanent & temporary exhibitions.
Hours & Admission Prices: By appointment. No charge; donations accepted.
Attendance: 200 (estimated)

Narrowsburg

FORT DELAWARE MUSEUM OF COLONIAL HISTORY, 6615 State Rt. 97, Narrowsburg, NY 12764. Mailing Address: Sullivan County DPW, P.O. Box 5012, Monticello, NY 12701-5192. Tel.: 845-252-6660. Fax: 845-791-8462.
Web Site: co.sullivan.ny.us
Founded: 1957.
Congressional District: 27
Key Personnel: Dir., Linda Dexter.
Personnel Profile: Part-Time Paid 12; Part-Time Volunteers 6.
Governing Authority: county. Operated by the Sullivan County Board of Supervisors. Tax-exempt.
History Museum: 1755-1785 a reconstruction of Cushetunk, the first stockaded settlement in the upper Delaware Valley.
Collections: stout stockade; cabins; blockhouses; gun platform; store house; blacksmith shed; candle shed; armory; animal yard; flintlock muskets; rifles; cannon; fowling pieces; 18th-century household furnishings; farm tools & implements; early gravestones; herb & vegetable garden; Loom Shed; log cabins; Lenape Indian dwelling.
Research Fields: genealogy.
Facilities: picnic ground; vending machines. Local handcrafts & museum-related items for sale.
Activities: guided tours; lectures; daily demonstrations including candlemaking, spinning & carding wool, weaving, musket & cannon firing; slide & taped programs; 18th-century military tactics, woodworking techniques, & basketmaking; summer military encampment; workshops in spinning & quilting.
Publications: book, Cushetunk, 1754-1784 a brief history of the early settlers who called themselves, The Delaware Company; Letters to Sarah: A Year in the Life of A Settlers Family, 1769-1770.
Hours & Admission Prices: Memorial Day to June Sat. 10-5, Sun. 12-5; late June to Labor Day Mon. & Fri.-Sat. 10-5, Sun. 12-5. Adults $7, seniors $5, children 5-14 $4. ♿
Attendance: 5,000

New City

HISTORICAL SOCIETY OF ROCKLAND COUNTY, (M), 20 Zukor Rd., New City, NY 10956-4388. Tel.: 845-634-9629. Fax: 845-634-8690.
E-mail: info@rocklandhistory.org
Web Site: www.rocklandhistory.org
Founded: 1965.
Congressional District: 26
Key Personnel: Exec. Dir., Erin L. Martin; Pres. (V), Dr. Thomas F.X. Casey.
Personnel Profile: Full-Time Paid 4; Part-Time Paid 4; Part-Time Volunteers 175; Interns 2.
Governing Authority: nonprofit organization. Tax-exempt.
History Museum.
Collections: furniture; decorative arts; paintings; prints; photographs; documents; genealogical papers; historical materials. Historic House & Structures: restored 1832 Dutch farmhouse & outbuildings belonging to Jacob Blauvelt.
Research Fields: local & regional history.
Facilities: 500-vol. library of local history books, photographs & archives for research on premises; museum, historic house; genealogical records, available for use by appointment. Publications & reproductions for sale.
Activities: guided tours; permanent & temporary exhibitions; lecture series; educational outreach programs; folklife programs.
Publications: quarterly pamphlet, South of the Mountains; books, Gleanings from Rockland History; Now & Then & Long Ago in Rockland County; The Way it Was in North Rockland; Wine & Bitters; The Tonnetti Years At Snedens Landing; How Things Began in Rockland County; Ladies Lib; How Rockland Women Got the Vote; Bicentennial Gleanings; Politics in the Gilded Age: A Biography of Clarence Lexow; Cole's History of Rockland County; Camp Shanks & Shanks Village; Haiti on the Hudson; Green's History of Rockland County; Growing Up in New City/Rockland in the 1790s; Adventures from the Past; Blossom; Rockland County 1900-2000, Century of History: True Stories From Mine Hole; A Catch of Grand Mothers.
Hours & Admission Prices: Daily 1-5. Adults $7, children $3; members no charge. Closed major holidays. ♿
Attendance: 12,000 (estimated)
Membership: New Members $15; Student & Senior Citizen $25; Individual $35; Family $40; Foreign $50; Sustaining $75; Libraries $100; Centurion $100-$249; Blauvelt Fellow $250-$499; President's Circle $500-$999; Patron $1,000-$2,500.

New Hartford

NEW HARTFORD HISTORICAL SOCIETY, Village Point Apt. Bldg., 2 Paris Rd., New Hartford, NY 13413. Mailing Address: P.O. Box 238, New Hartford, NY 13413-0238. Tel.: 315-724-7258.
Web Site: www.newhartfordpubliclibrary.org/history.html
Founded: 1941.
Key Personnel: Pres. (V) & Museum Shop Mgr., Barbara Couture; Archivist, Joanne Kujawski.
Personnel Profile: Full-Time Volunteers 1; Part-Time Volunteers 1.
Governing Authority: Tax-exempt.
Historical Museum.
Collections: area history; Elliott Hugh Colonial collection.
Hours & Admission Prices: Mon. 1-3, Sat. 10-2. No charge; donations accepted.
Attendance: 45 (estimated)
Membership: Student $1; Individual $10; Family $15; Contributing $25; Corporate $50.

New Paltz

THE HUGUENOT HISTORICAL SOCIETY, 18 Broadhead Ave., New Paltz, NY 12561-1403. Tel.: 845-255-1660. Fax: 845-255-0376.
E-mail: info@huguenotstreet.org
Web Site: www.huguenotstreet.org
Founded: 1894.
Congressional District: 27
Key Personnel: Exec. Dir., Eric J. Roth; Pres. (V), Mary Etta Schneider; Cur., Leslie LeFevre-Stratton; Museum Shop Mgr., Cheryl Schmidt.
Personnel Profile: Full-Time Paid 6; Part-Time Paid 12; Part-Time Volunteers 30; Interns 3.
Governing Authority: nonprofit organization. Branch Museums: Locust Lawn & Terwilliger House, Route 32, Gardiner, NY. 12525; 1818 Friends Meeting House, Plattekill, NY. Tax-exempt: 501(c)(3).
Historic Site & Historic House Museum: c.1680-1890, stone houses.
Collections: 17th to 18th-century French and Dutch documents; manuscripts; 17th to 18th-century furnishings. Historic Houses: 1678; 1721 Jean (Jacob) Hasbrouck House; 1721 Abraham (Daniel) Hasbrouck house; 1698-1735 Bevier-Elting; 1692-1894 Deyo house; French Church; 1694-1735 Hugo Freer house; 1799 LeFevre house; 1705 DuBois Fort.
Research Fields: 17th-century documents; items of French Huguenot & Dutch families; genealogy & history of New York state.
Facilities: 6,000-vol. library of Huguenot history, genealogy, & local history; literature available by appointment for use on the premises; reception facilities; reading room. Books & other museum-related items for sale.
Activities: guided tours; lectures; formally organized educational programs; training programs for professional museum workers; special events.
Publications: newsletter, On Huguenot Street.
Hours & Admission Prices: Grounds: year round. Visitor's Center: April & Nov.-Dec. Sat.-Sun. 11-3; May-Oct. Mon.-Tues. & Thurs.-Sun. 10:30-5. Deluxe Tour: $12. Standard Tour: $9; discounts to AAM members; children under 6 & members no charge. ♿
Attendance: 14,702 (accurate)
Membership: Individual $35; Household $50; Business & Contributor $100; Donor $250; Patron $500; Benefactor $1,000.

SAMUEL DORSKY MUSEUM OF ART, STATE UNIVERSITY OF NEW YORK AT NEW PALTZ, (M), 1 Hawk Dr., New Paltz, NY 12561-2447. Tel.: 845-257-3844. Fax: 845-257-3854.
E-mail: sdma@newpaltz.edu
Web Site: www.newpaltz.edu/museum
Founded: 1963.
Congressional District: 28
Key Personnel: Neil C. Trager Dir., Sara J. Pasti; Chm. (V), David A. Dorsky; Art Collections Mgr., Wayne Lempka; Museum Educator, Judi Esmond; Cur., Brian Wallace; Assoc. Cur. Collections, Dr. Jaimee Uhlenbrock; Preparator, Robert Wagner; Coord. Visitor Svcs., Amy Pickering.
Personnel Profile: Full-Time Paid 3; Part-Time Paid 3; Part-Time Volunteers 2; Interns 2.
Governing Authority: university. Parent Institution: State University of New York at New Paltz. Tax-exempt.
Art Gallery.
Collections: 19th & 20th-century American prints & paintings; regional art; Asian prints; pre-Columbian artifacts; contemporary & historical photography; metals; posters.
Activities: lectures; concerts; video screenings; temporary & traveling exhibitions; gallery talks; docent tours.
Publications: two annual catalogues.
Hours & Admission Prices: Wed.-Sun. 11-5. No charge; donations accepted. Closed legal & school holidays. ♿
Attendance: 16,000 (estimated)
Membership: Student $15; Seniors $25; Friend $50; Donor $100; Sponsor $250; Patron $500; Benefactor $1,000; Director's Circle $2,500.

New Rochelle

THOMAS PAINE MUSEUM AND ARCHIVES, 983 North Ave., New Rochelle, NY 10804-3609. Tel.: 914-632-5376.
Historic Building: housed in the former home of Thomas Paine.
Collections: Paine's life & history; personal artifacts; books; pamphlets photographs; manuscripts.
Hours & Admission Prices: Call for hours.

New Windsor

NATIONAL TEMPLE HILL ASSOCIATION, INC., Edmonston House, Headquarters, 1042 Rte. 94, New Windsor, NY 12553. Mailing Address: Edmonston House, Headquarters, P.O. Box 315, Vails Gate, NY 12584-0315. Tel.: 845-561-5073. Fax: 845-561-5073.
Founded: 1933.
Congressional District: 21
Key Personnel: Pres. (V), Daniel S. Lucia.
Personnel Profile: Part-Time Paid 5; Part-Time Volunteers 15.
Governing Authority: nonprofit organization. Subsidiary Institution: Last Encampment of the Continental Army. Tax-exempt: 501(c)(3).
Historic House: c.1755 Edmonston House served as headquarters during Revolutionary War for General Horatio Gates & Maj. Gen. Arthur St. Clair.
Collections: period furnishings; 18th-century architectural artifact with significant connection to the American Revolutionary events.
Research Fields: Colonial & Revolutionary Period of local area.
Facilities: meeting & research rooms.
Activities: open house; crafts workshops; programs & interpretation at the Last Encampment of the Continental Army on Rte. 300.
Publications: quarterly bulletin.
Hours & Admission Prices: Edmonston House: July-Sept. Sun. 2-5. Last Encampment of the Continental Army: late April to Oct. daylight hours; Guides Thurs.-Sun. 12-4:30. No charge; donations accepted.
Attendance: 1,200 (estimated)
Membership: Student $5; Individual $15; Couple $25; Business $50; Corporate $100; Life $1,000.

New York

ABRONS ARTS CENTER/HENRY STREET SETTLEMENT, 466 Grand St., New York, NY 10002-4804. Tel.: 212-598-0400. Fax: 212-505-8329.
E-mail: jdurham@henrystreet.org
Web Site: www.abronsartscenter.org
Formerly: The Main Gallery of Henry Street Settlement/Abrons Art Center
Founded: 1893.
Key Personnel: Dir. Abron Arts Center, Jay Wegman; C.E.O. & Dir., Verona Middleton Jeter; Chm. (V), Robert Harrison; Pres. (V), Dale Burch; House & Night Mgr., Carl Johnson; Deputy Dir. & Visual Arts Dir., Susan Flemmger; Dir. Visual Arts, Jonathan Durham; Administrative Asst., Wanda Egipciaco; Registrar, Sonia Diaz.
Personnel Profile: Full-Time Paid 3; Part-Time Volunteers 2; Interns 3.
Governing Authority: nonprofit. Parent Institution: Henry Street Settlement; Subsidiary Institution: Abrons Arts Center. Tax-exempt.
Arts Center.
Collections: changing thematic group exhibits of contemporary art, in all media; changing solo photography exhibits.
Major Exhibits: Malichi Farrel: The Shops Are Closed (T), 11/09-1/10.
Activities: gallery tours; workshops; family programs; instruction in all arts disciplines (visual arts, dance, theater & music); artist-in-residence workspace program.
Hours & Admission Prices: Tues.-Sat. 12-6. No charge; donations accepted. Closed national holidays. ♿
Attendance: 40,000 (accurate)
Membership: Balcony $55-$120; Mezzanine $200; Orchestra $500; Stage $1,000.

AMERICAN ACADEMY OF ARTS AND LETTERS, (M), 633 W. 155th St., New York, NY 10032-7501. Tel.: 212-368-5900. Fax: 212-491-4615.
E-mail: academy@artsandletters.org
Web Site: www.artsandletters.org
Founded: 1898.
Congressional District: 16
Key Personnel: Exec. Dir., Virginia Dajani; Pres., J.D. McClatchy; Music Programs, Ardith Holmgrain; Exec. Asst., Kristen Stevens; Archivist, Kathleen Kienholz; Library & Publications, Kathleen Dinah Trocino; Art & Architecture Awards, Exhibitions & Collections, Souhad Rafey; Literature & Richard Rodgers Awards, Jane Bolster; Asst. to Dir., Cody Upton; Program Asst., Hannah Blake.

Personnel Profile: Full-Time Paid 7; Part-Time Paid 6.
Governing Authority: nonprofit organization. Tax-exempt: 501(c)(3).
Art Museum & Library.
Collections: works by & about members of the American Academy of Arts & Letters; works by Childe Hassam & Eugene Speicher; art; archives; painting; sculpture; graphics; music; decorative arts.
Major Exhibits: Invitational Exhibition of Visual Arts, 3/11/10-4/11/10; Exhibition of Work by Newly Elected Members and Recipients of Honors and Awards, 5/20/10-6/13/10.
Research Fields: art; literature; music; architecture.
Facilities: 22,000-vol. library including musical scores & books of the works of or about the artists, architects, writers & composers who have been members of the American Academy of Arts & Letters. Archives containing correspondence & manuscripts relating to members. Open to scholars by appointment.
Activities: rotating exhibitions of art and manuscripts. Organization Sponsors: yearly cash awards for painting, sculpture, graphics, architecture, music & literature; all awards by nomination of the membership with no applications accepted; annual purchase of contemporary paintings, drawings and graphics for donation to museums.
Publications: catalogs of exhibitions, Proceedings of the American Academy of Arts & Letters.
Hours & Admission Prices: Galleries: Thurs.-Sun. 1-4, when exhibitions are held. No charge. Office: Mon.-Fri. 9:30-5. Closed holidays. ♿

AMERICAN FOLK ART MUSEUM, 45 W. 53rd St., New York, NY 10019-5401. Mailing Address: 49 E. 52nd St., New York, NY 10022-5965. Tel.: 212-265-1040; 800-421-1220. Fax: 212-977-8134. TDD: 800-662-1220.
E-mail: info@folkartmuseum.org
Web Site: www.folkartmuseum.org
Founded: 1961.
Congressional District: 17
Key Personnel: Dir., Maria Ann Conelli; Chief Administrative Officer, Linda Dunne; C.F.O., Robin Schlinger; Pres., Laura Parsons; Assoc. Dir. Individual Giving, Christine Corcoran; Dir. Devel., Blair Hartley; Dir. Exhibitions & Sr. Cur., Stacy Hollander; Dir. & Cur. The Contemporary Center, Brooke Davis Anderson; Dir. Publications, Tanya Heinrich; Registrar, Ann-Marie Reilly; Receptionist, Katya Ullmann; Museum Shop Mgr., Marie DiManno; Dir. Public Rels., Susan Flamm.
Personnel Profile: Full-Time Paid 41; Full-Time Volunteers 70; Part-Time Paid 32; Part-Time Volunteers 60; Interns 2.
Governing Authority: nonprofit organization. Tax-exempt: 501(c)(3).
Folk Art Museum.
Collections: American 18th- to 20th-century folk sculpture & painting; work of 20th-century self-taught artists; textile arts; decorative arts; environmental folk art; history.
Research Fields: folk & decorative arts; work of 20th-century self-taught artists; history.
Facilities: library; classroom. Books, gifts & reproductions for sale.
Activities: gallery talks; inter-museum loan, temporary & traveling exhibitions; craft classes; outreach programs to schools & interested groups, including lectures, workshops & folk art slide presentations; docent program including classes in folk art & decorative arts; internship program; Folk Art Explorers' Club; tours; antique show previews.
Publications: members' journal, Folk Art; exhibition catalogues; permanent collection catalogues; folk art books.
Hours & Admission Prices: Tues.-Thurs. & Sat.-Sun. 10-6, Fri. 10-7:30; guided tours by appointment. Adults $9; discounts to AAM & ICOM members; members no charge. ♿
Attendance: 165,000 (accurate)
Membership: Quilt Connection $20; Student & Senior Citizen $40; Individual $55; Dual & Family $75; Contributing $125; Sustaining $250; Benefactor $500; Director's Circle $1,000; Collector's Circle $2,500.

AMERICAN IRISH HISTORICAL SOCIETY, 991 5th Ave., New York, NY 10028-0101. Tel.: 212-288-2263. Fax: 212-628-7927.
E-mail: aihs@aihs.org
Web Site: www.aihs.org
Founded: 1897.
Key Personnel: Pres. Gen., Kevin M. Cahill, M.D.; Exec. Dir., Christopher P. Cahill.
Personnel Profile: Part-Time Volunteers 4.
Governing Authority: historical society; nonprofit organization. Subsidiary Institution: AIHS, California. Tax-exempt: 501(c)(3).
Research Library: housed in c.1900 townhouse.
Collections: Irish history & culture; history of Irish in America.
Facilities: 10,000-vol. library of Irish & American Irish references, available for use by public by appointment; reading rooms.
Activities: concerts; lectures; readings; recitals; play readings; receptions; presentations; permanent & temporary exhibits; concerts.
Publications: biannual literary magazine, The Recorder; quarterly events newsletter.
Hours & Admission Prices: Mon.-Fri. 10-5.
Attendance: 3,000 (estimated)
Membership: Individual $100; Sustaining $250; Contributing $500; Sponsor $1,000; Benefactor $2,000; Patron $2,500.

AMERICAN JEWISH HISTORICAL SOCIETY, 15 W. 16th St., New York, NY 10011-6301. Tel.: 212-294-6160. Fax: 212-294-6161.
E-mail: info@ajhs.org
Web Site: www.ajhs.org
Founded: 1892.
Congressional District: 4
Key Personnel: Pres. (V), Dan Kaplan; Exec. Dir., Evan Kingsley; Dir. Library & Archives, Susan Malbin; Membership Sec., Brian Hartmann.
Personnel Profile: Full-Time Paid 8; Part-Time Paid 1; Interns 3.
Governing Authority: nonprofit. Branch Museum: 160 Herrick Rd., Newton, MA 02459. Tel.: 617-559-8880. Tax-exempt: 501(c)(3).
Ethnic History Museum.
Collections: archival & library holdings relating to the American Jewish experience from the 16th century to present; colonial & early Federal portraits; family materials; Yiddish theatre collections of posters, music & actors; objects of daily life; works on paper; photographs; silhouettes; textiles; 9,000 manuscript items; 10,000 museum items.
Research Fields: American Jewish history.
Facilities: 40,000-vol. library of books, pamphlets, bulletins, periodicals & newspapers of the history of American Jews; reading room; exhibition galleries.
Activities: guided tours; lectures; films; inter-museum loan, permanent & temporary exhibits.
Publications: quarterly journal, American Jewish History; newsletter; books; tours in Europe & America on sites of Jewish interest; catalogs.
Hours & Admission Prices: Mon.-Thurs. 9-5, Fri. 9-2, Sun. 11-5. No charge. Closed national holidays & major Jewish holidays.
Attendance: 2,000 (estimated)
Membership: Student $18; Library & Regular $50; Centennial $100; Preservation Fellow $360; Patron $540; American Jewish Heritage Fellow $1,000.

* **AMERICAN MUSEUM OF NATURAL HISTORY, (M), (I),** Central Park West at 79th St., New York, NY 10024-5193. Tel.: 212-769-5100. Fax: 212-769-5018.
E-mail: communications@amnh.org
Web Site: www.amnh.org
Founded: 1869.
Congressional District: 17
Key Personnel: Pres., Ellen V. Futter; Chm. Bd. Trustees, Lewis W. Bernard; Sr. Vice Pres. & Provost, Dr. Michael J. Novacek; Sr. Vice Pres. Operations & Govt. Rels., Barbara D. Gunn; Sr. Vice Pres. & C.F.O., John Rorer; Gen. Counsel, Gerald R. Singer; Sr. Vice Pres. Devel. & Membership, Lynn DeBow; Sr. Vice Pres. Exhibition, David Harvey; Sr. Vice Pres. Education, Government Rels. & Strategic Planning, Lisa J. Gugenheim; Sr. Vice Pres. & Chief Digital Officer, Linda Perry-Lube; Sr. Vice Pres. Communications & Mktg., Charles D. McLean; Assoc. Dean Science Education and Exhibition, & Assoc. Cur. Div. Vertebrate Zoology, Dr. Christopher Raxworthy; Assoc. Dean Science Collections & Cur. Division Vertebrate Zoology, Dr. Darrel Frost; Chm. & Cur. Division Anthropology, Dr. Charles S. Spencer; Frederick P. Rose Dir., Hayden Planetarium, Dr. Neil deGrasse Tyson; Chm. & Cur. Division Invertebrate Zoology, Dr. Ward Wheeler; Chm. & Cur. Division Physical Sciences, Dr. Mordecai-Mark MacLow; Chm. & Cur. Division Paleontology, Dr. Mark Norell; Chm. & Cur. Division Vertebrate Zoology, Dr. Nancy B. Simmons; Dir. Center for Biodiversity & Conservation, Dr. Eleanor J. Sterling.
Personnel Profile: Full-Time Paid 1,052; Part-Time Paid 260; Part-Time Volunteers 850.
Governing Authority: board of trustees. Tax-exempt: 501(c)(3).
Natural History Museum.
Collections: amphibians; anthropology; arthropods; birds; dinosaurs; films;

fishes; frozen DNA tissue; gems; invertebrates; mammals; manuscripts; meteorites; minerals; photographs; prints; books; reptiles; rocks; shells; scanning electron microscope.
Major Exhibits: Extreme Mammals (T), 11/09-1/10; Frogs: A Chorus of Color, 11/09-1/10; The Butterfly Conservatory, 11/09-5/10; Traveling the Silk Road, 11/09-8/10.
Research Fields: anthropology; biodiversity conservation; comparative biology; genomics; invertebrate zoology; paleontology; physical sciences; vertebrate zoology.
Facilities: 487,000-vol. research library; The Rose Center for Earth & Space including the Hayden Planetarium; The Richard Gilder Graduate School; The Sackler Institute for Comparative Genomics; Parallel Computing Cluster; The Center for Biodiversity and Conservation; molecular laboratories; National Center for Science, Literacy, Education and Technology; Discovery room; Natural Science Center; classrooms; conservation laboratories; remote field research station; 1,000-seat LeFrak IMAX theater; 150-seat & 300-seat auditoriums; food court; cafe. Museum-related items for sale.
Activities: field expeditions; Ph.D. graduate program, undergraduate, doctoral & post-doctoral science training programs; temporary & traveling exhibitions; teacher training & professional development programs; web-based curricula & educational resources; formally organized education programs for children, families & adults; scientific conferences & symposia; inter-museum loan; AMNH Expeditions travel program; film & video festival; Moveable Museum program.
Publications: Novitates; The Bulletin of the American Museum of Natural History; Anthropological Papers of the American Museum of Natural History; quarterly calendar; scholarly books; textbooks; hall guides; teacher training material; brochures.
Hours & Admission Prices: Museum: daily 10-5:45. Rose Center: daily 10-5:45. Library: Tues.-Thurs. 2-5:30. Special Collections: by appointment. Suggested Donations: adults $16, students & seniors $12, children 2-12 $9; discounts to NYC Cultural Institutions Group members; members no charge. Additional fees for special exhibitions. Closed Thanksgiving; Christmas. ♿
Attendance: 4,000,000 (estimated)
Membership: Individual $70; Dual $90; Family $115; Contributor $195; Supporter $400; Sponsor $800; Friend $1,000; Patron $1,750 & up.

AMERICAN NUMISMATIC SOCIETY, (M), 75 Varick St., 11 Fl., New York, NY 10013-1917. Tel.: 212-571-4470. Fax: 212-571-4479.
Web Site: www.numismatics.org
Founded: 1858.
Congressional District: 8
Key Personnel: Exec. Dir., Dr. Ute Wartenberg; Pres. (V), Roger Siboni; American Cur., Robert Hoge; Greek Cur., Dr. Peter van Alfen; Collections Mgr., Dr. Elena Stolyarik; Research Scientist, Dr. Sebastian Heath; Dir. Finance & Operations, Anna Chang; Librarian, Elizabeth Hahn; Membership Assoc., Megan Fenselau; Museum Admin., Joanne Isaac; Deputy Dir., Andrew Meadows.
Personnel Profile: Full-Time Paid 15; Part-Time Paid 1; Part-Time Volunteers 6; Interns 4.
Governing Authority: society. Tax-exempt.
Numismatics History Museum.
Collections: numismatics; history; archaeology; manuscripts; books.
Research Fields: history; art history; economics related to numismatic evidence.
Facilities: 100,000-vol. library of books on numismatics available for use on premises; reading room.
Activities: guided tours; lectures; formally organized education programs for graduate students; training programs for professional museum workers; inter-museum loan, permanent, temporary & traveling exhibitions; numismatic conversation; webcasts. Annual Events: Coinage of the Americas Conference; Krause-Mishler Forum; Archer M. Huntington Award; The Groves Forum; The Sylvia Mani Hunter Memorial Lecture; The Mark M. Salton Memorial Lecture; The Harry W. Fowler Memorial Lecture.
Publications: magazine, American Numismatic Society; American Journal of Numismatics; Numismatic Literature; Colonial Newsletter; Series, Ancient Coins in North American Collections; Numismatic Notes and Monographs; Coinage of the Americas Conference Proceedings.
Hours & Admission Prices: Library: Tues.-Fri. 9:30-12 & 1-4:30 by appointment. Coin Research: Tues.-Fri. 9:30-4:30 by appointment. No charge. Federal Reserve Bank exhibit, 33 Liberty St.: Mon.-Fri. 10-4. Closed New Year's Day; Martin Luther King Jr. Day; Presidents' Day; Memorial Day; Independence Day; Labor Day; Thanksgiving & day after; Christmas. ♿
Attendance: 40,000 (estimated)
Membership: Student $35; Basic Associate $55; Full Associate $80; Foreign Associate $100; Fellow $110; Library Associate $150; Corporate Associate $500; Life Fellow & Life Associate $7,500.

AMERICAS SOCIETY, (M), 680 Park Ave., (at 68th St.), New York, NY 10065-5072. Tel.: 212-249-8950. Fax: 212-249-5868.
E-mail: arts@americas-society.org
Web Site: www.americas-society.org
Formerly: Center for Inter-American Relations
Founded: 1965.
Congressional District: 15
Key Personnel: Honorary Chm., David Rockefeller; Chm. (V), William Rhodes; Pres., Susan Segal; Dir. Visual Arts, Gabriela Rangel; Asst. Cur. & Exhibition Coord., Isabela Villanueva.
Personnel Profile: Full-Time Paid 39; Part-Time Paid 12; Part-Time Volunteers 1.
Governing Authority: nonprofit organization. Tax-exempt: 501(c)(3).
Art Gallery.
Collections: Latin American paintings & drawings; Latin America, Canada & the Caribbean cultures.
Research Fields: Latin American, Caribbean and Canadian art & culture.
Facilities: 3,000-vol. library of catalogues & books on Latin American art; 4,000 artists registry files with biographical information and/or slides. Exhibitions catalogs for sale.
Activities: temporary exhibits; inter-museum loans; lectures; educational programming; concerts; films; videos; panel discussions; symposia.
Publications: biannual, Review: Latin American Literature and Arts; exhibition catalogues.
Hours & Admission Prices: Wed.-Sat. 12-6. Gallery & Public Programs: no charge; donations accepted. Concerts: adults $15, students & senior citizens $10; discounts to members. Closed major holidays. ♿
Attendance: 10,000 (estimated)
Membership: Student & Senior Citizen $35; Individual $85; Sustaining $500; Donor $1,000; Patron $5,000.

ANTHOLOGY FILM ARCHIVES, 32 Second Ave., New York, NY 10003-8631. Tel.: 212-505-5181. Fax: 212-477-2714.
E-mail: robert@anthologyfilmarchives.org
Web Site: www.anthologyfilmarchives.org
Founded: 1970.
Congressional District: 15
Key Personnel: Pres. (V) & Dir., Jonas Mekas; Bd. Chm., Barney Oldfield; Financial Dir., John Mhiripiri; Membership, Wendy Dorsett; Public Rels., Stephanie Grey; Archivist, Andrew Lampert.
Personnel Profile: Full-Time Paid 8; Part-Time Paid 3; Part-Time Volunteers 6; Interns 5.
Governing Authority: private; nonprofit organization. Tax-exempt: 501(c)(3).
Film Museum.
Collections: over 12,000 avant-garde, classic films & documentaries; 6,000 photographs.
Research Fields: Jim Davis; Storm DeHirsch; Marie Menken.
Facilities: 8,000-vol. library; 190-seat large screen theater. Museum-related items for sale.
Activities: films. Annual Event: Film Preservation Honors Dinner.
Publications: quarterly film exhibition schedule; Annual Film Preservation Honors Dinner Journal; catalogs; books.
Hours & Admission Prices: Jan. to 3rd week in Aug. & Sept. to 3rd week in Dec. Film Screenings: Mon.-Fri. 6-11, Sat.-Sun. 3-11. Adults $9, senior citizens & students $5; members no charge.
Attendance: 50,000 (estimated)
Membership: Student & Senior $30; Adult $50; Dual Adult $75; Donor $250; Preservation Donor $1,500.

APERTURE FOUNDATION, 547 W. 27th St., 4th Fl., New York, NY 10001-5511. Tel.: 212-505-5555. Fax: 212-979-7759.
E-mail: info@aperture.org
Web Site: www.aperture.org
Founded: 1952.
Key Personnel: Dir., Juan Garcia de Oreyza; Book Publisher, Lesley A. Martin; Chm. (V), Celso Gonzalez-Falla; Dir. Limited Edition Prints, Kelly Mclaughlin.
Personnel Profile: Full-Time Paid 35; Part-Time Paid 2; Interns 10.
Governing Authority: private; nonprofit. Tax-exempt: 501(c)(3).
Photography Foundation.
Collections: Paul Strand archive.
Research Fields: photography; fine arts.
Facilities: Limited edition prints & books for sale.
Activities: educational programs; work scholars; portfolio reviews; traveling exhibitions; special events.
Publications: magazine, Aperture; photography books.
Hours & Admission Prices: Mon.-Sat. 10-6. No charge. ♿
Attendance: 16,887 (accurate)
Membership: Art Circle $1,000; Art Net $2,500; Art Council $5,000; Art Alliance $10,000.

ARTHUR A. HOUGHTON JR. GALLERY & THE GREAT HALL GALLERY, 7 E. 7th St., Foundation Bldg., New York, NY 10003-8128. Mailing Address: 30 Cooper Square, New York, NY 10003-7120. Tel.: 212-353-4200.
Founded: 1859.
Key Personnel: Dean of Art School, Saskia Bos
Art Gallery.
Collections: graphic design; fine arts; painting; sculpture; engineering.
Hours & Admission Prices: Mon.-Fri. 12-7, Sat. 12-5. No charge.

ARTISTS SPACE, 38 Greene St., 3rd Fl., New York, NY 10013-2505. Tel.: 212-226-3970. Fax: 212-966-1434.
Founded: 1972.
Key Personnel: Exec. Dir., Stefan Kalmar
Art Gallery.
Collections: works by contemporary artists.
Hours & Admission Prices: Tues.-Sat. 12-6. No charge. Closed Independence Day.

ASIA SOCIETY MUSEUM, (M), 725 Park Ave., New York, NY 10021-5088. Tel.: 212-288-6400. Fax: 212-517-7246 & 8315.
Web Site: www.asiasociety.org
Formerly: Asia Society Galleries
Founded: 1956.
Congressional District: 14
Key Personnel: Pres., Vishakha N. Desai; Exec. Vice Pres., Jamie Metzl; Interim Chm. (V), Charles R. Kaye; Museum Dir., Melissa Chiu; Assoc. Dir., Marion Kocot; Cur. Traditional Art, Adriana Proser; Assoc. Cur. Contemporary Art, Miwako Tezuka; Museum Shop Mgr., Anne Godshall.
Personnel Profile: Full-Time Paid 100; Part-Time Paid 5; Part-Time Volunteers 50.
Governing Authority: nonprofit organization. Dept. of The Asia Society, Inc. Tax-exempt: 501(c)(3).
Asian Art Museum.
Collections: Mr. & Mrs. John D. Rockefeller 3rd collection of Asian art.
Major Exhibits: Arts of Ancient Vietnam (T), 2/10-5/10; Pilgrimage & Buddhist Art (T), 3/10-6/10; Yoshimoto Nara (T), 9/10-1/11.
Research Fields: Asian art.
Facilities: conference & lecture rooms; 258-seat auditorium. Publications, books, catalogs & gift items for sale.
Activities: guided tours of current exhibitions; conferences; symposia; performances; lectures & films; inter-museum loan & traveling exhibitions.
Publications: Archives of Asian Art; exhibition catalogs; collection catalogue; brochures.
Hours & Admission Prices: July to Labor Day Tues.-Thurs. & Sat.-Sun. 11-6; Sept.-June Tues.-Thurs. & Sat.-Sun. 11-6, Fri. 11-9. Adults $10, seniors $7, students $5; discounts to AAM & ICOM members; members, children under 16 accompanied by a parent & Fri. 6-9 no charge. Closed New Year's Day; Independence Day; Thanksgiving; Christmas. ♿
Attendance: 95,000 (estimated)
Membership: Student, Senior & Associate $40; Individual $65; Dual & Family $120; Asia Circle $150; Contributing $250; Sustaining $500; President's Circle $1,000; Friends of Asian Arts $1,500.

ASIAN AMERICAN ARTS CENTRE, 26 Bowery, 3rd Fl., New York, NY 10013-5159. Tel.: 917-923-8118. Fax: 360-283-2154.
E-mail: aaacinfo@artspiral.org
Web Site: www.artspiral.org
Founded: 1974.
Congressional District: 15
Key Personnel: C.E.O. & Cur., Robert Lee; Chm. (V), Eleanor Yong.
Personnel Profile: Full-Time Paid 1; Full-Time Volunteers 1; Part-Time Paid 1; Part-Time Volunteers 5; Interns 5.
Governing Authority: nonprofit. Tax-exempt: 501(c)(3).
Contemporary American Culture Art Museum.
Collections: June 4th Movement; artist archive; folk arts; contemporary visual art works; folk art.
Research Fields: Milieu (the Asian American artists from 1945-1965); Asian folk art.
Facilities: 500-vol. Asian American artist library; archive of Asian American art.
Activities: Museum Sponsors: folk & contemporary art exhibition; panel discussions; slide shows.
Publications: biannual newsletter, Art-Spiral.
Hours & Admission Prices: Tues.-Fri. 12:30-6:30, Sat. 1:30-4:30. No charge; donations accepted.
Attendance: 5,000 (estimated)
Membership: Individual $35.

BARD GRADUATE CENTER: DECORATIVE ARTS, DESIGN HISTORY, & MATERIAL CULTURE, (M), 18 W. 86th St., New York, NY 10024-3602. Tel.: 212-501-3000. Fax: 212-501-3079. TDD: 212-501-3012 (for public programs only).
E-mail: Mulligan@BGC.bard.edu
Web Site: www.bgc.bard.edu
Founded: 1993.
Congressional District: 6
Key Personnel: Dir., Dr. Susan Weber; Dean & Chm. Academic Programs, Dr. Peter N. Miller; Dean Academic Admin. & Student Affairs, Elena Pinto Simon; Dir. Finance & Admin., Lorraine Bacalles; Dir. Exhibitions, Nina Stritzler-Levine; Editor Studies in the Decorative Arts, Paul Stirton; Dir. Devel., Susan Wall; Dir. External Affairs, Tim Mulligan.
Personnel Profile: Full-Time Paid 73; Part-Time Paid 2.
Governing Authority: nonprofit. Parent Institution: Bard College, Annandale-on-Hudson, NY. Tax-exempt: 501(c)(3).
Decorative Art Academic Institution & Gallery.
Collections: decorative arts, design, & culture.
Research Fields:
Facilities: library.
Activities: formally organized educational programs; guided gallery tours; symposia; continuing education courses; seminars; lectures; walking tours; trips; family programs; senior programs.
Publications: Studies In the Decorative Arts, semiannual journal; exhibition catalogues.
Hours & Admission Prices: Tues.-Wed. & Fri.-Sun. 11-5, Thurs. 11-8. Adults $8, senior citizens & students $5; discounts to AAM & ICOM members and museum staff; Thurs. after 5pm & children under 12 no charge. Closed New Year's Day; Martin Luther King Jr.'s Day; Easter; Memorial Day; Independence Day; Labor Day; Thanksgiving & day after; Christmas. ♿
Attendance: 3,000 (estimated)

BELVEDERE CASTLE-HENRY LUCE NATURE OBSERVATORY, mid-Central Park at 79th St., New York, NY 10021. Mailing Address: Central Park Conservancy, The Arsenal, 830 5th Ave., New York, NY 10065-7001. Tel.: 212-772-0210. Fax: 212-772-0214.
Web Site: www.centralparknyc.org
Key Personnel: Dir. Public Programs, Terry Carta.
Governing Authority: nonprofit. New York Dept. of Parks & Recreation & Central Park Conservancy. Tax-exempt: 501(c)(3).
Historic Site & Preservation Project: 1872 Gothic tower within 843 acre landmark park designed by Frederick Law Olmsted and Calvert Vaux.
Collections: hands-on workshops; science, natural history & ecology; National Weather Service station.
Activities: school group & weekend family workshops; tours.
Publications: quarterly calendar of events; map; guide.
Hours & Admission Prices: Nov.-March Wed.-Sun. 10-5; April-Oct. Tues.-Sun. 10-5. No charge.
Attendance: 100,000 (accurate)

BERNARD JUDAICA MUSEUM, CONGREGATION EMANU-EL OF THE CITY OF NEW YORK, (M), 1 E. 65th St., New York, NY 10065-6501. Tel.: 212-744-1400. Fax: 212-570-0826.
E-mail: info@emanuelnyc.org
Web Site: www.emanuelnyc.org
Formerly: The Herbert & Eileen Bernard Museum, Congregation Emanu-El of the City of New York
Founded: 1948.
Key Personnel: Pres., Marcia Waxman; Dir. Devel., Robyn W. Cimbol; Sr. Cur., Elka Deitsch.
Governing Authority: synagogue. Parent Institution: Congregation Emanu-El of the City of New York. Tax-exempt: 501(c)(3).
Judaica Museum: housed in 1929 synagogue.
Collections: liturgical items for synagogue & home; art; commemorative items commissioned by & for the synagogue; historical documents, photographs & graphics pertaining to the congregation; collections from the Jewish communities throughout the United States, Europe, North Africa & the Near East.
Research Fields: history of the congregation & its members; Judaica.
Activities: docent guided tours by appointment; gallery lecture series.
Publications: collection catalog, A Temple Treasury: The Judaica Collection of Congregation Emanu-El of the City of New York; exhibition pamphlets; museum checklist; exhibition catalogs; Maps of the Holy Land; To Have & To Hold: Decorated Jewish Marriage Contracts.
Hours & Admission Prices: Sun.-Thurs. 10-4:30, Fri. 10-4, Sat. 1-4:30. Docent tours are available by appointment. No charge. ♿

BOXING HALL OF CHAMPIONS, (M), 9 E. 40th St., New York, NY 10016-0402. Tel.: 212-532-1717.
E-mail: steve@bhoc.com

Web Site: www.bhoc.com
Boxing History Museum.
Collections: boxing champions; photographs.
Hours & Admission Prices: Call for hours.

CASTLE CLINTON NATIONAL MONUMENT, Battery Park, New York, NY 10004. Mailing Address: 26 Wall St., New York, NY 10005-1996. Tel.: 212-825-6992. Fax: 212-285-6874.
Web Site: www.nps.gov
Founded: 1950.
Congressional District: 8
Key Personnel: Supt., Shirley McKinney.
Personnel Profile: Full-Time Paid 8; Part-Time Paid 4.
Governing Authority: federal. Administered by National Park Service, U.S. Dept. of the Interior. Tax-exempt.
Historic Site.
Collections: collections & archives relating to Castle Clinton Fort; Castle Garden Entertainment Center; immigration depot; miniature dioramas depicting 19th century Manhattan.
Research Fields: 1855-1890 immigration; 1800-1825 Harbor defense.
Facilities: visitor information center; Statue of Liberty & Ellis Island ticketing.
Activities: conducted tours; special events.
Publications: site brochure.
Hours & Admission Prices: Daily 8:30-5. No charge. Closed Christmas. ♿
Attendance: 2,433,250 (accurate)

THE CATHEDRAL OF ST. JOHN THE DIVINE, 1047 Amsterdam Ave. & 112st., New York, NY 10025-1798. Tel.: 212-932-7347. Fax: 212-316-7424.
E-mail: info@stjohndivine.org
Web Site: www.stjohndivine.org
Founded: 1892.
Congressional District: 19
Key Personnel: C.E.O., Very Rev. Dr. James A. Kowalski.
Personnel Profile: Full-Time Paid 60; Part-Time Paid 70; Part-Time Volunteers 35; Interns 5.
Governing Authority: church. Parent Institution: Diocese of the State of New York. Tax-exempt: 501(c)(3).
Historic Building & Religious Museum: housed in a Gothic Cathedral.
Collections: art; religious artifacts; tapestries; stone & masonry; stained glass; plants & herbs mentioned in the Bible.
Research Fields: Biblical plants; history; architecture; Middle Ages.
Facilities: cathedral & its 11.6 acres.
Activities: guided tours; educational programs; family programs; school programs; medieval arts workshop; temporary exhibitions; concerts; events; services.
Publications: newsletter; booklets.
Hours & Admission Prices: Daily 8-6. Suggested Donation $5; members no charge. ♿
Attendance: 800,000 (estimated)
Membership: Society of Regents: Young Regents 21-40 $250; Portal Circle $2,500-$4,999; Arch Circle $5,000-$9,999; Rose Window Circle $10,000 & up.

CENTER FOR BOOK ARTS, 28 W. 27th St., 3rd Fl., New York, NY 10001-6906. Tel.: 212-481-0295. Fax: 866-708-8994.
E-mail: info@centerforbookarts.org
Web Site: centerforbookarts.org
Founded: 1974.
Key Personnel: Chm., Michael Held; Exec. Dir., Alexander Campos; Program Mgr., Sarah Nicholls; External Affairs Mgr., James Copeland.
Personnel Profile: Full-Time Paid 3; Part-Time Paid 40; Part-Time Volunteers 35; Interns 10.
Governing Authority: private; nonprofit organization. Tax-exempt: 501(c)(3).
Book Craft Museum.
Collections: contemporary artists' & historical books.
Facilities: 500-vol. library on bookmaking & related arts; 900 sq. ft. exhibit space; fully-equipped book bindery & letterpress printshop.
Activities: guided tours; lectures; formal education programs; participatory exhibits; workspace rentals program for book artists; book artists slide registry & book publication programs; apprentice & internship programs; outreach program for school groups. Annual Event: Open House & Sale in December.
Publications: exhibition catalogues; member newsletters; course catalogues.
Hours & Admission Prices: Mon.-Fri. 10-6, Sat. 10-4. No charge; donations accepted. Closed New Year's Day; Passover-Easter weekend; Memorial Day; Independence Day; Labor Day; Yom Kippur; Christmas. ♿
Attendance: 18,000 (estimated)
Membership: Associate $50; Friend $100; Patron $250: Supporter $500; Sustainer $1,000; Benefactor $2,500; Master Benefactor $5,000.

CENTER GALLERY, FORDHAM UNIVERSITY, Lincoln Center Campus, 113 W. 60th St., New York, NY 10023-7484. Tel.: 212-636-6000.
Art Gallery.
Collections: photographs; paintings; sculpture; drawings.
Hours & Admission Prices: Call for hours. No charge.

CHANCELLOR ROBERT R. LIVINGSTON MASONIC LIBRARY & MUSEUM, (M), 71 W. 23rd St., New York, NY 10010-4102. Tel.: 212-337-6620. Fax: 212-633-2639.
E-mail: info@nymasoniclibrary.org
Web Site: www.nymasoniclibrary.org
Founded: 1856.
Key Personnel: Dir., Thomas M. Savini; Pres. (V), Barry Mallah; Treas., Aldo Ghirarduzzi.
Personnel Profile: Full-Time Paid 3; Part-Time Paid 1; Part-Time Volunteers 12.
Governing Authority: private; nonprofit organization. Parent Institution: Grand Lodge of New York. Subsidiary Institution: Livingston Library, Utica Branch, Utica, NY. Tax-exempt: 501(c)(3).
History Museum: located in Masonic Hall.
Collections: concentration on Masonic history in New York state; strong holdings in Hermetic & esoteric thought; focus on New York state with items from around the world, 16th-century to present; American fraternalism history.
Facilities: 45,000-vol. library of bound books; 15,000-vol. library of Masonic periodicals.
Activities: films; lectures; study clubs; temporary exhibitions.
Publications: annual report.
Hours & Admission Prices: Mon. & Wed.-Fri. 8:30-4:30, Tues. 12-8. No charge; donations accepted. Closed legal holidays. ♿
Attendance: 3,200 (accurate)

CHILDREN'S MUSEUM OF MANHATTAN, The Tisch Building, 212 West 83rd St., New York, NY 10024-4901. Tel.: 212-721-1223. Fax: 212-721-1127.
Web Site: www.cmom.org
Founded: 1973.
Congressional District: 20
Key Personnel: C.E.O. & Exec. Dir., Andrew S. Ackerman; Honorary Chm., Laurie Tisch Sussman; Co. Chm., halley k. harrisburg; Co. Chm., John B. Rhea; Deputy Dir. Exhibits, Karen Snider; Deputy Dir. Education, Leslie Bushara; Comptroller, Candice Carnage; School & Outreach Programs Mgr., Jennifer Kozel; Museum Shop Mgr., Devon Jairam.
Personnel Profile: Full-Time Paid 40; Part-Time Paid 40; Part-Time Volunteers 75; Interns 20.
Governing Authority: nonprofit organization. Tax-exempt: 501(c)(3).
Children's Museum: housed in former elementary school building.
Collections: hands-on & participatory exhibits: literacy; science & the environment; arts, media & communications; early childhood education.
Research Fields: education & curriculum through the arts.
Facilities: environmental center; performing arts center; early childhood center; adventure center; children's birthday party program & facilities available by reservation. Museum-related items for sale.
Activities: guided tours; lectures; films; gallery talks; concerts; dance recitals; art festivals; workshops; formally organized education programs for children, adults, undergraduate & graduate students; docent program; training programs for museum workers; loan, permanent, temporary & traveling exhibitions; summer program; research.
Publications: calendars; brochures; posters; event schedules; publicity materials.
Hours & Admission Prices: Tues.-Sun., Mon. holidays & school vacations 10-5; school groups by appointment. Admission $10, senior citizens $7; children under one & members no charge. Closed New Year's Day; Thanksgiving; Christmas. ♿
Attendance: 340,000 (estimated)
Membership: Family $210; Friend $295; Supporter $395; Corporate $5,000 & up.

CHILDREN'S MUSEUM OF THE ARTS, 182 Lafayette St., New York, NY 10013-3276. Tel.: 212-274-0986. Fax: 212-274-1776.
Web Site: www.cmany.org
Founded: 1988.
Key Personnel: Exec. Dir., Keats Myer; Asst. Dir., Robin Parks Lockwood; Mgr. Art Programs, Claire Marcus; Mgr. Special Events, Lori Feren; Mktg. Mgr., Lucy Ofiesh; Cur., Prescott Trudeau; Mgr. Exhibitions & Collections, Sophie Kamin.
Personnel Profile: Full-Time Paid 10; Part-Time Paid 3; Interns 5.

Governing Authority: private; nonprofit organization. Tax-exempt: 501(c)(3).
Children's Museum.
Collections: 2,000 pieces of children's art from around the world; interactive exhibits.
Facilities: classrooms; 1,000 sq. ft. exhibit space. Museum-related items for sale.
Activities: formal education programs for children; temporary exhibitions; training programs for professional museum workers & educators. Annual Event: family fundraiser in spring; adult fundraiser in winter.
Publications: quarterly newsletter.
Hours & Admission Prices: Wed. & Fri.-Sun. 12-5, Thurs. 12-6. Adults $10; discounts to groups, AAM, AYM members & corporate sponsors, cool culture members; Thurs. 4-6 pay as you wish; members, children under 1 & seniors over 65 no charge. Closed Memorial Day; Independence Day; Labor Day; Thanksgiving; Christmas. ♿
Attendance: 35,000 (accurate)
Membership: CMA: Family $200; Friend $250; Patron $500.

CHILDREN'S MUSEUM OF THE NATIVE AMERICAN, 550 W. 155th St., New York, NY 10032-7801. Tel.: 212-694-2240.
Founded: 1976.
Key Personnel: Dir., Norman Ernsting
Children's Museum.
Collections: hands-on exhibits; Native American artifacts; tipi; canoe; Native American life & culture; photographs.
Activities: demonstrations; educational programs; Indian games; puppet show; workshops.
Hours & Admission Prices: Mon.-Fri. 8-2. Adults $5.

CHINA INSTITUTE GALLERY, CHINA INSTITUTE IN AMERICA, 125 E. 65th St., New York, NY 10065-7088. Tel.: 212-744-8181. Fax: 212-628-4159.
E-mail: gallery@chinainstitute.org
Web Site: www.chinainstitute.org
Founded: 1926.
Key Personnel: Dir., Willow Hai Chang; Chm., Virginia A. Kamsky; Pres., Sara Judge McCalpin; Registrar & Mgr., Sara Tam; Gallery Coord., Myoungsook Park; Gallery Asst. & Art Education, Yue Ma.
Personnel Profile: Full-Time Paid 34; Part-Time Paid 45; Part-Time Volunteers 10; Interns 10.
Governing Authority: nonprofit organization. Parent Institution: China Institute in America. Tax-exempt: 501(c)(3).
Art Gallery.
Collections: Chinese paintings, calligraphy & artifacts.
Major Exhibits: Confucious (T), 2/10-6/10; Woodcuts in Modern China, 1937-2008: Towards A Universal Pictorial Language (T), 9/10-12/10.
Facilities: 5,000-vol. library pertaining to Chinese; classrooms; 1,000 sq. ft. exhibit space. Museum-related items for sale.
Activities: concerts; films; guided tours; lectures; loan & traveling exhibitions; formal education programs.
Publications: exhibition catalogs.
Hours & Admission Prices: Tues. & Thurs. 10-8, Wed. & Fri.-Mon. 10-5. Adults $7, students & seniors $4; discounts to NYC Channel Thirteen members; Tues. & Thurs. 6pm-8pm, members & children under 12 no charge. Closed major holidays; between exhibitions.
Attendance: 9,150 (accurate)
Membership: Individual $55; Dual & Family $95.

THE CLOISTERS, 99 Margaret Corbin Dr., New York, NY 10040-1198. Tel.: 212-923-3700. Fax: 212-795-3640.
E-mail: cloisters@metmuseum.org
Web Site: www.metmuseum.org
Founded: 1938.
Congressional District: 20
Key Personnel: Cur. in Charge & Dept. Medieval Art & The Cloisters, Peter Barnet; Mgr. Administration, Christina Alphonso; Cur., Timothy Husband; Cur., Barbara Boehm; Conservator, Lucretia Kargere; Librarian, Michael Carter; Assoc. Mgr. Visitor Svcs., Keith Glutting; Museum Educator, Nancy Wu; Assoc. Security Mgr., Theodosios Kypriotis; Horticulturist, Deirdre Larkin; Museum Shop Mgr., Sheryl Ali.
Personnel Profile: Full-Time Paid 75; Part-Time Paid 20; Part-Time Volunteers 20.
Governing Authority: nonprofit organization. Parent Institution: The Metropolitan Museum of Art, 1000 5th Ave., New York, NY 10028. Tax-exempt: 501(c)(3).
Art Museum.
Collections: medieval art; cloisters & other European architectural elements; stained-glass windows; tapestries; sculpture; decorative arts; paintings; medieval-style gardens.
Research Fields: medieval art & architecture.
Facilities: 13,500-vol. library of books, 20,000 slides & 30,000 photographs on medieval art & architecture available to scholars & accredited graduate students by appointment; papers of Summer McKnight Crosby & George Grey Barnard; archives. Books, art reproductions & other museum-related items for sale.
Activities: guided tours; lectures; gallery talks; concerts; drama; formally organized education programs for children, adults & graduate students; permanent exhibitions; garden tours.
Publications: The Unicorn Tapestries; The Cloisters Cross; Medieval Tapestries; The Cloisters: Medieval Art and Architecture.
Hours & Admission Prices: March-Oct. Tues.-Sun. 9:30-5:15; Nov.-Feb. Tues.-Sun. 9:30-4:45. Recommended Admission: adults $20, seniors $15, students $10; discounts to AAM, ICOM & NY Museum council members; members & children under 12 accompanied by an adult no charge. Touch tours & sign language interpreter available on request. ♿
Attendance: 240,000 (estimated)
Membership: Associate $50; Met Net $60; Individual $95; Family/Dual $190; Friend $275; Sustaining $500; Apollo Circle $1,000; Contributing $1,200; Donor $1,800; Sponsor & Met Family Circle $4,000; Patron $8,000; Patron Circle $12,000; President's Circle $20,000.

THE COLLECTORS CLUB, INC., 22 E. 35th St., New York, NY 10016-3806. Tel.: 212-683-0559. Fax: 212-481-1269.
E-mail: collectorsclub@verizon.net
Web Site: www.collectorsclub.org
Founded: 1896.
Key Personnel: Pres., Roger Brody; Treas., Mark Banchik; Club. Sec., Dr. David Steidley.
Governing Authority: society. Tax-exempt: 501(c)(3).
Historic House and Library: housed in 1902, five-story brownstone rowhouse, former residence of Thomas B. Clark; neo-Georgian architecture designed by Stanford White.
Collections: medals & awards; 19th-century engraving & printing implements; early postal equipment; U.S. Classic Society's trophies; numerous philatelic collections including Harry M. Deggett's International reply coupons; Charles L. Pack's Brazil & Canada; photographic archives of Edward Knapp postal history covers; 130,000-vol. library of hard books, journals & periodicals from 18th-century to present day; maps; manuscripts; Philately: A Catalogue of The Collectors Club Library, New York City: Author Catalogue, Subject Catalogue, Title Catalogue, and Periodical Catalogue.
Research Fields: postal & philatelic history.
Facilities: library available for research & inter library loan; reading room; 65-capacity auditorium.
Activities: lectures; study clubs; hobby workshops; formally organized education programs for adults; loan & permanent exhibitions; guest speakers twice monthly. Museum Sponsors: International Philatelic Awards.
Publications: Books for philatelists, United States: The Ten Cents Stamps of 1855-59; A Census of United States Classic Plate Blocks 1851-1882. Afghanistan: Its Twentieth Century Postal Issues. Central America: Its Pre-Stamp History. Ecuador: Its Postmarks & Postal History. French Morocco: The 1943-44 Tour Hassan Issues. Honduras: The Black Air Mail. The Stamps of Jammu & Kashmir. Philatelic Handbook for Korea 1884-1905. Newfoundland Postal History. The New Hebrides: Postal Stamps & their History. New Zealand: 1898-99, Great Barrier Island Pigeon Post Stamps. Postal Stamps of Lithuania. Postal History & Postage Stamps of Serbia, 1841-1921. Catalogues, 71st Anniversary Philatelic Exhibition Commemorating the 75th Year of the Collectors Club (1971); Cumulative Index to Collectors Club Philatelist, 1922-71.
Hours & Admission Prices: Mon.-Fri. 10-5. No charge. Closed major holidays.
Membership: Non-Resident $75; Overseas $95; Resident $190.

THE CONSERVATORY GARDEN, Fifth Ave. at 105th St., New York, NY 10029. Mailing Address: Central Park Conservancy, 830 5th Ave., New York, NY 10065-7001. Tel.: 212-860-1382. Fax: 212-360-1388.
Web Site: www.centralparknyc.org
Key Personnel: Garden Dir., Lynden Miller; Garden Cur., Diane Schaub; Central Park Admin., Douglas Blonsky.
Personnel Profile: Full-Time Paid 4; Part-Time Volunteers 25.
Governing Authority: nonprofit. New York City Dept. of Parks & Recreation and Central Park Conservancy. Tax-exempt: 501(c)(3).
Botanical & Aquatic Gardens: six acre formal garden.
Collections: 20,000 tulips; 5,000 chrysanthemums; 175 different species of English-style perennials; annuals; bulbs; Woodland garden; Italian & French style gardens with seasonal tulip & Korean mum displays; 3 fountains.
Activities: garden tours; concerts. Annual Event: art exhibit.
Publications: Conservatory Garden Highlights, seasonal guides to plantings.
Hours & Admission Prices: Daily 8-dusk. No charge. ♿
Attendance: 10,000 (estimated)

COOPER-HEWITT, NATIONAL DESIGN MUSEUM, SMITHSONIAN INSTITUTION, 2 E. 91st St., New York, NY 10128-0669. Tel.: 212-849-8400. Fax: 212-849-8401.
Web Site: www.cooperhewitt.org
Founded: 1897.
Congressional District: 15
Key Personnel: Dir., Paul Warwick Thompson; Chm., Paul Herzan; Pres., James Rosenthal; Cur. Dir., Cara McCarty; Cur. Drawings & Prints, Gail Davidson; Cur. Product Design & Decorative Arts, Sarah Coffin; Cur. Textiles, Matilda McQuaid; Cur. Contemporary Design, Ellen Lupton; Cur. Wallcoverings, Gregory Herringshaw; Cur. Socially Responsible Design, Cynthia Smith; Dir. Communications, Jennifer Northrop; Deputy Dir., Caroline Baumann; Dir. Devel, Sophia Amaro; Librarian, Stephen H. Van Dyk; Dir. Education, Caroline Payson; Dir. Shop, Greg Krum; Museum Shop Mgr., Jocelyn Crapo.
Personnel Profile: Full-Time Paid 72; Part-Time Paid 13; Part-Time Volunteers 50; Interns 40.
Governing Authority: nonprofit organization. Parent Institution: Smithsonian Institution, Washington, D.C. Tax-exempt: 501(c)(3) & 170(b)(1)(A).
Design Museum: housed in 1901 Andrew Carnegie Mansion.
Collections: design & decorative arts of all periods & countries; architecture & design drawings; textiles; wallpaper; prints; graphics; woodwork; metalwork; ceramics; glass; furniture; graphic design; industrial design.
Major Exhibits: Design USA: Contemporary Innovation, 11/09-4/10/10; Why Design Now? National Design Triennial 2010, 4/10-12/10.
Research Fields: permanent collection; architecture; urban & graphic design.
Facilities: 70,000-vol. library pertaining to design, decorative arts design and architecture available for inter-library loan & research on the premises.
Activities: guided tours; lectures; gallery talks; formally organized education programs for children, adults, undergraduate & graduate college students; inter-museum loan, permanent, temporary & traveling exhibitions; home study programs; workshops; design information service. Museum Sponsors: Masters Degree program with Parson School of Design/New School in NYC & Washington, D.C.
Publications: exhibition catalogs; book, The Smithsonian Illustrated Library of Antiques; magazine.
Hours & Admission Prices: Mon.-Fri. 10-5, Sat. 10-6, Sun. 12-6. Adults $15, senior citizens & students $10; children under 12 & members no charge. Closed New Year's Day; Thanksgiving; Christmas. ♿
Attendance: 154,000 (accurate)
Membership: Student & Senior Citizen $50; National & International $55; Individual $75; Dual & Family $120; Contributing $200; Design Watch $500; Patron $1,000; National Design Council $2,500.

CZECH CENTER NEW YORK, 321 E. 73rd St., New York, NY 10021. Tel.: 646-422-3399. Fax: 646-422-3383.
E-mail: info@czechcenter.com
Web Site: www.czechcentres.cz/newyork/novinky.asp
Founded: 1995.
Key Personnel: Acting Dir., Marcel Sauer.
Personnel Profile: Full-Time Paid 7; Part-Time Paid 2; Part-Time Volunteers 2.
Governing Authority: foreign; nonprofit organization.
Civic Art & Culture Center Museum.
Collections: works of Czech artists.
Facilities: 1,250-vol. of books & magazines; 500 sq. ft. exhibit space.
Activities: concerts; dance recitals; films; traveling exhibitions; theater. Annual Event: Street Fair.
Publications: bimonthly newsletter, Ahoy.
Hours & Admission Prices: Mon.-11-5, Tues.-Wed. & Fri. 10-5, Thurs. 10-7. No charge; donations accepted. Closed New Year's Day; Christmas Eve, Day & day after.
Attendance: 10,000 (estimated)
Membership: Senior & Academic $30; Individual $40.

DAHESH MUSEUM OF ART, New York, NY 10022. Mailing Address: 45 E. Putnam Ave., Ste. 105, Greenwich, CT 06830-5428. Tel.: 212-759-0606. Fax: 203-861-9634.
Web Site: www.daheshmuseum.org
Founded: 1987.
Congressional District: 14
Key Personnel: Chm. (V), Mervat Zahid; C.F.O., William Ignatowich; Retail Sales Mgr., Martin Angeles.
Personnel Profile: Full-Time Paid 20; Part-Time Paid 17; Part-Time Volunteers 12; Interns 9.
Governing Authority: nonprofit organization. Tax-exempt: 501(c)(3).
Art Museum.
Collections: European art of the 19th & 20th centuries with emphasis on the academic tradition.
Research Fields: 19th & early 20th-century European academic art.
Activities: symposia; lectures; gallery talks; concerts.
Publications: Highlights from the Dahesh Museum Collection; newsletter; exhibition brochures.
Hours & Admission Prices: Temporarily closed for relocation. ♿
Membership: Student & Senior $40; Individual $70; Household $90; Contributing $150; Patron $300; Sustaining $600; Fellow $1,000; Director's Circle $2,500.

THE DRAWING CENTER, 35 Wooster St., New York, NY 10013-5300. Tel.: 212-219-2166, ext. 214. Fax: 212-966-2976.
E-mail: info@drawingcenter.org
Web Site: www.drawingcenter.org
Founded: 1977.
Congressional District: 8
Key Personnel: Exec. Dir., Brett Littman; Co Chm., Frances Beatty Adler; Co Chm., Eric Rudin; Exec. Editor of the Drawing Center's Publications, Jonathan T.D. Neil; Dir. Education, Aimee Good; Mng. Editor, Joanna Berman; Cur., Joao Ribas; Cur. Viewing Program, Nina Katchadourian; Public Rels. & Mktg. Officer, Emily Gaynor; Coord. Operations, Dan Gillespie; Visitor Svcs. & Bookstore Mgr., Chris Rose; Registrar, Anna Martin.
Personnel Profile: Full-Time Paid 10; Part-Time Paid 6; Part-Time Volunteers 10; Interns 22.
Governing Authority: nonprofit organization. Tax-exempt.
Art Museum: housed in c.1866 historic cast iron building.
Collections: drawings.
Major Exhibits: Selections, 1/15/10-4/5/10; Iannis Xenakis: Composer, Architect, Visionary (T), 1/15/10-4/8/10; Drawing Out: Student Artwork from Drawing Connections, 4/10/10-4/16/10; Leon Golub: Live & Die Like a Lion? (T), 4/23/10-7/23/10.
Research Fields: contemporary & historical drawing.
Facilities: 3,630 sq. ft. exhibit space. Exhibition catalogues & books for sale.
Activities: lectures; traveling & loan exhibitions; formally organized education programs for children, undergraduates & graduates; internship programs. Museum Sponsors: Artist Symposia; online registry featuring the work of 1,000 artists; literary series featuring new literature & poetry; ongoing Viewing Program where emerging artists' works are reviewed for possible inclusion in The Drawing Center Exhibitions.
Publications: exhibition catalogues; The Drawing Papers.
Hours & Admission Prices: Wed. & Fri.-Sun. 12-6, Thurs. 12-8. Suggested Admission: $3. Closed New Year's Day; Thanksgiving; Christmas. ♿
Attendance: 55,000 (accurate)
Membership: Artist $35; Individual $50; Dual $85; Contributor $150; Supporter $300; Associate $500; Donor $1,000; Friend $2,500; Corporate $5,000.

DYCKMAN FARMHOUSE MUSEUM AND PARK, 4881 Broadway, (at 204th St.), New York, NY 10034-3101. Tel.: 212-304-9422. Fax: 212-304-0635.
E-mail: info@dyckmanfarmhouse.org
Web Site: www.dyckmanfarmhouse.org
Founded: 1916.
Congressional District: 16
Key Personnel: Dir., Susan DeVries.
Personnel Profile: Full-Time Paid 3; Part-Time Volunteers 10; Interns 2.
Governing Authority: municipal. Parent Institution: Historic House Trust of New York City Parks & Recreation. Tax-exempt: 170(b) & 150(c)(3).
Historic House: 1784 Dyckman House, old Dutch-American farmhouse.
Collections: 18th-19th century furniture & furnishings; decorative art; Revolutionary War uniforms; Hessian hut; smokehouse.
Activities: guided tours; craft workshops; wine tastings.
Publications: brochures; newsletters; guide to historic sites of New York City.
Hours & Admission Prices: Wed.-Sat. 11-4, Sun. 12-4. Admission 10 & over $1.
Attendance: 12,924 (accurate)
Membership: Annual $25-$1,000.

EL MUSEO DEL BARRIO, (M), (I), 1230 Fifth Ave., New York, NY 10029-9962. Tel.: 212-831-7272. Fax: 212-831-7927.
E-mail: info@elmuseo.org
Web Site: www.elmuseo.org
Founded: 1969.
Congressional District: 15
Key Personnel: Dir., Julian Zugazagoitia; Chm. (V), Tony Bechara; Dir. Finance, Georgina Nichols; Chief Cur., Deborah Cullen; Dir. Education & Public Programs, Gonzalo Casals; Registrar, Noel Valentin; Mktg. Mgr., Rose Mary Cortes; Museum Shop Mgr., Myra Pineda; Dir. External Affairs, Susan Delvalle.
Personnel Profile: Full-Time Paid 35; Full-Time Volunteers 2; Part-Time Paid 1; Part-Time Volunteers 15; Interns 5.

Governing Authority: Operated by Amigos del Museo del Barrio, Inc. Tax-exempt.
Caribbean, Latino and Latin American Art Museum.
Collections: works on paper; sculptures; prints; paintings; films; photography; Santos & pre-Colombian collection with focus on Taino culture.
Major Exhibits: Nexus New York: Latin/American Artists in the Modern Metropolis, 11/09-2/10; Voces y Visiones: Highlights from El Museo del Barrio's Permanent Collection, 11/09; Phantom Sightings: Art After the Chicano Movement (T), 3/10-6/10; Retro/Active: The Works of Rafael Ferrer, 6/10-9/10; Nueva York, 9/10-2/11.
Research Fields: Puerto Rican & Latin American heritage, culture, history, art, music, literature & statistics.
Facilities: El Teatro, El Cafe, courtyard; Blackbox Theater & El Museo's Rooftop.
Activities: guided tours; lectures; films; performances; literary readings; symposia; educational programs; inter-museum loan; permanent, temporary & traveling exhibitions. Museum Sponsors: workshop in folk art, graphic arts, painting, drawing, sculpture, installation, art history lectures.
Publications: monthly e-newsletter; annual gala journal.
Hours & Admission Prices: Wed.-Sun. 11-6. Suggested Donation: adults $9, senior citizens & students $4; discount to AAM & ICOM members; members & children under 12 accompanied by parents no charge. ♿
Attendance: 300,000 (estimated)
Membership: Neighbor $25; Amigo $50; Familia $75; Supporter $100; Aficionado $500; Padrino $1,000; Patrons Circle $2,500; Corporation $10,000.

FEDERAL HALL NATIONAL MEMORIAL, 26 Wall St., New York, NY 10005-1996. Tel.: 212-825-6888. Fax: 212-825-6874.
Web Site: www.nps.gov/feha/
Founded: 1939.
Congressional District: 8
Key Personnel: Supt., Maria Burks.
Personnel Profile: Full-Time Paid 25.
Governing Authority: federal. Administered by National Park Service, Dept. of the Interior. Tax-exempt.
History Museum.
Collections: artifacts relating to George Washington; evolution of the Bill of Rights; historical development of New York City; evolution of Federal Hall; constitutional government; Custom House, sub-treasury.
Research Fields: 18th-19th century American history.
Facilities: Museum-related items for sale.
Activities: tours for groups; education programs; special events.
Publications: site brochure; booklet, John Peter Zenger.
Hours & Admission Prices: Mon.-Fri. 9-5. No charge. Closed New Year's Day; Martin Luther King Jr. Day; Memorial Day; Independence Day; Labor Day; Columbus Day; Veterans Day; Thanksgiving; Christmas. ♿
Attendance: 148,601 (accurate)

* **FRAUNCES TAVERN MUSEUM,** 54 Pearl St., New York, NY 10004-4300. Tel.: 212-425-1778, ext. 30. Fax: 212-509-3467.
E-mail: curator@fraucestavernmuseum.org
Web Site: www.fraucestavernmuseum.org
Founded: 1907.
Congressional District: 17
Key Personnel: Dir. & Cur., Suzanne Prabucki; Chm. (V), Charles C. Lucas, Jr., M.D.; Admin., Margaret O'Shaughnessy; Accounting, Cecelia Mahnken; Educator, Jennifer Patton; Security, Lindsford Bennett.
Personnel Profile: Full-Time Paid 5; Part-Time Paid 2; Part-Time Volunteers 15; Interns 1.
Governing Authority: society. Parent Institution: Sons of the Revolution in the State of New York. Tax-exempt: 501(c)(3).
History Museum: housed in 1907 renovated & restored 18th-century tavern & four adjacent 19th-century buildings.
Collections: 18th & 19th-century decorative arts; textiles; paintings; prints; manuscripts; Revolutionary War memorabilia; period rooms; five historic buildings.
Research Fields: early American history & culture; New York City history; historic preservation; American art, architecture & decorative arts.
Facilities: library; auditorium. Museum-related items for sale.
Activities: lectures; concerts; films; workshops; organized tours & programs; American history audio-visual presentations; permanent & temporary exhibitions.
Publications: monthly e-newsletter, The Patriot.
Hours & Admission Prices: Mon.-Sat. 12-5. Adults $10, seniors, students with ID & children 6-18 $5; discounts to AAM & ICOM members; children under 6 & members no charge. Closed New Year's Day; Martin Luther King Jr. Day; Good Friday; Labor Day; Christmas. ♿
Attendance: 14,658 (accurate)
Membership: Senior Citizen & Student $30; Individual $40; Family $60; Sustaining $125; Supporting $250; George Washington Fellow $500.

* **THE FRICK COLLECTION, (M), (I),** 1 East 70th St., New York, NY 10021-4981. Tel.: 212-288-0700. Fax: 212-628-4417.
E-mail: info@frick.org
Web Site: www.frick.org
Founded: 1920.
Congressional District: 14
Key Personnel: Dir., Anne L. Poulet; Pres. (V), Margot Bogert; Assoc. Dir. & Chief Cur., Colin Bailey; Cur., Susan Grace Galassi; Deputy Dir., Robert B. Goldsmith; Registrar, Diane Farynyk; Museum Shop Mgr., Kate Gerlough; Mgr. Devel., Lynne Rutkin; Mgr. Operations, Dennis F. Sweeney.
Personnel Profile: Full-Time Paid 166; Part-Time Paid 39; Part-Time Volunteers 74; Interns 15.
Governing Authority: nonprofit organization. Subsidiary Institution: Frick Art Reference Library. Tax-exempt: 501(c)(3).
Art Museum: formerly private home, c.1913-1914 building designed by Carrere & Hastings.
Collections: paintings; sculpture; furniture; decorative arts; prints & drawings.
Major Exhibits: European Paintings from Dulwich Picture Gallery, 3/10-5/10; Spanish Manner: Drawings from Ribera to Goya, 10/10-1/11.
Research Fields: areas related to works of art in the Frick Collection.
Facilities: approx. 3,000-vol. in house library of basic publications relating to works of art in The Frick Collection; also Frick Art Reference library: Founded 1920, housed in 1934 building designed by John Russell Pope, became division of the collection in 1984. 250,000 books; 78,000 sales catalogues; 3,650 serial titles; 1.2 million photographs; microforms collection. Museum-related items for sale.
Activities: lectures; concerts; symposium for graduate students affiliated with the art history departments; temporary exhibitions; seminars & gallery talks.
Publications: The Frick Collection: An Illustrated Catalogue, Vols. I-IX; Handbook of Paintings; The Frick Collection: An Introduction (video); Ingres & the Comtesse d'Haussonville; Art in the Frick Collection. A Guide to Works of Art on Exhibition; Paintings from the Frick Collection; Building The Frick Collection.
Hours & Admission Prices: Collection: Tues.-Sat. 10-6, Sun. & minor holidays 11-5. Reference Library: Sept.-May. Mon.-Fri. 10-5, Sat. 9:30-1; June-July Mon.-Fri. 10-5. Adults $18, seniors 62 & over $12, students $5; Sun. 11-1 pay what you wish; discounts to AAM & ICOM members and museum staff. Children under 10 not admitted. Closed New Year's Day; Independence Day; Thanksgiving; Christmas. ♿
Attendance: 282,061 (accurate)
Membership: Student $25; Non-Resident $40; Individual $60; Dual $90; Contributing $200; Supporting $400; Young Fellow $500; Sustaining $600; Non-Resident Fellow $800; Fellow $1,000; Contributing Fellow $2,500; Supporting Fellow $5,000; Sustaining Fellow $10,000; Director's Circle $25,000.

GENERAL GRANT NATIONAL MEMORIAL, Riverside Dr. & 122nd St., New York, NY 10027-2522. Tel.: 212-666-1640 & 1668. Fax: 212-932-9631.
Web Site: www.nps.gov/gegr/
Founded: 1897.
Congressional District: 17
Key Personnel: Supt., Shirley Mckinney; Cur., Judith Muller.
Personnel Profile: Full-Time Paid 5; Part-Time Volunteers 7.
Governing Authority: federal. Parent Institution: Manhattan Sites Unit, National Park Service, Dept. of the Interior. 212-825-6990. Tax-exempt.
Historical Museum: housed in 1897 building.
Collections: history; sarcophagi of Gen. Grant and his wife; memorabilia of Ulysses S. Grant; military.
Research Fields: Pres. Ulysses S. Grant; Civil War.
Facilities: 150-vol. library of biographies of Gen. Grant & Civil War history; exhibit rooms. Postcards & booklets for sale.
Activities: guided & self-guided tours; programs honoring Grant's birthday; rotating special exhibits; Civil War programs.
Publications: NPS site brochure.
Hours & Admission Prices: Daily 9-5. No charge. Closed New Year's Day; Thanksgiving; Christmas.
Attendance: 118,000 (accurate)

THE GRACIE MANSION CONSERVANCY, 88th St. & East End Ave., New York, NY 10028-8024. Tel.: 212-570-4751. Fax: 212-570-4493.
E-mail: dcarroll@cityhall.nyc.gov
Web Site: www.nyc.gov
Founded: 1981.
Key Personnel: Dir., Susan Danilow; Cur., Diana Carroll.

Governing Authority: municipal. Tax-exempt: 501(c)(3).
Historic House: 1799 Archibald Gracie country house. Designated the mayoral residence of New York City in 1942.
Collections: decorative arts of New York; paintings & prints by New York artists.
Research Fields: original residents of the mansion; New York City in the Federal period.
Facilities: 200-vol. library of decorative arts, American crafts & historic architecture books; garden; conservation center. Gift items for sale.
Activities: guided tours; docent program.
Hours & Admission Prices: Tours by reservation only. School Tours: Tues. & Thurs. mornings. No charge. Special Tours: Tues. & Thurs. afternoon. Public Tours: Wed. 10-2 hourly. Adults $7, senior citizens $4. ♿
Attendance: 30,000

GREY ART GALLERY, NEW YORK UNIVERSITY ART COLLECTION, (M), 100 Washington Square E., New York, NY 10003-6688. Tel.: 212-998-6780. Fax: 212-995-4024.
E-mail: greygallery@nyu.edu
Web Site: www.nyu.edu/greyart
Founded: 1975.
Congressional District: 17
Key Personnel: Deputy Dir., Frank Poueymirou; Gallery Mgr. & Registrar, Michele Wong; Asst. to Dir., Alyssa Plummer; Gallery Dir., Lynn Gumpert; Preparator, Philip Hall; Asst. Preparator, David Colossi; Asst. to Deputy Dir., Laurie Duke.
Personnel Profile: Full-Time Paid 7; Part-Time Paid 6; Interns 1.
Governing Authority: university. Parent Institution: New York University. Tax-exempt: 501(c)(3).
Fine Arts Museum: housed in Main Building of New York University on Washington Square, historic center of early New York City.
Collections: 19th & 20th-century paintings, sculpture & graphics; Abby Weed Grey Collection of Asian & Middle Eastern Art.
Research Fields: New acquisitions; paintings; sculpture; graphics; exhibition catalogue research.
Activities: lectures; films; gallery talks; education programs for children & adults, undergraduate & graduate college students affiliated with N.Y.U. & other Colleges in vicinity; inter-museum loan; permanent, temporary & traveling exhibitions.
Publications: exhibition catalogues.
Hours & Admission Prices: Tues. & Thurs.-Fri. 11-6, Wed. 11-8, Sat. 11-5. Suggested Donation: $3 per person. Closed holidays. ♿
Attendance: 25,000 (estimated)

HAMILTON GRANGE NATIONAL MEMORIAL, St. Nicholas Park, 100 St. Nicholas Terr., New York, NY 10026-2883. Mailing Address: c/o Federal Hall NM, 26 Wall St., New York, NY 10005. Tel.: 212-666-1640.
Web Site: www.nps.gov/hagr
Founded: 1924.
Congressional District: 15
Key Personnel: Park Supt., Jim Pepper; Technician, Cathy Hanson.
Governing Authority: federal. Administered by National Park Service, U.S. Dept. of Interior. Tax-exempt.
History Museum & Historic House: home of Alexander Hamilton.
Collections: early 19th-century furnishings; building's history; Hamilton memorabilia.
Activities: conducted tours; slide show.
Hours & Admission Prices: Closed for renovations until summer 2010.
Attendance: 11,478 (accurate)

HAMPDEN-BOOTH THEATRE LIBRARY AT THE PLAYERS, 16 Gramercy Park, New York, NY 10003-1705. Tel.: 212-228-1861. Fax: 212-253-6473.
E-mail: hampdenboo@aol.com
Web Site: hampden-booth.org
Founded: 1888.
Congressional District: 18
Key Personnel: Pres., Robert Winter-Berger; Cur., Raymond Wemmlinger.
Governing Authority: society. Affiliated with the Players. Tax-exempt: 501(c)(3).
Art & Theater Museum: housed in remodeled Gothic Revival townhouse.
Collections: American & English stage; manuscripts.
Research Fields: theater.
Facilities: 8,000-vol. library of published works on the performing arts available by appointment only; reading room.
Activities: guided tours; permanent & temporary exhibitions.
Hours & Admission Prices: By appointment. No charge; donations accepted.

THE HISPANIC SOCIETY OF AMERICA, (M), (I), 155th St. & Broadway, New York, NY 10032. Mailing Address: 613 W. 155th St., New York, NY 10032-7597. Tel.: 212-926-2234. Fax: 212-690-0743.
E-mail: info@hispanicsociety.org
Web Site: www.hispanicsociety.org
Founded: 1904.
Congressional District: 17
Key Personnel: Dir., Mitchell A. Codding; Asst. Dir. & Cur. Decorative Arts, Margaret E. Connors McQuade; Cur. Modern Books, Edwin Rolon; Cur. Prints & Photographs, Patrick Lenaghan; Cur. Paintings, Marcus B. Burke; Cur. Manuscripts & Rare Books, John O'Neill; Cur. Sculpture & Textiles, Constancio del Alamo; Education, Ricardo Hernandez.
Personnel Profile: Full-Time Paid 28; Part-Time Paid 13; Part-Time Volunteers 2; Interns 3.
Governing Authority: nonprofit organization. Tax-exempt: 501(c)(3).
Art Museum & Cultural Center.
Collections: culture of Iberian Peninsula from prehistoric times to present; paintings; sculpture; ceramics; textiles; archaeology; decorative arts; costumes; glass; art & culture from Spain, Portugal, Latin America, Philippines.
Research Fields: culture & history of Hispanic world: Spain, Portugal, Latin America & the Philippines.
Facilities: 350,000-vol. library of books, manuscripts, maps, photographs, archives, graphics & music related to the literature, language, history & arts of the Hispanic world: Spain, Portugal, Latin America and the the Philippines available for reference by scholars; reading room. Books & other museum-related items for sale.
Activities: recorded education program for children, adults & undergraduate college students; permanent & temporary exhibitions.
Publications: books & articles on bibliography; literature & art of the Hispanic world: Spain, Portugal, Latin America & the Philippines; catalogs of library collections & exhibitions.
Hours & Admission Prices: Museum: Tues.-Sat. 10-4:30, Sun. 1-4. No charge. Donations accepted. Reading Room: Tues.-Sat. 10-4:30. Closed holidays; Thanksgiving weekend; Christmas to New Year's Day.
Attendance: 25,000 (estimated)
Membership: Friends of the Hispanic Society $50.00 and up.

HISTORIC HOUSE TRUST OF NEW YORK CITY, (M), The Arsenal, 830 Fifth Ave., Rm. 203, New York, NY 10065-7001. Tel.: 212-360-8282. Fax: 212-360-8201.
E-mail: hht@parks.nyc.gov
Web Site: www.historichousetrust.org
Founded: 1989.
Congressional District: 14
Key Personnel: Exec. Dir., Franklin D. Vagnone; Co Chm., Deborah Krulewitch; Co Chm., Frances Eberhart; Sec., Richard Southwick; Treas., Lisa Ackerman.
Personnel Profile: Full-Time Paid 10.
Governing Authority: municipal government; nonprofit. Subsidiary Institutions: Bartow-Pell Mansion Museum, 895 Shore Rd., Pelham Bay Park, Bronx, NY 10464; Edgar Allan Poe Cottage, Poe Park, 2460 Grand Concourse at Kingsbridge, Rd., Bronx, NY 10467; Valentine-Varian House, Varian Park, 3266 Bainbridge Ave. at E. 208th St., Bronx, NY 10467; Van Cortlandt House Museum, Van Cortlandt Park, Broadway at 246th St., Bronx, NY 10471; Lefferts Homestead, Prospect Park, Flatbush Ave. at Empire Blvd., Brooklyn, NY 11215; Pieter Claesen Wyckoff House Museum, Wyckoff Park, Clarendon Rd. at Ralph Ave., Brooklyn, NY 11210; Dyckman Farmhouse Museum, Dyckman House Park, 4881 Broadway at 204th St., New York 10034; Gracie Mansion, Carl Schurz Park, 89th St. & East End Ave., New York 10128; Morris-Jumel Mansion, Roger Morris Park, 17-65 Jumel Terrace at 160th St., New York 10032; King Manor Museum, King Park, 150th St. & Jamaica Ave., Jamaica, NY 11432; Kingsland House, Weeping Beech Park, 143-35 37th Ave., Flushing, NY 11354; Queens County Farm Museum, 73-50 Little Neck Parkway, Floral Park, NY 11004; Alice Austen House Museum, Alice Austen Park, 2 Hylan Blvd., Staten Island, NY 10305; Conference House, Conference House Park, 7455 Hylan Blvd., Staten Island, NY 10307; Historic Richmond Town, LaTourette Park, 441 Clarke Ave., Staten Island, NY 10306; Seguine House, 441 Seguine Ave., Staten Island, NY 10307; The Old Stone House, Historic Interpretive Center, J.J. Byrne Park, 3rd St. btw. 4th & 5th Ave., Brooklyn, NY 11215; Little Red Lighthouse, Fort Washington Park, New York, NY; Merchant's House Museum, 29 E. 4th St. New York, NY 10003. Swedish Cottage Marionette Theatre, 79th St. & West Dr., Central Park, New York, NY 10024; Hendrick I. Lott House, 1940 E. 36th St., Brooklyn, NY 11234; Lewis H. Latimer House Museum, 34-41 137th St., Flushing, NY 11354. Tax-exempt.
Historic Agency: created in 1989 to preserve and promote 22 Historic House museums located on Park land in the five boroughs.

Collections: 22 historic houses throughout New York City; historical furnishings; personal artifacts.
Research Fields: early history of New York City; historical homes.
Activities: restoration & maintenance of 22 houses; curatorial restoration of house interiors to original styles; development of education programs & exhibitions; recreation of period gardens & landscapes.
Publications: guidebook, Historic Houses in New York City Parks; quarterly newsletter & calendar of events, Historic House News; brochure, Historic Houses in New York City Parks.
Hours & Admission Prices: Visit website for information.
Attendance: 600,000 (accurate)
Membership: Friend of the Trust: Friend $50; Associate $75; Family Friend $125; Patron $250; Fellow $500; Guardian $1,000; Cornerstone $5,000.

HUNTER COLLEGE ART GALLERIES, (M), 695 Park Ave., New York, NY 10065-5085. Tel.: 212-772-4991. Fax: 212-772-4554.
E-mail: tadler@hunter.cuny.edu
Founded: 1984.
Congressional District: 14
Key Personnel: Dir., Tom Weaver; Cur., Tracy L. Adler; Preparator, Phi Nguyen; Asst. Cur., Kristin Saroyan; Studio Supvr. MFA Bldg., Tim Laun.
Personnel Profile: Full-Time Paid 3; Part-Time Paid 12; Interns 10.
Governing Authority: public college; nonprofit. Parent Institution: City University of New York. Subsidiary Institutions: The Bertha and Karl Leubsdorf Art Gallery at Hunter College, 68th St. & Lexington Ave. S.W. Corner, New York, NY 10021; Hunter College/Times Square Gallery, 450 W. 41st St., New York, NY 10036. Tax-exempt: 501(c)(3).
Art Galleries.
Collections: American art since 1945.
Activities: loan exhibitions; temporary exhibitions.
Publications: exhibition catalogues; 8-10 annual catalogue publications; Exotic Representation; Doug Ohlson: Twenty Years of Painting, 1982-2002; Mark Feldstein: Recent Work, 1999-2001; Seeing Red; Vincent Longo: Reflections on Abstraction; Strange Worlds; Moved
Hours & Admission Prices: Sept.-June: Bertha and Karl Leubsdorf Art Gallery: Tues.-Sat 1-6. Times Square Gallery: Tues.-Sat. 1-6. No charge. Closed Christmas; New Year's Day. ♿
Attendance: 10,000 (estimated)
Membership: Associate Member $50; Friend $250; Sponsor $500; Founder $1,000; Life $10,000.

THE INTERCHURCH CENTER, 475 Riverside Dr., Rm. 253, New York, NY 10115-0003. Tel.: 212-870-2200. Fax: 212-870-2440.
Web Site: www.interchurch-center.org
Founded: 1959.
Congressional District: 15
Key Personnel: Pres. & Exec. Dir., Paula M. Maya; Chm. (V), Joanne Fernandez; Cur., Dorothy Cochran; Librarian, Tracey Del Duca.
Personnel Profile: Full-Time Paid 1; Part-Time Paid 2.
Governing Authority: nonprofit. Tax-exempt: 501(c)(3).
Library with Exhibits.
Collections: Revised Standard Version of the Bible exhibit; temporary exhibits of contemporary art.
Facilities: 11,000-vol. library of ecumenical & denominational religious books & periodicals, general reference material; slide registry of artists who have exhibited at TIC; 350-seat auditorium; cafeteria.
Activities: internet access; guided tours upon advance request; loan & permanent exhibitions.
Hours & Admission Prices: Mon.-Fri. 10-5. No charge. Closed legal holidays; Good Friday; day after Thanksgiving; Christmas Eve. ♿
Attendance: 5,000

* **INTERNATIONAL CENTER OF PHOTOGRAPHY, (M),** 1133 Avenue of the Americas at 43rd St., New York, NY 10036-7703. Mailing Address: 1114 Avenue of the Americas at 43rd St., New York, NY 10036-7703. Tel.: 212-857-0000. Fax: 212-857-0090.
E-mail: info@icp.org
Web Site: www.icp.org
Founded: 1974.
Congressional District: 14
Key Personnel: Dir., Willis E. Hartshorn; Chm. Bd. (V), Caryl S. Englander; Pres. (V), Jeffrey A. Rosen; Dir. Operations, Charles Barrett; Controller, Victor Quinones; Deputy Dir. Programs & Education, Phillip Block; Deputy Dir. External Affairs, Colleen Criste; Deputy Dir. Administration, Steve Rooney; Dir. Administration, Linda Freitag; Dir. Communications, Phyllis Levine; Dir. Retail Operations, Gigi Loizzo; Dir. Devel., Marie R. Spiller; Dir. Publications, Philomena Mariani; Membership Mgr., Lucig Kebranian; Deputy Dir. Exhibitions & Collections and Chief Cur., Brian Wallis; Cur., Christopher Phillips; Cur., Carol Squiers; Cur. Collections, Edward Earle; Dir. Special Projects, Ann Doherty; Registrar, Barbara Woytowicz; Librarian, Deirdre Donohue.
Personnel Profile: Full-Time Paid 80; Part-Time Paid 50; Part-Time Volunteers 20; Interns 40.
Governing Authority: private; nonprofit organization. Tax-exempt.
Photography Museum.
Collections: approx. 150,000 photographic prints, primarily 20th-century; over 4,000 hours of original audio recordings; collection of video tapes & films related to the Center's activities, photographers & photography.
Major Exhibits: Miroslav Tichy, 1/10-5/10; Twilight Visions: Surrealism, Photography, & Paris, 1/10-5/10; Alan B. Stone and the Senses of Place, 1/10-5/10; The Documents of Eugene Atgert, 1/10-5/10; Perspectives, 5/10-9/10; For All the World to See: Visual Culture and the Struggle for Civil Rights, 5/10-9/10; Jasper, Texas, 5/10-9/10; Take Me to the Water, 5/10-9/10; The Mexican Suitcase (T), 9/10-1/11; Chim, 9/10-1/11.
Research Fields: photography as art, communication, with concentration in documentary & photojournalism.
Facilities: 18,000-vol. library of photographic books & related materials; screening room; classrooms; archive study room available to researchers, students & museum professionals by appointment; black & white & color photo labs & digital media labs. Photographic books, portfolios, audio visuals & other museum-related items for sale.
Activities: changing exhibitions; guided tours; lectures; films; gallery talks; formally organized education programs; MFA program in conjunction with Bard College; docent program; loan & traveling exhibitions.
Publications: books; exhibition catalogs; program guides; annual report; posters; portfolios; brochures.
Hours & Admission Prices: Tues.-Thurs. & Sat.-Sun. 10-6, Fri. 10-8. Adults $12, students & senior citizens $8; discounts to AAM members; Fri. 5-8 admission by voluntary contribution; staff from NYC museums, children under 12, members & school group tours no charge. Closed New Year's Day; Independence Day; Thanksgiving; Christmas. ♿
Attendance: 148,904 (accurate)
Membership: Senior $55; Senior Citizen Double $70; Individual $75; Double $100; Supporting $200; Focus $300; Photography Circle $350; Silver Patron $650; Gold Patron $1,350; Benefactor Patron $3,500.

INTERNATIONAL PRINT CENTER NEW YORK (IPCNY), (M), 526 W. 26th St., Rm. 824, New York, NY 10001-5538. Tel.: 212-989-5090. Fax: 212-989-6069.
Web Site: www.ipcny.org
Founded: 1995.
Congressional District: 8
Key Personnel: C.E.O., Pres. & Dir., Anne Coffin; Chm. (V), Janice Oresman.
Personnel Profile: Full-Time Paid 3; Part-Time Paid 1; Part-Time Volunteers 20; Interns 9.
Governing Authority: state; nonprofit organization. Tax-exempt: 501(c)(3).
Print Exhibition Space.
Collections: fine art prints.
Research Fields: national directory of print workshops; participating artists' biographies.
Facilities: library.
Activities: internship program; lectures; loan, traveling & participatory exhibits; member events. Annual Events: Exhibition Openings; workshop visit.
Publications: exhibition catalogues; brochures; informational hand-outs.
Hours & Admission Prices: July Mon.-Fri. 11-6; Sept.-June Tues.-Sat. 11-6. No charge. Closed national holidays. ♿
Attendance: 24,000 (estimated)
Membership: Artist & Student $50; Basic $100; Contributing $250; Benefactor $500; Patron $1,000.

INTREPID SEA, AIR & SPACE MUSEUM, (M), Pier 86, W. 46th St. & 12th Ave., New York, NY 10036-4103. Tel.: 212-245-0072. Fax: 212-245-1547.
E-mail: dscialpi@intrepidmuseum.org
Web Site: www.intrepidmuseum.org
Founded: 1982.
Congressional District: 17
Key Personnel: Pres., Bill White; Exec. Dir., Susan Marenoff; Dir. Devel. & External Affairs, Lisa Yaconiello; Asst. Vice Pres. Mktg., Mike Onysko.
Personnel Profile: Full-Time Paid 126; Part-Time Paid 146; Part-Time Volunteers 50; Interns 16.
Governing Authority: nonprofit organization. Parent Institution: Intrepid Museum Foundation. Tax-exempt: 501(c)(3).
Armed Forces Museum: 900 ft. long aircraft carrier.
Collections: carrier history; Vietnam era destroyer Edson; destroyer escort Slater; guided missile submarine Growler; Polish MIG-21; British Scimitar; French Etendard; F-14 Super Tomcast; Coast Guard cutter Tamaroa; light ship Nantucket; research ship Elizabeth M. Fisher; Soviet missile corvette

Hiddensee; A-12 Blackbird; over 40 aircraft, helicopters, missiles, rockets & space vehicles; photographs.
Research Fields: 20th-century history & technology; aviation history; New York Marine history; naval history.
Facilities: 5,000-vol. library pertaining to sea, air & space history & technology; theater; educational facilities; cafe. Gift items for sale.
Activities: guided tours of smaller ships; organized education programs for children; docent program; elementary; secondary schools in science & social science; participatory, loan & temporary exhibitions; in-house volunteer programs; flight simulators; group tours; birthday parties for children; rental facilities; Growler submarine & Concorde tours.
Publications: membership newsletter, Intrepid Times.
Hours & Admission Prices: Mon.-Fri. 10-5, Sat.-Sun. 10-6. Closed Thanksgiving; Christmas. ♿
Attendance: 700,000 (estimated)
Membership: Intrepid Net $25; Student $30; Individual $90; Dual $120; Family $140; Patron $300; Friend $600.

ITALIAN AMERICAN MUSEUM, (M), 155 Mulberry St., New York, NY 10013-4721. Tel.: 212-965-9000. Fax: 347-810-1028.
E-mail: info@italianamericanmuseum.org
Web Site: www.italianamericanmuseum.org
Founded: 2001.
Congressional District: 14
Key Personnel: C.E.O., Chm. (V), Pres. (V) & Cur., Dr. Joseph V. Scelsa; Devel., Maria Fosco; Treas., Robert Ciofalo; Museum Shop Mgr., Dolores Jacome.
Personnel Profile: Full-Time Paid 3; Part-Time Paid 3; Part-Time Volunteers 7; Interns 2.
Governing Authority: public college. Parent Institution: The City University of New York. Tax-exempt: 501(c)(3).
Cultural Heritage Museum.
Collections: Italian artifacts; cultural heritage of Italy; contributions of Italians & Italian Americans to American culture.
Facilities: 6,000-vol. library; 2,000 sq. ft. exhibit space.
Activities: lectures; temporary & traveling exhibitions.
Publications: quarterly newspaper, America Italia Review.
Hours & Admission Prices: Wed., Thurs. & Sat.-Sun. 11-6, Fri. 11-8; other times by appointment. No charge; donations accepted. Closed legal holidays. ♿
Attendance: 2,000 (estimated)
Membership: $100.

JAPAN SOCIETY GALLERY, (M), 333 E. 47th St., New York, NY 10017-2399. Tel.: 212-832-1155. Fax: 212-715-1262.
E-mail: gallery@japansociety.org
Web Site: www.japansociety.org
Founded: 1907.
Congressional District: 15
Key Personnel: Pres., Motoatsu Sakurai; Vice Pres. & Gallery Dir., Joe Earle.
Personnel Profile: Full-Time Paid 3; Part-Time Paid 2; Part-Time Volunteers 1; Interns 1.
Governing Authority: society. A part of the Japan Society, Inc. Tax-exempt: 501(c)(3).
Art Museum.
Collections: Japanese art.
Major Exhibits: Serizawa: Master Japanese Textile Design, 11/09-1/10; Tales of Old Japan: Woodblock Prints by Utagawa Kuniyoshi from the Arthur R. Miller Collection from the Royal Academy of Arts, London (T), 3/10-6/10; Nui: Patchwork Garments from a Sheltered Community, 7/10-8/10; The Sounf of One Hand Clapping: Painting and Calligraphy by Zen Master Hakvin New Orleans Museum of Art (T), 10/10-1/11.
Research Fields: Japanese art here & abroad.
Facilities: 4,500-vol. library; auditorium; garden; classrooms. Museum-related items for sale.
Activities: guided tours; lectures; films; gallery talks; concerts; dance recitals; arts festivals; drama; traveling exhibitions; language classes.
Publications: exhibition catalogs; 2-3 scholarly catalogues per year.
Hours & Admission Prices: Spring & Fall: Tues.-Thurs. 11-6, Fri. 11-9, Sat.-Sun. 11-5; Summer: Tues.-Fri. 11-6, Sat.-Sun. 11-5. Spring & Fall: adults $12, seniors & students $10; discounts to AAM, ICOM & NYC Council of Museums; members no charge. Summer: adults $5. Closed major holidays. ♿
Attendance: 25,000 (accurate)
Membership: Student, Senior & Assoc. (those living beyond 100 miles from NYC) $40; Individual $60; Dual $95; Contributing $150; Sustaining $250; Sponsor $500; Patron Circle $1,000 & up.

*** THE JEWISH MUSEUM, (M),** 1109 Fifth Ave., New York, NY 10128-0118. Tel.: 212-423-3200. Fax: 212-423-3232.
E-mail: info@thejm.org
Web Site: www.thejewishmuseum.org
Founded: 1904.
Congressional District: 18
Key Personnel: Dir. & C.E.O., Joan Rosenbaum; Chm. (V), Joshua Nash; Pres. (V), Robert Prozan; Deputy Dir. External Affairs, Lynn Thommen; C.O.O., Mary A. Walling; Deputy Dir. Programs, Ruth Beesch; Dir. Education, Nelly Silagy Benedek; Assoc. Dir. Devel. & Institutional Giving, Sarah Himmelfarb; Assoc. Dir. Devel. & Special Events, Linda Padawer; Sr. Cur., Susan Goodman; Chief Cur., Norman Kleeblatt; Cur. Archaeology & Judaica and Chm. Curatorial Affairs, Susan L. Braunstein; Dir. Mktg., Grace Rapkin; Dir. Communications, Anne Scher; Dir. Business Devel., Debbie Schwab-Dorfman; Dir. Merchandising, Stacey Zaleski; Dir. Collecting & Exhibitions, Jane Rubin; Museum Shop Mgr., Pamela Elias.
Personnel Profile: Full-Time Paid 120; Part-Time Paid 5; Part-Time Volunteers 140; Interns 13.
Governing Authority: university. Parent Institution: The Jewish Theological Seminary of America, 3080 Broadway, New York, NY 10027. Tax-exempt: 501(c)(3).
Art Museum: housed in 1908 Felix Warburg Mansion, a six-story French Gothic structure.
Collections: Judaica collection spanning forty centuries; ceremonial objects; paintings; sculpture; prints; drawings; textiles; antiquities; photographs; decorative arts; coins; medals; historic manuscripts; artifacts; broadcast material; multimedia.
Major Exhibits: Curious George, 3/14/10-8/1/10; David Goldblatt (T), 5/4/10-9/26/10; Houdini (T), 10/10-3/11.
Research Fields: archaeology; Jewish history; Jewish art.
Facilities: library of Judaica references available by special permission to research scholars; 232-seat auditorium; renovated Warburg Mansion & new annex in June 1993. Books, Israeli and other contemporary crafts, ceremonial objects & other museum-related items for sale.
Activities: gallery tours; interpretive guide program for special & permanent exhibitions; participatory workshops for children; lecture series; film programs; concerts; inter-museum loans, permanent & temporary exhibitions; community outreach program; interpreters for the hearing-impaired (24 hrs. notice).
Publications: calendars of exhibitions & events; exhibition catalogs; posters; brochures; newsletters; New Year's graphics; biennial report.
Hours & Admission Prices: Thurs. & Sat.-Tues. 11-5:45, Fri. 11-4. Adults $12, senior citizens $10, students $7.50; discounts to members, AAM & ICOM members; members no charge. Closed New Year's Day; Martin Luther King Jr. Day; Thanksgiving; Jewish holidays. ♿
Attendance: 192,000 (accurate)
Membership: Senior Citizen $55; Individual, Dual Senior Citizen & Out of Town $70; Dual $120; Family $135; Friend $150; Contributing $250; Supporting $500; Sustaining $750.

KEHILA KEDOSHA JANINA SYNAGOGUE & MUSEUM, 280 Broome St., New York, NY 10002-3702. Mailing Address: P.O. Box 72, Cooper Station, New York, NY 10276-0072. Tel.: 212-431-1619. Fax: 631-367-3905.
E-mail: kehila_kedosha_janina@netzero.net
Web Site: www.kkjsm.org
Founded: 1997.
Key Personnel: Dir., Marcia Haddad Ikonomopoulos; Chm. (V), Sol Kofinas; 2nd Vice Pres., Rose Eskononts.
Governing Authority: Tax-exempt.
Jewish History Museum.
Collections: Jewish history & culture.
Hours & Admission Prices: Museum: Sun. 11-4; other times by appointment. Synagogue: Sat. 9am & holidays.
Attendance: 5,000 (accurate)

LACRASIA'S GLOVE MUSEUM, 1181 Broadway, 8th Fl., New York, NY 10001-7431. Tel.: 212-803-1600. Fax: 212-686-5250.
E-mail: glovesla@aol.com
Web Site: www.wegloveyou.com
Founded: 1986.
Congressional District: 8
Key Personnel: Dir., Jay G. Ruckel; Museum Shop Mgr., Lacrasia Duchein
General Museum.
Collections: the collection of a 20 year veteran glove maker; antique gloves; vintage clothes; tools.
Research Fields: glove history; glovemaking technology.
Facilities: 2,000 sq. ft. exhibition area.
Activities: New York City museum educators' roundtable; student tour groups.
Publications: the glove letter.

Hours & Admission Prices: By appointment only. No charge; donations accepted.
Attendance: 1,000 (estimated)

*** LOWER EAST SIDE TENEMENT MUSEUM,** 91 Orchard St., New York, NY 10002-3132. Tel.: 212-431-0233, ext. 0. Fax: 212-431-0402. TTY: 212-431-0714.
E-mail: lestm@tenement.org
Web Site: www.tenement.org
Founded: 1988.
Congressional District: 12
Key Personnel: Pres., Morris Vogel; Chm., Bruce A. Menin; Vice Pres. & C.O.O., Barry Roseman; Vice Pres. Education, Annie Polland; Vice Pres. Public Affairs, David Eng; Vice Pres., Museum Shop & Events, Helene Silver; Dir. Institutional Giving, Erica Raven; Dir. Education, Sarah Pharaon.
Personnel Profile: Full-Time Paid 36; Part-Time Paid 40; Part-Time Volunteers 13.
Governing Authority: nonprofit organization. Tax-exempt: 501(c)(3).
Immigrant History Museum: housed in c.1863 pre Old-Law tenement building.
Collections: historical immigrant documents; artifacts.
Research Fields: immigrant & urban history.
Facilities: 500-vol. library of material on history; 60-seat lecture hall. Books on historical subjects & other museum-related items for sale.
Activities: guided tours; lectures; loan exhibitions; ESOL workshops; training programs for professional museum workers; docent program; art exhibits; digital media projects; film screenings; school group tours.
Publications: monthly e-newsletter, News from the Tenement Museum; books, A Tenement Story; What Might Have Been: The Story of the Moores; 97 Orchard Street.
Hours & Admission Prices: Daily 10-6. Adults $20, senior citizens & students $17; discounts to Museum Council of NY & AAM members; children under 5 no charge. Closed New Year's Day; Thanksgiving; Christmas.
Attendance: 170,000 (accurate)
Membership: Senior & Student $45; Educator $45; Individual $55; Dual $90; Family $150; Tenement Friend $250; Tenement Contributor $500; Mutual Aid Society $1,000-$5,000.

MERCHANT'S HOUSE MUSEUM, (M), 29 E. Fourth St., New York, NY 10003-7003. Tel.: 212-777-1089. Fax: 212-777-1104.
E-mail: pi@merchantshouse.com
Web Site: www.merchantshouse.com
Founded: 1936.
Congressional District: 12
Key Personnel: Chm., Nicholas B.A. Nicholson; Exec. Dir., Margaret Halsey Gardiner; Sec., Anne Fairfax.
Personnel Profile: Full-Time Paid 2; Part-Time Paid 1; Part-Time Volunteers 54.
Governing Authority: nonprofit organization. Parent Institution: Historic House Trust - NYC Parks & Recreation. Tax-exempt: 501(c)(3).
Historic House: 1832 example of late Federal & Greek Revival architecture.
Collections: Seabury Tredwell family collections; 19th-century furniture, decorative arts & textiles.
Research Fields: lighting; clothing; china & porcelain; family books; garden plot.
Facilities: 350-vol. library; garden. Postcards & other museum-related items for sale.
Activities: docent program; formal education programs for adults, children, undergraduate & graduate students affiliated with NYU, FIT, Bardy, Parson's & New York School of Design; guided tours; lectures; study clubs; temporary exhibitions; training programs for professional museum workers; dramatic period readings.
Publications: quarterly newsletter, The Merchant's House Museum.
Hours & Admission Prices: Thurs.-Mon. 12-5. Adults $8, senior citizens & students $5; children under 12 & members no charge. Closed New Year's Eve & Day; Easter; Independence Day; Thanksgiving; Christmas Eve & Day.
Attendance: 6,000 (estimated)
Membership: Student & Senior $25; Good Neighbor $50; Family & Household $75; Protector $125; Cultural Hero $250; Princely Supporter $500; Leading Light $1,000; Paragon of Virtue $2,500.

*** THE METROPOLITAN MUSEUM OF ART, (M), (I),** 1000 Fifth Ave., (at 82nd St.), New York, NY 10028-0113. Tel.: 212-535-7710. Fax: 212-570-3879. TTY: 212-650-2551 & 570-3828.
E-mail: webmaster@metmuseum.org
Web Site: www.metmuseum.org
Founded: 1870.
Congressional District: 18
Key Personnel: Dir. & C.E.O., Thomas P. Campbell; Chm. Bd., James Houghton; Pres., David McKinney; Chm. (V), Lucinda Ballard; Sr. Vice Pres. External Affairs, Emily K. Rafferty; Sr. Vice Pres. & C.F.O., Deborah Winshel; Vice Pres. Merchandising Activities, Sally Pearson; Vice Pres. Communications & Mktg., Harold Holzer; Vice Pres. Sec. & Gen. Counsel, Sharon H. Cott; Vice Pres. Facilities Mgmt., Philip T. Venturino; Vice Pres. Construction, J. Nicholas Cameron; Assoc. Dir. Administration, Doralynn S. Pines; Assoc. Dir. Education, Kent Lydecker; Assoc. Dir. Exhibitions, Mahrukh Tarapor; Sr. Assoc. Counsel, Cristina Del Valle; Cur. in Charge, Arts of Africa, Oceania & the Americas, Julie Jones; Lawrence A. Fleischman Chm. Am. Wing, Morrison H. Heckscher; Cur., American Decorative Arts & Admin. of the American Wing, Peter M. Kenny; Anthony W. & Lulu C. Wang Cur. American Decorative Arts, Alice Cooney Frelinghuysen; Alice Pratt Brown Cur. American Paintings & Sculpture, H. Barbara Weinberg; Cur. in Charge, Ancient Near Eastern Art, Joan Aruz; Arthur Ochs Sulzberger Cur. in Charge, Arms & Armor, Stuart Pyhrr; Brooke Russell Astor Chm. Asian Art, James C.Y. Watt; Cur. in Charge Costume Institute, Harold Koda; Drue Heinz Chm. Drawings & Prints, George R. Goldner; Lila Acheson Wallace Cur. in Charge Egyptian Art, Dorothea Arnold; John Pope-Hennessy Chm. European Paintings, Everett Fahy; Iris & B. Gerald Cantor Cur. in Charge, European Sculpture & Decorative Arts, Ian Wardropper; Henry R. Kravis Cur. European Sculpture & Decorative Arts, James David Draper; Distinguished Research Cur., Olga Raggio; Cur. in Charge Greek & Roman Art, Carlos Picon; Distinguished Research Cur., Dietrich von Bothmer; Patty Cadby Birch Cur. in Charge Islamic Art, Daniel Walker; Cur. in Charge, Robert Lehman Collection, Laurence B. Kanter; Michel David-Weill Cur. in Charge Medieval Art & the Cloisters, Peter Barnet; Frederick P. Rose Cur. in Charge, Musical Instruments, J. Kenneth Moore; Cur. in Charge, Photographs, Maria Morris Hambourg; Acting Cur. in Charge, Photographs, Malcolm Daniel; Jacques & Natasha Gelman Chm. Modern Art, William S. Lieberman; Sherman Fairchild Chm. Paintings Conservation, Hubert von Sonnenburg; Sherman Fairchild Conservator in Charge, Objects Conservation, Lawrence Becker Sherman Fairchild Conservator in Charge, Sherman Fairchild Center for Works on Paper and Photographs Conservation Majorie Shelley; Acting Conservator in Charge Textile Conservation, Florica Zaharia; Arthur K. Watson Chief Librarian, Kenneth Soehner; Chief Librarian Photo & Slide Library, Priscilla F. Farah; Chief Registrar, Herb Moskowitz; Editor-in-Chief & Gen. Mgr. Publications, John P. O'Neill; Mgr. Visitor Svcs., Kathleen Arffmann; Chief Designer, Jeffrey L. Daly; Museum Shop Mgr., Will Sullivan.
Personnel Profile: Full-Time Paid 1,783; Part-Time Paid 744; Part-Time Volunteers 1,215; Interns 50.
Governing Authority: nonprofit organization. Branch Museum: The Cloisters Museum of European Medieval Art. Tax-exempt: 501(c)(3).
Art Museum.
Collections: ancient through modern art of Egypt, Greece, Rome, the Near & Far East, Europe, Africa, Oceania, pre-Columbian cultures & the U.S.; painting; sculpture; architecture; prints; photographs; drawings; glass; ceramics; metalwork; manuscripts; furniture; period rooms; textiles; costumes; arms & armor; musical instruments; decorative arts.
Research Fields: American decorative arts; ancient Near Eastern art; arms & armor; drawings; Egyptian art; European paintings & sculpture; European decorative arts; Asian art; Greek & Roman art; Robert Lehman Collection; medieval art; musical instruments; prints & photographs; African art, Oceanic art, pre-Columbian art; costumes; American paintings & sculpture; Islamic art; 20th-century art.
Facilities: 500,000-vol. library of art & related reference materials available for use by scholars & graduate students; 708- & 246-seat auditoriums; classrooms; restaurant & cafeteria. Books, reproductions & other museum-related items for sale.
Activities: guided tours; lectures; films; gallery talks; concerts; formally organized education programs for children & adults; docent program or council; training programs for professional museum workers; inter-museum loan, permanent, temporary & traveling exhibitions. Museum Sponsors: guided tours in Spanish, French, Italian, Japanese & other languages.
Publications: quarterly bulletin; bimonthly calendar; annual journal; annual report; exhibition catalogues; collection catalogues; scholarly books; popular books & calendars; brochures; educational publications.
Hours & Admission Prices: Tues.-Thurs. & Sun. 9:30-5:30, Fri.-Sat. 9:30-9. Suggested Donation: adults $20, senior citizens 65 & over $15, students $10; discount to AAM & ICOM members; members no charge. Closed New Year's Day; Thanksgiving; Christmas. ♿
Attendance: 5,400,000 (accurate)
Membership: Student $45; Associate $50; Met National $55; Individual $85; Dual $175; Friend $250; Sustaining $450; Contributing $1,000; Donor $1,350; Sponsor $3,500; Patron $7,000; Upper Patron $10,000.

MIRIAM & IRA D. WALLACH ART GALLERY, (M), 116th St. & Broadway, Schermerhorn Hall, 8th Fl., New York, NY 10027. Mailing Address: Columbia University, 826 Schermerhorn Hall, MC 5517, 1190 Amsterdam Ave., New York, NY 10027-7054. Tel.: 212-854-7288. Fax: 212-854-7800.
E-mail: wallach@columbia.edu
Web Site: www.columbia.edu/cu/wallach
Founded: 1986.
Congressional District: 16
Key Personnel: Dir. & Cur. Art Properties, Sarah Elliston Weiner.
Personnel Profile: Full-Time Paid 4; Part-Time Paid 2; Interns 2.
Governing Authority: private university. Parent Institution: Columbia University. Tax-exempt: 501(c)(3).
Art Gallery: housed in Schermerhorn Hall.
Collections: (collection is the property of Columbia University).
Research Fields: pertaining to student & faculty research.
Facilities: 2,300 sq. ft. exhibit space.
Activities: lectures; films; symposia; tours.
Publications: exhibition catalogs.
Hours & Admission Prices: During the academic year Wed.-Sat. 1-5. No charge. ♿
Attendance: 5,000 (estimated)

* **THE MORGAN LIBRARY & MUSEUM, (M),** 225 Madison Ave., New York, NY 10016-3405. Tel.: 212-685-0008. Fax: 212-481-3484.
E-mail: media@themorgan.org
Web Site: www.themorgan.org
Founded: 1924.
Congressional District: 15
Key Personnel: Dir., William M. Griswold; Pres., S. Parker Gilbert; Deputy Dir., Brian Regan; Dir. Finance & Administration, Kristina W. Stillman; Dir. Library & Museum Svcs., Robert E. Parks; Cur. Robert H. Taylor & Dept. Head, Declan Kiely; Cur. & Dept. Medieval & Renaissance Manuscripts, William M. Voelkle; Cur. Charles Engelhard & Head Dept. Drawings & Prints, Rhoda Eifel-Porter; Astor Cur. & Dept. Head, Printed Books & Bindings, John Bidwell; Dir. Member Svcs., Nadine Slowik; Assoc. Cur. Seals & Tablets, Sidney H. Babcock, IV; Controller, Loretta Greaney; Dir., Thaw Conservation Center, Margaret Holben Ellis; Mellon Conservator, Patricia Reyes; Dir. Education, Linden Chubin; Dir. Communications & Mktg., Patrick Milliman; Dir. Merchandising Svcs., Sean Hayes; Publications Mgr., Karen Banks.
Personnel Profile: Full-Time Paid 124; Part-Time Paid 41; Part-Time Volunteers 23; Interns 9.
Governing Authority: nonprofit organization. Tax-exempt: 170(b)(1)(A).
Library & Art Museum: housed in the 1906 library built by McKim, Mead, & White for Pierpont Morgan.
Collections: paintings; art objects; ancient Near Eastern seals & tablets; medieval & Renaissance manuscripts; printed & children's books; bindings; literary, historical & music manuscripts; Gilbert & Sullivan collection; old master to 20th-century drawings & prints.
Major Exhibits: Demons and Devotion: The Hours of Catherine of Cleves (T), 1/22/10-5/2/10; Rome After Raphael, 1/22/10-5/9/10; Flemish Illumination in the Era of Catherine of Cleves, 1/22/10-5/23/10; Palladio and His Legacy, 4/2/10-7/4/10; Romantic Gardens: Nature, Art and Landscape Design, 5/21/10-9/12/10; Albrecht Durer: What Beauty Is, 6/4/10-9/26/10; Mark Twain, 9/17/10-1/23/11; Roy Lichtenstein, 9/24/10-1/2/11.
Research Fields: all fields of collections.
Facilities: library collections available for scholarly use upon written application; reading room. Museum-related items for sale.
Activities: lectures; concerts; photographic services.
Publications: books; pamphlets; exhibition catalogs; facsimiles; guide to collections.
Hours & Admission Prices: Tues.-Thurs. 10:30-5, Fri. 10:30-9, Sat. 10-6, Sun. 11-6. Adults $12; discounts to AAM & ICOM members; members no charge. Closed New Year's Day; Thanksgiving; Christmas. ♿
Attendance: 154,000
Membership: Intro Individual $75; Individual $100; Dual & Family $150; Contributor $250; Sustainer & Young Associate $500; Conservator $1,000; Fellow $2,000; Patron Fellow $6,000; Pierpont Fellow $12,500.

* **MORRIS-JUMEL MANSION, (M),** 65 Jumel Ter., New York, NY 10032-5360. Tel.: 212-923-8008. Fax: 212-923-8947.
Web Site: www.morrisjumel.org
Founded: 1904.
Congressional District: 15
Key Personnel: Pres. (V), Nancy Goshow, A.I.A.; Vice Pres. (V), James Daly, Esq.; Dir., Kenneth Moss; Asst. Dir., Sheena Brown; Dir. Education, Sarah Mellace.
Personnel Profile: Full-Time Paid 3; Full-Time Volunteers 1; Part-Time Paid 4; Part-Time Volunteers 15; Interns 2.
Governing Authority: private; nonprofit. Tax-exempt: 501(c)(3).
Historic House: 1765 Morris-Jumel Mansion, oldest residence in Manhattan; used as Gen. Washington's headquarters during the Revolution; purchased by the Jumel family in 1810; Eliza Jumel married Aaron Burr in the front parlor.
Collections: archives; Chippendale, Federal & Empire furniture; silver, china, crystal, prints & paintings from the Colonial, Federal & Empire periods.
Research Fields: history; preservation; decorative arts; architecture.
Facilities: archives for use by appointment.
Activities: guided tours; lectures; gallery talks; concerts; educational programs; docent program; group tours by appointment only.
Publications: semi-annual newsletter; quarterly program calendar.
Hours & Admission Prices: Wed.-Sun. 10-4. Adults $5, students & senior citizens $4, school groups $1.50 per child; Historic House Trust of New York City, Museum Council of New York City, museum, children under 12, AAM & ICOM members no charge. Group tours available.
Attendance: 35,000 (estimated)
Membership: Friend $35; Family $55; Madame Jumel Circle $100; Roger Morris Circle $250; Aaron Burr Circle $500; George Washington Circle $1,000; Octagon Society & Cornerstone Corporate Circle $2,500.

* **MOUNT VERNON HOTEL MUSEUM & GARDEN, (M),** 421 E. 61st St., New York, NY 10065-8736. Tel.: 212-838-6878. Fax: 212-838-7390.
E-mail: info@mvhm.org
Web Site: www.mvhm.org
Formerly: Abigail Adams Smith Museum
Founded: 1939.
Congressional District: 15
Key Personnel: Dir., Rosalind Muggeridge; Dir. Education, Deborah O'Neill; Education Coord., Jamie Auriemma; Dir. Devel., Lisa Delmonico; Public Programs Coord., Amanda Wheeler.
Personnel Profile: Full-Time Paid 3; Part-Time Paid 6; Part-Time Volunteers 26; Interns 2.
Governing Authority: nonprofit organization. Parent Institution: Colonial Dames of America. Tax-exempt.
Historic House Museum: Built in 1799 interiors from 1826.
Collections: American decorative arts; 18th- & 19th-century documents & letters; period rooms represent the c.1830 Mount Vernon Hotel.
Research Fields: American Decorative Arts; federal Jacksonian New York.
Facilities: 200-seat auditorium. Museum-related items for sale.
Activities: school programs for K-12 students; seminars for adults; concerts; lectures & workshops for adults & families; outreach program for senior citizens.
Hours & Admission Prices: Tues.-Sun. 11-4. Adults $8, students & senior citizens $7; discounts to AAM & ICOM members & employees of local museums; children under 12 & members no charge. Closed New Year's Day; Independence Day; Thanksgiving; Christmas.
Attendance: 35,950 (accurate)
Membership: Senior/Student $30; Individual $35; Friend $40; Dual $65; Family $80; Supporter $120; Patron $250; Benefactor $500.

THE MUNICIPAL ART SOCIETY OF NEW YORK, 457 Madison Ave., New York, NY 10022-6843. Tel.: 212-935-3960, ext. 227. Fax: 212-753-1816.
E-mail: info@mas.org
Web Site: www.mas.org
Founded: 1893.
Congressional District: 15
Key Personnel: Pres., Vin Cipolla; Sr. Vice Pres., Frank Emile Sanchis, III; Dir. Planning Center, Eve Baron; Dir. Programs & Tours, Tamara Coombs.
Personnel Profile: Full-Time Paid 21; Part-Time Paid 8; Part-Time Volunteers 5; Interns 10.
Governing Authority: nonprofit organization. Tax-exempt: 501(c)(3).
Advocacy, planning & preservation organization dedicated to improving New York's environment. Located in the historic Villard House c.1892, arranged around an Italian Renaissance style courtyard opening onto Madison Ave.
Collections: paintings; photographs; sculpture.
Research Fields: historic preservation, planning, open space & livability issues focused on New York City.
Facilities: 2,000-vol. library available to public; lecture halls; meeting rooms; 2,647 sq. ft. exhibit space.
Activities: guided tours; films; organized education programs; loan & traveling exhibitions.
Publications: bimonthly newsletter; Juror's Guide; journal, Livable City.
Hours & Admission Prices: Mon.-Wed. & Fri.-Sat. 11-5. No charge. Closed federal holidays. ♿
Attendance: 65,000 (estimated)
Membership: Student & Senior $25; Individual $50; Family $75; Sustaining $125; Contributing $250; Sponsoring $500; Patron $1,000.

MUSEUM AT ELDRIDGE STREET, 12 Eldridge St., New York, NY 10002-6204. Tel.: 212-219-0888. Fax: 212-966-4782.
E-mail: contact@eldridgestreet.org
Web Site: www.eldridgestreet.org
Founded: 1986.
Congressional District: 12
Key Personnel: Exec. Dir., Bonnie Dimun; Chm. (V), Michael Weinstein; Pres. (V), Lorinda Ash Ezersky; Dir. Public Programs, Hanna Griff; Education Coord., Annie Polland; Dir. Devel., Eva Brune; Deputy Dir., Amy Milford.
Personnel Profile: Full-Time Paid 7; Part-Time Paid 2; Part-Time Volunteers 40; Interns 3.
Governing Authority: private; nonprofit organization. Tax-exempt: 501(c)(3).
Historic Site, Cultural Center & Museum: a national historic landmark.
Collections: concentration on New York Jewish history with special emphasis on the Lower East Side.
Research Fields: history of the Eldridge Street Synagogue & its congregation in the context of the development of American Judaism.
Facilities: 150-vol. library of materials relating to New York history, immigration to the United States and Judaica & Jewish history; educational facilities; 5,000 sq. ft. exhibit space. Museum-related items for sale.
Activities: concerts; docent program; formal education programs; guided tours; lectures; participatory & temporary exhibitions.
Publications: biannually, News from Eldridge Street.
Hours & Admission Prices: Synagogue Tours: Sun.-Thurs. 10-4. Adults $10, senior citizens & students $8, children 5-18 $6; discounts to AAM & ICOM members; members & children under 5 no charge. Closed Jewish & national holidays. ♿
Attendance: 20,000 (accurate)

THE MUSEUM AT FIT, Seventh Ave., (at 27th St.), New York, NY 10001-5992. Tel.: 212-217-4533. Fax: 212-217-4531.
E-mail: museuminfo@fitnyc.edu
Web Site: www.fitnyc.edu/museum
Founded: 1967.
Key Personnel: Dir. & Chief Cur., Dr. Valerie Steele; Head Conservator, Ann Coppinger; Deputy Dir., Patricia Mears; Registrar, Sonia Dingilian; Mgr. Exhibits, Fred Dennis.
Personnel Profile: Full-Time Paid 28; Part-Time Paid 2.
Governing Authority: university. Parent Institution: Fashion Institute of Technology (SUNY). Tax-exempt: 170(b)(1)(A).
Fashion Museum.
Collections: over 50,000 garments & accessories dating from the mid-18th century to the present, with a focus on 20th-century fashion, including: couture & ready-to-wear women's clothing; menswear ranging from formal to activewear; swimwear; lingerie; knitwear; children's clothing; Halston designs, patterns & related records documenting designer's life work; 15,000 accessories including shoes, hats & bags; over 30,000 textiles, dating from the 6th century to the present illustrating techniques & traditions from around the world.
Major Exhibits: Japan Fashion Now, 9/10-12/10.
Research Fields: history of fashion & textile; history of the design industries & professions.
Activities: guided tours; organized education programs for undergraduate or graduate college students; internships; programs relating to exhibitions; loan, temporary & traveling exhibitions.
Publications: Madame Gres; Gothic: Dark Glamour; Ralph Rucci: The Art of Weightlessness; Isabel Toledo: Fashion From the Inside Out.
Hours & Admission Prices: Tues.-Fri. 12-8, Sat. 10-5. No charge. Closed legal holidays. ♿
Attendance: 100,000
Membership: Under 35 $350; Couture Council $1,000.

MUSEUM OF AMERICAN FINANCE, 48 Wall St., New York, NY 10005-2903. Tel.: 212-908-4110. Fax: 212-908-4601.
E-mail: kaguilera@financialhistory.org
Web Site: www.financialhistory.org
Formerly: Museum of American Financial History
Founded: 1988.
Congressional District: 27
Key Personnel: Chm. (V), John E. Herzog; Pres. & C.E.O., David J. Cowen; Dir. Devel., Jeanne Driscoll; Dir. Communications, Kristin Aguilera; Mgr. Collections, Leena Akhtar; Dir. Visitor Svcs., Linda Rapacki; Business Mgr., Arturo Gomez.
Personnel Profile: Full-Time Paid 9; Part-Time Paid 5; Part-Time Volunteers 10; Interns 2.
Governing Authority: nonprofit organization. Tax-exempt: 501(c)(3).
Financial Museum and de facto Visitor Center for the New York Stock Exchange.
Collections: American financial history from the mid-18th century to present day; stock & bond certificates; books; periodicals; associated items.
Facilities: library; education center; 250-seat auditorium; exhibition space; archives; rental gallery. Museum-related items for sale.
Activities: permanent exhibitions on the capital markets; banking & money; entrepreneurship; Alexander Hamilton will open in 2007.
Publications: quarterly magazine, Financial History; books, Scripophily; Financing the American Revolution; exhibit catalogs.
Hours & Admission Prices: Exhibits: Tues.-Sat. 10-4. Adults $8, students & seniors $5; discounts to AAM, ICOM members & NYC museum employees; children 6 & under and members no charge. Closed major holidays. ♿
Attendance: 75,000 (estimated)
Membership: Student & Senior $45; Individual $55; International $65; Institutional $75; Family $85; Smithsonian Affiliate $150; Hamilton Society $500; Donor $1,000.

THE MUSEUM OF AMERICAN ILLUSTRATION AT THE SOCIETY OF ILLUSTRATORS, (M), 128 E. 63rd St., New York, NY 10065-7303. Tel.: 212-838-2560. Fax: 212-838-2561.
E-mail: info@societyillustrators.org
Web Site: www.societyillustrators.org
Formerly: Society of Illustrators Museum of American Illustration
Founded: 1901.
Congressional District: 18
Key Personnel: Pres., Dennis Dittrich; Dir., Anelle Miller.
Personnel Profile: Full-Time Paid 9; Interns 1.
Governing Authority: board of directors. Tax-exempt: 501(c)(3).
Art Museum & Gallery.
Collections: various forms of art media & books.
Major Exhibits: 52nd Illustrator's Annual Exhibit (T), 1/10-3/10; Student Scholarship Competition (T), 5/10; Earth: Fragile Planet (T), 6/10-7/10.
Research Fields: American Illustration.
Facilities: library & archives available by appointment only.
Activities: lectures; permanent & temporary exhibitions.
Publications: Annual of American Illustration; Library of American Illustration.
Hours & Admission Prices: Gallery: Sept.-July Tues. 10-8, Wed.-Fri. 10-5, Sat. 12-4. No charge; donations accepted. Closed legal holidays.
Attendance: 30,000 (estimated)
Membership: Student $35; Associate $500.

* **MUSEUM OF ARTS AND DESIGN, (M),** 2 Columbus Circle, New York, NY 10019-1800. Tel.: 212-299-7777. Fax: 212-299-7701.
E-mail: heidi.riegler@madmuseum.org
Web Site: www.madmuseum.org
Formerly: American Craft Museum
Founded: 1956.
Congressional District: 15
Key Personnel: Dir., Holly Hotchner; Chm., Barbara Tober; Pres., Nanette Laitman; Chief Cur. & Vice Pres. Programs & Collections, David McFadden; Cur., Ursula Ilse-Neuman; Registrar, Ellen Haldorf; Facility Mgr., Cesar Negron; Assoc. Vice Pres. Mktg., Liz Samurovich.
Personnel Profile: Full-Time Paid 38; Part-Time Paid 11; Part-Time Volunteers 15.
Governing Authority: nonprofit organization. Tax-exempt: 501(c)(3).
Art Museum.
Collections: American 20th-century crafts by artists working in ceramic, glass, fiber, metal, wood, mixed media, paper & plastic; traveling exhibition program.
Major Exhibits: Slash: Paper Under the Knife, 11/09-6/10/10; Bigger, Better, More: Arts of Viola Frey, 1/27/10-5/10/10.
Research Fields: 20th-century international craft, design & architecture.
Facilities: theater; event space; lecture & symposia facilities. Museum-related items for sale.
Activities: tours; lectures; symposia; workshops; audiovisual programs; Meet-the-Artist program; travel opportunities for support group members; temporary exhibits.
Publications: exhibition catalogs; newsletter.
Hours & Admission Prices: Wed. & Fri.-Sun. 11-6, Thurs. 11-9. Adults $15, students & seniors $12; members & children under 12 no charge. ♿
Attendance: 600,000 (estimated)
Membership: Students $50; Individual $75; Dual $100; Family $125; 360 Young Collectors $200; Contributing $250; Supporting $500.

MUSEUM OF BIBLICAL ART

MOBIA

MUSEUM OF BIBLICAL ART, (M), 1865 Broadway, New York, NY 10023-7503. Tel.: 212-408-1500 & 1495. Fax: 212-408-1292.
E-mail: info@mobia.org
Web Site: www.mobia.org
Founded: 2004.
Congressional District: 14
Key Personnel: Exec. Dir., Dr. Ena Heller; Chm. (V), Roberta Ahmanson; Dir. Operations & Museum Shop Mgr., Ute Keyes; Dir. External Affairs, Lisa Dierbeck; Museum Coord., Kate Williamson; Public Rels. & Devel. Assoc., Debbie Bujosa; Devel. Assoc., Megan R. Whitman; Asst. Cur. & Registrar, Adrianne Rubin; Cur. Education, Laura McManus; Dir. Exhibitions, Paul Tabor; Lead Art Handler, Dean Ebben.
Personnel Profile: Full-Time Paid 9; Part-Time Paid 4; Part-Time Volunteers 1; Interns 4.
Governing Authority: board of trustees. Tax-exempt: 501(c)(3).
Art Museum.
Collections: art in the Jewish & Christian traditions.
Major Exhibits: Tobi Kahn: Sacred Spaces for the 21st Century, 11/09-1/24/10; An Uneasy Communion: Jews, Christians, and the Altar Pieces of Medieval Aragon, 2/18/10-5/30/10; Ukrainian Icons (T), 6/18/10-9/12/10; Tiffany Ecclesiastical Designs (T), 10/10-1/30/11.
Facilities: education center. Books for sale.
Activities: films; adult workshops; family workshops; walking tours; audio guided tours; family days.
Publications: scholarly books on art & religion; exhibition catalogs; educational brochures & booklets; e-newsletter.
Hours & Admission Prices: Tues.-Wed. & Fri.-Sun. 10-6, Thurs. 10-8. Suggested Donations: adults $7, senior citizens & students $4; discounts to Museum Council of NY, AAM & ICOM members; members & children under 12 no charge. Closed New Year's Day; Independence Day; Thanksgiving; Christmas. ♿
Attendance: 21,932 (accurate)
Membership: Individual $50; Dual & Family $75; Contributor $125; Sponsor & Young Benefactor $250; Patron $500; Benefactor $1,000; Director's Circle $2,500; Trustees' Circle $5,000.

MUSEUM OF BUSINESS, COMMERCE & WEALTH, 177 W. 26 St., Loft 200, New York, NY 10001-6811. Tel.: 212-366-1447 & 613-3242. Fax: 413-375-0206.
Governing Authority: Tax-exempt: 501(c)(3).
History Museum.
Collections: business & corporate history.
Hours & Admission Prices: Call for hours.

MUSEUM OF CHINESE IN THE AMERICAS, 211-215 Centre St., New York, NY 10013-3601. Mailing Address: 70 Mulberry St., 2nd Fl., New York, NY 10013. Tel.: 212-619-4785. Fax: 212-619-4720.
E-mail: info@mocanyc.org
Web Site: www.mocanyc.org
Founded: 1980.
Congressional District: 15
Key Personnel: Exec. Dir., S. Alice Mong; Cur. Education, Beatrice Chen; Devel. Mgr., Jenny Wong; Dir. Devel., Carolyn Antonio.
Personnel Profile: Full-Time Paid 6; Part-Time Volunteers 20; Interns 6.
Governing Authority: nonprofit organization. Archives, 70 Mulberry St., 2nd Fl., New York, NY 10013. Tax-exempt: 501(c)(3).
History Museum: housed in 1893 former public school.
Collections: related to Chinese-American history & culture: archives; photographs; oral histories; Cantonese opera costumes; scripts; musical instruments; Chinatown store signs; local business-related artifacts; Chinese laundry collection; World War II Chinese-American veterans collection.
Research Fields: history and culture of the Chinese diaspora in North and South America.
Facilities: 1,800-vol. library on Asian-American history & culture, available for use by public; 1,025 sq. ft. exhibit space. Asian American-related books for sale.
Activities: guided gallery tours; Chinatown walking tours by appointment; workshops; lectures; literary, performing & visual arts presentations; traveling & participatory exhibits; media productions for rental; multidisciplinary, multimedia public programs; family programs.
Publications: biannual newsletter, Bu Gao Ban; bimonthly, calendar of events.
Hours & Admission Prices: Mon. & Fri. 11-5, Thurs. 11-9, Sat.-Sun. 10-5; other times by appointment. Adults $7, seniors 65 & over and students $4; children under 12 in groups less than 8 & members no charge.
Attendance: 50,000 (accurate)
Membership: Student & Senior Citizens $25; Individual $60; Red Envelope Friend $100; Lion Dancer $500; Museum Benefactor $1,000 & up; Legacy Builder $10,000.

MUSEUM OF COMIC AND CARTOON ART, 594 Broadway, Ste. 401, New York, NY 10012. Tel.: 212-254-3511. Fax: 212-254-3590.
E-mail: info@moccany.org
Founded: 2001.
Congressional District: 8
Key Personnel: Dir., Karl Erickson; Chm. (V), Ellen S. Abramowitz.
Personnel Profile: Full-Time Paid 1; Part-Time Volunteers 10.
Art Museum.
Collections: comics; cartoons; animation.
Major Exhibits: Archie Comics, 11/09-2/10.
Activities: special events.
Hours & Admission Prices: Tues.-Sun. 12-5. Adults $5; discounts to groups; children 12 & under no charge.
Membership: Student & Senior $25; Individual $35; Individual Plus $50; Family $75; Patron $100.

MUSEUM OF JEWISH HERITAGE-A LIVING MEMORIAL TO THE HOLOCAUST, 36 Battery Place, New York, NY 10280-1502. Tel.: 646-437-4200. Fax: 646-437-4311.
E-mail: aspilka@mjhnyc.org
Web Site: www.mjhnyc.org
Founded: 1984.
Congressional District: 8
Key Personnel: Chm. (V), Hon. Robert M. Morgenthau; Vice Chm. (V), George Klein; Vice Chm. (V), Manfred Ohrenstein; Vice Chm. (V), Howard J. Rubenstein; Dir., David Marwell; Cur. Collections, Esther Brumberg; Registrar, Erica Blumfeld; Dir. Operations, Michael Minerva; Dir. Education, Elizabeth Edelstein; Dir. Communications, Abby R. Spilka; Dir. Devel. Grants & Annual Giving, Jilian Gersten; Dir. Devel. Special Gifts, Felica Kobylanski; Dir. Finance, Mohad Athar; Dir. Human Resources, Tammy Chiu; Dir. Public Programs, Elissa Schein; Museum Shop Mgr., Warren Shalewitz; Deputy Dir., Ivy Barsky.
Personnel Profile: Full-Time Paid 63; Part-Time Paid 12; Part-Time Volunteers 250; Interns 90.
Governing Authority: nonprofit organization. Parent Institution: New York Holocaust Memorial Commission. Tax-exempt: 501(c)(3).
Jewish History Museum: 20th-century memorial to the Holocaust.
Collections: early 20th-century Jewish life; war against the Jews; Jewish renewal since 1945; multi-media installation; core exhibit.
Major Exhibits: The Morgenthaus: A Legacy of Service, 11/09-12/10.
Research Fields: the Holocaust; late 19th- to early 20th-century Jewish history; aspects of Jewish immigration to the U.S.
Facilities: 6,300-vol. library of books on Jewish history, Holocaust, reference material, memoirs; classrooms; Edmond J. Satra Hall.
Activities: tours for school groups; curriculum material; family programs; outreach; speakers bureau; programs on Wed., Sun. & evenings.
Publications: quarterly, Museum Newsletter; visitor's brochure; calendar of events; annual report; program brochures; educational workbooks; Daring to Resist: Jewish Defiance in the Holocaust (2007); Dominican Haven: The Jewish Refugee Settlement in Sosua 1940-1945 (2008).
Hours & Admission Prices: Daylight Savings Time: Sun.-Tues. & Thurs. 10-5:45, Wed. 10-8, Fri. 10-5; Eastern Standard Time & Eve of Jewish Holidays: Sun.-Tues. & Thurs. 10-5:45, Wed. 10-8, Fri. 10-3. Adults $12, seniors $10, students $7; discounts to AAM & ICOM members; members, children under 12 & Wed. 4-8 no charge. Closed Jewish holidays; Thanksgiving. ♿
Attendance: 150,223 (accurate)
Membership: Students $18; Senior & Contributing $36; Young Friends $50; Individual $54; Senior Dual $70; Young Friends Dual $90; Dual $100; National & International $150; Family $180; Sustaining & Tribute $360; Circle of Hope $500; Circle of Memory $750; Curator's Circle $1,000; Director's Circle $2,500; Chairman's Circle $5,000 & up.

* **THE MUSEUM OF MODERN ART,** 11 W. 53rd St., New York, NY 10019-5401. Tel.: 212-708-9400. Fax: 212-708-9889. TDD: 212-247-1230.
E-mail: comments@moma.org
Web Site: www.moma.org
Founded: 1929.
Congressional District: 14
Key Personnel: Chm., Jerry Speyer; Pres., Marie-Josee Kravis; Dir., Glenn Lowry; C.O.O., James Gara; Chief Cur. Photography, Peter Galassi; Sr. Deputy Dir. External Affairs, Michael Margitich; Dir. Human Resources,

Trish Jeffers; Sr. Deputy Dir. Exhibitions, Collections & Programs, Jennifer Russell; Deputy Dir. Education, Wendy Woon; Chief Cur. Prints & Illustrated Books, Deborah Wye; Gen. Counsel, Patty Lipshutz; Chief Cur. at Large, Kynaston McShine; Chief Cur. Painting & Sculpture, John Elderfield; Chief Cur. Architecture & Design, Barry Bergdoll; Chief Cur. Media, Klaus Biesenbach; Chief Cur. Dept. Drawings, Cornelia Butler; Chief Cur. Film, Rajendra Roy; Deputy Dir. Policy, Planning & Administration, Karen Davidson.

Personnel Profile: Full-Time Paid 766; Part-Time Paid 35; Part-Time Volunteers 314; Interns 58.

Governing Authority: nonprofit corporation. Tax-exempt: 501(c)(3).

Art Museum.

Collections: modern & contemporary art from 1880-present; painting; sculpture; drawings; prints; architecture & design; photography; film; video; posters; illustrated books; manuscripts.

Research Fields: pertaining to collections.

Facilities: 300,000-vol. library; archives; study centers; reading room; Edward John Noble Education Center; Abby Aldrich Rockefeller Sculpture Garden; 460-seat theater; 225-seat theater; restaurants; 2 cafes. Museum-related items for sale.

Activities: theaters; symposia; lecture series; films; gallery talks; conversations with contemporary artists; internship programs; inter-museum loan, permanent, temporary & traveling exhibitions; brown bag lunch lectures; courses at MoMA; weekend family programs; virtual visits & audio programs; high school programs; weekend teachers workshops; access programs; community programs.

Publications: books; exhibition catalogs; posters; cards; monthly members calendars & e-newsletter.

Hours & Admission Prices: Wed.-Thurs. & Sat.-Mon. 10:30-5:30, Fri. 10:30-8. Museum: adults $20, seniors 65 & over $16, full-time students with ID $12; discounts to AAM & ICOM members; children 16 & under, MoMA members & Fri. 4-8 no charge. Additional charge for film & media programs. Closed Thanksgiving; Christmas. ♿

Attendance: 2,219,554 (estimated)

Membership: Student $35; National & International $60; Individual $75; Family & Dual $150; Fellow $300; Supporting $500; Sustaining $1,000; Patron $1,500; Benefactor $2,500.

MUSEUM OF THE CITY OF NEW YORK, 1220 Fifth Ave. at 103rd St., New York, NY 10029. Mailing Address: 1220 Fifth Ave., New York, NY 10029-9958. Tel.: 212-534-1672. Fax: 212-423-0758.

E-mail: info@mcny.org

Web Site: www.mcny.org

Founded: 1923.

Congressional District: 19

Key Personnel: Dir., Susan Henshaw Jones; Chm. (V), Newton P.S. Merrill; Deputy Dir. Programs, Dr. Sarah Henry; Head of Education, Franny Kent; Vice Pres. Devel., Jennifer Juzaitis; Vice Pres. Finance & Admin. & C.F.O., Carl Dreyer; Chief Registrar, Caitlin Corrigan; Dir. Communications, Barbara Livenstein; Cur. Decorative Arts & Head of Collections Svcs., Deborah D. Waters; Cur. Costumes, Phyllis Magidson; Cur. Theatre, Marty Jacobs; Cur. Paintings & Sculpture, Andrea Henderson Fahnestock; Mgr. Human Resources, Marcy Mirkin; Mgr. Collections Access, Melanie Bower; Museum Shop Mgr., Thomas Price.

Personnel Profile: Full-Time Paid 70; Part-Time Paid 10; Part-Time Volunteers 50; Interns 10.

Governing Authority: nonprofit organization. Tax-exempt: 501(c)(3).

History Museum.

Collections: presentation relating to present & past social, economic, intellectual & political history of New York; costumes; furniture; silver; paintings; prints & photographs; decorative arts; manuscripts; fire-fighting equipment; maps; marine & military items; theatrical & musical items; toys; period rooms; archives; sculpture; graphics; textiles.

Research Fields: archives; painting; sculpture; graphics; decorative arts; costumes; general history; textiles; theatre.

Facilities: 248-seat auditorium.

Activities: guided tours available by appointment; lectures; gallery talks; formally organized education programs; family workshops; performances; inter-museum loan; temporary, traveling & permanent exhibitions: New York Toy Stories; Broadway!; Furniture of Distinction, 1780-1890. Museum Sponsors: Community programs; junior historical program.

Publications: quarterly; trimonthly; historical monopaths; Our Town: Images & Stories from the Museum of the City of New York; Berenice Abott's Changing New York: 1935-1939.

Hours & Admission Prices: Tues.-Sun. 10-5. Suggested Donations: families $20, adults $10, senior citizens, students & children $6; discounts to AAM, ICOM members, corporate members employees & employees of NYC Museum Council Institutions; children under 12 & members no charge. Closed New Year's Day; Thanksgiving; Christmas. ♿

Attendance: 163,964 (accurate)

Membership: Senior Citizen & Student $35; Individual $50; Dual $70; Family $75; Associate $100; Sustainers $250; Fellow $500.

NATIONAL ACADEMY MUSEUM AND SCHOOL OF FINE ARTS, 1083 Fifth Ave., (& 89th St.), New York, NY 10128-0114. Tel.: 212-369-4880. Fax: 212-360-6795.

Web Site: www.nationalacademy.org

Founded: 1825.

Congressional District: 15

Key Personnel: Exec. Dir., Carmine Branagan; Cur., Bruce Weber; Asst. Cur., Marshall Price; Conservator, Lucie Kinsolving; Cur. Education, Sandy Martiny; Asst. Paintings Conservator, Monica Griesbach; Dir. School, Nancy Little; Registrar, Athena Latocha; Artist Membership Coord., Nancy Malloy; Controller, Michael McKay; Dir. Communications, Mary Fichter; Dir. Operations & Security, Charles Biada; Museum Shop Mgr., John Ravet.

Personnel Profile: Full-Time Paid 20; Part-Time Paid 64; Part-Time Volunteers 6; Interns 6.

Governing Authority: nonprofit organization. Branch Museums: Gallery; School of Fine Arts. Tax-exempt: 501(c)(3).

Art Museum & School of Fine Arts.

Collections: American painting, sculpture, graphic arts, drawings; architectural renderings; archives pertaining to academy proceedings & members of academy.

Major Exhibits: 185th Annual Invitational, 2/17/10-6/8/10.

Research Fields: 19th-21st centuries American art.

Facilities: over 7,000-vol. library.

Activities: exhibitions from permanent collection; loan exhibitions; lectures; classes & workshops in the fine arts; annual juried exhibition; public programs.

Publications: catalogs of exhibitions & school; biannual, The Bulletin.

Hours & Admission Prices: Wed.-Thurs. 12-5, Fri.-Sun. 11-6. Adults $10, senior citizens & students $5; discounts to groups; NYC museum staff, AAM members, Channel 13, Central Park Conservancy & NY Times cardholders. ♿

Attendance: 60,000 (estimated)

Membership: Students & Seniors $25; Friend $50; Family $75; Contributor $125; Sponsor $250; Patron $500; Director's Circle $1,000; Benefactor $1,500; Fellow $2,500.

NATIONAL ARTS CLUB, 15 Gramercy Park S., New York, NY 10003-1796. Tel.: 212-475-3424. Fax: 212-475-3692.

Web Site: www.nationalartsclub.org

Founded: 1898.

Congressional District: 18

Key Personnel: Pres. (V), O. Aldon James, Jr.; Treas., Jason de Montmorency; Cur. National Arts Club Permanent Collection, Dr. Carol Lowrey; Chm. Exhibitions Committee, Diane Bernnhard.

Governing Authority: nonprofit organization. Tax-exempt: 501(c)(3).

Art Museum: housed in 1840s, former mansion of Governor Samuel Tilden.

Collections: late 19th & 20th-century American painting; sculpture; works on paper; decorative arts.

Research Fields: late 19th & early 20th-century American art.

Facilities: 150-vol. personal library of Robert Henri available for research upon request; public exhibitions.

Publications: brochure; Carol Lowrey, A Noble Tradition; exhibit catalogue, American Painting from the National Arts Club Permanent Collection.

Hours & Admission Prices: Call for confirmation of hours of exhibition galleries. No charge.

NATIONAL AUDUBON SOCIETY, 225 Varick St., Fl. 7, New York, NY 10014-4396. Tel.: 212-979-3000. Fax: 212-979-3188.

Web Site: www.audubon.org

Founded: 1905.

Congressional District: 8

Key Personnel: Chm., B. Holt Thrasher; Pres. & C.E.O., John Flicker; Dir. Mktg. & Communications, Nancy Severance.

Personnel Profile: Full-Time Paid 284; Part-Time Paid 44.

Governing Authority: not-for-profit organization. Tax-exempt: 501(c)(3).

Wildlife & Wildlife Habitat Protection Society.

Collections: wildlife & their habitats.

Research Fields: energy alternatives; ancient forests of the Northwest; wildlife trade; migratory bird program with Latin America; developing Beringia Wilderness Park; Everglades & wetlands preservation; local work.

Facilities: educational facilities; field research stations; nature centers. Environmentally associated items for sale.

Activities: formal education programs for children, adults, & undergraduate or graduate college students; guided tours; lectures; slide shows; TV & cable programs; Audubon Adventures student & teacher programs; 514 national chapters.

Publications: monthly news journal, Activist; periodic wildlife identification & information guides; bimonthly magazine, Audubon; grassroots action toolkits; Audubon Adventures curriculum.
Hours & Admission Prices: Contact individual sanctuaries for hours. ♿
Attendance: 125,000
Membership: Introductory $20; Regular $35.

THE NATIONAL MUSEUM OF CATHOLIC ART & HISTORY, 443 E. 115th St., New York, NY 10029-1702. Tel.: 212-828-5209. Fax: 212-828-5208.
E-mail: info@nmcah.org
Web Site: www.nmcah.org
Founded: 1995.
Congressional District: 15
Key Personnel: Chm., Edward J. Malloy; Exec. Dir., Christina Cox; Treas., Albert Luongo; Sec., Sister Jean DeMana, O.P., Ph.D.; Cur. Art, Mariavelia Savino; Graphic Artist, Marisol de los Santos; Special Events Coord., Helen Gonzales; Registrar, Oscar Augura.
Personnel Profile: Full-Time Paid 7; Part-Time Paid 4; Part-Time Volunteers 5; Interns 5.
Governing Authority: private; nonprofit. Tax-exempt: 501(c)(3).
Religious Art & Christian History Museum.
Collections: old master & contemporary religious paintings, sculpture, prints; liturgical vestments & objects; photographs.
Research Fields: Catholic History; Liturgical objects & vestments; religious painting, sculpture & decorative arts; contemporary Catholic artists; contribution of Catholicism to the Judeo-Christian tradition in the arts; dialogue between Christianity, other world religions, & the cultures they arise in.
Facilities: library; theater. Museum-related items for sale.
Activities: lectures; Catholic book club; rental facilities; educational programs; guest speakers.
Publications: exhibition catalogues; newsletter; class schedules; quarterly, Arts for the Millennium.
Hours & Admission Prices: Closed for renovations ♿
Attendance: 10,000 (estimated)

* **NATIONAL MUSEUM OF THE AMERICAN INDIAN, SMITHSONIAN INSTITUTION, (M),** George Gustav Heye Center, Alexander Custom House, One Bowling Green, New York, NY 10004-1415. Tel.: 212-514-3700 (New York); 301-238-1435 (Maryland); 202-287-2020 (Exec. Offices). Fax: 212-514-3800 (New York); 301-238-3203 (Maryland); 202-287-3528 (Exec. Offices).
Web Site: www.americanindian.si.edu
Founded: 1916.
Congressional District: 16
Key Personnel: Dir., W. Richard West; Deputy Dir., Douglas E. Evelyn; Dir. External Affairs & Develop., Elizabeth Duggal; Assoc. Dir. Mall Museum Transition, James Volkert; Asst. Dir. Public Programs, Helen Scheirbeck; Asst. Dir. Admin., Donna A. Scott; Asst. Dir. Cultural Resources, Bruce Bernstein; Asst. Dir. Exhibitions & Public Spaces, Kerry Boyd; Asst. Dir. Community Svcs. & Training Coord., James Pepper Henry; Deputy Asst. Dir. Public Programs, Carolyn Rapkievian; Deputy Asst. Dir. Administration, Kelly Bennett; Deputy Asst. Dir. Cultural Resources, Gerald McMaster; Deputy Asst. Dir. Exhibitions & Public Spaces, Karen Fort; Deputy Dir. External Affairs & Devel., Maggie Bertin; Head of Publications, Terence Winch; Dir. Public Affairs, Thomas W. Sweeney; Sr. Devel. Officer, Virginia Elwell; Membership Program Mgr., Edison Wato; Information Resource Mgr., Jane E. Sledge; Web Mgr., Cheryl Wilson; Resource Center Mgr., Marty Kreipe de Montano; Head of Conservation, Marian Kaminitz; Registrar, Ann M. Drumheller; Supervisory Photographer, Cynthia Frankenburg; Archivist, Sheree Bonaparte; Head Cur., M. J. Lenz; Head Cur. Research, Ann McMullen; Human Resources, Carol Belovitch; Budget Officer, Cynthia Smith; CRC Administrative Officer, Janice Cole; CRC Bldg. Mgr., John Standish; Dir. George Gustav Heye Center, NY, John Haworth; Devel. & External Affairs Officer, NY, Catherine Morrison; Head of Exhibitions, NY, Peter S. Brill; Education Dept. Mgr., NY, Johanna Gorelick; Resource Center Mgr., NY, Gaetana DeGennaro; Head of Film & Video Center, NY, Elizabeth Weatherford; Collections Move Mgr., NY, Scott Merritt; Museum Shop Mgr., NY, Lilli Liell; GGHC Facilities Mgr., NY, Myroslaw Riznyk.
Personnel Profile: Full-Time Paid 293; Part-Time Paid 21; Part-Time Volunteers 135.
Governing Authority: nonprofit, federally-chartered corporation. Parent Institution: Bureau of the Smithsonian Institution, 1000 Jefferson Dr., S.W., Washington, DC 20560. Subsidiary Institution: Cultural Resources Center, 4220 Silver Hill Rd., Suitland, MD 20746-2863; George Gustav Heye Center, One Bowling Green, New York, NY 10004. Tax-exempt: 501(c)(3).
Anthropology & Indian Museum.
Collections: American Indian archaeology & ethnology from North, Central, South America & Caribbean; artifacts; textiles; agriculture; anthropology; paintings; sculpture; decorative arts; costumes; numismatics; music; medical; literature; history; arts; language; Eskimo culture; photograph archives; manuscript collections.
Research Fields: prehistoric, historic & contemporary native people of the Western Hemisphere.
Facilities: New York: 20,000 sq. ft. exhibition galleries; Film & Video Center; resource center; contemporary Indian arts, crafts & books sale. Maryland: 145,000 sq. ft. collections and research facility; 86,000 archival prints & negatives; 3,500 color slide photographic collection; library; paper archives; research facilities.
Activities: New York: guided tours; interpretive programs; Expressive Culture series; inter-museum loans; permanent, temporary & traveling exhibitions; film & video programs; off-site lectures; information services; internship program; services to Native American groups. Maryland: collections storage & management; conservation; inter-museum loans; repatriation; collections & archival research; library; community outreach programs; internship program.
Publications: books; recordings; exhibition catalogues; brochures; quarterly magazine, American Indian.
Hours & Admission Prices: Thurs. 10-8, Fri.-Wed. 10-5. No charge; discounts & complimentary magazine subscriptions to charter members. Closed Christmas. ♿
Attendance: 334,506 (accurate)
Membership: Charter Circles: Golden Prairie $20; Riverbed $35; Everglades $50; Sky Meadows $100; Boundary Waters $250; Desert Sands $500.

NEW MUSEUM, 235 Bowery, New York, NY 10002-1218. Tel.: 212-219-1222, ext. 200. Fax: 212-431-5328.
E-mail: info@newmuseum.org
Web Site: www.newmuseum.org
Founded: 1977.
Congressional District: 18
Key Personnel: Dir., Lisa Phillips; Pres. Bd. of Trustees (V), Saul Dennison; Deputy Dir., John Hatfield; Chief Cur., Richard Flood; Operations Mgr., Tom Brumley; Bookstore Mgr., Daniel Thiem.
Personnel Profile: Full-Time Paid 50; Part-Time Paid 10; Part-Time Volunteers 5.
Governing Authority: nonprofit organization. Tax-exempt: 501(c)(3).
Art Museum.
Collections: contemporary art.
Major Exhibits: Urs Fischer: Marguerite de Ponty, 11/09-1/10; Nikhil Chopra, 11/09-2/2/10; The Imaginary Museum, Spring 2010.
Research Fields: contemporary art.
Facilities: Books for sale.
Activities: guided tours; lectures; performances; temporary & traveling exhibitions; educational programs; video.
Publications: catalogs, Barry LeVa; John Baldessari: Work 1966-80; Art & Ideology; Earl Staley 1973-1983; New Work: Golub; Hans Haacke; Fake, 1987; Pat Steir; Choices: Making an Art of Everyday Life; Ana Mendieta; Markus Raetz: In the Realm of the Possible; Impressario: Malcolm McLaren & the British New Wave; Christian Boltanski; brochures; Alfred Jensen: Paintings from the Years 1957-1977; New Work/New York, 1978; Barry LeVa, The Invented Landscape; Sustained Visions, 1979; Dimensions Variable; New Work/New York, 1979; Outside New York: Ohio, 1980; Deconstruction/Reconstruction: The Transformation of Photographic Information Into Metaphor, 1980: Events: Fashion Moda, Taller Boricua, Artists Invite Artists, 1980; Al Souza; Mary Stoppert; The Reverend Howard Finster; Candace Hill-Montgomery; Joseph Hilton; Kenneth Schorr; Brad Melamed; Anne Turyn; Gary Falk; books, Art after Modernism: Rethinking Representation; Bruce Nauman, Marcus Raetz, The Decade Show: Frameworks of Identity in the 1980's; Blasted Allegories: An Anthology of Writings by Contemporary Artists; Out There: Marginalization & Contemporary Cultures; The Interrupted Life, 1991; Rhetorical Image, 1990-91; Cadences: Icon & Abstraction in Contemporary Art, 1991; homo video, Where We Are Now; Discourses: Conversations in Post-Modern Art & Culture; Bad Girls, 1994; Contemporary Art and Multicultural Education, 1996; A Labor of Love, 1996; Carolee Schneemann: Up To And Including Her Limits, 1997; Remota: Airmail Paintings by Eugenio Dittborn, 1997; Mona Hatoum, 1997; Doris Salcedo, 1998; Martin Wong, 1998; Faith Ringgold, 1998; Temporarily Possessed, 1995; Marcel Odenbach, 1998; David Wojnarowicz, 1998; Time of Our Lives, 1999; Picturing the Modern Amazon, 2000; Cildo Meireles, 1999; Pierre et Gilles, 2001; William Kentridge, 2001; Black President, The Art and Legacy of Fela Kuti, 2003; East Village, 2004; John Waters Change of Life, 2004.
Hours & Admission Prices: Wed. & Sat.-Sun. 12-6, Thurs.-Fri. 12-9. Adult $12, seniors $10, students $8; members and children 18 & under no charge. Closed all major holidays. ♿
Attendance: 300,000
Membership: Student & Senior $35; Advocate $60; Dual $100; Deluxe $400; Premium $1,000.

NEW YORK CITY FIRE MUSEUM, 278 Spring St., New York, NY 10013-1405. Tel.: 212-691-1303. Fax: 212-924-0430.
Web Site: nycfiremuseum.org
Founded: 1987.
Congressional District: 17
Key Personnel: Pres., John Bower; Vice Pres., Dorothy Marks; Dir., Linda Burke; Treas., Paul Magda; Museum Shop Mgr., Noemi Bourdier.
Personnel Profile: Full-Time Paid 5; Part-Time Paid 2; Part-Time Volunteers 8; Interns 1.
Governing Authority: public; nonprofit organization. Parent Institution: The Friends of the NYCFD Collection, Inc. Tax-exempt.
Fire-Fighting Museum: housed in 1904 firehouse.
Collections: fire-related art & artifacts dating from 18th-century to the present including horse, hand-drawn & motorized pieces of apparatus; fire buckets; trumpets; toy & working models; helmets; parade hats; presentation silver; portraits; photographs; Currier & Ives & other prints; an important collection of fire insurance marks.
Research Fields: history of fire fighting in New York City, U.S. & world.
Facilities: audiovisual room; fire safety education Hazard House.
Activities: guided & educational tours; group tours by appointment.
Publications: member newsletter, The Housewatch.
Hours & Admission Prices: Tues.-Sat. 10-5, Sun. 10-4. Suggested Donations: adults $5, senior citizens & students $2, children $1. Closed holidays. ♿
Attendance: 43,685 (accurate)
Membership: Fire Dept. Personnel, Senior Citizens & Students $15; Individual $20; Family & Dual $25; Supporting $65; Patron $100; Contributor $250; Donor $500; Director's Circle $1,000; President's Club $2,500; Museum Sponsor $10,000.

THE NEW YORK CITY POLICE MUSEUM, (M), 100 Old Slip, New York, NY 10005-3539. Tel.: 212-480-3100, ext. 105. Fax: 212-480-9757.
E-mail: jbose@nycpolicemuseum.org
Web Site: www.nycpolicemuseum.org
Founded: 1998.
Key Personnel: C.E.O., Julie Bose; Pres. & Chm. (V), Carol Safir; Museum Shop Mgr., Iris Stephen.
Personnel Profile: Full-Time Paid 7; Part-Time Paid 3; Part-Time Volunteers 10; Interns 4.
Governing Authority: Affiliated with New York City Police Dept., #1 Police Plaza, NY. 10001. Parent Institution: SUNY Dept. of Education. Tax-exempt: 501(c)(3).
Police History Museum.
Collections: police artifacts; police lanterns; carved wooden night sticks; ivory night sticks; guns; knives; other unusual weapons; handcuffs; photographs; uniform articles dating from 1870 to present day; badges & shields from 1845-present day; antiques; firearms simulator; police vehicles.
Activities: permanent & loan exhibitions; family programs; adult education programs; mystery author series.
Publications: quarterly newsletter.
Hours & Admission Prices: Mon.-Sat. 10-5; school groups by appointment. Adults $7; discounts to AAM members; NYPD personnel & members no charge. Closed New Year's Day; Thanksgiving; Christmas. ♿
Attendance: 54,450 (accurate)
Membership: Out of Town $20; Silver Shield $25; Police Protectors $25; Family $45; Gold Shield $150; Chief $300; Commissioner's Circle $1,000.

NEW-YORK HISTORICAL SOCIETY, (M), 170 Central Park West, New York, NY 10024-5194. Tel.: 212-873-3400, ext. 273. Fax: 212-595-5253.
E-mail: lmirrer@nyhistory.org
Web Site: www.nyhistory.org
Founded: 1804.
Congressional District: 19
Key Personnel: Pres. & C.E.O., Louise Mirrer; Chm. (V), Roger Hertog; Exec. Vice Pres. & Dir. Library, Jean Ashton; Dir. Library Administration, Nina Nazionale; Sr. Art Historian, Linda S. Ferber; Chief Cur. Museum Div., Stephen Edidin; Vice Pres. Operations, Andrew Buonpastore; Vice Pres. Communications, Laura Washington; Vice Pres. Education, Adrienne Kupper; Vice Pres. Public Programs, Dale Gregory; Vice Pres. Devel., Mary Kilbourn; C.F.O., Richard Shein; Gen. Counsel & Chief Administrative Officer, Jennifer Schantz; Dir. Exhibitions, Gerhard Schlanzky; Dir. Merchandise Operations, Ione Saroyan; Dir. Security, Tony Christoforou; Dir. Special Events, Brooke Botwinick; Dir. Visitor Svcs., Chris Catanese; Dir. IT, Drew Sterling; Dir. Human Resources, Valerie Crane.
Personnel Profile: Full-Time Paid 106; Part-Time Paid 46; Part-Time Volunteers 191; Interns 33.
Governing Authority: nonprofit organization. Tax-exempt: 501(c)(3).
Historical Society.
Collections: Audubon watercolors; paintings; portraits; Hudson River School landscapes; genre paintings; silver; furniture; Tiffany lamps & glass; ceramics & glass; sculpture; toys; folk art; carriages; military & naval history collections; prints; photographs; architectural drawings; American imprints; broadsides; newspapers; sheet music; rare books & documents; maps; manuscripts; Henry Luce III Center for the Study of American Culture includes 46,000 artifacts spanning the 17th through the 21st centuries.
Major Exhibits: Lincoln & New York, 11/09-3/10; FDR's Brain Trust and the Beginning of the New Deal, 11/09-3/10; John Brown: the Abolitionist & His Legacy in Collaboration with Gilder Lehrman Institute, 11/09-3/10; Nature and the American Vision: The Hudson River School, 11/09-3/10; New York Painting Begins: Eighteenth Century Portraits, 11/09-3/25/10; The Grateful Dead: Now Playing at the New-York Historical Society, 3/3/10-9/6/10; Life for a Child, 10/1/10-12/10.
Research Fields: American & New York history; American fine arts & decorative arts.
Facilities: 700,000-vol. library of books pertaining to 17th- to 19th-century American history, with emphasis on New York City & State; reading room; 325-seat auditorium. Books & other museum-related items for sale.
Activities: guided tours; lectures; inter-museum loan, permanent & temporary exhibitions; concerts; plays; living history days; reenactments; family days; films.
Publications: books; guides to collections; catalogs of exhibitions; New-York Journal of American History.
Hours & Admission Prices: Museum: Tues.-Sat. 10-5, Fri. 10-8, Sun. 11-5:45. Library: Winter Tues.-Sat. 11-5; Summer Tues.-Fri. 11-5. Adults $12, seniors & educators $9, students $7; Empire State Museums reciprocal program; members & children no charge. Fri. 6pm-8pm pay as you wish. Closed Memorial Day; Labor Day; Thanksgiving; Christmas. ♿
Attendance: 350,000 (accurate)
Membership: Student, Senior Citizens & Educator $40; Individual $55; Dual Senior $70; Dual & Family $100; Young Friends $175; Friend $250; 1804 League $500; Benefactor $1,000; Gotham Fellow $2,500; Chairman's Council $5,000, $10,000, $25,000.

THE NEW YORK PUBLIC LIBRARY, ASTOR, LENOX AND TILDEN FOUNDATIONS, 476 Fifth Ave., Rm. 210, New York, NY 10018-2788. Tel.: 212-930-0800. Fax: 212-930-9299.
Web Site: www.nypl.org
Founded: 1895.
Key Personnel: Chm. Bd. Trustees, Catherine C. Marron; Pres. & C.E.O., Paul LeClerc; Sr. Vice Pres. & Administrative Officer, David Offensend; Dir. & Chief Exec. The Andrew W. Mellon, The Research Libraries, David Ferriero; Dir. Public Rels., Herb Scher; Mgr. Special Events, Kathryn Laino; Mgr. Public & Education Programs, Paul Holdengraber; Mgr. Exhibitions, Susan Rabbiner; Mgr. Public Rels., Anne Conty; Sr. Vice Pres. External Affairs, Catherine Carver Dunn; Deputy Dir. Public Svcs., The Branch Libraries, Mary Frances Cooper; Vice Pres. Budget & Planning, Jeffrey Roth; Deputy Dir. Administrative Svcs., The Branch Libraries, Anne Coriston; Dir. Humanities & Social Sciences, Heike Kordish; Brooke Russell Astor Librarian for Special Collections, H. George Fletcher; Vice Pres. Human Resources, Priscilla J. Southon; Mgr. Publications, Karen Van Westering; Dir. Science, Industry, Business Library, Kristin McDonough; Museum Shop Mgr., Sara Abraham; Dir. Performing Arts Library, Jacqueline Davis; Dir. Schomburg Ctr. Research Black Culture, Howard Dodson.
Personnel Profile: Full-Time Paid 2,272; Part-Time Paid 267.
Governing Authority: nonprofit organization. Branch Landmarks: 1905 Mott Haven Branch; 1911 The New York Public Library's Central Building; 1832 Jefferson Market Branch; 1884 Ottendorfer Branch; 1908 115th Street Branch; 1907 Hamilton Grange Branch; 1902 Yorkville Branch. Tax-exempt: 501(c)(3).
Public Library: housed in 1911 Central Building on the site of the Croton Reservoir.
Collections: 85 Branch Libraries & 4 Research Libraries housing over 54 million items. 1,000 public access computer terminals providing free internet access, free access to a wide range of electronic data bases, and access to the RL catalog (CATNYP) and the BL catalog (LEO). Features new Science, Industry & Business Library (SIBL), Library for the Performing Arts (LPA), Schomburg Center: The Study of Black Culture, and Center for the Humanities and Social Sciences (HSSL) with world renowned special collections as well as wide-ranging basic research & reference materials.
Research Fields: all areas except medicine, law, theology.
Facilities: library; reading room.
Activities: lectures; films; concerts; drama; formally organized educational programs; inter-museum loan, permanent & temporary exhibitions.
Publications: Biblion, Bulletin of the New York Public Library; New Technical Books; Children's Books; newsletter, Library Lines; Directory of Community Services. For a complete list of publications, contact The New York Public Library.
Hours & Admission Prices: Daily. Call for branch hours. No charge; donations accepted. Closed holidays. ♿
Attendance: 13,000,000 (accurate)

Membership: Friend $40; Participating Friend $65; Supporting Friend $100; Patron $250; Sustainer $500; Conservator $1,250.

THE NEW YORK PUBLIC LIBRARY FOR THE PERFORMING ARTS, 40 Lincoln Center Plaza, New York, NY 10023-7486. Tel.: 212-870-1830. Fax: 212-870-1870.
E-mail: bcohenstratyner@nypl.org
Web Site: www.nypl.org
Founded: 1965.
Congressional District: 17
Key Personnel: Pres., Paul LeClerc; Chm. (V), Katie Marron; Exec. Dir. Performing Arts, Jacqueline Z. Davis; Sr. Designer, Donald J. Vlack; Sr. Illustrator, Robert McGlynn; Head Exhibitions, Barbara Cohen-Stratyner; Theatre Cur., Karen Nickeson; Music Cur., George Boziwick; Cur. Recorded Sound, Sara Velez; Cur. Dance, Jan Schmidt; Museum Shop Mgr., Sara Abraham.
Personnel Profile: Full-Time Paid 112; Part-Time Paid 17; Part-Time Volunteers 20; Interns 8.
Governing Authority: nonprofit organization. Parent Institution: New York Public Library, 5th Ave. at 42nd St., New York, 10016. Tel.: 212-930-0800. Tax-exempt: 170(b)(1)(A).
History Museum of Performing Arts.
Collections: prints; letters; manuscripts; documents; photographs; posters, films; video tapes; memorabilia; dance; recordings.
Major Exhibits: Katharine Hepburn, 11/09-1/10; Lincoln Center at 50, 11/09-1/10; Performance & Revolution Central Europe, 11/09-4/10; Loft Jazz, 2/10-5/10; Social Dance in NYC, 5/10-9/10.
Research Fields: performing arts.
Facilities: library of circulating & reference books available for inter-library loan during building hours; reading rooms; 202-seat auditorium in addition to 8 wheelchair stations; 7 galleries.
Activities: free lectures and classes on research computer skills for teachers & general public; films; concerts; dance recitals; drama; formally organized education programs for teachers; loan, temporary & traveling exhibitions.
Publications: season brochures; calendars; free exhibition brochures.
Hours & Admission Prices: Mon. & Thurs. 12-8, Tues.-Wed. & Fri. 11-6, Sat. 10-6. No charge. Closed national holidays. ♿
Attendance: 350,000 (accurate)

THE NEW YORK STUDIO SCHOOL OF DRAWING, PAINTING & SCULPTURE, 8 W. 8th St., New York, NY 10011-9084. Tel.: 212-673-6466. Fax: 212-777-0996.
E-mail: info@nyss.org
Web Site: www.nyss.org
Founded: 1964.
Congressional District: 17
Key Personnel: Chm. (V), Maria Antonia Paterno-Castello; Dean, Graham Nickson; Acting Treas., Peter Krulewitch; C.O.O., Loree Jacquet; Registrar, Darcey Merante; Dir. Gallery, David Cohen.
Personnel Profile: Full-Time Paid 6; Part-Time Paid 13.
Governing Authority: private; nonprofit organization. Tax-exempt: 501(c)(3).
Art Institute: located in a federally landmarked building, site of studios of sculptors Daniel Chester French & Gertrude Vanderbilt Whitney; original site of the Whitney Museum of American Art.
Collections: paintings; sculpture; photographs; sculpture.
Facilities: 3,000-vol. library, 2,500 slide archive; classrooms; studios; 1,000 sq. ft. exhibit space.
Activities: weekly evening lecture series Oct.-May; loan exhibits; formal education programs for adults; non-affiliated certificate programs for undergraduate & graduate students.
Publications: annual newsletter, New York Studio School; illustrated brochures on selected exhibitions.
Hours & Admission Prices: Daily 10-10. Weekly Evening Lecture Series: Tues.-Wed. 6:30 pm-8 pm. No charge; donations accepted. Closed national holidays & school vacations, depending on exhibition schedule.
Attendance: 10,000 (estimated)

NICHOLAS ROERICH MUSEUM, (M), 319 W. 107th St., New York, NY 10025-2799. Tel.: 212-864-7752. Fax: 212-864-7704.
E-mail: director@roerich.org
Web Site: www.roerich.org
Founded: 1958.
Congressional District: 15
Key Personnel: Exec. Dir., Daniel Entin; Pres. (V), Edgar Lansbury; Directors Asst., Aida Tulskaya; Dir. Cultural Programs, Jean Fletcher.
Personnel Profile: Full-Time Paid 4; Part-Time Volunteers 4; Interns 1.
Governing Authority: nonprofit organization. Tax-exempt: 501(c)(3).
Art Museum.
Collections: paintings of Tibet, India, Himalayas by Nicholas Roerich.
Research Fields: Eastern art.
Activities: gallery talks; concerts; permanent exhibition; poetry readings.
Publications: books, The Invincible; Shambala, The Roerich Pact and Banner of Peace; Altai-Himalaya.
Hours & Admission Prices: Tues.-Sun. 2-5. No charge; donations accepted. Closed select holidays. ♿
Attendance: 10,000 (estimated)
Membership: Associate $25; Contributing $50; Sustaining $100.

THE PALEY CENTER FOR MEDIA, 25 W. 52nd St., New York, NY 10019-6104. Tel.: 212-621-6600. Fax: 212-621-6700.
Web Site: www.paleycenter.org
Formerly: The Museum of Television & Radio
Founded: 1975.
Congressional District: 18
Key Personnel: Chm. Bd., Frank A. Bennack, Jr.; Pres. & C.E.O., Pat Mitchell; Vice Pres. Public Affairs & Programs, Diane Lewis; Vice Pres. Business Affairs, John Wolters; Vice Pres. Dir. Los Angeles Museum, Craig Hitchcock; Cur., Ronald Simon; Cur., David Bushman; Dir. Devel., Jennifer Juzaitis; Dir. Technical Operation & Engineering, Doug Warner; Dir. Library & Information Svcs., Douglas F. Gibbons; Mgr. Public Rels., Amy Douthett; Museum Shop Mgr., Robert Eng.
Personnel Profile: Full-Time Paid 75; Part-Time Paid 55; Part-Time Volunteers 6; Interns 10.
Governing Authority: nonprofit organization. Branch Location: 465 N. Beverly Dr., Beverly Hills, CA 90210. Tel.: 310-786-1000. Tax-exempt: 170(b)(1)(A).
Digital Media Museum.
Collections: over 100,000 radio & television programs and advertisements from the 1920s to the present.
Facilities: NY: 64 television & 31 radio consoles; four screening theaters; radio listening room; radio broadcast studio; satellite up & down links. LA: 64 television & radio consoles; one screening room; one screening theater; radio listening room; radio broadcast studio; satellite up & down links.
Activities: TV & radio viewing; programs; formally organized education programs for students; seminars on various aspects of media; programs for industry professionals.
Publications: exhibition catalogs; seminar transcripts; catalogue of events.
Hours & Admission Prices: NY: Wed. & Fri.-Sun. 12-6, Thurs. 12-8. LA: Wed.-Sun 12-5, Thurs. 12-8. Suggested Donation: adults $10, senior citizens & students $8, children under 14 $5; discounts to AAM & ICOM members; members & California museum no charge. Closed New Year's Day; Independence Day; Thanksgiving; Christmas. ♿
Attendance: 120,000 (accurate)
Membership: Senior Citizen & Student $50; Individual $70; Dual & Family $100; Supporting $250; Sustaining $500; Patrons Circle $1,000 & up; Assoc. PaleyAfterDark Cir. $3,000; PAD $6,000.

PRATT MANHATTAN GALLERY, 144 W. 14th St., 2nd Fl., New York, NY 10011-7301. Tel.: 212-647-7778. Fax: 212-367-2484.
E-mail: exhibits@pratt.edu
Web Site: www.pratt.edu/exhibitions
Founded: 2002.
Key Personnel: Dir., Nick Battis; Asst. Dir., Jen Osborne; Exhibit Designer, Katherine Davis.
Personnel Profile: Full-Time Paid 2; Part-Time Paid 8; Interns 2.
Governing Authority: nonprofit. Parent Institution: Pratt Institute. Tax-exempt: 501(c)(3).
Art Museum & Center.
Collections: 19th- & 20th-century paintings, sculpture, prints, decorative arts & graphic arts by European & American artists.
Major Exhibits: Design Jazz: Improvizations on the Urban Street, 9/25/09-11/7/09; Ethics & Aesthetics: Sustainable Fashion Here and Now, 11/20/09-2/6/10; Envelopes, 2/19/10-5/1/10.
Research Fields: contemporary fine arts, design & architecture.
Facilities: 2,200 sq. ft. exhibit space; classrooms; lecture room.
Activities: lectures; continuing education & degree programs.
Publications: exhibition announcements & catalogs; posters; newsletter; biannual exhibitions & events calendar.
Hours & Admission Prices: Mon.-Fri. 10:30-5:30, Sat. 12-5. No charge. Closed major holidays. ♿
Attendance: 30,000

PUSH PIN GALLERY, FORDHAM UNIVERSITY, Lincoln Center Campus, Visual Arts Complex, New York, NY 10023-6594. Tel.: 212-636-6000.
Art Gallery.
Collections: works by student artists including paintings, drawings, & sculpture.
Hours & Admission Prices: Call for hours.

THE RENEE AND CHAIM GROSS FOUNDATION, 526 LaGuardia Place, New York, NY 10012-1401. Tel.: 212-529-4906. Fax: 212-529-1966.
E-mail: info@rcgrossfoundation.org
Web Site: www.rcgrossfoundation.org
Founded: 1995.
Congressional District: 8
Key Personnel: Pres., Miriam Gross; Exec. Dir. & Cur., Susan Greenberg Fisher, Ph.D.; Treas., Leah Gross-Hutchison; Catalogue Asst., Sarah Locke.
Personnel Profile: Full-Time Paid 1; Part-Time Paid 5.
Governing Authority: private; nonprofit. Parent Institution: Renee and Chaim Gross Foundation. Tax-exempt: 501(c)(3).
Art Museum: housed in a late 19th century structure with cast iron facade that served as Chaim Gross' home and studio for more than 30 years.
Collections: sculpture in wood, stone & bronze as well as drawings, watercolors and prints, 1921-1991, demonstrating the continuity of Chaim Gross' personal vision; wire armatures; clay & plaster maquettes; tools; photographs documenting the life of Chaim Gross.
Research Fields: the life & work of Chaim Gross and the historical context surrounding it.
Facilities: 2,500-vol. library of art & art history books, relating to the life of Gross and his contemporaries; photographic reference & representation of every sculpture as is known in library binders; Chaim Gross Archives for scholarly research on premises; biographies of artists; reference works, periodicals & exhibition catalogues; 2,500 sq. ft. exhibit space; skylight roofed working studio; video viewing room.
Activities: book & poetry readings; films; videos; guided tours; lectures; loan, temporary & traveling exhibitions. Annual Event: bus tour showing Gross sculpture in fall.
Publications: exhibition catalogues; exhibit brochures.
Hours & Admission Prices: Tues.-Fri. 10-5 by appointment. No charge; donation requested. Closed national holidays. ♿
Attendance: 12,000 (estimated)

THE ROSE MUSEUM AT CARNEGIE HALL, 154 W. 57th St., 2nd Fl., New York, NY 10019-3321. Mailing Address: 881 7th Ave., New York, NY 10019-3210. Tel.: 212-903-9629.
E-mail: archives@carnegiehall.org
Web Site: www.carnegiehall.org
Founded: 1991.
Key Personnel: C.E.O. Carnegie Hall, Clive Gillinson; Dir. & Archivist, Gino Francesconi; Chm. (V), Sanford I. Weill; Museum Shop Mgr., Sean Morrow; Assoc. Archivist, Robert Hudson.
Governing Authority: nonprofit organization.
Theatre Museum: housed in c.1891 Carnegie Hall building.
Collections: artifacts & photographs depicting history & development of the building; history of the studios; chronology of events from the main hall.
Facilities: 2,800-seat theatre. Souvenirs & other museum-related items for sale.
Activities: guided tours. Museum Sponsors: temporary exhibits reflecting an anniversary or festival on stage.
Hours & Admission Prices: Sept. 15-June daily 11-4:30, open to concert-goers before concerts & during intermission. No charge. ♿
Attendance: 25,000 (estimated)

RUBIN MUSEUM OF ART, 150 W. 17th St., New York, NY 10011-5402. Tel.: 212-620-5000.
E-mail: info@rmanyc.org
Web Site: www.rmanyc.org
Founded: 1999.
Congressional District: 8
Key Personnel: Dir., Donald Rubin; Museum Shop Mgr., Sherab Norpa.
Personnel Profile: Full-Time Paid 62; Part-Time Paid 10; Part-Time Volunteers 122; Interns 54.
Governing Authority: Tax-exempt.
Art Museum.
Collections: paintings, sculptures & textiles relating to the Himalayas.
Publications: exhibition catalogs.
Hours & Admission Prices: Mon. & Thurs. 11-5, Wed. 11-7, Fri. 11-10, Sat.-Sun. 11-6. Adults $10, seniors & artists with ID $7, college students with ID $2; discounts to AAM & ICOM memers; children under 12, members & Fri. 7pm-10pm no charge. ♿
Attendance: 140,000 (accurate)
Membership: Artist, Neighbor, Student and Senior 60 & over $35; Individual $55; Dual & Family $75; Friend $125; Sustaining $250; Benefactor $500; Chairman's Circle $1,000; Sponsor $2,500; Collector's Circle $5,000; Donors Circle $10,000.

SALMAGUNDI MUSEUM OF AMERICAN ART, 47 5th Ave., New York, NY 10003-4396. Tel.: 212-255-7740. Fax: 212-229-0172.
Web Site: www.salmagundi.org
Founded: 1871.
Key Personnel: Chm., Pamela Singleton; Pres., Claudia Seymour; Cur., Robert Mueller.
Governing Authority: nonprofit. Tax-exempt: 501(c)(3).
Art Gallery.
Collections: American art; paintings; photographs; artist's palettes.
Research Fields: art.
Facilities: library.
Activities: temporary exhibitions.
Publications: exhibition folders.
Hours & Admission Prices: Daily 1-5. No charge; donations accepted.
Attendance: 3,000 (estimated)

THE SCHOMBURG CENTER FOR RESEARCH IN BLACK CULTURE, The New York Public Library, 515 Malcolm X. Blvd., New York, NY 10037-1801. Tel.: 212-491-2200. Fax: 212-491-6760.
Web Site: www.schomburgcenter.org
Founded: 1925.
Congressional District: 16
Key Personnel: Chief, Howard Dodson; Head Reference, Genette McLaurin; Head Moving Image & Recorded Sound, James Briggs Murray; Head Archives, Diana Lachatenere; Devel. Officer, Roberta Yancy; Museum Shop Mgr., Bibi Uddin.
Governing Authority: nonprofit. Parent Institution: The New York Public Library. Research Center of The New York Public Library/Astor, Lenox & Tilden Foundations, 42nd & 5th Ave., New York, NY. 10018. Tel.: 212-790-6254. Tax-exempt: 170(b)(1)(A).
History Museum & Reference Library.
Collections: books by & about Afro-American, African Diasporan & African life & history; periodicals; pamphlets; manuscripts; personal papers; photographs; prints & drawings; paintings; sculpture; historical artifacts; clippings; playbills; programs; broadsides sheet music; audio-video recordings; films; phonorecords.
Research Fields: black history & culture throughout the world.
Facilities: 220,000-vol. library of print and non-print materials & art objects by or about people of African descent, available for use on-site; microfilm reading area; archives area; oral & video facilities.
Activities: exhibitions mounted on premises; book parties; symposia; scholarly research; lectures & receptions for authors; concerts; film; theater.
Publications: journal, The Schomburg Center; exhibition catalog.
Hours & Admission Prices: Mon.-Wed. 12-8, Thurs.-Fri. 11-6, Sat. 10-5. Exhibits: Tues.-Sat. 10-6, Sun. 1-5. No charge; donations accepted. ♿
Attendance: 120,000
Membership: Individual $35-$2,500; Organizational & Institutional $250-$2,500; Corporate $1,000-$25,000.

SIDNEY MISHKIN GALLERY OF BARUCH COLLEGE, 135 E. 22nd St., New York, NY 10010-5505. Mailing Address: Box D-0100, New York, NY 10010-5505. Tel.: 646-660-6652. Fax: 212-802-2693.
Web Site: www.baruch.cuny.edu/mishkin/gallery.html
Founded: 1981.
Congressional District: 15
Key Personnel: Dir., Sandra Kraskin, Ph.D.
Personnel Profile: Full-Time Paid 1; Part-Time Paid 2.
Governing Authority: Parent Institution: Baruch College, The City University of New York. Tax-exempt: 501(c)(3).
University Gallery: housed in 1939 Family Court Building erected by WPA.
Collections: 20th & 21st century paintings, sculpture, prints, & photographs.
Research Fields: modernism 1930-1960; self-taught artists; interdisciplinary; multicultural.
Activities: organized education programs for the public, undergraduate & graduate college students affiliated with Baruch College, City University of New York; temporary exhibitions of our own collections; traveling & loan exhibitions.
Publications: exhibition catalogues; brochures.
Hours & Admission Prices: Feb.-June & Sept.-Dec. Mon.-Wed. & Fri. 12-5, Thurs. 12-7. No charge. Closed university holidays. ♿

THE SKYSCRAPER MUSEUM, (M), 39 Battery Place, New York, NY 10280-1501. Tel.: 212-968-1961 & 945-6324. Fax: 212-732-3039.
E-mail: info@skyscraper.org
Web Site: www.skyscraper.org
Founded: 1997.
Congressional District: 8
Key Personnel: C.O.O., William Havemeyer; C.E.O., Dir. & Pres. (V), Carol Willis; Chm. (V), Jed Marcus; Treas., Owen Gutfreund; Museum Shop Mgr., Darnella Lewis.

Personnel Profile: Full-Time Paid 4; Part-Time Paid 5; Part-Time Volunteers 2; Interns 1.
Governing Authority: private; nonprofit organization. Tax-exempt: 501(c)(3).
Architecture Museum.
Collections: construction photographs & film; architectural & engineering drawings; contracts; builders' records; financial reports; advertising materials; periodicals; models; building tools & artifacts.
Major Exhibits: China Prophecy: Shanghai, 11/09-3/10; At The Corner of Capital: Wall Street, 4/10.
Research Fields: future exhibitions, including core exhibition, SKYSCRAPER/CITY; building document collection for virtual archive; international skyscrapers; urban density.
Facilities: 5,000 sq. ft. exhibit space; audiovisual room. Museum-related items for sale.
Activities: films; guided tours; lectures; rental gallery; walking tours outside of museum. Museum Sponsors: Making New York History award.
Publications: book, Building the Empire State; Form Follows Finance: Skyscrapers and Skylines in NY & Chicago; Lower Manhattan Plan.
Hours & Admission Prices: Wed.-Sun. 12-6. Adults $5, students & seniors $2.50; discounts to AAM & ICOM members; members no charge. ♿
Attendance: 25,000 (estimated)
Membership: Basic $35; Friend $50; Contributor $100; Supporter $500; Donor $1,000; Corporate $1,000 and up.

∗ **SOLOMON R. GUGGENHEIM MUSEUM, (M),** 1071 Fifth Ave. at 89th St., New York, NY 10128-0112. Tel.: 212-423-3500. Fax: 212-423-3787.
E-mail: info@guggenheim.org
Web Site: www.guggenheim.org
Founded: 1937.
Congressional District: 20
Key Personnel: Dir. Solomon R. Guggenheim Foundation, Richard Armstrong; C.O.O. Solomon R. Guggenheim Museum, Marc Steglitz; Chief Counsel, Sarah Austrain; Deputy Dir, External Affairs, Eleanor Goldhar; Chief Cur., Nancy Spector; Assoc. Cur. Contemporary Art & Mgr. Curatorial Affairs, Joan Young; Sr. Cur. Asian Art, Alexandra Monroe; Cur. Photography, Jennifer Blessing; Assoc. Cur. Collections & Exhibitions, Tracy Bashkoff; Dir. Education, Kim Kanatani; Exec. Dir., Major Gifts, Adrienne Hines; Exec. Dir. Corporate & Institutional Devel., John Wielk; Dir. Finance, Amy West; Chief Information Officer, Alexander Pasik; Dir. Media & Public Rels., Betsy Ennis; Dir. Mktg., Laura Miller; Dir. Registration, Mary Louise Napier; Project Mgr., Jessica Ludwig; Dir. Photographic Svcs. & Chief Photographer, David M. Heald; Dir. Publications, Beth Levy; Chief Graphic Designer, Marcia Fardella; Dir. Visitor Svcs., Maria Celi; Dir. & Counsel Administration, Brendan Connell; Dir. Security, Steve Ursell; Chm. Bd., William Mack; Pres. Bd., Jennifer Blei Stockman.
Personnel Profile: Full-Time Paid 289; Part-Time Paid 36.
Governing Authority: nonprofit organization. Operated by the Solomon R. Guggenheim Foundation, 527 Madison Ave., New York, NY 10022; Guggenheim Museum Bilbao, Bilbao, Spain. Sister Institutions: Peggy Guggenheim Collection in Venice, Italy; Guggenheim Museum Bilbao, Bilbao, Spain; Deutsche Guggenheim, Berlin Germany. Tax-exempt.
Art Museum: housed in building designed by Frank Lloyd Wright.
Collections: paintings; sculpture; video; works on paper of last 100 years including concentrations of works by Picasso, Chagall, Brancusi, Delaunay, Dubuffet, Pollock, Modigliani, Max Ernst, Mondrian, Miro, Rothko, Giacometti, Leger, Marc & an extensive representation of paintings by Kandinsky & Klee; broad range of post World War II painting & sculpture from the U.S. & Europe.
Research Fields: late 19th- & 20th-century art.
Facilities: 20,000-vol. library of modern art; documentation of the collection of Solomon R. Guggenheim Museum available for research by appointment only; auditorium. Catalogs, slides, posters, note cards, exhibition-related monographs for sale.
Activities: permanent, temporary & traveling exhibitions; inter-museum loan exhibitions; guided tours; lectures; films; music, dance & theater performances; symposia; panel discussions; gallery talks; internship programs for graduate & college students.
Publications: catalogues of exhibitions; handbook, The Guggenheim Museum Collection A to Z.
Hours & Admission Prices: Fri. 10-7:45, Sat.-Wed. 10-5:45. Adults $18, seniors & students $12; discounts to AAM & ICOM members; children under 12 & members no charge. ♿
Attendance: 1,000,000 (estimated)
Membership: Individual $75; Dual $125; Family $135; Fellow Associate $250; Supporting Associate $500.

SONY WONDER TECHNOLOGY LAB, (M), 56th St. & Madison Ave., New York, NY 10022. Mailing Address: 550 Madison Ave., Annex, New York, NY 10022-3211. Tel.: 212-833-8100. Fax: 212-833-4445.
E-mail: timothy_foster@sonyusa.com
Web Site: www.sonywondertechlab.com
Founded: 1994.
Key Personnel: Senior Dir., Karen Kelso.
Personnel Profile: Full-Time Paid 22; Part-Time Paid 8; Interns 1.
Governing Authority: corporation. Parent Institution: Sony Corporation of America.
Technology, Media & Science Museum.
Collections: technology & entertainment.
Facilities: 14,000 sq. ft. interactive, hands-on science & technology center; high definition theater.
Activities: special events; screenings; tours & teacher development; workshops; early learner programs.
Hours & Admission Prices: Tues.-Sat. 10-5, Sun. 12-5. No charge. Closed major holidays. ♿
Attendance: 220,000 (accurate)

SOUTH STREET SEAPORT MUSEUM, 12 Fulton St., New York, NY 10038-2109. Tel.: 212-748-8786. Fax: 212-748-8610.
E-mail: reservations@southstseaport.org
Web Site: www.southstreetseaportmuseum.org
Founded: 1967.
Congressional District: 8
Key Personnel: Chm. Bd. (V), Frank J. Sciame, Jr.; Pres. & C.E.O., Mary Ellen Pelzer; C.F.O., Terry Polcaro; Dir. Institutional Advancement, Carol Rauscher.
Personnel Profile: Full-Time Paid 23; Full-Time Volunteers 35; Part-Time Volunteers 107; Interns 10.
Governing Authority: nonprofit organization. Satellite Facility: New York Unearthed, 17 State St., New York, NY. Tel.: 212-748-8753. Tax-exempt: 501(c)(3).
Maritime History Museum.
Collections: documents; photographs; paintings; ship models; ship artifacts; navigational instruments; tools; printing presses; fishmarket artifacts; scrimshaw. Historic Ships: fourmasted bark, Peking; square rigged ship, Wavertree; wood fishing schooner, Lettie G. Howard; Ambrose Light Ship; schooner, Pioneer; tugboat W.O. Decker; harbor lighter, Marion M; tugboat Helen McAllister.
Major Exhibits: Treasures of a President: FDR & the Sea (T), 11/09-1/10; Normandie and Art Deco, 2/10-12/10; Alfred Steiglitz's New York, 6/10-12/10.
Research Fields: naval history; New York maritime commercial history; transportation; printing history; architectural history; 19th-century trade, economy & transportation; maritime history & technology.
Facilities: Books, prints & other museum-related items for sale.
Activities: demonstrations on ships & piers in summer; craft demonstrations; guided tours; lectures; films; classes; educational programs; children's workshops; school tours; public sailing aboard 1885 schooner Pioneer; teacher workshops.
Publications: magazine, Seaport includes Broadside Calendar of Events.
Hours & Admission Prices: Galleries & Ships: Jan.-March Fri.-Sun. 10-5; April-Dec. Tues.-Sun. 10-6. Adults $10, seniors & students $8, children 5-12 $5; discounts to Council of American Maritime Museums, International Congress of Maritime Museums, groups, AAM, ICOM, AAA & CAMM members; children under 5 & members no charge. Schooner Pioneer: May-Oct. three times daily, call for reservations & fee. ♿
Attendance: 235,011 (accurate)
Membership: Student & Senior Citizen $45; National & International $50; Individual $60; Dual $75; Family $125; Boatswain $300; Captain $500; Cape Horn Society $1,000; Navigator Society $2,500; Pilot Society $5,000; Commodore Society $10,000.

THE SPANISH INSTITUTE, 684 Park Ave., New York, NY 10065-5043. Tel.: 212-628-0420. Fax: 212-734-4177.
Web Site: www.queensofiaspanishinstitute.org
Founded: 1954.
Key Personnel: Chm., Oscar de la Renta; Pres. & C.E.O., Inmaculada de Habsburgo; Dir. Programs, Paloma Jimenez.
Personnel Profile: Full-Time Paid 12; Part-Time Paid 30; Part-Time Volunteers 2.
Governing Authority: nonprofit organization. Tax-exempt: 170(b)(1)(A).
Spanish Cultural Institute: housed in c.1920 building designed by McKim, Mead & White.
Collections: temporary exhibitions of Spanish art.
Research Fields: Spanish art in all media; collecting & patronage of Spanish art.

Facilities: 500-vol. library on Spanish art available to the public; 150-seat auditorium; classrooms; 2,200 sq. ft. exhibit space. Exhibition catalogs for sale.
Activities: recitals; films; videos; formal educational programs; guided tours; lectures; loan & traveling exhibitions.
Publications: annual report; newsletter; monthly calendar of events, exhibition catalogues; Spanish Polychrome Sculpture (1500-1800) in United States Collections; Spain, Espagne, Spanien: Foreign Artists Discover Spain 1800-1900; Iberian Antiquities in the Collection of Leon Levy & Shelby White; Valencian Painters 1865-1936; Matta's Quijote; Italian Drawings from the Biblioteca Nacional, Madrid; Ignacio Zuloaga in America.
Hours & Admission Prices: Mon.-Thurs. 10-6, Fri. 10-8, Sat. 11-5. Closed major holidays.
Attendance: 30,000
Membership: Student $25; Individual $50; Family $75; Sponsor $100; Supporter $500; Sustainer $1,000; Patron & Corporate Member $3,500; Benefactor & Corporate Patron $5,000; Corporate Benefactor $10,000.

SPORTS MUSEUM OF AMERICA, 1675 Broadway, Fl. 34, New York, NY 10019-5849. Tel.: 212-747-0900. Fax: 212-747-0911.
E-mail: info@thesportsmuseum.com
Web Site: www.thesportsmuseum.com
Founded: 2008.
Key Personnel: Dir., Philip Schwalb; Pres., John Urban; C.F.O., Sameer Ahuja; Cur., Laura Purcell; Museum Shop Mgr., Marcy Davis.
Personnel Profile: Interns 8.
Sports Museum.
Collections: American sports history; local, national & global sports; films; sports memorabilia.
Facilities: 28,000 exhibit space. Museum-related items for sale.
Activities: special events; lectures; participatory exhibits.
Publications: monthly newsletter.
Hours & Admission Prices: Daily 9-7. Adults $24, senior citizens 65 & over and students $21, children 6-15 $17; discounts to groups; children under 6 no charge. ♿

* **STATUE OF LIBERTY NATIONAL MONUMENT & ELLIS ISLAND IMMIGRATION MUSEUM, (M), (I),** Liberty Island, New York, NY 10004-1418. Tel.: 212-363-3200. Fax: 212-363-6304. TDD: 212-363-3301.
E-mail: stli_info@nps.gov
Web Site: www.nps.gov/stli
Founded: 1924.
Congressional District: 17
Key Personnel: Supt., Dave Luchsinger; Deputy Supt., John Hnedack; Chief Museum Svcs. Div., Diana Pardue; Cur. Exhibits & Media, Judith Giuriceo; Cur. Collections, Geraldine Santoro; Chief Maintenance, Peter O'Dougherty; Acting Administrative Officer & Contractor, Linda Deveau; Concessions Specialist, Ben Hanslin; Contract Specialist, Yeny Reyes; Chief Interpretation Div., Daniel Brown; Supervisory Archivist, George Tselos; Library, Jeff Dosik; Library, Barry Moreno; Concessioner, Brad Hill.
Personnel Profile: Full-Time Paid 177; Full-Time Volunteers 5; Part-Time Volunteers 128; Interns 10.
Governing Authority: federal. Parent Institution: U.S. Dept. of the Interior, National Park Service. Tax-exempt.
Statue of Liberty: housed in 1886 151-ft. copper statue bearing torch of freedom was gift of French people to commemorate alliance of U.S. & France; monument includes two exhibits on the Statue of Liberty: World Heritage Site. Ellis Island: over 12 million immigrants were processed here between 1892-1954; exhibits on Ellis Island, American immigration, film, learning center, library & oral history program; access to both islands by ferry.
Collections: history; folk art; archival & other materials pertaining to the Statue of Liberty & Ellis Island; Augustus F. Sherman photographs; immigrant oral histories with transcripts; contemporary art; photographs; film & video.
Research Fields: Statue of Liberty; Ellis Island; U.S. immigration.
Facilities: research library & oral history collection; two movie theatres; oral history recording studio; learning center for groups; restaurant. Gift items for sale.
Activities: temporary exhibitions; films; ranger tours; living history presentations.
Publications: brochures; NPS research reports.
Hours & Admission Prices: Liberty Island: daily 9:30-5. Time Pass required for visiting inside the monument. Advanced reservations suggested. Call: 866-782-8834. Ellis Island: daily 9:30-5:15. No charge; donations accepted. Circle Line Ferry Boats: call (212) 269-5755. Closed Christmas. ♿
Attendance: 3,408,560 (accurate)

* **THE STUDIO MUSEUM IN HARLEM, (M),** 144 W. 125th St., New York, NY 10027-4423. Tel.: 212-864-4500. Fax: 212-864-4800.
E-mail: pr@studiomuseum.org
Web Site: www.studiomuseum.org
Founded: 1967.
Congressional District: 19
Key Personnel: Dir. & Chief Cur., Thelma Golden; Asst. Cur., Naomi Beckwith; Asst. Dir. Education & Public Programs, Ayeshah Wiltshire.
Personnel Profile: Full-Time Paid 42; Part-Time Paid 9; Interns 6.
Governing Authority: private; nonprofit organization. Tax-exempt: 501(c)(3).
Contemporary Art Museum: sculpture garden; collection, documentation, preservation & interpretation of the art & artifacts of Black American & the African Diaspora.
Collections: 19th-21st century African American art; traditional & contemporary African art; Caribbean art; archives.
Research Fields: 19th & 20th-century African American art; African art; art of the African diaspora.
Facilities: classrooms. Books, African textiles, exhibition catalogues, African jewelry, posters & other museum-related items for sale.
Activities: temporary & traveling exhibitions; artist-in-residence program; public programs; guided tours; workshops. Museum Sponsors: Target Free Sundays.
Publications: exhibition catalogs; studio magazine.
Hours & Admission Prices: Wed.-Fri. & Sun. 12-6, Sat. 10-6. Suggested Donation: adults $7, students & senior citizens $3; discounts to AAM & ICOM members; members & children under 12 no charge. Closed major holidays. ♿
Attendance: 116,159 (estimated)
Membership: Individual $50; Family/Partner $75; Supporter $100; Contemporary Friends Individual $200; Associate $250; Contemporary Friends $300; Donor $500; Benefactor $1,000.

TAIPEI GALLERY/CHINESE INFORMATION AND CULTURE CENTER, (M), (I), McGraw-Hill Bldg., 1221 Ave. of the Americas, New York, NY 10020-1001. Mailing Address: 1 E. 42nd St., 7th Fl., New York, NY 10017-6904. Tel.: 212-373-1854.
Art Gallery.
Collections: period Chinese & contemporary arts from Taiwan; Chinese history & culture.
Hours & Admission Prices: Mon.-Fri. 10:30-5:30.

T.F. CHEN CULTURAL CENTER, 250 Lafayette St., New York, NY 10012-4040. Tel.: 212-966-4363. Fax: 212-966-5285.
E-mail: chen@tfchen.org
Web Site: www.tfchen.org
Founded: 1996.
Key Personnel: C.E.O. & Pres. (V), Lucia Chen; Chm. (V), Dr. T.F. Chen; Financial Dir., Ted Chen; Public Rels. & Cur., Julie Chen; Public Rels. & Cur., Louise Lu Chen.
Personnel Profile: Full-Time Paid 2; Full-Time Volunteers 4; Part-Time Paid 1; Part-Time Volunteers 4; Interns 3.
Governing Authority: private; nonprofit organization. Tax-exempt: 501(c)(3).
Art Museum.
Collections: art collection dating from 1951; multicultural; universal humanism; east & west.
Research Fields: artists in the Neo-Iconography style group shows.
Facilities: 500-vol. library on art history; 14,000 sq. ft. exhibit space. Museum-related items for sale.
Activities: arts festival; lectures; loan, traveling, exchange, participatory & temporary exhibitions.
Publications: annual newsletter.
Hours & Admission Prices: By appointment only. No charge. Closed New Year's Day; Christmas.
Attendance: 5,000 (estimated)

THEODORE ROOSEVELT BIRTHPLACE NATIONAL HISTORIC SITE, 28 E. 20th St., New York, NY 10003-1311. Tel.: 212-260-1616. Fax: 212-677-3587.
Web Site: www.nps.gov/thrb/
Founded: 1923.
Congressional District: 15
Key Personnel: Site Mgr., Michael Darden; Park Ranger, Michael Amato; Park Ranger, Daniel Prebatt.
Personnel Profile: Full-Time Paid 4; Part-Time Paid 1; Part-Time Volunteers 5; Interns 1.
Governing Authority: federal. Administered by National Park Service, Dept. of Interior. Tax-exempt.
Historic Site Museum: housed in 1919-1923 reconstructed Theodore Roosevelt birthplace.
Collections: mid-19th century period rooms; Theodore Roosevelt memorabilia & historical items.

Research Fields: Theodore Roosevelt; American history.
Facilities: auditorium. Books for sale.
Activities: guided tours; films; permanent exhibitions. Chamber music concerts Sept.-May.
Publications: site brochures.
Hours & Admission Prices: Tues.-Sat. 9-5. Tours: 10-11 & 1-4 on the hour. No charge. Closed federal holidays.
Attendance: 40,000 (accurate)
Membership: National Park Service: Golden Age 62 & over $10.

TRIBUTE WTC VISITOR CENTER, (M), 120 Liberty St., New York, NY 10006-1008. Tel.: 866-737-1184; 212-393-9160, ext. 138.
E-mail: visitorservices@tributewtc.org
Web Site: www.tributewtc.org
History Museum.
Collections: September 11th history; photographs.
Activities: special programs.
Hours & Admission Prices: Mon. & Wed.-Sat. 10-6, Tues. 12-6, Sun. 12-5. Adults $10. Closed New Year's Day; Easter; Thanksgiving; Christmas Eve, Day & week.

TRINITY MUSEUM OF THE PARISH OF TRINITY CHURCH, Broadway & Wall St., New York, NY 10006. Mailing Address: 74 Trinity Place, 4th Fl., New York, NY 10006-2003. Tel.: 212-602-0800 & 0872. Fax: 212-602-9648.
E-mail: archives@trinitywallstreet.org
Web Site: www.trinitywallstreet.org/history/museum
Founded: 1966.
Congressional District: 17
Key Personnel: C.E.O., Rev. Dr. James H. Cooper; Cur., Gwynedd Cannan; Museum Shop Mgr., David Jette.
Personnel Profile: Full-Time Paid 3; Part-Time Paid 2.
Governing Authority: church; nonprofit. Parent Institution: Trinity Church. Tax-exempt: 501(c)(3).
Religious & History Museum: housed in 1846 Trinity Church, on site first used in 1697.
Collections: 1644-present, church archives including documents, books; prints; photographs; paintings; artifacts & religious objects. Historic Building: 1766 St. Paul's Chapel.
Research Fields: religious history; New York City history; English history.
Facilities: 1,000-vol. library of religious, New York City & state history & English history available for research by appointment by qualified scholars and students; parish archives. Books, religious objects & museum-related items for sale.
Activities: self-guided tours; temporary & permanent exhibits; guided tours by appointment; educational video.
Publications: brochures; videos; A Guide to Trinity Church; Trinity, A Church, A Parish, A People.
Hours & Admission Prices: Mon.-Fri. 9-11:45 & 1-5:30, Sat.-Sun. 9-3:45; St. Paul's: Mon.-Sat. 10-6, Sun. 7-6. No charge; donations accepted. Closed holidays. ♿
Attendance: 33,000 (estimated)

THE UKRAINIAN MUSEUM, 222 E. 6th St., New York, NY 10003-8201. Tel.: 212-228-0110. Fax: 212-228-1947.
E-mail: info@ukrainianmuseum.org
Web Site: www.ukrainianmuseum.org
Founded: 1976.
Congressional District: 14
Key Personnel: Dir., Maria Shust; Pres. (V), Jaroslav Leshko; Admin. Dir., Daria Bajko; Museum Shop Mgr., Chrystyna Pevny.
Personnel Profile: Full-Time Paid 4; Part-Time Paid 9; Part-Time Volunteers 50.
Governing Authority: nonprofit. Tax-exempt: 501(c)(3).
Culturally Specific Museum.
Collections: fine art; folk art; archives; photographs; documents; Ukrainian culture, history & immigration to the U.S.; numismatics & philatelic.
Research Fields: Ukrainian ethnology; ethnography; fine arts; history.
Facilities: 3,000-vol. library; auditorium; 80-seat lecture & conference room. Museum-related items for sale.
Activities: guided tours; lectures; films; formally organized educational programs; permanent & temporary exhibitions.
Publications: exhibitions catalogues; brochures, books, annual reports.
Hours & Admission Prices: Wed.-Sun. 11:30-5. Adults $8, students & senior citizens $6; discounts to AAM & ICOM members; members & children under 12 no charge. Closed New Year's Day; Ukrainian Christmas & Easter; Easter; Independence Day; Labor Day; Thanksgiving; Christmas. ♿
Attendance: 25,000 (estimated)

Membership: Students $10; Senior Citizens $15; Regular $40; Family $75; Contributing $100; Life $7,500 & up.

UNION FOR REFORM JUDAISM, 633 Third Ave., New York, NY 10017-6706. Tel.: 212-650-4040. Fax: 212-650-4239.
E-mail: urj@urj.org
Web Site: www.urj.org
Formerly: Union of American Hebrew Congregation
Founded: 1957.
Key Personnel: Pres., Rabbi Eric H. Yoffie; Dir. Mktg. & Comm., Emily Grotta.
Governing Authority: denominational group. Operated by the Joint Commission on Synagogue Administration Union of American Hebrew Congregations and Central Conference of American Rabbis.
Religious Library & Museum.
Collections: books on Synagogue architecture; books on Synagogue art, ceremonial objects & works of Jewish artists; 2,500 slides on the collection.
Facilities: 200-vol. library on Synagogue architecture, art & ceremonial objects available on premises only.
Activities: reading room; slide rental service.
Publications: books, An American Synagogue for Today & Tomorrow; Contemporary Synagogue Art.
Hours & Admission Prices: Mon.-Thurs. 9-4, Fri. 9-5. Closed Jewish holidays & festivals.

THE VILCEK FOUNDATION, 167 E. 73rd St., New York, NY 10021. Tel.: 212-472-2500. Fax: 212-472-4720.
E-mail: info@vilcek.org
Web Site: www.vilcek.org
Founded: 2000.
Congressional District: 14
Key Personnel: Dir., Rick Kinsel; Pres., Jan Vilcek.
Personnel Profile: Full-Time Paid 3; Part-Time Paid 1.
Governing Authority: private; nonprofit organization. Tax-exempt: 501(c)(3).
History Museum.
Collections: works of immigrant artists, designers, & filmmakers.
Major Exhibits: Installation by Toshiko Nishi Kawa, 6/10-7/10; Fashion Exhibition by Madina Vadache, 9/10; Installation by Camilo Ontiveros, 11/10-12/10.
Facilities: 837 sq. ft. exhibit space.
Activities: concerts; dance recitals; films; lectures. Annual Event: off-site dinner reception to celebrate the Vilcek prizes in biomedical research and the arts and humanities.
Publications: biannual e-newsletter, The Vilcek Foundation.
Hours & Admission Prices: During Exhibitions: Wed.-Sat. 12-6; other times by appointment. No charge.
Attendance: 750

VISUAL ARTS MUSEUM, (M), 209 E. 23rd St., New York, NY 10010-3901. Tel.: 212-592-2144. Fax: 646-638-2110.
E-mail: fditommaso@sva.edu
Web Site: www.schoolofvisualarts.edu
Founded: 1971.
Congressional District: 14
Key Personnel: Dir., Francis Di Tommaso; Asst. Dir., Richard Brooks.
Personnel Profile: Full-Time Paid 6; Part-Time Paid 4.
Governing Authority: private college. Parent Institution: School of Visual Arts, New York.
Photography, Arts & Graphic Design Museum.
Collections: digital & new media.
Facilities: 180-seat auditorium; educational facilities; 2,000 sq. ft. exhibit space.
Activities: lectures; traveling exhibitions. Annual Event: The Masters Series.
Publications: exhibition brochures & catalogs.
Hours & Admission Prices: Mon.-Fri. 9-7, Sat. 10-6. No charge. ♿
Attendance: 9,700 (estimated)

*** WHITNEY MUSEUM OF AMERICAN ART, (M), (I),** 945 Madison Ave., New York, NY 10021-2790. Tel.: 212-570-3600. Fax: 212-606-0207.
Web Site: www.whitney.org
Founded: 1930.
Congressional District: 18
Key Personnel: Alice Pratt Brown Dir., Adam D. Weinberg; Assoc. Dir. Human Resources, Hillary Blass; Chief Cur. & Assoc. Dir. Programs, Donna DeSalvo; Deputy Dir., John Stanley; Assoc. Dir., Kathryn Potts; Chm. Education, Helena Rubinstein; Assoc. Dir. Conservation & Research, Carol Mancusi-Ungaro; Assoc. Dir. Collections & Exhibitions Management, Christy Putnam; Chief Mktg. & Communications Officer, Jeffrey Levine; Adjunct Cur., Andy Warhol Film Project, Callie Angell; Cur. & Cur.

Drawings, Carter Foster; Cur., Barbara Haskell; Anne and Joel Ehrenkranz Cur., Chrissie Iles; Cur. & Cur. Prints, David Kiehl; Cur. Permanent Collection, Dana Miller; Adjunct Cur. New Media Arts, Christiane Paul; Cur. & Sandra Gilman Cur. Photography, Elisabeth Sussman; Adjunct Cur. Performance, Limor Tomer; Dir. Devel., Alexandra Wheeler; Dir. Security, John Baliestri; Dir. Independent Study Program, Ron Clark; Dir. Foundation & Government Rels., Hillary Strong; Dir. Special Events, Gina Rogak; Dir. Corporate Partnerships, Amy Roth; Head Registrar (Collection), Barbi Spieler; Controller, John Collins; Irma & Benjamin Weiss Librarian, Carol Rusk; Head Publications, Rachel Wixom; Dir. Retail Operations, Jennifer Heslin; Mgr. Visitor Svcs., Wendy Borbee-Louvell.

Personnel Profile: Full-Time Paid 185; Part-Time Paid 27; Part-Time Volunteers 100; Interns 70.

Governing Authority: nonprofit organization. Branch Museums: Whitney Museum of American Art at Altria, 120 Park Ave., New York NY 10017. Tax-exempt.

Art Museum.

Collections: paintings; sculpture; drawings, prints & photography; film & video.

Research Fields: 20th-21st century American art.

Facilities: 37,000-vol. library; art available for study by appointment only; 120-seat film & video gallery; restaurant.

Activities: symposia; lectures; panel discussions; film & video programs; gallery talks; performances; formally organized education programs; training programs; temporary & traveling exhibitions; public school outreach programs & teachers workshops; public programs.

Publications: exhibition catalogs, brochures & books, posters, reproductions, cards, quarterly calendar; bulletin; gallery guides; brochures; education & membership materials; museum-related websites.

Hours & Admission Prices: Wed.-Sun. 11-6. Adults $18, senior citizens 62 & over with valid ID and youth 19-25 $12; discounts to groups, ICOM & AAM members; Fri. 6-9 pay what you wish; members, NYC public high school students & youth under 19 no charge. Closed New Year's Day; Thanksgiving; Christmas. ♿

Attendance: 650,000 (estimated)

Membership: Artist, Student & Educator $40; National & International $50; Individual $75; Dual $100; Family Contributor $150; Friend $250; Patron $500; Whitney Circle $1,000; Whitney Fellow $2,500.

YESHIVA UNIVERSITY MUSEUM AT THE CENTER FOR JEWISH HISTORY, (M), 15 W. 16th St., New York, NY 10011-6301. Tel.: 212-294-8330. Fax: 212-294-8335.

E-mail: info@yum.cjh.org

Web Site: www.yumuseum.org

Founded: 1973.

Congressional District: 8

Key Personnel: Vice Chair., Michael Jesselson; Vice Chair., Ted Mirvis; Dir., Dr. Jacob Wisse; Institutional Advancement Dir., Rachel Lazin; Assoc. Dir. Administration, Jody Heher; Assoc. Dir. Programs & Exhibitions, Gabriel M. Goldstein; Collection Cur., Bonni-Dara Michaels; Education Cur., Rachelle Bradt; Cur. Contemporary Exhibitions, Reba Wulkan.

Personnel Profile: Full-Time Paid 9; Part-Time Volunteers 35; Interns 2.

Governing Authority: Parent Institution: Yeshiva University. 500 W. 185 St., New York. Tel. 212-960-5400. Tax-exempt: 501(c)(3).

Religious & Cultural Museum: with the purpose of preserving, enriching & interpreting Jewish life as it is reflected in the arts, history & sciences.

Collections: Jewish ceremonial objects of silver & other metals; textile collection of ceremonial costumes & clothes; rare scrolls & books; manuscripts; archival materials; slides; photographs; 10 scale models of historic synagogues; photographs; fine art; sculpture & ethnographic material.

Research Fields: Jewish history, ethnography, art & culture.

Facilities: library of books on art, Jewish history & crafts available to scholars or researchers on premises; oral history archive. Ceremonial objects, books & other museum-related items for sale.

Activities: guided tours; lectures; concerts; arts festivals; craft workshops; formally organized education programs for children, adults & undergraduate college students; docent program; loan, permanent, temporary & traveling exhibitions.

Publications: books, The Jewish Wedding; Purim, The Face & The Mask; See and Sanctify: Exploring Jewish Symbols; Daily Life in Ancient Israel; Terezin 1942-1945: Through the Eyes of Norbert Troller; Tradition and Fantasy In Jewish Needlework; Raban Remembered: Jerusalem's Forgotten Master; Ashkenaz: The German Jewish Heritage; Lights/Orot; Medieval Justice: The Trial of the Jews of Trent; Mordecai Manuel Noah: The First American Jew; The Sephardic Journey: 1492-1992; Aishet Hayil: A Woman of Valor; Sacred Realm: The Emergence of the Synagogue in the Ancient World; Theodor Herzl: If You Will It, It Is Not A Dream; Siegmund Forst: A Lifetime in Arts and Letters; Ina Golub: The Work of the Weaver In Colors; Treasures of Dubrovnik; Major Intersections; Schwebel, David's Journey; Moritz Daniel Oppenheim: Jewish Identity in 19th Century Art; Komar & Melamid: Symbols of the Big Bang; Tobi Kahn: Microcosmos; Stories Untold: Jewish Pioneer Women, 1850-1910; Art Against Forgetting: Paintings by Leonard Meiselman; Journey to No End of the World: Judaica from the Gross Family Collection, Tel Aviv; Portion of the People: 300 Years of Southern Jewish Life; Stage & Page: Jewish Theater and Book Designs of Emanuele Luzzati; Fruits of a Lifetime: The Kathryn Yochelson Collection; A Perfect Fit: The Garment Industry and American Jewelry 1860-1960; Printing the Talmud: From Bomberg to Schottenstein; Ebrei Piemontesi: The Jews of Piedmont.

Hours & Admission Prices: Tues.-Thurs. & Sun. 11-5. Tours available by appointment. Adults $8, senior citizens & students $6; discounts to AAM & ICOM members; students, staff & alumi of Yeshiva University, members, Mon. 3:30-7:30 & Fri. 11-2:30 no charge. Closed Jewish holidays. ♿

Attendance: 40,000 (accurate)

Membership: Individual $50; Dual $72; Family $100; Supporting $150; Sustaining $250; Sponsor $500; Patron $l,000.

ZABRISKIE GALLERY, 41 E. 57th St., 4th Fl., New York, NY 10022-1907. Tel.: 212-752-1223. Fax: 212-752-1224.

E-mail: info@zabriskiegallery.com

Web Site: www.zabriskiegallery.com

Founded: 1954.

Key Personnel: Dir., Virginia M. Zabriskie

Art Gallery.

Collections: Dada; Surrealism; American Modernism; photographs; contemporary art.

Hours & Admission Prices: Memorial Day-Labor Day Mon.-Fri. 10-5:30; Sept. to mid-May Tues.-Sat. 10-5:30.

Newark Valley

BEMENT-BILLINGS FARMSTEAD, 9142 Rte. 38, Newark Valley, NY 13811. Mailing Address: P.O. Box 222, Newark Valley, NY 13811-0222. Tel.: 607-642-9516. Fax: 607-642-9516.

E-mail: nvhistory@stny.rr.com

Web Site: nvhistory.org

Founded: 1977.

Congressional District: 28

Key Personnel: Bd. Trustee, Ethel Curkendall; Bd. Trustee, Marcia Kiechler; Bd. Trustee, Doug Gorsline; Pres. (V), Ross McGraw.

Personnel Profile: Full-Time Paid 1; Part-Time Paid 1; Part-Time Volunteers 220; Interns 2.

Governing Authority: nonprofit organization. Parent Institution: Newark Valley Historical Society Inc. Subsidiary Institution: Binghamton University. Tax-exempt.

Historic Site: c.1840 Bement-Billings Farmstead.

Collections: 1840s furniture; cookware; utensils; furnishings; tools; 19th-century ledgers & daybooks of N. Tioga County.

Research Fields: early 19th-century farmers & tradesmen.

Facilities: 50-vol. library pertaining to local history, genealogy, folklife, antiques & preservation.

Activities: educational programming; interpreter training; youth program; summer workshops. Museum Sponsors: Spring Festival in June: plowing, wool & herb market, live music, craft vendors & demonstrations; Apple Fest in October; Civil War reenactment & encampment.

Publications: bimonthly newsletters; annual reports.

Hours & Admission Prices: July 5 to Oct. 6 Sat.-Sun. 12-4; other times by appointment. Adults $2, students $1; museum members no charge.

Attendance: 10,000 (estimated)

Membership: Senior Citizen $10; Individual $15; Family $25; Contributing $50; Professional Corporate & Sponsor $100; Sustaining $200; Patron $300.

NEWARK VALLEY DEPOT MUSEUM, Depot St., Newark Valley, NY 13811. Mailing Address: P.O. Box 222, Newark Valley, NY 13811-0222. Tel.: 607-642-9516. Fax: 607-642-9516.

E-mail: info@nvhistory.org

Web Site: www.nvhistory.org

Founded: 1977.

Congressional District: 28

Key Personnel: Pres., Ross McGraw; Treas., Doug Gorline.

Personnel Profile: Full-Time Paid 1; Part-Time Paid 1; Part-Time Volunteers 100.

Governing Authority: nonprofit organization. Parent Institution: Newark Valley Historical Society Inc. Tax-exempt.

Railroad Museum; 1869 Depot restored in 1910.

Collections: model railroad; railroad artifacts & memorabilia.

Facilities: depot for riding Tioga Scenic Railroad; snack bar. Museum-related items for sale.

Activities: Museum Sponsors: Depot Days in June to September.

Publications: bimonthly newsletter; annual report.
Hours & Admission Prices: July to 1st week of Oct. Sat.-Sun. 1:30-3. No charge; donations accepted. ♿
Attendance: 5,000 (estimated)
Membership: Senior Citizen $10; Individual $15; Family $25; Contributing $50; Professional $100; Corporate $100 & up.

Newburgh

HISTORICAL SOCIETY OF NEWBURGH BAY & THE HIGHLANDS - DAVID CRAWFORD HOUSE, 189 Montgomery St., Newburgh, NY 12550-3636. Tel.: 845-561-2585.
E-mail: historicalsocietynb@yahoo.com
Web Site: www.newburghhistoricalsociety.com
Founded: 1884.
Congressional District: 21
Key Personnel: Bd. Pres., Carla Decker; 1st Vice Pres., Justin Rider; 2nd Vice Pres., Carla Decker; Dir., Lisa Silverstone.
Personnel Profile: Part-Time Paid 1; Part-Time Volunteers 15.
Governing Authority: nonprofit organization. Parent Institution: Historical Society of Newburgh Bay and the Highlands. Tax-exempt: 501(c)(3).
Historic House: 1830 home of David Crawford.
Collections: 19th-century period furniture, decorative arts, toys & dolls; Hudson River School paintings; ship models of Hudson River crafts; local historical archives, photographs & artifacts.
Research Fields: middle 19th-century architecture, landscape design & commercial life.
Facilities: 3,000-vol. library pertaining to local & state history. Prints, crafts, reproductions & gift items for sale.
Activities: guided tours; lectures; concerts; organized education programs; loan & temporary exhibitions. Museum Sponsors: Community House tours in December; Biennial Benefit Art Auction.
Publications: newsletter; booklet, Andrew Jackson Downing. Prints, publications, book on local history & architecture & gift items for sale.
Hours & Admission Prices: April-Oct. Sun. 1-4; other times by appointment. Suggested Donation: Adults $5; members & children under 18 no charge. Closed major holidays. ♿
Attendance: 1,000 (estimated)
Membership: Senior $35; Individual $50; Family $75; Century Club $100; Crawford Club $250; 1830 Society $500; Captain's Circle $1,000.

WASHINGTON'S HEADQUARTERS STATE HISTORIC SITE, Corner of Liberty & Washington Sts., Newburgh, NY 12551-1476. Mailing Address: P.O. Box 1783, Newburgh, NY 12551-1783. Tel.: 845-562-1195.
Web Site: nysparks.state.ny.us/historic-sites/17/details.aspx
Founded: 1850.
Congressional District: 26
Key Personnel: Historic Site Mgr., Elyse B. Goldberg.
Personnel Profile: Full-Time Paid 12; Part-Time Paid 5.
Governing Authority: state. Parent Institution: New York State Office of Parks, Recreation & Historic Preservation; Palisades Interstate Park Commission. Tax-exempt: 501(c)(3).
Historic House Museum: 1750-1770 Jonathan Hasbrouck House, used as Gen. George Washington's headquarters, 1782-1783.
Collections: period furnishings; firearms; documents & military artifacts of the American Revolution; local history; Martha Washington's pocket watch; portraits of the Washingtons by Asher B. Durand; statuary; audiovisuals; Hasbrouck House preservation history. Historic Monument: 1887 Centennial Monument, Tower of Victory; early museum building: 1910.
Research Fields: American Revolution in the Hudson River Valley; George & Martha Washington and their staff.
Facilities: archives of 1,500 documents including deeds from 1648-1900 of land transactions, regional history, military service & the American Revolution in the Hudson Valley available on premises by advance request; 6 1/2 acre park Hudson Highland vistas; Historical Resource Repository # (NIC) NYOR 599-880.
Activities: guided tours; lectures; videos; concerts; permanent & temporary exhibitions; school programs; special programs & demonstrations; three-day Washington's Birthday Celebration.
Publications: site brochures, Inside Washington's Headquarters; historical research series, no charge; newsletter to members, Friends.
Hours & Admission Prices: mid-April to Oct. Wed.-Sat. 10-5, Sun. 1-5; Nov.-March by appointment. Adults $4, seniors 62 & over $3, children 5-12 $1; discount to groups; children under 12 & FSHSHH members no charge. Braille tours available. ♿
Attendance: 21,203 (accurate)
Membership: Friends of the State Historic Sites of the Hudson Highlands, Inc.: Individual $15; Household $25; Contributing $25-$99; Business & Corporate $100; Sustaining $100-$499; Patron $500-$999; Benefactor $1,000 & up.

Niagara Falls

AQUARIUM OF NIAGARA, 701 Whirlpool St., Niagara Falls, NY 14301-1094. Tel.: 716-285-3575, ext. 205. Fax: 716-285-8513.
E-mail: aquariumnf@aol.com
Web Site: www.aquariumofniagara.org
Founded: 1965.
Congressional District: 32
Key Personnel: Dir., Nancy A. Chapin; Pres. (V), Steven Czarnecki; Cur. Education, Jeanette Brunner; Museum Shop Mgr., Simone Russell.
Personnel Profile: Full-Time Paid 17; Part-Time Paid 14; Part-Time Volunteers 20; Interns 7.
Governing Authority: nonprofit. Niagara Aquarium Foundation. Tax-exempt.
Aquarium.
Collections: marine mammals; marine & freshwater fishes; penguins; invertebrates; outdoor seal & sea lion pool.
Research Fields: water quality; dietary supplements; marine mammal husbandry & skin properties.
Facilities: 150-vol. library of books on zoology; oceanography; natural history with emphasis on aquatic animals. Marine-related articles for sale.
Activities: marine mammal demonstrations; classes on aquatic biology for school groups, members; lectures; hands-on interactive displays for children; penguin & shark feeding demonstrations; animal interaction programs.
Publications: membership newsletter, Sea Star; teacher's manual; factsheets.
Hours & Admission Prices: July-Labor Day daily 9-6:30; Sept.-June daily 9-5. Adults $9.50, senior citizens $7, children 4-12 $6; discounts to AAA members & special groups; children under 4 & members no charge. State Park Pass Program. Closed Thanksgiving; Christmas. ♿
Attendance: 168,000 (accurate)
Membership: Senior Citizen $25; Individual & Senior Couple $35; Grandparent $45; Family $50.

NIAGARA GORGE DISCOVERY CENTER, New York State Parks, Niagara Region, Robert Moses State Pkwy. near Main St., Niagara Falls, NY 14303-0132. Mailing Address: New York State Parks, Western Dist., Niagara Region, Niagara Falls State Park, P.O. Box 1132, Niagara Falls, NY 14303-0132. Tel.: 716-278-1070 & 1796. Fax: 716-278-0838.
E-mail: angela.berti@oprhp.state.ny.us
Web Site: www.niagarafallsstatepark.com
Formerly: Schoellkopf Geological Museum
Founded: 1971.
Key Personnel: Park Mgr., Cindy Harris; Environmental Educator 2, Barry Virgilio; Mktg. & Public Affairs, Angela P. Berti.
Personnel Profile: Full-Time Paid 4; Part-Time Paid 6.
Governing Authority: state. Parent Institution: New York State Parks. Administered by Niagara Frontier State Park, Recreation and Historic Preservation Commission, Niagara Falls, NY. Tax-exempt.
Natural & Local History Museum: located on the brink of the Niagara Gorge.
Collections: marine invertebrates from middle Silurian & Devonian periods; minerals of local varieties; historical artifacts from the Niagara Gorge.
Facilities: theater; live gorge & falls camera; Time Portal & Gorge Elevator Experience Interactives; trailhead building; gorge hiking trails.
Activities: permanent exhibitions; Q & A sheet.
Hours & Admission Prices: Call for hours. Adults $3, children 6-12 $1.50; children 5 & under no charge. Closed New Year's Day; Thanksgiving; Christmas. ♿
Attendance: 68,551 (accurate)

Niagara University

CASTELLANI ART MUSEUM OF NIAGARA UNIVERSITY, (M), Niagara University, Niagara University, NY 14109. Mailing Address: P.O. Box 1938, Niagara University, NY 14109-1938. Tel.: 716-286-8200. Fax: 716-286-8289.
E-mail: kjk@niagara.edu
Web Site: www.niagara.edu/cam/
Founded: 1978.
Congressional District: 36
Key Personnel: Dir., Kate Koperski; Gallery & Installation Mgr., Kurt Von Voetsch; Cur. Collections & Exhibitions, Michael Beam; Registrar, Kathleen Fraas; Educ. Coord., Marian Granfield; Coord. Events, Public Rels. & Membership, Susan Clements; Museum Shop Mgr., Carla Castellani; Museum Shop Asst. Mgr., Anne LaBarbera; Office Coord., Regina Cecconi; Weekend & Special Events Mgr., Celia Rodino.
Personnel Profile: Full-Time Paid 6; Part-Time Paid 3; Part-Time Volunteers 68; Interns 3.
Governing Authority: Parent Institution: Niagara University. Tax-exempt.
University & Art Museum.

Collections: 4,000 works features paintings, sculpture, prints & drawings by artists active in the 19th & 20th centuries; pre-Columbian pottery; Underground Railroad.
Research Fields: 19th & 20th centuries.
Facilities: 4,200 sq. ft. exhibit space; classroom. Museum-related items for sale.
Activities: permanent & temporary exhibitions; art workshops for families; educational programs; docent guided tours.
Publications: exhibition catalogs; Arcadia Revisited; newsletter; In Company: Robert Creeley's Collaborations.
Hours & Admission Prices: Tues.-Sat. 11-5, Sun. 1-5. No charge; donations accepted. Closed Good Friday; Easter; Thanksgiving; Christmas; university holidays. ♿
Attendance: 20,000 (accurate)
Membership: Teacher $14; Senior Citizen, Student & Artist $15; Senior Citizen Couple and NU Faculty & Staff $25; Individual $30; Family $40; Contributor $100; Benefactor $500; Life $1,000; Life Fellow $5,000.

North Blenheim

LANSING MANOR HOUSE MUSEUM, 1378 State Rte. 30, North Blenheim, NY 12131. Mailing Address: P.O. Box 898, N. Blenheim, NY 12131-0898. Tel.: 800-724-0309. Fax: 518-287-6381.
E-mail: steve.ramsey@nypa.gov
Web Site: www.nypa.gov/html/vcblenhe.html
Founded: 1977.
Congressional District: 23
Key Personnel: Dir., Steve Ramsey.
Personnel Profile: Part-Time Paid 5.
Governing Authority: society; nonprofit. Parent Institution: New York Power Authority. Subsidiary Institution: Schoharie County Historical Society, P.O. Box 69, Old Stone Fort, Schoharie, NY 12157. Tax-exempt: 501(c)(3).
Historic House: 1819 Lansing Manor House, Federal Manor house built by Chancellor John Lansing Jr., occupied by his son-in-law Jacob Sutherland as manager of the Blenheim Patent 1783-1853.
Collections: Federal & Empire furniture, textiles, ceramics, pictures & manuscripts; hydro-electric power. Historic Buildings: 1819 carriage barn; 1804-1819 outbuildings; c.1790 tenant house.
Facilities: visitors center; educational center.
Activities: guided tours.
Hours & Admission Prices: May-Oct. Wed.-Mon. 10-5 by appointment. No charge. ♿
Attendance: 12,400 (accurate)

North Salem

HAMMOND MUSEUM AND JAPANESE STROLL GARDEN, (M), 28 Deveau Rd., North Salem, NY 10560-2115. Mailing Address: P.O. Box 326, 28 Deveau Rd., North Salem, NY 10560-2115. Tel.: 914-669-5033. Fax: 914-669-8221.
E-mail: gardenprogram@yahoo.com
Web Site: www.hammondmuseum.org.
Founded: 1957.
Congressional District: 2
Key Personnel: Dir., Lorraine Laken; Chm. Bd. (V), Stomu Miyazaki; Business Mgr., Judy Schurmacher.
Personnel Profile: Full-Time Paid 2; Part-Time Paid 1; Part-Time Volunteers 20; Interns 1.
Governing Authority: nonprofit. Tax-exempt: 170(B)(1)(A)(vi).
Cross-Cultural Center.
Collections: Asian art; decorative arts; Japanese stroll garden.
Major Exhibits: Brush With Nature, 4/10-6/10; Kohei O. Kamuto (caligraph), 6/10-9/10.
Facilities: botanical garden; restaurant. Art, crafts of different countries & other museum-related items for sale.
Activities: films; concerts; drama; lectures; workshops; formally organized education programs.
Hours & Admission Prices: Wed.-Sat. 12-4. Adults $5, seniors & students $4; discounts to AAM & AAA members; members no charge. ♿
Attendance: 13,000 (accurate)
Membership: Individual $35; Senior Family $40; Family $50; Contributing $100; Sustaining $250; Patron $500; Fellow $1,000; Corporate $2,000; Sponsor $2,500.

North Tonawanda

HERSCHELL CARROUSEL FACTORY MUSEUM, (M), 180 Thompson St., North Tonawanda, NY 14120-5420. Mailing Address: P.O. Box 672, North Tonawanda, NY 14120-0672. Tel.: 716-693-1885. Fax: 716-743-9018.
E-mail: hcfm@carrouselmuseum.org
Web Site: www.carrouselmuseum.org
Founded: 1983.
Congressional District: 26
Key Personnel: Pres. (V), Charles W. Proefrock; Museum Shop Mgr., Maureen Schumacher.
Personnel Profile: Full-Time Paid 2; Full-Time Volunteers 1; Part-Time Paid 3; Part-Time Volunteers 43; Interns 1.
Governing Authority: nonprofit organization. Parent Institution: Carousel Society of the Niagara Frontier. Tax-exempt: 501(c)(3).
Company Museum: housed in 1916 Allan Herschell Company factory building.
Collections: concentration on the history of the Herschell Company with emphasis on different types of amusement rides produced, marketing & design of rides, factory workers' lives, impact of factory on local economy.
Activities: woodcarving classes; carrousel chats; special events. Museum Sponsors: Victorian Tea in April; Renaissance Festival in June; Halloween Spooktacular in October; Lunch With Santa in November & December.
Publications: quarterly, Carrousel Newsletter.
Hours & Admission Prices: April-June 11 & Sept.-Dec. Wed.-Sun. 12-4; June 14 to Labor Day Mon.-Sat. 10-4, Sun. 12-4. Adults $5, senior citizens $4, children 2-12 $2.50; discounts to AARP & AAA members; members no charge. Closed Easter; Thanksgiving; Christmas. ♿
Attendance: 11,000 (estimated)
Membership: Senior Citizen $15; Senior Couple $20; Individual $25; Family $45.

NORTH TONAWANDA HISTORY MUSEUM, 54-60 Webster St., North Tonawanda, NY 14120-5814. Tel.: 716-213-0554.
E-mail: nthistorymuseum@aol.com
Web Site: www.nthistorymuseum.org
Founded: 2004.
Congressional District: 26
Key Personnel: Exec. Dir., Donna Zellner Neal; Pres. (V), Carl Tamburlin; Asst. Exec. Dir., John Zellner Neal; Archival Records Coord., Jane Garis; Research Coord., Walter Wozniak.
Personnel Profile: Full-Time Paid 1; Full-Time Volunteers 2; Part-Time Volunteers 3.
Governing Authority: private; nonprofit organization. Tax-exempt.
History Museum.
Collections: area ethnic heritage; Erie Canal & Niagara River influence and it's role as a lumber & industrial center during the 19th-20th centuries; photographs.
Research Fields: German, Polish, Italian, Irish, Hungarian, Lebanese, Syrian, & Slovak heritage; cemetery records; industrial & lumber heritage; Erie Canal heritage.
Facilities: library.
Activities: formal educational programs; group tours; guided tours; lectures; oral history program ghost walks; publications. Museum Sponsors: Historic Treasures Tour; Historic Homes Tour & Garden Walks; Ethnic Heritage Festival; Erie Canal music & vaudeville.
Publications: newsletter; annual report; book, North Tonawanda Ethnic Heritage Cookbook; Historic Treasures Guide 2005; North Tonawanda: The First 100 Years; North Tonawanda: The Lumber City; Historic Gardens Tour; The Rand Family Left A Lasting Imprint on North Tonawanda And The World; North Tonawanda: A Celebration of Our Diversity; North Tonawanda Families & Their Favorite Recipes; North Tonawanda: The Lumber City Tour Guide; Historic Treasures Guide 2007; Niagara Historic Trail Guide Book.
Hours & Admission Prices: Mon. 9-9, Tues.-Sat. 9-5. Museum: no charge; donations accepted. Seaway Trail Walks: adult $8, children $4, school groups $2 per student. Historic Treasures Tour $18. Ethnic Heritage Festival $5. Closed New Year's Eve & Day; Memorial Day; Independence Day; Thanksgiving; Christmas Eve & Day. ♿
Attendance: 8,000 (accurate)
Membership: Senior $10; Individual $15; Family $25; Business & Civic $50; Contributing $100; Life $250.

Northport

NORTHPORT HISTORICAL SOCIETY, (M), 215 Main St., Northport, NY 11768-1730. Mailing Address: P.O. Box 545, Northport, NY 11768-0545. Tel.: 631-757-9859. Fax: 631-757-9398.
Web Site: www.northporthistorical.org
Founded: 1962.
Congressional District: 3
Key Personnel: Dir., Rosemary S. Feeney; Pres. (V), Lois O'Hara; Museum Educator, Kari-Ann Carr; Museum Shop Mgr., Lois Howe.
Personnel Profile: Part-Time Paid 3; Part-Time Volunteers 85.
Governing Authority: society. Tax-exempt.
History Museum.

Collections: ship building tools; domestic utensils; clothing; ephemera & documents; photographs; maps.
Research Fields: history of Northport; genealogy; architecture & industry.
Facilities: research library; meeting room. Museum-related items for sale.
Activities: education programs; lectures; self-guided recorded walking tour; special events; guided walking tours. Museum Sponsors: Parading Down Main Street (monthly walking tours).
Publications: books, A Light House of Stone; Faded Laurel's History of Eaton's Neck and Asharoken; seasonal member newsletter; quarterly newsletter.
Hours & Admission Prices: Tues.-Sun. 1-4:30. Suggested Donation: $3; discounts to Smithsonian Museum Day members. Closed New Year's Day; Easter; Independence Day; Thanksgiving; Christmas.
Attendance: 4,342 (accurate)
Membership: Senior Citizen & Student $20; Individual $25; Senior Family $30; Family $40; Business $60; Supporting Friend $100; Patron $250; Sustainer $500; Conservator $1,000.

Norwich

CHENANGO COUNTY HISTORICAL SOCIETY MUSEUM, 45 Rexford St., Norwich, NY 13815-1121. Tel.: 607-334-9227. Fax: 607-334-7809.
E-mail: drdavecchs@roadrunner.com
Web Site: chenango.history.museum
Founded: 1939.
Congressional District: 24
Key Personnel: C.E.O. & Dir., R. David Drucker, Ph.D.; Pres., Mary C. Weidman; Vice Pres., Robert Cleveland; Treas., Tom Knapp; Sec., L. Joanne French; Education & Exhibits, Diane Hamblin.
Personnel Profile: Full-Time Paid 2; Full-Time Volunteers 5; Part-Time Volunteers 30.
Governing Authority: private society. Tax-exempt: 501(c)(3).
Historical Society Museum.
Collections: costumes; folklore; folkart; Native American artifacts; local early artifacts; documents; tools; Chenango County cultural history; Norwich Pharmacal Company.
Research Fields: folklore; archaeology; cemeteries of Chenango County; genealogy; manuscripts; local history publications.
Facilities: library of local history information available for use by permission of society.
Activities: guided tours; lectures; films; formally organized education programs for children; permanent & traveling exhibitions.
Publications: various booklets & books, list available upon request.
Hours & Admission Prices: Jan.-March Mon.-Fri. 1-5; April-Dec. Sun. 1-4, Mon.-Fri. 1-5; other times by appointment. No charge; donations accepted.
Attendance: 5,000 (estimated)
Membership: Senior Citizen 60 & over $15; Individual $20; Family $30; Supporting $100; Patron $200; Angel $300; Maydole $500; Chenango Circle $1,000.

NORTHEAST CLASSIC CAR MUSEUM, 24 Rexford St., Norwich, NY 13815-1172. Tel.: 607-334-2886. Fax: 607-336-6745.
E-mail: doreen@classiccarmuseum.org
Web Site: www.classiccarmuseum.org
Founded: 1997.
Key Personnel: Exec. Dir., Doreen Bates; Pres. (V), Sewain Conklin.
Personnel Profile: Full-Time Paid 3; Part-Time Volunteers 100.
Governing Authority: state; nonprofit. Tax-exempt: 501(c)(3).
Classic Car Museum.
Collections: vintage cars; Franklin luxury cars.
Hours & Admission Prices: Daily 9-5. Adults $9, children 6-18 $4; discounts to AAM members; members & children under 6 no charge. Closed New Year's Day; Thanksgiving; Christmas. ♿
Attendance: 12,000 (estimated)
Membership: Individual $25; Family $40; Business $50; Cord $100; Packard $250; Auburn $500; Pierce-Arrow $1,000; Franklin $2,500; Duesenberg $5,000.

Norwood

NORWOOD HISTORICAL ASSOCIATION AND MUSEUM, 39 N. Main St., Norwood, NY 13668-1123. Mailing Address: P.O. Box 163, Norwood, NY 13668-0163. Tel.: 315-353-2751.
E-mail: glacomb@twcny.rr.com
Founded: 1968.
Key Personnel: Dir., Richard Boprey; Chm. (V), Dick Boyle; Sec., Rose Valyo.
Personnel Profile: Part-Time Paid 1; Part-Time Volunteers 7.
Governing Authority: nonprofit organization. Tax-exempt: 501(c)(3).
General Museum.
Collections: railroad articles; folklore; history; industrial; Norwood Brass Fireman; official 1984 Olympic Band; manuscript collections.
Research Fields: local history.
Facilities: 75-vol. library of assorted legal documents; pamphlets; original programs of local events; newspapers; bound ledgers; text books; atlas & maps available by special arrangement for use on the premises.
Activities: guided tours; lectures; arts festivals; formally organized education programs; inter-museum loan, permanent & temporary exhibitions. Museum Sponsors: museum interest group for adults.
Publications: handbooks, Rails into Racquetteville; The Story of Norwood, NY.
Hours & Admission Prices: May-Oct. Tues. & Thurs. 2-4, other times by appointment. No charge; donations accepted.
Attendance: 300
Membership: Junior $.50; General $2.

Nyack

EDWARD HOPPER LANDMARK PRESERVATION FOUNDATION, 82 N. Broadway, Nyack, NY 10960-2628. Tel.: 845-358-0774. Fax: 845-358-0774.
E-mail: info@hopperhouse.org
Web Site: www.hopperhouse.com
Founded: 1971.
Key Personnel: Exec. Dir., Carole Perry; Pres., Ginger Stoltze.
Personnel Profile: Part-Time Paid 1; Part-Time Volunteers 40; Interns 1.
Governing Authority: private; nonprofit organization. Tax-exempt: FEX-160198.
Art Center: boyhood home of renowned American Realist painter, Edward Hopper.
Collections: photographs; sculpture.
Research Fields: Edward Hopper.
Facilities: 950 sq. ft. exhibit space. Books, prints, postcards, notecards, exhibited art & museum-related items for sale.
Activities: summer jazz concerts; lectures; tours; educational videos on Hopper's life & work; life drawing classes. Annual Events: Book Fairs in December; National Juried Small Works Show; Figure Show; Biennial Photography Show.
Publications: pamphlet.
Hours & Admission Prices: Thurs.-Sun. 1-5. Adults $2, students & retiree $1; members no charge. ♿
Attendance: 4,000 (estimated)
Membership: Student & Retiree $20; Individual $30; Family $50; Supporting $100; Sustaining $250; Patron $500; Benefactor $1,000.

Ogdensburg

* **FREDERIC REMINGTON ART MUSEUM, (M),** 303 Washington St., Ogdensburg, NY 13669-1517. Tel.: 315-393-2425. Fax: 315-393-4464.
E-mail: info@fredericremington.org
Web Site: www.fredericremington.org
Founded: 1923.
Congressional District: 26
Key Personnel: Exec. Dir., Ed LaVarnway; Administrative Aide, Shannon Wells; Pres., Ann Spies; Cur., Laura Foster; Dir. Youth Programs, Mary LaCombe; Museum Shop Mgr., Ray Barney; Account Clerk, Debbie Ormasen.
Personnel Profile: Full-Time Paid 7; Part-Time Paid 8; Part-Time Volunteers 16.
Governing Authority: municipal. Tax-exempt.
Art Museum: housed in 1809-10 Mansion with modern gallery addition.
Collections: Frederic Remington's paintings, sculpture, drawings, manuscripts; archives; decorative arts.
Research Fields: Frederic Remington.
Facilities: 4,500-vol. of Remington's personal library & family books; manuscript collections; Albert and Addie Priest Newell galleries. Museum-related items for sale.
Activities: guided tours; lectures; gallery talks; inter-museum loan, permanent & temporary exhibitions.
Publications: quarterly newsletter, Remington Related; catalog, Frederic Remington Memorial Collection; special exhibition catalogs.
Hours & Admission Prices: May-Oct. Mon.-Sat. 10-5, Sun. 1-5; Nov.-April Wed.-Sat. 11-5, Sun. 1-5. Adults $8, students 6-22 & senior citizen 65 & over $7; discounts to AAM members; children 5 & under and members no charge. Closed New Year's Day; Easter; Thanksgiving; Christmas. ♿
Attendance: 10,000 (accurate)
Membership: Student $15; Individual $30; Family & Dual $45; Dragoon $84; Sergeant $120; Trooper $240; Cheyenne $480; Ingleneuk Club $1,000.

Old Bethpage

OLD BETHPAGE VILLAGE RESTORATION, 1303 Round Swamp Rd., Old Bethpage, NY 11804-1199. Tel.: 516-572-8401. Fax: 516-572-8439.
Web Site: www.nassaucountyny.gov/parks
Founded: 1970.
Congressional District: 2
Key Personnel: Site Dir., James McKenna; Asst. Site Dir., Geraldine Jordan; Dir. Historic Interpretation, Henry Clark; Supvr. Volunteers, Judy Pockriss.
Personnel Profile: Full-Time Paid 9; Part-Time Paid 16; Part-Time Volunteers 40; Interns 6.
Governing Authority: county. Nassau County Dept. of Parks, Recreation & Museums, Museum Svcs., East Meadow, NY 11554. Tax-exempt.
Living History Village Museum: 15 historic site units which include houses, shops, barns, outbuildings, tavern, church & schoolhouse.
Collections: Americana including tools, utensils, furnishings & decorative arts.
Research Fields: local history.
Facilities: library of books related to historic interpretations of Long Island; 200-seat auditorium; cafeteria. Museum-related items for sale.
Activities: tours; formally organized education programs; lectures; concerts; seasonal special events & activities.
Publications: interpretive leaflet, Chronicle; seasonal leaflet, Enquirer; folder, Old Bethpage Village Restoration Schedule; Old Bethpage Guidebook.
Hours & Admission Prices: March-May & Nov.-Dec. Wed.-Sun. 10-4; June-Oct. Wed.-Sun. 10-5. Adults $10, seniors & children $7; discounts to groups; children under 5 no charge. Closed New Year's Eve; Veterans Day; Thanksgiving & day after; Christmas Eve & Day.
Attendance: 89,505 (accurate)

Old Chatham

* **THE SHAKER MUSEUM AND LIBRARY,** 88 Shaker Museum Rd., Old Chatham, NY 12136-2601. Tel.: 518-794-9100, ext. 218. Fax: 518-794-8621.
E-mail: contact@shakermuseumandlibrary.org
Web Site: www.shakermuseumandlibrary.org
Founded: 1950.
Congressional District: 24
Key Personnel: Pres., David Stocks; Chm. (V), Jeff Daly; Dir. Research, Jerry Grant.
Personnel Profile: Full-Time Paid 4; Part-Time Paid 11; Part-Time Volunteers 200.
Governing Authority: nonprofit corp. Subsidiary Institution: North Family Site at the Mount Lebanon Shaker Village. Tax-exempt: 501(c)(3).
Shaker History & Culture Museum.
Collections: furniture; baskets; textiles; woodworking tools & machinery; metal working machinery; household equipment; personal items; books; manuscripts; photographs; craft industries; clothing; tools.
Research Fields: Shaker history; philosophy & religion; decorative arts; folklore; industry; textiles; utopian & communal studies; material culture.
Facilities: research library; education center; herb garden. Museum-related items for sale.
Activities: permanent exhibits; public programs for adults, children & family groups; curriculum-based school program; guided tours by appointment; docent program; membership program.
Publications: newsletter, Broadside; Shaker Series of Monographs; catalogue, Making His Mark: The Work of Shaker Craftsman Orren Haskins.
Hours & Admission Prices: late May to mid-Oct. Wed.-Mon. 10-5. Adults $8, students 8-17 $4; discounts to groups & AAM members; children under 8 & members no charge. Library by appointment. Mount Lebanon Shaker Society National Historic Landmark: call for hours.
Attendance: 18,000 (estimated)
Membership: Individual $40; Family & Dual $60; Sustaining $100; Sponsor $250; Patron $500; Shaker Circle $1,000 & up.

Old Westbury

OLD WESTBURY GARDENS, 71 Old Westbury Rd., Old Westbury, NY 11568-1603. Mailing Address: P.O. Box 430, Old Westbury, NY 11568-0430. Tel.: 516-333-0048. Fax: 516-333-6807.
E-mail: emccauley@oldwestburygardens.org
Web Site: oldwestburygardens.org
Founded: 1958.
Congressional District: 4
Key Personnel: C.E.O. & Pres., John Norbeck; Chm. (V), Mary S. Phipps; Dir. Devel., Doreen Banks; Dir. Visitor Svcs. & Collections Mgmt., Paul Hunchak; Dir. Public Rels., Vincent Kish; Dir. Horticulture, Maura M. Brush; Museum Shop Mgr., Linda Holmes; Walled Garden Supvr., Kimberly Johnson; Greenhouse Supvr., Scott Lucas.
Personnel Profile: Full-Time Paid 27; Full-Time Volunteers 1; Part-Time Paid 40; Part-Time Volunteers 250; Interns 2.
Governing Authority: nonprofit organization. Parent Institution: Old Westbury Gardens, Inc. Tax-exempt: 501(c)(3).
Historic House & Public Horticultural Display Garden: 1906 Charles II style mansion furnished with 18th-century decorative & fine arts.
Collections: English 18th-century furniture & decorations & paintings; Chinese porcelains; formal gardens; family papers & documents; photographs.
Research Fields: horticulture; decorative arts; social history; landscape design.
Facilities: library of books on architecture, horticulture, natural sciences & art; botanical garden. Books & other museum-related items for sale.
Activities: guided tours; lectures; films; concerts; hobby workshops; temporary exhibitions.
Publications: newsletter, Old Westbury Gardens; Old Westbury Gardens Guidebook; Old Westbury Gardens Picture Book; Halcyon Days; Book of Days.
Hours & Admission Prices: April to mid-Dec. Wed.-Mon. 10-5. House & Gardens: Adults $10, senior citizens 62 & over $8, children 6-12 $6; discounts to seniors 62 & over on Mon.; museum members no charge, except during special events where noted. ♿
Attendance: 80,000 (accurate)
Membership: Basic Membership: Individual $40; Family & Dual $60; Supporting $100 ($25 tax deductible). Supporting Membership: Friends $250 ($165 tax deductible); Patron $500 ($330 tax deductible); Donor $1,000 ($815 tax deductible).

Onchiota

SIX NATIONS INDIAN MUSEUM, 1462 County Rte. 60, Onchiota, NY 12989-2102. Tel.: 518-891-2299.
E-mail: info@sixnationsindianmuseum.com
Web Site: www.sixnationsindianmuseum.com
Founded: 1954.
Key Personnel: Dir., John Fadden; Museum Shop Mgr. & Asst., Elizabeth E. Fadden.
Governing Authority: individual operation.
Indian Museum, with emphasis on Iroquois.
Collections: Six Nations Indians artifacts; ancient & modern Iroquois utensils, clothing, beaded record belts, wampum belts replicas; art work & dwellings; types of fires & exhibits; Iroquois culture & history; paintings reflecting Iroquois culture.
Facilities: Indian-related items, charts & pamphlets on the Iroquois for sale.
Activities: guided tours; lectures; formally organized education programs for children, adults & undergraduate and graduate college students.
Hours & Admission Prices: July-Aug. Tues.-Sun. 10-5; June & Sept. by appointment. Adults $4, children $2; Indians & special non-Indian friends no charge.
Attendance: 2,000 (estimated)

Oneida

MADISON COUNTY HISTORICAL SOCIETY-COTTAGE LAWN, (M), 435 Main St., Oneida, NY 13421-2440. Tel.: 315-363-4136 & 361-9735. Fax: 315-361-9735.
E-mail: history@mchs1900.org
Web Site: www.mchs1900.org
Founded: 1900.
Congressional District: 25
Key Personnel: C.E.O. & Exec. Dir., Sydney L. Loftus; Pres. (V), Mishell Magnusson.
Personnel Profile: Full-Time Paid 1; Full-Time Volunteers 1; Part-Time Paid 2; Part-Time Volunteers 15.
Governing Authority: nonprofit organization. Tax-exempt: 501(c)(3).
Historical Society Museum: housed in Gothic Revival 1849 Cottage Lawn designed by Alexander Jackson Davis.
Collections: 19th-century furnishings including paintings; furniture; glassware; ceramics; textiles; 19th-century tools including agriculture; woodworking; blacksmithing; tinsmithing; 1862 stage coach, carriages, carts & wagons; archival collections; traditional crafts.
Research Fields: Madison County & central New York history; genealogy; restoration resources & folklife; 18th- & 19th-century costuming & textiles; 19th-century conservations; folk & traditional crafts.
Facilities: 2,500-vol. library of historical books available for research; traditional crafts archives containing 20,000 slides, 180 tapes & 42 8 mm movies documenting traditional crafts & folklife. Museum-related items for sale.
Activities: guided tours; lectures; formally organized education programs for children & adults; membership programs. Museum Sponsors: annual Traditional Craft Days; annual Victorian Christmas celebration; annual Hop Festival; historic walking tours; historic house tours in fall.
Publications: annual journal, Madison County Heritage; County Roads Revisited; The Cultural Imprint of Madison County; annual, Studies in Traditional American Crafts; newsletters; annual report; pamphlets; videos.

Hours & Admission Prices: Mon.-Fri. 10-4. Tours: adults $5, seniors $2; discount to AAM members; children 12 & under and members no charge. Research: adults $5; members no charge.
Attendance: 12,000 (estimated)
Membership: Junior $5; Senior $15; Adult $20; Family $30; Supporting $75; Patron $125; Corporate & Life $300.

ONEIDA COMMUNITY MANSION HOUSE, (M), 170 Kenwood Ave., Oneida, NY 13421-2820. Tel.: 315-363-0745. Fax: 315-361-4580.
E-mail: ocmh@oneidacommunity.org
Web Site: www.oneidacommunity.org
Founded: 1987.
Congressional District: 23
Key Personnel: Exec. Dir., Patricia A. Hoffman; Cur. Interpretation & Collections, Anthony Wonderley.
Personnel Profile: Full-Time Paid 5; Part-Time Paid 7; Part-Time Volunteers 63; Interns 1.
Governing Authority: private; nonprofit organization. Subsidiary Institution: Mansion House Service Corp. Tax-exempt: 501(c)(3).
Historic House Museum: housed in the 93,000 sq. ft. brick Mansion House, constructed between 1861 & 1914.
Collections: furniture; clothing; decorative arts; paintings; works of art on paper; approx. 2,500 utilitarian objects made in or brought to the Oneida Community; books, pamphlets, sheet music & ephemera that illustrate the intellectual, cultural & business life of the community, approx. 10,500 items; a photographic archive documenting the life of the Mansion House during the days since the Oneida Community.
Research Fields: Oneida Community; communal societies.
Facilities: 200-seat auditorium. Museum-related items for sale.
Activities: tours; educational programs; musical performances; special events.
Publications: quarterly newsletter, Oneida Community Journal.
Hours & Admission Prices: Self-Guided Tours: Mon.-Sat. 10-4, Sun. 1-4. Guided Tours: Wed.-Sat. 10 & 2, Sun. 2; groups by appointment. Adults $5, students $3; discounts to AAM, AASLH & VHA members & groups; children & members no charge. Closed major holidays. ♿
Attendance: 8,900 (accurate)
Membership: Individual $40; Family $50; Associate $100; Contributor $250; Donor $500; Benefactor $1,000.

SHAKO:WI CULTURAL CENTER, Oneida Indian Nation, 5 Territory Rd., Oneida, NY 13421-9304. Tel.: 315-829-8801. Fax: 315-829-8805.
Web Site: www.oneida-nation.net
Founded: 1993.
Congressional District: 23
Key Personnel: Dir., Kandice Watson.
Personnel Profile: Full-Time Paid 2; Part-Time Paid 2.
Governing Authority: Oneida Indian Nation. Tax-exempt.
Tribal Museum.
Collections: Native Americans; photo archives of Oneida residents on disc; ethnographic; beadwork.
Activities: beading group; dance workshops; language instruction; painting classes.
Hours & Admission Prices: Daily 9-5. No charge. Closed holidays; American Indian Day.
Attendance: 3,600 (estimated)

Oneonta

THE NATIONAL SOCCER HALL OF FAME, Wright Soccer Campus, 18 Stadium Cir., Oneonta, NY 13820-1068. Tel.: 607-432-3351. Fax: 607-432-8429.
E-mail: info@soccerhall.org
Web Site: www.soccerhall.org
Founded: 1981.
Congressional District: 25
Key Personnel: Pres. & C.O.O., Stephen H. Baumann; Chm. (V), Douglas B. Willies; Vice Pres. Business Devel. & Operations, Jonathan Ullman; Dir. Devel., Kathryn Dailey; Dir. Museum & Archives, Jack Huckel; Museum Shop Mgr., Mary Myers.
Personnel Profile: Full-Time Paid 8; Full-Time Volunteers 1; Part-Time Paid 20; Part-Time Volunteers 20; Interns 5.
Governing Authority: nonprofit organization. Tax-exempt: 501(c)(3).
Sports History Museum.
Collections: soccer history; uniforms; balls; trophies; league records; archives; videotapes; photographs; media guides; films; paintings.
Research Fields: history of soccer.
Facilities: 13,500-vol. library pertaining to soccer; 40,000 sq. ft. exhibit space. Museum-related items for sale.
Activities: temporary exhibitions; organized education programs for undergraduate or graduate college students affiliated with State University of New York at Oneonta. Annual Events: Soccer Tournaments & Clinics; Hall of Fame Induction; Soccer Camps.
Publications: newsletter, Hall of Famer; online newsletter.
Hours & Admission Prices: Call for hours. Adults $12.50, students $9.50, senior citizens & veterans $8.50, youth 6-12 $7.50; discounts to military, AAM, NSCAA, NISOA, AYSO card members; children under 6 no charge. ♿
Attendance: 44,000 (estimated)

SCIENCE DISCOVERY CENTER OF ONEONTA, State University College, Oneonta, NY 13820-4015. Tel.: 607-436-2011. Fax: 607-436-2654.
E-mail: scdisc@oneonta.edu
Web Site: www.oneonta.edu/academics/sdc
Founded: 1987.
Congressional District: 25
Key Personnel: Dir., Hugh Gallagher, Jr.
Personnel Profile: Full-Time Volunteers 1; Part-Time Paid 1; Part-Time Volunteers 15.
Governing Authority: nonprofit. State University of New York, College of Oneonta. Tax-exempt: 501(c)(3).
Science Museum.
Collections: concentration on physics & physical science; interactive science exhibits.
Facilities: 200-vol. library on science experiments & activities available to the public; 3,000 sq. ft. exhibit space.
Activities: informal science activities for elementary, secondary & college classes; some formal instruction for science education majors on use of center's facilities & occasional formal science workshops for elementary teachers.
Publications: quarterly newsletter, Science Discovery Center of Oneonta Newsletter.
Hours & Admission Prices: July-Aug. Mon.-Sat. 12-4; Sept.-June Thurs.-Sat. 12-4. Groups by appointment only. No charge; donations accepted. Closed Thanksgiving; Christmas. ♿
Attendance: 5,720 (accurate)
Membership: Individual $25; Family $40; Benefactor $100; Life $400.

THE YAGER MUSEUM OF ART & CULTURE, One Hartwick Dr., West St., Oneonta, NY 13820-4000. Tel.: 607-431-4480. Fax: 607-431-4468.
E-mail: museum@hartwick.edu
Web Site: www.hartwick.edu/museum.xml
Founded: 1929.
Congressional District: 32
Key Personnel: College Pres., Dr. Margaret L. Drugovich; Cur. Anthropological Collection, Dr. David Anthony; Collections Mgr., Gary Norman; Museum Shop Mgr., Nancy Martin-Mathewson; Sec., Denise Wagner.
Personnel Profile: Full-Time Paid 1; Part-Time Paid 23.
Governing Authority: college board of trustees. Parent Institution: Hartwick College. Branch Museums: American Indian Collection & Fine Arts Collection. Tax-exempt: 501(c)(3).
General Museum.
Collections: Yager: Upper Susquehanna Indian artifacts, Southwest basketry & pottery; Furman collection of Mexican, Central American & South American artifacts; Sandell collection of Ecuadorian & Peruvian artifacts; Friess collection of Mexican masks; Marks collection of Pre-Columbian art. Van Ess Fine Arts collection of renaissance, baroque & American 19th century paintings, prints & sculpture; American Indians. Russian icons.
Research Fields: archaeological excavations in the Upper Susquehanna region; 19th-century fine arts.
Facilities: 800-vol. library of American Indian history books available on premises.
Activities: changing exhibitions; programs; seminars.
Publications: post cards; catalogues.
Hours & Admission Prices: Tues.-Sat. 12-4:30; collection research by appointment only. No charge, donations accepted. Closed school holidays. ♿
Attendance: 6,050 (accurate)
Membership: Student $10; Senior $25; Individual $30; Senior Couple $40; Family & Couple $50; Van Ess $500; Hassam $1,000; Yager $2,500 & up.

Ontario

HERITAGE SQUARE MUSEUM, 7147 Ontario Center Rd., Ontario, NY 14519. Mailing Address: P.O. Box 462, Ontario, NY 14519-0462. Tel.: 315-524-5356.
Web Site: heritagesquaremuseum.org
Formerly: Town of Ontario Historical & Landmark Preservation Society, Inc. Heritage Square
Founded: 1969.
Congressional District: 29

Key Personnel: Pres., Vera Graves; Vice Pres., Beth Howard; Sec., Jim Graves; Treas., Jean Tsepas.
Personnel Profile: Part-Time Volunteers 125.
Governing Authority: society. Parent Institution: Town of Ontario Historical & Landmark Preservation Society. Tax-exempt. 501(c)(3).
Historical Society Museum Complex.
Collections: iron ore mining; artifacts; furniture; agriculture; farm machinery & tools; education. Historic 1800's Buildings: c.1860 schoolhouse; c.1834 farmhouse; c.1840 meeting house; church; c.1860 log cabin; c.1890 miner's home; Ore Mivera house; barn; dry house (apples); lockup (jail); 1874 train station.
Research Fields: local Ontario history from 1807-1993.
Facilities: 100-seat auditorium.
Activities: guided tours; formally organized educational programs; video; slide shows.
Publications: newsletter, Town of Ontario Historical & Landmark Society; books, History of the Town of Ontario 1807-1993; Heritage Corners.
Hours & Admission Prices: June 6-Oct. 4 Sat.-Sun. 1:30-4; other times by appointment. School & group tours by bus are welcome. Call for admission prices; members no charge. Closed Memorial Day weekend; Independence Day weekend. ♿
Attendance: 1,550 (estimated)
Membership: Senior Citizens 62 & over $10; Individual $15; Family $25; Patron $50.

Orangeburg

ORANGETOWN HISTORICAL MUSEUM AND ARCHIVES - SALYER HOUSE AND DEPEW HOUSE, 196 Blaisdell Rd., Orangeburg, NY 10962-2011. Mailing Address: 26 Orangeburg Rd., Orangeburg, NY 10962-1706. Tel.: 845-398-1302. Fax: 845-398-8919.
E-mail: otownmuseum@optonline
Web Site: www.orangetownmuseum.com
Founded: 1992.
Congressional District: 20
Key Personnel: C.E.O., Mary R. Cardenas; Supvr., Thom Kleiner; Cur., Elizabeth Skrabonja; Public Rels., Laura Davie; Registrar, Ann Lively; Museum Shop Mgr., Jo Winograd.
Personnel Profile: Part-Time Paid 3; Part-Time Volunteers 11; Interns 1.
Governing Authority: nonprofit. Parent Institution: Town of Orangetown. Branch Museum: DePew House, 196 Blaisdell Rd., Orangeburg, NY 10962; The Salyer House, 213 Blue Hill Rd., Pearl River, NY 10965. Tax-exempt.
History Museum.
Collections: photographs; period artifacts; archives; books, newspaper articles & magazines containing articles pertaining to Orangetown history from the Colonial era to present. Historic Houses: Salyer House c.1779; De Pew House c.1777.
Major Exhibits: Our Lives In Their Hands, Spring 2010.
Facilities: 410-vol. library available for use on site by appointment; archives; 1,280 sq. ft. exhibit space. Museum-related items for sale.
Activities: school programs.
Publications: newsletter, Orangetown Crier.
Hours & Admission Prices: Sun. 1-4, Tues. 10-2; other times by appointment. No charge; donations accepted. Closed holidays. ♿
Attendance: 750 (accurate)
Membership: Student & Senior Citizen $10; Single $15; Family $20; Life $150; Corporate $500.

Orchard Park

ORCHARD PARK HISTORICAL SOCIETY, S-4287 S. Buffalo St., Orchard Park, NY 14127. Mailing Address: 4100 N. Freeman Rd., Orchard Park, NY 14127-2525. Tel.: 716-662-2185.
Founded: 1951.
Congressional District: 38
Key Personnel: C.E.O. & Pres., Dennis J. Mill; Cur., Yasabel N. Gibson.
Personnel Profile: Part-Time Volunteers 10; Interns 2.
Governing Authority: society. Tax-exempt: 501(c)(3).
General Museum.
Collections: artifacts; agricultural items; dolls; dishes; maps; deeds; clothing; utensils; toys; loom; early household items; furniture; Indian artifacts; Quaker artifacts.
Facilities: 150-vol. library of historic books available for research on premises.
Activities: lectures; permanent & temporary exhibitions; school loan service.
Hours & Admission Prices: Spring-Oct. 1st & 3rd Sat. 2-4; Nov. 28-Dec. 20 Sat.-Sun. 2-4; groups by appointment. Admission: $2. ♿
Attendance: 425 (estimated)
Membership: Single $10; Family $15. Life membership: Single $250; Family $350.

Orient

OYSTERPONDS HISTORICAL SOCIETY: MUSEUM & ARCHIVE OF ORIENT & EAST MARION HISTORY, (M), 1555 Village Lane, Orient, NY 11957. Mailing Address: P.O. Box 70, Orient, NY 11957-0070. Tel.: 631-323-2480. Fax: 631-323-3719.
E-mail: ohsorient@optonline.net
Web Site: www.oysterpondshistoricalsociety.org
Founded: 1944.
Congressional District: 1
Key Personnel: Exec., Ellen M. Cone Busch; Pres. (V), Tazewell Smith.
Personnel Profile: Full-Time Paid 1; Part-Time Paid 2; Part-Time Volunteers 50; Interns 1.
Governing Authority: board of trustees; society. Parent Institution: Oysterponds Historical Society, Inc. Tax-exempt: 501(c)(3).
History Village Museum Complex.
Collections: Indian artifacts; marine paintings; photographs; manuscripts & early documents; whaling & fishing artifacts; ship models & navigating instruments; spinning & weaving tools; clothing; furniture; toys; dolls; period tools; quilts; agricultural tools. Historical Houses: 1860s Village House; 1888 Old Point School House; 1860 Amanda Brown House; 1870 Seine House: sleighs & carriages; c.1780 Webb House; 1870 Vail House.
Research Fields: local history; genealogy; school books; costumes; local architecture.
Facilities: 1,000-vol. library containing 6,000 photos, 2,000 glass plate negatives; 10,000 documents available on premises for research. Museum-related items for sale.
Activities: guided tours; lectures; permanent & temporary exhibits; grade school program.
Publications: newsletter; books, Historic Orient Village; Griffin's Journal (reprint); She Went A-Whaling; Captain's Daughter; A Sense of Place.
Hours & Admission Prices: July-Oct. Thurs. & Sat.-Sun. 2-5; other times by appointment. Adults $5, children under 16 $.50; discounts to AASLH members; members no charge. ♿
Attendance: 5,000 (estimated)
Membership: Individual $30; Family $50; Associate $100; Sponsor $250; Patron $500; Benefactor $1,000.

Oriskany

ORISKANY BATTLEFIELD STATE HISTORIC SITE, 7801 State Rt. 69, Oriskany, NY 13424-4115. Tel.: 315-768-7224. Fax: 315-337-3081.
E-mail: nancy.demyttenaere@oprhp.state.ny.us
Web Site: www.nysparks.com
Founded: 1927.
Congressional District: 31
Key Personnel: Regl. Historic Preservation Supvr., Nancy Demyttenaere; Second in Command, Bill Acomb.
Personnel Profile: Full-Time Paid 3; Part-Time Paid 3; Part-Time Volunteers 1.
Governing Authority: state. Parent Institution: New York State Office of Parks, Recreation & Historic Preservation. Tax-exempt: 501(c)(3).
Historic Site: Revolutionary War Battlefield & Memorial Park, site of Aug. 6, 1777 ambush of Colonial Militia & Oneida allies by Loyalist forces.
Collections: Large memorial obelisk & other smaller monuments from 1884-1929; historic landscape & archives; commemorative souvenirs.
Facilities: battlefield site; visitor center; picnic area.
Activities: guided tours; special events.
Hours & Admission Prices: mid-May to mid-Oct. Wed.-Sat. & Mon. holidays 9-5, Sun. 1-5. No charge; donations accepted.
Attendance: 23,000 (accurate)

Ossining

OSSINING HISTORICAL SOCIETY MUSEUM, 196 Croton Ave., Ossining, NY 10562-4504. Tel.: 914-941-0001. Fax: 914-941-0001.
E-mail: ohsm@bestweb.net
Web Site: www.ossininghistorical.org
Founded: 1931.
Congressional District: 24
Key Personnel: Exec. Dir., Roberta Y. Arminio; Pres. (V), Norman T. MacDonald; Vice Pres., Raymond A. Barlaam; Treas., Greg Fratianni.
Personnel Profile: Full-Time Volunteers 5; Part-Time Volunteers 5; Interns 2.
Governing Authority: society; nonprofit organization. Tax-exempt: 501(c)(3).
Local History Museum & Fine Arts Collection.
Collections: costumes; paintings; Indian artifacts; war relics; doll collection; fine arts; books; bottles; china; photographs; portraits & paintings depicting culture of the 17th & 18th century residents; oral history collection; manuscript collections; VHS; newspaper collection, 1799 to present; photographs; microfilm; genealogy; maps; documents; toys; glass plates & negatives.
Research Fields: Sing Sing Prison; Hudson River; local & county history;

genealogy; school records; Croton Dam; Croton aqueduct; architecture; local government records.
Facilities: library; local newspapers 1799-present, magazines & journals; clipping file on local history; reference material; maps; reading room; video viewing center; oral history center; research room; archives.
Activities: guided tours; lectures; gallery talks; permanent & temporary exhibitions; genealogy information.
Publications: Sing Sing Prison Electrocutions; Civil War Directory - Local; War Memorial - All Wars; Images of America: Ossining Remembered; The 1950s in Ossining, NY; The 1940s in Ossining, NY; William Dolphins Civil War Diary; book, Sparta Cemetery; The Sparta Letters, The Record of Ossining's Earliest Residents; A Primer of Ossining History.
Hours & Admission Prices: Sun.-Thurs. 1-4, Sat. by appointment. No charge; donations accepted. Closed holidays. ♿
Attendance: 1,500 (estimated)
Membership: Student & Senior Citizen $10; Individual $20; Family $30; Sustaining & Civic $50; Patron & Commercial $100.

Oswego

FORT ONTARIO STATE HISTORIC SITE, One E. 4th St., Oswego, NY 13126-1233. Mailing Address: P.O. Box 5379, Oswego, NY 13126. Tel.: 315-343-4711.
Web Site: www.fortontario.com
Founded: 1949.
Congressional District: 30
Key Personnel: Pres. (V), Charles Harrington; Site Mgr., Paul Lear; Asst., Richard LaCrosse; Cur., Jennifer Emmons; Sec., Roberta Elmer; Maintenance Supvr., Robert Clarke.
Personnel Profile: Full-Time Paid 8; Part-Time Paid 12; Part-Time Volunteers 135.
Governing Authority: state. New York State Office of Parks, Recreation & Historic Preservation, & Central New York State Parks, Recreation & Historic Preservation Commission. Tax-exempt: 501(c)(3).
Military Museum: housed in 1839-1844 fortifications situated at the outlet of Oswego River into Lake Ontario.
Collections: military furnishings, firearms, equipment, uniforms, accoutrements, prints, paintings. Historic Buildings: 1842-1844 enlisted men's barracks, a magazine, two officers' quarters with outbuildings, post headquarters; 1863-1872 two guardhouses & five casemates; 1821 post hospital; 18th-century artifacts; photographs.
Research Fields: military & naval activities on the Great Lakes frontier from the French & Indian Wars through World War II; fortification design & construction; related political, economic & diplomatic events & personalities.
Facilities: 500-vol. collection of books & periodicals dealing with regional, military & social history available for use on premises by advance appointment; maps & plans; classroom; picnic area.
Activities: self-guided & guided tours; lectures; concerts; encampments; Civil War Artillery, Infantry and Engineer schools; kite festival & more.
Publications: folders, Fort Ontario; Fort Ontario: A Self-Guided Tour; "Welcome to Fort Ontario".
Hours & Admission Prices: May-Oct. 15 Tues.-Sun. & Mon holidays 10-4:30; groups by appointment. Adults $4, seniors & students with I.D. $3; children 12 & under & Friends of Fort Ontario no charge.
Attendance: 15,000 (accurate)
Membership: Senior $10; Individual $15; Family $25; Small Business $50; Benefactor $100; Patron $250; Sponsor $500; Corporate $1,000.

H. LEE WHITE MARINE MUSEUM, (M), W. 1st St. Pier, Oswego, NY 13126. Mailing Address: P.O. Box 101, Oswego, NY 13126-0101. Tel.: 315-342-0480. Fax: 315-343-5778.
E-mail: info@hleewhitemarinemuseum.com
Web Site: hleewhitemarinemuseum.com
Founded: 1982.
Key Personnel: Dir., Mercedes Niess.
Governing Authority: Tax-exempt.
Marine Museum.
Collections: maritime artifacts; photographs; boats.
Hours & Admission Prices: July-Aug. daily 10-5; Sept.-June daily 1-5. Adults $7, youth 5-12 $3; discounts to museum, AAM & ICOM members; children under 5 no charge. Closed New Year's Eve & Day; Easter; Thanksgiving; Christmas Eve, Day & week.
Attendance: 21,000 (estimated)
Membership: $25-$49; $50-$99; $100-$249; $250-$499; $500-$99; $1,000 & up.

RICHARDSON-BATES HOUSE MUSEUM, 135 E. 3rd St., Oswego, NY 13126-2655. Tel.: 315-343-1342.
E-mail: ochs@rbhousemuseum.org
Web Site: www.rbhousemuseum.org
Founded: 1896.
Congressional District: 24
Key Personnel: Dir., Terrance M. Prior; Pres. (V), Margaret McKinstry.
Personnel Profile: Full-Time Paid 1; Part-Time Paid 1; Part-Time Volunteers 3.
Governing Authority: nonprofit organization; Oswego County Historical Society. Tax-exempt: 509(a)(1); 501(c)(3).
Historic House Museum: Richardson-Bates house, built 1867-90.
Collections: Oswego County artifacts, photographs & documents; 19th-century furnishings, paintings & decorative arts; Native American artifacts.
Research Fields: local, regional & state history; Victorian decorative arts.
Facilities: 500-vol. library of material on local, regional & state history available for use upon application.
Activities: guided museum tours; permanent & changing exhibitions; outreach in-school lectures/demonstrations; lectures; special events.
Publications: Historical Journal, 1939-1977; monthly newsletter.
Hours & Admission Prices: Tues.-Fri. 10-5, Sat. 1-5; research library by appointment. Family $10; adults $4, students & seniors $2; discounts to American Assoc. for State & Local History, NY State Historical Assoc. & AAM members; members no charge. Closed holidays.
Attendance: 5,000 (accurate)
Membership: Senior Citizen & Student $10; Individual $20; Family $25; Order of the Sphinx $50-$99; Friends of Harriet $100-$248; Norman's Fellows $250-$499; Naomi's Circle $500-$999; Giving to the Max $1,000 & Up.

SAFE HAVEN MUSEUM AND EDUCATION CENTER, 2 E. 7th St., Oswego, NY 13126-1197. Mailing Address: P.O. Box 846, Oswego, NY 13126-0846. Tel.: 315-342-3003. Fax: 315-342-1411.
E-mail: safehaven@cnymail.com
Web Site: www.oswegohaven.org
Founded: 1990.
Congressional District: 24
Key Personnel: C.E.O. & Pres., Ronald Tascarella; Site Admin., Christine M. Sugrue.
Personnel Profile: Part-Time Paid 1.
Governing Authority: private; nonprofit organization. Tax-exempt.
History Museum.
Collections: photographs, memorabilia, primary source documents & oral history videotapes associated with the Fort Ontario World War II Refugee Center, only facility in the U.S. to shelter European World War II Holocaust refugees.
Publications: quarterly newsletter, New Ontario Chronicle.
Hours & Admission Prices: Memorial Day to Labor Day Tues.-Sun. 10-4; Winter: Wed.-Sun. 11-4. Adults $4, seniors $2, students $1; members no charge. ♿
Attendance: 2,500 (estimated)
Membership: Individual $20; Family $35.

TYLER ART GALLERY, State University of New York College of Arts & Science, 7060 State Rte. 104, Oswego, NY 13126-3599. Tel.: 315-312-2113. Fax: 315-312-5642.
E-mail: mail.dorsey@oswego.edu
Web Site: www.oswego.edu/other_campus/tylerart/index.html
Congressional District: 24
Key Personnel: Asst. Dir., Michael Flanagan; Administrative Aide, Mali Dorsey.
Personnel Profile: Full-Time Paid 2; Part-Time Paid 1; Interns 11.
Governing Authority: college. State University of New York, College of Arts & Science at Oswego. Tax-exempt.
Art Gallery.
Collections: teaching collection of 19th & 20th-century European & American drawings, prints, paintings & sculpture.
Activities: inter-museum loan exhibitions; temporary & traveling exhibitions; lectures; gallery talks.
Publications: brochures; checklists; posters.
Hours & Admission Prices: Sept.-May Tues.-Sat. 11:30-3. No charge; donations accepted. Closed during college vacation periods. ♿
Attendance: 18,650 (accurate)

Owego

TIOGA COUNTY HISTORICAL SOCIETY MUSEUM, 110 Front St., Owego, NY 13827-1519. Tel.: 607-687-2460. Fax: 607-687-2460.
E-mail: info@tiogahistory.org
Web Site: www.tiogahistory.org
Founded: 1914.
Congressional District: 22 & 24
Key Personnel: C.E.O. & Pres. (V), Gae Crosby; Exec. Dir., Roger Sharp.
Personnel Profile: Full-Time Paid 1; Part-Time Paid 3; Part-Time Volunteers 12.

Governing Authority: nonprofit. Tax-exempt: 501(c)(3).
History Museum.
Collections: Indian artifacts; firearms; pioneer crafts; early commerce, industry, transportation & agriculture exhibits; primitive paintings; textiles; photography.
Research Fields: genealogy; local history.
Facilities: 2,500-vol. library on area history, genealogy & newspaper files available on the premises; reading room.
Activities: guided tours; lectures; education programs; permanent & temporary exhibitions; school loan service; summer walking tours.
Publications: monthly newsletter; books & videotapes on local history.
Hours & Admission Prices: Tues.-Sat. 10-4. No charge; donations accepted. Closed New Year's Day; Independence Day; Thanksgiving; Christmas. ♿
Attendance: 3,900 (accurate)
Membership: Member $25; Family & Household $45; Supporter $100-$250; Corporate $250; Patron $500.

Oyster Bay

COE HALL, 1395 Planting Fields Rd., Oyster Bay, NY 11771-1302. Mailing Address: P.O. Box 660, Oyster Bay, NY 11771-0660. Tel.: 516-922-9210. Fax: 516-922-9226.
Web Site: plantingfields.org
Founded: 1979.
Congressional District: 3
Key Personnel: Exec. Dir., Henry Joyce; Chm. (V), Michael D. Coe; Pres. (V), G. Morgan Brown; Business Mgr., Sherley Cherenfant; Cur., Marianne Della Croce; Volunteer Coord. & Museum Shop Mgr., Katherine Sterner; Weekend Coord., Elsa Eisenberg; Coord. Membership & Dir. Devel., Patrice Panza; Field Trip Coord., Melissa Valencia; Garden Librarian, Rose Marie Papayanopulos; Asst. Cur., Kristy Caratzola; Dir. Special Events, Jennifer Lavella; Education Asst., Tracy Potavin.
Personnel Profile: Full-Time Paid 10; Part-Time Paid 2; Part-Time Volunteers 300; Interns 7.
Governing Authority: nonprofit organization. Parent Institution: Planting Fields Foundation, P.O. Box 660, Oyster Bay 11771. Tax-exempt: 501(c)(3).
Historic House: 1918-1921 Tudor Revival Mansion.
Collections: original & period furnishings; Baroque & Renaissance paintings; archival collection of Walker & Gillette drawings; Olmsted Brothers plans & drawings; medieval stained glass; family papers & manuscripts.
Major Exhibits: Long Island Gold Coast Weddings, 6/10-9/10.
Research Fields: Tudor revival architecture in England & United States with emphasis on Long Island; development of American studies programs throughout universities in the United States.
Facilities: library; 200-seat auditorium; visitor center; cafe.
Activities: guided tours; lectures; concerts; arts festivals; archives; docent program or council. Special Events: Arbor Day Festival; Dahlia Show; Winter Festival; Rhododendron Days; Fall Foliage Walks.
Publications: newsletter, Evergreen.
Hours & Admission Prices: April-Sept. daily 12-3:30; groups by appointment. Guided Tours: adults $3.50; discounts to AAM & AAA members; children 6-12 & members no charge. Arboretum: $6 per car. Closed legal holidays. ♿
Attendance: 200,000 (accurate)
Membership: Individual $50; Family $85; Contributor $150; Sponsor $300; Sustainer $500.

OYSTER BAY HISTORICAL SOCIETY, 20 Summit St., Oyster Bay, NY 11771-2317. Mailing Address: P.O. Box 297, Oyster Bay, NY 11771-0297. Tel.: 516-922-5032. Fax: 516-624-7291.
E-mail: obhistory@aol.com
Web Site: www.oysterbayhistory.org
Founded: 1960.
Congressional District: 3
Key Personnel: Dir., Thomas A. Kuehhas; Pres., Maureen Monck; Treas., Linda Morgan; Librarian, Stacie Hammond; Cur., Yvonne Cifarelli.
Personnel Profile: Full-Time Paid 1; Part-Time Paid 2; Part-Time Volunteers 18; Interns 2.
Governing Authority: society; nonprofit. Tax-exempt: 501(c)(3).
Historical Society Museum: housed in c.1720 Earle-Wightman House.
Collections: 18th-19th century household furnishings & decorative arts; books; manuscripts; maps; photographs; Reichman collection of early American tools & trades.
Research Fields: Long Island history from colonial period to the 20th century with emphasis on Oyster Bay.
Facilities: 1,150-vol. library containing 2,000 manuscripts, 2,500 photographs, 75 atlases & maps pertaining to local area history available for public use; botanical garden.
Activities: guided tours; lectures; films; concerts; organized education programs for children; participatory & temporary exhibitions.
Publications: books, The Diary of Mary Cooper: Life on a Long Island Farm 1768-1773; The Walls Have Tongues: Oyster Bay Houses and their Stories; Walking Tour of Old Oyster Bay; quarterly magazine, The Freeholder; What Kind of Noise Annoys An Oyster: An Oyster Songster.
Hours & Admission Prices: Tues.-Fri. 10-2, Sat. 9-1, Sun. 1-4. No charge; donations requested. Closed Christmas-New Year's Day. ♿
Attendance: 4,000 (estimated)
Membership: Individual $35; Family $45; Contributing $75; Sponsor $100; Sustaining $250; Patron $500; Benefactor $1,000 & up. Business $75; Business Sponsor $100; Business Friend $300; Business Patron $500 & up.

PLANTING FIELDS ARBORETUM STATE HISTORIC PARK, 1395 Planting Fields Rd., Oyster Bay, NY 11771-1302. Mailing Address: P.O. Box 58, Oyster Bay, NY 11771-0058. Tel.: 516-922-8600. Fax: 516-922-8610.
Web Site: www.plantingfields.org
Founded: 1955.
Congressional District: 3
Key Personnel: Dir., Vincent Simeone; Chm. Planting Fields Foundation, G. Morgan Browne; Horticulturist, Paul Dose; Asst. Dir., Peter Atkins; Volunteer Coord., Katherine Sterner.
Personnel Profile: Full-Time Paid 18; Part-Time Paid 24; Part-Time Volunteers 240; Interns 8.
Governing Authority: Parent Institution: New York State Office of Parks, Recreation & Historic Preservation. Subsidiary Institution: Planting Fields Foundation. Tax-exempt: 509(a)(3).
Arboretum.
Collections: rhododendron species & cultivars including deciduous and evergreen azaleas; herbarium; specimen trees; deciduous magnolias; synoptic shrub garden; greenhouse collections of camellias, orchids, cacti & economic plants.
Research Fields: arboretum.
Facilities: 5,000-vol. library of horticultural & botanical books; nature trails; formal gardens; tea house; play house; two restored glass house ranges. Historic Building: Coe Hall.
Activities: guided tours; lectures; films; formally organized educational programs; temporary exhibitions.
Publications: quarterly newsletter.
Hours & Admission Prices: Daily 9-5. Adults $6.50, senior citizens & students with I.D. $5, children 7-12 $2; children 6 & under no charge. Coe Hall: see separate listing. Closed Christmas Day. ♿
Attendance: 262,360 (estimated)
Membership: General $40.

* **RAYNHAM HALL MUSEUM, (M),** 20 W. Main St., Oyster Bay, NY 11771-2216. Tel.: 516-922-6808. Fax: 516-922-7640.
E-mail: info@raynhamhallmuseum.org
Web Site: www.raynhamhallmuseum.org
Founded: 1953.
Congressional District: 3
Key Personnel: Exec. Dir., Harriet Gerard Clark; Asst. Dir., Theresa Skvarla; Pres. (V), Kay Hutchins Sato; Coord. Education, Jessica M. Semins; Collections Mgr., Jennifer Ladd.
Personnel Profile: Full-Time Paid 2; Part-Time Paid 8; Part-Time Volunteers 30; Interns 1.
Governing Authority: nonprofit organization. Friends of Raynham Hall, Inc. Tax-exempt: 501(c)(3).
c.1738 Historic House Museum: 1851 Gothic Revival addition.
Collections: 18th & 19th-century household furnishings & decorative arts; textiles; archives; Townsend family furnishings; United States military; costumes; toys.
Research Fields: Townsend family; life in Oyster Bay, 1738-1880.
Facilities: Museum-related items for sale.
Activities: guided tours; audio tour of house & grounds; educational programs; lecture series; temporary exhibitions; local historic preservation; cooking & craft programs for boy and girl scouts.
Publications: brochures; annual report; quarterly newsletter; historic comic book-based.
Hours & Admission Prices: Tues.-Sun. 1-5; group tours by appointment. Adults $5, students with ID & senior citizens $3; discounts to AAM members; children under 6 & members no charge. Closed New Year's Day; Thanksgiving; Christmas; most national holidays.
Attendance: 10,032 (accurate)
Membership: Junior Culper, Jr. $5; Student $10; Individual $35; Family $45; Business Friend $75; 1740 Society & Business Sponsor $100; Culper Spy Ring & Business Benefactor $250; Victorian Society & Business Patron $500; Raynham Society $1,000.

SAGAMORE HILL NATIONAL HISTORIC SITE, 20 Sagamore Hill Rd., Oyster Bay, NY 11771-1899. Tel.: 516-922-4788. Fax: 516-922-4792.
E-mail: sahi_information@nps.gov
Web Site: www.nps.gov/sahi
Founded: 1963.
Congressional District: 3
Key Personnel: Supt., Thomas Ross; Cur., Amy Verone; Museum Shop Mgr., Debbie Bulck.
Personnel Profile: Full-Time Paid 16; Part-Time Paid 10; Part-Time Volunteers 35; Interns 2.
Governing Authority: federal. Administered by the National Park Service, U.S. Dept. of Interior, Washington, DC 20240. Tax-exempt.
Historic House Museum: 1885 Sagamore Hill, home of Theodore Roosevelt.
Collections: personal & household effects of Theodore Roosevelt & Roosevelt family.
Research Fields: life & presidency of Theodore Roosevelt.
Facilities: 350-vol. library of books written by or about Theodore Roosevelt available for study by prior arrangement with supt.
Activities: ranger-led tours of Theodore Roosevelt's home; self-guided tour of Old Orchard Museum; audiovisual programs.
Publications: guide book, Sagamore Hill.
Hours & Admission Prices: Memorial Day to Labor Day daily 9:30-5; Winter: Wed.-Sun. 9:30-5; groups by appointment. Adults $5; children under 16 & scheduled educational groups no charge. Closed New Year's Day; Thanksgiving; Christmas. ♿
Attendance: 65,000 (accurate)
Membership: Associate $35; Family $65; Sustaining $100; Patron $250; Sponsor $500; Benefactor $1,000; Corporate $5,000.

Painted Post

PAINTED POST - ERWIN MUSEUM AT THE DEPOT, 277 Steuben St., Painted Post, NY 14870. Mailing Address: 73 W. Pulteney St., Corning, NY 14830-2212. Tel.: 607-962-0249. Fax: 607-962-0249.
E-mail: ppemuseum@aol.com
Web Site: www.pattersonmuseum.org
Founded: 1945.
Congressional District: 29
Key Personnel: Pres., Sheri Golder; Vice Pres., Ron Nemy; Dir., Jessica Cunningham.
Personnel Profile: Part-Time Paid 20; Part-Time Volunteers 8.
Governing Authority: municipal. Parent Institution: Corning-Painted Post Historic Society. Subsidiary Institution: Conning Painted Post Historical Society. Tax-exempt.
General Museum.
Collections: Indian lore; historic artifacts; newspapers; books; 1930's local history, composed of artifacts related to regional land formation, occupation, settlement, commerce, industry, transportation, recreation, society, tradition.
Research Fields: Local & Indian history; Stenben County census records 1825-1925, painted Post, Erwin & regional history.
Facilities: 400-vol. library of local, state & national history available for research on premises; reading room, listed in the National Register of Historic places.
Activities: self-guided tours.
Publications: Erwin Town Cemeteries Records 1793-1979.
Hours & Admission Prices: June-Aug. Mon.-Fri. 10-4, Sat. 10-2; Sept.-May call for appointment; No charge, donations accepted. ♿
Attendance: 1,500

Palmyra

ALLING COVERLET MUSEUM, 122 William St., Palmyra, NY 14522-1030. Mailing Address: P.O. Box 96, Palmyra, NY 14522-0096. Tel.: 315-597-6737. Fax: 315-597-6981.
E-mail: bjfhpinc@rochester.rr.com
Web Site: www.historicpalmyrany.com
Founded: 1976.
Congressional District: 29
Key Personnel: Chm., Les Thomas; Exec. Dir., Bonnie J. Hays; Museum Shop Mgr., Steve Hays.
Personnel Profile: Full-Time Paid 1; Part-Time Paid 1.
Governing Authority: Parent Institution: Historic Palmyra, Inc. Tax-exempt.
American Coverlet Museum.
Collections: coverlets; quilts; looms; weaving materials.
Facilities: Museum-related items for sale.
Activities: tours; hands-on activities.
Publications: pamphlets; books.
Hours & Admission Prices: June to mid-Sept. daily 1-4. No charge; donations accepted. ♿
Attendance: 7,000 (accurate)
Membership: Students $5; Individual $15; Family $25.

HILL CUMORAH VISITORS CENTER & HISTORIC SITES, 603 State Rte. 21, Palmyra, NY 14522-9301. Tel.: 315-597-5851. Fax: 315-597-0165.
Web Site: www.hillcumorah.org
Founded: 1830.
Congressional District: 33
Key Personnel: Dir., Bryan Weston.
Personnel Profile: Full-Time Volunteers 44; Part-Time Volunteers 20.
Governing Authority: church; The Church of Jesus Christ of Latter-day Saints (Mormon), 50 E. North Temple, Salt Lake City, UT 84150. Tax-exempt.
Religious Museums & Historic Sites: 5 historical sites & places of historic significance in connection with the founding of the Church of Jesus Christ of Latter-day Saints.
Collections: household furnishings typical of 1820s western New York. Historic Structures and Sites: c.1825, home of Joseph Smith, founder of the LDS church; The Sacred Grove; c.1825, The Grandin Building, 217 E. Main St.; c.1850, Martin Harris House, Maple Ave.; c.1805, Peter Whitmer log farm house, Aunkst Rd., Waterloo.
Research Fields: LDS church history.
Facilities: visitors' center; historic homes.
Activities: guided tours of visitor center. Annual Event: Hill Cumorah Pageant, America's Witness For Christ in July.
Publications: books, Book of Mormon; Doctrine and Covenants; pamphlets.
Hours & Admission Prices: Winter: Mon.-Sat. 9-6, Sun. 12:30-6, Summer: Mon.-Sat. 9-7, Sun. 12:30-7. No charge. Closed New Year's Day; Thanksgiving; Christmas. ♿
Attendance: 150,000 (estimated)

HISTORIC PALMYRA'S PRINT SHOP, (M), 140 1/2 Market St., Palmyra, NY 14522. Mailing Address: P.O. Box 96, Palmyra, NY 14522-0096. Tel.: 315-597-6981. Fax: 315-597-6981.
Web Site: www.historicpalmyrany.com
Founded: 1967.
Congressional District: 29
Key Personnel: C.E.O. & Chm. (V), Les Thomas; Exec. Dir., Bonnie J. Hays; Museum Shop Mgr., Steve Hays.
Personnel Profile: Full-Time Paid 1; Part-Time Paid 1.
Governing Authority: nonprofit. Parent Institution: Historic Palmyra. Subsidiary Institutions: Alling Coverlet Museum, Phelps Store Museum, Palmyra Historical Museum. Tax-exempt: 501(c)(3).
History Museum: housed in an Erie Canal store & home.
Collections: textiles; decorative arts; weaving & spinning equipment; country store merchandise; home furnishings; dolls & toys; tools; quilts; 1800s printing press & cutters; printing blocks; type; advertisements; books; typewriters; comptometers; signs; lead type equipment.
Research Fields: textiles; history of Palmyra.
Facilities: 1,500-vol. library, available for use on premises. Books & items on weaving & textiles for sale.
Activities: guided tours; lectures; concerts; permanent & temporary exhibitions; school tours; cemetery tours; monthly programs.
Publications: newsletter; brochure; local information sheet.
Hours & Admission Prices: Print Shop: June to mid-Sept. Tues.-Sat. 11-4. Alling Museum: June to mid-Sept. daily 1-4. Palmyra Historical Museum & William Phelps General Store: June to mid-Sept. Tues.-Thurs. & Sat. 1-4. Donations: adults $2; members no charge. ♿
Attendance: 2,000 (estimated)
Membership: Students $5; Senior Citizens $10; Individual $15; Family $25; Supporting & Sustaining $50; Patron $100; Benefactor $1,000 & over.

HISTORIC PALMYRA'S - WM. PHELPS GENERAL STORE, 140 Market St., Palmyra, NY 14522-1136. Mailing Address: P.O. Box 96, Palymyra, NY 14522-0096. Tel.: 315-597-6981. Fax: 315-597-6981.
E-mail: bjfhpinc@rochester.rr.com
Web Site: www.historicpalmyrany.com
Formerly: Historic Palmyra Inc.
Founded: 1964.
Congressional District: 29
Key Personnel: Chm. & Pres. (V), Les Thomas; Exec. Dir., Bonnie J. Hays; Museum Shop Mgr., Steve Hays.
Personnel Profile: Full-Time Paid 1; Part-Time Paid 1; Part-Time Volunteers 2.
Governing Authority: Parent Institution: Historic Palmyra, Inc. Tax-exempt.
Erie Canal Store & Home: housed in c.1826 building.
Collections: period fixtures & furniture; personal artifacts. Historic Building: general store.
Research Fields: local archives; industry; religion; local residents; business.
Activities: school tours; cemetery tours; monthly programs.
Publications: newsletter; brochure; local information sheet.
Hours & Admission Prices: June to mid-Sept. Tues.-Sat. 11-4; Winter: by

appointment. Adults $2, senior citizens $1.50, students 12-17 $1; members no charge. Closed Independence Day; Labor Day. ♿
Attendance: 7,000 (accurate)
Membership: Student $5; Senior Citizen $10; Individual $15; Family $25; Organization $35; Supporting $50; Patron $100.

PALMYRA HISTORICAL MUSEUM, 132 Market St., Palmyra, NY 14522-1136. Mailing Address: P.O. Box 96, Palmyra, NY 14522-0096. Tel.: 315-597-6981. Fax: 315-597-6981.
Web Site: www.historicpalmyrany.com
Key Personnel: C.E.O. & Chm. (V), Les Thomas; Exec. Dir., Bonnie J. Hays; Museum Shop Mgr., Steve Hays.
Personnel Profile: Full-Time Paid 1.
Governing Authority: Parent Institution: Historic Palmyra. Tax-exempt: 501(c)(3).
Historic Building: housed in a former 26 room hotel, c.1826.
Collections: period furnishings; personal artifacts; photographs.
Activities: ghost hunts; cemetery walks; history programs; UGRR programs.
Publications: newsletters; walking brochure.
Hours & Admission Prices: June to mid-Sept. Tues.-Sat. 11-4. Adults $5; members no charge.
Attendance: 7,000
Membership: $5; $10; $15; $25; $150.

Parishville

PARISHVILLE MUSEUM, 1785 Main St., Parishville, NY 13672. Mailing Address: Box 534, Parishville, NY 13672-0534. Tel.: 315-265-7619.
Founded: 1964.
Key Personnel: Pres., Joseph McGill; Vice Pres., Sherry Remington.
Personnel Profile: Part-Time Paid 1.
Governing Authority: society. Tax-exempt: 501(c)(3).
History Museum: located in 1800 home.
Collections: items pertaining to early days of Parishville; 1850 & 1865 census; cemetery listings for each cemetery; obituary scrap books.
Research Fields: genealogy.
Facilities: library of history books available for research on premises.
Activities: guided tours; permanent exhibitions.
Publications: sketches of Parishville.
Hours & Admission Prices: July-Aug. Tues. & Thurs. 1-3; other times by appointment. No charge; donations accepted.
Attendance: 250 (estimated)
Membership: Annual $2; Life $15.

Paul Smiths

ADIRONDACK PARK VISITOR INTERPRETIVE CENTER, 8023 State Rte. 30, Paul Smiths, NY 12970-2107. Tel.: 518-327-3000.
Web Site: adkvic.org
Founded: 1989.
Key Personnel: Environmental Educator & Facility Mgr., Mike Brennan.
Personnel Profile: Full-Time Paid 7; Part-Time Paid 5; Part-Time Volunteers 30.
Governing Authority: state. Parent Institution: Adirondack Park Agency.
Nature Center.
Collections: natural history.
Facilities: hiking trails; butterfly house; educational programs. Museum Sponsors: live raptor demonstrations in summer.
Activities: slide presentations.
Publications: Adirondack Observer.
Hours & Admission Prices: Tues.-Sat. 9-5. No charge; donations accepted. Closed Thanksgiving; Christmas. ♿
Attendance: 68,000 (accurate)

Pawling

GUNNISON MUSEUM OF NATURAL HISTORY, 378 Old Quaker Hill Rd., Pawling, NY 12564-3449. Mailing Address: P.O. Box 345, Pawling, NY 12564-0345. Tel.: 845-855-5099.
Founded: 1960.
Key Personnel: Pres., Thomas Schroth; Cur., Mrs. James Mandracchia.
Personnel Profile: Part-Time Paid 1.
Governing Authority: Akin Hall Association. Tax-exempt: 501(c)(3).
Natural History Museum.
Collections: Gunnison collection of rocks, minerals, native birds & flora; agriculture; anatomy; entomology; geology; Indian artifacts; African & Asian musical instruments; mineralogy; natural history.
Facilities: 100-vol. library of natural history reference books available for use on premises.
Hours & Admission Prices: May-Oct. Fri.-Sun. 1-4. No charge; donations accepted.
Attendance: 1,000

HISTORICAL SOCIETY OF QUAKER HILL & PAWLING, 126 E. Main St., Pawling, NY 12564-1428. Mailing Address: P.O. Box 99, Pawling, NY 12564-0099. Tel.: 845-855-9316.
E-mail: nadadavis@msn.com
Web Site: www.pawling-history.org
Formerly: Historical Society of Quaker Hill & Pawling/John Kane House
Founded: 1910.
Congressional District: 19
Key Personnel: Pres. (V), Nada Davis; Membership, Charlotte Whaley; Museum Shop Mgr., Mrs. Jeanne Kelly.
Personnel Profile: Part-Time Volunteers 84.
Governing Authority: private; nonprofit organization. Tax-exempt: 501(c)(3).
Historical Society.
Collections: John Kane House: George Washington's headquarters in Autumn 1778, memorabilia from Lowell Thomas, radio broadcaster, lecturer & world traveler; the 1764 Oblong Meeting House: Gen. Washington used as a hospital for his troops in 1778; Akin Free Library: containing a Quaker Museum & Natural History Museum.
Facilities: library; botanical garden. Gift items for sale.
Activities: arts festivals; docent program; lectures; temporary exhibitions; Heirloom Day, bring your antiques to be appraised; Quilt Show; Art Exhibition, local artists. Annual Events: Tag Sale; Holiday Open House.
Publications: three times a year newsletter, Historical Society Newsletter.
Hours & Admission Prices: May 15-Oct. 15 Sat.-Sun. 2-4. Special opening 2nd weekend in Dec. No charge; donations accepted.
Attendance: 418 (accurate)

Peekskill

THE PEEKSKILL MUSEUM, 124 Union Ave., Peekskill, NY 10566-3429. Mailing Address: P.O. Box 84, Peekskill, NY 10566-0084. Tel.: 914-736-0473.
Web Site: www.peekskillmuseum.com
Founded: 1946.
Congressional District: 21
Key Personnel: Pres. (V), John Curran; Vice Pres., William Stillman; Treas., Paula Connolly; Corresponding Sec., Dolores Ubben.
Personnel Profile: Part-Time Volunteers 10.
Governing Authority: nonprofit organization. Tax-exempt.
Historic Building & History Museum: housed in 1876-77 Dwight Herrick House.
Collections: Peekskill memorabilia from Colonial period to present day; paintings; furniture; delftware; tureens; prints; period dresses; spinning wheels & looms; local newspapers; local stoves & plows; Revolutionary War cannon. Historic House: 1870s William Rutherford Mead house.
Research Fields: coal stove manufacturers; local & county history 1830-present.
Facilities: archives; research room.
Activities: lectures; formally organized education programs for children; permanent & temporary exhibitions.
Publications: quarterly newsletter, The Peekskill Museum.
Hours & Admission Prices: May-Dec. Sat. 1-3, weekdays by appointment. Adults $2, children $1; members no charge. ♿
Attendance: 500
Membership: Senior Citizen & Student $15; Family $25; Supporting $50; Benefactor $100; Corporate, Business & Contributor $150; Donor $250; Patron $500 and up.

Pelham

PELHAM ART CENTER, 155 Fifth Ave., Pelham, NY 10803-1503. Tel.: 914-738-2525. Fax: 914-738-2686.
E-mail: info@pelhamartcenter.org
Web Site: www.pelhamartcenter.org
Founded: 1972.
Congressional District: 20
Key Personnel: Dir., Lisa Robb; Chm. (V), Andrea Bayer; Pres. (V), Nancy Davis.
Personnel Profile: Full-Time Paid 3; Part-Time Paid 3; Part-Time Volunteers 3; Interns 1.
Governing Authority: nonprofit. Tax-exempt: 501(c)(3).
Art Center.
Collections: annual visual art & craft exhibitions; all forms of art media represented.
Facilities: 2 educational studios; darkroom; kilns. Museum-related items for sale.
Activities: guided tours; lectures; concerts; art classes; outreach programs.

Publications: class catalogs; summer camp catalog; calendar of events; Neighbor to Neighbor Discount Program; Birthday Flyer; Invitation to Exhibits.
Hours & Admission Prices: Tues.-Fri. 10-5, Sat. 10-4. No charge; donations accepted. Closed New Year's Day; Memorial Day; Independence Day; Columbus Day; Thanksgiving; Christmas. ♿
Attendance: 13,000 (estimated)
Membership: Senior & Educator $25; Individual $40; Family $60; Patron $125; Sponsor $250; Benefactor $500; Ansel $1,000.

Penn Yan

THE AGRICULTURAL MEMORIES MUSEUM, 1110 Townline Rd., Penn Yan, NY 14527-9002. Tel.: 315-536-1206.
E-mail: jrjensen@copper.net
Web Site: www.agriculturalmemoriesmuseum.com
Founded: 1997.
Key Personnel: Owner, Jennifer R. Jensen; Asst., Hilbert J. Jensen.
Governing Authority: private.
Agricultural Museum.
Collections: horse-drawn carriages & sleighs; period tractors; gasoline engines; toys; signs; pedal tractors & cars.
Research Fields: collection.
Facilities: library; 6,500 sq. ft. exhibit space.
Activities: films; guided tours; lectures.
Hours & Admission Prices: June-Oct. by appointment. Adults $4, students & children 2-12 $1; discounts to groups; children under 2 no charge.
Attendance: 250 (estimated)

YATES COUNTY GENEALOGICAL AND HISTORICAL SOCIETY AND OLIVER HOUSE MUSEUM AND L. CAROLINE UNDERWOOD MUSEUM, 107 Chapel St., Penn Yan, NY 14527-1128. Tel.: 315-536-7318. Fax: 315-536-0976.
E-mail: ycghs@yatespast.org
Web Site: www.yatespast.org
Founded: 1860.
Congressional District: 31
Key Personnel: Exec. Dir, John Potter; Association Pres., Bruce Warfield; Cur., Charles Mitchell; Administrative Asst., Greta Mickey.
Personnel Profile: Part-Time Paid 4; Part-Time Volunteers 50.
Governing Authority: society; nonprofit. Yates County Genealogical & Historical Society, Inc. Tax-exempt: 501(c)(3).
History Museum: housed in 1852 Oliver House.
Collections: 19th-century home furnishings; period rooms; costumes; portraits; photographs; manuscripts; maps & documents; tools & agricultural implements; material relating to Jemima Wilkinson; Indian artifacts; genealogical & local history research materials.
Research Fields: historic preservation; genealogical; architecture & archaeology; cultural impact of Indians & early white settlers on area; county history.
Facilities: research library, archival material & collections in storage available for research use upon approval of director; work rooms. Publications & gift items for sale.
Activities: guided tours; permanent & temporary exhibitions; slide shows; school outreach service; historic craft classes; genealogical classes; lectures; historical programs.
Publications: monthly newsletter, Yates Past.
Hours & Admission Prices: Tues.-Fri. 9-4. Museum: no charge; donations accepted. Research Room: $5 per hr.; discounts to YCGHS members. Closed major holidays. ♿
Attendance: 5,000 (estimated)
Membership: Individual $20; Family $30; Patron $75; Business Partner $100; Sustaining $200; Business Sustaining $250.

Pittsford

HISTORIC PITTSFORD, 18 Monroe Ave., Pittsford, NY 14534-1928. Tel.: 585-381-2941.
E-mail: kliklyjr@rochester.rr.com
Web Site: www.historicpittsford.com
Founded: 1966.
Congressional District: 30
Key Personnel: Dir., Kenneth Likly.
Personnel Profile: Part-Time Paid 1; Part-Time Volunteers 18.
Governing Authority: nonprofit corp. Tax-exempt: 501(c)(3).
Historic House: 1820 lawyer's office.
Collections: local history & culture; period furnishings.
Research Fields: local architecture.
Facilities: 200-vol. library of old law books available for research by appointment. Books & museum-related items for sale.
Activities: lectures; formally organized education programs for adults; architectural consultant program; permanent exhibitions.
Publications: biannual, Historic Pittsford Newsletter; folder, A Walking Tour Map of Historic Pittsford; book, Architecture Worth Saving in Pittsford, Elegant Village; Pittsford Scrapbook (stories of early Pittsford).
Hours & Admission Prices: Wed. & Sat. 9-12; other times by appointment. No charge.
Attendance: 450 (estimated)
Membership: Family $25; Business, Professional & Patron $100; Life $300.

Plattsburgh

CLINTON COUNTY HISTORICAL ASSOCIATION & MUSEUM, 98 Ohio Ave., Plattsburgh, NY 12903-4401. Tel.: 518-561-0340. Fax: 518-561-0340.
E-mail: director@clintoncountyhistorical.org
Web Site: www.clintoncountyhistorical.org
Founded: 1945.
Congressional District: 24
Key Personnel: Pres., Roger Harwood; Vice Pres., William Laundry; Sec., Jan Couture; Treas., Maurica Gilbert; Dir., Carol Blakeslee-Collin; Museum Shop Mgr., James Bailey.
Personnel Profile: Part-Time Paid 1; Part-Time Volunteers 4.
Governing Authority: nonprofit organization. Parent Institution: Clinton County Historical Association. Tax-exempt: 501(c)(3).
Historical Society Museum.
Collections: local history; paintings; maps; firearms; glass; ceramics; textiles; photographs; furniture; costumes; period clothing; negatives of late 19th & early 20th-century citizens & scenery.
Research Fields: Redford glass; iron mining in Clinton County; 18th & 19th-century military & naval warfare in the Champlain Valley; maritime culture of Lake Champlain.
Facilities: Local history publications for sale.
Activities: guided tours; lectures; docent program; organized education programs for adults, children & undergraduate or graduate college students affiliated with State University College at Plattsburgh; loan & temporary exhibitions.
Publications: semiannual newsletter, North Country Notes.
Hours & Admission Prices: Wed.-Sat. 10-3. Adults $4, seniors $3, children $2; discounts to AAA, AAM & ICOM members; school groups, Historical Association & members no charge. Closed legal holidays. ♿
Attendance: 1,000 (estimated)
Membership: Student $10; Individual $30; Family $50; Friend $90; Patron $150; Sponsor $300; Sustaining $600; Life $1,500.

KENT-DELORD HOUSE MUSEUM, (M), 17 Cumberland Ave., Plattsburgh, NY 12901-1849. Tel.: 518-561-1035. Fax: 518-562-1893.
E-mail: jkruegervt@msn.com
Web Site: www.kentdelordhouse.org
Founded: 1924.
Congressional District: 26
Key Personnel: Pres., Patricia Loughan; Dir., John Krueger.
Personnel Profile: Part-Time Paid 1; Part-Time Volunteers 25.
Governing Authority: Kent-Delord Corporation. Tax-exempt.
Historic House Museum: c.1797, Kent-Delord home.
Collections: period furnishings; paintings; 18th & 19th century decorative arts; manuscripts; photographs; textiles.
Research Fields: War of 1812; Civil War; Woman's Christian Temperance Union; 19th & early 20th century social work; domestic life in the 19th-century.
Facilities: off site access to manuscript collection.
Activities: guided tours; special exhibits; cultural events; educational programs; garden club.
Publications: book, Henry Delord & His Family; newsletter/journal, The Kent-Delord Quarterly; Love & Duty: Letters & Diaries of the Delord-Webb Women.
Hours & Admission Prices: Tues.-Fri. 12-2, Sat. call for hours; guided tours & group tours by appointment. Adults $5, students $3, children under 12 $2; discounts for groups; members no charge. ♿
Attendance: 8,000 (accurate)
Membership: Quartermaster Club $35; Bellevue Avenue Club $60; Carriage Club $100; Third Century Society $300.

PLATTSBURGH STATE ART MUSEUM S.U.N.Y., State University of New York, 101 Broad St., Plattsburgh, NY 12901-2637. Mailing Address: State University of New York, Myers Room 235, 101 Broad St., Plattsburgh, NY 12901-2637. Tel.: 518-564-2474 & 2178. Fax: 518-564-2473.
E-mail: ceil.esposito@plattsburgh.edu
Web Site: clubs.plattsburgh.edu/museum
Founded: 1952.
Congressional District: 26

Key Personnel: C.E.O., John Ettling; Dir., Cecilia M. Esposito; Mgr. Collections, David Driver.
Personnel Profile: Full-Time Paid 3; Part-Time Paid 2.
Governing Authority: university. Parent Institution: State University of New York. Tax-exempt: 170(b)(1)(A).
Art Museum & Galleries.
Collections: paintings, drawings, prints & sculptures; Rockwell Kent collection including 36 paintings, 100 prints, 1,500 drawings, sketches, proofs & designs; books owned by Kent; books about the artist; a set of first editions written or illustrated by Kent; bookplates, stationery, trademarks; Christmas cards; commercial illustration proofs; exhibition catalogs; Nina Winkel sculptures; Millet Asian collection; Ackerman modern art; Regina Slatkin art; 19th-century drawing, prints & sculptures.
Research Fields: Rockwell Kent; Nina Winkel; American Art 20th & 21st centuries.
Facilities: changing exhibition gallery; permanent collection gallery; work room, curatorial room; special collections reference room where Kent material is available for research upon request; Winkel sculpture court; Regina Slatkin Art Collection study room.
Activities: guided tours; visiting artist lectures; gallery talks; formally organized education programs for undergraduate students at the university, also available to elementary, secondary schools & community groups in the geographic area; 24 exhibitions each year; antique & contemporary, all media.
Publications: exhibition catalogs; quarterly journal, Kent Collector; monthly exhibition announcements; semiannual calendar of events.
Hours & Admission Prices: Jan. 2-Dec. 23 daily 12-4. No charge; donations accepted. Closed legal holidays. ♿
Attendance: 17,614 (estimated)

Port Jefferson

HISTORICAL SOCIETY OF GREATER PORT JEFFERSON, 115 Prospect St., Port Jefferson, NY 11777-1812. Mailing Address: Box 586, Port Jefferson, NY 11777-0586. Tel.: 631-473-2665.
E-mail: info@portjeffhistorical.org
Web Site: www.portjeffhistorical.org
Founded: 1967.
Congressional District: 1
Key Personnel: Pres. (V), Nick Acampora; Museum Shop Co-Mgr., Eileen Coen.
Personnel Profile: Part-Time Paid 3; Part-Time Volunteers 100.
Governing Authority: nonprofit organization. Tax-exempt.
Maritime Museum: housed in c.1840 John R. Mather homestead & out buildings.
Collections: maps; books; half hulls; paintings; sailmaker's tools & loft; shipbuilding artifacts & tools; tin items; looms; c.1900 diorama of Port Jefferson Harbor; maritime art, photographs, artifacts & memorabilia depicting the shipping industry of Port Jefferson; country store, butcher shop & barber shop replicas.
Research Fields: marine history; local artists and history.
Facilities: 175-vol. library of records, deeds, logs, ships records, maps, craft house, perennial garden, books, histories & newspapers available for inter-library loan & by appointment; gardens.
Activities: permanent & temporary exhibitions; educational tours for children; regular meetings.
Publications: catalogue; booklet, Port Jefferson-Story of a Village.
Hours & Admission Prices: Memorial Day to June Sat.-Sun. 1-4; July-Aug. Tues.-Wed. & Sat.-Sun. 1-4. Family $5, adults $3; children & members no charge. ♿
Attendance: 1,600 (estimated)
Membership: Single $25; Family, Business, & Professional $35; Contributing $50.

Port Jervis

MINISINK VALLEY HISTORICAL SOCIETY, 125-133 W. Main St., Port Jervis, NY 12771. Mailing Address: P.O. Box 659, Port Jervis, NY 12771-0659. Tel.: 845-856-2375. Fax: 845-856-1049.
E-mail: history@minisink.org
Web Site: www.minisink.org
Founded: 1889.
Congressional District: 20
Key Personnel: Exec. Dir., Peter Osborne, III; Pres., Robert Shultz; Treas., Nancy Conod.
Personnel Profile: Full-Time Paid 1; Part-Time Volunteers 15.
Governing Authority: nonprofit organization. Tax-exempt: 501(c)(3).
Historical Society Museum: housed in 1793 stone home.
Collections: genealogical data; family files; photographs; local history.
Research Fields: Delaware & Hudson Canal; railroads; Civil War; Indians.
Facilities: 50,000-vol. library for public use. Books and other related items for sale.
Activities: guided tours; lectures; broadcast programs; loan, temporary & traveling exhibitions. Society Sponsors: Christmas program for local groups.
Publications: triannual newsletter.
Hours & Admission Prices: Library: Thurs. 1-4; other times by appointment. Suggested Donation $4; discounts to members. Museum: July-Oct. Sat. 10-4. No charge; donations accepted. ♿
Attendance: 15,000
Membership: Individual $15; Family $20; Business $50.

Port Washington

COW NECK PENINSULA HISTORICAL SOCIETY SANDS-WILLETS HOUSE, 336 Port Washington Blvd., Port Washington, NY 11050-4530. Tel.: 516-365-9074.
E-mail: info@cowneck.org
Web Site: www.cowneck.org
Founded: 1962.
Congressional District: 6
Key Personnel: Pres. (V), Fred Blumlein; Treas., Richard Coyle; Cur., Harrison Hunt; Dir. Education, Mary Alice Puglise; Museum Shop Mgr., Evelyn Fitzsimmons.
Personnel Profile: Part-Time Paid 3; Part-Time Volunteers 25.
Governing Authority: nonprofit organization. Branch Museum: Thomas Dodge House, 58 Harbor Rd., Port Washington, NY 11050. Tax-exempt: 501(c)(3).
Historical Society Museum.
Collections: Port Washington history; 18th-century costumes; 19th-century quilts; 18th to early 20th-century decorative arts; toys; dolls; manuscript archives; photographs. Historic Buildings: c.1735 Sands-Willets House; c.1721 Thomas Dodge House; c.1690 Dutch Barn.
Research Fields: Port Washington history; Long Island history; Dodge and Sands family history.
Facilities: 100-vol. library of books on Long Island available for research on premises only. Museum-related items for sale.
Activities: guided tours; lectures; hobby workshops; formally organized education programs; temporary exhibitions. Annual Events: Dodge House Day in summer; Fall Fair in September; Holiday Fair in November; Christmas Party in December.
Publications: annual journal, Cow Neck Peninsula Historical Society; publications, The Mill Pond; Lower Main Street; Sketchbook of Cow Neck Houses; How to Research Your House; Historic Mitchell Farms.
Hours & Admission Prices: Sands-Willets House: Sun. 2-4, Wed. 10-2; other times by appointment. Dodge House: April-Nov. 2nd Sat. of month 1-5; other times by appointment. Adults $3, children $1; discount to groups & AAM members; members no charge. Closed holidays.
Attendance: 3,000 (estimated)
Membership: Student $10; Individual $25; Family $35; Sustaining $50; Sponsor $100; Life $500.

POLISH AMERICAN MUSEUM, 16 Belleview Ave., Port Washington, NY 11050-3607. Tel.: 516-883-6542.
Founded: 1977.
Congressional District: 3
Key Personnel: Pres., Barbara Szydlowski; 1st Vice Pres., Julian S. Jurus; 2nd Vice Pres., Steve Szachacz; Treas., Michael Levchuck; Recording Sec., Wilma Wierbicki; Historian, Irene Wierzbicki; Cur., Gerald Kochan.
Personnel Profile: Part-Time Volunteers 25.
Governing Authority: nonprofit organization. Polish American Museum Admin., 16 Belleview Ave, Port Washington, NY 11050. Tax-exempt: 501(c)(3).
Folk Art Museum & Library.
Collections: woodcarvings; glass; art; china; tapestry all from Poland; Polish language library; Archacki archives; history display.
Research Fields: Polish & Polish American history.
Facilities: 15,000-vol. library pertaining to Polish history & culture available for research on premise; photocopy available; reading room; classrooms. Items imported from Poland for sale.
Activities: lectures; films; hobby workshops; permanent exhibitions; historical & educational videotapes.
Publications: quarterly newsletter; annual journal.
Hours & Admission Prices: Wed.-Fri. 10-2, Sat.-Sun. by appointment. No charge; donations accepted. Closed legal holidays.
Attendance: 1,200 (estimated)
Membership: Active $25; Supporting $50; Life $500; Founder $1,000.

THE SALGO TRUST FOR EDUCATION, 95 Middle Neck Rd., Port Washington, NY 11050-1218. Tel.: 516-767-3654. Fax: 516-767-7881.
Founded: 1994.

Key Personnel: Trustee, Miklos Salgo; Trustee, Christina Salgo; Collection Mgr., Eileen Baral.
Governing Authority: Tax-exempt.
Art Museum.
Collections: Hungarian paintings, sculpture & silver 15th-18th century, saddles, saddle rugs & horse covers; French & European furniture & decorations; Chinese art; game boards & draughtsmen.
Research Fields: Hungarian painting & sculpture.
Facilities: library.
Hours & Admission Prices: By appointment only. No charge.

Potsdam

POTSDAM PUBLIC MUSEUM, (M), Civic Center at Park St., Potsdam, NY 13676. Mailing Address: P.O. Box 5168, Potsdam, NY 13676-5168. Tel.: 315-265-6910. Fax: 315-265-3149.
E-mail: museum@vi.potsdam.ny.us
Web Site: www.potsdampublicmuseum.org
Founded: 1940.
Congressional District: 30
Key Personnel: Dir. & Cur., Mimi Van Deusen; Pres. (V), Sharon Pickard.
Personnel Profile: Full-Time Paid 1; Part-Time Paid 4; Part-Time Volunteers 3.
Governing Authority: municipal. Parent Institution: Village of Potsdam. Tax-exempt: 170(b)(A)(IV).
Decorative Arts & History Museum: housed in 1876 sandstone church.
Collections: decorative arts including Burnap collection of English pottery; glass; American china; costumes; local historical artifacts & furniture; archives on local & county history; manuscripts; ceramics; glass; textiles; photographs; tools; paintings.
Research Fields: English pottery; glass; 19th & 20th-century costumes; American decorative arts; history of state, county, town & village; textiles.
Facilities: 50-vol. library.
Activities: guided tours; lectures; films; gallery talks; formally organized education programs for children, adults & undergraduate college students affiliated with State University College at Potsdam & Clarkson University; inter-museum loan, permanent & temporary exhibitions; self-guided architectural walking tour of Potsdam; school loan service.
Publications: Potsdam Museum Newsletter; booklets, Early History of Potsdam; Gallantry in the Field, Potsdam & the Civil War; Burnap Collection of Potsdam Museum; Clarkson Family of Potsdam; book, Images of America: Potsdam.
Hours & Admission Prices: Tues.-Sat. 12-6. No charge; donations accepted. Closed state & national holidays. ♿
Attendance: 15,300 (estimated)

ROLAND GIBSON GALLERY, (M), 44 Pierrepont Ave., State Univ. of New York at Potsdam, Potsdam, NY 13676-2200. Tel.: 315-267-3290. Fax: 315-267-4884.
E-mail: vasherak@potsdam.edu
Web Site: www.potsdam.edu/gibson/gibson.html
Founded: 1968.
Congressional District: 30
Key Personnel: Dir., April Vasher-Dean; Cur. Collections, Margaret Price; Registrar, Romi Sebald-Chudzinski; Dept. Sec., Claudette Fefee.
Personnel Profile: Full-Time Paid 4; Part-Time Paid 6; Interns 1.
Governing Authority: state. Affiliated with the State University of New York, University Plaza, Albany, NY 12246. Parent Institution: SUNY College at Potsdam. Tax-exempt.
University Art Museum.
Collections: contemporary sculpture, prints, ceramics, drawings & paintings; the Roland Gibson collection of 20th-century contemporary art.
Research Fields: pertaining to exhibitions & collections.
Facilities: 300-vol. library of catalogs from previous shows & catalogs from other galleries and museums, available on request; changing exhibition galleries; work & study room.
Activities: lectures; films; gallery talks; workshops; concerts; arts festivals; formally organized education programs; museum studies courses & internships; permanent, temporary, traveling & loan exhibitions.
Publications: catalogs on individual exhibitions; newsletter; brochures; posters; monthly bulletin.
Hours & Admission Prices: Summer: Wed.-Sat. 12-4; Academic Year: Mon. & Fri. 12-5, Tues. & Thurs. 12-7, Sat. 12-4. No charge; donations accepted. Closed college recesses; public holidays. ♿
Attendance: 14,000 (estimated)
Membership: Senior Citizen $10; Individual $15; Family $25; Contributing $100; Supporting $250; Patron $500; Benefactor $1,000.

Poughkeepsie

ART GALLERY MARIST COLLEGE, 3399 North Rd., Poughkeepsie, NY 12601-1387. Tel.: 845-575-3000, ext. 2308. Fax: 845-471-6213.
E-mail: edward.smith@marist.edu
Web Site: www.marist.edu/commarts/art/gallery.html
Founded: 1995.
Key Personnel: Dir., Edward Smith; Chm. Art Dept., Richard Lewis.
Personnel Profile: Interns 5.
Governing Authority: Parent Institution: Marist College. Tax-exempt.
Art Museum.
Collections: paintings; sculptures; photographs; contemporary work of artists from the Hudson Valley region & New York City.
Facilities: 3,500 sq. ft. exhibit space.
Activities: lectures; artist talks.
Publications: gallery announcements; occasional exhibition catalogues.
Hours & Admission Prices: Sept.-May Mon.-Sat. 12-5. No charge. ♿
Attendance: 2,000 (estimated)

DUTCHESS COUNTY HISTORICAL SOCIETY, Clinton House, 549 Main St., Poughkeepsie, NY 12601. Mailing Address: P.O. Box 88, Poughkeepsie, NY 12602-0088. Tel.: 845-471-1630. Fax: 845-471-8777.
E-mail: dchistorical@verizon.net
Web Site: www.dutchesscountyhistoricalsociety.org
Founded: 1914.
Congressional District: 25
Key Personnel: Pres. (V), Stephen Mann; Research Coord., Stephanie Mauri.
Personnel Profile: Part-Time Paid 2; Part-Time Volunteers 8; Interns 1.
Governing Authority: society; nonprofit. Building owned by the N.Y. State Office of Parks & Recreation & Historic Preservation. Branch Museum: 1767 Glebe House Museum, Poughkeepsie, NY 12601. Tax-exempt: 501(c)(3).
Historical Society Museum: housed in c.1765 Clinton House, used as NY state capitol during the Revolutionary War.
Collections: manuscripts & artifacts relating to the history of Dutchess County; photographs.
Research Fields: local history; oral history; genealogy; material culture.
Facilities: library of 500-volumes of printed local history, 25,000 manuscripts & 50,000 images, available for use under supervised conditions.
Activities: tours; temporary & traveling exhibitions; meetings; seminars; symposia.
Publications: Yearbook; newsletter, Dutchess Historian; 18th Century Documents of the Nine Partners Patent; County at Large; Family Vista; Portraits of Dutchess County; Glebe House; 150th Anniversary of the Ratification of the United States Constitution; 250th Anniversary of Poughkeepsie; Dutchess County 1778 - Year of Trial, Year of Transition; FDR at Home.
Hours & Admission Prices: Tues.-Fri. 10-3 by appointment only. Library: $20; members no charge. Closed New Year's Eve & Day; Memorial Day; Independence Day; Labor Day; Thanksgiving & day after; Christmas Eve & Day. ♿
Attendance: 4,236 (estimated)
Membership: Individual $50; Family & Contributor $75; Sustaining $100; Patron $250; Sponsor $500; Millennial Circle $1,000.

* **THE FRANCES LEHMAN LOEB ART CENTER, (M),** 124 Raymond Ave., Vassar College, Poughkeepsie, NY 12604-0001. Mailing Address: Box 703, Vassar College, Poughkeepsie, NY 12604-0001. Tel.: 845-437-5237 & LOEB (5632). Fax: 845-437-5955.
E-mail: jamundy@vassar.edu
Web Site: fllac.vassar.edu
Founded: 1864.
Congressional District: 25
Key Personnel: Ann Hendricks Bass Dir., James Mundy; The Phlip & Lynn Strauss Cur. Prints & Drawings, Patricia Phagan; Registrar & Collections Mgr., Joann Potter; Asst. Registrar, Karen Hines; Preparator, Bruce Bundock; Coord. Membership, Special Events & Volunteer Svcs., Jennifer Cole; Office Specialist, Francine Brown; Membership & Accounting Asst., Bev Doppel; The Emily Hargroves Fisher '57 & Richard B. Fisher Cur., Mary-Kay Lombino; Coord. Public Education & Information, Nicole M. Roylance.
Personnel Profile: Full-Time Paid 12; Part-Time Paid 2; Part-Time Volunteers 20; Interns 1.
Governing Authority: college. Parent Institution: Vassar College. Tax-exempt: 501(c)(3).
Art Museum.
Collections: American & European painting & sculpture, medieval to modern; Magoon collection of Hudson River School & other 19th-century American paintings; Greek & Roman antiquities; Asian art; drawings & watercolors; photographs; Old Master & modern prints.
Research Fields: all fields pertaining to the collection.

Facilities: 25,000-vol. library of books pertaining to art available for interlibrary loan & for use on the premises. Catalogues, posters & other art-related items for sale.
Activities: gallery talks; permanent & temporary exhibitions.
Publications: occasional catalogues; members' quarterly newsletter.
Hours & Admission Prices: Tues.-Wed. & Fri.-Sat 10-5, Thurs. 10-9, Sun. 1-5. No charge. Closed New Year's Eve & Day; Thanksgiving Day; Christmas Eve, Day & week. ♿
Attendance: 36,000 (estimated)
Membership: Friends of the Frances Lehman Loeb Art Center: Student $10; Participating $35; Contributing $100; Sustaining $250; Donor $500; Patron $1,000.

LOCUST GROVE, THE SAMUEL MORSE HISTORIC SITE, 2683 South Rd., Poughkeepsie, NY 12601-5275. Tel.: 845-454-4500, ext. 10. Fax: 845-485-7122.
E-mail: info@lgny.org
Web Site: www.lgny.org
Founded: 1979.
Congressional District: 25
Key Personnel: Exec. Dir., Kenneth Snodgrass.
Personnel Profile: Full-Time Paid 7; Part-Time Paid 20; Part-Time Volunteers 50.
Governing Authority: nonprofit organization. Private trust. Tax-exempt: 501(c)(3).
Historic Site: 1847 residence of Samuel F.B. Morse.
Collections: furniture; china; costumes; dolls; documents; manuscripts; telegraph equipment.
Research Fields: life of Samuel F.B. Morse.
Facilities: 3,000-vol. library of history & literature books; wildlife sanctuary; hiking trails; visitor center.
Activities: guided tours; lectures; formally organized education programs; training programs for professional museum workers; temporary exhibitions.
Publications: newsletters; brochures.
Hours & Admission Prices: Visitor Center: March-Dec. daily 10-5. Tours: May-Nov. daily 10-5; Dec. call for hours; groups by appointment only. Adults $10, youth 6-18 $6; discounts to AAM members; Friends members no charge.
Attendance: 20,000 (accurate)

MID-HUDSON CHILDREN'S MUSEUM, 75 N. Water St., Poughkeepsie, NY 12601-1720. Tel.: 845-471-0589. Fax: 845-471-0415.
E-mail: info@mhcm.org
Web Site: www.mhcm.org
Founded: 1989.
Congressional District: 19
Key Personnel: Exec. Dir., Ed Glisson; Pres. (V), Tracy Cass MacKenzie, Esq.; Treas., Steve Loehr; Dir. Devel., Rena Ann Hill; Interpretive Educator, Lisa diMarzo.
Personnel Profile: Full-Time Paid 4; Part-Time Paid 13; Part-Time Volunteers 7.
Governing Authority: private; nonprofit organization. Tax-exempt: 501(c)(3).
Children's Museum.
Collections: hands-on exhibits.
Facilities: 12,000 sq. ft. exhibit space; planetarium.
Activities: concerts; formal education programs for children; guided tours; hobby workshops; lectures; loan, traveling & participatory exhibitions; school loan service. Annual Event: Golf Tournament Fundraising event.
Publications: quarterly newsletter; calendar of events; annual report.
Hours & Admission Prices: Mon. school holidays call for hours; Tues.-Fri. 9:30-5; Sat.-Sun. 11-5. Private Tours: Tues.-Fri. 9 am. Admission $6.50; members & children under 2 no charge. Closed New Year's Day; Easter; Memorial Day; Independence Day; Labor Day; Thanksgiving; Christmas. ♿
Attendance: 60,000 (estimated)
Membership: Scholarship $40; Family $70; Family Plus $85; Reciprocal $100.

Pound Ridge

POUND RIDGE SOCIETY/MUSEUM, 255 Westchester Ave., Pound Ridge, NY 10576. Mailing Address: P.O. Box 51, Pound Ridge, NY 10576-0051. Tel.: 914-764-4333 (museum). Fax: 914-764-1778.
Web Site: www.prhsmuseum.org
Founded: 1983.
Congressional District: 20
Key Personnel: Pres. (V), Richard Major; Treas., Norman Tunnell.
Personnel Profile: Part-Time Volunteers 21.
Governing Authority: private; nonprofit organization. Parent Institution: Pound Ridge Historical Society. Tax-exempt: 501(c)(3).
Historical Society Museum: housed in an 1853 wooden frame building.
Collections: concentration on items pertaining to Pound Ridge; prehistoric remains; Native American articles; early tools; archives; letters; diaries; costumes & textiles; maps; documents; furniture; photographs.
Research Fields: railroading, history of Pound Ridge in all its facets.
Facilities: 50-vol. library on local history; 600 sq. ft. exhibit space. Gift items for sale.
Activities: docent program; educational programs, lectures, walking tours; oral history; exhibitions & publications. Annual Events: bus tours, antiques show; annual April meeting.
Publications: newsletter; booklets concerning Pound Ridge history.
Hours & Admission Prices: March-Dec. Sat.-Sun. 2-4; groups by appointment. No charge; donations accepted.
Attendance: 350 (estimated)
Membership: Youth under 18 $3; Individual $15; Family $25; Business $30; Patron $50; Sponsor $100; Sustaining $250; Lifetime $300;

Prattsburgh

NARCISSA PRENTISS HOUSE, 7225 County Rte. 75, Prattsburgh, NY 14873. Mailing Address: P.O. Box 307, Prattsburgh, NY 14873-0384. Tel.: 607-522-4537.
Founded: 1940.
Congressional District: 39
Key Personnel: Dir. & Pres. (V), Charlene Wilson; Chm. (V), Vicki Kopylczak.
Personnel Profile: Part-Time Paid 1; Part-Time Volunteers 10.
Governing Authority: nonprofit organization. Parent Institution: Committee to Preserve the Narcissa Prentiss House. Tax-exempt.
Historic House: c.1805 birthplace of Narcissa Prentiss Whitman, missionary.
Collections: period furnishings; books on the Whitman-Spalding expedition & related historical-religious matters.
Activities: guided tours.
Publications: pamphlet; books.
Hours & Admission Prices: mid-June to Sept. Sat.-Sun. 1-4; other times by appointment. No charge; donations accepted. Closed Independence Day; Labor Day.
Attendance: 250 (estimated)
Membership: Annual $10.

Prattsville

ZADOCK PRATT MUSEUM, Main St., Rte. 23, Prattsville, NY 12468-0333. Mailing Address: P.O. Box 333, Prattsville, NY 12468-0333. Tel.: 518-299-3395.
Historic House: housed in the former home of Zadock Pratt, Prattsville town founder; built in c.1828. Listed on the National Register of Historic Places.
Collections: Pratt family life & history; local history & culture; period furnishings; photographs; tannery artifacts; Civil War.
Facilities: Museum-related items for sale.
Hours & Admission Prices: Memorial Day to Columbus Day Thurs.-Sun. 1-5. Suggested Donation: $3.

Purchase

* **NEUBERGER MUSEUM OF ART, PURCHASE COLLEGE, STATE UNIVERSITY OF NEW YORK, (M),** 735 Anderson Hill Rd., Purchase, NY 10577-1402. Tel.: 914-251-6100. Fax: 914-251-6101.
E-mail: neuberger@purchase.edu
Web Site: www.neuberger.org
Founded: 1974.
Congressional District: 24
Key Personnel: Dir., Thom Collins; Chm., Helen Stambler Neaberger; Vice Chair, Wendy Gold; Vice Chair, Rachel Stern; Dir. Devel., Lea Emery; Chief Cur., Helaine Posner; Cur. African Art, Marie Therese Brincard; Head Museum Education, Eleanor P. Brackbill; Public Programs, Elena Pelligrini; Registrar, Patricia Magnani; Mktg., Kristi McKee; Public Rels., Carolyn Mandelker; Museum Shop Mgr., Jane Barry.
Personnel Profile: Part-Time Paid 3; Part-Time Volunteers 120; Interns 6.
Governing Authority: state. Parent Institution: Purchase College, State University of New York. Tax-exempt.
University Art Museum.
Collections: 20th & 21st century art in all media; African art.
Research Fields: 20th-century art; contemporary & African arts.
Facilities: 25,000 sq. ft. exhibit space; cafe. Museum-related items for sale.
Activities: guided tours; biennial series of Yaseen lectures; concerts; films; seminars; educational programs for elementary & secondary school students; docent council; temporary exhibitions; interdepartmental projects with other divisions of the State University of New York at Purchase; internships; lectures; dance recitals; family programs; art workshops.
Publications: exhibition catalogues; The Language of Art, a looking guide for teachers; CD ROM on selected works in permanent collection; quarterly calendar of events.

Hours & Admission Prices: Tues.-Sun. 12-5. Adults $5, seniors $3; discounts to AAM, ICOM, AAMD & Channel 13; members no charge. Closed major holidays. ♿
Attendance: 56,500 (accurate)
Membership: Senior $40; Individual $50; Family $75; Contributor $150; Donor $250-$300; Patron $500; Sustainer $1,000; Director's Circle $2,500; Neuberger Circle $5,000.

Queens

NEW YORK HALL OF SCIENCE, 47-01 111th St., Queens, NY 11368-2999. Tel.: 718-699-0005. Fax: 718-699-1341.
E-mail: cnordin@nyscience.org
Web Site: www.nyscience.org
Founded: 1964.
Congressional District: 7
Key Personnel: Pres. & C.E.O., Margaret Honey; Dir. & Chief Content Officer, Eric Siegel; Exec. Vice Pres. & C.O.O., Rober Logan; Dir. Communications, Mary Record; Sr. Vice Pres. Education & Family Programs, Preeti Gupta.
Personnel Profile: Full-Time Paid 80; Part-Time Paid 180; Part-Time Volunteers 40; Interns 5.
Governing Authority: nonprofit organization. Tax-exempt: 501(c)(3).
Science Museum.
Collections: more than 400 hands-on science exhibits pertaining to biology, chemistry, sound, light & physics.
Research Fields: informal science education.
Facilities: library containing a multimedia interdisciplinary collection of science books; 60,000 sq. ft. outdoor science playground; space-themed miniature golf course; educational facilities. Science-related items for sale.
Activities: lectures; films; workshops; organized education programs for children & adults; teacher training; science career access program; participatory exhibits. Equipment for rent.
Publications: monthly e-newsletter.
Hours & Admission Prices: April-June Mon.-Thurs. 9:30-2, Fri. 9:30-5, Sat.-Sun. 10-6; July-Aug. Mon.-Fri. 9:30-5, Sat.-Sun. 10-6; Sept.-March Tues.-Thurs. 9:30-2, Fri. 9:30-5, Sat.-Sun. 10-6. Adults $11, children, senior citizens & college students $8; discounts to AAM & ASTC members; members no charge; groups by reservation Mon.-Fri. Closed Labor Day; Thanksgiving; Christmas. ♿
Attendance: 500,000 (estimated)
Membership: Individual $40; Senior $55; Corporate Plus $75; Family $85; Family Plus $110; Donor $175; Supporter $300.

QUEENS MUSEUM OF ART, New York City Bldg., Flushing Meadows Corona Park, Queens, NY 11368-3398. Tel.: 718-592-9700. Fax: 718-592-5778.
Web Site: www.queensmuse.org
Founded: 1972.
Congressional District: 8
Key Personnel: Exec. Dir., Tom Finkelpearl; Pres., Daniel Murphy; Dir. Finance, Julie Lou; Dir. Education, Lauren Schloss; Dir. Exhibitions, Hitomi Iwasaki; Museum Shop Mgr., Betty Abramowitz.
Personnel Profile: Full-Time Paid 40; Part-Time Paid 13; Part-Time Volunteers 120; Interns 4.
Governing Authority: nonprofit organization. Satellite Gallery: Queens Museum Art Bulova Corporate Center. Tax-exempt: 501(c)(3).
Art & Cultural Center.
Collections: paintings; sculpture; prints & photographs; The Panorama of the City of New York architectural scale model; Tiffany lamps from Egon & Hildegard Neustadt Museum collection.
Major Exhibits: Duke Riely & O Zhang, 11/09-1/10.
Research Fields: art history; American cultural history.
Facilities: theatre; workshops. Museum-related items for sale.
Activities: special exhibits, 25-30 per year; tours; lectures; films; education & community service programs for children & adults; programs for the handicapped; intern & docent volunteer programs.
Publications: catalogs & brochures of exhibitions; quarterly QMA mail.
Hours & Admission Prices: Wed.-Fri. 10-5, Sat.-Sun. 12-5. Suggested Donations: adults $5, senior citizens & students $2.50; discounts to AAM & ICOM members; members & children under 5 no charge. Closed New Year's Day; Thanksgiving; Christmas. ♿
Attendance: 85,216 (accurate)
Membership: Student & Senior Citizen $25; Individual $35; Family $55; Supporting $100; Friend $200; Sponsor $500; Collector's Circle $750.

Remsen

STEUBEN MEMORIAL STATE HISTORIC SITE, Starr Hill Rd., Remsen, NY 13438. Mailing Address: c/o Oriskany Battlefield SHS, 7801 State Rte. 69, Oriskany, NY 13424-4115. Tel.: 315-768-7224. Fax: 315-337-3081.
E-mail: nancy.demyttenaere@oprhp.state.ny.us
Web Site: www.nysparks.com
Founded: 1930.
Congressional District: 31
Key Personnel: Regl. Historic Preservation Supv., Nancy Demyttenaere; Second in Command, Bill Acomb.
Personnel Profile: Full-Time Paid 3; Part-Time Paid 2; Part-Time Volunteers 6.
Governing Authority: state. Parent Institution: New York State Office of Parks, Recreation and Historic Preservation. Tax-exempt: 501(c)(3).
Historic Site: burial site of Baron Friederich Wilhelm von Steuben, Drillmaster of American Army, located on land granted by New York State for services in the American Revolution.
Collections: reproduction log cabin; furniture; tomb; sacred grave; historic archives.
Facilities: picnic area.
Activities: guided tours; special programs.
Hours & Admission Prices: mid-May to Labor Day Wed.-Sat. 10-5, Sun. 1-5. No charge; donations accepted. ♿
Attendance: 6,785 (accurate)

Rensselaer

CRAILO STATE HISTORIC SITE, 9 1/2 Riverside Ave., Rensselaer, NY 12144-2927. Tel.: 518-463-8738. Fax: 518-433-1860.
E-mail: maryellen.grimaldi@oprhp.state.ny.us
Founded: 1924.
Congressional District: 29
Key Personnel: Historic Site Mgr., Heidi Hill.
Personnel Profile: Full-Time Paid 2; Part-Time Paid 2; Part-Time Volunteers 10; Interns 1.
Governing Authority: state. Parent Institution: New York State Office of Parks, Recreation & Historic Preservation; Saratoga/Capital District State Park, Recreation & Historic Preservation Commission. Tax-exempt: 501(c)(3).
Historic Building: c.1704, brick dwelling belonging to the Van Rensselaer family; used as museum of Dutch culture in the upper Hudson Valley.
Collections: history; Dutch colonial period artifacts; 17th-century archaeological materials; models; reproductions.
Research Fields: 17th & 18th century Dutch culture in the Hudson River Valley.
Facilities: picnic area.
Activities: permanent exhibitions; school programs; summer program for children; guided tours; special programs & demonstrations. Museum Sponsors: summer concerts; preservation day open house.
Publications: Clothing the Colonists.
Hours & Admission Prices: Nov.-March Mon.-Fri. 11-4 by appointment. Adults $5, seniors & students $4; discounts to groups; children 12 & under no charge. ♿
Attendance: 10,000 (accurate)
Membership: Friends of Crailo: Student & Senior $5; Individual $10; Family $15; Sustaining $25; Corporate Member $100; Patron $200.

Rhinebeck

RHINEBECK AERODROME MUSEUM, 9 Norton Rd., Rhinebeck, NY 12572. Mailing Address: P.O. Box 229, Rhinebeck, NY 12572-0229. Tel.: 845-752-3200. Fax: 845-758-6481.
E-mail: info@oldrhinebeck.org
Web Site: www.oldrhinebeck.org
Founded: 1977.
Congressional District: 19
Key Personnel: Public Rels., Don Fleming; Pres. (V), Jim Reckard; Museum Shop Mgr., Saja Lindsey.
Personnel Profile: Full-Time Paid 3; Full-Time Volunteers 5; Part-Time Paid 20; Part-Time Volunteers 30.
Governing Authority: private; nonprofit organization. Subsidiary Institution: Old Rhinebeck Aerodrome Airshows, Stone Church Rd. & Norton Rd., Rhinebeck, NY 12572. Tax-exempt: 501(c)(3)
Aeronautics & Space Museum.
Collections: period airplanes covering the pioneer, World War I & Lindbergh eras; vintage clothing; period cars & motorcycles; Spirit of St. Louis memorabilia.
Research Fields: early aircraft designs & aviation pioneers, from 1900 through 1940.

Facilities: 300-vol. set of aircraft technical manuals and early aviation books; restaurant; 28,000 sq. ft. exhibit space. Gift items for sale.
Activities: loan, temporary & traveling exhibitions; barnstorming rides. Museum Sponsors: Air Shows June-Oct; Golden Age Biplane Fly-In; Pioneer Day; Radio Control Model Meet; Dehavilland Tiger Moth Fly-In; vintage car shows & antique machinery exhibits.
Publications: quarterly newsletter, Rotary Ramblings
Hours & Admission Prices: Museum: daily 10-5. Air Show: Sat.-Sun. 2pm. Mon.-Fri.: adults 18-64 $10, children 13-17 and seniors 65 & over $8, children 6-12 $3, children 5 & under no charge; Sat.-Sun.: adults $20, children 13-17 and seniors 65 & over $15, children 6-12 $5; children 5 & under no charge.
Attendance: 40,000 (estimated)
Membership: Basic $25; Participating $50; Supporting $100; Sustaining $500; Benefactor $1,000.

Richfield Springs

PETRIFIED CREATURES MUSEUM OF NATURAL HISTORY, (M), U.S. Rte. 20, Richfield Springs, NY 13439. Mailing Address: P.O. Box 751, Richfield Springs, NY 13439-0751. Tel.: 315-858-2868. Fax: 315-858-2868.
E-mail: petrifiedcreaturesmuseum@yahoo.com
Web Site: www.petrifiedcreatures.com
Founded: 1934.
Congressional District: 25
Key Personnel: C.E.O., Dir. & Museum Shop Mgr., Stella C. Mlecz; Education & Cur., Richard S. Mlecz; Public Rels. & Treas., Sally E. Kennedy; Archivist, Frank Maiocco; Security, Michael Vesely.
Personnel Profile: Full-Time Paid 1; Full-Time Volunteers 3; Part-Time Paid 1; Part-Time Volunteers 15.
Governing Authority: private; nonprofit organization. Tax-exempt: 501(c)(3).
Nature & Science Museum.
Collections: life size restorations of dinosaurs; prehistoric animal life; petrified fossils.
Research Fields: paleontology.
Facilities: Fossils, minerals, stoneware & butterflies for sale.
Activities: digging for fossils; formally organized educational programs; narrated exhibits.
Hours & Admission Prices: May 15-June & Sept. 1-Sept. 15 Thurs.-Mon. 10-5; July-Aug. daily 10-5. Adults $9, senior citizens $7, children 5-11 $5; discount to AAM & ICOM members; children under 5 no charge. ♿
Attendance: 7,500 (estimated)

Riverdale

DERFNER JUDAICA MUSEUM + THE ART COLLECTION AT THE HEBREW HOME AT RIVERDALE, 5901 Palisade Ave., Riverdale, NY 10471-1253. Tel.: 718-581-1596. Fax: 718-581-1980.
E-mail: judaicamuseum@hebrewhome.org
Web Site: hebrewhome.org/art.asp
Founded: 1982.
Congressional District: 17
Key Personnel: Dir. & Chief Cur., Susan Chevlowe; Preparator, Kevin Kane; Asst. Cur., Emily O'Leary; Admin., Yonina Langer; Educator, Arlene Braunstein; Educator, Elana Kaplan.
Personnel Profile: Full-Time Paid 2; Part-Time Paid 4; Part-Time Volunteers 15; Interns 2.
Governing Authority: nonprofit organization. Parent Institution: The Hebrew Home for the Aged at Riverdale. Tax-exempt: 501(c)(3).
Judaica and Modern/Contemporary Art Museum.
Collections: Ralph & Leuba Baum collection of ceremonial objects in silver, gold, pewter; textiles; amulet collection; modern art collection including 20th century prints, paintings, photographs, works on paper.
Major Exhibits: Tradition and Remebrance: Treasures of the Derfner Judaica Museum, 11/09-12/31/10.
Research Fields: amulets.
Facilities: Hebraica & manuscripts; educational facilities; lecture room/spaces; sculpture garden.
Activities: guided tours; lectures; concerts; organized educational programs; docent program; loan exhibitions.
Hours & Admission Prices: Mon.-Fri. 10:30-4:30. No charge; donations accepted. Closed federal & Jewish holidays. ♿
Attendance: 5,000 (accurate)
Membership: Friends $30; Contributing $100; Sustaining $500; Patron $1,000.

Riverhead

HALLOCKVILLE MUSEUM FARM, 6038 Sound Ave., Riverhead, NY 11901-5609. Tel.: 631-298-5292. Fax: 631-298-0144.
E-mail: hallockv@optonline.net
Web Site: www.hallockville.com
Founded: 1975.
Congressional District: 1
Key Personnel: Exec. Dir., Herbert Strobel; Pres. (V), Richard Wines.
Personnel Profile: Full-Time Paid 1; Part-Time Paid 3; Part-Time Volunteers 60.
Governing Authority: not-for-profit organization. Hallockville, Inc., Riverhead, NY 11901. Tax-exempt: 501(c)(3).
Historic Site: located on c.1765 Hallock Homestead.
Collections: rural & agricultural lifestyle of the Hallock family & the north fork of Long Island, NY, from 1880-1910.
Research Fields: North Fork vernacular architecture; Hallock family genealogy; North Fork agricultural history; North Fork & Northville social & community history.
Facilities: 200-vol. library of material culture reference books; Long Island local history, available to the public; educational building with four classrooms; historic farmstead. Books & museum-related items for sale.
Activities: arts festivals; formal education programs for children; guided tours; hobby workshops; lectures. Annual Events: Fall Festival & Craft Fair; Demonstration series.
Publications: quarterly newsletter, Hallockville Happenings; occasional booklets.
Hours & Admission Prices: May-Nov. Fri.-Sun. 11-4. Adults $7, seniors & children $4; members no charge. Closed New Year's Day; Easter; Thanksgiving; Christmas Eve & Day. ♿
Attendance: 10,000 (estimated)
Membership: Individual $20; Family $35; Sponsor $60; Contributor $125.

THE LONG ISLAND SCIENCE CENTER, (M), 11 W. Main St., Riverhead, NY 11901-2822. Tel.: 631-208-8000. Fax: 631-208-8304.
E-mail: programs@lisciencecenter.org
Web Site: www.lisciencecenter.org
Key Personnel: Exec. Dir., Delia Gibbs
Science Center.
Collections: hands-on exhibits.
Activities: educational programs; special events.
Hours & Admission Prices: July 9-Aug. 24 Wed.-Sun. 11-4; Sept.-June Mon.-Fri. 10-2, Sun. 11-4. Children $5, adults $2.

RAILROAD MUSEUM OF LONG ISLAND, 416 Griffing Ave., Riverhead, NY 11901-3012. Mailing Address: P.O. Box 726, Greenport, NY 11944-0726. Tel.: 631-727-7920 (Riverhead) & 477-0439 (Greenport). Fax: 631-261-6545.
E-mail: info@rmli.org
Web Site: www.rmli.org
Founded: 1990.
Congressional District: 1
Key Personnel: Pres. & Chm., Don Fisher; Exec. Dir., Liz Irwin; Trustee, Dennis Harrington; Vice Pres., George Faeth; Sec., James Werner; Treas., Al Schick; Devel., Don Fisher; Security, Bill Raynor; Museum Shop Mgr., Bonnie Cornett.
Personnel Profile: Full-Time Volunteers 300; Part-Time Volunteers 260.
Governing Authority: board of trustees. Branch Museum: 440 Fourth St., Greenport, NY 11944. Tax-exempt: 501(c)(3).
Railroad Museum.
Collections: railroading history of Long Island; photographs; artifacts; HO gauge layout; 3 steam engines; 1 diesel engine; 8 historic railroad cars; 2 railroad speeders; 2 railroad cars in Greenport, LI. Historic Station: 1890s restored freight depot; official headquarters in Riverhead.
Facilities: Greenport Location: Museum-related items for sale. Riverhead location: Museum & gift related items for sale & Bulk of Railroad collection.
Activities: guided tours. Museum Sponsors: benefit dinner; Railfest in August (Riverhead); Santa Claus weekend in December (Greenport).
Publications: quarterly newsletter, The Postboy.
Hours & Admission Prices: Riverhead: Memorial Day to Columbus Day Sat.-Sun. 10-4; Oct.-May Sat. 10-4. Greenport: Memorial Day to Oct. Sat.-Sun. 11-4. Adults $5, children 5-12 $3; discounts to NRHS members; children under 5 & members no charge. ♿
Attendance: 8,000 (estimated)
Membership: Senior Citizen & Student $20; Associate $25; Regular $40; Corporate $150.

SUFFOLK COUNTY HISTORICAL SOCIETY, (M), 300 W. Main St., Riverhead, NY 11901-2894. Tel.: 631-727-2881. Fax: 631-727-3467.
E-mail: schsociety@optonline.net
Web Site: www.suffolkcountyhistoricalsociety.org
Founded: 1886.
Congressional District: 1

Key Personnel: Pres., John Sprague, III; Dir., Wallace W. Broege; Exhibition Devel. Coord. & Public Programs, Kathryn Curran; Museum Shop Mgr., Julie Governale.
Personnel Profile: Full-Time Paid 3; Part-Time Paid 7; Part-Time Volunteers 25.
Governing Authority: society. Tax-exempt: 501(c)(3).
Historical Museum.
Collections: primarily Suffolk County; Long Island Indian artifacts; Revolutionary & Civil War firearms; vehicles; boat models; china & glass; whaling artifacts; textiles; costumes; ceramics & glassware; decorative arts.
Research Fields: Suffolk County history & genealogy.
Facilities: research library & archives. Museum-related items for sale.
Activities: guided group tours; school education program; monthly programs & seasonal workshops for children; genealogy section.
Publications: newsletter; quarterly booklet, The Register.
Hours & Admission Prices: Museum: Tues.-Sat. 12:30-4:30. Library: Wed.-Sat. 12:30-4:30. Library: $2. Closed legal holidays.
Attendance: 18,000 (estimated)
Membership: Individual $30; Family $35; Corporate $100; Sustaining $500; Life $1,000.

Rochester

DAR-HERVEY ELY HOUSE, 11 Livingston Park, Rochester, NY 14608-2047. Mailing Address: 138 Troup St., Rochester, NY 14608-2032. Tel.: 585-232-4509.
Founded: 1894.
Congressional District: 34
Key Personnel: Regent, Carol D. Levering; Chm. House & Grounds (V), Beverly D. Henning.
Personnel Profile: Part-Time Volunteers 30.
Governing Authority: private. Owned by Irondequoit Chapter of the D.A.R. Tax-exempt.
Historic House Museum: 1837 Hervey Ely House, example of Greek revival architecture.
Collections: furniture of early 1800s; china; glass; silver; Washington sideboard; Lafayette mirror; antiques; George Washington's drummer boy's drum; manuscripts.
Research Fields: conservation.
Facilities: 2,200-vol. library of genealogical books & periodicals available for research on premises by appointment; genealogical records; lineage research records; records of Revolutionary soldiers in area; reading room.
Activities: guided tours; lectures; films; formally organized education programs for children; permanent & temporary exhibitions.
Publications: year books, Genealogical Records; Lineage Research Records; Record Listing of All Revolutionary Soldiers.
Hours & Admission Prices: Second Wed. of month 10-12, Third Wed. of month 10:30-3:30; other times by appointment; Genealogical Library: Fri. 11-3. Adults $1.50, children $.75. ♿
Membership: Individual $55.

* **GEORGE EASTMAN HOUSE/INTERNATIONAL MUSEUM OF PHOTOGRAPHY AND FILM, (M),** 900 East Ave., Rochester, NY 14607-2298. Tel.: 585-271-3361. Fax: 585-271-3970.
E-mail: info@geh.org
Web Site: www.eastmanhouse.org
Founded: 1947.
Congressional District: 29
Key Personnel: Chm. (V), Susan Robfogel; Dir., Anthony Bannon; Sr. Cur. Motion Picture Collection, Edward Stratmann; Cur. Photography Collection, Alison Nordstrom; Cur. George Eastman Collection, Kathy Connor; Cur. Tech., Todd Gustavson; Dir. Devel., Pamela Reed Sanchez; Publications Mgr., Amy Van Dussen; Librarian, Rachel Stuhlman; Mgr. Operations & Finance, Daniel Y. McCormick; Dir. Communications & Visitor Svcs., Eliza Benington Kozlowski; Controller, Paul Piazza; Museum Shop Mgr. & Travel Exhibitions Coord., Peter Briggs; Dir. Interpretation, Roger Bruce; Dir. Conservation, Grant Romer; Registrar, Wataru Okada.
Personnel Profile: Full-Time Paid 64; Part-Time Paid 38; Part-Time Volunteers 200.
Governing Authority: nonprofit organization. Tax-exempt: 501(c)(3).
Photography and Cinematography Museum: housed in 1905 George Eastman home; historic house museum & gardens.
Collections: 400,000 photographs & negatives; 56,000 books & periodicals on photography & film; world's largest collection of cinematographic equipment; 28,000 motion pictures from 1895 to present with emphasis on silent era films from all countries; over 3 million motion picture stills of both silent & sound periods; restored 1905 colonial revival mansion & gardens; 20,000 cameras & other technology.
Research Fields: photographic & cinematographic history.
Facilities: 80-seat auditorium; 535-seat theater; photographic archives by appointment. Publications for sale.
Activities: formally organized education programs; inter-museum loan; permanent & traveling exhibitions house & garden tours; symposia; senior citizen programming; photographic & film exhibitions.
Publications: newsletter; catalogues; photographic history books & portfolios, Image.
Hours & Admission Prices: Tues.-Wed. & Fri.-Sat. 10-5, Thurs. 10-8, Sun. 1-5. Adults $10, senior citizens $8, students $6, children 5-12 $4; discounts to AAM & ICOM members; children under 5 & members no charge. Closed Mondays, Christmas Day, New Year's Day & Thanksgiving. ♿
Attendance: 155,000 (accurate)
Membership: Student $35; Senior $45; Individual & National $50; International $60; Dual & Household $70; Contributor $100; Sustainer $150; Patron $250; Benefactor $500.

HIGHLAND BOTANICAL PARK, 171 Reservoir Ave., Rochester, NY 14620-2728. Tel.: 585-753-7270. Fax: 585-753-7287.
E-mail: tpollock@monroecounty.gov
Web Site: www.monroecounty.gov/parks
Founded: 1888.
Key Personnel: Dir., Thomas Pollock; Park Supvr., Mark Quinn.
Personnel Profile: Full-Time Paid 8; Part-Time Volunteers 20.
Governing Authority: Parent Institution: Monroe County Dept. of Parks, 171 Reservoir Ave., Rochester, NY 14620. Tax-exempt.
Arboretum.
Collections: 500 varieties of flowering shrubs; trees; flowers; rock garden.
Facilities: ice-skating rink; warming shelter; softball field; hiking paths.
Activities: tours. Annual Event: Lilac Festival in May.
Hours & Admission Prices: Daily 10-4. Adults $1, children 12 & over & seniors $.50; children under 12 no charge. ♿
Attendance: 50,000

THE LANDMARK SOCIETY OF WESTERN NEW YORK, 133 S. Fitzhugh St., Rochester, NY 14608-2204. Tel.: 585-546-7029, ext. 10. Fax: 585-546-4788.
E-mail: info@landmarksociety.org
Web Site: www.landmarksociety.org
Founded: 1937.
Congressional District: 37
Key Personnel: Exec. Dir., Joanne Arany; Dir. Museum & Education, Cindy Boyer; Pres. (V), Jerry Ludwig; Cur., William Keeler.
Personnel Profile: Full-Time Paid 10; Part-Time Paid 4; Part-Time Volunteers 400.
Governing Authority: nonprofit corporation. Branch Museums: Campbell-Whittlesey House, 123 S. Fitzhugh St.; Stone-Tolan House, 2370 East Ave.; 1867, Ellwanger Garden, 625 Mt. Hope Ave. Tax-exempt: 501(c)(3).
Preservation Project: housed in 1840 Hoyt-Potter House. Historic House Museums: Campbell-Whittlesey & Stone-Tolan Houses.
Collections: art, furnishings & decorative arts of the early 19th-century; country-style architecture. Historic Houses: 1835-1836 Campbell-Whittlesey House; c.1792 Stone-Tolan House; 1867 Ellwanger Garden.
Research Fields: architecture; history; archaeology; preservation; historic landscaping & horticulture.
Facilities: 1,000-vol. library of reference books on architecture; decorative arts. Books, crafts & other museum-related items for sale.
Activities: guided tours; lectures; workshops; formally organized educational programs; docent program; inter-museum loan, permanent & temporary exhibitions; guided bus tours of historic districts.
Publications: Landmarks of Rochester and Monroe County; quarterly newsletter; booklets; brochures; guides; books, 200 Years of Rochester Architecture & Gardens, The City of Frederick Douglass: Rochester's African-American People & Places, Walking Tours of Downtown Rochester: Images of History; Rehab Rochester: A Sensible Guide for Old-House Maintenance, Repair & Rehabilitation; Historic New York: Architectural Journeys in the Empire State; Ghost Walk: Chilling Tales from Rochester's Past.
Hours & Admission Prices: Campbell-Whittlesey House: March-Dec. Thurs.-Fri. 12-4. Stone-Tolan House: March-Dec. Fri.-Sat. 12-4; groups by appointment. Adults $3, children 8-18 $1; discounts to AAM members; members no charge. Ellwanger Garden: 2nd week in May (lilac festival) by appointment. Wenrich Library: by appointment; no charge. Closed national holidays. ♿
Attendance: 21,420 (estimated)
Membership: Individual $35; Family $45; Patron $75; Pillar $125; Cornerstone $250; Keystone $500; Corinthian $1,000.

* **MEMORIAL ART GALLERY OF THE UNIVERSITY OF ROCHESTER, (M),** 500 University Ave., Rochester, NY 14607-1484. Tel.: 585-276-8900. Fax: 585-473-6266. TDD: 585-473-6152.
E-mail: maginfo@mag.rochester.edu
Web Site: mag.rochester.edu

Founded: 1913.
Congressional District: 34
Key Personnel: Dir., Grant Holcomb, III; Chief Cur., Marjorie Searl; Dir. Exhibitions, Marie Via; Cur. European Art, Nancy Norwood; Librarian & Webmaster, Lu Harper; Registrar Permanent Collection, Monica Simpson; Registrar Exhibitions, Daniel Knerr; Dir. Gallery Advancement, Joseph Carney; McPherson Dir. Education, Susan Dodge-Peters Daiss; Asst. Dir. for Admin., Kim Hallatt; Mktg. & Communications Mgr., Patti Giordano; Area Mgr., Debbie Smith; Museum Shop Mgr., Colleen Griffin-Underhill.
Personnel Profile: Full-Time Paid 45; Part-Time Paid 20; Part-Time Volunteers 1,701.
Governing Authority: university. Parent Institution: University of Rochester. Tax-exempt: 501(c)(3).
Art Museum: housed in 1913 Italian Renaissance style building with additions in 1926, 1968 & 1987, located on the site of the original campus of University of Rochester.
Collections: ancient, classical, medieval, Renaissance, baroque, 18th to 20th-century American, 19th & 20th-century French, American folk, Ancient American, African, Oriental art including paintings, sculpture, prints, drawings and decorative arts.
Research Fields: pertaining to collections.
Facilities: 38,000-vol. library of art and art history books, reference works, periodicals, exhibition catalogs & museum bulletins available for inter-library loan and for use on premises; restaurant; reading room; 300-seat auditorium; classrooms. Art books, reproductions, original paintings, sculpture & other museum-related items for sale.
Activities: guided tours; lectures; films; gallery talks; concerts; rental gallery; formally organized educational programs; docent program; inter-museum loan, permanent, temporary & traveling exhibitions; school loan service.
Publications: biennial financial report; bimonthly newsletter, MAGazine; calendar; exhibition catalogs; biennial scholarly bulletin; bimonthly newsletter, ARTiculate.
Hours & Admission Prices: Wed.& Fri.-Sun. 11-5, Thurs. 11-9. Adults $10, senior citizens, military & college students $6, children 6-18 $4; discounts to AAM & New York Consortium members and Thurs. 5-9pm; members & children under 6 no charge. Closed national holidays. ♿
Attendance: 245,512 (accurate)
Membership: Student $35; Out of Town $45; Associate: Individual $50, Family $65; Supporter: Individual $70, Family $85; Friend $140; Patron $300; Benefactor $600; Director's Circle $1,500 & up.

MONROE COMMUNITY COLLEGE, MERCER GALLERY, (M), 1000 E. Henrietta Rd., Brighton Campus, Rochester, NY 14623-5701. Tel.: 585-292-2021. Fax: 585-292-3120.
E-mail: kfarrell@monroecc.edu
Web Site: www.monroecc.edu
Congressional District: 52
Key Personnel: Dir., Ms. Kathleen Farrell.
Personnel Profile: Full-Time Paid 1; Part-Time Volunteers 4; Interns 3.
Governing Authority: public college; nonprofit. Tax-exempt: 501(c)(3).
Art Gallery.
Collections: student & faculty art.
Hours & Admission Prices: Mon.-Thurs.10-7, Fri. 10-5; other times by appointment. No charge.

ROCHESTER HISTORICAL SOCIETY, 115 South Ave., Rundel Memorial Building, Rochester, NY 14604-1817. Tel.: 585-428-8470. Fax: 716-271-9089.
E-mail: mkeller@rochesterhistory.org
Web Site: www.rochesterhistory.org
Founded: 1861.
Congressional District: 34
Key Personnel: Interim Exec. Dir., Meredith Keller; Pres. (V), Patrick Malgieri.
Personnel Profile: Full-Time Paid 3; Part-Time Paid 3; Part-Time Volunteers 62; Interns 1.
Governing Authority: society. Tax-exempt: 501(c)(3).
Historical Society Museum.
Collections: books; manuscripts; paintings; costume collection; silver; 15,000 photographs; architectural drawings; firearms, children's toys; furnishings; ceramics; perennial garden.
Research Fields: local history.
Facilities: 10,000-vol. library of books, 20,000 photographs, over 500 portraits of Rochesterians, genealogical & local history research files.
Activities: lecture series; permanent exhibitions; publications; research.
Publications: Rochester history.
Hours & Admission Prices: Temporarily closed.
Membership: Individual $35; Family $50; Sustaining $100; Patron $250; Benefactor & Corporate $500 & up.

ROCHESTER MEDICAL MUSEUM & ARCHIVES, (M), 333 Humboldt St., Rochester, NY 14610-1044. Tel.: 585-922-1847. Fax: 585-922-0018.
E-mail: kathleen.britton@rochestergeneral.org
Web Site: rochestergeneral.org/archives
Formerly: ViaHealth Archives Consortium
Founded: 1947.
Congressional District: 29
Key Personnel: Chm. (V), Betsy Morse; Interim Dir., Kathleen E. Britton.
Personnel Profile: Full-Time Paid 1; Part-Time Paid 3; Part-Time Volunteers 7.
Governing Authority: nonprofit. Parent Institution: Rochester General Hospital. Tax-exempt.
Medical Museum.
Collections: Rochester regional healthcare history including Rochester General Hospital & its affiliated agencies; nursing; medical; military medicine; costumes; archives; photographs.
Research Fields: Rochester General Hospital's contributions to the field of medicine & its development.
Facilities: 300-vol. library; 285 ft. of archival material pertaining to the hospital, available for use by public; 400 sq. ft. exhibit space.
Activities: guided tours; loan, temporary & traveling exhibitions; organized education programs for undergraduate or graduate college students affiliated with LPN Nursing School, primary & secondary school. Museum Sponsors: Century of Service Awards.
Publications: semiannual newsletter, Baker-Cederberg Notebook; occasional monographs.
Hours & Admission Prices: Research: Mon.-Fri. 9-4 ; other times by appointment. No charge; donations accepted. ♿
Attendance: 1,000 (estimated)
Membership: Associate $10; Contributor $25; Supporter $50; Patron $100; Benefactor $250; Legacy $500.

*** ROCHESTER MUSEUM & SCIENCE CENTER, (M),** 657 East Ave., Rochester, NY 14607-2177. Tel.: 585-271-4320. Fax: 585-271-5935.
E-mail: kate_bennett@rmsc.org
Web Site: www.rmsc.org
Founded: 1912.
Congressional District: 28
Key Personnel: C.E.O. & Pres., Kate Bennett; Chm. Bd. (V), Victor E. Salerno; Dir. Mktg. & Community Affairs, Debra Jacobson; Vice Pres. Business Devel. & Strategic Mktg., Philip F. Lentini; Vice Pres. Finance & Administration, Barbara Sauer; Vice Pres. Operations, Joseph R. Graves; Dir. Planetarium, Steven Fentress; Dir. Nature Center, David Gotham; Dir. Collections, George McIntosh; Dir. Visitor Satisfaction, Heidi Luizzi; Dir. Education, Calvin Uzelmeier; Mgr. Welcome Center & Museum Shop, Colleen McBride.
Personnel Profile: Full-Time Paid 64; Part-Time Paid 161; Part-Time Volunteers 547; Interns 2.
Governing Authority: nonprofit educational corporation. Divisions: Rochester Museum, 657 East. Ave., Rochester, NY; Rochester Museum-Strasenburgh Planetarium-see separate listing; Rochester Museum-Cumming Nature Center, Gulick Rd., Naples, NY. Tax-exempt: 501(c)(3).
Science & Technology, Natural Sciences & Cultural Heritage Museum.
Collections: over 1.2 million objects of regional science & technology, nature environments, & cultural heritage with emphasis on archaeological & contemporary Upstate New York Native cultures.
Research Fields: anthropology; regional culture & history; natural sciences; technology; environment.
Facilities: 30,000-vol. library of books on science, history, technology, anthropology, astronomy available for use on premises; 225-seat planetarium with large-format film; reading room; 400- & 100-seat auditoriums; classrooms. 900-acre Cumming Nature Center containing year-round trails, reconstructed pioneer homestead, log sugarhouse & outdoor exhibits; 100-seat theatre; wildlife viewing area; restaurant. Educational items pertaining to program fields for sale.
Activities: guided tours; lecture series; films; education programs; undergraduate & graduate internships; professional development for teachers; inter-museum loan; long-term & temporary exhibitions. Cumming Nature Center: cross country skiing & snowshoeing; maple sugaring; nature walks.
Publications: quarterly news & programs; research records; catalogs; annual report; educator guide.
Hours & Admission Prices: Rochester Museum: Mon.-Sat. 9-5, Sun. & holidays 11-5. Adults $10, senior citizens & college students $9, children 3-18 $8; discounts to AAM members; ASTC reciprocal membership; members & children under 3 no charge. Additional fee charged for some special exhibits. Strasenburgh Planetarium: call for hours. Adults $10, college students & senior citizens $9, children 3-18 $8; members & children under 3 no charge. Cumming Nature Center: Jan.-Oct. Sat.-Sun. 9-5. Suggested Donation: $3; members no charge. Museum & Planetarium: closed Thanksgiving; Christmas. ♿
Attendance: 408,258 (accurate)

Membership: Individual $58; Family $83; Family Plus $108; Patron $150 & up.

SENECA PARK ZOO, 2222 St. Paul St., Rochester, NY 14621-1097. Tel.: 585-266-6591. Fax: 585-266-5775.
E-mail: lsorel@monroecounty.gov
Web Site: www.senecaparkzoo.org
Founded: 1894.
Congressional District: 29
Key Personnel: C.E.O. & Dir., Lawrence Sorel; Exec. Dir. Seneca Park Zoo Society, Rachel Baker August; Veterinarian, Jeffrey Wyatt, D.V.M.; Museum Shop Mgr., Sue DeCaro.
Personnel Profile: Full-Time Paid 49; Part-Time Paid 23; Part-Time Volunteers 100; Interns 2.
Governing Authority: county. Parent Institution: County of Monroe, Dept. of Parks, 171 Reservoir Ave., Rochester 14620. Tax-exempt.
Zoo.
Collections: zoology; aviary; herpetology.
Research Fields: public education on live animal behavior; pathology; herpetology.
Facilities: 750-vol. library of books on zoos and zoology available on premises; cafeteria. Zoo-related items for sale.
Activities: guided tours; lectures; films; study clubs; docent program or council.
Publications: quarterly newsletter.
Hours & Admission Prices: April-Oct. daily 10-5; Nov.-March daily 10-4. April-Oct. adults $9, seniors 63 & over $8, youth 3-11 $6; children 2 & under no charge. Nov.-March: adults $7, seniors 63 & over $6, youth 3-11 $4; children 2 & under no charge. Closed New Year's Day; Thanksgiving; Christmas. ♿
Attendance: 345,981 (accurate)
Membership: Individual $39; Senior Couple $49; Family $69; Penguin Circle $125; Special Friend $250 & up.

* **STRONG NATIONAL MUSEUM OF PLAY, (M),** One Manhattan Square, Rochester, NY 14607-3941. Tel.: 585-263-2700. Fax: 585-263-2493. TDD: 585-423-0746.
E-mail: info@strongmuseum.org
Web Site: www.museumofplay.org
Founded: 1968.
Congressional District: 34
Key Personnel: Pres. & C.E.O., G. Rollie Adams, Ph.D.; Chm., William D. Rice; Vice Pres. Finance & Operations, Earl F. Johnson; Vice Pres. Institutional Advancement, Laura J. Sadowski; Vice Pres. Interpretation, Scott G. Eberle, Ph.D.; Vice Pres. Exhibit Devel. & Research, Jon-Paul Dyson, Ph.D.; Vice Pres. Education, Joan Hoffman; Vice Pres. Guest Svcs. & Human Resources, Kathleen Dengler; Museum Shop Mgr., Bobbi Price.
Personnel Profile: Full-Time Paid 90; Part-Time Paid 226; Part-Time Volunteers 19; Interns 1.
Governing Authority: private foundation. Tax-exempt.
History Museum.
Collections: reflect the cultural history of play; how play illuminates individual identity & the American experience; the role of play in learning, creativity & discovery.
Major Exhibits: Art of the Brick, 12/09-3/10; Lego Castle Adventure (T), 1/10-5/10; America's Favorite Doll, 1/10-12/10; American Comic Book Heroes, 1/10-12/10; Mind Bender Mansion (T), 5/10-9/10; National Geographic Maps, 10/10-1/11.
Research Fields: 19th-21st century American cultural history & material as it relates to play.
Facilities: 70,000 vol. library; butterfly garden; food court. Museum-related items for sale.
Activities: interactive learning environments: family & children's programs; concerts; dramatic presentations; lectures; workshops; community forums; school lessons; curriculum materials; inner-city outreach programs.
Publications: quarterly newsletter; American Journal of Play.
Hours & Admission Prices: Mon.-Thurs. 10-5, Fri.-Sat. 10-8, Sun. 12-5. Museum: adults $10, senior citizens $9, children 2-15 $8; discounts for AAM members, school groups & groups of 20 or more by appointment; children under 2 & members no charge. Museum & Butterfly Garden: adults $13, senior citizens $12, children 2-15 $11; children under 2 no charge. Closed Thanksgiving; Christmas. ♿
Attendance: 562,210 (accurate)
Membership: Dual $69; Family & Grandparent $89; Patron $125; Benefactor $250; Sustaining $500; Leading $1,000.

SUSAN B. ANTHONY HOUSE, (M), 17 Madison St., Rochester, NY 14608-1928. Tel.: 585-235-6124. Fax: 585-235-6212.
E-mail: czarcone@susanbanthonyhouse.org
Web Site: www.susanbanthonyhouse.org
Founded: 1946.
Congressional District: 32
Key Personnel: Chm. Bd. Directors, Clay C. Arnold; Exec. Dir., Deborah L. Hughes; Dir. Devel. & Public Rels., Ellen K. Wheeler; Dir. Program & Visitor Svcs., Annie Callanan; Volunteer Liaison & Weekend Coord., Sue Gaffney; Weekend Coord., Lenny Polizzi; Museum Shop Operations, Barbara Bleier; Administrative Asst., Claire Hawley Zarcone; Custodian, Doug Thompson.
Personnel Profile: Full-Time Paid 4; Full-Time Volunteers 1; Part-Time Paid 4; Part-Time Volunteers 100.
Governing Authority: society. Tax-exempt: 501(c)(3).
Historic House Museum: home of Susan B. Anthony; National Historic Landmark.
Collections: personal belongings of Susan B. Anthony; pictures & writings of famous women associated with Susan B. Anthony.
Research Fields: Women's Suffrage Movement.
Facilities: carriage house (education lecture hall).
Activities: tours, teas, and lunches; special exhibits; speaker program; According to Anthony Luncheon - Lecture Series September-June; educational programs for students, girl scouts, and seniors; special celebrations: NYS Day of Recognition & Susan B. Anthony Birthday Luncheon in February; 19th Amendment Festival in August; Election Day & Arrest Day commemorations in November; slide showing the 2nd & 3rd floor available for viewing.
Publications: newsletter.
Hours & Admission Prices: Tues.-Sun. 11-5. Adults $6, seniors $5, students & children 12 & under $3; discounts to AAM & AAA members; members no charge. Closed major holidays. ♿
Attendance: 7,000 (accurate)
Membership: Student $15; Individual $25; Family & Dual $35; 1872 League $50-$99; Red Shawl Club $100-$249; Suffragist Society $250-$499; Leadership Council $500-$999; Susan B. Anthony Circle $1,000 & up.

Rome

ERIE CANAL VILLAGE, 5789 Rome-New London Rd., Rte. 46 & 49, Rome, NY 13440-8338. Tel.: 315-337-3999. Fax: 315-339-7142.
E-mail: mandm2000@twcny.rr.com
Web Site: www.eriecanalvillage.net
Founded: 1973.
Congressional District: 31
Key Personnel: Owner, Ronad Trottier; Mgr., Melody Milewski.
Personnel Profile: Full-Time Paid 2; Part-Time Paid 15; Part-Time Volunteers 25.
Governing Authority: private.
Outdoor Living History Museum.
Collections: agricultural equipment; domestic objects; textiles; costumes; archival material; tools; decorative art objects related to canal history & village life in 19th-century upstate NY; cheese manufacturing.
Research Fields: Erie Canal; cheesemaking; transportation; agriculture; village life.
Facilities: 550-vol. library of agriculture, canal, cheesemaking & 19th-century culture available to the public; 100-seat auditorium. Books, publications, pottery, food stuffs, village craft products, gift items & toys for sale.
Activities: guided tours; docent program; participatory exhibits. Museum Sponsors: annual Canal Festival, Harvest Festival & Holiday Activities.
Hours & Admission Prices: Memorial Day to Labor Day Wed.-Sat. 10-5, Sun. 12-5. Adults $15, senior citizens & students 13-17 $12, children 5-12 $10; discounts to groups, AAM & ICOM members; children under 4 & members no charge. ♿
Attendance: 20,000 (estimated)
Membership: Adult $35; Senior $30; Family $130.

FORT STANWIX NATIONAL MONUMENT, 112 E. Park St., Rome, NY 13440-5816. Tel.: 315-338-7730. Fax: 315-334-5051.
E-mail: fost_superintendent@nps.gov
Web Site: www.nps.gov/fost
Founded: 1935.
Congressional District: 24
Key Personnel: Dir. & Supt., Debbie Conway; Chief Interpretation & Resources Management, Michael Kusch; Cur., Keith Routley.
Personnel Profile: Full-Time Paid 11; Part-Time Paid 10; Part-Time Volunteers 35.
Governing Authority: federal. Parent Institution: National Park Service, Dept. of the Interior. Tax-exempt.
National Monument.
Collections: 18th, 19th and 20th-century archaeological collection including arms & accoutrements, clothing, hardware, utensils, glassware and pottery; manuscript collection.
Facilities: 400-vol. library; theater. Museum-related items for sale.

Activities: living history; guided tours; historical education; permanent exhibits.
Publications: informational brochure, historical studies.
Hours & Admission Prices: Fort: April-Dec. daily 10-4. No charge. Closed Thanksgiving; Christmas. Visitor Center: daily 9-5. No charge. Closed New Year's Day; Thanksgiving; Christmas. ♿
Attendance: 71,263 (accurate)

ROME ART AND COMMUNITY CENTER, 308 W. Bloomfield St., Rome, NY 13440-4197. Tel.: 315-336-1040. Fax: 315-336-1090.
E-mail: executivedirector@romeart.org
Web Site: www.romeart.org
Founded: 1967.
Congressional District: 31
Key Personnel: Exec. Dir., Lauren Marie Getek; Fin. Mgr., Janice Connors.
Personnel Profile: Full-Time Paid 2; Part-Time Paid 2; Part-Time Volunteers 15.
Governing Authority: nonprofit organization. Tax-exempt: 501(c)(3).
Art Center.
Collections: all types of art media exhibits changing every month.
Facilities: classrooms; community meeting rooms. Art-related items for sale.
Activities: guided tours; lectures; films; gallery talks; concerts; hobby workshops; formally organized educational programs.
Publications: bimonthly newsletter; quarterly, class schedules; quarterly, Community Cultural Calendar.
Hours & Admission Prices: Summer: Tues.-Thurs. 10-6, Fri. 10-4, Sat. 10-2, Winter: Tues.-Thurs. 10-6, Fri. 10-4, Sat. 10-2. No charge; donations accepted. Closed National holidays. ♿
Attendance: 25,000 (estimated)
Membership: Green $5; Children 3-12 $18; Student & Senior $20; Individual $25; Household $40; Patron $100; Endowment $500.

ROME HISTORICAL SOCIETY MUSEUM, 200 Church St., Rome, NY 13440-5872. Tel.: 315-336-5870. Fax: 315-336-5912.
E-mail: info@romehistorical.org
Web Site: www.romehistorical.org
Founded: 1936.
Congressional District: 31
Key Personnel: Dir., Robert Avery; Pres. (V), Virginia Batchhelder; Cur., Ann Swanson; Museum Shop Mgr. & Admin., Mary Centro.
Personnel Profile: Full-Time Paid 2; Part-Time Paid 4; Part-Time Volunteers 12; Interns 2.
Governing Authority: Society. Parent Institution: Rome Historical Society. Tax-exempt.
Historical Society Museum.
Collections: domestic objects; furniture; tools; textiles; photographs; maps; primary source documents dating from 18th century to present; Rome Turney Radiator Co. records; archives of local history and genealogical documents.
Major Exhibits: Griffiss Air Force Base, 11/09-12/10.
Research Fields: local history; genealogy.
Facilities: 2,000-vol. library of Rome area & Central NY materials & documents available for research on premises with authorization; reading room; auditorium. Museum-related items for sale.
Activities: guided tours; lectures; films; permanent & temporary exhibitions; outreach programs.
Publications: quarterly Annals & Recollections; quarterly newsletter, RHS News.
Hours & Admission Prices: Museum: Tues.-Thurs. 10-5, Fri. 10-3; other times by appointment. No charge; donations accepted. Library by appointment. Research Fee: $15; students no charge. Closed major holidays. ♿
Attendance: 22,376 (accurate)
Membership: Senior $15; Individual $25; Family $35; Supporting $50; Sustaining $100; Sponsor $250; Patron $500; Benefactor $1,000.

Rosendale

CENTURY HOUSE HISTORICAL SOCIETY, 668 Rte. 213, A.J. Snyder Estate, Rosendale, NY 12472-0150. Mailing Address: P.O. Box 150, Rosendale, NY 12472-0150. Tel.: 845-658-9900.
E-mail: info@centuryhouse.org
Web Site: www.centuryhouse.org
Founded: 1988.
Congressional District: 26
Key Personnel: Pres. (V), Dietrich Werner; Museum Shop Mgr., Althea Doris Werner.
Personnel Profile: Part-Time Volunteers 24.
Governing Authority: state; New York State Education Dept. Tax-exempt.
Historic House: 1809 old stone Century House, built by Christopher Snyder for his son, Jacob L. Snyder, pioneer in cement manufacturing; Historic Site: Snyder Estate Natural Cement Historic District, on state & national registers of historic places.
Collections: period furnishings; antiques; barn; carriage house; 20 carriages; 1820s-1940s sleighs.
Activities: history tours; special cultural events; music, art & performance events.
Publications: brochures; quarterly newsletter, Natural News.
Hours & Admission Prices: April-Nov. Wed. & Sat.-Sun. 1-4; other times by appointment. Suggested Donation $3; members no charge. ♿
Attendance: 4,325 (accurate)
Membership: Annual $15; Family $25.

Roslyn

ROSLYN LANDMARK SOCIETY, 221 Main St., Roslyn, NY 11576-2168. Mailing Address: Roslyn Landmark Society, Box 234, 36 Main St., Roslyn, NY 11576. Tel.: 516-625-4363. Fax: 516-625-4363.
E-mail: info@roslynlandmarks.org
Web Site: www.roslynlandmarks.org/index.html
Formerly: Van Nostrand Starkins House
Founded: 1960.
Congressional District: 15
Key Personnel: Pres., Robert Sargent; Dir., Franklin H. Perrell.
Personnel Profile: Part-Time Paid 1; Part-Time Volunteers 2.
Governing Authority: nonprofit organization; Roslyn Landmark Society. Tax-exempt.
Historical Building & Site: c.1680 earliest surviving building in Roslyn; site contains a 17th-century well & has had 4 archaeological investigations.
Collections: architectural exhibit showing framing & construction of a 17th-century house; American decorative arts; period rooms; artifacts.
Activities: guided tours; lectures; participatory exhibits; children's programs.
Publications: annual, House Tour Guide.
Hours & Admission Prices: June-Oct. Sat.-Sun. 1-4. Adults $4, children $2.
Attendance: 600 (estimated)
Membership: Outside Long Island $15; Contributing $25; Sustaining $50; Supporting $100; Fellowship $200; Patron $1,000; Benefactor $2,000; Life $5,000.

Roslyn Harbor

NASSAU COUNTY MUSEUM OF ART, (M), One Museum Dr., Roslyn Harbor, NY 11576-1138. Tel.: 516-484-9337. Fax: 516-484-0710.
Web Site: www.nassaumuseum.org
Founded: 1989.
Congressional District: 6
Key Personnel: Dir., Constance Schwartz; Asst. Dir. & Registrar, Fernanda Bennett; Chief Cur., Franklin Hill Perrell; Office Mgr., Rita Mack; Pres. (V), H. Brooks Smith; Dir. Devel., Matthew Campo; Comptroller, Lisa Oosterom; Education Coord., Jean Henning; Membership Coord., Patricia Carpenter; Curatorial Asst., Brooke Dellapi; Grant Writer, Alison Carley; Receptionist, Dorothy Underwood; Weekend Coord., Julius Harris; Weekend Coord., Amby Lyman; Maintenance Engineer, Reynaldo Castillo; Gift Shop Mgr., Helen Green; Volunteer Coord., Nancy Barone; Docent Coord., Joan Brenner.
Personnel Profile: Full-Time Paid 14; Part-Time Paid 10; Part-Time Volunteers 275; Interns 10.
Governing Authority: bd. trustees; nonprofit. Tax-exempt.
Art Museum: housed in c.1900 three story neo-Georgian brick mansion, former estate of Childs Frick.
Collections: 19th & 20th-century American prints; drawings; 19th & 20th-century paintings; outdoor sculpture garden; formal gardens designed by Marion Cruger Coffin; architectural blueprints & drawings relating to the museum building & property; Tee Ridder Miniatures.
Research Fields: all fields of art; 20th-century American sculpture.
Facilities: 145-acres of lawns, ponds & wooded areas; hiking trails; pinetum; formal gardens; studio art classrooms; bookshop. Museum-related items for sale.
Activities: guided tours; lectures; gallery talks; docent programs; formally organized education programs for adults, children & undergraduate college students; loan, temporary & traveling exhibitions.
Publications: quarterly, exhibition catalogs; newsletter.
Hours & Admission Prices: Tues.-Sun. 11-5. Adults $10, seniors $8, children & students $4; discounts to AAM members & corporate sponsors, Newsday, Channel 13 & radio station WLUS members; members no charge. Closed county holidays. ♿
Attendance: 200,000 (accurate)
Membership: Senior Citizen & Student $30; Individual $40; Family & Dual $65; Supporting $110; Contemporary Collector's Circle $200; Sustaining $250; Friend $500; Council Member $1,000; Corporate $1,000 and up; Council Circle $2,500; Director's Circle $5,000.

Rotterdam Junction

MABEE FARM HISTORIC SITE, 1080 Main St., Rotterdam Junction, NY 12150. Tel.: 518-887-5073. Fax: 518-887-5746.
E-mail: mabee@nycap.rr.com
Web Site: www.mabeefarm.org
Formerly: Historic Mabee Farm Site
Congressional District: 21
Key Personnel: Pres., Ed Reilly; Chm., Merritt Glennon.
Personnel Profile: Full-Time Paid 2; Part-Time Volunteers 40; Interns 2.
Governing Authority: Tax-exempt. Parent Institution: Schenectady County Historical Society.
History Museum: housed in an 18th-century farm.
Collections: furnishings; textiles; farming implements; cemetery; gardens. Historic Buildings: pre-revolutionary Dutch barn; 18th century buildings including house; inn; slave quarters; carriage shed; black smith; wood shop; corn crib.
Research Fields: Mabee family; farming history; colonial life; enslaved peoples.
Facilities: gardens.
Activities: classes; music festival; workshops: blacksmithing; timber framing; spinning; knitting; Dutch oven cooking; soap making; make a gourd birdhouse; school programs. Museum Sponsors: Revolutionary War encampment; Community Day; Early Technologies Day; Craft Fair; Canal Festival in August; History Fair.
Publications: society newsletter.
Hours & Admission Prices: May-Sept. Tues.-Sat. 10-4. Adults $4, seniors & children $3; children under 12 no charge. ♿
Attendance: 17,000 (estimated)
Membership: Individual $25; Family $40; Donor $50; Sponsor $100; Patron $500; Life $1,000.

Roxbury

JOHN BURROUGHS MEMORIAL STATE HISTORIC SITE, Burroughs Memorial Rd., Roxbury, NY 12474. Mailing Address: Mine Kill State Park, Rte. 30, P.O. Box 923, North Blenheim, NY 12131-0923. Tel.: 518-827-6111, ext. 91. Fax: 518-827-6782.
E-mail: brian.strasavich@oprhp.state.ny.us
Web Site: www.nysparks.com
Founded: 1964.
Congressional District: 27
Key Personnel: Park Mgr., Brian Strasavich.
Governing Authority: state. Parent Institution: New York State Office of Parks, Recreation & Historic Preservation. Tax-exempt: 501(c)(3).
Historic Site: burial site of naturalist John Burroughs.
Hours & Admission Prices: April-Sept. daily 1:30pm to dusk; Oct.-March daily 7:30-4:30. No charge, donations accepted.

Rye

* **THE RYE HISTORICAL SOCIETY AND SQUARE HOUSE MUSEUM, (M),** One Purchase St., Rye, NY 10580-3002. Tel.: 914-967-7588. Fax: 914-967-6253.
Web Site: ryehistoricalsociety.org
Founded: 1964.
Congressional District: 18
Key Personnel: Exec. Dir., Dr. Ruth Smalt; Bd. Pres., Laura Brett.
Personnel Profile: Full-Time Paid 4; Part-Time Paid 1; Part-Time Volunteers 70; Interns 3.
Governing Authority: society; nonprofit organization. Parent Institution: The Rye Historical Society. Subsidiary Institution: Knapp House Library & Archives, 265 Rye Beach Ave., Rye, NY 10580. Tel.: 914-967-8657. Tax-exempt: 501(c)(3) & 170(b)(1)(A).
History Museum: housed in c.1730 Square House.
Collections: decorative arts; furniture; costumes & textiles; 17th-20th century manuscripts; local history; photographs; archaeology.
Research Fields: 17th-20th century manuscripts; 17th-18th century wills, inventories & deeds; regional history; photographs.
Facilities: 1,000-vol. library of local history available for research on premises; 80-seat meeting room. Historic Buildings: Square House c.1730, Knapp House c.1670-1750.
Activities: guided tours; adult & family programs; school programs; Junior Volunteer summer camp for 4th-7th graders.
Publications: quarterly calendar of events; cookbook, My Grandmother Had a Woodburning Stove; Colonial Cooking at the Square House; Silent Companions: Dummy Board Figures of the 17th through 19th Centuries; The Art of Lauren Ford; Read about Rye; Estates of Grace: The Architectural Heritage of Religious Structures in Rye; 100 Years of Health Care; Father Burke's Dream to Rescue Children of the Inner City: St. Benedict's Home, Rye, New York, 1841-1941; Views of Rye: 1907-1997.
Hours & Admission Prices: Tues.-Fri. 9-4, Sat. 10-3. No charge; donations accepted.
Membership: Student $15; Individual $45; Family $75; Sustainer $125; Sponsor $250; Benefactor $500; Patron $1,000; Angel $5,000.

Sackets Harbor

SACKETS HARBOR BATTLEFIELD STATE HISTORIC SITE, 504 W. Main St., Sackets Harbor, NY 13685. Mailing Address: P.O. Box 27, Sackets Harbor, NY 13685-0027. Tel.: 315-646-3634. Fax: 315-646-1203.
E-mail: constance.barone@oprhp.state.ny.us
Web Site: www.nysparks.com
Founded: 1933.
Congressional District: 30
Key Personnel: Site Mgr., Constance B. Barone; Interpretive Programs Asst., Stephen Wallace.
Personnel Profile: Full-Time Paid 4; Part-Time Paid 16; Part-Time Volunteers 30.
Governing Authority: state. Parent Institution: New York State. Subsidiary Institution: New York State Office of Parks, Recreation & Historic Preservation and Thousand Islands State Park, Recreation & Historic Preservation Commission; Sackets Harbor Battlefield Alliance Support Group. Tax-exempt: 501(c)(3).
Historic U.S. Navy Yard & Battlefield complex: housed in six buildings, 1818 Union Hotel; restored 1849 Commandant's & Master's houses; 1848 stable; 1850 ice house; 1832 farmhouse; located on site of 19th-century U.S. naval base, which played an important part in the War of 1812; Maritime Museum; restored 1850-60 navy yard building complex; War of 1812 battlefield in upstate N.Y.
Collections: War of 1812 weapons, armament accessories military clothing accessories; photographs; 1811-1860 microfilm on U.S. Navy; 19th-century household furniture & accessories; 1814 artifacts from Brig Jefferson, 1812-1815 Fort Tompkins. Historic Building: 1850 Commandant's house.
Research Fields: War of 1812 on Lake Ontario & in northern New York; life on a mid-19th century naval station; army life 1812-1816; ships built at Sackets Harbor; 1810-1820 military uniforms; field fortifications; 1750-1850 heirloom vegetable garden plants.
Facilities: 850-vol. library on local & military history; visitor center; reading room; picnic area.
Activities: guided tours; self-guided tours; temporary & permanent exhibits; educational programs; school lecture service; living history program; summer programs.
Publications: Archaeological Walking Tour of Sackets Harbor Battlefield; museum brochure; occasional pamphlets; Guide to 1813 Battlefield/Walking Tour.
Hours & Admission Prices: May-Sept. Thurs.-Mon.; other times for research only. Adults $3, seniors $2; Navy Yard Restoration: children under 12 no charge. ♿
Attendance: 112,280 (accurate)
Membership: Individual $25; Dual & Family $40; Business $50 & up; Corporate $100 & up.

Sag Harbor

SAG HARBOR WHALING & HISTORICAL MUSEUM, 200 Main St., Sag Harbor, NY 11963-3009. Mailing Address: P.O. Box 1327, Sag Harbor, NY 11963-0050. Tel.: 631-725-0770. Fax: 631-725-5638.
E-mail: info@sagharborwhalingmuseum.org
Web Site: www.sagharborwhalingmuseum.org
Founded: 1936.
Congressional District: 1
Key Personnel: Exec. Dir., Zachary N. Studenroth; Asst. Dir., Lynnette Pintauro.
Personnel Profile: Full-Time Paid 2; Part-Time Paid 4; Part-Time Volunteers 7.
Governing Authority: public corporation. Tax-exempt.
Whaling Museum: housed in 1845 Greek Revival mansion, Benjamin Huntting House.
Collections: whaling tools; scrimshaw; period fishing rods, reels & lures; books; models; clocks; dinnerware; antiques; guns; toys; oil paintings; ship models; pianos & fine furniture.
Research Fields: Sag Harbor whale ships & whaling.
Facilities: children's museum; whaleboat. Maritime & museum-related items for sale.
Activities: special Sunday events; educational talks; demonstrations.
Publications: Whales & Whaling; Tales of Sag Harbor; Sag Harbor History; A Walking Tour of Sag Harbor.
Hours & Admission Prices: mid-May to mid-Oct. Mon.-Sat. 10-5, Sun. 1-5. Adults $5, senior citizens & students $4, children 3-11 $1; discount to groups; tour guides, members & bus drivers no charge.
Attendance: 8,500 (estimated)
Membership: Individual $25; Family $30; Life $1,000.

Saint Bonaventure

THE REGINA A. QUICK CENTER FOR THE ARTS, (M), St. Bonaventure Univ., Rte. 417, Cornelius Welch Dr., Saint Bonaventure, NY 14778. Mailing Address: 285 E. College St., Oberlin, OH 44074-1354. Tel.: 716-375-2494. Fax: 716-375-2690.
E-mail: quick@sbu.edu
Web Site: www.sbu.edu/quickcenter.aspx?id=2012
Formerly: St. Bonaventure Art Collection
Founded: 1856.
Congressional District: 39
Key Personnel: Exec. Dir., Joseph A. LoSchiavo.
Personnel Profile: Full-Time Paid 11; Part-Time Paid 5; Part-Time Volunteers 40; Interns 3.
Governing Authority: St. Bonaventure University. Tax-exempt: 501(c)(3).
Art Museum.
Collections: paintings; sculpture; prints & drawings; Native American & Pre-Columbian pottery; Asian porcelain; Asian art; photography; creches.
Facilities: print & drawing study, & reading room (open by appointment).
Activities: guided tours; permanent & temporary exhibitions.
Publications: newsletter, QuickAccess.
Hours & Admission Prices: Summer: Tues.-Sat. 12-5. Winter: Mon.-Fri. 10-5, Sat.-Sun. 12-4. No charge; donations accepted. Closed New Year's Day; Easter; Thanksgiving; Christmas. ♿
Attendance: 20,000 (accurate)
Membership: Individual $45; Family/Dual $75; Contributing $100-$499; Sustaining $500-$999; Sponsor $1,000-$4,999; Patron $5,000-$9,999.

Saint Johnsville

FORT KLOCK HISTORIC RESTORATION, 7214 State Hwy. 5, Saint Johnsville, NY 13452-4502. Mailing Address: P.O. Box 42, Saint Johnsville, NY 13452-0042. Tel.: 518-568-7779.
E-mail: fortklock@gmail.com
Web Site: fortklock.org
Founded: 1954.
Congressional District: 105
Key Personnel: Chm. (V), Olof Jansson; Pres. (V), Cindy Sinchak.
Personnel Profile: Part-Time Volunteers 1.
Governing Authority: nonprofit organization. Tax-exempt: 501(c)(3).
Historic House Museum: 1750 Klock Homestead.
Collections: early Dutch architecture; farmhouse furnishings. Historic Buildings: restored Little Red Schoolhouse; Carriage House; Blacksmith Shop; Dutch Barn; 1750 Farmhouse; cheese house.
Research Fields: Dutch barns.
Facilities: picnic area. Museum-related items for sale.
Activities: guided tours; opening day colonial craft demonstrations. Museum Sponsors: Strawberry Festival in July; Stone Soup Musical Concert in July; Klock Family Reunion in August; Young Pioneer Program in August; Craft Fair in September; Interrupted Harvest in September; Fort Klock Haunted House in October; Open House for St. Nicholas Day in December.
Hours & Admission Prices: Memorial Day to mid-Oct. Tues.-Sun. 9-5; tours & special demonstration by appointment. Small admission charge. ♿
Attendance: 2,000 (estimated)
Membership: Junior 14-18 $1; Active $10; Supporting $15.

Salamanca

SALAMANCA RAIL MUSEUM, 170 Main St., Salamanca, NY 14779-1574. Tel.: 716-945-3133. Fax: 716-945-3133.
E-mail: salarail@verizon.net
Web Site: mysite.verizon.net/bizxyrad/salamancarailmuseumassociation/
Founded: 1980.
Congressional District: 31
Key Personnel: C.E.O., Chm. (V) & Cur., Gerald J. Fordham; Treas., Robert W. Irwin; Public Rels., Kevin Burleson; Museum Shop Mgr., Barbara A. Fordham.
Personnel Profile: Full-Time Paid 2; Part-Time Paid 1; Part-Time Volunteers 12.
Governing Authority: private; nonprofit organization. Tax-exempt: 501(c)(3).
Transportation Museum: housed in a 1912 restored passenger depot constructed by the Buffalo, Rochester and Pittsburgh Railway.
Collections: artifacts; photographs; videos; early 20th-century office furniture; telegraph keys; railroad memorabilia; train cars; nostalgic railroad pieces with emphasis on the three railroads that served the region: The Erie, the Baltimore and Ohio (BR & P), and the Pennsylvania Railroads.
Research Fields: local railroad history.
Facilities: 1,200-vol. library; 30-seat theater; 2,700 sq. ft. exhibit space. Museum-related items for sale.
Activities: docent program; films; formal education programs for children; guided tours; lectures; loan exhibitions; broadcast programs.
Publications: calendar, Salamanca Rail Museum; quarterly newsletter, The Junction Express; weekly newspaper column, Tracks From The Past.
Hours & Admission Prices: April-Dec. Mon.-Sat. 10-5, Sun. 12-5. Tours: $1 donation per person. Closed Thanksgiving; Christmas. ♿
Attendance: 6,205 (accurate)
Membership: Senior Citizens $5; Regular $8.

SENECA-IROQUOIS NATIONAL MUSEUM, (M), 814 Broad St., Salamanca, NY 14779-1378. Mailing Address: 252 Rochester St., Salamanca, NY 14779-1509. Tel.: 716-945-1760. Fax: 716-945-1624.
E-mail: sue.grey@sni.org
Web Site: www.senecamuseum.org
Founded: 1977.
Congressional District: 49
Key Personnel: Dir., Jare Cardinal; Public Rels. & Mktg. Mgr., Sue Grey; Museum Shop Mgr., Eva Aidman.
Personnel Profile: Full-Time Paid 7.
Governing Authority: nonprofit organization. Tax-exempt: 501(c)(3).
Anthropology & Ethnology Museum.
Collections: period cultural ancestral artifacts; Seneca & other Iroquois Nations of the Northeast; archaeology; history; modern art.
Research Fields: Seneca-Iroquois studies.
Facilities: Native made items and artworks for sale.
Activities: guided tours; docent program; inter-museum, permanent & temporary exhibitions.
Publications: catalogue of collections; data sheets; bibliographies.
Hours & Admission Prices: May-Oct. daily 9-5; Nov.-Dec. & Feb.-April Mon.-Fri. 9-5. Adults $5, senior citizens & college students $3.50, children 7-16 $3; discounts to AAM & AAA members; children under 7 no charge. Closed SNI observed holidays. ♿
Attendance: 15,000 (estimated)

Sanborn

SANBORN AREA HISTORICAL SOCIETY, (M), 2822 Niagara St., Sanborn, NY 14132-9282. Mailing Address: P.O. Box 172, Sanborn, NY 14132-0172. Tel.: 716-731-9510.
E-mail: sanborngerry@juno.com
Web Site: sanbornhistory.org
Founded: 1996.
Congressional District: 28
Key Personnel: Dir. & Pres. (V), Gary Townsend; Chm. (V), Marcia Rivers; Devel., Gerald E. Treichler; Public Rels. & Treas., Glenn Wienke; Archivist, Jane Schultz; Cur., Linda Jackson.
Personnel Profile: Part-Time Volunteers 76.
Governing Authority: private; nonprofit organization. Tax-exempt: 501(c)(3).
Agriculture Museum.
Collections: early farm equipment; kitchen; dolls; glassware; tools; toys; household artifacts; business advertising.
Facilities: library; 600 sq. ft. exhibit space; 58 acre farm.
Activities: programs; school & organization groups. Annual Events: Farm Festival; Ice Cream Social; Antique Show & Sale; Annual Program at High School.
Publications: quarterly newsletter, Salubris.
Hours & Admission Prices: School House Museum: April-Nov. Sun. 2-4; Dec.-March 1st Sun. 2-4; other times by appointment. Farm Museum: April-Oct. Wed. 1-4, Sun. 2-4; other times by appointment. No charge; donations accepted. ♿
Attendance: 400 (estimated)
Membership: Individual $10; Family $15; Patron, Business & Professional $100.

Saranac Lake

ROBERT LOUIS STEVENSON MEMORIAL COTTAGE, 44 Stevenson Lane, Saranac Lake, NY 12983-1975. Tel.: 518-891-1462.
Founded: 1916.
Congressional District: 30
Key Personnel: Pres., William Delahant; Vice Pres., Les Hershhorn; Cur., Mike Delahant; Sec., Rita Leonard; Treas., Wilhelm Tissot.
Personnel Profile: Full-Time Volunteers 1; Part-Time Volunteers 3.
Governing Authority: society. Operated by The Delahant Family. Tax-exempt.
Literary Museum: housed in 1887 home of Robert Louis Stevenson.
Collections: personal mementos; childhood photographs; original letters & articles of Stevenson lore.
Facilities: 125-vol. library of books on the life of Robert Louis Stevenson available for research by special request.
Activities: guided tours.
Publications: book, The Penny Piper of Saranac - An Episode in the Life of Robert Louis Stevenson.

Hours & Admission Prices: July to mid-Sept. Tues.-Sun. 9:30-12 & 1-4:30; other times by appointment. Adults $5; children under 12 & members no charge.
Attendance: 500 (estimated)
Membership: Individual/Family $25; Business/Organization $50; Supporter $100 & up; Patron $500 & up; Benefactor $1,000 & up.

Saratoga Springs

THE CHILDREN'S MUSEUM AT SARATOGA, 69 Caroline St., Saratoga Springs, NY 12866-3202. Tel.: 518-584-5540. Fax: 518-584-6059.
E-mail: info@cmssny.org
Web Site: www.cmssny.org
Founded: 1989.
Congressional District: 21 & 22
Key Personnel: Chm. (V), James Carminucci; Museum Shop Mgr., Ashley Terwilliger.
Personnel Profile: Full-Time Paid 2; Part-Time Paid 10.
Governing Authority: private; nonprofit. Tax-exempt: 501(c)(3).
Children's Museum.
Collections: interactive exhibits for children ages 2-7.
Facilities: educational facilities; 6,000 sq. ft. exhibit space. Shirts, caps & museum-related items for sale.
Activities: participatory exhibits; school outreach programs. Annual Events: luncheon fundraiser; golf tournament; gala in August.
Publications: quarterly newsletter, Interact.
Hours & Admission Prices: July-Labor Day Mon.-Sat. 9:30-4:30; Labor Day-June Tues.-Sat. 9:30-4:30, Sun. 12-4:30. Admission $6; children under one no charge. Closed New Year's Day; Easter; Memorial Day; Independence Day; Thanksgiving; Christmas Eve & Day. ♿
Attendance: 60,000 (accurate)
Membership: You & Me $30-$50; Top Trio $40-$65; Family Fun $50-$85; Traveler $125.

FRANCES YOUNG TANG TEACHING MUSEUM AND ART GALLERY, (M), Skidmore College, 815 N. Broadway, Saratoga Springs, NY 12866-1632. Tel.: 518-580-8080. Fax: 518-580-5069.
E-mail: tang@skidmore.edu
Web Site: www.skidmore.edu/tang
Founded: 2000.
Congressional District: 22
Key Personnel: Dayton Dir., John Weber; Education, Susi Kerr; Registrar, Elizabeth Karp; Cur., Ian Berry; Museum Shop Mgr., Barbara Schrade.
Personnel Profile: Full-Time Paid 14; Part-Time Paid 19; Part-Time Volunteers 4; Interns 4.
Governing Authority: private college; nonprofit. Parent Institution: Skidmore College. Tax-exempt: 501(c)(3).
Art Museum.
Collections: drawings; paintings; prints; sculptures; video, audio & installation art.
Major Exhibits: Arlene Shechet, 11/09-1/3/10; Nicole Eisenman, 11/09-1/10; Lives of the Hudson, 11/09-3/10; Amazement Park, 11/09-4/10; Fred Tomaselli, 2/6/10-6/6/10.
Research Fields: interdisciplinary teaching with artwork and objects of material culture.
Facilities: 200-seat auditorium; educational facilities. Museum-related items for sale.
Activities: concerts; docent program; films; formal education programs for children; guided tours; lectures; participatory, traveling & temporary exhibitions.
Publications: newsletter, Tang Talks; exhibit catalogues.
Hours & Admission Prices: Tues.-Fri. 10-5, Sat.-Sun. 12-5. Suggested Donations: adults $5; discounts to AAM & ICOM members; members no charge. Closed New Year's Day; Thanksgiving; Christmas Day. ♿
Attendance: 50,000 (accurate)
Membership: See website for information.

HISTORICAL SOCIETY OF SARATOGA SPRINGS, The Casino, Congress Park, Saratoga Springs, NY 12866. Mailing Address: P.O. Box 216, Saratoga Springs, NY 12866-0216. Tel.: 518-584-6920. Fax: 518-581-1477.
E-mail: info@saratogahistory.org
Web Site: www.saratogahistory.org
Founded: 1883.
Congressional District: 21
Key Personnel: Dir., James D. Parillo; Pres., Lisa Millis; Cur., Becky Codner; Research Asst., John Conors; Archivist, Doris Lamont; Museum Shop Mgr., Ted Waite.
Personnel Profile: Full-Time Paid 1; Part-Time Paid 3; Part-Time Volunteers 40; Interns 1.
Governing Authority: society. Parent Institution: George S. Bolster Collection. Branch Museum: Walworth Memorial Museum. Tax-exempt: 101(6) & 501(c)(3).
Local History Museum: housed in 1871 gambling casino, a designated National Landmark.
Collections: relating to the springs, hotels, gambling & other facets of Saratoga Springs history; Walworth Museum: furnishings of Reuben Hyde Walworth, last Chancellor of New York; papers of Frank Sullivan.
Research Fields: 19th-century resort life; spas & mineral springs; early history of the D.A.R.; Frank Sullivan; history of 19th- & 20th-century Saratoga Springs; hydrotherapy; New York State chancellors & Court of Chancery; 19th-century law & legal codes; Roman Catholic Paulist Order.
Facilities: 2,000-vol. library of books on the history of Saratoga Springs, newspapers, guidebooks, clippings, manuscripts, photographs; manuscripts, diaries, journals & correspondence of the Walworth family (1820-1950) & writer Frank Sullivan available by appointment; Ann Grey Gallery for changing exhibitions.
Activities: formally organized educational programs; monthly meetings & programs.
Publications: monthly newsletter, Chips; George S. Bolster (monograph), The Casino; exhibit catalogues.
Hours & Admission Prices: Memorial Day to Labor Day daily 10-4; Sept.-May Wed.-Sun. 10-4. Adults $5, students & senior citizens $4; discounts to AAM members; children, members, Ann Grey Gallery, Bolster Collection Archives no charge.
Attendance: 12,000 (estimated)
Membership: Senior Citizen & Student $15; Individual $25; Family $35; Sustaining $50; Patron $100.

NATIONAL MUSEUM OF DANCE & HALL OF FAME, 99 S. Broadway, Saratoga Springs, NY 12866-4557. Tel.: 518-584-2225, ext. 3001. Fax: 518-584-4515.
E-mail: donna@dancemuseum.org
Web Site: www.dancemuseum.org
Founded: 1986.
Congressional District: 22
Key Personnel: Interim Dir., Donna Skiff; Chm. Bd. Directors (V), Michele Riggi; Coord. Grants & Exhibits, Sarah Hall Weaver; Rental Coord., Jo Ambrosio; Museum Shop Mgr., Susan Buesing.
Personnel Profile: Full-Time Paid 3; Part-Time Paid 3; Part-Time Volunteers 30; Interns 5.
Governing Authority: private; nonprofit organization. Parent Institution: Saratoga Performing Arts Center, Saratoga, NY. Tax-exempt: 501(c)(3).
Dance Museum.
Collections: photographs; personal items of dancers; dance & dance history; costumes; videos; audio; clippings; ephemera; 19th-20th century American professional dance artifacts; dance archives.
Major Exhibits: The Man Can Move, 6/10; Postage Paid, 6/10.
Research Fields: relationships between dance and socio-economical, political & cultural aspects of society at large.
Facilities: 3 dance studios; 75,000 sq. ft. exhibit space; resource room. Gift items for sale.
Activities: dance school; dance workshops; lectures; showings; interactive children's corner; live performances; arts festivals; dance concerts; guided tours; workshops; rental facilities; special events. Annual Events: Hall of Fame Induction; exhibit openings.
Publications: biannual newsletter, Foot Notes.
Hours & Admission Prices: Seasonal Hours: Tues.-Sun. 10-4:30. Adults $6.50, senior citizens & students $5, children under 12 $3; members no charge. Closed New Year's Eve, day & week; Christmas Eve, Day & week. ♿
Attendance: 9,000 (estimated)
Membership: Student & Senior $25; Enthusiast $40; Family Dance Troupe $60; Corps Dancer $100; Soloist $250; Principal $500; Choreographer $1,000; Patron $2,000; Benefactor $5,000.

NATIONAL MUSEUM OF RACING AND HALL OF FAME, (M), 191 Union Ave., Saratoga Springs, NY 12866-3556. Tel.: 518-584-0400; 800-562-5394. Fax: 518-584-4574.
E-mail: info@racingmuseum.org/nmrmedia@racingmuseum.net
Web Site: racingmuseum.org
Founded: 1950.
Congressional District: 29
Key Personnel: Dir., Joseph E. Aulisi; Pres., Stella F. Thayer; Asst. Dir. & Membership, Cathy Maguire.
Personnel Profile: Full-Time Paid 10; Part-Time Paid 5; Part-Time Volunteers 15.
Governing Authority: nonprofit organization. Tax-exempt: 501(c)(3).
National Thoroughbred Racing Museum.
Collections: equine paintings; sporting art; thoroughbred racing trophies; racing colors; sculpture; racing memorabilia; hall of fame.

Research Fields: thoroughbred horses; thoroughbred racing.
Facilities: library available for use by appointment; 250-seat auditorium; theater; films; video equipment. Items pertaining to thoroughbred horses & racing, books, prints & other museum-related items for sale.
Activities: guided tours for groups by advance appointment; audiovisuals; films; inter-museum & permanent exhibitions. Museum Sponsors: gala; Hall of Fame induction ceremonies.
Publications: Quarterly Member Newsletter.
Hours & Admission Prices: Racing Season daily 9-5; Off Season: Mon.-Sat. 10-4, Sun. 12-4. Adults $7, students & senior citizens with ID $5; discounts to groups, AAM & ICOM members; members & children under 5 no charge. Closed New Year's Day; Easter; Thanksgiving; Christmas. ♿
Attendance: 60,000 (accurate)
Membership: Individual $50; Family $75; Contributor $100; Donor $250; Associate $500; Patron $1,000; Benefactor $1,500; Gold Cup $2,500.

NEW YORK STATE MILITARY MUSEUM AND VETERANS RESEARCH CENTER, 61 Lake Ave., Saratoga Springs, NY 12866-2315. Tel.: 518-581-5100. Fax: 518-581-5111.
E-mail: historians@ny.ngb.army.mil
Web Site: www.nysmm.org
Founded: 1863.
Congressional District: 20
Key Personnel: Dir., Michael Aikey; Registrar, Christopher Morton; Chief Cur., Courtney Burns; Archivist, Jim Gandy; Museum Shop Mgr., Harold Sheffer.
Personnel Profile: Full-Time Paid 12; Part-Time Paid 1; Part-Time Volunteers 50; Interns 3.
Governing Authority: state.
Military Museum.
Collections: New York State's military history from colonial times to the present; New York State's battle flag; State's veterans oral history; military equipment.
Facilities: 3,000-vol. library of military books; 70-seat auditorium; 9,000 sq. ft. exhibit space. Museum-related items for sale.
Activities: docent program; formal education programs; guided tours; lectures; temporary exhibitions.
Hours & Admission Prices: Tues.-Sat. 10-4, Sun. 12-4. No charge; donations accepted. Closed New York State holidays. ♿
Attendance: 12,000 (estimated)

SARATOGA AUTOMOBILE MUSEUM, 110 Avenue of the Pines, Saratoga Springs, NY 12866-6220. Tel.: 518-587-1935. Fax: 518-587-4149.
Web Site: www.saratogaautomuseum.org
Founded: 2002.
Congressional District: 21
Key Personnel: Dir., Jean Hoffman; Dir. Devel., Richard Selikoff; Education & Public Rels., Alan Edstrom.
Personnel Profile: Full-Time Paid 4; Full-Time Volunteers 15; Part-Time Paid 2; Part-Time Volunteers 140; Interns 4.
Governing Authority: private; nonprofit organization. Tax-exempt: 501(c)(3).
Automobile Museum.
Collections: automobile history; automobiles; racing cars.
Major Exhibits: 50 Years of Corvette, 11/09-3/10; Designs of Dutch Darrin, 3/10-10/10.
Activities: formal education programs; car restoration classes for VOTEC students; guided tours; lectures; participatory exhibits. Annual Events: Auto Show in spring; Lawn Shows in summer.
Publications: quarterly newsmagazine, Horsepower; gallery guides; show program.
Hours & Admission Prices: June-Sept. daily 10-5; Columbus Day to May Tues.-Sun. 10-5. Adults $8, senior citizens, active military & students 17 & over $5, children 6-16 $3.50; discounts to groups; children under 6 no charge. Closed New Year's Eve & Day; Thanksgiving; Christmas. ♿
Attendance: 30,000 (accurate)
Membership: Student & Senior $25; Single $35; Family $50; Patron $250; Silver Arrow $1,000.

THE SCHICK ART GALLERY, SKIDMORE COLLEGE, 815 N. Broadway, Saisselin Art Bldg., Fl. 2, Saratoga Springs, NY 12866-1698. Tel.: 518-580-5049 & 5000. Fax: 516-580-5029.
E-mail: mjablons@skidmore.edu
Web Site: www.skidmore.edu/schick
Founded: 1926.
Key Personnel: Asst. to Dir., Mary Jablonski.
Personnel Profile: Full-Time Paid 1; Part-Time Paid 4.
Governing Authority: college. Parent Institution: Skidmore College. Tax-exempt.
Art Gallery.
Collections: paintings; graphics; ceramics; sculpture.
Facilities: gallery for changing exhibits.
Activities: lectures; films; gallery talks; temporary exhibitions.
Publications: exhibition brochures; catalogues.
Hours & Admission Prices: Sept.-May Mon.-Fri. 9-5, Sat.-Sun. 1-4:30; Summer: hours variable according to summer class schedules. No charge. ♿
Attendance: 25,000 (estimated)

Saugerties

OPUS 40 AND THE QUARRYMAN'S MUSEUM, 50 Fite Rd., Saugerties, NY 12477-3260. Tel.: 845-246-3400. Fax: 845-246-1997.
E-mail: tad@opus40.org
Web Site: www.opus40.org
Founded: 1978.
Congressional District: 26
Key Personnel: C.E.O., Pat Richards; Pres. (V), Tad Richards.
Personnel Profile: Part-Time Volunteers 30.
Governing Authority: nonprofit organization. Tax-exempt: 501(c)(3).
Sculpture/Earthwork & History Museum.
Collections: 6.5-acre environmental bluestone sculpture; 19th-century quarrymen's tools & artifacts.
Facilities: 12-acres of grounds; performing arts center. Gift items for sale.
Activities: lectures; concerts; performing, visual & literary arts events.
Publications: monograph, Harvy Fite's OPUS 40; brochure.
Hours & Admission Prices: Memorial Day-Columbus Day Fri.-Sun. 11:30-6. Adults $10, senior citizens & students $7, school age children $3; discounts to AAM & ICOM members; members & children under 5 no charge.
Attendance: 15,000
Membership: Individual $25; Family $40; Supporting $75; Sustaining $100; Sponsor $500; Patron $1,000.

Sayville

SAYVILLE HISTORICAL SOCIETY, Edwards St. & Collins Ave., Sayville, NY 11782. Mailing Address: P.O. Box 41, Sayville, NY 11782-0041. Tel.: 631-563-0186 & 567-1289.
Founded: 1944.
Congressional District: 2
Key Personnel: Admin., Linda Conron; Pres. (V), Constance Currie; Treas., John Wells.
Personnel Profile: Part-Time Paid 2; Part-Time Volunteers 8.
Governing Authority: board of directors; not-for-profit organization. Tax-exempt.
Historical Society Museum.
Collections: local history from colonial times to present.
Facilities: library available to public only upon request; 2,900 sq. ft. exhibit space; herb garden.
Activities: guided tours; lectures; loan & temporary exhibits. Annual Events: Christmas Open House; Holiday House Tour; An Afternoon on the Edwards Farm.
Publications: quarterly newsletter, Homestead Happenings.
Hours & Admission Prices: Oct.-June 1st & 3rd Sun. 2-4. No charge; donations accepted. Closed when holiday falls on Open House Sunday.
Attendance: 830 (accurate)
Membership: Junior $5; Individual $15; Family $25; Life $200.

Scarsdale

THE GREENBURGH NATURE CENTER, 99 Dromore Rd., Scarsdale, NY 10583-1705. Tel.: 914-723-3470. Fax: 914-725-6599.
E-mail: khundgen@greenburghnaturecenter.org
Web Site: www.greenburghnaturecenter.org
Founded: 1975.
Congressional District: 23
Key Personnel: C.E.O., Kurt Hundgen; Chm. (V), Margaret Goldberg; Mng. Dir., Penny Berman; Education, John Mancuso; Cur., Travis Brady; Naturalist, Jenn Sloan; Data Mgr., Jocelyn Lim.
Personnel Profile: Full-Time Paid 12; Part-Time Paid 2; Part-Time Volunteers 50; Interns 4.
Governing Authority: bd. of directors; nonprofit organization. Tax-exempt: 501(c)(3).
Nature Center: located on a 33-acre greenspace, former Nunataks Estate.
Collections: wildlife; working & observational honeybees hives; pond life aquaria & brook; 25 acres of woodlands & wetland; 2-acre lawn with specimen shrubs & trees; rock outcrops of Fordham Gneiss; live animal museum consisting of about 140 exotic & local fauna; glacial boulders; nature discovery room with hands-on exhibits; rock garden; apple orchard; herb garden; natural history artifacts; Native American & colonial farm artifacts.
Research Fields: bird & reptile behavior; natural history; insects; arachnids; forest ecology.

Facilities: 700-vol. nature library pertaining to zoology, botany, natural history & ecology; oasis for spring & fall migrating song birds; aquarium; 60-seat auditorium; botanical garden; exhibit space apart from museum; nature center; greenhouse with educational exhibits; training site for outdoor education specialists; zoological park; meeting rooms; nature trails. Nature-related items for sale.
Activities: guided tours; natural trails; lectures; outdoor concerts; hobby workshops; organized educational programs; outreach program; participatory exhibits; mobile van; temporary & changing exhibitions. Museum Sponsors: Springfair; Halloween Walks; Fall Festival.
Publications: quarterly newsletter; calendar; annual illustrated natural history booklets; various guides to gardens, grounds & trails.
Hours & Admission Prices: July 7-June 20 Grounds: daily dawn-dusk. Manor House: Sat.-Thurs. 9:30-5. Adults $7, children 2-12 $5; discounts to NYSAM members; Greenburgh residents, Westchester County Parks Pass; members no charge. ♿
Attendance: 78,000 (estimated)
Membership: Senior Citizen $30; Individual $40; Senior Family $50; Family $60.

THE SCARSDALE HISTORICAL SOCIETY, 937 Post Rd., Scarsdale, NY 10583-5656. Mailing Address: P.O. Box 431, Scarsdale, NY 10583-0431. Tel.: 914-723-1744. Fax: 914-723-2185.
E-mail: history@cloud9.net
Web Site: scarsdalehistory.org
Founded: 1973.
Congressional District: 20
Key Personnel: Pres., Bill Doescher; Exec. Dir., Cindy Krossman; Treas., Gloria Forte; Museum Shop Mgr., Greta Fisher; Museum Shop Mgr., Etta Parker.
Personnel Profile: Full-Time Paid 1; Part-Time Paid 3; Part-Time Volunteers 20.
Governing Authority: nonprofit organization. Tax-exempt: 501(c)(3).
Historical Society: housed in 1828 Quaker Meeting House, a 19th-century farm house of modest means.
Collections: 19th-century textiles, costumes, furniture, rugs, farm equipment, documents, paintings, kitchen utensils, maps, photographs. Historic House: 18th-century Cudner-Hyatt Farm House.
Research Fields: architecture; furnishings; gardens; cooking; costumes; decorative arts; local history; oral history; archaeology.
Facilities: 2,500-vol. library pertaining to history, architecture, costumes, furniture, cooking & gardening available on premises only; slides; tapes; maps; photographs; paintings; documents. Books & other publications for sale.
Activities: guided tours; audiovisual slide presentation; lectures; organized educational programs; docent program; temporary, loan, traveling & participating exhibitions.
Publications: brochures; booklets, Scarsdale Heritage Homes; A Celebration of Westchester Arts & Decorations of Three Hundred Years; Bronx River Retrospective; Did you Know your Roof had a Name?; The Cudner-Hyatt House-The Story of its Two Families; A Century of Ceramics in the Hudson Valley; Summer Pleasures: Suburban Leisure in the 19th Century.
Hours & Admission Prices: Mon.-Fri. 9-4; other times by appointment. Museum: adults $3, senior citizens & students $2; discounts to AAM members; members no charge. Cudner Hyatt House: adults $5, seniors & students $3; discounts to AAM members; members no charge. Closed national holidays.
Attendance: 10,000 (accurate)
Membership: Student $10; Senior Citizen $25; Business $25 and up; Senior Couple $35; Family $50; Donor $75; Sponsor $100; Associate $125; Sustainer $150; Patron $300; Benefactor $600.

WEINBERG NATURE CENTER, 455 Mamaroneck Rd., Scarsdale, NY 10583-7727. Tel.: 914-722-1289. Fax: 914-723-4784 (call first).
E-mail: support@weinbergnaturecenter.org
Web Site: www.weinbergnaturecenter.org
Founded: 1958.
Key Personnel: Exec. Dir., Walter D. Terrell, Jr.; Pres., Dr. Melissa Grigione.
Personnel Profile: Full-Time Paid 1; Part-Time Paid 3; Part-Time Volunteers 10.
Governing Authority: municipal. Parent Institution: The Scarsdale Parks & Recreation Dept. Tax-exempt.
Nature Center.
Collections: rocks; shells; leaves; pictures of birds & wild flowers; live exhibits; wildlife exhibits; taxidermy specimens of native wildlife.
Facilities: 500-vol. library of books & research notes available for use by special permission; nature trails.
Activities: guided tours; lectures; formally organized educational programs; temporary exhibitions; workshops.
Publications: newsletter format, calendar of events.
Hours & Admission Prices: Summer: Mon.-Fri. 9-5; Fall, Winter & Spring: Wed.-Sun. 9-5. Charge for some weekend programs. Closed village holidays. ♿
Attendance: 20,000 (estimated)
Membership: Friends of the Weinberg Nature Center Inc.: Individual $15; Family $25; Institutional $100; Sustaining $250; Life $1,000; Best Friend $5,000.

Schenectady

MANDEVILLE GALLERY, UNION COLLEGE, Nott Memorial, Schenectady, NY 12308. Mailing Address: 807 Union St., Union College, Schaffer Library, Schenectady, NY 12308-3103. Tel.: 518-388-6729. Fax: 518-388-8340.
Web Site: www.union.edu/gallery
Founded: 1995.
Congressional District: 21
Key Personnel: Dir., Rachel Seligman.
Personnel Profile: Full-Time Paid 2.
Governing Authority: private; nonprofit organization. Parent Institution: Union College, Schenectady, NY 12308-3155. Tax-exempt: 170(b)(1)(A).
Art Museum.
Collections: 19th & 20th century European & American works on paper; portraits; Asian art; early scientific & mathematical apparatus; period artifacts.
Activities: lectures; loan, participatory, traveling & temporary exhibitions.
Hours & Admission Prices: Daily 10-6. No charge; donations accepted. Closed New Year's Eve & Day; Independence Day; Thanksgiving & day after; Christmas week. ♿
Attendance: 5,000 (estimated)

SCHENECTADY COUNTY HISTORICAL SOCIETY, 32 Washington Ave., Schenectady, NY 12305-1600. Tel.: 518-374-0263. Fax: 518-688-2825.
E-mail: curator@schist.org
Web Site: www.schist.org
Founded: 1905.
Congressional District: 21
Key Personnel: Vice Pres., Merritt Glennon; Pres. (V), Edwin D. Reilly, Jr.; Cur., Kate Weller; Librarian, Katherine Chansky; Site Mgr. Mabee Farm, Pat Barrot; Office Mgr., Jennifer Hanson; Treas., Mary Treanor; Museum Shop Mgr., Kim Mabee.
Personnel Profile: Full-Time Paid 6; Part-Time Volunteers 50; Interns 4.
Governing Authority: society. Subsidiary Institution: 18th-century farm site, Mabee Farm Historic Site, 1080 Main St. (Rt. 5S), Rotterdam Junction, NY 12150. Tax-exempt: 501(c)(3).
General Museum & Historic House Site: located within area of original Schenectady stockade built by the Dutch in 1661.
Collections: paintings; guns; toys and dolls; furniture; household goods; Indian artifacts; decorative arts; various collections pertaining to Schenectady County; books; manuscripts; genealogical data; maps; photographs; recordings.
Research Fields: genealogy; Schenectady County history; early colonial (Dutch, English & Palatine) settlement in New York, Erie Canal; American Locomotive Co.; General Electric.
Facilities: 2,500-vol. library of books available on premises; reading room; 50-seat auditorium. Books for sale.
Activities: guided tours; lectures; courses; inter-museum loan, permanent & temporary exhibitions; research guidance & training; Walkabout & Waterfront Fair.
Publications: bimonthly, Schenectady County Historical Society Newsletter. Arcadia publications: Rotterdam; Glenville; Niskayuna.
Hours & Admission Prices: Museum: Mon.-Fri. 1-5, Sat. 10-4. Library: Mon.-Fri. 9-5, Sat. 10-2. Mabee Farm: Tues.-Sat. 10-4. Museum: adults $5, children $2. Library: adults $4; members & students no charge. Closed national holidays. ♿
Attendance: 17,000 (accurate)
Membership: Individual $25; Family $50; Donor $75; Sponsor $100; Benefactor $250; Patron $500; Life $1,000.

SCHENECTADY MUSEUM AND SUITS-BUECHE PLANETARIUM, (M), 15 Nott Terrace Heights, Schenectady, NY 12308-3198. Tel.: 518-382-7890. Fax: 518-382-7893.
E-mail: schdymuse@schenectadymuseum.org
Web Site: www.schenectadymuseum.org
Founded: 1934.
Congressional District: 21
Key Personnel: Exec. Dir., Kerry M. Orlyk; Co-Pres. (V), Jane N. Golub; Co-Pres. (V), Denise V. Gonick; Museum Shop Coord., Twila White.
Personnel Profile: Full-Time Paid 15; Part-Time Paid 9; Part-Time Volunteers 23; Interns 5.

Governing Authority: nonprofit organization. Tax-exempt: 501(c)(3).
History, Science & Technology Museum and Planetarium.
Collections: area science & technology including General Electric; Charles Steinmetz & American Locomotive Company photographs; WRGB television station artifacts; technology artifacts including early home appliances, radios, televisions, experimental electric equipment, medical imaging equipment, & 1978 prototype electric car; 19th-20th century textiles; technology-related art.
Major Exhibits: Trains, 11/09-4/10; Invention Convention, 5/10.
Research Fields: history of regional science & technology; urban studies; contemporary art.
Facilities: 20,000 sq. ft. exhibit space; 70-seat auditorium; classrooms; planetarium; archives; radio stations WZIR & WBZCRZ; SMARA Amateur Radio Club. Museum related items for sale.
Activities: lectures; films; gallery talks; permanent & temporary exhibits in science & regional history; adult classes; workshops; education programs for children & adults; planetarium programs; docent program; outreach programs.
Publications: quarterly newsletters; monthly member updates; annual report.
Hours & Admission Prices: Tues.-Sat. 10-5. Adults $6.50, seniors $5.25, children 4-12 $4; discounts to AAM members; ASTC, Empire State Reciprocal Program members, museum members & children under 4 no charge. Planetarium Programs: Tues.-Fri. 2 pm, Sat. 1, 2 & 3. Additional $3.75 per person. Closed New Year's Day; Memorial Day; Independence Day; Labor Day; Thanksgiving; Christmas. ♿
Attendance: 44,688 (accurate)
Membership: Senior & Student $30; Senior Couple & Individual $45; Grandparents $50; Couple $60; Family $65.

Schoharie

OLD STONE FORT MUSEUM COMPLEX, (M), 145 Fort Rd., Schoharie, NY 12157-4705. Tel.: 518-295-7192. Fax: 518-295-7187.
E-mail: office@schohariehistory.net
Web Site: www.theoldstonefort.org
Founded: 1889.
Congressional District: 22, 23
Key Personnel: C.E.O. & Dir., Carle J. Kopecky; Pres., Jeff O'Connor; Treas., Anne Hendrix; Cur. & Education, Daniel Beams; Museum Shop Mgr. & Public Rels., Laura Spickerman.
Personnel Profile: Full-Time Paid 4; Part-Time Paid 12; Part-Time Volunteers 80.
Governing Authority: society. Parent Institution: Schoharie County Historical Society. Subsidiary Institution: Lansing Manor Museum. Tax-exempt: 501(c)(3).
General Museum: housed in 1772 church, later used as a fort.
Collections: Indian artifacts; deeds; manuscripts; documents; local genealogies; 18th-century land grants; maps; church records; cemetery records; local newspapers; tools; vehicles; furniture; household items; firearms; arts & crafts; clothing; quilts; agriculture; technology; military history; transportation; archaeology; natural history; textiles; folk art; decorative arts.
Research Fields: local history; genealogy; folklore.
Facilities: 2,500-vol. library of NY State & Schoharie County history available for use on the premises May-Oct.; reading room. Books & other museum-related items for sale.
Activities: guided tours; lectures; permanent & temporary exhibitions; living history demonstrations; concerts; formal education programs; school loan service. Museum Sponsors: Revolutionary War & Civil War reenactments; Strawberry Festival.
Publications: semiannual pamphlet, Schoharie County Historical Review.
Hours & Admission Prices: May-June & Sept.-Oct. Tues.-Sat. 10-5, Sun. 12-5; July.-Aug. Mon.-Sat. 10-5, Sun. 12-5. Adults $5, senior citizens $4.50, children $1.50; discounts to AAM & ICOM members; Schoharie County Schools & members no charge. ♿
Attendance: 4,900 (accurate)
Membership: Students & Senior Citizens $20; Regular $25; Family $40; Sustaining $50 & up; Supporting $75; Life $1,000.

SCHOHARIE COLONIAL HERITAGE ASSOCIATION, 1743 Palatine House, Spring St., Schoharie, NY 12157. Mailing Address: P.O. Box 554, Schoharie, NY 12157-0554. Tel.: 518-295-7505 & 7585. Fax: 518-295-6001.
E-mail: scha@midtel.net
Web Site: www.midtel.net/~scha
Founded: 1963.
Congressional District: 31
Key Personnel: C.E.O., Sarah Sherman; Pres., Jean Harra; Vice Pres., Ruth Anne Keese; Treas., Donna McCabe.
Personnel Profile: Part-Time Paid 3; Part-Time Volunteers 5.
Governing Authority: society; nonprofit organization. Branch Museum: Depot Lane Center, Depot Lane, Schoharie, NY 12157. Tax-exempt: 501(c)(3).
Historic Building: housed in 1743 Palatine House, old Lutheran parsonage.
Collections: 18th-century articles used by ministers at home & in church; pictures; documents; articles pertaining to 19th century Middleburgh & Schoharie Railroad. Historic Structure: 1891 railroad depot.
Research Fields: German Palatine life.
Facilities: architectural design; digs; gardens; cemetery.
Activities: guided tours; lecture series; weaving demonstrations. Association Sponsors: Wool Day, spinning & weaving lessons and workshops, dyeing & herb workshops.
Publications: pamphlet, Visit The 1743 Palatine House & 1891 Train Car Museum.
Hours & Admission Prices: May group tours only; June-Oct. Thurs.-Sun. 1-4. Adults $2.50, students $1; discounts to groups; members first visit no charge. RR Museum: Memorial Day to Columbus Day Sat.-Sun. 12-4.
Attendance: 750 (estimated)
Membership: Individual $10; Family $15; Donor $25; Sustaining $50; Patron $100; Life Benefactor $1,000.

Scotia

FLINT HOUSE, 421 Reynolds St., Scotia, NY 12302-1601. Tel.: 518-374-2371.
Founded: 1997.
Personnel Profile: Part-Time Volunteers 4.
Governing Authority: municipal.
Historic House & Museum: housed in a 1735 salt box house.
Collections: village history; broom corn industry from 1860-2007.
Facilities: library.
Activities: guided tours; lectures.
Hours & Admission Prices: Call for a guided tour, 518-374-2871. No charge; donations accepted.
Attendance: 875 (accurate)

SCOTIA-GLENVILLE CHILDREN'S MUSEUM, 303 Mohawk Ave., Scotia, NY 12302-1815. Tel.: 518-346-1764. Fax: 518-377-6593.
E-mail: dbennett@travelingmuseum.org
Web Site: www.travelingmuseum.org
Founded: 1978.
Congressional District: 23
Key Personnel: Exec. Dir., Diana Bennett.
Personnel Profile: Full-Time Paid 3; Part-Time Paid 27; Part-Time Volunteers 125.
Governing Authority: nonprofit organization. Tax-exempt: 501(c)(3).
Traveling Children's Museum.
Collections: artifacts illustrating concepts in natural science; physical science; archaeology; history; decorative arts; fine arts & crafts.
Facilities: meeting room.
Activities: concerts; family workshops; organized education programs for children & families; participatory exhibits; traveling museum presentations; community-wide special events.
Publications: quarterly newsletter; annual report; resource handbooks.
Hours & Admission Prices: Office: Mon.-Fri. 8:30-4:30. Traveling Museum daily. Program Fee: $99.
Attendance: 76,610 (accurate)
Membership: Supporter $25; Organization $75; Patron $50; Sponsor $75; Contributor $100.

Sea Cliff

SEA CLIFF VILLAGE MUSEUM, 95 Tenth Ave., Sea Cliff, NY 11579-1127. Tel.: 516-671-0090. Fax: 516-671-2530.
E-mail: seacliffmuseum@aol.com
Founded: 1979.
Key Personnel: Dir. & Cur., Sara Reres; Chm. (V), Patricia F. Smith; Museum Technician, James Reres.
Personnel Profile: Part-Time Paid 2; Part-Time Volunteers 50; Interns 2.
Governing Authority: municipal.
Village Museum: housed in the former Sea Cliff Methodist Church, built in 1913.
Collections: Sea Cliff history, 1870 to mid-twentieth century including documents, photographs, artifacts, & costumes.
Major Exhibits: Sea Cliff Classics, 1/10-5/10.
Research Fields: Carpenter family; Henry Otto Korten glass negatives.
Facilities: library; 500 sq. ft. exhibit space; garden. Museum-related items for sale.
Activities: docent program; lectures. Annual Event: Friends Exhibit Opening Reception.
Publications: annual newsletter.
Hours & Admission Prices: Oct.-June Sat.-Sun. 2-5. No charge; donations accepted.
Attendance: 1,000 (accurate)

Membership: Seniors $10; Individual $15; Family $25.

Seaford

SEAFORD HISTORICAL MUSEUM, 3890 Waverly Ave., Seaford, NY 11783-2614. Mailing Address: Seaford Historical Society, P.O. Box 1254, Seaford, NY 11783. Tel.: 516-781-5184.
E-mail: seafordhistoric@optonline.net
Web Site: www.seafordhistoricalsociety.org
Founded: 1968.
Congressional District: 4
Key Personnel: Pres., Charles Wroblewski.
Governing Authority: society; chartered by NY board of regents; nonprofit. Tax-exempt: 501(c)(3).
History Museum: housed in 1893 two-room schoolhouse.
Collections: farm tools; local memorabilia; maritime artifacts associated with life of area Baymen & farmers; old photographs.
Research Fields: local history.
Activities: lectures; hobby workshops; permanent & temporary exhibitions.
Publications: newsletter, Seaford Historical Society Quarterly.
Hours & Admission Prices: By appointment. No charge; donations accepted. ♿
Attendance: 2,000
Membership: Individual $10; Family $25; Individual Life & Business $50; Family Life $125.

Selden

SUFFOLK CENTER ON THE HOLOCAUST, DIVERSITY & HUMAN UNDERSTANDING, (M), Suffolk County Community College, Huntington Library, 2nd Fl., 533 College Rd., Selden, NY 11784-2851. Tel.: 631-451-4700. Fax: 631-451-4697.
E-mail: chdhu@sunysuffolk.edu
Web Site: www.chdhu.org
History Museum.
Collections: Holocaust history; slavery; photographs; documents; period artifacts.
Activities: special events; educational programs.
Hours & Admission Prices: Mon.-Thurs. 10-2; other times by appointment.

Selkirk

BETHLEHEM HISTORICAL ASSOCIATION, 1003 River Rd., Selkirk, NY 12158-4033. Mailing Address: P.O. Box 263, Selkirk, NY 12158-0263. Tel.: 518-767-9432.
Web Site: bha1965.webs.com
Founded: 1965.
Congressional District: 28
Key Personnel: Pres., Susan Haswell; Registrar, Joseph Allgaier.
Governing Authority: nonprofit organization. Tax-exempt: 501(c)(3).
General Museum: housed in 1859 Cedar Hill school.
Collections: tools for farming; ice-harvesting; railroading; fruit-growing; dolls; toys; early school material; early items from the home; clothing from the home; clothing from Town of Bethlehem; 1851 Albany Plank Road Toll Gate.
Research Fields: local industries of past; early arts & crafts; genealogy.
Facilities: library on Bethlehem history & resource material used in setting up temporary exhibits available by request; genealogy library; herb garden.
Activities: guided tours; lectures; films; formally organized education programs for children; historic sites survey including taped interviews; permanent & temporary exhibitions.
Publications: annual membership booklet; newsletter; book, Records of People of the Town of Bethlehem, Albany County, NY 1698-1880.
Hours & Admission Prices: June-Aug. Sun. 2-5. No charge; donations accepted. ♿
Attendance: 375 (accurate)
Membership: Single $20; Family $30; Business $50.

Seneca Falls

NATIONAL WOMEN'S HALL OF FAME, 76 Fall St., Seneca Falls, NY 13148-1451. Mailing Address: P.O. Box 335, Seneca Falls, NY 13148-0335. Tel.: 315-568-8060. Fax: 315-568-2976.
E-mail: greatwomen@greatwomen.org
Web Site: www.greatwomen.org
Founded: 1969.
Congressional District: 29
Key Personnel: Exec. Dir., Christine Moulton; Bd. Pres., Beth Quillen Thomas.
Personnel Profile: Full-Time Paid 4; Part-Time Paid 4; Part-Time Volunteers 40; Interns 2.
Governing Authority: nonprofit. Tax-exempt: 501(c)(3).
Historic Building & Site: 1920s Victorian style bank building.
Collections: photographs; artifacts; audio loops; history related letters; personal memorabilia of honorees; suffrage items; biographies & correspondence of Inductees.
Research Fields: women nominated for induction into the hall; files on other women of accomplishment.
Facilities: 3,000-vol. library available for use pertaining to women's history. Museum-related items for sale.
Activities: guided tours; lectures; film; organized education programs for undergraduate or graduate college students; internship program; essay & new media contest; participatory, loan, temporary & traveling exhibitions; school loan service; honors ceremonies; special monthly programs.
Publications: quarterly newsletter; education kit.
Hours & Admission Prices: Feb.-April & Oct.-Dec. Wed.-Sat. 11-5; May-Sept. Mon.-Sat. 10-5, Sun 12-5. Family $7, adults $3, students & seniors $1.50; members & children under 5 no charge. Closed New Year's Day; Easter; Memorial Day; Independence Day; Labor Day; Thanksgiving; Christmas. ♿
Attendance: 15,000 (accurate)
Membership: Students & Senior Citizens $15; Individual $25; Family $50; Sponsor $100; Friend $250; Patron $500; President's Circle $2,500.

SENECA FALLS HISTORICAL SOCIETY, (M), 55 Cayuga St., Seneca Falls, NY 13148-1222. Tel.: 315-568-8412. Fax: 315-568-8426.
E-mail: sfhs@rochester.rr.com
Web Site: www.sfhistoricalsociety.org
Founded: 1896.
Congressional District: 24
Key Personnel: Exec. Dir., Philomena M. Cammuso; Dir. Education, Frances T. Barbieri; Pres. Bd. Trustees, John E. Becker, II; Collections Mgr., Kathleen Jans-Duffy.
Personnel Profile: Full-Time Paid 3; Full-Time Volunteers 4; Part-Time Volunteers 100; Interns 2.
Governing Authority: society. Tax-exempt: 170(b)(1)(A).
Local History Museum: 23 room Victorian Mansion.
Collections: 19th-century American decorative & fine art; local history artifacts; costumes; toys; pre- & post-Industrial tools; photographs; children's room; Silsby steam fire engine; manuscripts; memorabilia of the first Women's Rights Convention held in 1848; apparel from early 1800s to the turn of the century; industry; archives; Indian artifacts; paintings of Carlos Bellows.
Research Fields: local history; fire apparatus; pump manufacturing; Woman's Rights Movement; genealogy; county & canal history.
Facilities: 2,000-vol. research library & archives for use on premises; 23 room Victorian house with period rooms. Museum-related items for sale.
Activities: guided tours; lectures; docent programs; permanent & temporary exhibitions; craft classes; school loan service.
Publications: bimonthly newsletters; maps; booklets: Cowing Story (fire-engines); Silsby Mfg. Story; Debut of Women's Rights; Sad Irons, The Seneca Falls of David Lum 1806-1875; As We Were, Vol. I & II, 19th & 20th Century Photographs of Seneca Falls; The Flats: Including the Canal and Early Industries of Seneca Falls; Finding Aids: Women's Rights; Gould's Pumps, Inc.
Hours & Admission Prices: Business: Mon.-Fri. 9-4. Tours: June-Sept. Mon.-Fri. hourly 10-3 , Sat.-Sun. 1-3. Adults $5, students $2.50, families $10; discounts to AAM, ICOM, AAA & AARP members; members no charge. Closed New Year's Day; Memorial Day; Independence Day; Thanksgiving; Christmas week.
Attendance: 18,000 (accurate)
Membership: Student (under 18) $10; Associate $30; Contributor (Individual & Family) $50; Supporter $75; Sustainer $125; Subscriber $250; Sponsor $500; Patron $1,000; Corporate $2,000; Benefactor $5,000.

Setauket

GALLERY NORTH, 90 N. Country Rd., Setauket, NY 11733-1352. Tel.: 631-751-2676. Fax: 631-751-0180.
E-mail: info@gallerynorth.org
Web Site: www.gallerynorth.org
Founded: 1965.
Congressional District: 1
Key Personnel: Pres. & Chm., Paul Lamb; Dir. & Cur., Colleen Hanson; Asst., Carolyn Fell.
Personnel Profile: Full-Time Paid 1; Part-Time Paid 4; Part-Time Volunteers 2.
Governing Authority: nonprofit organization. Tax-exempt.
Art Gallery.
Collections: contemporary works by Long Island artists & crafts people.
Facilities: 1,200 sq. ft. exhibit space.
Activities: annual outdoor art show; lectures; trips; studio tours; adult painting workshops; children's art workshops.

Publications: quarterly newsletter for members only, Gallery North News.
Hours & Admission Prices: mid-Jan. to Dec. Tues.-Sat. 10-5, Sun. 12-5. No charge. Closed Easter; Thanksgiving; Christmas. ♿
Attendance: 17,500 (estimated)
Membership: Friends $50-$500 & up.

THREE VILLAGE HISTORICAL SOCIETY, 93 N. Country Rd., Setauket, NY 11733-1347. Tel.: 631-751-3730. Fax: 631-751-3936.
E-mail: info@tvhs.org
Web Site: threevillagehistoricalsociety.org
Founded: 1964.
Congressional District: 1
Key Personnel: Pres. (V), Peter Paul Ostapow; Archivist, Karen Martin; Office Asst., Dianne Trautmann.
Personnel Profile: Part-Time Paid 3; Part-Time Volunteers 350; Interns 1.
Governing Authority: private; nonprofit organization. Tax-exempt.
Historical Society.
Collections: related to the history, from earliest settlement to present, of the Three Village area of Long Island's North Shore.
Research Fields: 19th-century seafaring women; 19th-century culture, folklore; 20th-century development issues; 17th- to 20th-century deed search & property development.
Facilities: Books for sale.
Activities: docent program; formal educational programs; guided tours; lectures; loan exhibitions. Annual Events: Apple Festival; Spirits of Three Villages Cemetery Tour; Candlelight House Tour; Walk Through History.
Publications: annual research volume; quarterly newsletter; local history books.
Hours & Admission Prices: Mon.-Fri. 10-3, Sat.-Sun. by appointment. No charge; donations accepted.
Attendance: 30,000 (estimated)
Membership: Individual $30; Family $50; Patron $100; Benefactor $250; Major Contributor $500; Founder $1,000.

Shelter Island

SHELTER ISLAND HISTORICAL SOCIETY, (M), 16 S. Ferry Rd., Shelter Island, NY 11964. Mailing Address: P.O. Box 847, Shelter Island, NY 11964-0847. Tel.: 631-749-0025. Fax: 631-749-1825.
E-mail: sihissoc@optonline.net
Web Site: shelterislandhistory.org
Founded: 1965.
Congressional District: 1
Key Personnel: Dir., Louise Green; Pres., Belle Lareau; Sec., A. Krauss; Museum Shop Mgr., Patricia Yourdon.
Personnel Profile: Full-Time Paid 1; Part-Time Paid 3; Part-Time Volunteers 64; Interns 1.
Governing Authority: society. Tax-exempt.
Historic House Museum: 1743 James Havens house.
Collections: period documents, photographs, memorabilia & furniture pertaining to the town of Shelter Island.
Research Fields: historical data concerning the town of Shelter Island.
Activities: monthly meetings; changing exhibits; lectures; educational programs.
Publications: monthly newsletter; book, History of Shelter Island: The Smallest Village; The Story of Shelter Island in the Revolution; A Chronicle of Shelter Island Churches; A Woman Named Matilda & Other True Accounts of Old Shelter Island; God's Summer Cottage; History of the Union Chapel-1875-1980.
Hours & Admission Prices: June 24-Sept. 3 Mon.-Sat. 10-2. No charge; donations accepted.
Attendance: 5,500 (estimated)
Membership: Individual $30; Family $45; Corporate $400; Individual Life $1,000; Joint Life $1,500.

Sidney

SIDNEY HISTORICAL ASSOCIATION, 21 Liberty St., Rm. 218, Sidney, NY 13838-1246. Mailing Address: 21 Liberty St., Box 8, Sidney, NY 13838-1266. Tel.: 607-563-2542.
Web Site: www.sidneyonline.com/sha.htm
Founded: 1945.
Congressional District: 25
Key Personnel: Pres., Erin Andrews; Vice Pres., Joelene Cole; Cur., Graydon Ballard; Treas., Russell Luce; Sec., Bonnie Curtis.
Personnel Profile: Part-Time Volunteers 14.
Governing Authority: association; nonprofit organization. Tax-exempt.
Regional History Museum.
Collections: history; archaeology; archives; photographs; Indian artifacts; Troop C, Capt. Fox picture & trophy collection 1920-1992; genealogies; manuscripts; wooden horse sleigh made in Sidney by Cortland, Cart & Carriage Co. 1890s.
Research Fields: local history; Indian artifacts & sites; genealogy.
Facilities: library of historical books, records, newspapers, diaries & microfilm; reports available for research upon request with member of association in attendance.
Activities: guided tours; lectures; films; formally organized educational programs; temporary exhibitions; antique appraisal clinics.
Publications: Organizational Histories; Sidney - Then & Now - 1772-1972; Lest We Forget; newspaper articles; community calendar; microfilming; quarterly newsletter; reproductions of historic maps.
Hours & Admission Prices: Sept.-May Tues. 1-4, Wed. 6pm-8pm, Thurs. 9-11:30; other times by appointment. No charge; donations accepted. Closed holidays. ♿
Attendance: 750 (accurate)
Membership: Individual $10; Life $50.

Skaneateles

THE JOHN D. BARROW ART GALLERY, Skaneateles Library, 49 E. Genesee St., Skaneateles, NY 13152-1314. Tel.: 315-685-5135.
Web Site: www.johndbarrowgallery.com
Art Gallery.
Collections: 435 paintings highlighting the historical & cultural aspects of the local community in the mid to late 1800s.
Facilities: Museum-related items for sale.
Hours & Admission Prices: Memorial Day to Labor Day Mon.-Fri. 1-4, Sat. 11-4; Sept.-May Thurs.-Fri. 10-3. Tours by appointment. No charge; donations accepted. Closed holidays.

Smithtown

SMITHTOWN HISTORICAL SOCIETY, (M), 239 Middle Country Rd., Smithtown, NY 11787-2807. Tel.: 631-265-6768. Fax: 631-979-4694.
E-mail: info@smithtownhistorical.org
Web Site: www.smithtownhistorical.org
Founded: 1955.
Congressional District: 1
Key Personnel: Dir., Kiernan Lannon; Pres. (V), Brad Harris; Dir. Education, Elizabeth Jenks.
Personnel Profile: Full-Time Paid 4; Part-Time Paid 7; Part-Time Volunteers 30; Interns 2.
Governing Authority: society. Tax-exempt.
Historical Society Museums.
Collections: documents, books, decorative arts, costumes relating to the history of Smithtown. Historic Houses: 1700 Obadiah Smith house; 1750 Epenetus Smith Tavern; 1750 Franklin O. Arthur Farm; 1819 Caleb Smith house; 1790 Judge J. Lawrence Smith Homestead; 1870 Reading Room; 1900 Brush barn; 1918 Roseneath Cottage; 1860 Rockwell Barn & Carriage House.
Research Fields: preservation; genealogy; local history.
Facilities: library of history & genealogy books available for use on premises. Museum-related items for sale.
Activities: films; exhibit & demonstration programs; school educational programs; changing exhibits; special events.
Publications: books, Genealogy of Smith Family; Smithtown 1660-1929: Looking Back Through the Lens; Old Houses in Smithtown-Rockwell's Scrapbook; map, Early Residents of Smithtown 1660-1885.
Hours & Admission Prices: Caleb Smith House: Mon.-Fri. 9-5, Sat. by appointment. Historic Houses: by appointment. No charge; donations accepted. ♿
Attendance: 25,000 (estimated)
Membership: Individual $25; Family $35; Sustaining $75; Patron $100; Life $1,000.

Sodus Point

SODUS BAY HISTORICAL SOCIETY, 7606 N. Ontario St., Sodus Point, NY 14555-9536. Mailing Address: P.O. Box 94, Sodus Point, NY 14555-0094. Tel.: 315-483-4936. Fax: 315-483-1398.
E-mail: bmccreary@soduspointlighthouse.org
Web Site: www.soduspointlighthouse.org
Founded: 1972.
Congressional District: 27
Key Personnel: Exec. Dir., Bradley D. McCreary; Pres. (V), Fran Klaver; Chm. (V) & Museum Shop Mgr., Alice Bill; Vice Pres. (V), Jack Kelly.
Personnel Profile: Full-Time Paid 1; Part-Time Paid 1; Part-Time Volunteers 125.
Governing Authority: nonprofit organization. Tax-exempt: 501(c)(3).
Lighthouse Museum: 1870 Sodus Bay Lighthouse & two outbuildings.
Collections: concentration on Great Lakes maritime history with major emphasis on Lake Ontario & Sodus Bay.

Research Fields: Great Lakes Lighthouse Service; US Lighthouse Service; US Lighthouse Board; US Coast Guard.
Facilities: 1870 Lighthouse.
Activities: Independence Day gala & 10 free concerts; guided tours; lectures.
Publications: monthly newsletter (nine issues).
Hours & Admission Prices: May-Oct. Tues.-Sun. & Mon. holidays 10-5. Adults $3, children $1. ♿
Attendance: 20,000 (estimated)
Membership: Individual $15; Family $20; Contributing $50; Patron $100; Sustaining $250; Life $500.

Somers

SOMERS HISTORICAL SOCIETY, Elephant Hotel, Rte. 100 & 202, Somers, NY 10589. Mailing Address: P.O. Box 336, Somers, NY 10589-0336. Tel.: 914-277-4977.
E-mail: dianaart@msn.com
Web Site: www.somersmuseum.org
Formerly: Somers Historical Society Museum and Museum of the Early American Circus
Founded: 1956.
Congressional District: 25
Key Personnel: Pres. (V), Emil Antonaccio.
Personnel Profile: Part-Time Volunteers 15.
Governing Authority: society; board of trustees. Tax-exempt: 990-A.
Circus & Local History Museum: housed in 1825 Elephant Hotel built by Hachaliah Bailey.
Collections: early American circus history; furniture, artifacts & manuscripts relating to local history; couriers, posters, lithographs, manuscripts, route books & other memorabilia relating to pioneer circus; Rowell Miniature Circus.
Research Fields: pioneer circus; genealogy; local history.
Facilities: 1,000-vol. library of local history & circus available for research by appointment. Museum-related items for sale.
Activities: guided tours; permanent & temporary exhibitions; special events.
Publications: books, The Elephant Hotel; America; reprint, History of Somers (1886); reprint, Journal of Dr. Elias Cornelius, Rev. War; Somers Remembered; Somers Confederates: James Wright & his Nephews.
Hours & Admission Prices: Thurs. 2-4; other times by appointment. No charge; donations accepted.
Attendance: 1,000 (estimated)
Membership: Regular: Student $5; Single $15; Family $25. Sustaining: Single $35; Family $50; Patron $100; Life $250 & $350.

Southampton

* **THE PARRISH ART MUSEUM, (M),** 25 Job's Lane, Southampton, NY 11968-5393. Tel.: 631-283-2118, ext. 12. Fax: 631-283-7006.
E-mail: info@parrishart.org
Web Site: www.parrishart.org
Founded: 1898.
Congressional District: 1
Key Personnel: Dir., Terrie Sultan; Co-Chm., Carlo Beonzini Vender; Co-Chm., Douglas Polley; Dir. Public Rels., Mark Segal; Asst. Dir., Anke Jackson; Deputy Dir. Special Events & Membership, Nina Madison; Deputy Dir. Education, Cara Conklin-Wingfield; Asst. Finance, Susan Swiatocha; Chief Cur. Art & Education, Alicia Longwell; Bldg. Mgr., Walter Gallagher; Robert Lehman Cur., Klaus Ottmann.
Personnel Profile: Full-Time Paid 20; Part-Time Paid 4; Part-Time Volunteers 156; Interns 2.
Governing Authority: nonprofit organization. Tax-exempt: 501(c)(3).
Art Museum: built in 1897, under the direction of Grosvenor Atterbury, in the style of the Latin Cross.
Collections: American art from the 19th century to present; paintings & archives of William Merritt Chase; Fairfield Porter paintings.
Major Exhibits: Students View American Views, 12/5/09-1/3/10; Alex Katz: Seeing, Drawing, Making (T), 2/7/10-4/11/10; Fairfield Porter Raw (T), 4/18/10-6/20/10; Rackstraw Downes: Onsite Paintings, 1974-2009, 6/27/10-9/19/10; Chuck Close Prints: Process and Collaboration (T), 9/26/10-11/28/10; Students Print Up Close, 12/4/10-1/2/11.
Research Fields: William Merritt Chase; Fairfield Porter; 19th century American etchings.
Facilities: 5,300-vol. library of art & rare books, including 3,800-volume personal library of Aline B. Saarinen; 200-vols. of catalogs & periodicals; 250-seat auditorium; arboretum. Art books, publications, original prints & other museum-related items for sale.
Activities: guided tours; films; concerts; lectures; performing arts events; workshops for children; formally organized education programs for children; inter-museum loan, permanent & temporary exhibitions; school loan service.
Publications: exhibition catalogs; quarterly newsletter; interpretive brochures.
Hours & Admission Prices: June to mid-Sept. Mon.-Sat. 11-5, Sun. 1-5; mid-Sept. to June Mon. & Thurs.-Sat. 11-5, Sun. 1-5. Adults $7, senior citizens & students w/ID $5; discounts to AAM & ICOM members; children 18 & under and members no charge. Closed New Year's Day; Easter; Independence Day; Thanksgiving; Christmas. ♿
Attendance: 40,000 (estimated)
Membership: Individual $45; Family $75; Associate $125; Sponsor $250; Contributor $500.

SHINNECOCK NATION CULTURAL CENTER AND MUSEUM, 100 Montauk Hwy. & W. Gate Rd., Southampton, NY 11969. Mailing Address: P.O. Box 5059, Southampton, NY 11969-5059. Tel.: 631-287-4923. Fax: 631-287-7153.
E-mail: office@shinnecockmuseum.org
Web Site: www.shinnecockmuseum.org
Native American Museum.
Collections: Shinnecock heritage, culture & history; paintings; murals; sculptures.
Hours & Admission Prices: Fri.-Sat. 11-4, Sun. 12-4; tours by appointment.

SOUTHAMPTON HISTORICAL MUSEUMS AND RESEARCH CENTER, (M), 17 Meeting House Lane, Southampton, NY 11968-4911. Mailing Address: P.O. Box 303, Southampton, NY 11969-0303. Tel.: 631-283-2494. Fax: 631-283-4540.
E-mail: info@southamptonhistoricalmuseum.org
Web Site: southamptonhistoricalmuseum.org
Formerly: Southampton Colonial Society
Founded: 1898.
Congressional District: 1
Key Personnel: Exec. Dir., Tom Edmonds; Co Pres., Anne Bishop Rachel; Co Pres., Elizabeth DeBarto Skinner; Museum Shop Mgr., Millie DeMarco; Asst. to Dir. & Registrar, Blaine Phelps; Mgr. Research Center, Mary Cummings; Registrar, Carol Hammel; Dir. Programs, Lynn Egan.
Personnel Profile: Full-Time Paid 1; Part-Time Paid 5; Part-Time Volunteers 2; Interns 2.
Governing Authority: nonprofit organization. Parent Institution: Colonial Society of the Town of Southampton. Subsidiary Institution: Halsey House Museum; Pelletreau Shop. Tax-exempt: 170(b)(1)(A).
History Museum.
Collections: local history with changing exhibits focusing on South Fork culture including folk art, Native American, whaling, rural tools, area ethnic history. Historic Sites: 1843 Roger Mansion; 1660 Thomas Halsey; c.1750 Pelletreau goldsmith shop; Conscience Point Historic Site & Nature Walk.
Research Fields: Southampton history.
Facilities: 10,000-vol. library of material on South Fork history.
Activities: education programs; craft workshops; guided tours; temporary exhibitions.
Publications: newsletter; brochures.
Hours & Admission Prices: Rogers Mansion & Pelletreau Shop: Tues.-Sat. 11-4. Thomas Halsey House: July to mid-Oct. Fri.-Sun. 11-4. Adults $4; discounts to AAM & ICOM members; children 17 & under and members no charge. ♿
Attendance: 25,253 (accurate)
Membership: Individual $25; Family & Couple $45; Sustaining $150; Contributing $250; Sponsor $500; Patron $1,000; President's Circle $5,000.

Southold

SOUTHOLD HISTORICAL SOCIETY AND MUSEUM, (M), 54325 Main Rd., Southold, NY 11971-4646. Mailing Address: P.O. Box 1, Southold, NY 11971-0001. Tel.: 631-765-5500 & 5551. Fax: 631-765-8510.
E-mail: sohissoc@optonline.net
Web Site: southoldhistoricalsociety.org
Founded: 1960.
Congressional District: 1
Key Personnel: Dir. & Museum Shop Mgr., Geoffrey Fleming; Pres. (V), Ronald Rossi; Museum Shop Mgr., Susi Young.
Personnel Profile: Full-Time Paid 2; Part-Time Paid 2; Part-Time Volunteers 155.
Governing Authority: society. Parent Institution: Southold Historical Society. Subsidiary Institution: Horton Point Nautical Museum. Tax-exempt: 900.
General Museum.
Collections: farm implements; china; silver; quilts; textiles; costumes; hats; furniture; maritime collection; archives; paintings; decorative arts; agriculture; paintings; costumes; 19th century overton corncrib; glass; manuscript collections. Historic Buildings: 1899 Hallock Currie-Bell House; middle 18th-century Pine Neck barn; c.1790 Thomas Moore House; c.1845 Irving Downs Carriage House; c.1845 Henry Cleveland blacksmith shop; 1857 Horton's Point Lighthouse & Nautical Museum; 1875 Bayview Icehouse.
Research Fields: genealogy; local history.

Facilities: 1,000-vol. library of historical books available for research on the premises.
Activities: guided tours; formally organized education programs for children; permanent & temporary exhibitions.
Publications: annual report; newsletter.
Hours & Admission Prices: July-Aug. Wed. & Sat.-Sun. 1-4. Adults $2; members & children no charge; donations accepted. ♿
Attendance: 9,000 (estimated)
Membership: Annual $20; Contributing $50; Sustaining $100; Business $100-$250; Patron $750; Benefactor $1,000.

SOUTHOLD INDIAN MUSEUM, (M), 1080 Bayview Rd., Southold, NY 11971. Mailing Address: P.O. Box 268, Southold, NY 11971-0268. Tel.: 631-765-5577. Fax: 631-765-5577.
E-mail: indianmuseum@aol.com
Web Site: southoldindianmuseum.org
Founded: 1925.
Congressional District: 1
Key Personnel: Chm. (V), Audrey Watson-Wigley; Pres. (V), Ellen Barcel; Membership, Martha Waide; Education, Margaret Waide; Museum Shop Mgr., Lisa Cordani-Stevenson.
Personnel Profile: Part-Time Paid 1.
Governing Authority: Incorporated Long Island Chapter of the New York State Archaeological Association; nonprofit organization. Tax-exempt: 501(c)(3).
Archaeology & Indian Museum.
Collections: spear heads; murals; Algonquin ceramic pottery; soapstone pots & bowls; arrow heads; knife blades; hoe blades; hammers; gouges; drills; aborigine vegetables, foods & herbs for medical purposes; toys; fishing tackle with net & sinkers; jewelry; ornaments; smoking pipes; clothing; religious relics; handiworks of Eskimos.
Research Fields: Long Island archaeology.
Facilities: 1,500-vol. archaeological library; 100-seat auditorium; 1,600 sq. ft. exhibit space. Publications & other museum-related items for sale.
Activities: guided tours; lectures; organized education programs for children; monthly meetings; trips; traveling exhibitions.
Publications: quarterly newsletter, Southold Indian Museum News; Archaeology leaflets; museum guide.
Hours & Admission Prices: Sun. 1:30-4:30. Suggested Donation: adults $2. Closed New Year's Day; Easter; Thanksgiving; Christmas.
Attendance: 3,000 (estimated)
Membership: Active $38; Active Husband-Wife $50.

Spencerport

OGDEN HISTORICAL SOCIETY, 568 Colby St., Spencerport, NY 14559. Mailing Address: P.O. Box 777, Adams Basin, NY 14410-0777. Tel.: 585-352-0660 & 4214.
Founded: 1958.
Congressional District: 34
Key Personnel: Pres., Ted Rogers; Vice Pres., Edgar White; Program Dir. & Chm. (V), Betty Spencer; Sec., Irene Rogers.
Governing Authority: board of trustees. Tax-exempt.
Historic House: 1811 Eastman-Colby House.
Collections: furnishings; clothing; implements of early 19th-century farm house.
Facilities: local history & general information on Erie Canal.
Activities: lectures; films; inter-museum loan; craft demonstrations.
Hours & Admission Prices: Memorial Day to Thanksgiving Sun. 2-4, group tours by appointment. No charge; donations accepted. ♿
Attendance: 500 (estimated)
Membership: Individual $6; Family $10.

Springville

CONCORD HISTORICAL SOCIETY, WARNER MUSEUM, 23 N. Buffalo St., Springville, NY 14141-1335. Mailing Address: P.O. Box 425, Springville, NY 14141-0425. Tel.: 716-592-0094.
E-mail: lucybensley@townofconcordnyhistoricalsociety.org
Web Site: www.townofconcordnyhistoricalsociety.org
Founded: 1953.
Key Personnel: Pres., Donald Orton; Vice Pres., Jeanne Fornes; Treas., Pam Batterson; Sec., Jane Neureuther; Historian, David Batterson.
Governing Authority: municipal; society. Subsidiary Institution: Concord Historical Society Genealogical Library, 23 N. Buffalo St., Springville, NY 14141. Tax-exempt: 501(c)(3).
Local History Museum.
Collections: carpenter tools; pictures; Pop Warner's Indian artifact collection; pump organ; china; furniture; local historical items.
Facilities: library of history & school books, maps & photographs available for research by appointment on premise; reading room.
Activities: temporary exhibitions; tours.
Publications: newsletter.
Hours & Admission Prices: 2nd & 4th Sun. & Thurs. 2-4; other times by appointment. No charge; donations accepted. ♿
Attendance: 650 (estimated)
Membership: Senior Citizen $5; Individual $10; Life $50.

Staatsburg

STAATSBURGH STATE HISTORIC SITE, Old Post Road, Staatsburg, NY 12580-5911. Mailing Address: P.O. Box 308, Staatsburg, NY 12580-0308. Tel.: 845-889-8851. Fax: 845-889-8321.
E-mail: melodye.moore@oprhp.state.ny.us
Web Site: www.staatsburgh.org
Formerly: Mills Mansion State Historic Site
Founded: 1938.
Congressional District: 25
Key Personnel: Historic Site Mgr., Melodye Moore; Pres. (V), Caroline Carey; Museum Shop Mgr., Brenda Juarez.
Personnel Profile: Full-Time Paid 10; Part-Time Paid 8; Part-Time Volunteers 75.
Governing Authority: state. Parent Institution: New York State Office of Parks, Recreation & Historic Preservation Taconic Region. Tax-exempt: 501(c)(3).
Historic House Museum: 1895 65-room Neo-classical Revival mansion designed by Stanford White.
Collections: 19th & 20th-century furnishings belonging to the Mills family; fine & decorative arts.
Research Fields: Livingston & Mills families; fine & decorative arts.
Facilities: golf course; picnic area; cross-country skiing trails; camp ground; state park.
Activities: guided tours; concerts; lectures; special events; school programs.
Publications: map of grounds; Great Estates of the Hudson Valley.
Hours & Admission Prices: House: Jan.-March Sat.-Sun. 11-4; April-Oct. Tues.-Sat. 10-5, Sun. 12-5; Dec. call for hours. Grounds: daily 8-dusk. Adults $5, senior citizens, students & groups $4; discount to Friends & groups; children 12 & under and members no charge. ♿
Attendance: 24,206 (accurate)
Membership: Student & Senior Citizen $15; Individual $20; Family $35; Contributor $50; Sustainer $100; Sponsor $250; Patron $500; Benefactor $1,000.

Staten Island

ALICE AUSTEN HOUSE MUSEUM, (M), Alice Austen Park, 2 Hylan Blvd., Staten Island, NY 10305-2002. Tel.: 718-816-4506. Fax: 718-815-3959.
E-mail: eaausten@aol.com
Web Site: www.aliceausten.org
Founded: 1979.
Congressional District: 14
Key Personnel: Exec. Dir., Carl Rutberg; Chm. & Pres. (V), Donna Hakim; Project Coord., Jean Creagan; Educator, Annmarie McDonnel; Educator, Sara Signorely.
Personnel Profile: Full-Time Paid 3; Full-Time Volunteers 2; Part-Time Paid 2; Part-Time Volunteers 20.
Governing Authority: nonprofit historical & preservation organization. Parent Institutions: Friends of Alice Austen House, Inc. Tax-exempt.
Historic House: c.1690 one of the oldest in New York, home of photographer Alice Austen.
Collections: Victorian furniture & furnishings; photographs by Alice Austen; archival holdings; architectural elements; gardens.
Research Fields: photography & life of Alice Austen; New York City history; aspects of Victoriana & early 20th-century social history.
Facilities: garden; lawns; meeting room; VCR viewing room. Gift items for sale.
Activities: lectures; concerts; walking tours; gallery tours.
Publications: quarterly newsletter; museum guidebook; exhibition catalogs & checklists; walking tour booklet; Street Types of New York photograph portfolio reprint.
Hours & Admission Prices: March-Dec. Thurs.-Sun. 12-5. Adults $2; discounts to AAM & ICOM members; members no charge. Closed major holidays. ♿
Attendance: 19,000 (estimated)
Membership: Senior & Student Friend $15; Friend $25; Family Friend $40; Supporting Friend $100; Business Friend $101 & up; Sustaining Friend $250; Guardian of Clear Comfort $500.

THE CONFERENCE HOUSE, 298 Satterlee St., Staten Island, NY 10307. Tel.: 718-984-6046. Fax: 718-984-7760.
E-mail: info@conferencehouse.org
Web Site: www.conferencehouse.org
Founded: 1927.

Key Personnel: Pres., Gerard Lacagnino; Museum Shop Mgr., Catherine Castell.
Personnel Profile: Full-Time Paid 2; Part-Time Volunteers 12; Interns 1.
Governing Authority: municipal. Parent Institution: The Conference House Association. Tax-exempt.
Historic House Museum: housed in 1675 Conference House or Billopp House, built by Capt. Christopher Billopp, English Navy. Site of peace conference during Revolutionary War between Ben Franklin, John Adams & Edward Rutledge with Lord Admiral Richard Howe, Sept. 11, 1776.
Collections: 18th century furnishings & accessories.
Facilities: 50-seat 17th century kitchen used as classroom. Museum-related items for sale.
Activities: guided tours; permanent exhibitions; formally organized education programs for children; slide presentation; open-hearth cooking demonstration & spinning & weaving demonstrations. Museum Sponsors: Art Show; Peace Conference Celebration; Craft Sale & Open House; October Harvest Festival; Yuletide Celebration.
Publications: quarterly newsletter; brochures.
Hours & Admission Prices: April to mid-Dec. Fri.-Sun. 1-4. Adults $3, children & seniors $2; members no charge. Closed New Year's Day; Independence Day; Thanksgiving; Christmas.
Attendance: 3,906 (accurate)
Membership: Senior & Student $20; Individual $25; Family $40; Supporting $100; Corporate $250.

GARIBALDI-MEUCCI MUSEUM, (M), 420 Tompkins Ave., Staten Island, NY 10305-1704. Tel.: 718-442-1608. Fax: 718-442-8635.
E-mail: info@garibaldimeuccimuseum.org
Web Site: garibaldimeuccimuseum.org
Formerly: Garibaldi and Meucci Museum of the Order Sons of Italy In America
Founded: 1956.
Congressional District: 14
Key Personnel: Dir. & Admin., Nicole Fenton; Chm., Robert Necci; Pres. & C.E.O., John Dabbene; Coord. Publicity, Bonnie McCourt.
Personnel Profile: Full-Time Paid 1; Part-Time Paid 7; Part-Time Volunteers 6.
Governing Authority: nonprofit organization. Tax-exempt: 501(c)(3).
Historic House: 1845 country home of Antonio Meucci, Italian Patriot, General Giuseppe Garibaldi also occupied house 1850-53.
Collections: life & work of Meucci & Garibaldi, the Risorgimento, Italian history & culture; prints; paintings; medals; coins; military uniforms; artifacts; personal artifacts; period restored Garibaldi bedroom; contemporary Italian & Italian American culture & heritage.
Major Exhibits: Memories of Italy by Loren Ellis, 1/9/10-4/4/10; Italian-American Visual Artists Network (I.A.V.A.N.E.T.), 4/10/10-7/4/10; Going Green by Antonio DeSantis, 7/10/10-10/3/10.
Research Fields: history of house; Italian American history & culture; the Italian Risorgimento (unification of Italy); history of the telephone.
Facilities: 1,200-vol. research library; 35-seat auditorium.
Activities: guided tours; culture & history lectures; films; concerts; Italian language classes; daily school program K-12.
Publications: book, Antonio Meucci; Italian language text & work books; children's books; Anita Garibaldi Biography; Heritage Publications; Italian culture & heritage publications.
Hours & Admission Prices: Tues.-Sun. 1-5. School Programs: daily 10-11:30. Suggested Donation: $5; discounts to AAM & ICOM members; children under 10 & members no charge. Closed bank holidays.
Attendance: 100,000 (estimated)
Membership: Student & Senior $25; Individual $40; Household $50-$99; Sponsor $100-$499; Benefactor $500-$999; Patron $1,000 & up.

HISTORIC RICHMOND TOWN, 441 Clarke Ave., Staten Island, NY 10306-1196. Tel.: 718-351-1611. Fax: 718-351-6057.
E-mail: squadrino@historicrichmondtown.org
Web Site: www.historicrichmondtown.org
Founded: 1856.
Congressional District: 14
Key Personnel: Exec. Dir., Ed Wiseman; Pres. (V), John Gustafsson; Vice Pres. Devel., Mktg. & Administration, David Picerno; Chief Cur., Maxine Friedman; Dir. Education, Felicity Beil; Museum Shop Mgr., Adria Scaduto.
Personnel Profile: Full-Time Paid 25; Part-Time Paid 15; Part-Time Volunteers 250; Interns 2.
Governing Authority: nonprofit. Parent Institution: Staten Island Historical Society. Tax-exempt.
Historic Village: 28 historic buildings on 100 acres dating from late 17th century, Staten Island's first county seat.
Collections: tools; costumes; furnishings; toys; folk art; textiles; rare Stansbury press; china & glass; military; archives; manuscripts. 28 Historic Structures including oldest surviving school in U.S., Voorlezer's House c.1695; Decker Farm.
Research Fields: Staten Island history; genealogy; trades; occupations; crafts; architectural history; local history.
Facilities: 15,000-vol. library; archives; 75-seat auditorium; snack bar; cafe; rental facilities. Museum-related items for sale.
Activities: loan & permanent exhibitions; craft demonstrations; concerts; lectures; films; summer day camp; curriculum based educational tours. Annual Events: Civil War Encampment; Autumn Celebration; Big Apple Wine Fest in May; Richmond County Fair; October pumpkin-picking program at Decker Farm (shuttle bus available); Christmas festivities.
Publications: biannual, Staten Island Historian; calendar.
Hours & Admission Prices: July-Aug. Wed.-Sun. 10-5; Sept.-June Wed.-Sun. 1-5, call to confirm. Adults $5, senior citizens $4, children 5-16 $3.50; discounts to AAM members; children under 5 & members no charge. Closed New Year's Day; Easter; Thanksgiving; Christmas.
Attendance: 85,000 (accurate)
Membership: Senior $30; Individual $35; Family $50; Sponsor $75; Contributing $100; Patron $500; Benefactor $1,000; Corporate $2,500.

JACQUES MARCHAIS MUSEUM OF TIBETAN ART, 338 Lighthouse Ave., Staten Island, NY 10306-1217. Tel.: 718-987-3500. Fax: 718-351-0402.
E-mail: mventrudo@tibetanmuseum.org
Web Site: www.tibetanmuseum.org
Founded: 1945.
Congressional District: 14
Key Personnel: C.E.O., Meg Ventrudo; Chm. (V), Beverly Garcia-Anderson; Cur., Sarah Johnson, Ph.D.; Bookkeeper, Jayne Catalfo; Maintenance, Clem Palumbo; Visitor Svcs. & Program Mgr., Amy Hitchoff.
Personnel Profile: Full-Time Paid 1; Part-Time Paid 4; Part-Time Volunteers 6; Interns 2.
Governing Authority: nonprofit. Tax-exempt.
Tibetan Art Museum: Buddhist art, primarily Tibetan, as well as other Asian objects exhibited in a traditional Tibetan style building.
Collections: Tibetan & Buddhist art.
Major Exhibits: Tibetan Portrait: The Power of Compassion, 3/10-12/10.
Research Fields: oriental art & religion.
Facilities: 1,100-vol. library; gardens. Gift-related items for sale.
Activities: public lectures & performances; permanent exhibition; children's art workshops, guided tours; participatory workshops for senior citizens & students.
Publications: booklet, The Dalai Lama at the Jacques Marchais Tibetan Museum; calendar of events; brochure; posters; catalogue of collections, Treasures of Tibetan Art.
Hours & Admission Prices: Wed.-Sun. 1-5; other times by appointment. Adults $5, seniors & students $3; discounts to AAM & ICOM members; members no charge. Closed majors holidays.
Attendance: 5,098 (accurate)
Membership: Student & Senior $25; Individual $30; Family $45; Sponsor $75.

THE NOBLE MARITIME COLLECTION, (M), 1000 Richmond Terr., Staten Island, NY 10301-1114. Tel.: 718-447-6490. Fax: 718-447-6056.
E-mail: erinurban@noblemaritime.org
Web Site: www.noblemaritime.org
Formerly: The John A. Noble Collection
Founded: 1986.
Congressional District: 14
Key Personnel: Exec. Dir., Erin Urban; Asst. Dir., Ciro Galeno; Dir. Programs, D.B. Lampman.
Personnel Profile: Full-Time Paid 4; Part-Time Paid 2; Part-Time Volunteers 150; Interns 2.
Governing Authority: nonprofit organization. Tax-exempt: 501(c)(3).
Art & Maritime History Museum.
Collections: lithographs; paintings; formal & plein ain drawings; photographs; writings; marine artifacts; furnishings; memorabilia; teak saloon houseboat.
Research Fields: art history; maritime history.
Facilities: 4,900-vol. library of material reflecting maritime concerns & history available to the public on premises. John A. Noble (1913-1983) lithographs, reproductions, books & catalogues for sale.
Activities: guided tours; lectures; films; organized education programs for children and adults; loan, temporary & traveling exhibitions.
Publications: quarterly newsletter, Hold Fast!; books, John A. Noble: The Rowboat Drawings; Hulls & Hulks in the Tide of Time: The Life & Work of John A. Noble; The Fight for Sailor's Snug Harbor; The Terrible Captain Jack Visits the Museum; Caddell Dry Dock: 100 Years Harborside.
Hours & Admission Prices: Thurs.-Sun. 1-5. Adults $5, seniors, students &

educators $3; discounts to AAM members; children under 10 & members no charge. Closed New Year's Day; Thanksgiving & Day after; Christmas. ♿

Attendance: 30,000 (estimated)

Membership: Senior Citizen & Educator $25; Individual $40; Family $75; Sail $250; Mast $500; Rowboat Society $1,000; Quarterdeck $2,500; Crow's Nest $5,000.

SEGUINE-BURKE PLANTATION, 440 Seguine Ave., Staten Island, NY 10309-3936. Mailing Address: 830 Fifth Ave., The Arsenal, Rm. 203, New York, NY 10065-7001. Tel.: 718-967-3542.

Web Site: www.historichousetrust.org

Formerly: Seguine House

Founded: 1989.

Congressional District: 13

Key Personnel: Exec. Dir. Historic House Trust, Franklin D. Vagnone.

Governing Authority: nonprofit historical agency. Parent Institutions: Historic House Trust of New York City, The Arsenal, Room 203, Central Park, New York; New York City Dept. of Parks & Recreation.

Historic House: 1837 two-story Greek Revival mansion built by businessman Joseph A. Seguine.

Collections: historic structure; stable; barn; carriage house; antique furnishings.

Research Fields: early Staten Island history.

Activities: guided tours.

Hours & Admission Prices: By appointment only.

Membership: Friends $35; Associate $75; Patron $250.

SNUG HARBOR CULTURAL CENTER AND BOTANICAL GARDEN, 1000 Richmond Ter., Staten Island, NY 10301-1114. Tel.: 718-448-2500, ext. 509. Fax: 718-815-0198.

E-mail: info@snug-harbor.org

Web Site: www.snug-harbor.org

Founded: 1976.

Congressional District: 14

Key Personnel: C.E.O., Frances X. Paulo Huber; Chm. (V), Mark Lauria; Museum Shop Mgr., Nick Dowen; Dir. Visual Art & Exhibit Cur., Frank Verpoorten.

Personnel Profile: Full-Time Paid 30; Part-Time Paid 15; Part-Time Volunteers 25; Interns 1.

Governing Authority: nonprofit. Subsidiary Institution: Smithsonian affiliate. Tax-exempt: 501(c)(3).

Cultural Center: founded in 1831 as a home for sailors, located in National Historic Landmark District encompassing 28 historic buildings & structures on 80 acres.

Collections: artifacts of Sailors Snug Harbor; nautical theme stained glass, wood & iron work; business & architectural records; contemporary art; landscapes; gardens; photographs.

Research Fields: visual & performing arts.

Facilities: botanical garden; auditorium; classrooms; 80-acre park; 700-seat music hall; 150-seat recital hall; banquet hall; outdoor theatre; conference facilities. Museum-related items for sale.

Activities: guided tours; lectures; films; gallery talks; concerts; dance recitals; arts festivals; drama; artist studios & residencies; education programs for school children; performing arts shows & workshops for children; children's educational programs in architecture & horticulture.

Publications: book, Sailors Snug Harbor; art catalogues; calendar of events.

Hours & Admission Prices: Center: daily 10-5. Grounds: daily 8-dusk. Galleries: daily 10-5. Gardens & Galleries Tour: adults $6, seniors, students & members $5, children under 12 $3. Special Events Days & Performance Events: varied admission fees. ♿

Attendance: 450,000 (accurate)

Membership: The Sailor's Society: Senior Citizen Ensign, Student Ensign, City of NY Employee, Veteran, Maritime &/or Building Trade Employee Ensign $30; Ensign $35; Captain $50; Admiral $100. The Randall Society: Randall Society Member $500; Randall Society Benefactor $1,000; Randall Society Supporter $2,500.

STATEN ISLAND CHILDREN'S MUSEUM, (M), 1000 Richmond Terr. at Snug Harbor, Staten Island, NY 10301. Tel.: 718-273-2060. Fax: 718-273-2836.

E-mail: drosenthal@sichildrensmuseum.org

Web Site: www.statenislandkids.org

Founded: 1974.

Congressional District: 24

Key Personnel: Exec. Dir., Dina R. Rosenthal; Business Mgr., Margherita Monck; Dir. Education, Addy Manipella; Volunteer & Intern Coord., Carl Jackman; Dir. External Affairs, Marjorie Waxman; Exhibits Mgr., Michael Shanley.

Personnel Profile: Full-Time Paid 14; Part-Time Paid 37; Part-Time Volunteers 20.

Governing Authority: nonprofit organization. Tax-exempt: 501(c)(3).

Children's Museum.

Collections: arts & sciences; interactive exhibitions reflecting themes in arts, humanities & sciences; pre-school exhibit; insects.

Research Fields: visitor evaluation; art education; use of arts in teaching science.

Facilities: art workshop; performance space. Museum-related items for sale.

Activities: school & community youth group tours; public programs; workshop services; guest artist demonstrations & workshops; cooperative programming with the school district, community groups & other cultural organizations; outreach programs; science theater productions for museum & school audiences; teacher enhancement programs.

Publications: quarterly, activity calendars; events newsletter; brochures; exhibit catalogues.

Hours & Admission Prices: School Year: Tues.-Sun. 12-5; Summer: Tues.-Sun. 10-5. Admission: over 1 $6; discounts to AAM, AYM & ASTC members; members no charge. Closed New Year's Day; Easter; Memorial Day; Independence Day; Labor Day; Thanksgiving; Christmas. ♿

Attendance: 180,000 (accurate)

Membership: Family $75; Companionship $100; Friendship $150 & up.

STATEN ISLAND HISTORICAL SOCIETY, 441 Clarke Ave., Staten Island, NY 10306-1125. Tel.: 718-351-1611. Fax: 718-351-6057.

E-mail: Sihs-secretary@Si.rr.com

Web Site: www.historicrichmondtown.org

Founded: 1856.

Congressional District: 14

Key Personnel: Exec. Dir., Ed Wiseman; Pres. (V), John Gustafsson; Vice Pres. Devel., Mktg. & Administration, David Picerno; Dir. Education, Felicity Beil; Chief Cur., Maxine Friedman; Museum Shop Mgr., Adria Scaduto.

Personnel Profile: Full-Time Paid 25; Full-Time Volunteers 4; Part-Time Paid 15; Part-Time Volunteers 350; Interns 4.

Governing Authority: private; nonprofit society. Subsidiary Institution: Historic Richmond Town. Tax-exempt: 501(c)(3).

History Museum: housed in 1848-1917 County Clerk's & Surrogate's office, part of historic 100-acre village & museum complex.

Collections: furniture; china; glass; costumes; military; archives; manuscripts; tools; toys; folk art; textiles; Stansbury press; 28 historic buildings.

Research Fields: genealogy; local history; trades; occupations; crafts; architectural history.

Facilities: 15,000-vol. library of books on local history & genealogy available on premises for research by appointment; archives; 75-seat auditorium; snack bar. Books, crafts & other museum-related items for sale.

Activities: guided tours; lectures; films; formally organized educational programs; inter-museum loan, permanent exhibitions; craft demonstration; summer day camp.

Publications: half-yearly journal, Staten Island Historian; calendar.

Hours & Admission Prices: June-Aug. Wed.-Sun. 10-5; Sept.-May Wed.-Sun. 1-5. Adults $5, senior citizens $4, students & children 5-16 $3.50; discounts to AAM members; society members & museum professionals no charge. Closed New Year's Day; Easter; Thanksgiving; Christmas. ♿

Attendance: 88,000 (accurate)

Membership: Seniors $30; Individual $35; Family $50; Sponsor $75; Contributing $100; Patron $500; Benefactor $1,000; Corporate $2,500.

STATEN ISLAND MUSEUM, (M), 75 Stuyvesant Place, Staten Island, NY 10301-1998. Tel.: 718-727-1135, ext. 114. Fax: 718-273-5683.

E-mail: hbehnke@statenislandmuseum.org

Web Site: www.statenislandmuseum.org

Formerly: Staten Island Institute of Arts & Sciences (SIIAS)

Founded: 1881.

Congressional District: 17

Key Personnel: C.E.O., Elizabeth Egbert; Chm., Henry Arlin Salmon; Cur. History, Patricia Salmon; Vice Pres. Mktg. & Devel., Henryk Behnke; Dir. Science, Edward Johnson; School Programs Asst., Loretta Lonecke; Public Rels. & Mktg. Asst., Rachel Somma; Dir. Devel., Cheryl Adolph.

Personnel Profile: Full-Time Paid 12; Part-Time Paid 30; Part-Time Volunteers 25; Interns 5.

Governing Authority: private; nonprofit organization. Tax-exempt: 501(c)(3).

General Museum.

Collections: artworks; natural science specimens; local history archives; paintings; decorative arts; sculpture; archaeology; manuscripts; photographs; maps; prints; costumes & textiles; graphics; natural history of Staten Island & region; minerals; botany; ornithology; herpetology; entymology; Staten Island Ferry collection.

Research Fields: area art, natural science & history; decorative arts; environmental concerns; preservation of natural resources; photography; 19th-century American painting; American portraits.

Facilities: 16,000-vol. library; classroom; 80-seat auditorium. Maritime history publications, nautical gifts & ferry-related items for sale.
Activities: workshops; demonstrations; academic internships; permanent & temporary exhibitions; study clubs; formally organized educational programs for children & adults; guided Staten Island Ferry tours; nature & neighborhood walks.
Publications: quarterly newsletter; special exhibition catalogues; publications on natural science & local history of Staten Island.
Hours & Admission Prices: Sun.-Fri. 12-5, Sat. 10-5. Adults $2, students & seniors $1; discounts to AAM & ICOM members; members no charge. Closed New Year's Day; Memorial Day; Independence Day; Thanksgiving; Christmas. ♿
Attendance: 65,000 (estimated)
Membership: Senior (62 & up) $25; Individual $35; Family $50; Collector's Club $100; Connoiseur's Club $150; Curator's Circle $250; President's Circle $500; Trustees Circle $1,000.

STATEN ISLAND ZOO, 614 Broadway, Staten Island, NY 10310-2896. Tel.: 718-442-3100 & 3101. Fax: 718-981-8711.
Web Site: www.statenislandzoo.org
Founded: 1936.
Congressional District: 17
Key Personnel: C.E.O., John J. Caltabiano; Pres., William J. Frew, Jr.; Assoc. Cur., Peter Laline.
Personnel Profile: Full-Time Paid 41; Part-Time Paid 9; Part-Time Volunteers 44; Interns 2.
Governing Authority: society. Staten Island Zoological Society. Tax-exempt: 501(c)(3).
Zoo.
Collections: herpetology; mammalogy; avian; aquarium.
Facilities: 1,000-vol. library of books on zoology and biology; snack bar. Books & other museum-related items for sale.
Activities: lectures; films; zoomobile outreach program; formally organized education programs for children.
Publications: quarterly newsletter, What's Happening at the Zoo?
Hours & Admission Prices: Daily 10-4:45. Adults $8, seniors 60 & over $6, children 3-14 $5, disabled $3; members, children under 3, members of reciprocal zoos & every Wed. 2-4:45 no charge. Closed New Year's Day; Thanksgiving; Christmas. ♿
Attendance: 175,387 (accurate)
Membership: Individual $45; Family $85; Gold Card $160; Corporate Donor $250; Life $500; Corporate Sponsor $1,000; Corporate Benefactor $2,500.

Sterling Center

STERLING HISTORICAL SOCIETY AND LITTLE RED SCHOOLHOUSE MUSEUM, Rte. 104A, Sterling Center, NY 13156. Mailing Address: 14352 Woods Rd., Sterling, NY 13156-4116. Tel.: 315-947-6461 & 564-6189.
E-mail: sterlinghistory@lakeontario.net
Web Site: www.lakeontario.net/sterlinghistory
Founded: 1976.
Congressional District: 33
Key Personnel: Pres., Don H. Richardson; Sec. & Trustee, Susan Parsons; Treasurer & Trustee, Judith Snyder; Trustee, H. Lucille Flack; Trustee, Carl Dates; Town Clerk, Lisa Cooper; Museum Shop Mgr., Susan Allen.
Personnel Profile: Full-Time Volunteers 1; Part-Time Volunteers 14; Interns 1.
Governing Authority: society. Parent Institution: Town of Sterling. Subsidiary Institution: Cayuga Museum. Branch Museum: C.C.C. (Civilian Conservation Corps.) mini museum & monuments in Fairhaven Beach State Park. Tax-exempt.
Historical Society Museum: housed in The Little Red School House, an original wood frame, two-story structure.
Collections: personal artifacts; cameras & developing equipment; glass negatives; typewriters; Doctor's bag including medical items; Civil War; Indian artifacts; railroad signal tower; period store; barber shop; period kitchen; old blacksmith shop.
Research Fields: genealogy.
Facilities: classroom.
Activities: temporary exhibitions; special crafts display; special exhibits; movie presentation; special speakers.
Publications: brochure; newsletters; books; annual community calendars.
Hours & Admission Prices: mid-June to Aug. Sat.-Sun. 1-5. No charge; donations accepted. ♿
Attendance: 375 (estimated)
Membership: Single $5; Family $10; Life $75.

Stillwater

SARATOGA NATIONAL HISTORICAL PARK, 648 Route 32, Stillwater, NY 12170-1604. Tel.: 518-664-9821, ext. 224. Fax: 518-664-3349.
E-mail: sara_info@nps.gov
Web Site: www.nps.gov/sara
Founded: 1938.
Congressional District: 24
Key Personnel: Supt., Joe Finan; Program Dir., Gina Johnson.
Personnel Profile: Full-Time Paid 16; Part-Time Paid 6; Part-Time Volunteers 20; Interns 1.
Governing Authority: federal. Administered by the Dept. of Interior, National Park Service, Interior Bldg., Washington, DC 20240.
Military Museum: located on the site of the Battles of Saratoga, Sept. 19 and Oct. 7, 1777.
Collections: military history and the Burgoyne Campaign.
Research Fields: Burgoyne Campaign; the Battles of Saratoga.
Facilities: 600-vol. library of books, microfilm and research reports related to the American Revolution, Burgoyne Campaign and the Battles of Saratoga available for use by researchers on premises; 80-seat auditorium; theater; battlefield unit; visitor center; tour road; picnic areas; Saratoga Monument Unit; Philip Schuyler House. History-related educational items for sale.
Activities: orientation films; tours; talks & walks; period demonstrations.
Publications: brochure, Saratoga National Historical Park.
Hours & Admission Prices: Daily 9-5; tour rates available. No charge for park; $5 for use of tour road; $3 for hiking & biking. Closed New Year's Day; Thanksgiving; Christmas. ♿
Attendance: 150,000 (accurate)

Stony Brook

* **LONG ISLAND MUSEUM OF AMERICAN ART, HISTORY & CARRIAGES, (M),** 1200 Rte. 25A, Stony Brook, NY 11790-1992. Tel.: 631-751-0066, ext. 0. Fax: 631-751-0353.
E-mail: mail@longislandmuseum.org
Web Site: www.longlslandmuseum.org
Formerly: The Museums at Stony Brook
Founded: 1935.
Congressional District: 1
Key Personnel: Pres. & C.E.O., Jacqueline Day; Chm. (V), Albert A. Brayson, II; Chief Cur., William S. Ayres; Dir. Devel., Deirdre Doherty; Dir. Admin., William Clark; Dir. Education, Betsy Radecki; Dir. Communications, Julie Diamond; Cur. History, Joshua Ruff.
Personnel Profile: Full-Time Paid 21; Part-Time Paid 5; Part-Time Volunteers 205; Interns 10.
Governing Authority: nonprofit organization. Tax-exempt: 501(c)(3).
General Museum.
Collections: 200 carriages & horse-drawn vehicles, carriage accoutrements; 19th- & 20th-century American art including the William Sidney Mount collection of paintings, drawings, memorabilia; costumes & accessories; dolls; toys; wildfowling decoys; decorative arts; miniature rooms; local archives; early photographs; painter William Sidney Mount, including archives. Historic Buildings: 18th-century Hawkins-Mount house; 18th-century barn; 19th-century schoolhouse; 19th-century blacksmith shop; carriage shed.
Major Exhibits: William Sidney Mount Exhibition, 11/09-6/10; America's Kitchens (T), 2/10-10/10.
Research Fields: horse-drawn transportation; 19th- & 20th-century American art; history; costumes & textiles; wildfowling decoys.
Facilities: 2,000-vol. library of American art & Long Island history; classroom; meeting room
Activities: formally organized education programs for children, adults & families; permanent & temporary exhibitions; training program for museum guides; internship programs; special events; concerts; seminars; workshops.
Publications: annual report; quarterly newsletter; exhibition catalogs; brochures; books related to collections.
Hours & Admission Prices: Call for hours. Adults $9, senior citizens $7, children $4; discounts to AAM members; members no charge. Closed New Year's Day; Thanksgiving; Christmas Eve & Day. ♿
Attendance: 40,839 (accurate)
Membership: Students & Senior Citizens $25; Individual $40; Dual & Family $60; Contributor $100; Sponsor $250; Patron $500; President's Council $1,000; Carriage Circle $2,500.

MUSEUM OF LONG ISLAND NATURAL SCIENCES, Earth & Space Sciences Bldg.-State University of New York at Stony Brook, Stony Brook, NY 11794-0001. Tel.: 631-632-8230. Fax: 631-632-8240.
E-mail: Pamela.Stewart@sunysb.edu
Web Site: www.geosciences.stonybrook.edu/museum
Founded: 1973.
Congressional District: 1

Key Personnel: Dir., Pamela Stewart; Cur. Geology, Steven E. Englebright.
Personnel Profile: Full-Time Paid 1; Part-Time Paid 1; Part-Time Volunteers 18.
Governing Authority: university; nonprofit organization. Parent Institution: State University of New York at Stony Brook. Tax-exempt.
Natural Science Museum.
Collections: worldwide modern & fossil marine invertebrates especially Mollusca; natural history collections of Long Island, especially insects & their host plants; general herbarium; minerals & fossils; modern marine invertebrates.
Research Fields: geology of Long Island; ecology; marine science; science education; botany.
Facilities: classrooms; meeting rooms; nature trails.
Activities: guided tours; lectures; films; gallery talks; formally organized education programs for children, adults, college students affiliated with State University of New York; loan, permanent & temporary exhibitions; field trips.
Publications: calendar of events; A Beachcombers Guide to Long Island Shores; The Pine Barrens; Our Fragile Wilderness; Tall Grass by the Sea: A Guide to Long Islands Salt Marshes; film, Long Island Wilderness. . .The Pine Barrens; books, The Mashomack Preserve Study, 3 vols; Long Island Water Resources Curriculum Guide, 2 vols; A Field Guide to Long Island Woodlands; A Field Guide to Long Island's Freshwater Wetlands; A Field Guide to Long Island's Seashores.
Hours & Admission Prices: Mon.-Fri. 9-5. No charge; donations accepted. Closed national holidays. ♿
Attendance: 20,000 (estimated)
Membership: Student $10; Individual $15; Dual & Family $25; Supporting $30; Associate $50; Contributor $60; Sustainer $100; Affiliate $250; Patron $500; Supporter $1,000; Benefactor $2,500.

UNIVERSITY ART GALLERY, STATE UNIVERSITY OF NEW YORK AT STONY BROOK, Staller Center for the Arts, Stony Brook, NY 11794-0001. Tel.: 516-632-7240. Fax: 516-632-1976.
E-mail: rcooper@notes.cc.sunysb.edu
Founded: 1975.
Congressional District: 1
Key Personnel: Dir., Rhonda Cooper.
Personnel Profile: Full-Time Paid 2; Interns 5.
Governing Authority: university; nonprofit. Parent Institution: SUNY at Stony Brook. Tax-exempt.
University Art Gallery.
Collections: paintings; sculpture; photographs.
Research Fields: modern & contemporary art.
Facilities: 4,700 sq. ft. exhibit space; educational facilities.
Activities: formal education programs; traveling exhibitions.
Publications: exhibition catalogues 4 times annually.
Hours & Admission Prices: early Sept. to May Tues.-Fri. 12-4, Sat. 7-9. No charge. Closed holidays. ♿
Attendance: 12,000 (estimated)

Stony Point

STONY POINT BATTLEFIELD STATE HISTORIC SITE, 44 Battlefield Rd., Stony Point, NY 10980. Mailing Address: Box 182, Stony Point, NY 10980-0182. Tel.: 845-786-2521. Fax: 845-786-0463.
Web Site: www.nysparks.com
Founded: 1897.
Congressional District: 26
Key Personnel: Historic Site Mgr., Julia M. Warger.
Personnel Profile: Part-Time Paid 5; Part-Time Volunteers 3.
Governing Authority: state. Parent Institution: New York State Office of Parks, Recreation & Historic Preservation & Palisades Interstate Park Commission. Tax-exempt: 501(c)(3).
Historic Site & Military Museum: located on the site of raid on British stronghold by Brigadier Gen. Anthony Wayne on July 15, 1779.
Collections: Revolutionary War equipment & artifacts. Historic Structure: c.1826 lighthouse.
Research Fields: American Revolution in Hudson Valley; lighthouses of the Hudson River Valley.
Facilities: outdoor walking tour; picnic areas.
Activities: permanent exhibit; special programs & living history demonstrations.
Hours & Admission Prices: mid-April to Oct. Wed.-Sun. 10-5, Sun. 12-5. Museum & Lighthouse: Sat.-Sun. & Mon. holidays $5 per vehicle. Additional Fees Charged: evening tours, lantern walks, special events, & programs. ♿
Attendance: 27,500 (estimated)

Syracuse

THE COMMUNITY FOLK ART CENTER, (M), 805 E. Genesee St., Syracuse, NY 13210-1507. Tel.: 315-442-2230. Fax: 315-442-2972.
E-mail: cfac@syr.edu
Web Site: communityfolkartcenter.org
Key Personnel: Exec. Dir., Kheli Willetts
Art Center.
Collections: African American culture & art.
Activities: gallery talks; workshops; studio arts, ceramics & dance classes.
Hours & Admission Prices: Tues.-Fri. 10-5, Sat. 11-5.

* **ERIE CANAL MUSEUM, (M),** 318 Erie Blvd., E., Syracuse, NY 13202-1106. Tel.: 315-471-0593. Fax: 315-471-7220.
E-mail: contactus@eriecanalmuseum.org
Web Site: www.eriecanalmuseum.org
Founded: 1962.
Congressional District: 25
Key Personnel: Interim Exec. Dir., Diana Goodsight; Pres. (V), Kathleen Rapp; Cur., Daniel Franklin Ward; Devel. & Public Rels. Dir., Rory Lawrence; Operations Mgr., Steve Caraccuo.
Personnel Profile: Full-Time Paid 4; Part-Time Paid 4; Part-Time Volunteers 40.
Governing Authority: nonprofit organization. Tax-exempt: 501(c)(3).
History Museum: housed in 1850 Greek Revival style Weighlock Building, a monument to Erie Canal architecture; Syracuse Heritage Area Visitors Center.
Collections: patent models; commemorative china; textiles; 19th-century household items & tools; paintings; photographs; manuscripts; maps; final account journals; engineering records; prints of the canal era. Historic Building: Weighlock Building, used for collection of tolls & administration of a division of the 19th & 20th-century Erie Canal network; the impact of Erie Canal on United States history in the 19th century; Syracuse history; 65 ft. long canal boat replica.
Research Fields: history, use & operation of the canal; economics of construction & impact on surrounding territories; life of canal era; construction of boats; development of Erie Canal Park.
Facilities: 6,000-vol. library of state legislative records, 900,000 manuscripts, 30,000 photos, negatives & slides, secondary historical works & primary sources available by appointment; towpath trail; orientation center.
Activities: guided museum tours; lectures; graduate student internships; inter-museum exhibitions; school loan service; walking tours; motor coach tours; education programs; festival for children.
Publications: quarterly newsletter, A Canal Boat Primer; books, A Novel Look at the Erie Canal; Photos From the Collection; Syracuse; An Urban Landscape; Always Know Your Pal; Children of the Erie Canal; Syracuse Architecture: A City Rises from the Banks of the Canal; Those Among Us: Uncovering the Story of Who Built the Erie Canal.
Hours & Admission Prices: Mon.-Sat. 10-5, Sun. 10-3. No charge; donations accepted. Library by appointment only. Closed New Year's Day; Independence Day; Thanksgiving; Christmas. ♿
Attendance: 25,000 (estimated)
Membership: General $35; Family $50; Canaller $100; Weighmaster $500 & up.

* **EVERSON MUSEUM OF ART, (M),** 401 Harrison St., Syracuse, NY 13202-3091. Tel.: 315-474-6064. Fax: 315-474-6943.
E-mail: everson@everson.org
Web Site: www.everson.org
Formerly: Everson Museum of Art of Syracuse & Onodaga County
Founded: 1896.
Key Personnel: Pres. (V), Jack Rudnick; Dir., Steven Kern; Pres. (V), Lucia Whisenand; Sr. Cur., Debora Ryan; Cur. Education, Pam McLaughlin; Archivist & Librarian, Mary Iversen; Dir. Public Rels., Sarah Massett; Museum Shop Mgr., Sheila Goldie; Museum Shop Mgr., Karen Williams.
Personnel Profile: Full-Time Paid 17; Part-Time Paid 1; Part-Time Volunteers 324; Interns 7.
Governing Authority: nonprofit organization. Tax-exempt: 501(c)(3).
Art Museum.
Collections: 18th-20th century American paintings, sculpture, drawings & graphics; American ceramics A.D. 1100-21st century; ceramics of the world, 3000 B.C.-21st century; photography; study collections of Asian, African and Oceanic art & artifacts.
Research Fields: American painting & sculpture; 19th, 20th & 21st century American ceramics.
Facilities: 10,000-vol. library of art history, art criticism, biography & exhibition catalogs, available for research on premise & for inter-library loan; 299-seat auditorium; classrooms; cafe. Museum-related items for sale.
Activities: guided tours; docent program; lectures; films; gallery talks; concerts; dance recitals; arts festivals; education programs for school children,

students, families, and adults; outreach programs; training programs for professional museum workers; inter-museum loan exhibitions; permanent, traveling & temporary exhibitions.
Publications: handbooks; guides to various collections; catalogues of major exhibitions; quarterly newsletter.
Hours & Admission Prices: Tues.-Fri. & Sun. 12-5, Sat. 10-5. Suggested Donation: $5 per person. Closed New Year's Day; Independence Day; Thanksgiving; Christmas. ♿
Attendance: 82,105 (estimated)
Membership: Senior Citizen & Student $25; Participating $35; Family $50; Fellow $100; Patron $250; Guarantor $500; Everson Circle $1,000; George Fisk Comfort Society $5,000; Fernando Carter Friends $10,000; Director's Circle $15,000; President's Circle $25,000 & up.

MILTON J. RUBENSTEIN MUSEUM OF SCIENCE & TECHNOLOGY, 500 S. Franklin St., Syracuse, NY 13202-1245. Tel.: 315-425-9068, ext. 0. Fax: 315-425-9072.
Web Site: www.most.org
Founded: 1978.
Congressional District: 25
Key Personnel: Pres., Larry R. Leatherman; Chm. (V), Richard Sykes; Vice Pres. (V), Edgar Galson; Treas., Patrick Dooher; Museum Shop Mgr., Nancy Allison.
Personnel Profile: Full-Time Paid 20; Part-Time Paid 22; Part-Time Volunteers 140; Interns 2.
Governing Authority: nonprofit organization. Parent Institution: Discover Center of Science & Technology. Tax-exempt: 501(c)(3).
Science & Technology Museum.
Collections: concept oriented exhibits on a wide range of scientific & technological topics aimed at visitor participation involving hands-on techniques.
Research Fields: history of science.
Facilities: meeting rooms; teachers resource center; Silverman Planetarium; classrooms; Bristol Omnitheater (IMAX Dome). Science-related kits & specimens for sale.
Activities: demonstrations; lectures; films; hobby workshops; planetarium presentations; in-school science programs; hands-on exhibits; formally organized education programs; docent program or council; loan, permanent, temporary & traveling exhibitions; field trips.
Publications: quarterly newsletter.
Hours & Admission Prices: Wed.-Sun. 10-5. Adults $5, seniors 65 & over and children under 11 $4; discounts to ASTC members; members no charge. ♿
Attendance: 160,000 (estimated)
Membership: Senior $24; Individual $49; Grandparent $59; Family $69; Enhanced Family $79.

MUSEUM OF AUTOMOBILE ART AND DESIGN, 6710 Brooklawn Pkwy., Syracuse, NY 13211-2104. Tel.: 315-432-8282. Fax: 315-432-8256.
Web Site: www.moaaad.org
Formerly: The Museum of Automobile History
Founded: 1996.
Key Personnel: C.E.O., Walter Miller.
Personnel Profile: Full-Time Paid 1.
Governing Authority: private.
Automobile Art Museum.
Collections: artwork pertaining to advertising, styling & memorabilia of the history of automobiles from the 19th-century to the present.
Facilities: 9,000 sq. ft. exhibit space. Museum-related items for sale.
Activities: films; guided tours; lectures; participatory & traveling exhibitions.
Hours & Admission Prices: Call for hours.
Attendance: 20,000 (estimated)

ONONDAGA HISTORICAL ASSOCIATION MUSEUM & RESEARCH CENTER, 321 Montgomery St., Syracuse, NY 13202-2098. Tel.: 315-428-1864. Fax: 315-471-2133.
E-mail: ohamail2002@yahoo.com
Web Site: www.cnyhistory.org
Founded: 1862.
Congressional District: 27
Key Personnel: Exec. Dir., Gregg Tripoli; Asst. Dir. & Cur. Collections, Thomas Hunter; Pres. (V), Thomas Riley; Cur. History, Dennis Connors; Dir. Devel., Adrienne Kelley; Education Assoc., Scott Peal; Archivist & Museum Shop Mgr., Pamela Priest; Administrative Asst., Karen Cooney.
Personnel Profile: Full-Time Paid 7; Part-Time Paid 2; Part-Time Volunteers 40; Interns 2.
Governing Authority: society. Tax-exempt: 170(b)(1)(A).
Local Historical Museum.
Collections: Syracuse, Onondaga County & area history; Underground Railroad artifacts; New York State canal history; landscapes & portraits by local artists; archaeology; archives; graphics; costumes; ethnology; transportation; stained glass; pottery; manuscripts; architectural drawings, newspapers, imprints, decorative arts, photographs; typewriters; Franklin automobiles & other locally manufactured products; sports history; extensive library; manuscripts; maps.
Research Fields: Onondaga County & area history.
Facilities: library of photographs, maps, documents & other reference materials available on premises; classroom; auditorium. Books & museum-related items for sale.
Activities: guided tours; lectures; workshops; craft demonstrations; temporary & traveling exhibitions; bus tours. Museum Sponsors: Ghost Walk; National History Day Competition.
Publications: quarterly newsletter, History Highlights; Syracuse Landmarks; Images of America: Syracuse, local photographs from 1854; Images of America: Greater Syracuse, local photographs from 1900; Crossroads In Time: An Illustrated History of Syracuse; Historic Photos of Syracuse.
Hours & Admission Prices: Museum: Wed.-Fri. 10-4, Sat.-Sun. 11-4. No charge; donations accepted. Research Center: Wed.-Fri. 10-2; Mon. & Tues. by appointment. Adults $7. Closed national holidays. ♿
Attendance: 30,000 (estimated)
Membership: Student & Senior Citizen $25; Individual $30; Family $40; Researcher $50; Archivist $100; Corporation $500; Scholar $1,000.

ROSAMOND GIFFORD ZOO AT BURNET PARK, 1 Conservation Place, Syracuse, NY 13204-2590. Tel.: 315-435-8511. Fax: 315-435-8517.
E-mail: info@rosamondgiffordzoo.org
Web Site: www.rosamondgiffordzoo.org
Formerly: Burnet Park Zoo
Founded: 1914.
Congressional District: 23
Key Personnel: Dir., Chuck Doyle; Dir. Devel., Holly Karker; Exhibit Artist, Kate Woodle; Dir. Retail Sales, Sharon DeGaramo; Cur. Animals, Ted Fox; Cur. Animals, Tom LaBarge; Coord. Volunteer Svcs., Ellen Vaughn.
Personnel Profile: Full-Time Paid 41; Part-Time Paid 3; Part-Time Volunteers 259; Interns 35.
Governing Authority: county. Parent Institution: Onondaga County Parks. Tax-exempt: 170(b)(1)(A).
Zoo.
Collections: invertebrates; fish; amphibians; reptiles, birds & mammals.
Research Fields: mammalian, avian, reptilian & fish behavior.
Facilities: 45 acres of grounds.
Activities: tours; seminars; film series; summer camp. Museum Sponsors: educational programs through extensive volunteer program; 4-H program.
Publications: teacher's guide to zoo; map; training materials; animal briefs; multimedia presentations; bimonthly publication, Tracks; monthly docent newsletter, The Inside Track; membership newsletter.
Hours & Admission Prices: Daily 10-4:30. Adults $6.50, senior citizens & students 15-21 $4.50, children 3-15 $4; discounts to groups; children 2 & under, AZA, IZE & AAZK members no charge. Closed New Year's Day; Thanksgiving; Christmas. ♿
Attendance: 332,115 (accurate)
Membership: Senior $10; Senior plus one $12; Individual $23; Couple $45; Family $59; Patron $125; Supporting $225; Sustaining $325.

SUART GALLERIES - SYRACUSE UNIVERSITY, Shaffer Art Bldg., Syracuse University, Syracuse, NY 13244-0001. Tel.: 315-443-4097. Fax: 315-443-9225.
E-mail: suart@syr.edu
Web Site: suart.syr.edu
Formerly: Syracuse University Art Collection
Founded: 1871.
Congressional District: 27
Key Personnel: Dir., Domenic J. Iacono; Assoc. Dir., David Prince; Registrar, Laura Wellner; Designer & Preparator, Andrew J. Saluti; Coord. Collection & Exhibition, Emily Dittman; Administrative Asst., Joan Recuparo; Sec. & Office Coord., Alex Hahn.
Personnel Profile: Full-Time Paid 8; Part-Time Paid 5; Part-Time Volunteers 2.
Governing Authority: private university; nonprofit. Parent Institution: Syracuse University. Tax-exempt.
Art Gallery.
Collections: 20th-century American graphics, painting, sculpture & decorative arts; prehistoric to modern Western art; textiles; history of illustration.
Research Fields: art between the World Wars.
Facilities: 3,200-vol. library of catalog raisonnes; general art history; American art monographs; indexes & listings of artists; educational facilities.
Activities: formal education programs for undergraduate or graduate college students; loan, temporary & traveling exhibitions.
Publications: highlight special collection; semi-annual collection exhibitions catalog.
Hours & Admission Prices: Tues.-Sun. 11-4:30; other times by appointment. No charge. ♿

Attendance: 12,000 (estimated)

Tappan

TAPPANTOWN HISTORICAL SOCIETY, (M), Tappan, NY 10983. Mailing Address: Box 71, Tappan, NY 10983-0071. Tel.: 845-359-1149 & 2730.
Web Site: tappantown.org
Founded: 1965.
Congressional District: 47
Key Personnel: Pres., Carol LaValle; Vice Pres., John Morton; Treas., Gerri McCauley.
Governing Authority: nonprofit organization.
Historical Society & Historic District: approximately 20 18th- & 19th-century homes.
Collections: American architecture; preservation project; architectural heritage.
Research Fields: local history.
Activities: educational programs; 1-mile walking tours; guided tours; dating of houses.
Publications: annual booklet, Drummer Boy; quarterly newsletter.
Hours & Admission Prices: No charge.
Membership: Individual $10; Family $15.

Tarrytown

HISTORIC HUDSON VALLEY, (M), 150 White Plains Rd., Tarrytown, NY 10591-5535. Tel.: 914-631-8200. Fax: 914-631-0089. TDD: 800-448-4007.
E-mail: mail@hudsonvalley.org
Web Site: www.hudsonvalley.org
Founded: 1951.
Congressional District: 22
Key Personnel: Chm. (V), Michael Hegarty; Pres., Waddell W. Stillman; Dir. Finance & Administration, David M. Parsons; Dir. Public Rels., Rob Schweitzer; Dir. Historic Structures, Geoffrey Carter; Cur., Kathleen E. Johnson; Dir. Retail Sales, Henri Corbacho.
Personnel Profile: Full-Time Paid 106; Part-Time Paid 214; Part-Time Volunteers 430; Interns 10.
Governing Authority: private operating foundation. Tax-exempt: 501(c)(3).
Preservation Project.
Collections: maps; prints; photographs; architectural plans; slides & films; fine & decorative arts; manuscripts & memorabilia. Historic Houses: mid-18th century Philipsburg Manor, Upper Mills, Sleepy Hollow, NY; 1790-1812 Van Cortlandt Manor, Croton-on-Hudson; 1835-1859 Sunnyside, Tarrytown home of author Washington Irving; 1805-1985 Montgomery Place, Annandale on Hudson; Union Church of Pocantico Hills, housing stained glass works of art by Matisse & Chagall; Kykuit, the Rockefeller Estate (1900-1913).
Research Fields: life in the lower Hudson Valley.
Facilities: 30,000-vol. library of books; 100-seat auditorium. Books & museum-related items for sale.
Activities: guided tours; films; formally organized education programs; demonstrations; special events; permanent & temporary exhibitions; intermuseum loans; interpretive programming; visitation program for Kykuit, the Rockefeller house and gardens, a property of the National Trust for Historic Preservation.
Publications: books; booklets; exhibition catalogs.
Hours & Admission Prices: Philipsburg Manor: Feb.-March by appointment; April-Sept. Wed.-Mon. 10-6, Oct. daily 10-6; Nov.-Dec. Sat.-Sun. & Fri. after Thanksgiving 10-4; groups by appointment. Adults $12, senior citizens $10, children $6. Sunnyside: March by appointment; April-Oct. Wed.-Mon. 11-6; Nov.-Dec. Sat.-Sun. & Fri. after Thanksgiving 10-4; groups by appointment. Adults $12, senior citizens $10, children $6. Van Cortlandt Manor: March-May 22 by appointment; May 23-Sept. 7 Thurs.-Sun. 11-6; Oct. call for hours; Nov.-Dec. Sat.-Sun. & Fri. after Thanksgiving 10-4; groups by appointment. Adults $12, senior citizens $10, children $6. Kykuit: May 9-Dec. call for hours. Classic Tour: adults $23, senior citizens & children $21. Grand Tour: adults $40. Union Church: April-Sept. Mon. & Wed.-Sat. 10-6, Sun. 2-6; Oct. Mon.-Sat. 10-6, Sun. 2-6; Nov.-Dec. 13 Mon. & Wed.-Sat. 10-4, Sun. 2-4. Adults $5, children $3. Montgomery Place: temporarily closed. ♿
Attendance: 190,000 (accurate)
Membership: Senior 62 & over $50; Individual $60; Dual $100; Family $140; Family Plus $200; Premier $350; Sponsor $500; Pocantico Society $2,500-$5,000.

THE HISTORICAL SOCIETY, SERVING SLEEPY HOLLOW AND TARRYTOWN, One Grove St., Tarrytown, NY 10591-4122. Tel.: 914-631-8374.
E-mail: historyatgrove@aol.com
Web Site: www.sleepyhollowchamber.com/history.html
Formerly: The Historical Society of Tarrytowns, Inc.
Founded: 1889.
Congressional District: 23
Key Personnel: Pres., Scott Monje; Admin. & Cur., Sara Mascia.
Personnel Profile: Full-Time Paid 1; Part-Time Volunteers 12.
Governing Authority: society. Bd. of Trustees. Tax-exempt: 170(b)(1)(A).
General History Museum.
Collections: Native American artifacts; early Dutch history of the region; photographs; artifacts from local archaeological dig; local memorabilia; military papers; land records; wills; American Revolution: 1780 capture of Major John Andre at Tarrytown; Washington Irving & other men and women of letters; paintings; costumes; manuscripts; early military artifacts; art collections of Evart Duychinck III, Ezra Ames, John Mare, Emily N. Hatch, DeWitt C. Hay, & Edgar Mayhew Bacon; jewelry; clothing; textiles; dolls; toys; household implements.
Research Fields: genealogy; local history-social, economic, political, geographical, & architectural.
Facilities: 3,500-vol. library of material on local & New York State history & genealogy, 715 maps, records of Ward B. Burnett Post, G.A.R.; Civil War papers of Cap. Charles H. Rockwell; microfilm of local newspapers; reading room. Museum-related items for sale.
Activities: guided tours; lectures; permanent & temporary exhibitions. Society Sponsors: annual Strawberry Festival; historic house tours.
Publications: Images of America Tarrytown and Sleepy Hollow.
Hours & Admission Prices: Sept.-July Tues.-Thurs. & Sat. 2-4. No charge; donations accepted. Closed holidays.
Membership: Student $10; Individual $30; Family $40; Sustaining $50; Contributing $100; Business & Organization $100; Life $500.

LYNDHURST, (M), 635 S. Broadway, Tarrytown, NY 10591-6499. Tel.: 914-631-4481, ext. 0. Fax: 914-631-5634.
E-mail: lyndhurst@nthp.org
Web Site: www.lyndhurst.org
Founded: 1964.
Congressional District: 22
Key Personnel: Dir., John H. Braunlein; Asst. Dir., Cathryn McElroy Anders; Business Mgr., Virginia Cassell; Interim Chm. Bd., Stephen Tilly; Education Cur., Judith Beil; Head Visitor Svcs., Ira Stein; Mktg. Coord., Stephania Brown; Restoration Projects Mgr., Krystyn Hastings-Silver; Buildings & Grounds Mgr., David Ware; Museum Shop Mgr., Joy Smith.
Personnel Profile: Full-Time Paid 8; Part-Time Paid 35; Part-Time Volunteers 75; Interns 20.
Governing Authority: nonprofit organization. Parent Institution: National Trust for Historic Preservation, 1785 Massachusetts Ave. N.W., Washington, DC 20036. Tax-exempt: 501(c)(3).
Historic House Museum: 19th-century Gothic revival residence of William Paulding, George Merritt & Jay Gould family, designed by A.J. Davis.
Collections: 19th- & early 20th-century decorative arts; fine arts; textiles; A.J. Davis-designed Gothic furniture; rare book library; specimen trees. Historic Building: carriage house.
Research Fields: architecture; decorative arts; landscape; local history; archives consisting of family & estate records; photographs.
Facilities: cafe; meeting space. Museum-related items for sale.
Activities: guided tours; lectures; audio tour; concerts; special events; educational programs.
Publications: Lyndhurst guidebook; exhibit catalogues; newsletters.
Hours & Admission Prices: May-Oct. Mon. holidays & Tues.-Sun. 10-5; Nov.-April Sat.-Sun. 10-4. Adults $12, senior citizens $11; children 6-16 $6; discounts to AAM members; members, National Trust for Historic Preservation members & children under 5 no charge. ♿
Attendance: 67,510 (accurate)
Membership: Senior Citizens $35; Individual $40; Dual Senior $60; Family $65; Contributing $100; Supporting $250; Benefactor $500; Talleyrand Society $1,000; Tower Society $2,500; Gould Society $5,000.

Ticonderoga

* **FORT TICONDEROGA,** 30 Ti Fort Rd., Rte 74 E., Ticonderoga, NY 12883. Mailing Address: P.O. Box 390, Ticonderoga, NY 12883-0390. Tel.: 518-585-2821. Fax: 518-585-2210.
E-mail: fort@fort-ticonderoga.org
Web Site: www.fort-ticonderoga.org
Founded: 1908.
Congressional District: 20
Key Personnel: Acting Dir., Kelly O'Neil-Teer; Pres. (V), Edward W. Pell; Dir. Mktg & Communications, Marci Hall; Supt. Bldgs. & Grounds, Lyle St. Jean; Cur. Collections, Christopher D. Fox; Cur. Landscape, Katie Elzer-Peters; Dir. Interpretation & Education, Richard Strum; Museum Shop Mgr., Margaret Shaw.
Personnel Profile: Full-Time Paid 18; Full-Time Volunteers 1; Part-Time Paid 62; Part-Time Volunteers 1,054; Interns 1.

Governing Authority: nonprofit organization. Parent Institution: Fort Ticonderoga Assoc.; Mt. Independence, Orwell, VT; Mt. Hope Battery, Ticonderoga; Mount Defiance, NY. Tax-exempt: 170(b)(1)(A).
Military History Museum: housed in 1755 barracks of now reconstructed Colonial & Revolutionary fortress; restored formal garden c.1920.
Collections: 300 manuscripts; books; maps; prints; engravings; guns; cannon; swords; uniforms; engraved power horns; 18th-century military accoutrements; military manuals & biographies; paintings of 18th-century military scenes & 19th-century landscapes depicting the Fort; 1756-1920 King's Garden.
Research Fields: Colonial & Revolutionary American history; 19th-century tourism.
Facilities: 13,000-vol. library of Colonial & Revolutionary military history available for research by appointment in the Thompson-Pell Research Center; restaurant. Museum-related items for sale.
Activities: guided tours; lectures; films; formally organized educational programs; temporary exhibitions; artillery and musket demonstrations; fife & drum corps performances; garden tours.
Publications: newsletter, The Haversack; annual brochure; annual report; Fort Ticonderoga and Its Dependencies; Lake Champlain and The Upper Hudson Valley; Robert Rogers of the Rangers; Fort Ticonderoga: Key to a Continent; Madison & Jefferson's Journey to the Northern Lakes; archives on CD-ROM, The King's Garden at Fort Ticonderoga; other books on regional military history; pictorial guide to Fort Ticonderoga.
Hours & Admission Prices: early May to late Oct. daily 9:30-5. Adults $15, seniors $13.50, children 7-12 $7; children under 7 & members no charge. ♿
Attendance: 86,102 (accurate)
Membership: Individual $45; Family $60; Supporter $100; Aide-de-camp $250; Enseigne $500; Brigade Major $1,000; Marechal $5,000; Chevalier $10,000.

Tonawanda

HISTORICAL SOCIETY OF THE TONAWANDAS, INC., 113 Main St., Tonawanda, NY 14150-2129. Tel.: 716-694-7406.
E-mail: tonahist@localnet.com
Web Site: www.tonawandashistory.org
Founded: 1961.
Congressional District: 36
Key Personnel: Pres. (V), Patrick Barnany; Museum Shop Mgr., Robert Schweitzer.
Personnel Profile: Part-Time Volunteers 50.
Governing Authority: society. Affiliated with Board of Regents, State University of New York. Branch Museum: Long Homestead, 24 E. Niagara St. Tax-exempt: 501(c)(3).
Historical Society Museums: housed in 1870 brick New York Central Railroad Station & 1829 Long Homestead.
Collections: museum industry; transportation; military; history; Indian artifacts; lumber; medical; costumes; archives; Erie Canal; barber shop; firemen; manuscripts; furnishings. Historic Building: Long Homestead.
Research Fields: local history.
Facilities: 15,000-vol. library of books, bound newspapers, maps, atlas, county histories, scrapbooks, diaries, business & church records, genealogies, obituary files, microfilm of early United States census & Civil War period newspapers available on premises by appointment; reading room. Booklets & other museum-related items for sale.
Activities: guided tours; permanent & temporary exhibitions.
Publications: monthly newsletter, The Lumber Shover; booklets, Civil War Veterans of the Tonawandas; Recollections of the Erie Canal; Tolerable Tales of the Tonawandas; Trolley Days in the Tonawandas; Historical Society Cookbook.
Hours & Admission Prices: Museum: Wed.-Fri. 12-4:30, Thurs. 10-6, Sat. 10-2. No charge. Long Homestead: May & Sept. Sun.1-4; June to Labor Day Sat.-Sun. 1-4; other times by appointment. Admission $4; children under 12 & members no charge. Closed holidays.
Attendance: 4,000 (estimated)
Membership: Single $15; Family $25.

Troy

THE CHILDREN'S MUSEUM OF SCIENCE AND TECHNOLOGY, 250 Jordan Rd., Troy, NY 12180-8394. Tel.: 518-235-2120. Fax: 518-235-6836.
Web Site: www.cmost.org
Formerly: The Junior Museum
Founded: 1954.
Congressional District: 23
Key Personnel: Dir., John Graydon Smith; Chm. (V), M. Lynn Bradley; Museum Shop Mgr., Laurie Miedema.
Personnel Profile: Full-Time Paid 6; Part-Time Paid 6; Part-Time Volunteers 10; Interns 6.
Governing Authority: nonprofit organization. Tax-exempt: 501(c)(3).
Children's Museum & Science Center.
Collections: live animals; science & natural history; rocks; minerals; environmental; reusable fuels; weather & meteorology.
Facilities: Digistar II planetarium. Museum-related items for sale.
Activities: interpretations of exhibits presented to school groups, other groups & individual visitors by museum teachers; weekend workshops; college workstudy program; school break workshops; summer workshops; special school programs & classes on environmental education; festivals; family gallery of multiple participatory science exhibits; summer camp.
Publications: annual teacher brochure.
Hours & Admission Prices: July-Aug. Mon.-Sat. 10-5; Sept.-June Thurs.-Sun. 10-5; other times by appointment. Admission 2 & over $5; discounts to ASTC members; members & children under 2 no charge. Closed New Year's Day; Easter; Memorial Day; Independence Day; Labor Day; Thanksgiving; Christmas. ♿
Attendance: 65,000 (accurate)
Membership: Grandparents $75-$105; Family $80-$110; Family Explorer $120; Sponsor $250; Shooting Star $500; Hendrick Hudson $1,000.

* **RENSSELAER COUNTY HISTORICAL SOCIETY, (M),** 57 Second St., Troy, NY 12180-3928. Tel.: 518-272-7232. Fax: 518-273-1264.
E-mail: info@rchsonline.org
Web Site: www.rchsonline.org
Founded: 1927.
Congressional District: 23
Key Personnel: Pres., Joyce Chupka; Cur., Stacy Pomeroy Draper; Registrar, Kathryn Sheehan; Dir. Education, Mari Shopsis.
Personnel Profile: Full-Time Paid 4; Part-Time Paid 1; Part-Time Volunteers 50; Interns 2.
Governing Authority: society. Subsidiary Institution: 1827 Hart-Cluett House. Tax-exempt: 501(c)(3).
History & Art Museum: 1927 Hart-Cluett House;
Collections: early to mid-19th century furnishings; portraits; manuscripts; maps; photographs; American decorative arts; objects & archives related to the area's history; genealogy. Historic Building: 1827 Hart-Cluett House.
Research Fields: local history & American decorative arts.
Facilities: local history research library; meeting room. Museum-related items for sale.
Activities: school education program; guided tours; lectures; gallery talks; educational & family programming; inter-museum loan, permanent, temporary & traveling exhibitions.
Publications: newsletter.
Hours & Admission Prices: Feb.-Dec. 23 Tues.-Sat. 12-5. Adults $5; members no charge. ♿
Attendance: 10,000 (estimated)
Membership: Student $20; Individual $40; Family & Sustainer $60; Sponsor $125; Patron $250; Fellow $500; Benefactor $1,000.

Tupper Lake

NATURAL HISTORY MUSEUM OF THE ADIRONDACKS/THE WILD CENTER, (M), 45 Museum Dr., Tupper Lake, NY 12986-9712. Tel.: 518-359-7800. Fax: 518-359-3253.
Web Site: www.wildcenter.org
Founded: 1998.
Congressional District: 20
Key Personnel: Exec. Dir., Stephanie Ratcliffe; Pres. Bd. Trustees (V), Donald K. Clifford, Jr.; Dir. Devel., Diana Fortune; Dir. Programs, Jennifer Kretser; Public Rels., Susan Arnold; Cur., Dave Gross; Facilities Mgr., Christopher Rdzanek; Archivist, Betty Woods; Museum Shop, Sara Tagliarino.
Personnel Profile: Full-Time Paid 28; Full-Time Volunteers 50; Part-Time Paid 17; Part-Time Volunteers 140; Interns 6.
Governing Authority: private; nonprofit organization. Tax-exempt: 501(c)(3).
Natural History Museum.
Collections: zoological; paleontological; botanical; geological.
Facilities: 600-vol. library; aquarium; cafeteria; 13,000 sq. ft. exhibit space; 165-seat theater. Museum-related items for sale.
Activities: docent program; films; guided tours; lectures; participatory & temporary exhibits; theater; informal learning programs. Annual Event: Wildfest.
Publications: biannual newsletter, The Otter.
Hours & Admission Prices: May & Nov.-March Fri.-Sun. 10-5; Memorial Day to Labor Day daily 10-6; Sept.-Oct. daily 10-5. Adults & students $15, senior citizens $13, children $9; discounts to groups; members & children under 3 no charge. Closed New Year's Day; Thanksgiving; Christmas. ♿
Attendance: 92,000
Membership: Individual $45; Individual Plus One $85; Family $85; Family Sponsor $100; Grandparents $125; Family Deluxe $250; Adirondack Family Camp $500; Patron's Circle $1,000.

Ulster Park

KLYNE ESOPUS MUSEUM, 764 Rte. 9W, Ulster Park, NY 12487. Mailing Address: P.O. Box 751, Port Ewen, NY 12466-0751. Tel.: 845-226-8221.
E-mail: info@klyneesopusmuseum.org
Web Site: klyneesopusmuseum.org
Founded: 1969.
Congressional District: 26
Key Personnel: Pres. (V), Alexander F. Contini; Museum Shop Mgr., Dorothy Savaria.
Personnel Profile: Part-Time Paid 1; Part-Time Volunteers 30.
Governing Authority: nonprofit; state chartered educational facility. Subsidiary Institution: Perrine's Covered Bridge. Tax-exempt: 501(c)(3).
Local History Museum: housed in c.1827 Old Dutch Church.
Collections: 10,000 BC to 20th century historical artifacts; local & regional history; genealogical & historical records; special emphasis on town of Esopus, Hudson River, Sojourner Truth, Alton B. Parker, John Burroughs & Attilio J. Contini.
Research Fields: local property history; Black & American Indian genealogy from 18th to 19th centuries.
Facilities: 161-vol. library of genealogical & historical materials available to the public; 50-seat lecture hall; 1,200 sq. ft. exhibit space. Museum-related items for sale.
Activities: arts festival; guided tours; lectures; loan & temporary exhibitions.
Publications: quarterly newsletter.
Hours & Admission Prices: last week of May to 1st week of Dec. Fri.-Tues. 1-4; groups by appointment only. No charge; donations accepted. ♿
Attendance: 650 (estimated)
Membership: Individual $15; Family $20; Individual Life $200; Family Life $400.

Upton

BROOKHAVEN NATIONAL LABORATORY-SCIENCE LEARNING CENTER, Brookhaven National Laboratory, Upton, NY 11973-5000. Mailing Address: P.O. Box 5000, Bldg. 400, Upton, NY 11973-5000. Tel.: 631-344-2838 & 4495. Fax: 631-344-5832.
E-mail: oep@bnl.gov
Web Site: www.bnl.gov/slc
Formerly: BNL Science Museum
Founded: 1977.
Congressional District: 1
Key Personnel: Supr., Gail Donoghue; Coord., Bernadette Uzzi.
Personnel Profile: Full-Time Paid 3; Part-Time Paid 3.
Governing Authority: federal; nonprofit. Tax-exempt.
Science Museum: dedicated to using inquiry methods to teach science to students in grades K-12.
Collections: objects relating to scientific research.
Research Fields: high energy physics; chemistry; medicine; biology; chemistry, environmental & applied technologies.
Facilities: educational facilities; 5,000 sq. ft. exhibit space.
Activities: onsite & outreach science programs for students; participatory exhibits; workshops. Center Sponsors: Elementary School Science Fair & Magnetic Levitation competition.
Hours & Admission Prices: Open to school groups, scouts & teachers by appointment only. No charge. ♿
Attendance: 37,000 (accurate)

Utica

CHILDREN'S MUSEUM OF HISTORY, NATURAL HISTORY AND SCIENCE AT UTICA, NEW YORK, 311 Main St., Utica, NY 13501-1282. Tel.: 315-724-6129. Fax: 315-724-6120.
E-mail: marlenebrown@adelphia.net
Web Site: museum4kids.net
Founded: 1963.
Congressional District: 31
Key Personnel: Exec. Dir., Marlene Brown; Chm. (V), David Pendergast; Prog. Mgr., James P. Castilla; Maintenance, Donald Zyga.
Personnel Profile: Full-Time Paid 1; Part-Time Paid 2; Part-Time Volunteers 3.
Governing Authority: nonprofit organization. Parent Institution: New York State Board of Regents. Tax-exempt: 501(c)(3).
Children's Museum.
Collections: Indian artifacts; historic dioramas; rocks; minerals; shells; bird & animal mounts; outdoor railroad display; wax dinosaur models & paintings; period toys; NASA exhibit.
Facilities: classrooms; 5-story historic building. Museum-related items for sale.
Activities: formally organized education programs; school loan service; permanent & temporary exhibits; music & storytelling programs for children; culturally diverse programs.
Publications: monthly newsletter; brochure.
Hours & Admission Prices: Mon. & Thurs.-Fri. 9:30-2:30, Sat. 10-3:45. Adults $9, seniors $8, youth 2-17 $7; discounts to groups; children under 2 & members no charge. ♿
Attendance: 18,000 (accurate)
Membership: Individual & Student $30; Family $45; Family Plus $60; Corporate $250 & up.

*** MUNSON-WILLIAMS-PROCTOR ARTS INSTITUTE MUSEUM OF ART, (M),** 310 Genesee St., Utica, NY 13502-4799. Tel.: 315-797-0000, ext. 2168. Fax: 315-797-5608.
Web Site: www.mwpai.org
Founded: 1919.
Congressional District: 25
Key Personnel: Dir. Museum of Art, Dr. Paul D. Schweizer; Pres., Dr. Daniel E. O'Leary; Dir. Communications, John Bach; Art Shop Mgr., Bona Starring; Vice Pres. Operations, Anthony Spiridigloizzi; Dir. Physical Plant, Barton Rasmus; Cur. Modern & Contemporary Art, Mary Murray; Registrar, Maggie Mazzullo; Cur. Decorative Arts, Anna T. D'Ambrosio; Head Librarian, Kathryn Corcoran; Museum Educator, April Oswald; Exhibition Coord., Elena G.P. Lochmatow.
Personnel Profile: Full-Time Paid 11; Part-Time Paid 10; Part-Time Volunteers 42; Interns 2.
Governing Authority: private; nonprofit organization. Tax-exempt.
Art Museum.
Collections: 18th- & 19th-century American paintings; 20th-21st century European & American paintings & sculpture; European, Japanese, American prints; 19th-century American decorative arts; Proctor watch collection; manuscript collections; Historic House: 1850 Fountain Elms, restored mid-Victorian, Italian villa style house designed by William L. Woolett, Jr., four rooms in 1850 decor.
Major Exhibits: James E. Freeman, 1808-1884: An American Painter in Italy, 11/09-1/10.
Research Fields: 18th- to 21st-century American & European Art; 19th century decorative arts.
Facilities: 25,000 books & 25,000 color slides, 500 videos plus 800 compact discs; lending library of originals; exhibition space; school of art; meeting-house; 271-seat auditorium. Original paintings, sculpture, pottery, prints & jewelry by area artists, jewelry reproductions, art books & other museum-related items for sale.
Activities: guided tours; lectures; films; gallery talks; interactive gallery; concerts; dance recitals; arts festival; drama; rental gallery; formally organized education programs for children, adults & undergraduate students; docent program inter-museum loan, permanent, temporary & traveling exhibitions.
Publications: Order & Enigma: American Art Between the Wars; The Voyage of Life by Thomas Cole: Paintings, Drawings & Prints; 200 Years of American Art (w/AFA); Watches: The Proctor Collection; The Blue & Gray: Oneida County Stoneware; From Drawing to Dwelling: the Planning & Construction of Fountain Elms; The Art of Trenton Falls; Alex Katz: A Drawing Retrospective; John Monti: The Sculpture Court Project; The Distinction of Being Different: Joseph P. McHugh and the American Arts & Crafts Movement; Life Lines: American Master Drawings; Sculpture Space: Celebrating 20 Years; Artistry in Rosewood: Furniture by Elijah Galusha; Masterpieces of American Furniture from the Munson-Williams Proctor Institute; American Twentieth-Century Watercolors at the Munson-Williams-Proctor Arts Institute; Jewels of Time: Watches from the Munson-Williams-Proctor Collection; Collecting Modernism: European Masterworks from the MWPAI; Ferdinand Richardt: Drawings of America, 1855-1859 (2007); A Brass Menagerie: Metalwork of the Aesthetic Movement (2006); Auspicious Vision: Edward Wales Root and American Modernism (2007); James E. Freeman, 1808-1884: An American Painter in Italy.
Hours & Admission Prices: Tues.-Sat. 10-5, Sun. 1-5. No charge. Closed New Year's Day; Martin Luther King Jr. Day; Independence Day; Thanksgiving; Christmas. ♿
Attendance: 64,861 (accurate)
Membership: Student $25; Individual $35; Family $50; Contributor $100; Associate $150; Patron $250; President's Circle $500; Heritage Group $1,000. Business: Colleague $100; Affiliate $200; Sustainer $500; Leader $1,000.

ONEIDA COUNTY HISTORICAL SOCIETY, 1608 Genesee St., Utica, NY 13502-5425. Tel.: 315-735-3642. Fax: 315-732-0806.
E-mail: ochs@midyork.org
Web Site: www.oneidacountyhistory.org
Founded: 1876.
Congressional District: 25
Key Personnel: Exec. Dir., Brian J. Howard; Chm. Bd. (V), Richard D. Allen.

Personnel Profile: Full-Time Paid 1; Full-Time Volunteers 1; Part-Time Paid 1; Part-Time Volunteers 30; Interns 2.
Governing Authority: nonprofit organization. Tax-exempt: 501(c)(3).
History Museum: housed in former First Church of Christ, Scientist.
Collections: local history books, pamphlets, photographs, maps, manuscripts & artifacts pertaining to the history of Utica, Oneida County & the Mohawk Valley.
Research Fields: local history; Mohawk Valley.
Facilities: library of books, pamphlets, documents, manuscripts, maps, photographs available for research on premises; copies or photostats may be ordered; reading room.
Activities: lectures; permanent & temporary exhibitions.
Publications: quarterly newsletter, Oniota.
Hours & Admission Prices: Tues.-Fri. 10-4, Sat. 11-3. Adults $2; members no charge. Research Library: $5 per day. Closed national holidays. ♿
Attendance: 5,000 (accurate)
Membership: Student $25; Individual $40; Family $70; Corporate $150.

UTICA ZOO, 99 Steele Hill Rd., Utica, NY 13501-5090. Tel.: 315-738-0472. Fax: 315-738-0475.
E-mail: info@uticazoo.org
Web Site: www.uticazoo.org
Founded: 1914.
Congressional District: 31
Key Personnel: Exec. Dir., Elizabeth G. Irons; Mgr. Education, Mary Hall; Coord. Devel., Erin Bonk; Cur. Animals, Michael Bates; Supt. Bldgs. & Grounds, Gary Mundschenk; Veterinarian, Ellen Hilton, D.V.M; Revenue Center Mgr., Patricia Jones.
Personnel Profile: Full-Time Paid 13; Part-Time Volunteers 50; Interns 12.
Governing Authority: nonprofit organization. Parent Institution: Utica Zoological Society. Tax-exempt: 501(c)(3).
Zoo.
Collections: exotic & domestic animals, birds, reptiles & vertebrates.
Research Fields: veterinary medicine; animal behavior.
Facilities: library of natural history, zoology, zoo management reference material available for research on premises only; 300-seat amphitheater; 50-seat auditorium/classroom; picnic grove. Books & other items with animal themes for sale.
Activities: lectures; films; study clubs; formally organized educational programs; docent program; permanent exhibitions; travel program; zoomobile presentations; Zoo Parents program.
Publications: quarterly newsletter, Zoo News; annual report.
Hours & Admission Prices: Daily 10-5. Adults $6.50, seniors 60 & up $5, children 4-12 $3.50, students in groups of 10 or more $2; AZA & reciprocal zoo society members no charge. ♿
Attendance: 73,000 (accurate)
Membership: Associate $20; Individual $45; Senior Family $50; Family $55; Extended Family $65; Honor Roll $75; Silver $125; Gold $275; Platinum $500; Diamond $1,000.

Vails Gate

KNOX HEADQUARTERS STATE HISTORIC SITE, Forge Hill Rd. at Rte. 94, Vails Gate, NY 12584. Mailing Address: P.O. Box 207, Vails Gate, NY 12584-0207. Tel.: 845-561-5498. Fax: 845-561-5498.
E-mail: Michael.Clark@oprhp.state.ny.us
Web Site: www.friendsofpalisades.org
Founded: 1922.
Congressional District: 26
Key Personnel: C.E.O., Michael J. Clark.
Personnel Profile: Full-Time Paid 1; Part-Time Paid 2.
Governing Authority: state government. Parent Institution: New York State Office of Parks, Recreation & Historic Preservation. Palisades Interstate Park Commission. Tax-exempt: 501(c)(3).
Historic House Museum: 1754 John Ellison home, used as Continental Army officers' headquarters.
Collections: period furnishings; orientation exhibit; research collection. Historic Structure: c.1741 mill ruins.
Research Fields: American Revolution in Hudson Valley; Gen. Henry Knox & Horatio Gates; the Ellison family; General Nathanael Greene, Slavery in the Mid-Hudson Valley.
Facilities: library of research files available for use by appointment; nature trail.
Activities: guided tours; lectures; school programs; special programs & demonstrations; hiking trails.
Hours & Admission Prices: Memorial Day-Labor Day Wed.-Sat. 10-5, Sun. 1-5; special events & other times by appointment. No charge.
Attendance: 8,500 (estimated)
Membership: Friends of the State Historic Sites of the Hudson Highlands: Individual $15; Household $25; Contributing $50; Business, Corporate & Sustaining $100; Patron $500; Benefactor $1,000.

NATIONAL PURPLE HEART HALL OF HONOR, 374 Temple Hill Rd., Vails Gate, NY 12584-0207. Mailing Address: P.O. Box 207, Vails Gate, NY 12584-0207. Tel.: 845-561-1765; 877-284-6667. Fax: 845-569-0382.
Key Personnel: Dir., Anita Pidala; Program Dir., Peter Bedrossian
Military History Museum: commemorates America's military personnel that were wounded or killed in combat.
Collections: Purple Heart recipients; military artifacts; photographs; films; hands-on exhbits.
Research Fields: Purple Heart recipients & their stories
Facilities: theater; ceremonial grounds.
Activities: interactive exhibits; interactive computer terminals; educational programs.
Hours & Admission Prices: Mon.-Sat. 10-5, Sun. 1-5. No charge; donations accpeted. Closed most holidays. ♿

NEW WINDSOR CANTONMENT STATE HISTORIC SITE, 374 Rt. 300, Temple Hill Rd., Vails Gate, NY 12584. Mailing Address: P.O. Box 207, Vails Gate, NY 12584-0207. Tel.: 845-561-1765. Fax: 845-561-6577.
Web Site: www.nysparks.com
Founded: 1918.
Congressional District: 26
Key Personnel: Historic Site Mgr., Michael J. Clark.
Personnel Profile: Full-Time Paid 5; Part-Time Paid 5; Part-Time Volunteers 200.
Governing Authority: state government. Parent Institution: New York State Office of Parks, Recreation & Historic Preservation. Palisades Interstate Park Commission. Tax-exempt: 501(c)(3).
Historic Site: living history museum located on site of last encampment of Washington's northern Continental Army, 1782-1783.
Collections: Revolutionary War; original & reproduction military equipment & artifacts; local history documents from late 18th century to early 1800s; reconstruction of the Temple Building; Temple Hill Monument; Continental Army artillery; Continental Artillery Park of 1780-81.
Research Fields: American Revolution encampments.
Facilities: 750-vol. library of history available by advance request; 150-seat program area; picnic area.
Activities: living history; blacksmithing & military demonstrations daily; special events; school groups.
Hours & Admission Prices: mid-April to mid-Nov. Wed.-Sat. 10-5, Sun. 1-5. Admission for group tours & educational programs. ♿
Attendance: 23,000 (accurate)
Membership: Friends of the State Historic Sites of the Hudson Highlands: Individual $15; Household $25; Contributing $50; Business Corporate $100; Sustaining $100-$499; Patron $500-$999; Benefactor $1,000 & up.

Vestal

THE VESTAL MUSEUM, 328 Vestal Pkwy. E., Vestal, NY 13850. Mailing Address: 605 Vestal Pkwy. W., Vestal, NY 13850-1437. Tel.: 607-748-1432.
E-mail: vmuseum@vestalny.com
Founded: 1976.
Congressional District: 27
Key Personnel: Dir., Jan Roosa; Cur., Virginia Wood; Museum Shop Mgr., Cathy Roosa.
Personnel Profile: Part-Time Paid 2; Part-Time Volunteers 8; Interns 1.
Governing Authority: municipal. Parent Institution: Town of Vestal. Tax-exempt: 170(b)(1)(A).
Historic Building: 1881 DL&W Vestal Railroad Depot.
Collections: tools of past eras; railroad memorabilia; graphic illustrations; period clothing; artifacts of past lifestyles of area.
Facilities: Gift items for sale.
Activities: guided tours; lectures; films; gallery talks; arts festivals; loan, permanent & temporary exhibitions.
Publications: monthly, Vestal Historical Society Newsletter.
Hours & Admission Prices: Feb.-March & Nov.-Dec. Tues.-Sat. 11-3; April & Oct. Tues.-Sat. 10-3; group tours by appointment. No charge; donations accepted. ♿
Attendance: 4,000 (accurate)
Membership: Students $1; Individual $8; Family $10; Patron $25.

Victor

GANONDAGAN STATE HISTORIC SITE, 1488 Victor Bloomfield Rd. at State Rte. 444, Victor, NY 14564. Mailing Address: P.O. Box 239, Victor, NY 14564-0239. Tel.: 585-924-5848 & 5414. Fax: 585-742-1732.
Web Site: www.ganondagan.org
Founded: 1972.
Congressional District: 33
Key Personnel: Historic Site Mgr., G. Peter Jemison; Interpretive Programs, Michael Galban; Pres. Friends Ganondagan (V), Perry Groung.
Personnel Profile: Full-Time Paid 4; Part-Time Paid 1.

Governing Authority: state. New York State Office of Parks, Recreation & Historic Preservation, and Finger Lakes State Parks, Recreation & Historic Preservation Commission. Tax-exempt.
Historic Site: late 17th-century Seneca Indian town settlement.
Collections: Seneca artifacts; trade items of European manufacture.
Research Fields: Seneca Indians.
Facilities: visitors center; 3 walking trails.
Activities: Handenosaunee Cultural events in summer & fall.
Publications: Art from Ganondagan: War Against the Seneca.
Hours & Admission Prices: Trails: 8-sunset, weather permitting. Guided Walks: Sat.-Sun. 12 & 2. Visitors Center: May-Oct. Tues.-Sun. 9-5. Adults $3, children $2; discounts to AAM members.
Attendance: 37,000 (accurate)
Membership: Friends of Ganondagan: Students & Senior Citizens $10; Single $15; Family $30; Patron $75; Longhouse Friends $100 & up; Earthkeeper $250 & up.

VALENTOWN MUSEUM, 7370 Valentown Sq., Victor, NY 14564. Mailing Address: Victor Historical Society, P.O. Box 472, Victor, NY 14564-0472. Tel.: 585-924-4170. Fax: 585-924-0523.
E-mail: info@valentown.org
Web Site: valentown.org
Founded: 1940.
Congressional District: 33
Key Personnel: Pres. (V), Carol Finch.
Personnel Profile: Full-Time Volunteers 2; Part-Time Volunteers 20.
Governing Authority: society. Parent Institution: Victor Historical Society. Tax-exempt.
History Museum: housed in 1879 Valentown Hall, 19th century community center, located on site of camp area for War of 1812 soldiers & on Seneca Indian Trail of the 1600s used by fur traders, explorers & missionaries.
Collections: stores furnished with original material; local Civil War material; archaeological Indian artifacts; early Mormon artifacts.
Research Fields: local history; folk lore.
Activities: guided tours; lectures.
Publications: newsletter.
Hours & Admission Prices: May-Oct. Tues., Thurs. & Sat.-Sun. 12-4. Tours: by appointment. Adults $5, seniors & students $3; discount to members; children under 5 no charge.
Attendance: 4,000 (estimated)
Membership: Senior Citizens 60 & over $18; Individual $20; Family $30; Sponsor $100; Benefactor $250; Life $500.

Walden

HISTORICAL SOCIETY OF WALDEN & WALLKILL VALLEY, 34 N. Montgomery St., Walden, NY 12586-1117. Mailing Address: P.O. Box 48, Walden, NY 12586-0048. Tel.: 845-778-1173.
E-mail: magic318@hvc.rr.com
Web Site: www.thewaldenhouse.org
Founded: 1958.
Congressional District: 97
Key Personnel: Pres. (V), Barbara Imbasciani.
Personnel Profile: Part-Time Volunteers 15.
Governing Authority: Parent Institution: Historical Society of Walden & Wallkill Valley, Inc. Tax-exempt: 509(a)(2).
Historic House Museum: late 18th-century Jacob Walden House.
Collections: furnishings; local history.
Research Fields: local history.
Facilities: 500-vol. library of local history & genealogy available by appointment.
Activities: guided tours; lectures; slides; permanent & temporary exhibitions; monthly lectures on local history April-June & Sept.-Nov.
Publications: newsletter.
Hours & Admission Prices: Open by appointment only. No charge; donations requested.
Attendance: 150 (estimated)
Membership: Student $3; Senior over 65 $7.50; Senior Family & Single $10; Family $15.

Wantagh

WANTAGH HISTORICAL & PRESERVATION SOCIETY, 1700 Wantaugh Ave., Wantagh, NY 11793. Mailing Address: P.O. Box 132, Wantagh, NY 11793-0132. Tel.: 516-826-8767.
Web Site: wantagh.li/museum/index.htm
Founded: 1965.
Key Personnel: Pres., Jeffrey Saporito; 1st Vice Pres., Joshua Soren; 2nd Vice Pres., Ellen Cook.
Personnel Profile: Full-Time Volunteers 16.
Governing Authority: Nassau County Department of Parks & Recreation. Tax-exempt.
History Museum.
Collections: former railroad station built in 1885; restored turn of the century ticket agent's booth; Wantagh's first Post Office c.1908; Long Island railroad parlor car c.1912; telegraph apparatus; photographs.
Activities: craft fairs; period auto displays.
Publications: The Information Window.
Hours & Admission Prices: Sun. 2-4. No charge; donations accepted.
Attendance: 1,000 (estimated)
Membership: Individual $6; Family $12; Friend $25; Patron $50; Fellow $100.

Wappinger Falls

SPORTS MUSEUM OF DUTCHESS COUNTY, Wheeler Hill Rd., Wappinger Falls, NY 12590. Mailing Address: P.O. Box 7, Poughkeepsie, NY 12602-0007. Tel.: 845-297-9308.
Sports Museum.
Collections: sports equipment & memorabilia; photographs; hall of fame.
Activities: special events; induction ceremony.
Hours & Admission Prices: Summer: Sat. 11-4, Sun. 1-4.

Warsaw

WARSAW HISTORICAL MUSEUM, 15 Perry Ave., Warsaw, NY 14569-1205. Tel.: 585-786-5240.
E-mail: gateshouse@basicisp.com
Web Site: warsawhistory.org
Founded: 1938.
Congressional District: 31
Personnel Profile: Part-Time Volunteers 12.
Governing Authority: society. Parent Institution: Warsaw Historical Society. Tax-exempt: 501(c)(3).
Historic Building Museum: c.1824 building.
Collections: period furniture; local history; military items; clothing, farm & carpentry tools; dishes; manuscripts.
Research Fields: genealogy & local history.
Facilities: 500-vol. library of various old school historical books, pamphlets, old newspapers available for research upon application.
Activities: lectures & discussions; guided tours; walking tours of historic district; permanent & temporary exhibitions.
Publications: periodic newsletter.
Hours & Admission Prices: Mon.-Fri. 10-2; other times by appointment. No charge; donations accepted.
Attendance: 50 (estimated)
Membership: Individual $2; Life $25.

Warwick

THE HISTORICAL SOCIETY OF THE TOWN OF WARWICK, Main St. & Forester Ave., Warwick, NY 10990. Mailing Address: P.O. Box 353, Warwick, NY 10990-0353. Tel.: 845-986-3236.
E-mail: info@warwickhistoricalsociety.org
Web Site: www.warwickhistoricalsociety.org
Founded: 1906.
Congressional District: 26
Key Personnel: Pres., Sheila Warner.
Personnel Profile: Part-Time Paid 2; Part-Time Volunteers 60.
Governing Authority: society. Tax-exempt: 501(c)(3).
General Museum.
Collections: furniture from Queen Anne through Duncan Phyfe periods; examples of work done by local cabinet makers of 1810-1830; hunting & trapping equipment used by sportsman-author, William Henry Herbert (pen name Frank Forester); old carriages; sleighs; ploughs; ice-cutting equipment; old farm tools; 1890 Lehigh & Hudson River Railways four-wheeled caboose; herb garden; archaeology; costumes; history. Historic Buildings: 1810 house; 1764 old shingle house; 1810 old school Baptist meeting house; 1810 Ketchum house; 1825 barn; Baird tavern 1766, featuring ballroom.
Facilities: over 200-vol. library of history books & biographies.
Activities: guided tours; permanent exhibitions; restoration committee involved in restoring old houses for interested citizens; fundraising.
Publications: books, People of the Valleys, A History of Warwick 1700-1976; Days Gone By-A History in Pictures, Town of Warwick, NY 1827-1945; monthly newsletter.
Hours & Admission Prices: July-Aug. Tues. & Sat. 2-4:30. No charge; donations accepted.
Attendance: 1,000 (estimated)
Membership: Student $10; Senior $20-$39; Individual $25-$49; Senior Dual $40-$99; Household $50-$99; Business $100 & up; Friend $100-$249; Donor $250-$499; Patron $500-$999; Benefactor $1,000 & up; Lifetime $5,000 & up.

PACEM IN TERRIS, 96 Covered Bridge Rd., Warwick, NY 10990-2854. Tel.: 845-986-4329. Fax: 845-986-4329.
Founded: 1972.
Congressional District: 19
Key Personnel: Pres. & Dir., Lukas Franck; Mentor-in-Chief, Claske Berndes; Asst., Frances Jennick.
Personnel Profile: Part-Time Paid 2; Part-Time Volunteers 4.
Governing Authority: nonprofit corporation under the Education Laws of the State of New York. Tax-exempt.
Historic House: c.1780 water mill ruin & c.1840 country inn, McCanns Hotel & Saloon.
Collections: drawings; paintings; sculptures.
Facilities: sculpture garden.
Activities: classical chamber music concerts; spiritual drama & poetry readings; temporary exhibitions.
Publications: visitors guide; newsletter, The Shoestring.
Hours & Admission Prices: May-Oct. Sat.-Sun. & holidays 11-6. No charge; donations accepted.
Attendance: 3,000 (estimated)

Water Mill

WATER MILL MUSEUM, (M), 41 Old Mill Rd., Water Mill, NY 11976. Mailing Address: P.O. Box 63, Water Mill, NY 11976-0063. Tel.: 631-726-4625.
Web Site: www.watermillmuseum.org
Founded: 1942.
Congressional District: 1
Key Personnel: Pres., Faye Andreasen; Museum Shop Mgr., Joan Wilson.
Personnel Profile: Part-Time Paid 1; Part-Time Volunteers 30.
Governing Authority: nonprofit organization. Parent Institution: NYS Board of Regents. Tax-exempt.
Historic Building Museum: oldest commercial structure on the east end of Long Island. A water-powered working grist mill.
Collections: exhibits & tools relating to milling and 19th-century community life; tools of the ice harvester, blacksmith, farmer, cooper, wheelwright, baymen & carpenter; extensive photographic record of early 20th-century Water Mill.
Research Fields: local history; milling; tools.
Facilities: herb garden. Museum-related items for sale.
Activities: guided tours; lectures; arts festivals; children's activities. Museum Sponsors: art exhibition; school tours; quilt shows.
Publications: booklets, Harvest of Water Mill History; Mill Primer; 17th & 18th-Century Recipes Recommended by Master Millers; The Millers Meal-Corn Wheat & Rye Recipes; Quilts at the Water Mill Museum; Oral History Of Water Mill; Celebrating Community, History of a Long Island Hamlet, 1644-1994.
Hours & Admission Prices: May 30-Oct. 1 Mon. & Thurs.-Sat. 11-5, Sun. 1-5. Adults $3, seniors $2.50; children & members no charge.
Attendance: 3,000 (estimated)
Membership: Individual $20; Family $25; Supporting $50; Sponsor $100.

Waterford

NEW YORK STATE BUREAU OF HISTORIC SITES, Peebles Island, Waterford, NY 12188. Mailing Address: P.O. Box 219, Waterford, NY 12188-0219. Tel.: 518-237-8643, ext. 3202. Fax: 518-235-4248.
Web Site: www.nysparks.state.ny.us
Founded: 1972.
Key Personnel: Acting Dir., John Lovell; Scientist Archaeology, Paul Huey; Exhibit Specialist, David Meyersburg; Interpretive Programs Coord., Audrey Nieson; Restoration Coord., Chris Flagg; Assoc. Cur., Susan Walker; Collections Mgr., Anne R. Cassidy; Painting Conservator, Joyce Zucker; Decorative Arts Conservator, Heidi Miksch; Textiles Conservator, Deborah Trupin; Furniture Conservator, David L. Bayne; Gilded Objects Conservator, Eric Price; Flag Conservator, Sarah Stevens; Paper Conservator, Michele Phillips; Chief Protective Svcs., Alton Malcolm.
Personnel Profile: Full-Time Paid 45; Part-Time Paid 5; Part-Time Volunteers 10; Interns 2.
Governing Authority: state. New York State Office of Parks, Recreation & Historic Preservation. Tax-exempt.
State Agency.
Collections: The Bureau of Historic Sites, together with park regions, administers the following state historic sites: Bennington Battlefield, Hoosick Falls; Clermont, Germantown; Crailo, Rensselaer; Crown Point, Crown Point; Fort Ontario, Oswego; Ganondagan, Victor; Guy Park, Amsterdam; Herkimer Home, Little Falls; Hyde Hall, East Springfield; John Brown Farm, Lake Placid; John Jay Homestead, Katonah; John Burroughs Memorial, Roxbury; Johnson Hall, Johnstown; Knox's Headquarters, Vails Gate; Lorenzo, Cazenovia; Staatsburgh, Staatsburg; New Windsor Cantonment, Vails Gate; Olana, Hudson; Oriskany Battlefield, Oriskany; Philipse Manor Hall, Yonkers; Rexford Aqueduct, Rexford; Sackets Harbor Battlefield, Sackets Harbor; Schoharie Crossing, Fort Hunter; Schuyler Mansion, Albany; Senate House, Kingston; Stony Point Battlefield, Stony Point; Steuben Memorial, Remsen; Walt Whitman Birthplace, Huntington Station; Washington's Headquarters, Newburgh; Planting Fields Arboretum, Oyster Bay. Clinton House, Poughkeepsie, is a state historic site under lease agreement with the Dutchess County Historical Society; Old Fort Niagara, Youngstown, is a state historic site under lease agreement with the Old Fort Niagara Association; Grant Cottage, Wilton, is a state historic site under lease agreement with the Friends of Grant College; Old Erie Canal, Kirkville; Old Croton Aqueduct, Dobbs Ferry; Caumsett, Huntington; Sonnenberg Gardens & Mansion, Canandaigua.
Research Fields: state history; archaeology; historic structures; collections management; military history & technology; decorative arts; conservation of collections.
Facilities: Collections Care Center: laboratories for conservation of paintings, paper items, decorative arts objects, furniture, archaeological material & textiles.
Activities: Bureau of Historic Sites provides technical services to state historic sites & state parks; research; interpretation; restoration of buildings; archaeology; exhibit design & fabrication; collections management. Bureau Sponsors: Annual Open House; Historic Preservation Week in September.
Publications: technical reports; papers related to activities; site-related promotional & interpretive literature.
Hours & Admission Prices: Office: Mon.-Fri. 8-5. Refer to individual site listings for hours & admission fees. ♿
Attendance: 1,708,000

WATERFORD HISTORICAL MUSEUM AND CULTURAL CENTER, 2 Museum Lane, Waterford, NY 12188-2639. Tel.: 518-238-0809. Fax: 518-238-0809.
E-mail: info@waterfordmuseum.com
Web Site: www.waterfordmuseum.com
Founded: 1964.
Key Personnel: Dir., Brad L. Utter; Pres. (V), Nancy Spretty.
Personnel Profile: Full-Time Paid 1; Part-Time Paid 1; Part-Time Volunteers 60; Interns 2.
Governing Authority: museum. Parent Institution: NY State Regents, Bd. of Directors. Tax-exempt: 501(c)(3).
Local History Museum & Cultural Center: Housed in 1830 Hugh White homestead.
Collections: dresses; kitchenware; kitchen tools & implements; quilts; china; tinware; Champlain & Erie Canal photos & artifacts; medical collections; tools; objects related to history of Waterford & surrounding area.
Major Exhibits: Making Waterford Our Home: French Canadians, 5/10-4/11.
Facilities: library of books, microfilm & newspapers pertaining to local history & barge canal; meeting room; kitchen facilities available.
Activities: guided tours; lectures; educational programs for children; permanent & temporary exhibitions; day trips; outreach programs. Museum Sponsors: Community Heritage Day; Old Fashioned Firemen's Master.
Publications: bimonthly newsletter, The Homestead; White Homestead on Wheels; Waterford to Whitehall; The Waterford Flight; Standard of the Age: A Brief History of the Button Fire Engine Works Waterford, NY.
Hours & Admission Prices: See website for current hours. No charge; donations accepted. Closed major holidays. ♿
Attendance: 1,000 (estimated)
Membership: Student $10; Individual $15; Family $25; Contributor $50; Sustainer $75; Patron $100.

Waterloo

NATIONAL MEMORIAL DAY MUSEUM, 35 E. Main St., Waterloo, NY 13165-1430. Mailing Address: 31 E. William, Waterloo, NY 13165-1410. Tel.: 315-539-0533. Fax: 315-539-7798.
E-mail: terwilliger@fltg.net
Web Site: waterloony.com
Founded: 1966.
Congressional District: 29
Key Personnel: C.E.O., William H. Sigrist; Dir., James T. Hughes.
Personnel Profile: Full-Time Paid 2; Part-Time Paid 1; Part-Time Volunteers 20.
Governing Authority: society. Parent Institution: Waterloo Library & Historical Society. Tax-exempt.
Memorial Day Museum: housed in c.1836 home.
Collections: mementos of first Memorial Day & its founders; Civil War artifacts; U.S. war archives.
Activities: guided tours; historical programs; school programs; archival research.
Publications: The History and Origin of Memorial Day in Waterloo, New York.

Hours & Admission Prices: April 15-May 22 & Sept. 8-Dec. 15 Tues.-Sat. 10-5, May 23-Sept. 4 Tues.-Sun. 10-5. Tours by request. Requested Donations: family $5, adults $3, senior citizens $2, students $1; members & children under 12 no charge. Closed Labor Day.
Attendance: 1,300 (accurate)
Membership: Senior 60 & over $10; Individual $20; Family $35; Friend $100; Contributor $200; Sponsor $300; Patron $500; Benefactor $1,000.

PETER WHITMER SR. HOME AND VISITORS CENTER, 1451 Aunkst Rd., Waterloo, NY 13165-9736. Mailing Address: Hill Cumorah Visitors Center, 603 State, Rte. 21, Palmyra, NY 14522-9301. Tel.: 315-539-2552. Fax: 315-597-0165.
E-mail: info@hillcumorah.org
Web Site: www.hillcumorah.org
Founded: 1980.
Congressional District: 29
Key Personnel: Dir., A. Bryan Weston.
Personnel Profile: Full-Time Volunteers 28.
Governing Authority: church. Parent Institution: Church of Jesus Christ of Latter-Day Saints, 50 E. North Temple, Salt Lake City, UT 84150. Tax-exempt.
Historic House: located on site of organization of The Church of Jesus Christ of Latter-Day Saints (Mormon), 1830.
Collections: household furnishings typical of Western New York, 1820-1830; artwork depicting events leading to church organization.
Research Fields: Latter-Day Saints Church history.
Facilities: visitor center; displays.
Activities: guided tours.
Publications: books, Book of Mormon; Doctrine & Covenants; pamphlets.
Hours & Admission Prices: Summer: Mon.-Sat. 9-6, Sun. 12:30-6; Winter: Mon.-Sat. 9-5, Sun. 12:30-5. No charge. Closed New Year's Day; Thanksgiving; Christmas. ♿
Attendance: 70,000 (estimated)

TERWILLIGER MUSEUM, 31 E. Williams St., Waterloo, NY 13165-1410. Tel.: 315-539-0533. Fax: 315-539-7798.
E-mail: terwilliger@fltg.net
Web Site: waterloony.com
Founded: 1960.
Congressional District: 33
Key Personnel: C.E.O., William H. Sigrist; Dir., James T. Hughes.
Personnel Profile: Full-Time Paid 2; Part-Time Paid 1; Part-Time Volunteers 20.
Governing Authority: society. Parent Institution: Waterloo Library & Historical Society. Tax-exempt: 501(c)(3).
Local History Museum.
Collections: local history; industry; genealogy; period autos; agriculture; period displays; manuscripts; village store; 1914 mural of downtown Waterloo; long house; Indian artifacts; 5 period rooms, from early log house room to Roaring Twenties.
Research Fields: local history.
Facilities: 16,000-vol. library of general material & local history available to public & inter-library loan; reading room; 100-seat auditorium.
Activities: guided tours; lectures; films; formally organized education programs for children; permanent & temporary exhibitions.
Publications: A Story of the Seneca River; 200 Year History of Volunteer Firefighters in Waterloo, NY; Early History of Waterloo.
Hours & Admission Prices: Tues.-Fri. 1-4. Tours by appointment. Donation requested: family $5, adults $3, seniors $2, students $1; members & children under 12 no charge.
Attendance: 1,318 (accurate)
Membership: Senior 60 & over $10; Individual $20; Family $35; Friend $100; Contributor $200; Sponsor $300; Patron $500; Benefactor $1,000.

Watertown

JEFFERSON COUNTY HISTORICAL SOCIETY, 228 Washington St., Watertown, NY 13601-3379. Tel.: 4. Fax: 315-782-2913.
E-mail: director@jeffersoncountyhistory.org
Web Site: jeffersoncountyhistory.org
Founded: 1886.
Congressional District: 30
Key Personnel: Dir., William G. Wood; Pres. (V), Roxanne M. Burns; Cur. Education, Melissa Widrick; Cur. Collections, Lenka Walldroff; Business Mgr., Elaine Bock.
Personnel Profile: Full-Time Paid 3; Full-Time Volunteers 1; Part-Time Paid 2; Part-Time Volunteers 60.
Governing Authority: nonprofit organization. Tax-exempt: 501(c)(3).
History Museum: housed in 1878 Paddock Mansion.
Collections: local history & culture; period furnishings; 19th-century Americana; handmade agricultural & woodworking tools; early machinery; clothing; portraits; archives & photographs; northern New York Indian artifacts; Tyler coverlets 1834-1858; water turbines; restored 1910 Babcock automobile; Victorian garden; log cabin; one-room schoolhouse; house.
Research Fields: local history and prehistory.
Facilities: 2,200-vol. library of local & northern New York history available for research on premises; classroom; gallery; Victorian garden. Period furnishings, regional literature & museum-related items for sale.
Activities: guided tours; lectures; formally organized education programs; docent program; permanent, temporary & traveling exhibits.
Publications: annual, Jefferson County Historical Society Bulletin; newsletter, Museum Musings.
Hours & Admission Prices: May-Dec. Tues.-Fri. 10-5, Sat. 10-4, Jan.-April Tues.-Fri. 10-5. No charge; donations accepted. Closed national holidays. ♿
Attendance: 11,000 (estimated)
Membership: Senior Citizen $25; Individual $30; Family $45; Sustaining $60; Institution $75; Patron $100; Life $500. Business: Individual $50; Contributing $100; Sustaining $250; Patron $500; Sponsor $1,000; Partner $5,000.

SCI-TECH CENTER OF NORTHERN NEW YORK, 154 Stone St., Watertown, NY 13601-3250. Tel.: 315-788-1340. Fax: 315-788-2738 (call first).
E-mail: scitech@scitechcenter.org
Web Site: www.scitechcenter.org
Founded: 1982.
Congressional District: 26
Key Personnel: C.E.O., Stephen Karon; Pres. (V), Todd Vincent.
Personnel Profile: Full-Time Paid 1; Part-Time Volunteers 25; Interns 1.
Governing Authority: nonprofit organization. Tax-exempt: 501(c)(3).
Science & Technology Museum.
Collections: interactive science & technology exhibits from the fields of physics, biology & computer technology, including skeletons, garden of smells, electrical dollhouse & shadow room.
Facilities: 3,500 sq. ft. exhibit space; classrooms. Gift items for sale.
Activities: guided tours; hands-on workshops for children & adults; participatory exhibits; birthday parties; chess club; lego club; regional science fair; astronomy observing sessions.
Publications: quarterly newsletter, Sci-Tech Scope; monthly update of programming.
Hours & Admission Prices: Tues. 9-1, Wed.-Sat. 10-4. Adults $4, children $3, seniors $2; discounts to reciprocal partners, AAM members, ICOM members & groups with reservations; children under 3 & members no charge. Closed Thanksgiving; Christmas. ♿
Attendance: 9,000 (estimated)
Membership: Senior $15; Individual $30; Military Family $40; Family $45.

Watervliet

WATERVLIET ARSENAL'S MUSEUM OF THE BIG GUNS, (M), Watervliet Arsenal, 1 Buffington St., Watervliet, NY 12189-4003. Tel.: 518-266-5805. Fax: 518-266-5859.
E-mail: robert.pfeil@conus.army.mil
Web Site: www.wva.army.mil
Founded: 1975.
Congressional District: 23
Key Personnel: Dir. & Cur., Robert Pfeil.
Personnel Profile: Full-Time Paid 2; Part-Time Volunteers 5.
Governing Authority: federal government. Parent Institution: Watervliet Arsenal. Subsidiary Institution: Chief of Military History. Tax-exempt.
Military Museum: housed in 1859 cast iron warehouse for artillery factory.
Collections: military materials & equipment; 1600s-present cannon & related ordnance; early 1900 machine shop.
Research Fields: cannon development.
Facilities: 1,000-vol. library of military books & technical manuals; 5,000 photographs of the arsenal & cannon; 10,000 sq. ft. exhibit space.
Activities: videos; slide shows; permanent & temporary exhibitions; guided tours.
Publications: booklets, The Big Deterrent, The 16-inch Gun; Watervliet Arsenal, Civil War Years 1861-1865; Arsenal History.
Hours & Admission Prices: Sun.-Thurs. 10-3; group tours by appointment. No charge; donations accepted. Closed federal holidays. ♿
Attendance: 2,000 (accurate)

Watkins Glen

INTERNATIONAL MOTOR RACING RESEARCH CENTER AT WATKINS GLEN, 610 S. Decatur St., Watkins Glen, NY 14891-1613. Tel.: 607-535-9044. Fax: 607-535-9039.
E-mail: research@racingarchives.org
Web Site: www.racingarchives.org
Formerly: Watkins Glen Motor Racing Research Library

Founded: 1998.
Key Personnel: Pres., J.C. Argetsinger; Chm. (V), Syd Silverman; Dir. Archives & Admin., Mark Steigerwald.
Personnel Profile: Full-Time Paid 2; Part-Time Paid 3; Part-Time Volunteers 3.
Governing Authority: private; nonprofit organization.
Sports Museum & Research Library.
Collections: motorsport archives; paintings; photographs.
Research Fields: women in motorsport; West Coast racing; general motor racing history.
Facilities: 2,500-vol. library; 25-seat auditorium; 3,000 sq. ft. exhibit space.
Activities: films; lectures; broadcast programs. Annual Events: receptions; art shows.
Publications: quarterly newsletter, From the Racing Archives.
Hours & Admission Prices: Mon.-Sat. 9-5; other times by appointment. No charge; donations accepted. ♿
Attendance: 4,000 (estimated)
Membership: Green Flag $25; White Flag $100; Checkered Flag $500; Victory Flag $1,000; Grand Prix Champion $2,500.

Weedsport

HALL OF FAME & CLASSIC CAR MUSEUM, 1 Speedway Dr., Weedsport, NY 13166-9544. Mailing Address: P.O. Box 240, Weedsport, NY 13166-0240. Tel.: 315-834-6606. Fax: 315-834-9734.
Founded: 1992.
Key Personnel: Treas., Gary Spaid; Cur., Jack Speno; Museum Shop Mgr., Harry Elkema.
Personnel Profile: Full-Time Paid 1; Part-Time Paid 3.
Governing Authority: municipal.
Motorsports Museum.
Collections: race cars from 40s to present; classic cars from 30s-70's .
Facilities: 10-vol. library; 10-seat theater. Museum-related items for sale.
Activities: guided tours; broadcast programs; weekly races. Museum Sponsors: Hall of Fame Induction Ceremonies in May.
Hours & Admission Prices: Memorial Day to Columbus Day Sat.-Sun. 12-6; other times by appointment. Adults $5, senior citizens & students $4; discounts to groups of 10 or more, AAM & ICOM members. Closed Easter; Mother's Day. ♿
Attendance: 5,000 (estimated)

OLD BRUTUS HISTORICAL SOCIETY, INC., 8943 N. Seneca St., Weedsport, NY 13166. Mailing Address: P.O. Box 516, Weedsport, NY 13166-0516. Tel.: 315-834-6285.
Founded: 1967.
Congressional District: 33
Key Personnel: C.E.O. & Pres. (V), William Saroodis; Dir. (V), Dennis Randall; Historian, Jeanne Baker; Treas., Jean Saroodis; Sec., Barbara Ward.
Personnel Profile: Part-Time Volunteers 50.
Governing Authority: society; nonprofit organization. Parent Institution: Old Brutus Historical Society. Tax-exempt: 501(c)(3).
Local Historical Society & Museum.
Collections: genealogy; local history; agricultural items & implements; furnishings & memorabilia; local manufactured artifacts; maps; photographs; household items & artifacts; manuscripts; newspaper clips; 1850-1990 clothing; room & school and canal boat cabin mock up; genealogy file on local families.
Major Exhibits: You CAN Get There From Here, 11/09-1/10.
Research Fields: genealogy; local history; Erie Canal.
Facilities: 2,000-vol. library of books & atlases pertaining to history & genealogy available for research on premises by appointment; 50-seat auditorium. Museum-related items for sale.
Activities: guided tours; lectures; films; formally organized education programs for children; permanent & temporary exhibitions; public programs.
Hours & Admission Prices: Memorial Day-Labor Day Sun. & Wed. 2-4, Mon.-Tues. 9:30-12; other times by appointment. No charge; donations accepted. ♿
Attendance: 2,500 (estimated)
Membership: Individual $5; Life $50.

Wellsville

THE MATHER HOMESTEAD MUSEUM, LIBRARY AND MEMORIAL PARK, 343 N. Main St., Wellsville, NY 14895-1016. Mailing Address: P.O. Box 531, Wellsville, NY 14895-0531. Tel.: 585-593-1636.
Founded: 1981.
Congressional District: 29
Key Personnel: Dir., Mrs. Glenn Williams.
Personnel Profile: Part-Time Volunteers 28.
Governing Authority: private; nonprofit.
Historic House Museum.
Collections: 1930s artifacts, music, books, games, catalogues, & toys.
Research Fields: 1930s artifacts.
Facilities: library.
Activities: special events; concerts; films. Museum Sponsors: Easy Egg Hunt; Reading Declaration of Independence in July; Halloween Paint-Out in October.
Publications: newsletter, The Homestead Hoot; music, original scores; articles; Sound Adventures.
Hours & Admission Prices: by appointment. No charge. Special accommodations for the blind or poorly sighted. ♿
Attendance: 200 (estimated)

West Henrietta

NEW YORK MUSEUM OF TRANSPORTATION, 6393 E. River Rd., West Henrietta, NY 14586-9575. Mailing Address: P.O. Box 136, West Henrietta, NY 14586-0136. Tel.: 585-533-1113.
Web Site: www.nymtmuseum.org
Founded: 1975.
Congressional District: 35
Key Personnel: Pres., Theodore H. Strang, Jr.; Sec., James E. Dierks; Treas., Robert Nesbitt; Museum Shop Mgr., Douglas Anderson.
Personnel Profile: Part-Time Volunteers 35.
Governing Authority: nonprofit organization. Tax-exempt: 501(c)(3).
Transportation Museum.
Collections: 1867-1955, elements & evidence from the transportation facilities in Western New York; transportation history; street cars; interurbans; railroad equipment; trucks; maps; printed matter; gas, steam & diesel electric locomotives; operational railroad line; horse drawn & highway vehicles. Historic Building: 1904 Rochester & Eastern Rapid Railway Way Station.
Research Fields: sociological impacts of changes in the transportation patterns in Western New York from 1880-1955; area trolley line history.
Facilities: 6,000-vol. library available for research by appointment; one & three-fourths mile demonstrational railway; 15,000 sq. ft. exhibit space; 25-seat theater. Rochester & Genesee Valley Railroad Museum Country Depot. Museum-related items for sale.
Activities: guided tours; lectures; permanent, temporary & traveling exhibitions; special events; off-site slide talks; interurban trolley rides on museum railroad.
Publications: quarterly newsletter, Head End.
Hours & Admission Prices: Sun. 11-5; groups and other times by appointment. Mid-May to Oct. adults $7, seniors 65 & over $6, students 3-15 $5; members no charge; Nov. to mid-May call for admission fees. Closed New Year's Day; Easter; Christmas. ♿
Attendance: 5,600 (accurate)
Membership: Student $10; Individual $25; Family $35; Sustaining $50; Sponsor $100; Benefactor $250; Patron $500.

West Park

JOHN BURROUGHS ASSOCIATION, INC., Off John Burroughs Dr., West Park, NY 12493. Mailing Address: John Burroughs Assoc., Inc., 15 W. 77th St., New York, NY 10024-5153. Tel.: 212-769-5169. Fax: 212-313-7182.
E-mail: breslof@amnh.org
Web Site: research.amnh.org/burroughs/
Formerly: Slabsides
Founded: 1921.
Key Personnel: Pres., David Liddell; Sec., Lisa Breslof.
Personnel Profile: Part-Time Volunteers 25.
Governing Authority: nonprofit organization. Parent Institution: John Burroughs Association, c/o American Museum of Natural History, Central Park West, New York, NY. 10024. Tax-exempt: 501(c)(3).
Historic House Museum: 1895-1896 house built by naturalist John Burroughs in Nature Sanctuary.
Collections: china & housekeeping equipment used by John Burroughs.
Facilities: nature center. Museum-related items for sale.
Activities: guided walks on sanctuary trails; lectures. Museum Sponsors: open house in May & October.
Publications: brochure, Wakerobin Newsletter published three times annually; indexes to the collected works of John Burroughs.
Hours & Admission Prices: By appointment. Trails: dawn to dusk daily. No charge; donations accepted.
Attendance: 800 (estimated)
Membership: Senior & Student $15; Annual $25; Family $35; Patron $50; Life $500.

West Point

CONSTITUTION ISLAND ASSOCIATION, (M), South Dock, West Point, NY 10996-0041. Mailing Address: P.O. Box 41, West Point, NY 10996-0041. Tel.: 845-446-8676. Fax: 845-622-6022.
E-mail: info@constitutionisland.org
Web Site: www.constitutionisland.org
Founded: 1916.
Congressional District: 21
Key Personnel: Exec. Dir., Richard de Koster; Chm. (V), Elizabeth Pugh.
Personnel Profile: Part-Time Paid 3; Part-Time Volunteers 70.
Governing Authority: nonprofit corporation. Chartered by University of the State of New York. Tax-exempt.
Historic House Museum: c.1800 Victorian home of writers Susan & Anna Warner on Constitution Island, site of several Revolutionary War fortification ruins; traditional 19th century gardens.
Collections: Warner House collection including 15 rooms of Warner family furnishings; furniture; art; china; glass; kitchen & gardening utensils; memorabilia.
Research Fields: Warner family and books; Revolutionary War period & relationship of Constitution Island to the war.
Facilities: 2,000-vol. library of books, documents & correspondence of the Warner family; Anna B. Warner Memorial Garden. Booklets on local history for sale.
Activities: guided tours; lectures; slide program; special education program for children; permanent exhibitions; Little American Program.
Publications: annual report; local history booklet; books, Susan Warner; Gardening by Myself; Light in the Morning; Defense of the Hudson Highlands.
Hours & Admission Prices: late April to June 15 schools only, by reservation; June 21 to early Oct. Wed.-Thurs. 1-2. Adults $10, senior citizens & children under 16 $9; discounts to AAM & ICOM members; children 6 & under no charge.
Attendance: 6,200 (accurate)
Membership: Individual $25; Family $40; Patron $500; Benefactor $1,000.

* **WEST POINT MUSEUM, (M),** United States Military Academy, Bldg. 2110, West Point, NY 10996. Tel.: 845-938-2203 & 3590. Fax: 845-938-7478.
E-mail: museum@usma.edu
Web Site: www.usma.edu (selected site MUSEUM)
Founded: 1854.
Congressional District: 19
Key Personnel: Dir., David M. Reel; Cur. Art, Gary Hood; Cur. Arms, Leslie D. Jensen; Cur. Uniforms & Military History, Michael J. McAfee; Cur. Design, Richard H. Clark; Museum Specialist Conservator, Paul R. Ackermann; Admin., Jean Cumming; Registrar, Marlana Cook; Museum Shop Mgr., Brandi Stokes; Museum Technician, Arnold Cecchini; Collection Analyst, Brian Rayca; Security Chief, Gloria Johnson.
Personnel Profile: Full-Time Paid 14; Full-Time Volunteers 2; Part-Time Paid 2; Part-Time Volunteers 2; Interns 1.
Governing Authority: federal. Parent Institution: Dept. of Defense, Dept. of Army & U.S. Military Academy. Tax-exempt: 401(c)(3).
Military History Museum.
Collections: history of military events & personalities; collection of weapons, military art; artifacts, paintings, sculpture, prints, photographs, American & European uniforms, documents; Fort Putman, historic restoration of Revolutionary War fort overlooking U.S. Military Academy.
Research Fields: history of American & European profession of arms & uniforms; European & American paintings; West Point historical artifacts, portraits & archival material.
Facilities: 1,600-vol. library of arms, armor & military reference books available for use on premises by appointment. West Point and Army related gift items for sale.
Activities: formally organized education programs for undergraduate & graduate college students; inter-museum loan, permanent & temporary exhibitions; lectures.
Publications: The West Point Museum: A Guide to the Museum.
Hours & Admission Prices: Daily 10:30-4:15. No charge; donations accepted. Closed New Year's Day; Thanksgiving; Christmas. No charge; donations accepted. ♿
Attendance: 215,000 (accurate)

West Sayville

LONG ISLAND MARITIME MUSEUM, (M), 86 West Ave., West Sayville, NY 11796-1908. Mailing Address: P.O. Box 184, West Sayville, NY 11796-0184. Tel.: 631-854-4974. Fax: 631-854-4979.
E-mail: limaritime@verizon.net
Web Site: www.limaritime.org
Founded: 1966.
Congressional District: 2
Key Personnel: Chm., Michael Sacca; Dir., Natasha S. Alexenko; Deputy Dir., Jo Anne Brintrup; Registrar, Arlene Balcewicz; Librarian, Barbara Forde; Coord. Programming, Michelle Hausman.
Personnel Profile: Full-Time Paid 2; Part-Time Paid 8; Part-Time Volunteers 100; Interns 1.
Governing Authority: New York State Board of Regents; chartered by University of the State of New York Education Dept. Tax-exempt: 501(c)(3).
Maritime History Museum.
Collections: maritime history; small craft collection; United States Life Saving service equipment; shipwreck artifacts. Historic Buildings: Penney Boatshop; Rudolph Oyster House; 1890 Bayman's Cottage. Historic Ships: Priscilla, 1888 oyster vessel; Modesty, 1923 oyster sloop; Charlotte c.1880 sandbagger converted to a tugboat 1915.
Research Fields: pertaining to collections; Long Island South Shore Boat Builders; oyster & clamming; yachting; waterfowl hunting; duck decoys.
Facilities: library of books, documents, photographs, press clippings & periodicals relating to maritime history available for research by appointment.
Activities: lectures; oral history sessions. Museum Sponsors: maritime, folkcraft demonstrations. Museum Sponsors: Nautical Festival; Seafood Festival; Art Show in June.
Hours & Admission Prices: Mon.-Sat. 10-4, Sun. 12-4. Adults $4, senior citizens & children under 12 $2; discounts for CAMM, AAM & ICOM members; members no charge. ♿
Attendance: 85,000 (estimated)
Membership: Over 65 $25; Individual $40; Family $75; Privileged $150; Organizational $200; Small Business $250; Corporate $500.

Westfield

CHAUTAUQUA COUNTY HISTORICAL SOCIETY, MCCLURG MUSEUM, Rts. 20 & 394 (Main & Portage Sts.), Westfield, NY 14787. Mailing Address: P.O. Box 7, Westfield, NY 14787-0007. Tel.: 716-326-2977.
E-mail: mcclurg@fairpoint.net
Web Site: www.westfieldantiqueshow.com
Founded: 1883.
Congressional District: 150
Key Personnel: Pres. (V) & Dir., James O'Brien; Vice Pres., Dr. David Brown; Office Mgr., Shari Golnitz.
Personnel Profile: Part-Time Paid 1; Part-Time Volunteers 18.
Governing Authority: state regents; society board of trustees. Tax-exempt.
County History Museum: housed in 1818 Mansion, built by James McClurg, an early settler.
Collections: agriculture; history; military; Native American artifacts; archives; costumes; furniture; genealogy of Chautauqua County.
Major Exhibits: Lincoln Legacy, 11/09-12/10.
Research Fields: genealogy; Tourgee papers; Foote papers.
Facilities: 2,000-vol. library of history books; 16-room restored period house.
Activities: guided tours; permanent exhibits; quarterly meetings.
Publications: quarterly newsletter; books, Updated County History 1938-1978; Patriot Soldiers of 1775-1783, Update; James McClurg, Pioneer; Chautauqua County Regiments and Soldiers in the Civil War 1861-1865.
Hours & Admission Prices: Tues.-Sat. 10-4; tours by appointment. Adults $5, seniors & students $1; children & members no charge. Closed holidays.
Attendance: 2,500 (estimated)
Membership: Individual $20; Family $30; Benefactor $100; Business $250.

Wilson

WILSON HISTORICAL MUSEUM, 645 Lake St., Wilson, NY 14172. Mailing Address: P.O. Box 830, Wilson, NY 14172-0830. Tel.: 716-751-9886. Fax: 716-751-6141.
E-mail: agaffiliat@aol.com
Web Site: www.wilsonnewyork.com/hist_society.html
Founded: 1972.
Congressional District: 36
Key Personnel: Pres. & C.E.O. (V), Wallace Goodman; Cur., Dorothy Maxfield.
Personnel Profile: Part-Time Volunteers 132.
Governing Authority: nonprofit society. Affiliated with the Wilson Historical Society. Tax-exempt: 501(c)(3).
General & Historical Society Museum: housed in 1912 Railroad Depot.
Collections: woodworking tools; dresses; quilts; railroad artifacts; books; wood carvings; farm tools; farm implements; genealogical records; period cars; 1903 caboose.
Research Fields: local history; genealogy.
Facilities: 100-vol. library of books available for research on premises only. Ceramics, booklets & postcards for sale.

Activities: guided tours; loan, permanent & temporary exhibitions. Annual Event: Memorial Day Fair.
Publications: monthly newsletter, W.H.S. Newsletter; booklets, Story of Billy Sherman; Tall Tales and Legends; Churches of Wilson; Land of Cobblestones; The Valiant Men of Battery M; Postal Service in the Town of Wilson; Wilson Historical Society Cookbook; Wilson's Vanishing Heritage; The Albright Opera House; Story of Sunset Island; The Wilson Free Library; Wilson Sketchbook.
Hours & Admission Prices: May-Nov. Sun. 2-4. No charge; donations accepted.
Attendance: 1,200 (estimated)
Membership: Juniors under 18 $1; Single $5; Couple $10; Life $150; Honorary (85 yrs. & over) no charge.

Wilton

ULYSSES S. GRANT COTTAGE STATE HISTORIC SITE, Mount McGregor, Wilton, NY 12831. Mailing Address: P.O. Box 2294, Wilton, NY 12831-5294. Tel.: 518-587-8277.
E-mail: info@grantcottage.org
Web Site: www.grantcottage.org
Founded: 1890.
Congressional District: 22
Key Personnel: Admin., Beverly Clark; Pres. (V), R. Frank Glew.
Personnel Profile: Part-Time Paid 3; Part-Time Volunteers 25.
Governing Authority: Tax-exempt.
Historic House: 1878 cottage where Gen. Ulysses S. Grant spent the last six weeks of his life in June/July 1885; completed his personal memoirs.
Collections: period furnishings; Grant memorabilia; funeral floral pieces.
Facilities: visitor center. Museum-related items for sale.
Activities: reenactments; tours; student programs; music; view of the Hudson Valley; lectures; demonstrations.
Publications: The Grant Cottage Chronicles
Hours & Admission Prices: Memorial Day-Labor Day Wed.-Sun. 10-4; Sept. to Columbus Day Sat.-Sun. 10-4. Adults $4, senior citizens & students $3, youth 6-12 $2; children 5 & under and members no charge. ♿
Attendance: 2,500 (estimated)
Membership: $15; $25; $40; $50; $100; $250 & up.

Windsor

OLD STONE HOUSE MUSEUM, 22 Chestnut St., Windsor, NY 13865-4105. Tel.: 607-655-1491.
Founded: 1970.
Congressional District: 124
Key Personnel: Dir., Louella F. English.
Personnel Profile: Part-Time Volunteers 3.
Governing Authority: individual operation.
History Museum: housed in Federal period house of Major Jed Hotchkiss, C.S.A.
Collections: Civil War artifacts, weapons, accoutrements pertaining to men of area; historical objects of local interest from local homes, businesses & industries; local Indian relics; old pictures; books & maps; tools; implements; lamps; furniture; bottles; whips of local manufactures.
Research Fields: local military history; local history.
Facilities: 300-vol. library of books, primarily Civil War & local history, available for inter-library loan by arrangement with owner on premises only.
Activities: guided tours; lectures; films; permanent exhibitions.
Hours & Admission Prices: Sat.-Sun. 10-5; other times by appointment. No charge; donations accepted.
Attendance: 700 (estimated)

Woodstock

CENTER FOR PHOTOGRAPHY AT WOODSTOCK, 59 Tinker St., Woodstock, NY 12498-1236. Tel.: 845-679-7747 & 9957. Fax: 845-679-6337.
E-mail: info@cpw.org
Web Site: www.cpw.org
Founded: 1977.
Key Personnel: Exec. Dir., Ariel Shanberg; Program Assoc., Akemi Hiatt; Operations Mgr., Larry Lewis; Coord. Education, Liz Unteman.
Personnel Profile: Full-Time Paid 4; Part-Time Paid 1; Part-Time Volunteers 10; Interns 10.
Governing Authority: Tax-exempt: 501(c)(3).
Photography Museum.
Collections: fine art photography.
Facilities: library.
Activities: workshops; lectures; internships available; 1 or 2-day workshops available; residencies for artists.
Publications: Photography Quarterly.
Hours & Admission Prices: Wed.-Sun. 12-5. Lecture series: adults $7; discount to members, seniors & students. Gallery: no charge; donations accepted. ♿
Attendance: 50,000 (estimated)
Membership: Subscribing $25; Student $30; Individual $45; Family $50; Supporting $60; Friend $100; Patron $250-$1,250.

WOODSTOCK ARTISTS ASSOCIATION & MUSEUM, (M), 28 Tinker St., Woodstock, NY 12498-1233. Tel.: 845-679-2940. Fax: 845-679-2198.
E-mail: info@woodstockart.org
Web Site: www.woodstockart.org
Founded: 1919.
Key Personnel: Exec. Dir., Josephine Bloodgood; Chm., Lee Sider; Coord. Gallery & Museum Shop, Patricia Seminara.
Personnel Profile: Full-Time Paid 4; Part-Time Paid 3; Part-Time Volunteers 30; Interns 1.
Art Association & Museum.
Collections: work of American artists associated with the Woodstock Art Colony; archives of original documents & photographs.
Facilities: archives.
Activities: exhibitions; adult and school programs.
Publications: exhibition catalogs, Woodstock's Art Heritage: The Permanent Collection of the WAA; The Maverich Art Colony.
Hours & Admission Prices: Fri.-Sun. 12-5; other times by appointment. Suggested donation $5; discounts to AAM & ICOM members; members no charge. Closed New Year's Day; Thanksgiving; Christmas. ♿
Attendance: 25,000 (accurate)
Membership: Youth $40; Individual & Supporting Friend $100; Artist $135; Family Friends$150.

Wyoming

MIDDLEBURY HISTORICAL SOCIETY, 22 S. Academy St., Wyoming, NY 14591-9801. Mailing Address: P.O. Box 198, Wyoming, NY 14591-0198.
Founded: 1941.
Congressional District: 35
Key Personnel: Pres., Mr. Douglas Norton; 1st Vice Pres., Keith Kruppner; 2nd Vice Pres., Doris Bannister; Sec., Sallie Herrendeen; Cur., Karen Aman.
Personnel Profile: Part-Time Volunteers 12.
Governing Authority: historical society; nonprofit. Parent Institution: Middlebury Historical Society. Tax-exempt.
Historical Society Museum: housed in 1817 Middlebury Academy.
Collections: military equipment; musical instruments; farm tools; photographs; local history records; women's costumes & accessories; textiles.
Research Fields: local town & village history.
Facilities: 450-vol. library of material on the 18th- & 19th-centuries available for use upon application.
Activities: guided tours; permanent & temporary exhibitions; demonstrations; meetings.
Publications: A History of Middlebury; From Middlebury to Middlebury; Village of Wyoming Historic Tours-1985; Town of Middlebury's; Wyoming - The Town Where I Grew Up.
Hours & Admission Prices: June-Sept. Sun. 2-5. No charge; donations accepted. ♿
Attendance: 691 (accurate)
Membership: Senior $2.50; Single $5; Family $25.

Yonkers

* **HUDSON RIVER MUSEUM, (M),** 511 Warburton Ave., Yonkers, NY 10701-1899. Tel.: 914-963-4550. Fax: 914-963-8558.
E-mail: info@hrm.org
Web Site: www.hrm.org
Founded: 1919.
Congressional District: 17
Key Personnel: Dir., Michael Botwinick; Trustee Chm., Jan Adelson; Asst. Dir. Finance & Administration, Jared Hammond; Cur. Collections, Laura Vookles; Cur. Exhibitions, Bartholomew Bland; Asst. Dir. Exhibitions & Programs, Jean Paul Maitinsky; Asst. Dir. Devel., Kimberly Woodward; Dir. Public Rels., Linda Locke.
Personnel Profile: Full-Time Paid 28; Part-Time Paid 41; Part-Time Volunteers 100.
Governing Authority: nonprofit organization. Tax-exempt: 501(c)(3).
General Museum.
Collections: 19th-, 20th- & 21st-century American painting, sculpture, photography, furniture, decorative arts, historical documents, costumes, local & regional memorabilia; planetarium. Historic House: 1877 Victorian Glenview.
Major Exhibits: Bakelite in Yonkers: Pioneering the Age of Plastics, 1/10-5/30/10; Jacob Lawrence Prints (T), 2/6/10-5/1/10; Collecting for a New

Millennium, 2/6/10-5/1/10; Susan Wides: Kaaterskill Mannahatta, 6/26/10-9/6/10; Richard Deon: Paradon & Conformity for 20 Years - Paintings & Prints, 6/26/10-9/6/10.
Research Fields: 19th, 20th & 21st-century American fine & decorative arts; architecture; astronomy; technology; Hudson River Valley art, history & natural science.
Facilities: 200-seat auditorium; 127-seat planetarium; education center.
Activities: tours; planetarium shows; cultural programs for seniors; family weekend craft programs; docent programs; research by appointment; permanent, temporary & traveling exhibitions; public programs.
Publications: monthly calendar of events; newsletter; exhibition catalogs; annual camp and teacher guides.
Hours & Admission Prices: Museum: Wed.-Thurs. & Sat.-Sun. 12-5, Fri. 12-8. Planetarium Fri. 7, Sat.-Sun. 12:30, 1:30, 2:30, 3:30; school groups & tours by appointment. Adults $5, senior citizens & children 5-16 $3; discounts for Metro-North Rail Road commuters, AAM & Channel 13 members; members no charge. Closed New Year's Day; Thanksgiving; Christmas. ♿
Attendance: 51,500 (estimated)
Membership: Senior Citizen $25; Dual Senior $35; Individual $40; Dual $50; Family $60; Supporter $100; Director's Circle $250.

PHILIPSE MANOR HALL STATE HISTORIC SITE, 29 Warburton Ave., (& Dock St.), Yonkers, NY 10701-2721. Tel.: 914-965-4027. Fax: 914-965-6485.
Web Site: www.nysparks.state.ny.us/historic-sites/37/details.aspx
Founded: 1911.
Congressional District: 23
Key Personnel: Dir., Kimberly Flook; Commissioner, Carol Ash; Pres. (V), Joan Jennings.
Personnel Profile: Full-Time Paid 5; Part-Time Paid 3; Part-Time Volunteers 50.
Governing Authority: state. Parent Institution: New York State Office of Parks, Recreation & Historic Preservation. Tax-exempt.
Art & History Museum: housed in early 18th-century Georgian style manor house.
Collections: paintings; photographs; structures; architecture.
Research Fields: Philipse family; landholding in colonial New York; Loyalists in the American Revolution; American art.
Facilities: changing exhibits; 80-seat auditorium.
Activities: guided tours; concerts; lectures; gallery talks; demonstrations; craft workshops; children's theatre; permanent & temporary exhibitions; special programs; school programs; educational program.
Publications: booklet: An American Loyalist; The Ordeal of Frederick Philipse III; semiannual newsletter.
Hours & Admission Prices: April-Oct. Tues.-Sun. 12-4; Nov.-March Tues.-Sun. 12-3; other times by appointment. Adults $5, seniors $3; members & children under 12 no charge. Closed holidays. ♿
Attendance: 25,000 (estimated)
Membership: Associate $15; Individual $25; Family $50; Contributing $100; Sponsor $250; Patron $500; Benefactor $1,000.

Yorktown Heights

TOWN OF YORKTOWN MUSEUM, YCCC Building - Top Fl., 1974 Commerce St., Yorktown Heights, NY 10598-4433. Tel.: 914-962-2970. Fax: 914-962-4379.
E-mail: museum@yorktownny.org
Web Site: www.yorktownmuseum.org
Founded: 1966.
Congressional District: 19
Key Personnel: C.E.O., Alice Roker; Chm. (V), Vishnu V. Patel; Tour Coord., Nancy Augustowski; Asst. Cur., Adele Hobby.
Personnel Profile: Part-Time Paid 2; Part-Time Volunteers 5; Interns 1.
Governing Authority: municipal. Subsidiary Institution: Yorktown Museum Research Center, 1974 Commerce St., Yorktown, NY 10598. Tax-exempt.
General Museum.
Collections: agricultural tools; household tools & equipment; costumes; manuscripts; textiles; dollhouses; toys & dolls; ephemera; photographs; Indian artifacts; spinning & weaving equipment; newspapers; Sylvia Newton Thorne marionettes, Old Put Line of New York Central R.R; Woodlands Room featuring items of the Mohican Indian; holiday decorations; period school books & cookbooks; period fashion magazines & ladies magazines; family genealogical files & photos; letters; documents; Bible records.
Research Fields: history of township.
Facilities: library of books of local history, antiques, architecture, collectibles & genealogy; research room. Gift & museum related items for sale.
Activities: guided tours; lectures; inter-museum loan, permanent & temporary exhibitions; school loan service; slide lectures & mini-exhibits to local school & civic organizations; genealogical & historical research; typescripts available for use to the public.
Publications: museum newsletter; art exhibit catalog.
Hours & Admission Prices: Call for hours & appointments. Tours: adults $2. Closed Easter; Thanksgiving; Christmas. ♿
Attendance: 5,000 (accurate)

Youngstown

OLD FORT NIAGARA, 2 Scott Ave., Fort Niagara State Park, Youngstown, NY 14174. Mailing Address: P.O. Box 169, Youngstown, NY 14174-0169. Tel.: 716-745-7611. Fax: 716-745-9141.
E-mail: ofn@oldfortniagara.org
Web Site: www.oldfortniagara.org
Founded: 1927.
Congressional District: 28
Key Personnel: C.E.O., Robert L. Emerson; Pres. (V), Richard Shick, Ph.D.; Interpretive Program Mgr., Eric Bloomquist; Cur., Jerome Brubaker; Museum Shop Mgr., Patricia Fitzpatrick.
Personnel Profile: Full-Time Paid 9; Full-Time Volunteers 1; Part-Time Paid 45; Part-Time Volunteers 1,750.
Governing Authority: nonprofit corporation. Tax-exempt: 501(c)(3).
Military Historic Site.
Collections: military; history; archaeology; site-related.
Research Fields: archaeology; military; history.
Facilities: 3,000-vol. library of history books & manuscripts available for specific research. Museum-related items for sale.
Activities: guided tours; living history demonstrations; permanent exhibitions.
Publications: brochures, Old Fort Niagara; Visitor's Guide; History & Guide to Old Fort Niagara; books: Seige-1759: The Campaign Against Niagara, The Gold-Laced Coat; Green Coats & Glory; Old Fort Niagara, An Illustrated History; A New System of Domestic Cookery; The Battle of Fort George; Navy Island: Historic Treasure of the Niagara; Molly Brant: A Legacy of Her Own; 1812 Sailor's Diaries; Memoirs of Pierre Pouchot.
Hours & Admission Prices: July-Aug. daily 9-7; Sept.-June daily 9-5. Adults $10, senior citizens $9, children 6-12 $6; discounts to groups, AAM & ICOM members; members no charge. Closed New Year's Day; Thanksgiving; Christmas. ♿
Attendance: 85,000 (accurate)
Membership: Individual $30; Family $50; Life & Sustaining $1,000; Endowing $2,000 & up.

NORTH CAROLINA

(286 listings)

Albemarle

MORROW MOUNTAIN STATE PARK, 49104 Morrow Mountain Rd., Albemarle, NC 28001-7886. Tel.: 704-982-4402. Fax: 704-982-5323.
E-mail: morrow.mountain@ncmail.net
Web Site: www.ncparks.gov
Founded: 1962.
Congressional District: 5
Key Personnel: Park Supt., Timothy McCree.
Governing Authority: state. A branch of North Carolina Dept. of Environment and Natural Resources, North Carolina Division of Parks & Recreation, P.O. Box 27687, Raleigh, NC 27611. Tax-exempt.
Park Museum.
Collections: geological history; Indian civilization; artifacts of Morrow Mountain area; reversion to a climax forest area; mounted animals of the area; local plant species.
Facilities: 16-vol. library of nature books available for use by special request only on premises; nature center.
Activities: lectures; slides; guided nature hikes.
Hours & Admission Prices: Daily 10-5. No charge. Closed Christmas. ♿
Attendance: 201,970 (estimated)

STANLY COUNTY HISTORIC PRESERVATION COMMISSION AND MUSEUM, (M), 245 E. Main St., Albemarle, NC 28001-4919. Tel.: 704-986-3777. Fax: 704-986-3778.
E-mail: junderwood@co.stanly.nc.us
Web Site: www.stanlycountymuseum.com
Founded: 1973.
Congressional District: 8
Key Personnel: Dir., Jonathan A. Underwood; Chm., Christy Stoner; Cur., Lessie Huneycutt.
Personnel Profile: Full-Time Paid 2; Part-Time Paid 1; Part-Time Volunteers 45; Interns 4.
Governing Authority: county. Parent Institution: County of Stanly. Tax-exempt.
History Museum & Visitor Center.
Collections: local history; period clothing; period furniture; textiles; photographs; documents. Historic Houses: c.1847 Freeman-Marks House; c.1852 I.W. Snuggs House.

Research Fields: local history.
Facilities: 100-vol. library of local history; visitors center. Museum-related items for sale.
Activities: guided tours; lectures; films; workshops; organized educational programs; docent program; participatory, loan & temporary exhibitions.
Publications: brochure, Badin: A Town at the Narrows; books: The Stanly County Folklife Tour - 1991, Stanly County, The Architectural Legacy of a Rural North Carolina County (1992); Images of America: Stanly County (2000).
Hours & Admission Prices: Tues.-Fri. 10-5, Sat. 10-4. No charge; donations accepted. Closed major holidays. ♿
Attendance: 5,881 (accurate)
Membership: Senior Citizen $10; Individual $20; Household $35; Bronze Circle $50-$99; Silver Circle $100-$199; Gold Circle $200-$499; Platinum Circle $500 & up.

Asheboro

NORTH CAROLINA ZOOLOGICAL PARK, 4401 Zoo Pkwy., Asheboro, NC 27205-1425. Tel.: 800-488-0444; 336-879-7000. Fax: 336-879-2891.
Web Site: www.nczoo.org
Founded: 1972.
Congressional District: 4
Key Personnel: Chm. Zoological Park Council, Scott Reed; Dir., Dr. David M. Jones; Business Officer, Mary Joan Pugh; Human Resources Officer, Cami Bunting; Gen. Cur., Ken Reininger; Cur. Horticulture, Virginia Wall; Design Cur., Ellen Greer; Cur. Mammals, Terry Webb; Assoc. Cur. Mammals, Guy Lichty; Cur. Herpetology, John Groves; Public Rels. Mgr., Rod Hackney; Mktg. Officer, Chris Bulla; Veterinarian, Michael R. Loomis; Gift Shop Mgr., Sharon McIntoch.
Personnel Profile: Full-Time Paid 260; Full-Time Volunteers 70; Part-Time Paid 200; Part-Time Volunteers 70.
Governing Authority: state. North Carolina Dept. of Environment & Natural Resources, 512 Salisbury St., Archdale Bldg., Raleigh, NC 27611; Tel. 919-733-4984. Tax-exempt: 170(b)(1)(A).
Zoo.
Collections: 800 African animals; 300 North American animals; 30,000 introduced plants.
Research Fields: chimpanzee behavior; primate husbandry; rhinoceros behavior; primate reproduction; elephant migration patterns in Cameroon, Africa; Cross River gorilla behavior in Cameroon, Africa.
Facilities: 1,800 vol. library of zoo management, wildlife ecology, zoology, botany; outdoor theater; fast food facility; picnic area. Zoo-related items for sale.
Activities: formally organized education programs for children & college students affiliated with UNC-Greensboro & N.C. State Univ. School of Veterinary Medicine; docent program; special events.
Publications: brochure; society newsletter; educators tour booklet; visitor guide; self-guided aviary tour; school packets for grades K-12.
Hours & Admission Prices: Daily 9-5; groups by appointment. Adults $10, senior citizens & college students $8, children 2-12 $6; discounts for groups, AZA, AAM & selected zoological institutions AAA members; North Carolina school groups in grades K-12, members & children under 2 no charge. ♿
Attendance: 710,637 (accurate)
Membership: Individual $29; Individual-plus $39; Family $59; Family-plus $69; Zookeeper $100; Curator $250; Director's Guild $1,500.

Asheville

* **ASHEVILLE ART MUSEUM,** 2 S. Pack Square, Asheville, NC 28801-3521. Mailing Address: P.O. Box 1717, Asheville, NC 28802-1717. Tel.: 828-253-3227. Fax: 828-257-4503.
E-mail: mailbox@ashevilleart.org
Web Site: www.ashevilleart.org
Founded: 1948.
Congressional District: 11
Key Personnel: C.E.O., Pamela L. Myers; Chm. (V), Rob Pulleyn; Immediate Past Chm., Phillip Broughton; Cur., Frank E. Thomson; Mgr. Devel., Scott Bunn; Mgr. Membership, Rebecca Lynch-Maass; Mgr. School & Family Programs, Erin Shope; Museum Shop Mgr., Hillary Frye.
Personnel Profile: Full-Time Paid 11; Part-Time Paid 2; Part-Time Volunteers 174; Interns 7.
Governing Authority: nonprofit organization. Parent Institution: Asheville Art Museum Association, Inc.
Art Museum.
Collections: American art in all media from 1900 to present: painting, prints, drawings, sculpture photography; contemporary art & studio craft, southeastern regional works & works related to Black Mountain College.
Major Exhibits: Looking Forward: Celebrating New Works and New Directions for the Permanent Collection, 11/09-12/10; Lorna Blaine Halper: Spiral Man and Other Patterns, 12/11/09-5/9/10; Children's Book Illustrations, 2/12/10-7/11/10; Tim Barnwell: Musical Portraits, 2/5/10-5/16/10; Richard Serra Graphic Works, 7/16/10-12/5/10; Artists and Tourists in the Land of the Sky, 1855-1929, 7/30/10-1/9/11; Lasting Gifts V: Recent Aquisitions to the Permanent Collection, 10/15/10-3/13/11; The Olmstead Project: Photographs by Lee Friedlander, 12/9/10-4/24/11.
Research Fields: Black Mountain College; contemporary crafts; regional artists; architecture.
Facilities: art library; classroom & studio; art resource center; 525-seat theater; multipurpose room. Museum-related items for sale.
Activities: guided tours; lectures; films; gallery demonstrations; formally organized educational programs; permanent & temporary exhibitions; slide programs; rural outreach program; adult & family programs; artist programs; summer camps & workshops.
Publications: newsletters; exhibition catalogues.
Hours & Admission Prices: Tues.-Sat. 10-5, Sun. 1-5; special evening hours available. Adults $6, senior citizens & students $5; discounts to AAM & ICOM members; members no charge; Southeastern & North American reciprocal members. Closed New Year's Day; Independence Day; Labor Day; Thanksgiving; Christmas. ♿
Attendance: 103,216 (accurate)
Membership: Student $25; Artists, Educator & Senior $40; Individual $50; Family & Dual $70; Patron $150; Sustaining $300; Benefactor $600; Director's Forum $1,000.

BILTMORE ESTATE, One Approach Rd., Asheville, NC 28803-8900. Tel.: 828-255-1333; 800-411-3812. Fax: 828-225-6383.
E-mail: rking@biltmore.com
Web Site: www.biltmore.com
Founded: 1930.
Congressional District: 11
Key Personnel: C.E.O., William A.V. Cecil, Jr.; Exec. Vice Pres., Richard Presby; Exec. Vice Pres., Steven Miller; Vice Pres., Richard King; Sr. Vice Pres. Attraction, Tom Ruff; Exec. Vice Pres., George W. Pickering, III; Vice Pres. Finance & Controller, Stephen Watson; Vice Pres. Agricultural Svcs., Ted Katsigianis; Sr. Vice Pres. Mktg., Jerry Douglass; Vice Pres. Winemaker, Bernard Delille; Vice Pres. Sales, Jim Owens; Public Rels. Mgr., Elizabeth Sims; Group Sales Mgr., Paula Wilbur.
Personnel Profile: Full-Time Paid 584; Part-Time Paid 500.
Governing Authority: company.
Historic House, Conservatory & Gardens: 1895 Biltmore House.
Collections: paintings; tapestries; prints; sculpture; furniture; rugs & related decorative art. Conservatory & Gardens: azaleas, roses, orchids, tropical collections.
Research Fields: 19th-century arts & furniture; tapestries; conservation; preservation; architecture; landscape design.
Facilities: gardens; three restaurants; winery; conservatory. Museum-related items for sale.
Activities: self-guided tours. Museum Sponsors: Festival of Flowers; Christmas at Biltmore; candlelight evenings (by reservation); chamber music; summer evening concerts (by reservation); fall fair.
Publications: guidebook.
Hours & Admission Prices: Welcome Center: Mon.-Thurs. 8:30-3, Fri.-Sat. 8:30-4. House: Mon.-Thurs. 9-3:30, Fri.-Sat. 9-4:30. See website for admission fees. ♿
Attendance: 902,000 (accurate)

BILTMORE HOMESPUN SHOPS - GROVEWOOD GALLERY, 111 Grovewood Rd., Asheville, NC 28804-2858. Tel.: 828-253-7651. Fax: 828-254-2489.
E-mail: homespun@grovewood.com
Web Site: grovewood.com
Founded: 1901.
Congressional District: 11
Key Personnel: Mgr., Allison Mills; Pres., Barbara Blomberg; Pres., Marilyn Patten.
Personnel Profile: Full-Time Paid 11; Part-Time Paid 8.
Governing Authority: company, Biltmore Industries. Branch Museum: Estes-Winn Antique Automobile Museum. Tax-exempt.
Textile Museum: complex of six buildings c.1917 operating as Biltmore handwoven homespun industries.
Collections: 1920 tools, looms, machinery & other items related to homespun.
Facilities: Local handcrafted items, woodcarvings & other related items for sale.
Activities: film demonstrating homespun transformed from fleece to finished cloth; films; permanent exhibitions.
Publications: brochure.
Hours & Admission Prices: April-Dec. Mon.-Sat. 10-5, Sun. 11-5. No charge; donations accepted. Closed Thanksgiving; Christmas. ♿
Attendance: 22,635 (accurate)

BLACK MOUNTAIN COLLEGE MUSEUM & ARTS CENTER, 56 Broadway, Asheville, NC 28801-2916. Mailing Address: P.O. Box 18912, Asheville, NC 28814-0912. Tel.: 828-350-8484. Fax: 828-350-8484.
E-mail: bmcmac@bellsouth.net
Web Site: www.blackmountaincollege.org
Founded: 1993.
Key Personnel: Program Dir., Alice Sebrell.
Personnel Profile: Part-Time Paid 2; Part-Time Volunteers 50; Interns 1.
Governing Authority: private; nonprofit organization. Tax-exempt: 501(c)(3).
Art Museum.
Collections: documents; artwork; photographs; books related to Black Mountain College & those who taught or attended it.
Major Exhibits: From BMC to NYC: The Tutelary Years of Ray Johnson (1948-1962), 2/10-5/10; Kenneth Snelson, 6/10-9/10.
Research Fields: educational programs for public primary & elementary schools; oral histories of Black Mountain College members.
Activities: formal education programs for children; guided tours; lectures; participatory, temporary & traveling exhibitions.
Publications: Black Mountain College Dossier; newsletter; exhibit catalogues.
Hours & Admission Prices: Wed.-Sat. 12-4. Adults $3; discounts to AAM & ICOM members; members no charge. ♿
Membership: Student $15; Individual $35; Family $60; Affiliate $125; Donor $500; Patron $1,000.

BLUE RDIGE PARKWAY VISITOR CENTER, 195 Hemphill Knob Rd., Asheville, NC 28803-8686. Tel.: 828-298-5330.
Key Personnel: Exec. Dir., Penn Dameron
History Museum.
Collections: local history, heritage & culture; economic traditions; photographs; personal artifacts; hands-on exhibits.
Facilities: 70-seat theater. Museum-related items for sale.
Activities: interactive exhibits; listening stations; family events.
Hours & Admission Prices: Daily 9-5. Closed New Year's Day; Thanksgiving; Christmas.

BOTANICAL GARDENS AT ASHEVILLE, 151 W. T. Weaver Blvd., Asheville, NC 28804-3414. Tel.: 828-252-5190.
E-mail: bgardens@bellsouth.net
Web Site: ashevillebotanicalgardens.org
Founded: 1960.
Congressional District: 11
Key Personnel: Pres., Suzanne Wodek; Vice Pres., Lou Dwarshuis; Horticulture Chm., Jay Kranyik; Administrative Asst., Heather Rayburn.
Personnel Profile: Part-Time Paid 3; Part-Time Volunteers 100.
Governing Authority: nonprofit corp. Tax-exempt: 501(c)(3).
Botanical Gardens: includes site of earthen battlements of the Civil War, Battle of Asheville.
Collections: native flora of Southern Appalachians. Historical House: The Hayes Cabin, Smoky Mountain log cabin furnished with primitive furniture of the early settlers.
Research Fields: preservation of endangered species of plants.
Facilities: botanical library & garden; visitor center; Cole Botany Library; Butler Lecture Hall.
Activities: guided tours; lectures; childrens' programs; formally organized education programs for undergraduate college students affiliated with the Univ. of North Carolina. Botanical Gardens Sponsors: special events for the public in the area of conservation, botany & nature study.
Publications: quarterly newsletter, The New Leaf; brochures.
Hours & Admission Prices: Visitor Center: mid-March-Dec. daily 10-4. Grounds: daily. No charge; donations accepted. Closed Thanksgiving; Christmas. ♿
Attendance: 65,000 (estimated)
Membership: Student $15; Individual $25; Family & Club $35; Contributor $50; Sustaining $100; Benefactor $500.

COLBURN EARTH SCIENCE MUSEUM, (M), Pack Place Education, Arts & Science Center, 2 S. Pack Square, Asheville, NC 28801. Mailing Address: P.O. Box 1617, Asheville, NC 28802-1617. Tel.: 828-254-7162. Fax: 828-257-4505.
E-mail: info@colburnmuseum.org
Web Site: www.packplace.org
Formerly: Colburn Gem & Mineral Museum, Inc.
Founded: 1960.
Congressional District: 11
Key Personnel: Dir., Kathleen O. Davis; Museum Shop Mgr., Jessica Varney.
Personnel Profile: Full-Time Paid 4; Part-Time Paid 2.
Governing Authority: nonprofit; bd. directors. Tax-exempt.
Geology, Mineralogy & Paleontology Museum & Earth Science.
Collections: North Carolina & worldwide minerals; gems; North Carolina rocks, micromount minerals; Perloff slides; mining photos; Owen gems; mining artifacts; history of mining; meteorology.
Research Fields: mineralogy.
Facilities: library; permanent & temporary exhibit galleries; lecture hall; research lab; star lab planetarium. Gift items for sale.
Activities: self-directed & guided tours; lectures; field trips; organized educational programs; permanent & temporary exhibition.
Hours & Admission Prices: Tues.-Sat. 10-5, Sun. 1-5. Adults $4, senior citizens & children $3; discount to groups; children under 4, AAM members & members no charge. Closed major holidays. ♿
Attendance: 25,000 (accurate)
Membership: Junior $15; Individual $35; Family $50; Patron $100; Sponsor $250; Contributor $500; Benefactor $1,000.

ESTES-WINN ANTIQUE AUTOMOBILE MUSEUM, 111 Grovewood Rd., Asheville, NC 28804-2858. Tel.: 828-253-7651. Fax: 828-254-2489.
E-mail: automuseum@grovewood.com
Web Site: www.grovewood.com
Founded: 1970.
Congressional District: 11
Key Personnel: Mgr., Allison Mills; Pres., Marilyn Patton; Pres., Barbara Blomberg; Business Officer, Shirley Dobbs.
Personnel Profile: Part-Time Paid 2.
Governing Authority: nonprofit organization. Affiliated with Biltmore Indus. Tax-exempt: 501(c)(3).
Transportation Museum: located on the grounds of c.1917 Biltmore Homespun Shops.
Collections: 19 rare & period cars.
Publications: brochure.
Hours & Admission Prices: April-Dec. Mon.-Sat. 10-5, Sun. 11-5. No charge; donations accepted. ♿
Attendance: 22,635 (accurate)

* **THE HEALTH ADVENTURE, (M),** 2 S. Pack Square, Asheville, NC 28801-3521. Mailing Address: P.O. Box 180, Asheville, NC 28802-0180. Tel.: 828-254-6373. Fax: 828-257-4521.
E-mail: info@thehealthadventure.org
Web Site: www.thehealthadventure.org
Founded: 1968.
Congressional District: 11
Key Personnel: C.E.O., Paige Johnson; Chm. Bd., Joe Brumit; Dir. Education, Myra Lynch; Health Educator, Jenny Mercer; Health & Science Educator, Heather Wieler; Vice Pres. Programs & Exhibits, Jim Taylor; Dir. Volunteers & Events, Jessica Lane; Dir. Exhibits, Jesse Paden; School Reservationist, Stefanie Kompathoum; Devel. Asst., Donna Anderson; Accounting Mgr., Mitzi Morris; Museum Shop Mgr., Diana Bowen; Vice Pres. Mktg. & Devel., Tracie Perkins; Membership Coord., Allison Dyer.
Personnel Profile: Full-Time Paid 15; Part-Time Paid 11; Part-Time Volunteers 265.
Governing Authority: nonprofit organization. Tax-exempt.
Science Museum.
Collections: bones, nutrition, digestion, muscles, circulation, dental, respiration; life patterns; substance abuse; brains; senses; creativity; sports health; general anatomy; transparent anatomical mannequin.
Research Fields: hands-on science & health education.
Facilities: 20,000 sq. ft. exhibit space; 70-seat theatre; 60-seat theatre; classrooms. Science-related items for sale.
Activities: self-directed & guided tours; lectures; films; formally organized educational programs; docent program; permanent & traveling exhibitions.
Publications: newsletter, Brainstorm.
Hours & Admission Prices: Mon.-Sat. 10-5, Sun. 1-5. Adults $8.50, students & seniors $7.50, children 2-11 $6; discount to ASTC members; members & children under 2 no charge. Closed holidays. ♿
Attendance: 132,120 (accurate)
Membership: Individual $30; Family $60; Bodyworks $100; Heartthrob $250; Backbone $500; Tam Society $1,000.

THE NORTH CAROLINA ARBORETUM, 100 Frederick Law Olmsted Way, Asheville, NC 28806-9315. Tel.: 828-665-2492. Fax: 828-665-2371.
Arboretum.
Collections: plants; trees; flowers.
Facilities: nature trails. Museum-related items for sale.
Activities: research; demonstrations; educational programs; workshops; tours; classes; nature walks.
Hours & Admission Prices: Mon.-Sat. 9-5, Sun. 12-5. Closed New Year's Day; Thanksgiving; Christmas.

SMITH-MCDOWELL HOUSE MUSEUM, (M), 283 Victoria Rd., Asheville, NC 28801-4817. Tel.: 828-253-9231. Fax: 828-253-5518.
E-mail: smh@wnchistory.org
Web Site: www.wnchistory.org
Founded: 1981.
Congressional District: 11
Key Personnel: Pres., Dan Huger; Coord. Education, Lisa Whitfield.
Personnel Profile: Part-Time Paid 3; Part-Time Volunteers 30; Interns 1.
Governing Authority: nonprofit organization. Parent Institution: Western North Carolina Historical Assn. Tax-exempt: 501(c)(3).
Historic Building & Local History Museum: housed in 1840 Smith-McDowell House.
Collections: 19th-century decorative arts & artifacts relating to Western North Carolina.
Major Exhibits: 19th-Century Wedding Gowns, 3/10-4/10; Victorian Christmas, 11/10-12/10.
Research Fields: Western North Carolina history.
Facilities: 500-vol. library; classroom.
Activities: guided tours; formally organized educational programs; docent program. Museum Sponsors: Victorian Christmas Celebration; Heritage Festival, Buncombe County Chautauqua.
Publications: quarterly newsletter.
Hours & Admission Prices: Wed.-Sat. 10-4, Sun. 12-4. Adults $7, children $3; discounts to groups, AAA & AASLH members; members no charge. Additional fee for Christmas exhibit. ♿
Attendance: 2,500 (estimated)
Membership: Individual $35; Family $50; Supporting $75; Patron $100; Sponsor $250; Benefactor $500.

THE SOUTHERN APPALACHIAN RADIO MUSEUM, Elm Bldg., Rm. 315, Victoria Rd., Asheville, NC 28801. Tel.: 828-299-1276.
Founded: 1999.
Key Personnel: Pres., John Travis; Vice Pres., Norman Harrill; Sec. & Treas., Clint Gorman.
Personnel Profile: Part-Time Volunteers 7.
Governing Authority: nonprofit. Tax-exempt: 501(c)(3).
History Museum.
Collections: radio history; test instruments; Atwater Kent; Philco; Silvertone; Crosley; Hammarlund; Harvey Wells; spark gap transmitters; keys; period QSL cards; amateur radio station, W4AFM.
Hours & Admission Prices: Feb.-Nov. Fri. 1-3; other times by appointment. No charge; donations accepted. Closed school holidays.

SOUTHERN HIGHLAND CRAFT GUILD AT THE FOLK ART CENTER, (M), Milepost 382, Blue Ridge Pkwy., Asheville, NC 28805. Mailing Address: P.O. Box 9545, Asheville, NC 28815-0545. Tel.: 828-298-7928. Fax: 828-298-7962.
E-mail: info@craftguild.org
Web Site: www.southernhighlandguild.org
Formerly: Folk Art Center
Founded: 1930.
Congressional District: 11
Key Personnel: Exec. Dir., Tom Bailey.
Personnel Profile: Full-Time Paid 20; Part-Time Paid 10; Part-Time Volunteers 60.
Governing Authority: jointly: private; nonprofit. Parent Institution: Southern Highland Handicraft Guild, in association with National Park Svcs. Tax-exempt.
Southern Appalachian Craft Museum.
Collections: traditional & contemporary crafts & trades.
Research Fields: traditional crafts; American crafts; folk art; Southern Appalachian culture.
Facilities: library; information center. Publications & crafts for sale.
Activities: demonstration; craft related.
Publications: quarterly newsletter, Highland Highlights.
Hours & Admission Prices: Jan.-March daily 9-5; April-Dec. daily 9-6. No charge; donations accepted. Closed New Year's Day; Thanksgiving; Christmas. ♿
Attendance: 281,000 (accurate)
Membership: Donor Recognition Categories $50 & $150.

THOMAS WOLFE MEMORIAL, 52 N. Market St., Asheville, NC 28801-8105. Tel.: 828-253-8304. Fax: 828-252-8171.
E-mail: contactus@wolfememorial.com
Web Site: www.wolfememorial.com
Founded: 1949.
Congressional District: 11
Key Personnel: Dir., Steve Hill; Museum Shop Mgr., Jesse Cox.
Personnel Profile: Full-Time Paid 5; Part-Time Paid 5; Part-Time Volunteers 5.
Governing Authority: state. North Carolina Dept. of Cultural Resources, 109 E. Jones St., Raleigh, NC. 27611. Parent Institution: North Carolina Historic Sites.
Historic House: built in 1883 Thomas Wolfe boarding house, The Old Kentucky Home.
Collections: early 20th century boarding house furnishings; Thomas Wolfe memorabilia.
Research Fields: 20th-century American Literature; early 20th century Asheville, NC.
Facilities: visitors center. Museum-related items for sale.
Activities: guided tours of house; AV(isual) program in Visitors Center.
Publications: brochure; A Literary Journey; The Lost World of Thomas Wolfe; article, Historic Homes; newsletter.
Hours & Admission Prices: April-June 2 Tues. Tues.-Sat. 9-5; June 3-Oct. Tues.-Sat. 9-5, Sun. 1-5; Nov.-March Tues.-Sat. 10-4, Sun. 1-4. Adults $1, students $.50. ♿
Attendance: 18,000 (accurate)
Membership: Friend $25-$49; Boarder $50-$99; Scholar $100-$149; Angel $150 & up.

WESTERN NORTH CAROLINA NATURE CENTER, 75 Gashes Creek Rd., Asheville, NC 28805-2529. Tel.: 828-298-5600, ext. 303. Fax: 828-298-2644.
E-mail: staff@wildwnc.org
Web Site: www.wncnaturecenter.org
Founded: 1977.
Congressional District: 11
Key Personnel: Dir., Chris Gentile; Supt. Recreation, Diane Ruggiero; Dir. Education, Keith Mastin; Cur. of Animal Collections, Tim Hunter; Museum Shop Mgr., Mischa Trinks.
Personnel Profile: Full-Time Paid 16; Part-Time Paid 3; Part-Time Volunteers 80; Interns 6.
Governing Authority: nonprofit. Parent Institution: City of Asheville. Tax-exempt.
Nature Center & Botanical Garden.
Collections: living animals & plants.
Research Fields: red wolf captive breeding program.
Facilities: gardens; nature trail; zoological park; aquarium; classrooms. Gift items for sale.
Activities: guided tours; lectures; films; gallery talks; study clubs; hobby workshops; TV programs; formally organized education programs for children; docent program; permanent exhibitions.
Publications: newsletter.
Hours & Admission Prices: Daily 10-5. Adults $8, senior citizens $7, children 3-14 $4; discounts to ASTC & AZA members; members and children 2 & under no charge. Closed major winter holidays. ♿
Attendance: 91,503 (accurate)
Membership: Individual $30; Couple $45; Family $60; Wildlife Guardian $100; Nature Benefactor $250.

Atlantic Beach

FORT MACON STATE PARK, 2300 E. Fort Macon Rd., Atlantic Beach, NC 28512-5638. Mailing Address: P.O. Box 127, Atlantic Beach, NC 28512-0127. Tel.: 252-726-3775. Fax: 252-726-2497.
E-mail: fort.macon@ncmail.net
Web Site: www.clis.com/friends
Founded: 1924.
Congressional District: 1
Key Personnel: Park Supt., Jody A. Merritt; Chief Park Ranger, Randall Newman; Park Ranger, R. Scott Crocker; Park Ranger, Paul R. Branch; Park Ranger, John Iullwood; Chief Maintenance, Barry Smith; Maintenance Mechanic, Larry Stover; Gen. Utility Worker, Thomas Coombs; Office Asst. III, Cleta Buck.
Personnel Profile: Full-Time Paid 9; Part-Time Paid 13; Part-Time Volunteers 25.
Governing Authority: state. NC Div. of Parks & Recreation, Box 27687, Archdale Bldg., Raleigh, NC 27611. Tel. 919-733-4181.
Museum & Historic Building: 1834 brick casemated, irregular pentagon shape, outer & inner walls with moat, Fort Macon.
Collections: 1834-1944 military artifacts; Civil War, Spanish American War & World War II artifacts & equipment; artillery projectiles; soldier & garrison life relics; two replica barbette cannons; two original mortars & a field gun.
Facilities: library pertaining to American military history, Civil War & coastal ecology available for research on premises only.
Activities: guided tours; lectures; permanent exhibitions; living history programs.
Hours & Admission Prices: Daily 9-5:30. No charge. Closed Christmas. ♿
Attendance: 1,250,000 (estimated)

Aurora

AURORA FOSSIL MUSEUM, 400 Main St., Aurora, NC 27806-0352. Mailing Address: P.O. Box 352, Aurora, NC 27806-0352. Tel.: 252-322-4238. Fax: 252-322-2220.
E-mail: aurfosmus@yahoo.com
Web Site: aurorafossilmuseum.com
Founded: 1976.
Congressional District: 1
Key Personnel: Dir., Andrea W. Stilley.
Personnel Profile: Full-Time Paid 2; Part-Time Paid 2.
Governing Authority: nonprofit. Tax-exempt.
Geology & Paleontology Museum.
Collections: geology & paleontology from coastal plains of North Carolina; pleistocene, pliocene, & miocene marine fossils.
Facilities: picnics. Museum-related items for sale.
Activities: outreach programs; field studies; fossil pile; school groups.
Publications: AFM teacher's packet.
Hours & Admission Prices: March to Labor Day Mon.-Sat. 9-4:30, Sun. 12:30-4:30; Sept.-Feb. Mon.-Sat. 9-4:30; groups of 10 or more by appointment. No charge; donations accepted. ♿
Attendance: 25,000 (accurate)
Membership: Individual $50; Family $75.

Bailey

THE COUNTRY DOCTOR MUSEUM, 6642 Peele Rd., Bailey, NC 27807. Mailing Address: P.O. Box 34, Bailey, NC 27807-0034. Tel.: 252-235-4165. Fax: 252-235-2372.
Web Site: www.countrydoctormuseum.org
Founded: 1967.
Congressional District: 2
Personnel Profile: Full-Time Paid 1; Part-Time Paid 3.
Governing Authority: nonprofit organization. Parent Institution: Medical Foundation of East Carolina University. Managed by Laupus Library of ECU. Tax-exempt: 501(c)(3).
Rural Medical & Pharmacology Museum with emphasis on Eastern North Carolina from 1850-1960.
Collections: 19th- & early 20th-century medical and pharmacy instruments, furnishings & supplies of country doctors.
Research Fields: 19th- & early 20th-century medicine and pharmacy.
Facilities: 1,000-vol. library of medical books available for inter-library loan through Laupus Library, East Carolina University Medical School and to doctors, nurses, pharmacists, nursing & research students; medicinal herb garden.
Activities: guided tours; lectures.
Publications: book, The Country Doctor Museum; Medicinal Herb Garden of the C.D. Museum; Tarheel Doctors and Patients; Patent Medicines in North Carolina; Blackberries to Fishing Worms; A Nurse's Education.
Hours & Admission Prices: Tues.-Sat. 10-4. Adults $5, senior citizens & AAA members $4, students $3. Closed holidays. ♿
Attendance: 2,000 (estimated)

Bath

HISTORIC BATH STATE HISTORIC SITE, 207 Carteret St., Bath, NC 27808. Mailing Address: P.O. Box 148, Bath, NC 27808-0148. Tel.: 252-923-3971. Fax: 252-923-3971.
E-mail: bath@ncdcr.gov
Web Site: www.bath.nchistoricsites.org
Founded: 1963.
Congressional District: 3
Key Personnel: Site Mgr., Leigh Swane; Gift Shop Mgr., Robyn Jackson.
Personnel Profile: Full-Time Paid 5; Part-Time Paid 4; Part-Time Volunteers 6; Interns 1.
Governing Authority: state. Parent Institution: North Carolina Dept. of Cultural Resources, Historic Sites Section 4620 Mail Service Center Raleigh, NC 27699-4620. Tax-exempt: 170(b)(1)(A).
Visitor Center.
Collections: history. Historic Houses: 1751 Palmer-Marsh House; 1830 Bonner House; 1790 Van Der Veer House.
Research Fields: Bath & colonial North Carolina.
Facilities: Colonial publications & museum-related items for sale.
Activities: guided tours; lectures; films; formally organized education programs for children; permanent exhibitions.
Publications: guide book; brochure.
Hours & Admission Prices: Tues.-Sat. 9-5. Two house tour: adults $2, students $1; discount to groups. Closed winter holidays. ♿
Attendance: 30,600 (estimated)

Beaufort

BEAUFORT HISTORIC SITE, 138 Turner St., Beaufort, NC 28516-2139. Mailing Address: P.O. Box 363, Beaufort, NC 28516-0363. Tel.: 252-728-5225. Fax: 252-728-4966.
E-mail: beaufortshistoricsite@earthlink.net
Web Site: www.beauforthistoricsite.org
Founded: 1960.
Congressional District: 2
Key Personnel: Exec. Dir., Patricia Suggs; Chm. (V), Polly Hagle; Pres. (V), Doug Brady; Vice Pres., Fred McCune; Vice Pres., John Hagle; Treas., Whit Procter; Museum Shop Mgr., Diane Donovan.
Personnel Profile: Full-Time Paid 4; Part-Time Paid 11; Part-Time Volunteers 300.
Governing Authority: private volunteer board; nonprofit organization. Parent Institution: Beaufort Historical Association. Tax-exempt.
Historical & Preservation Society.
Collections: period furnishings; historic documents; c.1709 Old Burying Ground. Historic Houses: c.1825 John C. Manson House; c.1825 Josiah Bell House; c.1796 Carteret County Courthouse; c.1829 Carteret County Jail; c.1859 Apothecary Shop; c.1778 Samuel Leffer Cottage; c.1732 Rustell House.
Research Fields: architectural history; collections research; county & North Carolina coastal history; family history; old Burying Ground of 1731 history.
Facilities: 2 acre site; herb garden; Welcome Center. Gift items for sale.
Activities: guided tours; lectures; docent program; exhibits; traditional crafts & living history; English bus tours; weaving demonstrations. Site Sponsors: Publick Day in April; Old Homes Tour & Antiques show Fundraiser in June; harvest time exhibition in October; Jumble Sale & Community Thanksgiving Feast in November; Christmas Walk in December.
Publications: newsletter, Historic Times.
Hours & Admission Prices: Mon.-Sat. 9:30-5; group tours by appointment. Adults $8, children under 12 $4. English Bus Tours: Mon. & Wed.-Sat. Adults $8. Old Burying Ground Tour: Tues.-Thurs. 2:30 Adults $8; discounts to AAA members & groups of 30 or more. Closed Easter; Thanksgiving; Christmas Eve & Day. ♿
Attendance: 65,000 (estimated)
Membership: Senior & Student $15; Family & Contributor $25; Donor $50; Business $25-$1000; Sponsor $100; Patron $250; Benefactor $500; Heritage Club $1,000.

* **NORTH CAROLINA MARITIME MUSEUM, (M),** 315 Front St., Beaufort, NC 28516-2124. Tel.: 252-728-7317. Fax: 252-728-2108.
E-mail: maritime@ncdcr.gov
Web Site: www.ncmaritimemuseum.org
Founded: 1975.
Congressional District: 1
Key Personnel: Dir., Joe Schwarzer; Pres. Friends of the Museum, Eddy Myers; Cur. Education, Allison Besch; Assoc. Cur., Laurie Streble; Coord. Group Programs, Allison Gleason; Registrar Collections, Frances Hayden; Collections Mgr., Darlene Perry; Watercraft & Maritime Research Cur., Paul Fontenoy; Exhibit Designer, Mike Carraway; Exhibit Technician, Larry Copeland; Exhibit Technician, Terry Greene; Boatshop Mgr., William Prentice; Boatbuilder, Craig Wright; Coord. Cape Lookout Studies, Keith Rittmaster; Business Mgr., Bobby Springle; Nautical Archaeologist, David Moore; Artist & Illustrator, Michelle McConnell; Building & Grounds Supt., Denny Hailey; Museum Shop Mgr., Sharon Resor; Southport Branch Mgr., Mary Strickland; Program Coord., Lori Duppstadt.
Personnel Profile: Full-Time Paid 20; Full-Time Volunteers 115; Part-Time Paid 6; Part-Time Volunteers 125.
Governing Authority: state. Parent Institution: North Carolina Dept. of Cultural Resources, Office of Archives & History. Subsidiary Institution: Division of State History Museums. Tax-exempt.
Natural & Maritime History Museum.
Collections: marine specimens; seashells; ship models; marine artifacts; traditional small watercraft collection.
Research Fields: development & history of small craft of North Carolina.
Facilities: ship's library of plans, charts & volumes on traditional boat building; boatshop. Books, prints, pamphlets for sale.
Activities: lectures; year-round field trips; boatbuilding skills program; junior sailing program; adult learn to sail program. Museum Sponsors: the summer school of science for children; Traditional Wooden Boat Show.
Publications: newsletter, The Waterline; field guide, Seacoast Life; calendar, Guide to Salt Marsh Plants; Guide to Dune Plants; Construction Plans for Traditional North Carolina Watercraft; N.C. Traditional Work Boats; Discover Maritime North Carolina.
Hours & Admission Prices: Mon.-Fri. 9-5, Sat. 10-5, Sun. 1-5. No charge. Closed New Year's Day; Thanksgiving; Christmas Eve & Day. ♿
Attendance: 260,756 (accurate)

Membership: Individual $25; Family $50; Supporter $100; Patron $250; Sustaining $500; Benefactor $1,000; Lifetime $2,500.

Belhaven

BELHAVEN MEMORIAL MUSEUM, INC., 211 E. Main St., Belhaven Town Hall, 2nd Fl., Belhaven, NC 27810-1413. Mailing Address: P.O. Box 220, Belhaven, NC 27810-0220. Tel.: 252-943-6817. Fax: 252-943-2357.
Web Site: www.beaufort-county.com/Belhaven/museum/Belhaven.htm
Founded: 1965.
Congressional District: 3
Key Personnel: Pres., Ed Harris.
Personnel Profile: Part-Time Paid 2.
Governing Authority: nonprofit corporation. Tax-exempt.
Local History Museum.
Collections: 19th- to 20th-century historical items of coastal Carolina; early phonographs; Indian artifacts; marine.
Publications: quarterly newsletter.
Hours & Admission Prices: Thurs.-Tues. 1-5. No charge; donations accepted.
Attendance: 5,000 (estimated)
Membership: Supporter $10; Explorer $25; Archivist $50; Special Contributor $100; Corporate Sponsor $200.

Belmont

DANIEL STOWE BOTANICAL GARDEN, 6500 S. New Hope Rd., Belmont, NC 28012-8788. Tel.: 704-825-4490. Fax: 704-829-1240.
Web Site: www.dsbg.org
Key Personnel: Exec. Dir., Kara Newport; Dir. Grounds, Jim Summey; Dir. Mktg. & Guest Svcs., Jim Hoffman, APR
Botanical Garden.
Collections: themed gardens; fountains.
Facilities: gardens; nature trail. Museum-related items for sale.
Activities: special events; educational community classes.
Publications: quarterly newsletter, The Garden Path; e-news, Garden Buzz.
Hours & Admission Prices: Daily 9-5. Adults $10, seniors 60 & over $9, children 4-12 $5; discounts to AAA members; members & children under 4 no charge. Closed New Year's Day; Thanksgiving; Christmas. ♿
Membership: Individual $5; Household $75; Premier Household $125.

Black Mountain

SWANNANOA VALLEY MUSEUM, 223 W. State St., Black Mountain, NC 28711-3408. Mailing Address: P.O. Box 306, Black Mountain, NC 28711-0306. Tel.: 828-669-9566.
E-mail: info@swannanoavalleymuseum.org
Web Site: www.swannanoavalleymuseum.org
Founded: 1989.
Congressional District: 11
Key Personnel: Dir., Jill Jones; Chm. (V), Wendell Begley.
Personnel Profile: Part-Time Paid 1; Part-Time Volunteers 80.
Governing Authority: Parent Institution: Swannanoa Valley Historical & Preservation Assoc., Inc. Tax-exempt.
History Museum.
Collections: area history & culture.
Activities: school, community & senior outreach; special events; guided tours. Museum Sponsors: Heritage Roundtables.
Hours & Admission Prices: April-Oct. Tues.-Fri. 10-5, Sat. 12-4, Sun. 2-5. No charge; donations accepted. ♿
Attendance: 5,000 (estimated)
Membership: Individual $25; Family $40; Booster $100; Sponsor $250; Patron $500; Benefactor $1,000 & up.

Blowing Rock

APPALACHIAN HERITAGE MUSEUM, 175 Mystery Hill Lane, Blowing Rock, NC 28605. Tel.: 828-264-2792. Fax: 828-262-3292.
Founded: 1989.
Congressional District: 5
History Museum.
Collections: local history & culture; period artifacts; photographs.
Hours & Admission Prices: June-Aug. daily 9-8; Sept.-May daily 9-5. Adults 13-59 $8, seniors 60 & over $7, children 5-12 $6; discounts to groups; children 4 & under no charge.

MYSTERY HILL - HERITAGE & NATIVE ARTIFACT MUSEUM, 129 Mystery Hill Lane, Blowing Rock, NC 28605-9549. Tel.: 828-264-2792.
E-mail: info@mysteryhill-nc.com
Historic House Museum: built in 1903.
Collections: local history & culture; arrowheads; Native American artifacts; period furnishings; personal artifacts.
Activities: hands-on exhibits, experiments & illusions.
Hours & Admission Prices: June-Aug. daily 9-8; Sept.-May 9-5. Adults 13-59 $8, seniors 60 & over $7, children 5-12 $6; discounts to groups; children 4 & under no charge.

Boone

THE CHILDREN'S PLAYHOUSE, 400 Tracy Circle, Boone, NC 28607-3846. Tel.: 828-263-0011.
Web Site: www.goplayhouse.org/
Key Personnel: Exec. Dir., Kathy Parham
Children's Museum.
Collections: hands-on exhibits.
Activities: workshops; educational programs.
Hours & Admission Prices: Tues.-Fri. 10-5, Sat. 10-3. Admission $5; children one & under and members no charge.

DANIEL BOONE NATIVE GARDENS, 651 Horn in the West Dr., Boone, NC 28607. Mailing Address: P.O. Box 1705, Boone, NC 28607. Tel.: 828-264-6390.
Native Gardens.
Collections: native Appalachian trees, shrubs, & wildflowers; plants.
Activities: rental facilities; special events.
Hours & Admission Prices: May-Oct. daily 10-6. Adults 16 & over $2.

HICKORY RIDGE HOMESTEAD, 591 Horn in the West Dr., Boone, NC 28607-4283. Mailing Address: P.O. Box 295, Boone, NC 28607-0295. Tel.: 704-264-2120.
History Museum.
Collections: local history & culture; hands-on exhibits; period furnishings & artifacts; historic buildings.
Activities: educational programs; special events; hands-on exhibits; workshops; live-in programs; summer day camps.
Hours & Admission Prices: May-Oct. Tues.-Sun. 1-8:30; other times by appointment.

TURCHIN CENTER FOR THE VISUAL ARTS, 423 W. King St., Boone, NC 28607-3523. Mailing Address: ASU Box 32139, Boone, NC 28608. Tel.: 828-262-3017. Fax: 828-262-7546.
Key Personnel: Dir., Hank T. Foreman
Art Gallery.
Collections: works by regional, national & international artists.
Hours & Admission Prices: Tues.-Thurs. & Sat. 10-6, Fri. 12-8. No charge.

Brevard

SILVERMONT MANSION, E. Main St., Brevard, NC 28712. Tel.: 828-884-3156.
Historic House Museum: built in 1902. Listed on the National Register of Historic Places.
Collections: family history; personal artifacts; period furnishings; photographs.
Activities: rental facilities.
Hours & Admission Prices: Call for hours.

SPIERS GALLERY, Sims Art Center, Brevard College, 1 Brevard College Dr., Brevard, NC 28712-4283. Tel.: 828-883-8292, ext. 8188. Fax: 828-884-3790.
E-mail: bbyers@brevard.edu.
Web Site: www.Brevard.edu
Key Personnel: Dir., Bill Byers.
Personnel Profile: Full-Time Paid 4; Part-Time Paid 2; Part-Time Volunteers 1.
Governing Authority: university; nonprofit. Parent Institution: Brevard College.
Art Gallery.
Collections: American art.
Activities: temporary exhibitions; arts festivals; lectures; poetry readings; musical performances.
Publications: exhibition notices.
Hours & Admission Prices: Sept.-May Mon.-Fri. 8-3. No charge. ♿
Attendance: 1,000 (estimated)

TRANSYLVANIA HERITAGE MUSEUM, 40 W. Jordan St., Brevard, NC 28712-3641. Mailing Address: P.O. Box 2347, Brevard, NC 28712-2347. Tel.: 828-884-2347.
Key Personnel: Exec. Dir., Rebecca Suddeth
History Museum.
Collections: local history & culture; personal artifacts; photographs; period furnishings.
Facilities: Museum-related items for sale.

Activities: special events.
Hours & Admission Prices: Wed.-Sat. 10-5. No charge.

Bryson City

SMOKY MOUNTAIN TRAINS, 100 Greenlee St., Bryson City, NC 28713. Mailing Address: P.O. Box 1490, Bryson City, NC 28713-1490. Tel.: 828-488-5200; 866-914-5200. Fax: 828-488-3162.
E-mail: info@smokymountaintrains.com
Web Site: www.smokymountaintrains.com
Founded: 2002.
Key Personnel: C.E.O. & Cur., Timothy O. Cooper.
Personnel Profile: Full-Time Paid 1; Part-Time Paid 4.
Train Museum.
Collections: 7,000 Lionel (TM) engines, cars & accessories; 1934 Blue Comet Passenger set; Joshua Lionel Cowen Challenger steam locomotives; 3,000 trains dating from 1918-2003.
Facilities: 7,000 sq. ft. exhibit space; children's activity center. Museum-related items for sale.
Activities: children's activities.
Publications: semiannual newsletter.
Hours & Admission Prices: Mon.-Sat. 8:30-5:30. Adults $9, members $7, children 4-11 $5; discount to groups; children under 3 no charge. Closed New Year's Day; Thanksgiving; Christmas. ♿
Attendance: 30,000 (accurate)

Burgaw

PENDER COUNTY MUSEUM, 200 W. Bridgers St., Burgaw, NC 28425. Mailing Address: P.O. Box 1380, Burgaw, NC 28425-1380. Tel.: 910-259-8543.
Governing Authority: private; nonprofit organization. Parent Institution: Pender County Historical Society. Tax-exempt.
Local History Museum.
Collections: WWII veterans' oral history transcripts; farm implements; tools; furniture; genealogy; photographs.
Publications: quarterly newsletter.
Hours & Admission Prices: Thurs.-Fri. 1-4, Sat. 10-2. No charge; donations accepted.
Membership: Individual $10; Family $25; Sustaining $50; Patron $75; Benefactor & Life $100; Corporate & Business $150.

Burlington

ALAMANCE BATTLEGROUND STATE HISTORIC SITE, 5803 South N.C. 62, Burlington, NC 27215. Tel.: 336-227-4785. Fax: 336-227-4787.
E-mail: alamance@ncmail.net
Web Site: www.alamancebattleground.nchistoricsites.org
Founded: 1955.
Congressional District: 6
Key Personnel: Site Mgr., Bryan Dalton; Historic Site Asst. & Museum Shop Mgr., Bill Thompson; Historic Interpreter, Kerri Clavette.
Personnel Profile: Full-Time Paid 3; Part-Time Paid 2; Part-Time Volunteers 6.
Governing Authority: state. Parent Institution: North Carolina Dept. of Cultural Resources, Office of Archives & History, Div. of State Historic Sites. Tax-exempt: 170(b)(1)(A).
Historic Site.
Collections: military; area history. Historic House: c.1780 Allen House.
Research Fields: Colonial era.
Facilities: Publications relating to Colonial period & museum-related items for sale.
Activities: guided tours; lectures; films; formally organized education programs; permanent exhibitions.
Publications: brochure.
Hours & Admission Prices: Mon.-Sat. 9-5. No charge; donations accepted. Closed major holidays. ♿
Attendance: 10,530 (accurate)

ALAMANCE COUNTY HISTORICAL MUSEUM, 4777 S. Hwy. 62, Burlington, NC 27215-9295. Tel.: 336-226-8254.
E-mail: achminfo@alamancemuseum.org
Web Site: www.alamancemuseum.org
Founded: 1976.
Key Personnel: C.E.O. & Dir., William Vincent, Ph.D.; Chm. (V), Nathan Adams; Pres. (V), Mr. David Sellers.
Personnel Profile: Full-Time Paid 2; Part-Time Paid 1; Part-Time Volunteers 20; Interns 1.
Governing Authority: Tax-exempt.
Historic House Museum: housed in the former home of E.M. Holt.
Collections: period artifacts & furnishings; local history; quilts; Native American artifacts; pottery; clothing; toys; 19th century military artifacts.
Activities: temporary & permanent exhibits.
Hours & Admission Prices: Tues.-Fri. 9-4, Sat. 10:30-4, Sun. 1-4. No charge; donations accepted.
Attendance: 15,000 (accurate)
Membership: $25; $35; $50; $100; $250; $500; $1,000; $5,000.

Burnsville

YANCEY HISTORY ASSOCIATION - RUSH WRAY MUSEUM, McElroy House, 11 Academy St., Burnsville, NC 28714. Mailing Address: 3 Academy St., Burnsville, NC 28714-2944. Tel.: 828-682-3671.
History Museum: housed in the McElroy House.
Collections: Yancey County history & heritage.
Activities: educational programs.
Hours & Admission Prices: Wed.-Sat. 10-4.

Buxton

HATTERAS ISLAND VISITOR CENTER, Cape Hatteras Light Station, Buxton, NC 27920. Mailing Address: 1401 National Park Dr., Manteo, NC 27954-9451. Tel.: 252-473-2111 & 995-4474. Fax: 252-473-2595.
E-mail: caha_information@nps.gov
Web Site: www.nps.gov/caha
Founded: 1953.
Congressional District: 1
Key Personnel: Supt., Mike Murray.
Personnel Profile: Full-Time Paid 2; Part-Time Paid 10; Part-Time Volunteers 37; Interns 2.
Governing Authority: federal. Parent Institution: National Park Service. Affiliated with Cape Hatteras National Seashore. Tax-exempt.
Park Museum.
Collections: history; natural history. Historic Houses: 1854 Double Keeper's Quarters; 1870 Cape Hatteras Lighthouse; 1870 Cape Hatteras Lighthouse Keeper's dwellings.
Facilities: Maps, charts & books for sale.
Activities: guided tours; lectures; permanent exhibitions.
Publications: park brochure; park newspaper; site bulletins.
Hours & Admission Prices: Center: daily 9-5. No charge. Lighthouse: Easter weekend to Columbus Day. Adults $6, seniors 62 & over and children 12 & under $4; members no charge. Closed Christmas. ♿
Attendance: 4,500,000 (estimated)

Canton

CANTON AREA HISTORICAL MUSEUM, 36 Park St., Canton, NC 28716-4324. Tel.: 828-646-3412.
E-mail: cantonvisitorcenter@charterinternet.com
Key Personnel: Dir., Wayne Carson
History Museum.
Collections: area history & culture; photographs; inventor, Fillmore Christopher; author, Fred Chappell.
Hours & Admission Prices: Mon. & Fri. 9-1, Wed. & Sat. 10-12; other times by appointment. No charge; donations accepted.

Carrboro

THE ARTSCENTER, 300-G E. Main St., Carrboro, NC 27510-2359. Tel.: 919-929-2787, ext. 201. Fax: 919-969-8574.
E-mail: info@artscenterlive.org
Web Site: www.artscenterlive.org
Art Gallery.
Collections: paintings; photographs; sculpture.
Hours & Admission Prices: Call for hours.

Cashiers

ZACHARY-TOLBERT HOUSE, 1940 Hwy. 107 S., Cashiers, NC 28717. Mailing Address: P.O. Box 104, Cashiers, NC 28717-0104. Tel.: 828-743-7710. Fax: 828-743-0732.
E-mail: info@cashiershistoricalsociety.org
Web Site: www.cashiershistoricalsociety.org/
Key Personnel: Exec. Dir., Tim Osment
Historic House Museum.
Collections: period furnishings; personal artifacts.
Hours & Admission Prices: May-Oct. Fri.-Sat. 11-3. Tours: $5 per person; members no charge.

Chadbourn

1910 A.C.L. DEPOT, 1st Ave. & Colony St., Chadbourn, NC 28431. Mailing Address: P.O. Box 100, Chadbourn, NC 28431-0100.
Key Personnel: Dir., Edna T. Yates; Treas., Hilda Bullard.
Personnel Profile: Part-Time Volunteers 2.
Governing Authority: private; nonprofit organization. Tax-exempt: 501(c)(3).
History Museum: housed in a former train depot built in 1910. Listed on the Register of Historic Places.
Collections: depot & train history; paintings; period artifacts.
Activities: guided tours; temporary exhibitions; train rides; tours; school group tours. Annual Event: Strawberry Festival.
Hours & Admission Prices: Tues. 1-5, Sun. 2-5; other times by appointment. No charge; donations accepted.
Attendance: 1,000 (estimated)

Chapel Hill

* **ACKLAND ART MUSEUM, (M),** University of North Carolina at Chapel Hill, South Columbia St. at Franklin St., Chapel Hill, NC 27514. Mailing Address: Campus Box 3400, University of North Carolina at Chapel Hill, Chapel Hill, NC 27599-3400. Tel.: 919-966-5736. Fax: 919-966-1400. TDD: 919-962-0837.
E-mail: ackland@email.unc.edu
Web Site: www.ackland.org
Founded: 1958.
Congressional District: 4
Key Personnel: Dir., Emily Kass; Conservator, Lyn Koehnline; Cur. Collection, Timothy Riggs; Sr. Museum Educator, Beth Shaw McGuire; Registrar, Anita Heggli.
Personnel Profile: Full-Time Paid 19; Part-Time Paid 3; Part-Time Volunteers 200; Interns 2.
Governing Authority: Parent Institution: The University of North Carolina at Chapel Hill. Tax-exempt: 501(c)(3).
Art Museum.
Collections: European & American painting, sculpture & drawings from ancient times-20th century; 15th- to 20th-century prints; photographs; North Carolina folk art; Far Eastern art; Indian miniatures & sculpture.
Research Fields: ancient, medieval, Renaissance through modern art.
Facilities: 39,000-vol. library of art books, periodicals & 154,000 slides available through university art department.
Activities: guided tours; lectures; gallery talks; permanent & temporary exhibitions; community outreach program.
Publications: newsletter 3 times a year; exhibition catalogues
Hours & Admission Prices: Wed.-Sat. 10-5, Sun. 1-5. No charge; donations accepted. ♿
Attendance: 39,210 (accurate)
Membership: Student $15; Individual $30; Dual & Family $50; Contributor $100; Sponsor $250; Sustaining $500; Patron $1,000; Leadership $2,500; Vanguard $5,000.

COKER ARBORETUM OF THE NORTH CAROLINA BOTANICAL GARDEN, Raleigh St. & Cameron Ave. UNC Campus, Chapel Hill, NC 27514. Mailing Address: The University of North Carolina at Chapel Hill, CB #3375 Totten Center, Chapel Hill, NC 27599-3375. Tel.: 919-962-0522. Fax: 919-962-3531.
E-mail: ncbg@unc.edu
Web Site: www.ncbg.unc.edu
Founded: 1903.
Congressional District: 4
Key Personnel: Dir., Dr. Peter White; Cur., Dan Stern.
Personnel Profile: Full-Time Paid 2; Part-Time Paid 1; Part-Time Volunteers 4.
Governing Authority: state. Parent Institution: North Carolina Botanical Garden. Tax-exempt.
Arboretum.
Collections: dwarf conifers; southeastern U.S. native species; Asian species; daffodils; daylilies; grasses.
Activities: seasonal tours
Publications: brochure; newsletter, North Carolina Botanical Garden Newsletter.
Hours & Admission Prices: mid-March to early Nov. Sat. 9-5, Sun. 1-5; early Nov. to mid-March Mon.-Fri. 8-5, Sat. 9-6, Sun. 1-6. No charge; donations accepted. ♿
Attendance: 10,000 (estimated)
Membership: Volunteer, Student & Senior $10; Individual $35; Family $45; Organization $50.

MOREHEAD PLANETARIUM AND SCIENCE CENTER, 250 E. Franklin St., Chapel Hill, NC 27599-0001. Mailing Address: CB #3480 UNC, Chapel Hill, NC 27599-0001. Tel.: 919-962-1236. Fax: 919-962-1238.
E-mail: mhplanet@unc.edu
Web Site: www.moreheadplanetarium.org
Founded: 1949.
Congressional District: 4
Key Personnel: Dir., Todd Boyette; Dir. External Rels., Jeff Hill; Dir. Education Programs, Denise Young; Dir. Devel., Carol Vorhaus; Reservations, Adam Phelps; Retail, Ron Risch; Mktg. Mgr., Karen Kornegay; Dir. Finance, Susan Durham; Dir. Star Theater, Richard McColman; Camp Programs, Jonathan Frederick; Dir. Outreach Programs, Betty Brown; Exhibits, Michele Kloda.
Personnel Profile: Full-Time Paid 32; Part-Time Paid 80; Part-Time Volunteers 40.
Governing Authority: university. Parent Institution: University of North Carolina, Chapel Hill. Tax-exempt.
Planetarium and Science Center.
Collections: hands-on exhibits.
Facilities: 240-seat planetarium with Carl Zeiss Model VI star projector; sundial; digital movie theater. Science-related items for sale.
Activities: lectures; classes for children & adults; permanent & temporary exhibitions; planetarium shows; skywatching sessions; summer camps; current science programs.
Publications: eNews magazine, "Sundial".
Hours & Admission Prices: Tues.-Thurs. 10-3:30, Fri.-Sat. 10-3:30 & 6:30-11:30, Sun. 1-4:30. Adults $6, students, children & senior citizens $5; members no charge. Closed Thanksgiving; Christmas Eve & Day. ♿
Attendance: 198,535 (accurate)
Membership: Household $60; Friend $100; Lunar Circle $250; Solar Circle $500; Stellar Circle $1,000.

NORTH CAROLINA BOTANICAL GARDEN, 100 Old Mason Farm Rd., Chapel Hill, NC 27517. Mailing Address: The University of North Carolina at Chapel Hill, CB 3375, Chapel Hill, NC 27599-3375. Tel.: 919-962-0522. Fax: 919-962-3531.
E-mail: ncbg@unc.edu
Web Site: www.ncbg.unc.edu
Founded: 1952.
Congressional District: 17
Key Personnel: C.E.O. & Dir., Dr. Peter S. White; Pres. (V), Bill Bracey; Assoc. Dir. Devel., Charlotte Jones-Roe; Asst. Dir., Frances Allen; Asst. Dir. Conservation, John L. Randall.
Personnel Profile: Full-Time Paid 25; Part-Time Paid 4; Part-Time Volunteers 225; Interns 10.
Governing Authority: state; university. Parent Institution: The University of North Carolina at Chapel Hill. Subsidiary Institution: Botanical Garden Foundation, Inc. Tax-exempt: 501(c)(3).
Botanical Garden.
Collections: living native plants of the Southeastern United States; nature center; woody plants; herb garden; garden of flowering plant families; native perennial borders; accessible gardening demonstration raised beds; Coker Arboretum on UNC campus; over 660,000 plant specimens; carnivorous plants of the southeastern U.S; herbarium.
Research Fields: plant taxonomy, propagation & evolution; pollination biology; ecology.
Facilities: herbarium & botanical reference library; 800 acres; research plots; greenhouse; classroom; nature trails. Museum-related items for sale.
Activities: guided tours; horticultural therapy services; lectures; formally organized education programs; plant rescues; educational trips within US and abroad; summer nature program for children; bimonthly botanical art exhibits; certificate programs.
Publications: bimonthly newsletter.
Hours & Admission Prices: Daylight Savings Time: Mon.-Fri. 8-5, Sat. 9-6, Sun. 1-6; Eastern Standard Time: Mon.-Fri. 8-5, Sat. 9-5, Sun. 1-5. No charge; donations accepted. Closed New Year's Day; Martin Luther King Jr. Day; Thanksgiving; Christmas. ♿
Attendance: 85,000 (estimated)
Membership: Volunteer, Student & Senior $25; Individual $45; Family $60; Organization $100.

Charlotte

BILLY GRAHAM LIBRARY, 4330 Westmont Dr., Charlotte, NC 28217-1001. Tel.: 704-401-3200.
Web Site: www.billygraham.org/library
Founded: 2007.
Library & Historic Home: childhood home of Billy Graham has been restored & moved to this location.
Collections: Graham's family history; personal artifacts; photographs; films.
Facilities: library; cafe. Museum-related items for sale.
Hours & Admission Prices: Mon.-Sat. 9:30-5; call to confirm; groups of 15 or more by appointment. No charge. ♿

CAROLINAS HISTORIC AVIATION MUSEUM, Charlotte-Douglas Intl. Airport, 4108 Minuteman Way, Charlotte, NC 28208-6891. Tel.: 704-359-8442. Fax: 704-359-0057.
E-mail: chaclibrary@yahoo.com
Web Site: www.carolinasaviation.org
Founded: 1991.
Congressional District: 8
Key Personnel: Dir., Randall Breedlove; Pres. (V), Shawn Dorsch; Museum Shop Mgr. & Office Mgr., Fred Gunther.
Personnel Profile: Part-Time Paid 2; Part-Time Volunteers 150.
Governing Authority: private; nonprofit organization. Tax-exempt: 501(c)(3).
Aviation Museum: housed in the original Charlotte Airport Hangar on the grounds of the Charlotte/Douglas International Airport; restoration is in progress to restore to its original 1937 condition.
Collections: focus on aviation history & artifacts pertaining to North Carolina and South Carolina from Wright Brothers first flight at Kitty Hawk, North Carolina, to present; World War II military aircraft; Piedmont Airlines DC-3 & two OV-1D Mohawk turbo-prop aircraft, all flyable & taken to airshow & aviation events; restored KC-97 cockpit; restored F-4 cockpit & fuselage; World War II aircraft service manuals & aircraft around the world; 10,000 aviation magazines; 1,000 pilot biographies.
Research Fields: restoration of aircrafts using research of military records that indicate whether originally was Navy, Marine or Air Force, original paint scheme, nose art & tail numbers
Facilities: 4,000-vol. aviation library ; 11,000 sq. ft. exhibit space. Aviation-related items for sale.
Activities: guided tours; temporary exhibitions; birthday packages; scout programs; view aircraft restoration. Annual Event: public open house in autumn.
Publications: monthly newsletter, Contact.
Hours & Admission Prices: Tues.-Sat. 10-4, Sun. 1-5. Adults $8, senior citizens and children 6 & over $5; children under 5 no charge. Closed New Year's Day; Easter; Thanksgiving; Christmas Eve & Day. ♿
Attendance: 25,000 (accurate)
Membership: Individual $25; Family $40; Patron $100; Benefactor $500; Corporate $1,000 & up.

CHARLOTTE MUSEUM OF HISTORY, (M), 3500 Shamrock Dr., Charlotte, NC 28215-3297. Tel.: 704-568-1774. Fax: 704-566-1817.
E-mail: info@charlottemuseum.org
Web Site: www.charlottemuseum.org
Founded: 1976.
Congressional District: 9
Key Personnel: C.E.O. & Pres., Mary Davis Smart; Chm. (V), Mark Henriques; Museum Shop Mgr., Meredith Olan.
Personnel Profile: Full-Time Paid 16; Part-Time Paid 6; Part-Time Volunteers 50; Interns 7.
Governing Authority: Parent Institution: Charlotte Museum of History, Inc. Tax-exempt.
History Museum.
Collections: furnishings from 1774-1820; regional artifacts & colonial to modern objects; archives; American Freedom Bell; hands-on exhibits Historic Building: 1774 rock house.
Research Fields: early history of the North Carolina Piedmont; genealogy of Alexander family; ancillary genealogy of Charlotte-Mecklenberg area.
Facilities: library. Gift items for sale.
Activities: guided tours; lectures; films; docent programs, loan, traveling & changing exhibitions. Annual Events: Revolutionary Charlotte Haunted Homesite; Twelfth Night; Colonial Fair; Independence Day Celebration.
Publications: newsletter.
Hours & Admission Prices: Museum: Tues.-Sat. 10-5, Sun. 1-5. Homesite Tours: Tues.-Sun. 1:15 & 3:15. Adult $6; discounts to senior citizens, AAA, AAM, ICOM, Time Travelers, Smithsonian Affiliates & groups with advance reservations; members no charge. ♿
Attendance: 54,928 (accurate)
Membership: Individual $35; Dual Senior $55; Household $65; Keystone $125; Patriot $250; Patron $500.

CHARLOTTE NATURE MUSEUM, 1658 Sterling Rd., Charlotte, NC 28209-1599. Mailing Address: 301 N. Tryon St., Charlotte, NC 28202-2138. Tel.: 704-372-6261, ext. 300; 800-935-0553. Fax: 704-333-8948.
Web Site: www.discoveryplace.org
Founded: 1947.
Congressional District: 9
Key Personnel: C.E.O. & Pres., John L. Mackay; Chm. (V), Gay Dorsey; Sr. Vice Pres. Operations & C.F.O., Linda Quinn; Vice Pres. Education & Programs, Deborah Curry; Vice Pres. Exhibits & Creative Svc., Dean Briere; Dir., Lisa Hoffman.
Personnel Profile: Full-Time Paid 4; Part-Time Paid 6; Part-Time Volunteers 15; Interns 1.
Governing Authority: nonprofit organization; board of trustees. Parent Institution: Discovery Place, Inc., 301 N. Tryon St., Charlotte, NC 28202. Tax-exempt: 501(c)(3) & 170(b)(1)(A).
Nature Museum.
Collections: teaching collection of biological material used with school classes; live collection of indigenous animals; live butterfly exhibit.
Facilities: early childhood teaching facility; nature center; puppet theater; classrooms, including outside teaching deck; 5 acres of nature trails; planetarium. Museum-related items for sale.
Activities: lectures; hobby workshops; formally organized educational programs; docent program or council; permanent & temporary exhibitions.
Publications: quarterly workshop bulletin.
Hours & Admission Prices: Tues.-Fri. 9-5, Sat. 10-5, Sun. 12-5. Admission $6; discounts to groups of 15 or more; children 2 & under and members no charge. Closed New Year's Day; Easter; Independence Day; Thanksgiving; Christmas Eve & Day. ♿
Attendance: 68,519 (accurate)
Membership: Individual $35; Family & Grandparent $75; Sponsor $125; Adventurer $150; Voyager $250; Explorer $500; Pioneer $1,000-2,500.

* **DISCOVERY PLACE, INC., (M),** 301 N. Tryon St., Charlotte, NC 28202-2138. Tel.: 704-372-6261. Fax: 704-337-2670.
Web Site: www.discoveryplace.org
Founded: 1981.
Congressional District: 12
Key Personnel: Pres. & C.E.O., John L. Mackay; Chm. (V), Larry Polski; Sr. Vice Pres. Operations & C.F.O., Linda Quinn; Vice Pres. Education & Programs, Deborah Curry; Dir. Mktg., Jim Hoffman; Dir. Devel., Kara Newport; Dir. Operations, Sandi Blakely; Vice Pres. Exhibits & Creative Svcs., Dean Briere; Dir. Omnimax Theatre, Danny Blakely; Dir. School Svcs., Deb Emmans; Dir. Human Resources & Volunteer Svcs., Ervin Gourdine; Museum Shop Mgr., Laura Palacio; Dir. Outreach, Tiffernay White; Collections Mgr., Dawn Cobb.
Personnel Profile: Full-Time Paid 74; Part-Time Paid 101; Part-Time Volunteers 250.
Governing Authority: board of trustees; nonprofit organization. Tax-exempt: 501(c)(3) & 170(b)(1)(A).
Science & Technology Center, Omnimax Theater & Planetarium.
Collections: ethnological; geological; technological; archaeology; entomology; ethnology; herpetology; mineralogy; paleontology; malacology; ornithology; rainforest with tropical bird species.
Research Fields: entomology; ichthyology; archaeology; paleontology; history of technology.
Facilities: restaurant; aquarium; Omnimax; planetarium. Museum-related items for sale.
Activities: lectures; films; science festivals; formally organized education programs for children & adults; docent program; internship program; school classes offered for kindergarten through college; permanent & temporary exhibitions; school loan service; outreach program; touch pool.
Publications: quarterly workshop bulletin; quarterly newsletter; annual teacher's guide; annual report.
Hours & Admission Prices: Mon.-Wed. 9-5, Thurs.-Sat. 9-6, Sun. 12-6. Adults $10, senior citizens 60 & over and youth 2-13 $8. Closed Easter; Thanksgiving; Christmas Eve & Day. ♿
Attendance: 525,000 (accurate)
Membership: Individual $35; Family & Grandparent $75; Sponsor $125; Adventurer $250-$500; Voyager $501-$1,000; Explorer $1,001-$2,500; Pioneer $2,501-$5,000.

HARVEY B. GANTT CENTER, 551 S. Tryon St., Charlotte, NC 28202. Tel.: 704-547-3700.
Web Site: www.aacc-charlotte.org
Formerly: Afro-American Cultural Center
Founded: 1974.
Congressional District: 12
Key Personnel: Pres. & C.E.O., David R. Taylor; Senior Dir. Operations, Carolyn Mints.
Governing Authority: private; nonprofit organization. Tax-exempt: 501(c)(3).
Cultural Center: housed in the former Little Rock AME Zion Church, c.1910.
Collections: African & African American art.
Activities: visual arts; performance arts; arts education.
Hours & Admission Prices: Tues.-Sat. 10-5, Sun. 1-5. Admission: $3.50. Closed New Year's Day; Easter; Independence Day; Thanksgiving; Christmas. ♿
Attendance: 50,000 (estimated)
Membership: Student & Senior Citizen $35; Individual $50; Professional Investor $55; Family $100; Community Investor $150; Ebony Society Bronze $250; Ebony Society Silver $500; Organizational Investor $600; Corporate & Ebony Society Gold $1,000.

HISTORIC ROSEDALE, 3427 N. Tryon St., Charlotte, NC 28206-2052. Tel.: 704-335-0325. Fax: 704-335-0384.
E-mail: roseplan@historicrosedale.org
Web Site: historicrosedale.org
Founded: 1989.
Congressional District: 12
Key Personnel: Exec. Dir., Deborah A. Hunter; Co Pres. (V), Agnes B. Weisiger; Co Pres. (V), James H. Williams; Dir. Education & Vol. Coord., Sara Craig.
Personnel Profile: Full-Time Paid 1; Part-Time Paid 4; Part-Time Volunteers 35; Interns 1.
Governing Authority: private; nonprofit organization. Parent Institution: Historic Rosedale Foundation. Tax-exempt.
General Museum.
Collections: period furniture; family items.
Research Fields: decorative arts of the Catawba River Valley; family history; African-American slaves on the plantation; mapping of area; use of herbs in medicinal practices; regional history.
Facilities: 150-vol. library; 400 sq. ft. exhibit space.
Activities: docent program; formal education programs for children; guided tours; lectures. Museum Sponsors: Spring Frolic With Dancing in the Gardens; Christmas at Rosedale; major guest speaker fundraiser.
Publications: quarterly newsletter, Historic Rosedale.
Hours & Admission Prices: Tours: Thurs.-Sun. 1:30-3; groups of 15 or more by appointment. Adults $5, senior citizens & children 4-18 $4; members and children 3 & under no charge. Closed major holidays.
Attendance: 7,500 (accurate)
Membership: Individual $35; Family $75; Patron $150; Sponsor $300; Benefactor $250; Silver $500; Gold $1,000; 1815 Society (3 Years) $1,000 & up.

LEVINE MUSEUM OF THE NEW SOUTH, (M), 200 E. Seventh St., Charlotte, NC 28202-2508. Tel.: 704-333-1887. Fax: 704-333-1896.
Web Site: www.museumofthenewsouth.org
Founded: 1991.
Congressional District: 12
Key Personnel: Pres. & C.E.O., Emily F. Zimmern; Chm., Rob Harrington; Treas., Ben Maffitt.
Personnel Profile: Full-Time Paid 15; Part-Time Paid 1; Part-Time Volunteers 20; Interns 4.
Governing Authority: nonprofit organization. Tax-exempt: 501(c)(3).
History Museum.
Collections: history of American South from the Civil War to present.
Major Exhibits: Changing Places, 11/09-2/11.
Research Fields: local history.
Facilities: education & social program areas.
Activities: formal educational programs for adults, children & students; guided tours; lectures; loan & participatory exhibitions; training programs for professional museum workers; oral & multi-media history presentation.
Publications: newsletter; book.
Hours & Admission Prices: Mon.-Sat. 10-5, Sun. 12-5. Adults $6; discounts to AAM & ICOM members; members no charge. Closed New Year's Day; Memorial Day; Independence Day; Labor Day; Thanksgiving; Christmas. ♿
Attendance: 57,000 (estimated)
Membership: Individual $35; Household $60.

THE LIGHT FACTORY - CONTEMPORARY MUSEUM OF PHOTOGRAPHY & FILM, 345 N. College St., Spirit Square, Ste. 211, Charlotte, NC 28202-2113. Tel.: 704-333-9755. Fax: 704-333-5910.
E-mail: info@lightfactory.org
Web Site: www.lightfactory.org
Founded: 1972.
Congressional District: 12
Key Personnel: Exec. Dir., Marcie Kelso; Chm. (V), Steve Cohen; Treas., Steve Menaker; Chief Cur., Dennis Kiel.
Personnel Profile: Full-Time Paid 8; Part-Time Paid 1; Part-Time Volunteers 150; Interns 5.
Governing Authority: private; nonprofit organization. Tax-exempt: 501(c)(3).
Art Museum.
Collections: light-generated media including photography, video & film.
Research Fields: contemporary photography; interactive new media.
Facilities: 500-vol. library of art & photography books available to the public; 3,500 sq. ft. exhibit space; classroom; darkroom.
Activities: educational programs; films; guided tours; hobby workshops; lectures; traveling exhibitions; community outreach; special events.
Publications: quarterly newsletter; quarterly calendar; catalogues.
Hours & Admission Prices: Mon.-Sat. 9-6, Sun. 1-6. No charge; donations accepted. Closed New Year's Day; Easter; Independence Day; Thanksgiving; Christmas; major holidays. ♿
Attendance: 70,000 (estimated)
Membership: Students & Senior Citizens $25; Individual $40; Family $75; Associate $125; Patron $250; Collector's Circle $500; Corporate $1,000.

MINT MUSEUM OF ART, 2730 Randolph Rd., Charlotte, NC 28207-2031. Tel.: 704-337-2000. Fax: 704-337-2101. TDD: 704-337-2096.
E-mail: info@mintmuseum.org
Web Site: www.mintmuseum.org
Founded: 1936.
Congressional District: 9
Key Personnel: Exec. Dir., Phil Kline; Chm., Beverly Hance; C.F.O., Mike Smith; Chief Cur. Fine Art, Charles Mo; Dir. Education, Cheryl Palmer; Chief Cur. Craft & Design, Annie Carlano; Cur. American Art, Jonathan Stuhlman; Cur. Contemporary Art, Carla Hanzal; Cur. Decorative Arts, Brian D. Gallagher; Asst. Cur. Craft + Design, Allie Farlowe; Mgr. Public Rels., Elizabeth Isenhour; Head Design & Installation, Kurt Warnke; Registrar, Martha T. Mayberry; Librarian, Joyce Weaver; Museum Shop Mgr., Sandy Fisher; Facility Mgr., Hank McKiernan.
Personnel Profile: Full-Time Paid 45; Part-Time Paid 25; Part-Time Volunteers 2,313; Interns 20.
Governing Authority: nonprofit organization. Parent Institution: The Mint Museums. Tax-exempt.
Art Museum: housed in 1835 first branch of the U.S. Mint, expanded in 1967 & 1985.
Collections: American & European paintings, furniture & decorative arts; African, pre-Columbian & Spanish Colonial art; porcelain & pottery; historic costumes; North Carolina pottery; contemporary art.
Research Fields: European, American & pre-Columbian art; Delhom Gallery devoted to research & study in ceramics.
Facilities: 15,000-vol. library of art books & periodicals available for use on premises; 180-seat auditorium. Paintings, sculpture, pottery, prints, art books, reproductions of jewelry, sculpture & postcards for sale.
Activities: guided tours; lectures; gallery talks; concerts; formally organized educational programs; docent program; inter-museum loan, permanent, temporary & traveling exhibitions.
Publications: bimonthly, Mint Museum Member News; catalogs of major exhibitions; books, North Carolina Pottery; Experience Art at the Mint Museums: A Look at the Collections; bi-weekly email, Mint e-News.
Hours & Admission Prices: Tues. 10-9, Wed.-Sat. 10-5. Adults $10, seniors & college students $8, children 5-16 $5; discounts to Southeastern & North American Reciprocal members; members and children 4 & under no charge. Closed holidays. ♿
Attendance: 150,000 (estimated)
Membership: Student & Teach $45; Individual $60; Family $100; Silver Circle $1,000; Gold Circle $2,500; Platinum Circle $5,000; Chairman's Circle $10,000.

* **MINT MUSEUM OF CRAFT + DESIGN, (M),** 220 N. Tryon St., Charlotte, NC 28202-2137. Tel.: 704-337-2000. Fax: 704-337-2101. TDD: 704-337-2096.
E-mail: info@mintmuseum.org
Web Site: www.mintmuseum.org
Founded: 1999.
Congressional District: 9
Key Personnel: Exec. Dir., Phil Kline; Chm. (V), Beverly Hance; Chief Cur. Craft + Design, Annie Carlano; Chief Cur. Fine Art, Charles Mo; Cur. Contemporary Art, Carla Hanzal; Cur. American Art, Jonathan Stuhlman; Asst. Cur. Craft + Design, Allie Farlowe; Cur. Decorative Arts, Brian D. Gallagher; Mgr. Public Rels., Elizabeth Isenhour; Dir. Education, Cheryl Palmer; Facility Mgr., Hank McKiernan; Head Design & Installation, Kurt Warnke; Registrar, Martha T. Mayberry; Librarian, Joyce Weaver; Museum Shop Mgr., Irene Balboni.
Personnel Profile: Full-Time Paid 45; Part-Time Paid 25; Part-Time Volunteers 2,313; Interns 20.
Governing Authority: nonprofit organization. Parent Institution: The Mint Museum. Tax-exempt.
Craft Museum.
Collections: ceramics; fiber; glass; metal; wood.
Research Fields: studio crafts.
Activities: guided tours; gallery talks; lectures; artist demonstrations; temporary & traveling exhibitions.
Publications: Allan Chasanoff Ceramic Collection; Constructing Elozua: A Retrospective in 2004; The Nature of Craft and the Penland Experience; Spectrum: The Sculpture of John Kuhn.
Hours & Admission Prices: Tues.-Sat. 10-5. Adults $10, seniors & college students $8, children 5-17 $5; children 4 & under, Tues. 10-2 & third Thurs. 5-8 no charge. Closed major holidays. ♿
Attendance: 150,000 (estimated)
Membership: Student & Teacher $45; Individual $60; Dual $80; Family $100;

Silver Circle & Founders' Circle $1,000; Gold Circle $2,500; Platinum Circle $5,000; Chairman's Circle $10,000.

PUBLIC LIBRARY OF CHARLOTTE AND MECKLENBURG COUNTY, 310 N. Tryon St., Charlotte, NC 28202-2139. Tel.: 704-416-0100.
Web Site: www.plcmc.org
Founded: 1903.
Congressional District: 9
Key Personnel: Mgr., Patrice Ebert.
Governing Authority: nonprofit. Tax-exempt: 170(b)(1)(A).
Public Library.
Collections: books; films.
Research Fields: local history; genealogy.
Facilities: library; reading room; 200-seat auditorium.
Activities: guided tours; films; local artist gallery.
Publications: Friends of Library newsletter; Business Information newsletter; bibliographies; PLCMC News; Annual Report.
Hours & Admission Prices: Mon.-Thurs. 9-9, Fri.-Sat. 9-6, Sun. 1-6. No charge. Closed national holidays. ♿

SPIRIT SQUARE CENTER FOR ARTS AND EDUCATION, 345 N. College St., Charlotte, NC 28202-2113. Mailing Address: North Carolina Blumenthal Performing Arts Center, P.O. Box 37322, Charlotte, NC 28237. Tel.: 704-372-1000.
Web Site: www.blumenthalcenter.org
Key Personnel: Pres., Tom Gabbard; Public Rels. & Media, Kathy Scott Rummage.
Personnel Profile: Full-Time Paid 84; Part-Time Paid 17; Part-Time Volunteers 447; Interns 9.
Art Gallery.
Collections: paintings.
Facilities: 720-seat theater.
Activities: classes.
Hours & Admission Prices: Call for hours.
Attendance: 298,729 (estimated)

WING HAVEN GARDENS AND BIRD SANCTUARY, 248 Ridgewood Ave., Charlotte, NC 28209-1632. Tel.: 704-331-0664.
E-mail: winghavengardens@carolina.rr.com
Web Site: www.winghavengardens.com
Founded: 1927.
Congressional District: 9
Key Personnel: Exec. Dir., Dia Steiger; Pres. (V), Al Waugh; Cur. Garden, Jeffrey Drum.
Personnel Profile: Full-Time Paid 5; Part-Time Paid 4; Part-Time Volunteers 400.
Governing Authority: Parent Institution: Wing Haven Foundation, Inc. Tax-exempt.
Arboretum.
Collections: living plants; garden statuary.
Facilities: nature conservation center; gardens. Plants & nursery-related items for sale.
Activities: guided tours; programs.
Publications: newsletter: Wing Haven; Birds of Charlotte and Mecklenburg County; Verses from the Garden; Guide to Wing Haven; A Bird in the House.
Hours & Admission Prices: Tues. 3-5, Wed. 10-12, Sat. 10-5; groups by appointment. Suggested Donation: $5. ♿
Attendance: 7,300 (accurate)
Membership: Individual $35; Family $65; Patron $100; Grand Patron $250; Sponsor $500; Benefactor $1,000; Founder $2,500; Clarkson Society $5,000.

Cherokee

MOUNTAIN FARM MUSEUM-GREAT SMOKY MOUNTAINS NATIONAL PARK, 1194 Newfound Gap Rd., Cherokee, NC 28719-8249. Tel.: 828-497-1900 & 1904. Fax: 828-497-1910.
E-mail: grsm_smokies_information@nps.gov
Web Site: nps.gov/grsm
Founded: 1953.
Congressional District: 11
Key Personnel: Site Supvr., Lynda Doucette.
Personnel Profile: Full-Time Paid 1; Part-Time Volunteers 6.
Governing Authority: federal. Parent Institution: Great Smoky Mountains National Park Service, Gatlinburg, TN 37738; Tel. 865-436-1256; 436-1200 (automated information). Tax-exempt.
Park Visitor Center.
Collections: 10 historic farm buildings, including dwellings moved to current location from throughout Great Smoky Mountains National Park.
Facilities: Postcards, slides & books for sale.
Activities: permanent exhibitions.
Publications: self guiding booklet, Mountain Farm Museum.
Hours & Admission Prices: Call for hours. No charge; donations accepted. Closed Christmas. ♿

MUSEUM OF THE CHEROKEE INDIAN, 589 Tsali Blvd., Cherokee, NC 28719. Mailing Address: P.O. Box 1599, Cherokee, NC 28719-1599. Tel.: 828-497-3481. Fax: 828-497-4985.
E-mail: littlejohn@cherokeemuseum.org
Web Site: www.cherokeemuseum.org
Founded: 1948.
Congressional District: 11
Key Personnel: Dir., Ken Blankenship; Administrative Mgr. & Museum Shop Mgr., Sharon Littlejohn; Facilities Mgr., Driver Pheasant, Jr.; Financial, Wendy McRay.
Personnel Profile: Full-Time Paid 12.
Governing Authority: nonprofit organization. Owned by the Eastern Band of Cherokee Indians. Tax-exempt: 501(c)(3).
Cherokee Indian Museum.
Collections: Indian artifacts; relics; archives; 16th century Cherokee homestead exhibit.
Research Fields: Cherokee Culture; history; language.
Facilities: 3,000-vol. rare document reference library.
Activities: self-guided tours; interactive exhibit.
Publications: annual, Journal of Cherokee Studies.
Hours & Admission Prices: Memorial Day to Labor Day Mon.-Sat. 9-7, Sun. 9-5; Sept.-May daily 9-5. Adults $9, children 6-14 $6; complimentary subscription to Journal for members; discounts for AAA & AARP members Jan.-May, groups & AAM members; members & children 5 & under no charge. Closed New Year's Day; Thanksgiving; Christmas. ♿
Attendance: 150,000
Membership: Individual & Institution $30; Family $50; Friend $100; Clan $250; Tsali $500; Chief $1,000.

Cherryville

C. GRIER BEAM TRUCK MUSEUM, 111 N. Mountain St., Cherryville, NC 28021-2940. Mailing Address: P.O. Box 238, Cherryville, NC 28021-0238. Tel.: 704-435-3072. Fax: 704-445-9010.
E-mail: jdismukes@carolina.rr.com
Web Site: www.beamtruckmuseum.com
Founded: 1982.
Congressional District: 10
Key Personnel: C.E.O. & Chm. (V), Michael N. Beam; Pres., Sandra B. Dismukes; Museum Shop Mgr., Joseph C. Dismukes.
Personnel Profile: Full-Time Paid 2; Part-Time Paid 4; Part-Time Volunteers 6.
Governing Authority: board of directors. Tax-exempt.
Transportation Museum.
Collections: 14 trucks; history of Carolina trucking company.
Facilities: Museum-related items for sale.
Activities: Museum Sponsors: Annual Spring Antique Car Show; Antique Farm Tractor Show in August; Open House during Christmas.
Hours & Admission Prices: Thurs. & Sat. 10-3, Fri. 10-5. No charge; donations accepted. Closed New Year's Day; Independence Day; Christmas. ♿
Attendance: 3,000 (estimated)
Membership: Annual $15.

CHERRYVILLE HISTORICAL MUSEUM, 109 E. Main St., Cherryville, NC 28021-3406. Mailing Address: P.O. Box 307, Cherryville, NC 28021-0307. Tel.: 704-435-8011.
Historic Building: built in 1911.
Collections: local history & culture; fire truck; photographs; art; medical instruments; farm equipment; period artifacts.
Facilities: library. Museum-related items for sale.
Hours & Admission Prices: Sat. 10-2.

Columbus

POLK COUNTY HISTORICAL ASSOCIATION MUSEUM, 60 Walker St., Columbus, NC 28722. Mailing Address: P.O. Box 503, Columbus, NC 28722-0503. Tel.: 828-894-3351.
Web Site: www.polkcounty.org
Founded: 1980.
History Museum.
Collections: Cherokee Indian artifacts; early settlers; Revolutionary War; Civil War; WWI & WWII; settlers' tools & clothing; railroad memorabilia; personal artifacts; photographs; paintings.
Hours & Admission Prices: Tues. & Thurs. 10-1, Sat. 10-4; other times by appointment. ♿

Membership: Individual $15-$25; Corporate $50; Lifetime $150.

Concord

BACKING UP CLASSICS AUTO MUSEUM, 4545 Concord Pkwy. S., Concord, NC 28027-4618. Tel.: 704-788-9500.
E-mail: info@morrisonmotorco.com
Web Site: www.morrisonmotorco.com
Key Personnel: Dir., Lindsay Morrison Hartman
Classic Car Museum.
Collections: over 50 vehicles including classics, 50s, 60s, & period cars; photographs.
Facilities: 18,000 sq. ft. exhibit space. Museum-related items for sale.
Activities: rental facilities.
Hours & Admission Prices: Spring-Summer: Mon.-Fri. 9-6, Sat. 9-5, Sun. 11-5; Fall-Winter: Mon.-Fri. & Sun. 10-5, Sat. 9-5.

Corolla

THE WHALEHEAD CLUB, (M), 1100 Club Rd., Corolla, NC 27927. Mailing Address: P.O. Box 307, Corolla, NC 27927-0307. Tel.: 252-453-9040. Fax: 252-457-0129.
Founded: 1992.
Key Personnel: Dir. & Devel., Edna Baden; Pres. (V), Horace Bell; Public Rels., Vickie Schreffler; Treas., Kimberley Hoey; Cur., Jill Landen; Museum Shop Mgr., Terry Blocher.
Personnel Profile: Full-Time Paid 6; Part-Time Paid 16; Part-Time Volunteers 9; Interns 2.
Governing Authority: private; nonprofit organization. Tax-exempt: 501(c)(3).
Historic House Museum: listed on the National Register of Historic Sites.
Collections: Art Nouveau; 1920s-1930s decorative arts; Hunt Club history. Historic Structures: house; boathouse; bridge.
Research Fields: history of the Knight family & their servants; Art Nouveau; Tiffany; Hunt Club's on the Northern Outer Banks of North Carolina.
Facilities: 21,000 sq. ft. exhibit space. Museum-related items for sale.
Activities: arts festivals; concerts; docent program; guided tours. Annual Events: Spring Social Fundraising Event; Excursion Day; Independence Day; Haunted Village; Wine Festival.
Publications: seasonal newsletter, The Whalehead Window.
Hours & Admission Prices: March-Nov. daily 9-5; Dec.-Feb. Mon.-Sat. 9-5. Adults $7; children 8 & under no charge. Closed New Year's Day; Martin Luther King Jr. Day; Easter; Thanksgiving; Christmas Eve, Day & day after.
Attendance: 20,000 (accurate)
Membership: Senior $20; Individual $50; Family $100; Contributor $250; Donor $500; Sustainer $1,000; Knight's Circle $5,000.

Creswell

SOMERSET PLACE STATE HISTORIC SITE, 2572 Lake Shore Rd., Creswell, NC 27928-9174. Tel.: 252-797-4560. Fax: 252-797-4171.
E-mail: somerset@ncdcr.gov
Web Site: www.nchistoricsites.org/somerset
Founded: 1969.
Congressional District: 1
Key Personnel: Site Mgr., Karen Hayes; Museum Shop Mgr., Lisa Biggs.
Personnel Profile: Full-Time Paid 4; Part-Time Paid 1.
Governing Authority: state. Parent Institution: North Carolina Department of Cultural Resources, 109 E. Jones St., Raleigh, NC. 27601-2807. Tax-exempt: 501(c)(3).
Plantation.
Collections: agriculture; dairy; ice house; smoke house; kitchen storehouse; kitchen-laundry; 1790-1910 plantation slave records & federal population census schedules for Chowan, Tyrrell & Washington counties. Historic Houses include c.1820 Colony House, 1830 Collins Mansion House, excavated dwellings in slave community; two-story four room slave quarter; one room slave quarter; slave hospital.
Research Fields: African-American history; agriculture; archaeology; 19th-century decorative arts.
Facilities: visitor center; historic plantation buildings.
Activities: guided tours; lectures; permanent exhibitions.
Publications: brochure; newsletter.
Hours & Admission Prices: April-Oct. Mon.-Sat. 9-5, Sun. 1-5; Nov.-March Mon.-Sat. 10-4, Sun. 1-4. No charge, donations accepted. Closed holidays. ♿
Attendance: 23,407 (accurate)
Membership: Individual $20; Family $30; Donor $50; Patron $100; Friend $500; Benefactor $1,000.

Crossnore

CROSSNORE WEAVERS AND GALLERY: A WORKING MUSEUM, 205 Johnson Lane, Crossnore, NC 28616. Mailing Address: P.O. Box 249, Crossnore, NC 28616-0249. Tel.: 828-733-4660. Fax: 828-733-3250.
E-mail: mhill@crossnoreschool.org
Web Site: crossnoreweavers.org
Formerly: The Weaving Room
Founded: 1920.
Congressional District: 11
Key Personnel: Dir., Martha Hill; Chm. (V), Freda Nichols.
Personnel Profile: Full-Time Paid 1; Part-Time Paid 2; Part-Time Volunteers 4.
Governing Authority: bd. of trustees. Parent Institution: Crossnore School. Subsidiary Institution: Crossnore Weavers. Tax-exempt.
History Museum: listed on the National Register of Historical Places.
Collections: early American life; period furnishings & looms.
Activities: handweaving demonstrations.
Publications: newsletter, The Crossnore School; catalogue, Crossnore Weavers: A Working Museum.
Hours & Admission Prices: Mon.-Sat. 9-5. No charge.Closed Easter; Thanksgiving; Christmas. ♿
Attendance: 5,500 (estimated)

Cullowhee

FINE ARTS MUSEUM - WESTERN CAROLINA UNIVERSITY FINE & PERFORMING ARTS CENTER, Cullowhee, NC 28723. Tel.: 828-227-2479 & 3591. Fax: 828-227-7632.
E-mail: lormand@wcu.edu
Web Site: www.wcu.edu/fapac/Galleries/
Key Personnel: Dir., Paul Lormand
Fine Arts Museum.
Collections: works by contemporary artists.
Facilities: 10,000 sq. ft. exhibit space.
Hours & Admission Prices: Tues.-Fri. 10-4, Sat. 1-4. No charge; donations accepted. Closed university holidays; academic breaks.

MOUNTAIN HERITAGE CENTER, (M), Western Carolina University, 150 H. F. Robinson Bldg., Cullowhee, NC 28723. Tel.: 828-227-7129.
Web Site: www.wcu.edu/mhc
Founded: 1975.
Congressional District: 11
Key Personnel: Dir., L. Scott Philyaw; Cur., Trevor Jones; Education Specialist, Peter Koch; Historic Interpreter, David Brewin; Coord. Events, Trina Royar; Office Mgr., Sona Norton; Digital Projects, Christie Osborne.
Personnel Profile: Full-Time Paid 6; Part-Time Paid 2; Part-Time Volunteers 7; Interns 3.
Governing Authority: university. Parent Institution: Western Carolina University, Cullowhee. Tel.: 828-227-7211. Tax-exempt: 170(b)(1)(A).
History Museum.
Collections: Center: Cherokees & the European pioneer artifacts; tools; photographs; oral history; folklore recordings. Library: manuscripts & records.
Major Exhibits: Our State Dog: North Carolina's Plott Hound (T), 11/09-4/10; Decoration Day (T), 11/09-5/10.
Research Fields: Scotch-Irish migration; Appalachian culture; folklore; regional history; Cherokee Indian history.
Facilities: research room; 91-seat auditorium.
Activities: guided tours; lectures; films; permanent exhibits; formally organized educational programs; permanent, temporary & traveling exhibitions. Museum Sponsors: Migration of the Scotch-Irish; Mountain Heritage Day in September.
Publications: book, Our Western North Carolina Mountain Heritage; Leave-taking: The Scotch Irish Come to Western North Carolina.
Hours & Admission Prices: June-Oct. Mon.-Wed. & Fri. 8-5, Thurs. 8-8, Sat. 10-5; Nov.-May Mon.-Wed. & Fri. 8-5, Thurs. 8-8. No charge. Closed Christmas to New Year's Day. ♿
Attendance: 30,000 (estimated)
Membership: Annual $25.

Currie

MOORES CREEK NATIONAL BATTLEFIELD, 40 Patriots Hall Dr., Currie, NC 28435. Tel.: 910-283-5591. Fax: 910-283-5351.
Web Site: www.nps.gov/mocr
Founded: 1926.
Congressional District: 1 & 3
Key Personnel: Park Ranger, Timothy Boyd.
Personnel Profile: Full-Time Paid 4; Part-Time Paid 1; Part-Time Volunteers 3; Interns 1.
Governing Authority: federal. Parent Institution: U.S. Dept. of the Interior, National Park Service.

Military Museum: located on the site of the Feb. 27, 1776 Battle of Moores Creek Bridge.
Collections: weapons; diorama.
Research Fields: history of the park, including period before park establishment in 1926.
Facilities: library of North Carolina, Revolutionary War history; parks; environment books, available for use on premises. Historical booklets, books, cards & museum-related items for sale.
Activities: two self-guiding trails: History Trail; Tarheel Trail.
Publications: brochure, Moores Creek National Battlefield; Moores Creek Bridge Campaign; Roster of the Loyalists at the Battle of Moores Creek; Roster of the Patriots at the Battle of Moores Creek; poster, Colonial Militia; video, Moores Creek Bridge.
Hours & Admission Prices: Daily 9-5. No charge. Closed New Year's Day; Christmas. ♿
Attendance: 48,988 (accurate)
Membership: Student $5; Individual $10; Family & Group $25; Corporate $100; Patron $125; Life Individual $150; Life Family $200; Life Benefactor $500.

Dallas

* **GASTON COUNTY MUSEUM OF ART AND HISTORY, (M),** 131 W. Main St., Dallas, NC 28034-2021. Mailing Address: P.O. Box 429, Dallas, NC 28034-0429. Tel.: 704-922-7681. Fax: 704-922-7683.
E-mail: museum@co.gaston.nc.us
Web Site: www.gastoncountymuseum.org
Founded: 1975.
Congressional District: 10
Key Personnel: Dir., Elizabeth E. Dampier; Vice Chm., Charles Lineberger; Administrative Asst., Elaine Jackson; Programs Coord., Jeffery Pruett; Registrar, Regan Brooks.
Personnel Profile: Full-Time Paid 5; Part-Time Paid 2; Part-Time Volunteers 25; Interns 1.
Governing Authority: county; nonprofit. Tax-exempt: 501(c)(3).
Art and History Museum: housed in 1852 Hoffman Hotel.
Collections: art; regional history; carriage & sleigh collection; textiles; 19th-century parlors, including hands-on parlor. Historic Buildings: 1901 Dallas Depot; 1852 Hoffman Hotel; 1848 Gaston County Jail.
Research Fields: regional history; textile history.
Facilities: classrooms. Museum-related items for sale.
Activities: guided tours; lectures; workshops; educational programs; loan, permanent, temporary & traveling exhibitions.
Publications: walking tour guide for historic district, Historic Dallas: A Stroll Through 19th Century America; Patchwork.
Hours & Admission Prices: Tues.-Fri. 10-5, Sat. 10-3, 1st Sun. of month 2-5; other times by appointment. No charge. Closed holidays. ♿
Attendance: 27,000 (estimated)
Membership: Student & Senior $15; Gaston County Individual $25; Non-resident Individual $30; Gaston County Family $40; Non-resident Family $50; Benefactor $100; Sustainer $250; Patron $500; Gaston Gold Society $1,000.

Davidson

VAN EVERY/SMITH GALLERIES, (M), 315 N. Main St., Davidson College Visual Arts Center, Davidson, NC 28036-9404. Mailing Address: P.O. Box 7117, Davidson, NC 28035-7117. Tel.: 704-894-2520 & 2519. Fax: 704-894-2691.
E-mail: brthomas@davidson.edu
Web Site: www.davidson.edu
Founded: 1962.
Congressional District: 9
Key Personnel: Dir., Brad Thomas.
Personnel Profile: Full-Time Paid 1; Part-Time Paid 11.
Governing Authority: college. Parent Institution: Davidson College. Subsidiary Institution: William H. Van Every & Edward M. Smith Galleries. Tax-exempt.
College Art Gallery.
Collections: 15th- to 20th-century graphics; painting; sculpture; photography.
Activities: lectures; gallery talks; temporary exhibitions.
Publications: exhibition brochures with essay & posters.
Hours & Admission Prices: Sept.-May Mon.-Fri. 10-5, Sat.-Sun. 12-4. No charge. Closed college & national holidays. ♿
Attendance: 4,000 (accurate)

Durham

BENNETT PLACE STATE HISTORIC SITE, 4409 Bennett Memorial Road, Durham, NC 27705-2307. Tel.: 919-383-4345. Fax: 919-383-4349.
E-mail: bennett@ncdcr.gov
Web Site: www.bennettplace.nchistoricsites.org
Formerly: Bennett Farm
Founded: 1961.
Congressional District: 2
Key Personnel: Site Mgr., John Guss; Pres. Support Group, Karen Edwards.
Personnel Profile: Full-Time Paid 3; Part-Time Paid 1; Part-Time Volunteers 12; Interns 1.
Governing Authority: state. Parent Institution: North Carolina Dept. of Cultural Resources, 109 E. Jones St., Raleigh, NC 27611. Tax-exempt: 170(b).
Military Museum & Historic Farm: reconstructed c.1850 Bennett House.
Collections: log kitchen; history; Civil War; military uniforms & civilian clothing; historic structures; weaponry; farm implements; paintings.
Research Fields: Civil War & Agriculture in North Carolina.
Facilities: library; visitor center; nature trail; picnic area. Gift-related items for sale.
Activities: guided tours; costumed interpretation; special events; theater presentation; school programs.
Publications: brochure; newsletter; Bennett Place Courier.
Hours & Admission Prices: Tues.-Sat. 9-5. No charge; donations accepted. Closed major holidays. ♿
Attendance: 22,000 (estimated)

DUKE HOMESTEAD STATE HISTORIC SITE, 2828 Duke Homestead Rd., Durham, NC 27705-2726. Tel.: 919-477-5498. Fax: 919-479-7092.
E-mail: duke@ncdcr.gov
Web Site: www.ibiblio.org/dukehome
Founded: 1974.
Congressional District: 2
Key Personnel: Site Mgr. & Museum Shop Mgr., Jennifer Farley; Pres. (V), Walker Stone; Pres. (V), David Welsh.
Personnel Profile: Full-Time Paid 4; Part-Time Paid 4; Part-Time Volunteers 50.
Governing Authority: state. North Carolina Dept. of Cultural Resources, 109 E. Jones St., Raleigh 27611. Tax-exempt: 501(c)(3) & 170(b)(1)(A).
Historic House: 1852 homestead of Washington Duke, founder of the American Tobacco Co.
Collections: furnished house of early 1870s; tobacco barn; well house; packhouse; 1870 third factory; reconstructed first factory; tobacco history.
Research Fields: tobacco history.
Facilities: visitor center; historic house; barns.
Activities: guided tours; lectures; audiovisual program; craft workshops; participatory demonstrations; special events; formally organized education program for children.
Publications: guide book; biannual publication.
Hours & Admission Prices: Tues.-Sat. 9-5. No charge; donations accepted. Closed Thanksgiving; Christmas Eve & Day. ♿
Attendance: 18,000 (accurate)
Membership: Family $25-$49; Hander $50-$99; Stringer $100-$249; Primer $250-$499; Grower $500-$999; Corporate & Charter $1,000 & up.

HISTORIC STAGVILLE, 5828 Old Oxford Hwy., Durham, NC 27712-9758. Tel.: 919-620-0120.
E-mail: info@stagville.org
Web Site: www.stagville.org
Founded: 1977.
Congressional District: 4
Key Personnel: Site Mgr., Frachele Scott.
Personnel Profile: Full-Time Paid 2; Part-Time Paid 2; Part-Time Volunteers 3; Interns 5.
Governing Authority: state; nonprofit corporation. Parent Institution: North Carolina, Div. of Archives & History, Dept. of Cultural Resources, 4610 Mail Service Center, Raleigh, NC 27699-4610. Tax-exempt.
Historic House.
Collections: furniture & furnishings of the period; farm implements; tools. Historic Buildings: 1787 Plantation House; 1860 Slave Cabins; 1860 Barn; late 18th-century Cottage.
Research Fields: African-American history; oral history; preservation education; southern & plantation history.
Facilities: classroom building.
Activities: guided tours; classes in historic architecture, preservation, African-American history; historic landscapes; restoration.
Publications: newsletter, The Key.
Hours & Admission Prices: Tours: Tues.-Sat. 10-3. No charge; donations accepted. Closed New Year's Day; Martin Luther King Jr. Day; Good Friday; Memorial Day; Independence Day; Labor Day; Veterans Day; Thanksgiving; Christmas. ♿
Attendance: 7,000 (estimated)
Membership: Individual $25; Joint $30; Contributing $50; Sustaining $100; Patron $200; Benefactor $500.

HISTORY OF MEDICINE COLLECTIONS, Duke University Medical Center Library, Durham, NC 27710-0001. Mailing Address: DUMC 3702, Durham, NC 27710-0001. Tel.: 919-660-1143 & 1144. Fax: 919-681-7599.
E-mail: mclhistory@mc.duke.edu
Web Site: www.mclibrary.duke.edu/hmc
Founded: 1930.
Key Personnel: Cur., Suzanne Porter.
Personnel Profile: Full-Time Paid 1; Part-Time Paid 1.
Governing Authority: university. Parent Institution: Duke University. Tax-exempt: 501(c)(3).
University Library.
Collections: books; journals; manuscripts; medical instruments & artifacts; prints; photographs.
Research Fields: history of medicine.
Facilities: 33,000-vol. library of medical & scientific books, journals, manuscripts, reference material on the history of medicine & biology available for research on premises; reading room; medicinal herb garden.
Activities: lectures; formally organized education programs for graduate students; temporary exhibitions.
Publications: newsletter, Trent Associates Report.
Hours & Admission Prices: Tues.-Fri. 10-4; appointments encouraged. No charge. ♿
Attendance: 2,000 (estimated)
Membership: Trent Associates: Member $25; Contributing $50; Sustaining $100.

MUSEUM OF LIFE AND SCIENCE, 433 W. Murray Ave., Durham, NC 27704-3101. Tel.: 919-220-5429. Fax: 919-220-5575.
E-mail: contactus@ncmls.org
Web Site: www.ncmls.org
Formerly: North Carolina Museum of Life and Science
Founded: 1946.
Congressional District: 2
Key Personnel: C.E.O. & Pres., Barry Van Deman; Vice Pres. Exhibits & Planning, Roy Griffiths; Dir. Sales & Guest Svcs., Julie Lucier; Publicity Dir., Allison Savicz; Dir. Mktg., Greg Tenhover; Animal Dir., Sherry Samuels; Dir. Butterfly House & Insectarium, Uli Hartmond; Vice Pres. External Rels., Julie Ketner Rigby; Interim Vice Pres. Education, Shawntel Landavazo.
Personnel Profile: Full-Time Paid 58; Part-Time Paid 14; Part-Time Volunteers 350; Interns 4.
Governing Authority: nonprofit organization. Tax-exempt: 501(c)(3).
Science & Technology Center.
Collections: hands-on science exhibits; wildlife & flora indigenous to North Carolina; small railway; weather; communications; physics; geology; paleontology; aerospace; animal habitats; biology; children's exhibits; physical & natural science discovery rooms; classrooms; farmyard & animals; moonrook; meteorite; large animals including bears & red wolves; Magic Wings Butterfly House: 1,000 exotic butterflies from Africa, Asia, Central & South America; Aventis CropScience Insectarium: live insects & their predators, specimens, interactive exhibits, murals; insect environments.
Research Fields: science & technology education.
Facilities: butterfly house & insectarium; discovery rooms; lab & classrooms; meeting room with A/V booth; catering kitchen; 70-acre outdoor campus features outdoor exhibit areas, farmyard, small railway, nature park with animals & outdoor maze; cafe. Museum-related items for sale.
Activities: classes; lectures; science-in-suitcase outreach program; after-school programs; teacher training; special events; demonstrations. Annual Event: science camp in summer.
Publications: bimonthly newsletter; teacher's guide; school guide; visitor's guide; corporate newsletter.
Hours & Admission Prices: Jan-Sept. 13 & Dec. 15-Dec. 31 Mon.-Sat. 10-5, Sun. 12-5; Sept. 14-Dec. 14 Tues.-Sat. 10-5, Sun. 12-5. Adults $12.50, senior citizens 65 & over and military with ID $10.50, children 3-12 $9.50; discounts to AAA members; members & children under 3 no charge. Train Rides $2.50. Closed New Year's Day; Thanksgiving; Christmas. ♿
Attendance: 300,000 (accurate)
Membership: Couple $65; Four People $95; Six People $125; Eight People $145.

NCCU ART MUSEUM, (M), North Carolina Central University, Lawson St. (Btw. Fine Arts Bldg. & Music Bldg.), Durham, NC 27707. Mailing Address: P.O. Box 19555, Durham, NC 27703. Tel.: 919-530-6211. Fax: 919-560-5649.
Web Site: web.nccu.edu/artmuseum
Founded: 1971.
Congressional District: 4
Key Personnel: Dir., Kenneth G. Rodgers; Registrar, Pat Jones.
Governing Authority: state; nonprofit. Parent Institution: University of North Carolina. Subsidiary Institution: North Carolina Central University. Tax-exempt: 501(c)(3); 170(b)(1)(A); 509(A)(1).
University Art Museum.
Collections: contemporary painting, sculpture, & original prints with a focus on the works by African American artists; traditional African sculpture & artifacts.
Research Fields: minority artists; exhibition subjects.
Activities: lectures; gallery talks; formally organized education programs for undergraduate college students; loan, permanent, temporary & traveling exhibitions.
Publications: catalogue; American Landscape East & West: 1820-1920; Duncanson: A British-American Connection; Geoffrey Holder, Painter; Gullah Life Reflections: A Traveling Exhibition of the Paintings of Jonathan Green; Joy of Living: Romare Bearden's Late Work.
Hours & Admission Prices: Tues.-Fri. 9-5, Sun. 2-5. No charge. ♿

* **NASHER MUSEUM OF ART AT DUKE UNIVERSITY, (M),** 2001 Campus Dr., Durham, NC 27705-1003. Mailing Address: P.O. Box 90732, Durham, NC 27708-0732. Tel.: 919-684-5135. Fax: 919-681-8624.
E-mail: nasherinfo@duke.edu
Web Site: www.nasher.duke.edu
Formerly: Duke University Museum of Art
Founded: 1969.
Congressional District: 2
Key Personnel: C.E.O., Pres. & Pres. of Duke University, Richard H. Brodhead; Dir., Dr. Kimerly Rorschach; Pres., Peg Palmer; Pres., Margie Satinsky; Coord. Membership, Amy Weaver; Cur., Dr. Sarah W. Schroth; Dir. Devel., Kristen Greenaway; Mgr. Mktg. & Communications, Wendy Hower Livingston; Registrar, Myra Scott; Coord. Special Events, Kathleen Wright; Cur., Trevor Schoonmaker; Cur., Anne Schroder; Deputy Dir. Operations, Dorothy Clark; Museum Shop Mgr., Arienne Cheek.
Personnel Profile: Full-Time Paid 29; Part-Time Paid 2; Part-Time Volunteers 100; Interns 12.
Governing Authority: university. Parent Institution: Duke University. Tax-exempt: 501(c)(3).
Art Museum.
Collections: modern & contemporary art; African art; Greek & Roman period artifacts; early American art; American & European paintings, sculpture & works on paper; medieval sculpture.
Research Fields: pertaining to collections.
Activities: guided tours; gallery talks; poetry readings; concerts; plays; film series; docent program; inter-museum loan, permanent & temporary exhibitions; lectures; symposia; student art volunteer program; available for rental to nonprofit organizations, member corporations & Duke Univ. departments.
Publications: exhibition catalogs; newsletter; annual report.
Hours & Admission Prices: Tues.-Wed. & Fri.-Sat. 10-5, Thurs. 10-9, Sun. 12-5. Suggested Donation: adults $5, seniors & Duke Alumni $4, non-Duke students $3; children under 16, members, Duke students, faculty & staff no charge. ♿
Attendance: 131,450 (accurate)
Membership: Friends of the Art Museum: Student $20; Individual $50; Duke Faculty & Staff $40; Family $60; Sponsor $100; Patron $50; Director's Circle $500; Brummer Society Bronze $1,000; Brummer Society Silver $2,500; Brummer Society Gold $5,000.

Edenton

HISTORIC EDENTON STATE HISTORIC SITE, 108 N. Broad St., Edenton, NC 27932-1903. Mailing Address: P.O. Box 474, Edenton, NC 27932-0474. Tel.: 252-482-2637. Fax: 252-482-3499.
E-mail: edenton@ncdcr.gov/linda.eure@ncdcr.gov
Web Site: www.edenton.nchistoricsites.org
Formerly: James Iredell House State Historic Site
Founded: 1951.
Congressional District: 3
Key Personnel: Site Mgr., Linda Jordan Eure; Operations Mgr., Judith W. Chilcoat; Office Asst., Ann T. Byrum; Historic Interpreter, Keith Furlough; Historic Interpreter, Sharon K. Keeter; Historic Interpreter, Charles Boyette; Historic Interpreter, Carolyn A. Owens; Bldg. & Environmental Svcs., George S. Lassiter; Maintenance Mechanic, Blake S. Harmon.
Personnel Profile: Full-Time Paid 9; Part-Time Paid 4; Part-Time Volunteers 35.
Governing Authority: state. Parent Institution: North Carolina Office of Archives & History, 4610 Mail Service Center, Raleigh, NC 27699-4610. Subsidiary Institution: James Iredell Historical Association, Inc. Tax-exempt.
Historic House Museum.
Collections: period furnishings; kitchen utensils; formal gardens; 1756 kitchen; c.1827 dairy. Historic Buildings: c.1827 Bandon Schoolhouse; c.1827 Bandon Smokehouse; carriage house; 1800/1827 James Iredell

House; 18th century necessary house; 1886 Roanoke River Lighthouse; 1767 Chowan County Courthouse National Historic Landmark.
Research Fields: James Iredell; period furnishings; architecture; 18th century history of U.S. Supreme Court; 18th century legal & social history.
Facilities: visitor center; information services. Local history books, local handicrafted items & guidebooks for sale.
Activities: guided tours; formally organized education programs; audiovisual program; permanent exhibitions; special events & programs.
Publications: brochure; town map; Harriet Jacobs Self-Guided Brochure; Edenton Architecture Self-Guided Brochure.
Hours & Admission Prices: Mon.-Sat. 9-5, Sun. 1-4. Guided walking and trolley tours: $10, $6, or $4 per person. Visitor Center: no charge. Closed New Year's Day; Martin Luther King Jr. Day; Easter Sunday; Veterans Day; Thanksgiving Day; Christmas Eve & Day. ♿
Attendance: 23,439 (accurate)

Elizabeth City

MUSEUM OF THE ALBEMARLE, (M), 501 S. Water St., Elizabeth City, NC 27909-4863. Tel.: 252-335-1453. Fax: 252-335-0637.
E-mail: moa@ncdcr.gov
Web Site: www.museumofthealbemarle.com
Founded: 1967.
Congressional District: 1
Key Personnel: Admin., Ed Merrell; Administrative Sec., Mary Cherry; Cur., Tom Butchko; Coord. Education, Charlotte Patterson; Facilities Mgr., Wayne Mathews; Exhibits Chief, Don Pendergraft; Lighting, Electronics & Interactive Technician, Lynette Sawyer; Educator, Lori Meads; Educator, Meg Puckett; Utility Worker, William Seymore; Museum Shop Mgr., Suzanne Sears; Office Asst., Gina Cappellano; Public Information Asst., Lisa Doepker; Exhibit Designer, Jamie McCargo; Carpenter, Matthew Ferrell; Housekeeper, Ben Shipley; Processing Asst., Fay Leary; Registrar, Darroll Midgette; Public Rels., Thom Spagnol; Collections Specialist, Wanda Stiles.
Personnel Profile: Full-Time Paid 20; Part-Time Paid 7; Part-Time Volunteers 40.
Governing Authority: Parent Institution: North Carolina Museum of History. Dept. of Cultural Resources, 5 E. Edenton St., Raleigh, NC 27601-1011. Tax-exempt.
History Museum.
Collections: regional history; Indian artifacts; agricultural exhibits; lumbering items; decoys; farming; fishing; military featuring U.S. Coast Guard.
Major Exhibits: America's Secret Warriors: The Oss (T), 11/09-6/10; Barbie's Golden Anniversary, 11/09-4/10; Gates County Celebration, 12/09-5/10; Camden County Celebration, 4/10-6/10; New Harmonies: Celebrating American Roots Music (T), 6/10-7/10; Tending the Still: A.N.C. Tradition, 9/10-4/11.
Research Fields: regional history; area industries & lifestyle.
Facilities: 1,000-vol. library of historical information available for use on premises by appointment (Tues.-Fri.). Museum-related items for sale.
Activities: guided tours; changing exhibitions; formally organized educational programs; living history; hands-on history programs.
Publications: brochure; quarterly newsletter; annual school programs brochure; exhibit catalog, A Taste of the Past: Foodways of the Albemarle 1585-1830.
Hours & Admission Prices: Tues.-Sat. 9-5, Sun. 2-5. No charge; donations accepted. Closed state holidays. ♿
Attendance: 40,000 (estimated)
Membership: Student $15; Individual $30; Family $50; Patron $100-$499; Sponsor $500-$999; Benefactor $1,000-$4,999; Duke of Albemarle Society $5,000 & up.

Ellerbe

RANKIN MUSEUM OF AMERICAN HERITAGE, 131 W. Church St., Ellerbe, NC 28338. Mailing Address: P.O. Box 499, Ellerbe, NC 28338-0499. Tel.: 910-652-6378.
Web Site: www.rankinmuseum.com
Founded: 1986.
Congressional District: 19
Key Personnel: Founder, Dr. P.R. Rankin, Jr.; Art Cur. & Supvr., Gail Benson; Pres., Julian Carter; Vice Pres., Judy Richardson; Financial Dir., Amy Kesler.
Personnel Profile: Full-Time Paid 1; Part-Time Paid 3; Part-Time Volunteers 2.
Governing Authority: private; nonprofit organization. Parent Institution: Rankin Museum of American Heritage, Box 499, Ellerbe, NC 28338. Tax-exempt: 501(c)(3).
General Museum.
Collections: Native Americans of North, Central & South American; natural history including animal studies, geology & paleontology; heritage & history of North Carolina, South Carolina, & Richmond County; Civil War artifacts; paintings; medical artifacts from 1800 to early 1900s.
Facilities: classroom; 6,500 sq. ft. exhibit space. Museum-related items for sale.
Activities: adult art & craft workshops; summer student workshops; seasonal festivals; guided tours; education programs with schools. Museum Sponsors: annual fundraiser barbeque; Meet the Artist Series.
Publications: annual newsletter.
Hours & Admission Prices: Mon.-Tues. & Thurs.-Fri. 10-4, Sat. 1-5, Sun. 2-5. Adults $4, students $1; discounts to school & adult groups & AAA members; children 4 & under no charge. Closed New Year's Day; Thanksgiving; Christmas. ♿
Attendance: 4,000 (estimated)
Membership: Student $5; Adult $15; Family $25; Contributor $50; Sustaining $100; Patron $1,000.

Farmville

MAY MUSEUM & PARK, 3802 S. Main, Farmville, NC 27828-8548. Mailing Address: P.O. Box 86, Farmville, NC 27828-0086. Tel.: 252-753-6725. Fax: 252-753-7313.
E-mail: maymuseum@farmville-nc.com
Founded: 1991.
Congressional District: 1
Key Personnel: Cur., Donna Kemp.
Personnel Profile: Full-Time Paid 2; Part-Time Paid 1; Part-Time Volunteers 4.
Governing Authority: municipal; nonprofit. Parent Institution: Town of Farmville. Tax-exempt.
History Museum.
Collections: quilts; furniture; photographs; books; documents; sketches & artwork.
Facilities: 500-vol. library; botanical garden.
Activities: Annual Event: Community Dogwood Festival.
Hours & Admission Prices: Mon.-Fri. 9-5. No charge; donations accepted.
Attendance: 1,000 (estimated)

Fayetteville

THE AIRBORNE & SPECIAL OPERATIONS MUSEUM, (M), 100 Bragg Blvd., Fayetteville, NC 28301-4806. Tel.: 910-643-2766. Fax: 910-643-2792.
E-mail: jamesh.huggins@us.army.mil
Web Site: www.asomf.org
Founded: 2000.
Congressional District: 8
Key Personnel: C.E.O. & Chm., Paul Galloway; Dir., James H. Huggins; Chm. (V), Gen. James J. Lindsay, (U.S.A.) (R); Pres. (V), Henry Holt; Cur. Collections, Mary Dennings; Collections, George Stefanski; Museum Shop Mgr., Amanda Swan.
Personnel Profile: Full-Time Paid 17; Part-Time Paid 4; Part-Time Volunteers 97.
Governing Authority: federal; nonprofit organization. Parent Institution: U.S. Army. Tax-exempt: 501(c)(3).
Military Museum.
Collections: 1940-present military artifacts; uniforms; equipment; weapons; soldering equipment; C-47 WWII airplane; CG4A WACO glider; Huey helicopter; AH-6 helicopter; HUMMV.
Major Exhibits: First Special Service Force - The Devil's Brigade, 12/09-10/10.
Facilities: 22,000 sq. ft. exhibit space; 200-seat theater. Museum-related items for sale.
Activities: docent program; films; rental gallery; temporary exhibitions; theater; 24-seat motion simulator; paver stones available to memorialized veterans. Annual Event: National Airborne Day in August.
Publications: newsletter; annual report; gift shop catalog.
Hours & Admission Prices: Mon. Federal holidays & Tues.-Sat. 10-5, Sun. 12-5. No charge; donations accepted. Closed New Year's Day; Easter; Thanksgiving; Christmas. ♿
Attendance: 164,639 (accurate)
Membership: Friend: Student under 18 & military; Individual $35; Student & Military Family $40; Family $50. Contributor $100-$499; Donor $500-$599; Patron $1,000-$2,499; Sponsor $2,500-$4,999.

AIRBORNE & SPECIAL OPERATIONS MUSEUM, 100 Bragg Blvd., Fayetteville, NC 28301-4806. Tel.: 910-643-2766. Fax: 910-643-2793.
Key Personnel: Dir., Dr. John S. Duvall
Military Museum.
Collections: military history & artifacts; photographs; personal artifacts.
Facilities: theater. Museum-related items for sale.
Activities: simulator.

Hours & Admission Prices: Tues.-Sat. 10-5, Sun. 12-5. No charge; donations accepted. Closed New Year's Day; Easter; Thanksgiving; Christmas. ♿

ARTS COUNCIL OF FAYETTEVILLE/CUMBERLAND COUNTY, 301 Hay St., Fayetteville, NC 28301-5535. Mailing Address: P.O. Box 318, Fayetteville, NC 28302-0318. Tel.: 910-323-1776. Fax: 910-323-1727.
E-mail: admin@theartscouncil.com
Web Site: www.theartscouncil.com
Founded: 1974.
Congressional District: 7
Key Personnel: Exec. Dir., Deborah Martin Mintz; Gen. Mgr., Nancy Silver; Dir. Arts Education, Elaine Bryant; Dir. Devel. & Mktg., Margo Jarvis; Exec. Asst., Jennifer Gilbertson.
Personnel Profile: Full-Time Paid 10; Part-Time Paid 2; Part-Time Volunteers 400; Interns 1.
Governing Authority: nonprofit organization. Tax-exempt: 501(c)(3).
Arts Center: housed in c.1910 former Post Office & Library.
Collections: paintings.
Facilities: dark room.
Activities: self-guided tours; concerts; dance recitals; arts festivals; theatrical productions; temporary exhibitions. Gallery Sponsors: exhibits by & competitions for local & trade area artists.
Publications: monthly newsletter.
Hours & Admission Prices: Mon.-Thurs. 8:30-5, Fri. 8:30-Noon; other times by appointment. No charge. Closed New Year's Day; Good Friday; Memorial Day; Independence Day; Labor Day; Thanksgiving; Christmas. ♿
Attendance: 85,000 (estimated)
Membership: Apprentice $25; Bottega $50; Avant-Garde $75; Patron $100; Bread & Cheese Club $250; Curator $500; Model $1,000; Connoisseur $2,500; Muse $5,000.

FASCINATE-U CHILDREN'S MUSEUM, 116 Green St., Fayetteville, NC 28301-5024. Mailing Address: P.O. Box 2671, Fayetteville, NC 28302-2671. Tel.: 910-829-9171. Fax: 910-433-1639.
E-mail: webmail@fascinate-u.com
Web Site: www.fascinate-u.com
Children's Museum.
Collections: hands-on exhibits.
Hours & Admission Prices: Tues. & Thurs.-Fri. 9-5, Wed. 9-7, Sat. 10-5, Sun. 12-5. Children $3, adults $1.

FAYETTEVILLE MUSEUM OF ART, (M), 839 Stamper Rd., Fayetteville, NC 28303-4135. Mailing Address: P.O. Box 35134, Fayetteville, NC 28303-0134. Tel.: 910-485-5121. Fax: 910-485-5233.
E-mail: receptionist@faymoa.org
Web Site: www.fayettevillemuseumart.org
Founded: 1971.
Congressional District: 7
Key Personnel: Pres. (V), Menno Pennink, M.D.; Exec. Dir., Tom Grubb; 1st Vice Pres., John "Mac" Healy; Asst. Dir. & Cur., Michele Horn.
Personnel Profile: Full-Time Paid 6; Part-Time Paid 3; Part-Time Volunteers 80; Interns 1.
Governing Authority: nonprofit organization. Tax-exempt.
Art Museum.
Collections: works of contemporary North Carolina artists; contemporary Russian art; African artifacts; pottery; sculpture garden; paintings & sculpture.
Facilities: reference & slide library; educational facilities; six-acre garden.
Activities: lectures; arts festivals; children's art classes & workshops; jewelry workshops; docent programs; intern programs; volunteer opportunities; temporary exhibitions including a biannual statewide competition; premiere parties; outreach. Museum Sponsors: Fayetteville After Five Concert Series May to October; Annual Gala; Museum Miles 5K; Arts Festival for Special Needs Children.
Publications: exhibition brochure; member's bulletin.
Hours & Admission Prices: Jan. 2-Dec. 23 Mon.-Fri. 10-5. No charge; donations accepted. Closed New Year's Day; Martin Luther King Jr. Day; Good Friday; Memorial Day; Independence Day; Labor Day; Thanksgiving. ♿
Attendance: 180,000 (estimated)
Membership: Individual $35; Family $50; Sustainer $100; Patron $250; Director $500; Benefactor $1,000; Corporate Leader $1,500; Corporate Associate $2,500; Corporate Partner $5,000.

MUSEUM OF THE CAPE FEAR HISTORICAL COMPLEX, 801 Arsenal Ave., Fayetteville, NC 28305. Mailing Address: P.O. Box 53693, Fayetteville, NC 28305-3693. Tel.: 910-486-1330. Fax: 910-486-1585.
E-mail: david.reid@ncdcr.gov
Web Site: museumofthecapefear.ncdcr.gov
Founded: 1985.
Congressional District: 7
Key Personnel: Admin., David E. Reid; Assoc. Cur. Education, Leisa Greathouse; Exhibit Designer, Margaret Shearin; Carpenter & Exhibit Builder, Jim Frederickson; Assoc. Cur. Research, Kathryn A. Beach; 1897 Poe House Educator, Heidi Bleazey; Arsenal Park Educator, Chris Woodson; Historic Interpreter, Jim Brisson; Collections Asst., Bill Surface.
Personnel Profile: Full-Time Paid 13; Part-Time Paid 4; Part-Time Volunteers 80.
Governing Authority: Division of State History Museums, N.C. Dept. of Cultural Resources, 5 E. Edenton St., Raleigh, NC 27601. Tax-exempt.
History Museum: octagonal structure & building foundations from the federal arsenal in Arsenal Park.
Collections: artifacts pertaining to history & culture of southern North Carolina. Historic Building: 1897 historic house.
Research Fields: regional history.
Facilities: reference & slide library; 6,900 sq. ft. exhibit galleries; classroom. Museum-related items for sale.
Activities: changing exhibitions; educational programs; guided tours; lectures & film series; workshops; special events.
Publications: brochure; quarterly newsletter, the Longleaf; quarterly calendar of events.
Hours & Admission Prices: Tues.-Sat. 10-5, Sun. 1-5. No charge; donations accepted. Closed New Year's Day; Easter; Independence Day; Thanksgiving; Christmas Eve & Day. ♿
Attendance: 25,000 (accurate)
Membership: Individual $25; Family & Patron $100; Benefactor $500; Sustainer $1,000. Corporate: Bronze $250; Silver $500; Gold $1,000.

Ferguson

WHIPPOORWILL ACADEMY AND VILLAGE, 11928 NC Hwy. 268 W., Ferguson, NC 28624. Tel.: 336-973-3237.
History Museum.
Collections: local history & culture; period furnishings; one-room schoolhouse; Daniel Boone's replica cabin; Chapel of Peace; blacksmith shop; country store; jail; tavern.
Facilities: Museum-related items for sale.
Activities: Museum Sponsors: Old Fashioned Day Worship Service in September; Christmas Open House.
Hours & Admission Prices: April-Dec. Sat.-Sun. 3-5; other times by appointment. No charge; donations accepted.

Flat Rock

CARL SANDBURG HOME NATIONAL HISTORIC SITE, 81 Carl Sandburg Lane, Flat Rock, NC 28731-8635. Tel.: 828-693-4178. Fax: 828-693-4179.
E-mail: carl_administration@nps.gov
Web Site: www.nps.gov/carl
Founded: 1968.
Congressional District: 11
Key Personnel: Park Supt., Ms. Connie Backlund; Museum Shop Mgr., Ms. Sharon Stepp.
Personnel Profile: Full-Time Paid 2; Part-Time Paid 1; Part-Time Volunteers 10.
Governing Authority: federal. Parent Institution: National Park Service, U.S. Dept. of Interior. Tax-exempt.
Historic House: 1838 Connemara Farm of Confederate Sec. of Treasury C. G. Memminger & later acquired by Carl Sandburg in 1945.
Collections: Carl Sandburg's working library; books; letters; papers; photographs.
Research Fields: Carl Sandburg; American literature.
Facilities: 8,000-vol. library of American literature, history, biography; summer outdoor auditorium. Carl Sandburg works for sale.
Activities: guided tours; films; permanent exhibitions.
Hours & Admission Prices: Daily 9-5. Adults $5; children under 17 no charge. ♿
Attendance: 100,000 (estimated)

Fontana Dam

FONTANA DAM, Hwy. 28 S., Fontana Dam, NC 28733-9700. Tel.: 800-467-1388; 828-498-2226.
History Museum.
Collections: history of the dam; hydroelectric power; photographs.
Facilities: visitor center.
Activities: guided tours.
Hours & Admission Prices: May-Nov. Visitor Center: daily 9-7. Electric Plant Tours: daily 10-6:30.

Forest City

RUTHERFORD COUNTY FARM MUSEUM, 240 Depot St., Forest City, NC 28043-3654. Tel.: 828-248-1248.
Key Personnel: Dir., Wilbur Burgin
Farm Museum.
Collections: farm equipment; period artifacts; murals.
Hours & Admission Prices: Wed.-Sat. 10-3. Adults $2; children no charge.

Fort Bragg

82ND AIRBORNE DIVISION WAR MEMORIAL MUSEUM, Building C-6841 Ardennes St., Fort Bragg, NC 28310-0001. Mailing Address: P.O. Box 70119, Fort Bragg, NC 28307-0119. Tel.: 910-432-3443 & 5307. Fax: 910-432-1642.
Web Site: www.bragg.army.mil/18abn/museums.htm
Founded: 1946.
Congressional District: 7
Key Personnel: Chm. (V), Richard O'Hore; Dir. & Cur., John W. Aarsen; Registrar, Betty J. Rucker; Archivist, Jimmie Hallis; Museum Shop Mgr., Ami Cooper.
Personnel Profile: Full-Time Paid 4; Part-Time Paid 1; Part-Time Volunteers 20.
Governing Authority: federal government. Parent Institution: Museum Branch, Training Division. Affiliated with the 82nd Airborne Historical Society. Tax-exempt: 501(c)(3).
Military Museum.
Collections: history of World War I & II, history of 82nd Division from World War I to present, Desert Storm & Desert Shield, Panama, Dominican Republic, Grenada, Vietnam; history of 82nd Airborne Division from WWI to present; U.S. & foreign materials, weapons, uniforms, equipment, flags, vehicles, aircraft, art.
Research Fields: history of airborne units & warfare.
Facilities: library; 5,000 sq. ft. exhibit space; educational facilities; 65-seat theater. Museum-related gifts for sale.
Activities: lectures; films; permanent & temporary exhibitions. Annual Event: All American Week in May.
Publications: 82nd Abn. Div. History: 1917 to Present.
Hours & Admission Prices: Tues.-Sat. 10-4:30 (valid photo ID required). No charge; donations accepted. Closed New Year's Day; Thanksgiving; Christmas. ♿
Attendance: 65,000 (accurate)
Membership: Lifetime $5.

JFK SPECIAL WARFARE MUSEUM, (M), Ardennes & Marion Sts., Bldg. D-2502, Fort Bragg, NC 28307. Mailing Address: Commander, USA JFK SWCS, Attn: AOJK-MU, Fort Bragg, NC 28310-0001. Tel.: 910-432-1533 & 4272. Fax: 910-432-4062.
E-mail: merrittr@soc.mil
Founded: 1963.
Key Personnel: Cur., Roxanne M. Merritt; Museum Assn. Pres., Col. William Palmer, (USA Ret.); Museum Specialist, Clenon "Gene" Freeman; Gift Shop Mgr., Betty Amaker.
Personnel Profile: Full-Time Paid 7; Part-Time Volunteers 1.
Governing Authority: federal. Parent Institution: U.S. Army Special Warfare Center & School. Subsidiary Institution: JFK Special Warfare, SF Branch Historical & Memorial Association. Tax-exempt: 501(c)(3).
U.S. Army Military Museum.
Collections: unconventional warfare, military & ethnographic collection; U.S. Army JFK Special Warfare Center; U.S. Army Special Operations Command; U.S. Army Special Forces; U.S. Army Psychological Operations Groups; U.S Army Ranger & Civil Affairs units.
Research Fields: unconventional warfare; unit histories of special groups including Darby's Rangers, Merrill's Marauders; 1st Special Service Force, OSS & Alamo Scouts; Special Forces involvement in Vietnam conflict; Airborne Rangers; Special Operations in Latin America & Desert Storm.
Facilities: Hall of Heroes; U.S. Army Special Operations Command Headquarters. Items dealing with Special Forces, Rangers, 4th Psyops, Civil Affairs, Airborne & Ft. Bragg for sale.
Activities: permanent & traveling exhibitions.
Publications: quarterly newsletter, Museum Musings; gift shop catalog; brochure.
Hours & Admission Prices: Tues.-Sun. 11-4. No charge; donations accepted. Closed most federal holidays. ♿
Attendance: 56,750 (accurate)
Membership: Individual $20; Supporting $50; Sponsor $100; Friend $500; President's Council $1,000.

Four Oaks

BENTONVILLE BATTLEFIELD STATE HISTORIC SITE, 5466 Harper House Rd., Four Oaks, NC 27524-9125. Tel.: 910-594-0789. Fax: 910-594-0027.
E-mail: bentonville@ncdcr.gov
Web Site: www.bentonvillebattlefield.nchistoricsites.org
Founded: 1961.
Congressional District: 3
Key Personnel: Site Mgr., Donald B. Taylor; Site Asst. Mgr., Derrick Brown; Site Interpreter, Jeff Fritzinger.
Personnel Profile: Full-Time Paid 4; Part-Time Paid 6.
Governing Authority: state. North Carolina Dept. of Cultural Resources, 109 E. Jones St., Raleigh 27611. Parent Institution: North Carolina Division of Archives & History. Subsidiary Institution: North Carolina Historic Sites Section. Tax-exempt: 170(b).
Historic Site.
Collections: military artifacts; history items. Historic House: c.1855 Harper House, used by Union army as field hospital during Battle of Bentonville.
Facilities: visitor center; audiovisual room; picnic areas.
Activities: guided tours; lectures; walking trail to union trenches; artillery demonstrations; audiovisual programs; seasonal living history; self guided driving tour; fiber optic map of the first day's fighting (6 minute presentation). Annual Events: living history events.
Publications: brochure.
Hours & Admission Prices: April-Sept. Mon.-Sat. 9-5; Oct.-March Tues.-Sat. 9-5. No charge; donations accepted. Closed most major holidays.
Attendance: 28,000 (accurate)
Membership: Bentonville Battleground Historical Association: Annual $20.

Franklin

FRANKLIN GEM & MINERAL MUSEUM, 25 Phillips St., Franklin, NC 28734-3029. Tel.: 828-369-7831 & 342-6360.
Founded: 1974.
Congressional District: 11
Key Personnel: Mgr., Ray Behr; Pres. (V), Tom Sterrett; Museum Shop Mgr., Wally Smith.
Personnel Profile: Part-Time Volunteers 110.
Gem & Mineral Museum: housed in the former Macon County Public Jail; built in 1850.
Collections: gems; minerals; mining; fossils; Native American artifacts; sea shells.
Activities: special events. Annual Events: Gemboree in July & October.
Publications: The Mountain Gem.
Hours & Admission Prices: May-Oct. Mon.-Sat. 12-4; Nov.-April Sat. 12-4; groups by appointment. No charge; donations accepted. Closed Independence Day.
Attendance: 9,000 (estimated)
Membership: Adult $15, $10 each additional adult, $3 additional per child under 18.

MACON COUNTY HISTORICAL SOCIETY & MUSEUM, 36 W. Main, Franklin, NC 28734. Tel.: 828-524-9758.
History Museum: housed in the Pendergrass Building, c.1904.
Collections: period artifacts; photographs; county history.
Research Fields: genealogical & historical.
Facilities: Museum-related items for sale.
Activities: public programs.
Publications: quarterly newsletter; books.
Hours & Admission Prices: May-Oct. Tues.-Fri. 10-5, Sat. 1-5; other times by appointment; Nov.-April Tues.-Fri. 10-4, Sat. 1-4. No charge; donations accepted.

THE SCOTTISH TARTANS MUSEUM, 86 E. Main St., Franklin, NC 28734-3026. Tel.: 828-524-7472.
E-mail: tartans@scottishtartans.org
Web Site: www.scottishtartans.org/
General Museum.
Collections: origins, history & development of tartans; Scottish culture, history, dress, migration & military; over 500 tartans.
Facilities: Museum-related items for sale.
Activities: special events; tours.
Hours & Admission Prices: Mon.-Sat. 10-5. Adults $2, children $1.

WILDERNESS TAXIDERMY & OUTFITTERS MUSEUM, 5040 Highlands Rd., Franklin, NC 28734-4009. Tel.: 828-524-3677. Fax: 828-349-4200.
Taxidermy Museum.
Collections: animals from around the world; wildlife art.

Hours & Admission Prices: Mon.-Tues. & Thurs.-Fri. 8-5, Sat. 8 am-12 pm.

Fremont

CHARLES B. AYCOCK BIRTHPLACE STATE HISTORIC SITE, 264 Governor Aycock Rd., Fremont, NC 27830. Mailing Address: P.O. Box 207, Fremont, NC 27830-0207. Tel.: 919-242-5581. Fax: 919-242-6668.
E-mail: aycock@ncdcr.gov
Web Site: www.ah.dcr.state.nc.us/hs/Aycock/Aycock.htm
Founded: 1959.
Congressional District: 3
Key Personnel: Site Mgr., Leigh V. Strickland; Museum Shop Mgr., Sarah Pittman.
Personnel Profile: Full-Time Paid 5; Part-Time Volunteers 20.
Governing Authority: state. Parent Institution: North Carolina Dept. of Cultural Resources, 4601 Mail Service Center, Raleigh, NC 27699-4601. Tax-exempt: 170(b).
History Museum.
Collections: history. Historic Houses: c.1846 Charles B. Aycock Birthplace; 1893 schoolhouse.
Major Exhibits: Blind & Deaf Education in North Carolina, 11/09-1/10; School Intergration in North Carolina, 1/10-7/10.
Research Fields: C.B. Aycock; 19th-century farm life; 19th-century education in North Carolina.
Facilities: visitor center.
Activities: guided tours; lectures; films; formally organized education programs for children; permanent exhibitions; special living history program.
Publications: brochure; semi-annual newsletter, The Orator.
Hours & Admission Prices: Mon.-Sat. 9-5. No charge; donations accepted. Closed Martin Luther King Jr. Day; Memorial Day; Independence Day; Labor Day; Veterans Day; Thanksgiving; Christmas Eve & Day. ♿
Attendance: 19,198 (accurate)

Frisco

FRISCO NATIVE AMERICAN MUSEUM AND NATURAL HISTORY CENTER, (M), 53536 Hwy. 12, Frisco, NC 27936. Mailing Address: P.O. Box 399, Frisco, NC 27936-0399. Tel.: 252-995-4440. Fax: 252-995-4030.
E-mail: bfriend1@embarqmail.com
Web Site: www.nativeamericanmuseum.org
Founded: 1986.
Congressional District: 3
Key Personnel: Exec. Dir., Carl Bornfriend; Chm. & Pres., James Goes; Chm. (V), Elvin Hooper; Education & Public Rels., Joyce Bornfriend; Museum Shop Mgr., Grace Peele; Maintenance, Manuel Gonzalez.
Personnel Profile: Full-Time Paid 1; Full-Time Volunteers 2; Part-Time Paid 2; Part-Time Volunteers 35; Interns 1.
Governing Authority: private; nonprofit organization. Tax-exempt: 501(c)(3).
History Museum: located on Hatteras Island, the central building is more than 100 years old with a history of use as a village post office & general store.
Collections: concentration on Native American artifacts from North America including the Algonquian Tribe of Hatteras Island.
Major Exhibits: Northwest Coast "Dancing Mask", 11/09-12/10.
Research Fields: Chiricahua, Apache Photo Collection; women's roles in Native American culture; representative samples of Native American dress.
Facilities: 4,000-vol. library; educational facilities; 2,445 sq. ft. exhibit space; nature center. Museum-related items for sale.
Activities: docent program; formal educational programs; guided tours; lectures; participatory exhibits; study clubs. Museum Sponsors: seminars & workshops on Native American culture; Annual Inter-Tribal PowWow, Journey Home; summer programs including beginning archaeology & beginning birding classes every Friday June-August.
Publications: annual brochure; semiannual newsletter, Museum Update.
Hours & Admission Prices: Summer: Tues.-Sun. 11-5, Mon. by appointment; Winter: call for hours. Family $15, adults $5, senior citizens $3; discount to AAM members. Closed Thanksgiving; Christmas. ♿
Attendance: 35,000 (estimated)
Membership: Student $5; Individual $10; Family $25; Charter $100; Sponsoring $200; Life $1,000.

Gastonia

* **SCHIELE MUSEUM OF NATURAL HISTORY AND LYNN PLANETARIUM, (M),** 1500 E. Garrison Blvd., Gastonia, NC 28054-5133. Tel.: 704-866-6908. Fax: 704-866-6041.
E-mail: carried@cityofgastonia.com
Web Site: www.schielemuseum.org
Founded: 1960.
Congressional District: 9
Key Personnel: Dir., Dr. V. Ann Tippitt; Chm. (V), Larry Brannock; Asst. Dir., Karl McKinnon; Dir. Advancement, Debbie Windley; Dir. Mktg., Mary Alice Rogers; Collections Mgr., Carrie V. Duran; Cur. Life Sciences, Duane Flynn; Research Coord., Dr. J. Alan May; Head Education, Tony Pasour; Museum Shop Mgr., Nancy Hagerman; Dir. Planetarium, Jim Craig; Security, Lanny Cook.
Personnel Profile: Full-Time Paid 26; Full-Time Volunteers 78; Part-Time Paid 7; Part-Time Volunteers 138; Interns 5.
Governing Authority: municipal. Parent Institution: City of Gastonia. Subsidiary Institution: Board of Trustees of Schiele Museum, Inc. Tax-exempt: 501(c)(3).
Natural History Museum.
Collections: North American mammals; birds; reptiles & amphibians; fishes; invertebrate; fossils; rocks, minerals & gems; anthropology; insects; bird eggs; natural history art; Native American objects.
Major Exhibits: A Natural View, 3/10-4/10; Pirates, 5/10-12/10; Ancient Carolinians, 9/10-12/10.
Research Fields: anthropology; archaeology; mycology; paleontology; Colonial & Native American lifestyles; entomology; regional ecosystem change; malacology.
Facilities: 5,000-vol. library; auditorium; environmental classroom; planetarium; nature trail & composite late 18th-century farm; Catawba Indian village.
Activities: lectures; films; formally organized educational programs; environment program; docent programs; traveling exhibits; travel programs; education expeditions; museum internship; summer workshops in astronomy, geology, ecology & conservation; Native American studies; Aboriginal studies program; outdoor environmental studies; living history programs in Native American studies & Colonial lifestyles. Museum Sponsors: Colonial Christmas & Thanksgiving Outdoor learning site program.
Publications: annual report; quarterly newsletter, Bobcat Tales; exhibition guides; catalogues; brochures.
Hours & Admission Prices: Mon.-Sat. 9-5, Sun. 1-5. Museum: City Residents: adults $5, students & seniors $4; members no charge. Non-Residents: adults $7, students & seniors $6; members no charge. Planetarium: adults $3; discounts to AAM, ASTC & ICOM members; members no charge. Closed Easter; Thanksgiving; Christmas Eve & Day. ♿
Attendance: 76,506 (accurate)
Membership: Individual $50; Family $75; Business Partner $150; Corporate Partner & Benefactor $250; Executive Partner & Schiele Society $500; President's Partner $1,000; Schiele Guardian $2,000; Chairman's Partner $2,500.

Goldsboro

ARTS COUNCIL OF WAYNE COUNTY, 2406 E. Ash St., Goldsboro, NC 27534-7511. Tel.: 919-736-3300. Fax: 919-736-3335.
E-mail: artscouncil@artsinwayne.org
Web Site: artsinwayne.org
Formerly: Community Arts Council, Inc.
Founded: 1963.
Congressional District: 3
Key Personnel: Exec. Dir., Sarah Merritt; Gallery & Education Dir., Becca Scott Reynolds.
Personnel Profile: Full-Time Paid 2; Part-Time Paid 1.
Governing Authority: nonprofit. Tax-exempt.
Art Museum.
Collections: permanent collection works by contemporary artists.
Facilities: exhibit gallery; art market; studios; classrooms. Art & fine crafts for sale.
Activities: adult & children's art classes; art demonstrations; workshops; film showings; lectures; tours; monthly exhibits; county-wide outreach programs working with senior citizen groups, headstart children, nursing home residents and the mentally & physically handicapped.
Publications: newsletter, Artwise.
Hours & Admission Prices: Mon.-Fri. 9-5. No charge; donations accepted. Closed New Years Day & day after; Good Friday; Easter; Memorial Day; Independence Day; Labor Day; Thanksgiving & day after; Christmas Eve, Day & week. ♿
Membership: Friends of the Arts: Individual $10; Family $15; Contributing $25; Supporting $50; Patron $100; Sustaining Patron $250; Benefactor $500; Sustaining Benefactor $1,000.

Greensboro

AFRICAN AMERICAN ATELIER, Greensboro Cultural Center, 200 N. Davie St., Greensboro, NC 27401. Tel.: 336-333-6885. Fax: 336-373-4826.
E-mail: info@africanamericanatelier.org
Art Gallery.
Collections: African American history & culture; paintings; photographs.
Facilities: 2,000 sq. ft. exhibit space.
Activities: youth programs; educational programs.

Hours & Admission Prices: Tues. & Thurs.-Sat. 10-5, Wed. 10-7, Sun. 2-5.

BLANDWOOD MANSION, 447 W. Washington St., Greensboro, NC 27401-2348. Mailing Address: P.O. Box 13136, Greensboro, NC 27415-3136. Tel.: 336-272-5003. Fax: 336-271-8049.
E-mail: apoteat@blandwood.org
Web Site: www.blandwood.org/
Key Personnel: Dir. & Cur., Ashley Poteat
Historic House: former home of North Carolina Governor John Motley Moorehead, c.1790. A National Historic Landmark.
Collections: period furnishings; personal artifacts; photographs.
Hours & Admission Prices: Feb.-Dec. Tues.-Sat. 11-4, Sun. 2-5; groups of 20 or more by appointment. Adults $8, seniors $7, children under 12 $5; discounts to AAA members & groups; school groups no charge. Closed holiday.

CENTER FOR VISUAL ARTISTS - GREENSBORO, 200 N. Davie St., Greensboro, NC 27401-2819. Mailing Address: P.O. Box 13, Greensboro, NC 27401-2865. Tel.: 336-333-7485. Fax: 336-333-7477.
E-mail: info@greensboroart.org
Web Site: www.greensboroart.org
Formerly: Greensboro Artists' League
Founded: 1956.
Congressional District: 6
Key Personnel: Pres., George Odom; Dir. Devel., Robin Reid; Dir. Education, Katie Lank; Cur., Kristy Thomas; Programming Asst., Melanie Greene.
Personnel Profile: Part-Time Paid 4; Part-Time Volunteers 1.
Governing Authority: nonprofit organization. Parent Institution: United Arts Council of Greensboro. Tax-exempt: 501(c)(3).
Art Gallery: located in the Greensboro Cultural Center.
Collections: works by artists of the Triad & beyond.
Facilities: gallery.
Activities: lectures; gallery talks; juried competition; workshops; special projects.
Publications: monthly member newsletter.
Hours & Admission Prices: Tues. & Thurs.-Sat. 10-5, Wed. 10-7, Sun. 2-5. No charge; donations accepted. Closed legal holidays. ♿
Attendance: 90,000 (estimated)
Membership: Seniors 55 & over and Students 18 & over $30; Individual 18 & over $40; Family & Supportive $75; Patron $100; Benefactor $250; Sustaining Benefactor $500; Business Sponsorships $1,000.

COLONIAL HERITAGE CENTER AT GUILFORD COURTHOUSE NATIONAL MILITARY PARK, 2200 New Garden Rd., Greensboro, NC 27410-2354. Tel.: 336-545-5315. Fax: 336-545-5314.
E-mail: guco_administration@nps.gov
Web Site: www.nps.gov/guco
Formerly: Tannenbaum Historic Park
Founded: 1988.
Congressional District: 6
Key Personnel: Dir., Charles Cranfield.
Personnel Profile: Full-Time Paid 3; Part-Time Paid 6; Part-Time Volunteers 20; Interns 2.
Governing Authority: municipal. Parent Institution: City of Greensboro, NC. Tax-exempt.
Historic Site.
Collections: graphic arts; furnishings; structures; 18th century maps; 1976 American Revolution Bicentennial.
Research Fields: colonial backcounty.
Facilities: Colonial Heritage Center Museum; historic buildings; picnic facilities.
Activities: living history programs.
Hours & Admission Prices: Fri.-Sun. 8:30-5. No charge.
Attendance: 20,000 (estimated)
Membership: Guilford Battleground Company: Student $10; Individual $20; Family $35; Contributor $50; Donor $100; Benefactor $1,000.

GREEN HILL CENTER FOR NORTH CAROLINA ART, 200 N. Davie St., Greensboro, NC 27401. Mailing Address: 200 N. Davie St., Box 4, Greensboro, NC 27401. Tel.: 336-333-7460. Fax: 336-333-2612.
E-mail: info@greenhillcenter.org
Web Site: www.greenhillcenter.org
Formerly: Green Hill Art Gallery
Founded: 1974.
Key Personnel: Dir., Laura Way; Mgr. Sales Gallery, Lu Dickson; Curatorial Asst. & Graphic Design, Mario Gallucci; Assoc. Exec. Dir., Mary Young; Dir. Education, Jaymie Meyer; ArtQuest Operations Mgr., Verna Fricke; Cur., Edie Carpenter; Coord. Devel. & Membership, Courtney Whittington; Receptionist, Cheryl Daniels; Receptionist, Delois Bynum; Business Mgr., Evelyn Nadler.
Personnel Profile: Full-Time Paid 9; Part-Time Paid 5; Part-Time Volunteers 40; Interns 5.
Governing Authority: nonprofit organization. Tax-exempt: 501(c)(3).
Art Gallery.
Collections: visual arts of North Carolina; focus on North Carolina art, solo & group shows; interactive children's gallery focusing on process of making art; hands-on exhibits.
Research Fields: contemporary North Carolina Art.
Facilities: Sales gallery with North Carolina art & fine crafts for sale.
Activities: guided tours; lectures; gallery talks; concerts; formally organized educational programs.
Publications: newsletter; calendar; catalogs of exhibitions.
Hours & Admission Prices: Gallery: Tues.-Wed. & Fri.-Sat. 10-5, Thurs. 10-7, Sun. 2-5. Gallery: Suggested Donation: $5. ArtQuest: Mon. 9:30-12:30, Tues. & Thurs.-Sat. 12:30-5, Wed. 12:30-7. ArtQuest: $5 per person; members no charge. Closed legal holidays. ♿
Attendance: 68,652 (accurate)
Membership: Student $25; Senior $30; Individual $40; Family $75; Friend $150; Supporter $250; Donor $500; Patron $1,000; Benefactor $2,500; Leadership $5,000; Champion $10,000.

GREENSBORO CHILDREN'S MUSEUM, 220 N. Church St., Greensboro, NC 27401-2918. Tel.: 336-574-2898. Fax: 336-574-3810.
E-mail: info@gcmuseum.com
Web Site: www.gcmuseum.com
Founded: 1999.
Key Personnel: C.E.O., Betsy Grant; Chm. (V), John Cross; Mktg., Steffany Reeve.
Personnel Profile: Full-Time Paid 9; Part-Time Paid 5; Part-Time Volunteers 20; Interns 8.
Governing Authority: Tax-exempt: 501(c)(3).
Children's Museum.
Collections: hands-on exhibits.
Facilities: Museum-related items for sale.
Activities: rental facilities; educational programs; special events; birthday parties; teacher workshops.
Hours & Admission Prices: Mon. 9-12 (members only), Tues.-Thurs & Sat. 9-5, Fri. 9-8, Sun. 1-5. Adults $6, seniors $5; discounts to groups of 10 or more, Fri. 5-8 & Sun. 1-5; members & children under one no charge. Closed New Year's Day; Easter; Memorial Day; Independence Day; Labor Day; Thanksgiving; Christmas Eve & Day. ♿
Attendance: 140,000 (accurate)
Membership: Family $95; Grandparent $80; ACM $150.

* **GREENSBORO HISTORICAL MUSEUM, INC., (M),** 130 Summit Ave., Greensboro, NC 27401-3016. Tel.: 336-373-2043 & 2982 (before 10am & Mon.). Fax: 336-373-2204.
E-mail: fred.goss@greensboro-nc.gov
Web Site: www.greensborohistory.org
Founded: 1924.
Congressional District: 6
Key Personnel: Dir., Fred Goss; Pres., Ken Bethea; Cur. & Registrar, Susan Webster; Cur. Collections, Jon Zachman; Cur. Education, Betty K. Phipps; Community Historian, Linda Evans; Archivist, Stephen Catlett.
Personnel Profile: Full-Time Paid 9; Part-Time Paid 22; Part-Time Volunteers 214; Interns 6.
Governing Authority: municipal & historical society. Parent Institution: City of Greensboro. Tax-exempt: 501(c)(3).
History Museum: housed in 1892 First Presbyterian Church building built in Richardson Romanesque style.
Collections: transportation; military; Confederate longarms; Dolley Madison; O. Henry; pharmacy & medical artifacts; decorative arts including large collection of American historical glass; local ethnic & religious groups exhibits including the Greensboro lunch counter civil rights sit-ins; room interiors; turn-of-the-century Greensborough Village; changing exhibits. Historic Houses: Christian Isley House & McNairy House; Hockett Blacksmith Shop.
Research Fields: county history; decorative arts.
Facilities: 800-vol. library of books on local & regional history available for use on premises with proper identification; 150-seat auditorium; archival collections for use on premises. Postcards, military miniatures, books, city flags, pewter miniatures, handmade mountain toys, reproduction antique toys, North Carolina pottery & museum approved reproductions for sale.
Activities: guided tours; lectures; films; gallery talks; heritage travel program; formally organized education programs for children; docent program; permanent & temporary exhibitions. Museum Sponsors: intern programs with local universities; traveling exhibitions to schools.
Publications: bimonthly, newsletter; annual report.
Hours & Admission Prices: Tues.-Sat. 10-5, Sun. 2-5. No charge; donations accepted. Closed city holidays. ♿

Attendance: 42,885 (accurate)
Membership: Student $20; Senior Citizen $25; Individual $30; Family $50; Contributor $75; Sponsor $125; Sustainer $250; Patron $500; Benefactor $1,000 & up.

GUILFORD COLLEGE ART GALLERY, (M), 5800 W. Friendly Ave., Greensboro, NC 27410-4108. Tel.: 336-316-2438. Fax: 336-316-2950.
E-mail: thammond@guilford.edu
Web Site: www.guilford.edu/artgallery
Founded: 1990.
Congressional District: 6
Key Personnel: Dir. & Cur., Theresa N. Hammond.
Personnel Profile: Full-Time Paid 1; Interns 2.
Governing Authority: private college. Parent Institution: Guilford College. Tax-exempt: 501(c)(3).
College Art Gallery: located in Hege Library.
Collections: fine art & crafts representing a variety of periods, styles & cultures.
Major Exhibits: Alumni Art Exhibition, 1/10-2/10; African Art from the Collection of Dr. Bobbie Person, 3/10-4/10.
Facilities: 5,000 sq. ft. exhibit space.
Activities: guided tours; temporary exhibitions; student internships.
Hours & Admission Prices: Main Gallery: Mon.-Fri. 9-5, Sun. 2-5. Atrium Galleries: Mon.-Thurs. 8:30-2, Fri. 8:30-6, Sat. 10-9, Sun. 12-2. No charge. Closed college holidays. ♿
Attendance: 7,500 (estimated)

GUILFORD COURTHOUSE NATIONAL MILITARY PARK, 2332 New Garden Rd., Greensboro, NC 27410-2355. Tel.: 336-288-1776. Fax: 336-282-2296.
E-mail: guco_administration@nps.gov
Web Site: www.nps.gov/guco
Founded: 1917.
Congressional District: 13
Key Personnel: Supt., Charles Cranfield; Museum Shop Mgr., Nancy Stewart.
Personnel Profile: Full-Time Paid 10; Part-Time Paid 1; Part-Time Volunteers 20; Interns 1.
Governing Authority: federal. Parent Institution: Dept. of Interior. Subsidiary Institution: National Park Service. Tax-exempt.
Military Museum.
Collections: Revolutionary War weapons; soldier mannequins; RW equipment; artifacts; introductory movie; battle map.
Research Fields: battle & Southern campaign of Revolutionary War.
Facilities: 700-vol. library of microfilm, military reports, books pertaining to the American Revolution, books & pamphlets concerning the state of North Carolina available for research on premises. Booklets pertaining to the Revolutionary War, reproductions of the Declaration of Independence, postcards & reproductions of 1781 Tarleton Map of the Battle of Guilford Courthouse for sale.
Activities: special programs & lectures by appointment; audiovisual program of the Battle of Guilford Courthouse.
Publications: books, Another Such Victory, The Monuments at Guilford Courthouse National Military Park; Battlemap.
Hours & Admission Prices: Daily 8:30-5. No charge; donations accepted. Closed New Year's Day; Thanksgiving; Christmas Eve & Day. ♿
Attendance: 39,450 (accurate)

IRENE CULLIS GALLERY, GREENSBORO COLLEGE, 815 W. Market St., Greensboro, NC 27401-1875. Tel.: 336-272-7102. Fax: 336-217-7245.
Web Site: www.gborocollege.edu
Founded: 1838.
Congressional District: 6
Key Personnel: Gallery Dir., James Langer.
Governing Authority: college. Greensboro College.
College Art Gallery.
Collections: paintings; photographs; sculpture.
Facilities: gallery.
Activities: monthly exhibitions: professional, faculty & student shows.
Hours & Admission Prices: Sept.-April Mon.-Fri. 10:30-4, Sun. 2-5 during exhibitions. No charge. Closed college holidays. ♿
Attendance: 3,000 (estimated)

*** THE NATURAL SCIENCE CENTER OF GREENSBORO, INC., (M),** 4301 Lawndale Dr., Greensboro, NC 27455-1899. Tel.: 336-288-3769. Fax: 336-288-2531.
E-mail: info@natsci.org
Web Site: www.natsci.org
Founded: 1957.
Congressional District: 6
Key Personnel: Exec. Dir., Glenn Dobrogosz; Business Mgr., Steve Fogarty; Cur. Naturalist, Richard G. Bolling; Cur. Collections, Ken Schneidmiller; Cur. Zoo, Peggy V. Ferebee; Cur. Planetarium, Roger D. Joyner; Cur. Volunteers, Marion Gilligan; Cur. Education, Richard A. Betton; Museum Shop Mgr., Clay Kirkman; Asst. Cur. Education, Ron Settle; Dir. Mktg., Roxanna Burkhart; Mgr. Visitor Svcs., Marcia Farrow.
Personnel Profile: Full-Time Paid 25; Full-Time Volunteers 450; Part-Time Paid 39.
Governing Authority: board of trustees; nonprofit organization. Tax-exempt: 501(c)(3).
Natural History, Science Museum, Planetarium & Zoo.
Collections: geology; ornithology; entomology; mammals; reptiles; paleontology; conchology; period scientific documents & instruments.
Facilities: marine aquarium; solar observatory; nature trails; auditorium; digital dome theater. Museum reproductions & gifts for sale.
Activities: lectures; TV & radio programs; Junior Museum Council; college intern programs; workshops.
Publications: brochure; newsletters; educator's guide; annual report.
Hours & Admission Prices: Museum: Mon.-Sat. 9-5, Sun. 12:30-5. Zoo: Mon.-Sat. 10-4, Sun. 12:30-4. Adults $8, seniors 65 & over and children 2-13 $7; discounts to Greensboro residents; children under 2 no charge. OmniSphere Theater: $5. Closed New Year's Day; Thanksgiving; Christmas. ♿
Attendance: 276,000 (accurate)
Membership: City Taxpayer Individual $50; Individual & City Grandparent $55; Non City Grandparent & City Taxpayer Family $70; Family $75; Associate $100; Patron $250; Benefactor $500; President's Circle $1,000.

NORTH CAROLINA A&T STATE UNIVERSITY GALLERIES, Corner of Bluford and Dudley Sts., Greensboro, NC 27411-0001. Mailing Address: Dudley Bldg., 1601 E. Market St., Greensboro, NC 27411-0002. Tel.: 336-334-3209. Fax: 336-334-4378.
E-mail: sharris@ncat.edu
Web Site: www.ncat.edu/~museum/
Formerly: Mattye Reed African Heritage Center
Founded: 1968.
Congressional District: 6
Key Personnel: Dir., Shawnya Harris; Cur., Christi Pemberton; Administrative Asst., Lisa Phillips.
Governing Authority: university. Tax-exempt.
University Museum.
Collections: arts & history from over 31 African nations, Mattye Reed African collection; H.C. Taylor contemporary art.
Research Fields: African art history, culture & heritage.
Facilities: education room; artist studio; resource room.
Activities: guided tours; lectures; education programs for students; permanent & traveling exhibitions; community & university departmental partnership programs; artist in residency program; Friends of the Galleries Committee.
Publications: brochures; exhibition catalogues; museum & cultural sites directories.
Hours & Admission Prices: Mon.-Fri. 10-5; other times by appointment. No charge; donations accepted. Closed university holidays.
Attendance: 10,000 (estimated)

*** WEATHERSPOON ART MUSEUM, (M),** Spring Garden & Tate St., Univ. of NC at Greensboro, Greensboro, NC 27402-6170. Mailing Address: P.O. Box 26170, Greensboro, NC 27402-6170. Tel.: 336-334-5770. Fax: 336-334-5907.
E-mail: weatherspoon@uncg.edu
Web Site: weatherspoon.uncg.edu
Formerly: Weatherspoon Art Gallery
Founded: 1941.
Congressional District: 6
Key Personnel: Dir., Nancy Doll; C.E.O., Dr. David Perrin; Pres. (V), Gay Dillard; Public & Community Rels. Officer, Loring Martensen; Cur. Collections, Elaine D. Gustafson; Cur. Education, Ann Grimaldi; Cur. Exhibitions, Xandra Eden; Museum Shop Mgr., Tina Hundley; Asst. Cur. Education, Terri Dowell-Dennis.
Personnel Profile: Full-Time Paid 15; Part-Time Paid 2; Part-Time Volunteers 110; Interns 6.
Governing Authority: state; university. Parent Institution: The University of North Carolina at Greensboro. Tax-exempt: 501(c)(3).
University Art Museum.
Collections: American modern & contemporary paintings; sculpture; works on paper; Dillard collection of art on paper; Claribel & Etta Cone collection including Matisse lithographs & bronzes; Lenoir C. Wright Japanese prints.
Major Exhibits: Art on Paper 2010, 11/09-1/10; Taryn Simon, 1/17/10-4/18/10; Tom LaDuke (T), 1/24/10-4/18/10; Existed: Leonardo Drew (T), 2/7/10-5/9/10; Andy Warhol Polaroids (T), 7/4/10-10/17/10.
Research Fields: American modern & contemporary art.
Facilities: sculpture court; lecture hall. Museum-related items for sale.

Activities: guided tours; lectures; gallery talks; docent program; temporary, traveling & permanent exhibitions; youth programs; membership activities including Contemporary Collectors trips to art venues; performances; film screenings.
Publications: exhibition catalogs; biennial bulletin; newsletters; gallery guides.
Hours & Admission Prices: Tues.-Wed. & Fri. 10-5, Thurs. 10-9, Sat.-Sun. 1-5. No charge; donations accepted. Closed university holidays. ♿
Attendance: 30,192 (accurate)
Membership: Student $15; Artist $20; Senior Citizen $25; Individual $35; Family $50; Supporter $100; Contributor $250; Friend; $500; Benefactor $1,000; Patron $2,500.

Greenville

*** GREENVILLE MUSEUM OF ART, INC., (M),** 802 S. Evans St., Greenville, NC 27834-3268. Tel.: 252-758-1946.
E-mail: info@gmoa.org
Web Site: www.gmoa.org
Founded: 1956.
Congressional District: 1
Key Personnel: C.E.O., Dir. & Dir. Education, Charlotte Fitz; Bd. Pres., Heather Stepp; Exhibit Designer, Christopher Daniels.
Personnel Profile: Full-Time Paid 2; Part-Time Paid 3; Part-Time Volunteers 10; Interns 1.
Governing Authority: nonprofit organization. Tax-exempt: 501(c)(3).
20th-century American Art & Visual Arts Museum.
Collections: oils; water colors; sculpture; graphic arts; ceramics; education & children's collections; 20th-century American art.
Research Fields: North Carolina visual art; 1900-1940, American drawings & paintings.
Facilities: classrooms; studios; reception room.
Activities: guest artists series; gallery talks; seminars; docent program; museum tour trips; Artist Association programs; art classes & workshops for adults & children; multicultural programs for children 6 & over.
Publications: quarterly newsletter; monthly exhibition announcements.
Hours & Admission Prices: Tues.-Fri. 10-4:30, Sat. 1-4. Tours: Wed.-Fri. between 10 & 12. No charge; donations accepted. Closed major holidays. ♿
Attendance: 12,000 (accurate)
Membership: Individual $45; Family $60; Sponsor $100; Donor $150; Patron $250; Benefactor $600; Honorary Trustee $1,200.

WELLINGTON B. GRAY GALLERY, East Carolina Univ., Jenkins Fine Arts Cntr., Greenville, NC 27858-4353. Tel.: 252-328-6336. Fax: 252-328-6441.
E-mail: braswellg@ecu.edu
Web Site: www.ecu.edu/art/home/html
Founded: 1978.
Congressional District: 1
Key Personnel: Dir., Tom Braswell.
Personnel Profile: Full-Time Paid 3; Part-Time Paid 14; Part-Time Volunteers 10; Interns 1.
Governing Authority: university. Parent Institution: East Carolina University. Subsidiary Institution: East Carolina University School of Art. Tax-exempt.
Art Gallery.
Collections: contemporary & African art.
Research Fields: contemporary art.
Facilities: 6,000 sq. ft. exhibit space.
Activities: lectures; films; gallery talks; temporary & traveling exhibitions; international, national & regional exhibitions of contemporary works, installations & site-specific work.
Publications: catalogs for selected exhibitions; Fiber: Fabrication/Revelation; Jacob Lawrence: An American Master; Minnie Evans: Artist; Anders Knutsson: A Retrospective; Baltic Ceramist: 1996; Robert Lee Humber: A Collector Creates; International Photography & Digital Image Exhibition.
Hours & Admission Prices: Mon.-Fri. 10-4, Sat. 10-2. No charge; donations accepted. Closed for university holidays. ♿
Attendance: 20,102 (accurate)

Halifax

HISTORIC HALIFAX STATE HISTORIC SITE, St. David & Dobb Sts., Halifax, NC 27839. Mailing Address: P.O. Box 406, Halifax, NC 27839-0406. Tel.: 252-583-7191. Fax: 252-583-9421.
E-mail: halifax@ncdcr.gov
Web Site: www.halifax.nchistoricsites.org
Founded: 1955.
Congressional District: 2
Key Personnel: Sites Mgr., Monica Moody; Chm., Wrenn Phillips; Museum Shop Mgr., Vivian Price.
Personnel Profile: Full-Time Paid 5; Part-Time Volunteers 10.
Governing Authority: state. Parent Institution: North Carolina Historic Sites, 109 E. Jones St., Raleigh, NC 27611. Tax-exempt: 170(b)(1)(A).
Preservation Project & Visitor Center.
Collections: archaeology; history. Historic Houses: 1760 Owens House; 1810 Burgess House; 1833 Clerk's office; 1838 Jail; 1790 Tap Room; 1790 Eagle Tavern; 1808 Sally-Billy House; 1783 William R. Davie House.
Research Fields: archaeology; history; preservation project.
Facilities: visitor center; picnic area.
Activities: guided tours; lectures; permanent exhibitions.
Publications: brochure.
Hours & Admission Prices: Call for hours. No charge; donations accepted. Closed holidays. ♿
Attendance: 27,000 (estimated)
Membership: Individual $10; Contributing $25; Donor $50; Patron $100.

Hamlet

NATIONAL RAILROAD MUSEUM AND HALL OF FAME, INC., Business Hwy. 74 E., Hamlet, NC 28345. Mailing Address: P.O. Box 1583, Hamlet, NC 28345-1583. Tel.: 910-582-2383.
Founded: 1976.
Key Personnel: C.E.O., Chm. (V) & Pres. (V), Bill Williams; Treas., Education & Museum Shop Mgr., Larry Mercer; Public Rels., Bobbie Williams.
Personnel Profile: Part-Time Volunteers 9.
Governing Authority: private; nonprofit organization. Tax-exempt: 501(c)(3).
Railroad Museum.
Collections: photographs; maps; model railroad layout; four pieces of rolling stock; recreated telegraph office; SAL locomotive 1114 SDP 35 & caboose SAL 5241; 1892 Tornado replica.
Facilities: library. Museum-related items for sale.
Activities: formal education programs for children; guided tours; lectures; facility rental for special groups. Annual Event: Seaboard Festival Day in October.
Publications: brochures.
Hours & Admission Prices: Sat. 11-4, Sun. 1-4; other times by appointment. No charge; donations accepted. Closed Christmas.
Attendance: 5,000 (estimated)
Membership: Student $5; Adult $10.

Harkers Island

CORE SOUND WATERFOWL MUSEUM & HERITAGE CENTER, 1785 Island Rd., Harkers Island, NC 28531-9670. Mailing Address: P.O. Box 556, Harkers Island, NC 28531-0556. Tel.: 919-728-1500. Fax: 919-728-1742.
E-mail: museum@coresound.com
Web Site: www.coresound.com
Founded: 1992.
Congressional District: 3
Key Personnel: Dir., Karen Willis Amspacher; Chm. (V), Charles S. Jones; Museum Shop Mgr., Jennifer Taylor.
Personnel Profile: Full-Time Paid 2; Part-Time Paid 8; Part-Time Volunteers 425.
Governing Authority: private; nonprofit organization. Tax-exempt.
Heritage Center.
Collections: local history & culture; waterfowling traditions.
Research Fields: local history; coastal culture.
Facilities: library; archives; community center. Museum-related items for sale.
Activities: carving demonstrations; boatbuilding & restoration; oral histories; community documentary projects; foodways.
Hours & Admission Prices: Mon.-Sat. 10-5, Sun. 2-5. No charge; donations accepted. Closed New Year's Day; Easter; Thanksgiving; Christmas. ♿
Attendance: 25,000 (estimated)
Membership: Individual $30; Family $50; Businesses $75.

Hatteras

GRAVEYARD OF THE ATLANTIC MUSEUM, 59200 Museum Dr., Hatteras, NC 27943. Mailing Address: P.O. Box 191, Hatteras, NC 27943-0191. Tel.: 252-986-2995. Fax: 252-986-1212.
E-mail: museum@graveyardoftheatlantic.com
Web Site: www.graveyardoftheatlantic.com
Governing Authority: Parent Institution: State of North Carolina Museum of History. Tax-exempt.
Maritime History Museum.
Collections: maritime history; North Carolina Outer Banks shipwrecks; seafaring history.
Hours & Admission Prices: Mon.-Fri. 10-4. No charge; donations accepted. ♿
Attendance: 50,000 (accurate)

Hayesville

CLAY COUNTY HISTORICAL AND ARTS COUNCIL MUSEUM, 21 Davis Loop, Hayesville, NC 28904. Mailing Address: P.O. Box 5, Hayesville, NC 28904-0005. Tel.: 828-389-6814.
History Museum: housed in a former county jail; built in 1912.
Collections: Native American artifacts; photographs; early farm kitchen; 1800s loom & clothing; 1916 switchboard; 1838 quilt.
Hours & Admission Prices: Memorial Day to Labor Day Tues.-Sat. 10-4; Sept.-Oct. Fri.-Sat. 10-4. No charge; donations accepted.
Attendance: 800

Hendersonville

HISTORIC JOHNSON FARM, 3346 Haywood Rd., Hendersonville, NC 28791-9721. Tel.: 828-891-6585. Fax: 828-890-7001.
Historic Farm: housed on a late 19th-century tobacco farm. Listed on the National Register of Historic Places.
Collections: family & farm history; personal artifacts; period furnishings. Historic Buildings: 10 farm buildings.
Facilities: nature trails.
Activities: guided tours.
Hours & Admission Prices: May-Oct. Tues.-Sat. 9-2:30; Nov.-April Tues.-Fri. 9-2:30. Adults $3, students $2.

HOLMES EDUCATIONAL STATE FOREST, 1299 Crab Creek Rd., Hendersonville, NC 28739-8440. Tel.: 828-692-0100.
State Forest.
Collections: plants; trees; flowers; ecology.
Facilities: nature trails.
Activities: audio stations; classes; picnic area; hiking trails; educational programs.
Hours & Admission Prices: mid-March to late Nov. Tues.-Sun.

MINERAL AND LAPIDARY MUSEUM OF HENDERSON COUNTY INC., 400 N. Main St., Hendersonville, NC 28792-4901. Tel.: 828-698-1977. Fax: 828-698-1977.
E-mail: info@mineralmuseum.org
Web Site: www.mineralmuseum.org
Founded: 1996.
Congressional District: 11
Key Personnel: C.E.O. & Pres., Helen Hauser; Treas., Zeb Palmer; Museum Shop Mgr., Diane Lapp.
Personnel Profile: Part-Time Volunteers 65.
Governing Authority: private; nonprofit. Tax-exempt.
Mineral & Lapidary Museum.
Collections: minerals from USA & world, mostly from North Carolina.
Facilities: 1,100 sq. ft. exhibit space. Items related to minerals, gems, fossils, fluorescents, jewelry for sale.
Activities: formal education programs for children; hobby workshops.
Hours & Admission Prices: Mon.-Fri. 1-5, Sat. 10-5. No charge; donations accepted. Closed New Year's Day; Thanksgiving; Christmas. ♿
Attendance: 31,300 (accurate)

MOUNTAIN FARM AND HOME MUSEUM, 101 Brookside Camp Rd., Hendersonville, NC 28792-1101. Tel.: 828-697-8846.
Key Personnel: Pres., A.B. Wexler
History Museum.
Collections: period farm machinery & tools.
Activities: educational programs.
Hours & Admission Prices: Mon.-Fri. 8-4. No charge; donations accepted.

WESTERN NORTH CAROLINA AIR MUSEUM, (M), Brooklyn Ave., Hendersonville, NC 28793. Mailing Address: P.O. Box 2343, Hendersonville, NC 28793-2343. Tel.: 828-698-2482.
Founded: 1990.
Key Personnel: Dir. Docents, Chet Phillips; Pres. (V), Steve Lyons; Museum Shop Mgr., Jim Granere.
Personnel Profile: Part-Time Volunteers 30.
Governing Authority: private. Tax-exempt: 501(c)(3).
Aviation Museum.
Collections: aviation heritage of North Carolina; period aircraft; flight manuals; engines; photographs; models.
Facilities: Museum-related items for sale.
Activities: special events.
Hours & Admission Prices: April-Oct. Sun. & Wed. 12-5, Sat. 10-5; Nov.-March Wed. & Sat.-Sun. 12-5. No charge; donations accepted. ♿
Membership: Individuals $30; Family $40.

Hertford

NEWBOLD WHITE HOUSE HISTORIC SITE, 151 Newbold-White Rd., Hertford, NC 27944-8240. Mailing Address: P.O. Box 103, Hertford, NC 27944-0103. Tel.: 252-426-7567.
Key Personnel: Dir., Glenda Maynard
Historic Building: c.1730.
Collections: period furnishings; 18th-19th century artifacts; 18th century smokehouse; kitchen garden; 17th century Quaker cemetery.
Facilities: nature trail; picnic area. Museum-related items for sale.
Hours & Admission Prices: March-Nov. Tues.-Sat. 10-4; other times by appointment. Adults $5, child $3; children under 6 no charge.

Hickory

CATAWBA SCIENCE CENTER, 243 3rd Ave., N.E., Hickory, NC 28601-5168. Mailing Address: P.O. Box 2431, Hickory, NC 28603-2431. Tel.: 828-322-8169, ext. 300. Fax: 828-322-1585.
E-mail: info@catawbascience.org
Web Site: www.catawbascience.org
Founded: 1975.
Congressional District: 10
Key Personnel: Dir., Alan Barnhardt; Asst. Dir., Tricia Little; Pres. (V), George McCretz; Dir. Exhibits, Tom Prendergast; Dir. Visitor Svcs., Bruce Beerbower; Dir. Programs, Erin Graves; Museum Shop Mgr., Nadia Scopes.
Personnel Profile: Full-Time Paid 18; Part-Time Paid 20; Part-Time Volunteers 50.
Governing Authority: nonprofit organization. Tax-exempt: 501(c)(3).
Science & Technology Center.
Collections: teaching collections.
Facilities: digital planetarium; aquarium exhibits (saltwater & freshwater)
Activities: informal education programs for children; permanent & temporary exhibitions; pre-school outreach program.
Publications: newsletter; brochure.
Hours & Admission Prices: Tues.-Fri. 10-5, Sat. 10-4, Sun. 1-4. Adults $6, senior citizens 62 and over, military with ID & youth 3-18 $4; children under 3, members & ASTC Passport Program Participants no charge. Closed major holidays. ♿
Attendance: 101,000 (accurate)
Membership: Senior Citizen $25; Individual $50; Family/Grandparents $65; Donor $75; Patron $100; Benefactor $250; Stellar Society $500; Angel $1,000; President's Circle $2,000; Philanthropist $5,000.

HICKORY LANDMARKS SOCIETY-PROPST HOUSE AND MAPLE GROVE MUSEUMS, 542 2nd Ave., Hickory, NC 28601. Mailing Address: P.O. Box 2341, Hickory, NC 28603-2341. Tel.: 828-322-4731. Fax: 828-327-9096.
E-mail: info@hickorylandmarks.org
Web Site: www.hickorylandmarks.org/
Founded: 1968.
Congressional District: 10
Key Personnel: Exec. Dir. & C.E.O., Patrick T. Daily; Cur. Collections, Leslie Keller.
Personnel Profile: Full-Time Paid 1; Part-Time Paid 2; Part-Time Volunteers 40.
Governing Authority: nonprofit organization. Affiliated of the Catawba County Council for the Arts. Tax-exempt: 501(c)(3).
Three Victorian House museums (1882-1895).
Collections: Victorian period furniture.
Research Fields: 19th century local history.
Activities: house tours, special events.
Publications: newsletter, Landmarkings.
Hours & Admission Prices: Propst St. House Museum: March 15-Dec. 15 Thurs. & Sun. 1:30-4:30. Maple Grove Museum: Mon.-Fri. 9-5. No charge; donations accepted.
Attendance: 6,300 (estimated)
Membership: Individual $25; Family $35.

* **THE HICKORY MUSEUM OF ART, (M),** 243 Third Ave., N.E., Hickory, NC 28601-5168. Mailing Address: P.O. Box 2572, Hickory, NC 28603-2572. Tel.: 828-327-8576. Fax: 828-327-7281.
E-mail: info@hickorymuseumofart.org
Web Site: www.hickorymuseumofart.org
Founded: 1944.
Congressional District: 10
Key Personnel: Exec. Dir., Lise C. Swensson; Dir. Education, Virginia Zellmer; Dir. Communications & Mktg., Kristina Allen; Dir. Membership, Lauren Gallion; Museum Shop Mgr., Ronni Smith.
Personnel Profile: Full-Time Paid 3; Part-Time Paid 13; Part-Time Volunteers 80; Interns 2.
Governing Authority: board of trustees. Tax-exempt: 501(c)(3).

Art Museum.
Collections: 1850 to present American art; American art pottery; NC glass & pottery; outsider art.
Major Exhibits: NC Traveling Waterclor (T), 1/10-3/1/10; Elizabeth Catlett in Mexico, 1/16/10-5/2/10; Paul Whitener Student Art, 3/6/10-5/2/10; Joel Urruty Sculpture, 5/8/10-9/19/10; Carl Moser Photography, 9/25/10-1/16/11; NC Watercolor Show, 10/10-1/11.
Research Fields: American art.
Facilities: 1200-vol. library of art; research books; classrooms.
Activities: guided tours; lectures; films; gallery talks; permanent & traveling exhibitions; art classes.
Publications: quarterly newsletter; monthly announcements; catalogues on Museum collections; exhibition catalogues.
Hours & Admission Prices: Tues.-Sat. 10-4, Sun. 1-4. No charge. Closed New Year's Day; Easter; Independence Day; Thanksgiving; Christmas. ♿
Attendance: 37,056 (accurate)
Membership: Individual $40; Family $50; Contributor $100; Patron $150; Sustainer $250; Benefactor $500; Sponsor $1,000; President's Circle $2,500.

HICKORY MUSEUM OF ART, 243 Third Ave., N.E., Hickory, NC 28601. Mailing Address: P.O. Box 2572, Hickory, NC 28603. Tel.: 828-327-8576. Fax: 828-327-7281.
Key Personnel: Exec. Dir., Lise C. Swensson
Art Museum.
Collections: paintings; photographs.
Facilities: Museum-related items for sale.
Hours & Admission Prices: Tues.-Sat. 10-4, Sun. 1-4. No charge. Closed holidays.

Hiddenite

HIDDENITE CENTER, INC., 316 Church St., Hiddenite, NC 28636. Mailing Address: P.O. Box 311, Hiddenite, NC 28636-0311. Tel.: 828-632-6966. Fax: 828-632-5756.
E-mail: hidnight@aol.com
Web Site: www.hiddenitecenter.com
Founded: 1981.
Congressional District: 5
Key Personnel: Pres., Robert Snead; Exec. Dir., Dwaine C. Coley; Administrative Asst. & Public Rels., Karen B. Walker; Dir. Education, Allison S. Houchins; Custodial & Security, Robert Walker; Museum Shop Mgr., Peggy Martin.
Personnel Profile: Full-Time Paid 2; Part-Time Paid 6; Part-Time Volunteers 60.
Governing Authority: state. Tax-exempt: 501(c)(3).
General Museum & Art Center: housed in 1900 James Paul Lucas Mansion.
Collections: dolls; gem & mineral display; pottery; basketry; quilts; visual arts; paintings; woven works; multicultural exhibits; house furnishings.
Major Exhibits: Arts & Crafts from Around the World, 1/10; My Irish Heritage, 2/10; Alexander County's Local Artists Exhibition, 3/10; Sisters: Rita Ledford & Alva Hoke, 6/10-7/10; Brushy Mountain Quilters Exhibition, 11/10; Victorian Christmas, 12/10.
Research Fields: quilt documentation; historic architecture; folklorist research of local tradition.
Facilities: 250-seat auditorium; educational facilities; theatre. Handcrafted items, books & pens for sale.
Activities: lectures; guided tours; concerts; dance recitals; arts festivals; theatre; organized educational programs; docent program; participatory, loan & temporary exhibitions; hobby workshops. Center Sponsors: Celebration of Arts; Local Art Competition; Heritage Fair; Christmas Show; Quilt Symposium.
Publications: monthly newsletter, Friendsletter.
Hours & Admission Prices: Mon.-Fri. 9-4:30. Museum: adults $2.50, seniors & students $1.50; discounts to AAM members & NC Museums Council; children under 6, members, Art Center, gallery & doll collection no charge. Closed Easter & day after; Independence Day; Labor Day; Thanksgiving; Christmas. ♿
Attendance: 45,000 (accurate)
Membership: Individual, Senior & Family $25; Patron $50; Grand Patron $100; Sponsor $500; Endowment Donor $1,000.

High Point

DOLL & MINIATURE MUSEUM OF HIGH POINT, 101 W. Green Dr., High Point, NC 27260-6620. Tel.: 336-885-3655. Fax: 336-887-2159.
E-mail: dollandminiature@northstate.net
Web Site: dollandminiaturemuseum.org
Formerly: Angela Peterson Doll & Miniature Museum
Founded: 1983.
Congressional District: 6
Key Personnel: Admin., Marlene Hedrick; Museum Shop Mgr., Margaret Starrett.
Governing Authority: Tax-exempt.
Toy Museum.
Collections: dolls; dollhouses; costumes; miniatures; nativity scenes.
Facilities: meeting room.
Activities: Girl Scout Patch program; themed birthday parties & tea parties.
Hours & Admission Prices: Tues.-Sun. Call for hours. Adults $5; discount to military & AAA members; members no charge. Closed holidays. ♿
Membership: Individual $25; Family $50; Patron $100; Advocate $250; Angel $500; Benefactor $1,000; Champion $5,000.

HIGH POINT MUSEUM & HISTORICAL PARK, (M), 1859 E. Lexington Ave., High Point, NC 27262-3499. Tel.: 336-885-1859. Fax: 336-883-3284.
E-mail: hpmuseum@highpointnc.gov
Web Site: www.highpointmuseum.org
Founded: 1966.
Congressional District: 6
Key Personnel: Dir., Edith Brady; Chm. (V), Deane Belk; Registrar, Corinne Midgett; Community Rel., Teresa Loflin; Museum Shop Mgr., Mary Barnett; Cur. Collections, Jennifer Burns; Education Asst., Sarah DeYoung.
Personnel Profile: Full-Time Paid 6; Full-Time Volunteers 1; Part-Time Paid 12; Part-Time Volunteers 40.
Governing Authority: society; nonprofit organization. Parent Institution: High Point Historical Society, Inc. Tax-exempt: 501(c)(3).
History Museum.
Collections: 18th-19th century tools, textiles, ceramics, furniture; industrial, social, civic, military; local area history; photographs; history of High Point, including Native Americans, Quakers, development of furniture & textile industries from settlement to present. Historic Buildings: 1786 John and Phebe Haley House; 1824 Richard Mendenhall Store; 1819 Jamestown Friends Meeting House; blacksmith shop c.1841; 1801 Hoggatt house; High Point, home of John Coltrane & Fantasia Barrino: personal artifacts including his piano; The Little Red Schoolhouse; 1929.
Major Exhibits: High Point's Furniture Heritage, 11/09-12/10.
Research Fields: history of Piedmont; Quaker settlement; High Point local history; economic & technological history of local industries.
Facilities: reference library; 150-seat lecture hall; 25-seat meeting room; 50-seat educational classroom; 40-seat meeting room. Museum-related items for sale.
Activities: guided tours; lectures; films; temporary exhibitions; school & community educational outreach programs; 18th-century skills & crafts hands-on exhibits; museum classes.
Publications: quarterly newsletter; Time Piece, When Racing was Racing; exhibit related pamphlets; African-American Gallery Guide.
Hours & Admission Prices: Museum: Tues.-Sat. 10-4:30, Sun. 1-4:30. Historical Park: Sat. 10-4, Sun. 1-4. No charge. Closed New Year's Day; Martin Luther King Jr. Day; Easter; Memorial Day; Independence Day; Labor Day; Thanksgiving & day after; Christmas Eve & Day. ♿
Attendance: 16,000 (estimated)
Membership: Educator & Student $20; Individual $30; Family $60; Benefactor $110; 1859 Club Member $150; 1859 Club Patron & Friend of History $300; Founder $500; Plank Road Society $1,000; 1859 Club Visionary $1,859;

PIEDMONT ENVIRONMENTAL CENTER, 1220 Penny Rd., High Point, NC 27265-9182. Tel.: 336-883-8531. Fax: 336-883-8537.
E-mail: info@piedmontenvironmental.com
Web Site: www.piedmontenvironmental.com
Founded: 1973.
Congressional District: 6
Key Personnel: Exec. Dir., Richard Thomas; Pres., Steve Hall; Vice Pres., Gary Sturgill.
Personnel Profile: Full-Time Paid 4; Part-Time Volunteers 10; Interns 1.
Governing Authority: nonprofit organization. Tax-exempt: 501(c)(3).
Environmental & Nature Center.
Collections: rocks & minerals of Eastern U.S.; insects; native animals; area reptiles.
Facilities: educational facilities; wildflower meadow.
Activities: public programming; local & extended field trips; school programming; international ecotours.
Publications: bimonthly newsletter.
Hours & Admission Prices: Mon.-Fri. 9-5. No charge; donations accepted. Closed New Year's Day; Easter; Independence Day; Thanksgiving; Christmas. ♿
Attendance: 15,000 (accurate)
Membership: Students $15; Seniors $20; Individual $25; Family $35; Club $50; Leadership $200.

SPRINGFIELD MUSEUM OF OLD DOMESTIC LIFE, 555 E. Springfield Rd., High Point, NC 27263-1843. Mailing Address: 803 Kingston Dr., High Point, NC 27262-7047. Tel.: 910-889-4911; 336-882-3054.
Founded: 1935.
Key Personnel: Dir. & Chief Cur., Brenda Haworth; Asst. Cur., Dan Warren.
Governing Authority: church. Parent Institution: Springfield Memorial Assoc. Tax-exempt.
General Museum: housed in 1858 3rd meeting house located on the site of one of the first Normal schools in North Carolina.
Collections: items used by early settlers: cooking utensils, woodworking tools, shoe making items, old plank road material; loom; Indian artifacts.
Activities: guided tours.
Publications: booklet; book of photographs.
Hours & Admission Prices: By appointment. No charge; donations accepted.
Attendance: 100 (estimated)

Highlands

MUSEUM OF AMERICAN CUT AND ENGRAVED GLASS, 472 Chestnut St., Highlands, NC 28741. Mailing Address: 218 Whiteside Mountain Rd., Highlands, NC 28741-7357. Tel.: 828-526-3415 & 3427.
E-mail: geobon@hcgexpress.net
Founded: 1996.
Key Personnel: Dir., George E. Siek.
Personnel Profile: Full-Time Volunteers 1; Part-Time Volunteers 6.
Governing Authority: Tax-exempt.
Glass Museum.
Collections: American Brilliant Period cut & engraved glass from 1876-1916.
Hours & Admission Prices: May-Oct. Tues., Thurs. & Sat. 1-4; Nov. Sat. 1-4; Dec.-April by appointment. Closed Independence Day unless it falls on Tues., Thurs., or Sat. No charge.
Attendance: 1,500 (estimated)

Hillsborough

ORANGE COUNTY HISTORICAL MUSEUM, 201 N. Churton St., Hillsborough, NC 27278-2535. Tel.: 919-732-2201.
E-mail: info@orangenchistory.org
Web Site: www.orangecountymuseum.org
Founded: 1957.
Congressional District: 4
Key Personnel: Exec. Dir., Darcie Martin; Docent, Cheryl Caskey; Docent, Carol Yavelak; Museum Shop Mgr., Gus St. John.
Personnel Profile: Part-Time Paid 3; Part-Time Volunteers 15; Interns 1.
Governing Authority: board of directors. Tax-exempt.
Local History Museum.
Collections: crafts of early settlers; Indian artifacts; 20-piece set of King's Standard weights & measures; china; silver; loom, spinning wheels & home spun bed spreads & costumes; guns; pump organ.
Research Fields: Orange County history.
Facilities: Museum-related items for sale.
Activities: guided tours; permanent & temporary exhibitions; heritage education program.
Hours & Admission Prices: Jan.-March Tues.-Sun. 1-4; April-Dec. Tues.-Sat. 11-4, Sun. 1-4; group tours by appointment. No charge; donations accepted.
Attendance: 7,300 (accurate)
Membership: Basic $40.

Huntersville

HISTORIC LATTA PLANTATION, 5225 Sample Rd., Huntersville, NC 28078-9107. Tel.: 704-875-2312. Fax: 704-875-1724.
Web Site: www.lattaplantation.org
Founded: 1972.
Key Personnel: Exec. Dir., Kristin Toler; Bd. Pres., Lawrence Kimbrough; Dir. Education, Blair Elder; Visitor Svcs. Mgr., Nicole Glinski.
Personnel Profile: Full-Time Paid 7; Part-Time Paid 2; Part-Time Volunteers 35.
Governing Authority: nonprofit educational institution. Tax-exempt.
Historic House Museum: 1800 house.
Collections: Federal period furniture; decorative arts; agricultural artifacts; back country items; plantation outbuildings; working kitchen; farm animals; period cooking utensils. Historic Buildings: 1800 house; barns; log house.
Research Fields: slavery in Mecklenburg County; 19th century clothing; Latta family; 19th century agriculture; Yeoman farmers.
Facilities: 200-vol. library available to volunteers, Latta descendents & history scholars. Museum-related items for sale.
Activities: self guided tours; educational programs for children; historic craft workshops; living history demonstrations; docent program; membership program; Civil War & Revolutionary War encampments; Back of the Big House program; special events; living history summer camp for children. Museum Sponsors: Folk Life Festival; Backcountry Christmas.
Publications: quarterly newsletter; The Latta Journal; monthly volunteer newsletter, Around the Plantation.
Hours & Admission Prices: Tues.-Sat. 10-5, Sun. 1-5. Adults $6, seniors 62 & over and students $5; discount to groups of 15 or more & AAM members; members & children under 5 no charge. Closed major holidays.
Attendance: 30,000 (accurate)
Membership: Individual $35; Family $60; Patron $100; Sponsor $250; Sustainer $500; Benefactor $1,000.

Kannapolis

THE CANNON VILLAGE VISITOR CENTER, 200 West Ave., Kannapolis, NC 28081-4335. Tel.: 704-938-3200. Fax: 704-932-4188.
Founded: 1974.
Congressional District: 9
Key Personnel: Pres., Lynn Scott Safirt; Mktg. Dir., Phyllis W. Beaver.
Personnel Profile: Part-Time Paid 4.
Governing Authority: company. Parent Institution: Atlantic American Properties, 200 West Ave., Kannapolis, NC. 28081. Subsidiary Institution: Fieldcrest Cannon, Inc.
Company Museum.
Collections: photographs; documents; products; artifacts; textile art; historic artifacts; period handloom; 1,200 year-old samples of textiles; Sam Bass tribute to Dale Earnhardt.
Facilities: 4,500 sq. ft. exhibit area; visitor center.
Activities: multi-image slide show highlighting the textile manufacturing process.
Hours & Admission Prices: Closed for renovations. ♿
Attendance: 42,000 (estimated)

Kenansville

COWAN MUSEUM, 411 S. Main St., Kenansville, NC 28349. Mailing Address: P.O. Box 950, Kenansville, NC 28349-0950. Tel.: 910-296-2149.
Web Site: www.cowanmuseum.com
Key Personnel: Cur., Mrs. Ila O. Cowan
History Museum.
Collections: local history & culture; photographs; period artifacts.
Hours & Admission Prices: Tues.-Sat. 10-4, Sun. 2-4. No charge. Closed holidays. ♿

Kenly

TOBACCO FARM LIFE MUSEUM, INC., Hwy. 301 N., 709 Church St., Kenly, NC 27542. Mailing Address: P.O. Box 88, Kenly, NC 27542-0088. Tel.: 919-284-3431; 800-965-1437. Fax: 919-284-9788.
E-mail: director@tobaccofarmlifemuseum.org
Web Site: www.tobaccofarmlifemuseum.org.
Founded: 1983.
Congressional District: 3
Key Personnel: Mgr., Elaine Richardson; Chm. (V), Pender Sharp; Cur., Melony Johnson; Visitor Svcs. Coord. & Museum Shop Mgr., Elaine Richardson.
Personnel Profile: Full-Time Paid 2; Full-Time Volunteers 1; Part-Time Paid 5; Part-Time Volunteers 50; Interns 1.
Governing Authority: Tax-exempt: 501(c)(3).
Agriculture Museum.
Collections: farm tools, implements & equipment used to produce, harvest & market flue-cured tobacco and other native NC products; agricultural tools & items; rural household furnishings; textiles; personal papers & documents. Historic Buildings: c.1900 farmhouse; detached kitchen; smoke house; log tobacco curing barn; blacksmith shop; one room schoolhouse.
Research Fields: eastern North Carolina farming families.
Facilities: 4,000 sq. ft. exhibit space; 50-seat theatre. Gifts, books & museum-related items for sale.
Activities: tours; films; organized educational programs; hands-on children's exhibit; intern program; farmers market. Museum Sponsors: Festival; Anniversary Celebration; Christmas Celebration.
Publications: annual report; newsletter.
Hours & Admission Prices: mid-Jan. to Dec. Mon.-Sat. 9:30-5, Sun. 2-5. Adults $6, senior citizens $5, students $4; discounts to AAM, AAA & NCMC members; members & children 2 & under no charge. Closed Easter; Thanksgiving; Christmas & day after. ♿
Attendance: 13,000 (accurate)
Membership: Senior $15; Individual $25; Family $50; Grower $120; Harvester $240; Producer $600; Planter $1,000; Corporate $1,000 & up.

Kernersville

KORNER'S FOLLY, 413 S. Main St., Kernersville, NC 27284-2737. Tel.: 336-996-7922. Fax: 336-996-1199.
E-mail: bruce@kornersfolly.org
Web Site: www.kornersfolly.org
Founded: 1996.
Congressional District: 5
Key Personnel: Exec. Dir., Bruce Frankel; Pres., Norma Pearman; Treas., Laurie McDaniel.
Personnel Profile: Full-Time Paid 1; Part-Time Paid 2; Part-Time Volunteers 85.
Governing Authority: private; nonprofit organization. Parent Institution: Korner's Folly Foundation. Tax-exempt: 501(c)(3).
Historic House: c.1880 Victorian home.
Collections: furnishings; smoke house; Aunt Dealy's house.
Research Fields: construction & restoration 1880-1900.
Activities: formal education programs & tours for school children; guided tours; theater; monthly children's puppet show. Annual Events: Christmas at Korner's Folly; Founder's Day; Kenersville Little Theater's Annual Fall Production; Annual Winetasting Fundraiser.
Publications: quarterly newsletter, The Kornerstone.
Hours & Admission Prices: Thurs.-Sat. 10-4, Sun. 1-4. Adults $8, children $4; discounts to groups of 20 or more; children under 6 no charge. Closed New Year's Day; Easter; Thanksgiving; Christmas Eve.
Attendance: 10,000 (estimated)
Membership: Individual $35; Family $50; Friend of Folly $100; Jule Korner: Founder $300, Visionary $500, Preservationist $1,000.

Kill Devil Hills

WRIGHT BROTHERS NATIONAL MEMORIAL, 1000 Croatan Hwy., Kill Devil Hills, NC 27948. Mailing Address: 1400 National Park Dr., Manteo, NC 27954. Tel.: 252-441-7430, ext. 0. Fax: 252-473-2595.
Web Site: www.nps.gov/wrbr
Founded: 1927.
Congressional District: 3
Key Personnel: Supt., Mike Murray.
Personnel Profile: Full-Time Paid 6; Part-Time Volunteers 12.
Governing Authority: federal. Parent Institution: Dept. of the Interior. Subsidiary Institution: U.S. National Park Service, Interior Building, Washington, DC 20240. Tax-exempt.
Located on the site of the Wright Brothers first powered flight in 1903. Centennial Pavilion: reconstructed Wright camp buildings & 60 ft. memorial shaft atop Big Kill Devil Hill.
Collections: replicas of 1903 flyer; 1902 glider & wind tunnel moon cloth that Neil Armstrong took to the moon in 1969; original parts of the Wright Flyer, tools used by the Wright brothers; Wright Brothers sculpture.
Research Fields: aviation library; photographs.
Facilities: Books & museum-related items for sale.
Activities: guided tours; lectures. Annual Event: celebration of first successful powered flight by Orville & Wilbur Wright; Wilbur Wright's Birthday in April; 29th Annual Wright Kite Festival in July; National Aviation Day & Orville Wright's Birthday in August; Anniversary of the First Flight in Dec.
Hours & Admission Prices: mid-June to Labor Day daily 9-6; Sept. to mid-June daily 9-5. Adults $4; seniors with Golden Age Card Federal Pass & children under 16 no charge. Closed Christmas Day. ♿
Attendance: 496,500 (accurate)

Kings Mountain

CROWDERS MOUNTAIN STATE PARK, 522 Park Office Lane, Kings Mountain, NC 28086-7902. Tel.: 704-853-5375. Fax: 704-853-5391.
Founded: 1993.
Congressional District: 10
Key Personnel: Park Supt., Larry Hyde.
Personnel Profile: Full-Time Paid 12; Part-Time Paid 7; Part-Time Volunteers 10.
Governing Authority: Parent Institution: NC State Parks. Tax exempt.
Park & Visitors Center.
Collections: wildlife & their habitats; mounted wildlife; plants; environment.
Facilities: classroom; auditorium; nature trails.
Activities: hiking.
Hours & Admission Prices: Park: March-April & Sept.-Oct. daily 8-8; May-Aug. daily 8-9; June-Aug. daily 8-9; Nov.-Feb. daily 8-6. No charge. ♿
Attendance: 349,000 (accurate)

Kinston

CSS NEUSE STATE HISTORIC SITE AND GOV. RICHARD CASWELL MEMORIAL, U.S. Hwy. 70 Business, 2612 W. Vernon Ave., Kinston, NC 28504. Tel.: 252-522-2091. Fax: 252-527-7036.
E-mail: cssneuse@ncdcr.gov
Web Site: www.cssneuse.nchistoricsites.org
Founded: 1965.
Congressional District: 4
Key Personnel: Historic Site Mgr., Guy Smith; Historic Interpreter III, Morris Bass; Historic Interpreter II & Museum Shop Mgr., Holly Weaver; Historic Site Asst., Thomas R. Dawson; Office Asst. III, Sharon Clements; Maintenance Mechanic II, Gaston Davis.
Personnel Profile: Full-Time Paid 6; Part-Time Paid 3.
Governing Authority: state. North Carolina Dept. of Cultural Resources, 4601 Mail Service Center, Raleigh, NC 27699-4601. Tax-exempt: 170(b).
Historic Site.
Collections: artifacts from the ram Neuse; sunken Confederate iron clad gunboat c.1862-65; hull of ship; items depicting life of Richard Caswell, first elected governor of N.C., 1776-1780 & 1784-1787.
Facilities: picnic facility.
Activities: guided tours; lectures; audiovisual program; formally organized education programs; living history demonstrations; hands-on ropemaking & demonstrations.
Publications: brochure; The CSS NEUSE: A Question of Iron & Time.
Hours & Admission Prices: Call for hours. No charge; donations accepted. Closed major state holidays. ♿
Attendance: 13,000 (estimated)

COMMUNITY COUNCIL FOR THE ARTS, 400 N. Queen St., Kinston, NC 28501-4328. Tel.: 252-527-2517. Fax: 252-527-8280.
E-mail: slandis@kinstoncca.com
Web Site: www.kinstoncca.com
Formerly: Kinston Arts Council, Inc.
Founded: 1965.
Congressional District: 1
Key Personnel: Exec. Dir., Sandy Landis; Pres., Vickie Robinson; Dir. Gallery, Niki Litts; Financial Svcs. Dir., Elaine Carmon.
Personnel Profile: Full-Time Paid 2; Part-Time Paid 3; Part-Time Volunteers 15.
Governing Authority: nonprofit. Affiliated with North Carolina Arts Council, Raleigh, NC 27611. Tel.: 919-733-7897. Tax-exempt.
Arts Council: housed in historic building.
Collections: works by North Carolina & international artists; model trains.
Facilities: meeting room; children's gallery; classrooms. Museum-related items for sale.
Activities: guided tours; arts festivals; competitive art exhibition; permanent & temporary exhibitions; classes; workshops; special projects & events; performing arts programs.
Publications: monthly newsletter, Kaleidoscope.
Hours & Admission Prices: Tues.-Fri. 10-6, Sat. 10-2. No charge, donations accepted. Closed state holidays. ♿
Attendance: 10,000
Membership: Individual $50; Family $100; Donor $150; Sponsor $250; Patron $500; Sustainer $1,000; Renaissance $5,000.

Kure Beach

FORT FISHER STATE HISTORIC SITE, U.S. Hwy. 421-1610 Fort Fisher Blvd., S. of Kure Beach, Kure Beach, NC 28449. Mailing Address: Box 169, Kure Beach, NC 28449-0169. Tel.: 910-458-5538. Fax: 910-458-0477.
E-mail: fisher@ncdcr.gov
Web Site: www.fortfisher.nchistoricsites.org
Founded: 1961.
Congressional District: 7
Personnel Profile: Full-Time Paid 5; Part-Time Paid 3; Part-Time Volunteers 15; Interns 1.
Governing Authority: state. North Carolina Dept. of Cultural Resources, 109 E. Jones St., Raleigh, 27611. Tax-exempt: 170(b).
Historic Site & Visitor Center.
Collections: underwater archaeology; military accoutrements; memorabilia; Civil War fort ruins & remains; Civil War artifacts; findings from sunken blockade runners.
Research Fields: Civil War Coastal Defenses.
Facilities: visitor center; Civil War military earthworks; trails.
Activities: guided tours; lectures; formally organized education programs; living history events.
Publications: brochure.
Hours & Admission Prices: April-Sept. Mon.-Sat. 9-5, Sun. 1-5; Oct.-March Tues.-Sat. 10-4. No charge; donations accepted. Closed major holidays. ♿
Attendance: 700,000 (accurate)

NORTH CAROLINA AQUARIUM AT FORT FISHER, 900 Loggerhead Rd., Kure Beach, NC 28449-3786. Tel.: 910-458-8257. Fax: 910-458-6812.
E-mail: kathy.pinnick@ncdenr.gov
Web Site: www.ncaquariums.com
Founded: 1976.
Congressional District: 7
Key Personnel: Dir., Donna D. Moffitt; Dir. Operations & Husbandry, Paul Barrington; Cur. Exhibits, David Barney; Cur. Education, Peggy Sloan; Aquariology Cur., Hap Fatzinger; Dive Coord., Brian Germick; Aquarist, Melissa Johnson; Aquarist, Michael Suchy; Aquarist, Rich Bamberger; Aquarist, Keith Farmer; Aquarist, Julie Johnson; Aquarist, Marc Neill; Bldg. Supt., Tom Coit; Business Mgr., Nancy Peterson; Visitor Svcs. Coord., Martha Latta; Media Technician, Bob Griffin; Events Coord., Terry Bryant; Publicity & Mktg., Amy Kilgore.
Personnel Profile: Full-Time Paid 39; Part-Time Paid 38; Part-Time Volunteers 200; Interns 6.
Governing Authority: state. Parent Institution: North Carolina Dept. of Environment & Natural Resources, Aquariums Division, 3125 Poplarwood Ct., Ste. 160, Raleigh, NC 27604. Tel. 919-877-5500. Other Aquariums: North Carolina Aquarium-Roanoke Island, P.O. Box 967, Manteo, NC 27954. Tel. 252-473-3493; North Carolina Aquarium-Pine Knoll Shores, P.O. Box 580, Atlantic Beach, NC 28512. Tel. 252-247-4003.
Aquarium: aquatic life & habitats of North Carolina.
Collections: live saltwater & freshwater fishes; sea turtles; sharks; stingrays; alligators; lion fish.
Research Fields: marine sciences, with emphasis on marine biology.
Facilities: freshwater conservatory; gardens; aquarium; auditorium; classrooms. Educational items & aquarium-related items for sale.
Activities: lectures; films; formally organized education programs by appointment; docent programs or council; field trips; summer camps; outreach programs.
Publications: monthly online Calendar of Events; teachers guide, The Aquarium News; various information folders.
Hours & Admission Prices: Daily 9-5. Adults $8, seniors $7, children 6-17 $6; discount to AZA members; children under 6, registered school groups, Aquarium Society & AZA members no charge. Closed New Year's Day; Thanksgiving Day; Christmas Day. ♿
Attendance: 408,000 (accurate)
Membership: Individual $30; Family $50; Donor $100; Patron $300; Benefactor $1,000.

Lake Junaluska

WORLD METHODIST MUSEUM, 575 N. Lakeshore Dr., Lake Junaluska, NC 28745-9742. Mailing Address: P.O. Box 518, Lake Junaluska, NC 28745-0518. Tel.: 828-456-9432, ext. 4. Fax: 828-456-9433.
Web Site: www.worldmethodistcouncil.org
Founded: 1954.
Congressional District: 11
Key Personnel: Gen. Sec. World Methodist Council, Dr. George Freeman; Asst. to Gen. Sec., Roma Wyatt; Museum Dir., Dianne N. Mills.
Personnel Profile: Full-Time Paid 1; Part-Time Paid 1; Interns 1.
Governing Authority: church. Parent Institution: World Methodist Council. Tax-exempt.
Religious History Museum.
Collections: items of early Methodism from 18th century England including original letters by John Wesley, Francis Asbury & Thomas Coke; traveling pulpit used by Wesley; pottery busts of John Wesley & other Staffordshire artisans; John Hurst Watercolors of Wesley's England; Frank O. Salisbury portraits.
Major Exhibits: Francis Asbury & Frontier Methodism, 11/09-12/09.
Research Fields: Methodist Church history & the 74 member churches of Council.
Facilities: library of rare books.
Activities: guided & self-guided tours; video tape introduction.
Publications: newsletter of World Methodist Council, World Parish; newsletter, WMC First Friday Newsletter.
Hours & Admission Prices: Summer: Mon.-Fri. 9-5, Sat. 10-2; Fall, Winter, & Spring Mon.-Fri. 9-5. No charge; donations accepted. Closed holidays. ♿
Attendance: 6,000 (accurate)
Membership: Friends of the Museum: Contributor $25; Sustainer $50; Sponsor $100; Patron $500; Benefactor $1,000; Grand Benefactor $3,000.

Lake Waccamaw

LAKE WACCAMAW DEPOT MUSEUM, 201 Flemington Ave., Lake Waccamaw, NC 28450. Mailing Address: P.O. Box 386, Lake Waccamaw, NC 28450-0386. Tel.: 910-646-1992.
E-mail: lwdm@ncez.net
Founded: 1977.
Congressional District: 7
Key Personnel: Chm. (V), Nancy Sigmon; Treas., Martha Lowe; Cur., Ginger Littrell; Museum Shop Mgr., Lynn Cain.
Personnel Profile: Part-Time Paid 1.
Governing Authority: nonprofit organization. Tax-exempt: 501(c)(3).
Marine Science & History Museum: housed in c.1904 railroad station.
Collections: photographs; deeds; artifacts; fossils; tools; mounted birds; railroad & logging industry artifacts; Waccamaw-Siouan Indians from Archaic Period (8,000-500 B.C.).
Activities: guided tours; lectures; films; formally organized educational programs; permanent exhibitions; slide presentation; canoeing; camping; hiking; fossil hunts; field trips. Museum Sponsors: The Way It Was; chartered bus tours; Indian dance teams.
Publications: brochures; quarterly program, Calendar of Events.
Hours & Admission Prices: Wed.-Fri. 10-3, Sun. 3-5. No charge; donations accepted. ♿
Attendance: 3,600 (estimated)
Membership: Individual $15; Family $25; Associate $35; Patron $50; Sustaining $100; Benefactor $500 & up.

Laurinburg

ST. ANDREWS PRESBYTERIAN COLLEGE ART GALLERY, 1700 Dogwood Mile, Laurinburg, NC 28352-5521. Tel.: 910-277-5555. Fax: 910-277-5020.
Art Gallery.
Collections: paintings; photographs; sculpture.
Hours & Admission Prices: Mon.-Fri. 9-4:30. No charge.

Lenoir

CALDWELL ARTS COUNCIL, 601 College Ave., Lenoir, NC 28645-5406. Mailing Address: P.O. Box 1613, Lenoir, NC 28645-1613. Tel.: 828-754-2486. Fax: 828-754-2440.
E-mail: info@caldwellarts.com
Web Site: www.caldwellarts.com
Founded: 1976.
Key Personnel: Dir., Lee Carol Giduz
Cultural Arts Museum.
Collections: paintings; sculpture.
Activities: art classes; arist competitions; grants to community; temporary exhibitions.
Hours & Admission Prices: Tues.-Fri. 9-5, Sat. by appointment.

CALDWELL HERITAGE MUSEUM, (M), 112 Vaiden St., Lenoir, NC 28645-5670. Tel.: 828-758-4004.
Web Site: www.caldwellheritagemuseum.org
Founded: 1991.
Key Personnel: Dir., John O. Hawkins; Chm. (V), Bob Booth.
Personnel Profile: Full-Time Volunteers 1; Part-Time Paid 1.
Governing Authority: Tax-exempt.
History Museum.
Collections: Caldwell County history; photographs.
Hours & Admission Prices: Tues.-Fri. 10-4:30, Sat. 10-3. No charge.

FORT DEFIANCE, 1792 Fort Defiance Dr., Lenoir, NC 28645-6606. Tel.: 828-758-1671.
Historic Building: former home of Revolutionary War hero, Gen. William Lenoir; built in 1792.
Collections: military history; personal artifacts; period furnishings; military uniforms; clothing.
Hours & Admission Prices: Call for hours.

TUTTLE EDUCATIONAL STATE FOREST, 3420 Playmore Beach Rd., Lenoir, NC 28655. Tel.: 828-757-5608.
Governing Authority: nonprofit organization.
Park Museum.
Collections: local history; ecosystems; plants; trees; flowers.
Facilities: nature trail.
Activities: classes; workshops; picnic area; hiking.
Hours & Admission Prices: Call for hours.

Lexington

DAVIDSON COUNTY HISTORICAL MUSEUM, (M), 2 S. Main St.-Old Courthouse, Lexington, NC 27292-3320. Tel.: 336-242-2035. Fax: 336-242-2871.
E-mail: choffmann@co.davidson.nc.us
Web Site: www.co.davidson.nc.us/museum
Founded: 1976.
Congressional District: 6

Key Personnel: Cur., Catherine Matthews Hoffmann; Registrar, Pamela Daniel.
Personnel Profile: Full-Time Paid 1; Part-Time Paid 2; Part-Time Volunteers 4; Interns 1.
Governing Authority: county. Parent Institution: Davidson County. Subsidiary Institution: Davidson County Historical Association. Tax-exempt: 501(c)(3).
Local History Museum: housed in c.1858 county's oldest existing courthouse. Listed on the Naional Register of Historic Places.
Collections: local history. Historic Building: 1858 courthouse building.
Research Fields: local history.
Facilities: courtroom; balcony; jury room & holding room.
Activities: guided tours; lectures; formally organized education programs; temporary & traveling exhibitions.
Publications: quarterly newsletter.
Hours & Admission Prices: Tues.-Fri. 10-4, first Sun. of month 2-4. No charge; donations accepted. Closed holidays. ♿
Attendance: 18,000 (accurate)

Lincolnton

LINCOLN COUNTY MUSEUM OF HISTORY, (M), 403 E. Main St., Lincolnton, NC 28092-3305. Tel.: 704-748-9090. Fax: 704-732-9057.
E-mail: lcmh@bellsouth.net
Web Site: www.lincolncountyhistory.com
Founded: 1955.
Congressional District: 10
Key Personnel: Exec. Dir., Jason L. Harpe; Cur. Archaeology & Collections, January W. Porter; Administrative Asst., Tina Guffey.
Personnel Profile: Full-Time Paid 1; Part-Time Paid 2; Part-Time Volunteers 20.
Governing Authority: Tax-exempt.
History Museum.
Collections: Lincoln County heritage & history; Native American artifacts; early immigrants; the Battle of Ramsour's Mill; Civil War; archaeological artifacts; ceramics; archives.
Activities: seminars & programs; cemetery preservation; Tarheel Junior Historian Camp; digital photography courses; archaeology camp.
Publications: The Lincoln Sentinel.
Hours & Admission Prices: Tues. & Thurs. 1-5, Sun. 2-5. No charge; donations accepted. ♿
Attendance: 4,000 (estimated)

Linville

GRANDFATHER MOUNTAIN, 2050 Blowing Rock Hwy., Linville, NC 28646. Mailing Address: P.O. Box 129, Linville, NC 28646. Tel.: 800-468-7325. Fax: 828-733-2608.
E-mail: nature@grandfather.com
Nature Center.
Collections: black bears; river otters; cougars; bald eagles; golden eagles; white-tailed deer.
Facilities: nature trails. Museum-related items for sale.
Activities: hiking.
Hours & Admission Prices: Spring & Fall daily 8-6, Summer: daily 8-7; Winter: daily 9-5. Adults 13-59 $15, seniors 60 & over $13, children 4-12 $7; children under 4 no charge.

Louisburg

LOUISBURG COLLEGE ART GALLERY, 501 N. Main St., Louisburg, NC 27549-2399. Tel.: 919-496-2521. Fax: 919-496-1788.
Web Site: www.louisburg.edu/news/art.html
Founded: 1957.
Key Personnel: Dir. & Cur., William Hinton; Business Officer, Belinda Faulkner; Public Rels. & Publications Dir., Amy McManus.
Governing Authority: college; nonprofit organization. Affiliated with Louisburg College. Tax-exempt.
Art Gallery: housed in 1787 Louisburg College auditorium theatre complex.
Collections: primitive, American impressionist & contemporary art.
Facilities: classrooms.
Activities: guided tours; lectures; gallery talks; arts festivals; loan, permanent, & temporary exhibitions.
Publications: Alumni Review.
Hours & Admission Prices: Aug.-April Mon.-Fri. 9-5. No charge. Closed holidays. ♿
Attendance: 10,000

Lumberton

ROBESON PLANETARIUM AND SCIENCE CENTER, 410 Caton Rd., Lumberton, NC 28358. Tel.: 910-735-2147.
E-mail: brandt@uncp.edu
Web Site: www.robesonsky.com
Key Personnel: Dir., Ken Brandt
Planetarium & Science Center.
Collections: geology; space science.
Activities: educational programs & shows.
Hours & Admission Prices: Call for hours & admission.

Maggie Valley

WHEELS THROUGH TIME MUSEUM, INC., 62 Vintage Lane, Maggie Valley, NC 28751. Mailing Address: P.O. Box 790, Maggie Valley, NC 28751-0790. Tel.: 828-926-6266. Fax: 828-926-9158.
E-mail: info@wheelsthroughtime.com
Founded: 2002.
Congressional District: 11
Motorcycle & Automobile Museum.
Collections: over 230 period motorcycles & automobiles from 1903 to present; factory lithographs; photographs; posters; clothing; trophies; autographed photos.
Research Fields: Blue Ridge transportation history.
Facilities: Museum-related items for sale.
Hours & Admission Prices: April-Nov. daily 9-5; Dec.-March daily 10-5. Adults $12, seniors 65 & over $10, children 6-12 $6. ♿
Attendance: 50,000
Membership: Annual $100; Lifetime $300.

Manteo

FORT RALEIGH NATIONAL HISTORIC SITE, 1401 National Park Dr., Manteo, NC 27954-9451. Tel.: 252-473-5772. Fax: 252-473-2595.
E-mail: milagros_flores@nps.gov
Web Site: www.nps.gov/fora
Founded: 1941.
Congressional District: 3
Key Personnel: Supt., Mike Murray; Volunteer Coord., Mary Doll; Museum Shop Mgr., Rulaine Kegerris.
Personnel Profile: Full-Time Paid 3; Part-Time Paid 2; Part-Time Volunteers 3.
Governing Authority: federal. Parent Institution: National Park Service. Tax-exempt.
Historic Park Museum: located on the site of the 1585-1587 Roanoke Island Colony attempts.
Collections: relics from period of first colony; history; archaeology; Indian artifacts.
Facilities: 70-seat auditorium. Museum-related items for sale.
Activities: guided tours; lectures; films; permanent exhibitions. Park Sponsors: The Lost Colony in summer.
Publications: handbook, Fort Raleigh.
Hours & Admission Prices: Park: daily sunrise to sunset. Visitor Center: daily 9-5. Closed Christmas. ♿
Attendance: 170,780 (estimated)

NORTH CAROLINA AQUARIUM ON ROANOKE ISLAND, 374 Airport Rd., Manteo, NC 27954-9485. Mailing Address: P.O. Box 967, Maneto, NC 27954-0967. Tel.: 252-473-3494. Fax: 252-473-1980.
E-mail: rlmail@ncaquariums.com
Web Site: www.ncaquariums.com
Founded: 1976.
Congressional District: 3
Key Personnel: Dir., Joe Malat; Business Mgr., Carol Smith; Dir. Operations & Husbandry, Frank Hudgins; Cur. Education, Pat Raves.
Personnel Profile: Full-Time Paid 40; Part-Time Paid 15; Part-Time Volunteers 20; Interns 7.
Governing Authority: state government. Parent Institution: N.C. Aquariums.
Aquarium.
Collections: over 300 species of native/regional fish, reptiles & amphibians and invertebrates; over 2000 specimens; concentration in coastal northeastern North Carolina habitats & aquatic life.
Research Fields: aquatic animal (sea turtle & marine mammal) rehabilitation.
Facilities: 800-vol. library of books & reports of coastal nature; extensive vertical files of coastal North Carolina topics covering over 20 years. Educational items of marine & aquatic nature for sale.
Activities: docent program; films; formal education programs for adults, children & college students; lectures; participatory & temporary exhibitions; training programs; rental gallery. Annual Events: Wild Foods Weekend; Shark Discovery Day; Earth Day Festival.
Publications: quarterly, Events Calendar & Newsletter.

Hours & Admission Prices: Daily 9-5. Adults $8, senior citizens $7, children 6-17 $6; children 5 & under, members, NC aquarium society, NC school groups, Martin Luther King Day, & Veterans Day no charge. Closed New Year's Day; Thanksgiving; Christmas. ♿
Attendance: 350,000 (accurate)
Membership: Individual $25; Family $40; Donor $100; Patron $300; Director $500; Benefactor $1,000.

ROANOKE ISLAND FESTIVAL PARK, One Festival Park, Manteo, NC 27954-9396. Tel.: 252-475-1500. Fax: 252-475-1507.
E-mail: rifp.information@ncmail.net
Web Site: www.roanokeisland.com
Founded: 1983.
Congressional District: 2
Key Personnel: Acting Exec. Dir., Kim Sawyer; Chm. (V), Dr. Tom Brooks; Pres. (V), Friends of Elizabeth II, Tod Clissold; Operations Mgr., Amy Hinnant; Facilities Mgr., Carroll Williams; Communications Mgr., Tanya Young.
Personnel Profile: Full-Time Paid 39; Part-Time Paid 20; Part-Time Volunteers 52; Interns 1.
Governing Authority: state. Parent Institution: North Carolina Dept. of Cultural Resources, Raleigh, NC 27611. Subsidiary Institution: Roanoke Island Commission. Tax-exempt: 170(b)(1)(A).
History Museum: living history 1585 settlement site & replica 16th century ship.
Collections: reproductions of 16th-century artifacts; tools; equipment; personal artifacts & furnishings; Outer Banks history; working reproduction of 16th-century English sailing vessel.
Research Fields: Elizabethan England & exploration; 16th-century life in coastal North America; Roanoke Island Civil War; Roanoke Island Freedman's Colony; Outer Banks; maritime history; national cultures of Roanoke Island.
Facilities: theater; 3,500-seat outdoor pavilion; maritime boatshop; visitor center; nature boardwalk & trails. Museum-related items for sale.
Activities: tours; audiovisual program; living history presentation; volunteer sailing program.
Publications: brochures; quarterly newsletter, The Voyager.
Hours & Admission Prices: Daily 9-5. Adults $8, students $5; members & children under 5 no charge. ♿
Attendance: 150,000 (accurate)
Membership: Individual $25; Dual $40; Family $50; Participating $100; Corporate $200.

Marion

HISTORIC CARSON HOUSE, 1805 US Hwy. 70 W., Marion, NC 28752. Tel.: 828-724-4948.
Web Site: www.historiccarsonhouse.com
Founded: 1964.
Congressional District: 11
Key Personnel: Chm. (V) & Pres., Dr. James Haney; Treas., Richard Buchanan; Sec., Ann McNutt; Exec. Dir., Sara Bryant.
Personnel Profile: Part-Time Paid 1; Part-Time Volunteers 30.
Governing Authority: nonprofit organization. Parent Institution: Carson House Restoration Inc. Tax-exempt: 501(c)(3); 170(b)(1)(A).
History Museum: housed in 1793 Col. John Carson House.
Collections: 350 artifacts dating back to pioneer times; manuscripts; hand woven coverlets; three quilts made & quilted by slaves; quilt woven by a Princess slave; hand woven towels; clocks; period furniture; grand piano; organ; musical instruments.
Major Exhibits: Barn Exhibit, 4/10-11/10; Art of Farm Life, 4/10-11/10; Pieces of the Heart (Quilts), 4/10-11/10.
Research Fields: family histories; Civil War; Revolutionary War.
Facilities: library of genealogy, family histories, national, state & local books available for use on premises; reading room.
Activities: guided tours; study clubs; formally organized educational programs; permanent & temporary exhibitions.
Publications: book, Stories Not Told in History Books; Where Early Settlers Made Their Homes; Life of Samuel Price Carson; Research Study of Carson House; McDowell County Pictorial History; book, Everything That's All.
Hours & Admission Prices: April-Nov. Wed.-Sat. 10-4, Sun. 2-5; groups by appointment. Adults $5, children $1.50; discounts to groups of 10 or more; children under 12 no charge. ♿
Attendance: 4,000 (estimated)

LINVILLE CAVERNS, 19929 US 221 N., Marion, NC 28752. Tel.: 800-419-0540. Fax: 828-756-4171.
E-mail: info@linvillecaverns.com
Geology Museum.
Collections: geology; local history; science.
Facilities: visitors center.
Activities: guided tours.
Hours & Admission Prices: Call for hours.

Mars Hill

RURAL LIFE MUSEUM, Mars Hill College, Montague Bldg., 100 Athletic St., Mars Hill, NC 28754. Mailing Address: Mars Hill College, P.O. Box 6706, Mars Hill, NC 28754-5000. Tel.: 828-689-1262.
History Museum.
Collections: Southern Appalachian culture & history.
Hours & Admission Prices: By appointment. No charge.

Midland

REED GOLD MINE STATE HISTORIC SITE, 9621 Reed Mine Rd., Midland, NC 28107-9673. Tel.: 704-721-4653. Fax: 704-721-4657.
E-mail: johnreed1799@gmail.com
Web Site: www.nchistoricsites.org/reed
Founded: 1971.
Congressional District: 8
Key Personnel: Site Mgr., Sharon Robinson; Museum Shop Mgr., Susan Smith.
Personnel Profile: Full-Time Paid 6; Part-Time Paid 8; Part-Time Volunteers 6.
Governing Authority: state. Parent Institution: North Carolina Department of Cultural Resources, 109 E. Jones St., Raleigh, NC 27611. Tax-exempt: 501(c)(3); 170(b)(1)(A).
Historic Site: 1799 site of the first documented discovery of gold in the United States.
Collections: 19th- to 20th-century mining machinery; coins; steam engines; artifacts; c.1895 operating stamp mill.
Research Fields: local history; gold mining.
Facilities: library; visitor center; trails; panning station; stamp mill; picnic area.
Activities: guided tours; lectures; formally organized educational programs for children; instruction in gold panning; film; underground workings.
Publications: guidebook; brochure; biannual newsletter, Golden Gazette; The Story of John Reed.
Hours & Admission Prices: Tues.-Sat. 9-5. No charge; donations accepted. Gold panning: $2, group panning $1.50. Closed state holidays. ♿
Attendance: 47,000 (accurate)
Membership: Iron $25; Nickel $50; Copper $100; Silver $250; Gold $500; Midas Club $1,000.

Montreat

PRESBYTERIAN HERITAGE CENTER, (M), 318 Georgia Ter., Montreat, NC 28757. Mailing Address: P.O. Box 207, Montreat, NC 28757-0207. Tel.: 828-669-6556.
Key Personnel: Pres., Frank L. Arnold
Heritage Center.
Collections: Presbyterian history; photographs; period furnishings; religious artifacts.
Hours & Admission Prices: Tues.-Fri. 10-4, Sat. 1-4, Sun. 1:30-4.

Mooresville

NORTH CAROLINA AUTO RACING HALL OF FAME, 119 Knob Hill Rd., Lakeside Park, Mooresville, NC 28117-6847. Tel.: 704-663-5331.
E-mail: donna@ncarhof.com
Web Site: www.ncarhof.com
Key Personnel: Mgr., Donna DeNardo
Auto Racing Museum.
Collections: heritage of motorsports; over 35 race cars; Hall of Fame Inductees.
Facilities: theater. Museum-related items for sale.
Activities: Museum Sponsors: Induction Ceremony.
Hours & Admission Prices: Mon.-Fri. 10-5, Sat. 10-3. Adults $6, seniors 55 & over and children 6-12 $3.

Morehead City

THE HISTORY PLACE, (M), The History Place, 1008 Arendell St., Morehead City, NC 28557-4143. Tel.: 252-247-7533. Fax: 252-247-2756.
E-mail: historyplace@starfishnet.com
Web Site: www.thehistoryplace.org
Formerly: Carteret County Museum of History & Art
Founded: 1971.
Key Personnel: Pres. (V), Janet Eshleman; Librarian, David Montgomery;

Exec. Dir., Cindi Hamilton; Museum Shop Mgr., Grace Ewen; Museum Shop Mgr., Stacey Veros.
Personnel Profile: Full-Time Paid 1; Part-Time Paid 1; Part-Time Volunteers 120.
Governing Authority: Tax-exempt.
History & Art Museum.
Collections: local genealogy; memorabilia of Carteret County; pictures & artifacts.
Facilities: research library; tea room; auditorium; banquet facility; conference room. Museum-related items for sale.
Activities: walking tours; programs; bus tours; genealogy seminars; monthly meetings; Sunday Supplement programs; concerts; children's programs; antique shows; concerts; lunch with Rodney - history lectures.
Publications: history journal, The Researcher; local books.
Hours & Admission Prices: Tues.-Sat. 10-4. No charge; donations accepted. Closed holidays. ♿
Attendance: 38,000 (accurate)
Membership: $10; $25; $30; $35; $250; Business $100.

Morganton

MCDOWELL HOUSE AT QUAKER MEADOWS, 119 St. Mary's Church Rd., Morganton, NC 28680. Mailing Address: P.O. Box 915, Morganton, NC 28680-0915. Tel.: 828-437-4104.
E-mail: historicburkefou@bellsouth.net
Web Site: www.historicburke.org
Historic House Museum: built in 1812 by Captain Charles McDowell, Jr.
Collections: area history; 19th century life.
Hours & Admission Prices: April-Oct. Sun. 2-4; other times by appointment. No charge.

SENATOR SAM J. ERVIN, JR. LIBRARY AND MUSEUM, Western Piedmont Community College, 1001 Burkemont Ave., Morganton, NC 28655. Mailing Address: 1001 Burkemont Ave., Morganton, NC 28655-4504. Tel.: 828-438-6152.
E-mail: library@wpcc.edu
Web Site: www.samervinlibrary.org
Founded: 1990.
Congressional District: 10
Key Personnel: Cur., Daniel R. Smith; Asst. Cur., Nancy Daniel.
Personnel Profile: Part-Time Paid 4.
Governing Authority: Parent Institution: Western Piedmont Foundation. Subsidiary Institution: Ervin Library Fund. Tax-exempt.
History Museum.
Collections: replica of Senator Ervin's home library; books; correspondence; photographs; furniture; memorabilia.
Hours & Admission Prices: Mon.-Fri. 8-5. No charge.

Mount Airy

GERTRUDE SMITH HOUSE, (M), 708 N. Main St., Mount Airy, NC 27030. Mailing Address: 615 N. Main St., Mount Airy, NC 27030-3723. Tel.: 336-786-6856; 800-576-0231. Fax: 336-786-9193.
E-mail: visitandy@visitmountairy.com
Web Site: www.visitmountairy.com
Founded: 1984.
Congressional District: 5
Key Personnel: Chm., Edward N. Swanson; Exec. Dir., Ann L. Vaughn; Sec. Foundation, David Beal.
Personnel Profile: Full-Time Paid 1; Part-Time Paid 7; Part-Time Volunteers 6; Interns 1.
Governing Authority: nonprofit organization. Parent Institution: Gilmer-Smith Foundation. Tax-exempt: 501(c)(3).
Cultural & Enrichment Center: housed in the former Jefferson Davis Smith family home; built in 1903. Listed on the National Register of Historic Places.
Collections: family history & personal artifacts; period furnishings; paintings.
Facilities: 20-seat lecture room; park. Garden for the Senses, (for the visually impaired) with Braille labels.
Activities: guided tours; lectures; concerts; outreach programs. Open House: Thanksgiving to Christmas Eve.
Hours & Admission Prices: Dec. Mon., Wed. & Fri.-Sat. 11-4; other times by appointment, call 336-789-4636. No charge; Closed holidays. ♿
Attendance: 8,947 (accurate)

MOUNT AIRY MUSEUM OF REGIONAL HISTORY, (M), 301 N. Main St., Mount Airy, NC 27030-3811. Tel.: 336-786-4478; 336-786-1666.
E-mail: mamrh@northcarolinamuseum.org
Web Site: www.northcarolinamuseum.org
Key Personnel: Dir., Matthew J. Edwards; Cur. Collections, Amy Snyder; Museum Shop Mgr., Nancy Davis
History Museum.
Collections: regional history; personal artifacts.
Hours & Admission Prices: April-Oct. Tues.-Sat. 10-4; Nov.-March Tues.-Sat. 10-2. Adults $4, senior citizens $3, students $2; discounts to groups

Mount Gilead

TOWN CREEK INDIAN MOUND STATE HISTORIC SITE, 509 Town Creek Mound Rd., Mount Gilead, NC 27306-8506. Tel.: 910-439-6802. Fax: 910-439-6441.
E-mail: towncreek@ncdcr.gov
Web Site: www.towncreek.nchistoricsites.org
Founded: 1937.
Congressional District: 8
Key Personnel: Site Mgr., Rich Thompson.
Personnel Profile: Full-Time Paid 4; Part-Time Paid 4; Part-Time Volunteers 6; Interns 1.
Governing Authority: state. North Carolina Dept. of Cultural Resources, 4620 Mail Service Center, Raleigh, NC 27699-4620. Tax-exempt: 170(b).
Historic Site & Visitor Center: Mississippian period Ceremonial Center restored; temple on top of earth mound, priest's dwelling, burial house & mud-plastered palisade surrounding temple.
Collections: anthropology; archaeology; Indian artifacts; Indian mound; reconstructed Indian structures.
Research Fields: Woodland Indians of North Carolina; archaeology.
Facilities: visitor center.
Activities: guided tours; lectures; formally organized education programs.
Publications: brochure; guidebook.
Hours & Admission Prices: Tues.-Sat. 9-5, Sun. 1-5. No charge; donations accepted. Closed holidays. ♿
Attendance: 36,000 (estimated)

Murfreesboro

MURFREESBORO HISTORICAL ASSOCIATION, 116 E. Main St., Murfreesboro, NC 27855-1407. Mailing Address: P.O. Box 3, Murfreesboro, NC 27855-0003. Tel.: 252-398-5922. Fax: 252-398-5871.
E-mail: mha@murfreesboronc.org
Web Site: www.murfreesboronc.org
Formerly: Rea Museum
Founded: 1967.
Congressional District: 1
Key Personnel: Tour Dir. & Administrator, Kay Thomas; Museum Shop Mgr., SuEllen Askew.
Personnel Profile: Full-Time Paid 1; Part-Time Paid 1; Part-Time Volunteers 150.
Governing Authority: society. Parent Institution: Murfreesboro Historical Assoc. Tax-exempt: 501(c)(3).
Preservation Projects.
Collections: agriculture; history; American Indian artifacts; early educational materials; manuscripts & photographs; Richard J. Gatling Room; Gatling artifacts; Gatling family. Historic Building: 1790 William Rea Store; 1790 Roberts-Vaughan House; 1814 Wheeler House; 1870 Winborne County Store & Law Office.
Research Fields: religion; agriculture; education; American Indian artifacts.
Facilities: Gifts for sale.
Activities: guided tours; lectures; permanent & temporary exhibitions.
Publications: books, Renaissance In Carolina 1971-1976; Renaissance in Carolina II; Murfreesboro, NC Plan Alternatives for the National Register Historic District; brochures; The Tuscaroras Vol. I & II.
Hours & Admission Prices: Mon.-Fri. 9-5. Roberts-Vaughan House no charge. Tours: Sat. 11-4. William Rea Store, Wheeler House & Winborne Country Store & Law Office: adults $8, students $5; children under 6 no charge. Jefcoat Museum $8.
Attendance: 15,000 (estimated)
Membership: Individual $25; Family $35; Sponsor $100; Patron $300; Life $1,000; Benefactor $1,500.

Murphy

CHEROKEE COUNTY HISTORICAL MUSEUM, INC., 87 Peachtree St., Murphy, NC 28906-2940. Tel.: 828-837-6792. Fax: 828-837-6792.
E-mail: cchm@webworkz.com
Founded: 1977.
Congressional District: 11
Key Personnel: Dir. & Museum Shop Mgr., Wanda Stalcup; Chm. (V), Glenda Sanders; Vice Chm., Mary Ann Thompson.
Personnel Profile: Full-Time Paid 1; Part-Time Paid 2; Part-Time Volunteers 2.
Governing Authority: nonprofit organization; museum council. Tax-exempt: 501(c)(3) & 170(b)(1)(A).
History Museum.

Collections: Indian artifacts; early American housewares; primitives; minerals; firearms; musical instruments; local history items; manuscripts; over 500 dolls; Cherokee culture. Historic Building: c.1800 Cherokee house.
Research Fields: local history.
Facilities: library of books about the Cherokee Indian Nation & local history; reading room. Postcards & notepaper for sale.
Activities: guided tours; lectures; permanent & temporary exhibitions.
Publications: brochures, The History & Architecture of Cherokee County, NC.; books, Cherokee County Heritage, Vol. I & II, Pictorial History of Cherokee County; Heritage & Cherokee County, Vol. III.
Hours & Admission Prices: Mon.-Fri. 9-5; group tours by appointment. Adults $3, children $1; students no charge. Closed New Year's Day; Good Friday through Easter Monday; Memorial Day; Independence Day; Labor Day; Thanksgiving; Christmas. ♿
Attendance: 7,000 (estimated)

New Bern

FRIENDS OF FIREMEN'S MUSEUM, 408 Hancock St., New Bern, NC 28560-4923. Tel.: 252-636-4087 & 4020. Fax: 252-636-4087.
E-mail: firechief-nb@admin.ci.new-bern.nc.us
Formerly: New Bern Firemen's Museum
Founded: 1955.
Key Personnel: C.E.O., Charles Williams; Sec. & Treas., Richard M. Register; Museum Shop Mgr., Ben Gaskill.
Personnel Profile: Full-Time Paid 1; Part-Time Paid 1; Part-Time Volunteers 1.
Governing Authority: municipal. Tax-exempt.
Fire-Fighting Museum.
Collections: history; firematic display; Civil War display; preservation project; world record 1884 horse-drawn steamer; horse-drawn hose wagons & handreel; steam engines; 1914 fire engine; 1800s leather fire helmets; preserved 1900s fire horse; period fire fighting equipment; photographs.
Research Fields: permanent exhibits.
Facilities: Firematic-related materials for sale.
Activities: guided tours; permanent exhibitions.
Publications: newsletter, Museum Sparks.
Hours & Admission Prices: Mon.-Sat. 10-4. Adults $5, children $2.50; children under 6 no charge. Closed New Year's Day; Thanksgiving; Christmas.
Attendance: 14,000 (estimated)

* **TRYON PALACE HISTORIC SITES & GARDENS, (M),** 610 Pollock St., New Bern, NC 28562-5614. Mailing Address: P.O. Box 1007, New Bern, NC 28563-1007. Tel.: 252-514-4900; 800-767-1560. Fax: 252-514-4876.
E-mail: info@tryonpalace.org
Web Site: www.tryonpalace.org
Founded: 1945.
Congressional District: 1
Key Personnel: Dir., Kay P. Williams; Pres. (V), Bob Mattocks; Deputy Dir., Philippe Lafargue; Mgr. Communications & Mktg., Nancy Hawley; Human Resources Coord., Nancy Perlman; Cur. Interpretation, Katie Brightman; Cur. Education, Rebecca Reimer; Exhibit Developer, Nancy Gray; Group Sales Mgr., Karen R. Pierson; Controller, Susan L. Flowers; Conservator, David Taylor; Registrar, J. Dean Knight; Council of Friends Membership Devel. & Special Events Coord., Karen O'Connell; Public Svcs. & Dir. Devel., Cheryl Kite; African American Outreach Coord., Sharon C. Bryant; Volunteer Coord., Fran Campbell; Security Coord., Orlando Venters; Museum Shop Mgr., Paul Brown; Visitor Center Mgr., Carl Simms; Horticulture Branch Head, Lisa Wimpfheimer; Greenhouse Mgr., Timothy Minch.
Personnel Profile: Full-Time Paid 48; Part-Time Paid 40; Part-Time Volunteers 300; Interns 3.
Governing Authority: state; nonprofit organization. Affiliated with The Tryon Palace Commission, Office of Archives & History, North Carolina Dept. of Cultural Resources. Tax-exempt.
History Museum.
Collections: 18th, 19th, & 20th century English & American objects, including furniture, paintings, books, porcelains, textiles, sculptures & metalwork; heritage plants; architectural fragments; prints; currency; maps. Historic Buildings: c.1830 George W. Dixon House; c.1779 John Wright Stanly House; c.1810 Daves House; c.1809 Jones House; c.1890 Commission House; c.1880 Disosway House; c.1809 New Bern Academy; c.1785 Gaston House; c.1804 Robert Hay House; c.1842 William Hollister House.
Major Exhibits: Hats Off to the Dreamers, 11/09-12/12; Old Bern/New Bern (T), 7/20/10-12/10; John Lawson: A Naturalist Who Documented the Carolinas at the Point of Settlement (T), 7/20/10-6/11.
Research Fields: North Carolina history; 18th- &19th-century material culture; African-American history of the central North Carolina coast; African American artisans of 18th & 19th centuries, New Bern.
Facilities: 4,000-vol. library of reference books & books on history & decorative arts, available for research by scholars by advance appointment; 200-seat auditorium; 14 period gardens; classrooms; 2 theatres; cafe. Museum-related items for sale.
Activities: guided tours; lectures; conservation, preservation & educational programs; domestic skills & craft demonstrations; garden workshops & events; daily living history programs; character interpretation program; African American history program; interactive children's exhibits. Museum Sponsors: New Bern's 300th Anniversary Celebration; Independence Day Celebration; Tryon Palace Decorative Arts Symposium in March; Garden events; Fife & Drum Corps events; recreating African American Celebration of Christmas in eastern North Carolina; Christmas Candlelight Tours.
Publications: guidebook; periodic pamphlets & leaflets; books, History of the New Bern Academy; A Candlelight Christmas; Tryon Treasury; A New Bern Album; Profile of a Patriot; Historic Architecture of New Bern & Craven County; Singleton Slave Narrative; magazine, Palace.
Hours & Admission Prices: Jan.-June Mon.-Sat. 9-5, Sun. 1-5, last tour at 4. Gardens: June-Aug. Mon.-Sat. 9-7, Sun. 1-7, last tour at 4. Adults $15, children $6; discounts to families, AAM & AAA members and groups of 20 or more scheduled two weeks in advance. Closed New Year's Day; Thanksgiving; Christmas Eve, Day & day after. ♿
Attendance: 94,878 (accurate)
Membership: Student $20; Associate $50; Supporter $100; Family & Grandparent $125; Sponsor $250; Sustainer $500; Patron $1,000; Benefactor $2,500; Champion $5,000 & up.

Newland

AVERY COUNTY MUSEUM, 1829 Schultz Circle, Newland, NC 28657. Mailing Address: P.O. Box 266, Newland, NC 28657-0266. Tel.: 828-733-7111.
E-mail: averymuseum@interlink-caf[00e9].com
Web Site: averymuseum.com
Founded: 1977.
Congressional District: 10
Key Personnel: Exec. Dir., Cindy Peters.
Personnel Profile: Part-Time Volunteers 10.
Governing Authority: nonprofit organization. Subsidiary Institution: Avery County Historical Society. Tax-exempt: 501(c)(3).
County Museum.
Collections: local genealogies; artifacts of prominent citizens of the past; local minerals.
Activities: guided tours; lectures; formally organized education programs for children; permanent & temporary exhibitions; group tours.
Publications: Avery County Heritage: Biographies, Genealogies, Church Histories, Vols. I, II & III; Avery County Heritage: Historic Sites, Vol. IV.
Hours & Admission Prices: May-Oct. Fri. 10-4, Sat. 11-3; other times by appointment. No charge; donations accepted.
Attendance: 1,000 (estimated)
Membership: Student $2; Adults $15; Family $20; Business $50.

Newton

CATAWBA COUNTY MUSEUM OF HISTORY, (M), 30 N. College Ave., Newton, NC 28658. Mailing Address: P.O. Box 73, Newton, NC 28658-0073. Tel.: 828-465-0383. Fax: 828-465-9813.
E-mail: info@catawbahistory.org
Web Site: www.catawbahistory.org
Founded: 1949.
Congressional District: 10
Key Personnel: C.E.O. & Dir., Melinda Herzog; Asst. Dir. & Cur., Jason L. Toney; Pres. (V) & Chm. (V), Dr. Allen Huffman; Cur., Carroll Clark; Registrar, Jennifer Marquart-Leach; Business Officer, Donald W. Norwood.
Personnel Profile: Full-Time Paid 4; Part-Time Paid 2; Part-Time Volunteers 123.
Governing Authority: nonprofit. Parent Institution: Catawba County Historical Association. Subsidiary Institution: Harper House/Hickory History Center; Bunker Hill Covered Bridge, Claremont, NC; Murray's Mill Historic Site, Catawba, NC. Tax-exempt: 501(c)(3).
History Museum: housed in former 1924 Catawba Courthouse.
Collections: Upper Piedmont history including household utensils, tools, weapons, textiles, folk art; agricultural implements; furniture; objects

relating to the development of furniture industry; manuscripts; manufacturing. Historic Buildings: 1900 Grist Mill Complex; 1894 Bunker Hill Covered Bridge; 1887 Historic Harper House; 1790 Huffman Plantation House; Lyerly House 1912.
Research Fields: local, family & architectural history.
Facilities: Historic Murray's Mill: 7,800-vol. library of rare books & books on local history available for use on premises only; reading room; botanical garden; 1913 overshot waterwheel-powered grist mill; 1890s country store; 1880 wheat house-folk art gallery; 1913 miller's residence; located 2 miles west of Catawba, NC. Historic Bunker Hill Covered Bridge: 1895 Haupt truss design; located 2 miles east of Claremont, NC; 1887 Harper House; Hickory History Center housed in 1912 Bonniwell Lyerly House containing five exhibit galleries & archive.
Activities: guided tours; lectures; films; gallery talks; formally organized educational programs; docent program or council; permanent & temporary exhibitions; school loan service.
Publications: books, A History of Catawba County; Tombstone Inscriptions of Old St. Paul's Church; Grandmother's House; A History of the Yount Family; Blackburn Family History; Catawba County: An Architectural History; The Catawbans, Vol. I & II.
Hours & Admission Prices: Museum of History: Wed.-Sat. 9-4, Sun. 1:30-4:30; other times by appointment. No charge; donations accepted. Murray's Mill Site: Thurs.-Sat. 9-4, Sun. 1:30-4:30. Admission 6 & over $3. Bunker Hill Covered Bridge: daily sunrise to sunset. No charge. Harper House & Hickory History Center: admission $5. Closed major holidays. ♿
Attendance: 43,480 (estimated)
Membership: Senior $25; Individual $30; Family $50; Friend $100; Sponsor $150; Donor $250; Patron $500; Corporate $2,500; Institutional $5,000.

North Wilkesboro

WILKES ART GALLERY, 913 C St., North Wilkesboro, NC 28659-4119. Tel.: 336-667-2841. Fax: 336-667-9264.
E-mail: info@wilkesartgallery.org
Web Site: wilkesartgallery.org
Founded: 1962.
Congressional District: 5
Key Personnel: C.E.O., Kara Minton-Elmore; Pres., Madeline Johnson; Vice Pres., John Harwell; Office Mgr., Eric Blahnik.
Personnel Profile: Full-Time Paid 1; Full-Time Volunteers 2; Part-Time Paid 3; Part-Time Volunteers 2; Interns 1.
Governing Authority: nonprofit organization. Tax-exempt: 501(c)(3).
Art Gallery.
Collections: contemporary paintings, graphics, sculpture, primarily of North Carolina artists.
Facilities: classrooms. Original crafts & artwork for sale.
Activities: guided tours; lectures; films; gallery talks; arts festivals; formally organized education programs; docent program or council; permanent, temporary & traveling exhibitions; school & community loan service.
Publications: monthly newsletter, Wilkes Art Gallery Newsletter; monthly brochures & catalogues, Title of Exhibition.
Hours & Admission Prices: Tues. 10-8, Wed.-Fri. 10-5, Sat. 10-2. No charge; donations accepted. Closed New Year's Day; Easter & day after; Memorial Day; Independence Day; Labor Day; Thanksgiving; Christmas Eve & Day. ♿
Attendance: 12,000 (estimated)
Membership: Student & Senior Citizen $25; Individual $35; Family $50; Friend $125-$299; Advocate $300-$499; Benefactor $500 & up. Call for information about higher levels of membership.

Ocracoke

DAVID WILLIAMS HOUSE MUSEUM, (M), 49 Water Plant Rd., Ocracoke, NC 27960. Mailing Address: P.O. Box 1240, Ocracoke, NC 27960-1240. Tel.: 252-928-7375.
Governing Authority: nonprofit organization.
Historic House Museum: c.1900. Listed on the National Register of Historic Places.
Collections: period furnishings; photographs.
Facilities: library. Museum-related items for sale.
Activities: porch talks. Museum Sponsors: Educational Programs June, July & August; Wassail Party in December.
Publications: biannual membership newsletter, The Mullet Wrapper.
Hours & Admission Prices: Call for hours. No charge; donations accepted.
Membership: Individual $15.

OCRACOKE ISLAND VISITOR CENTER, Hwy. 12, Ocracoke, NC 27960. Mailing Address: 1401 National Park Dr., Manteo, NC 27954-9451. Tel.: 252-473-2111 & 928-4531. Fax: 252-473-2595.
E-mail: caha_information@nps.gov
Web Site: www.nps.gov/caha
Founded: 1956.
Congressional District: 1
Key Personnel: Supt., Mike Murray.
Personnel Profile: Full-Time Paid 1; Part-Time Paid 3.
Governing Authority: federal. Affiliated with Cape Hatteras National Seashore. Parent Institution: Dept. of the Interior. Subsidiary Institution: U.S. National Park Service. Tax-exempt.
Park Museum & Visitor Center.
Collections: wall panel exhibits; history; natural history.
Facilities: Maps & books for sale.
Activities: programs by interpretive park rangers June-Aug.
Publications: park brochure; park newspaper; site bulletins.
Hours & Admission Prices: Mid-June to Labor Day daily 9-6; Sept.-June daily 9-5. No charge. ♿
Attendance: 54,600 (accurate)

Old Fort

MOUNTAIN GATEWAY MUSEUM, 102 Water St., Old Fort, NC 28762. Mailing Address: P.O. Box 1286, Old Fort, NC 28762-1286. Tel.: 828-668-9259. Fax: 828-668-0041.
E-mail: mgm@ncmail.net
Founded: 1971.
Congressional District: 11
Key Personnel: C.E.O., Dir. & Cur., Sam Gray.
Personnel Profile: Full-Time Paid 3; Part-Time Paid 5.
Governing Authority: Parent Institution: N.C. Dept. of Cultural Resources. Branch: North Carolina Museum of History, North Carolina Dept. of Cultural Resources, Div. of Archives & History, 109 E. Jones St., Raleigh, NC 27611. Tax-exempt.
History Museum.
Collections: mountain life artifacts; pottery; farm implements; history & culture of Western North Carolina; log cabins.
Research Fields: local history.
Facilities: Museum-related items for sale.
Activities: guided tours; education programs.
Hours & Admission Prices: Mon. 12-5, Tues.-Sat. 9-5, Sun. 2-5. No charge. Closed state holidays.
Attendance: 20,000 (accurate)

Oxford

GRANVILLE COUNTY HISTORICAL SOCIETY MUSEUM, 1 Museum Lane, Oxford, NC 27565. Mailing Address: P.O. Box 1433, Oxford, NC 27565-1433. Tel.: 919-693-9706. Fax: 919-693-9706.
E-mail: webmail@granvillemuseumnc.org
Web Site: www.granvillemuseumnc.org
Founded: 1996.
Congressional District: 78
Key Personnel: Dir. & Museum Shop Mgr., Pam Thornton; Asst. Dir., Valerie Heinssen; Pres. (V), Michael Currin.
Personnel Profile: Full-Time Paid 1; Part-Time Paid 5; Part-Time Volunteers 70.
Governing Authority: private; nonprofit. Parent Institution: Granville County Historical Society. Branch Museum: Harris Exhibit Hall, 110 Count St., Oxford, NC. Tax-exempt: 501(c)(3).
History & Science Museum.
Collections: Granville County history, art & science. Harris Exhibit Hall: science, arts, cultural topics & history exhibits.
Facilities: 75-vol. library on local history & historic preservation; 2 1,500 sq. ft. exhibit spaces. Harris Hall: museum-related items for sale.
Activities: docent program; films; formal education program for children; guided tours; lectures; loan, temporary & traveling exhibitions.
Publications: quarterly, Granville County Historical Society Newsletter; monthly, Docent Diary.
Hours & Admission Prices: Wed.-Fri. 10-4, Sat. 11-3. No charge; donations accepted. Closed Easter; Thanksgiving; Christmas. ♿
Attendance: 6,000 (accurate)
Membership: Individual $25; Double $40; Business $75; Lifetime $300.

Pembroke

NATIVE AMERICAN RESOURCE CENTER, (M), University of North Carolina at Pembroke, Pembroke, NC 28372. Mailing Address: P.O. Box 1510, Pembroke, NC 28372-1510. Tel.: 910-521-6282.
E-mail: nativemuseum@uncp.edu
Web Site: www.uncp.edu/nativemuseum/
Founded: 1979.
Congressional District: 7
Key Personnel: Dir., Dr. Stanley Knick; Business Officer, Neil R. Hawk; Publications & Public Rels. Dir., Amber Rach.

Governing Authority: college. University of North Carolina at Pembroke. Tax-exempt: 170 (b)(1)(A).
Native American Museum: housed in 1923 Old Main Building.
Collections: Indian artifacts; handicrafts; art, books, cassettes, record albums & films pertaining to Native Americans & Lumbee Indians.
Research Fields: Lumbee history & culture; prehistory of southeastern North Carolina; Indian health & educational issues.
Facilities: 350-vol. library pertaining to Native Americans available for use on premises; reading room; 90-seat auditorium.
Activities: guided tours; lectures; films; traveling exhibitions.
Publications: newsletter, Spirit!; book, Robeson Trails Archaeological Survey: Reconnaissance in Robeson County; reader, Along the Trail: A Reader About Native Americans; brochure; The Lumbee in Context; River Spirits: A Collection of Lumbee Writings; Fine in the World: Lumbee Language in Time and Place; DVDs: Indian By Birth; Lumbee By Grace; In The Heart of Tradition; Our People: The Sappony; Dancing In The Gardens of the Lord; Listen to the Drum; DVDs: Our People: The Lumbee; Our People: The Occaneechi Band of Saponi Nation; VHS: A Healing Faith.
Hours & Admission Prices: Mon.-Sat. 8-5; groups by appointment. No charge. Closed state holidays. ♿
Attendance: 10,000 (accurate)
Membership: Student $5; Subscriber $15; Teacher $20; Sustainer $30; Sponsor $60; Benefactor $100; Patron $250; Angel $500.

Pine Knoll Shores

NORTH CAROLINA AQUARIUM AT PINE KNOLL SHORES, One Roosevelt Dr., Pine Knoll Shores, NC 28512. Mailing Address: P.O. Box 580, Public Relations Dept., Atlantic Beach, NC 28512-0580. Tel.: 252-247-4003. Fax: 252-247-0663.
E-mail: pksmail@ncaquariums.com
Web Site: www.ncaquariums.com
Founded: 1976.
Key Personnel: Dir., Jay Barnes; Dir. Husbandry & Operations, Stuart May; Cur. Education, Windy Arey Kent; Coord. Public Rels., Julie Powers.
Personnel Profile: Full-Time Paid 45; Part-Time Paid 45; Part-Time Volunteers 230; Interns 6.
Governing Authority: state; nonprofit. Parent Institution: North Carolina Aquariums, 3125 Poplarwood Ct., Ste. 160, Raleigh, NC 27604. Tax-exempt: 501(c)(3).
Aquarium.
Collections: live displays & supportive artifacts that focus on the natural history of North Carolina's aquatic life.
Facilities: 300-vol. library of books related to coastal & aquatic natural history; 150-seat auditorium; educational facilities; nature trails. Books, educational games, shirts & museum-related items for sale.
Activities: films; formal educational programs; lectures; day camps; family programs; field trips; participatory exhibits; conservation special events. Museum Sponsors: Surf Fishing School.
Publications: magazine, Aquarium News; seasonal calendar of activities & events.
Hours & Admission Prices: Adults $8, seniors 62 & over $7, children 6-17 $6; children under 5 & members no charge. Closed New Year's Day; Thanksgiving; Christmas. ♿
Attendance: 444,521 (accurate)
Membership: Individual $30; Family $50; Donor $100; Patron $300; Benefactor $1,000.

Pineville

PRESIDENT JAMES K. POLK STATE HISTORIC SITE, 12031 Lancaster Hwy., Pineville, NC 28134. Mailing Address: P.O. Box 475, Pineville, NC 28134-0475. Tel.: 704-889-7145. Fax: 704-889-3057.
E-mail: polk@ncdcr.gov
Web Site: www.polk.nchistoricsites.org
Founded: 1968.
Congressional District: 9
Key Personnel: Site Mgr., Scott Warren; Pres. (V), Sharon Van Kuren.
Personnel Profile: Full-Time Paid 3; Part-Time Paid 2; Part-Time Volunteers 30; Interns 1.
Governing Authority: state. Parent Institution: North Carolina Dept. of Cultural Resources, 109 E. Jones St., Raleigh, NC 27611. Subsidiary Institution: J.K. Polk Memorial Support Fund, Inc. Tax-exempt: 170(b)(1)(A).
Historic Buildings & Visitor Center.
Collections: life & times of James K. Polk; late 18th- & early 19th-century furnishings. Historic Buildings: main house, barn, separate kitchen.
Major Exhibits: Political Life of Henry Clay, 1/10-12/10; The Journey of the USS James K. Polk, 1/10-12/10.
Research Fields: life & times of James K. Polk 1795-1849.
Facilities: visitor center.
Activities: guided tours; films; formally organized education programs for students; permanent exhibitions; audiovisual programs; lectures & demonstrations for organized school groups & special events.
Publications: brochure (available in braille); exhibit text in braille; The Young Hickory News.
Hours & Admission Prices: Tues.-Sat. 9-5. No charge; donations accepted. Closed New Year's Day; Memorial Day; Independence Day; Labor Day; Thanksgiving; Christmas Eve & Day. ♿
Attendance: 13,000 (estimated)
Membership: Congressman $20; Governor $25; Speaker of the House $40; President $100.

Pinnacle

HORNE CREEK LIVING HISTORICAL FARM, 308 Horne Creek Farm Rd., Pinnacle, NC 27043. Tel.: 336-325-2298. Fax: 336-325-3150.
E-mail: hornecreek@ncmail.net
History Museum.
Collections: North Carolina's rural heritage & history; photographs; historic buildings.
Facilities: nature trails. Museum-related items for sale.
Activities: special events; hands-on working farm.
Hours & Admission Prices: Tues.-Sat. 9-5. No charge; donations accepted. Closed most major holidays.

Pisgah Forest

ALLISON-DEAVER HOUSE MUSEUM, 200 Hwy. 280, Pisgah Forest, NC 28768. Mailing Address: Transylvania County Historical Society, P.O. Box 2061, Brevard, NC 28712-2061. Tel.: 828-884-5137 & 8570.
Web Site: www.preservingourpast.org
Historic House Museum: listed on the National Register of Historic Places.
Collections: period furnishings; personal artifacts.
Facilities: Museum-related items for sale.
Hours & Admission Prices: May-Oct. by appointment.

Plymouth

PORT-O-PLYMOUTH MUSEUM, 302 E. Water St., Plymouth, NC 27962. Mailing Address: P.O. Box 296, Plymouth, NC 27962-0296. Tel.: 252-793-1377.
E-mail: porto@plymouthnc.com
Web Site: www.livinghistoryweekend.com/port_o.htm
Key Personnel: Cur., Harry Thompson.
Governing Authority: private; nonprofit organization.
History Museum.
Collections: local history & culture; photographs; Civil War memorabilia; paintings.
Facilities: Museum-related items for sale.
Activities: Museum Sponsors: Living History Weekend.
Hours & Admission Prices: Tues.-Sat. 9-4.

Raleigh

AFRICAN AMERICAN CULTURAL COMPLEX, 119 Sunnybrook Rd., Raleigh, NC 27610-1827. Tel.: 919-250-9336. Fax: 919-212-3598.
Governing Authority: nonprofit organization.
History Museum.
Collections: African American history, culture, & inventions; documents; personal artifacts; period furnishings; Hall of Fame inductees.
Facilities: amphitheater; nature trails.
Hours & Admission Prices: By appointment.

ARTSPACE, 201 E. Davie St., Raleigh, NC 27601-1869. Tel.: 919-821-2787. Fax: 919-821-0383.
Web Site: www.artspacenc.org
Founded: 1986.
Key Personnel: Exec. Dir., Mary Poole; Devel., Anna Spell Miller; Dir. Programs & Exhibitions, Lia Newman.
Personnel Profile: Full-Time Paid 7; Part-Time Paid 5; Part-Time Volunteers 350; Interns 1.
Governing Authority: private; nonprofit organization. Tax-exempt: 501(c)(3).
Art Museum & Gallery.
Collections: works by regional, national & international artists.
Major Exhibits: Looking Back, Part 2, 12/09-1/10; Work by Howard Sherman, 1/10-3/10; New Works, 3/10-5/10; Work by Jim Henkel, 4/10-5/10; Work by Hedwig Brouckaert, Shaun Cassidy, and Israel Davis, 5/10-6/10; Summer Artist-in-Residence, 7/10-9/10; Fine Contemporary Craft, 11/10-1/11.
Facilities: educational facilities. Museum-related items for sale.
Activities: formal education programs; docent program; guided tours; lectures; rental gallery.

Publications: bimonthly newsletter; monthly e-newsletter; course catalogs; exhibition brochures.
Hours & Admission Prices: Tues.-Sat. 10-6. No charge; donations accepted. Closed New Year's Day; Christmas. ♿
Attendance: 150,000 (estimated)
Membership: Students & Seniors $30; Individual $40; Family $60; Art Lovers $100-$249; Art Advocates $250-$499; Art Collectors $500-$999; Sponsors $1,000 & up.

CAM CONTEMPORARY ART MUSEUM, (M), Jay Gates, Raleigh, NC 27603-1819. Mailing Address: NC State Univ. College of Design, Campus #7701, Raleigh, NC 27695-0001. Tel.: 919-513-0946. Fax: 919-515-7330.
Web Site: www.cam.ncsu.edu
Founded: 1983.
Congressional District: 4
Key Personnel: Interim Dir., Jay Gates; Cur. Education, Nicole Welch.
Personnel Profile: Full-Time Paid 3; Part-Time Paid 2; Interns 3.
Governing Authority: nonprofit organization. Tax-exempt: 501(c)(3).
Contemporary Art.
Collections: national, regional & international contemporary art & design; performance & public art projects.
Research Fields:
Activities: guided tours; lectures; films; concerts; performances; broadcast programs; organized education programs; docent program; traveling exhibitions.
Publications: exhibition catalogues.
Hours & Admission Prices: Closed for relocation until 2010. ♿
Attendance: 30,000 (estimated)
Membership: Student $15; Artist, Senior & Teacher $20; Individual $25; Double & Family $40; Sponsor $100; Business Sponsor $150-$500; Associate $250; Patron & Contemporary Arts Forum $500; Contemporary Arts Fellow $1,000; Business Associate $1,000-$4,900; Friend of Contemporary Art $5,000; Business Friend $5,000-$9,000; Benefactor $10,000 & up.

GREGG MUSEUM OF ART & DESIGN AT NORTH CAROLINA STATE UNIVERSITY, (M), 3302 Talley Student Center, 2610 Cates Ave., Raleigh, NC 27695-0001. Mailing Address: Box 7306, Raleigh, NC 27695-0001. Tel.: 919-515-3503. Fax: 919-515-6163.
E-mail: gregg@ncsu.edu
Web Site: www.ncsu.edu/gregg
Formerly: North Carolina State University Gallery of Art & Design
Founded: 1979.
Congressional District: 4
Key Personnel: Interim Dir. & Cur. Collection, Dr. Lynn J. Ennis; Cur. Education & Resources, Zoe Starling; Art Preparator, Matt Gay; Registrar, Mary Hauser; Asst. Registrar, Chris Gannon; Program Asst., Hilary Kinlaw; Security, Clara Ray.
Personnel Profile: Full-Time Paid 4; Part-Time Paid 3; Part-Time Volunteers 4; Interns 8.
Governing Authority: university. Parent Institution: North Carolina State University. Tax-exempt: 170(b)(1)(A).
Art Museum.
Collections: contemporary & historic textiles, ceramics, photography, glass, furniture, metals, outsider art as well as work by faculty of the NCSU College of Design.
Major Exhibits: With Lathe and Chisel: North Carolina Wood Turners and Carvers, 1/21/10-5/15/10; Faces and Mazes (T), 1/21/10-5/15/10.
Research Fields: textiles; ceramics pertaining to North Carolina & the South; product design; furniture; material culture; photography.
Facilities: auditorium; theater; classrooms; cafeteria.
Activities: formally organized education programs for undergraduate & graduate college students; loan, permanent, temporary & traveling exhibitions.
Publications: newsletter, Friends of the Gregg; exhibition catalogues.
Hours & Admission Prices: Wed.-Fri. 12-8, Sat.-Sun. 2-8. No charge; donations accepted. Closed university holidays. ♿
Attendance: 36,500 (estimated)
Membership: Friends of the Gregg: Student $10; Individual $25; Family $35; Donor $100; Patron $250; Sponsor $500; Benefactor $1,000.

HAYWOOD HALL HOUSE AND GARDEN, 211 New Bern Place, Raleigh, NC 27601. Tel.: 919-832-8357 & 4158.
Governing Authority: Parent Institution: The National Society of the Colonial Dames of America.
Historic House: housed in the former home of State Treasurer John Haywood; built in 1799.
Collections: Haywood family history; personal artifacts; period furnishings; photographs; paintings.
Facilities: gardens.
Activities: rental facilities.
Hours & Admission Prices: March to mid-Dec. Thurs. 10:30-1:30; other times by appointment.

HISTORIC OAK VIEW COUNTY PARK, (M), 4028 Carya Dr., Raleigh, NC 27610-2913. Tel.: 919-250-1013. Fax: 919-250-1119.
E-mail: oakview@wakegov.com
Web Site: www.wakegov/parks/oakview
Personnel Profile: Full-Time Paid 2; Part-Time Paid 5.
Governing Authority: Parent Institution: Wake County Parks, Recreation and Open Space.
Historic Farmstead.
Collections: agricultural heritage; local history. Historic Structures: 1855 farmhouse; plank kitchen; c.1900 cotton gin house; livestock barn; carriage house.
Facilities: visitor's center.
Activities: educational programs; special events; permanent exhibits.
Hours & Admission Prices: Park: Mon.-Sat. 8:30-5, Sun. 1-5. No charge. Closed New Year's Day; Thanksgiving; Christmas Eve & Day. ♿
Attendance: 100,000 (estimated)

JC RAULSTON ARBORETUM AT NC STATE UNIVERSITY, 4415 Beryl Rd., Raleigh, NC 27695-0001. Mailing Address: Dept. Horticultural Science, Box 7522, Raleigh, NC 27695-0001. Tel.: 919-515-3132. Fax: 919-515-5361.
Web Site: www.ncsu.edu/jcraulstonarboretum
Founded: 1976.
Key Personnel: Interim Dir., Ted Bilderbeck
Arboretum.
Collections: over 6,000 plants.
Activities: teaching & research programs.
Hours & Admission Prices: April-Oct. daily 8-8; Nov.-March daily 8-5. No charge; donations accepted. ♿

JOEL LANE MUSEUM HOUSE, 160 S. St. Mary's St., Raleigh, NC 27603-1618. Mailing Address: P.O. Box 10884, Raleigh, NC 27605-0884. Tel.: 919-833-3431. Fax: 919-833-9431.
E-mail: joellane@bellsouth.net
Web Site: www.joellane.org
Founded: 1972.
Key Personnel: Pres. (V), Margaret Rolfsen; Cur., Isabella Long.
Personnel Profile: Full-Time Paid 2; Part-Time Paid 3.
Governing Authority: Parent Institution: NSCDA in North Carolina. Tax-exempt.
Historic House Museum: housed in the former home of Colonel Joel Lane. Listed on the National Register of Historic Places.
Collections: Lane family history; personal artifacts; period furnishings; hands-on exhibits; local history.
Research Fields: African Americans 18th century in Wake County, NC.
Facilities: Museum-related items for sale.
Activities: educational programs; hands-on activities.
Publications: Chameleon on the Crabtree: The Story of Joel Lane.
Hours & Admission Prices: Tours: March to mid-Dec. Wed.-Fri. 10, 11, 12 & 1, Sat. 1, 2 & 3; other times by appointment. Adults $5, seniors 65 & over $4, students $3; children under 6 no charge.
Attendance: 3,000 (accurate)
Membership: Individual $40; Family $50; Colonial Patron $100.

MARBLES KIDS MUSEUM, 201 E. Hargett St., Raleigh, NC 27601-1437. Tel.: 919-834-4040 & 857-1085. Fax: 919-834-3516.
E-mail: info@marbleskidsmuseum.org
Web Site: www.marbleskidsmuseum.org
Formerly: Exploris
Founded: 2007.
Key Personnel: Chm. Bd. (V), Blount Williams; Pres., Sally Edwards; Dir. Finance, Andy Kleitsch; Dir. Mktg., Deidre Albert; Dir. Education & Training, Lori Barnes; Vice Pres. Exhibits, Pam Hartley; Vice Pres. Facilities & IT, Tim Hazlehurst; Vice Pres. Sales, Britt Thomas; Museum Shop Mgr., Toni Strickland.
Personnel Profile: Full-Time Paid 35; Part-Time Paid 50; Part-Time Volunteers 65; Interns 2.
Governing Authority: private; nonprofit organization. Tax-exempt: 501(c)(3).
Children's Museum.
Collections: interactive exhibits.
Facilities: 267-seat IMAX theatre; classrooms & rental spaces.
Activities: summer camps; school's out camps; daily & weekly programming; special events; birthday parties; IMAX films; traveling exhibits.
Publications: monthly newsletter; annual report; educators guide; brochures; e-blasts; calendars.

Hours & Admission Prices: Tues.-Sat. 9-5, Sun. 12-5. Adults $5; members no charge. ACM reciprocity. Closed Easter; Thanksgiving; Christmas. ♿
Attendance: 372,000 (estimated)
Membership: IMAX $60; Marbles Grand $90; Family $100; Family Plus $150.

MORDECAI HISTORIC PARK, 1 Mimosa St., Raleigh, NC 27604-1203. Mailing Address: P.O. Box 28072, Raleigh, NC 27611-8072. Tel.: 919-857-4364. Fax: 919-834-7314.
E-mail: info@cappresinc.org
Web Site: www.raleighnc.gov/mordecai
Founded: 1972.
Congressional District: 2
Key Personnel: Pres. & C.E.O., Gary G. Roth.
Personnel Profile: Full-Time Paid 3; Part-Time Paid 7; Part-Time Volunteers 225.
Governing Authority: Parent Institution: Capital Area Preservation, Inc. Tax-exempt.
Historic Houses: housed in the birthplace of Andrew Johnson.
Collections: period furnishings; period linens. Historic Houses: early Raleigh office; Badger/Iredell law office; c.1785 Mordecai house; 2 original plantation dependencies; 1830 Ellen Mordecai garden; c.1842 Allen kitchen.
Facilities: Museum-related items for sale.
Activities: guided tours; special events.
Publications: interpretive brochure, Gleanings From Long Ago.
Hours & Admission Prices: Tues.-Sat. 10-3, Sun. 1-3, last tour 3. Adults $5, youth 7-17 & seniors $3; children 6 & under no charge. ♿
Attendance: 11,000 (accurate)
Membership: Annual Membership: Individual $30; Family $50. President's Circle Membership: Sustainer $100; Contributor $250; Patron $500; Benefactor $1,000.

* **NORTH CAROLINA MUSEUM OF ART, (M), (I),** 2110 Blue Ridge Rd., Raleigh, NC 27607-6494. Mailing Address: 4630 Mail Service Center, Raleigh, NC 27699-4600. Tel.: 919-839-6262. Fax: 919-733-8034.
E-mail: cwoodrum@ncmamail.dcr.state.nc.us
Web Site: www.ncartmuseum.org
Founded: 1956.
Congressional District: 4
Key Personnel: Dir., Lawrence J. Wheeler; Deputy Dir. Art & Cur. Modern Art, John Coffey; Cur. Ancient Art, David H. Steel; Chief Deputy Dir. & C.F.O., Caterri Woodrum; Cur. Northern European, Dennis P. Weller; Cur. Ancient Art, Mary Ellen Soles; Dir. Mktg., Melanie Davis-Jones; Dir. Education, Susan Glasser; Dir. Devel. & Membership, Ellen Stone; Chief Registrar, Maggie Gregory; Librarian, Natalia Lonchyna; Mgr. Communications, Jennifer Bahus; Chief Conservator, Bill Brown; Chief Cur. & Cur. Contemporary Art, Linda Dougherty; Assoc. Cur. Contemporary Art, Kinsey Katchka; Mgr. Exhibitions, Tiara L. Paris; Dir. Planning & Design, Dan Gottlieb.
Personnel Profile: Full-Time Paid 140; Full-Time Volunteers 500; Part-Time Paid 8; Part-Time Volunteers 320; Interns 4.
Governing Authority: state. Parent Institution N.C. Dept. of Cultural Resources. Subsidiary Institution: N.C. Museum of Art Foundation, Inc. Tax-exempt.
Art Museum.
Collections: European & American art; ancient art; African, Oceanic & pre-Columbian art; Kress collection; Mary Duke Biddle Education Gallery; North Carolina art; Judaic art.
Facilities: 34,000-vol. art reference library; restaurant. Museum-related items for sale.
Activities: guided tours; lectures; films; concerts; workshops; teacher seminars; art consultation; art reference library; state extension program; permanent & temporary exhibitions.
Publications: bulletin; magazine; exhibition & permanent collection catalogues & brochures; calendar of events.
Hours & Admission Prices: Temporarily closed till April 2010. Charge for special exhibitions only. ♿
Attendance: 400,000 (estimated)
Membership: Student $24; Senior Citizen $30; Individual $40; Senior Couple $50; Dual $65; Family $75; Patron $125; Sustainer $250; Benefactor $500; Fellow $1,000; Director's Circle $2,500; Humber Society $5,000; Collectors Cabinet/Gold $10,000; Collectors Cabinet & Platinum $25,000.

* **NORTH CAROLINA MUSEUM OF HISTORY, (M),** 5 E. Edenton St., Raleigh, NC 27601-1011. Mailing Address: 4650 Mail Service Center, Raleigh, NC 27699-4650. Tel.: 919-807-7900. Fax: 919-733-8655.
E-mail: ken.howard@ncdcr.gov
Web Site: ncmuseumofhistory.org
Founded: 1902.
Congressional District: 4
Key Personnel: Dir. N.C. Museum of History & Div. of State History Museums, Kenneth B. Howard; Assoc. Dir., Bill McCrea; Assoc. Dir., Jackson Marshall; Exec. Dir. No. Carolina Museum of History Assoc., Walker Mabe; C.O.O., Heyward McKinney; Admin. Mountain Gateway Museum & Heritage Center, Terrell Finley; Admin. Museum of the Cape Fear Historical Complex, David Reid; Admin. Museum of the Albemarle, Ed Merrell; Chief Cur., Dr. Joseph Porter; Chief Collections Management, John Campbell; Chief Administrative Svcs., Thom Swindell; Museum Store Mgr., Lynn Brower; Public Information Officer, Susan Friday Lamb; Dir. NC Maritime Museums & The Graveyard of the Atlantic Museum, Joseph K. Schwarzer.
Personnel Profile: Full-Time Paid 73; Part-Time Paid 5; Part-Time Volunteers 127; Interns 10.
Governing Authority: state. Parent Institution: North Carolina Dept. Cultural Resources, Office of Archives and History. Subsidiary Institutions: Mountain Gateway Museum and Heritage Center; Museum of the Albemarle; Museum of the Cape Fear Historical Complex; North Carolina Maritime Museum in Beaufort with a branch in Southport; Graveyard of the Atlantic Museum. Affiliate of the Smithsonian Institution. Tax-exempt.
North Carolina History Museum.
Collections: decorative arts; furnishings; costumes; uniforms; tools & equipment; industry; folklife; numismatics; currency; weapons; textiles; anthropology; paintings; graphics; military; medicine; transportation; toys; tobacco; North Carolina history & material culture.
Research Fields: culture, social, military, economic, political history & folk life of North Carolina.
Facilities: 3,000-vol. library; 315-seat auditorium; classrooms; conference rooms. Museum-related items for sale.
Activities: guided tours; hands-on museum classroom program; lecture series; workshops for children, adults & teachers; films; traditional music presentations; festivals; symposia; permanent & temporary exhibitions; media center including videos; hands-on classroom kits; online workshops; distance learning classes; interactive website; virtual field trips; video presentations & podcasts on web site. Museum Sponsors: Tar Heel Junior Historian Association; consultant services for in-state history museums.
Publications: docent newsletter; program-related educational leaflets & pamphlets; magazine & newsletter, Tar Heel Junior Historian Association; exhibition-related publications; e-newsletter; biennial magazine, Circa; bimonthly program calendar.
Hours & Admission Prices: Mon.-Sat. 9-5, Sun. 12-5. No charge; donations accepted. Closed New Year's Day; Thanksgiving; Christmas. ♿
Attendance: 319,942 (accurate)
Membership: Scribe $40; Archivist $60; Patriot $100; Enthusiast $150; Historian $250; Curator's Assembly $500; Benefactor $1,000; Sterling Benefactor $1,500; Fred Olds Society $2,500; Executive Gallery $5,000.

* **NORTH CAROLINA MUSEUM OF NATURAL SCIENCES, (M),** 11 W. Jones St., Raleigh, NC 27601-1029. Mailing Address: Mail Service Center 1626, Raleigh, NC 27699-1600. Tel.: 919-733-7450. Fax: 919-733-1573.
Web Site: www.naturalsciences.org
Founded: 1879.
Congressional District: 4
Key Personnel: Dir., Dr. Betsy Bennett; Deputy Dir. Museum Operations, Alvin L. Braswell; Dir. Devel., Bonnie L. Smith; Dir. Exhibits, Roy G. Campbell; Deputy Dir. Research & Strategic Planning and Interim Dir. Nature Museum Research Center, Dr. Karen Giroux; Dir. School Programs, Liz Baird; Dir. Prairie Ridge, Mary Ann Brittain; Dir. Public Programs, Jesse P. Perry, III; Mktg. Dir., Jeff Williford; Dir. Communications, Jonathan Pishney; Dir., Friends of the Museum, Angela Baker-James; Cur. Mammals, Lisa J. Gatens; Cur. Birds, John Gerwin; Cur. Terrestrial Invertebrates, Dr. Rowland Shelley; Cur. Paleontology, Vince Schneider; Cur. Herpetology, Dr. Bryan Stuart; Cur. Crustaceans, Dr. John Cooper; Cur. Fishes, Dr. Wayne Starnes; Cur. Geology, Dr. Christopher Tacker; Cur. Aquatic Invertebrates, Dr. Arthur Bogan; Museum Shop Mgr., Heather Heath.
Personnel Profile: Full-Time Paid 111; Part-Time Paid 55; Part-Time Volunteers 297; Interns 28.
Governing Authority: state. Division of North Carolina Department of Environment Natural Resources, 412 Salisbury St., Raleigh. Subsidiary Institution: N.C. Museum of Forestry, Whiteville, NC. Tax-exempt: 170(c)(1).
Natural Science Museum.
Collections: zoology, geology, paleontology, with emphasis on North Carolina & the southeastern United States.
Major Exhibits: The National Geographic Society's A Journey Through the Arctic Refuge, 11/09-1/10; Megalodon, Largest Shark That Ever Lived, 2/10-5/10.
Research Fields: mammalogy; ornithology; herpetology; ichthyology; invertebrate zoology; ecology; endangered species; systematics.

Facilities: 7,000-vol. library of natural history books available for use on premises; 262-seat auditorium; naturalist center; cafe; laboratory; rental facilities; 38 acre outdoor education facility. Nature study & natural history books for sale.
Activities: permanent, temporary & traveling exhibits; statewide teacher workshops & outreach programs; classes; trips to local & international natural areas; adult, children & family events; high definition films; resource box loans; self-guided tours; lectures; school & group programs; presentations; internships; meeting place for natural history groups; faunal surveys; advisory services for government agencies. Annual Events: Astronomy Day; A Natural History Halloween; Bugfest; Groundhog Day; Reptile & Amphibian Day; Planet Earth Celebration.
Publications: quarterly popular natural history magazine & program calendar; information leaflets; special publications; educator guide.
Hours & Admission Prices: Mon.-Sat. 9-5, Sun. 12-5, 1st Fri. of month 9-9. No charge; donations accepted. ♿
Attendance: 724,000 (accurate)
Membership: Individual $45; Family $55; Discovery Club $100; Naturalist Society $250; Explorers Society $500; Adventure Society $1,000.

NORTH CAROLINA OFFICE OF ARCHIVES AND HISTORY, 109 E. Jones St., Raleigh, NC 27601-1023. Mailing Address: 4610 Mail Service Center, Raleigh, NC 27699-4610. Tel.: 919-807-7280. Fax: 919-733-8807.
E-mail: webmaster@ncmail.net
Web Site: www.ah.dcr.state.nc.us/
Founded: 1903.
Congressional District: 4
Key Personnel: Deputy Sec., Dr. Jeffrey J. Crow; Chief Division of Historical Resources, Dr. David Brook; Chief Historic Sites Section, Keith Hardison; Chief State Capitol Visitor Svcs. Section, Deanna Kerrigan; Chief Historic Preservation, Peter Sandbeck; Chief Historical Publications Section, Donna Kelly; Chief Tryon Palace Section, Kay P. Williams; Chief Archives & Records, Jesse Lankford; Chief North Carolina Maritime Museum, Dr. Joseph Schwarzer; Chief Archaeology, Steve Claggett.
Personnel Profile: Full-Time Paid 407.
Governing Authority: state. Parent Institution: North Carolina Dept. of Cultural Resources. Subsidiary Institutions: NC Transportation Museum; Tobacco Museum at Duke Homestead; North Carolina Maritime Museum. Tax-exempt: 170(b)(1)(A).
Historic House & Site.
Collections: decorative arts & furnishings; costumes; uniforms; manuscripts; photography; industry; archaeology; folklore; numismatics; weapons; textiles; anthropology; paintings; graphics; military; medicine; transportation. Sites & Historic Houses: 1744 Palmer-Marsh House, Bath; 1759 James Iredell House, Edenton; 1760 Owens House, Halifax; 1770 Constitution House, Halifax; 1770 Tryon Palace, New Bern; 1770 House in the Horseshoe, Carthage; 1782 Allen House, Burlington; 1799 Stagville Plantation, Durham; 1825 Bonner House, Bath; 1830 Collins House, Creswell; 1833 Clerk of Court's office, Halifax; 1838 colonial jail, Halifax; 1840 State Capitol, Raleigh; 1840 Aycock birthplace, Fremont; 1850 Harper House, Newton Grove; 1852 Duke Homestead, Durham; 1883 Thomas Wolfe House, Asheville; reconstructed 1960 Vance birthplace, Weaverville; reconstructed 1962 Bennett House, Durham; reconstructed 1968 Polk Homestead Pineville; 1880 Hauser Farmhouse Pinnacle; 1924 Roundhouse, Spencer; 1926 Canary cottage (Palmer Memorial Institute), Sedalia; 1726-1830 Brunswick town remains Winnabow; 1864 confederate seaboat wooden hull, Kinston; site of 1756 log Fort Dobbs, Statesville; 1862-1865 Ft. Fisher earthworks Kure Beach; 1850-1912 restored underground workings of Reed Gold Mine, stanfield; 1300-1500 Town Creek Indian mound with reconstructed temples, Mt. Gilead.
Research Fields: museology; decorative arts; architecture; archaeology; historic preservation; genealogy; North Carolina history; maritime history.
Facilities: archives.
Activities: guided tours; lectures; films; special events: such as encampments, living history & reenactments; docent programs; inter-museum loan, permanent, temporary & traveling exhibitions.
Publications: quarterly scholarly journal, NC. Historical Review; bimonthly newsletter, Carolina Comments; Federation Bulletin.
Hours & Admission Prices: Archives Research Room: Tues.-Fri. 8-5, Sat. 9-4. State Historic Sites: call for hours. State Capitol: Mon.-Fri. 8-5, Sat. 9-5, Sun. 1-5. Admission at most sites no charge. Closed national holidays. ♿

RALEIGH CITY MUSEUM, Briggs Bldg., Ste. 100, 220 Fayetteville St. Mall, Raleigh, NC 27601-1310. Tel.: 919-832-3775. Fax: 919-832-3085.
E-mail: jlitzelman@raleighcitymuseum.org
Web Site: www.raleighcitymuseum.org
Founded: 1993.
Key Personnel: Dir. & C.E.O., Wade Carmichael; Chm. (V), Martha H. Waters; Pres. Bd., Greg Paul; Dir. Education & Outreach, Jenny Litzelman; Treas., Gary Blum; Cur., Ladye Jane Vickers; Museum Shop Mgr., Donna Martin Devine.
Personnel Profile: Full-Time Paid 4; Part-Time Volunteers 12; Interns 7.
Governing Authority: private; nonprofit organization. Tax-exempt.
History Museum.
Collections: artifacts & photographs originating in or related to the city of Raleigh.
Major Exhibits: The Revolution of Media, 11/09-9/10.
Facilities: 5,000 sq. ft. exhibit space; classroom. Museum-related items for sale.
Activities: docent program; guided tours; lectures; rental gallery; school loan service; temporary exhibitions; broadcast programs.
Publications: exhibit catalogs, Let Us March On: Raleigh's Journey Toward Civil Rights; Businesses That Built Raleigh; Historic Raleigh.
Hours & Admission Prices: Tues.-Fri. 10-4, Sat. 1-4. No charge; donations accepted. Closed New Year's Day; Thanksgiving; Christmas Eve & Day. ♿
Attendance: 16,097 (accurate)
Membership: Student & Senior $20; Individual $25; Family $35; Patron $100; Sponsor $250; Benefactor $500; Heritage $1,000; Founder $2,500; Golden Oak $5,000; Capital Society $10,000.

Randleman

RICHARD PETTY MUSEUM, 142 W. Academy St., Randleman, NC 27317-1502. Tel.: 336-495-1143. Fax: 336-495-1543.
E-mail: bdavis@pettyracing.com
Founded: 1988.
Key Personnel: Museum Shop Mgr., Doris Gammons.
Personnel Profile: Full-Time Paid 4.
Car Racing Museum.
Collections: race cars; awards; photographs; fan memorabilia; videos; personal artifacts; family history.
Facilities: Museum-related items for sale.
Hours & Admission Prices: Mon.-Sat. 9-5. Adults $8, seniors $4.50, students $3; discounts to groups; children 6 & under no charge. Closed Thanksgiving; Christmas. ♿
Attendance: 25,000 (estimated)

Reidsville

CHINQUA PENN PLANTATION, 2138 Wentworth St., Reidsville, NC 27320-7304. Mailing Address: PO Box 161, Wentworth, NC 27375-0161. Tel.: 336-349-4576, ext. 21. Fax: 336-342-4863.
Web Site: www.chinquapenn.com
Founded: 1966.
Congressional District: 5
Key Personnel: Dir., Lisa Phelps; Dir., Calvin Phelps; Cur., Ann Toler; Museum Shop Mgr., Amy Huber.
Personnel Profile: Full-Time Paid 13; Part-Time Paid 18; Part-Time Volunteers 30.
Governing Authority: private; nonprofit organization.
General Museum.
Collections: art; furniture; personal artifacts from around the world; farm, garden & household tools & equipment; exotic & native horticulture. Historic Buildings: 27-room mansion built in 1920s; 1923 lodges; 1928 greenhouse & clock tower; 1930 pagoda.
Research Fields: history of the Penn & Schoellkopf families; Chinqua-Penn Plantation.
Facilities: botanical garden; 40-seat theater; greenhouse; wine tasting room. Museum-related items for sale.
Activities: guided tours; temporary exhibitions; jazz festivals. Annual Events: Spring Flower Days March-May; Gatsby Day in September; Halloween & Easter special events for children; Stew Day in November; Holidays at Chinqua-Penn in November & December.
Hours & Admission Prices: Wed.-Sat. 10-5, Sun. 1-5. Adults $20. Closed Easter; Thanksgiving; Christmas.
Attendance: 28,000 (estimated)
Membership: Adults $25.

Richlands

ONSLOW COUNTY MUSEUM, 301 S. Wilmington St., Richlands, NC 28574-8326. Tel.: 910-324-5008. Fax: 910-324-2897.
E-mail: museum@onslawcountync.gov
Web Site: www.co.onslow.nc.us/museum
Founded: 1976.
Congressional District: 3
Key Personnel: Division Head, Lisa Whitman-Grice; Pres., Jeff Morton; Chm., Brock Ridge; Collections Mgr., Patricia Hughey; Education Coord., Brandie K. Cline-Baggett; Public Information Asst., JoAnn Becker; Exhibits Facilitator, Kenneth Barbee.

Personnel Profile: Full-Time Paid 5; Part-Time Paid 1; Part-Time Volunteers 75; Interns 1.
Governing Authority: nonprofit organization. Parent Institution: Onslow County Government & Museum Foundation Board, Inc. Tax-exempt.
General Museum.
Collections: 19th- & early 20th-century tools & farm implements, woodworking tools, 19th-century costumes; Native American artifacts & quilts.
Research Fields: Onslow County history, architectural history in area, surrounding counties; genealogical research.
Facilities: multi-purpose classroom & meeting room; research room.
Activities: guided tours; lectures; musical performances; changing exhibits. Annual Events: Living History Weekend in April; Summer Art Program for Youth June & July; Annual Art Craft Festival in November.
Publications: brochures: A Brief History of Onslow; Historic Sites in Onslow; Richlands Historic District: Walking & Driving Tour; books, The Architectural History of Onslow County, North Carolina; The Water and the Wood, the history of Onslow County.
Hours & Admission Prices: Tues.-Fri. 10-4:30, Sat. 10-4; school groups by appointment. Adults $2, students & youth 3-18 $1; children 3 & under no charge. Closed New Year's Day; Martin Luther King Jr. Day; Good Friday; Easter; Independence Day; Labor Day; Veterans Day; Thanksgiving & day after; Christmas. ♿
Attendance: 17,500 (estimated)
Membership: Individual $10; Family $25; Contributor $50; Sponsor $100; Patron $500 & up.

Roanoke Rapids

ROANOKE CANAL MUSEUM AND TRAIL, (M), 15 Jackson St. Ext., Roanoke Rapids, NC 27870-1901. Tel.: 252-537-2769.
E-mail: canalmuseum@roanokerapidsnc.com
Web Site: www.roanokecanal.com/museum
Key Personnel: Mgr., Harold Jacobson
History Museum: listed on the National Register of Historic Places.
Collections: Roanoke River Valley history; engineering of the canal; hydroelectric power; photographs.
Facilities: nature trails. Museum-related items for sale.
Activities: educational programs; guided tours; hiking.
Hours & Admission Prices: Museum: Tues.-Sat. 9-4. Trail: daily dawn to dusk. Admission: $9; children 8 & under no charge.

Robbinsville

JUNALUSKA MEMORIAL AND MUSEUM, 1 Junaluska Dr., Hwy. 143, Robbinsville, NC 28771. Mailing Address: P.O. Box 1547, Robbinsville, NC 28771-1547. Tel.: 828-479-4727.
E-mail: friendsofjuno@dnet.net
Web Site: www.junaluska.com
Key Personnel: Mgr., Thomas Holland
History Museum.
Collections: Cheoah Valley artifacts, art & crafts; arrowheads & spearheads; gravesite of Cherokee Warrior Junaluska.
Facilities: Museum-related items for sale.
Hours & Admission Prices: Mon.-Fri. 8-4. No charge.

Rocky Mount

ROCKY MOUNT ARTS CENTER, 270 Gay St., Rocky Mount, NC 27804-5442. Tel.: 252-972-1163. Fax: 252-972-1563.
E-mail: maureen.daly.@rockymountnc.gov
Web Site: www.imperialcentre.org
Founded: 1956.
Congressional District: 4
Key Personnel: Cultural Arts Admin., Maureen Daly; Visual Arts Specialist, Catherine Coulter; Arts Education Specialist, Jennifer Rankin; Administrative Sec., Felicia Murphy; Box Office Mgr., Adrienne Lynch; Dir. Theatre, David Nields; Preparator, Neil Coleman; Theatre Technical Dir., Michael Baggesi; Program Asst., Andre Jenkins; Theatre Costumer, Pat Allen.
Personnel Profile: Full-Time Paid 7; Part-Time Paid 12; Part-Time Volunteers 24; Interns 1.
Governing Authority: municipal; nonprofit organization. Parent Institution: City of Rocky Mount, NC. Tax-exempt: 501(c)(3).
Civic Art & Cultural Center.
Collections: 2 & 3 dimensional works predominantly by North Carolina artists 1950-present.
Major Exhibits: Japanese Wood Block Prints by Keiji Shinohara, 1/10-5/10; Handcrafted: A Juried Exhibition of Ceramics, Fiber, Glass, Metal, Wood, 1/10-5/10; 53 National Juried Art Exhibition, 5/10-9/10; Beauty Shop Series by Michael Dorsey, 5/10-9/10; Paintings by Cathy Lees, 5/10-9/10; Anne Lemanski, 5/10-9/10; Jan Ru-Wan, 9/10-12/10; Vintage Selections from the Costume Shop, 9/10-12/10; Salmagundi Sculpture Competition, 10/10-8/11.
Activities: guided tours; lectures; films; gallery talks; arts festivals; community theatre & other theatrical productions; concerts; formally organized educational programs; loan, permanent & traveling exhibitions.
Publications: newsletter, Arty Facts; brochure, The Arts Center Season; exhibition catalogs; ceramic programs.
Hours & Admission Prices: Tues.-Sat. 10-5, Sun. 1-5. Gallery: no charge; donations accepted. Productions: call for prices. Closed Easter; Thanksgiving; Christmas. ♿
Attendance: 45,000 (accurate)
Membership: Friends of the Arts Center, Inc.: Jefferson $25; Shakespeare $50; Davinci $100; Einstein $500.

ROCKY MOUNT CHILDREN'S MUSEUM AND SCIENCE CENTER, INC., 270 Gay St., Rocky Mount, NC 27804-5442. Tel.: 252-972-1167. Fax: 252-972-1535.
E-mail: museum@imperialcentre.org
Web Site: museum.imperialcentre.org
Founded: 1952.
Congressional District: 2
Key Personnel: Dir., Candy L. Madrid; Space Science Educator, Steve Schmidt; Cur. Education, Leigh Lasher White; Cur. Exhibits, Steve Armstrong; Sec., Tabitha Richardson.
Personnel Profile: Full-Time Paid 7; Part-Time Paid 14; Part-Time Volunteers 50.
Governing Authority: municipal. Parent Institution: City of Rocky Mount. Tax-exempt: 501(c)(3).
Science Museum.
Collections: hands-on science & technology exhibits; health exhibits; natural history; early childhood; digital planetarium; live animal habitats.
Activities: hands-on classes; on-floor science demonstrations; puppet shows for school & day care groups; permanent & temporary exhibitions; science camps; field trips; docent training & outreach programs; digital planetarium; laser light shows.
Publications: newsletter, Star Stuff.
Hours & Admission Prices: Tues.-Sat. 10-5, Sun. 1-5. Adults 16-59 $4, senior citizens 60 & over and children 3-15 $3; Sun. 1-5, members, ASTC and children 2 & under no charge. Planetarium: $3.50. Closed Thanksgiving; Christmas. ♿
Attendance: 100,000 (accurate)
Membership: Individual $25; Family & Grandparent $50; Out-of-State $100; Patron $500; Guardian Angel $1,000.

STONEWALL MANOR, 1331 Stonewall Lane, Rocky Mount, NC 27804. Mailing Address: P.O. Box 9028, Rocky Mount, NC 27804. Tel.: 252-442-0063. Fax: 252-443-0137.
E-mail: stonewalllf@embarqmail.com
Web Site: www.stonewallmanor.org
Founded: 1970.
Congressional District: 2
Key Personnel: Pres. (V), Morris Wilder; Nash County Historical Coord., Lauren Fillietaz; Tour Guide, Mary Dyer; Tour Guide, Barbara Hardisen Privette; Treas., Stewart Gibson.
Personnel Profile: Part-Time Volunteers 8.
Governing Authority: nonprofit organization. Parent Institution: Nash County Historical Association, Inc. Tax-exempt: 501(c)(3).
Historic House & Site.
Collections: local historical memorabilia. Historic House: c.1830 Stonewall, late Federal Manor House.
Facilities: Museum-related items for sale.
Activities: guided tours; lectures; films; permanent exhibitions.
Hours & Admission Prices: Call for hours. Adults $5, seniors $3, children under 12 $2; discounts to groups of 6 or more; children 4 & under no charge. ♿
Attendance: 1,000 (estimated)
Membership: Individual $10; Family $15; Associate $25; Corporate $35; Sustaining $50; Life $100.

Roxboro

PERSON COUNTY MUSEUM OF HISTORY, (M), 309 N. Main St., Roxboro, NC 27573-5326. Mailing Address: P.O. Box 1792, Roxboro, NC 27573-1792. Tel.: 336-597-2884.
E-mail: pcmuseum@roxboro.net
Web Site: www.visitroxboronc.com/heritage/museum.htm
History Museum.
Collections: local history; dolls; china; military uniforms; Native American artifacts; period furnishings; photographs.
Hours & Admission Prices: Wed.-Fri. 10-4, Sat. 10-2; other times by appointment.

Rutherfordton

KIDSENSES CHILDREN'S MUSEUM, 172 N. Main St., Rutherfordton, NC 28139-2502. Mailing Address: P.O. Box 150, Rutherfordton, NC 28139-0150. Tel.: 828-286-2120.
E-mail: info@kidsenses.com
Web Site: www.kidsenses.com
Children's Museum.
Collections: hands-on exhibits.
Activities: workshops.
Hours & Admission Prices: Tues.-Thurs. & Sat. 9-5, Fri. 9-8. Adults $5, seniors 55 & over and Mon.-Fri. after 3 pm $3.

Salisbury

DAN NICHOLAS PARK NATURE CENTER, 6800 Bringle Ferry Rd., Salisbury, NC 28146-7144. Tel.: 704-216-7803. Fax: 704-639-0947.
E-mail: bringled@co.rowan.nc.us
Web Site: www.dannicholas.net
Founded: 1975.
Congressional District: 7
Key Personnel: Parks & Recreation Dir., Dan Bringle; County Mgr., Gary Page; Nature Center Dir., Bob Pendergrass; Asst. Naturalist, David Jones.
Personnel Profile: Full-Time Paid 3; Part-Time Paid 4.
Governing Authority: county. Parent Institution: County of Rowan. Tax-exempt.
Zoo & Nature Center Museum.
Collections: over 50 species of native wildlife; marine room with salt water aquarium tank. Historic Building: 1858 log cabin.
Facilities: 100-seat auditorium & classroom; 500-seat amphitheater; petting barn; outdoor animal area; nature trails; 13 acre lake.
Activities: lectures; films; arts festivals; study clubs; formally organized education programs; permanent & temporary exhibitions.
Hours & Admission Prices: Park: March daily 9-6, April-June daily 8-8, July-Aug. daily 8-9, Sept.-Oct. daily 9-7; Nov.-Feb. daily 9-5. Petting Barn $.50. ♿
Attendance: 100,000

HORIZONS UNLIMITED SUPPLEMENTARY EDUCATIONAL CENTER, 1636 Parkview Circle, Salisbury, NC 28144-2461. Tel.: 704-639-3004. Fax: 704-639-3015.
Web Site: www.rss.k12.nc.us/horizons/HU1/home.html
Founded: 1967.
Congressional District: 8
Key Personnel: Dir. & Space Science Specialist, Lisa Wear; Science Specialist & Dir. Planetarium, Patsy Wilson; History Specialist, Theresa Pierce.
Governing Authority: public school district. Tax-exempt.
General Museum.
Collections: natural science; astronomy; wildlife. Historic Buildings: 1842 One Room Log School; 1850 Chilean Ore Mill; Apollo Lunar Lander (1/3 scale model); Indian artifacts.
Facilities: 300-vol. library of material on visual art, space science, natural science, history available on premises or to be checked out by local residents, students or teachers; nature center; planetarium; classrooms; 24-acre wetlands natural area; aquariums; touch tanks; rain forest aviary; health museum.
Activities: guided tours; lectures; films; gallery talks; formally organized education programs for children, adults & undergraduate students; temporary & traveling exhibitions; school loan service.
Publications: monthly bulletins.
Hours & Admission Prices: By appointment. County Nonresident $3. ♿
Attendance: 21,850

ROWAN MUSEUM, INC., 202 N. Main St., Salisbury, NC 28144-4356. Tel.: 704-633-5946. Fax: 704-633-9858.
E-mail: rowanmuseum@carolina.rr.com
Web Site: rowanmuseum.org
Founded: 1953.
Congressional District: 12
Key Personnel: Exec. Dir., Kaye Brown Hirst; Pres., Paul Brown.
Personnel Profile: Full-Time Paid 2; Full-Time Volunteers 50; Part-Time Paid 12; Part-Time Volunteers 6; Interns 1.
Governing Authority: corporate trustees. Tax-exempt: 501(c)(3).
History Museum.
Collections: artifacts of region from 1700s-1900s. Historic Houses: 1766 Old Stone House, residence of Michael Braun; 1819 Utzman-Chambers House.
Activities: guided tours. Museum Sponsors: History Summer Day Camp; Heritage Celebration at Old Stone House; Colonial Christmas; Antiques Show.
Publications: biannual newsletter.
Hours & Admission Prices: Utzman-Chambers House: April-Nov. Sat.-Sun. 1-4. Rowan Museum: Mon.-Fri. 10-4, Sat.-Sun.1-4; other times by appointment. Old Stone House: April-Dec. Thurs.-Sun. 1-4. Adults $3, students $1.50, children $1; discounts to AAM members. ♿
Attendance: 5,000 (estimated)
Membership: Individual $35-$59; Family $60-$100; Sustaining $100-$249; Donor $250-$499; Business $250 & up; Patron $500-$999; Maxwell Chambers Society $1,000 & up.

* **WATERWORKS VISUAL ARTS CENTER, (M),** 123 E. Liberty St., Salisbury, NC 28144-5038. Tel.: 704-636-1882. Fax: 704-636-1895.
E-mail: info@waterworks.org
Web Site: waterworks.org
Founded: 1959.
Congressional District: 12
Key Personnel: Pres. (V), Tim Proper; Exec. Dir., Anne Scott Clement.
Personnel Profile: Full-Time Paid 3; Part-Time Paid 20; Part-Time Volunteers 110; Interns 2.
Governing Authority: nonprofit organization. Waterworks Visual Arts Center, Inc. Tax-exempt: 501(c)(3).
Art Museum.
Collections: paintings; photographs; sculpture.
Facilities: art library; sculpture studio; 2 general use studios; young people's gallery; conference room; sensory gardens.
Activities: guided tours; lectures; gallery talks; formally organized education programs for children, adults & special populations; docent program.
Publications: Exhibition catalogue.
Hours & Admission Prices: Mon.-Wed. & Fri. 10-5, Thurs. 10-7, Sat. 10-4. No charge; donations accepted. Closed major holidays. ♿
Attendance: 13,106 (accurate)
Membership: Individual & Family $50 & up; Friend $200; Affiliate $500 & up; Patron $1,000 & up; Fellow $2,500 & up; Benefactor $5,000 & up.

Sanford

HOUSE IN THE HORSESHOE STATE HISTORIC SITE, 288 Alston House Rd., Sanford, NC 27330-8712. Tel.: 910-947-2051. Fax: 910-947-2051.
E-mail: horseshoe@ncmail.net
Web Site: www.houseinthehorseshoe.nchistoricsites.org
Founded: 1955.
Congressional District: 8
Key Personnel: Site Mgr., John Hairr.
Personnel Profile: Full-Time Paid 3; Part-Time Paid 2; Part-Time Volunteers 12.
Governing Authority: state. North Carolina Dept. of Cultural Resources, Historic Sites Section, 532 N. Wilmington St., 4620 Mail Service Center, Raleigh, NC 27699-4620. Tax-exempt.
Historic House: housed in the former home of North Carolina Governor Benjamin Williams; built in 1772.
Collections: colonial artifacts & furnishings.
Research Fields: North Carolina agricultural history; Revolutionary War & local history.
Facilities: picnic area. Gift items for sale.
Activities: guided tours; lectures; formally organized education programs; musket demonstrations for organized groups; special events. Museum Sponsors: A Living History Encampment in April; Battle Reenactment in August; Christmas Open House in December.
Publications: brochure; electronic newsletter.
Hours & Admission Prices: Tues.-Sat. 9-5. No charge; donations accepted. Closed state holidays. ♿
Attendance: 16,745 (accurate)

RAILROAD HOUSE HISTORICAL ASSOCIATION MUSEUM, 110 Charlotte Ave., Sanford, NC 27330-4304. Mailing Address: P.O. Box 1023, Sanford, NC 27331-1023. Tel.: 919-776-7479.
Founded: 1962.
Congressional District: 3
Key Personnel: Pres. (V), Worth Pickard.
Personnel Profile: Part-Time Volunteers 40; Interns 10.
Governing Authority: society; nonprofit. Tax-exempt.
Historic House: 1872 Railroad House, Gothic Revival, oldest house in Sanford, home of the first mayor & site of first school.
Collections: local historical artifacts & documents; railroad history; artifacts from Endor Iron Furnace; Cole pottery, collection of one of the last hand kiln potters; soil exhibit; fossils; uniforms from WW I & II.
Research Fields: restoration of the c.1859 stack of the Endor Iron Furnace, a Civil War site for smelting pig iron; archaeological studies at Endor Site.
Activities: reading room; permanent & temporary exhibitions.
Publications: newsletter; The History & Architecture of Lee Co.; Men of

Endor; Sanford and Lee County, North Carolina; Images of America Series; In Celebration of the 2007 Centennial of Lee County, North Carolina.
Hours & Admission Prices: Sat.-Sun. 1-5; other times by appointment. No charge; donations accepted.
Attendance: 4,000 (estimated)
Membership: Family $25; Corporate Donation.

Seagrove

NORTH CAROLINA POTTERY CENTER, 233 East Ave., Seagrove, NC 27341-0531. Tel.: 336-873-8430. Fax: 336-873-8530.
E-mail: ncpc@atomic.net
Web Site: www.ncpotterycenter.com
Founded: 1998.
Congressional District: 6
Key Personnel: Pres., Timothy Blackburn; Mgr., Paulett Badgett.
Personnel Profile: Full-Time Paid 2; Part-Time Paid 3; Part-Time Volunteers 45; Interns 1.
Governing Authority: private; nonprofit organization. Tax-exempt: 501(c)(3).
Pottery Center.
Collections: North Carolina pottery from prehistoric to contemporary; regional, national, & international clay traditions; southern pottery & related tools, equipment & documentation; photographs.
Research Fields: North Carolina & Southern pottery; pottery techniques & technology.
Facilities: 100-vol. library; classrooms; multipurpose room; 2,300 sq. ft. exhibit space. Museum-related items for sale.
Activities: lectures; workshops; demonstrations; outreach programs. Annual Events: Catawba Valley Pottery Festival; Seagrove Pottery Festival.
Publications: newsletter, North Carolina Pottery Center Newsletter.
Hours & Admission Prices: Tues.-Sat. 10-4. Adults $2, students 9th-12th grade $1; students K-8th grade & members no charge. ♿
Attendance: 12,000 (accurate)
Membership: Individual $35; Family $50; Contributor $100; Donor $500; Benefactor $1,000.

Sedalia

CHARLOTTE HAWKINS BROWN MUSEUM, 6136 Burlington Rd., Sedalia, NC 27249. Mailing Address: P.O. Box B, Sedalia, NC 27342-0190. Tel.: 336-449-4846. Fax: 336-449-0176.
Web Site: www.nchistoricsites.org/chb/chb.htm
Personnel Profile: Full-Time Paid 5; Part-Time Paid 1; Part-Time Volunteers 5; Interns 5.
Governing Authority: Parent Institution: North Carolina Department of Cultural Resources. Subsidiary Institution: Division of State Historic Sites.
History Museum.
Collections: African American history & culture; women's history; period furnishings; personal artifacts. Historic Buildings: house; school.
Major Exhibits: African American Stamps & Coins, 2/10-3/10.
Activities: Museum Sponsors: Heritage Day in July.
Hours & Admission Prices: Mon.-Sat. 9-5. No charge; donations accepted. Closed most major state holidays. ♿
Attendance: 13,000 (accurate)

Seven Springs

CLIFFS OF THE NEUSE STATE PARK, 345A Park Entrance Rd., Seven Springs, NC 28578-8971. Tel.: 919-778-6234. Fax: 919-778-7447.
E-mail: cliffs.neuse@ncmail.net
Web Site: www.ncparks.gov/Visit/parks/clne/main.php
Founded: 1979.
Key Personnel: Park Supt., Lyden Sutton; Dist. Naturalist, Jeanne Peacock.
Governing Authority: state. Affiliated with the North Carolina Div. of Parks & Recreation, 1615 Mail Service Center, Raleigh, NC 27699-1615. Tax-exempt.
Park Museum.
Collections: American Indian pottery & arrowheads; herbarium; insects; mammals.
Research Fields: geology; botany; paleontology; archaeology; zoology.
Facilities: guide books.
Activities: guided tours; lectures; films; permanent exhibitions; audiovisuals.
Publications: environmental educational learning experience: The Cliffs of Time, designed for grades 6-8.
Hours & Admission Prices: March-May & Sept.-Nov. daily 8-8; June-Aug. daily 8-9; Dec.-Feb. daily 8-6. No charge. Closed Christmas.
Attendance: 70,000 (estimated)

Shelby

CLEVELAND COUNTY HISTORICAL MUSEUM, Court Square, Shelby, NC 28150. Mailing Address: P.O. Box 1210, Shelby, NC 28151-1210. Tel.: 704-482-8186. Fax: 704-482-8186.
Founded: 1976.
Congressional District: 10
Key Personnel: Dir. & Cur., Lamar Wilson; Museum Shop & Office Mgr., Ginger DuBre.
Personnel Profile: Full-Time Paid 2; Part-Time Paid 1; Interns 3.
Governing Authority: nonprofit organization. Parent Institution: Cleveland County Historical Association, Inc. Tax-exempt: 501(c)(3).
Historical Society Museum: housed in 1907 classical revival courthouse.
Collections: photographs; documents; clothing; textiles; tools; furniture; housewares; medical; communication; military; agricultural; religious; manuscripts; live living history displays at Peeler Mill cabin & Broadriver cabin.
Research Fields: local history.
Facilities: historical books available for research on premises; reading room. Historical, general & hand-crafted items for sale.
Activities: guided tours; lectures; films; gallery talks; arts festivals; study clubs; hobby workshops; docent program; formally organized education programs for undergraduate & graduate college students of Gaston College; training programs; permanent & temporary exhibitions; living history cabin.
Publications: quarterly newsletters.
Hours & Admission Prices: Tues.-Fri. 9-4. Discounts to AAM members. Closed all national & county holidays. ♿
Attendance: 25,000
Membership: Individual $15; Family $25; Patron $50; Professional $100; Corporate $200; Individual Life $500.

Smithfield

AVA GARDNER MUSEUM, 325 E. Market St., Smithfield, NC 27577-3919. Tel.: 919-934-5830. Fax: 919-934-6998.
E-mail: avainfo@avagardner.org
Web Site: www.avagardner.org
Founded: 1996.
Key Personnel: Dir., Jessica Meadows; Chm. (V), Rick Lotz.
Personnel Profile: Full-Time Paid 1; Part-Time Paid 4.
Governing Authority: Tax-exempt.
Film Museum.
Collections: artifacts reflecting the movie career & private life of Ava Gardner including photographs, newspaper articles, personal artifacts, & portraits.
Hours & Admission Prices: Mon.-Sat. 9-5, Sun. 2-5. Adults $6, seniors 65 & over, military and children 13-16 $5, children 6-12 $4; discounts to members; children under 3 no charge. ♿
Attendance: 12,000 (accurate)
Membership: Student $20; Individual $25; Family $30; Military & Senior Citizen Family $40.

Snow Camp

SNOW CAMP HISTORICAL SOCIETY, 1 Drama Rd., Snow Camp, NC 27349. Mailing Address: P.O. Box 535, Snow Camp, NC 27349-0535. Tel.: 336-376-6948. Fax: 910-376-6849.
E-mail: snowcampot@aol.com
Web Site: www.snowcampdrama.com
History Museum.
Collections: local history; personal artifacts; photographs.
Hours & Admission Prices: Mon.-Fri. 9-5. No charge.

South Nags Head

BODIE ISLAND LIGHT STATION, Bodie Island Lighthouse, South Nags Head, NC 27959. Mailing Address: 1401 National Park Dr., Manteo, NC 27954-9451. Tel.: 252-473-2111 & 441-5711. Fax: 252-473-2595.
E-mail: caha_information@nps.gov
Web Site: www.nps.gov/caha
Formerly: Bodie Island Visitor Center
Founded: 1956.
Congressional District: 3
Key Personnel: Supt., Mike Murray.
Personnel Profile: Full-Time Paid 1; Part-Time Paid 3; Part-Time Volunteers 8.
Governing Authority: federal. Affiliated with Cape Hatteras National Seashore. Parent Institution: National Park Service. Tax-exempt.
Park Museum & Visitor Center.
Collections: Historic Building: 1872 Bodie Island Light Station includes lighthouse & keeper dwelling.
Facilities: Books & theme-related items for sale.
Publications: park brochure; various related site bulletins.

Hours & Admission Prices: Daily 9-5. No charge; donations accepted. ♿

Southern Pines

ARTS COUNCIL OF MOORE COUNTY - CAMPBELL HOUSE, 482 E. Connecticut Ave., Southern Pines, NC 28387-5624. Mailing Address: P.O. Box 405, Southern Pines, NC 28388-0405. Tel.: 910-692-2787. Fax: 910-693-1217.
E-mail: acmc@mooreart.net
Web Site: www.mooreart.net
Founded: 1973.
Art Museum.
Collections: works by local, regional & national artists.
Hours & Admission Prices: Mon.-Fri. 9-5, 3rd Sat.-Sun. of month 2-4. No charge.

WEYMOUTH WOODS-SANDHILLS NATURE PRESERVE MUSEUM, 1024 Fort Bragg Rd., Southern Pines, NC 28387-7319. Tel.: 910-692-2167. Fax: 910-692-8042.
E-mail: weymouth@pinehurst.net
Web Site: www.sandhillsonline.com/attractions/weymouthwoods/
Founded: 1969.
Congressional District: 8
Key Personnel: Ranger & Naturalist, Kim Hyre; Supt. & Naturalist, Scott Hartley; Maintenance Mechanic, Ed McCrimmon; Maintenance Mechanic, Cledus Miller.
Personnel Profile: Full-Time Paid 6; Part-Time Paid 1.
Governing Authority: state. Parent Institution: N.C. Dept. of Environment, Natural Resources, Division of Parks & Recreation, P.O. Box 27687, Raleigh, NC 27611. Tax-exempt.
Natural History & Science Museum.
Collections: study specimens; Indian artifacts; turpentine industry artifacts; herbarium; wildlife refuge & bird sanctuary.
Research Fields: archaeological; ethnological; botanical; zoological; interpretive planning.
Facilities: 800-vol. library of natural history available on premises; nature center; field search station; separate laboratory operation; auditorium.
Activities: guided tours; lectures; films; formally organized education programs for children; permanent & temporary exhibits.
Publications: brochure; bird & wildflower checklist.
Hours & Admission Prices: Daily 8-6. No charge; donations accepted.
Attendance: 22,295 (estimated)

Spencer

NORTH CAROLINA TRANSPORTATION MUSEUM, 411 S. Salisbury Ave., Spencer, NC 28159-2238. Tel.: 704-636-2889; 877-NCTM-FUN. Fax: 704-639-1881.
E-mail: nctrans@nctrans.org
Web Site: www.nctrans.org
Founded: 1977.
Congressional District: 12
Key Personnel: Exec. Dir., Elizabeth Smith; Advisory Foundation Pres. (V), Ray Johnson; Facility Mgr., Brian Howell; Visitor Svcs. Mgr., Larry Neal; Public Information Officer, Mark Brown; Administrative Svcs. Mgr., Marlene Minshew; Interim Historic Interpreter III, LeAnne Johnson; Historic Interpreter II & Group Coord., Vickie Peacock; Sec., Alane Mills; Exhibits Coord., Bob Hopkins; Historian, Walter Turner.
Personnel Profile: Full-Time Paid 16; Part-Time Paid 5; Part-Time Volunteers 100; Interns 1.
Governing Authority: state. Parent Institution: Historic Sites Section, Dept. of Cultural Resources, 109 E. Jones St., Raleigh, NC. 27611. Tel. 919-733-7862. Tax-exempt.
Historic Transportation Museum: housed in 1896, Southern Railway steam primary staging & repair facility complex containing 20 structures, 37 bay roundhouse, turntable & 90,000 feet back shop.
Collections: 8 steam locomotives; 10 diesel locomotives (6 operating); 50 assorted rolling stock; transportation artifacts & memorabilia; Conestoga wagon; 1896 mail buggy. Historic Cars: 1902 Loretto Rail Car; 1907 Ford Model R Roadster; 1917 Doris private rail car; 1919 Dodge Brothers Roadster; 1959 Edsel Corsair.
Research Fields: transportation.
Facilities: 500-vol. library pertaining to transportation; 30-seat auditorium. Books, Transportation items & other museum-related items for sale.
Activities: guided tours; lectures; films; docent program; formally organized education for adults & undergraduate students; permanent exhibitions. Museum Sponsors: car shows; special events. Annual Events: Rail Days; A Day Out with Thomas the Tank Engine.
Publications: brochures; history publications; semiannual magazine, Shop Talk.
Hours & Admission Prices: Jan.-Feb. Tues.-Sat. 9-5, Sun. 1-4; March-April & Nov.-Dec. Tues.-Sat. 9-5, Sun. 1-5; May-Oct. Mon.-Sat. 9-5, Sun. 1-5. No charge; donations accepted. Train Ride: adults $6, seniors 60 & over and children 3-12 $5; discounts to AAA members. Closed New Year's Day; Easter; Veterans Day; Thanksgiving; Christmas. ♿
Attendance: 120,000 (estimated)
Membership: Students & Junior Engineers $10; Seniors over 60 $20; Individual $25; Family $35; Supporting $50.

Spruce Pine

MUSEUM OF NORTH CAROLINA MINERALS, Milepost 331, Blue Ridge Pkwy. at Hwy. 226, Spruce Pine, NC 28777. Mailing Address: Blue Ridge Pkwy. Foundation, 717 S. Marshall St., Ste. 105 B, Winston-Salem, NC 27101-5865. Tel.: 828-765-2761. Fax: 828-765-0202.
Founded: 1955.
Congressional District: 11
Key Personnel: District Ranger, Tim Francis.
Personnel Profile: Full-Time Paid 2; Part-Time Paid 4; Part-Time Volunteers 5; Interns 2.
Governing Authority: federal. Parent Institution: National Park Service. Subsidiary Institution: Blue Ridge Parkway. Tax-exempt.
Mineral & Mineral Industry Museum.
Collections: geology; study collection; industry.
Research Fields: mineralogy; mineral industries.
Activities: permanent exhibitions; lapidary demonstrations. Museum Sponsors: revolutionary military encampment in September.
Hours & Admission Prices: Daily 9-5. No charge. Closed New Year's Day; Thanksgiving; Christmas. ♿
Attendance: 254,000 (estimated)

Statesville

FORT DOBBS STATE HISTORIC SITE, 438 Fort Dobbs Rd., Statesville, NC 28625-1915. Tel.: 704-873-5882. Fax: 704-873-5995.
E-mail: info@fortdobbs.org
Web Site: www.fortdobbs.org
Founded: 1969.
Congressional District: 9
Key Personnel: Historic Site Mgr., Beth Hill; Chm. (V), Ralph Bentley; Historic Interpreter, Scott Douglas.
Personnel Profile: Full-Time Paid 3; Full-Time Volunteers 20; Part-Time Paid 5; Part-Time Volunteers 40.
Governing Authority: state. North Carolina Dept. of Cultural Resources, 109 E. Jones St., Raleigh, NC 27611. Tax-exempt: 501(c)(3); 170(b)(1)(A).
Historic Site.
Collections: mid-18th century frontier fort; French & India War.
Research Fields: French & Indian War archaeology; NC frontier; back country settlement.
Facilities: picnic shelter; visitor center; nature trail.
Activities: special events; living history programming; daily interpretive programs.
Publications: brochure; Fort Dobbs Gazette.
Hours & Admission Prices: Tues.-Sat. 9-5. No charge; donations accepted. ♿
Attendance: 20,000 (estimated)
Membership: Cadet $10; Sentinel $20; Corporal $50; Sergeant $60; Ensign $150; Lieutenant $200; Captain $500; Major $1,000; Colonel $5,000.

IREDELL MUSEUMS - HERITAGE FARMSTEAD & LEARNING CENTER, 1335 Museum Rd., Statesville, NC 28625-8377. Mailing Address: P.O. Box 223, Statesville, NC 28687-0223. Tel.: 704-873-4734. Fax: 704-873-4407.
E-mail: tgolas@iredellmuseums.org
Web Site: www.iredellmuseums.org/
Formerly: Iredell Museum of Arts & Heritage
Founded: 1956.
Congressional District: 9
Key Personnel: Exec. Dir., Theresa Golas; Office Asst., Terry Lutar.
Personnel Profile: Part-Time Paid 4; Part-Time Volunteers 15.
Governing Authority: nonprofit organization. Parent Institution: Tax-exempt.
General Museum: housed in c.1900 Statesville Pump Station.
Collections: local history & culture; period artifacts & furnishings. Historic Buildings: Pioneer Log Cabin & Farmstead; c.1750 smoke house; 1800 pioneer cabin; WWI, WWII, Korea, Vietnam war artifacts; 1750's-1800 furniture; textiles.
Research Fields: Statesville history; art; culture.
Facilities: nature trails.
Activities: guided tours; lectures; films; temporary exhibitions; educational programs; classes; nature trails. Annual Events: Art on the Green; Art in Bloom; Christmas at the cabins.
Publications: newsletter; pamphlets.
Hours & Admission Prices: By appointment & special events. ♿

Attendance: 25,000 (estimated)
Membership: Student & Senior Citizen $15; Individual $25: Family $40; Patron $100; Benefactor $500.

Tarboro

BLOUNT-BRIDGERS HOUSE/HOBSON PITTMAN MEMORIAL GALLERY, 130 Bridgers St., Tarboro, NC 27886-3868. Tel.: 252-823-4159. Fax: 252-823-6190.
E-mail: edgecombearts@embarqmail.com
Web Site: edgecombearts.com
Formerly: Blount-Bridgers House/Edgecombe Country Art Museum
Founded: 1982.
Congressional District: 2
Key Personnel: Mgr., Carol Banks.
Personnel Profile: Full-Time Paid 1; Part-Time Paid 1; Part-Time Volunteers 14.
Governing Authority: nonprofit organization. Parent Institution: Edgecombe County Arts Council. Tax-exempt: 501(c)(3).
Art Museum: housed in c.1808 Blount-Bridgers plantation house.
Collections: Hobson Pittman 20th-century art; 20th-century American art; 19th-century silver; 19th-century ceramics; 19th-century American furniture.
Research Fields: Hobson Pittman; Blount Family history; Edgecombe County history.
Facilities: 2,000-vol. library; 75-seat gallery; 3,400 sq. ft. exhibit space. Arts & crafts by local artists for sale.
Activities: guided tours; lectures; arts festivals; organized educational programs; docent program; loan, traveling & temporary exhibitions; walking tours of historic district.
Publications: newsletter; annual report; brochure; book, The Poet's Pallette, Selected Works by Hobson Pittman.
Hours & Admission Prices: Tues.-Fri. 10-4, Sat.-Sun. 2-4; groups by appointment. Adults $5, children under 12 $2; members no charge . Closed New Year's Day; Good Friday; Easter; Memorial Day; Independence Day; Labor Day; Thanksgiving; Christmas. ♿
Attendance: 4,000 (estimated)
Membership: Student & Teacher $15; Individual $25; Family & Couple $45; Donor $50-$249; Sponsor $250-$499; Patron $500-$999; Benefactor $1,000 & up.

Valdese

WALDENSIAN HERITAGE MUSEUM, 208 Rodoret St., S., Valdese, NC 28690-2841. Mailing Address: P.O. Box 111, Valdese, NC 28690-0111. Tel.: 828-874-1111; 879-2531. Fax: 828-874-1111.
E-mail: museum@waldensianpresbyterian.org
Web Site: www.waldensianpresbyterian.org
Formerly: Museum of Waldensian History
Founded: 1955.
Congressional District: 10
Key Personnel: Exec. Dir. & Museum Shop Mgr., Gretchen Costner; Pres. (V), Jewell Bounous.
Personnel Profile: Full-Time Paid 1; Part-Time Volunteers 15.
Governing Authority: church. Parent Institution: Waldensian Presbyterian Church. Tax-exempt: 170(b)(1)(A).
Religious Museum.
Collections: late 19th & early 20th-century clothing & household furnishings; farm implements & construction tools related to the Waldensians; church furnishings & religious items related to the Waldensian Presbyterian Church; photographs of church people, events & early homes; World War I & II uniforms & artifacts.
Facilities: 500-vol. library of books related to Waldensian history, including Bibles & services dating back to the 16th century, available for research on premises; reading room. Books on Waldensian history & language & gift items for sale.
Activities: guided tours; lectures; docent program or council; outdoor theatre.
Publications: books, The Waldenses of Valdese; The Provencal Speech of The Waldensian Colonists of Valdese, NC; Genealogy of the Waldensian Settlers in Valdese, NC 1893-1990; booklets, The Waldenses of Burke County; The History of the Waldenses; The History & Heritage of the Waldensian Presbyterian Church in Valdese (first 100 years).
Hours & Admission Prices: Summer during outdoor drama: Fri.-Sat. 4-6. Tours: Tues.-Fri. 11 & 2; other times by appointment. Adults $2, students $1. Closed New Year's Day; Easter; Memorial Day; Labor Day; Thanksgiving; Christmas. ♿
Attendance: 2,000 (estimated)

Wadesboro

ANSON COUNTY HISTORICAL SOCIETY, INC., 206 E. Wade St., Wadesboro, NC 28170-2229. Tel.: 704-694-6694. Fax: 704-694-3763.
E-mail: ansonhistorical@windstream.net
Web Site: www.ansonhistoricalsociety.org
Founded: 1962.
Congressional District: 8
Key Personnel: Dir., John Jennings Dunlap, III
Personnel Profile: Part-Time Volunteers 10.
Governing Authority: society. Tax-exempt: 170(b)(1)(A), 501(c)(3).
General Museum.
Collections: period furniture; agriculture; paintings; colonial garden; Indian artifacts; Ashe-Covington Medical Museum (medical artifacts). Historic Houses: 1783 Boggan-Hammond House; 1839 Alexander Little Wing.
Research Fields: paintings; colonial garden.
Activities: guided tours; lectures; arts festivals; permanent & temporary exhibitions.
Publications: quarterly newsletter; pamphlets; books, A Pictorial Tribute; History of Anson County 1750-1976; Cemeteries of Anson County, Volume I; Cemeteries of Anson County, Volume II; Eastview Cemetery, Wadesboro, NC.
Hours & Admission Prices: Mon.-Fri. 9-5; groups by appointment only. No charge; donations accepted. ♿
Attendance: 850 (estimated)
Membership: Individual $25; Family $50; Business $100; Life $2,000.

Wake Forest

WAKE FOREST COLLEGE BIRTHPLACE SOCIETY, INC., 414 N. Main St., Wake Forest, NC 27587. Mailing Address: P.O. Box 494, Wake Forest, NC 27588-0494. Tel.: 919-556-2911. Fax: 919-556-2911.
E-mail: morriscc@wfu.edu
Web Site: www.wakeforestbirthplace.org
Founded: 1956.
Congressional District: 4
Key Personnel: Exec. Dir., Ed Morris; Pres. (V), Susan Brinkley; Vice Pres., Durward Matheny; Sec., Jennifer Smart; Cur. Exhibits, E.C. Crow, III
Personnel Profile: Full-Time Paid 1; Part-Time Paid 1; Part-Time Volunteers 50; Interns 1.
Governing Authority: nonprofit organization. Parent Institution: Wake Forest University. Tax-exempt: 501(c)(3).
Historic Society Museum: housed in 1820 building, first home of Wake Forest College in 1834.
Collections: memorabilia of Wake Forest College & town of Wake Forest; period furniture; publications; archives.
Research Fields: college & town history; history of education in NC; Baptist heritage; sports; medical school.
Activities: formally organized educational programs for children.
Publications: brochure describing house; newsletter; research journal.
Hours & Admission Prices: Tues.-Fri. 10-12 & 1:30-4:30, Sun. 3-5; tours by appointment. No charge; donations accepted. Closed major holidays. ♿
Attendance: 5,000 (estimated)
Membership: Individual $35; Family $50; Patron $250; Samuel Wait Society $500.

Waxhaw

THE MUSEUM OF THE ALPHABET, 6409 Davis Rd., The JAARS Center, Waxhaw, NC 28173. Mailing Address: P.O. Box 248, Waxhaw, NC 28173-0248. Tel.: 704-843-6066. Fax: 704-843-6200.
E-mail: info@jaars.org
Web Site: www.jaars.org/museum/alphabet/index.htm
Founded: 1990.
Congressional District: 8
Key Personnel: Dir., LaDonna Mann; Financial Dir., Kevin Golding; Public Rels. Dir., John Hutchinson.
Personnel Profile: Part-Time Volunteers 9; Interns 1.
Governing Authority: nonprofit organization. Tax-exempt: 501(c)(3) & 170(b)(1)(A).
Alphabet Museum.
Collections:
Facilities: 750-vol. library of art; history; linguistics books; 5,000 sq. ft. exhibit space. Museum-related items for sale.
Activities: films; guided tours; participatory exhibits.
Publications: booklet, The Alphabet Makers, Alphabet Roots; Alphabet Account, Past Masters, Old Lamp Lighters.
Hours & Admission Prices: Mon.-Sat. 9-12 & 1-4. No charge; donations accepted. Closed government holidays. ♿
Attendance: 8,300 (accurate)

MUSEUM OF THE WAXHAWS & ANDREW JACKSON MEMORIAL, 8215 Waxhaw Hwy. - Hwy. 75, Waxhaw, NC 28173. Mailing Address: P.O. Box 7, Waxhaw, NC 28173-1038. Tel.: 704-843-1832. Fax: 704-843-1832.
E-mail: mwaxhaw@museumofthewaxhaws.com
Web Site: www.museumofthewaxhaws.com/
Founded: 1996.
Congressional District: 8
Key Personnel: Dir., Sharon Murrer; Pres. (V), Mary Alice Wilson.
Personnel Profile: Part-Time Paid 1; Part-Time Volunteers 25.
Governing Authority: private; nonprofit organization. Parent Institution: Andrew Jackson Historical Foundation. Tax-exempt: 501(c)(3).
Regional History Museum focus on settlement period, American Revolution & Andrew Jackson's life.
Collections: civilian & military related artifacts associated with the Waxhaw Settlement & President Andrew Jackson; time line 1650-1900 tells the story of The Waxhaws a border region along NC/SC line; Andrew Jackson, 7th US President was born in the area (1767), serves as a living memorial to President Jackson; areas of focus are the American Revolution & the Civil War.
Research Fields: area study of Scots-Irish immigration & culture; Andrew Jackson.
Facilities: 8,500 sq. ft. exhibit space; 66-seat theater. Museum-related items for sale.
Activities: guided tours; lectures; theater & outdoor drama company located with museum; craft workshops; youth reenactment days. Annual Events: two living history days; Outdoor drama in June.
Publications: quarterly newsletter, Museum Monitor.
Hours & Admission Prices: Fri.-Sat. 10-5, Sun. 2-5. Adults $5, seniors 60 & over $4, children 6-12 $2; members and children 5 & under no charge. Closed New Year's Day; Thanksgiving; Christmas. ♿
Attendance: 3,000 (accurate)
Membership: Patron's Society $1-$99; Director's Society $100-$249; Scotch-Irish Society $250-$499; William R. Davie Society $500-$749; Waxhaw Heritage Society $750-$999; "Old Hickory" Society $1,000-$2,499; Elizabeth Jackson Society $2,500-$4,999; President Andrew Jackson Society $5,000 & up.

Waynesville

MUSEUM OF NORTH CAROLINA HANDICRAFTS IN THE HISTORIC SHELTON HOUSE, 49 Shelton St., Waynesville, NC 28786-5795. Mailing Address: P.O. Box 145, Waynesville, NC 28786. Tel.: 828-452-1551.
E-mail: museumnc@bellsouth.net
Web Site: www.haywood-nc.com
Founded: 1977.
Handicraft Museum: housed in the former home of Stephen Jehn Shelton and then to his son, William Taylor Shelton, founder of the Shiprock New Mexico Navajo Indian Reservation & School; built in 1875. Listed on the National Register of Historic Places.
Collections: 18th-21st century handicrafts & furniture; Cherokee & Navajo artifacts.
Hours & Admission Prices: May-Oct. Tues.-Sat. 10-4; Winter: call for hours. Adults $5, students $3; discounts to groups of 10 or more; children under 5 no charge.
Attendance: 600 (estimated)

Weaverville

ZEBULON B. VANCE BIRTHPLACE STATE HISTORIC SITE, 911 Reems Creek Rd., Weaverville, NC 28787-8710. Tel.: 828-645-6706. Fax: 828-645-0936.
Web Site: www.nchistoricsites.org/vance/vance.htm
Founded: 1961.
Congressional District: 11
Key Personnel: Site Mgr., David Tate.
Personnel Profile: Full-Time Paid 3; Part-Time Paid 3; Part-Time Volunteers 1.
Governing Authority: state. Parent Institution: North Carolina Department of Cultural Resources, 109 E. Jones St., Raleigh, NC 27611. Tax-exempt: 170(b).
Park Museum Visitor Center.
Collections: Historic House: 1795 reconstructed log house & out buildings.
Research Fields: Zebulon B. Vance.
Facilities: visitor center.
Activities: guided tours; lectures; formally organized education programs for children; permanent exhibitions; participatory demonstrations.
Publications: brochure.
Hours & Admission Prices: Tues.-Sat. 9-5. No charge; donations accepted. Closed major holidays. ♿
Attendance: 9,665 (accurate)

Whiteville

NORTH CAROLINA MUSEUM OF FORESTRY, 415 S. Madison St., Whiteville, NC 28472-4125. Tel.: 910-914-4185. Fax: 910-641-0385.
E-mail: forestry.museum@ncmail.net
Founded: 2000.
Congressional District: 7
Key Personnel: Dir., Harry Warren; Pres. Bd., Harold Blanchard; Exhibit Coord., Sara Capps; Educator, Kellie Lewis; Administrative Asst., Rhonda Billeaud.
Personnel Profile: Full-Time Paid 4; Part-Time Paid 3; Part-Time Volunteers 33; Interns 1.
Governing Authority: state. Parent Institution: North Carolina Museum of Natural Sciences, Raleigh, NC. Tax-exempt: 501(c)(3).
Natural History Museum.
Collections: North Carolina forest history & natural history.
Facilities: 164-vol. library; educational facilities; 8,000 sq. ft. exhibit space.
Activities: docent program; guided tours; lectures; loan, participatory & traveling exhibitions; rental gallery. Annual Events: George Washington Birthday tree giveaway; Festival of Trees; Wildlife Encounters; Pecan Festival.
Hours & Admission Prices: Mon.-Fri. 9-5, Sat. 1-4, Sun. 2-5. No charge. Closed state holidays. ♿
Attendance: 13,421 (accurate)

Wilkesboro

WILKES HERITAGE MUSEUM, 100 E. Main St., Wilkesboro, NC 28697. Mailing Address: P.O. Box 935, Wilkesboro, NC 28697-0935. Tel.: 336-667-3171.
E-mail: info@wilkesheritagemuseum.com
Web Site: www.wilkesheritagemuseum.com
Key Personnel: Dir., Jennifer Furr
History Museum.
Collections: early settlers; pottery; education; religion; NASCAR; moonshine; industry; military. Historic Buildings: Old Wilkes Jail; Robert Cleveland Log Home.
Hours & Admission Prices: Tues.-Sat. 10-4. Adults $5, students and seniors 55 & over $4; children 4 & under no charge. Closed major holidays.

Willard

PENDERLEA HOMESTEAD MUSEUM, 284 Garden Rd., Willard, NC 28478-6780. Tel.: 910-285-3490.
E-mail: info@penderleahomesteadmuseum.org
Web Site: www.penderleahomesteadmuseum.org
Key Personnel: Pres. Bd. Dirs., Al Owens; Vice Pres., Jimbo Robbins; Chm., Ann Southerland Cottle
History Museum.
Collections: local history & culture; early settlers; farming; photographs; period artifacts.
Hours & Admission Prices: Sat. 1-4. Adults $3, senior citizens $2; children under 12 no charge.

Wilmington

AIRLIE GARDENS, 300 Airlie Rd., Wilmington, NC 28403-3706. Tel.: 910-798-7700.
Gardens.
Collections: plants; trees; flowers; sculpture; over 130 bird species; works of Minnie Evans; mosaics.
Facilities: nature trails.
Activities: hiking; summer camp.
Hours & Admission Prices: Jan. 2-March 19 Mon.-Sat. 9-5; March 20-April 2 & May 18-Dec. daily 9-5; April 3-May 17 Sun.-Wed. 9-5, Thurs.-Sat. 9-7.

BATTLESHIP NORTH CAROLINA, (M), Eagles Island, #1 Battleship Rd., Wilmington, NC 28401. Mailing Address: P.O. Box 480, Wilmington, NC 28402-0480. Tel.: 910-251-5797. Fax: 910-251-5807.
E-mail: museum@battleshipnc.com
Web Site: www.battleshipnc.com
Founded: 1961.
Congressional District: 7
Key Personnel: Exec. Dir., Capt. Terry Bragg; Chm. (V), Michael Fox; Asst. Dir. Maintenance, Roger Miller; Dir. Promotions, Heather Loftin; Dir. Museum Svcs., Kim Robinson Sincox; Cur. Collections, Mary Ames Sheret; Dir. Sales, Leesa McFarlane; Comptroller, Elizabeth Rollinson; Dir. Programs, Danielle Wallace.
Personnel Profile: Full-Time Paid 25; Part-Time Paid 15; Part-Time Volunteers 12.
Governing Authority: state. Subsidiary Institution: Friends of the Battleship NC. Tax-exempt.

Historic Ship Museum.
Collections: World War II & U.S. Navy paintings & photographs; Kingfisher float plane; naval artifacts of the World War II era; artifacts & archival materials from ships named North Carolina, 1818-1947; SSN777 attack submarine North Carolina (2008-); archival material from U.S.S. NORTH CAROLINA (BB-55); early 20th century U.S. Navy archival material.
Research Fields: ships named NORTH CAROLINA.
Facilities: auditorium; visitor's orientation center; picnic grounds; rental spaces; river taxi (seasonal). Gifts, postcards & books for sale.
Activities: self-guided tours; permanent & changing exhibitions; school group presentations; volunteer program. Annual Events: Memorial Day service; Independence Day; Living History Weekends; $1 Fantail Film Festivals.
Publications: books, revised & expanded second edition - Battleship North Carolina; USS North Carolina Ship's Data I; newsletter.
Hours & Admission Prices: Memorial Day to Labor Day daily 8-8; Sept.-May daily 8-5. Adults $12, seniors & military $10, children 6-11 $6; discounts to groups, Historic Naval Ships Assoc. & Tin Can Sailors Assoc. members; Friends of the Battleship & children under 5 no charge.
Attendance: 200,200 (accurate)
Membership: Midshipman (college student) $15; Ensign (out-of-state) $20; Lieutenant (individual) $25; Lieutenant (couple) $35; Lieutenant Commander $45; Commander $100; Captain $250; Commodore $500; Admiral $1,000.

BELLAMY MANSION MUSEUM OF HISTORY AND DESIGN ARTS, 503 Market St., Wilmington, NC 28401-4634. Mailing Address: P.O. Box 1176, Wilmington, NC 28402-1176. Tel.: 910-251-3700, ext. 102. Fax: 910-763-8154.
E-mail: info@bellamymansion.org
Web Site: www.bellamymansion.org
Founded: 1993.
Congressional District: 1
Key Personnel: Exec. Dir., Beverly Ayscue; Chm., Sharon Stone; Dir. Mktg. & Facilities, Gene Ayscue; Dir. Public Education, Madeline Flagler.
Personnel Profile: Full-Time Paid 2; Part-Time Paid 3; Part-Time Volunteers 75.
Governing Authority: private; nonprofit organization. Parent Institution: The Historic Preservation Foundation of North Carolina. Tax-exempt: 501(c)(3).
Historic House Museum: housed in c.1861 Bellamy Mansion, a 22-room Greek Revival and Italianate residence built by free and enslaved African Americans that includes original slave quarters.
Collections: original furnishings; textiles; family material; archeological finds; structures.
Research Fields: history and design arts.
Facilities: 5,000 sq. ft. exhibit space.
Activities: guided tours; temporary & traveling exhibitions.
Publications: quarterly newsletter, Bellamy Mansion News.
Hours & Admission Prices: Tues.-Sat. 10-5, Sun. 1-5. Adults $10, children 5-12 $4; discounts to groups, Preservation North Carolina & Friends of Bellamy Mansion Museum members; members & National Trust for Historic Preservation members no charge. Closed New Year's Day; Easter; Memorial Day; Independence Day; Thanksgiving; Christmas.
Attendance: 15,000 (accurate)
Membership: Individual $35; Contributor $50; Family $60; Friend $125; Supporter $150; Sponsor $250; Benefactor $500; Cornerstone $1,000; Heritage Leader $2,500.

THE BURGWIN-WRIGHT MUSEUM, 224 Market St., Wilmington, NC 28401-4444. Tel.: 910-762-0570. Fax: 910-762-8650.
E-mail: jackie.m@burgwinwrighthouse.com
Web Site: www.burgwinwrighthouse.com
Formerly: The Burgwin-Wright Museum and Gardens
Founded: 1770.
Congressional District: 7
Key Personnel: Pres. (V), Ginger Finley.
Personnel Profile: Full-Time Paid 1; Part-Time Paid 6; Part-Time Volunteers 5.
Governing Authority: society. Parent Institution: The National Society of the Colonial Dames of America in the State of North Carolina, Wilmington, NC 28401. Tax-exempt: 501(c)(3).
Historic House Museum: housed in 1771 Burgwin-Wright House & Garden.
Collections: 18th & early 19th-century furnishings, gardens & orchard; colonial kitchen.
Activities: guided tours; open hearth cooking demonstrations in colonial kitchen.
Hours & Admission Prices: Tues.-Sat. 10-4, last tour at 3. Adults $10, children 5-12 $5; children under 5 no charge. Closed national holidays; Christmas week.
Attendance: 4,500 (estimated)

CAMERON ART MUSEUM, (M), 3201 S. 17th St., Wilmington, NC 28412-6554. Tel.: 910-395-5999. Fax: 910-395-5030.
Web Site: www.cameronartmuseum.com
Formerly: St. John's Museum of Art
Founded: 1962.
Congressional District: 7
Key Personnel: Dir., Deborah Velders; Cur. Public Programs, Daphne Holmes; Property Mgr., Johnnie McKoy; Cur. Education, Georgia Mastroieni; Curatorial Assoc., Ashley Standera; Resident Master Artist, Hiroshi Sueyoshi; Registrar, Holly Tripman.
Personnel Profile: Full-Time Paid 10; Part-Time Paid 10; Part-Time Volunteers 100.
Governing Authority: nonprofit organization. Tax-exempt: 501(c)(3).
Art Museum: housed on the grounds of the last battle of the Civil War.
Collections: fine art; design & crafts.
Research Fields: folk art (Minnie Evans Study Center).
Facilities: art library; cafe; auditorium; reception hall. Museum-related items for sale.
Activities: permanent & temporary exhibitions; artist & gallery talks; interdisciplinary programs; classes; workshops; tours; monthly children's programs; child docent program; artist-in-residence program (Clay Studio).
Publications: member bulletin; exhibition catalogues, Gwathmey Siegel: Inspiration and Transformation; Robert Delford Brown: Meat, Maps and Militant Metaphysics.
Hours & Admission Prices: Tues.-Fri. 11-2, Sat.-Sun. 11-5. Adults $8; discount to NARM members; members no charge. Closed holidays. ♿
Attendance: 40,000 (estimated)
Membership: Students & Seniors $30; Individual $50; Household $100; Friend $150; Sustainer $500; Donor $1,000.

*** CAPE FEAR MUSEUM OF HISTORY AND SCIENCE, (M),** 814 Market St., Wilmington, NC 28401-4752. Tel.: 910-798-4350. Fax: 910-798-4382.
E-mail: jrudolph@nhcgov.com
Web Site: www.CapeFearMuseum.com
Founded: 1898.
Congressional District: 7
Key Personnel: Dir., Ruth Haas; Advisory Bd., Bill Terrell; Pres. (V) CFM Associates, Inc., Chris Reid; Administrative Asst., Jane O'Brien; Volunteer Coord. & Museum Shop Mgr., Karen Smith; Cur., Barbara L. Rowe; Mgr. Education, Rebecca Dotterer; Public Rels. Specialist, Jacob Rudolph; Educator, Jeff Zuege; Educator, Virginia Howell; Educator, Jameson McDermott; Educator, Pepper Hill; Mgr. Exhibits, Jenean Todd; Exhibits Designer, John Timmerman; Receptionist, Gayle Oliver; Registrar, Terri Hudgins; Historian, Dr. Janet Davidson.
Personnel Profile: Full-Time Paid 12; Part-Time Paid 8; Part-Time Volunteers 95.
Governing Authority: county-appointed museum advisory bd.; administrative. Parent Institution: New Hanover County. Subsidiary Institution: Cape Fear Museum Associates, Inc. Tax-exempt.
Natural & Regional History Museum.
Collections: objects, documents & photographs representing the history, science & cultures of lower Cape Fear, including business & industry; natural history; household items; costumes & textiles; decorative arts; agriculture; military; maritime; forestry & lumbering; collection from former Blockade Runner Museum; model of 1863 Wilmington Water Front.
Research Fields: Lower Cape Fear history & natural history.
Facilities: library of books, pamphlets, research files & media on local, state, regional history, natural history & museum practice available on museum premises by appointment; 10,000 + sq. ft. exhibition space; photo reproduction; collection-based research also available by appointment.
Activities: long-term & changing exhibitions; K-12 school programs; outreach programs & classroom kits; public programs & events for children, family, adult & community groups.
Publications: member newsletters; brochures & rack cards; calendars; educational program guides; publicity materials.
Hours & Admission Prices: Memorial Day-Labor Day Mon.-Sat. 9-5, Sun. 1-5; Sept.-May Tues.-Sat. 9-5, Sun. 1-5. Adults $6, seniors, college students & military $5, children 3-17 $3; children under 3 & members no charge. Closed major holidays ♿
Attendance: 40,420 (accurate)
Membership: Individual $30; Family $45; Donor $100; Patron $250; Director $500; Benefactor & Corporate Contributor $1,000; Corporate Patron $2,500; Corporate Benefactor $5,000.

THE CHILDREN'S MUSEUM OF WILMINGTON, 116 Orange St., Wilmington, NC 28401-4421. Tel.: 910-254-3534.
E-mail: info@playwilmington.org
Web Site: www.playwilmington.org
Children's Museum.

Collections: hands-on exhibits.
Activities: rental facilities; birthday parties; school field trips.
Hours & Admission Prices: Summer: Mon.-Sat. 10-5, Sun. 1-5; Winter: Mon.-Fri. 9-5, Sat. 10-5, Sun. 1-5. Admission $8; ACM reciprocal program; children under one no charge. Closed Easter; Thanksgiving; Christmas Eve & Day. ♿
Attendance: 50,000 (accurate)
Membership: Grandparent $75; Family Fun Pass $95; Family Passport $125.

LOWER CAPE FEAR HISTORICAL SOCIETY, INC., 126 S. Third St., Wilmington, NC 28401-4556. Tel.: 910-762-0492 & 2976. Fax: 910-763-5869.
E-mail: info@latimerhouse.org
Web Site: www.latimerhouse.org
Founded: 1956.
Congressional District: 7
Key Personnel: Exec. Dir., Candace McGreevy; Pres. (V), Dee Eicher; Chm. (V), Pat Hardee; Office Mgr., Diane Laursen; Archives Representative, James Rush Beeler; Archivist, Shannon SanCartier.
Personnel Profile: Full-Time Paid 1; Full-Time Volunteers 40; Part-Time Paid 3; Part-Time Volunteers 50.
Governing Authority: nonprofit corporation. Tax-exempt.
Decorative Arts Museum: housed in 1852 Latimer House, on National Register of Historic Places.
Collections: original furnishings, artifacts & portraits; Cape Fear region lifestyle in 1850s.
Research Fields: archives.
Facilities: books & material relating to Wilmington archives available for research by application.
Activities: guided tours; walking tour of historic district. Museum Sponsors: three annual formal lectures.
Publications: newsletter; journal; bulletins; brochure; short stories on Cape Fear area.
Hours & Admission Prices: Mon.-Fri. 10-4, Sat. 12-5. Adults $10, children & students $5; discounts to AAM, AAA & AARP members; members no charge.
Attendance: 3,000 (accurate)
Membership: Individual $35; Family $50.

MUSEUM OF WORLD CULTURES/UNIVERSITY OF NORTH CAROLINA AT WILMINGTON, 601 College Rd., Wilmington, NC 28403-5649. Tel.: 910-962-7233. Fax: 910-962-7439.
Web Site: www.uncwil.edu/mwc
Key Personnel: Interim Dir., Betsy Bilger
University Museum: displays in 16 buildings.
Collections: artifacts from around the world; clothing; textiles; jewelry; pottery; furniture; figures; drawings; photographs; prints; scrolls.
Hours & Admission Prices: Call for hours.

POPLAR GROVE HISTORIC PLANTATION, 10200 U.S. Hwy. 17 N., Wilmington, NC 28411-6854. Tel.: 910-686-4868, ext. 26. Fax: 910-686-4309.
E-mail: pgp@poplargrove.com
Web Site: www.poplargrove.com
Founded: 1980.
Congressional District: 7
Key Personnel: Pres. (V), Chris Wilcox; Dir., Nancy Simon; Museum Shop Mgr., Nancy Kroeger; Volunteer Coord., Jeanne Walker.
Personnel Profile: Full-Time Paid 9; Part-Time Paid 6; Part-Time Volunteers 100; Interns 1.
Governing Authority: nonprofit organization. Tax-exempt.
Historic House & Site: housed in 1850 Greek Revival Plantation Manor House.
Collections: 19th-century furnishings; agricultural implements; historic buildings: 1850 manor house; kitchen; smoke house; 1875 tenant house.
Research Fields: agriculture; archaeology; Black history; genealogy; 19th-century trades & crafts.
Facilities: plantation house & buildings; cultural arts center; picnic area; restaurant. Gift items for sale.
Activities: guided tours; organized educational programs; classes; craft workshops. Special Events: Summer Fair; Antique Fair in May; Halloween Festival; Christmas open house.
Publications: newsletter.
Hours & Admission Prices: Feb.-Dec. Mon.-Sat. 9-5, Sun. 12-5. Adults $8, senior citizens $6, students 6-16 $3; discount to groups of 15 or more, AAM, ICOM & AAA members; members & children under 5 no charge. Closed Easter; Thanksgiving; Christmas.
Attendance: 40,000 (estimated)
Membership: Patron $25; Dozier Society $50; Goober Society $100; Mumford Society $500; Foy Society $500 and up.

WILMINGTON RAILROAD MUSEUM, (M), 505 Nutt St., Wilmington, NC 28401-3347. Tel.: 910-763-2634.
E-mail: wrrmnc@bellsouth.net
Web Site: www.wrrm.org
Founded: 1979.
Key Personnel: Exec. Dir., Mark W. Koenig; Pres. (V), David Nurd.
Personnel Profile: Full-Time Paid 1; Part-Time Paid 4; Part-Time Volunteers 40.
Governing Authority: not-for-profit organization. Tax-exempt: 501(c)(3).
Railroad Museum: housed in 1883 freight warehouse building.
Collections: late 19th-century to middle 20th-century railroad artifacts; photographs; tools; manuals; textiles; china; silver; railroad memorabilia; rolling stock. Historic Buildings: c.1882 & 1883 freight warehouses.
Facilities: 1,000-vol. library of railroad related material; 6,500 sq.ft. exhibit space; archival material from Atlantic Coast Line RR.
Activities: guided tours; programs for children & adults.
Publications: quarterly newsletter, The Dispatcher.
Hours & Admission Prices: April 1-Sept. 30 Mon.-Sat. 10-5, Sun. 1-5; Oct. 1-March 31 Mon.-Sat. 10-4. Adults $7, military & seniors 60 & over $6, children 2-12 $3; discounts to members, groups, AAM & ICOM members; members & children under 2 no charge. Closed New Year's Eve & Day; Easter; Thanksgiving; Christmas Eve & Day. ♿
Attendance: 17,452 (accurate)
Membership: Coach $40; Club Car $60; Pullman $125; Private Car $250; RR Baron $500.

Wilson

BARTON ART GALLERIES, Whitehead & Gold St., Wilson, NC 27893. Mailing Address: Art Dept., Barton College, P.O. Box 5000, Wilson, NC 27893-7000. Tel.: 252-399-6477 & 6300.
Web Site: www.barton.edu
Founded: 1965.
Congressional District: 2
Key Personnel: Dir., Gerard Lange.
Personnel Profile: Part-Time Paid 5; Interns 3.
Governing Authority: college. Parent Institution: Barton College. Tax-exempt.
Art Gallery.
Collections: various art media & other works donated to the college or purchased by the museum.
Facilities: 4,000-vol. library pertaining to art history available for research & for inter-library loan.
Activities: lectures; gallery talks; arts festivals; formally organized education programs for undergraduate college students; temporary exhibitions.
Publications: gallery programs; exhibition catalogues.
Hours & Admission Prices: Mid-Aug. to mid-May Mon.-Fri. 10-3. No charge. Closed New Year's Day; Good Friday; Thanksgiving; Christmas; fall & spring breaks. ♿
Membership: Student, Faculty, & Staff $10; Individual $25; Family $50; Hirsham $100; Guggenheim $250; Metropolitan $500; Louvre $1,000 & up.

IMAGINATION STATION SCIENCE MUSEUM, 224 E. Nash St., Wilson, NC 27893. Mailing Address: P.O. Box 2127, Wilson, NC 27894-2127. Tel.: 252-291-5113. Fax: 252-291-2968.
E-mail: mail@imaginescience.org
Web Site: www.imaginescience.org
Founded: 1989.
Congressional District: 1
Key Personnel: C.E.O., Jonathan Brooks; Pres., Sam Lanier; Dir. Education, Laura Dameron; Educator, Drew Hackney; Educator, Kristy Owens; Educator, Tameka Dickens; Museum Shop Mgr., Stephanie Cherry.
Personnel Profile: Full-Time Paid 3; Part-Time Paid 5.
Governing Authority: private; nonprofit organization. Tax-exempt: 501(c)(3)
Science Museum.
Collections: interactive science exhibits; reptiles.
Facilities: 14,000 sq. ft. exhibit space; 100-seat auditorium; education facilities; planetarium. Museum-related items for sale.
Activities: mobile vans; school loan service; traveling exhibition; training for teachers. Annual Events: Spooky Science Carnival in October; Independence Day celebration; Earth Day celebration.
Publications: quarterly newsletter, Lab Notes.
Hours & Admission Prices: Mon.-Sat. 9-5. Adults $5, seniors & students $4; discounts to AAM & ASTC members; children under 4 & members no charge. Closed Thanksgiving; Christmas. ♿
Attendance: 20,000 (accurate)
Membership: Family $60.

Windsor

HISTORIC HOPE FOUNDATION, INC., 132 Hope House Rd., Windsor, NC 27983-7458. Tel.: 252-794-3140. Fax: 252-794-5583.
E-mail: hopeplantation@coastalnet.com
Web Site: www.hopeplantation.org
Founded: 1965.
Congressional District: 1
Key Personnel: Pres. (V), Dr. John L. Hill; Administrative Asst., Belinda Winborne; Cur., Gregory Tyler.
Personnel Profile: Full-Time Paid 1; Part-Time Paid 10; Part-Time Volunteers 50; Interns 1.
Governing Authority: nonprofit organization. Tax-exempt: 501(c)(3).
Historic House Museum: located on the Hope Plantation.
Collections: period furniture; decorative arts; fine art. Historic Houses: 1763 King-Bazemore House; 1800 Samuel Cox House; 1803 Hope Mansion; Roanoke-Chowan Heritage Center: history; art; African American; Native American.
Research Fields: gardening; African American heritage.
Facilities: research library; nature trails.
Activities: guided tours; lectures; films; decorative arts symposium; permanent exhibitions.
Publications: semi-annual newsletter.
Hours & Admission Prices: Late Oct.-March Mon.-Sat. 10-4, Sun. 2-5, April-late Oct. Mon.-Sat. 10-5, Sun. 2-5. Adults $8, senior $7, children & students $3; discount to AAA members; members no charge. Closed Thanksgiving; Christmas.
Attendance: 17,500 (estimated)
Membership: Individual $30; Family $50; Donor $75; Contributing $100; Corporate/Business $125; Patron $500; Benefactor $1,000.

Winnabow

BRUNSWICK TOWN/FORT ANDERSON STATE HISTORIC SITE, 8884 St. Philips Rd., S.E., Winnabow, NC 28479-5035. Tel.: 910-371-6613. Fax: 910-383-3806.
E-mail: brunswick@ncdcr.gov
Web Site: www.nchistoricsites.org/brunswic/brunswic.htm
Founded: 1958.
Congressional District: 7
Key Personnel: Regl. Supvr. East Region, James A. Bartley.
Personnel Profile: Full-Time Paid 5; Part-Time Paid 6.
Governing Authority: state. Parent Institution: North Carolina Division of Archives & History. Subsidiary Institution: North Carolina Dept. of Cultural Resources, 109 E. Jones St., Raleigh, NC 27611. Tax-exempt: 170(b)(1)(A).
Historic Site: 1726-1776 excavated foundations of port town; earthen Confederate Fort Anderson.
Collections: 18th-century English & Civil War artifacts; colonial.
Research Fields: local history.
Facilities: visitor center.
Activities: guided tours; lectures; school programs.
Publications: brochure.
Hours & Admission Prices: Tues.-Sat. 9-5. No charge; donations accepted. Closed Thanksgiving; Christmas Eve & Day. ♿
Attendance: 54,680 (accurate)

Winston-Salem

CHARLOTTE AND PHILIP HANES ART GALLERY, WAKE FOREST UNIVERSITY, Art Dept., Winston-Salem, NC 27109. Mailing Address: P.O. Box 7232, Winston-Salem, NC 27109. Tel.: 336-758-5795 & 5585. Fax: 336-758-6014.
E-mail: faccinto@wfu.edu
Web Site: www.wfu.edu/Academic-departments/Art/gall_index.html
Formerly: Wake Forest University Fine Arts Gallery
Founded: 1976.
Key Personnel: Dir., Victor Faccinto; Asst. Dir., Paul Bright.
Personnel Profile: Full-Time Paid 2; Part-Time Paid 6.
Governing Authority: university; nonprofit. Tax-exempt.
Art Museum.
Collections: paintings; drawings; sculpture.
Major Exhibits: Dongoski-Olsen-Scobel, 2/10-3/10.
Facilities: educational facilities.
Activities: lectures; loan & traveling exhibitions; curating contemporary & historical exhibitions in various media.
Publications: catalogues for exhibitions.
Hours & Admission Prices: Sept.-May Mon.-Fri. 10-5, Sat.-Sun. 1-5. No charge. Closed university holidays. ♿
Attendance: 6,500

CHILDREN'S MUSEUM OF WINSTON-SALEM, 390 S. Liberty St., Winston-Salem, NC 27101-5260. Tel.: 336-723-9111. Fax: 336-723-9469.
E-mail: info@childrensmuseumofws.org
Web Site: www.childrensmuseumofws.org
Founded: 2004.
Key Personnel: Interim Exec. Dir., Eva Wu; Dir. Finance & Mktg., A.J. Wolff Edge; Program Mgr., Mary Mollitt; Dir. Guest Svcs., Lesa Pierce.
Governing Authority: nonprofit organization. Tax-exempt: 501(c)(3).
Children's Museum.
Collections: hands-on exhibits.
Facilities: Museum-related items for sale.
Activities: special events. Museum Sponsors: Annual Gala.
Hours & Admission Prices: Memorial Day to Labor Day Mon.-Sat. 10-4, Sun. 1-5; Sept.-May Tues.-Sat. 10-4, Sun. 1-5. Adults $7, seniors 62 & over $6; discounts to groups of 15 or more; educators & children under one no charge. Closed New Year's Day; Easter; Thanksgiving; Christmas. ♿

DELTA ARTS CENTER, 2611 New Walkertown Rd., Winston-Salem, NC 27101-1948. Tel.: 336-722-2625.
E-mail: delta2611@bellsouth.net
Web Site: www.deltafinearts.org/
Key Personnel: Exec. Dir., Dianne Caesar
Arts Center.
Collections: paintings & sculpture by African-American artists from North Carolina.
Hours & Admission Prices: Tues.-Fri. 10-5, Sat. 11-3; groups by appointment. No charge. Closed New Year's Eve, Day & day after; Thanksgiving & day after; Christmas Eve, Day & week.

DIGGS GALLERY AT WINSTON-SALEM STATE UNIVERSITY, 601 Martin Luther King Jr. Dr., Winston-Salem, NC 27110-0003. Tel.: 336-750-2458. Fax: 336-750-2463.
E-mail: diggsinfo@wssu.edu
Web Site: www.wssu.edu
Founded: 1990.
Congressional District: 12
Key Personnel: Dir., Cur. & Devel., Belinda Tate; Chm. (V), Sylvia Sprinkle Hamlin; Cur. Education, Dara Silver; Office Asst., Monica Scott.
Personnel Profile: Full-Time Paid 3; Part-Time Paid 1; Part-Time Volunteers 8; Interns 2.
Governing Authority: public university; nonprofit. Parent Institution: Winston-Salem State University. Tax-exempt: 501(c)(3).
University Art Gallery.
Collections: African-American art; sculptures by Mel Edwards, Tyrone Mitchell, Beverly Buchanan & Dennis Peacock; John Biggers murals; paintings, prints & sculptures by Romare Bearden, Stephanie Pogue, Samuel Brown, Selma Burke & William Artis; emphasis on North Carolina & southeastern African-American artists.
Research Fields: African art; African-American art (historical & contemporary); art of the African diaspora; memory jugs: African-American grave markers.
Facilities: 100-vol. African & African-American library.
Activities: arts festivals; concerts; films; formal education programs for adults, children & college students at Winston-Salem State University; guided tours; lectures; loan, traveling & participatory exhibits; temporary exhibits of our own collection; training programs for professional museum workers.
Publications: exhibition catalogs.
Hours & Admission Prices: Gallery: Tues.-Sat. 11-5. Office: Mon.-Fri. 8-5. No charge. Closed New Year's Eve & Day; Martin Luther King Jr. Day; Good Friday; Memorial Day; Independence Day; Labor Day; Veterans Day; Thanksgiving; Christmas Eve, Day & week. ♿
Attendance: 14,700 (accurate)
Membership: Annual $25.

HISTORIC BETHABARA PARK, 2147 Bethabara Rd., Winston-Salem, NC 27106-2701. Tel.: 336-924-8191. Fax: 336-924-0535.
Web Site: www.bethabarapark.org
Founded: 1966.
Congressional District: 5
Key Personnel: Dir., Ellen M. Kutcher.
Personnel Profile: Full-Time Paid 4; Part-Time Paid 21; Part-Time Volunteers 250; Interns 1.
Governing Authority: board of trustees. Parent Institution: Historic Bethabara Park, Inc., City of Winston-Salem Recreation & Parks Dept. Tax-exempt: 501(c)(3).
Historic Site & Wilderness Preserve: 1753 site of the first Moravian Settlement in North Carolina.
Collections: Moravian pottery, furniture. Historic Buildings: 1782 Potter's House; 1788 Gemeinhaus (church); 1803 Distiller's House; 1756-1763

Reconstructed Palisade Fort; stabilized archaeological foundations of original buildings in 1753 community; reconstructed 1759 community garden; 1761 medical garden; reconstructed 1754 village.
Research Fields: Moravian history; archaeology.
Facilities: wildlife preserve; restored colonial gardens; theater; 15 km. of nature trails; picnic area; visitor center.
Activities: guided tours; lectures; special events; audiovisual presentation; volunteers wildlife preserve trails.
Publications: brochures; Historic Bethabara Park Field Guide.
Hours & Admission Prices: Visitor Center & Buildings: April to mid-Dec. Tues.-Fri. 10:30-4:30, Sat.-Sun. 1:30-4:30. Grounds: daily. Adults $2, children $1. ♿
Attendance: 131,000 (estimated)

* **HISTORIC TOWN OF SALEM, (M),** 600 S. Main St., Winston-Salem, NC 27101-5329. Tel.: 336-721-7300; 888-653-7253. Fax: 336-721-7335.
E-mail: webmaster@oldsalem.org
Web Site: www.oldsalem.org
Formerly: Old Salem Inc.
Founded: 1950.
Congressional District: 5
Key Personnel: Pres., Paul G. Reber; Chm. (V), F. Borden Hanes; C.F.O., Allyson Brown; Vice Pres., Horton Center, Paula Locklair; Vice Pres. & Dir. Restoration, John Larson; Vice Pres. Devel., Norma Pearman; Vice Pres. Retail, Gail Carpenter; Vice Pres. Interpretation, John Caramia; Dir. Mktg., Renee Boyd; Cur. Collections, Johanna Brown; Coord. Crafts, Nat Norwood; Museum Shop Mgr., Ann Johnson.
Personnel Profile: Full-Time Paid 100; Part-Time Paid 100; Part-Time Volunteers 40; Interns 2.
Governing Authority: nonprofit organization. Branch Museum: The Museum of Early Southern Decorative Arts; The Children's Museum at Old Salem; The Toy Museum at Old Salem. Tax-exempt: 501(c)(3).
Historic Restoration Village: 1766 Moravian Congregation Town.
Collections: 18th, early 19th-century Moravian artifacts; authentic furnishings; tools for craft shops in Single Brothers House; history; outdoor museum; gardens; music; decorative arts. Historic Buildings: 1769-1786 Single Brothers House; 1771 Miksch Tobacco Shop; 1784 Salem Tavern; 1794 Boys School; 1800 Winkler Bakery; 1802 Vierling House; 1803 Market Fire House; 1819 John Vogler House; 1827 Shultz Shoemaker Shop; 1833 Vogler Gunsmith Shop; 1861 St. Philips Church.
Research Fields: architecture; crafts; community life of the early Moravians & enslaved African Americans.
Facilities: 2,000-vol. library of books, articles, & periodicals; reading room; auditoriums; restaurants. Reproductions, gifts & bakery goods for sale.
Activities: guided tours; lectures; films; concerts; formally organized education programs for children, adults & undergraduate college students; permanent exhibitions.
Publications: books, Candle Lovefeast; An Adventure in Historic Preservation; The Moravian Potters in North Carolina; The Quiet People of the Land; The Three Forks of Muddy Creek; Johann Ludwig Eberhardt & His Salem Clocks; Moravian Decorative Arts in North Carolina.
Hours & Admission Prices: Visitor Center: Tues.-Sat. 9-5, Sun. 12:30-5. Town: Tues.-Sat. 9:30-4:30, Sun. 1-4:30. Adults $21, children $10; discounts to AAM & ICOM members. Closed Easter; Thanksgiving; Christmas Eve & Day. ♿
Attendance: 111,211 (accurate)
Membership: Student & Senior Citizen $30; Individual $40; Family $50; Sustaining $100; Benefactor $250; Patron $500; Marshall Society $1,000 & up.

MUSEUM OF ANTHROPOLOGY, (M), Wingate Rd., Winston-Salem, NC 27109-7267. Mailing Address: P.O. Box 7267, Winston-Salem, NC 27109-7267. Tel.: 336-758-5282. Fax: 336-758-5116.
Web Site: www.wfu.edu/MOA
Formerly: Museum of Man
Founded: 1963.
Congressional District: 5
Key Personnel: Dir., Dr. Stephen Whittington; Pres. (V), William Evans; Educator, Tina Smith; Registrar & Collections Mgr., Kyle Elizabeth Bryner; Shop Assoc., Anne Gilmore; Public Rels., Mktg. & Membership Coord., Sara Cromwell.
Personnel Profile: Full-Time Paid 4; Part-Time Paid 1; Part-Time Volunteers 29.
Governing Authority: university. Parent Institution: Wake Forest University. Tax-exempt.
Anthropology Museum.
Collections: anthropological and archaeological collections from the Americas, Africa, Asia & the Pacific.
Major Exhibits: Tattooing Traditions, 1/10-8/10.
Research Fields: archaeology; physical anthropology; Native American art; cultural ecology.
Facilities: small library. Museum-related hand-crafted items from around the world for sale.
Activities: formally organized education programs for kindergarten-12th grade; museum studies courses for undergraduate students; permanent & temporary exhibitions; lecture series; college classes; tours & outreach programs; summer camps; family days.
Publications: MOA newsletter.
Hours & Admission Prices: Tues.-Sat. 10-4:30; groups by appointment only. No charge; donations accepted. ♿
Attendance: 20,268 (accurate)
Membership: Student, Teacher & Senior $15; Individual $25; Family $40; Supporting $50-$99; Patron $100-$499; Banks Founder's Circle $500 & up.

MUSEUM OF EARLY SOUTHERN DECORATIVE ARTS (MESDA), 924 S. Main St., Winston-Salem, NC 27101-5335. Tel.: 336-721-7360. Fax: 336-721-7367.
E-mail: research@oldsalem.org
Web Site: www.mesda.org
Founded: 1965.
Congressional District: 5
Key Personnel: C.E.O. & Pres., Lee French; C.F.O., Eric Hoyle; Vice Pres. & Chief Cur., Robert Leath; Dir. Research, June Lucas; Dir. Education & Special Programs, Sally Gant; Assoc. Cur., Daniel Ackermann; Dir. Devel., Frances Beasley; Dir. Collections & Cur., Johanna M. Brown; Collections Mgr., Abigail Linville; Office Admin., Martha Ashley; Photographer, Wes Stewart; Librarian, Michele Doyle; Vice Pres. Publications, Gary Albert.
Personnel Profile: Full-Time Paid 14; Part-Time Paid 40.
Governing Authority: nonprofit organization. Parent Institution: Old Salem, Inc., 600 S. Main St., Winston-Salem, NC 27101. Tax-exempt: 501(c)(3).
Decorative Arts Museum.
Collections: architecture; furniture; paintings; ceramics; textiles; prints; metalwares used or made in the South through 1820.
Research Fields: southern decorative arts through 1820 in Maryland, Virginia, Kentucky, Tennessee, the Carolinas, & Georgia.
Facilities: library; 30 period room settings; research center; auditorium. Museum-related items for sale.
Activities: guided tours; lectures; formally organized programs for adults & undergraduate college students; annual graduate Summer Institute in coordination with the University of Virginia; temporary exhibitions.
Publications: magazine, Old Salem Museum & Gardens.
Hours & Admission Prices: Tues.-Sat. 9:30-4:30, Sun. 1-5. Adults $21, children 6-16 $10; discounts to AAM & ICOM members. Closed Easter; Thanksgiving; Christmas Eve & Day. ♿
Attendance: 19,176 (accurate)
Membership: Annual $50 & up.

REYNOLDA GARDENS OF WAKE FOREST UNIVERSITY, 100 Reynolda Village, Winston-Salem, NC 27106-5123. Tel.: 336-758-5593. Fax: 336-758-4132.
E-mail: gardens@wfu.edu
Web Site: www.reynoldagardens.org
Founded: 1962.
Congressional District: 5
Key Personnel: Mgr., Preston Stockton; Asst. Mgr., John Kiger; Cur. Education, Camilla Wilcox.
Personnel Profile: Full-Time Paid 6; Part-Time Volunteers 30.
Governing Authority: nonprofit. Reynolda Gardens Committee of Wake; Forest University. Tax-exempt.
Conservatory: housed in 1912 building.
Collections: tropical plants; roses; cactus; orchids.
Research Fields: botany.
Facilities: garden; nature trails; 60-seat auditorium.
Activities: lectures; concerts; formally organized educational programs; volunteer program.
Publications: biannual gardeners journal; biannual calendar; web publication, Naturalist's Notebook for K-5 educators.
Hours & Admission Prices: Greenhouses: Jan. Mon.-Fri. 10-4; Feb.-Dec. Mon.-Sat. 10-4. Grounds: daily sunrise-sunset. No charge. ♿
Attendance: 100,000 (estimated)
Membership: Friend $30; Donor $50; Family $100; Sponsor $250; Patron $500; Benefactor $1,000.

* **REYNOLDA HOUSE MUSEUM OF AMERICAN ART, (M),** 2250 Reynolda Rd., Winston-Salem, NC 27106-5117. Mailing Address: P.O. Box 7287, Winston-Salem, NC 27109-7287. Tel.: 336-758-5150; 888-663-1149. Fax: 336-758-5704.
Web Site: reynoldahouse.org

Founded: 1964.
Congressional District: 5
Key Personnel: C.E.O., Allison C. Perkins; Chm. Bd., J.D. Wilson; Pres. (V), Judy Watson; Founding Dir., Barbara B. Millhouse; Dir. Devel., Marty Edwards; Business Mgr., Kim Hampton; Cur. Education, Kathleen F.G. Hutton; Dir. Collections Management, Rebecca Eddins; Archivist, Todd Crumley; Museum Shop Mgr., Cindy Byrd.
Personnel Profile: Full-Time Paid 26; Part-Time Paid 52; Part-Time Volunteers 240; Interns 8.
Governing Authority: nonprofit charitable organization. Affiliated with Wake Forest University. Tax-exempt: 501(c)(3).
Art Museum: housed in 1917 Reynolda House, home of R.J. Reynolds, founder of Reynolds Tobacco Company.
Collections: American paintings, sculpture & prints; costumes; decorative arts; archives.
Major Exhibits: William Christenberry: Photographs (T), 2/13/10-6/27/10.
Research Fields: American art; American Country House.
Facilities: library of books & pamphlets pertaining to American art available for research; botanical gardens. Museum-related items for sale.
Activities: guided tours; lectures; films; concerts; arts festivals; drama; formally organized education programs children & adults as well as undergraduate & graduate college students; American Foundations, interdisciplinary summer program for graduate, and continuing education classes; January College Intern Program; docent program; inter-museum loan & permanent exhibitions.
Publications: catalog, American Originals: Selections from Reynolda House, Museum of American Art; Reynolda: A History of an American Country House, 1997; The Reynolda House Aeolian Organ; The Paris Gowns in the Reynolda House Collection; A World of Her Own Making Katharine Smith Reynolds & the Landscape of Reynolda; Log of Aeroplane NR-898W; Reynolda Farms; American Wilderness: The Hudson River School of Painting.
Hours & Admission Prices: Tues.-Sat. 9:30-4:30, Sun. 1:30-4:30. Adults $10, senior citizens $9; discounts to AAM, ICOM & AAA members; children, students with current ID & members no charge. Closed New Year's Day; Thanksgiving; Christmas. ♿
Attendance: 36,379 (accurate)
Membership: Educator $35; Individual $50; Dual/Family $75; Patron $150; Benefactor $250; Sustainer $500; The Reynolda Society $1,000 & up.

SCIWORKS, (M), 400 Hanes-Mill Rd., Winston-Salem, NC 27105-9667. Tel.: 336-767-6730. Fax: 336-661-1777.
E-mail: bssanford@sciworks.org
Web Site: www.sciworks.org
Founded: 1964.
Congressional District: 5
Key Personnel: C.E.O., Dr. Beverly Sanford; Bd. Chm., Jimmy T. Flythe; Vice Pres. Finance, Sam Hancock; Vice Pres. Programs & Education, Kelli Johnson; Vice Pres. Exhibits, Tom Wilson; Vice Pres. Devel. & Mktg., Debbie Cesta; Vice Pres. Facilities, Carl Nisbet; Science Shop Mgr., Bobbie Tucker.
Personnel Profile: Full-Time Paid 17; Part-Time Paid 13; Part-Time Volunteers 60; Interns 10.
Governing Authority: nonprofit organization. Tax-exempt: 501(c)(3).
Science & Technology Museum.
Collections: hands-on exhibits relating to the physical sciences, natural sciences, health sciences; natural history includes rocks, minerals, sea shells & mounts; planetarium; 15-acre environmental park.
Facilities: 30,000 sq. ft. exhibit space; 150-seat science theatre; 120-seat planetarium; classrooms; 32 acres of grounds; 15-acre environmental park; picnic area. Science museum-related items for sale.
Activities: education science programs for walk-in visitors & organized groups of children, students & adults; outreach programs; permanent & traveling exhibits; workshops for children & teachers; volunteer program; annual special events & festivals; laser shows.
Publications: quarterly newsletter.
Hours & Admission Prices: Mon.-Fri. 10-4, Sat. 11-5. Exhibits: adults $10, students & seniors $8, children 2-5 $6; discounts for ASTC & AAM members; children under 2 & members no charge. Closed New Year's Day; Thanksgiving; Christmas. ♿
Attendance: 100,000 (accurate)
Membership: Cardholder $50; Cardholder +1 $65; Cardholder +2 $80; Cardholder +3 $95; Cardholder +4 $110; Large Family $120; supersize any level $15.

SOUTHEASTERN CENTER FOR CONTEMPORARY ART, (M), 750 Marguerite Dr., Winston-Salem, NC 27106-5861. Tel.: 336-725-1904. Fax: 336-722-6059.
E-mail: general@secca.org
Web Site: www.secca.org
Founded: 1956.
Congressional District: 5
Key Personnel: Dir., Mark R. Leach; Bd. Advisory Chm., Joia Johnson; Cur. Art, Steven Matijcio; Dir. Finance & Operations, Karin Burnette; Mktg. & Public Rels., Ellen Wallace.
Personnel Profile: Full-Time Paid 9; Part-Time Paid 5; Interns 1.
Governing Authority: nonprofit; board of directors. Parent Institution: North Carolina Dept. of Cultural Resources. Subsidiary Institution: North Carolina Museum of Art. Tax-exempt: 501(c)(3).
Contemporary Art.
Collections: year round changing exhibitions of contemporary art-interior & exterior installations.
Facilities: library; auditorium; 32-acres of wooded grounds & sculpture sites.
Activities: lectures; panels; films; gallery talks; education programs for children & adults in arts & humanities; music, dance, drama performances; traveling exhibitions; special events. Museum Sponsors: Artists in the Community II.
Publications: quarterly newsletter; gallery notes; exhibition catalogs.
Hours & Admission Prices: Closed for renovations until March 2010. ♿
Attendance: 60,000 (estimated)

Wrightsville Beach

WRIGHTSVILLE BEACH MUSEUM OF HISTORY, 303 W. Salisbury St., Wrightsville Beach, NC 28480-1819. Mailing Address: P.O. Box 584, Wrightsville Beach, NC 28480-0584. Tel.: 910-256-2569. Fax: 910-256-2569.
E-mail: info@wbmuseum.com
Web Site: www.wbmuseum.com
Key Personnel: Dir., Madeline Flagler.
Governing Authority: private; nonprofit organization.
History Museum: housed in Myer's Cottage.
Collections: local history & culture; personal artifacts; photographs.
Hours & Admission Prices: Tues.-Fri. 10-4, Sat. 12-5, Sun. 1-5. No charge.

NORTH DAKOTA

(147 listings)

Abercrombie

FORT ABERCROMBIE STATE HISTORIC SITE, 935 Broadway, Abercrombie, ND 58001. Mailing Address: P.O. Box 148, Abercrombie, ND 58001-0148. Tel.: 701-553-8513 & 328-2666. Fax: 701-328-3710.
E-mail: histsoc@nd.us
Web Site: www.history.nd.gov
Founded: 1905.
Key Personnel: Dir. State Historical Society of ND, Merlan E. Paaverud, Jr.; Dir. Historic Preservation Division, Fern Swenson; Mgr. Eastern Regl. Sites, Vance E. Nelson; Mgr. Historic Sites, Diane Rogness; Site Supvr., James V. Acker.
Personnel Profile: Full-Time Paid 3; Part-Time Paid 6.
Governing Authority: society. Parent Institution: State Historical Society of North Dakota. Subsidiary Institution: Friends of Fort Abercrombie. Tax-exempt: 501(c)(3).
Historic Site: This site preserves the military post that served from 1857 to 1877 as the gateway to the Dakota frontier. It was besieged by the Sioux during the Dakota conflict of 1862.
Collections: Red River ox cart; relics from pioneer days & early history of Fort; flagpole. Historic Buildings: 2 reconstructed blockhouses; original guardhouse (restored); ghosted building sites & palisade.
Facilities: Museum-related items for sale.
Activities: summer programs: Dutch Oven demos; quilting demos; hide tanning demos; Memorial Day & Independence Day programs; living history demos Saturday & Sunday May-September; children's story time; arts & crafts for children. Museum Sponsors: Aber Days community celebration in June.
Publications: brochure.
Hours & Admission Prices: May 16-Sept. 15 Thurs.-Mon. 8-5. Adults $5, children 6-15 $2.50, student in groups $1; children 5 & under no charge. Season Pass: Individual $10, Family $20, bus group rate $2 per person for groups of 20 or more. ♿
Attendance: 10,000 (estimated)
Membership: North Dakota Heritage Foundation.

Adams

KNUDT SALLE LOG CABIN, Rt. 1, Adams, ND 58210. Mailing Address: Rte. 1, Box 10, Adams, ND 58210. Tel.: 701-944-2792.
Founded: 1970.

Congressional District: 11
Governing Authority: society. Affiliated with The Walsh Co. Historical Society & Adams Community Club. Tax-exempt.
Preservation Project: housed in 1884 log cabin located in city park.
Collections: cast iron kitchen range; cast iron cookware; 1880 furnishings; working plow; trip hammer.
Research Fields: 1880s household furnishings & utensils.
Activities: permanent exhibitions.
Publications: brochure, History of Cabin.
Hours & Admission Prices: Memorial Day-Labor Day Sun. 2-5; other times by appointment. No charge; donations accepted. ♿
Attendance: 60 (estimated)

Alexander

LEWIS AND CLARK TRAIL MUSEUM, US Hwy. 85, Alexander, ND 58831. Mailing Address: P.O. Box 343, Alexander, ND 58831-0343. Tel.: 701-828-3157.
History Museum: housed in 1914 school building.
Collections: scale model of Fort Mandan; historical artifacts on North Dakota's homestead days; photographs.
Hours & Admission Prices: Call for hours.

Almont

ALMONT HERITAGE PARK AND MUSEUM, Main St., Almont, ND 58520. Tel.: 701-843-7927.
Key Personnel: Chm. (V) & Pres. (V), Tracy Larson; Co-Chm. (V), Nancy Doll.
Governing Authority: Parent Institution: Almont Historical Society.
History Museum.
Collections: local history; photographs; historic buildings.
Hours & Admission Prices: Memorial Day to Labor Day. No charge.

Ashley

MCINTOSH COUNTY HISTORICAL SOCIETY, 615 Center Ave. N., Ashley, ND 58413-7011. Tel.: 701-288-3374.
Founded: 1977.
Key Personnel: Pres. (V), Ronald J. Meidinger.
Personnel Profile: Part-Time Volunteers 15.
Governing Authority: county.
Historical Museum.
Collections: Lutheran Church; sod house; outdoor baking oven; schoolhouse; domestic equipment; furniture; clothing; farm machinery; blacksmith equipment; 500-line railroad depot; 500-line railroad caboose; 500-line railroad baggage & freight wagons.
Facilities: McIntosh County Heritage Center.
Hours & Admission Prices: June-Sept. Sun. 2-4; other times by appointment. No charge; donations accepted. ♿
Attendance: 250 (estimated)
Membership: Single $10; Family $15; Business $35; Contributing $50; Patron $100; Life $1,000.

Beach

GOLDEN VALLEY COUNTY MUSEUM, 185 1st Ave., S.E., Beach, ND 58621. Mailing Address: P.O. Box 384, Beach, ND 58621-0384. Tel.: 701-872-3938.
Congressional District: 39
Key Personnel: Pres. (V), Judy M. Ridenhower.
Personnel Profile: Part-Time Paid 1.
Governing Authority: county. Parent Institution: Golden Valley County Historical Society. Tax-exempt.
History Museum.
Collections: area history; personal artifacts; period tractors & farm equipment; fossils; Indian arrowheads; wagons. Historic Building: 1909 schoolhouse.
Hours & Admission Prices: May 30 to Labor Day Mon.-Fri. 1-4; other times by appointment. No charge; donations accepted. ♿
Attendance: 500
Membership: 3 Years $15; 5 Years $20; Life $100.

Belcourt

TURTLE MOUNTAIN CHIPPEWA HISTORICAL SOCIETY, Hwy. 5, Belcourt, ND 58316. Mailing Address: P.O. Box 257, Belcourt, ND 58316-0257. Tel.: 701-477-2639 & 2600. Fax: 701-477-0065.
Web Site: www.chippewa.utma.com/two.html
Formerly: Turtle Mountain Chippewa Heritage Center
Founded: 1985.
Key Personnel: Exec. Dir., Sheldon Williams; Chm., Jeremy Laducer.
Personnel Profile: Part-Time Paid 1; Part-Time Volunteers 2.
Governing Authority: board of directors. Turtle Mountain Indian Historical Society. Tax-exempt.
History Museum & Art Gallery.
Collections: Chippewa Indian artifacts; contemporary art.
Research Fields: Chippewa-Metis history.
Facilities: archives; classroom; reading room. Gift items for sale.
Activities: temporary exhibitions.
Publications: quarterly newsletter for members, Singing Bird.
Hours & Admission Prices: Mon.-Fri. 10-5. No charge; donations accepted. ♿
Attendance: 1,000
Membership: Single $10; Family $15; Supporting $25; Company $50; Organizational $100; Life $500.

Berthhold

UPPER SOURIS NATIONAL WILDLIFE REFUGE, 17705 212th Ave., N.W., Berthhold, ND 58718-9666. Tel.: 701-468-5467.
E-mail: uppersouris@fws.gov
Web Site: www.fws.gov/uppersouris
Wildlife Refuge.
Collections: waterfowl; nesting cormorants & great blue herons; birds; white-tailed deer.
Hours & Admission Prices: Refuge: daily 5am-10pm. Visitor Center: Mon.-Fri. 8-4:30.

Beulah

HELMUTH PFENNIG WILDLIFE MUSEUM, 6148 3rd St., N.W., Beulah, ND 58523-9488. Tel.: 701-873-4889.
Natural History Museum.
Collections: over 175 animal specimens from around the world.
Hours & Admission Prices: Call for hours.

MERCER COUNTY MUSEUM, 108 Seventh St., N.E., Beulah, ND 58523. Mailing Address: P.O. Box 1134, Beulah, ND 58523-1134. Tel.: 701-873-5070.
Founded: 1979.
General Museum.
Collections: local history & culture; frontier life; personal artifacts; period furnishings; military artifacts.
Publications: quarterly newsletter, Bits & Pieces.
Hours & Admission Prices: Memorial Day to Labor Day Sun. 1-4; other times by appointment. No charge; donations accepted. ♿
Membership: Individual $5; Business $25; Life $100.

Bismarck

BISMARCK ART & GALLERIES ASSOCIATION, 422 E. Front Ave., Bismarck, ND 58504-5641. Tel.: 701-223-5986. Fax: 701-223-8960.
E-mail: baga@midconetwork.com
Web Site: bismarck-art.org
Key Personnel: Exec. Dir., Linda Christman; Program Dir., Sherry Niesar; Administrative Asst., Kathy Fettig
Art Gallery.
Collections: local history & culture; art exhibits.
Hours & Admission Prices: Tues.-Fri. 10-5, Sat. 1-3.
Membership: Student & Senior $20; Artist $25; Individual $40; Family $50; Contributor $100-$499; Donor $500-$999; Supporter $1,000-$4,499; Sustainer $2,500-$4,999; Benefactor $5,000-$9,999; Patron $10,000 & up.

BUCKSTOP JUNCTION, E. Bismarck Expwy., Bismarck, ND 58501. Mailing Address: P.O. Box 941, Bismarck, ND 58502-0941. Tel.: 701-250-8575.
Web Site: www.BuckstopJunction.org
Founded: 1992.
Key Personnel: Pres. (V), Judith M. Fried; Museum Shop Mgr., Marlette Pittman.
Personnel Profile: Part-Time Volunteers 35.
Governing Authority: Parent Institution: Missouri Valley Historical Society. Tax-exempt.
Historic Village.
Collections: town history; period furnishings; historic buildings.
Activities: rental facilities. Annual Event: Old Settlers' Day & Corn Feed in August.
Publications: quarterly newsletter, The Sentinel.
Hours & Admission Prices: May to mid-Sept. Office & Shoppe Tues.-Sat. 10-3. Guided Tours: Fri.-Sat. 1:30; mid-Sept. to April Office & Shoppe Tues.-Fri. 10-3. Guided Tours: by appointment. Adults $5; members no charge.

Attendance: 4,500 (estimated)
Membership: Single $25; Family $35; Donor $50; Business & Organization $75.

CAMP HANCOCK STATE HISTORIC SITE, 1st & Main St., Bismarck, ND Mailing Address: c/o North Dakota Heritage Center, 612 East Boulevard Ave., Bismarck, ND 58505-0612. Tel.: 701-328-9664 & 2666.
Web Site: www.discovernd.com/hist
Founded: 1951.
Key Personnel: Dir., State Historical Society of ND, Merlan E. Paaverud, Jr.; Dir. Historic Sites, Fern Swenson; Mgr. Historic Sites., Diane Rogness.
Personnel Profile: Full-Time Paid 1.
Governing Authority: state. Parent Institution: State Historical Society of North Dakota.
Historic Site: preserves part of military installation originally established as Camp Greeley in 1872 to protect work gangs building the Northern Pacific Railroad.
Collections: artifacts about local history; railroad steam engine; oldest existing building in Bismarck; local 1880s era church.
Publications: quarterly, North Dakota History and Plains Talk.
Hours & Admission Prices: mid-May to mid-Sept. Wed.-Sun. 1-5. No charge; donations accepted. Discount to members at the State Historical Society's museum stores.
Attendance: 2,000 (accurate)
Membership: For membership information, call (701) 222-1966.

THE CLELL AND RUTH GANNON GALLERY AT BISMARCK STATE COLLEGE, Library Bldg., 1500 Edwards Ave., Bismarck, ND 58501-1276. Tel.: 701-391-9840.
E-mail: andrea.fagerstrom@bsc.nodak.edu
Web Site: www.bismarckstate.edu/faculty/art/gallery
Key Personnel: Dir., Andrea Fagerstrom.
Personnel Profile: Part-Time Paid 1.
Art Museum.
Collections: works by local, regional & national artists.
Major Exhibits: Annual Art Faculty Exhibition, 3/10; Annual Student Art Exhibit, 4/10.
Hours & Admission Prices: Mon.-Thurs. 7am-9pm, Fri. 7-4, Sun. 4-8. No charge.

DAKOTA ZOO, Sertoma Park Rd., Bismarck, ND 58502. Mailing Address: P.O. Box 711, Bismarck, ND 58502-0711. Tel.: 701-223-7543. Fax: 701-258-8350.
E-mail: director@dakotazoo.org
Web Site: www.dakotazoo.org
Founded: 1961.
Key Personnel: Dir., Terry Lincoln; Pres. (V), Randy Bieber; Museum Shop Mgr., Diana Lincoln.
Personnel Profile: Full-Time Paid 9; Part-Time Paid 16; Part-Time Volunteers 75.
Governing Authority: private. Parent Institution: Dakota Zoological Society. Tax-exempt.
Zoo.
Collections: mammals; reptiles; birds; insects; amphibians, fish.
Research Fields: mountain lions; wild horses & elk.
Facilities: meeting room; Discovery Center; Gazebo.
Activities: adopted animal program; volunteer docent program; lectures; school visits; slide presentations.
Publications: Zoo guides.
Hours & Admission Prices: May-Sept. daily 10-7. Adults $6.50, children 12 & under $3.50; discounts to AZA members; members no charge. ♿
Attendance: 121,600 (accurate)
Membership: Individual $35; Family & Grandparent $55; Family Plus $85.

THE ELSE FORDE GALLERY AT BISMARCK STATE COLLEGE, Schafer Hall, 1500 Edwards Ave., Bismarck, ND 58501-1276. Tel.: 701-224-5601.
E-mail: barbara.jirges@bsc.nodak.edu
Web Site: www.ndga.org/galleries/bscg.html
Key Personnel: Dir., Barbara Jirges
Art Gallery.
Collections: student artwork; works by local , regional & national artists.
Hours & Admission Prices: Mon.-Thurs. 7am-9pm, Fri. 7-4, Sun. 6pm-9pm.

FORMER GOVERNORS' MANSION STATE HISTORIC SITE, 320 Ave. B East, Bismarck, ND 58501-3676. Mailing Address: State Historical Society of North Dakota, North Dakota Heritage Center, 612 E. Boulevard Ave., Bismarck, ND 58505. Tel.: 701-255-3819 & 328-2666. Fax: 701-328-3710.
Web Site: www.discovernd.com/hist
Founded: 1895.
Key Personnel: Dir. SHSND, Merlan E. Paaverud, Jr.; Dir. Historic Preservation Div., Fern Swenson; Historic Sites Mgr., Diane Rogness.
Personnel Profile: Full-Time Paid 2; Part-Time Paid 1; Part-Time Volunteers 20.
Governing Authority: state. Parent Institution: State Historical Society. Subsidiary Institution: Society for the Preservation of the Former Governors' Mansion. Tax-exempt: 501(c)(3).
Historic Site: consists of a two and one-half story restored Victorian house and Carriage house, constructed in 1884 it was the residence for 21 governors of North Dakota from 1893 to 1960.
Collections: original furnishings; gubernatorial memorabilia.
Activities: summer programs. Museum Sponsors: Annual Lawn Party every August.
Publications: brochures.
Hours & Admission Prices: mid-May to mid-Sept. Wed.-Sun. 1-5. No charge; donations accepted.
Attendance: 3,500
Membership: State Historical Society of North Dakota Foundation: Individual $30; Family $40.

GARY'S GALLERY, 305 E. Broadway, Bismarck, ND 58501-4007. Tel.: 701-258-0060.
E-mail: info@garypmillerart.com
Web Site: www.garymillerart.com
Founded: 1974.
Art Museum.
Collections: paintings; illustrations; prints.
Hours & Admission Prices: Call for hours.

GATEWAY TO SCIENCE, 1810 Schafer St., Ste. 1, Bismarck, ND 58501-1218. Tel.: 701-258-1975. Fax: 701-222-7515.
E-mail: gscience@gscience.org
Web Site: www.gscience.org
Founded: 1994.
Key Personnel: Exec. Dir., Elisabeth Demke; Pres. (V), Arthur Carlson.
Personnel Profile: Part-Time Paid 9; Part-Time Volunteers 100.
Governing Authority: private; nonprofit organization. Tax-exempt: 501(c)(3).
Science Museum.
Collections: hands-on science exhibits.
Facilities: 2,200 sq. ft. exhibit space.
Activities: formal education programs for children; workshops; guided tours; traveling & participatory exhibits; school loan service; summer science camps. Annual Events: Einstein on Wine in fall; Environmental Festival in spring; A Day for the Birds in June; Family Rocket Day in July; Bubble Bliss in August.
Publications: newsletter, Gateway to Science News.
Hours & Admission Prices: Mon.-Thurs. 12-7, Fri.-Sat. 12-5. Adults $5, students 4-18 $2; members, ASTC members, Gateway to Science members & children under 4 no charge. Closed New Year's Eve & Day; Easter; Independence Day; Thanksgiving; Christmas Eve & Day. ♿
Attendance: 12,238 (accurate)
Membership: Student & Senior Citizen (62 & Up) $20; Individual $30; Grandparents $45; Family $50; Family Plus $70; Sustaining $125.

LATITUDES GALLERY, 107 N. 5th St., Bismarck, ND 58501-4026. Tel.: 701-224-9034. Fax: 701-224-5177.
E-mail: latitudes@latitudesgallery.com
Web Site: www.latitudesgallery.com
Art Gallery.
Collections: paintings by North Dakota artists; hand-blown art glass from Seattle & Portland.
Facilities: Museum-related items for sale.
Hours & Admission Prices: Mon.-Fri. 10-5:30, Sun. 10-5.

NORTH DAKOTA HERITAGE CENTER, 612 East Blvd. Ave., Bismarck, ND 58505-0660. Tel.: 701-328-2666. Fax: 701-328-3710.
Web Site: www.history.nd.gov
Founded: 1895.
Congressional District: 1
Key Personnel: Dir., Merlan E. Paaverud, Jr.; Pres. (V), Chester Nelson; Museum Shop Mgr., Rhonda Brown.
Personnel Profile: Full-Time Paid 62; Full-Time Volunteers 12; Part-Time Paid 2; Part-Time Volunteers 215; Interns 8.
Governing Authority: state. Tax-exempt.
History Museum.
Collections: local history & culture; photographs; artifacts; paleontology.
Major Exhibits: Lincoln's Legacy in North Dakota (T), 11/09-1/10; Sakakawea

Statue Centennial, 11/09-4/10; How Does Your Garden Grow? (T), 11/09-11/11; North Dakota Remembers World War II (T), 10/10-10/12.
Research Fields: North Dakota history.
Facilities: state archives.
Publications: North Dakota History; Plains Talk.
Hours & Admission Prices: Exhibit Galleries: Mon.-Fri. 8-5, Sat.-Sun. 10-5. No charge; donations accepted. Closed New Year's Day; Easter; Thanksgiving; Christmas. ♿
Attendance: 100,000
Membership: Individual $35; Family $45; Sustaining $100; Patron $250; Corporate $500; Founder $1,000; Trustee $2,002; Director $5,000; Benefactor $10,000.

NORTH DAKOTA STATE CAPITOL, 600 E. Boulevard Ave., Bismarck, ND 58505. Tel.: 701-328-2480 & 2471. Fax: 701-328-0121.
Historic Building: built in 1933.
Collections: U.S. history & culture; photographs; paintings; period furnishings.
Hours & Admission Prices: Tours: Memorial Day to Labor Day Mon.-Fri. 8-4, Sat. 9-4, Sun. 1-4; Sept.-May Mon.-Fri. 8-4. No charge.

*** STATE HISTORICAL SOCIETY OF NORTH DAKOTA, (M),** North Dakota Heritage Center, 612 E. Blvd., Bismarck, ND 58505. Tel.: 701-328-2666. Fax: 701-328-3710. TDD: 800-366-6888.
E-mail: histsoc@state.nd.us
Web Site: www.discovernd.com/hist
Founded: 1895.
Key Personnel: Dir., Merlan E. Paaverud, Jr.; Asst. Dir., David C. Skalsky; Dir. Communications, Richard E. Collin; Museum & Education Dir., Claudia J. Berg; Dir. State Archives, Gerald Newborg; Dir. Historic Preservation & Deputy State Historic Preservation Officer, Fern Swenson; Museum Shop Mgr., Rhonda Brown.
Personnel Profile: Full-Time Paid 60; Part-Time Paid 35; Part-Time Volunteers 200; Interns 6.
Governing Authority: State Historical Board. Branch Museums: Fort Abercrombie, Abercrombie, ND; Chateau de Mores, Medora, ND; Camp Hancock, Bismarck, ND; Fort Buford, Buford, ND; De Mores State Historic Site, Medora, ND; Former Governors' Mansion, Bismarck, ND; Fort Totten, near Devils Lake, ND; Gingras Trading Post, Walhalla, ND; Whitestone Hill, Kulm, ND; Missouri-Yellowstone Confluence Interpretive Center, Buford, ND; Pembina State Museum, Pembina, ND. Tax-exempt.
History Museum.
Collections: 50,000 history, natural history & ethnology artifacts; 1.5 million archeological items; 150,000 photographic images; 1,650 historical manuscripts; 2,800 archival records series; 1,400 newspaper titles; 1,200 recorded oral histories; 115,000 books & periodicals; 10,000 maps; 3.5 million ft. of film.
Research Fields: archaeology; architectural; railroad; North Dakota history.
Facilities: 100,000-vol. library with reading room, archives, manuscripts, maps & photographs available for use on premises.
Activities: permanent & temporary exhibits; gallery demonstrations; public programming for adults & children; lectures; film workshops; docent & volunteer programs; traveling exhibition program; youth, family & school programs including suitcase exhibits; annual workshops for county & local historical societies; annual history conference; teacher workshops; outdoor adventures.
Publications: quarterly journal, North Dakota History; quarterly newsletter, Plains Talk; books, Sacred Beauty: Quillwork of Plains Women (1998); A Traveler's Companion to North Dakota's State Historic Sites (2003); Lewis and Clark in North Dakota (2003); Fort Totten (2nd Ed. 2004); No Two Horns: A Gallery of Art and Exploits (2003).
Hours & Admission Prices: Heritage Center: Mon.-Fri. 8-5, Sat.-Sun. 10-5. Research Library: Mon.-Fri. 8-4:30, 2nd Sat. every month. No charge; donations accepted. Closed New Year's Day; Easter; Thanksgiving; Christmas. ♿
Attendance: 100,000 (accurate)
Membership: Individual $35; Family $45; Sustaining $100; Patron $250; Corporate $500; Founder $1,000; Director $5,000; Benefactor $10,000.

UTTC CULTURAL ARTS INTERPRETIVE CENTER, United Tribes Technical College, Bismarck, ND 58504. Tel.: 701-255-3285.
Native American Museum.
Collections: Native American history & culture; personal artifacts; photographs; art.
Hours & Admission Prices: Mon.-Fri. 8-5 by appointment.

Bottineau

BOTTINEAU COUNTY HISTORICAL MUSEUM, N. Main St., Bottineau, ND 58318. Tel.: 701-228-3800.
Founded: 1982.
Key Personnel: Pres. (V), Twilla Glinz.
Governing Authority: Tax-exempt.
History Museum.
Collections: life in 19th & 20th centuries; pioneer families; period artifacts; farm machinery; schoolhouse; 1900s cars & trucks; tractors & engines from the early 1900s.
Hours & Admission Prices: Memorial Day to Labor Day Sat.-Sun. 1:30-4:30; other times by appointment. No charge; donations accepted. ♿
Membership: Annual $5; Life $100.

Bowdon

BOWDON CENTENNIAL MUSEUM, 232 40th Ave., N.E., Bowdon, ND 58418. Tel.: 701-962-3736.
E-mail: lindawidicker@daktel.com
Founded: 1989.
Key Personnel: Treas., Vivian Miller; Public Rels., Rod L. Widicker; Security, Laurel Jones.
Governing Authority: private; nonprofit organization.
History Museum.
Collections: local history & culture; period furnishings; personal artifacts; photographs.
Facilities: 5,000-vol. library.
Activities: guided tours; fundraisers.
Hours & Admission Prices: late May to late Oct. Wed.-Sun. 1-5; other times by appointment. No charge; donations accepted. ♿
Attendance: 350 (estimated)

Bowman

PIONEER TRAILS REGIONAL MUSEUM, 12 First Ave., N.E., Bowman, ND 58623-4010. Mailing Address: P.O. Box 78, Bowman, ND 58623-0078. Tel.: 701-523-3600. Fax: 701-523-3600.
E-mail: ptrm@ptrm.org
Founded: 1992.
Key Personnel: Pres. (V), Dean Pearson.
Governing Authority: Parent Institution: Bowman County Historical and Genealogical Society. Tax-exempt.
History Museum.
Collections: area history; ranching; Native American artifacts; military; fossils.
Facilities: garden. Museum-related items for sale.
Hours & Admission Prices: May-Sept. Mon.-Fri. 9-5; Labor Day-Memorial Day Mon.-Fri. 10-4. Adults 14 & over $3; children under 14 & members no charge. Closed New Year's Eve & Day; Easter; Memorial Day; Independence Day; Labor Day; Thanksgiving; Christmas Eve & Day. ♿
Attendance: 3,600 (estimated)
Membership: Single $20; Family $30.

Cando

CANDO ARTS CENTER, 1115 4th Ave., Cando, ND 58324-6161. Tel.: 701-968-4501.
E-mail: sblordtwo@gondtc.com
Key Personnel: Dir., Shelley Lord
Art Center.
Collections: student artwork.
Hours & Admission Prices: Tues.-Sun. 1-4.

CANDO PIONEER FOUNDATION, INC., 502 Main St., Cando, ND 58324. Mailing Address: P.O. Box 142, Cando, ND 58324-0104. Tel.: 701-968-3943 & 3490.
E-mail: slarson@gondte.com
Formerly: Pioneer Museum
Founded: 1976.
History Museum.
Collections: local history & culture; newspapers; photographs. Historic Building: one room school.
Hours & Admission Prices: By appointment. No charge. ♿

Carrington

FOSTER COUNTY MUSEUM, 2nd St. & 16th Ave. S., Carrington, ND 58421. Tel.: 701-652-1313.
History Museum.
Collections: photographs; display cases; agricultural equipment.

Hours & Admission Prices: By appointment.

Carson

GRANT COUNTY MUSEUM, 9260 56th Ave. SW, Carson, ND 58529-9596. Tel.: 701-522-3437.
E-mail: gcn@westriv.com
Founded: 1970.
Congressional District: 35
Key Personnel: Chm. & Pres., Dennis Roth; Treas., Arlene Wells.
Governing Authority: county; nonprofit. Parent Institution: the Elgin Commercial Club. Tax-exempt.
Historical Society Museum: housed in old railroad depot.
Collections: railroad equipment; bedroom & kitchen display; pioneer items; old school desks; printing equipment; post office display.
Activities: guided tours.
Publications: yearly brochure, Elgin Commercial Club Project.
Hours & Admission Prices: Open by appointment only. Open during Grant Co. Fair, 3rd. week of Aug. No charge; donations accepted.
Attendance: 43,000 (estimated)
Membership: Individual $5.

Cavalier

PEMBINA COUNTY HISTORICAL SOCIETY AND MUSEUM, 13572 Hwy. 5, Cavalier, ND 58220. Tel.: 701-265-4941.
E-mail: pchsm@polarcomm.com
Web Site: ndpchs.com/museum.htm
Founded: 1968.
Key Personnel: Admin., Zelda Hartje
Historical Society Museum.
Collections: Pembina County history; pioneer farm machinery; historic buildings.
Activities: Museum Sponsors: Annual Pioneer Machinery Show and Tractor Pull in September.
Publications: newsletter.
Hours & Admission Prices: May-Oct. daily 1-4; Winter: Tues.-Thurs. 10-4; tours by appointment. No charge.
Membership: Individual $10.

PIONEER HERITAGE CENTER, 13571 Hwy. 5, Cavalier, ND 58220-9545. Tel.: 701-265-4561. Fax: 701-265-4443.
E-mail: isp@nd.gov
Web Site: www.parkrec.nd.gov
Founded: 1989.
Key Personnel: Pres. (V), Rosemarie Myrdal; Park Mgr., Justin Robinson; Park Ranger & Interpretive Coord., Dennis Clark; Museum Shop Mgr., Lorraine Schroeder.
Personnel Profile: Full-Time Paid 2; Part-Time Paid 1; Part-Time Volunteers 25.
Governing Authority: Parent Institution: Northeastern North Dakota Heritage Association. Subsidiary Institution: Icelandic State Park. Tax-exempt.
State Park Museum.
Collections: historical, dealing with settlement period 1870-1920.
Facilities: homestead; nature preserve; nature trail; interpretive center. Pioneer Heritage Buildings: church; town hall; one room school; log cabin.
Activities: guided tours; special events.
Publications: Home Quarter Newsletter.
Hours & Admission Prices: Center: Memorial Day-Labor Day Mon.-Fri. 9-8, Sat.-Sun. 9-6; Fall, Winter & Spring Mon.-Fri. 9-5, Sun. 1-5. $5 per vehicle; $25 per year. ♿
Attendance: 12,000 (accurate)
Membership: Individual $15; Organization $20.

Cayuga

TEWAUKON NATIONAL WILDLIFE REFUGE, 9754 143 1/2 Ave., S.E., Cayuga, ND 58013-9764. Tel.: 701-724-3598.
E-mail: tewaukon@fws.gov
Web Site: www.fws.gov/tewaukon
Wildlife Refuge.
Collections: migratory birds & other wildlife.
Facilities: 8,363-acre refuge.
Activities: recreational activities.
Hours & Admission Prices: Refuge: daily 5am-10pm. Office & Visitor Center: Mon.-Fri. 8-4:30.

Center

FORT CLARK TRADING POST STATE HISTORIC SITE, 1074 27th Ave., S.W., Center, ND 58530-9429. Tel.: 701-328-2666.
Web Site: www.state.nd.us/hist
Founded: 1965.
Key Personnel: Agency Dir., Merlan E. Paaverud, Jr.; Dir. Historic Preservation, Fern Swenson; Historic Sites Mgr., Diane Rogness.
Personnel Profile: Full-Time Paid 1; Part-Time Paid 1.
Governing Authority: state. Parent Institution: State Historical Society of North Dakota.
Historic Site Museum: built in 1830-1831, the fort was burned down in 1861.
Collections: archeological Mandan Indian villages; Fort Clark fur trading post eras covering the period 1822-1862.
Publications: quarterly, North Dakota History and Plains Talk.
Hours & Admission Prices: Daily 8-5. No charge; donations accepted. Society's Museum Stores: discounts to members.
Attendance: 10,000 (accurate)
Membership: For membership information, please call (701) 222-1966.

Coleharbor

AUDUBON NATIONAL WILDLIFE REFUGE, 3275 11th St., N.W., Coleharbor, ND 58531-9419. Tel.: 701-442-5474. Fax: 701-442-5546.
E-mail: audubon@fws.gov
Web Site: audubon.fws.gov
Key Personnel: Project Leader, Lloyd James
Wildlife Refuge.
Collections: birds; mammals; reptiles; amphibian; fish.
Facilities: 14,735 acres.
Hours & Admission Prices: Daily 8-4:30. No charge.

Cooperstown

GRIGGS COUNTY HISTORICAL MUSEUM, 203 12th St., S.E., Cooperstown, ND 58425. Mailing Address: P.O. Box 242, Cooperstown, ND 58425-0242.
History Museum.
Collections: Griggs County history; period artifacts; newspapers; blacksmith shop; one-room school; Rhodes animated collection.
Activities: Museum Sponsors: Pioneer Days in July; Old Fashioned Christmas in December.
Hours & Admission Prices: May-Sept. Sun. 1-4:30; other times by appointment.

Crosby

DIVIDE COUNTY HISTORICAL SOCIETY MUSEUM, 300 Second Ave., N.E., Crosby, ND 58730. Mailing Address: P.O. Box 130, Crosby, ND 58730-0130. Tel.: 701-965-6705.
Founded: 1969.
Key Personnel: Chm. (V), Donna Hazlett-Nelson.
Governing Authority: nonprofit organization. Tax-exempt.
Village Museum.
Collections: pioneer artifacts; farm implements: vehicles; stationary gas engines; miniature trains. Historic Buildings: bank; Lutheran church; homestead claim shack; schools; stores; blacksmith shop; saw mill; car club displays.
Activities: temporary exhibitions. Annual Event: Threshing Bee & parades in July.
Hours & Admission Prices: Tours by appointment, call for information. No charge; donations accepted. Facilities: $12 for 3 days.
Attendance: 3,600 (estimated)

Devils Lake

LAKE REGION HERITAGE CENTER, 502 4th St., Devils Lake, ND 58301-0245. Tel.: 701-662-3701. Fax: 701-662-2810.
Web Site: lrhs.homestead.com
Key Personnel: Cur., Jim Schiele
Heritage Center.
Collections: local history & culture; personal artifacts; photographs; paintings; automobiles.
Activities: guided tours.
Hours & Admission Prices: Summer: Mon.-Fri. 7-5, Sat.-Sun. 12-5; Sept.-June Mon.-Fri. 8:30-5.

LAKE REGION HERITAGE HOUSE MUSEUM, 416 Sixth St., Devils Lake, ND 58301-0626. Mailing Address: P.O. Box 245, Devils Lake, ND 58301-0245. Tel.: 701-662-3701 & 7080.
Historic House Museum.
Collections: local history; period furnishings; photographs; personal artifacts.
Hours & Admission Prices: Wed.-Sun. 1-4; other times by appointment. Adults $3, seniors & students $2; children under 6 no charge.

NORTH DAKOTA MARITIME MUSEUM, Fifth St. & Fourth Ave., Devils Lake, ND 58301-0626. Mailing Address: P.O. Box 626, Devils Lake, ND 58301-0626. Tel.: 701-662-7031. Fax: 701-662-7049.
Maritime Museum.
Collections: maritime history; photographs; uniforms; posters; books; military artifacts.
Hours & Admission Prices: Sun. 2-5 by appointment.

SULLYS HILL NATIONAL GAME PRESERVE, 221 2nd St., W., Devils Lake, ND 58301-2963. Tel.: 701-662-8612.
Web Site: sullyshill.fws.gov
Wildlife Preserve.
Collections: migratory birds & big game including elk, deer, prairie dogs; waterfowl; foxes; raccoons; skunks; weasels; mink; beaver; rabbits, wild turkey.
Facilities: theater; classroom; visitor center; aquarium. Museum-related items for sale.
Activities: waterfowl observation; birdwatching; special events; educational programs.
Hours & Admission Prices: Auto Tour: May-Oct. daily 8 am to sunset. $2 per vehicle.

Dickinson

DSU ART GALLERY, Klinefelter Hall, Dickinson State Univ., Dickinson, ND 58601-4896. Mailing Address: Klinefelter Hall, Box 28, Dickinson State Univ., Dickinson, ND 58601-4896. Tel.: 800-279-HAWK.
Art Gallery.
Collections: paintings; sculpture; drawings.
Hours & Admission Prices: Mon.-Fri. 8-5. No charge.

DAKOTA DINOSAUR MUSEUM, (M), 200 E. Museum Dr., Dickinson, ND 58601-4000. Tel.: 701-225-3466. Fax: 701-227-0534.
E-mail: info@dakotadino.com
Web Site: www.dakotadino.com
Founded: 1991.
Key Personnel: C.E.O. & Museum Shop Mgr., Alice League; Pres. (V), Richard Johnson.
Personnel Profile: Full-Time Paid 2; Part-Time Volunteers 2.
Governing Authority: private; nonprofit organization. Tax-exempt: 501(c)(3).
Paleontology, Mineral & Geology Museum.
Collections: 12,000 paleontology & mineral specimens; complete triceratops skeleton collected in the Hell Creek formation; seashells; 14 full scale dinosaurs (11 inside and 3 outside); 10,000-year old bison; rhinoceros.
Hours & Admission Prices: May to Labor Day daily 9-5; call for off-season hours. Adults $7, seniors 65 & over $6, children 3-12 $4; discounts to groups. ♿
Attendance: 10,480 (accurate)
Membership: Individual $20; Family $40; Contributor $100; Sponsor $250.

DICKINSON MUSEUM CENTER, 188 Museum Dr. E., Dickinson, ND 58601-4088. Tel.: 701-456-6225.
E-mail: info@dickinsonmuseumcenter.org
Web Site: www.dickinsonmuseumcenter.org
Formerly: Joachim Regional Museum
Founded: 1983.
Key Personnel: Dir., Danielle Stuckle; Pres. (V), Kristen Steffan; Museum Asst., Emily Bradbury.
Personnel Profile: Full-Time Paid 2; Part-Time Paid 5; Part-Time Volunteers 30; Interns 2.
Governing Authority: Parent Institution: Southwestern North Dakota Museum Foundation, Inc. Tax-exempt: 501(c)(3).
History Museum.
Collections: history; art archives.
Research Fields: local history.
Hours & Admission Prices: Memorial Day to Labor Day daily 9-5; Winter: Mon.-Fri. 9-5. No charge; donations accepted. ♿
Attendance: 6,000 (estimated)
Membership: Individual $10; Family $20.

UKRAINIAN CULTURAL INSTITUTE, 1221 W. Villard, Dickinson, ND 58601-4849. Mailing Address: P.O. Box 6, Dickinson, ND 58602-0006. Tel.: 701-483-1486. Fax: 701-483-4366.
Ukrainian History Museum.
Collections: Ukrainian history & culture; hand-crafted Ukrainian eggs; folk art; religious artifacts.
Facilities: Museum-related items for sale.
Hours & Admission Prices: Mon.-Thurs. 8-4:30, Fri.-Sun. by appointment. No charge; donations accepted.

Dunn Center

DUNN COUNTY HISTORICAL SOCIETY & MUSEUM, Dunn Center, ND 58626. Mailing Address: P.O. Box 86, Dunn Center, ND 58626-0086. Tel.: 701-548-8111.
E-mail: dunncountymuseum@ndsupernet.com
Web Site: www.dunncountymuseum.org
Historical Society Museum
Collections: local history & culture; Native American display; 1929 Nash; old time kitchen; Western display; photographs.
Hours & Admission Prices: May-Sept. Tues.-Sat. 11-4, Sun. 12-4; Oct.-April by appointment. Family $3, adults $1; students & children no charge.

Dunseith

INTERNATIONAL PEACE GARDEN, 10939 Hwy. 281, Dunseith, ND 58329-9445. Mailing Address: R.R. 1 Box 116, Dunseith, ND 58329-9445. Tel.: 701-263-4390; 888-432-6733. Fax: 701-263-3169.
E-mail: kathy@peacegarden.com
Web Site: www.peacegarden.com
Founded: 1932.
Key Personnel: C.E.O. & C.O.O., Doug Hevenor; Pres. (V), Ed Anderson; Vice Pres., Tyrone Langager; Finance Mgr., Leonard Richard.
Personnel Profile: Full-Time Paid 5; Part-Time Paid 40.
Governing Authority: nonprofit. Tax-exempt.
Arboretum.
Collections: garden history; Carillion Bell Tower; floral clock; gardens; photographs; 911 memorial.
Research Fields: botanical.
Facilities: garden; chapel; camp grounds; concessions; interpretive center; convention & wedding reception facilities. Gift-related items for sale.
Activities: tours; International Music camp; Legion Athletic camp; concerts; bird watching. Annual Event: International Country Gospel Fest.
Publications: Annual Visitors Guide.
Hours & Admission Prices: Garden: daily; Peak time for flowers: July 15-Aug. 15. Gate: late May to mid-Sept. daily 9-7. Office: Mon.-Fri. 80-4. Donations: $125 per tour bus, $25 season pass, $20 per vehicle a season, $10 per vehicle a day, $5 pedestrian. ♿
Attendance: 150,000
Membership: Foundation $150.

Edmore

WHEATLAND MANOR, 405 S. Grant St., Edmore, ND 58330. Mailing Address: P.O. Box 8, Edmore, ND 58330-0008. Tel.: 701-644-2291 & 2453.
History Museum.
Collections: local history & culture; furnishings of early 1900s; photographs.
Hours & Admission Prices: Memorial Day-Labor Day Sun. 1-3; other times by appointment.

Egeland

TOWNER COUNTY HISTORICAL MUSEUM, Main St., Egeland, ND 58331. Tel.: 701-682-5106.
Founded: 1974.
Personnel Profile: Part-Time Paid 3; Part-Time Volunteers 10.
Historical Society Museums.
Collections: horse-drawn hearse; antique automobiles; Bavarian crystal; dolls; Soo Line Railroad depot equipped with period furnishings.
Hours & Admission Prices: By appointment. Adults $5.
Membership: Individual $5; Life $100.

Ellendale

COLEMAN MUSEUM, Southeast Corner of Main St. & Railroad Ave., Ellendale, ND 58436. Mailing Address: P.O. Box 385, Ellendale, ND 58436-0385.
Governing Authority: Parent Institution: Ellendale Historical Society.
Historical Society Museum.
Collections: artifacts & memorabilia of the Ellendale area; photographs.

Hours & Admission Prices: June-Sept. Tues. & Fri. 1-5.

Epping

BUFFALO TRAILS MUSEUM, Main St., Epping, ND 58843. Mailing Address: P.O. Box 22, Epping, ND 58843-0022. Tel.: 701-859-4361 (June-Aug.).
E-mail: buffalotrails@epping.govoffice.com
Web Site: epping.govoffice.com
Founded: 1966.
Key Personnel: Pres., Duane Syverson.
Personnel Profile: Part-Time Paid 2; Part-Time Volunteers 6.
Governing Authority: nonprofit organization. Parent Institution: Williams County Historical Society. Tax-exempt: 501(c)(3).
Regional History Museum.
Collections: regional history; Indian artifacts; geology; mineralogy; archaeology; natural history. Historic Buildings: 1903 Fosse Barber shop; 1906 O. E. Ellingson general merchandise store; 1906 C. F. Carpenter harness & hardware store; 1908 homestead log cabin; 1926 one-room rural school.
Research Fields: regional history; archaeology.
Facilities: cafe; park; picnic area.
Activities: guided tours; permanent & temporary exhibitions; camping.
Publications: museum brochure; tour guide.
Hours & Admission Prices: May-July Tues.-Sat. 10-4, Sun. 12-5. Adults $3.50, students & groups over 10 $2; discounts to groups; life members no charge.
Attendance: 275 (estimated)
Membership: Life $200.

Fargo

THE CHILDREN'S MUSEUM AT YUNKER FARM, 1201 28th Ave. N., Fargo, ND 58102-1337. Tel.: 701-232-6102. Fax: 701-232-4605.
E-mail: info@childrensmuseum-yunker.org
Web Site: www.childrensmuseum-yunker.org
Founded: 1989.
Congressional District: 45
Key Personnel: Exec. Dir., Yvette Nasset; Chm. (V), Sharon Syrdal.
Personnel Profile: Full-Time Paid 3; Full-Time Volunteers 1; Part-Time Paid 5; Part-Time Volunteers 300; Interns 4.
Governing Authority: nonprofit. Tax-exempt: 501(c)(3).
Children's Museum
Collections: hands-on exhibits.
Facilities: nature trail; playground; picnic shelter; carousel miniature train. Museum-related items for sale.
Activities: annual events: Party in the Pumpkin Patch, Halloween Party, Easter Celebration; classes & workshops: Kidcology Camp, Yunkie Club, Think Thursday; Children's Musical Theater; monthly special events.
Publications: quarterly newsletter, Museum Mania.
Hours & Admission Prices: Sept.-June Tues.-Wed. & Fri.-Sat. 10-5, Thurs. 1-8, Sun. 1-5; Summer: Mon.-Wed. & Fri.-Sat. 10-5, Thurs. 1-8, Sun. 1-5. Admission $4; children under one & members no charge. Closed New Year's Day; Easter; Thanksgiving, Christmas Eve & Day. ♿
Attendance: 46,000 (estimated)
Membership: Individual $30; Family $60; Contributor $100; Patron $250.

FARGO AIR MUSEUM, 1609 19th Ave. N., Fargo, ND 58102-1886. Tel.: 701-293-8043. Fax: 701-293-8103.
Web Site: fargoairmuseum.org
Founded: 2001.
Key Personnel: Exec. Dir., Fran Brummund; Chm., Steve Blazek.
Personnel Profile: Full-Time Paid 1; Part-Time Paid 1; Part-Time Volunteers 29; Interns 1.
Governing Authority: private; nonprofit organization. Tax-exempt: 501(c)(3).
Air & Space Museum.
Collections: 20 civilian & military aircraft; 4 murals depicting a century of aviation & agricultural aviation; aviation artifacts & history; air racing; Happy Hooligan.
Facilities: 2,000-vol. library; 1,800 sq. ft. exhibit space. Museum-related items for sale.
Activities: films; swing dances. Annual Events: Amelia Earhardt; Santa Fly-In; Air Racing.
Publications: newsletter, Legends.
Hours & Admission Prices: Memorial Day to Labor Day Mon.-Sat. 9-5, Sun. 12-4; Sept.-May Tues.-Sat. 9-5, Sun 12-4. Adults $6, senior citizens $5, children 5-12 $4; discounts to groups; members no charge. Closed New Year's Day; Easter; Thanksgiving; Christmas.
Attendance: 30,000 (estimated)
Membership: Senior, Student & Military $15; Individual $25; Dual $35; Family $55.

FARGO THEATRE, 314 Broadway, Fargo, ND 58102-4715. Tel.: 701-239-8385.
Historic Building: housed in a fully-restored art deco theatre built in 1926 to host Vaudeville & silent movies.
Collections: theatre history; Wurlitzer pipe organ; statue commemorating the film Fargo.
Facilities: 870-seat theatre.
Activities: tours; independent & art films; live stage events; special events & performances; concerts; guest speakers. Theatre Events: Midnight Movie Series; Classic Film Series; Silent Movie nights; Fargo Film Festival.
Hours & Admission Prices: Tours: call for hours. Films: Mon.-Fri. 5, 7 & 9pm, Sat.-Sun. 1, 3, 5, 7, & 9pm.

GALLERY 4, LTD, 114 Broadway, Fargo, ND 58102-4942. Tel.: 701-237-6867.
Web Site: www.gallery4fargo.com
Founded: 1975.
Art Gallery.
Collections: paintings; drawings; sculpture; glass; wood.
Hours & Admission Prices: Tues.-Wed. & Fri.-Sat. 11-5, Thurs. 11-7. ♿

MAURY WILLS MUSEUM, 1515 15th Ave. N., Ground Fl., Fargo, ND 58102-5701. Tel.: 701-235-6161.
Sports Museum.
Collections: Maury Wills' life & career; personal artifacts; baseball history & artifacts; photographs.
Hours & Admission Prices: Mon.-Fri. 9-5. No charge.

MEMORIAL UNION GALLERY, 258 Memorial Union, North Dakota State Univ., Fargo, ND 58105-5476. Mailing Address: North Dakota State University, Dept. 5340, P.O. Box 6050, Fargo, ND 58108-6050. Tel.: 701-231-8239. Fax: 701-231-7866.
Web Site: www.mu.ndsu.edu/gallery/exhibits_and_artists
Founded: 1975.
Key Personnel: Gallery Coord., Esther Hockett.
Personnel Profile: Full-Time Paid 1; Part-Time Paid 12.
Governing Authority: university. Parent Institution: North Dakota State University. Tax-exempt.
Art Gallery.
Collections: contemporary works of art by regional & local American artists; works by prominent artists including Andy Warhol, Pablo Picasso, & Salvador Dali; 1977 edition of prints from Lakeside Studios.
Activities: guided tours; lectures; gallery talks; loan, permanent, temporary & traveling exhibitions; student exhibits.
Publications: exhibit mailers & posters.
Hours & Admission Prices: mid-May to July 15 Tues.-Sat. 11-5; Sept. to mid-May Tues.-Wed. & Fri.-Sat. 11-5, Thurs. 11-4; other times by appointment. No charge; donations accepted. Closed holidays. ♿
Attendance: 2,300 (accurate)

* **PLAINS ART MUSEUM, (M),** 704 First Ave. N., Fargo, ND 58102-4904. Mailing Address: P.O. Box 2338, Fargo, ND 58108-2338. Tel.: 701-232-3821, ext. 101. Fax: 701-293-1082.
E-mail: museum@plainsart.org
Web Site: www.plainsart.org
Founded: 1973.
Key Personnel: Chm., Michael J. Olsen; Pres. & C.E.O., Colleen Sheehy, Ph.D.; C.F.O., Mark Henze; Devel., Joni Janz; Vice Pres. & Curatorial, Rusty Freeman; Public Rels., Sue Petry; Vice Pres. Registration & Collections, Mark Ryan.
Personnel Profile: Full-Time Paid 21; Part-Time Paid 9; Part-Time Volunteers 135.
Governing Authority: private; nonprofit organization. Tax-exempt: 501(c)(3).
Art Museum.
Collections: over 3,000 objects including fine art, Native American & ethnographic with an emphasis on art of the upper Midwest.
Facilities: 7,400 sq. ft. exhibit space; cafe. Museum-related items for sale.
Activities: outreach art education programs to North Dakota & Minnesota; concerts; dance recitals; docent program; guided tours; lectures; mobile gallery; participatory, loan, temporary & traveling exhibitions. Annual Events: Trash or Treasure in April; Spring Gala Fundraiser in May.
Publications: quarterly newsletter, Museum News; triannual education newsletter, Experiences for Life!
Hours & Admission Prices: Galleries: Tues.-Wed. & Fri.-Sat. 10-5, Thurs. 10-8, Sun. 1-5. Adults $5, seniors & educators w/ID $4; discounts to AAM & MPMA members; members, children & students with ID no charge. Closed New Year's Day; Memorial Day; Independence Day; Labor Day; Thanksgiving; Christmas. ♿
Attendance: 52,837 (accurate)

Membership: Senior & Student $25; Individual $40; Household $75; Friend $100; Enthusiast $250; Advocate $500; Curator $1,000; Director $2,500; President $5,000.

RED RIVER ZOO, 4220 21st Ave., S.W., Fargo, ND 58104-8603. Tel.: 701-277-9240. Fax: 701-277-9238.
Zoo.
Collections: over 300 animals representing 75 species; exotic plants.
Activities: special events; rental facilities; educational programs.
Hours & Admission Prices: May 2 to Labor Day daily 10-8; Sept.-May 1 Sat.-Sun. 12-4 (weather permitting). Adults $7, seniors over 60 $6, children 2-14 $4; members & children under 2 no charge.
Membership: Individual $35; Household $55.

ROGER MARIS MUSEUM, West Acres Shopping Center, 3902 13th Ave. S., Fargo, ND 58103-3357. Tel.: 701-282-2222; 800-783-6450.
Web Site: www.rogermarismuseum.com
Founded: 1984.
Sports Museum.
Collections: personal artifacts; replica of Roger's Yankee Stadium monument & 1961 locker; video.
Hours & Admission Prices: Mon.-Sat. 7am-9 pm, Sun. 10-6. No Charge. Closed Easter; Thanksgiving; Christmas.

Fessenden

WELLS COUNTY MUSEUM, Wells County Fairgrounds, Fessenden, ND 58438. Mailing Address: P. O. Box 282, Fessenden, ND 58438-0282. Tel.: 701-547-3403.
Founded: 1972.
Congressional District: 1
Key Personnel: Pres., Carol Beck; Vice Pres., Judy Marlin; Sec., Vernon Pranke; Museum Shop Mgr., Leonard Martin.
Personnel Profile: Part-Time Paid 1; Part-Time Volunteers 10.
Governing Authority: county; nonprofit society. Affiliated with Wells County Historical Society. Branch Museum: Hurd Round House. Tax-exempt: 501(c)(3).
Historic Building: housed in a 1919 2-room school house.
Collections: period agriculture implements; period automobiles; horse drawn vehicles; ethnic artifacts; pioneer tools & utensils; manuscripts; clothing; photographs; early home & church furnishings; early school textbooks & furnishings; complete county newspaper archives; various documents & ledgers of early businesses in the county.
Research Fields: local history.
Activities: guided tours; lectures; films; permanent exhibitions. Annual Event: Fair Days in June. Museum Sponsors: business meetings in May & Oct.
Publications: monthly newsletter, Wells County History.
Hours & Admission Prices: By appointment. No charge; donations accepted.
Attendance: 350 (estimated)

Forbes

SCHULSTAD STONE HOUSE MUSEUM, 320 Lewis St., Forbes, ND 58439. Tel.: 701-357-7281.
Historic House Museum: built in 1907.
Collections: period furnishings; personal artifcts; photographs.
Hours & Admission Prices: May-Sept. 1 by appointment.

SHIMMIN TVEIT MUSEUM, Forbes, ND 58439. Mailing Address: P.O. Box 85, Forbes, ND 58439-0085. Tel.: 701-357-7281.
American Indian Museum.
Collections: American Indians; early settlers.
Hours & Admission Prices: Call for hours.

Forman

SARGENT COUNTY MUSEUM, 8987 Hwy. 32, Forman, ND 58032. Mailing Address: 13443 88th St., S.E., Forman, ND 58032-9709. Tel.: 701-724-3194.
Personnel Profile: Part-Time Volunteers 6.
Governing Authority: Tax-exempt.
History Museum.
Collections: local history & culture; photographs; personal artifacts; newspapers from mid 1880s to 1970s on microfilm.
Hours & Admission Prices: Memorial Day to Labor Day Sun.-Fri. 1-4; other times by appointment. Adults $5. ♿
Attendance: 700 (accurate)
Membership: Single $7.50; Family $15.

Fort Ransom

RANSOM COUNTY HISTORICAL SOCIETY, 101 Mill Road, S.E., Fort Ransom, ND 58033-9740. Mailing Address: 12512 85th St., S.E., Gwinner, ND 58040-9743. Tel.: 701-678-2045. Fax: 701-678-2045.
Web Site: members.tripod.com/rchsmuseum
Founded: 1972.
Key Personnel: Pres. (V), Richard Birklid.
Personnel Profile: Part-Time Paid 3; Part-Time Volunteers 10; Interns 1.
Governing Authority: society; nonprofit organization. Parent Institution: State Historical Society of North Dakota, Bismarck, ND 58505. Tax-exempt: 501(c)(3).
History Museum: housed in 1867-1872 U.S. Military Fort.
Collections: pictures; books; records; clothing; tools; household items. Historic Building: 1881 T.J. Walker Flour Mill.
Activities: tours.
Publications: Starting a Cookbook.
Hours & Admission Prices: Memorial Day-Oct. daily 1-5; other times by appointment. Adults $1; members & children no charge.
Attendance: 5,000
Membership: Active $1; Individual $5; Family $10; Business Institutional $25; Contributing & Sustaining $50; Lifetime over 60 $50; Lifetime $100.

Fort Totten

FORT TOTTEN STATE HISTORIC SITE, 417 Cavalry Circle, Fort Totten, ND 58335. Mailing Address: P.O. Box 224, Fort Totten, ND 58335-0224. Tel.: 701-766-4441. Fax: 701-766-1382.
E-mail: jmattson@state.nd.us
Web Site: www.discovernd.com/hist
Founded: 1960.
Key Personnel: Dir. State Historical Society of North Dakota, Merl Paaverud; Div. Dir. Historic Sites, Fern Swenson; Eastern Rgnl. Site Mgr., Diane Rogness; Site Supvr. & Museum Store Mgr., Jack Mattson.
Personnel Profile: Full-Time Paid 2; Part-Time Paid 8; Part-Time Volunteers 15.
Governing Authority: state. Parent Institution: State Historical Society of ND. Subsidiary Institution: Fort Totten State Historic Site Foundation & Pioneer Daughters. Tax-exempt: 501(c)(3).
Historic Site & Outdoor Museum: 1868-1890 Military Post; Pioneer Daughters Museum; 1891-1959 Indian School, consisting of 17 structures.
Collections: artifacts pertaining to Native American & pioneer heritage of Devils Lake & North Dakota region. Historic Structures: officers row; enlisted men's barracks; commissary; quartermaster storehouse; powder magazine; hospital; bakery; adjutant's office.
Research Fields: military history; Indian School history; pioneers of Devil's Lake region history.
Facilities: interpretive center; 300-seat auditorium. Books, postcards & other native American & military-related items for sale.
Activities: self-guided tours; organized group guided tours; organized educational programs for children & adults; tours with catered meals on request. Annual Event: Living History Field Day in September. For more information call (701) 766-4441.
Publications: booklet, Fort Totten: Military Post & Indian School, 1867-1959; video, Images of Fort Totten.
Hours & Admission Prices: Site: Visitor Center & P.W. Museum Facilities: mid-May to mid-Sept. daily 8-5; mid-Sept to mid-May Mon.-Fri. by appointment. Adults $4, children 6-15 $1.50; discounts to school groups, NDHF & FFTHS members; members & children under 6 no charge. Season Passes: Individual $10; Family $20. Bus tour $40 per bus. ♿
Attendance: 15,000 (estimated)
Membership: Friends of Ft. Totten Historic Site: Raccoon $15; Star $26; Turtle $201; Deer $501; Buffalo $1,001; Storyteller $5,001.

Fullerton

ROSEBUD SCHOOL MUSEUM, Main St., Fullerton, ND 58441. Mailing Address: P.O. Box 27, Fullerton, ND 58441-0027. Tel.: 701-375-7521.
Historic Building: housed in a former one-room schoolhouse; built in 1901.
Collections: local history; period furnishings; personal artifacts; photographs; local school artifacts.
Hours & Admission Prices: May-Oct. by appointment.

Garrison

HERITAGE PARK MUSEUM, First St. & First Ave. NW, Garrison, ND 58540. Mailing Address: P.O. Box 850, Garrison, ND 58540-0850. Tel.: 701-463-2631.
History Museum.
Collections: local history & culture; railroad depot; homestead house & blacksmith shop.

Hours & Admission Prices: Call for hours.

NORTH DAKOTA FIRE FIGHTERS MUSEUM, 52 N. Main St., Garrison, ND 58540. Tel.: 701-463-2099; 800-799-4242.
Fire Fighters Museum.
Collections: fire fighting history; firefighters records, personal artifacts & memorabilia; uniforms; photographs; fire apparatus & equipment.
Activities: educational programs; induction ceremony; Hall of Fame. Museum Sponsors: Fire Prevention Week.
Hours & Admission Prices: Mon.-Fri. 8-5. No charge.

NORTH DAKOTA FISHING HALL OF FAME AND MUSEUM, N. Main St. City Park, Garrison, ND 58540. Mailing Address: P.O. Box 459, Garrison, ND 58540-0459.
Personnel Profile: Part-Time Paid 1.
Fishing Museum.
Collections: fishing memorabilia; native fishermen.
Hours & Admission Prices: Mon.-Fri. 1-6, Sat.-Sun. 11-5.

Glen Ullin

GLEN ULLIN MUSEUM, 207 S. 10th St., Glen Ullin, ND 58631. Mailing Address: 6315 46th St., Glen Ullin, ND 58631-9734. Tel.: 701-348-3295.
Founded: 1983.
Key Personnel: Pres. (V), Lance Gartner.
Personnel Profile: Part-Time Volunteers 6.
Governing Authority: Tax-exempt.
Historic Buildings.
Collections: local history & culture; period furnishings; personal artifacts; photographs. Historic Buildings: house, 1884; Bethany church, 1896, schoolhouse, 1920.
Hours & Admission Prices: Sept. 3rd Sat.-Sun.; other times by appointment. No charge; donations accepted. ♿
Attendance: 750 (estimated)
Membership: Individual $2; Life $50.

Grafton

HISTORIC ELMWOOD HOUSE, Stephen Ave. & 2nd St., Grafton, ND 58237. Mailing Address: Chamber of Commerce, 432 Hill Ave., Grafton, ND 58237-1002. Tel.: 701-352-0152.
Historic House Museum: housed in the former home of North Dakota's second Attorney General, Cam Spencer; built in 1895. Listed on the National Register of Historic Places.
Collections: family history; personal artifacts; period furnishings; photographs.
Activities: rental facilities.
Hours & Admission Prices: By appointment.

JUGVILLE MUSEUM, 695 W. 12th St., Grafton, ND 58237-2115. Tel.: 701-520-1273.
Governing Authority: Parent Institution: Walsh County Heritage Village, 695 Hwy. 17 W., Grafton, ND 58237.
History Museum.
Collections: village & farm implements; monuments; gazebos.
Hours & Admission Prices: Call for hours. No charge; donations accepted.

Grand Forks

THE ARTSPLACE, 1110 2nd Ave. N., Grand Forks, ND 58203-3620. Tel.: 701-746-6479.
Founded: 1988.
Art Gallery.
Collections: works by local, regional & national artists; prints; paintings; photographs.
Hours & Admission Prices: Mon.-Sat. 10-5; other times by appointment. No charge; donations accepted.
Attendance: 950 (accurate)

BROWNING ARTS, 23 S. Fourth St., Grand Forks, ND 58201-4733. Tel.: 701-746-5090.
Art Gallery.
Collections: ceramics; painting; drawings; photography; computer art; sculpture; jewelry.
Facilities: Museum-related items for sale.
Hours & Admission Prices: Jan. to late Nov. Mon.-Fri. 9-5:30; Thanksgiving to Christmas Mon.-Sat. 9-5:30.

GRAND FORKS COUNTY HISTORICAL SOCIETY, 2405 Belmont Rd., Grand Forks, ND 58201-7505. Tel.: 701-775-2216.
E-mail: gfhistory@midconetwork.com
Web Site: grandforkshistory.com
Founded: 1970.
Congressional District: 17 & 18
Key Personnel: Pres., Suellen Bateman; Dir., Leah Byzewski; Treas., Gene Monson.
Personnel Profile: Full-Time Paid 1; Part-Time Paid 3; Part-Time Volunteers 2.
Governing Authority: society; nonprofit organization. Owned & operated by Grand Forks County Historical Society, 2405 Belmont Rd., Grand Forks 58201. Tel.: 701-775-2216. Branch Museums: Campbell House; Myra Museum; Grand Forks Post Office; one-room schoolhouse; Carriage House; Myra Centennial Pavilion. Tax-exempt: 501(c)(3).
Historical Society Museum: located on former farmsite belonging to Tom Campbell, the agriculturalist.
Collections: historic objects mostly from Grand Forks County area. Buildings: Campbell House; Myra Museum; Grand Forks Post Office; one-room schoolhouse; Carriage House; Myra Centennial Pavilion.
Research Fields: local history.
Facilities: browsing library; craftroom; meeting room.
Activities: guided tours; permanent & temporary exhibitions. Museum Sponsors: ice cream social; craft sale; antique show & sale.
Publications: newsletter, The Paddlewheel Press.
Hours & Admission Prices: Grounds: May 15-Sept. 15 daily 1-5. Office: Summer Mon.-Fri. 9-12; Winter Sat.-Sun. 1-5. Adults $3; members no charge. Closed Independence Day. ♿
Attendance: 5,000 (estimated)
Membership: Individual $10; Family $25; Business $150, $250, $500.

NORTH DAKOTA MUSEUM OF ART, 261 Centennial Dr., Stop 7305, Grand Forks, ND 58202-6003. Mailing Address: 261 Centennial Dr., Stop 7305, Grand Forks, ND 58202-6003. Tel.: 701-777-4195. Fax: 701-777-4425.
E-mail: ndmoa@ndmoa.com
Web Site: www.ndmoa.com
Founded: 1970.
Congressional District: 1
Key Personnel: Dir. & Chief Cur., Laurel J. Reuter; Chm. Bd. Trustees, David Hasbargen; Exhibition Coord. & Registrar, Greg Vettel; Dir. Education, Sue Fink; Dir. Rural Art, Matthew Wallace; Asst. to Dir., Brian Lofthus; Business Mgr., Amy Hovde; Office Mgr., Elizabeth Glouatsky; Dir. Installation Tech, Justin Dalzell; Mgr. Cafe, Justin Welsh.
Personnel Profile: Full-Time Paid 10; Part-Time Paid 10; Part-Time Volunteers 80.
Governing Authority: private cultural institution. Tax-exempt: 501(c)(3).
Art Museum.
Collections: national & international contemporary art; Northern Plains art; national American Indian since 1950.
Research Fields: contemporary art; American Indian art, contemporary & historical.
Facilities: outdoor sculpture garden; video viewing room; lecture room; cafe. Museum-related items for sale.
Activities: concerts; readings; performances; films, as well as special events for both children & adults.
Publications: quarterly newsletter; occasional catalogs of specific exhibitions.
Hours & Admission Prices: Mon.-Fri. 9-5, Sat.-Sun. 1-5. No charge; donations accepted. ♿
Attendance: 50,000 (estimated)
Membership: Student $10; Individual $35; Household $50; Sustaining $100; Supporting $250; Sponsor $500; Patron $1,000; Benefactor $5,000; Barton Benes Donor Wall $10,000.

UNIVERSITY OF NORTH DAKOTA HUGHES FINE ARTS CENTER GALLERY, Hughes Fine Arts Center, Rm. 127, 3350 Campus Rd., Stop 7099, Grand Forks, ND 58202-7099. Tel.: 701-777-2257. Fax: 701-777-2903.
E-mail: art.jones@und.nodak.edu
University Art Gallery.
Collections: paintings; photographs.
Hours & Admission Prices: Mon.-Fri. 11-4.

UNIVERSITY OF NORTH DAKOTA ZOOLOGY MUSEUM, Dept. of Biology, Grand Forks, ND 58202. Tel.: 701-777-2621. Fax: 701-777-2623.
E-mail: katherine.mehl@und.nodak.edu
Web Site: www.und.edu/dept/biology/undergrad
Founded: 1883.
Congressional District: 1
Key Personnel: Cur. Vertebrates, Katherine R. Mehl; Cur. Invertebrates, Dr. Jefferson Vaughan.

Governing Authority: university. Affiliated with University of North Dakota. Tax-exempt: 170(b)(1)(A).
Natural History Museum.
Collections: birds; fishes; mammals; insects; reptiles & amphibians; parasite of Aquatic Invertebrates.
Research Fields: pertaining to collections.
Facilities: 3,000-vol. library of taxonomy & history books available for inter-library loan; field research station; laboratories; classrooms.
Activities: guided tours; formally organized education programs for undergraduate & graduate students affiliated with University of North Dakota; permanent & temporary exhibits.
Hours & Admission Prices: Mon.-Fri. 8-4:30. Call for appointment. No charge. Closed national holidays.
Attendance: 200 (estimated)

Grand Rapids

LAMOURE COUNTY MUSEUM, Memorial Park, Grand Rapids, ND 58458. Mailing Address: P.O. Box 128, LaMoure, ND 58458-0128. Tel.: 701-883-5301.
Historical Building.
Collections: personal artifacts; period furnishings; Senator Milton Young.
Hours & Admission Prices: Memorial Day to Labor Day Sat.-Sun. 1-8; other times by appointment.

Grassy Butte

OLD SOD POST OFFICE, 101 Museum Dr., Grassy Butte, ND 58634. Tel.: 701-863-6769 & 6570.
E-mail: crranch@ndsupernet.com
Key Personnel: Pres. (V), Gail Chinn.
Personnel Profile: Part-Time Paid 2; Part-Time Volunteers 2.
Governing Authority: Parent Institution: McKenzie County Historic Society. Tax-exempt.
History Museum: built in 1912 of logs & sod, housed Grassy Butte Post Office from 1914 to 1964. Listed on the National Register of Historic Places.
Collections: period artifacts from 1800s & 1900s.
Hours & Admission Prices: Memorial Day to June Sat.-Sun. 9-4; July to Labor Day daily 9-4. No charge; donations accepted.

Hanks

PIONEER TRAILS MUSEUM, 9 miles west junction Hwy. 85 & Hwy. 50, Hanks, ND 58856. Tel.: 701-572-4759.
History Museum.
Collections: local history & culture; photographs; historical area artifacts from the early settlement days.
Hours & Admission Prices: June-Sept. Mon.-Fri. by appointment; Sun. 1-5.

Hatton

HATTON-EIELSON MUSEUM & HISTORICAL ASSOCIATION, 403 Durham Ave., Hatton, ND 58240. Mailing Address: P.O. Box 278, Hatton, ND 58240-0278. Tel.: 701-543-3615. Fax: 701-543-4013.
E-mail: mlc@gra.midco.net
Web Site: www.eielson.org
Founded: 1973.
Congressional District: 20
Key Personnel: C.E.O., Terry Fladeland; Vice Pres., Jerry Pederson; Asst. Cur., Eileen Mork; Public Rels., Eileen Holt; Public Rels. & Sec., Gary Lillemoen; Treas. & Museum Shop Mgr., Eileen Holt.
Personnel Profile: Part-Time Volunteers 20.
Governing Authority: society; nonprofit organization. Tax-exempt.
Historic Building: c.1900 Victorian home of aviator-explorer Carl Ben Eielson.
Collections: photographs; local history items; pioneer artifacts; mail service items; aviation memorabilia pertaining to Alaska & Antarctica; newspapers; Victorian furnishings; glassware; manuscripts; 1921 FOKKER airplane fuselage that Eielson flew in Alaska.
Research Fields: local history.
Facilities: 500-vol. library of historical books available for research on premises. Museum-related items for sale.
Activities: guided tours; formally organized education programs for children & adults; permanent exhibitions. Museum Sponsors: annual barbeque. Annual Event: Sweetheart Dinner for six.
Hours & Admission Prices: Spring & Summer: Sun. 1-4:30; Winter: by appointment. Adults $5, children $1; preschool no charge.
Attendance: 3,000 (estimated)
Membership: Individual $5; Family $10; Business $25; Booster $100; Top of the World $1,000.

Hebron

HEBRON HISTORICAL AND ART SOCIETY, 606 Lincoln Ave., Hebron, ND 58638. Tel.: 701-878-4644.
Web Site: www.hebronnd.org/live_historical.html
Founded: 1979.
Key Personnel: Pres. (V), Jack Hauser; Vice Pres., Ken Johnson; Museum Shop Mgr., Henry Mische.
Governing Authority: Tax-exempt.
History Museum.
Collections: area history; over 2,000 artifacts & memorabilia; 1929 Model A Ford Snowmobile; hand drawn horse cart; period stationary engines; photographs; 900 dolls from 57 countries.
Major Exhibits: St. Paul-based TRACES Center for History (T), 4/26/10-5/7/10; Chautauqua (T), 7/1/10-7/4/10.
Hours & Admission Prices: By appointment. No charge; donations accepted.
Attendance: 200
Membership: Annual $3.

Hillsboro

TRAILL COUNTY HISTORICAL SOCIETY, 306 Caledonia W. Ave., Hillsboro, ND 58045. Mailing Address: Box 173, Hillsboro, ND 58045-0173. Tel.: 701-636-5571.
Founded: 1965.
Congressional District: 1
Key Personnel: Pres. (V), Shirley Nysveen; Cur., Marilu Person.
Personnel Profile: Part-Time Volunteers 200.
Governing Authority: Traill County. Affiliated with North Dakota State Historical Society, Bismarck. Tax-exempt.
General Museum: housed in 1897 three-story brick mansion.
Collections: household furnishings of the 1800s; Indian artifact room & basement of early agricultural implements; Norwegian immigrant items; rare Red River fur trader's cart; old farm equipment & machinery. Historic Buildings: Pioneer Agricultural building; St. Olaf's Chapel; 1870 log cabin; 1920s rural one-room school.
Research Fields: local Indian archaeology.
Hours & Admission Prices: June-Aug. Sat.-Sun. 2-5; appointments available year-round. Adults $2; members & children no charge when accompanied by an adult.
Attendance: 1,000 (estimated)
Membership: Individual $5; Family $10.

Hope

STEELE COUNTY HISTORICAL SOCIETY, 301 Steele Ave., Hope, ND 58046. Mailing Address: P.O. Box 144, Hope, ND 58046-0144. Tel.: 701-945-2394. Fax: 701-945-2394.
E-mail: scmuseum@invisimax.com
Web Site: www.steelecomuseum.com
Formerly: Steele County Museum
Founded: 1966.
Congressional District: 23
Key Personnel: Pres. (V), Homer Wennerston; Dir., Sue Johnson.
Personnel Profile: Full-Time Paid 1; Part-Time Volunteers 15.
Governing Authority: nonprofit organization. Parent Institution: North Dakota State University. Tax-exempt: 501(c)(3).
Historical Society Museum: housed in 1882 Baldwin Arcade; listed on National Register; one-room schoolhouse; cultural center; Enger Log House c.1872.
Collections: clothing; furniture; archival materials; photographs; newspapers; farm machinery; Indian artifacts; manuscripts; 4 historic buildings; quilts; looms; folk art.
Research Fields: local history; agriculture; rural life.
Facilities: 13,000 sq. ft. in 7 buildings.
Activities: guided tours; lectures; films; arts & holiday festivals; permanent & temporary exhibitions; permanent weaving studio; traditional arts workshops; costume rentals.
Publications: annual report.
Hours & Admission Prices: Summer: Tues.-Fri. 9-5, Sun. 2-5; Sept.-June Tues.-Fri. 9-5. Suggested Donation: adults $5, seniors $3, children $3; students & members no charge. ♿
Attendance: 1,800 (estimated)
Membership: Individual $10; Family $15 & up; Friend $50-$99; Supporter $100-$499; Sustaining $500-$999; Benefactor $1,000 & up.

Jamestown

THE ARTS CENTER, 115 2nd St., S.W., Jamestown, ND 58401-4114. Mailing Address: P.O. Box 363, Jamestown, ND 58402-0363. Tel.: 701-251-2496.
E-mail: artscenter@csicable.net
Web Site: www.jamestownartscenter.org
Key Personnel: Dir., Taylor Barnes; Gallery Dir., Sally Jeppson.
Personnel Profile: Full-Time Paid 1; Part-Time Paid 3.
Governing Authority: Parent Institution: Jamestown Fine Arts Association. Tax-exempt.
Art Museum.
Collections: works by local artists.
Major Exhibits: Obsessed With North Dakota - Photography of Clint Saunders & Daron Krueger (T), 1/10; Laura Wennstrom, 2/10; Animals: Them & Us (T), 3/10; St. Johns Bible Project, 4/10; 46th Annual JFAA Spring Art Show, 5/10.
Facilities: theater.
Activities: classes; performances; workshops; art shows; holiday quilt & fiber show; temporary exhibitions.
Hours & Admission Prices: Mon.-Fri. 9-5, Sat. 10-1. No charge; donations accepted. ♿
Membership: Senior $20; Individual $35; Family $50.

FRONTIER VILLAGE ASSOCIATION, INC., 17th St., S.E., Jamestown, ND 58401. Mailing Address: P.O. Box 324, Jamestown, ND 58402-0324. Tel.: 701-251-9145. Fax: 701-251-9146.
Founded: 1959.
Congressional District: 48
Key Personnel: Pres. (V), Mitzy Hagar; Vice Pres., Charles Tamata; Sec., Lila Slokkeland.
Personnel Profile: Part-Time Paid 5; Part-Time Volunteers 4.
Governing Authority: nonprofit organization. Parent Institution: City of Jamestown. Tax-exempt: 501(c)(3).
History Museum.
Collections: general items of early Pioneer days.
Activities: guided tours; arts festival; theater; stagecoach rides, pony rides, stagecoach hold-up (acting).
Publications: brochure.
Hours & Admission Prices: Memorial Day-Labor Day daily 9-9. No charge; donations accepted. ♿
Attendance: 150,000 (estimated)

NATIONAL BUFFALO MUSEUM, 500 17th St., S.E., Jamestown, ND 58401-6456. Tel.: 701-252-8648; 800-807-1511.
E-mail: director@buffalomuseum.com
Web Site: www.buffalomuseum.com/index.htm
Founded: 1993.
Key Personnel: Dir., Felicia Sargeant.
Personnel Profile: Full-Time Paid 2; Part-Time Paid 6; Part-Time Volunteers 15.
Governing Authority: nonprofit organization.
Buffalo Museum.
Collections: cultural & natural history of bison and the Great Plains; Plains Indian artifacts; paintings; sculpture; Native American art; 19th century firearms; North Dakota wildlife; Lewis & Clark; live bison herd.
Facilities: Museum-related items for sale.
Activities: educational programs; video presentation; community events; school & youth programs. Annual Events: White Cloud's birthday celebration; Potholes and Prairies Birding Festival.
Hours & Admission Prices: May & Sept.-Oct. Mon.-Fri. 9-5, Sat. 10-5, Sun. 12-5; Memorial Day to Labor Day daily 8-8; Nov.-April Mon.-Fri. 9-5, Sat. 10-5. Adults $5, seniors $4, students 7-18 $1; discounts to groups of 15 or more & AAA members; members and children 6 & under no charge. ♿
Attendance: 18,898 (accurate)
Membership: Individual $15; Family $25; Lifetime $250. Business: Pewter $50; Silver $100; Gold $150; Diamond $200.

STUTSMAN COUNTY MEMORIAL MUSEUM, 321 3rd Ave., S.E., Jamestown, ND 58401-4208. Mailing Address: P.O. Box 1002, Jamestown, ND 58402-1002. Tel.: 701-252-6741 & 4809.
Web Site: jamestownnd.com
Founded: 1964.
Congressional District: 12
Key Personnel: C.E.O. & Pres. (V), Alden Kollman; Cur., Leah Mitchell.
Personnel Profile: Part-Time Paid 2; Part-Time Volunteers 18.
Governing Authority: nonprofit organization. Tax-exempt: 501(c)(3).
General Museum: Museum is housed in three story brick building; Built in 1907 and most items are from before 1930.
Collections: agriculture; costumes; dolls; dishes; equipment; Indian artifacts; medical; military; music; railroad room; country store; chapel; homesteaders shanty.
Facilities: 300-vol. library of local and state history books & 35 scrap books available for inter-library loan & historical research; reading room.
Activities: Museum Sponsors: annual ice cream social fun night.
Publications: biannual newsletter.
Hours & Admission Prices: Memorial Day to Sept. Mon.-Fri. 10-5, Sat.-Sun. 1-5; tours by appointment. No charge; donations accepted.
Attendance: 1,700 (estimated)
Membership: Individual $10-$500.

Kulm

WHITESTONE HILL BATTLEFIELD STATE HISTORIC SITE, 7310 86th St., S.E., Kulm, ND 58456-9555. Mailing Address: 612 E. Boulevard Ave., Bismarck, ND 58505-0660. Tel.: 701-328-2666. Fax: 701-328-3710.
Web Site: www.discovernd.com/hist
Founded: 1904.
Key Personnel: Dir., State Historical Society of ND, Merl Paaverud; Historic Sites Mgr., Diane Rogness.
Personnel Profile: Part-Time Paid 2.
Governing Authority: state. Parent Institution: State Historical Society of North Dakota. Subsidiary Institution: Friends of Whitestone Hill Battlefield State Historic Site. Tax-exempt: 501(c)(3).
Historic Site Museum: army troops under General Alfred Sully battled Sioux warriors in 1863.
Collections: artifacts; graves; monuments commemorating the Battle of Whitestone Hill.
Facilities: 2 monuments; park, picnic & recreational sites.
Publications: quarterly, North Dakota History and Plains Talk.
Hours & Admission Prices: May 16 to Sept. 15 Thurs.-Mon. 10-5. No charge; donations accepted. Discounts to members at the State Historical Society's museum stores.
Attendance: 2,000 (accurate)
Membership: For membership information, please call 701-222-1966.

LaMoure

TOY FARMER MUSEUM, 7496 106th Ave., SE, LaMoure, ND 58458-9404. Tel.: 701-883-5206; 800-533-8293. Fax: 701-883-5209.
E-mail: info@toyfarmer.com
Web Site: www.toyfarmer.com
Toy Farmer Museum.
Collections: toy memorabilia.
Facilities: Museum-related items for sale.
Hours & Admission Prices: May-Sept. Mon.-Fri. 10-6, Sat.-Sun. 12-5; Oct-April Mon.-Fri. 10-5, Sat.-Sun. 12-5. No charge. Closed New Year's; Easter; Thanksgiving; Christmas.

Larimore

LARIMORE COMMUNITY MUSEUM, 310 Towner Ave., Larimore, ND 58251. Mailing Address: P.O. Box 524, Larimore, ND 58251-0524. Tel.: 701-397-5723.
Key Personnel: Pres., Helen Welte; Treas., B. Jean Swanson
History Museum.
Collections: local history & culture; photographs; personal artifacts.
Hours & Admission Prices: Memorial Day to Labor Day. Suggested Donations: adults $1, students $.50.

Lidgerwood

LIDGERWOOD COMMUNITY MUSEUM, 10 Third Ave., SE, Lidgerwood, ND 58053. Tel.: 701-538-4466.
E-mail: lmuseum@rrt.net
History Museum.
Collections: local history & culture; antique furnishings; works of North Dakota native sculptor & artist Ida Prokop.
Hours & Admission Prices: First & third Sun. of the month 1-5. No charge; donations accepted.

Linton

EMMONS COUNTY MUSEUM, NW First and Oak, Linton, ND 58552. Tel.: 701-782-4228.
Governing Authority: county. Parent Institution: Emmons County Historical Society.
History Museum: housed in St. James Episcopal Church.
Collections: household items; military items; antique buggy, sleigh & tools; leather tack.

Hours & Admission Prices: Fri. & Sun. 2-4; other times by appointment. No charge; donations accepted.

Makoti

MAKOTI THRESHERS' MUSEUM, South edge of Town, Makoti, ND 58756. Mailing Address: 30000 338th St. S.W., Ryder, ND 58779-9522. Tel.: 701-726-5656.
Web Site: www.makoti.net
Founded: 1961.
Key Personnel: Pres. (V), Mehrl Breher
History Museum.
Collections: over 250 stationary engines; 150 period farm tractors; prairie community including post office, church, blacksmith shop, & school; cars; trucks.
Hours & Admission Prices: June-Sept. by appointment. Donations accepted.
Attendance: 3,000

Mandan

FORT ABRAHAM LINCOLN STATE PARK, 4480 Ft. Lincoln Rd., Mandan, ND 58554-7947. Mailing Address: 2204 Sommer Dr. N., Mandan, ND 58554-8257. Tel.: 701-667-6340. Fax: 701-667-6349.
E-mail: falsp@nd.gov
Web Site: www.parkrec.nd.gov
Founded: 1936.
Key Personnel: Supt., Chuck Erickson; Historian, Kevin Kirkey; Park Mgr, Dan Schelske.
Personnel Profile: Full-Time Paid 3; Part-Time Paid 20.
Governing Authority: state. Affiliated with North Dakota Parks & Recreation Dept., 1835 Bismarck Expwy., Bismarck, ND 58504. Tax-exempt.
State Park Museum.
Collections: Mandan Indian artifacts; 1870s military; 7th Cavalry & Custer. Historic Sites: Slant Indian village; cavalry post; blockhouses.
Facilities: Books & other museum-related items for sale.
Activities: slide-tape program; movies on area; outdoor interpretive programs; guided & self-guided tours; interpretive markers.
Publications: brochures.
Hours & Admission Prices: April & Oct. daily 1-5; May & Sept. daily 9-5; Memorial Day-Labor Day daily 9-7; Nov.-March open upon request. Park fee (includes visits to all interpretive sites & tours): adults $6, students $4; members no charge. Closed winter holidays. ♿
Attendance: 150,000 (estimated)
Membership: Family $35.

NORTH DAKOTA STATE RAILROAD MUSEUM, 3102 37th St., N.W., Mandan, ND 58554-7001. Mailing Address: P.O. Box 1001, Mandan, ND 58554-7001. Tel.: 701-663-9322.
Founded: 1985.
Railroad History Museum.
Collections: train cars; HO models; photographs; timetables.
Facilities: Museum-related items for sale.
Hours & Admission Prices: Memorial Day to Labor Day daily 1-5. ♿

Manvel

MANVEL MUSEUM, Main St., Manvel, ND 58256. Mailing Address: P.O. Box 2057, Bismarck, ND 58502-2057. Tel.: 701-696-2279.
History Museum.
Collections: personal items of former state representative Dagne Olson; antique furnishings; books.
Hours & Admission Prices: By appointment.

Mayville

GOOSE RIVER HERITAGE CENTER, Main St. & 1st Ave., S.E., Mayville, ND 58257. Mailing Address: 320 1st St NW, Mayville, ND 58257-1107. Tel.: 701-788-4115.
Key Personnel: Pres., Betty Karaim.
Personnel Profile: Part-Time Volunteers 15.
Governing Authority: Tax-exempt.
History Museum.
Collections: local history & culture; photographs; personal artifacts.
Hours & Admission Prices: Memorial Day to Labor Day Sat.-Sun. 1-4; other times by appointment. No charge; donations accepted.

Medora

CHATEAU DE MORES STATE HISTORIC SITE, 3448 Chateau Rd., Medora, ND 58645. Mailing Address: P.O. Box 106, Medora, ND 58645-0106. Tel.: 701-623-4355. Fax: 701-623-4921.
E-mail: shschateau@nd.gov
Web Site: www.nd.gov/list/chateau
Founded: 1936.
Key Personnel: Dir. State Historical Society of ND, Merl Paaverud; Dir. Historic Sites, Fern Swenson; Mgr. State Sites, Diane Rogness; Museum Shop Mgr., Rhonda Brown.
Personnel Profile: Full-Time Paid 1; Part-Time Paid 24; Part-Time Volunteers 12; Interns 2.
Governing Authority: state. Parent Institution: State Historical Society of North Dakota.
Historic Site: the life and activities of a French nobleman and entrepreneur, the Marquis de Mores, who came west in 1883. This 26 two-story chateau was built as the summer residence of the Marquis's family.
Collections: personal items belonging to the Marquis de Mores, French nobleman and entrepreneur; original furnishings; riding tack, coaches & clothing.
Major Exhibits: The Art of Einar Olstead (T), 11/09-10/10; The Photos of Frank Fisk, 11/09-10/11.
Facilities: visitor center; interpretive center. Video & museum-related items for sale.
Activities: self-guided tours; summer programs, including De Mores Day & History Alive.
Publications: books, Aristocracy on the Western Frontier: The Legacy of the Marquis de Mores (1994); The Career of the Marquis de Mores in the Badlands of North Dakota (1994).
Hours & Admission Prices: mid-May to mid-Sept. daily 8:30-6:30. Interpretive Center: Sept. 16-May 15 Wed.-Sun. 9-5. Adults $7, children 6-15 $3; discounts to school groups; children under 6 no charge. Season Pass: $20. Closed Easter; Thanksgiving; Christmas. ♿
Attendance: 85,000 (accurate)
Membership: Individual $35; Family $45.

MEDORA DOLL HOUSE, 485 Broadway, Medora, ND 58645. Mailing Address: P.O. Box 198, Medora, ND 58645-0198. Tel.: 800-633-6721.
E-mail: medora@medora.com
Web Site: www.medora.com/attractions/dollhouse.html
Doll Museum.
Collections: period dolls.
Hours & Admission Prices: Memorial Day to Labor Day daily 10-7. Adults $2.79, students grades 2-12 $.93; pre-school children no charge.

THEODORE ROOSEVELT NATIONAL PARK-VISITOR CENTER, 315 2nd Ave., Medora, ND 58645. Mailing Address: P.O. Box 7, Medora, ND 58645-0007. Tel.: 701-623-4730. Fax: 701-623-4840.
E-mail: bruce_kaye@nps.gov
Web Site: www.nps.gov/thro
Founded: 1959.
Congressional District: 1
Key Personnel: Park Supt., Val Naylor; Chief Interpretation, Bruce M. Kaye.
Personnel Profile: Full-Time Paid 3; Full-Time Volunteers 1; Part-Time Paid 9; Part-Time Volunteers 4; Interns 4.
Governing Authority: federal government. Parent Institution: Theodore Roosevelt National Park. Tax-exempt.
Visitor Center & National Park.
Collections: partial collection of Theodore Roosevelt's ranching effects; herbarium; anthropology; archaeology; botany; geology; Indian artifacts; industry; natural history, as it relates to Theodore Roosevelt National Park. Historic Building: 1883 Maltese Cross cabin.
Facilities: 2,500-vol. library of history & natural history books available for use on premises; visitors center. Publications for sale.
Activities: guided tours; permanent exhibitions; evening campfire programs.
Publications: Natural history handbooks; book, Theodore Roosevelt in the Dakota Badlands.
Hours & Admission Prices: Park: daily. South Unit Visitor Center: daily 8-4. Painted Canyon Visitor Center: April-June & Sept.-Nov. 8:30-4:30; Summer: call for extended hours. North Unit Visitor Center: daily 9-5:30. Park: Vehicle $10, Individual $5. Annual Pass $80. Closed New Year's Day; Thanksgiving; Christmas. ♿
Attendance: 441,936 (accurate)

Minnewaukan

MINNEWAUKAN MUSEUM, 210 Elm St., W., Minnewaukan, ND 58351.
History Museum. Listed in the National Register of Historic Places.
Collections: pioneer artifacts; clothing; military displays from the Civil War, WWI & WWII.

Hours & Admission Prices: May-Sept. Sun. 2-5. No charge; donations accepted.

Minot

DAKOTA TERRITORY AIR MUSEUM, 100 34th Ave., N.E., Minot, ND 58703. Mailing Address: P.O. Box 195, Minot, ND 58702-0195. Tel.: 701-852-8500.
E-mail: airmuseum@minot.com
Web Site: dakotaterritoryairmuseum.com/
Founded: 1986.
Key Personnel: Chm. (V), Don Larson; Cur., Glenn Blackaby.
Personnel Profile: Full-Time Paid 1; Part-Time Paid 2; Part-Time Volunteers 40.
Governing Authority: Tax-exempt: 501(c)(3).
Aviation History Museum.
Collections: Lockheed T-33 Jet Trainer (U.S. Air Force's first jet trainer); Douglas C-47 (DC-3) World War II Transport.; Douglas C-47 Cockpit; L-T-V (Chance Vought) A-7 Corsair 2; Curtis P-40 Warhawk; '34 Stinson Reliant; North American T-28; '34 Fairchild 24; '32 Monocoupe 110; '28 Waco 10; '40 Waco UPF-7; '30 Pietenpol; '37 J-2 Cub; '79 Vari-eze; '67 Volksplane; '51 Luscombe; '89 Rotorway Exec helicopter; '29 Arrow Sport; T-6 Texan Twin Beech D-18; '31 Waco QCF-2; '67 Starduster; '45 Taylorcraft; '46 Ercoupe; '42 Piper J-3 Cub; '47 A-3 Callair; '49 Cessna 195; '67 Breezy; literature & periodicals; area military aviation service flight gear & equipment; photographs; aviation's role in the region's agriculture and transportation needs; Minot Fire Department trucks from 1920s & 1930s.
Activities: special events.
Publications: members' newsletter, Dakota Territory Air Museum.
Hours & Admission Prices: mid-May to mid-Oct. Mon.-Sat. 10-5, Sun. 1-5; other times by appointment. Family $10, adults $4, children 6-17 $2; members no charge. ♿
Attendance: 3,600 (estimated)
Membership: Individual $35; Family $45; Individual Lifetime $200; Family Lifetime & Business Lifetime $300.

NORTH DAKOTA ART GALLERY ASSOCIATION, (M), 412 19th Ave., S.W., Minot, ND 58701-6420. Tel.: 701-858-3242. Fax: 701-858-3894.
E-mail: ndaga@ndaga.org
Web Site: www.ndaga.org
Founded: 1977.
Key Personnel: Dir., Linda A. Olson.
Personnel Profile: Part-Time Paid 2; Part-Time Volunteers 2; Interns 2.
Art Gallery.
Collections: works by local & regional artists.
Major Exhibits: Absolute Dot - Ewa Tarsia, 11/09-6/10; Sculpted Landscapes - Ken Dulgarno, 11/09-6/10; Cris Fulton Prairie Pastels, 11/09-7/10; Arts Dakota, 11/09-10/10; Bill Nybo - Cardoodles, 11/09-11/10; Anne Coreenwood - Winter Court, 11/09-1/11.
Activities: children's programs; performances; workshops; student art show; student traveling show; arts trunks; cultural encounters & games; story telling; arts trunks.
Hours & Admission Prices: Mon.-Fri. 9-5.

NORTHWEST ART CENTER, Minot State University, 11th Ave. N.W., Minot, ND 58707-0001. Mailing Address: 500 University Ave. W., Minot, ND 58707-0001. Tel.: 701-858-3264.
E-mail: nac@minotstateu.edu
Web Site: www.minotstateu.edu/nac
Formerly: Hartnett Hall Gallery
Founded: 1976.
Key Personnel: Dir., Avis Veikley.
Personnel Profile: Part-Time Paid 4; Interns 2.
Governing Authority: Parent Institution: Minot State University. Tax-exempt.
Art Center.
Collections: contemporary & traditional art by local, regional & national artists.
Facilities: library.
Activities: art exhibitions; lecture series.
Publications: Americas 2000.
Hours & Admission Prices: Mon.-Fri. 8-4:30; other times by appointment. No charge; donations accepted. ♿
Attendance: 5,000
Membership: Student & Senior Citizen $10; Individual $20; Household $25; Sponsor $50-$99; Patron $100-$999; Benefactor $1,000.

OLD SOO DEPOT TRANSPORTATION MUSEUM, 15 N. Main St., Minot, ND 58703-3103. Mailing Address: P.O. Box 2148, Minot, ND 58702. Tel.: 701-852-2234.
Founded: 2000.
Historic Building: housed in the restored 1912 Soo Line Depot.
Collections: American West transportation history including railroads, automobiles, buses, & aviation.
Hours & Admission Prices: Call for hours. No charge.

RAILROAD MUSEUM OF MINOT, 19 First St., N.E., Minot, ND 58701-3960. Mailing Address: P.O. Box 74, Minot, ND 58702-0074. Tel.: 701-852-7091.
E-mail: info@railroadmuseumofminot.org
Web Site: www.railroadmuseumofminot.org
Founded: 1986.
Key Personnel: Dir., James Huston; Museum Shop Mgr., Roger Burchill
Railroad Museum.
Collections: over 100 years of regional rail history; photographs; memorabilia; communication systems.
Activities: train rides.
Hours & Admission Prices: Sat. 10-2; other times by appointment. No charge; donations accepted. ♿
Attendance: 2,000 (estimated)
Membership: Porter $25; Switchmen $50; Conductor $75; Engineer $100; Yard Foreman $200; B.L.E. $500; Jim Hill $1,000.

ROOSEVELT PARK ZOO, 1219 Burdick Expwy., E., Minot, ND 58701. Mailing Address: P.O. Box 549, Minot, ND 58702-0549. Tel.: 701-857-4166. Fax: 701-857-4169.
E-mail: gmzszoo@ndak.net
Web Site: www.rpzoo.com
Founded: 1918.
Key Personnel: Chm., Bob Petry; Dir., Dana Pritschet; Pres. (V), Jenny Steckler; Museum Shop Mgr., Becky Dewitz.
Personnel Profile: Full-Time Paid 7; Full-Time Volunteers 2; Part-Time Paid 20; Part-Time Volunteers 100.
Governing Authority: municipal. Parent Institution: Minot Park District. Subsidiary Institution: Greater Minot Zoological Society. Tax-exempt: 501(c)(3).
Zoo.
Collections: animals; birds; reptiles.
Activities: guided tours; organized education programs for children & adults.
Publications: quarterly newsletter, Inside Tracks.
Hours & Admission Prices: May-Sept. daily 10-8. Adults $6, children 4-12 $3.50; discounts to groups; AZA members and children 3 & under no charge. Season passes available. ♿
Attendance: 75,000 (accurate)
Membership: Individual $20; Family & Grandparent $55; Family Plus $75; Patron $100.

SCANDINAVIAN HERITAGE PARK, 1020 S. Broadway, Minot, ND 58701-4660. Mailing Address: P.O. Box 862, Minot, ND 58702-0862. Tel.: 701-852-9161.
E-mail: scandha@srt.com
Web Site: www.scandinavianheritage.org
Key Personnel: Pres., Mark Anderson
Cultural Heritage Museum.
Collections: Scandinavian heritage & culture; early area settlers; statues; historic house.
Hours & Admission Prices: Memorial Day to Labor Day Mon.-Fri. 8-7, Sat. 10-4, Sun. 12-4. No charge.

TAUBE MUSEUM OF ART, 2 N. Main St., Minot, ND 58703-3104. Tel.: 701-838-4445. Fax: 701-838-6471.
E-mail: taube@srt.com
Web Site: www.taubemuseum.org
Formerly: Taube Museum of Art and Minot Art Association
Founded: 1970.
Congressional District: 2
Key Personnel: Exec. Dir. & Museum Shop Mgr., Nancy F. Brown; Pres. (V), Zoe Spooner.
Personnel Profile: Full-Time Paid 1; Part-Time Paid 1; Part-Time Volunteers 25; Interns 1.
Governing Authority: nonprofit organization. Tax-exempt: 501(c)(3).
Art Museum: housed in renovated bank building.
Collections: paintings; sculptures; photos.
Major Exhibits: Arts Dakota (T), 1/10; ND Student Art Show, 4/10; Small Works, 6/15/10-7/22/10; Mike Marth, 7/27/10-8/27/10; Black & White

Photo Show, 9/10-10/8/10; Brian Taylor Landscapes, 10/19/10-11/19/10; Festival of the Season, 11/26/10-12/24/10.
Facilities: 2,346 sq. ft. main gallery. Original artworks & museum-related items for sale.
Activities: art auction; North Dakota student art show; art festivals; art classes for all ages; participation in local festivals & fund-raisers.
Publications: quarterly newsletter.
Hours & Admission Prices: Tues.-Fri. 10:30-5:30, Sat. 11-4; other times by appointment. Suggested Donation: adults $2. Closed holidays. ♿
Attendance: 77,500 (estimated)
Membership: Students & Senior Citizens $25; Adult $45; Family $60; Sustainer $100; Business $200; Business Patron $500; Benefactor $1,000; Corporate $1,500.

WARD COUNTY HISTORICAL SOCIETY, 2005 Burdick Expwy. E., Minot, ND 58702. Mailing Address: P.O. Box 994, Minot, ND 58702-0994. Tel.: 701-839-0785.
E-mail: wchs@wchsnd.org
Web Site: www.wchsnd.org
Founded: 1951.
Key Personnel: Pres. (V), Paul P. Robinette, Jr.
Personnel Profile: Part-Time Volunteers 7; Interns 1.
Governing Authority: county. Tax-exempt.
Historic Building & Site.
Collections: farm implements; church; blacksmith shop; county courthouse; pioneer barber shop; dental facility; rail depot & artifacts; homesteader cabin; two schoolhouses; print shop.
Research Fields: genealogical.
Facilities: research facility.
Activities: various seasonal programs.
Publications: bimonthly newsletter, Prairie Perspectives.
Hours & Admission Prices: June-Aug. Wed. & Fri.-Sat. 10-3. Adults $2, children 7-12 $1; active duty military & spouses, children under 6 and members no charge. ♿
Attendance: 6,000 (accurate)
Membership: Single $15; Family $25; Business $50.

Mohall

RENVILLE COUNTY HISTORICAL SOCIETY, 504 First St., N.E., Mohall, ND 58761-4200. Mailing Address: P.O. Box 213, Sherwood, ND 58782-0213. Tel.: 701-756-6195.
Founded: 1978.
Congressional District: 1
Key Personnel: Pres., Oran Keith; Vice Pres., Nina Engh; Sec., Betty Johnson; Treas., Joyce Lunde.
Personnel Profile: Part-Time Paid 1; Part-Time Volunteers 4.
Governing Authority: nonprofit organization. Tax-exempt: 170(b)(1)(A).
General Museum: housed in a pioneer church from Norma, ND & first depot built in Mohall, ND.
Collections: local items used in the area during homestead days; historic buildings.
Research Fields: history of governmental subdivisions.
Activities: guided tours; permanent exhibitions.
Hours & Admission Prices: June-Aug. Sun. 2-5. No charge; donations accepted. ♿
Attendance: 50 (estimated)
Membership: Annual $5; Life $100.

Mooreton

BAGG BONANZA HISTORICAL FARM, I-29 S., Mooreton, ND 58061. Mailing Address: P.O. Box 702, Mooreton, ND 58061. Tel.: 701-274-8989 & 642-2411.
Web Site: www.baggfarm.com
History Museum.
Collections: farming era of the 1800s to early 1900s; restored 21-bedroom main house.
Facilities: 15-acre farm.
Hours & Admission Prices: Summer: Fri.-Sun. 12-6; other times by appointment. Adults $5, children under 12 $3.50; children under 6 no charge. ♿

Napoleon

LOGAN COUNTY MUSEUM, 207 Lake St. W., Napoleon, ND 58561. Mailing Address: 208 E. 5th St., Napoleon, ND 58561-7217. Tel.: 701-754-2640.
Founded: 1984.
Congressional District: 1
Key Personnel: Dir., Joe A. Fettig.
Personnel Profile: Part-Time Volunteers 20.
Governing Authority: county. Parent Institution: Logan County Historical Society.
Historical Society Museum.
Collections: local history & culture; photographs.
Hours & Admission Prices: Call for hours. No charge; donations accepted.
Attendance: 150
Membership: Annual $2; Life $50.

New Rockford

EDDY COUNTY MUSEUM, 6840 18th St., N.E., New Rockford, ND 58356. Tel.: 701-947-5490.
History Museum.
Collections: local history & culture; photographs; historic furnishings & exhibits.
Hours & Admission Prices: May-Sept. Sun. & holidays 1:30-5; other times by appointment. No charge.

New Town

THREE TRIBES MUSEUM, 302 Frontage Rd., New Town, ND 58763. Mailing Address: P.O. Box 147, New Town, ND 58763-0147. Tel.: 701-627-4477. Fax: 701-627-3805.
E-mail: tatmuseum@restel.net
Founded: 1964.
Personnel Profile: Part-Time Paid 3; Part-Time Volunteers 2.
Native American Museum.
Collections: Mandan, Hidatsa & Arikara Indian history & culture; photographs; personal artifacts.
Facilities: Museum-related items for sale.
Activities: tours.
Hours & Admission Prices: May-Oct. Mon.-Sat. 10-4, Sun. 1-4. Adults $3, seniors & children 12-18 $2; children 11 & under no charge.
Attendance: 5,000 (accurate)

Oakes

DICKEY COUNTY HISTORICAL PARK, Oakes, ND 58474. Tel.: 701-742-2843. Fax: 701-783-4361.
History Museum.
Collections: local history & culture; Burlington Northern caboose & depot; photographs.
Hours & Admission Prices: By appointment.

Parshall

PAUL BROSTE ROCK MUSEUM, Main St., Parshall, ND 58770. Mailing Address: P.O. Box 184, Parshall, ND 58770-0184. Tel.: 701-862-3264.
Founded: 1964.
Rock Museum.
Collections: rocks; crystals.
Hours & Admission Prices: May to Labor Day Wed.-Sun. 12-4. Adults $4, students $2. ♿
Membership: Life $100.

Pembina

PEMBINA STATE MUSEUM, 805 State Hwy. 59, Pembina, ND 58271-0456. Mailing Address: P.O. Box 456, Pembina, ND 58271-0456. Tel.: 701-825-6840. Fax: 701-825-6383.
E-mail: jblanchard@nd.gov
Web Site: history.nd.gov
Founded: 1996.
Congressional District: 1
Key Personnel: Dir. S.H.S. of ND, Merlan E. Paaverud, Jr.; Dir. Historic Preservation Div., Fern Swenson; Museum Site Supvr., Jeff Blanchard; Museum Shop Mgr., Betty Pelletier.
Personnel Profile: Full-Time Paid 1; Part-Time Paid 5.
Governing Authority: state; nonprofit organization. Parent Institution: State Historical Society of North Dakota. Tax-exempt.
History Museum.
Collections: Barry Collection; archeology of region, Metis, Red River Valley of the North settlement, military; transportation.
Major Exhibits: Lincoln's Legacy (T), 2/10-2/12.
Research Fields: fur trade; agricultural history; settlement; transportation history; frontier military-Fort Pembina; American Indian: Metis.
Facilities: public meeting room; 110 ft. observation tower; travel information center. Museum-related items for sale.
Activities: bimonthly interpretive programming.
Publications: North Dakota History; Plains Talk.

Hours & Admission Prices: Summer: May 16-Sept. 15 Mon.-Sat. 9-6, Sun. 1-6; Winter: Sept. 16-May 15 Mon.-Sat. 9-5, Sun. 1-5. Museum: no charge; donations accepted. Tower: $2; SHSND Foundation no charge. Closed New Year's Day; Easter; Thanksgiving; Christmas. ♿
Attendance: 5,208 (accurate)
Membership: State Historical Society of ND Foundation: Individual $35; Family $45.

Plaza

PLAZA COMMUNITY MUSEUM, Main St., Plaza, ND 58771. Mailing Address: P.O. Box 65, Plaza, ND 58771-0065. Tel.: 701-497-3454.
E-mail: tusentat@restel.net
History Museum: housed in a church.
Collections: historic items from the Plaza community; photographs.
Hours & Admission Prices: By appointment. No charge; donations accepted.

Powers Lake

BURKE COUNTY HISTORICAL POWERS LAKE COMPLEX, 8334 Hwy. 50, Powers Lake, ND 58773-9111. Tel.: 701-546-4491.
Founded: 1986.
Congressional District: 4
Key Personnel: C.E.O., Larry Tinjum; Chm. (V) & Pres. (V), Dennis Dosch; Education, Financial Dir. & Devel., Phillip Wienmann; Cur., Calvin Myers; Archivist, Harold Jorgenson; Public Rels., Margaret Nelson; Registrar, Donna Fredrickson; Security, Joan Thompson; Museum Shop Mgr., Orris Enget.
Personnel Profile: Part-Time Volunteers 15.
Governing Authority: private; nonprofit organization.
History Museum.
Collections: school; church; homestead shack; parsonage & depot; period artifacts.
Activities: guided tours. Annual Events: City Days in July; church service in August; Variety Show, fund-raiser in spring.
Hours & Admission Prices: Call for hours. No charge; donations accepted.
Attendance: 93 (accurate)
Membership: Individual $1; Life Membership $100.

Ray

RAY OPERA HOUSE MUSEUM, 119 Main St., Ray, ND 58849. Mailing Address: 416 4th Ave. E., Ray, ND 58849-4913. Tel.: 701-568-3437.
Founded: 1989.
Key Personnel: Pres. (V), Nyla Jean Kellar.
Governing Authority: Tax-exempt.
History Museum.
Collections: local history; period furnishings; school memorabilia.
Hours & Admission Prices: June-Oct. Sun. 2-4; other times by appointment. No charge; donations accepted. ♿
Attendance: 50 (estimated)
Membership: Annual $1.

Regent

HETTINGER COUNTY HISTORICAL SOCIETY, Main Street, Regent, ND 58650. Mailing Address: P.O. Box 151, Regent, ND 58650-0151. Tel.: 701-563-4543. Fax: 701-563-4602.
Founded: 1962.
Congressional District: 35
Key Personnel: Chm. (V), Jess Kouba; Pres. (V), Gary Greff; Sec. & Treas., Ruth Fitterer.
Personnel Profile: Part-Time Paid 10; Part-Time Volunteers 7.
Governing Authority: society. Affiliated with State Historical Society of North Dakota. Bismarck, ND 58501. Tax-exempt.
Local History Museum.
Collections: Pioneer Street: blacksmith shop; barber shop; rural church; print shop; schoolhouse; harness shop; bar; bank; insurance co.; general merchandise store; post office; hotel; jail; meat market; pioneer machinery & farm tools; written histories; genealogical sheets of county residents; artifacts & collectibles; 1911-1965 Dr. S. W. Hill Drug Store; with equipment & tools; Hettinger County area furniture & antiques; Indian room; two period cars; home-built airplane; American Indian artifacts; antique store & merchandise; shell collection; stuffed birds & animals; army uniforms, WWI, WWII & Gulf War; artifacts from wars; two-year old German-Hungarian building full of authentic Banat (Germany) artifacts. Genealogies of Hettinger County residents
Research Fields: pioneer antiques; Indian relics; genealogical study.
Facilities: approx. 300-vol. library of medical books, newspapers, old books, maps & periodicals.
Activities: guided tours; annual meetings.
Publications: brochure; postcard.
Hours & Admission Prices: Memorial Day to Labor Day daily 9-5; other times by appointment. Adults $5, teenager $3; discount to groups; children no charge. ♿
Attendance: 700 (estimated)
Membership: Individual $5.

Rugby

GEOGRAPHICAL CENTER HISTORICAL MUSEUM, 1 Block E. Hwy. U.S. #2 & ND #3, Rugby, ND 58368. Mailing Address: 102 Hwy 2 S.E., Rugby, ND 58368-2424. Tel.: 701-776-6414.
Web Site: www.prairievillagemuseum.com
Founded: 1964.
Key Personnel: Pres. (V), Hubert Seiler; Vice Pres., Delmer Ostrem; Treas., Linda Lysne; Museum Shop Mgr., Pamela Schmitt; Sec., Vicky Harmel.
Personnel Profile: Full-Time Paid 3; Full-Time Volunteers 1; Part-Time Paid 4; Part-Time Volunteers 6.
Governing Authority: bd. directors; nonprofit organization. Parent Institution: Geographical Center Historical Society. Tax-exempt: 501(c)(3).
Historical Society Museum Complex: located at geographical center of North America.
Collections: farm machinery; cars; buggies; wagons. Pioneer Village with 27 furnished structures.
Activities: loan, permanent & temporary exhibitions.
Publications: quarterly newsletter.
Hours & Admission Prices: May-Sept. Mon.-Sat. 8-7, Sun. 1-7. Adults $7, youth 12-15 $3, children 6-11 $1; discounts to AAA & ARP members & groups; children under 6 no charge. ♿
Attendance: 5,027 (estimated)
Membership: Individual $10; Family $20.

PRAIRIE VILLAGE MUSEUM, 102 Hwy. 2 S.E., Rugby, ND 58368-2424. Tel.: 701-776-6414 & 542-3813.
Web Site: www.prairievillagemuseum.com
Founded: 1964.
Key Personnel: Dir., Pam Schmitt; Pres. (V), Dr. Hubert Seiler.
Personnel Profile: Full-Time Paid 2; Full-Time Volunteers 1; Part-Time Paid 3; Part-Time Volunteers 2.
Governing Authority: Tax-exempt.
History Museum.
Collections: area history & culture; period cars; general store; guns; early train travel; Native American & Eskimo artifacts.
Hours & Admission Prices: May-Sept. Mon.-Sat. 8-7, Sun. 1-7. Adults 16 & over $7, children 12-15 $3, children 6-11 $1; discounts to senior citizens, AAA members & military; children 5 & under no charge. ♿
Attendance: 4,000 (estimated)
Membership: Single $10; Family $20.

Ryder

RYDER HISTORICAL SOCIETY MUSEUM, 20510 184th St., S.W., Ryder, ND 58779-9547. Tel.: 701-758-2527.
Founded: 1978.
Key Personnel: Pres. (V), Glen Warner
Historical Society Museum.
Collections: local history & culture; photographs; dolls; salt-n-pepper shakers; pens; military uniforms; school room & clothing; old irons; license plates; cameras; dental equipment; dishes; old tools; barb wire.
Hours & Admission Prices: June-Aug. Wed. 10-4; other times by appointment. No charge; donations accepted. ♿
Membership: Life $35.

St. John

ROLETTE COUNTY HISTORICAL SOCIETY MUSEUM, Main St., St. John, ND 58369. Tel.: 701-477-3026.
Governing Authority: county. Parent Institution: Rolette County Historical Society.
Historical Society Museum.
Collections: local & regional exhibits; clothing; photography; household & agricultural tools; machinery.
Hours & Admission Prices: Sun. 2-4.

Stanley

FLICKERTAIL VILLAGE AND MUSEUM, 5th St., S.E. off U.S. 2, Stanley, ND 58784. Mailing Address: P.O. Box 718, Stanley, ND 58784-0718. Tel.: 701-628-3335 & 2802.
Key Personnel: Dir., Robert G. Liebl

History Museum.
Collections: 18 buildings including depot, jail, school, church, homestead, & country store; Girl Scout artifacts; restored dolls.
Hours & Admission Prices: June-Aug. Wed. 6:30pm-7:30pm, Sun. 2-4; other times by appointment. Adults $3, children 11 & under $1.

Stanton

KNIFE RIVER INDIAN VILLAGES NATIONAL HISTORIC SITE, 564 County Rd. 37, Stanton, ND 58571-9422. Mailing Address: P.O. Box 9, Stanton, ND 58571-0009. Tel.: 701-745-3300. Fax: 701-745-3708.
E-mail: knri_information@nps.gov
Web Site: www.nps.gov/knri
Founded: 1974.
Congressional District: 1
Key Personnel: Supt., Brian McCutchen; Museum Shop Mgr., Dorothy Cook.
Personnel Profile: Full-Time Paid 8; Part-Time Paid 12; Part-Time Volunteers 18; Interns 2.
Governing Authority: federal. Parent Institution: Dept. of the Interior. Subsidiary Institution: National Park Service, Washington, D.C. Tax-exempt: 501(c)(3).
Historic Site.
Collections: Hidatsa & Mandan Cultural Artifacts; Native Americans of the Northern Plains.
Facilities: visitor center; full-scale furnished earth lodge. Books for sale.
Activities: tours; special events; self-guided nature & cross-country ski trails. Museum Sponsors: Northern Plains Indian Culture Festival last weekend in July.
Hours & Admission Prices: Memorial Day to Labor Day 8-6, tours available; Sept.-May 8-4:30. No charge. Closed New Year's Day; Thanksgiving; Christmas. ♿
Attendance: 24,704 (accurate)

Strasburg

PIONEER HERITAGE, INC., 845 88th St., S.E., Strasburg, ND 58573. Mailing Address: P.O. Box 52, Strasburg, ND 58573-0052. Tel.: 701-336-7103 & 7777.
E-mail: tscj@bektel.com
Formerly: Ludwig Welk Farmstead
Personnel Profile: Part-Time Paid 6.
Historic House Museum: housed in the boyhood home of Lawrence Welk.
Collections: personal artifacts; period furnishings.
Hours & Admission Prices: Memorial Day to Labor Day Fri.-Mon. 10-5; other times by appointment. Adults $5, children 6-12 $3. ♿

Tioga

NORSEMAN MUSEUM, Corner of Second St. N. & Welo, Tioga, ND 58852. Mailing Address: P.O. Box 671, Tioga, ND 58852-0671. Tel.: 701-664-2702.
History Museum.
Collections: local history & culture; photographs & artifacts of early settlers homes & farms.
Hours & Admission Prices: June-Aug. Sun. 2-4; other times by appointment.

Valley City

BARNES COUNTY HISTORICAL MUSEUM, 315 Central Ave. N., Valley City, ND 58072-2954. Tel.: 701-845-0966. Fax: 701-845-4282 (Attn: Wes).
E-mail: bchistoricalsociety@hotmail.com
Web Site: www.hellovalley.com
Founded: 1930.
Congressional District: 24
Key Personnel: Cur., Wes Anderson; Museum Shop Mgr., Nancy Bartz.
Personnel Profile: Full-Time Paid 1; Part-Time Volunteers 40.
Governing Authority: society. Parent Institution: Barnes County Historical Society. Tax-exempt.
History Museum.
Collections: historical exhibits; military items; costumes; tools; glasswares; dolls; Far Eastern artifacts.
Research Fields: genealogy; county history.
Facilities: newspaper research files.
Activities: historical tours; member study of county history; lectures.
Publications: book, History of Barnes County.
Hours & Admission Prices: Mon.-Sat. 10-4, Sun. by appointment. No charge; donations accepted. Closed national holidays. ♿
Attendance: 10,000 (accurate)
Membership: Individual $20; Family $25; Friends Club $100-$1,000.

Wahpeton

CHAHINKAPA ZOO, 1004 R.J. Hughes Dr., Wahpeton, ND 58075. Mailing Address: P.O. Box 1325, Wahpeton, ND 58074-1325. Tel.: 701-642-8709. Fax: 701-642-9285.
Web Site: www.wahpetonpark.com/zoo.htm
Key Personnel: Zoo Dir., Kathy Diekman; Foreman, Tom Schmaltz; Zookeeper, Nick Terfehr
Zoo.
Collections: over 200 animals & birds representing 60 species including fossa, otters, bison, monkeys, gibbon apes, camels, snow leopards, grizzly bears, wallabies, cougars, gemsbok, llamas, elk & Bengal tigers.
Hours & Admission Prices: May-Sept. daily 10-7; Oct. daily 10-5. Adults $6, seniors $5.50, children 4-12 $2.50.

RICHLAND COUNTY HISTORICAL MUSEUM, 2nd St. and 7th Ave. N., Wahpeton, ND 58075. Mailing Address: P.O. Box 1292, Wahpeton, ND 58074-1292. Tel.: 701-642-3075.
Founded: 1946.
Congressional District: 25
Key Personnel: Pres. (V), Lois Berndt; Museum Shop Mgr., Marjo Johnson.
Personnel Profile: Full-Time Paid 4; Part-Time Paid 2; Part-Time Volunteers 5.
Governing Authority: county. Affiliated with Richland County Historical Society. Tax-exempt.
Historical Society Museum.
Collections: archives; Indian artifacts; Rosemeade pottery; Roger's statues; manuscripts; genealogical; land records; cemetery records; 1885 census.
Research Fields: local history.
Facilities: Museum-related items for sale.
Activities: guided tours; permanent exhibitions; historical society meets monthly.
Publications: History of Richland County.
Hours & Admission Prices: mid-April to Oct. Tues., Thurs. & Sat.-Sun. 1-4. No charge; donations accepted. Closed Easter; Independence Day; Labor Day.
Attendance: 1,300 (estimated)
Membership: Life $25 & up.

Walhalla

GINGRAS TRADING POST STATE HISTORIC SITE, 12882 129 Ave., N.E., Walhalla, ND 58282. Mailing Address: Pembina State Museum, P.O. Box 456, Pembina, ND 58271-0456. Tel.: 701-549-2775. Fax: 701-328-3710.
E-mail: jblanchard@nd.gov
Web Site: history.nd.gov
Founded: 1956.
Congressional District: 1
Key Personnel: Dir., State Historical Society of ND, Merlan E. Paaverud, Jr.; Historic Site Supvr., Jeff Blanchard; Dir. Archaeology & Historic Preservation, Fern Swenson; Mgr. Historic Sites, Diane Rogness.
Personnel Profile: Full-Time Paid 1; Part-Time Paid 2.
Governing Authority: state. Parent Institution: State Historical Society of North Dakota.
Historic Site Museum.
Collections: fur trade hand-hewn oak log store & home of Antoine Gingras.
Facilities: Fur trade store.
Activities: monthly interpretive programming.
Publications: quarterly, North Dakota History and Plains Talk.
Hours & Admission Prices: May 16-Sept. 15 daily 10-5. No charge; donations accepted.
Attendance: 802 (accurate)
Membership: State Historical Society of ND Foundation: Individual $35; Family $45.

Washburn

MCLEAN COUNTY HISTORICAL SOCIETY MUSEUM, 610 Main St., Washburn, ND 58577. Mailing Address: P.O. Box 345, Washburn, ND 58577-0345. Tel.: 701-462-3744.
E-mail: vmerkel@westriv.com
Web Site: www.wrtc.com/vmerkel/McleanCountyMuseum
Founded: 1967.
Congressional District: 4
Key Personnel: Pres., Dan Wicklander; Cur., Vivian Merkel.
Personnel Profile: Full-Time Paid 1; Part-Time Paid 3; Part-Time Volunteers 3.
Governing Authority: society. Affiliated with the McLean County Historical Society. Tax-exempt.
Historical Society Museum: housed in 1905, County Courthouse & separate building adjacent.
Collections: pioneer & Indian artifacts; office machine; threshing machine;

steam engine; birds & small animals; audiovisual & film; photo equipment & prints; keelboat; medical equipment; geological; farm tools; fishing equipment.
Research Fields: newspapers; pioneer books; town centennial books; family histories.
Facilities: 300-vol. library of old books, diaries, papers, historical materials, available for research on premises. Books for sale.
Activities: guided tours; research.
Publications: book, McLean County Heritage; reprints, Fifty Pioneer Mothers; Pioneer Days of Washburn.
Hours & Admission Prices: June-Aug. Tues.-Sat. 1-5; other times by appointment. No charge; donations accepted. ♿
Attendance: 950 (estimated)
Membership: Individual $5; Family $10; Life $100.

THE NORTH DAKOTA LEWIS & CLARK INTERPRETIVE CENTER, 2876 N. 8th St., S.E., Washburn, ND 58577. Mailing Address: P.O. Box 607, Washburn, ND 58577-0607. Tel.: 701-462-8535; 877-462-8535. Fax: 701-462-3316.
E-mail: info@fortmandan.org
Web Site: www.fortmandan.org
Founded: 1997.
Key Personnel: Dir., David Borlaug
History Museum.
Collections: Lewis & Clark expedition; Native American artifacts; wood canoe; Karl Bodmer watercolors.
Activities: facility rental.
Hours & Admission Prices: Memorial Day to Labor Day daily 9-5; Sept.-May Mon.-Sat. 9-5, Sun. 12-5; groups by appointment. Adults $7.50, students $5; member no charge. ♿
Membership: Standard $40; Sustaining $100; Core $250.

Watford City

PIONEER MUSEUM OF MCKENZIE COUNTY, 100 2nd Ave., S.W., Watford City, ND 58854. Mailing Address: P.O. Box 126, Watford City, ND 58854-0126. Tel.: 701-444-2990. Fax: 701-444-5804.
E-mail: museum@ruggedwest.com
Web Site: www.4eyes.net
Founded: 1968.
Congressional District: 39
Key Personnel: Pres. (V), Jennifer Sorenson; Dir., Charlotte Schilke; Sec. & Treas., Jan Dodge; Cur., Sylvia Leiseth.
Personnel Profile: Full-Time Paid 1; Part-Time Paid 3; Part-Time Volunteers 3.
Governing Authority: nonprofit organization. Parent Institution: McKenzie County Historical Society, Watford City, ND 58854. Tax-exempt: 501(c)(3).
Pioneer Museum.
Collections: pioneer furnishings & clothing; photographs.
Activities: permanent exhibitions.
Hours & Admission Prices: Mon.-Sat. 10-6. Adults $2, students $1; pre-school children no charge. ♿
Attendance: 1,000 (estimated)

West Fargo

CASS COUNTY HISTORICAL SOCIETY AT BONANZAVILLE, 1351 W. Main Ave., West Fargo, ND 58078-1321. Mailing Address: P.O. Box 719, West Fargo, ND 58078-0719. Tel.: 701-282-2822. Fax: 701-282-7606.
E-mail: info@bonanzaville.com
Web Site: www.bonanzaville.com
Formerly: Red River & Northern Plains Regional Museum
Founded: 1954.
Key Personnel: Pres., Virginia Dambach; Exec. Dir., Bruce Whitmarsh; Cur., Alison Ostgarden; Cur., Andrew Nielson; Facilities Mgr., Rich Asleson.
Personnel Profile: Full-Time Paid 4; Full-Time Volunteers 2; Part-Time Paid 3; Part-Time Volunteers 100; Interns 1.
Governing Authority: society. Tax-exempt: 501(c)(3) & 170(b).
Pioneer Village & Museum Complex: consisting of 44 buildings.
Collections: Indian artifacts; pioneer home equipment; crafts; textiles; maps & atlas; city directories; historical North Dakota history from 1869-1920s; publications; limited genealogical material; minerals; period cars; cameras; dolls; farm machinery; Rosemeade pottery. Historic Structures: 1920 log cabin; 1890 Arthur Town Hall; 1887 saw mill; 1880 grainery; 1897 Hagen House; 1881 Houston House; 1884 farm house; 1895 one-room school; 1898 St. John's Church; 1890 homestead; 1900 barber shop.
Research Fields: local & regional history.
Facilities: 10,384 sq. ft. exhibit space apart from museum; banquet & wedding facilities. Museum-related items for sale.
Activities: self-guided tours; special events; rotating & permanent exhibitions. Annual Events: Pioneer Days in August; Living History events in summer.
Publications: quarterly newsletter; bimonthly newsletter, Bonanzaville Times.
Hours & Admission Prices: May & Oct. Sat. 10-5, Sun. 12-5; June-Sept. Mon.-Sat. 10-5, Sun. 12-5. Village: May-Oct. Mon.-Fri. 9-5; other times by appointment. Adults $8, children $4; discounts to groups, AAA & AAM members; children under 5 & members no charge.
Attendance: 19,414 (accurate)
Membership: Individual $30; Family $50; Patron $100; Supporter $250; Sustainer $500.

Williston

FORT BUFORD STATE HISTORIC SITE, 15349 39th Lane, N.W., Williston, ND 58801-8677. Tel.: 701-572-9034. Fax: 701-572-9033.
E-mail: shsbuford@nd.gov
Web Site: www.nd.gov/hist
Founded: 1931.
Key Personnel: Dir. State Historical Society of ND, Merl Paaverud; Div. Dir. Historic Sites, Fern Swenson; Mgr. Historic Sites, Diane Rogness; Site Supvr., Mark Sundlov; Asst. Site Supvr., Jean Turcotte; Museum Shop Mgr., Rhonda Brown.
Personnel Profile: Full-Time Paid 2; Part-Time Paid 7; Part-Time Volunteers 3.
Governing Authority: state. nonprofit organization. Parent Institution: State Historical Society of North Dakota. Subsidiary Institution: Friends of Fort Union/Fort Buford. Tax-exempt: 170(b)(1)(A).
Historic Site: housed in 1871 officers quarters of Fort Buford, at confluence of Yellowstone and Missouri Rivers; site of Sitting Bull's surrender July 20, 1881.
Collections: military uniforms, weapons, furnishings used at the site during this era; history of confluence region & North Dakota; reconstructed barracks.
Facilities: officers' quarters; magazine buildings; post cemetery sites; picnic area; campground; visitor center; meeting room. Museum-related items for sale.
Activities: permanent & temporary exhibits.
Publications: book, The Last Years of Sitting Bull, by Herbert T. Hoover & Robert C. Hollow (second printing, 1985); North Dakota history journal.
Hours & Admission Prices: May 16-Sept. 15 daily 8-6. Confluence Center: Sept. 16 to May 15 Wed.-Sun. 9-4. Adults $5, children 6-15 $2.50, school groups $1 each; discounts to SHSND foundation members; members and children 5 & under no charge. Tour Bus: $40 per bus. Annual Site Pass: $20. Closed New Year's Day, Easter, Thanksgiving, Christmas. ♿
Attendance: 14,753 (accurate)
Membership: Individual $35; Family $45.

FORT UNION TRADING POST NATIONAL HISTORIC SITE, 15550 Hwy. 1804, Williston, ND 58801-8680. Tel.: 701-572-9083. Fax: 701-572-7321.
E-mail: audrey_barnhart@nps.gov
Web Site: www.nps.gov/fous
Founded: 1966.
Key Personnel: Supt., Andrew Banta; Historian, Randy Kane; Cur., Audrey Barnhart.
Personnel Profile: Full-Time Paid 7; Part-Time Paid 1.
Governing Authority: federal. Affiliated with U.S. National Park Service, Dept. of the Interior. Tax-exempt.
Historic Site: site of American Fur Company reconstructed fur trading fort at the historic confluence of the Missouri & Yellowstone Rivers.
Collections: archaeological specimens & field records; fur trade related artifacts; Ben Innis book & manuscript collection; Union-Buford Council papers.
Research Fields: Northern Plains fur trade era including the Anglo European influence & the Native American influence; Lewis & Clark.
Facilities: 3,000-vol. library of books & microfilms on Northern Plains Indians, military, & fur trade of the upper Missouri Region including North Dakota, Montana & Saskatchewan, available on site. Books on the Upper Missouri River Region & its history for sale.
Activities: guided tours; lectures; summer living history programs.
Publications: newsletter, Confluence News.
Hours & Admission Prices: Winter daily 9-5:30; Summer daily 8-8. No charge. Closed New Year's Day; Thanksgiving; Christmas Day. ♿
Attendance: 20,000 (accurate)
Membership: Individual $10.

FRONTIER MUSEUM, 6330 2nd Ave. W., Williston, ND 58801. Mailing Address: P.O. Box 285, Williston, ND 58802-0285.
E-mail: jimr@co.williams.nd.us
Founded: 1958.
Congressional District: 1
Key Personnel: Pres., Jim Ryen; Bd. Member, Jean Bartlett.
Governing Authority: historical society. Parent Institution: Williams County Historical Society; nonprofit organization. Tax-exempt: 501(c)(3).

General Museum.
Collections: history; paintings; sculpture; graphics; decorative arts; archaeology; military; numismatic; philatelic; textiles; transportation. Historic Buildings: 1890 Log Cabin; 1906 old judge's home; 1906 country church; 1906 grocery store; Great Northern caboose; 1914 country school; old time doctor's & dentist's office.
Research Fields: frontier living; Indian artifacts; rock identification.
Facilities: 300-vol. library of material on history; biography; exploration; general available for use on premises. Locally-made crafts & other museum-related items for sale.
Activities: guided tours; lectures; tapes; permanent exhibitions.
Hours & Admission Prices: By appointment. Adults $3, children $1.50. ♿
Attendance: 2,000 (estimated)
Membership: Annual $3; Patron $10; Sustaining $25; Life $100.

Wolford

DALE & MARTHA HAWK MUSEUM, 4839 78 St., Wolford, ND 58385-9402. Tel.: 701-583-2381.
E-mail: dmhawk@gondtc.com
Web Site: www.hawkmuseum.org
Founded: 1981.
Key Personnel: Dir., Lowell Johnson; Cur., Gordon Thingvold
History Museum.
Collections: period cars, farm equipment & threshers; personal artifacts; steam engines; period tractors; early furniture; general store; church; one-room school; black smith shop; motorcycles.
Activities: camping. Annual Events: Farm Show in June; Dog Show in June.
Hours & Admission Prices: May-Oct. daily 9-5. Adults $5, youth 12-17 $2, children under 12 $1.50. ♿
Attendance: 3,500 (estimated)
Membership: Lifetime $500.

Woodworth

MELZER MUSEUM, Main St., Woodworth, ND 58476. Tel.: 701-752-4119.
History Museum.
Collections: local history & culture; American Indian photography; office of Dr. Melzer, an early settlement physician.
Hours & Admission Prices: By appointment.

OHIO

(386 listings)

Akron

* **AKRON ART MUSEUM, (M),** One South High, Akron, OH 44308-1801. Tel.: 330-376-9185. Fax: 330-376-1180.
E-mail: mail@akronartmuseum.org
Web Site: www.akronartmuseum.org
Founded: 1922.
Congressional District: 14
Key Personnel: Dir. & C.E.O., Mitchell Kahan, Ph.D.; Pres. (V), Myriam Altieri Haslinger; Dir. Education, Melissa Higgins; Assoc. Educator, Alison Caplan; Dir. Curatorial Affairs, Barbara Tannenbaum; Dir. Devel., Susan Schweitzer; Dir. Mktg. Communication, Elizabeth Wilson; Collections Mgr., Arnold Tunstall; Cur. Exhibitions, Ellen Rudolph; C.O.O., Gail Wild; Museum Shop Mgr., Laura Firestone.
Personnel Profile: Full-Time Paid 24; Part-Time Paid 20; Part-Time Volunteers 250; Interns 3.
Governing Authority: nonprofit organization. Tax-exempt: 501(c)(3).
Art Museum.
Collections: paintings & sculpture by Philip Guston, Frank Stella, Claes Oldenburg, Donald Judd, David Salle, Richard Deacon, Lari Pittman, Sol LeWitt & Doris Salcedo; works by photographers Lewis Hine, Robert Frank, Harry Callahan, Lee Friedlander, Gilbert & George, Hiroshi Sugimoto, Sopie Calle & Carrie Mae Weems.
Major Exhibits: Familiar Faces: Chuck Close in Ohio Collections, 11/09-1/3/10; The Legend of John Brown, 11/09-2/14/10; Nucler Enchantment: Photograph+s by Patrick Nagatani, 11/09-2/14/10; Pattern ID, 1/23/10-5/9/10; Andrew Borowiec: Photographs, 2/20/10-6/20/10; Isaac Julien's True North, 6/5/10-9/26/10; Andrew Moore: Detroit, 6/26/10-10/10; Who Shot Rock, 10/23/10-1/23/11.
Facilities: 10,000-vol. library of technical art books & publications available to students & teachers from area universities.
Activities: lectures; concerts; video programs; formally organized educational programs; docent program.
Publications: biennial report; quarterly magazine; gallery guides; exhibition catalogues.
Hours & Admission Prices: Administrative Office: Mon.-Fri. 9-5. Gallery: Wed. & Fri.-Sun. 11-5, Thurs. 11-9. Adults $7, students & seniors 65 & over $5; discounts to AAM & ICOM members; 1st Sun., children 12 & under and members no charge. Closed New Year's Day; Memorial Day; Independence Day; Labor Day; Thanksgiving; Christmas Eve & Day. ♿
Attendance: 99,547 (accurate)
Membership: Single $50; General & Family $65; Contributor $100; Sponsor $250; Sustainer $500; Benefactor $1,000 & up.

AKRON ZOOLOGICAL PARK, 500 Edgewood Ave., Akron, OH 44307-2199. Tel.: 330-375-2550 & 2525. Fax: 330-375-2575.
Web Site: www.akronzoo.org
Founded: 1953.
Congressional District: 14
Key Personnel: Pres. & C.E.O., L. Patricia Simmons; Chm. (V), Mike Stark; Vice Pres. Collections & Grounds, Doug Piekarz; Vice Pres. Business, Chuck Craig; Vice Pres. Communications, Linda Troutman; Museum Shop Mgr., Joan Hummel.
Personnel Profile: Full-Time Paid 71; Part-Time Paid 22; Part-Time Volunteers 125; Interns 5.
Governing Authority: board of trustees; nonprofit. Tax-exempt: 501(c)(3).
Zoo.
Collections: lions; tigers; jaguars; snow leopards; condors; bats; penguins; Komodo dragons; flamingos; Chinese alligators; Galapagos tortoises; eagles; river otters; bears; gibbons; waterfowl; Ohio farmland; parrots.
Research Fields: animal behavior.
Facilities: food concession; picnic grounds. Zoo-related items for sale.
Activities: school programs & orientations; docent program; train rides; temporary, traveling & permanent exhibits; guided tours; formally organized education programs. Zoo Sponsors: Animal Show in summer; Halloween Trick or Treat adventure.
Publications: quarterly newsletter, Zoo Tales; brochure.
Hours & Admission Prices: May-Oct. daily 10-5; Nov.-April daily 11-4. May-Oct. adults $9, senior citizens $7.50, children 2-14 $5.50; discounts to groups & AZA members; members & children under 2 no charge. Parking $2. Nov.-April adults $5.50. Parking $1.50. Closed New Year's Day; Thanksgiving; Christmas Eve & Day. ♿
Attendance: 255,000 (estimated)
Membership: Companion $55; Family & Grandparent $65; Donor $200; Patron $300.

HOWER HOUSE, University of Akron, 60 Fir Hill, Akron, OH 44325-0001. Tel.: 330-972-6909. Fax: 330-384-2635.
E-mail: sylvia5@uakron.edu
Web Site: www3.uakron.edu/howerhse/
Historic House Museum: former home of John Henry Hower, a leading Akron industrialist; c.1871.
Collections: Howard family artifacts; period furnishings; personal artifacts.
Activities: summer programs; holiday festivities; speakers; special events.
Hours & Admission Prices: Feb.-Dec. Wed.-Sat. 12-3:30, Sun. 1-4; groups by appointment. Adults $5, senior citizens 65 & over $4, students $2; discounts to groups; children under 6 no charge. Closed major holidays.

NATIONAL INVENTORS HALL OF FAME, 221 S. Broadway, Akron, OH 44308-1505. Tel.: 800-968-4332; 330-762-6565 & 4463. Fax: 330-762-6313.
E-mail: museum@invent.org
Web Site: www.invent.org
Founded: 1973.
Congressional District: 13
Key Personnel: Dir. Facilities, Vince Greczanik; Public Rels., Rini Paiva; Museum Shop Mgr. & Exhibits Designer, Mitch Scott.
Personnel Profile: Full-Time Paid 60; Part-Time Paid 25; Part-Time Volunteers 100; Interns 5.
Governing Authority: private; nonprofit. Parent Institution: National Inventors Hall of Fame Foundation. Tax-exempt: 501(c)(3).
Science Museum.
Collections: personal artifacts; hall of fame.
Research Fields: inventors.
Facilities: 5,000 sq. ft. exhibit space.
Activities: participatory & traveling exhibits. Annual Events: Induction Ceremony; Collegiate Inventors Competition; Camp Invention; Club Invention.
Hours & Admission Prices: Closed for renovation until 2010. ♿
Attendance: 50,000 (accurate)

* **STAN HYWET HALL AND GARDENS, INC.,** 714 N. Portage Path, Akron, OH 44303-1399. Tel.: 330-836-5533 & 315-3284. Fax: 330-836-2680.
E-mail: mheppner@stanhywet.org

Web Site: www.stanhywet.org
Founded: 1957.
Congressional District: 14
Key Personnel: Exec. Vice Pres. & C.O.O., William R.M. Binnie; Vice Pres. Devel., Susan D. Van Vorst; Vice Pres. Museum Svcs. Division & Cur. Collections, Mark J. Heppner; Museum Shop Mgr., Cynthia Kennard.
Personnel Profile: Full-Time Paid 50; Part-Time Paid 70; Part-Time Volunteers 1,300; Interns 7.
Governing Authority: nonprofit. Affiliated with Stan Hywet Hall Foundation, Inc. Tax-exempt: 501(c)(3).
Historic House Museum: 1912-15 65-room Tudor Revival: manor house and country estate of Frank A. Seiberling, founder of Goodyear Tire & Rubber Co.
Collections: English & American period artifacts; 16th- to 18th-century European tapestries; 18th- to 20th-century American & British fine art; 19th- to 20th century glass, ceramics, textiles & other decorative arts.
Research Fields: American landscape architecture, 20th-century architecture & interior design; 20th-century social history; decorative arts; historic preservation.
Facilities: 260-seat auditorium; conservatory & greenhouses; 70 acres of landscaped gardens & grounds; cafe; rentals. Museum-related items for sale.
Publications: Stan Hywet Hall & Gardens Magazine; Calendar of Events; Annual Report & Honor Roll of Donors; volunteer newsletter.
Hours & Admission Prices: April-Dec. Tues.-Sun. 11-4:30. Adults $12, seniors $11, youth 13-17 $6; discounts to groups & AAM members; members, children 12 & under no charge. Corbin Conservatory Exhibit: additional fee. Closed New Year's Eve & Day; Easter; Nov. 13; Thanksgiving; Christmas Eve & Day. ♿
Attendance: 200,000 (accurate)
Membership: Single $50; Dual $60; Family $65; Contributing $100.

SUMMIT COUNTY HISTORICAL SOCIETY, 550 Copley Rd., Akron, OH 44320-2398. Tel.: 330-535-1120. Fax: 330-535-0250.
E-mail: schs@summithistory.org
Web Site: summithistory.org
Founded: 1924.
Congressional District: 14
Key Personnel: Exec. Dir., Paula G. Moran; Pres. (V), Dr. Lynn Metzger, Ph.D.; Business Mgr., Sandra Pecimon; Cur., Leianne Heppner; Education Coord., Alison First.
Personnel Profile: Full-Time Paid 4; Part-Time Paid 4; Part-Time Volunteers 60; Interns 4.
Governing Authority: society. Tax-exempt: 501(c)(3).
History Museum.
Collections: early Americana; transportation; pottery; costumes; glass; manuscript collections. Historic Houses: 1830 John Brown House; 1840 Old Stone School; 1837 Simon Perkins Mansion.
Research Fields: transportation; pottery; industrial & urban history.
Facilities: Museum-related items for sale.
Activities: guided tours; lectures; films; study clubs; permanent & temporary exhibitions; preservation efforts; outreach programs for elementary schools & older adults.
Publications: quarterly bulletin, Old Portage Trail Review; books; pamphlets.
Hours & Admission Prices: Tours: Wed.-Fri. 12:30 & 2:30; mornings for school groups & tours by appointment. Adults $5, seniors & children under 16 $4; members no charge. Closed national holidays.
Attendance: 5,000 (estimated)
Membership: Individual $40; Family $50; Summit Sponsor $100; John Brown Benefactor $250; Simon Perkins Benefactor $500.

Alliance

MABEL HARTZELL HISTORICAL HOME, 840 N. Park Ave., Alliance, OH 44601-1728. Mailing Address: P.O. Box 2044, Alliance, OH 44601-0044. Tel.: 330-823-1677.
Web Site: www.alliancehistory.org/house.html
Founded: 1939.
Congressional District: 16
Key Personnel: Dir. & C.E.O., Leigh Mainwaring; Pres., Don Shaffer; Treas., Lucy Harrison; Sec., Jennifer Crist.
Personnel Profile: Part-Time Volunteers 30.
Governing Authority: private; nonprofit. Tax-exempt: 501(c)(3).
Historic House: an 1867 Italianate built by Matthew Earley, a prominent businessman & politician; restored to 1880s period with original furnishings.
Collections: life in the Victorian era; Renaissance revival furniture; curved staircase; sitting room parlor.
Research Fields: Isaac Taylor Headland, missionary to China, 1880-1910, & professor at Mount Union College, 1910-1935; Alliance Woman's Club 75th Anniversary retro; preparation for Sesquicentennial of Alliance in the year 2000.
Facilities: library of photographs related to the Alliance community & Morgan Engineering.
Activities: docent program; guided tours; lectures. Annual Event: Victorian Christmas in December.
Hours & Admission Prices: By appointment only. Admission $2; children under 12 & members no charge.
Attendance: 3,300 (estimated)
Membership: Regular $10; Family $15; Patron $25; Mabel Hartzell Club $100; Life $300.

Antwerp

EHRHART MUSEUM, 118 N. Main St., Antwerp, OH 45813-9348. Mailing Address: 14745 State Rt. 49, Antwerp, OH 45813-9348. Tel.: 419-258-2665. Fax: 419-258-1875.
Founded: 1963.
Congressional District: 5
Key Personnel: Pres. (V), Randy Shaffer; Vice Pres. (V), Judy Snook.
Personnel Profile: Part-Time Volunteers 4.
Governing Authority: society; nonprofit organization. Parent Institution: Otto E. Ehrhart-Paulding County Historical Society. Tax-exempt: 501(c)(3).
Natural History Museum.
Collections: archaeology; ethnology; geology; philatelic; mounted birds & animals; insects; historical artifacts.
Research Fields: Local genealogical; history of county.
Facilities: 500-vol. library of local history books available for use on premises with 10 days prior written permission & presence of librarian; nature center. Rocks & minerals, and museum-related items for sale.
Activities: guided tours; slide shows; restoration of the Antwerp Depot Railroad Station.
Publications: newsletter.
Hours & Admission Prices: Temporarily closed. ♿
Attendance: 1,000 (accurate)
Membership: Student $1; Contributing $10; Merchant & Organization $40; Life $100.

Archbold

HISTORIC SAUDER VILLAGE, 22611 State Rte. 2, Archbold, OH 43502-9452. Mailing Address: P.O. Box 235, Archbold, OH 43502-0235. Tel.: 419-446-2541; 800-590-9755. Fax: 419-445-5251. TDD: 419-445-9610.
E-mail: info@saudervillage.org
Web Site: www.saudervillage.org
Founded: 1971.
Congressional District: 5
Key Personnel: Chm. (V), Sharon Fellers; Exec. Dir., Debbie Sauder David; Dir. Historic Operations, Kris Jemmott; Cur. Collections, Sara Feldbawer; Business Officer, Denny Shannon; Dir. Public Rels., Kim Krieger; Museum Shop Mgr., Leslie Hartman.
Personnel Profile: Full-Time Paid 22; Part-Time Paid 240; Part-Time Volunteers 480; Interns 1.
Governing Authority: nonprofit organization. Tax-exempt.
Living History Village.
Collections: farm equipment; woodworking tools; household items; blacksmith; potter; glassblower; spinning & weaving; broommaking; cooper; tinsmith; basket maker; grist mill; herbalist.
Facilities: 37-building pioneer village; visitors center; exhibition hall; 350-seat restaurant; cafe; 35 room Country Inn; 37 site campground; Native American Village & trading post. Gift items for sale.
Activities: tours; lectures; arts & music festivals; workshops; working mill; permanent exhibitions; pioneer craft demonstrations; educational programming. Museum Sponsors: monthly festivals April-Oct.
Publications: quarterly member's magazine
Hours & Admission Prices: April 29-May Tues.-Fri. 10-3:30, Sat. 10-5, Sun. 12-4; Memorial Day to Labor Day Tues.-Sat. 10-5, Sun. 12-4; Sept.-Oct. Tues.-Fri. 10-3:30, Sat. 10-5, Sun. 12-4. Adults $12.50, students 6-16 $6.25; discount to seniors, AAA members & groups; members and children 5 & under no charge. Call for restaurant information. ♿
Attendance: 100,000 (accurate)
Membership: Single $40; Single Plus & Couple $65; Family & Grandparent $75. Expanded level: Single $80; Couple $130; Family & Grandparent $150.

Ashland

ASHLAND COUNTY HISTORICAL SOCIETY, 420 Center St., Ashland, OH 44805-3247. Tel.: 419-289-3111.
Key Personnel: Dir. Operations, Chris Box

Historical Society Museum.
Collections: county history & culture; photographs; personal artifacts; quill baskets; art glass tumblers; pressed glass goblets.
Hours & Admission Prices: Tours: April-Dec. Sun., Wed. & Fri. 1-4; other times by appointment. No charge.

Ashtabula

ASHTABULA ARTS CENTER, 2928 West 13th St., Ashtabula, OH 44004-2498. Tel.: 440-964-3396. Fax: 440-964-3396.
E-mail: aac@suite224.net
Web Site: www.artscenternews.com
Founded: 1953.
Congressional District: 11
Key Personnel: Exec. Dir., Elizabeth Koski; Pres. (V), Judy Robson; Art Coord., Meeghan Humphrey; Business Mgr., Cindy Rimplela; Music Coord., Lyn Rocco; Dance Dept. Coord., Shelagh Dubsky.
Personnel Profile: Full-Time Paid 8; Part-Time Paid 3; Part-Time Volunteers 125.
Governing Authority: nonprofit organization. Tax-exempt: 501(c)(3).
Art Museum Center.
Collections: contemporary art.
Research Fields: local history.
Facilities: classrooms; performance area; theater.
Activities: lectures; gallery talks; dance recitals; arts festivals; hobby workshops; formally organized education programs for children & adults in visual arts, dance, drama, music; outreach program in schools; permanent, temporary & traveling exhibitions; performance ensembles & repertory groups.
Publications: bimonthly newsletter; annual report; general brochure.
Hours & Admission Prices: Mon.-Thurs. 9-9, Fri.-Sat. 9-5. No charge. Closed holidays. ♿
Attendance: 15,000 (estimated)
Membership: Individual $25; Family $50; Supporters $100; Friends $200; Patrons $500; Donors $1,000; Benefactors $2,000; Golden Investors $5,000 & up.

ASHTABULA MARINE MUSEUM, 1071 Walnut Blvd., Ashtabula, OH 44004-3249. Mailing Address: P.O. Box 36, Jefferson, OH 44047-0036.
Web Site: www.ashtabulamarinemuseum.org
Marine Museum: housed in the former residence of the Lighthouse Keepers and the Coast Guard Chief, built in 1871/1898.
Collections: models; paintings; marine artifacts; photographs of early Ashtabula Harbor, ore boats & tugs; miniature hand-made brass tools; scale model of a Hulett Ore Unloading Machine.
Hours & Admission Prices: Memorial Day weekend-Aug. Fri.-Sun. & holidays 12-5; Sept. Sat.-Sun. 12-5. Adults $4, children 6-16 $3; children under 6 no charge.

Athens

ATHENS COUNTY HISTORICAL SOCIETY AND MUSEUM, 65 N. Court St., Athens, OH 45701-2506. Tel.: 740-592-2280. Fax: 740-594-8352.
Founded: 1980.
Key Personnel: Dir., Keke Riesbeck; Pres. (V), Tom O'Grady; Museum Shop Mgr., Laura Farrell.
Personnel Profile: Full-Time Paid 2; Part-Time Paid 2; Part-Time Volunteers 20; Interns 15.
Governing Authority: private; nonprofit organization. Tax-exempt.
Historical Society Museum.
Collections: county history & culture; photographs; personal artifacts; hands-on exhibits.
Major Exhibits: Please Touch, 11/09-11/10.
Facilities: library; meeting & lecture hall; exhibit space.
Activities: school programs; hands-on exhibits; history camp; movie night; history lectures; genealogy classes.
Publications: birth, death, marriage, cemetery, & township history records; local history.
Hours & Admission Prices: Tues.-Sat. 12-4. Adults $4, seniors, children & university students $2, children 12 & under $1; members & 3rd Sat. of month no charge. ♿
Attendance: 3,220 (accurate)
Membership: Individual $15; Family $30; Friend $100; Business Club $175; Sponsoring $250; Life $500; Patron $1,000.

THE DAIRY BARN ARTS CENTER, 8000 Dairy Lane, Athens, OH 45701-9393. Mailing Address: P.O. Box 747, Athens, OH 45701-0747. Tel.: 740-592-4981. Fax: 740-592-5090.
Founded: 1978.
Congressional District: 6
Key Personnel: Dir., Andrea Lewis.
Personnel Profile: Full-Time Paid 5; Part-Time Paid 2.
Governing Authority: Tax-exempt.
Arts Center: housed in a former daily barn; built in 1914. Listed on the National Register of Historic Places.
Collections: works by contemporary artists.
Major Exhibits: OH+5, 1/15/10-2/20/10; Transcending the Figure: Contemporary Ceramics, 3/12/10-4/25/10; Quilting Traditions: The Art of the Amish, 5/28/10-9/6/10; Appalachia!, 9/24/10-11/21/10.
Facilities: performance area; classroom.
Activities: festivals; educational programs; special events.
Publications: exhibition catalogs, Quilt National; Bead International; Beyond Basketry; Contemporary Ceramics.
Hours & Admission Prices: Winter: Tues.-Wed. & Fri.-Sat. 12-5, Thurs. 12-8, Sun. 1-5; Summer: call for extended hours. Adults $6, students & seniors $5; members & children under 12 no charge. ♿
Attendance: 22,000 (accurate)
Membership: Student & Senior $25; Individual $50; Family $100; Sustainer $250.

KENNEDY MUSEUM OF ART, (M), Ohio University, Lin Hall, Athens, OH 45701-2979. Tel.: 740-593-1304. Fax: 740-593-1305.
Web Site: www.ohiou.edu/museum
Founded: 1993.
Congressional District: 10
Key Personnel: Cur. Education, Sally Delgado; Cur., Petra Kralickova; Registrar, Jeffrey Carr; Administrative Asst., Beth Tragert.
Personnel Profile: Full-Time Paid 5; Part-Time Paid 2; Part-Time Volunteers 150; Interns 12.
Governing Authority: university. Parent Institution: Ohio University. Tax-exempt.
University Art Museum.
Collections: southwest Native American Collection of Edwin L. & Ruth E. Kennedy; works on paper; American painting, sculpture; photography; ceramics; non western art.
Major Exhibits: Biennial School of Art Faculty Exhibit, 1/10-3/10; Sun Koo Yuh: Sculptures & Drawings, 4/10-7/10.
Research Fields: American art; contemporary prints; southwest Native American textiles.
Activities: guided tours; lectures; symposiums; gallery talks; performances; organized education programs; docent programs; school programs; teacher training; internships; permanent, temporary & traveling exhibitions.
Publications: newsletter, Kennedy Museum of Art Magazine.
Hours & Admission Prices: Gallery: Tues.-Wed. & Fri. 12-5, Thurs. 12-8, Sat.-Sun. 1-5. No charge; donations accepted. ♿
Attendance: 10,000 (estimated)
Membership: Individual $25; Household $35; Patron $50; Benefactor $100; Sustaining $250; Partner $500; Director's Circle $1,000.

OHIO UNIVERSITY ART GALLERY, 528 Seigfred Hall, Athens, OH 45701. Tel.: 740-593-0796. Fax: 740-593-1305.
E-mail: kralicko@ohio.edu
Web Site: www.ohiou.edu/art/ougallery.html
Key Personnel: Dir. Exhibition, Petra Kralickova
University Art Gallery.
Collections: works by national & regional artists.
Facilities: 2,500 sq. ft. exhibit space.
Activities: Annual Events: Graphic Design Bachelor of Fine Arts exhibition; juried show of undergraduate artwork.
Hours & Admission Prices: Mon.-Sat. 10-4. No charge.

Aurora

AURORA HISTORICAL SOCIETY, (M), 115 E. Pioneer Trail, Aurora Memorial Library Bldg., Aurora, OH 44202-7922. Tel.: 330-995-3336.
E-mail: aurorahist@alltel.net
Founded: 1968.
Congressional District: 14
Key Personnel: Pres., Tim Holder; Dir., Marcelle R. Wilson, Ph.D; Museum Shop Mgr., Josephine Smalley.
Personnel Profile: Full-Time Paid 1; Interns 1.
Governing Authority: society; nonprofit organization. Affiliated with Library Trust-Aurora Memorial Library. Tax-exempt: 501(c)(3).
General Museum.
Collections: church, family & business records; cheese-making equipment; farm implements; home furnishings; photo records; genealogies; WWII.
Research Fields: century homes; genealogy.
Facilities: library.

Activities: guided tours; lectures; gallery talks; permanent exhibitions; local research; century homes recognition; antique show.
Publications: Aurora Story 1 and 2, The Pioneer; Images of America: Aurora; Tastes of Aurora: Favorite Recipes From The Past & From Today.
Hours & Admission Prices: Tues.-Wed. 2-4; other times by appointment. No charge. ♿
Attendance: 650 (accurate)
Membership: Individual $25; Family $35; Contributing $50; Benefactor $100; Life $1,000.

Bainbridge

DR. JOHN HARRIS DENTAL MUSEUM, 208 West Main St., Bainbridge, OH 45612. Mailing Address: Bainbridge Historical Society, P.O. Box 424, Bainbridge, OH 45612-0424. Tel.: 740-634-2228.
Founded: 1939.
Key Personnel: Chm. (V), Mrs. Cherry Miller; Museum Shop Mgr., Dr. Jack C. Weinrich.
Personnel Profile: Part-Time Volunteers 10.
Governing Authority: Parent Institution: Bainbridge Historical Society. Tax-exempt: 501(c)(3).
Dental History Museum: housed in 1827 former office of Dr. John Harris.
Collections: dental artifacts from 1627-present.
Facilities: library of dental literature.
Activities: guided tours.
Hours & Admission Prices: April-May & Sept.-Oct. Sat.-Sun. 12-4; June-Aug. Tues.-Sun. 12-4. Adults $2; children under 12 & members no charge. ♿
Attendance: 350 (estimated)
Membership: Bainbridge Historical Society: Individual $5.

Barnesville

BELMONT COUNTY VICTORIAN MANSION MUSEUM, 532 N. Chestnut St., Barnesville, OH 43713-1274. Mailing Address: P.O. Box 434, Barnesville, OH 43713-0434. Tel.: 740-484-4716 & 425-2926.
Formerly: Gay 90's Mansion Museum
Founded: 1966.
Congressional District: 20
Key Personnel: C.E.O. & Pres., Judy Jenewein; Dir. & Treas., Rebecca J. Thomas.
Personnel Profile: Part-Time Volunteers 35.
Governing Authority: county; society. Operated by Belmont County Historical Society. Tax-exempt: 501(c)(3).
General Museum: housed in 1890 Richardsonian mansion.
Collections: glass; china; utensils; furniture; clothing; manuscripts; quilts.
Facilities: 150-vol. library of old books available for use on premises; reading room.
Activities: guided tours; formally organized education programs for children. Annual Event: Victorian Christmas Show.
Publications: annual brochures & fact sheets.
Hours & Admission Prices: May-Sept. Wed.-Sun. & holidays 1-4; special tours by appointment. Adults $5, children 6-18 $2; discounts to groups.
Attendance: 1,058 (accurate)
Membership: Single $15; Couple $25; Sustaining $25; Life $150; Life Couple $200.

Bath

HALE FARM AND VILLAGE, 2686 Oak Hill Rd., Bath, OH 44210. Mailing Address: P.O. Box 296, Bath, OH 44210-0296. Tel.: 330-666-3711. Fax: 330-666-9497.
E-mail: kfalconc@wrhs.org
Web Site: www.halefarm.org
Founded: 1956.
Congressional District: 14
Key Personnel: C.E.O. & Pres., Dr. Gainor B. Davis; Vice Pres., Kelly Falconc-Hall.
Personnel Profile: Full-Time Paid 12; Part-Time Paid 20; Part-Time Volunteers 70.
Governing Authority: Parent Institution: The Western Reserve Historical Society, 10825 East Blvd., Cleveland, OH. 44106. Tax-exempt: 170(b)(1)(A).
Village Museum.19th century agrarian & village communities in the Western Reserve.
Collections: agriculture; crafts. Historic Buildings: 1816 log schoolhouse; 1825 Hale House; 1825 Wade law office; 1825 Franklin glassworks; steam sawmill; 1830 salt box house; 1832 Goldsmith House; 1832 Brown Land Office; 1844 Greek revival house; 1845 stone Herrick House; carriage museum; 1850 Stow House; 1851 meetinghouse.
Research Fields: Midwestern glass; mid-19th century rural costumes.
Facilities: restaurant; visitor center. Museum-related items for sale.
Activities: guided self-guided tours; lectures; permanent exhibitions; craft demonstrations.
Publications: The Jonathan Hale Farm.
Hours & Admission Prices: June-Oct. Wed.-Sun. 11-5; Nov.-Dec. Wed.-Fri. 9:30-2, Sat.-Sun. 11-5. Adults $10, children 3-12 $5; discounts to groups, AAM & ICOM members; members no charge. Closed New Year's Day; Thanksgiving; Christmas. ♿
Attendance: 65,000 (accurate)
Membership: Individual $50; Family & Couple $70; Sustaining $150; Fellow $250; Special Fellow $500.

Bay Village

BAYARTS, 28795 Lake Rd., Bay Village, OH 44140-1399. Tel.: 440-871-6543 & 5678. Fax: 440-871-0452.
E-mail: info@bayarts.net
Web Site: www.bayarts.net
Formerly: Baycrafters, Inc.
Founded: 1948.
Congressional District: 23
Key Personnel: Exec. Dir., Nancy Heaton; Mgr. Gallery & Dir. Education, Erin Stack; Chm. Bd. Directors, Ray Young; Chm. (V), Julie Holmes.
Personnel Profile: Part-Time Paid 2; Part-Time Volunteers 46.
Governing Authority: nonprofit organization. Tax-exempt.
Art Association: housed in original Huntington Estate. Visual arts organization with consignment shop for members in 1882 Nickel Plate Bay Village Railway Station with a Norfolk & Western Caboose.
Collections: works by regional artists.
Facilities: 200-vol. library of arts & crafts reference & instruction books & materials available for research with membership in BAYarts; classrooms. Arts & crafts by regional artists & craftsmen for sale.
Activities: gallery talks; arts festivals; workshops; formally organized education programs; consignment shop.
Publications: periodical, Brochure of Classes & Events; Artists Entry Form for Juried Competitions.
Hours & Admission Prices: Mon.-Sat. 10-5, Sun. 12-5. No charge; donations accepted. Closed holidays.
Attendance: 100,000
Membership: Individual $25; Family $45.

LAKE ERIE NATURE & SCIENCE CENTER, 28728 Wolf Rd., Bay Village, OH 44140-1350. Tel.: 440-871-2900. Fax: 440-871-2901.
Web Site: www.lensc.org
Founded: 1945.
Congressional District: 10
Key Personnel: C.E.O. & Dir., Larry D. Richardson; Pres. (V), Patrick Mazur; Museum Shop Mgr., Sheryl Caine.
Personnel Profile: Full-Time Paid 14; Part-Time Paid 15; Part-Time Volunteers 100; Interns 4.
Governing Authority: nonprofit organization. Tax-exempt.
Nature Center.
Collections: astronomy; botany; geology; physical science; zoology; live wildlife; ecological & environmental.
Facilities: library; wild flower & teaching garden; classrooms; planetarium; aquariums.
Activities: natural & physical science classes for school children; weekend family programs; adult workshops; nature films; nature art shows; travelogues. Center Sponsors: Nature classes, traveling programs for hospitalized children, the handicapped & senior citizens.
Publications: LENSC program guide; activities schedule; informational brochure, newsletter, WREN Wildlife Rehab Education; annual report.
Hours & Admission Prices: Daily 10-5; groups by appointment only. No charge; donations accepted. Closed New Year's; Easter; Memorial Day; Independence Day; Labor Day; Thanksgiving; Christmas. ♿
Attendance: 180,000 (accurate)
Membership: Individual $25; Family $50; Contributing $200; Supporting $500.

ROSE HILL MUSEUM, 27715 Lake Rd., Bay Village, OH 44140. Mailing Address: P.O. Box 40187, Bay Village, OH 44140-0187. Tel.: 440-871-7338 & 835-2718.
E-mail: mail@bayhistorical.com
Web Site: www.bayhistorical.com
Founded: 1960.
Congressional District: 23
Key Personnel: Pres. (V), Carole Roske; Corresponding Sec., Kari Eckel; Treas., Tom Phillips; Museum Shop Mgr., Cheryl Leece; Accessions, Janet Zvara.
Personnel Profile: Part-Time Volunteers 12.

Governing Authority: society. Parent Institution: Bay Village Historical Society. Tax-exempt: 501(c)(3).
History Museum: housed in 1818 Western Reserve farmhouse belonging to the Cahoon Family, first settlers in Dover Township.
Collections: clothing; children's toys; Wischmeyer boats; primitive furniture of the earliest settlers; Empire & Victorian furniture belonging to the Cahoon family; 1818 bedroom; roped bed; cornhusk mattress; Victorian bedroom; cellar containing a furnished summer kitchen & food storerooms; Cleveland history; local genealogy; 1810 replica log cabin with furnishings.
Research Fields: history of the Dover Township-Western Reserve area.
Facilities: 200-vol. library of genealogy, Cahoon & local history books available for research on premises only; smoke house; cabin-replica of cahoons. Books & other museum-related items for sale.
Activities: outreach to school & other organizations; guided tours; hobby workshops; formally organized education programs for children; temporary exhibitions; school tour service by appointment. Museum Sponsors: Huntington Heritage Days in October.
Publications: book, Bay Village, A Way Of Life; coloring book, Patchwork Quilt; Bay Village Historical Society Cook Book.
Hours & Admission Prices: Sun. 2-4:30, call for special tours. No charge; donations accepted. ♿
Attendance: 1,500
Membership: Senior $7.50; Single $10; Family $15; Patron $25.

Beachwood

MALTZ MUSEUM OF JEWISH HERITAGE, (M), 2929 Richmond Rd., Beachwood, OH 44122-3270. Tel.: 216-593-0575. Fax: 216-593-0576.
E-mail: info@mmjh.org
Web Site: maltzmuseum.org
Founded: 2005.
Congressional District: 16
Key Personnel: Chm. Bd., Milton Maltz; Pres., Tamar Maltz; Exec. Dir., Judith Feniger; Devel., Laura Whay Klein; Education, Lynda Bender; Media Rels., Adam Teresi; Registrar, Amber Anderson; Mgr. Special Exhibits, Stacy Singerman; Admin., Laurie Hughes; Archivist, Sean Martin; Museum Shop Mgr., Martha Sivertson.
Personnel Profile: Full-Time Paid 10; Part-Time Paid 5.
Governing Authority: private; nonprofit organization. Tax-exempt: 501(c)(3).
Jewish Heritage Museum.
Collections: Jewish heritage; films; personal artifacts; oral histories; art; photographs.
Facilities: 60-seat theater; 12,000 sq. ft. exhibit space.
Hours & Admission Prices: Tues., Thurs.-Fri. & Sun. 11-5, Wed. 11-9, Sat. 12-5. Adults $7, students & seniors $5; children under 12 no charge. ♿

Bedford

BEDFORD HISTORICAL SOCIETY MUSEUM AND LIBRARY, (M), 30 S. Park St. (Squire Place), Bedford, OH 44146. Mailing Address: P.O. Box 46282, Bedford, OH 44146-0282. Tel.: 440-232-0796.
Web Site: www.bedfordohiohistory.org
Formerly: Bedford Museum
Founded: 1955.
Congressional District: 21
Key Personnel: C.E.O., Janet Caldwell; Pres., Betsy Lee; Archivist, Joyce Maruna; Librarian, Paul Pojman; Mgr., Doris Shriver.
Personnel Profile: Full-Time Paid 1; Part-Time Paid 3; Part-Time Volunteers 12; Interns 1.
Governing Authority: society; Bedford Historical Society. Tax-exempt: 501(c)(3).
History Museum.
Collections: Americana; archaeology; archives; period furniture; glass; local & Ohio history; Indian artifacts; Jacka 1876 Centennial collection; Siegel railway collection; numismatic; manuscripts; the Squire Lincoln collection; the Barnum Civil War library. The art of Archibald Willard & Richard Sedlon. Historic Building: 1874 Bedford Township Hall; 1832 Hezekiah Dunham House; 1882 Bedford Railroad Depot; 1893 Gothic Church.
Research Fields: local history; genealogy.
Facilities: 12,000-vol. library of local & state history books available for use on premises. Used books & other museum-related items for sale.
Activities: guided tours; permanent & temporary exhibitions. Museum Sponsors: annual Strawberry Festival.
Publications: quarterly bulletin; book, Bedford Vignettes; Bedford Village Views-1992; children's activity book, All About Bedford, Ohio.
Hours & Admission Prices: Mon. & Wed. 7:30pm-10pm, Thurs. 10am-4pm; Second Sun. of the month 2-5. No charge; donations accepted. ♿
Attendance: 4,000 (accurate)
Membership: Junior (17 & under) $5; Annual $10; Family $20; Contributing $25; Life $150; Corporate $250.

Bellaire

THE NATIONAL GLASS IMPERIAL MUSEUM, 3200 Belmont St., Bellaire, OH 43906-1521. Mailing Address: P.O. Box 534, Bellaire, OH 43906-0534. Tel.: 740-671-3971.
E-mail: info@imperialglass.org
Web Site: www.imperialglass.org/museum.htm
Founded: 2003.
Congressional District: 6
Key Personnel: Admin., Rosalie Wenckoski; Chm. (V), Paul Douglas.
Personnel Profile: Part-Time Paid 1; Part-Time Volunteers 25.
Governing Authority: Parent Institution: National Imperial Glass Collectors' Society, Inc. Tax-exempt.
Glass Museum.
Collections: Imperial glassware.
Research Fields: glass.
Facilities: research room.
Activities: school groups.
Publications: The Imperial Collectors Glasszette.
Hours & Admission Prices: April-Oct. Thurs.-Sat. 11-3. Admission: $3; NIGCS members no charge. Closed Independence Day. ♿
Attendance: 350 (estimated)

Bellbrook

BELLBROOK HISTORICAL MUSEUM, 42 N. Main St., Bellbrook, OH 45305-2009. Mailing Address: P.O. Box 285, Bellbrook, OH 45305-0285. Tel.: 937-848-4666.
Personnel Profile: Part-Time Paid 1.
Governing Authority: city.
History Museum: housed in The Crowl Building, a former mortuary.
Collections: artifacts that portray the story of Bellbrook from 1816.
Hours & Admission Prices: Sat. 12-5. No charge; donations accepted. Closed holidays. ♿
Attendance: 100 (estimated)

Bellefontaine

LOGAN COUNTY HISTORICAL SOCIETY MUSEUM, 521 E. Columbus Ave., Bellefontaine, OH 43311-2401. Tel.: 937-593-7557.
E-mail: logancomuseum@embarqmail.com
Web Site: www.logancountymuseum.org
Founded: 1945.
Congressional District: 7
Key Personnel: Dir. & Cur., Todd McCormick.
Personnel Profile: Full-Time Paid 2; Part-Time Paid 1; Part-Time Volunteers 62.
Governing Authority: nonprofit. Affiliated with Logan County Historical Society, 521 E. Columbus Ave., Bellefontaine. Tax-exempt.
Historical Society Museum.
Collections: household appliances; tools; clothing; cameras; communications; music; firearms; uniforms & other insignia; railroad artifacts; autos; military & pioneer costumes; geology; Warren Cushman art; American Indian relics; manuscripts; agriculture.
Research Fields: local history; genealogy.
Facilities: 300-vol. library available for use on premises; 40-seat auditorium; reading room.
Activities: guided tours; lectures; permanent & temporary exhibitions.
Publications: brochure, Tour Guide of the County; booklets, First Concrete Street in America; leaflet, Welcome to Our Museum; Pictorial History Book; Historic Glimpses of Logan County, Ohio; Life in Rebel Prisons; quarterly newsletter.
Hours & Admission Prices: May-Oct. Wed. & Fri.-Sun. 1-4; Nov.-April Fri.-Sat. 1-4. No charge; donations accepted. ♿
Attendance: 5,000 (estimated)
Membership: Young Historians $2; Adult $15; Family $20; Business $30.

Bellevue

HISTORIC LYME VILLAGE ASSOCIATION, 5001 State Rte. 4, Bellevue, OH 44811. Mailing Address: P.O. Box 342, Bellevue, OH 44811-0342. Tel.: 419-483-4949.
Web Site: www.lymmevillage.com
Founded: 1972.
Congressional District: 5
Key Personnel: Pres., Roger Kinney; Vice Pres., Gail Frederick; Treas., Dennis Bauer; Dir. & Museum Shop Mgr., Raymond Parker.
Personnel Profile: Part-Time Volunteers 40; Interns 0.
Governing Authority: private; nonprofit organization. Tax-exempt: 501(c)(3).
History Museum.
Collections: early-1800s to early-1900s houses, buildings & furnishings.

Activities: guided tours of village; Pioneer Days in September; Murder Mystery & Dinner in October; Victorian Dinners and Christmas tours in December.
Publications: newsletter, Lyme Lines.
Hours & Admission Prices: June-Aug. Tues.-Sat. 11-4, Sun. 1-4; Sept.-Oct. Sun 1-4. Adults $8, senior citizens (60 & over) $7, children 6-12 $4. ♿
Attendance: 7,000 (estimated)
Membership: Student & Senior Citizen 60 & over $10; Individual $20; Family $45; Corporate $200 & up; Individual Life $300.

MAD RIVER & NKP RAILROAD MUSEUM, 253 Southwest St., Bellevue, OH 44811-1377. Mailing Address: 233 York St., Bellevue, OH 44811-1377. Tel.: 419-483-2222.
Railroad History Museum.
Collections: Mad River & Lake Erie Railroad history; railroad artifacts; photographs; tools; china; linens; badges; uniforms; lanterns; drawings; rolling stock.
Facilities: picnic area. Museum-related items for sale.
Activities: hands-on exhibits; group tours.
Hours & Admission Prices: May & Sept.-Oct. Sat.-Sun. 12-4; Memorial Day to Labor Day daily 12-4. Adults $7, seniors 60 & over $6, children 3-12 $4; children under 3 no charge.

Beverly

THE OLIVER TUCKER MUSEUM, 441 5th St., Beverly, OH 45715. Mailing Address: 70 Maple Circle, Waterford, OH 45786-5321. Tel.: 740-984-2489.
Web Site: olivertuckermuseum.com
Founded: 1971.
Congressional District: 11
Key Personnel: Pres. (V), Susan Trotter; Bd. Trustee, Wayne Fansworth; Bd. Trustee & Vice Pres., Francis M. Sampson.
Personnel Profile: Part-Time Volunteers 10.
Governing Authority: society; nonprofit organization. Parent Institution: Lower Muskingum Historical Society, P.O. Box 191, Waterford, OH 45786. Tax-exempt.
Historic Buildings.
Collections: Mary Tucker Townsend artifacts; photogaphs; documents; doctor's office furnishings & instruments; early furniture & clothing; period church alter c.1800; early settlers of the Lower Muskingum Valley area; riverboat items; log cabin containing period furnishings including working loom, weaving items, spinning wheels; hardware; letter distribution box from late 1700 post office Waterford, OH 45786; Civil War artifacts. Historic Buildings: 1835 John Dodge Home & 1886 Oliver Tucker Home; barn.
Research Fields: genealogy.
Facilities: Museum-related items for sale.
Activities: guided tours, with appointment 740-984-2489; permanent exhibitions.
Publications: magazine, Reflections Along The Muskingum; historical booklets on cemetery lots; Bicentennial magazines.
Hours & Admission Prices: June-Aug. Sat.-Sun. 1-4 other times by appointment. No charge; donations accepted. ♿
Attendance: 425 (estimated)
Membership: Lower Muskingum Historical Society: Student $1; Individual $3; Family $5; Life $100.

Bexley

BEXLEY HISTORICAL SOCIETY, 2080 Clifton Ave., Bexley, OH 43209-1405. Mailing Address: P.O. Box 9285, Bexley, OH 43209-0285. Tel.: 614-559-4360. Fax: 614-235-3420.
E-mail: info@bexleyhistory.org
Web Site: www.bexleyhistory.org
Founded: 1974.
Congressional District: 12
Key Personnel: Pres., David Baker; Recording Sec., Nancy Beck; Treas., Gary Seckel; Museum Shop Mgr., Edie Mae Herrel.
Personnel Profile: Part-Time Volunteers 17.
Governing Authority: nonprofit organization. Tax-exempt.
Local History Museum.
Collections: local memorabilia.
Research Fields: local history.
Facilities: 150-vol. library of historical books available for research on premises.
Activities: formally organized education programs for children; loan, permanent & temporary exhibitions.
Hours & Admission Prices: 2nd Mon. of month 6:30pm-8pm; other times by appointment. No charge; donations accepted. Closed holidays. ♿
Attendance: 200 (estimated)
Membership: Senior Citizens $15; General $25; Supporter $50; Patron $100.

Bluffton

THE LION AND LAMB PEACE ARTS CENTER, Bluffton University, 1 University Dr., Bluffton, OH 45817-2104. Tel.: 419-358-3207.
E-mail: lionlamb@bluffton.edu
Web Site: www.bluffton.edu/lionlamb
Founded: 1987.
Key Personnel: Dir., Louise Matthews.
Personnel Profile: Part-Time Paid 1.
Governing Authority: Parent institution: Bluffton University. Tax-exempt.
Arts & Literature Center.
Collections: peace & peace related items; children's literature; book illustrations; children's art; music.
Publications: yearly, 2 newsletters.
Hours & Admission Prices: Call for hours. No charge. ♿

Bolivar

FORT LAURENS STATE MEMORIAL, 11067 Fort Laurens Rd., N.W., Bolivar, OH 44612. Mailing Address: P.O. Box 508, Zoar, OH 44697-0508. Tel.: 330-874-2059. Fax: 330-874-2936.
E-mail: fortlaurens@wilkshire.net
Web Site: ohsweb.ohiohistory.org/places/ne02/index.shtml
Founded: 1972.
Congressional District: 18
Key Personnel: Dir., Victoria Branson.
Personnel Profile: Full-Time Paid 1; Part-Time Paid 2.
Governing Authority: nonprofit. Parent Institution: The Ohio Historical Society, Ohio Historical Center, 1982 Velma Ave., Columbus, OH 43211. Tax-exempt.
Military Fort Museum: site of the only Revolutionary War fort in Ohio; the site of the Tomb of the Unknown Patriot of the Revolutionary War.
Collections: archaeological artifacts from the fort; costumed mannequins; weapons; accoutrements of the American Revolution; video of fort's history.
Facilities: theater; picnic area; 3-mile nature trail.
Activities: audiovisual program.
Hours & Admission Prices: Memorial Day-Labor Day Wed.-Sat. 9:30-5, Sun. & holidays 12-5; Sept.-Oct. Sat. 9:30-5, Sun. 12-5; groups by appointment April-Oct. Adults $3, students $2; discounts to groups, AAM & ICOM members; members & Ohio Historical Society members no charge. ♿
Attendance: 3,873 (accurate)
Membership: Senior Individual $55; Individual $60; Senior Family $70; Family $75.

Bowling Green

AMERICAN CIVIL WAR MUSEUM OF OHIO, 123 E. Court St., Bowling Green, OH 43402. Mailing Address: 21200 Hull Prairie Rd., Bowling Green, OH 43402-8772. Tel.: 419-352-0209.
E-mail: myoungacwmo@aol.com
Governing Authority: Tax-exempt: 501(c)(3).
Civil War History Museum.
Collections: Civil War history; war memorabilia; photographs.
Facilities: Museum-related items for sale.
Publications: newsletter.
Hours & Admission Prices: Tues., Thurs. & Fri. 11-6, Sat. 10-5, Sun. 12-4; other times by appointment. Adults $5, seniors $4, students $2.50.

BOWLING GREEN STATE UNIVERSITY FINE ARTS CENTER GALLERIES, Fine Arts Center, Bowling Green State University, Bowling Green, OH 43403-0001. Tel.: 419-372-8525. Fax: 419-372-2544.
E-mail: galleries@bgsu.edu
Web Site: gallery.bgsu.edu
Founded: 1960.
Congressional District: 5
Key Personnel: Dir., Jacqueline S. Nathan.
Personnel Profile: Full-Time Paid 1; Part-Time Paid 8; Part-Time Volunteers 50; Interns 3.
Governing Authority: public university; nonprofit. Tax-exempt.
Art Gallery.
Collections: prints.
Facilities: glass, sculpture, printmaking, ceramics, photography, design & computer art studios; drawing and painting, fibers & art history lecture room.
Activities: student & faculty exhibits; guided tours; lectures; school loan service; temporary exhibitions of gallery collections; loan & traveling exhibition; National & Regional Invitational Exhibitions. Annual Event: New Music & Art Festival.

Publications: catalogs once or twice a year.
Hours & Admission Prices: May-Aug. call for hours; Sept.-April Tues.-Wed. & Fri.-Sat. 11-4, Thurs. 11-4 & 6pm-9pm, Sun. 1-4. No charge; donations accepted. Closed Yom Kippur; university holidays. ♿
Attendance: 9,000 (estimated)
Membership: Medici Circle $25 & up.

WOOD COUNTY HISTORICAL CENTER AND MUSEUM, (M), 13660 County Home Rd., Bowling Green, OH 43402-9281. Tel.: 419-352-0967. Fax: 419-352-6220.
E-mail: director@woodcountyhistory.org
Web Site: www.woodcountyhistory.org
Founded: 1955.
Congressional District: 5
Key Personnel: Dir., Christie Raber; Education Coord., Michael McMaster; Asst. to Dir., Kelli Kling; Cur., Randolph Brown; Volunteer Coord., Heather Sloane.
Personnel Profile: Full-Time Paid 4; Part-Time Paid 1; Part-Time Volunteers 100; Interns 4.
Governing Authority: society. Parent Institutions: Wood County Commissioners. Tax-exempt: 501(c)(3).
Regional History Museum: housed in a former county infirmary or poor farm on 50-acre site.
Collections: family & regional history; poor farm history; photography; oil boom history; working derrick; drilling equipment; farm & community life; period furniture; decorative arts; farm machinery; medical instruments; crime evidence; Native American artifacts.
Research Fields: Wood County History & Infirmary.
Facilities: arboretum; shelter house; herb garden; nature trails; picnic areas & meeting rooms.
Activities: tours; programs on local history; historical displays; monthly tea series; monthly curator program series. Museum Sponsors: Antique Appraisal Clinic in March; Spring Open House in April; Wood County Heritage Days in June; Power of Yesteryear Antique Tractor Show in June; Historical Society BBQ Fundraiser in June; Vintage Base Ball - Wood County Inmates in August; Halloween Folklore & Funfest in October; Old Home Holiday Tours in December.
Publications: quarterly newsletter, The Black Swamp Chanticleer; book, The Wood County Atlases, 1875-1912, A Century or So of Wood County Weather, 1787-1991; booklet, The Home; A Kid's History of the Wood County Infirmary; Wood County Fields.
Hours & Admission Prices: Tours: April-Oct. & Dec. Tues.-Fri. 9:30-4:30, Sat.-Sun. 1-4; other times by appointment. Suggested Donation: adults $4; discounts to AAM & AAA members; members no charge. Closed holidays. ♿
Attendance: 25,000 (estimated)
Membership: Seniors & Students $10; Individual $15; Family $25; Business $45; Sustaining $60; Patron $100; Life Individual $300; Life Couple $500.

Bradford

BRADFORD OHIO RAILROAD MUSEUM, 200 N. Miami Ave., Bradford, OH 45308-1164. Mailing Address: P.O. Box 101, Bradford, OH 45308-0101. Fax: 740-654-0505.
E-mail: mkosier@brhio.com
Web Site: bradfordrrmuseum.org
Founded: 2002.
Congressional District: 49
Key Personnel: C.E.O. & Pres. (V), Gloria Shafer; Devel., Marilyn Kosier; Chm. (V), Don Wick; Education, Jeremy Martin; Public Rels., Sue Vickroy; Treas., Jordon Ingle; Archivist, Leora Shell; Museum Shop Mgr., Gail Shafer.
Governing Authority: private; nonprofit organization. Tax-exempt: 501(c)(3).
History & Railroad Museum.
Collections: historic railyards; railroad artifacts & tower; photographs.
Activities: walking tour. Annual Events: Salute to the Railroaders; Railroad Days; Hobo Days.
Hours & Admission Prices: April-Dec. Sat. 10-4, Sun. 1-4. Adults $4, seniors $2; members no charge. ♿
Membership: Individual $20.

Brecksville

CUYAHOGA VALLEY NATIONAL PARK, 15610 Vaughn Rd., Brecksville, OH 44141-3097. Tel.: 216-524-1497. Fax: 216-524-2604.
Web Site: www.nps.gov/cuva
Formerly: Cuyahoga Valley National Recreation Area
Founded: 1974.
Congressional District: 10, 11, 13, 14 & 17
Key Personnel: Deputy Supt., Paul J. Stoehr; Chief, Interpretation & Visitor Svcs., Jennie Vasarhelyi.
Governing Authority: federal. National Park Service, Dept. of the Interior, Washington, D.C. Tax-exempt.
Park Museum.
Collections: historic archaeology; historic structures.
Research Fields: zoology; biology; aquatic ecosystems; history; archeology; oral history.
Facilities: reference library; environmental education center; visitor centers.
Activities: interpretive programs; special cultural art events.
Publications: brochures; quarterly, calendar of events.
Hours & Admission Prices: Park: daily. Towpath Trail daily 24 hours; other trails dawn to dusk. Park Visitor Centers: call for hours. No charge; donations accepted. ♿
Attendance: 2,800,000 (accurate)

Brooklyn

BROOKLYN HISTORICAL SOCIETY, 4442 Ridge Rd., Brooklyn, OH 44144-3353. Mailing Address: P.O. Box 44422, Brooklyn, OH 44144-0422. Tel.: 216-941-0160.
E-mail: groundhogsgarden@wowway.com
Founded: 1970.
Congressional District: 10
Key Personnel: Pres. (V), Barbara Stepic; Vice Pres., Elaine Schmidt; Museum Shop Mgr., Ardyce Elaine Steck.
Personnel Profile: Part-Time Volunteers 30; Interns 2.
Governing Authority: society; nonprofit organization. Tax-exempt.
Local History Museum.
Collections: clothes; glass; hair receivers; tools; furniture; period artifacts & memorabilia of Victorian era; clothes; furniture & memorabilia of 1920s; perennials; herb garden including over 60 varieties; World War I; 1941 fire truck; early schools in Brooklyn; Brooklyn High School yearbooks; area high school & college yearbooks; period city records; 1930s-1940s toys; medical artifacts.
Research Fields: genealogy; early school history; city records; voting records; yearbooks.
Facilities: research library. Crafts, herbs & museum-related items for sale.
Activities: guided tours; permanent & temporary exhibitions; school tours; school 25th & 50th reunion tours; talks on history; quilting & rug loom demonstrations. Museum Sponsors: Old-Time Craft Sale in September.
Publications: brochure; tour guide; annual newsletter; docent guide; History of Schools in Brooklyn.
Hours & Admission Prices: Tues. 10-2. No charge; donations accepted. Closed holiday weekends. ♿
Attendance: 1,200 (estimated)
Membership: Student $1.50; Single $5; Couple $7; Life $100.

Bryan

SPANGLER STORE & MUSEUM, 400 N. Portland St., Bryan, OH 43506-1200. Tel.: 419-633-6439; 888-636-4221.
Company Museum.
Collections: company & family history; photographs; machinery; equipment; tools; candy industry.
Facilities: Museum-related items for sale.
Activities: guided tours.
Hours & Admission Prices: Memorial Day to Labor Day Tues.-Fri. 12-5; Winter: Wed.-Fri. 12-5; other times by appointment. Museum: no charge. Tours: adults $5, seniors $4, children 6-18 $3; children 5 & under no charge. Closed New Year's Eve & Day; Good Friday; Memorial Day; Independence Day; Thanksgiving & day after; Christmas Eve & Day.

Bucyrus

BUCYRUS HISTORICAL SOCIETY, 202 S. Walnut St., Bucyrus, OH 44820-2326. Mailing Address: P.O. Box 493, Bucyrus, OH 44820-0493. Tel.: 419-562-6386 & 9073.
Web Site: www.bucyrusonline.com/bhs
Founded: 1969.
Congressional District: 4
Key Personnel: C.E.O., Dr. John K. Kurtz; Cur., Mary Ellen Lust; Cur., Don Lust.
Governing Authority: society; nonprofit. Tax-exempt.
Historical Society Museum: housed in 1839 Scroggs Family Home.
Collections: furniture & furnishings of the period; restored Niagra horse-drawn steam engine c.1826 & Silby hose cart c.1869.
Facilities: library of books available for research on premises.
Activities: guided tours; permanent exhibitions.
Hours & Admission Prices: Mon. 1-4; tours by appointment. No charge; donations accepted. Closed holidays.
Attendance: 600 (estimated)
Membership: Single $7; Life $100; Patron $500.

CRAWFORD AGRICULTURAL MUSEUM, 610 Whetstone St., Bucyrus, OH 44820. Tel.: 419-562-0723.
Agricultural Museum.
Collections: local history & culture; period farm equipment & machinery; farm life.
Activities: guided tours.
Hours & Admission Prices: May-Sept. 1st & 3rd Sun. 1-4.

Burton

CENTURY VILLAGE MUSEUM, 14653 E. Park St., Burton, OH 44021. Mailing Address: P.O. Box 153, Burton, OH 44021-0153. Tel.: 440-834-1492. Fax: 440-834-4012.
Web Site: geaugahistorical.org
Founded: 1938.
Congressional District: 11
Key Personnel: Pres. (V), Kurt Updegraff; Site Mgr. & Museum Shop Mgr., Cheryl McNulty; Office Mgr., Cathy McNeill; Dir. Tours, Rosemary Kneale; Maintenance Supvr., William Troyer.
Personnel Profile: Full-Time Paid 4; Part-Time Paid 12; Part-Time Volunteers 150.
Governing Authority: private; nonprofit organization. Parent Institution: Geauga County Historical Society. Tax-exempt: 501(c)(3).
Historic Village Museum.
Collections: history & development of Geauga County within the Western Reserve; furniture & artifacts of Geauga County; historic homes & buildings forming a recreated 19th-century village; railroad station; caboose; 19th-century farming operation; archival material of local & genealogical interest. Historic Buildings: 1817 William Law House; 1834 Boughton House; 1824 Hitchcock House; 1838 Hickox Brick; 1872 one room schoolhouse; 1850 country store; 1825 blacksmith shop; 1806 Cook House; 1856 red barn; 1850-1889 white barn; 1846 church; 1870 ladies' apparel shop.
Research Fields: genealogy & local history.
Facilities: research library. Country store, gift & craft items for sale.
Activities: guided tours; formally organized education programs for youth. Museum Sponsors: 12 special event weekends during the summer; Apple Butter Festival in October.
Publications: Geauga County Historical Society Quarterly; brochures; pamphlets.
Hours & Admission Prices: April-Nov. Public Tours: Sat.-Sun. 1 & 3. School Tours: by appointment. Adults $7, children 6-12 $4; discounts to AAA & Golden Buckeye members; children under 6 no charge.
Attendance: 47,000 (estimated)
Membership: Senior Citizens $25; Individual $35; Family $55; Silver $100; Gold $250; Platinum $500.

Cadiz

CLARK GABLE MUSEUM, 138 Charleston St., Cadiz, OH 43907. Tel.: 740-942-4989.
Historic House Museum: housed in the birthplace of Clark Gable.
Collections: Clark Gable's personal artifacts; period furnishings; photographs; 1954 Cadillac.
Facilities: Museum-related items for sale.
Hours & Admission Prices: May Tues.-Sat. 10-4; June-Sept. Tues.-Sat. 10-4, Sun. 1:30-4; Oct.-April Tues.-Fri. 10-4. Adults $5.50, seniors $4.75, children $3; discounts to groups of 10 or more. Closed major holidays.

HARRISON COUNTY HISTORY OF COAL MUSEUM, Puskarich Public Library, 200 E. Market St., Cadiz, OH 43907-1214. Tel.: 740-942-2623.
History Museum.
Collections: early mining tools; heavy machinery; working scale model of a dragline; historic photographs.
Hours & Admission Prices: Mon.-Sat. 9-5, Sun. by appointment. No charge.

Cambridge

DEGENHART PAPERWEIGHT & GLASS MUSEUM, INC., 65323 Highland Hills Rd., Intersection of I-77 & Rte. 22, Cambridge, OH 43725. Mailing Address: P.O. Box 186, Cambridge, OH 43725-0186. Tel.: 740-432-2626.
E-mail: degmus@verizon.net
Web Site: degenhartglass.com
Founded: 1978.
Congressional District: 18
Key Personnel: Pres. (V), James Caldwell; Cur. & Membership Coord., Jennifer Hatcher; Staff Asst., Betty Sivard; Staff Asst., Lindsey Hatcher; Staff Asst., Pat Bennett; Staff Asst., Sandra Hill.
Personnel Profile: Full-Time Paid 1; Part-Time Paid 3.
Governing Authority: nonprofit organization. Tax-exempt: 501(c)(3).
Glass & Paperweight Museum.
Collections: Ohio Valley midwestern pattern glass; 20th-century paperweights; blown & cut artglass; decorative items.
Research Fields: art of making glass objects; Ohio Valley glass & paperweights.
Facilities: library of primary & secondary literature of glassware, personal correspondence with reference to glass industry in Pittsburgh & Wheeling, Ohio region c.1920-1950; available by prior arrangements on premises; reading room. Glass novelties, tableware & books on glass for sale.
Activities: films; permanent & temporary exhibitions; workshops.
Publications: quarterly newsletter, Heartbeat.
Hours & Admission Prices: Jan.-May Mon.-Fri. 10-4; mid-May to Dec. Mon.-Sat. 9-5; groups by appointment. Adults $1.50, seniors over 55 & AAA members $1; children under 18 & bus groups of 10 or more no charge. Closed major holidays. ♿
Membership: Individual $5; Family $10; Patron $25.

GUERNSEY COUNTY MUSEUM, 218 N. 8th St., Cambridge, OH 43725-1840. Mailing Address: P.O. Box 741, Cambridge, OH 43725-0741. Tel.: 740-439-5884.
E-mail: curator@gcohmuseum.org
Web Site: www.gcohmuseum.org
Founded: 1963.
Congressional District: 18
Key Personnel: Pres., Linda Atkins; Vice Pres., Hanley Starr; Sec., Paula Murphy; Treas., Mary Jane Downerd; Cur., Kurt Tostenson.
Personnel Profile: Part-Time Paid 1.
Governing Authority: society. Guernsey County Historical Society. Tax-exempt.
General Museum: housed in 1831 McFarland Home.
Collections: glass; military; china; pottery; hand tools; furniture; kitchen ware; Victorian Parlor, Hall of Fame room; ladies boutique; John Glenn room.
Research Fields: genealogy.
Activities: quilt shows; class tours; historical slide programs throughout the county; portrayals of historical men, The Legend of Fighting Bill Reed; Chaplain McFarland.
Publications: brochures.
Hours & Admission Prices: mid-March to mid-Dec. Tues., Thurs. & Sat. 12-3; tours by appointment. Adults $3, children $2; members no charge.
Attendance: 189 (accurate)
Membership: Individual $5; Family $10; Business $25; Life $100.

NATIONAL MUSEUM OF CAMBRIDGE GLASS, 136 S. Ninth St., Cambridge, OH 43725-2453. Mailing Address: P.O. Box 416, Cambridge, OH 43725-0416. Tel.: 740-432-4245.
Web Site: www.cambridgeglass.org
Key Personnel: Chm. (V), Cynthia Arent; Pres. (V), Richard D. Jones.
Governing Authority: Tax-exempt.
Glass Museum.
Collections: glassmaking history; Cambridge glass; period furniture.
Facilities: Museum-related items for sale.
Hours & Admission Prices: April-Oct. Wed.-Sat. 9-4, Sun. 12-4. Adults $4, senior citizens $3; discounts to AAA members; children under 12 no charge. Closed Easter; Independence Day. ♿

Canal Fulton

CANAL FULTON HERITAGE SOCIETY, 116 S. Canal St., Canal Fulton, OH 44614-1104. Tel.: 330-854-3808; 1-800-Helena 3. Fax: 330-854-2013.
E-mail: cfhs@discovercanalfulton.com
Web Site: www.discovercanalfulton.com
Founded: 1968.
Congressional District: 16
Key Personnel: Pres., John Hatfield.
Personnel Profile: Part-Time Paid 1.
Governing Authority: board of trustees; nonprofit organization. Tax-exempt: 501(c)(3).
Historical & Preservation Society.
Collections: furnishings; canal artifacts; photographs; maps. Historic Houses: 1847 Oberlin House; 1870s Heritage House; 1900 Blank House.
Research Fields: local history; Ohio canals.
Facilities: Canal-related items & books & historical books for sale.
Activities: guided tours; lectures; films; docent program or council; canal boat ride on St. Helena III; permanent exhibitions.
Hours & Admission Prices: Heritage House: by appointment. St. Helena III: Summer: Tues.-Sun. 1, 2:30; Fall: Sat.-Sun. 1, 2:30. Oberlin House & Old Canal Days Museum by appointment only. Adults $7, senior citizens $6, children $5, members $1.
Attendance: 10,000

Membership: Student & Single Senior $5; Individual & Senior Couple $10; Family $15; Business $50 & up; Sustaining $50; Contributing $100; Life $1,000.

Canal Winchester

SLATE RUN LIVING HISTORICAL FARM, METRO PARKS, 1375 State Rte. 674 N., Canal Winchester, OH 43110-9406. Tel.: 614-833-1880. Fax: 614-834-1220. TDD: 614-895-6240.
Web Site: www.metroparks.net/ParksSlateRunFarm.aspx
Founded: 1981.
Key Personnel: C.E.O., John O'Meara; Dir. Farm Program, Ann Culek.
Personnel Profile: Full-Time Paid 5; Part-Time Paid 2; Part-Time Volunteers 60; Interns 1.
Governing Authority: Franklin County Metro Parks. Tax-exempt.
Historic Site: 1856 house; 1881 barn.
Collections: agricultural implements & machinery; household goods; buildings; livestock.
Research Fields: 1880-1900 mid-Ohio agriculture & social life; local history.
Activities: guided & self-guided tours; organized education programs; docent program.
Publications: monthly newsletter, Slate.
Hours & Admission Prices: April-May & Sept.-Oct. Tues.-Sat. 9-4, Sun. 11-4; June-Aug. Tues.-Thurs. 9-4, Fri.-Sat. 9-6, Sun. 11-6; Nov.-March Wed.-Sat. 9-4, Sun. 11-4. No charge. Closed New Year's Day; Thanksgiving; Christmas. ♿
Attendance: 40,000 (estimated)

Canfield

THE WAR VET MUSEUM, 23 E. Main St., Canfield, OH 44406-1360. Tel.: 330-533-6311.
E-mail: warvetmuseum@gmail.com
Web Site: www.warvetmuseum.org
Key Personnel: Owner & Operator, Lew Speece
Military Museum.
Collections: over 36,000 artifacts from all periods of U.S. history; model trains; photographs.
Hours & Admission Prices: Call for hours.

Canton

CANTON CLASSIC CAR MUSEUM, 555 Market Ave. S., Canton, OH 44702-2111. Mailing Address: 612 Market Ave. S., Canton, OH 44702-2114. Tel.: 330-455-3603. Fax: 330-455-0363.
E-mail: char@cantonclassiccar.org
Web Site: www.cantonclassiccar.org
Founded: 1978.
Congressional District: 14
Key Personnel: Dir., Char Lautzenheiser; Chm. (V), Florence Belden; Pres. (V), Marshall Belden, Jr.; Financial Dir., Timothy Belden; Operations Mgr., Gary Pelger; Sr. Cur., Al Parsons; Cur., Norman Munson; Admissions, Dennis Dickey.
Personnel Profile: Full-Time Paid 2; Part-Time Paid 5; Part-Time Volunteers 6; Interns 1.
Governing Authority: private; nonprofit organization. Tax-exempt.
Automobile Museum.
Collections: pre-World War II domestic vehicles; memorabilia; post World War II vehicles.
Research Fields: study of Lincoln Highway.
Facilities: 1,000-vol. library of automotive history; 20,000 sq. ft. exhibit space. Gift items for sale.
Activities: formal education programs; guided tours.
Publications: quarterly newsletter, CCCM News.
Hours & Admission Prices: Daily 10-5. Adults $7.50, senior citizens $6, children 6-18 $5; discounts to AAA, tour & family groups; members & children under 6 no charge. Closed New Year's Day; Easter; Thanksgiving; Christmas. ♿
Attendance: 10,000 (estimated)
Membership: Individual $25; w/Spouse $35; Family $50; Sustaining $250; Life $1,000; Corporate $5,000.

* **THE CANTON MUSEUM OF ART, (M),** 1001 Market Ave. N., Canton, OH 44702-1075. Tel.: 330-453-7666. Fax: 330-453-1034.
E-mail: staff@cantonart.org
Web Site: www.cantonart.org
Founded: 1935.
Congressional District: 16
Key Personnel: Exec. Dir., M. J. Albacete; Pres. (V), Joseph Lapinski; Business Mgr., Kay McAllister; Mktg. Mgr., Mary Byrne; Coord. Education, Lauren Kuntzman.
Personnel Profile: Full-Time Paid 6; Full-Time Volunteers 1; Part-Time Paid 7; Part-Time Volunteers 125; Interns 2.
Governing Authority: nonprofit organization. Tax-exempt: 501(c)(3).
Art Center and Museum.
Collections: 19th-20th century American art; watercolors; works on paper; contemporary ceramics; European art.
Research Fields: American watercolor.
Facilities: 2,500-vol. library; education wing; sculpture courtyard.
Activities: lectures; films; formally organized education programs; docent program; permanent, temporary & traveling exhibits. Museum Sponsors; arts & craft festival.
Publications: class schedules; exhibition catalogs; annual report.
Hours & Admission Prices: Tues.-Thurs. 10-8, Fri. 10-5, Sat. 10-3, Sun. 1-5. Adults $6, senior citizens & college students $4; discounts to AAM members; children 12 & under and members no charge. Closed New Year's Day; Memorial Day; Independence Day; Labor Day; Thanksgiving; Christmas. ♿
Attendance: 35,121 (accurate)
Membership: Student $15; Individual $30; Family $55; Gallery Circle $100; Director's Circle $300; Life $2,500.

MCKINLEY PRESIDENTIAL LIBRARY & MUSEUM, 800 McKinley Monument Dr., N.W., Canton, OH 44708-4832. Mailing Address: P.O. Box 20070, Canton, OH 44701-0070. Tel.: 330-455-7043. Fax: 330-455-1137.
E-mail: mmuseum@neo.rr.com
Web Site: www.mckinleymuseum.org
Founded: 1946.
Congressional District: 16
Key Personnel: Dir., Joyce Yut; Pres. (V), Robert F. Belden; Vice Pres., Don Deitemyer; Cur., Kimberly Kenney; Sec., Robert Leibensperger; Treas., Dennis Fulmer; Asst. Sec., Treas. & Museum Shop Mgr., Cindy Sober; Dir. Planetarium, David Richards; Dir. Education, Chris Kenney; Dir. Science, Lynette Reiner; Volunteer Dir., Stephanie Span; Librarian, Karl Ash; Office Mgr., Rita Zwick.
Personnel Profile: Full-Time Paid 6; Part-Time Paid 22; Part-Time Volunteers 130.
Governing Authority: nonprofit organization. Parent Institution: Stark County Historical Society. Tax-exempt: 501(c)(3).
History, Science & Comprehensive Family Museum.
Collections: archives; astronomy; glass; natural and physical science; architecture; ceramics; clocks & watches; decorative arts; industrial & natural history; transportation; Street of Shops; 96 ft. replica of HO train; Foucault Pendulum; dolls; toys; Dueber-Hampden watches; McKinley memorabilia & history; Discover World: natural history; current ecosystem; Space Ship Earth.
Major Exhibits: Life in Miniature, 1/10-2/14/10; Quilt Exhibit, 2/26/10-6/6/10; The Victorian Age, 6/18/10-11/21/10; White House Gardens (T), 12/3/10-1/30/11.
Research Fields: astronomy; Stark County history; Pres. William McKinley; Paleo-Indians.
Facilities: 5,000-vol. library of books on McKinley, Stark County, Ohio, Civil War, Spanish American War available on premises; planetarium; science center; 250-seat auditorium; classrooms; McKinley National Memorial & grounds. Museum-related items for sale.
Activities: guided tours; lectures; films; formally organized education programs for children; interactive science exhibits,
Publications: bimonthly newsletter; brochure, Discover World; planetarium brochure; teacher's guide; schedule of classes; books, The McKinley Monument A Tribute to a Fallen President; Canton's West Lawn Cemetery; Canton A Journey Through Time; The Wm. McKinley Presidential Library & Museum; Canton Pioneers in Flight.
Hours & Admission Prices: Mon.-Sat. 9-4, Sun. 12-4. Adults $7, senior citizens $6, children 3-18 $5; discounts to adult groups over 20 & ASTC reciprocity members; museum members & children under 3 no charge. Closed New Year's Day; Easter; Memorial Day; Labor Day; Thanksgiving; Christmas Day. ♿
Attendance: 45,000 (accurate)
Membership: Individual $37; Family $49; Celestial $80; Silver $140; Gold $300; Diamond $575; William McKinley Circle $1,700; Individual Lifetime $5,000.

NATIONAL FIRST LADIES' LIBRARY, (M), 331 S. Market Ave., Canton, OH 44702-2107. Tel.: 330-452-0876. Fax: 330-445-2008.
E-mail: pkrider@firstladies.org
Web Site: www.firstladies.org
Founded: 1998.
Congressional District: 16
Key Personnel: Exec. Dir., Patricia Krider; Pres. (V), Mary Regula; Education, Lucinda Frailly; Museum Shop Mgr., Mary Rhodes.

Personnel Profile: Full-Time Paid 6; Part-Time Paid 5; Part-Time Volunteers 28; Interns 1.
Governing Authority: private; nonprofit organization. Tax-exempt: 501(c)(3).
History Museum.
Collections: contributions by First Ladies to our nation; clothing; photographs; letters; audiovisual.
Facilities: 3,000-vol. library; 90-seat auditorium; educational facilities; 10,000 sq. ft. exhibit space. Museum-related items for sale.
Activities: formal education programs; guided tours; lectures; participatory & temporary exhibits; auditorium.
Publications: biannual newsletter.
Hours & Admission Prices: Guided Tours: June-Aug. Tues.-Sat. 9:30, 10:30, 12:30, 1:30 & 2:30, Sun. 12:30, 1:30 & 2:30; Sept.-May Tues.-Sat. 9:30, 10:30, 12:30, 1:30 & 2:30. Adults $7, senior citizens $6, students $5. Closed major holidays. ♿
Attendance: 8,500 (estimated)
Membership: Individual $50; Inaugural Circle $100; Ida Saxton McKinley Circle $250; Executive Circle $500; First Ladies' Inner Circle $1,000; Heritage Circle $5,000.

NATIONAL FOOTBALL MUSEUM, INC., (M), 2121 George Halas Dr., N.W., Canton, OH 44708-2630. Tel.: 330-456-8207. Fax: 330-456-8175 & 9080 (Library).
Web Site: www.profootballhof.com
Founded: 1963.
Congressional District: 16
Key Personnel: Pres. & Exec. Dir., Stephen Perry; Chm. (V) & Cur. Collections, Jason Aikens; Vice Pres. Retail Sales & Licensing, Steve Strawbridge; Vice Pres. & C.F.O., D. William Allen; Vice Pres. Communications & Exhibits, Joe Horrigan; Vice Pres. Mktg. & Operations, Dave Motts; Registrar, Christy Lake; Information Svcs. Mgr., Pete Fierle; Operations Mgr., Kevin Shiplet; Education Program Coord., Jerry Csaki; Researcher, Saleem Choudhry; Museum Shop Mgr., Michelle Hunt; Communications Asst., Chris Schilling; Information Svcs. Specialist, Chad Reese; Event Mktg. Specialist, Gail McLaughlin.
Personnel Profile: Full-Time Paid 34; Part-Time Paid 40; Part-Time Volunteers 300; Interns 6.
Governing Authority: nonprofit organization. Tax-exempt: 501(c)(3).
Professional Football Museum.
Collections: mementoes from the games & players including equipment, photos, films; videotapes; material pertinent to the development of pro football in the U.S.; printed game accounts; files on players, games & circumstances contributing to football's growth; artists' works, illustrations, photos & paintings; Hall of Fame Enshrinement; enshrinee mementoes room; historical displays.
Research Fields: professional football history.
Facilities: 3,000-vol. library of material on professional football, available for use on premises or through correspondence with personnel by mail; 350-seat theater; turnable theater featuring NFL action in Cinemascope; snack shop. Officially licensed National Football League items for sale.
Activities: films; fan activated videos; interactive exhibits.
Publications: annual magazine, Pro Football Hall of Fame Yearbook; newsletter 3 times a year, Insider.
Hours & Admission Prices: Memorial Day-Labor Day daily 9-8; Sept.-May daily 9-5. Adults $18, senior citizens $15, children 6-14 $12; discount to groups & AAM members; children 5 & under, members and Insider's Club members no charge. Closed Christmas. ♿
Attendance: 196,351 (accurate)
Membership: Youth $25; Player $50; Team $100; Coach $500; Owner $1,000.

Carrollton

BLUEBIRD FARM TOY MUSEUM, 190 Alamo Rd., Carrollton, OH 44615-9581. Tel.: 330-627-7980.
Toy Museum.
Collections: toys from the 1700s to present; wooden, wax, china, French & German bisque, mechanical papier-mache, & cloth dolls; Teddy bears; stuffed animals; Raggedy Ann & Andy; Shirley Temple; Mickey & Minnie Mouse; toy china sets; period dollhouses.
Facilities: Museum-related items for sale.
Hours & Admission Prices: Call for hours.

MCCOOK HOUSE, CIVIL WAR MUSEUM, Public Square (west side), Carrollton, OH 44615. Mailing Address: P.O. Box 174, Carrollton, OH 44615-0174. Tel.: 330-627-3345; 800-600-7172. Fax: 330-627-5366.
Web Site: www.ohiohistory.org/places/mcookhse/
Founded: 1963.
Congressional District: 18
Key Personnel: Mgr., Cur. & Museum Shop Mgr., Shirley Anderson; Pres. (V), Thomas Konst; Vice Pres., Marcia Stertzbach; Sec., Diane George.
Personnel Profile: Part-Time Paid 1; Part-Time Volunteers 10.
Governing Authority: state; nonprofit. Parent Institution: Ohio Historical Society. Subsidiary Institution: Carroll County Historical Society. Tax-exempt: 501(c)(3).
History Museum.
Collections: local history; military items; period medical instruments and textiles; local pottery. Historic House: 1837 McCook house.
Research Fields: military.
Facilities: 35-vol. collection of local newspapers.
Activities: guided tours.
Publications: quarterly newsletter, Carroll County Historical Society News.
Hours & Admission Prices: Memorial Day to Labor Day Fri.-Sat. 10-5, Sun. 1-5; Sept. to mid-Oct. Sat. 10-5, Sun. 1-5; tours by appointment. Adults $3, senior citizens & AAA members $2.50, children 6-12 $1; Carroll Co. Historical Society & Ohio Historical Society members no charge.
Attendance: 1,195 (accurate)
Membership: Student $2; Individual $6; Family $10; Institutional $50; Life Individual $100; Life Couple $150; Life Business $200.

Celina

MERCER COUNTY HISTORICAL MUSEUM, THE RILEY HOME, 130 E. Market, Celina, OH 45822-1731. Mailing Address: P.O. Box 512, Celina, OH 45822-1731. Tel.: 419-678-2614.
E-mail: histalig@bright.net
Founded: 1959.
Congressional District: 8
Key Personnel: Pres. (V), Joyce L. Alig.
Personnel Profile: Part-Time Volunteers 125.
Governing Authority: society; nonprofit. Parent Institution: Mercer County Historical Society. Tax-exempt: 501(c)(3).
Historical Society Museum: housed in 1896 the Riley home.
Collections: archives of Mercer County history; agriculture; carpenter's & blacksmith's tools; period furniture; school display; costume collections; glassware; guns; Indian artifacts; medical, dental & health display; art; archival collections of Mercer County history & Capt. James Riley heritage; 1898-1900 Ohioans in Alaska gold rush.
Research Fields: Mercer County history & genealogy; Captain James Riley & the Riley family; James Zura Riley, Alaska & Yukon Gold rush, 1898-1900.
Facilities: 1,000-vol. library of books on Mercer County history, Ohio & American history.
Activities: guided tours; lectures; films; gallery talks; study clubs; TV programs; formally organized education programs; temporary & permanent exhibitions.
Publications: quarterly, Mercer County Historical Society Newsletter; museum brochure; books: 1978 Mercer County History; History of Celina, Ohio, 1834-1984; History of St. Henry, Ohio, 1837-1987; Coldwater Sesquicentennial 1838-1988; Native Americans & Early Settlers; The Meeting of Cultures, 1780's-1980's; Those Magnificent Big Barns of Mercer County of Western Ohio; Mercer County Centennial Buildings; Ohio's Last Frontiersman, Captain James Riley; Mercer County, Ohio's Courthouses 1824-1998; Mercer County, Ohio: History of the Land Between the St. Marys & Wabash River Valleys; Old Gold Rush to Alaska Diaries, 1898-1900, A True Story; Mercer County, Ohio Fair, 1852-2002; German-American Death Card Collection, 2 Vols.; Celina, Ohio, Our Post Card Past; Rockford, Ohio, Our Post Card Past; Mercer County, Ohio, Our Post Card Past; Grand Lake St. Marys, Ohio, Our Post Card Past; Passport to Mercer County, Ohio History: Granville Township; St. Henry, Burkettsville, Cranberry Prairie, Himmelgarten Convent & St. Marys Novitiate (2007).
Hours & Admission Prices: by appointment only. No charge. ♿
Attendance: 6,000 (accurate)
Membership: Membership fee voluntary.

Centerville

CENTERVILLE - WASHINGTON TOWNSHIP HISTORICAL SOCIETY & ASAHEL WRIGHT COMMUNITY CENTER, 26 N. Main St., Centerville, OH 45459-4619. Tel.: 937-291-2223. Fax: 937-432-9296.
Web Site: www.mvcc.net/centerville/histsoc
Founded: 1966.
Key Personnel: Pres., Ray Turton; Admin., Vickie Bondi; Administrative Asst., Peggy Brooker; Coord. Education, Marcia Rouse.
Personnel Profile: Part-Time Paid 4; Part-Time Volunteers 30.
Governing Authority: private; nonprofit corporation. Parent Institution: Centerville - Washington Township Historical Society, 89 W. Franklin St., Centerville, OH 45459. Tax exempt: 501(c)(3).
Historic House Museum: housed in the former home of the Wright Brothers great uncle.
Collections: furnishings & personal artifacts depicting life in the early 1800s.
Facilities: library; classroom. Museum-related items for sale.

Activities: formal education programs; guided tours; lectures; broadcast programs. Annual Events: Victorian Tea; July 4th Americana Festival; Autumn Ball.
Publications: monthly newsletter, The Curator.
Hours & Admission Prices: Tues.-Fri. 12-4. Gift Shop: Tues.-Sat. 12-4. No charge; donations accepted. Closed New Year's; Thanksgiving; Christmas.
Attendance: 1,500 (estimated)
Membership: Individual Senior over 60 $20; Individual: $25; Family $35; Business: $45; Sustaining $50; Patron: $100; Life $500; Angel $1,000; Benefactor $5,000.

CENTERVILLE - WASHINGTON TOWNSHIP HISTORICAL SOCIETY & WALTON HOUSE MUSEUM, 89 W. Franklin St., Centerville, OH 45459-4735. Tel.: 937-433-0123. Fax: 937-424-4629.
E-mail: cwths@sbcglobal.net
Web Site: www.mvcc.net/centerville/histsoc
Founded: 1966.
Congressional District: 3
Key Personnel: Dir., Vickie Bondi; Pres. (V), Roy Turton; Museum Shop Mgr., Cherie Nelson.
Personnel Profile: Part-Time Paid 7; Part-Time Volunteers 50.
Governing Authority: private; nonprofit organization. Branch Museums: Walton House Museum, Centerville, OH; Asahel Wright Community & Visitor Center, Centerville, OH. Tax-exempt.
History Museum.
Collections: area artifacts, data & information; family histories; landmark files; society archives.
Facilities: library; research center.
Activities: summer youth classes; monthly speaker series; spring and fall fundraising events.
Publications: local historical books & publications; monthly newsletter.
Hours & Admission Prices: Tues.-Fri. 12-4, Sat. by appointment. No charge; donations accepted.
Attendance: 5,000 (estimated)
Membership: Individual $25; Family $35; Business $50; Friend $100; Patron $250; Supporter $500; Benefactor $1,000.

Chagrin Falls

CHAGRIN FALLS HISTORICAL SOCIETY, 21 Walnut St., Chagrin Falls, OH 44022-3125. Tel.: 440-247-4695.
Founded: 1949.
Congressional District: 22
Key Personnel: Co Pres., S.R. Zalba; Co Pres., JoAnn Roeder; Cur., Pat E. Zalba; Photograph Collection, Zo Sykora; Librarian, Arline Moore.
Personnel Profile: Part-Time Volunteers 50.
Governing Authority: society. Tax-exempt: 501(c)(3).
Historical Society Museum.
Collections: doll collection of Marian Jencick; costumes; household articles; china; Bullard butter molds; glassware; regional art & artifacts; Ober, Williams & Chagrin Falls Manufacturing Co. sad irons & stands; paintings & information on primitive artist Henry Church, Jr. paintings & history, native of Chagrin Falls; Max Barnard paintings, birdhouses & history; photographs of early C.F. industries; village; homes; schools; transportation; people; organizations (1870s to present day); Williams cast iron banks.
Research Fields: village history; genealogy; relating to items in museum.
Facilities: library of c.1874-1964 newspapers, The Chagrin Falls Exponent available.
Activities: guided tours; formally organized education programs; permanent & temporary exhibitions; monthly program meeting open to public; old-time baseball games played by 1860s rules, featuring The Forest Citys versus other historical society sponsored teams throughout the region. Museum Sponsors: biennial house tour; Christmas Season Open House.
Publications: monthly newsletter; pamphlet, Village Victorian; books, Annie's Anecdotes; The Drawings of Max Barnard; cookbook, Taste of the Past; Chagrin Falls; Whence the Name; pamphlet, How to Care for Your Historic Home; video, Chagrin Falls: A Look at Our Past; book, Chagrin Falls: An Ohio Village History; books, The Stranahan Folding Canvas Boat Company of Chagrin Falls; The History of the Ober Manufacturing Company of Chagrin Falls, 1862-1959; History of the Chagrin Hardware Company.
Hours & Admission Prices: Thurs. 2-4; other times by appointment. No charge; donations accepted. Closed holidays.
Attendance: 2,500 (estimated)
Membership: Annual $10; Family $15; Sustaining $25; Corporate $50; Life $100.

Chillicothe

ADENA MANSION AND GARDENS, 847 Adena Rd., Chillicothe, OH 45601-1380. Mailing Address: P.O. Box 831, Chillicothe, OH 45601-0831. Tel.: 740-772-1500; 800-319-7248. Fax: 740-775-2746.
E-mail: jrupp@ohiohistory.org
Web Site: www.ohiohistory.org/places/adena/
Formerly: Adena State Memorial, The Home of Thomas Worthington
Founded: 1946.
Congressional District: 6
Key Personnel: Operations Mgr., R. Warnock.
Personnel Profile: Full-Time Paid 4; Part-Time Paid 5; Part-Time Volunteers 30.
Governing Authority: society; nonprofit. Parent Institution: Ohio Historical Society, Ohio Historical Center, Columbus, OH 43211-2497. Tax-exempt.
Historic House Restoration: 1806-1807 original mansion of Ohio's sixth governor & first senator, Thomas Worthington.
Collections: American furniture & furnishings, 1760-1830; settlement of Ohio; Ohio's path to statehood; Thomas Worthington family artifacts; outbuildings.
Research Fields: history of Worthington & Swearingen families.
Facilities: education center; gardens.
Activities: guided tours; public programs. Annual Event: Heirloom Plant Sale.
Hours & Admission Prices: June-Sept. Wed.-Sat. 10-5, Sun. 12-5; Oct. Sat. 10-5, Sun. 12-5. Adults $8, children 6-12 $4; discounts to senior citizens, AAM & AAA members; OHS members and children 5 & under no charge. Closed New Year's Day; Memorial Day; Independence Day; Labor Day; Thanksgiving; Christmas. ♿
Attendance: 11,000 (accurate)
Membership: See separate listing for Ohio Historical Center.

THE FRIENDS OF LUCY HAYES HERITAGE CENTER, 90 W. Sixth St., Chillicothe, OH 45601-3838. Mailing Address: P.O. Box 1790, Chillicothe, OH 45601-5790. Tel.: 740-775-5829 (center). Fax: 740-775-5829.
E-mail: lucy@lucyhayes.org
Web Site: www.lucyhayes.org
Founded: 1996.
Congressional District: 6
Key Personnel: Pres. (V), Jane Friedman; Treas., Linda Barrett; Sec., Melody Smith.
Personnel Profile: Part-Time Volunteers 20.
Governing Authority: private; nonprofit organization. Tax-exempt: 501(c)(3).
General Museum: restored birthplace of First Lady Lucy Hayes.
Collections: pictures; pamphlets of speeches; White House invitations; civil war memorabilia; postcards; letters; Hayes family personal artifacts; Empire Style furniture; replica of the birthplace; 1876 newspapers; hooked rug, Lucy doll.
Activities: guided tours; loan exhibitions; meeting room. Annual Events: Ohio Statehood Day; open house & program; bus tours to historical sites; ice cream & cake social in August; Annual Holiday Dinner.
Publications: quarterly newsletter, News From The Board - Lucy Hayes Heritage Center.
Hours & Admission Prices: April-Sept. Mon. 10-2, Sat. 1-4; other times by appointment. Adults $4, children $2; members no charge. Closed Good Friday; Memorial Day weekend.
Attendance: 425 (accurate)
Membership: Individual $10; Family $20; Organization $25.

HOPEWELL CULTURE NATIONAL HISTORICAL PARK, 16062 State Rte. 104, Chillicothe, OH 45601-9701. Tel.: 740-774-1126. Fax: 740-774-1140.
E-mail: hocu_superintendent@nps.gov
Web Site: www.nps.gov/hocu
Founded: 1923.
Congressional District: 7
Governing Authority: federal. Parent Institution: U.S. Dept. of the Interior, National Park Service. Tax-exempt.
Park Museum: 200 B.C.-500 A.D., Hopewell Indian earthwork.
Collections: archaeological artifacts from Hopewell culture who built earthen mounds & embankments between 200 B.C. and A.D. 500; items from World War I army training facility, Camp Sherman.
Research Fields: archaeological; local history.
Facilities: 1,000-vol. library on Native American culture, particularly the Hopewell culture, and National Park Service; Visitor Center; environmental study area. Printed material, postcards, booklets, replicas of artifacts for sale.
Activities: guided tours; lectures; formally organized education programs for children; permanent & temporary exhibitions.
Publications: biannual newsletter, Hopewell Happenings; newsletter, Hopewell Archeology.

Hours & Admission Prices: Visitor's Center: Memorial Day to Labor Day daily 8:30-6; Sept.-May daily 8:30-5. No charge. Closed New Year's Day; Thanksgiving; Christmas. ♿
Attendance: 30,000 (accurate)
Membership: Senior $10; Annual $80.

ROSS COUNTY HISTORICAL SOCIETY, INC., 45 W. 5th St., Chillicothe, OH 45601-3227. Tel.: 740-772-1936.
E-mail: info@rosscountyhistorical.org
Web Site: www.rosscountyhistorical.org
Founded: 1896.
Congressional District: 6
Key Personnel: C.E.O. & Museum Shop Mgr., Thomas G. Kuhn; Pres. (V), Pat Medert.
Personnel Profile: Full-Time Paid 2; Part-Time Paid 6; Part-Time Volunteers 25.
Governing Authority: society; nonprofit. Parent Institution: Ross County Historical Society. Tax-exempt: 501(c)(3).
General Museum.
Collections: prehistoric artifacts; manuscripts; pioneer tools; household furnishings; 19th to 20th-century toys & costumes; naval paintings of Admiral Henry W. Walke; Ohio's Constitution Table from 1800-1816 when Chillicothe was capital of the Northwest Territory & first capital of Ohio; pioneer crafts; early state & local history; Civil War & WWII vehicles; portrait gallery. Historic Houses: 1838 William T. & Elizabeth A. McClintick Home; 1838 David McCandless McKell Library; 1901 Marianne & Charles Franklin Home devoted to the role of the 19th-century woman; 1827 Knoles Log House.
Research Fields: Indian artifacts; early statehood documents.
Facilities: 12,000-vol. library of 19th-century books & manuscripts with emphasis on Ohio History; McKell collection of early children's books, illuminated manuscripts, incunabula & prints available for use by request. Postcards & other museum-related items for sale.
Activities: guided tours; lectures; films; permanent & temporary exhibitions.
Publications: postcards; booklets; newsletter.
Hours & Admission Prices: Jan.-March by appointment only; April-Dec. Tues.-Sat. 1-5. Adults $4, senior citizens & students $2; discounts to AAM, ICOM & AAA members; members & Ross County School classes no charge. Closed major holidays. ♿
Attendance: 5,000 (accurate)
Membership: Youth $10; Individual $20; Family $30; Contributing $75; Business $100; Life $500; Patron $750; Benefactor $1,000.

Cincinnati

AMERICAN CLASSICAL MUSIC HALL OF FAME AND MUSEUM, 1225 Elm St., Cincinnati, OH 45202-7531. Tel.: 800-499-3263. Fax: 513-621-1563.
Founded: 1995.
Congressional District: 1
Key Personnel: Exec. Dir., Stefan A. Skirtz; Pres. Bd. Trustees (V), Robert Fitzpatrick; Trustee Treas., Richard M. Adams.
Personnel Profile: Full-Time Paid 2.
Governing Authority: private; nonprofit organization. Tax-exempt: 501(c)(3).
Music History Museum.
Collections: artifacts reflecting the many facets of classical music in U.S.
Facilities: 100-seat auditorium.
Activities: interactive exhibits & displays.
Publications: annual commemorative book of current inductees.
Hours & Admission Prices: Mon.-Fri. 9-4:30. No charge. Closed New Year's Day; Independence Day; Thanksgiving; Christmas; major holidays.
Attendance: 2,500 (estimated)
Membership: Ambassador $50 & up.

AMERICAN SIGN MUSEUM, 2515 Essex Place, Cincinnati, OH 45206-1955. Mailing Address: 11262 Cornell Park Dr., Cincinnati, OH 45242-1812. Tel.: 513-258-4020. Fax: 513-421-5144.
E-mail: tod@signmuseum.org
Web Site: www.signmuseum.org
Founded: 1999.
Key Personnel: Dir. & Pres., Tod Swormstedt; Devel., John Johnson; Treas., Brian Foos.
Personnel Profile: Full-Time Paid 1; Part-Time Paid 1; Part-Time Volunteers 4.
Governing Authority: private; nonprofit organization. Tax-exempt: 501(c)(3).
Sign Museum.
Collections: signs from all over the United States; history of technology & advertising in America; photographs.
Facilities: library; 5,500 sq. ft. exhibit space. Museum-related items for sale.
Activities: guided tours; participatory & temporary exhibitions; receptions.
Publications: quarterly newsletter, American Sign Museum.
Hours & Admission Prices: By appointment. Adults $10; discounts to groups. Closed Thanksgiving week. ♿
Attendance: 2,196 (accurate)
Membership: Basic $35; Family $50; Friend $100; Supporter $500; Corporate $1,000; Sustaining $2,500.

BETTS HOUSE RESEARCH CENTER, 416 Clark St., Cincinnati, OH 45203-1423. Tel.: 513-651-0734. Fax: 513-651-0734.
E-mail: bettshouserc@fuse.net
Web Site: bettshouse.org
Founded: 1995.
Congressional District: 1
Key Personnel: Exec. Dir., Julie Carpenter; Pres. (V), Murray Monroe, Jr.; Treas., Sam Minkarah; Sec., Laura Chace.
Personnel Profile: Part-Time Paid 1; Part-Time Volunteers 15.
Governing Authority: private; nonprofit. Tax-exempt: 501(c)(3).
Historic Building: 1804 farm house with mid- & late-19th-century additions.
Collections: items relating to the history of the building & building materials.
Major Exhibits: Multi Family Housing in Cincinnati (T), 4/10-9/10.
Research Fields: evolution of building materials from 1800 to present.
Activities: guided tours; lectures. Museum Sponsors: Bond At The Betts House, a taste of trades mini-camp for youth.
Hours & Admission Prices: Tues.-Thurs. 11-2; other times by appointment. Adults $2; discounts to AAM & ICOM members; members no charge. Closed federal holidays.
Attendance: 929 (accurate)
Membership: Individual $35.

CARY COTTAGE, Clovernook Center for the Blind and Visually Impaired, 7000 Hamilton Ave., Cincinnati, OH 45231-5240. Tel.: 513-522-3860. Fax: 513-728-3946. TDD: 513-522-3860.
E-mail: clovernook@clovernook.org
Web Site: www.clovernook.org
Founded: 1903.
Congressional District: 1
Key Personnel: Pres. & C.E.O., Robin Usalis.
Governing Authority: nonprofit organization. Parent Institution: The Clovernook Center for the Blind. Tax-exempt.
Historic House: 1832 home of poets Alice & Phoebe Cary.
Collections: 1832-1850 period furnishings; kitchen herb garden; literature pertaining to Cary sisters.
Activities: guided tours by appt.; permanent exhibitions; special events.
Publications: brochures.
Hours & Admission Prices: Tours by appointment. No charge; donations accepted.
Attendance: 150 (estimated)

CINCINNATI ART GALLERIES, 225 E. Sixth St., Cincinnati, OH 45202-3209. Tel.: 513-381-2128. Fax: 513-381-7527.
E-mail: sandlers@cincyart.com
Web Site: www.cincinnatiartgalleries.com
Art Gallery.
Collections: 19th & 20th century American and European paintings; sculpture; pottery; art glass.
Hours & Admission Prices: Winter: Mon.-Fri. 9-5, Sat. 10-4. Summer: Mon.-Fri. 9-4, Sat. 10-4.

* **CINCINNATI ART MUSEUM, (M),** 953 Eden Park Dr., Cincinnati, OH 45202-1596. Tel.: 513-639-2954. Fax: 513-639-2888.
E-mail: information@cincyart.org
Web Site: www.cincinnatiartmuseum.org
Founded: 1881.
Congressional District: 1
Key Personnel: Dir., Aaron Betsky; Deputy Dir. Institutional Advancement, Patricia Hynes; Deputy Dir. Operations, Debbie Bowman; Deputy Dir. Curatorial, Anita Ellis; Deputy Dir. Presentation, Stephen Jaycox; Cur. Prints, Kristin Spangenberg; Cur. Contemporary Art, Jessica Flores Garcia; Cur. American Art, Julie Aronson; Cur. Decorative Arts & Designs, Amy Dehan; Cur. Fashion Arts & Textiles, Cindy Amneus; Cur. Asian Art, Hou-mei Sung; Museum Shop Mgr., Deborah Molzberger.
Personnel Profile: Full-Time Paid 107; Part-Time Paid 115; Interns 10.
Governing Authority: nonprofit organization. Parent Institution: Cincinnati Museum Assoc. Tax-exempt: 501(c)(3).
Art Museum.
Collections: ancient art; Egyptian, Greek, Roman, Indian, Chinese, Japanese, Islamic, Nabatean, near & far Eastern and medieval art; 16th- to 20th-century European painting & sculptures; 18th- to 20th-century American

paintings; 18th- to 19th-century portrait miniatures; decorative arts; costumes; textiles; musical instruments; contemporary art; African & Native American art.
Facilities: 53,000-vol. library of material pertaining to art available for inter-library loan & use on premises; auditorium; lecture hall; restaurant. Museum-related items for sale.
Activities: guided tours; lectures; gallery talks; formally organized education programs; inter-museum loan, permanent & special exhibitions; evenings for educators; speakers bureau.
Publications: exhibition catalogues; permanent collection catalogues; publications brochure.
Hours & Admission Prices: Tues.-Sun. 11-5. No charge; donations accepted. Closed New Year's Day; Independence Day; Thanksgiving; Christmas. ♿
Attendance: 228,745 (accurate)
Membership: Individual $45; Dual $60; Family $75; Supporting $125; Associate $250; Fellow $500; Founders Society $1,000.

CINCINNATI CHRISTIAN UNIVERSITY, 2700 Glenway Ave., Cincinnati, OH 45204-1738. Tel.: 513-244-8100 & 8445. Fax: 513-244-8140.
E-mail: sara.fudge@ccuniversity.edu
Key Personnel: Dir., Sara Fudge.
Governing Authority: private; nonprofit organization.
Religious Museum.
Collections: period Near Eastern, Greek & Roman artifacts; minerals.
Facilities: library; educational facilities; 100 sq. ft. exhibit space.
Activities: temporary exhibitions.
Hours & Admission Prices: Mon.-Fri. 8-4:30. No charge. Closed Memorial Day; Labor Day; Thanksgiving; Christmas & week after. ♿
Attendance: 300 (estimated)

CINCINNATI FIRE MUSEUM, (M), 315 W. Court St., Cincinnati, OH 45202-1073. Tel.: 513-621-5553. Fax: 513-621-1456.
Web Site: www.cincyfiremuseum.com
Founded: 1979.
Congressional District: 2
Key Personnel: Chief Exec. Dir., Barbara M. Hammond; Pres., Tom Hardy.
Personnel Profile: Full-Time Paid 1; Part-Time Paid 5; Part-Time Volunteers 40.
Governing Authority: nonprofit organization. Tax-exempt: 501(c)(3).
History & Fire-Fighting Museum: housed in 1906 firehouse.
Collections: fire-fighting artifacts dating from mid 19th century to present; photographs; documents; manuscripts.
Research Fields: history of fire-fighting.
Facilities: 90-seat auditorium; 18-seat theater. Museum-related items for sale.
Activities: guided tours; lectures; films; formally organized education programs for children; docent program; permanent & temporary exhibitions; Safe House fire prevention & safety education programs; hands-on exhibits.
Publications: A Guide to Cincinnati's Historic Firehouses.
Hours & Admission Prices: Tues.-Fri. 10-4, Sat.-Sun. 12-4. Adults $7, senior citizens $6, children 6-12 $5; discounts to AAM members & groups; children 5 & under and members no charge. Closed holidays. ♿
Attendance: 20,000 (accurate)
Membership: Individual $30; 2 Alarm $40; 3 Alarm $50; 4 Alarm $75; 5 Alarm $150. Firefighters: Individual $25; Family $35. Corporate: 2 Alarm $100; 3 Alarm $250; 4 Alarm $500; 5 Alarm $1,000.

CINCINNATI MUSEUM CENTER AT UNION TERMINAL, (M), 1301 Western Ave., Cincinnati, OH 45203-1123. Tel.: 513-287-7000. Fax: 513-287-7002.
E-mail: dmcdonald@cincymuseum.org
Web Site: www.cincymuseum.org
Founded: 1818.
Congressional District: 1
Key Personnel: C.E.O. & Pres., Douglass W. McDonald; Past Pres., George Vincent; Chm. (V), Keith Harrison; Vice Pres. Exhibits & Museum Planning, Sandra Shipley; Vice Pres. Administration & C.F.O., Victoria Chester; Vice Pres. Featured Experiences, David Duszynski; Vice Pres. Museums, Tonya M. Matthews, Ph.D.; Vice Pres. Mktg. & Public Rels., Elizabeth Wiecher Pierce; Vice Pres. Institutional Advancement, Elizabeth Lee Hoffheimer; Asst. Vice Pres. Natural History & Science, Glenn Storrs; Asst. Vice Pres. Duke Energy Children's Museum & Education, Kesha Williams; Dir. Cincinnati Historical Society Library, Ruby Rogers; Dir. Sales, Andrea Howard; Dir. Volunteer Svcs., Angie Smorey; Dir. Facilities, Steve Terheiden; Registrar, Jane MacKnight; Dir. Traveling Exhibits, Chris Novy; Dir. Nature Preserve, Christopher Bedel; Dir. Customer Rels., Violet Rae Downey; Dir. Retail Operations, Barbara Witschger.
Personnel Profile: Full-Time Paid 160; Part-Time Paid 140; Part-Time Volunteers 1,365.
Governing Authority: private; nonprofit organization. Subsidiary Institution: Cincinnati History Museum; The Cincinnati Historical Society Library; Robert D. Lindner Family OMNIMAX Theater; Museum of Natural History & Science; Duke Energy Children's Museum; Children's & Youth Museum. Tax-exempt: 501(c)(3).
Natural & Regional History Museum.
Collections: historical regional ephemera; invertebrate paleontology; conchology; entomology; ethnology; geology; mineralogy; vertebrate paleontology; prehistoric & historic archaeology; ornithology; mammology; herpetology; photographs; manuscripts; broadcast archives; regional business history archives.
Research Fields: archaeology; zoology; paleontoglogy; Cincinnati area history.
Facilities: library; 225-seat auditorium; 13,000-acre nature preserve; research center; theater. Books, art objects, shells, rocks & other museum-related items for sale.
Activities: lectures; films; formally organized education programs; docent program; permanent, traveling & temporary exhibitions; field trips; outreach (school-site visits); producer of touring exhibits & Omnimax films; audiovisual aids.
Publications: books, Elementary Guide to the Fossils & Strata of the Ordovician; Archaeology of Hamilton County, Ohio; Turpin Indians; Black Island Paradise; First Farmers of the Middle Ohio Valley; Remembering Ruth Lyons: 1905-1988; Cincinnati: The Queen City; Picnics in the Park Cookbook; quarterly publication catalog, Reflections; production of 70mm IMAX-format films; quarterly journal, Ohio Valley History.
Hours & Admission Prices: Mon.-Sat. 10-5, Sun. 11-6. Adults $8, senior citizens 60 & over $7, children 3-12 $6; discounts to seniors; members no charge. Closed Thanksgiving; Christmas. ♿
Attendance: 1,300,000 (accurate)
Membership: Duke Energy Children's Museum, Cincinnati History Museum or Museum of Natural History & Science: Explorer Basic: Individual $79; Family $99. Explorer Plus: Individual $95; Family $115. Explorer Premium: Individual $120; Family $140. Explorer Platinum: Individual $275; Ambassador $500.

* **CINCINNATI ZOO & BOTANICAL GARDEN,** 3400 Vine St., Cincinnati, OH 45220-1333. Tel.: 513-281-4700, ext. 0 & 559-7724. Fax: 513-487-3336. TDD: 513-559-2730.
E-mail: info@cincinnatizoo.org
Web Site: www.cincinnatizoo.org
Founded: 1875.
Congressional District: 01
Key Personnel: Exec. Dir., Thane Maynard; C.O.O., Dave Jenike; Dir. Mktg. & Public Rels., Chad Yelton; Veterinarian, Mark Campbell, D.V.M.; Museum Shop Mgr., Lisa Sparks; Dir. Human Resources, Jeff Walton; Mgr. Guest Rels., T.R. Amrine; Mktg., Tiffany Sands.
Personnel Profile: Full-Time Paid 196; Part-Time Paid 430; Part-Time Volunteers 1,100; Interns 35.
Governing Authority: society. Tax-exempt: 501(c)(3).
Zoo.
Collections: aviary; aquarium; herpetology; arboretum; 3,000 taxa of plants; botanical garden; mammals; invertebrates; carnivore house.
Research Fields: aviary; aquarium; herpetology-amphibian research; mammals; reproductive research.
Facilities: 2,500-vol. library of books available for inter-library loan; CREW (Center for Reproduction of Endangered Wildlife) Research Dept. dedicated to preservation & propagation of endangered wildlife; children's zoo; jungle trials; Asian & African rainforest.
Activities: guided tours; lectures; films; concerts; study clubs; formally organized education programs for children & undergraduate college students; inter-museum loan, permanent & temporary exhibitions.
Publications: book, Cincinnati Zoo Official Guide Book; annual report; newsletter, Wildlife Explorer.
Hours & Admission Prices: Winter: daily 9-5; Summer: daily 9-6. Adults $13, seniors $9, children $8, parking $6.50; discounts to groups of 25 or more, AAM & ICOM members; museum members & AZA members no charge. ♿
Attendance: 1,200,000 (estimated)
Membership: Individual $47; Single Parent $65; Family $79.

CIVIC GARDEN CENTER OF GREATER CINCINNATI, 2715 Reading Rd., Cincinnati, OH 45206-1617. Tel.: 513-221-0981. Fax: 513-221-0961.
E-mail: vciotti@civicgardencenter.org
Web Site: www.civicgardencenter.org
Founded: 1942.
Key Personnel: Exec. Dir., Vickie Ciotti; Volunteer Coord., Connie Booth; Coord. Youth Education, Corina Bullock; Horticulturist I, Cara Hague; Exec. Asst., Terry Houston; Coord. Neighborhood Gardens, Peter Huttinger; Horticulturist III, Paul Koloszar; Finance Mgr., Judy Rahm.

Personnel Profile: Full-Time Paid 7; Part-Time Paid 2; Part-Time Volunteers 550; Interns 2.
Governing Authority: private; nonprofit organization. Tax-exempt.
Horticultural Center.
Collections: gardening; botanical; horticulture.
Facilities: library.
Activities: formal education programs; gardening classes; Community Garden training & programming for inner city youths & adults.
Publications: Gardener's Quarterly.
Hours & Admission Prices: Mon.-Fri. 9-4. No charge; donations accepted. ♿
Attendance: 10,000 (estimated)
Membership: Student, Teacher & Senior Citizens $25; Individual $35; Family $50.

THE CONTEMPORARY ARTS CENTER, 44 E. Sixth St., Cincinnati, OH 45202-3998. Tel.: 513-345-8400. Fax: 513-721-7418.
E-mail: admin@cacmail.org
Web Site: www.contemporaryartscenter.org
Founded: 1939.
Congressional District: 1
Key Personnel: Dir., Raphaela Platow; Asst. to Dir., Bettina Bellucci; Chm., Otto M. Budig, Jr.; Pres., Jennie Rosenthal Berliant; Dir. External Affairs, Melodee DuBois; Dir. Finance, Margaux Higgins; Sr. Cur., Toby Kamps; Curatorial Asst., Clare Norwood; Curatorial Asst., Maiza Hixson; Dir. Facilities, Dave Gearding; Cur. Education, Scott Boberg; Dir. Devel., Kathryn Brass; Dir. Mktg., Peggy Shannon; Mgr. Membership, Merrilee Luke-Ebbeler; Visitor Svcs. Mgr., Melanie Derrick.
Personnel Profile: Full-Time Paid 28; Part-Time Paid 15; Part-Time Volunteers 59; Interns 10.
Governing Authority: nonprofit organization. Tax-exempt.
Art Museum.
Collections: works by contemporary artists.
Research Fields: contemporary art.
Facilities: 1,000-vol. library. Catalogues, booklets & other museum-related items for sale.
Activities: guided tours; lectures; films; gallery talks; dance performances; docent & educational programs; traveling exhibitions; video programs; artists' residences.
Publications: newsletters; gallery guides; exhibition catalogues; brochures; audio guides.
Hours & Admission Prices: Mon. 10-9, Wed.-Fri. 10-6, Sat.-Sun. 11-6. Adults $7.50, senior citizens $6.50, students $5.50, children 3-13 $4.50; discounts to AAM members; children under 3, Mon. after 5pm & members no charge. ♿
Attendance: 177,000 (accurate)
Membership: Student $25; Individual $45; Individual Plus One $60; Family $65; Collector's Connection $125; Patron's Circle $250; Curator's Circle $500; Director's Circle $1,000; Trustee Circle $2,500.

DAAP GALLERIES, University of Cincinnati, 2624 Clifton Ave., Cincinnati, OH 45221-0001. Mailing Address: Univ. of Cincinnati, P.O. Box 210016, Cincinnati, OH 45221-0016. Tel.: 513-556-2839. Fax: 513-556-3288.
E-mail: DAAP.galleries@uc.edu
Web Site: www.daap.uc.edu/Gallery/gallery.htm
Founded: 1993.
Key Personnel: Dir., Anne Timpano; Collections Asst., Jonathan Nolting; Curatorial Asst., Sandra Geiser; Gallery Asst., Forest Harman; Mgr. Meyers Gallery, Rob Anderson; Mgr. Reed Gallery, Tijana Antonic; Mgr. University Galleries on Sycamore, Maria Seda-Reeder.
Governing Authority: public university; nonprofit. Parent Institution: University of Cincinnati, Cincinnati 45221. Tax-exempt: 170(b)(1)(A).
Art Gallery.
Collections: art of ancient Greece, Europe, Asia & the Americas; art of the United States emphasizing late 19th- & early 20th-century paintings, sculpture & works on paper.
Research Fields: American art, especially the late 19th & early 20th centuries.
Activities: formal education programs for undergraduate & graduate students affiliated with the Univ. of Cincinnati; lectures; loan, temporary & traveling exhibitions.
Publications: exhibition announcements; exhibition catalogues.
Hours & Admission Prices: Reed Gallery & Meyers Gallery: Mon.-Fri. 10-5. University Galleries on Sycamore Tues.-Fri. 11-5, Sat. 11-4. No charge. Closed university holidays. ♿
Attendance: 10,000 (estimated)

THE DELHI HISTORICAL SOCIETY MUSEUM, 468 Anderson Ferry Rd., Cincinnati, OH 45238-5281. Tel.: 513-451-4313. Fax: 513-451-4300.
Web Site: delhihistoricalsociety.org
Historical Society Museum: formerly the Joe Witterstaetter Homestead, built in the 1880s.
Collections: local history & culture; exhibits pertaining to Delhi history.
Hours & Admission Prices: Tues., Thurs. & Sun. 12-3.

INDIAN HILL HISTORICAL SOCIETY, 8100 Given Rd., Cincinnati, OH 45243-1520. Tel.: 513-891-1873. Fax: 513-891-1873.
E-mail: ihhist@cinci.rr.com
Web Site: www.indianhill.org
Founded: 1973.
Congressional District: 26
Key Personnel: Pres. (V), Barbara Hauck; Admin., Helen Verkamp.
Personnel Profile: Part-Time Paid 3; Part-Time Volunteers 35.
Governing Authority: society; nonprofit. Tax-exempt.
Local History Museum & Genealogies: housed in 1873 one-room school building & 1860 house.
Collections: monthly rotating collections.
Research Fields: local history.
Facilities: 500-vol. library of books available for inter-library loan.
Activities: monthly programs; lectures; concerts; arts festivals; study clubs; hobby workshops; formally organized education programs.
Publications: monthly newsletter, The Sampler.
Hours & Admission Prices: Open by appointment only. No charge. ♿
Attendance: 1,500 (estimated)
Membership: Individual $40; Family $50; Sustaining $90; Patron $175.

KROHN CONSERVATORY, 1501 Eden Park Dr., Cincinnati, OH 45202-6030. Tel.: 513-421-4086 & 5707. Fax: 513-421-6007. TDD: 513-352-3380.
E-mail: andrea.schepmann@cincinnati.oh.gov
Web Site: www.cineypark.com
Founded: 1933.
Congressional District: 2
Key Personnel: Dir. & Museum Shop Mgr., Andrea Schepmann; District Supvr., Ruth Spears; Volunteer Coord., Christyl Johnson.
Personnel Profile: Full-Time Paid 6; Part-Time Paid 8; Part-Time Volunteers 270.
Governing Authority: municipal. Affiliated with City of Cincinnati, Board of Park Commissioners. Tax-exempt.
Botanical Garden & Conservatory.
Collections: tropical & warm climate plants; cacti; succulents; palms; ferns; aroids; orchids; crotons; carnivorous display - Bonsai.
Research Fields: horticulture.
Facilities: 50-vol. library on horticulture available for inter-library loan; 30-seat meeting room. Museum-related items for sale.
Activities: guided tours; lectures; study clubs; permanent & temporary exhibitions.
Publications: map; self-guiding walking tour; tour brochure.
Hours & Admission Prices: Daily 10-5; special evening hours during Christmas Show. Charge for special events and shows only. ♿
Attendance: 185,000 (accurate)
Membership: Individual $25; Family $40; Patron $100; Founder $1,000.

MOUNT AIRY ARBORETUM, 5083 Colerain Ave., Cincinnati, OH 45223-1072. Tel.: 513-541-8176. Fax: 513-541-8176.
E-mail: paula.miller@cincinnati-oh.gov
Web Site: www.cincinnati-oh.gov/parks
Founded: 1932.
Congressional District: 23
Key Personnel: Dir. Parks, William Carden; Supvr. Mt. Airy, Larry Parker.
Personnel Profile: Full-Time Paid 1; Part-Time Volunteers 2.
Governing Authority: municipal. Affiliated with Cincinnati Bd. of Park Commissioners, 950 Eden Park Dr., 45202. Tax-exempt.
Botanical Garden: located on the site of Mount Airy Forest, the first municipal reforestation project in the U.S., started in 1911.
Collections: native hardwoods; evergreens; lilacs; azaleas; viburnums; perennial gardens; dwarf conifer garden; quince; crabapples; ground covers; clematis vine display garden.
Research Fields: plant trials.
Facilities: campsites available for Scout troops; 2 rustic lodges-75, 150 or 200 person capacity, available for meetings or receptions; reserved picnic area.
Activities: guided tours; lectures.
Publications: guide, Mount Airy Arboretum Plant Guide Map.
Hours & Admission Prices: Forest: daily 6am-10pm. Arboretum daily 7:30-dark. No charge. All facilities require reservations; call 513-352-4080.

NATIONAL UNDERGROUND RAILROAD FREEDOM CENTER, 50 E. Freedom Way, Cincinnati, OH 45202-3414. Tel.: 513-333-7500; 877-648-4838 (toll free).
Web Site: www.freedomcenter.org
Founded: 1995.
Key Personnel: Pres., Donald Murphy; Chm. (V), John Pepper; Museum Shop Mgr., James Tecco.
Personnel Profile: Full-Time Paid 52; Part-Time Paid 29; Interns 3.
History Museum.
Collections: slavery; resistance movements; achievement of freedom.
Facilities: cafe. Museum-related items for sale.
Activities: interactive educational programs; research.
Hours & Admission Prices: Tues.-Sun. 11-5. Adults $12, students and seniors 60 & over $10, children 6-12 $8; discounts to groups of 10 or more with reservation. Closed Thanksgiving; Christmas. ♿

SKIRBALL MUSEUM CINCINNATI HEBREW UNION COLLEGE-JEWISH INSTITUTE OF RELIGION, 3101 Clifton Ave., Cincinnati, OH 45220-2488. Tel.: 513-487-3053. Fax: 513-221-0321.
E-mail: outreach@huc.edu
Web Site: www.huc.edu/museums/cn
Founded: 1913.
Congressional District: 1
Key Personnel: Pres, Rabbi David Ellenson, P.h.D.
Personnel Profile: Part-Time Paid 1; Part-Time Volunteers 25.
Governing Authority: college. Parent Institution: Hebrew Union College. Tax-exempt: 501(c)(3).
Art and Jewish History Museum.
Collections: ceremonial objects relating to Jewish customs, rituals & life cycle events; biblical archaeology; textiles; decorative arts; prints; paintings; photographs.
Facilities: Archaeology Center; conference room; auditorium.
Activities: guided tours; docent program; permanent exhibits.
Hours & Admission Prices: By appointment. Suggested Donation. ♿
Attendance: 4,000 (estimated)
Membership: Participating $35; Supporting $100; Sustaining $250; Patron $500.

STUDIO SAN GIUSEPPE ART GALLERY, College of Mt. St. Joseph, 5701 Delhi Rd., Cincinnati, OH 45233-1670. Tel.: 513-244-4314. Fax: 513-244-4942.
E-mail: Jerry_Bellas@mail.msj.edu
Web Site: www.msj.edu
Founded: 1962.
Congressional District: 2
Key Personnel: Dir. & Chm. Art Dept., Gerald M. Bellas.
Personnel Profile: Part-Time Paid 1; Interns 2.
Governing Authority: private college; nonprofit. Parent Institution: College of Mount St. Joseph. Tax-exempt: 501(c)(3).
Art Gallery: housed in the Dorothy Meyer Ziv Art Building.
Collections: art works & crafts donated to the school over the years.
Facilities: 1,500 sq. ft. exhibit space.
Activities: temporary exhibits relating to art curriculum; guided tours; lectures; participatory exhibit; films.
Hours & Admission Prices: Academic year: Mon.-Fri. 10-5, Sat.-Sun. 1:30-4:30. No charge. Closed major holidays. ♿
Attendance: 5,000 (estimated)
Membership: Individual $10; Associate $25; Sponsor $50; Patron $100.

* **TAFT MUSEUM OF ART, (M),** 316 Pike St., Cincinnati, OH 45202-4293. Tel.: 513-241-0343. Fax: 513-241-7762.
E-mail: taftmuseum@taftmuseum.org
Web Site: www.taftmuseum.org
Founded: 1932.
Congressional District: 2
Key Personnel: Acting Dir., Phillip C. Long; Chm. (V), Paul Chellgren; Chief Cur., Lynne D. Ambrosini, Ph.D.; Membership & Web Mgr., Elizabeth Skipper; Dir. Organizational Resources & Planning, Cynthia M. Kearns; Dir. Institutional Advancement, Nathan J. Smallwood; Assoc. Cur. Docent & School Svcs., Jean Graves; Asst. Cur. Family Studio, Anne S. Arenstein; Mgr. Special Events, Barbara J. Lenhardt; Exhibition Coord. & Curatorial Asst., Tammy Muente; Collections Technician, Mark J. Allen; Dir. Security, Alan Jones; Mgr. Devel., Natalie N. Mathis; Assoc. Cur. Public Programs & Publications, Catherine O'Hara; Chief Preparator & Exhibition Designer, Mark Rohling; Museum Shop Mgr. & Visitor Svcs., Brooke Sherritt; Volunteer Coord. & Scheduling Mgr., Lynne Staat; Mgr. Facility Rentals, Kitty Paschall; Registrar & Collections Mgr., Joan C. Hendricks; Mktg. & Public Rels. Mgr., Tricia Suit; Asst. to Dir., Christine Miller; Asst. Preparator, Sherri Besso; Exec. Chef, Mark Bowers; Dir. Finance, Patricia B. Hassel, CPA
Personnel Profile: Full-Time Paid 28; Part-Time Paid 12; Part-Time Volunteers 179; Interns 8.
Governing Authority: nonprofit organization. Subsidiary Institution: Taft Publications, Inc. Tax-exempt: 170(b)(1)(A).
Art Museum: housed in 1820 Baum-Longworth-Taft House.
Collections: Dutch, English, Spanish & French Old Master paintings; Kangxi, Yongzheng, Qianlong Chinese porcelains; Limoges enamels; Italian 16th-century Maiolica & engraved rock crystals; European & English 17th-& 18th-century watches; 19th-century European & American paintings; decorative arts; Federal furniture.
Major Exhibits: Drawn by New York: Drawings and Watercolors from the NY Historical Society (T), 11/20/09-1/17/10; An Antique Christmas, 11/27/09-1/10/10; Small Paintings-Keystone Gallery, 1/15/10-5/23/10; Dutch Utopia: American Artists in Holland 1880-1914, 2/5/10-5/2/10; Truth Beauty: Pictorialism and Photograph as Art, 1845-1945 (T), 5/21/10-8/8/10; Turner Watercolors-Keystone Gallery, 5/28/10-7/25/10; American Elegance: Chintz Applique Quilts, 1780-1850 (T), 8/27/10-11/7/10.
Research Fields: pertaining to collections.
Facilities: 2,000-vol. library of books available for use on premises by appointment. Catalogs, booklets & other museum-related items for sale.
Activities: guided tours; lectures; gallery talks; concerts; formally organized education programs for children, students & adults; docent program or council; inter-museum loan, permanent & temporary exhibitions; Duncanson Artist-in-Residence; film series.
Publications: books, J.M.W. Turner: The Foundations of Genius; Louise Bourgeois; The Taft Museum: Its History & Collections; Night Lights; Skating in the Arts of 17th Century Holland; The American Weigh; Masterworks/Enamel/87; Paul Ashbrook; Nicholas Longworth-Art Patron of Cincinnati; China in 1700: Kangxi Porcelains at the Taft Museum; Christmas in Naples; At the Table; William Wegman: History of Travel; Tyrone Geter, Artist Face to Face: Two Centuries of Self-Portraits; Patterns in a Revolution: French Printed Textiles, 1759-1821; Oliver Newberry Chaffee (1881-1944); Fin de Siecle, Prints, Posters & Prose; An Exhibition of Tang Sancai Pottery from the collection of Alan & Simone Hartman; Tributes to the Tafts; Cavaliers & Cardinals: 19th Century French Anecodotal Painting; Master Dutch Drawings & Watercolors of the 19th Century from Haags Gemeentemuseum; Tell Me A Story; Tarleton Blackwell; Looking for Leonardo: Native & Folk Art Objects Found in America by Bates & Isabel Lowry; Dutch Drawings & Watercolors from the Kharkiv Art Museum; The Vanishing Frontier: Henry F. Varny, 1847-1916; East Meets West: Chinese Export and Design; The Great Migration: The Evolution of African American Art, 1790-1945; TAFT Museum of Art, An Illustrated Guide; Hiram Powers: Genius in Marble; Brush, Clay & Wood: The Nancy & Ed Rosenthal Collection of Chinese Art Portico; members newsletter, Portico.
Hours & Admission Prices: Tues.-Sun. 11-5. Adults $8, students & senior citizens $5; discounts to AAM & ICOM members; members and children 18 & under no charge. Closed New Year's Day; Independence Day; Thanksgiving; Christmas. ♿
Attendance: 59,139 (accurate)
Membership: Individual $45; Family & Dual $60; Patron $125; Sustaining $250; Fellow $500.

TRAILSIDE NATURE CENTER, Brookline Dr., Burnet Woods Park, Cincinnati, OH 45220. Mailing Address: 4 Beech Lane, Cincinnati, OH 45208-2614. Tel.: 513-321-6070 & 751-3679. Fax: 513-321-6218.
E-mail: vivian.wagner@cincinnati-oh.gov
Web Site: www.cinci-parks.org
Formerly: Trailside Nature Center & Museum
Founded: 1930.
Congressional District: 1
Key Personnel: C.E.O. & Dir. Parks, Willie F. Carden, Jr.; Dir. Outdoor Centers, Erin Morris; Coord. Education, Vivian Wagner.
Personnel Profile: Full-Time Paid 1; Part-Time Paid 2.
Governing Authority: municipal. Parent Institution: City of Cincinnati, Bd. of Park Commissioners, Interpretive Services Div. Subsidiary Institution: Wolff Plantation. Tax-exempt.
Park Museum.
Collections: local birds, insects & other animals; tree & plant specimens; rocks & fossils; surface, underground & water habitats; exhibits displaying components of the park; sky chart exhibit.
Facilities: 50-seat auditorium; 30-seat auditorium; classrooms; planetarium; nature library.
Activities: lectures; field trips; nature clubs; summer day camp; adult education classes; handicraft classes; weather & night sky information; planetarium programs; teacher & youth-leader education.
Publications: calendar of Nature Activities.
Hours & Admission Prices: No charge; donations accepted. Closed holidays. ♿
Attendance: 20,000 (estimated)

WILLIAM HOWARD TAFT NATIONAL HISTORIC SITE, 2038 Auburn Ave., Cincinnati, OH 45219-3025. Tel.: 513-684-3262. Fax: 513-684-3627.
Web Site: www.nps.gov/wiho/index.html
Founded: 1969.
Congressional District: 2
Key Personnel: Supt., Reggie Tiller; Museum Shop Mgr. & Chief of Interpretation & Resources Mgmt., Ray Henderson.
Personnel Profile: Full-Time Paid 8; Part-Time Paid 4; Part-Time Volunteers 20.
Governing Authority: federal government. Parent Institution: National Park Service/Dept. of Interior. Tax-exempt.
Historic House Museum: c.1857 birthplace & boyhood home of William Howard Taft, 27th President of the U.S. & 10th Chief Justice. Taft Education Center, 2038 Auburn Ave., Cincinnati, OH 45219-3025.
Collections: furnishings; memorabilia of President Taft & his family.
Research Fields: history of William Howard Taft & his birthplace.
Facilities: library related to William Howard Taft, his family, his birthplace.
Activities: guided tours; lectures; temporary exhibitions; educational programs for school groups.
Publications: brochure; newsletter.
Hours & Admission Prices: Daily 8-4. No charge; donations accepted. Closed New Year's Day; Thanksgiving; Christmas. ♿
Attendance: 17,000 (accurate)
Membership: Friends of the William Howard Taft Birthplace: Individual $25.

XAVIER UNIVERSITY ART GALLERY, 3800 Victory Pkwy., Cincinnati, OH 45207-1035. Tel.: 513-745-3811. Fax: 513-745-1098. TDD: 513-745-3811.
Web Site: xavier.edu/art/gallery.cfm
Founded: 1831.
Key Personnel: Dir., Katherine Uetz.
Governing Authority: private university; nonprofit. Parent Institution: Xavier University. Tax-exempt.
Art Gallery.
Collections: paintings; sculpture; photographs.
Activities: student & professional art exhibitions; films.
Hours & Admission Prices: Academic year: Mon.-Fri. 10-4. No charge. Closed official & university holidays. ♿
Attendance: 1,800

Cleveland

THE CHILDREN'S MUSEUM OF CLEVELAND, 10730 Euclid Ave., Cleveland, OH 44106-2200. Tel.: 216-791-7114 & 791-KIDS. Fax: 216-791-8838.
E-mail: info@clevelandchildrensmuseum.org
Web Site: clevelandchildrensmuseum.org
Formerly: Rainbow Children's Museum and TRW Early Learning Center
Founded: 1981.
Congressional District: 21
Key Personnel: Dir., Jeffrey Saxon; Pres. Bd. (V), Richard J. Maicki; Coord. Membership & Group Tours, Lisa Merk; Mgr. Guest Svcs. & Coord. Volunteers, Kelley McClelland; Facility & Exhibit Maintenance, Dennis Bunch; Dir. Operations, Leland Merk; Interpretation & Intern Mgr., Rachel Smucker; Dir. Education, Colleen Cross; Mgr. Business & Devel., Andrea Ranta; Coord. Exhibits, Maria Campanelli; Dir. Finance, Patrick Conroy.
Personnel Profile: Full-Time Paid 8; Part-Time Paid 9; Part-Time Volunteers 3; Interns 7.
Governing Authority: nonprofit organization. Tax-exempt: 501(c)(3).
Children's Museum.
Collections: hands-on participatory exhibits.
Research Fields: pertaining to exhibits.
Facilities: Museum-related items for sale.
Activities: organized education programs for children & volunteers; loan exhibitions; hands-on family learning.
Publications: monthly calendar; quarterly newsletter; brochures; rack cards; curriculum guides.
Hours & Admission Prices: Daily 10-5. Children 1-12 $7, adults $6; members no charge. Closed major holidays. ♿
Attendance: 70,588 (accurate)
Membership: Individual Plus (1 adult/1 child) $40; Family of four $60 (over 4 members $10 extra per person).

CLEVELAND BOTANICAL GARDEN, 11030 East Blvd., Cleveland, OH 44106-1706. Tel.: 216-721-1600, ext. 194. Fax: 216-721-2056.
E-mail: nronayne@cbgarden.org
Web Site: www.cbgarden.org
Founded: 1930.
Congressional District: 11
Key Personnel: Dir., Natalie Ronayne; Pres., Ruth Eppig; Vice Pres., Matthew V. Crawford; Devel. Officer, Lynne Feighan; Museum Shop Mgr., Kate Fox.
Personnel Profile: Full-Time Paid 53; Part-Time Paid 26; Part-Time Volunteers 350; Interns 12.
Governing Authority: nonprofit organization. Tax-exempt: 501(c)(3).
Botanical Garden.
Collections: Japanese, herb, rose, perennial & wild flower gardens; reading garden; Hershey children's garden. Glasshouse: Costa Rica & Madagascar ecosystems.
Facilities: 16,000-vol. library of books on gardening & horticulture, 125 videos on gardening & landscape design, nursery catalogs, available for research in library & circulation to members; reading room; 325-seat auditorium; classrooms; Hershey Children's Garden for children 2-12. Institution related items for sale.
Activities: lectures; classes; workshops; formally organized education programs for adults, children & special populations. Annual Events: Cleveland Botanical Garden Flower Show in May; Winter Show in December.
Publications: quarterly magazine, The Bulletin; annual report; schedule of events; visitor brochure; visitor map.
Hours & Admission Prices: April-Oct. Mon.-Tues. & Thurs.-Sat. 10-5, Wed. 10-9, Sun. 12-5; Nov.-March Tues. & Thurs.-Sat. 10-5, Wed. 10-9, Sun. 12-5. Adults $7; members no charge. Closed federal holidays. ♿
Attendance: 140,000 (accurate)
Membership: Individual $55; Family $65; Friend $100; Partner $250; Sponsor $500; Director's Circle $1,000; Founder's Society $5,000.

CLEVELAND METROPARKS ZOO, (M), 3900 Wildlife Way, Cleveland, OH 44109-3132. Tel.: 216-661-6500, ext. 0. Fax: 216-661-3312. TDD: 216-661-1090.
E-mail: zooinfo@clevelandmetroparks.com
Web Site: www.clemetzoo.com
Founded: 1882.
Congressional District: 20
Key Personnel: Dir., Steve H. Taylor; Facilities Mgr., Todd Kinzer; Guest Svcs. Mgr., Edith Ricchiuto; Mktg. Mgr., Susan Allen; Cur. Education, Victoria Searles; Exec. Dir. Zoo Society, Elizabeth Fowler; Gen. Cur., Geoffrey Hall.
Personnel Profile: Full-Time Paid 168; Part-Time Paid 40; Part-Time Volunteers 522; Interns 20.
Governing Authority: Cleveland Metroparks Board, 4101 Fulton Pkwy., Cleveland, OH 44144. Parent Institution: Cleveland Metroparks.
Zoo.
Collections: mammals; birds; reptiles; fish; invertebrates.
Research Fields: animal behavior & social structures of primates.
Facilities: 4,401-vol. library of zoology books available on premises during office hours; aquarium. Museum-related items for sale.
Activities: lectures; formally organized education programs for children; permanent & traveling exhibitions; runs; walks; simulator ride.
Publications: quarterly magazine, Z to U; semiannual magazine, Z; monthly magazine, The Emerald Necklace.
Hours & Admission Prices: Memorial Day-Labor Day Mon.-Fri. 10-5, Sat.-Sun. & holidays 10-7; Sept.-May daily 10-5. Zoo & Rainforest: adults $10, children 2-11 $7; Mon. residents of Cuyahoga County & Hinckley Township, children under 2 no charge. Closed New Year's Day; Christmas. ♿
Attendance: 1,208,379 (accurate)
Membership: Senior Plus $40; Individual Plus $53; Family $68; Family Plus $88; Sustaining $125; Contributing $250.

* **THE CLEVELAND MUSEUM OF ART, (M), (I),** 11150 East Blvd., Cleveland, OH 44106-1797. Tel.: 216-421-7340. Fax: 216-421-0411. TDD: 216-421-0018.
E-mail: info@clevelandart.org
Web Site: www.clevelandart.org
Founded: 1913.
Congressional District: 21
Key Personnel: Co. Chm., James T. Bartlett; Co Chm., Michael J. Horvitz; Pres. (V), Alfred M. Rankin, Jr.; Dir., Timothy Rub; Deputy Dir. Admin. & Treas., Janet G. Ashe; Chief Cur., C. Griffith Mann; Editor Publications, Laurence Channing; Dir. Collections Mgmt., Mary Suzor; Dir. Mktg. & Communications, Cindy Fink; Deputy Dir. Devel. & External Affairs, Susan Jaros; Dir. Library & Archives, Elizabeth Lantz; Dir. Design & Architecture, Jeffrey W. Strean; Cur. Chinese Art, Anita Chung; Cur. Greek & Roman Art, Michael J. Bennett; Cur. Prints, Jane Glaubinger; Cur. Modern European Art, William H. Robinson; Cur. Medieval Art, Stephen N. Fliegel; Cur. European Painting & Sculpture, 1500-1800, Jon Seydl; Cur. Textiles & Islamic Art, Louise W. Mackie; Cur. Photography, Tom Hinson; Cur. Decorative Art & Design, Stephen A. Harrison; Assoc. Cur. Art of the Ancient Americas, Susan Bergh; Cur. African Art, Constantine Petridis; Assoc. Cur. American Painting & Sculpture, Mark Cole; Assoc. Cur. of

Prints & Drawings, Heather Lemonedes; Paintings Conservator, Marcia Steele; Dir. Education & Public Programs, Marjorie Williams; Dir. Exhibitions, Heidi Domine Strean; Dir. Performing Arts, Music & Film, Massoud Saidpour; Dir. Human Resources, Sharon Reaves; Assoc. Dir. Volunteer Initiatives, Diane DeBevec; Mgr. Retail & Merchandising, Catherine Surratt.

Personnel Profile: Full-Time Paid 282; Part-Time Paid 95; Part-Time Volunteers 397; Interns 23.

Governing Authority: nonprofit organization. Tax-exempt: 501(c)(3).

Art Museum.

Collections: art from all cultures & periods; paintings; sculpture; graphics; decorative arts; music; numismatic; textiles; photography; digital images; microfilm; slides.

Research Fields: paintings; sculpture; graphics; decorative arts; music; textiles; photography.

Facilities: 442,039-vol. library of art books & periodicals; 765-seat auditorium; two 160-seat halls; restaurant. Books, postcards, print reproductions, color slides, paper goods, small decorative objects & jewelry for sale.

Activities: Parade the Circle, June 2008.

Publications: monthly, Members Magazine; annual report; annual volume, Cleveland Studies in the History of Art; Handbook of the Cleveland Museum of Art; exhibition catalogs; books relating to museum collections; guide to the galleries, collection catalogues, Masterpieces in Asian Art 19th-Century European Paintings; Knockouts: A Pocket Guide to the CMA (2002).

Hours & Admission Prices: Tues., Thurs. & Sat.-Sun. 10-5, Wed. & Fri. 10-9. No charge; donations accepted. Closed New Year's Day; Independence Day; Thanksgiving; Christmas. ♿

Attendance: 269,808 (accurate)

Membership: CMA Annual: Student $25; Senior Citizen $35; Senior Couple $45; Individual $50; Family $65; Classic $100; Fellow $225; Patron $300; Contributing $500; Director's Circle $1,000; President's Circle $2,500; Founder's Society $5,000; Collector's Circle $10,000; Patron Sponsor $25,000.

* **THE CLEVELAND MUSEUM OF NATURAL HISTORY, (M),** 1 Wade Oval Dr., University Circle, Cleveland, OH 44106-1767. Tel.: 216-231-4600. Fax: 216-231-5919. TDD: 216-231-7777.

E-mail: info@cmnh.org

Web Site: www.cmnh.org

Founded: 1920.

Congressional District: 21

Key Personnel: Interim C.E.O. & C.O.O., Bonnie Cummings; Pres. (V), Nathaniel T. Smith; Dir. Communications & Mktg., Marie Graf; C.F.O., Doug Stelzer; Dir. Science & Cur. Archaeology, Dr. Joe Keiper; Registrar, Carole Camillo; Cur. Invertebrate Paleontology, Dr. Joseph Hannibal; Cur. Vertebrate Zoology, Dr. Timothy Matson; Cur. Paleobotany, Dr. Shya Chitaley; Cur. Vertebrate Paleontology, Dr. Michael Ryan; Cur. Invertebrate Zoology, Dr. Joe Keiper; Cur. Mineralogy, Dr. David Saja; Cur. Ornithology, Dr. Andrew Jones; Dir. Education, Carin Miller; Dir. Conservation & Cur. Botany, Dr. James Bissell; Dir. Wildlife Resources, Harvey Webster; Cur. Archaeology, Dr. Brian Redmond; Dir. GreenCityBlueLake Institute, David Beach; Dir. Human Health, Dr. Linda Spurlok; Museum Store Mgr., Susan Rozman.

Personnel Profile: Full-Time Paid 103; Part-Time Paid 87; Part-Time Volunteers 300; Interns 30.

Governing Authority: nonprofit corporation. Branch Museum: Mentor Marsh Nature Center. Tax-exempt: 501(c)(3).

Natural History Museum.

Collections: archives; archaeology; ethnography; physical anthropology; natural history arts; entomology; herbarium; herpetology; mammalogy; ornithology; ichthyology; mineralogy; invertebrate paleontology; vertebrate paleontology; paleobotany.

Major Exhibits: Dinosaurs: Ancient Fossils, New Discoveries (T), 11/09-11/31/10; Wild Music (T), 5/29/10-8/29/10.

Research Fields: archaeology; cultural anthropology; physical anthropology; botany; entomology; herpetology; mammalogy; invertebrate paleontology; mineralogy; astronomy; vertebrate paleontology; paleobotany; ornithology; wildlife research.

Facilities: 60,000-vol. library of natural history; 500-seat auditorium; Discovery Center; observatory; planetarium; conservation lab; casting lab; environmental garden; captive wildlife area; 27 off-site natural areas; classrooms; meeting & banquet room; cafe. Museum-related items for sale.

Activities: guided tours; lectures; films; TV & radio programs; formally organized education programs for children, adults, undergraduate & graduate college students; permanent, temporary & traveling exhibitions; astronomy programming; live animal programs; Science Resource Center; Future Scientists Program; summer internships.

Publications: members newsletter, Tracks; scientific papers; scientific journal, Kirtlandia; annual report; Cleveland Bird Calendar; Dragon Flies and Damsel Flies.

Hours & Admission Prices: Mon.-Tues. & Thurs.-Sat. 10-5, Wed. 10-10, Sun. 12-5. Adults $9, students, senior citizens & children 7-18 $7, children 3-6 $6; discount to AAM members; children 2 & under, Tues. & Thurs. 3-5, museum & Ohio Museums Assoc. members no charge. Planetarium: $3. Closed New Year's Day; Memorial Day; Independence Day; Labor Day; Thanksgiving; Christmas. ♿

Attendance: 265,000 (accurate)

Membership: Individual Senior $40; Individual $45; Couple Senior $55; Family $65; Participating & Nature League $85; Friend $150; Associate $250; Mentor $500.

CLEVELAND POLICE HISTORICAL SOCIETY & MUSEUM, (M), 1300 Ontario St., Cleveland, OH 44113-1600. Tel.: 216-623-5055 & 5056. Fax: 216-623-5145.

E-mail: clevelandpolicemus@roadrunner.com

Web Site: www.clevelandpolicemuseum.org

Founded: 1983.

Congressional District: 11

Key Personnel: Museum Shop Mgr., Geraldine Diemert; Office Mgr., Marilyn Jech.

Personnel Profile: Part-Time Paid 3; Part-Time Volunteers 1.

Governing Authority: nonprofit organization. Tax exempt: 501(c)(3).

Police Museum: presently housed in Cleveland police headquarters.

Collections: history of the Cleveland Police Dept. from 1866-present; incomplete files of annual reports, case files, city & state codes, criminology texts, directories, manuals, police blotters & orders, scrapbooks; over 13,000 photographs including police personnel, buildings, equipment, selected criminal cases & Cleveland events; memorabilia includes badges, patches, uniforms, equipment, firearms, call boxes, police motorcycles, a jail, fingerprint table.

Research Fields: Cleveland Ohio law enforcement history.

Activities: guided tours; traveling museums in boxes; living history outreach program; slide programs; preservation research.

Publications: newsletter, CPHS; newsletter, The Hot Sheet.

Hours & Admission Prices: Mon.-Fri. 10-4. No charge; donations accepted. Closed New Year's Day; Memorial Day; Independence Day; Labor Day; Thanksgiving; Christmas. ♿

Attendance: 6,722 (accurate)

Membership: CPD Retired $25; Individual $52.

CLEVELAND STATE UNIVERSITY ART GALLERY, 2307 Chester Ave., Cleveland, OH 44114-3607. Mailing Address: 2121 Euclid Ave. AB 101, Cleveland, OH 44115-2226. Tel.: 216-687-2103 & 2000. Fax: 216-687-9340. TDD: 216-687-2000.

E-mail: t.knapp@csuohio.edu

Web Site: www.csuohio.edu/artgallery

Founded: 1973.

Congressional District: 10

Key Personnel: Dir. & Cur., Robert Thurmer; Chm., George Mauersberger; Pres., Michael Schwartz; Vice Pres. Finance, Roy L. Ray; Devel., Craig Zullig; Public Rels., Mary Grodek.

Personnel Profile: Full-Time Paid 2; Full-Time Volunteers 1; Part-Time Paid 7; Part-Time Volunteers 18; Interns 4.

Governing Authority: state government & public university; nonprofit. Parent Institution: Cleveland State University. Subsidiary Institution: Art Gallery. Tax-exempt: 501(c)(3).

University Art Gallery.

Collections: works by traditional & contemporary artists.

Major Exhibits: The Human Subject, 11/09-1/10; 60 X 60 (T), 1/10-3/10; Islamic Contemporary Art, 5/10-6/10; Ken Nevadomi Retrospective, 9/10-10/10; 19th People's Art Show, 10/10-12/10.

Research Fields: critical analysis of the relationship of art & society.

Facilities: educational facilities; 4,500 sq. ft. exhibit space.

Activities: formal education programs for undergraduate & graduate college students; guided tours; lectures; workshops by artists, performance art presentations.

Publications: exhibition catalogs published 1-3 times annually.

Hours & Admission Prices: Sept.-May Mon.-Fri. 10-5, Sat. 12-4. No charge; donations accepted. Closed federal, state & university holidays. ♿

Attendance: 18,231 (accurate)

Membership: Students $10; $25; $40; $200; $500; $1,000.

CRAWFORD AUTO-AVIATION MUSEUM, 10825 East Blvd., Cleveland, OH 44106-1703. Tel.: 216-721-5722. Fax: 216-721-0891.

Web Site: www.wrhs.org

Founded: 1963.

Congressional District: 21

Key Personnel: Pres., Gainor B. Davis, Ph.D.; Chm. (V), Becky Carlino; C.F.O., John Holzhouser; Vice Pres. Museums, Dr. Edward Jay Pershey; Vice Pres. Institutional Advancement, Kelly Falcone Hall; Education, Janice Ziegler; Public Rels., Angie Lowrie; Security, Mark Corcoran.
Governing Authority: private; nonprofit organization. Parent Institution: Western Reserve Historical Society, Cleveland, OH. Tax-exempt: 501(c)(3).
Automobile & Aircraft Museum.
Collections: 200 autos & aircraft transportation documents.
Facilities: library; 75,000 sq. ft. exhibit space.
Activities: guided tours; hobby workshops; lectures; rental gallery; participatory & temporary exhibitions.
Publications: quarterly newsletter; monthly eBlasts.
Hours & Admission Prices: Mon.-Sat. 10-5, Sun. 12-5. Adults $8.50, senior citizens $7.50, students 3-12 $5; discounts to tours & groups; members no charge. Closed New Year's Day; Independence Day; Thanksgiving; Christmas Eve & Day. ♿
Membership: Individual $50; Family & Couple $70; Sustaining $150; Fellow $500.

DITTRICK MUSEUM OF MEDICAL HISTORY, 11000 Euclid Ave., Cleveland, OH 44106-1714. Tel.: 216-368-3648. Fax: 216-368-0165.
E-mail: james.edmonson@case.edu
Web Site: www.case.edu/artsci/dittrick/site2
Founded: 1926.
Congressional District: 21
Key Personnel: Chief Cur., James M. Edmonson; Museum Registrar & Archivist, Jennifer K. Nieves; Website Design & Photography, Laura Travis.
Personnel Profile: Full-Time Paid 3; Part-Time Volunteers 2.
Governing Authority: Case Western Reserve University. Affiliated with College of Arts & Sciences. Tax-exempt: 509(a)(1).
Medical History Museum.
Collections: over 75,000 historical objects related to the practice of medicine, dentistry, pharmacy & nursing; exhibits emphasize medicine in the 19th- & early 20th-centuries including recreation of doctors' offices & a 19th-century pharmacy; contraception history; manuscript collections.
Research Fields: history of the health sciences.
Facilities: 10,000-vol. library of medical history available for inter-library loan; 450-seat auditorium.
Activities: guided tours; education programs for undergraduate & graduate students; inter-museum loan, temporary exhibits.
Publications: biannual newsletter, Newsletter of the Cleveland Medical Library Association.
Hours & Admission Prices: Mon.-Fri. 10-5. No charge. Closed New Year's Day; Memorial Day weekend; Independence Day; Labor Day weekend; Thanksgiving; Christmas Eve & Day. ♿
Membership: Partners in Medical History: Associate Partner $25; Partner $50; Sustaining Partner $100; Sponsoring Partner $250; Senior Partner $500; Fellow for Life $1,000.

DUNHAM TAVERN MUSEUM, 6709 Euclid Ave., Cleveland, OH 44103-3913. Tel.: 216-431-1060.
E-mail: dunhamtavern@sbcglobal.net
Web Site: www.dunhamtavern.org
Founded: 1939.
Congressional District: 22
Key Personnel: Pres. (V), Marsha French; Treas., Garrit Wamelink.
Personnel Profile: Part-Time Paid 1; Part-Time Volunteers 40.
Governing Authority: society. Tax-exempt: 501(c)(3).
General Museum: housed in 1824 Dunham Tavern.
Collections: folklore; glass; textiles; mocha ware; pewter; lustre ware; Ohio room; early American artifacts; herb garden; Queen Ann & Chippendale furniture; McIntire mantel; historic log cabin located on heritage trail.
Research Fields: Cleveland & Western Reserve history taverns; transportation.
Facilities: 2,000-vol. library of Ohio & Cleveland history books available for use by application to the Board of Trustees or librarian; outdoor trail of 19th-century life; picnic area; English garden.
Activities: guided tours; lectures; films; permanent & temporary exhibitions.
Publications: monthly bulletin.
Hours & Admission Prices: Wed. & Sun. 1-4. Adults $3, children under 12 $2; discounts to AAM members; members no charge; group tours call for appointment. Closed New Year's Day; Easter; Thanksgiving; Christmas. ♿
Attendance: 4,200 (estimated)
Membership: Single $30; Family $50; Corporate $150; Life $1,000.

GREAT LAKES SCIENCE CENTER, 601 Erieside Ave., Cleveland, OH 44114-1021. Tel.: 216-694-2000. Fax: 216-696-2140. TDD: 216-696-3823.
Web Site: www.greatscience.com
Founded: 1988.
Congressional District: 21
Key Personnel: Pres. & C.E.O., Linda Abraham-Silver; Chm. Bd., Jeanette Grasselli Brown; C.O.O. & C.F.O., Don Paterson; Dir. Exhibits, Valence Davillier; Vice Pres. Mktg. & Guest Svcs., Jamie Finley; Vice Pres. Devel., Joel Fox; Dir. Facilities & Security, Gordon Milne; Special Events Mgr., Amanda Bowen; Vice Pres. Strategic Initiatives, Blake Andres; Dir. Human Resources, Renee Jones.
Personnel Profile: Full-Time Paid 42; Part-Time Paid 103; Part-Time Volunteers 169; Interns 1.
Governing Authority: private; nonprofit organization. Subsidiary Institution: Steamship William G. Mather Museum, 305 Mather Way, Cleveland, OH 44114. Tax-exempt: 501(c)(3).
Technology & Science Museum.
Collections: hands-on exhibits.
Major Exhibits: Water: H2O=Life (T), 11/14/09-4/11/10; Strange Matter (T), 5/29/10-1/3/11.
Facilities: 200-seat auditorium; 157,458 sq. ft. exhibit space; cafe; 320-seat OMNIMAX theater.
Activities: hands-on exhibits; omnimax theater; education programs; traveling exhibitions; workshops; summer, spring, & winter science camps; birthday parties; space rentals.
Hours & Admission Prices: Daily 10-5. Adults $9.50, senior $8.50, youth 12-17 $7.50; members no charge. Closed Thanksgiving; Christmas. ♿
Membership: Individual Max & Family $85; Family Plus $100; Family Max $150; Sustaining Family Max $250; Patron Family Max $500; President's Circle $1,000.

INTERNATIONAL WOMEN'S AIR & SPACE MUSEUM, INC., (M), 1501 N. Marginal Rd., Rm. 165, Cleveland, OH 44114-3726. Tel.: 216-623-1111. Fax: 216-623-1113.
E-mail: cluhta@iwasm.org
Web Site: www.iwasm.org
Founded: 1976.
Congressional District: 10
Key Personnel: Pres. (V), Caroline Luhta; Exec. Dir., Toni Mullee; Office Mgr., Heather Alexander.
Personnel Profile: Part-Time Paid 3; Part-Time Volunteers 6.
Governing Authority: nonprofit organization. Tax-exempt: 501(c)(3).
Women's Aeronautics Museum: housed at an airport.
Collections: photos; military uniforms; personal papers; clothing & costumes; trophies & plaques; aviation art; posters; aircraft components; First Day covers; Ruth Nichols collection of papers; Smith mini-plane; history of women in aviation & space.
Research Fields: All areas of women in aviation & aerospace.
Facilities: 1,000-vol. library of aviation & women in aeronautics material available to the public; study area available for researchers. Books & other museum-related items for sale.
Activities: loaned exhibits; tours; local speakers. Annual Events: career fair; pre-air show event; wine tasting event.
Publications: quarterly newsletter, IWASM Quarterly.
Hours & Admission Prices: Mon.-Fri. 10-4; exhibits accessible daily. No charge; donations accepted. Closed holidays. ♿
Attendance: 10,000 (estimated)
Membership: Student $10; Senior 65 & over $25; Individual $30; International $35; Individual Gold $100; Corporation $500.

MUSEUM OF CONTEMPORARY ART CLEVELAND, 8501 Carnegie Ave., Cleveland, OH 44106-2919. Tel.: 216-421-8671. Fax: 216-421-0737.
E-mail: info@mocacleveland.org
Web Site: www.mocacleveland.org
Formerly: Cleveland Center for Contemporary Art
Founded: 1968.
Congressional District: 21
Key Personnel: Dir., Jill Snyder; Bd. Pres., Harriet Warm; Community Rels. Mgr., Jude Goergen; Emily Hall Tremaine Curatorial Fellow, Megan Lykins; Dir. Mktg. & Communications, Kelly Bird; Dir. Finance, Grace Garver; Sr. Cur., Margo Crutchfield; Graphic Designer, Danielle Rini Uva; Visitor Svcs. Mgr. & Museum Shop Mgr., Heather Young; School Programs & Tour Coord., Dara Sepkoski; Dir. Devel., John Grayson; Registrar & Cur. Coord., Ann Albano; Mgr. Member Rels., Rob Sikora; Exhibitions Mgr., Ray Juaire; Asst. Preparator, Paul Sydorenko; Finance Asst. & IT Mgr., Terri Tokar; Asst. Cur., Ana Vejzovic; Administrative Asst., Andrea Kormos.
Personnel Profile: Full-Time Paid 13; Part-Time Paid 5; Part-Time Volunteers 10; Interns 10.
Governing Authority: nonprofit organization. Tax-exempt: 501(c)(3).
Art Museum.
Collections: contemporary visual art.
Research Fields: contemporary visual arts.
Facilities: Artspace. Museum-related items for sale.

Activities: lectures; tours; multi-arts programs; films; loan & traveling exhibitions.
Publications: catalogues; newsletter, invitations; brochures.
Hours & Admission Prices: Tues. & Thurs.-Sun. 11-5, Wed. 11-8. Adults $4, students & seniors $3; discounts to AAM & ICOM members; children under 12, members and MOCA members no charge. Closed New Year's Day; Easter; Independence Day; Thanksgiving; Christmas. ♿
Attendance: 20,000
Membership: Student, Senior & Artist $25; Individual $40; Household $50; Plus $75; MOCA Society $150; MOCA Fellow $250; Patron $500-$10,000.

NASA GLENN RESEARCH CENTER'S VISITOR CENTER, 21000 Brookpark Rd., Cleveland, OH 44135-3127. Tel.: 216-433-2005. Fax: 216-433-3061. TDD: 216-433-9834.
Web Site: www.nasa.gov/centers/glenn/home/index.html
Formerly: NASA Lewis Research Center's Visitor Center
Founded: 1976.
Congressional District: 20
Key Personnel: Project Mgr., Danielle Woodson; Exhibits Mgr., Bill Buckingham; Educational Programs Mgr. & Volunteer Coord., Monica Boyd; Teacher Resource Coord., Renee Yoder; Speakers Bureau Coord., Heidi Toledo; Aerospace Lecturer, Ray Storey; Aerospace Lecturer & Tour Scheduler, Brenda Morgan.
Personnel Profile: Full-Time Paid 9; Part-Time Paid 2; Part-Time Volunteers 54.
Governing Authority: federal. Parent Institution: NASA Glenn Research Center. Tax-exempt.
Aeronautics & Space Museum.
Collections: displays pertaining to nation's space program, including terrestrial energy, materials research, space shuttle & Earth study satellites; space station.
Research Fields: power systems; propulsion.
Facilities: auditorium; resource center.
Activities: grade school programs; guided tours; audiovisual programs.
Publications: NASA publications.
Hours & Admission Prices: Museum: Mon.-Fri. 9-4, Sat. 10-3, Sun. 1-5. No charge. Research Facility Tours: Wed. 2-3; advanced reservations requested. Closed New Year's Eve & Day; Easter; Thanksgiving; Christmas Eve & Day. ♿
Attendance: 100,000

THE NATURE CENTER AT SHAKER LAKES, 2600 S. Park Blvd., Cleveland, OH 44120-1699. Tel.: 216-321-5935, ext. 227. Fax: 216-321-1869.
E-mail: naturecenter@shakerlakes.org
Web Site: www.shakerlakes.org
Founded: 1966.
Congressional District: 22
Key Personnel: Exec. Dir., Kay Carlson; Bd. Pres., Gail Arnold; Dir. Devel., Molly Walsh; Financial Officer, Chrissy Maharg; Mgr. Welcome Desk, Beverly Barr.
Personnel Profile: Full-Time Paid 11; Part-Time Paid 9; Part-Time Volunteers 12.
Governing Authority: nonprofit organization. Tax-exempt: 501(c)(3).
Nature Center.
Collections: marsh & stream habitat; plants; trees; geology.
Facilities: nature center; stewardship center; nature trails; 2,000 sq. ft. exhibit space; 90-seat auditorium; classrooms; wildflower & butterfly gardens; outdoor pavilion. Museum-related items for sale.
Activities: lectures; films; arts festivals; study clubs; hobby workshops; TV programs; formally organized earth education programs for a variety of children & adult audiences; docent program; temporary exhibitions; self-guided trails; wildlife viewing area.
Publications: bimonthly letter, The Rookery; quarterly, program schedule; annual report; School Program Topics Guide.
Hours & Admission Prices: Mon.-Sat. 10-5, Sun. 1-5. No charge; donations accepted. Closed New Year's Day; Easter; Memorial Day; Independence Day; Labor Day; Thanksgiving; Christmas. ♿
Attendance: 17,935 (accurate)
Membership: Student $25; Senior $40; Individual $45; Senior Couple & Supporter $60; Family $65; Sustainer $100; Sponsor $250; Teal $500; Heron $1,000; Green Heron $2,500; Blue Heron $5,000; Great Blue Heron $10,000.

REINBERGER GALLERIES AT THE CLEVELAND INSTITUTE OF ART, 11141 East Blvd., Gund Bldg., Cleveland, OH 44106-1710. Tel.: 216-421-7000.
Web Site: www.cia.edu/galleries/galleries.php
Key Personnel: Dir., Bruce Checefsky
Art Gallery.
Collections: art exhibitions.
Hours & Admission Prices: Tues.-Sat. 10-6, Sun. 12-6.

THE ROCK AND ROLL HALL OF FAME AND MUSEUM, 751 Erieside Ave., Cleveland, OH 44114-1023. Mailing Address: 1100 Rock and Roll Blvd., Cleveland, OH 44114. Tel.: 216-781-7625. Fax: 216-781-1832.
E-mail: tmesek@rockhall.org
Web Site: www.rockhall.com
Founded: 1985.
Congressional District: 10
Key Personnel: C.E.O. & Pres., Terry Stewart; Pres. & C.E.O. Rock and Roll Hall of Fame Foundation, Joel Peresman; Co Chm., Jann Wenner; Co Chm., Frank Sullivan; Exec. Vice Pres. & C.F.O., Brian Kenyon; Vice Pres. Exhibitions & Curatorial Affairs, James Henke; Vice Pres. Education & Public Programs, Lauren Onkey; Vice Pres. Planning & Institutional Rels., Jacklyn Chisholm; Vice Pres. Devel., Gregory Harris; Vice Pres. Mktg. & Communications, Todd Mesek; Exec. Dir. New York Rock and Roll Hall of Fame Foundation, Suzan I. Evans; Vice Pres. Education & Public Programs, David Spiro; Museum Store Mgr., Catherine E. Surratt; Vice Pres. Sales & Mktg., Larry Benders; Vice Pres. Planning & Devel., Janis Purdy; Vice Pres. Finance & Administration, Brian Kenyon.
Personnel Profile: Full-Time Paid 90; Part-Time Paid 20; Part-Time Volunteers 56; Interns 9.
Governing Authority: private; nonprofit. Parent Institution: Rock and Roll Hall of Fame Foundation, Cleveland Rock & Roll Inc. Tax-exempt: 501(c)(3).
Rock and Roll Music Museum.
Collections: musical instruments; stage props; costumes; vehicles; promotional artifacts; artwork; documents; ephemera; photographs; sound recordings; periodicals.
Major Exhibits: From Asbury Park to the Promised Land: The Life and Music of Bruce Springsteen, 11/09-8/10; 2010 Inductees Exhibit, 4/10-2/11.
Research Fields: history of rock and roll from its earliest roots in folk, blues, country, R&B, & gospel music to present; Hall of Fame inductees; music business; rock music journalism & criticism.
Facilities: research library & archives; 200-seat multi-media theater; 50,000 sq. ft. exhibit space; cafe. Museum-related items for sale.
Activities: lectures; concerts; films; formally organized education programs for children & adults including distance learning & teacher education; permanent, temporary & traveling exhibitions; community festivals; facility rentals; docent & volunteer program. Annual Event: Induction Ceremony.
Publications: biannual member newsletter; exhibit guidebook; annual report; catalogs; exhibition catalog, From Asbury Park to the Promised Land: The Life and Music of Bruce Springsteen (2009).
Hours & Admission Prices: Memorial Day to Labor Day Wed. & Sat. 10-9, Thurs.-Tues. 10-5:30; Sept.-May Wed. 10-9, Thurs.-Tues. 10-5:30. Adults $22, senior citizens 65 & over $17, children 9-12 $13; members no charge. Closed Thanksgiving; Christmas. ♿
Attendance: 435,000 (accurate)
Membership: Rocker $50; Roller $140; Inductee $250; Headliner $500; Platinum $1,000; Chairman's Club $2,500; Rock Star $5,000; Legend $10,000.

ROMANIAN ETHNIC ART MUSEUM, St. Mary's Romanian Orthodox Cathedral, 3256 Warren Rd., Cleveland, OH 44111-1144. Mailing Address: Dobrea & Associates, 5500 S. Marginal Rd., Cleveland, OH 44103-1072. Tel.: 216-521-8449. Fax: 216-941-3068.
E-mail: st.mary.cathedral@sbcglobal.net
Web Site: smroc.link2net.net/culture.html#ream
Founded: 1960.
Congressional District: 20
Key Personnel: Pres., George Dobrea.
Personnel Profile: Part-Time Volunteers 25.
Governing Authority: church; nonprofit. Affiliated with Romanian Orthodox Episcopate, 2522 Grey Tower Rd., Jackson, MI 49201. Tax-exempt.
Folk Art Museum.
Collections: Anisoara Stan folk art; Dr. O.K. Cosla Romanian art; Gunther books, art & costume; Romanian artist paintings.
Research Fields: Romanian folk art & culture.
Facilities: 3,000-vol. library of books on Romanian culture, available for use on premises; reading room; classrooms. Religious & Romanian articles for sale.
Activities: guided tours; lectures; films; reading room; study clubs; permanent exhibitions.
Hours & Admission Prices: Museum: by appointment. Office: Mon.-Fri. 9-5. No charge; donations accepted.
Attendance: 1,500 (estimated)

STEAMSHIP WILLIAM G. MATHER MUSEUM, 305 Mather Way, Cleveland, OH 44114. Tel.: 216-574-9053 & 6262 (Programs). Fax: 216-574-2536.
E-mail: wgmather@aol.com
Web Site: wgmather.nhlink.net
Founded: 1991.
Congressional District: 21
Key Personnel: Exec. Dir., Holly Holcombe; Pres., James Ireland; Deputy Dir., Robert Catalano; Accountant, William McDonald; Cur., Loucinda Holt.
Personnel Profile: Full-Time Paid 4; Part-Time Paid 5; Part-Time Volunteers 180; Interns 1.
Governing Authority: private; nonprofit organization. Parent Institution: Harbor Heritage Society, Cleveland, OH. Tax-exempt: 501(c)(3).
Maritime Museum: housed in 1925 Great Lakes freighter.
Collections: 618 ft. former Great Lakes freighter & flagship; personal & transportation artifacts related to Great Lakes shipping; onboard tools, workstations, machinery & instruments needed to power, maintain, navigate, load/unload a working freighter (1925-1980).
Facilities: 300 person open deck area; dining rooms available for small groups (10-15).
Activities: docent program; tours & related activities for children; guided tours; lectures; demonstrations; special events. Annual Events: Whistle Pull in July; Air Show Deck Party Labor Day weekend.
Publications: quarterly newsletter, The MATHER Matters.
Hours & Admission Prices: May & Sept.-Oct. Fri.-Sun. 10-5; June-Aug. daily 10-5. Adults $5.50, senior citizens $4.50, students $3.50; discount to AAM members; children under 4 no charge. Closed Labor Day weekend.
Attendance: 30,697 (accurate)
Membership: Individual $20; Couple $35; Family $50; Sustaining $100; Small Business $125; Corporate $250.

THE TEMPLE MUSEUM OF RELIGIOUS ART, (M), University Circle at Silver Park, 1855 Ansel Rd., Cleveland, OH 44106. Mailing Address: 26000 Shaker Blvd., Beachwood, OH 44122-7199. Tel.: 216-831-3233. Fax: 216-831-4216.
Web Site: www.ttti.org
Founded: 1950.
Congressional District: 21
Key Personnel: Dir., Bob Allenick; Museum Dir., Sue Koletsky.
Personnel Profile: Full-Time Paid 1; Part-Time Paid 3; Part-Time Volunteers 10; Interns 1.
Governing Authority: denominational group. Parent Institution: The Temple - Tifereth Israel, 26000 Shaker Blvd., Beachwood, OH 44122. Branch gallery: The Maltz Museum of Jewish Heritage, 2929 Richmond Rd., Beachwood, OH 44122. Tax-exempt.
Religious Judaica Museum.
Collections: religious objects; ritual silver; paintings; sculpture; graphics; decorative arts; archaeology.
Research Fields: Judaic ritual; decorative & folk art.
Facilities: 45,000-vol. library.
Activities: guided tours; special exhibits.
Publications: bulletin, The Temple.
Hours & Admission Prices: Museum tours available by appointment Mon.-Fri. 9-4. No charge; donations accepted. Closed Jewish & legal holidays.
Attendance: 4,000 (estimated)

UKRAINIAN MUSEUM-ARCHIVES, INC., (M), 1202 Kenilworth Ave., Cleveland, OH 44113-4417. Tel.: 216-781-4329. Fax: 216-781-5844.
E-mail: staff@umacleveland.org
Web Site: www.umacleveland.org
Founded: 1952.
Congressional District: 10
Key Personnel: Dir., Andrew Fedynsky; Chm. Bd. Dirs., Taras Szmagala, Sr.; Sec. Bd. Dirs., Marta Mudri; Treas. Bd. Dirs., Borys Pakush; Cur., Aniza Kraus.
Personnel Profile: Full-Time Paid 1; Part-Time Paid 2; Part-Time Volunteers 35.
Governing Authority: nonprofit organization. Tax-exempt: 501(c)(3).
Ukrainian History, Culture & Art Museum.
Collections: artifacts, documents, books, sculptures, newspapers, pictures, Easter eggs & other items pertaining to Ukrainian culture & history, particularly in the United States.
Research Fields: Ukrainian press outside the Ukraine.
Facilities: 21,000-vol. library of Ukrainian books, books on the Ukraine in other languages & periodical titles including many historical publications, available for use on premises only; reading room.
Activities: community discussion.
Publications: Ukrainian books; bibliographical indexes; pamphlets; chronicles; private stamps.
Hours & Admission Prices: Tues.-Sat. 10-3. No charge; donations accepted. Closed holidays.
Attendance: 2,500 (estimated)
Membership: Regular Senior & Student $10; Regular $25; Sustaining $50; Sponsor $100; Silver $250; Gold $500.

WESTERN RESERVE HISTORICAL SOCIETY, 10825 East Blvd., Cleveland, OH 44106-1788. Tel.: 216-721-5722. Fax: 216-721-0891.
Web Site: www.wrhs.org
Founded: 1867.
Congressional District: 21
Key Personnel: Pres. & C.E.O., Gainor B. Davis, Ph.D.; Dir. Research, John Grabowski; Dir. Sales & Mktg., Angie Lowrie; Vice Pres. Museums & Historical Properties, Ed Pershey; Vice Pres. Finance & Administration, John Holtzhauser; Vice Pres. Institutional Advancement, Kelly Hall; Vice Pres. Education, Janice Ziegler.
Personnel Profile: Full-Time Paid 150; Part-Time Paid 80; Part-Time Volunteers 400; Interns 40.
Governing Authority: society. Branch Museums: History Museum - Crawford Auto-Aviation Museum; Hale Farm & Village, 2686 Oakhill Rd., Bath, OH 44210, Tel. 330-666-3711; Shandy Hall, 6333 S. Ridge W., Geneva, OH 44041, Tel. 440-466-3680; Loghurst, 3067 Boardman-Canfield, Canfield, OH 44406, Tel. 330-533-4330. Tax-exempt: 501(c)(3).
General Museum.
Collections: costumes; textiles; glassware; porcelain; early aircraft; 1895-1976 automobiles; 1770-1920 furnished rooms. Historic Buildings: 1812-1850 Hale Farm & Village, Bath, Ohio, working farm & restored village buildings; 1815 Shandy Hall, pioneer home in Unionville, Ohio; 1803 Loghurst.
Research Fields: United States, Ohio & local history; automotive history; regional aviation history.
Facilities: research library covering national & regional history, genealogical sources.
Activities: guided tours; lectures; special exhibitions; musical concerts; receptions; special events; craft demonstrations.
Publications: books, Merging Traditions; Birth of Modern Cleveland; Town to Tower; Cleveland Architecture, 1876-1976; Treasures by the Bay; James E. Taylor Sketchbook; Guide to Archives; The Jonathan Hale Farm; A Tour to New Connecticut in 1811; The Narrative of Henry Leavitt Ellsworth; Golden Wheels; If Elected; Balanced in the Wind; The Frances Payne Bolton Papers; The Terminal Tower: Tower City Center-A Historical Perspective; The Frederick C. Crawford Collection: The Automobile in American Culture; Showplace of America: Cleveland's Euclid Avenue 1850-1910; Cleveland-The Making of a City; The Western Reserve: The Story of New Connecticut in Ohio; The Encyclopedia of Cleveland History 2nd edition (in cooperation with Case Western Reserve University) & The Dictionary of Cleveland Biographies (in cooperation with Case Western Reserve University); There Are No Strangers At the Feast: Catholicism & Community in Northeastern Ohio.
Hours & Admission Prices: Wed. 1-9, Thurs.-Sat. 10-5, Sun 1-5. Adults $8.50, senior citizens $7.50, students $5; members no charge. ♿
Attendance: 205,000 (accurate)
Membership: Individual $50; Family & Couple $70; Sustaining $150; Fellow $500.

Clyde

CLYDE HISTORICAL MUSEUM, 124 W. Buckeye St., Clyde, OH 43410-1934. Mailing Address: PO Box 97, Clyde, OH 43410-0097. Tel.: 419-547-7946.
E-mail: clydeheritageleague@yahoo.com
History Museum.
Collections: local history & culture; Native American artifacts; military; personal artifacts; photographs.
Activities: summer family programs.
Hours & Admission Prices: April-Sept. Thurs. 1-4; other times by appointment.

Columbiana

THE LOG HOUSE MUSEUM OF THE HISTORICAL SOCIETY OF COLUMBIANA-FAIRFIELD TOWNSHIP, 10 E. Park Ave., Columbiana, OH 44408-1350. Tel.: 330-482-2983.
Formerly: The Historical Society of Columbiana-Fairfield Township
Founded: 1953.
Congressional District: 19
Key Personnel: Pres., Helen Gormley; Cur. & Historian, Nora Salmen; Genealogist, Joan Beatty.
Governing Authority: society; nonprofit organization. Tax-exempt.
Local History Museum: housed in original log house on site of 1807 post office.

Collections: Civil War & World War I artifacts; 8 bound volumes of letters written by General E. Holloway; bound volumes of early Columbiana newspapers; dolls; wool coverlets with dates; quilts; display of dinosaur bones; period furniture; clothing; wooden tools; books; pottery; Harvey S. Firestone.
Major Exhibits: Indian Artifacts, 4/10-4/12.
Research Fields: genealogy; local history.
Facilities: 300-vol. library of Bibles, ledgers, early local newspapers, local histories available for research on premises; reading room. Museum-related items for sale.
Activities: guided tours; permanent & temporary exhibitions.
Publications: History of Columbiana & Fairfield Township; brochure; DVD on Columbiana.
Hours & Admission Prices: Memorial Day to early Sept. Sat.-Sun. 2-4. Tours by appointment. No charge; donations accepted.
Attendance: 1,000 (estimated)
Membership: Individual $7.50; Family $10; Contributing $20; Lifetime $250.

Columbus

BUNTE GALLERY, Franklin University-Alumni Hall, 301 E. Rich St., Columbus, OH 43215-4960.
Art Gallery. Built in honor of Dr. Frederick J. Bunte, Franklin University's second president.
Collections: artwork of local & regional artists; Emerson Burkhart Collection; Elijah Pierce Piece sculpture.
Hours & Admission Prices: Mon.-Thurs. 8-5.

COSI COLUMBUS, 333 W. Broad St., Columbus, OH 43215-2738. Tel.: 614-228-2674. Fax: 614-629-3226.
E-mail: call_center@mail.cosi.org
Web Site: www.cosi.org
Founded: 1964.
Congressional District: 15
Key Personnel: Pres. & C.E.O., David E. Chesebrough, Ed.D.; Chm. Bd., Dr. Carl F. Kohrt; Vice Pres. Admin. & Finance & C.F.O., Rick Dodsworth; Vice Pres. Experience Div., Steve Langsdorf.
Personnel Profile: Full-Time Paid 137; Part-Time Paid 55.
Governing Authority: board of trustees. Tax-exempt: 501(c)(3).
Science/Technology Center.
Collections: over 300 hands-on exhibits; science; technology; industry; history.
Research Fields: science; technology; industry; history; early childhood development; learning in informal settings.
Facilities: 300,000 sq. ft. exhibit space; rental facilities; 7-story extreme screen theater; cafe. Museum-related items for sale.
Activities: hands-on exhibits; curriculum oriented programs for schools, teachers & groups; workshops; formally organized education programs; permanent, traveling & temporary exhibits; rental facilities.
Publications: quarterly stakeholder newsletter & annual report, COSI News; programming brochures; teacher newsletter, Teacher e-news; member newsletter & enews.
Hours & Admission Prices: Wed.-Sat. 10-5, Sun. 12-6. Adult $12.50, senior 60 & over $10.50, youth $7.50; discounts to ASTC members; teachers & members no charge. Extreme Screen Theater: $7.50 film only, $6 with general admission pass. Closed New Year's Day; Easter; Independence Day & day before; Thanksgiving; Christmas Eve & Day. ♿
Attendance: 536,308 (accurate)
Membership: Family Access $20; Student $25; Military, Teacher & Single Adult Family $60; Family & Grandparent $80; Donor Society $150 & up.

CENTRAL OHIO FIRE MUSEUM, 260 N. 4th St., Columbus, OH 43215-2511. Tel.: 614-464-4099.
Founded: 1982.
Personnel Profile: Full-Time Paid 4; Part-Time Volunteers 6.
Governing Authority: Tax-exempt.
Fire Museum: housed in restored 1908 engine house. Listed on the National Register of Historic Places.
Collections: hand-drawn, horse-drawn & early motorized fire apparatus; hands-on exhibits.
Activities: fire safety education programs for all ages.
Hours & Admission Prices: Tues.-Sat. 10-4; groups by appointment. Adults $6; members no charge. Closed hoildays. ♿
Attendance: 10,000 (estimated)

COLUMBUS CULTURAL ARTS CENTER, 139 W. Main St., Columbus, OH 43215-5064. Tel.: 614-645-7047. Fax: 614-645-5862. TDD: 614-645-3317.
Web Site: www.culturalartscenteronline.org
Founded: 1978.
Congressional District: 15
Key Personnel: Arts Admin., Jennifer L. Johnson; Pres. Support Organization, Richard Wissler; Mktg. Mgr., Sheri-Lynn Caffey.
Personnel Profile: Full-Time Paid 7; Part-Time Paid 6.
Governing Authority: municipal. Parent Institution: A Division of Columbus Recreation & Parks Dept. Tax-exempt.
Center for Cultural & Visual Arts.
Collections: paintings.
Facilities: meeting rooms & studios for jewelry, enameling, stone carving, ceramics, sculpture, weaving, bronze casting, painting, drawing & surface design.
Activities: organized classes; temporary & touring exhibits; concerts; poetry readings; workshops; community outreach through public art.
Publications: quarterly catalogue of class & program offerings.
Hours & Admission Prices: Gallery: Mon. 1-4 & 7pm-9:30pm, Tues. & Wed.-Fri. 9-4, Thurs. 9-4 & 7pm-9:30pm, Sat. 1-4:30. No charge; donations accepted. ♿
Attendance: 50,000
Membership: General $10.

∗ **COLUMBUS MUSEUM OF ART, (M),** 480 E. Broad St., Columbus, OH 43215-3886. Tel.: 614-221-6801. Fax: 614-221-0226.
E-mail: info@cmaohio.org
Web Site: www.columbusmuseum.org
Founded: 1878.
Congressional District: 12
Key Personnel: Pres., D. Scott Owens; First Vice Pres., John C. Vorys; Second Vice Pres., Patricia M. Jurgensen; Exec. Dir., Nannette V. Maciejunes; Chief Cur., Catherine Evans; Cur. European Art, Dominique Vasseur; Assoc. Cur. American Art, Melissa Wolfe; Assoc. Cur. Contemporary Art, Lisa Dent; Dir. Education, Cynthia Foley; Chief Registrar & Exhibitions Mgr., Melinda Knapp; Exhibition Designer, Greg Jones; Deputy Dir. Operations, Rod Bouc; Dir. Devel., Norma Sexton; Dir. Mktg. & Communications, Melissa Ferguson; Dir. Visitor Svcs. & Volunteers, Pam Edwards; Volunteer Mgr., Nancy Johnson; Museum Shop Mgr., David Tweet.
Personnel Profile: Full-Time Paid 63; Part-Time Paid 70; Part-Time Volunteers 1,400; Interns 30.
Governing Authority: nonprofit organization. Tax-exempt: 501(c)(3).
Art Museum.
Collections: late 19th & early 20th-century European & American paintings, sculpture and works on paper; photography; contemporary art; 20th-century folk art; 19th-century American textiles; 16th to 18th-century European paintings; Philip & Suzanne Schiller collection of American Social Commentary Art, 1930-1970.
Research Fields: pertaining to collection.
Facilities: 300-seat auditorium; community lecture room; sculpture garden; Derby Court; The Palette Cafe. Museum-related items for sale.
Activities: guided tours; lectures; seminars; gallery talks; films; concerts; workshops; self-guided tours; permanent, temporary & traveling exhibitions; family programs; studio classes; interactive exhibition for children & families.
Publications: bimonthly members' magazine, Artbytes; annual report; exhibition & permanent collection catalogs; gallery guides.
Hours & Admission Prices: Tues.-Wed. & Fri.-Sun. 10-5:30 & Thurs.10-8:30. Adults $8, senior citizens, students, children 6-18 $5; discounts to AAM members; children 5 & under, members and Sun. no charge. Closed New Year's Day; Independence Day; Thanksgiving; Christmas. ♿
Attendance: 209,000 (accurate)
Membership: Student $25; Member & Guest $60; Household $75; Reciprocal $115; Supporter $250; Patron $500; Benefactor $1,000.

FRANKLIN PARK CONSERVATORY, 1777 E. Broad St., Columbus, OH 43203-2040. Tel.: 614-645-TREE; 800-214-PARK. Fax: 614-645-5921.
Founded: 1895.
Key Personnel: Dir., Bruce Harkey; Museum Shop Mgr., Barb Carruthers.
Personnel Profile: Full-Time Paid 60; Part-Time Paid 15.
Conservatory.
Collections: botanical garden; plants; flowers; trees; butterflies; Chimly artwork.
Facilities: butterfly emergence center.
Hours & Admission Prices: Tues. & Thurs.-Sun. 10-5, Wed. 10-8. Adults $7.50, students & seniors $6, children 2-12 $4; discounts to AAM members; children under 2 & members no charge. Closed Thanksgiving; Christmas. ♿
Attendance: 275,000
Membership: Senior Individual & Student $25; Individual $30; Add a Guest $45; Household $55; Grandparent $55; Supporting $85; Centennial $100; Patron $250.

HERITAGE MUSEUM OF KAPPA KAPPA GAMMA, 530 E. Town St., Columbus, OH 43215-4820. Mailing Address: P.O. Box 38, Columbus, OH 43216-0038. Tel.: 614-341-2129; 866-554-1870. Fax: 614-228-6303.
E-mail: ktowers@kkg.org
Web Site: www.kappa.org/museum
Founded: 1980.
Key Personnel: Archivist & Cur., Kylie Towers.
Personnel Profile: Full-Time Paid 1; Part-Time Volunteers 12; Interns 1.
Governing Authority: Parent Institution: Kappa Kappa Gamma Foundation. Tax-exempt: 501(c)(3).
History Museum: former home of an Ohio governor, built in 1852. Listed on the National Register of Historic Places.
Collections: period furnishings; photographs.
Hours & Admission Prices: Wed.-Thurs. 1-4; other times by appointment. No charge; donations accepted.
Attendance: 1,000 (estimated)
Membership: Donor $100; Partner $250; Sponsor $500; Patron $1,000; Benefactor $5,000.

HISTORIC COSTUME & TEXTILES COLLECTION, (M), 1787 Neil Ave., Columbus, OH 43210-1220. Tel.: 614-292-3090. Fax: 614-688-8133.
E-mail: strege.2@osu.edu
Web Site: costume.osu.edu
Congressional District: 15
Key Personnel: Cur., Gayle Strege; Volunteer Coord., Harriet McBride; Museum Librarian, Leta Hendricks.
Personnel Profile: Full-Time Paid 2; Part-Time Paid 4; Part-Time Volunteers 6; Interns 1.
Governing Authority: Parent Institution: The Ohio State University. Tax-exempt.
Costume & Textile Museum.
Collections: costumes & textiles.
Major Exhibits: Fashion & Flora, 1/10-5/10.
Research Fields: costume history.
Activities: tours; lectures; research.
Publications: past & present exhibit catalogs.
Hours & Admission Prices: Wed.-Thurs. 11-6, Fri.-Sat. 12-4; other times by appointment. No charge, donations accepted. Closed university holidays. ♿
Attendance: 1,000 (estimated)
Membership: Senior $25; Active $35; Sustaining $50; Patron $100; Trendsetter $250; Couture $500; Corporate $1,000.

JACK NICKLAUS MUSEUM, 2355 Olentangy River Rd., Columbus, OH 43210-1074. Tel.: 614-247-5959. Fax: 614-247-5906.
E-mail: info@nicklausmuseum.org
Web Site: www.nicklausmuseum.org
Key Personnel: Cur., Steve Auch; Events Mgr., Barbara Hartley
Sports Museum.
Collections: Jack Nicklaus' life & career including trophies, photographs, & mementos from his 20 major championships & 100 worldwide professional victories; golf history.
Facilities: 24,000 sq. ft. exhibit space; theater. Museum-related items for sale.
Activities: corporate functions; banquets; receptions; rehearsal dinners; special events.
Hours & Admission Prices: Tues.-Sat. 9-5. Adults $10, students $5.

JUBILEE MUSEUM AND CATHOLIC CULTURAL CENTER, 57 S. Grubb St., Columbus, OH 43215-2747. Tel.: 614-461-6204. Fax: 614-221-9818.
E-mail: jubileemuseum@columbus.rr.com
Web Site: www.jubileemuseum.org
Formerly: Jubilee Museum at Holy Family
Founded: 1998.
Key Personnel: Cur., Rev. Kevin F. Lutz.
Personnel Profile: Full-Time Paid 2; Part-Time Paid 2; Part-Time Volunteers 10.
Governing Authority: Parent Institution: Diocese of Columbus.
Religious Museum: housed in the former Holy Family High School.
Collections: Holy Land & Catholic religious artifacts; paintings; statues; vestments; altars; personal artifacts.
Publications: newsletter.
Hours & Admission Prices: Mon.-Fri. 9:30-2:30 by appointment. No charge; donations accepted.
Attendance: 3,500 (estimated)

KELTON HOUSE MUSEUM & GARDEN, (M), 586 E. Town St., Columbus, OH 43215-4888. Tel.: 614-464-2022. Fax: 614-464-3346.
E-mail: keltonhouse@cs.com
Web Site: www.keltonhouse.com
Founded: 1976.
Congressional District: 15
Key Personnel: Dir. Devel. & Membership, Georgeanne Reuter; Chm. (V), Molly Dobbins; Chm. Elect, Debbie Wilkins; Pres., Melissa Kirtley.
Personnel Profile: Part-Time Paid 3; Part-Time Volunteers 35.
Governing Authority: nonprofit organization. Parent Institution: Junior League of Columbus. Tax-exempt: 501(c)(3).
Historic House Museum.
Collections: period furniture; decorative arts; china & ceramics; Victorian toys & clothing; music boxes; Civil War items; items emphasizing Columbus history.
Research Fields: local history.
Facilities: 200-vol. library; archives; rental meeting rooms & banquet facilities. Gift items for sale.
Activities: guided tours; lectures; underground railroad learning station; docent program; organized education programs; intern program for college students. Museum Sponsors: Victorian Christmas.
Publications: biannual newsletter, Keltonian.
Hours & Admission Prices: Sun. 1-4; Mon.-Fri. by appointment. Adults $6, senior citizens $4, children over 6 $2; members no charge. Closed Easter; Christmas. ♿
Attendance: 7,000 (accurate)
Membership: Friend $35; Educator $50; Preservationist $100; Ketlon Society $250 & up.

THE OHIO CRAFT MUSEUM, 1665 W. Fifth Ave., Columbus, OH 43212-2315. Tel.: 614-486-4402.
Craft Museum.
Collections: exhibits on fine craft.
Hours & Admission Prices: Mon.-Fri. 10-5, Sat.-Sun. 1-4 (during exhibitions). Closed major holidays.

* **OHIO HISTORICAL SOCIETY, (M),** 1982 Velma Ave., Columbus, OH 43211-2497. Tel.: 614-297-2300; 800-686-6124. Fax: 614-297-2352. TDD: 800-750-0750.
Web Site: www.ohiohistory.org
Formerly: Ohio Historical Center
Founded: 1885.
Congressional District: 15
Key Personnel: C.E.O., Burt A. Logan; Pres. Bd., Richard T. Prasse; Cur. Archaeology, Brad Lepper; Cur. Natural History, Robert Glotzhober; Cur., Cliff Eckle; Education & Interpretation Svcs., Connie Bodner; Chief Devel. Officer, Tomy Barry; Timeline Editor, David Simmons; Historic Sites & Facilities, George Kane; Dir. Outreach & Historic Preservation Svcs., James Strider; Mgr. Public Rels., Kim Schuette.
Personnel Profile: Full-Time Paid 180; Part-Time Paid 74; Part-Time Volunteers 1,158.
Governing Authority: nonprofit organization. Branch Museums: Adena, Chillicothe; Neil Armstrong Air & Space Museum, Wapakoneta; Buckeye Furnace, Jackson County; Campus Martius Museum of the Northwest Territory, Marietta; Wahkeena Nature Preserve, Lancaster; Cedar Bog, Urbana; Paul L. Dunbar House, Dayton; Flint Ridge Museum, Brownsville; Fort Ancient, Lebanon; Fort Hill, Hillsboro; Fort Laurens, Bolivar; Fort Meigs, Perrysburg; Fort Recovery, Fort Recovery; Glendower, Lebanon; U.S. Grant Birthplace, Point Pleasant; U.S. Grant Boyhood Home, Georgetown; U.S. Grant Schoolhouse, Georgetown; Benjamin R. Hanby House, Westerville; Rutherford B. Hayes Museum, Fremont; Indian Mill Museum, Upper Sandusky; McCook House, Carrollton; National Road-Zane Grey Museum, Norwich; Our House Tavern, Gallipolis; Piqua Historical Area & Historic Indian Museum, Piqua; Museum of Ceramics, East Liverpool; Schoenbrunn, New Philadelphia; Serpent Mound, Peebles; Zoar Village, Zoar; Ohio State House Visitor Center; Ohio Village, Columbus; Warren G. Harding Home & Memorial, Marion. Youngstown Center of Industry and Labor, Youngstown; National Afro-American Museum & Cultural Center, Wilberforce; Cooke House, Sandusky; Shaker Historical Museum, Shaker Heights. Tax-exempt: 501(c)(3).
History Museum.
Collections: prehistoric archaeology of Midwest; pre-Columbian Indian artifacts & art objects; natural history: invertebrates, insects, fish, reptiles, birds, mammals, minerals; historical objects: paintings, decorative arts, drawings, prints, craft tools & products, textiles, clothing, glass & ceramics of Ohio; industrial & military artifacts; library & manuscript collections; state archives; artifacts from the Zoar & Schoenbrunn religious groups.
Major Exhibits: Soul! Art from the National Afro-American Museum & Cultural Center, 11/09-2/10; To Have and To Hold: Treasures from the Christopher Collection, 11/09-4/10; Quilts with Soul, 12/09-2/10; Were You There? An Illustrated Spiritual by Allan Rohen Crite, 12/09-2/10; Quilting African American (T), 4/10-5/10.
Research Fields: archaeology; natural history & environmental studies; architectural; business; industrial; labor; military; political & social history.

Facilities: 142,000-vol. library on Ohio history, prehistory, & natural history available for inter-library loan & on premises; reading room; 280-seat auditorium; restaurant. Reproductions, publications & other museum-related items for sale.
Activities: permanent & temporary exhibitions; guided tours; gallery talks; films; lectures; school loan service; TV & radio programs; volunteer program & council; formally organized education programs for undergraduate & graduate college students; state historic preservation program; training programs for professional museum workers; field services to other historical organizations.
Publications: bimonthly magazine, Timeline; bimonthly newsletters, Echoes, The Local Historian & Ohio Preservation.
Hours & Admission Prices: Ohio Historical Center: Thurs. 9-9, Fri.-Sat. 9-5, Sun. 1-5. Ohio Village & Branch Sites: call 800-686-6124 for hours. Archives-Library: Thurs. 1-9, Fri.-Sat. 9-5. Adults $8, students $4; discounts to Golden Buckeye, Ohio Farm Bureau Western Reserve, OAHSM, society, AAA, AARP, AAM & ICOM members; OHS members & children under 6 no charge. Closed New Year's Day; Thanksgiving; Christmas Day. ♿
Attendance: 409,130 (accurate)
Membership: Individual $35; Family $55; History Lover $85; Supporter $235.

ORTON GEOLOGICAL MUSEUM, OHIO STATE UNIVERSITY, 155 S. Oval Mall, Columbus, OH 43210-1308. Tel.: 614-292-6896. Fax: 614-292-1496.
E-mail: gnidovec@geology.ohio-state.edu
Founded: 1892.
Congressional District: 11
Key Personnel: Dir. & Professor, Bill Ausich; Collection Mgr. & Cur., Dale Gnidovec.
Personnel Profile: Full-Time Paid 2; Part-Time Volunteers 1.
Governing Authority: university; nonprofit organization. Parent Institution: Ohio State University, School of Earth Sciences. Tax-exempt.
College Geology Museum: housed in Orton Hall.
Collections: fossils; minerals; rocks; meteorites.
Research Fields: paleontology; mineralogy.
Facilities: Fossils, minerals & rocks for sale.
Activities: guided tours; permanent & temporary exhibitions.
Hours & Admission Prices: Mon.-Fri. 9-5. No charge; donations accepted. ♿
Attendance: 12,000

THE SCHUMACHER GALLERY, CAPITAL UNIVERSITY, (M), 1 College and Main, Columbus, OH 43209-2394. Tel.: 614-236-6319. Fax: 614-236-6490.
Web Site: www.schumachergallery.org
Founded: 1964.
Congressional District: 12
Key Personnel: Dir., Dr. Cassandra Tellier; Asst. to Dir., David Gentilini.
Personnel Profile: Full-Time Paid 2; Part-Time Paid 12; Part-Time Volunteers 6; Interns 2.
Governing Authority: university. Parent Institution: Capital University. Tax-exempt: 170(b)(1)(A).
University Art Museum.
Collections: Ohio artists; graphics; contemporary painting & sculpture; period works, 16th-19th century; ethnic art; Asian art; Inuit art; African & Oceanic Art.
Facilities: library.
Activities: guided tours; lectures; films; gallery talks; concerts; formally organized education programs for undergraduate & graduate college students; permanent, temporary & traveling exhibitions.
Hours & Admission Prices: Sept.-May Mon.-Sat. 1-5. No charge; donations accepted. ♿
Attendance: 10,000

WEXNER CENTER FOR THE ARTS, The Ohio State University, 1871 N. High St., Columbus, OH 43210-1393. Tel.: 614-292-0330. Fax: 614-292-3369 & 2827.
E-mail: info@wexarts.org
Web Site: www.wexarts.org
Founded: 1989.
Congressional District: 15
Key Personnel: Dir., Sherri Geldin; Pres., C. Robert Kidder; Deputy Dir., Jack Jackson; Dir. Mktg. & Communications, Jerry Dannemiller; Exhibitions Mgr., Jill Davis; Dir. Public Rels. & Media Rels., Karen Simonian; Cur. Media Arts, William Horrigan; Dir. Performing Arts, Charles Helm; Dir. Education, Shelly Casto; Chief Exhibitions Designer, Larry Heller; Chief Cur. Exhibitions, Helen Molesworth; Chm. (V), Leslie H. Wexner; Dir. Devel., Jeff Byars; Head Registrar, Megan Cavanaugh.
Personnel Profile: Full-Time Paid 70; Part-Time Paid 63; Part-Time Volunteers 129; Interns 5.
Governing Authority: Ohio State University. Tax-exempt.
Contemporary Arts Center.
Collections: painting, sculpture, photography & graphic arts of 1960-1970s; sub-collections of graphic & Asian arts; multi-disciplinary, contemporary arts center.
Facilities: film & video auditorium; 2 performing arts theaters; video & audio production & editing; print viewing room; cafe. Museum-related items for sale.
Activities: performing arts; film & video programs; lectures; gallery talks; formally organized education programs; loan, permanent, & temporary circulating exhibitions.
Publications: monthly calendar; catalogues; gallery guides.
Hours & Admission Prices: Tues.-Wed. & Sun. 11-6, Thurs.-Sat. 11-8. No charge. ♿
Attendance: 190,380 (accurate)
Membership: Friend $50; Patron $125; Sponsor $250; Fellow $500; Vanguard Circle $1,000; Director's Circle $1,500; Producers Circle $2,500; Armory Circle $5,000; Benefactors Circle $10,000; Trustees Circle $25,000.

Conneaut

CONNEAUT RAILROAD MUSEUM, Depot St., Conneaut, OH 44030. Mailing Address: P.O. Box 643, Conneaut, OH 44030-0643. Tel.: 440-599-7878.
E-mail: ronbgrumpy@suite224.net
Founded: 1962.
Congressional District: 11
Key Personnel: Natl. Dir. & Chm. (V), Jim Clancy; Pres. (V), & Museum Shop Mgr., Ronald F. Brundage, Jr.; Vice Pres., James Scott; Sec., Polly Sauerwein; Treas., Norman Gross.
Personnel Profile: Part-Time Paid 10; Part-Time Volunteers 5.
Governing Authority: municipal. Affiliated with the National Railway Historical Society. Tax-exempt: 501(c)(3) & 170(b)(1)(A).
Antique Railroad Museum: housed in 1900 former New York Central depot.
Collections: engines; hopper car; wood caboose; 1866 stock certificate of Red River Line, N.Y.C.; relics of Ashtabula disaster 1876; scale models of locomotives & equipment; lanterns; photos; timetables; watches; passes; steam era display.
Activities: guided tours; formally organized education programs for children; temporary & traveling exhibitions.
Publications: monthly newsletter, The Semaphore.
Hours & Admission Prices: Memorial Day-Labor Day daily 12-5. No charge; donations accepted. ♿
Attendance: 10,000 (estimated)
Membership: Sustaining $8; International $35.

Coshocton

* **JOHNSON-HUMRICKHOUSE MUSEUM, (M),** Roscoe Village, 300 N. Whitewoman St., Coshocton, OH 43812-1061. Tel.: 740-622-8710. Fax: 740-622-8710 *51.
E-mail: JHMuseum@sbcglobal.net
Web Site: www.jhmuseum.org/default.htm
Founded: 1931.
Congressional District: 18
Key Personnel: Dir., Patti Malenke; Chm. (V), Hilma Thomas; Pres. (V), Carolyn Simpson; Dir. Devel., Terry Reddick; Museum Shop Mgr., Phyllis Cotterman.
Personnel Profile: Full-Time Paid 2; Part-Time Paid 5; Part-Time Volunteers 4.
Governing Authority: county. Administered by Board of Trustees, Coshocton County Public Library. Tax-exempt: 170(b)(1)(A).
General Museum.
Collections: American Indian basketry, beadwork, pottery, Inuit carvings & artifacts; Ohio prehistoric points & tools; Japanese & Chinese fine & decorative arts, porcelains, lacquer ware, metal & wood sculptures, cloisonne, textiles, and Japanese prints, armor & weaponry; 19th- & 20th-century American & European textiles, period firearms, 19th-century American; cut glass, ceramics & decorative arts; tools, numismatics & items of local history; Newark Holy Stones.
Facilities: community meeting room. Museum-related items for sale.
Activities: guided tours; lectures; gallery talks; formally organized education programs for children; inter-museum loan, permanent & temporary exhibitions.
Publications: quarterly newsletter.
Hours & Admission Prices: May-Oct. daily 12-5; Nov.-April Tues.-Sun. 1-4:30. Adults $3, youth $2; members no charge. Closed New Year's Day; Easter; Thanksgiving; Christmas Eve & Day. ♿
Attendance: 16,000 (accurate)

Membership: Individual $20; Dual & Family $30; Contributing $50; Supporting $100; Sustaining $200; Benefactor $350; Founder $500.

POMERENE CENTER FOR THE ARTS, 317 Mulberry St., Coshocton, OH 43812-2037. Tel.: 740-622-0326.
E-mail: acornell@pomerenearts.org
Web Site: www.pomerenearts.org/index.htm
Key Personnel: Dir., Anne Cornell
Art Museum: housed in an 1836 Greek Revival home.
Collections: works by local, regional & national artists.
Hours & Admission Prices: Tues.-Fri. 1-5; Sat.-Sun. by appointment. No Charge.

ROSCOE VILLAGE FOUNDATION, 600 N. Whitewoman St., Coshocton, OH 43812-1072. Tel.: 740-622-9310; 800-877-1830. Fax: 740-623-6555.
E-mail: rvmarketing@roscoevillage.com
Web Site: www.roscoevillage.com
Founded: 1968.
Congressional District: 18
Key Personnel: C.E.O., Joel L. Hampton; Dir. Landscaping, Connie Miller; Dir. Facilities, Chad A. Miller; Dir. Operations, Rhonda Hanes; Historian, Wilma Hunt.
Personnel Profile: Full-Time Paid 50; Part-Time Paid 55; Part-Time Volunteers 60; Interns 2.
Governing Authority: nonprofit organization. Parent Institution: Roscoe Village Foundation, Inc. Tax-exempt: 501(c)(3).
Historic Site: more than 30 restored buildings; Greek Revival structures.
Collections: living history buildings with emphasis on Ohio's canal-era period; period furniture; clothing; crafts; decorative arts; glass; photos; household utensils; canal-era artifacts; maps; deeds; scrip; rules; tools; tin smith shop; spinning wheel; interactive display for children: water wheel & woodworking.
Research Fields: Ohio & Erie Canal history.
Facilities: 800-vol. library; 65-seat auditorium; educational facilities; meeting rooms; two restaurants; country inn. Museum-related items for sale.
Activities: self-guided tours; lecture series; festivals; hobby workshops; craft demonstrations; rental gallery; organized education programs; participatory exhibits. Village Sponsors: Dulcimer Days; Coshocton Canal Festival; Apple Butter Stirrin'; Christmas Candlelightings; Civil War Reenactment; Heritage Craft and Old Time Music Festival.
Publications: brochures; quarterly, Roscoe Village News; books, The Big Ditch; Twenty-Five Miles to Nowhere; Around the Stove in Roscoe's General Store; Plan & Profile Map of Ohio & Erie Canal; Business Meeting Planners; Tour Meeting Planners; map, canals of Ohio.
Hours & Admission Prices: Visitor's Center: daily 10-5. Building Tour: family $29.95, adults $9.95, student $4.95; discounts to seniors, AAA members & groups. Closed New Year's Day, Easter, Thanksgiving, Christmas. ♿
Attendance: 334,000 (estimated)
Membership: Individual $30; Family $50; Patron $75; Sustaining $100; Contributing $250; Fellow $500; William Roscoe Society $10,000; Corporate $500, $750, $1,000, $2,500, $4,000, $5,000.

Crestline

CRESTLINE SHUNK MUSEUM, 211 N. Thoman St., Crestline, OH 44827-1444. Mailing Address: P.O. Box 456, Crestline, OH 44827-0456. Tel.: 419-683-3410.
Founded: 1947.
Key Personnel: Pres. (V), Ray Holland.
Governing Authority: society; nonprofit organization. Parent Institution: Crestline Historical Society. Tax-exempt: 501(c)(3).
Local History Museum: housed in 1860 Victorian home.
Collections: railroad artifacts; summer kitchen; Victorian parlor & bedroom; glassware; silver; china; toys; dolls; early school memorabilia; Crawford Indian room.
Activities: guided tours; lectures.
Publications: annual booklet, Crestline Historical Society.
Hours & Admission Prices: Memorial Day-Labor Day Sat.-Sun. 2-4; other times by appointment. No charge; donations accepted.
Attendance: 200 (estimated)
Membership: Individual $6; Family $10; Life $150.

LOWE-VOLK PARK NATURE CENTER, Crawford Park District, 2401 St. Rt. 598, Crestline, OH 44827. Tel.: 419-683-9000. Fax: 419-683-6281.
Key Personnel: Dir., Bill Fisher
Nature Center.
Collections: local natural history & culture; murals; wildlife; photographs; stained glass.
Facilities: Museum-related items for sale.
Activities: educational programs; special events.
Hours & Admission Prices: Mon.-Sat. 9-4, Sun. 12-4.

Dayton

AULLWOOD AUDUBON CENTER AND FARM, (M), 1000 Aullwood Rd., Dayton, OH 45414-1198. Tel.: 937-890-7360. Fax: 937-890-2382.
E-mail: ckrueger@audubon.org
Web Site: aullwood.center.audubon.org
Founded: 1957.
Congressional District: 3
Key Personnel: Exec. Dir., Charity Krueger; Pres. (V), Cindy Garner; Education Coord., Tom Hissong; Naturalist Teacher, John Wilson; Naturalist Teacher, Mikell Kloeters; Naturalist Teacher, Nicole Conrad; Volunteer Coord., Nina Lapitan; Farm Mgr., John Stedman; Maintenance Supvr., Pat Rice; Resource Technician, Gary Reibert; Devel. Coord., Ardith Hamilton; Office Mgr., Barb Trick; Museum Shop Mgr., Wendy Jacoby; Membership & Naturalist Teacher, Larry Brown; Outreach Naturalist, Chris Rowlands; Center Maintenance Worker, Lonny Kidd; Housekeeper, Melissa Nicely.
Personnel Profile: Full-Time Paid 14; Part-Time Paid 35; Part-Time Volunteers 900; Interns 12.
Governing Authority: nonprofit organization. Parent Institution: National Audubon Society, 225 Varick St., 7th Fl., New York, NY 10014. Subsidiary Institution: Friends of Aullwood. Tax-exempt: 501(c)(3).
Environmental Education Facility & Working Educational Farm.
Collections: natural history; energy conservation; agricultural material; working farm includes buildings, pasture, croplands, livestock & machinery; 200 acres of natural & agricultural land, interpretative buildings & exhibits including stores, restored & created tall-grass prairie.
Major Exhibits: Photographs by Ray Mueller, 5/10-6/10; Art Quilt Exhibit, 7/10-8/10; Amish Quilt Exhibit, 9/10.
Research Fields: energy; agriculture; organic agriculture; birds; butterflies; plants; environmental education techniques.
Facilities: 2,000-vol. library of natural history, conservation & environmental books available for staff & selected public use; nature center. Museum-related items for sale.
Activities: guided tours; lectures; films; consulting services to schools; formally organized education programs; professional teachers; permanent & temporary exhibitions; special events.
Publications: Aullwood Audubon Center & Farm Newsletter.
Hours & Admission Prices: Mon.-Sat. 9-5, Sun. 1-5. Adults $4, students $2; ANCA, National Audubon Society & Friends of the Aullwood members no charge. Closed winter holidays. ♿
Attendance: 110,000 (accurate)
Membership: Student $20; Individual & Senior Couple $40; Family & Household or Grandparent & Grandchild $50-$124; Sustainer $125-$249; Sponsor $250-$499; Patron $500 & up.

*** BOONSHOFT MUSEUM OF DISCOVERY, (M),** 2600 DeWeese Pkwy., Dayton, OH 45414-5400. Tel.: 937-275-7431. Fax: 937-275-5811.
E-mail: info@boonshoftmuseum.org
Web Site: www.boonshoftmuseum.org
Founded: 1893.
Congressional District: 3
Key Personnel: Pres. & C.E.O., Mark J. Meister; Chm. (V), Steve Zofkie; C.F.O., Ken Betche; Vice Pres. Collections & Research, Lynn Simonelli; Vice Pres. Education, Susan Pion; Dir. Astronomy, Cheri Adams; Dir. Admin., Karen Finlay; Vice Pres. External Rels., Diane Farrell; Museum Shop Mgr., Angela Shaffer; Dir. Facilities Management, Mike McFann; Cur. Anthropology, William Kennedy; Sun Water Indian Village/Archaeological Park Site Mgr. & Site Anthropologist, Andrew Sawyer; Cur. Live Animals, Mark Mazzei.
Personnel Profile: Full-Time Paid 50; Part-Time Paid 29; Part-Time Volunteers 400; Interns 10.
Governing Authority: nonprofit organization. Parent Institution: Dayton Society of Natural History. Subsidiary Institutions: Sunwatch Indian Village/Archaeological Park. Tax-exempt: 501(c)(3) & 170(b)(1)(A).
Natural History Museum & Archaeological Park.
Collections: archaeology; ornithology; ethnology; entomology; geology; herpetology; invertebrates; mammals; paleontology; live animals; archives.
Major Exhibits: Too Small to See (T), 1/10-5/10; How People Make Things (T), 5/10-9/10; Amazing Sea (T), 9/10-1/11.
Research Fields: biology; paleontology; archaeology; astronomy.
Facilities: Caryl D. Philips Space Theater; Bieser Discovery Center; Wild Ohio; Apollo Observatory; The Food Chain Cafe; Boonshoft Science Central; Mead Treehouse; EcoTrek; Reynold & Reynolds Exploration Computer Center; Science of a Sphere. Branch Museum: Visitors' Center at SunWatch, a reconstructed 12th century Indian village. Museum-related items for sale at both locations.
Activities: guided school tours; lectures; films; study clubs; formally organized education programs; weekend demonstrations; permanent & temporary exhibitions; daily planetary programs; weekend laser shows.

Publications: annual report; monthly calendar, Quick E Bytes; monthly newsletter, Smart-E-News; biannual newsletter.
Hours & Admission Prices: Mon.-Sat. 9-5, Sun. 12-5. Adults $8.50, senior citizens & children 2-12 $7.50; discount to seniors & AAM members; members, ACM, AZA & ASTC members no charge. Call 937-275-7431 for times & titles of shows. Laser programs available on some weekends, call for information. SunWatch is open Tues.-Sat. 9-5, Sun. 12-5. Adults $5, children $3. Call 937-268-8199 for program information. Both locations closed New Year's Eve & Day; Easter; Thanksgiving; Christmas Eve & Day. ♿
Attendance: 240,563 (accurate)
Membership: Military $59; Voyager $69; Adventurer $100; Explorer $250; Discoverer $500; John B. Greene Society $1,000 & up.

COX ARBORETUM METROPARK, 6733 Springboro Pike, Dayton, OH 45449-3496. Tel.: 937-434-9005. Fax: 937-438-1221. TDD: 937-275-PARK.
E-mail: jwoodhull@metroparks.org
Web Site: www.coxarboretum.org
Formerly: Cox Arboretum & Gardens MetroPark
Founded: 1963.
Congressional District: 6
Key Personnel: Dir. Arboretum, Jay Woodhull; Park Mgr., Rick Stanforth; Horticulturist, Richmond Pearson; Family & Children's Education, Katrina Arnold; Adult Education, Yvonne Dunphe.
Personnel Profile: Full-Time Paid 15; Part-Time Paid 7; Part-Time Volunteers 378; Interns 3.
Governing Authority: county. Parent Institution: Five Rivers Metro Park, 1375 E. Siebenthaler, Dayton, OH 45414. Tel: 937-275-7275. Branch Museum: Aullwood Gardens. Tax-exempt.
Arboretum & Gardens.
Collections: rock garden; shrub garden; crabapple allee; water garden; wildflower garden; clematis arbor; conifer knoll; edible landscape garden; herb garden; conservation corner - prairie; butterfly meadow; magnolia collection; children's boxwood maze; meditation garden; nature trails; butterfly house.
Research Fields: magnolia, lilacs.
Facilities: 750-vol. library of books on horticultural & gardening available for research by staff or public on premises; botanical garden; reading room; 50-seat auditorium; 175-seat conference center; edible landscape demonstration garden; herb garden; propagation greenhouses; rock garden. Horticultural-related items, gifts & books for sale.
Activities: guided tours; lectures; group talks; study clubs; formally organized education programs for children & adults; docent programs; permanent exhibitions. Museum Sponsors: Butterfly & Garlic Festivals.
Publications: newsletter, Arb News; program schedule; brochures & mailers.
Hours & Admission Prices: Grounds: April-Oct. daily 8am-10pm; Nov.-March daily 8am-8pm. Buildings: Mon.-Fri. 8-5, Sat.-Sun. 11-4. No charge; donations accepted. Closed New Year's Day; Christmas. ♿
Attendance: 360,000 (estimated)
Membership: Crabapple $40; Dogwood $75; Lilac $100; Cherry $250; Magnolia $500; Founders Society $1,000.

* **DAYTON ART INSTITUTE, (M),** 456 Belmonte Park N., Dayton, OH 45405-4700. Tel.: 937-223-5277. Fax: 937-223-3140.
E-mail: info@daytonartinstitute.org
Web Site: www.daytonartinstitute.org
Founded: 1919.
Congressional District: 3
Key Personnel: Dir. & C.E.O., Janice Driesbach; Chm., Michael Gretizer; Dir. Planned Gifts & Membership Coord., Laura Letton; Dir. Public Rels. & Mktg., Dona Vella; Dir. Educational Resources & Svcs., Susan Anable; Chief Cur., Will South; Museum Shop Mgr., Diane Haskell.
Personnel Profile: Full-Time Paid 22; Part-Time Paid 55; Part-Time Volunteers 355; Interns 7.
Governing Authority: nonprofit organization. Tax-exempt.
Art Museum.
Collections: European & American paintings & sculpture, classical, Asian, pre-Columbian primitive objects; prints; graphic arts; ceramics & decorative arts; contemporary art collection.
Research Fields: all fields of art history.
Facilities: 500-seat auditorium; conference & meeting space; classrooms; cafe. Books, reproductions, jewelry, sculpture & postcards for sale.
Activities: guided tours; lectures; gallery talks; concerts; formally organized education programs; docent program; participatory gallery; permanent, temporary & traveling exhibitions. Museum Sponsors: annual Oktoberfest; annual Art Ball.
Publications: quarterly members magazine; annual report; exhibition catalogs.
Hours & Admission Prices: Tues.-Wed. & Fri. 10-4, Thurs. 10-8, Sat.-Sun. 12-5. Special exhibition fee charged. Closed major holidays. ♿
Attendance: 147,000 (accurate)
Membership: Student $25; Senior $30; Individual $40; Senior Couple 65 & over $45; Family $60; Sponsoring $125; Sustaining $250; Cantilever Society $500; Jefferson Patterson Society $1,300 & up.

DAYTON HISTORY AT CARILLON PARK, (M), 1000 Carillon Blvd., Dayton, OH 45409-2023. Tel.: 937-293-2841, ext. 100. Fax: 937-293-5798.
E-mail: bkress@carillonpark.org
Web Site: www.carillonpark.org
Formerly: Carillon Historical Park
Founded: 1950.
Congressional District: 3
Key Personnel: Chm. (V), Rob Connelly; Pres. & C.E.O., Brady Kress; Mgr. Community Collections, Nancy Horlacher; Dir. Education & Program Svcs., Alex Heckman; Mgr. Events, Teresa Beachler; Dir. Grounds & Maintenance, Lloyd Miller; Lead Interpreter, Danny Schlegal; Lead Interpreter, Angela Neimie; Communications Mgr., Christopher Jones; Exec. Asst., Pamela Ribic; Museum Shop Mgr. & Visitors Svcs. Mgr., Linda Vanover; Dir. Business Operations, Gail Hamer; Mgr. Devel. Technology, Joy McMeekin.
Personnel Profile: Full-Time Paid 15; Part-Time Paid 12; Part-Time Volunteers 175.
Governing Authority: nonprofit organization. Parent Institution: Dayton Foundation. Tax-exempt.
Historical Museum Complex.
Collections: Wright brothers' 1905 airplane; camera; tools; bicycles; engine; printing items; locally made antique automobiles & bicycles; train car; bridges; canal lock; 1835 locomotive; interurban car; trolley bus; caboose; Conestoga wagon; Concord coach; 1776 Newcom tavern; 1815 stone cottage; 1895 canal superintendent's office; 1896 railway station; 1896 one-room school; 1924 gas station; 1930s print shop equipment; Deeds Carillon bell tower.
Research Fields: Wright brothers; local printing; industry companies.
Facilities: 23 buildings with exhibits information. Museum-related items for sale.
Activities: interpreters in buildings; special events; concerts; one-room schoolhouse program for fourth graders; three videos; student workshops.
Publications: booklets; pamphlets.
Hours & Admission Prices: Mon.-Sat. 9:30-5, Sun. 12-5. Adults $8, senior citizens $7, students 3-16 $5; discounts to AASLH members; children under 3 & members no charge. ♿
Attendance: 160,000 (estimated)
Membership: Individual $30; Family $40; Supporter $50; Sponsor $100; Patron $200.

DAYTON INTERNATIONAL PEACE MUSEUM, (M), 208 W. Monument Ave., Dayton, OH 45402-3015. Tel.: 937-227-3223.
E-mail: info@daytonpeacemuseum.org
Web Site: www.daytonpeacemuseum.org
Founded: 2004.
Congressional District: 3
Key Personnel: Dir., Steve Fryburg.
Personnel Profile: Part-Time Volunteers 35; Interns 3.
Governing Authority: nonprofit organization. Tax-exempt: 501(c)(3).
Peace Museum.
Collections: history of peace, nonviolence, & peaceful cultures; cultural & religious tolerance; photographs.
Activities: educational programs; special events.
Hours & Admission Prices: Tues.-Sat. 10-5, Sun. 1-5. No charge; donations accepted. Closed major holidays.
Membership: Student $25; Individual $45; Family $65; Peace Promoter $100; Organization $150; Peace Advocate $500; Peace Sustainer $1,000; Peace Patron $5,000; Founder's Club $10,000.

DUNBAR HOUSE STATE MEMORIAL, 219 N. Paul Laurence Dunbar St., Dayton, OH 45402-6502. Mailing Address: 1982 Velma Ave., Columbus, OH 43211-2453. Tel.: 937-293-2841, ext. 101.
E-mail: aheckman@daytonhistory.org
Web Site: www.ohiohistory.org/places/dunbar
Formerly: Paul Laurence Dunbar State Memorial
Founded: 1936.
Congressional District: 3
Key Personnel: Pres. (V), Benette DeCoux.
Personnel Profile: Full-Time Paid 1; Part-Time Paid 2; Part-Time Volunteers 15; Interns 1.
Governing Authority: society. Parent Institution: The Ohio Historical Society, 1985 Velma Ave., Columbus, OH. 43211. Tax-exempt.
Historic House: home of Negro poet, Paul Laurence Dunbar.
Collections: Paul Laurence Dunbar collection; clothing worn by Paul Laurence

& Mrs. Dunbar; family paintings & photographs; Dunbar family bible, his typewriter, publications & personal library; Dunbar's fishing poles & other recreational items.
Research Fields: American history.
Activities: Annual Event: Dunbar's Birthday Commemoration in June.
Hours & Admission Prices: April-May Sat. 9-5, Sun. 12-5; Memorial Day to Labor Day Thurs.-Sun. 9-5, holidays 12-5; Sept.-Oct. Sat. 9:30-5, Sun. 12-5. Adults $6, children 6-12 $3; discounts to active military, AAA members, seniors & groups; children 5 & under no charge. ♿
Attendance: 5,000 (accurate)
Membership: Annual $47.

PATTERSON HOMESTEAD, 1815 Brown St., Dayton, OH 45409-2414. Mailing Address: 1000 Carillon Blvd. #D, Dayton, OH 45409-2023. Tel.: 937-222-9724. Fax: 937-222-0345.
Founded: 1953.
Congressional District: 3
Key Personnel: Dir., Denise L. Darling; Cur., Ray Shook; Rental Supvr., Mike Smoot; Maintenance Supvr., Bill LaFeur.
Personnel Profile: Full-Time Paid 1; Part-Time Paid 4; Part-Time Volunteers 12; Interns 2.
Governing Authority: municipal. Affiliated with Montgomery County Historical Society, 224 N. St. Clair St., Dayton, OH 45402. Tax-exempt.
Historic House: Patterson Homestead, a vernacular Ohio Federal style farmhouse built between 1816-1850.
Collections: period furniture, ranging from the hand-made to machine produced products including Queen Anne, Chippendale, Federal, American Empire, Eastlake & the classical revival style of the Victorian period, several oil portraits of members of the Patterson family; manuscript; furniture textiles, & books belonging to Pattersons.
Research Fields: Kentucky & Ohio pioneers: Col. Robert Patterson, founder of Lexington, KY; Frank & John H. Patterson, founders of National Cash Register Co.
Facilities: 110-seat rental facility available for public & private events.
Activities: guided tours; lectures; formally organized education programs for children & graduate students affiliated with Wright State University; docent program or council; permanent & temporary exhibitions; rental facilities.
Publications: Montgomery County Historical Society newsletter, Ionic Columns.
Hours & Admission Prices: May-Oct. Thurs.-Sat. 10-4. Suggested Donation: $2 per person. Closed legal holidays. ♿
Attendance: 1,280 (accurate)
Membership: Seniors $15; Individual $25; Family $40; Sustaining $100; Patron $500; Benefactor $1,000 and up.

ROBERT AND ELAINE STEIN GALLERIES, 3640 Colonel Glenn Hwy., 128-CAC, Dayton, OH 45435-0001. Tel.: 937-775-2978. Fax: 937-775-4082.
E-mail: tess.cortes@wright.edu
Web Site: www.wright.edu/artgalleries/
Formerly: Wright State University Art Galleries
Founded: 1974.
Congressional District: 7
Key Personnel: Gallery Coord., Tess Cortes.
Personnel Profile: Full-Time Paid 1; Part-Time Paid 12; Part-Time Volunteers 10; Interns 1.
Governing Authority: university. Parent Institution: Wright State University. Tax-exempt.
University Art Gallery.
Collections: contemporary works of art; works on paper; paintings; sculpture; visual documentations.
Research Fields: all areas of contemporary art.
Facilities: preparation areas.
Activities: contemporary art exhibitions; lectures; films; gallery talks; formally organized education programs for undergraduate & graduate students affiliated with Wright State Univ.
Publications: exhibition catalogs; artists' books; print editions; CD-ROM multimedia catalogues.
Hours & Admission Prices: Tues.-Fri. 10-4, Sat.-Sun. 12-5, special hours on WSU Theatre nights. No charge. Closed holidays. ♿
Attendance: 12,000 (accurate)
Membership: Student $25; Alumni $50; Artist $100; Educator $150; Friend $500.

SUNWATCH INDIAN VILLAGE/ARCHAEOLOGICAL PARK, 2301 W. River Rd., Dayton, OH 45417. Tel.: 937-268-8199. Fax: 937-268-1760.
E-mail: sunwatch@sunwatch.org
Web Site: www.sunwatch.org
Formerly: Sunwatch Prehistoric Indian Village
Founded: 1988.
Congressional District: 3
Key Personnel: Pres. & C.E.O., Mark Meister; Bd. Chm., Steve Zofkie; Dir. Education, Jean Copas; Museum Shop Mgr., Janet Williams; Site Mgr., Andrew Sawyer.
Personnel Profile: Full-Time Paid 3; Part-Time Paid 3; Part-Time Volunteers 20; Interns 8.
Governing Authority: private; nonprofit organization. Parent Institution: Dayton Society of Natural History, Dayton. Tax-exempt: 501(c)(3).
Historic Site: reconstruction of an 800-year-old village built by the Fort Ancient Indians; designated a National Historic Landmark in 1990.
Collections: more than one million artifacts discovered from the Fort Ancient Indian culture of the AD 1200s.
Research Fields: Archaeology.
Facilities: visitor center; reconstructed 800 year old village; restored native prairie; lecture rooms.
Activities: family days; scout days; overnights; pow wow; nature flute gathering. Museum Sponsors: Keeping The Tradition Pow Wow; Sun Watch Flute & Art Gathering; Summer Lore.
Publications: Adventures.
Hours & Admission Prices: Tues.-Sat. 9-5, Sun. 12-5. Adults $5, senior citizens & students 6-17 $3; members no charge. Closed New Year's Eve & Day; Easter; Thanksgiving; Christmas Eve & Day. ♿
Attendance: 21,000 (accurate)
Membership: Military $59; Family & Grandparent $69; Adventurer $100; Explorer $250; Discoverer $500; John B. Greene Society $1,000 & up.

Defiance

AU GLAIZE VILLAGE, 12296 Krouse Rd., Defiance, OH 43512. Mailing Address: P.O. Box 801, Defiance, OH 43512-0801. Tel.: 419-782-7255.
Founded: 1966.
Congressional District: 5
Key Personnel: Pres., Lynn Lantz; Vice Pres., Jerry DeLong.
Personnel Profile: Full-Time Volunteers 3; Part-Time Volunteers 12.
Governing Authority: county; nonprofit. Parent Institution: Defiance County Historical Society. Branch Museums: William Bensinger Military Museum; Charles Slocum Natural History Museum. Tax-exempt.
Village Museum.
Collections: local history; farm implements & equipment; household items; clothing; military uniforms; natural history; archaeology; model trains & equipment. Historic Buildings: 1875 Mark Center Post Office; 1854 Jewell R.R. Station; 1875 St. John Lutheran Church; Ayersville Telephone Office; 1850 Sherry School House; Vaughn's Lockkeepers House; Kinner cabin; Kieffer cabin; 1875 Chapel of the Crosses; Meyers Cider Mill.
Research Fields: local history.
Facilities: food service available. Museum-related items for sale.
Activities: docent program or council; permanent & temporary exhibitions; special events. Museum Sponsors: Days of Yesteryear in May; Black Swamp Steam Show in June; Car Show in July; Herb and Art Show in July; Johnny Appleseed Festival in October; Halloween Lantern Tours in October.
Publications: annual newsletter, Village Guide; newspaper listing buildings; self-guided tour book; Justice in Defiance.
Hours & Admission Prices: May-Oct. event weekends & by appointment. Adults $3, children 6-16 $1; discounts for Ohio Pass, senior citizens $2 on event days; children 6 and under & members no charge.
Attendance: 6,000 (estimated)
Membership: Individual $5; Family $10; Supporting $25; Sustaining $50; Life $100.

Delaware

DELAWARE COUNTY HISTORICAL SOCIETY - NASH HOUSE MUSEUM, 157 E. William St., Delaware, OH 43015-2165. Tel.: 740-369-3831.
Founded: 1955.
Historic House. Built in the 1878.
Collections: local history & culture; photographs; furnishings; period artifacts.
Publications: semiannual newsletter, Delaware Historian.
Hours & Admission Prices: Mid-March to Mid-Nov. Wed., Sat. & Sun. 2-4:30, Thurs. 10-4:30; Nov.-March. Sun. 2-4:30. No charge. Closed legal holidays.
Membership: Individual $10; Household $15; Patron $35; Sponsor $100; Silver Sponsor $250; Gold Sponsor $500; Platinum Sponsor $1,000.

RICHARD M. ROSS ART MUSEUM, (M), Ohio Wesleyan University, 61 S. Sandusky St., Delaware, OH 43015-2333. Tel.: 740-368-3606.
Art Museum.
Collections: paintings; sculpture; photographs.
Hours & Admission Prices: Tues.-Wed. & Fri. 10-5, Thurs. 10-9, Sun. 1-5. No charge.

Delphos

DELPHOS CANAL COMMISSION MUSEUM, 241 Main St., Delphos, OH 45833-1764. Mailing Address: P.O. Box 256, Delphos, OH 45833-0256. Tel.: 419-695-7737.
History Museum.
Collections: canal & canal boat history; local history & culture; photographs; personal artifacts; period furnishings; 1902 Sears Buggy Roadster; period tools & manufacturing equipment; business; industry; schools; churches.
Hours & Admission Prices: 1st & 3rd Sun. of month 1-3; 2nd & 4th Mon. of month 7pm-9pm; groups by appointment. No charge.

DELPHOS POSTAL MUSEUM, 339 N. Main St., Delphos, OH 45833-0174. Mailing Address: P.O. Box 174, Delphos, OH 45833-0174. Tel.: 419-303-5482.
History Museum.
Collections: postal history; period artifacts; mail processing; stamps; 1906 Harrington coach; mail sled; jeep; 1963 Westcoaster; 1957 Cushman mailster.
Hours & Admission Prices: Call for hours. No charge.

Dennison

THE DENNISON RAILROAD DEPOT MUSEUM, 400 Center St., Dennison, OH 44621-1402. Mailing Address: P.O. Box 11, Dennison, OH 44621-0011. Tel.: 740-922-6776; 877-278-8020 (toll free). Fax: 740-922-4929.
E-mail: depot@tusco.net
Web Site: www.dennisondepot.org
Founded: 1984.
Congressional District: 18
Key Personnel: C.E.O., Wendy R. Zucal; Cur. Model Railroad, Paul Stratton; Chm. Bd., Bob Michels; Finance Chm., Mike Connor; Treas. & Public Rels., Rose Wanosik; Experience Coord., Ian Wamboldt; Dir. Mktg., Laura Milarcik; Coord. Membership, Carrie Callahan; Teachers Advisory Comm., Lorrie Wheeler; Museum Shop Mgr., Mary Galbreath; Railroad Restoration, Jason Johnson; Women's Society, Kim Peters; Trax Diner Inc., Sandy Armitt; Trax Diner Inc., Michael Smith; Property, Ed Griffin; Volunteer Coord., Peg Henry.
Personnel Profile: Full-Time Paid 2; Full-Time Volunteers 51; Part-Time Paid 5; Part-Time Volunteers 150.
Governing Authority: municipal; private; nonprofit organization. Tax-exempt: 501(c)(3).
Railroad Depot Museum: housed in 1873 Pennsylvania Railroad Depot.
Collections: artifacts; railroad; World War II Canteen Site; local history; model train display; Keystone exhibition hall; rolling stock; railroad cars.
Facilities: library; 70-seat restaurant; 2,564 sq. ft. exhibit space. Museum-related items for sale.
Activities: docent program; guided tours; lectures; loan exhibitions; broadcast programs; Polar Express train rides; children's interactive train car. Museum Sponsors: Railroad Festival; Railroad Symposium; Christmas Tour of Homes; Spring Ball; Garden Tour; American Soldiers Homecoming Festival.
Publications: quarterly newsletter, The Timetable.
Hours & Admission Prices: Tues.-Fri. 10-5, Sat. 11-4, Sun. 11-3. Adults $8, senior citizens $6, students 7-17 $4; discounts to AAM & AAA members; children under 7 & members no charge. Closed New Year's Day; Easter; Independence Day; Thanksgiving; Christmas. ♿
Attendance: 75,000 (estimated)
Membership: Student $5; Individual $10; Family $20; Corporate $40; Individual Life $100; Married Life $150; Corporate Life $200; Benefactor $500.

Dover

J.E. REEVES HOME & MUSEUM, 325 E. Iron Ave., Dover, OH 44622-2105. Tel.: 330-343-7040; 800-815-2794. Fax: 330-343-6290.
E-mail: reeves@tusco.net
Web Site: web.tusco.net/reeves
Founded: 1958.
Congressional District: 18
Key Personnel: Chm. Bd., Sue Rees; Pres., Greg Bair; Vice Pres., Patti Feller; Dir. J.E. Reeves Home, Matt Lautzenheiser.
Personnel Profile: Full-Time Paid 1; Part-Time Paid 10; Part-Time Volunteers 20.
Governing Authority: nonprofit. Affiliated with the Dover Historical Society. Tax-exempt.
General Historical Society Museum: housed in 19th-century restored Victorian mansion, home of J.E. Reeves.
Collections: historical maps; agriculture; archaeology; archives; paintings; costumes; geology; glass; music players; Civil War artifacts; original draperies; chandeliers; carved & tufted period furniture; decorative arts; mineralogy; vehicles; carriages; 1922 Rauch & Lang electric car; restored 19th-century Victorian Mansion with original furnishings & Carriage House Museum holding historic artifacts, including the family sleigh and carriage, and memorabilia surrounding Dover born guerrilla Civil War leader, William Clark Quantrill.
Research Fields: birthplace of William Clark Quantrill.
Facilities: over 500-vol. library of books available by permission; reading room.
Activities: guided tours; lectures; permanent & temporary exhibitions.
Publications: quarterly newsletter; books.
Hours & Admission Prices: June-Oct. Tues.-Sun. noon-4; Nov. 11-Dec. 22 daily 1-7. Adults $6, seniors & AAA members $5, children 13-18 $2; discounts to AAM members.
Attendance: 6,000 (estimated)
Membership: Student $2; Individual Participating $13; Couple Participating $18; Family $20; Life $175; Corporate $300.

WARTHER MUSEUM INC., 331 Karl Ave., Dover, OH 44622-2767. Tel.: 330-343-7513.
E-mail: info@warthers.com
Web Site: www.warthers.com
Founded: 1936.
Key Personnel: C.E.O., David R. Warther; Pres., Mark Warther; Museum Shop Mgr., Carol Moreland.
Personnel Profile: Full-Time Paid 2; Part-Time Paid 8.
Governing Authority: individual operation.
Arts & Crafts Museum.
Collections: hand-carved works of art by Ernest Warther; history of steam engines from 250 B.C.-present day in ivory, ebony & pearl; 8 ft. ebony & ivory replica of the Lincoln funeral train; 50,000 buttons arranged in designs on walls & ceiling; telegraph station; railroad park.
Facilities: picnic facilities; Swiss gardens; 3-acre landscaped grounds.
Activities: guided tours; formally organized education programs for children.
Hours & Admission Prices: Daily 9-5. Adults $11.50, students $6; discounts to groups. Closed New Year's Day; Easter; Thanksgiving; Christmas. ♿
Attendance: 100,000 (estimated)
Membership: Single $17; Couple $27; Family $37.

Dublin

WORLD'S FIRST WENDY'S RESTAURANT, One Dave Thomas Blvd., Dublin, OH 43017-5452. Tel.: 614-764-3100.
General Museum: housed in the first Wendy's Restaurant opened in 1969; named after his daughter Melinda (Wendy) Thomas, a nickname given to her by her siblings.
Collections: original test griddle; ad campaigns; photographs; personal artifacts; trophies; grand opening memorabilia.
Facilities: restaurant.
Hours & Admission Prices: Mon.-Fri. 10-8, Sat. 10-7, Sun. 11-6. No charge.

East Liverpool

LOU HOLTZ/UPPER OHIO VALLEY HALL OF FAME, 120 E. Fifth St., East Liverpool, OH 43920-3031. Tel.: 330-386-5443. Fax: 330-382-0244.
E-mail: director@louholtzhalloffame.com
Web Site: www.louholtzhalloffame.com
Founded: 1998.
Congressional District: 6
Key Personnel: Pres., Frank C. Dawson; Treas., Jackman Vodrey; Dir., Robin Webster.
Personnel Profile: Full-Time Paid 1; Part-Time Paid 1; Part-Time Volunteers 2.
Governing Authority: private; nonprofit organization. Tax-exempt: 501(c)(3).
Hall of Fame.
Collections: memorabilia related to Coach Lou Holtz & other inductees; communities of the Upper Ohio Valley.
Facilities: 3,500 sq. ft. exhibit space. Books & sports-related items for sale.
Activities: films; guided tours. Museum Sponsors: Hall of Fame weekend in summer; Induction banquet; celebrity golf tournament.
Publications: quarterly newsletter.
Hours & Admission Prices: Mon.-Fri. 10-5, Sat. 10-1. No charge; donations accepted. Closed legal holidays.
Attendance: 2,500 (estimated)
Membership: Varsity $15; MVP $50; All-Conference $100; All-State $250; All-American $500; Coaches Club $1,000; Hall of Fame $5,000; Inductee Cubicle $10,000; Naming Opportunities $12,500 & up.

MUSEUM OF CERAMICS, 400 E. 5th St. at Broadway, East Liverpool, OH 43920-3134. Tel.: 330-386-6001; 800-600-7180.
E-mail: museumofceramics@gmail.com

Web Site: www.themuseumofceramics.org
Founded: 1980.
Congressional District: 18
Key Personnel: Dir. & Museum Shop Mgr., S.W. Vodrey; Historic Site Technician, Philip L. Rickerd.
Personnel Profile: Part-Time Paid 3; Part-Time Volunteers 6.
Governing Authority: Parent Institution: Museum of Ceramics Foundation. Tax-exempt.
History Museum: housed in 1909 Old City Post Office.
Collections: East Liverpool ceramics; 1930s paintings; WPA era mural; Lotus ware; art pottery.
Major Exhibits: Hidden Beauties 2010 Exhibit, 5/10-12/10.
Research Fields: pertaining to collections.
Facilities: Museum-related items for sale.
Activities: guided tours; special events; lectures; temporary exhibitions; audiovisual shows; school outreach programs.
Hours & Admission Prices: Tues.-Sat. 9:30-3:30. Adults $4, students $2; discounts to AAA members & Time Travelers; children 5 & under and members no charge. Closed federal holidays.
Attendance: 1,900 (estimated)
Membership: Ironstone $25; Rockingham $50; Parian $100.

Eastlake

CROATIAN HERITAGE MUSEUM & LIBRARY, 34900 Lakeshore Blvd., Eastlake, OH 44095-3575. Tel.: 440-946-2044 (museum); 440-327-9498 (Pres.). Fax: 216-991-2310.
E-mail: croatianmuseum@sbcglobal.net
Web Site: www.croatianmuseum.com
Founded: 1983.
Congressional District: 19
Key Personnel: Pres. & Cur., Branka M. Malinar; Treas., Kathy Kuhar; Archivist & Librarian, Jerry Malinar; Devel., Judith Zivic; Public Rels., Suzanne Jerin.
Personnel Profile: Part-Time Volunteers 15.
Governing Authority: nonprofit. Parent Institution: American Croatian Lodge. Tax-exempt: 501(c)(3).
Folk Art Museum.
Collections: Croatian artifacts; folk art & dress; textiles; folk costumes; wood carvings; sculpture; metal work; leather work; paintings.
Research Fields: Croatian textiles, customs, & architecture; folk art; wedding customs.
Facilities: 13,500 library of books & Croatian journals; restaurant; educational facilities. Museum-related items for sale.
Activities: guided tours; school loan service; traveling exhibitions. Museum Sponsors: Easter event; Christmas event.
Publications: brochures for weaving exhibit; Croatian Castles of Zagorje, Croatia; Croatian Christmas Customs; Croatian Easter Customs Croatian Wedding Customs.
Hours & Admission Prices: Fri. 3-8, Sat. 1-5; other times by appointment. No charge; donations accepted. Closed New Year's Day; Christmas. ♿
Attendance: 9,000 (estimated)
Membership: Individual $20; Family $30; Supporting $50; Supporter Family $100; Patron $101-$499; Benefactor $500 & up.

Elmore

SCHEDEL ARBORETUM & GARDENS, 19255 W. Portage River S. Rd., Elmore, OH 43416-9743. Tel.: 419-862-3182.
Web Site: www.schedel-gardens.org/schedel/
Key Personnel: Dir., Reginald D. Noble.
Governing Authority: nonprofit organization.
Arboretum.
Collections: 17 acre gardens include 15,000 annuals; perennials; flowering trees; shrubs. Schedel Home: period Persian rugs; carved jade; bronze; personal artifacts; paintings; photographs; furnishings.
Facilities: botanical garden. Museum-related items for sale.
Activities: arts festivals; guided tours; temporary exhibits; weddings; receptions; workshops; concerts.
Publications: quarterly newsletter, The Torii.
Hours & Admission Prices: May-Oct. Tues.-Sat. 10-4, Sun. 12-4. Adults $8, seniors $7, children $6; members no charge.
Attendance: 15,000 (accurate)

Elyria

THE HICKORIES MUSEUM OF THE LORAIN COUNTY HISTORICAL SOCIETY, 509 Washington Ave., Elyria, OH 44035-5128. Tel.: 440-322-3341. Fax: 440-322-2817.
E-mail: thehickories@alltel.net
Web Site: lchs.org
Founded: 1889.
Congressional District: 13
Key Personnel: Exec. Dir., William Bird; Pres. (V), John Musson; Office Mgr., Linda Greenaway; Librarian, Karis Lyon; Education Coord., Janet Bird; Education Coord., Jim Smith; Archivist, Eric Greenly; Preservation Consultant, Marilyn Fedelchak-Harley.
Personnel Profile: Full-Time Paid 1; Part-Time Paid 5; Part-Time Volunteers 70.
Governing Authority: society. Parent Institution: Lorain County Historical Society, Inc. Tax-exempt: 501(c)(3).
History Museum.
Collections: photographic images 1842-present; costumes & textiles 1860-1950; original artwork representing local people & scenes and by local artists; artifact collection, 1800-1950; late 19th- & early 20th-century household furnishings, woodworking & textile production tools & equipment, glassware; toys. Historic Building: 1894-95 The Hickories, Elyria.
Research Fields: genealogy; local history; family history; social history (family & home) 1890-1920.
Facilities: library & local history archives.
Activities: museum tours; permanent & temporary exhibitions; school programs on & off site; workshops & seminars for members, guests & area historical groups; special events & fundraisers.
Publications: quarterly newsletter, Hickory Leaves.
Hours & Admission Prices: Tours: Tues.-Fri. 1-4, Sat. 1-3; group & school tours by appointment. Adults $5, youth 13-18 $3, children 6-12 $2; discounts to groups, AAM & ICOM members; members of Northeastern Ohio Inter Museum Council, LCHS members & employees & immediate family no charge. Closed holidays.
Attendance: 4,000 (estimated)
Membership: Student (with ID) $15; Individual $25; Family $35; Sustaining $60; Patron $125; Heritage $250; Garford Club $500.

Fairport Harbor

FAIRPORT MARINE MUSEUM, 129 Second St., Fairport Harbor, OH 44077-5816. Tel.: 440-354-4825.
E-mail: fhhs@ncweb.com
Web Site: www.fairportlighthouse.com
Founded: 1945.
Congressional District: 11
Key Personnel: Pres. (V), Dan Maxson; Treas. (V), Kathy Nurminen.
Personnel Profile: Part-Time Volunteers 20.
Governing Authority: society. Affiliated with Fairport Harbor Historical Society. Tax-exempt.
Marine Museum: housed in 1871 Fairport Lighthouse & keeper's residence.
Collections: navigation instruments; marine charts; manuscript collections; pictures & paintings of ships; lanterns; lighthouse lens; ship carpenters' tools; models & half-hulls of ships; iron ore; Indian relics; pilot house from Laker Frontenac.
Research Fields: local history; Great Lakes merchant vessels.
Facilities: 250-vol. library of marine books available for use by appointment; lighthouse tower.
Activities: guided tours; permanent exhibitions.
Publications: newsletter; brochure.
Hours & Admission Prices: Memorial Day to mid-Sept. Wed., Sat.-Sun. & legal holidays 1-6; group tours by appointment. Adults $3, senior citizens & children 6-12 $2; members & children under 6 no charge. ♿
Attendance: 5,000 (accurate)
Membership: Regular $10; Couple $15; Benefactor $25; Life $250.

Findlay

HANCOCK HISTORICAL MUSEUM, 422 W. Sandusky St., Findlay, OH 45840-3222. Tel.: 419-423-4433. Fax: 419-423-2154.
Web Site: www.hancockhistoricalmuseum.org
Founded: 1970.
Congressional District: 4
Key Personnel: Dir., Sue Tucker; Pres. (V), Rosalinda Paul; Cur. & Archivist, Adam Criblez; Accountant, Carrie Glass; Volunteer & Education Coord., Renee Smith.
Personnel Profile: Full-Time Paid 2; Part-Time Paid 4; Part-Time Volunteers 75; Interns 5.
Governing Authority: nonprofit organization. Branch Museums: Log Cabin; Red School House; De Wald-Funk House. Tax-exempt.
Local History Museum.
Collections: 1875-1900, art glass; 1886-1889, pattern glass made in Findlay, Ohio; 1916 Grant car; camera & dolls; miniature train. Historic Buildings: 1880 Hull House; one room schoolhouse; log house; De Wald-Funk House; Little Red Schoolhouse.

Research Fields: Findlay Glass, Andrews Raiders (Civil War), women of Hancock County; Hancock County history; ethnic roots of Hancock County.
Activities: guided tours; permanent & temporary exhibitions; miniature train rides.
Publications: newsletter; reprints of local histories, atlases; Museum Herstory: Voices From the Past Women of Hancock County, Ohio; pictorial history of Hancock Co.; Ethnic Roots of Hancock County, Ohio; Families and Facades, Divided By A River.
Hours & Admission Prices: Wed.-Fri. 12:30-4:30, Sun. 1-4; tours available by appointment. Adults $5, seniors $2; children & members no charge. ♿
Attendance: 40,000 (accurate)
Membership: Individual $40-$74; Contributing $75-$249; Sustaining Friends $250-$499; Supporting Friends $500-$999; Heritage $1,000.

MAZZA MUSEUM, Gardner Fine Arts Pavilion, University of Findlay, Findlay, OH 45840-3653. Mailing Address: The University of Findlay, 1000 N. Main St., Findlay, OH 45840-3653. Tel.: 800-472-9502, ext. 5521.
Key Personnel: Museum Shop Mgr., Jan Miller; Museum Shop Mgr., Lee Myers.
Personnel Profile: Full-Time Paid 4.
Governing Authority: Parent Institution: The University of Findlay. Tax-exempt.
Art Museum.
Collections: over 4,000 works of art; children's picture book art; literacy.
Activities: guided tours; special events.
Hours & Admission Prices: Wed.-Fri. 12-5, Sun. 1-4; other times by appointment. No charge; donations accepted. Closed major holidays. ♿
Attendance: 10,000
Membership: Individual $25.

Fort Recovery

FORT RECOVERY MUSEUM, 1 Fort Site St., Fort Recovery, OH 45846. Mailing Address: 1318 Fox Rd., Fort Recovery, OH 45846-9756. Tel.: 419-375-4649.
E-mail: hlefevre@bright.net
Web Site: www.fortrecoverymuseum.com
Founded: 1982.
Congressional District: 8
Key Personnel: Pres. (V), Helen LeFevre.
Personnel Profile: Part-Time Paid 2; Part-Time Volunteers 10.
Governing Authority: society. Parent Institution: Ohio Historical Society, Columbus, 43211. Tel.: 614-466-1500. Tax-exempt: 170(b)(1)(A).
Military & Indian Museum: housed in partially reconstructed Anthony Wayne fort with two blockhouses.
Collections: relics from 1791, battle of St. Clair's defeat; relics of 1794, Wayne's victory; accoutrements; military artifacts; Indian artifacts. Historic Structures: two blockhouses; partial fort buildings; blacksmith shop.
Activities: school tours. Museum Sponsors: Indian Artifacts Show in June.
Publications: Ft. Recovery Historical Sketch; VHS documentary, St. Clair's Defeat.
Hours & Admission Prices: May & Sept. Sat.-Sun. 12-5; June-Aug. daily 12-5. Adults $3, students $1; members, OHS members, children 5 & under no charge.
Attendance: 3,346 (estimated)
Membership: Richard Butler Patron $10; Anthony Wayne Patron $25; St. Clair Patron $50; Presidential Patron $100.

Fostoria

FOSTORIA AREA HISTORICAL MUSEUM, 123 W. North St., Fostoria, OH 44830-2232. Mailing Address: P.O. Box 142, Fostoria, OH 44830-0142.
Founded: 1972.
Congressional District: 26
Key Personnel: C.E.O. & Treas., Leonard Skonecki; Pres. (V), George A. Gray.
Personnel Profile: Part-Time Volunteers 13.
Governing Authority: private; nonprofit organization. Parent Institution: Fostoria Area Historical Society. Tax-exempt.
General Museum.
Collections: furniture; personal artifacts; fire equipment.
Facilities: 14,000 sq. ft. exhibit space. Museum-related items for sale.
Activities: films; guided tours; lectures; broadcast programs. Annual Events: 8 monthly meetings open to members & public.
Publications: monthly bulletin, Historical Activities Summary.
Hours & Admission Prices: Temporarily closed. ♿
Attendance: 1,000 (estimated)
Membership: Individual $15; Family $25; Corporate $30; Life $200.

GLASS HERITAGE GALLERY, 109 N. Main St., Fostoria, OH 44830-2215. Tel.: 419-435-5077.
Glass Museum.
Collections: glassmaking history & industries; local industry glass, 1887-1920; vases; lamps; pitchers.
Hours & Admission Prices: Spring: Thurs.-Sat. 10-4.

Franklin

HARDING MUSEUM, 302 Park Ave., Franklin, OH 45005-3549. Tel.: 937-746-8295.
Founded: 1965.
Congressional District: 6
Key Personnel: Pres., Dan Darragh; Museum Shop Mgr., Mary Nenninger.
Personnel Profile: Part-Time Paid 1; Part-Time Volunteers 6.
Governing Authority: society; nonprofit. Parent Institution: Franklin Area Historical Society. Subsidiary Institution: 1804 Log Post Office, Franklin, OH. Tax-exempt: 170(b)(1)(A).
Local History Museum: housed in 1901 home of Major General E.F. Harding.
Collections: Franklin area history; Gen. E. Forrest Harding's personal artifacts.
Major Exhibits: Franklin in the Civil War, 4/10-11/10.
Research Fields: history of Franklin & Clear Creek Townships; military history; World War II; Nuremberg Trials.
Facilities: library of local history & military books available for research on premises.
Activities: guided tours; permanent exhibitions. Annual Event: Franklin's Amazing Historical Race first Sunday in June.
Publications: newsletter; books, History of Franklin in the Great Miami Valley; tour pamphlets for city and Mackinaw Historic District.
Hours & Admission Prices: April-Nov. Sun. 2-5; other times by appointment. Suggested Donation: adults $3, children $1.
Attendance: 1,000 (estimated)
Membership: Individual $15; Family $22.50; Business $50; Life $225.

Fremont

* **RUTHERFORD B. HAYES PRESIDENTIAL CENTER, (M),** Spiegel Grove, Fremont, OH 43420-2796. Tel.: 419-332-2081. Fax: 419-332-5424.
E-mail: tculbertson@rbhayes.org
Web Site: www.rbhayes.org
Founded: 1916.
Congressional District: 5
Key Personnel: Exec. Dir., Thomas J. Culbertson; Pres. (V), Stephen A. Hayes; Cur. Manuscript, Nan Card; Head Librarian, Rebecca Hill; Head Photographic Resources, Gilbert Gonzalez; Dir. Devel., Kathy Boukissen; Museum Shop Mgr., Merry May.
Personnel Profile: Full-Time Paid 16; Part-Time Paid 22; Part-Time Volunteers 145.
Governing Authority: nonprofit organization. Affiliated with The Ohio Historical Society, Columbus, OH 43211. Tax-exempt: 501(c)(3).
U.S. Library & Museum.
Collections: Hayes family memorabilia including Mrs. Hayes' wedding gown & White House reception gowns; the President's carriage; Civil War relics; Fanny Hayes's two doll houses; Hayes family portraits; 5,000 linear ft. of manuscripts; Indian relics; weapons; White House dining room sideboard; White House china; 75,000 photographs from 1840-present; memorabilia collected by Colonel Webb C. Hayes; 240 periodicals & newsletters; 6,300 newspaper volumes; 6,100 reels of microfilm. Historic Buildings: 1859 Hayes residence; 1873 Dillon House; 1870s carriage house, service buildings; White House gates 1873; tomb of Lucy & Rutherford B. Hayes.
Major Exhibits: Croquet, 2/10-8/10; Christmas Train, 11/10-12/10.
Research Fields: American history 1865-1914, emphasis on Gilded Age; Ohio & local history; Spanish-American War; monetary & prison reform; African American history.
Facilities: 70,000-vol. library of material on American history available for inter-library loan, including 12,000-vol. of President Hayes' personal library for use under staff supervision; reading room; auditorium; 25-acre estate; gardens; walking & jogging paths; Indian portage & Harrison military trail. Museum-related items for sale.
Activities: guided tours; lecture series; school programs; slide presentations; music programs; nature walks.
Publications: quarterly newsletter, The Statesman; monthly newsletter for members & volunteers, Billet.
Hours & Admission Prices: Museum & Residence: Tues.-Sat. 9-5, Sun. & holidays 12-5. Adults $13, children 6-12 $5; discounts to groups with appointment, senior citizens, active military & their families, AAA members, Civil War Trust & Natl. Historical Society; children under 6, AAM, AASLH, OHS & HPC members & grounds no charge. Closed New Year's Day; Easter; Thanksgiving; Christmas. Library: Tues.-Sat. 9-5. No charge. Closed holidays. ♿
Attendance: 38,891 (accurate)

Membership: Student $20; Individual $30; Individual Plus $45; Family & Grandparent $50; Patron $100; Representative $250; Cabinet $500; Advisor $1,000; Executive $1,500.

Galion

BROWNELLA COTTAGE, 132 S. Union St., Galion, OH 44833-2524. Mailing Address: P.O. Box 125, Galion, OH 44833-0125. Tel.: 419-468-9338 & 5567.
Web Site: www.galionhistory.com
Founded: 1981.
Congressional District: 8
Key Personnel: Pres., Craig Clinger; Vice Pres., Doug Osborne; Treas., Jerry Lantz; Record Sec., Bill DeBolt.
Governing Authority: society; nonprofit. Branch Museum: Galion Historical Society, Inc. Tax-exempt: 501(c)(3).
Historic House: Home & Study of Bishop William Montgomery Brown.
Collections: artifacts; personal belongings; furniture; area historical items.
Facilities: study containing printed works of Bishop William Montgomery Brown.
Activities: guided tours; lectures.
Publications: quarterly newsletter, The Historian.
Hours & Admission Prices: June-Oct. Sun. Tours 1:30, 2:15 & 3; groups by appointment. Adults $5, students $3.
Attendance: 500 (accurate)
Membership: Students $5, Individual $10, Family $15, Sustaining $25, Contributing $50, Patron & Corporate $100.

GALION HISTORICAL MUSEUM, 132 S. Union St., Galion, OH 44833-2524. Mailing Address: P.O. Box 125, Galion, OH 44833-0125. Tel.: 419-468-1026.
Web Site: www.galionhistory.com
Founded: 1956.
Congressional District: 8
Key Personnel: Acting Dir., Dr. Bernard M. Mansfield.
Governing Authority: nonprofit. Parent Institution: Galion Historical Society, Inc. Tax-exempt: 501(c)(3).
History Museum.
Collections: Galion & Crawford county history from prehistoric to modern times; Indian artifacts; pioneer items; local industrial items; 1906 horse-drawn fire engine.
Facilities: Museum-related items for sale.
Activities: guided tours; temporary exhibitions of your own collections; regularly changing exhibitions.
Publications: weekly newspaper columns on local history; quarterly newsletter.
Hours & Admission Prices: June-Oct. Sun. 2-4. No charge; donations accepted. ♿
Attendance: 500 (estimated)
Membership: Students $5, Individual $10, Family $15, Sustaining $25, Contributing $50, Patron & Corporate $100.

Gallipolis

FRENCH ART COLONY, 530 First Ave., Gallipolis, OH 45631-1245. Mailing Address: P.O. Box 472, Gallipolis, OH 45631-0472. Tel.: 740-446-3834. Fax: 740-446-3834.
E-mail: fac-office@att.net
Web Site: www.frenchartcolony.org
Founded: 1971.
Congressional District: 6
Key Personnel: Bd. Member, Jan Thaler; Bd. Member, Peggy Evans; Program Dir., Carrie Napora.
Personnel Profile: Full-Time Paid 1; Full-Time Volunteers 4; Part-Time Paid 1; Part-Time Volunteers 20.
Governing Authority: nonprofit organization. Tax-exempt: 501(c)(3).
Art Gallery: housed in 1855 Holzer Family Home.
Collections: private collections of fine art & antiques.
Research Fields: design arts; OAC pilot study.
Facilities: library of visual art; classrooms; gardens.
Activities: guided tours; lectures; gallery talks; concerts; classes; dance recitals; arts festivals; hobby workshops; educational programs; dance classes; rental facilities.
Publications: bimonthly newsletter, Currents.
Hours & Admission Prices: Galleries: Tues.-Fri. 10-6, Sat. 10-3, Sun. 1-5. No charge; donations accepted. ♿
Attendance: 7,000 (estimated)
Membership: Student $15; Senior Citizen $27; Individual $30; Family $50; Supporter $100; Donor $500; Benefactor $1,000.

OUR HOUSE STATE MEMORIAL, 432 First Ave., Gallipolis, OH 45631. Mailing Address: P.O. Box 607, Gallipolis, OH 45631-0607. Tel.: 740-446-0586.
Web Site: ohiohistory.org/places/ourhouse
Founded: 1933.
Congressional District: 10
Key Personnel: Pres., Sara Sheets; Chm. (V), Carol Warren; Site Mgr., Dwetta Gay.
Personnel Profile: Full-Time Paid 1; Part-Time Paid 1; Part-Time Volunteers 17.
Governing Authority: society. Parent Institution: Ohio Historical Society, Columbus, OH 43211. Subsidiary Institution: Friends of Our House. Tax-exempt.
History Museum: housed in 1819 restored Ohio River tavern.
Collections: period furnishings.
Research Fields: history of Gallipolis; Ohio French settlement.
Activities: guided tours; special events; Victorian teas; birthday parties; luncheons & dinners; children's day camp. Museum Sponsors: History Day & Colonial Days.
Hours & Admission Prices: Memorial Day-Labor Day Wed.-Sat. 10-4, Sun. 1-4. Adults $4, senior citizens $3, children $1; discounts to AAM, OHS members, the Armed Forces & seniors; members no charge.
Attendance: 5,000 (estimated)

Gambier

KENYON COLLEGE OLIN ART GALLERY, Olin Library, Gambier, OH 43022. Tel.: 740-427-5346.
E-mail: youngerd@kenyan.edu
Web Site: www2.kenyon.edu/artgallery/info/general.htm
Key Personnel: Dir., Dan Younger
Art Gallery.
Collections: works by regional, national & international artists.
Activities: permanent & temporary exhibits; educational programs; lectures.
Publications: brochures; exhibition catalogues.
Hours & Admission Prices: Mon.-Fri. 10-8, Sat.-Sun. 10-5.

Garfield Heights

CLEVELAND METROPARKS OUTDOOR EDUCATION DIVISION, 11350 Broadway Ave., Garfield Heights, OH 44125-1664. Tel.: 216-341-9225. Fax: 216-341-8528.
E-mail: outdooreduc@clevelandmetroparks.com
Web Site: www.clemetparks.com
Founded: 1917.
Congressional District: 20
Key Personnel: C.E.O. & Exec. Dir., Vern J. Hartenburg; Chief Outdoor Education, Robert D. Hinkle, Ph.D.; Div. Sec., Maryellen Dombek; Naturalist & Artist, Jennifer Brumfield; Interpretive Technology Specialist, Louisa Kreider; Mgr. Nature Center (Brecksville), Sharon Hosko; Naturalist-Brecksville, Debra Shankland; Naturalist-Brecksville, Jenny McClain; Naturalist-Brecksville, Kelly McGinnis; Naturalist-Brecksville, John Miller; Naturalist-Brecksville, Pam Taylor; Mgr. Visitor Center (Canal Way), Foster Brown; Naturalist (Canal Way), Jill Hauger; Historical Interpreter (Canal Way), William Mallery; Historical Interpreter (Canal Way), Doug Kusak; Mgr. Nature Center (Garfield Park), Carl Casavecchia; Naturalist (Garfield Park), Stacey Allen; Naturalist (Garfield Park), Valerie Fetzer; Cultural History Interpreter (Garfield Park), Sherrie Tolliver; Mgr. Outdoor Recreation (IGO), Dana Smith; Outdoor Recreation Inclusion Specialist (IGO), Philip Brekke; Mgr. Look About Lodge, Barb Holtz; Naturalist (Look About Lodge), Carly Martin; Naturalist (Look About Lodge), Stefanie Verish; Outreach Mgr., Nature Tracks, Ray Hereford; management Trainee (Nature Tracks), Demetrius Lambert-Falconer; Mgr. Nature Center (North Chagrin), Barbara Burko; Naturalist (North Chagrin), Timothy Krynak; Naturalist (North Chagrin), Angelec Hillsman; Naturalist (North Chagrin), Deborah Marcinski; Naturalist (North Chagrin), Mindy Murdock; Naturalist (North Chagrin), Jeffrey Riebe; Naturalist (North Chagrin), Traci Williams; Mgr. Nature Center (Rocky River), Wendy Weirich; Naturalist (Rocky River), Chris Larson-McKenzie; Naturalist (Rocky River), David Dvorak; Naturalist (Rocky River), Min Sui Keung; Naturalist (Rocky River), Gretchen Motts; Naturalist (Rocky River), Joni Norris; Naturalist (Rocky River), Kathleen Schmidt; Mgr. Youth Outdoors, John Rode; Recreation Specialist (Youth Outdoors), Sheri Williamson; Recreation Specialist (Youth Outdoors), Brian Fyfe; Recreation Specialist (Youth Outdoors), Valerie Hearst; Recreation Specialist (Youth Outdoors), Joseph Lehner.
Personnel Profile: Full-Time Paid 31; Part-Time Paid 36; Part-Time Volunteers 497.
Governing Authority: political subdivision, State of Ohio. Cleveland Metroparks System. Nature Centers & Services: Brecksville Nature Center; Canal Way Visitor Center; North Chagrin Nature Center at North Chagrin; Rocky

River Nature Center; Garfield Park Nature Center; Look-About Lodge; Nature Tracks mobile nature center. Tax-exempt.
Nature Center & Conservation Area.
Research Fields: white-tailed deer population dynamics; oak-hickory forest restoration; prairie restoration; marsh restoration.
Facilities: six nature & visitor centers located in regional parks; education complex at Cleveland Metroparks Zoo.
Activities: guided tours; lectures; gallery talks; study clubs; TV & radio programs; formally organized education programs; temporary exhibitions.
Publications: monthly newsletter, The Emerald Necklace; quarterly, Naturalist Almanac; trail maps.
Hours & Admission Prices: Trails: daily 6am-11pm. Nature Centers: daily 9:30-5. No charge. Nature Centers: closed New Year's Day; Easter; Thanksgiving; Christmas. ♿
Attendance: 438,941 (estimated)

Gates Mills

GATES MILLS HISTORICAL SOCIETY, 7580 Old Mill Rd., Gates Mills, OH 44040. Mailing Address: P.O. Box 191, Gates Mills, OH 44040-0191. Tel.: 440-423-4808.
Founded: 1946.
Congressional District: 22
Key Personnel: Pres., Sally Burke; Treas., Helen Gelbach; Sec., Raymond Burke.
Governing Authority: society. Tax-exempt: 501(c)(3).
History Museum.
Collections: interior furnishings; kitchen utensils; Native Indian.
Research Fields: Local genealogy & Western Reserve.
Facilities: library. Decorative maps, postcards & books for sale.
Activities: permanent exhibitions.
Publications: books, 1826-1976 A Pictorial History of Gates Mills; 1920-1970, George Brown of Gates Mills; Bill Henderson's Gates Mills.
Hours & Admission Prices: Mon.-Fri. 9-5, Sat. 9-1. No charge; donations accepted.
Attendance: 1,500
Membership: Regular $15; Family $20; Sustaining $30.

Geneva

PLATT R. SPENCER MEMORIAL ARCHIVES AND SPECIAL COLLECTIONS AREA, Geneva Public Library, 860 Sherman St., Geneva, OH 44041-9101. Tel.: 440-466-4521, ext. 107 & 109. Fax: 440-466-0162.
Web Site: www.acdl.info/archives
Founded: 1988.
Congressional District: 19
Key Personnel: Dir., William Tokarczyk; Asst. Dir., Donna Wall; Archivist, Louise Legeza.
Personnel Profile: Part-Time Paid 3; Part-Time Volunteers 3.
Governing Authority: county government. Parent Institution: Ashtabula Co. District Library.
Archive.
Collections: Ashtabula County history & genealogy including over 2,200 family files; postcards; phonetic spelling movement books; Platt R. Spencer family memorabilia, penmanship items & business artifacts; Archie Bell manuscripts & published travel books; letters & photos of turn-of-the-century actors, opera singers & authors; Edith M. Thomas poetry; children's texts; newspapers; court house records; obituaries.
Research Fields: local history; genealogy; local authored poetry; phonetic spelling movement; Platt R. Spencer & penmanship.
Facilities: 2,500-vol. collection of selected U.S., foreign history & biographical/history books, bound periodicals, 1723-1774.
Activities: participatory exhibits.
Publications: brochures.
Hours & Admission Prices: Archives: Tues. & Thurs. 11-6. Genealogy: Summer: Mon.-Thurs. 9:30-8, Fri. 9:30-4, Sat. 9:30-1:30. Winter: Mon.-Thurs. 9:30-8, Fri. 9:30-4, Sat. 10-4, Sun. 1-4. Call first to verify availability. No charge; donations accepted. Closed New Year's Eve & Day; Easter; Memorial Day; Independence Day; Labor Day; Thanksgiving; Christmas Eve & Day. ♿

SHANDY HALL, 6333 S. Ridge Rd., Geneva, OH 44041-8377. Tel.: 440-466-3680.
Web Site: www.wrhs.org
Founded: 1937.
Congressional District: 11
Key Personnel: Cur., Byron Robertson.
Personnel Profile: Full-Time Paid 1; Part-Time Paid 3.
Governing Authority: society. Affiliated with Western Reserve Historical Society, 10825 East Blvd., Cleveland 44106. Tax-exempt: 170(b)(1)(A).
Historic House: 1815 Shandy Hall, early Western Reserve home.
Collections: original Harper family furnishings; clothes; books; toys.
Activities: guided tours.
Hours & Admission Prices: By appointment. Adults $3, seniors & children $2; discounts to groups; preschoolers no charge.
Attendance: 2,000 (estimated)
Membership: Individual $40; Family $55; Sustaining $75; Special Sustaining $150; Fellow $250; Special Fellow $500; Fellow for Life $2,000-$5,000.

Geneva-on-the-Lake

ASHTABULA COUNTY HISTORICAL SOCIETY, 5685 Lake Rd., Geneva-on-the-Lake, OH 44041-9427. Mailing Address: P.O. Box 36, Jefferson, OH 44047-0036. Tel.: 440-466-7337.
E-mail: nan@alltel.net
Web Site: www.ashtcohs.com
Founded: 1838.
Congressional District: 11
Key Personnel: Pres., Cher Shepard.
Personnel Profile: Part-Time Volunteers 10.
Governing Authority: society. Tax-exempt: 501(c)(3).
House Museum & Landmark: 1811 Blakeslee Log Cabin, 1823 Jennie Munger Gregory Memorial Museum, Geneva-on-The Lake; 1823 Joshua R. Giddings law office.
Collections: period furnishings 1850-1900; office furnishings & library; manuscripts; documents; pictures; postcards; archival papers.
Research Fields: historical.
Facilities: 1800-1860 Congressional documents; museum library of historical books.
Activities: guided tours; lectures; permanent & temporary exhibitions; dedications of century plaques on century homes, buildings & businesses. Museum Sponsors: Log Cabin days in September.
Publications: quarterly bulletin, Ashtabula County History.
Hours & Admission Prices: May & Sept. Wed.-Fri. 12-4; Memorial Day to Labor Day Wed.-Sat. 12-4. Adults $4, youth $1; children 12 & under and members no charge. Closed Memorial Day; Labor Day.
Attendance: 1,000 (estimated)
Membership: Individual $15; Family $20; Corporate $50; Life $200.

Glenford

FLINT RIDGE STATE MEMORIAL MUSEUM, 7091 Brownsville Rd., S.E., Glenford, OH 43739-9639. Tel.: 740-787-2476; 800-283-8707.
E-mail: meweingartner@ohiohistory.org
Web Site: ohsweb.ohiohistory.org/places/c01/index.shtml
Founded: 1933.
Congressional District: 10
Key Personnel: Mgr., M.E. Weingartner; Education Specialist, Hapi Cummons.
Personnel Profile: Full-Time Paid 4.
Governing Authority: society. Parent Institution: The Ohio Historical Society, Ohio Historical Center Site Operations, 1985 Velma Ave., Columbus, OH 43211. Tax-exempt.
Natural History Museum: located on the site of prehistoric flint pit.
Collections: geology exhibits; flint deposits; geologic time scale; flint relics & artifacts; displays on prehistoric man.
Facilities: nature trails; facilities & trail for visually impaired & disabled; picnic area. Museum-related items for sale.
Publications: pamphlet.
Hours & Admission Prices: Memorial Day-Labor Day Sat.-Sun. 12-5. Adults $4, children 6-12 $3; discounts to school groups, seniors & AAA members; members and children 5 & under 6 no charge. ♿
Attendance: 7,158 (accurate)
Membership: Student $25; Senior 60 & over $35; Individual $40; Full Senior 60 & over and up to 8 guests $42; Full $47; Life $1,000.

Gnadenhutten

GNADENHUTTEN HISTORICAL PARK & MUSEUM, 352 S. Cherry St., Gnadenhutten, OH 44629. Mailing Address: 400 E. Main St., Gnadenhutten, OH 44629-9750. Tel.: 740-254-4143. Fax: 740-254-4992.
E-mail: gnadmuse@tusco.net
Web Site: www.gnaden.tusco.net
Founded: 1963.
Congressional District: 18
Key Personnel: Pres., Kenneth Long; Dir., Chm. (V) & Museum Shop Mgr., Debi Long.
Personnel Profile: Full-Time Volunteers 2; Part-Time Volunteers 25.
Governing Authority: society. Parent Institution: Gnadenhutten Historical Society. Tax-exempt.
Historical Park Museum.
Collections: c.1772-1875 Indian artifacts; historical manuscripts of missions &

village; memorial monument; replica of log cabin church & Indian leader's cabin; mannikin, John Heckwelder.
Activities: lectures; permanent exhibitions.
Publications: Massacre At Gnadenhutten.
Hours & Admission Prices: May to Labor Day Mon.-Sat. 10-5, Sun. 1-5; Labor Day to Oct. Sat. 10-5, Sun. 1-5; other times by appointment. Adults $3. ♿
Attendance: 10,000 (estimated)
Membership: Individual $5; Family $10; Business $25.

Gomer

GOMER WELSH COMMUNITY MUSEUM, 7365 Gomer Rd., Gomer, OH 45809. Tel.: 419-999-5820 & 642-5911.
History Museum.
Collections: Welsh family history, heritage, & culture; personal artifacts; oral histories; photographs.
Hours & Admission Prices: 2nd & 4th Sun. of month 1:30-4. No charge.

Granville

DENISON MUSEUM, (M), 240 W. Broadway, Burke Hall, Granville, OH 43023-1120. Mailing Address: P.O. Box 810, 240 W. Broadway, Granville, OH 43023-0810. Tel.: 740-587-6255. Fax: 740-587-5628.
E-mail: schotta@denison.edu
Web Site: www.denison.edu/museum
Formerly: Denison University Art Gallery
Founded: 1946.
Congressional District: 17
Key Personnel: Dir., Dr. Natalie Marsh.
Personnel Profile: Full-Time Paid 2; Part-Time Paid 1; Interns 6.
Governing Authority: university. Affiliated with Denison University. Tax-exempt.
Art & Ethnology Museum.
Collections: Asian textiles, paintings, sculpture, lacquerware and ceramics; European and American prints, paintings & drawings; Kuna Indian artifacts; special strength in Burmese art.
Research Fields: Asian, European, American & Kuna Indian art.
Facilities: museum laboratory.
Activities: traveling & permanent exhibitions; national & state arts councils & exhibiting artists; lectures; guided tours.
Publications: exhibition catalogs.
Hours & Admission Prices: Thurs. 12-7, Fri.-Wed. 12-5. No charge. Closed university holidays. ♿
Attendance: 2,800 (estimated)

GRANVILLE HISTORICAL SOCIETY MUSEUM, 115 E. Broadway, Granville, OH 43023-1303. Mailing Address: P.O. Box 129, Granville, OH 43023-0129. Tel.: 740-587-3951.
E-mail: office@granvillehistory.org
Web Site: www.granvillehistory.org
Founded: 1885.
Congressional District: 19
Key Personnel: Pres. (V) & Cur., Cynthia Cort; Vice Pres., Don Schilling.
Personnel Profile: Part-Time Paid 2; Part-Time Volunteers 40; Interns 1.
Governing Authority: nonprofit. Parent Institution: Granville Historical Society. Tax-exempt: 501(c)(3).
History Museum: housed in 1816 Alexandrian Bank.
Collections: village records; artifacts of local nature; family & business papers; carpenter tools prior to 1850; history; industry; agriculture; archaeology; costumes; glass; decorative arts; geology; military; textiles.
Research Fields: limited archival research.
Facilities: Publications for sale.
Activities: guided tours; permanent exhibitions.
Publications: pamphlets & books on local subjects of interest; quarterly newsletter, Historical Times.
Hours & Admission Prices: Mid-April to mid-Oct. Fri. 12-3, Sat. 10-4, Sun. 1-4; other times by appointment. No charge; donations accepted.
Attendance: 1,500 (estimated)
Membership: Individual $25; Family $35.

ROBBINS HUNTER MUSEUM, AVERY-DOWNER HOUSE, 221 E. Broadway, Granville, OH 43023-1305. Mailing Address: P.O. Box 183, Granville, OH 43023-0183. Tel.: 740-587-0430. Fax: 740-587-0430.
E-mail: annlowder@windstream.net
Web Site: www.robbinshunter.org
Founded: 1981.
Congressional District: 12
Key Personnel: Pres., Jim Jung; Chm. Bd., Don DeSapri.
Personnel Profile: Part-Time Paid 2; Part-Time Volunteers 50.
Governing Authority: bd. of governors. Parent Institution: Licking County Historical Society, P.O. Box 785, 6th St. Park, Newark, OH 43055. Tel.: 614-345-4898. Subsidiary Institution: Board of Governors of Robbins Hunter Museum. Tax-exempt: 501(c)(3).
Historic House: 1842 American Greek Revival house, designed by Minard Lafever.
Collections: period furnishings; artifacts pertaining to the 19th century, life & times of Granville, Ohio 1840-1870.
Research Fields: 19th-century decorative arts & furnishings; American Greek Revival architecture & interior design.
Activities: guided tours; loan, permanent & traveling exhibitions.
Publications: brochures; local history newsletter, exhibit catalogs; quarterly newsletter.
Hours & Admission Prices: March 2-Dec. 20 Wed.-Sat. 1-3. No charge; donations accepted. Closed Independence Day; Thanksgiving; Christmas. ♿
Attendance: 7,500 (estimated)
Membership: Senior & Student $25; Individual $35; Family & Grandparent $50; Contributor $100; Supporter $200; Patron $500.

Greenville

GARST MUSEUM, (M), 205 N. Broadway, Greenville, OH 45331-2222. Tel.: 937-548-5250. Fax: 937-548-7645.
E-mail: garstmuseum@embarqmail.com
Web Site: www.garstmuseum.org
Formerly: Darke County Historical Society
Founded: 1903.
Congressional District: 8
Key Personnel: Pres. (V), John F. Marchal; Vice Pres., Richard Brown; Dir., Penny Perry; Treas., Allen Hauberg; Museum Shop Mgr., Brenda Arnett.
Personnel Profile: Full-Time Paid 2; Part-Time Paid 12; Part-Time Volunteers 30; Interns 1.
Governing Authority: society. Parent Institution: The Darke County Historical Society, Inc. Tax-exempt: 2954.
History Museum: housed in 1852 Inn.
Collections: Annie Oakley; Native American; Treaty of Greenville; Lowell Thomas; American antiques; military history; 1890s to 1940s shops; farm equipment.
Research Fields: Greenville history; Annie Oakley & Treaty of Greenville; genealogy; Native Americans.
Facilities: library.
Activities: guided tours; films; arts festivals; permanent & temporary exhibitions; educational field trips; docent tours; speakers. Annual Events: Veterans Day Panel; Annie Oakley Days; Christmas Open House.
Publications: books, newsletters & pamphlets relating to Annie Oakley; Anthony Wayne & Treaty of Greenville; The Autobiography of Annie Oakley; Frank Butler, The Man Behind the Woman.
Hours & Admission Prices: Feb.-Dec. Tues.-Sat. 10-4, Sun. 1-4. Adults $5, senior citizens 60 & over $3, youth 6-18 $2; discounts to AAM & AAA members; members no charge. Closed New Year's Eve & Day; Easter; Independence Day; Thanksgiving; Christmas Eve & Day. ♿
Attendance: 11,200 (accurate)
Membership: Individual $25; Family $50; Family Plus One $250; Family Plus Two $500; Sustaining $1,000; Corporate $1,500.

Groveport

MOTTS MILITARY MUSEUM, (M), 5075 S. Hamilton Rd., Groveport, OH 43125-9336. Tel.: 614-836-1500. Fax: 614-836-5110.
E-mail: info@mottsmilitarymuseum.org
Web Site: www.mottsmilitarymuseum.org
Founded: 1988.
Congressional District: 12
Key Personnel: Dir. & Archivist, Warren E. Motts; Financial Dir., Ronald Albers; Devel., Gerrit Vanstraten; Public Rels. & Museum Shop Mgr., Daisy Motts.
Personnel Profile: Full-Time Paid 1; Full-Time Volunteers 4; Part-Time Volunteers 36.
Governing Authority: nonprofit. Tax-exempt: 501(c)(3).
Military Museum.
Collections: historical military items from the Civil War, WWI, WWII, Korea, Vietnam & Desert Storm.
Research Fields: Vietnam soldiers' graves to place grave stones.
Facilities: 1,000-vol. library of military history books; video histories, research classrooms. Museum-related items for sale.
Activities: guided tours; temporary, traveling & loan exhibitions. Annual Events: Community, Veteran & Educational programs; Christmas Party.
Publications: quarterly newsletter, From the Trenches.
Hours & Admission Prices: Tues.-Sat. 9-5, Sun. 1-5. Adults $5, senior citizens $4, students $3; members and children 5 & under no charge. Closed national holidays. ♿

Attendance: 4,500 (estimated)
Membership: Student $15; Individual $35; Family $45; Corporate $100; Individual Lifetime $500; Family Lifetime $750; Veterans Corporate Life $1,000; Corporate Life $1,500.

Hamilton

BUTLER COUNTY HISTORICAL SOCIETY, (M), 327 N. 2nd St., Hamilton, OH 45011-1651. Tel.: 513-896-9930. Fax: 513-896-9936.
E-mail: bcomuseum@fuse.net
Web Site: www.bchistoricalsociety.com
Formerly: Butler County Museum
Founded: 1934.
Congressional District: 8
Key Personnel: Pres. (V), James E. Schwartz; Dir., Michael Riesenberg.
Personnel Profile: Part-Time Paid 2; Part-Time Volunteers 15.
Governing Authority: nonprofit organization. Parent Institution: Butler County Historical Society. Tax-exempt.
History Museum: housed in Benninghofen mansion; built 1861.
Collections: glassware; china; musical instruments; toys; dolls; Indian artifacts; original interior architectural elements; period furnishings from mid-19th century through the 1900s; local & regional history; industry; military artifacts.
Research Fields: genealogy.
Facilities: 300-vol. library pertaining to history & genealogy; reading room.
Activities: guided tours; permanent & temporary exhibitions; local history programs.
Publications: newsletter, Benninghofen Post.
Hours & Admission Prices: Tues.-Wed. & Fri. 11-4, Sat. 9-2; groups by appointment. Adults $3; members no charge. Closed major holidays. ♿
Attendance: 2,500 (estimated)
Membership: Senior $12; Individual $15; Household $25; Organizational $50; Life $250.

PYRAMID HILL SCULPTURE PARK & MUSEUM, 1763 Hamilton Cleves Rd., St. Rd. 128, Hamilton, OH 45013-9601. Tel.: 513-868-8336. Fax: 513-868-3585.
E-mail: pyramid@pyramidhill.org
Web Site: www.pyramidhill.org
Founded: 1997.
Congressional District: 8
Key Personnel: Dir., H.T. Wilks.
Personnel Profile: Full-Time Paid 6; Full-Time Volunteers 1; Part-Time Paid 8; Part-Time Volunteers 15; Interns 1.
Governing Authority: Tax-exempt.
Sculpture Park & Museum.
Collections: large monumental works of sculpture; over 90 pieces of ancient sculpture.
Facilities: amphitheater; pavilion; tea room.
Activities: concert series; children's programs.
Publications: quarterly newsletter.
Hours & Admission Prices: April-Oct. Mon.-Fri. 8-5, Sat.-Sun. 8-6; Nov.-March Mon.-Fri. 8-5, Sat.-Sun. 10-5. Adults $5, children $1.50. ♿
Attendance: 112,366 (accurate)
Membership: Individual $35; Family $40; Contributor $125; Patron $250; Sponsor $500; Benefactor $1,000; Ambassador $2,500; Founder's Society $5,000.

Harrison

AMERICAN WATCHMAKERS-CLOCKMAKERS INSTITUTE, 701 Enterprise Dr., Harrison, OH 45030-2164. Tel.: 513-367-9800. Fax: 513-367-1414.
E-mail: jlubic@awi-net.org
Web Site: www.awci.com
Founded: 1960.
Congressional District: 2
Key Personnel: Exec. Dir., James E. Lubic.
Governing Authority: nonprofit organization. Subsidiary Institution: Education Library Charitable Trust. Tax-exempt: 501(c)(6).
Horological Display.
Collections: watches; clocks; tools of the trade; chronometers.
Facilities: 3,000-vol. library pertaining to horology.
Activities: guided tours by appointment only.
Publications: Horological Times.
Hours & Admission Prices: Mon.-Fri. 8-5 by appointment only. Adults $3, senior citizens $2; school groups, children 12 & under, AWCI members no charge. Closed national holidays. ♿
Attendance: 200 (estimated)
Membership: Individual $137; Industry $300.

VILLAGE HISTORICAL SOCIETY OF HARRISON, INC., Governor Othniel Looker Home, 10580 Marvin Rd., Harrison, OH 45030. Mailing Address: P.O. Box 419, Harrison, OH 45030-0419. Tel.: 513-367-9285.
E-mail: mlsmith6@cinci.rr.com
Founded: 1962.
Congressional District: 2
Key Personnel: Pres., Mary Lou Smith; Vice Pres., John Anthony; Recording Sec., Robert Welsh; Corresponding Sec., Ann L. Woelfel; Treas., Linda Losekamp.
Personnel Profile: Part-Time Volunteers 10.
Governing Authority: society. Tax-exempt: 501(c)(3).
Historic House: 1804 Othniel Looker Home. Listed on the National Register of Historic Places.
Collections: local history & culture; period furnishings; photographs.
Facilities: Museum-related items for sale.
Activities: monthly speakers; displays; films; readings.
Hours & Admission Prices: May-Sept. third Sun. of each month 1:30-4; other times & tours by appointment. No charge; donations accepted.
Membership: Single $7.50; Family $10.

Hillsboro

HIGHLAND HOUSE MUSEUM, 151 E. Main St., Hillsboro, OH 45133-1450. Tel.: 937-393-3392.
Founded: 1965.
Governing Authority: society. Parent Institution: Highland County Historical Society. Tax-exempt.
Historic House: 1844 Highland House.
Collections: furnished typically of the era; furniture; china; glassware; tools; documents; newspapers; Indian relics; early memorabilia from the 1874, Crusade Against Intoxicating Liquid; receipts of trade oddities.
Activities: rental facilities.
Publications: books, Blackburns: Today & Yesterday; Bearers of the Pioneer Spirit, The McAnallys.
Hours & Admission Prices: Fri. 1-5, Sun. 1-4; other times by appointment. No charge; donations accepted.
Attendance: 1,500 (estimated)
Membership: Single $10; Family $25; Sustaining $25.

Hudson

HUDSON LIBRARY AND HISTORICAL SOCIETY, 96 Library St., Hudson, OH 44236-5122. Tel.: 330-653-6658. Fax: 330-650-3373.
E-mail: archives3@hudson.lib.oh.us
Web Site: www.hudson.lib.oh.us
Founded: 1910.
Congressional District: 14
Key Personnel: Dir. & Cur., E. Leslie Polott; Pres. Bd. Trustees (V), Deborah Baker-Hall; Archivist, Gwendolyn Mayer.
Personnel Profile: Full-Time Paid 26; Part-Time Paid 20; Part-Time Volunteers 15; Interns 1.
Governing Authority: society. Tax-exempt.
Regional History Museum.
Collections: historical objects & documents relating to the history of Hudson Township; archives; manuscripts; John Brown family papers. Historic House: 1833 Frederick Baldwin House.
Facilities: 4,000-vol. library of history & genealogy books available for use on premises only.
Activities: guided local history tours.
Publications: Books to Bytes; Yesterday In Hudson.
Hours & Admission Prices: Mon.-Thurs. 9-9, Fri.-Sat. 9-5, Sun. 12-5. No charge. Closed New Year's Eve & Day; Easter; Memorial Day; Independence Day; Labor Day; Thanksgiving; Christmas Eve & Day.

Ironton

LAWRENCE COUNTY GRAY HOUSE MUSEUM, 506 S. 6th St., Ironton, OH 45638-1825. Mailing Address: P.O. Box 73, Ironton, OH 45638-0073. Tel.: 740-532-1222.
Founded: 1988.
Congressional District: 10
Key Personnel: Pres. (V), Patricia Arrington; Treas., Herbert Brown; Museum Shop Mgr., Peggy Karshner.
Personnel Profile: Part-Time Volunteers 30.
Governing Authority: nonprofit organization. Parent Institution: Lawrence County Historical Society. Tax-exempt.
General Museum.
Collections: charcoal iron furnaces; Hanging Rock Iron region artifacts; stone cutting tools; Indian cooking utensils; vintage clothing; period furniture; Lyons railroad photos; Lawrence Co. sports legends; Capt. Brotherton riverboats; Nannie Kelly Wright collection; Oros sheet music; John Rankin room; Col. & Mrs. George Gray furniture; vintage photographs.

Research Fields: old country cemeteries.
Activities: auctions; appraisal fairs. Annual Events: Easter Egg Hunt; Spring Tea in April; Christmas Walk in Dec.
Publications: monthly newsletters; books, 1892 in Ironton; Folk Lore & Legends; local poetry.
Hours & Admission Prices: mid-April to mid-Dec. Fri.-Sun. 1-4. No charge, donations accepted. ♿
Attendance: 1,723 (accurate)
Membership: Single $10; Family $15; Friend $50; Patron $100; Life $1,000; Joint Life $1,100.

Jackson

LILLIAN JONES MUSEUM, (M), 75 Broadway St., Jackson, OH 45640-1610. Tel.: 740-286-2556.
E-mail: lillianjones@dragonbbs.com
Web Site: lillianjones.museum.com/home.html
Key Personnel: Cur., Rhonda Woolum
History Museum.
Collections: period artifacts; furnishings; Jackson County history.
Activities: special events; research.
Hours & Admission Prices: Museum: Jan.-April Tues.-Wed. 1-4; May-Dec. Tues.-Wed. & Sat. 1-4; other times by appointment. Genealogy Center: Wed. 1-4; other times by appointment. No charge. ♿

Kalida

PUTNAM COUNTY HISTORICAL SOCIETY MUSEUM, 201 E. Main St., Kalida, OH 45853. Mailing Address: P.O. Box 264, Kalida, OH 45853-0264. Tel.: 419-532-3008. Fax: 419-532-2944.
E-mail: pchs@bright.net
Web Site: www.bright.net/~pchs/
Founded: 1873.
Congressional District: 5
Key Personnel: Pres., Joe Balbaugh; Vice Pres., Janis Lentz; Chm. (V) & Cur., Carol Wise; Recording Sec., Ruth Oglesbee; Corresponding Sec., Lori Ann Hemenway; Treas., Ron Edelbrock; Membership, Dorothy VonderEmbse.
Personnel Profile: Part-Time Paid 2; Part-Time Volunteers 35.
Governing Authority: nonprofit organization. Parent Institution: Putnam County Historical Society. Tax-exempt.
Historical Building: housed in 1901 old Methodist church.
Collections: c.1900 local artifacts; items for genealogical research.
Research Fields: genealogy; historical.
Facilities: 250-vol. library of local history & adjoining counties available for research on premises.
Activities: guided tours; speeches. Society Sponsors: Christmas Open House; work shops; fair booth; bicentennial program.
Publications: quarterly newsletter, Putman County Heritage; books, Centennial History 1873-1973; Blizzard of 1978 in Putnam County, Ohio; Historical History 1880 & Historical Atlas of Putnam County 1895; Pioneer Reminiscences 1878 & 1887; 1896 Portrait & Biographical Record of Putnam County; One-Room Schools in Putnam County 1985; Oral History; 1834-1934 Centennial of Putnam County.
Hours & Admission Prices: Sun. 1-4, Wed. 9-12. No charge; donations accepted. ♿
Attendance: 2,000 (estimated)
Membership: Individual $10; Life $150.

Kent

THE KELSO HOUSE MUSEUM, 4158 State Route 43, Kent, OH 44240-6916. Mailing Address: P.O. Box 1231, Kent, OH 44240-0024. Tel.: 330-673-1058.
E-mail: kelsohouse1@aol.com
Web Site: www.kelsohouse.org
Founded: 1963.
Congressional District: 11
Key Personnel: Cur., Judi Allen.
Personnel Profile: Part-Time Paid 1; Part-Time Volunteers 9.
Governing Authority: society; nonprofit organization. Affiliated with Brimfield Memorial House Association, Inc. Tax-exempt: 501(c)(3).
Regional History Museum: housed in 1833 William R. Kelso House or Union House as it was later called.
Collections: 1833 Kelso House: furniture; household items; tools; photographs. Grounds: 1845 New England style barn; corn crib; granary; 1870 Sylvester B. Jones House. The Edgar L. McCormack local history collection, located in special collections, Kent State University Library includes manuscripts of local origin; records of Brimfield churches & schools; diaries; account books.
Research Fields: local history.
Facilities: auditorium.
Activities: guided tours; lectures; permanent & temporary exhibitions.
Publications: newsletter, The Kelso Courier.
Hours & Admission Prices: Thurs. & Sat. 12-4; other times by appointment. No charge; donations accepted.
Attendance: 300 (estimated)
Membership: Individual $10; Contributing $15; Sustaining $25; Sponsoring $50; Life (one name) $200.

KENT STATE UNIVERSITY MUSEUM, (M), Rockwell Hall, Corner of E. Main & S. Lincoln Sts., Kent, OH 44242-0001. Mailing Address: P.O. Box 5190, Kent, OH 44242-0001. Tel.: 330-672-3450. Fax: 330-672-3218.
E-mail: museum@kent.edu
Web Site: www.kent.edu/museum/
Founded: 1981.
Congressional District: 17
Key Personnel: Dir., Jean Druesedow; Registrar, Joanne Fenn; Administrative Asst., Carol Gaj.
Personnel Profile: Full-Time Paid 6; Part-Time Paid 13; Part-Time Volunteers 52.
Governing Authority: university. Parent Institution: Kent State University. Subsidiary Institution: KSU Foundation. Tax-exempt: 501(c)(3).
Costume & Decorative Arts Museum: housed in 1927 building, first library of the University.
Collections: history of Western dress, 1750 to present; 19th-20th century American glass; Asian & African regional dress; 18th-20th century ceramics; 17th-20th century furniture; 17th-century to modern textiles; 19th-century English, French & German fashion periodicals.
Research Fields: costume history; textiles.
Facilities: 2,500-vol. costume & decorative art reference library; 120-seat auditorium; nine galleries. Museum-related items for sale.
Activities: guided tours; docent program; loan & temporary exhibitions; organized educational programs for undergraduate college students affiliated with Kent State University.
Publications: brochures; catalogues.
Hours & Admission Prices: Wed. & Fri.-Sat. 10-4:45, Thurs. 10-8:45, Sun. 12-4:45. Adults $5, senior citizen $4, children $3; discounts to AAM & ICOM members; children under 7 no charge. Annual pass $25. Closed university & national holidays. ♿
Attendance: 8,714 (accurate)
Membership: Annual $25; Platinum Circle $1,000.

KENT STATE UNIVERSITY, SCHOOL OF ART GALLERIES, Kent, OH 44242-. Mailing Address: P.O. Box 5190, Kent, OH 44242-0001. Tel.: 330-672-7853. Fax: 330-672-4729.
E-mail: galleries@kent.edu
Web Site: galleries.kent.edu
Founded: 1950.
Congressional District: 11
Key Personnel: Dir., Christine Havice.
Personnel Profile: Full-Time Paid 1; Part-Time Paid 12; Part-Time Volunteers 1; Interns 2.
Governing Authority: state. Parent Institution: Kent State University. Branch Galleries: Michener Gallery; Downtown Gallery; William H. Eells Art Gallery; Collection Gallery; Student Galleries. Tax-exempt: 501(c)(3).
Art School and Gallery.
Collections: paintings; sculpture; prints; graduate theses; decorative arts; Hazel Janicki & William Schock collection; James A. Michener collection; Milton Adams collection.
Research Fields: contemporary American art.
Facilities: lectures; guided tours.
Activities: performances; lectures; special events; formally organized education programs; undergraduate & graduate students exhibitions.
Publications: booklets: Contemporary American, Canadian & European Enamelists; Leadership Artifacts of West Africa; Objects in Clay, Fiber, Glass & Metal; Indonesian Textiles; Contemporary Platinum Prints & Photographs; An Interview with Patrick Ireland; West African Textiles & Dress; A New Generation of Ohio Artists; Contemporary Woven Work: America & Abroad; European Glass; Akron & Kent Painters: 1940-1970; The Cleveland Enamelists: 1930-1955; Response to the City: Photography & Sculpture; Robert Smithson's Partially Buried Woodshed; 15th Annual Collage National Exhibit; Print in Enamel; West African Men's Wearing: Design & Technique.
Hours & Admission Prices: Tues.-Fri. 11-5. No charge; donations accepted. Closed school holidays. ♿
Attendance: 26,000 (accurate)
Membership: Student & Senior Citizen $10; Individual $15; Family $25; Sponsor $50; Benefactor $100; Patron $500.

Kenton

HARDIN COUNTY HISTORICAL MUSEUMS, INC., 223 N. Main St., Kenton, OH 43326-1505. Tel.: 419-673-7147.
E-mail: hardincountymuseums@windstream.net
Web Site: www.hardinmuseums.org
Founded: 1991.
Congressional District: 4
Key Personnel: Admin., Linda Iams.
Personnel Profile: Part-Time Paid 1; Part-Time Volunteers 100.
Governing Authority: nonprofit. Parent Institution: Hardin County Historical Museums, Inc. Tax-exempt.
History Museum.
Collections: local history; Native American artifacts; military artifacts; Kenton Hardware toys; 1st Medal of Honor winner Jacob Parrott militaria; pioneer crafts & tools; D.A.R. memorabilia; Charles Shanafelt Collection of relics & natural curiosities; farming implements; one-room schoolhouse; Fred Machetanz Alaskan art & literature.
Research Fields: local history.
Facilities: archives.
Activities: guided tours; lectures; audiovisual programs; walking tours; permanent & temporary exhibitions; school visitation.
Hours & Admission Prices: Mon.-Fri. 1-4. No charge; donations accepted. Closed holidays. ♿
Attendance: 500 (estimated)
Membership: Individual $25; Family $35; Business $100; Life $500.

THE ORGANETTE HOUSE MECHANICAL MUSIC MUSEUM, 15577 US Hwy. 68, Kenton, OH 43326-9306. Tel.: 419-674-4312.
E-mail: todd@organettehouse.com
Web Site: www.organettehouse.com
Mechanical Music Museum.
Collections: over 50 organettes & other mechanical music.
Hours & Admission Prices: By appointment. No charge.

Kirtland

* **THE HOLDEN ARBORETUM,** 9500 Sperry Rd., Kirtland, OH 44094-5172. Tel.: 440-946-4400. Fax: 440-602-3857.
E-mail: holden@holdenarb.org
Web Site: www.holdenarb.org
Founded: 1931.
Congressional District: 11
Key Personnel: Dir., Clem Hamilton; Chm. Bd. (V), Joe Mahovlic; Dir. Finance, Jim Ansberry; Dir. Horticulture & Conservation, Roger Gettig; Dir. Education, Paul C. Spector; Dir. Devel., Pam Eichenaur; Dir. Research, Mary A. Topa; Dir. Guest Svcs., David A. Desimone; Dir. Human Resources, Jack Blackwell; Museum Shop Mgr., Kristie Hawley.
Personnel Profile: Full-Time Paid 75; Part-Time Paid 10; Part-Time Volunteers 700; Interns 4.
Governing Authority: nonprofit organization. Subsidiary Institution: David G. Leach Research Station. Tax-exempt: 501(c)(3).
Arboretum.
Collections: native & cultivated woody plants, wildflowers, rare books & nutcrackers.
Research Fields: stress biology of urban forests.
Facilities: 9,000-vol. library on horticulture & botany available on premises by request; nature center; bird observation blind; classrooms. Educational literature & museum-related items for sale.
Activities: guided tours; lectures; formally organized education programs.
Publications: bimonthly magazine, Leaves, The Holden Arboretum Class & Events Magazine.
Hours & Admission Prices: Daily 9-5. Adults $6, senior citizens $5, children 6-12 $3; discounts to groups & AAM members; seniors on Tues., members & children under 6 no charge. Closed Thanksgiving; Christmas. ♿
Attendance: 90,607 (accurate)
Membership: Aspen & Buckeye $40; Maple $50.

Lakewood

CLEVELAND ARTISTS FOUNDATION AT BECK CENTER FOR THE ARTS, 17801 Detroit Ave., Lakewood, OH 44107-3413. Tel.: 216-227-9507. Fax: 216-228-6050.
E-mail: laurenhansgen@clevelandartists.org
Web Site: www.clevelandartists.org
Founded: 1984.
Congressional District: 23
Key Personnel: Interim Dir., Lauren Hansgen; Pres., William Lipscomb.
Personnel Profile: Full-Time Paid 1; Part-Time Paid 2; Part-Time Volunteers 40; Interns 2.
Governing Authority: nonprofit. Tax-exempt: 501(c)(3).
Art Museum.
Collections: contemporary & historic art from Northeast Ohio.
Facilities: auditorium; theater; classrooms; gallery for Cleveland artists foundation.
Activities: gallery talks; workshops; lectures.
Hours & Admission Prices: Summer: Tues.-Fri. 1-5; Sept.-May Tues.-Thurs. 1-5, Fri.-Sat. 1-8. No charge; donations accepted. Closed major holidays. ♿
Attendance: 30,000 (estimated)
Membership: CAF Member $35; Family $50; Patron $100; Sponsor $250; Corporate Sponsor $1,000; Show Sponsor $5,000.

OLDEST STONE HOUSE MUSEUM, (M), 14710 Lake Ave., Lakewood, OH 44107-1353. Tel.: 216-221-7343. Fax: 216-221-0320.
E-mail: lakewoodhistory@bge.net
Web Site: www.lakewoodhistory.org
Founded: 1952.
Congressional District: 19
Key Personnel: Exec. Dir., Mazie M. Adams; Pres. (V), Paula Reed.
Personnel Profile: Full-Time Paid 1; Part-Time Volunteers 50.
Governing Authority: board of trustees; municipal; society; Lakewood Historical Society; nonprofit organization. Tax-exempt: 501(c)(3).
Historic House Museum: 1838 Old Stone House.
Collections: period furnishings of the 1830s & 40s; slide collection of early photographs.
Research Fields: local landmark houses & early settlers.
Facilities: 300-vol. library of the early history of Ohio, research books relating to antiques & early textbooks available for use by members & on premises; herb gardens. Museum-related items for sale.
Activities: guided tours; lectures; formally organized education programs for children; permanent & temporary exhibitions; school loan service.
Publications: books, Romance in Lakewood Streets; A Child's Journal of Early Lakewood; Lakewood, The First Hundred Years; quarterly, Lakewood Historical Society Newsletter; Lakewood Lore.
Hours & Admission Prices: Feb.-Nov. Wed. 1-4, Sun. 2-5. No charge; donations accepted. Closed national holidays.
Attendance: 2,500 (accurate)
Membership: Senior Citizens $8; Family & Individual $15; Contributing $25; Sustaining $50; Patron $100; Benefactor $250.

Lancaster

DECORATIVE ARTS CENTER OF OHIO, (M), 145 E. Main St., Lancaster, OH 43130-3713. Mailing Address: P.O. Box 845, Lancaster, OH 43130-0845. Tel.: 740-681-1423. Fax: 740-681-2713.
Web Site: www.decartsohio.org
Founded: 1997.
Congressional District: 7
Key Personnel: C.E.O., Julia C. Parke; Pres. (V), Dave Hareum; Administrative Asst., Emily C. Dawson; Asst. Dir. Education, Trisha Clifford-Sprouse; Dir. Programming, Becky Dungan; Dir. Devel. & External Affairs, Mandi Custer; Dir. Operations, Andrea Brookover; Museum Shop Mgr., Betty Arnsbarger; Weekend Mgr., Maggie Conrad.
Personnel Profile: Full-Time Paid 3; Part-Time Paid 5; Part-Time Volunteers 50; Interns 2.
Governing Authority: private; nonprofit organization. Tax-exempt.
Decorative Arts Museum.
Collections: 19th & 20th-centuries decorative arts.
Research Fields: decorative arts; crafts; domestic architecture.
Facilities: library; art studios & classrooms.
Activities: lectures; concerts; workshops; classes; temporary exhibitions.
Publications: semiannual member newsletter, New From the Center.
Hours & Admission Prices: Tues.-Fri. 12-4, Sat. 10-4, Sun. 1-4. Groups of 10 or more $3. Closed major holidays. ♿
Attendance: 12,800 (estimated)
Membership: Student K-12 and Senior 55 & over $25; Individual $35; Grandparent, Family & Household $55; Contributor $100; Supporter $250; Patron $500.

THE GEORGIAN MUSEUM, 105 E. Wheeling St., Lancaster, OH 43130-3706. Tel.: 740-654-9923. Fax: 740-654-9121.
E-mail: info@fairfieldheritage.org
Web Site: www.fairfieldheritage.org
Founded: 1976.
Congressional District: 10
Key Personnel: Dir., Myrna Figgins; Pres. (V), Joyce Harvey; Office Mgr., Karen S. Smith; Museum Shop Mgr., Janet McCafferty; Museum Shop Mgr., Delores Troup.
Personnel Profile: Part-Time Paid 6; Part-Time Volunteers 125.

Governing Authority: nonprofit organization. Owned & Operated by The Fairfield Heritage Association, Inc., 105 E. Wheeling St. Tax-exempt: 107(b)(1)(A).
Historical Society Museum: housed in 1830-1832 The Georgian, Federal-style house with Regency features.
Collections: furniture; silver; costumes; tools; glass; Indian artifacts found in Fairfield county; Fairfield County historical items depicting lifestyle of affluent families from 1820-1850.
Research Fields: county survey of historic structures over 100 years old; preservation.
Facilities: reference library available for use on premises. Gift items including books pertaining to Fairfield County for sale.
Activities: lectures; films; gallery talks; tours of the museum, Square 13 historical district & early churches; reading room; hobby workshops; docent program; permanent, temporary & traveling exhibitions. Museum Sponsors: oral histories; fifth grade week; Christmas Candlelight Tour.
Publications: reprints of early histories; quarterly, Fairfield Heritage; books, Cross Roads & Fence Corners; Architecture & Arts of Fairfield County; Campfire to Courthouse; Sherman Family Chronicle; Covered Bridges of Fairfield County.
Hours & Admission Prices: Jan.-March by appointment only; April to mid-Dec. Tues.-Sun. 1-4. Adults $6, students 6-18 $1; discount to groups & seniors; children under 6 & members no charge. Closed holidays. ♿
Attendance: 7,500 (estimated)
Membership: Student 6-18 $10; Senior Citizen $15; Individual $20; Family $40; Sustaining $50; Fellow $75; Patron $100; Historian $150; Supporter $250; Curator $350; Partner $500; Archivist $650; Preservationist $1,000; Executive $1,500.

OHIO GLASS MUSEUM, 124 W. Main St., Lancaster, OH 43130. Tel.: 740-687-0101.
Founded: 2002.
Glass Museum.
Collections: glass industry & history; glass from local & national artists and companies including Heisey, Fenton, Imperial, Cambridge, Anchor-Hocking/Lancaster Glass, Lancaster Lens/Lancaster Glass, Gay-Fad, and Erickson.
Facilities: theater.
Activities: film.
Hours & Admission Prices: March-Oct. Tues.-Sun. 1-4; Nov.-Feb. Tues.-Sat. 1-4; other times by appointment. Adults $4, seniors $3, students 6-18 $2.
Membership: Individual $35; Couple $50; Family $60; Patron $100; Sponsor $250; Benefactor $400.

SHERMAN HOUSE MUSEUM, 137 E. Main St., Lancaster, OH 43130-3713. Mailing Address: 105 E. Wheeling St., Lancaster, OH 43130-3706. Tel.: 740-687-5891. Fax: 740-654-9121.
E-mail: fairheritage@greenapple.com
Web Site: www.shermanhouse.com
Congressional District: 7
Key Personnel: Dir., Laura Bullock; Office Mgr., Karen S. Smith; Exec. Sec., Betty Ann Boone; Museum Shop Mgr., Janet McCafferty; Museum Shop Mgr., Delores Troup.
Personnel Profile: Part-Time Paid 1; Part-Time Volunteers 100.
Governing Authority: nonprofit organization. Parent Institution: The Fairfield Heritage Association, 105 E. Wheeling St. Tax-exempt: 107(b)(1)(A).
Historical House.
Collections: furniture; silver; costumes; tools; glass; Indian artifacts found in Fairfield County; Fairfield County historical items; Civil War artifacts; Sherman family items; Civil War era art; quilts; coverlets; veteran & GAR artifacts; garden history.
Activities: lectures; films; gallery talks; tours of the museum; Square 13 historical district & early churches; oral histories; reading room; hobby workshops; docent program; permanent, temporary & traveling exhibitions. Museum Sponsors: Civil War Roundtable; Annual Garden Party; fifth grade week; Christmas Candlelight tour.
Publications: reprints of early histories; quarterly, Fairfield Heritage; books, Cross Roads & Fence Corners; Architecture & Arts of Fairfield County; Campfire to Courthouse; Covered Bridges of Fairfield County; combination atlas map of Fairfield County, OH 1875; Fifty Six Miles into the Hills, The story of Lancaster Lateral & Hocking Canals; William T. Sherman Activity & Coloring Book.
Hours & Admission Prices: April to mid-Dec. Tues.-Sun. 1-4. Adults $6; discount to groups, seniors, students and AAA & AAM members; children under 6 & members no charge. Closed holidays. ♿
Attendance: 11,000 (estimated)
Membership: Senior Citizen $15; Individual $20; Family $40; Sustaining $50; Fellow $75; Patron $100; Historian $150; Supporter $250; Curator $350; Partner $500; Archivist $650; Preservationist $1,000; Executive $1,500.

Lebanon

GLENDOWER STATE MEMORIAL, 105 Cincinnati Ave., Lebanon, OH 45036-2117. Mailing Address: 105 S. Broadway, Lebanon, OH 45036-1707. Tel.: 513-932-1817. Fax: 513-932-8560.
E-mail: wchs@wchsmuseum.org
Web Site: wchsmuseum.org
Founded: 1944.
Congressional District: 7
Personnel Profile: Part-Time Paid 1; Part-Time Volunteers 12.
Governing Authority: Tax-exempt.
Historic Building Museum: restored Greek revival house.
Collections: 19th-century furniture & furnishings.
Hours & Admission Prices: June to Labor Day Wed.-Sun. 12-4; Sept.-Oct. Sat.-Sun. 12-4; school groups by appointment. Adults $5, children $3.50; WCHS members no charge.
Attendance: 1,384 (estimated)

WARREN COUNTY HISTORY CENTER, (M), 105 S. Broadway, Lebanon, OH 45036-1707. Tel.: 513-932-1817. Fax: 513-932-8560.
E-mail: wchs@wchsmuseum.org
Web Site: wchsmuseum.org
Founded: 1940.
Congressional District: 7
Key Personnel: Exec. Dir., Victoria V.H. Tappy; Pres. (V), J. William Duning; Asst. Dir. & Historian, John J. Zimkus; Cur., Mary Klei.
Personnel Profile: Full-Time Paid 1; Part-Time Paid 3; Part-Time Volunteers 40.
Governing Authority: society; nonprofit organization. Tax-exempt: 501(c)(3).
Local History Museum.
Collections: early artifacts from southwestern Ohio; paleontology; Shaker furniture and household articles; Native American artifacts; genealogy library.
Research Fields: genealogy; Shaker history.
Facilities: 2,000-vol. library of local history, biographies and genealogy books available for use on premises; reading room. Books, museum publication & hand-crafted items for sale.
Activities: guided tours; lectures; temporary & traveling exhibitions.
Publications: quarterly newsletter, Historicalog; local history booklets.
Hours & Admission Prices: Tues.-Sat. 9-4, Sun. 12-4. Adults $5, senior citizens 65 & over $4.50, children 5-18 $3.50; members no charge. Closed national holidays. ♿
Attendance: 3,057 (estimated)
Membership: Student 18 & under $15; Individual $20; Family $30; Sustaining $60; Patron $125; Gold Card $500.

Lexington

RICHLAND COUNTY MUSEUM, 51 Church St., Lexington, OH 44904-1258. Mailing Address: P.O. Box 3153, Lexington, OH 44904-0153. Tel.: 419-884-2230.
E-mail: woodsiewoman@yahoo.com
Web Site: www.richlandcountymuseum.org
Founded: 1966.
Congressional District: 4
Key Personnel: Pres., Jeffrey Mandeville; Treas., Loretta Hilliard; Sec., Shirley Addlesperger.
Personnel Profile: Part-Time Volunteers 20; Interns 1.
Governing Authority: society. Tax-exempt: 501(c)(3).
General Museum: housed in 1800 school building.
Collections: history; agriculture; art; children's toys; Indian; medical; Jacquard coverlets; Richland County weavers.
Activities: guided tours; permanent exhibitions.
Publications: one-room schools booklet.
Hours & Admission Prices: May-Oct. Sun. 1:30-4:30; group tours by appointment. No charge; donations accepted. ♿
Attendance: 2,000 (estimated)
Membership: Individual $5; Family $10; Associate $25-$49; Benefactor $50-$99; Distinguished $100 & up; Corporate $1,000.

Lima

∗ **ALLEN COUNTY MUSEUM, (M),** 620 W. Market St., Lima, OH 45801-4665. Tel.: 419-222-9426. Fax: 419-222-0649.
Web Site: www.allencountymuseum.org
Founded: 1908.
Congressional District: 4
Key Personnel: Dir., Patricia Smith; Pres., William C. Timmermeister; Chm. (V), Sue Clover; Cur. Manuscripts & Archives, Anna B. Selfridge; Cur.

Collections, John Carnes; Cur. Education, Sarah Rish; Asst. Cur., Charles Bates; Museum Shop Mgr., Joann Park; Admin. Asst. & Bookkeeper, Donna Collins.
Personnel Profile: Full-Time Paid 5; Part-Time Paid 15; Part-Time Volunteers 60; Interns 1.
Governing Authority: society. Parent Institution: Allen County Historical Society. Tax-exempt: 501(c)(3).
History Museum.
Collections: Indian relics; minerals; fossils; documents; manuscripts; photographs; drawings pertaining to steam & electric railroads; files from old Lima locomotive works; pioneer rooms; tools; furniture; 19th century fire-fighting equipment; Lincoln Park railroad exhibit; furnished miniature model of Mount Vernon. Historic Houses: 1848 log house; 1890 MacDonell house.
Research Fields: local history; railroad history.
Facilities: 5,000-vol. general library of books available for use on premises; reading room; 150-seat auditorium.
Activities: guided tours; lectures; films; gallery talks; concerts; arts festivals; formally organized education programs for children; permanent & temporary exhibitions.
Publications: quarterly newsletter, Museum Musings; biannual local history periodical, The Allen County Reporter.
Hours & Admission Prices: Museum: Tues.-Sun. 1-5. Children's Discovery Center: Tues.-Sun. 1-5. No charge; donations accepted. MacDonell House: No charge; donations accepted. Closed holidays. ♿
Attendance: 64,000 (estimated)
Membership: Individual $20; Family $30; Patron $50; Corporate $75.

ARTSPACE/LIMA, 65 Town Square, Lima, OH 45801-4950. Tel.: 419-222-1721.
Key Personnel: Operations Mgr., Bill Sullivan
Art Gallery.
Collections: paintings; photographs; sculpture.
Facilities: Museum-related items for sale.
Activities: classes; permanent & temporary exhibits.
Hours & Admission Prices: Tues.-Fri. 10-5, Sat. 10-2.

LIMA FIRE FIGHTERS MEMORIAL MUSEUM, Lincoln Park, Elm St. & Shawnee St., Lima, OH 45804. Tel.: 419-221-5164.
Fire Fighters Museum.
Collections: Lima's fire fighting history & heroes; 19th century horse-drawn steam pumper; photographs; equipment; uniforms; newspaper clippings.
Hours & Admission Prices: By appointment. No charge.

Lisbon

LISBON HISTORICAL SOCIETY, 117/119 E. Washington St., Lisbon, OH 44432. Mailing Address: P.O. Box 191, Lisbon, OH 44432-0191. Tel.: 330-424-9000. Fax: 330-424-1861.
E-mail: lisbonhs@epohi.com
Web Site: www.lisbonhistory.org
Founded: 1938.
Congressional District: 6
Key Personnel: Pres. (V), Tom McKenna; Head Cur., Gene Krotky.
Personnel Profile: Part-Time Volunteers 8.
Governing Authority: nonprofit organization. Subsidiary Institutions: Old Stone House, 117 E. Washington St., Lisbon 44432; Erie Railroad Station Museum, 119 E. Washington St. Tax-exempt: 501(c)(3).
General Museum.
Collections: early items of local history; New Lisbon, Lisbon history; early records; genealogical materials.
Facilities: 100-vol. library of early Ohio & local history, including probate records 1803-1920, available on request.
Activities: guided tours; permanent & temporary exhibitions; research; children's programs; educational programs.
Publications: quarterly newsletter; books, Reflections of a Village: Lisbon 1803-2003; The First Baptist Church of New Lisbon 1806-1825; A Proud Heritage.
Hours & Admission Prices: Tues. 10-3; other times by appointment. Donation: $2. Closed holidays.
Attendance: 1,500 (estimated)
Membership: Individual $15; Family $25; Patron $75; Life $500.

Lithopolis

THE WAGNALLS MEMORIAL FOUNDATION, 150 E. Columbus St., Lithopolis, OH 43136. Mailing Address: P.O. Box 217, Lithopolis, OH 43136-0217. Tel.: 614-837-4765, ext. 104. Fax: 614-833-4767.
E-mail: pdrodofsky@wagnalls.org
Web Site: www.wagnalls.org
Founded: 1924.
Congressional District: 10
Key Personnel: Dir., M. Ellen Gruber; Pres. (V), David Wyakoop.
Personnel Profile: Full-Time Paid 2; Part-Time Paid 2.
Governing Authority: nonprofit organization. Tax-exempt: 501(c)(3).
Library & Community Center; Foundation.
Collections: paintings of John Ward Dunsmore; poems of Edwin Markham; books & personal items of Mabel Wagnalls Jones; letters from O'Henry
Research Fields: Ohio history.
Facilities: 35,000-vol. library; reading room; 400-seat auditorium; dining hall; recreation room.
Activities: guided tours; lectures; permanent exhibits; rotating & special exhibits; displays; musical programs; education class; children's acting classes; theatre productions.
Publications: newsletter, Wagnalls Digest.
Hours & Admission Prices: Library & Museum: June-Aug. Mon.-Thurs. 10-8, Sat. 10-2; Sept.-May Mon.-Thurs. 10-8, Sat. 10-2, Sun. 1-5. No charge; donations accepted. Closed national holidays. ♿

Lorain

BLACK RIVER HISTORICAL SOCIETY OF LORAIN, 309 W. 5th St., Lorain, OH 44052-1611. Tel.: 440-245-2563. Fax: 440-245-3591.
E-mail: brhsmoore@centurytel.net
Web Site: www.loraincityhistory.org
Founded: 1981.
Congressional District: 13
Key Personnel: Vice Pres., Rosemary Balchak; Chm. (V), John McGarvey; Treas., Pam Szucs; Cur., Dee Trifiletti; Education, Rodney Beals; Museum Shop Mgr., Carolyn Sipkovsky.
Personnel Profile: Full-Time Paid 1; Part-Time Volunteers 25.
Governing Authority: municipal; nonprofit. Tax-exempt: 501(c)(3).
General Museum.
Collections: artifacts; photographs; stories; histories of businesses & industries of Lorain.
Facilities: 100-vol. library. Museum-related items for sale.
Activities: guided tours; school service.
Publications: quarterly newsletter, Black River Historical Society Newsletter; Moore Memos.
Hours & Admission Prices: Mon.-Fri. 10-4:30, Sun. 1-4:30. Adults $3, students $1; children under 5 & members no charge. Closed major holidays. ♿
Attendance: 420 (estimated)
Membership: Youth $5; Historian $15; Archivist $50; Benefactor $100; Life $400; Corporate Benefactor $150; Corporate Life $3,000.

Loudonville

CLEO REDD FISHER MUSEUM, 203 E. Main St., Loudonville, OH 44842-1214. Tel.: 419-994-4050.
Founded: 1973.
Congressional District: 17
Key Personnel: Pres., John Leininger.
Personnel Profile: Part-Time Volunteers 15.
Governing Authority: society. Mohican Historical Society. Tax-exempt.
Local History Museum.
Collections: Indian relics; pioneer & Victorian rooms, ceramics; Charles Kettering & Hugo Young memorabilia; early photographs of town & area; coverlets; records.
Facilities: 400-vol. library; 150-seat meeting room.
Activities: guided tours; lectures; loan exhibitions.
Hours & Admission Prices: May to mid-Oct. Sat.-Sun. 2-5; tour groups at other times by appointment. Adults $.50, children $.25.
Attendance: 500 (estimated)
Membership: Society Membership $2.

Loveland

GREATER LOVELAND HISTORICAL SOCIETY MUSEUM, 201 Riverside Dr., Loveland, OH 45140-2303. Tel.: 513-683-5692. Fax: 513-683-7409.
E-mail: glhsm@fuse.net
Web Site: www.lovelandmuseum.org
Founded: 1975.
Congressional District: 6
Key Personnel: Dir., Janet Beller; Pres., Robert Bauer; Librarian, Jo Funke; Museum Shop Co-Mgr., Nancy Garfinkel.
Personnel Profile: Part-Time Paid 1; Part-Time Volunteers 75.
Governing Authority: society; nonprofit organization. Parent Institution: Greater Loveland Historical Society. Tax-exempt: 501(c)(3).
Local History Museum: housed in c.1861 two-story frame structure, 1797 log house & herb garden.

Collections: dolls; costumes; photographs; genealogy library; 35-volumes of Loveland newspapers; local history from Indian habitation to present time; Victorian furnishings; 1920's kitchen; textiles; Nancy Ford Cones photographs. Historic Structures: 1797 log cabin & herb garden; 1897 Bishop-Coleman Gazebo.
Research Fields: homes; genealogy; Loveland High School annuals; bound local newspapers; local history.
Facilities: library; archives, 5,400 sq. ft. exhibit space. Museum-related items for sale.
Activities: school & group guided tours; membership & community programs; rotating, loan & permanent exhibits; spring bazaars; films; hobby workshops; docent programs; special events; lectures; antiques auction; rental facilities. Annual Events: banquet; picnic; heritage weekend in spring; Victorian bazaar in fall; Christmas programs.
Publications: quarterly newsletter, Reflections; books: Passages Through Time: A Loveland History; 25th Anniversary Cookbook, a collection of favorite recipes from members; Loveland Memorabilia.
Hours & Admission Prices: Sat.-Sun. 1-4:30; groups & other times by appointment. No charge; donations accepted. Closed Christmas. ♿
Attendance: 2,000 (estimated)
Membership: Individual $10; Family $15; Contributing $25; Sustaining $50; Supporting $100; Life $1,000 & up; Corporate $50-$1,000 & up.

Lucas

MALABAR FARM STATE PARK, 4050 Bromfield Rd., Lucas, OH 44843-9745. Tel.: 419-892-2784. Fax: 419-892-3988.
E-mail: malabar.farm.parks@dnr.state.oh.us
Web Site: www.malabarfarm.org
Founded: 1939.
Congressional District: 4
Key Personnel: C.E.O. & Museum Shop Mgr., Jason Wefley; Museum Shop Mgr., Sybil Burskey.
Personnel Profile: Full-Time Paid 6; Full-Time Volunteers 1; Part-Time Paid 9; Part-Time Volunteers 150; Interns 1.
Governing Authority: state. Parent Institution: Malabar Farm Foundation. Subsidiary Institution: Columbus Community Foundation. Tax-exempt.
Park Museum: housed in The Big House, former home of author Louis Bromfield.
Collections: original furnishings; 2 Grandma Moses paintings. Historic Building: 1820 Malabar Inn.
Facilities: 6,500-vol. library of ecology books; campground; restaurant; domestic animal zoo; picnic area.
Activities: guided tours; nature programs; seasonal special events.
Publications: guide, Malabar Farm Tour; maps; Ohio State Park brochures.
Hours & Admission Prices: Nov.-April Sat.-Sun. 11-5; call for additional hours. Adults $4, seniors $3.60, children 6-18 $2; Farm Wagon Tours: $2 per person; discounts to Golden Buckeye Card Holders; children under 6 & members no charge. Closed New Year's Day; Martin Luther King Jr. Day; Presidents' Day; Columbus Day; Thanksgiving; Christmas. ♿
Attendance: 352,600 (estimated)
Membership: Individual $50.

Mansfield

KINGWOOD CENTER, 900 Park Ave., W., Mansfield, OH 44906-2999. Tel.: 419-522-0211. Fax: 419-522-0211.
E-mail: info@kingwoodcenter.org
Web Site: www.kingwoodcenter.org
Founded: 1953.
Congressional District: 4
Key Personnel: C.E.O., Charles T. Gleaves; Dir. Education, William W. Collins; Museum Shop Mgr., Heather McClain.
Personnel Profile: Full-Time Paid 17; Part-Time Paid 10; Part-Time Volunteers 240; Interns 2.
Governing Authority: nonprofit organization. Tax-exempt: 501(c)(3).
Botanical Garden.
Collections: display gardens; greenhouse.
Research Fields: horticulture.
Facilities: 8,500-vol. library on botany, horticulture, gardening and nature; reading room; 250-seat auditorium; classrooms. Gift items for sale.
Activities: guided tours; lectures; films; concerts; study clubs; hobby workshops; formally organized education programs; docent program.
Publications: monthly newsletter, Kingwood Center News.
Hours & Admission Prices: Gardens: March-Nov. daily 8am to sunset. Kingwood Hall: March-Nov. Sat. 10-5, Sun. 1-5. Greenhouse: March-Nov. daily 8-4:30. No charge, donations accepted. Closed holidays. ♿
Attendance: 250,000 (estimated)
Membership: Member $25; Friend $50; Donor $100; Patron $500; Benefactor $1,000.

LIVING BIBLE MUSEUM, 500 Tingley Ave., Mansfield, OH 44905-1234. Tel.: 800-222-0139. Fax: 419-524-2002.
E-mail: lbmjulia@richnet.net
Web Site: www.livingbiblemuseum.org/
Key Personnel: Dir., Julia Mott-Hardin
Religious Museum.
Collections: life-sized Bible re-creations; woodcarvings; Bibles; paintings.
Activities: tours.
Hours & Admission Prices: Mon.-Sat. 9-6, Sun. 3-7. Various tours available. Call for prices. ♿

THE MANSFIELD ART CENTER, 700 Marion Ave., Mansfield, OH 44906-5006. Tel.: 419-756-1700. Fax: 419-756-0860.
E-mail: info@mansfieldartcenter.org
Web Site: www.mansfieldartcenter.org
Founded: 1946.
Congressional District: 17
Key Personnel: Exec. Dir., Paul Kemerling; Dir. Education, Jodi Burgholder; Museum Shop Mgr., Judy Francl.
Governing Authority: nonprofit. Tax-exempt: 501(c)(3).
Art Gallery.
Collections: changing exhibitions.
Facilities: 500-vol. library of fine arts books; classrooms. Fine arts & crafts by artists for sale.
Activities: guided tours; lectures; films; gallery talks; group & theme shows; competitive exhibitions; workshops; formally organized education programs; docent program; inter-museum loan & traveling exhibitions.
Publications: monthly newsletter; quarterly class schedules; annual members report; annual report; special exhibit guides.
Hours & Admission Prices: Tues.-Sat. 11-5, Sun. 12-5. No charge; donations accepted. Closed national holidays. ♿
Attendance: 80,000
Membership: Individual $40; Family $50; Patron $100; Friend $250; Contributor $500; Corporate $500-$1,000; Sponsor $750; Benefactor $1,000.

MANSFIELD MEMORIAL MUSEUM, 34 Park Ave., W., Mansfield, OH 44902-1603. Tel.: 419-525-2491.
Key Personnel: Owner, Julia Hardin; Gen. Mgr., Scott Cater
History Museum.
Collections: local history & culture; military history; photographs; period artifacts.
Hours & Admission Prices: Feb.-Dec. Sat. 10-4, Sun. 12-4. No charge; donations accepted.

Marblehead

JOHNSON'S ISLAND MUSEUM & INFORMATION CENTER, 414 W. Main St., Marblehead, OH 43440. Mailing Address: P.O. Box 1865, Marblehead, OH 43440-0495.
E-mail: jipres@johnsonsisland.org
History Museum.
Collections: island's history; Civil War POW Depot; Pleasure Resort; quarry operations; photographs; personal artifacts.
Hours & Admission Prices: Memorial Day to Labor Day Sat.-Sun. & holidays 12-5; other times by appointment.

Marietta

CAMPUS MARTIUS MUSEUM, 601 2nd St., Marietta, OH 45750-2122. Tel.: 740-373-3750; 800-860-0145. Fax: 740-373-3680.
E-mail: cmmoriv@ohiohistory.org
Web Site: www.ohiohistory.org/places/campus
Founded: 1929.
Congressional District: 6
Key Personnel: C.E.O. Ohio Historical Society, William Laidlaw; Site Mgr., L Hendershot.
Personnel Profile: Full-Time Paid 3; Part-Time Paid 1; Part-Time Volunteers 60.
Governing Authority: private; nonprofit; educational organization. Parent Institution: The Ohio Historical Society, Ohio Historical Center, 1982 Velma Ave., Columbus, OH 43211. Tax-exempt: 501(c)(3); 509(a).
History Museum.
Collections: items pertaining to history of early Northwest Territory & Marietta, Ohio; 19th- & early to mid-20th century farming, transportation & industry; steamboat photographs; area genealogical information; migration of farmers to cities of Ohio from 1880-1920; migration of Appalachian people to Ohio's urban centers from 1917-1970. Historic Houses: 1788 Ohio Company Land Office; 1789 Rufus Putnam House.
Research Fields: history of Northwest Territory; pioneer life and settlement; the Ohio River.

Facilities: 3,000-vol. library of historical, genealogical & river material available for use on premises; auditorium; audiovisual programs; interactive video programs. Ohio-made crafts & other museum-related items for sale.
Activities: guided tours; permanent & temporary exhibits; special educational programs, including school workshops; summer day camp.
Hours & Admission Prices: Mon. & Wed.-Sat. 9:30-5, Sun. 12-5. Adults $7, students $4; discounts to senior citizens, groups, military & AAA members; OHS members and children 5 & under no charge. Closed New Year's Day; Easter; Thanksgiving; Christmas. ♿
Attendance: 9,500 (accurate)
Membership: See separate listing for Ohio Historical Society. Friends of the Museum: Student $10; Individual $15; Family $30; Special Friend $50.

THE CASTLE, 418 Fourth St., Marietta, OH 45750-2003. Tel.: 740-373-4180. Fax: 740-373-4233.
E-mail: castle@mariettacastle.org
Web Site: www.mariettacastle.org
Founded: 1992.
Key Personnel: Dir., Lynne Shuman; Pres., Larry Hawn; Treas., Matt Pottmeyer.
Personnel Profile: Full-Time Paid 2; Part-Time Paid 5; Part-Time Volunteers 44.
Governing Authority: private; nonprofit organization. Parent Institution: Betsey Mills Corp. Tax-exempt: 501(c)(3).
Historic House: c.1855 Gothic Revival-style home.
Collections: Victorian furnishings.
Research Fields: history of site & families that occupied the house.
Activities: guided tours; workshops; lectures; history camp; concerts; docent program; ghost tours. Annual Events: Herb Sale; storytelling; Victorian Christmas; Victorian Funeral.
Publications: quarterly newsletter, The Calling Card.
Hours & Admission Prices: Jan.-March group tours only; April-May & Sept.-Dec. Mon. & Thurs.-Fri. 10-4, Sat.-Sun. 1-4; June-Aug. daily. Adults $6, senior citizens $5.50, students $3; discounts to groups, AARP, AAM & AAA members; children under 6 & members no charge. Closed New Year's Day; Easter; Thanksgiving; Christmas. ♿
Attendance: 6,023 (accurate)
Membership: Individual $25; Family $40; Contributing $50; Patron $100.

THE CHILDREN'S TOY & DOLL MUSEUM, 206 Gilman St., Marietta, OH 45750-2837. Mailing Address: P.O. Box 4034, Marietta, OH 45750-7034. Tel.: 740-373-8820.
Personnel Profile: Part-Time Volunteers 15.
Governing Authority: Tax-exempt.
Children's Museum.
Collections: international dolls; period toys; doll houses; miniature circus; toy transportation.
Activities: children's playroom.
Hours & Admission Prices: May-Nov. Mon. & Sat. 1-4; other times by appointment. Family $5, adults $3, children $1; discount to families; members no charge.
Membership: Regular $10; Family $15; Bronze Patron $25; Silver Patron $50; Gold Patron $100; Platinum Patron $200.

OHIO RIVER MUSEUM, 601 Front St., Marietta, OH 45750. Mailing Address: 601 Second St., Marietta, OH 45750-2122. Tel.: 740-373-3750; 800-860-0145. Fax: 614-373-3680.
E-mail: cmmoriv@ohiohistory.org
Web Site: www.ohiohistory.org/places/ohriver
Founded: 1941.
Congressional District: 6
Key Personnel: C.E.O. Ohio Historical Society, William Laidlaw; Pres. (V), Richard D. Ruppart; Interim Mgr., Le Ann Hendershot.
Personnel Profile: Full-Time Paid 1; Part-Time Paid 2; Part-Time Volunteers 12.
Governing Authority: private; nonprofit; educational organization. Parent Institution: Ohio Historical Society, 1982 Velma Ave. Columbus, OH 43211. Tax-exempt: 501(c)(3); 509(a).
History Museum & Historic Ship: 1918 stern-wheel Steamer, W.P. Snyder Jr., a National Historic Landmark.
Collections: ecological, recreational & commercial history of the Ohio River from its origin-present day; river history exhibits.
Research Fields: river history.
Facilities: library of river information material; auditorium. Museum-related items for sale.
Activities: guided tours; lectures; permanent exhibits; summer day camp; special educational programs; audiovisual program.
Hours & Admission Prices: Please call ahead to verify admission and hours. Museum & Steam Towboat WP SNYDER, JR: Memorial Day to Sept. 20 Mon. & Wed.-Sat. 9:30-5, Sun 12-5; school groups by appointment. Adults $7, students 6-18 $3; discounts to groups & AAM members; OHS members & children under 5 no charge. ♿
Attendance: 4,200 (estimated)
Membership: see separate listing for Ohio Historical Society. Friends of the Museum: Student $10; Individual $15; Family $30; Special Friend $50.

Marion

HARDING HOME AND MUSEUM, 380 Mt. Vernon Ave., Marion, OH 43302-4120. Tel.: 740-387-9630; 800-600-6894. Fax: 740-387-9630 (call first).
E-mail: mgilpin@ohiohistory.org
Web Site: www.ohiohistory.org
Founded: 1925.
Congressional District: 7
Key Personnel: Site Mgr., Melinda Gilpin.
Personnel Profile: Full-Time Paid 2; Part-Time Paid 2; Part-Time Volunteers 1.
Governing Authority: nonprofit organization. Parent Institution: Ohio Historical Society, Inc. I-71 & 17th Ave., Columbus, OH 43211. Tax-exempt: 501(c)(3).
History Museum: housed in 1920 cottage, press corps center for Harding's Campaign.
Collections: mementos of Harding's life from boyhood to presidency; presidential memorabilia; original furniture & furnishings. Historic House: 1890 Harding Home.
Activities: guided tours; formally organized education programs for children; permanent exhibitions.
Publications: Ohio Historical Society, Time Line.
Hours & Admission Prices: April-May & Sept.-Oct. Sat. 9:30-5, Sun. 12-5; Memorial Day-Labor Day Thurs.-Sat. 9:30-5, Sun. 12-5. Adults $6, children 6-12 $3; discount to active military, AAA members & groups; children 5 & under and members no charge. ♿
Attendance: 6,000 (estimated)
Membership: Student Membership $25; Individual Membership: Age 60 & over $30; Individual $35; Full Membership: Age 60 & over $37; up to 8 people $42.

THE MARION COUNTY HISTORICAL SOCIETY MUSEUM, 169 E. Church St., Marion, OH 43302-3825. Tel.: 740-387-4255. Fax: 740-387-0117.
E-mail: mchs@marionhistory.com
Web Site: www.marionhistory.com
Founded: 1969.
Congressional District: 4
Key Personnel: C.E.O. & Museum Shop Mgr., Gale E. Martin; Pres., Jan Augenstein; Treas., Diane Mault.
Personnel Profile: Full-Time Paid 1; Part-Time Paid 3; Part-Time Volunteers 36; Interns 1.
Governing Authority: private; nonprofit organization. Tax-exempt: 501(c)(3).
History Museum.
Collections: Marion County area history & artifacts; Warren G. Harding presidential artifacts & documents.
Major Exhibits: Enriching Our Lives: Arts & Culture, 11/09-12/27/09; Dreaming a Better Life: Pioneers & Early Settlers, 3/5/10-12/18/11; Inventors, Entrepreneurs & Laborers, 3/6/10-12/26/10.
Research Fields: history of individual townships in Marion County, Ohio; genealogy; Warren G. Harding.
Facilities: 1,000-vol. library of history & genealogy books; 50-seat auditorium. Museum-related items for sale.
Activities: guided tours; lectures; temporary exhibitions; in-school programs. Annual Event: Marion County Fair; Night at Heritage Hall; Saturday in the Park; Blasst From the Past.
Publications: quarterly newsletter, Hallmarks.
Hours & Admission Prices: March-April & Nov.-Dec. Sat.-Sun. 1-4; May-Oct. Wed.-Sun. 1-4; group tours by appointment. Adults $4, seniors $3, children $1.50; discounts to Golden Buckeye members; members no charge. ♿
Attendance: 8,000 (accurate)
Membership: Student $10; Regular $25; Family $35; Sustaining $60; Pride $100-$3,000.

STENGEL-TRUE MUSEUM, 504 S. State St., Marion, OH 43302-5036. Mailing Address: P.O. Box 3, Marion, OH 43301-0003. Tel.: 740-387-6000.
Founded: 1973.
Congressional District: 7
Key Personnel: Chm. (V), John Bartram; Dir. & Museum Shop Mgr., Jim Ballinger.
Governing Authority: nonprofit organization. Tax-exempt: 501(c)(3).
Historical Society Museum: housed in c.1860 Judge Ozias Bowen home.
Collections: period artifacts; glass; Victorian bric-a-brac; table zither; John

Miller family paintings; china; guns; Indian artifacts; pewter; copper; silver; timepieces; eyeglasses.
Activities: guided tours.
Hours & Admission Prices: By appointment. No charge; donations accepted. Closed holidays.
Attendance: 2,400 (estimated)

WYANDOT POPCORN MUSEUM, Heritage Hall, 169 E. Church St., Marion, OH 43302-3825. Tel.: 740-387-4255.
Founded: 1981.
Key Personnel: Dir., Gale E. Martin; Pres. (V), Brooks Brown; Museum Shop Mgr., Velenda Mackay.
Personnel Profile: Full-Time Paid 1; Part-Time Paid 2.
Popcorn Museum.
Collections: restored popcorn antiques.
Hours & Admission Prices: May-Oct. Wed.-Sun. 1-4; Nov.-April Sat.-Sun. 1-4. Adults $4, seniors $3, children 6-12 $1.50; discounts to AAA & Golden Buckeye members; members no charge. Closed New Year's Day; Easter; Memorial Day; Independence Day; Labor Day; Thanksgiving; Christmas.
Attendance: 6,000 (estimated)

Marysville

THE UNION COUNTY HISTORICAL SOCIETY, 246 W. Sixth St., Marysville, OH 43040-1531. Mailing Address: P.O. Box 303, Marysville, OH 43040-0303. Tel.: 937-644-0568.
Founded: 1949.
Congressional District: 7
Key Personnel: Pres., Robert W. Parrott; Vice Pres., William Mc Carthy; Treas., John Woerner.
Personnel Profile: Part-Time Paid 2; Part-Time Volunteers 12.
Governing Authority: society. Tax-exempt.
General Museum: housed in 1870 Henry W. Morey home.
Collections: farm tools; furniture; china; glass; silver; clothing; manuscripts; war relics pertaining to Union County; Indian arrowheads, chisels and hammers.
Facilities: reading room.
Activities: guided tours; gallery talks; formally organized education programs for children; permanent, temporary & traveling exhibitions.
Hours & Admission Prices: April-Nov. Wed. 1-4; other times by appointment. No charge. Closed New Year's Day; Thanksgiving; Christmas.
Membership: Individual $10; Life $150.

Massillon

* **THE MASSILLON MUSEUM, (M),** 121 Lincoln Way, E., Massillon, OH 44646-6633. Tel.: 330-833-4061. Fax: 330-833-2925.
Web Site: www.massillonmuseum.org
Founded: 1933.
Congressional District: 16
Key Personnel: Dir. & C.E.O., Christine Fowler Shearer; Chm. (V), Nancy Gessner; Archivist, Mandy Altimus; Cur., Alexandra Nicholis; Museum Shop Mgr., Judy Paquelet.
Personnel Profile: Full-Time Paid 3; Part-Time Paid 4; Part-Time Volunteers 120; Interns 4.
Governing Authority: private; nonprofit organization. Tax-exempt: 501(c)(3).
History & Art Museum.
Collections: American folk art; glass; china; pottery; metal; American & European fine & decorative arts; costumes; graphics; Indian artifacts; war items; tools & utensils; photographs; quilts & coverlets.
Research Fields: Ohio artists; local history.
Facilities: library of local history manuscripts & books available to qualified graduate students & adults for use on premises; classrooms. Arts & crafts for sale.
Activities: guided tours; lectures; arts festivals; workshops; docent program; permanent, temporary & traveling exhibitions; formally organized education programs; lecture series; music series.
Publications: pamphlets, show catalogs.
Hours & Admission Prices: Tues.-Sat. 9:30-5, Sun. 2-5; evenings by appointment. No charge; donations accepted. Closed legal holidays. ♿
Attendance: 15,425 (accurate)
Membership: Student $10; Individual $25; Family $35; Contributing $75-$199; Sustaining $200-$499; Benefactor $500-$999; Director's Circle $1000 & up.

Maumee

WOLCOTT HOUSE MUSEUM COMPLEX, 1031 River Rd., Maumee, OH 43537-3460. Tel.: 419-893-9602 & 1840. Fax: 419-893-3108.
E-mail: mvhs@buckeye-access.com
Web Site: www.maumee.org/recreation/wolcott.htm
Founded: 1961.
Congressional District: 9
Key Personnel: Pres., Barbara Dennis; Exec. Dir., Jack Hiles; Museum Shop Mgr., Tonya Haynes.
Personnel Profile: Part-Time Paid 7; Part-Time Volunteers 50.
Governing Authority: society. Parent Institution: Maumee Valley Historical Society. Tax-exempt.
Historic Structures: 1836 Wolcott House; c.1850 log cabin; c.1840 saltbox style farmhouse; c.1880 train depot; c.1901 country church; c.1840 Greek Revival townhouse.
Collections: mid-19th century items pertaining to Maumee Valley History; house furnishings; clothing.
Research Fields: local history; historic preservation.
Facilities: Museum-related items for sale.
Activities: guided tours; lectures; slides; special events.
Publications: Northwest Ohio History Journal.
Hours & Admission Prices: Museum Guided Tours: Thurs.-Sun. 12:30 & 2:30. Adults $5, seniors $4, students $2.50; discounts to AAA members; members no charge. Gift Shop: April-Dec. Thurs.-Sun. 12-4:30.
Attendance: 10,000 (estimated)
Membership: Senior, Student & Teacher $25; General $35; Legacy Club $50; Founder's Club $100; Heritage Club $150; Curator's Club $250.

McCutchenville

MCCUTCHEN OVERLAND INN, 283 State Hwy. 53 N., McCutchenville, OH 44844. Mailing Address: P.O. Box 372, Upper Sandusky, OH 43351-0372. Tel.: 419-981-2052.
Founded: 1967.
Key Personnel: Pres. (V), Robin Schuster; Cur., Anna Bea Heilman.
Personnel Profile: Part-Time Paid 2.
Governing Authority: nonprofit. Tax-exempt: 501(c)(3).
Historic House: housed in a former stage coach stop built by Col. Joseph McCutchen in 1829.
Collections: Victorian furniture; kitchen items; quilts; coverlets; tea leaf ironstone; primitive furniture; china; rope beds; toys.
Facilities: Gift items for sale.
Activities: guided tours.
Publications: bimonthly newsletter.
Hours & Admission Prices: June-Oct. Sat.-Sun. 1-4:30. Adults $2, children 13 & under $1. ♿
Membership: Annual $15.

Medina

AMERICA'S ICE CREAM & DAIRY MUSEUM, 1050 Lafayette Rd., Medina, OH 44256-3549. Mailing Address: 317 Forest Meadows Dr., Medina, OH 44256-1611. Tel.: 330-722-3839.
E-mail: elmfarm1934@aol.com
Web Site: www.elmfarm.com
Formerly: Elm Farm Ice Cream & Dairy Museum
Founded: 1999.
Key Personnel: C.E.O., Sherry S. Abell; Cur., Carl T. Abell.
Governing Authority: private corporation.
Ice Cream & Dairy Museum.
Collections: ice cream memorabilia; dispensers; signs; advertising; 1905 soda fountain; photographs; prints; period toys; prototype scooper; full-size rare trucks & bottles; cream separators; butter churns; advertising; milk wagon; milk trucks.
Research Fields: historical facts on ice cream.
Facilities: reference library on ice cream history & manufacturing; ice cream parlor; outside courtyard seating. Gift items for sale.
Activities: guided tours.
Hours & Admission Prices: March-Dec. Tues.-Sun. 12-5. Adults $4.50, senior citizens $4, students $3; discounts to groups, AAM members; children under 5 no charge. ♿
Attendance: 5,000 (estimated)

MEDINA COUNTY HISTORICAL SOCIETY, THE JOHN SMART HOUSE, 206 N. Elmwood St., Medina, OH 44256-1829. Mailing Address: P.O. Box 306, Medina, OH 44258-0306. Tel.: 330-722-1341.
E-mail: info@medinahistorical.org
Web Site: www.medinahistorical.com
Founded: 1922.
Congressional District: 17
Key Personnel: C.E.O., Brian Feron; Pres. (V), Judy Davanzo; Cur., Thomas D. Hilberg.
Personnel Profile: Part-Time Paid 1; Part-Time Volunteers 20.
Governing Authority: independent; nonprofit. Tax-exempt.
Historical Society Museum: located in 14-room Victorian home.
Collections: Levitt & Wolbach collections; Indian & Civil War artifacts; Victorian furnishings.

Research Fields: genealogy & history of Medina County.
Facilities: library available for use on premise only.
Activities: guided tours; seminars; field trips for members.
Publications: monthly, report of events; quarterly, newsletter.
Hours & Admission Prices: Tues. & Thurs. 9-5, 1st Sun. of the month 1-4; other times by appointment. No charge; donations accepted.
Attendance: 2,300 (estimated)
Membership: Seniors & Students $8; Individual $15; Family $20; Organization $25; Patron $35; Corporate $75.

MEDINA TOY AND TRAIN MUSEUM, 7 Public Square, Medina, OH 44256-2203. Tel.: 330-764-4455.
Toy & Train Museum.
Collections: railroad memorabilia; model trains; hands-on exhibits; model cars & airplanes; toys; dolls; 500 train engines.
Facilities: library.
Hours & Admission Prices: Mon.-Sat. 10-5, Sun. 12-5. No charge; donations accepted.

PORTHOLES INTO THE PAST, 4450 Poe Rd., Medina, OH 44256-9742.
Founded: 1984.
Congressional District: 13
Key Personnel: Pres. & Dir., Merle H. Mishne.
Governing Authority: individual operation.
History, Art & Transportation Museum: located on site over 16 acres, including a 3/4 acre bass & bluegill stocked pond, farmed fields & woods.
Collections: vintage cars, including Alfa Romeo, Alta, American LaFrance, Bugatti, Citroen, Elva, Ferrari, Lotus & Maserati; over 2,000 framed examples of car art, blue prints & cutaway drawings; over 200 images of Bugatti cars; over 60, c.1910 Montaut-Gamy lithographs; over 500 framed images of airplanes, emphasis on the Beech Staggering, Flying Tigers & Curtis P-40s Bell P-39; impressionist art; models; American Indian artifacts; original World War II posters; paintings; prints; drawings; photographs; advertising art.
Research Fields: history of auto racing, Bugatti automobiles, airplane racing. Beech Staggering airplanes, Toulouse-Lautrec, Claude Monet & early photographers.
Facilities: 10,000-vol. library of books & magazines pertaining to autos, airplanes, art, photography, racing, Western America, Paris-France & history.
Activities: guided tours; lectures; films; rental gallery; participatory, loan, temporary & traveling exhibitions.
Publications: biannual brochure, Portholes.
Hours & Admission Prices: By appointment. No charge. Closed New Year's Day; Christmas. ♿

Mentor

JAMES A. GARFIELD NATIONAL HISTORIC SITE, 8095 Mentor Ave., Mentor, OH 44060-5753. Tel.: 440-255-8722. Fax: 440-974-2045.
E-mail: sherda_williams@nps.gov
Web Site: ww.nps.gov/jaga
Founded: 1936.
Congressional District: 14
Key Personnel: Site Mgr., Sherda Williams.
Personnel Profile: Full-Time Paid 6; Part-Time Paid 7; Part-Time Volunteers 20.
Governing Authority: Parent Institution: National Park Service.
Historic House: c.1880 home of former Pres. James Garfield.
Collections: Garfield memorabilia; furniture; photographs; campaign office; presidential library.
Facilities: picnic area; visitors center. Horse Barn: education facility.
Activities: guided tours; organized education programs for children; video; special events.
Hours & Admission Prices: May-Oct. Mon.-Sat. 10-5, Sun. 12-5; Nov.-April Sat.-Sun. 10-5. Admission $5; children 15 & under and NPS Pass holders no charge. Closed New Year's Day; Thanksgiving; Christmas. ♿
Attendance: 22,479 (accurate)

Miamisburg

MIAMISBURG HISTORICAL SOCIETY, 4 N. Main St., Miamisburg, OH 45342-2313. Mailing Address: P.O. Box 774, Miamisburg, OH 45343-0774. Tel.: 937-859-5000.
Key Personnel: Dir., Cathy Oberer; Cur., Joe Steffen.
Governing Authority: Branch Museum: Daniel Gebhart Tavern Museum, Lock St. & Old Main St., Miamisburg, OH.
Historical Society Museum.
Collections: local history & culture; photographs.
Facilities: Museum-related items for sale.
Activities: rental facilities; research.
Hours & Admission Prices: Wed. & Sat. 1-4; other times by appointment.

Milan

MILAN HISTORICAL MUSEUM, INC., (M), 10 Edison Dr., Milan, OH 44846-9319. Mailing Address: P.O. Box 308, Milan, OH 44846-0308. Tel.: 419-499-2968. Fax: 419-499-9004.
E-mail: museum@milanhistory.org
Web Site: www.milanhistory.org
Founded: 1930.
Congressional District: 2
Key Personnel: Pres. (V), Dr. David Berckmueller; C.E.O. & Dir., Ann R. Basilone.
Personnel Profile: Full-Time Paid 2; Part-Time Paid 20; Part-Time Volunteers 40.
Governing Authority: nonprofit. Tax-exempt: 170(c).
General Museum: housed in 1846 home of Dr. Lehman Galpin who assisted in the birth of Thomas A. Edison.
Collections: folklore; textiles; history; costumes; decorative arts; Indian artifacts; marine; natural history; outdoor museum; transportation; 1,500 pieces of art glass; 400 period dolls. Historic House & Structures: 1843, Sayles House; Newton Arts Building; general store; blacksmith shop.
Research Fields: art glass.
Facilities: seven buildings; four historic structures; reconstructed general store; Newton Memorial Arts Building; Doll & Toy House. Museum-related items for sale.
Activities: guided tours; permanent exhibitions.
Publications: self-guided walking tours; newsletter, New Milan Ledger.
Hours & Admission Prices: April-May & Sept.-Oct. Sat.-Sun. 1-5; June-Aug. Tues.-Sat. 10-5, Sun. 1-5; other times by appointment. Adults $7, Senior Citizens $6, children 6-12 $4; discount to AAM members & groups; members no charge. Closed Labor Day weekend. ♿
Attendance: 5,700
Membership: Active $20; Family $40; Sponsor $50; Patron $100; Business $200; Lifetime $1,000.

THOMAS EDISON BIRTHPLACE MUSEUM, (M), 9 N. Edison Dr., Milan, OH 44846-9321. Mailing Address: P.O. Box 451, Milan, OH 44846-0451. Tel.: 419-499-2135. Fax: 419-499-2135 (call first).
E-mail: edisonbp@accnorwalk.com
Web Site: www.tomedison.org
Founded: 1947.
Key Personnel: C.E.O. & Pres. (V), Robert K.L. Wheeler; Dir., Annette Kluding; Cur., Laurence J. Russell.
Personnel Profile: Full-Time Paid 2; Part-Time Paid 10; Part-Time Volunteers 2.
Governing Authority: nonprofit organization. Tax-exempt.
Historic House Museum: 1841 birthplace & home of Thomas A. Edison.
Collections: family furnishings from 1780-1870; inventions; personal memorabilia; photographs; documents.
Facilities: Books & postcards for sale.
Activities: guided tours; formally organized education programs for children.
Publications: book, Edison-Inspiration to Youth.
Hours & Admission Prices: Feb.-March & Nov.-Dec. Wed.-Sun. 1-4; April-May & Sept.-Oct. Tues.-Sun. 1-5; June-Aug. Tues.-Sat. 10-5, Sun. 1-5. Last tour is at 4:30. Adults $6, senior citizens $5, children $3; discount to groups of 12 or more. Closed New Year's Day; Easter; Labor Day; Thanksgiving; Christmas.
Attendance: 7,968 (accurate)
Membership: Single $25; Family $50; Special Friends $100; Lifetime $1,000; Corporate Sponsor $5,000.

Milford

PROMONT HOUSE MUSEUM, Greater Milford Area Historical Society Inc., 906 Main St., Milford, OH 45150-1767. Tel.: 513-248-0324. Fax: 513-248-2304.
E-mail: promonthouse@fuse.net
Web Site: www.milfordhistory.net
Founded: 1967.
Congressional District: 6
Key Personnel: C.E.O. & Pres. (V), Dick Nordloh; Museum Shop Mgr., Tracy Lanham.
Personnel Profile: Part-Time Paid 1; Part-Time Volunteers 80.
Governing Authority: society; nonprofit organization. The Greater Milford Area Historical Society, Inc. Tax-exempt: 501(c)(3).
Historical Society Museum: housed in 1865, Italianate 3-story brick home.
Collections: artifacts; documents; furnishings of the area; black history vintage wedding gowns 1864-1995; Indian items.

Facilities: library of papers & documents, miscellaneous subject matter pertaining to the area.
Activities: guided tours; special exhibits.
Publications: newsletter.
Hours & Admission Prices: Fri.-Sun. 1:30-4:30; special groups by appointment. Adults $5, children $1; members no charge.
Attendance: 2,500 (estimated)
Membership: Single $25; Family $35; Patron Single $50; Patron Family $100; Lifetime $1,000. Business: Small $500; Large $1,000.

Millersburg

HOLMES COUNTY HISTORICAL SOCIETY, (M), 484 Wooster Rd., Millersburg, OH 44654. Mailing Address: P.O. Box 126, Millerburg, OH 44654-0126. Tel.: 330-674-0022; 888-201-0022. Fax: 208-439-8675.
E-mail: hchs@valkyrie.net
Web Site: www.victorianhouse.org
Founded: 1965.
Congressional District: 17
Key Personnel: Exec. Dir., Mark Boley; Pres., Joyce Cotton; Vice Pres., Ted Money; Sec., Mary Grace Engisch; Treas., Bonnie Self; Cur., Helen Smith.
Personnel Profile: Full-Time Paid 1; Part-Time Volunteers 50.
Governing Authority: society; nonprofit organization. Tax-exempt.
Historical Society Museum: housed in 1902 Victorian-style house.
Collections: period furniture, furnishings & artifacts; early medical equipment; war mementoes; early law office; pioneer tools.
Research Fields: oral history project of Holmes County.
Facilities: 1,000-vol. library of antique books.
Activities: guided tours; lectures.
Hours & Admission Prices: April Sat.-Sun. 1-4; May-Oct. Tues.-Sun. 1-4; group tours by appointment. Adults $7, seniors 65 & over $3, students $3; discounts to AAA members & groups; children under 12 & members no charge.
Attendance: 5,000 (estimated)
Membership: Single $15; Family $20; Supporting $20-$99; Life $500.

Minerva

STEAM RAILROAD MUSEUM, 177 Curry St., Minerva, OH 44657-1817. Mailing Address: P.O. Box 21175, Canton, OH 44701-1175. Tel.: 330-868-8814.
Web Site: www.steamrrmuseum.net/
Railroad Museum.
Collections: raliroad signals; signal tower equipment; railroad lanterns, tools, books, bells, whistles, photographs, & motion pictures; Pennsylvania Railroad safe; Wheeling and Lake Erie Railway steam locomotive #3960.
Hours & Admission Prices: Call for hours.

Minster

LAKE LORAMIE HERITAGE MUSEUM, Lake Loramie State Park, State Rte. 362, 4401 Fort Loramie Swanders Rd., Minster, OH 45865-9306. Tel.: 937-295-2011.
History Museum.
Collections: local history, heritage, & culture; photographs; harvesting ice tools; documents; wood & canvas kayak; personal artifacts; period furnishings.
Hours & Admission Prices: Summer: Sat. 10-5, Sun. 10-2.

Montpelier

WILLIAMS COUNTY HISTORICAL MUSEUM, 611 E. Main St., Williams County Fairgrounds, Montpelier, OH 43543. Mailing Address: P.O. Box 415, Montpelier, OH 43543-0415. Tel.: 419-485-8200.
Web Site: williamscountyhistory.org
Founded: 1956.
Congressional District: 5
Key Personnel: Pres., Robert Bauer; Dir., Lisa Oberlin; Cur., Kara Dreher.
Personnel Profile: Full-Time Paid 1.
Governing Authority: county; society. Tax-exempt.
General Museum.
Collections: American prehistoric & historic Indian artifacts; agricultural items; anthropology; archaeology; archives; history; Indian artifacts; Hopewell Indian Mounds; railroad memorabilia. Historic Houses: 1850 Lett log cabin; c.1845 Kunkle Log House; 1883 Edon; 1880 Wabash Caboose.
Research Fields: local history.
Facilities: 300-vol. library of local history books available for use only on premises. Museum-related items for sale.
Activities: guided tours; lectures; formally organized education programs for adults; docent program & council; Jr. Historian Summer Program.
Publications: quarterly newsletter, Northwest Historian.
Hours & Admission Prices: May-Nov. Sun.-Thurs. 1-4; Dec.-April Mon.-Fri. 10-5; other times & tours by appointment. Adults 2, children 6-18 $1; members no charge. Closed holidays. ♿
Attendance: 7,200
Membership: Student $7; Senior $24; Individual $29; Senior Couple $34; Family $39; Life $399; Professional $299; Life $399; Life Couple $549.

Mount Pleasant

FRIENDS (QUAKER) YEARLY MEETING HOUSE STATE MEMORIAL, 298 Market St., Mount Pleasant, OH 43939. Mailing Address: P.O. Box 35, Mount Pleasant, OH 43939-0035. Tel.: 740-769-2893; 800-752-2631.
Founded: 1814.
Congressional District: 18
Key Personnel: Site Operations Mgr., Sherry Sawchuk.
Personnel Profile: Part-Time Volunteers 20.
Governing Authority: nonprofit. Parent Institution: The Ohio Historical Society, I 71 & 17th Ave., Columbus, 43211. Subsidiary Institution: Mt. Pleasant Historical Society.
Historic House Museum: built in 1814.
Collections: local history & culture; Quaker's history & artifacts; tools; period furnishings; archives; religious items.
Activities: guided tours. Annual Event: Garden Tour in August.
Hours & Admission Prices: May-Oct. by appointment. Meeting House: adults $4, children 6-12 $2; discounts to groups; OHS members & children under 5 no charge. Six Building Tour: adults $10, students 6-12 $5; discounts to groups; children under 5 no charge.
Attendance: 500 (estimated)

MOUNT PLEASANT HISTORICAL SOCIETY, 342 Union St., Mount Pleasant, OH 43939-9800. Mailing Address: Union St. Box 35, Mount Pleasant, OH 43939-9800. Tel.: 740-769-2893; 800-752-2631.
Web Site: users.lst.net./gudzent/
Founded: 1948.
Congressional District: 18
Key Personnel: C.E.O. & Pres. (V), Sherry Sawchuk.
Personnel Profile: Full-Time Volunteers 15; Part-Time Volunteers 20.
Governing Authority: society. Branch Museums: Friends (Quaker) Meeting House, 298 Market St., Mount Pleasant, OH; P. L. Bone Store Museum; The Elizabeth House Mansion Museum; Historical Center: The Burriss Store Museum; The Tin Shop Museum. Tax-exempt: 501(c)(3).
General Museum.
Collections: books; tools; documents; records; period clothing; pictures; photos; dolls; bottles & jars; historic store.
Research Fields: local history; Quaker genealogy; underground railroad.
Facilities: library of local & Quaker history books available for research on premises; reading room.
Activities: guided tours; permanent & temporary exhibitions.
Publications: newsletter, The Town Crier; educational workbook, Discover Historic Mount Pleasant, Ohio.
Hours & Admission Prices: May-Oct. by appointment. Adults $15, children 6-12 $6; discount to groups of 20 or more; children under 5 no charge.
Attendance: 500 (estimated)
Membership: Individual $15.

Mount Vernon

KNOX COUNTY HISTORICAL SOCIETY, 875 Harcourt Rd., Mount Vernon, OH 43050-4325. Mailing Address: P.O. Box 522, Mount Vernon, OH 43050-0522. Tel.: 740-393-5247.
E-mail: kchs@knoxhistory.org
Web Site: www.knoxhistory.org/about.htm
Key Personnel: Dir., James K. Gibson
Historical Society Museum.
Collections: local history & culture; photographs.
Activities: educational programs.
Publications: newsletter.
Hours & Admission Prices: Wed. 6pm-8pm, Thurs.-Sun. 2-4.

Nelsonville

STUART'S OPERA HOUSE, 52 Public Sq., Nelsonville, OH 45764-1133. Mailing Address: P.O. Box 217, Nelsonville, OH 45764-0217. Tel.: 740-753-1924. Fax: 740-753-1982.
Web Site: www.stuartsoperahouse.org
Formerly: Hocking Valley Museum of Theatrical History, Inc.
Founded: 1978.
Congressional District: 10
Key Personnel: Pres., Miki Brooks; Dir., Tim Peacock; C.O.O., Adam Fischer.
Personnel Profile: Full-Time Paid 3; Full-Time Volunteers 1; Part-Time Volunteers 20; Interns 1.

Governing Authority: nonprofit organization. Tax-exempt: 501(c)(3).
Theater Museum: housed in 1879 Stuart's Opera House.
Collections: scenery; chairs; dressing rooms.
Activities: guided tours; lectures.
Publications: brochures.
Hours & Admission Prices: Mon.-Fri. 10-5. No charge; donations accepted. ♿
Attendance: 20,000 (estimated)

New Bremen

THE BICYCLE MUSEUM OF AMERICA, 7 W. Monroe St., New Bremen, OH 45869-1146. Tel.: 419-629-2311. Fax: 419-629-3256.
E-mail: annette.thompson@crown.com
Web Site: www.bicyclemuseum.com
Founded: 1997.
Key Personnel: C.E.O., James F. Dicke, II; Cur., Public Rels. & Museum Shop Mgr., Annette Thompson.
Personnel Profile: Full-Time Paid 1; Part-Time Paid 2.
Governing Authority: private; nonprofit. Tax-exempt: 501(c)(3).
Bicycle Museum.
Collections: 200 bicycles from 1816 to present.
Facilities: library; cafeteria; educational facilities; 13,000 sq. ft. exhibit space. Museum-related items for sale.
Activities: films; guided tours; lectures; loan & traveling exhibitions; training programs for professional museum workers; study clubs.
Hours & Admission Prices: Sept.-June Mon.-Fri. 11-5, Sat. 11-2; Summer: Mon.-Fri. 11-7, Sat. 11-2. Adults $3, senior citizens $2, students $1; discount to groups of 15 or more; children under 6 no charge. ♿
Attendance: 20,000 (estimated)
Membership: Single $10; Family $20.

New Philadelphia

HISTORIC SCHOENBRUNN, 1984 W. High Ave., New Philadelphia, OH 44663. Mailing Address: P.O. Box 11, Dennison, OH 44621-0011. Tel.: 330-339-3636; 877-278-8020. Fax: 740-922-4929.
E-mail: schoenbrunnvillage@ymail.com
Web Site: www.ohiosfirstvillage.com
Formerly: Schoenbrunn Village State Memorial
Founded: 1928.
Congressional District: 18
Personnel Profile: Full-Time Paid 1; Part-Time Paid 4; Part-Time Volunteers 20.
Governing Authority: society. Parent Institution: Ohio Historical Society, Columbus, OH 43211. Tax-exempt: 170(b)(1)(A).
Museum Village Complex.
Collections: 17 reconstructed log structures of Moravian Indian Mission, Ohio's first Christian settlement.
Research Fields: Native American history; American mission & religious history.
Facilities: picnic area. Museum-related items for sale.
Activities: Special Events: June-Oct.
Publications: calendar of special events.
Hours & Admission Prices: Memorial Day-Labor Day Wed.-Sat. 9-5, Sun. 12-5: Sept.-Oct. Sat. 9-5, Sun. 12-5. Adults $7, seniors $5, children $4; discounts to groups & AAM members; members no charge. ♿
Attendance: 11,000 (estimated)
Membership: see separate listing for Ohio Historical Center.

Newark

THE DAWES ARBORETUM, 7770 Jacksontown Rd., S.E., Newark, OH 43056-9380. Tel.: 740-323-2355 & 800-44-DAWES.
E-mail: laappleman@dawesarb.org
Web Site: www.dawesarb.org
Founded: 1929.
Congressional District: 17
Key Personnel: Co Chm., Josephine Jacobsmeyer; Co Chm., Teresa Young; Dir., Luke Messinger; Public Information Officer, Laura Appleman; Horticulturist, Michael E. Ecker; Naturalist, Lori A. Totman; Supt. Grounds, Darrell Romine; Historian, David A. Vermilion; Business Mgr., Beverly Telepchak.
Personnel Profile: Full-Time Paid 36; Part-Time Paid 12; Part-Time Volunteers 312; Interns 5.
Governing Authority: private; nonprofit foundation. Tax-exempt: 501(c)(3); 509(a).
Arboretum & Nature Center.
Collections: over 3,000 varieties trees, shrubs & vines; gardens; natural history. Historic Building: Daweswood House.
Research Fields: botanical; zoological.
Facilities: 2,000-vol. library of books on horticulture, history & natural history available for use on premises; 175-seat auditorium; 1,790 acres; nature center; classrooms; history center. Museum-related items for sale.
Activities: guided tours; lectures; classes; films; workshops; formally organized education programs for children, adults and undergraduate college students; temporary exhibitions.
Publications: monthly newsletter; biannual journal/magazine; annual report; various brochures, pamphlets & information sheets; web site materials.
Hours & Admission Prices: Grounds: daily dawn-dusk. No charge. Daweswood House Museum: Sat.-Sun. 3:15. Museum: adults $2, children 6-12 $1. Closed New Year's Day; Thanksgiving; Christmas. ♿
Attendance: 275,000 (estimated)
Membership: Friend $20; Friend Plus One $30; Partnership $40; Contributing $100; Sustaining $250; Patron $500.

THE GREAT CIRCLE EARTHWORKS, 99 Cooper Ave., Newark, OH 43055-2422. Mailing Address: 1982 Velma Ave., Columbus, OH 43211-2453. Tel.: 800-752-2602.
Web Site: www.ohiohistory.org/places/moundld/
Formerly: Moundbuilders State Memorial & Museum
Congressional District: 10
Personnel Profile: Full-Time Paid 4; Part-Time Volunteers 4.
Governing Authority: society. The Ohio Historical Society. Ohio Historical Center, 1982 Velma Ave., Columbus, OH 43211. Tax-exempt.
Prehistoric Indian Art Museum & Historical Site: embankment 1,200 feet in diameter with earthen walls 8-14 feet in height enclosing 26 acres; comprise The Great Circle Earthworks, ceremonial grounds of prehistoric Hopewell Indians, 1000 B.C.-700 A.D.
Collections: art objects & other media representing achievements of the Adena & Hopewell cultures 1000 B.C.-700 A.D; prehistoric knives, pottery, pipes & jewelry.
Facilities: picnic area.
Hours & Admission Prices: Mon.-Fri. 8:30-5, Sat. 10-5, Sun. 1-5. No charge; donations accepted. Closed New Year's Eve & Day; Thanksgiving & day after; Christmas Eve & Day. ♿
Attendance: 7,000 (estimated)
Membership: Student $25; Individual Senior 60 & over $35; Individual $40; Full Senior 60 & over $42 (admits up to 8 guests); Full $47(admits up to 8 guests); Life $1,000.

LICKING COUNTY ARTS, 2431 W. Audrey Dr., Newark, OH 43055-8636. Tel.: 740-349-8031 & 350-7490.
E-mail: lcaa@mainstreetaccess.net
Web Site: www.lickingcountyarts.org
Founded: 1959.
Congressional District: 10
Key Personnel: Museum Shop Cur., Mary Helen Fernandez Stewart.
Personnel Profile: Part-Time Paid 1; Part-Time Volunteers 30.
Governing Authority: federal; nonprofit organization. Parent Institution: Licking County Art Assoc. Tax-exempt: 501(c)(3).
Art Gallery; Exhibition Gallery.
Collections: 19th- & 20th-century prints & paintings; ceramics; fiber pieces; hand-blown glass; wood sculpture.
Facilities: studio; class rooms. Gallery-related items for sale.
Activities: traveling & temporary exhibitions; guided tours; art workshops; art class series; gallery talks.
Publications: monthly newsletter, Art Print; monthly docent news.
Hours & Admission Prices: Mon.-Fri. 11-4, Sat. call for hours; school tours by appointment. No charge; donations accepted. Closed holidays. ♿
Attendance: 2,500
Membership: Individual $20; Family $30; Patron $50; Business & Sustaining $100; Life $500; Benefactor $1,000 & up.

LICKING COUNTY HISTORICAL SOCIETY, Veterans Park, N. 6th St., Newark, OH 43058. Mailing Address: P.O. Box 785, Newark, OH 43058-0785. Tel.: 740-345-4898. Fax: 740-345-4898 (call first).
Web Site: www.lchsohio.org
Founded: 1947.
Congressional District: 17
Key Personnel: Pres., Jim Hostetter; Cur., Emily Larson.
Personnel Profile: Part-Time Paid 5; Part-Time Volunteers 10.
Governing Authority: nonprofit organization. Subsidiary Institutions: Sherwood Davidson House, Webb House Museum, Buckingham Meeting House, Newark, OH; Robbins-Hunter Museum, Granville, OH. Tax-exempt: 501(c)(3).
Historic Buildings.
Collections: 18th- & 19th-century artifacts; early 20th-century items. Historic Buildings: c.1820 Sherwood-Davidson House; 1835 Buckingham Meeting House; 1842 Avery Downer House; 1907 Webb House.
Research Fields: local artists.

Facilities: 1,000-vol. library of books & newspapers, available to the public; 100-seat restaurant; 5,000 sq. ft. exhibit space. Locally made items for sale.
Activities: docent program; films; formal education programs for children; guided tours; lectures; participatory & temporary exhibitions; school loan service; trips; 4 traveling trunk museums. Annual Events: John Clem Drummer Boy Breakfast; Graveyard Walk at Cedar Hill Cemetery; Christmas Open House.
Publications: quarterly newsletter, Licking County Historical Society Quarterly.
Hours & Admission Prices: Office & Library: by appointment.
Attendance: 3,200 (estimated)
Membership: Student $10; Senior Citizen $20; Individual $25; Joint Senior $30; Family $35; Contributing $60; Sustaining $125; Life $1,000.

NATIONAL HEISEY GLASS MUSEUM, (M), 169 W. Church St., Newark, OH 43055-4945. Tel.: 740-345-2932. Fax: 740-345-9638.
E-mail: business@heisaymuseum.org
Web Site: www.heiseymuseum.org
Founded: 1974.
Congressional District: 18
Key Personnel: Pres., Bryan Baker; Museum Shop Mgr., Shelly Hoberg; Cur., Walter Ludwig; Clerk, Mary Jo Kochendorfer; Clerk, Alisha Tilley; Clerk, Justin Church.
Personnel Profile: Full-Time Paid 2; Part-Time Paid 3; Part-Time Volunteers 5.
Governing Authority: nonprofit organization; private collectors' club. Parent Institution: Heisey Collectors of America, Inc., 169 W. Church St., Newark. Tax-exempt: 501(c)(3).
Glass Museum: housed in 1831 King House.
Collections: Heisey glassware; glassmakers' tools; 4,000 Heisey glass moulds; 700 Heisey etching plates; 7,000 Heisey mould drawings; Heisey factory memorabilia; original Heisey factory records & catalogs.
Research Fields: history, production & preservation of Heisey Glassware; history of glassmaking.
Facilities: library of original catalogs & factory records of the A.H. Heisey & Co.; materials on other glass factories, available for private use by members of the Heisey Collectors of America; media center; conference room; reading room. Museum-related items for sale.
Activities: guided tours; lectures; films; study clubs; TV programs; docent program; permanent, temporary & loan exhibitions; film & slide shows available on rental basis.
Publications: monthly newsletter, Heisey News.
Hours & Admission Prices: Tues.-Sat. 10-4, Sun. 1-4. Adults $4; discount to groups of 10 or more; members & children under 18 accompanied by adult no charge. Closed holidays. ♿
Attendance: 3,500 (estimated)
Membership: Associate & Voting Member $30; Individual Contributing $50; Joint Contributing $60 (two people in the same household); Family Contributing $75 (parents & children under 18); Patron $125; Sponsor $250; Benefactor $500.

SHERWOOD-DAVIDSON HOUSE, Veterans Park 6th St., Newark, OH 43058-0785. Mailing Address: P.O. Box 785, Newark, OH 43058-0785. Tel.: 740-345-4898. Fax: 740-345-4898 (call first).
E-mail: sherwooddavidson@yahoo.com
Web Site: www.lchsohio.org
Founded: 1947.
Congressional District: 17
Key Personnel: Pres., Ryan Mecdanl; Cur., Emily Larson.
Personnel Profile: Part-Time Paid 1; Part-Time Volunteers 15.
Governing Authority: society. Parent Institution: Licking County Historical Society. Tax-exempt: 501(c)(3).
Historic House Museum: c.1820 Sherwood-Davidson house-a federal style home built by Buckingham Sherwood.
Collections: Federal & early Victorian furnishings; historical costumes; toys; antique books; glass.
Research Fields: Licking County history.
Facilities: 1835 Buckingham House, available for meetings & receptions.
Activities: guided tours; lectures; films; concerts; arts festivals; TV & radio programs; docent program; permanent, temporary & traveling exhibitions.
Publications: brochures; quarterly newsletter, The Quarterly.
Hours & Admission Prices: May to mid-Dec. Tues., Thurs. & Sat. 1-4. Adults $3; members no charge. Closed holidays.
Attendance: 900 (estimated)
Membership: Student $10; Senior Citizens 65 & over $20; Individual $25; Joint Senior Citizens $30; Family $35; Contributing $60; Sustaining $125; Life $1,000.

WEBB HOUSE MUSEUM, 303 Granville St., Newark, OH 43055-4480. Tel.: 740-345-8540.
E-mail: webbhouse@lchsohio.org
Web Site: lchsohio.org
Founded: 1978.
Congressional District: 17
Key Personnel: Cur., Mindy Honey Nelson.
Personnel Profile: Part-Time Paid 4; Part-Time Volunteers 2.
Governing Authority: society; nonprofit. Licking County Historical Society, P.O. 785, 6th St. Park, Newark, OH 43055. Tel. 740-345-4898. Tax-exempt: 501(c)(3).
Historic House Museum & Gardens.
Collections: period furnishings, art, silver, china, glass, photographs by Clarence White & Ema Spencer; carriage house.
Research Fields: Arts & Crafts Movement.
Facilities: lawns & gardens with a 1900 atmosphere.
Activities: guided tours; craft classes. Museum Sponsors: Herbal Luncheon in summer; Midsummer Twilight Garden Tour in July; Holiday Open House in December.
Publications: newsletter, Licking County Historical Society Quarterly.
Hours & Admission Prices: Thurs.-Fri. & Sun. 1-4; other times by appointment. No charge. Tour groups $2 per person.
Attendance: 466 (accurate)

THE WORKS: OHIO CENTER FOR HISTORY, ART & TECHNOLOGY, 55 S. First St., Newark, OH 43055-5429. Mailing Address: P.O. Box 721, Newark, OH 43058-0721. Tel.: 740-349-9277. Fax: 740-345-7252.
Web Site: www.attheworks.org
Formerly: Institute of Industrial Technology
Founded: 1996.
Congressional District: 18
Key Personnel: C.E.O., Marcia W. Downes; Chm., Michael Menzer; Museum Shop Mgr., Tawna England.
Personnel Profile: Full-Time Paid 14; Part-Time Paid 4; Part-Time Volunteers 90; Interns 5.
Governing Authority: Parent Institution: Howard E. Lefevre Foundation. Subsidiary Institution: Ohio State University at Newark. Tax-exempt.
Science & History Museum.
Collections: Licking County Ohio history; glass blowing studio; working letterpress; interurban train; 1881 steam engine factory; wood turning shop; car barn; wood working shop.
Facilities: Museum-related items for sale.
Activities: tours; glass blowing demonstrations; school field trips; home school programs; artist-in-residence program in glass & print.
Publications: quarterly newsletter, The Works; quarterly class schedules; annual report.
Hours & Admission Prices: May 2-Sept. Mon.-Fri. 9-5, Sat. 10-4; Oct.-May Mon.-Fri. 9-5, Sat. 10-4, Sun. 12-5. Adults $6, senior citizens $4, children $2; discounts to ASTC members; members no charge. Closed Labor Day; Memorial Day; Thanksgiving; Christmas. ♿
Attendance: 60,631 (accurate)
Membership: Individual $30; Family & Grandparent $60; Partner $100; Sustaining $200; Sponsor $500; Patron $1,000.

Newcomerstown

OLDE MAIN STREET MUSEUM & SOCIAL CENTER, 213 W. Canal St., Newcomerstown, OH 43832-1101. Mailing Address: P.O. Box 443, Newcomerstown, OH 43832-0443. Tel.: 740-498-7735.
Founded: 2007.
Congressional District: 16
Key Personnel: Pres., Mary Watts; Vice Pres., Ray McFadden; Sec., Ellen Pickrell; Treas., Don Fenton; Coord. Social Events, Marlene Ross; Historian, Elaine Mayenschien.
Governing Authority: society. Parent Institution: Newcomerstown Historical Society. Tax-exempt.
History Museum.
Collections: local history; period furnishings; personal artifacts.
Facilities: banquet facilities.
Activities: rental facilities.
Hours & Admission Prices: Memorial Day to Labor Day Tues.-Sat. 10-3, Sun. 1-4; tours by appointment. Adults $3. ♿
Membership: Regular $10; Business $20.

TEMPERANCE TAVERN, 221 W. Canal St., Newcomerstown, OH 43832-1101. Mailing Address: P.O. Box 443, Newcomerstown, OH 43832-0443. Tel.: 614-498-7735.
Founded: 1974.
Congressional District: 16
Key Personnel: Pres., Mary Watts; Vice Pres., Ray McFadden; Sec., Ellen

Pickrell; Treas., Don Fenton; Coord. Social Events, Marlene Ross; Historian, Elaine Mayenschien.
Personnel Profile: Part-Time Volunteers 30.
Governing Authority: society. Newcomerstown Historical Society. Tax-exempt.
Historical Society Museum: housed in c.1841 Temperance Tavern.
Collections: local history; Indian artifacts; period furniture; archaeology display; 1827-1930 costumes; Cy Young monuments; Woody Hayes.
Research Fields: local history; Indian artifacts.
Facilities: library of local history books available for inter-library loan & for research.
Activities: guided tours; films.
Hours & Admission Prices: Memorial Day to Labor Day Tues.-Sat. 10-3, Sun. 1-4; tours by appointment. Adults $3; donations accepted.
Attendance: 800 (estimated)
Membership: Regular $10; Business $20.

USS RADFORD NATIONAL NAVAL MUSEUM, 238 W. Canal St., Newcomerstown, OH 43832-1102. Mailing Address: 132 W. Canal St., Newcomerstown, OH 43832-1102. Tel.: 740-498-4446. Fax: 740-498-8803.
Web Site: www.ussradford446.org
Founded: 2001.
Key Personnel: Pres. (V), Vane Scott; Museum Shop Mgr., Gayle Opphile.
Personnel Profile: Full-Time Paid 1; Part-Time Volunteers 3.
Governing Authority: Parent Institution: USS Radford 446, Inc. Tax-exempt.
Naval Military Museum.
Collections: WWII, Korea, Vietnam & Cold War memorabilia; Admirals original uniforms; QH 50 D.A.S.H.; pre WWII dress whites; personal artifacts; weapons; Japanese War memorabilia; part of USS Helena CL 50; DesRon 21 ship displays.
Publications: quarterly Radford newsletter.
Hours & Admission Prices: Memorial Day to Labor Day Tues.-Sat. 10-3, Sun. 1-3; bus & family tours by appointment. Donation: adults $3, children $1; discounts to tour groups. ♿

Niles

MCKINLEY BIRTHPLACE HOME, 40 S. Main St., Niles, OH 44446-5012. Tel.: 330-652-5788. Fax: 330-652-5788.
Web Site: www.mckinley.lib.oh.us
Founded: 1911.
Congressional District: 17
Key Personnel: Pres. (V), William Jensen; Chm. (V), Delores Macalf; Dir. Library, Patrick Finan.
Personnel Profile: Full-Time Paid 16; Part-Time Paid 3.
Governing Authority: nonprofit organization.
History Museum: housed in Memorial Building located on the site formerly occupied by Little White School House attended by Pres. McKinley.
Collections: William McKinley memorabilia & artifacts.
Facilities: 500-seat auditorium. Museum-related items for sale.
Activities: guided tours; gallery talks; permanent exhibitions.
Hours & Admission Prices: Museum: Mon.-Thurs. 9-8, Fri.-Sat. 9-5:30. Home: Memorial Day to Labor Day Wed.-Sat. 9-5, Sun. 1-5; Sept.-May Sat. 9-5, Sun. 1-5. No charge. Closed holidays. ♿
Attendance: 8,000 (estimated)
Membership: Associate $10; Sustaining $25; Patron $50; Life $100.

North Canton

HOOVER HISTORICAL CENTER, 1875 E. Maple St., North Canton, OH 44720-3331. Tel.: 330-499-0287.
E-mail: ahaines@walsh.edu
Web Site: www.walsh.edu/hooverhistoricalcent.htm
Founded: 1978.
Congressional District: 16
Key Personnel: Operations Coord. & Museum Shop Mgr., Ann Haines; Center Rep., Patty Garber.
Personnel Profile: Full-Time Paid 1; Part-Time Paid 6; Part-Time Volunteers 75; Interns 2.
Governing Authority: company. Parent Institution: Walsh University. Tax-exempt.
Company & History Museum: housed in 1853 Hoover family home.
Collections: tanning & leather craft tools; vacuum cleaners; Victorian furniture, decor, clothing & ABC plates; vintage clothing & accessories; photographs; Hoover Company memorabilia; vintage advertisements; Hoover family; company; advertising; World War II artifacts by Hoover Company; herb gardens; 1800-1980s ladies fashion. Historic Buildings: c.1840 Tannery; 1853 farmhouse with 1870 Victorian Italianate style addition.
Major Exhibits: Walsh University: 50 Golden Years in the Making, 3/10-11/10; "Sew Many Memories" Quilts Reflecting Community History, 3/10/11/10.
Research Fields: German heritage in Stark County; Victorian customs 1870-1900; Hoover Company history; vacuum cleaner technology; Victorian architecture & decor; herbs; North Canton Community; Walsh University history.
Facilities: 150-vol. library available for use by public; herb gardens.
Activities: docent program; videos; guided tours. Annual Events: 1860s baseball matches May-September; Tales in Thyme (outdoor storytelling) in August; Christmas Open House in December; Summer Garden Tea & Tours.
Publications: quarterly newsletter, Center News.
Hours & Admission Prices: Feb. Wed.-Fri. 1-4; March-Dec. Wed.-Sat. 1-4. Groups of 8 or more require advance reservations; morning reservations available Tues.-Fri. Adults $3; children 12 & under no charge. Closed holidays. ♿
Attendance: 2,000 (estimated)

Northfield

PALMER HOUSE, HISTORICAL SOCIETY OF OLDE NORTHFIELD, 9390 Olde Eight Rd., Northfield, OH 44067. Mailing Address: P.O. Box 99, Northfield, OH 44067. Tel.: 330-467-8538. Fax: 330-467-8322.
E-mail: hson@worldnet.att.net
Web Site: www.hson.ifo
Founded: 1956.
Congressional District: 13
Key Personnel: Vice Pres., Arch Milani; Sec., Jesse Nehaz; Treas., Jill Potter.
Personnel Profile: Part-Time Volunteers 10.
Governing Authority: society. Parent Institution: Historical Society of Olde Northfield. Tax-exempt: 501(c)(3).
Historical Society Museum.
Collections: agriculture; costumes; folklore; glass; Indian artifacts; kitchen ware; toys; tools; records; pictures. Historical House: 1844 Vertical Plank Western Reserve House.
Research Fields: history of Western Reserve lands.
Facilities: 100-vol. library of local & county history books available for use on premises. Surplus books & museum-related items for sale.
Activities: guided tours; lectures; films; formally organized education programs for adults; temporary exhibitions.
Publications: quarterly tertiary newsletter.
Hours & Admission Prices: 2nd & 4th Sun. of month 2-4; other times by appointment. No charge; donations accepted.
Attendance: 500
Membership: Individual $7; Husband & Wife $10; Contributing $25; Life $100.

Norwalk

FIRELANDS HISTORICAL SOCIETY MUSEUM, 4 Case Ave., Norwalk, OH 44857-1404. Mailing Address: P.O. Box 572, Norwalk, OH 44857-0572. Tel.: 419-668-6038.
Founded: 1857.
Congressional District: 13
Key Personnel: Pres., Patricia Mak.
Personnel Profile: Part-Time Paid 1; Part-Time Volunteers 3.
Governing Authority: society. Parent Institution: Firelands Historical Society. Tax-exempt: 501(c)(3).
History Museum: housed in 1836 Preston-Wickham House.
Collections: archaeology; archives; primitive paintings; costumes; decorative arts; folklore; geology; glass; Indian artifacts; numismatic collections; manuscripts; paleontology; transportation; weapons.
Facilities: 4,000-vol. library of historical and genealogical books available for research on premises; reading room. Museum-related items for sale.
Activities: guided tours; lectures; study clubs; permanent & temporary exhibitions.
Publications: annual magazine, Firelands Pioneer.
Hours & Admission Prices: Sun. 12-4, Tues.-Sat. 10-3. Adults $4, youth 12-18 $3; members & children under 12 no charge.
Attendance: 550 (estimated)
Membership: Single $12; Husband and Wife $20; Personal Life $250; Business Life $500.

Norwich

NATIONAL ROAD/ZANE GREY MUSEUM, 8850 E. Pike, Norwich, OH 43767-9785. Mailing Address: c/o John & Annie Glenn Museum Foundation, P.O. Box 107, New Concord, OH 43762. Tel.: 740-872-3143. Fax: 740-872-3510.
Web Site: ohiohistory.org
Founded: 1973.
Congressional District: 10
Key Personnel: Mgr., Mary Ellen Weingartner.

Personnel Profile: Full-Time Paid 1; Part-Time Paid 1.
Governing Authority: society. Parent Institution: The Ohio Historical Society, Ohio Historical Center, 1985 Velma Ave., Columbus, OH 43211. Tax-exempt: 170(b)(1)(A).
General Museum.
Collections: items pertaining to transportation; vehicles; Ohio art pottery; personal items of Zane Grey.
Facilities: Publications & other items relating to transportation for sale.
Activities: guided tours; permanent exhibitions.
Hours & Admission Prices: May-Sept. Wed.-Sat. 10-4, Sun. 1-4. Adult $7, seniors $6, students $3; discounts to groups and AAA, AAM & ICOM member; children 5 & under and member no charge. ♿
Attendance: 20,000 (estimated)
Membership: Individual $35; Family $55; History Lover $85; Supporter $235.

Norwood

DRAKE PLANETARIUM, 2020 Sherman Ave., Norwood, OH 45212-2616. Tel.: 513-396-5578. Fax: 513-396-6486.
E-mail: csteger@drakeplanetarium.org
Web Site: www.drakeplanetarium.org
Key Personnel: Dir., Pamela Bowers; Business Mgr., Carolyn Steger.
Governing Authority: nonprofit organization.
Planetarium.
Collections: astronomy-related exhibits.
Activities: educational programs.
Hours & Admission Prices: Call for hours.

DRAKE SCIENCE CENTER, (M), 2060 Sherman Ave., Norwood, OH 45212-3100.
E-mail: csteger@drakeplanetarium.org
Web Site: www.drakeplanetarium.org/contact.html
Key Personnel: Business Mgr., Carolyn Steger
Science Center.
Collections: hands-on exhibits.
Activities: summer camp; educational programs.
Hours & Admission Prices: Call for hours.

Oak Hill

WELSH-AMERICAN HERITAGE MUSEUM, 412 E. Main St., Oak Hill, OH 45656-1229. Tel.: 740-682-7057.
Web Site: jacksonohio.org/welshmuseum.htm
Founded: 1971.
Key Personnel: Cur., Mildred Bangert.
Governing Authority: nonprofit organization.
History Museum.
Collections: Welsh culture & traditions; records; artifacts; books; photographs.
Hours & Admission Prices: June-Aug. Sat.-Sun. 2-4; other times by appointment. No charge; donations accepted.

Oberlin

* **ALLEN MEMORIAL ART MUSEUM - OBERLIN COLLEGE, (M),** 87 N. Main St., Oberlin, OH 44074-1161. Tel.: 440-775-8665. Fax: 440-775-6841.
E-mail: melissa.duffes@oberlin.edu
Web Site: www.oberlin.edu/amam
Founded: 1917.
Congressional District: 13
Key Personnel: Dir. The John G.W. Cowles, Stephanie Wiles; Cur. Western Art, Andria Derstine; Media & Publications, Melissa Duffes; Registrar, Lucille Stiger; Cur. Education, Jason Trimmer; Cur. Academic Programs, Liliana Milkova; Administrative Asst., Laura Winters.
Personnel Profile: Full-Time Paid 10; Part-Time Volunteers 15; Interns 1.
Governing Authority: college; board of trustees. Parent Institution: Oberlin College. Tax-exempt: 501(c)(3).
Art Museum.
Collections: Egyptian, Greek & Roman sculpture & decorative arts; East Asian & South Asian sculpture, painting & prints, including the Mary A. Ainsworth collection of Japanese woodblock prints; Islamic carpets; medieval art; 14th to 20th-century European paintings, sculpture & decorative arts; 19th to 20th-century American paintings, sculpture & decorative arts; African & pre-Columbian art; contemporary painting, sculpture & video; European & American prints, drawings & photographs; textiles.
Research Fields: all fields related to collections; Eva Hesse Archives; Frantisek Kupka.
Facilities: 82,000-vol. Clarence Ward Art Library; Wolfgang Stechow Print Study Room. Slides, catalogues & AMAM Bulletin publications for sale.
Activities: guided tours; lectures; gallery talks; adult & children's classes; temporary exhibitions; concerts; domestic & international loans.
Publications: biannual newsletter; Allen Memorial Art Museum News; annual bulletin, Allen Memorial Art Museum Bulletin; exhibition catalogues & brochures; permanent collection catalogue on CD-Rom; cards; postcards.
Hours & Admission Prices: Tues.-Sat. 10-5, Sun. 1-5. No charge; donations accepted. Closed major holidays. ♿
Attendance: 22,533 (accurate)
Membership: Senior Citizen & Student $20; Individual $40; Family $50; Contributing $100; Supporting $500; Director's Circle $1,000 & up.

* **OBERLIN HERITAGE CENTER, (M),** 73-1/2 S. Professor St., Oberlin, OH 44074. Mailing Address: P.O. Box 0455, Oberlin, OH 44074-0455. Tel.: 440-774-1700. Fax: 440-774-8061.
E-mail: history@oberlinheritage.org
Web Site: www.oberlinheritage.org
Formerly: Oberlin Heritage Center/O.H.I.O. (Oberlin Historical and Improvement Organization)
Founded: 1964.
Congressional District: 13
Key Personnel: C.E.O., Patricia Murphy; Pres. (V), James W. White.
Personnel Profile: Full-Time Paid 2; Part-Time Paid 3; Part-Time Volunteers 250; Interns 5.
Governing Authority: nonprofit organization. Parent Institution: The Oberlin Historical & Improvement Organization. Tax-exempt.
Historic House: 1866 Italianate villa, originally the home of Giles Shurtleff, leader of the first African American regiment from Ohio in the Civil War & the home of James Monroe, occupied by Monroe family 1870-1930, a college professor, important abolitionist, U.S. Congressman & colleague of Frederick Douglass and President Lincoln's ambassador to Brazil; part of the National Park Service's Underground Railroad Network to Freedom program.
Collections: 19th-century furniture & furnishings; local history materials. Historic Buildings: The 1836 Little Red Schoolhouse was Oberlin's first public school, now restored as a pioneer era one-room school. The 1884 Jewett House, a brick Victorian house, was the home of Oberlin College chemistry professor Frank Fanning Jewett & his wife Frances, an author of school textbooks on public health. The Jewetts rented out second floor rooms to male Oberlin college students. It is listed on the National Register of Historic Places.
Research Fields: abolitionists; Oberlin College; underground railroad; temperance movement; women's history; Civil War; building inventories; Oberlin family histories.
Activities: public programs on aspects of local history; heritage preservations & civic affairs.
Publications: Newsletter, Oberlin Heritage Center Gazette.
Hours & Admission Prices: Guided Tours: Tues., Thurs. & Sat. 10:30 & 1:30; other times by appointment. Adults $6; discounts to AAM, ICOM, AAA, AASLH & Time Traveler's members; members & children accompanied by adult no charge. Closed Christmas-New Year's Day; all major holidays. Gift Shop Office (at Monroe House): Tues.-Sat. 10-3.
Attendance: 11,601 (accurate)
Membership: Senior & Student $15; Individual $25; Family & Dual $40; Heritage Collector $50; Heritage Rescuer $100; Heritage Leader $250; Heritage Ambassador $500; Heritage Champion $1,000. Business or Organization Membership: Active $25; Heritage Collector $50; Heritage Rescuer $100; Heritage Leader $250; Heritage Ambassador $500; Heritage Champion $1,000.

Oregon

OREGON-JERUSALEM HISTORICAL SOCIETY, 1133 Grasser St., Oregon, OH 43616-7632. Mailing Address: P.O. Box 167632, Oregon, OH 43616-7632. Tel.: 419-693-7052. Fax: 419-693-7052.
Web Site: www.ojhs.org
Founded: 1963.
Congressional District: 9
Key Personnel: C.E.O. & Pres. (V), Connie Isbell.
Personnel Profile: Part-Time Volunteers 30.
Governing Authority: society. Parent Institution: Oregon Jerusalem Historical Society. Tax-exempt.
General Museum.
Collections: school records; maps; old farm equipment; musical instruments; office equipment; old household furniture; Indian artifacts; china; glass; costumes; country store; 1900 one-room school; barber shop; doctor's office; Civil War artifacts: oil paintings, clothes, swords, drums, medical instruments, flags, cannon balls, shells, bayonets; Spanish-American War; World War I; World War II; Korean; Vietnam military. Historic Building: Red Brick Schoolhouse.
Research Fields: historical sites for markers.
Facilities: elementary school.
Activities: guided tours; genealogy assistance available to visitors.
Publications: bimonthly newsletter.

Hours & Admission Prices: Thurs. 11-2; other times by appointment. No charge; donations accepted. ♿
Attendance: 1,500 (accurate)
Membership: Individual $15; Family $30; Contributing $100 & up & Individual Life; Family Life $200.

Oregonia

FORT ANCIENT MUSEUM, 6123 State Rt. 350, (Exit 32 & 36 off I-71), Oregonia, OH 45054-9708. Tel.: 513-932-4421. Fax: 513-932-4843; 800-860-0141.
E-mail: jblosser@ohiohistory.org
Web Site: ohiohistory.org
Founded: 1891.
Congressional District: 6
Key Personnel: Area Mgr., Jack K. Blosser.
Personnel Profile: Full-Time Paid 4; Part-Time Paid 4; Part-Time Volunteers 20.
Governing Authority: nonprofit organization. Parent Institution: Ohio Historical Society, I-71 & 17th Ave., Columbus, OH. 43211. Tax-exempt.
Prehistoric Site Museum.
Collections: artifacts of prehistoric Indian life & culture.
Research Fields: ceremonial sites; habitation areas; Ohio Valley prehistory; hilltop enclosure.
Facilities: 9,000 sq. ft. exhibit space; garden; picnic area; classroom. Literature & other museum-related items for sale.
Activities: trails. Museum Sponsors: Annual American Indian Gathering in June.
Hours & Admission Prices: April-Oct. Wed.-Sat. 10-5, Sun. 12-5; other times by appointment. Adults $6, seniors 60 & over $5, children 6-12 $4; discounts to AAA members; OHS members and children 5 & under no charge. ♿
Attendance: 25,000 (accurate)

Oxford

HEFNER ZOOLOGY MUSEUM, (M), 100 Upham Hall, Miami Univ., Oxford, OH 45056. Tel.: 513-529-4617. Fax: 513-529-6900.
E-mail: kaufmadg@muohio.edu
Web Site: www.environmentaleducationohio.org
Founded: 1951.
Key Personnel: C.E.O., Donald G. Kaufman; Education, Steve Eshbaugh; Public Rels., Cecilia Berg.
Personnel Profile: Full-Time Paid 4.
Governing Authority: public university; nonprofit. Parent Institution: Miami University, Oxford, OH. Tax-exempt: 501(c)(3).
Natural History Museum.
Collections: fauna of southwest Ohio.
Facilities: 350-vol. library; 1,800 sq. ft. exhibit space; educational facilities.
Activities: formal education programs; guided tours; lectures; temporary exhibitions.
Hours & Admission Prices: June-Aug. Mon.-Fri. 9-5; Sept.-May Mon.-Fri. 9-5, Sun. 1-4. No charge; donations accepted. Closed university holidays. ♿
Attendance: 5,000 (estimated)

* **MIAMI UNIVERSITY ART MUSEUM, (M),** 801 S. Patterson Ave., Oxford, OH 45056-3435. Tel.: 513-529-2232. Fax: 513-529-6555. TDD: 513-529-1541.
E-mail: wicksrs@muohio.edu
Web Site: www.muohio.edu/artmuseum
Founded: 1978.
Congressional District: 8
Key Personnel: Dir., Robert S. Wicks, Ph.D.; Cur. Exhibitions, Lena Vigna; Cur. Education, Cynthia C. Collins; Registrar, Laura B. Henderson; Program Assoc., Susan V. Gambrell; Preparator & Operations Mgr., Mark DeGennaro; Audience Devel., Kelly E. Wilson.
Personnel Profile: Full-Time Paid 7; Part-Time Paid 11; Part-Time Volunteers 120; Interns 3.
Governing Authority: university. Parent Institution: Miami University. Subsidiary Institution: McGuffey Museum. Tax-exempt: 501(c)(3).
University Museum.
Collections: ancient; Islamic; Native American; pre-Columbian; 19th-20th century American & European painting, sculpture & works on paper; African; European & American decorative arts; Leica cameras; international folk art & textiles; contemporary American folk art & outsider art; Chinese, oceanic & ancient art.
Research Fields: pertaining to collection.
Facilities: library of exhibition catalogues, reference books related to permanent collection available for research by appointment; 150-seat auditorium; five galleries of changing exhibitions. Museum-related items for sale.
Activities: guided tours; lectures; films; gallery talks; concerts; docent program; formally organized education programs for undergraduate & graduate college students affiliated with Miami University; art education program for school children; loan, permanent, temporary & traveling exhibitions; educational outreach program; diverse volunteer & intern program; membership association activities.
Publications: brochure, Calendar of Events; occasional exhibition catalogues, Major Exhibitions; newsletter; annual report.
Hours & Admission Prices: Tues.-Fri. 10-5, Sat. 12-5. Galleries open during evening programs & events. No charge. Closed national & university holidays. ♿
Attendance: 30,000 (estimated)
Membership: Student $20; Faculty & Staff $25; Individual $30; Family $60; Sponsor $100-$499; Sustaining $500-$999; Major Patron $10,000; Benefactor $100,000; Major Benefactor $500,000.

WILLIAM HOLMES MCGUFFEY MUSEUM, 410 E. Spring St., Oxford, OH 45056-3646. Tel.: 513-529-8380. Fax: 513-529-2637.
E-mail: mcguffeymuseum@muohio.edu
Web Site: www.units.muohio.edu/mcguffeymuseum
Founded: 1960.
Congressional District: 8
Key Personnel: Pres. (V), Jenny Presnell; Cur., Stephen C. Gordon.
Personnel Profile: Full-Time Paid 1; Part-Time Paid 5; Part-Time Volunteers 25.
Governing Authority: university. Parent Institution: Miami University. Tax-exempt: 501(c)(3).
Historic House Museum: 1833 home of William Holmes McGuffey.
Collections: McGuffey Eclectic Readers; McGuffey memorabilia, furniture & other decorative arts of the 19th century.
Facilities: 19th century restored home.
Activities: guided tours; permanent exhibitions; special volunteer group.
Publications: leaflets, William Holmes McGuffey; The McGuffey Museum of Miami University, Oxford, Ohio; newsletter, The McGuffey Report Card.
Hours & Admission Prices: Tues.-Fri. 1-5, Sat.-Sun. 1-4. No charge; donations accepted. Closed university holidays. ♿
Attendance: 2,500 (accurate)

Painesville

LAKE COUNTY HISTORICAL SOCIETY, 415 Riverside Dr., Painesville, OH 44077-5321. Tel.: 440--639-2945. Fax: 440-255-8980.
Web Site: www.lakehistory.org
Founded: 1936.
Congressional District: 19
Key Personnel: Exec. Dir., Kathie Purmal; Pres. Bd. Trustees, Mark Welch.
Personnel Profile: Full-Time Paid 3; Full-Time Volunteers 2; Part-Time Paid 2; Part-Time Volunteers 225.
Governing Authority: nonprofit organization. Tax-exempt.
History Museum.
Collections: 19th- & 20th-century decorative arts, costumes, photographs, archival material, tools, implements & manuscripts.
Research Fields: local history; architecture; genealogy; family history.
Facilities: 2,350-vol. research library of history & genealogy books available to researchers. Museum-related items, books, quarterly journal & pamphlets for sale.
Activities: Historic Home register; plaques for structures at least 50 years old; in-school & on-site education programs. Museum Sponsors: Little Mountain Heritage Festival in July.
Publications: quarterly newsletter.
Hours & Admission Prices: Museum: Tues.-Fri. 10-4, Sat.-Sun. 1-4. Research Library: Tues.-Fri. 9-4, Sat.-Sun by appointment. Museum: $3. Library: adults $7; discount to AAM & ICOM members. ♿
Attendance: 28,000 (estimated)
Membership: Student $10; Senior Citizen $15; Senior Couple (over 60) $20; Individual $25; Family $35; Patron $50; Golden Patron $100; Life Member $500.

Peebles

SERPENT MOUND MUSEUM, 3850 State Rte. 73, Peebles, OH 45660-9128. Tel.: 937-587-2796. Fax: 937-587-1116.
E-mail: serpentmound@arcofappalachia.org
Web Site: www.arcofappalachia.org
Founded: 1900.
Congressional District: 6
Key Personnel: Site. Mgr., Bruce Lombardo; Dir., Nancy Stranahan.
Personnel Profile: Full-Time Paid 1; Part-Time Paid 2; Interns 1.
Governing Authority: Parent Institution: Ohio Historical Society, 1985 Velma Ave., Columbus, OH. 43211. Subsidiary Institution: Arc of Appalachia Preserve System (AAPS). Tax-exempt.
Indian Museum.

Collections: Adena Indian culture.
Hours & Admission Prices: Ground: daily dawn to dusk. Museum: April-May & Sept.-Oct. Sat.-Sun. 10-5; Memorial Day to Labor Day daily 10-5. Grounds: Wed.-Sun. 10-5. Parking: car & vans $7, campers & RVs $9; OHS members no charge.
Attendance: 40,000 (accurate)
Membership: Student $25; Individual Senior 60 & over $38; Individual $43; Family Senior 60 & over (8 members) $45; Family (8 members) $75; Lifetime $1,000.

Perrysburg

FORT MEIGS STATE MEMORIAL, 29100 W. River Rd., Perrysburg, OH 43551-6019. Mailing Address: 29100 W. River Rd., P.O. Box 3, Perrysburg, OH 43551-6019. Tel.: 419-874-4121.
E-mail: rfinch@ohiohistory.org
Web Site: www.fortmeigs.org/
Founded: 1950.
Congressional District: 5
Key Personnel: Historic Site Mgr., Rick Finch.
Personnel Profile: Full-Time Paid 4; Full-Time Volunteers 3; Part-Time Paid 1.
Governing Authority: The Ohio Historical Society. Ohio Historical Center Site Operations, 1985 Velma Ave., Columbus, OH. 43211. Tax-exempt.
Military Fort Museum: reconstructed 1813 fort from the War of 1812; History Museum.
Collections: cannon batteries; earthen traverses; seven block houses; dioramas; artifacts & weapons of the war; history displays.
Research Fields: War of 1812.
Facilities: permanent exhibitions; 3,000 sq. museum exhibit.
Activities: tours; lectures; living history demonstrations.
Publications: books, Men of Patriotism, Courage, and Enterprise; Fort Meigs in the War of 1812.
Hours & Admission Prices: Museum & Visitors Center: daily. Fort: April-Oct. Wed.-Sat. 9:30-5, Sun. 12-5. Adults $8, seniors 60 & over $7, students $4; members & children 5 and under no charge.
Attendance: 20,000 (accurate)

OWENS COMMUNITY COLLEGE/WALTER E. TERHUNE GALLERY, (M), 30335 Oregon Rd., Perrysburg, OH 43551-4593. Mailing Address: P.O. Box 10000, Toledo, OH 43699-1947. Tel.: 567-661-2721. Fax: 567-661-7687.
E-mail: wynn_perry@owens.edu
Web Site: www.owens.edu/
Founded: 2003.
Key Personnel: Dir. & Cur., Wynn Perry.
Personnel Profile: Part-Time Paid 1; Interns 4.
Governing Authority: public college.
Art Museum.
Collections: works by students & faculty including paintings, photography, ceramics & sculpture.
Major Exhibits: Installation: Debra Davis, 1/8/10-2/13/10; 3 Kruegers, 2/22/10-3/27/10; Student Show, 4/10-5/1/10; Friends of Photography, 5/19/10-6/3/10; Toledo Emerges, 6/13/10-7/29/10; Owens Designs, 8/16/10-9/18/10; Arturo Rodrquez Prints, 9/24/10-10/23/10; Eigth Annual Faculty Exhibition, 11/1/10-12/10/10.
Facilities: 50-seat cafeteria; 1,880 sq. ft. exhibit space; 513-seat theater.
Activities: concerts; dance recitals; films; formal education programs for adults & college students; guided tours; hobby workshops; lectures; loan, participatory, traveling & temporary exhibitions.
Hours & Admission Prices: Mon.-Tues. & Fri. 10-4, Wed.-Thurs. 10-8, Sat. 10-3. No charge. Closed major holidays; school breaks. ♿
Attendance: 7,000 (accurate)

Pickerington

MOTORCYCLE HALL OF FAME MUSEUM, 13515 Yarmouth Dr., Pickerington, OH 43147-8214. Tel.: 614-856-2222, ext. 1234. Fax: 614-856-2221.
E-mail: info@motorcyclemuseum.org
Web Site: www.motorcyclemuseum.org
Formerly: Motorcycle Heritage Museum.
Founded: 1990.
Congressional District: 12
Key Personnel: Operations Mgr., Katy Wood; Dir. Mktg., Don Argento; Dir. Resource Devel., Dan Smith; Chm., Oscar Scofield; Treas., Tom White; Annual Fund Mgr., Toni Shoap; Museum Shop Mgr., Beth Myers.
Personnel Profile: Full-Time Paid 5; Part-Time Paid 4; Part-Time Volunteers 6.
Governing Authority: society; nonprofit. Parent Institution: American Motorcyclist Association. Subsidiary Institution: American Motorcycle Heritage Foundation. Tax-exempt: 501(c)(3).
Sports Museum; Transportation Museum.
Collections: motorcycles; riding clothing & accessories; racing gear; competition memorabilia; archives; photographs; film; video; Hall of Fame.
Research Fields: motorcycle history.
Facilities: 8,000 sq. ft. exhibit space. Museum & motorcycle-related items for sale.
Activities: theme, loan & temporary exhibitions; guided tours. Museum Sponsors: Vintage Motorcycle Days (fundraiser)
Publications: annual report; annual update newsletter.
Hours & Admission Prices: Daily 9-5. Adults $10, seniors $8, students 12-17 $3; discounts to members, National Motorcycle Association, AMA, AMCA & AHRMA members. Closed New Year's Day; Easter; Thanksgiving; Christmas. ♿
Attendance: 23,000 (accurate)
Membership: AMA $39.

Piqua

PIQUA HISTORICAL AREA STATE MEMORIAL, 9845 N. Hardin Rd., Piqua, OH 45356-9707. Tel.: 937-773-2522. Fax: 937-773-4311.
E-mail: ahite@ohiohistory.org
Web Site: www.ohiohistory.org/places/piqua
Founded: 1972.
Congressional District: 8
Key Personnel: Site Mgr., Andy Hite; Groundskeeper, Rob Cline; Museum Shop Mgr., Diana Jacobs; Lead Interpreter, Sheri L. Barhorst.
Personnel Profile: Full-Time Paid 2; Part-Time Paid 8; Part-Time Volunteers 60.
Governing Authority: society. Parent Institution: Ohio Historical Society, 1982 Velma Ave., Columbus, OH 43211. Tax-exempt: 170(b)(1)(A).
History Museum.
Collections: early 18th- & 19th-century furnishings & tools; historic American Indian tools; weapons; costumes; art; canoes; trade items; graphic art; miscellaneous historic & theme-related material; historic woodland culture in Ohio; interprets changes in agriculture from Native American beginnings to the present European style farms; the Eastern Woodland Indians of Ohio. Historic Buildings: Johnston home & farm.
Facilities: barn & other outbuildings; picnic area. Museum-related items for sale.
Activities: demonstrations of early 19th-century crafts; guided tours for school groups; canal boat ride; permanent exhibits.
Publications: Ohio Agricultural History 1800-1900; Native American History 1700-1900; Transportation-Canal History 1830-1900.
Hours & Admission Prices: April-May. & Sept.-Oct. Mon.-Fri. 9-2 by appointmet; June-Aug. Thurs.-Fri. 10-5, Sat.-Sun. 12-5. Adults $8, senior citizens $7, children 6-12 $4; discounts to groups with advanced reservation; OHS, members no charge. ♿
Attendance: 20,000 (accurate)
Membership: Individual $35; Family $55; History Lover $85; Supporter $235.

Point Pleasant

GRANT'S BIRTHPLACE STATE MEMORIAL, 1551 State Rte. 232, Point Pleasant, OH 45153-9301. Mailing Address: P.O. Box 2, New Richmond, OH 45157-0002. Tel.: 513-553-4911; 800-283-8932. Fax: 614-297-2352.
Web Site: www.ohiohistory.org/places/grantbir
Congressional District: 2
Key Personnel: Museum Attendant, Loretta Fuhrman.
Governing Authority: society. Affiliated with Ohio Historical Society. Columbus, OH. 43211. Tax-exempt: 170(b)(1)(A).
Historic House: 1821 restored cottage, birthplace of Ulysses S. Grant.
Collections: artifacts relative to Ulysses S. Grant.
Hours & Admission Prices: April-Oct. Wed.-Sat. 9:30-12 & 1-5, Sun. 1-5; groups by appointment. Adults $2.50, seniors $2, children 6-12 $1.50; children 5 & under and OHS members no charge. ♿
Attendance: 6,000

Pomeroy

MEIGS COUNTY MUSEUM, 144 Butternut Ave., Pomeroy, OH 45769-1260. Mailing Address: P.O. Box 145, Pomeroy, OH 45769-0145. Tel.: 740-992-3810 & 2264. Fax: 740-992-3810.
Web Site: meigscohistorical.org
Founded: 1960.
Congressional District: 6
Key Personnel: Pres., Margaret Parker.
Personnel Profile: Part-Time Paid 2; Part-Time Volunteers 3.
Governing Authority: society. Parent Institution: Meigs County Pioneer & Historical Society. Tax-exempt.
Local History Museum.
Collections: history exhibits; artifacts & memorabilia; history items of Meigs County.

Research Fields: Ohio & river history; genealogy.
Facilities: 3,500-vol. library of material on local history; theater; meeting rooms.
Activities: guided tours; hobby workshops; seminars; oral history project.
Publications: books, Meigs County History 1979; reprints, Wilkesville-Salem 1874; Hardesty Meigs History 1883; Pioneer History-Larkin 1908; Poll Book Records 1800s; Pioneer Annual Meetings; Bedford Township; Meigs County History 1987; Index to Meigs County, OH death records: 1867-1908; Meigs County Birth and Death Records: 1867-1908; Pictorial History of Meigs County; Meigs County History Vol. II & Vol. III; Pictorial History of Portland, Ohio.
Hours & Admission Prices: Mon.-Fri. 10-3. Adults $1, children $.50. ♿
Attendance: 3,000
Membership: Individual $10; Family $18; Contributing $100.

Port Clinton

OTTAWA COUNTY HISTORICAL MUSEUM, 126 W. 3rd. St., Port Clinton, OH 43452-1842. Mailing Address: P.O. Box 845, Port Clinton, OH 43452-0845. Tel.: 419-732-2273.
E-mail: ochm@cros.net
Founded: 1932.
Congressional District: 5
Key Personnel: Cur., Peggy Debien.
Personnel Profile: Part-Time Paid 1; Part-Time Volunteers 8.
Governing Authority: nonprofit. Parent Institution: Area Heritage Foundation Inc. Tax-exempt.
History Museum.
Collections: Indian relics; early household items; hand machine equipment; clothing; guns; rocks; toys; china; cameras; historical photos; local photographs; newspaper clippings.
Research Fields: local history.
Facilities: genealogical & historical library.
Activities: permanent exhibitions.
Publications: book, The Heritage of Port Clinton, Ohio.
Hours & Admission Prices: Winter: Wed. 12-3; Summer: Tues.-Thurs. 12-3; other times by appointment. No charge; donations accepted. ♿
Attendance: 600 (estimated)
Membership: Annual $15; Family $20; Life $1,000.

Portsmouth

SOUTHERN OHIO MUSEUM, (M), 825 Gallia St., Portsmouth, OH 45662-4137. Mailing Address: P.O. Box 990, Portsmouth, OH 45662-0990. Tel.: 740-354-5629. Fax: 740-354-4090.
E-mail: info@somacc.com
Web Site: www.somacc.com
Founded: 1979.
Congressional District: 2
Key Personnel: Dir., Sara Johnson; Gallery & Collections Mgr., Darren Baker; Cur. Performing Arts., Pegi Wilkes.
Personnel Profile: Full-Time Paid 4; Part-Time Paid 6; Part-Time Volunteers 65.
Governing Authority: nonprofit organization. Parent Institution: Southern Ohio Museum Corp. Tax-exempt: 501(c)(3).
Museum & Cultural Center.
Collections: American Art; folk art; decorative arts; prehistoric Native American artifacts.
Research Fields: local history; American Art; Contemporary Art; prehistoric American artifacts
Facilities: theater; reading room; classrooms. Crafts, toys & museum publications for sale.
Activities: guided tours; lectures; films; concerts; drama; formally organized education programs; docent program; temporary, traveling & loan exhibitions.
Publications: quarterly newsletter; exhibition catalogues.
Hours & Admission Prices: Tues.-Fri. 10-5, Sat. 1-5. Adults $2, students & children under 12 $1; discount to AAM members; members & Fri. no charge. Closed national holidays. ♿
Attendance: 18,000 (estimated)
Membership: Student & Senior $15; Individual $25; Family $35; Sustaining $50; Supporting $100; Donor $500; Patron $1,000.

Powell

COLUMBUS ZOO AND AQUARIUM, 4850 W. Powell Rd., Powell, OH 43065-0400. Mailing Address: P.O. Box 400, Powell, OH 43065-0400. Tel.: 614-645-3400. Fax: 614-645-3465.
E-mail: jeff.swanagan@columbuszoo.org
Web Site: www.columbuszoo.org
Formerly: Columbus Zoological Park Association, Inc.
Founded: 1927.
Congressional District: 12
Key Personnel: Dir., Jeffery S. Swanagan; Chm. (V), Bill Hoy; Pres. (V), Connie Woodburn; C.O.O., Dale Schmidt; Gen. Cur., Dusty Lombardi; Dir. Veterinary Medicine, Michael T. Barrie, D.V.M.; Asst. Zoo Dir. Conservation & Animal Care, Lewis Greene; Assoc. Zoo Dir. Mktg., Pete Fingerhut; Museum Shop Mgr., Lisa Jones.
Personnel Profile: Full-Time Paid 250; Part-Time Paid 400; Part-Time Volunteers 325.
Governing Authority: association. Tax-exempt.
Zoology Museum.
Collections: aquarium; aviary; herpetology; mammals.
Research Fields: behavioral, reproductive & physiology behavior, artificial breeding; education on endangered & exotic animals.
Facilities: library of zoology books available for use by staff or volunteers.
Activities: lectures; docent tours; train rides; formally organized education programs; permanent & traveling exhibitions.
Publications: quarterly magazine, Beastly Banner; annual report.
Hours & Admission Prices: Memorial Day-Labor Day 9-6; Sept.-May 9-5. Admission 10-59 $12, children 2-9 and senior citizens 60 & over $7; discounts to members of reciprocating zoos; members & children under 2 no charge. ♿
Attendance: 1,862,433 (accurate)
Membership: Individual $39; Family $89; Family Plus $109; Gold $99.99; Member's Club $150; Keeper's Club $250; Curator's Club $500; Director's Club $750; Colo Club $1,000.

Put-in-Bay

ANTIQUE CAR MUSEUM, 979 Catawba Ave., Put-in-Bay, OH 43456-0708. Mailing Address: P.O. Box 708, Put-in-Bay, OH 43456-0708. Tel.: 419-285-2283.
Car Museum.
Collections: period cars including Model Ts; snow mobiles; gasoline memorabilia.
Hours & Admission Prices: April & Oct. Sat.-Sun. 11-5; May-Sept. daily 10:30-6. No charge.

THE BUTTERYFLY HOUSE, 979 Catawba Ave., Put-in-Bay, OH 43456. Mailing Address: P.O. Box 708, Put-in-Bay, OH 43456-0708. Tel.: 419-285-4855.
Butterfly Museum.
Collections: over 500 species of butterflies from around the world; flowers; plants; trees; gardens.
Facilities: Museum-related items for sale.
Activities: educational program.
Hours & Admission Prices: April & Oct. Sat.-Sun. 10-5; May-Sept. daily 9-6. Adults $7.50, children 6-12 $4.50; children under 6 no charge.

CHOCOLATE MUSEUM, 820 Catawba Ave., Put-in-Bay, OH 43456. Tel.: 419-734-7114.
History Museum.
Collections: history of chocolate & chocolate making; period chocolate collectibles.
Hours & Admission Prices: May-Sept. daily.

LAKE ERIE ISLANDS HISTORICAL SOCIETY, 25 Town Hall Place, Put-in-Bay, OH 43456. Mailing Address: P.O. Box 25, Put-in-Bay, OH 43456-0025. Tel.: 419-285-2804.
Historical Society Museum.
Collections: local history & culture; photographs; personal artifacts; period furnishings.
Activities: educational programs; special events.
Hours & Admission Prices: mid-May to June & Sept. daily 11-5; July-Aug. daily 10-6; Oct. Sat.-Sun. 11-5; groups by appointment. Adults $2, youth 12 & over $1; children 11 & under no charge.

PERRY'S CAVE, 979 Catawba Ave., Put-in-Bay, OH 43456. Mailing Address: P.O. Box 708, Put-in-Bay, OH 43456-0708. Tel.: 419-285-2283.
Geology Museum: an Ohio Natural Landmark.
Collections: local history & geology; natural limestone cave; underground lake.
Facilities: Museum-related items for sale.
Activities: guided tours; private lantern tours.
Hours & Admission Prices: April & Oct. Sat.-Sun. 11-5; May-Sept. daily 10-6. Adults $7.50, children 6-12 $4.50; children under 6 no charge.

PERRY'S VICTORY & INTERNATIONAL PEACE MEMORIAL, 93 Delaware Ave., Put-in-Bay, OH 43456. Mailing Address: P.O. Box 549, Put-in-Bay, OH 43456-0549. Tel.: 419-285-2184. Fax: 419-285-2516.
Web Site: www.nps.gov/pevi/
Founded: 1936.
Congressional District: 9
Key Personnel: Supt., Andrew J. Ferguson; Ranger, Sue Judis.
Governing Authority: federal. Parent Institution: National Park Service, Dept. of the Interior Washington D.C. Tax-exempt.
Park Museum; History Museum.
Collections: weapons & equipment from the War of 1812; War of 1812 naval ordnance; paintings; engravings; lithographs; items relating to the construction & early history of Perry's Victory & International Peace Memorial.
Research Fields: War of 1812 in the Northwest; Battle of Lake Erie; Memorial Column; international peace between U.S. & Canada.
Facilities: 1,000-vol. library of books & pamphlets pertaining to the War of 1812 & the Battle of Lake Erie; papers of the Perry Centennial Commission available for research; 317 ft. observation deck; visitor contact station. Books & other museum-related items for sale.
Activities: interpretive talks; living history demonstrations; tour of Memorial Column.
Publications: Deep Water Sailors-Shallow Water Soldiers: Manning the U.S. Fleet on Lake Erie, 1913; Oliver Hazard Perry & The Battle of Lake Erie; Amongst My Best Men; African Americans & the War of 1812.
Hours & Admission Prices: late April to mid-May & late Sept. to mid-Oct. daily 10-5; mid-May to mid-June & early Sept. daily 10-6; mid-June-Aug. daily 10-7; late Oct. to mid-April by appointment. Adults $3; National Park Service Day, senior citizens over 62 w/Golden Age Passport & children under 16 no charge.
Attendance: 204,161 (accurate)

STONEHENGE ESTATE, 808 Langram Rd., Put-in-Bay, OH 43456. Mailing Address: P.O. Box 599, Put-in-Bay, OH 43456-0599. Tel.: 419-285-6134 & 2585.
Historic House Museum: housed in a stone farmhouse. Listed on the National Register of Historic Places.
Collections: local history & culture; photographs; period furnishings; personal artifacts; wine cellar. Historic Building: Wine Press Cottage.
Facilities: Museum-related items for sale.
Hours & Admission Prices: Memorial Day to Labor Day daily 11-5. Adults 16 & over $7, children 6-15 $4; children 5 & under no charge.

Ravenna

PORTAGE COUNTY HISTORICAL SOCIETY, 6549 N. Chestnut St., Ravenna, OH 44266-3907. Tel.: 330-296-3523.
Web Site: history.portage.oh.us
Founded: 1951.
Congressional District: 11
Key Personnel: Pres., Guy Pernetti; Museum Shop Mgr., Barbara Petroski.
Personnel Profile: Part-Time Volunteers 3.
Governing Authority: trustees & society; nonprofit organization. Tax-exempt: 501(c)(3).
General Museum.
Collections: history artifacts; archives; archaeology finds; glassware. Historic Homes: c.1829, 1832, 1869.
Research Fields: Portage county history; archaeology; genealogy; glass.
Facilities: 150-vol. library of genealogy; history books; court records available for use by appointment; reading room.
Activities: guided tours; monthly lectures; temporary exhibitions.
Publications: book, Portage Heritage; 1874-1978, Bicentennial Atlas; quarterly, newsletter; Ravenna, A Bicentennial Album of 19th Century Photographs; History of Portage County Ohio Illustrated 1885.
Hours & Admission Prices: Tues., Thurs. & Sun. 2-4. No charge; donations accepted. Closed holidays. ♿
Attendance: 1,700 (accurate)
Membership: Student & Senior Citizen $5; Individual $10; Family $15; Sustaining $20; Patron $30; Contributing $60; Life $150 & up.

Reading

READING HISTORICAL SOCIETY MUSEUM, 22 W. Benson St., Reading, OH 45215-3202. Tel.: 513-761-8535.
Founded: 1988.
Congressional District: 2
Key Personnel: Pres. (V), James J. Lichtenberg.
Personnel Profile: Part-Time Volunteers 9.
Governing Authority: nonprofit organization. Tax-exempt.
Historical Society Museum; 1905 house built by local tinsmith.
Collections: furnishings; personal artifacts; marching band uniforms; military uniforms; replica of Doughboy statue from WWI monument; 2 period pianos.
Facilities: library; reading room.
Activities: lectures to seniors & school groups. Museum Sponsors: Memorial Day open house; Annual Settlement Day Dinner; Reading Cross Roads Celebration.
Publications: quarterly newsletter, Bridging Time; 2001 History of Reading - Sesquicentennial of Incorporation; 1994 History of Reading - Bicentennial of Founding.
Hours & Admission Prices: first Sun. of each month 1-3; other times by appointment. No charge; donations accepted.
Attendance: 100 (estimated)
Membership: Annual $5; Patron $25, $50, $100, $500

Ripley

RANKIN HOUSE STATE MEMORIAL, 6152 Rankin Hill Rd., Ripley, OH 45167-1044. Mailing Address: P.O. Box 176, Ripley, OH 45167-0176. Tel.: 937-392-1627.
E-mail: ripleyohio@aol.com
Web Site: www.ripleyohio.net
Founded: 1938.
Congressional District: 2
Key Personnel: Dir., Betty Campbell.
Governing Authority: Affiliated with Ohio Historical Society, Columbus, OH. Tel.: 614-297-2610. Tax-exempt: 170(b)(1)(A).
Historic Site: restored home of abolitionist Rev. John Rankin, 1828; underground railroad site.
Collections: period furnishings.
Hours & Admission Prices: May to mid-Dec. Tues.-Sat. 10-5, Sun. 12-5; groups by appointment. Adults $3, students 6-18 $1; members and children 5 & under no charge.
Attendance: 5,000
Membership: Annual $47.

Rittman

RITTMAN HISTORICAL SOCIETY, 393 W. Sunset Dr., Rittman, OH 44270-1054. Mailing Address: P.O. Box 583, Rittman, OH 44270-0583. Tel.: 330-925-7572.
Founded: 1960.
Congressional District: 16
Key Personnel: Co Pres., Anita Frase; Co Pres., Robert Frase; Treas., Betty Montgomery.
Governing Authority: society. Tax-exempt.
Historic House Museum.
Collections: Historic Houses: 1817 Old Knupp Church; 1859 Gish house, built on old tobacco farm.
Facilities: 200-vol. library of historical books available to society members for use on premises.
Activities: geology study of pioneer families.
Hours & Admission Prices: By appointment only. No charge; donations accepted.
Membership: Student $5; Single $7; Couple $10; Business $25; Lifetime $100.

Roseville

NATIONAL CERAMIC MUSEUM AND HERITAGE CENTER, 7327 Ceramic Rd., N.E., Roseville, OH 43777-9694. Mailing Address: P.O. Box 200, Crooksville, OH 43731-0200. Tel.: 740-697-7021. Fax: 740-697-0171.
E-mail: natceramicmuseum@yahoo.com
Web Site: www.ceramiccenter.info
Formerly: Ohio Ceramic Center
Founded: 1970.
Key Personnel: Dir., Kathy Campbell; Pres. (V), Kent Papageorge; Vice Pres., Joan Spring; Museum Shop Mgr., Betty Larabee.
Personnel Profile: Full-Time Paid 1; Part-Time Paid 1.
Governing Authority:
Arts & Crafts Museum.
Collections: development of pottery from Ohio Bluebird potteries from 1750 to modern ceramic industry; Roseville, Crooksville & Zanesville, Ohio manufacturers.
Major Exhibits: 1910, 3/10-6/10; Hull Pottery - The Business, 4/10-9/10; Proud of Our Own, 5/10-10/10; Star Stoneware, 7/10-9/10.
Research Fields: pottery in Crooksville, Roseville & surrounding areas.
Facilities: Pottery & other museum-related items for sale.
Activities: pottery demonstrations; research; ceramic classes. Annual Events: Pottery Festival in July; Theme Is Pottery Judged Show in September.
Hours & Admission Prices: March-Dec. Wed.-Sat. 10-5, Sun. 12-5; other times by appointment. Adults $4, senior citizens $3.50, students $2; discounts to

AAM & ICOM members; children under 5 & members no charge. Closed Memorial Day; Independence Day; Labor Day. ♿
Attendance: 10,000
Membership: Seniors & Students $10; Individual $15; Family $25; Business $50.

Saint Marys

AUGLAIZE COUNTY HISTORICAL SOCIETY, Daniel Mooney Museum, 223 S. Main St., Saint Marys, OH 45885-2208. Tel.: 419-393-8532 & 738-9328.
Web Site: www.auglaizecountyhistory.org/
Founded: 1963.
Key Personnel: Pres. (V), Karen Dietz; Vice Pres., George Neargarder; Treas., James Heinrich.
Personnel Profile: Part-Time Paid 1; Part-Time Volunteers 15.
Governing Authority: county; nonprofit organization. Subsidiary Institution: Wapakoneta Local History Museum, 206 W. Main St., Wapakoneta, OH. Tax-exempt.
General Museum: housed in c.1876 home of Civil War Officer Major Charles Hipp.
Collections: Fort St. Marys, Fort Amanda & Fort Barbee artifacts; American Indian artifacts; Miami Erie Canal; oil wells; Gordon State Park; early industry; Civil War; local manufacturing. Historic Building: Gary Log House - Auglaize County Fair Grounds; churns; military exhibits.
Research Fields: archaeological dig at Fort St. Marys.
Activities: guided tours; traveling exhibitions by mobile home to schools. Museum Sponsors: Log House at County Fair.
Publications: newsletter, Auglaize County Newsletter.
Hours & Admission Prices: Mon. & Wed.-Fri. 8-5, Tues. 8-7, Sat. 1-4. No charge; donations accepted. Closed holidays.
Attendance: 1,500 (estimated)
Membership: Basic $25.

Salem

THE BUTLER INSTITUTE OF AMERICAN ART - SALEM BRANCH, 343 E. State St., Salem, OH 44460-2846. Tel.: 330-332-8213. Fax: 330-337-8286.
E-mail: info@butlerart.com
Key Personnel: Exec. Dir. & Chief Cur., Dr. Louis A. Zona
Art Museum.
Collections: works by regional artists.
Facilities: classroom. Museum-related items for sale.
Hours & Admission Prices: Wed.-Sat. 11-4. No charge.

SALEM HISTORICAL SOCIETY AND MUSEUM, 208 S. Broadway Ave., Salem, OH 44460-3004. Tel.: 330-337-8514.
E-mail: historicalsociety@salemohio.com
Web Site: www.salemohio.com/historicalsociety/
Founded: 1947.
Congressional District: 18
Key Personnel: Pres. (V), David J. Shivers; Museum Dir., David C. Stratton; Cur., Janice Lesher; Museum Shop Mgr., Dixie Gordon.
Personnel Profile: Part-Time Volunteers 10.
Governing Authority: nonprofit organization. Parent Institution: Salem Historical Society. Tax-exempt: 501(c)(3).
Local History Museum.
Collections: abolitionist artifacts & exhibits; Ohio Women's Rights exhibit; Civil War collection; carpenter shop; woodworking tools & artifacts; coal mine exhibit; Fire Department exhibit; Quaker exhibit; Romanian & Saxon exhibits; Salem China Co.; 50s barbershop display; early china & glass; Mullin's Manufacturing history; photographs; valentines; postcards; toy room; kitchen utensils; loom; spinning wheels; anti-slavery history, pictures; one-room schoolhouse; local artifacts.
Research Fields: local history; early businesses.
Facilities: library of general, history & rare books available for use on premises; reading room. Local publications & other museum-related items for sale.
Activities: guided tours; formally organized education programs for children; permanent exhibitions; ice cream social in June; annual tea in November. Museum Sponsors: Founders Day Dinner; City Celebration in the Fall.
Publications: quarterly newsletter, Bugle.
Hours & Admission Prices: May-Oct. Sun. 1-4; other times call for appointment. Adults $4, groups of 25 or more $3, children $2; members no charge. Closed major holidays. ♿
Attendance: 3,500 (estimated)
Membership: Single $20; Family $40; Life $1,000.

Sandusky

MARITIME MUSEUM OF SANDUSKY, 125 Meigs St., Sandusky, OH 44870-2834. Tel.: 419-624-0274.
E-mail: smmuseum@accsandusky.com
Founded: 1995.
Congressional District: 9
Personnel Profile: Full-Time Paid 1; Part-Time Paid 3; Part-Time Volunteers 150; Interns 1.
Governing Authority: Parent Institution: Sandusky Area Maritime Association. Tax-exempt.
Maritime History Museum.
Collections: maritime history; ship models; tools; boat building; photographs.
Facilities: Museum-related items for sale.
Activities: educational programs; model making; outreach programs; birthday parties; classes; boat building & restoration.
Publications: newsletter, The Messenger.
Hours & Admission Prices: June-Aug. Tues.-Sat. 10-4, Sun. 12-4; Sept.-May Fri.-Sat. 10-4, Sun. 12-4. Adults $4, senior citizens & children under 12 $3. Closed major holidays. ♿
Attendance: 24,417 (accurate)
Membership: Student & Senior $20; Individual $25; Family $50; Contributor $100; Life $1,000.

MUSEUM OF CAROUSEL ART & HISTORY, 301 Jackson St., Sandusky, OH 44870-2621. Tel.: 419-626-6111. Fax: 419-626-1297.
E-mail: merrygoround39@peoplepc.com
Web Site: www.merrygoroundmuseum.org
Formerly: Merry Go Round Museum
Founded: 1990.
Key Personnel: C.E.O., Veronica Vanden Bout; Pres. (V) & Chm. (V), Gary Mortus; Financial Dir., Bridget Castle; Museum Shop Mgr., Carol Brown.
Personnel Profile: Full-Time Paid 2; Part-Time Paid 3; Part-Time Volunteers 105; Interns 1.
Governing Authority: private; nonprofit organization. Tax-exempt: 501(c)(3).
Carousel Art & History Museum.
Collections: American & International carousel art & history; tools & partially carved pieces from G.A. Dentzel carving shop; fully restored & operational Herschell carousel.
Major Exhibits: Where the Wild Things Are, 3/10-12/11.
Research Fields: carousel art & history.
Facilities: 200-vol. library on carousel art & history; 10,000 sq. ft. exhibit space. Gift items for sale.
Activities: wood carving classes; public art program; local artist exhibits. Annual Events: New Year's Eve Gala; Follies; Carving Weekend; Toast of Ohio Wine Festival.
Publications: quarterly newsletter, Stargazer; monthly volunteer newsletter, Ponytales.
Hours & Admission Prices: Jan.-Feb. Sat. 11-5, Sun. 12-5; March-May & Sept.-Dec. Wed.-Sat. 11-5, Sun. 12-5; Memorial Day-Labor Day Mon.-Sat. 10-5, Sun. 12-5. Adults $5, senior citizens $4, children $3, discounts to groups of 10 or more; member adults no charge. Closed New Year's Eve & Day; Easter; Thanksgiving; Christmas Eve & Day. ♿
Attendance: 21,232 (estimated)
Membership: Senior & Student $20; Individual $25; Family $40; Jumpers $100; Prancers $250; Standers $500; Chariot $1,000; Brass Ring $5,000; Lead Horse $150,000.

SANDUSKY LIBRARY FOLLETT HOUSE MUSEUM, 404 Wayne St., Sandusky, OH 44870-2751. Mailing Address: Sandusky Library, 114 W. Adams St., Sandusky, OH 44870-2751. Tel.: 419-625-3834. Fax: 419-625-4574.
E-mail: museumservices@sandusky.lib.oh.us
Web Site: www.sandusky.lib.oh.us/
Founded: 1902.
Congressional District: 5
Key Personnel: Cur., Maggie Marconi; Admin. Reference & Museum Svcs., Dennis McMullen; Archives Librarian, Ron Davidson.
Personnel Profile: Full-Time Paid 3; Part-Time Paid 3; Part-Time Volunteers 1; Interns 1.
Governing Authority: nonprofit association. Parent Institution: Sandusky Library Association, 114 W. Adams. Tax-exempt.
Local History Museum: housed in the 1834-37 Greek Revival home of Oran Follett.
Collections: household objects; furniture; toys; artifacts of Sandusky, Erie County & Johnson's Island Civil War Confederate Officers Prison; 1834-37 Greek Revival home of Oran Follett.
Research Fields: Sandusky & Erie county history; Johnson's Island prison.
Facilities: Sandusky Library: archives.

Activities: guided tours by appointment; traveling exhibits to local schools; speakers available.
Publications: books, At Home in Early Sandusky; From The Widow's Walk: A View of Sandusky Vol. I & II; Images of America: Sandusky, Ohio; Erie County and The Erie Isles: A Pictorial History of The Early Years; Erie County & The Erie Isles: A Pictoral History 1940-1975; Erie County & The Erie Isles: A Pictoral History 1975-Today.
Hours & Admission Prices: April & May Sat. 12-4, Sun. 1-4; June-Aug. Wed. & Fri. 12-4, Sat. 10-1; Sept.-Dec. Sat. 10-1; group tours by appointment. No charge; donations accepted. Closed Easter; Thanksgiving; Christmas.
Attendance: 3,000 (estimated)

Shaker Heights

THE SHAKER HISTORICAL SOCIETY, 16740 S. Park Blvd., Shaker Heights, OH 44120-1641. Tel.: 216-921-1201. Fax: 216-921-2615.
E-mail: shakerhistory@shakerhistory.com
Web Site: www.shakerhistory.org
Founded: 1947.
Congressional District: 22
Key Personnel: Pres. (V), Linda Lissauer; Exec. Dir., Sabine Kretzschmar; Devel. & Mktg. Mgr., Danielle Andrews; Museum Shop Mgr., Carol Saluppo.
Personnel Profile: Full-Time Paid 1; Part-Time Paid 3; Part-Time Volunteers 75.
Governing Authority: society; nonprofit. Tax-exempt: 501(c)(3).
Historical Society Museum: located on land once owned by North Union Colony of Shakers, in a historic 1910 house.
Collections: furniture & artifacts of North Union & other Shaker communities; materials; books; maps; memorabilia related to Shaker Heights; an early 'garden city' community; the Shaker Rapid Transit and Warrensville Township.
Research Fields: local history.
Facilities: 2,000-vol. library of Shakers, Northern Ohio history with emphasis on Shaker Heights & the Van Sweringen Brothers available for research by appointment and fee. Miniature furniture & other items related to Shakers for sale.
Activities: guided tours; video; lectures and programs; educational program for schools by arrangement; permanent and special exhibits; special events.
Publications: quarterly journal, The JOURNAL.
Hours & Admission Prices: Tues.-Fri. & Sun. 2-5; other times by appointment. Suggested Donations: adults $2, children 6-18 $1; members no charge. Closed holidays.
Attendance: 2,500 (accurate)
Membership: Individual $25; Family $35; Sustaining $50; Patron $100; Life $500.

Sharonville

HISTORIC SOUTHWEST OHIO, INC., Heritage Village, 11450 Lebanon Pike, Rte. 42, Sharonville, OH 45241. Mailing Address: P.O. Box 62475, Cincinnati, OH 45262-0475. Tel.: 513-563-9484. Fax: 513-563-0914.
E-mail: jmmccone@heritagevillagecincinnati.org
Web Site: www.heritagevillagecincinnati.org
Founded: 1964.
Congressional District: 1
Key Personnel: Pres. (V), Nadine Friedmann; Dir. Education, Lisa Egan.
Personnel Profile: Full-Time Paid 4; Full-Time Volunteers 1; Part-Time Paid 3; Part-Time Volunteers 70; Interns 1.
Governing Authority: private; nonprofit corporation. Parent Institution: Historic Southwest Ohio, Inc. Subsidiary Institution: Heritage Village Museum. Tax-exempt: 501(c)(3).
Historic Village Museum.
Collections: Historic Structures. Heritage Village: Medical Office; 1852 Hayner House; 1815 Gatch Barn; 1818 Elk Lick House & dependencies; 1872 Chester Park Railroad Station; 1825 Vorches House; 1804 Kemper Log House; 1860 Owensville Store. 19th century furniture & decorative arts; farm equipment & vehicles.
Research Fields: history; decorative arts of the 19th-century southwestern Ohio.
Facilities: Resource Center. Gifts & books for sale in Heritage Village.
Activities: tours; lectures; continuing education; school tours, outreach, kids camp, special events.
Publications: monthly newsletter; survey booklets; walking tour brochures.
Hours & Admission Prices: Heritage Village: May-Sept. Tues.-Sat. 10-5, Sun. 1-5. Adults $5, children $3; members no charge. ♿
Attendance: 22,000 (accurate)
Membership: Individual $30; Family $50; Hayner Society $1,000 & up.

Sheffield Lake

103RD OHIO VOLUNTEER INFANTRY CIVIL WAR MUSEUM, 5501 E. Lake Rd., Sheffield Lake, OH 44054-1900. Tel.: 440-949-2790 & 2976.
Web Site: 103ovi.org
Formerly: 103rd Ohio Volunteer Infantry Memorial Foundation
Founded: 1972.
Key Personnel: Pres., Connie Parker; Cur., Deborah Wagner; Museum Shop Mgr., Darlene Grubaugh.
Personnel Profile: Part-Time Volunteers 10.
Governing Authority: nonprofit organization. Tax-exempt: 501(c)(3).
Military Museum: housed in c.1900 Elfordilno frame structure located on 4-acre site purchased in 1866 by the 103rd Ohio Volunteer Infantry.
Collections: historic Civil War relics; furniture; camp lamps; uniforms; fife & drum; flags; photographs; guns; trade items; books; monographs; biographies; manuscripts.
Research Fields: the Civil War; 103rd Ohio Volunteer Infantry.
Facilities: 300-vol. library of documented Civil War histories; 300-seat hall. Museum-related items for sale.
Activities: guided tours; lectures; temporary exhibitions.
Publications: quarterly newsletter, Assembly Call.
Hours & Admission Prices: Call for appointment. Suggested Donation: adults $2, students $1; members no charge.
Attendance: 500 (estimated)
Membership: Individual $10; Family $25.

Springfield

CLARK COUNTY HISTORICAL SOCIETY - HERITAGE CENTER OF CLARK COUNTY, (M), 117 S. Fountain Ave., Springfield, OH 45502-1207. Tel.: 937-324-0657. Fax: 937-324-1992.
Web Site: www.heritagecenter.us
Founded: 1897.
Congressional District: 7
Key Personnel: C.E.O., Roger Sherrock; Pres. (V), William MacGregor; Cur., Kasey Eichensehr.
Personnel Profile: Full-Time Paid 8; Part-Time Paid 4; Part-Time Volunteers 75; Interns 2.
Governing Authority: county; society; nonprofit. Restoration Sites: 1826, The David Crabill House, 3000 Croft Rd; 1856, Clark County, OH. Tax-exempt.
History Museum.
Collections: 1829-1970 newspaper files; furniture; pioneer utensils; early tools & farm equipment; documents, government records & periodicals.
Research Fields: local & area history.
Facilities: 2,500-vol. library of early newspapers & other material pertaining to 19th-century Clark County & general Americana available for use on premises; archives; reading room.
Activities: gallery talks; permanent & temporary exhibitions; lectures.
Publications: annual monographs; quarterly newsletter.
Hours & Admission Prices: Gallery: Tues.-Sat. 9-5. Library & Archives: Wed.-Sat. 10-5. Suggested Donations: Gallery & Museum $10 per family, $5 per person. Library & Archives: $4 per day; members no charge. Closed national holidays. ♿
Attendance: 28,401 (accurate)
Membership: Individual $25; Family $35.

PENNSYLVANIA HOUSE MUSEUM, 1311 W. Main St., Springfield, OH 45504-2815. Tel.: 937-322-7668.
Web Site: www.pennsylvaniahousemuseum.info
Governing Authority: Parent Institution: Lagonda Chapter of the Daughters of the American Revolution.
Historic House Museum: housed in a Federal-style home built by David Snively in 1839; former home of Dr. Isaac K. Funk of Funk & Wagnalls.
Collections: period furnishings; personal artifacts; photographs.
Hours & Admission Prices: March-Dec. Sat.-Sun. 1-3; groups by appointment. Adults $5, students $2. Closed holidays.

* **SPRINGFIELD MUSEUM OF ART, (M),** 107 Cliff Park Rd., Springfield, OH 45504-2501. Tel.: 937-325-4673. Fax: 937-325-4674.
E-mail: smoa@main-net.com
Web Site: www.springfieldart.museum
Founded: 1946.
Congressional District: 7
Key Personnel: Exec. Dir., Angus Randolph; Bd. Pres., Andy Inck; Cur., Charlotte Gordon; Dir. Mktg., Katherine Denney; Facilities Mgr., James Brewer; Systems Mgr., Ken Pinkham.
Personnel Profile: Full-Time Paid 3; Part-Time Paid 5; Part-Time Volunteers 95.
Governing Authority: nonprofit organization. Parent Institution: Springfield Art Association. Tax-exempt: 501(c)(3) & 170(b)(1)(A).
Art Museum.

Collections: 19th & 20th-century American art.
Major Exhibits: Bounty or Burden: Installation by Gretchen Stevens Cochran, 11/09-3/7/10; Form, Figure and Function: Contemporary Ohio Clay (T), 1/23/10-4/4/10; Japanese American Print Exchange, 3/13/10-4/25/10; 64th Annual Juried Members Exhibition, 4/17/10-6/12/10; Regional Dialect, 6/26/10-9/6/10; Fragile Nature (T), 9/19/10-10/30/10; Ohio Plein Air Society, 11/13/10-1/3/11.
Research Fields:
Facilities: 4,300-vol. library of fine arts books available for use on premises. Original works, paintings, sculpture, drawings & museum-related items for sale.
Activities: lectures; gallery talks; formally organized education programs; art workshops; studio art classes.
Publications: bimonthly newsletters; exhibition catalogues; gallery handouts; quarterly class schedules.
Hours & Admission Prices: Tues.-Sat. 9-5, Sun. 12:30-4:30. Adults $5; discounts to AAM members; members & Sun. no charge. Closed New Year's Day; Memorial Day; Independence Day; Labor Day; Christmas. ♿
Attendance: 39,989 (accurate)
Membership: Student $25; Individual $40; Family $60; Supporter $100; Sustainer $250; Patron $500; Gallery Circle $1,000.

THE WESTCOTT HOUSE FOUNDATION, 1340 E. High St., Springfield, OH 45505-1166. Tel.: 937-327-9291. Fax: 937-327-9074.
E-mail: info@westcotthouse.org
Web Site: www.westcotthouse.org
Founded: 2001.
Key Personnel: Chm., Mark Chepp; Dir. Devel., Jenny Montgomery; Cur., Marta Wojcik; Volunteer Coord., Erik Lindsjo; Facilities Mgr., Tom Fyffe.
Personnel Profile: Full-Time Paid 4; Full-Time Volunteers 1; Part-Time Paid 1; Part-Time Volunteers 100.
Governing Authority: private; nonprofit organization. Tax-exempt: 501(c)(3).
Historic House Museum: housed in Frank Lloyd Wright's only Prairie Style home in Ohio.
Collections: period furnishings; personal artifacts.
Research Fields: history & architecture of the house and community.
Activities: concerts; docent program; films; school programs; guided tours; lectures; temporary exhibitions; summer arts camp. Annual Events: Annual Fundraiser; Donor Recognition Night; Volunteer Recognition Night.
Publications: quarterly, the Westcott House Foundation Newsletter.
Hours & Admission Prices: Wed.-Sat. 11-5, Sun. 1-5. Adults $8.50; members no charge. Frank Lloyd Wright reciprocal membership. ♿
Attendance: 9,003 (accurate)
Membership: Student $25; Single $35; Family $55; Family Plus $85; Apprentice $150; Journeyman $250; Craftsman $500; Masterbuilder $1,000; Designer $2,500.

Steubenville

THE JEFFERSON COUNTY HISTORICAL ASSOC., 426 Franklin Ave., Steubenville, OH 43952-1818. Mailing Address: Box 4268, Steubenville, OH 43952-8268. Tel.: 740-283-1133 & 282-9776. Fax: 740-282-9161.
E-mail: jmusm@att.net
Web Site: rootsweb.com/~ohjcha
Founded: 1973.
Congressional District: 18
Key Personnel: Pres., Judy Brancazio; 1st Vice Pres., Eleanor Naylor; 2nd Vice Pres. & Library Dir., Charles Green.
Personnel Profile: Full-Time Volunteers 5; Part-Time Volunteers 15.
Governing Authority: society; nonprofit organization. Subsidiary Institution: Vivian Snyder Genealogical Library. Tax-exempt: 501(c)(3).
Historical Society Museum: housed in 1918 mansion.
Collections: Jefferson County history; transportation gallery; riverboat room; trains; bridal room; bridal gowns, some 200 years old; president's room; feature memorabilia & photos, books, presidents born in Ohio; Civil War; WWI & WWII; Steubenville Pottery Company history; Russell Wright.
Research Fields: genealogy; history.
Facilities: 5,000-vol. library of genealogical & history books available for research on premises. Area history & museum related items for sale.
Activities: guided tours; lectures; permanent exhibitions.
Publications: quarterly newsletter.
Hours & Admission Prices: April-Nov. by appointment. Library: March-Dec. Tues.-Fri. 10-3. Office: April-Nov. Tues.-Fri. 10-3. Suggested Donation: adults $2; members no charge. Closed holidays.
Attendance: 1,000 (estimated)
Membership: Annual $15; Sponsor $50; Life $200.

Strongsville

GARDENVIEW HORTICULTURAL PARK, 16711 Pearl Rd. Rte. 42, 1 1/2 miles S. of Rte. 82, Strongsville, OH 44136-6048. Tel.: 440-238-6653.
E-mail: grhp@raex.com
Web Site: www.geocities.com/heartland/cottage/9303
Founded: 1949.
Key Personnel: Dir., Henry A. Ross; Asst. Dir., Mark LaRosa.
Personnel Profile: Full-Time Volunteers 2.
Governing Authority: nonprofit corporation. Tax-exempt: 501(c)(3).
Public Horticultural Park.
Collections: 6 acres of English Cottage gardens; 10-acre arboretum containing 2,500 flowering trees, 100,000 daffodils, underplanted with spring bulbs & wildflowers.
Facilities: 6,000-vol. library of reference books on gardening, birds, animals, travel; crafts available for use by members only.
Activities: guided tours by appointment for groups.
Publications: annual report to members.
Hours & Admission Prices: April 15-Oct. 15 Sat.-Sun. 12-6; groups & members year-round by appointment. Adults $5, children $3.
Membership: Annual $25; Sustaining $50 & up.

Sugar Grove

WAHKEENA NATURE PRESERVE, 2200 Pump Station Rd., Sugar Grove, OH 43155-9665. Tel.: 740-746-8695; 800-297-1883.
Web Site: ohsweb.ohiohistory.org/places/c13/
Founded: 1957.
Congressional District: 10
Key Personnel: Site Mgr., Thomas Shisler.
Personnel Profile: Full-Time Paid 1.
Governing Authority: society. The Ohio Historical Society. Site Operations 1982 Velma Ave., Columbus, OH. 43211. Tax-exempt.
Nature Center.
Collections: 100 species of birds; eight species native orchids; 15 species mammals; rhododendron & mountain laurel; 30 types of ferns.
Research Fields: botany; zoology; ecology.
Facilities: nature center; hiking trails.
Activities: nature guides & trails; interpretation area; seminars; walks; formally organized education program.
Publications: Timeline.
Hours & Admission Prices: April-Oct. Sat.-Sun. 8-4:30. $2 per car; AAM & ICOM members no charge.
Attendance: 3,500
Membership: Ohio Historical Society: Family $50.

Sugarcreek

ALPINE HILLS HISTORICAL MUSEUM, 106 W. Main St., Sugarcreek, OH 44681. Mailing Address: P.O. Box 293, Sugarcreek, OH 44681-0293. Tel.: 888-609-7592.
E-mail: ldyoungen@verizon.net
Founded: 1977.
Personnel Profile: Part-Time Volunteers 9.
Governing Authority: Tax-exempt.
History Museum.
Collections: local history & culture; Swiss & Amish heritage; Amish kitchen; cheese making; photographs; period furnishings; audio-visuals.
Activities: audio-visual presentations.
Hours & Admission Prices: April-Nov. Mon.-Sat. 9:30-4:30. Suggested Donation: $2 per person; children no charge.
Attendance: 7,500 (accurate)
Membership: Annual $15; Life $100; Memorial $500.

Tiffin

SENECA COUNTY MUSEUM, 28 Clay St., Tiffin, OH 44883-2259. Tel.: 419-447-5955. Fax: 419-443-7940.
Founded: 1942.
Congressional District: 5
Key Personnel: Dir., Rosalie Adams; Pres. (V), Barry Porter.
Personnel Profile: Full-Time Paid 1; Part-Time Paid 1; Part-Time Volunteers 25; Interns 1.
Governing Authority: museum foundation. Parent Institution: Seneca County. Subsidiary Institution: Seneca County Museum Foundation Inc. Tax-exempt.
Historic House: 1853 Rezin W. Shawhan residence & carriage house.
Collections: costumes; glass; porcelain history; pressed glass; art glass; Tiffin glassware; weapons; folk craft pieces; historical items; primitive farm tools; period fire equipment.
Research Fields: state & local history.

Facilities: library of local history; educational center.
Activities: guided tours; lectures; films.
Hours & Admission Prices: Wed.-Thurs. 1-4; other times by appointment. Admission $1. Closed holidays.
Attendance: 7,000
Membership: Individual $10; Family $15.

TIFFIN GLASS MUSEUM, 25 S. Washington St., Tiffin, OH 44883-2347. Tel.: 419-448-0200.
Glass Museum.
Collections: over 2,000 pieces of glass including stemware, lamps, vases, & bowls; factory history & documents.
Facilities: Museum-related items for sale.
Hours & Admission Prices: Tues.-Sat. 1-5; other times by appointment. No charge.

Toledo

BLAIR MUSEUM OF LITHOPHANES, (M), 5403 Elmer Dr., Toledo, OH 43615-2803. Tel.: 419-245-1356. Fax: 419-535-5770.
E-mail: margaretcarney@sbcglobal.net
Web Site: www.lithophanemuseum.org
Founded: 1966.
Key Personnel: Dir. & Cur., Margaret Carney, Ph.D.
Governing Authority: municipal. Tax-exempt: 501(c)(3).
Decorative Arts Museum.
Collections: over 2,340 19th century porcelain lithophanes; engravings.
Research Fields: lithophanes; 19th century engravings.
Publications: biannual membership newsletter, The Blair Museum of Lithophanes Bulletin.
Hours & Admission Prices: May-Sept. Sat.-Sun. 1-4; other times by appointment. No charge; donations accepted. Special Tours: $5 per person. ♿
Attendance: 5,000 (estimated)

COSI TOLEDO, 1 Discovery Way, Toledo, OH 43604-1579. Tel.: 419-244-2674. Fax: 419-255-2674.
E-mail: cosi@cositoledo.org
Web Site: www.cositoledo.org
Founded: 1997.
Key Personnel: Dir. Operations, Lori Hauser; Chm. (V), David Waterman; Treas., Brent Cousinio; Dir. Exhibitions, Carl Nelson; Dir. Devel., Deborah Caldwell; Dir. Education, Dante Centouri; Mgr. Visitor Svcs., Tina Hicks; Museum Shop Mgr., Alex Gonzales.
Personnel Profile: Full-Time Paid 36; Part-Time Paid 58; Part-Time Volunteers 186; Interns 3.
Governing Authority: private; nonprofit organization. Tax-exempt: 501(c)(3).
Science Museum.
Collections: hands-on science exhibits.
Facilities: restaurant; labs. Museum-related items for sale.
Activities: formal education programs; participatory exhibits; broadcast progams; temporary exhibitions. Annual Events: Bash (fundraiser); various week long events.
Publications: quarterly newsletter, Discover.
Hours & Admission Prices: Tues.-Sat. 10-5, Sun. 12-5. Adults 13 & over $8.50, seniors 65 & over $7.50, children 3-12 $6.50; children 2 & under no charge. ♿
Attendance: 209,430 (accurate)
Membership: Individual & Teacher $55; Grandparent $60; Family $65; Family Plus $80; Supporting $100; Sustaining $250; Founder's Circle $500 & $1,000.

TOLEDO BOTANICAL GARDEN, 5403 Elmer Dr., Toledo, OH 43615-2803. Tel.: 419-536-5566. Fax: 419-536-5574.
E-mail: receptionist@toledogarden.org
Web Site: www.toledogarden.org
Formerly: Crosby Gardens
Founded: 1982.
Congressional District: 5
Key Personnel: Dir., Janet Schroeder.
Personnel Profile: Full-Time Paid 11; Part-Time Paid 20; Interns 6.
Governing Authority: Tax-exempt.
Botanical Garden.
Collections: Gardens: herbs; perennial; pioneer; vegetable; hosta; hemerocallis.
Activities: special events; weddings; rental facilities.
Publications: magazine, Cultivation.
Hours & Admission Prices: Daily dawn to dusk. No charge. ♿
Attendance: 130,000 (estimated)
Membership: Senior $30; Individual $40; Family & Grandparent $50; Friend $75; Sustaining $100; Supporting $250; Patron $500; Toledo Botanical Society $1,000.

TOLEDO FIREFIGHTERS MUSEUM, 918 Sylvania Ave., Toledo, OH 43612-1343. Tel.: 419-478-3473.
E-mail: toledofiremuseum@bex.net
Governing Authority: nonprofit organization. Tax-exempt: 501(c)(3).
Firefighters Museum: housed in Old Number 18 Fire House.
Collections: over 150 years of Toledo fire fighting history; period fire fighting equipment & uniforms; 1837 Neptune, Toledo's first fire pumper; 1927 American-LaFrance pumper; 1929 Pirsch pumper; 1936 Schacht service ladder truck; 1969 Willy's Fire Jeep; firehouse gongs; helmets; period fire toys; photographs.
Facilities: library.
Activities: children's educational activities.
Publications: newsletter.
Hours & Admission Prices: Sat. 12-4; other times by appointment. No charge. ♿

* **THE TOLEDO MUSEUM OF ART, (M), (I),** 2445 Monroe St., Toledo, OH 43620-1500. Mailing Address: P.O. Box 1013, Toledo, OH 43697-1013. Tel.: 419-255-8000. Fax: 419-255-5638. TDD: 419-255-8000.
E-mail: info@toledomuseum.org
Web Site: www.toledomuseum.org
Founded: 1901.
Congressional District: 9
Key Personnel: Pres., Elizabeth Brady; Dir., Don Bacigalupi, Ph.D.; C.O.O., Rod A. Bigelow; Chief Cur., Carolyn Putney; Cur. William Hutton European Paintings & Sculpture before 1900, Lawrence W. Nichols; Cur. Glass, Jutta-Annette Page; Assoc. Cur. Modern & Contemporary, Amy Gilman; Assoc. Cur. Ancient Art, Sandra Knudsen; Registrar, Patricia Whitesides; Head Librarian, Anne O. Morris; Controller, Tim Szymanski.
Personnel Profile: Full-Time Paid 110; Part-Time Paid 103; Part-Time Volunteers 250; Interns 10.
Governing Authority: nonprofit organization. Tax-exempt: 501(c)(3).
Art Museum.
Collections: European & American painting, sculpture, decorative arts; ancient, European & American glass; early ancient glass; ancient & medieval art; books & manuscripts; prints; photography; jewelry; modern & contemporary art.
Major Exhibits: Storybook Stars: Award Winning Illustrations from the Mazza Collection, 11/09-1/10; Bare Witness: Photographs by Gordon Parks (T), 2/10-4/10; Mexico's Toledo, 3/10-5/10; Psychadelic 60s: Posters from the Rock Era, 6/10-9/10; 92nd Toledo Area Artists, 7/10-8/10; Small Worlds, 11/10-2/11.
Research Fields: pertaining to collections.
Facilities: over 60,000-vol. library of books, slides & periodicals on art & music available for use on premises; reading room; 165-seat lecture hall; classrooms; restaurant; 1,750-seat concert hall; sculpture garden. Books on art, postcards, reproductions of art & original works by area artists for sale.
Activities: guided tours; lectures; films; gallery talks; concerts; formally organized education programs for children, young adults, adults; docent program or council; inter-museum loan, permanent, temporary & traveling exhibitions; rental facilities.
Publications: quarterly members magazine; exhibition & collection catalogues; information guides for campus architecture.
Hours & Admission Prices: Tues.-Thurs. 10-4, Fri. 10-10, Sat. 10-6, Sun. 12-6. No charge. Closed occasional holidays. ♿
Attendance: 430,000 (accurate)
Membership: Senior Citizens $35-$50; Individual $50; Family/Dual $75; Contributing $125; Reciprocal $250; Supporting $500; President's Council $1,000.

THE TOLEDO ZOO, 2700 Broadway St., Toledo, OH 43609-3100. Mailing Address: P.O. Box 140130, Toledo, OH 43614-0130. Tel.: 419-385-5721. Fax: 419-389-8670.
Web Site: www.toledozoo.org
Founded: 1900.
Congressional District: 9
Key Personnel: Exec. Dir., Anne Baker, Ph.D; Pres., Gary Smith; Veterinarian, Dr. Wynona Shellabarger; Dir. Visitor Svcs., David DiCola; Dir. Human Resources, Nancy Foley; Conservation Biologist, Dr. Peter Tolson; Dir. Horticulture & Maintenance, Nancy Bucher; Cur. Fishes, Jay F. Hemdal; Cur. Interpretive Svcs., Vanessa Neeb; Cur. Herpetology, Andy Odum; Coord. (V), Bill Davis; Registrar, Glenous Favata; Merchandise Buyer, Deborah L. Noward; Cur. Birds, Robert Webster; Cur. Education, Mitchell Magdich; Cur. Mammals, Randi Meyerson; Construction Mgr., Rick Payeff.

Personnel Profile: Full-Time Paid 158; Part-Time Paid 353; Part-Time Volunteers 541; Interns 15.
Governing Authority: society; nonprofit organization. Tax-exempt: 501(c)(3).
Zoo.
Collections: natural history; greenhouse; botanical gardens; mammals, birds; fish; reptiles; herptiles; polar bears; seals.
Research Fields: SSP programs; Aruba Island rattlesnake; Bali starling; cheetah; chimpanzee; Dumeril's ground boa; elephants; lion-tailed macaque; lowland gorilla; orangutan; Puerto Rican crested toad; radiated tortoise; snow leopard; Virgin Islands boa; white rhinoceros; Wyoming toad, cinereous vulture; Karner blue butterfly; Mitchell's Satyr butterfly; Purplish Copper butterfly; Swamp Metalmark butterfly.
Facilities: botanical garden; aquarium; outdoor amphitheater; classrooms; theaters; children's petting zoo; cafe. Zoo-related items for sale.
Activities: summer concerts; formally organized education programs; docent program or council; educational outreach (schools, nursing homes & libraries); distance learning; summer camp; children's zoo; teacher workshops; interpretive programming; home school; gifted & talented; rental facilities.
Publications: quarterly magazine, Safari!; souvenir guidebook.
Hours & Admission Prices: May-Sept. daily 10-5; Oct.-April daily 10-4. Adults $10, seniors 60 & over and children 2-11 $7; discounts to groups & AZA members; members with card & children under 2 no charge. Parking fee $5. Closed New Year's Day; Thanksgiving; Christmas. ♿
Attendance: 1,022,869 (accurate)
Membership: Single $35; Individual Plus $45; Grandparent $50; Family $60; Supporting Family $85; Contributor $125; President's Silver Circle $250; President's Gold Circle $500; President's Diamond Circle $1,000; President's Platinum Circle $2,500.

UNIVERSITY OF TOLEDO STRANAHAN ARBORETUM, 4131 Tantara Dr., Toledo, OH 43623. Tel.: 419-841-1007.
Key Personnel: Dir., Dr. Daryl Dwyer
Arboretum.
Collections: trees; plants; flowers; ponds; wetlands.
Facilities: 47-acre site.
Hours & Admission Prices: Mon.-Fri. 8-5.

WILDWOOD MANOR HOUSE, 5100 W. Central Ave., Toledo, OH 43615-2106. Tel.: 419-407-9700; 419-407-9784.
Web Site: www.metroparkstoledo.com
Founded: 1975.
Key Personnel: Mgr. Historical Dept., Janet Rozick; Facilities Coord., Erin Moss
Historic House: c.1938.
Collections: period furnishings; photographs.
Activities: special events; educational programs.
Hours & Admission Prices: Jan.-March Sat.-Sun. 12-5; April-Dec. Wed.-Sun. 12-5. No charge; donations accepted. Closed holidays.

Trenton

CHRISHOLM HISTORIC FARMSTEAD, 2070 Woodsdale Rd., Trenton, OH 45067-9752. Mailing Address: P.O. Box 276, Trenton, OH 45067-0276. Tel.: 513-276-5265.
Key Personnel: Dir., Anne Jantzen
Historic Site: housed in the Samuel Augspurger farmhouse, built in 1874. Listed on the National Register of Historic Places.
Collections: period furnishings; Amish-Mennonite settlers; county history.
Facilities: picnic area.
Activities: educational programs; special events; rental facilities.
Hours & Admission Prices: Park: daily 8am to dusk. Home: Summer call for hours; other times by appointment.

Troy

BRUKNER NATURE CENTER, 5995 Horseshoe Bend Rd., Troy, OH 45373-9485. Tel.: 937-698-6493.
E-mail: info@bruknernaturecenter.com
Web Site: www.bruknernaturecenter.com
Governing Authority: nonprofit organization.
Nature Center.
Collections: wetland; forest; prairie; wildlife. Historic Building: 1804 Idding's log home.
Facilities: nature trails; 165 acre nature preserve; auditorium.
Activities: educational programs.
Hours & Admission Prices: Mon.-Sat. 9-5, Sun. 12:30-5. Adults $1, children $.25.

OVERFIELD TAVERN MUSEUM, 201 E. Water St., Troy, OH 45373-3438. Tel.: 937-335-4019.
E-mail: info@overfieldtavernmuseum.com
Web Site: www.overfieldtavernmuseum.com/index.htm
Founded: 1966.
Congressional District: 4
Key Personnel: Dir., Robert Patton; Asst. Cur., Busser Howell; Cur., Kelly Smith.
Governing Authority: nonprofit organization. Tax-exempt: 501(c)(3).
Historic Building Museum: housed in 1808 Overfield Tavern a 2-story, hewed-log building, which served as the first courthouse in Troy, Ohio.
Collections: late 18th & early 19th century artifacts; pewter; redware; slipware; wrought-iron accessories; brass; copper & tin primitives; fireplace equipment; tavern tables; Windsor chairs; lighting devices; old leather-bound books.
Research Fields: period pioneer artifacts; the pioneer tavern & how it was operated; genealogy.
Activities: guided tours; lectures; arts festivals; formally organized education programs for children. Museum Sponsors: arts & crafts demonstrations, such as spinning, weaving, fireplace cookery; historic displays at Troy-Hayner Cultural Center.
Hours & Admission Prices: April-Oct. Sat.-Sun. 1-5; other times by appointment. No charge; donations accepted. Closed New Year's Eve & Day; Easter; Independence Day; Thanksgiving.
Membership: Individual $5; Family $10; Life $100.

TROY-HAYNER CULTURAL CENTER, 301 W. Main St., Troy, OH 45373-3241. Tel.: 937-339-0457. Fax: 937-335-6373.
E-mail: troyhaynercenter@troyhayner.org
Web Site: www.troyhayner.org
Founded: 1976.
Congressional District: 8
Key Personnel: Pres. (V), Bruce Davidson; Dir., Linda Lee Jolly; Asst. Dir., Terri Boehringer.
Personnel Profile: Full-Time Paid 4; Part-Time Paid 8; Part-Time Volunteers 119; Interns 1.
Governing Authority: Troy-Hayner Board of Governors. Parent Institution: Troy City School District, 500 N. Market St., Troy, OH 45373. Tel.: 513-332-6700. Tax-exempt.
Cultural Center: housed in c.1914 Mary Jane Hayner House, built in the Norman-Romanesque Revival style of architecture.
Collections: 1800's Hayner Distillery exhibit & Mary Jane Hayner Family memorabilia; Mary Coleman Allen miniatures; distillery artifacts.
Major Exhibits: Young Masters - Student Art Show, 1/10/10-2/28/10; Enamel & Metal Sculpture, 3/7/10-4/25/10; Strawberry Festival Historical Exhibit, 5/2/10-6/20/10; So. Ohio Forge & Anvil, 6/27/10-8/15/10; Watercolorist: Angela Chang & Sharon Stolzberger, 8/22/10-10/3/10; Through Our Eyes - Miami Cty. Photography, 10/10/10-11/28/10; Annual Holiday Exhibition, 12/3/10-1/9/11.
Facilities: rental facilities.
Activities: guided tours; lectures; concerts; recitals; classes & workshops; temporary exhibits; formally organized education programs; community events; private parties.
Publications: newsletter; brochures; annual report.
Hours & Admission Prices: Mon. 7pm-9pm, Tues.-Thurs. 9-5 & 7pm-9pm, Fri.-Sat. 9-5, Sun. 1-5. No charge; donations accepted. Closed holidays. ♿
Attendance: 41,534 (estimated)
Membership: Friends of Hayner: Annual $30.

Twinsburg

TWINSBURG HISTORICAL SOCIETY, 8996 Darrow Rd., Twinsburg, OH 44087-2127. Mailing Address: P.O. Box 7, Twinsburg, OH 44087-0007. Tel.: 330-487-5565.
Web Site: lwkweb.com/twinsburghistoricalsociety/
Founded: 1963.
Congressional District: 2
Key Personnel: Pres., Audrey Kancler; Vice Pres., Ed Ponter; Sec., Bonnie Williams; Corresponding Sec., Lea Bissell; Treas., Dan Simecek.
Personnel Profile: Part-Time Volunteers 12.
Governing Authority: nonprofit organization. Tax-exempt: 501(c)(3).
General Museum: housed in 1865 school.
Collections: 19th-century furniture; tools; clothes; toys; local artifacts.
Activities: guided tours; demonstrations; permanent exhibitions; information programs; special programs. Museum Sponsors: Ice Cream Social in July; Olde Thyme Fayre in September; Cemetery Walk in October.
Publications: monthly newsletter.
Hours & Admission Prices: Feb.-Dec. last Sun. of month; other times by appointment. No charge; donations accepted. ♿
Attendance: 300 (estimated)

Membership: Active Single $8; Active Family & Contributing Single $15; Contributing Couple $25; Professional $35; Life $100.

Uhrichsville

UHRICHSVILLE CLAY MUSEUM, 30 N. Main St., Uhrichsville, OH 44683. Mailing Address: P.O. Box 11, Dennison, OH 44621. Tel.: 740-922-6776 & 5455. Fax: 740-922-4929.
E-mail: claydirector@tusco.net
Founded: 2008.
Congressional District: 18
Key Personnel: Dir., Reba Allen.
Personnel Profile: Full-Time Paid 1.
Governing Authority: Parent Institution: Dennison RK Depot Museum. Tax-exempt.
History Museum.
Collections: clay history; clay brick; industrial history; clay sewer pipes; folk art; sewer pipes; period tools; photographs.
Facilities: facility rental.
Activities: Museum Sponsors: Clay Workers Picnic; Clay Queen's Tea.
Hours & Admission Prices: Thurs.-Fri. 9-5, Sat. 11-4. Adults $3, seniors $2, students $1; discounts to groups of 20 or more. Closed major holidays.

Upper Sandusky

INDIAN MILL MUSEUM STATE MEMORIAL, 7417 Wyandot Co. Rd. 47, Upper Sandusky, OH 43351-1430. Mailing Address: c/o Upper Sandusky Chamber of Commerce, 108 E. Wyandot Ave., Upper Sandusky, OH 43351-1430. Tel.: 419-294-3349 & 4022.
Web Site: www.ohiohistory.org/places/indian
Founded: 1967.
Congressional District: 4
Key Personnel: Dir., Denise Clark.
Governing Authority: society. Affiliated with Ohio Historical Society, 1985 Velma Ave., Columbus, OH. 43211.
Historic Site.
Collections: grist mill.
Hours & Admission Prices: Memorial Day to Labor Day Fri.-Sun. 1-6; Sept.-Oct. Sat.-Sun. 1-6; groups by appointment. Adults & children 13 & over $1, children 6-12 $.50; children under 6 & Ohio Historical Society members no charge. ♿
Attendance: 2,245 (accurate)

WYANDOT COUNTY HISTORICAL SOCIETY, 130 S. 7th St., Upper Sandusky, OH 43351-1339. Mailing Address: P.O. Box 372, Upper Sandusky, OH 43351-0372. Tel.: 419-294-3857.
E-mail: curator@wyandothistory.org
Web Site: www.wyandothistory.org
Founded: 1929.
Key Personnel: Pres., Robin Schuster; Cur., Kris Lininger.
Governing Authority: nonprofit organization. Tax-exempt: 501(c)(3).
General Museum.
Collections: agriculture; arboretum; archives; paintings; children's museum; manuscripts; costumes; glass; history; Indian artifacts; marine; medical; musical instruments. Historic House: 1852 McCutchen Overland Inn.
Activities: lectures; formally organized education programs for children; permanent & temporary exhibitions.
Publications: bimonthly newsletter.
Hours & Admission Prices: May-Oct. Thurs.-Sun. 1-4:30. Adults $2, students & children $1. ♿
Membership: Annual $15.

Urbana

CEDAR BOG NATURE PRESERVE, 980 Woodburn Rd., Urbana, OH 43078-9417. Mailing Address: P.O. Box 510, Urbana, OH 43078-0510. Tel.: 937-484-3744; 800-860-0147.
Web Site: www.ohiohistory.org/places/cedarbog
Founded: 1942.
Congressional District: 1
Key Personnel: Site Mgr., E. Doerzbacher.
Governing Authority: society. The Ohio Historical Society, Ohio Historical Center Museums Division, 1982 Velma Ave., Columbus, OH 43211. Tax-exempt.
Nature Preserve: post-glacial alkaline bog in Ohio.
Collections: plants typical of a boreal fen; fish; endangered spotted turtles; endangered massasauga rattlesnakes; butterflies; birds; trees in the bog from the Ice Age.
Research Fields: geology; botany, ecology.
Facilities: nature & observation area.
Publications: books, Ohio Journal of Science; Cedar Bog Symposium.
Hours & Admission Prices: April-Oct. Wed.-Sun. 9-4:30; Nov.-March by appointment. Adults $4, children 6-12 & school groups $3; children 5 & under and members no charge. ♿
Attendance: 5,000 (accurate)
Membership: Cedar Bog Association: $10 & up; Ohio Historical Society: $30 & up.

CHAMPAIGN COUNTY HISTORICAL MUSEUM, 809 E. Lawn Ave., Urbana, OH 43078-1256. Mailing Address: P.O. Box 65, Urbana, OH 43078-0065. Tel.: 937-653-6721.
E-mail: champhistmus@ctcn.net
Web Site: www.champaigncountyhistoricalmuseum.org
Founded: 1934.
Congressional District: 7
Key Personnel: Pres. (V), Anne Mayer; Treas., Howard Brust.
Personnel Profile: Part-Time Volunteers 7; Interns 1.
Governing Authority: nonprofit organization. Parent Institution: Champaign County Historical Society. Tax-exempt: 501A.
Historical Society Museum: housed in 1912 school for Champaign County Children's Home.
Collections: Civil War; Brand Whitlock; manuscripts; period artifacts; Simon Kenton collection; local photographs; early farm implements; Native American diorama.
Facilities: 100-vol. library of historical books available upon request.
Activities: guided tours; lectures; films; arts festivals; formally organized education programs for adults; permanent & temporary exhibitions. Annual Event: Octoberfest & craft show in October
Publications: A Brief History of Simon Kenton; A Brief History of Richard Stanhope.
Hours & Admission Prices: Tues. 10-4, 1st Sun. of month 1-4; other times by appointment. No charge; donations accepted. ♿
Attendance: 4,000 (accurate)
Membership: Family $10.

JOHNNY APPLESEED SOCIETY MUSEUM, (M), Bailey Hall, Urbana University, Urbana, OH 43078-2081. Tel.: 937-484-1303. Fax: 937-484-1322.
E-mail: jbesecker@urbana.edu
Web Site: www.urbana.edu/index.php/alumni_and_friends/appleseed_society/museum/
Personnel Profile: Full-Time Paid 1.
Governing Authority: Tax-exempt.
History Museum.
Collections: Johnny (Appleseed) Chapman memorabilia & written materials.
Hours & Admission Prices: Tues.-Fri. 10-2, Sat. 12-4; other times by appointment.

Van Wert

CENTRAL INSURANCE FIRE MUSEUM, 800 S. Washington St., Van Wert, OH 45891-2381. Tel.: 419-238-1010.
Web Site: www.central-insurance.com/docs/museum.htm
Fire-Fighting Museum.
Collections: leather fire buckets dating back to the 1700s; over 600 antique fire toys; fire extinguishers & glass fire "grenades" from the 1850's; antique firman helmets & uniforms; hand-drawn pumper used in 1871; Ahrens horse-drawn steam pumper; 1926 Ahrens-Fox pumper.
Hours & Admission Prices: 3rd Fri. of each month 1-3; other times by appointment.

VAN WERT COUNTY HISTORICAL SOCIETY, 602 N. Washington St., Van Wert, OH 45891-1265. Mailing Address: P.O. Box 621, Van Wert, OH 45891-0621. Tel.: 419-771-9851.
Historic House Museum: housed in the former home of John O. & Tacey Viella Clark; built in 1895.
Collections: local history & culture; photographs; period furnishings; personal artifacts; Native American artifacts. Historic Buildings: 1906 one-room school; 1860 log house; 1875 gazebo.
Activities: special events.
Hours & Admission Prices: March-Nov. Sun. 2-4:30; groups by appointment.

Vandalia

TRAPSHOOTING HALL OF FAME & MUSEUM, 601 W. National Rd., Vandalia, OH 45377-1036. Tel.: 937-898-4638, ext. 528. Fax: 937-898-5541.
E-mail: hof@shootata.com
Web Site: www.traphof.org/index2.htm
Trapshooting Museum.
Collections: trapshooting artifacts & memorabilia; photographs.

Hours & Admission Prices: Mon.-Fri. 9-3. No charge. Closed New Year's; Memorial Day; Independence Day; Labor Day; Thanksgiving; Christmas.

Vermilion

INLAND SEAS MARITIME MUSEUM, 480 Main St., Vermilion, OH 44089-1015. Mailing Address: P.O. Box 435, Vermilion, OH 44089-0435. Tel.: 440-967-3467. Fax: 440-967-1519.
E-mail: glhs1@inlandseas.org
Web Site: www.inlandseas.org
Founded: 1944.
Congressional District: 5
Key Personnel: Exec. Dir., Christopher H. Gillcrist; Chm., Frank Samsel; Business Mgr., Nancy Blanton; Museum Shop Mgr., Noelle McFarland.
Personnel Profile: Full-Time Paid 5; Part-Time Paid 6; Part-Time Volunteers 12.
Governing Authority: society; nonprofit. Affiliated with the Great Lakes Historical Society. Tax-exempt: 501(c)(3).
Maritime Museum: housed in 1909 residence of Commodore F.W. Wakefield. Museum is contained in 1968 addition to former residency of Commodore F.W. Wakefield. Home is now administration offices and The Clarence S. Metcalf library.
Collections: Great Lakes ship models; paintings; photographs; marine artifacts & relics; marine engines; yachting & racing artifacts; lighthouse lens; model steam engines; artifacts from recreational & commercial vessels; shipbuilding tools & equipment; naval architecture plans; artifacts from lighthouses, life saving, Coast Guard; library.
Research Fields: shipping and passenger vessels on the Great Lakes; ship wrecks on the Great Lakes.
Facilities: 2,400-vol. library contains information, photos, log books, books & manuscripts on the history of shipping on the Great Lakes available on premises to members; photographs of lake vessels & related facilities; mail order service; reading room. Journal, ship building books for sale.
Activities: guided tours; permanent, temporary & traveling exhibitions; model boatshows, fairs & exhibitions; shipwrights group; living history program; dinner programs featuring speakers & other programs relating to the Great Lakes.
Publications: quarterly journal, Inland Seas; annual magazine, Index for Inland Seas; quarterly newsletter, Chadburn.
Hours & Admission Prices: Jan. 2-April Mon.-Fri. 11-4, Sat.-Sun. 10-5; May -Aug. daily 10-5; Sept.-Dec. Mon.-Fri. 11-5, Sat.-Sun. 10-5; groups by appointment. Family $14, adults $6, seniors & youths 12 & under $5; discounts to AAM, AAA & NE Ohio Intermuseum Council members; members no charge. Closed New Year's Day; Easter; Thanksgiving, Christmas.
Attendance: 13,000 (estimated)
Membership: Student $15; Senior Citizen 65 & over $32; Regular $49; Sustaining $64; Contributing $100; Benefactor $200; Patron $500; Life $2,500; Corporate memberships available.

Wapakoneta

ARMSTRONG AIR & SPACE MUSEUM, I-75 & Bellefontaine Rd., Wapakoneta, OH 45895. Mailing Address: P.O. Box 1978, Wapakoneta, OH 45895-0978. Tel.: 419-738-8811. Fax: 419-738-3361.
Web Site: www.ohiohistory.org
Founded: 1972.
Congressional District: 4
Key Personnel: Dir. Historical Society, Dr. Gary C. Ness; Museum Dir., Rebecca Moor.
Personnel Profile: Full-Time Paid 3; Part-Time Paid 4.
Governing Authority: Parent Institution: Ohio Historical Society, 1982 Velma Ave., Columbus, OH 43211. Tax-exempt.
Aeronautics & Space Museum.
Collections: symbols & relics of Ohio air & space achievements; moon rock display; space shuttle display; space flight suits; memorabilia from Neil Armstrong's boyhood interest in aviation; space shuttle landing simulator; lunar landing simulator. Historic Aircrafts: 1946 Aeronca 7AC Champion; 1966 Gemini VIII; c.1960 F5D Skylancer.
Facilities: theater. Aeronautical & other museum-related items for sale.
Activities: film & art exhibits; audiovisual; infinity cube; permanent & loan exhibitions.
Hours & Admission Prices: Mon.-Sat. 9:30-5, Sun. & holidays 12-5. Adults $7, students $2; discount to groups, Golden Buckeye, AAA & AAM members; members & children under 5 no charge. Closed New Year's Day, Thanksgiving & Christmas. ♿
Attendance: 50,000 (accurate)
Membership: Annual $50.

Warren

JOHN STARK EDWARDS HOUSE, 303 Monroe St., N.W., Warren, OH 44483-4812. Mailing Address: P.O. Box 1907, Warren, OH 44482-1907. Tel.: 330-394-4653.
E-mail: museum@trumbullcountyhistory.org
Web Site: www.trumbullcountyhistory.org
Founded: 1938.
Congressional District: 19
Key Personnel: Pres. (V), Don M. Hazel; Chm. (V), Marti Gilbert; Museum Shop Mgr., Nancy Brant.
Personnel Profile: Part-Time Volunteers 30.
Governing Authority: society. Trumbull County Historical Society. Tax-exempt.
Historic House: 1807 John Stark Edwards house.
Collections: 1800 quilts; old tools; 1800s clothing; musical instruments; old books.
Facilities: 100-vol. library of historical data on the Connecticut Western Reserve & Trumbull County, Warren, Ohio, available for research on premises. History books & other museum-related items for sale.
Activities: guided tours.
Publications: quarterly newsletter, Trump of Fame.
Hours & Admission Prices: April-Nov. Sat.-Sun. 1-4; Dec.-April Sun. 2-4; groups by appointment. No charge; donations accepted. Closed holidays.
Attendance: 2,100 (accurate)
Membership: Students $10; Individual $25; Family $40; Corporation $100; Life $250.

NATIONAL PACKARD MUSEUM, 1899 Mahoning Ave., N.W., Warren, OH 44483-2081. Tel.: 330-394-1899. Fax: 330-394-7796.
E-mail: national@packardmuseum.org
Web Site: www.packardmuseum.org
Founded: 1989.
Key Personnel: C.E.O., Cur. & Archivist, Mary Ann Porinchak; Pres. (V), Mike Yost; Treas., Scott Masters; Devel., Charlie Ohlin; Museum Shop Mgr., Gail Stark.
Personnel Profile: Full-Time Paid 2; Full-Time Volunteers 2; Part-Time Paid 2; Part-Time Volunteers 75; Interns 1.
Governing Authority: private; nonprofit organization. Tax-exempt: 501(c)(3).
History Museum.
Collections: Packard family history; motor car memorabilia; Packard Electric, Packard Motor Car & Ohio Lamp history; Packard motor cars 1900-1958.
Research Fields: Packard Motor Car Company & their involvement in the war effort; building of the PT boat, fighter plane & war machine engines.
Facilities: classroom; court yard; 7,500 sq. ft. exhibit space. Museum-related items for sale.
Activities: docent program; guided tours; hobby workshops; lectures; loan, temporary & participatory exhibitions; internships with Kent State & YSU; school tours with scavenger hunt; facility rental. Annual Events: Car Shows: All Packard; All Makes & Models.
Publications: quarterly newsletter, Time Machine.
Hours & Admission Prices: Tues.-Sat. 12-5, Sun. 1-5; varied hours for special events & prearranged tours. Adults $5, senior citizens & students $3; discounts to groups; members & children under 7 no charge. Closed New Year's Eve & Day; Easter; Memorial Day; Independence Day; Labor Day; Thanksgiving; Christmas Eve & Day. ♿
Attendance: 20,000 (estimated)
Membership: Senior Citizen 65 & over $18; Individual $30; Family $60; Supporter $120. Life: Packard Live Wire $500; Packard Old Pacific $750; Packard No One $1,000; Packard Phaeton $5,000.

Washington Court House

FAYETTE COUNTY MUSEUM, 517 Columbus Ave., Washington Court House, OH 43160-1427. Tel.: 740-335-2953.
Founded: 1948.
Key Personnel: Pres. (V), Warren Craig; Financial Dir., Craig Breedlove; Sec. Bd. Trustees, Donald J. Moore.
Personnel Profile: Part-Time Paid 1; Part-Time Volunteers 25.
Governing Authority: private; nonprofit organization. Tax-exempt: 501(c)(3).
History Museum: housed in a 14 room Victorian mansion.
Collections: period furnishings; artifacts; memorabilia depicting history & heritage of Fayette County, Ohio.
Research Fields: history of local schools.
Facilities: 200-vol. library of County & Ohio history; 1,400 sq. ft. exhibit space.
Activities: lectures; school loan service; temporary exhibitions. Museum Sponsors: Ice Cream Social; Holiday Open House.
Publications: county-wide tour map; 2010 calendar.
Hours & Admission Prices: May-Aug. Sat.-Sun. 1-4. No charge; donations accepted.

Attendance: 1,350 (accurate)
Membership: Student $1; Adult $10; Business $50; Life $100.

Wauseon

FULTON COUNTY HISTORICAL MUSEUM, 229 Monroe St., Wauseon, OH 43567-1127. Mailing Address: P.O. Box 104, Wauseon, OH 43567-0104. Tel.: 419-337-7922.
E-mail: museum@fultoncountyhs.org
Web Site: www.fultoncountyhs.org
Founded: 1883.
Congressional District: 5
Key Personnel: Pres. (V), Carl Buehrer; Dir., John D. Swearingen, Jr.
Personnel Profile: Part-Time Paid 1; Part-Time Volunteers 10.
Governing Authority: society. Fulton County Historical Society, Inc. Tax-exempt.
History Museum.
Collections: artifacts of Fulton County from 1830-1976. Historic Buildings: 1838 Log Cabin; 1896 Lake Shore & Michigan Southern Railroad Depot; 1861 blacksmith shop; Swan Creek Township building.
Publications: quarterly newsletter, Fulton County Pioneer.
Hours & Admission Prices: March-Dec.Tues. 4-7, Thurs. 10-4, Sat. 10-2; other times by appointment. Closed holidays. ♿
Attendance: 850 (estimated)
Membership: Individual $20; Senior Couple $25; Family $30; Life $350.

Waynesville

CAESAR'S CREEK PIONEER VILLAGE, Caesar's Creek State Park, 3999 Pioneer Village Rd., Waynesville, OH 45068-9719. Mailing Address: P.O. Box 652, Waynesville, OH 45068-0652. Tel.: 513-897-1120.
E-mail: ccpv@embarqmail.com
Web Site: www.caesarscreekvillage.org
Key Personnel: Dir., Kathy Sewell.
Governing Authority: nonprofit organization.
History Museum.
Collections: Southwestern Ohio frontier history from 1793-1812; Ohio's heritage.
Activities: school programs; rental facilities. Museum Sponsors: festivals.
Hours & Admission Prices: Call for hours.

Wellington

SPIRIT OF '76 MUSEUM, 201 N. Main St., Wellington, OH 44090. Mailing Address: P.O. Box 76, Wellington, OH 44090-0076. Tel.: 440-647-4367 & 4576.
Founded: 1968.
Congressional District: 5
Key Personnel: Pres., John Perry.
Personnel Profile: Part-Time Volunteers 14.
Governing Authority: nonprofit. Parent Institution: Southern Lorain County Historical Society. Tax-exempt: 501(c)(3).
Historical Society Museum: housed in 1872 building.
Collections: items associated with Archibald M. Willard's painting The Spirit of '76; 16 Willard oils, water colors and murals; artifacts associated with the history of Southern Lorain County.
Facilities: reading room; 100-seat auditorium; classrooms. Gift items for sale.
Activities: guided tours; lectures; films; formally organized education programs for adults.
Publications: newsletters.
Hours & Admission Prices: April-Oct. Sat.-Sun. 2:30-5 by appointment; groups of 10 or more by appointment. No charge; donations accepted. ♿
Attendance: 950 (accurate)
Membership: 18 & Under $1; Single $5; Couple & Patron $10; Life $50.

Wellston

BUCKEYE FURNACE STATE MEMORIAL, 123 Buckeye Park Rd., T167, Wellston, OH 45692-9511. Mailing Address: Friends of Buckeye Furnace, Inc., P.O. Box 475, Jackson, OH 45640-0475. Tel.: 740-384-3537.
Web Site: ohsweb.ohiohistory.org/places/se02
Founded: 1976.
Congressional District: 6
Key Personnel: Museum Attendant, Pat Hollingshead.
Governing Authority: society. The Ohio Historical Society. Ohio Historical Center Site Operations Office, 1985 Velma Ave., Columbus, OH. 43211.
Historic Buildings: 1851 restored Iron Furnace Complex.
Collections: Historic Structures: casting shed; company store; office; charging house; engine house.
Facilities: picnic area; nature trails.
Activities: multimedia presentation; Spring wildflower walks.
Publications: site brochures.
Hours & Admission Prices: Memorial Day to Oct. Wed.-Fri. by appointment, Sat.-Sun. 12-5. Adults $4, children 6-12 $3; children 5 & under and members no charge.

Wellsville

RIVER MUSEUM, 1003 Riverside Ave., Wellsville, OH 43968-1374. Mailing Address: P.O. Box 13, Wellsville, OH 43968-0013.
Founded: 1955.
Congressional District: 18
Key Personnel: Pres., Robert J. Beresford; Vice Pres., Bonny Beresford; Treas, Pat Lawrence; Sec., Joan Davidson.
Personnel Profile: Part-Time Volunteers 8; Interns 7.
Governing Authority: private; nonprofit organization. Tax-exempt.
History Museum: housed in c.1870 home of Dr. John Hammond.
Collections: period furnishings; 1953 Pennsylvania Railroad Cabin Car; Civil War memorabilia, saber; Indian artifacts; pottery; period kitchen utensils; railroad displays; boat display room; military room; French Indian WWI & II memorabilia; vintage clothing; hatpins & holders; quilts; original Pretty Boy Death Mask.
Facilities: 100-vol. library of genealogy.
Activities: guided tours.
Hours & Admission Prices: June-Sept. Sun. 1-4:30; private tours available all year. Charge for special tours only. ♿
Attendance: 1,200 (estimated)
Membership: Individual $5.

West Liberty

PIATT CASTLES, 10051 Township Rd. 47, West Liberty, OH 43357. Mailing Address: P.O. Box 497, West Liberty, OH 43357-0497. Tel.: 937-465-2821. Fax: 937-465-7774.
E-mail: macochee@logan.net
Web Site: www.piattcastles.org
Founded: 1912.
Congressional District: 7
Key Personnel: C.E.O. & Pres., Margaret Piatt; Vice Pres. & Museum Shop Mgr., James White.
Personnel Profile: Full-Time Paid 1; Part-Time Paid 20; Part-Time Volunteers 8; Interns 2.
Governing Authority: private.
Historic House Museums: Mac-A-Cheek completed in 1871; Norman-French style home with several generations of Piatt Family furnishings & objects; Mac-O-Chee Castle completed in 1881 Flemish style home with American furnishings & objects.
Collections: Piatt family furnishings & objects; firearms; archival & library holdings; American furnishings & objects.
Research Fields: Piatt family; Donn Piatt; General A. Sanders Piatt.
Facilities: library; archives.
Activities: guided tours; school & adult programs; summer evening performances. Annual Event: Christmas Open House.
Publications: brochures.
Hours & Admission Prices: Spring & Fall Fri.-Sun. 11-4; Memorial Day-Labor Day daily 11-5. Adults $9 per castle, students & children 5-15 $6; discounts to seniors, AAA & AAM members.
Attendance: 1,200 (accurate)
Membership: Friend $30; Patron $50; Contributor $100; Supporter $250.

Westerville

ANTI-SALOON LEAGUE MUSEUM, Westerville Public Library, 126 S. State St., Westerville, OH 43081-2029. Tel.: 614-882-7277, ext. 160. Fax: 614-882-5369.
E-mail: bweinhar@westervillelibrary.org
Web Site: www.wpl.lib.oh.us/antisaloon/
Founded: 1990.
Key Personnel: Archivist, Beth Weinhardt.
Personnel Profile: Full-Time Paid 2; Part-Time Volunteers 2.
Governing Authority: nonprofit. Parent Institution: Westerville Public Library, 126 S. State St., Westerville, OH 43081.
History Museum: housed in the building that served as League headquarters.
Collections: publications; fliers; posters; song books; microfilm; archives of community history from the first settlement to modern times.
Facilities: 225-vol. library.
Activities: formal education programs; guided tours; lectures.
Hours & Admission Prices: Mon.-Fri. 9-6. No charge. ♿
Attendance: 3,000 (estimated)

HANBY HOUSE, 160 W. Main St., Westerville, OH 43081. Mailing Address: P.O. Box 1063, Westerville, OH 43086-7063. Tel.: 614-891-6289; 800-600-6843.
Web Site: ohsweb.ohiohistory.org/places/c02/
Founded: 1937.
Congressional District: 12
Key Personnel: Chm. (V), Margaret Baker; Pres., Bill Merriman; Sec., Mary Bigham.
Personnel Profile: Part-Time Volunteers 50.
Governing Authority: state. Parent Institution: Ohio Historical Society, 1982 Velma Ave., Columbus, OH 43211. Subsidiary Institution: Westerville Historical Society, P.O. Box 1063, Westerville, OH 43081. Tax-exempt.
Historic House: 1853 pre-Civil War home of Bishop William Hanby, father of composer & author Benjamin R. Hanby. Underground railroad.
Collections: music; furniture; household items of the Hanby family; underground railroad site.
Research Fields: life in Civil War times; underground railroad in Ohio; genealogy of the Hanby Family.
Facilities: library of Hanby music & family history books available for use on premises.
Activities: permanent exhibitions; audiovisual; demonstrations of household crafts of 1860s; tour guides in costume; presentation of life of the Hanby family.
Publications: books, Choose You This Day, The Legacy of The Hanbys; A Hundred Years with Dacia Custer Shoemaker; The House of Brotherhood, Story of Hanby House.
Hours & Admission Prices: May-Sept. Sat.-Sun. 1-4; other times by appointment. Adults $2, children 6-12 $.75; discounts to senior citizens, AAA, AAM, Golden Buckeye & Ohio Historical Society members; Hanby Club members & children under 6 no charge. ♿
Attendance: 2,600 (accurate)
Membership: Annual $10.

INNISWOOD METRO GARDENS, 940 S. Hempstead Rd., Westerville, OH 43081-3612. Tel.: 614-895-6216. Fax: 614-895-6352.
Web Site: www.inniswood.org
Botanical Garden: former estate of Grace and Mary Innis.
Collections: more than 2,000 species of plants; specialty collections of hostas, daffodils & daylilies.
Hours & Admission Prices: Daily 7-dusk. No charge.

WEITKAMP OBSERVATORY AND PLANETARIUM, Otterbein College, 155 W. Main St., Westerville, OH 43081-1430. Tel.: 614-823-1316. Fax: 614-823-1968.
E-mail: ewerwa@otterbein.edu
Web Site: www.otterbein.edu/physics/weitkamp.asp
Founded: 1955.
Congressional District: 15
Key Personnel: Dir., Uwe Trittmann.
Personnel Profile: Part-Time Volunteers 1.
Governing Authority: college. Affiliated with the Otterbein College. Tax-exempt: 501(c)(3).
Observatory & Planetarium.
Collections: astronomy; 14 & 8 inch Celestron Schmidt-Cassegrain telescopes; Meade CCD camera & guidance system; Spitz planetarium projector.
Facilities: planetarium; observatory deck.
Activities: lectures; formally organized education programs.
Hours & Admission Prices: By appointment only. No charge; donations accepted.
Attendance: 200 (estimated)

Whitehouse

THE BUTTERFLY HOUSE, 11455 Obee Rd., Whitehouse, OH 43571-9205. Tel.: 419-877-2733.
Butterfly House.
Collections: over 1,000 butterflies from around the world; butterfly life cycle.
Hours & Admission Prices: April-Sept. Mon.-Sat. 10-5, Sun. 12-5; Oct. Sat.-Sun. Adults 13-64 $6, seniors 65 & over $5, children 4-12 $4.50; children 3 & under no charge.

Wilberforce

NATIONAL AFRO-AMERICAN MUSEUM & CULTURAL CENTER, 1350 Brush Row Rd., Wilberforce, OH 45384-0578. Mailing Address: P.O. Box 578, Wilberforce, OH 45384-0578. Tel.: 937-376-4944, ext. 122. Fax: 937-376-2007.
E-mail: wbillingsley@ohiohistory.org
Web Site: www.blackohio.org
Founded: 1972.
Congressional District: 7
Key Personnel: Site Mgr., William Billingsley; Chm. (V), Dr. Kenneth Goings; Cur., Dr. Floyd R. Thomas; Registrar, Wendy Felder.
Personnel Profile: Full-Time Paid 7; Part-Time Paid 1.
Governing Authority: nonprofit organization. Parent Institution: Ohio Historical Society. Tax-exempt: 501(c)(3).
African American History Museum: located on grounds of c.1856 Wilberforce University campus.
Collections: African American life between 1945 & the passage of the Voting Rights Act of 1965; objects & images reflecting African-American families, jobs, schools, churches, organizations, music; African-American published serials; 2,147 slides; 1,551 recordings.
Facilities: 6,481-vol. library of books on all aspects of African-American experience; 40-seat theatre. Gift items for sale.
Activities: guided tours; rental gallery; theatre; traveling exhibitions.
Hours & Admission Prices: Tues.-Sat. 9-5. Adults $4, seniors $3.60, children & students $1.50; discounts to AAM & Assoc. of African American Museum members; members no charge. Closed major holidays. ♿
Attendance: 2,500 (accurate)
Membership: Basic $30; Family $50; Contributing $75; Basic Plus $130; Supporting $125; Family Plus $150.

PAUL ROBESON CULTURAL AND PERFORMING ARTS CENTER, Central State University, U.S. 42, Wilberforce, OH 45384. Mailing Address: P.O. Box 1004, Wilberforce, OH 45384-1004. Tel.: 937-376-6403.
Web Site: www.centralstate.edu/academics/art_science/fine_performing_arts
Key Personnel: Chm., Assoc. Prof. William Caldwell Asst. Prof. Kenneth Pointer Assoc. Prof. Abner Cope Assoc. Prof. Dr. Ronald Claxton Assoc. Prof. Dwayne Daniel
Art Gallery.
Collections: paintings.
Facilities: 850-seat auditorium; recital hall.
Activities: convocations; lectures; recitals; workshops; temporary exhibitions.
Hours & Admission Prices: Call for hours. No charge.

Willoughby

INDIAN MUSEUM OF LAKE COUNTY, OHIO, (M), 25 Public Sq.-Technical Center, Bldg. B, Willoughby, OH 44094. Mailing Address: P.O. Box 883, Willoughby, OH 44096-0883. Tel.: 440-951-3813.
Web Site: indianmuseumoflakecounty.org
Founded: 1980.
Congressional District: 11
Key Personnel: Dir. & Museum Shop Mgr., Ann L. Dewald; Pres. (V), Douglas R. Divish; Treas., John Brewster.
Personnel Profile: Full-Time Volunteers 1; Part-Time Paid 2; Part-Time Volunteers 21; Interns 2.
Governing Authority: nonprofit organization. Parent Institution: Lake County Chapter of Archaeological Society of Ohio. Tax-exempt: 501(c)(3).
Native American Museum.
Collections: 10,000 B.C.-1650 A.D. pre-contact artifacts of Ohio; 1800 A.D.-present crafts & art of North American Native Americans.
Research Fields: pre-contact Native Americans of northeastern Ohio; Tarahumara, an Huichol of Mexico; The Southwest: (Hopi, Navaho, Apache, Papago); Natives of Alaska; Natives of the Pacific Northwest; Plains Indians; Native Americans of the Eastern Woodlands; Navajo weaving; pictographs & petroglyphs.
Facilities: 900-vol. library pertaining to anthropology, art, history of Native Americans for public use. Books for sale.
Activities: guided tours; lectures; films; organized education programs; docent program.
Publications: newsletter.
Hours & Admission Prices: May-Aug. Mon.-Fri. 10-4, Sat.-Sun. 1-4; Sept.-April Mon.-Fri. 9-4, Sat.-Sun. 1-4. Adults $2, seniors $1.50. Closed major holiday weekends; winter & spring breaks. ♿
Attendance: 3,000 (estimated)
Membership: Regular $20-$29; Contributing $30-$49; Donor $50-$99; Sustainer $100-$149; Patron $150-$249; Benefactor $250-$999; Honors $1,000 & up.

KIRTLAND TEMPLE HISTORIC CENTER, 7809 Joseph St., Willoughby, OH 44094-9255. Tel.: 440-256-1830. Fax: 440-256-1929.
E-mail: info@kirtlandtemple.org
Web Site: www.kirtlandtemple.org
Key Personnel: C.E.O., Barbara B. Walden; Pres., Stephen Veazey.
Personnel Profile: Full-Time Paid 3; Full-Time Volunteers 3; Part-Time Paid 2; Part-Time Volunteers 2; Interns 6.
Governing Authority: Community of Christ. Tax-exempt: 501(c)(3).
Historic Site: 1833, house of worship.
Collections: 1830s tools & furnishings; museum display space with period publications.

Facilities: Visitor Center.
Activities: guided tours; school programs; reserved services.
Publications: Restoration Trail Forum.
Hours & Admission Prices: Jan.-Feb. Sat. 10-4, Sun. 1-4; March-April Mon.-Sat. 10-4, Sun. 1-5; May-Oct. Mon.-Sat. 9-5, Sun. 1-5; Nov.-Dec. Mon.-Sat. 10-4, Sun. 1-4; groups by appointment. Tours: $2. Closed New Year's Day; Easter; Thanksgiving; Christmas Eve & Day.
Attendance: 45,000 (accurate)

Wilmington

CLINTON COUNTY HISTORICAL SOCIETY, (M), 149 E. Locust St., Wilmington, OH 45177-2338. Mailing Address: P.O. Box 529, Wilmington, OH 45177-0529. Tel.: 937-382-4684. Fax: 937-382-5634.
E-mail: cchs@core.com
Web Site: clintoncountyhistory.org
Founded: 1948.
Key Personnel: Dir., Kay Fisher.
Personnel Profile: Full-Time Paid 1; Part-Time Paid 1; Part-Time Volunteers 25.
Governing Authority: private; nonprofit organization. Tax-exempt: 501(c)(3).
Historical Society Museum: housed in an 1835 Greek Revival mansion and Victorian home.
Collections: Quaker heritage & settlement of the county; sculpture; paintings.
Major Exhibits: Play Dates: A Toy Exhibit, 12/10.
Facilities: 700-vol. library. Museum-related items for sale.
Activities: guided tours; lectures; formal education programs.
Publications: newsletter, History Center News.
Hours & Admission Prices: Museum: March-Dec. Wed.-Fri. 1-4. Library: March-Dec. Wed.-Sat. 1-4. Adults $5; members no charge. ♿
Attendance: 750
Membership: Single $20; Family $30; Patron & Business $100; Benefactor $1,000.

Wilmot

THE WILDERNESS CENTER INC., 9877 Alabama Ave., S.W., Wilmot, OH 44689. Mailing Address: P.O. Box 202, Wilmot, OH 44689-0202. Tel.: 330-359-5235. Fax: 330-359-7898.
E-mail: gordon@wildernesscenter.org
Web Site: www.wildernesscenter.org
Founded: 1964.
Congressional District: 16
Key Personnel: Exec. Dir., Gordon T. Maupin; Pres., Daniel Buehler; Dir. Education, Joann L. Ballbach; Naturalist, Kenneth R. Schlegel, Jr.; Naturalist, Carrie Elvey; Naturalist, Lynda A. Price; Dir. Devel., Tamara Seikel; Dir. Land Stewardship, Gary Popotnik; Bookstore & Office Mgr., Rebecca Cyphert; Staff Accountant, Laurie Howard; Auction Coord., Gina Rodi; Custodian, Frederick Heline; Mktg. & Public Rels., Vicki L. Capps.
Personnel Profile: Full-Time Paid 11; Full-Time Volunteers 5; Part-Time Paid 6; Part-Time Volunteers 685; Interns 1.
Governing Authority: board of trustees; nonprofit organization. Tax-exempt: 501(c)(3).
Nature Center & Land Trust.
Collections: fauna; local insects.
Research Fields: bird banding; insects; endangered plants; box turtles.
Facilities: 1,000-acre nature center; seven nature trails; 7.5 acre lake; planetarium; observation tower; picnic area; auditorium; meeting rooms; astronomical observatory.
Activities: guided tours; lectures; films; hobby & natural history workshops; formally organized education programs; interactive exhibits; bird viewing room. Special Interest Clubs: astronomy, birding, backpacking, nature photography, storytellers, woodcarvers, fly fishing; geology, cavers & climbers; botanizers artistic endeavors.
Publications: monthly, Members' Newsletter; quarterly newsletter, Teacher Trails; annual report.
Hours & Admission Prices: Interpretive Building: Tues.-Sat. 9-5, Sun. 1-5. Nature Center: daily dawn-dusk. No charge; donations accepted. ♿
Attendance: 80,000 (accurate)
Membership: Individual $25; Family $35; Supporting $60; Sustaining $90; Fellow $150; Donor & Annual Benefactor $275; Life $1,250; Endowment Benefactor $2,000.

Wooster

THE COLLEGE OF WOOSTER ART MUSEUM, Ebert Art Center, 1220 Beall Ave., Wooster, OH 44691. Tel.: 330-263-2495. Fax: 330-263-2633.
E-mail: kzurko@wooster.edu
Web Site: www.artmuseum.wooster.edu
Founded: 1930.
Congressional District: 16
Key Personnel: Dir., Kitty McManus Zurko; Preparator, Douglas McGlumphy.
Personnel Profile: Full-Time Paid 1; Part-Time Paid 2.
Governing Authority: The College of Wooster. Tax-exempt: 101(A).
College Art Gallery.
Collections: John Taylor Arms Collection of European & American prints; Persian decorative arts; Chinese bronzes; African art; ancient Middle Eastern pottery.
Major Exhibits: World At War (T), 1/12/10-2/10; Andy Warhol: Photographs, 3/23/10-5/10/10; Chinese & Japanese Calligraphy & Painting, 8/29/10-11/20/10.
Research Fields: American, African, Asian & European graphics; decorative arts.
Activities: lectures; films; gallery talks; programs for undergraduate college students; temporary exhibitions; music.
Publications: exhibition brochures & catalogues.
Hours & Admission Prices: Tues.-Fri. 10:30-4:30, Sat.-Sun. 1-5. No charge. ♿
Attendance: 9,500 (accurate)

WAYNE CENTER FOR THE ARTS, 237 S. Walnut St., Wooster, OH 44691-4753. Tel.: 330-264-2787. Fax: 330-264-9314.
E-mail: waynectr@wayneartscenter.org
Web Site: www.wayneartscenter.org
Founded: 1973.
Congressional District: 16
Key Personnel: Exec. Dir., Robb Hyde; Bookkeeper, Marge Yochheim; Education Coord., Liza Zemancik.
Personnel Profile: Full-Time Paid 2; Part-Time Paid 5; Part-Time Volunteers 30; Interns 1.
Governing Authority: Tax-exempt.
Art Center.
Collections: works by regional & national artists; pottery by international potters.
Hours & Admission Prices: Mon. 12-9, Tues.-Thurs. 9-9, Fri. 9-7, Sat. 9-2. No charge; donations accepted.
Membership: Annual $75.

WAYNE COUNTY HISTORICAL SOCIETY, 546 E. Bowman St., Wooster, OH 44691-3110. Tel.: 330-264-8856. Fax: 330-264-8823.
E-mail: host@waynehistorical.org
Web Site: www.waynehistorical.org
Founded: 1954.
Congressional District: 16
Key Personnel: Pres., Charles Kennedy; Sec., Margo Stafford; Treas., Dan Garrison; Office Admin., Susan K. Mykrantz.
Personnel Profile: Part-Time Paid 1; Part-Time Volunteers 100.
Governing Authority: society. Tax-exempt.
General Museum: Housed in the original home of General Reasin Beall built between 1815 & 1817 on a land grant signed by Pres. James Madison.
Collections: earlly lustre ware; pressed glass; china; mounted birds & animals; guns & other militaria; portraits of Wayne County & Wooster citizens; Indian artifacts from Wayne County; period tools, household artifacts, furniture, dolls & toys; fire equipment; transportation; military; farm tools; taxidermy. Historic buildings: General Reasin Beall Homestead; 1873 one-room schoolhouse; Kister Building containing 1880's carpenter; blacksmith; farm; tools; general store including early 1900s furnishings; general mercantile store; ladies dress shop; Carriage House, including original Gerstenslager carriages; Relief Co. No.4 firehouse.
Research Fields: archaeological investigations of local sites.
Facilities: 1,000-vol. documents, letters & manuscripts pertaining to Ohio & Wayne County local history & pioneer families.
Activities: guided tours; formally organized education programs for children; permanent exhibitions; special quarterly exhibits.
Publications: maps, abstracts of court records; quarterly newsletter.
Hours & Admission Prices: Feb.-Oct. Wed.-Sun. 2-4:30; Nov.-Jan. by appointment. Adults $5; members & students no charge. Closed national holidays; Christmas. ♿
Attendance: 10,000 (estimated)
Membership: Seniors 60 & over $15; Individual $20; Family $25; Patron $50; Benefactor $100; Life - Single Payment $350. Business & Corporate Memberships: Silver $100; Gold $250; Platinum $500.

Worthington

OHIO RAILWAY MUSEUM, 990 Proprietors Rd., Worthington, OH 43085. Mailing Address: P.O. Box 777, Worthington, OH 43085-0777. Tel.: 614-885-7345.
E-mail: info@ohiorailwaymuseum.net
Web Site: www.ohiorailwaymuseum.org
Founded: 1945.
Congressional District: 15

Key Personnel: Pres., Bill Wahl; Vice Pres. (V), Jack Hilborn; Treas., Don McKelvey.
Governing Authority: nonprofit organization. Tax-exempt: 501(c)(3).
Transportation Museum.
Collections: historic steam & electric railway equipment operating on 1 mile of track; artifacts; manuscripts; Ohio interurbans; Columbus Streetcar; electric streetcars & interurbans; Pullmans, 1929 The John Greenleaf Whittier; 1925 Time Square; 1928 Williamsport business car; 1920 mail car; 1924 Vulcan steam engine; 1910 Norfolk & Western #578 steam engine; 1918 passenger & baggage cars.
Facilities: library. Museum-related items for sale.
Activities: guided tours; organized education programs for children; permanent exhibitions; electric train, streetcar & interurban rides. Museum Sponsors: State Fair in August; Twilight Trolleys; Old Worthington Market Day; Ghost Train; Santa Trolley.
Publications: newsletter, Rail Fax.
Hours & Admission Prices: May 27-Sept. Sun. 1-5; groups by appointment. Adults $6, seniors 55 & over $5, children 4-12 $4; children 3 & under no charge.
Attendance: 4,000
Membership: Regular $20.

WORTHINGTON HISTORICAL SOCIETY, 50 W. New England Ave., Worthington, OH 43085-3536. Tel.: 614-885-1247. Fax: 614-885-1040.
E-mail: worthhsoc@aol.com
Web Site: www.worthington.org/history
Founded: 1955.
Congressional District: 15
Key Personnel: Pres. Worthington Historical Society (V), Jutta C. Pegues; Cur., Sue Whitaker; Public Rels., Carol Little; Museum Shop Mgr., Gloria Newman; Membership, Henrietta Nichols.
Personnel Profile: Part-Time Paid 4; Part-Time Volunteers 100.
Governing Authority: society; nonprofit organization. Branch Museums: Orange Johnson House, 956 High St., Worthington, OH 43085. Tel.: 614-885-1274; The Doll Museum, 50 W. New England Ave., Worthington 43085. Tax-exempt.
Historic House Museums: 1811-1819, Orange Johnson House & Garden; The Doll Museum, 1845 Classical Revival Manse & Society Headquarters.
Collections: Worthington Indian Mound; 19th & 20th century dolls; lace; early community memorabilia; manuscripts; period clothing.
Facilities: 300-vol. library of books on local history available for inter-library loan by special arrangement. Craft items for sale.
Activities: guided tours; lectures; study clubs; formally organized education programs; docent training; permanent & special exhibitions.
Publications: monthly newsletter, The Intelligencer.
Hours & Admission Prices: Orange Johnson House: April-Dec. Sun. 2-5; other times by appointment. Adults $3, seniors & children $2; members no charge. The Doll Museum: Tues.-Fri. 1-4, Sat. 10-2. Library: 1st & 3rd Wed. 1:30-4. Gift Shop: Tues.-Fri. 1-4, Sat. 10-2. Closed holidays.
Attendance: 3,900 (accurate)
Membership: Senior Citizen $20; Individual & senior couple $25; Family $30; Contributing $50; Patron $100; Golden Patron $200. Business: Pioneer $35; Settler $50; Town Crier $100; Town Marshal $200; Village Founder $500.

Wright-Patterson Air Force Base

* **NATIONAL MUSEUM OF THE UNITED STATES AIR FORCE,** 1100 Spaatz St., Wright-Patterson Air Force Base, OH 45433-7102. Tel.: 937-255-3286. Fax: 937-255-0523.
E-mail: nationalmuseum.usaf@wpafb.af.mil
Web Site: www.nationalmuseum.af.mil
Founded: 1923.
Congressional District: 3
Key Personnel: Dir., Maj. Gen. Charles D. Metcalf, USAF Ret.; Senior Cur., Terry Aitken; Education, Judith Wehn; Public Rels., Diana Bachert; Collection Mgr., Krista Strider; Research/Archives, Wes Henry; Operations, Daniel Dobbyn; Air Force Museum Foundation, Col. Richard Johnson, USAF Ret.; Museum Shop Mgr., Kim Pierre.
Personnel Profile: Full-Time Paid 96; Part-Time Volunteers 450.
Governing Authority: federal. Parent Institution: United States Air Force, The Pentagon, Washington, DC. Tax-exempt.
Military Aviation Museum: located at historic Wright Field, site of early aviation pioneering.
Collections: over 400 aerospace vehicles; 400,000 photos & 8.9 million documents, books, test reports, operational manuals, aircraft drawings & unit histories related to the history of military aviation; video & audio tapes; uniforms; personal military memorabilia; aviation guns & instruments; aircraft squadron insignia; military badges; space hardware & foods; models; WWII Control Tower.
Research Fields: aeronautical technology; military apparel & air force history.
Facilities: 1.2 million sq. ft. of exhibit space on 450 acre campus; outdoor airpark & memorial park; 500-seat auditorium; 500-seat IMAX theater; restaurant. Museum-related items for sale.
Activities: guest lectures; in house & outreach educational programs; school tours for children grades 4-12; self-guided tours; daily heritage tours; limited behind the scenes public tours for adults; special exhibit openings; concerts; flying events.
Publications: brochures; illustrated exhibit guide; quarterly journal, Friends Journal; annual report; e-newsletter; calendar of events.
Hours & Admission Prices: Daily 9-5. Museum: no charge. IMAX Theatre: call for admission prices. Closed New Year's Day; Thanksgiving; Christmas. ♿
Attendance: 1,000,000 (estimated)
Membership: Senior over 65 $28; Friends $32; Family $40; Sustaining $50; Associate $75; Contributing $150; Supporting $500.

Xenia

GREENE COUNTY HISTORICAL SOCIETY, 74 W. Church St., Xenia, OH 45385-2902. Tel.: 937-372-4606. Fax: 372-372-5660 (call first).
E-mail: GCHSXO@sbcglobal.net
Founded: 1929.
Congressional District: 7
Key Personnel: Pres., Ben Thompson; Exec. Dir., Catherine Wilson.
Personnel Profile: Part-Time Paid 2; Part-Time Volunteers 30.
Governing Authority: society. Tax-exempt: 501(c)(3).
Historical Society Museum.
Collections: Cosley coverlets; period furniture; paintings; agricultural implements; dolls. Historic Houses: 1798 Galloway Log House; 1877 Victorian style home; Carriage House Museum: military, farming, railroad, Indian exhibits.
Facilities: Books pertaining to Greene County history for sale.
Activities: guest speakers; special events. Museum Sponsors: Model Railroad workshops; Old Fashioned Days open house; annual tour of private homes.
Publications: monthly newsletter, Our Heritage; books on Greene County History.
Hours & Admission Prices: Tues.-Fri. 9-12 & 1-3:30; call for weekend hours. Suggested Donations: $3 per person; members no charge. ♿
Attendance: 3,000 (estimated)
Membership: Student $5; Senior Citizen Single $10; Regular Single $15; Senior Citizen Double $20; Family $30; Lifetime $250.

Yellow Springs

GLEN HELEN ECOLOGY INSTITUTE TRAILSIDE MUSEUM, 405 Corry St., Yellow Springs, OH 45387-1843. Mailing Address: 1075 State Rt. 343, Yellow Springs, OH 45387. Tel.: 937-767-7648. Fax: 937-767-6655.
E-mail: rjaramillo@antioch-college.edu
Web Site: www.glenhelen.org
Founded: 1951.
Congressional District: 7
Key Personnel: Asst. Dir., Rebecca Jaramillo.
Governing Authority: college. Antioch University. Operated by Glen Helen Ecology Institute. Tax-exempt.
Natural History Museum & Nature Center.
Collections: natural history. Historic Buildings: 1814 Grinnell Mill; covered bridge.
Facilities: 500-vol. library of natural history books available on premises; nature preserve. Publications for sale.
Activities: guided tours; lectures; formally organized education programs for children.
Publications: Guide to Historical Sites in Glen Helen; Map of Glen Helen; quarterly newsletter, In the Glen.
Hours & Admission Prices: Call for hours.
Attendance: 12,000
Membership: Contributing $25; Supporting $40; Sustaining $65; Sponsoring $125; Benefactor $500; Patron & Corporate $1,000.

Youngstown

* **THE ARMS FAMILY MUSEUM OF LOCAL HISTORY, (M),** 648 Wick Ave., Youngstown, OH 44502-1289. Tel.: 330-743-2589. Fax: 330-743-7210.
E-mail: mvhs@mahoninghistory.org
Web Site: www.mahoninghistory.org
Founded: 1961.
Congressional District: 17
Key Personnel: Pres., J. David Sabine; Dir., H. William Lawson; Mgr. Education & External Rels., Leann Rich; Registrar, T. Lea Mollman; Mgr. Collections & Curatorial Svcs., Jessica D. Trickett; Archivist, Pamela Speis; Museum Shop Mgr., Leann Rich.

Personnel Profile: Full-Time Paid 9; Part-Time Paid 17; Part-Time Volunteers 15; Interns 2.
Governing Authority: nonprofit organization; society. Parent Institution: Mahoning Valley Historical Society. Tax-exempt: 501(c)(3) & 509(a)(1).
Local History Museum.
Collections: Arms family house & contents; Native American history; furnishings; costumes; archives; B.F. Wirt Eclectic collection includes books, manuscripts, art works & antiquities from a Youngstown attorney, public official & world traveler of the late 19th & early 20th centuries; business & media archives of the Mahoning Valley collection includes business records, broadcasting equipment & film & videotape library from WKBN, Youngstown's CBS network affiliate & radio & television pioneers.
Major Exhibits: The Mahoning Valley Collects, 11/09-9/10; Holiday in Motion, 12/09-1/10.
Research Fields: local history.
Facilities: local history museum in preserved arts & crafts mansion; archives collections housed in carriage house on site; primary & secondary local history resources especially strong on family history, cultural history, development of built environment, local steel manufacturing material, local newspapers.
Activities: guided tours; programs; slide presentations; lectures; traveling suitcase museums for elementary schools.
Publications: pamphlet, Discover Greystone; quarterly newsletter, Historical Happenings; A Read & Color Book about the Mahoning Valley.
Hours & Admission Prices: Tues.-Sun. 1-5. Adults $4, college students & senior citizens $3, students under 18 $2; discounts for AAM, ICOM; members no charge. Closed national holidays. ♿
Attendance: 15,000 (accurate)
Membership: Student $10; Individual $30; Family $50; Sustaining $75; Preservation Society $100 & up.

* **THE BUTLER INSTITUTE OF AMERICAN ART, (M),** 524 Wick Ave., Youngstown, OH 44502-1286. Tel.: 330-743-1711. Fax: 330-743-9567.
E-mail: info@butlerart.com
Web Site: www.butlerart.com
Founded: 1919.
Congressional District: 19
Key Personnel: Dir., Louis A. Zona; Pres. (V), John MacIntosh; Asst. Dir., M. Susan Carfano; Dir. Education, Carole O'Brien; Business Mgr., Martha Merk; Dir. Information, Kathy Earnhart; Museum Shop Mgr., Renee Sheakoski.
Personnel Profile: Full-Time Paid 20; Part-Time Paid 10; Part-Time Volunteers 150; Interns 10.
Governing Authority: nonprofit. Tax-exempt: 501(c)(3).
American Art Museum.
Collections: American art from Colonial to present times; 5,000 works including major paintings by Copley, Earl, Homer, Eakins, Heade, Henri, Sheeler, Hopper, Koch, Gottleib, Mitchell, Warhol, Nevelson, Rockwell, Rauschenberg & Leslie; Western & Marine collections; survey of American watercolor paintings & works on paper; Americana ceramics, sculpture & contemporary photographs; holograms & other technological work.
Major Exhibits: Jedd Novatt, 1/10-3/10; Donald Woodman, 1/24/10-3/14/10; Jules Olitski: An Inside View (T), 3/21/10-5/16/10; Andy Warhol's Wild Raspberries, 4/18/10-6/27/10; Robert Vonnoh, 5/2/10-6/27/10; Twentieth Century Photography, 9/10-12/10; A Salute to Women: Portrait Painters, 9/12/10-10/10.
Research Fields: American art.
Facilities: library of American art books available on premises; The Beecher Center Wing for Technology Art; electronic archive center. Art publications for sale.
Activities: guided tours; lectures; films; gallery talks; concerts; permanent & temporary exhibitions; children & adult art classes.
Publications: biennial report; annual, National Midyear Show Catalog; catalogues of permanent collection; brochures; postcards; individual exhibition catalogues.
Hours & Admission Prices: Tues. & Thurs.-Sat. 11-4, Wed. 11-8, Sun. 12-4. No charge; donations accepted. Closed New Year's Day; Easter; Independence Day; Thanksgiving; Christmas. ♿
Attendance: 140,000 (estimated)
Membership: Student $10; Individual $35; Family $45; Sustaining $60; Donor $100; Trustees Circle: Sponsor $300; Patron $500; Collector $1,000; Connoisseur $3,000 & up.

CHILDREN'S CENTER FOR SCIENCE & TECHNOLOGY, 139 E. Boardman St., Youngstown, OH 44503-1828. Tel.: 330-744-5914. Fax: 330-746-7806.
E-mail: info@valleykids.org
Web Site: www.valleykids.org
Formerly: Children's Museum of the Valley
Founded: 2001.
Congressional District: 17
Key Personnel: Dir., Suzanne Barbati.
Personnel Profile: Full-Time Paid 4; Part-Time Paid 3; Part-Time Volunteers 20.
Governing Authority: private; nonprofit organization. Tax-exempt: 501(c)(3).
Children's Museum.
Collections: hands-on exhibits.
Facilities: classroom; 10,000 sq. ft. exhibit space; cafeteria. Museum-related items for sale.
Activities: special events; weekly programs; participatory exhibits; storytime programs. Annual Events: Halloween Spooktacular; Spring Fling; CMV Birthday Party.
Publications: quarterly newsletter, Play Matters.
Hours & Admission Prices: Tues.-Fri. 10-4:30, Sat. 12-4:30. Adults $5, senior citizens $4; discounts to groups & ACM reciprocal members; first Wed. of month & children under 3 no charge. Closed New Year's Day; Independence Day; Christmas Eve & Day. ♿
Attendance: 18,000 (estimated)
Membership: Individual $35; Family $50; Grandparent $60; Sponsor $100.

FORD NATURE EDUCATION CENTER, 840 Old Furnace Rd., Youngstown, OH 44511-1470. Mailing Address: Mill Creek MetroParks, P.O. Box 596, Canfield, OH 44406. Tel.: 330-740-7107. Fax: 330-740-7133.
Web Site: www.millcreekmetroparks.com
Founded: 1972.
Congressional District: 17
Key Personnel: Mgr. Interpretive Svcs., Mindy Henning; Asst. Mgr. Interpretive Svcs., Raymond Novotny; Pres., Virginia Daily.
Personnel Profile: Full-Time Paid 3; Part-Time Paid 6.
Governing Authority: Parent Institution: Mill Creek Metropolitan Park District. Tel. 330-702-3000. Tax-exempt: 501(c)(3).
Nature Center: housed in 1912, 13-room stone mansion.
Collections: zoology, botany & geology specimens from Northeast Ohio.
Facilities: 2,000-vol. library pertaining to natural history material available to the public; classroom & meeting room; nature & conservation center; nature trail. Nature book & supplies for sale.
Activities: guided tours; lectures; films; hobby workshops; organized education programs for children and adults; docent program; participatory exhibits; organized education programs for undergraduate or graduate college students affiliated with Youngstown State University. Annual Event: Photography Competition.
Hours & Admission Prices: Daily 9-5. No charge; donations accepted. Closed New Year's; Thanksgiving; Christmas. ♿
Attendance: 20,000 (accurate)

MCDONOUGH MUSEUM OF ART, Youngstown State University, 525 Wick Ave., Youngstown, OH 44555-0001. Tel.: 330-941-1400.
Key Personnel: Dir., Leslie A. Brothers; Asst. Dir., Angela DeLucia; Exhibition Design & Production Mgr., Robyn Maas; Media & Membership Coord., Christy Kamperman
Art Museum.
Collections: student artwork.
Hours & Admission Prices: Tues., Thurs., Fri. & Sat. 11-4, Wed. 11-8. No charge ♿

YOUNGSTOWN HISTORICAL CENTER OF INDUSTRY & LABOR, 151 W. Wood St., Youngstown, OH 44503-1034. Mailing Address: P.O. Box 533, Youngstown, OH 44501-0533. Tel.: 330-743-5934; 800-262-6137.
Key Personnel: Site Mgr., N. Haraburda
History Museum.
Collections: workers' tools & clothing; "last heats", the last batches of steel; photographs.
Hours & Admission Prices: Wed.-Fri. 10-4, Sat.-Sun. 12-4. Adults $7, children 6-12 $3; discount to AAA members, seniors & active military; children 5 & under and Ohio Historical Society members no charge. Closed New Year's Day; Independence Day; Labor Day; Thanksgiving; Christmas. ♿

Zanesville

DR. INCREASE MATHEWS HOUSE, 304 Woodlawn Ave., Zanesville, OH 43701-4940. Mailing Address: 115 Jefferson St., Zanesville, OH 43701-4905. Tel.: 740-454-9500.
Web Site: www.muskinghumhistory.org
Founded: 1970.
Congressional District: 18
Key Personnel: Dir., Jim Geyer; Pres., Bob Jenkins.
Personnel Profile: Part-Time Paid 1; Part-Time Volunteers 20.
Governing Authority: nonprofit organization. Parent Institution: Pioneer & Historical Society of Muskingum County. Tax-exempt.

Historical Society Museum: housed in 1805 Dr. Increase Matthews House.
Collections: material owned by early settlers & local townspeople; costumes; furniture; military; portraits; kitchen implements; art pottery; textiles; primitive paintings.
Research Fields: Muskingum County furniture, history, geography, & archeology.
Facilities: library of local history books, papers & pamphlets available for research by special request. Books & local history items for sale.
Activities: guided tours; lecture series; formally organized education programs for children; temporary exhibitions.
Publications: quarterly, Muskingum Journal; booklets, Muskingum County Courthouse 1877-1977; Dr. Increase Mathews House; Zanesville & Muskingum County Bicentennial Military History; Historic Homes of Zanesville; Muskingum Annuals, Vols. I-V.
Hours & Admission Prices: April-May & Oct. 1st & 3rd Sun. 1-5; June-Sept. Sat.-Sun. 1-4; other times by appointment. Adults $2, students $1; discounts to groups, AAM & ICOM members; members no charge.
Attendance: 534 (estimated)
Membership: Senior Citizen $10; Individual $15; Family $30; Life $300.

THE STONE ACADEMY, 115 Jefferson St., Zanesville, OH 43701. Tel.: 740-454-9500.
Governing Authority: Parent Institution: Pioneer and Historical Society Office.
Historic House Museum: housed in the childhood home of Elizabeth Robins, late 19th century actress, author & activist; built in 1809.
Collections: local history & culture; period documents, clothing, & furnishings; fine art; personal artifacts; photographs.
Facilities: archives.
Hours & Admission Prices: Tues.-Fri. 12-4.

ZANESVILLE MUSEUM OF ART, (M), 620 Military Rd., Zanesville, OH 43701-1533. Tel.: 740-452-0741. Fax: 740-452-0797.
Web Site: www.zanesvillemuseumofart.org
Formerly: Zanesville Art Center
Founded: 1936.
Congressional District: 10
Key Personnel: Dir., Susan Talbot-Stanaway; Pres. (V), Donald Weitmarschen; Preparator, Gary Strawser; Sec., Vanessa Brosie; Education Coord., Steven Dressler; Registrar, Amy Kesting.
Personnel Profile: Full-Time Paid 4; Part-Time Paid 3; Part-Time Volunteers 70.
Governing Authority: nonprofit. Tax-exempt: 501(c)(3).
Art Museum.
Collections: paintings; drawings; prints; photography; sculpture; American, European, Asian, Indian, Pre-Columbian, African Oceanic art; Ohio, national & international ceramics & glass.
Major Exhibits: The Photographs of Jane Reece, 12/12/09-2/6/10; Watercolors from the Permanent Collection, 1/7/10-2/27/10; Paintings & Illustrations by Chris Leeper, 2/14/10-4/17/10; Art Quilts by Susan Nash, 4/24/10-6/19/10; Deco Ceramics Ohio, 5/29/10-8/14/10; National Watercolor Society Annual (T), 6/13/10-8/1/10; The 69th Ohio Show, 8/14/10-10/30/10; Form, Figure, Function: Ohio Pottery (T), 11/6/10-1/8/11.
Research Fields: American paintings & pottery.
Facilities: 6,000-vol. library of art books; reading room; 100-seat auditorium; classrooms.
Activities: guided tours; lectures; gallery talks; workshops; education programs; permanent, temporary & traveling exhibitions.
Publications: quarterly bulletin; brochures.
Hours & Admission Prices: Tues.-Wed. & Fri. 10-5, Thurs. 10-8:30, Sat. 9-5. Adults $4; discount to AAM members; members no charge. Closed holidays. ♿
Attendance: 15,000 (estimated)
Membership: Individual $30; Household $45 & up; Sustaining $75 & up; Fellow $100 & up; Contributing $200 & up; Patron $300 & up; Benefactor $500 & up; Masterpiece Society $1,000 & up.

Zoar

ZOAR STATE MEMORIAL, 198 Main St., Zoar, OH 44697. Mailing Address: P.O. Box 508, Zoar, OH 44697-0508. Tel.: 330-874-4336; 800-874-4336. Fax: 330-874-2936.
Web Site: ohiohistory.org/places/zoar
Founded: 1930.
Congressional District: 18
Personnel Profile: Full-Time Paid 4; Part-Time Paid 12; Part-Time Volunteers 60.
Governing Authority: nonprofit organization. Parent Institution: Ohio Historical Society, 1982 Velma Ave., Columbus, OH 43211. Tax-exempt.
Historic Site: 10 restored buildings of 1817 German village founded by communal religious sect.
Collections: Germanic-American folk arts & crafts; tools; furniture; greenhouse; textiles.
Research Fields: communal societies; German-American studies; religious history; 19th-century agrarian community.
Facilities: meeting room.
Activities: guided tours; demonstrations & interpretive staff.
Publications: book, Zoar: An Ohio Experiment in Communalism.
Hours & Admission Prices: April-May & Sept.-Oct. Sat. 9:30-5, Sun. 12-5; Memorial Day-Labor Day Wed.-Sat. 9:30-5, Sun. & holidays 12-5. April-Oct. groups by appointment. Adults $6, students $2; discount to senior citizens, AAM, AAA & ICOM members; members & Ohio Historical Society members no charge.
Attendance: 17,243 (accurate)
Membership: Student $25; Senior Citizen Individual $55; Annual Individual $60; Senior Citizen Family $70; Annual Family $75.

OKLAHOMA

(201 listings)

Afton

NATIONAL ROD & CUSTOM CAR HALL OF FAME MUSEUM, 55251 E. Hwy. 85A, Afton, OK 74331-2774. Tel.: 918-257-4234 & 8073. Fax: 918-257-8224.
E-mail: dstarbird@wavelinx.net
Web Site: darrylstarbird.com
Founded: 1995.
Automobile Museum.
Collections: over 50 custom built cars.
Hours & Admission Prices: March-Oct. Wed. 11-5; other times by appointment. Adults 13 & over $7, children 8-12 $4.

Aline

SOD HOUSE MUSEUM, State Hwy. 8, N. of Cleo Springs, Aline, OK 73716. Mailing Address: Rte. 3, P.O. Box 28, Aline, OK 73716-0028. Tel.: 580-463-2441.
E-mail: sodhouse@okhistory.org
Web Site: www.okhistory.org
Founded: 1968.
Congressional District: 6
Key Personnel: Historic Properties Mgr., Renee Mitchell; Cur., Jana Brown.
Governing Authority: state. Parent Institution: Oklahoma Historical Society. (See separate listing). Tax-exempt.
Historic House: built 1894, following the opening of the Cherokee Outlet.
Collections: period artifacts from 1889-1918; household & farm equipment; cellar built in 1911; homesteader sod house furnishings; farm equipment.
Facilities: picnic tables.
Activities: monthly public programs; trunk programs for students.
Hours & Admission Prices: Tues.-Sat. 9-5. No charge; donations accepted. Closed legal holidays. ♿
Attendance: 6,500 (accurate)
Membership: Annual $10; Lifetime $200.

Altus

MUSEUM OF THE WESTERN PRAIRIE, 1100 Memorial Dr., Altus, OK 73521-2600. Tel.: 580-482-1044.
E-mail: muswestpr@okhistory.org
Web Site: www.okhistory.org
Founded: 1970.
Congressional District: 4
Key Personnel: Pres. (V), Dennis Vernon; Dir., Bart McClenny; Museum Shop Mgr., Mary Jane Winsett.
Personnel Profile: Full-Time Paid 1; Part-Time Paid 2; Part-Time Volunteers 47.
Governing Authority: state. Parent Institution: Oklahoma Historical Society. (see separate listing). Tax-exempt: 501(c)(3) & 170(b)(1)(A).
General & Historical Society Museum.
Collections: agricultural & ranching tools; fossils; Native American artifacts; local history; archives.
Research Fields: prairie lifestyles; local history.
Facilities: library; theater.
Activities: self-guided tours; guided tours by appointment; permanent & temporary exhibitions.
Hours & Admission Prices: Tues.-Sat. 9-5. No charge; donations accepted. Closed state holidays. ♿
Attendance: 4,037 (accurate)
Membership: Oklahoma Historical Society: Individual $25; Family & Institutional $40; Supporting $75; Life $500; Benefactor $1,000.

Alva

CHEROKEE STRIP MUSEUM, 901 14th St., Alva, OK 73717-2500. Tel.: 580-327-2030.
Founded: 1961.
Congressional District: 6
Key Personnel: C.E.O., Rose Blunk.
Personnel Profile: Part-Time Paid 2; Part-Time Volunteers 15.
Governing Authority: society; nonprofit organization. Tax-exempt.
General Museum.
Collections: costumes; Indian sculptures with bow & headdress; post office; washing machine room; rock & natural science; farm machinery & equipment; guns; prisoner-of-war artifacts; American Indian; nursery; telephones; newspapers; flags of Oklahoma; dolls; dishes; furniture; war uniforms; clocks; spinning wheel; general store & kitchen. Historic Structures: wooden windmills; 1932 schoolhouse.
Research Fields: genealogy & history of the area; schools; churches; professions; founding of neighboring towns.
Facilities: 50-vol. library of Abraham Lincoln historical publications, historical & biographical books on Cherokee Strip, early settler poems & cattle brands available for research on premises.
Activities: guided tours; docent program or council; permanent & temporary exhibitions; special tours for children's classes, scout groups & handicapped persons. Museum Sponsors: Annual Festival of Trees in December.
Publications: brochures.
Hours & Admission Prices: Tues.-Sun. 2-5; groups by appointment. No charge; donations accepted. Closed Easter; Christmas. ♿
Attendance: 3,000 (estimated)
Membership: Annual $15; Lifetime $100.

NORTHWESTERN OKLAHOMA STATE UNIVERSITY MUSEUM, Jesse Dunn Bldg., 709 Oklahoma Blvd., Alva, OK 73717-2749. Tel.: 580-327-1700, ext. 8513 & 8564. Fax: 580-327-8556.
E-mail: sdthompson@nwosu.edu
Web Site: www.nwosu.edu
Founded: 1902.
Congressional District: 6
Key Personnel: Co Dir., Dr. Steven Thompson; Co Dir., Dr. Aaron Place.
Personnel Profile: Part-Time Paid 6; Part-Time Volunteers 2.
Governing Authority: university. Parent Institution: Northwestern Oklahoma State University. Tax-exempt: 170(b)(1)(A).
Natural History Museum.
Collections: mounted bird & mammal specimens; study skins of birds & mammals; pleistocene fossils; Indian artifacts; natural science; paleontology; mineralogy; geology; entomology; ichthyology; vascular plants; historical & archival material about NWOSU.
Facilities: 115,000-vol. library; 220,000 microfiche units; 5,000 microfilm reels.
Activities: occasional guided tours; permanent exhibitions.
Hours & Admission Prices: Call for hours. No charge; donations accepted. Closed college holidays.
Attendance: 600 (accurate)

Anadarko

ANADARKO HERITAGE MUSEUM, 311 E. Main St., Anadarko, OK 73005-3023. Tel.: 405-247-3240.
Formerly: Philomathic Museum
Founded: 1936.
Congressional District: 6
Key Personnel: C.E.O. & Pres. (V), Betty Bell; Cur., Robin Willis.
Personnel Profile: Part-Time Paid 2.
Governing Authority: society. Parent Institution: Philomathic Club. Subsidiary Institution: City of Anadarko. Tax-exempt: 501(c)(3).
General Museum.
Collections: toys & dolls; doctor's office; country store; Indian Agency; Caddo County history; railroad memorabilia; military equipment & uniforms; American Indian dolls, paintings, clothing & artifacts; glassware & period household items; photographs including photographers Horrace Poolaw & Mrs. Annette Ross Hume.
Major Exhibits: Riverside Indian School, 1/10-4/10; Indian Musical Instrument, 1/10-4/10; Ladies Dresses & Undergarments, 1/10-5/10; Indian Artist, 4/10-9/10.
Activities: off-site presentations for schools, clubs, & organizations by request.
Hours & Admission Prices: Tues.-Fri. 10-5, Sat.-Sun. 1-5. No charge; donations accepted. Closed legal holidays. ♿
Attendance: 1,000 (estimated)

DELAWARE NATION MUSEUM, 31064 State Hwy. 281, Anadarko, OK 73005. Tel.: 405-247-2448, ext. 1181. Fax: 405-247-8905.
Web Site: www.delawarenation.com
Formerly: Delaware Tribal Museum
Key Personnel: Pres., Kerry Holton
Native American Museum.
Collections: Native American artifacts; beadwork; clothing.
Facilities: Museum-related items for sale.
Hours & Admission Prices: Mon.-Fri. 9-5. No charge; donations accepted.

INDIAN CITY U.S.A. CULTURAL CENTER, 2 1/2 Miles S. on Hwy. 8, Anadarko, OK 73005. Mailing Address: P.O. Box 626, Anadarko, OK 73005-0626. Tel.: 405-247-5661. Fax: 450-247-2467.
Founded: 1955.
Personnel Profile: Full-Time Paid 12.
Governing Authority: Parent Institution: Kiowa Tribe of Oklahoma.
Natural History Museum: located on 1887 site of Tonkawa Massacre.
Collections: Indian artifacts; pottery; dance costumes; cradles, bags; moccasins; leggings; rugs; Indian dolls; paintings; arrowheads; Indian dressed mannequins; early American Indian articles.
Activities: guided tours; dance recitals.
Publications: brochures.
Hours & Admission Prices: Temporarily closed. ♿
Attendance: 38,471 (estimated)

NATIONAL HALL OF FAME FOR FAMOUS AMERICAN INDIANS, Hwy. 62, E., Anadarko, OK 73005. Mailing Address: P.O. Box 548, Anadarko, OK 73005-0548. Tel.: 405-247-5555 & 3331. Fax: 405-247-5571.
Founded: 1952.
Congressional District: 6
Key Personnel: C.E.O. (V), Joe McBride, Jr.; Sec., Carolyn N. McBride.
Personnel Profile: Part-Time Volunteers 4.
Governing Authority: bd. of directors. Parent Institution: State Historical Society of Oklahoma. Tax-exempt: 501(c)(3).
Native American Museum.
Collections: sculptured bronze busts of famous Native Americans in outdoor landscaped area.
Research Fields: historians.
Facilities: Visitor's Information Center.
Activities: dedication ceremonies for honorees.
Publications: self-tour brochure, The National Hall of Fame for Famous American Indians.
Hours & Admission Prices: Mon.-Sat. 9-5, Sun. 1-5. No charge; donations accepted. Closed New Year's Day; Thanksgiving; Christmas. ♿
Attendance: 20,000 (estimated)
Membership: Annual Individual $10; Family $25; Life $100.

SOUTHERN PLAINS INDIAN MUSEUM, 715 E. Central Blvd., Anadarko, OK 73005-4437. Mailing Address: P.O. Box 749, Hwy. 62, E., Anadarko, OK 73005-0749. Tel.: 405-247-6221. Fax: 405-247-7593.
Founded: 1947.
Congressional District: 4
Key Personnel: Cur., Eva Williams.
Personnel Profile: Full-Time Paid 3.
Governing Authority: federal. Parent Institution: Indian Arts & Crafts Board, Rm. 4004, U.S. Department of the Interior, Washington, DC 20240. Tax-exempt.
Indian Art Museum.
Collections: historic & contemporary arts of the southern Plains Indian peoples; paintings; sculpture.
Research Fields: historic & contemporary Native American art.
Facilities: Paintings, jewelry, suede handbags, beaded jewelry, accessories, books & audio cassettes for sale (operated by Oklahoma Indian Arts & Crafts Coop).
Activities: lectures; gallery talks; permanent & temporary exhibitions.
Publications: exhibition brochures; catalogs.
Hours & Admission Prices: Tues.-Sat. 9-5. No charge. Closed New Year's Day; Thanksgiving; Christmas. ♿
Attendance: 25,000 (estimated)
Membership: Student $2; Indian Artist & Craftsman $5; Individual $6; Family $10; Business $100.

Apache

APACHE HISTORICAL SOCIETY MUSEUM, 101 W. Evans, Apache, OK 73006. Mailing Address: P.O. Box 101, Apache, OK 73006-0101. Tel.: 580-588-3392.
Founded: 1971.
Congressional District: 3
Key Personnel: Chm. & Pres. (V), Danny Swanda; Museum Shop Mgr., Mary Joyce Swanda.
Personnel Profile: Part-Time Paid 1; Part-Time Volunteers 1.

Governing Authority: Tax-exempt.
Historical Society Museum.
Collections: period furnishings; records; photographs; town history; Indian art. Historic Building: 1901 State Bank.
Publications: weekly, historical column.
Hours & Admission Prices: Tues.-Fri. 12-5. No charge; donations accepted. Closed holidays.
Attendance: 400
Membership: Annual $10.

Ardmore

CHARLES B. GODDARD CENTER FOR VISUAL AND PERFORMING ARTS, 401 First Ave., S.W., Ardmore, OK 73401-4725. Mailing Address: P.O. Box 1624, Ardmore, OK 73402-1624. Tel.: 580-226-0909. Fax: 580-226-8891.
Web Site: www.goddardcenter.org
Founded: 1969.
Congressional District: 3
Key Personnel: C.E.O., Bill Rahhal; Dir., Maria Parrott; Treas. (V), Charles Williams; Maintenance & Preparator, Eric Blongren.
Personnel Profile: Full-Time Paid 3; Part-Time Paid 3; Part-Time Volunteers 50.
Governing Authority: nonprofit. Tax-exempt: 501(c)(3).
Center for Visual & Performing Arts.
Collections: contemporary paintings; lithographs; graphics; sculptures; photographs; contemporary printmaking & paintings; Native American & western painting; western & contemporary sculpture.
Facilities: 313-seat theatre; classroom/studio; art studio.
Activities: plays; concerts; dance performances; education programs in art & dance; art classes; temporary & permanent art exhibits; theatre.
Publications: quarterly newsletter.
Hours & Admission Prices: Tues.-Fri. 9-4, Sat. 1-4. No charge. Closed national holidays. ♿
Attendance: 10,000 (estimated)
Membership: Student $15; Single $25; Couple $50; Patron $250; Personal Benefactor $525; Business Benefactor $775.

ELIZA CRUCE HALL DOLL COLLECTION, 320 E. St., N.W., Ardmore, OK 73401-4304. Tel.: 580-223-8290.
Founded: 1971.
Congressional District: 3
Key Personnel: Dir., Daniel R. Gibbs.
Governing Authority: municipal. Parent Institution: The Ardmore Public Library. Tax-exempt: 170(b)(1)(A).
Antique Doll Museum.
Collections: 300 dolls dating back to early 1700s; three original French Court dolls depicting members of the court of Marie Antoinette; English pedlars; French fashion dolls; Lenci; Kruse, Kestner, Ravca, Klumpe, Montanari, Schoenhut & Bye-lo dolls; miniature tea services.
Facilities: 50-vol. library of books on antique dolls, toys & costuming.
Activities: guided tours; lectures.
Hours & Admission Prices: Mon.-Thurs. 10-8, Fri. 10-6, Sat.-Sun. 1-5. No charge; donations accepted. Closed legal holidays. ♿
Attendance: 10,000

GREATER SOUTHWEST HISTORICAL MUSEUM, (M), 35 Sunset Dr., Ardmore, OK 73401-2852. Tel.: 580-226-3857. Fax: 580-226-3357.
Web Site: www.gshm.org
Key Personnel: Dir., Michael W. Anderson; Museum Shop Mgr., Rena Tibbits.
Personnel Profile: Full-Time Paid 3; Part-Time Paid 2.
History Museum.
Collections: South-Central Oklahoma history & culture; Native American artifacts; photographs; military artifacts.
Facilities: research library. Museum-related items for sale.
Activities: educational programs.
Publications: quarterly newsletter.
Hours & Admission Prices: Tues.-Sat. 10-5. No charge; donations accepted. ♿
Attendance: 10,000 (estimated)
Membership: Student $10; Senior $15; Individual $25; Couple $35; Family & Business $50; Sustaining $100; Patron $250; Benefactor $500.

TUCKER TOWER NATURE CENTER, c/o Lake Murray State Park, 18407 Scenic State Hwy. 77, Ardmore, OK 73401-7083. Tel.: 580-223-2109. Fax: 580-223-4052.
Web Site: www.oklahomaparks.com
Founded: 1952.
Congressional District: 3
Key Personnel: Park Naturalist, Mark Teders.
Personnel Profile: Full-Time Paid 1; Part-Time Paid 3; Part-Time Volunteers 10.
Governing Authority: state. Parent Institution: Oklahoma Tourism & Recreation. Subsidiary Institution: Lake Murray State Park. Tax-exempt: 170(b)(1)(A).
Park Museum: built 1933-35 by WPA & CCC for a Governor's Retreat.
Collections: fossils; minerals; meteorite; nature exhibits.
Research Fields: pertaining to collection.
Activities: guided tours; lectures; audiovisual programs; outdoor activities; permanent & temporary exhibitions.
Hours & Admission Prices: Feb.-May & Sept.-Nov. Wed.-Sun. 9-5; Memorial Day-Labor Day daily 9-7. Admission $.50.
Attendance: 30,000 (accurate)

Atoka

CONFEDERATE MEMORIAL MUSEUM, US Hwy. 69 N., Atoka, OK 74525. Mailing Address: P.O. Box 245, Atoka, OK 74525-0245. Tel.: 580-889-7192.
E-mail: atokamuseum@yahoo.com
Founded: 1986.
Key Personnel: Site Mgr., Gwen Walker; Museum Dir., Cindy Wallis; Pres. (V), Paula Hardman.
Personnel Profile: Full-Time Paid 1; Full-Time Volunteers 1; Part-Time Volunteers 1.
Governing Authority: Parent Institution: Atoka County Historical Society. Tax-exempt.
Military Museum.
Collections: military artifacts; personal artifacts; uniforms; photographs; U.S. & Confederate Battle Flags.
Facilities: Museum-related items for sale.
Activities: reenactments. Annual Event: Living History Presentations.
Publications: quarterly newsletter; Tales of Atoka County Heritage; Civil War in the Western Choctaw Nation; Old Boggy Depot, 1838-1883; Father Murrow, The Life of J.S. Murrow; Confederate Volunteers of Atoka County; Down the Texas Road.
Hours & Admission Prices: Mon.-Fri. 9-4. No charge; donations accepted. Closed national holidays. ♿
Attendance: 9,000 (estimated)
Membership: Individual $10; Family $15.

Barnsdall

BIGHEART MUSEUM, 616 W. Main, Barnsdall, OK 74002. Mailing Address: P.O. Box 475, Barnsdall, OK 74002-0475. Tel.: 918-847-2397.
Key Personnel: Cur., Joe Williams; Cur., Faye Wickware
History Museum: named after Osage Chief James Bigheart.
Collections: Native American history & culture; town history.
Hours & Admission Prices: Tues.-Fri. 12-4, Sat. 9-1. No charge.

Bartlesville

BARTLESVILLE AREA HISTORY MUSEUM, 401 S. Johnstone Ave., City Bldg., 5th Fl., Bartlesville, OK 74003-6619. Tel.: 918-338-4290. Fax: 918-338-4264.
E-mail: history@cityofbartlesville.org
Web Site: www.bartlesvillehistorycom
Founded: 1964.
Congressional District: 5
Key Personnel: Dir., Joan Singleton; Registrar, Matthew Clapper; Volunteer Coord. & Public Rels., Jo Crabtree; Education Coord., Kay Little.
Personnel Profile: Full-Time Paid 1; Part-Time Volunteers 60.
Governing Authority: municipal government. Tax-exempt: 501(c)(3).
History Museum.
Collections: early settlers & Native Indian tribes living in the western frontier from late 1800s to present with major focus on early 1900s.
Research Fields: commerce & trade; early city residents.
Facilities: 8,000 sq. ft. exhibit space.
Activities: guided tours; lectures; traveling exhibitions; school presentations; civic organization speaker.
Hours & Admission Prices: Tues.-Sat. 10-4. No charge; donations accepted. Closed major holidays. ♿
Attendance: 8,000 (estimated)

FRANK PHILLIPS HOME, 1107 S. Cherokee, Bartlesville, OK 74003-5027. Tel.: 918-336-2491. Fax: 918-336-3529.
E-mail: jgoss@okhistory.org
Web Site: www.frankphillipshome.org
Founded: 1973.
Congressional District: 2
Key Personnel: Dir. & Cur., Jim L. Goss.

Personnel Profile: Full-Time Paid 2; Part-Time Paid 4; Part-Time Volunteers 25.
Governing Authority: state. Parent Institution: Oklahoma Historical Society. (See separate listing). Tax-exempt.
Historic House: 1909 Frank Phillips home.
Collections: 1930s period furniture.
Research Fields: Phillips family history; history of F. Phillips, founder of Phillips Petroleum Co.; Oklahoma oil industry.
Facilities: 2,000-vol. library of books.
Activities: guided tours; arts festivals; temporary & permanent exhibitions.
Hours & Admission Prices: Wed.-Sat. 10-5, 2nd Sun. 1-5; final tour 4; other times by appointment. Requested Donation: $3. Closed major holidays. ♿
Attendance: 6,591 (accurate)
Membership: Friend $33-$65; '66er $66-$165; Roustabout $166-$265; Driller $266-$365; Wildcatter $366-$665; Gusher $666-$1,065; Oil Baron/Baroness $1,066 & up.

PHILLIPS PETROLEUM COMPANY MUSEUM, 410 Keeler, Bartlesville, OK 74004. Tel.: 918-661-8687.
E-mail: lorrie.l.rockman@conocophillips.com
Web Site: www.phillips66museum.com
Key Personnel: Dir., Lorrie Rockman
History and Technology Museum.
Collections: artifacts & memorabilia pertaining to the Phillips Petroleum Company.
Hours & Admission Prices: Mon.-Sat. 10-4. No charge. Closed holidays.

PRICE TOWER ARTS CENTER, (M), 510 S. Dewey, Bartlesville, OK 74003-3560. Mailing Address: P.O. Box 2464, Bartlesville, OK 74005-2464. Tel.: 918-336-4949. Fax: 918-336-7117.
E-mail: info@pricetower.org
Web Site: www.pricetower.org
Founded: 1985.
Congressional District: 5
Key Personnel: Exec. Dir., Timothy Boruff; Cur. Collections & Exhibitions, Scott Perkins; Docent Coord., Cynthia Naylor; Dir. Operations, Laura Riley; Dir. Mktg. & Public Rels., Debra Woodall; Mgr. Retail Operations, Christine Staton; Chm. (V), C.J. Silas; Pres. (V), Robbie A. Morris; Coord. Devel., Amanda Herwig.
Personnel Profile: Full-Time Paid 16; Part-Time Paid 2; Part-Time Volunteers 40; Interns 2.
Governing Authority: nonprofit organization. Subsidiary Institution: Inn at Price Tower, Inc. Tax-exempt: 501(c)(3).
Art, Architecture & Design Museum: housed in Price Tower, designed by Frank Lloyd Wright.
Collections: Frank Lloyd Wright, Bruce Goff, Dennis Oppenheim, & Karim Rashid; art, architectural & design objects of the 20th & 21st centuries.
Major Exhibits: The Film Costumes of Edith Head, 1/10-5/10; Fellowship: 75 Years of Box Projects (T), 5/10-9/10; William Schickel: Spirit Manifest (T), 10/10-12/10.
Research Fields: permanent collection; 20th-century & contemporary art, architecture and design.
Facilities: library; 7,000 sq. ft. exhibit space; restaurant; rental facilities. Museum-related items for sale.
Activities: guided tours; lectures; docent program; traveling & permanent exhibitions.
Publications: newsletter, The View.
Hours & Admission Prices: Gallery: Tues.-Sat. 10-5, Sun. 12-5. Adults $4, seniors $3; discounts to AAM, ICOM, NARM members, & Frank Lloyd Wright public sites; members and students 16 & under no charge. Tower Tours: Tues.-Sat. 11 & 2, Sun. 2; reservations recommended. Tours: adults $10, seniors $8, students $5. Closed New Year's Day; Thanksgiving; Christmas. ♿
Attendance: 25,000 (accurate)
Membership: Artist, Educator & Student $30; Personal $40; Family $66; Contributing $100; Supporter $250; Associate $1,000. Giving Societies: Director's Circle $2,500; Chairman's Council $5,000.

WOOLAROC MUSEUM, (M), 1925 Woolaroc Ranch Rd., Bartlesville, OK 74003-7171. Tel.: 918-336-0307, ext. 10; 888-WOOLAROC. Fax: 918-336-0084.
E-mail: lstone@woolaroc.org
Web Site: www.woolaroc.org
Founded: 1929.
Congressional District: 5
Key Personnel: Dir., Kenneth Meek; C.E.O., Bob Fraser; Cur. Art, Linda Stone; Bldg. Supt., Tim Sydebotham; Museum Shop Mgr., Beth Greene.
Personnel Profile: Full-Time Paid 5; Part-Time Paid 1; Part-Time Volunteers 70.
Governing Authority: nonprofit organization. Parent Institution: The Frank Phillips Foundation, Inc., Woolaroc Ranch, P.O. Box 1647, Bartlesville, OK 74005. Tax-exempt.
Art & History Museum.
Collections: Indian artifacts; paintings; sculpture; ethnology; archaeology; anthropology; guns.
Facilities: historic log lodge; nature trails; snack bar. Books, reproductions & Indian handicrafts for sale.
Activities: docent program or council; permanent exhibitions; school loan service of slides & film about Woolaroc; provides color transparencies for educational purposes.
Publications: guidebook, Woolaroc; coffee table book, Woolaroc.
Hours & Admission Prices: Memorial Day to Labor Day Tues.-Sun. 10-5; Sept.-May Wed.-Sun. 10-5. Adults 12-64 $8, senior citizens $6; discounts to AAM members, special needs groups & organized school groups; members & children under 12 no charge. Closed Thanksgiving; Christmas. ♿
Attendance: 100,000 (accurate)
Membership: Partner $100; Associate Sponsor $250; Sponsor $500; Sustaining $1,000; Benefactor $2,500; Patron $5,000; Grand Patron $10,000 & up.

Bixby

BIXBY HISTORICAL SOCIETY MUSEUM, 24 E. McKennon Ave., Bixby, OK 74008-4332. Mailing Address: P.O. Box 1046, Bixby, OK 74008-1046. Tel.: 918-366-1200.
E-mail: bixby.okhs@cox.net
Web Site: www.rootsweb.ancestry.com/~okbhs/index.html
Historical Society Museum.
Collections: artifacts & memorabilia pertaining to the Bixby area.
Hours & Admission Prices: Wed. & 1st Sat. of each month 11-2.

Blackwell

TOP OF OKLAHOMA HISTORICAL MUSEUM, 303 S. Main St., Blackwell, OK 74631-3347. Tel.: 580-363-0209.
Founded: 1972.
Congressional District: 6
Key Personnel: Dir., Louise Akers; Pres., Pam Campbell; Sec., Fredda Ganer; Gift Shop Mgr., Eloise Reser.
Personnel Profile: Part-Time Paid 1; Part-Time Volunteers 100.
Governing Authority: society. Tax-exempt.
Local History Museum: housed in c.1912 Electric Park Pavilion.
Collections: personal artifacts; period pioneer equipment & house furnishings; local school history of Maroon Spirit; church; military artifacts; industrial exhibits; historical documents; period photographs; articulture; early 1900s bedroom, parlor & kitchen; audiovisual room; seminar room; military room; 1893 Cherokee outlet land run to 1920; period school artifacts; Indian artifacts; music room.
Facilities: library of land records & historical documents; club room.
Activities: lectures; films; traveling exhibitions.
Publications: quarterly newsletter.
Hours & Admission Prices: Mon.-Sat. 10-4, Sun. 1-4. No charge; donations accepted. Closed major holidays. ♿
Attendance: 3,000 (estimated)
Membership: Children $1; Adults $5; Lifetime $100.

Boley

BOLEY HISTORICAL MUSEUM, 10 W. Grant St., Boley, OK 74829. Mailing Address: P.O. Box 158, Boley, OK 74829-0158. Tel.: 918-667-9790.
History Museum.
Collections: local history & culture.
Hours & Admission Prices: By appointment.

Bristow

BRISTOW HISTORICAL MUSEUM, 1 Railroad Place, Bristow, OK 74010-3040. Mailing Address: P.O. Box 127, Bristow, OK 74010-0127. Tel.: 918-367-5151.
Web Site: www.visitbristowok.com/museums.htm
History Museum: housed in 1923 restored depot.
Collections: local history & culture; railroad memorabilia.
Hours & Admission Prices: Mon.-Fri. 9-4.

Broken Bow

OKLAHOMA FOREST HERITAGE CENTER, (M), Beavers Bend Resort Park, US-259A, Broken Bow, OK 74728. Mailing Address: P.O. Box 157, Broken Bow, OK 74728-0157. Tel.: 580-494-6497. Fax: 580-494-6689.
E-mail: fhc@beaversbend.com
Web Site: www.beaversbend.com
Founded: 1976.
Congressional District: 2
Key Personnel: Dir., Doug Zook; Museum Shop Mgr., Vicki Taylor.
Personnel Profile: Full-Time Paid 2.
Governing Authority: state.
Forestry Museum.
Collections: historical documents; forestry tools; wood art; homestead memorabilia; historic photo murals; papermaking; 1940s lumbering; dioramas.
Major Exhibits: Best of Texoma Woodcarver, 3/7/10-5/2/10; Masters at Work, 9/10/10-10/17/10.
Activities: formal education programs.
Publications: newsletter, Forest Heritage; book, Traveling Timber Towns; Civilian Conservation Corps of McCurtain County.
Hours & Admission Prices: Daily 8-8. No charge; donations accepted. ♿
Attendance: 150,000 (estimated)
Membership: Forest Friend $25; Forest Patron $100; Forest Benefactor $500.

Cache

QUANAH PARKER STAR HOUSE/EAGLE PARK GHOST TOWN, Rte. 2 (SH-115 at US-62), Cache, OK 73527. Mailing Address: 810 N. 8th St., Cache, OK 73527-9630. Tel.: 580-429-3420.
Key Personnel: Mgr., Kathy Threadwell; Mgr., Wayne Gipson.
Governing Authority: Parent Institution: Trading Post, Inc.
History Museum.
Collections: period furnishings. Historic Buildings: 1884 home of Comanche Chief Quanah Parker; 1869 log building; Saddle Mountain Indian Baptist Church.
Hours & Admission Prices: By appointment only.

Carnegie

KIOWA CULTURE PRESERVATION AUTHORITY, Hwy. 9 W., Carnegie, OK 73015. Mailing Address: P.O. Box 885, Carnegie, OK 73015-0885. Tel.: 580-654-2300, ext. 370.
Formerly: Kiowa Tribe Museum and Resource Center
Key Personnel: Chm. (V), David Sullivan; Sec. & Treas., Tommie Louise Doyebi.
Personnel Profile: Part-Time Volunteers 2.
Governing Authority: Parent Institution: Kiowa Tribe of Oklahoma. Tax-exempt.
American Indian Museum.
Collections: Kiowa art, language & cultural heritage; paintings; native crafts; Kiowa Sundance teepee; warriors memorial.
Hours & Admission Prices: Mon.-Fri. 8-4:30. No charge; donations accepted. ♿
Attendance: 1,500 (accurate)
Membership: Sponsor $5,000; Associate $1,000; Friend $2,500.

Catoosa

ARKANSAS RIVER HISTORICAL SOCIETY MUSEUM, 5350 Cimarron Rd., Catoosa, OK 74015-3027. Tel.: 918-266-2291. Fax: 918-226-7678.
Historical Society Museum.
Collections: area navigation system history; photographs; waterway memorabilia; Native American artifacts; Lock and Dam motorized model.
Hours & Admission Prices: Mon.-Fri. 8-4:30. No charge; donations accepted.

Chandler

LINCOLN COUNTY HISTORICAL SOCIETY AND MUSEUM OF PIONEER HISTORY, 717-719 Manvel Ave., Chandler, OK 74834-2842. Tel.: 405-258-2425. Fax: 405-258-2809.
E-mail: lincolncountyhs@sbcglobal.net
Web Site: pioneermuseumolh.org
Founded: 1954.
Congressional District: 6
Key Personnel: Chm. (V), Sandra Bailey; Pres. (V), Virginia Frazier; Dir., Amanda Cagle; Museum Shop Mgr., Tom Feherenbach.
Personnel Profile: Full-Time Paid 1; Part-Time Paid 1; Part-Time Volunteers 7.
Governing Authority: society. Tax-exempt: 501(c)(3).
Local History Museum.
Collections: local artifacts, relics & history of pioneer families in 1897 building; cemetery records; county census on microfilm; land record; county papers on microfilm; family files; old telephone books; school yearbooks; manuscripts; memorabilia of Sheriff Bill Tilghman, the last of the frontier Marshalls & Times man, Benny Kent, frontier movie news photographer; hand operated printing press; military artifacts; mural depicting growth in Lincoln County; doctor's office; school room.
Research Fields: genealogy.
Facilities: microfilm & microfilm reader & printer for county newspapers; auditorium; fiche reader.
Activities: guided tours; lectures; permanent & temporary exhibitions.
Publications: quarterly newsletter; booklet, History of Lincoln County.
Hours & Admission Prices: Tues.-Sat. 10-4. No charge. ♿
Attendance: 3,954 (accurate)
Membership: Individual $15; Family $25; Patron $50; Sustaining & Corporate $100.

Claremore

J.M. DAVIS ARMS & HISTORICAL MUSEUM, 333 N. Lynn Riggs Blvd., Claremore, OK 74017-6817. Mailing Address: P.O. Box 966, Claremore, OK 74018-0966. Tel.: 918-341-5707. Fax: 918-341-5771.
E-mail: rohrgary@sbcglobal.net
Web Site: www.thegunmuseum.com
Founded: 1965.
Congressional District: 2
Key Personnel: Exec. Dir., Gary Rohr; Cur., Jason Schubert; Chm. (V), William Higgins; Tourism Coord., Kimberly Thompson; Gift Shop, David Cuttler.
Personnel Profile: Full-Time Paid 5; Part-Time Paid 5.
Governing Authority: state. Parent Institution: State of Oklahoma. Tax-exempt: 170(b)(1)(A).
Firearms & Historical Museum.
Collections: 35,000 artifacts; 13,000 firearms; western memorabilia; Native American artifacts; statuaries; knives and swords; World War I posters; music boxes from 1880's; steins from around the world; replica 1800's gunsmith shop & gun store.
Research Fields: firearms; edged weapons; steins.
Facilities: 2,050-vol. library of research books available for use on premises or removed by special permission; reception room. Indian-made items, books & other museum-related items for sale.
Activities: guided tours; lectures; special events. Children's Museum: teaching gun safety; classic western movies; arcade.
Publications: brochures & museum legends.
Hours & Admission Prices: Mon.-Sat. 8:30-5, Sun. 10-5. No charge; donations requested. Closed Thanksgiving; Christmas. ♿

WILL ROGERS MEMORIAL MUSEUM, 1720 W. Will Rogers Blvd., Claremore, OK 74017-3208. Mailing Address: P.O. Box 157, Claremore, OK 74018-0157. Tel.: 918-341-0719. Fax: 918-343-8119.
E-mail: wrinfo@willrogers.org
Web Site: www.willrogers.org
Founded: 1938.
Congressional District: 2
Key Personnel: Dir., Steven K. Gragert; Museum Shop Mgr., Julie Luna.
Personnel Profile: Full-Time Paid 7; Part-Time Paid 9; Part-Time Volunteers 17; Interns 2.
Governing Authority: state. Parent Institution: Will Rogers Memorial Commission. Subsidiary Institution: Will Rogers Birthplace. Tax-exempt: 170(b)(1)(A).
History Museum.
Collections: statue of Will Rogers by Jo Davidson; personal items; documents; saddle collection; dioramas; archives; sculpture; history; manuscripts; paintings by Charles Banks Wilson, Torres Rojas, Count Tambourini & Wayne Cooper; Will Rogers films.
Research Fields: life & career of Will Rogers; Will Rogers' genealogy.
Facilities: 2,500-vol. library of books, films, manuscripts available for research by appointment only; 175-seat theater. Copies of Will Rogers' writing & other museum-related items for sale.
Activities: guided tours; lectures; films; permanent exhibitions; gallery talks by appointment.
Publications: booklet, Will Rogers Memorial Booklet; copies of all Will Rogers' writings; books, Will Rogers & Wiley Post in Alaska; Radio Broadcasts of Will Rogers; There's Not a Bathing Suit in Russia; Ether and Me; Never Met a Man I Didn't Like; The Life and Writings of Will Rogers; Will Rogers at the Ziegfeld Follies; the Genealogy of Will Rogers; The Papers of Will Rogers.
Hours & Admission Prices: Daily 8-5. No charge; donations accepted. ♿
Attendance: 117,082 (accurate)
Membership: Student $20; Senior $25; Individual $30; Family & Senior Couple $45; Roper $100; Performer $250; Communicator $500; Ambassador $750; Will's Lariat of Friends $1,000.

Clinton

MOHAWK LODGE INDIAN STORE, 22702 Rte. 66 N., Clinton, OK 73601-7526. Tel.: 580-323-2360.
Key Personnel: Owner, Pat Henry
American Indian Museum: trading post opened in 1892.
Collections: Plains & western tribe history; 1890s Native American artifacts; Indian art & crafts supplies.
Hours & Admission Prices: Mon.-Sat. 9-5. No charge.

OKLAHOMA ROUTE 66 MUSEUM, 2229 W. Gary Blvd., Clinton, OK 73601-5305. Tel.: 580-323-7866. Fax: 580-323-2870.
Web Site: www.route66.org
Founded: 1967.
Congressional District: 6
Key Personnel: C.E.O., Bob Blackburn; Dir., Pat Smith; Cur., Andy Watson.
Personnel Profile: Full-Time Paid 4; Part-Time Paid 2; Part-Time Volunteers 20.
Governing Authority: Parent Institution: Oklahoma Historical Society. Tax-exempt.
History Museum.
Collections: historical artifacts.
Research Fields: history of Rte. 66 in Oklahoma.
Facilities: library & archives; park with picnic facilities; meeting room. Museum-related items for sale.
Activities: permanent & temporary exhibitions.
Hours & Admission Prices: Mon.-Sat. 9-5, Sun. 1-5. Adults $3, senior citizens $2.50, students 6-18 $1. ♿
Attendance: 34,000 (accurate)
Membership: Friends of Oklahoma Rte. 66 Museum: Individual $15; Family $25; Student 18 & under, Seniors 55 & over $10; Organizations & Clubs $50; Corporate $100.

Collinsville

COLLINSVILLE DEPOT MUSEUM, 115 S. 10th St., Collinsville, OK 74021-3124. Tel.: 918-371-3540.
Founded: 1975.
Congressional District: 1
Key Personnel: Pres. Historical Society, William Terrill Thomas.
Governing Authority: nonprofit organization. Collinsville Historical Society. Tax-exempt.
Antiques Museum: housed in 90-year-old depot.
Collections: early 1800 living room & kitchen; local & railroad artifacts; World War I & II uniforms, photos; caboose; memorial brick sidewalk; time capsule in burial vault.
Activities: guided tours; arts festivals; permanent exhibitions.
Hours & Admission Prices: by appointment only. No charge; donations accepted. ♿
Membership: $15 per person or family; Life $100.

NEWSPAPER MUSEUM, 1110 W. Main St., Collinsville, OK 74021-3113. Tel.: 918-371-1901.
Web Site: www.cvilleok.com/museum.html
History Museum.
Collections: artifacts & memorabilia pertaining to The Collinsville News.
Hours & Admission Prices: By appointment. Tours: adults $1.

Coweta

MISSION BELL MUSEUM, 204 S. Bristow Ave., Coweta, OK 74429-2301. Mailing Address: P.O. Box 850, Coweta, OK 74429-0850. Tel.: 918-486-2189. Fax: 918-486-2513.
Founded: 1977.
Congressional District: 2
Personnel Profile: Part-Time Volunteers 1.
Governing Authority: nonprofit organization. Tax-exempt.
Historical Society Museum: housed in a former Presbyterian Church; built in 1907.
Collections: local history & culture; photographs; period furnishings.
Activities: guided tours.
Hours & Admission Prices: Tues. & Thurs. open four hours & by appointment only. No charge; donations accepted.
Attendance: 200 (estimated)
Membership: Historical Society $4.

Cushing

CIMARRON VALLEY RAILROAD MUSEUM, South Kings Hwy., Cushing, OK 74023. Mailing Address: P.O. Box 844, Cushing, OK 74023-0844. Tel.: 918-225-3936.
Founded: 1970.
Congressional District: 4
Key Personnel: Cur. & Owner, Eric Miller; Chm. (V), Lawrence Gibbs John Kirk Garry Smith Woodrow Morehouse Dora Clayton.
Personnel Profile: Part-Time Volunteers 2.
Governing Authority: private; nonprofit organization.
Transportation Museum.
Collections: railroad artifacts: lanterns, china, silver, tools, books, furniture, signals, station items; 1917 oil tank car; 1897 box car; diesel switch locomotive.
Facilities: 250-vol. library of railroad books; 3,200 sq. ft. exhibit space.
Activities: group and Individual tours.
Hours & Admission Prices: By appointment only. No charge; donations accepted. ♿
Attendance: 240 (estimated)

Dewey

DEWEY HOTEL MUSEUM, 801 N. Delaware, Dewey, OK 74029-1609. Mailing Address: P.O. Box 255, Bartlesville, OK 74005-0255. Tel.: 918-534-0215.
Founded: 1899.
Congressional District: 2
Key Personnel: Pres. (V), Gary Mackey.
Personnel Profile: Full-Time Paid 1; Part-Time Paid 1; Part-Time Volunteers 12; Interns 5.
Governing Authority: nonprofit; society. Parent Institution: Washington County Historical Society, Inc.
Historic Building: 1899 Victorian-style wood frame hotel built for Jacob H. Bartles.
Collections: furniture & furnishings from 1890-1910; photographs from 1880-1930; Delaware, Cherokee & Osage Indian artifacts; white furniture & furnishings; western articles including saddles, chaps, & spurs.
Research Fields: period clothing, furniture & furnishing.
Activities: guided tours; lectures; meeting room.
Publications: newsletter.
Hours & Admission Prices: April-Nov. daily 10-4, Sun. 1-4. Adults $1; members & children under 13 with an adult no charge. Closed holidays.
Attendance: 6,000 (accurate)
Membership: Annual $10; Life $250.

TOM MIX MUSEUM, 721 N. Delaware, Dewey, OK 74029-2307. Mailing Address: P.O. Box 190, Dewey, OK 74029-0190. Tel.: 918-534-1555.
Founded: 1968.
Congressional District: 2
Key Personnel: Museum Shop Mgr., Peggy Berryhill; Museum Shop Mgr., Iris Myers.
Personnel Profile: Part-Time Paid 2.
Governing Authority: state. Parent Institution: Oklahoma Historical Society (see separate listing). Tax-exempt.
History Museum.
Collections: personal belongings of silent movie star, Tom Mix; his career & horse including clothing, saddles, & guns.
Research Fields: life of Tom Mix.
Facilities: small movie theater.
Activities: tours; permanent exhibitions; Tom Mix films; cowboy program; scavenger hunts. Museum Sponsors: Annual Festival.
Hours & Admission Prices: Feb. Sat.-Sun.; March-Dec. Tues.-Sat. 10-4:30, Sun. 1-4:30. Suggested Donation: adults $2, children $.50. Closed legal holidays. ♿
Attendance: 5,500 (estimated)
Membership: Individual $25; Family & Institutional $40; Supporting $75; Life $500; Benefactor $1,000.

Drumright

DRUMRIGHT COMMUNITY HISTORICAL MUSEUM, 301 E. Broadway, Drumright, OK 74030-3802. Mailing Address: 301 E. Broadway, Drumright, OK 74030-3805. Tel.: 918-352-3002.
Founded: 1969.
History Museum: housed in a 1916 Santa Fe Depot. Listed on the National Register of Historic Places.
Collections: local history; oil industry; equipment; photographs; period artifacts.
Hours & Admission Prices: Wed.-Fri. 12-4, Sat. 9-5; groups by appointment. No charge.

Attendance: 1,000
Membership: Member $10; Lifetime $500; Corporate Sponsor $250.

Duncan

CHISHOLM TRAIL HERITAGE CENTER, 1000 N. Chisholm Trail Pkwy., Duncan, OK 73533-1539. Tel.: 580-252-6692 & 6563. Fax: 580-252-6567.
E-mail: info@onthechisholmtrail.com
Web Site: www.onthechisholmtrail.com
Formerly: On The Chisholm Trail Statue & Museum
Founded: 1998.
Congressional District: 4
Key Personnel: Exec. Dir., Bill Benson; Bd. Pres., Marilyn Hugon; Museum Shop Mgr., Syvonna Davis.
Personnel Profile: Full-Time Paid 3; Part-Time Paid 14; Part-Time Volunteers 1.
Governing Authority: private; nonprofit organization. Parent Institution: On the Chisholm Trail Association. Tax-exempt: 501(c)(3).
History Museum.
Collections: hands-on exhibits; cowboy, cavalry & Native American clothing & personal artifacts; photographs; artifacts & memorabilia of the Chisholm & other cattle trails; sculptures including a full-scale bronze cattle drive scene.
Facilities: 3,000 sq. ft. exhibit space; 45-seat theater; Statuary Park. Museum-related items for sale.
Activities: films; guided tours; lectures; loan exhibitions. Annual Event: Chuckwagon Cooking Contest and Festival.
Hours & Admission Prices: Mon.-Sat. 10-5, Sun. 1-5. Adults $6, seniors 55 & over $5, youth 5-17 $4; discount to groups. Closed New Year's Day; Easter; Thanksgiving; Christmas. ♿
Attendance: 20,000 (estimated)
Membership: Individual $30; Family $50; Family & Friends $100; Sustaining $250; Patron $500; Corporate $500 & up; Benefactor $1,000.

STEPHENS COUNTY HISTORICAL SOCIETY AND MUSEUM, Hwy. 81 & Beech, Fuqua Park, Duncan, OK 73533. Mailing Address: P.O. Box 1294, Duncan, OK 73534-1294. Tel.: 580-252-0717; 800-782-7167. Fax: 580-251-3195.
Founded: 1971.
Congressional District: 3
Key Personnel: C.E.O., John Jennings; Chm. & Asst. Dir. (V), Vickie Zimmerman; Dir., Pee Wee Cary; Assoc. Dir., Louise Elliott; Assoc. Dir., Marge Rigdon; Assoc. Dir., Sharleen Johns; Museum Shop Mgr., Patty Woolf.
Personnel Profile: Full-Time Paid 1; Part-Time Volunteers 7.
Governing Authority: municipal & county. Tax-exempt: 501(c)(3) & 170(b).
History Museum.
Collections: anthropology; archaeology; paintings; sculpture; graphics; decorative art; costumes; ethnology; geology; American Indian artifacts; mineralogy; numismatics; panorama of the oil industry depicting exploration, drilling, completion & refining of oil; manuscript collection; dioramas, 3 dimensional models of research & development 1920-1980; philatelic; technical; transportation; gems & lapidary.
Research Fields: oil industry, Halliburton Services; Sun Petroleum; Mack Oil Co.
Facilities: library of material on Oklahoma history; genealogical research; Halliburton Cementers available on premises only.
Activities: guided tours; lectures; films; gallery talks; custom hand quilting by special order; arts festivals; study clubs; formally organized education programs for adults, children, undergraduate & graduate students; inter-museum, permanent & temporary exhibitions; archives of pioneer historical research.
Publications: Pictorial history of Stephens County.
Hours & Admission Prices: Tues. & Thurs.-Sat. 1-5. No charge; donations accepted. Closed New Year's Eve & Day; Easter; Thanksgiving; Christmas. ♿
Attendance: 6,894 (accurate)
Membership: Individual $15; Family $25; Organizations $35; Reunion $100; Sustaining $250-$500; Life $500.

Durant

FORT WASHITA, 15 miles east of Madill on SH-199, Durant, OK 74701. Mailing Address: 3348 State Rd. 199, Durant, OK 74701-8503. Tel.: 580-924-6502. Fax: 580-924-6502.
E-mail: ftwashita@okhistory.org
Web Site: www.texoma-ok.com/trooper/1842.htm
Founded: 1967.
Congressional District: 3
Key Personnel: C.E.O., Dr. Bob Blackburn; Pres. (V), Marie Brearley; Property Mgr., Larry Marcy; Museum Shop Mgr., Ron Petty.
Personnel Profile: Full-Time Paid 3; Part-Time Paid 1; Part-Time Volunteers 15.
Governing Authority: state. Parent Institution: Oklahoma Historical Society. (See separate listing). Tax-exempt.
Historic Site: 1842-1865 frontier military fort.
Collections: frontier maps; ruins; restoration of historical building.
Activities: military & civilian living history demonstrations.
Publications: quarterly newsletter, Chronicles of Oklahoma; monthly newsletter, Mistletoe Leaves.
Hours & Admission Prices: Mon.-Sat. 9-4:30, Sun. 1-4:30. No charge; donations accepted. Closed national holidays.
Attendance: 25,000 (accurate)
Membership: Annual $10; Lifetime $200.

THREE VALLEY MUSEUM, 401 W. Main St., Durant, OK 74701-5026. Mailing Address: P.O. Box 1191, Durant, OK 74702-1191. Tel.: 580-920-1907.
Key Personnel: Pres., Leslie Webster
History Museum.
Collections: Choctaw Nation & Bryan County history.
Activities: Annual Event: quilt show in March.
Hours & Admission Prices: Mon.-Fri. 1-5; tours by appointment. No charge; donations accepted. Closed Thanksgiving; Christmas.

Edmond

EDMOND HISTORICAL SOCIETY MUSEUM, (M), 431 S. Boulevard, Edmond, OK 73034-3873. Tel.: 405-340-0078. Fax: 405-340-2771.
E-mail: edmondhistory@coxinet.net
Web Site: edmondhistory.org
Founded: 1983.
Congressional District: 5
Key Personnel: Exec. Dir., Jena Mottola; Pres. (V), Jennifer Hibbard; Treas., Sabrina Thompson; Museum Collection Coord., Gregory Zornes; Cur., Jarod Atkins.
Personnel Profile: Full-Time Paid 4; Full-Time Volunteers 1; Part-Time Volunteers 100; Interns 1.
Governing Authority: private; nonprofit organization. Tax-exempt: 501(c)(3).
Historical Society Museum: housed in 1936 native stone armory.
Collections: concentration on the history of Edmond & the surrounding area from prehistoric to modern times.
Research Fields: Edmond 1889ers who made the land run into Oklahoma in 1889; Route 66 in Edmond.
Facilities: research library; 7,500 sq. ft. exhibit space; childrens hands-on center. Items related to Edmond for sale.
Activities: docent program; formal education program; scholary lectures; guided tours; workshops; temporary & traveling exhibitions. Annual Events: 1889er Homestead Fair; Heritage Dinner, Preservation Awards & Roll of Honor.
Publications: triannual newsletter, The Society Report.
Hours & Admission Prices: Tues.-Fri. 10-5, Sat. 1-4. No charge; donations accepted. Closed New Year's Eve & Day; Thanksgiving weekend; Christmas Eve, Day & week. ♿
Attendance: 25,000 (estimated)
Membership: Student & Super Senior 75 & over $10; Senior 62-74 $20; Individual $35; Family $50; Contributing $90; Business $175.

LABORATORY OF HISTORY MUSEUM, (M), University of Central Oklahoma, Department of History & Geography, 100 N. University Dr., Edmond, OK 73034-5207. Tel.: 405-974-4669.
Founded: 1915.
Key Personnel: Dir., Heidi Vaughn.
Governing Authority: Parent Institution: University of Central Oklahoma. Tax-exempt.
History Museum.
Collections: local history & culture.
Hours & Admission Prices: Call for hours. No charge; donations accepted.

El Reno

CANADIAN COUNTY HISTORICAL MUSEUM, 300 S. Grand, El Reno, OK 73036-3610. Tel.: 405-262-5121. Fax: 405-262-9397.
E-mail: vptrishane@aol.com
Web Site: www.elreno.org
Founded: 1969.
Congressional District: 5
Key Personnel: Pres., Vicki Proctor; Cur., Pat Reuter; Gift Shop Mgr., Marguerite Stoakes.

Personnel Profile: Full-Time Paid 1; Full-Time Volunteers 1; Part-Time Paid 2; Part-Time Volunteers 5.
Governing Authority: historical society; nonprofit organization. Tax-exempt.
Historical Society Museum: housed in 1906 Rock Island Railway Station on 98th Meridian.
Collections: railway artifacts; Native American artifacts & history; Ft. Reno; Darlington Indian Agency; pioneer furniture & kitchen; barbed wire; tools; vehicles; fire fighting equipment; U.S. Reformatory; Red Cross Canteen; farm machinery; business equipment; clothing; rural school; mounted wildlife; Canadian County cowboys.
Research Fields: county history; rural schools; local towns; ghost towns.
Facilities: 200-vol. library of historical material for use on premises. Indian-related gift items for sale (gift shop located in El Reno Hotel).
Activities: guided tours; lectures; temporary exhibits; historical programs; trolley rides.
Publications: letters.
Hours & Admission Prices: Wed.-Sat. 10-5, Sun. 1-5. No charge. Closed New Year's Day; Independence Day; Thanksgiving; Christmas. ♿
Membership: Youth Under 12 $2; Annual $10; Life $100.

Elk City

NATIONAL ROUTE 66 MUSEUM AND OLD TOWN COMPLEX, 2717 W. Hwy. 66, Elk City, OK 73644. Mailing Address: P.O. Box 5, Elk City, OK 73648-0005. Tel.: 405-225-6266. Fax: 580-225-3234.
Founded: 1966.
Congressional District: 6
Key Personnel: Chm., Jack Bonny; Cur., Lucy Stansberry; Museum Shop Mgr., Gary Dumas.
Personnel Profile: Full-Time Paid 5; Part-Time Paid 3; Part-Time Volunteers 25.
Governing Authority: municipal; nonprofit organization. Tax-exempt.
General Museum.
Collections: pioneer artifacts; costumes; glass; medical equipment; Rock Bluff School; caboose & depot; wagon yard; pioneer chapel; schoolhouse; Western rodeo; Indian artifacts; period cars; motorcycles. Historic Buildings: 1912 museum building; grist mill; bank. Store Fronts: mercantile, furniture, grocery, jewelry, barber shop, land office, post office, doctor's office, opera house.
Facilities: 400-vol. library of school & history books; 200-seat Opera House.
Activities: guided tours; summer series. Museum Sponsors: old-fashioned Christmas.
Publications: newspaper, weekly feature in local newspaper.
Hours & Admission Prices: Memorial Day to Labor Day Mon.-Sat. 9-7, Sun. 2-5; Sept.-May Mon.-Sat. 9-5, Sun. 2-5. Adults $5, seniors & children over 6 $4; discounts to groups, AAA members, bus tours, members, senior & school groups. Closed New Year's Day; Easter; Thanksgiving; Christmas Eve & Day. ♿
Attendance: 35,000 (accurate)

Enid

CHEROKEE STRIP REGIONAL HERITAGE CENTER, 507 S. 4th St., Enid, OK 73701-5835. Tel.: 580-237-1907 & 234-8999. Fax: 580-234-8703.
E-mail: aholland@okhistory.org
Web Site: regionalheritagecenter.org
Formerly: Museum of the Cherokee Strip
Founded: 1951.
Congressional District: 5
Key Personnel: Pres., Andrea Holland; Dir., Dr. Sally Soelle; Chm. (V), Yami Maruicsin; Dir., Pam Leavengood; Museum Shop Mgr., Dorothy Bourgo.
Personnel Profile: Full-Time Paid 3; Part-Time Paid 2; Part-Time Volunteers 18.
Governing Authority: state. Parent Institution: Oklahoma Historical Society. Subsidiary Institution: Sons & Daughters of the Cherokee Strip Pioneers. Tax-exempt.
Regional History Museum.
Collections: farm implements; Native American artifacts; regional history; 1893 land run & development of Northwest Oklahoma.
Research Fields: regional history & opening of Cherokee Outlet.
Facilities: library; auditorium; theater; research center.
Activities: guided tours; permanent & traveling exhibitions; special events.
Publications: newsletter, Deeds of '93; Journal of the Cherokee Strip Pioneers.
Hours & Admission Prices: Closed for renovation until fall 2010. ♿
Attendance: 15,000 (accurate)

Erick

ROGER MILLER MUSEUM, Corner of Roger Miller Blvd. & Sheb Wooley Ave., Erick, OK 73645. Mailing Address: P.O. Box 464, Erick, OK 73645-0464. Tel.: 580-526-3833.
Web Site: www.rogermillermuseum.com
History Museum.
Collections: artifacts & memorabilia pertaining to singer & songwriter Roger Miller.
Hours & Admission Prices: Wed.-Sat. 10-5, Sun. 1-5; other times by appointment.

Fort Gibson

FORT GIBSON HISTORIC SITE, 907 N. Garrison Ave., Fort Gibson, OK 74434. Mailing Address: P.O. Box 457, Fort Gibson, OK 74434-0457. Tel.: 918-478-4088. Fax: 918-478-4089.
E-mail: fortgibson@okhistory.org
Web Site: www.fortgibson.com/historical_sites.htm
Founded: 1936.
Congressional District: 2
Key Personnel: Dir., Chris Morgan; Museum Shop Mgr., Cody Joliff.
Personnel Profile: Full-Time Paid 5; Part-Time Paid 2.
Governing Authority: state. Parent Institution: Oklahoma Historical Society, Historical Bldg., Oklahoma City 73105. Tax-exempt.
Military Museum Complex.
Collections: photographs; military artifacts; accoutrements; weapons; replicas of 1824 log fort. Historic Structures: 1845 barracks; 1871 post hospital; 1867 adjutant's office; 1867 blacksmith's shop; 1863 powder magazine; 1846 commissary.
Research Fields: Oklahoma military history.
Facilities: visitor center. Books & museum-related items for sale.
Activities: tours; education programs. Special Events: living history event; Public Bake Day in March; Mexican War Encampment in October; Candlelight Tour in December.
Hours & Admission Prices: April 15-Oct. 14 Tues.-Sat. 10-5; Oct. 15-April 14 Thurs.-Sun. 10-5. Adults $3, senior citizens $2.50, students 6-18 $1; discounts to AAM & CAMM members; children 5 & under and members no charge.
Attendance: 25,706 (accurate)
Membership: Friends of Ft. Gibson $10.

Fort Sill

FORT SILL NATIONAL HISTORIC LANDMARK, 437 Quanah Rd., Fort Sill, OK 73503-5100. Tel.: 580-442-5123. Fax: 580-442-8120.
E-mail: towana.spivey@conus.army.mil
Web Site: sill-www.army.mil/museum/home%20page.htm
Formerly: Fort Sill Museum
Founded: 1934.
Congressional District: 4
Key Personnel: Dir. & Chief Cur., Towana Spivey; Administrative Asst., Michele Burnett-Mabry; Museum Specialist, Lee Gibson; Museum Specialist, Mark Megehee; Exhibit Specialist, Dave Herndon; Operations Chief, Thierry Lescasse; Museum Aid, John Chadwick; Museum Specialist, John Beckman.
Personnel Profile: Full-Time Paid 9; Part-Time Volunteers 60.
Governing Authority: federal. Parent Institution: U.S. Army. Affiliated with U.S. Army Center of Military History. Tax-exempt: 501(c)(3).
Military Museum: housed in the 1869-75 original stone buildings of Fort Sill's Indian Territory.
Collections: U.S. Army field artillery from all periods; U.S. Cavalry, Infantry & Indian items from Western frontier period; military ordnance; uniforms; equipment; horse furnishings; vehicles; Native American artifacts; paintings; photographs & archives; African American Buffalo Soldiers in the west; 50 historic buildings of frontier army posts.
Research Fields: history of field artillery & cavalry; South Plains frontier; Kiowa, Apache & Comanche Indians; frontier law enforcement.
Facilities: 10,000-vol. reference library & 60,000 photo archive on history & development of U.S. Field Artillery, Fort Sill & the South Plains frontier available for research by appointment; visitor center.
Activities: guided tours; education programs; permanent exhibitions; Pass in Review: A History of Fort Sill, a multimedia production shown daily.
Publications: brochure, Warriors in Blue; Cannoneers from the Past; Fort Sill-Crossroads of the West; A Time Before Nature & Man in the Fort Sill Vicinity; The Long Journey-Satanta's Shield; The Spirit of the Past Lives On; pamphlets, Parade of Quarters; Volunteer Handbook; NCO-Backbone of the Army; book, Sherman House, The History of the Commander's Quarters; booklets, Missile Park; Fort Sill Heritage Fair; The Buffalo Soldiers; newsletter, The Fort Sill Dispatch; booklet, Rockets and Missiles of the Field Artillery; brochure, The French 75.

Hours & Admission Prices: Tues.-Sat. 8:30-5. No charge; donations accepted. Closed New Year's Eve & Day; Thanksgiving; Christmas Eve & Day. ♿
Attendance: 210,000 (estimated)

Fort Towson

FORT TOWSON HISTORIC SITE, HC 63, Fort Towson, OK 74735-9273. Mailing Address: P.O. Box 1580, Fort Towson, OK 74735-9273. Tel.: 580-873-2634. Fax: 580-873-9385.
E-mail: fttowson@okhistory.org
Web Site: www.okhistory.org/military/forttowson.html
Formerly: Fort Towson Military Park
Founded: 1972.
Congressional District: 3
Key Personnel: Site Mgr. & Dir., John Davis; Interim Cur., Keith Reese.
Personnel Profile: Full-Time Paid 3; Part-Time Volunteers 1.
Governing Authority: state. Parent Institution: Oklahoma Historical Society, Oklahoma City, OK (see separate listing). Tax-exempt.
Historic Site & Ruins.
Collections: local history; personal artifacts; period furnishings; photographs.
Activities: tours & lectures by appointment.
Hours & Admission Prices: Mon.-Fri. 9-5, Sat.-Sun. 1-5. No charge; donations accepted. Closed state holidays.
Attendance: 29,454 (accurate)
Membership: Please see separate listing for Oklahoma Historical Society, Oklahoma City.

Gate

GATEWAY TO THE PANHANDLE, Main St., Gate, OK 73844. Mailing Address: P.O. Box 27, Gate, OK 73844-0027. Tel.: 580-934-2004.
E-mail: emaphet@ptsi.net
Founded: 1975.
Congressional District: 6
Key Personnel: Dir., Pres. (V) & Museum Shop Mgr., L. Ernestine Maphet; Cur. & Librarian, Audrey Wilson; Deputy Dir., Karen Bond; Deputy Dir., Diane Hein; Asst. Dir., Louise Hein.
Personnel Profile: Part-Time Paid 1; Part-Time Volunteers 9.
Governing Authority: nonprofit organization. Parent Institution: Gateway to the Panhandle Museum Association & Library. Tax-exempt: 501(c)(3).
Historic Buildings.
Collections: farm implements & equipment; household items; dishes; Civil War artifacts; prehistoric bones; painted murals; historical Gate School & Gym; school artifacts; decorative arts. Historic Buildings: 1912 depot; 1912 school (listed on the National Register of Historic Places).
Research Fields: local history; genealogy.
Facilities: library of books available for the town & community use. Museum-related items for sale.
Activities: guided tours; permanent & temporary exhibitions.
Publications: book, Gate History & Vigalente's; Family Lost; Climb a Mountain; You Can't Buy a Home; Gate School History 1892-1992; Hangman's Tree; historical calendars.
Hours & Admission Prices: Mon.-Sat. 1-6, Sun. & holidays by appointment. No charge; donations accepted. Closed Thanksgiving; Christmas. ♿
Attendance: 450 (estimated)
Membership: Annual donations requested.

Gene Autry

GENE AUTRY OKLAHOMA MUSEUM, 47 Prairie St., Gene Autry, OK 73436. Mailing Address: P.O. Box 44, Gene Autry, OK 73436-0044. Tel.: 580-294-3047. Fax: 580-294-3454.
E-mail: townofgeneautry@brightok.net
Web Site: geneautryokmuseum.com
Founded: 1990.
Key Personnel: Dir., Elvin R. Sweeten; Museum Shop Mgr., Flora R. Sweeten.
Personnel Profile: Part-Time Volunteers 2.
Governing Authority: Tax-exempt.
General Museum.
Collections: Gene Autry, Roy Rogers, Rex Allen, Tex Ritter, Jimmy Wakely, Eddie Dean, & others who appeared in musical Western movies of the 1930s & 1940s.
Facilities: Museum-related items for sale.
Activities: Annual Event: Film & Music Festival.
Hours & Admission Prices: Jan. 6-Dec. 22 Mon.-Sat. 10-4. No charge; donations accepted. ♿
Attendance: 15,000 (estimated)
Membership: $25; $50; $75; $100; $200; $500; $700.

Goodwell

NO MAN'S LAND HISTORICAL SOCIETY, 207 W. Sewell St., Goodwell, OK 73939. Mailing Address: P.O. Box 278, Goodwell, OK 73939-0278. Tel.: 580-349-6697. Fax: 580-349-2670.
E-mail: nmlhs@ptsi.net
Founded: 1934.
Congressional District: 6
Key Personnel: Dir., Debbie Colson; Pres. (V), Ron Kincannon.
Personnel Profile: Full-Time Paid 1; Part-Time Paid 2.
Governing Authority: society. Parent Institution: Panhandle State University & Oklahoma Historical Society. Tax-exempt: 501(c)(3).
Historical Society Museum.
Collections: Hal Clark & William B. Baker Indian artifacts; Duckett Alabaster carvings; anthropology; archaeology; geology; mineralogy; paleontology; archives; zoology; agriculture; costumes; art; No Man's Land history; pioneer history; Dust Bowl history; natural history; flora & fauna.
Research Fields: Indian artifacts; Western history.
Facilities: 500-vol. library of Western & local history documents available for use on premises; reading room.
Activities: guided tours; lectures.
Publications: newsletter.
Hours & Admission Prices: May-Sept. Tues.-Fri. 10-12 & 1-3, Sat. 10-12 & 1-5; Oct.-April Tues-Sat. 10-12 & 1-3. No charge; donations accepted. Closed legal holidays. ♿
Attendance: 4,000 (estimated)
Membership: Individual $15; Life $100.

Gore

CHEROKEE COURTHOUSE VISITORS INFORMATION CENTER & MUSEUM, 2 1/2 miles S.E. of Gore on Hwy. 64, Gore, OK 74435. Mailing Address: Rte. 2, Box 37-1, Gore, OK 74435-9414. Tel.: 918-489-5663. Fax: 918-489-2217.
E-mail: fsg@crosstel.net
Founded: 1973.
Congressional District: 2
Key Personnel: Museum Shop Mgr., Frankie Sue Gilliam.
Personnel Profile: Full-Time Volunteers 1; Part-Time Paid 1; Part-Time Volunteers 10.
Governing Authority: state. Parent Institution: Cherokee Nation, Box 948, Tahlequah, OK 74465. Tax-exempt.
History Museum: replicas of the original capital of the Cherokee Nation.
Collections: period Cherokees Indians.
Facilities: Gift items & Cherokee handmade items for sale.
Hours & Admission Prices: Mon.-Sat. 9-5; other times by appointment. No charge; donations accepted. Closed major holidays.

Grove

HAR-BER VILLAGE, 4404 W. 20th St., Grove, OK 74344-5136. Tel.: 918-786-6446 & 3488. Fax: 918-787-6213.
E-mail: harbervil@aol.com
Web Site: www.har-bervillage.com
Founded: 1968.
Congressional District: 2
Key Personnel: Co-Founder, Mrs. Bernice Jones; Exec. Dir., Jan Norman; C.E.O. & Pres., Gary Smith.
Personnel Profile: Full-Time Paid 7; Part-Time Paid 2; Part-Time Volunteers 23.
Governing Authority: individual operation. Tax-exempt.
Historic Village Museum.
Collections: pottery; china; toys; natural history; furniture; lamps; dolls; farm machinery; stagecoaches; prairie schooner; steam engines; wagons; buggies; guns; musical instruments; clothing. Historic Buildings: approx. 112 buildings on Grand Lake of the Cherokees, including doctors office, drug store & bank; Sweet Annie Herb Garden; Ecology Center.
Facilities: visitor center.
Activities: self-guided tours; permanent exhibitions.
Publications: brochures.
Hours & Admission Prices: March-Oct. 15 Mon.-Sat. 9-6, Sun. 12:30-5. Oct. 16-Nov.15 Mon.-Sat. 9-5, Sun. 12:30-5. Adults 14-62 $3.50, seniors $2.50; discounts to groups; children under 14 no charge. Season Pass $10. ♿
Attendance: 300,125 (accurate)

Guthrie

NATIONAL LIGHTER MUSEUM, 5715 S. Sooner Rd., Guthrie, OK 73044-6739. Tel.: 405-282-3025.
E-mail: tballard8@cox.net
Web Site: www.nationallightermuseum.com

Key Personnel: Owner & Cur., Ted C. Ballard
History Museum.
Collections: fire-making devices.
Hours & Admission Prices: By appointment. No charge.

OKLAHOMA FRONTIER DRUG STORE MUSEUM, 214 W. Oklahoma, Guthrie, OK 73044-3132. Tel.: 405-282-1895.
Web Site: www.drugmuseum.org
Founded: 1992.
Governing Authority: Tax-exempt.
Drugstore & Pharmacy Museum.
Collections: period artifacts; 1923 soda fountain; 1890s pharmaceutical memorabilia.
Facilities: Museum-related items for sale.
Hours & Admission Prices: Tues.-Sat. 10-5. No charge; donations accepted. Closed New Year's Day; Christmas.

OKLAHOMA SPORTS MUSEUM, 315 W. Oklahoma Ave., Guthrie, OK 73044-3107. Tel.: 405-260-1342. Fax: 405-260-1342.
E-mail: oklahomasportsmuseum@sbcglobal.net
Web Site: oklahomasportsmuseum.com
Founded: 1993.
Key Personnel: Dir., Richard Hendricks
Sports Museum.
Collections: artifacts & memorabilia of professional & Olympic athletes from Oklahoma.
Activities: rental facility; interactive exhibit.
Hours & Admission Prices: Mon.-Thurs. 1-5, Fri.-Sat. 10-5, Sun. by appointment. No charge; donations accepted.

OKLAHOMA TERRITORIAL MUSEUM, 406 E. Oklahoma Ave., Guthrie, OK 73044-3317. Tel.: 405-282-1889.
E-mail: guthriecomplex@okhistory.org
Web Site: www.oklahomaterritorialmuseum.org
Founded: 1970.
Congressional District: 6
Key Personnel: Dir., Nathan Turner; Cur. Collections, Erin Brown; Main Tech, James Ray; Clerk, Sharen Bowers.
Personnel Profile: Full-Time Paid 4; Part-Time Volunteers 20.
Governing Authority: state. Parent Institution: Oklahoma Historical Society (see separate listing). Tax-exempt.
History Museum: housed in the Fred Pfeiffer Memorial Museum building & the Carnegie Library.
Collections: items relating to Oklahoma 1889 Land run & territorial urban period.
Research Fields: territorial Oklahoma.
Facilities: 4,000-vol. library from 1900-1910.
Activities: arts festivals; permanent & temporary exhibitions; special activities; educational programs.
Hours & Admission Prices: Tues.-Sat. 9-5. No charge; donations accepted. Closed holidays. ♿
Attendance: 16,685 (accurate)
Membership: Student & Senior Citizen $10; Individual $15; Family & Institutional $25; Supporting $50; Life $300; Benefactor $500.

STATE CAPITAL PUBLISHING MUSEUM, 301 W. Harrison Ave., Guthrie, OK 73044-4414. Tel.: 405-282-4123.
E-mail: scpm@okhistory.org
Web Site: www.guthrieok.com/museums.html
Founded: 1976.
Congressional District: 5
Key Personnel: Dir., Justin Lenhart; C.E.O., Bob Blackburn; Cur., Stephanie Fields; Site Attendant, Phillip Washburn; Clerk, Sharen Bowers.
Personnel Profile: Full-Time Paid 3; Part-Time Volunteers 25.
Governing Authority: state. Parent Institution: Oklahoma Historical Society. (See separate listing). Tax-exempt.
Publishing Museum: housed in 1902 State Capital Co. Building, originally constructed by frontier editor & publisher Frank Hilton Greer.
Collections: original printing & publishing artifacts; company records; working vintage printing presses; 1889-1910 newspapers published by the State Capital Co. on microfilm; manuscript collection.
Research Fields: history of printing & newspaper publishing with emphasis on the Oklahoma territorial 1890-1907 & early statehood period.
Facilities: library of 1889-1910, microfilm newspapers.
Activities: printing; permanent & temporary exhibitions; educational programs.
Hours & Admission Prices: Thurs.-Sat. 9-5. No charge; donations accepted. Closed holidays. ♿
Attendance: 13,389 (accurate)
Membership: Student & Senior Citizen $10; Individual $15; Family & Institutional $25; Supporting $50; Life $300; Benefactor $500.

Healdton

HEALDTON OIL MUSEUM, 315 E. Main St., Healdton, OK 73438-1836. Tel.: 580-497-3929. Fax: 580-229-0900.
E-mail: healdtonchamber@suddenlinkmail.com
Web Site: www.okhistory.org/outreach/affiliates/healdtonoil.html
Founded: 1973.
Congressional District: 3
Key Personnel: Mgr., Melanie Williams.
Personnel Profile: Part-Time Paid 1.
Governing Authority: state. Branch of Oklahoma Historical Society. Tax-exempt.
Technology Museum.
Collections: oil field rigs; equipment; tools, photographs; documents related to Oklahoma oil industry.
Research Fields: oil industry.
Activities: tours; permanent exhibitions.
Hours & Admission Prices: Mon.-Fri. 9-4. No charge; donations accepted. Closed legal holidays. ♿
Attendance: 2,411 (estimated)
Membership: Individual $25; Family & Institutional $40; Supporting $75; Life $500; Benefactor $1,000.

Heavener

HEAVENER RUNESTONE STATE PARK, 18365 Runestone Rd., Heavener, OK 74937-7493. Tel.: 918-653-2241. Fax: 918-653-3435.
E-mail: heavener@oklahomaparks.com
Founded: 1967.
Congressional District: 3
Key Personnel: Park Mgr., Rick Sanders; Maintenance & Repair Tech., William Rowland.
Personnel Profile: Full-Time Paid 3.
Governing Authority: state. Affiliated with Oklahoma Tourism and Recreation Dept., 500 Will Rogers Building, Oklahoma City, OK 73105. Tax-exempt.
Historic Site: Runestone inscription, Glome Valley.
Collections: local history & culture; photographs.
Facilities: visitor center; interpretive center & trail; nature trail; playground & picnic area; community building.
Activities: Annual Events: Easter Sunrise Service; Easter Egg Hunt; Trash Off Day; July 4th Musical; Car Show in August.
Publications: brochure.
Hours & Admission Prices: March-Oct. daily 8-dusk; Nov.-Feb. daily 8-dusk. No charge; donations accepted. ♿
Attendance: 90,000 (accurate)

PETER CONSER HOUSE, 47114 Conser Creek Rd., Heavener, OK 74937-9022. Tel.: 918-653-2493.
Founded: 1970.
Congressional District: 3
Key Personnel: C.E.O., Dr. Bob Blackburn; Site Mgr., A.G. Hembree.
Governing Authority: state. Parent Institution: Oklahoma Historical Society. Tax-exempt.
Historic House: 1894 Peter Conser House; a captain of the Lighthorsemen of the Moshulatubbe District, a noted law enforcement group of the Choctaw nation.
Collections: furnishings & artifacts from 1894-1910.
Research Fields: Choctaw history, particularly that of the Lighthorsemen.
Facilities: library.
Activities: tours.
Publications: Mistletoe Leaves; Chronicles.
Hours & Admission Prices: Wed.-Sat. 10-5, Sun. 1-5. No charge; donations accepted. Closed national holidays. ♿
Attendance: 6,000 (estimated)
Membership: Student & Retired $10; Individual $15; Family & Institution $25; Supporting $50; Life $300; Benefactor $500.

Henryetta

HENRYETTA TERRITORIAL MUSEUM, (M), 410 W. Moore, Henryetta, OK 74437-5255. Mailing Address: P.O. Box 220, Henryetta, OK 74437-0220. Tel.: 918-652-7112.
Web Site: www.territorialmuseum.net
Founded: 1982.
Congressional District: 2
Key Personnel: Pres., Marsha Smith; Pres. (V), Mike Doak.
Personnel Profile: Part-Time Paid 1.

Governing Authority: Parent Institution: Henryetta Historical Society. Tax-exempt.
History Museum.
Collections: area history; photographs.
Hours & Admission Prices: Wed.-Sat. 10-3; other times by appointment. No charge; donations accepted. Closed holidays.
Attendance: 1,500 (estimated)
Membership: Individual $15; Family $25; Business $50, $100, $250.

Hobart

GENERAL TOMMY FRANKS LEADERSHIP INSTITUTE AND MUSEUM, 507 S. Main, Hobart, OK 73651. Mailing Address: P.O. Box 222, Hobart, OK 73651-0222. Tel.: 580-726-5900. Fax: 580-726-5901.
E-mail: museum@tommyfranksmuseum.org
Web Site: tommyfranksmuseum.org
Governing Authority: Tax-exempt.
History Museum.
Collections: General Tommy Franks life; military history; photographs; uniforms; personal artifacts; medals; challenge coins.
Facilities: Museum-related items for sale.
Activities: special events; educational programs.
Hours & Admission Prices: Mon.-Sat. 10-12 & 1-5. No charge; donations accepted. Closed holidays. ♿
Attendance: 3,000 (estimated)

Hominy

DRUMMOND HOME, 305 N. Price, Hominy, OK 74035-1007. Tel.: 918-885-2374.
Founded: 1986.
Key Personnel: Site Mgr., Beverly Whitcomb.
Personnel Profile: Full-Time Paid 1; Part-Time Paid 1.
Governing Authority: state. Parent Institution: Oklahoma Historical Society (see separate listing). Tax-exempt.
Historic House: 1905 Drummond Home.
Collections: original furnishings; clothing; documents; photographs; decorative arts.
Major Exhibits: Doll Exhibits, 2/10; Quilt Exhibit, 4/10; Drummond Heirloom Exhibit, 7/10.
Research Fields: Drummond family & their relations with the Osage; cattle industry; period furnishings.
Activities: tours; Christmas decoration. Annual Event: Christmas Tour of Homes; Parade of Historical Santas in December; Christmas Open House in December.
Publications: Mistletoe Leaves (Oklahoma Historical Society); Friend's newsletter.
Hours & Admission Prices: Wed.-Sat. 9-5, Sun. 1-5. No charge; donations accepted. Closed state holidays.
Attendance: 1,800 (estimated)
Membership: Please see separate listing for Oklahoma Historical Society.

FIELD HISTORICAL PRINTING MUSEUM, 109 W. Main St., Hominy, OK 74035-1031. Tel.: 918-885-2688.
History Museum.
Collections: two 1930 linotypes; 12 printing presses; engraver; ludlow; strip caster; cameras; brass; foundry & wood type; engravings; teletypesetter; Western Union equipment; Dow Jones machines.
Hours & Admission Prices: By appointment. No charge.

Hugo

CHOCTAW COUNTY HISTORICAL SOCIETY, 309 North B St., Hugo, OK 74743-3325. Mailing Address: P.O. Box 577, Hugo, OK 74743-0577. Tel.: 580-326-6630.
E-mail: friscodepot@live.com
Web Site: www.friscodepot.org
Founded: 1978.
Congressional District: 3
Key Personnel: Chm. (V), Noel Pence; Treas. & Museum Shop Mgr., Norman Pence.
Personnel Profile: Part-Time Volunteers 12.
Governing Authority: society; nonprofit organization. Parent Institution: Choctaw County Historical Society. Subsidiary Institution: Frisco Depot Museum. Tax-exempt.
Railroad Museum: housed in 1912 Frisco Railroad Depot; original Harvey House restaurant.
Collections: railroad items; local history; newspaper stories of early day events; two early fire trucks. Historic Structure: restored Harvey House restaurant, dormitory rooms & manager's apartment; working miniature trains with various engines of Frisco models; early day farm equipment display; hand made miniature circus display; large collection of early day photos of area, building & surrounding towns; restored kitchen, includes early day gas, kerosene & wood cook stoves; first long distance telephone switchboard in area; 250 year-old spinning wheel & loom; telegraph equipment; hand crank wooden washing machines; ladies turn-of-the-century apparel & accessories; country school room; doctor's office; old barber shop c.1900.
Research Fields: local history of towns in surrounding area.
Facilities: library of books on history of towns & early day events before statehood; 150-seat auditorium. Books on local history, reprints of early day pictures for sale.
Activities: guided tours; arts festivals; rental gallery. Annual Events: Homecoming days in June.
Publications: book, Hugo, 1916.
Hours & Admission Prices: Tues.-Sat. 10-4; tours by appointment. Museum: no charge; donations accepted. ♿
Attendance: 3,000 (accurate)
Membership: Annual $25.

Idabel

MUSEUM OF THE RED RIVER, (M), 812 E. Lincoln Rd., Idabel, OK 74745-7815. Tel.: 508-286-3616. Fax: 508-286-3616.
E-mail: motrr@hotmail.com
Web Site: www.museumoftheredriver.org
Founded: 1974.
Congressional District: 3
Key Personnel: Dir., Henry Moy; Pres. (V) Herron Foundation, Donald A. Herron; Pres. (V) Idabel Museum Society, Judy Petre; Keeper of Collections, Daniel Vick; Program Cur., Paulette LaGasse; Cur. Assoc., Mario Rivera; Public Rels., Michelle Finch Walker; Business Mgr., Sue Coffman; Museum Shop Mgr., Sherron Mitchell.
Personnel Profile: Full-Time Paid 6; Full-Time Volunteers 2; Part-Time Paid 3; Part-Time Volunteers 10; Interns 3.
Governing Authority: municipal; owned and maintained by Herron Foundation on behalf of the city of Idabel; operated by Idabel Museum Society, Inc. Tax-exempt.
General Museum.
Collections: prehistoric to contemporary American Indian collections, emphasis on local Indian history, Caddo, Choctaw; interpretive exhibits material culture of the Americas; Native American art & archaeology; regional natural history; regional paleontological & geological specimens.
Research Fields: Caddoan archaeology.
Facilities: library & archaeological study collections available for research on premises. Indian & folk crafts for sale.
Activities: rotating & permanent exhibits & occasional special exhibitions; gallery lectures; films; childrens programs.
Publications: archeological survey reports; educational leaflets.
Hours & Admission Prices: Tues.-Sat. 10-5, Sun. 1-5. No charge; donations accepted. Closed New Year's Day; Memorial Day; Independence Day; Thanksgiving; Christmas. ♿
Attendance: 11,900 (accurate)

Indiahoma

WICHITA MOUNTAINS WILDLIFE REFUGE, 32 Refuge Headquarters, Indiahoma, OK 73552-2478. Tel.: 580-429-3222.
Wildlife Refuge.
Collections: wildlife & their habitats; plants; ecology.
Facilities: nature trails.
Activities: hiking; camping; fishing.
Hours & Admission Prices: Mon.-Fri. 8-4:30.

Jay

DELAWARE COUNTY HISTORICAL SOCIETY & MARIEE WALLACE MUSEUM, 538 Krause St., Jay, OK 74346. Mailing Address: P.O. Box 855, Jay, OK 74346-0855. Tel.: 918-253-4345; 866-253-4345.
E-mail: delcohsmuseum@brightok.net
Historical Society Museum.
Collections: local history & culture; toy trains; buggies; wagons; American Indian & Trail of Tears artifacts.
Hours & Admission Prices: Mon.-Tues. & Thurs.-Fri. 9-5, Wed. 1:30-5. No charge.

Jenks

OKLAHOMA AQUARIUM AND THE KARL AND BEVERLY WHITE NATIONAL FISHING TACKLE MUSEUM, 300 Aquarium Dr., Jenks, OK 74037-4148. Mailing Address: P.O. Box 910, Jenks, OK 74037-0910. Tel.: 918-296-3474. Fax: 918-296-3467.
Web Site: okaquarium.org
Key Personnel: Exec. Dir., Teri Bowers
Aquarium.
Collections: over 200 salt & fresh water species and mammals; 20,000 pieces of fishing tackle.
Facilities: deli. Museum-related items for sale.
Activities: summer camp; educational programs; special events.
Hours & Admission Prices: Tues. 10-9, Wed.-Mon. 10-6. Adults $13.95, senior citizens & military $11.95, children 3-12 $9.95; children 2 & under no charge. Closed Christmas.

Keota

OVERSTREET-KERR HISTORICAL FARM, 29186 Kerr-Overstreet Rd., Keota, OK 74941-6560. Tel.: 918-966-3396. Fax: 918-966-3396.
E-mail: okhfarm@crosstel.net
Web Site: www.kerrcenter.com
Founded: 1990.
Congressional District: 2
Key Personnel: Dir., Alan Ware; Education, Registrar & Museum Shop Mgr., Jeremy Henson; Pres. (V), Jim Horne; Public Rels., Maura McDermott; Treas., Ann Ware; Farm Devel. Mgr., Jim Combs.
Personnel Profile: Full-Time Paid 2; Part-Time Paid 1; Part-Time Volunteers 2.
Governing Authority: private; nonprofit organization. Parent Institution: Kerr Center, P.O. Box 588, Poteau, OK 74953.
Farm Museum.
Collections: lifestyle of the Native American & Pioneer farmer from 1871 to 1952; endangered livestock breeds; 1890-1940 farm equipment; outbuildings.
Research Fields: John Deere hay making & grain production equipment from 1890-1940.
Facilities: 324 sq. ft. exhibit space; nature trail; heirloom orchard. Museum-related items for sale.
Activities: formal education programs for children; guided tours; hobby workshops; demonstrations. Annual Event: Fall Farm Fest in October.
Publications: monthly newsletter, Field Notes; promotional brochures.
Hours & Admission Prices: Mon.-Sat. by appointment. Adults $3; children under 6 & students no charge. ♿
Attendance: 5,000 (estimated)

Kingfisher

CHISHOLM TRAIL MUSEUM, 605 Zellers Ave., Kingfisher, OK 73750-4228. Tel.: 405-375-5176.
E-mail: chisholmtrail@okhistory.org
Web Site: www.chisholmandseay.com
Founded: 1970.
Congressional District: 6
Key Personnel: Pres., Jeremy Ingle; Dir., Renee Mitchell; Museum Shop Mgr., Marvin Reames.
Personnel Profile: Full-Time Paid 2; Part-Time Paid 1.
Governing Authority: state. Parent Institution: Oklahoma Historical Society, Wiley Post Bldg., 2401 N. Laird Ave., Oklahoma City, OK 73105. Tax-exempt.
General Museum.
Collections: agriculture; archaeology; arrowheads; barbed wire; photographs; newspapers; cowboy & old farm equipment; parts of restored frontier town; early days stores; Indian artifacts; Dalton Cabin; First Bank of Kingfisher; Gant schoolhouse (one room); Harmony Church; log cabin (two room).
Research Fields: Pioneer Kingfisher; Chisholm Trail; Jesse Chisholm; J.V. Admire.
Facilities: wildlife diorama; meeting room. Museum-related items for sale.
Activities: guided tours. Museum Sponsors: Living History in Spring; Christmas at Governor Seay Mansion & Pioneer Village in December.
Publications: brochures.
Hours & Admission Prices: Tues.-Sat. 10-5. No charge; donations accepted. Closed state holidays. ♿
Attendance: 8,500 (estimated)
Membership: Annual $10; Life $100.

GOVERNOR SEAY MANSION, 605 Zellers Ave., Kingfisher, OK 73750-4228. Tel.: 405-375-5176. Fax: 405-375-5176.
E-mail: reneem@okhistory.org
Web Site: www.chisholmandseay.com
Founded: 1967.
Congressional District: 6
Key Personnel: C.E.O., Bob Blackburn; Pres., Jeremy Ingle; Cur., Renee Mitchell; Museum Shop Mgr., Marvin Reames.
Personnel Profile: Full-Time Paid 2; Part-Time Volunteers 30.
Governing Authority: state. Parent Institution: Oklahoma Historical Society, Wiley Post Bldg., 2401 N. Laird Ave., Oklahoma City, OK 73105-7914. Subsidiary Institution: Chisholm Trail Museum, Inc. Tax-exempt.
Historic House: Built-in 1892 restored mansion of second territorial Gov. A.J. Seay.
Collections: period furniture.
Research Fields: Governor A.J. Seay.
Activities: guided tours.
Publications: brochure.
Hours & Admission Prices: Tues.-Sat. 10-5. No charge; donations accepted. Closed state holidays. ♿
Attendance: 7,000 (estimated)
Membership: Annual $10; Life $100.

Krebs

KREBS HERITAGE MUSEUM, 85 S. Main St., Krebs, OK 74554. Mailing Address: P.O. Box 1519, Krebs, OK 74554-1519. Tel.: 918-426-0377.
Founded: 1997.
Congressional District: 2
Key Personnel: C.E.O., Dir. & Chm. (V), Steve DeFrange; Museum Shop Mgr., Julia Hancock.
Governing Authority: bd. dirs. Tax-exempt.
Historical Museum.
Collections: Civil War; coal mining; general military; Krebs City artifacts; area family booths; horse-drawn vehicles; early American tools.
Hours & Admission Prices: Call for hours. No charge; donations accepted. ♿
Attendance: 875

Langston

MELVIN B. TOLSON BLACK HERITAGE CENTER, Langston University, Sanford Hall, Langston, OK 73050. Tel.: 405-466-3346. Fax: 405-466-2979.
Black Heritage Center.
Collections: African American books, newspapers, videos & film; paintings; photographs; sculpture.
Hours & Admission Prices: Sun. 2-10, Mon., Wed. & Fri. 8-5, Tues. & Thurs. 8-10.

Laverne

LAVERNE COMMUNITY MUSEUM, 1st & Broadway, Laverne, OK 73848. Mailing Address: P.O. Box 5, Laverne, OK 73848-0005. Tel.: 580-921-3941.
E-mail: rogers@ptsi.net
Key Personnel: Pres., Shellie Rogers; Vice Pres., Linda Rogers; Sec. & Treas., Dante Bebilaqua
History Museum: housed in a 1912 hotel.
Collections: Native American artifacts; dolls; period furnishings; Jane Jayroe, Miss America of 1967; shoes.
Hours & Admission Prices: By appointment only. No charge.

Lawton

CAMERON UNIVERSITY ART GALLERY, 2800 Gore Blvd., Lawton, OK 73505-6377. Tel.: 580-581-2211.
Art Gallery.
Collections: paintings; photographs; sculpture.
Hours & Admission Prices: No charge.

COMANCHE NATIONAL MUSEUM AND CULTURAL CENTER, (M), 701 N.W. Ferris Ave., Lawton, OK 73507-5442. Tel.: 580-353-0404.
E-mail: comanchemuseum@gmail.com
Web Site: comanchemuseum.com

Founded: 2007.
Key Personnel: Dir., Phyllis Wahahrockah-Tasi; Collections Mgr., Amber Davis; Program Asst., Candy Morgan; Historian Aide, Zona RedElk Suminski; Program Asst., Vanessa Tomahsah; Receptionist, Bambi Allen
Native American Museum.
Collections: local history & culture relating to the Comanche Indians.
Hours & Admission Prices: Mon.-Fri. 8-5, Sat. 10-2. No charge. Closed Thanksgiving; Christmas. ♿

LESLIE POWELL FOUNDATION AND GALLERY, 620 S.W. D Ave., Lawton, OK 73501-4508. Tel.: 580-357-9526. Fax: 580-357-9526.
E-mail: lpartgallery@sbcglobal.net
Web Site: www.lpgallery.org
Founded: 1986.
Key Personnel: Exec. Dir. & Cur., Nancy P. Anderson.
Personnel Profile: Full-Time Paid 1; Part-Time Paid 1; Interns 1.
Governing Authority: Tax-exempt.
Art Gallery.
Collections: works by noted artists; paintings; sculptures; 44 works of Leslie Powell Japanese wood cut collection on display.
Facilities: 80-seat lecture hall.
Activities: concerts; lectures; openings.
Publications: online newsletter; biennial show catalog, even years in November.
Hours & Admission Prices: Mon.-Sat. 12-4.
Attendance: 3,000 (accurate)

* **MUSEUM OF THE GREAT PLAINS, (M),** 601 Ferris N.W. Ave., Lawton, OK 73507-5443. Tel.: 580-581-3460. Fax: 580-581-3458.
Web Site: www.museumgreatplains.org
Founded: 1960.
Congressional District: 4
Key Personnel: Dir. & Cur. Exhibits, John Hernandez; Chm., Juanita Pahdopony; Head Cur., Deborah Baroff; Living History Interpreter, Tim Poteete; Registrar, Jim Whiteley; Registrar Asst., Rebecca Royal; Educator, Jana Brown; Dir. Technical Svcs., Brian Smith; Dir. Devel., Rex Givens; Museum Shop Mgr., Peggy Brown; Administrative Asst., Mary Owensby; Bldg. Mgr., Larry Holland; Receptionist & Weekend Clerk, Dean Keiser; Receptionist, Lora Moffet.
Personnel Profile: Full-Time Paid 10; Part-Time Paid 3; Part-Time Volunteers 20; Interns 1.
Governing Authority: Museum of the Great Plains Authority. Tax-exempt: 501(c)(3).
Regional History Museum.
Collections: primary documents pertaining to Great Plains region; agricultural & hardware catalogs; 1869-2000 photographs and microfilm of blacksmith & carriage periodicals and wagon catalogs; archives; photographs of Plains Indians & white settlement; exhibits and artifacts representing the material culture of man from prehistoric times to the present; outdoor exhibits of agriculture machinery; 300 ton Baldwin steam locomotive. Historic Buildings: 1902 depot & Blue Beaver one room schoolhouse; 1830s Red River Trading Post & living history program; Tingley Indian store collections from Anadarko, OK are described in Vol. 17 (1978) Great Plains Journal, published by the Institute of the Great Plains.
Research Fields: history & archeology of Great Plains region.
Facilities: 20,000-vol. library, 200,000 documents, 30,000 photographs for research; 150-seat auditorium; outdoor amphitheater; laboratories.
Activities: guided tours; art shows; special films; lectures; demonstrations.
Publications: annual, Great Plains Journal; The Writings of J. Frank Dobie: A Bibliography; Domebo: A Paleo-Indian Mammoth Kill in the Prairie Plains; Early Indian Trade Guns 1625-1775; A Historical Guide to Wagon Hardware & Blacksmith Supplies; Test Excavations in the Mangum Reservoir Area of Southwestern Oklahoma; An Archaeological Reconnaissance of Fort Sill, Oklahoma; Archaeological Investigations of the Kiowa & Comanche Indian Agency Commissaries; an Archaeological Survey in the Gypsum Breaks on the Elm Fork of Red River; an Archaeological Reconnaissance of the Salt Plains Areas of Northwestern Oklahoma; Archaeological Investigations Along the Waurika Pipeline; MGP Record Newsletter.
Hours & Admission Prices: Mon.-Sat. 10-5, Sun. 1-5. Adults $6, senior citizens $5, children 7-11 $2.50; members & children under 7 no charge. ♿
Attendance: 30,000 (accurate)
Membership: Institutional $25; Individual $30; Family $50; Contributing $100; Star $200; Corporate $250-$1,000.

Lindsay

MURRAY-LINDSAY MANSION & PIKES PEAK SCHOOL, Hwy. 76 S., Lindsay, OK 73052-0282. Mailing Address: P.O. Box 282, Lindsay, OK 73052-0282. Tel.: 405-756-2121.
Founded: 1971.
Congressional District: 4
Key Personnel: Pres. (V), Shawn Bridwell.
Personnel Profile: Part-Time Volunteers 30.
Governing Authority: society. Parent Institution: City of Lindsay. Subsidiary Institution: Lindsay Community Historical Society. Tax-exempt.
Historic Buildings.
Collections: local history & culture; Chickasaw setters; period school furnishings; 187-piece teapot collection; photographs; personal artifacts. Historic Buildings: 1879 Murray-Lindsay Mansion; 1908 Pikes school.
Research Fields: period furnishings & Murray family history; one & two room schools of Garvin County.
Activities: guided tours; replicate 1908 school classes.
Publications: From Pioneers to Progress; Pikes Peak School History 1908 to Present; Military History - Lindsay History Book, 1902-2002.
Hours & Admission Prices: Wed.-Fri. & Sun. 1-4, Sat. 10-2; other times by appointment. No charge; donations accepted. Closed all holidays. ♿
Attendance: 2,500 (estimated)
Membership: Annual $10; Lifetime $200.

Mangum

OLD GREER COUNTY MUSEUM & HALL OF FAME, 222 W. Jefferson St., Mangum, OK 73554-4000. Mailing Address: P.O. Box 2, Mangum, OK 73554-0002. Tel.: 580-782-2851.
E-mail: museum222@att.net
Web Site: oldgreercountymuseum.com
Founded: 1972.
Congressional District: 6
Key Personnel: Pres. (V), Dick Stickle; Chm., Mgr. & Museum Shop Mgr., Judy Forehand.
Personnel Profile: Part-Time Paid 2; Part-Time Volunteers 3.
Governing Authority: nonprofit. Tax-exempt: 501(c)(3).
History Museum.
Collections: quilts; replica of rooms including a millinery store, barber shop, optometrist office, Masonic Hall, civic room; mementoes of schools; photographs; dolls; salt & pepper shakers; Indian artifacts; farming items; horse drawn plow; barbed wire; music; military artifacts; cowboy memorabilia; medical equipment; local art; bird collection; replica of half-dugout; Fire Station; 1928 Seagrave Fire Truck; tax records from 1896-1950.
Research Fields: local artifacts.
Facilities: 60 rooms of Old Greer County history; tax record books from 1890's; 50-vol. library of history books available for research on premises; reading room.
Activities: guided tours; school projects; reenactments.
Publications: History of Old Greer County & Its Pioneers; weekly newspaper column; quarterly newsletter.
Hours & Admission Prices: Mon.-Sat. 9-12 & 1-4. Adults $3, children 6-12 $1; members no charge. Closed legal holidays. ♿
Attendance: 700 (estimated)
Membership: Individual $25; Sustaining $100 & up.

McAlester

J.G. PUTERBAUGH HOUSE & GARRARD ARDENEUM, 345 E. Adams, McAlester, OK 74501-4651. Mailing Address: P.O. Box 759, McAlester, OK 74502. Tel.: 918-423-8555.
Historic House Museum: housed in the former home of J.G. Puterbaugh, one of the founding fathers of McAlester's coal business.
Collections: furnishings; maps; photographs; period artifacts.
Hours & Admission Prices: By appointment.

J. J. MCALESTER MANSION, 14 E. Smith, McAlester, OK 74501-2648. Tel.: 918-423-8620.
Historic House Museum: built in 1870. Listed on the National Register of Historic Places.
Collections: period furnishings; personal artifacts; photographs.
Hours & Admission Prices: Fri. by appointment. $2 per person.

MCALESTER SCOTTISH RITE MASONIC CENTER, 305 N. 2nd St., McAlester, OK 74501-4648. Mailing Address: P.O. Box 609, McAlester, OK 74502-0609. Tel.: 918-423-6360. Fax: 918-423-6362.
History Museum.

Collections: Scottish history & culture; photographs; costumes; 1930 custom-built Kimball organ.
Facilities: library.
Hours & Admission Prices: Masonic Center: Mon.-Fri. 8-12 & 1-5. Tours: Mon.-Fri. 9-12 & 1-4. No charge.

OKLAHOMA PRISONS' HISTORICAL MUSEUM, Stonewall & West St., McAlester, OK 74501-4651. Mailing Address: P.O. Box 97, McAlester, OK 74502-0097. Tel.: 918-423-4700.
Prison History Museum.
Collections: prison history; photographs; Oklahoma's electric chair.
Hours & Admission Prices: Call for hours.

OKLAHOMA TROLLEY MUSEUM, 21 E. Monroe, McAlester, OK 74501-4651. Mailing Address: P.O. Box 145, McAlester, OK 74502-0145. Tel.: 918-423-2446.
Trolley Museum.
Collections: restored trolley cars from 1907 to 1933; local history; photographs.
Hours & Admission Prices: Call for hours.

PITTSBURGH COUNTY GENEALOGICAL AND HISTORICAL SOCIETY, INC., 113 E. Carl Albert Pkwy., McAlester, OK 74501-5039. Tel.: 918-426-0388.
Web Site: www.pittsburghcogenealogical.org
Formerly: Pittsburgh County Historical Museum
Key Personnel: Pres., Tom Crowl
History Museum.
Collections: books; genealogy; mining; Native American artifacts; local history.
Facilities: library.
Hours & Admission Prices: Mon.-Fri. 9-3. No charge; donations accepted. Closed major holidays.

TANNEHILL MUSEUM, 500 W. Stonewall, McAlester, OK 74501-2346. Tel.: 918-423-5953.
Gun Museum.
Collections: guns; weapons; local history.
Hours & Admission Prices: By appointment.

Medford

GRANT COUNTY MUSEUM, Main & Cherokee Sts., Medford, OK 73759. Mailing Address: P.O. Box 31, Medford, OK 73759-0031. Tel.: 580-395-2342. Fax: 580-395-2343.
Founded: 1965.
Congressional District: 6
Governing Authority: county. Parent Institution: Oklahoma State Historical Society. Tax-exempt.
General Museum.
Collections: artifacts; archives; sod plow; wheel; wheat cradle; churns; pictures; old fashioned kitchen; local history & genealogy.
Research Fields: memorabilia; family histories; genealogies.
Activities: lectures; monthly programs; quilt & antique show.
Publications: books, Vol. I, Family Histories of Grant County; Early Legends of Osage Creek; Vol. 2, Family Histories, Land Marks, Schools, Churches; Historical Tales of the Cherokee Strip and the Rhubarb Farm; Glimmer on the Hill; Chisholm Trail.
Hours & Admission Prices: By appointment only. No charge; donations accepted. ♿
Membership: Active $10; Life $150.

Miami

DOBSON MUSEUM, 110 A S.W., Miami, OK 74354-6806. Tel.: 918-542-5388.
History Museum.
Collections: local history & culture; Native American artifacts; photographs; paintings; mining; woodworking tools; furniture; period newspapers.
Hours & Admission Prices: Sun., Wed. & Fri. 1-4. No charge.

Muskogee

ATALOA LODGE MUSEUM, 2299 Old Bacone Rd., Muskogee, OK 74403-1568. Tel.: 918-683-4581, ext. 283; 888-682-5514, ext. 7283. Fax: 918-687-5913.
Web Site: www.bacone.edu/ataloa
Founded: 1932.
Congressional District: 2
Key Personnel: Museum Dir., John Timothy.
Personnel Profile: Interns 4.
Governing Authority: private; college. Parent Institution: Bacone College. Tax-exempt: 501(c)(3).
Indian Artifacts Museum.
Collections: Native American material, stone artifacts; rugs; blankets; basketry; pottery; beadwork; quillwork. Historic Building: 1932 Ataloa Lodge.
Facilities: Bacone College Research Library available for use by appointment.
Activities: guided tours; lectures; permanent & rotating exhibitions.
Publications: booklets, Baconian; Smoke Signals.
Hours & Admission Prices: Mon.-Sat. 8-5, Sun. 1-5. Adults $3, Students $2, Elders $1.50; children under 6 no charge. Closed national holidays except by appointment. ♿
Attendance: 6,000

THE FIVE CIVILIZED TRIBES MUSEUM, (M), 1101 Honor Heights Dr., Muskogee, OK 74401-1321. Tel.: 918-683-1701; 877-587-4237. Fax: 918-683-3070.
E-mail: 5civilizedtribes@sbcglobal.net
Web Site: www.fivetribes.org
Founded: 1966.
Congressional District: 2
Key Personnel: Pres., Dr. J.W. Wiggins; Dir., Mary Robinson.
Personnel Profile: Full-Time Paid 3; Full-Time Volunteers 1; Part-Time Paid 3; Part-Time Volunteers 100.
Governing Authority: nonprofit organization; board of directors. Tax-exempt.
American Indian Museum & Art Gallery: housed in 1875 Union Indian Agency Building; pertains to the Cherokee, Chickasaw, Choctaw, Creek & Seminole tribal histories & American Indian Territory History.
Collections: paintings in traditional American Indian art style & sculpture by Cherokee, Choctaw, Chickasaw, Creek & Seminole tribe artists on tribal subjects; artifacts; photographs; books; documents; manuscripts; maps.
Research Fields: history; literature; traditions; cultures; genealogy; theater; music; biography; artifacts; source correspondence; sculpture.
Facilities: library; art gallery. Items created by members of the Five Civilized Tribes for sale.
Activities: guided tours; gallery talks; formally organized education programs for children; annual art show, student art competition, craft show, competitive art show, masters art show.
Publications: newsletter; book, Poems of Alexander Lawrence Posey-Creek Indian Bard, Art Prints, Cherokee Book, Muskogee Book, Pow Wow Chow Cookbook.
Hours & Admission Prices: Mon.-Sat. 10-5, Sun. 1-5. Adults $3, senior citizens $2, students $1.50; discounts to NHS members & groups; children under 6 no charge. Closed New Year's Day; Thanksgiving; Christmas. ♿
Attendance: 28,728 (accurate)
Membership: Senior Citizens $20; Associate $30; Sustaining $50; DA-CO-TAH $100; Sequoyah $300; Osceola $500; The Golden Eagle $1,000; The Council $2,500.

MUSKOGEE WAR MEMORIAL PARK & MILITARY MUSEUM, 3500 Batfish Rd., Muskogee, OK 74401. Mailing Address: P.O. Box 253, Muskogee, OK 74402-0253. Tel.: 918-682-6294. Fax: 918-682-1642.
E-mail: ussbatfish@sbcglobal.net
Web Site: www.ussbatfish.com
Formerly: USS Batfish
Founded: 1972.
Congressional District: 2
Key Personnel: Park Mgr., Rick Dennis; Chm. Bd., Jim Ritchie; Sec., Pam Bush.
Personnel Profile: Full-Time Paid 1; Full-Time Volunteers 8; Part-Time Volunteers 20; Interns 2.
Governing Authority: municipal; nonprofit. Tax-exempt.
Maritime Naval Museum: War Memorial & WWII Submarine, U.S.S. Batfish.
Collections: artifacts from all branches of service: Army, Navy, Marine, & Air Force; memorial to 52 subs lost in World War II; Civil War to present; USS Batfish submarine.
Facilities: Museum-related items for sale.
Activities: self-guided submarine tours; picnic area.
Publications: tour guide, Batfish.
Hours & Admission Prices: mid-March to mid-Oct. Wed.-Sat. 10-6, Sun. 1-6. Adult $6, senior citizens $4, children $3; discounts available for groups, military & AAA and AAM members. Closed Easter; Thanksgiving; Christmas.
Attendance: 25,000 (estimated)
Membership: Senior, Student & Veteran $20; Individual $30; Couples $35; Family $40.

THOMAS-FOREMAN HOME, 1419 W. Okmulgee, Muskogee, OK 74401-6740. Tel.: 918-686-6624. Fax: 918-682-3477.
E-mail: staff@3riversmuseum.com
Web Site: www.3riversmuseum.com
Founded: 1970.
Congressional District: 2
Key Personnel: Chm. (V), Linda Moore; Pres. (V), Jerry Marshall.
Personnel Profile: Part-Time Volunteers 8.
Governing Authority: Parent Institution: Three Rivers Museum, 220 Elgin, Muskogee, OK 74401. Supporting Organization: Friends of Thomas-Foreman Home. Tax-exempt.
Historic House: 1898 Home of Judge John R. Thomas and Grant & Carolyn Thomas Foreman.
Collections: original furnishings; private collections of Thomas & Foreman families.
Research Fields: pre-statehood Oklahoma.
Activities: guided tours. Museum Sponsors: Azalea Festival in April.
Hours & Admission Prices: Fri.-Sat. 10-5; tours by appointment. Adults $2, seniors & students $1. Closed national holidays.
Attendance: 1,200
Membership: Individual $20; Family $30; Builder $100; Friend $250; Sustainer $500.

THREE RIVERS MUSEUM, 220 Elgin, Muskogee, OK 74401-7019. Tel.: 918-686-6624. Fax: 918-682-3477.
E-mail: staff@3riversmuseum.com
Web Site: www.3riversmuseum.com
Founded: 1985.
Congressional District: 2
Key Personnel: Chm., Roger Bell; Dir., Sue Tolbert.
Personnel Profile: Full-Time Paid 1; Part-Time Paid 2; Part-Time Volunteers 20.
Governing Authority: Parent Institution: City of Muskogee. Subsidiary Institution: Three Rivers Museum of Muskogee, Inc.
History Museum: housed in restored 1916 Midland Valley Railroad Depot.
Collections: photographs; letters & documents; furnishings; clothing; military; railroad; area memorabilia.
Research Fields: Three Rivers region.
Facilities: conference room. Museum-related items for sale.
Activities: tours; special programs.
Publications: quarterly newsletter, 3 Rivers Historian.
Hours & Admission Prices: Wed.-Sat. 10-5. Adults $3, students $1.50; children under 6 no charge. ♿
Attendance: 2,000 (estimated)
Membership: Individual $25; Family $35; Builder $100; Sponsor $250; Sustainer $500.

Newkirk

NEWKIRK COMMUNITY HISTORICAL MUSEUM, 101 S. Maple, Newkirk, OK 74647-4026. Tel.: 580-362-2377. Fax: 580-362-3390.
History Museum.
Collections: Kay County artifacts from 1893 to 1940; local history & culture; restored mail buggy; period furnishings; photographs; Native American artifacts.
Facilities: Museum-related items for sale.
Hours & Admission Prices: Sun. 2-4; other times by appointment. No charge.

Noble

TIMBERLAKE ROSE ROCK MUSEUM, 419 S. Hwy. 77, Noble, OK 73068-0663. Mailing Address: P.O. Box 663, Noble, OK 73068-0663. Tel.: 405-872-9838.
Natural History Museum.
Collections: barite rose rocks; quartz crystals.
Activities: Museum Sponsors: Rose Rock Festival in May.
Hours & Admission Prices: Tues.-Fri. 10-6, Sat. 10-4.

Norman

FIREHOUSE ART CENTER, 444 S. Flood Ave., Norman, OK 73069-5513. Tel.: 405-329-4523. Fax: 405-292-9763.
E-mail: info@normanfirehouse.com
Web Site: www.normanfirehouse.com
Founded: 1971.
Key Personnel: Exec. Dir., Douglas Shaw Elder; Operations Coord., Carla Chew.
Personnel Profile: Full-Time Paid 3; Part-Time Paid 4.
Governing Authority: nonprofit organization.
Art Center.
Collections: paintings.
Major Exhibits: Paintings of Bobbie Anderson & Sharon Burchette, 1/15/10-3/5/10; Elyse Bogart (Jewelry) & Douglas Shaw Elder (Sculptures), 3/12/10-4/30/10; 24 Works on Paper, 5/21/10-6/18/10; 33rd Annual Midsummer Nights Fair, 7/9/10-7/10/10; Faculty Art Show, 7/9/10-7/30/10; Children's Art Program Exhibit, 8/13/10-8/20/10.
Hours & Admission Prices: Mon.-Fri. 9:30-5:30, Sat. 10-4. No charge. Closed federal holidays.
Membership: Basic $45; Family $70; Patron $120; Associate $300; Benefactor $500; Silver $1,000; Gold $1,500; Platinum $2,500; Sponsor $5,000.

* **THE FRED JONES JR. MUSEUM OF ART, (M), (I),** University of Oklahoma, 555 Elm Ave., Norman, OK 73019-0001. Tel.: 405-325-3272; 405-325-0843. Fax: 405-325-7696.
Web Site: www.ou.edu/fjjma
Founded: 1936.
Congressional District: 4
Key Personnel: The Wylodean & Bill Saxon Dir., Ghislain d'Humieres; Deputy Dir., Gail Kana Anderson; Mgr. Administration & Operations, Becky Z. Trumble; Community Rels. Officer, Mary Jane Rutherford; Registrar, Kim Moinette; Cur. Education, Susan G. Baley; Asst. Cur. Education, Karen McWilliams; Cur. Adkins, Mark A. White; Preparator, Brad Stevens; Preparator, Clay Little; Administrative Asst., Brigid Brink; Security & Facilities Mgr., Joyce Cummins; Security Asst., Josh Puckett; Security Asst., Roberta Santa Cruz; Asst. Registrar, Miranda Callander; Customer Rels., Tracy Bidwell; Customer Rels., Hetty Strong; Tour Coord., Amber Hasbrook.
Personnel Profile: Full-Time Paid 23; Part-Time Paid 4; Part-Time Volunteers 100; Interns 6.
Governing Authority: state; university. Parent Institution: University of Oklahoma. Tax-exempt: 501(c)(3).
Art Museum.
Collections: French impressionism; American art; Native American art; photography; contemporary art; Asian art; European graphics from the 16th century to present.
Research Fields: French impressionism; 20th century American art; contemporary art; Native American art; art of the American West; photography.
Facilities: Museum-related items for sale.
Activities: guided tours; lectures; films; gallery talks; concerts; inter-museum loan; permanent, temporary & traveling exhibitions.
Publications: exhibition calendar; posters; catalogs; brochures; postcards.
Hours & Admission Prices: Tues.-Thurs. & Sat. 10-5, Fri. 10-9, Sun. 1-5. Adults $5; discounts to AAM & ICOM members; members & Tues. no charge. ♿
Membership: Student $15; Single, Faculty & Educator $20; Family & Dual $35; Associate $50; Supporter $100; Sustainer $250; Patron $500; Benefactor $1,000.

LITTLE RIVER ZOO, 3405 S.E. 120th, Norman, OK 73026-8563. Tel.: 405-366-7229. Fax: 405-366-6302.
E-mail: brittany@littleriverzoo.com; jszoo@littleriverzoo.com
Web Site: www.littleriverzoo.com
Founded: 1996.
Key Personnel: Dir., Janet Schmid.
Personnel Profile: Full-Time Paid 7; Part-Time Paid 32; Part-Time Volunteers 200; Interns 15.
Governing Authority: Tax-exempt.
Zoo.
Collections: animals from around the world.
Facilities: Museum-related items for sale.
Activities: petting zoo; guided tours; special animal program; special events; birthday parties. Museum Sponsors: Junior Zookeeper Camps (animal) Wildchild Adoptions.
Hours & Admission Prices: Daily 10-5. Adults $7, senior citizens $5, children 3-11 $4; discounts to military, Oklahoma University faculty, & groups of 20 or more; members no charge. ♿
Membership: Individual $25; Family $50.

MOORE-LINDSAY HOUSE HISTORICAL MUSEUM, (M), 508 N. Peters, Norman, OK 73069-7251. Tel.: 405-321-0156.
E-mail: cchs@coxinet.net
Web Site: www.normanhistorichouse.com
Formerly: The Norman Cleveland County Historical Museum
Founded: 1973.
Congressional District: 4
Key Personnel: Dir., Stephen Martin; Pres., Vernon Maddux.
Personnel Profile: Full-Time Paid 1; Part-Time Paid 2; Part-Time Volunteers 6; Interns 1.
Governing Authority: nonprofit organization. Tax-exempt: 501(c)(3).
Historical Society Museum: housed in 1899 Queen Anne style urban house.

Collections: furniture; furnishings; decorative arts; textiles; toys; books; photographs; documents relating to Cleveland County history, particularly during the territorial period; Victorian artifacts.
Major Exhibits: Football Exhibit, 9/11/10-10/29/10.
Research Fields: documentation of collections.
Facilities: library of books, photos, documents focusing on Cleveland county history c.1900, available for use on premises.
Activities: guided tours; formally organized education programs for children; adult evening programs; local history slide programs; temporary exhibitions.
Publications: quarterly newsletter, The Round Tower.
Hours & Admission Prices: Wed.-Sat. 10-4; other times by appointment. No charge; donations accepted. Closed holidays.
Attendance: 2,000 (estimated)
Membership: Individual $20; Family $25; Sustaining $50; Corporate $100.

ROBERT BEBB HERBARIUM, 770 Van Vleet Oval, Rm. 206, Norman, OK 73019-6155. Mailing Address: Department of Botany & Microbiology, Univ. of Oklahoma, 206 Cross Hall, Norman, OK 73019-0001. Tel.: 405-325-7533. Fax: 405-325-7619.
E-mail: bebbherbarium@ou.edu
Web Site: www.biosurvey.ou.edu/bebb/bebbhome.html
Founded: 1920.
Congressional District: 4
Key Personnel: Cur., Wayne J. Elisens; Collections Mgr., Amy Buthod.
Personnel Profile: Full-Time Paid 2; Part-Time Paid 1.
Governing Authority: university. Parent Institution: University of Oklahoma. Tax-exempt.
Herbarium.
Collections: botany; herbarium with emphasis on vascular plants of the Great Plains, Southwestern & Southeastern U.S. & Oklahoma.
Research Fields: molecular systematics; pollination ecology; floristics; phylogenetics; palynology; orchid phylogeny; flora of Oklahoma.
Facilities: associated with Noble Laboratory of Electron Microscopy & Oklahoma Natural Heritage Inventory.
Activities: inter-institutional loans for study; exchange of specimens.
Hours & Admission Prices: Daily 9-5. No charge. Closed university holidays. ♿

* **SAM NOBLE OKLAHOMA MUSEUM OF NATURAL HISTORY, (M), (I),** University of Oklahoma, 2401 Chautauqua, Norman, OK 73072-7029. Tel.: 405-325-8978. Fax: 405-325-7699.
E-mail: snomnh@ou.edu
Web Site: www.snomnh.ou.edu
Founded: 1899.
Congressional District: 4
Key Personnel: Dir. & Cur. Mammals, Dr. Michael A. Mares; Cur. Vertebrate Paleontology, Dr. R.L. Cifelli; Cur. Reptiles, Dr. L.J. Vitt; Cur. Amphibians, Dr. J.P. Caldwell; Cur. Archeology, Dr. D. Wyckoff; Cur. Invertebrate Paleontology, Dr. S. Westrop; Asst. Cur. Mammals, Dr. J.K. Braun; Cur. Vertebrate Paleontology, Dr. N.J. Czaplewski; Assoc. Dir., Peter B. Tirrell; Coord. Dept. Computing Systems, Patrick Fisher; Head Admin. & Finance, Melanie Davidson; Registrar & Repatriation Specialist, Julie Droke; Security & Facilities Operations, David Dagg; Cur. Ichthyology, Dr. E. Marsh-Matthews; Cur. Ornithology, Dr. G. Schnell; Cur. Native American Languages, Dr. M. Linn; Head Education, Dr. Holly Hughes; Museum Shop Mgr., Mary Ann Roe.
Personnel Profile: Full-Time Paid 93; Part-Time Paid 53; Part-Time Volunteers 304.
Governing Authority: university. Parent Institution: University of Oklahoma. Tax-exempt: 501(c)(3).
General Museum.
Collections: mammals; birds; fish; amphibians; reptiles; insects; invertebrates; botany; anthropology; ethnology; archaeology; history; classical art; paleontology; paleobotany; minerals; textiles; Indian artifacts.
Research Fields: zoology; mammalogy; anthropology; ornithology; ichthyology; geology; entomology; ethnology; plants; herpetology; history; mineralogy; classical art; archaeology; paleontology; textiles; museology.
Facilities: research labs; 174-seat auditorium; discovery room; teaching lab; classroom; cafe. Museum-related items for sale.
Activities: films, & guided tours of exhibits for school & other groups; summer workshops; public lectures; field trips for members & other adults; school programs & educational loans; inter-museum loan, traveling, temporary & permanent exhibits; special events; volunteer program.
Publications: newsletter, Sam Noble Oklahoma Museum of Natural History; miscellaneous publications; Occasional Papers of the Sam Noble Oklahoma Museum of Natural History.
Hours & Admission Prices: Museum: Mon.-Sat. 10-5, Sun. 1-5. Office: Mon.-Fri. 8-5. Adults $5, seniors $4, children $3; discounts for AAM & ICOM members, military and AAA members; members & children under 5 no charge. Closed major holidays. ♿
Attendance: 170,431 (accurate)
Membership: Senior $20; Individual $30; Family $45; Supporter $250; Patron $500; Benefactor $1,000.

Nowata

NOWATA COUNTY HISTORICAL SOCIETY MUSEUM, 121 S. Pine St., Nowata, OK 74048-3413. Mailing Address: P.O. Box 87, Nowata, OK 74048-0087. Tel.: 918-273-1191.
Founded: 1969.
Congressional District: 2
Key Personnel: C.E.O. & Pres. (V), Raymond Cline; Vice Pres., Caroll Carun; Treas., James Arnold; Sec., Fred Barrowman.
Governing Authority: society; nonprofit. Parent Institution: Nowata County Historical Society Board of Trustees. Tax-exempt: 501(c)(3).
Historical Society Museum: housed in former Nowata Clinic Hospital Building.
Collections: cowboy room; tools; art; old dentist office; dining room with dishes; school rooms; 3 bedrooms with quilts, chambers cradle & old clothing; trophies & pictures; furniture; equipment; Indian Suite; Army & Navy display; wood carvings from all over the world; salt & pepper collections; doll room; oil field equipment.
Research Fields: history of the county & surrounding area.
Facilities: library of historical, fiction & non-fiction books available for research on premises. Museum-related items for sale.
Activities: tours.
Publications: quarterly newsletter, Nowata Historical Society Newsletter.
Hours & Admission Prices: Tues.-Sat. 1-4; other times by appointment. No charge; donations accepted. ♿
Attendance: 2,050 (estimated)
Membership: Annual $5; Lifetime $50.

Okemah

TERRITORY TOWN, five miles west of Okemah I-40, Exit 217, N. Hwy. 48, Okemah, OK 74859. Mailing Address: Rte. 2, Box 297-A, Okemah, OK 74859-9802. Tel.: 918-623-2599.
Founded: 1967.
Key Personnel: Owner, Louise Parsons.
Governing Authority: individual operation.
General Museum.
Collections: guns; Indian relics; Civil War relics; documents; early pictures; gun display.
Research Fields: local history.
Facilities: Gift items for sale.
Activities: tours.
Hours & Admission Prices: March-Sept. daily 9-7; Winter: daily 9-5. Adults $2, children 5-12 & student groups $1; children under 5 no charge.
Attendance: 933 (accurate)

Oklahoma City

ASA NATIONAL SOFTBALL HALL OF FAME AND MUSEUM COMPLEX, 2801 N.E. 50th, Oklahoma City, OK 73111-7200. Tel.: 405-424-5266. Fax: 405-424-3855.
E-mail: bplummer@softball.org
Web Site: www.asasoftball.com
Founded: 1957.
Congressional District: 6
Key Personnel: Exec. Dir., Ron Radigonda; Pres. (V), Joey Rich; Hall of Fame Svcs. Mgr., Bill Plummer, III
Personnel Profile: Full-Time Paid 28.
Governing Authority: nonprofit organization. Parent Institution: Amateur Softball Assoc. of America. Tax-exempt.
Sports Museum.
Collections: plaques; oil paintings; uniforms; softball registry; memorabilia pertinent to softball; Hall of Fame memorabilia; Olympic team displays; softball video displays.
Activities: guided tours; films; video cassettes; permanent exhibitions.
Publications: brochures; pamphlets; manuals; bimonthly, USA Softball Magazine; quarterly newsletter.
Hours & Admission Prices: March-Sept. Mon.-Fri. 8-4:30, Sat. 10-4, Sun. 1-4; Oct.-Feb. Mon.-Fri. 8-5. Adults $6, children 15 & under $3; discount to groups; teams no charge. ♿
Attendance: 150,000 (estimated)
Membership: Life $150.

AMERICAN BANJO MUSEUM, (M), 9 E. Sheridan Ave., Oklahoma City, OK 73104-2424. Mailing Address: 116 E. Oklahoma Ave., Guthrie, OK 73044. Tel.: 405-604-2793.
E-mail: info@banjomuseum.org
Formerly: National Four-String Banjo Hall of Fame Museum
Key Personnel: Exec. Dir., Johnny Baier
Musical Instrument Museum.
Collections: Banjo history & music; instruments; recordings; film; video; printed music; instructional materials; photographs.
Hours & Admission Prices: Tues.-Sat. 11-6, Sun. 12-5. Family $15, adults $6, seniors $5, children 6-17 $4.

CITY ARTS CENTER, (M), 3000 General Pershing Blvd., Oklahoma City, OK 73107-6202. Tel.: 405-951-0000. Fax: 405-951-0003.
E-mail: sherry@cityartscenter.org
Web Site: www.cityartscenter.org
Founded: 1989.
Congressional District: 5
Key Personnel: Chm. (V), Christian K. Keesee; Pres. (V), Lori Tyler; Exec. Dir., Mary Ann Prior; Administrative Dir., Sherry Fair; Artistic Dir., Clint Stone.
Personnel Profile: Full-Time Paid 9; Part-Time Paid 2; Part-Time Volunteers 100.
Arts Center.
Collections: contemporary works.
Activities: performances; classes; special events; demonstrations; meetings; social events.
Hours & Admission Prices: Mon.-Thurs. 9am-10pm, Fri.-Sat. 9-5. No charge; donations accepted. Closed major holidays. ♿
Attendance: 8,000 (estimated)

45TH INFANTRY DIVISION MUSEUM, 2145 N.E. 36th, Oklahoma City, OK 73111-5396. Tel.: 405-424-5313 & 5393. Fax: 405-424-3748.
E-mail: curator@45thdivisionmuseum.com
Web Site: www.45thdivisionmuseum.com
Founded: 1976.
Congressional District: 5
Key Personnel: Chm. Bd. (V), William G. Evans; Cur., Michael E. Gonzales; IT Specialist, Leon Shackelford; Museum Shop Mgr., Mr. Chuck Willits.
Personnel Profile: Full-Time Paid 2; Part-Time Paid 1; Part-Time Volunteers 36.
Governing Authority: state. Branch of Oklahoma Military Dept., 3501 Military Circle, Oklahoma City, OK 73111. Tel.: 405-425-8000. Tax-exempt: 501(c)(3).
Military History Museum.
Collections: military arms including the American Civil War; personal property of Adolf Hitler; original Willie & Joe cartoons created by Bill Mauldin for which he received the Pulitzer prize; uniforms; accoutrements; vehicles; photos; maps; drawings; manuscripts; technical manuals; field manuals; charts; sound recordings; film; video tape.
Research Fields: military history of Oklahoma & the Southwestern United States.
Facilities: 7,000-vol. library of general military history; vehicle identification, technical manuals available for research; auditorium; theater; classrooms. Museum-related items for sale.
Activities: lectures; films; loan, permanent & temporary exhibitions.
Publications: occasional pamphlet, Thunderbird Imprints, Historical Monographs; unit histories; authorized Bill Mauldin prints.
Hours & Admission Prices: Tues.-Fri. 9-4:15, Sat. 10-4:15, Sun. 1-4:15. No entry within 45 minutes of closing, park gates locked no later than 5. No charge; donations accepted. Closed holidays; open patriotic holidays. ♿
Attendance: 37,955 (accurate)

GAYLORD-PICKENS OKLAHOMA HERITAGE MUSEUM, (M), 1400 Classen Dr., Oklahoma City, OK 73106-6614. Tel.: 405-235-4458. Fax: 405-235-2714.
E-mail: oha@oklahomaheritage.com
Web Site: www.oklahomaheritage.com
Founded: 1971.
Congressional District: 5
Key Personnel: Pres., Shanon L. Nance; Chm. (V), Glen D. Johnson.
Personnel Profile: Full-Time Paid 13; Part-Time Paid 8.
Governing Authority: private. Tax-exempt.
Heritage Museum.
Collections: Oklahoma Hall of Fame portraits, busts, & archives.
Activities: special exhibits; tours of center. Museum Sponsors: statewide scholarship history contest; essay & poster contest; Oklahoma Hall of Fame in November; Statewide Music Contest.
Publications: magazine, Oklahoma; newsletter, Legacy; Oklahoma Trackmakers Series; Oklahoma Horizons Series.
Hours & Admission Prices: Tues.-Fri. 9-5, Sat. 10-5. Adults $7, seniors citizens 62 & up and students 6-17 $5; discounts to groups of 15 or more; members no charge. Closed New Year's Day; Thanksgiving; Christmas. ♿
Attendance: 5,000
Membership: Regular $35; Centennial $100; Sponsor $250; Pioneer $500; Honor $1,000; Corporate Circle $2,500; President's Circle $5,000; Chairman's Circle $10,000.

HARN HOMESTEAD AND 1889ER MUSEUM, 1721 N. Lincoln Blvd., Oklahoma City, OK 73105-4911. Tel.: 405-235-4058. Fax: 405-235-4041.
E-mail: cgolding@harnhomestead.com
Web Site: www.harnhomestead.com
Founded: 1986.
Congressional District: 6
Key Personnel: Chm. (V), David Sapper; Exec. Dir., Cher Lucewicz Golding; Pres. (V), Taylor Currie.
Personnel Profile: Full-Time Paid 4; Full-Time Volunteers 3; Part-Time Paid 2; Part-Time Volunteers 10; Interns 2.
Governing Authority: William Fremont Harn Gardens, Inc. Tax-exempt: 170(b)(1)(A).
Historic House: housed in 1904 Victorian house & barn located on the site of 10-acre tract which was part of 1889 Land Run.
Collections: pre-1907 furnishings; 6 historic buildings; exhibit barn.
Facilities: 10-acre facility; gazebo; picnic grounds.
Activities: guided tours; lectures; formally organized education programs for children & adults; docent program & council; permanent & temporary exhibits.
Publications: Children Today, Oklahoma Yesterday; Teachers Guide to Territorial History Activities.
Hours & Admission Prices: Mon.-Fri. 10-4. Adults $5, seniors & military $4; members and children 3 & under no charge. Closed Federal holidays. ♿
Attendance: 25,000 (accurate)
Membership: Boomer $35-$49; Stake Holder $50-$99; Homesteader $100-$249; Wagon Master $250-$749; Marshal $750-$1,499; Territorial Governor $1,500 & up.

INTERNATIONAL PHOTOGRAPHY HALL OF FAME & MUSEUM, 2100 NE 52nd St., Oklahoma City, OK 73111-7107. Tel.: 405-424-4055. Fax: 405-424-4058.
E-mail: info@iphf.org
Web Site: www.iphf.org
Founded: 1963.
Key Personnel: Exec. Dir., Michael Scalf, Sr.; Pres. (V), John Nagel
Photography Museum.
Collections: cameras, darkroom & studio equipment from the 20th century; 20th century photographic images.
Hours & Admission Prices: Mon.-Fri. 9-5, Sat. 9-6, Sun. 11-6. Adults $9.50, seniors 65 & over and children 3-12 $8.25. Closed Thanksgiving; Christmas Eve & Day.
Membership: Student $20; Introduction $35; Supporting $50; Exhibitor $150; Elector $250; Patron $500.

MELTON ART REFERENCE LIBRARY, 4300 N. Sewell, Oklahoma City, OK 73118-8010. Tel.: 405-525-3603. Fax: 405-525-0396.
E-mail: MeltonArt@aol.com
Web Site: www.marl-okc.org
Founded: 1979.
Congressional District: 6
Key Personnel: C.E.O. & Pres., Robynne Mulcahy; Dir., Suzanne Silvester.
Personnel Profile: Part-Time Paid 1; Part-Time Volunteers 1; Interns 1.
Governing Authority: nonprofit organization. Tax-exempt: 501(c)(3).
Art Resource Library.
Collections: monographs, raisonnes & biographies of artists; original art.
Research Fields: lesser known artists & their works.
Facilities: 6,000-vol. library of raisonnes, biographies & autobiographies of artists, art reference & resource books & catalogs available for use by the public; educational facilities.
Activities: guided tours; lectures; organized education programs for children & adults; loan, temporary & traveling exhibitions; study access for art students.
Publications: resource book; Artists and Their Museums - Vol. I & II; Progress on the Land; Legacy Collection; Directory of Oklahoma Artists; History of the Art Renaissance Club; Directory of Oklahoma Artists.
Hours & Admission Prices: Mon.-Fri. 10-5. No charge; donations accepted. Closed holidays. ♿
Attendance: 1,500

MYRIAD BOTANICAL GARDENS, 301 W. Reno, Oklahoma City, OK 73102-5014. Mailing Address: 100 Myriad Gardens, Oklahoma City, OK 73102-5014. Tel.: 405-297-3995. Fax: 405-297-3620.
Web Site: www.myriadgardens.com
Founded: 1975.
Key Personnel: Mgr., Allan Storjohann; Chm. (V), James R. Tolbert, III; Pres. (V), James A. Pickel; Mgmt. Specialist, Janna Beth Tipton; Myriad Gardens Foundation, Debora Morey; Cur., Janet Latham; Public Rels., Jennifer Lindsey-McClintock; Registrar, Sandy Wilson; Coord. Education, Kenton Peters; Museum Shop Mgr., Julie Pyle; Building Operations Mgr., Kendle Riley.
Personnel Profile: Full-Time Paid 16; Part-Time Paid 15; Part-Time Volunteers 80.
Governing Authority: municipal. Parent Institution: City of Oklahoma City Parks & Recreation Dept.
Botanical Gardens.
Collections: over 1,000 species of plants.
Major Exhibits: Save the Plants, Save the Planet, 1/10-4/10.
Facilities: library; 17 acres; botanical garden. Museum-related items for sale.
Activities: arts festival; concert; docent program; formal education programs for children; guided tours; hobby workshops; lectures; theater; temporary & traveling exhibitions; radio programs; plant sales; rentals; meetings. Annual Events: Holiday Lights; Independence Day; Mother & Father's Day.
Publications: quarterly newsletter, Crystal Connection.
Hours & Admission Prices: Museum: Mon.-Sat. 9-6, Sun. 12-6. Adults $6, seniors 62 & over and students 13-18 $5, children 4-12 $3; children 3 & under and members no charge. Gardens: daily 6am-11pm. No charge. Closed New Year's Day; Thanksgiving; Christmas.
Attendance: 1,000,000
Membership: Individual $25; Family & Grandparents $35; Contributor $50; Sustainer $100.

* **NATIONAL COWBOY & WESTERN HERITAGE MUSEUM,** 1700 N.E. 63rd St., Oklahoma City, OK 73111-7997. Tel.: 405-478-2250. Fax: 405-478-4714.
E-mail: info@nationalcowboymuseum.org
Web Site: www.nationalcowboymuseum.org
Formerly: National Cowboy Hall of Fame and Western Heritage Center
Founded: 1955.
Congressional District: 6
Key Personnel: Exec. Dir., Chuck Schroeder; Asst. Dir., Mike Leslie; C.F.O., Denny Zimmerman; Dir. Devel., Mary Lurry; Dir. Mktg. & Editor-in-Chief, Leslie Baker; Dir. Research Center, Chuck Rand; Dir. Education, Gretchen Jeane; Dir. Operations, Doug Lane; Mgr. Information Systems, Sharon Szymanski; Cur. Art, Ed Muno; Cur. History, Richard Rattenbury; Cur. Native American Collections, Steve Grafe; McCasland Chair Cowboy Culture, Don Reeves; Dir. Tourism Mktg., Aaron Martin; Dir. Publications, Judy Hilovsky; Dir. Public Rels. & Museum Events, Shayla Simpson; Registrar, Melissa Owens; Museum Shop Mgr., Laney Carey; Facility Sales Mgr., Charlene Ferris.
Personnel Profile: Full-Time Paid 108; Part-Time Paid 17; Part-Time Volunteers 300.
Governing Authority: nonprofit organization. Tax-exempt: 501(c)(3).
Art & History Museum.
Collections: contemporary Western & Native American fine arts including works by Russell, Remington, Schreyvogel & Fechin; Arthur & Shifra Silberman Native American Fine Arts Collection; Joe Grandee Collection of the Frontier West; cowboys & ranching; rodeo history; western popular culture; frontier military history materials; Native American material cultural; Weitzenhoffer Fine American firearms; Glenn D. Shirley Western Americana Collection.
Major Exhibits: When Animals Attack: Humorous Hunting Tableaux, 1/10-7/10; The Guitar as Art, 2/10-5/10; The Power of Music, 2/10-5/10; Earnest Spy Buck: Mother Earth Taught Me, 2/10-5/10; Prix de West, 6/10-9/10; Spectacular Building Wrecks, 7/10-12/10; TCAA, 9/10-12/10; Sole Mates: Cowboy Boots and Art, 10/10-12/10.
Research Fields: fine arts (Western & Native American); Native American material culture; cowboy culture & ranching; rodeo history; western popular culture; frontier military; social history; firearms; Western Americana; popular western imagery.
Facilities: 31,000-vol. library & archives at research center; restaurant; gardens; education center; theatre; banquet facilities. Museum-related items for sale.
Activities: guided tours; Prix de West seminars & demonstrations; after school program; docent program; chuckwagon gathering; art education workshops; Western Heritage Awards; rental facilities. Museum Sponsors: Tuesdays at Sundown; Cowboy Christmas Ball; Traditional Cowboy Arts Association Seminar.
Publications: quarterly magazine, Persimmon Hill; quarterly, The Ketchpen.
Hours & Admission Prices: Daily 9-5. Adults $10, senior citizens $8.50, children 6-12 $4.50; discount to groups; members no charge. Closed New Year's Day; Thanksgiving; Christmas. ♿
Attendance: 203,529 (accurate)
Membership: Premium Family $75; Golden Spike Society $250; Pony Express Society $500; Grand Canyon Society $1,000; Prix De West Society $3,500; American West Society $5,000; Remington & Russell Society $10,000.

* **OKLAHOMA CITY MUSEUM OF ART, (M),** 415 Couch Dr., Oklahoma City, OK 73102-2214. Tel.: 405-236-3100, ext. 200. Fax: 405-236-3122.
E-mail: ggentele@okcmoa.com
Web Site: www.okcmoa.com
Founded: 1945.
Key Personnel: C.E.O. & Pres., Glen Gentele; Chm., Frank D. Hill; Chief Cur., Hardy George, Ph.D.; Assoc. Cur., Alison Amick; Curatorial Asst., Jennifer Klos; Film Cur., Brian Hearn; Senior Assoc. Educator, Chandra Boyd; Exec. Asst., Susie Bauer; Dir. Finance, Rodney L. Lee; Facilities Operations Mgr., Jack Madden; Information Systems Admin., Garrett Cullum; Devel. Dir., Ken Lindquist; Membership & Sr. Devel. Officer, Jim Eastep; Event & Tour Coord., Whitney Cross; Communications Mgr., Leslie Spears; Chief Preparator & Photographer, James Meeks; Assoc. Preparator & Exhibit Designer, Ernesto Sanchez Villareal; Asst. Registrar, Christina Hicks; Visitor Svcs. Assoc., Talitha Clemmons; Visitor Svcs. Assoc., Sidney Moore; Chief Safety & Security, Adam Edwards; Museum Store Mgr., Christen Conger; Administrative Assoc., Diane Glenn; Editor, Nicole Emmons.
Personnel Profile: Full-Time Paid 34; Part-Time Paid 28; Part-Time Volunteers 200; Interns 8.
Governing Authority: nonprofit organization. Tax-exempt: 501(c)(3).
Art Museum: housed in the Donald W. Reynolds Visual Arts Center.
Collections: modern & contemporary late 19th to 20th-centuries American paintings; 18th to 20th centuries European paintings; American & European prints; historical maps; photography; Chihuly glass.
Research Fields: 19th & 20th-century American & European art.
Facilities: library; 250-seat theatre; 110-seat cafe; 3 classrooms; print study room; education center. Museum-related items for sale.
Activities: guided tours; lectures; films; education programs for children & adults; docent program; loan, temporary & traveling exhibitions. Museum Sponsors: Renaissance Ball; Beaux Arts Society; Friends Society; Allied Arts Foundation; museum school classes & camps.
Publications: quarterly newsletter; exhibition brochures & catalogues; annual report; permanent collection catalogues; audio guides.
Hours & Admission Prices: Tues.-Wed. & Fri.-Sat. 10-5, Thurs. 10-9, Sun. 12-5. Adults $12, senior citizens & students $9; discounts to groups of 15 or more & AAM members; members and children 5 & under no charge. Closed New Year's Day; Easter; Independence Day; Thanksgiving; Christmas. ♿
Attendance: 130,000 (accurate)
Membership: Individual $50; Family & Dual $75; Fellow $100; Friend $300; Supporter $500; Sustainer $1,000.

* **OKLAHOMA CITY NATIONAL MEMORIAL & MUSEUM, (M),** 620 N. Harvey, Oklahoma City, OK 73102-3032. Mailing Address: P.O. Box 323, Oklahoma City, OK 73101-0323. Tel.: 405-235-3313. Fax: 405-235-3315.
E-mail: kariwatkins@oklahomacitynationalmemorial.org
Web Site: www.oklahomacitynationalmemorial.org
Founded: 1995.
Congressional District: 6
Key Personnel: C.E.O., Kari F. Watkins; Dir., Joanne Riley; Chm. (V), John Richels; Museum Shop Mgr., Joyce Andrews.
Personnel Profile: Full-Time Paid 22; Part-Time Paid 3; Part-Time Volunteers 65.
Governing Authority: private; nonprofit organization. Parent Institution: Oklahoma City National Memorial Foundation. Tax-exempt: 501(c)(3).
Historic Foundation.
Collections: terrorism & the bombing of Oklahoma City's Alfred P. Murrah Federal Building; photographs; audio recordings; damaged furnishings & building pieces; personal artifacts; videos; memorial tribute.
Research Fields: terrorism; psychology; crime & punishment.
Facilities: archives; reading room.
Publications: Walking Tour of the Oklahoma National Memorial & Museum.
Hours & Admission Prices: Mon.-Sat. 9-6, Sun. 1-6. Adults $10, seniors & students $8; discounts to groups. Closed New Year's Day; Thanksgiving; Christmas Eve & Day. ♿
Attendance: 545,699 (accurate)

* **OKLAHOMA CITY ZOO, (M),** 2101 N.E. 50th St., Oklahoma City, OK 73111-7199. Tel.: 405-425-0231 & 424-3344. Fax: 405-425-0207.
E-mail: bcastro@okczoo.com

Web Site: www.okczoo.com
Founded: 1904.
Congressional District: 97
Key Personnel: C.E.O. & Exec. Dir., Dwight Scott; Chm. (V), Bob Hammack; Dir. Animal Management, Brian Aucoin; Cur. Birds, Darcy Henthorn; Cur. Mammals, Bill Savage; Mgr., Public Rels. & Mktg., Tara Henson; Dir. Education Programs, Teresa Randall; Museum Shop Mgr., Karen Jones; Horticulturist, Pearl Pearson; Dir. Bldgs. & Grounds, Ernest Wilson; Dir. Financial Svcs., Mark Campbell.
Personnel Profile: Full-Time Paid 137; Part-Time Paid 120; Part-Time Volunteers 123.
Governing Authority: municipal; nonprofit organization. Parent Institution: Oklahoma City Zoological Trust. Tax-exempt.
Zoo.
Collections: over 2,100 animals representing 500 species; exotic horticultural collection.
Research Fields: ethology; reproduction; camouflage; husbandry.
Facilities: aquarium; aquatics center; 300-seat auditorium; classrooms; food concessions. Gift items for sale.
Activities: guided tours; lectures; concerts; formally organized education programs for children, adults, undergraduate & graduate students; docent program; zoomobiles.
Publications: weekly newsletter, Gnusweek.
Hours & Admission Prices: Summer: daily 9-6. Winter: daily 9-5. Adults $7, children 3-11 & senior citizens $4, Safari Tram $2. Closed New Year's Day; Thanksgiving; Christmas. ♿
Attendance: 787,717 (accurate)
Membership: Junior $10; Wildcard $40; Family & Grandparent $60; Family Plus & Grandparent Plus $85.

OKLAHOMA FIREFIGHTERS MUSEUM, 2716 N.E. 50th St., Oklahoma City, OK 73111-7299. Tel.: 405-424-3440; 800-308-5336. Fax: 405-425-1032.
E-mail: jims@osfa.info
Web Site: osfa.info
Founded: 1970.
Congressional District: 5
Key Personnel: Dir., Jim Sanders; Mgr., Mike Billingsley.
Personnel Profile: Full-Time Paid 2; Part-Time Paid 2; Part-Time Volunteers 6.
Governing Authority: nonprofit organization. Parent Institution: The Oklahoma State Firefighters Association. Tax-exempt: 501(c)(3).
Fire-Fighting History Museum.
Collections: fire-fighting apparatus & appliances. Historic Building: 1869 first fire station in Oklahoma.
Facilities: Fire service items & gifts for sale.
Activities: audio tours; guided tours; safety DVD; lectures; films; formally organized education programs for children; permanent exhibitions; rental facilities.
Publications: Oklahoma Firefighter; Oklahoma Chiefs Association.
Hours & Admission Prices: Mon.-Sat. 9-4:30, Sun. 1-4:30. Adults $5, senior citizens $4, children 6-12 $2; discounts to AAM, ICOM & AAA members; members & children under 6 no charge. Closed major holidays. ♿
Attendance: 7,000 (accurate)
Membership: Retired $22; Chief $45; Firefighter $56.

OKLAHOMA HISTORICAL SOCIETY, 2401 N. Laird Ave., Oklahoma City, OK 73105-7914. Tel.: 405-521-2491. Fax: 405-521-2492.
Web Site: www.okhistory.org
Founded: 1893.
Congressional District: 5
Key Personnel: Exec. Dir., Dr. Bob Blackburn; Pres., James Waldo; Deputy Dir., Dr. Tim Zwink; Dir. Research Div., William Welge; Oklahoma Museum of History Dir., Dan Provo; Dir. Museums & Historic Sites Div., Kathy Dickson; Dir. Publications, Diana Everett, Ph.D; Dir. Finance, Terry Howard; Dir. Personnel, Sherri Henderson; Deputy State Historic Preservation Officer, Melvena Thurman Heisch; Museum Shop Mgr., Mike Tippit.
Personnel Profile: Full-Time Paid 144; Part-Time Paid 45; Part-Time Volunteers 1,500; Interns 4.
Governing Authority: state. Branch Museums: Oklahoma Territorial Museum, Guthrie; Museum of the Western Prairie, Altus; Tom Mix Museum, Dewey; Fort Gibson; Cherokee Strip Regional Heritage Center, Enid; Cherokee Strip Museum, Perry; No Man's Land Museum, Goodwell; Oklahoma History Center, Oklahoma City; State Capital Publishing Museum, Guthrie; White Hair Memorial, Ralston Historic Sites & Houses: 1830 Fort Towson; 1842 Fort Washita; 1920's Jim Thorpe Home, Yale; 1898 Peter Conser House, Heavener; 1828 Sequoyah's Cabin, Sallisaw; 1894 Sod House, Aline; 1930s Frank Phillips' Mansion, Bartlesville; 1903 Overholser Mansion, Oklahoma City; 1905 Drummond Home, Hominy; Chisholm Trail & Seay Mansion, Kingfisher; Pioneer Woman Museum, Ponca City; Oklahoma Rte. 66 Museum, Clinton; Fort Supply, Fort Supply; George M. Murrell Home Site, Park Hill; Pawnee Bill Ranch Site, Pawnee; Spiro Mounds Archaeological Park, Spiro; T.B. Ferguson Home Site, Watonga. Tax-exempt.
State Historical Society Museums.
Collections: approx. 1,000,000 objects; Native American collections covering indigenous & removal tribes, Spiro Mounds objects, archeological material from early historic sites; military collections; political campaign material; clothing; decorative arts; printing equipment; farm & ranch implements; paintings; toys; textiles; business machines. For more specific information see individual listings.
Research Fields: Oklahoma history; U.S. Indian policy; Native American tribes in Oklahoma; genealogy; historic architecture; military in Oklahoma.
Facilities: 80,000-vol. library of history & genealogy material available for research on premises; newspapers; microfilm; three million manuscripts & documents. Museum-related items for sale.
Activities: lectures; films; gallery talks; formally organized education programs for children; permanent, temporary & traveling exhibitions.
Publications: quarterly journal, The Chronicles of Oklahoma; brochures; the Oklahoma Series; exhibition catalogs; monthly newsletter, Mistletoe Leaves.
Hours & Admission Prices: OKlahoma History Center: Mon.-Sat. 10-5. Administration Offices: Mon.-Fri. 8-5. Field Facilities: Tues.-Fri. 9-5, Sat.-Sun. 2-5. Adults $5; discounts to AAM members; members no charge. Closed New Year's Day; Thanksgiving; Christmas. ♿
Attendance: 415,377 (accurate)
Membership: Individual $35; Institutional $50; Friend $100; Associate $250; Fellow $500; Director's Circle $1,000; Benefactor $5,000.

OKLAHOMA MUSEUM OF HISTORY, (M), 2401 N. Laird Ave., Oklahoma City, OK 73105-7914. Tel.: 405-522-5248. Fax: 405-521-5402.
Web Site: www.ok-history.mus.ok.us
Formerly: The State Museum of History
Founded: 1893.
Congressional District: 5
Key Personnel: Exec. Dir. & C.E.O., Dr. Bob Blackburn; Bd. Pres. & Chm. (V), Jim Waldo; Museum Dir., Dan Provo; Asst. Museum Dir., Jeff Briley; Dir. Education, Mike Adkins; Dir. Exhibits, Jeff Moore; Research Dir., Bill Welge; Outreach Dir., Kathy Dickson; Museum Shop Mgr., Mike Tippit.
Personnel Profile: Full-Time Paid 29; Part-Time Paid 4; Part-Time Volunteers 150.
Governing Authority: state. Parent Institution: Oklahoma Historical Society (see separate listing). Tax-exempt.
State History Museum.
Collections: material pertaining to state history; decorative arts; textiles; costumes; Native American collection; research collections.
Major Exhibits: Another Hot Oklahoma Night, 1/10-12/1/10.
Research Fields: Oklahoma history; American Indian; firearms; furniture; textiles; photography; genealogy.
Facilities: library; auditorium; classroom; archives. Museum-related items for sale.
Activities: special exhibits; extension & group programs; student education.
Publications: newsletter, Mistletoe Leaves; Chronicles of Oklahoma.
Hours & Admission Prices: Mon.-Sat. 9-5, Sun. 12-5. Families $15, adults $5, seniors $4, students $3; discount to AAM members & Smithsonian affiliates; children 5 & under and members no charge. Closed New Year's Day; Thanksgiving; Christmas Day. ♿
Attendance: 175,000 (accurate)
Membership: Single/Individual $35; Family/Dual $50; Friend $100; Associate $250; Fellow $500; Director's Circle $1,000; Benefactor $5,000.

OKLAHOMA MUSEUMS ASSOCIATION, (M), 2100 NE 52nd St., Oklahoma City, OK 73111-7107. Tel.: 405-424-7757. Fax: 405-427-5068.
E-mail: info@okmuseums.org
Web Site: www.okmuseums.org
Founded: 1972.
Congressional District: 5
Key Personnel: Exec. Dir., Brenda Granger; Pres., Deborah Burke.
Personnel Profile: Full-Time Paid 2; Part-Time Volunteers 65; Interns 1.
Governing Authority: not-for-profit organization. Tax-exempt: 501(c)(3).
Museum Service Organization.
Facilities: library.
Activities: conferences; seminars; traveling exhibitions; consultations; workshops.
Publications: quarterly newsletter, Musenews; museum education programs; technical bulletins. ♿
Membership: Student $15; Member $25; Institutional $35-$500; Treasure $50; Classis $100; Corporate $100-$1,000; Gem $175; Masterpiece $250.

OKLAHOMA RAILWAY MUSEUM, 3400 N.E. Grand Blvd., Oklahoma City, OK 73111-4417. Tel.: 405-424-8222. Fax: 405-424-0504.
Web Site: www.oklahomarailwaymuseum.org
Founded: 1999.
Congressional District: 5
Key Personnel: Pres. (V), Stan Hall; Sec., Drake Rice
Railway Museum.
Collections: Oklahoma railroad history.
Activities: seasonal train rides.
Hours & Admission Prices: Sat. 10-4. Museum: no charge. Train Rides: adults 13 & over $8, children 3-15 $5; children under 3 no charge.
Attendance: 20,368 (estimated)
Membership: Student & Senior $25; Individual $30.

OKLAHOMA VISUAL ARTS COALITION, Stage Center, 400 W. Sheridan, Oklahoma City, OK 73102. Mailing Address: P.O. Box 1946, Oklahoma City, OK 73101-1946. Tel.: 405-232-6991. Fax: 405-316-5611.
E-mail: director@ovac-ok.org
Web Site: www.ovac-ok.org
Key Personnel: Exec. Dir., Julia Kirt; Prog. Asst., Stephanie Ruggles Winter; Publications & Mktg. Mgr., Kelsey Karper
Art Museum.
Collections: works by Oklahoma artists.
Hours & Admission Prices: Call for hours.

OVERHOLSER MANSION, 405 N.W. 15th, Oklahoma City, OK 73103-3503. Tel.: 405-528-8485.
E-mail: overholser@earthlink.net
Web Site: www.preserveok.org
Founded: 1972.
Congressional District: 5
Key Personnel: Exec. Dir., Preservation Oklahoma, Dr. Sheila Spurgeon; Site Admin., Liz Carr.
Personnel Profile: Full-Time Paid 1.
Governing Authority: state. Parent Institution: Oklahoma Historical Society (See separate listing.) Tax-exempt.
Historic House: 1902-04 Overholser Mansion.
Collections: original furnishings; costumes; articles; documents.
Research Fields: Urban history of Oklahoma Territory; social, cultural & economic.
Facilities: meeting room; interpretive center.
Activities: guided tours; permanent exhibitions; lectures; workshops; education programs.
Hours & Admission Prices: Feb.-Dec. Tues.-Sat. 10-3. Adults $3, senior citizens $2.50, students 6-18 $1; discounts to AAM & ICOM members; children under 6 no charge. Closed legal holidays.
Attendance: 21,000
Membership: See separate listing for Oklahoma Historical Society.

RED EARTH MUSEUM, 2100 N.E. 52nd St., Oklahoma City, OK 73111-7198. Tel.: 405-427-5228. Fax: 405-427-8079.
E-mail: info@redearth.org
Web Site: www.redearth.org
Founded: 1978.
Congressional District: 5
Key Personnel: Exec. Dir., Connie Hart Yellowman; Dir. Communications, Eric Oesch; Dir. Devel., Christy Alcox; Dir. Programs, Erin Merryweather
Native American Museum.
Collections: American Indian cultures & history; cradleboards; contemporary & traditional art; hands-on exhibits.
Facilities: library. Museum-related items for sale.
Activities: educational programs; special events.
Hours & Admission Prices: Mon.-Fri. 9-5, Sat. 9-6, Sun. 11-6. Adult 13-64 $13.50, children 3-12 $10.25. ♿
Attendance: 200,000 (estimated)

* **SCIENCE MUSEUM OKLAHOMA, (M),** 2100 N.E. 52 St., Oklahoma City, OK 73111-7107. Tel.: 405-602-OMNI (6664) & 3726. Fax: 405-602-3767.
E-mail: otto@sciencemuseumok.org
Web Site: sciencemuseumok.org
Formerly: Omniplex Science Museum
Founded: 1958.
Congressional District: 6
Key Personnel: Pres., Don Otto; Chm. (V), James W. Farris; Communications Dir., Karen Carney; Science Programs Coord., Chris Wilkerson; Dir. Human Resources, Jennifer Friend; Dir. Devel., Ashley Perkins; Dir. Oklahoma Museum Network, Sherry Marshall; Vice Pres. Operations & Finance, Kevin Wilson; Vice Pres. Programs & Interpretation, Suzette Ellison; Controller, Charles Davis; Visitor Rels. Specialist, Melody Muniz.
Personnel Profile: Full-Time Paid 50; Part-Time Paid 87; Part-Time Volunteers 30.
Governing Authority: nonprofit organization. Tax-exempt: 501(c)(3).
Science & Technology Museum.
Collections: hands-on exhibits.
Facilities: planetarium; classrooms; auditorium; Dome Theater; gardens; cafe. Gift items for sale.
Activities: demonstrations; merit badge classes; field trips; science; traveling labs; overnight camp-ins; camp-in science; science shows; education programs for children & adults.
Publications: general museum brochure; educational brochure; email member newsletter.
Hours & Admission Prices: Mon.-Fri. 9-5, Sat. 9-6, Sun. 11-6. Adults $10.95; discounts to ASTC members; members no charge. Closed Thanksgiving; Christmas Eve & Day. ♿
Attendance: 354,500 (accurate)
Membership: Silver 2 $60; Gold 2 $80; Silver 6 $100; Silver 8 $110; Gold 6 $160.

WORLD OF WINGS PIGEON CENTER, 2300 N.E. 63rd, Oklahoma City, OK 73111-8208. Tel.: 405-478-5155; 866-570-2473. Fax: 405-478-4552.
E-mail: pigeoncenter@aol.com
Web Site: www.pigeoncenter.org
Founded: 1973.
Congressional District: 5
Key Personnel: Dir., Randy Goodpasture; Office Mgr., Tammy Potter.
Personnel Profile: Full-Time Paid 2; Part-Time Paid 1.
Governing Authority: private; nonprofit organization. Parent Institution: American Homing Pigeon Institute, Oklahoma City, OK . Tax-exempt: 501(c)(3).
Pigeon Center Museum.
Collections: paintings; sketches; books; lithographs; scientific research papers & equipment; historic collections from World Wars I & II and European use of pigeons.
Facilities: 1,000-vol. library books on pigeon flying, breeding etc.
Activities: guided tours; temporary exhibitions. Annual Event: annual races.
Hours & Admission Prices: Museum/Library: Mon.-Fri. 8-5. Administrative Offices: Mon.-Fri. 8-5. No charge; donations accepted. Closed holidays. ♿
Membership: Individual $20; Family $35; Sustaining $100; Benefactor $500; Patron $1,000.

THE WORLD ORGANIZATION OF CHINA PAINTERS, 2641 N.W. 10th St., Oklahoma City, OK 73107-5407. Tel.: 405-521-1234. Fax: 405-521-1265.
E-mail: wocporg@theshop.net
Web Site: www.theshop.net/wocporg
Founded: 1967.
Key Personnel: Exec. Dir., Patricia Dickerson; World Show Pres., Paige Gray; World Show Vice Pres., Mary Ann Clarin; Museum Shop, Office & Property Mgr., Mary Early; Exhibit Clerk, Michelle Richardson.
Personnel Profile: Full-Time Paid 3; Part-Time Volunteers 20.
Governing Authority: not-for-profit organization. Tax-exempt: 501(c)(3).
Porcelain Museum.
Collections: 19th-20th century hand painted porcelain from around the world; hand-painted porcelain from 20th century artists.
Facilities: 500-vol. library; 4,000 sq. ft. exhibit space; educational facilities. Hand painted porcelain items for sale.
Activities: guided tours; formal education programs for children & adults; painting seminars & classes; temporary exhibitions; international guest artist teachers.
Publications: bimonthly porcelain art magazine, The China Painter.
Hours & Admission Prices: Mon.-Thurs. 9-5, Sat.-Sun. call for hours. No charge; donations accepted. Closed New Year's Eve & Day; Memorial Day; Independence Day; Labor Day; Thanksgiving; Christmas. ♿
Attendance: 2,500
Membership: Organization $27; Worldwide $34; International $39.

Okmulgee

CREEK COUNCIL HOUSE MUSEUM, Town Square, 106 W. 6th, Okmulgee, OK 74447-5014. Tel.: 918-756-2324. Fax: 918-756-3671.
E-mail: creekmuseum@sbcglobal.net
Founded: 1923.
Congressional District: 2
Key Personnel: Dir., David Anderson; Pres. (V), Mary Volturo; Museum Shop Mgr., Wayne Ramer.
Personnel Profile: Full-Time Paid 3; Part-Time Paid 1; Part-Time Volunteers 25.

Governing Authority: nonprofit organization. City of Okmulgee. Parent Institution: Creek Council House Museum Association. Tax-exempt.
Muscogee Creek History Museum: housed in 1878 Creek Council House.
Collections: Indian history; archives; archaeology; history of Muscogee Creek Nation.
Research Fields: Creek trade items in Indian territory; types of Creek ornamentation.
Facilities: Creek & Oklahoma history books available for research on premises. Indian arts & crafts for sale.
Activities: guided tours.
Publications: Creek/English Dictionary, 1st & 2nd Creek readers.
Hours & Admission Prices: Memorial Day to Labor Day Tues.-Sat. 10-4:30, Sun. 1-4. No charge, except for special exhibits; discounts to AAM, ICOM & CIMA members. Closed legal holidays. ♿
Attendance: 7,843 (accurate)
Membership: Alligator (Senior Citizen) $25; Deer $30; Bird $50; Panther $100; Beaver $300; Raccoon $500; Bear $1,000; Wind $2,500.

Oologah

OOLOGAH HISTORICAL SOCIETY, 148 W. Cooweescoowee Ave., Oologah, OK 74053. Mailing Address: P.O. Box 185, Oologah, OK 74053-0185. Tel.: 918-443-2790.
Founded: 1987.
Congressional District: 2
Key Personnel: Co Pres., Marian Clark.
Personnel Profile: Part-Time Paid 2; Part-Time Volunteers 10.
Historical Society Museum.
Collections: local history & culture; photographs; personal artifacts.
Hours & Admission Prices: Mon.-Fri. 9-5, Sat. 10-2. No charge; donations accepted. ♿
Attendance: 450 (estimated)

Owasso

OWASSO HISTORICAL MUSEUM, 26 S. Main St., Owasso, OK 74055-3109. Tel.: 918-272-4966.
E-mail: mboutwell@cityofowasso.com
Web Site: cityofowasso.com/museum/index.html
Key Personnel: Dir., Marcia Boutwell
Historical Society Museum: housed in the Komma Building, built in 1928.
Collections: historical artifacts & memorabilia pertaining to the city of Owasso.
Hours & Admission Prices: Tues.-Fri. 12-4, Sat. 10-4. No charge; donations accepted.

Park Hill

CHEROKEE NATIONAL MUSEUM, (M), 21192 S. Keeler Dr., Park Hill, OK 74451. Mailing Address: P.O. Box 515, Tahlequah, OK 74465-0515. Tel.: 918-456-6007. Fax: 918-456-6165.
E-mail: info@cherokeeheritage.org
Web Site: www.cherokeeheritage.org
Founded: 1963.
Congressional District: 2
Key Personnel: Exec. Dir., Carey Tilley; Cur., I. Mickel Yantz; Archivist, Tom Mooney; Museum Shop Mgr., Kathryn Roastingear.
Personnel Profile: Full-Time Paid 40; Part-Time Volunteers 10.
Governing Authority: board of directors; nonprofit organization. Parent Institution: Cherokee National Historical Society. Subsidiary Institution: Cherokee Heritage Center. Tax-exempt: 501(c)(3).
History Museum: site of 1851 Cherokee Female Seminary, burned in 1887.
Collections: artifacts; paintings; 42-structure ancient village; 9-structure rural village; Cherokee pottery & heritage arts.
Major Exhibits: Time of Transition A Cherokee Town in the 1700s, 2/1/10-4/4/10; 39th Annual Trail of Tears Art Show, 4/10/10-5/2/10; Trading Post Exhibit, 5/10/10-8/15/10; Homecoming Art Show, 8/21/10-9/26/10; National Treasure, 10/4/10-12/31/10.
Research Fields: Cherokee history and culture; Cherokee genealogy; Ancient Village.
Facilities: 2,500-vol. library on Cherokee heritage, archives, manuscripts, photographs; microfilm; 9,000 sq. ft. exhibit space; 1,800-seat outdoor theater; arboretum. Museum-related items for sale.
Activities: traditional art classes. Museum Sponsors: Indian Territory Days; Cherokee Heritage Gospel Sing; Trail of Tears Art Show; Cherokee Genealogy Conferences; Ancient Cherokee Days; Cherokee Homecoming Art Show.
Publications: quarterly, The Columns.
Hours & Admission Prices: Feb.-Dec. Sun. 1-5, Mon.-Sat. 10-5. Adults $8.50, seniors 55 & over and college students $7.50, youth 5-18 $5; discounts to groups of 10 or more; children 5 & under and Cherokee National Historical Society, Inc. members no charge. Closed New Year's Eve; Easter; Thanksgiving; Christmas Eve & Day. ♿
Attendance: 21,000 (estimated)
Membership: Learner $25; Elder $30; Adult $40; Family $75; Mentor $250; Provider Patron $1,000; John Ross Patron $2,500; Sequoyah Patron $5,000.

MURRELL HOME, 19479 E. Murrell Home Rd., Park Hill, OK 74451-2001. Tel.: 918-456-2751. Fax: 918-456-2751.
E-mail: murrellhome@okhistory.org
Web Site: www.okhistory.org
Founded: 1948.
Congressional District: 2
Key Personnel: Site Mgr., Shirley Pettengill; Museum Shop Mgr., Amanda Pritchett.
Personnel Profile: Full-Time Paid 2; Part-Time Paid 4; Part-Time Volunteers 1.
Governing Authority: society. Parent Institution: Oklahoma Historical Society, 2401 N. Laird Ave., Oklahoma City, OK 73105-7914. Tax-exempt.
Historic House: Murrell Home built c.1845.
Collections: out-buildings; Indian artifacts; archives; costumes; pre-Civil War period furnishings.
Research Fields: Cherokee-American history.
Facilities: 200-vol. library of Cherokee Indian history books; picnic area; nature trail.
Activities: guided tours; living history education program. Gift-related items for sale.
Publications: Friends of Murrell Home Newsletter, quarterly
Hours & Admission Prices: March-Oct. Tues.-Sat. 10-5, Sun. 1-5; Nov.-Feb. Wed.-Sat. 10-5, Sun. 1-5. No charge; donations accepted. Closed state legal holidays. ♿
Attendance: 29,073 (accurate)
Membership: Individual $10; Family $15; Business & Organization $25.

Pawhuska

OSAGE COUNTY HISTORICAL SOCIETY MUSEUM, 700 N. Lynn Ave., Pawhuska, OK 74056-3238. Tel.: 918-287-9119.
E-mail: ochs@att.net
Web Site: www.osagecohistoricalmuseum.com
Founded: 1964.
Congressional District: 2
Key Personnel: C.E.O., Dir. & Cur., Mrs. J.B. Smith; Museum Shop Mgr., Judy Taylor.
Personnel Profile: Full-Time Paid 1; Full-Time Volunteers 1; Part-Time Paid 2; Part-Time Volunteers 3.
Governing Authority: society. Tax-exempt.
Historic Building: 1923 Santa Fe Depot Building.
Collections: pioneer; Indian, Western & military artifacts; items pertaining to oil; memorabilia of the first Boy Scout troop in America, 1909, organized by Rev. Mitchell of London, England with British charter; Old Santa Fe depot; early oil and American Indian exhibits & pictures; stainless steel Santa Fe; combination passenger, mail & freight car; Santa Fe cattle freight car; 1900 era one-room furnished schoolhouse.
Facilities: Books & other museum-related items for sale.
Activities: guided tours; permanent & inter-museum loan exhibitions.
Publications: History book, Osage County Profiles; booklet, Pioneer Days with the Osage Indians.
Hours & Admission Prices: Mon.-Fri. 9-5. No charge; donations accepted. Closed Thanksgiving; Christmas. ♿
Attendance: 9,000 (estimated)
Membership: Individual $5; Sustaining $12; Lifetime $100; Business $250.

OSAGE TRIBAL MUSEUM, LIBRARY, AND ARCHIVES, 819 Grandview Ave., Pawhuska, OK 74056-3203. Mailing Address: P.O. Box 779, Pawhuska, OK 74056-0779. Tel.: 918-287-5441. Fax: 918-287-1060.
E-mail: kredkorn@osagetribe.org
Web Site: www.osagetribe.com/museum.html
Formerly: Osage Nation Tribal Museum
Founded: 1938.
Key Personnel: Dir., Kathryn Red Corn.
Personnel Profile: Full-Time Paid 3; Full-Time Volunteers 2; Part-Time Volunteers 6.
Native American Museum: listed on the National Register of Historic Places.
Collections: Osage culture & history; photographs from 1800s to present; John L. bird collection; documents; maps; paintings.
Facilities: Museum-related items for sale.
Activities: Osage heritage classes; videos; lectures; public programs.
Hours & Admission Prices: Tues.-Sat. 9-5. No charge; donations accepted.
Attendance: 5,000 (estimated)

Pawnee

PAWNEE BILL RANCH AND MUSEUM, (M), 1141 Pawnee Bill Rd., Pawnee, OK 74058-3563. Mailing Address: P.O. Box 493, Pawnee, OK 74058-0493. Tel.: 918-762-2513. Fax: 918-762-2514.
E-mail: pawneebill@okhistory.org
Web Site: www.pawneebillranch.org
Founded: 1962.
Congressional District: 1
Key Personnel: Dir., Ron Brown; C.E.O., Dr. Bob Blackburn; Chm. (V), Anna Davis; Historical Collections Specialist, Erin Brown; Museum Shop Mgr., Anna Davis.
Personnel Profile: Full-Time Paid 6; Part-Time Paid 3; Part-Time Volunteers 14; Interns 1.
Governing Authority: state. Parent Institution: Oklahoma Historical Society, 2100 N. Lincoln Blvd., Oklahoma City, OK 73105-4997. Tax-exempt.
Historic House: 1910 restored house. Home of Wild West showman and bison ranch.
Collections: 1910-1940, original furnishings of Pawnee Bill; photos & exhibits of Wild West Show days; calliope; stagecoach; 1900 billboard advertising Pawnee Bill's Wild West Show; Indian artifacts; early day farming, ranching equipment.
Research Fields: Pawnee Bill and his Wild West.
Facilities: drive through Longhorn & Buffalo pasture; picnic shelters; small meeting room; activity & camping area for organized youth groups.
Activities: seminars; workshops; mansion tours & special tours. Museum Sponsors: Wild West shows in June.
Publications: brochures; fact sheets.
Hours & Admission Prices: April-Oct. Sun.-Mon. 1-4, Tues.-Sat. 10-5 (last tour 4:15); Nov.-March Wed.-Sat. 10-5, Sun. 1-4. No charge; donations accepted. Closed state holidays. ♿
Attendance: 53,319 (accurate)
Membership: Individual $15; Family $25; Institutional $75.

Perkins

OKLAHOMA TERRITORIAL PLAZA, 750 N. Main St., Perkins, OK 74059. Mailing Address: P.O. Box 788, Perkins, OK 74059-0788. Tel.: 405-547-2777.
Formerly: Old Church Center and Museum
Key Personnel: Dir., W. David Sasser.
Personnel Profile: Full-Time Volunteers 1; Part-Time Volunteers 23.
Governing Authority: Parent Institution: Oklahoma Territorial Plaza Trust. Tax-exempt.
Historic Buildings.
Collections: Oklahoma history; period furnishings & artifacts; Cimarron Valley history. Historic Buildings: 1891 church; 1896 one-room schoolhouse; 1901 log cabin; 1907 barn; 1916 Santa Fe railroad depot; 1960s service station; restored home of Frank "Pistol Pete" Eaton.
Hours & Admission Prices: Buildings: Sat.-Sun.; other times by appointment. Park: daily. No charge; donations accepted. ♿
Attendance: 7,300 (estimated)

Perry

CHEROKEE STRIP MUSEUM AND ROSE HILL SCHOOL, 2617 W. Fir St., Perry, OK 73077-7903. Tel.: 580-336-2405. Fax: 580-336-2064.
Web Site: cherokee-strip-museum.org
Formerly: Cherokee Strip Museum and Henry S. Johnston Library
Founded: 1965.
Congressional District: 6
Key Personnel: Cur., Kaye Bond.
Governing Authority: state. Parent Institution: Oklahoma Historical Society, (See separate listing). Tax-exempt.
History Museum.
Collections: agricultural equipment, medical & historical artifacts; Otoe-Missouri collections; costumes; glass. Historic Building: Rose Hill School 1895.
Facilities: library of books & newspapers.
Activities: tours; traveling & temporary displays; permanent exhibits.
Hours & Admission Prices: mid-Jan. to Dec. Tues.-Fri. 9-5, Sat. 10-4. No charge; donations accepted. Closed legal holidays. ♿
Attendance: 9,000 (accurate)
Membership: Annual $15; Lifetime $300.

Ponca City

CANN MEMORIAL BOTANICAL GARDEN, 1500 E. Grand, Ponca City, OK 74604-5209. Mailing Address: 905 W. Hartford, Ponca City, OK 74601-1162. Tel.: 580-767-0430.
Botanical Garden.
Collections: wisteria arbors; sundials; water garden; perennials; herbs; annuals. Historic House: c.1908 home.
Facilities: 10 acre gardens; nature trails.
Activities: rental facilities.
Hours & Admission Prices: Daily dawn to dusk. No charge; donations accepted.

CONOCO MUSEUM, 501 W. South Ave., Ponca City, OK 74601-6105. Tel.: 580-765-8687.
E-mail: carla.m.o'neill@conocophillips.com
Web Site: www.conocomuseum.com
Key Personnel: Dir., Carla O'Neill
History Museum.
Collections: artifacts & memorabilia pertaining to the Conoco Oil Company.
Hours & Admission Prices: Mon.-Sat. 10-5, Sun. 1-5. No charge. Closed holidays.

MARLAND MANSION ESTATE, 901 Monument Rd., Ponca City, OK 74604-3600. Tel.: 580-767-0420; 800-422-8340. Fax: 580-763-8054.
E-mail: marlandmansion@poncacityok.gov
Web Site: www.marlandmansion.com
Key Personnel: Exec. Dir., David Keathly
Historic House Museum: housed in a 55-room Italian Renaissance villa, c.1925.
Collections: murals; mosaic ceiling; period furnishings; personal artifacts.
Activities: guided tours.
Hours & Admission Prices: Mon.-Sat. 10-5, Sun. 1-5. Adults $7, seniors 65 & over and students 12-17 $5, students 6-11 $4.

MARLAND'S GRAND HOME, 1000 E. Grand, Ponca City, OK 74601-5607. Tel.: 580-767-0427.
Web Site: marlandgrandhome.com
Formerly: Ponca City Cultural Center Museum
Founded: 1968.
Congressional District: 38
Key Personnel: Dir., David Keathly.
Personnel Profile: Full-Time Paid 1; Part-Time Paid 1; Part-Time Volunteers 20.
Governing Authority: municipal. Tax-exempt.
Cultural Center & Ethnology Museum.
Collections: cultural artifacts of five neighboring Native American tribes: Ponca, Kaw, Otoe, Osage & Tonkawa; 101 ranch & Wild West Show memorabilia; D.A.R. display; restored historic furnishings & decor.
Research Fields: American Indians; cowboys; ranch life; E.W. Marland.
Publications: museum brochure.
Hours & Admission Prices: Tues.-Sat. 10-5. Adults $3, children 6-16 $1. Closed holidays.
Attendance: 8,500 (accurate)
Membership: Pioneers $10; Land Seekers $25; Claim Stakers $100; Sod Busters $250; Homesteaders $500; Builders $1,000.

PIONEER WOMAN STATUE & MUSEUM, 701 Monument, Ponca City, OK 74604-3910. Tel.: 580-765-6108. Fax: 580-762-2498.
E-mail: info@pioneerwomanmuseum.com
Web Site: www.pioneerwomanmuseum.com
Founded: 1958.
Congressional District: 6
Key Personnel: Dir., Rebecca Larsen Brave.
Personnel Profile: Full-Time Paid 2; Part-Time Paid 1; Part-Time Volunteers 6.
Governing Authority: state. Affiliated with the Oklahoma Historical Society, 2100 Lincoln Blvd., Oklahoma City, OK 73105. Tax-exempt.
State Park Museum & Historical Museum.
Collections: 17' bronze statue of the Pioneer Woman by Bryant Baker; Oklahoma's pioneer women; E.W. Marland, Governor of Oklahoma 1935-39; important women of Oklahoma.
Research Fields: E. W. Marland; 101 Ranch & Miller brothers; women of Oklahoma.
Facilities: Museum-related items for sale.
Activities: guided tours; weaving demonstrations; traveling exhibitions; video on Oklahoma women; educational programming.
Publications: museum exhibits & Oklahoma women booklet.
Hours & Admission Prices: Tues.-Sat. 9-5, Sun. 1-5. Adults $3, senior citizens $2.50, students 6-18 $1; Oklahoma Historical Society members no charge. Closed state holidays. ♿
Attendance: 8,500 (accurate)

PONCA CITY ART CENTER, 819 E. Central, Ponca City, OK 74601-5506. Mailing Address: P.O. Box 1394, Ponca City, OK 74602-1394. Tel.: 580-765-9746.
E-mail: pcartcenter@sbcglobal.net
Web Site: www.poncacity.com/attractions/art_center.htm
Founded: 1966.
Key Personnel: Dir. & Office Mgr., Jerry Cathey.
Governing Authority: Tax-exempt.
Art Museum: housed in Soldani Mansion. Listed on the National Register of Historic Places.
Collections: paintings.
Facilities: Museum-related items for sale.
Activities: art classes; workshops. Annual Event: Fine Arts Festival.
Hours & Admission Prices: Wed.-Sun. 1-5. No charge; donations accepted. Closed Independence Day; Thanksgiving, Christmas.
Membership: Individual & Family $20; Sponsor $30; Donor $50; Fellow of the Arts $75; Founder $150; Life $1,000; Benefactor $5,000.

Poteau

ROBERT S. KERR MUSEUM, 23009 Kerr Mansion Rd., Poteau, OK 74953-8119. Tel.: 918-647-8221. Fax: 918-647-3952.
E-mail: cburleigh@carlalbert.edu
Web Site: www.casc.cc.ok.us/kerr_center
Founded: 1968.
Congressional District: 3
Key Personnel: Dir., Cheryl Burleigh.
Personnel Profile: Full-Time Paid 1; Part-Time Paid 1; Part-Time Volunteers 5.
Governing Authority: society. Parent Institution: Carl Albert State College. Tax-exempt: 501(c)(3).
Oklahoma History Museum.
Collections: Senator Robert S. Kerr pictures & mementoes; Spiro Mounds artifacts; farm & home implements; geology of east Oklahoma; barbed wire; pioneer artifacts; Choctaw Indian artifacts; Viking runestones.
Research Fields: prehistory.
Facilities: Kerr Country Mansion; conference rooms.
Activities: lectures; art & quilt exhibits.
Publications: newsletter; booklets; Butterfield Stage; Pre-Historic People; The Choctaw Story; The Edward's Store; When Coal Was King.
Hours & Admission Prices: Mon.-Fri. 9-5, Sat.-Sun. 1-5. No charge; donations accepted. Closed major holidays. ♿
Attendance: 3,556 (accurate)
Membership: Annual $10; Contributing $25; Lifetime $500.

Ripley

WASHINGTON IRVING TRAIL & MUSEUM, 3918 S. Mehan Rd., Ripley, OK 74062-6278. Tel.: 405-624-9130.
Founded: 1994.
Congressional District: 3
Key Personnel: Dir. & Museum Shop Mgr., Dale Chlouber.
Personnel Profile: Full-Time Volunteers 1; Part-Time Volunteers 12.
Governing Authority: Tax-exempt.
History Museum.
Collections: local, state & regional history; Civil War; Southwest Indian artifacts.
Publications: The Oklahoma Cowboy Band, 1908.
Hours & Admission Prices: Wed.-Sat. 11-5, Sun. 1-5. No charge; donations accepted. ♿
Attendance: 8,000 (estimated)

Sallisaw

14 FLAGS MUSEUM, 400 E. Cherokee, Sallisaw, OK 74955. Mailing Address: Rural Rte. 1, P.O. Box 103A, Sallisaw, OK 74955. Tel.: 918-775-2608. Fax: 918-775-9550.
E-mail: chamber@sallisawok.org
History Museum: housed in a log cabin; built in 1845.
Collections: Oklahoma's history & culture; period furnishings; general store; cattle brands; caboose.
Hours & Admission Prices: Daily 9-5. No charge.

SEQUOYAH CABIN, Rte. 1, Sallisaw, OK 74955-9744. Mailing Address: P.O. Box 141, Sallisaw, OK 74955-9744. Tel.: 918-775-2413.
E-mail: seqcabin@ipa.net
Formerly: Sequoyah Home Site
Founded: 1936.
Congressional District: 2
Key Personnel: C.E.O., Bob Blackburn; Cur. & Museum Shop Mgr., Jerry Dobbs.
Personnel Profile: Full-Time Paid 2; Full-Time Volunteers 1; Part-Time Volunteers 5.
Governing Authority: state. Parent Institution: Oklahoma Historical Society. Tax-exempt.
Historic Building & Site: housed in 1829, Sequoyah Log Cabin.
Collections: artifacts; house furnishings & exhibits relating to Native Americans (primarily Cherokee) & the inventor of the Cherokee Syllabary (Sequoyah); interpretative exhibit center.
Research Fields: Cherokee history.
Facilities: visitor center; picnic area.
Activities: various cultural & educational activities.
Publications: booklets: Mistletoe Leaves; quarterly newsletter, Chronicles of Oklahoma.
Hours & Admission Prices: Tues.-Fri. 9-5, Sat.-Sun. 2-5. No charge; donations accepted. Closed holidays. ♿
Attendance: 20,000 (estimated)
Membership: Student & Retired over 64 $15; Annual Individual $25; Institutional & Family $40; Supporting $75; Individual Life $500; Benefactor $1,000.

Sand Springs

SAND SPRINGS CULTURAL & HISTORICAL MUSEUM, 9 E. Broadway, Sand Springs, OK 74063. Tel.: 918-246-2509. Fax: 918-245-7101.
E-mail: museum@sandspringsok.org
Web Site: www.sandspringsmuseum.org
Founded: 1991.
Congressional District: 1
Key Personnel: C.E.O., Dir. & Museum Shop Mgr., Dr. Stacy Reaves; Chm. (V), Jerry Hanner; Chm. (V), Ed Dubie; Pres. (V), Cynthia Phillips; Public Events, Ruth Ellen Henry.
Personnel Profile: Full-Time Paid 2; Part-Time Volunteers 14.
Governing Authority: private; nonprofit organization. Parent Institution: City of Sand Springs. Tax-exempt.
Cultural and Historical Museum.
Collections: cultural heritage artifacts.
Facilities: Charles Pages Memorial Library.
Activities: genealogy workshops; children's art shows; art classes; tours.
Publications: quarterly, Sands Springs Reflections; annual, Sand Springs Cultural & Historical Museum History Calendar.
Hours & Admission Prices: Tues.-Wed. & Fri. 10-5, Thurs. 10-7, Sat. 10-2; other times by appointment. No charge; donations accepted. ♿
Attendance: 5,000 (estimated)
Membership: Senior $10; Individual $15; Family $20; Business $50; Contributing $100; Corporate $250; Sponsor $500; Patron $1,000.

Sapulpa

SAPULPA HISTORICAL MUSEUM, 100 E. Lee, Sapulpa, OK 74066-4216. Mailing Address: P.O. Box 278, Sapulpa, OK 74067-0278. Tel.: 918-224-4871. Fax: 918-224-7765.
E-mail: sapulpahistsoc@tulsacoxmail.com
Founded: 1968.
Congressional District: 1
Key Personnel: Pres., David Robertson; Vice Pres., Ron Gibson; Dir. & Treas., Doris R. Yocham; Sec., Darla Reed.
Personnel Profile: Full-Time Volunteers 1; Part-Time Paid 1; Part-Time Volunteers 55.
Governing Authority: nonprofit. Tax-exempt: 501(c)(3).
History Museum: housed in three-story, 1910 Wills Building, which was renovated in 1982.
Collections: early 1900s kitchen equipment; parlor furniture; hand-pulled ladder wagon; 1900s-1920s clothes; militaria; Frisco railroad items; glass industry items; Native American artifacts; Native American and African-American photographs; arrowheads; 1939 Fire Engine; Catfish String Band instruments; early oil field display; early schoolroom; general store; war artifacts.
Research Fields: local history.
Activities: guided tours.
Publications: quarterly, Our Heritage; Sapulpa History Books, Vols. I & II.
Hours & Admission Prices: Jan. to late Aug. & Sept. to late Dec. Mon.-Thurs. 10-3. No charge; donations accepted. Closed major holidays. ♿
Attendance: 1,800 (accurate)
Membership: Annual $15; Family $25; Life $125.

Sayre

SHORTGRASS COUNTRY MUSEUM SOCIETY, 106 E. Poplar Ave., Sayre, OK 73662-2933. Mailing Address: P.O. Box 260, Sayre, OK 73662-0260.
Founded: 1992.

Key Personnel: Dir., Joan Ellison; Business Advisor & Dir., Bunny Neff.
Personnel Profile: Part-Time Paid 1; Part-Time Volunteers 7.
Governing Authority: Tax-exempt.
Historic Building Museum: housed in the former Rock Island Depot; built in 1901.
Collections: western Oklahoma history; railroad history; personal artifacts.
Research Fields: local family histories.
Activities: reading program with school; outreach presentations. Museum Sponsors: Open Houses.
Publications: newsletter.
Hours & Admission Prices: Feb.-Nov. Tues.-Fri. 9-12; Dec.-Jan. call for hours; other times by appointment. No charge; donations accepted. ♿
Attendance: 350 (estimated)
Membership: Retired over 65 $10; Single $15; Family $20; Business $30; Donor $250; Support $500; Endowment $1,000; Patron $2,500.

Seminole

JASMINE MORAN CHILDREN'S MUSEUM, 1714 Hwy. 9 W., Seminole, OK 74868. Tel.: 405-382-0950. Fax: 405-382-3707.
Web Site: www.jasminemoran.com/frameset.html
Key Personnel: Exec. Dir., Marci Donato
Children's Museum.
Collections: hands-on exhibits.
Activities: train ride.
Hours & Admission Prices: Tues.-Sat. 10-5, Sun. 1-5. Admission 3-60 $8, seniors over 60 $7; children under 3 no charge. Closed major holidays.

Shattuck

SHATTUCK WINDMILL MUSEUM & PARK, 1100 S. Main, Shattuck, OK 73858. Mailing Address: P.O. Box 227, Shattuck, OK 73858-0227. Tel.: 580-938-5291.
Founded: 1994.
Key Personnel: Dir., Phillis Ballew; Chm. (V), Naomi Bradley
History Museum.
Collections: 51 restored mills from 1870 to 1970; wooden wheels; 18' railroad eclipse. Historic Buildings: 1901 homestead; Halladay standard mill; half dugout soddy, 1904.
Hours & Admission Prices: Daily. No charge. ♿
Attendance: 1,500 (accurate)

Shawnee

CITIZEN POTAWATOMI NATION CULTURAL HERITAGE CENTER, (M), 1899 S. Gordon Cooper Dr., Shawnee, OK 74801-9004. Tel.: 405-878-5830; 800-880-9880. Fax: 405-878-5840.
Web Site: www.potawatomi.org
Formerly: Citizen Potawatomi Museum
Founded: 2006.
Key Personnel: Chm., John A. "Rocky" Barrett; Mgr. Collections, Stacy S. Coon; Facilities & Operations Mgr., Cindy Stewart
Native American Museum.
Collections: Potawatomi history & cultural heritage; art; crafts; language; textiles.
Hours & Admission Prices: Tues.-Fri. 8-5, Sat. 10-3. No charge; donations accepted. Closed holidays. ♿
Attendance: 21,000

MABEE-GERRER MUSEUM OF ART, (M), 1900 W. MacArthur, Shawnee, OK 74804-2403. Tel.: 405-878-5300. Fax: 405-878-5133.
E-mail: info@mgmoa.org
Web Site: www.mgmoa.org
Founded: 1914.
Congressional District: 5
Key Personnel: Dir., Dane Pollei; Chm., Linda Peterson; Preparator, Clay Little; Cur. Education, Donna Merkt; Cur. Collections & Museum Shop Mgr., Delaynna Trim; Dir. Devel., Tonya Ricks.
Personnel Profile: Full-Time Paid 5; Part-Time Paid 3; Part-Time Volunteers 100; Interns 2.
Governing Authority: nonprofit corporation. Parent Institution: St. Gregory's Abbey. Tax-exempt: 501(c)(3).
Art Museum.
Collections: artifacts from ancient civilizations including: Egyptian, Babylonian, pre-Columbian, North, South and Central American Indians, African, South Pacific, Asian, European & American oil paintings; prints; drawings; watercolors; Persian & Chinese oriental rugs; bronze, ivory, marble and Romanesque wood sculpture.
Major Exhibits: Ancient Bronzes of the Asian Grasslands from the Arthur M. Sackler Foundation (T), 1/23/10-3/28/10; Objects of Devotion: Spanish Colonial Art 1650-1950, 4/30/10-6/13/10.
Facilities: 1,500-vol. library of art for public use; sculpture garden.
Activities: guided tours; lectures; organized education programs for children & adults, including art classes, art camp & programs with local schools; docent program; loan exhibitions.
Publications: catalogs with exhibitions.
Hours & Admission Prices: Tues.-Sat. 10-5, Sun. 1-4. Adults $5, Seniors $4, children 6-17 $3; discount to AAM members; children under 5 no charge. Closed major holidays. ♿
Attendance: 20,000 (estimated)
Membership: Student $15; Individual $35; Family $50; Hudson River League $100; Chase Studio League $250; Papyrus Guild $500; School of Raphael $1,000.

PRAGUE HISTORICAL MUSEUM, 1008 N. Broadway, Shawnee, OK 74801-5043. Tel.: 405-567-4750.
History Museum.
Collections: local history & culture; photographs; Olympian Jim Thorpe artifacts.
Activities: Annual Event: Kolache Festival in May.
Hours & Admission Prices: Mon., Wed. & Fri. 1-4; groups by appointment. No charge; donations accepted.

Skiatook

SKIATOOK MUSEUM, 115 S. Broadway, Skiatook, OK 74070-1540. Tel.: 918-396-7558.
Key Personnel: Pres., Donna Sue Jones; Vice Pres., John Reynolds
History Museum: housed in a former doctor's home, built in 1912.
Collections: Cherokee & Osage artifacts including clothing & drums; local history; personal artifacts; documents; furniture; photographs; newspapers; military uniforms & medals; WWI, WWII & Korean War; period doctor's equipment.
Hours & Admission Prices: Tues.-Fri. 1-4. No charge; donations accepted. Closed legal holidays.

Spiro

SPIRO MOUNDS ARCHAEOLOGICAL CENTER, 18154 1st St., Spiro, OK 74959-4463. Tel.: 918-962-2062. Fax: 918-962-2062.
E-mail: spiromds@ipa.net
Web Site: www.okhistory.org
Founded: 1978.
Congressional District: 3
Key Personnel: Historic Property Mgr., Dennis Peterson.
Personnel Profile: Full-Time Paid 2; Part-Time Paid 1.
Governing Authority: state. Parent Institution: Oklahoma Historical Society. Tax-exempt.
Archaeological Site.
Collections: original & reproductions of artifacts; 1250-1450, Spiro Phase period.
Research Fields: archaeology; Mississippian culture & art.
Facilities: interpretive center.
Activities: trail; group tours. Annual Events: Kite Flite Day; Winter Solstice, Summer Solstice, Vernal Equinox & Autumnal Equinox tours & programs.
Publications: brochures.
Hours & Admission Prices: Wed.-Sat. 9-5, Sun. 12-5. No charge; donations accepted. Closed New Year's Eve & Day; Thanksgiving; Christmas. ♿
Attendance: 10,000 (estimated)
Membership: Spiro Mounds Development Associates: Individual $10; Organization $25; Lifetime $500.

Stillwater

GARDINER ART GALLERY, Oklahoma State University, Stillwater, OK 74078-0001. Mailing Address: 108 Bartlett Center, Stillwater, OK 74078-4084. Tel.: 405-744-6016. Fax: 405-744-5767.
Web Site: art.okstate.edu
Founded: 1965.
Congressional District: 6
Key Personnel: Gallery Dir., Teresa Holder.
Personnel Profile: Full-Time Paid 1; Part-Time Paid 1; Interns 1.
Governing Authority: university. Parent Institution: Oklahoma State University, Dept. of Art. Tax-exempt.
Art Museum.
Collections: graphics.
Activities: rotating exhibitions.
Publications: calendar; occasional catalog.
Hours & Admission Prices: Mon.-Fri. 8-5. No charge. Closed national holidays. ♿
Attendance: 10,000 (estimated)

NATIONAL WRESTLING HALL OF FAME & MUSEUM, 405 W. Hall of Fame Ave., Stillwater, OK 74075-5025. Tel.: 405-377-5243. Fax: 405-377-5244.
E-mail: info@wrestlinghalloffame.org
Web Site: www.wrestlinghalloffame.org
Founded: 1976.
Congressional District: 3
Key Personnel: C.E.O., Lee Roy Smith; Chm. (V), James Keen; Museum Shop Mgr., April Chipman.
Personnel Profile: Full-Time Paid 3; Part-Time Paid 2.
Governing Authority: nonprofit corporation. Tax-exempt: 501(c)(3).
Sports Museum: located near campus of Oklahoma State University.
Collections: Wall of Champions display; Hall of Outstanding Americans; Hall of Distinguished Members; memorabilia including medals, trophies, scrapbooks, statues, photos & clothing pertaining to amateur wrestling.
Facilities: 10,000-vol. library available for research on premises; reading room; auditorium; theater. Wrestling-related gift items for sale.
Activities: films; lectures.
Publications: newsletter.
Hours & Admission Prices: Mon.-Fri. 9-4; other times by appointment. Adults $5, students $2 Closed holidays. ♿
Attendance: 10,000 (estimated)

OKLAHOMA STATE UNIVERSITY BOTANICAL GARDEN, (M), 360 Agricultural Hall, Stillwater, OK 74078-6025. Tel.: 405-744-5414. Fax: 405-744-9709.
Web Site: hortla.okstate.edu
Founded: 1935.
Congressional District: 3
Key Personnel: Dir., Dr. Dale M. Maronek; Education, Mr. David Hillock; Cur., Dr. Mike Schnelle.
Personnel Profile: Full-Time Paid 4; Part-Time Paid 6; Part-Time Volunteers 43; Interns 1.
Governing Authority: public university.
Botanical Garden.
Collections: theme gardens.
Research Fields: turfgrass; woody & herbaceous ornamental plants.
Facilities: botanical garden; educational facilities; field research station.
Activities: formal education programs for adults & university students. Annual Event: Garden Fest.
Hours & Admission Prices: Mon.-Fri. 8-5. No charge; donations accepted.
Attendance: 12,000 (estimated)
Membership: Student $20; Corporate Partner $125; Sustaining Partner $250; Garden Partner $500; Founding Partner $1,000.

THE SHEERAR AND CULTURAL HERITAGE CENTER, 702 S. Duncan St., Stillwater, OK 74074-4443. Tel.: 405-377-0395.
Web Site: www.sheerarmuseum.org
History Museum.
Collections: local history & culture; household articles; clothing; tools; 3,450 buttons from 1740-1930.
Hours & Admission Prices: Tues.-Fri. 11-4, Sat.-Sun. 1-4. No charge. Closed major holidays.

Sulphur

CHICKASAW NATIONAL RECREATION AREA, 1008 W. Second St., Sulphur, OK 73086-4814. Tel.: 580-622-7236 (Visitor Information Station); 7220 (Headquarters). Fax: 580-622-2296. TDD: 580-622-3165.
Web Site: www.nps.gov/chic
Formerly: Platt National Park
Founded: 1906.
Congressional District: 4
Key Personnel: Supt., Bruce Noble; Chief Interpreter, Ron Parker.
Personnel Profile: Full-Time Paid 4; Part-Time Paid 1.
Governing Authority: federal. Operated by National Park Service, U.S. Dept. of Interior. Tax-exempt.
Nature Center.
Collections: snakes; frogs; turtles; insects; plants; fish; mammals; birds; herbarium.
Research Fields: natural history
Facilities: 700-vol. library of books on natural history, conservation, ecology, environmental problems, history of the area, interpretation & education available for use on premises; reading room; 140-seat auditorium. Books for sale.
Activities: nature walks; films; children's programs; environmental education; evening interpretive programs; Junior Ranger program; living history program c.1906.
Publications: orientation brochures, trail guide, visitors guide.
Hours & Admission Prices: Park: daily. Nature Center: Memorial Day-Labor Day daily 9-5:30; Sept.-May daily 9-4:30. No charge. Closed New Year's Day; Thanksgiving; Christmas. ♿
Attendance: 95,167 (accurate)

Tecumseh

TECUMSEH HISTORICAL SOCIETY MUSEUM, 114 S. Broadway, Tecumseh, OK 74873-3206. Tel.: 405-598-8666.
Historical Society Museum: housed in the former Dixon Millinery.
Collections: local history & culture; photographs; period ledgers; Dixon Millinery company artifacts including hats.
Hours & Admission Prices: Sat. 10-2. No charge.

Tishomingo

CHICKASAW COUNCIL HOUSE MUSEUM, 209 N. Fisher, Tishomingo, OK 73460-1717. Mailing Address: P.O. Box 1548, Ada, OK 74821-1548. Tel.: 580-371-3351.
E-mail: museum@chickasaw.net
Web Site: www.chickasaw.net
Founded: 1970.
Congressional District: 3
Key Personnel: Mgr., Flora Fink.
Personnel Profile: Full-Time Paid 4; Interns 1.
Governing Authority: state. Parent Institution: Chickasaw Nation. Tax-exempt.
Native American Museum.
Collections: articles relating to the Chickasaws life in Oklahoma Indian territory; first Council House built & used by Chickasaws; Mississippi migration; Chickasaw works.
Research Fields: genealogy; local history; court records; Chickasaw Dawes Rolls cemetery records.
Facilities: library of Indian Territory Court records & material pertaining to history of the Chickasaws available for use on premises.
Activities: guided tours; lectures; study clubs; permanent exhibitions.
Hours & Admission Prices: Mon.-Fri. 9-6, Sat. 10-4. No charge; donations accepted. Closed legal holidays. ♿

Tonkawa

THE A.D. BUCK MUSEUM OF NATURAL HISTORY & SCIENCE, 1220 E. Grand, Tonkawa, OK 74653. Mailing Address: P.O. Box 310, Tonkawa, OK 74653-0310. Tel.: 580-628-6200. Fax: 405-628-6209.
E-mail: rex.ackerson@north-ok.edu
Founded: 1913.
Congressional District: 6
Key Personnel: Academic Dean, Judy Colwell; Faculty Dir. & Cur., Rex Ackerson.
Personnel Profile: Part-Time Paid 2.
Governing Authority: college. North Central Accreditations Association. Parent Institution: Northern Oklahoma College. Tax-exempt: 170(b)(1)(A).
History & Science Museum.
Collections: Indian; mineralogy; zoology; pioneer artifacts; Northern Oklahoma history.
Research Fields: local history.
Activities: guided tours; inter-museum loan, permanent & temporary exhibitions.
Hours & Admission Prices: Sept.-May Mon.-Fri. 2-5. No charge. ♿
Attendance: 117 (accurate)

Tulsa

ELSING MUSEUM, LRC 139B, 7777 S. Lewis Ave., Tulsa, OK 74171-0001. Tel.: 918-495-6262.
Web Site: elsing.oru.edu
Founded: 1975.
Key Personnel: Dir., Dr. Nate Meleen; Cur., Roger Bush; Geologist, Dr. Steve Herr.
Governing Authority: Parent Institution: Oral Roberts University. Tax-exempt.
Geology Museum.
Collections: gems; minerals; natural art; Indian artifacts; oriental artifacts.
Hours & Admission Prices: Wed.-Sat. 1:30-4:30. No charge; donations accepted. Closed holidays. ♿
Attendance: 600 (estimated)

* **GILCREASE MUSEUM, (M),** 1400 N. Gilcrease Museum Rd., Tulsa, OK 74127-2100. Tel.: 918-596-2700 & 2787; 888-655-2278 (Toll Free). Fax: 918-596-2770.
Web Site: www.gilcrease.utulsa.edu
Founded: 1949.
Congressional District: 1

Key Personnel: Exec. Dir., Duane H. King, Ph.D.; Rights & Reproduction, Rob Cross; Collections Mgr., Randy Ramer; Dir. Membership, Linda Galbraith; Registrar, Amanda Lett; Dir. Devel., Carolyn Dalton; Dir. Education, Lanette Coppage; Dir. Museum Shop, Amanda Burns; Event Coord., Kristin Licciardone; Public Information Officer, Anne Brockman; Cur. Exhibitions, David Newell.
Personnel Profile: Full-Time Paid 45; Part-Time Paid 7; Interns 2.
Governing Authority: Parent Institution: City of Tulsa. Subsidiary Institution: University of Tulsa. Tax-exempt: 501(c)(3).
American History & Art Museum.
Collections: American sculpture & painting; manuscripts; cultures of Five Civilized Tribes; American Indian artifacts from the Arctic to Mexico; the westward movement in U.S.; documents; graphics; artifacts from the cultures of Central & South America.
Major Exhibits: The Masterworks of Charles M. Russell: A Retrospective of Painting & Sculpture (T), 2/10-5/10; The West of Olaf Seltzer, 2/10-9/10; America: Life, Liberty & The Pursuits of a Nation, 6/10-1/11.
Research Fields: archaeology; ethnology; art history.
Facilities: 111,000-vol. library of documents, manuscripts, maps, books & photographs on trans-Mississippi west, Five Civilized Tribes, surveys & Western movement, colonial, Indian & Hispanic history available for use by appointment; reading room; 220-seat, state-of-the-art auditorium; restaurant; 470 adjacent acres; 23 acres landscaped with historic theme gardens. Books, prints of paintings, Indian jewelry & other museum-related items for sale.
Activities: guided tours; lectures; films; gallery talks; rental facilities; formal education programs for children, adults & undergraduate college students; docent program; permanent & temporary exhibitions.
Publications: biannual, Gilcrease Journal; bimonthly, Gilcrease Newsletter; books, Thomas Moran: The Field Sketches; A Guidebook to Manuscripts; First Artist of the West: George Catlin Paintings & Watercolors from the Collection of Gilcrease Museum; Catlin Catalogue; Visitor's Guide to Collections; Treasures of Gilcrease; Alfred Jacob Miller: Watercolors of the American West; George Catlin's Souvenir of the North American Indians; After Lewis and Clark: The Forces of Change 1806-1871; The Many Faces of Edward Sherriff Curtis; Charles Banks Wilson: An Oklahoma Life in Art.
Hours & Admission Prices: Tues.-Sun. 10-5. Adults $8, seniors 62 & over and military $6, college students $5; Univ. of Tulsa students, school tours, members, 1st Tues. of month and children 18 & under no charge. Closed Christmas. ♿
Attendance: 73,154 (accurate)
Membership: Student $25; Individual $50; Family & Dual $65; Friend $125; Supporter $250; Young Patron $400; Patron $500.

INTERNATIONAL LINEN REGISTRY MUSEUM, 4107 S. Yale Ave., Tulsa, OK 74135-6015.
General Museum.
Collections: period linens from around the world.
Activities: demonstrations; seminars.
Hours & Admission Prices: Mon.-Thurs. & Sat. 10-9, Fri. 10-4, Sun. 12-6. No charge.

MABLE B. LITTLE HERITAGE HOUSE MUSEUM, 322 N. Greenwood Ave., Tulsa, OK 74120-1026. Tel.: 918-596-1006. Fax: 918-583-2770.
E-mail: mlmackey@sbcglobal.net
Historic House.
Collections: period artifacts; early furnishings; personal artifacts.
Hours & Admission Prices: Mon.-Fri. 9-4:30, Sat. by appointment.

* **THE PHILBROOK MUSEUM OF ART, INC., (M),** 2727 S. Rockford Rd., Tulsa, OK 74114-4104. Mailing Address: P.O. Box 52510, Tulsa, OK 74152-0510. Tel.: 918-748-5300 & 5321. Fax: 918-743-4230. TDD: 918-749-7941 (public info. line).
E-mail: jdorsey@philbrook.org
Web Site: www.philbrook.org
Founded: 1938.
Congressional District: 1
Key Personnel: Exec. Dir., Pres. & C.E.O., Randall Suffolk; Chm., Bill Lobeck; Deputy Dir., David Singleton; Facility Mgr., Charisse Cooper; Dir. Exhibitions & Collections, Christine Knop Kallenberger; Librarian, Tom Young; Museum Shop Mgr., Susan Shrewder; Dir. Devel., Janice Updike Walker; Dir. Finance, Donna Durrin; Cur. Native American & Non Western Art, Christina Burke.
Personnel Profile: Full-Time Paid 60; Part-Time Paid 15; Part-Time Volunteers 400; Interns 2.
Governing Authority: state. nonprofit organization. Tax-exempt: 501(c)(3).
Art Museum & Gardens.
Collections: Samuel H. Kress Italian Renaissance paintings & sculptures; American & European paintings; Clark Field American Indian baskets & pottery; American Indian costumes & artifacts; American Indian paintings; African sculpture; Japanese screens & scrolls; Southeast Asian ceramics; American & European prints, Old Masters to present; contemporary art; Eugene B. Adkins Native American & western art.
Major Exhibits: A Passion for the West: Paintings from the Eugene B. Adkins Collection, 12/09-1/10; Hans Hofmann: Circa 1950 (T), 2/10-5/10; To Live Forever: Egyptian Treasures from the Brooklyn Museum (T), 6/10-9/10; Adaptation: Video Installations by Guy Ben-Ner, Arturo Herrera, Catherine Sullivan and Eve Sussman and the Rufus Corp. (T), 10/10-1/11.
Research Fields: American Indian art.
Facilities: 18,900-vol. library; classrooms; 23 acres of formal & natural gardens.
Activities: guided tours; lectures; concerts; special trips; films; gallery talks; docent program; speakers bureau; inter-museum loan, permanent, temporary & traveling exhibitions.
Publications: quarterly bulletins to members; catalogs of temporary exhibitions.
Hours & Admission Prices: Tues.-Wed. & Fri.-Sun. 10-5, Thurs. 10-8. Adults $7.50, senior citizens & students $5.50; discounts to groups of 10 or more; children 18 & under, members, and 2nd Sat. of month no charge. ♿
Attendance: 113,931 (accurate)
Membership: Individual $50; Family & Dual $65; Associate $125; Supporter $250; Sponsor $500; Contributor $750; Masters Society (under 40) $1,000; Masters Society $2,000; Masters Society Patron $5,000; Masters Society Benefactor $10,000.

RICHARDSON ASIAN ART MUSEUM, 4770 S. Harvard Ave., Tulsa, OK 74135-3056. Tel.: 918-747-9393.
Web Site: richardsonart.org
Art Museum.
Collections: asian art including jade figures, Quan Yen figures, Foo Dog traditional statuary & Buddhist temple jars.
Hours & Admission Prices: Thurs.-Sat. 10-5, Sun. 1-5.

SHERWIN MILLER MUSEUM OF JEWISH ART, (M), 2021 E. 71st St., Tulsa, OK 74136-5408. Tel.: 918-492-1818. Fax: 918-492-1888.
E-mail: info@jewishmuseum.net
Web Site: www.jewishmuseum.net
Formerly: Fenster Museum of Jewish Art
Founded: 1966.
Congressional District: 1
Key Personnel: Exec. Dir., Arthur M. Feldman; Pres., Gay Clarkson; Devel. & Mktg., Melissa Schnur; Cur., Dr. Karen York; Admin. Asst., Corey Wickersham.
Personnel Profile: Full-Time Paid 4; Part-Time Volunteers 25; Interns 1.
Governing Authority: nonprofit organization. Tax-exempt: 501(c)(3).
Judaica Art Museum.
Collections: Jewish history, culture & art from biblical times to present; ritual objects; synagogue textiles; ethographic artifacts; costumes; archaeological artifacts; documents; archival materials; photographs; prints; paintings; sculptures; architectural elements; Holocaust era artifacts, documents & photographs.
Research Fields: Jewish arts & crafts; regional & state Jewish history.
Facilities: 1,000-vol. library containing reference works for the study of Jewish art available to the public; educational facilities.
Activities: guided tours; lectures; organized education programs for children; docent program; participatory & loan exhibitions.
Publications: newsletter.
Hours & Admission Prices: Adults $5.50, senior citizens $4.50, students $3; discounts to law enforcement, uniform services, military, teachers & AAM members; members no charge. ♿
Attendance: 10,000 (estimated)
Membership: Student $25; Senior $35; General $40; Family $60; Friend $100; Contributing $250; Supporting $500; Sustaining $750; Patron $1,000; Sponsor $1,500; Benefactor $2,500; Director's Circle $5,000; Life $25,000.

SOCIETY OF EXPLORATION GEOPHYSICISTS - GEOSCIENCE CENTER, (M), 8801 S. Yale, Tulsa, OK 74137-3573. Mailing Address: P.O. Box 702740, Tulsa, OK 74170-2740. Tel.: 918-497-5555. Fax: 918-497-5557.
Earth Science Center.
Collections: earth science; geology; rocks; minerals; fossils.
Activities: educational programs.
Hours & Admission Prices: Call for hours.

TULSA AIR AND SPACE MUSEUM & PLANETARIUM, 3624 N. 74th E. Ave., Tulsa, OK 74115-3622. Tel.: 918-834-9900.
Space Museum & Planetarium.
Collections: history & future of aerospace; science & technology; hands-on

exhibits; photographs; military aircraft including 1931 Spartan C-2, the Rockwell Ranger 2000, the HuGo Craft, & the Grumman F-14A Tomcat.
Facilities: 19,000 sq. ft. exhibit space; planetarium.
Activities: special events; educational programs; hands-on activities.
Hours & Admission Prices: Tues.-Sat. 10-5, Sun. 1-5. Adults $6, seniors 62 & over, students and military $5, youth 4-12 $4; children 3 & under no charge. Closed holidays.

TULSA HISTORICAL SOCIETY MUSEUM, 2445 S. Peoria, Tulsa, OK 74114-1326. Tel.: 918-712-9484.
E-mail: ths@tulsahistory.org
Web Site: tulsahistory.org
Key Personnel: Exec. Dir., Sharon Terry; Office Mgr., Michelle Place; Dir. Education & Exhibits, Maggie Brown; Collections Mgr., Joshua Peck
Historical Society Museum: housed in the Samuel Travis Mansion.
Collections: 5,000 photographs; rare books; film & video archives; maps; historical costumes; decorative arts.
Hours & Admission Prices: Tues.-Sat. 10-2. No charge. Closed holidays.

* **TULSA ZOO & LIVING MUSEUM,** 5701 E. 36th St., N., Tulsa, OK 74115-2100. Tel.: 918-669-6600 & 6202. Fax: 918-669-6260.
E-mail: tulsazoo@ci.tulsa.ok.us
Web Site: tulsazoo.org
Founded: 1927.
Congressional District: 1
Key Personnel: Dir., Stephen Walker; Registrar, Gary Lunsford; Education Cur., Jennifer Haase; Exhibits Cur., Kathleen Buck-Miser; Horticultural Cur., Jay Ross; Living Museum Cur., Brett Fidler; Museum Shop Mgr., Paul Pearson.
Personnel Profile: Full-Time Paid 82; Part-Time Paid 4; Part-Time Volunteers 250.
Governing Authority: municipal. Parent Institution: Tulsa Park & Recreation Board, 1712 W. Charles Page Blvd. Tax-exempt.
Zoo & Natural History Museum.
Collections: live animals & plants; North American fossils, geological specimens; Native American, African American, tropical American, Asian cultural artifacts & displays.
Research Fields: cooperative animal behavior research; archaeological; palaeontological.
Facilities: 1,730-vol. library of zoological books available upon request; restaurant. Books & educational novelties for sale.
Activities: guided tours for schools, civic groups; lectures; TV & radio programs; semi-annual training programs for docents & zooteens; summer workshops in zoology, art, photography; in-school programs for grades 4 & 6; work experience in zoo management for college credit.
Publications: newsletter, Zoo News; Volunteer Newsletter; annual reports of zoo.
Hours & Admission Prices: Daily 9-5. Adults $8, senior citizens 65 & over $6, children 3-11 $4; discounts to AZA members; children 2 & under, Tulsa school groups & members no charge. Closed Christmas. ♿
Attendance: 630,000 (estimated)
Membership: Associate $45; Family & Grandparent $60; Family Plus $80; Penguin & Friends $125.

Vinita

EASTERN TRAILS MUSEUM, 215 W. Illinois, Vinita, OK 74301-3129. Tel.: 918-256-2115.
Web Site: www.vinitapl.okpls.org/museum.htm
Key Personnel: Cur., Wanda Norton
History Museum.
Collections: items pertaining to the history of the Cherokee, Shawnee & Delaware Indians.
Hours & Admission Prices: Mon.-Fri. 1:30-4, Sat. 1-3.

Wagoner

CITY OF WAGONER HISTORICAL MUSEUM, 122 S. Main, Wagoner, OK 74467-5221. Mailing Address: P.O. Box 406, Wagoner, OK 74477-0406. Tel.: 918-485-9111.
History Museum.
Collections: local history & culture; period clothing; Civil War artifacts; photographs.
Activities: guided tours.
Hours & Admission Prices: Tues.-Sat. 10-3. No charge. ♿

Wakita

TWISTER THE MOVIE MUSEUM, 101 W. Main St., Wakita, OK 73771. Mailing Address: P.O. Box 285, Wakita, OK 73771-0285. Tel.: 580-594-2312.
Web Site: www.twistercountry.com
Movie Museum: located in the town where the movie Twister was filmed.
Collections: film memorabilia; props; pictures; Twister pinball machine; original Dorothy machine.
Facilities: Museum-related items for sale.
Activities: tours.
Hours & Admission Prices: Call for hours. No charge.

Warner

WALLIS MUSEUM, 1000 College Rd., Warner, OK 74469-9700. Mailing Address: Rte. 1, Box 1000, Warner, OK 74469-9700. Tel.: 918-463-6236. Fax: 918-463-6314.
E-mail: mrigney@connorsstate.edu
Web Site: www.connorsstate.edu
Formerly: Rural Farming & Agriculture Museum
Founded: 1963.
Congressional District: 2
Key Personnel: C.E.O., Dr. Donnie Nero.
Personnel Profile: Part-Time Volunteers 1.
Governing Authority: college. Parent Institution: Connors State College. Tax-exempt: 501(c)(3).
University Museum.
Collections: Indian artifacts; local history; minerals; manuscripts; agriculture & farming artifacts.
Activities: permanent exhibitions.
Hours & Admission Prices: Closed for relocation. ♿

Watonga

T.B. FERGUSON HOME, 519 N. Weigel, Watonga, OK 73772. Tel.: 580-623-5069.
Founded: 1972.
Congressional District: 6
Key Personnel: Cur., Mary Deane.
Personnel Profile: Part-Time Paid 1; Part-Time Volunteers 6.
Governing Authority: state. Parent Institution: Oklahoma Historical Society, Oklahoma History Center, 2401 N. Laird Ave., Oklahoma City, OK 73105-7914. Tax-exempt.
Historic House: c.1901 T.B. Ferguson Home, home of sixth territorial Governor.
Collections: period furnishings; 1892-1921 early-day pioneer items; personal items of T.B. & Elva Ferguson; tax rolls; maps; books. Historical Buildings: c.1893 City Jail; c.1870 Federal Remount Station.
Research Fields: Governor Ferguson.
Activities: guided tours; political re-enactment. Museum Sponsors: Cheese Festival.
Publications: brochures; weekly news column in Watonga Republican Newspaper.
Hours & Admission Prices: Wed.-Fri. 12-4, Sat. 9-5. No charge; donations accepted. Closed state holidays.
Attendance: 4,320 (estimated)
Membership: Friends $10; Individual $15; Family $25; Institutional $35; Life $300; Benefactor $500.

Waurika

ROCK ISLAND DEPOT MUSEUM, 105 S. Meridian, Waurika, OK 73573. Mailing Address: 122 S. Main St., Waurika, OK 73573-3054. Tel.: 590-228-3274. Fax: 590-228-2907.
E-mail: museum@waurika.lib.ok.us
Congressional District: 4
Key Personnel: Museum Bd. Pres., Nancy Way; Librarian & Cur., Cathy Dumas.
Governing Authority: city of Waurika.
History Museum.
Collections: Rock Island Railroad memorabilia; authentic period caboose.
Facilities: library; meeting room.
Publications: Oklahoma flyer, Waurika; Post Offices in and near Jefferson County, Oklahoma.
Hours & Admission Prices: Mon.-Fri. 9-5.

Weatherford

STAFFORD AIR & SPACE MUSEUM, 3000 Logan Rd., Weatherford, OK 73096-2681. Tel.: 580-772-5871.
E-mail: director@staffordspacecenter.com
Web Site: www.staffordspacecenter.com
Air & Space Museum.
Collections: history of air & space flight; jet engines & equipment; model aircraft; General Staffords missions; rocket engines & equipment.
Hours & Admission Prices: Mon.-Sat. 9-5, Sun. 1-5. Adults 19 & over $5, children & students $2. Closed New Year's Day; Easter; Memorial Day; Independence Day; Labor Day; Thanksgiving; Christmas. ♿

Webbers Falls

WEBBERS FALLS HISTORICAL SOCIETY AND MUSEUM, Commercial & Main, Webbers Falls, OK 74470. Mailing Address: P.O. Box 5, Webbers Falls, OK 74470. Tel.: 918-464-2728.
Historical Society Museum: town named in honor of Chief Walter Webber who settled here in 1828.
Collections: local history & culture; Cherokee settlers; photographs; personal artifacts.
Hours & Admission Prices: Call for hours.

Wewoka

SEMINOLE NATION MUSEUM, 524 S. Wewoka Ave., Wewoka, OK 74884-3239. Mailing Address: Box 1532, Wewoka, OK 74884-1532. Tel.: 405-257-5580. Fax: 405-257-5580.
E-mail: semuseum@okplus.com
Web Site: www.theseminolenationmuseum.org
Founded: 1974.
Congressional District: 4
Key Personnel: C.E.O. & Pres. (V), William Wantland; Exec. Dir. & Chief Cur., Richard Ellwanger; Asst. Cur., Lewis Johnson; Physical Plant, Noah Hail; Registrar, Karen Smith.
Personnel Profile: Full-Time Paid 3; Part-Time Paid 1; Part-Time Volunteers 27.
Governing Authority: society. Parent Institution: The Seminole Nation Historical Society. Tax-exempt.
History Museum.
Collections: Seminoles; freedmen Blacks; pioneer history; Native American art gallery; Oklahoma Oil Boom & railroad history.
Research Fields: Seminole Indians; Freedman; Genealogy.
Facilities: reading room. Arts & crafts of the Seminole and Creek Indians, beadwork, needlepoint, Seminole dolls & paintings for sale.
Activities: guided tours; school programs.
Publications: quarterly newsletter.
Hours & Admission Prices: Feb.-Dec. Mon.-Sat. 10-4. No charge; donations accepted. Closed major holidays. ♿
Attendance: 10,000 (estimated)
Membership: Sustaining $25; Sponsor $50; Century Club $100 & up.

Wilburton

ROBBERS CAVE NATURE CENTER, Hwy. 2 N., Wilburton, OK 74578. Mailing Address: P.O. Box 9, Wilburton, OK 74578-0009. Tel.: 918-465-2565; 800-654-8240. Fax: 918-465-5763.
Web Site: www.touroklahoma.com/detail.asp?id=1+5U+3607
Key Personnel: Park Mgr., Merle Cox; Park Naturalist, Jacque Martin
Nature Center.
Collections: Native American history; natural history. Historic Building: 1930s natural stone bathhouse.
Facilities: nature trails. Museum-related items for sale.
Activities: haunted cave tours; hiking.
Hours & Admission Prices: Summer: Sat.-Thurs. 8-6, Fri. 8-8. Summer: daily 8-8, call to confirm.

Woodward

PLAINS INDIANS AND PIONEERS MUSEUM, (M), 2009 Williams Ave., Woodward, OK 73801-5717. Tel.: 580-256-6136. Fax: 580-256-2577.
E-mail: pipm@swbell.net
Web Site: www.pipm1.org
Founded: 1966.
Congressional District: 5
Key Personnel: Dir., Robert Roberson; Cur., Ian Swart; Special Projects, Courtney Jones.
Personnel Profile: Full-Time Paid 3; Full-Time Volunteers 20; Part-Time Paid 1; Part-Time Volunteers 20.
Governing Authority: foundation; nonprofit organization. Parent Institution: Plains Indians & Pioneers Historical Foundation. Tax-exempt.
Regional History Museum.
Collections: early day pioneer life & Indian artifacts; bank from Fargo; Fort Supply fire house & post office; Woodward's centennial; historic photographs & textiles; agricultural development in northwest Oklahoma featuring murals by Fred Olds & Jana Sol; Lee & Lienemann restored pioneer cabin; stable.
Research Fields: northwest Oklahoma local & regional history; Woodward tornado April 9, 1947.
Facilities: Books, art prints & museum-related items for sale.
Activities: permanent & changing exhibitions; lectures; tours; shows on hobbies & art; children's workshops & programming.
Publications: newsletter, Northwest Winds; books, Woodward County Pioneer Families Before 1915; Woodward County Family Histories; Below Devil's Gap; Northwest Oklahoma Territory Map; map, Woodward County Schools 1910.
Hours & Admission Prices: Tues.-Sat. 10-5. No charge; donations accepted. Closed major holidays. ♿
Attendance: 9,000 (accurate)
Membership: Individual $25; Family $35; Club & Business Basic $50; Individual & Business Bronze $100; Individual & Business Silver $250; Individual & Business Gold $500; Individual Lifetime $1,000.

Wynnewood

ESKRIDGE HOTEL MUSEUM, 114 E. Robert S. Kerr Blvd., Wynnewood, OK 73098-6621. Tel.: 405-207-0101. Fax: 405-665-5433.
Governing Authority: Parent Institution: Wynnewood Historical Society.
History Museum: built by Pinckney Reid Eskridge in 1907.
Collections: Oklahoma history; period artifacts; photographs; furnishings.
Facilities: Museum-related items for sale.
Activities: rental facilities.
Hours & Admission Prices: Mon.-Fri. 11-2, Sat.-Sun. 10-2. Adults $4, seniors 55 & over $3, students $2; discounts to groups; children 5 & under no charge.

Yale

JIM THORPE HOME, 706 E. Boston Ave., Yale, OK 74085-4004. Tel.: 918-387-2815.
E-mail: frick.linda@yahoo.com
Founded: 1973.
Congressional District: 33
Key Personnel: Cur., Linda C. Frick; Cur., Virginia Stanford.
Governing Authority: state. Parent Institution: Oklahoma Historical Society (see separate listing). Subsidiary Institution: Jim Thorpe Memorial Foundation. Tax-exempt.
History Museum.
Collections: 1920s furnishings & memorabilia; Jim Thorpe family photographs; replica of Jim Thorpe's boyhood cabin. Historic House: 1876 cabin.
Research Fields: Life of Jim Thorpe.
Hours & Admission Prices: Wed.-Sat. 10-5. No charge; donations accepted. Closed major holidays. ♿
Membership: Annual $10; Lifetime $200.

Yukon

YUKON HISTORICAL SOCIETY MUSEUM & ART CENTER, 601 Oak, Yukon, OK 73099-2538. Tel.: 405-354-5079.
Web Site: www.thestagedoorinc.org
Key Personnel: Pres., John Knuppel
History & Art Museum: housed in a 1910 school building.
Collections: period artifacts; Czech history; flour mill history.
Facilities: theater.
Activities: theater productions; fundraiser.
Hours & Admission Prices: By appointment. Museum: no charge. Art Center: call for admission prices.

YUKON'S BEST RAILROAD MUSEUM, 410 Oak Ave., Yukon, OK 73099-2640. Tel.: 405-354-5079.
Key Personnel: Pres. & Cur., John Knuppel; Cur., Jack Austerman
Railroad Museum.
Collections: model trains; Rock Island artifacts; railroad memorabilia.
Hours & Admission Prices: By appointment. No charge; donations accepted.

OREGON

(176 listings)

Agness

AGNESS-ILLAHE MUSEUM, 34470 Agness-Illaha Rd., Agness, OR 97406-9701. Tel.: 541-247-2014.
History Museum.
Collections: Native American artifacts; historical items.
Hours & Admission Prices: May-Sept. daily 11-2.

Albany

ALBANY REGIONAL MUSEUM, 136 Lyon St., S., Albany, OR 97321-2703. Tel.: 541-967-7122.
E-mail: armuseum@peak.org
Web Site: www.armuseum.com
Founded: 1980.
Congressional District: 5
Key Personnel: Chm. (V), Gerald L. Brenneman; Treas., Michael Kok; Admin. Coord., Tami Sneddon; Museum Asst., Melissa Schneider; Cataloger, Diane Frampton.
Personnel Profile: Part-Time Paid 3; Part-Time Volunteers 20.
Governing Authority: private; nonprofit organization. Tax-exempt: 501(c)(3).
Historical Museum.
Collections: cultural artifacts; memorabilia; photos.
Facilities: 200-vol. library; 4,000 sq. ft. exhibit space. Museum-related items for sale.
Activities: guided tours; temporary exhibitions. Annual Event: business meeting for public.
Publications: quarterly newsletter, Albany Old Times.
Hours & Admission Prices: Mon.-Sat. 12-4. No charge; donations accepted. Closed New Year's Day; Labor Day; Thanksgiving; Christmas.
Attendance: 4,156 (accurate)
Membership: Individual $10; Family $15; Business $50; Patron $100.

THE MONTEITH HOUSE MUSEUM, 518 Second Ave., S.W., Albany, OR 97321-2239. Mailing Address: Monteith Historic Society, P.O. Box 965, Albany, OR 97321-0362. Tel.: 541-928-0911.
Web Site: albanyvisitors.com/historic-albany/museums/monteith-house
Historic House: built in 1849. Listed on the National Register of Historic Places.
Collections: period artifacts & memorabilia dedicated to the pioneer ancestors.
Hours & Admission Prices: June 15-Sept. 15 Wed.-Sun. 12-4.

Ashland

SCHNEIDER MUSEUM OF ART, (M), Southern Oregon University, 1250 Siskiyou Blvd., Ashland, OR 97520-5001. Tel.: 541-552-8484. Fax: 541-552-8241.
E-mail: cranem@sou.edu
Web Site: www.sou.edu/sma
Founded: 1986.
Congressional District: 2
Key Personnel: Dir., Michael Crane; Chm. Bd., Gigi Morgan; Preparator & Registrar, Stephen Frazier; Office Mgr., Kim Hearon.
Personnel Profile: Full-Time Paid 2; Part-Time Paid 2; Part-Time Volunteers 48; Interns 8.
Governing Authority: nonprofit. Parent Institution: Southern Oregon University. Tax-exempt.
Art Museum.
Collections: contemporary art; Native American baskets; preColumbia artifacts; works on paper.
Activities: workshops; visiting artists; lectures; major fundraisers.
Publications: quarterly bulletin; catalogs.
Hours & Admission Prices: Mon.-Sat. 10-4. No charges; donations accepted. Closed state holidays; Thanksgiving weekend. ♿
Attendance: 15,000 (estimated)
Membership: Student $15; Individual $30; Family $60; Benefactor $100; Patron $250.

SCIENCEWORKS HANDS-ON MUSEUM, 1500 E. Main St., Ashland, OR 97520-1312. Tel.: 541-482-6767. Fax: 541-482-5716.
E-mail: info@scienceworksmuseum.org
Web Site: www.scienceworksmuseum.org
Founded: 2002.
Congressional District: 2
Key Personnel: Exec. Dir., Mark DiRienzo; Chm. (V), Sharon Javna; Museum Shop Mgr., Rachel Cardillo.
Personnel Profile: Full-Time Paid 7; Part-Time Paid 5; Part-Time Volunteers 100.
Governing Authority: Tax-exempt.
Science Museum.
Collections: hands-on exhibits.
Activities: special events; school groups; summer science camps; festivals; birthday parties; summer internship.
Hours & Admission Prices: Wed.-Sat. 10-4, Sun. 12-4. Adults $7.50, children 2-12 & senior 65 & over $5; discounts to groups of 10 or more & ASTEC members; children under 2 & members no charge. Closed New Year's Day; Memorial Day; Independence Day; Labor Day; Thanksgiving; Christmas. ♿
Attendance: 45,000 (accurate)
Membership: Family $60.

SOUTHERN OREGON UNIVERSITY MUSEUM OF VERTEBRATE NATURAL HISTORY, 1250 Siskiyou Blvd., Ashland, OR 97520-5001. Mailing Address: Southern Oregon University, Dept. of Biology, Ashland, OR 97520. Tel.: 541-552-6749 & 6341. Fax: 541-552-6415.
E-mail: stonek@sou.edu
Founded: 1969.
Congressional District: 52
Key Personnel: Cur., Dr. Karen Stone; Sec. Biology Dept., Colleen Martin.
Governing Authority: university. Parent Institution: Southern Oregon University.
Vertebrate Biology Museum.
Collections: vertebrate specimens; bird skins; mammal skins; reptiles; amphibians; fish.
Research Fields: vertebrate biology.
Activities: research; teaching.
Hours & Admission Prices: By appointment only. No charge; donations accepted.

Astoria

* **COLUMBIA RIVER MARITIME MUSEUM, (M),** 1792 Marine Dr., Astoria, OR 97103-3525. Tel.: 503-325-2323. Fax: 503-325-2331.
E-mail: information@crmm.org
Web Site: www.crmm.org
Founded: 1962.
Congressional District: 1
Key Personnel: Exec. Dir., Sam Johnson; Deputy Dir., David Pearson; Chm. (V), Tom Dulcich; Cur., Jeff Smith; Museum Shop Mgr., Blue Anderson.
Personnel Profile: Full-Time Paid 14; Part-Time Paid 10; Part-Time Volunteers 100.
Governing Authority: nonprofit organization. Tax-exempt: 501(c)(3).
History & Maritime Museum.
Collections: lightship (afloat); small craft; marine engines; naval weapons; nautical instruments; tools; miscellaneous marine artifacts; ship models; paintings; prints; photographs; maps; books; manuscripts; navigational aids; bridge from USS Knapp; charts commercial fishing craft and gear; Coast Guard craft and gear; cannery tools and gear.
Research Fields: Pacific Northwest maritime history.
Facilities: 8,000-vol. library of nautical books available for use on the premises & by appointment only.
Activities: permanent & temporary exhibitions; films; lectures; demonstrations of maritime skills; school programs; summer family programs; summer day camp.
Publications: quarterly newsletter, Quarterdeck.
Hours & Admission Prices: Daily 9:30-5. Adults $10, senior citizens $8, children $5; discounts to ICOM, AAM & Time Travelers Network members; members & children under 6 no charge; reciprocal admission with participating Council of American Maritime Museums. Closed Thanksgiving; Christmas. ♿
Attendance: 100,463 (accurate)
Membership: Statesman (individual senior 65 & up) $25; Ensign $30; Crew (family) $50; Helmsman $75; Boatswain $125; Pilot $250; Navigator $500; Captain $1,000; Commodore $2,500; Admiral $5,000.

FLAVEL HOUSE MUSEUM, (M), 441 8th St., Astoria, OR 97103-4620. Mailing Address: P.O. Box 88, Astoria, OR 97103-0088. Tel.: 503-325-2203. Fax: 503-325-7727.
E-mail: cchs@cumtux.org
Web Site: www.cumtux.org
Formerly: Captain George Flavel House Museum
Founded: 1951.
Congressional District: 1
Key Personnel: Exec. Dir., McAndrew Burns; Pres. (V), Kent Easom; Cur. & Archivist, Liisa Penner; Business Mgr., Martha L. Dahl; Dir. Mktg. & Devel., W. Sam Rascoe; Cur., Lisa Studts; Museum Maintenance, Chuck Bean.

Personnel Profile: Full-Time Paid 6; Part-Time Paid 2; Part-Time Volunteers 50.
Governing Authority: private; nonprofit organization. Parent Institution: Clatsop County Historical Society. Subsidiary Institution: Heritage Museum; Uppertown Fire Fighters Museum. Tax-exempt.
Historic House Museum.
Collections: furniture; art; Victorian era furnishings; household objects.
Research Fields: Victorian art; local & regional history; Flavel family history.
Facilities: Museum-related items for sale in the Carriage House.
Activities: guided tours by appointment.
Publications: quarterly journal, CUMTUX; newsletter; catalogue: John H. Trullinger Paintings; Historic Flavel House.
Hours & Admission Prices: May-Oct. daily 10-5; Nov.-April daily 11-4. Family $15, adults $5, youth 6-17 $2; discounts to senior citizens & AAA members; children under 6 & members no charge. Closed New Year's Day; Thanksgiving; Christmas Eve & Day.
Attendance: 23,000 (estimated)
Membership: Individual $35; Family & Foreign $50; Contributing $100-$499; Patron $500-$999; Benefactor & Corporate $1,000 & up.

THE HERITAGE MUSEUM, 1618 Exchange St., Astoria, OR 97103-3615. Mailing Address: P.O. Box 88, Astoria, OR 97103-0088. Tel.: 503-338-4849. Fax: 503-338-6265.
E-mail: cchs@cumtux.org
Web Site: www.cumtux.org
Founded: 1985.
Congressional District: 1
Key Personnel: Exec. Dir., McAndrew Burns; Bd. Pres., Kent Easom; Business Mgr., Martha L. Dahl; Dir. Mktg. & Devel., W. Sam Rascoe; Museum Maintenance, Chuck Bean; Archivist, Liisa Penner; Cur., Lisa Studts.
Personnel Profile: Full-Time Paid 6; Part-Time Paid 2; Part-Time Volunteers 50.
Governing Authority: private; nonprofit. Parent Institution: Clatsop County Historical Society. Subsidiary Institution: Flavel House, Uppertown Fire Fighters Museum. Tax-exempt.
Historical Society Museum.
Collections: natural history; geology; Native American artifacts; early immigrants & settlers of the region; nautical events; commerce in Clatsop County & along the Columbia River; logging; lumber; fish packing; ethnic exhibit.
Research Fields: Clatsop county history.
Facilities: research library; temporary & permanent archives; rental facility. Museum-related items for sale.
Activities: special events; lectures; guided tours.
Publications: quarterly, Cumtux; newsletter; oral history videos, Steam Whistle Logging; Remembering Uniontown; art catalogues, Legacy of John H. Trillinger.
Hours & Admission Prices: May-Oct. daily 10-5; Nov.-April Tues.-Sat. 11-4. Adults $4, senior citizens & AAA members $3, children 6-17 $2; discounts to AAA members & seniors; members no charge. Closed New Year's Eve & Day; Thanksgiving; Christmas Eve & Day. ♿
Attendance: 6,500 (estimated)
Membership: Individual $35; Family $55; Contributing $100-$499; Patron $500-$999; Benefactor & Corporate $1,000 and up.

LEWIS & CLARK NATIONAL HISTORICAL PARK, 92343 Fort Clatsop Rd., Astoria, OR 97103-8375. Tel.: 503-861-2471. Fax: 503-861-2585. TDD: 503-861-1620.
E-mail: deborah_s_wood@nps.gov
Web Site: www.nps.gov/lewi
Formerly: Fort Clatsop National Memorial
Founded: 1958.
Congressional District: 1
Key Personnel: Supt., David Szymanski; Cultural Resource Mgr., Deborah S. Wood.
Personnel Profile: Full-Time Paid 16; Part-Time Paid 12; Part-Time Volunteers 25.
Governing Authority: federal. Parent Institution: National Park Service, Washington, DC. Tax-exempt: 170(b).
Historic Fort: replica of the 1805-1806, winter encampment of the Lewis & Clark Expedition; objects relating to the Lewis & Clark expedition.
Collections: Lewis & Clark Expedition; research library; cultural & natural objects & specimens; Fort Clatsop replica.
Research Fields: Lewis & Clark Expedition.
Facilities: 2,000-vol. reference library; visitor center; canoe landing & fresh water spring site; hiking trails. Museum-related books for sale.
Activities: living history programs in summer; visitor center programs; audiovisual program; on & off-site school programs; environmental programs.
Publications: 75 titles on Lewis & Clark, natural & cultural history; 3 titles on the Charbonneau Family; Plants of Fort Clatsop & the Clatsop Indians.
Hours & Admission Prices: mid-June to Labor Day daily 8-6; Sept. to mid-June daily 8-5. April-Sept. Families $5, adults 17 & over $3; children 16 & under & Oct.-March no charge. Closed Christmas. ♿
Attendance: 226,000 (accurate)

UPPERTOWN FIREFIGHTERS MUSEUM, 30th & Marine Dr., Astoria, OR 97103. Mailing Address: Clatsop County Historical Society, P.O. Box 88, Astoria, OR 97103-0088. Tel.: 503-325-2203. Fax: 503-325-7727.
E-mail: cchs@cumtux.org
Web Site: www.cumtux.org
Founded: 1990.
Congressional District: 1
Key Personnel: Exec. Dir., McAndrew Burns; Pres. (V), Kent Easom; Business Mgr., Martha L. Dahl; Dir. Mktg. & Devel., W. Sam Rascoe; Archivist, Liisa Penner; Museum Maintenance, Chuck Bean; Cur., Lisa Studts.
Personnel Profile: Full-Time Paid 6; Part-Time Paid 2; Part-Time Volunteers 50.
Governing Authority: private; nonprofit organization. Parent Institution: Clatsop County Historical Society. Subsidiary Institutions: Heritage Museum; Flavel House. Tax-exempt.
Firefighters Museum.
Collections: fire-fighting equipment & memorabilia; photographs; fire pole; 1912 American LaFrance chemical wagon; 1921 Stutz; 1878 Hayes ladder wagon.
Facilities: meeting room.
Activities: children's activities.
Publications: Uppertown Fire Fighters' Museum.
Hours & Admission Prices: Wed.-Fri. 10-2, Sat. 10-3. $3 per person, cap of $15 per family; discounts to AAA members. Closed New Year's Eve & Day; Thanksgiving; Christmas Eve & Day. ♿
Attendance: 3,000 (estimated)
Membership: Individual $35; Family $55; Contributing $100-$499; Patron $500-$999; Benefactor $1,000 and up.

Aurora

AURORA COLONY HISTORICAL SOCIETY, (M), 15018 2nd St., N.E., Aurora, OR 97002. Mailing Address: P.O. Box 202, Aurora, OR 97002-0202. Tel.: 503-678-5754.
Founded: 1963.
Congressional District: 18
Key Personnel: Pres. (V), Gail Robinson; Museum Shop Mgr., Pamela Weninger.
Personnel Profile: Full-Time Paid 1; Part-Time Paid 5; Part-Time Volunteers 75.
Governing Authority: Parent Institution: Aurora Colony Historical Society. Subsidiary Institution: Old Aurora Colony Museum. Tax-exempt.
Historical Society Museum.
Collections: local history; personal artifacts; photographs; furniture; tools; music; instruments; textiles; quilts; clothing; legal documents; maps; letters; books; ledgers; household items; historic buildings.
Major Exhibits: We Have Everything Plenty, 2/10-6/27/10.
Activities: lectures; tours; living history demonstrations; 4th grade educational program. Annual Events: Quilt Show; Strawberry Social.
Publications: newsletter.
Hours & Admission Prices: Feb.-Dec. Tues.-Sat. 11-4, Sun. 12-4. Adults $6, seniors 60 & over $5, students $2; discounts to AAA & AAMA members; children 5 & under and members no charge. Closed major holidays. ♿
Attendance: 4,500 (accurate)
Membership: Seniors & Student $15; Friend $25; Family $35; Partner $50; Business $100; Corporate $250; Benefactor $500; Patron $1,000.

Baker City

BAKER HERITAGE MUSEUM, 2480 Grove St., Baker City, OR 97814-2719. Tel.: 541-523-9308. Fax: 541-523-9308.
E-mail: jjacobs@bakercounty.org
Web Site: www.bakerheritagemuseum.com
Formerly: Oregon Trail Regional Museum
Founded: 1982.
Congressional District: 59
Key Personnel: Dir., Joan Jacobs; Chm. (V), Peggi Timm; Museum Shop Mgr., Karen Carriere.
Personnel Profile: Full-Time Volunteers 40; Part-Time Paid 2; Part-Time Volunteers 35.
Governing Authority: county; nonprofit organization. Subsidiary Institution: Adler House Museum, Baker City, OR. Tax-exempt: 170(b)(1)(A).
History Museum.
Collections: artifacts of the original area settlers from 1800 to 1920s; photo

archives; historical research materials, texts & papers; rocks & minerals. Historic House: Adler House, a turn-of-the-century, Victorian-Italian style home.
Facilities: 300-vol. library; 25,000 sq. ft. exhibit space. Museum-related items for sale.
Activities: formal education programs for children; lectures.
Publications: quarterly newsletter, Museum Memo.
Hours & Admission Prices: last full week in March-Oct. daily 9-5; Winter: by appointment only. Office: Nov. to last full week in March Mon.-Fri. 9-5. Family $18, adults $5, senior citizens 60 & over $4.50; discounts to groups & AAM members; children under 16 & members no charge. Closed most winter holidays. ♿
Attendance: 20,000 (accurate)
Membership: Individual $20; Family $30; Partner $60; Patrons $100; Contributor $250; Steward $500.

NATIONAL HISTORIC OREGON TRAIL INTERPRETIVE CENTER, 22267 Oregon Hwy. 86, Baker City, OR 97814. Mailing Address: P.O. Box 987, Baker City, OR 97814-0987. Tel.: 541-523-1843. Fax: 541-523-1834.
E-mail: OR_NHOTIC_Mail@blm.gov
Web Site: www.blm.gov/or/oregontrail/
Founded: 1992.
Congressional District: 2
Key Personnel: Center Dir., Sarah LeCompte; Interpretive Specialist, Nancy Harms; Museum Shop Mgr., Gay Stackle; Volunteer Coord., Pamela Petterson; Heavy Equipment Operator, Don Chastain; Management Asst. & Support Supvr., Pamela Dugan; Visitor Information Specialist, Kelly Burns; Visitor Information Asst., Earl Scott; Visitor Information Asst., Phoebe Galvan; Mktg., Gary Koy.
Personnel Profile: Full-Time Paid 10; Full-Time Volunteers 40; Part-Time Paid 5; Part-Time Volunteers 100; Interns 3.
Governing Authority: federal government; nonprofit organization. Parent Institution: Bureau of Land Management. Tax-exempt: 501(c)(3).
History Museum & Interpretive Center: interpretive center along Oregon Trail; historic gold mining site.
Collections: personal, transportation, recreational & archaeological artifacts; historical photographs.
Research Fields: Oregon Trail 1840-1880.
Facilities: 750-vol. library; 150-seat auditorium; outdoor wagon encampment & lode mine site; interpretive overlook; outdoor lighted amphitheater; 4 mile hiking trail leading to Oregon Trail Ruts; picnic pavilion. Books & museum-related items for sale.
Activities: lectures; loan, participatory & temporary exhibitions; living history. Annual Events: Pioneer Festival; Holiday Open House; Mining Heritage Day.
Publications: newsletter, Trail Mix; Oregon Trail Education Resource Guide.
Hours & Admission Prices: April-Oct. daily 9-6; Nov.-March daily 9-4. Adults $5, senior citizens 62 & over, organized groups & tours $3.50; discounts to Golden Age, Golden Eagle & Golden Access members; schools & children 15 & under no charge. Closed New Year's Day; Thanksgiving; Christmas. ♿
Attendance: 69,852 (accurate)
Membership: Trail Tenders, no dues; Assoc. Trail Tenders $20.

Bandon

BANDON HISTORICAL SOCIETY MUSEUM, 270 Fillmore & Hwy. 101, Bandon, OR 97411. Mailing Address: P.O. Box 737, Bandon, OR 97411-0737. Tel.: 541-347-2164. Fax: 541-347-2164.
E-mail: bandonhistoricalmuseum@yahoo.com
Web Site: bandonhistoricalmuseum.org
Formerly: Coquille River Museum/Brandon Historical Society
Founded: 1977.
Congressional District: 24
Key Personnel: Exec. Dir. & Museum Shop Mgr., Judy Knox; Pres. (V) & Museum Shop Mgr., Kathy Dornath; Treas., John Gamble; Vice Pres. & Sec., Betty Hiley; Education, Carol Acklin; Cur., Reg Pullen.
Personnel Profile: Full-Time Paid 1; Part-Time Volunteers 40.
Governing Authority: private; nonprofit organization. Tax-exempt: 501(c)(3).
History Museum.
Collections: area history & artifacts; local Native American artifacts; over 1,500 photographs; Bandon's two fires 1914 & 1936; 1920-1960s period clothing; early businesses; local area schools; pioneer family stories & memorabilia; natural history; local military; fishing; farming; cheese making; timber industry; maritime boat building; riverboats; sculling vessels & commerce of the area from 1800s-1960.
Research Fields: local cemeteries & obituaries; newspaper; school students; old business; Pioneer families genealogy; Bandon School class annuals.
Facilities: library & research center; classroom; 4,000 sq. ft. exhibit space. Gift-related items for sale.
Activities: docent program; educational programs; tours; lectures; training for volunteers; book signings; special displays. Museum Sponsors: Veterans Day; Cranberry Festival activities; Christmas activity.
Publications: newsletter 3 times annually, The Bandon Light; books, Woodenships & Master Craftsmen; Shipbuilding & Their Builders; Bandon Then and Now; Bandon by the Sea.
Hours & Admission Prices: Feb.-Dec. Mon.-Sat. 10-4. Adults $2; children under 12 & Bandon Historical Society members no charge. Closed New Year's Day; Thanksgiving; Christmas. ♿
Attendance: 4,250 (accurate)
Membership: Individual $15; Family $25; Business $35; Life $250; Benefactor $500; Patron $1,000.

COQUILLE RIVER LIGHTHOUSE/BULLARDS BEACH STATE PARK, 2 miles N. of Bandon, Hwy. 101, Bandon, OR 97411. Mailing Address: P.O. Box 569, Bandon, OR 97411-0569. Tel.: 541-347-2209. Fax: 541-347-4656.
Web Site: www.oregonstateparks.org/park_71.php
Founded: 1896.
Key Personnel: Park Mgr., Frank D. Arnold; Park Ranger, Pam Stevens.
Personnel Profile: Full-Time Paid 2; Part-Time Volunteers 22.
Governing Authority: state. Tax-exempt.
Historic Building Museum: housed in 1896 lighthouse.
Collections: interpretive display.
Facilities: 300 sq. ft. exhibit space. Gift items for sale.
Activities: formal education programs for children; guided tours; lectures; temporary exhibitions. Museum Sponsors: OPRD Day in June.
Publications: brochure, Coquille River Lighthouse.
Hours & Admission Prices: Coquille River Lighthouse: May & Oct. daily 10-4; June-Sept. Mon.-Tues. 10-4, Wed.-Sun. 9-6; No charge; donations accepted.
Attendance: 28,380 (accurate)

Bend

DES CHUTES HISTORICAL MUSEUM, 129 N.W. Idaho Ave., Bend, OR 97701-2602. Tel.: 541-389-1813. Fax: 541-317-9345.
E-mail: info@deschuteshistory.org
Web Site: www.deschuteshistory.org
Founded: 1975.
Congressional District: 5
Key Personnel: Exec. Dir., Kelly Cannon-Miller; Pres. (V), Les Joslin.
Personnel Profile: Part-Time Paid 4; Part-Time Volunteers 40.
Governing Authority: private; nonprofit organization. Parent Institution: Deschutes Cuonty Historical Society. Tax-exempt: 501(c)(3).
History Museum: housed in 1914 Reid School.
Collections: county history; veterans & soldiers of central Oregon; photographs; Bend Bulletin archives; county history.
Facilities: 1,000-vol. library; meeting facilities. Museum-related items for sale.
Activities: arts festivals; films; formal education programs; guided tours; loan exhibitions; school loan service; study clubs.
Publications: monthly newsletter, The Homesteader; books on Central Oregon History.
Hours & Admission Prices: Tues.-Sat. 10-4:30; other times by appointment. Adults $5, children 13-17 $2; Independence Day, children 12 & under and members no charge. Closed New Year's Day; Thanksgiving; Christmas. ♿
Attendance: 8,000 (estimated)
Membership: Single $15; Family $25; Business $40; Donor $50; Patron & Business Plus $100; Benefactor & President's Club $500.

∗ **HIGH DESERT MUSEUM, (M),** 59800 S. Hwy. 97, Bend, OR 97702-7963. Tel.: 541-382-4754. Fax: 541-382-5256.
Web Site: www.highdesertmuseum.org
Founded: 1974.
Congressional District: 2
Key Personnel: Pres., Janeanne A. Upp; Human Resources & Volunteer Program Coord., Tracy Suckow; Vice Pres. Programs, Greta Brunschwyler; Cur. Western History, Robert Boyd; Cur. Education, Wildlife, Nolan Harvey; Cur. Education, School Programs, Linda Rhine; Facilities Mgr., Arnie Tronson; Mgr. Guest Svcs. & Museum Shop Mgr., Nicole Swarts.
Personnel Profile: Full-Time Paid 43; Part-Time Paid 2; Part-Time Volunteers 250; Interns 7.
Governing Authority: nonprofit organization. Tax-exempt: 501(c)(3).
Natural & Cultural History Museum.
Collections: over 120 live animals representing regional wildlife; local & natural history; Great Basin prehistory & cultural history; historic artifacts; Native American ethnographic objects, especially Columbia River plateau clothing & bags; historic, landscape & wildlife art & photographs; Plateau Native Americans; forest ecosystem; turn-of-the-century sawmill; U.S. Forest Service.

Major Exhibits: Art Through Ancestry, 11/09-2/10; Year of the Forest (T), 1/10-9/11; Stones from the Sky (T), 2/10-6/10; Sin in the Sagebrush (T), 2/10-9/10.
Research Fields: onsite monitoring of free-roaming wildlife.
Facilities: library; classrooms; cafe. Museum-related items for sale.
Activities: lectures; educational programs for schools & special events; adult & teen volunteer program; field excursions; permanent & temporary exhibitions; daily presentations & demonstrations.
Publications: quarterly newsletter; brochures; educational materials.
Hours & Admission Prices: May-Oct. daily 9-5; Nov.-Sept. daily 10-4. May-Oct. adults 13-64 $15, seniors 65 & over $12, children 5-12 $9; discounts to groups; members and children 4 & under no charge. Nov.-Sept. adults 13-64 $10, seniors 65 & over $9, children 5-12 $6; children 4 & under no charge. Closed New Year's Day; Thanksgiving; Christmas. ♿
Attendance: 176,070 (accurate)
Membership: Individual $50; Individual Plus $60; Family & Grandparents $75; Family Plus $120; Silver Spurs $300; Fellow/Business $1,000; Curator's Circle $2,500; Museum Associate $5,000; President's Council $10,000; Founder's Circle $25,000.

WORKING WONDERS CHILDREN'S MUSEUM, 520 S.W. Powerhouse Dr. #624, Bend, OR 97702-1297. Tel.: 541-389-4500.
E-mail: info@workingwonders.org
Web Site: www.workingwonders.org
Founded: 2004.
Key Personnel: Exec. Dir., DeeDee Erhard; Bd. Pres. (V), Lucinda Fournier.
Personnel Profile: Full-Time Paid 3; Part-Time Paid 5; Part-Time Volunteers 200.
Governing Authority: Tax-exempt.
Children's Museum.
Collections: hands-on exhibits; science; art.
Activities: birthday parties; workshops.
Hours & Admission Prices: Wed.-Sat. 10-5, Sun. 11-5. Admission $6, seniors over 60 $5; children under one & over 99 no charge. ♿
Attendance: 37,000

Brookings

CHETCO VALLEY HISTORICAL MUSEUM, 15461 Museum Rd., Brookings, OR 97415. Mailing Address: P.O. Box 2096, Brookings, OR 97415-0303. Tel.: 541-469-6651.
E-mail: pattymcvay@gmail.com
Historic House Museum: housed in the Blake house; built in 1857.
Collections: early pioneer life; local history & culture; Native American artifacts; photographs; period furnishings.
Hours & Admission Prices: Winter: Sat.-Sun. 12-4; Summer: call for extended hours.
Membership: Annual $25.

Brooks

ANTIQUE CATERPILLAR MACHINERY MUSEUM, 3995 Brooklake Rd., N.E., Brooks, OR 97303-9732. Mailing Address: P.O. Box 3377, Portland, OR 97208-3377. Tel.: 503-538-3935.
E-mail: jplongtin@msn.com
Web Site: www.antiquecaterpillarmuseum.com
Key Personnel: Pres., Don Leffler.
Governing Authority: nonprofit organization. Tax-exempt: 501(c)(3).
Machinery Museum.
Collections: caterpillar history & equipment; period trucks, tractors & steamrollers.
Activities: demonstrations; educational programs.
Hours & Admission Prices: Call for hours.

PACIFIC NORTHWEST TRUCK MUSEUM, 3995 Brooklake Rd., N.E., Brooks, OR 97305. Mailing Address: P.O. Box 9087, Brooks, OR 97305-0087. Tel.: 503-312-0039 & 463-8701.
E-mail: office@pacificnwtruckmuseum.org
Web Site: www.pacificnwtruckmuseum.org
Founded: 1989.
Key Personnel: Pres. (V), Terry Dovre; Chm. (V), Doug Delano; Treas., Craig Vogel; Archivist, Ken Goudy, Jr.; Museum Shop Mgr., Red Nelson.
Personnel Profile: Part-Time Volunteers 100.
Governing Authority: nonprofit. Tax-exempt: 501(c)(3).
Truck Museum.
Collections: 1912-1993 Class 6 & larger trucks; truck manufacturing & transportation industries; artifacts; photographs; drawings; manuals; patents; literature; biographies; monkey wrenches.
Facilities: library; 30,500 sq. ft. exhibit space. Museum-related items for sale.
Activities: guided tours; hobby workshops; lectures; loan exhibitions. Museum Sponsors: Truck Show in August; parades; festivals; road tours.
Publications: bimonthy newsletter, Pacific Northwest Truck Museum.
Hours & Admission Prices: April-Sept. Sat.-Sun. 10-4:30; other times by appointment. Donation: adults $5; members no charge. Closed New Year's Day; Christmas. ♿
Attendance: 18,000 (estimated)
Membership: Individual $25; Household $35.

Brownsville

LINN COUNTY HISTORICAL MUSEUM AND MOYER HOUSE, 101 Park Ave., Brownsville, OR 97327. Mailing Address: Box 607, Brownsville, OR 97327-0607. Tel.: 541-466-3390 & 3070. Fax: 541-466-3390.
E-mail: jmoyer@peak.org
Web Site: www.co.linn.or.us/museum
Founded: 1962.
Congressional District: 37
Key Personnel: C.E.O., Brian Carrol; Chm. Trust (V), Glenn Harrison; Pres. Friends (V), Myrna Baughman; Museum Coord., Gary Timms; Museum Shop Mgr., Joni Nelson.
Personnel Profile: Part-Time Paid 3; Part-Time Volunteers 15.
Governing Authority: county; nonprofit. Parent Institution: Linn County Parks & Recreation. Subsidiary Institution: Linn County Museum Friends. Tax-exempt.
Local History Museum: arranged to represent 1800s city with exhibits of businesses operating in the community showing life-style pursuits in other fields such as agriculture, mining & timber; early travel 1850-1920s. Historic House: 1881 Italianate Victorian, Moyer House.
Collections: Linn County history; industry; commerce; domestic arts; furnishings; documents; photographs; genealogical records; family books; Linn County files; reference books; pioneer artifacts; Native American artifacts.
Research Fields: genealogy; architectural; local history; early pioneer life.
Facilities: 9,290 sq. ft. exhibit space; 30-seat theater. Moyer House: 2,450 sq. ft. Historical pamphlets, books & other museum-related items for sale.
Activities: guided tours; lectures; organized educational programs for children; participatory, loan & temporary exhibitions. Museum Sponsors: Living History drama at Moyer House.
Publications: biannual newsletter: guidebook: Take a Walk; semi-annual newsletter published by Friends of the Museum.
Hours & Admission Prices: Mon.-Sat. 11-4, Sun. 1-5. Guided Tours $2. Closed New Year's Day; Easter; Thanksgiving; Christmas. ♿
Attendance: 8,298 (estimated)
Membership: Pioneer Descendant $10; Individual $15; Family $25; Patron $40; Benefactor $100.

Burns

HARNEY COUNTY HISTORICAL MUSEUM, 18 W. D St., Burns, OR 97720-1226. Mailing Address: P.O. Box 388, Burns, OR 97720-0388. Tel.: 541-573-5618. Fax: 541-573-7225.
Web Site: www.burnsmuseum.com/
Founded: 1960.
Congressional District: 2
Key Personnel: Pres., Bill Renwick; Vice Pres., Emery Ferguson.
Personnel Profile: Full-Time Volunteers 24; Part-Time Volunteers 25.
Governing Authority: society. Parent Institution: Harney County Historical Society. Tax-exempt.
General Museum.
Collections: archaeology; history; natural history; pioneer kitchen; geology; Indian artifacts; mineralogy; zoology; costumes; Indian headdress; butterfly collection; paintings; clothing; pioneer kitchen; Ilda Mae Hayes room; wagon shed room; bird showcase; Hanley room; salt & pepper shakers; guns; Dan Opie quarter horse trophy collection; early historical photographs; civilian conservation corps display; wildlife diorama; mounted displays; ancestor trade and skills.
Research Fields: agriculture; Indian artifacts; timber; genealogy.
Activities: guided tours; occasional demonstrations of pioneer crafts; permanent & temporary exhibitions.
Publications: quarterly newsletter, Harney County Historical Highlights; Harney County, Oregon and Its Rangeland, George Francis Brimlow; Harney County: An Historical Inventory, Royal Jackson & Jennifer Lee.
Hours & Admission Prices: April -Sept. Mon.-Sat. 10-4. Suggested Donation: Family of 4 $6 (additional children $.50 each), couples $5, adults $4, senior citizens $3, children 6-12 $1; discounts to groups; members no charge. ♿
Attendance: 1,024 (accurate)
Membership: Individual $10; Family & Business $20; Supporting $25; Single Life $100; Couple Life $150.

Canby

CANBY HISTORICAL SOCIETY, 888 N.E. 4th Ave., Canby, OR 97013-2300. Mailing Address: P.O. Box 160, Canby, OR 97013-0160. Tel.: 503-266-6712.
E-mail: depotmuseum@canby.com
Web Site: www.canbyhistoricalsociety.org
Formerly: Canby Depot Museum
Founded: 1968.
Key Personnel: Pres., Sue Carson; Vice Pres., Cheryl Rahn.
Personnel Profile: Part-Time Paid 1; Part-Time Volunteers 50.
Governing Authority: private; nonprofit organization. Parent Institution: Canby Historical Society. Tax-exempt: 501(c)(3).
History Museum: housed in an 1891 railroad depot.
Collections: Oregon history from prehistoric to modern; history of Canby & the surrounding area; caboose; speeder car; railroading, agriculture & daily living of early Oregon pioneers.
Research Fields: genealogical.
Facilities: 100-vol. library; 2,000 sq. ft. exhibit space. Museum-related items for sale.
Activities: formal education programs for children; guided tours; temporary exhibitions. Museum Sponsors: Antique Appraisal Day; Pioneer Breakfast in July; semiannual flea market.
Publications: quarterly newsletter, Canby Historical Society; annual historical calendar.
Hours & Admission Prices: March-Dec. Thurs.-Sun. 1-4. Suggested Donation: adults $2. Closed holidays; holiday weekends. ♿
Attendance: 1,100 (estimated)
Membership: Individual $15; Family $25; Supporter $100-$249; Contributor $250-$499; Sponsor $500-$999; Depot Patron $1,000 & up.

Cannon Beach

CANNON BEACH HISTORY CENTER AND MUSEUM, 1387 S. Spruce St., Cannon Beach, OR 97110. Mailing Address: P.O. Box 1005, Cannon Beach, OR 97110-1005. Tel.: 503-436-9301.
Web Site: www.cbhistory.org
History Museum.
Collections: historical artifacts & memorabilia pertaining to Cannon Beach.
Hours & Admission Prices: Wed.-Sun. 1-5.

Canyon City

GRANT COUNTY HISTORICAL MUSEUM, 101 S. Canyon City Blvd., Hwy. 395, Canyon City, OR 97820. Mailing Address: P.O. Box 464, Canyon City, OR 97820-0464. Tel.: 541-575-0362. Fax: 541-575-0515.
E-mail: museum@ortelco.net
Web Site: www.gchistoricalmuseum.com
Founded: 1953.
Congressional District: 2
Personnel Profile: Part-Time Paid 1; Part-Time Volunteers 11.
Governing Authority: municipal.
Local History Museum: located in Canyon City, site of active gold mining area in 1862.
Collections: pioneer artifacts & relics; native rock display; Indian artifacts; gold mining; newspapers 1884-1903. Historic Buildings: 1864 Home of Joaquin Miller; 1910 Greenhorn City Jail.
Facilities: library of books & pictures on county history available for research on premises.
Activities: permanent exhibitions.
Hours & Admission Prices: May-Sept. Mon.-Sat. 9-4:30; other times by appointment. Adults $4, senior citizens $3.50, children 7-17 $2; children 6 & under no charge.
Attendance: 1,200 (accurate)

Cascade Locks

CASCADE LOCKS HISTORICAL MUSEUM, 1 Marine Dr., Cascade Locks, OR 97014. Mailing Address: P.O. Box 307, Cascade Locks, OR 97014-0307. Tel.: 541-374-8619.
Web Site: www.portofcascadelocks.org/marinepark.htm
History Museum.
Collections: local transportation history including the Oregon Pony, the first steam engine in the Pacific Northwest.
Hours & Admission Prices: May-Oct. daily 12-5.

Central Point

CRATER ROCK MUSEUM, 2002 Scenic Ave., Central Point, OR 97502-2185. Mailing Address: P.O. Box 3999, Central Point, OR 97502-0041. Tel.: 541-664-6081.
History Museum.
Collections: rocks; fossils; petrified wood; arrowheads.
Hours & Admission Prices: Tues.-Sat. 10-4. Adults $4, seniors, students & children $2.

Chiloquin

COLLIER MEMORIAL STATE PARK & LOGGING MUSEUM, Hwy. 97, (30 mi. north of Klamath Falls), Chiloquin, OR 97624-9631. Mailing Address: 46000 Hwy. 97. N., Chiloquin, OR 97624-9631. Tel.: 541-783-2471. Fax: 541-783-2707.
Web Site: www.oregonstateparks.org/park_228.php
Founded: 1945.
Congressional District: 4
Key Personnel: Cur. & Park Mgr., James Beauchemin.
Personnel Profile: Full-Time Paid 4; Part-Time Paid 6.
Governing Authority: state. Parent Institution: Oregon State Parks. Tax exempt.
Logging, Pioneer & Lumber Museum & Village.
Collections: logging & lumbering artifacts; Dolbeer Donkey Engine; 1929 Hines sawmill; Beloit Tree Harvester; Romeo & Juliet Bridge; Sumner Sash gang saw; photographs; locomotives; track layer; trout spawning beds; giant Corliss twin steam engine; Indian artifacts; mid-1800 pioneer log houses; ox shoeing blacksmith shop; wooden wheeled wagons; caterpillars; high wheels; lumber trucks; logging trucks; McVay Log loader; snag pushers; 85 ft. steel spar poles simulating log transfer; steam logging equipment; railroad logging equipment; logging arches; 1880-1980 logging equipment & artifacts; pioneer surveying instruments.
Research Fields: millwright, machine & logging tools.
Facilities: camp & picnic grounds; Spring Creek; 650-acre Pine Forest; overnight trailer camp.
Activities: fishing; beaver aspen harvest; permanent exhibitions; hiking; canoeing; equestrian.
Publications: pamphlets; Collier State Park-Logging Museum-Walking Tour Guide.
Hours & Admission Prices: Museum: daily 8-4. Park: daily dawn-dusk. Office: Mon.-Fri. 8-4:30. No charge; donations accepted. ♿
Attendance: 88,164
Membership: Friends of Collier Memorial State Park $5.

Clackamas

OREGON MILITARY MUSEUM, Camp Withycombe, 10101 S.E. Clackamas Rd., Clackamas, OR 97015-9180. Tel.: 503-557-5359. Fax: 503-557-6713.
E-mail: tracy.thoennes@us.army.mil
Web Site: www.ormilmuseum.org
Founded: 1974.
Congressional District: 5
Key Personnel: Cur., Tracy Thoennes.
Personnel Profile: Full-Time Paid 2; Part-Time Paid 1; Part-Time Volunteers 15; Interns 1.
Governing Authority: State of Oregon Military Department, National Guard. Tax-exempt.
Military History Museum.
Collections: Oregon's military history from mid-19th century to present; aircraft; artwork; equipment; insignia; ordnance; tanks; uniforms; vehicles. Historic Buildings: WWII Quonset Hut; 1911 Artillery Barn.
Research Fields: Oregon National Guard in major American Wars 1898-present; Oregon casualties & necrology in WWI & WWII.
Facilities: 20,000-vol. reference library by appointment.
Activities: docent tours; educational activities; research; outreach programs for community & National Guard events. Museum Sponsors: Annual Living History Day.
Publications: Annual Report; brochure.
Hours & Admission Prices: Temporarily closed for relocation. No charge; donations accepted. Closed federal holidays. ♿
Attendance: 3,500 (accurate)
Membership: Foundation $10.

Columbia City

CAPLES HOUSE MUSEUM, 1915 1st St., Columbia City, OR 97018. Mailing Address: Caretaker, Caples Museum, P.O. Box 263, Columbia City, OR 97018-0263. Tel.: 503-397-5390.
Web Site: www.rootsweb.com/~orossdar/Caples.htm
Historic House Museum.
Collections: personal artifacts; period furnishings.
Hours & Admission Prices: March-Oct. Fri.-Sun. & holidays 1-5; other times by appointment. Adults $3; discounts to members.

Condon

GILLIAM COUNTY HISTORICAL SOCIETY - DEPOT MUSEUM COMPLEX, Hwy. 19 at Burns Park, Condon, OR 97823. Mailing Address: P.O. Box 377, Condon, OR 97823-0377. Tel.: 503-384-4233.
Founded: 1985.
Congressional District: 59
Key Personnel: Pres. (V), Karen Wilde; Treas., Kay Hassing; Exec. Sec., Lois Blessington.
Personnel Profile: Part-Time Paid 1; Part-Time Volunteers 30.
Governing Authority: private; nonprofit organization. Tax-exempt: 501(c)(3).
History Museum.
Collections: Gilliam County history; farm machinery.
Research Fields: genealogy.
Facilities: library; 10,000 sq. ft. exhibit space.
Activities: films; guided tours; loan & temporary exhibitions. Annual Events: Independence Day parade float; County Fair booth; banquet; Appreciation Day.
Publications: biannual newsletter.
Hours & Admission Prices: May-Oct. Wed.-Sun. & holidays 1-5. Suggested Donations: adults $2.50, high school students $.50, children $.25. ♿
Attendance: 650 (accurate)
Membership: Single $15; Couple & Family $25.

Coos Bay

COOS ART MUSEUM, (M), 235 Anderson, Coos Bay, OR 97420-1610. Tel.: 541-267-3901 & 4877. Fax: 541-267-4877 (please call 267-3901).
E-mail: adavenport@coosart.org
Web Site: www.coosart.org
Founded: 1950.
Congressional District: 4
Key Personnel: Pres. (V), Jan Delimont.
Personnel Profile: Full-Time Paid 1; Part-Time Paid 7; Part-Time Volunteers 15.
Governing Authority: nonprofit organization. Tax-exempt: 501(c)(3).
Art Museum: housed in 1935 Post Office building.
Collections: contemporary American prints; historical maritime photography; Northwest art in various media.
Research Fields: 20th-century art.
Facilities: classrooms.
Activities: classes; workshops; lectures; films; tours; special art events; rental & sales program. Museum Sponsors: Fundraiser in July & September.
Publications: exhibition announcements; class schedules.
Hours & Admission Prices: Tues.-Fri. 10-4, Sat. 1-4. Adults $5, seniors & students $2; members no charge. ♿
Attendance: 20,254 (estimated)
Membership: Student $15; Individual $45; Family $70; Business/Active Supporter $150; Gallery Club $250; Curator's Circle $500; President's Circle $1,000; Benefactor $2,500.

MARSHFIELD SUN PRINTING MUSEUM, Front & Bayshore, Coos Bay, OR 97420. Mailing Address: P.O. Box 783, Coos Bay, OR 97420-0148. Tel.: 541-267-3762.
E-mail: lionel@wildblue.net
Founded: 1975.
Key Personnel: Pres. (V), Marty Giles.
Personnel Profile: Full-Time Paid 1; Part-Time Paid 1; Part-Time Volunteers 5.
Governing Authority: Parent Institution: Marshfield Sun Association. Tax-exempt.
Historic Building Museum: housed in the former Marshfield Sun newspaper building.
Collections: printing & local history; printing equipment.
Hours & Admission Prices: Memorial Day to Labor Day Tues.-Sat. 10-4; other times by appointment. No charge; donations accepted. ♿
Attendance: 280 (accurate)
Membership: Senior $20; Regular $35; Donor $50; Benefactor $150; Life $200; Business $500.

Corbett

FRIENDS OF VISTA HOUSE, Crown Point State Park, 40700 E. Historic Columbia River Hwy., Corbett, OR 97019. Mailing Address: Friends of Vista House, P.O. Box 204, Corbett, OR 97019-0204. Tel.: 503-695-2230. Fax: 503-695-2250.
E-mail: friends@vistahouse.com
Web Site: www.vistahouse.com
Founded: 1982.
Key Personnel: Dir., Louise P. Yarbrough.
Personnel Profile: Full-Time Paid 1; Part-Time Paid 12.
Historic Building Museum: built in 1916. Listed on the National Register of Historic Places.
Collections: Oregon pioneer history; photographs; sculpture; observatory.
Facilities: cafe. Museum-related items for sale.
Publications: newsletter.
Hours & Admission Prices: March-Oct. daily 9-6; Nov.-Feb. Sat.-Sun. No charge; donations accepted. ♿
Attendance: 1,000,000 (estimated)
Membership: Individual $25; Family $50; Emerald $100; Diamond $250; Crown Jewel $500; Lancaster Circle $1,000; Lazarus Society $2,500; Thor's Crown $5,000.

Corvallis

OREGON STATE UNIVERSITY MEMORIAL UNION CONCOURSE GALLERY, Jefferson St., OSU, Corvallis, OR 97331. Mailing Address: 10 Memorial Union E., Corvallis, OR 97331-8592. Tel.: 541-737-6371. Fax: 541-737-1565.
E-mail: susan.bourque@oregonstate.edu
Web Site: www.osumu.org/about_art.htm
Founded: 1927.
Congressional District: 1
Key Personnel: Dir., Kent Sumner; Coord. Exhibits, Susan Bourque.
Personnel Profile: Full-Time Paid 1; Part-Time Paid 1; Part-Time Volunteers 2.
Governing Authority: state; university. Affiliated with the Oregon State Board of Higher Education. Tax-exempt.
Art Institute.
Collections: paintings; sculpture; prints.
Activities: guided tours; lectures; films; gallery talks; concerts; arts festivals; hobby workshops; permanent & temporary exhibitions.
Hours & Admission Prices: June-Aug. Mon.-Fri. 8-5; Sept.-May Mon.-Thurs. 7-11, Fri. 7-12, Sat. 7:30-12, Sun. 8:30-11. No charge; donations accepted. Closed national holidays. ♿
Attendance: 36,000 (estimated)

Cottage Grove

COTTAGE GROVE MUSEUM & ANNEX, 147 H St. & Birch Ave., Cottage Grove, OR 97424. Mailing Address: P.O. Box 142, Cottage Grove, OR 97424-0005. Tel.: 541-942-3832. Fax: 541-942-9804.
E-mail: ronairvine1@aol.com
Founded: 1961.
Congressional District: 4
Key Personnel: Chm. (V), Joe Griggs; Museum Shop Mgr., Jo Anne Skelton.
Personnel Profile: Part-Time Paid 1; Part-Time Volunteers 12.
Governing Authority: C.G. Museum Perpetuation Corp. Tax-exempt.
General Museum: housed in former 1896 octagonal Roman Catholic Church.
Collections: pioneer articles; farm & industry artifacts; Indian artifacts; mining tools; firearms; Civil War items; Italian stain glass windows; original Oregon covered bridge prints; Titanic display; quilts; military uniforms.
Facilities: 130-vol. library pertaining to the War of the Rebellion available to the public.
Hours & Admission Prices: Summer: Wed.-Sun. 1-4; Winter: Sat.-Sun. 1-4. No charge; donations accepted.
Attendance: 1,500 (estimated)

Crater Lake

CRATER LAKE NATIONAL PARK, (M), Hwy. 62, Crater Lake, OR 97604. Mailing Address: P.O. Box 7, Crater Lake, OR 97604-0007. Tel.: 541-594-3095. Fax: 541-594-3010.
E-mail: mary_benterou@nps.gov
Founded: 1902.
Congressional District: 2
Key Personnel: Supt., Craig Ackerman; Park Cur., Mary Benterou.
Personnel Profile: Full-Time Paid 1.
Governing Authority: federal. Parent Institution: U.S. Dept. of the Interior. Subsidiary Institution: National Park Service. Tax-exempt.
Park Museum.
Collections: natural history; period artifacts; herbarium; zoology; geology.

Research Fields: Crater Lake, geology; botany; zoology.
Facilities: 1,500-vol. library of natural science & history & 8,000 natural resource specimens available for research by appointment on premises. Books & slides for sale.
Activities: guided tours June-September; lectures.
Publications: leaflet, Nature Trail; Birds of Crater Lake; Crater Lake Trails; A Guide To Crater Lake; annual, Nature Notes from Crater Lake.
Hours & Admission Prices: Visitor Center: daily 9-4:30. Entry fee. ♿
Attendance: 500,000
Membership: Individual $10; Family $15; Supporting $100; Benefactor $250; Life $500; Corporate $500 & up.

Depoe Bay

OREGON COAST SPORTS MUSEUM & INTERNATIONAL SPORTS HALL OF FAME AND OLYMPIC MUSEUM, 110 N.E. Hwy. 101, Depoe Bay, OR 97341. Mailing Address: P.O. Box 166, Depoe Bay, OR 97341-0166. Tel.: 541-765-2923; 702-346-1776.
E-mail: enash327@yahoo.com
Web Site: www.olympicsource.org
Founded: 1980.
Key Personnel: Exec. Dir. & Museum Shop Mgr., Eric Nash
Sports Museum.
Collections: Olympic memorabilia 1896 to present; pins; medals; posters; stamps; uniforms; porcelain; torches; books; photographs; personal artifacts.
Research Fields: Olympic history.
Hours & Admission Prices: By appointment. Adults $8, children under 12 $5; discounts to groups, AAM & ICOM members; members no charge.

Echo

CHINESE HOUSE/O.R. & N. MUSEUM & ST. PETER'S CATHOLIC CHURCH, 230 W. Bridge & 33208 Marble, Echo, OR 97826. Mailing Address: P.O. Box 426, Echo, OR 97826-0426. Tel.: 541-376-8411. Fax: 541-376-8218.
E-mail: ecpl@centurytel.net
Web Site: www.echo-oregon.com
Founded: 1987.
Congressional District: 2
Key Personnel: C.E.O., Diane Berry.
Personnel Profile: Part-Time Paid 1; Part-Time Volunteers 7.
Governing Authority: private; nonprofit organization. Tax-exempt: 501(c)(3).
History Museum.
Collections: artifacts; photographs; documents; tools; early Catholic relics; statuary.
Activities: guided tours; temporary exhibitions.
Publications: Echo Story: Part I Early Days to Arrival of the Railroad.
Hours & Admission Prices: Call for hours & appointment. No charge; donations accepted.
Attendance: 75 (estimated)
Membership: Individual/Library $20; Contributing $50; Patron $100.

FORT HENRIETTA INTERPRETIVE PARK, 10 W. Main, Echo, OR 97826. Mailing Address: P.O. Box 9, Echo, OR 97826-0009. Tel.: 541-376-8411. Fax: 541-376-8218.
E-mail: ecpl@centurytel.net
Web Site: www.echo-oregon.com
Founded: 1985.
Congressional District: 2
Key Personnel: C.E.O. & Records, Diane Berry; Chm. (V), Mayor Richard Winter, Ph.D.
Personnel Profile: Part-Time Volunteers 2.
Governing Authority: municipal; nonprofit. Tax-exempt.
History Museum & Interpretive Center.
Collections: covered wagon; replica of Fort Block House; interpretive panels; covered wagon museum; fire equipment c.1905-1915; hook & ladder; chemical wagon; 1st Umatilla County jail.
Activities: self-guided tours.
Publications: Echo Cultural Inventory; The Echo Story - Part I Early Days to Arrival of the Railroad.
Hours & Admission Prices: Park: Mon.-Fri. dawn-dusk. Library: Mon.-Fri. 8:30-4:30. No charge; donations accepted. ♿

OREGON TRAIL ARBORETUM, 1 Neely Lane, Echo, OR 97826. Mailing Address: 20 S. Bonanza, P.O. Box 9, Echo, OR 97826-0009. Tel.: 541-376-8411. Fax: 541-376-8218.
E-mail: ecpl@centurytel.net
Web Site: www.echo-oregon.com
Founded: 1993.
Congressional District: 2
Key Personnel: C.E.O. & Records, Diane Berry; Mayor, Richard Winter, Ph.D.
Personnel Profile: Part-Time Volunteers 2.
Governing Authority: municipal. Parent Institution: City of Echo. Tax-exempt.
Arboretum.
Collections: over 130 trees & shrubs; history of trees in Echo.
Research Fields: northeastern Oregon ornamental nursery trade.
Facilities: nature trails.
Activities: self guided tours; educational programs for children. Annual Events: Tree Fair in April; Arbor Day Poster contest.
Publications: brochure, Echo Historical & Cultural Inventory.
Hours & Admission Prices: Mon.-Fri. dawn-dusk. No charge; donations accepted. ♿

Eugene

* **JORDAN SCHNITZER MUSEUM OF ART, (M),** 1430 Johnson Lane, Eugene, OR 97403. Mailing Address: 1223 University of Oregon, Eugene, OR 97403-1223. Tel.: 541-346-3027 & 0973. Fax: 541-346-0976.
E-mail: jsma@uoregon.edu
Web Site: jsma.uoregon.edu
Formerly: University of Oregon Museum of Art
Founded: 1932.
Congressional District: 4
Key Personnel: Exec. Dir., Jill Hartz; Cur. American Rgnl. Art, Lawrence Fong; Assoc. Dir. Operations & Exhibits, Kurt Neugebauer; Dir. Education, Lisa Abia-Smith; Registrar, Jean Nattinger; Chief Preparator, Rick Gehrke; Dir. Communications, Erick Hoffman; Dir. Devel., Deidre Sandvick; Visitor Svcs., Jamie Leaf.
Personnel Profile: Full-Time Paid 13; Part-Time Paid 7; Part-Time Volunteers 50; Interns 5.
Governing Authority: university. Parent Institution: University of Oregon. Tax-exempt: 170(b)(1)(A).
Art Museum.
Collections: American & regional art; European, Korean, Chinese & Japanese; Russian icons.
Major Exhibits: Amazonia: Photographs by Sam Abell (T), 1/15/10-4/8/10; Gus Van Sant & Andy Warhol, Summer 2010; Guiseppe Vasi's Rome (T), 9/25/10-1/2/11.
Research Fields: Asian, contemporary northwest & American art.
Facilities: garden & sculpture court; cafe. Museum-related items for sale.
Activities: guided tours; gallery talks & demonstrations; student practica; inter-museum loan exhibitions; rental space available; exhibition interpreter program; studio classes; interactive exhibits; art-making studio.
Publications: collections catalog; brochure; newsletters; annual report; exhibition catalogs.
Hours & Admission Prices: Wed. 11-8, Thurs.-Sun. 11-5. Adults $5, seniors $3; discounts to AAM & ICOM members; North American reciprocal members, Univ. of Oregon students, faculty & staff; high school & non-UO college students, children 13 & under and members no charge. ♿
Attendance: 51,000 (accurate)
Membership: Student & Teacher $25; Active $45; Family $55; Contributor $100; Sustainer $250; Fellow $500; Director's Circle $1,000.

LANE COMMUNITY COLLEGE ART GALLERY, 4000 E. 30th Ave., Eugene, OR 97405-0640. Tel.: 541-463-5409. Fax: 541-463-4185.
Founded: 1970.
Key Personnel: Dir., Rick Williams.
Personnel Profile: Part-Time Paid 1.
Governing Authority: public college; nonprofit.
Art Gallery.
Collections: paintings; photographs; sculpture.
Facilities: educational facilities; 875 sq. ft. exhibit space.
Activities: lectures.
Hours & Admission Prices: Sept.-June Mon.-Thurs. 8-9, Fri. 8-4. No charge. Closed New Year's Day; Presidents' Day; Memorial Day; Labor Day; Thanksgiving; Christmas. ♿
Attendance: 6,000 (estimated)

LANE COUNTY HISTORICAL SOCIETY & MUSEUM, 740 W. 13th Ave., Eugene, OR 97402-4010. Tel.: 541-682-4242. Fax: 541-682-7361.
E-mail: info@lanecountyhistoricalsociety.org
Web Site: www.lanecountyhistoricalsociety.org
Founded: 1951.
Congressional District: 4
Key Personnel: Dir., Robert L. Hart; Office Mgr., Linda Bright.
Personnel Profile: Full-Time Paid 1; Part-Time Paid 6; Part-Time Volunteers 40.
Governing Authority: nonprofit organization. Tax-exempt: 501(c)(3).
History Museum.

Collections: 1850s-1950s textiles, tools, vehicles, household furnishings; 14,000 photographs; early settlement period; transportation artifacts; 1920s & 1930s trades; children's exhibits. Historic Building: 1853 county clerk's building.
Research Fields: Lane County history.
Facilities: 2,500-vol. library & archives on Lane County history.
Activities: guided tours; formally organized education programs for children; permanent & temporary exhibitions; slide programs; school loan service; nitrate negative digitization project. Museum Sponsors: Annual Quilt Exhibition in April.
Publications: booklet, Oregon Trail & 19th Century Lane County; books on Lane County & Oregon history; Oregon Trail published material & diary reprints; triannual newsletter, The Lane County Historian; quarterly newsletter, The Artifact.
Hours & Admission Prices: Tues.-Sat. 10-4. Adults $3, seniors $2, youth 15-17 $.75; children under 14 & members no charge. Closed national holidays.
Attendance: 8,638 (accurate)
Membership: Senior Citizen $15; Individual $25; Supporter & Family $40; Sponsor $75-$199; Business & Patron $200-$999; Benefactor $1,000 & up.

MAUDE I. KERNS ART CENTER, 1910 E. 15th Ave., Eugene, OR 97403-2094. Tel.: 541-345-1571. Fax: 541-345-6248.
E-mail: staff@mkartcenter.org
Web Site: www.mkartcenter.org
Founded: 1962.
Key Personnel: Bd. Pres. (V), Deborah Watkins; Exec. Dir., Karen Pavelec; Administrative Asst., Sarah Kemp; Education Coord., Shayann Hoffer; Exhibition Dir., Tina Schrager; Exhibits Asst., Nick Cook; Dir. Publications, Marsha Shankman.
Personnel Profile: Full-Time Paid 3; Part-Time Paid 3; Part-Time Volunteers 400; Interns 20.
Governing Authority: nonprofit organization. Tax-exempt: 501(c)(3).
Art Museum: housed in 1895 historic landmark church building.
Collections: work of Maude Kerns.
Facilities: classroom; printmakers studio; ceramics cooperative.
Activities: arts festivals; Art & the Vineyard; formal education programs for adults & children; guided tours; lectures. Museum Sponsors: Art and the Vineyard; Independence Day Weekend in July.
Publications: quarterly newsletter; quarterly class schedules.
Hours & Admission Prices: Mon.-Fri. 10-5:30, Sat. 12-4. Suggested Donations: family $5, individual $2. ♿
Attendance: 60,000 (estimated)
Membership: Students & Seniors $25; Adult $35; Family $55; Business $75; Patron $100; Benefactor $250 and up.

MOUNT PISGAH ARBORETUM, 34901 Frank Parrish Rd., Eugene, OR 97405-9673. Tel.: 541-747-3817. Fax: 541-747-1504 (call first).
E-mail: mtpisgah@efn.org
Web Site: www.mountpisgaharboretum.org
Founded: 1973.
Congressional District: 4
Key Personnel: Exec. Dir., Brad van Appel; Pres. Bd., Jon Stafford; Chm. Site Overview Committee, Theodore Palmer; Operations Mgr., Tom LoCascio; Education Mgr., Fran Rosenthal.
Personnel Profile: Full-Time Paid 5; Full-Time Volunteers 10; Part-Time Paid 1; Part-Time Volunteers 500.
Governing Authority: nonprofit organization. Parent Institution: Friends of Mount Pisgah Arboretum. Tax-exempt: 501(c)(3).
Arboretum-Botanical Garden.
Collections: native vegetation; 200 species of exotics.
Research Fields: natural habitat rehabilitation.
Facilities: 500-vol. library pertaining to botany & horticulture available for research on premises; nature trails & guides; 200-acre site.
Activities: guided tours; formally organized education programs for children; permanent exhibitions. Arboretum Sponsors: Wildflower Festival in Spring; Arbor Week celebrations in April; Mushroom Festival in Fall.
Publications: newsletter; pamphlets; brochure; mushroom cookbook; nature guide; newsletter, Tree Time.
Hours & Admission Prices: Daily dawn-dusk. No charge; donations accepted. ♿
Attendance: 177,000 (estimated)
Membership: Student & Senior Citizen $30; Individual $40; Family $50; Nonprofit Organization $50; Business $100; Life $1,000.

OREGON AIR & SPACE MUSEUM, 90377 Boeing Dr., Eugene, OR 97402-9536. Tel.: 541-461-1101.
Founded: 1991.
Congressional District: 4
Key Personnel: Pres. (V), Bruce Lamont; Dir. Operations & Museum Shop Mgr., Thomas Winn.
Personnel Profile: Part-Time Paid 1; Part-Time Volunteers 40.
Governing Authority: nonprofit organization. Tax-exempt: 501(c)(3).
Aviation & Space Museum.
Collections: aircraft; engines; uniforms; photographs; history of flight; Oregon aviation history; space program; display of over 1,000 scale model aircraft; women in aviation.
Facilities: library of books & video on aviation & space topics; classrooms; 8,500 sq. ft. exhibit space; 85-seat theatre. Museum-related items for sale.
Activities: guided tours; lectures; organized education programs; temporary & traveling exhibitions. Museum Sponsors: banquet; air show; USO style hangar dances.
Publications: quarterly newsletter, Wings of Oregon.
Hours & Admission Prices: April-Oct. Wed.-Sun. 12-4; Nov.-March Wed.-Sat. 12-4. Adults $5, senior citizens 62 & up $4, children 13-18 $3, children 6-11 $2; discounts to AAM & ICOM members; children under 6, members, Pearson Air Museums, and Seattle Museums of Flight members no charge. Closed some holidays. ♿
Attendance: 9,000 (estimated)
Membership: Individual & Senior Family $35; Family $45; Sustaining $60; Contributing $150.

SCIENCE FACTORY CHILDREN'S MUSEUM & PLANETARIUM, 2300 Leo Harris Pkwy., Eugene, OR 97401-8834. Mailing Address: P.O. Box 1518, Eugene, OR 97440-1518. Tel.: 541-682-7887. Fax: 541-484-9027.
E-mail: bobreeves@sciencefactory.org
Web Site: www.sciencefactory.org
Formerly: Willamette Science & Technology Center (WISTEC)
Founded: 1961.
Congressional District: 4
Key Personnel: Exec. Dir., Bob Reeves; Chm. (V), Joyce Berman; Museum Shop Mgr., Sara Pritt.
Personnel Profile: Full-Time Paid 4; Full-Time Volunteers 1; Part-Time Paid 3; Part-Time Volunteers 50.
Governing Authority: nonprofit organization. Tax-exempt: 501(c)(3).
Science Museum.
Collections: interactive science exhibits.
Facilities: planetarium; classrooms; computer labs. Museum-related items for sale.
Activities: interactive exhibits; planetarium shows; after school workshops; summer science camp; special events; birthday parties; science workshops; formally organized education programs; permanent & temporary exhibitions; preschool discovery days; science clubs; speakers.
Publications: newsletter, Update; monthly e-news; exhibit catalogues.
Hours & Admission Prices: Call or visit website; groups by appointment. Adults $4; discounts to AAA, KRVM, Oregon Public Broadcasting members, ASTC Passport Program members & University of Oregon Alumni Association; members no charge. Reciprocal admission, donations accepted. Closed Independence Day; Thanksgiving; Christmas. ♿
Attendance: 35,000 (estimated)
Membership: Individual $30; Family $55; Premier $100.

UNIVERSITY OF OREGON MUSEUM OF NATURAL AND CULTURAL HISTORY, (M), 1680 E. 15th Ave., Eugene, OR 97403-1224. Mailing Address: 1224 University of Oregon, Eugene, OR 97403-1224. Tel.: 541-346-3024 & 1671. Fax: 541-346-5334.
E-mail: mnh@uoregon.edu
Web Site: natural-history.uoregon.edu
Founded: 1932.
Congressional District: 4
Key Personnel: Dir., Jon Erlandson; Dir. Prog., Patricia Krier; Dir. Research, Thomas Connolly; Dir. Collections, Pamela Endzweig; Asst. Dir. Exhibitions, Cynthia Budlong; Museum Shop Mgr., Terry Church; Asst. Dir. Visitors Svcs., Judith Pruitt; Asst. Dir. Education & Outreach, Ann Craig.
Personnel Profile: Full-Time Paid 14; Part-Time Paid 17; Part-Time Volunteers 65; Interns 4.
Governing Authority: state; university. Parent Institution: University of Oregon. Subsidiary Institution: Oregon State Museum of Anthropology. Tax-exempt: 170(c)1.
Natural History Museum. (Association of Science - Associated member with ASTC Technology Centers).
Collections: Oregon natural & cultural history & archaeology; worldwide ethnology.
Research Fields: Oregon archaeology & anthropology.
Facilities: 1,000-vol. library of technical reports & documentation; 3,500 sq. ft. exhibit space; research area. Museum-related items for sale.
Activities: guided tours; lectures; organized education programs; temporary exhibitions; docent program.
Publications: quarterly newsletter, Fieldnotes; scholarly special publications.

Hours & Admission Prices: Wed.-Sun. Family $8, adults $3, seniors & youth $2; ASTC & MNCH & museum members, UO faculty, students & staff no charge. Closed New Year's Day; Independence Day; Thanksgiving; Christmas. ♿
Attendance: 22,000 (estimated)
Membership: Individual $40; Family $50; Supporter $100; Director's $500 & up.

Florence

SIUSLAW PIONEER MUSEUM, 278 Maple St., Florence, OR 97439. Mailing Address: P.O. Box 2637, Florence, OR 97439-0164. Tel.: 541-997-7884.
Founded: 1970.
Key Personnel: Cur., Louis Campbell.
Personnel Profile: Part-Time Volunteers 35.
Governing Authority: nonprofit organization. Tax-exempt.
History Museum.
Collections: local history & culture; photographs.
Hours & Admission Prices: Feb.-Nov. Tues.-Sun. 12-4. Adults $3; children under 16 & members no charge. Closed Easter; Thanksgiving; Christmas.

Forest Grove

PACIFIC UNIVERSITY MUSEUM, Pacific University, 2043 College Way, Forest Grove, OR 97116-1756. Tel.: 503-352-2211. Fax: 503-352-2252.
Web Site: www.pacificu.edu
Founded: 1949.
Congressional District: 1
Key Personnel: Pres., Dr. Lesley M. Hallick.
Personnel Profile: Part-Time Volunteers 12.
Governing Authority: university. Tax-exempt: 101(6).
History Museum housed in: 1850 Old College Hall.
Collections: artifacts relating to the history of Pacific University & Tualatin Academy; Asian cultures & missionary activity.
Research Fields: biographical; institutional history of Pacific University; development of higher education in the Pacific Northwest.
Facilities: meeting & reception room; chapel.
Activities: guided tours.
Publications: Splendid Audacity: The Story of Pacific University; On Your Own Two Feet: A Self Guided Tour of Our Historic Campus.
Hours & Admission Prices: First Wed. 1-4, or by appointment. No charge; donations accepted. Closed university vacations & holidays.
Attendance: 1,500 (estimated)

Fort Rock

FORT ROCK VALLEY HISTORICAL HOMESTEAD MUSEUM, 64696 Fort Rock Rd., Fort Rock, OR 97735. Mailing Address: Fort Rock Valley Historical Society, P.O. Box 84, Fort Rock, OR 97735-0084. Tel.: 541-576-2207.
Historic Buildings: eleven buildings in a village setting.
Collections: local history & culture; photographs; period furnishings. Historic Buildings: homestead houses; church; school buildings.
Facilities: rental facilities. Museum-related items for sale.
Hours & Admission Prices: Memorial Day to Labor Day Fri.-Sun. 10-4. Admission 12 & over $1.

Fossil

FOSSIL MUSEUM, First & Main, Fossil, OR 97830. Mailing Address: P.O. Box 465, Fossil, OR 97830-0465. Tel.: 541-763-2113. Fax: 541-763-2026.
Founded: 1966.
Congressional District: 2
Key Personnel: Chm. (V), Donna D. Hopper; Pres. (V), Marilyn G. Garcia.
Personnel Profile: Part-Time Volunteers 27.
Governing Authority: municipal government; nonprofit.
History Museum.
Collections: photographs; local newspapers; household & personal items from 1840-present.
Facilities: 2,400 sq. ft. exhibit space.
Activities: guided tours; loan exhibitions; school loan service; community schools partner. Museum Sponsors: Quilt Show; Music in the Park; Christmas tour of Home.
Publications: annual newsletter; Fossil Museum; Days of Yore and Then Some More; Book of Local History.
Hours & Admission Prices: Memorial Day to Labor Day Mon. 9-4, Wed.-Sun. 1-4. No charge; donations accepted ♿
Attendance: 1,616 (accurate)

Garibaldi

GARIBALDI MUSEUM, 112 Garibaldi Ave., Garibaldi, OR 97118. Mailing Address: 112 Hwy. 101, Garibaldi, OR 97118. Tel.: 503-322-8411.
E-mail: cherylevans@comcast.net
Web Site: www.garibaldimuseum.com
Founded: 1986.
Congressional District: 5
Key Personnel: Dir., Cheryl P. Evans.
Personnel Profile: Full-Time Volunteers 2; Part-Time Paid 1; Part-Time Volunteers 16.
Governing Authority: bd. of directors. Tax-exempt.
Maritime Museum.
Collections: local maritime heritage & history; Captain Robert Gray's life & historic vessels including models of the Columbia Redivivia & Lady Washington; reproductions of seafarers clothing & musical instruments; photographs.
Hours & Admission Prices: May-Oct. Thurs.-Mon. 12-4. Adults $3, seniors & children 5-17 $.50; discounts to groups; children under 5 no charge. ♿
Membership: Friends $25.

Gold Beach

ROGUE RIVER MUSEUM, 29880 Harbor Dr., Gold Beach, OR 97444. Mailing Address: P.O. Box 1011, Gold Beach, OR 97444-1011. Tel.: 541-247-4571.
Web Site: www.roguejets.com/museum.php
History Museum.
Collections: historical artifacts; photographs; taxidermy.
Hours & Admission Prices: Call for hours.

Government Camp

MT. HOOD CULTURAL CENTER & MUSEUM, 88900 E. Hwy. 26, Business Loop, Government Camp, OR 97028. Mailing Address: P.O. Box 55, Government Camp, OR 97028-0055. Tel.: 503-272-3301.
E-mail: mthoodmuseum@centurytel.net
Web Site: www.mthoodmuseum.org
Founded: 1998.
Congressional District: 3
Key Personnel: Pres. (V), Bing Sheldon.
Personnel Profile: Full-Time Paid 1; Part-Time Paid 2; Part-Time Volunteers 80; Interns 2.
History Museum.
Collections: history of winter sports; early exploration; settlement & natural history of Mt. Hood.
Facilities: community meeting room.
Activities: arts & crafts school; historic home tours.
Publications: quarterly newsletter.
Hours & Admission Prices: Daily 10-5. No charge; donations accepted. Closed Thanksgiving; Christmas. ♿
Attendance: 12,000 (accurate)
Membership: Individual $20; Family $35; Patron $100; Benefactor $250; Summit Club $1,000.

Grand Ronde

CONFEDERATED TRIBES OF GRAND RONDE CULTURAL RESOURCES DEPARTMENT, (M), 9615 Grand Ronde Rd., Grand Ronde, OR 97347-9712. Tel.: 503-879-2248. Fax: 503-879-2126.
E-mail: lindy.trolan@grandronde.org
Web Site: www.grandronde.org
Founded: 1995.
Congressional District: 5
Key Personnel: Coord. Education, Tony A. Johnson; Coord. Cultural Collections, Lindy Trolan; Coord. Site Protection, Khani Schultz; Language Teacher, Jackie Whisler; Language & Cultural Specialist, Bobby Mercier; Language Teacher, Crystal Szczepanski; Language Teacher, Richard So-Happy; Language Teacher, Kathy Cole; Language Teacher, Shawn Bobb; Asst. Language Teacher, Ali Holsclaw; Cultural Resources Specialist, Eirik Thorsgard; Cultural Education Specialist, Leslie Riggs; Cultural Resource Technician, Daniel Haug; Cultural Resource Mgr., David Lewis; Receptionist, Angella McCallister.
Personnel Profile: Full-Time Paid 16.
Governing Authority: The Confederated Tribes of the Grand Ronde Community of Oregon.
Tribal Museum.
Collections: Indian artifacts; manuscripts; oral histories; traditional Indian crafts & art; archival materials; photographs & language materials related to Grand Ronde tribal community.
Research Fields: Indian culture & history, specifically of the Confederated Tribes of the Grand Ronde Community of Oregon & related tribes.

Facilities: 100-vol. library of culture & history of Grand Ronde Tribes & related tribes; tribal repository.
Activities: cultural protection & cultural language programs for tribal community; cultural education classes.
Publications: Tribal newspapers, Smoke Signals; virtual gallery, Ntsayka Ikanum: Our Story.
Hours & Admission Prices: Offices: Mon.-Fri. 8-5. Closed New Year's Day; Presidents' Day; Independence Day; Labor Day; Veterans Day; Thanksgiving; Christmas; National Indian Day; Restoration Day.

Grants Pass

GRANTS PASS MUSEUM OF ART, 229 S.W. G St., Grants Pass, OR 97526-2415. Mailing Address: P.O. Box 966, Grants Pass, OR 97528-0081. Tel.: 541-479-3290. Fax: 541-479-1218.
E-mail: museum@gpmuseum.com
Web Site: www.gpmuseum.com
Founded: 1979.
Congressional District: 2
Key Personnel: Exec. Dir., Chris Pondelick; Pres. (V), Bill Lowe; Treas. (V), Don Stocking; Museum Shop Mgr., Carissa Moddison.
Personnel Profile: Part-Time Paid 2; Part-Time Volunteers 32; Interns 2.
Governing Authority: nonprofit organization. Tax-exempt: 501(c)(3).
Art Museum.
Collections: contemporary regional art.
Major Exhibits: Grants Pass Museum of Art Permanent Collection, 1/12/10-1/29/10; Studio Art Quilt Association (T), 6/1/10-6/16/10; Abstract Paintings by Randy Johnson, 7/20/10-8/27/10; American Watercolor Society (T), 8/31/10-10/8/10; American Art & Culture; The 1940s, 10/12/10-11/19/10; GPMA Members Exhibit, 11/30/10-12/17/10.
Facilities: workshops; classrooms.
Activities: guided tours; lectures; gallery talks; formally organized education programs for children; traveling exhibitions; workshops; permanent exhibitions.
Publications: quarterly newsletter; exhibit announcements.
Hours & Admission Prices: Summer: Tues.-Sat. 12-4; Winter: Tues.-Fri. 12-4, Sat. 10-1:30. No charge; donations accepted. Closed Easter; Memorial Day; Independence Day; Labor Day; Thanksgiving weekend. ♿
Attendance: 17,000 (accurate)
Membership: Student & Teacher $20-$29; Individual $30-$59; Family $60-$99; Guild $100-$249; Patron $250-$499; Benefactor $500 & up.

SCHMIDT HOUSE MUSEUM & RESEARCH LIBRARY, 508 & 512 S.W. 5th St., Grants Pass, OR 97526-2804. Mailing Address: 512 S.W. 5th St., Grants Pass, OR 97526-2804. Tel.: 541-479-7827. Fax: 888-488-5410.
E-mail: josephinehistorical@charter.net
Web Site: www.josephinehistorical.org
Founded: 1960.
Key Personnel: C.E.O. & Museum Shop Mgr., Rose Scott; Chm. (V), Jean Boling; Pres. (V) & Devel., Joan Momsen; Financial Dir., Marilyn Luttrell; Education, Janet Lane.
Personnel Profile: Part-Time Paid 2; Part-Time Volunteers 50.
Governing Authority: private; nonprofit organization. Parent Institution: Josephine County Historical Society, Grants Pass, OR. Tax-exempt: 501(c)(3).
Historic House & Research Library.
Collections: 1885-1925 furniture; toys; clothes; photos; documents; books; microfilm; magazines; newspapers.
Research Fields: genealogy; local history.
Facilities: library. Museum-related items for sale.
Activities: films; guided tours; lectures; temporary exhibitions. Museum Sponsors: Pie Social; Heritage Events.
Publications: quarterly newsletter, The Oldtimer.
Hours & Admission Prices: Tues.-Fri. 10-4. Adults $3, children $1; members no charge.
Attendance: 1,500 (estimated)
Membership: Individual $15; Family $25; Business $55; Sustaining $100; Newsletter $195; Lifetime $1,000.

WISEMAN & FIREHOUSE GALLERIES, ROGUE COMMUNITY COLLEGE, (M), 3345 Redwood Hwy., Grants Pass, OR 97527-9291. Tel.: 541-956-7339. Fax: 503-471-3588.
E-mail: tdrake@roguecc.edu
Web Site: www.roguecc.edu/galleries
Founded: 1985.
Key Personnel: Dir., Ms. Tommi Drake; Pres. Rogue Community College, Peter Angsadt; Gallery Asst., Heather Green.
Personnel Profile: Full-Time Paid 2; Part-Time Paid 4; Part-Time Volunteers 15.
Governing Authority: municipal; nonprofit. Parent Institution: Rogue Community College. Tax-exempt.
Art Galleries: the FireHouse Gallery is housed in the firehouse portion of historic city hall; the Wiseman Gallery is located on the Redwood Campus & Rogue Community College campus in the Wiseman Center.
Collections: contemporary art including paintings, prints, drawings, sculpture & photographs.
Facilities: educational facilities; 250-seat theater.
Activities: volunteer program; formal education programs for adults & children; temporary & traveling exhibitions. Annual Events: Art Auction & Dance; Black, White and the Blues.
Publications: annual directory exhibits listing for each gallery; catalogues that accompany exhibits.
Hours & Admission Prices: Wiseman Gallery: Mon.-Thurs. 8am-7pm, Fri. 8-3, Sat. 9-12. FireHouse Gallery: Tues.-Fri. 11:30-4:30, Sat. 10-1. No charge. Closed national holidays & between college quarters. Call for summer hours. ♿
Attendance: 19,000 (estimated)

Gresham

FAIRVIEW-ROCKWOOD-WILKES HISTORICAL SOCIETY, 17111 N.E. Sandy Blvd., Gresham, OR 97030. Mailing Address: P.O. Box 946, Fairview, OR 97024-0946. Tel.: 503-261-8078.
Formerly: Zimmerman House and Heslin House Museums
Founded: 1987.
Key Personnel: Pres. (V), Dodi Davies.
Personnel Profile: Part-Time Volunteers 25.
Governing Authority: Parent Institution: Fairview-Rockwood-Wilkes Historical Society. Branch Museum: Heslin House Museum, 60 Main St., Fairview, OR 97024.
Historic Houses: Zimmerman House built in 1874. Heslin House: built in 1893.
Collections: local history & culture; period furnishings; personal artifacts; photographs.
Activities: educational programs; group tours.
Publications: Reflections.
Hours & Admission Prices: Zimmerman House: 3rd Sat. of month 10-3. Heslin House: 3rd Sat. of month 10-3. Adults $3; members no charge.

GRESHAM HISTORY MUSEUM, 410 N. Main Ave., Gresham, OR 97030-7212. Mailing Address: P.O. Box 65, Gresham, OR 97030-0011. Tel.: 503-661-0347.
Web Site: community.gorge.net/ghs/
Formerly: Gresham Pioneer Museum
Founded: 1976.
Key Personnel: Pres. (V), Jack Horner; Security, Larry Kerr; Education, Utahna Kerr; Archivist & Museum Shop Mgr., Pat Stone.
Personnel Profile: Part-Time Volunteers 35.
Governing Authority: nonprofit organization. Parent Institution: Gresham Historical Society. Tax-exempt: 501(c)(3).
Historical Society Museum: housed in 1913 Carnegie library.
Collections: photographs; historical artifacts; ephemera.
Activities: lectures; organized education programs; school loan service; loan, temporary & traveling exhibitions.
Publications: monthly, Gresham Historical Society Newsletter.
Hours & Admission Prices: Tues.-Sat. 12-4. No charge; donations accepted. ♿
Attendance: 400 (estimated)
Membership: Student & Senior $10; Regular $25; Family $50.

Haines

EASTERN OREGON MUSEUM, 3rd & Wilcox, Haines, OR 97833-6388. Mailing Address: 14514 Muddy Creek Lane, Haines, OR 97833-6388. Tel.: 541-856-3233.
Web Site: www.hainesoregon.com/eomuseum
Formerly: Eastern Oregon Museum on the Old Oregon Trail
Founded: 1958.
Congressional District: 2
Key Personnel: Pres., Linda Smith; Vice Pres., Viola Perkins; Treas., Mary Rider; Sec., Julie Johnson.
Personnel Profile: Part-Time Volunteers 20.
Governing Authority: board of directors; nonprofit organization. Tax-exempt: 501(c)(3).
General Museum: housed in a 1931 old school gym.
Collections: over 10,000 artifacts; farm implements; blacksmith shop; authentic parlor; buggies; cutters; hacks & a surrey; musical instruments; bells; dolls & toys; replica kitchen; washing & sewing machines; old newspapers; old school books; uniforms; guns; arrowheads. Historic Building: late 1880s railroad depot.
Facilities: approx. 100-vol. library of local & Oregon history, available for use on the premises by appointment. Craft items, jewelry, handmade items for sale.
Activities: guided tours for schools, club groups & senior citizens groups.

Publications: brochures.
Hours & Admission Prices: May 15-Sept. 15 Wed.-Mon.; other times by appointment. Requested Donation: family $5, adult $2. ♿
Attendance: 4,000 (accurate)
Membership: Individual $3; Family $5; Life $100.

Hammond

FORT STEVENS HISTORIC MILITARY SITE & MUSEUM, Fort Stevens State Park, 100 Peter Iredale Rd., Hammond, OR 97121-9712. Tel.: 503-861-1671.
Historic Site.
Collections: artifacts & interpretive displays pertaining to the history of Fort Stevens.
Hours & Admission Prices: June-Sept. daily 10-4; Oct.-May daily 10-6.

Hillsboro

CLASSIC AIRCRAFT AVIATION MUSEUM, (M), 3005 N.E. Cornell Rd., Hillsboro, OR 97124-6316. Mailing Address: P.O. Box 91430, Portland, OR 97291-0008. Tel.: 503-693-1414.
E-mail: donkel@classicaircraft.org
Web Site: www.classicaircraft.org
Key Personnel: Dir., Doug Donkel, Ph.D.
Governing Authority: nonprofit organization. Tax-exempt: 501(c)(3).
Aviation Museum.
Collections: aviation history, technology, & engineering; aircraft.
Activities: air shows; historical reunions; aviation events; flight demonstrations.
Hours & Admission Prices: Mon.-Thurs. 9-4; other times by appointment. No charge.

RICE NORTHWEST MUSEUM OF ROCKS AND MINERALS, 26385 N.W. Groveland Dr., Hillsboro, OR 97124-9351. Tel.: 503-647-2418. Fax: 503-647-5207.
E-mail: info@ricenwmuseum.org
Web Site: www.ricenwmuseum.org
Founded: 1996.
Key Personnel: Dir., S. Jane Guariniello.
Personnel Profile: Full-Time Paid 3; Full-Time Volunteers 1; Part-Time Paid 13; Part-Time Volunteers 4.
Governing Authority: Tax-exempt.
Geology Museum.
Collections: northwest minerals; crystalized minerals; meteorites; petrified wood; fossils; agates; lapidary arts; synthetics; fluorescents; gemstones.
Major Exhibits: Tualatin Valley Gem Club Exhibit, 1/10-12/10; Mt. Hood Rock Club Exhibit, 1/10-12/10.
Facilities: banquet facilities.
Activities: research; rental facilities.
Hours & Admission Prices: Wed.-Sun. 1-5; groups by appointment. Adults $7, seniors $6, students 5-17 $5; discounts to AAA members; members & children under 5 no charge. Closed New Year's Day; Independence Day; Thanksgiving; Christmas. ♿
Attendance: 30,000 (accurate)
Membership: Individual $50; One + One $75; Family $90; Family Plus $100.

Hood River

THE HISTORY MUSEUM OF HOOD RIVER COUNTY, 300 E. Port Marina Dr., Hood River, OR 97031-1198. Mailing Address: P.O. Box 781, Hood River, OR 97031-0026. Tel.: 541-386-6772. Fax: 541-386-6772.
E-mail: thehistorymuseum@hrecn.net
Web Site: www.co.hood-river.or.us/museum
Formerly: Hood River County Historical Museum
Founded: 1907.
Congressional District: 2
Key Personnel: C.E.O., Dave Meriwether; Chm. (v), Carol Faull; Dir., Connie Nice; Museum Shop Mgr., Nellie Hjalatin.
Personnel Profile: Full-Time Paid 1; Full-Time Volunteers 15; Part-Time Volunteers 50.
Governing Authority: county; nonprofit organization. Parent Institution: Hood River County. Subsidiary Institution: Hood River County Historical Society. Tax-exempt.
General Museum.
Collections: biographical files dating from early pioneers; photographic history of Hood River.
Major Exhibits: Farm Life: A Century of Change for Farm Families and Their Neighbors (T), 3/25/10-6/20/10.
Research Fields: early pioneer; family; Hood River & area.
Facilities: library; picnic area. Museum-related items for sale.
Activities: Museum Sponsors: Cemetery Tales in September.
Hours & Admission Prices: April & Oct. daily 1-5; May-Sept. Mon.-Sat. 10-5, Sun. 1-5; July-Aug. Tues. & Thurs. 10-7. No charge; donations accepted. ♿
Attendance: 5,300 (estimated)
Membership: Senior & Student $20; Individual $30; Family $45; Supporter $250.

WESTERN ANTIQUE AEROPLANE & AUTOMOBILE MUSEUM, Ken Jernstedt Airfield 4S2, 1600 Air Museum Rd., Hood River, OR 97031-9800. Tel.: 541-308-1600. Fax: 541-308-1601.
E-mail: info@waaamuseum.org
Web Site: www.waaamuseum.org
Key Personnel: Pres. & Founder, Terry Brandt; Dir., Jeremy Young; Dir. Restorations, Thomas Murphy
Transportation History Museum.
Collections: transporation artifacts & memorabilia.
Hours & Admission Prices: Daily 9-5. Adults $12, senior citizens & veterans $10, students 5-18 $6; children 4 & under and active military with ID no charge.

Jacksonville

CHILDREN'S MUSEUM, 206 N. Fifth St., Jacksonville, OR 97530. Tel.: 541-773-6536. Fax: 541-776-7994.
E-mail: publicrelations@sohs.org
Web Site: www.sohs.org/page.asp?navid=71
Key Personnel: Exec. Dir., John Enders; Cur. Collections & Exhibits, Steve Wyatt.
Governing Authority: Parent Institution: Southern Oregon Historical Society.
Children's Museum.
Collections: hands-on history exhibits.
Hours & Admission Prices: Temporarily closed until spring 2010.

SOUTHERN OREGON HISTORICAL SOCIETY, 5th & C Sts., Jacksonville, OR 97530. Mailing Address: P.O. Box 1570, Jacksonville, OR 97530-1570. Tel.: 541-773-6536. Fax: 541-776-7994.
E-mail: communicate@sohs.org
Web Site: www.sohs.org
Founded: 1946.
Congressional District: 2
Key Personnel: Exec. Dir., John Enders; Dir. Finance & Operations, Maureen Smith; Education & Programs Coord., Stephanie Butler; Devel. Coord., Richard Seidman; Cur. Collections, Suzanne M.M. Warner; Library Mgr., Carol Samuelson.
Personnel Profile: Full-Time Paid 17; Part-Time Paid 10; Part-Time Volunteers 250.
Governing Authority: society. Parent Institution: Southern Oregon Historical Society, Inc. Branch Institutions: Research Center, Medford; Jacksonville Museum of Southern Oregon History, Children's Museum, Beekman House, Beekman Bank, Catholic Rectory, U.S. Hotel, History Store, Jacksonville; Hanley Farm, Central Point. Tax-exempt: 501(c)(3).
History Museum & Historic Sites.
Collections: historical artifacts; textiles; clothing; Peter Britt collection; 19th- & 20th-century photographic equipment; furnishings; firearms; Dorland Robinson artwork; tools & equipment from regional businesses & industries; manuscripts; maps; oral histories; photographs. Historic Buildings: 1883 Jackson County courthouse; 1910 Children's Museum; 1873 CC Beekman house; 1863 Beekman bank; 1860s Hanley Farm.
Research Fields: local & southwestern Oregon history.
Facilities: library of books on local & Southwestern Oregon history; meeting rooms. Museum-related items for sale.
Activities: tours of permanent & temporary exhibits; walking, cemetery tours; adult, family, youth education programs; educational outreach programs; living history program.
Publications: quarterly popular history magazine, Southern Oregon Heritage Today; A Century of the Photographic Arts in Southern Oregon: A Directory of Jackson County Photographers, 1856-1956; brochures, Historic Discovery Drives; Spirit of Ashland.
Hours & Admission Prices: Call 541-773-6536 for hours & admission prices. Members no charge. Closed New Year's Day; Thanksgiving; Christmas. ♿
Attendance: 269,867 (accurate)
Membership: Individual $35; Family $50; Patron $100; Curator $200; Business $250; Director $500; Historian's Circle $1,000; Lifetime $2,500.

John Day

KAM WAH CHUNG STATE HERITAGE SITE, Ing Hay Way, John Day, OR 97845. Mailing Address: P.O. Box 115, John Day, OR 97845-0115. Tel.: 541-575-2800; 800-551-6949.
Formerly: Kam Wah Chung & Co. Museum
Key Personnel: Cur., Christina Sweet.

Governing Authority: Parent Institution: Oregon Parks & Recreation Dept.
Chinese Heritage Museum.
Collections: Oregon's Chinese heritage, history & culture.
Hours & Admission Prices: May-Oct. daily 9-5. No charge.
Attendance: 6,000 (accurate)

Joseph

WALLOWA COUNTY MUSEUM, 110 S. Main, Joseph, OR 97846. Mailing Address: P.O. Box 430, Joseph, OR 97846-0430. Tel.: 541-432-6095.
Key Personnel: Bd. Chm., Caryl Coppin; Cur., Ann Hayes
History Museum.
Collections: county history; Native American artifacts; early settlers.
Hours & Admission Prices: Memorial Day to late Sept. daily 10-5.

Junction City

JUNCTION CITY HISTORICAL SOCIETY, 655 Holly St., Junction City, OR 97448-1631. Tel.: 541-952-0900. Fax: 541-998-2924.
E-mail: cgoodin253@msn.com
Web Site: www.junctioncity.com/history
Founded: 1971.
Congressional District: 4
Key Personnel: Pres., Linda VanOrden; Vice Pres., Dale Rowe; Cur., Kitty Goodin.
Personnel Profile: Part-Time Volunteers 30.
Governing Authority: nonprofit organization. Branch Museum: 1874 vintage Mary Pitney House, 289 W. 4th St., Junction City, OR. Tax-exempt: 170(b)(1)(3).
History Museum & House: housed in 1872 Dr. Norman Lee house, first doctor in Junction City.
Collections: furnishings belonging to Dr. Lee; medical tools; dental tools; Indian artifacts, including the war bonnet of Chief Red Cloud; clothing & household items belonging to Clarence Pitney; artifacts donated by local citizens; Junction City's first jail.
Activities: guided tours; formal & informal education programs; oral history; walking tour. Special Event: Scandinavian Festival in August.
Publications: quarterly newsletter.
Hours & Admission Prices: Thurs. 3-5, first Sat. of month 1-4. No charge; donations accepted.
Attendance: 1,424 (accurate)
Membership: Annual $10.

Keizer

THE KEIZER HERITAGE MUSEUM, 980 Chemawa Rd., N.E., Keizer, OR 97307-3716. Mailing Address: P.O. Box 20845, Keizer, OR 97307-0845. Tel.: 503-393-9660.
Web Site: www.wvi.com/~heritage/museum.html
History Museum.
Collections: historical artifacts & memorabilia pertaining to the city of Keizer.
Hours & Admission Prices: Tues. & Thurs. 2-4, Sat. 10-4.

Kerby

KERBYVILLE MUSEUM, 24195 Redwood Hwy., Kerby, OR 97531. Mailing Address: P.O. Box 3003, Kerby, OR 97531-3003. Tel.: 541-592-5252.
Founded: 1959.
Congressional District: 4
Key Personnel: Pres., Dennis Strayer; Vice Pres., Lloydeen K. Davis; Sec., Donna Tellyer; Treas., Chuck Rigby.
Personnel Profile: Part-Time Volunteers 9.
Governing Authority: nonprofit. Parent Institution: Kerbyville Museum & History Center. Subsidiary Institution: Kerbyville Museum board of directors. Tax-exempt: 501(c)(3).
History Museum: part of which is housed in 1880s Old Naucke Residence located on the site of the Old Town of Kerbyville.
Collections: military items of World War I & II; Indian artifacts; pioneer home furnishings; mining, farming, logging equipment; drugs; medicines; bottles; glassware; dishes; costumes; country store; American Express Office; old Post Office facade; picture gallery; dolls; tools; musical instruments. Historic Building: 1898 Grimmett School House.
Facilities: research library.
Activities: local tours, temporary exhibitions.
Hours & Admission Prices: April-Nov. 1 Mon.-Tues. & Thurs.-Sun. 11-3. Adults $4, seniors $3, children 6-16 $2; discount to school groups & families; children under 6 no charge. ♿
Attendance: 1,000 (estimated)

Kimberly

JOHN DAY FOSSIL BEDS NATIONAL MONUMENT, 32651 Hwy. 19, Kimberly, OR 97848-6228. Tel.: 541-987-2333 (administrative). Fax: 541-987-2336. TDD: 541-987-2334.
E-mail: joda_paleontology@nps.gov
Web Site: www.nps.gov/joda
Founded: 1975.
Congressional District: 2
Key Personnel: Chm. (V), Lia Vella; Supt., James Hammett; Chief Interpreter, J. Fiedor; Cur., Chris Schierup; Paleobotanist, Liz Lovelock; Preparator, Jennifer Cavin.
Personnel Profile: Full-Time Paid 4; Part-Time Paid 5.
Governing Authority: federal. Parent Institution: National Park Service. Branch Museum: Visitor Information Station. Tax-exempt.
Park Museum: housed in 1917-18 ranch house.
Collections: fossils from Clarno, John Day, Mascall & Rattlesnake geologic formations of Eastern Oregon; rock samples.
Research Fields: geology; paleontology; fossil preservation; paleo-climates, paleoenvironments of related formations.
Facilities: 500-vol. library of books, numerous research papers on geology, paleontology, modern natural history & history of Eastern Oregon & National Parks available for research on premises; Thomas Condon Paleontology Center. Books on general geology & natural history of area for sale.
Activities: guided tours; formally organized education programs for children; permanent exhibitions.
Hours & Admission Prices: Museum: March to late Nov. daily 9-5; late Nov. to Feb. Mon.-Fri. 9-5. No charge. ♿
Attendance: 43,000 (accurate)

Klamath Falls

FAVELL MUSEUM INC., 125 W. Main St., Klamath Falls, OR 97601-4287. Tel.: 541-882-9996. Fax: 541-850-0125.
E-mail: pat@favellmuseum.org
Web Site: www.favellmuseum.org
Formerly: Favell Museum of Western Art and Indian Artifacts
Founded: 1972.
Congressional District: 53
Key Personnel: Dir., Patsy H. McMillan; Chm. (V), Richard Wendt.
Personnel Profile: Full-Time Paid 2; Full-Time Volunteers 1; Part-Time Paid 3.
Governing Authority: nonprofit foundation. Tax-exempt.
Indian History & Fine Arts Museum: located on an old Indian camp.
Collections: Indian artifacts including 60,000 arrowheads, stonework, bonework, pottery, beadwork & quillwork; contemporary Western art; paintings; bronzes; dioramas; woodcarvings; 125 miniature firearms; guns; rocks & minerals including fire opal display.
Research Fields: Oregon archaeology.
Facilities: 150-seat auditorium. Original Western art, lithographs of paintings, Indian crafts, books related to Indians & Indian jewelry for sale.
Activities: lectures; gallery talks; TV programs; radio programs.
Publications: book, A Treasury Of Our Western Heritage; The Favell Museum: A Treasury of Our American Heritage.
Hours & Admission Prices: Tues.-Sat. 9:30-5:30. Family $20, adults $7, children 6-16 $4; members no charge. ♿
Attendance: 14,000 (estimated)
Membership: Single $20; Family $50; Patron $100; Small Business $500; Business $1,000; Corporate $5,000.

KLAMATH COUNTY MUSEUM, (M), 1451 Main St., Klamath Falls, OR 97601-5989. Tel.: 541-883-4208. Fax: 541-883-5710.
E-mail: tkepple@co.klamath.or.us
Web Site: www.co.klamath.or.us/museum/index.htm
Founded: 1954.
Congressional District: 53
Key Personnel: Mgr., Todd Kepple; Cur., Lynn Jeche; Museum Shop Mgr., Nancy Sieverts; Museum Asst., Susan Rambo.
Personnel Profile: Full-Time Paid 2; Part-Time Paid 4; Part-Time Volunteers 20.
Governing Authority: county. Parent Institution: Klamath County, Oregon. Branch Museums: Baldwin Hotel Museum, 31 Main St.; Ft. Klamath Museum, Ft. Klamath, OR. Tax-exempt.
History & Natural History Museum.
Collections: anthropology; local history; natural history.
Research Fields: pertaining to local history & items in collection.
Facilities: 7,000-vol. library of history books, maps, manuscripts, microfilms & documents available on premises. Books & museum-related items for sale.
Activities: tours; lectures; films; workshops; inter-museum, permanent, temporary & traveling exhibitions.

Publications: research papers; book, Guardhouses, Gallows, & Graves; Historical coloring book.
Hours & Admission Prices: Klamath County Museum: Tues.-Sat. 9-5. Adults $4. Baldwin Hotel Museum: Wed.-Sun. 10-4. Adults $10. Ft. Klamath Museum: June to Labor Day Thurs.-Mon. 10-6. No charge; donations accepted. Closed major holidays.
Attendance: 15,000 (estimated)

SENATOR GEORGE BALDWIN HOTEL, 31 Main St., Klamath Falls, OR 97601-3174. Mailing Address: 1451 Main St., Klamath Falls, OR 97601-5915. Tel.: 541-883-4208. Fax: 541-883-5170.
Founded: 1954.
Congressional District: 53
Key Personnel: Mgr., Todd Kepple; Cur., Lynne Jeche.
Personnel Profile: Full-Time Paid 2; Part-Time Paid 3; Part-Time Volunteers 20.
Governing Authority: county; nonprofit.
Historic Houses & Historic Buildings Museum: Victorian 3 story structure built in 1906.
Collections: furnishings; structures; personal artifacts.
Facilities: 250-vol. library. Museum-related items for sale.
Activities: school loan service; monthly antique appraisals. Annual Event: Antique Toy Show.
Hours & Admission Prices: June-Sept. Tues.-Sat. 10-4. Adults $2, seniors & students $1; children 6 and under & members no charge.
Attendance: 4,500 (estimated)

La Grande

EASTERN OREGON FIRE MUSEUM & LEARNING CENTER, 102 Elm St., La Grande, OR 97850-2621. Tel.: 541-963-8588. Fax: 541-963-3936.
Fire Museum: housed in the former fire station of downtown La Grande. Listed on the National Register of Historic Places.
Collections: firefighting history; period fire trucks; firefighting equipment; photographs.
Hours & Admission Prices: Memorial Day to Labor Day Mon.-Fri. 9-5, Sat. 9-3; Sept.-May Mon.-Fri. 9-5; other times by appointment. No charge; donations accepted.

Lakeview

SCHMINCK MEMORIAL MUSEUM, 128 S. E St., Lakeview, OR 97630-1721. Tel.: 541-947-3134.
E-mail: schminck@centurytel.net
Founded: 1938.
Congressional District: 2
Key Personnel: Dir., Monica Lawson.
Personnel Profile: Full-Time Paid 1; Part-Time Volunteers 1.
Governing Authority: society. Administered by Oregon State Society Daughters of American Revolution. Tax-exempt.
History Museum: housed in the former home of pioneers, Dalph & Lula Schminck; home is a Sears Craftsmen Built house ordered from Sears Catalog 1922.
Collections: clothing; household implements; furniture; tools; quilts; Native American artifacts; toys; saddles; ranching implements; personal artifacts including belonging that came over with Lula Schminck's mother on the Applegate Wagon Train in 1846; rose garden.
Facilities: 750-vol. library; rose garden.
Activities: guided tours; permanent & temporary exhibitions; tours for classes & related children's groups.
Publications: Tri & fold brochure.
Hours & Admission Prices: March-Oct. Wed.-Sat. 11-4. Adults & teens $3; children under 13 no charge. Closed holidays.
Attendance: 800 (estimated)

Lincoln City

NORTH LINCOLN COUNTY HISTORICAL MUSEUM, 4907 S.W. Hwy. 101, Lincoln City, OR 97367-1417. Tel.: 541-996-6614.
E-mail: director@wcn.net
Web Site: northlincolncountyhistoricalmuseum.org
Founded: 1987.
Congressional District: 5
Key Personnel: Dir., Anne Hall; Museum Shop Mgr., Ann Murdock.
Personnel Profile: Full-Time Paid 1; Part-Time Paid 1; Part-Time Volunteers 19.
Governing Authority: Tax-exempt.
History Museum.
Collections: county history & culture; personal artifacts; photographs; Native American artifacts; fishing; logging; tools; period artifacts.
Research Fields: North Lincoln County.
Facilities: research library; meeting room.
Activities: historical programs. Annual Event: Pioneer Picnic.
Publications: quarterly newsletter; monograph, Lincoln City and the Twenty Miracle Miles.
Hours & Admission Prices: May 16-Oct. 15 Wed.-Sun. 12-5; Oct. 16-May 15 Wed.-Sat. 12-5. Closed holidays. ♿
Attendance: 5,000 (accurate)
Membership: Individual $15; Sustaining $50; Supporter & Business $100; Benefactor $100 & up.

Marylhurst

THE ART GYM, Marylhurst University, 17600 Pacific Hwy. 43, Marylhurst, OR 97036-0261. Mailing Address: P.O. Box 261, Marylhurst, OR 97036-0261. Tel.: 503-699-6243 & 636-8141. Fax: 503-636-9526.
E-mail: artgym@marylhurst.edu
Web Site: www.marylhurst.edu
Formerly: The Art Gym at Marylhurst University
Founded: 1980.
Congressional District: 1
Key Personnel: Dir. & Cur., Terri M. Hopkins.
Personnel Profile: Part-Time Paid 3; Part-Time Volunteers 15; Interns 1.
Governing Authority: private; university; nonprofit. Parent Institution: Marylhurst University. Tax-exempt.
University Museum.
Collections: contemporary northwest art.
Research Fields: contemporary Northwest art & artists; art in the Northwest since 1900.
Facilities: 2,500 sq. ft. exhibit space.
Activities: guided tours; lectures; loan exhibitions; formal education programs for undergraduate & graduate students affiliated with Marylhurst University.
Publications: exhibition catalogs; exhibition announcements published six times annually.
Hours & Admission Prices: Jan.-June & Sept.-Nov. Tues.-Sun. 12-4. No charge; donations accepted. Closed on holidays. ♿
Attendance: 5,000 (accurate)
Membership: Artists & Students $15-$34; General $35-$74; Sponsor $75 & up; Patron $150 & up; Guarantor $250 & up; Visionary $500 & up.

McMinnville

EVERGREEN AVIATION MUSEUM, 500 N.E. Captain Michael King Smith Way, McMinnville, OR 97128-8877. Tel.: 503-434-4180 & 4185. Fax: 503-434-4058.
E-mail: phil.jaeger@evergreenaviation.com
Web Site: www.sprucegoose.org
Formerly: Evergreen Airventure Museum
Founded: 1992.
Congressional District: 1
Key Personnel: C.E.O., William Schaub; Exec. Dir., Tom A. Wiggins; Exec. Dir., Jereme Coker; Chm. (V), Delford M. Smith; Pres. (V), Denny Smith; Dir. Opers., Phil Jaeger; Museum Shop Mgr., Kelvin Johnson.
Personnel Profile: Full-Time Paid 18; Part-Time Paid 4; Part-Time Volunteers 215; Interns 4.
Governing Authority: private; nonprofit, bd. of trustees. Tax-exempt: 501(c)(3).
Aeronautics & Space Museum.
Collections: period commercial, military & general aviation with emphasis on warbirds (fighters, bombers, trainers, recon) restored and flown regularly; collection includes historic HK-1 Hughes Flying Boat, the largest aircraft ever to fly, an SR71 & Sixty other Vintage aircraft.
Research Fields: restoration techniques for period furnishings; HK-1 assembly; HK-1 disassembly & move from Long Beach, CA to McMinnville, OR.
Facilities: 150-seat auditorium; 121,000 sq. ft. exhibit space; cafe; children's exhibit area. Museum-related items for sale.
Activities: films; guided tours; hobby & restoration workshops; lectures; temporary exhibitions. Annual Events: airshow; fly-in events; military & patriotic celebrations.
Publications: quarterly newsletter.
Hours & Admission Prices: Daily 9-5. Adults 17-64 $13, seniors 65 & over, veterans & active duty military, reservists $12, students with ID $7; discounts to AAA members & student groups; children 5 & under and members no charge. Closed holidays. ♿
Attendance: 167,500 (accurate)
Membership: Military $10; Student & Teacher $20; Individual $30; Dual $50; Family $75; Patron $100; Supporter $250; Sponsor $500; Sustainer $1,000. Corporate: Crew Chief $100; Flight Leader $250; Squadron Commander $500; Group Commander $1,000; Wing Commander $2,500.

Medford

KID TIME!, 226 N. Ross Lane, Medford, OR 97501-2220. Tel.: 541-772-9922.
Web Site: www.kid-time.org
Formerly: Kids' Imagination Discovery Space
Children's Museum.
Collections: hands-on exhibits.
Activities: birthday parties; special events.
Hours & Admission Prices: Mon.-Sat. 10-5, Sun. 11-4. Children $6, adults $3.
Membership: Family: 3 month $40; 6 month $65; 1 Year $95.

ROGUE GALLERY & ART CENTER, 40 S. Bartlett, Medford, OR 97501-7216. Tel.: 541-772-8118. Fax: 541-772-0294.
Web Site: www.roguegallery.org
Founded: 1959.
Congressional District: 2
Key Personnel: Exec. Dir., Judy Barnes; Office Mgr. & Volunteer Coord., Janice Alderman; Dir. Devel., Heather Crow; Dir. Education, Holly Kilpatrick.
Personnel Profile: Full-Time Paid 1; Full-Time Volunteers 2; Part-Time Paid 2; Part-Time Volunteers 65; Interns 3.
Governing Authority: nonprofit organization. Parent Institution: Rogue Valley Art Association. Tax-exempt: 501(c)(3).
Visual Art Center & Art Gallery.
Collections: regional prints, printmakers, Oregon sculpture; regional paintings & artworks.
Facilities: classroom; boardroom. Museum-related items for sale.
Activities: guided tours; lectures; films; gallery talks; rental gallery; formally organized education programs for children; docent program or council; temporary & traveling exhibitions.
Publications: bimonthly newsletters.
Hours & Admission Prices: Tues.-Fri. 10-5, Sat. 11-3. No charge; donations accepted. Closed national holidays. ♿
Attendance: 20,000 (estimated)
Membership: Youth (under 21) $25; Individual $35; Family & Dual $50; Patron $100; Sustainer $250; Benefactor $500. Business $100-$1,000.

Milwaukie

MILWAUKIE MUSEUM, 3737 S.E. Adams St., Milwaukie, OR 97222-5917. Tel.: 503-659-5780.
E-mail: milwaukiemuseum@juno.com
Web Site: milwaukiemuseum.tripod.com
Founded: 1975.
Personnel Profile: Full-Time Volunteers 1; Part-Time Volunteers 15.
Governing Authority: Parent Institution: Milwaukie Historical Society. Tax-exempt.
Historic House Museum: housed in the former home of the George Wise family, built in 1865.
Collections: period furnishings; personal artifacts.
Publications: Milwaukie history.
Hours & Admission Prices: Sat.-Sun. 11-3. No charge; donations accepted. Closed Easter; Christmas. ♿
Attendance: 650 (accurate)
Membership: Individual $10; Lifetime $100.

Monmouth

JENSEN ARCTIC MUSEUM, 590 W. Church St., Western Oregon University, Monmouth, OR 97361-1395. Tel.: 503-838-8468. Fax: 503-838-8289.
E-mail: arctic@wou.edu
Web Site: www.wou.edu/arctic
Founded: 1985.
Congressional District: 5
Key Personnel: Pres. Friends of the Jensen Arctic Museum, Peter Burke; Cur., Roben Jack Larrison; Public Rels., Lisa Pulliam; Security, Jay Carey.
Personnel Profile: Part-Time Paid 1; Part-Time Volunteers 24; Interns 2.
Governing Authority: public college. Parent Institution: Western Oregon University. Subsidiary Institution: Western Foundation. Tax-exempt.
Arctic Ecology & Culture Museum.
Collections: cultural artifacts of the peoples of the Arctic region.
Research Fields: bilingual education; preparation of teachers.
Facilities: 2,400-vol. library of history & culture of the peoples in the Arctic available for use by the public; 4,000 sq. ft. exhibit space. Photos of the Arctic regions, native Alaskan handcrafts & art for sale.
Activities: docent program; films; formal education programs for children & undergraduate & graduate students; guided tours; children's activities. Annual Events: Birthday Celebration in May; Salmon Bake Fundraiser in September.
Publications: quarterly newsletter; annual, Hunters on the Arctic Rim.
Hours & Admission Prices: Wed.-Sat. 10-4. Suggested Donation: adults $2, children under 12 $1. Closed federal holidays. ♿
Attendance: 4,500 (accurate)
Membership: Senior Citizen & Student $15; Family $40; Supporter $50; Business $100; Sponsor $200; Patron $500; President's Club $1,000.

Myrtle Point

COOS COUNTY LOGGING MUSEUM, 705 Maple St., Myrtle Point, OR 97458. Mailing Address: P.O. Box 325, Myrtle Point, OR 97458-0325. Tel.: 541-572-1014.
Key Personnel: Pres. (V), Gary Dickenson.
Governing Authority: nonprofit organization. Tax-exempt.
Logging Museum.
Collections: period logging equipment; chain saws; spring boards; rigging equipment; axes; railroad artifacts; photographs; myrtlewood carvings.
Facilities: Museum-related items for sale.
Hours & Admission Prices: Mon.-Sat. 10-4, Sun. 1-4. No charge; donations accepted. ♿
Attendance: 4,800 (estimated)

Newberg

HOOVER-MINTHORN HOUSE MUSEUM, 115 S. River St., Newberg, OR 97132-3153. Tel.: 503-538-6629.
Governing Authority: Parent Institution: The National Society of The Colonial Dames of America in the State of Oregon.
Historic House Museum: housed in the boyhood home of President Herbert Hoover, 1885-1889; built in 1881. Listed on the National Register of Historic Places.
Collections: local & family history; Hoover's bedroom furniture; personal artifacts; period furnishings; photographs.
Hours & Admission Prices: March-Nov. Wed.-Sun. 1-4; Dec.-Feb. Sat.-Sun. 1-4. Closed holidays.

Newport

HATFIELD MARINE SCIENCE CENTER, OREGON STATE UNIVERSITY, (M), 2030 Marine Science Dr., Newport, OR 97365-5296. Tel.: 541-867-0100.
E-mail: lynne.wright@oregonstate.edu
Web Site: hmsc.oregonstate.edu/visitor
Founded: 1965.
Congressional District: 1
Key Personnel: Marine Education Specialist, Bill Hanshumaker; Volunteer Coord., Katherine Fuller; Museum Shop Mgr. & Visitor Svcs. Mgr., Lynne Wright.
Personnel Profile: Full-Time Paid 9; Part-Time Paid 12; Part-Time Volunteers 70; Interns 2.
Governing Authority: university. Affiliated with Oregon State University, Corvallis; On-Site Oregon Dept. of Fish & Wildlife Marine Lab; Marine Div. U.S. Environmental Protection Agency; NMFS Newport Aquaculture Lab; Marine Resources Research Division of NOAA. Tax-exempt.
Aquarium.
Collections: marine fish & invertebrates of Oregon's coastal waters; marine research.
Research Fields: oceanography; fisheries; toxicology; pharmacology; physiology; biochemistry; geophysics.
Facilities: salt water aquarium. Marine & natural sciences bookstore.
Activities: interactive exhibits; summer lectures; films; permanent & temporary exhibitions; volunteers & docents; graduate internships; summer estuary guided walks. Museum Sponsors: Seafest event in June.
Publications: monthly volunteer newsletter; quarterly, Friends of HMSC; pamphlets.
Hours & Admission Prices: Memorial Day to Labor Day daily 10-5; Winter: Thurs.-Mon. 10-4. No charge; donations requested. Closed New Year's Day; Christmas. ♿
Attendance: 141,000 (estimated)

OREGON COAST AQUARIUM, 2820 S.E. Ferry Slip Rd., Newport, OR 97365-5269. Tel.: 541-867-3474.
E-mail: info@aquarium.org
Web Site: www.aquarium.org
Founded: 1992.
Congressional District: 5
Key Personnel: Dir., Dale A. Schmidt; Chm. (V), George Borhlert.
Personnel Profile: Full-Time Paid 67; Full-Time Volunteers 350; Part-Time Paid 3; Interns 3.
Governing Authority: Tax-exempt.
Aquarium.
Collections: turtles; sea otters; seals & sea lions; sea bird aviary.

Research Fields: rockfish reproduction.
Hours & Admission Prices: Memorial Day to Labor Day daily 9-6; Sept.-May daily 10-5. Adult 13-64 $14.25, seniors 65 & over $12.25, youth 3-12 $8.75; children 2 & under no charge. ♿
Attendance: 448,579 (accurate)
Membership: Individual $39; Couple $55; Family $70; Family Plus $100; Sponsor $250; Patron $500; Rockfish Society $1,000.

OREGON COAST HISTORY CENTER, 545 S.W. Ninth, Newport, OR 97365-4726. Tel.: 541-265-7509. Fax: 541-265-3992.
E-mail: coasthistory@newportnet.com
Web Site: www.oregoncoast.history.museum
Founded: 1948.
Congressional District: 1
Key Personnel: C.E.O., Loretta Harrison; Pres. (V), Carol Jones; Museum Shop Mgr., Brenda Baker.
Personnel Profile: Full-Time Paid 2; Full-Time Volunteers 25; Part-Time Paid 6; Part-Time Volunteers 12; Interns 1.
Governing Authority: society; bd. of directors. Parent Institution: Lincoln County Historical Society. Affiliated with Oregon Historical Society. Tax-exempt: 501(c)(3).
History Museum.
Collections: Log cabin: Copeland collection of Siletz Reservation artifacts including basketry, points, beads & dance skirts; pioneer artifacts; logging, agricultural, maritime, recreational fishing & hunting; military artifacts. Burrows House: domestic life from 1860s-1950s including furniture, dishware, toys, appliances, clothing & other personal artifacts.
Research Fields: Oregon coast history; Lincoln County history; Siletz Reservation & Tribe; biographies & genealogies of local inhabitants & families; local industries & railroads.
Facilities: 150-vol. library of Oregon historical publications & books; Carriage House Storage building; reading room.
Activities: guided tours; gallery talks; permanent, temporary & traveling exhibitions.
Publications: books, The Land That Kept Its Promise; Pacific Spruce Corp.; Pictorial History of Otter Rock; Steam Towards The Sunset; Siletz Indian Reservation 1855-1900; School District #61; At Rest in Lincoln County; Yaquina Bay 1778-1978; Lincoln County Anthology; Pictorial Toledo, OR; reprint of 1923 Pacific Spruce Corp. & Subsidiaries; Lincoln County Kitchen Memories; Pathfinder: The First Automobile Trip from Newport to Siletz Bay; Siletz-Survived for an Artifact; When Time Seemed to Pause; Tragedy on Yaquina Bar; The Voyage of the Prairie Schooner; video, Lincoln County's Road from Mud to Glory.
Hours & Admission Prices: June-Sept. Tues.-Sun. 10-5; Oct.-May Tues.-Sun. 11-4. No charge; donations accepted. Closed New Year's Day; Independence Day; Thanksgiving; Christmas. ♿
Attendance: 15,000 (accurate)
Membership: Student $1; Annual $10; Family & Organization $25; Contributor $100; Sponsor $101-$499; Benefactor $500 & up.

North Bend

COOS HISTORICAL & MARITIME MUSEUM, 1220 Sherman, North Bend, OR 97459-3666. Tel.: 541-756-6320. Fax: 541-756-6320.
E-mail: cmuseum@verizon.net
Web Site: www.coohistory.org
Formerly: Coos County Historical Society Museum
Founded: 1891.
Congressional District: 47
Key Personnel: C.E.O. & Dir., Annie Donnelly; Pres., Jennifer Groth; Pres. (V), Steve Greif.
Personnel Profile: Full-Time Paid 2; Part-Time Paid 2; Part-Time Volunteers 50.
Governing Authority: nonprofit organization. Owned & operated by Coos County Historical Society. Tax-exempt: 501(c)(3).
General History Museum.
Collections: artifacts relating to the tidewater highways of Coos County & Southwestern Coastal Oregon; the Fahy collection of Indian artifacts; the Magee collection of international artifacts; steam donkey engine used for logging in Coos County; historic photographs & negatives.
Research Fields: Coos County history.
Facilities: 1,100-vol. library of regional print and manuscript material, photographs & maps.
Activities: permanent & temporary exhibits; educational programs; book signings; research assistance; group tours.
Publications: Waterways newsletter quarterly; books, A Century of Coos and Curry; Coos Bay Region.
Hours & Admission Prices: Tues.-Sat. 10-4. Adults $2; members no charge. Closed Thanksgiving; Christmas. ♿
Attendance: 2,500 (accurate)
Membership: Individual $25; Family $35; Business & Corporate $100; Benefactor $250.

Nyssa

OREGON TRAIL AGRICULTURAL MUSEUM, 117 Good Ave., Nyssa, OR 97913-3833. Mailing Address: P.O. Box 2303, Nyssa, OR 97913-0303. Tel.: 541-372-3712.
Governing Authority: Parent Institution: Nyssa Historical Society.
Agriculture Museum.
Collections: local history; agricultural heritage; early farm & ranch equipment; restored sheep wagons; photographs; Oregon Trail history.
Activities: demonstrations.
Hours & Admission Prices: Summer: Fri.-Sat. 10-4, Sun. 1-4. No charge; donations accepted.

Oakland

OAKLAND MUSEUM, 130 Locust St., Oakland, OR 97462. Mailing Address: P.O. Box 624, Oakland, OR 97462-0624. Tel.: 541-459-3087.
E-mail: oaklandinfo@makewebs.com
Web Site: www.makewebs.com/oakland/Things_to_Do/Museum/museum.html
Key Personnel: Dir., Louise J. Stearns
History Museum.
Collections: historical artifacts & memorabilia pertaining to the city of Oakland.
Hours & Admission Prices: Daily 12:30-3:30. No charge; donations accepted.

Oakridge

OAKRIDGE-WESTFIR PIONEER MUSEUM, 76433 Pine St., Oakridge, OR 97463. Mailing Address: P.O. Box 807, Oakridge, OR 97463-0807. Tel.: 541-782-2402.
History Museum.
Collections: local history & culture; photographs; period artifacts.
Hours & Admission Prices: Call for hours.

Ontario

FOUR RIVERS CULTURAL CENTER & MUSEUM, 676 S.W. 5th Ave., Ontario, OR 97914-3436. Tel.: 541-889-8191. Fax: 541-889-7628.
Web Site: www.4rcc.com
Founded: 1987.
Key Personnel: Pres. (V) & Chm. (V), Nancy Bent; Exec. Dir., John Gaskill; Museum Shop Mgr., Shawn Maggar.
Personnel Profile: Full-Time Paid 3; Part-Time Paid 2; Part-Time Volunteers 60; Interns 3.
Governing Authority: private; nonprofit organization. Tax-exempt: 501(c)(3).
History Museum.
Collections: historical artifacts; clothing; first settlers to the eastern Oregon area including Basque, Northern Paiutes, Japanese-American, Hispanic & Euro American.
Research Fields: Western Treasure Valley (east Oregon/southwest Idaho) history with special emphasis on the history of local Japanese-Americans, Basque-Americans, Hispanic Americans, Native Americans & other cultural and ethnic groups represented in the area & the relationship of these people to the land over time; agriculture.
Facilities: botanical garden; 542-seat theater; 16,000 sq. ft. exhibit space; conference center. Museum-related items for sale.
Activities: lectures; temporary exhibits; classes.
Publications: quarterly newsletter, Four Rivers Cultural Center; Shining Water News.
Hours & Admission Prices: Mon.-Sat. 10-5. Adults $4, seniors $3; discounts to groups over 20; members no charge. ♿
Attendance: 7,693 (accurate)
Membership: Students $10; Individual $30; Family $50; Contributor $125; Corporate $275.

Oregon City

MCLOUGHLIN HOUSE, McLoughlin Park, 713 Center St., Oregon City, OR 97045-1948. Tel.: 503-656-5146.
Governing Authority: Parent Institution: National Park Service.
Historic House Museum: housed in the former home of Dr. John McLoughlin, Chief Factor of the Hudson Bay Company; built in 1846. Listed on the National Register of Historic Places.
Collections: family & local history; period furnishings; photographs; personal artifacts.
Activities: special events; demonstrations.

Hours & Admission Prices: Feb.-Dec. Wed.-Sat. 10-4, Sun. 1-4. No charge.

MUSEUM OF THE OREGON TERRITORY, 211 Tumwater Dr., Oregon City, OR 97045-2900. Tel.: 503-655-5574. Fax: 503-655-0035.
History Museum.
Collections: local history & culture; photographs; Lady Justice statue.
Facilities: rental facilities.
Hours & Admission Prices: Daily 11-4. Adults $7, children 5-17 $5; children under 5 no charge.

ROSE FARM MUSEUM, 915 Rilance Lane, Oregon City, OR 97045-3730.
Historic House Museum: housed in the former home of William & Louisa Holmes; built in 1847.
Collections: local & family history; furnishings; photographs.
Hours & Admission Prices: May-Sept. Sat. 10-4, Sun. 1-5. Adults $3, seniors $2, youth 6-17 $2; children 6 & under no charge.

STEVENS CRAWFORD MUSEUM, 603 6th St., Oregon City, OR 97045-2232. Tel.: 503-655-2866.
Historic House Museum: built in 1908.
Collections: family & local history; period furnishings & toys; photographs.
Hours & Admission Prices: Wed.-Fri. 12-4, Sat. 1-4. Adults $4, seniors $3, students $2; children under 5 no charge.

Parkdale

INTERNATIONAL MUSEUM OF CAROUSEL ART, 4976 Alexander Dr., Parkdale, OR 97041-7604. Mailing Address: P.O. Box 468, Mount Hood, OR 97041-0468. Tel.: 541-352-7663. Fax: 541-387-8797.
E-mail: osperron@gmail.com
Web Site: www.carouselmuseum.com
Founded: 1982.
Key Personnel: Dir., Mark Reed; Chm. (V), Duane Perron.
Governing Authority: nonprofit organization. Tax-exempt: 501(c)(3).
General Museum.
Collections: period carousels; carousel art & history.
Activities: classes.
Hours & Admission Prices: Temporarily closed. Adults $5, students & seniors $4, children 5-10 $2; members and children 4 & under no charge. ♿

Pendleton

CHILDREN'S MUSEUM OF EASTERN OREGON, 400 S. Main St., Pendleton, OR 97801-2248. Tel.: 541-276-1066.
Web Site: www.cmeo.org
Founded: 1996.
Key Personnel: Exec. Dir., Jill Gregg; Pres., Sarah Haug
Children's Museum.
Collections: hands-on exhibits.
Activities: birthday parties; special events; educational programs; classes.
Hours & Admission Prices: Tues.-Sat. 10-5; groups by appointment. Admission $3; discounts to groups of 15 or more; children under one no charge.
Membership: Family $50; Family + 2 $80.

HERITAGE STATION, UMATILLA COUNTY HISTORICAL SOCIETY MUSEUM, (M), 108 S.W. Frazer, Pendleton, OR 97801-2138. Mailing Address: P.O. Box 253, Pendleton, OR 97801-0253. Tel.: 541-276-0012. Fax: 541-276-7989.
E-mail: info@heritagestationmuseum.org
Web Site: www.heritagestationmuseum.org
Founded: 1974.
Congressional District: 2
Key Personnel: Exec. Dir., Barbara Lund-Jones; Pres. (V), Tim Mabry; Treas., Tom Winn; Museum Shop Mgr., Amy Rosenberg.
Personnel Profile: Full-Time Paid 2; Part-Time Volunteers 375.
Governing Authority: private; nonprofit. Parent Institution: Umatilla County Historical Society. Tax-exempt: 501(c)(3).
Historical Society Museum: located in a 1909 train depot.
Collections: prehistory & history of Umatilla County & its population; refurbished 1879 one-room school; hand-hewn log cabin.
Research Fields: Umatilla County history.
Facilities: library; 4,200 sq. ft. exhibit space. Museum-related items for sale.
Activities: guided tours; lectures; temporary & traveling exhibitions. Museum Sponsors: spring & fall series of informal educational events.
Publications: triannual periodical, Pioneer Trails; triannual, The UCHS Newsletter.
Hours & Admission Prices: Adults $6, students $2; discount to AAM members & groups; children under 5 & members no charge. Closed New Year's Day; Thanksgiving; Christmas. ♿
Attendance: 5,500 (estimated)
Membership: Individual $40; Family $50; Business $75.

TAMASTSLIKT CULTURAL INSTITUTE, 72789 Hwy. 331, Pendleton, OR 97801-3379. Tel.: 541-966-9748. Fax: 541-966-9927.
Web Site: www.tamastslikt.org
Founded: 1998.
Congressional District: 2
Key Personnel: C.E.O., Roberta Conner; Devel., John Chess; Chm. Tribal Council, Antone Minthorn; Education, Susan Sheoships; Public Rels., Charles Denight; Treas., Les Minthorn; Exhibits Mgr., Randall Melton; Security, Steve Wynn; Archivist, Malissa Minthorn; Museum Shop Mgr., Joan Deroko.
Personnel Profile: Full-Time Paid 20; Part-Time Paid 10.
Governing Authority: Tribal Government. Parent Institution: Confederated Tribes of the Umatilla Indian Reservation.
History Museum.
Collections: history & culture of American Indian Tribes, the Cayuse, Umatilla & Walla Walla; their relationship with Lewis & Clark, early fur traders, missionaries, Oregon Trail immigrants & modern members of the surrounding areas; artifacts; photographs; video & interactive multimedia.
Major Exhibits: A Litany of Salmon (T), 1/15/10-4/18/10; Here Forever Art Show, 8/6/10-9/23/10; Forget Me Not: Mothers and Sons (T), 10/8/10-12/10.
Facilities: 14,000 sq. ft. exhibit space. Museum-related items for sale.
Publications: As Days Go By; Our History, Our Land, and Our People; The Coyuse, Umatilla and Walla Walla.
Hours & Admission Prices: April-Oct. daily 9-5; Nov.-March Mon.-Sat. 9-5. Adults $8; discounts to AAM members. Closed New Year's Day; Thanksgiving; Christmas.
Attendance: 34,000 (estimated)
Membership: Friend $50; Advocate $75; Patron $150; Sponsor $250; Benefactor $500.

Philomath

BENTON COUNTY HISTORICAL MUSEUM, (M), 1101 Main St., Philomath, OR 97370. Mailing Address: P.O. Box 35, Philomath, OR 97370-0035. Tel.: 541-929-6230. Fax: 541-929-6261.
Web Site: www.bentoncountymuseum.org
Founded: 1980.
Congressional District: 5
Key Personnel: Exec. Dir., Irene Zenev.
Personnel Profile: Full-Time Paid 4; Part-Time Paid 4; Part-Time Volunteers 50; Interns 3.
Governing Authority: nonprofit organization. Parent Institution: Benton County Historical Society. Tax-exempt: 501(c)(3).
History Museum & Art Gallery: housed in c.1867 brick building, originally used as the Philomath College building.
Collections: local history & culture; photographs; archives.
Major Exhibits: Can You Hear Me? Now?, 11/09-11/10; Ekphrastic Poetry & Photography, 1/10-2/10; Art: The 4th R, 3/10-4/10; WVHS Art Competition, 4/10-5/10; Artists Honor Historic Preservation, 5/10-7/10; Philomath Open Studios, 9/10-11/10.
Research Fields: local history.
Facilities: 300-vol. library of local history; 150-seat auditorium. Books for sale.
Activities: lectures; organized education programs for children & adults; participatory, loan & traveling exhibitions; temporary exhibitions of your own collections; school loan service.
Publications: quarterly newsletter, The Society Record.
Hours & Admission Prices: Philomath: Tues.-Sat. 10-4:30. No charge; donations accepted. Closed New Year's Day; Independence Day; Thanksgiving; Christmas. ♿
Attendance: 8,000 (estimated)
Membership: Senior Citizen $15; Individual $20; Family $30; Sponsor $60; Patron $120; Basic Business $150; Benefactor $365; Sustaining & Business Plus $500; History-Maker & Corporate $1,000.

Port Orford

PORT ORFORD LIFEBOAT STATION, 92331 Coast Guard Hill Rd., Port Orford, OR 97465. Mailing Address: Point Orford Heritage Society - Heads State Park, P.O. Box 1132, Port Orford, OR 97465-1132. Tel.: 541-332-0521.
Web Site: www.portorfordlifeboatstation.org
Founded: 2000.
Key Personnel: Pres., Steve Roemen
Coast Guard History Museum.
Collections: local history; Coast Guard artifacts; photographs; model ships; newspapers; nautical artifacts.

Hours & Admission Prices: April-Oct. Thurs.-Mon. 10-3:30; other times by appointment. No charge.

Portland

THE BERRY BOTANIC GARDEN, 11505 S.W. Summerville Ave., Portland, OR 97219-8309. Tel.: 503-636-4112, ext. 0. Fax: 503-636-7496.
E-mail: bbg@berrybot.org
Web Site: www.berrybot.org
Founded: 1978.
Congressional District: 1
Key Personnel: Pres. (V), Kailla Platt; Exec. Dir., Margaret Eickmann.
Personnel Profile: Full-Time Paid 5; Part-Time Paid 2; Part-Time Volunteers 190; Interns 2.
Governing Authority: individual operation. Tax-exempt: 501(c)(3).
Botanical Garden: located on the wooded 6 acre site developed as a private garden in the 1930s. Listed in the National Register of Historic places.
Collections: rhododendrons; primulas; alpines; plants native to the Pacific Northwest emphasizing rare & endangered plants.
Research Fields: seed bank for rare & endangered plants of the Pacific Northwest; population status & biology of rare & endangered native plants.
Facilities: 2,000-vol. library pertaining to horticulture & botany, emphasizing the Garden's plant collections; available for members or by prior arrangement on site.
Activities: guided group tours; classes; biannual plant sales; seed exchange; no cost seeds for members, interns, volunteers & docent program.
Publications: brochure; membership brochure; quarterly newsletter; class & event listing, Berry Buzz.
Hours & Admission Prices: Garden: daylight hours by appointment only. Office: Mon.-Fri. 9-4:30. Adults $5; discounts to AABGA members; members no charge. ♿
Attendance: 3,000 (estimated)
Membership: Individual $40; Club $50; Family & Dual $60; Supporter $75; Friends $100; Trillium Associate $250; Cliff Penstemon $500; Western Lily $1,000.

THE DOUGLAS F. COOLEY MEMORIAL ART GALLERY, REED COLLEGE, 3203 S.E. Woodstock Blvd., Portland, OR 97202-8138. Tel.: 503-771-1112 & 7251. Fax: 503-788-6691 (Reed College).
E-mail: snyders@reed.edu
Web Site: web.reed.edu/gallery
Founded: 1989.
Congressional District: 3
Key Personnel: Dir. & Cur., Stephanie Snyder; Asst. Dir., Silas Cook.
Personnel Profile: Full-Time Paid 1; Part-Time Paid 2.
Governing Authority: college. Parent Institution: Reed College. Tax-exempt: 501(c)(3).
Exhibition Gallery.
Collections: 20th-century American, 19th-century European & other works on paper.
Activities: lectures; gallery talks; symposia; temporary & traveling exhibitions.
Publications: exhibition catalog, The Serpentine Lattice; Ree Morton; Modern Art in America; Documenting a Myth; Robert Adams; What is a Man.
Hours & Admission Prices: Sept.-June Tues.-Sun. 12-6. No charge. ♿
Attendance: 5,500
Membership: Cooley Gallery Art Assoc. $100; $250.

THE HAT MUSEUM, 1928 S.E. Ladd Ave., Portland, OR 97214-4737. Tel.: 503-232-0433.
E-mail: justalyce@usa.net
Web Site: www.thehatmuseum.com
Founded: 2005.
Key Personnel: Dir., Alyce Cornyn-Selby; Museum Shop Mgr., Gracie Zusman
Hat Museum: housed in the Ladd-Reingold House; built in 1910. Listed on the National Register of Historic Places.
Collections: over 1,000 hats; photographs; period furnishings.
Facilities: Museum-related items for sale.
Hours & Admission Prices: By appointment. Admission $10. Closed New Year's Day; Christmas.

HELLENIC AMERICAN CULTURAL CENTER & MUSEUM, (M), 3131 N.E. Glisan, Portland, OR 97232-2501. Tel.: 503-234-0468.
Web Site: www.hellenicamericancc.org
Founded: 2006.
Key Personnel: Chm. (V), Stefanos Vertopoulos; Pres. (V), Katherine Karafotias.
Governing Authority: nonprofit organization. Tax-exempt: 501(c)(3).
Cultural Center.
Collections: Hellenic (Greek) history & culture in Oregon & SW Washington; photographs; personal artifacts.
Hours & Admission Prices: Call for hours. No charge. ♿
Attendance: 1,500 (estimated)

HOYT ARBORETUM, 4000 S.W. Fairview Blvd., Portland, OR 97221-2706. Tel.: 503-865-8733. Fax: 508-823-4213.
E-mail: info@hoytarboretum.org
Web Site: www.hoytarboretum.org
Founded: 1928.
Congressional District: 1
Key Personnel: Exec. Dir. Hoyt Arboretum Friends Foundation, Matt Sinclair; Pres. Bd., Leslie Campbell; City Nature West Natural Resources Supvr. Portland Parks & Recreation, Dan Moeller.
Personnel Profile: Full-Time Paid 6; Part-Time Paid 1; Part-Time Volunteers 150; Interns 1.
Governing Authority: municipal. Parent Institution: City of Portland. Subsidiary Institution: Hoyt Arboretum Friends Foundation. Tax-exempt.
Arboretum.
Collections: 1,100 species of trees & shrubs.
Facilities: library; self-guided trails. Museum-related items for sale.
Activities: guided & self-guided tours; lectures; workshops & education sessions; international seed exchange.
Publications: trail guides; maps; educational brochures.
Hours & Admission Prices: Park: daily 6am-10pm. Visitor Center: Mon.-Fri. 9-4, Sat. 9-3. No charge; donations accepted. ♿
Attendance: 350,000 (estimated)
Membership: Individual & Fir Society $25; Family & Contributing $35; Sponsor & Magnolia Society $50; Maple Society $75; Friend & Spruce Society $100; Cedar Society $250; Benefactor & Pine Society $500; Founder & Oak Society $1,000.

LITTMAN & WHITE GALLERIES, 1825 SW Broadway #250, Portland, OR 97201-3256. Mailing Address: P.O. Box 751-SD, Portland, OR 97207. Tel.: 503-725-5656. Fax: 503-725-5680.
E-mail: artcom@pdx.edu
Formerly: Portland State University Galleries
Founded: 1976.
Key Personnel: C.E.O. & Coord., Emilie Gerber; Coord., Theresa Tate.
Personnel Profile: Full-Time Paid 2.
Art Gallery .
Collections: original prints; paintings; sculpture.
Facilities: Littman Gallery: 1,300 sq. ft. exhibit space.
Activities: lectures; gallery talks; loan exhibitions.
Hours & Admission Prices: Littman Gallery: Mon.-Fri. 12-4. No charge. White Gallery: Mon.-Fri. 8-10, Sat. 9-7. No Charge. ♿

MUSEUM OF CONTEMPORARY CRAFT, 724 Northwest Davis St., Portland, OR 97209-3663. Tel.: 503-223-2654. Fax: 503-223-0190.
E-mail: communications@museumofcontemporarycraft.org
Web Site: www.museumofcontemporarycraft.org
Formerly: Contemporary Crafts Museum & Gallery
Founded: 1937.
Congressional District: 5
Key Personnel: Cur., Namita Gupta Wiggers; Gallery Dir., John Reynolds.
Personnel Profile: Full-Time Paid 10; Part-Time Paid 1; Part-Time Volunteers 65; Interns 12.
Governing Authority: private; nonprofit corporation. Tax-exempt.
Contemporary Craft Museum.
Collections: 20th century arts & crafts; wood; clay; glass; metal; textiles.
Research Fields: craft; museology; contemporary practice.
Facilities: library; event facilities. Museum-related items for sale.
Activities: guided tours; artist & curator talks; panel discussions; films; workshops; hands-on art activities; special events.
Publications: Unpacking the Collection: Selections from the Museum of Contemporary Craft; exhibition catalogues.
Hours & Admission Prices: Tues.-Wed. & Fri.-Sat. 11-6, 1st Thurs. of month 11-8. No charge; donations accepted. Closed New Year's Day; Independence Day; Thanksgiving; Christmas. ♿
Attendance: 75,000 (accurate)
Membership: Artist, Student & Senior $35; Individual $40; Household $65; Friend $125; Supporter $250; Sustainer $500; Patron $1,000; Benefactor $2,500.

THE OLD CHURCH SOCIETY, INC., 1422 S.W. 11th Ave., Portland, OR 97201-3304. Tel.: 503-222-2031. Fax: 503-222-2981.
E-mail: staff@oldchurch.org
Web Site: www.oldchurch.org
Founded: 1968.
Key Personnel: Pres., Kelli Fields; Gen. Mgr., Trish Augustin; Restoration Architect, Bill Hawkins, III; Historian, Lannie Hurst.

Personnel Profile: Part-Time Paid 5; Part-Time Volunteers 3.
Governing Authority: society; nonprofit organization. Tax-exempt: 501(c)(3).
Historical Society: housed in 1882 Calvary Presbyterian Church.
Collections: Lannie Hurst Parlor restored & furnished with Victorian furnishings; 1883 Hook & Hastings tracker action pipe organ.
Facilities: 350-seat auditorium. Note paper & posters for sale.
Activities: Gallery Sponsors: Wed. sack lunch recitals.
Publications: quarterly newsletter, The Old Church Organ.
Hours & Admission Prices: Mon.-Fri. 11-3, Sat. by appointment. No charge; donations accepted. Closed New Year's Day; Memorial Day; Independence Day; Labor Day; Thanksgiving; Christmas. ♿
Attendance: 50,000 (estimated)
Membership: Individual $20; Family $35; Sustaining $50; Guarantor $100 Patron $500; Life $1,000; Benefactor $5,000.

* **OREGON HISTORICAL SOCIETY,** 1200 S.W. Park Ave., Portland, OR 97205-2483. Tel.: 503-222-1741. Fax: 503-221-2035. TDD: 503-241-1173.
E-mail: orhist@ohs.org
Web Site: www.ohs.org
Founded: 1898.
Congressional District: 1
Key Personnel: Pres., John Herman; Exec. Dir., George Vogt; Dir. Devel. & Mktg., Sue Metzler; Dir. Artifact Collections & Exhibits, Marsha Matthews; Editor Oregon Historical Quarterly, Eliza Canky-Jones; Museum Shop Mgr., Kell Smith.
Personnel Profile: Full-Time Paid 27; Part-Time Paid 11; Part-Time Volunteers 240; Interns 2.
Governing Authority: society; nonprofit organization. Parent Institution: Oregon Historical Society. Tax-exempt: 501(c)(3).
History Museum.
Collections: anthropological; ethnographic; archaeological artifacts of Oregon Country & Pacific Rim; maritime collection; paintings; costumes; textiles; furnishings; tools; political memorabilia; advertising; manuscripts; rare books; oral histories; films; videos; photographs; maps; periodicals; microfilm & fiche; architectural drawings; government documents.
Research Fields: Oregon history; Pacific Rim exploration & settlement; native American history; genealogical; prehistory to present; Oregon business history; Northwest artists; Oregon quilts & textiles.
Facilities: research library of books, maps, pamphlets, manuscripts, sound recordings, statewide newspaper microfilm collection, two million plus photographs, diaries & journals, early films. Books & other museum-related items for sale.
Activities: lectures; guided tours; organized educational programs for children; films; reading room; permanent, temporary & traveling exhibits; Oregon Geographic Names Board; OHS Affiliate program.
Publications: Oregon Historical Quarterly.
Hours & Admission Prices: Museum: Tues.-Sat. 10-5, Sun. 12-5. Library: Thurs.-Sat. 1-5. Adults $11, students & seniors $9, youth 6-18 $5; members and children 5 & under no charge. ♿
Attendance: 40,000 (estimated)
Membership: Student $25; Individual $60; Family $80; Contributor $100; Grantor $250; Steward $500.

OREGON JEWISH MUSEUM, 310 N.W. Davis St., Portland, OR 97209-3925. Tel.: 503-226-3600. Fax: 503-226-1800.
E-mail: museum@ojm.org
Web Site: www.ojm.org
Founded: 1989.
Congressional District: 1
Key Personnel: Dir., Judith Margles; Pres. (V), Craig Wollner.
Personnel Profile: Full-Time Paid 2; Part-Time Paid 4; Part-Time Volunteers 27; Interns 5.
Governing Authority: Tax-exempt.
Jewish Museum.
Collections: Jewish life & culture; documents; family & business histories; photographs.
Major Exhibits: The Shape of Time: Accumulations of Place and Memory, 11/09-3/28/10; A Journey Through Generation, 4/6/10-4/22/10; Jews @ Work: The Professions, 5/6/10-9/5/10; Ernest Bloch Photographs, 9/26/10-1/2/11.
Research Fields: Oregon Jewish history.
Facilities: library & archives.
Publications: quarterly newsletter.
Hours & Admission Prices: Tues.-Fri. 10:30-3, Sun. 1-4. Adults $3; members no charge. Closed holidays.
Attendance: 5,500 (estimated)
Membership: Friend $50-$99; Sponsor $100-$249; Donor $250-$499; Patron $500 & up.

OREGON MARITIME MUSEUM, (M), S.W. Pine St. & Naito Pkwy., Portland, OR 97204. Mailing Address: 115 S.W. Ash St., Ste. 400C, Portland, OR 97204-3568. Tel.: 503-224-7724.
E-mail: info@oregonmaritimemuseum.org
Founded: 1980.
Personnel Profile: Part-Time Paid 2; Part-Time Volunteers 100.
Maritime Museum.
Collections: maritime heritage; river history; maritime records & artifacts; paintings; nautical instruments; photographs; local shipyard history.
Activities: educational programs.
Hours & Admission Prices: Wed.-Sat. 11-4, Sun. 12:30-4:30. Adults $5, seniors 62 & over $4, students 6-17 $3; members & children under 6 no charge. ♿
Membership: Seniors $20; Adults $25; Family $35; Supporting $50; Sustaining $100; Grantor $250; Steward $500; Life $1,000.

OREGON MUSEUM OF SCIENCE AND INDUSTRY, (M), 1945 S.E. Water Ave., Portland, OR 97214-3356. Tel.: 503-797-4000. Fax: 503-797-4566.
E-mail: bmolony@omsi.edu
Web Site: www.omsi.edu
Founded: 1944.
Congressional District: 3
Key Personnel: Pres., Nancy Stueber; Chm. Bd. Trustees, Steve Cox; Sr. Vice Pres. Support & Administration, Paul Carlson; Vice Pres. Mktg., Retail & Sales, Doug Orloff; Vice Pres. New Project Devel., Ray Vandiver; Vice Pres. Facility, Rod McDowell; Vice Pres. Finance, Human Resources & Volunteer Svcs., Tim Mack; Dir. Retail Operations, Russ Repp; Museum Shop Buyer & New Product Designer, Arlana Burke.
Personnel Profile: Full-Time Paid 152; Part-Time Paid 86; Part-Time Volunteers 340; Interns 10.
Governing Authority: nonprofit organization. Tax-exempt: 501(c)(3).
Science & Technology Center.
Collections: mineralogy; paleontology; zoology; natural history; archaeology; computers; electricity; health; fine art; historical objects; 219-ft. submarine, USS Blueback.
Research Fields: physical & natural sciences; education.
Facilities: field research station; 330-seats OMNIMAX Theater; 200-seat planetarium; 15-person motion simulator; 300-seat auditorium; classrooms; field research center; nature center; riverfront restaurant. Books, science supplies, telescopes, science kits & souvenirs for sale.
Activities: guided tours; lectures; films; study clubs; hobby workshops; organized education classes for children & adults; school loan service; outdoor education programs; temporary exhibits; submarine; residential camp programs throughout Oregon & Pacific Northwest. Museum Sponsors: research facilities for high school students.
Publications: quarterly, OMSI Member Magazine; annual catalogs: Fieldtrip Planner, Outreach; Camps; Classes.
Hours & Admission Prices: mid-June to Labor Day daily 9:30-7; Sept. to mid-June Tues.-Sun. 9:30-5:30. Adults $11, youth 3-13 and seniors 63 & over $9; discounts to AAA members; children under 3 & ASTC members no charge. Closed Thanksgiving; Christmas. Call 503-797-4661 for group information & reservations. Special pricing for premier featured exhibits. ♿
Attendance: 950,000 (estimated)
Membership: OMSI for 2 $75; Family & Grandparent $90; Family Plus & Grandparent Plus $115; Friend $135; Patron $250-$499; Benefactor $500-$999; President's Circle $1,000 & up.

OREGON NIKKEI LEGACY CENTER, 121 N.W. 2nd Ave., Portland, OR 97209-3903. Tel.: 503-224-1458.
Japanese Heritage Museum.
Collections: Japanese history & culture; photographs; art; personal artifacts.
Facilities: library. Museum-related items for sale.
Activities: summer internships; special events; educational programs
Hours & Admission Prices: Tues.-Sat. 11-3, Sun. 12-3. Adults $3; members no charge.

OREGON SPORTS HALL OF FAME AND MUSEUM, Portland, OR 97222. Mailing Address: 8500 S.E. McLoughlin Blvd. Ste. 101, Portland, OR 97222-6370. Tel.: 503-227-7466. Fax: 503-235-5688.
E-mail: info@oregonsportshall.org
Web Site: www.oregonsportshall.org
Formerly: State of Oregon Sports Hall of Fame
Founded: 1978.
Key Personnel: Pres. (V), Chuck Richards; Exec. Dir., Mike Rose.
Personnel Profile: Full-Time Paid 2.
Governing Authority: nonprofit organization. Tax-exempt: 501(c)(3).
Sports Museum.

Collections: athletic memorabilia; photos; implements; posters; written descriptions; uniforms; videos; shoes.
Research Fields: sports & athletic achievement.
Hours & Admission Prices: Temporarily closed for relocation. ♿
Attendance: 10,000 (estimated)
Membership: Individual $35; Family $50; Contributor $100; All League $500; All State $1,000; All American $2,500; MVP $5,000.

OREGON ZOO, 4001 S.W. Canyon Rd., Portland, OR 97221-2799. Tel.: 503-226-1561. Fax: 503-226-6836.
Web Site: www.oregonzoo.org
Founded: 1887.
Congressional District: 1
Key Personnel: Council Pres., David Bragdon; Deputy Dir. Living Collections, Mike Keele; Finance Mgr., Craig Stroud; Gen. Cur., Chris Pfefferkorn; Asst. Zoological Cur., Michael Illig; Asst. Zoological Cur., Gilbert Gomez; Asst. Zoological Cur., Shawn St. Michael; Mng. Dir. Oregon Zoo Foundation, Kregg Hanson; Dir. Devel. Oregon Zoo Foundation, Karen Lloyd; Mktg. Mgr., Jane Hartline; Veterinarian, Mitch Finnegan, D.V.M.; Veterinarian, Lisa Harrenstien, D.V.M.; Deputy Dir. Operations, Carmen Hannold; Mgr. Operations, Ivan Ratcliff; Exhibits Mgr., Brent Shelby; Media Rels. Officer, Bill LaMarche; Construction & Maintenance Mgr., Steve Chaney; Volunteer Mgr., Jennifer Payne; Education Mgr. Programs, Charis Henrie; Conservation Mgr., Anne Warner; Guest Svcs. Mgr., Jim Gilbert; Retail Shop Mgr., Terri Pelham; Security Mgr., Dan Lorenzen.
Personnel Profile: Full-Time Paid 145; Part-Time Paid 13; Part-Time Volunteers 2,100; Interns 20.
Governing Authority: regional government. Parent Institution: Metro.
Zoo.
Collections: mammals; birds; reptiles; amphibians; insects; fish; invertebrates.
Research Fields: studies of ecology of zoo animals; captive breeding & insemination; animal behavior.
Facilities: library; classrooms; research center; animal hospital; railway; band shell; animal exhibits; elephant museum.
Activities: formally organized education programs; volunteer programs; permanent & traveling exhibitions; mobile vans; field trips; classes for pre-school thru college age level; programs for disabled & senior citizens; birds of prey.
Publications: brochures; quarterly members newsletter; research publications.
Hours & Admission Prices: April 15-Sept. 15 daily 9-6; Sept. 16-April 14 daily 9-4. Adults $10.50, senior citizens 65 & over $9, youth 3-11 $7.50; 2nd Tues. each month $2; discounts to groups & AZA members; children 2 & under no charge. Closed Christmas. ♿
Attendance: 1,621,521 (accurate)
Membership: Individual $44; Zoo4Two $54; Individual Plus $59; Family $69; Zoo4Two Plus $74; Family Plus $94; Patron $125; Benefactor $250; Sponsor $500; Conservation Circle $1,000.

PITTOCK MANSION, (M), 3229 N.W. Pittock Dr., Portland, OR 97210-5099. Tel.: 503-823-3623. Fax: 503-823-3626.
E-mail: mbones@pittockmansion.org
Web Site: www.pittockmansion.org
Founded: 1965.
Key Personnel: Exec. Dir., Marta Bones; Pres. (V), Randall Stevens; Mgr. Visitor Svcs., Elizabeth Marcum; Program & Collection Mgr., Patricia Larkin.
Personnel Profile: Full-Time Paid 4; Part-Time Paid 8; Part-Time Volunteers 120.
Governing Authority: Parent Institution: Pittock Mansion Society. Subsidiary Institution: City of Portland, Bureau of Parks, 1120 S.W. Fifth Ave., Portland, OR 97204. Tax-exempt: 501(c)(3) & 170(b)(1)(A).
Historic House: 1909-1914 French Renaissance, Pittock Mansion.
Collections: period furnishings; fine art; decorative art.
Facilities: Museum-related items for sale.
Activities: guided tours; special tours; docent program; discovery program; permanent & temporary exhibitions.
Publications: Society Membership Newsletter; promotion flyer & brochure.
Hours & Admission Prices: Feb.-Dec. daily 11-4. Adults $7, senior citizens $6, children 6-18 $4; discounts to military & AAA members; members no charge. Closed New Year's Day; Thanksgiving; Christmas. ♿
Attendance: 50,000 (estimated)
Membership: Individual $30; Dual $45; Family $60; Supporter $100-$249; Contributor $250-$499; Sponsor $500-$999; Patron $1,000 & up. Corporate: Bronze $250; Silver $750; Gold $1,500.

* **PORTLAND ART MUSEUM, (M),** 1219 S.W. Park Ave., Portland, OR 97205-2486. Tel.: 503-226-2811. Fax: 503-226-4842.
E-mail: info@pam.org
Web Site: www.portlandartmuseum.org
Founded: 1892.
Congressional District: 1
Key Personnel: Dir., Brian Ferriso; C.F.O., Gareth Nevitt; Dir. Mktg., Beth Heinrich; Dir. Devel., J.S. May; Chief Cur., Bruce Guenther; Dir. Northwest Film Center, Bill Foster; Cur. Native American Art, Anna Strankman; Cur. Prints & Drawings, Dr. Annette Dixon; Dir. Education, Tina Olsen; Dir. Collections Mgmt., Donald Urquhart; Conservator, Elizabeth Chambers; Librarian, Debra Royer; Museum Shop Mgr., Michelle Betcone.
Personnel Profile: Full-Time Paid 127; Part-Time Paid 67; Part-Time Volunteers 865; Interns 31.
Governing Authority: nonprofit organization. Subsidiary Institution: Northwest Film Center. Tax-exempt: 501(c)(3).
Art Museum.
Collections: American: 19th & 20th century paintings, sculpture, decorative arts; Asian: sculptures, paintings, bronzes, ceramics, decorative arts; European: paintings, sculpture, silver, decorative arts; Graphics: Vivian & Gordon Gilkey Graphics Art, Japanese prints; Photography: 19th & 20th-century, Northwest regional collection; Modern & Contemporary Art: 20th-century paintings, sculpture, decorative arts, Clement Greenberg collection; Native American: Elizabeth Cole Butler collection of Native American art, Rasmussen collection of Northwest Coast Indian & Eskimo arts, Cameroon art; pre-Columbian art; Northwest Art: paintings, sculptures, decorative arts.
Facilities: art reference library; 115,000 sq. ft. gallery space; conservation laboratory; film study center; rental sales gallery; multimedia resource center; 380-seat auditorium; classrooms; 2 ballrooms. Museum-related items for sale.
Activities: guided tours; lectures & symposia; films; gallery talks & activities; permanent, temporary & traveling exhibitions; classes for adults, youth & families.
Publications: quarterly newsletter.
Hours & Admission Prices: Mon. holidays, Tues.-Wed. & Sat. 10-5, Thurs.-Fri. 10-8, Sun. 12-5. Adults $10, seniors & students 18 & over $9; discounts for groups, AAM & Western Reciprocal members; children 17 & under and members no charge. Additional fee for special exhibitions. Closed Christmas. ♿
Attendance: 350,000 (estimated)
Membership: Individual $45; Family & Dual $75; Friend $100; Young & Art $150; Sponsor $250; Sustainer $500; Patron $1,000 & up.

PORTLAND CHILDREN'S MUSEUM, 4015 S.W. Canyon Rd., Portland, OR 97221-2759. Tel.: 503-223-6500. Fax: 503-223-6600.
E-mail: mwright@portlandcm.org
Web Site: www.portlandchildrensmuseum.org
Formerly: CM2-Children's Museum 2nd Generation
Founded: 1949.
Congressional District: 1
Key Personnel: Pres. Bd., Brendan O'Scannlain; Exec. Dir., Sarah Orleans; Dir. Education & Research, Judy Graves; Dir. Mktg. & Communications, Shannon Grosswiler; Accountant, Brenda Smith; Dir. Visitor Svcs. & Human Resources, Christine Hinrichs.
Personnel Profile: Full-Time Paid 20; Part-Time Paid 40; Part-Time Volunteers 35; Interns 6.
Governing Authority: municipal; nonprofit corporation. Parent Institution: Portland Bureau of Parks & Recreation, 1120 S.W. Fifth Ave., Portland 97204. Jointly administered by Friends of the Children's Museum. Tax-exempt: 501(c)(3) & 170(c)(1).
Children's Museum.
Collections: natural history; paleontology; cultural history; transportation; toys; dolls; stuffed animals of North America; hands-on exhibit; children's art.
Research Fields: early childhood education; playground games; multicultural artifacts of childhood.
Facilities: ceramic & arts classrooms; hands-on museum for children; presentation facilities.
Activities: drop-in art activities; presentations on ceramic & multicultural subjects; birthday parties; presentations to school groups.
Publications: quarterly newsletter; members' newsletters; annual report; tourist guides & flyers.
Hours & Admission Prices: March-Aug. Mon.-Sun. 9-5; Sept.-Feb. Tues.-Sun. 9-5. Adults $8, military & seniors 55 & over $7; members & children under 1 no charge. ♿
Attendance: 250,000 (estimated)
Membership: 2 Person $35; 3 Person $55; Family & Grandparent $75; Premier $125; Premier Plus $250; A Cut Above $500; A Cut Above Plus $750; A Cut Above Ultimate $1,000.

PORTLAND POLICE MUSEUM, 1111 S.W. 2nd Ave., 16th Fl., Portland, OR 97204-3231. Tel.: 503-823-0019.
Police Museum.

Collections: police history & memorabilia; photographs; uniforms; equipment; documents; police officers memorial.
Facilities: Museum-related items for sale.
Hours & Admission Prices: Tues.-Fri. 10-3. No charge.

VELVETERIA - MUSEUM OF VELVET PAINTINGS, 2448 E. Burnside St., Portland, OR 97214-1752. Tel.: 503-233-5100.
Art Museum.
Collections: over 300 velvet paintings.
Hours & Admission Prices: Thurs.-Sun. 12-5. Admission $5.

WASHINGTON COUNTY HISTORICAL SOCIETY, 17677 N.W. Springville Rd., Portland, OR 97229-1743. Tel.: 503-645-5353. Fax: 503-645-5650 (call first).
E-mail: info@washingtoncountymuseum.org
Web Site: www.washingtoncountymuseum.org
Founded: 1956.
Congressional District: 1
Key Personnel: Exec. Dir., Samuel Shogren; Pres., Gary J. Imbrie; Treas., Devon Reese; Collections & Programs Mgr., Jennifer Kozik; Museum Research Asst., Winnifred Herrschaft.
Personnel Profile: Full-Time Paid 2; Part-Time Paid 2; Part-Time Volunteers 75; Interns 1.
Governing Authority: private; nonprofit organization. Tax-exempt: 501(c)(3).
History Museum.
Collections: artifacts; photo images; manuscripts; documents; Washington County, Oregon maps: Native American through high technology.
Research Fields: Washington County history; census; genealogy; Oregon trail; pioneer life; schools.
Facilities: 550-vol. library; 2,000 sq. ft. exhibit space. Museum-related items for sale.
Activities: Mobile Museum visits schools; guided tours; traveling exhibits; workshops; monthly lecture series; Scout Saturdays program; summer camp. Museum Sponsors: Annual Draft Horse Plowing Exhibition.
Publications: semi-annual, The Washington County Historian; pictorial history of Washington County, This Far Off Sunset Land; guide to historic sites & attractions of Washington County, Hidden Treasures.
Hours & Admission Prices: Museum: Mon.-Sat. 10-4:30. Adults $3, senior citizens & children 6-17 $2; members, faculty, staff, students of PCC & children under 6 no charge. Research Library: Fri.-Sat. 10-4:30, call first. Closed major holidays. ♿
Attendance: 4,839 (accurate)
Membership: Individual $20; Couples $30; Family & Grandparent $40; George Ebbert Society $50 & up; Joseph Gale Society $100 & up; Joseph Meek Society $250 & up; Tabitha Brown Society $500 & up; Director's Circle $1,000 & up.

WELLS FARGO HISTORY EXHIBIT, 1300 S.W. Fifth Ave., Portland, OR 97201-5688. Mailing Address: Wells Fargo Historical Services, 420 Montgomery St., MAC-A0101-106, San Francisco, CA 94163-0001. Tel.: 503-886-1102.
Founded: 2001.
Key Personnel: Exhibit Interpreter, Steve Greenwood.
Governing Authority: profit-making organization. Affiliated with Wells Fargo Bank.
Company History Exhibit.
Collections: Concord Stagecoach; Wells Fargo banking & express history; mining; staging.
Activities: guided group tours; audiovisual programs.
Publications: scholarly pamphlets.
Hours & Admission Prices: Mon.-Fri. 9-6. No charge. Closed bank holidays. ♿

WORLD FORESTRY CENTER DISCOVERY MUSEUM, 4033 S.W. Canyon Rd., Portland, OR 97221-2798. Tel.: 503-228-1367. Fax: 503-228-4608.
E-mail: info@worldforestry.org
Web Site: www.worldforestry.org
Founded: 1964.
Congressional District: 1
Key Personnel: C.E.O. & Pres., Gary Hartshorn; Chm. (V), Harry Merlo; Pres. (V), Eric Schooler; Operations Dir., Mark Reed; Museum Shop Mgr., Louise George.
Personnel Profile: Full-Time Paid 30; Part-Time Paid 7; Part-Time Volunteers 250; Interns 5.
Governing Authority: nonprofit organization. Parent Institution: World Forestry Center. Subsidiary Institution: World Forest Institute. Tax-exempt: 501(c)(3).
Global Forestry Museum.
Collections: forest & forestry artifacts including the Pacific NW & forests of the world; global petrified woods; books; photographs; interactive exhibits.
Research Fields: world forestry.
Facilities: 160 acres demonstration forests & nature center; visitor center; classrooms; 250-seat auditorium & 400-seat auditorium; information center.
Activities: guided tours; lectures; permanent & temporary exhibits; forestry classes for youths; ecology classes; tree planting lessons; Boy Scout campouts; interpretive hikes; international fellowship program; computer simulations; canopy lift ride; summer camp; teachers summer camp; international educators institute; tree farm guided hikes. Annual Events: Chocolate Fest; Coffee Fest; Veterans Day Week; Smithsonian Museum Day; Girl Scout's Day; Day of the African Child.
Publications: WFI newsletter.
Hours & Admission Prices: Daily 10-5. Adult $8, senior citizens $7, youth 5-18 $5; discounts to groups; children 4 & under and members no charge. Closed Thanksgiving; Christmas Eve & Day. ♿
Attendance: 70,000 (accurate)
Membership: Individual $35; Individual Plus $40; Family $45; Family Plus $50.

Princeton

BENSON MEMORIAL MUSEUM, MALHEUR NATIONAL WILDLIFE REFUGE, 36391 Sodhouse Lane, Princeton, OR 97721-9523. Tel.: 541-493-2612. Fax: 541-493-2405.
Web Site: fws.gov/malheur
Founded: 1954.
Congressional District: 2
Key Personnel: Asst. Mgr., Chad Karges; Outdoor Planner, Carey Goss.
Governing Authority: federal. Tax-exempt.
Wildlife Refuge & Bird Sanctuary.
Collections: representative specimens of species of birds & small mammals; zoology.
Activities: self-guided tours.
Publications: general leaflet, bird list.
Hours & Admission Prices: Daily sunrise-sunset. Visitor Center: Mon.-Fri. 8-4, Sat.-Sun. call for hours. No charge; donations accepted. ♿
Attendance: 60,000 (estimated)

Prineville

A.R. BOWMAN MEMORIAL MUSEUM, (M), 246 N. Main St., Prineville, OR 97754-1852. Tel.: 541-447-3715. Fax: 541-447-3715 (call first).
E-mail: bowmuse@netscape.net
Web Site: www.bowmanmuseum.org
Founded: 1971.
Key Personnel: Dir. & C.E.O., Gordon Gillespie; Pres., Terry Holtyapple.
Personnel Profile: Full-Time Paid 1; Full-Time Volunteers 2; Part-Time Paid 2; Part-Time Volunteers 11.
Governing Authority: county; society. Parent Institution: Crook County Historical Society. Tax-exempt.
Local History Museum: housed in 1910 bank building.
Collections: personal artifacts of local pioneers; American Indian artifacts; local mineral society's rocks; genealogy; newspaper index; photographs.
Research Fields: history of area.
Facilities: Local historical books & other museum-related articles for sale.
Activities: local history field trips; quarterly meetings; historical programs.
Publications: quarterly newsletter.
Hours & Admission Prices: Feb.-May & Sept.-Dec. Tues.-Fri. 10-5, Sat. 11-4; June-Aug. Mon.-Fri. 10-5, Sat.-Sun. 11-4. No charge; donations accepted. Closed major holidays.
Attendance: 10,882 (estimated)
Membership: Senior 65 & over $6; Adult $10; Family $15; Business $25; Sustaining $50.

Reedsport

UMPQUA DISCOVERY CENTER, 409 Riverfront Way, Reedsport, OR 97467-1495. Tel.: 541-271-4816. Fax: 541-271-4816.
E-mail: umpquadiscoverycenter@charterinternet.com
Web Site: www.umpquadiscoverycenter.com
Founded: 1993.
Congressional District: 4
Key Personnel: Dir. & Museum Shop Mgr., Diane Novak.
Personnel Profile: Full-Time Paid 1; Part-Time Paid 2; Part-Time Volunteers 25.
Governing Authority: municipal; nonprofit organization. Tax-exempt: 501(c)(3).
History Museum.
Collections: Oregon coast history with emphasis on the city of Reedsport and the Lower Umpqua area; dioramas & natural sounds of tidewater towns;

history of towns where life, commerce & transportation depended on the ebb & flow of the tides; paintings; simulated indoor trail of the natural history of the area.
Research Fields: local Umpqua Valley area history.
Facilities: 140-vol. library; 7,000 sq. ft. interpretive center; 50-seat theater. Museum-related items for sale.
Activities: permanent & temporary exhibits; concerts; films; formal education programs; guided tours; lectures; rental gallery; simulated indoor trail. Center Sponsors: Riverfront Rhythms Concerts in Summer; Tsalia Festival, The Umpqua River in September.
Publications: quarterly newsletter, News of Discovery.
Hours & Admission Prices: June-Sept. daily 9-5; Oct.-May daily 10-4. Adults $8, senior citizens 65 & up $7, children 6-15 $4; discounts to families & groups; members no charge. Closed New Year's Day; Thanksgiving; Christmas. ♿
Attendance: 24,000 (estimated)
Membership: Individual $25; Family (one household) & Grandparent (4 grandchildren per visit) $45; Business $125, $250, $500 &, $1,000.

Rickreall

POLK COUNTY MUSEUM, 560 S.W. Pacific Hwy., Rickreall, OR 97371. Mailing Address: P.O. Box 67, Monmouth, OR 97361-0067. Tel.: 503-623-6251.
Governing Authority: Parent Institution: Polk County Historical Society.
History Museum.
Collections: local history & culture; photographs; Native American artifacts; natural history; personal artifacts; period furnishings.
Facilities: library. Museum-related items for sale.
Activities: educational programs.
Hours & Admission Prices: Mon. & Wed.-Sat. 1-5. Adults $3, seniors $2, students $1; children under 5 no charge.

Rogue River

WOODVILLE MUSEUM, INC., 199 First St., Rogue River, OR 97537. Mailing Address: P.O. Box 128, Rogue River, OR 97537-0128. Tel.: 541-582-3088.
Founded: 1986.
Congressional District: 2
Key Personnel: Chm., Samuel D. Evensizer; Treas., Shirley O. Allen.
Personnel Profile: Full-Time Volunteers 12; Part-Time Volunteers 3.
Governing Authority: private; nonprofit organization.
History Museum: housed in Hatch House, c.1909.
Collections: local history & culture; photographs; personal artifacts.
Facilities: 2,500 sq. ft. exhibit space.
Activities: concerts; temporary exhibitions. Museum Sponsors: Rooster Crow.
Hours & Admission Prices: Tues.-Sat. 12-4. No charge; donations accepted. Closed legal holidays.
Attendance: 2,000 (estimated)
Membership: Regular $10.

Roseburg

DOUGLAS COUNTY HISTORICAL SOCIETY - LANE HOUSE, 533 S.E. Douglas Ave., Roseburg, OR 97470. Mailing Address: P.O. Box 2534, Roseburg, OR 97470-0430. Tel.: 541-673-0466.
Founded: 1953.
Key Personnel: Pres. (V), John Robertson; Chm. (V), Gwen Bates.
Personnel Profile: Full-Time Volunteers 30.
Governing Authority: society. Parent Institution: Douglas County Historical Society. Tax-exempt: 501(c)(3).
Historic House: Floed-Lane House.
Collections: period furnishings; history of house, General Joseph Lane & Lane family.
Facilities: 200-vol. library of old books available for use on premises.
Publications: quarterly magazine, Umpqua Trapper; book, Historic Douglas County; 620 stories of families.
Hours & Admission Prices: Sat.-Sun. 1-4; other times by appointment. No charge; donations accepted. Closed Easter; Independence Day; Labor Day; Thanksgiving; Christmas.
Attendance: 320 (accurate)
Membership: Individual $25.

DOUGLAS COUNTY MUSEUM OF HISTORY AND NATURAL HISTORY, (M), 123 Museum Dr., Roseburg, OR 97471-5308. Tel.: 541-957-7007. Fax: 541-957-7017.
E-mail: museum@co.douglas.or.us
Web Site: www.co.douglas.or.us/museum
Founded: 1968.
Congressional District: 4
Key Personnel: C.E.O., Stacy B. McLaughlin; Cur., Jena Mitchell; Cur., Dennis Ruley; Research Librarian & Museum Shop Mgr., Karen Bratton.
Personnel Profile: Full-Time Paid 5; Part-Time Paid 1; Part-Time Volunteers 75.
Governing Authority: county. Parent Institution: Douglas County. Tax-exempt: 501(c)(3).
General Museum.
Collections: Native Indian artifacts; manuscripts; pioneer tools; guns; utensils; railroad equipment; agricultural equipment; marine artifacts; vehicles; machinery; 20,000 historic photographs; native birds, animals & herbarium.
Research Fields: county history of Indians; settlers; agriculture; logging & milling; railroads & forest service Oregon & California grant lands; transportation; fur trade; mining; natural science; exploration.
Facilities: 2,600-vol. library of Oregon & Pacific Northwest history available for use on premises only; microfilm & oral histories; reading room.
Activities: guided tours; lectures; films; TV & radio programs; permanent, temporary & traveling exhibitions; genealogy. Museum Sponsors: slide programs presented to groups at any outside location on request.
Publications: newsletter.
Hours & Admission Prices: Jan.-Oct. Mon.-Fri. 9-5, Sat. 10-5, Sun. 12-5; Nov.-Dec. Tues.-Fri. 9-5, Sat. 10-5. Adults $4, seniors $3, children 4-17 & college students $2; children under 4 & members no charge. Closed legal holidays. ♿
Attendance: 12,000 (accurate)
Membership: Individual $15; Couple & Family $30; Patron $50; Contributor $100; Sponsor $250.

Saint Helens

HISTORICAL SOCIETY OF COLUMBIA COUNTY, 2194 Columbia Blvd., Saint Helens, OR 97051-1739. Tel.: 503-366-3650.
E-mail: rj@historyofcc.org
Web Site: www.historyofcc.org
Formerly: Columbia County Historical Society Museum
Founded: 1930.
Congressional District: 1
Key Personnel: Pres. (V), Cathy Taylor.
Personnel Profile: Part-Time Paid 1; Part-Time Volunteers 5; Interns 1.
Governing Authority: nonprofit historical society; affiliated with Oregon Historical Society, 1230 S.W. Park, Portland, OR 97205. Tax-exempt 501(c)(3).
General Museum: housed in historic train depot.
Collections: period furniture; books; records: Columbia County marriages 1856-1900, alphabetical listing of tombstones in Columbia County: 1850-1984; photos; Indian artifacts; historical relics; pottery; bottles; quilts; pioneer equipment.
Research Fields: family records; early history; cemetery records.
Facilities: 22-vol. library of history & scrapbooks available for use at the museum; reading space. Postcards & booklets for sale.
Activities: self-guided tours.
Publications: Columbia County Historical Booklets; monthly newsletters; periodicals.
Hours & Admission Prices: Tues.-Sat. 10-2. No charge; donations accepted. ♿
Attendance: 250 (estimated)
Membership: Single $15; Couple $21; Family $27.

Saint Paul

CHAMPOEG STATE HERITAGE AREA VISITOR CENTER, 8239 Champoeg Rd., N.E., Saint Paul, OR 97137-9796. Mailing Address: 7679 Champoeg Rd. NE, St. Paul, OR 97137-9525. Tel.: 503-678-1251. Fax: 503-678-6142.
Web Site: www.oregonstateparks.org/park_113.php
Founded: 1901.
Key Personnel: Park Mgr., Dennis Wiley; Pres. (V), Barry Freeman.
Personnel Profile: Full-Time Paid 1; Part-Time Paid 4; Part-Time Volunteers 4.
Governing Authority: Parent Institution: Oregon Parks & Recreation Dept. Tax-exempt.
Park Museum Visitor Center: at location of first provisional government in the Pacific Northwest (1843).
Collections: tools; artifacts; furniture; implements; dishes; transportation; riverboats; portraits of pioneers; American Indian artifacts.
Research Fields: history; archeology.
Facilities: visitor center featuring interpretive displays relating Champoeg significance in the settlement of the Oregon Territory.
Activities: summer living history demonstrations; school living history programming; videos.
Publications: brochure, Champoeg State Park; leaflet, History of Champoeg; brochure, French Prairie Loop.
Hours & Admission Prices: Mon.-Fri. 11-4, Sat.-Sun. 10-4. Car parking $3

(covers visitor center admission). No charge; donations accepted. Closed major holidays Oct.-April. ♿
Attendance: 17,250
Membership: Individual $12; Family $25; Life $1,000.

PIONEER MOTHERS MEMORIAL CABIN, 8035 Champoeg Rd., N.E., Saint Paul, OR 97137-9709. Tel.: 503-633-2237.
Web Site: www.newellhouse.com/pioneercabin.htm#DAR
History Museum.
Collections: period pioneer furnishings; collapsible Hudson's Bay heating stove; guns & muskets from 1777-1853; hair wreath; feather & yarn wreaths; fife play at Lincoln's funeral; china & glassware.
Activities: group tours; special events.
Hours & Admission Prices: March-Oct. Fri.-Sun. & holidays 1-5 or by appointment. Adults $4, seniors & DAR members $3, children $2.

ROBERT NEWELL HOUSE, DAR MUSEUM, 8089 Champoeg Rd., N.E., Saint Paul, OR 97137-9709. Tel.: 503-266-3944.
E-mail: newellhousemuseum@centurytel.net
Web Site: www.newellhouse.com/index.htm
Founded: 1959.
Key Personnel: Dir., Judy Van Atta; DAR State Chm. Buildings & Grounds, Barbara Kieffer; Chm. Grounds, Donna Biggs; State Cur., Terry Maloney.
Personnel Profile: Part-Time Paid 1; Part-Time Volunteers 3.
Governing Authority: society. Parent Institution: Oregon State Society DAR. Subsidiary Institution: Pioneer Mothers Memorial Cabin Museum. Tax-exempt.
Historic House: 1959 restoration of 1852 Robert E. Newell House and 1931 pioneer cabin.
Collections: Indian artifacts; quilts & hand work; Oregon's governors wives' inaugural gowns; furniture & furnishings; Masonic items; guns & muskets, 1777-1853. Historic Buildings: 1850 Butteville jail; two-room schoolhouse.
Facilities: Stationery, books & periodicals for sale.
Activities: guided tours including school groups (at Newell House); hands-on demonstrations.
Publications: books, Men of Champoeg; Historic Houses in Oregon; Oregon Landmark Books; brochure on museum.
Hours & Admission Prices: March-Sept. Fri.-Sun. 1-5; private tours by appointment. Adults $4, children under 12 $2; discounts to members & seniors.
Attendance: 4,500 (estimated)

Salem

A.C. GILBERT'S DISCOVERY VILLAGE, 116 Marion St., N.E., Salem, OR 97301-3437. Tel.: 503-371-3631; 800-208-9514. Fax: 503-316-3485.
E-mail: info@acgilbert.org
Web Site: www.acgilbert.org
Formerly: Gilbert House Children's Museum
Founded: 1987.
Congressional District: 5
Key Personnel: Exec. Dir., Pamela Vorachek; Pres. (V), Shannon Martinez.
Personnel Profile: Full-Time Paid 5; Part-Time Paid 20; Part-Time Volunteers 35.
Governing Authority: nonprofit. Tax-exempt: 501(c)(3).
Historic Houses: home of Andrew T. Gilbert, banker; home of C.S. Rockenfield, nurseryman; home of J.L. Parrish, businessman & minister.
Collections: toys & inventions of Alfred Carlton Gilbert; contemporary hands-on exhibits in arts, sciences & humanities.
Facilities: classroom; resource center; gardens; outdoor discovery center.
Activities: tours; arts festivals; hobby workshops; organized education programs for children; outreach educational programs; participatory & traveling exhibitions; organized education programs with students affiliated with Western Oregon University & Willamette University.
Publications: quarterly newsletter, Discovery.
Hours & Admission Prices: Mon.-Sat. 10-5, Sun. 12-5. Adults 3-59 $5.75, seniors 60 & over $4.25, children 1-2 $2.75; discounts to AAA members; members no charge. Closed New Year's Day; Easter; Thanksgiving; Christmas Day. ♿
Attendance: 80,000 (accurate)
Membership: You & Me $45; Grandparent $55; Family $65.

HALLIE FORD MUSEUM OF ART, (M), Willamette University, 700 State St., Salem, OR 97301. Mailing Address: Willamette University, 900 State St., Salem, OR 97301-3922. Tel.: 503-370-6855. Fax: 503-375-5458.
E-mail: museum-art@willamette.edu
Web Site: www.willamette.edu/museum_of_art/
Founded: 1998.
Congressional District: 5
Key Personnel: Dir. & C.E.O., John Olbrantz; Cur. Collections, Jonathan Bucci; Cur. Education, Elizabeth Garrison; Designer & Preparator, David Andersen.
Personnel Profile: Full-Time Paid 8; Part-Time Paid 2; Part-Time Volunteers 12; Interns 4.
Governing Authority: private university; nonprofit. Parent Institution: Willamette University. Tax-exempt: 501(c)(3).
Art Museum.
Collections: archives; American, European, Asian, Native American & regional art.
Research Fields: University's art collection with emphasis on historic & contemporary regional art.
Facilities: print study center; lecture hall; 9,000 sq. ft. exhibit space. Museum-related items for sale.
Activities: concerts; docent program; films; formal education programs for Willamette University students; guided tours; lectures; loan, temporary & traveling exhibitions; poetry readings; artist demonstrations. Museum Sponsors: Symposia.
Publications: biannual calendar of events, Brushstrokes; quarterly alumni magazine, Willamette Scene; temporary exhibitions catalogues.
Hours & Admission Prices: Tues.-Sat. 10-5, Sun. 1-5. Adults $3, senior citizens & students $2; discounts to AAM members; members & children under 13 no charge. Closed Easter; Independence Day; Thanksgiving & day after; Christmas Eve-New Year's Day. ♿
Attendance: 30,000 (estimated)
Membership: Individual $25; Family & Dual $50; Sponsor $100; Donor $250; Benefactor $500; Patron $1,000.

HISTORIC DEEPWOOD ESTATE, 1116 Mission St., S.E., Salem, OR 97302-6207. Tel.: 503-363-1825. Fax: 503-363-3586.
E-mail: visit@historicdeepwoodestate.org
Web Site: www.historicdeepwoodestate.org
Founded: 1974.
Key Personnel: Exec. Dir., Lois M. Cole.
Personnel Profile: Full-Time Paid 1; Part-Time Paid 2; Part-Time Volunteers 60; Interns 1.
Governing Authority: private; nonprofit organization.
Historical Museum.
Collections: personal artifacts; furnishings.
Hours & Admission Prices: Tours: Memorial Day to Labor Day Sun.-Fri. 12-4; Sept.-May. Wed.-Thurs. & Sat. 11-3. Adults $4, senior citizens & students $3, children $2; children under 5 no charge.
Attendance: 17,106
Membership: Student and Senior 55 & over $20; Individual $30; Family $50; Patron $50; Business & Photographer $100; Corporate $250; Sustaining $500; Benefactor $1,000.

MARION COUNTY HISTORICAL SOCIETY, (M), 260 12th St., S.E., Salem, OR 97301-2287. Tel.: 503-364-2128. Fax: 503-391-5356.
E-mail: mchs@marionhistory.org
Web Site: www.marionhistory.org
Founded: 1950.
Congressional District: 5
Key Personnel: C.E.O., Ross Sutherland; Pres. (V), Coburn Grabenhorst; Dir., Amy Vandegrift.
Personnel Profile: Full-Time Paid 2; Part-Time Volunteers 50.
Governing Authority: private; nonprofit organization. Tax-exempt: 501(c)(3).
General Museum.
Collections: history of Marion County from the Kalapuya Indians to present.
Major Exhibits: 150 Miles of History: A Trip Around Marion County, 11/09-12/10.
Facilities: 1,500-vol. library; 1,500 sq. ft. exhibit space. Museum-related items for sale.
Activities: formal education programs for adults; lectures; school loan service; traveling exhibitions.
Publications: quarterly historical journal, Historic Marion; quarterly program newsletter, Member Matters.
Hours & Admission Prices: Tues.-Sat. 12-4. Adults $4, senior citizens $3.50, children $2.50; discount to military, AAA & AAM members; members no charge.
Attendance: 2,500 (estimated)
Membership: Seniors & Student $35; Family $50; Kalapuya $100; Pudding $250; Santiam $500; Willamette $1,000; Heritage $2,500.

MISSION MILL MUSEUM ASSOCIATION, 1313 Mill St., S.E., Salem, OR 97301-6307. Tel.: 503-585-7012. Fax: 503-588-9902.
E-mail: info@missionmill.org
Web Site: www.missionmill.org
Founded: 1964.

Congressional District: 5
Key Personnel: Exec. Dir., Peter Booth; Pres., Bobbie Clyde; Rental & Special Events Coord., Laura Cruz; Bookkeeper, Linda Langham.
Personnel Profile: Full-Time Paid 9; Part-Time Paid 6; Part-Time Volunteers 200; Interns 4.
Governing Authority: nonprofit organization. Tax-exempt: 501(c)(3).
History Museum.
Collections: 1896 brick woolen mill with attendant machine shop, turbine, & other outbuildings; plus mill equipment, archives; Methodist mission & settlers' houses from 1840s & 1850s.
Major Exhibits: Facing Statehood, 11/09-5/22/10; Wrapped in Pride: Ghanaian Kente & African American Identity (T), 6/16/10-8/11/10; Art and Oregon Agriculture, 10/8/10-12/26/10.
Research Fields: The Methodist mission to the Oregon country & its impact. The Thomas Kay Woolen Mill & woolen industry in the Pacific Northwest.
Facilities: Thomas Kay Woolen Mil; turbine machine shop; three mission houses, pioneer era house & church, archives pertaining to textile technology; Methodist Mission; rental spaces, shops, picnic grounds. Museum-related items for sale.
Activities: guided-tours; speaker series; docent program; intern program; textile art classes; special exhibits. Museum Sponsors: Sheep to Shawl Festival; Quilt & Textile Festival; Magic at the Mill holiday lighting; Heritage Awards.
Publications: quarterly newsletter.
Hours & Admission Prices: Mon.-Sat. 10-5. Museum: no charge; donations accepted. Tours: adults $6; discounts to AAM & AAA members; members no charge. Closed New Year's Day; Martin Luther King Jr. Day; Thanksgiving; Christmas. ♿
Attendance: 35,000 (estimated)
Membership: Senior Citizen & Student $25; Individual $35; Family $40; Contributor $50; Business, Professional & Donor $100; Corporate Sponsor $250; Patron $500; Benefactor $1,000.

OREGON ELECTRIC RAILWAY HISTORICAL SOCIETY, INC., 3395 Brooklake Rd., N.E., Salem, OR 97303. Tel.: 503-888-4014.
Web Site: www.oregonelectricrailway.org
Founded: 1957.
Congressional District: 1
Key Personnel: Museum Dir., Greg Bonn; Pres., Bob Terkelsen; Chm. (V), Charles Philpot; Museum Shop Mgr., John Nagy.
Personnel Profile: Full-Time Volunteers 3; Part-Time Volunteers 25.
Governing Authority: society. Parent Institution: Oregon Electric Railway Historical Society. Trolley Operations: Willamette Shore Trolley, 311 N. State St., Lake Oswego, OR, 97034. Tax-exempt: 501(c)(3).
Electric Railway Museum.
Collections: light electric streetcars of 1899-1977; interurban cars; railroad lore; operating tramway with all related equipment & facilities themed to 1910; videos of historic street railway.
Research Fields: tramway technology.
Facilities: 100-vol. library of historical & technical street railway subjects available by request. Gift items for sale.
Activities: guided tours; trolley car rides.
Publications: bulletin, The Transfer.
Hours & Admission Prices: Museum: adults $6. Williamette Shore: adults $10; members no charge. ♿
Attendance: 6,856 (accurate)
Membership: Active $30; Family $40.

SALEM ART ASSOCIATION-BUSH HOUSE MUSEUM AND BUSH BARN ART CENTER, 600 Mission St., S.E., Salem, OR 97302-6203. Tel.: 503-581-2228. Fax: 503-371-3342.
E-mail: info@salemart.org
Web Site: www.salemart.org
Founded: 1919.
Congressional District: 5
Key Personnel: Exec. Dir., Sandra Burnett; Pres. (V), Catherine Jarmin Miller; Community Arts Education Dir., Kathleen Dinges; Program Dir. Bush House Museum, Sara Heil Swanborn; Operations Mgr., Kerry Jackson.
Personnel Profile: Full-Time Paid 9; Part-Time Paid 6; Part-Time Volunteers 1,000.
Governing Authority: society. Parent Institution: Salem Art Association. Tax-exempt: 501(c)(3).
Historic House Museum: housed in 1877 Asahel Bush, II house. Historic Barn: home of the Salem Art Association.
Collections: costumes; decorative arts completely furnished in the period.
Research Fields: costumes; decorative arts.
Facilities: classroom; print studio; sales & rental gallery for NW artists; conservatory, ceramics studio.
Activities: guided tours; lectures; gallery talks; concerts; formally organized education programs for children, adults & undergraduate college students; permanent & temporary exhibitions. Annual Event: Salem Art Fair & Festival in July.
Publications: exhibit announcements; class schedules; newsletters, prospectus for special exhibits & the Salem Art Fair & Festival; brochures.
Hours & Admission Prices: Bush House: Jan.-Feb. call for hours; April & Oct.-Dec. Tues.-Sun. 1-4; May-Sept. Tues.-Sun. 12-5. Adults $4, seniors & students 13-21 $3, children 6-12 $2; discounts to AAA members; Salem Art Association, BBAC & BHM members no charge. Bush Barn Art Center: Tues.-Fri. 11-6, Sat.-Sun. 12-5. No charge. ♿
Attendance: 40,000 (estimated)
Membership: Artist $25; Individual $30; Family $50; Patron $100; Business $150; Sponsor $500.

Scio

SCIO HISTORICAL SOCIETY & DEPOT MUSEUM, 39004 N.E. 1st Ave., Scio, OR 97374. Mailing Address: P.O. Box 226, Scio, OR 97374-0226. Tel.: 503-394-2199.
History Museum.
Collections: historical items, printed material & memorabilia.
Hours & Admission Prices: May-Oct. Sat.-Sun. 1-4.

Seaside

SEASIDE AQUARIUM, 200 N. Prom, Seaside, OR 97138-5945. Tel.: 503-738-6211.
E-mail: aquarium@seasideaquarium.com
Web Site: www.seasideaquarium.com
Aquarium.
Collections: marine wildlife.
Hours & Admission Prices: Call for hours. Adults $7.50, senior citizens 64 & over $6.25, children 6-13 $3.75; children 5 & under no charge.

SEASIDE MUSEUM & HISTORICAL SOCIETY, 570 Necanicum Dr., Seaside, OR 97138-6040. Tel.: 503-738-7065. Fax: 503-738-7065.
E-mail: smhs@seasurf.net
Web Site: www.seasidemuseum.org/
Founded: 1974.
Congressional District: 1
Key Personnel: Pres., Chris Gonzales; Chm. (V), Roger Waller; Museum Shop Mgr., Val Smith.
Personnel Profile: Part-Time Paid 1; Part-Time Volunteers 25.
Governing Authority: Tax-exempt.
History Museum.
Collections: history of Seaside; period artifacts. Historic House: c.1912 Butterfield Cottage.
Facilities: research library; gardens. Museum-related items for sale.
Activities: special events.
Publications: quarterly newsletter.
Hours & Admission Prices: May-Sept. Mon.-Sat. 10-4; Oct.-April Mon.-Sat. 10-3; groups by appointment. Adults $3, senior citizens $2, students $1; members and children 6 & under no charge. Closed New Year's Day; Easter; Mother's Day; Memorial Day; Father's Day; Labor Day; Thanksgiving; Christmas. ♿
Attendance: 1,777 (accurate)
Membership: Students $2; Adult $10; Couple $15; Family $18.75; Business $25-$49; Supporting $50-$99; Corporate $100-$299; Patron $300-$499; Benefactor $500-$999; Life $1,000.

Springfield

SPRINGFIELD MUSEUM, 590 Main St., Springfield, OR 97477-5469. Tel.: 541-726-3677. Fax: 541-726-3688.
E-mail: dgruell@ci.springfield.or.us
Web Site: www.springfieldmuseum.com
Founded: 1981.
Congressional District: 4
Key Personnel: Dir., David Staton; Pres., Dione Young; Cur. & Registrar, Jan McKee.
Personnel Profile: Full-Time Paid 1; Part-Time Volunteers 45.
Governing Authority: municipal; nonprofit organization. Parent Institution: City of Springfield. Tax-exempt.
General Museum: housed in 1911 building.
Collections: costumes; photographs; documents; tools.
Research Fields: Springfield, Oregon's history.
Facilities: 2,300 sq. ft. exhibit space. Museum-related items for sale.
Activities: guided tours; organized education programs for children; temporary exhibitions; Historic Springfield Interpretive Center.
Publications: quarterly newsletter, Museum Notes; annual exhibit schedule; Historic Springfield Interpretive Center pamphlet.

Hours & Admission Prices: Tues.-Fri. 10-4, Sat. 12-4. Adults $2; discounts to OMA & AAM members; members no charge. Closed legal holidays. ♿
Attendance: 8,978 (accurate)
Membership: Individual & Senior Family $25; Family $50; Sponsor $75; Donor $100; Benefactor $250; Patron $500; Sustaining $1,000.

Sweet Home

EAST LINN MUSEUM, 746 Long St., Sweet Home, OR 97386-3303. Tel.: 541-367-4580.
Founded: 1976.
Congressional District: 4
Key Personnel: Pres. (V), Gail Gregory; Museum Shop Mgr., Glenda Hopkins.
Personnel Profile: Part-Time Volunteers 19.
Governing Authority: Tax-exempt.
History Museum.
Collections: local history & culture; photographs; personal artifacts; tools & equipment.
Hours & Admission Prices: Feb.- May & Sept. 8-Nov. Thurs.-Sat. 11-4, Sun. 1-4; June-Sept. Wed.-Sat. 11-4, Sun. 1-4. No charge; donations accepted. Closed Easter. ♿
Attendance: 2,500 (estimated)
Membership: Family $10; Supporting $25; Contributing $50.

The Dalles

* **COLUMBIA GORGE DISCOVERY CENTER AND WASCO COUNTY MUSEUM, (M),** 5000 Discovery Dr., The Dalles, OR 97058-9755. Tel.: 541-296-8600. Fax: 541-298-8660.
E-mail: collins@gorgediscovery.org
Web Site: www.gorgediscovery.org
Founded: 1997.
Congressional District: 2
Key Personnel: Chm. (V), William G. Dick, II; Exec. Dir., Carolyn Purcell; Museum Shop Mgr., Karen Austin; Asst. Dir., Kathleen Collins; Coord. Membership, Lori Fiegenbaum; Dir. Education, Steve Thompson.
Personnel Profile: Full-Time Paid 8; Part-Time Paid 10; Part-Time Volunteers 42.
Governing Authority: private; nonprofit. Tax-exempt: 501(c)(3).
Interpretive Center & Museum.
Collections: geologic history of the Columbia River Gorge; wildlife & natural history; Native American artifacts; Lewis and Clark; local industry; pioneer artifacts; photographs; documents; manuscripts; textiles; furnishings; petroglyphs.
Research Fields: cultural, historical & natural resources of the north & central Oregon region and the Columbia River Gorge; settlement history; Lewis and Clark archaeology.
Facilities: research library; cafe; classroom; picnic area; nature trails. Museum-related items for sale.
Activities: organized educational programs; permanent, temporary & traveling exhibits; special guest lectures; volunteer program & training; live raptor programs.
Publications: Fort Dalles Military Map; Plant and Animal Guide; quarterly newsletter; books, Celilo Falls: Remembering Thunder by Wilma Roberts; The Columbia Gorge Discovery Center and Wasco County Historical Museum Exhibit Book; A Road, a Railroad, and a Country Store: The Story of Boyd, Oregon by Nancy Ward; annual report; Cargo Exhibit Catalog.
Hours & Admission Prices: Daily 9-5. Adults $8, senior citizen & groups of 10 or more $6.50, children $4; discounts to AAM & AAA members; members no charge. Closed New Year's Day; Thanksgiving; Christmas. ♿
Attendance: 39,709 (accurate)
Membership: College Student, Teacher & Senior $25; Individual $35; Family Dual $50; Discovery $125; Business $125-$500.

THE DALLES ART ASSOCIATION, 220 E. 4th St., The Dalles, OR 97058-2206. Tel.: 541-296-4759.
E-mail: thedallesart@earthlink.net
Web Site: thedallesartcenter.org
Founded: 1967.
Congressional District: 2
Key Personnel: Dir., Carolyn Wright.
Personnel Profile: Part-Time Paid 1; Part-Time Volunteers 50.
Governing Authority: private; nonprofit organization. Tax-exempt: 501(c)(3).
Art Association Gallery.
Collections: paintings; photographs; sculpture.
Facilities: classroom.
Activities: student show; art auctions; monthly exhibits.
Publications: bimonthly newsletter; monthly showcard.
Hours & Admission Prices: mid-Jan. to Dec. Tues.-Sat. 11-5. No charge; donations accepted. Closed New Year's Day; Independence Day; Thanksgiving; Christmas. ♿
Attendance: 5,000 (estimated)
Membership: Student & Senior $25; Individual $35; Family $45; Business & Friend $75; Sponsor $100; Corporate & Sustaining $250; Benefactor $500; Associate $1,000.

FORT DALLES MUSEUM/ANDERSON HOMESTEAD, 500 W. 15th St., The Dalles, OR 97058-1527. Mailing Address: Box 806, The Dalles, OR 97058-0806. Tel.: 541-296-4547.
Web Site: www.historicthedalles.org/fort_dalles
Founded: 1951.
Congressional District: 2
Key Personnel: Chm. (V), Sam Woolsey; Museum Shop Mgr., Hilary Hines.
Personnel Profile: Part-Time Paid 7; Part-Time Volunteers 4.
Governing Authority: municipal; county. Parent Institution: Wasco County - City of The Dalles. Tax-exempt.
Historic Building Museum: 1856 Fort Dalles Surgeon's quarters.
Collections: history; military; vehicles.
Facilities: Gift items for sale.
Activities: permanent exhibitions.
Hours & Admission Prices: May 15-Sept. 15 daily 10-5. Call for off-season hours. Adults $5, seniors 55 & over $4, students 7-17 $1; discounts to groups; members no charge. Closed winter holidays.
Attendance: 2,750 (accurate)
Membership: Individual $15; Family $35; Rifle Regiment $100; Medical Officer $250; Commanding Officer $500; Inspector General $1,000 & up.

Tillamook

LATIMER QUILT AND TEXTILE CENTER, 2105 Wilson River Loop Rd., Tillamook, OR 97141. Tel.: 503-842-8622.
Textile Museum.
Collections: quilts; quilt blocks & templates; fabric samples; clothing; hand-woven coverlets; looms; spinning wheels; quilting & weaving textile tools & implements.
Facilities: library. Museum-related items for sale.
Activities: demonstrations; educational programs. Museum Sponsors: Tidal Treasures Quilt and Fiber Arts Festival in June.
Hours & Admission Prices: May-Sept. daily 10-5; Oct. & April Tues.-Sat. 10-4, Sun. 12-4; Nov.-March Tues.-Sat. 10-4. Admission $3; discounts to groups; members & children under 6 no charge. Closed New Year's Day; Independence Day; Thanksgiving; Christmas.

TILLAMOOK AIR MUSEUM, 6030 Hangar Rd., Tillamook, OR 97141-9641. Tel.: 503-842-1130. Fax: 503-842-3054.
E-mail: info@tillamookair.com
Web Site: www.tillamookair.com
Formerly: Tillamook Naval Air Station Museum
Founded: 1994.
Key Personnel: C.E.O., Mike Oliver; Cur., Christian Gurling; Museum Shop Mgr., Michelle Forster.
Personnel Profile: Full-Time Paid 6; Part-Time Paid 12.
General Museum.
Collections: top 5 U.S. war birds; aircraft 1917 to present; use of blimps in WWII.
Facilities: 47-seat restaurant; 300,000 sq. ft. exhibit space; 50-seat theater. Museum-related items for sale.
Activities: docent program; films.
Hours & Admission Prices: Daily 9-5. Adults $11.50, senior citizens $10.50, military with active ID $9, youth 6-17 $7; children 5 & under no charge. Closed Thanksgiving; Christmas. ♿
Attendance: 80,000 (accurate)

TILLAMOOK CHEESE FACTORY & VISITOR'S CENTER, 4175 Hwy. 101 N., Tillamook, OR 97141-7770. Tel.: 503-815-1300.
Web Site: www.tillamookcheese.com
Visitor Center.
Collections: artifacts & memorabilia pertaining to the history of the cheese-making process.
Hours & Admission Prices: mid-June to Labor Day daily 8-8; Sept.-June daily 8-6. No charge. Closed Thanksgiving; Christmas. ♿
Attendance: 950,000

TILLAMOOK COUNTY PIONEER MUSEUM, 2106 Second St., Tillamook, OR 97141-2399. Tel.: 503-842-4553. Fax: 503-842-4553.
E-mail: clb@tcpm.org
Web Site: www.tcpm.org
Founded: 1935.
Congressional District: 1
Key Personnel: Dir., Carol L. Brown.

Personnel Profile: Full-Time Paid 2; Part-Time Paid 2; Part-Time Volunteers 15.
Governing Authority: nonprofit association. Parent Institution: Tillamook County Pioneer Museum Foundation. Tax-exempt.
Historical Museum: housed in 1905 Old Courthouse.
Collections: pioneer artifacts; archaeology; natural history; dishes; rocks; minerals; zoology; mounted animals, birds & fish; wildlife & natural history dioramas; logging displays; great grandmother's kitchen; Victorian parlor; blacksmith shop; 1870s photos; genealogical files.
Facilities: library of county & state history books available for use on premises.
Activities: permanent exhibitions.
Publications: yearly historical calendar.
Hours & Admission Prices: Tues.-Sat. 9-5, Sun. 11-5. Research Library: Tues.-Fri. 9-5, Sat. 10-4 or by appointment. Families $7, adults $3, seniors $2.50, students 12-17 $.50; discounts to AAM members; children under 12 no charge. Closed major holidays.
Attendance: 36,000 (estimated)

Toledo

TOLEDO HISTORICAL MUSEUM AT TOLEDO CITY HALL, 206 N. Main St., Toledo, OR 97391-1536. Tel.: 541-265-7509.
History Museum.
Collections: historical photographic exhibits pertaining to logging, railroad & settlement history of the area.
Hours & Admission Prices: Mon.-Fri. 8-5, Sat.-Sun. by appointment.

YAQUINA PACIFIC RAILROAD HISTORICAL SOCIETY, 100 N.W. A St., Toledo, OR 97391-1570. Mailing Address: P.O. Box 119, Toledo, OR 97391-0119. Tel.: 541-336-5256.
E-mail: office@yaquinapacificrr.org
Web Site: www.yaquinapacificrr.org
Key Personnel: Pres. (V), Bill Bain.
Personnel Profile: Part-Time Paid 1.
Railroad History Museum.
Collections: railroad & timber history; period railroad rolling stock & equipment.
Publications: monthly, Yaquina Shortline.
Hours & Admission Prices: Tues.-Sat. 10-2. No charge; donations accepted. ♿
Attendance: 1,500 (accurate)
Membership: Participating $38; Supporting $58; Sustaining $100; Bronze Spike $250; Silver Spike $500; Golden Spike $1,000; Platinum Spike $3,000.

YAQUINA RIVER MUSEUM OF ART, 151 N.E. Alder St., Toledo, OR 97391-1521. Tel.: 541-336-1907. Fax: 541-336-1907.
E-mail: yrartmuseum@charter.net
Web Site: www.michaelgibbons.net/museum.htm
Key Personnel: Cur., Michael Gibbons
Art Museum.
Collections: artwork by Michael Gibbons & other local artists.
Hours & Admission Prices: Fri.-Sun. 11-6.

Trail

TRAIL TAVERN MUSEUM, 144 Old Hwy. 62, Trail, OR 97541. Mailing Address: P.O. Box 245, Trail, OR 97541-0245. Tel.: 541-621-4462.
History Museum: housed in a former tavern.
Collections: historical artifacts & memorabilia pertaining to the life on the Upper Rogue River.
Hours & Admission Prices: April-Oct. Wed.-Sun. 11:30-4:30; Nov.-March Sat.-Sun. 11:30-4:30; other times by appointment.

Troutdale

TROUTDALE HISTORICAL SOCIETY, 726 E. Historic Columbia River Hwy., Troutdale, OR 97060-2061. Mailing Address: 104 S.E. Kibling, Troutdale, OR 97060-2012. Tel.: 503-661-2164. Fax: 503-674-2995.
E-mail: info@troutdalehistory.org
Web Site: www.troutdalehistory.org
Founded: 1968.
Key Personnel: Pres., Scott Cuningham; Vice Pres. & Museum Shop Mgr., Mona Mitchoff; Cur., Mary Bryson; Historian, Sharon Nesbit.
Personnel Profile: Full-Time Volunteers 2; Part-Time Paid 1; Part-Time Volunteers 45.
Governing Authority: private; nonprofit organization. Branch Museums: Rail Depot Museum, 473 E. Historic Columbia River Hwy., Troutdale, OR; Harlow House Museum, 726 E. Historic Columbia River Hwy., Troutdale, OR; Barn Museum, 732 E. Historic Columbia River Hwy., Troutdale, OR. Tax-exempt: 501(c)(3).
Historical Society Museum.
Collections: photographs; furnishings; structures. Historic Buildings: Harlow House, 1900 historic home containing period furnishings; Rail Depot Museum, 1907 Depot (Union Pacific) containing local railroad related artifacts; Barn Museum.
Research Fields: Lewis & Clark.
Facilities: library. Museum-related items for sale.
Activities: monthly education programs. Annual Events: Historic Tea & Tour in May; Cemetery Tour in May; Ice Cream Social in June; Trek in September.
Publications: monthly newsletter, Bygone Times.
Hours & Admission Prices: Depot: Tues.-Fri. 10-4. Harlow House & Barn: call for hours. No charge; donations accepted. ♿
Attendance: 2,500 (estimated)
Membership: Individual $20; Family $30. Lovers Oak Club: Individual $100; Family $150. Business Sponsor $250.

Umatilla

UMATILLA MUSEUM & HISTORICAL FOUNDATION, 911 Sixth St., Umatilla, OR 97882. Mailing Address: P.O. Box 975, Umatilla, OR 97882-0975. Tel.: 541-922-0209.
Founded: 1992.
Key Personnel: Pres. (V), Jodi Hansen.
Personnel Profile: Part-Time Volunteers 12.
Governing Authority: Tax-exempt.
History Museum.
Collections: Umatilla history & culture; period furnishings; military artifacts; photographs.
Activities: special events; educational programs.
Hours & Admission Prices: Call for hours. No charge; donations accepted. ♿
Membership: Student $5; Senior 60 & over $10; Senior Couple $18; Individual $20; Couple $35; Business $50; Patron $100; Donor $250.

Union

UNION COUNTY MUSEUM, 311 S. Main St., Union, OR 97883. Mailing Address: P.O. Box 190, Union, OR 97883-0190. Tel.: 541-562-6003.
Founded: 1969.
Congressional District: 2
Key Personnel: Pres. (V), Sharon Hohstadt; Museum Shop Mgr., Carol Mulvany.
Governing Authority: society; nonprofit. Tax-exempt: 501(c)(3).
History Museum: housed in 1881 former First National Bank of Union building.
Collections: settlement & development of Union County, including artifacts, photographs & manuscripts dating from 1830-present.
Research Fields: development of Union County oral history & historic buildings & sites.
Facilities: 100-vol. library of local and regional history & environment, maps, photos & unpublished research, available for use upon application to the curator; reading room; 50-seat auditorium.
Activities: guided tours; lectures; reading room; educational programs for schools.
Publications: quarterly newsletter, The Scout.
Hours & Admission Prices: Mother's Day-Columbus Day Mon.-Sat. 10-4; other times by appointment. Adults $4, senior citizens $3, students $2; members no charge. ♿
Attendance: 300 (estimated)
Membership: Annual $10; Family $20; Business $50; Life $300.

Vale

MALHEUR HISTORICAL PROJECT, STONEHOUSE MUSEUM, (M), 255 Main St., Vale, OR 97918. Mailing Address: P.O. Box 413, Vale, OR 97918-0413. Tel.: 541-473-2070.
Founded: 1995.
Key Personnel: Pres., Gary Fugate; Treas., Charlotte Fugate.
Personnel Profile: Part-Time Volunteers 30.
Governing Authority: private; nonprofit organization. Tax-exempt: 501(c)(3).
Historic House: 1872 stone house built as a wayside house on the Oregon Trail.
Collections: ancient Indian artifacts & local historical artifacts, documents & photographs of Malheur County & the Oregon Trail and the Northern Piautes & Bannock Indians.
Research Fields: survey of historical sites in Malheur County.
Facilities: library; botanical garden; 800 sq. ft. exhibit space; research facility.
Activities: docent programs; guided tours; lectures; temporary exhibitions. Annual Event: Independence Day celebrations.
Publications: quarterly newsletter, Stone House.
Hours & Admission Prices: May-Oct. Tues.-Sat. 12-4. No charge; donations accepted. ♿
Attendance: 3,000 (estimated)

Membership: Seniors & Students $10; Individuals $12; Family $25.

Vernonia

VERNONIA PIONEER MUSEUM, 511 E. Bridge St., Vernonia, OR 97064-1406. Mailing Address: P.O. Box 26, Vernonia, OR 97064-0026. Tel.: 503-429-3713. Fax: 503-429-9411.
E-mail: VPMA@agalis.net
Web Site: vernonia-or.gov
Formerly: Vernonia Historical Museum
Founded: 1962.
Key Personnel: Pres. (V), Carol Davis; Vice Pres., Ralph Keasey; Sec., Barbara Larsen.
Personnel Profile: Part-Time Volunteers 12.
Governing Authority: county. Affiliated with Oregon State Historical Society. Parent Institution: Veronia Arts & Heritage Association. Tax-exempt.
Historical Museum: housed in the old Oregon American Mill office built in the late 1920s; listed on the National Register of Historic Places.
Collections: history of Nehalem Valley pioneers; logging; photographs; 1930s sawmill.
Publications: bimonthly newsletter.
Hours & Admission Prices: June-Aug. Fri.-Sun. 1-4; Sept.-May Sat.-Sun. 1-4. No charge; donations accepted. Closed New Year's Day; Easter; Mother's Day; Independence Day; Independence Day; Christmas. ♿
Attendance: 1,000 (accurate)
Membership: Single $15; Couple $20; Family $25.

Waldport

WALDPORT HERITAGE MUSEUM, 320 N.E. Grant St., Waldport, OR 97394. Mailing Address: P.O. Box 822, Waldport, OR 97394-0822. Tel.: 541-563-7092.
E-mail: waldportmuseum@peak.org
Founded: 1997.
Key Personnel: Pres., Colleen Nickerson; Pres. (V), Judy Gibbs.
Governing Authority: Managed by the Alsi Historical & Genealogical Society.
History Museum.
Collections: historical artifacts & memorabilia; genealogy.
Major Exhibits: Pioneer of the Year, 9/10.
Hours & Admission Prices: Wed.-Fri. 12-4, Sat.-Sun. 10-4. No charge; donations accepted. ♿
Attendance: 797 (accurate)
Membership: Single $5; Family $10; Business $25; Lifetime $50.

Warm Springs

THE MUSEUM AT WARM SPRINGS, 2189 Hwy. 26, Warm Springs, OR 97761. Mailing Address: P.O. Box 909, Warm Springs, OR 97761-0909. Tel.: 541-553-3331. Fax: 541-553-3338.
E-mail: carol@redmond-net.com
Web Site: www.warmsprings.com/museum/
Founded: 1991.
Congressional District: 2
Key Personnel: Exec. Dir., Carol Leone; Office Mgr. & Bd. Sec., Beulah N. Tsumpti; Pres. (V), Roberta Kirk; Vice Pres., Hon. Victor Atiyeh; Devel. Officer, Dora Goudy-Smith; Receptionist, Leanne Blueback; Cur., Natalie Kirk; Archivist, Evaline Patt; Museum Shop Mgr., Debra Stacona.
Personnel Profile: Full-Time Paid 13; Part-Time Volunteers 18; Interns 1.
Governing Authority: private; nonprofit organization. Parent Institutions: The Confederated Tribes of the Warm Springs Reservation of Oregon. Tax-exempt: 501(c)(3).
Tribal Museum.
Collections: artifacts & archival material that explain the culture & heritage of the Warm Springs, Wasco & Paiute Tribes that comprise the Confederated Tribes of the Warm Springs Reservation of Oregon; teepee.
Facilities: library; photo archives; river walkway. Museum-related items for sale.
Activities: educational programs; cultural workshops; storytelling for school tours; demonstrations; crafts; lectures; permanent & temporary exhibitions. Museum Sponsors: living traditions all summer; community craft fairs, Memorial & Labor Day weekends.
Publications: quarterly newsletter, TWANAT.
Hours & Admission Prices: mid-March to mid-Nov. daily 9-5; mid-Nov. to mid-March Wed.-Sun. 9-5. Adults $6, seniors $5, children $3; discount to groups; AAM, ICOM, Western Museums Assoc., OMA, AASLH members & members no charge. Closed New Year's Day; Thanksgiving; Christmas. ♿
Attendance: 20,000 (estimated)
Membership: Senior Citizen $25; Individual $35; Family $45; Fellow $65; Sponsor $100; Sustainer $250; Contributor $500; Patron $1,000; Benefactor $2,500.

Woodburn

WOODBURN MUSEUM, 455 N. Front St., Woodburn, OR 97071-3931. Tel.: 503-980-2416.
Web Site: www.woodburn-or.gov/communitydevelopment/history/default.aspx
History Museum.
Collections: Woodburn's history, agriculture, farming, railroad, social, educational & civic heritage.
Hours & Admission Prices: March-Dec. Fri.-Sat. 11-3; other times by appointment.

Yachats

LITTLE LOG CHURCH & MUSEUM, 328 W. Third St., Yachats, OR 97498. Mailing Address: P.O. Box 712, Yachats, OR 97498-0712. Tel.: 541-547-3976.
Key Personnel: Dir., Karl Christianson
Historic Building Museum: housed in the former Little Log Church; built in the shape of a cross.
Collections: local history; books; photographs; sculptures; personal artifacts; drawings; paintings.
Activities: weddings; memorials; special events.
Hours & Admission Prices: Fri.-Wed. 12-3.

PENNSYLVANIA

(452 listings)

Abington

BRIAR BUSH NATURE CENTER, 1212 Edge Hill Rd., Abington, PA 19001-3203. Tel.: 215-887-6603. Fax: 215-887-9079.
Web Site: www.briarbush.org
Founded: 1962.
Congressional District: 13
Key Personnel: Exec. Dir., Dede Long; Pres., Henry Geyer; Devel. Coord., Anne-Marie D'Onofrio; Environment Education-Outreach, Jeffrey Moore; Environmental Educator & Public Rels. Coord., Kristen Facente; Treas., Kathy Moore; Sr. Naturalist, Mark Fallon.
Personnel Profile: Full-Time Paid 7; Part-Time Paid 10; Part-Time Volunteers 150; Interns 3.
Governing Authority: municipal; nonprofit organization. Parent Institution: Abington Township. Subsidiary Institution: Friends of Briar Bush. Tax-exempt: 501(c)(3).
Nature Center.
Collections: ecology of the mid-Atlantic states; live animals; active beehive; pond fed by windmill pump; wildflowers; plants of woodland; seeds; shells; rocks.
Facilities: 1,000-vol. library pertaining to science & nature; nature & conservation center; bird observatory; 60-seat meeting room; nature trails. Museum-related items for sale.
Activities: guided tours; lectures; films; organized environmental education programs; docent program; participatory exhibits; school programs; after school programs; birding trips; crawl through cave; seasonal butterfly house; Nature Playscape.
Publications: newsletter, Briar Flyer; blog, The Briar Blog.
Hours & Admission Prices: Observatory & Museum: Mon.-Sat. 9-5, Sun. 1-5. Nature Trails sunrise-sunset. No charge; donations accepted. Closed holidays. ♿
Attendance: 65,000 (accurate)
Membership: Senior Citizen $20; Individual $25; Family $40.

Alexandria

HARTSLOG HERITAGE MUSEUM, Alexandria Public Library, 2nd Fl., Main St., Alexandria, PA 16611. Mailing Address: P.O. Box 3, Alexandria, PA 16611-0003. Tel.: 814-669-4313.
History Museum.
Collections: area history; carpentry & blacksmith tools; period furniture & clothing; paintings; tableware; photographs; business records.
Hours & Admission Prices: 1st Sun. of month 2-4; other times by appointment. No charge; donations accepted.

Allentown

* **ALLENTOWN ART MUSEUM, (M),** 31 N. Fifth St., Allentown, PA 18101-1616. Mailing Address: P.O. Box 388, Allentown, PA 18105-0388. Tel.: 610-432-4333. Fax: 610-434-7409.
E-mail: info@allentownartmuseum.org
Web Site: allentownartmuseum.org

Founded: 1934.
Congressional District: 15
Key Personnel: Interim Exec. Dir., Robert Metzger; Pres. (V), Gary L. Millenbruch; Dir. Devel., Elsbeth Haymon; Mgr. Government & Foundations Rels., Rhonda K. Mauk; The Kate Fowler Merle-Smith Textile Cur., Dr. Jacqueline M. Atkins; Registrar, Karen Barlow; Museum Shop Mgr., Sharon Yurkanin; Bldg. Operations Mgr., Douglas Bowerman.
Personnel Profile: Full-Time Paid 31; Part-Time Paid 18; Part-Time Volunteers 300; Interns 12.
Governing Authority: nonprofit organization. Tax-exempt.
Art Museum.
Collections: European & American paintings & sculpture; prints; drawings; textiles; decorative arts.
Research Fields: pertinent to collection.
Facilities: 15,000-vol. library; 150-seat auditorium; cafe. Catalogs, reproductions & postcards for sale.
Activities: guided tours; lectures; films; gallery talks; concerts; permanent, temporary & traveling exhibitions; school loan service.
Publications: quarterly newsletter; exhibition catalogues.
Hours & Admission Prices: Wed.-Sat. 11-5, Sun. 12-5. Adults $6, senior citizens $4, children & students (with valid ID) $3; discounts to AAM members; children under 6, members & Sun. no charge; additional fee for special exhibitions. Closed national holidays. ♿
Attendance: 103,500 (accurate)
Membership: Student $20; Senior $35; Individual $45; Household $60; Contributor $100; Sustainer $200; Patron $500; Kress $1,000 & up.

AMERICA ON WHEELS, 5 N. Front St., Allentown, PA 18102-5303. Tel.: 610-432-4200. Fax: 610-432-3670.
Web Site: www.americaonwheels.org
Founded: 1994.
Congressional District: 15
Key Personnel: Exec. Dir., Linda Merkel; Pres. (V), Jack Curcio.
Personnel Profile: Full-Time Paid 3; Part-Time Paid 2; Part-Time Volunteers 50.
Governing Authority: private; nonprofit organization. Tax-exempt: 501(c)(3).
Transportation Museum.
Collections: vehicles; transportation history & artifacts.
Major Exhibits: Custom and Concept Cars, 1/10-4/10.
Facilities: 300-vol. library; classroom; 23,000 sq. ft. exhibit space; 40-seat theater; rental facilities. Museum-related items for sale.
Activities: group tours; educational programs; workshops; corporate events & symposiums; birthday parties; anniversary & wedding receptions.
Publications: newsletter, Spoke & Word.
Hours & Admission Prices: Tues.-Sat. 10-5, Sun. 12-5. Adults $7, seniors 62 & over $5, children 6-16 $3.50; discount to AOW & AAA members. Closed New Year's Day; Independence Day; Thanksgiving; Christmas. ♿
Attendance: 75,000
Membership: Annual $35-$2,500.

DA VINCI SCIENCE CENTER, 3145 Hamilton Blvd. Bypass, Allentown, PA 18103-3686. Tel.: 484-664-1002. Fax: 484-664-1022.
Key Personnel: Exec. Dir., Troy A. Thrash
Science Center.
Collections: hands-on science exhibits; photographs; videos; Hall of Fame.
Activities: special events; educational programs.
Hours & Admission Prices: Mon.-Sat. 9:30-5, Sun. 12-5. Adults $9.95, seniors 62 & over, military, and children 4-12 $7.95; children 3 & under no charge.

LEHIGH VALLEY HERITAGE MUSEUM, 432 W. Walnut St., Allentown, PA 18102-5428. Tel.: 610-435-1074, ext. 19. Fax: 610-435-9812.
Web Site: www.lchs.museum
Formerly: Lehigh County Historical Society
Founded: 1904.
Congressional District: 15
Key Personnel: Exec. Dir., Joseph Garrera; Museum Cur., Dir. Library & Archives, Jill Youngken; Reference Librarian, Carol Herrity; Dir. Education, Sarah Thayer Nelson.
Personnel Profile: Full-Time Paid 10; Full-Time Volunteers 5; Part-Time Paid 32; Part-Time Volunteers 125; Interns 2.
Governing Authority: society; nonprofit corporation. Branch Museums & Historic Sites: (1756) Troxell-Steckel House & Farm Museum, Egypt, PA; (1768) George Taylor House, Catasauqua, PA; (1770) Trout Hall, Allentown, PA; (1760) Haines Mill, Allentown, PA; (1817) Lehigh County Museum, Allentown, PA; (1892) David O. Saylor Cement Industry Museum, Coplay, PA; (1868) Lock Ridge Furnace Museum, Alburtis, PA; (1893) One-Room Schoolhouse, Claussville. Tax-exempt: 501(c)(3).
Historical Society.
Collections: 35,000 objects of decorative arts; furniture; textiles; architectural elements; agricultural & industrial tools & equipment; fine & folk art; domestic equipment; Lenni Lenape Indian materials; horse-drawn & motorized vehicles; 3 million documents, maps, government records, personal papers, business & commercial records; religious & social manuscripts & printed texts; genealogical materials; Pennsylvania German decorative texts & fraktur; 65,000 photographs & negatives; 10,000 books. Historic Buildings: Reninger House (c.1860); Gruber House (c.1912).
Research Fields: Lehigh Valley social, economic, cultural, architectural history; genealogy.
Facilities: 10,000-vol. research library; classrooms; 250-seat lecture hall; 13,000 sq. ft. exhibit space. Museum-related items for sale.
Activities: permanent & temporary exhibitions; inter-museum loans; guided tours; formally organized education programs for students K-12; undergraduate & graduate internships; lectures; films; workshops; bus tour travel program; special events; holiday programs; outdoor festivals & concerts.
Publications: quarterly newsletter; semiannual bulletins; biennial book, Proceedings of the Lehigh County Historical Society; occasional papers; newsletter, Town Crier; books, Allentown 1762-1987: A 225-Year History; Yuscht fer Schee: Architectural Ornament in Allentown; Hidden From History: The Latino Community of Allentown, Pennsylvania.
Hours & Admission Prices: Museum: Tues.-Sat. 10-4, Sun. 11-4. Adults $6, children $3; members no charge. Taylor House & Troxell-Steckel House & Barn: June-Oct. Sat.-Sun. 1-4. Adults $5. Trout Hall: April-Nov. Tues.-Sat. 12-3, Sun. 1-4. Adults $5; discounts to groups. Lock Ridge Furnace Museum & Haines Mill: May-Sept. Sat.-Sun. 1-4. No charge. Claussville Schoolhouse: by appointment. Adults $5. Saylor Cement Museum: daily. No charge. Research $6. Closed major holidays. ♿
Attendance: 36,500 (estimated)
Membership: Student $15; Individual $35; Family $50; Patron $100; Contributing $250; Sustaining $500; Benefactor $1,000.

MARTIN ART GALLERY, Baker Center for the Arts, Muhlenberg College, Allentown, PA 18104. Tel.: 484-664-3467. Fax: 484-664-3633.
E-mail: kburke@muhlenberg.edu
Web Site: www.muhlenberg.edu/cultural/gallery
Founded: 1976.
Personnel Profile: Full-Time Paid 1; Part-Time Paid 3; Interns 1.
Governing Authority: Parent Institution: Muhlenberg College. Tax-exempt.
College Art Gallery.
Collections: paintings; works on paper; sculpture.
Major Exhibits: Exploring the Etching Revival, 1/20/10-2/20/10; Lehigh Art Alliance 75th Anniversary Juried Exhibition, 6/4/10-7/10; Joseph Elliott: New Work, 9/10.
Publications: exhibition booklets.
Hours & Admission Prices: Tues.-Sat. 12-8. No charge. Closed all major holidays; semester breaks. ♿
Attendance: 7,000 (estimated)

MUSEUM OF INDIAN CULTURE, 2825 Fish Hatchery Rd., Allentown, PA 18103-9214. Tel.: 610-797-2121. Fax: 610-797-2801.
E-mail: info@museumofindianculture.org
Web Site: www.museumofindianculture.org
Formerly: Lenni Lenape Historical Society
Founded: 1980.
Key Personnel: C.E.O., Pat Rivera; Cur., Archivist & Registrar, Lee Hallman.
Personnel Profile: Full-Time Volunteers 5; Part-Time Volunteers 12; Interns 2.
Governing Authority: private; nonprofit organization. Tax-exempt: 501(c)(3).
Historical Society & Museum.
Collections: concentration on Northeast Woodland Indians & Inter Tribal with some early Pennsylvania German artifacts.
Research Fields: Northeast Woodland Indians.
Facilities: 3,100-vol. library; 18th-century farm house. Gift items for sale.
Activities: arts festivals; formal educational programs; guided tours; hobby workshops; lectures; participatory, loan & traveling exhibitions. Annual Events: Spring Corn Festival in May; Roasting Ears of Corn Food Festival in August; A Time of Thanksgiving in October.
Publications: quarterly newsletter, Indian Culture Quarterly.
Hours & Admission Prices: Jan.-Feb. Sat.-Sun. 12-4; March-Dec. Fri.-Sun. 12-4. Adults $5, seniors & children 12-17 $4; members no charge. Closed national holidays. ♿
Attendance: 14,000 (estimated)
Membership: Senior Citizen, Students & Teachers $20; Individual $30; Family $50; Sponsor $100-$499; Patron $500-$999; Benefactor $1,000 & up.

Allenwood

CLYDE PEELING'S REPTILAND, 18628 U.S. Route 15, Allenwood, PA 17810-9731. Tel.: 570-538-1869. Fax: 570-538-1714.
E-mail: info@reptiland.com
Web Site: www.reptiland.com

Founded: 1964.
Key Personnel: C.E.O., Clyde Peeling; Cur., Chad Peeling; Office Mgr. & Museum Shop Mgr., Chris Peeling; Exhibit Designer, Elliot Peeling.
Personnel Profile: Full-Time Paid 19; Part-Time Paid 6; Part-Time Volunteers 3; Interns 2.
Governing Authority: individual operation organized for profit.
Zoo.
Collections: reptiles; amphibians; birds.
Major Exhibits: Butterfly Greenhouse, 5/10-10/10.
Facilities: botanical garden; 250-seat theatre; zoological park. Jewelry, books & other zoo-related items for sale.
Activities: lectures; theatre; formally organized education programs for children; traveling exhibitions; TV & radio programs.
Publications: newsletter, Reptiletter.
Hours & Admission Prices: April-May & Sept.-Oct. daily 10-6; Memorial Day-Labor Day daily 9-7; Nov.-March daily 10-5. Adults $12, children 3-11 $10; children under 3 & members no charge. Closed New Year's Day; Thanksgiving; Christmas. ♿
Attendance: 35,000 (estimated)
Membership: Individual $39; Family of Two $49 (each additional member $12).

Allison Park

DEPRECIATION LANDS MUSEUM, 4743 S. Pioneer Rd., Allison Park, PA 15101-2400. Mailing Address: P.O. Box 174, Allison Park, PA 15101-0174. Tel.: 412-486-0563.
Founded: 1974.
Congressional District: 14
Key Personnel: Chm. (V), Glenn Jones; Pres. (V), Judy Tutino; Treas. Assoc., Susan Love; Treas. & Sec. Commission, Jessie N. Wink; Museum Shop Mgr., Susan Addis-Stanny.
Personnel Profile: Part-Time Volunteers 15.
Governing Authority: municipal. Parent Institution: Hampton Township. Affiliated with The Hampton Historical Commission, 3101 McCully Rd., Allison Park 15101. Tax-exempt.
History Museum: housed in c.1839 Covenanter Church, a Greek Revival church, located on The Depreciation Lands.
Collections: The Depreciation Lands history; log house; herb & dye gardens; cemetery; wagon (Kramer); tool barn; 1-room schoolhouse, furnishings including pot-bellied stove; old desks-different sizes for children; teacher's desk; books; slates; blacksmith shop; gunsmithing shop; forge; tools; old time sleigh; period bake oven.
Research Fields: Indian Wars of 1784-1795; causes of the financial problems of the Revolutionary War soldiers; history of the soldiers who took up tracts in these lands.
Facilities: Nature & Conservation Center; library includes reports related to the Depreciation Lands, old school books & township histories and maps; the Indian Wars. Museum-related items for sale.
Activities: tours; lectures; education programs; permanent & temporary exhibitions. Annual Events: Colonial Teas in February; Fall Festival in October; Halloween Tours in October; Colonial Market & Settlers' Christmas in December.
Publications: monthly newsletter.
Hours & Admission Prices: Jan.-March by appointment only; April-Dec. Sun. 1-4. Adults $3; members no charge. ♿
Attendance: 8,000 (estimated)
Membership: Single $15; Family & Group $50.

Altoona

QUAINT CORNER CHILDREN'S MUSEUM, 2000 Union Ave., Altoona, PA 16601-2059. Tel.: 814-944-6830.
Web Site: www.quaintcorner.org
Key Personnel:
Governing Authority: nonprofit organization. Tax-exempt: 501(c)(3).
Children's Museum: housed in the former home of Daniel O'Rorke; built 1893.
Collections: hands-on exhibits.
Activities: birthday parties; classes; programs.
Hours & Admission Prices: Fri.-Sat. 10-5. Family $5.

RAILROADERS MEMORIAL MUSEUM, 1300 9th Ave., Altoona, PA 16602-2487. Tel.: 814-946-0834. Fax: 814-946-9457.
E-mail: admin@railroadcity.com
Web Site: www.railroadcity.com
Founded: 1972.
Congressional District: 9
Key Personnel: C.E.O. & Exec. Dir., Larry Salone; Chm. (V), Dr. Andy Mulhollen; Museum Shop Mgr., Cyndi Hershey.
Personnel Profile: Full-Time Paid 4; Part-Time Paid 10; Part-Time Volunteers 60.
Governing Authority: nonprofit organization. Subsidiary Institution: Horseshoe Curve National Historic Landmark. Tax-exempt: 501(c)(3).
Railroad Museum.
Collections: railroading artifacts; paintings; photographs; documents; communications equipment; uniforms; models; tools; rolling stock; GG-1; RPO car; dining car; K-4 & 0-4-0 steam locomotives.
Research Fields: Walter L. Main circus wreck; oral history research; ethnicity.
Facilities: 2,000-vol. library available for public use; 45,000 sq. ft. interpretive center; 80-seat auditorium. Museum-related items for sale.
Activities: guided tours; lectures; films; hobby workshops; docent program; loan & temporary exhibitions; school loan service.
Publications: books, The Wreck of the Red Arrow; Great Circus Train Wreck of 1893; quarterly newsletter, The Standard.
Hours & Admission Prices: Museum: May-Oct. daily 10-5; Nov.-Dec. Fri.-Mon. 10-5. Horseshoe Curve: April & Oct. daily 10-4; May daily 10-5; June-Sept. daily 10-6. Museum & Horseshoe Curve: adults $9, seniors $7, children 4-12 $5. Horseshoe Curve: $5. Closed Thanksgiving; Christmas. ♿
Attendance: 113,356 (accurate)
Membership: Associate $25; Contributing $50; Trustee $150; Benefactor $500; Patron $1,000. Corporate: Silver $500; Gold $1,000; Diamond $2,500; Platinum $5,000.

SOUTHERN ALLEGHENIES MUSEUM OF ART AT ALTOONA, 1210 11th Ave., Altoona, PA 16601. Tel.: 814-946-4464. Fax: 814-946-3131.
Key Personnel: Dir., Gary Moyer
Art Museum.
Collections: photographs; prints; paintings.
Major Exhibits: Antique Dolls, 11/13/09-1/10; Steve Gilbert, 1/15/10-4/10/10; Ken Cotlar, 2/19/10-5/16/10; Forbidden: Forever Cuba, 4/16/10-8/14/10; Ben Jones, 5/28/10-8/22/10.
Activities: special events; permanent & temporary exhibitions. Museum Sponsors: Summer Art Camp in July; The Art of Wine in November.
Hours & Admission Prices: Tues.-Fri. 10-5, Sat. 1-5. No charge; donations accepted. ♿
Membership: Student & Senior Citizen $25; Individual & Artist $35; Family $50-$99; Sponsor $100-$249; Sustaining $250-$499; Benefactor $500-$999; Connoisseur $1,000-$1,499; Exhibition Sponsor $1,500; Education Sponsor $2,500; Museum Associate $5,000; Director's Circle $10,000.

Ambler

THE STOOGEUM, 904 Sheble Lane, Ambler, PA 19002. Mailing Address: P.O. Box 747, Gwynedd Valley, PA 19437-0747. Tel.: 267-468-0810.
E-mail: garystooge@aol.com
Web Site: www.stoogeum.com
Key Personnel: Cur., Gary Lassin
Comedy Museum.
Collections: Three Stooges memorabilia from 1918 to present; personal artifacts; movie props & costumes; photographs; movie posters; toys; games; artwork; hands-on exhibits.
Facilities: library; 85-seat theater.
Activities: films; lectures; special presentations. Annual Event: Three Stooges Fan Club meeting.
Publications: journal, The Three Stooges.
Hours & Admission Prices: Open one Sat. per month (check website for dates) 10-3. No charge. ♿
Attendance: 2,500 (estimated)

Ambridge

OLD ECONOMY VILLAGE, 270 Sixteenth St., Ambridge, PA 15003-2225. Tel.: 724-266-4500. Fax: 724-266-3010.
E-mail: mlandis@state.pa.us
Web Site: www.oldeconomyvillage.org
Founded: 1919.
Congressional District: 4
Key Personnel: Site Dir., Mary Ann Landis; Pres. (V), Brian Hayden; Devel. Mgr., Linda Thomas; Office Coord., Elaine Voss; Museum Shop Mgr., Lynn Popovich.
Personnel Profile: Full-Time Paid 12; Part-Time Paid 3; Part-Time Volunteers 150.
Governing Authority: state. Commonwealth of Pennsylvania. Parent Institution: Pennsylvania Historical & Museum Commission, Box 1026, Harrisburg, PA 17108. Tax-exempt.
Historic Village Museum: 18 buildings of the original town of Economy (now Ambridge), PA, built between 1824 & 1831.
Collections: history; communitarian society; textiles; technology; manuscript collections; industrial; decorative arts; archives. Historic Buildings: George & Frederick Rapp Houses; 1826 grotto; 1826 Baker House (family dwelling); 1826 cabinet shop; 1827 store; 1827 granary; 1828 feast hall, mechanics' building; 1831 pavilion.

Major Exhibits: Harmony in Wood, 11/09-12/31/09.
Research Fields: textiles & textile manufacturing; religion; furniture; early 19th century methods of life in communal society; 19th century business history of Western PA.
Facilities: 5,000-vol. library of the Harmony Society available by appointment on premises; classrooms; outdoor museum. Handicrafts & museum-related items for sale.
Activities: guided tours; lectures; films; concerts; formally organized educational programs; docent program; permanent & temporary exhibitions. Museum Sponsors: Young Harmonists.
Publications: newsletter, Bibliography of Harmony Society; guidebook, manuals for guides & docents.
Hours & Admission Prices: EST: Tues.-Sat. 9-5, Sun. 12-5. Adults 12-64 $9, senior citizens 65 & over $8, children 3-11 $6; discount to AAA members; children under 2 & members no charge. Closed New Year's Day; Martin Luther King Jr. Day; Presidents Day; Columbus Day; Veterans Day; Thanksgiving; Christmas. ♿
Attendance: 24,500 (accurate)
Membership: Student $15; Individual $25; Family & Grandparent $40; Friends $100; Patron $250; Benefactor $500; Sustaining $1,000.

Annville

SUZANNE H. ARNOLD ART GALLERY, LEBANON VALLEY COLLEGE, (M), 101 N. College Ave., Annville, PA 17003-1404. Tel.: 717-867-6445. Fax: 717-867-6124.
Web Site: www.lvc.edu/gallery
Founded: 1994.
Congressional District: 17
Key Personnel: Dir., Lisa Tice; Co Chm., Richard Charles; Registrar & Cur., Crista Detweiler.
Personnel Profile: Full-Time Paid 2; Part-Time Volunteers 6.
Governing Authority: private college. Tax-exempt: 501(c)(3).
Art Museum.
Collections: Pennsylvania Fraktur, Chinese, African & Inuit art; prints; paintings; sculpture; photographs.
Major Exhibits: Carol Brown Goldberg, 1/15/10-2/21/10; Piranesi: The Grandeur of Rome, 3/5/10-4/25/10; 39th Annual Juried Exhibition, 4/30/10-5/9/10.
Facilities: 200-seat auditorium; 1,000 sq. ft. exhibit space.
Activities: concerts; formal education programs for college students; guided tours; lectures; loan exhibitions. Annual Event: Artist's Demonstrations.
Publications: biannual newsletter, Friends of the Gallery.
Hours & Admission Prices: Wed. 5-8pm, Thurs.-Fri. 1-4:30, Sat.-Sun. 11-5. No charge; donations accepted. Closed during college holidays. ♿
Attendance: 4,500 (estimated)
Membership: Individual $35-$59; Family $60-$99; Sustainer $100-$249; Sponsor $250-$499; Patron $500-$999; Director $1,000-$4,999; Benefactor $5,000 & up.

Ashland

PIONEER TUNNEL COAL MINE & STEAM TRAIN, 19th & Oak Sts., Ashland, PA 17921. Tel.: 570-875-3850 & 3301.
E-mail: ashpa@ptd.net
Web Site: www.pioneertunnel.com
Founded: 1962.
Key Personnel: Gen. Mgr., Howard Smith; Business Mgr., Kathy Lattis
Mining Museum.
Collections: history of mining; 1920s steam locomotive.
Activities: coal mine tour; train ride; festivals. Annual Event: Pioneer Day in August.
Hours & Admission Prices: Mine Tours: April daily 11, 12:30 & 2; May & Sept.-Oct. Mon.-Fri. 11, 12:30 & 2, Sat.-Sun. 10-6; Memorial Day to Labor Day: daily 10-6. Coal Mine Tours: adult $9, children 2-11 $6.50; discounts to groups. Steam Train Ride: adult $7, children 2-11 $5.50; discounts to groups.

Athens

TIOGA POINT MUSEUM, 724 S. Main St., Athens, PA 18810-1000. Mailing Address: P.O. Box 143, Athens, PA 18810-0143. Tel.: 570-888-7225.
E-mail: tpointmuseum@stny.rr.com
Web Site: www.tiogapointmuseum.com
Founded: 1895.
Congressional District: 23
Key Personnel: Dir. & Cur., Jaime A. Anderson; Pres. (V), Dr. Donald W. Hunt.
Personnel Profile: Full-Time Paid 1; Part-Time Paid 1; Part-Time Volunteers 5.
Governing Authority: nonprofit organization. Tax-exempt: 101.
General Museum.
Collections: local & natural history; fine arts; early canals; railroads; Revolutionary War; Civil War; Native American archaeology & ethnography; local history archives; rare books with decorated bindings.
Research Fields: local genealogy; local history; French Azilum; Native American archaeology.
Facilities: 500-vol. library of rare books available by appointment on premises; reading room. Pamphlets for sale.
Activities: guided tours; lectures; permanent & temporary exhibitions.
Publications: newsletter.
Hours & Admission Prices: Tues. & Thurs. 12-8, Sat. 10-1; other times by appointment. No charge; donations accepted. Closed national holidays. ♿
Attendance: 1,423 (accurate)
Membership: Junior $5; Student & Senior Individual $15; Individual & Senior Family $25; Family $40; Research Sponsor $60; Contributing $100; Supporting $500; Sustaining $1,000.

Audubon

JOHN JAMES AUDUBON CENTER AT MILL GROVE, 1201 Pawlings Rd., Audubon, PA 19403-2242. Tel.: 610-666-5593. Fax: 610-630-2209.
E-mail: millgrove@audubon.org
Web Site: pa.audubon.org/centers_mill_grove.html
Formerly: Mill Grove, The Audubon Wildlife Sanctuary
Founded: 1951.
Congressional District: 13
Key Personnel: Dir., Jean Bochnowski; Chm. (V), Leigh Altadonna; Cur. Collections & Exhibitions, Nancy S. Powell; Facilities Coord., Susannah Conard; Museum Shop Mgr. & Volunteer Coord., Sue Tarzwell.
Personnel Profile: Full-Time Paid 6; Part-Time Paid 1; Part-Time Volunteers 80; Interns 2.
Governing Authority: private; nonprofit. Parent Institution: National Audubon Society. Tax-exempt.
Art Museum; Wildlife Refuge; Historic Site: built in 1762; first American home of John James Audubon (1803-1806), a National Historic Landmark.
Collections: examples of every major artwork published by John James Audubon; complete, original 19th-century editions; natural history.
Research Fields: J.J. Audubon; ornithology; natural history.
Facilities: nature trails; feeding stations; nesting boxes. Museum-related items for sale.
Activities: formal educational programs for children & adults; seasonal guided nature walks; seasonal special events; permanent & temporary exhibits; self-guided tours.
Publications: newsletter, calendar of events.
Hours & Admission Prices: Tues.-Sat. 10-4, Sun. 1-4; guided tours by appointment. Grounds: 7am to dusk. Adults $4, seniors 60 & over $3, children 4-17 $2; members no charge. Closed New Year's Eve & Day; Easter; Independence Day; Thanksgiving; Christmas Eve & Day; major holidays.
Attendance: 20,000 (accurate)
Membership: Senior $35; Individual $40; Senior Family $50; Family $55; Supporter $100.

Avella

MEADOWCROFT ROCKSHELTER AND MUSEUM OF RURAL LIFE, 401 Meadowcroft Rd., Avella, PA 15312-2759. Tel.: 724-587-3412. Fax: 724-587-3414.
Web Site: www.heinzhistorycenter.org
Founded: 1969.
Congressional District: 18
Key Personnel: Dir., David R. Scofield; Cur., Bonnie Reese; Education Mgr., Dr. John Boback; Museum Shop Mgr., Fran Skariot.
Personnel Profile: Full-Time Paid 5; Part-Time Paid 9; Part-Time Volunteers 5; Interns 2.
Governing Authority: Tax-exempt.
History Museum.
Collections: local history & culture; photographs; personal artifacts.
Facilities: 275-acre history village with 19th century rural village recreation; 17th century eastern woodlands Indian village recreation; National Historic Landmark-Meadowcroft Rockshelter.
Activities: educational programming; public programming.
Publications: quarterly, Western PA History.
Hours & Admission Prices: May & Sept.-Oct. Sat. 12-5, Sun. 1-5; Memorial Day to Labor Day Wed.-Sat. 12-5, Sun. 1-5. Adults $10, children 6-16 $5; members & children under 6 no charge.
Attendance: 14,049 (accurate)
Membership: Individual $57; Grandparents $80; Family $85; Contributor $125; Patron $250; Benefactor $500; President's Circle $1,000; 1879 Society $1,879.

Beaver Falls

AIR HERITAGE, 35 Piper St., Beaver Falls, PA 15010-1043. Tel.: 724-843-2820.
E-mail: airheritage1@verizon.net
Web Site: www.airheritage.org
Aviation History Museum.
Collections: civilian, commercial & military aviation history; aviation artifacts.
Facilities: Museum-related items for sale.
Hours & Admission Prices: Mon.-Sat. 10-5, Sun. by appointment. No charge; donations accepted. Closed major holidays.
Membership: Individual $30.

BEAVER FALLS HISTORICAL SOCIETY AND MUSEUM, 1301 7th Ave., Beaver Falls, PA 15010-4219. Tel.: 724-846-4340.
Historical Society Museum.
Collections: local history & culture; photographs; genealogy; personal artifacts.
Activities: research.
Hours & Admission Prices: 10-3 Mon.-Wed. & Fri. 10-3.

Bedford

BEDFORD COUNTY HISTORICAL SOCIETY, 6441 Lincoln Hwy., Bedford, PA 15522. Tel.: 814-623-2011.
E-mail: bedfordhistory@embarqmail.com
Web Site: www.bedfordpahistory.com
Historical Society Museum.
Collections: local history & culture; photographs; personal artifacts.
Facilities: library.
Activities: research.
Hours & Admission Prices: Mon.-Fri. 9-4, 3rd Sat. of month 9-2.

FORT BEDFORD MUSEUM, 110 Fort Bedford Dr., Bedford, PA 15522. Tel.: 814-623-8891.
E-mail: info@fotbedfordmuseum.org
Web Site: www.fortbedfordmuseum.org
Founded: 1958.
Congressional District: 9
Key Personnel: Dir., Huston Godwin; Cur., Larry Yantz.
Personnel Profile: Full-Time Paid 1; Part-Time Paid 1; Part-Time Volunteers 1.
Governing Authority: municipal. Affiliated with the Bedford Boro Council, West Penn St. Parent Institution: Pioneer Historical Society, 814-623-2011. Tax-exempt.
History Museum.
Collections: Indian artifacts; period vehicles & furnishings.
Research Fields: local area artifacts.
Facilities: Museum-related items for sale.
Activities: guided tours; temporary special exhibits.
Publications: descriptive brochures.
Hours & Admission Prices: April-Oct. Wed.-Sun. 11-7; other times by appointment. Adults $5, senior citizens 65 & over $4.50, students 6-18 $2; children under 6 no charge.
Attendance: 2,870 (accurate)

THE NATIONAL MUSEUM OF THE AMERICAN COVERLET, 322 S. Juliana St., Bedford, PA 15522-1734. Tel.: 814-623-1588.
E-mail: info@coverletmuseum.org
Web Site: www.coverletmuseum.org
Founded: 2006.
Key Personnel: Museum Dir., Melinda Zongor.
Governing Authority: nonprofit organization. Tax-exempt.
Coverlet Museum.
Collections: American woven coverlet history; period American woven coverlets.
Major Exhibits: Stay at Home & Use Me Well, 11/09-9/10.
Facilities: Museum-related items for sale.
Activities: special programs.
Publications: membership newsletter, Yarns.
Hours & Admission Prices: Mon.-Sat. 10-5, Sun. 12-4. Adults $6, senior citizens 60 & over $5; members no charge.
Membership: Individual $40; Family $50; Sponsor $100; Corporate $250; Patron $500; Benefactor $1,000.

Bellefonte

CENTRE COUNTY LIBRARY AND HISTORICAL MUSEUM, 203 N. Allegheny St., Bellefonte, PA 16823-1601. Tel.: 814-355-1516. Fax: 814-355-2700.
E-mail: paroom@centrecountylibrary.org
Web Site: www.centrecountylibrary.org
Founded: 1939.
Congressional District: 23
Key Personnel: Cur., Kathleen Wunderly.
Personnel Profile: Full-Time Paid 1; Part-Time Paid 1; Part-Time Volunteers 8; Interns 4.
Governing Authority: board of directors. Parent Institution: Centre County Library. Tax-exempt.
Historic Library & Local History Museum.
Collections: furniture; china; county artifacts. Historic House: 1814-1816 Miles-Humes House.
Research Fields: local history; genealogy.
Facilities: 3,000-vol. library of Pennsylvania historical & genealogical books, records, letters & manuscripts available for use by public.
Activities: guided tours; temporary exhibitions.
Publications: books, Centre County Marriages, 1800-1850; Centre County Marriages, 1851-1873; Centre County Marriages 1874-1885; Deaths of Centre County 1821-1869.
Hours & Admission Prices: Mon.-Fri. 10-5, Sat. 10-4. No charge; donations accepted. Closed national holidays.
Attendance: 2,360 (accurate)

Bethlehem

BANANA FACTORY, 25 W. Third St., Bethlehem, PA 18015-1238. Tel.: 610-332-1300.
E-mail: info@fest.org
Web Site: www.bananafactory.org
Founded: 1998.
Key Personnel: Dir., Janice Lipzin; Museum Shop Mgr., Steve Ott.
Governing Authority: Parent Institution: ArtsQuest. Tax-exempt.
Art Gallery.
Collections: paintings; photographs; sculpture.
Major Exhibits: Family Pictures...Untold Stories, 3/27/10-5/23/10; Russel Hart: Infrared Images, 7/10-10-9/5/10; Ellen Slupe: Intersections, 8/28/10-10/24/10; Bethlehem Palette Club, 9/11/10-11/14/10.
Activities: guided tours; art programs; adult & children's classes.
Publications: quarterly, Quest.
Hours & Admission Prices: Gallery: daily 11-4. Building: Mon.-Fri. 8am-9:30pm, Sat.-Sun. 8:30-5. No charge. Closed New Year's Day; Thanksgiving; Christmas. ♿

BURNSIDE PLANTATION, INC., 1461 Schoenersville Rd., Bethlehem, PA 18018-1889. Mailing Address: 459 Old York Rd., Bethlehem, PA 18018-5862. Tel.: 610-868-5044. Fax: 610-882-5044.
Web Site: www.historicbethlehem.org
Founded: 1986.
Congressional District: 15
Key Personnel: Exec. Dir., Charlene Donchez Mowers; Finance, Tom Homanick; Pres., Robert Windolph; Education & Collections, Marsha Fritz; Cur. Collections, Bonnie Stacy.
Personnel Profile: Full-Time Paid 8; Part-Time Paid 10; Part-Time Volunteers 50.
Governing Authority: Parent Institution: Historic Bethlehem Partnership. Tax-exempt: 501(c)(3).
Historic Site.
Collections: farming practices, domestic crafts, & decorative arts from 1748-1848. Historic Buildings: c.1748 farm house with 1818 addition; c.1825 summer kitchen; mid 19th-century bank barn with horsepower wheel, corn crib & wagon shed.
Research Fields: Moravian agricultural practices; Pennsylvania German rural furnishings.
Facilities: educational facilities; nature center.
Activities: docent program; formal education programs for children; lectures. Annual Events: Blueberry Festival in July; Harvest Festival in Fall; Colonial Winter Festival in December.
Publications: Historic Bethlehem Partnership Newsletter.
Hours & Admission Prices: July-Aug. Sat. 12-4; call for additional hours; tours by appointment. Self-guided walking tours: daily. No charge; donations accepted.
Attendance: 4,000 (estimated)
Membership: Student $15; Individual $50; Family $75; deSchweinitz Club

$125; J.S. Goundie Club $250; James Burnside Society $500; Annie Kemerer Society $1,000; 1741 Society $2,000-$5,000.

COLONIAL INDUSTRIAL QUARTER, 459 Old York Rd., Bethlehem, PA 18018-5862. Tel.: 610-882-0450. Fax: 610-882-0460.
Web Site: www.historicbethlehem.org
Formerly: Historic Bethlehem Inc.
Founded: 1957.
Congressional District: 15
Key Personnel: Exec. Dir., Charlene Donchez Mowers; Finance, Thomas Homanick; Pres. (V), Jean Theman; Cur. Collections, Bonnie Stacy; Education & Collections, Marsha L. Fritz.
Personnel Profile: Full-Time Paid 6; Part-Time Paid 20; Part-Time Volunteers 35.
Governing Authority: Parent Institution: Historic Bethlehem Partnership. Subsidiary Institutions: Burnside Plantation, Bethlehem, PA; Kemerer Museum of Decorative Arts, Bethlehem, PA; Moravian Museum of Bethlehem, Bethlehem, PA; Historic Bethlehem, Inc. Tax-exempt: 501(c)(3).
Historical Site.
Collections: historic artifacts from 1700-1885 with special emphasis on Moravian industrial history. Historic Buildings: 1761 Tannery; 1762 Waterworks; 1869 Luckenbach Mill; 1782-1831 Miller's House; reconstructed Springhouse; 1750 Smithy. Historic House: 1810 Goundie House.
Research Fields: Bethlehem history; Moravian history; 18th-century industry & trades; crafts.
Activities: Museum Sponsors: demonstrations from June to September.
Publications: Historic Bethlehem Partnership Newsletter.
Hours & Admission Prices: Colonial Industrial Quarter Smithy: Summer & Fall Fri.-Sun. 12-4. Grounds: daily. Goundie House & Welcome Center: Tues.-Sat. 10-5, Sun. 12-5. Christmas Season: Mon.-Sat. 10-5, Sun. 12-5. No charge; donations accepted. ♿
Attendance: 10,000 (estimated)
Membership: Student $20; Individual $50; Family & deSchweinitz Club $125; J.S. Goundie Club $250; James Burnside Society $500; Annie Kemerer Society $1,000; 1741 Society $2,000-$5,000.

KEMERER MUSEUM OF DECORATIVE ARTS, 427 N. New St., Bethlehem, PA 18018-5802. Mailing Address: 459 Old York Rd., Bethlehem, PA 18018-5862. Tel.: 610-868-6868. Fax: 610-332-2459.
Web Site: www.historicbethlehem.org
Founded: 1954.
Congressional District: 15
Key Personnel: Museum Site Coord., Mary Meilinger.
Personnel Profile: Full-Time Paid 10; Part-Time Paid 20; Part-Time Volunteers 50; Interns 2.
Governing Authority: nonprofit organization. Parent Institution: Historic Bethlehem Partnership. Tax-exempt: 501(c)(3).
Regional Decorative Arts Museum.
Collections: 18th- & 19th-century American decorative arts; photographs, prints & stereographic views of regional interest; regional 19th-century oil landscape paintings.
Research Fields: design influences on regional decorative arts, local craftsman & artists life & collecting activities of Annie S. Kemerer.
Facilities: 750-vol. library of history books by appointment.
Activities: guided tours; lectures; educational programs, permanent & temporary exhibitions.
Publications: newsletter, Historic Bethlehem Partnership.
Hours & Admission Prices: Fri.-Sun. 12-4. Youth $5, senior citizens $4; discount to AAA members; HBP members no charge. ♿
Attendance: 10,000 (estimated)
Membership: Student $15; Individual $50; Family $75; deSchweinitz Club $125; J.S. Goundie Club $250; James Burnside Society $500; Annie Kemerer Society $1,000; 1741 Society $2,000-$5,000.

LEHIGH UNIVERSITY ART GALLERIES/MUSEUM OPERATIONS, (M), Zoellner Arts Center, 420 E. Packer Ave., Bethlehem, PA 18015-3010. Tel.: 610-758-3615. Fax: 610-758-4580.
E-mail: db01@lehigh.edu
Web Site: www.luag.org
Founded: 1864.
Congressional District: 15
Key Personnel: Dir. & Cur., Ricardo Viera; Coord. Collections & Exhibitions, Mark Wonsidler; Asst. Dir., Denise Stangl; Editor, Patricia Kandianis; Collections Asst., Amanda Hannon Davis; Asst. Collections Mgr. & Preparator, Jeffrey W. Ludwig.
Personnel Profile: Full-Time Paid 4; Part-Time Paid 4; Part-Time Volunteers 35.
Governing Authority: university. Parent Institution: Lehigh University. Tax-exempt.
University Museum.
Collections: 18th- & 19th-century American, English & French paintings; prints & photography; 20th-century American, Ashcan & contemporary paintings; contemporary Latin American photography; 20th-century contemporary prints; European, American & Oriental prints & artist's books 19th- & 20th-century & contemporary photography; Etruscan Bronzes; 19th- & 20th-century African goldweights; pre-Columbian artifacts; contemporary American folk art; public contemporary sculpture garden collection.
Major Exhibits: disFUNcional: Challenge VII. 31 Artists From Wood Turning Center, Philadelphia, 12/09-3/14/10; Calder and Dali Portfolios from the Lehigh University Collection, 1/10-2/10; Lehigh University Art, Architecture & Design Faculty Show, 3/10-5/10; Concurrent: Natalie Alper, Tom McFarlane, Diane Simpson, Larry Webb, 6/10-8/10; Andy Warhol Photography, 9/10-12/10; Joe Elliott: Beyond Bethlehem, Vintage Prints, 9/10-12/10; Harry Bertoia: Drawings, 9/10-11/10.
Research Fields: methodology; Hispanic American art; contemporary art & photography.
Facilities: library of books & catalogs, available for staff & museum studies reference only.
Activities: guided tours; lectures; gallery talks; formally organized education programs for undergraduate college students; museum studies; inter-museum loan; permanent, traveling & temporary exhibitions; interactive children's workshop.
Publications: exhibition catalogs; current exhibitions calendar; announcements; posters.
Hours & Admission Prices: Zoellner Arts Center, upper & lower level galleries: Wed.-Sat. 11-5, Sun. 1-5. DuBois Gallery, Maginnes Hall: Mon.-Fri. 9-10, Sat. 9-12. Siegel Gallery, Iacocca Hall: Mon.-Thurs. 9-10, Fri. 9-5. Gallery at Rauch Business Center: Mon.-Fri. 8-10, Sat. 8-5. Call for Summer hours. No charge; donations accepted. Closed national holidays; school holidays. ♿
Attendance: 5,402 (accurate)

* **MORAVIAN MUSEUM OF BETHLEHEM, INC., (M),** 66 W. Church St., Bethlehem, PA 18018-5805. Mailing Address: 459 Old York Rd., Bethlehem, PA 18018-5862. Tel.: 610-867-0173. Fax: 610-694-0960.
Web Site: www.historicbethlehem.org
Founded: 1938.
Congressional District: 15
Key Personnel: Exec. Dir., Charlene Donchez Mowers; Finance, Thomas Homanick; Pres., David Rabaut; Site Mgr., Megan VanRavenswaay; Devel., Sophia Chishty; Collections & Education, Marsha Fritz; Cur. Collections, Bonnie Stacy.
Personnel Profile: Full-Time Paid 9; Part-Time Paid 21; Part-Time Volunteers 70; Interns 2.
Governing Authority: private; nonprofit. Parent Institution: Historic Bethlehem Partnership. Tax-exempt: 501(c)(3).
Historic Site Museum: housed in 1741 Gemeinhaus, a National Historic Landmark; religious; apothecary museum; missionary work.
Collections: domestic objects; religious items; tools; textiles that document the Moravian community of Bethlehem. Historic Buildings: maintained by the museum include 1741 Gemeinhaus, 1752 Apothecary, 1758 Nain House.
Research Fields: Moravian history & decorative arts.
Activities: guided & self-guided tours; Moravian Community walking tour; docent program; lectures; musical programs.
Publications: book, Gemeinhaus; Historic Bethlehem Partnership e-newsletter.
Hours & Admission Prices: March to Thanksgiving & Christmas Season Fri.-Sun. 12-4. HBP Pass: adults $10, children 6-12 $6; discounts to AAM members; members & children under 6 no charge. Closed New Year's Day; Memorial Day; Independence Day; Labor Day; Thanksgiving; Christmas Eve & Day.
Attendance: 10,000 (estimated)
Membership: Student $20; Teachers $40; Individual $50; Family $75; deSchweinitz Club $125; J.S. Goundie Club $250; James Burnside Society $500; Annie Kemerer Society $1,000; 1741 Society $2,000-$5,000.

NATIONAL MUSEUM OF INDUSTRIAL HISTORY, (M), 530 E. Third St., Bethlehem, PA 18015-1314. Tel.: 610-694-6644. Fax: 610-694-6641.
E-mail: nmih@fast.net
Web Site: www.nmih.org
Founded: 1997.
Congressional District: 15
Key Personnel: C.E.O. & Pres., Stephen G. Donches; Chm. (V), Priscilla Payne Hurd; Treas., Theodore W. Harlan.
Personnel Profile: Full-Time Paid 2; Part-Time Volunteers 7; Interns 2.
Governing Authority: private; nonprofit organization. Tax-exempt: 501(c)(3).
History Museum: housed on the site of the former Bethlehem Steel plant.
Collections: steam engines; slate industry equipment; short-line railroad memorabilia; machine tools.
Hours & Admission Prices: Closed for construction.

SUN INN PRESERVATION ASSOCIATION INC., 556 Main St., 2nd Fl., Bethlehem, PA 18018-5861. Tel.: 610-866-1758. Fax: 610-866-3360.
E-mail: buckysz@aol.com
Web Site: www.suninnbethlehem.org/
Founded: 1982.
Congressional District: 15
Key Personnel: Pres., John Howard; Vice Pres., Anne McGeady; Financial Dir., Forrest O'Brien; Innkeeper, Bucky Szwborski.
Personnel Profile: Part-Time Paid 2; Part-Time Volunteers 15.
Governing Authority: private; nonprofit organization. Tax-exempt: 501(c)(3).
Historical Museum: housed in a Germanic stone building which hosted the military leaders, statesmen and the Founding Fathers during the American Revolution.
Collections: guest registers & inventory records of The Inn; furnishings; photographs.
Activities: school tours; guided tours; lectures. Annual Events: Lantern Tours; Strawberry Festival; Christmas Tour & Film.
Publications: brochure three times a year, Sonnenschein; newsletter, Sonnenschein.
Hours & Admission Prices: Fri.-Sun. 12-4. Adults $7, family $5, members $4, students $1; children under 5 no charge. ♿
Attendance: 3,000 (estimated)
Membership: Senior Citizen $25; Individual $40; Family $55; Benefactor $125; Preservationist $250; Sponsor $500; Presidential $1,000.

Biglerville

NATIONAL APPLE MUSEUM, 154 W. Hanover St., Biglerville, PA 17307. Mailing Address: P.O. Box 656, Biglerville, PA 17307-0656. Tel.: 717-677-4556.
E-mail: info@nationalapplemuseum.com
Web Site: nationalapplemuseum.com
Founded: 1990.
Congressional District: 19
Key Personnel: Pres. (V), Harold L. Griffie; Archivist, Tim Smith.
Personnel Profile: Part-Time Volunteers 30.
Governing Authority: society; nonprofit. Owned & managed by Biglerville Historical and Preservation Society. Tax-exempt: 501(c)(3).
Local History & Agriculture Museum: housed in restored Civil War barn.
Collections: apple production, processing & utilization history; associated cultural life artifacts; home furnishings; community memorabilia; photo collections; genealogy; land records; maps; farm equipment.
Research Fields: apple & related fruit production; processing & utilization history; land ownership patterns; genealogy.
Facilities: library of research material available to the public; 150-seat auditorium; 9,500 sq. ft. exhibit space; banquet facilities. Fruit gift packs, books, jewelry & other novelty items for sale.
Activities: guided tours; lectures; films; concerts; temporary exhibitions. Museum Sponsors: Apple Blossom Festival; Apple Harvest Festival; Flea Market Day; Founders Day Festival.
Hours & Admission Prices: May-Oct. Sat. 12-4, Sun. 1-4; groups by appointment anytime. Adults $2, students $1, children under 12 $.75; discounts to senior citizens, AAM & ICOM members. ♿
Attendance: 3,500 (estimated)
Membership: Annual $5; Associate $10; Sustaining $25; Life $100.

Bird-in-Hand

AMERICANA MUSEUM OF BIRD-IN-HAND, 2705 Old Philadelphia Pike, Bird-in-Hand, PA 17505. Tel.: 717-391-9780.
History Museum.
Collections: history & culture; period artifacts; barber shop; woodworking shop; tea parlor; print shop; millinery; toy store; blacksmith shop; tobacco shop; apothecary; wheelwright shop; general store.
Hours & Admission Prices: April-Nov. Tues.-Sat. 10-5. Adults $4, seniors 60 & over $3, children 6-12 $2; children 5 & under no charge.

Birdsboro

DANIEL BOONE HOMESTEAD, 400 Daniel Boone Rd., Birdsboro, PA 19508-8735. Tel.: 610-582-4900. Fax: 610-582-1744.
E-mail: jlewars@state.pa.us
Web Site: www.danielboonehomestead.org
Founded: 1937.
Congressional District: 6
Key Personnel: Historic Site Admin., James Lewars; Pres. (V), Dan Berg.
Personnel Profile: Full-Time Paid 4; Part-Time Paid 3; Part-Time Volunteers 75; Interns 3.
Governing Authority: state. Administered by Pennsylvania Historical & Museum Commission, Box 1026, Harrisburg, PA 17120. Tax-exempt.
Open Air Museum: located on site of Daniel Boone's birth.
Collections: rural decorative arts; furniture; agricultural & blacksmithing tools. Historic Buildings: 1730-1779 Boone House; smokehouse; barn; blacksmith shop; Bertolet log house; bake house; Bertolet Sawmill.
Research Fields: Pennsylvania History.
Facilities: wildlife sanctuary; visitor center; 579-acres of grounds; camping facilities for youth groups; youth hostel; lake; trails. Publications relating to Daniel Boone & Pennsylvania history for sale.
Activities: tours; education programs; living history programs; lectures; environmental education.
Publications: Pennsylvania Historical & Museum Commission publications; site brochures; site booklet; newsletter, Friends.
Hours & Admission Prices: Tues.-Sat. 9-5, Sun. 12-5. Adult $4, senior citizens & prearranged groups $3.50, children 6-12 $2; discounts to AAM & AAA members & Friends of PHMC; members & children under 6 no charge. Closed New Year's Day; Martin Luther King Jr. Day; Presidents Day; Easter; Columbus Day; Veterans Day; Thanksgiving; Christmas. ♿
Attendance: 90,000 (estimated)
Membership: Junior $5; Individual $20; Family $30; Patron $75; Sustaining $150; Benefactor $500.

Bloomsburg

THE CHILDREN'S MUSEUM, INC., (M), 2 W. Seventh St., Bloomsburg, PA 17815-2603. Tel.: 570-389-9206.
E-mail: info@the-childrens-museum.org
Web Site: www.the-childrens-museum.org
Personnel Profile: Full-Time Paid 2; Part-Time Paid 4; Part-Time Volunteers 100.
Governing Authority: nonprofit organization. Tax-exempt.
Children's Museum.
Collections: hands-on exhibits.
Facilities: Museum-related items for sale.
Hours & Admission Prices: Jan.-Feb. Fri.-Sat. 10-4; March 6 to June 9 Tues.-Fri. 12-4, Sat. 10-4; June 12 to Dec. 20 Tues.-Sat. 10-4. Adults $5; discounts to AAM members; children under 2 no charge. Closed major holidays. ♿
Attendance: 11,000 (accurate)
Membership: Individual $35; Just the 2 of US $60; Family & Grandparents $75; Contributing $100.

COLUMBIA COUNTY HISTORICAL AND GENEALOGICAL SOCIETY, 225 Market St., Bloomsburg, PA 17815-1726. Mailing Address: P.O. Box 360, Bloomsburg, PA 17815-0360. Tel.: 570-784-1600.
E-mail: research@colcohist-gensoc.org
Web Site: www.colcohist-gensoc.org
Founded: 1914.
Congressional District: 11
Key Personnel: Pres., William Baillie; Exec. Dir., Bonnie Farver; Museum Dir., Barbara Parker.
Personnel Profile: Part-Time Volunteers 20.
Governing Authority: society; board of directors. Tax-exempt: 501(c)(3).
Historical Society Museum.
Collections: local & state history; Indian artifacts; agricultural implements; 1870-1915 household items; newspapers; genealogies; photographs; microfilm.
Research Fields: genealogy; local county history & photos.
Facilities: 2,000-vol. library; reading room.
Activities: lectures; research services; courthouse research.
Publications: quarterly newsletter series on local subjects.
Hours & Admission Prices: Tues. & Fri. 9-3, Thurs. 9-7:30, Sat. 9-11:30. Library Research: $2 per hour; members no charge. ♿
Attendance: 2,298 (accurate)
Membership: Individual $18; Husband & Wife $25; Family $30; Life $200.

HAAS GALLERY OF ART - BLOOMSBURG UNIVERSITY, Haas Center for the Arts & Mitrani Hall, 2nd Fl., Bloomsburg, PA 17815. Mailing Address: Dept. of Art & Art History, 400 E. Second St., Bloomsburg, PA 17815. Tel.: 570-389-4708.
Key Personnel: Gallery Assoc., Lee S. Millard
Art Gallery.
Collections: paintings; photographs; drawings; sculpture.
Activities: temporary exhibits.
Hours & Admission Prices: Mon.-Fri. 9-4, Sat. 1-4. No charge. Closed university holidays.

Blue Bell

WISSAHICKON VALLEY HISTORICAL SOCIETY, 799 Skippack Pike, Blue Bell, PA 19422. Mailing Address: P.O. Box 96, Ambler, PA 19002-0096. Tel.: 215-646-6541.
Founded: 1976.
Governing Authority: Tax-exempt.
Historical Society Museum: housed in the former Whitpain Public School; built 1895. Listed on the National Register of Historic Places.
Collections: local history & culture; photographs; personal artifacts; early furnishings.
Activities: Annual Event: Fall Market Day in October.
Hours & Admission Prices: Call for hours.

Boalsburg

COLUMBUS CHAPEL, BOAL MANSION MUSEUM, 163 Boal Estate Dr., Boalsburg, PA 16827. Mailing Address: P.O. Box 116, Boalsburg, PA 16827-0116. Tel.: 814-466-6210. Fax: 814-466-9266 (call first).
E-mail: office@boalmuseum.com
Web Site: boalmuseum.com
Founded: 1952.
Congressional District: 23
Key Personnel: C.E.O. & Pres. (V), Christopher Lee.
Personnel Profile: Full-Time Paid 1; Part-Time Paid 4; Part-Time Volunteers 15; Interns 1.
Governing Authority: society; nonprofit organization. Parent Institution: Penn State University. Tax-exempt: 501(c)(3).
Historic House Museum: 1789, Boal Mansion.
Collections: 16th-century Christopher Columbus Chapel interior brought from Spain in 1909; history; art; weapons from Colonial period through World War I; period furnishings; Columbus relics; decorative arts; farm implements; carriages.
Research Fields: Centre County 1789-present; Christopher Columbus family 1451-present; American cultural history 1789-present.
Facilities: 750-vol. library of historical books available for research by written permission of director; Columbus & related family archives (1451-1902) on micro-film. Color slides & historical pamphlets for sale.
Activities: concerts; docent program; lectures; guided tours; formal education programs for children; stations tour for school students; Action Learning Experience for grades 4-6; rental facilities. Museum Sponsors: Memorial Day Festival; Columbus Day Ball; annual benefit musicale.
Publications: semi-annual, Columbus Chapel & Boal Mansion Museum Newsletter.
Hours & Admission Prices: May-Oct. Tues.-Sun. 1:30-5; Summer: Tues.-Sat. 10-5, Sun. 12-5. Adults $10, children $6; discount to prearranged group tours over 10. ♿
Attendance: 25,000
Membership: Patron $100; Sponsor $250; Benefactor $500; Grand Benefactor $1,000.

PENNSYLVANIA MILITARY MUSEUM AND 28TH DIVISION SHRINE, (M), 602 Boalsburg Pike, Boalsburg, PA 16827-1251. Mailing Address: P.O. Box 160A, Boalsburg, PA 16827-0660. Tel.: 814-466-6263. Fax: 814-466-6618.
E-mail: wleech@state.pa.us
Web Site: www.pamilmuseum.org
Founded: 1969.
Congressional District: 5
Key Personnel: Dir. & Cur., William J. Leech; Pres., Gil Steele; Business Mgr. & Museum Shop Mgr., Karla Thurston; Museum Educator, Joseph Horvath.
Personnel Profile: Full-Time Paid 5; Part-Time Paid 3; Part-Time Volunteers 10; Interns 2.
Governing Authority: state. Parent Institution: Pennsylvania Historical and Museum Commission, Box 1026; William Penn Memorial Museum, Harrisburg, PA 17108. Tax-exempt: 170(c)(1).
Military Museum.
Collections: Pennsylvania military history & artifacts from 1747 to present; personal histories of Pennsylvania veterans.
Research Fields: military equipment, clothing, arms & related items; Pennsylvania militia units since 1747; Civil War regiment histories with unit rosters.
Facilities: 400-vol. library of books & pamphlets on military history available for inter-library loan & for research on premises.
Activities: guided tours; lectures; formally organized education programs for children; permanent & temporary exhibitions.
Publications: brochures.
Hours & Admission Prices: Museum: call for hours. Shrine & Museum Grounds: Summer Tues.-Sat. 9-5, Sun. 12-5; Winter call for hours. Adults 12-64 $6, seniors & groups $5.50, youths 3-11 $4; discounts to AAM members; children under 3 & members no charge. Closed New Year's Day; Thanksgiving; Christmas. ♿
Attendance: 15,000 (estimated)
Membership: Individual $20; Family $25.

Bolivar

ANTIOCHIAN HERITAGE MUSEUM, (M), Antiochian Village Conference and Retreat Center, 140 Church Camp Tr., Bolivar, PA 15923-2512. Tel.: 724-238-3677. Fax: 724-238-2102.
E-mail: sales@antiochianvillage.org
Web Site: www.antiochianvillage.org/center/heritage/museum.html
Key Personnel: Cur., Julia Ritter
History Museum.
Collections: over 750 items including textiles, inlaid woodwork, metal crafts, jewelry & religious art of the Near East.
Hours & Admission Prices: Mon.-Fri. 10-4; Sat.-Sun. by appointment.

Boyertown

BOYERTOWN AREA HISTORICAL SOCIETY, 43 S. Chestnut St., Boyertown, PA 19512-1508. Tel.: 610-367-5255.
Key Personnel: Dir. Collections, Lindsay Dierolf.
Governing Authority: nonprofit organization. Tax-exempt: 501(c)(3).
Historical Society Museum: housed in the former home of George Unger & later the St. Columbkill Roman Catholic Church; built in 1902.
Collections: local history & culture; period furnishings; personal artifacts; photographs.
Hours & Admission Prices: Thurs. 1-9; other times by appointment. ♿
Membership: Individual $10; Family $15; Patron $25; Life $150; Corporate $250.

BOYERTOWN MUSEUM OF HISTORIC VEHICLES, (M), 85 S. Walnut St., Boyertown, PA 19512-1462. Tel.: 610-367-2090. Fax: 610-367-9712.
E-mail: mail@boyertownmuseum.org
Web Site: boyertownmuseum.org
Founded: 1965.
Congressional District: 6
Key Personnel: Exec. Dir., Kenneth D. Wells, II; Chm. Exec. Committee (V), Robert H. Dare; Pres. (V), Bernard Hofmann; Operations Mgr., Sandi Miller.
Personnel Profile: Full-Time Paid 3; Full-Time Volunteers 1; Part-Time Paid 1; Part-Time Volunteers 4.
Governing Authority: nonprofit organization. Tax-exempt: 501(c)(3).
Transportation Museum.
Collections: horse drawn, gas, steam, & electric powered autos, trucks; fire apparatus; tools used by vehicle builders; art; models; S.E. Pennsylvania memorabilia.
Research Fields: horse drawn & mechanized vehicles and their builders.
Facilities: meeting room; banquet facilities. Museum-related items for sale.
Activities: self-guided & directed group tours; education program in schools; lectures; special exhibits; production of a one hour TV program seen on cable. Museum Sponsors: annual Duryea Days, antique & classic auto show; & other events.
Publications: book, A Century of Vehicle Craftsmanship; newsletter for members.
Hours & Admission Prices: Tues.-Sun. 9:30-4. Adults $6, seniors $5, students $4; discounts to AAA & AAM members; children under 6 no charge. Closed major holidays. ♿
Attendance: 4,900 (accurate)
Membership: Individual $20; Family $40; Associate $50; Sponsor $100; Sustaining $250; Patron $500; Benefactor $1,000.

Bradford

ZIPPO/CASE VISITORS CENTER, 1932 Zippo Dr., Bradford, PA 16701-5414. Mailing Address: 33 Barbour St., Bradford, PA 16701-1998. Tel.: 814-368-1932 & 2711. Fax: 814-368-2874.
E-mail: lmeabon@zippo.com
Web Site: www.zippo.com
Founded: 1994.
Congressional District: 5
Key Personnel: C.E.O. & Pres. Zippo Mfg. Co., Gregory W. Booth; Dir., Patrick Grandy; Cur. & Archivist, Linda Meabon; Museum Shop Mgr., Joshua Gleason.
Personnel Profile: Full-Time Paid 4; Part-Time Paid 6.
Governing Authority: private organization. Parent Institution: Zippo Manufacturing Co., 33 Barbour St., Bradford, PA 16701.
Company Museum.
Collections: Zippo lighters and other Zippo products & company history from the founding of the company in 1932 to present day; Case knives & Case

company history from 1889 to present day; interactive exhibits; re-creation of the 1947 Chrysler Saratoga Zippo Car.
Facilities: Zippo & Case Cutlery products for sale.
Activities: guided tours-motorcoach.
Publications: annual reference guide, Zippo Lighter Collectors Guide.
Hours & Admission Prices: Mon.-Sat. 9-5, Sun. 11-4. Closed New Year's Day; Easter; Thanksgiving. ♿
Attendance: 50,000 (estimated)

Bryn Athyn

GLENCAIRN MUSEUM: ACADEMY OF THE NEW CHURCH, 1001 Cathedral Rd., Bryn Athyn, PA 19009-0757. Mailing Address: Box 757, Bryn Athyn, PA 19009-0757. Tel.: 267-502-2600 & 2990. Fax: 267-502-2986.
E-mail: info@glencairnmuseum.org
Web Site: www.glencairnmuseum.org
Founded: 1878.
Congressional District: 8
Key Personnel: Dir., Stephen H. Morley; Cur., C. Edward Gyllenhaal; Registrar & Collection Mgr., Bret Bostock; Operations Admin., Doreen F. Carey; Coord. Education, Diane M. Fehon; Outreach & Public Rels. Coord., Joralyn Echols; Asst. Operations Admin., Edwin Steiner; Collections Asst. & Concert Coord., Peter Childs.
Personnel Profile: Full-Time Paid 8; Part-Time Paid 12; Part-Time Volunteers 20; Interns 5.
Governing Authority: Parent Institution: The Academy of the New Church. Subsidiary Institutions: Glencairn Archives. Tax-exempt: 170(b)(1)(A).
Religious Art Museum: housed in a Romanesque style building crafted in stained glass, mosaic, & sculptured granite; c.1939.
Collections: Native American artifacts; Egyptian sculpture & artifacts; Far Eastern; furniture; Greek & Roman sculpture, jewelry & artifacts; medieval stained glass, ivories, enamels, sculpture, arms & armor; 19th- & 20th-century art; oriental rugs; coins; tapestries; Mesopotamian sculpture & artifacts; model of tabernacle of Israel.
Research Fields: medieval art; classical archeology.
Facilities: 1,000-vol. library pertaining to art & medieval architecture; education facilities.
Activities: guided tours; concerts; organized education programs for schools, undergraduate & graduate students; interpreter program; temporary exhibitions; lecture series; workshops. Museum Sponsors: quarterly Open Houses.
Publications: newsletter; collection catalogs; exhibition catalogs.
Hours & Admission Prices: Mon.-Fri. 9-5 by appointment only. Guided Tours: Sat. 11, 11:30, 12:30 & 1; reservations suggested. Adults $8, seniors $6, students $4; discounts for members, AAM & ICOM members; children 4 & under, alumni & Sat. no charge. Fees subject to change. Closed national holidays.
Attendance: 21,475 (accurate)
Membership: Single $25; Family $35; Frequent Visitor $75.

Bushkill

POCONO INDIAN MUSEUM, Rte. 209, Bushkill, PA 18324. Tel.: 570-588-9338.
American Indian Museum.
Collections: Delaware Indian history & culture; period artifacts; weapons; tools; sculpture.
Facilities: Museum-related items for sale.
Hours & Admission Prices: Memorial Day to Labor Day 10-7; Winter: 10-5:30. Adults $5, children 6-12 $2.50; children under six no charge.

Butler

MARIDON MUSEUM, (M), 322 N. McKean St., Butler, PA 16001-4913. Fax: 724-282-0567.
Web Site: www.maridon.org
Founded: 2004.
Key Personnel: Pres. Bd., George J. Kelly, Jr.; Vice Pres. & Treas., Kenneth Bronder; Mktg. & Public Rels., Larry Berg.
Personnel Profile: Full-Time Paid 1; Part-Time Paid 2.
Governing Authority: private; nonprofit organization. Tax-exempt: 501(c)(3).
History Museum.
Collections: Chinese & Japanese history including jade; ivory; paintings; precious stones; bronzes; 18th-19th century German Meissen porcelain figures.
Facilities: library; classrooms. Museum-related items for sale.
Activities: guided tours; educational workshops; lectures; temporary exhibits. Annual Events: Chinese New Year Celebration; Meissen Fest; Hinamatsuri Girl's Festival; 753 Shichi Go San Festival for Children.
Publications: brochures; booklet, The Meridon Museum: A New Window on the World.
Hours & Admission Prices: Tues.-Sat. 11-5, Sun. 12-5. Adults $4, senior citizens & students $3; members and children 8 & under no charge. Closed New Year's Day; Easter; Memorial Day; Independence Day; Labor Day; Thanksgiving; Christmas. ♿
Attendance: 2,100 (estimated)
Membership: Student & Senior $20; Individual $25; Family $35; Contributor $100; Friend $250; Donor $500; Sustaining Patron $1,000; Museum Circle $2,500 & up; Lifetime $25,000.

California

THE GALLAGHER HOUSE - CALIFORNIA AREA HISTORICAL SOCIETY, 429 Wood St. @ 5th St., California, PA 15419. Mailing Address: P.O. Box 624, California, PA 15419-0624. Tel.: 724-938-3250.
Key Personnel: Pres. (V), Patricia Cowen.
Governing Authority: Parent Institution: California Area Historical Society. Tax-exempt.
Historic House: built in 1903.
Collections: local history & culture; photographs; period artifacts; obituaries 1900 to present; local funeral home & cemetery records; tax records; maps.
Research Fields: genealogy; local history.
Activities: research.
Publications: newsletter, The California Crier.
Hours & Admission Prices: Tues.-Thurs. 9-4; other times by appointment. No charge; donations accepted. Closed holidays.
Membership: Single $20; Couple $25; Corporate $100; Life $300.

Camp Hill

THE FRIENDS OF PEACE CHURCH, St. John's and Trindle Roads, Camp Hill, PA 17011. Mailing Address: P.O. Box 3034, Shiremanstown, PA 17011-3034. Tel.: 717-737-6492.
Web Site: www.historicpeacechurch.org
Founded: 1979.
Congressional District: 19
Key Personnel: Pres., James Bower; Vice Pres., D'Arcy Wagonhurst; Treas., Vernon Cleary; Sec., Earnest Kepner; Property Placement Officer, Robert Sieber; Museum Shop Mgr., Betty O'Neill.
Personnel Profile: Part-Time Paid 3; Part-Time Volunteers 25.
Governing Authority: state. Administered by the Pennsylvania Historical and Museum Commission, P.O. Box 1026, Harrisburg, PA 17120. Tax-exempt.
Historic Site & Building: 1799 Georgian style stone church.
Collections: pewter communion service; 1807 Conrad Doll Organ made with wooden & pewter pipes; 19th-century German Bible & hymnbook; funeral bier; whale oil lamps; hanging oil lamps; 10 plate stoves; original pews; hourglass pulpit.
Facilities: Museum-related items for sale.
Activities: organ concerts; site interpretation; craft demonstrations; concerts; lectures; weddings; Good Friday service; Christmas Carol Sing; Easter Sunrise Candlelight Service.
Publications: quarterly newsletter, The Sounding Board.
Hours & Admission Prices: June-Sept. Sun. 2-5. No charge; donations accepted. ♿
Attendance: 9,290 (accurate)
Membership: Regular $5; Sustaining $10; Patron $25.

Carlisle

CUMBERLAND COUNTY HISTORICAL SOCIETY, THE HAMILTON LIBRARY AND THE TWO MILE HOUSE, 21 N. Pitt St., Carlisle, PA 17013-2945. Mailing Address: P.O. Box 626, Carlisle, PA 17013-0626. Tel.: 717-249-7610. Fax: 717-258-9332.
E-mail: info@historicalsociety.com
Web Site: www.historicalsociety.com
Founded: 1874.
Congressional District: 19
Key Personnel: Exec. Dir., Linda F. Witmer; Librarian, Cara Holtry; Museum Shop Mgr., Kim Laidler.
Personnel Profile: Full-Time Paid 8; Part-Time Paid 15; Part-Time Volunteers 250; Interns 8.
Governing Authority: society; nonprofit. Subsidiary Institution: Two Mile House, 1189 Walnut Bottom Rd., Carlisle, PA. Tax-exempt.
Local History Library & Museum.
Collections: Library: papers; books; newspapers; county records; genealogy; photo archives; publications; Indian School materials. Museum: provides visitors with a glimpse of early life & crafts of county; children's touch gallery; Indian School gallery.
Research Fields: Cumberland County history; Indian School materials; genealogy.
Facilities: 7,000-vol. library; genealogical files; AV aids; reading room.
Activities: guided tours; lectures; permanent & special exhibitions.

Publications: quarterly newsletter; biannual journal; annual photo essay book on county topic.
Hours & Admission Prices: Mon. 3-9, Tues.-Fri. 10-4, Sat. 10-3. Library: adults $5. Museum & Exhibits no charge; donations accepted. Closed New Year's Day; Memorial Day; Independence Day; Labor Day; Martin Luther King, Jr. Day; Presidents' Day; Thanksgiving; Christmas & day after. ♿
Attendance: 36,000 (accurate)
Membership: Individual $40; Family $45; Supporter $50; Patron $150; Business $250; Corporate $500; James Hamilton $500; Heritage Circle $1,000.

THE TROUT GALLERY, (M), W. High St., between College & West Sts., Carlisle, PA 17013. Mailing Address: Dickinson College, P.O. Box 1773, Carlisle, PA 17013-2896. Tel.: 717-245-1344. Fax: 717-254-8929.
E-mail: trout@dickinson.edu
Web Site: www.dickinson.edu/trout
Founded: 1983.
Congressional District: 19
Key Personnel: Dir., Dr. Phillip Earenfight; Registrar & Exhibition Preparator, James Bowman; Cur. Education, Wendy Pires; Asst. Dir. Publications, Patricia Pohlman; Dir. Publications, Kimberley Nichols.
Personnel Profile: Full-Time Paid 4; Part-Time Paid 10; Interns 1.
Governing Authority: college; nonprofit. Parent Institution: Dickinson College. Tax-exempt.
Art Museum.
Collections: art history; Gerofsky African art; Potamkin collection; Cole Oriental & decorative arts; Carnegie prints; 5,000 Old Master & modern prints.
Research Fields: pertaining to collections.
Facilities: 230-capacity auditorium; educational facilities; print study.
Activities: guided tours; lectures; films; concerts; organized education programs for area school and adult groups in addition to undergraduate college students affiliated with course work towards a Bachelor's of Art in Art history & studio art; internships; loan, temporary & traveling exhibitions; symposia.
Publications: catalogues, Toshiko Takaezu Ceramics Textiles & Bronzes; Wayne Thiebaud, Paintings, Drawings & Graphics 1961-1983; Homage to Alumni & Friends, Recent Gifts to Dickinson College's Fine Arts Collection; Etruscan Pottery: The Meeting of Greece & Etruria; 11 Contemporary Latin American Artists: Works On Paper; Rauschenberg's Surface Series; The Bible & 20th-Century Artists; Joseph Priestley in America, 1794-1804; A Historical Sculpture of Africa; The Grand Tradition: Nineteenth-Century Landscapes from the Permanent Collection; Objects of Diversity: Process and Interpretation; Fields of Vision: Selected Works by Contemporary Irish Artists; African Objects of Prestige & Personal Adornment from the Permanent Collection; A Decade of Giving, The Trout Gallery 1983-1993; Unraveling the Mask: Portraits of Twentieth-Century Experience; Visions of Home: American Impressionist Images of Suburban Leisure and Country Comfort; brochures, Calendar of Shows per semester; 20th century American women artists: Selections from the Permanent Collection at Dickinson College; Vessels: Selections from the Permanent Collection; Writing on Hands: Memory and Knowledge in Early Modern European; Selective Visions: The Art of Ralston Crawford; 19th Century Life: A Closer Look; Images of Transience: Nature and Culture in Art; Grace Hartigan: Painting Art History; Woodcuts to Wrapping Paper: Concepts of Originality in Contemporary Prints; Quincy: Selected Paintings; Within the Landscape: Essays on Nineteenth-Century American Art and Culture; Inked Impressions: Ellen Day Hale and the Painter-Etcher Movement; A Kiowa's Odyssey: A Sketchbook from Fort Marion; America en plein air: Impressions by Henry Ryan MacGinnis; New Lives for Asian Images; Handentanden: Senior Studio Art Majors Exhibition; Joyce Kozloff: Co+Ordinates; Through the Lens: Studies in Photography; LIMINAL.
Hours & Admission Prices: Tues.-Sat. 10-4. No charge. Closed national holidays; Thanksgiving break; Christmas break. ♿
Attendance: 8,437 (accurate)
Membership: Supporter: Student $15; Individual $30; Dual $45; Family $60. Sustainer $250; Partner $500; Benefactor $1,000; The John DicKinson Society $2,500.

UNITED STATES ARMY HERITAGE AND EDUCATION CENTER - ARMY HERITAGE MUSEUM, (M), 950 Soldiers Dr., Carlisle, PA 17013-5021. Tel.: 717-245-3972. Fax: 717-245-4370 (COM) & 242-4370 (DSN).
E-mail: usamhi@carlisle.army.mil
Web Site: www.usahec.org
Founded: 1967.
Congressional District: 17
Key Personnel: Dir., Col. James G. Pierce; Dir. Operations, Lt. Col. Mark A. Viney; Dir. US Army Military History Institute, Dr. Conrad Crane; Dir. Army Heritage Museum, Jay Graybeal.
Personnel Profile: Full-Time Paid 73; Part-Time Paid 1; Part-Time Volunteers 39; Interns 3.
Governing Authority: federal. Parent Institution: U.S. Army War College. Tax-exempt.
Military Museum.
Collections: US Army history, culture & personal artifacts; books; manuscripts; diaries & letters; photographs; Hessian Guard House.
Research Fields: history of U.S. army; world military history.
Facilities: military research facility.
Activities: self-guided tours.
Publications: brochures, descriptions of main collection & special programs.
Hours & Admission Prices: Hessian: Mon.-Fri. 9-4:45, Sat. 10-4, Sun. 12-4. Institute Research Collections: Mon.-Fri. 9-4:45, Sat. 9-1. No charge. Closed federal holidays. ♿
Attendance: 10,000 (accurate)

Castle Shannon

CASTLE SHANNON HISTORICAL SOCIETY, 1003 Castle Shannon Blvd., Castle Shannon, PA 15234-1803. Tel.: 412-561-7909.
Historical Society Museum.
Collections: local history & culture; photographs; period artifacts.
Hours & Admission Prices: Call for hours.

Catawissa

CATAWISSA RAILROAD CO., 119 Pine St., Catawissa, PA 17820-1239. Tel.: 570-356-2345. Fax: 570-356-7876.
Web Site: caboosenut.com
Founded: 1980.
Railroad Museum.
Collections: 14 railroad cabooses; 1931 Davenport steam engine & tender; 400 ft. of track; railroad memorabilia.
Hours & Admission Prices: Daily 8-5.

Centre Hall

PENN'S CAVE & WILDLIFE PARK, 222 Penns Cave Rd., Centre Hall, PA 16828-8103. Tel.: 814-364-1664. Fax: 814-364-8778.
Cavern & Wildlife Park.
Collections: North American wildlife including bears, wolves, elk, deer, bobcats, bison, longhorn cattle, mustangs, & cougar; local natural history; geology; biology.
Facilities: Museum-related items for sale.
Activities: motorboat cave & wildlife tours; special events; guided tours.
Hours & Admission Prices: Call for hours. Wildlife Park: adults $19, senior citizens 65 & over $18, children 2-12 $11; children one & under no charge. Cave: adults $14,95, senior citizens 65 & over $13.95, children 2-12 $7.95; children one & under no charge. Cave & Park: adults $29.95, seniors citizens 65 & over $28.95, children 2-12 $15.95; children one & under no charge.

Chadds Ford

BRANDYWINE BATTLEFIELD PARK, 1491 Baltimore Pike, Chadds Ford, PA 19317. Mailing Address: Box 202, Chadds Ford, PA 19317-0202. Tel.: 610-459-3342, ext. 3001. Fax: 610-459-9586.
Web Site: www.brandywinebattlefield.org
Founded: 1947.
Congressional District: 5
Key Personnel: Pres., Linda Kaat; Site Admin., Michael Bertheaud.
Personnel Profile: Full-Time Paid 3; Part-Time Paid 5; Part-Time Volunteers 75; Interns 2.
Governing Authority: state. Parent Institution: Pennsylvania Historical & Museum Commission. Tax-exempt.
Historic Site: site of the Battle of the Brandywine.
Collections: history; costumes; period furnishings; prints; Revolutionary War equipment & firearms. Historic Houses: Gen. Washington's headquarters; Lafayette's quarters.
Research Fields: Revolutionary War; Battle of Brandywine, 1777; Quakers' Lifestyles.
Facilities: picnic areas; Visitor Center with exhibits. Museum-related items for sale.
Activities: guided tours; inter-museum loan & permanent exhibitions; military reenactments; organized educational programs; special events.
Publications: booklet, Driving Tour of Brandywine Battlefield.
Hours & Admission Prices: March-Nov. Wed.-Sat. 9-4, Sun. 12-4; Dec.-Feb. Thurs.-Sat. 9-4, Sun. 12-4. Adults $5, senior citizens & groups $3.50, youth 6-17 $2.50; discounts Dec.-Feb.
Attendance: 50,000 (accurate)
Membership: Brandywine Battlefield Associates: Individual $25; Family $35; Contributor $60; Benefactor $125; Patron $250; Guardian $500.

* **BRANDYWINE RIVER MUSEUM, (M),** U.S. Rte. 1, at Hoffman's Mill Rd., Chadds Ford, PA 19317. Mailing Address: P.O. Box 141, Chadds Ford, PA 19317-0141. Tel.: 610-388-2700. Fax: 610-388-1197.
E-mail: inquiries@brandywine.org
Web Site: www.brandywinemuseum.org.
Founded: 1971.
Congressional District: 7
Key Personnel: C.E.O. & Dir., James H. Duff; Chm. (V), George A. Weymouth; Pres. (V), Wendell Fenton, Esq.; Cur. Collections, Virginia H. O'Hara; Assoc. Cur., Audrey Lewis; Assoc. Cur. N.C. Wyeth Collections, Christine B. Podmaniczky; Registrar, Jean A. Gilmore; Dir. Finance & Administration, Joel E. Necowitz; Dir. Public Rels., Hillary Holland; Museum Shop Mgr., Erika G. Bucino; Supvr. Education, Mary W. Cronin; Asst. Educator, Jane V. Flitner; Chief of Security, Robert Booker; Dir. Devel., Suzanne M. Regnier; Volunteer Coord., Donna M. Gormel.
Personnel Profile: Full-Time Paid 78; Part-Time Paid 52; Part-Time Volunteers 358; Interns 2.
Governing Authority: nonprofit organization. Parent Institution: Brandywine Conservancy. Branch Museum: N.C. Wyeth House & Studio; Kuerner Farm. Tax-exempt: 501(c)(3).
Art Museum: housed in 1864 Hoffman's Mill located on the Brandywine River.
Collections: American art with emphasis on art of Brandywine region; still-life painting & illustration; artists' memorabilia.
Major Exhibits: N.C. Wyeth & The Philadelphia Sketch Club, 3/20/10-5/23/10; Selected Caldecott Winners, 3/20/10-5/23/10; John Haberle: Master of Illusion (T), 4/17/10-7/11/10; American Stoneware, 5/29/10-7/18/10; Portraits from the Collection, 6/12/10-9/6/10; Reality Check: Contemporary American Trompe L'oeil, 9/11/10-11/21/10; The Imaginary Beasts of Royal Lacey Scoville, 11/26/10-1/9/11.
Research Fields: art history of the region; American illustration & still-life painting.
Facilities: 11,000-vol. library on American art available by appointment; 150-seat lecture room; 120-seat restaurant. Books, reproductions & museum-related items for sale.
Activities: permanent & temporary exhibitions; guided tours; gallery talks; formally organized education programs; docent program; concerts.
Publications: exhibition catalogs; quarterly newsletter, Catalyst; Catalogue of the Permanent Collection.
Hours & Admission Prices: Daily 9:30-4:30. Adults $10, senior citizens, students & children 6-12 $6; discounts to AAM, ICOM & AAMD members; children under 6 & members no charge. Closed Christmas. ♿
Attendance: 110,345 (accurate)
Membership: Senior & Educator $40; Individual $45; Dual $60; Family $65; Donor $100; Patron $250; Sponsor $500; Benefactor $1,000; Preservation Fellow $5,000; Trustee Circle $10,000.

CHADDS FORD HISTORICAL SOCIETY, (M), 1736 Creek Rd., Chadds Ford, PA 19317. Mailing Address: P.O. Box 27, Chadds Ford, PA 19317-0027. Tel.: 610-388-7376. Fax: 610-388-7480.
E-mail: info@chaddsfordhistoricalsociety.org
Web Site: www.chaddsfordhistory.org
Founded: 1968.
Key Personnel: Exec. Dir., Ginger Tucker; Pres. (V), Dr. George Franz; Education Coord. & Collections Mgr., Lynda Gillow; Office Mgr., Matt DiFilippo; Museum Shop Mgr., Cheryl Trozzi.
Personnel Profile: Part-Time Paid 3; Part-Time Volunteers 3; Interns 3.
Historical Society Museum.
Collections: local history; photographs.
Major Exhibits: From Moo to You: Dairying Around Chadds Ford, 11/09-12/09; Tom Burke's Birdhouses, 11/09-12/10.
Activities: permanent exhibitions; young adult & adult educational programs; school programs; demonstrations; special events; interpretive videos.
Publications: newsletter, Notes From the Ford.
Hours & Admission Prices: House Tours: May-Sept. Sat.-Sun. 1-5; other times by appointment. Barn Visitor's Center: Mon.-Fri. 9-2, Sat.-Sun. 1-5. Barn: no charge. Each House: $5 per person.
Attendance: 10,000
Membership: Individual $25; Family $40; Contributor $75; Patron $125; Sustaining $250; Benefactor $500; Lifetime $3,000.

THE CHRISTIAN C. SANDERSON MUSEUM, 1755 Creek Rd. (Old Rte. 100), Chadds Ford, PA 19317. Mailing Address: P.O. Box 153, Chadds Ford, PA 19317-0153. Tel.: 610-388-6545.
E-mail: info@sandersonmuseum.org
Web Site: www.sandersonmuseum.org
Founded: 1967.
Congressional District: 5
Key Personnel: Pres. (V), Sally Jane Denk; Cur., Charles E. Ulmann.
Personnel Profile: Full-Time Volunteers 26; Part-Time Volunteers 26.
Governing Authority: nonprofit organization. Tax-exempt: 501(c)(3).
History Museum.
Collections: American Revolution to WWII; personal & family items; historical artifacts; early Andrew Wyeth items.
Hours & Admission Prices: March-Nov. Sat.-Sun. 12-4; groups by appointment. No charge; donations accepted. Closed Easter; Thanksgiving; Christmas.
Attendance: 1,000 (estimated)
Membership: Annual $5; Life $50.

Chester

WIDENER UNIVERSITY ART COLLECTION AND GALLERY, (M), 14th & Chestnut Sts. (University Center), Chester, PA 19013. Mailing Address: One University Pl., Chester, PA 19013-5792. Tel.: 610-499-1189 & 4000. Fax: 610-499-4425.
E-mail: rmwarda@widener.edu
Web Site: www.widener.edu/artgallery
Founded: 1970.
Congressional District: 7
Key Personnel: Collections Mgr., Rebecca M. Warda.
Governing Authority: university. Tax-exempt: 501(c)(3).
University Art Museum.
Collections: 19th- & 20th-century American paintings & sculpture; Alfred O. Deshong Collection: 18th- & 19th-century European genre paintings; 18th- & 19th-century Oriental art objects; 19th-century American paintings.
Research Fields: American impressionism; DeShong genealogy.
Activities: lectures; temporary exhibitions.
Publications: pamphlets.
Hours & Admission Prices: Sept.-May Tues. 10-7, Wed.-Sat. 10-4:30; June-Aug. call for hours. No charge. Closed major holidays. ♿
Attendance: 4,000 (estimated)

Clarion

CLARION COUNTY HISTORICAL SOCIETY, SUTTON-DITZ HOUSE MUSEUM, 17 S. Fifth Ave., Clarion, PA 16214-1501. Tel.: 814-226-4450. Fax: 814-226-7106.
Founded: 1955.
Congressional District: 23
Key Personnel: Dir. & Cur., Mary Lea Lucas.
Personnel Profile: Full-Time Paid 1; Part-Time Paid 1; Part-Time Volunteers 10.
Governing Authority: society; nonprofit organization. Tax-exempt: 501(c)(3).
County History Museum: located in c. 1850 home, renovated in 1909.
Collections: local history; manuscripts; 1800-present historical photographs.
Research Fields: Western Pennsylvania history.
Facilities: 3,000-vol. library of books of genealogical & local historical interest available on premises.
Activities: guided tours of the Museum; lectures; & historical programs; temporary & permanent exhibits; bus tours.
Publications: Century Homes & Buildings of Clarion County, Vols. I, II & III; quarterly newsletter, Clarion County & Its Beginnings.
Hours & Admission Prices: Museum: Tues.-Fri. 10-4; other times by appointment. No charge; donations accepted. Closed major holidays.
Attendance: 1,800 (estimated)
Membership: Individual $10; Family $18; Sustaining $35; Patron $50; Life $200.

UNIVERSITY GALLERIES, Clarion Univ. of Pennsylvania, Carlson Library A-4, Clarion, PA 16214. Tel.: 814-393-2523. Fax: 814-393-2168.
E-mail: gallery@clarion.edu
Formerly: Sandford Gallery
Founded: 1982.
Congressional District: 23
Key Personnel: Dir., Vicky A. Clark.
Personnel Profile: Part-Time Paid 7.
Governing Authority: university. Tax-exempt: 501(c)(3).
Art Gallery.
Collections: 19th- & 20th-century American art; Kuba textiles.
Major Exhibits: Pennsyltucky, 1/10-3/10.
Facilities: 1,120 sq. ft. exhibit space.
Activities: lectures; organized educations programs for students affiliated with Clarion University; participatory, temporary & traveling exhibitions.
Publications: show brochures.
Hours & Admission Prices: Mon.-Thurs. 10-3. No charge. Closed university holidays.
Attendance: 1,500 (estimated)
Membership: Annual $25; University Club $1,000.

Clearfield

CLEARFIELD COUNTY HISTORICAL SOCIETY, 104 E. Pine St., Clearfield, PA 16830-2517. Tel.: 814-765-6125.
Web Site: www.clfdhistory.com
Founded: 1955.
Congressional District: 23
Key Personnel: Pres., Denny Shaffner; 1st Vice Pres., Mort Landy; Sec., Jane Elling; Membership, Cathie Hughes; Treas., Brent Thomas; Museum Shop Mgr., Warren Fox.
Personnel Profile: Part-Time Volunteers 21.
Governing Authority: society. Tax-exempt.
Local History Museum: housed in c.1880, 3-story brick building.
Collections: Indian flints; built-in mine mouth; lumbering display; PA primitives; comprehensive library of Central PA history; genealogy records; carriage house; Bloody Knox log cabin.
Research Fields: family genealogy; local history.
Activities: guided tours; lectures; annual dinner.
Publications: semi-annual bulletin; pamphlets; reprints; fall & spring bulletin.
Hours & Admission Prices: May-Oct. Thurs. & Sun. 1:30-4:30; other times by appointment. No charge; donations accepted.
Attendance: 1,300 (accurate)
Membership: Student $2; Individual $10; Business, Club, Industry $35; Life $150.

Coalport

COALPORT AREA COAL MUSEUM, 961 Forest St., Coalport, PA 16627. Mailing Address: P.O. Box 248, Coalport, PA 16627-0248. Tel.: 814-672-4378.
Key Personnel: Pres. & Cur., Richard W. Snyder, II
History Museum.
Collections: coal mining industry, heritage & history; photographs; personal artifacts; tools; company documents; genealogy.
Hours & Admission Prices: Call for hours.

Collegeville

* **PHILIP AND MURIEL BERMAN MUSEUM OF ART AT URSINUS COLLEGE, (M),** 601 E. Main St., Collegeville, PA 19426-1000. Mailing Address: P.O. Box 1000, Collegeville, PA 19426-1000. Tel.: 610-409-3500. Fax: 610-409-3664.
E-mail: lhanover@ursinus.edu
Web Site: www.ursinus.edu/berman
Founded: 1987.
Congressional District: 13
Key Personnel: Pres., Dr. John Strassburger; Chm. Art Advisory Bd., Robert L. Brant, Esq.; Dir., Lisa Tremper Hanover; Administrative Asst., Suzanne Calvin; Collections Mgr., Julie Choma; Assoc. Dir. Education, Susan Shifrin.
Personnel Profile: Full-Time Paid 4; Part-Time Volunteers 10; Interns 12.
Governing Authority: private university; nonprofit. Parent Institution: Ursinus College. Tax-exempt: 501(c)(3).
Art Museum.
Collections: 19th- & early 20th-century American landscape, portrait & genre paintings, prints & watercolors, emphasis on Pennsylvania Impressionist & regional schools; Old Master & contemporary Japanese woodcut prints, scrolls & artifacts; 18th- & 19th-century European portraits; 1950-1990 American painting & graphics; Pennsylvania German Fraktur; documents; artifacts; eastern European paintings; contemporary sculpture; private collection of British sculptor Lynn Chadwick.
Research Fields: 19th-century Pennsylvania regional painting (New Hope school); Pennsylvania German history & culture.
Facilities: 1,200-vol. library of art material available for inter-library loan & to the public; educational facilities. Museum-related items for sale.
Activities: guided tours; lectures; films; loan, temporary & traveling exhibitions; organized education programs for undergraduate & graduate students affiliated with Ursinus College. Museum Sponsors: Friends Annual Event.
Publications: quarterly calendar of events; exhibition catalogues; Friends of the Museum Newsletter.
Hours & Admission Prices: Tues.-Fri. 10-4, Sat.-Sun. 12-4:30. No charge; donations accepted. Closed college holidays. ♿
Attendance: 32,000 (estimated)
Membership: Patron $50; Sponsor $100; Collector Club $250; Connoisseur Club $750; American Impressionists $1,500; Chadwick Society $2,500; Old Master Association $5,000.

Columbia

COLUMBIA MUSEUM OF HISTORY, 21 N. Second St., Columbia, PA 17512.
Key Personnel: Dir., Florence Miller
History Museum: housed in the former First Evangelical Lutheran Church; built in 1850.
Collections: local history & culture; photographs; personal artifacts; period furnishings.
Activities: genealogy research; educational programs. Museum Sponsors: Underground Railroad in October.
Hours & Admission Prices: Sun. 1:30-4:30; other times by appointment. No charge.

FIRST NATIONAL BANK MUSEUM, 170 Locust St., Columbia, PA 17512-1109. Tel.: 717-684-8864. Fax: 717-684-8048.
History Museum.
Collections: bank history; period artifacts & furnishings including teller cages, the President's office, walk-in vault, & check canceller.
Hours & Admission Prices: Call for hours. Adults $6, seniors $5, students $4; discounts to groups; children under 12 no charge.

THE NATIONAL WATCH & CLOCK MUSEUM, (M), 514 Poplar St., Columbia, PA 17512-2124. Tel.: 717-684-8261. Fax: 717-684-0878.
Web Site: www.nawcc.org
Founded: 1971.
Congressional District: 16
Key Personnel: Exec. Dir., J. Steven Humphrey; Museum Dir., Noel Poirier; Cur., Carter Harris; Library Dir., Sharon Gordon; Librarian, Nancy Dyer.
Personnel Profile: Full-Time Paid 20; Part-Time Paid 13; Part-Time Volunteers 27.
Governing Authority: nonprofit organization. Parent Institution: NAWCC, Inc. Tax-exempt: 501(c)(3).
Horological Museum.
Collections: American & foreign clocks, watches, horological tools; timekeeping from the sundial to GPS; NYU & James Arthur collection.
Research Fields: horology; watch & clock industry.
Facilities: 5,000-vol. library of reference books; 2,000-vol. lending library for members only; pamphlets, catalogues & ephemera on horology & file of 40,000 U.S. & foreign horological patents; rare book collection of horological material including some formerly in the Franklin Institute; Hamilton Watch Company records.
Activities: special exhibitions. School of Horology: clock repair, watch repair, reverse painting on glass techniques; school programs; public programs.
Publications: bimonthly Bulletin; bimonthly Mart.
Hours & Admission Prices: April-Nov. Tues.-Sat. 10-5, Sun. 12-4; Dec.-March Tues.-Sat. 10-4. Adults $7; discounts to children, senior citizens, groups, AAA & AAM members; ASTC passport & NAWCC members no charge. Closed holidays. ♿
Attendance: 15,000 (estimated)
Membership: Annual $70; Lifetime under 40 $3,000; Lifetime 40 & over $2,000.

WRIGHT'S FERRY MANSION, (M), 38 S. Second St., Columbia, PA 17512-1402. Mailing Address: P.O. Box 68, Columbia, PA 17512-0068. Tel.: 717-684-4325.
Founded: 1974.
Congressional District: 16
Key Personnel: Exec. Dir., Thomas Cook; Cur., Elizabeth Meg Schaefer.
Personnel Profile: Full-Time Paid 2; Part-Time Paid 3.
Governing Authority: nonprofit organization. Parent Institution: The von Hess Foundation. Tax-exempt: 501(c)(3) & 509(a).
Historic House: 1738 Susanna Wright House.
Collections: early 18th-century Philadelphia furniture, English ceramics, glass, textiles & metals.
Research Fields: early 18th-century decorative arts, architecture & interiors; early 18th-century Philadelphia; Susanna Wright; Quaker social & cultural life.
Activities: guided tours; lectures.
Publications: brochure; two-vol. set of books, Wright's Ferry Mansion: The House and the Collection.
Hours & Admission Prices: May-Oct. Tues.-Wed. & Fri.-Sat. 10-3 (last tour begins at 3). Adults $5, children 6-18 $2.50; discount to groups. Closed holidays.
Attendance: 2,000

Coolspring

COOLSPRING POWER MUSEUM, 179 Coolspring Rd., Coolspring, PA 15730. Mailing Address: P.O. Box 19, Coolspring, PA 15730-0019. Tel.: 814-849-6883. Fax: 814-849-5495.
E-mail: cpm@coolspringpowermuseum.org
Web Site: www.coolspringpowermuseum.org
Founded: 1985.
Congressional District: 5
Key Personnel: C.E.O. & Pres., Vance Packard; Dir., Paul Harvey, M.D.; Dir., Chris Austin; Dir., Douglas Fye, Jr.; Dir. & Financial Dir., Jennifer Fye; Dir., Clark Colby; Dir., John Hanley; Dir., Kim Himes; Dir., Edward Kuntz; Dir., Brad Miller; Chm. (V) & Membership, Gail Lavender; Dir. & Newsletter, Vance Packard; Museum Shop Mgr., Fran Colby.
Personnel Profile: Part-Time Paid 1; Part-Time Volunteers 171.
Governing Authority: nonprofit organization. Tax-exempt: 501(c)(3).
Historical Museum.
Collections: internal combustion engines; pumps; electrical generation equipment; oil field artifacts; oil pipeline equipment; machine tools.
Research Fields: early builders of internal combustion engines; oil line & petroleum production companies; developmental technology of the internal combustion engine.
Facilities: 1,490-vol. library of patent drawings, engineering drawings for several early engine manufactures, internal combustion texts, equipment catalogs & related periodicals, available for use by the public; 25,100 sq. ft. exhibit space; 41-acres of outside display area. Museum-related items for sale.
Activities: guided tours; lectures; films; docent program; participatory & loan exhibitions. Annual Event: Antique Power Exhibition & Show.
Publications: annual technical journal, Bores & Strokes; bimonthly newsletters, CPM News, Iron & Oil Review.
Hours & Admission Prices: April-Oct. 3rd. full weekend of month 10-5; other times by appointment. Adult $5, senior citizen, children under 12 & students $1; discounts to groups; children & members no charge.
Attendance: 19,125 (estimated)
Membership: Individual $25; Family $35; Patron $1,000; Cornerstone Patron $5,000; Endowment Patron $10,000.

Cornwall

CORNWALL IRON FURNACE, 94 Rexmont Rd., Cornwall, PA 17016. Mailing Address: P.O. Box 251, Cornwall, PA 17016-0251. Tel.: 717-272-9711. Fax: 717-272-0450.
E-mail: ssomers@state.pa.us
Web Site: www.cornwallironfurnace.org
Founded: 1932.
Congressional District: 16
Key Personnel: Historic Site Admin., Stephen G. Somers.
Personnel Profile: Full-Time Paid 2; Part-Time Paid 1; Part-Time Volunteers 15.
Governing Authority: state. Parent Institution: Pennsylvania Historical & Museum Commission, 300 North St., Harrisburg, PA 17120. Subsidiary Institution: Cornwall Iron Furnace Associates, Inc. Tax-exempt.
Industrial Museum.
Collections: charcoal process; ironmaking artifacts; geology; 19th-century horse-drawn vehicles.
Facilities: charcoal house; preserved 19th-century furnace complex; visitor center on 18th-century site; roasting oven; blacksmith shop; smokehouse; picnic area.
Activities: guided tours; film series; lectures; craft demonstrations; changing exhibits.
Publications: books, booklets on industrial state & local history.
Hours & Admission Prices: Tues.-Sat. 9-5, Sun. 12-5. Adults $6, senior citizens 65 & over $5.50, youth 3-12 $4; discounts to AAM members; children under 6 no charge. Closed New Year's Day; Martin Luther King Jr. Day; Presidents' Day; Columbus Day; Veterans Day; Thanksgiving & day after; Christmas. ♿
Attendance: 9,000 (estimated)
Membership: Cornwall Iron Furnace Associates: Student $15; Senior Citizen $18; Individual $20; Family $30.

Corry

CORRY AREA HISTORICAL SOCIETY, 945 Mead Ave., Corry, PA 16407. Mailing Address: P.O. Box 107, Corry, PA 16407-0107. Tel.: 814-664-4749.
Web Site: www.tbscc.com
Founded: 1965.
Congressional District: 24
Key Personnel: C.E.O., James R. Nelson; Vice Pres., John Silvis; Sec., Karen Silvis; Treas. & Cur., Robert Lindsey; Treas., John Lutz.
Personnel Profile: Part-Time Volunteers 20.
Governing Authority: Parent Institution: City of Cory. Tax-exempt.
Local History Museum.
Collections: industry; transportation; costumes; agriculture; music.
Research Fields: Corry area.
Facilities: library of books, newspapers & deeds available on premises.
Activities: permanent exhibitions; Mead Park Days; monthly exhibit meetings.
Publications: book, Everyone A Hero.
Hours & Admission Prices: Memorial Day-Labor Day Sat.-Sun. & holidays 2-4, groups & tours at other times by appointment. No charge; donations accepted. ♿
Attendance: 5,500 (accurate)
Membership: Individual $3; Contributing $5; Sustaining $50; Life $100.

Coudersport

POTTER COUNTY HISTORICAL SOCIETY, 308 N. Main St., Coudersport, PA 16915-1626. Mailing Address: P.O. Box 605, Coudersport, PA 16915-0605. Tel.: 814-274-4410.
E-mail: pottercohist@zitomedia.net
Web Site: history.pottercountypa.net
Founded: 1919.
Congressional District: 23
Key Personnel: Pres., Leon B. Reed; Vice Pres. & Program Chm., Roger Gartside; 2nd Vice Pres., David Castano; Sec. & Treas., James Centanni; Asst. Sec. & Treas., Lucille Church; Cur., Robert K. Currin.
Personnel Profile: Part-Time Volunteers 9.
Governing Authority: society. Tax-exempt.
Historical Society Museum.
Collections: pioneer artifacts; prints; paintings; Bliss Indian collection; newspapers; books; materials covering local area & the industrial, political and cultural development of Potter County from pre-history to the present; photograph collection Civil War-present.
Research Fields: local history; genealogy.
Facilities: 1,200-vol. library on history, genealogy and census records available for use on premises; reading room.
Activities: guided tours; research.
Publications: quarterly bulletin.
Hours & Admission Prices: Museum: Mon. & Fri. 1-4, Thurs. 6:30pm-8:30pm. Research: Oct.-May Mon. & Fri. 1-4, Thurs. 6:30pm-8:30pm or by appointment. No charge; donations accepted.
Attendance: 1,800 (estimated)
Membership: Individual $5.

Cresson

ADMIRAL PEARY MONUMENT, 7468 Admiral Peary Hwy., Rte. 2014, Cresson, PA 16630-1717. Mailing Address: Bureau of Historic Sites & Museums-Commonwealth Keystone Building, 400 North St., Harrisburg, PA 17120-0053. Tel.: 717-705-0559.
Founded: 1945.
Congressional District: 12
Key Personnel: Property Placement Div. Chief, Robert N. Sieber.
Governing Authority: state. Administered by Pennsylvania Historical and Museum Commission, Box 1026, Harrisburg, PA. 17108. Tel.: 717-783-5406.
State Monument: dedicated to Admiral Robert E. Peary, discoverer of the North Pole in 1909.
Collections: sculpture.
Facilities: picnic area.
Hours & Admission Prices: Daily dawn-dusk. No charge.

Dallas

PAULY FRIEDMAN ART GALLERY, Misericordia University, 301 Lake St., Dallas, PA 18612-1008. Tel.: 570-674-6250. Fax: 570-674-6416.
E-mail: dposatko@misericordia.edu
Web Site: www.misericordia.edu
Formerly: MacDonald Art Gallery
Founded: 2009.
Key Personnel: Dir., Brian J. Benedetti; Cur. & Gallery Asst., Dona Posatko.
Personnel Profile: Full-Time Paid 1; Part-Time Paid 1.
Governing Authority: Parent Institution: Misericordia University. Tax-exempt.
Art Gallery.
Collections: paintings; photography; sculpture; decorative arts; prints; drawings.
Major Exhibits: La Tinta Grita-The Ink Shoots: The Art of Social Resistance in Oaxaca, Mexico (T), 1/25/10-2/27/10; Robert Capa WWII Photographs, 3/8/10-4/17/10; Modern Masters in Print, 4/26/10-6/26/10.
Hours & Admission Prices: Mon.-Thurs. 10:30-8, Sat.-Sun. 1-5. No charge. ♿

Delaware Water Gap

ANTOINE DUTOT MUSEUM & GALLERY, S. Main St., (Rte. 611), Delaware Water Gap, PA 18327. Mailing Address: P.O. Box 484, Delaware Water Gap, PA 18327-0484. Tel.: 570-476-4240.

History Museum & Art Gallery: housed in a former school house; c.1850.

Collections: local history & culture; period furnishings; personal artifacts; paintings; photographs.

Hours & Admission Prices: Memorial Day to Columbus Day Sat.-Sun. 1-5. Suggested Donation: adults $2; children under 12 no charge.

Devon

JENKINS ARBORETUM, 631 Berwyn Baptist Rd., Devon, PA 19333-1001. Tel.: 610-647-8870.

Web Site: www.jenkinsarboretum.org

Founded: 1974.

Congressional District: 5

Key Personnel: Dir., Dr. Harold E. Sweetman.

Personnel Profile: Full-Time Paid 6; Part-Time Paid 1; Part-Time Volunteers 15; Interns 2.

Governing Authority: nonprofit organization. Tax-exempt.

Arboretum: on grounds of former home of H. Lawrence Jenkins & Elisabeth Phillippe Jenkins.

Collections: living collection of azaleas, rhododendrons & wildflowers; naturalistic landscape design emphasizing native flora.

Facilities: botanical garden.

Publications: annual newsletter.

Hours & Admission Prices: Daily 8am to sunset. No charge; donations accepted.

Attendance: 20,000

Membership: Regular $45; Donor $100; Patron $250; Circle of Friends $1,000.

Doylestown

BUCKS COUNTY CIVIL WAR LIBRARY & MUSEUM, (M), 32 N. Broad St., Doylestown, PA 18901-4317. Mailing Address: 197 W. Court St., Doylestown, PA 18901-4144. Tel.: 215-348-8293. Fax: 215-348-8293.

E-mail: streckerb@netreach.net

Web Site: buckscivilwar.com

Founded: 2003.

Congressional District: 8

Key Personnel: Exec. Dir., Treas. & Public Rels., Betty J. Strecker; Pres., Tim Linehan, Jr.

Personnel Profile: Full-Time Paid 1; Full-Time Volunteers 5; Part-Time Volunteers 4; Interns 1.

Governing Authority: private; nonprofit organization. Tax-exempt: 501(c)(3).

History Museum.

Collections: Civil War & 104th Volunteer PA Regiment artifacts; manuscripts; books; articles.

Facilities: library. Museum-related items for sale.

Activities: guided tours; lectures; loan, participatory & temporary exhibits; study clubs. Annual Events: Community Open House in May.

Publications: quarterly newsletter, Swamp Angel II News.

Hours & Admission Prices: Sat. 10:30-2; other times by appointment. No charge; donations accepted.

Attendance: 260 (estimated)

Membership: Student $5; Individual $18; Family $30; Friend $50; Corporate $100.

DOYLESTOWN HISTORICAL SOCIETY, 56 S. Main St., Doylestown, PA 18901-0550. Mailing Address: P.O. Box 1634, Doylestown, PA 18901-0550. Tel.: 215-345-9430.

Historical Society Museum.

Collections: local history & culture; photographs; personal artifacts.

Hours & Admission Prices: Sat. 10-4; other times by appointment.

FONTHILL MUSEUM OF THE BUCKS COUNTY HISTORICAL SOCIETY, E. Court St. & Rte. 313, Doylestown, PA 18901. Mailing Address: 84 S. Pine St., Doylestown, PA 18901-4930. Tel.: 215-348-9461. Fax: 215-348-9462.

E-mail: fhmail@fonthillmuseum.org

Web Site: www.fonthillmuseum.org

Founded: 1930.

Congressional District: 8

Key Personnel: C.E.O., Doug Dolan; Chm., Brian McLeod; Site Admin., Edward L. Reidell.

Personnel Profile: Full-Time Paid 2; Part-Time Paid 29; Part-Time Volunteers 37; Interns 2.

Governing Authority: nonprofit organization. Governed by Fonthill Trust. Administered by Bucks County Historical Society. Tax-exempt: 501(c)(3).

Historic House Museum & National Historic Landmark: Fonthill, a 44-room concrete castle-like building built 1908-1912, was the home of Henry C. Mercer (1856-1930), noted archaeologist, collector and arts & crafts movement tilemaker.

Collections: Mercer's Moravian tiles; Persian, Spanish & Delft tiles; 7,000 prints & engravings; ceramics; anthropology; costumes; photographs; archives.

Research Fields: arts & crafts movement; tile manufacturing; early concrete construction.

Facilities: 6,000-vol. library of Henry Mercer with limited availability to the public through Bucks County Historical Society Library. Publications, & postcards for sale.

Activities: guided tours; organized education programs for children; guide program. Museum Sponsors: special events; rental program.

Hours & Admission Prices: Mon.-Sat. 10-5, Sun. 12-5; guided tour only, reservations requested. Adults $10, senior citizens $9, students $4; discounts to AAM & ICOM members; children under 5 & members no charge. Closed New Year's Day; Thanksgiving; Christmas. ♿

Attendance: 30,000 (estimated)

Membership: Student $20; Senior $30; Individual $35; Household & Grandparent $55; Sustaining $75; Sponsor $150.

HERITAGE CONSERVANCY, 85 Old Dublin Pike, Doylestown, PA 18901-2468. Tel.: 215-345-7020. Fax: 215-345-4328.

E-mail: info@heritageconservancy.org

Web Site: www.heritageconservancy.org

Founded: 1958.

Congressional District: 8

Key Personnel: Pres., Clifford C. David, Jr.; Chm., Honorable William Hart Rufe, III

Governing Authority: nonprofit membership organization.

Headquarters housed in 1927, Tudor Revival Style Aldie Mansion; emphasis on land conservation and historic preservation.

Collections: artwork of local artists; decorative arts; photographs.

Research Fields: Bucks County; Pennsylvania history & architecture.

Facilities: archives on Bucks County architecture & nature areas.

Activities: guided tours; lectures; films; organized education programs.

Publications: newsletter, Environs.

Hours & Admission Prices: By appointment only. Adults $4; children 12 & under no charge. ♿

Membership: Student $15; Individual $30; Family $50; Advocate $100; Benefactor $250; Conservator $500; Guardian $1,000. Business membership categories available.

* **JAMES A. MICHENER ART MUSEUM, (M),** 138 S. Pine St., Doylestown, PA 18901-4931. Tel.: 215-340-9800, ext. 113. Fax: 215-340-9807.

E-mail: jamam1@michenerartmuseum.org

Web Site: www.michenerartmuseum.org

Founded: 1987.

Congressional District: 8

Key Personnel: Dir. & C.E.O., Bruce Katsiff; Chm. Bd. Trustees (V), William Aichele; Pres. Bd. Trustees (V), Kevin Putman; Senior Cur., Brian Peterson; Accounting Mgr., Dorothy Landes; Exhibitions Registrar, Sean Wells; Librarian & Database Coord., Birgitta Bond; Preparator, Bryan Brems; Membership Coord. & Systems Network Admin., Joan Welcker; Dir. Mktg., Kathleen McSherry; Exec. Asst., Candace Clarke; Dir. Programs, Zoriana Siokalo; Cur. Education, Adrienne Romano; Cur. Collections, Constance Kimmerle, Ph.D.; Facility Mgr., Gilbert Winner; Visitors Svcs. & Museum Shop Mgr., Pamela Sergey; Dir. Operations & Visitor Svcs., Hollie Brown.

Personnel Profile: Full-Time Paid 20; Part-Time Paid 22; Part-Time Volunteers 229; Interns 2.

Art Museum.

Collections: Impressionists artists including Edward Redfield, Daniel Garber, William Lathrop & John Folinsbee; American abstract expressionists; 19th & 20th-century American paintings.

Research Fields: 19th & 20th-century Bucks County artists.

Facilities: 32,000 sq. ft. exhibit space; educational facilities; sculpture gardens.

Activities: guided tours; lectures; films; concerts; arts festivals; organized educational programs; docent program; permanent & temporary exhibitions.

Publications: exhibition catalogues.

Hours & Admission Prices: Doylestown: Memorial Day to Labor Day Tues. & Thurs.-Fri. 10-4:30, Wed. 10-9, Sat. 10-5, Sun. 12-5; Sept.-May Tues.-Fri. 10-4:30, Sat. 10-5, Sun. 12-5. Adults $6.50, seniors $6, children 6-18 $4; members & children under 6 no charge. ♿

Attendance: 132,001 (accurate)

Membership: Student $15; Seniors $30; Individual $36; Grandparent, Dual & Family $60; Key & Contributor $100; Sponsor $250; Donor $500; Michener Circle $1,000.

Publications: Journal of the Historical Society of the Cocalico Valley; biannual book of historical photographs.
Hours & Admission Prices: Museum: Sat. 10-4. No charge; donations accepted. Library & Research Center: Mon. & Wed.-Thurs. 9:30-6, Sat. 8:30-5. Research: $3.
Attendance: 900 (estimated)
Membership: Regular $20; Family Membership $30; Life $500.

Erie

ERIE ART MUSEUM, 411 State St., Erie, PA 16501-1106. Tel.: 814-459-5477. Fax: 814-452-1744.
E-mail: contact@erieartmuseum.org
Web Site: www.erieartmuseum.org
Founded: 1898.
Congressional District: 21
Key Personnel: Exec. Dir., John L. Vanco; Pres. (V)., Stephen Porter; Dir. Mktg. & Devel., Tammy Roche; Dir. Administration & Finance, Jenae Gary; Dir. Education & Folk Art Coord., Kelly Armor; Frame Shop Mgr., Joseph Popp; Coord. Publications, Andrea Krivak; Education Coord., Stephanie Campbell; Building & Events Operations, Sam Ansbro; Registrar, Vance Lupher.
Personnel Profile: Full-Time Paid 10; Part-Time Paid 3; Part-Time Volunteers 150; Interns 12.
Governing Authority: nonprofit organization. Tax-exempt: 501(c)(3).
Art Museum Center.
Collections: paintings; sculpture; graphics; decorative arts; photography; American ceramics; Indian bronze & stone sculpture; oriental porcelains & jade; contemporary baskets; Tibetan paintings.
Major Exhibits: Ancient Alloy: Bronzes From The Collection, 1/10-12/10; Making It Better: Folk Art in PA, 1/5/10-4/11/10; Malcolm Christhilf, 1/22/10-4/24/10; 87th Annual Spring Show, 4/24/10-6/20/10; Anne Marie Magenau, 4/30/10-7/24/10.
Research Fields: American ceramic art.
Facilities: studios; classrooms.
Activities: guided tours; lectures; films; gallery talks; formally organized educational programs; temporary & traveling exhibitions; circulating exhibitions; jazz & new music concerts. Museum Sponsors: Annual Spring Show competition.
Publications: monthly e-newsletter; members' newsletter; exhibition announcements; exhibition catalogs.
Hours & Admission Prices: Tues.-Sat. 11-5, Sun. 1-5. Adults $4, students & senior citizens $3, children $2; discounts to AAM & ICOM members; members & Wed. no charge. New Year's Day; Easter; Independence Day; Thanksgiving; Christmas. ♿
Attendance: 36,000 (estimated)
Membership: Green $10; Student & Senior Citizen $15; Individual $35; Family $65; Patron $100; Sustaining $250; Sponsor $500.

ERIE COUNTY HISTORY CENTER & CASHIER'S HOUSE, 417-419 State St., Erie, PA 16501. Mailing Address: 419 State St., Erie, PA 16501-1106. Tel.: 814-454-1813. Fax: 814-454-6890.
E-mail: echs@eriecountyhistory.org
Web Site: www.eriecountyhistory.org
Founded: 1903.
Congressional District: 3
Key Personnel: Operations Dir., Melanie Keubel-Stankey; Pres. (V), Charles Scalise.
Personnel Profile: Full-Time Paid 4; Part-Time Paid 2; Part-Time Volunteers 10; Interns 8.
Governing Authority: society. Parent Institution: Erie County Historical Society. Tax-exempt: 501(c)(3).
Historical Society Museum.
Collections: 1735-present, northwestern Pennsylvania & Great Lakes history.
Research Fields: history of Erie County area, industry & architecture.
Facilities: 3,500-vol. library containing books, documents, manuscripts, dealing with Erie County & northwest Pennsylvania history.
Activities: lectures; formally organized educational programs; temporary exhibitions.
Publications: Journal of Erie Studies; books; periodic newsletter.
Hours & Admission Prices: Tues.-Sat. 11-4. Family $10, Adults $4, seniors $3, children $2; discounts to AAM & AASLH members; members no charge. Closed holidays. ♿
Attendance: 4,526 (accurate)
Membership: Student $10; Individual $35; Family & Grandparent $50; Patron $75; Sustaining $100; Sponsor $250; Corporate $500.

ERIE MARITIME MUSEUM & FLAGSHIP NIAGARA, Bayview Commons, 150 E. Front St., Ste. 100, Erie, PA 16507-1594. Tel.: 814-452-2744 Fax: 814-455-6760.
E-mail: sail@flagshipniagara.org
Web Site: www.flagshipniagara.org
Formerly: Erie Maritime Museum, Homeport U.S. Brig Niagara
Founded: 1998.
Congressional District: 3
Key Personnel: Chm. PHMC, Wayne Spilove; Exec. Dir. PHMC, Barbar Franco; Chm. (V) & Pres. Flagship Niagara League, Brian Scott; Sit Admin. & Sr. Captain, Walter Rybka; Dir. Flagship Niagara League Barbara Johnson; Museum Shop Mgr., Timothy McLaughlin.
Personnel Profile: Full-Time Paid 10; Part-Time Paid 2; Part-Time Volunteer 160; Interns 4.
Governing Authority: state. Administered by Pennsylvania Historical & Museum Commission, Box 1026, Harrisburg, PA 17108. Subsidiary Institution: Flagship Niagara League. Tax-exempt.
Historic Ship & History Museum: Erie maritime; 1813 U.S. Brig Niagara commanded by Comdr. Oliver Hazard Perry.
Collections: Battle of Lake Erie; War of 1812; 19th-century sailing & region maritime history; homeport to the U.S. Brig Niagara; live fire exhibit of th U.S. Brig Lawrence; U.S.S. Michigan/U.S.S. Wolverine; photograph video.
Research Fields: War of 1812; Battle of Lake Erie; naval architecture; Lak Erie maritime history; U.S.S. Michigan/U.S.S. Wolverine.
Facilities: library on Lake Erie maritime history available to scholars members; visitor center; theater; 299-seat auditorium. Museum-relate items for sale.
Activities: guided tours; special programs; on-board ship demonstration hands-on & interactive exhibits; concerts; films; lectures; one day sailir school vessel; 2-4 week live-aboard sail training; educational programs.
Publications: quarterly newsletter, Niagara League News.
Hours & Admission Prices: Jan.-March Thurs.-Sat. 9-5, Sun. 12-5; April-De Mon.-Sat. 9-5, Sun. 12-5; call for ships schedule. Adults $8, senior citize $5, youth 6-17 $3; discounts to AAM & ICOM members; children under & league members no charge. Closed New Year's Day; Martin Luther Ki Jr. Day; Presidents' Day; Columbus Day; Veterans Day; Thanksgivin Christmas.
Attendance: 24,869 (accurate)
Membership: Individual $25; Family $40; Captain $60; Commodore $12 Admiral $275; Perry's Company $500; Fleet Commander $1,000.

ERIE PLANETARIUM, 356 W. Sixth St., Erie, PA 16507-1245. Mailir Address: 419 State St., Erie, PA 16501-1106. Tel.: 814-871-5790 454-1813. Fax: 814-454-6890.
E-mail: echs@eriecountyhistory.org
Web Site: www.eriecountyhistory.org/erie-planetarium
Founded: 1959.
Congressional District: 3
Key Personnel: Dir. Operations & Visitor Member Svcs., Melanie Kuebe Stankey; Planetarium Coord., Jim Gavio.
Personnel Profile: Part-Time Paid 1; Part-Time Volunteers 6.
Governing Authority: private; nonprofit organization. Parent Institution: Er County Historical Society. Tax-exempt: 501(c)(3).
Planetarium.
Collections: geology; astronomy.
Facilities: Spitz A3P projector; 20 ft. dome.
Activities: planetarium shows; scout programs; birthday parties; special eve programs; hands-on activities.
Hours & Admission Prices: Call for hours. Family $10, adult $4, senior $ children $2; discounts to AAM members & groups; members no charge.
Attendance: 5,500 (estimated)
Membership: Student $10; Individual $35; Family & Grandparent $50; Patro $75; Sustaining $100; Sponsor $250; Corporate $500.

ERIE ZOOLOGICAL PARK & BOTANICAL GARDENS OF NORTH WESTERN PENNSYLVANIA, 423 W. 38th St., Erie, PA 16508-2701 Mailing Address: P.O. Box 3268, Erie, PA 16508-0268. Tel.: 814-864-4091 Fax: 814-864-1140.
E-mail: info@eriezoo.org
Web Site: www.eriezoo.org
Founded: 1962.
Key Personnel: Pres. & C.E.O., Scott Mitchell; Coord. Mktg. & Events Ainslie Brosig.
Personnel Profile: Full-Time Paid 27; Part-Time Paid 70; Part-Time Volunteer 412.
Governing Authority: society. Parent Institution: Erie Zoological Society Tax-exempt.
Zoo & Botanical Garden.

*** MERCER MUSEUM OF THE BUCKS COUNTY HISTORICAL SOCIETY, (M),** 84 S. Pine St., Doylestown, PA 18901-4930. Tel.: 215-345-0210. Fax: 215-230-0823.
E-mail: info@mercermuseum.org
Web Site: www.mercermuseum.org
Founded: 1916.
Congressional District: 8
Key Personnel: C.E.O. & Pres., Douglas C. Dolan; Chm., Brian McLeod; Exec. Vice Pres., Molly W. Lowell; Vice Pres. Collections & Interpretation, Cory Amsler.
Personnel Profile: Full-Time Paid 10; Part-Time Paid 25; Part-Time Volunteers 250; Interns 1.
Governing Authority: society. Parent Institution: Bucks County Historical Society. Tax-exempt: 501(c)(3).
History, Historical Technology & Folk Art Museum: housed in 1916 concrete castle-like National Historic Landmark building.
Collections: 40,000 tools & products of early handcraft; artifacts of everyday life; Pennsylvania German material culture; folk art; local history items.
Research Fields: pre-industrial technology; material culture; local history; genealogy.
Facilities: Spruance Library: 20,000-vol. library of Bucks Countiana genealogical materials & historical technology books, maps, periodicals and pamphlets available for use during library hours.
Activities: workshops; education programs; family programs; permanent & temporary exhibitions; digital audio guide; summer camp.
Publications: newsletter, Penny Lots; various books & pamphlets.
Hours & Admission Prices: Museum: Sun. 12-5, Mon. & Wed.-Sat. 10-5, Tues. 10-9. Spruance Library: Tues. 1-9, Wed.-Fri. 1-5, Sat. 10-5. Adults $9, senior citizens $8, students $4; discounts to groups, AAA, AAM & ICOM members; children under 5 & members no charge. Closed New Year's Day; Thanksgiving; Christmas. ♿
Attendance: 65,000 (estimated)
Membership: Student $20; Senior $30; Individual $35; Family & Grandparent $55; Sustaining $75; Sponsor $150; Contributor $250; Distinguished Donor $500; President's Circle $1,000.

MORAVIAN POTTERY & TILE WORKS, 130 Swamp Rd., Doylestown, PA 18901-2451. Tel.: 215-345-6722. Fax: 215-345-1361.
E-mail: mptw@buckscounty.org
Web Site: www.buckscounty.org/visitors
Founded: 1969.
Congressional District: 8
Key Personnel: Dir., Charles Yeske.
Personnel Profile: Full-Time Paid 12; Part-Time Paid 4.
Governing Authority: county. Tax-exempt.
Historic Building: a National Historic Landmark.
Collections: tile industry, production, & installation; tiles; mosaics.
Activities: factory tours.
Hours & Admission Prices: Tours: daily 10-4:45. Adults $4.50, senior citizens $3.50, children 7-17 $2.50; discounts to AAM members. Tile Shop: no charge. Closed major holidays. ♿
Attendance: 26,387 (accurate)
Membership: Individual $35.

DuBois

WINKLER GALLERY OF FINE ART, 36 N. Brady St., DuBois, PA 15801-2256. Tel.: 814-375-5834.
Art Gallery.
Collections: paintings; photography; mosaics; blown glass; sculpture.
Hours & Admission Prices: Tues.-Thurs. 11-5, Fri.-Sat. 11-8.

Easton

LAFAYETTE COLLEGE ART GALLERIES, WILLIAMS CENTER FOR THE ARTS, 317 Hamilton St., Easton, PA 18042-1768. Tel.: 610-330-5361. Fax: 610-330-5642.
E-mail: okayam@lafayette.edu
Web Site: lafayette.edu/williamsgallery
Founded: 1983.
Congressional District: 136
Key Personnel: Pres. Lafayette College, Dan Weiss; Dir. Williams Center for the Arts, H. Ellis Finger; Vice Pres. & Treas., Mitchell Wein; Dir. Lafayette Art Galleries, Michiko Okaya; Skillman Library Archivist, Diane Windham Shaw; Dir. Security, Hugh Harris.
Personnel Profile: Full-Time Paid 1; Part-Time Paid 1.
Governing Authority: private college; not-for-profit. Parent Institution: Lafayette College. Tax-exempt.
College Art Gallery.
Collections: 19th- & 20th-century American & British portrait & historical paintings; photographs; Abraham Lincoln & Marquis de Lafayette memorabilia & artwork; 20th-century contemporary prints; Kirby paintings.
Research Fields: pertaining to collections.
Facilities: 2,400 sq. ft. exhibit space.
Activities: lectures; in-house loan & temporary exhibitions.
Publications: triannual, exhibit catalogs & brochures; newsletter.
Hours & Admission Prices: Sept.-May Mon.-Tues.-Wed. & Fri. 10-5, Thurs. 10-8, Sat.-Sun. 12-5. No charge. Closed school holidays. ♿
Attendance: 7,000 (estimated)

*** NATIONAL CANAL MUSEUM, HUGH MOORE HISTORICAL PARK AND MUSEUMS,** 30 Centre Square, Easton, PA 18042-7743. Tel.: 610-559-6613. Fax: 610-250-6686.
E-mail: ncm@canals.org
Web Site: canals.org
Founded: 1970.
Congressional District: 15
Key Personnel: Chm. (V), Jack Krissinger; Museum Principal, Shelly Wiles; Operations Coord., Jonathan Markloff.
Personnel Profile: Full-Time Paid 8; Part-Time Paid 30; Part-Time Volunteers 104; Interns 4.
Governing Authority: municipal & nonprofit corporation. Tax-exempt.
Transportation and Industrial Museum.
Collections: canal related artifacts; manuscripts; photo archives; industrial artifacts & records. Historical House: 1923 Locktenders House Museum.
Research Fields: Towpath canals; canal-related industries; early railroads; canal folklore; oral history; recreational use of canals; anthracite coal mining; anthracite iron production; industrial history, technology, steel production & research; communication; technology.
Facilities: 10,000-vol. library of books on canals of the Towpath Era & canal related industries available for research on premises only; archives; reading room; research center; 50-seat auditorium. Transportation-related books & items for sale.
Activities: tours; lectures; films; formally organized education programs; loan & temporary exhibitions; hiking trails; boat rentals; mule-drawn canal boat rides.
Publications: quarterly, biannual books; Canal Currents; quarterly, Locktender; annual, Proceedings of Canal History and Technology Proceedings.
Hours & Admission Prices: National Canal Museum: Tues.-Fri. 9:30-3, Sat. 9:30-5, Sun. 12-5. Adults & children $9.50, senior citizens $9. Admission includes The Crayola Factory. Canal Boat Ride: May Sat. 9:30-5, Sun. 12-5; Memorial Day to Labor Day daily; Sept. Sat. 9:30-5, Sun. 12-5. Adults $7, seniors $6.50, children 3-15 $5; discounts to AAM members & groups of 15 or more. Technology Center: May Sat. 12-5; Memorial Day to Labor Day daily 12-4. Admission $5. ♿
Attendance: 300,000 (accurate)
Membership: Associate $25; Contributing $40; Supporting $60; Sustaining $100; Sponsoring $500; Patron $1,000; Benefactor $2,500. Corporate: Supporting $100-$499; Sponsoring $500-$999; Patron $1,000-$2,500; Benefactor $2,500 & up.

NORTHAMPTON COUNTY HISTORICAL AND GENEALOGICAL SOCIETY, 107 S. 4th St., Easton, PA 18042-4597. Mailing Address: 101-107 S. Fourth St., Easton, PA 18042. Tel.: 610-253-1222. Fax: 610-253-4701.
E-mail: director@northamptonctymuseum.org
Web Site: northamptonctymuseum.org
Founded: 1906.
Congressional District: 15
Key Personnel: Exec. Dir., Colleen Cunningham Lavdar; Pres. (V), L. Anderson Daub; Librarian (V), Mrs. Roland S. Moyer; Cur., Andria Zaia.
Personnel Profile: Full-Time Paid 1; Full-Time Volunteers 2; Part-Time Paid 4; Part-Time Volunteers 70.
Governing Authority: society; nonprofit. Subsidiary Institutions: History Learning Center; Illick Research Library; Nicholas Children's Museum; Kressler Memorial Gardens; Northampton County Museum. Tax-exempt: 501(c)(3).
Historical Society Museum: housed in 1832 Jacob Mixsell House.
Collections: 19th-century portraits; Native American artifacts; period dolls; military equipment & uniforms; 19th-century costumes; folk art items; manuscripts; early craft & trade implements; furniture, food prep implements.
Research Fields: genealogy; 18th- to 20th-century local history.
Facilities: 5,000-vol. library of local history & genealogical books available for use by request.
Activities: guided tours; lectures; permanent & changing exhibitions.
Publications: approx. 20 books & pamphlets on subjects related to local history.
Hours & Admission Prices: Museum: Mon.-Fri. 9-4. Library: Tues.-Fri. 9-2. Adults $3.
Attendance: 3,000 (estimated)

Membership: Young Historian (Student) $10; Museum Protector (Individual) $40-$49; Penn's Kinfolk (Family) $50-$99; Historic Circle $100-$149; Mixsell Circle $150-$499; Pacesetters $500-$999; Benefactors $1,000 & up.

Ebensburg

CAMBRIA COUNTY HISTORICAL SOCIETY, 615 N. Center, Ebensburg, PA 15931-1122. Mailing Address: P.O. Box 278, Ebensburg, PA 15931-0278. Tel.: 814-472-6674.
Web Site: www.cambriacountyhistorical.com
Founded: 1925.
Congressional District: 12
Key Personnel: C.E.O. & Pres. (V), Fremont McKenrick; Cur., Kathy Jones.
Personnel Profile: Part-Time Paid 1.
Governing Authority: private; nonprofit organization. Tax-exempt: 501(c)(3).
General Museum: housed in the 1889 A.W. Buck house.
Collections: 19th-20th century artifacts; history; agriculture; archives; Indian artifacts; industry; numismatic; toys; military; county census; newspapers from 1831.
Research Fields: genealogy; county history.
Facilities: approx. 3,000-vol. library of archives, State's history, biography, genealogy, Indian history, county censuses & newspapers available on premises; reading room.
Activities: guided tours; lectures; films.
Publications: reprint of 1890 Caldwell Atlas of Cambria County; quarterly newsletter, The Cambria County Heritage.
Hours & Admission Prices: Tues.-Fri. 10-4, Sat. 9-1. No charge; donations accepted; Research Library $3 non members. ♿
Attendance: 2,000
Membership: Annual $20; Family $25; Donor $30; Patron $50; Life $250; Benefactor $500.

Eckley

ECKLEY MINERS' VILLAGE, Main St., Eckley, PA 18255. Mailing Address: 2 Eckley Main St., Weatherly, PA 18255-5030. Tel.: 570-636-2070. Fax: 570-636-2938. TDD: 800-654-5988.
Web Site: www.eckleyminers.org
Founded: 1969.
Congressional District: 11
Key Personnel: Dir., David Dubick; Cur., Richard Stanislau; Pres., Pasco Schiavo, Esq.; Museum Shop Mgr., Mellisa Sanchez.
Personnel Profile: Full-Time Paid 8; Part-Time Paid 4; Part-Time Volunteers 55; Interns 3.
Governing Authority: state. Pennsylvania Historical & Museum Commission, P.O. Box 1026, Harrisburg, 17120. Tax-exempt: 170(c)(1).
Historic Village: 54 houses built in the 1850s as coal patch town including Roman Catholic Church, Episcopal Church, doctor's office; coal breaker, visitor's center & mule barn.
Collections: miner's houses; mine owner's homes; churches; artifacts relating to mining & life of the anthracite families.
Research Fields: anthracite coal mining & social & cultural history of anthracite region.
Facilities: library of research material; visitors center; theater. Museum-related items for sale.
Activities: guided tours; lectures; films; plays; education programs for primary, secondary & college students; permanent exhibitions. Special Events: Christmas program; Patch Town Days; Civil War Encampment.
Publications: quarterly newsletter; pamphlets.
Hours & Admission Prices: Mon.-Sat. 9-5, Sun. 12-5. Adults $6, senior citizens 60 & over $5.50, children 6-12 $4; discounts to AAM, ICOM members & all professional organizations; children under 6 & members no charge. Closed Martin Luther King Jr. Day; Veterans Day; Columbus Day; Thanksgiving, Christmas. ♿
Attendance: 20,000 (estimated)
Membership: Individual $15; Family $20; Contributor $30; Sponsor $50; Benefactor $100; Patron $500.

Eldred

ELDRED WORLD WAR II MUSEUM, 201 Main St., Eldred, PA 16731. Mailing Address: P.O. Box 273, Eldred, PA 16731-0273. Tel.: 814-225-2220; 866-686-9944 (Toll Free). Fax: 814-225-4407.
Founded: 1996.
Key Personnel: Dir., Jay P. Tennies
Military History Museum.
Collections: WWII history; military equipment, uniforms, & personal stories; photographs; personal artifacts.
Activities: special events.
Hours & Admission Prices: Sun. 1-4, Tues.-Sat. 10-4. Adults $5; discounts to groups; children 18 & under no charge. Closed New Year's Eve & Day; Independence Day; Thanksgiving & day after; Christmas Eve, Day & day after.

Elizabethtown

WINTERS HERITAGE HOUSE MUSEUM, 41-47 E. High St., Elizabethtown, PA 17022. Mailing Address: P.O. Box 14, Elizabethtown, PA 17022-0014. Tel.: 717-367-4672. Fax: 717-367-9991.
Web Site: www.elizabethtownhistory.org
Founded: 1988.
Congressional District: 16
Key Personnel: Exec. Dir., Lori B. Donofrio-Galley; Pres. (V), Dr. Michael A. Worman.
Personnel Profile: Full-Time Volunteers 100; Part-Time Paid 2; Part-Time Volunteers 3; Interns 1.
Governing Authority: Parent Institution: Elizabethtown Preservation Assoc. Tax-exempt.
Historic House Museum: c.1750.
Collections: family histories; maps; deeds; obituaries; local history & memorabilia; oral histories; yearbooks; photographs; architecture.
Major Exhibits: Quilt Show, 5/10; Traditional Arts, Fall 2010.
Research Fields: genealogy; local history.
Facilities: genealogy library.
Activities: hands-on demonstrations; classes; workshops; research; walking tours; mural interpretation. Annual Events: Appraisal Fair; Holiday Craft Show.
Publications: member newsletter.
Hours & Admission Prices: March-May & Sept.-Dec. Thurs.-Fri. 9:30-3:30, Sat. 9:30-12; June-Aug. Thurs.-Fri. 9:30-3:30. Museum: no charge; donations accepted. Research: non-members $5 daily. Closed holidays.
Attendance: 1,000 (estimated)
Membership: Individual $15; Family $30; Sustaining $50; Patron $100; Sponsor $250; Benefactor $500; Associate & Life $1,000.

Elkins Park

RICHARD WALL HOUSE MUSEUM, 1 Wall Park Dr., Elkins Park, PA 19027. Tel.: 215-887-9159 & 6200, ext. 114.
Founded: 1980.
Congressional District: 2
Key Personnel: Chm. (V), Stephen Banks; Vice Chm., David Harrower; Cur., Dorothy Spruill
Historic House Museum: listed on the National Register of Historic Places.
Collections: local history & culture from late 1700s to 1950s; period furnishings; personal artifacts; springhouse; carriage house.
Hours & Admission Prices: Sun. 1-4; other times by appointment. No charge; donations accepted.

THE TEMPLE JUDEA MUSEUM OF REFORM CONGREGATION KENESETH ISRAEL, 8339 Old York Rd., Elkins Park, PA 19027-1515. Tel.: 215-887-2027. Fax: 215-887-1070.
E-mail: tjmuseum@aol.com
Web Site: www.kenesethisrael.org/museum.html
Founded: 1984.
Congressional District: 2
Key Personnel: Dir. & Cur., Rita Rosen Poley; Chm. (V), Karen Shain Schloss.
Personnel Profile: Part-Time Paid 1; Part-Time Volunteers 20.
Governing Authority: denominational group; nonprofit. Tax-exempt: 501(c)(3).
Religious Museum.
Collections: over 1,000 Jewish artifacts from around the world; fabrics crafted for religious ceremonial, folk & cultural use; paintings; prints; lithographs; photographs; silver ceremonial objects; embroidered Torah binder, 1695; second oldest American ketubah (marriage contract) PA, 1778; Jewish music & performing arts; ephemera.
Facilities: 500-vol. library; 197 sq. ft. exhibit space.
Activities: guided tours; lectures; loan & temporary exhibitions. Annual Event: Artisans' Festival.
Publications: newsletter, Friends of the Museum.
Hours & Admission Prices: Mon.-Fri. 1-4; other times by appointment. No charge. Closed Jewish holidays; legal holidays. ♿
Attendance: 2,000 (estimated)
Membership: Friend $36; Patron $90; Benefactor $180.

Elverson

HOPEWELL FURNACE NATIONAL HISTORIC SITE, 2 Mark Bird Lane, Elverson, PA 19520-9535. Tel.: 610-582-8773. Fax: 610-582-2768.
E-mail: hofu_superintendent@nps.gov
Web Site: www.nps.gov/hofu
Formerly: Hopewell Village National Historic Site

Founded: 1938.
Congressional District: 16
Key Personnel: Supt., Edie Shean-Hammond; Facility Mgr., George Martin; Pres. Friends of Hopewell Furnace NHS, Terry Stauffer; Cultural Resource Mgr., Rebecca Ross; Chief Interpretation, Frances Delmar; Chief Natural Resources, Steven Ambrose; Coord. Arts & Crafts Program, Helen Seguin; Administrative Officer, Eleanor Martin; Museum Shop Mgr., Christine Rogers; Volunteer Coord., Frank Hebblethwaite.
Personnel Profile: Full-Time Paid 14; Part-Time Paid 11; Part-Time Volunteers 434; Interns 2.
Governing Authority: federal. Parent Institution: National Park Service, Dept. of Interior, Washington, DC. Tax-exempt.
Industrial Museum.
Collections: 1770-1880 structures with period furniture; tenant houses; operating water-wheel; restored furnace structures; office; store; barn; archives with microfilm of original records & documents; history of iron business; manuscripts; CCC records; WPA & WWII records; CCC structures & artifacts; living history farm; apple orchard; ethnographic database 1771-1930s.
Major Exhibits: Black History Month Exhibit, 2/10; Women's History, 3/10; Volunteer Exhibit, 4/10; Memorial Day, 5/10; Farm Animals of Hopewell Furnace, 6/10; Fueling the Furnace, 8/10; Apple Harvest Exhibit, 9/10; Christmas Exhibit, 12/10.
Research Fields: late 18th- & 19th-century history of iron production & village life in Pennsylvania; CCC & WPA history; African American history including underground railroad.
Facilities: 700-vol. library of books, microfilm & dissertations pertaining to the history of iron business; auditorium; nature trails; 848-acre site; apple orchard. Postcards, furnace collectibles, books, arts & crafts for sale.
Activities: pre-arranged guided tours; permanent exhibitions; film & slide presentation; school loan service of films; curriculum-based interactive school programs; research; sheep shearing; living history costumed interpretation; charcoal-making demonstrations; apple picking; arts & crafts demonstrations.
Publications: handbook, Hopewell Furnace; American Charcoal Making; newsletter, Hopewell Volunteer Reporter; video, Hopewell Furnace Demonstration; A Summer Day at a Charcoal Iron Furnace; Junior History Guide to Hopewell Furnace NHS; Hopewell Village - The Dynamics of a 19th Century Iron Making Community; Hopewell Furnace Educational Jigsaw Puzzle.
Hours & Admission Prices: Grounds: daily 9-5. Visitor Center & Village: Wed.-Sun. 9-5. Adults $4; National Parks Pass, Access Pass, Senior Pass, Hopewell Furnace Park Pass holders & Jan.-Feb. no charge. Closed New Year's Day; Martin Luther King Jr. Day; Presidents' Day; Thanksgiving; Christmas. ♿
Attendance: 60,000 (estimated)
Membership: Hopewell Furnace Park Pass $20; National Park Pass $80.

Emlenton

PUMPING JACK MUSEUM, Crawford Center on Hill St., Hill St., Emlenton, PA 16373. Mailing Address: P.O. Box 25, Emlenton, PA 16373-0025. Tel.: 724-867-0030.
E-mail: pumpingjackmuseum@csonline.com
Web Site: www.pumpingjack.com
Key Personnel: Pres. (V), Joyce Beikert.
Personnel Profile: Full-Time Volunteers 8.
History Museum.
Collections: oil history; local heritage; equipment; personal artifacts; photographs.
Research Fields: genealogy.
Publications: book, Emlenton Walking Tour; Allegheny River guide, Oil On The Brain.
Hours & Admission Prices: May-Oct. Sat.-Sun. 12-3; other times by appointment. No charge; donations accepted. ♿
Attendance: 100 (estimated)
Membership: Student $3; Individual $10; Family $15.

Emmaus

SHELTER HOUSE SOCIETY, 601 S. 4th St., Emmaus, PA 18049-3934. Mailing Address: Box 254, Emmaus, PA 18049-0254. Tel.: 610-965-9258 & 5280.
Founded: 1951.
Congressional District: 15
Key Personnel: Chm., Jeanette Lehman; Pres., Noreen Yamamoto; Sec., Jane Maulfair.
Governing Authority: board of directors. Tax-exempt.
Historic House: 1734-1741 Shelter House.
Collections: history.
Research Fields: history.
Facilities: 500-vol. library of books & material pertaining to local & family history available for use on premises; reading room; pavilion for cultural group meetings; outdoor fireplaces & recreation areas.
Activities: cultural gatherings.
Publications: annual magazine, The Hearthstone.
Hours & Admission Prices: Daily by appointment only. No charge; donations accepted.
Attendance: 400 (estimated)
Membership: Individual $15; Family $25; Patriots $50; Life (Founders) $100.

Ephrata

EICHER ARTS CENTER AND INDIAN MUSEUM, 407 Cocalico St., Ephrata, PA 17522. Mailing Address: P.O. Box 601, Ephrata, PA 17522. Tel.: 717-738-3084.
Web Site: www.virtualephrata.org
Key Personnel: Coord., James DeFilippis
History Museum: built in 1733 by members of the Ephrata Cloister Brotherhood.
Collections: local history & culture; Native American artifacts; period furnishings; photographs.
Facilities: Museum-related items for sale.
Activities: rental facilities.
Hours & Admission Prices: By appointment. No charge.

* **EPHRATA CLOISTER,** 632 W. Main St., Ephrata, PA 17522-1717. Tel.: 717-733-6600. Fax: 717-733-4364.
E-mail: info@ephratacloister.org
Web Site: www.ephratacloister.org
Founded: 1732.
Congressional District: 16
Key Personnel: Dir., Elizabeth Bertheaud; Pres., Gloria Meiskey; Museum Shop Mgr., Susan Shober.
Personnel Profile: Full-Time Paid 9; Full-Time Volunteers 1; Part-Time Paid 6; Part-Time Volunteers 120.
Governing Authority: state. Parent Institution: Pennsylvania Historical and Museum Commission, Keystone Bldg., Plaza Level, 400 North St., Harrisburg, PA 17120-0053. Subsidiary Institution: Ephrata Cloister Associates. Tax-exempt.
Historic Site: comprising of twelve mid-18th century buildings of Germanic architectural style, located on original site of a celibate religious community.
Collections: books printed here in 18th & early 19th centuries; furniture produced by 18th century society; buildings representative of unique architectural significance.
Research Fields: archaeological; architectural; calligraphy & music; religion.
Facilities: 600-vol. library; 100-seat auditorium; 450-seat outdoor ampitheatre. Cloister inspired reproductions & folk art items for sale.
Activities: guided tours; lectures; concerts; formally organized educational programs; docent program or council; history classes; visitor orientation video.
Publications: books, booklets on Pennsylvania history.
Hours & Admission Prices: Jan.-Feb. Tues.-Sat. 9-5, Sun. 12-5; March-Dec. Mon.-Sat. 9-5, Sun. 12-5. Adults $7, senior citizens 60 & over $6.50, youth 6-17 $5; discounts to groups, all motor clubs, National Historical Society, AAM & ICOM members; members no charge. Closed New Year's Day; Easter; Veterans Day; Thanksgiving & day after; Christmas.
Attendance: 30,000 (estimated)
Membership: Individual $18; Contributing (2 person) $28; Family $43; Business, Civic & Professional $100; Benefactor $500.

HISTORICAL SOCIETY OF THE COCALICO VALLEY, 237/249 W. Main St., Ephrata, PA 17522. Mailing Address: P.O. Box 193, Ephrata, PA 17522-0193. Tel.: 717-733-1616.
E-mail: cjmarquet@gmail.com
Web Site: www.cocalicovalleyhs.org
Founded: 1957.
Congressional District: 16
Key Personnel: Pres. (V), Clarence Spohn; Librarian, Cynthia J. Marquet.
Personnel Profile: Part-Time Paid 1.
Governing Authority: society. Tax-exempt.
History Museum.
Collections: history of Cocalico Valley; reference library; manuscripts; papers of Col. George S. Howard, 1st Dir. of U.S.A.F. Band; Harry F. Stauffer photographs; Pennsylvania German art & culture.
Research Fields: genealogy; local history; U.S.A.F. Band history; history & culture of Pennsylvania Germans.
Facilities: library of books on genealogy & history available for use on premises.
Activities: lectures; films; permanent & temporary exhibitions.

Collections: 2,500 specimens representing 600 species of plants; over 500 animals from 118 species.
Publications: member newsletter, ZooNews.
Hours & Admission Prices: Daily 10-5. Adults $7, senior citizens $6, children 2-11 $4; children under 2, members and physically & mentally challenged no charge. ♿
Attendance: 280,000 (estimated)
Membership: Individual, Single Parent, Grandparent & Family $50; Family Plus & Grandparent Plus $60.

EXPERIENCE CHILDREN'S MUSEUM, 420 French St., Erie, PA 16507-1541. Tel.: 814-453-3743. Fax: 814-459-9735.
E-mail: junep@eriechildrensmuseum.org
Web Site: www.eriechildrensmuseum.org
Founded: 1992.
Congressional District: 21
Key Personnel: Exec. Dir., June Pintea.
Personnel Profile: Full-Time Paid 1; Part-Time Paid 5; Part-Time Volunteers 471; Interns 2.
Governing Authority: nonprofit; board of directors. Tax-exempt.
Children's/Youth Museum.
Collections: 55 hands-on exhibits designed for children ages 2-12.
Facilities: theater. Gift items for sale.
Publications: newsletter, Kaleidoscope.
Hours & Admission Prices: June-Aug. Tues.-Sat. 10-4, Sun. 1-4; Sept.-May Wed.-Sat. 10-4, Sun. 1-4; tours by appointment. Admission $5; children under 2 & members no charge. ♿
Attendance: 37,200 (accurate)
Membership: Single & Single Grandparent Plus $40; Single Plus One & Grandparent $45; Family & Grandparent Plus $50; Family Plus $55.

WATSON-CURTZE MANSION, 356 W. Sixth St., Erie, PA 16507-1245. Mailing Address: 419 State St., Erie, PA 16501-1106. Tel.: 814-871-5790 & 454-1813. Fax: 814-454-6890.
E-mail: echs@eriecountyhistory.org
Web Site: www.eriecountyhistory.org
Formerly: Erie Historical Museum and Planetarium
Founded: 1999.
Congressional District: 3
Key Personnel: Operating Dir., Melanie Kuebel-Stankey.
Personnel Profile: Full-Time Paid 3; Part-Time Volunteers 15.
Governing Authority: private; nonprofit organization. Parent Institution: Erie County Historical Society. Tax-exempt: 501(c)(3).
Historic House.
Collections: 19th- to 20th-century Victorian & American Renaissance decorative arts, Eugene Iverd paintings & prints; textiles & costumes; civil war history; Moses Billings paintings; planetarium. Historic House: 1891 Watson-Curtze Mansion.
Research Fields: 19th-century decorative arts.
Activities: guided tours; lectures; educational programs; permanent & temporary exhibitions; special events. Annual Events: Victorian Holiday exhibit mid-November to mid-January.
Publications: brochures; flyers, pamphlets on events that occur at the museum & planetarium; Guide to the Mansion.
Hours & Admission Prices: Call for hours. Family $10, Adults $4, seniors $3, children 2-12 $2; discounts to AAM members & Wed.; members & children under 2 no charge.
Attendance: 5,075 (accurate)
Membership: Student $10; Individual $35; Family & Grandparent $50; Patron $75; Sustaining $100; Sponsor $250; Corporate $500.

Fallsington

HISTORIC FALLSINGTON, INC., 4 Yardley Ave., Fallsington, PA 19054-1117. Tel.: 215-295-6567. Fax: 215-295-6567.
E-mail: info@historicfallsington.org
Web Site: www.historicfallsington.org
Founded: 1953.
Congressional District: 8
Key Personnel: Exec. Dir., Erica Armour; Pres. (V), Robert L.B. Harman.
Personnel Profile: Full-Time Paid 1; Part-Time Paid 3; Part-Time Volunteers 90; Interns 2.
Governing Authority: board of trustees. Tax-exempt: 501(c)(3).
17th to 20th-Century Quaker Village.
Collections: furnishings & documents; local history. Historic Houses: 1809 Burges-Lippincott House; 1700s Stage-Coach Tavern; 1760s Moon-Williamson Log House; 1758 schoolmaster's house; 1728 former Friends' Meeting House.
Research Fields: local village & Quaker history & culture, 1685-present.
Facilities: picnic area. Museum-related items for sale.
Activities: guided tours; programs & special events; lectures; crafts groups.
Publications: booklet, Historic Fallsington.
Hours & Admission Prices: mid-May to mid-Oct. Tues.-Sat. 10:30-3:30; mid-Oct. to mid-May Tues.-Fri. by appointment. Adults $6, senior citizens $5, children 6-18 $3; discounts to AAA members; members & children 5 and under no charge. Closed New Year's Day; Presidents' Day; Easter; Memorial Day; Independence Day; Labor Day; Christmas.
Attendance: 7,500 (estimated)
Membership: Individual $25; Family $45; Donor $100; Benefactor $250; Patron $1,000; Preservationist $2,500.

Farmington

FORT NECESSITY NATIONAL BATTLEFIELD, One Washington Pkwy., Farmington, PA 15437-9501. Tel.: 724-329-5512. Fax: 724-329-8682.
E-mail: lawren_dunn@nps.gov
Web Site: www.nps.gov/fone
Founded: 1931.
Congressional District: 12
Key Personnel: C.E.O., Joanne Hanley; Acting Site Mgr., Mary Ellen Snyder; Cultural Resource Mgr. & Cur., Lawren Dunn; Museum Shop Mgr., James Tomasek.
Personnel Profile: Full-Time Paid 18; Part-Time Paid 5; Part-Time Volunteers 25; Interns 4.
Governing Authority: federal. Parent Institution: Dept. of the Interior. Subsidiary Institution: National Park Service.
History Museum.
Collections: history; 1820s stage tavern; 1827 Mount Washington Tavern; 1754 French & Indian war site; George Washington's first battle; reconstructed Fort Necessity Stockade.
Research Fields: history.
Facilities: 1200-vol. library of historic source material pertaining to the Great Meadows & Braddock's Campaigns along with material on the National Road & early transportation and the French & Indian War; visitor center; audiovisual program.
Activities: permanent exhibits; guided tours & living history programs during summer months.
Publications: Park Handbook, A Charming Field; park folders & inserts.
Hours & Admission Prices: Summer: daily 9-5; Winter: Tues.-Sat. 9-5. Adults 16 & over $5. Closed federal holidays. ♿
Attendance: 125,000 (estimated)

Fort Loudoun

STATE HISTORIC SITE OF FORT LOUDOUN, 1720 Brooklyn Rd., Fort Loudoun, PA 17724. Mailing Address: P.O. Box 181, Fort Loudoun, PA 17224-0181. Tel.: 717-369-3318. Fax: 717-783-1073.
E-mail: secretary@fortloudoun-pa.com
Web Site: www.fortloudoun-pa.com/
Founded: 1968.
Congressional District: 9
Key Personnel: Property Placement Officer, Robert N. Sieber.
Governing Authority: state. Peters Township Board of Supervisors. Operated by the Fort Loudon Historical Society in agreement with the Pennsylvania Historical and Museum Commission, Box 1026, Harrisburg, PA 17120.
Historic Site: site of Fort Loudoun, erected in 1756 by the British.
Collections: historical displays of the fort occupation.
Facilities: picnic facilities.
Activities: reenactments.
Hours & Admission Prices: Memorial Day to Labor Day Sat.-Sun. 12-5; other times by appointment. No charge; donations accepted.
Membership: Individual $5; Family $10; Life $100.

Fort Washington

THE HIGHLANDS, 7001 Sheaff Lane, Fort Washington, PA 19034-2005. Tel.: 215-641-2687. Fax: 215-641-2556.
E-mail: mbb@highlandshistorical.org
Web Site: www.highlandshistorical.org
Founded: 1975.
Congressional District: 13
Key Personnel: Pres., Gary N. Smith; Dir., Margaret Bleecker Blades; Cur. Education, Elizabeth Gavrys.
Personnel Profile: Full-Time Paid 3; Part-Time Paid 11; Part-Time Volunteers 45.
Governing Authority: state. Administered by the Highlands Historical Society in cooperation with the Pennsylvania Historical & Museum Commission, Box 1026, Harrisburg, PA 17120. Tax-exempt.
Historic House: 1796 Georgian Country House built by Anthony Morris, Speaker of the Pennsylvania Senate.

Collections: historic house; nine outbuildings; 44 acre estate; landscape features a number of architectural elements closely linked to the 2 acre formal gardens.
Facilities: formal gardens.
Activities: restoration & public programs.
Publications: quarterly newsletter.
Hours & Admission Prices: Tours: Mon.-Fri. 1:30 & 3, Sat.-Sun. by appointment. Adults $5; discounts to AAM members; AABGA members no charge. ♿
Attendance: 12,000 (accurate)
Membership: Young Friend $25; Individual $40; Family $60; Friend $100; Sheaff Society $250; Sinkler/Roosevelt Society $500; Anthony Morris Circle $1,000.

HISTORICAL SOCIETY OF FORT WASHINGTON, c/o The Clifton House, 473 Bethlehem Pike, Fort Washington, PA 19034-2313. Tel.: 215-646-6065.
Web Site: www.amblerhistory.com
Founded: 1935.
Congressional District: 13
Key Personnel: Pres. (V), Robin Costa; Treas., Lewis Keen; Librarian, Elizabeth Sadler.
Personnel Profile: Part-Time Volunteers 25.
Governing Authority: executive board. Tax-exempt.
Historical Society & Genealogical Library: housed in 1801 Clifton House.
Collections: 1,800-vol. library.
Research Fields: county history; genealogy; biography; Revolutionary War, Civil War, state & U.S. history.
Facilities: research library & reading room.
Activities: lectures; formally organized educational programs; permanent exhibitions.
Publications: newsletter; brochure.
Hours & Admission Prices: Sept.-June Wed. 2-4; other times by appointment. No charge; donations accepted. Closed holidays.
Attendance: 800 (estimated)
Membership: Students $10; Single $25; Couple $40; Business $100; Business Sponsor & Life Individual $200; Life Couple $300.

HOPE LODGE AND MATHER MILL, 553 S. Bethlehem Pike, Fort Washington, PA 19034. Tel.: 215-646-1595. Fax: 215-628-9471.
E-mail: jhauger@state.pa.us
Web Site: www.ushistory.org/hope
Founded: 1957.
Congressional District: 13
Key Personnel: Site Admin., Joan Hauger; Pres. (V) Friends of Hope Lodge, Jack Gumbrecht; Museum Shop Mgr., Wanda Rauch.
Personnel Profile: Full-Time Paid 2; Part-Time Volunteers 60.
Governing Authority: state. Parent Institution: Pennsylvania Historical & Museum Commission, Commonwealth Keystone Building, Plaza Level, 400 North St., Harrisburg, PA 17120-0053. Tax-exempt.
Historic Buildings: 1743, Hope Lodge, built for Samuel Morris; c.1820 Mather mill, stone grist mill built on the site of former 17th-century mill by Edward Farmar.
Collections: 18th & 19th century furnishing & decorative arts, paintings & prints.
Research Fields: social & labor history; architecture; agriculture.
Facilities: landscape gardens. Museum-related items for sale.
Activities: guided tours; lectures; craft demonstrations; school tours. Museum Sponsors: traditional music events; reenactment of 1777 Whitemarsh Encampment; British Car Show.
Publications: cookbook, Hope Lodge Favorite Recipes; History of Mather Mill; biography of Samuel Morris. Hope Lodge and Mather Mill: a Pennsylvania Trail of History Guide; History of William & Alice Degin (Preservers of a National Treasure); Lime Industry at Hope Lodge.
Hours & Admission Prices: Fri.-Sat. 10-5, Sun. 12-5. Adults $6, senior citizens $5, youth 3-11 $3; discounts to AAM members, groups, PA Trail of History; Travel & Motor Club members; active military & their families, children under 3, museum professionals, PA Heritage Society members & members no charge. Closed New Year's Day; Martin Luther King Jr. Day; Presidents' Day; Columbus Day; Veterans Day; Thanksgiving & day after; Christmas. ♿
Attendance: 8,300 (accurate)
Membership: Individual $20; Family $35; Patron $50; Sponsor $100.

Forty Fort

NATHAN DENISON ADVOCATES, 35 Denison St., Forty Fort, PA 18704-4311. Tel.: 570-288-5531 & 5623.
Founded: 1970.
Congressional District: 11
Key Personnel: Pres. (V), Mrs. Louise Robinson; Property Placement Officer PA Historic & Museum Commission, Robert Sieber.
Personnel Profile: Part-Time Volunteers 22.
Governing Authority: state; nonprofit. Managed by the Denison Advocates. Supported by the Pennsylvania Historical & Museum Commission, Box 1026, Harrisburg, PA 17108-1026. Tax-exempt.
Historic House: 1790 Denison House, Connecticut style architecture, built in the Wyoming Valley; home of Col. Nathan Denison, 1790-1809.
Collections: 18th-century furnishings of house, authentic & reproductions; quill pen; ink well; sealing wax & stamp molds; red ware sand blotter shaker; pictures; paintings; 1684 land sale document.
Facilities: Gift items for sale.
Activities: guided tours. Special Events: May-October.
Publications: booklet, Nathan Denison In The Wyoming Valley, The Nathan Denison Story: A Coloring Booklet; video, The Battle of Wyoming.
Hours & Admission Prices: Tours by appointment. Adults $3, children $2.
Attendance: 1,000 (accurate)

Franklin

VENANGO COUNTY HISTORICAL SOCIETY, 301 S. Park St., Franklin, PA 16323-1238. Tel.: 814-437-2275.
E-mail: vchistory@csonline.net
Key Personnel: Pres., Rainy Linn; Archivist, Marianne Battista
Historical Society: housed in the Hoge-Osmer House, built c.1865.
Collections: local history & culture; photographs; personal artifacts.
Hours & Admission Prices: Jan.-April Sat. 10-2; May-Dec. Tues.-Thurs. & Sat. 10-2.

Galeton

PENNSYLVANIA LUMBER MUSEUM, 5600 U.S. 6 West, Galeton, PA 16922. Mailing Address: P.O. Box 239, Galeton, PA 16922-0239. Tel.: 814-435-2652. Fax: 814-435-6361.
Web Site: www.lumbermuseum.org
Founded: 1970.
Congressional District: 5
Key Personnel: Historic Site Admin., Dolores Buchsen; Pres., Robert Miller; Museum Shop Mgr., Gloria Harris.
Personnel Profile: Full-Time Paid 3; Part-Time Paid 2; Part-Time Volunteers 14.
Governing Authority: state. Pennsylvania Historical and Museum Commission, 3rd & North Sts., P.O. Box 1026, Harrisburg, PA. 17120. Tax-exempt: 170(c)1.
History and Lumber Museum.
Collections: logging tools & equipment; sawmill; logging camp; outdoor museum; two locomotive engines; log loader; railroad log cars; 1917 Model-T Ford Runabout.
Research Fields: pertaining to collections.
Facilities: 2,000-vol. library of books on forestry, natural history & lumbering history available for use on premises; auditorium. Gift items for sale.
Activities: guided tours; lectures; films; festivals; formally organized educational programs; permanent & temporary exhibitions.
Publications: walking guide to the museum.
Hours & Admission Prices: April-Nov. daily 9-5. Adults $4, senior citizens $3:50, children 6-17 $2; museum, AAM & ICOM members no charge. Closed winter holidays. ♿
Membership: Single $10; Family $15; Patron $30; Supporting $50; Corporate $75; Benefactor $100.

Gallitzin

ALLEGHENY PORTAGE RAILROAD NATIONAL HISTORIC SITE AND JOHNSTOWN FLOOD NATIONAL MEMORIAL, 110 Federal Park Rd., Gallitzin, PA 16641-2000. Tel.: 814-886-6116. Fax: 814-884-0206.
E-mail: nancy_smith@nps.gov
Web Site: www.nps.gov/alpo
Founded: 1964.
Congressional District: 12
Key Personnel: Supt., Keith Newlin; Cur., Nancy Smith; Museum Shop Mgr., Doug Bosley.
Personnel Profile: Full-Time Paid 10; Part-Time Paid 5.
Governing Authority: federal. Parent Institution: U.S. Dept. of the Interior, National Park Service, Washington, DC 20240. Tax-exempt: 501(c)(3).
Visitor Center:
Collections: books, articles, books; photographs; 1889 Johnstown flood artifacts; photographs & other artifacts relating to Allegheny Portage Railroad, Pennsylvania Mainline Canal, transportation; Lemon House: transportation, social & economic story.
Research Fields: Allegheny Portage Railroad; Pennsylvania Mainline Canal; Johnstown flood of 1889; 19th century relief efforts; immigrants.

Facilities: 35-vol. library of secondary source material on Pennsylvania Main Line Canal; Allegheny Portage Railroad; 1889 Johnstown Flood available for use on premises; 50-seat auditorium; picnic area; theater. Leaflets & books for sale.
Activities: guided walks; permanent & temporary exhibits; audiovisual programs; period costume demonstrations; hiking.
Publications: park folders; park inserts; park handbook, The Lemon House, A Place in History; The Sylvester Welch's Report on the Allegheny Portage Railroad; Allegheny, Old Portage Railroad 1834-1854; books.
Hours & Admission Prices: Daily 9-5. Adults $4; children under 16 no charge. Closed holidays in winter. ♿
Attendance: 140,000

Gettysburg

ADAMS COUNTY HISTORICAL SOCIETY, (M), 111 Seminary Ridge, Gettysburg, PA 17325-1718. Mailing Address: P.O. Box 4325, Gettysburg, PA 17325-4325. Tel.: 717-334-4723, ext. 201. Fax: 717-334-0722.
E-mail: info@achs-pa.org
Web Site: www.achs-pa.org
Founded: 1940.
Congressional District: 19
Key Personnel: C.E.O., Wayne E. Motts.
Personnel Profile: Full-Time Paid 2; Part-Time Paid 4; Part-Time Volunteers 50; Interns 6.
Governing Authority: nonprofit organization. Tax-exempt: 501(c)(3).
General Museum: housed in 1832 Schmucker Hall, on campus of Lutheran Theological Seminary located on Gettysburg battlefield.
Collections: art; archives; Indian artifacts; genealogy; Civil War artifacts; photographs.
Facilities: 5,000-vol. library of local history, genealogy, newspapers, tax records, estate papers; Civil War books available for research on premises during public hours; reading room.
Activities: lectures; temporary & permanent exhibits; monthly meetings; museum tours; workshops; classes.
Publications: bimonthly newsletter; annual volume.
Hours & Admission Prices: Wed. & Fri.-Sat. 9-12 & 1-4, Thurs. 6pm-9pm. Museum Tours: by appointment. Adults $3; discounts to groups & AAM members; children & students no charge. Research: adults $5; members no charge. Closed holidays.
Attendance: 2,100 (estimated)
Membership: Individual $25; Supporting $35; Family $50; Bermudian Settlement $100; Carroll's Delight $500; Digges Choice $1,000; Corporate $100-$10,000.

THE DAVID WILLS HOUSE, 8 Lincoln Sq., Gettysburg, PA 17325-2205. Tel.: 866-486-5735. Fax: 717-334-5796.
E-mail: info@davidwillshouse.org
Web Site: www.davidwillshouse.org
Founded: 2009.
Congressional District: 19
Key Personnel: Mgr., Jennifer Roth; Chm. (V), Brad Hoch.
Personnel Profile: Full-Time Paid 1; Part-Time Paid 4; Part-Time Volunteers 12.
Governing Authority: Parent Institution: National Park Service & Main Street Gettysburg. Tax-exempt.
History Museum.
Collections: local history & culture; Abraham Lincoln's Gettysburg Address; replicas of Lincoln's bedroom & David Wills' law office.
Hours & Admission Prices: March-April & Sept.-Nov. Wed.-Mon. 9-5; May-Aug. daily 10-6; Dec.-Feb. Thurs.-Mon. 9-5. Adults $6.50, seniors & groups $5.50, youth 6-18 $4. ♿
Membership: Single $50; Couple $75; Family $100; Business $250.

EISENHOWER NATIONAL HISTORIC SITE, 1195 Baltimore Pike, Gettysburg, PA 17325-7034. Mailing Address: 250 Eisenhower Farm Lane, Gettysburg, PA 17325-7108. Tel.: 717-338-9114. Fax: 717-338-0821. TDD: 717-334-1382.
E-mail: eise_site_manager@nps.gov
Web Site: www.nps.gov/eise
Founded: 1967.
Congressional District: 19
Key Personnel: Supt., Dr. John A. Latschar; Museum Cur., Michael R. Florer; Supervisory Historian, Carol A. Hegeman; Museum Shop Mgr., Lisa Kamps.
Personnel Profile: Full-Time Paid 7; Part-Time Paid 4; Part-Time Volunteers 609; Interns 5.
Governing Authority: federal. Parent Institution: National Park Service, U.S. Dept. of Interior, Washington, DC 20240. Tax-exempt: 501(c)(3).
Historic Site: presidential & retirement home of Dwight D. Eisenhower, 34th President of the U.S. & Supreme Commander of Allied forces in Europe during World War II.
Collections: historic structures; furnishings; farm equipment & other vehicles; Eisenhower personal possessions; Eisenhower presidential memorabilia; World War II memorabilia; archaeology.
Research Fields: Eisenhower presidency; 20th-century presidential history.
Facilities: information & visitor center. Museum-related items for sale.
Activities: self-guided tours of home & grounds; farm walking tour; Junior Secret Service Agent program; audiovisual program; conducted tours and programs.
Publications: brochure.
Hours & Admission Prices: Visitor Center: daily 8-4. House: daily 9-4. Tours via shuttle bus only. Adults $6.50, children 6-12 $4; discounts to groups of 16 or more. Closed New Year's Day; Thanksgiving; Christmas. . ♿
Attendance: 70,000 (accurate)

GETTYSBURG NATIONAL MILITARY PARK, 1195 Baltimore Pike, Ste. 100, Gettysburg, PA 17325-7034. Tel.: 717-334-1124. Fax: 717-334-1891. TDD: 717-334-1382.
Web Site: www.nps.gov/gett
Founded: 1895.
Congressional District: 19
Key Personnel: Chief Museum Cur., Greg Goodell.
Personnel Profile: Full-Time Paid 90; Part-Time Volunteers 1,929.
Governing Authority: federal. Parent Institution: National Park Service, Dept. of the Interior. Tax-exempt.
Military Museum & Battlefield.
Collections: Gettysburg Museum of the Civil War; Paul Philippoteaux's Gettysburg Cyclorama. Historic Site: Gettysburg National Cemetery.
Research Fields: Civil War & related topics.
Facilities: 2,700-vol. library primarily on the Battle of Gettysburg, Civil War & environmental books, available for use on premises by appointment; Cyclorama Center. Books, postcards & slides for sale.
Activities: guided tours; films; permanent exhibits; site talks; campfire programs; Electric Map orientation program of the Battle of Gettysburg.
Hours & Admission Prices: April-May & Sept.-Oct. daily 8-6; June-Aug. daily 8-7; Nov.-March daily 8-5. Closed New Year's Day; Thanksgiving; Christmas. ♿
Attendance: 1,900,000 (accurate)

LINCOLN TRAIN MUSEUM, 425 Steinwehr Ave., Gettysburg, PA 17325-2930. Tel.: 717-334-5678. Fax: 717-334-9100.
E-mail: gbgtours@embarqmail.com
Web Site: www.gettysburgbattlefieldtours.com
Congressional District: 19
Key Personnel: Museum Shop Mgr., Pam Jones.
Personnel Profile: Full-Time Paid 2; Part-Time Paid 4.
Governing Authority: private; profit organization.
History Museum.
Collections: model train of Abe Lincoln; numerous operating layouts; railroad dioramas.
Facilities: cafeteria. Museum-related items for sale.
Hours & Admission Prices: March-May & Sept. to late Nov. daily 9-5; June to mid-Aug. daily 9-7. Adults $7.25, seniors $6.95, children 6-12 $3.50; discounts to AAA members. Closed Thanksgiving.
Attendance: 30,000 (estimated)

SCHMUCKER ART GALLERY, Gettysburg College, 300 N. Washington St., Gettysburg, PA 17325-1483. Mailing Address: Box 2452, Gettysburg, PA 17325. Tel.: 717-337-6080. Fax: 717-337-6099.
E-mail: segan@gettysburg.edu
Web Site: www.gettysburg.edu/gallery
Key Personnel: Dir., Shannon Egan, Ph.D.
Personnel Profile: Full-Time Paid 1; Part-Time Paid 1; Part-Time Volunteers 1; Interns 8.
Governing Authority: Parent Institution: Gettysburg College. Tax-exempt.
Art Gallery.
Collections: works by local, national & international contemporary artists.
Activities: temporary & traveling exhibitions.
Hours & Admission Prices: Tues.-Sat. 10-4. No charge; donations accepted. Closed college holidays. ♿

SHRIVER HOUSE MUSEUM, 309 Baltimore Ave., Gettysburg, PA 17325-2602. Tel.: 717-337-2800.
Founded: 1996.
Key Personnel: Dir., Nancie W. Gudmestad
Historic House Museum: housed in the former home of George & Hettie Shriver; built in 1860.
Collections: family & local history; period furnishings; photographs.

Facilities: Museum-related items for sale.
Activities: rental facilities.
Hours & Admission Prices: Feb.-March Sat.-Sun. 12-5; April-Nov. Mon.-Sat. 10-5, Sun. 12-5; other times by appointment. Adults $7.50, seniors $7.25, children 12 & under $5; discounts to groups.
Attendance: 18,000

SOLDIERS NATIONAL MUSEUM, 777 Baltimore St., Gettysburg, PA 17325-2600. Tel.: 717-334-4890. Fax: 717-334-9100.
E-mail: gbgtours@embarqmail.com
Web Site: www.gettysburgbattlefieldtours.com
Founded: 1950.
Congressional District: 19
Key Personnel: Administrative Asst., Bonnie Jacoby.
Personnel Profile: Full-Time Paid 3.
Governing Authority: private. Parent Institution: Heritage Inns, Inc., Gettysburg, PA.
Military Museum.
Collections: artifacts; military memorabilia; confederate encampment; miniature dioramas.
Facilities: Museum-related items for sale.
Activities: guided tours; loan exhibitions.
Hours & Admission Prices: March-June & Sept. to late Nov. 9-5; July to mid-Aug. 9-7. Adults $7.25, senior citizens $6.95, children 4-11 $3.50. Closed Thanksgiving & week after.
Attendance: 5,000 (estimated)

Girard

THE BATTLES MUSEUMS OF RURAL LIFE, 436 Walnut St., Girard, PA 16417-1650. Mailing Address: 419 State St., Erie, PA 16501-1106. Tel.: 814-454-1813. Fax: 814-454-6890.
E-mail: echs@eriecountyhistory.org
Web Site: www.eriecountyhistory.org
Founded: 1989.
Congressional District: 6
Key Personnel: Operations Dir., Melanie Keubel-Stankey; Pres. (V), Charles Scalise.
Personnel Profile: Full-Time Paid 1; Part-Time Paid 1; Part-Time Volunteers 14.
Governing Authority: private; nonprofit organization. Parent Institution: Erie County Historical Society, 417 State St., Erie, PA 16501. Tax-exempt: 501(c)(3).
Historic & Agriculture Museum: housed on 130 acres of farmland & woodland.
Collections: 2 & 3 dimensional artifacts from the Battles family of Girard, PA & from the region 1840-1952.
Research Fields: 1920's costumes; 1860 Lifestyles.
Facilities: 1858 & 1861 farmhouses; ecology trail.
Activities: docent program; formal education programs for adults, children & under-graduate or graduate archaeology students with Edinboro University; guided tours; lectures; temporary exhibitions.
Hours & Admission Prices: By appointment. Family $10, Adults $4, senior citizens $3, children $2; discounts to AAM members; members & children under 6 no charge. ♿
Attendance: 3,562 (accurate)
Membership: Student $10; Individual $35; Family & Grandparent $50; Patron $75; Sustaining $100; Sponsor $250; Corporate $500.

HAZEL KIBLER MEMORIAL MUSEUM, 522 Main St., Girard, PA 16417-1713. Tel.: 814-774-4168.
E-mail: swinick@aol.com
Web Site: westcountyhistorical.com
Key Personnel: Pres., Stephanie Wincik.
Governing Authority: Parent Institution: West County Historical Society.
History Museum.
Collections: Marx toys; clown & circus owner, Dan Rice memorabilia; period furnishings; photographs; newspapers.
Hours & Admission Prices: mid-May to Sept. Sun. 2-5; groups by appointment. Adults $2, children $1.

Gladwyne

HENRY FOUNDATION FOR BOTANICAL RESEARCH, 801 Stony Lane, Gladwyne, PA 19035-1460. Mailing Address: P.O. Box 7, Gladwyne, PA 19035-0007. Tel.: 610-525-2037. Fax: 610-525-4024.
Founded: 1949.
Key Personnel: Pres. & Exec. Dir., Susan P. Treadway; Cur., Betsey W. Davis.
Personnel Profile: Full-Time Paid 2; Part-Time Paid 1; Part-Time Volunteers 8; Interns 3.
Governing Authority: nonprofit. Tax-exempt.
Botanical Garden.
Collections: Native American Flora; Mary G. Henry Collection.
Research Fields: Native American flora.
Facilities: library pertaining to botany; botanical garden.
Activities: guided tours; lectures; organized educational programs; special events; classes.
Publications: newsletter.
Hours & Admission Prices: Tues.-Thurs. 10-3 by appointment. Admission $5.
Attendance: 8,000 (estimated)
Membership: Individual $25; Dual $40; Contributor $100; Sustainer $250; Patron $500; Benefactor $1,000; Guardian $2,500.

RIVERBEND ENVIRONMENTAL EDUCATION CENTER, 1950 Spring Mill Rd., Gladwyne, PA 19035-1000. Tel.: 610-527-5234. Fax: 610-527-1161.
E-mail: info@riverbendeec.org
Web Site: www.riverbendeec.org
Founded: 1974.
Congressional District: 13
Key Personnel: Exec. Dir., Laurie Bachman; Chm. (V) & Pres. (V), Beverly Galloway.
Personnel Profile: Full-Time Paid 6; Part-Time Paid 12; Part-Time Volunteers 10; Interns 5.
Governing Authority: nonprofit organization. Tax-exempt: 501(c)(3), 170(b)(1)(A).
Nature Center.
Collections: taxidermy; live animals in tanks.
Facilities: 1,000-vol. library; 30 acres of open space with ponds, streams, meadow & wooded areas; nature center with teaching & meeting space.
Activities: school & camp educational programs; public programs; special events; organized educational programs; summer day camp; internship program; Native American program; birthday parties; barn rentals.
Publications: newsletter, Round the Bend; camp brochure; school program brochure; general brochure on mission.
Hours & Admission Prices: Grounds: daily dawn to dusk. Center: Mon.-Fri. 9-5. Fee for camp & school programs. Walking Trails: no charge. Closed national holidays. ♿
Attendance: 12,000 (estimated)
Membership: Basic Family & Individual $50; Family & Individual Plus $100; Birdwatcher $250; Nature Lover $500; Riverkeeper $1,000.

Glenside

ARCADIA UNIVERSITY ART GALLERY, (M), Church & Easton Rds., Glenside, PA 19038. Mailing Address: 450 S. Easton Rd., Glenside, PA 19038-3295. Tel.: 215-572-2133, 2131 & 2900. Fax: 215-881-8774.
E-mail: torchiar@arcadia.edu
Web Site: www.arcadia.edu
Formerly: Beaver College Art Gallery
Founded: 1853.
Congressional District: 135
Key Personnel: Pres., Jerry Griener; Dir., Richard Torchia; Vice Pres. Institutional Advancement, Nick Costa; Public Rels., Lori Bauer.
Personnel Profile: Full-Time Paid 1; Part-Time Paid 9; Part-Time Volunteers 13.
Governing Authority: college; nonprofit. Parent Institution: Arcadia University. Tax-exempt: 501(c)(3).
Art Gallery: housed in c.1893 historic building.
Collections: paintings; sculpture; prints; works by regional artists; works by Benton Spruance, long time chair of the Fine Arts Dept.
Major Exhibits: Ai Weiwei: Dropping the Urn (T), 2/17/10-4/18/10.
Research Fields: contemporary visual art.
Facilities: 1,200 sq. ft. exhibit space; 150-seat theatre. Exhibition catalogues for sale.
Activities: guided tours; lectures. Annual Events: Exhibitions & Symposia.
Publications: exhibition catalogues.
Hours & Admission Prices: Sept.-May Tues.-Wed. & Fri. 10-3, Thurs. 10-8, Sat.-Sun. 12-4. No charge; donations accepted. Closed Thanksgiving; Christmas.
Attendance: 6,500 (estimated)
Membership: Artist & Senior Citizen $25; Friend $50; Family $100; Patron $200; Benefactor $500.

Grantham

M. LOUISE AUGHINBAUGH GALLERY AT MESSIAH COLLEGE, One College Ave., Grantham, PA 17027-9800. Mailing Address: P.O. Box 3004, One College Ave., Grantham, PA 17027. Tel.: 717-766-2511, ext. 2486.
E-mail: sbiddle@messiah.edu

Web Site: messiah.edu
Founded: 1979.
Key Personnel: Dir., Christine A. Forsythe.
Governing Authority: private college. Tax-exempt.
Art Museum.
Collections: paintings.
Activities: lectures; education programs.
Hours & Admission Prices: Mon.-Thurs. 9-4, Fri. 9-9, Sun. 2-5. No charge. ♿

THE OAKES MUSEUM AT MESSIAH COLLEGE, (M), One College Ave., Grantham, PA 17027-9800. Mailing Address: Box 3029, Grantham, PA 17027-9800. Tel.: 717-691-6082. Fax: 717-691-6046.
E-mail: oakesmuseum@messiah.edu
Web Site: www.messiah.edu/Oakes
Founded: 2002.
Key Personnel: Dir., Kenneth A. Mark; Education Coord., Helena Cicero; Education Coord., Beth Erikson; Treas., Lois Voigt; Cur. Herpetology & Ornithology, Dr. Erik Lindquist; Cur. Botany & Entomology, Dr. David Foster; Cur. Geology, Mr. Edwin Charles; Cur. Concology, Mrs. Ruth Bierbower; Cur. Mycology, Dr. Gary Emberger; Cur. Archaeology, Dr. David Pettegrew.
Personnel Profile: Full-Time Paid 2; Part-Time Paid 6; Part-Time Volunteers 12; Interns 1.
Governing Authority: private college. Tax-exempt: 501(c)(3).
Natural History Museum.
Collections: African & North American mammals, including a full body elephant skeleton; bird eggs & nests, seashells, minerals, insects, fungi, snakes & frogs; Native American artifacts.
Research Fields: vernal pool study; Project Golden Frog; Yellow Breeches Restoration Project.
Facilities: 10,000 sq. ft. exhibit space; 75 acre outdoor program area; classrooms; labs. Museum-related items for sale.
Activities: formal education programs for college students, adults & children; guided tours; lectures; participatory & temporary exhibits; scout programs; seniors citizen customized programming to meet education requirements for Pennsylvania state standards.
Hours & Admission Prices: Sat. 1-5. Adults $6, senior citizens, students and children 3-12 $3; discounts to groups. Closed major holidays. ♿
Attendance: 11,284 (accurate)

Green Lane

GOSCHENHOPPEN FOLKLIFE LIBRARY AND MUSEUM, 116 Gravel Pike, Red Men's Hall, Green Lane, PA 18054-0476. Mailing Address: P.O. Box 476, Green Lane, PA 18054-0476. Tel.: 215-234-8953.
E-mail: redmens_hall@goschenhoppen.org
Web Site: www.goschenhoppen.org
Founded: 1965.
Congressional District: 15
Key Personnel: C.E.O. & Chm., George Spotts; Pres. (V), Edward C. Johnson; Chm. Museum & Library, D.F. Abe Roan; Historian & Cur., Alan Keyser; Sec., Susan Cook.
Personnel Profile: Part-Time Paid 1; Part-Time Volunteers 800; Interns 150.
Governing Authority: society. Parent Institution: Goschenhoppen Historians, Inc. Tax-exempt: 501(c)(3).
Folklife Museum: housed in c.1900 three-story brick Red Men's Hall; Country Store Museum: a recreation of a country store c.1870-1930; Henry Antes House: a restored 1736 Germanic house containing two floors in the attic & located on the site of the Pottsgrove encampment of the Continental Army, September, 1777.
Collections: Pennsylvania German folklore & folkculture; local history, & archaeology; archives; agriculture; costumes; 1864 & 1820 pipe organ; decorative arts; textiles; weaver's shop; hearth kitchen; PA German Parlor; blacksmith shop; country store museum.
Research Fields: folklore; PA German folk culture; regional history from 1683 on.
Facilities: 700-vol. library of Pennsylvania history & folk culture available for use on premises; 250-seat auditorium; meeting & conference rooms; Goschenhoppen Folklife Museum; Henry Antes House-1736 National Historic Landmark, under restoration, available for tours by appointment.
Activities: guided tours; concerts; lectures; formally organized educational programs; permanent & temporary exhibitions. Annual Event: Goschenhoppen Folk Festival in August.
Publications: monthly newsletter, Goschenhoppen Newsletter; cookbook, Goschenhoppen Recipes; annual festival program, The Goschenhoppen Intelligencer, a reproduction of the German newspaper, Bauren-Freund; books, Just a Quilt, local oral history & local designs; Lest I Shall Be Forgotten-color photos, anecdotes & traditions of quilts from the Montgomery County Quilt Documentation; James E. Frill's Music Book, 1830s; Berks Co. Fiddle Tunes.
Hours & Admission Prices: Museum: April-Oct. Sun. 1:30-4; other times by appointment, call 215-234-8953. No charge; donations accepted. Folk Festival: adults $10; children 6-12 $2. Children under 6 no charge. ♿
Attendance: 7,850 (estimated)
Membership: Single $20; Family $30; Contributing $50; Patron $80; Life $250.

Greencastle

ALLISON-ANTRIM MUSEUM, INC., (M), 365 S. Ridge Ave., Greencastle, PA 17225-1157. Tel.: 717-597-9010.
E-mail: aamuseum@greencastlemuseum.org
Web Site: www.greencastlemuseum.org
Founded: 1995.
Congressional District: 9
Key Personnel: Pres., Bonnie A. Shockey; Treas., David McCarney.
Personnel Profile: Full-Time Volunteers 1; Part-Time Volunteers 45.
Governing Authority: public; nonprofit organization. Tax-exempt: 501(c)(3).
General Museum.
Collections: 20th-century paintings by African American artist, Walter Washington Smith; memorabilia of Henry P. Fletcher, a U.S. ambassador and diplomat to six countries for 51 years under eight presidents; Pennsylvania governors' signatures on primary documents dating back to 1715; Civil War collection, including primary documents, letters and uniforms; the Carl's Drugstore collection of medical and drug store items; early agricultural equipment and implements.
Facilities: 200-vol. library Greencastle & Antrim Township local history & genealogy; 634 sq. ft. exhibit space; a reconstructed 1860s German bank barn with climate-controlled storage and additional exhibit area.
Activities: docent program; guided tours; lectures; temporary exhibitions; monthly speaker series; monthly special exhibits.
Publications: bimonthly newsletter, Allison-Antrim Annals.
Hours & Admission Prices: Call for hours. No charge; donations accepted. Closed New Year's Day; Easter; Thanksgiving; Christmas. ♿
Attendance: 3,000 (accurate)
Membership: Student $5; Individual $10; Family $25; Patron $26-$99; Supporting & Business $100-$199; Sustaining $200-$800.

Greensburg

* **WESTMORELAND MUSEUM OF AMERICAN ART, (M),** 221 N. Main St., Greensburg, PA 15601-1898. Tel.: 724-837-1500. Fax: 724-837-2921.
E-mail: info@wmuseumaa.org
Web Site: www.wmuseumaa.org
Founded: 1949.
Congressional District: 20
Key Personnel: Dir. & C.E.O., Judith H. O'Toole; Pres. (V), Bruce M. Wolf; Chief Cur., Barbara L. Jones; Asst. Dir. Advancement, Amy B. Baldonieri; Asst. Public & Financial Devel., Pat Erdelsky; Dir. Education & Visitor Svcs., Katie Barnard; Dir. Mktg. & Information Technology, Judy Linz Ross; Preparator, P.J. Zimmerlink; Mgr. Collections, Douglas W. Evans; Museum Shop Mgr., Ginnie Leiner.
Personnel Profile: Full-Time Paid 14; Part-Time Paid 16; Part-Time Volunteers 185; Interns 4.
Governing Authority: nonprofit organization. Tax-exempt: 501(c)(3) & 4942(j)(3).
American Art Museum.
Collections: 18th- to 20th-century American paintings; sculpture; drawings; prints; furniture & decorative arts; 19th & 20th-century toy collection.
Major Exhibits: Celebrating the Art of the Thirties: Paintings from the Jason Schoen Collection, 1/24/10-5/16/10; The Westmoreland Juried Biennial, 6/6/10-7/4/10; Rooted in Tradition: Art Quilts from the Rocky Mountain Quilt Museum (T), 7/25/10-9/4/10; Associated Artists of Pittsburgh: Celebrating a Century of Art, 10/10/10-2/2/11.
Research Fields: paintings by Southwestern Pennsylvania & American artists.
Facilities: cafe. Museum-related items for sale.
Activities: docent guided tours; in-house lectures & gallery talks; educational outreach programs for grades K-12; children art classes & art camp; internships; inter-museum loans; ongoing educational activities; permanent & temporary exhibitions; symposia.
Publications: book, 250 Years of Art in Pennsylvania; catalogs, George Hetzel & the Scalp Level Tradition; The Permanent Collection of the Westmoreland Museum of Art; Southwestern Pennsylvania Painters, 1800-1945; Penn's Promise: Still Life Painting in Pennsylvania, 1795-1930; Southwestern Pennsylvania Painters From the Westmoreland Museum of Art Permanent Collection; exhibition catalogs; gallery guides; Born of Fire: The Valley of Work; American Scenery: Different Views in Hudson River School Painting; Samuel Rosenberg: Portrait of a Painter; Made in Pennsylvania: A Folk Art Tradition; Painting in the United States 2008.
Hours & Admission Prices: Wed. & Fri.-Sun. 11-5, Thurs. 11-9. Suggested

Donation: adults $5; discounts to AAM members; members, students & children under 12 no charge. Closed New Year's Day; Easter; Thanksgiving; Christmas. ♿
Attendance: 23,300 (accurate)
Membership: Student & Senior $25; Individual $40; Dual & Family $60; Donor $125; Patron's Circle $450; Director's Circle $1,000; President's Circle & Corporate $2,000. Small Business $125, $450 or $1,000.

Greenville

GREENVILLE RAILROAD PARK AND MUSEUM, 314 Main St., Greenville, PA 16125-2615. Tel.: 724-588-4009.
E-mail: greenvillerailroadpark@gmail.com
Web Site: www.greenvilletrainmuseum.org
Railroad Museum.
Collections: railroad history; switch engines; coal tender; hopper car; 1913 Empire touring car; 1952 caboose.
Hours & Admission Prices: May & Sept.-Oct. daily 1-5; mid-June to Labor Day Tues.-Sun. 1-5.

Hamburg

READING RAILROAD HERITAGE MUSEUM, 500 S. Third St., Hamburg, PA 19526. Mailing Address: P.O. Box 15143, Reading, PA 19612-5143.
Web Site: www.readingrailroad.org
Founded: 1976.
Key Personnel: Devel., John Brown; Pres. (V), Duane E. Engle; Treas., Jim Adams; Archivist, Richard Bates.
Personnel Profile: Part-Time Volunteers 100.
Governing Authority: private; nonprofit organization. Tax-exempt: 501(c)(3).
Transportation Museum.
Collections: Reading Railroad history & equipment, artifacts & paperwork; operational equipment.
Facilities: library; 41,200 sq. ft. exhibit space. Museum-related items for sale.
Activities: guided tours; loan, temporary & traveling exhibitions; operating train trips; equipment restoration.
Publications: monthly newsletter, Crusader; quarterly magazine, Beeline.
Hours & Admission Prices: Sat. 10-5, Sun. 12-5. Adults $5; members no charge.
Attendance: 2,000 (estimated)
Membership: Student $15; Individual $35; Family $43; Contributing $55; Sustaining $100; Corporate $150.

Harleysville

MENNONITE HERITAGE CENTER, 565 Yoder Rd., Harleysville, PA 19438-1020. Tel.: 215-256-3020. Fax: 215-256-3023.
E-mail: info@mhep.org
Web Site: www.mhep.org/
Founded: 1974.
Congressional District: 5
Key Personnel: Dir., Sarah Wolfgang Heffner; Asst. Dir., Rose A. Moyer; Cur. & Librarian, Joel D. Alderfer; Volunteer Coord. & Museum Shop Mgr., Janice Godshall.
Personnel Profile: Full-Time Paid 3; Full-Time Volunteers 4; Part-Time Volunteers 50.
Governing Authority: nonprofit organization. Parent Institution: Mennonite Historians of Eastern Pennsylvania. Tax-exempt: 501(c)(3).
Heritage Center.
Collections: Pennsylvania German Fraktur (illuminated writing); costumes; tools; archival materials; 16th to 19th-century books & Bibles; ethnology; photographs; needlework; quilts & coverlets; ceramics; pottery; glassware; local history & genealogy; early southeastern Pennsylvania German & Mennonite history.
Research Fields: local genealogy.
Facilities: library; archives; 3,000 sq. ft. exhibit space. Mennonite-Anabaptist history books, Pennsylvania German culture books, local cookbooks, Fraktur prints & local genealogy books for sale.
Activities: audiovisual presentations; educational, interpretive & slide lectures; educational programs for adults; religious programs. Museum Sponsors: Apple Butter Frolic; Croquet Away Tournament; Pennsylvania German Folk Art Sale.
Publications: quarterly newsletter.
Hours & Admission Prices: Tues.-Fri. 10-5, Sat. 10-2. Donation requested. Closed New Year's Day; Good Friday; Easter; Independence Day; Thanksgiving; Christmas. ♿
Attendance: 4,700
Membership: Student & Senior $25; Individual $35; Family $50; Contributing $75; Supporting $100; Sustaining $250; Associate $1,000.

Harrisburg

ART ASSOCIATION OF HARRISBURG, 21 N. Front St., Harrisburg, PA 17101-1625. Tel.: 717-236-1432. Fax: 717-236-6631.
E-mail: carrie@artassocofhbg.com
Web Site: www.artassocofhbg.com
Founded: 1926.
Key Personnel: Dir., Pres. & Museum Shop Mgr., Carrie Wissler Thomas; Chm. (V), Rick LeBlanc.
Personnel Profile: Full-Time Paid 1; Part-Time Paid 4.
Governing Authority: not-for-profit organization. Tax-exempt.
Art: 1810 four-story Italianate-style home housing the Art Association building.
Collections: paintings; graphics.
Major Exhibits: Figuratively Speaking, 1/15/10-2/11/10; Invitational, 2/19/10-3/25/10; Invitational, 4/2/10-5/6/10; 82nd Juried Exhibition, 5/15/10-6/17/10; Art School Annual, 6/26/10-7/22/10; Invitational, 7/30/10-9/2/10; Fall Membership, 9/12/10-10/14/10; Invitational, 10/22/10-11/24/10; Invitational, 12/3/10-1/6/11.
Facilities: 400-vol. art library; educational facilities. Museum-related items for sale.
Activities: formal educational programs; guided tours; concerts; community exhibitions. Annual Events: Juried Exhibition; Meet the Artist in summer; Gallery Walk in September; Costume Ball.
Publications: quarterly newsletter; school catalogue; monthly show invitations.
Hours & Admission Prices: Mon.-Thurs. 9:30-9, Fri. 9:30-4, Sat. 10-4, Sun. 2-5. No charge. Closed New Year's Day; Easter; Thanksgiving; Christmas.
Attendance: 12,000 (estimated)
Membership: Student $25; Artist & Supporter $40; Promoter $60; Patron $125; Benefactor $250; Sponsor $500; Gold $750; Friend $1,000.

FORT HUNTER MANSION & PARK, (M), 5300 N. Front St., Harrisburg, PA 17110-1718. Tel.: 717-599-5751. Fax: 717-599-5838.
Web Site: www.forthunter.org
Founded: 1933.
Key Personnel: Mansion Mgr., Mary Trost; Park Mgr., Julia Hair; Educator, Elizabeth Johnson.
Personnel Profile: Full-Time Paid 1; Part-Time Paid 7.
Governing Authority: county; board of trustees; nonprofit organization. Parent Institution: County of Dauphin. Subsidiary Institution: Board of Trustees for Fort Hunter. Tax-exempt: 501(c)(3).
Historic House & Park: housed in 1814 Federal style stone mansion, on the site of French & Indian War fort.
Collections: carriages; photographs; clothing; china; correspondence; elliptical staircase; Early American, Empire and Victorian furnishings. Historic Structures: historic barns; icehouse; tavern; springhouse.
Facilities: 8,000 sq. ft. exhibit space; nature area; 19th-century boxwood garden; herb gardens; pavilion for picnics; trails. Museum-related items for sale.
Activities: guided tours; lectures; arts festivals; organized educational programs for children; docent program; temporary exhibitions; performing arts; nature walks; military reenactments. Museum Sponsors: Fort Hunter Day in September; Yuletide celebrations; seasonal fairs & craft shows; Christmas celebration.
Publications: quarterly newsletter, The Chronicler.
Hours & Admission Prices: May-Dec. Tues.-Sat. 10-5, Sun. 12-5. Adults $5, senior citizens $4, children $3; discounts to AAM members; members no charge. ♿
Attendance: 9,000 (estimated)
Membership: Student & Senior Citizen $20; Individual $25; Family & Organization $35; Supporting $50; Patron $100; Sponsor & Corporate $250.

THE HISTORICAL SOCIETY OF DAUPHIN COUNTY, The John Harris/Simon Cameron Mansion, 219 S. Front St., Harrisburg, PA 17104-1619. Tel.: 717-233-3462. Fax: 717-233-6059.
Web Site: www.dauphincountyhistory.org
Founded: 1869.
Congressional District: 17
Key Personnel: Exec. Dir., Kathryn W. McCorkle; Pres. (V), Frank Pinto; Cur., Stephen Bachmann; Librarian, Ken Frew.
Personnel Profile: Part-Time Paid 7; Part-Time Volunteers 45; Interns 1.
Governing Authority: board of trustees. Tax-exempt.
Historic House Museum: 1766 built by John Harris, Jr., founder of Harrisburg; enlarged by Simon Cameron, Lincoln's first secretary of war.
Collections: decorative arts; household items; tools; toys; textiles; Indian artifacts; ceramics; glass; clocks; John Harris furniture; Simon Cameron furniture.
Research Fields: genealogy; county history.

Facilities: library; reception & meeting rooms.
Activities: guided tours; research; school programs; workshops; bus tours; weddings; community events; adult programs.
Publications: newsletter, The Oracle; annual publication, The Susquehanna Journal.
Hours & Admission Prices: Tours: Tues.-Fri. 1-4, last tour begins at 3. Tour: adults $8, senior citizens $7, children 5-12 $5; discounts to groups; children under 4 & members no charge. Library: Tues.-Fri. 1-4. Adults $10. Closed most holidays. ♿
Attendance: 2,500 (estimated)
Membership: Individual $30; Family $40; Heritage Circle $50; Haldeman Circle $100; Cameron Circle $250; Harris Circle $500; Penn Circle $1,000.

THE NATIONAL CIVIL WAR MUSEUM, (M), One Lincoln Center at Reservoir Park, Harrisburg, PA 17103. Tel.: 717-260-1861. Fax: 717-260-9599.
E-mail: info@nationalcivilwarmuseum.org
Web Site: www.nationalcivilwarmuseum.org
Key Personnel: Dir., Janice I. Mullin; Founder, Stephen R. Reed
Military Museum.
Collections: personal & military artifacts; manuscripts; documents; photographs.
Facilities: Museum-related items for sale.
Activities: special events.
Hours & Admission Prices: Winter: Mon.-Sat. 10-5, Sun. 12-5. Summer: Mon.-Tues. & Thurs.-Sat. 10-5, Wed. 10-8, Sun. 12-5. Adults $10, seniors 60 & over $8, students and children 6 & over $7. Closed New Year's Day; Easter; Thanksgiving & day after; Christmas; most federal holidays.

PENNSYLVANIA FEDERATION OF MUSEUMS AND HISTORICAL ORGANIZATIONS, (M), 234 N. 3rd St., Harrisburg, PA 17101-1516. Tel.: 717-909-4950. Fax: 717-909-3996.
E-mail: pamuseums@pamuseums.org
Web Site: www.pamuseums.org
Founded: 1907.
Congressional District: 17
Key Personnel: Exec. Dir., Deborah M. Filipi; Deputy Dir., Janet MacGregor.
Personnel Profile: Full-Time Paid 3; Part-Time Paid 1.
Governing Authority: nonprofit organization.
Museum Service Organization.
Activities: training programs for volunteer & professional museum staff.
Publications: quarterly newsletter, Tapestry; Keystone Treasures: Guide to Museums and Historical Organizations in Pennsylvania.
Hours & Admission Prices: Mon.-Fri. 8:30-5. Closed federal & state holidays. ♿
Membership: Individual $35; Affiliate $95; Institutional $55-$225.

PENNSYLVANIA HISTORICAL & MUSEUM COMMISSION, 300 North St., Harrisburg, PA 17120-0101. Tel.: 717-787-2891. Fax: 717-783-1073.
Web Site: www.phmc.state.us/
Founded: 1945.
Congressional District: 17
Key Personnel: Chm. (V), Wayne Spilove; Dir. Bureau of Historic Sites & Museums, Stephen Miller; Dir. Bureau of Archives & History, David Haury; Dir. Bureau of The State Museum of Pennsylvania, John Leighow; Dir. Bureau for Historic Preservation, Jean H. Cutler; Dir. Bureau of Management Svcs., Thomas Leonard; Div. Chief Historic Sites & Museums, Nadine Steinmetz; Div. Chief Historic Sites & Museums, Bruce Bazelon; Chief Div. Architecture & Preservation, Barry Loveland.
Personnel Profile: Full-Time Paid 306; Part-Time Paid 96; Part-Time Volunteers 2,900.
Governing Authority: state. Branch Museums & Historic Sites: State Museum of Pennsylvania, Harrisburg; Landis Valley Museum, Lancaster; Pennsylvania Military Museum, Boalsburg; Ft. Pitt Museum, Pittsburgh; Pennsylvania Lumber Museum, Galeton; Somerset Historical Center, Somerset; Old Economy Village, Ambridge; Daniel Boone Homestead, Birdsboro; Conrad Weiser Homestead, Womelsdorf; French Azilum, Wysox; Brandywine Battlefield Park, Chadds Ford; Pennsbury Manor, Morrisville; Historic Peace Church, Camp Hill; Morton Homestead, Prospect Park; United States Brig Niagara & Erie Maritime Museum, Erie; Ft. LeBoeuf, Waterford; Judson House, Waterford; Old Mill Village, New Milford; Railroad Museum of Pennsylvania, Strasburg; Scranton Iron Furnaces, Scranton; Old Chester Court House, Chester; Tuscarora Academy, Academia; Ephrata Cloister, Ephrata; Robert Fulton Birthplace, Quarryville; Cornwall Iron Furnace, Cornwall; McCoy House, Lewistown; Graeme Park, Horsham; Hope Lodge, Mather Mill, Ft. Washington; Joseph Priestley House, Northumberland; Historic Warrior Run Church, McEwensville; Drake Well Museum, Titusville; Historic Pithole City, Pithole; David Bradford House, Washington; Bushy Run Battlefield, Jeannette; The Highlands, Whitemarsh Township; Washington Crossing Historic Park, Washington Crossing; Pennsylvania State Archives, Harrisburg; Pennsylvania Anthracite Heritage Museum, Scranton; Eckley Miners' Village, Eckley; Museum of Anthracite Mining, Ashland; Nathan Denison House, Forty Fort; Bowman's Hill Wildflower Preserve, Washington Crossing. Tax-exempt.
State Agency; Conservation Center.
Collections: arts & crafts; china; glass; silver; folk arts; textile; military; preservation project; anthropology; ethnology; Indian artifacts; archaeology; entomology; insects; geology; mineralogy; paleontology; herbarium; medical; dental; health; natural history; natural science; science; agriculture; antiques; forestry; guns; industrial; logging & lumber; mining; religious; technology; transportation; rural life history; maritime; railroad; historic houses; ruins; industrial sites; religious & political history.
Research Fields: history; archaeology; geology; natural science; exhibits technology; science & technology; fine arts; decorative arts; museology; genealogy; military history; maritime.
Facilities: 99,000-vol. library of history, science, natural history, art, folk art, archaeology available for inter-library loan & on premises by written request; nature/conservation center; planetarium; reading room; 400-seat auditorium; theater; classrooms. Reproductions & items relating to collections for sale.
Activities: guided tours; lectures; films; concerts; dance recitals; arts festivals; study clubs; hobby workshops; TV & radio programs; formally organized education programs; inter-museum loan, permanent, temporary & traveling exhibitions.
Publications: books; leaflets; post cards; monographs; reproductions; calendars; posters; history magazine; rack cards.
Hours & Admission Prices: See individual listings for museums, historic sites, & houses; discounts for AAM & ICOM members; PA Heritage Society, State Legislature, media, State Museum of Pennsylvania members, teachers, tour leaders & children under 6 no charge. ♿
Attendance: 1,100,000 (estimated)
Membership: Individual $40; Family $55; Contributor $100.

THE PENNSYLVANIA NATIONAL FIRE MUSEUM, 1820 N. 4th St., Harrisburg, PA 17104. Tel.: 717-232-8915. Fax: 717-232-8916.
E-mail: info@pnfm.org
Key Personnel: Pres., Dave Warren, Jr.
Fire Museum: housed in the 1899 Victorian firehouse Reily Hose Company No. 10.
Collections: firefighting history & equipment from hand-drawn fire apparatus to modern tools.
Hours & Admission Prices: Tues.-Sat. 10-4, Sun. 1-4. Adults $6, seniors $5, student $4; discounts to groups. Closed holidays.

ROSE LEHRMAN ART GALLERY, (M), Rose Lehrman Art Center, Harrisburg Area Community College, 1 HACC Dr., Harrisburg, PA 17110-2903. Tel.: 717-780-2435.
E-mail: kebanist@hacc.edu
Web Site: www.hacc.edu/RoseLehrmanArtsCenter/ArtGallery/index.cfm
Key Personnel: Cur., Kim Banister
Art Gallery.
Collections: art exhibitions.
Hours & Admission Prices: Summer & Fall: Mon., Wed. & Fri. 11-3, Tues. & Thurs. 11-3 and 5-7 or by appointment.

*** THE STATE MUSEUM OF PENNSYLVANIA,** 300 North St., Harrisburg, PA 17120-0101. Tel.: 717-787-4980. Fax: 717-783-4558.
E-mail: hpollman@state.pa.us
Web Site: www.statemuseumpa.org
Founded: 1905.
Congressional District: 17
Key Personnel: PHMC Exec. Dir., Barbara Franco; Dir., John C. Leighow; PHMC Chm. (V), Wayne Spilove; Operations Section, Dwight Lindenberger; Education Section, Ruth M. Arnold; Exhibition Management, Robert Bullock; Chief Curatorial Programs Div., William A. Sisson; Asst. to the Dir., Janee Concepcion; Mktg. Dir., Howard Pollman; Press Sec., Kirk Wilson; Sr. Cur. Popular Culture, Curt Miner; Sr. Cur. Zoology & Botany, Dr. Walter Meshaka; Sr. Cur. Paleontology & Geology, Dr. Robert M. Sullivan; Sr. Cur. Art Collections, N. Lee Stevens; Sr. Cur. Industry & Technology, Military & Political History, John Zwierzyna; Sr. Cur. Archaeology, Dr. Kurt Carr; Librarian, Paula Heiman; Planetarium Educator, Linda Powell; Educator, Candee Farrell; Educator, Cherie Trimble; Educator, Christine Yanick; Museum Shop Mgr., Morgan Muth.
Personnel Profile: Full-Time Paid 43; Part-Time Paid 23; Part-Time Volunteers 59; Interns 5.
Governing Authority: state. Parent Institution: Pennsylvania Historical and Museum Commission. Tax-exempt: 170(c)(1).
General Museum.

Collections: Pennsylvania collections of fine arts; native American & historic archaeology; natural science including birds, fish, mammals, insects, plants; science; technology including vehicles, appliances, tools, machinery; military & political history; community & domestic life; geology & paleontology.
Research Fields: Pennsylvania art history, history, mammals & plants; archaeology; technology; decorative art; geology & paleontology.
Facilities: 25,000-vol. library of material on general & Pennsylvania archaeology, technology, military history, Pennsylvania biography & natural science available for use on premises or by arrangement; reading room; planetarium; 395-seat auditorium; classrooms. Museum-related items for sale.
Activities: tours; lectures; films; gallery talks; concerts; arts festivals; TV & radio programs; formally organized education programs; docent program; inter-museum loan & temporary exhibitions.
Publications: Susquehanna Indians; quarterly Calendar of Events; Natural History Notes; Ephrat Archaeology Series.
Hours & Admission Prices: Museum: Tues.-Sat. 9-5, Sun. 12-5. No charge. Planetarium & Curiosity Connection: adults $5; discount to Heritage Society members. Closed New Year's Day; Martin Luther King Jr. Day; Presidents' Day; Memorial Day; Independence Day; Labor Day; Columbus Day; Veterans Day; Thanksgiving; Christmas. ♿
Attendance: 300,000 (estimated)

SUSQUEHANNA ART MUSEUM, (M), 301 Market St., Harrisburg, PA 17101-2224. Tel.: 717-233-8668. Fax: 717-233-8155.
Web Site: www.sqart.org
Founded: 1989.
Key Personnel: Exec. Dir., Corinne Topper.
Personnel Profile: Full-Time Paid 4; Part-Time Volunteers 10; Interns 3.
Governing Authority: Tax-exempt.
Art Museum.
Collections: works by regional & international artists.
Hours & Admission Prices: Tues.-Wed. & Fri. 10-4, Thurs. 4-8, Sat. 10-4, Sun. 1-4. Adults $5; discount to AAM members; members no charge. Closed holidays. ♿
Attendance: 10,000 (estimated)
Membership: Individual $30; Family $50; Supporter $100; Patron $250; Benefactor $500; Sustainer Circle $1,000.

WHITAKER CENTER FOR SCIENCE AND THE ARTS, 222 Market St., Harrisburg, PA 17101-2113. Mailing Address: 225 Market St., Harrisburg, PA 17101-2126. Tel.: 717-214-ARTS (2787). Fax: 717-221-8208.
E-mail: info@whitakercenter.org
Web Site: www.whitakercenter.org
Formerly: Museum of Scientific Discovery
Founded: 1993.
Congressional District: 17
Key Personnel: Pres. & C.E.O., Michael L. Hanes; Vice Pres. Science & IMAX Programs, Steve Bishop; Vice Pres. Sales & Mktg., Kathleen Keller; C.F.O., Natalie Sandel; Bd. Chm., Jack M. Stover, Esq.; Controller, Margaret Freedman; Vice Pres. Operations, Lisa Kreider; Museum Shop Mgr., Teresa Griffin; Exhibits Mgr., Deborah Peters; Dir. Education, Lori Lauver.
Personnel Profile: Full-Time Paid 30; Part-Time Paid 30; Part-Time Volunteers 200; Interns 12.
Governing Authority: private; not-for-profit organization. Tax-exempt: 501(c)(3).
Science Museum.
Collections: physical, natural & life science exhibits.
Major Exhibits: Tech City (T), 1/10-3/10; Titanic: The Artifact Exhibition (T), 3/10-9/10.
Facilities: 200-seat IMAX(R) theater; 664-seat performing arts theater; children's hall; classrooms. Museum-related items for sale.
Activities: interactive exhibits; live science theatre & demonstrations; outreach program; workshops for children, families & adults; teacher professional development workshops; programs for schools, scouts & groups; volunteer programs.
Publications: members newsletter, Passport; Educator's Planning Guide; theater program, Spotlight; monthly events guides.
Hours & Admission Prices: Science Center: Tues.-Sat. 9:30-5, Sun. 11:30-5. Adults $13.75, senior citizens, students & children 3-12 $11.75; discounts to ASTC members; members & children under 3 no charge. IMAX: adults $9.50, seniors, students & children 3-12 $8; discounts to members. Combo: adults $17.75, seniors, students & children 3-12 $15.75. Holiday hours vary. ♿
Attendance: 400,000 (estimated)
Membership: Individual $59; Family/Grandparent $89; Friend $150.

Hartsville

MOLAND HOUSE, 1641 Old York Rd., Hartsville, PA 18974. Mailing Address: P.O. Box 107, Jamison, PA 18929-0107. Tel.: 215-343-1936 & 918-1754.
E-mail: events@moland.org
Web Site: moland.org
Key Personnel: Pres., David Mullen.
Governing Authority: Parent Institution: Warwick Township. Tax-exempt.
Historical House Museum: housed in Moland family's farmhouse which was used as George Washington's headquarters from August 10, 1777 to August 23, 1777.
Collections: photographs; historical records.
Activities: Museum Sponsors: reenactment in August.
Publications: Moland Gazette.
Hours & Admission Prices: Call for hours. Adults $3.
Attendance: 1,000 (estimated)
Membership: Individual $10; Family $15; Corporate $50.

Haverford

HAVERFORD COLLEGE ARBORETUM, 370 Lancaster Ave., Haverford, PA 19041-1392. Tel.: 610-896-1101. Fax: 610-896-1095.
E-mail: arbor@haverford.edu
Web Site: www.haverford.edu/Arboretum/home.htm
Founded: 1834.
Congressional District: 13
Key Personnel: Dir., William Astifan; Cur., Martha Van Artsdalen; Pres. (V), Lathrop B. Nelson, Jr.
Personnel Profile: Full-Time Paid 5; Part-Time Volunteers 3.
Governing Authority: college. Parent Institution: Haverford College. Tax-exempt: 501(c)(3).
Arboretum: Haverford College is a Quaker institution, the architecture reflects a simple style starting in 1831.
Collections: oak & beech trees, many trees date back to the 1840s; azaleas; rhododendrons; ornamental fruit trees; pinetum; Japanese Zen garden.
Facilities: 216 acres; gardens; nature trail.
Activities: self-guided tours; lectures; seasonal guided tours; garden bus trips.
Publications: self-guided tree tours; newsletters; annual report.
Hours & Admission Prices: Daily dawn-dusk. No charge; donations accepted. ♿
Membership: Students $10; Individual $25; Family $40; Sustaining $60; Supporter $100; Benefactor $250; Patron $500; Life Member $1,000.

Havertown

HAVERFORD TOWNSHIP HISTORICAL SOCIETY, Karakung Dr., Powder Mill Valley Park, Havertown, PA 19083. Mailing Address: Box 825, Havertown, PA 19083-0825. Tel.: 610-446-7988.
E-mail: info@haverfordhistoricalsociety.org
Web Site: www.haverfordhistoricalsociety.org
Founded: 1939.
Congressional District: 7
Key Personnel: Cur., Carolyn Joseph; Pres., Amy Wolfe.
Personnel Profile: Part-Time Volunteers 12.
Governing Authority: society. Tax-exempt.
Local History Museum: housed in c.1710 Lawrence Cabin, adjoining c.1810 Nitre Hall home of the Powder Master & c.1797 Federal School.
Collections: period furnishings; costumes; glass photographic plates of Philadelphia & Westchester Traction Co., 1903-1915; railroads; engines; paper archives of township historical sites, buildings, organizations & government.
Research Fields: history of Haverford Township, powder mills & manufacture of black powder.
Facilities: 75-vol. library of local & Pennsylvania history, architecture & preservation, available by appointment.
Activities: guided tours; lectures; permanent & temporary exhibitions; a full day of life, work &/or school in the 1700s & 1800s programs. Museum Sponsors: Craft Days; A Day in a One-Room School; Heritage Festival in Spring.
Publications: brochure; newsletter.
Hours & Admission Prices: May-Sept. 1st Sat.-Sun. each month 1-4. Adults $2, children 6-18 $1. ♿
Attendance: 1,000 (estimated)
Membership: Student $5; Individual $10; Family $15; Contributing Organization $25.

Hazleton

GREATER HAZLETON HISTORICAL SOCIETY, 55 N. Wyoming St., Hazleton, PA 18201-6069. Tel.: 570-455-8576. Fax: 570-455-8576.
E-mail: museum@youronline.net
Web Site: www.hazletonhistory.8m.com
Founded: 1983.
Congressional District: 11
Key Personnel: Pres., Thomas Gabos; Vice Pres., Antonio Rodriguez; Treas., Walter Throne; Sec., Joan Sacco.
Personnel Profile: Full-Time Paid 1; Full-Time Volunteers 2; Part-Time Volunteers 25; Interns 1.
Governing Authority: nonprofit organization. Tax-exempt.
Historical Society Museum.
Collections: Indian artifacts; local historical & industrial items; photographs; mining industry items; anthropology.
Research Fields: Pennsylvania newspaper project; local history.
Facilities: local history library including newspapers & genealogical research materials; 100-seat auditorium; 1,850 sq. ft. exhibit space.
Activities: guided tours; films; temporary exhibitions.
Publications: quarterly newsletter.
Hours & Admission Prices: Museum: Mon.-Fri. 9:30-1:30, Sat.-Sun. by appointment. Tours: Summer: Mon.-Fri. 9:30-1:30, Sat.-Sun. by appointment only; Sept.-June daily 1-5. Adults $5, students & children $2; members no charge. Closed New Year's Day; Easter; Christmas. ♿
Attendance: 1,000 (estimated)
Membership: Individual $15; Family $20.

Hellertown

GILMAN MUSEUM, at the Cave, 726 Durham St., Hellertown, PA 18055. Mailing Address: P.O. Box M, Hellertown, PA 18055-0220. Tel.: 610-838-8767. Fax: 610-838-2961.
E-mail: info@lostcave.com
Web Site: www.lostcave.com
Founded: 1955.
Congressional District: 15
Key Personnel: Dir., C.E.O. & Chief Cur., Beverly L. Rozewicz.
Governing Authority: nonprofit.
Natural History & Antique Weapons: located on the site of an old Limestone Quarry, at the entrance of a natural underground series of caverns.
Collections: guns; mounted natural history specimens from around the world; gem stones; mineral specimens; early colonial items; fossils.
Research Fields: weaponry; gems; minerals; plants; ancient curios.
Facilities: botanical garden. Museum-related items for sale.
Activities: guided cave tours; permanent exhibitions.
Hours & Admission Prices: Memorial Day to Labor Day daily 9-6; Sept.-May daily 9-5. Cavern Tours: adults $10.50, children 3-12 $6.50. Closed New Year's Day; Thanksgiving; Christmas.
Attendance: 25,000 (estimated)

Hershey

ANTIQUE AUTO MUSEUM, 161 Museum Dr., Hershey, PA 17033-2462. Tel.: 717-566-7100. Fax: 717-566-7300.
Key Personnel: Exec. Dir., Holly Bedsole
Automobile Museum.
Collections: automobile history; period automobiles & buses.
Major Exhibits: Camaros & Firebirds, 11/09-4/4/10; GM Futurliner #10 (T), 11/09-4/10; Fast From the Past: Competition Motorcycles of Yesteryear, 11/09-5/11; AACA Museum Collectors Series - Muscle Cars, 4/23/10-9/6/10; AACA 75th Anniversary Exhibit, 9/24/10-12/10.
Facilities: Museum-related items for sale.
Activities: hands-on activities; license plate rubbing; village mat with cars. Annual Event: Model Railroad November to December.
Publications: e-newsletter, Rumble Seat.
Hours & Admission Prices: Daily 9-5. Adults $10, seniors 61 & over $9, children 4-12 $7; members and children 3 & under no charge. Closed New Year's Day; Thanksgiving; Christmas Eve & Day. ♿
Attendance: 48,000 (accurate)
Membership: Individual $55; Family $80; Supporting $120; Life $1,000.

* **HERSHEY GARDENS, (M),** 170 Hotel Rd., Hershey, PA 17033-9507. Tel.: 717-534-3492. Fax: 717-533-5095.
E-mail: info@hersheygardens.org
Web Site: www.hersheygardens.org
Founded: 1937.
Congressional District: 17
Key Personnel: Dir., Marta Howell; Dir. Horticulture, Barbara Whitcraft; Dir. Public Rels. & Mktg., Jill Manley; Ground Mgr., Jamie Shiffer; Coord. Special Events, Tammy Harris.
Personnel Profile: Full-Time Paid 9; Part-Time Paid 22; Part-Time Volunteers 350; Interns 4.
Governing Authority: private; nonprofit organization. Parent Institution: The M.S. Hershey Foundation, 1 W. Chocolate Ave., Ste. 200, Hershey, PA 17033. Tax-exempt: 501(c)(3).
Arboretum/ Botanical Gardens & Horticultural Society: retains original 1937 landscape design & structures.
Collections: over 7,000 roses; more than 75,000 spring bulbs; rare trees & plants; summer flowering annuals; horticulturally themed gardens; mature specimen trees; seasonal butterfly house of North American species; children's garden; giant sequoia.
Facilities: 23-acres exhibit space; botanical gardens. Museum-related items for sale.
Activities: formal education programs; lectures; temporary exhibits; special tours; member's reception; volunteer reception. Annual Events: Hershey Community Gardenfest; Fall Family Fun Fest; A Day of Wines & Roses; Jack-O-Lantern Jamboree; Biergarten; Brick and Bench Dedication Ceremonies.
Publications: quarterly newsletter, Twigs & Gigs.
Hours & Admission Prices: Jan.-Feb. Fri.-Sun. 10-4; March & Nov.-Dec. daily 10-4; April-May & Sept.-Oct. daily 9-5; June-Aug. daily 9-8. Adults $10, seniors 62 & over $9, children 3-12 $6; discounts to AAA members & groups; children under 3 & members no charge. Closed Thanksgiving; Christmas. ♿
Attendance: 120,800 (accurate)
Membership: Individual $35; Household $60; Crocus $150; Tulip $250; Lily $500; Rose $1,000.

THE HERSHEY STORY, 63 W. Chocolate Ave., Hershey, PA 17033-1558. Tel.: 717-534-3439. Fax: 717-534-8940.
E-mail: info@hersheymuseum.org
Web Site: www.hersheystory.org
Formerly: Hershey Museum
Founded: 1933.
Congressional District: 17
Key Personnel: Interim Dir., Don Papson; Assoc. Dir., Amy Bischof; Mgr. Public Programs, Lois Miklas; Dir. Education, Mariella Trosko; Mgr. Chocolate Lab, Kyle Nagurny; School Programs Supvr., Beth Hiner; Mgr. Collections, Valerie Seiber; Mgr. Visitor Experience, Lisa Morelli; Trips & Excursions Consultant, Janet Hester; Mgr. Systems, Information & Accounting, Sharon Smith; Coord. Membership, Barb Latz.
Personnel Profile: Full-Time Paid 10; Part-Time Paid 17; Part-Time Volunteers 86.
Governing Authority: foundation. Parent Institution: The M.S. Hershey Foundation. Tax-exempt: 501(c)(3).
History Museum.
Collections: Milton Hershey's life & legacy.
Major Exhibits: 1968 in America (T), 6/10-10/10.
Research Fields: Milton S. Hershey; Hershey chocolate history; Pennsylvania German life & arts; North American Indian ethnographic & archeological materials.
Facilities: 10,500 sq. ft. museum experience space; 2,000 sq. ft. special exhibit gallery.
Activities: chocolate lab; chocolate tasting; Museum EduQuests for school groups.
Publications: book, Built on Chocolate: The Story of the Hershey Chocolate Company.
Hours & Admission Prices: Daily 9-5:30. Adults $10, senior citizens 62 & over $9, youth 3-12 $7.50; discounts to groups, ICOM, AAM & AAA members; members no charge. Closed Thanksgiving; Christmas. ♿
Attendance: 90,215 (accurate)
Membership: Individual $50; Senior 60 & over $40; Couple $75; Family $100.

THE MUSEUM OF BUS TRANSPORTATION, INC., 161 Museum Dr., Hershey, PA 17033-2462. Tel.: 717-566-7100, ext. 119. Fax: 717-566-7300.
E-mail: thebusmuseum@yahoo.com
Web Site: www.busmuseum.org
Key Personnel: C.E.O., Pres. & Mgr., J. Thomas Collins; Vice Pres., Robert Smith; Treas., Edwin P. Wolf; Museum Shop Mgr., O.J. Ogden.
Personnel Profile: Part-Time Volunteers 12.
Governing Authority: private; nonprofit organization. Tax-exempt: 501(c)(3).
Transportation Museum.
Collections: 12 buses from 1912-1987; photographs; scale models; bus stop signs; bus station signs.
Facilities: library; 6,000 sq. ft. exhibit space. Museum-related items for sale.
Activities: guided tours; lectures; special events. Annual Events: meeting and open house in October.
Publications: quarterly newsletter, Bus Musings.
Hours & Admission Prices: Summer: daily 9-5; Labor Day to Memorial Day

Wed.-Sun. 9-5. Adults $7; discount to members. Closed New Year's Day; Thanksgiving; Christmas.
Attendance: 40,000 (accurate)
Membership: Annual $25; Lifetime $500.

ZOOAMERICA NORTH AMERICAN WILDLIFE PARK, 100 W. Hershey Park Dr., Hershey, PA 17033. Mailing Address: P.O. Box 866, Hershey, PA 17033-2727. Tel.: 717-534-3900. Fax: 717-534-3151.
E-mail: zooamerica@hersheypa.com
Web Site: www.zooamerica.com
Founded: 1978.
Congressional District: 17
Key Personnel: Dir., Troy E. Stump; Cur., Dale Snyder; Supvr. Everglades Exhibits, Pat McCann; Supvr. Desert Exhibits, Katie Fessler; Supvr. Education Programs, Elaine Gruin; Supvr. Exterior Exhibits, Tal Wenrich; Supvr. Exterior Exhibits, Tim Becker; Administrative Support, Dee Nixon.
Personnel Profile: Full-Time Paid 11; Part-Time Paid 25; Part-Time Volunteers 12.
Governing Authority: Parent Institution: Hershey Entertainment and Resorts.
Zoological Park.
Collections: wild animals & plants of North America.
Research Fields: veterinary medicine.
Facilities: zoological park; aquarium; outdoor snack shop. Materials relating to natural history of North America for sale.
Activities: guided tours; lectures; films; gallery talks; formally organized education programs for children.
Publications: biannual, ZooAmerica Newsletter.
Hours & Admission Prices: Call for hours. Adults $9, senior citizens, children 3-8 $7.50; children under 2 no charge. Closed New Year's Day; Thanksgiving; Christmas. ♿
Membership: Individual $30; Family $90.

Honesdale

WAYNE COUNTY HISTORICAL SOCIETY, (M), 810 Main, Honesdale, PA 18431-1847. Mailing Address: P.O. Box 446, Honesdale, PA 18431-0446. Tel.: 570-253-3240. Fax: 570-253-5204.
Web Site: www.waynehistorypa.org
Founded: 1917.
Congressional District: 10
Key Personnel: Exec. Dir., Sally Talaga; Pres., Elaine Hillier; 1st Vice Pres., Carol Dunn; 2nd Vice Pres., Linda Lee; Sec., Ann Kovatch; Treas., Joan Litzenbauer; Museum Shop Mgr., Kay Stephenson; Librarian, Gloria McCullough.
Personnel Profile: Full-Time Paid 1; Part-Time Paid 3; Part-Time Volunteers 100.
Governing Authority: society. Tax-exempt.
History Museum.
Collections: archives; paintings; costumes; cut glass; history; Indian artifacts; 1829 The Stourbridge Lion steam locomotive replica; D&H Canal Co. exhibit; Native American exhibit including 4,600 pieces archaeology collection of Dr. Vernon Leslie.
Research Fields: genealogy & general Wayne County history.
Facilities: library of historical records & genealogy books available for use on premises.
Activities: permanent & rotating exhibitions.
Publications: quarterly newsletter; D & H Canal, A History by Edwin LeRoy; Canal Town-Honesdale 1850-1875 & Honesdale, the Early Years; Things Forgotten-Wayne Co. 1876-89; Honesdale & The Sturbridge Lions, History of Wayne Co. PA 1788-1998, Of Pulley, Ropes and Gear.
Hours & Admission Prices: Call for hours. Adults $5, children 12-18 $3; discounts to groups; members & students no charge. Closed New Year's Day; Thanksgiving; Christmas. ♿
Attendance: 5,000 (estimated)
Membership: Junior $10; Individual $35; Family $50; Life Member $1,000.

Horsham

GRAEME PARK, 859 County Line Rd., Horsham, PA 19044-1401. Tel.: 215-343-0965, ext. 3001. Fax: 215-343-2223.
E-mail: ra-graemepark@state.pa.us
Web Site: www.ushistory.org/graeme
Founded: 1958.
Congressional District: 13
Key Personnel: Pres. (V), Beth McCausland; Dir., Office Mgr, Historic Site Admin. & Museum Educator, Joan Hauger; Museum Shop Mgr., Carol Brunner.
Personnel Profile: Part-Time Paid 3; Part-Time Volunteers 50.
Governing Authority: state. Parent Institution: Pennsylvania Historical & Museum Commission, Keystone Bldg., 400 North St., Harrisburg, PA 17108. Subsidiary Institution: Friends of Graeme Park. Tax-exempt.
Historic House: 1721, Keith Mansion, located within 42 acres at Graeme Park.
Collections: period furnishings; Georgian style wood paneling installed by Dr. Thomas Graeme, the son-in-law of Gov. Keith, in 1760; reproduction of an outdoor kitchen. Historic Buildings: 19th-century barn; The Keith House.
Research Fields: 18th-century architecture; social history; food preparation; herb gardens; labor history; gender history; African American history; slavery.
Facilities: visitor center; picnic area; pond. Museum-related items for sale.
Activities: guided tours; organized education programs for adults & school groups. Museum Sponsors: Sweethearts Tour in February; Charter Day in March; Anniversary Tour in April; Mother's Day Brunch in May; Living History Days in summer; Celtic Heritage Festival in July; summer history camp in July; Halloween Tours in October; Holiday Event in November.
Publications: brochure, Graeme Park; books; The Penrose Family at Graeme Park; newsletter, Graeme park Gazette; Monograph on Sir William Keith; Trail of History Guide to Graeme Park.
Hours & Admission Prices: Fri.-Sat. 10-4, Sun. 12-4; last tours are one hour before closing. Adults $6, seniors 65 & over and groups $5, youth 3-11 $3; discounts to PHMC Trail of History, AAM, ICOM & AAA members; PA Heritage members, members & children under 3 no charge. Closed New Year's Day; Martin Luther King Jr. Day; Presidents' Day; Columbus Day; Veterans Day; Thanksgiving; Christmas. ♿
Attendance: 8,311
Membership: The Friends of Graeme Park: Youth $5; Individual $15; Family $25; Patron $50; Sponsor $100; Corporation $500 Silver Corporate $1,000; Gold Corporate $2,500.

THE HAROLD F. PITCAIRN WINGS OF FREEDOM AVIATION MUSEUM, 1155 Easton Rd., Horsham, PA 19044. Mailing Address: Delaware Valley Historical Aircraft Association, Naval Air Station, Joint Reserve Base, 1155 Easton Rd., Willow Grove, PA 19090-5200. Tel.: 215-275-2277.
E-mail: dvhaa@comcast.net
Web Site: www.dvhaa.org
Key Personnel: Chm. (V), Ronald Nelson; Cur., Susan Halteman.
Personnel Profile: Part-Time Volunteers 45.
Governing Authority: Parent Institution: Delaware Valley Historical Aircraft Assoc. Tax-exempt.
Aviation Museum.
Collections: 17 aircrafts; World War I; Pitcairn Era' World War II; Tuskegee Airmen; Cold War; women in aviation; Korea; Southeast Asia; contemporary aviation; space exploration; over 200 hand-crafted scale models; videos; films.
Facilities: 5,000-vol. library; archives.
Hours & Admission Prices: Wed.-Fri. 10:30-3, Sat.-Sun. 10:30-4. No charge; donations accepted. ♿
Attendance: 12,000 (accurate)
Membership: Individual $25; Corporate $500.

Hummelstown

HUMMELSTOWN AREA HISTORICAL SOCIETY MUSEUM AND PARISH HOUSE, N. Rosanna & N. Alley, Hummelstown, PA 17036. Mailing Address: 28 W. Main St., Hummelstown, PA 17036-1515. Tel.: 717-566-6314.
Web Site: www.hummelstownhistorical.org
Founded: 1970.
Congressional District: 17
Key Personnel: Pres. (V), William S. Jackson.
Personnel Profile: Part-Time Paid 1.
Governing Authority: Tax-exempt.
Historical Society Museum: housed in a former Zion Lutheran Church; built in 1815.
Collections: local history & culture; period furnishings; personal artifacts; photographs; clothing; Susquehannock Indian artifacts.
Facilities: research library.
Activities: monthly membership meetings & speakers; annual member picnic; period bus trips to historic locations.
Publications: quarterly member's newsletter.
Hours & Admission Prices: Museum: Mon. 12-4; other times by appointment. Library: Mon. 9-3, Tues.-Wed. 12-5:30. Museum: no charge. Library: $5.
Membership: Annual $10; Contributing $20; Life $200; Business & Professional $40.

Huntingdon

HUNTINGDON COUNTY HISTORICAL SOCIETY, 106 4th St., Huntingdon, PA 16652-1418. Mailing Address: P.O. Box 305, Huntingdon, PA 16652-0305. Tel.: 814-643-5449. Fax: 814-643-2711.
E-mail: mail@huntingdonhistory.org
Web Site: www.huntingdonhistory.org

Founded: 1938.
Congressional District: 9
Key Personnel: Exec. Dir., Jennifer Stahl; Pres., Thomas A. Yoder.
Personnel Profile: Part-Time Paid 1; Part-Time Volunteers 23; Interns 1.
Governing Authority: society. Tax-exempt.
History Museum.
Collections: county historical materials; photographs; house furnishings; military artifacts; fine arts; costumes; manuscripts.
Research Fields: Local Sites Survey; county history; genealogy; industrial & Civil War history of county.
Facilities: research library; historic house.
Activities: programs; permanent & temporary exhibits; tours; research projects; workshops.
Publications: genealogy; quarterly newsletter; Glazier Stoneware; Atlas Blair & Huntingdon Counties; Second Century: A Huntingdon County Bicentennial Album; Two Centuries in Huntingdon; Along the Raystown; Huntingdon County Cemetery Guide.
Hours & Admission Prices: Victorian House Museum: Wed. & Fri. 9-4, Thurs. 9-5. Library: mid-March to mid-Nov. Wed. & Fri. 9-4, Thurs. 9-5; other times by appointment. Office: Tues.-Fri. 9-4. No charge; donations accepted.
Attendance: 1,800 (estimated)
Membership: Individual $25; Family $30; Supporter $60; Benefactor $125; Life $500.

JUNIATA COLLEGE MUSEUM OF ART, (M), Moore & 17th St., Huntingdon, PA 16652. Tel.: 814-641-3505. Fax: 814-641-3607.
E-mail: maloney@juniata.edu
Web Site: www.juniata.edu/services/museum
Founded: 1998.
Congressional District: 9
Key Personnel: Dir., Judy Maloney; Cur., Jennifer Streb.
Personnel Profile: Full-Time Paid 2; Interns 4.
Governing Authority: private college. Tax-exempt: 501(c)(3).
Art Museum: housed in former Carnegie Library built in 1906; Beaux-Arts style, Greek cross with rotunda & stained glass windows.
Collections: American & European paintings, drawings & prints from the 17th-20th centuries; emphasis on the Hudson River School & American portrait miniatures; local history.
Research Fields: Hudson River School; American portrait miniatures.
Facilities: 2,000 sq. ft. exhibit space.
Activities: loan, traveling & temporary exhibitions.
Hours & Admission Prices: May-Aug. Wed.-Fri. 12-4; Sept.-April Mon.-Fri. 10-4, Sat. 12-4. No charge. Closed major holidays; college holidays. ♿
Attendance: 2,000 (estimated)
Membership: Student & Senior Citizen $15; Family $35; Contributor $100; Supporter $250; Patron $500.

SWIGART MUSEUM, (M), 12031 William Penn Hwy., Museum Park, Rte. 22 E., Huntingdon, PA 16652. Mailing Address: P.O. Box 214, Huntingdon, PA 16652-0214. Tel.: 814-643-0885. Fax: 814-643-2857.
E-mail: tours@swigartmuseum.com
Web Site: www.swigartmuseum.com
Founded: 1927.
Congressional District: 9
Governing Authority: individual operation.
Automotive Museum.
Collections: 2 Tuckers - The Tin Goose & #1013 Herbie The Love Bug; 1920 Carroll; 1916 Scripps-Booth; 1908 Studebaker Electric; license plates; name plates; toys; photographs; paintings; automobiliana.
Research Fields: automobile history; development of automotive transportation.
Facilities: 20,000-vol. library of manuscripts, books, manuals, journals, catalogs, sales literature available for research upon application. Transportation & automobile-related books & items for sale.
Activities: guided tours; lectures; special programs for schools.
Hours & Admission Prices: Memorial Day-Oct. daily 10-5. Adults $6, senior citizens $5.50, children 6-12 $3; discounts to groups; children under 6 no charge. ♿

Indiana

HISTORICAL AND GENEALOGICAL SOCIETY OF INDIANA COUNTY, 621 Wayne Ave., Indiana, PA 15701-3072. Tel.: 724-463-9600. Fax: 724-463-9899.
E-mail: ichistoricalsociety@gmail.com
Web Site: www.rootsweb.ancestry.com/~paicgs/
Founded: 1938.
Congressional District: 12
Key Personnel: Pres., Herb Gledifsch; Chm., JoAnne McQuilkin.
Personnel Profile: Full-Time Paid 2; Part-Time Paid 1; Part-Time Volunteers 30.
Governing Authority: private; nonprofit. Tax-exempt: 501(c)(3).
Local History Museum.
Collections: genealogy; county history; archives relating to local history; artifacts of local manufacture & use; fine arts; tools; underground railroad in Indiana County, PA.
Research Fields: genealogy; county history; historic preservation; western Pennsylvania history.
Facilities: 10,000-vol. library of genealogy & local history books available for use on premises; reading room; research artifact collection; artifact & archival conservation. Magazines, postcards, booklets, genealogical supplies for sale.
Activities: meetings; workshops; tours; seminars; historic preservation consultation.
Publications: annual magazine; monthly newsletter, The Clark House News.
Hours & Admission Prices: Tues.-Fri. 9-4, Sat. 10-3. Library: $3 per person; members & students no charge. ♿
Attendance: 2,300 (accurate)
Membership: Individual $25; Family $30; Sustaining & Small Business $60; Corporate $125; Life $500; Life (Husband & Wife) $750; Society Benefactor $1,000.

THE JIMMY STEWART MUSEUM, (M), 835 Philadelphia St., Indiana, PA 15701-3907. Mailing Address: P.O. Box One, Indiana, PA 15701. Tel.: 724-349-6112; 800-83-JIMMY. Fax: 724-349-6140.
E-mail: tharley@jimmy.org
Web Site: www.jimmy.org
Founded: 1994.
Congressional District: 12
Key Personnel: C.E.O., Timothy F. Harley; Pres. (V), Carson Greene, Jr.; Vice Pres., Dr. John Butzow; Treas., Gregor Young, IV, J.D.; Museum Shop Mgr., Elizabeth Leeper.
Personnel Profile: Full-Time Paid 1; Part-Time Paid 1; Part-Time Volunteers 25.
Governing Authority: private; nonprofit. Parent Institution: The James M. Stewart Museum Foundation, Indiana, PA. Tax-exempt: 501(c)(3).
History & Audio-Visual Film Museum.
Collections: artifacts documenting the history of the Stewart family in western Pennsylvania; original movie posters & stills; personal & professional memorabilia of Jimmy Stewart, including awards, movie props, military artifacts, photographs, correspondence from directors & actors.
Facilities: 40-vol. library of books on Stewart's career, military service, family history, correspondence, radio, theater, film and TV career; classrooms; 5,000 sq. ft. exhibit space; 50-seat theater. Videos, posters, books, lobby cards, half sheets, film memorabilia, postcards and T-shirts for sale.
Activities: docent program; films; formal education programs for children and Indiana (PA) University students; guided tours; lectures; temporary exhibitions; broadcast programs. Annual Events: Harvey Award in May; It's A Wonderful Life Celebration in December.
Publications: The Stewart Sentinel - The Newsletter of The Jimmy Stewart Museum.
Hours & Admission Prices: Mon.-Sat. 10-5, Sun. & holidays 12-5. Adults $5, senior citizens $4, students $3; children under 7 & members no charge. Closed New Year's Day; Easter; Independence Day; Labor Day; Thanksgiving; Christmas. ♿
Attendance: 8,200 (estimated)
Membership: Individual Student & Senior $25; Individual Adult $35; Senior Couple $45; Family $50.

KIPP GALLERY AT INDIANA UNIVERSITY OF PENNSYLVANIA, College of Fine Arts, Sprowls Hall, 1st Fl., 470 S. 11th St., Indiana, PA 15705-0001. Tel.: 724-357-2530. Fax: 724-357-7778.
Web Site: www.arts.iup.edu/kipp
Founded: 1971.
Congressional District: 12
Key Personnel: Dean College of Fine Arts, Michael Hood; Dir., Kyle Houser.
Personnel Profile: Full-Time Paid 1; Part-Time Paid 4; Interns 3.
Governing Authority: university; not for profit organization. Parent Institution: Indiana University of Pennsylvania. Subsidiary Institution: IUP Student Cooperative Association.
University Art Gallery.
Collections: paintings; photographs; sculpture.
Publications: quarterly bulletin, Insight.
Hours & Admission Prices: Tues.-Fri. 11-4, Sat. 1-4. No charge. ♿

THE UNIVERSITY MUSEUM, (M), Sutton Hall, Indiana University of Pennsylvania, 1011 South Dr., Indiana, PA 15705-0001. Mailing Address: Sutton Hall, Indiana Univ. of Penn., Room 111, Indiana, PA 15705-0001. Tel.: 724-357-2397. Fax: 724-357-7778.
E-mail: mhood@iup.edu
Web Site: www.iup.edu/museum
Founded: 1981.
Congressional District: 12
Key Personnel: Pres., William Double; Dean, Michael Hood.
Personnel Profile: Part-Time Paid 1; Part-Time Volunteers 40; Interns 3.
Governing Authority: university. Parent Institution: The Foundation For IUP. Tax-exempt: 501(c)(3).
Art & History Museum: National Historic Landmark Site.
Collections: art & cultural history; folk art; 19th & 20th-century American art works; American Indian artifacts; 185 paintings & drawings by Milton Bancroft; Inuit Indian sculptures.
Major Exhibits: Emerging Artists: Grad Exhibit, 2/6/10-3/6/10; Paint & Pixels, 3/25/10-5/1/10.
Research Fields: Collections: Milton Bancroft; Wilbur Coffman Photographs; James & Mary Jack Inuit; Ros Purdy Memorial Graphics.
Activities: guided tours; docent programs; lectures; seminars; participatory, loan & temporary exhibitions.
Publications: Insight University Museum quarterly bulletin.
Hours & Admission Prices: Tues.-Wed. & Fri. 2-6:30, Thurs. 12-7:30, Sat. 12-4. No charge. Closed university holidays. ♿
Attendance: 8,000
Membership: Museum Friends: Student $5; Senior Citizen $15; Individual $25; Supporting $50; Active $100; Patron $250; Show Sponsorship $500; Benefactor $1,000 & up.

Jeannette

BUSHY RUN BATTLEFIELD, 1253 Bushy Run Rd., Jeannette, PA 15644. Mailing Address: P.O. Box 468, Harrison City, PA 15636-0468. Tel.: 724-527-5584. Fax: 724-527-5610.
E-mail: brbns@winbeam.com
Web Site: www.bushyrunbattlefield.com
Founded: 1933.
Congressional District: 12
Key Personnel: Pres. (V), Jean Loughry; Museum Shop Mgr., Kelly Ruoff.
Personnel Profile: Full-Time Paid 1; Part-Time Paid 1; Part-Time Volunteers 35; Interns 1.
Governing Authority: state. Parent Institution: Pennsylvania Historical & Museum Commission, Box 1026, Harrisburg, PA 17108-1026. Subsidiary Institution: Bushy Run Battlefield Heritage Society. Tax-exempt.
Military Museum: located on the site of Bushy Run Battlefield, used during Pontiac's Rebellion, 1763.
Collections: 18th-century military artifacts.
Research Fields: middle 18th-century military.
Facilities: amphitheatre; Flour Sak Battle Discovery Trail; Environmental trails; picnic area; visitor's center. Military publications for sale.
Activities: military reenactments; education programs; lectures; special events; permanent exhibitions.
Publications: book, War for Empire in Western Pennsylvania; Bushy Run Battlefield: Pennsylvania Trail of History Guide, The Battle of Bushy Run.
Hours & Admission Prices: Visitor's Center: April-Oct. Wed.-Sun. 9-5. Park: Wed.-Sun. 9-5; groups by appointment. Adults $5, seniors & AAA members $4.50, children 6-17 $3; discounts to AAM members; members no charge. ♿
Attendance: 52,600 (estimated)
Membership: Active Individual $15; Family $25; Sponsor $50; Corporate $100-$499; Endowment $500-$999; Lifetime $1,000.

Jenkintown

ABINGTON ART CENTER, 515 Meetinghouse Rd., Jenkintown, PA 19046-2964. Tel.: 215-887-4882. Fax: 215-887-5789.
E-mail: info@abingtonartcenter.org
Web Site: www.abingtonartcenter.org
Founded: 1939.
Congressional District: 13
Key Personnel: Exec. Dir., Laura Burnham; Asst. Dir., Heather Rutledge; Chm. (V), Arlen Shenkman.
Personnel Profile: Full-Time Paid 6; Part-Time Paid 6; Part-Time Volunteers 32.
Governing Authority: private; nonprofit. Tax-exempt: 501(c)(3).
Art Center & Sculpture Park.
Collections: regional contemporary art & sculpture park.
Research Fields: outdoor contemporary sculpture.
Facilities: studio school; sculpture park.
Activities: formal educational program; guided tours; lectures; rental facility. Museum Sponsors: Outreach programs to many organizations including 500 school children. Annual Event: concert series, Festival for young artists in August.
Publications: a combined quarterly newsletter and class listing.
Hours & Admission Prices: Tues.-Wed. & Fri. 10-5, Thurs. 10-7, Sat.-Sun. 10-3. No charge; donations accepted. Closed New Year's Eve & Day; Independence Day; Thanksgiving; Christmas week. ♿
Attendance: 36,210 (accurate)
Membership: Individual $50; Dual & Family $65; Member Plus $75; Patron $125 & up.

OLD YORK ROAD HISTORICAL SOCIETY, 460 Old York Rd., Jenkintown, PA 19046-2895. Tel.: 215-886-8590.
E-mail: info@oyrhs.org
Web Site: www.oyrhs.org
Founded: 1936.
Congressional District: 13
Key Personnel: Pres. (V), David B. Rowland; Photo Archivist, Joyce Root; Archivist, Shannon Lefevre; Archivist, Linda Stanley.
Personnel Profile: Part-Time Paid 1; Part-Time Volunteers 7; Interns 1.
Governing Authority: society. Tax-exempt.
Local History Research Library.
Collections: local historical items; 165,000 photographic images, vertical files; property atlas collection; journals; books, newspapers, magazines, & manuscripts pertaining to Old York Road area of southeastern Pennsylvania (Eastern Montgomery County).
Research Fields: genealogy; preservation of historical buildings.
Facilities: rent research room and archival storage space from the Jenkintown Library.
Activities: lecture series (5 events); organized tours of local historic sites.
Publications: annual journal, Old York Road Historical Society Bulletin; semiannual newsletter, The Corridor.
Hours & Admission Prices: Mon. 7pm-9pm, Tues. 11-2, Wed. 11-3; other times by appointment. No charge; donations accepted.
Attendance: 465 (accurate)
Membership: Individual $30; Family $45; Patron $75; Patron Plus $125; Contributor $250; Sustainer $500; Benefactor $1,000.

Jersey Shore

JERSEY SHORE HISTORICAL SOCIETY, 200 S. Main St., Jersey Shore, PA 17740-1812. Tel.: 717-398-1973.
Founded: 1963.
Historical Society Museum.
Collections: local history & heritage; photographs; personal artifacts; period furnishings.
Hours & Admission Prices: Call for hours.
Membership: Individual $15; Life $100.

Jim Thorpe

ASA PACKER MANSION, Packer Hill, Jim Thorpe, PA 18229-0108. Mailing Address: P.O Box 108, Jim Thorpe, PA 18229-0108. Tel.: 570-325-3229.
E-mail: abretzik@yahoo.com
Web Site: www.asapackermansion.com
Founded: 1913.
Congressional District: 11
Key Personnel: Dir. & Historian, Ava Bretzik.
Governing Authority: municipal; society. Parent Institution: Borough of Jim Thorpe. Subsidiary Institution: Jim Thorpe Lions Club.
Historic Building: 1860 Victorian mansion.
Collections: furnishings.
Facilities: 500-vol. library of owner's personal library available for use by reference. Museum-related items for sale.
Activities: guided tours; lectures; permanent & temporary exhibitions.
Hours & Admission Prices: April-May Sat.-Sun. 11-4:15; Memorial Day-Nov 1. daily 11-4:15. Adults $8, senior citizens 55 & over $7, students & children 6-18 $5; children under 5 no charge. ♿
Attendance: 30,000

Johnstown

JOHNSTOWN AREA HERITAGE ASSOCIATION, 201 6th Ave., Johnstown, PA 15906-2500. Mailing Address: P.O. Box 1889, Johnstown, PA 15907-1889. Tel.: 814-539-1889. Fax: 814-535-1931.
E-mail: info@jaha.org
Web Site: www.jaha.org
Formerly: Johnstown Flood Museum
Founded: 1971.
Congressional District: 12

Key Personnel: Exec. Dir., Richard A. Burkert; Pres. (V), Ronald Carnevali; Designer, Marcia Kelly; Dir. Devel., Patti Genovese; Dir. Visitor Svcs., Melissa Bacon; Controller, Paul Jucha; Cur., Daniel Ingram; Archivist, Robin Rommel.
Personnel Profile: Full-Time Paid 12; Part-Time Paid 8; Part-Time Volunteers 30; Interns 3.
Governing Authority: nonprofit organization. Parent Institution: Johnstown Area Heritage Association. Tax-exempt: 501(c)(3).
History Museum.
Collections: industry, transportation & flooding; manuscripts; photographs; Academy Award-winning film portray the legendary 1889 Johnstown Flood. Heritage Discovery Center: interactive media & exhibits on life in industrial Johnstown.
Research Fields: influence of flooding in the development of Johnstown; early transportation; steel industry in the area; coal industry in Western Pennsylvania; immigration & ethnicity.
Facilities: library of local history manuscripts & photographic collection available for research. Books & museum-related items for sale.
Activities: guided tours; lectures; films; loan, permanent & temporary exhibitions; ethnic festival; walking tours.
Publications: 8 or more misc. local history publications; quarterly newsletter, Walking Tours.
Hours & Admission Prices: May-Oct. Sun.-Thurs. 10-5, Fri.-Sat. 10-7; Nov.-April daily 10-5. Two Sites: Adults $6, senior citizens $5, students $4; discounts to AAM & ICOM members; members & children no charge. ♿
Attendance: 68,000 (accurate)
Membership: Individual $25; Family $35; Contributor $50; Supporter $100; Benefactor $250; Patron $500; Sustaining Patron $1,000.

SOUTHERN ALLEGHENIES MUSEUM OF ART AT JOHNSTOWN, Pasquerilla Performing Arts Center, University of Pittsburgh at Johnstown, 450 Schoolhouse Rd., Johnstown, PA 15904-2912. Tel.: 814-269-7234. Fax: 814-269-7240.
E-mail: johnstown@sama-art.org
Web Site: www.sama-art.org
Founded: 1982.
Congressional District: 72
Key Personnel: Exec. Dir., G. Gary Moyer; Coord. & Education Admin., Tina Lehman.
Personnel Profile: Full-Time Paid 1; Part-Time Paid 2; Part-Time Volunteers 2.
Governing Authority: nonprofit organization. Parent Institution: Southern Alleghenies Museum of Art, Saint Francis University Mall, Loretto, PA 15940. Tax-exempt: 501(c)(3).
Art Museum.
Collections: paintings; photographs; sculpture.
Activities: changing exhibitions; gallery tours; lectures; artists in residence; classes & workshops; performing arts; summer children's events; art film festival.
Publications: exhibition catalogues.
Hours & Admission Prices: Mon.-Fri. 9:30-4:30. No charge; donations accepted. Closed major holidays. ♿
Attendance: 50,428 (accurate)
Membership: See separate listing for Southern Alleghenies Museum of Art.

Kempton

ALBANY TOWNSHIP HISTORICAL SOCIETY, 404 Old Philly Pike, Kempton, PA 19529-9306. Mailing Address: P.O. Box 95, Kempton, PA 19529. Tel.: 610-756-6144.
Web Site: albanyths.org
Historical Society Museum: housed in a former grain & feed warehouse; built in 1917.
Collections: local history & culture; photographs; personal artifacts; period furnishings.
Activities: special events.
Publications: quarterly newsletter; book, Folk Art and Foodways of the Pennsylvania Dutch.
Hours & Admission Prices: 3rd Sun. of month 1-4. No charge.
Membership: Student $10; Individual $20; Family $25; Corporate $100; Lifetime $300; Lifetime Family $375.

HAWK MOUNTAIN SANCTUARY, 1700 Hawk Mountain Rd., Kempton, PA 19529-9379. Tel.: 610-756-6961. Fax: 610-756-4468.
E-mail: info@hawkmountain.org
Web Site: www.hawkmountain.org
Founded: 1934.
Congressional District: 6
Key Personnel: Pres., Lee Schisler, Jr.; Dir. Devel. & Communications, Celeste Voyer.
Personnel Profile: Full-Time Paid 20; Part-Time Paid 5; Part-Time Volunteers 250; Interns 10.
Nature Center.
Collections: natural area; plant garden; observation point; visitor center.
Research Fields: ornithology & ecology.
Facilities: visitor center; 8 miles of trails & picnic lookouts; 2,600 acre natural area famous for eye-level views of raptors during their autumn migration.
Activities: public programs & year-round special events.
Publications: Raptor Watch: a global directory of raptor migration sites; Hawks Aloft by Maurice Brown; Hawk Mountain 1,000: A Species Checklist; Raptors of Hawk Mountain Coloring Book; Flight Guide.
Hours & Admission Prices: Sept.-Nov. daily 8-5; Dec.-Aug. daily 9-5. Adults $7, children 6-12 $3; members no charge. ♿
Attendance: 70,000 (estimated)
Membership: Individual $35; Family $40; Family Plus $50; Sustaining $75; Broadwing Club $100.

Kennett Square

LONGWOOD GARDENS, Rte. 1, Kennett Square, PA 19348. Mailing Address: P.O. Box 501, Kennett Square, PA 19348-0501. Tel.: 610-388-1000. Fax: 610-388-2294.
Web Site: www.longwoodgardens.org
Founded: 1906.
Congressional District: 5
Key Personnel: C.E.O., Nathan Hayward; Dir., Paul Redman; Head Horticulture Dept., Sharon Loving; Head Maintenance Dept., Mark Winnicki; Head Administration Dept., Dennis Fisher; Cur. Plants, Tomasz Anisko; Mgr. Mktg., Marnie Conley; Performing Arts Coord., Dara Gordon.
Personnel Profile: Full-Time Paid 160; Part-Time Paid 170; Part-Time Volunteers 350; Interns 55.
Governing Authority: nonprofit. Parent Institution: Longwood Gardens, Inc., P.O. Box 501, Kennett Square, PA 19348. Cooperates with University of Delaware. Tax-exempt: 501(c)(3).
Arboretum & Horticultural Display Garden.
Collections: 11,000 tropical & hardy woody & herbaceous plants. Historic House: Peirce-du Pont House containing the Longwood Heritage exhibit.
Major Exhibits: Making Scents: The Art and Passion of Fragrance, 4/10-12/10.
Research Fields: hybridization, selection of ornamental plants; studies of improved horticultural techniques.
Facilities: 21,500-vol. library of books on gardening, horticulture, floras, landscape design available for inter-library loan & for research to qualified persons; 1,050 acres of developed gardens; 4 acres under glass; 20 indoor gardens; open air theater; 400-seat restaurant. Books, videos, items for sale.
Activities: guided tours; lectures; concerts; formally organized programs for adults, undergraduate & graduate college students; professional gardener training program; Idea Garden for home gardeners; horticultural exhibitions; arts & crafts exhibits; evening holiday displays; performing arts events.
Publications: picture book, Longwood Gardens; video, Longwood Gardens/A Video Visit Throughout the Year; books, The Planning Vision; Tulip Trees & Quaker Gentlemen; booklets on various plant groups; compact discs of the Longwood Organ; video, Horticultural Career Training at Longwood Gardens.
Hours & Admission Prices: April-Aug. daily 9-6; Sept.-March daily 9-5. Illuminated evening fountain display: June-Aug. Thurs.-Sat. evenings at dusk. Adults $16. ♿
Attendance: 853,100 (accurate)
Membership: Garden Passes: Adult (Individual) $60; Family & Grandparent $105.

King of Prussia

VALLEY FORGE NATIONAL HISTORICAL PARK, 1400 N. Outer Line Dr., King of Prussia, PA 19406-1009. Tel.: 610-783-1077. Fax: 610-783-1060.
Web Site: www.nps.gov/vafo
Founded: 1893.
Congressional District: 7
Key Personnel: Supt., Michael A. Caldwell; Volunteer Coord., Ernestine White; Cur., Dona McDermott; Museum Shop Mgr., Daria Fink.
Personnel Profile: Full-Time Paid 72; Part-Time Volunteers 124.
Governing Authority: federal. Parent Institution: Dept. of Interior, National Park Service. Tax-exempt.
Historic Site: c.1777-1778 site of Continental Army winter encampment.
Collections: period furnishings, 1770-1780; original headquarters of George Washington & other generals; replica huts of the Continental soldiers; archaeological artifacts from encampment; George C. Neumann collection of revolutionary arms & accoutrements; military manuscripts; 18th century military weaponry.
Research Fields: George Washington; encampments of Revolutionary army; military history of the period.

Facilities: visitor center; tour road; picnic areas; bicycle, hiking & bridle trails; research library; museum & visitor center. Publications & postcards for sale.
Activities: guided walks & tours; living history demonstrations; orientation film; special events.
Hours & Admission Prices: Daily 9-5. No charge. Closed New Year's Day; Thanksgiving; Christmas. ♿
Attendance: 1,200,000

Kinzers

ROUGH & TUMBLE ENGINEERS HISTORICAL ASSOCIATION, Rte. 30, Kinzers, PA 17535. Mailing Address: Box 9, Kinzers, PA 17535-0009. Tel.: 717-442-4249.
Web Site: www.roughandtumble.org
Founded: 1948.
Key Personnel: Pres., Harvey Bashore; Cur., David Adams.
Governing Authority: society. Tax-exempt: 501(c)(3).
Agricultural & Mechanical Technology & History.
Collections: steam engines; tractors; generators; small models; covered wagon; gas engines; sawmill; trains; large industrial trailers, commercial vehicles (trucks, construction equipment) agricultural & household.
Research Fields: history of technology.
Facilities: 200-vol. library pertaining to steam power, traction engines & early gas power for public use. Museum-related items for sale.
Activities: guided tours; lectures; broadcast programs; participatory, loan & temporary exhibitions.
Publications: quarterly newsletter, Whistle; book, Rough and Tumble Engineering.
Hours & Admission Prices: Call for hours & admission. ♿
Membership: Individual $20; Family $25; Life $200.

Knoxville

KNOXVILLE PUBLIC LIBRARY, 112 Main St., Knoxville, PA 16928-0277. Mailing Address: P.O. Box 277, Knoxville, PA 16928-0277. Tel.: 814-326-4448. Fax: 814-326-4448.
E-mail: kplibrary@verizon.net
Web Site: www.knoxvillepubliclibrary.com
Founded: 1921.
Congressional District: 10
Key Personnel: Pres., Eugene A. Seelye; Librarian, Ellen Williams; Asst. Librarian, Elaine Van Sickle.
Personnel Profile: Part-Time Paid 2; Part-Time Volunteers 2.
Governing Authority: nonprofit organization. Tax-exempt: 501(c)(3).
History Museum.
Collections: local history; ephemera; photographs.
Facilities: 200-vol. library of Tioga County, manuscripts, Pennsylvania & southern tier New York history.
Activities: permanent & temporary exhibitions.
Hours & Admission Prices: Mon. 9-8:30, Wed. 9-6:30, Fri.-Sat. 9-4. No charge.

Kutztown

PENNSYLVANIA GERMAN CULTURAL HERITAGE CENTER AT KUTZTOWN UNIVERSITY, 22 Luckenbill Rd., Kutztown, PA 19530-9203. Tel.: 610-683-1589; 484-646-4165 (Library) & 4172 (Store). Fax: 610-683-1330.
E-mail: heritage@kutztown.edu
Web Site: www.kutztown.edu/community/PGCHC
Formerly: Pennsylvania Dutch Folk Culture Society, Inc.
Founded: 1992.
Congressional District: 187
Key Personnel: Dir., Dr. Robert Reynolds; Information Technology, Patty Frandsen; Pres. (V), Paul Kunkel; Chm. (V), William Bender.
Personnel Profile: Full-Time Paid 1; Full-Time Volunteers 2; Part-Time Paid 3; Part-Time Volunteers 4; Interns 1.
Governing Authority: nonprofit organization. Parent Institution: Kutztown University Foundation. Tax-exempt: 501(c)(3).
Folk Culture Museum.
Collections: folk items and art; taufscheins; agriculture; general; costumes; colonial period & turn of the century exhibits; third generation tinsmith shop; tools & items made by former tinsmith; 1800-1910 PA German culture; one-room schoolhouse; 19th century farmhouse; summerhouse with wash house & home butchering equipment: Swiss bank barn with barn stars; painted furniture & dower chest. Historic Buildings: 2 log cabins, c.1700.
Research Fields: folklore; genealogy & local history; PA German culture.
Facilities: library of books, tapes, pictures, slides pertaining to genealogy folklore; historic house c. 1810; Swiss bank barn c. 1860's; summerhouse; washhouse & butchering shop; one room schoolhouse c.1850's. Handmade, local & regional history & culture & museum-related items for sale.
Activities: guided tours; lectures; formally organized education programs for children & adults; folklife demonstrations; children's cultural camp.
Publications: newsletter, Heritage Center News.
Hours & Admission Prices: Mon.-Fri. 10-12 & 1-4; other times by appointment. Adults & tours $5; members no charge. Closed most holidays. ♿
Attendance: 12,000 (estimated)
Membership: Adult $25-$500.

Lackawaxen

ZANE GREY MUSEUM, 135 Scenic Dr., Lackawaxen, PA 18435. Mailing Address: 274 River Rd., Beach Lake, PA 18405-4046. Tel.: 570-685-4871. Fax: 570-685-4874.
E-mail: upde_interpretation@nps.gov
Web Site: www.nps.gov/upde
Founded: 1978.
Congressional District: 10
Key Personnel: Supt., Vidal Martinez; Chief Interpretation, Loren Goering; Museum Cur., Dorothy Moon; Museum Shop Mgr., Connie Lloyd.
Personnel Profile: Full-Time Paid 3; Part-Time Paid 3.
Governing Authority: federal government. Parent Institution: National Park Service, Dept. of the Interior, Washington, DC. Tax-exempt.
History Museum.
Collections: books, archival; Zane Grey memorabilia.
Research Fields: life & writing of Zane Grey.
Facilities: archives.
Activities: guided tours.
Publications: brochures; Zane Grey novels; audiotapes; videotapes.
Hours & Admission Prices: Memorial Day-Labor Day Fri.-Sun. 10-5; Sept. to mid-Oct. Sat.-Sun. 10-5. No charge; donations accepted.
Attendance: 8,000 (accurate)

Lake Ariel

CLAWS 'N' PAWS WILD ANIMAL PARK, 1475 Ledgedale Rd., Lake Ariel, PA 18436-5589. Tel.: 570-698-6154.
Zoo.
Collections: over 300 animals representing 120 species.
Facilities: Museum-related items for sale.
Activities: animal shows; special events.
Hours & Admission Prices: May to mid-Oct. daily 10-6. Adults 12 & over $13.95, seniors 65 & over $12.95, children 2-11 $9.95; children one & under no charge.

Lancaster

DEMUTH MUSEUM, (M), 120 E. King St., Lancaster, PA 17602-2832. Tel.: 717-299-9940. Fax: 717-299-9749.
E-mail: info@demuth.org
Founded: 1981.
Key Personnel: Dir., Anne M. Lampe.
Personnel Profile: Full-Time Paid 3; Part-Time Paid 1.
Governing Authority: Tax-exempt.
Art Museum.
Collections: Charles Demuth's artwork; archive.
Facilities: library; archives.
Hours & Admission Prices: Feb.-Dec. Tues.-Sat. 10-4, Sun. 1-4. No charge; donations accepted.

EDWARD HAND MEDICAL HERITAGE MUSEUM, 881 Rockford Rd., Lancaster, PA 17602-1225. Tel.: 717-393-9588.
Medical Museum.
Collections: period medical artifacts.
Hours & Admission Prices: Fri. 10am to noon; other times by appointment. No charge.

HANDS-ON HOUSE, CHILDREN'S MUSEUM OF LANCASTER, 721 Landis Valley Rd., Lancaster, PA 17601-4888. Tel.: 717-569-KIDS. Fax: 717-581-9283.
E-mail: info@handsonhouse.org
Web Site: handsonhouse.org
Founded: 1987.
Key Personnel: Exec. Dir., Lynne Morrison.
Personnel Profile: Full-Time Paid 4; Part-Time Paid 12.
Governing Authority: nonprofit. Tax-exempt: 501(c)(3).
Children's Museum.
Collections: hands-on exhibits.
Facilities: Children's toys for sale.

Activities: organized education programs for children; participatory exhibits.
Publications: quarterly newsletter, Handprints.
Hours & Admission Prices: Labor Day to Memorial Day Tues.-Thurs. 11-4, Fri. 11-8, Sat. 10-5, Sun. 12-5; Memorial Day to Labor Day Mon.-Thurs. & Sat. 10-5, Fri. 10-8, Sun. 12-5. Admission $7; discounts to groups & ACM members; members no charge. Closed New Year's Day; Easter; Memorial Day; Independence Day; Labor Day; Thanksgiving; Christmas. ♿
Attendance: 60,000 (estimated)
Membership: Individual $20; Grandparent $25; Family $60; Family Plus $70; Contributing $100.

HERITAGE CENTER OF LANCASTER COUNTY, INC., 13 W. King St., Lancaster, PA 17603-3813. Tel.: 717-299-6440. Fax: 717-299-6916.
Web Site: www.lancasterheritage.com
Founded: 1973.
Congressional District: 16
Key Personnel: Vice Pres., Kimberly Fortney; Cur., Wendell Zercher; Museum Shop Mgr., Sue Schumann.
Personnel Profile: Full-Time Paid 7; Full-Time Volunteers 3; Part-Time Paid 15; Part-Time Volunteers 450; Interns 2.
Governing Authority: nonprofit organization. Tax-exempt: 501(c)(3).
General Museum.
Collections: Lancaster County decorative arts; furniture; quilt & textiles; fraktur; paintings; ceramics; glass; iron; silver; pewter; regional history.
Research Fields: 18th, 19th & 20th-century decorative arts of Lancaster County; Pennsylvania & mid-Atlantic region.
Facilities: Museum-related items for sale.
Activities: lectures; loan, permanent & temporary exhibitions; special events.
Publications: newsletter; exhibit catalogs.
Hours & Admission Prices: Quilt Museum: March-Dec. Mon.-Sat. 9-5. Heritage Center: March-Dec. Mon.-Sat. 9-5, Sun. 10-3. Quilt Museum: adults $6; children no charge. Heritage Center: no charge. Closed New Year's Day; Memorial Day; Thanksgiving; Christmas. ♿
Attendance: 75,000 (accurate)
Membership: Single $25; Family $50; Collector Circle $75; Curator Circle $100; Museum Guild $250; Heritage Guild $500; Benefactor $1,000.

LANCASTER COUNTY HISTORICAL SOCIETY, 230 N. President Ave., Lancaster, PA 17603-3125. Tel.: 717-392-4633. Fax: 717-293-2739.
E-mail: info@lancasterhistory.org
Web Site: www.lancasterhistory.org
Founded: 1886.
Congressional District: 16
Key Personnel: Pres. & C.E.O., Thomas R. Ryan; Vice Pres., Robin Sarratt-Cohen; Cur., Barry Rauhauser; Dir. Library Svcs., Robert K. Weber; Archivist, Heather Tennies; Genealogist, Kevin Shue.
Personnel Profile: Full-Time Paid 13; Full-Time Volunteers 1; Part-Time Paid 8; Part-Time Volunteers 273.
Governing Authority: private; nonprofit corporation. Tax-exempt: 501(c)(3).
Historical Society Archives, Library & Exhibitions.
Collections: Lancaster County history; glass; pewter; costumes; books; Judge Yeates Law library with 1,500 vols.; county archives 1729-1850; local newspapers 1787-1936; manuscript material; Jacob Eichholtz portraits; Arthur Armstrong portraits; local history.
Research Fields: economic, political, social, genealogical & technological history of Lancaster County.
Facilities: 15,000-vol. library & archives; reading room; meeting room; research facilities; classroom; bookstore. Museum-related items for sale.
Activities: tours; lectures; living history events; temporary exhibits; arboretum walk.
Publications: Journal of the Lancaster County Historical Society; newsletter, The Historian.
Hours & Admission Prices: Tues. & Thurs. 9:30-9:30, Wed. & Fri.-Sat. 9:30-4:30. Research Library: adults $8, senior citizens 65 & over $7, students $6, children 6-11 $3; discounts to AAA, AAM & ICOM members; members no charge. Exhibitions: no charge; donations accepted. Closed national holidays. ♿
Attendance: 22,000 (estimated)
Membership: High School Students free upon application; College Students $5 (semester); Regular $40; Family $50; Contributing $75; Benefactor $100; Business $100 & up; Sustainer $250; Director's Circle $500; President's Circle $1,000; Historian's Circle $5,000.

LANCASTER MUSEUM OF ART, (M), 135 N. Lime St., Lancaster, PA 17602-2952. Tel.: 717-394-3497. Fax: 717-394-0101.
E-mail: info@Lmapa.org
Web Site: www.Lmapa.org
Founded: 1965.
Congressional District: 16
Key Personnel: Exec. Dir., Stanley I. Grand, Ph.D.; Bd. Pres., Claudia Himes.
Personnel Profile: Full-Time Paid 5; Part-Time Paid 3; Part-Time Volunteers 25; Interns 3.
Governing Authority: nonprofit organization. Tax-exempt: 501(c)(3).
Regional Visual Arts Museum.
Collections: various media of art.
Major Exhibits: Zeuxis: The Common Object (T), 1/11/10-2/28/10; Lancaster County Young Artists Exhibition, 3/5/10-3/28/10; Seymour Remenick: A Retrospective, 4/2/10-5/30/10; 48th Annual Open Art Award Exhibition, 6/4/10-7/25/10; Echo Valley Art Group @ 65, 8/6/10-9/26/10; Rafael Ferrer, 10/10-11/21/10; Trees Galore!, 12/3/10-12/20/10.
Research Fields: The Grubb Family; Lancaster City Mansion.
Activities: changing exhibitions; guided tours; lectures; concerts; arts festivals; organized education programs.
Publications: newsletter; exhibitions catalogues; e-mail newsletters.
Hours & Admission Prices: Moving to: 201 N. Queen St., Lancaster, PA; call for information. Tues.-Sat. 10-4, Sun. 12-4. Donations Requested. Closed national holidays.
Attendance: 35,000 (estimated)
Membership: Individual $35; Family $65; Sponsor $125; Patron $250; Curator's Circle $500; Director's Circle $1,250.

LANDIS VALLEY MUSEUM, 2451 Kissel Hill Rd., Lancaster, PA 17601-4809. Tel.: 717-569-0401, ext. 216 & 208. Fax: 717-560-2147.
E-mail: stemiller@state.pa.us
Web Site: landisvalleymuseum.org
Founded: 1925.
Congressional District: 16
Key Personnel: Bd. Pres., Andrew Esbenshade; Dir., Russell M. Swody; Museum Shop Mgr., Mary Parelli; Business, Patricia Frey; Events Coord., Cindy Kirby-Reedy; Maintenance & Security, William Morrow; Farm & Garden Mgr., Joseph Schott; Coord. Heirloom Seed Project, Beth Leensvaart; Cur., Bruce Bomberger; Interpretation Supvr., Karen Duvall; Museum Educator, Tim Essig; Museum Educator, Mike Emery; Museum Preparator, Donna Horst; Dir. Group Sales, Joyce Perkinson; Scholar in Residence, Dr. Irwin Richman.
Personnel Profile: Full-Time Paid 25; Full-Time Volunteers 2; Part-Time Paid 44; Part-Time Volunteers 409; Interns 3.
Governing Authority: state. Parent Institution: Pennsylvania Historical and Museum Commission. Subsidiary Institution: Landis Valley Assoc. Tax-exempt: 501(c)(3).
Rural Life & Culture Village Museum Complex.
Collections: agriculture; Pennsylvania German decorative arts; folk culture; textiles; transportation. Historic Buildings: Mennonite & Amish religion; tavern; gun shop; craft building; 1870s Isaac Landis farm complex; late 1700 Log Farm; 1830s-1840s Brick Farmstead; 1870s Pierce Landis complex; 1890 Schoolhouse; 1857 Landis Valley Hotel.
Research Fields: agriculture; Pennsylvania German history & material culture; folk culture; science & technology; textiles; transportation.
Facilities: 12,000-vol. library of agricultural journals & texts, folk art, farm & history books available for use on premises by written request. Publications, gift items, museum reproductions & ceramics for sale.
Activities: guided tours; lectures; films; formally organized education programs; permanent & temporary exhibitions; workshops; youth classes; holiday events. Museum Sponsors: Harvest Days; Pennsylvania Institute of Rural Life & Culture.
Publications: history & guidebook, Landis Valley; Heirloom Seed Catalog (annual); quarterly The Valley Gazette; PA German Food & Traditions; PA German Farms, Gardens & Seeds: 400 Years at Landis Valley; book, The Art of Seeds; Lancaster County postcards; the Landis family album.
Hours & Admission Prices: Mon.-Sat. 9-5, Sun. 12-5. Adults $11, senior citizens $8.50, youth 6-12 $7; discount to groups, AAA, AAM & ICOM members, student groups & for tickets from other state sites & local museums; children under 6 & members no charge. Closed New Year's Day; Thanksgiving; Christmas. ♿
Attendance: 65,737 (accurate)
Membership: Student $20; Senior Citizen $25; Individual $35; Family & Grand Family $55; Patron $100; Heirloom Club $250; Landis Club $500.

THE PHILLIPS MUSEUM OF ART, FRANKLIN & MARSHALL COLLEGE, (M), 700 College Ave., Lancaster, PA 17604. Mailing Address: P.O. Box 3003, Lancaster, PA 17604-3003. Tel.: 717-291-3879. Fax: 717-358-4441.
E-mail: claire.giblin@fandm.edu
Web Site: www.fandm.edu/phillipsmuseum.xml
Founded: 2000.
Congressional District: 16
Key Personnel: Interim Dir., Eliza J. Reilly; Acting Cur., Claire Giblin; Exhibition Coord. & Preparator, Russell O'Connell.

Personnel Profile: Full-Time Paid 2; Part-Time Paid 2; Part-Time Volunteers 2; Interns 17.
Governing Authority: nonprofit; private college. Parent Institution: Franklin & Marshall College, Lancaster, PA. Tax-exempt: 501(c)(3).
Art Museum.
Collections: 19th-20th century American paintings; 20th century photographs; American decorative arts; Pennsylvania folk art; African art.
Major Exhibits: Wright, 11/12/09-12/11; Faculty, 1/19/10-3/7/10; Kingerlee (T), 2/26/10-4/18/10; OH, 3/11/10-4/11/10; Senior Show, 4/12/10-5/15/10; Student Show, 4/19/10-5/7/10.
Facilities: cafeteria; educational facilities.
Activities: lectures; loan, temporary & traveling exhibitions.
Publications: exhibition catalogues.
Hours & Admission Prices: Academic Year: Tues.-Fri. 11:30-4:30, Sat.-Sun. 12:30-4:30; Summer: call for hours. No charge. Closed legal holidays. ♿
Attendance: 5,000 (estimated)
Membership: General $35; Contributor $100; Franklin $500; Trustee Assoc. $1,000; Fellow $5,000.

ROCK FORD PLANTATION, 881 Rockford Rd., Lancaster, PA 17602-1225. Tel.: 717-392-7223. Fax: 717-392-7283 (call first).
Web Site: www.rockfordplantation.org
Formerly: Historic Rock Ford
Founded: 1958.
Congressional District: 97
Key Personnel: Exec. Dir., Samuel C. Slaymaker; Pres. (V), Stephanie Rieker; Museum Shop Mgr., Lisa A. Haldy.
Personnel Profile: Full-Time Paid 1; Part-Time Paid 3; Part-Time Volunteers 50; Interns 3.
Governing Authority: nonprofit organization. Parent Institution: Rock Ford Foundation, Inc. Tax-exempt: 501(c)(3).
Historic House: 1794 Georgian mansion of Gen. Edward Hand.
Collections: late 18th & early 19th century American furnishings; art belonging to General Edward Hand & his family.
Research Fields: Hand family.
Facilities: Gift items for sale.
Activities: guided tours; school programs; permanent exhibitions. Museum Sponsors: Yuletide Tours; Revolutionary War Encampment; Halloween program.
Publications: Rock Ford Guidebook; school packets, Gen. E. Hand biographies.
Hours & Admission Prices: April-Oct. Wed.-Sun. 11-3; last tour begins at 3; Nov.-March by appointment. Adults $6, seniors $5, students 6-12 $4; discounts to AAM, ICOM, AAA members, groups & senior citizens; members & children under 6 no charge. ♿
Attendance: 3,000 (estimated)
Membership: Individual $15; Family $25; Associate $35; Sponsor $50; Patron $100; Sustaining $200.

SEHNER-ELLICOTT-VON HESS HOUSE, 123 N. Prince St., Lancaster, PA 17603-3525. Tel.: 717-291-5861. Fax: 717-291-2251.
E-mail: tas@hptrust.org
Web Site: www.hptrust.org
Founded: 1966.
Key Personnel: Exec. Dir., Timothy Smedick.
Governing Authority: Parent Institution: Historic Preservation Trust of Lancaster County.
Historic House: c.1787.
Collections: county history & culture; period furnishings; photographs.
Facilities: library.
Hours & Admission Prices: Mon.-Fri. 9-3:30. No charge; donations accepted. Closed holidays.
Membership: Individual $35; Family $50; Business $100.

WOLF MUSEUM OF MUSIC AND ART, 423 W. Chestnut Ave., Lancaster, PA 17603-3405. Tel.: 717-392-6382.
Music & Art Museum: housed in the former home & studio of Dr. William A. Wolf & his wife Frances; built in 1886.
Collections: family history; period furnishings; personal artifacts; two 1915 Knabe concert grand pianos; paintings.
Activities: public recitals.
Hours & Admission Prices: By appointment & for public recitals.

Landisville

AMOS HERR HOUSE FOUNDATION AND HISTORIC SOCIETY, 1756 Nissley Rd., Landisville, PA 17538-1360. Mailing Address: P.O. Box 52, Landisville, PA 17538-0052. Tel.: 717-898-8822.
E-mail: info@herrhomestead.org
Web Site: www.herrhomestead.org
Founded: 1990.
Key Personnel: Pres. (V) & Museum Shop Mgr., John Houston; Treas., Gerald Albright; Cur. & Archivist, Eileen Johns; Sec., Mrs. Millie Brubaker.
Personnel Profile: Part-Time Volunteers 90.
Governing Authority: private; nonprofit organization. Tax-exempt.
History Museum.
Collections: furnishings; 19th-20th century farm equipment.
Facilities: library; nature center. Museum-related items for sale.
Activities: docent program; guided tours; hobby workshops; lectures; school loan service; participatory & temporary exhibitions. Annual Events: historic lectures; Amos Herr 5K Honey Run.
Publications: newsletter, three times a year, AHHF newsletter.
Hours & Admission Prices: April-Oct. Sat.-Sun. 1-4; private tours by appointment. No charge; donations accepted. Closed New Year's Day; Easter; Memorial Day; Independence Day; Labor Day; Thanksgiving; Christmas. ♿
Attendance: 750 (estimated)
Membership: Individual $15; Family $20; Friend $25; Supporting $50; Contributing $100; Sustaining $250; Guarantor $500; Benefactor $1,000.

Langhorne

HISTORIC LANGHORNE ASSOCIATION, 160 W. Maple Ave., Langhorne, PA 19047-2820. Tel.: 215-757-1888 & 6158. Fax: 215-741-5767.
E-mail: historiclanghorne1@verizon.net
Web Site: hla.buxcom.net
Founded: 1965.
Congressional District: 8
Key Personnel: Pres., James Maier; Vice Pres. & Archivist, Lawrence Langhans; Treas., Jack Fulton; Librarian, Jean Noble; Archivist, Museum Shop Mgr. & Recording Sec., Evelyn Aicher.
Personnel Profile: Part-Time Volunteers 15.
Governing Authority: nonprofit organization. Tax-exempt: 501(c)(3).
Historical Association.
Collections: early Quaker heritage & Bucks County pre-Revolutionary War to present, history; artifacts; clothing; quilts; art; architecture.
Research Fields: homes & other buildings of historic value in Langhorne; genealogy.
Facilities: 275-vol. library on American, Pennsylvania & Bucks County history; colonial artifacts available to the public; 75-seat auditorium; 1,600 sq. ft. exhibit space. Museum-related items for sale.
Activities: guided tours; lectures; loan & temporary exhibitions; monthly general meeting with guest speaker. Annual Events: Walking tour of Langhorne; Spring porch & patio tour; Memorial Day Open House; Christmas house tour of Langhorne; Santa's visit & carol sing-a-long.
Publications: monthly newsletter.
Hours & Admission Prices: Wed. & Sat. 10-12 & 7-9; other times by appointment. No charge; donations accepted.
Attendance: 1,200 (accurate)
Membership: Member $20; Family $25; Patron $50; Century $100; Historic $250; Worthington $500; Williamson $1,000.

Laughlintown

COMPASS INN MUSEUM, 1382 Rte. 30 E., Laughlintown, PA 15655. Mailing Address: P.O. Box 167, Laughlintown, PA 15655-0167. Tel.: 724-238-4983.
Web Site: www.compassinn.com
Founded: 1972.
Congressional District: 18
Key Personnel: Pres. (V), Christen Mizikar; Inn Keeper & Museum Shop Mgr., Jim Koontz; Office Mgr., Tina Yandrick.
Personnel Profile: Full-Time Paid 2; Part-Time Paid 3; Part-Time Volunteers 40.
Governing Authority: Parent Institution: Ligonier Valley Historical Society. Tax-exempt.
History Museum: housed in a restored stagecoach stop; built in 1799. Listed on the National Register of Historic Places.
Collections: early 1800s life; period furnishings; Conestoga wagon; stagecoach; blacksmith tools; pots & utensils; 1790 beehive oven; cookhouse; blacksmith shop; barn; carpenter shop.
Facilities: Museum-related items for sale.
Activities: school programs; tours. Museum Sponsors: Grand Tea in April; Living History Weekends June to August; Halloween Storytelling Event in October; Candlelight Tours November to mid-December.
Publications: quarterly newsletter.
Hours & Admission Prices: May-Oct. Tues.-Sat. 11-4, Sun. 1-5; groups of 10 or more by appointment. Adults $9, students $6; discounts to senior citizens & AAA members; children 5 & under no charge.
Attendance: 5,000 (estimated)

Membership: Student $5; Senior $10; Individual $15; Household $25; Institution & Professional $50; Patron $70; Friend $100; Benefactor $250.

Lebanon

THE LEBANON COUNTY HISTORICAL SOCIETY, 924 Cumberland St., Lebanon, PA 17042-5186. Tel.: 717-272-1473. Fax: 717-272-7474.
E-mail: staff@lchsociety.org
Web Site: lchsociety.org
Formerly: The Stoy Museum of the Lebanon County Historical Society
Founded: 1898.
Congressional District: 17
Key Personnel: Pres., John B. Hoffman; Vice Pres., Barbara Gaffney; Treas., Carol Christ; Librarian, Christine Mason; Sec., Louise Bours.
Personnel Profile: Full-Time Paid 2; Part-Time Volunteers 82.
Governing Authority: nonprofit organization. Subsidiary Institution: Union Canal Tunnel Park, 25th St. & Union Canal Dr., Lebanon, PA. Tax-exempt.
Historical Society Museum.
Collections: historical interest; period items. Historic Site: Union Canal Tunnel, oldest existing transportation tunnel in the U.S.
Research Fields: local history & genealogy.
Facilities: 3,000-vol. library of genealogy, Civil War and history books available for use on premises; microfilms of local newspapers from 1838-present; reading room.
Activities: guided tours; lectures; field trips; permanent & temporary exhibitions; historical information. Society Sponsors: Union Canal Tunnel Fair; Scare Affair in October.
Publications: annual booklet; bimonthly newsletter, Seeds of History.
Hours & Admission Prices: Mon. 1-8, Tues.-Thurs. 11-4:30, 1st & 3rd Sun. 1-4:30. Groups by appointment. Adults $5, senior citizens $4, children 9-18 $2; members & children under 9 no charge. Library: adults $5; students & members no charge. Union Canal Tunnel: Adults $5, children 6-14 $3. Closed national holidays.
Attendance: 2,000 (accurate)
Membership: Student $5; Individual $35; Family $50; Friend $75; 1898 Circle Individual $150; 1898 Circle Family $200; Patron $300; Historian $500; Benefactor $1,000 & up.

Lewisburg

PACKWOOD HOUSE MUSEUM, (M), 8 Market St., Lewisburg, PA 17837. Mailing Address: 15 N. Water St., Lewisburg, PA 17837-1569. Tel.: 570-524-0323. Fax: 570-524-0548.
E-mail: info@packwoodhousemuseum.com
Web Site: www.packwoodhousemuseum.com
Founded: 1972.
Congressional District: 10
Key Personnel: C.E.O. & Dir., Dr. Richard A. Sauers; Chm. (V), Lois Vandenhauvel; Museum Shop Mgr., Sue Hornberger.
Personnel Profile: Full-Time Paid 2; Part-Time Paid 1; Part-Time Volunteers 50; Interns 4.
Governing Authority: nonprofit organization. Parent Institution: The Fetherston Foundation. Tax-exempt: 501(c)(3).
Tour Center & History Museum originally constructed as a two-story log cabin, 1796-1799. Andrew Shearer's Tavern 1806-1817, renamed 1848-1886 American House Hotel by Adam J. Weidensaul.
Collections: decorative arts, including American 18th- to 20th-century furniture, glassware, stoneware, chinaware, quilts, coverlets; primitive farm accessories; Oriental rugs & objects; central Pennsylvania pieces.
Research Fields: decorative arts from the central Susquehanna Valley.
Facilities: botanical garden; rental facilities available. Museum-related items for sale.
Activities: guided tours; lectures; bus trips; changing exhibits; special seasonal programs; craft classes.
Publications: three newsletters per year; annual report.
Hours & Admission Prices: Tues.-Sat. 10-5, last tour daily 3:30; other times by appointment only. Adults $10, senior citizens $8, students $7; discounts to AAM, ICOM & AASLH members; members & children under 12 no charge. Closed holidays.
Attendance: 6,000 (estimated)
Membership: Student $5; Individual $30; Family $45; Business $100; Sponsor $125; Patron $250; Benefactor $500; Life $2,500.

SAMEK ART GALLERY, (M), Elaine Langone Center, Bucknell University, Lewisburg, PA 17837. Tel.: 570-577-3981. Fax: 570-577-3215.
E-mail: peltier@bucknell.edu
Web Site: www1.bucknell.edu/samek/
Formerly: Bucknell Art Gallery
Founded: 1979.
Congressional District: 5
Key Personnel: Dir., Dan Mills; Operations Mgr., Cynthia Peltier.
Personnel Profile: Full-Time Paid 3; Part-Time Paid 12; Interns 2.
Governing Authority: university. Parent Institution: Bucknell University. Tax-exempt: 501(c)(3).
University Art Museum.
Collections: Kress Collection: Renaissance Art, 19th- & 20th-century European & American Art; The Sordoni Collection of Japanese Art; Cook Collection of Musical Instruments.
Major Exhibits: Concurrent (T), 1/15/10-5/15/10; Strokes & Expressions (T), 3/10-5/10; Xiaoze Xie: Amplified Moments Spring 2010-Fall 2011 (T); Strokes & Expressions (T), 6/10-7/3/10; Fransje Killaars: Color At The Center (T), 6/10-5/11; Strokes & Expressions (T), 8/15/10-9/3/10.
Research Fields: contemporary & 20th-century American art; photography.
Facilities: 125-seat auditorium.
Activities: guided tours; lectures; films; concerts; dance recitals; arts festivals; organized education programs; docent program; loan, temporary & traveling exhibitions.
Publications: exhibition catalogues.
Hours & Admission Prices: Aug.-May Mon.-Wed. & Fri. 11-5, Thurs. 11-8, Sat.-Sun. 1-5; call to confirm show. No charge. Closed major holidays; university breaks. ♿
Attendance: 24,853 (accurate)

SLIFER HOUSE, 80 Magnolia Dr., Lewisburg, PA 17837-6312. Tel.: 570-524-2245. Fax: 570-524-2245.
E-mail: gary.parks@albrightcare.org
Web Site: www.albrightcare.org/slifer-house
Founded: 1976.
Congressional District: 5
Key Personnel: Dir., Gary W. Parks; Chm. (V), Paul Mauger; C.F.O., Jackie Dancho.
Personnel Profile: Full-Time Paid 1; Part-Time Paid 1; Part-Time Volunteers 40; Interns 2.
Governing Authority: private; nonprofit organization. Parent Institution: Albright Care Services. Tax-exempt: 501(c)(3).
Historic House: 1861 Tuscan villa, designed by architect Samuel Sloan.
Collections: Victorian furnishings & decorative arts representative of life in a country estate in central Pennsylvania.
Research Fields: life of Colonel Eli Slifer; Victorian era; decorative arts; political history.
Facilities: library & archives; 400 sq. ft. exhibit space. Postcards, books, prints, other museum-related items for sale.
Activities: guided tours; lectures; concerts; docent program; garden tour. Annual Events: Lincoln Program; Ice Cream Socials; band concerts; Holiday Soiree; Murder Mystery; Civil War Encampment; Garden Party & Art Auction.
Publications: quarterly newsletter, The Victorian Times.
Hours & Admission Prices: Jan.-April Tues.-Fri. 1-4; Easter to Christmas Tues.-Sun. 1-4. Adults $6, senior citizens 60 & over $5, children 10-16 $3; members & children 10 & under no charge. ♿
Attendance: 5,000 (accurate)
Membership: Basic $20; Patron $40; Family $75; Contributing $100; Business; Associate Member $125; Corporate Member $250.

UNION COUNTY HISTORICAL SOCIETY, Union County Courthouse, 2nd and St. Louis Sts., Lewisburg, PA 17837-1903. Mailing Address: Union County Courthouse, 103 S. 2nd St., Lewisburg, PA 17837-1903. Tel.: 570-524-8666. Fax: 570-524-8743.
E-mail: hstoricl@ptd.net
Web Site: www.unioncountyhistoricalsociety.org
Founded: 1908.
Congressional District: 5
Key Personnel: Pres., M. Lois Huffines; Vice Pres., Jeannette Lasansky; Sec., Diane Meixell; Treas,, David Milne.
Personnel Profile: Part-Time Paid 3; Part-Time Volunteers 10.
Governing Authority: society; nonprofit organization. Branch Museum: small museum at the Union County Court House, Lewisburg. Tax-exempt.
Historical Society Museum.
Collections: local historical items; manuscripts; slides; local pictures, early county school records; genealogy; oral traditions.
Research Fields: oral traditions; genealogy; history.
Facilities: office.
Activities: house tours; lectures; films; permanent & temporary exhibitions; oral tradition project.
Publications: Union County Pennsylvania: A Celebration in History by Charles M. Synder; Study Guide for elementary students of Union County, PA; Union County Heritage paperback collections of research in county, published every two years since 1968; annual calendar with historic county scenes from 1976 to present; local postcards; Oral Traditions publications: Willow Oak and Rye, Buggy Town, Central Pennsylvania Redware, etc.

Hours & Admission Prices: Mon.-Fri. 8:30-12 & 1-4:30. Suggested Donation: adults $5. ♿
Attendance: 1,300 (estimated)
Membership: Individual $30; Family $45; Contributor $60; Patron $100; Sponsor $150; Life $400.

Lewistown

MCCOY HOUSE, 17 N. Main St., Lewistown, PA 17044-1746. Mailing Address: One W. Market St., Lewistown, PA 17044. Tel.: 717-242-1022 & 248-4711. Fax: 717-242-3488.
E-mail: mchistory@verizon.net
Web Site: www.mccoyhouse.com
Founded: 1921.
Congressional District: 9
Key Personnel: Property Placement Officer, Michael A. Bertheaud; Pres., Stephen J. Rynkewitz, Jr.; Sec., Karen L. Aurand.
Personnel Profile: Part-Time Paid 1; Part-Time Volunteers 54.
Governing Authority: state. Operated by the Mifflin County Historical Society for the Pennsylvania Historical & Museum Commission, Box 1026, Harrisburg, PA 17120. Tax-exempt.
Historic House: birthplace of Major General Frank McCoy, who served in the Army from the Spanish-American War through World War II.
Collections: General McCoy memorabilia; furniture & furnishings of the family; Mifflin County Historical Society artifacts.
Facilities: publications for sale.
Activities: bus trips; banquets.
Publications: local history & genealogy books; society newsletter, "Notes From Monument Square".
Hours & Admission Prices: Museum: May-Dec. Sun. 1:30-4. No charge; donations accepted. Library: Tues.-Wed. 10-4, 1st & 3rd Sat. 10-3. Admission $5; members no charge.
Attendance: 1,500 (estimated)
Membership: Individual $15; Family $20; Supporting $35; Social $50; Individual Life $150.

Ligonier

FORT LIGONIER ASSOCIATION, 200 S. Market St., Ligonier, PA 15658-1242. Tel.: 724-238-9701. Fax: 724-238-9732.
E-mail: office@fortligonier.org
Web Site: www.fortligonier.org
Founded: 1946.
Congressional District: 12
Key Personnel: Dir., J. Martin West; Cur. Education, Penelope A. West.
Personnel Profile: Full-Time Paid 6; Part-Time Paid 18; Part-Time Volunteers 60; Interns 2.
Governing Authority: nonprofit foundation. Tax-exempt.
History Museum.
Collections: archaeology; decorative arts; fine arts; military arms & equipment.
Research Fields: archaeology; French & Indian War; 18th-century military & fortifications; Native Americans; local history; original art by Reynolds, Ramsay & Morier.
Facilities: 150-seat auditorium; reconstructed 18th-century fort. Museum-related items for sale.
Activities: military interpretation programs; living history interpretation programs; formal educational programming & classes; folkcrafts.
Publications: booklets & pamphlets.
Hours & Admission Prices: April 15-Nov. 15 Mon.-Sat. 10-4:30, Sun. 12-4:30. Adults $7, seniors $6, children 6-14 $4; discounts to groups, AAM & ICOM members; children under 5 & members no charge. ♿
Attendance: 37,112 (accurate)
Membership: Individual $35; Family $45; Sponsor $200.

SOUTHERN ALLEGHENIES MUSEUM OF ART AT LIGONIER VALLEY, One Boucher Lane, Rte. 711, Ligonier, PA 15658-2110. Tel.: 724-238-6015. Fax: 724-238-6281.
E-mail: ligonier@sama-art.org
Web Site: ww.sama-art.org
Art Museum.
Collections: paintings; paperweights.
Activities: permanent & temporary exhibitions; special events.
Hours & Admission Prices: Tues.-Fri. 10-5, Sat.-Sun. 1-5. No charge; donations accepted. Closed holidays.

Lititz

CANDY AMERICANA MUSEUM, 48 N. Broad St., Lititz, PA 17543-1005. Mailing Address: Wilbur Chocolate Co., Candy Store, 48 N. Broad St., Lititz, PA 17543. Tel.: 888-294-5287 (Toll Free); 717-626-3249 (Store).
Key Personnel: Mgr., Louise Brown
Candy Museum.
Collections: company history; period chocolate memorabilia; early candy machinery & molds; tins & boxes; marble slabs; starch trays; copper kettles; over 150 hand-painted European & Oriental porcelain chocolate pots; video.
Activities: video tour; see candy being made in the working kitchen.
Hours & Admission Prices: Mon.-Sat. 10-5. No charge.

LITITZ MUSEUM AND JOHANNES MUELLER HOUSE, 137-145 E. Main St., Lititz, PA 17543-2009. Tel.: 717-627-4636.
E-mail: ihf@dejazzd.com
Web Site: www.lititzhistoricalfoundation.com
Key Personnel: Pres., Randy Weit
Historic House Museum: built in 1793.
Collections: local history & culture; period furnishings; personal artifacts.
Hours & Admission Prices: Mon.-Fri. 10-4. Museum: adults $1.50. House: adults $5, senior citizens $4, students $3; discount to AAA members; children under 10 & members no charge.

Lock Haven

HEISEY MUSEUM, CLINTON COUNTY HISTORICAL SOCIETY, (M), 362 E. Water St., Lock Haven, PA 17745-1418. Tel.: 570-748-7254.
E-mail: heisey@clintoncountyhistory.com
Web Site: www.clintoncountyhistory.com
Founded: 1921.
Congressional District: 23
Key Personnel: Exec. Dir., Anne M. McCloskey; Museum Shop Mgr., Arlene Hoffman.
Personnel Profile: Part-Time Paid 5; Part-Time Volunteers 15; Interns 4.
Governing Authority: society; nonprofit organization. Parent Institution: Clinton County Historical Society. Subsidiary Institutions: Heisey Museum, Lock Haven, PA. Tax-exempt: 501(c)(3).
Historical Society Museum.
Collections: Victorian period clothing; furniture; artifacts.
Research Fields: Victorian period; canal & lumber history; local history.
Facilities: 500-vol. non-circulating library on local & Clinton County history. Gift items for sale.
Activities: guided tours; lectures; public archaeological digs.
Publications: quarterly newsletter, News & Notes.
Hours & Admission Prices: Tues.-Fri. 10-4. Family $10, adults $5; discounts to AAA members; military & members no charge. Closed Thanksgiving; Christmas.
Attendance: 4,850 (estimated)
Membership: Annual: Single $20; Family $30; Life: $150-$500.

PIPER AVIATION MUSEUM FOUNDATION, One Piper Way, Lock Haven, PA 17745-2266. Tel.: 570-748-8283. Fax: 570-893-8357.
E-mail: piper@kcnet.org
Web Site: www.pipermuseum.com
Founded: 1986.
Congressional District: 76
Key Personnel: Pres. & Security, John R. Merinar; Treas., John B. Bryerton; Cur., Dr. Ira Masemore; Historian, Harry Mutter; Public Rels., Stacy Young; Registrar, Peg McCloskey.
Personnel Profile: Full-Time Paid 1; Full-Time Volunteers 3; Part-Time Paid 3; Part-Time Volunteers 12; Interns 2.
Governing Authority: private; nonprofit organization. Tax-exempt: 501(c)(3).
Aviation Museum.
Collections: Piper Aircraft history from 1937 to modern times; early Piper Company including archives; aviation history.
Research Fields: history of Piper aircraft.
Facilities: library & archives of photographs, company records, slides, movies & scrapbooks available to the public by appointment; 27,700 sq. ft. exhibit space. Museum-related items for sale.
Activities: temporary exhibitions; Tomahawk flight simulator. Annual Events: Sentimental Journey to Cub Heaven; Armed Forces Day Open House in May; 5 day Fly-In in June; 3 day Wing & Things summer camp; Veterans Day Open House in November.
Publications: quarterly newsletter, The Cub Reporter.
Hours & Admission Prices: Mon.-Fri. 9-4, Sat. 10-4, Sun. 12-4. Adults $6, seniors $5, children 7-15 $3; children under 6 & members no charge. Closed major holidays. ♿
Attendance: 3,500 (estimated)
Membership: Personal $20; Family $30; Brick $75; Personal with Brick $80; Family with Brick $100; Life $300.

Loretto

*** SOUTHERN ALLEGHENIES MUSEUM OF ART AT LORETTO,** Saint Francis University Mall, 110 Franciscan Way, Loretto, PA 15940-9709. Mailing Address: P.O. Box 9, Loretto, PA 15940-0009. Tel.: 814-472-3920. Fax: 814-472-4131.
E-mail: loretto@sama-art.org
Web Site: www.sama-art.org
Founded: 1975.
Congressional District: 12
Key Personnel: Exec. Dir., G. Gary Moyer; Pres. (V), John K. Duggan, Jr.; Interim Cur. & Collections Mgr., Bobby J. Moore.
Personnel Profile: Full-Time Paid 12; Part-Time Paid 13; Part-Time Volunteers 25; Interns 10.
Governing Authority: nonprofit organization. Branch Museums: Southern Alleghenies Museum of Art, 1210 11th Ave., Altoona, PA. Tel.: 814-946-4464. Southern Alleghenies Museum of Art, University of Pittsburgh at Johnstown, Johnstown, PA. Tel.: 814-269-7234. Southern Alleghenies Museum of Art at Ligonier Valley, One Boucher Lane, Rte. 711 S., Ligonier, PA. Tel.: 724-238-6015. Tax-exempt: 501(c)(3).
Visual Art Museum: located on the Mall of St. Francis University.
Collections: 19th- & 20th-century American art.
Research Fields: American art.
Facilities: library; 250-seat auditorium; two classrooms; two painting studios; photography studio; community arts center; three community outreach centers & galleries off-site.
Activities: guided tours; lectures; concerts; formally organized education programs for children, adults & college students affiliated with St. Francis University; inter-museum loan; permanent & temporary exhibitions.
Publications: catalogues of special exhibitions & the permanent collection; Friends material; calendars; newsletter.
Hours & Admission Prices: Tues.-Fri. 10-5, Sat.-1-5. No charge. Closed holidays. ♿
Attendance: 75,000 (estimated)
Membership: Student & Senior Citizen $25; Individual Artist $35; Family $50-$99; Sponsor $100-$249; Sustaining $250-$499; Benefactor $500-$999; Connoisseur $1,000-$1,499; Exhibition Sponsor $1,500; Education Sponsor $2,500 & up.

Malvern

THE WHARTON ESHERICK MUSEUM, (M), 1520 Horseshoe Trail, Malvern, PA 19355. Mailing Address: P.O. Box 595, Paoli, PA 19301-0595. Tel.: 610-644-5822. Fax: 610-644-2244.
E-mail: whartonesherickmuseum@netzero.net
Founded: 1971.
Congressional District: 6
Key Personnel: Pres. (V), Laurence A. Liss; Exec. Dir., Robert Leonard; Cur., Dir. Programs & Membership, Paul Eisenhauer.
Personnel Profile: Full-Time Paid 2; Part-Time Paid 2; Part-Time Volunteers 24.
Governing Authority: nonprofit organization. Tax-exempt: 501(c)(3).
Art & Woodworking Museum: housed in Wharton Esherick's handcrafted residence & studio, a national historic landmark for architecture.
Collections: 200 pieces of the artist's work including oil & watercolor paintings, woodcuts & prints, sculpture in wood, stone & ceramic, furniture, utensils & furnishings.
Facilities: library of catalogs, clippings & correspondence relative to Wharton Esherick, available for use on premises on request by scholars. Catalogs, postcards, slides, note cards, restrikes of woodcuts for sale.
Activities: guided tours; permanent & changing exhibitions; outside lectures.
Publications: quarterly newsletter; catalog.
Hours & Admission Prices: Guided Tours: March-Dec. Sat. 10-5, Sun. 1-5; groups weekdays 10-4; reservations required for all tours. Adults $10, children under 12 $5; discounts to ICOM members; AAM & museum members no charge. Closed holidays. ♿
Attendance: 4,904 (accurate)
Membership: Individual $40; Family $75; Supporting $150; Contributing $250.

Marietta

LE PETIT MUSEUM OF MUSICAL BOXES, 255 W. Market St., Marietta, PA 17547-1413. Tel.: 717-426-1154.
Music Box Museum.
Collections: period musical boxes.
Hours & Admission Prices: March-Dec. Mon.-Sat. 10-4, Sun. 12-4; other times by appointment. Admission $3.

Meadville

ALLEGHENY COLLEGE ART GALLERIES (BOWMAN, PENELEC & MEGAHAN GALLERIES), N. Main St., Meadville, PA 16335-3902. Mailing Address: Box 23, Meadville, PA 16335. Tel.: 814-332-4365.
E-mail: darren.miller@allegheny.edu
Web Site: www.allegheny.edu
Founded: 1970.
Congressional District: 21
Key Personnel: Dir., Darren Miller.
Personnel Profile: Full-Time Paid 1; Part-Time Paid 5.
Governing Authority: private college; nonprofit. Parent Institution: Allegheny College. Tax-exempt: 501(c)(3).
Art Gallery.
Collections: 20th-century prints & photos; miscellaneous art works.
Major Exhibits: In Between, 1/26/10-2/16/10; The Art of Persuasion, 2/23/10-3/16/10; Annual Student Show, 4/6/10-4/25/10; Senior Projects, 5/4/10-5/15/10.
Research Fields: contemporary American art.
Facilities: classrooms; theater; 4,000 sq. ft. exhibit space.
Activities: guided tours; lectures; loan, temporary & traveling exhibitions.
Publications: brochures; catalogs.
Hours & Admission Prices: Tues.-Fri. 12:30-5, Sat. 1:30-5, Sun. 2-4. No charge. ♿
Attendance: 5,000 (estimated)

BALDWIN-REYNOLDS HOUSE MUSEUM, 639 Terrace St., Meadville, PA 16335-1733. Mailing Address: P.O. Box 411, Meadville, PA 16335-2902. Tel.: 814-333-9882. Fax: 814-724-6080.
E-mail: museum@baldwinreynolds.org
Web Site: www.baldwinreynolds.org
Founded: 1883.
Congressional District: 21
Key Personnel: Chm. (V), Bruce Barrett; Pres. (V), Beth Rekas; Cur., Joshua F. Sherretts.
Personnel Profile: Full-Time Volunteers 1; Part-Time Paid 1; Part-Time Volunteers 40; Interns 1.
Governing Authority: society. Parent Institution: Crawford County Historical Society. Tax-exempt: 501(c)(3).
Historic House: 1841-43 Baldwin-Reynolds Mansion.
Collections: paintings; costumes; history; medicine; numismatic; genealogy books & artifacts; newspapers; maps; manuscripts. Historic House: Dr. J. R. Mosier Medical Office.
Research Fields: Holland Land Co., Pennsylvania Population Co., Reynolds Papers; Shadeland Papers; genealogy; Henry Baldwin; rural medicine.
Facilities: 3,000-vol. library of history books.
Activities: guided tours; lectures; films; permanent exhibitions; bus tours. Annual Event: Trees of Christmas in November & December.
Publications: books, In French Creek Valley; 1841 Diary of William Reynolds; Crawford County Cemetery Inscriptions, Vol. I, II, III, IV; Stories from French Creek Valley; The First 100 Years; Pioneers of Crawford County, 1788-1800; Atlas of the Oil Region of Pennsylvania, 1865; John Wilkes Booth; Atlas of Crawford County Penna. 1876; David Mead: Pennsylvania's Last Frontiersman; The Baldwin-Reynolds House; reprint, Tribune 1888 Centennial Edition; biannual newsletter, Crawford County History; The Civil War Diaries of Seth Waid III; The Lake As It Was (A History of Connezut Lake, Penns.); Pioneer Life In Crawford County, Pennsylvania; Images of America: Meadville.
Hours & Admission Prices: Mid-May to Aug. Wed.-Sun. 12-4. Tours: June-Aug. 12, 1, 2, 3. Adults $5, children $3; members no charge.
Attendance: 4,000 (estimated)
Membership: Individual $15; Family $30; Patron $40; Benefactor $75; Sustaining $150; Lifetime $450.

Mechanicsburg

MECHANICSBURG MUSEUM ASSOCIATION, (M), 2 W. Strawberry Alley, Mechanicsburg, PA 17055-6213. Tel.: 717-697-6088. Fax: 717-697-6285.
Founded: 1975.
Congressional District: 19
Key Personnel: Dir., Steven B. Zimmerman; Pres. (V), Ruth N. Wrightstone, Ph.D.; Devel., Donna Nailor; Education, Nancy Cassel; Public Rels., James Quick; Registrar, Jerry Reid; Cur., Fern Oram; Security, Gerald Forry.
Personnel Profile: Full-Time Paid 1; Full-Time Volunteers 1; Part-Time Paid 1; Part-Time Volunteers 75.
Governing Authority: private; nonprofit organization. Tax-exempt: 501(c)(3).
Local History Museum.
Collections: photographs; decorative arts; local industry & business; oral histories; manuscripts; advertising signs; railroad artifacts; musical instruments; clothing; Civil War; military; fine arts. Historic Buildings: Passenger

Station; Museum at the Freight Station; Frankeberger Tavern; Stationmasters House; Washington Street Station.
Major Exhibits: Trains - Christmas, 11/09-1/10.
Research Fields: local history & chronology; building & property history; oral history of local people; community history; Cumberland Valley Railroad.
Facilities: 500-vol. library; educational facilities. Museum-related items for sale.
Activities: concerts; docent program; formal education programs; guided tours; lectures; participatory & temporary exhibits. Annual Events: auction; Holly Trolley Tour; Garden Tour; Quilt Show; Golf Tournament; occasional papers.
Publications: newsletter, Mechanicsburg Museum Association Newsletter; annual book, A Walk Through Mechanicsburg's Past.
Hours & Admission Prices: Tues.-Sat. 12-3; other times by appointment. Frankeberger Tavern: May-Sept. Sat. 12-3. No charge; donations accepted. Closed holidays. ♿
Attendance: 7,391 (accurate)
Membership: Family $35; Sustaining $75; Benefactor $100; Corporate $250; Patron $1,000.

Media

COLONIAL PENNSYLVANIA PLANTATION, Ridley Creek State Park, Rte. 3, Media, PA 19063. Tel.: 610-566-1725. Fax: 610-566-4252.
E-mail: info@colonialplantation.org
Web Site: www.colonialplantation.org
Founded: 1973.
Congressional District: 7
Key Personnel: Pres., Patricia A. Theodore; Treas., David Stitely; Dir. Public Rels., James Adams; Sales Shop Mgr., Karyn Confer.
Personnel Profile: Full-Time Paid 3; Part-Time Paid 18; Part-Time Volunteers 50.
Governing Authority: nonprofit organization. Tax-exempt: 501(c)(3).
Historical Museum: housed in c.18th-century Quaker farm.
Collections: 18th-century household furnishings; farm implements; farm animals.
Research Fields: food preservation; farm techniques; animal breeding.
Facilities: 2,000-vol. library pertaining to colonial history. Museum-related items for sale.
Activities: guided tours; hobby workshops; organized education programs for children; docent program.
Publications: Inside the Colonial Pennsylvania Plantation; An Activity Book of Colonial Times.
Hours & Admission Prices: April to mid-Nov. Mon.-Fri. 9-4, Sat.-Sun. 11-4. Adults $6, children 4-12 $4; members & children under 4 no charge. ♿
Attendance: 27,000 (accurate)
Membership: Individual $35; Family $50; Benjamin Franklin $100; Joseph Pratt $250.

DELAWARE COUNTY INSTITUTE OF SCIENCE, 11 Veterans Sq., Media, PA 19063-3201. Tel.: 610-566-5126.
Web Site: www.delcoscience.com
Founded: 1837.
Key Personnel: Pres., Alfred C. Palmer
Science Museum.
Collections: mounted birds & animals; herbarium; fossils; shells; corals; microscopes; minerals.
Facilities: library.
Hours & Admission Prices: Mon., Thurs. & Sat. 9-1. No charge.

TYLER ARBORETUM, 515 Painter Rd., Media, PA 19063-4424. Tel.: 610-566-9134. Fax: 610-891-1490.
E-mail: info@tylerarboretum.org
Web Site: tylerarboretum.org
Founded: 1946.
Congressional District: 5
Key Personnel: Exec. Dir., Richard A. Colbert; Dir. Horticulture, Mike Karkowski.
Personnel Profile: Full-Time Paid 9; Part-Time Paid 15; Part-Time Volunteers 275; Interns 3.
Governing Authority: nonprofit educational institution. Tax-exempt.
Arboretum.
Collections: plant collections from mid-1800s by Painter brothers and 1950s by Dr. Wister: rhododendron, cherry, crab apple, lilac, magnolia; 85-acre pinetum; contemporary specialty gardens: fragrant herb garden, bird habitat garden, butterfly garden, newly redesigned native woodland walk; meadow maze; 200 acres of special plant collections; 450 acres of forest & fields. Historic Buildings: c.1738 Lachford Hall, home of the Painter brothers; c.1863 Painter Library; c.1833 barn.
Facilities: visitors center; 20 miles of marked trails. Books & gift items for sale.
Activities: permanent exhibitions; educational lectures & workshops; informal walks.
Publications: quarterly newsletter; educational event schedule; various brochures; visitors map & guide; annual report.
Hours & Admission Prices: Seasonal hours, see website. Adults $7, seniors 65 & over $6, children 3-15 $4; discounts to AABGA members; children under 3 & members no charge; participates in AHS reciprocal admissions program.
Attendance: 52,000 (estimated)
Membership: Individual $50; Family $60; Contributing $130; Organizational $200; Circle of Friends $300-$3,000.

Mercer

MERCER COUNTY HISTORICAL SOCIETY, 119 S. Pitt St., Mercer, PA 16137-1211. Tel.: 724-662-3490.
E-mail: info@mchspa.org
Web Site: www.mchspa.org
Founded: 1946.
Congressional District: 21
Key Personnel: Exec. Dir., William C. Philson; Pres. & C.E.O., David M. Miller.
Personnel Profile: Full-Time Paid 1; Full-Time Volunteers 1; Part-Time Paid 5; Part-Time Volunteers 13.
Governing Authority: society; nonprofit organization. Tax-exempt.
Historical Society Museum: housed in 1825 Magoffin House.
Collections: papers of Dr. John W. Goodsell, Griff Nichols, Junkin Estate; manuscripts; church & cemetery records; archives of local materials; Indian artifacts; restored church; restored print shop. Historic Buildings: Caldwell School; log cabin.
Facilities: 3,000-vol. library of history & genealogy available for use on premises or through photocopy; reading room; microfilm; archive material.
Activities: guided tours; films.
Publications: quarterly newsletter; manuscript, on Polar Trails.
Hours & Admission Prices: Tues.-Fri. 10-4:30, Sat. 10-3; group tours by appointment only. No charge; donations accepted. Closed national holidays. ♿
Attendance: 3,000 (estimated)
Membership: Student & Senior Citizen $6; Regular $10; Family $15; Contributing $25; Patron $50; Sustaining $100; Life $200.

Merion

BARNES FOUNDATION, 300 N. Latch's Lane, Merion, PA 19066-1729. Tel.: 610-667-0290. Fax: 610-664-4026.
E-mail: info@barnesfoundation.org
Web Site: www.barnesfoundation.org
Founded: 1922.
Congressional District: 13
Key Personnel: Dir., Derek Gillman; Chm., Dr. Bernard Watson; Museum Shop Mgr., Julie Steiner.
Personnel Profile: Full-Time Paid 40; Full-Time Volunteers 80; Part-Time Paid 37; Part-Time Volunteers 77; Interns 2.
Governing Authority: Tax-exempt.
Art Foundation: 18th-century historic site.
Collections: impressionist; post-impressionist; early modern; old masters; African sculpture; Native American art; American decorative art.
Facilities: 12 acre arboretum.
Activities: ongoing classes in art appreciation & horticulture.
Publications: books, Great French Paintings; The Art of Renoir; The Art of Matisse; The Art of Painting; CD-ROM, A Passion for Art.
Hours & Admission Prices: June-Aug. Wed.-Sun. 9:30-5; Sept.-May Thurs.-Sun. 9:30-5. Adults $15; children under 3 & members no charge. ♿
Attendance: 62,400 (estimated)
Membership: $40 & up.

Middleburg

THE SNYDER COUNTY HISTORICAL SOCIETY, 30 E. Market St., Middleburg, PA 17842-1017. Mailing Address: P.O. Box 276, Middleburg, PA 17842-0276. Tel.: 570-837-6191. Fax: 570-837-4282.
E-mail: schs@snydercounty.org
Founded: 1898.
Congressional District: 10
Key Personnel: C.E.O. & Pres. (V), Teresa J. Berger; Editor, Ruth Roush; Sec., Lee E. Knepp.
Personnel Profile: Part-Time Volunteers 20; Interns 1.
Governing Authority: society. Tax-exempt: 501(c)(3).
Historical Society Museum.

Collections: archives; genealogy; Indian artifacts; Civil War relics; history books & old newspapers available for use on premises.
Research Fields: history; genealogy; Pennsylvania German heritage.
Facilities: auditorium; library.
Activities: tours; meetings; presentations.
Publications: annual book, Snyder County Historical Bulletin; 5-vol. set of bulletins.
Hours & Admission Prices: Museum: May-Sept. Sun. 1:30-5; other times by appointment. Library: March-April & Oct.-Dec. Mon. & Thurs.-Fri. 10-3.30; May-Sept. Sun. 1:30-5, Mon. & Thurs.-Fri. 10-3:30. No charge; donations accepted. ♿
Attendance: 2,000 (estimated)
Membership: Junior $7.50; Individual $15; Life $200.

Mifflinburg

MIFFLINBURG BUGGY MUSEUM ASSOCIATION, INC., 598 Green St., Mifflinburg, PA 17844-1241. Tel.: 570-966-1355. Fax: 570-966-9231.
E-mail: buggymuseum@jlink.net
Web Site: www.buggymuseum.org
Founded: 1978.
Congressional District: 10
Key Personnel: Dir., Bronwen Sanders; Pres. (V), Fred N. Swader, Ph.D.
Personnel Profile: Full-Time Paid 1; Part-Time Volunteers 65; Interns 1.
Governing Authority: private; nonprofit organization. Tax-exempt: 501(c)(3).
Industrial Museum.
Collections: tools & equipment of the William A. Heiss Coachworks; Heiss family furnishings, documents & photographs; buggy industry in Mifflinburg; late 19th to early 20th century transportation.
Research Fields: history of Mifflinburg Buggy makers.
Facilities: library; auditorium. Museum-related items for sale.
Activities: guided tours; temporary exhibitions; trips for members; bingo; monthly walks. Annual Events: Buggy Day (Heritage); Battle of Chambers Ridge (Civil War Encampment); Garden Tour.
Publications: biannual newsletter, Coachwork Chronicle.
Hours & Admission Prices: Museum: April-Oct. Thurs.-Sat. 10-5, Sun. 1-5. Visitor Center: April-Oct. Thurs.-Sat. 10-5, Sun. 1-5; Nov.-Dec. Sat. 10-5. Adults $8, students & children $4; discounts to AAA & AARP members; members no charge. Closed major holidays. ♿
Attendance: 3,133 (accurate)
Membership: Student $10; Individual $20; Family $35; Friend $50; Sponsor $100; Patron $250; Benefactor $500.

Mifflintown

TUSCARORA ACADEMY MUSEUM - JUNIATA COUNTY HISTORICAL SOCIETY, 498 Jefferson St., Ste. B, Mifflintown, PA 17059-1431. Tel.: 717-436-5152.
E-mail: jchs1931@pa.net
Web Site: www.rootsweb.com/~pajchs
Founded: 1931.
Congressional District: 9
Key Personnel: Pres., Terry L. Wheeler; Vice Pres., Audrey Sizelove.
Personnel Profile: Full-Time Volunteers 2; Part-Time Volunteers 6.
Governing Authority: state. Operated by the Juniata County Historical Society. Tax-exempt.
Historic Building: housed in a former boarding school; built in 1816.
Collections: boarding school dormitory rooms; WWI & II military artifacts; Indian artifacts; geology; early home furnishings; country store; post office.
Activities: guided tours; special programs.
Publications: quarterly magazine; society newsletter, Juniata Jottings.
Hours & Admission Prices: June-Aug. Sun. 1:30-4; other times by appointment. No charge; donations accepted.
Attendance: 200 (estimated)
Membership: Juniata County Historical Society: Individual $15; Family $20; Life $100.

Milford

PIKE COUNTY HISTORICAL SOCIETY, 608 Broad St., Milford, PA 18337-1704. Tel.: 570-296-8126.
E-mail: pikemuse@ptd.net
Web Site: www.pikecountyhistoricalsociety.org
Founded: 1930.
Congressional District: 12
Key Personnel: C.E.O. & Pres. (V), Dick Daddis; Dir., Lori Strelicki.
Personnel Profile: Part-Time Paid 1; Part-Time Volunteers 30.
Governing Authority: society; executive committee. Tax-exempt.
Local History Museum.
Collections: period farm & home implements; Lincoln assassination tableau; Lincoln Flag; Civil War exhibit; Indian relics; old photos; early schoolhouse memorabilia; restored Abbot & Downing Coucard Coach. Historic Building: restored one-room schoolhouse.
Facilities: 30-vol. collection of forestry materials available for use on premises by arrangement.
Activities: guided tours; lectures; permanent exhibitions.
Publications: cassette tapes, Ride Through Time.
Hours & Admission Prices: Colums Museum: July-Aug. Wed.-Sun. 1-4; Sept.-June Wed. & Sat.-Sun. 1-4; other times by appointment. Adults $5, students $3; children & members no charge.
Attendance: 3,000 (estimated)
Membership: Junior Historian $5; Regular $15; Patron $50; Grand Patron $150; Museum Sponsor $500.

Mill Run

FALLINGWATER, 1478 Mill Run Rd., Mill Run, PA 15464-1542. Mailing Address: P.O. Box R, Mill Run, PA 15464-0167. Tel.: 724-329-8501. Fax: 724-329-0881.
E-mail: fallingwater@paconserve.org
Web Site: www.fallingwater.org
Founded: 1964.
Congressional District: 12
Key Personnel: Pres., Thomas Saunders; Dir. & Vice Pres., Lynda S. Waggoner; Museum Shop Mgr., Betsy Poole.
Personnel Profile: Full-Time Paid 56; Part-Time Paid 52; Part-Time Volunteers 65; Interns 4.
Governing Authority: nonprofit organization. Parent Institution: Western Pennsylvania Conservancy. Tax-exempt: 501(c)(3).
Historic House: designed by Frank Lloyd Wright in 1935 for the Edgar Kaufmann family, built over a waterfall.
Collections: decorative arts, including furniture by Frank Lloyd Wright; glass; ceramics; textiles; sculpture by Lipchitz, Arp & Voulkos; painting & graphic works by Picasso, Diego Rivera; 19th-century Japanese printmakers, J.J. Audubon.
Facilities: 500-vol. library of art & architecture; in-door restaurant; nature center; rental facilities. Books, contemporary & traditional crafts, slides & cards for sale.
Activities: general guided tours, in-depth tours, family & Land of Fallingwater tours; week-long residency programs for teachers & students; lectures; school programs; hiking; camping.
Publications: annual brochure; newsletter, Conserve.
Hours & Admission Prices: mid-March to Nov. Thurs.-Tues. 10-4; reservations essential. Adults $18. Grounds only: adults $8. In-depth tours by appointment only: adults $55; discounts to school groups, AAM members, Western Pennsylvania Conservancy & Frank Lloyd Wright Building Conservancy members. ♿
Attendance: 152,872 (accurate)
Membership: Individual $25; Dual $50; Contributing $100; Patron $250; Benefactor $500; Leadership $1,000.

Millersburg

HISTORICAL SOCIETY OF MILLERSBURG & UPPER PAXTON TOWNSHIP MUSEUM, 330 Center St., Millersburg, PA 17061. Mailing Address: P.O. Box 171, Millersburg, PA 17061-0171. Tel.: 717-692-4084.
Founded: 1980.
Congressional District: 17
Key Personnel: Dir., Don Smith; Dir., Leslie Smith.
Governing Authority: nonprofit organization. Tax-exempt: 501(c)(3).
Local History Museum: housed in 1919 fire house & municipal building.
Collections: local life from prehistoric to modern times; pre-Indian & Indian artifacts; clothing; photographs; archives; paintings. Historic Building: 1898 railroad station.
Facilities: 100-vol. library of historical & genealogical material available to the public; 1,500 sq. ft. exhibit space. Books & other gift items for sale.
Activities: guided tours; temporary exhibitions. Museum Sponsors: Arts & Crafts Show.
Publications: quarterly newsletter, The Herald.
Hours & Admission Prices: May-Oct. Sat. 10-2, Sun. 2-4. No charge; donations accepted.
Attendance: 1,000 (accurate)
Membership: Student $5; Individual $10; Family $18; Life $200.

Montrose

SUSQUEHANNA COUNTY HISTORICAL SOCIETY & FREE LIBRARY ASSOCIATION, Two Monument Sq., Montrose, PA 18801-1115. Tel.: 570-278-1881. Fax: 570-278-9336.
E-mail: info@susqcohistsoc.org
Web Site: www.susqcohistsoc.org
Founded: 1890.

Congressional District: 10
Key Personnel: Administrator & Librarian, Susan Stone; Chm. Historical Committee, Sue Bennett Dyson; Chm. Bd., Cathy Chiarella; Cur., Elizabeth A. Smith.
Personnel Profile: Full-Time Paid 2; Part-Time Paid 2; Part-Time Volunteers 10.
Governing Authority: nonprofit organization. Tax-exempt.
History Museum.
Collections: Susquehanna County history & culture; period artifacts.
Research Fields: Susquehanna County history & genealogy.
Facilities: 500-vol. library of genealogy, marriage, death, cemetery & local DAR records, complete genealogies, microfilms of county newspapers from 1816-present & census reports of Susquehanna County & neighboring counties from 1790-1930, available for use on premises with staff member present.
Activities: guided tours on request; permanent & rotating exhibitions. Museum Sponsors: special exhibit in December.
Publications: reprints, Centennial History of Susquehanna County, 1887; History of Susquehanna County, 1873; 1872 Beer's Atlas of Susquehanna County with complete index; Susquehanna County Historical Society Journal of Genealogy and Local History; Waiting for the Lord: Nineteenth Century Black Communities in Susquehanna County, PA.
Hours & Admission Prices: Museum & Genealogy Reference Room: May-Sept. Mon.-Fri. 9-5; Oct.-April Mon. & Thurs.-Fri. 9-5, Tues.-Wed. 12-5. Public Library: Mon.-Fri. 9-9, Sat. 9-4. No charge; donations accepted. Genealogy Reference Room: $5 research fee for visiting non-members; $65 for all mailed requests. Closed national holidays. ♿
Attendance: 2,700 (estimated)
Membership: Public Library: Contributing Individual $20; Family $30. Historical Society; Genealogy & Journal: Individual $20; Dual $25.

Morrisville

* **PENNSBURY MANOR,** 400 Pennsbury Memorial Rd., Morrisville, PA 19067-6797. Tel.: 215-946-0400. Fax: 215-310-1011. TDD: 215-310-1016.
E-mail: willpenn17@aol.com
Web Site: www.pennsburymanor.org
Founded: 1939.
Congressional District: 8
Key Personnel: Dir., Douglas Miller; Museum Education, Mary Ellyn Kunz; Pres., Mike Hall; Researcher, Lara Murphy; Cur., Kimberly McCarty; Volunteer Coord., Ann Clements; Horticulturist, Charles Thomforde; Mgr. The Pennsbury Society, Fern Wolff; Supt. Bldgs. & Grounds, Joseph Cameli; Public Rels., Tabitha Dardes; Museum Shop Mgr., Cindy Praria.
Personnel Profile: Full-Time Paid 11; Part-Time Paid 6; Part-Time Volunteers 125; Interns 2.
Governing Authority: state; nonprofit organization. Parent Institution: Pennsylvania Historical and Museum Commission, P.O. Box 1026, Harrisburg, PA. 17108-1026. Subsidiary: The Pennsbury Society. Tax-exempt.
Historic House Museum: 1683 Pennsbury Manor, residence of William Penn, reconstructed in 1939.
Collections: 17th century English furnishings; living collection of ornamental & useful plants; livestock.
Research Fields: William Penn; 17th-century Pennsylvania; Quaker social & cultural life; historic preservation movement.
Facilities: 1,100-vol. library of material pertaining to William Penn, decorative arts, & social history available on premises; 100-seat auditorium; farm; picnic pavilion; period gardens. Museum-related items for sale.
Activities: guided tours; programs for elementary, secondary schools, & families; formally organized education programs for adults; living history programs; craft workshops; temporary exhibitions. Museum Sponsors: Holly Nights.
Publications: A Pennsbury Manor Cookbook; Pennsbury Brewing Book; Chuse Thy Cloaths: Pennsbury Clothing; William Penn.
Hours & Admission Prices: Tues.-Sat. 9-5, Sun. 12-5. Adults 18-59 $7, senior citizens 65 & over $6, children 3-11 $4; discounts to AAM & ICOM members. Grounds Pass: $3. Closed New Year's Day; Veterans Day; Columbus Day; Thanksgiving & following day; Christmas. ♿
Attendance: 27,500 (accurate)
Membership: Basic $25; Individual $35; Family $45; Individual Passport $55; Family Passport $65; Heritage $250; Penn's Partners $500 & up.

Mountainhome

CRESCO STATION MUSEUM, Rte. 390 & Sand Spring Rd., Mountainhome, PA 18342. Mailing Address: P.O. Box 358, Mountainhome, PA 18342-0358. Tel.: 570-595-2279.
History Museum.
Collections: local history & culture; photographs; personal artifacts; period furnishings.
Activities: temporary exhibitions; research. Museum Sponsors: monthly art shows; musical programs June to September.
Hours & Admission Prices: Memorial Day to June & Sept.-Oct. 12 Sun. 1-4; July-Aug. Wed. & Sat.-Sun. 1-4.

Narberth

SWEET MABEL FOLK ART & FINE CRAFT GALLERY, 41 N. Narberth Ave., Narberth, PA 19072-2347. Tel.: 610-667-3041.
Art Gallery.
Collections: works by regional & national artists; carvings; paintings; photographs.
Activities: workshops; classes; receptions; birthday parties.
Hours & Admission Prices: Tues.-Sat. 11-6, Sun. 12-5.

Nazareth

MARTIN GUITAR MUSEUM, 510 Sycamore St., Nazareth, PA 18064. Mailing Address: P.O. Box 329, Nazareth, PA 18064-0329. Tel.: 610-759-2837. Fax: 610-759-5757.
Guitar Museum.
Collections: music history & culture; over 170 guitars; tools; guitarmaking.
Facilities: visitor center. Museum-related items for sale.
Activities: guided tours.
Hours & Admission Prices: Museum & Visitor Center: Mon.-Fri. 8-5. Factory: Mon.-Fri. 9-4. Closed national holidays.

MORAVIAN HISTORICAL SOCIETY, (M), 214 E. Center St., Nazareth, PA 18064-2209. Tel.: 610-759-5070. Fax: 610-759-2462.
E-mail: director@moravianhistoricalsociety.org
Web Site: www.moravianhistoricalsociety.org
Founded: 1857.
Congressional District: 15
Key Personnel: Exec. Dir., Wendy S. Weida; Pres., Rev. Dennis Rohn; Vice Pres., Dr. Linda Shay Gardner.
Personnel Profile: Full-Time Paid 1; Part-Time Paid 6; Part-Time Volunteers 50; Interns 3.
Governing Authority: society. Tax-exempt.
History Museum: housed in 1740 Whitefield House.
Collections: art & artifacts concerning the history of the Moravian Church; 18th century paintings by John Valentine Haidt; early musical instruments; manuscripts.
Research Fields: Moravian Church history.
Facilities: research library.
Activities: guided tours; permanent exhibitions.
Publications: Journal of Moravian History.
Hours & Admission Prices: Daily 1-4. Adults $5, children $3; children under 5, members, AAM & ICOM members no charge. Closed major holidays. ♿
Attendance: 5,000 (accurate)
Membership: Individual $50. Donor Clubs: Manor Club $100; Bicentennial Club $200; Whitefield Club $500; Spangenberg Club $1,000; Zinzendorf Club $5,000; Comenius Club $10,000 & up.

PENNSYLVANIA LONGRIFLE MUSEUM, 401 Henry Rd., Nazareth, PA 18064. Mailing Address: P.O. Box 345, Nazareth, PA 18064-0345. Tel.: 610-759-9029. Fax: 610-759-9029.
E-mail: jacobsburg@rcn.com
Web Site: www.jacobsburg.org
Key Personnel: Exec. Dir., Jan Ballard
History Museum.
Collections: early American firearms history; Henry family history.
Activities: school programs; lectures; youth history day camp; early American gunsmithing courses.
Hours & Admission Prices: May-Oct. Sun. 1-4. Adults $3; members & children under 12 no charge.

New Brighton

THE MERRICK ART GALLERY, 1100 Fifth Ave., New Brighton, PA 15066-2022. Mailing Address: P.O. Box 312, New Brighton, PA 15066-0312. Tel.: 724-846-1130.
E-mail: merrickart@comcast.net
Web Site: www.merrickartgallery.org
Founded: 1880.
Congressional District: 4
Key Personnel: Dir. & Education Dir., Cynthia A. Kundar; Trustee, Karen Capper.
Personnel Profile: Full-Time Paid 1; Part-Time Volunteers 35; Interns 1.
Governing Authority: nonprofit organization. Tax-exempt: 501(c)(3).
Art Museum.

Collections: French, English, German & American 18th- & 19th-century paintings; 225 European & American 19th-century paintings; manuscript collections; works by Prud'hon Courbet, Thomas Sully, Thomas Hill, A.B. Durand; geological, zoological & entomological specimen collections.
Research Fields: 19th century.
Facilities: 1,200-vol. library, available for use under director's supervision; classrooms.
Activities: guided tours; arts festivals; lectures; concerts; library; hobby workshops; docent program; formally organized education programs; permanent & temporary exhibits monthly.
Publications: quarterly newsletter, Merrick Gallery Associates Newsletter; catalogue of 19th-century European & American paintings; brochure, The Merrick Art Gallery, a self-guiding tour of the permanent collection.
Hours & Admission Prices: Winter & Spring: Tues.-Sat. 10-4:30, Sun. 1-4; Summer & Fall: Wed.-Sat. 10-4, every other Sun. 1-4. No charge; donations accepted; docent guided tours $2. Closed New Year's Eve & Day; Memorial Day; Independence Day; Labor Day; Thanksgiving; Christmas to mid-Jan.; holiday weekends. ♿
Attendance: 4,200 (estimated)
Membership: Student $5; Senior $10; Individual $20; Family & Nonprofit $25; Contributing $40; Business Level I $50; Business Level II & Gustave Courbet Society $100; Lifetime & Merrick Circle $500.

New Castle

THE HOYT INSTITUTE OF FINE ARTS, 124 E. Leasure Ave., New Castle, PA 16101-2398. Tel.: 724-652-2882. Fax: 724-657-8786.
E-mail: hoyt@hoytartcenter.org
Web Site: www.hoytartcenter.org
Founded: 1965.
Congressional District: 4
Key Personnel: C.E.O. & Exec. Dir., Kimberly B. Koller-Jones; Pres. (V), Eugene DeCaprio; Exhibitions Coord., Patricia McLatchy; Program Dir., Robert Presnar.
Personnel Profile: Full-Time Paid 2; Part-Time Paid 5; Part-Time Volunteers 3; Interns 1.
Governing Authority: nonprofit organization. Tax-exempt: 501(c)(3).
Art Museum: housed in two early 20th-century mansions, Greek Revival style & Tudor Revival style.
Collections: paintings; prints; ceramics; photographs; sculpture; furniture.
Facilities: 1,000-vol. library of fine arts books, available for use on premises only; classrooms. Art items for sale.
Activities: guided & self-guided tours; lectures; concerts; organized educational programs; temporary & traveling exhibitions. Institute Sponsors: Mid Atlantic Art Show; Regional Art Show.
Publications: quarterly newsletter.
Hours & Admission Prices: Tues. & Thurs. 11-8, Wed. & Fri.-Sat. 11-4, Sun. for special events; guided tours by appointment. East Mansion no charge. West Mansion Tours: Guided $5, Self-Guided $3; discounts to AAM members. Closed New Year's Day; Easter; Memorial Day; Independence Day; Labor Day; Thanksgiving; Christmas. ♿
Attendance: 22,500 (estimated)
Membership: Individual $30; Family $45; Associate $75; Century $100; Century II $200; Patron $300; Hoyt Donor $500; Director's Circle $1,000; Benefactor $2,500.

New Hope

* **BOWMAN'S HILL WILDFLOWER PRESERVE, (M),** 1635 River Rd. (PA Rte. 32), New Hope, PA 18938. Mailing Address: P.O. Box 685, New Hope, PA 18938-0685. Tel.: 215-862-2924. Fax: 215-862-1846.
E-mail: bhwp@bhwp.org
Web Site: www.bhwp.org
Founded: 1934.
Congressional District: 8
Key Personnel: Dir., Miles Arnott; Chm. (V), Sandy Ryon; Outreach, Nancy Beaubaire; Cur., Paul Teese, Ph.D.; Coord. Education, Amy Hoffmann; Museum Shop Mgr., Joyce Burian.
Personnel Profile: Full-Time Paid 5; Part-Time Paid 4; Part-Time Volunteers 110; Interns 2.
Governing Authority: state. Parent Institution: Pennsylvania Historical & Museum Commission. Subsidiary Institution: Bowman's Hill Wildflower Preserve Assoc. Tax-exempt: 501(c)(3).
Botanical Garden.
Collections: native plants of Pennsylvania.
Facilities: library; visitor & resource center; 2.5 miles of trails; 80-seat auditorium; indoor bird observatory; picnic pavilion. Museum-related items for sale.
Activities: guided tours; lectures; docent program; internship program; permanent & temporary exhibitions; symposia for professionals, classes, workshops, children's programs; Signature Plants self-guided tour.
Publications: newsletter; blooming guides; Ways With Wildflowers; seasonal calendar of events; Native Plant Information Sheets.
Hours & Admission Prices: Jan. 2-Dec. 23 daily 9-5. Adults $5, seniors 62 & over and students $3, children 4-14 $2; children under 4 & members no charge. Closed Thanksgiving. ♿
Attendance: 80,000 (estimated)
Membership: Student & Senior Citizen $20; Individual $25; Family $50; Benefactor $100; Patron $500; Sustaining $1,000.

THE PARRY MANSION MUSEUM, 45 S. Main St., New Hope, PA 18938. Mailing Address: P.O. Box 41, New Hope, PA 18938-0041. Tel.: 215-862-6729. Fax: 215-862-8227.
E-mail: newhopehs@verizon.net
Web Site: newhopehistoricalsociety.org
Founded: 1972.
Congressional District: 18
Key Personnel: Pres., Edwin Hild; Exec. Dir., Deborah Lang; Treas., Frank Policare; Archivist, Terry McNealy.
Personnel Profile: Full-Time Volunteers 6; Part-Time Paid 3; Part-Time Volunteers 3.
Governing Authority: nonprofit organization. Parent Institution: New Hope Historical Society. Tax-exempt.
Decorative Arts Museum.
Collections: 1775-1900 furniture & decorative arts.
Activities: guided tours; docent program.
Publications: A Walking Tour of New Hope; Guide to the Parry Mansion Museum; The Parry Legacy; A Quaker Lady's Cookbook.
Hours & Admission Prices: May-Oct. Sat.-Sun. 1:30-3. No charge. Group tours of 10 or more available year round by reservation.
Attendance: 2,300 (estimated)
Membership: Individual $30; Family $60; Business $100; Business Partner $250; Life $500.

Newtown

HICKS ART CENTER GALLERY - BUCKS COUNTY COMMUNITY COLLEGE, (M), 275 Swamp Rd., Newtown, PA 18940-4106. Tel.: 215-504-8531.
E-mail: orlandof@bucks.edu
Web Site: www.bucks.edu/gallery
Key Personnel: Exec. Dir., Fran Orlando
Art Gallery.
Collections: works by college students & county residents.
Activities: Annual Event: Bucks County High School Art Exhibition.
Hours & Admission Prices: Mon. & Fri. 9-4, Tues.-Thurs. 9-8, Sat. 9-12.

NEWTOWN HISTORIC ASSOCIATION, Court St. & Centre Ave., Newtown, PA 18940. Mailing Address: P.O. Box 303, Newtown, PA 18940-0303. Tel.: 215-968-4004. Fax: 215-968-8925.
Web Site: www.newtown.pa.us/historic/nha.html
Founded: 1964.
Congressional District: 8
Key Personnel: Pres. (V), Head Research Library & Security, David Callahan; Treas., Marjorie Torongo; Librarian, Rick Booream; Membership, Mary J. Callahan; Cur., Harriet Beckert; Museum Shop Mgr., Geno Peruzzi.
Personnel Profile: Part-Time Volunteers 26; Interns 2.
Governing Authority: nonprofit organization. Tax-exempt: 501(c)(3).
Local History Museum: housed in early 1700s Court Inn.
Collections: Edward Hicks artifacts; local artifacts of historical significance.
Facilities: 1,000-vol. library of Newtown & area history books, available for use on premises.
Activities: guided tours; lectures. Annual Events: Market Day Craft Fair; Christmas Open House Tour.
Publications: newsletter, The Half Moon.
Hours & Admission Prices: June-Aug. Tues. 9-3, Thurs. 7-9, Sun. 2-4; Sept.-May Tues. 9-3, Thurs. 7-9. No charge; donations accepted. Closed holidays.
Attendance: 1,900 (estimated)
Membership: Individual $25; Family $35; Contributing $75; Corporate $150; Life $500.

North Huntingdon

BIG MAC MUSEUM, 9051 Rte. 30, North Huntingdon, PA 15642-2792. Tel.: 724-863-9837.
Web Site: www.bigmacmuseum.com
Founded: 2007.
History Museum.
Collections: Big Mac history & advertising; photographs; memorabilia; 14 ft by 12 ft Big Mac.

Facilities: restaurant.
Hours & Admission Prices: Tours: by appointment.

North Wales

ROTH LIVING FARM MUSEUM OF DELAWARE VALLEY COLLEGE, 502 Dekalb Pike, North Wales, PA 19454-2236. Tel.: 215-699-3994.
E-mail: rothmuseum@delval.edu
Web Site: www.delval.edu/roth
Key Personnel: Mgr., George Gross.
Personnel Profile: Part-Time Paid 1; Part-Time Volunteers 4; Interns 4.
Living Farm Museum.
Collections: 19th century American farming; period equipment; hands-on exhibits; horses; cattle; sheep; goats; chickens.
Activities: special events; demonstrations; school programs; seasonal activities; 4H & scout programs.
Hours & Admission Prices: Call for hours. Prices vary by program.
Attendance: 1,153

Northumberland

JOSEPH PRIESTLEY HOUSE, 472 Priestley Ave., Northumberland, PA 17857-1226. Tel.: 570-473-9474. Fax: 570-473-7901.
E-mail: mBashore@state.pa.us
Web Site: www.josephpriestleyhouse.org
Founded: 1960.
Congressional District: 17
Key Personnel: Pres. (V), Amanda Kessler; Site Admin., Andrea Bashore.
Personnel Profile: Full-Time Paid 2; Part-Time Volunteers 20; Interns 1.
Governing Authority: state. Parent Institution: Pennsylvania Historical & Museum Commission, 300 North St., Harrisburg, PA 17120-0024. Tax-exempt.
Historic House: 1798 Joseph Priestley house.
Collections: period scientific equipment; decorative art & historic furniture of the period of Joseph Priestley.
Research Fields: 18th-century chemistry; dissenting 18th-century English religion; social history.
Facilities: visitor center. Museum-related items for sale.
Activities: tours; seminars; education programs; videos; summer history camp.
Publications: Friends Newsletter.
Hours & Admission Prices: Wed.-Sat. 9-4:30, Sun. 12-4:30. Tours: hourly 10-3 Adults $6, senior citizens & groups $5.50, youth 3-11 $4; discounts to PHMC, AAM, ICOM & Federation members; members and active military & their family no charge. Closed some federal holidays.
Attendance: 1,736 (accurate)
Membership: Individual $12; Family $25; Patron $100; Donor $500; Benefactor $1,000.

Oil City

VENANGO MUSEUM OF ART, SCIENCE & INDUSTRY, 270 Seneca St., Oil City, PA 16301-1304. Tel.: 814-676-2007. Fax: 814-678-6719.
E-mail: venangomuseum@venangomuseum.org
Web Site: www.venangomuseum.org
Founded: 1961.
Congressional District: 2
Key Personnel: Pres. (V), Mary Balas; Financial Dir., Ola Cox; Exec. Dir., Security & Museum Shop Mgr., Betsy Kellner.
Personnel Profile: Full-Time Paid 1; Part-Time Paid 3; Part-Time Volunteers 6; Interns 2.
Governing Authority: nonprofit organization. Parent Institution: Venango Museum Corporation. Tax-exempt: 501(c)(3).
Art, Science & Industry Museum: housed in c.1905 Beau Arts style Post Office Building.
Collections: archives; photographs; clocks; oil industry items & history; items relating to northwestern Pennsylvania history; 1928 Wurlitzer organ; 1937 Cord Automobile.
Research Fields: related to artifacts & individuals from Venango County.
Facilities: 750-vol. library of ledgers, stock certificates, periodicals & newspapers, for staff use only, includes records of early oil companies that developed in Venango County after Col. Edwin Drake discovered oil in Titusville; educational facilities. Museum-related items for sale.
Activities: guided tours; lectures; concerts; rental gallery; organized education programs for children; film documentaries.
Publications: quarterly newsletter, Venango Museum of Art, Science & Industry.
Hours & Admission Prices: April-Dec. Tues.-Fri. 10-4, Sat. 11-4, Sun. 2-5. Adults $4, senior citizens & students $2, children under 12 $1.50; members no charge. Closed New Year's Day; Easter; Memorial Day; Independence Day; Labor Day; Thanksgiving; Christmas. ♿

Attendance: 3,000 (estimated)
Membership: Senior Citizen $10; Individual $15; Family $25; Sustaining Friends Circle $100-$199; Director's Circle $250-$499; Trustees Circle $500-$999; Presidents' Circle $1,000-$2,999; Founders Circle $3,000 & up.

Paradise

NATIONAL CHRISTMAS CENTER, 3427 Lincoln Hwy., Paradise, PA 17562-9621. Tel.: 717-442-7950. Fax: 717-442-9304.
E-mail: info@nationalchristmascenter.com
Web Site: www.nationalchristmascenter.com; nationalchristmascenter-.blogspot.com
Founded: 1998.
Key Personnel: Exec. Dir., Mandy Brown; Cur. & Historian, Jim Morrison
Christmas Museum.
Collections: Christmas history & traditions from around the world; homes hand-painted in folk art of each country; life-sized figures; period Christmas china; ornaments; Santa Claus images & stories; Santa's workshop & the North Pole; trains; cookie cutters; American Christmas collection; vintage merchandise, signage, fixtures; wooden & cardboard toys, v-mail, ration books & stamps, period greeting cards; 1897 letter, photos, family history of letter's author; hand-blown glass ornaments; contemporary & period nativities from around the world.
Research Fields: Christmas customs, celebrations, lore, traditions.
Facilities: 20,000 sq. ft. exhibit space; cafe. Gift-related items for sale.
Activities: occasional lecture series with guided tours.
Hours & Admission Prices: March-April Sat.-Sun. 10-6; May-Jan. 3 daily 10-6; call for extended holiday hours. Adults $11, children 3-12 $5; members no charge. Closed New Year's Day; Thanksgiving; Christmas. ♿
Membership: Child 3-12 $12.50; Adult $27.

NATIONAL CHRISTMAS CENTER AND MUSEUM, 3427 Lincoln Hwy. E., Paradise, PA 17562-9621. Tel.: 717-442-7950.
Founded: 1998.
Key Personnel: Exec. Dir., Mandy Brown; Museum Dir., Jennifer McElhany; Cur., Jim Morrison; Museum Shop Mgr., Mandy Brown.
Personnel Profile: Full-Time Paid 1; Part-Time Paid 14.
Governing Authority: bd. of directors.
Christmas History Museum.
Collections: history & traditions of Christmas; Santas; ornaments; decorations; ephemera.
Hours & Admission Prices: March-April Sat.-Sun. 10-6; May-Jan. 1 daily 10-6; other times by appointment. Call for extended holiday hours. Adults $11, children 3-12 $5; members no charge. Closed New Year's Day; Easter; Thanksgiving; Christmas. ♿
Membership: Children $12.50; Adults $27.

Pennsburg

SCHWENKFELDER LIBRARY & HERITAGE CENTER, 105 Seminary St., Pennsburg, PA 18073-1898. Tel.: 215-679-3103. Fax: 215-679-8175.
E-mail: info@schwenkfelder.com
Web Site: schwenkfelder.com
Founded: 1913.
Congressional District: 15
Key Personnel: Administrative Asst., Michelle Pritt; Exec. Dir., David W. Luz; Pres., Jerry Heebner; Cur. Collections, Candace K. Perry; Archivist, Hunt Schenkel; Educator, Rebecca Lawrence; Assoc. Dir. Research, Dr. Allen Viehmeyer; Assoc. Dir. Theology, Dr. Peter C. Erb.
Personnel Profile: Full-Time Paid 5; Full-Time Volunteers 1; Part-Time Paid 3; Part-Time Volunteers 129.
Governing Authority: nonprofit organization. Tax-exempt: 501(c)(3).
History Museum.
Collections: European & American culture of the Schwenkfelders, a German Protestant sect, 1720-present; local history of Perkiomen Valley, PA.
Research Fields: Schwenkfelder history & culture; Upper Perkiomen Valley history.
Activities: guided tours; permanent & changing exhibitions.
Publications: newsletter, Fraktor; book, Fraktu - Writings and Folk Art Drawings.
Hours & Admission Prices: Tues.-Wed. & Fri. 9-4, Thurs. 9-8, Sat. 10-3, Sun. 1-4. No charge, donations accepted. ♿
Attendance: 10,466 (accurate)
Membership: Friends of the Schwenkfelder Library and Heritage Center: Student $3; Individual $10; Family $15; Life $150; Corporate $250.

Perkasie

THE PEARL S. BUCK HOUSE, (M), 520 Dublin Rd., Perkasie, PA 18944-3000. Tel.: 215-249-0100; 800-220-BUCK. Fax: 215-249-9657.
E-mail: pearlshouse@pearlsbuck.org

Web Site: www.psbi.org
Founded: 1964.
Congressional District: 8
Key Personnel: C.E.O., Janet C. Mintzer; Vice Pres. Operations, Teri Mandic; Cur., Donna C. Rhodes.
Personnel Profile: Full-Time Paid 1; Part-Time Paid 2; Part-Time Volunteers 150; Interns 2.
Governing Authority: nonprofit organization. Parent Institution: Pearl S. Buck International, Inc. Tax-exempt: 501(c)(3).
Historic House Museum: housed in pre-1825 stone farmhouse.
Collections: Asian & American art, artifacts & furniture; books, awards & personal items of Pearl S. Buck.
Facilities: 8,200-vol. library of fiction, history, biography, juvenile & foreign books; first editions & other copies of Pearl S. Buck's works; 1,600 sq. ft. exhibit space; 100-seat auditorium. Asian gift items for sale.
Activities: guided tours; cultural events; home office for international child & family development organization, Pearl S. Buck International, Inc. Annual Event: holiday festival tours in December.
Publications: Connections; annual report.
Hours & Admission Prices: March-Dec. Tours: Tues.-Sat. 11, 1 & 2, Sun. 1 & 2; group tours by appointment. Adults $7, senior citizens & students $6; discounts to AAA members; members no charge. Holiday Tours: call for admission prices. Closed legal holiday & holiday weekends.
Attendance: 10,000 (estimated)
Membership: Individual $30-$1,000.

Philadelphia

* **THE ACADEMY OF NATURAL SCIENCES, (M),** 1900 Ben Franklin Pkwy., Philadelphia, PA 19103-1195. Tel.: 215-299-1000. Fax: 215-299-1028.
Web Site: www.ansp.org
Founded: 1812.
Congressional District: 2
Key Personnel: Chm. Bd. Trustees, R. James Macaleer; Pres. & C.E.O., William Y. Brown, Ph.D.; Vice Pres. Systematics & Library, Edward Daeschler, Ph.D.; Vice Pres. Finance & Admin., David Rusenko; Vice Pres. Environmental Research & Dir. Patrick Center for Environmental Research, David Velinsky, Ph.D.; Vice Pres. Public Operations, Barbara Ceiga; Museum Shop Mgr., Henry Hejnar.
Personnel Profile: Full-Time Paid 120; Part-Time Paid 60; Part-Time Volunteers 320; Interns 20.
Governing Authority: nonprofit organization. Tax-exempt: 501(c)(3).
Natural Science Museum.
Collections: botany; diatoms; entomology; ichthyology; malacology; invertebrate paleontology; vertebrate paleontology; ornithology; mammalogy; herpetology; mineralogy; mounted specimens; ethnographic objects; art objects; portraits; ornithological photographic materials; live animal unit, including locally endangered & threatened species; dinosaurs; manuscripts; photographs; periodicals;
Research Fields: systematic & evolutionary biology; environmental research; ecology.
Facilities: library; cafe.
Activities: lectures; films; gallery talks; study clubs; hobby workshops; educational programs; graduate & undergraduate teaching with various universities; temporary & traveling exhibitions; school loan service in school programs; natural science expeditions; global scientific research.
Publications: scientific publications, Proceedings of the Academy of Natural Sciences; Monographs & Malacologia; members online newsletter; members magazine.
Hours & Admission Prices: Mon.-Fri. 10-4:30, Sat.-Sun. & holidays 10-5. Adults $12, senior citizens & military & college students $10, children 3-12 $8; discounts to groups and ICOM, AAA & AAM members; members & children under 3 no charge. Closed New Year's Day; Thanksgiving; Christmas. ♿
Attendance: 200,000 (accurate)
Membership: Individual $50; Family $70; Family Plus $80; Supporting $150; Partners Club $250-$499; Founders Club $500-$999.

THE AFRICAN AMERICAN MUSEUM IN PHILADELPHIA, 701 Arch St., Philadelphia, PA 19106-1504. Tel.: 215-574-0380, ext. 230. Fax: 215-574-3110.
E-mail: info@aampmuseum.org
Web Site: www.aampmuseum.org
Founded: 1976.
Congressional District: 1
Key Personnel: Pres. & C.E.O., Romona Riscoe Benson; Membership & Volunteer Coord., Shirley Mercer Browning; Dir. Devel., Kristina Palmer; Cur. Education & Public Programming, Leslie Willis-Lowry; Conservator & Cur. Collections, Leslie Guy; Cur. Exhibitions, Richard Watson; Museum Shop Mgr., Gladys M. Adams.
Personnel Profile: Full-Time Paid 25; Part-Time Paid 5; Part-Time Volunteers 80; Interns 6.
Governing Authority: municipal; nonprofit organization. Tax-exempt: 501(c)(3).
Historical & Cultural Museum. This African American Museum in Philadelphia (AAMP) is dedicated to collecting, preserving and interpreting the material and intellectual culture of African Americans.
Collections: paintings & prints by African American artists; artifacts & memorabilia relating to 19th- & 20th-century African American history; Jack Franklin Photographic Collection 1940-present; performing arts memorabilia; Philadelphia Hilldale Baseball Club; sports; local politics & civil rights; beauticians; military history; public school education; local community organizations; African artifacts.
Research Fields: African American history & culture in Philadelphia, the Delaware Valley, Pennsylvania & the Americas.
Facilities: 1,500-vol. library of African American books; 200-seat auditorium. Museum-related items for sale.
Activities: guided tours; seminars; film & lecture series; jazz concerts; arts festivals; docent programs; workshops; theater; loan & traveling exhibitions; radio programs; African American artists exhibitions; book signings; collecting workshops; gallery talks; family programs.
Publications: exhibition catalog; brochures.
Hours & Admission Prices: Tues.-Sat. 10-5, Sun. 12-5. Adults $10, youth 4-12, students with ID & senior citizens $8; discounts to groups, AAM & ICOM members; members no charge. Closed national holidays. ♿
Attendance: 60,000 (estimated)
Membership: Student & Senior Citizen $25; Individual $45; Family $60; other categories available.

AMERICAN CATHOLIC HISTORICAL SOCIETY, 263 S. 4th St., Philadelphia, PA 19106-3819. Tel.: 215-925-5752.
E-mail: americancatholichistsoc@gmail.com
Web Site: www.amchs.org
Founded: 1884.
Key Personnel: Exec. Dir., Rev. Msgr. James P. McCoy; Pres. (V), Edgar Welsh; Co-Editor, Roger Van Allen, Ph.D.; Co-Editor, Margaret Maginnis, Ph.D.; Sec., Louis N. Ferrero, P.E.; Archivist, Joseph J. Casino.
Personnel Profile: Part-Time Volunteers 20.
Governing Authority: nonprofit organization; bd. of managers of the American Catholic Historical Society of Philadelphia. Subsidiary Institution: Philadelphia Archdiocesan Historical Research Center, 100 E. Wynnewood Rd., Wynnewood, PA 19096-3001. Tax-exempt: 501(c)(3).
Religious & American History Museum.
Collections: archives; history.
Major Exhibits: ACHS-125 Years of Service, 11/09-9/10.
Research Fields: American & American Catholic history.
Facilities: 35,000-vol. library of Americana, newspapers, pamphlets, artifacts & original manuscripts pertaining to Catholic church in U.S., by appointment only.
Activities: guided tours; lectures; temporary exhibitions. Annual Event: Barry Award Dinner.
Publications: annual newsletter; quarterly, Journal: American Catholic Studies.
Hours & Admission Prices: by appointment. No charge; donations accepted.
Attendance: 1,000 (estimated)
Membership: Annual $40.

AMERICAN PHILOSOPHICAL SOCIETY MUSEUM (APS), (M), Philosophical Hall, 104 S. Fifth St., Philadelphia, PA 19106. Mailing Address: Richardson Hall, 431 Chestnut St., Philadelphia, PA 19106-2426. Tel.: 215-440-3440. Fax: 267-386-3491.
E-mail: museum@amphilsoc.org
Web Site: www.apsmuseum.org
Founded: 2001.
Key Personnel: C.E.O., Mary Patterson McPherson; Dir. & Cur., Sue Ann Prince; Chm. (V), Henry A. Millon; Pres., Baruch S. Blumberg; Devel., Nanette Holben; Education, Jenni Drozdek; Treas., John Wolfe.
Personnel Profile: Full-Time Paid 5; Part-Time Paid 3; Part-Time Volunteers 12; Interns 3.
Governing Authority: private; nonprofit organization. Parent Institution: American Philosophical Society, Philadelphia, PA. Tax-exempt: 501(c)(3).
History, Art & Science Museum.
Collections: 18th- & 19th-century history, art & science.
Major Exhibits: Dialogues With Darwin, 11/09-10/10.
Research Fields: exploration, surveying & mapping (18th-20th centuries); natural history.
Facilities: auditorium; 2,000 sq. ft. exhibit space; nature center.
Activities: docent program; formal education program for University of Arts students; guided tours; workshops; lectures; artist residencies; participatory & temporary exhibitions.
Publications: exhibitions catalogues.

Hours & Admission Prices: Summer: Thurs.-Sun. 10-4. Winter: Fri.-Sun. 10-4; additional Wed. evening hours. No charge; donations requested. Closed holidays. ♿
Attendance: 68,212 (accurate)

AMERICAN SWEDISH HISTORICAL FOUNDATION & MUSEUM, (M), 1900 Pattison Ave., Philadelphia, PA 19145-5999. Tel.: 215-389-1776. Fax: 215-389-7701.
E-mail: info@americanswedish.org
Web Site: www.americanswedish.org
Founded: 1926.
Congressional District: 3
Key Personnel: Exec. Dir., Tracey Beck; Assoc. Dir., Birgitta W. Davis; Chm. (V), Bob Savage; Cur., Carrie Hogan; Educator, Tricia Davies; Membership & Visitor Svcs., Caroline Rossy; Maintenance, Frank Sanders.
Personnel Profile: Full-Time Paid 6; Part-Time Paid 3; Part-Time Volunteers 200; Interns 2.
Governing Authority: nonprofit organization. Parent Institution: American Swedish Historical Foundation. Tax-exempt: 501(c)(3).
Swedish-American History & Art Museum: located on 17th-century Queen Christina land grant.
Collections: Swedish colonial & immigrant experience in the U.S. from 1638; manuscripts.
Research Fields: history of Swedes & American Swedes.
Facilities: 6,000-vol. reference library; meeting rooms; banquet facilities. Gift items for sale.
Activities: tours; lectures; films; concerts; reading room; inter-museum loan, permanent, temporary & traveling exhibitions.
Publications: newsletter; occasional & exhibition catalogs.
Hours & Admission Prices: Tues.-Fri. 10-4, Sat.-Sun. 12-4. Adults $6, senior citizens & students $5; discounts to AAM members; members & children under 12 no charge. Closed holidays. ♿
Attendance: 12,000 (accurate)
Membership: Individual $45; Family $55; Friend $100; Sustaining $250; Patron $500; Key Contributor $1,000.

ARTHUR ROSS GALLERY, UNIVERSITY OF PENNSYLVANIA, (M), 220 S. 34th St., Philadelphia, PA 19104-3808. Mailing Address: Box 5 College Hall, Philadelphia, PA 19105-0005. Tel.: 215-898-2083 & 1479. Fax: 215-573-2045.
E-mail: arg@pobox.upenn.edu
Web Site: www.upenn.edu/ARG
Founded: 1983.
Congressional District: 1
Key Personnel: Dir., Lynn Marsden-Atlass; Assoc. Dir., Dejay B. Duckett; Gallery Coord., Sara Stewart.
Personnel Profile: Full-Time Paid 3.
Governing Authority: private university. Parent Institution: University of Pennsylvania, Philadelphia. Tax-exempt: 501(c)(3).
Art Gallery: housed in a building designed by Frank Furness in 1891 as the University of Pennsylvania main library. A National Historical Landmark.
Collections: fine arts; historic & contemporary art; archaeological artifacts; textiles; sculpture.
Facilities: 1,700 sq. ft. exhibit space.
Activities: children's programs; lectures; symposia.
Publications: catalogues; annual exhibition schedule.
Hours & Admission Prices: Tues.-Fri. 10-5, Sat.-Sun. 12-5. No charge. Closed New Year's Day; Easter; Independence Day; Thanksgiving; Christmas. ♿
Attendance: 12,000 (estimated)
Membership: Contributing Friend $100-$999; Sustaining Friend $1,000 and up.

THE ATHENAEUM OF PHILADELPHIA, 219 S. 6th St., E. Washington Square, Philadelphia, PA 19106-3794. Tel.: 215-925-2688. Fax: 215-925-3755.
Web Site: www.philaathenaeum.org
Founded: 1814.
Congressional District: 1
Key Personnel: Exec. Dir., Dr. Sandra L. Tatman; Chm. (V), Lea C. Sherk; Cur. Architecture, Bruce Laverty; Circulation Librarian, Jill L. Lee; Asst. Dir. Programs, Eileen M. Magee; Digital Center Supvr., Michael Senaca.
Personnel Profile: Full-Time Paid 10; Part-Time Paid 2; Part-Time Volunteers 2; Interns 2.
Governing Authority: nonprofit corporation. Tax-exempt: 501(c)(3) & 509(a)(1).
Library with Art Collections: housed in 1845-1847, Athenaeum of Philadelphia (national historic landmark), John Notman (1810-1865), architect.
Collections: architecture & design; 300,000 architectural photographs; 250,000 architectural drawings, c.1790-1945.
Research Fields: 19th- & early 20th-century American architecture, literature & decorative arts.
Facilities: 75,000-vol. reference library; manuscripts available for use by qualified students upon application; architectural archives; reading room; Dorothy W. & F. Otto Haas Gallery.
Activities: lectures; inter-museum permanent & temporary exhibitions; provides research grants in American architectural history & building technology prior to 1860.
Publications: newsletter; booklist.
Hours & Admission Prices: Mon.-Fri. 9-5. Research: by appointment. No charge. Closed bank holidays. ♿
Attendance: 20,000 (estimated)
Membership: Annual $125; Patron $150; Sustaining $250; Supporting $500; Benefactor $1,000; Life $3,000.

ATWATER KENT MUSEUM OF PHILADELPHIA DBA PHILADELPHIA HISTORY MUSEUM, 15 S. 7th St., Philadelphia, PA 19106-2395. Tel.: 215-685-4830. Fax: 215-685-4837.
Web Site: www.philadephiahistory.org
Formerly: Atwater Kent Museum
Founded: 1938.
Congressional District: 1
Key Personnel: C.E.O. & Exec. Dir., Viki Sand; Senior Cur., Jeffrey R. Ray; Historian, Cynthia Little; Grants Mgr., Christine Davis; Registrar, Susan Drinan; Dir. Mktg. & Public Rels., Kate Bieg; Dir. Devel., Jennifer Fuges; Mgr. Membership, Jennifer Pratt; Exec. Asst., Emily Cooper.
Personnel Profile: Full-Time Paid 8; Part-Time Paid 6; Part-Time Volunteers 18; Interns 2.
Governing Authority: board of trustees. Philadelphia, PA. Tax-exempt.
History Museum: housed in 1826 building designed by John Haviland.
Collections: 50,000 prints, photographs & two-dimensional ephemera; 43,000 three-dimensional objects, including 2,700 textiles, 2,000 toys & 2,000 craft & industry artifacts; 7,500 books, pamphlets & manuscripts reflecting Philadelphia history 1680 to the present; Historical Society of Pennsylvania Art and Artifact Collection (11,400 items); Insurance Company of North America (CIGNA) (350 items); The Balch Institute for Ethnic Studies (250 items)
Major Exhibits: Experience Philadelphia! Fall 2010; Philadelphia's Reliquary Fall 2010; Community History Gallery Fall 2010; Philadelphia in the 1970s-80s Fall 2010; Sports and their Fans Fall 2010.
Research Fields: social, cultural, industrial history of Philadelphia.
Facilities: collection study center for research; gallery space.
Activities: Museum Sponsors: Community History Gallery; Capital City; Philadelphia in the 1970s; William Penn's Welcome Week; Holy Philly Works; Philadelphia Document Film Series; Sunday Suppers; Sports Talk; National History Day; Quest for Freedom.
Publications: books, Invisible Philadelphia: Community Through Voluntary Organizations; Rebels and Loyalists: The Revolutionary Soldier in Philadelphia; Magic Lantern of Dr. Thomas Story Kirkbridge.
Hours & Admission Prices: Museum is closed for planned renovations until Fall 2010. Visit www.philadelphiahistory.org or call 215-685-4830 for updated hours and admission information. ♿
Attendance: 13,857 (estimated)
Membership: Senior & Student $25; Individual $35; Household $55; Participating $75; Sustaining $125; Contributing $250; Sponsor $500; Director's Circle $1,000.

AWBURY ARBORETUM, Francis Cope House, One Awbury Rd., Philadelphia, PA 19138-1505. Tel.: 215-849-2855. Fax: 215-849-0213.
E-mail: awbury@awbury.org
Web Site: www.awbury.org
Founded: 1984.
Congressional District: 2
Key Personnel: C.E.O. & Exec. Dir., Gerald Kaufman; Chm. & Pres. (V), John Friedman; Dir. Outreach & Education, Mona Margarita, Ph.D.; Dir. Devel., Nicole Wolverton; Administrative Asst. & Museum Shop Mgr., Kathy Williamson.
Personnel Profile: Full-Time Paid 10; Full-Time Volunteers 1; Part-Time Paid 15; Part-Time Volunteers 12; Interns 15.
Governing Authority: two nonprofit organizations. City Parks Association, Trustees. Parent Institution: Awbury Arboretum Association; Subsidiary Institution: City Parks Association. Tax-exempt: 501(c)(3) & 509(a)(1).
Arboretum & Cultural Landscape: 1860 Francis Cope House.
Collections: 55-acre English landscaped park; noteworthy trees include beeches, river birch, bigleaf linden, alder, ginkgo, oaks & ailanthus; champion archives with Cope family records; arboretum plans & records; historic furnishings; plants; euphusage 19th-century plants typical to a Victorian country estate, as well as native species & local plant communities. Archives include correspondence, books & diaries of Cope family; 1,000 historic photographs of Awbury and its inhabitants; plans for the landscape and historic structures; records of the city Parks Association established in 1880. Maps.

* **MERCER MUSEUM OF THE BUCKS COUNTY HISTORICAL SOCIETY, (M),** 84 S. Pine St., Doylestown, PA 18901-4930. Tel.: 215-345-0210. Fax: 215-230-0823.
E-mail: info@mercermuseum.org
Web Site: www.mercermuseum.org
Founded: 1916.
Congressional District: 8
Key Personnel: C.E.O. & Pres., Douglas C. Dolan; Chm., Brian McLeod; Exec. Vice Pres., Molly W. Lowell; Vice Pres. Collections & Interpretation, Cory Amsler.
Personnel Profile: Full-Time Paid 10; Part-Time Paid 25; Part-Time Volunteers 250; Interns 1.
Governing Authority: society. Parent Institution: Bucks County Historical Society. Tax-exempt: 501(c)(3).
History, Historical Technology & Folk Art Museum: housed in 1916 concrete castle-like National Historic Landmark building.
Collections: 40,000 tools & products of early handcraft; artifacts of everyday life; Pennsylvania German material culture; folk art; local history items.
Research Fields: pre-industrial technology; material culture; local history; genealogy.
Facilities: Spruance Library: 20,000-vol. library of Bucks Countiana genealogical materials & historical technology books, maps, periodicals and pamphlets available for use during library hours.
Activities: workshops; education programs; family programs; permanent & temporary exhibitions; digital audio guide; summer camp.
Publications: newsletter, Penny Lots; various books & pamphlets.
Hours & Admission Prices: Museum: Sun. 12-5, Mon. & Wed.-Sat. 10-5, Tues. 10-9. Spruance Library: Tues. 1-9, Wed.-Fri. 1-5, Sat. 10-5. Adults $9, senior citizens $8, students $4; discounts to groups, AAA, AAM & ICOM members; children under 5 & members no charge. Closed New Year's Day; Thanksgiving; Christmas. ♿
Attendance: 65,000 (estimated)
Membership: Student $20; Senior $30; Individual $35; Family & Grandparent $55; Sustaining $75; Sponsor $150; Contributor $250; Distinguished Donor $500; President's Circle $1,000.

MORAVIAN POTTERY & TILE WORKS, 130 Swamp Rd., Doylestown, PA 18901-2451. Tel.: 215-345-6722. Fax: 215-345-1361.
E-mail: mptw@buckscounty.org
Web Site: www.buckscounty.org/visitors
Founded: 1969.
Congressional District: 8
Key Personnel: Dir., Charles Yeske.
Personnel Profile: Full-Time Paid 12; Part-Time Paid 4.
Governing Authority: county. Tax-exempt.
Historic Building: a National Historic Landmark.
Collections: tile industry, production, & installation; tiles; mosaics.
Activities: factory tours.
Hours & Admission Prices: Tours: daily 10-4:45. Adults $4.50, senior citizens $3.50, children 7-17 $2.50; discounts to AAM members. Tile Shop: no charge. Closed major holidays. ♿
Attendance: 26,387 (accurate)
Membership: Individual $35.

DuBois

WINKLER GALLERY OF FINE ART, 36 N. Brady St., DuBois, PA 15801-2256. Tel.: 814-375-5834.
Art Gallery.
Collections: paintings; photography; mosaics; blown glass; sculpture.
Hours & Admission Prices: Tues.-Thurs. 11-5, Fri.-Sat. 11-8.

Easton

LAFAYETTE COLLEGE ART GALLERIES, WILLIAMS CENTER FOR THE ARTS, 317 Hamilton St., Easton, PA 18042-1768. Tel.: 610-330-5361. Fax: 610-330-5642.
E-mail: okayam@lafayette.edu
Web Site: lafayette.edu/williamsgallery
Founded: 1983.
Congressional District: 136
Key Personnel: Pres. Lafayette College, Dan Weiss; Dir. Williams Center for the Arts, H. Ellis Finger; Vice Pres. & Treas., Mitchell Wein; Dir. Lafayette Art Galleries, Michiko Okaya; Skillman Library Archivist, Diane Windham Shaw; Dir. Security, Hugh Harris.
Personnel Profile: Full-Time Paid 1; Part-Time Paid 1.
Governing Authority: private college; not-for-profit. Parent Institution: Lafayette College. Tax-exempt.
College Art Gallery.
Collections: 19th- & 20th-century American & British portrait & historical paintings; photographs; Abraham Lincoln & Marquis de Lafayette memorabilia & artwork; 20th-century contemporary prints; Kirby paintings.
Research Fields: pertaining to collections.
Facilities: 2,400 sq. ft. exhibit space.
Activities: lectures; in-house loan & temporary exhibitions.
Publications: triannual, exhibit catalogs & brochures; newsletter.
Hours & Admission Prices: Sept.-May Mon.-Tues.-Wed. & Fri. 10-5, Thurs. 10-8, Sat.-Sun. 12-5. No charge. Closed school holidays. ♿
Attendance: 7,000 (estimated)

* **NATIONAL CANAL MUSEUM, HUGH MOORE HISTORICAL PARK AND MUSEUMS,** 30 Centre Square, Easton, PA 18042-7743. Tel.: 610-559-6613. Fax: 610-250-6686.
E-mail: ncm@canals.org
Web Site: canals.org
Founded: 1970.
Congressional District: 15
Key Personnel: Chm. (V), Jack Krissinger; Museum Principal, Shelly Wiles; Operations Coord., Jonathan Markloff.
Personnel Profile: Full-Time Paid 8; Part-Time Paid 30; Part-Time Volunteers 104; Interns 4.
Governing Authority: municipal & nonprofit corporation. Tax-exempt.
Transportation and Industrial Museum.
Collections: canal related artifacts; manuscripts; photo archives; industrial artifacts & records. Historical House: 1923 Locktenders House Museum.
Research Fields: Towpath canals; canal-related industries; early railroads; canal folklore; oral history; recreational use of canals; anthracite coal mining; anthracite iron production; industrial history, technology, steel production & research; communication; technology.
Facilities: 10,000-vol. library of books on canals of the Towpath Era & canal related industries available for research on premises only; archives; reading room; research center; 50-seat auditorium. Transportation-related books & items for sale.
Activities: tours; lectures; films; formally organized education programs; loan & temporary exhibitions; hiking trails; boat rentals; mule-drawn canal boat rides.
Publications: quarterly, biannual books; Canal Currents; quarterly, Locktender; annual, Proceedings of Canal History and Technology Proceedings.
Hours & Admission Prices: National Canal Museum: Tues.-Fri. 9:30-3, Sat. 9:30-5, Sun. 12-5. Adults & children $9.50, senior citizens $9. Admission includes The Crayola Factory. Canal Boat Ride: May Sat. 9:30-5, Sun. 12-5; Memorial Day to Labor Day daily; Sept. Sat. 9:30-5, Sun. 12-5. Adults $7, seniors $6.50, children 3-15 $5; discounts to AAM members & groups of 15 or more. Technology Center: May Sat. 12-5; Memorial Day to Labor Day daily 12-4. Admission $5. ♿
Attendance: 300,000 (accurate)
Membership: Associate $25; Contributing $40; Supporting $60; Sustaining $100; Sponsoring $500; Patron $1,000; Benefactor $2,500. Corporate: Supporting $100-$499; Sponsoring $500-$999; Patron $1,000-$2,500; Benefactor $2,500 & up.

NORTHAMPTON COUNTY HISTORICAL AND GENEALOGICAL SOCIETY, 107 S. 4th St., Easton, PA 18042-4597. Mailing Address: 101-107 S. Fourth St., Easton, PA 18042. Tel.: 610-253-1222. Fax: 610-253-4701.
E-mail: director@northamptonctymuseum.org
Web Site: northamptonctymuseum.org
Founded: 1906.
Congressional District: 15
Key Personnel: Exec. Dir., Colleen Cunningham Lavdar; Pres. (V), L. Anderson Daub; Librarian (V), Mrs. Roland S. Moyer; Cur., Andria Zaia.
Personnel Profile: Full-Time Paid 1; Full-Time Volunteers 2; Part-Time Paid 4; Part-Time Volunteers 70.
Governing Authority: society; nonprofit. Subsidiary Institutions: History Learning Center; Illick Research Library; Nicholas Children's Museum; Kressler Memorial Gardens; Northampton County Museum. Tax-exempt: 501(c)(3).
Historical Society Museum: housed in 1832 Jacob Mixsell House.
Collections: 19th-century portraits; Native American artifacts; period dolls; military equipment & uniforms; 19th-century costumes; folk art items; manuscripts; early craft & trade implements; furniture, food prep implements.
Research Fields: genealogy; 18th- to 20th-century local history.
Facilities: 5,000-vol. library of local history & genealogical books available for use by request.
Activities: guided tours; lectures; permanent & changing exhibitions.
Publications: approx. 20 books & pamphlets on subjects related to local history.
Hours & Admission Prices: Museum: Mon.-Fri. 9-4. Library: Tues.-Fri. 9-2. Adults $3.
Attendance: 3,000 (estimated)

Membership: Young Historian (Student) $10; Museum Protector (Individual) $40-$49; Penn's Kinfolk (Family) $50-$99; Historic Circle $100-$149; Mixsell Circle $150-$499; Pacesetters $500-$999; Benefactors $1,000 & up.

Ebensburg

CAMBRIA COUNTY HISTORICAL SOCIETY, 615 N. Center, Ebensburg, PA 15931-1122. Mailing Address: P.O. Box 278, Ebensburg, PA 15931-0278. Tel.: 814-472-6674.
Web Site: www.cambriacountyhistorical.com
Founded: 1925.
Congressional District: 12
Key Personnel: C.E.O. & Pres. (V), Fremont McKenrick; Cur., Kathy Jones.
Personnel Profile: Part-Time Paid 1.
Governing Authority: private; nonprofit organization. Tax-exempt: 501(c)(3).
General Museum: housed in the 1889 A.W. Buck house.
Collections: 19th-20th century artifacts; history; agriculture; archives; Indian artifacts; industry; numismatic; toys; military; county census; newspapers from 1831.
Research Fields: genealogy; county history.
Facilities: approx. 3,000-vol. library of archives, State's history, biography, genealogy, Indian history, county censuses & newspapers available on premises; reading room.
Activities: guided tours; lectures; films.
Publications: reprint of 1890 Caldwell Atlas of Cambria County; quarterly newsletter, The Cambria County Heritage.
Hours & Admission Prices: Tues.-Fri. 10-4, Sat. 9-1. No charge; donations accepted; Research Library $3 non members. ♿
Attendance: 2,000
Membership: Annual $20; Family $25; Donor $30; Patron $50; Life $250; Benefactor $500.

Eckley

ECKLEY MINERS' VILLAGE, Main St., Eckley, PA 18255. Mailing Address: 2 Eckley Main St., Weatherly, PA 18255-5030. Tel.: 570-636-2070. Fax: 570-636-2938. TDD: 800-654-5988.
Web Site: www.eckleyminers.org
Founded: 1969.
Congressional District: 11
Key Personnel: Dir., David Dubick; Cur., Richard Stanislau; Pres., Pasco Schiavo, Esq.; Museum Shop Mgr., Mellisa Sanchez.
Personnel Profile: Full-Time Paid 8; Part-Time Paid 4; Part-Time Volunteers 55; Interns 3.
Governing Authority: state. Pennsylvania Historical & Museum Commission, P.O. Box 1026, Harrisburg, 17120. Tax-exempt: 170(c)(1).
Historic Village: 54 houses built in the 1850s as coal patch town including Roman Catholic Church, Episcopal Church, doctor's office; coal breaker, visitor's center & mule barn.
Collections: miner's houses; mine owner's homes; churches; artifacts relating to mining & life of the anthracite families.
Research Fields: anthracite coal mining & social & cultural history of anthracite region.
Facilities: library of research material; visitors center; theater. Museum-related items for sale.
Activities: guided tours; lectures; films; plays; education programs for primary, secondary & college students; permanent exhibitions. Special Events: Christmas program; Patch Town Days; Civil War Encampment.
Publications: quarterly newsletter; pamphlets.
Hours & Admission Prices: Mon.-Sat. 9-5, Sun. 12-5. Adults $6, senior citizens 60 & over $5.50, children 6-12 $4; discounts to AAM, ICOM members & all professional organizations; children under 6 & members no charge. Closed Martin Luther King Jr. Day; Veterans Day; Columbus Day; Thanksgiving, Christmas. ♿
Attendance: 20,000 (estimated)
Membership: Individual $15; Family $20; Contributor $30; Sponsor $50; Benefactor $100; Patron $500.

Eldred

ELDRED WORLD WAR II MUSEUM, 201 Main St., Eldred, PA 16731. Mailing Address: P.O. Box 273, Eldred, PA 16731-0273. Tel.: 814-225-2220; 866-686-9944 (Toll Free). Fax: 814-225-4407.
Founded: 1996.
Key Personnel: Dir., Jay P. Tennies
Military History Museum.
Collections: WWII history; military equipment, uniforms, & personal stories; photographs; personal artifacts.
Activities: special events.
Hours & Admission Prices: Sun. 1-4, Tues.-Sat. 10-4. Adults $5; discounts to groups; children 18 & under no charge. Closed New Year's Eve & Day; Independence Day; Thanksgiving & day after; Christmas Eve, Day & day after.

Elizabethtown

WINTERS HERITAGE HOUSE MUSEUM, 41-47 E. High St., Elizabethtown, PA 17022. Mailing Address: P.O. Box 14, Elizabethtown, PA 17022-0014. Tel.: 717-367-4672. Fax: 717-367-9991.
Web Site: www.elizabethtownhistory.org
Founded: 1988.
Congressional District: 16
Key Personnel: Exec. Dir., Lori B. Donofrio-Galley; Pres. (V), Dr. Michael A. Worman.
Personnel Profile: Full-Time Volunteers 100; Part-Time Paid 2; Part-Time Volunteers 3; Interns 1.
Governing Authority: Parent Institution: Elizabethtown Preservation Assoc. Tax-exempt.
Historic House Museum: c.1750.
Collections: family histories; maps; deeds; obituaries; local history & memorabilia; oral histories; yearbooks; photographs; architecture.
Major Exhibits: Quilt Show, 5/10; Traditional Arts, Fall 2010.
Research Fields: genealogy; local history.
Facilities: genealogy library.
Activities: hands-on demonstrations; classes; workshops; research; walking tours; mural interpretation. Annual Events: Appraisal Fair; Holiday Craft Show.
Publications: member newsletter.
Hours & Admission Prices: March-May & Sept.-Dec. Thurs.-Fri. 9:30-3:30, Sat. 9:30-12; June-Aug. Thurs.-Fri. 9:30-3:30. Museum: no charge; donations accepted. Research: non-members $5 daily. Closed holidays.
Attendance: 1,000 (estimated)
Membership: Individual $15; Family $30; Sustaining $50; Patron $100; Sponsor $250; Benefactor $500; Associate & Life $1,000.

Elkins Park

RICHARD WALL HOUSE MUSEUM, 1 Wall Park Dr., Elkins Park, PA 19027. Tel.: 215-887-9159 & 6200, ext. 114.
Founded: 1980.
Congressional District: 2
Key Personnel: Chm. (V), Stephen Banks; Vice Chm., David Harrower; Cur., Dorothy Spruill
Historic House Museum: listed on the National Register of Historic Places.
Collections: local history & culture from late 1700s to 1950s; period furnishings; personal artifacts; springhouse; carriage house.
Hours & Admission Prices: Sun. 1-4; other times by appointment. No charge; donations accepted.

THE TEMPLE JUDEA MUSEUM OF REFORM CONGREGATION KENESETH ISRAEL, 8339 Old York Rd., Elkins Park, PA 19027-1515. Tel.: 215-887-2027. Fax: 215-887-1070.
E-mail: tjmuseum@aol.com
Web Site: www.kenesethisrael.org/museum.html
Founded: 1984.
Congressional District: 2
Key Personnel: Dir. & Cur., Rita Rosen Poley; Chm. (V), Karen Shain Schloss.
Personnel Profile: Part-Time Paid 1; Part-Time Volunteers 20.
Governing Authority: denominational group; nonprofit. Tax-exempt: 501(c)(3).
Religious Museum.
Collections: over 1,000 Jewish artifacts from around the world; fabrics crafted for religious ceremonial, folk & cultural use; paintings; prints; lithographs; photographs; silver ceremonial objects; embroidered Torah binder, 1695; second oldest American ketubah (marriage contract) PA, 1778; Jewish music & performing arts; ephemera.
Facilities: 500-vol. library; 197 sq. ft. exhibit space.
Activities: guided tours; lectures; loan & temporary exhibitions. Annual Event: Artisans' Festival.
Publications: newsletter, Friends of the Museum.
Hours & Admission Prices: Mon.-Fri. 1-4; other times by appointment. No charge. Closed Jewish holidays; legal holidays. ♿
Attendance: 2,000 (estimated)
Membership: Friend $36; Patron $90; Benefactor $180.

Elverson

HOPEWELL FURNACE NATIONAL HISTORIC SITE, 2 Mark Bird Lane, Elverson, PA 19520-9535. Tel.: 610-582-8773. Fax: 610-582-2768.
E-mail: hofu_superintendent@nps.gov
Web Site: www.nps.gov/hofu
Formerly: Hopewell Village National Historic Site

Publications: Journal of the Historical Society of the Cocalico Valley; biannual book of historical photographs.
Hours & Admission Prices: Museum: Sat. 10-4. No charge; donations accepted. Library & Research Center: Mon. & Wed.-Thurs. 9:30-6, Sat. 8:30-5. Research: $3.
Attendance: 900 (estimated)
Membership: Regular $20; Family Membership $30; Life $500.

Erie

ERIE ART MUSEUM, 411 State St., Erie, PA 16501-1106. Tel.: 814-459-5477. Fax: 814-452-1744.
E-mail: contact@erieartmuseum.org
Web Site: www.erieartmuseum.org
Founded: 1898.
Congressional District: 21
Key Personnel: Exec. Dir., John L. Vanco; Pres. (V)., Stephen Porter; Dir. Mktg. & Devel., Tammy Roche; Dir. Administration & Finance, Jenae Gary; Dir. Education & Folk Art Coord., Kelly Armor; Frame Shop Mgr., Joseph Popp; Coord. Publications, Andrea Krivak; Education Coord., Stephanie Campbell; Building & Events Operations, Sam Ansbro; Registrar, Vance Lupher.
Personnel Profile: Full-Time Paid 10; Part-Time Paid 3; Part-Time Volunteers 150; Interns 12.
Governing Authority: nonprofit organization. Tax-exempt: 501(c)(3).
Art Museum Center.
Collections: paintings; sculpture; graphics; decorative arts; photography; American ceramics; Indian bronze & stone sculpture; oriental porcelains & jade; contemporary baskets; Tibetan paintings.
Major Exhibits: Ancient Alloy: Bronzes From The Collection, 1/10-12/10; Making It Better: Folk Art in PA, 1/5/10-4/11/10; Malcolm Christhilf, 1/22/10-4/24/10; 87th Annual Spring Show, 4/24/10-6/20/10; Anne Marie Magenau, 4/30/10-7/24/10.
Research Fields: American ceramic art.
Facilities: studios; classrooms.
Activities: guided tours; lectures; films; gallery talks; formally organized educational programs; temporary & traveling exhibitions; circulating exhibitions; jazz & new music concerts. Museum Sponsors: Annual Spring Show competition.
Publications: monthly e-newsletter; members' newsletter; exhibition announcements; exhibition catalogs.
Hours & Admission Prices: Tues.-Sat. 11-5, Sun. 1-5. Adults $4, students & senior citizens $3, children $2; discounts to AAM & ICOM members; members & Wed. no charge. New Year's Day; Easter; Independence Day; Thanksgiving; Christmas. ♿
Attendance: 36,000 (estimated)
Membership: Green $10; Student & Senior Citizen $15; Individual $35; Family $65; Patron $100; Sustaining $250; Sponsor $500.

ERIE COUNTY HISTORY CENTER & CASHIER'S HOUSE, 417-419 State St., Erie, PA 16501. Mailing Address: 419 State St., Erie, PA 16501-1106. Tel.: 814-454-1813. Fax: 814-454-6890.
E-mail: echs@eriecountyhistory.org
Web Site: www.eriecountyhistory.org
Founded: 1903.
Congressional District: 3
Key Personnel: Operations Dir., Melanie Keubel-Stankey; Pres. (V), Charles Scalise.
Personnel Profile: Full-Time Paid 4; Part-Time Paid 2; Part-Time Volunteers 10; Interns 8.
Governing Authority: society. Parent Institution: Erie County Historical Society. Tax-exempt: 501(c)(3).
Historical Society Museum.
Collections: 1735-present, northwestern Pennsylvania & Great Lakes history.
Research Fields: history of Erie County area, industry & architecture.
Facilities: 3,500-vol. library containing books, documents, manuscripts, dealing with Erie County & northwest Pennsylvania history.
Activities: lectures; formally organized educational programs; temporary exhibitions.
Publications: Journal of Erie Studies; books; periodic newsletter.
Hours & Admission Prices: Tues.-Sat. 11-4. Family $10, Adults $4, seniors $3, children $2; discounts to AAM & AASLH members; members no charge. Closed holidays. ♿
Attendance: 4,526 (accurate)
Membership: Student $10; Individual $35; Family & Grandparent $50; Patron $75; Sustaining $100; Sponsor $250; Corporate $500.

ERIE MARITIME MUSEUM & FLAGSHIP NIAGARA, Bayview Commons, 150 E. Front St., Ste. 100, Erie, PA 16507-1594. Tel.: 814-452-2744. Fax: 814-455-6760.
E-mail: sail@flagshipniagara.org
Web Site: www.flagshipniagara.org
Formerly: Erie Maritime Museum, Homeport U.S. Brig Niagara
Founded: 1998.
Congressional District: 3
Key Personnel: Chm. PHMC, Wayne Spilove; Exec. Dir. PHMC, Barbara Franco; Chm. (V) & Pres. Flagship Niagara League, Brian Scott; Site Admin. & Sr. Captain, Walter Rybka; Dir. Flagship Niagara League, Barbara Johnson; Museum Shop Mgr., Timothy McLaughlin.
Personnel Profile: Full-Time Paid 10; Part-Time Paid 2; Part-Time Volunteers 160; Interns 4.
Governing Authority: state. Administered by Pennsylvania Historical & Museum Commission, Box 1026, Harrisburg, PA 17108. Subsidiary Institution: Flagship Niagara League. Tax-exempt.
Historic Ship & History Museum: Erie maritime; 1813 U.S. Brig Niagara, commanded by Comdr. Oliver Hazard Perry.
Collections: Battle of Lake Erie; War of 1812; 19th-century sailing & regional maritime history; homeport to the U.S. Brig Niagara; live fire exhibit of the U.S. Brig Lawrence; U.S.S. Michigan/U.S.S. Wolverine; photographs; video.
Research Fields: War of 1812; Battle of Lake Erie; naval architecture; Lake Erie maritime history; U.S.S. Michigan/U.S.S. Wolverine.
Facilities: library on Lake Erie maritime history available to scholars & members; visitor center; theater; 299-seat auditorium. Museum-related items for sale.
Activities: guided tours; special programs; on-board ship demonstrations; hands-on & interactive exhibits; concerts; films; lectures; one day sailing school vessel; 2-4 week live-aboard sail training; educational programs.
Publications: quarterly newsletter, Niagara League News.
Hours & Admission Prices: Jan.-March Thurs.-Sat. 9-5, Sun. 12-5; April-Dec. Mon.-Sat. 9-5, Sun. 12-5; call for ships schedule. Adults $8, senior citizens $5, youth 6-17 $3; discounts to AAM & ICOM members; children under 5 & league members no charge. Closed New Year's Day; Martin Luther King Jr. Day; Presidents' Day; Columbus Day; Veterans Day; Thanksgiving; Christmas.
Attendance: 24,869 (accurate)
Membership: Individual $25; Family $40; Captain $60; Commodore $125; Admiral $275; Perry's Company $500; Fleet Commander $1,000.

ERIE PLANETARIUM, 356 W. Sixth St., Erie, PA 16507-1245. Mailing Address: 419 State St., Erie, PA 16501-1106. Tel.: 814-871-5790 & 454-1813. Fax: 814-454-6890.
E-mail: echs@eriecountyhistory.org
Web Site: www.eriecountyhistory.org/erie-planetarium
Founded: 1959.
Congressional District: 3
Key Personnel: Dir. Operations & Visitor Member Svcs., Melanie Kuebel-Stankey; Planetarium Coord., Jim Gavio.
Personnel Profile: Part-Time Paid 1; Part-Time Volunteers 6.
Governing Authority: private; nonprofit organization. Parent Institution: Erie County Historical Society. Tax-exempt: 501(c)(3).
Planetarium.
Collections: geology; astronomy.
Facilities: Spitz A3P projector; 20 ft. dome.
Activities: planetarium shows; scout programs; birthday parties; special event programs; hands-on activities.
Hours & Admission Prices: Call for hours. Family $10, adult $4, senior $3, children $2; discounts to AAM members & groups; members no charge. ♿
Attendance: 5,500 (estimated)
Membership: Student $10; Individual $35; Family & Grandparent $50; Patron $75; Sustaining $100; Sponsor $250; Corporate $500.

ERIE ZOOLOGICAL PARK & BOTANICAL GARDENS OF NORTHWESTERN PENNSYLVANIA, 423 W. 38th St., Erie, PA 16508-2701. Mailing Address: P.O. Box 3268, Erie, PA 16508-0268. Tel.: 814-864-4091. Fax: 814-864-1140.
E-mail: info@eriezoo.org
Web Site: www.eriezoo.org
Founded: 1962.
Key Personnel: Pres. & C.E.O., Scott Mitchell; Coord. Mktg. & Events, Ainslie Brosig.
Personnel Profile: Full-Time Paid 27; Part-Time Paid 70; Part-Time Volunteers 412.
Governing Authority: society. Parent Institution: Erie Zoological Society. Tax-exempt.
Zoo & Botanical Garden.

Founded: 1938.
Congressional District: 16
Key Personnel: Supt., Edie Shean-Hammond; Facility Mgr., George Martin; Pres. Friends of Hopewell Furnace NHS, Terry Stauffer; Cultural Resource Mgr., Rebecca Ross; Chief Interpretation, Frances Delmar; Chief Natural Resources, Steven Ambrose; Coord. Arts & Crafts Program, Helen Seguin; Administrative Officer, Eleanor Martin; Museum Shop Mgr., Christine Rogers; Volunteer Coord., Frank Hebblethwaite.
Personnel Profile: Full-Time Paid 14; Part-Time Paid 11; Part-Time Volunteers 434; Interns 2.
Governing Authority: federal. Parent Institution: National Park Service, Dept. of Interior, Washington, DC. Tax-exempt.
Industrial Museum.
Collections: 1770-1880 structures with period furniture; tenant houses; operating water-wheel; restored furnace structures; office; store; barn; archives with microfilm of original records & documents; history of iron business; manuscripts; CCC records; WPA & WWII records; CCC structures & artifacts; living history farm; apple orchard; ethnographic database 1771-1930s.
Major Exhibits: Black History Month Exhibit, 2/10; Women's History, 3/10; Volunteer Exhibit, 4/10; Memorial Day, 5/10; Farm Animals of Hopewell Furnace, 6/10; Fueling the Furnace, 8/10; Apple Harvest Exhibit, 9/10; Christmas Exhibit, 12/10.
Research Fields: late 18th- & 19th-century history of iron production & village life in Pennsylvania; CCC & WPA history; African American history including underground railroad.
Facilities: 700-vol. library of books, microfilm & dissertations pertaining to the history of iron business; auditorium; nature trails; 848-acre site; apple orchard. Postcards, furnace collectibles, books, arts & crafts for sale.
Activities: pre-arranged guided tours; permanent exhibitions; film & slide presentation; school loan service of films; curriculum-based interactive school programs; research; sheep shearing; living history costumed interpretation; charcoal-making demonstrations; apple picking; arts & crafts demonstrations.
Publications: handbook, Hopewell Furnace; American Charcoal Making; newsletter, Hopewell Volunteer Reporter; video, Hopewell Furnace Demonstration; A Summer Day at a Charcoal Iron Furnace; Junior History Guide to Hopewell Furnace NHS; Hopewell Village - The Dynamics of a 19th Century Iron Making Community; Hopewell Furnace Educational Jigsaw Puzzle.
Hours & Admission Prices: Grounds: daily 9-5. Visitor Center & Village: Wed.-Sun. 9-5. Adults $4; National Parks Pass, Access Pass, Senior Pass, Hopewell Furnace Park Pass holders & Jan.-Feb. no charge. Closed New Year's Day; Martin Luther King Jr. Day; Presidents' Day; Thanksgiving; Christmas. ♿
Attendance: 60,000 (estimated)
Membership: Hopewell Furnace Park Pass $20; National Park Pass $80.

Emlenton

PUMPING JACK MUSEUM, Crawford Center on Hill St., Hill St., Emlenton, PA 16373. Mailing Address: P.O. Box 25, Emlenton, PA 16373-0025. Tel.: 724-867-0030.
E-mail: pumpingjackmuseum@csonline.com
Web Site: www.pumpingjack.com
Key Personnel: Pres. (V), Joyce Beikert.
Personnel Profile: Full-Time Volunteers 8.
History Museum.
Collections: oil history; local heritage; equipment; personal artifacts; photographs.
Research Fields: genealogy.
Publications: book, Emlenton Walking Tour; Allegheny River guide, Oil On The Brain.
Hours & Admission Prices: May-Oct. Sat.-Sun. 12-3; other times by appointment. No charge; donations accepted. ♿
Attendance: 100 (estimated)
Membership: Student $3; Individual $10; Family $15.

Emmaus

SHELTER HOUSE SOCIETY, 601 S. 4th St., Emmaus, PA 18049-3934. Mailing Address: Box 254, Emmaus, PA 18049-0254. Tel.: 610-965-9258 & 5280.
Founded: 1951.
Congressional District: 15
Key Personnel: Chm., Jeanette Lehman; Pres., Noreen Yamamoto; Sec., Jane Maulfair.
Governing Authority: board of directors. Tax-exempt.
Historic House: 1734-1741 Shelter House.
Collections: history.
Research Fields: history.
Facilities: 500-vol. library of books & material pertaining to local & family history available for use on premises; reading room; pavilion for cultural group meetings; outdoor fireplaces & recreation areas.
Activities: cultural gatherings.
Publications: annual magazine, The Hearthstone.
Hours & Admission Prices: Daily by appointment only. No charge; donations accepted.
Attendance: 400 (estimated)
Membership: Individual $15; Family $25; Patriots $50; Life (Founders) $100.

Ephrata

EICHER ARTS CENTER AND INDIAN MUSEUM, 407 Cocalico St., Ephrata, PA 17522. Mailing Address: P.O. Box 601, Ephrata, PA 17522. Tel.: 717-738-3084.
Web Site: www.virtualephrata.org
Key Personnel: Coord., James DeFilippis
History Museum: built in 1733 by members of the Ephrata Cloister Brotherhood.
Collections: local history & culture; Native American artifacts; period furnishings; photographs.
Facilities: Museum-related items for sale.
Activities: rental facilities.
Hours & Admission Prices: By appointment. No charge.

* **EPHRATA CLOISTER,** 632 W. Main St., Ephrata, PA 17522-1717. Tel.: 717-733-6600. Fax: 717-733-4364.
E-mail: info@ephratacloister.org
Web Site: www.ephratacloister.org
Founded: 1732.
Congressional District: 16
Key Personnel: Dir., Elizabeth Bertheaud; Pres., Gloria Meiskey; Museum Shop Mgr., Susan Shober.
Personnel Profile: Full-Time Paid 9; Full-Time Volunteers 1; Part-Time Paid 6; Part-Time Volunteers 120.
Governing Authority: state. Parent Institution: Pennsylvania Historical and Museum Commission, Keystone Bldg., Plaza Level, 400 North St., Harrisburg, PA 17120-0053. Subsidiary Institution: Ephrata Cloister Associates. Tax-exempt.
Historic Site: comprising of twelve mid-18th century buildings of Germanic architectural style, located on original site of a celibate religious community.
Collections: books printed here in 18th & early 19th centuries; furniture produced by 18th century society; buildings representative of unique architectural significance.
Research Fields: archaeological; architectural; calligraphy & music; religion.
Facilities: 600-vol. library; 100-seat auditorium; 450-seat outdoor ampitheatre. Cloister inspired reproductions & folk art items for sale.
Activities: guided tours; lectures; concerts; formally organized educational programs; docent program or council; history classes; visitor orientation video.
Publications: books, booklets on Pennsylvania history.
Hours & Admission Prices: Jan.-Feb. Tues.-Sat. 9-5, Sun. 12-5; March-Dec. Mon.-Sat. 9-5, Sun. 12-5. Adults $7, senior citizens 60 & over $6.50, youth 6-17 $5; discounts to groups, all motor clubs, National Historical Society, AAM & ICOM members; members no charge. Closed New Year's Day; Easter; Veterans Day; Thanksgiving & day after; Christmas.
Attendance: 30,000 (estimated)
Membership: Individual $18; Contributing (2 person) $28; Family $43; Business, Civic & Professional $100; Benefactor $500.

HISTORICAL SOCIETY OF THE COCALICO VALLEY, 237/249 W. Main St., Ephrata, PA 17522. Mailing Address: P.O. Box 193, Ephrata, PA 17522-0193. Tel.: 717-733-1616.
E-mail: cjmarquet@gmail.com
Web Site: www.cocalicovalleyhs.org
Founded: 1957.
Congressional District: 16
Key Personnel: Pres. (V), Clarence Spohn; Librarian, Cynthia J. Marquet.
Personnel Profile: Part-Time Paid 1.
Governing Authority: society. Tax-exempt.
History Museum.
Collections: history of Cocalico Valley; reference library; manuscripts; papers of Col. George S. Howard, 1st Dir. of U.S.A.F. Band; Harry F. Stauffer photographs; Pennsylvania German art & culture.
Research Fields: genealogy; local history; U.S.A.F. Band history; history & culture of Pennsylvania Germans.
Facilities: library of books on genealogy & history available for use on premises.
Activities: lectures; films; permanent & temporary exhibitions.

Research Fields: nature education; horticulture; local history.
Facilities: nature & conservation center.
Activities: guided tours; formally organized education programs; adult job training in horticulture.
Publications: newsletter, The Arbor; A Walk though Awbury with Sir Peter Shepheard; A History of Awbury; Awbury Memories; For Emancipation and Education: Black and Quakes,1680-1900.
Hours & Admission Prices: Daily dawn-dusk. No charge; donations accepted. ♿
Attendance: 10,000 (estimated)
Membership: Senior Citizen, Student & Individual $25; Family $50; Supporting $500; Sustaining $1,500.

BARTRAM'S GARDEN, 54th St. & Lindbergh Blvd., Philadelphia, PA 19143. Tel.: 215-729-5281. Fax: 215-729-1047.
E-mail: info@bartramsgarden.org
Web Site: www.bartramsgarden.org
Founded: 1893.
Congressional District: 1
Key Personnel: Pres., James Straw; Exec. Dir., Louise Turan; Museum Shop Mgr., Barbara Klein.
Personnel Profile: Full-Time Paid 7; Part-Time Paid 8.
Governing Authority: nonprofit organization. Affiliated with the John Bartram Assoc. Parent Institution: Fairmount Park. Tax-exempt: 501(c)(3); 170(b)(1)(A).
Historic House & Botanical Garden: c.1700 Bartram House.
Collections: 18th & early 19th-century furnishings & decorative arts that reflect the Bartram tenancy; early Bartram related books; manuscripts; publications, horticultural & ornithological works. Historic Buildings: outbuildings; stable; sheds; barn; icehouse; seed house; stone cider mill.
Research Fields: 18th & 19th-century horticultural & botanical practices; the Bartram family.
Facilities: library of books, papers, articles that relate to the Bartrams & horticulture in the 18th & 19th centuries available for research upon application to the John Bartram Assoc.; botanical garden. Museum-related items for sale.
Activities: guided tours; lectures; formally organized educational programs; loan, permanent, temporary & traveling exhibitions.
Publications: Bartram Broadside; Bartram Leaf.
Hours & Admission Prices: Jan.-Feb. by appointment only. House: March-Dec. call for hours. Gift Shop: March-Dec. Fri.-Sun. 10:30-4:30. Reservations for group tours available all year. Adults $10, senior citizens & students $8; discounts to AAM members; children 12 & under & members no charge. Garden: daily dawn-dusk. No charge. Closed holidays.
Attendance: 40,000 (estimated)
Membership: Individual $35; Household $50; Naturalist $100; Botanist $250; Explorer $500; Collector $1,000.

BETSY ROSS HOUSE, (M), 239 Arch St., Philadelphia, PA 19106-1999. Tel.: 215-686-1252. Fax: 215-686-1256.
E-mail: lisa@betsyrosshouse.org
Web Site: www.betsyrosshouse.org
Founded: 1898.
Congressional District: 1
Key Personnel: Dir., Lisa Moulder; Chm., Wayne Spilove; Mgr. Collections, Michelle Budeni; Facilities Mgr., Frank Fisher; Public Rels., Heather Kincaid; Museum Shop Mgr., Ashley Baney.
Personnel Profile: Full-Time Paid 6; Part-Time Paid 10; Part-Time Volunteers 3; Interns 2.
Governing Authority: private; nonprofit organization. Parent Institution: Historic Philadelphia, Inc. Tax-exempt: 501(c)(3).
Historic House: 1773-1786 home of Betsy Ross, seamstress of the first American flag.
Collections: craftsman's tools; furnishings; personal artifacts; restored 18th-century upholstery shop.
Research Fields: 18th-19th centuries historic Philadelphia; history of the Betsy Ross house; Betsy Ross.
Facilities: courtyard. Museum-related items for sale.
Activities: concerts. Museum Sponsors: playlets & reenactments June-August; Flag Day celebration; Independence Day activities.
Hours & Admission Prices: April to mid-Oct. daily 10-5; mid-Oct. to March Tues.-Sun. 10-5. Adults & seniors $3, children & students $2; discounts to AAM & ICOM members; members no charge. Audio Guide, includes admission $4. Closed New Year's Day; Thanksgiving; Christmas. ♿
Attendance: 315,459 (accurate)

CHESTNUT HILL HISTORICAL SOCIETY, 8708 Germantown Ave., Philadelphia, PA 19118-2717. Tel.: 215-247-0417. Fax: 215-247-9329.
E-mail: info@chhist.org
Historical Society Museum: housed in an 1870s Victorian house.
Collections: local history & culture; genealogy; architectural drawings & building records; photographs; maps; prints; drawings.
Activities: educational programs; tours.
Hours & Admission Prices: Tues.-Fri. 9:30-2:30, Sat. 11-4 by appointment. Research $15; members no charge.

CIVIL WAR AND UNDERGROUND RAILROAD MUSEUM OF PHILADELPHIA, (M), 3rd & Chestnut Sts., Philadelphia, PA 19103. Mailing Address: 2301 Market St., N1-1, Philadelphia, PA 19103-1338. Tel.: 215-405-8719. Fax: 215-735-3812.
E-mail: ddiberardo@cwurmuseum.org
Web Site: www.cwurmuseum.org
Formerly: The Civil War Library & Museum
Founded: 1888.
Congressional District: 2
Key Personnel: Pres. & C.E.O., Sharon A. Smith; Cur., Andrew Coldren.
Personnel Profile: Full-Time Paid 3; Part-Time Paid 2; Part-Time Volunteers 12.
Governing Authority: nonprofit. Tax-exempt.
History Museum: housed in 1857 building of the Civil War period.
Collections: Civil War uniforms; arms; accoutrements; personal memorabilia; standards; insignias; Lincoln items.
Research Fields: Civil War; Underground Railroad; genealogy.
Facilities: 10,000-vol. library pertaining to the Civil War available to the public.
Activities: living history performances; speakers; educational events.
Publications: quarterly newsletter.
Hours & Admission Prices: Closed until 2014.
Attendance: 4,000 (estimated)
Membership: Individual $35; Family $50.

CLIVEDEN OF THE NATIONAL TRUST, 6401 Germantown Ave., Philadelphia, PA 19144-1998. Tel.: 215-848-1777. Fax: 215-438-2892. TDD: 215-848-1777.
E-mail: info@cliveden.org
Web Site: www.cliveden.org
Founded: 1972.
Congressional District: 201
Key Personnel: Chm. (V), Robert A. MacDonnell; Exec. Dir., David W. Young; Cur. History, Phillip Sietz; Dir. Education, Rick Fink; Deputy Dir. Devel., Anne Roller; Museum Shop Mgr., Sandy Swark.
Personnel Profile: Full-Time Paid 4; Part-Time Paid 15; Interns 2.
Governing Authority: nonprofit organization. Operated by Cliveden, Inc. Parent Institution: The National Trust for Historic Preservation, 1785 Massachusetts Ave., N.W., Washington, DC 20036. Tax-exempt: 501(c)(3).
Historic House Museum: 1763-1767 residence built by Benjamin Chew & site of the Battle of Germantown, Oct. 4, 1777.
Collections: Philadelphia Chippendale furniture; Chew family memorabilia & papers; 18th to 19th-century decorative arts. Historic House: c.1798 Upsala home.
Research Fields: Chew Family; decorative arts; Germantown; historic preservation; Battle of Germantown; Philadelphia social history.
Facilities: meeting space; garden. Books & museum-related items for sale.
Activities: guided tours; lectures; school programs; special events; Upsala home available for rental. Museum Sponsors: Jazz Festival; Battle Reenactment.
Publications: newsletter.
Hours & Admission Prices: April-Dec. Thurs.-Sun. 12-4; other times by appointment. Adults $8, students $6; discounts to AAA & Mobil travel members; members & Friends of Cliveden & National Trust no charge. Closed New Year's Day; Easter; Thanksgiving; Christmas. ♿
Attendance: 15,883 (accurate)
Membership: Individual $35; Family $60; Sponsor $250.

THE DESIGN CENTER AT PHILADELPHIA UNIVERSITY, (M), 4200 Henry Ave., Philadelphia, PA 19144. Tel.: 215-951-5338. Fax: 215-951-2662.
E-mail: thedesigncenter@philau.edu
Web Site: www.philau.edu/designcenter
Formerly: The Design Center at Philadelphia University
Founded: 1978.
Congressional District: 2
Key Personnel: Dir., Hilary Jay; Asst. Dir., Carla Bednar; Cur. Collections, Nancy Packer.
Personnel Profile: Full-Time Paid 2; Part-Time Paid 6; Part-Time Volunteers 2; Interns 2.
Governing Authority: college; nonprofit organization. Parent Institution: Philadelphia University. Tax-exempt: 501(c)(3).
Design Museum.

Collections: international textiles dating from 4th-century A.D. to present; 200,000 indexed swatches; fashion; costumes; clothing accessories; interior fabrics; historic textiles; quilts; lace 16th-century to present; fringe collection; color swatch cards; textile tools & implements; dye sample books.
Research Fields: history of textiles; textile industry; historic clothing; international textiles & costumes; lace; color science; design; Philadelphia history.
Facilities: 500-vol. library.
Activities: guided tours; lectures; loan & temporary exhibitions; outreach materials.
Publications: Florabunda, The Evolution of Floral Design on Fabric; The Philadelphia System of Textile Manufacture, 1884-1984; Anything Goes: Textiles of the 20s & the 30s; The Art of the Textile Blockmaker; The Bauhaus Weaving Workshop: Source & Influence for American Textiles; Scalamandre: Preserving America's Textile Heritage, 1929-1989; The Art of African Textiles: Form and Function, 1995; Le Corbusier: Inside the Machine for Living 2001; Black & White 2002; What is Design Today? 2002.
Hours & Admission Prices: Galleries: Mon.-Fri. 10-4. Textile Collection: by appointment. No charge. Closed major & school holidays. ♿
Attendance: 6,000 (estimated)

EASTERN STATE PENITENTIARY HISTORIC SITE, 22nd & Fairmount Ave., Philadelphia, PA 19130. Mailing Address: 2027 Fairmount Ave., Philadelphia, PA 19130. Tel.: 215-236-3300 & 5111. Fax: 215-236-5289.
E-mail: info@easternstate.org
Web Site: www.easternstate.org
Key Personnel: Exec. Dir., Sara Jane Elk; Program Dir., Sean Kelley; Asst. Program Dir. Operations & Special Events, Brett Bertolino
Historic Site.
Collections: artifacts; inmate made crafts.
Hours & Admission Prices: Daily 10-5. Adults $12, senior citizens $10, students & children 8-17 $8; children under 7 not admitted. Closed New Year's Eve & Day; Easter; Thanksgiving; Christmas Eve & Day.
Attendance: 190,000 (estimated)

THE EBENEZER MAXWELL MANSION, INC., (M), 200 W. Tulpehocken St., Philadelphia, PA 19144-3210. Tel.: 215-438-1861. Fax: 215-438-0133.
E-mail: emaxwellmansion@yahoo.com
Web Site: www.ebenezermaxwellmansion.org
Founded: 1975.
Congressional District: 2
Key Personnel: Exec. Dir., Diane S. Richardson; Pres., Susan B. Harrison.
Personnel Profile: Full-Time Paid 1; Part-Time Paid 1; Part-Time Volunteers 40.
Governing Authority: nonprofit. Tax-exempt: 501(c)(3).
Historic House: 1859 Victorian Villa.
Collections: period rooms, furnishings & gardens reflecting mid- & late Victorian life of 1850-1890; hands-on exhibits.
Research Fields: 19th-century architecture; decorative arts; lifestyles; technical restoration information.
Facilities: 250-vol. library pertaining to Victorian history, artifacts & restoration processes; educational facilities; period gardens.
Activities: guided tours; lectures; organized educational programs; docent program; temporary exhibitions; workshops; classes;. Museum Sponsors: Old Fashioned Picnic in summer; Murder Mystery in October; Dickens Christmas Party in December.
Publications: brochure; semiannual newsletter; annual report; Max Fax; garden brochure; garden book.
Hours & Admission Prices: April-Dec. 15 Thurs. & Sat. 12-4; other times by appointment; groups by appointment. Adults $6, students $5; members no charge. Closed national holidays.
Attendance: 1,338 (accurate)
Membership: Ebenezer Maxwell Apprentice $15; Ebenezer Maxwell Associate $35; Hunter-Stevenson Circle $50; Hunter & Rommell Contributor $100; Stevenson & Bean Patron $200; Rosalie Hunter Charity League $500; Augusta Stevenson & Cotillion Society $1,000.

EDGAR ALLAN POE NATIONAL HISTORIC SITE, 532 N. Seventh St., Philadelphia, PA 19123. Mailing Address: 143 S. 3rd St., Philadelphia, PA 19106-2818. Tel.: 215-597-8780 & 8787. Fax: 215-861-4950. TDD: 215-597-8780.
Web Site: www.nps.gov/edal
Founded: 1978.
Congressional District: 3
Key Personnel: Mgr., Steve Sitarski; Cur., Karie Diethorn.
Personnel Profile: Full-Time Paid 3; Part-Time Paid 4; Part-Time Volunteers 6.
Governing Authority: federal. Parent Institution: Independence National Historical Park, 143 S. 3rd St., Philadelphia, PA 19106. Tax-exempt.
Historic Site: c.1843 Edgar Allan Poe brick house.
Collections: Poe's life & history; personal artifacts; period furnishings.
Research Fields: Poe's life; literary achievements.
Facilities: reference library of secondary materials on Edgar Allan Poe available for research on premises; reading room; theater. Books, tapes, cards on Edgar Allan Poe for sale.
Activities: Ranger guided tours offered with special theme events; lectures; films; formally organized education programs for children & college students; permanent exhibitions; Junior Ranger activities. Annual Events: Programs commemorating Poe's birth & death in January & October; Poetry in April; Mystery in July; science fiction in August; Ghostly Grip Horror Tales in October.
Publications: park folder; teacher's handbook.
Hours & Admission Prices: Wed.-Sun. 9-5. No charge; donations accepted. Closed New Year's Day; Veterans Day; Thanksgiving; Christmas.
Attendance: 18,500 (accurate)

ELFRETH'S ALLEY ASSOCIATION, 126 Elfreths Alley, Philadelphia, PA 19106-2006. Tel.: 215-574-0560. Fax: 215-922-7869.
E-mail: information@elfrethsalley.org
Web Site: www.elfrethsalley.org
Founded: 1934.
Congressional District: 1
Key Personnel: Pres., Erik William; Exec. Dir., Dena Ferrara.
Personnel Profile: Full-Time Paid 1; Part-Time Paid 3; Part-Time Volunteers 5; Interns 3.
Governing Authority: Tax-exempt.
Historic House.
Collections: 18th-century & early 19th-century historic structures; historic street featuring 28 buildings interpreting urban life; 2 historic 18th-century homes; archival documents; 18-century homewares & furniture.
Hours & Admission Prices: Tues.-Sat. 10-5, Sun. 12-5. Adults $5, children 6-18 & school groups $1; discount to AAM & ICOM mebers; Philadelphia schools and children under 6 no charge.
Attendance: 44,300 (accurate)

ESTHER M. KLEIN ART GALLERY AT UNIVERSITY CITY SCIENCE CENTER, 3600 Market St., Philadelphia, PA 19104-2641. Mailing Address: 3711 Market St., Ste. 800, Philadelphia, PA 19104-5504. Tel.: 215-966-6188. Fax: 215-966-6001.
E-mail: kleinart@sciencecenter.org
Web Site: www.kleinartgallery.org
Founded: 1976.
Congressional District: 2
Key Personnel: C.E.O. & Pres., Dr. Stephen Tang; Dir., Dan Schimmel; Cur., David Clayton.
Personnel Profile: Part-Time Paid 2; Part-Time Volunteers 10; Interns 2.
Governing Authority: private; nonprofit organization. Parent Institution: University City Science Center. Tax-exempt: 501(c)(3).
Art Gallery.
Collections: paintings; sculpture; photography; styles range from realism to abstraction, folk art to traditional.
Research Fields: development of new & creative technologies.
Facilities: library of exhibition catalogues; 60-seat auditorium; 1,000 sq. ft. exhibit space.
Activities: art education programs for students & adults; arranged tours; continuing changing exhibitions by well-known & emerging artists; multicultural exhibitions; Art-in-Science & community service exhibitions; gallery talks; slide & panel discussions; education programs; studio workshops.
Publications: catalogues; brochures.
Hours & Admission Prices: Mon.-Sat. 9-5. No charge; donations accepted. ♿
Attendance: 100,000 (estimated)

THE FABRIC WORKSHOP AND MUSEUM, (M), (I), 1214 Arch St., Philadelphia, PA 19107-2800. Tel.: 215-561-8888. Fax: 215-561-8887.
E-mail: info@fabricworkshopandmuseum.org
Web Site: www.fabricworkshopandmuseum.org
Founded: 1977.
Congressional District: 1
Key Personnel: Artistic Dir. & Founder, Marion Stroud; Pres. (V), Katherine Sokolnikoff; Project Technician, Jenn McTague; Asst. to Directors, Jeffrey Bussmann; Administrative Asst., Meg Baird; Museum Shop Mgr., Tracey Blackman; Project Coord., Andrea Landau; Master Printer & Project Coord., Mary Anne Friel; Videographer, Tyler Henry; Master Printer, Virgil Marti; Project Coord., Nami Yamamoto; Education & Outreach, Sophie Sanders; Education Dept. Coord., Apprentice Coord. & Master Printer,

Christina Roberts; IT Support, Jeremiah Misfeldt; Devel. Officer, Marie Coste; Coord. High School Apprentice, Lucy Lau Bigham.
Personnel Profile: Full-Time Paid 13; Part-Time Paid 7.
Governing Authority: nonprofit organization. Tax-exempt: 501(c)(3).
Contemporary Art Museum & Studio focusing on work in new material & new media.
Collections: contemporary art produced in the Artist-in-Residence program, including print multiples, video, monoprints, sculptural objects, installations, performance costumes, furniture, functional objects, preliminary drawings, paintings, related ceramics & sculpture; photographs; sculpture.
Facilities: 4,500 sq. ft. exhibit space. Museum-related items for sale.
Activities: artist-in-residence program; lectures; guided tours; organized educational programs; loan, temporary & traveling exhibitions; apprentice program; video programs; slide library.
Publications: An Industrious Art: Innovation in Pattern & Print; A Decade of Pattern; Donald Lipski: Who's Afraid of Red, White & Blue; Mel Chin: Soil and Sky; Carrie Mae Weems; Jorge Pardo; Glen Ligon and Gary Simmons; Comfort Zone; New Material as New Media; Lee Bul: Live Forever; On the Wall; Swarm.
Hours & Admission Prices: Mon.-Fri. 10-6, Sat.-Sun. 12-5; groups by appointment. Adults $3; members no charge. Closed federal holidays. ♿
Attendance: 10,000 (estimated)
Membership: Artist $20; Individual $35; Family $45; Patron $100; Sustaining $250; Friend $500; Benefactor $1,000; Director's Circle $2,000.

FAIRMOUNT PARK HORTICULTURE CENTER, 100 N. Horticultural Dr., West Park, Philadelphia, PA 19131. Mailing Address: One Park Way, 10th Fl., 1515 Arch St., Philadelphia, PA 19102-1511. Tel.: 215-685-0096. Fax: 215-685-0103.
Web Site: www.fairmountpark.org/hortcenter.asp
Formerly: The Horticulture Center
Founded: 1979.
Congressional District: 3
Key Personnel: Exec. Dir., Mark A. Focht; Pres., Robert N.C. Nix, III; District Mgr., Lori Hayes.
Personnel Profile: Full-Time Paid 19; Part-Time Volunteers 15.
Governing Authority: municipal. Parent Institution: Fairmount Park Commission. Tax-exempt.
Park Museum.
Collections: trees of Asian & North American origin.
Facilities: greenhouses; 32,000 sq. ft. exhibit space; 75-seat meeting room.
Activities: guided tours; lectures; hobby workshops.
Hours & Admission Prices: Display House: daily 9-3. Donation: adults $2. Grounds: daily 9-5. Closed national holidays. ♿
Attendance: 20,000 (estimated)

FIREMAN'S HALL MUSEUM, (M), 147 N. 2nd St., Philadelphia, PA 19106-2097. Tel.: 215-923-1438. Fax: 215-923-0479.
E-mail: firemus@aol.com
Founded: 1967.
Congressional District: 3
Key Personnel: Pres., Charles M. Lillie; Museum Shop Mgr., Henry J. Magee.
Personnel Profile: Full-Time Paid 1; Part-Time Paid 4; Part-Time Volunteers 14; Interns 1.
Governing Authority: municipal government; nonprofit. Parent Institution: Philadelphia Fire Department; Subsidiary: Philadelphia Fire Department Historical Corp. Tax-exempt.
Fire-Fighting Museum: housed in 1900 Philadelphia firehouse.
Collections: fire-fighting equipment & apparatus; tools; uniforms; prints; photographs; models; fire house furniture; fire marks.
Research Fields: history of fire fighting in Philadelphia & surrounding area.
Facilities: 1,000-vol. library of books, reports, log, ledgers & journals, available for use by public by appointment. Gift items for sale.
Activities: guided tours; lectures; films; organized educational programs.
Hours & Admission Prices: Tues.-Sat. 10-4:30. No charge; donations accepted. Closed city holidays. ♿
Attendance: 20,000
Membership: Individual $20; Family $30; Patron $100; Corporate $250-$5,000.

FORT MIFFLIN ON THE DELAWARE, Fort Mifflin & Hog Island Rds., Philadelphia, PA 19153-3990. Tel.: 215-685-4167. Fax: 215-685-4166.
E-mail: leeanderson@fortmifflin.us
Web Site: www.fortmifflin.us
Founded: 1984.
Congressional District: 1
Key Personnel: C.E.O., F. Traynor Breen; Exec. Dir., Lee Patrick Anderson.
Personnel Profile: Full-Time Paid 3; Part-Time Paid 7; Part-Time Volunteers 200.
Governing Authority: municipal; nonprofit organization. Tax-exempt: 501(c)(3).
Historic Site: 1777 fort.
Collections: 13 historic buildings; dungeons; moat; cannon.
Facilities: 3,000 sq. ft. exhibit space. Gift items for sale.
Activities: guided tours; lectures; weapons demonstrations; organized educational programs; docent program; Soldier Life; Revolutionary War & Civil War interpretation.
Publications: Ft. Mifflin: Valiant Defender; Fort Quarterly.
Hours & Admission Prices: April-Nov. Wed.-Sun. 10-4; other times by appointment. Adults $6, senior $5, children 6-12 $3; discounts to AAA members & groups; members and children 5 & under no charge. ♿
Attendance: 35,000 (accurate)
Membership: Basic $15; Family $25; Donor $50; Defender $100; Patriot $500; Sponsor $1,000.

* **THE FRANKLIN INSTITUTE, (M),** 222 N. 20th St., Philadelphia, PA 19103-1190. Tel.: 215-448-1200. Fax: 215-448-1109.
E-mail: dwint@fi.edu
Web Site: www.fi.edu
Founded: 1824.
Congressional District: 2
Key Personnel: Pres. & C.E.O., Dennis M. Wint, Ph.D.; Chm. (V), Marsha R. Perelman; Sec. Bd. & Vice Pres., Larry Dubinski; Innovation Center, Frederic Bertley, Ph.D.; Sr. Vice Pres. Finance & Administration, Jeff Perkins; Vice Pres. Operations, Richard Rabena; Vice Pres. Exhibit & Program Devel., Steven Snyder, Ph.D.; Vice Pres. Human Resources, Reid Styles; Vice Pres. Franklin Center, Philip Hammer, Ph.D.; Vice Pres. Information Technology, Paul Ricchiuti.
Personnel Profile: Full-Time Paid 148; Part-Time Paid 182; Part-Time Volunteers 351; Interns 18.
Governing Authority: nonprofit organization. Tax-exempt: 501(c)(3).
Science & Technology Museum, Planetarium & Omniverse Theater.
Collections: science; history; industry; technology; transportation; marine; naval; aeronautics; astronomy; space exploration; energy; mathematics; stamps & coins.
Research Fields: education; science; technology.
Facilities: 270-seat auditorium; 140-seat theatre for science demonstrations; 200-seat planetarium; 340-seat omniverse theater; 75-seat discovery theater; children's museum; classrooms; state-of-the-art video conferencing center; Benjamin Franklin National Memorial. Books, educational games & museum-related items for sale.
Activities: lectures; workshops; formally organized education programs for children; films; docent program or council; inter-museum loan, permanent, temporary & traveling exhibitions; traveling science shows; special educational programs with local school districts; museum-to-go; science activity kit & teacher training outreach programs; scout & group camp-in overnight programs.
Publications: bimonthly, Journal of The Franklin Institute; quarterly members' newsletter.
Hours & Admission Prices: Daily 9:30-5. IMAX Theater: Sun.-Thurs. 9:30-6, Fri.-Sat. 9:30-9. Adults $14.75, senior citizens, students & military $13.75, children $12; discounts to AAM members; members no charge. Closed New Year's Day; Thanksgiving; Christmas Eve & Day. ♿
Attendance: 1,000,000 (accurate)
Membership: Student $25; Individual $35; Family $65; Family Max $90; Premier $135.

FRED WOLF, JR. GALLERY/KLEIN BRANCH JEWISH COMMUNITY CENTER, 10100 Jamison Ave., Philadelphia, PA 19116-3832. Tel.: 215-698-7300. Fax: 215-673-7447.
E-mail: pactman@phillyjcc.com
Founded: 1975.
Congressional District: 3
Key Personnel: Dir. Klein Branch, Andre Krug; Co-Chair, Gary B. Freedman; Co-Chair, Max M. Berger; Dir. Art Gallery, Ruth Morley; Dir. Public Rels. & Mktg., Alison Polsky; Security, Ray Graham.
Personnel Profile: Full-Time Paid 1; Part-Time Volunteers 4.
Governing Authority: private; nonprofit Jewish community center. Parent Institution: Jewish Community Centers of Greater Philadelphia, Philadelphia, PA. Tax-exempt: 501(c)(3).
Art and Arts & Crafts Museum.
Collections: Judaic artifacts from the Obermayer collection dating back to the 18th century in the US; prints, paintings, photographs, & sculptures from the early 1900s to the present; millennium exhibit of Judaica.
Facilities: 250-seat auditorium; 150 sq. ft. exhibit space; 400-seat theater; educational facilities; restaurant. Museum-related items for sale.
Activities: lectures; formal education programs for adults; opening receptions; gallery talks; temporary exhibitions.
Publications: newsletter of programs, Impact; catalogue of events, Directions.

Hours & Admission Prices: Mon.-Thurs. 9-9, Fri. & Sun. 9-4. No charge. Closed Jewish holidays. ♿
Attendance: 45,000 (estimated)
Membership: Jewish Community Center: call for fees. Fred Wolf, Jr. Gallery: no charge.

FREE LIBRARY OF PHILADELPHIA RARE BOOK DEPARTMENT, 1901 Vine St., 3rd Fl., Philadelphia, PA 19103-1189. Tel.: 215-686-5416. Fax: 215-563-3628.
E-mail: dewaltj@library.phila.gov
Web Site: www.freelibrary.org
Founded: 1891.
Key Personnel: Dept. Head, Jim DeWalt.
Personnel Profile: Full-Time Paid 5.
Governing Authority: municipal. Tax-exempt: 170(b)(1)(A).
Public Library.
Collections: cuneiform tablets; European & Oriental manuscripts; incunabula; Pennsylvania German fraktur & imprints; early American children's books; Beatrix Potter, Kate Greenaway, Arthur Rackham, Charles Dickens and Palmer Cox collections; Carson collection on the Development of the Common Law; Gimbel collection of works of Edgar Allan Poe; Robert Lawson & Munro Leaf collections; Thornton Oakley collection of Howard Pyle and His Students; Biddle collection of Horace; Elkins collection of Americana and works of Oliver Goldsmith; Strouse collection of Letters of the Presidents; American Sunday School Union collection; Brewster collection of A.B. Frost.
Facilities: reading room; 400-seat auditorium.
Activities: lectures; temporary exhibitions.
Publications: books.
Hours & Admission Prices: Mon.-Fri. 9-5. ♿

THE GALLERIES AT MOORE, (M), 20th St. & The Parkway, Philadelphia, PA 19103. Tel.: 215-965-4027. Fax: 215-568-5921.
E-mail: galleries@moore.edu
Web Site: www.thegalleriesatmoore.org
Formerly: The Goldie Paley Gallery at Moore College of Art and Design
Founded: 1984.
Congressional District: 2
Key Personnel: Dir., Lorie Mertes; Asst. to Dir. & Office Mgr., Gabrielle Lavin.
Personnel Profile: Full-Time Paid 3; Part-Time Paid 6; Part-Time Volunteers 5; Interns 2.
Governing Authority: college. Parent Institution: Moore College of Art and Design. Tax-exempt: 501(c)(3).
Art Gallery.
Collections: paintings; photographs; drawings; sculpture.
Major Exhibits: Philagrafika 2010, 1/10-4/10; NCECA, 3/10-4/10.
Research Fields: paintings; sculpture; graphic design; architecture; photography; outsider art.
Facilities: 50,000-vol. library of visual arts books.
Activities: guided tours; lectures; films; gallery talks; concerts; symposia; workshops; temporary & traveling exhibitions.
Publications: exhibition catalogues.
Hours & Admission Prices: Mon.-Fri. 11-7, Sat. 11-5. No charge; donations accepted. Closed all academic & legal holidays. ♿
Attendance: 49,500 (estimated)
Membership: Basic $75; Contributor $100; Supporter $250; Patron $500; Benefactor $1,000; Director's Circle $2,500; Founder's Circle $5,000.

THE GENEALOGICAL SOCIETY OF PENNSYLVANIA, 1300 Locust St,. 2nd Fl., Philadelphia, PA 19107-5661. Tel.: 215-545-0391. Fax: 215-545-0936.
E-mail: execdir@genpa.org
Web Site: www.genpa.org
Founded: 1892.
Congressional District: 1
Key Personnel: Pres., Claire Keenan Agthe; Administrative Mgr., Joyce Homan.
Personnel Profile: Full-Time Paid 1; Part-Time Paid 2; Part-Time Volunteers 25.
Governing Authority: board of directors. Tax-exempt: 501(c)(3).
Genealogical Society Library.
Collections: genealogies; manuscripts; family, church & civil records.
Facilities: library.
Activities: lectures.
Publications: semiannual magazine, The Pennsylvania Genealogical Magazine; quarterly newsletter, Penn In Hand; 2-3 yearly monographs & special publications.
Hours & Admission Prices: Call for hours. ♿
Attendance: 900 (accurate)
Membership: Student, Teacher & Senior $50; Research $60; Patron $120; Philadelphia $500.

GERMANTOWN HISTORICAL SOCIETY, 5501 Germantown Ave., Philadelphia, PA 19144-2291. Tel.: 215-844-1683. Fax: 215-844-2831.
E-mail: info@germantownhistory.org
Web Site: www.germantownhistory.org
Founded: 1900.
Congressional District: 1
Key Personnel: Site Admin., Laura Beardsley; Librarian & Archivist, Sandra Chaff.
Personnel Profile: Full-Time Paid 1; Part-Time Paid 2; Part-Time Volunteers 30; Interns 2.
Governing Authority: corporation; nonprofit. Tax-exempt.
Local History Museum & Library.
Collections: 17th- to 20th-century artifacts relating to Germantown, Mt. Airy & Chestnut Hill (northwest Philadelphia); decorative arts; costumes; textiles; dolls; toys; household equipment; photographs spanning 300 years of Germantown's history.
Research Fields: genealogy; local railroads; industrial, commercial & architectural history; history of local organizations; gardening.
Facilities: 3,000-vol. library of local historical books; over 5,000 manuscripts, photographs & prints.
Activities: guided tours; lectures; seminars; school programs; facility rental.
Publications: magazine, Germantown Crier; pamphlets; small books on topics of local history; brochures; newsletter, Germantown Now and Then.
Hours & Admission Prices: Tues. 9-1, Thurs. & Sun. 1-5; other times by appointment. Museum: adults $5, seniors & students with ID $4, children under 12 $2. Library & Museum: adults $7.50, students with ID $5; discounts to Philadelphia card, AAM, AAA & ICOM members; members no charge. ♿
Attendance: 4,500 (estimated)
Membership: Individual $30; Household $40; Institution $60; Contributor $100; Sponsor $250; Patron $500; Founders Club $1,000.

GRAND ARMY OF THE REPUBLIC MUSEUM & LIBRARY, 4278 Griscom St., Philadelphia, PA 19124-3954. Tel.: 215-289-6484 & 673-1688.
E-mail: garmuslib@verizon.net
Web Site: www.garmuslib.org
Founded: 1926.
Key Personnel: Dir., Elmer F. Atkinson; Sec., Michael E. Peter.
Personnel Profile: Part-Time Volunteers 20.
Governing Authority: nonprofit organization. Tax-exempt: 501(c)(3).
Civil War Museum: housed in 1796 late Georgian-style house.
Collections: Civil War items, including guns, swords, drums, letters & pictures; war-related books.
Research Fields: Civil War historical & genealogical records.
Facilities: 3,000-vol. library pertaining to the Civil War for research on premises; 4,200 sq. ft. exhibit space.
Activities: guided tours; lectures; loan exhibitions; community outreach programs.
Publications: triannual newsletter.
Hours & Admission Prices: Tues. 12-4, first Sun. of month 12-5; other times by appointment. No charge; donations accepted. ♿
Attendance: 3,200
Membership: Individual $20; Family $30; Colonel's Guard $40; General's Staff $50.

HISTORICAL SOCIETY OF PENNSYLVANIA, 1300 Locust St., Philadelphia, PA 19107-5699. Tel.: 215-732-6200. Fax: 215-732-2680.
E-mail: library@hsp.org
Web Site: www.hsp.org
Founded: 1824.
Congressional District: 1
Key Personnel: Pres., Kim Sajet; Dir. Library, Lee Arnold.
Personnel Profile: Full-Time Paid 26; Part-Time Paid 10; Part-Time Volunteers 7; Interns 7.
Governing Authority: society. Tax-exempt: 501(c)(3).
Historical Research Library.
Collections: 20 million manuscripts, books, prints, drawings, maps & photographs; Balch Institute for Ethnic Studies and The Genealogical Society of Pennsylvania collections.
Research Fields: political, commercial & social history of the American colonies; mid-Atlantic & Southern states prior to the Civil War; Philadelphia, Commonwealth of Pennsylvania & Delaware Valley from colonial period to the present; immigration & ethnic studies.
Facilities: library of nongovernmental repositories of documentary materials

including 560,000 books, 312,000 graphic works, and 19 million manuscripts renowned for its 17th-, 18th- & 20th-century holdings on Philadelphia & southeastern Pennsylvania Collections are used for historical & genealogical research; xerox & photographic services, rights & reproduction services, fee-based research-by-mail services.
Activities: conferences; orientation to research; lectures.
Publications: Guide to the Manuscript Collections of the Historical Society of Pennsylvania; quarterly journal, The Pennsylvania Magazine of History & Biography; magazine, Pennsylvania Legacies; video, All Aboard for Philadelphia; members' newsletter, Sidelights.
Hours & Admission Prices: Tues. & Thurs. 12:30-5:30, Wed. 12:30-8:30, Fri. 10-5:30. Library: adults $6, students w/valid ID $3; 12 free visits for members per year. Closed national holidays. ♿
Attendance: 7,137 (accurate)
Membership: Student, Teacher, & Senior $50; Research $60; Patron $120; Philadelphian $500; Treasures Society $1,000.

* **INDEPENDENCE NATIONAL HISTORICAL PARK, (M),** 143 S. 3rd St., Philadelphia, PA 19106-2818. Tel.: 215-597-8787. Fax: 215-597-5556.
Web Site: www.nps.gov/inde
Founded: 1948.
Congressional District: 3
Key Personnel: Supt., Cynthia MacLeod; Chief Historian, Dr. James Meuller; Chief Cur., Karie Diethorn; Chief Cultural Resources Mgr., Dr. Doris Fanelli; Archivist, Karen D. Stevens; Chief Architect, Charles Tonetti; Chief of Interpretation, Steve Sitarski; Public Affairs Officer, Jane Cowley.
Personnel Profile: Full-Time Paid 216; Part-Time Paid 22; Part-Time Volunteers 57; Interns 2.
Governing Authority: federal. Parent Institution: National Park Service. Tax-exempt.
General Museum.
Collections: decorative arts; history; archaeology; American portraits from 1770-1830 by Peale, Sharples, West, Sully, Pine; 18th century American period furnishings; objects and documents relating to Independence Hall, Congress Hall; personal memorabilia relating to Revolution and early Federal period; archives; military; graphics. Historic Buildings and Sites: 1732-1800 Independence Hall; Liberty Bell Pavilion; 1790-1800 Congress Hall; 1791-1800 Old City Hall; Second Bank Portrait Gallery; 1722-1790 Franklin Court; 1787-1836 Bishop White House; 1791-1793 Todd House; 1774-1800 City Tavern; 1775-1805 New Hall Military Museum; 1797-1798 Kosciuszko House; 1777 Graff House; 1772-1794 Deshler-Morris House.
Research Fields: decorative arts; history.
Facilities: 6,000-vol. library of books, manuscripts & microfilm relating to Parks historic period available for inter-library loan and upon written request.
Activities: guided tours; off-site lectures; formally organized education programs for children; inter-museum loan, permanent & temporary exhibitions.
Publications: book, Treasures of Independence.
Hours & Admission Prices: Daily 9-5. Independence Hall: 8:30-6; tour ticket required. ♿
Attendance: 5,500,000 (accurate)

* **INDEPENDENCE SEAPORT MUSEUM, (M),** Penn's Landing Waterfront, 211 S. Columbus Blvd. at Walnut St., Philadelphia, PA 19106-3101. Tel.: 215-413-8655. Fax: 215-925-6713.
Web Site: www.phillyseaport.org
Founded: 1960.
Congressional District: 1
Key Personnel: Pres. & Dir., Lori Dillard Rech; Chm. (V), Peter McCausland; Coord. Devel. & Membership, Alexis Jeffcoat; Cur., Craig Bruns; Dir. Communication, Michele D. Girolamo; Librarian, Matt Herbison; Visitor Svcs. Mgr., Shonda Woods.
Personnel Profile: Full-Time Paid 23; Part-Time Paid 19; Part-Time Volunteers 40; Interns 36.
Governing Authority: nonprofit organization. Tax-exempt: 501(c)(3).
Maritime Museum.
Collections: USS Olympia; USS Becuna; ship models; historic small boats; figureheads; paintings; prints; drawings; weapons; memorabilia & artifacts related to ships & the sea; manuscripts; photographs; textiles.
Research Fields: maritime history with emphasis on Delaware Bay, River & tributaries.
Facilities: 10,000-vol. library available by appointment only; 530-seat concert hall. Museum-related items for sale.
Activities: lectures; films; permanent, temporary & traveling interactive exhibitions; boat conservation; boat building classes; inter-museum loans; community school & family.
Publications: newsletter, Masthead; Challenger Sketchbook; American Naval Broadsides; The Delaware Bay and River Defense of Philadelphia 1775-1777; George Robert Bonfield Marine Painter 1805-1898; The Titanic & Her Era; The Empress of China; Philadelphia on the River; The Tale of the Mermaid; Gone Fishing; Ironclad Intruder: U.S.S. MONITOR; Commerce & the Constitution; Marine Art & Antiques/Jack Tar/A Sailor's Life, 1750-1910; A Yachtsman's Eye/The Glen S. Foster Collection of Marine Paintings.
Hours & Admission Prices: Daily 10-5. Museum & Historic Ships: adults $12, seniors 65 & over $10, children, students & military $7; discounts to AAM, AAA & ICOM members, active military & groups of 10 or more; members & children under 2 no charge. Closed New Year's Day; Thanksgiving; Christmas. ♿
Attendance: 88,570 (accurate)
Membership: Individual $35; Family $45; Individual Plus & Family Plus $75; Navigator $150; First Mate $300; Pilot $500; Seaport Society $1,000-$5,000.

INSTITUTE OF CONTEMPORARY ART, UNIVERSITY OF PENNSYLVANIA, 118 S. 36th St., Philadelphia, PA 19104-3289. Tel.: 215-898-7108 & 5911. Fax: 215-898-5050.
E-mail: info@icaphila.org
Web Site: www.icaphila.org
Founded: 1963.
Congressional District: 1
Key Personnel: Dir., Claudia Gould; Senior Cur., Ingrid Schaffner; Curatorial Asst., Kate Kraczon; Asst. Cur., Jenelle Porter; Chief Devel. Officer, Marilyn Pollick; Business Admin., Mary Jo Ward; Dir. Mktg. & Communications, Jill Katz; Exhibitions Coord. & Registrar, Robert Chaney; Preparator, Shannon Bowser; Customer Svc. & Education Asst., William Hidalgo.
Personnel Profile: Full-Time Paid 15; Part-Time Paid 3; Interns 8.
Governing Authority: university. Tax-exempt.
Contemporary Art Gallery.
Collections: works by contemporary artists.
Major Exhibits: Maira Kalman - Exaltations Observations (T), 1/14/10-6/6/10; Queer Voice, 4/22/10-8/1/10.
Research Fields: contemporary art.
Facilities: archives of statements & notes by artists exhibited at ICA; Philadelphia artists registry; videotapes archives; auditorium.
Activities: public programs; readings; lectures; symposia; performances; films & videos.
Publications: exhibition catalogues; brochures; newsletters; limited art editions made specifically for the ICA.
Hours & Admission Prices: Wed.-Fri. 12-8, Sat.-Sun. 11-5. No charge; donations accepted. Closed New Year's Day; Easter; Thanksgiving; Christmas. ♿
Attendance: 21,000 (accurate)
Membership: Individual $40; Dual/Family $100; Contributor $250; Participant $500; Leadership Circle Benefactor $1,000; Director's Circle $2,500; Sustainer $5,000.

JOHNSON HOUSE UNDERGROUND RAILROAD MUSEUM, 6306 Germantown Ave., Philadelphia, PA 19144-1908. Tel.: 215-438-1768.
Historic House: built c.1768. Listed on the National Register of Historic Places.
Collections: local history & culture; period furnishings; photographs; personal artifacts.
Activities: educational programs; workshops.
Hours & Admission Prices: Thurs.-Fri. 10-4 by appointment, Sat. 1-4.

LA SALLE UNIVERSITY ART MUSEUM, (M), 1900 W. Olney Ave., Philadelphia, PA 19141-1199. Tel.: 215-951-1221. Fax: 215-951-5096.
E-mail: vendelin@lasalle.edu
Web Site: www.lasalle.edu/museum
Founded: 1975.
Congressional District: 1
Key Personnel: Dir. & Chief Cur., Madeleine Viljoen; Chm. (V), William E. Kelly, Jr.; Asst. Cur. Education, Miranda Clark-Binder; Asst. Cur. Art, Carmen Vendelin.
Personnel Profile: Full-Time Paid 4.
Governing Authority: university. A branch of La Salle University. Tax-exempt: 75243239.
Art Museum.
Collections: European & American 15th- to 20th-century paintings, drawings, watercolors, prints; sculpture; Japanese prints; African sculpture; ancient Greek terra-cotta vessels & Tanagra figurines; Pre-Columbian terra-cotta vessels.
Major Exhibits: Li Qin Tan, 1/10-2/10; Charles Willson Peale and His Family at Belfield, 3/10-4/10; Moe Brooker, 5/10-7/10; Faculty Art Exhibition, 8/30/10-9/12/10; Sidney Goodman, 9/10-12/10.
Activities: gallery talks; tours; temporary & special exhibitions; concerts; lectures; K-12 educational programming.

Publications: exhibit publications, LaSalle University Art Museum: Guide to the Collection (2002); survey.
Hours & Admission Prices: Mon.-Fri. 10-4, Sun. 2-4. Regular Tour: no charge; donations accepted. ♿
Attendance: 5,377 (accurate)
Membership: Hierarchy of Angels: Angels $25; Archangels $50; Principalities $75; Virtues $100; Powers $250; Dominations $500; Thrones $750; Cherubim $1,000; Seraphim $2,500 & up.

LEMON HILL MANSION, Lemon Hill & Sedgeley Dr., E., Fairmont Park, Philadelphia, PA 19130. Mailing Address: Colonial Dames of America, 303 W. Lancaster Ave., PMB 139, Wayne, PA 19087-3938. Tel.: 215-232-4337. Fax: 215-646-8472.
E-mail: epenniman149@gmail.com
Web Site: www.lemonhill.org
Founded: 1800.
Congressional District: 2
Key Personnel: Chm., Eleanor Penniman; Dir., Joyce Jones.
Personnel Profile: Part-Time Paid 1; Part-Time Volunteers 150.
Governing Authority: nonprofit organization. Affiliated with Colonial Dames of America, 421 E. 61st St., New York, NY 10021. Tax-exempt: 501(c)(3).
Historic House & Site: c.1800 Lemon Hill Mansion built by Henry Pratt on land that had belonged to Robert Morris.
Collections: 1800-1836 decorative arts & furnishings.
Activities: guided tours; lectures; permanent & temporary exhibitions.
Publications: The Diary of Harriet Manigault, 1813-16; brochure; postcard.
Hours & Admission Prices: April-Dec. Wed.-Sun. 10-4; other times by appointment. Adults $5, students & senior citizens 60 and over $3.
Attendance: 10,000 (estimated)
Membership: Friends of Lemon Hill: $35-$1,000.

LIBRARY COMPANY OF PHILADELPHIA, 1314 Locust St., Philadelphia, PA 19107-5698. Tel.: 215-546-3181. Fax: 215-546-5167.
E-mail: cking@librarycompany.org
Web Site: www.librarycompany.org
Founded: 1731.
Congressional District: 1
Key Personnel: Dir., John C. Van Horne; Pres. (V), Beatrice W.B. Garvan; Librarian, James N. Green; Cur. Prints, Sarah Weatherwax; Chief Conservation, Jennifer Woods Rosner; Chief Reference, Cornelia S. King; Chief Cataloguer & Systems Librarian, Ruth I. Hughes; Cur. Printed Books, Rachel D'Agostino.
Personnel Profile: Full-Time Paid 14; Part-Time Paid 9; Part-Time Volunteers 5; Interns 2.
Governing Authority: nonprofit organization. Tax-exempt: 170(b)(1)(A) & 501(c)(3).
Library of Rare Books.
Collections: libraries of James Logan, Benjamin Rush, William Byrd & Benjamin Franklin; books printed in or available in America before 1860; broadsides, manuscripts, newspapers, pamphlets & periodicals printed in & around Philadelphia; pamphlets of the American Revolution, Federal & Jacksonian Periods, and the Civil War; history of women, particularly of the 19th century; Afro-Americana; American Judaica; prints & photos of Philadelphia; 16th- & 17th-century European science, literature, history, classical language & religion books; paintings; sculpture; furniture.
Major Exhibits: Philadelphia on Stone, 3/10-10/10.
Research Fields: American & Anglo-American history to 1860; African American history; medical history; American architectural history; early American graphic arts; early American photography; American imprints; women's history, particularly 19th century.
Facilities: 500,000-vol. library of American history & literature, Afro-American history & other reference volumes for use by public for research on premises; works printed after 1880 available for inter-library loan; print department with 75,000 graphic items; reading rooms.
Activities: lectures; guided tours by appointment; permanent & temporary exhibitions; public programs; fellowship program.
Publications: Annual Report of the Library Company; public exhibition catalogs & special publications; newsletter.
Hours & Admission Prices: Mon.-Fri. 9-4:45. No charge. Closed major holidays. ♿
Attendance: 6,018 (accurate)
Membership: Friend $50; Shareholder $200 (one-time investment; dues $50 a year).

MARIO LANZA INSTITUTE/MUSEUM, 712 Montrose St., Philadelphia, PA 19147-3944. Mailing Address: P.O. Box 54624, Philadelphia, PA 19148-0624. Tel.: 215-238-9691. Fax: 215-238-9694.
E-mail: mariolanzamuseum@aol.com
Web Site: www.mario-lanza-institute.org
Founded: 1962.
Congressional District: 1
Key Personnel: Pres., Mary Galanti Papola; Publicity Dir., Vice Pres. & Sec., Bill Ronayne; Treas., Jeanette Frese; Bd. Member, Frank Briatico; Bd. Member, Alfred Gagliardi; Legal Counsel, Joseph Caruso, Esq.
Personnel Profile: Full-Time Volunteers 3; Part-Time Volunteers 1.
Governing Authority: private; nonprofit organization. Parent Institution: Mario Lanza Institute. Tax-exempt: 501(c)(3).
Specialized Museum: one block from museum is the Mario Lanza Birthplace.
Collections: concentration on Mario Lanza; film-related memorabilia; private photographs, movie stills & posters; private audio recordings; video movie & TV programming; commercial records, compact discs & cassette tapes; paintings; biographies; newsletters; costumes.
Research Fields: biographical & recordings.
Facilities: 40-vol. library of ball fundraising events, clippings & photographs; 1,000 sq. ft. exhibit space. Museum-related items for sale.
Activities: concerts; films; guided tours. Annual Events: Mario Lanza Ball; Spring Recital.
Publications: brochure; catalog; articles; newsletter.
Hours & Admission Prices: Mon.-Sat. 11-3. No charge; donations accepted.
Attendance: 2,500 (estimated)
Membership: Call for information.

MARVIN SAMSON CENTER FOR HISTORY OF PHARMACY/USP MUSEUM, 600 S. 43rd St., Philadelphia, PA 19104-4418. Tel.: 215-596-8721. Fax: 215-895-1113.
Web Site: www.usp.edu/museum
Founded: 1995.
Key Personnel: Dir. & Cur., Michael Brody
Pharmacy Museum.
Collections: history of pharmacy.
Hours & Admission Prices: Call for hours. No charge.
Attendance: 5,000

THE MASONIC LIBRARY AND MUSEUM OF PENNSYLVANIA, (M), Masonic Temple, One N. Broad St., Philadelphia, PA 19107-2520. Tel.: 215-988-1909 & 1900. Fax: 215-988-1953.
E-mail: azfrederick@pagrandlodge.org
Web Site: www.pagrandlodge.org
Founded: 1731.
Congressional District: 2
Key Personnel: Exec. Dir., Andrew A. Zellers-Frederick; Librarian, Glenys A. Waldman; Asst. Librarian, Catherine L. Giaimo; Cur., Dennis P. Buttleman, Jr.; Museum Shop Mgr., Carole Alpe.
Personnel Profile: Full-Time Paid 39; Part-Time Paid 2; Part-Time Volunteers 10.
Governing Authority: society. Parent Institution: Grand Lodge F. & A.M. of Pennsylvania. Tax-exempt.
History Museum: housed in c.1873 Masonic Temple.
Collections: historic Masonic objects; jewels; textiles; ceramics; glass; documents; books; prints.
Research Fields: history of Freemasonry; Pennsylvania Freemasonry; Masonic & fraternal symbolism & mysticism; religion; philosophy.
Facilities: 70,000-vol. library available to the public; building available for rental. Masonic books & other museum-related items for sale.
Activities: guided tours; temporary & permanent exhibitions.
Publications: quarterly magazine, The Pennsylvania Freemason.
Hours & Admission Prices: Tues.-Fri. 9-5, Sat. 9-12; other times by appointment. Admission $8, members $5; discounts to AAM members. Closed national holidays. ♿
Attendance: 30,000 (estimated)
Membership: Member $30; Fellow $100; Benefactor $1,000.

* **MORRIS ARBORETUM OF THE UNIVERSITY OF PENNSYLVANIA,** 100 E. Northwestern Ave., Philadelphia, PA 19118-2697. Tel.: 215-247-5777. Fax: 215-248-4439.
E-mail: cranesj@upenn.edu
Web Site: www.morrisarboretum.org
Formerly: The Gardens at Morris Arboretum
Founded: 1933.
Congressional District: 2
Key Personnel: Dir., Paul W. Meyer; Dir. Facilities & Finance, Kevin Schrecengost; Dir. Botany, Dr. Timothy Block; Dir. Mktg., Susan Crane; Dir. Public Programs, Robert Gutowski; Museum Shop Mgr., Adele Waerig.
Personnel Profile: Full-Time Paid 34; Part-Time Paid 15; Part-Time Volunteers 530; Interns 9.
Governing Authority: college. Parent Institution: University of Pennsylvania. Tax-exempt.
Arboretum.
Collections: mature specimens of native & introduced woody plants in landscape setting; herbarium; tropical fernery; modern sculpture.

Major Exhibits: Patrick Dougherty's The Summer Palace, 11/09-12/10.
Research Fields: adaptability of trees to urban sites; flora of Pennsylvania; plant introduction & evaluation; micro propagation research; bioassays of the living collection; integrated pest management.
Facilities: library; historic 166-acre arboretum; greenhouses; specialty gardens; herbarium; education center; plant pathology lab.
Activities: guided tours; lectures; educational programs; research programs; Center for Urban Forestry; permanent exhibits; special programs; seed exchange. Annual Events: Garden Railway late May to mid-October; Holiday Garden Railway late November to December.
Publications: quarterly newsletter; seed exchange list; interpretive brochures; annual report.
Hours & Admission Prices: April-Oct. Mon.-Fri. 10-4, Sat.-Sun. 10-5; Nov.-March 10-4 daily. Adults $14, senior citizens $12, students & youth 3-18 $7; discounts to PHS, AAA, WHYY, WXPN, PCVB members and Penn students, staff, & alumni; members no charge. Closed New Year's Day; Thanksgiving; Christmas Eve & Day. ♿
Attendance: 96,366 (accurate)
Membership: Far Away Friends $40; Individual $55; Dual $65; Regular Family $75; Beech $95; Chestnut $150; Holly $250; Oak $500; Laurel $1,000; Katsura $2,500.

THE MUSEUM OF NURSING HISTORY, INC., U.S. Rte. 1, Roosevelt Ave. & Adams Ave., Philadelphia, PA 19107. Mailing Address: 761 Sproul Road, #299, Springfield, PA 19064-1215. Tel.: 215-829-3971.
E-mail: sdavis10@earthlink.net
Web Site: www.nursinghistory.org
Founded: 1976.
Key Personnel: Pres. & Nurse Historian, Dr. Sandra Davis; Founder & Dir. Emeritus, Joan T. Large; Treas., Nancy J. Scheutz.
Personnel Profile: Part-Time Volunteers 15.
Governing Authority: volunteer board of directors. Tax-exempt: 501(c)(3).
Nursing History: located in Pennsylvania Hospital, the first hospital in the U.S. (1751).
Collections: nursing memorabilia from 1860-1960 with emphasis on nurses & nursing in Pennsylvania; military nurses uniform.
Research Fields: nurses & nursing in Pennsylvania, 1860-1960; nursing texts, biographies, papers & reports.
Facilities: 200-vol. library on nursing; 250-seat theater; 800 sq. ft. exhibit space.
Activities: formal education programs for all area nursing schools. Annual Events: Fall Educational Program; Spring Historical Presentation.
Publications: biannual newsletter, The Museum Muse.
Hours & Admission Prices: Mon.-Fri. 9-5, special arrangements for group tours. No charge.
Attendance: 120 (estimated)
Membership: Student & Retired $15; Individual $35; Organization $100; Patron $150 & up; Life $500.

MUTTER MUSEUM, COLLEGE OF PHYSICIANS OF PHILADELPHIA, (M), 19 S. 22nd St., Philadelphia, PA 19103-3097. Tel.: 215-563-3737, ext. 273. Fax: 215-561-6477.
Web Site: www.collphyphil.org
Founded: 1863.
Congressional District: 2
Key Personnel: Dir., Robert Hicks; C.E.O. College of Physicians of Philadelphia, George Wohlreich; Cur., Anna N. Dhody.
Personnel Profile: Full-Time Paid 4; Part-Time Volunteers 20; Interns 2.
Governing Authority: nonprofit organization. Parent Institution: College of Physicians of Philadelphia. Tax-exempt: 501(c)(3).
Medical Museum.
Collections: human anatomy & pathology; medical history & biography; development of medical instrumentation; development of fetus & anomalies; folklore; quackery; military medicine; nursing & apothecary artifacts; memorabilia of physicians; period medical items; oil portraits; prints; photographs; sculpture.
Research Fields: medical history & biography; pathology of bone & tissue; paleopathology; physical anthropology; biology; anatomy; military medicine; folklore; genetic defects; teratology; anomalies; medical specialties & instrumentation; medical art illustration.
Facilities: reference library with medical journals, documentation & bibliographic services available for inter-library use; herb garden; meeting rooms; audiovisual equipment. Reprints, slides, photographs of collections for sale.
Activities: audio guide; guided tours; lectures by appointment; permanent & temporary exhibits.
Publications: quarterly journal; Transactions & Studies of the College of Physicians of Philadelphia.
Hours & Admission Prices: Library: Tues.-Thurs. 10-4 by appointment. Museum: daily 10-5. Adults $14, senior citizens 65 & up, college students with I.D. & children 6-18 $10; discounts to groups, AAM & ICOM members; children under 6 no charge. Closed New Year's Day; Thanksgiving; Christmas Eve & Day. ♿
Attendance: 104,086 (accurate)
Membership: Non-Resident Fellows $200; Fellows of College (elected) $275; Resident Fellows $350.

NAOMI WOOD COLLECTION AT WOODFORD MANSION, 33rd & Dauphin St., E. Fairmount Park, Philadelphia, PA 19132. Tel.: 215-229-6115.
Web Site: woodfordmansion.org
Founded: 1926.
Key Personnel: Co-Trustee, Lawrence H. Berger; Co-Trustee, Mellon Bank; Site Mgr., Martha Moffat.
Personnel Profile: Full-Time Paid 1; Part-Time Paid 6; Part-Time Volunteers 30.
Governing Authority: nonprofit organization. Tax-exempt.
Historic House Museum: 1756 Woodford Mansion.
Collections: decorative arts; English Delftware; Colonial Philadelphia & American furnishings; pewter; silver; needlework; portraits.
Activities: guided tours. Annual Event: Holiday Tours in December.
Publications: book, The Story of The Naomi Wood Collection and Woodford Mansion.
Hours & Admission Prices: Tues.-Sun. 10-4. Adults $5, senior citizens $3, children $2. Closed major holidays.
Attendance: 5,000 (estimated)

NATIONAL ARCHIVES AND RECORDS ADMINISTRATION - MID-ATLANTIC REGION, (M), Chestnut St., between 9th & 10th Sts., Philadelphia, PA 19107-4292. Mailing Address: 900 Market St., Philadelphia, PA 19107-4228. Tel.: 215-606-0112 & 0100. Fax: 215-606-0116.
E-mail: philadelphia.archives@nara.gov
Web Site: www.archives.gov/midatlantic
Founded: 1934.
Congressional District: 1
Key Personnel: Regl. Admin., V. Chapman-Smith; Rgnl. Archives Dir., Leslie Simon; Asst. Rgnl. Admin., David Roland.
Personnel Profile: Full-Time Paid 8; Part-Time Paid 1; Part-Time Volunteers 12; Interns 5.
Governing Authority: federal government. Parent Institution: National Archives & Records Administration, Washington D.C. Tax-exempt.
Archives: housed in 1938 Works Project Administration Construction building.
Collections: photographs, documents & artifacts related to cultural, social, political & economic history of the Federal Government; Federal Government activities in the Mid-Atlantic region; archives; 1790-1965, documents, drawings & photographs; East Coast lighthouse drawings; records of Federal agencies & courts in Delaware, Maryland, Pennsylvania, Virginia & West Virginia.
Research Fields: Federal records; Chinese immigration & exclusion laws; Civil War; Confederate blockade running; patent materials; 19th-century military & federal arsenals; U.S. census; immigration & naturalization; Federal Court records; U.S. mint records; U.S. Corp. of Engineers; African-American history; women's history.
Facilities: 500-vol. guide to the archives; archives available for use by public; research & reference rooms; classroom; conference room; field research station; 600 sq. ft. exhibit space. Gift items for sale.
Activities: guided tours; lectures; films; organized education programs for children, adults & undergraduate or graduate college students; participatory, loan, temporary & traveling exhibitions; National History Day local coordinator.
Publications: periodic guides to various collections; periodical, Guide to Records in the National Archives-Mid Atlantic Region; exhibition catalogs.
Hours & Admission Prices: Mon.-Fri. 8-5, 2nd Sat. of month 8-4. No charge; donations accepted. Closed federal holidays. ♿
Attendance: 12,000 (accurate)

NATIONAL CONSTITUTION CENTER, (M), 525 Arch St., Independence Mall, Philadelphia, PA 19106-1595. Tel.: 866-917-1787; 215-409-6600.
Web Site: www.constitutioncenter.org
Key Personnel: Pres. & C.E.O., Linda E. Johnson; Sr. Public Rels. Mgr., Ashley Berke
History Museum.
Collections: the Constitution & its history; photographs.
Activities: special events.
Hours & Admission Prices: Mon.-Fri. 9:30-5, Sat. 9:30-6, Sun. 12-5. Adults $12, senior citizens 65 & over $11, children 4-12 $8; military & children under 4 no charge.

NATIONAL LIBERTY MUSEUM, 321 Chestnut St., Philadelphia, PA 19106-2707. Tel.: 215-925-2800. Fax: 215-925-3800.
E-mail: jgriesemer@libertymuseum.org

Web Site: www.libertymuseum.org
Founded: 2000.
Key Personnel: C.E.O. & Vice Pres., Gwen Borowsky; Founder & Chm. (V), Irvin J. Borowsky; Pres. (V), Douglas Tozour; Controller, Ronald Kroes; Devel., Sandra Kelly; Devel., Paggy Sweeney; Devel., Joanne Hirsh; Dir. Programs, Kevin O'Rangers; Mktg., Sherry Hawk; Public Rels., Jan Griesemer; Mktg., Bob Hawk; Museum Shop Mgr., Leroy Ford.
Personnel Profile: Full-Time Paid 24; Full-Time Volunteers 1; Part-Time Paid 7; Part-Time Volunteers 10.
Governing Authority: private; nonprofit organization. Tax-exempt: 501(c)(3).
Art Museum.
Collections: glass sculptures; film; artwork.
Facilities: education center; 30,000 sq. ft. exhibit space. Museum-related items for sale.
Activities: docent program; films; guided tours; participatory exhibits. Annual Events: Glass Weekend - includes dinner, auction & view of private collections; Heroes of Liberty dinner; Police & Firefighters awards of valor; International Interfaith awards; Inspirations award; Young Heroes award.
Publications: newsletters, National Liberty Museum; Coalition of Collectors and Artists; book, Heroes of Liberty From Around the World.
Hours & Admission Prices: Summer: daily 10-5. Sept.-June Tues.-Sun. 10-5. Adults $7, seniors $6, students $5; scheduled tours, members & Sunday no charge. Closed Christmas. ♿
Attendance: 62,000 (estimated)
Membership: Individual $35; Family $60; Committee to Difuse Violence $100; Supporters of Freedom $250; Liberty Circle $500; Founder's Committee $1,000; Wall of Honor Circle & Major Donor $10,000 & up.

NATIONAL MUSEUM OF AMERICAN JEWISH HISTORY, (M), Independence Mall East, 55 N. 5th St., Philadelphia, PA 19106-2197. Tel.: 215-923-3811. Fax: 215-923-0763.
E-mail: nmajh@nmajh.org
Web Site: www.nmajh.org
Founded: 1976.
Congressional District: 1
Key Personnel: Pres. & C.E.O., Michael Rosenzweig; Co-Chm., George M. Ross; Co-Chm., Ronald Rubin; Dir. Finance, Maureen Brusca; Deputy Dir. Programming & Museum Historian, Josh Perelman; Dir. Public Rels., Jay Nachman; Education Project Coord., Robert Levin; Museum Shop Mgr., Elaine Silverman; Museum Shop Mgr., Eva Schlanger.
Personnel Profile: Full-Time Paid 25; Part-Time Paid 6; Part-Time Volunteers 85; Interns 1.
Governing Authority: nonprofit. Tax-exempt: 501(c)(3).
Social & Ethnic History Museum: located on Independence Mall.
Collections: artifacts reflect the occupational, domestic, communal & religious aspects of Jewish life in America from Colonial times to the present.
Research Fields: History of Jews & Judaism in America.
Facilities: 1,500-vol. library of monographs & reference works on American Jewish history, books, pamphlets & other printed primary source material available to scholars & interested researchers with permission of the registrar; auditorium; classrooms; theater in gallery; film library focusing on American Jewish contributions to the cinema and American Jewish history. Books on American Jewish life & history, ceremonial objects, photos, graphics & reproductions of historical artifacts for sale.
Activities: guided tours; lectures; films; gallery talks; concerts; docent program or council; loan, permanent & temporary exhibitions.
Publications: newsletter; exhibition catalogs.
Hours & Admission Prices: Mon.-Thurs. 10-5, Fri. 10-3, Sun. 12-5. No charge; donations accepted. Closed New Year's Day; Memorial Day; Independence Day; Labor Day; Thanksgiving; major Jewish holidays & festivals. ♿
Attendance: 25,000 (accurate)
Membership: Student & Senior $20; Senior Couple $25; Individual $35; Couple $40; Family $60; Friends Circle Supporter $150; Friends Circle $300; Friends Sponsor $500; Friends Circle Benefactor $1,000.

PAINTED BRIDE ART CENTER, 230 Vine St., Philadelphia, PA 19106-1293. Tel.: 215-925-9914. Fax: 215-925-7402.
E-mail: info@paintedbride.org
Web Site: paintedbride.org
Key Personnel: Exec. Dir., Laurel Raczka; Assoc. Dir., Lisa Nelson-Haynes
Art Center.
Collections: works by local, national & international artists.
Facilities: performing arts theater.
Activities: performances.
Hours & Admission Prices: Tues.-Sat. 12-6 & during performances.

∗ **PENNSYLVANIA ACADEMY OF THE FINE ARTS, (M),** 128 N. Broad St., Philadelphia, PA 19102-1424. Tel.: 215-972-7600 & 7642. Fax: 215-972-5564, 567-2429 & 569-0153.
E-mail: pafa@pafa.org
Web Site: www.pafa.org
Founded: 1805.
Congressional District: 2
Key Personnel: Chm. (V), Donald R. Caldwell; Pres. & C.E.O., Edward T. Lewis; Edna S. Tuttleman Museum Dir., David R. Brigham; Sr. Vice Pres. Human Resources & Administration, Leslie Moody; Sr. Vice Pres. Mktg. & Communications, Marsha Braverman; Sr. Vice Pres. Devel., Louisa Hanshew; Mgr. Rights & Reproductions, Barbara Katus; Sr. Registrar, Gale Rawson; Assoc. Registrar, Robert Harman; Archivist, Cheryl Leibold; Cur. Contemporary Art, Julien Robson; Cur. Modern Art, Robert Cozzolino; Chief Conservator, Aella Diamantopoulos; Museum Shop Mgr., Mark De Lelys; Cur. Historical American Art, Anna Marley; Dir. Public Programs, Judy Ringold.
Personnel Profile: Full-Time Paid 66; Part-Time Paid 5; Part-Time Volunteers 60; Interns 5.
Governing Authority: nonprofit. Tax-exempt: 501(c)(3).
Art Museum & School: housed in 1876 Centennial building designed by Furness & Hewitt.
Collections: 18th- to 21st-century American paintings, drawings, sculpture & prints; works by Washington Allston, Benjamin West, the Peale Family, Gilbert Stuart, Thomas Sully, William Rush, William Sidney Mount, Thomas Eakins, Winslow Homer, Edward Hopper, Childe Hassam, Arthur B. Carles, Robert Henri, Cecilia Beaux, Horace Pippin, William Bailey, Alex Katz, William Merritt Chase, Richard Diebenkorn, Jacob Lawrence, Robert Motherwell, Sidney Goodman & Mary Frank.
Major Exhibits: Philagrafika: The Graphic Unconscious Prints at the Core of Contemporary Artistic Production, 1/27/10-4/11/10; 109th Annual Student Exhibition, 5/15/10-6/6/10.
Research Fields: American painting; sculpture; works on paper; architecture; archives.
Facilities: 9,000-vol. library of visual arts & Academy's archives open to public for reference by appointment; 130-seat auditorium; classrooms; cafe. Catalogs, books, jewelry, postcards, posters & other museum-related items for sale.
Activities: guided tours; lectures; permanent collection; studio classes; temporary & inter-museum traveling exhibitions; symposia; loan program.
Publications: exhibition catalogues; newsletter; brochures; quarterly magazine; annual report.
Hours & Admission Prices: Tues.-Sat. 10-5, Sun. 11-5. Permanent Collection: adults $10, senior citizens & students with ID $8, youth 5-18 $6; discounts to AAM & ICOM members; members no charge. Permanent & Special Exhibitions: adults $15, seniors & students with ID $12, youth 5-18 $10. Closed major holidays. ♿
Attendance: 37,787 (accurate)
Membership: Student $20; National $30; Individual $50; Young Friends $60; Family $75; Alumni Circle $100; Friend $150; Patron $300; Potamkin Society Young Collector's Under 40 $350; Benefactor $500; Potamkin Collector's Society $750; Potamin Collector's Society Connoisseur $5,000; Charles Willson Peale Society $1,000-$2,499; Mary Cassatt Circle $2,500-$4,999; Thomas Eakins Circle $5,000-$9,999; President's Circle $10,000-$24,999; Chairman's Circle $25,000 & up.

THE PHILADELPHIA ART ALLIANCE, 251 S. 18th St., Philadelphia, PA 19103-6168. Tel.: 215-545-4302. Fax: 215-545-0767.
E-mail: info@philartalliance.org
Web Site: www.philartalliance.org
Founded: 1915.
Congressional District: 2
Key Personnel: Exec. Dir., Gay Walling; Pres. (V), Carole Shanis; Dir. Exhibitions, Melissa Caldwell; Dir. Devel., Michael Burri; Dir. Programs, Alex Styer; Coord. Membership, Christine Manturuk; Receptionist, Joe Patterson.
Personnel Profile: Full-Time Paid 6; Part-Time Paid 3; Part-Time Volunteers 12; Interns 2.
Governing Authority: nonprofit organization. Tax-exempt: 501(c)(3).
Multi-Disciplinary Arts Center: housed in c.1906 home, designed by Klauder of the architectural firm Day & Klauder; located on Rittenhouse Square.
Collections: craft; drawings; paintings; prints; photography.
Activities: contemporary visual arts exhibitions program; guided tours; lectures; gallery talks; concerts; readings of screen plays; poetry readings; book launchings & signings; temporary exhibitions.
Publications: newsletter; exhibition catalogs.
Hours & Admission Prices: Tues.-Sun. 11-5. Adults $5, seniors $3; members no charge. Closed national holidays.
Attendance: 20,000 (estimated)

Membership: Student $35; Artist $45; Young Friend $50; Friend $75; Household $100; Patron $250; Benefactor $500; Wetherill $1,000.

PHILADELPHIA MUMMERS MUSEUM, 1100 South 2nd St., Philadelphia, PA 19147-5497. Tel.: 215-336-3050. Fax: 215-389-5630.
E-mail: mummersmus@aol.com
Web Site: www.mummersmuseum.org
Founded: 1976.
Congressional District: 1
Key Personnel: Exec. Dir., Palma B. Lucas; Pres., John Millaway; Cur. & Library Coord., Jack Cohen; Museum Shop Mgr., Eileen Garbarino.
Personnel Profile: Full-Time Paid 2; Full-Time Volunteers 1; Part-Time Paid 7; Part-Time Volunteers 30.
Governing Authority: municipal; nonprofit organization. Parent Institution: New Year's Shooters & Mummers Museum, Inc. Tax-exempt: 501(c)(3).
Audio-Visual Film & Costume Museum: located on 1600-1800s site of original route of Mummers.
Collections: memorabilia of Philadelphia Mummers including comic, fancy brigade & string band divisions; Mummer suits of present & past years; photographs of Mummers & past parades; ornamental organizational badges; video tapes & films of past and present parades; special events with Philadelphia Mummers as the main theme.
Research Fields: Philadelphia Mummery.
Facilities: library of past parade program books, old photographs, films, slides, recordings & tape interviews with veteran Mummers & newspaper clippings, available for use by museum members only; reading room; theater. Gift items for sale.
Activities: guided tours; films; permanent exhibitions; band concerts.
Publications: monthly newsletter, Mummers Museum News.
Hours & Admission Prices: May-Sept. Wed. & Fri-Sat. 9:30-4:30, Thurs. 9:30-9:30; Oct.-April Wed.-Sat. 9:30-4:30. Adults $3.50, senior citizens & children $2.50; discounts to international students, groups, AAA & AARP members; members no charge. Closed holidays. ♿
Attendance: 12,000 (estimated)
Membership: Individual $10; Family $25; Contributing $100; Patron $500; Corporate $1,000.

* **PHILADELPHIA MUSEUM OF ART, (M), (I),** 26th St. & Benjamin Franklin Pkwy., Philadelphia, PA 19130. Mailing Address: P.O. Box 7646, Philadelphia, PA 19101-7646. Tel.: 215-763-8100 & 235-SHOW (ticketing line). Fax: 215-236-4465.
E-mail: visitorservices@philamuseum.org
Web Site: www.philamuseum.org
Founded: 1876.
Congressional District: 3
Key Personnel: Chm. Bd., H.F. Gerry Lenfest; C.O.O. & Interim C.E.O., Gail M. Harrity; C.F.O., Robert Rambo; Dir. Operations, Robert Morrone; Dir. External Affairs, Cheryl McClenney-Brooker; Cur. European Painting Before 1900 & John G. Johnson Collection, Joseph J. Rishel; Cur. American Decorative Arts, David Barquist; Cur. European Decorative Arts After 1700, Kathryn B. Hiesinger; Cur. American Art, Kathleen Foster; Cur. Modern Art, Michael Taylor; Cur. East Asian Art, Felice Fischer; Cur. Indian & Himalayan Art, Darielle Mason; Sr. Cur. Prints, Drawings & Photographs, Innis H. Shoemaker; Cur. Drawings, Ann B. Percy; Cur. Prints, John Ittmann; Cur. Costume & Textiles, Dilys Blum; Sr. Conservator Decorative Arts & Sculpture, P. Andrew Lins; Cur. Education, Marla Shoemaker; Sr. Conservator Paintings, Mark S. Tucker; Interim Dir. Mktg. & Public Rels., Norman Keyes; Registrar, Irene Taurins; Conservator Furniture, David DeMuzio; Conservator Works of Art on Paper, Nancy Ash; Librarian, C. Danial Elliott; Conservation Scientist, Beth Price; Dir. Wholesale & Retail Operations, Stuart Gerstein; Interim Head Curatorial Affairs, Alice Beamesderfer.
Personnel Profile: Full-Time Paid 336; Full-Time Volunteers 525; Part-Time Paid 147; Part-Time Volunteers 632; Interns 20.
Governing Authority: municipal; nonprofit organization. Affiliated Museums: Rodin Museum, 22nd St. & The Parkway, 19130; Samuel S. Fleisher Art Memorial, 715-719 Catharine St., 19147; Mount Pleasant and Cedar Grove Fairmount Park Houses. Tax-exempt.
Art Museum: located in Fairmount Park.
Collections: Indian and Himalayan, Far & Near Eastern art; European medieval & Renaissance art including Foulc & Barnard; European painting, sculpture & decorative arts, including John G. Johnson; Eastern & Western period rooms from 12th- to 19th-centuries; American painting, sculpture & decorative arts, including Pennsylvania German arts & the Lorimer glass; 20th-century painting & sculpture, including Gallatin & Arensberg; contemporary art; prints & drawings; Alfred Stieglitz Center collection of photography; Kienbusch arms & armor. Historic Houses: 1721 Cedar Grove; 1761 Mount Pleasant.
Major Exhibits: Picasso and The School of Paris, 2/10-4/10; Renoir In The Twentieth Century, 6/10-8/10.
Research Fields: art history; conservation.
Facilities: 130,000-vol. library of art reference books available for inter-library loan & for use on premises; 395-seat auditorium; classrooms; restaurant & cafeteria. Art books, reproductions, jewelry, postcards for sale.
Activities: guided tours; lectures; films; gallery talks; concerts; arts festivals; formally organized education programs for children, adults, families & the handicapped; guide programs; inter-museum loan, special & traveling exhibitions; audio tours; Friday evening programs.
Publications: Bulletin Philadelphia Museum of Art; exhibition & collection catalogs; monthly calendar.
Hours & Admission Prices: Tues.-Thurs. & Sat.-Sun. 10-5, Fri. 10-8:45. Adults $16, senior citizens 65 & over $14, students & children 13-18 $12; discounts to AAM & ICOM members; members and children 12 & under no charge. General admission does not include special ticketed exhibitions. Closed Independence Day; Thanksgiving; Christmas. ♿
Attendance: 780,000 (estimated)
Membership: Student $40; Individual $65; Dual $100; Household $110; Family Plus $150; Supporter $175; Sustainer $300; Sponsor $600; Patron $1,000; Associates $2,000 & up.

PHILADELPHIA MUSEUM OF JEWISH ART/CONGREGATION RODEPH SHALOM, 615 N. Broad St., Philadelphia, PA 19123-2417. Tel.: 215-627-6747. Fax: 215-627-1313.
E-mail: pmja@rodephshalom.org
Web Site: www.rodephshalom.org
Founded: 1975.
Key Personnel: Chm., Gail S. Rosenberg; Advisor, Rabbi William I. Kuhn; Dir., Joan C. Sall; Registrar, Susan A. Popkin.
Governing Authority: synagogue; nonprofit.
Religious Museum: housed in the oldest German synagogue in the Western hemisphere.
Collections: Jewish art; religious ceremonials.
Facilities: 150 sq. ft. exhibit space.
Hours & Admission Prices: Mon.-Thurs. 10-4, Fri. 10-2. No charge; donations accepted. Closed Jewish & public holidays. ♿
Attendance: 6,000

PHILADELPHIA SOCIETY FOR THE PRESERVATION OF LANDMARKS, (M), 321 S. 4th St., Philadelphia, PA 19106-4218. Tel.: 215-925-2251. Fax: 215-925-7909.
E-mail: info@philalandmarks.org
Web Site: www.philalandmarks.org
Founded: 1931.
Congressional District: 1
Key Personnel: Exec. Dir., Brandi Levine; Chm. (V), George Haitsch; Admin., Jorja Fullerton.
Personnel Profile: Full-Time Paid 4; Full-Time Volunteers 8; Part-Time Paid 4; Part-Time Volunteers 80.
Governing Authority: nonprofit organization. Historic House Museums: 1744 Grumblethorpe, 5267 Germantown Ave.; 1765 Powel House, 244 S. 3rd St.; 1786 Physick House, 321 S. 4th St.; 1724 Historic Waynesborough, 2049 Waynesborough Rd., Paoli. Tax-exempt: 501(c)(3).
Historic Building/Site.
Collections: 1700-1840 Philadelphia & American-made furniture & decorative arts.
Research Fields: culinary history; medical history pre-1840; gardens 1744-1855.
Activities: tours; lectures; special events; annual meeting; programs; workshops; Elderhostel program in Philadelphia.
Publications: newsletter.
Hours & Admission Prices: Powel & Physick House: Thurs.-Sat. 12-4, Sun. 1-4. Grumblethorpe: by appointment. Waynesborough: mid-March to Dec. Wed.-Sun. 1-3. Family $12, Adults $5, students & senior citizens $4, groups of 10 or more $3; children under 6 & Landmarks' members no charge.
Attendance: 21,000 (estimated)
Membership: Individual $25; Household $50.

THE PHILADELPHIA ZOO, 3400 W. Girard Ave., Philadelphia, PA 19104-1139. Tel.: 215-243-1100, ext. 0. Fax: 215-243-5385.
E-mail: lastname.firstname@phillyzoo.org
Web Site: www.philadelphiazoo.org
Formerly: The Philadelphia Zoo and Zoological Garden
Founded: 1859.
Congressional District: 2
Key Personnel: Chm. Bd., Jay H. Calvert, Jr.; C.E.O. & Pres., Vikram Dewan; C.O.O., Dr. Andrew Baker; C.F.O., Joseph Steuer; C.M.O., Amy Shearer; Vice Pres. Animal Health, Keith C. Hinshaw, DVM; Vice Pres. Conservation, Kim Lengel; Vice Pres. Facilities, Nina Bisbee; Vice Pres. Community Affairs & Rgnl. Initiatives, Kenneth Woodson; Vice Pres. Devel., Sara Hertz.

Personnel Profile: Full-Time Paid 195; Part-Time Paid 178; Part-Time Volunteers 600; Interns 131.
Governing Authority: society; nonprofit corporation; board of directors. Parent Institution: Zoological Society of Philadelphia. Tax-exempt: 501(c)(3).
Zoo.
Collections: 1,500 species of wild animals; 30,000 species of plants; birds; mammals; reptiles; amphibians; invertebrates; pachyderm; bear. Historic Buildings: Solitude, 1785; Furness Gates; Bird House.
Research Fields: animal behavior; animal nutrition; exotic animal pathology; visitor behavior; animal husbandry.
Facilities: 1,400-vol. library of zoology & natural history available for use on premises; 42 acre Victorian garden; zoo.
Activities: guided tours; travel program; lectures; formally organized education programs for children, adults & graduate students affiliated with the University of Pennsylvania; children & adult workshops; docent programs; participatory, permanent exhibitions; mobile vans; zoo camp; junior zoo intern program; children's zoo volunteer program; education internships; live animal presentations; youth programming. Annual Events: Zoobilee; Adopt Day; Conservation Festival; World Cultures Fest; International Migratory Bird Days; Teach Fest.
Publications: monthly e-newsletter; member news.
Hours & Admission Prices: March-Nov. daily 9:30-5; Dec.-Feb. daily 9:30-4. March-Nov. adult $18, child 2-11 $15; Dec.-Feb. admission $12.95; discounts to groups with advanced reservations; children under 2 & members no charge. Closed New Year's Eve & Day; Thanksgiving; Christmas Eve & Day. ♿
Attendance: 1,200,000 (accurate)
Membership: Individual $54; Family $94; Family Plus $114; Family Deluxe $204; Contributor $280; Supporter $400; Benefactor $800; Associate $1,300; Patron $2,500; Presidents Circle $5,000; Leadership Partner $10,000; Founder $15,000; Keeper of the Kingdom $20,000.

* **PLEASE TOUCH MUSEUM, (M),** Memorial Hall, Fairmount Park, 4231 Ave. of the Republic, Philadelphia, PA 19131-3719. Tel.: 215-581-3181.
E-mail: ceo@pleasetouchmuseum.org
Web Site: www.pleasetouchmuseum.org
Founded: 1976.
Congressional District: 3
Key Personnel: Pres. & C.E.O., Nancy D. Kolb; Exec. Dir., Laura Foster; Vice Pres. Operations, John McDevitt; Chm. (V), Elizabeth Cartmell; Vice Pres. Finance & C.F.O., Concetta Bencivenga; Vice Pres. Devel., Stephanie Capello; Vice Pres. Exhibits, Willard Whitson; Vice Pres. External Rels., Lesly Attarian; Vice Pres. Education & Community Svcs., Andrea Hoffman Jelin; Cur., Stacey Swigart; Dir. Retail Operations, Tucker Hager.
Personnel Profile: Full-Time Paid 92; Part-Time Paid 106; Part-Time Volunteers 9; Interns 5.
Governing Authority: nonprofit organization. Tax-exempt: 501(c)(3).
Children's Museum.
Collections: contemporary American toys post-1945; period children's artifacts; archives; art & sculpture; photographs; 1876 Centennial.
Research Fields: play; value of play; cognitive learning in informal environments; toy history; toy safety; play behavior; 1876 Centennial exhibition; history of childhood in the Delaware Valley.
Facilities: 35,886 sq. ft. exhibit space; 130-seat theatre. Children's books, toys, games & other museum-related items for sale.
Activities: special events; educational programs; outreach to non-traditional museum audiences; theater performances; gallery programs; birthday parties; special exhibitions; traveling trunks (educational kits) available for rental; Community Partners Program with social service agencies.
Publications: annual report; newsletter.
Hours & Admission Prices: Mon.-Sat. 9-5, Sun. 11-5. Admission $15; discounts to AAM & ACM members; children under one no charge. Closed New Year's Day; Thanksgiving; Christmas. ♿
Attendance: 450,000 (estimated)
Membership: 4 People $150; 6 People $170; Super 6 Person $220.

PRESBYTERIAN HISTORICAL SOCIETY, 425 Lombard St., Philadelphia, PA 19147-1516. Tel.: 215-627-1852. Fax: 215-627-0509.
E-mail: refdesk@history.pcusa.org
Web Site: www.history.pcusa.org
Founded: 1852.
Congressional District: 1
Key Personnel: Dir., Frederick J. Heuser, Jr.
Governing Authority: church. Affiliated with the Dept. of History, office of General Assembly, Presbyterian Church. (U.S.A.). Tax-exempt: 501(c)(3).
Religious Museum.
Collections: oil portraits; communion tokens; silver; pewter; pictures; maps; manuscript collection of 400,000 letters; early European imprints before 1800; early Bibles; archives; numismatic.
Facilities: 117,000-vol. library of books on Presbyterian & Reformed Church history available for use on premises; reading room.
Activities: guided tours; lectures; permanent & temporary exhibitions.
Publications: quarterly journal, American Presbyterians: Journal of Presbyterian History; books, Presbyterian Historical Society Publication Series.
Hours & Admission Prices: Mon.-Fri. 8:30-4:30. No charge. Closed national holidays. ♿
Attendance: 1,000
Membership: Lois Harkrider Stair Associates $1-$99; Hallie Paxson Winsborough Club $100-$249; William H. Sheppard Council $250-$499; Lucy Craft Laney Scholars $500-$999; John Wanamaker Society $1,000-$4,999; John Chavis Fellows $5,000-$9,999; John Witherspoon Circle $10,000-$14,999; Francis Makemie Society $15,000 & up.

THE PRINT CENTER, 1614 Latimer St., Philadelphia, PA 19103-6308. Tel.: 215-735-6090. Fax: 215-735-5511.
E-mail: info@printcenter.org
Web Site: www.printcenter.org
Founded: 1915.
Congressional District: 2
Key Personnel: Exec. Dir., Elizabeth F. Spungen; Asst. Dir., Ashley Peel Pinkham; Pres. (V), Hester Stinnett; Cur., John Caperton; Gallery Store Mgr., Eli VandenBerg.
Personnel Profile: Full-Time Paid 4; Part-Time Paid 3; Part-Time Volunteers 50; Interns 10.
Governing Authority: nonprofit organization. Tax-exempt: 501(c)(3).
Arts Center.
Collections: permanent print collection at the Philadelphia Museum of Art; archive collection at the Historical Society of Pennsylvania.
Research Fields: prints & photographs.
Facilities: reference service. Museum-related items for sale.
Activities: lectures; workshops; temporary & traveling exhibitions; photography & print shows; consultations; referrals; consignment photo & print sales.
Publications: exhibition catalogs.
Hours & Admission Prices: Tues.-Sat. 11-5:30. No charge; donations accepted.
Attendance: 5,000,000 (estimated)
Membership: Student $30; Artist & Individual $40; Contributing (2 individuals) $75; Sustaining $150; Collector $300; Zinc $500; Copper $1,000; Silver $2,500; Corporate $3,500; Gold $5,000; Platinum $10,000.

RODIN MUSEUM, Benjamin Franklin Pkwy. at 22nd St., Philadelphia, PA 19130. Mailing Address: c/o Philadelphia Museum of Art, P.O. Box 7646, Philadelphia, PA 19101-7646. Tel.: 215-763-8100. Fax: 215-235-0050. TDD: 215-684-7600.
Web Site: www.rodinmuseum.org
Founded: 1926.
Congressional District: 3
Key Personnel: Sr. Cur. The Gisela & Dennis Alter European Paintings Before 1900 & The John G. Johnson Collection, Joseph J. Rishel; Museum Shop Mgr., Stuart Gerstein.
Governing Authority: municipal; nonprofit. Parent Institution: The Philadelphia Museum of Art, P.O. Box 7646, 19101. Tax-exempt.
Art Museum.
Collections: Auguste Rodin sculpture & drawings.
Research Fields: art history; conservation.
Facilities: Books & replicas of Rodin sculptures for sale.
Activities: guided tours; lectures; gallery talks; inter-museum loan & permanent exhibitions; audio tours.
Publications: handbook; catalog, The Sculpture of Auguste Rodin.
Hours & Admission Prices: Tues.-Sun. 10-5. Suggested Donation: adults $3. Closed holidays. ♿
Attendance: 52,480 (accurate)
Membership: Included in Philadelphia Museum of Art membership. Student $35; Individual $50; Household $85; Contributing $110; Supporting $150; Sustaining $250; Sponsor $500; Patron $1,000; Museum Associates $1,500 & up.

ROSENBACH MUSEUM & LIBRARY, (M), 2008-2010 DeLancy Place, Philadelphia, PA 19103-6584. Tel.: 215-732-1600. Fax: 215-545-7529.
E-mail: info@rosenbach.org
Web Site: www.rosenbach.org/home/home.html
Founded: 1954.
Congressional District: 2
Key Personnel: Chm., Susan B. Miller; Dir., Derick Dreher; Cur. & Dir. Collections, Judith M. Guston; Registrar, Karen Schoenewaldt; Librarian, Elizabeth E. Fuller; Facilities Mgr., Stacey Hendricks; Buyer & Museum

Shop Mgr., Candace Wilkin; Visitor Svcs. Mgr., Lauren Abshire; Exec. Asst., Cathleen Chandler; Publicist, Megan Wendell; Dir. Devel., Christina Deemel.
Personnel Profile: Full-Time Paid 13; Full-Time Volunteers 1; Part-Time Paid 6; Part-Time Volunteers 42.
Governing Authority: nonprofit corporation. Tax-exempt.
Rare Books & Library Museum.
Collections: rare books & manuscripts: British & American literature, Chaucer-present; Joyce's Ulysses manuscript; American history, 1504-1941; 18th- & 19th-century English, French & American furniture, paintings, silver & other decorative arts; incunabula; over 7,000 drawings & watercolors by Maurice Sendak; the Marianne Moore literary archives; prints, drawings, book illustrations & portrait miniatures.
Research Fields: bibliography; decorative arts; book illustrations; American & English literature; American history.
Facilities: gardens; banquet facility. Museum-related items for sale.
Activities: museum & gallery tours; public programs; children's programming; permanent & temporary exhibitions; museum membership program; volunteer docent program; rental space available. Museum Sponsors: Bloomsday celebration in June; special events in conjunction with exhibitions.
Publications: newsletter; brochure; catalog, A Selection From Our Shelves; publications of Maurice Sendak; Cook's Choice: A Selection of Recipes; Passing Through: Letters & Documents Written in Philadelphia by Famous Visitors; Rosenwald & Rosenbach: Two Philadelphia Bookmen; facsimile of James Joyce's autograph manuscript of Ulysses; facsimile of Poor Richard's Almanac by Benjamin Franklin; 18th-century French Book Illustration; Drawings of Jean-Baptiste LePrince; Marianne Moore: Vision Into Verse; Rosenbach Abroad; Blake to Beardsley; Rosenbach Redux: Further Book Adventures in England & Ireland; Sendak at the Rosenbach; The Poet's Progress: Robert Burns; Bram Stroker's Dracula: A Centennial Exhibition; The Advent of Alice: A Celebration of the Carroll Centenary; Nakahama Manjiro's Hyosen Kiryaku: A Companion Book; Ulysses in Hand: The Rosenbach Manuscript.
Hours & Admission Prices: Tues. & Fri. 12-5, Wed.-Thurs. 12-8, Sat. 12-6. Guided Tours: adults $10, senior citizens 65 & over $8, children & students with ID $5; discounts to groups, AAM & ICOM members and museum professionals; children under 5 & members no charge. Closed national holidays. ♿
Attendance: 13,000 (accurate)
Membership: Student & Senior Citizen $25; Friend $45; Household $75; Connoisseur $150; Patron $300; Aficionado $500; Bibliophile $1,000.

RYERSS MUSEUM & LIBRARY, Burholme Park, 7370 Central Ave., Philadelphia, PA 19111-3059. Tel.: 215-685-0544 & 0599.
E-mail: admin@ryerssmuseum.org
Web Site: ryerssmuseum.org
Founded: 1910.
Congressional District: 4
Key Personnel: Park Historian & Admin. Supvr., Theresa Stuhlman.
Personnel Profile: Part-Time Paid 5; Part-Time Volunteers 2.
Governing Authority: municipal; nonprofit. Parent Institution: City of Philadelphia, Fairmount Park Commission. Tax-exempt.
Decorative Art & General Museum: housed in 1859 Victorian House.
Collections: 18th- & 19th-century decorative arts; China Trade & Oriental collections; Victorian & period furnishings.
Research Fields: pertaining to the collections.
Facilities: 20,000-vol. library of general and Victorian era books; reading room.
Hours & Admission Prices: Fri.-Sun. 10-4. No charge; donations accepted. Closed New Year's; Easter; Thanksgiving; Christmas. ♿
Membership: Friends of Burholme $10.

ST. GEORGE'S UNITED METHODIST CHURCH, 235 N. Fourth St., Philadelphia, PA 19106-1194. Tel.: 215-925-7788.
E-mail: office@historicstgeorges.org
Web Site: www.historicstgeorges.org
Founded: 1767.
Key Personnel: Admin., Donna Miller.
Governing Authority: church. Tax-exempt.
Religious Museum: housed in 1763 St. George's United Methodist Church, built of British brick & located on the original site of construction.
Collections: original John Wesley Chalice Cup sent from England to Francis Asbury in 1784; Francis Asbury's personal Bible brought with him from England in 1771; manuscripts; Asbury watch.
Research Fields: British & American church history; records of closed churches.
Facilities: 7,000-vol. library of European & American books on Methodism available for research on premises; reading room.
Activities: guided tours; temporary exhibitions. Museum Sponsors: Associate Membership Program.
Publications: quarterly newsletter to associate members.
Hours & Admission Prices: Mon.-Fri. 10-3, Sat.-Sun. by appointment. No charge; donations accepted.
Attendance: 2,000 (estimated)

SAINT JOSEPH'S UNIVERSITY - UNIVERSITY GALLERY - BOLAND HALL, 5600 City Line Ave., Philadelphia, PA 19131-1376. Tel.: 610-660-1840. Fax: 610-660-2278.
E-mail: jbracy@sju.edu
Web Site: www.sju.edu/gallery
Founded: 1976.
Key Personnel: Chm. Fine & Performing Arts Dept., Deron Albright; Assoc. Dir. Gallery, Jeanne Bracy.
Governing Authority: private university; nonprofit. Tax-exempt: 501(c)(3).
University Art Museum.
Collections: Ceramics
Activities: arts festivals; concerts; films; formal education programs for undergraduate & graduate college students; lectures; participatory exhibits; theater.
Hours & Admission Prices: Sept.-May Mon.-Fri. 10-4. No charge; donations accepted. Closed national holidays. ♿
Attendance: 2,000 (estimated)

SAMUEL S. FLEISHER ART MEMORIAL, 719 Catharine St., Philadelphia, PA 19147-2811. Tel.: 215-922-3456, ext. 318.
E-mail: info@fleisher.org
Web Site: www.fleisher.org
Key Personnel: Bd. Pres., Liz Price; Exec. Dir., Matthew Braun; Exhibitions Mgr., Warren Angle.
Governing Authority: Parent Institution: Philadelphia Museum of Art.
Art Museum.
Collections: works by regional artists.
Activities: Annual Event: The Challenge (artists competition).
Hours & Admission Prices: Mon.-Fri. 11-5; call for additional hours.

THE SCHUYLKILL CENTER FOR ENVIRONMENTAL EDUCATION, 8480 Hagy's Mill Rd., Philadelphia, PA 19128-1998. Tel.: 215-482-7300, ext. 110. Fax: 215-482-8158.
E-mail: scee@schuylkillcenter.org
Web Site: www.schuylkillcenter.org
Founded: 1965.
Congressional District: 2
Key Personnel: Exec. Dir., Dennis Burton; Pres. Bd. Trustees, John Howard; Bd. Vice Pres., Anne Bower; Bd. Vice Pres., Jeffery Hayes; Bd. Vice Pres., Lara Herzig Malatests; Bd. Vice Pres., Wendy Willard; Bd. Sec., Ron Varnum; Dir. Education, Virginia Ranly; Dir. Wildlife Rehabilitation, Rick Schubert; Dir. Art Programs, Mary Salvante; Dir. Land Restoration, Fran Lawn; Grant Coord., Emily Simmons.
Personnel Profile: Full-Time Paid 15; Part-Time Paid 15; Part-Time Volunteers 108.
Governing Authority: nonprofit organization. Parent Institution: SCEE, Inc. Tax-exempt: 501(c)(3).
Nature Center.
Collections: Over 400-acres of the nature center; insect collection; taxidermied birds; mineral & herbarium; rare books; solar panel array & green roof.
Research Fields: educational process; ecological restoration; environmental education.
Facilities: nature center; field research station; educational facilities; 200-seat auditorium; K-8 charter school; interactive discovery center. Museum-related items for sale.
Activities: guided tours; lectures; arts festivals; organized education programs children, adults & undergraduate or graduate college students affiliated with Philadelphia, Arcadia & Temple Universities; school loan service.
Publications: quarterly newsletter, The Quill; seasonal brochures; annual report.
Hours & Admission Prices: Center: Mon.-Sat. 8:30-5. Trails: daily 8:30-4:30. No charge; donations accepted. Closed New Year's Day; Easter; Memorial Day; Independence Day; Labor Day; Thanksgiving; Christmas. ♿
Attendance: 55,500 (accurate)
Membership: Individual $40; Family $60; Wildlife $75; Contributing & Organizational $100; Fellows $250-$1,000.

SIMEONE FOUNDATION MUSEUM, (M), 6825-31 Norwitch Dr., Philadelphia, PA 19153-3412. Tel.: 215-365-7233. Fax: 215-365-8230.
Web Site: www.simeonefoundation.org
Key Personnel: Exec. Dir., Fred Simeone; Operations Admin., Volunteers, Amanda Bartley; Facilities Rental, Kristina Ford; Cur., Kevin Kelly; Retail Operations, Darryl Northington; Communications & Public Rels., Harry Hurst
Sports Museum.

Collections: car racing memorabilia.
Hours & Admission Prices: Tues.-Fri. 10-6, Sat.-Sun. 10-4. Adults $12, seniors $10, students $8; children under 8 no charge.

THE STEPHEN GIRARD COLLECTION, Girard College #116, 2101 S. College Ave., Philadelphia, PA 19121-4857. Tel.: 215-787-4434. Fax: 215-787-4404.
E-mail: elaurent@girardcollege.com
Web Site: www.girardcollege.com
Founded: 1831.
Congressional District: 2
Key Personnel: Dir. Historical Resources, Elizabeth M. Laurent; Pres. Girard College, Dominic M. Cermele.
Personnel Profile: Full-Time Paid 1; Part-Time Volunteers 4.
Governing Authority: Parent Institution: Board of Directors of City Trusts. Subsidiary Institution: Girard College. Tax-exempt.
Period Furniture & Decorative Arts Museum: located in Founder's Hall, Greek Revival Building designed by Thomas U. Walter, on the grounds of Girard College.
Collections: personal artifacts of Stephen Girard (1750-1831) including furniture by Trotter, Connelly & Haines; American, French & English Silver; China trade items; paintings, books, porcelain; S.G. papers: 1780-1831 correspondence, including U.S. presidents, statesmen, naval officers & diplomats; ledgers & journals; charts; maps; broadsides; drawings; ships & shipping; 1832 architectural competition drawings; T.U. Walter construction drawings for Founder's Hall.
Research Fields: Stephen Girard Papers are available for research & also on microfilm at the American Philosophical Society in Philadelphia.
Activities: guided tours.
Publications: Stephen Girard Collection; A Catalogue of the Personal Library of Stephen Girard; Monument to Philanthropy: The Design and Building of Girard College, 1832-1848; Girard College - A Living History.
Hours & Admission Prices: Thurs. 9-2; group tours available by appointment at other times. Call for group rates.
Attendance: 2,000 (accurate)

TEMPLE GALLERY, TYLER SCHOOL OF ART OF TEMPLE UNIVERSITY, 2001 N. 13th St., Philadelphia, PA 19122-6016. Tel.: 215-777-9144. Fax: 215-777-9143.
E-mail: exhibitions@temple.edu
Web Site: www.temple.edu/tyler/exhibitions
Founded: 1985.
Key Personnel: Interim Dir., Shayna V. McConville; Registrar, Nancy Lewis.
Personnel Profile: Full-Time Paid 2; Part-Time Paid 3.
Governing Authority: public university; nonprofit. Parent Institution: Temple University. Subsidiary Institution: Tyler School of Art. Tax-exempt.
Art Gallery.
Collections: works by contemporary artists.
Major Exhibits: Philagrafika 2010: The Graphic Unconscious, 1/10-4/10; Jack Wolgin Fine Arts Prize, 9/10-11/10.
Research Fields: contemporary art.
Activities: films; lectures; symposiums; traveling exhibitions.
Publications: exhibition catalogues.
Hours & Admission Prices: Wed.-Sat. 11-6; other times by appointment. No charge.
Attendance: 20,000 (estimated)
Membership: Friends of the Gallery $25; $100; $1,000; $5,000.

TREASURY OF FAITH MUSEUM, 810 N. Franklin St., Philadelphia, PA 19123. Tel.: 215-627-3389. Fax: 215-627-4225.
E-mail: tofmuseum@catholic.org
Religious Museum.
Collections: Ukrainian Catholic Church history & roots; religious artifacts; altar; paintings; signed antimensions; iconostas from the original Ukrainian Catholic Cathedral of the Immaculate Conception; bishop's throne; tabernacle; liturgical books; sacred vessels.
Facilities: classrooms.
Hours & Admission Prices: Call for hours.

* **UNIVERSITY OF PENNSYLVANIA MUSEUM OF ARCHAEOLOGY AND ANTHROPOLOGY, (M), (I),** 3260 South St., Philadelphia, PA 19104-6324. Tel.: 215-898-4000. Fax: 215-898-0657.
E-mail: info@museum.upenn.edu
Web Site: www.museum.upenn.edu
Founded: 1887.
Congressional District: 1
Key Personnel: Chm. (V), Bd. Overseers, Michael J. Kowalski; Dir., Richard Hodges, Ph.D.; Deputy Dir. & Cur. Mediterranean Section, Brian Rose, Ph.D.; C.O.O., Melissa Smith; Assoc. Dir. Admin. & Finance, Alan Waldt; Chief of Staff, James Mathieu; Asst. Dir. Public Information, Pam Kosty; Dir. Devel., Amanda Mitchell-Boyask; Assoc. Dir. Education, Gillian Wakely; Senior Archivist, Alex Pezzati; Head Librarian, John Weeks, Ph.D.; Head Exhibits & Lead Exhibit Designer, Kate Quinn; Asst. Dir. Special Events, Tena Thomason; Senior Registrar, Xiuqin Zhou; Interim Head Conservator, Lynn Grant; Assoc. Cur. Babylonian Section, Stephen Tinney, Ph.D.; Cur. American Section, Robert Preucel, Ph.D.; Cur. Egyptian Section, David Silverman, Ph.D.; Assoc. Cur. Near East Section, Richard Zettler, Ph.D.; Assoc. Cur. Historical Archaeology Section, Robert L. Schuyler, Ph.D.; Women's Committee Chair, Emily Starr; Coord. Docent, Doris Panzer; Asst. Dir. Education & Volunteer Coord., Jane Nelson; Volunteer Docents Chair, Geri Lifshey; Museum Shop Mgr., Susan West.
Personnel Profile: Full-Time Paid 101; Part-Time Paid 2; Part-Time Volunteers 250; Interns 12.
Governing Authority: university. Parent Institution: The University of Pennsylvania. Tax-exempt: 501(c)(3).
University Archaeology & Anthropology Museum.
Collections: Egyptian, Mediterranean, Near Eastern, African, South, Southeast & East Asian, Oceanic & Australian, American, Mesoamerican archaeological & ethnographic materials.
Major Exhibits: His Golden Touch: The Gordion Drawings of Piet de Jong, 11/09-1/10/10; Painted Metaphors: The Pottery and Politics of the Ancient Maya (T), 11/09-1/10; Fulfilling a Prophecy, 11/09-7/10; In Citizen's Garb: Southern Plains Native Americans, 1889-1891 (T), 3/26/10-6/20/10; Archaeologists and Travelers in Ottoman Lands, Fall 2010 (T).
Research Fields: fields related to collections.
Facilities: 80,000-vol. library on archaeology, anthropology & ethnology available for use of University of PA students, visiting scholars & staff; archives containing 2,000 linear feet and 300,000 photographs of expedition & administrative records for use by qualified researchers; 60,375 sq. ft. of exhibition space; two auditoriums; classrooms; cafeteria.
Activities: lectures; films; gallery talks; concerts; docent program; travel program; community school programs; formally organized education programs for undergraduate & graduate students; inter-museum loan, permanent, temporary & traveling exhibitions; school loan service; family-oriented world culture days.
Publications: magazine 3 times a year, EXPEDITION; quarterly calendar of events; quarterly membership newsletter; annual report; monographs; guide books; catalogues; edited volumns.
Hours & Admission Prices: Memorial Day-Labor Day: Tues.-Sat. 10-4:30; Sept.-May Tues.-Sat. 10-4:30, Sun. 1-5. Adults $10, senior citizens $7, children 6-17 & students $6; discounts to AAM & ICOM members; children under 6, Penn Card holders & members no charge. Closed New Year's Day; Easter; Memorial Day; Independence Day; Thanksgiving; Christmas. ♿
Attendance: 145,000 (estimated)
Membership: Student $40; Associate (Beyond 100 mile radius) $50; Individual $55; Dual $65; Household $80; Sustaining $150; Patron $250; Fellow $500; Loren Eiseley Society $1,500 & up.

THE UNIVERSITY OF THE ARTS - ROSENWALD-WOLF GALLERY, (M), 333 S. Broad St., Philadelphia, PA 19107-5839. Mailing Address: 320 S. Broad St., Philadelphia, PA 19102-4994. Tel.: 215-717-6480. Fax: 215-717-6468.
E-mail: ssachs@uarts.edu
Web Site: www.uarts.edu
Founded: 1876.
Congressional District: 1
Key Personnel: Pres. (V), Sean Buffington; Dir., Sid Sachs.
Personnel Profile: Full-Time Paid 2; Part-Time Paid 10.
Governing Authority: college; nonprofit organization. Parent Institution: University of the Arts. Tax-exempt: 501(c)(3).
University Art Gallery.
Collections: paintings.
Research Fields: contemporary design, fine arts and crafts.
Activities: temporary exhibitions, lectures & gallery talks; conferences; performances open to the public.
Publications: exhibition catalogues & illustrated brochures.
Hours & Admission Prices: Mon.-Fri. 10-5, Sat. 12-5. No charge. Closed academic holidays. ♿
Attendance: 30,000 (estimated)

U.S. MINT-PHILADELPHIA, 5th and Arch Sts., Philadelphia, PA 19106. Mailing Address: 151 N. Independence Mall E., Philadelphia, PA 19106-1886. Tel.: 215-408-0114. Fax: 215-408-2700. TDD: 215-597-0077.
Web Site: www.usmint.gov/
Founded: 1792.
Key Personnel: Dir., Edmund Moy; Public Rels. & Exhibits, Timothy Grant; Museum Shop Mgr., Renee Brooks.
Governing Authority: federal; nonprofit. Dept. of Treasury. Tax-exempt.
Numismatics Museum.

Collections: coin production equipment; mint artifacts; coins; medals.
Research Fields: coins & medals produced by the U.S. Mint.
Facilities: 500-vol. library of coins, medal and mint history material; 22,000 sq. ft. exhibit space. Current U.S. special coins and medals for sale.
Publications: tour brochure.
Hours & Admission Prices: Mon.-Fri. 9-3. No charge. Closed federal holidays. ♿
Attendance: 342,346 (accurate)

THE VICTORIAN SOCIETY IN AMERICA, 1636 Sansom St., Philadelphia, PA 19103-5404. Tel.: 215-636-9872. Fax: 215-636-9873.
E-mail: info@victoriansociety.org
Web Site: www.victoriansociety.org
Founded: 1966.
Key Personnel: Pres. (V), Bruce Davies; Business Mgr., Robert McCown.
Personnel Profile: Full-Time Paid 1; Part-Time Paid 1; Part-Time Volunteers 40.
Governing Authority: society. Tax-exempt: 501(c)(3).
Historical Society: housed in an1899 Victorian church.
Collections: documentary resources.
Research Fields: 19th-century America & Great Britain.
Facilities: library of 19th-century American History available for research in the Athenaeum only.
Activities: symposia; lectures; British & American summer schools; international & study tours; festivals.
Publications: quarterly newsletter, The Victorian; semiannual scholarly magazine, 19th Century.
Hours & Admission Prices: Mon.-Fri. 9-5. No charge. Closed New Year's Day; Memorial Day; Independence Day; Labor Day; Thanksgiving; Christmas.
Membership: Student $30; Library/Historic House & Museums/University $45; Individual $50; Household $60; Sustaining $100; Contributing & Business $250; Life $1,500.

WAGNER FREE INSTITUTE OF SCIENCE, (M), 1700 W. Montgomery Ave., Philadelphia, PA 19121-3227. Tel.: 215-763-6529. Fax: 215-763-1299.
E-mail: info@wagnerfreeinstitute.org
Web Site: www.wagnerfreeinstitute.org
Founded: 1855.
Congressional District: 3
Key Personnel: Dir., Susan Glassman; Museum Admin., Pat Warner; Librarian & Archivist, Lynn Dorwaldt; Dir. Children's Education, Dana Semos; Children's Educator, Holly Clark.
Personnel Profile: Full-Time Paid 9; Part-Time Paid 3; Part-Time Volunteers 60; Interns 8.
Governing Authority: nonprofit organization. Tax-exempt: 501(c)(3).
Natural History & Natural Science Museum.
Collections: mineralogy; paleontology; entomology; botany; shells; mammals; fish & reptiles; birds; 19th-century scientific instruments.
Research Fields: history of science; systematics.
Facilities: 42,000-vol. library; archives; reading room; 450-seat auditorium.
Activities: lectures; films; formally organized educational programs; permanent exhibitions; symposia; tours; special weekend programs.
Publications: bulletin, Transactions; course catalogue.
Hours & Admission Prices: Tues.-Fri. 9-4. Museum: $8 suggested donation. Guided Tours: adults $15, seniors $10, children $5; discounts to members & groups. Education Programs: no charge. Closed national holidays.
Attendance: 18,000 (estimated)
Membership: Individual Friend $25; Family Friends $35; Contributor $50; Donor $100; Sustainer $250; Patron $500; Benefactor $1,000 & up.

* **WOODMERE ART MUSEUM, (M),** 9201 Germantown Ave., Philadelphia, PA 19118-2618. Tel.: 215-247-0476. Fax: 215-247-2387.
Web Site: www.woodmereartmuseum.org
Founded: 1940.
Congressional District: 13
Key Personnel: C.E.O., Dir. & Cur., Michael W. Schantz, Ph.D.; Pres., Dianne Meyer, Esq.; Dir. Devel., Mary Agnes Williams; Cur. Education, Pamela Birmingham; Registrar, Sally Larson; Museum Educator, Hildy Tow; Museum Shop Mgr., Lori Hines.
Personnel Profile: Full-Time Paid 10; Part-Time Paid 5; Part-Time Volunteers 81.
Governing Authority: nonprofit organization. Tax-exempt: 501(c)(3).
Art Museum: housed in 1867 Victorian mansion with modern additions.
Collections: the Charles Knox Smith collection of European & American paintings & sculpture; porcelains, including Royal Sevres & Meissen ware; textiles & Oriental carpets; the Woodmere collection of paintings & prints, featuring artists of the Delaware Valley; Severo Antonelli photographs.
Research Fields: 19th- & 20th-century American Art.
Facilities: 2,000-vol. library of basic reference materials, including a collection of monographic volumes dedicated to artists represented in the collections. Works by regional artists including paintings, prints, ceramics & textiles for sale.
Activities: guided tours; gallery talks; lectures; concerts; permanent & temporary exhibitions; children's gallery.
Publications: exhibition catalogues; calendar of events; newsletter; program guide.
Hours & Admission Prices: Tues.-Sat. 10-5, Sun. 1-5. Suggested Donation: adults $5; discounts to AAM & ICOM members & Cultural Pass holders; members no charge. Closed selected holidays. ♿
Attendance: 48,000 (estimated)
Membership: Student $20; Individual $35; Family $60; Contributing $100; Supporting $250; Patron $500; Connoisseur $1,000.

WYCK, 6026 Germantown Ave., Philadelphia, PA 19144-2191. Tel.: 215-848-1690. Fax: 215-848-1612.
E-mail: wyck@wyck.org
Web Site: www.wyck.org
Founded: 1973.
Key Personnel: Exec. Dir., Eileen Rojas; Chm. (V), Rob Fleming; Vice Chm., Emily Lind Baker; Cur., Laura Keim; Horticulturist, Nicole Juday.
Personnel Profile: Full-Time Paid 1; Part-Time Paid 5; Part-Time Volunteers 20.
Governing Authority: nonprofit organization; administered by The Wyck Association. Tax-exempt: 170(b)(1)(A).
Historic Building Museum: housed in 18th-century building.
Collections: furniture; glass; ceramics; metals; textiles; archives with nine generations of family manuscripts; rose & vegetable garden.
Research Fields: Germantown gardens & houses; social history.
Facilities: 2,000-vol. library pertaining to history, religion & science. Museum-related items for sale.
Activities: guided tours; organized education programs for children & adults; intern program for gardening students. Museum Sponsors: Farmer's Market May to November.
Publications: pamphlet, Germantown & Its Founders; brochure, Wyck.
Hours & Admission Prices: April-Dec. 15 Tues., Thurs. & Sat. 1-4. Family $10, adults & children $5, senior citizens $4; discounts to AAM & ICOM members; members no charge. Closed New Year's Day; Independence Day; Christmas; Thanksgiving. ♿
Attendance: 3,681 (accurate)
Membership: Individual $50; Family $75; Donor $150; Contributor $250; Benefactor $500; Patron $1,000.

Phoenixville

HISTORICAL SOCIETY OF THE PHOENIXVILLE AREA, (M), 204 Church St., Phoenixville, PA 19460-3414. Tel.: 610-933-7646.
E-mail: hspa@verizon.net
Web Site: www.phoenixvillehistoricalsociety.org
Founded: 1980.
Congressional District: 6th
Key Personnel: Pres., Susan C. Marshall; Treas., Duane Parker; Devel., Richard Lusch; Public Rels., Martha Parker; Cur., Rebecca Manley; Archivist, Edgar Naratil; Office Mgr., Robert Deger.
Personnel Profile: Part-Time Volunteers 100.
Governing Authority: private; nonprofit organization. Tax-exempt: 501(c)(3).
Historical Society Museum.
Collections: local history; Native American; industrial history; Etruscan Majolica pottery; documents; photographs.
Research Fields: regional & community history; genealogy.
Facilities: 275-vol. library; archives; 1,700 sq. ft. exhibit space.
Activities: formal education programs for adults; guided tours; temporary exhibitions; broadcast programs. Annual Events: Strawberry Festival; Flea Market; town walk; banquet.
Publications: quarterly newsletter, Newsletter of the Historical Society of the Phoenix Area.
Hours & Admission Prices: Wed.-Fri. 9-3, 1st Sun. of month 1-4; other times by appointment. No charge; donations accepted. ♿
Attendance: 750 (accurate)
Membership: Student & Senior Citizen $15; Individual $20; Family $25; Business $50; Friend of HSPA $75; Contributor $150; Sponsor $250.

Pittsburgh

THE ANDY WARHOL MUSEUM, 117 Sandusky St., Pittsburgh, PA 15212-5890. Tel.: 412-237-8300. Fax: 412-237-8340.
Web Site: www.warhol.org
Founded: 1994.
Congressional District: 18
Key Personnel: Chm. Bd. Overseers, Randall Dearth; Pres. & C.E.O., David

M. Hillenbrand; Dir. AWM, Thomas Sokolowski; Deputy Dir., Colleen Russell Criste; Archivist, Matt Wrbican; Cur. Film & Video, Geralyn H. Huxley.
Governing Authority: nonprofit organization. Parent Institution: Carnegie Institute. Tax-exempt: 501(c)(3).
Art Museum: industrial warehouse with ornate terra cotta clad facade, built 1911-22.
Collections: concentrations on the works, creative process & life of Andy Warhol including paintings, prints, drawings, films, videos, audio-tapes, sculpture, photographs, installations & archival study center.
Research Fields: collections & cultural studies relating to the second half of the 20th-century.
Facilities: archives study center; education resource center & studio; 110-seat theater; cafe. Museum-related items for sale.
Activities: lectures; art activities for adults & children; films; temporary special exhibitions; rotating exhibitions of museum collections; group visits; teacher education workshops; opening and other events.
Publications: inaugural publication, The Andy Warhol Museum; Andy Warhol 1956-86: Mirror of His Time; The Warhol Look/Glamour Style Fashion; Andy Warhol: 365 Takes; magazine, CARNEGIE.
Hours & Admission Prices: Tues.-Thurs. & Sat.-Sun. 10-5, Fri. 10-10. Adults $15, senior citizens 55 & over $9, students & children 3-18 $8; discounts Fri. 5-10 and AAM & ICOM members; members of Carnegie Museums of Pittsburgh no charge. Closed legal holidays. ♿
Attendance: 92,000
Membership: Senior 65 & over $50; Individual $75; Dual $100; Family $130; Premium $200.

ASSOCIATED AMERICAN JEWISH MUSEUMS, 4905 Fifth Ave., Pittsburgh, PA 15213-2941. Tel.: 412-621-6566. Fax: 412-621-5475.
E-mail: jacob@rodefshalom.org
Founded: 1972.
Key Personnel: C.E.O. & Pres. (V), Walter Jacob; Financial Dir., Jeff Herzog; Education, F. Pomerantz; Public Rels., Francine Rickenbach.
Personnel Profile: Part-Time Volunteers 10.
Governing Authority: private; nonprofit organization. Tax-exempt: 501(c)(3).
Ethnic History Association.
Collections: historical & artistic Judaica; synagogue collections.
Research Fields: modern Ketubot; rural American synagogues; Samuel Rosenberg, the artist.
Activities: lectures; loan & traveling exhibitions. Annual Event: Symposia.
Publications: quarterly newsletter, Gallery.
Hours & Admission Prices: No charge.
Attendance: 5,000 (estimated)
Membership: Synagogues $25-$1,000.

AUGUST WILSON CENTER FOR AFRICAN AMERICAN CULTURE, 980 Liberty Ave., Pittsburgh, PA 15222-3736. Tel.: 412-258-2700. Fax: 412-258-2701.
E-mail: pquatchak@augustwilsoncenter.org
Web Site: www.augustwilsoncenter.org
Founded: 2002.
Congressional District: 14
Key Personnel: Pres. & C.E.O., Marva H. Harris; Chm. (V), Oliver W. Byrd.
Personnel Profile: Full-Time Paid 18; Part-Time Volunteers 140; Interns 3.
Governing Authority: Tax-exempt.
Cultural Center.
Collections: African American culture & history; photography; paintings; period artifacts; communication artifacts.
Major Exhibits: In My Father's House, 11/09-6/10; Looking Forward: Images of Children by Charles "Teenie" Harris, 11/09-12/09; Charles "Teenie" Harris: Rhapsody in Black and White, 11/09-12/09; Women of a New Tribe: Photography by Jerry Taliaferro, 11/09-12/09.
Facilities: 486-seat theater; education center; rehearsal hall; restaurant; meeting area. Museum-related items for sale.
Activities: visual & performing arts programs; educational programs.
Publications: season brochure; gallery guides; marketing collateral; curriculum guides.
Hours & Admission Prices: Tues.-Wed. & Fri.-Sat. 10-5, Thurs. 10-8, Sun. 12-5; additional hours on performance days. Adults $10, seniors $8, children & students $6; discounts to groups; member no charge. Cloed major holidays. ♿
Attendance: 19,839 (accurate)
Membership: Basic: Children and Youth 17 & under $15; Senior & Full-time Students $25; Individual $40; Couple & Dual $60; Family $75. Contemporary Friends: Individual $200; Couple & Dual $350. Donor Circle: Patron $150-$499; Leader $500-$1,944; August Wilson Circle $1,945-$2,499; Founders' Circle $2,500-$4,999; Institution Builder $5,000 & up.

* **CARNEGIE MUSEUM OF ART,** 4400 Forbes Ave., Pittsburgh, PA 15213-4080. Tel.: 412-622-3131. Fax: 412-622-3112.
Web Site: www.cmoa.org
Founded: 1896.
Congressional District: 14
Key Personnel: Chm., William Hunt; Pres. & C.E.O., David M. Hillenbrand; Dir. The Henry J. Heinz II, Lynn Zelevansky; Chief Cur. & Cur. Fine Arts, Louise Lippincott; Deputy Dir., Maureen Rolla; Cur. Decorative Arts, Jason Busch; Cur. Architecture, Tracy Myers; Cur. Architecture, Raymund Ryan; Cur. Education, Marilyn M. Russell; Chief Conservator, Ellen Baxter; Dir. Exhibitions, Christopher Rauhoff; Head, Publications, Katie Reilly; Dir. Technology Initiatives, Will Real; Registrar, Monika Tomko; Communications Mgr., Ellen James; Dir. Devel., Renee Pekor; Dir. Mktg., Kitty Julian; Vice Pres. Devel., Dolores F. Ellenberg.
Governing Authority: nonprofit organization. Parent Institution: Carnegie Institute. Tax-exempt: 501(c)(3).
Art Museum: housed in 1896-1907, Alden and Harlow American Renaissance-style building & 1974 Edward Larrabee Barnes addition.
Collections: European & American paintings with emphasis on 19th- & 20th-century American, French Impressionist & Post-Impressionist; sculpture; prints; drawings; watercolors; photographs; international & American contemporary art, including film & video; Asian & African art; European & American decorative arts; architectural & sculptural casts; architectural drawings & models.
Research Fields: pertaining to collections.
Facilities: library; outdoor sculpture court; theater; conservation laboratory; cafe. Museum-related items for sale.
Activities: guided & audio tours; lectures; classes; gallery talks; inter-museum loans; traveling exhibition program; special exhibitions; docent program; visiting filmmaker & video artist programs. Museum Sponsors: Carnegie International exhibition; Annual Associated Artists of Pittsburgh exhibition; Three Rivers Arts Festival.
Publications: exhibition & collection catalogues; educational materials; brochures; film program notes; CARNEGIE Magazine.
Hours & Admission Prices: July 4-Aug. Mon.-Wed. & Fri.-Sat. 10-5, Thurs. 10-8, Sun. 12-5; Sept.-July 3 Tues.-Wed. & Fri.-Sat. 10-5, Thurs. 10-8, Sun. 12-5, call to confirm. Adults $15, senior citizens $12, full-time students & children ages 3 and over $11; discounts to AAM & ICOM members; members no charge. Closed legal holidays. ♿
Attendance: 645,200 (accurate)
Membership: Senior 65 & over $50; Individual $75; Dual $100; Family $130; Premium $200.

CARNEGIE MUSEUM OF NATURAL HISTORY, 4400 Forbes Ave., Pittsburgh, PA 15213-4080. Tel.: 412-622-3131. Fax: 412-622-8837.
Web Site: www.carnegiemnh.org
Founded: 1896.
Congressional District: 14
Key Personnel: Bd. Chm., Joseph Guyaux; Pres. & C.E.O., David M. Hillenbrand; Dir., Samuel M. Taylor, Ph.D.; Deputy Dir., Ellen McCallie; Dir. Finance, Robert Querio; Assoc. Dir. Research & Collections, Zhe-Xi Luo; Cur. Vertebrate Paleontology, Dr. K. Christopher Beard; Head Minerals, Marc L. Wilson; Collection Mgr. Amphibians & Reptiles, Stephen Rogers; Cur. Birds, Dr. Bradley C. Livezey; Assoc. Cur. Botany, Dr. Cynthia Morton; Assoc. Cur., Invertebrate Zoology, Dr. John E. Rawlins; Cur. Anthropology, Dr. David R. Watters; Assoc. Cur. Mollusks, Timothy Pearce; Chair, Div. of Education, Diane Grzybek; Chair, Div. Exhibit Design & Production, James R. Senior; Dir. Powdermill Nature Reserve, Dr. David A. Smith; Mgr. Library, Xianghua Sun; Dir. Mktg., Kitty Julian; Dir. Devel., Alisa Braho; Vice Pres. CMP Devel., Dolores F. Ellenberg.
Governing Authority: nonprofit organization. Parent Institution: Carnegie Institute. Branch Station: Powdermill Nature Reserve, 1847, Rte. 381, Rector, PA 15677-9605. Tax-exempt: 501(c)(3).
Natural History & Anthropology Museum: housed in c.1896 American Renaissance style building.
Collections: geology & minerals; invertebrate & vertebrate paleontology; paleobotany; botany; herbarium; entomology; mollusks; amphibians; reptiles; ornithology; mammalogy; anthropology; archaeology; historic; wildlife art.
Research Fields: geology; invertebrate & vertebrate paleontology; paleobotany; botany; entomology; arachnids; amphibians; reptiles; ornithology; malacology; mammalogy; anthropology; archaeology; conservation; ecology.
Facilities: 150,000-vol. library of reference works on natural history & anthropology; maps; pamphlets, available for inter-library loan & to qualified students & research personnel; molecular & conservation laboratories; classrooms; lecture hall; cafe; 2,200-acre biological field station in western Pennsylvania. Reproductions, original objects & museum-related items for sale.
Activities: guided tours; teen docent program; lectures; films; gallery talks;

in-service programs for teachers; formally organized education programs for children & adults; outreach programs to schools, hospitals & institutions with special-needs populations; training programs for professional museum workers; pre- & postdoctoral fellowship program; permanent & temporary exhibitions; distance learning program; school loan service.
Publications: scientific journals, Annals of Carnegie Museum, Bulletin Series; Special Publications Series; CARNEGIE Magazine; exhibition catalogues; pamphlets; popular books for adults & children.
Hours & Admission Prices: July 5-Aug. Mon.-Wed. & Fri.-Sat. 10-5, Thurs. 10-8, Sun. 12-5; Sept.-July 3 Tues.-Wed. & Fri.-Sat. 10-5, Thurs. 10-8, Sun. 12-5, call to confirm. Adults $15, senior citizens $12, full-time students and children 3 & over $11; discounts to AAM & ICOM members; members no charge. Closed legal holidays. ♿
Membership: Senior 65 & over $50; Individual $75; Dual $100; Family $130; Premium $200.

CARNEGIE MUSEUMS OF PITTSBURGH (CARNEGIE INSTITUTE), 4400 Forbes Ave., Pittsburgh, PA 15213-4080. Tel.: 412-622-3131.
Web Site: www.carnegiemuseums.org
Founded: 1896.
Congressional District: 14
Key Personnel: Pres. & C.E.O., David M. Hillenbrand; C.F.O., Kevin D. Hiles; Vice Pres. Devel., Dolores F. Ellenberg; Vice Pres. Facilities, Planning & Operations, Timothy Mahaney; Dir. Corporate Human Resources, Eileen Meddis; Co-Dir. Henry Buhl, Jr., Carnegie Science Center, Ronald Baillie; Vice Pres. Mktg. & Co-Dir. Henry Buhl, Jr., Carnegie Science Center, Ann Metzger; Dir. Carnegie Museum of Natural History, Samuel M. Taylor; Dir. The Andy Warhol Museum, Thomas Sokolowski; The Henry J. Heinz II Dir. Carnegie Museum of Art, Lynn Zelevansky.
Governing Authority: nonprofit organization. Administers: The Andy Warhol Museum; Carnegie Museum of Art; Carnegie Museum of Natural History; Carnegie Science Center. Tax-exempt: 501(c)(3).
General Museum.
Collections: located at The Andy Warhol Museum; Carnegie Museum of Art; Carnegie Museum of Natural History; Carnegie Science Center.
Research Fields: pertaining to collections.
Facilities: see The Andy Warhol Museum, Carnegie Museum of Art, Carnegie Museum of Natural History and Carnegie Science Center for additional facilities.
Activities: permanent exhibitions; educational programs for adults & children; guided tours; lectures; concerts; public events; member activities; member trips. See The Andy Warhol Museum, Carnegie Museum of Art, Carnegie Museum of Natural History, and Carnegie Science Center for additional activities.
Publications: CARNEGIE Magazine. See The Andy Warhol Museum, Carnegie Museum of Art, Carnegie Museum of Natural History, and Carnegie Science Center for additional publications.
Hours & Admission Prices: See The Andy Warhol Museum, Carnegie Museum of Art, Carnegie Museum of Natural History and Carnegie Science Center for hours & admission prices. ♿
Attendance: 1,654,500
Membership: Senior 65 & up $50; Individual $75; Dual $100; Family $130; Premium $200. (All memberships subject to change).

* **CARNEGIE SCIENCE CENTER,** One Allegheny Ave., Pittsburgh, PA 15212-5895. Tel.: 412-237-3400. Fax: 412-237-3375.
Web Site: www.carnegiesciencecenter.org
Founded: 1991.
Congressional District: 18
Key Personnel: Pres. & C.E.O., David M. Hillenbrand; Henry Buhl, Jr. Co Dir., Ann Metzger; Henry Buhl, Jr. Co Dir. & Chief Program Officer, Ronald J. Baillie; Dir. Science & Education, John Radzilowicz; Dir. Visitor Experience, Jessica Lausch; C.F.O., Kevin D. Hiles; Dir. Finance, Nancy Weidle; Vice Pres. Devel., Dolores F. Ellenberg; Dir. Devel. & Science, Danni Piccolo.
Personnel Profile: Full-Time Paid 80; Part-Time Volunteers 120.
Governing Authority: nonprofit organization. Parent Institution: Carnegie Institute. Tax-exempt: 501(c)(3).
Science and Technology Center.
Collections: Cold War-era submarine; space artifacts; model railroad & village.
Facilities: 150-seat planetarium; 300-seat auditorium; 340-seat OMNIMAX theater; coral reef aquarium; classrooms; observatory; computer learning lab; cafe; concession stand. Museum-related items for sale.
Activities: interactive exhibits; demonstrations; sky shows; laser shows; workshops for children & adults; science & engineering fair; teacher education; outreach programs; volunteer program; lab programs; overnighters; birthday parties; science apprenticeships.
Publications: astronomical calendar; magazine, CARNEGIE.
Hours & Admission Prices: Sun.-Thurs. 10-5, Fri.-Sat. 10-7; call to confirm. Adults $14, senior citizens & children $10; discounts to groups, AAM, ASTC & ICOM members; members no charge. Closed Thanksgiving; Christmas; occasional Steeler home game days. ♿
Attendance: 730,000
Membership: Senior 65 & over $50; Individual $75; Dual $100; Family $130; Premium $200.

CENTER FOR AMERICAN MUSIC, University of Pittsburgh, Stephen Foster Memorial, 4301 Forbes Ave., Pittsburgh, PA 15260. Tel.: 412-624-4100. Fax: 412-624-7447.
E-mail: dir@pitt.edu
Web Site: www.pitt.edu/~amerimus/CAM1.htm
Founded: 1937.
Congressional District: 14
Key Personnel: Dir., Deane L. Root; Assoc. Dir., Kathryn Miller Haines.
Personnel Profile: Full-Time Paid 2; Part-Time Paid 1; Part-Time Volunteers 20; Interns 2.
Governing Authority: university. Parent Institution: University of Pittsburgh. Tax-exempt: 170(b)(1)(A).
Music History Museum.
Collections: material relating to music in American Life; composer Stephen Collins Foster, 1826-1864; manuscripts; musical instruments; photographs.
Research Fields: life & works of Stephen Collins Foster; American music history.
Facilities: 30,000-item research library relating to American music 1830s-1930s emphasis; Life & Works of Stephen Collins Foster; archives; reading room; 580-seat auditorium; classroom.
Activities: guided tours; permanent exhibitions; performances; radio broadcasts; concert series; educational programs; lectures; curriculum guides.
Publications: songbook, Songs of Stephen Foster; research pamphlets; scores; sound recordings; biographical sketch of Foster.
Hours & Admission Prices: By appointment only. Closed university holidays. ♿
Attendance: 3,497 (estimated)

CHILDREN'S MUSEUM OF PITTSBURGH, 10 Children's Way, Pittsburgh, PA 15212-5250. Tel.: 412-322-5058. Fax: 412-322-4932.
E-mail: stuffee@pittsburghkids.org
Web Site: www.pittsburghkids.org
Formerly: Pittsburgh Children's Museum
Founded: 1980.
Congressional District: 14
Key Personnel: Exec. Dir., Jane Werner; Deputy Exec. Dir., Chris Siefert; Pres., Tom Mole; Vice Pres., Evan Rosenberg; Vice Pres., Jennifer Broadhurst; Sec., Gratia Maley; Treas., Robert Denove; Dir. Finance, Rebecca McNeil; Dir. Education, Lois Winslow; Dir. Visitor Svcs., Admissions & Museum Shop Mgr., George Brzezinski; Dir. Mktg., Bill Schlageter; Dir. Devel., Deborah Ellwood; Dir. Exhibits, Penny Lodge.
Personnel Profile: Full-Time Paid 30; Part-Time Paid 120; Part-Time Volunteers 60; Interns 10.
Governing Authority: nonprofit organization. Tax-exempt: 501(c)(3).
Children's Museum.
Collections: hands-on exhibits; renewable & educational resources; Margo Lovelace puppet & mask collection; communication artifacts; Andy Warhol's Myths; 10 silkscreen prints; Jim Henson puppets & props; Fred Rogers puppets; kids' climber; shimmering wind sculpture. Historic Buildings: c.1897 Post Office; c.1939 Planetarium.
Major Exhibits: Pittsburgh!, 1/10-5/10; Curious George, 6/10-9/10; Tough Art, 10/10-12/10.
Research Fields: anthropological studies relevant to international artifacts contained in Margo Lovelace puppet & mask collection; printmaking in the contemporary U.S.; interactive artwork; artists.
Facilities: 125-seat theater; classrooms; party rooms; 31,000 sq. ft. exhibit space; cafe. Museum-related items for sale.
Activities: participatory exhibits including play with real stuff for children 2-14; guided tours; organized education programs for children, undergraduate & graduate college students; volunteer program; traveling, loan, permanent & temporary exhibitions; school rental programs; school outreach programs; performing arts; puppet shows; plays; storytelling; residencies; afterschool & overnight programs for adolescents; literacy program for families; school & outreach programs; birthday party program; brochures; kids' climbers; rental facilities; family learning studies.
Publications: bimonthly e-newsletter; brochures; posters; banners; eblasts.
Hours & Admission Prices: Mon.-Sat. 10-5, Sun. 12-5. Adults $11, senior citizens & children over 7 $10; discounts to ASTC & ACM reciprocal memberships. Closed New Year's Day; Easter; Memorial Day; Independence Day; Labor Day; Thanksgiving; Christmas. ♿
Attendance: 232,098 (accurate)
Membership: Family $99; Extended Family & Grandparents $130; Deluxe Family $199.

THE FORT PITT BLOCK HOUSE, Point State Park, Pittsburgh, PA 15222. Mailing Address: 101 Commonwealth Place, Point State Pk., Pittsburgh, PA 15222-1212. Tel.: 412-471-1764.
Founded: 1894.
Congressional District: 14
Key Personnel: Pres. (V), Barbara M. Foster; Cur. & Museum Shop Mgr., Kelly Linn.
Governing Authority: private; nonprofit organization. Parent Institution: Fort Pitt Society; Subsidiary Institution: Pittsburgh Chapter, NSDAR. The Fort Pitt Society of the Daughters of the American Revolution of Allegheny County, Pennsylvania; Pittsburgh Chapter DAR.
Historic Building: 1764 Fort Pitt Block House.
Collections: 1764 Fort Pitt Block House; military artifacts.
Research Fields: French & Indian War; early colonial, western Pennsylvania, & Pittsburgh history.
Facilities: private library for use by curators; lectures. Books & other museum-related items for sale.
Activities: lectures.
Publications: books, Fort Duquesne & Fort Pitt.
Hours & Admission Prices: Wed.-Sun. 10-5. No charge; donations accepted. Closed most legal holidays. ♿
Attendance: 10,000 (estimated)

FORT PITT MUSEUM, Point State Park, Pittsburgh, PA 15222. Mailing Address: 101 Commonwealth Place, Pittsburgh, PA 15222-1212. Tel.: 412-281-9284. Fax: 412-281-1417.
Web Site: www.fortpittmuseum.com
Founded: 1964.
Congressional District: 14
History Museum: located on the original site of Fort Pitt.
Collections: 1750-1800 historic artifacts from Pittsburgh; military & frontier objects; tools; muskets; cannon; furniture; maps; documents.
Research Fields: French & Indian War; the American frontier.
Facilities: 200-vol. library of history of western Pennsylvania & the French and Indian War period; 18th-century books on military subjects available on premises; 100-seat auditorium; classrooms. Reproduction tinware, books & other museum-related items for sale.
Activities: guided tours; lectures; formally organized education programs for children; docent program; permanent & temporary exhibits. Museum Sponsors: 18th-century music performances June to August; Royal American Regiment drills.
Hours & Admission Prices: Temporarily closed.

THE FRICK ART & HISTORICAL CENTER, (M), 7227 Reynolds St., Pittsburgh, PA 15208-2919. Tel.: 412-371-0600. Fax: 412-371-6104.
E-mail: info@thefrickpittsburgh.org
Web Site: www.thefrickpittsburgh.org
Founded: 1990.
Congressional District: 14
Key Personnel: Dir., William B. Bodine, Jr.; Chm. (V), David A. Brownlee; Dir. Admin. & Finance, Terri L. Chapman; Dir. External Affairs, Susan S. Neszpaul; Comptroller, Chris Chambers; Dir. Education, Pam St. John; Dir. Curatorial Affairs, Sarah Hall; Registrar of Clayton, Robin Pflasterer; Registrar of Car & Carriage Museum, Bill Sheerer; Museum Shop Mgr., Beth Regan.
Personnel Profile: Full-Time Paid 50; Part-Time Paid 110; Part-Time Volunteers 10; Interns 4.
Governing Authority: nonprofit organization. Subsidiary Institution: The Frick Art Museum; Clayton, The Henry Clay Frick Estate; Car & Carriage Museum. Tax-exempt: 501(c)(3).
Art & History Museums.
Collections: Frick Art Museum: European paintings with emphasis on Italian paintings of the early Renaissance; 18th- century French paintings & sculptures; bronze & terracotta sculpture; tapestries; decorative arts; Chinese porcelain. Clayton, The Henry Clay Frick Estate: Frick family heirlooms; decorative arts; period furniture & furnishings; 19th-century art; porcelain; glass; costumes & textiles. Car & Carriage Museum: period carriages & vintage automobiles.
Major Exhibits: Icons of American Photography: A Century of Photographs from the Cleveland Museum of Art (T), 11/09-1/3/10; Childrens Hospital 1951: Photographs by Esther Bubley, 11/09-1/3/10; 1934: A New Deal for Artists (T), 1/30/10-4/25/10.
Research Fields: pertaining to collections & programming.
Facilities: art museum: 165-seat auditorium; permanent & temporary exhibitions; sketching & workshop studio; historic house; transportation museum; greenhouse; education center; restaurant. Museum-related items for sale.
Activities: guided tours; educational programs; lectures; traveling & permanent exhibitions; member receptions; special events; concerts; public events; film & video programs; cell phone tours.
Publications: member's newsletter & calendar; books, The Frick Art & Historical Center; My Father, Henry Clay Frick; catalogues, Renaissance & Baroque Bronzes in the Frick Art Museum; Collecting in the Guilded Age: Art Patronage in Pittsburgh 1890-1910; Clayton Days - Picture Stories; Christian Milovanoff, Conversation Pieces; Aaronel de Roy Gruber: The Frick Landscapes; The Early Works of Henry Koerner; Hoka-Neni; Seldom Seen Creatures of the Frick; Pittsburgh Collects: European Drawings, 1500 to 1800; Artistry & Innovation in Pittsburgh Glass, 1808-1882: From Bakewell & Ensell to Bakewell, Pears & Co.
Hours & Admission Prices: Tues.-Sun. 10-5. Clayton Tour: adults $12, seniors & students $10; discounts to AAM & ICOM members; members no charge. Closed New Year's Day; Independence Day; Thanksgiving; Christmas Eve & Day. ♿
Attendance: 132,070 (accurate)
Membership: Senior $30; Individual & Teacher $45; Family & Double $60; Fellow $100; Patron $250; Benefactor $500; Founders' Circle $1,000.

HISTORIC HARTWOOD MANSION, 200 Hartwood Acres, Pittsburgh, PA 15238-1193. Tel.: 412-767-9200. Fax: 412-767-0171.
Web Site: www.county.allegheny.pa.us/parks
Key Personnel: Dir., Linda K. Joy.
Personnel Profile: Part-Time Paid 9; Part-Time Volunteers 25.
Governing Authority: Parent Institution: Allegheny County Parks. Tax-exempt.
Historic House Museum: built in 1929, estate of John and Mary Flinn Lawrence, daughter of state Sen. William Flinn.
Collections: period furniture; personal artifacts; family photographs.
Hours & Admission Prices: Mon.-Sat. 10-3, Sun. 12-4. Adults $6, senior citizens 60 & over and children 13-17 $3, children 6-12 $2, children 5 & under $1. Closed holidays.

HUNT INSTITUTE FOR BOTANICAL DOCUMENTATION, Carnegie Mellon University, 5000 Forbes Ave., Pittsburgh, PA 15213-3815. Tel.: 412-268-2434. Fax: 412-268-5677.
Web Site: huntbot.andrew.cmu.edu
Founded: 1961.
Congressional District: 21
Key Personnel: Dir., Dr. Robert W. Kiger; Asst. Dir., Dr. T. D. Jacobsen; Business Officer & Sales Mgr., Donna M. Connelly; Art Cur., James J. White; Librarian, Charlotte A. Tancin; Archivist, Angela L. Todd.
Personnel Profile: Full-Time Paid 17.
Governing Authority: university. Parent Institution: Research Division of Carnegie Mellon University. Tax-exempt.
Science Art Institute.
Collections: botanical art & illustrations; watercolors, drawings & original prints; autograph collection from 18th through the 20th century; private papers of botanists; iconographic collection; Strandell collection of Linnaeana; Michel Adanson's library; Torner collection of Sesse & Mocino biological illustrations.
Research Fields: history of botany.
Facilities: 25,000-vol. library of books & journals on botany & its history, especially systemic botany, emphasizing pre-1850, available for research on premises; gallery.
Activities: temporary & traveling exhibitions.
Publications: brochures; journal; books; exhibition catalogues; bulletin.
Hours & Admission Prices: Mon.-Fri. 8:30-12 & 1-5, Sun. 1-4. No charge. Closed holidays.
Membership: Associate $35; Patron $100 & up.

MATTRESS FACTORY, LTD., 500 Sampsonia Way, Pittsburgh, PA 15212-4444. Tel.: 412-231-3169. Fax: 412-322-2231.
E-mail: info@mattress.org
Web Site: www.mattress.org
Founded: 1977.
Congressional District: 14
Key Personnel: C.E.O. & Pres. (V), Barbara Luderowski; Cur., Michael Olijnyk; Asst. Dir., Catena Bahneman.
Personnel Profile: Full-Time Paid 12; Part-Time Paid 12; Part-Time Volunteers 40; Interns 5.
Governing Authority: nonprofit organization. Tax-exempt: 501(c)(3).
Art Museum.
Collections: works by James Turrell, Winifred Lutz, Rolf Julius, Jene Highstein, Bill Woodrow, Allan Wexler, William Anastasi; collector's prints by Julius, Jene Highstein, William Anastasi, & Jessica Stockholder; installation art.
Facilities: library, including videos, tapes, slides, & books, pertaining to installation & performance art; 7,820 sq. ft. exhibit space.
Activities: guided tours; youth & adult education workshops; lectures; participatory exhibits; performances by performance artists.
Publications: biannual newsletter, Installation & Performance; retrospective catalogue.

Hours & Admission Prices: Tues.-Sat. 10-5, Sun. 1-5; other times by appointment. Adults $10, senior citizens $8, students $7; discounts to North American Reciprocal Membership Program & AAM members; members & children under 6 no charge. Closed New Year's Day; Easter; Memorial Day; Thanksgiving; Christmas. ♿
Attendance: 35,000 (estimated)
Membership: Student $25; Senior $30; International $40; Household $125; Associate $250; Factory 500 $500; Patron $1,000.

THE MILLER GALLERY AT CARNEGIE MELLON, Purnell Center for the Arts, Carnegie Mellon University, Pittsburgh, PA 15213-3890. Mailing Address: 5000 Forbes Ave., Pittsburgh, PA 15213-3890. Tel.: 412-268-3618. Fax: 412-268-4746.
Web Site: www.cmu.edu/millergallery
Formerly: Regina Gouger Miller Gallery
Founded: 2000.
Key Personnel: Dir., Astria Suparak; Graphics & Office Coord., Margaret Cox.
Personnel Profile: Full-Time Paid 3; Part-Time Paid 15; Interns 2.
Governing Authority: Parent Institution: Carnegie Mellon. Tax-exempt.
Art Gallery.
Collections: paintings.
Facilities: 9,000 sq. ft. exhibit space.
Activities: special events.
Publications: exhibition catalogues & brochures.
Hours & Admission Prices: Tues.-Sun. 12-6. No charge; donations accepted. ♿
Attendance: 15,000 (estimated)
Membership: Student $10; Individual $40.

NATIONAL AVIARY IN PITTSBURGH, INC., Allegheny Commons West, 700 Arch St., Pittsburgh, PA 15212-5248. Tel.: 412-323-7235. Fax: 412-321-4364.
E-mail: info@aviary.org
Web Site: www.aviary.org
Founded: 1952.
Congressional District: 14
Key Personnel: Exec. Dir., Patrick T. Mangus; Museum Shop Mgr., Betsy Swartz.
Personnel Profile: Full-Time Paid 30; Part-Time Paid 5; Part-Time Volunteers 69; Interns 7.
Governing Authority: private. Parent Institution: National Aviary in Pittsburgh, Inc. Tax-exempt: 501(c)(3).
Aviary.
Collections: 883 live birds; plants.
Research Fields: bird behavior; diets; avian ecology; breeding & reproduction.
Facilities: library of natural history books available on premises by permission; zoological park; botanical garden. Bird guide books, nature oriented gift items for sale.
Activities: guided tours on special request; permanent exhibitions; live exhibits; volunteer program. Center Sponsors: special instruction for talented school children by arrangement.
Publications: member newsletter.
Hours & Admission Prices: Mon.-Sat. 10-5, Sun. 12-5. Adults $9, seniors $8, children 2-12 $7.50; discounts to AAZPA & AAA members, Giant Eagle Advantage & DUO Card Holders & groups of 15 or more; members & children 2 and under no charge. Closed Thanksgiving; Christmas Day. ♿
Attendance: 110,212 (accurate)
Membership: Senior $25; Individual $35; Family $45; Family Plus $60; Donor $100; Patron $250; Benefactor $500; Partner in Preservation $750 and up.

PHIPPS CONSERVATORY AND BOTANICAL GARDENS, 1 Schenley Park, Pittsburgh, PA 15213-3830. Mailing Address: 1059 Shady Ave., Pittsburgh, PA 15232-2912. Tel.: 412-622-6914. Fax: 412-622-7363.
E-mail: info@phipps.conservatory.org
Web Site: www.phipps.conservatory.org
Founded: 1892.
Congressional District: 14
Key Personnel: Chm., Joseph Lagana; Exec. Dir., Richard Piacentini.
Governing Authority: municipal; nonprofit organization. Tax-exempt.
Conservatory.
Collections: orchids; palms; cacti & succulents; tropical plants; ferns; bonsai; plants from all over the world.
Facilities: 200-vol. library on horticulture available for reference; botanical gardens; display gardens under glass; outdoor perennial, rose, Japanese, & aquatic gardens. Gardening, conservatory-related items for sale.
Activities: permanent exhibits; seasonal flower shows; educational classes; guided tours.
Publications: Phipps Magazine; schools & programs brochure.
Hours & Admission Prices: Sat.-Thurs. 9:30-5, Fri. 9:30-10. Adult $10, seniors & students $9, children 2-18 $7; discounts to groups of 15 or more & AAA members; children under 2 & members no charge; AABGA reciprocal admission. Closed Thanksgiving & Christmas. ♿
Attendance: 225,000 (estimated)
Membership: Student & Senior Citizen $40; Individual $45; Family & Household $70; Contributing $145; Supporter $245; Sustaining $495; Benefactor $995; Henry Phipps Associate $1,245.

PITTSBURGH FILMMAKERS/PITTSBURGH CENTER FOR THE ARTS, 6300 Fifth Ave., Pittsburgh, PA 15232-2922. Tel.: 412-361-0873 & 0455. Fax: 412-361-8338.
E-mail: info@pittsburgharts.org
Web Site: www.pittsburgharts.org
Founded: 1945.
Congressional District: 14
Key Personnel: Exec. Dir., Charlie Humphrey; Dir., Laura Domencic; Dir. Devel., Loretta Stanish; Cur., Adam Welch; Museum Shop Mgr., Jen Carter.
Personnel Profile: Full-Time Paid 38; Part-Time Paid 40; Part-Time Volunteers 50; Interns 4.
Governing Authority: nonprofit organization. Tax-exempt: 501(c)(3).
Contemporary Arts Center.
Collections: various forms of art media.
Facilities: artworks by more than 600 regional & national artists for sale.
Activities: guided tours; lectures; organized education programs for children & adults with special needs, high school program; regional, national, international & traveling exhibitions. Museum Sponsors: Holiday Sale; Art Camp.
Publications: class schedule; email announcements & updates.
Hours & Admission Prices: Tues.-Sat. 10-5, Sun. 12-5. Suggested Donation $5; members no charge. Closed Christmas. ♿
Attendance: 36,067 (accurate)
Membership: Associate: Individual $60; Family $90. Access: Individual $75; Family $150.

PITTSBURGH ZOO AND PPG AQUARIUM, One Wild Place, Pittsburgh, PA 15206. Tel.: 412-665-3639, ext. 0. Fax: 412-665-3661.
E-mail: djones@pittsburghzoo.org
Web Site: zoo.pgh.pa.us
Founded: 1898.
Key Personnel: C.E.O. & Pres., Dr. Barbara T. Baker; Chm. (V), Beverlynn Elliott; Zoo Veterinarian, Dr. Stephanie James; Education Coord., Margie Marks; Gift Shop Mgr., Eli Grill.
Personnel Profile: Full-Time Paid 110; Part-Time Paid 35; Part-Time Volunteers 165; Interns 6.
Governing Authority: Parent Institution: Zoological Society of Pittsburgh. Tax-exempt.
Zoo & Aquarium.
Collections: birds, reptiles fish & mammals from all over the world; 4,000 specimens; 434 species.
Research Fields: Inia management & biology; African elephant reproduction.
Facilities: 500-vol. library of reference books.
Activities: art classes; twilight tours; summer camp program; workshops. Zoo Sponsors: Members' Day; Radio Stations Day.
Publications: bimonthly, Zoo Insider; Zoo Explorer.
Hours & Admission Prices: Spring & Fall daily 9-5; Winter daily 9-4 (gates close at 3); Memorial Day to Labor Day daily 9-6 (gates close at 4:30). Adults $12, senior citizens $11, children 2-13 $10; discount to groups; members & AAZPA members no charge. Closed New Year's Day; Thanksgiving; Christmas. ♿
Attendance: 1,010,237 (accurate)
Membership: Individual & Senior Couple $50; Family & Grandparents $75; Family Plus $110; Contributing $160.

RODEF SHALOM BIBLICAL BOTANICAL GARDEN, 4905 5th Ave., Pittsburgh, PA 15213-2941. Tel.: 412-621-6566. Fax: 412-621-5475.
E-mail: jacob@rodefshalom.org
Web Site: www.biblicalgardenpittsburgh.org
Founded: 1987.
Key Personnel: C.E.O., Charles Deaktor; Dir., Irene Jacob.
Personnel Profile: Full-Time Volunteers 2; Part-Time Volunteers 45.
Governing Authority: nonprofit. Parent Institution: Rodef Shalom congregation. Tax-exempt: 501(c)(3).
Biblical Botanical Garden.
Collections: more than 200 temperate & tropical species of plants.
Major Exhibits: Dressing Well - Plants and Clothing - Ancient and Modern, 6/10-9/10.
Research Fields: biblical plants; near Eastern plants.
Facilities: gardens.
Activities: guided tours; lectures; organized education programs for adults; temporary exhibitions; annual events.

Publications: periodic newsletter, Papyrus; biannual papers of symposia; annual booklets; books.
Hours & Admission Prices: June to mid-Sept. Sun.-Tues. & Thurs. 10-2, Wed. 7-9, Sat. 12-1. No charge; donations accepted. ♿
Attendance: 3,500 (estimated)

SENATOR JOHN HEINZ HISTORY CENTER, (M), 1212 Smallman St., Pittsburgh, PA 15222-4200. Tel.: 412-454-6000. Fax: 412-454-6031.
E-mail: hswp@hswp.org
Web Site: www.heinzhistorycenter.org
Formerly: Senator John Heinz Pittsburgh Regional History Center
Founded: 1879.
Congressional District: 14
Key Personnel: Pres. & C.E.O., Andrew E. Masich; Chm. (V), Stephen Tritch; Controller, Lori Presto; Museum Div. Dir., Anne Madarasz; Acquisitions Archivist, Dave Grinnell; Senior Vice Pres., Betty Arenth; Dir. Education & Visitor Svcs., Ann Fortescue; Dir. Mktg. & Communications, Ned Schano; Registrar & Collections Mgr., Kathleen Wendell; Dir. Human Resources, Anne Marie Grzybek; Dir. Meadowcroft Rockshelter & Museum of Rural Life, David Scofield; Dir. Library & Archives, Alexis Macklin; Museum Shop Mgr., Debbie Rhoads.
Personnel Profile: Full-Time Paid 77; Part-Time Paid 40; Part-Time Volunteers 700; Interns 53.
Governing Authority: board of trustees. Parent Institution: Historical Society of Western Pennsylvania. Subsidiary Institution: Meadowcroft Museum of Rural Life, Avella, PA; Western Pennsylvania Sports Museum. Tax-exempt: 501(c)(3).
History Museum.
Collections: books; archives; costumes; tools; vehicles; industrial artifacts; glass & decorative arts; toys & other items related to Western Pennsylvania history.
Research Fields: western Pennsylvania & Pittsburgh history; American business & industry; ethnicity & folklife; urban & rural history; family history; women's history.
Facilities: 35,000-vol. library & archive of regional history books, manuscripts, maps, family history, music & newspapers, available for interlibrary loan & for public use; reading room; 80-seat restaurant; classrooms; 7,000 sq. ft. Children's Discovery Hall. Museum-related items for sale.
Activities: concerts; guided tours; dance recitals; docent program; formal education for children; lectures; hobby workshops; participatory, permanent, temporary & traveling exhibits; rental gallery; theater; library & archives research facilities. Annual Events: History Makers Dinner; History Uncorked; National History Day; 1879 Founders Circle Dinner; History Book Fair; Asian Heritage Festival; Glass Expo.
Publications: quarterly magazine, Western Pennsylvania History; quarterly newsletter, Making History; books, Boundless Lives: Italian Americans of Western Pennsylvania; Glass: Shattering Notions; Points in Time: Building a Life in Western Pennsylvania; Pittsburgh's Strip District: Around the World in a Neighborhood; Pittsburgh Born, Pittsburgh Bred; Soul Soldiers: African Americans and the Vietnam Era; local history curriculum kits.
Hours & Admission Prices: History Center: daily 10-5. Sports Museum: daily 10-5. Library & Archives: Thurs.-Sat. 10-5. Meadowcroft: Memorial Day-Labor Day Wed-Sat. 12-5, Sun. 1-5. History Center, Sports Museum, Library & archives: adults $10, seniors $9, children 4-17 $5; discounts to AAM members; children under 3 & Time Travelers no charge. Meadowcroft: Adults $10, seniors $9, children 4-17 $5; discounts to AAM members; children under 3 & members no charge. Call for group rates. Closed New Year's Day; Easter; Thanksgiving; Christmas. ♿
Attendance: 160,000 (estimated)
Membership: Student $25; Individual $57; Grandparent $80; Family $85; Contributor $125; Patron $250.

SOCIETY FOR CONTEMPORARY CRAFT, 2100 Smallman St., Pittsburgh, PA 15222-4440. Tel.: 412-261-7003. Fax: 412-261-1941.
E-mail: info@contemporarycraft.org
Web Site: www.contemporarycraft.org
Founded: 1971.
Congressional District: 14
Key Personnel: Exec. Dir., Janet L. McCall; Pres. Bd., Julia Sawyer; Dir. Exhibitions, Kate Lydon; Dir. Education, Laura Rundell; Mgr. Devel., Christina Bard; Dir. Finance, Bob Musca; Dir. Devel., Becky Berkey; Museum Store Mgr., Sharon Massey; Asst. Museum Store Mgr., Janet Darby; Studio Asst., Adrienne Borkowski.
Personnel Profile: Full-Time Paid 6; Part-Time Paid 4; Part-Time Volunteers 40; Interns 1.
Governing Authority: nonprofit organization. Tax-exempt.
Contemporary Craft Museum.
Collections: contemporary works of art by nationally known artists including clay, wood, metal, glass, jewelry, fiber & mixed media.
Research Fields: contemporary art with a focus on crafts.
Facilities: 1,700-vol. library; 3,000 sq. ft. exhibit space. Contemporary crafts for sale.
Activities: guided tours; artist lectures; adult studio classes; quarterly public opening receptions; drop-in studio for kids; artist demonstrations.
Publications: exhibition catalogs; quarterly newsletter.
Hours & Admission Prices: Tues.-Sat. 10-5. No charge; donations accepted. Closed major holidays. ♿
Attendance: 128,000 (estimated)
Membership: Friend $60; Patron $125; Sponsor $250; Benefactor $500; Collector's Circle $1,000.

UNIVERSITY ART GALLERY, UNIVERSITY OF PITTSBURGH, 104 Frick Fine Arts Bldg., University of Pittsburgh, Pittsburgh, PA 15260-7601. Tel.: 412-648-2400 & 2423. Fax: 412-648-2792.
Web Site: vrcoll.fa.pitt.edu/uag
Founded: 1966.
Key Personnel: Dept. Chm., Kirk Savage.
Personnel Profile: Full-Time Paid 1; Part-Time Paid 1; Interns 1.
Governing Authority: private university. Parent Institution: University of Pittsburgh. Tax-exempt.
Art Gallery: housed in 1965 building by Helen Clay Frick.
Collections: emphasis on western Pennsylvania; paintings; Callot prints; Asian decorative arts; western Pennsylvania paintings; Callot prints; works by Gertrude Quastler; Asian decorative arts.
Facilities: 200-seat auditorium; educational facilities.
Activities: lectures; loan, temporary & traveling exhibitions.
Hours & Admission Prices: Mon.-Wed. & Fri. 10-4, Thurs. 10-8. No charge. Closed holidays; when the University is not in session. ♿

WOOD STREET GALLERIES, 601 Wood St., Pittsburgh, PA 15222-2503. Tel.: 412-471-5605. Fax: 412-232-3262.
Web Site: www.woodstreetgalleries.org
Key Personnel: Cur., Murray Horne; Asst. Cur., Kate Little; Preparator, George Dun; Preparator, Chris Korch; Preparator, Chris Beauregard; Preparator, Ian Brill; Preparator, Marc Burgess; Preparator, Jonathan Chamberlain; Preparator, Ryan Emmett; Preparator, Curt Riegelnegg
Contemporary Gallery.
Collections: works by contemporary artists.
Hours & Admission Prices: Tues.-Thurs. 11-6, Fri.-Sat. 11-8. No charge; donations accepted.
Attendance: 1,500 (accurate)

Pleasantville

PITHOLE VISITOR CENTER, 14118 Pithole Rd., Pleasantville, PA 16341. Mailing Address: 202 Museum Lane, Titusville, PA 16354-7658. Tel.: 814-827-2797. Fax: 814-827-4888 (Drake Well).
E-mail: drakewell@verizon.net
Founded: 1975.
Congressional District: 23
Key Personnel: C.E.O., Barbara Franco; Chm., Stephen Miller; Site Mgr., Barbara Zolli; Pres. (V), Fred Sliter.
Personnel Profile: Part-Time Volunteers 6.
Governing Authority: state. Parent Institution: Pennsylvania Historical & Museum Commission, Commonwealth Keystone Bldg., 400 North St., Harrisburg, PA 17120. Tel.: 717-787-3115. Tax-exempt.
Oil Well Museum.
Collections: 1865-75 oil industry tools & equipment; model of former oil boom town.
Research Fields: 19th-century oil industry.
Facilities: visitor center; picnic area; archaeology site. Museum-related items for sale.
Activities: self-guided tours; multi-media programs.
Hours & Admission Prices: June to Labor Day Sat.-Sun. 12-6; other times by appointment. Adults 16 & over $2, students 6-15 $1.
Attendance: 2,000 (estimated)

Plymouth

PLYMOUTH HISTORICAL SOCIETY, INC., 115 Gaylord Ave., Plymouth, PA 18651-2200. Tel.: 570-779-5840.
Founded: 1986.
Key Personnel: Dir. & Pres. (V), Georgetta Potoski; Treas., Irene Hujick; Devel., Helen Yonells; Education, Pat Matthews; Public Rels., Chris Pagoda.
Governing Authority: private; nonprofit organization. Tax-exempt: 501(c)(3).
Historical Society Museum.
Collections: local artifacts; Native American; coal mining; genealogy; early 1900s kitchen; utensils; dishes; sewing machine; carpet loom; period furnishings.

Research Fields: church histories; genealogy; coal mining.
Facilities: 500-vol. library; 350-seat auditorium; 1,500 sq. ft. exhibit space; classrooms.
Activities: formal education programs for adults; guided tours; temporary exhibitions; lectures; special events.
Publications: annual newsletter, Plymouth Historical Society, Inc.
Hours & Admission Prices: Thurs. 6 pm-8 pm, Sat. 12-4; other times by appointment. No charge; donations accepted.
Attendance: 300
Membership: Individual $15; Family $25.

Point Marion

FRIENDSHIP HILL NATIONAL HISTORIC SITE, RD1, Point Marion, PA 15474. Mailing Address: 1 Washington Pkwy., Farmington, PA 15437-9501. Tel.: 724-725-9190. Fax: 724-725-1999.
E-mail: lawren_dunn@nps.gov
Web Site: www.nps.gov/frhi
Founded: 1978.
Congressional District: 20
Key Personnel: C.E.O., Joanne Hanley; Site Mgr., Mary Ellen Synder; Cultural Resource Mgr. & Cur., Lawren Dunn; Museum Shop Mgr., James Tomasek.
Personnel Profile: Full-Time Paid 5; Part-Time Paid 2; Part-Time Volunteers 7; Interns 1.
Governing Authority: federal. Parent Institution: Dept. of the Interior. Subsidiary Institution: National Park Service. Tax-exempt.
History Museum.
Collections: Albert Gallatin; whiskey rebellion.
Research Fields: career of Albert Gallatin; history of southwest Pennsylvania.
Facilities: library; visitor center; hiking trails.
Activities: guided tours; self-guided tours; trail guides for hiking & cross-country skiing.
Publications: park folders & inserts only.
Hours & Admission Prices: Summer: daily 9-5; Winter: Sat.-Sun. 9-5. No charge. Closed Federal holidays. ♿
Attendance: 50,000 (estimated)

Pottstown

POTTSGROVE MANOR, (M), 100 W. King St., Pottstown, PA 19464-6318. Tel.: 610-326-4014. Fax: 610-326-9618.
E-mail: pottsgrovemanor@montcopa.org
Web Site: www.historicsites.montcopa.org
Founded: 1988.
Congressional District: 5
Key Personnel: Dir. Parks & Heritage Svcs. Dept., Ronald Ahlbrandt; Site Supvr., Laura Daugherty; Cur., Amy Reis.
Personnel Profile: Full-Time Paid 3; Part-Time Paid 2; Part-Time Volunteers 60.
Governing Authority: Parent Institution: Parks & Heritage Services, Department of Montgomery County. Tax-exempt.
Historic House: 1752 Pottsgrove Manor.
Collections: 1752-1783 furnishings & interpretation; lifestyle.
Major Exhibits: So Long and Toilsome A Journey: Transportation in Colonial PA, 3/6/10-1/30/11.
Research Fields: early Pennsylvania iron industry; Potts family & 18th-century lifestyle; colonial Black history.
Facilities: colonial revival boxwood formal & flower gardens. Museum-related items, handcrafted colonial reproductions & books for sale.
Activities: guided tours; children's educational programs & special events.
Publications: volunteer newsletter.
Hours & Admission Prices: Tues.-Sat. 10-4, Sun. 1-4. No charge; donations accepted. Closed New Year's Day; Easter; Independence Day; Thanksgiving; Christmas. ♿
Attendance: 6,188 (accurate)

Pottsville

HISTORICAL SOCIETY OF SCHUYLKILL COUNTY, (M), 305 N. Centre St., Pottsville, PA 17901-2512. Mailing Address: P.O. Box 1356, Pottsville, PA 17901-7356. Tel.: 570-622-7540. Fax: 570-628-2012.
Key Personnel: Dir., Dr. Peter Yasenchak
Historical Society Museum.
Collections: county history & culture; photographs; personal artifacts.
Hours & Admission Prices: Wed. 1:30-7, Thurs.-Fri. 10-4, Sat. 9-1. Adults $3; members no charge.

Prospect Park

MORTON HOMESTEAD, 100 Lincoln Ave., Prospect Park, PA 19076. Mailing Address: P.O. Box 202, c/o Pennsylvania Historical & Museum Commission, Chadds Fond, PA 19317-0202. Tel.: 610-583-7221 & 459-3342. Fax: 610-583-2349.
E-mail: erump@state.pa.us
Founded: 1939.
Congressional District: 7
Key Personnel: Dir., Bob Sieber.
Governing Authority: state. Parent Institution: Pennsylvania Historical & Museum Commission. Tax-exempt.
History Museum: housed in late 17th-century Morton Homestead.
Collections: outdoor exhibits on history of the site.
Facilities: outdoor exhibits; picnic area.
Activities: tours.
Hours & Admission Prices: Temporarily closed. ♿
Attendance: 2,000 (estimated)

Punxsutawney

PUNXSUTAWNEY AREA HISTORICAL & GENEALOGICAL SOCIETY, 400-401 W. Mahoning St., Punxsutawney, PA 15767. Mailing Address: P.O. Box 286, Punxsutawney, PA 15767-0286. Tel.: 814-938-2555.
Founded: 1978.
Key Personnel: Chm. (V), Elmer Reed; Pres. (V), Martha A. Armstrong; Museum Shop Mgr., Karen Curry.
Personnel Profile: Full-Time Volunteers 2; Part-Time Volunteers 25.
Governing Authority: Tax-exempt.
Historical Society Museum.
Collections: local history & culture; Native American artifacts; period tools & utensils; regional lumbering; area coal mining & coke production; local railroading; clothing; quilts; radio & early televisions; photographs; Groundhog Day history; genealogy.
Major Exhibits: Objects of Costume, 11/09-7/11.
Facilities: Museum-related items for sale.
Activities: children's art workshops in the spring & fall; children's history camp in summer.
Publications: quarterly newsletter, Histo-Report.
Hours & Admission Prices: Bennis House & Lattimer House: Thurs.-Sun. 1-4. Genealogy: Lattimer House Thurs. & Sat. 10-1. No charge; donations accepted. ♿
Attendance: 1,000 (estimated)
Membership: Individual $15; Family $25; Life $300.

Quarryville

SOLANCO HISTORICAL SOCIETY, 1932 Robert Fulton Hwy., Quarryville, PA 17566. Mailing Address: Box 33, Quarryville, PA 17566-0033. Tel.: 717-548-2679.
E-mail: slchs@aol.com
Web Site: www.roots.com/~paslchs/index.html
Formerly: Robert Fulton Birthplace
Founded: 1970.
Congressional District: 16
Key Personnel: C.E.O., Mrs. Suzanne P. Lamborn; Museum Shop Mgr., Anita Reed; Museum Shop Mgr., Stan White.
Personnel Profile: Part-Time Volunteers 22.
Governing Authority: state. Parent Institution: Southern Lancaster County Historical Society for the Pennsylvania Historical & Museum Commission, Box 1026, Harrisburg, PA. 17120.
Historic House: c.1760 Robert Fulton birthplace.
Collections: local history; period furniture; genealogical material; 4 historic buildings.
Research Fields: agriculture & mining of the Soanco area; Lancaster Oxford Southern Railroad; genealogy; local history.
Activities: guided tours; permanent exhibitions.
Publications: annual calendar; quarterly, newsletter.
Hours & Admission Prices: Birthplace: Memorial Day-Labor Day Sat. 11-4, Sun. 1-5. Adults $4, children 6-12 $2; children under 6 no charge. ♿
Attendance: 750 (estimated)
Membership: Annual $10; Life $100.

Reading

BERKS COUNTY HERITAGE CENTER, 1102 Red Bridge Rd., Reading, PA 19605. Mailing Address: 2201 Tulpehocken Rd., Wyomissing, PA 19610-1020. Tel.: 610-374-8839. Fax: 610-373-7049.
E-mail: cwegener@countyobberks.com
Web Site: www.co.berks.pa.us/parks/cwp

Founded: 1981.
Congressional District: 17
Key Personnel: Dir., Cathy L. Wegener.
Personnel Profile: Full-Time Paid 1; Part-Time Paid 7; Part-Time Volunteers 125.
Governing Authority: Parent Institution: Berks County Parks & Recreation Dept. Tax-exempt.
History Museum.
Collections: local history & culture; wagon wheel manufacturing; period artifacts; canal transportation. Historic Building: Gruber Wagon Works.
Activities: lectures; workshops. Annual Event: Heritage Festival in October.
Publications: Gruber Wagon Works: The Place Where Time Stood Still.
Hours & Admission Prices: May-Oct. Tues.-Sat. 10-4, Sun. 12-5. Adults $5, senior citizens 60 & over $4, students 7-18 $3; children under 7 no charge.
Attendance: 10,000 (estimated)

FREEDMAN GALLERY-ALBRIGHT COLLEGE, (M), 13th St. & Bern St., Reading, PA 19604. Mailing Address: Box 15234, Reading, PA 19612-5234. Tel.: 610-921-7541. Fax: 610-921-7768.
E-mail: gallery@alb.org
Web Site: www.albright.edu/freedman
Founded: 1976.
Congressional District: 6
Key Personnel: Pres., Dr. Lex McMillan; Dir., Michael Howell; Provost, Dr. Andrea Chapdelaine; Vice Pres. Finance, Bill Wood; Dir. Public Information, Barbara Marshall.
Personnel Profile: Full-Time Paid 1; Part-Time Paid 5; Interns 1.
Governing Authority: college. Parent Institution: Albright College. Tax-exempt: 501(c)(3).
College Art Gallery.
Collections: paintings, drawings, photographs, sculpture & prints by contemporary American artists.
Research Fields: contemporary art in all mediums.
Facilities: 2,800 sq. ft. exhibit space; 250-seat auditorium; educational facilities.
Activities: guided tours; lectures; films; broadcast programs; organized education programs for undergraduate or graduate college students; participatory, loan, temporary & traveling exhibitions.
Publications: exhibition catalogs; brochures.
Hours & Admission Prices: Sept.-May Tues. 12-8, Wed.-Fri. 12-6, Sat.-Sun. 12-4; Call for summer hours. No charge; donations accepted. Closed major holidays & college breaks. ♿
Attendance: 10,715 (estimated)
Membership: Individual $25; Family & Contributing $50; Supporting $100; Patron $500; Benefactor $1,000.

HISTORICAL SOCIETY OF BERKS COUNTY, 940 Centre Ave., Reading, PA 19601-2198. Tel.: 610-375-4375. Fax: 610-375-4376.
E-mail: history@berkshistory.org
Web Site: www.berkshistory.org
Founded: 1869.
Congressional District: 6
Key Personnel: C.E.O., George M. Meiser, IX; Dir., Sime B. Bertolet.
Personnel Profile: Full-Time Paid 4; Part-Time Paid 7; Part-Time Volunteers 100; Interns 10.
Governing Authority: society. Tax-exempt: 501(c)(3).
History Museum.
Collections: agriculture items; archives; decorative arts; history; Indian artifacts; Pennsylvania German arts & crafts.
Research Fields: county history.
Facilities: 10,000-vol. library of local history books available on premises; 200-seat auditorium. Gift items for sale.
Activities: lectures; concerts; formally organized education programs for children; docent program permanent & temporary exhibitions; school loan service; children's hands-on room.
Publications: quarterly magazine, Historical Review of Berks County; The Passing Scene.
Hours & Admission Prices: Tues.-Sat. 9-4. Adults $4, senior citizens $3, children $2; discounts to AAM members; members no charge. Library: $5. ♿
Attendance: 15,000 (estimated)
Membership: Individual $40; Family $50; Contributing $75; Benefactor $100; Guarantor $500. Business & Professional: Sponsor $100; Supporting $250; Corporate Guarantor $500; Corporate Patron $1,000.

MID ATLANTIC AIR MUSEUM, 11 Museum Dr., Reading, PA 19605-9407. Tel.: 610-372-7333. Fax: 610-372-1702.
E-mail: maam@maam.org
Web Site: www.maam.org
Founded: 1980.
Congressional District: 14
Key Personnel: Chm. & Pres., Russell A. Strine; Cur. & Museum Shop Mgr., Linda T. Strine; Business Office Mgr., Brenda Saylor; Special Projects Coord., David Schott.
Personnel Profile: Full-Time Paid 5; Part-Time Paid 5; Part-Time Volunteers 150; Interns 1.
Governing Authority: private; nonprofit organization. Tax-exempt: 501(c)(3).
Aviation Museum.
Collections: 70 aircrafts; aviation with emphasis on Mid-Atlantic states history.
Research Fields: historic aviation.
Facilities: 10,000-vol. library available for use on the premises; field research station; classroom; 25-seat meeting room. Museum-related items for sale.
Activities: concerts; docent program; guided tours; hobby workshops; lectures; rental gallery; school loan service; loan, temporary & traveling exhibitions; training programs for professional museum workers; speakers bureau activities. Annual Events: World War II Weekend; Planes, Trains & Automobiles Weekend.
Publications: bimonthly newsletter, Museum Review.
Hours & Admission Prices: Daily 9:30-4. Adults $6, children $3; discounts to groups; members & children 5 and under no charge. Closed New Year's Day; Easter; Independence Day; Thanksgiving; Christmas. ♿
Attendance: 30,000 (accurate)
Membership: Individual $45; Sustaining $100; Corporate $500; Life $750.

PLANETARIUM AT THE READING PUBLIC MUSEUM, 1211 Parkside Dr. S., Reading, PA 19611-1441. Mailing Address: 500 Museum Rd., Reading, PA 19611-1425. Tel.: 610-371-5850, ext . 244. Fax: 610-371-5632.
E-mail: planetarium@readingpublicmuseum.org
Web Site: www.readingpublicmuseum.org/planetarium
Founded: 1967.
Congressional District: 6
Key Personnel: C.E.O. & Dir., Ronald C. Roth; Chm. (V), Rolf D. Schmidt; 1st Vice Chm. (V), Kathleen W. Kleppinger; 2nd Vice Chm. (V), Donald Bristol; Dir. Planetarium, Mark J. Mazurkiewicz.
Personnel Profile: Full-Time Paid 1; Part-Time Paid 3.
Governing Authority: Foundation. Parent Institution: Reading Public Museum. Tax-exempt: 170 (b)(1)(A).
Planetarium.
Collections: astronomical artifacts; meteorites; serigraphs.
Research Fields: planetarium production techniques.
Facilities: 1,000-vol. library of astronomical materials, tapes, records, films & 7,000 photographic slides; satellite weather station; spacesphere.
Activities: foreign language programs; special education classes; special provisions for the physically handicapped; college classes.
Publications: M.A.P.S.; Planetary Society; I.P.S.
Hours & Admission Prices: Tues.-Thurs. & Sat. 11-5, Fri. 11-8, Sun. 12-5. Museum: adults $7, children $5. Star Shows: adults $6, seniors, children & students $4; discounts to AAM & ICOM members; children under 4 & members no charge. Closed New Year's Day; Martin Luther King Jr. Day; Labor Day; Thanksgiving; Christmas. ♿
Attendance: 17,000 (accurate)
Membership: Full-time Student $20; Senior $25; Individual $35; Family Dual $60; Contributor $125.

* **READING PUBLIC MUSEUM, (M),** 500 Museum Rd., Reading, PA 19611-1425. Tel.: 610-371-5850, ext. 224. Fax: 610-371-5632.
Web Site: www.readingpublicmuseum.org
Founded: 1904.
Congressional District: 6
Key Personnel: Chm., Rolf Schmidt; Dir. & C.E.O., Ronald C. Roth; 1st Vice Chm., Kathleen W. Kleppinger; 2nd Vice Chm., Don Bristol; Sec., Sandi M. Abraham; Treas., Richard W. Zuidema; Asst. Sec., Leigh Rye; Museum Shop Mgr., Nancy Chapple.
Personnel Profile: Full-Time Paid 15; Part-Time Paid 7; Part-Time Volunteers 600; Interns 2.
Governing Authority: foundation. Parent Institution: Foundation for the Reading Public Museum. Tax-exempt: 501(c)(3).
Art & Science Museum.
Collections: anthropology; arboretum; archaeology; paintings; sculpture; graphics; decorative arts; entomology; Pennsylvania folk art; American Indian artifacts; mineralogy; natural history; paleontology.
Major Exhibits: The Magic of Hollywood: The Gene London Costume Collection, 11/09-5/30/10; Backyard Monsters (T), 4/13/10-7/5/10; Jun Kaneko, 6/26/10-9/5/10; William Baziotes Retrospective, 10/9/10-1/16/11; Raucous! Everything Raven (T), 10/10/10-1/12/11.
Research Fields: paintings; graphics; entomology.
Facilities: 18,000-vol. library of art & natural history books available on

premises by request; arboretum; 200-seat auditorium; planetarium. Fine art, local art, reproductions, crafts, museum-related items for sale.
Activities: guided tours; lectures; films; gallery talks; concerts; formally organized educational programs; gallery teachers program; outreach & collaborations with many local organizations; inter-museum loan, permanent, temporary & traveling exhibitions; school loan service; organized trips.
Publications: exhibit catalogues; Friends newsletter; Museum Road.
Hours & Admission Prices: Tues.-Thurs. & Sat. 11-5, Fri. 11-8, Sun. 12-5. Adults $7, children 4-17, seniors, & students $5; discounts as part of ASTC reciprocal agreement; members no charge. Closed New Year's Day; Thanksgiving; Christmas. ♿
Attendance: 50,326 (accurate)
Membership: Student $20; Senior Citizen & Educator $25; Individual $35; Dual Senior $ 50; Family $60; Contributor $125.

Rockhill Furnace

RAILWAYS TO YESTERDAY, INC., adjacent to East Broad Top Railroad, State Rte. 994, Rockhill Furnace, PA 17249. Mailing Address: P.O. Box 1601, Allentown, PA 18105-1601. Tel.: 717-821-2179; 814-447-9576.
Web Site: www.rockhilltrolley.org
Founded: 1960.
Congressional District: 9
Key Personnel: Chm. (V), Joel Salomon; Pres. (V), Matthew Nawn; Librarian, Douglas E. Peters; Treas., Judy Mullen; Museum Shop Mgr., Charles T. Kumpas.
Personnel Profile: Part-Time Volunteers 25.
Governing Authority: nonprofit organization. Tax-exempt: 501(c)(3).
Transportation Museum: specializes in collecting, restoring & maintaining cars that operated in Pennsylvania; trolley cars from Johnstown, Philadelphia, York, Scranton & other locations in operation.
Collections: seven operating passenger trolley cars; two operating electric snow sweepers; operating snowplow; operating maintenance of way trolley; ten non-operating trolleys; Septa subway car; four other railcars; photographs, books & artifacts related to railways.
Research Fields: history of electric railway transportation & related items.
Facilities: approx. 1,300-vol. library of railway-related material; restoration information & facilities available for use by contacting Douglas E. Peters, 706 Glenwood St., Emmaus, PA 18049. Tel. 610-965-4203. Railway books for sale.
Activities: guided tours; operating trolleys; temporary exhibitions; members restore & operate cars on weekends; new members welcome. Museum Sponsors: Christmas Holiday Events.
Publications: quarterly newsletter, The Trolley Museum Retriever.
Hours & Admission Prices: June-Oct. Sat.-Sun. 10:30-4:15. Adults $6, children 2-12 accompanied by adult $3; discounts to other railway museum members; members & children under 2 no charge.
Attendance: 5,000 (estimated)
Membership: Family & children under 18 $5; Associate $25; Sustaining $40.

ROCKHILL TROLLEY MUSEUM, 430 Meadow St., Rockhill Furnace, PA 17249. Mailing Address: P.O. Box 203, Rockhill Furnace, PA 17249. Tel.: 814-447-9576 (weekends); 610-437-0448 (weekdays).
E-mail: sgurley@prodigy.net
Web Site: www.rockhilltrolley.org
Founded: 1962.
Congressional District: 9
Key Personnel: Pres., Joel Salomon; Archivist, Douglas Peters; Museum Shop Mgr., Charles T. Kumpas.
Personnel Profile: Part-Time Volunteers 35.
Governing Authority: private; nonprofit organization. Parent Institution: Railways To Yesterday Inc., P.O. Box 1601, Allentown, PA 18105. Tax-exempt: 501(c)(3).
Transportation Museum.
Collections: 24 trolleys from 1899-1947 including cars from Pennsylvania; photographs.
Facilities: library. Seven operating passenger trolleys; two operating snowsweeper trolleys. Museum-related items for sale.
Activities: demonstration trolley ride; guided tours; restoration shop viewing area; special events. Museum Sponsors: Fall Spectacular; Member's Day; Santa's Trolley.
Publications: quarterly newsletter, The Retriever.
Hours & Admission Prices: June-Oct. Sat.-Sun. 11-4. Adults $6, children 2-12 $3; discounts to groups, AAA, AARP & AAM members; members no charge.
Attendance: 5,000 (estimated)
Membership: Associate $25; Sustaining $40.

Russell

SHED MUSEUM, 7159 Scandia Rd., Russell, PA 16345-6941. Tel.: 814-757-4443.
Key Personnel: Dir., Debbie Fitzsimmons
History Museum.
Collections: local history & culture; period artifacts; early cars; gas engines; photographs.
Facilities: Museum-related items for sale.
Hours & Admission Prices: May-Oct. Fri.-Sun. 11-5 & by appointment.

Saint Marys

HISTORICAL SOCIETY OF ST. MARYS AND BENZINGER TOWNSHIP, 99 Erie Ave., Saint Marys, PA 15857-1408. Tel.: 814-834-6525.
E-mail: stmaryshistoricalsociety@windstream.net
Web Site: smhistoricalsociety.com
Founded: 1960.
Congressional District: 5
Key Personnel: Pres., Jeanette Donachy; Sec., Donna M. Burgess; Cur., Alice Beimel.
Personnel Profile: Part-Time Volunteers 30.
Governing Authority: municipal; nonprofit organization. Tax-exempt.
History Museum.
Collections: photographic representation of early history of St. Marys; documents; artifacts; manuscript collections.
Research Fields: local history; videotaped interviews of older residents; family histories; photos; artifacts; deeds, maps & other documents.
Facilities: library of photographs, artifacts, deeds, maps & documents available for loan and on premises; reading room.
Activities: guided tours; lectures; formally organized educational programs; permanent exhibitions.
Publications: weekly historical column; annual member newsletter.
Hours & Admission Prices: Tues. 10-4, Thurs. 1-4 & 6-8; other times by appointment. No charge. ♿
Attendance: 1,500 (estimated)
Membership: Student $1; Single $6; Family $10; Patron $25; Benefactor $50; Corporate $100.

Schaefferstown

HISTORIC SCHAEFFERSTOWN, INC., 106 N. Market St., Schaefferstown, PA 17088. Mailing Address: P.O. Box 307, Schaefferstown, PA 17088-0307. Tel.: 717-949-2444.
E-mail: info@hsimuseum.org
Web Site: www.hsimuseum.org
Founded: 1965.
Congressional District: 17
Key Personnel: Pres., Alice Oskam; Museum Shop Mgr., Betty Fromm.
Personnel Profile: Part-Time Paid 1; Part-Time Volunteers 205.
Governing Authority: nonprofit organization. Tax-exempt: 501(c)(3).
Village Museum.
Collections: portrayal of 18th- & 19th-century Pennsylvania German life & culture; tools; implements; furniture; quilts; Indian artifacts. Historic Buildings: c.1740 Alexander Schaeffer Farm Museum; c.1740s Gemberling-Rex House; 1969 Thomas R. Brendle Memorial Library & Museum.
Research Fields: agricultural practices from 18th-19th century to present in Pennsylvania Dutch country; folklife of the Pennsylvania Germans.
Facilities: 700-vol. library of books on Pennsylvania history, the history of the Pennsylvania Germans, folklore & folklife of the Pennsylvania Germans available for use upon request; reading room.
Activities: guided tours; lectures; permanent & temporary exhibitions.
Publications: quarterly bulletin, Historic Schaefferstown Record; pamphlets; booklets, Volume I of the Brendle Collection of Pennsylvania German Folklore.
Hours & Admission Prices: Alexander Schaeffer Farm Museum: April-Oct. 4 1st Sat. of month 10-4. Festivals: 10-5. Adults $5; children under 12 & members no charge. Brendle Museum & Rex House: April 4 to Oct. 4 Tues.-Thurs. 1-4, 1st Sat. of month 10-4; Oct. 5 to April 3 Tues.-Thurs. 1-4. Adults $3 per site; discounts to AAM & ICOM members; members no charge.
Attendance: 4,863 (accurate)
Membership: Individual $17; Family $27.

Schnecksville

LEHIGH VALLEY ZOO, 5150 Game Preserve Rd., Schnecksville, PA 18078-0519. Mailing Address: P.O. Box 519, Schnecksville, PA 18078-0519. Tel.: 610-799-4171. Fax: 610-799-4170.
Zoo.

Collections: wildlife & their habitats.
Activities: special events; educational programs; rental facilities.
Hours & Admission Prices: April-Oct. daily 10-4; Nov.-March daily 10-3. April-Oct.: adults $9, seniors 65 & over $7.25, children 2-11 $6.50; Nov.-March: adults $6.50, seniors 65 & over and children 2-11 $6.50. Closed New Year's Day; Thanksgiving; Christmas.

Schwenksville

PENNYPACKER MILLS, 5 Haldeman Rd., Schwenksville, PA 19473-1844. Tel.: 610-287-9349. Fax: 610-287-9657.
E-mail: pennypackermills@montcopa.org
Web Site: www.montcopa.org
Founded: 1981.
Congressional District: 6
Key Personnel: Dir. Montgomery Co. (PA) Dept. of Parks & Heritage Svcs., Ronald H. Ahlbrandt; Park Site Supvr., Ella Aderman.
Personnel Profile: Full-Time Paid 6; Part-Time Paid 1; Part-Time Volunteers 50.
Governing Authority: county. Parent Institution: Montgomery Co. (PA) Dept. of Parks & Heritage Services, 1430 Dekalb St., Norristown, PA 19404. Tax-exempt.
Historic House: c.1901-1916 colonial revival building.
Collections: Pennypacker family memorabilia; 18th- to 20th-century furnishings; letters; books; photos; historic landscape.
Research Fields: 17th to early 20th-century family history; 20th-century landscape history; colonial revival architectural history; late 19th to early 20th-century Pennsylvania political history.
Facilities: 3,000-vol. library pertaining to local history; 50,000 Pennypacker letters; exhibit gallery; informal landscape garden; mansion; barn; 170 acre rural property.
Activities: guided tours; organized educational programs; docent program; workshops; nature walks; loan & temporary exhibitions. Special Events: Summer Social; Children's Halloween; Civil War Reunion; Christmas Open House.
Publications: bimonthly newletter.
Hours & Admission Prices: Tues.-Sat. 10-4, Sun. 1-4; last tour 3:30. Suggested Donation: $2. Closed New Year's Eve & Day; Easter; Independence Day; Thanksgiving; Christmas Eve & Day. ♿
Attendance: 25,000 (accurate)

Scottdale

WEST OVERTON MUSEUMS, 109 West Overton Rd., Scottdale, PA 15683. Tel.: 724-887-7910. Fax: 724-887-5010.
E-mail: info@westovertonvillage.org
Web Site: www.westovertonvillage.org
Founded: 1928.
Congressional District: 12
Key Personnel: Pres. Bd., Alisa Barnhart; Dir., Christopher Kline; Museum Shop Mgr., Connie Fox.
Personnel Profile: Full-Time Paid 4; Part-Time Paid 4; Part-Time Volunteers 60; Interns 1.
Governing Authority: society. Tax-exempt: 501(c)(3).
Museum Complex: c.1850 rural industrial village.
Collections: 1839-1939 household & farm implements; industrial implements; archives.
Facilities: auditorium; media center & reference library; archives; photographs. Museum-related items for sale.
Activities: guided tours; lectures; theater; organized education programs for children; participatory, permanent & temporary exhibitions.
Publications: Oberholtzer & Nash Family History; quarterly newsletter, The Village Progress; a collection of Civil War letters, Remember Your Friend Until Death.
Hours & Admission Prices: May-Oct. Fri.-Sat. 12-6, Sun. 1-5; other times by appointment. Adults $7, senior citizens & children $4; members & children under 6 no charge. Closed major holidays. ♿
Attendance: 5,000 (estimated)
Membership: Individual $15; Family $30; Bronze $50; Silver $75; Gold & Business $100; Platinum & Sponsor $250; Patron $500.

Scranton

EVERHART MUSEUM: NATURAL HISTORY, SCIENCE AND ART, (M), 1901 Mulberry St., Scranton, PA 18510-2390. Tel.: 570-346-7186. Fax: 570-346-0652.
E-mail: general.information@everhart-museum.org
Web Site: www.everhart-museum.org
Founded: 1908.
Congressional District: 10
Key Personnel: C.E.O. & Dir., Cara A. Sutherland; Chm. Bd., Mark H. De Stefano; Dir. Interpretive Programs, Terra Steele; Cur., Nezka Pfeifer; Dir. Devel. & Communications, Lauren White; Museum Shop Mgr., Deb Burke; Administrative Asst., Nancy Casey; Dir. Resources, Deborah L. Pann.
Personnel Profile: Full-Time Paid 6; Part-Time Paid 10; Part-Time Volunteers 60; Interns 10.
Governing Authority: nonprofit organization. Tax-exempt: 501(c)(3).
Art, Science & Natural History Museum.
Collections: 19th- & 20th-century American art; European paintings & works on paper; Dorflinger Glass; American folk art; Asian Art; Ethnographic Arts from Oceanic, African, Native American & Pre-Columbian cultures; natural history collection - animals, birds, insects, fossils, rocks, shells, vertebrates, minerals.
Research Fields: John Willard Raught (1857-1931) American Impressionist Painter; American folk art; geology; regional art; Dorflinger Glass.
Facilities: Museum-related items for sale.
Activities: lectures; gallery talks; educational programs; permanent & temporary exhibitions.
Publications: newsletter; brochures; catalogs.
Hours & Admission Prices: Feb.-Dec. Mon. & Thurs.-Fri. 12-4, Sat. 10-5, Sun. 12-5. Adults $5, students & seniors $3, children $2; discounts to AAM & ICOM members; children under 6 & members no charge. ♿
Attendance: 20,860 (accurate)
Membership: Student/Academic & Senior 60 and over $25; Individual $30; Dual Senior $40; Family $45; Sustainer $100; Patron $250; Curator's Circle $500; Artist's Circle $1,000; Director's Circle $2,000 & up.

THE HOUDINI MUSEUM & THEATER, 1433 N. Main Ave., Scranton, PA 18508-1822. Mailing Address: 229 Willow Ave., Olyphant, PA 18447-1443. Tel.: 570-342-5555.
Web Site: www.houdini.org
Founded: 1992.
Key Personnel: C.E.O. & Pres. (V), John Bravo; Chm. (V), Joann Englehardt; Financial Dir., Dorothy Krugger; Cur. & Archivist, Freida Schmidt; Devel., Penny Wilkes; Public Rels., Dick Brooks; Security & Museum Shop Mgr., Ray Carter; Education, Dorothy Dietrich.
Personnel Profile: Full-Time Volunteers 2; Part-Time Volunteers 10.
Governing Authority: private; nonprofit organization. Tax-exempt: 501(c)(3).
History Museum.
Collections: history room containing pictures & artifacts designed to map Houdini's life from birth to death; prop room displays artifacts & props belonging to Houdini; theater room displays posters; film & artifacts.
Research Fields: research is ongoing to uncover dates & significant appearances of Houdini as he traveled the world.
Facilities: 5,000-vol. library of books & documents on Houdini; educational facilities; 4,000 sq. ft. exhibit space; 150-seat large screen theater. Museum-related items for sale.
Activities: films; formal education programs for children; guided tours; lectures; theater; magic show. Museum Sponsors: Halloween Spooktacular Shows.
Hours & Admission Prices: Open Memorial Day to Labor Day daily for tours & magic shows, call for hours. Adults $14.95, children 11 & under $11.95; discounts to AAM & ICOM members and groups of 20 or more.
Attendance: 40,000 (estimated)
Membership: Individual $25; Patron $50; Silver $100; Gold $200.

THE LACKAWANNA HISTORICAL SOCIETY AT THE CATLIN HOUSE, 232 Monroe Ave., Scranton, PA 18510-2104. Tel.: 570-344-3841. Fax: 570-344-3815.
E-mail: maryann@lackawannahistory.org
Web Site: lackawannahistory.org
Founded: 1886.
Congressional District: 10
Key Personnel: Exec. Dir., Mary Ann Moran-Sarakinus; Pres., Donald J. Frederickson, Jr., Esq.; Treas., Douglas Forrer; Sec., Arlene Devereaux Ohara; Museum Asst., Ann Marie O'Hara.
Personnel Profile: Full-Time Paid 1; Part-Time Paid 2; Part-Time Volunteers 8.
Governing Authority: nonprofit organization. Tax-exempt: 501(c)(3).
Historic Society Museum: housed in The Catlin House, a late Victorian mansion in English Tudor Revival architecture.
Collections: archives containing manuscripts, letters, documents, maps, books, & photographs pertaining to the settlement of Lackawanna County, Pennsylvania & the development of the Iron, Coal, Railroad & Lace industries from 1840-present; period furnishings; clothing; paintings; agricultural items; Civil War items; bicycles; typewriters; local memorabilia.
Research Fields: iron manufacturing; anthracite coal mining; Pennsylvania railroads & street car lines; 19th-century architecture; photographic history; lace manufacture & genealogy.
Facilities: 2,000-vol. library of books; 322 manuscripts; archives of coal

companies, lace manufacturing company, railroads, genealogies, local histories, photographs, maps, letters, ledgers & reports available to the public.
Activities: guided tours by prior appointment; lectures; concerts; docent program; organized education programs for undergraduate or graduate college students affiliated with Marywood College & University of Scranton, Scranton, PA; loan, temporary & traveling exhibitions; traveling lectures to schools.
Publications: journal, The Lackawanna Historical Society Journal; brochure, Welcome to the Lackawanna Historical Society; book, Greetings from Scranton.
Hours & Admission Prices: Tues.-Fri. 10-5, Sat. 12-3. Guided Tours: Tues.-Fri. 1-3, Sat. 12-3 or by appointment. Museum: $2 per person; donations accepted. Library: $5 per person. Closed New Year's; Good Friday; Memorial Day; Independence Day; Labor Day; Thanksgiving; Christmas Eve & Day. ♿
Attendance: 4,000 (estimated)
Membership: Student $10; Individual $25; Family $35; Contributing $75; Sustaining $150; Organization & Business available.

PENNSYLVANIA ANTHRACITE HERITAGE MUSEUM, 22 Bald Mountain Rd., McDade Park, Scranton, PA 18504. Tel.: 570-963-4804 & 4845. Fax: 570-963-4194.
E-mail: ckulesa@state.pa.us
Web Site: www.anthracitemuseum.org
Founded: 1970.
Congressional District: 10
Key Personnel: Pres. (V), Mr. Francis Tartella; Admin., Chester J. Kulesa; Cur., Richard Stanislaus; Museum Shop Mgr., Margaret Reese.
Personnel Profile: Full-Time Paid 7; Part-Time Paid 3; Part-Time Volunteers 40; Interns 2.
Governing Authority: state. Pennsylvania Historical and Museum Commission, Bureau of Historic Sites and Museums Commonwealth Keystone Building, Plaza Level, 400 North St., Harrisburg, PA 17120-0053. Tax-exempt: 170(c)(1).
History Museum.
Collections: religious, medical & education materials; mining tools & machinery; silk & lace machinery; photographs; maps; vehicles; prints; paintings.
Research Fields: history of northeast Pennsylvania including transportation, urban, mining, textile, social & cultural areas, ethnicity, immigration.
Facilities: library of research materials; 25,000 sq. ft. exhibit hall; auditorium. Museum-related items for sale.
Activities: tours; films; lectures; education programs for students; arts fair; drama & music performances.
Publications: quarterly newsletter; pamphlets; books.
Hours & Admission Prices: April-Nov. Mon.-Sat. 9-5, Sun. 12-5; Dec.-March Tues.-Sat. 9-5, Sun. 12-5. Adults 12-64 $6, senior citizens 65 & over $5.50, youth 3-11 $4; discounts to AAM & ICOM; active military, family, children under 6 & members no charge. Closed New Year's Day; Civil Rights Day; Presidents' Day; Columbus Day; Veterans Day; Thanksgiving; Christmas. ♿
Attendance: 20,000 (accurate)
Membership: Senior Citizen & Student $15; Individual $20; Family $30.

STEAMTOWN NATIONAL HISTORIC SITE, 350 Cliff St. off Lackawanna Ave., Scranton, PA 18503. Mailing Address: 150 S. Washington Ave., Scranton, PA 18503-2079. Tel.: 570-340-5200 & 5201. Fax: 570-340-5309.
Web Site: www.nps.gov/stea
Founded: 1986.
Congressional District: 11
Key Personnel: C.E.O., Harold Hagen.
Personnel Profile: Full-Time Paid 60; Part-Time Paid 20; Part-Time Volunteers 80.
Governing Authority: federal. Parent Institution: National Park Service. Tax-exempt: 501(c)(3).
Transportation & Technology Museum; located in Scranton's DL&W railroad yard.
Collections: steam locomotives; passenger coaches; maintenance of way equipment; locomotive shop & turntable; small objects.
Research Fields: 20th-century steam railroading.
Facilities: two museums; visitor center; restored roundhouse.
Activities: steam excursions; tours conducted by park rangers.
Hours & Admission Prices: Jan. 6-March 29 daily 10-4; March 30-Jan. 5 daily 9-5. Adults $6; children 16 & under no charge. Train Excursion Ride: call for information. Closed New Year's Day; Thanksgiving; Christmas. ♿
Attendance: 120,000 (accurate)

SURACI GALLERY, MAHADY GALLERY, AND THE MASLOW COLLECTION, (M), 2300 Adams Ave., Scranton, PA 18509-1598. Tel.: 570-348-6278, ext. 2428. Fax: 570-340-6023.
E-mail: gallery@marywood.edu
Web Site: www.themaslow collection.org
Formerly: Marywood University Art Galleries (Suraci Gallery and Contemporary Gallery)
Founded: 1915.
Congressional District: 11
Key Personnel: C.E.O. & Pres., Sister Anne Munley, I.H.M., Ph.D.; Dir., Sandra Ward Povse.
Personnel Profile: Full-Time Paid 2; Part-Time Paid 14; Interns 1.
Governing Authority: private college; nonprofit. Parent Institution: Marywood University. Tax-exempt: 501(c)(3).
University Art Gallery.
Collections: Suraci Gallery: 19th-century Chinese trade furniture & Russian bronzes; European marble sculpture; Oriental decorative arts (ceramics & ivories); 19th-century European ceramics & American and European furniture. Mahady Gallery: contemporary art exhibits in all media. Maslow Collection: contemporary art including paintings, photographs, & major prints by Jasper Johns, Frank Stella, Robert Rauschenberg, & Andy Warhol; contemporary 2-dimensional.
Major Exhibits: Selections from the Maslow Collection, 11/09-12/10; Small Works: William Bramton, Betsey Garand, Brenda Garand & Maggie Shen, 1/16/10-2/14/10.
Research Fields: 19th-century Chinese trade furniture; Oriental decorative arts; Russian bronzes & European marble sculpture; 19th-century European & American furniture; 19th-century European ceramics; contemporary paintings by emerging NY artists from late 1970s to early 1990s.
Facilities: 5,500 sq. ft. exhibit space.
Activities: guided tours; lectures; temporary exhibitions; field experience & independent studies for undergraduate & graduate college students. Biennial Events: Regional Art Exhibition, a juried exhibit open to artists in northeastern Pennsylvania.
Publications: exhibition catalogs, Women's Work; Soul Full: the personal & the political; Transcending the Surface; The Poetic Object: Paintings of Rebecca Purdum; Zeuxis: Still Life Painting; Anne Tabachnick: Painting about Paintings; Rayuela/Hopscotch: 15 Contemporary Latin American Artists; Potter's Apprentice.
Hours & Admission Prices: Winter: Mon. & Thurs.-Fri. 9-4, Tues.-Wed. 9-8, Sat.-Sun. 1-4. Summer: Mon.-Fri. 12-3. No charge. Closed major holidays; semester breaks. ♿
Attendance: 17,525 (estimated)

Selinsgrove

LORE DEGENSTEIN GALLERY, Susquehanna University, 514 University Ave., Selinsgrove, PA 17870-1001. Tel.: 570-372-4059. Fax: 570-372-2775.
E-mail: olivetti@susqu.edu
Web Site: www.susqu.edu/art_gallery
Founded: 1993.
Congressional District: 17
Key Personnel: Dir., Daniel Olivetti.
Personnel Profile: Full-Time Paid 1; Part-Time Paid 15; Interns 2.
Governing Authority: private college; nonprofit. Parent Institution: Susquehanna University. Tax-exempt.
Art Gallery.
Collections: American & Pennsylvania regional art including paintings, sculpture, prints, drawings & photographs; French advertising posters from 1887-1990; French literary magazines from 1895-1905.
Research Fields: American art; French advertising posters.
Facilities: 450-seat auditorium; 2,500 sq. ft. exhibit space.
Activities: formal education programs for undergraduate students affiliated with Susquehanna University; guided tours; lectures; loan, temporary & traveling exhibitions.
Publications: exhibition catalog, Encountering the Narrative in the Recent Work of Florence Putterman; Hans Moller, Purveyor of Color: The Essence of Vision 1943-1995.
Hours & Admission Prices: Daily 12-4. No charge. Closed university holidays & breaks. ♿
Attendance: 3,592 (accurate)

Sewickley

SEWICKLEY VALLEY HISTORICAL SOCIETY, 200 Broad St., Sewickley, PA 15143-1525. Tel.: 412-741-5315.
E-mail: sewickleyhistory@verizon.net
Web Site: www.sewickleyhistory.org
Key Personnel: Pres., L. John Kroeck
Historical Society Museum.

Collections: local history & culture; period furnishings; personal artifacts; photographs.
Activities: lectures; seminars.
Hours & Admission Prices: Tues.-Fri. 10-2; other times by appointment.

Shippensburg

SHIPPENSBURG HISTORICAL SOCIETY MUSEUM, 52 W. King St., Shippensburg, PA 17257-0539. Mailing Address: P.O. Box 539, Shippensburg, PA 17257-0539. Tel.: 717-532-6727.
E-mail: info@shippensburghistory.org
Web Site: www.shippensburghistory.org
Founded: 1945.
Congressional District: 9
Key Personnel: Pres., John McCorriston; Vice Pres., John Gaughan; Collections Mgr., Trisha Grace; Cur., Jacob Crider.
Personnel Profile: Part-Time Paid 1; Part-Time Volunteers 50.
Governing Authority: society. Affiliated with Shippensburg Historical Society. Tax-exempt: 170(b).
General Museum.
Collections: area history; archives; material pertaining to local events & history; general items; Native American artifacts; WPA projects; medical related items; photographs; Laughlin postcards; clothing; goblets; toys; dolls; inkwells; miniature carousels; fans & ivory artifacts.
Research Fields: genealogy & local history.
Facilities: library of early first editions, Pennsylvania literature & history and historical society books available for research on premises.
Activities: guided tours; permanent & temporary exhibitions; programs & special events.
Publications: books, Forbes Expedition - Cowan's Gap to Juniata Crossing; 1821 & 1858 maps of Shippensburg; Shippen's Survey 1737-1762; Yesterday's Shippensburg 1994; Cemetery Lists: Records In Stone, Vols. I, II, III, IV & V; pictorial history, Shippensburg area; The Elusive Fort Morris; Do You Remember?; Clyde A. Laughlin, Postcard King of the Cumberland Valley; Shippensburg area historical postcards; The Caledonia Story; newsletter for members; The Shippensburg Historical Society: A Fifty Year Retrospective 1945-1995; Indians, Indians; 1860 U.S. Census of Shippensburg Borough, Cumberland Co., PA; Shippensburg in the Civil War; Black History of Shippensburg, Pennsylvania: 1860-1936; Samuel Davis Sturgis 1822-1889: Shippensburg's Forgotten Hero; Battle of the Bulge: One Small Corner.
Hours & Admission Prices: Wed. & Fri.-Sat. 1-4 & by appointment. No charge; donations accepted.
Attendance: 1,800 (estimated)
Membership: Single $20; Couple $30; Contributing $50; Business $100; Corporate $250; Life $300.

SHIPPENSBURG UNIVERSITY FASHION ARCHIVES AND MUSEUM, 1871 Old Main Dr., Harley Hall, Lower Level, Shippensburg, PA 17257-2299. Tel.: 717-477-1239.
Web Site: webspace.ship.edu/fasharch/
Founded: 1980.
Key Personnel: Dir., Dr. Karin J. Bohleke.
Personnel Profile: Part-Time Paid 5; Part-Time Volunteers 6.
Governing Authority: public university. Tax-exempt: 501(c)(3).
University Costume Museum.
Collections: 19th-20th century clothing & accessories.
Major Exhibits: Nineteenth Century Costume Treasures of the Fashion Archives and Museum, 2/4/10-12/8/10.
Facilities: 1,500-vol. library; 800 sq. ft. exhibit space.
Activities: lectures; temporary exhibitions.
Publications: annual newsletter, A Sense of Style.
Hours & Admission Prices: Academic Year: Mon.-Thurs. 12-4; other times by appointment. No charge; donations accepted. Closed holidays.
Attendance: 900 (estimated)

Somerset

HISTORICAL AND GENEALOGICAL SOCIETY OF SOMERSET COUNTY, 10649 Somerset Pike, Somerset, PA 15501-7357. Tel.: 814-445-6077. Fax: 814-443-6621.
E-mail: bsarver@state.pa.us
Web Site: www.somersethistoricalcenter.org
Founded: 1959.
Congressional District: 12
Key Personnel: Pres., George Kaufman; Cur., Carrie Blough; Asst. Cur., Gail Smith; Librarian, Susan Seese; Museum Shop Mgr., Mark Ware.
Personnel Profile: Full-Time Paid 2; Part-Time Paid 1; Part-Time Volunteers 35.
Governing Authority: nonprofit corporation. Tax-exempt: 501(c)(3).
Local History Museum; SW Pennsylvania rural history.
Collections: agriculture; archaeology; genealogy; archives; cider press; maple sugar camp. Historic Houses: 1804 log house; 1773 first settlers log cabin. Historic Site: covered bridge; agriculture
Research Fields: agriculture; archaeology; genealogy; manuscripts; archives.
Facilities: 1,000-vol. library of history books available for use on premises; reading room.
Activities: lectures; tours; craft workshops; genealogical research. Museum Sponsors: Mountain Craft Days in September.
Publications: quarterly magazine, Laurel Messenger.
Hours & Admission Prices: Tues.-Sat. 9-5, Sun. 12-5. Adults $6, seniors $3.50, children 6-17 $2; discounts with tickets from other PHMC sites & AAM members; members no charge. Closed most holidays. ♿
Attendance: 23,000 (accurate)
Membership: Student $5; Individual $25; Family $35; Sustaining $55; Life $1,000.

LAUREL ARTS, 214 S. Harrison Ave., Somerset, PA 15501-1803. Tel.: 814-443-2433. Fax: 814-443-3870.
E-mail: arts@laurelarts.org
Web Site: www.laurelarts.org
Founded: 1975.
Congressional District: 12
Key Personnel: Dir., Michael S. Knecht; Pres. (V), Sharon Clapper; Treas., Andy Burns.
Personnel Profile: Full-Time Paid 3; Part-Time Paid 10; Part-Time Volunteers 500.
Governing Authority: private; nonprofit organization. Tax-exempt: 501(c)(3).
Art Museum.
Collections: local & regional works of art including oils, watercolors, pastels, serigraphs, lithographs, weavings, mosaics, photographs, papercuttings, & bronzes.
Facilities: library; 1,600 sq. ft. exhibit space.
Activities: permanent & temporary exhibitions; art classes & workshops; performing arts programs; summer camps; arts festivals; dance recitals; formal education programs. Annual Event: Somerfest.
Publications: bimonthly newsletter, ArtLink.
Hours & Admission Prices: Mon.-Thurs. 10-8, Fri. 10-4, Sat. 12-4. No charge. Closed New Year's Day; Easter; Memorial Day; Independence Day; Labor Day; Thanksgiving & day after; Christmas week.
Attendance: 51,015 (estimated)
Membership: Single $25; Couple $35; Family $40; Associate $100; Platinum $250; Sustaining $500 & up.

SOMERSET HISTORICAL CENTER, 10649 Somerset Pike, Somerset, PA 15501-7357. Tel.: 814-445-6077. Fax: 814-443-6621.
E-mail: chfox@state.pa.us
Web Site: www.somersethistoricalcenter.org
Founded: 1969.
Congressional District: 12
Key Personnel: Admin., Charles Fox; Educator, Mark D. Ware; Clerk, Bernice Sarver; Maintenance, Eric Sadler.
Personnel Profile: Full-Time Paid 4; Part-Time Paid 2; Part-Time Volunteers 25; Interns 1.
Governing Authority: state. Parent Institution: Pennsylvania Historical and Museum Commission, Commonwealth Keystone Bldg., 400 North St., Harrisburg, PA. 17120-0053. Subsidiary: Historical & Genealogical Society of Somerset Co. Tax-exempt: 170(c)(1).
History Museum.
Collections: agriculture; rural history; 1880 cider press. Historic Buildings & Sites: 1798 two-story log house; 1860 maple sugar camp; 1850 covered bridge; 1773 reconstructed log cabin; comprehensive agricultural exhibits.
Research Fields: agriculture & rural life; southwest PA 1740-1940 genealogy; vernacular architecture.
Facilities: 300-vol. library of genealogical and history books available for use on premises only; 1,000 family history files; folklife center.
Activities: guided tours; lectures; films; formally organized educational programs; permanent & temporary exhibitions. Museum Sponsors: Mountain Craft Days.
Publications: quarterly newsletter, Laurel Messenger.
Hours & Admission Prices: Tues.-Sat. 9-5, Sun. 12-5. Adults 18-60 $6, seniors $5.50, youth $3; discounts to groups, tickets from other PHMC sites, AAA & AAM members; members no charge. Closed New Year's Day; Thanksgiving; Christmas. ♿
Attendance: 23,000 (accurate)
Membership: Single $25; Family $35.

South Fork

JOHNSTOWN FLOOD NATIONAL MEMORIAL, 733 Lake Rd., South Fork, PA 15956-3602. Tel.: 814-495-4643. Fax: 814-495-7463.
Web Site: www.nps.gov/jofl
Founded: 1964.
Congressional District: 12
Key Personnel: Supt., Keith Newlin; Chm. (V) & Museum Shop Mgr., Doug Richardson; Cur., Nancy Smith.
Personnel Profile: Full-Time Paid 4; Part-Time Volunteers 100.
Governing Authority: federal. U.S. Dept. of the Interior, National Park Service, Washington, DC 20240. Tax-exempt: 501(c)(3).
Park Museum Memorial: located at the site of the dam which collapsed May 31, 1889, causing the Johnstown Flood.
Collections: books; articles; photos; artifacts relating to 1889 Johnstown Flood.
Research Fields: Pennsylvania Mainline Canal; Lake Conemaugh; South Fork Fishing & Hunting Club; 1889 Johnstown Flood.
Facilities: visitor center; picnic area. Books for sale.
Activities: guided tours; hiking; costumed interpretation
Hours & Admission Prices: Memorial Day-Labor Day daily 9-5. Adults 15 & over $5. Closed New Year's Day; Martin Luther King Jr. Day; Presidents' Day; Veterans Day; Thanksgiving; Christmas. ♿
Attendance: 190,000

South Williamsport

PETER J. MCGOVERN LITTLE LEAGUE MUSEUM, (M), 525 Rte. 15 Hwy., South Williamsport, PA 17701. Mailing Address: P.O. Box 3485, Williamsport, PA 17701-0485. Tel.: 570-326-3607. Fax: 570-326-2267.
E-mail: museum@littleleague.org
Web Site: www.littleleague.org
Formerly: Peter J. McGovern Little League Baseball Museum
Founded: 1982.
Congressional District: 17
Key Personnel: C.E.O., Steven Keener; Dir., Janice L. Ogurcak; Financial Dir., David Houseknecht; Museum Shop Mgr., Adam Thompson.
Personnel Profile: Full-Time Paid 2; Part-Time Paid 6; Part-Time Volunteers 12.
Governing Authority: nonprofit organization. Parent Institution: Little League Baseball, Inc. Tax-exempt: 501(c)(3).
Little League Museum.
Collections: growth & development of Little League Baseball, 1939-present; equipment; uniforms; photos; 1954-present team rosters; 1947-present Little League World Series programs; magazines featuring youth baseball; films.
Major Exhibits: Roberto Clemente (T), 9/10-10/10.
Facilities: 110-vol. library pertaining to the sport of baseball & Little League, pamphlets, booklets, rule books, articles, archives tracing the growth & development of Little League, available for use by appointment; 100-seat theatre. Gift items for sale.
Activities: films; guided tours; loan, temporary & participatory exhibitions.
Publications: newsletter, Pieces of the Past.
Hours & Admission Prices: June Mon. & Thurs.-Sat. 10-5, Sun. 12-5; July-Aug. Mon.-Sat. 10-5, Sun. 12-5; Labor Day to Memorial Day Fri.-Sat. 10-5; other times by appointment. Call for admission prices. Closed New Year's Day; Easter; Thanksgiving; Christmas. ♿
Attendance: 18,000 (accurate)

Springdale

RACHEL CARSON HOMESTEAD, 613 Marion Ave., Springdale, PA 15144-1242. Mailing Address: P.O. Box 46, Springdale, PA 15144-0046. Tel.: 724-274-5459. Fax: 724-275-1259.
E-mail: carsonhomestead@verizon.net
Web Site: www.rachelcarsonhomestead.org
Founded: 1975.
Congressional District: 4
Key Personnel: Bd. Pres., Kathleen Wendell; Exec. Dir., Patricia DeMarco, Ph.D.
Personnel Profile: Full-Time Paid 4; Part-Time Volunteers 10; Interns 1.
Governing Authority: private; nonprofit. Tax-exempt: 501(c)(3).
Historic House: located at the birthplace & childhood home of ecologist & Silent Spring author Rachel Carson.
Collections: Carson family period artifacts; environmental history.
Facilities: 150-vol. library on Rachel Carson, environmental issues & history; educational facilities; 800 sq. ft. exhibit space; nature/conservation center. Museum-related items for sale.
Activities: formal education programs for children; summer camp grades K-8; guided tours; lectures; loan exhibitions; volunteer programs. Annual Event: Rachel Carson Day in May.
Publications: quarterly newsletter, The Spring.
Hours & Admission Prices: Call for reservation. Adults $5, senior citizens & children 5-12 $3; discounts to groups of ten or more; members no charge. Closed major holidays. ♿
Attendance: 2,000 (estimated)
Membership: Kid's Club $10; Student, Senior & Low Income $15; Individual $30; Family $50; Supporting Member $125; Sustaining Member $275; Patron $500; Benefactor $1,000.

Springs

SPRINGS MUSEUM, Rte. 669, Springs, PA 15562. Mailing Address: P.O. Box 62, Springs, PA 15562-0062. Tel.: 814-662-2625.
E-mail: jfb@qcol.net
Web Site: www.springspa.org
Founded: 1957.
Congressional District: 12
Key Personnel: Pres. (V), Joseph Bender.
Personnel Profile: Part-Time Paid 7; Part-Time Volunteers 6.
Governing Authority: society. Parent Institution: Spring Historical Society of Casselman Valley. Tax-exempt.
General Museum.
Collections: fossils; pioneer tools; furniture.
Facilities: library of scrapbooks of historical value available on premises.
Activities: guided tours. Society Sponsors: Folk Festival in October.
Publications: annual magazine, Casselman Chronicle.
Hours & Admission Prices: Memorial Day to Labor Day Wed.-Fri. 1-5, Sat. 9-2. No Charge; donations accepted. ♿
Attendance: 5,000 (estimated)
Membership: Individual $20; Family $30.

State College

CENTRE COUNTY HISTORICAL SOCIETY, (M), Centre Furnace Mansion, 1001 E. College Ave., State College, PA 16801-6898. Tel.: 814-234-4779.
E-mail: info@centrecountyhistory.org
Web Site: centrecountyhistory.org
Founded: 1904.
Congressional District: 5
Key Personnel: Pres. (V), Jacqueline J. Melander; Exec. Dir., Angela Breeden.
Personnel Profile: Full-Time Paid 2; Full-Time Volunteers 1; Part-Time Volunteers 50; Interns 1.
Governing Authority: private; nonprofit organization. Tax-exempt: 501(c)(3).
General Museum.
Collections: Victorian furnishings; 19th-20th century Centre County clothing, tools, business memorabilia & personal artifacts; area business history; Thompson family papers; photographs, manuscripts, ledgers & ephemera of area residents; sculptor, George Gray Barnard papers.
Research Fields: 19th-century Pennsylvania; historic gardens; Centre County social, cultural, economic & architectural history.
Facilities: 1,000-vol. library; 500 sq. ft. exhibit space. Museum-related items for sale.
Activities: docent program; guided tours; lectures; school curriculum materials & loan service; participatory & temporary exhibitions. Annual Events: Plant Celebration at the Mansion; Independence Day festivities; Family Holiday Open House; local & out-of-town bus tours.
Publications: quarterly newsletter, Mansion Notes; annual journal, Centre County Heritage; monographs.
Hours & Admission Prices: Sun.-Mon., Wed. & Fri. 1-4. No charge; donations accepted. Closed New Year's Day; Easter; Labor Day; Thanksgiving; Christmas week. ♿
Attendance: 7,000 (estimated)
Membership: Annual $25; Friend & Business $50; Patron $100; Life Member $250; Benefactor $500.

Strasburg

THE NATIONAL TOY TRAIN MUSEUM, (M), 300 Paradise Lane, Strasburg, PA 17579-0248. Mailing Address: P.O. Box 248, Strasburg, PA 17579-0248. Tel.: 717-687-8976 & 8623. Fax: 717-687-0742.
E-mail: jluppino@traincollectors.org
Web Site: www.nttmuseum.org
Founded: 1954.
Congressional District: 16
Key Personnel: Operations Mgr., John V. Luppino; Pres., Ronald A. Stowell; Past Pres., Richard C. Clement; Quarterly Editor, Mark Boyd; Publications Editor, Timothy Stier.
Personnel Profile: Full-Time Paid 8; Part-Time Paid 7; Part-Time Volunteers 20.

Governing Authority: nonprofit organization. Parent Institution: Train Collectors Association, P.O. Box 248, Paradise Lane, Strasburg, PA 17579. Tax-exempt: 501(c)(3).
Toy & Model Train Museum.
Collections: toy trains, primarily Tinplate dating from 1840's; model trains & related paraphernalia & accessories; railroadiana; manuscript collections.
Research Fields: toy trains; antique toys; railroadiana.
Facilities: library of books on toys, toy & model trains and railroads, hobby & train magazines, photos and prints, manufacturers' catalogues & archival material. Books, gifts & toys for sale.
Activities: five operating layouts; videos; changing exhibitions.
Publications: quarterly magazine, Train Collectors Quarterly; bimonthly newsletter, National Headquarters News; Train Collectors quarterly directory; online magazine, "e-train" at www.tcaetrain.org; book: Lionel, Standard of the World; ; pamphlets.
Hours & Admission Prices: April & Nov.-Dec. Sat.-Sun. & holidays 10-5; May-Oct. Fri.-Mon.; adults 13-64 $6, seniors 64+ $5, children 6-12 $3, family $15, season pass $18,; discount to AAA members; AAM members, members & children under 6 no charge. Tours: adults $2.50, children $1. Closed New Year's Day; Thanksgiving; Christmas. ♿
Attendance: 53,000 (accurate)
Membership: Individual & Junior $35; Family: additional $1 per family member.

RAILROAD MUSEUM OF PENNSYLVANIA, 300 Gap Rd., Strasburg, PA 17579. Mailing Address: P.O. Box 15, Strasburg, PA 17579-0015. Tel.: 717-687-8629 & 8628, ext. 3001. Fax: 717-687-0876.
E-mail: info@rrmuseumpa.org
Web Site: www.rrmuseumpa.org
Founded: 1963.
Congressional District: 16
Key Personnel: Acting Dir., Nadine Steinmetz; Pres. (V), Robert Lawrence; Education, Patrick Morrison; Cur., Bradley Smith; Librarian & Archivist, Kurt Bell; Restoration Mgr., Allan Martin; Security, Dennis Keperling; Gift Shop Mgr., Laura Martin.
Personnel Profile: Full-Time Paid 19; Part-Time Paid 8; Part-Time Volunteers 150; Interns 2.
Governing Authority: state. Parent Institution: Pennsylvania Historical and Museum Commission, The State Museum Bldg., 300 North St., Harrisburg, PA 17120-0090. Tax-exempt: 170(c)(1).
History & Transportation Museum.
Collections: transportation; railroad history; locomotives; railroad cars; railroad models; tools; telegraph equipment; lanterns; photographs; artwork; paper railroadiana.
Research Fields: railroad history & technology; photographs & negatives.
Facilities: 6,000-vol. library of reports, books, timetables on railroad history; 105,000 sq. ft. exhibit space; 4-acre exhibit space apart from museum; 30-seat theater; outdoor railyard. Museum-related items for sale.
Activities: guided tours; railroad skills demonstrations; live steam operations; orientation programs; children's programs; concerts; docent program; films; loan, participatory & traveling exhibitions.
Publications: quarterly journal, The Milepost; Pennsylvania Railroad Cookbook; booklet, The Broadway Limited; guidebook, The Railroad Museum of Pennsylvania; booklet, The Lancaster Locomotive Works; Baldwin Locomotive Works Negative Catalogue; Benkline Collection of Negatives.
Hours & Admission Prices: April-Oct. Mon.-Sat. 9-5, Sun. 12-5; Nov.-March Tues-Sat. 9-5, Sun. 12-5. Adults $8, senior citizens $7, children 6-17 $6; discounts to AAM & AAA members; children 5 and under & members no charge. Closed New Year's Day; Thanksgiving; Christmas. ♿
Attendance: 133,500 (accurate)
Membership: Student $20; Basic $35; Family $45; Supporting $60; Benefactor $70-$5,000.

Strongstown

DANE CASTLE, Frederick Rd., Strongstown, PA 15957. Mailing Address: P.O. Box 10, Strongstown, PA 15957-0010. Tel.: 814-749-7341.
History Museum.
Collections: medieval art; weapons; suits of armor; shields; helmets; photographs.
Activities: rental facilities.
Hours & Admission Prices: April-Oct. by appointment.

Stroudsburg

MONROE COUNTY HISTORICAL ASSOCIATION/STROUD MANSION, (M), 900 Main St., Stroudsburg, PA 18360-1604. Tel.: 570-421-7703. Fax: 570-421-9199.
E-mail: mcha@ptd.net
Web Site: www.monroehistorical.org
Formerly: Stroud Mansion/Monroe County Historical Association
Founded: 1921.
Congressional District: 10
Key Personnel: Pres., David Thomas; Exec. Dir., Amy Leiser.
Personnel Profile: Full-Time Paid 1; Part-Time Paid 2; Part-Time Volunteers 10.
Governing Authority: nonprofit organization. Parent Institution: Monroe County Historical Association. Tax-exempt: 501(c)(3).
Historical Society Museum: housed in a mansion built by Jacob Stroud, founder of Stroudsburg, for his son.
Collections: decorative arts; toys; textiles; costumes; textile working tools; weapons; Indian artifacts; Victorian paintings; prints; photographs.
Research Fields: Monroe County history & genealogy.
Facilities: 8,000-vol. library; 2,800 sq. ft. exhibit space. Historical Society publications for sale.
Activities: guided tours; lectures; hobby workshops; school loan service; outreach educational programs for schools & community groups.
Publications: quarterly newsletter, The Fan Light; brochure about sites & services.
Hours & Admission Prices: Tues.-Fri. 9-4, 1st & 3rd Sat. 10-4. Adults $8; discounts to AAM members; members no charge. Closed major holidays. ♿
Attendance: 1,895 (accurate)
Membership: Student $10; Senior Individual $15; Individual $25; Family $35; Patron $50; Century $100; Small Business $150; Corporate $250.

QUIET VALLEY LIVING HISTORICAL FARM, 1000 Turkey Hill Rd., Stroudsburg, PA 18360-9455. Tel.: 570-992-6161. Fax: 570-992-9587.
E-mail: farm@quietvalley.org
Web Site: www.quietvalley.org
Founded: 1963.
Congressional District: 15
Key Personnel: Pres. (V), Tom Bilheimer; Dir., Debra Seip.
Personnel Profile: Full-Time Paid 5; Part-Time Paid 20; Part-Time Volunteers 500.
Governing Authority: nonprofit organization. Tax-exempt: 501(c)(3).
Living Farm Museum: housed on the 1765 site of a Pennsylvania homestead.
Collections: furnishings; implements; Pennsylvania German agriculture. Historic Buildings: 14 buildings from 1765-1890.
Research Fields: early farm crafts; 18th-19th century agriculture; rural life.
Facilities: 500-vol. library of material relating to early farm life available to the staff only. Handmade history-related items, commercial items & books for sale.
Activities: guided tours for school groups; tours for general public; workshops; docent program; day camp. Annual Events: Harvest Festival; Farm Animal Frolic; Old Time Christmas.
Publications: newsletter, five times a year.
Hours & Admission Prices: June 20-Labor Day Tues.-Sat. 10-5, Sun. 1-5; school groups by appointment. Adults $7, children 3-12 $4; discounts to groups & AAA members; members no charge. Special Events: Summer Program $7, Harvest Festival & Old Time Christmas $6, Farm Animal Frolic $ 4, children $3. ♿
Attendance: 27,000 (estimated)
Membership: Junior $10; Senior $15; Individual $20; Family $50; Contributing $75; Sustaining $125; Donor $500; Life $1,000.

Sunbury

THE NORTHUMBERLAND COUNTY HISTORICAL SOCIETY, (M), 1150 N. Front St., Sunbury, PA 17801-1126. Tel.: 570-286-4083. Fax: 570-286-2140.
E-mail: director@northumberlandcountyhistoricalsociety.org
Web Site: www.northumberlandcountyhistoricalsociety.org
Founded: 1925.
Congressional District: 17
Key Personnel: Dir., Cynthia L. Inkrote; Pres. (V), Scott A. Heintzelman; Office Mgr., Charlotte Rhinehart.
Personnel Profile: Full-Time Paid 1; Part-Time Volunteers 12.
Governing Authority: Tax-exempt.
Historic Site: 1756-94, frontier outpost; 1852, Hunter Mansion.
Collections: military & Indian artifacts; documents; clothing.
Research Fields: genealogy; local history.
Facilities: library.
Activities: guided tours; special programs.
Publications: books & booklets on Pennsylvania history; Society proceedings & reprints.
Hours & Admission Prices: Mon., Wed. & Fri. 1-4. Museum: no charge; donations accepted. Library $5; members no charge. ♿
Attendance: 3,900 (estimated)
Membership: Individual $20; Family $35; Life $300.

Swarthmore

* **SCOTT ARBORETUM OF SWARTHMORE COLLEGE, (M),** 500 College Ave., Swarthmore, PA 19081-1306. Tel.: 610-328-8025. Fax: 610-328-7755.
E-mail: scott@swarthmore.edu
Web Site: www.scottarboretum.org
Formerly: The Scott Foundation
Founded: 1929.
Congressional District: 7
Key Personnel: Dir., Claire Sawyers; Pres. (V), Cindy Mead; Education Coord., Julie Jenny; Horticultural Coord., Jeff Jabco; Member & Visitor Svcs. Coord., Becky Robert; Collections Documentation & Project Mgr., Rhoda Maurer; Cur., Andrew Bunting; Office Mgr., Jacqui West.
Personnel Profile: Full-Time Paid 20; Part-Time Paid 8; Part-Time Volunteers 200; Interns 1.
Governing Authority: college. Parent Institution: Swarthmore College. Tax-exempt: 501(c)(3).
Arboretum.
Collections: horticulture; botany; arboretum; plants with significant ornamental value.
Research Fields: plant evaluation programs.
Facilities: 1,000-vol. library of reference & research books available on premises; classrooms.
Activities: guided tours; lectures; formally organized education programs; permanent & temporary exhibitions; Scott medal & award.
Publications: newsletter, Hybrid; class schedules, Year in Review, interpretive brochures on special collections; book, The Scott Arboretum of Swarthmore College: The First 75 Years.
Hours & Admission Prices: Arboretum: daily dawn-dusk. Main office: Mon.-Fri. 8:30-12 & 1-4:30. No charge; donations accepted. Office closed Thanksgiving; Christmas-New Year's Day; Independence Day. ♿
Attendance: 30,000 (estimated)
Membership: Student $10; Individual $40; Dual $55; Contributor $75; Organization $125; Sponsor $150; Benefactor $250; Patron $500; Director's Circle $1,000; Philanthropist $3,000.

Tidioute

SIMPLER TIMES MUSEUM, 45 Simpler Times Lane, U.S. Rte. 62, Tidioute, PA 16351. Mailing Address: 111 Simpler Times Lane, Tidioute, PA 16351. Tel.: 814-484-3483.
Founded: 1992.
Key Personnel: Chm. (V), Bruce E. Ziegler.
Governing Authority: Tax-exempt.
Local History Museum.
Collections: local oil, gas, timber, & agriculture history; 90 gasoline pumps; hit and miss engines; farm tractors & equipment; Ford cars from 1913 & up; gasoline signs, globes & containers.
Hours & Admission Prices: Call for hours. Adults $4; discounts to groups of 20 or more.
Attendance: 4,500 (estimated)

Tionesta

FOREST COUNTY HISTORICAL SOCIETY, 206 Elm St., Tionesta, PA 16353. Mailing Address: P.O. Box 546, Tionesta, PA 16353-0546. Tel.: 814-755-4422.
Historical Society Museum.
Collections: local history & culture; period artifacts; photographs.
Hours & Admission Prices: late May to late Sept. Mon.-Sat. 10-4; other times by appointment.

Titusville

* **DRAKE WELL MUSEUM,** 202 Museum Lane, Titusville, PA 16354-7658. Tel.: 814-827-2797. Fax: 814-827-4888.
E-mail: drakewell@verizon.net
Web Site: www.drakewell.org
Founded: 1934.
Congressional District: 23
Key Personnel: C.E.O., Barbara Franco; Bureau Dir., Stephen Miller; Pres. (V), Grant Carner; Historic Site Admin., Barbara T. Zolli; Museum Shop Mgr., Sheri Hamilton.
Personnel Profile: Full-Time Paid 8; Part-Time Paid 6; Part-Time Volunteers 10; Interns 3.
Governing Authority: state. Administered by the Pennsylvania Historical & Museum Commission, Commonwealth Keystone Bldg., 400 North St., Harrisburg, PA 17120. Tax-exempt: 170(b)(1)(A).
Industrial Oil Museum: located on site of first commercially successful oil well.
Collections: early lighting devices; oil well drilling & production tools and equipment; collodion wet plate negatives of development of Pennsylvania oil industry; replica of Drake's derrick & engine house.
Research Fields: oil industry history.
Facilities: approx. 5,000-vol. library on oil production & its history available for research; 140-seat auditorium; theater; picnic area. Museum-related items for sale.
Activities: guided & self-guided tours; concerts; formally organized education programs for children; permanent & temporary exhibitions; film & video programs.
Publications: newsletter, The Barker.
Hours & Admission Prices: May-Oct. Mon.-Sat. 9-5, Sun. 12-5; Nov.-April Tues.-Sat. 9-5, Sun. 12-5. Adults 12-64 $6, senior citizens 65 & over $5, youth 3-11 $3; discounts to AAA members; children under 3 no charge. Closed New Year's Day; Martin Luther King Jr. Day; Presidents' Day; Columbus Day; Veterans Day; Thanksgiving; Christmas. ♿
Attendance: 42,000 (estimated)
Membership: Individual $30; Corporate $250.

Towanda

BRADFORD COUNTY HISTORICAL SOCIETY, (M), 109 Pine St., Towanda, PA 18848-1701. Tel.: 570-265-2240.
E-mail: info@bradfordhistory.com
Web Site: www.bradfordhistory.com
Founded: 1870.
Congressional District: 10
Key Personnel: Dir., Matthew Carl.
Personnel Profile: Full-Time Paid 1; Part-Time Paid 1; Part-Time Volunteers 25.
Governing Authority: nonprofit organization. Tax-exempt: 501(c)(3).
Historical Society Museum: Bradford County jail building.
Collections: furniture & furnishings of the 19th century; Civil War memorabilia; Indian artifacts; boy & girl scouting items; toys; baby carriages; tools; handmade items. Replica: c.1905 log cabin.
Research Fields: genealogy & local history.
Facilities: 1,000-vol. library of books & microfilm pertaining to local history & genealogy available for research.
Activities: guided tours.
Publications: quarterly magazine, The Settler; 1995 History of Bradford County PA; book, Barclay MT - A History.
Hours & Admission Prices: Library: Wed.-Fri. 10-4, Sat. by appointment. Museum: June-Sept. Thurs.-Sat. 10-4; groups by appointment. No charge; donations accepted. Genealogy Research: $5 daily. Closed Federal holidays. ♿
Attendance: 1,500
Membership: Student $15; Basic $25; Sustaining $35; Family $45; Benefactor $100; Patron $500; Life $1,000.

FRENCH AZILUM, INC., R.R. 2, Towanda, PA 18848-9107. Mailing Address: Box 266, Towanda, PA 18848-9107. Tel.: 570-265-3376.
E-mail: frenchazilum@epix.net
Web Site: www.frenchazilum.net
Founded: 1954.
Congressional District: 10
Key Personnel: Pres. Bd., Bob Veleker; Site Mgr., Kate Angerson.
Personnel Profile: Full-Time Paid 1; Part-Time Volunteers 12.
Governing Authority: state. Parent Institution: Pennsylvania Historical & Museum Commission, Box 1026, Harrisburg, PA 17120. Tax-exempt.
Historic House & Site: 1793-1803 Refuge of the French Royalists; 1836 Laporte House.
Collections: heirlooms of the emigres; antique farm tools; blacksmith & carpenters tools; spinning & weaving implements; 18th- & 19th-century period furniture.
Research Fields: archaeological sites.
Facilities: library of material pertaining to French Revolution; Marie Antoinette; French Azilum & local history; nature trail. Museum-related items for sale.
Activities: site interpretation; craft fair.
Hours & Admission Prices: May 2-May 24 Sat.-Sun. 11-5; Memorial Day to Labor Day Wed.-Sun. 11-5; Sept.-Oct. Wed-Sun. 11-4. Adults $6, senior citizens 55 & over $5, students $3; children under 12 & members no charge. ♿
Attendance: 3,750 (estimated)
Membership: Individual $30; Family $40; Supporting $75; Contributing $100; Special Donor & Corporate $500.

Trappe

THE HISTORICAL SOCIETY OF TRAPPE, COLLEGEVILLE, PERKIOMEN VALLEY, INC., 301 W. Main St., Trappe, PA 19426. Mailing Address: P.O. Box 26708, Collegeville, PA 19426-0708. Tel.: 610-489-7560. Fax: 610-489-7560.
E-mail: info@trappehistoricalsociety.org
Web Site: www.trappehistoricalsociety.org
Founded: 1964.
Congressional District: 13
Key Personnel: Pres., Rev. Robert A. Meschke; Treas., Patricia A. Quinty; Historian, Rev. Judith A. Meier.
Personnel Profile: Part-Time Paid 1; Part-Time Volunteers 20; Interns 1.
Governing Authority: society; nonprofit organization. Branch Museum: Muhlenberg House, 201 W. Main St., Trappe, PA. Tax-exempt: 501(c)(3).
Local History Museum: housed in early 18th- & 19th-century Dewees Tavern.
Collections: archives; genealogy; history; preservation project; manuscript collections; historical markers.
Research Fields: genealogy; Muhlenberg & Revolutionary War period.
Facilities: 500-vol. library of research books & manuscripts on genealogy available for use on premises by appointment. Gifts & pamphlets for sale.
Activities: guided tours; lectures; permanent exhibitions; historical markers.
Publications: quarterly, The Chronicle; newsletter; map, Washington's Itinerary in Montgomery County Sept.-Dec. 1777; Registry of Historic Building in Trappe.
Hours & Admission Prices: House: June-Sept. Sun. 1:30-4. Museum: Tues. & Thurs. 9-12. Donations: $2.
Attendance: 1,100 (estimated)
Membership: Student $10; Individual $25; Family $50; Supporting $100-$249; Patron $250-$499; Sustaining $500-$999; Benefactor $1,000 & up.

University Park

EARTH & MINERAL SCIENCES MUSEUM AND ART GALLERY, 19 Deike Burrows Rd., University Park, PA 16802-5000. Mailing Address: 207 Deike Bldg., Pennsylvania State University, University Park, PA 16802-5000. Tel.: 814-865-6336.
E-mail: rgraham@ems.psu.edu
Web Site: www.ems.psu.edu/museum
Key Personnel: C.E.O. & Dir., Russell W. Graham.
Personnel Profile: Full-Time Paid 1; Part-Time Paid 1.
Governing Authority: Parent Institution: EMS College. Tax-exempt.
Natural History, Science & Art Museum.
Collections: rocks; minerals; fossils; glasses; ceramics; metals; plastics; synthetic materials; mining & scientific equipment; archaeological artifacts; paintings; sculptures; drawings.
Research Fields: mineralogy & paleontology.
Facilities: two exhibit galleries; research & collection facility; curator office; exhibits & collection office.
Activities: school tours & special programs.
Publications: annual report.
Hours & Admission Prices: Mon.-Fri. 9:30-5. No charge. Closed legal holidays; university's recess. ♿
Attendance: 8,000 (estimated)
Membership: Regular $20; Pyrite $100; Gypsum $500; Quartz & Gold $1,000.

THE FROST ENTOMOLOGICAL MUSEUM, DEPT. OF ENTOMOLOGY, THE PENNSYLVANIA STATE UNIVERSITY, Headhouse #3, Curtin Rd., University Park, PA 16802-1009. Tel.: 814-863-2865. Fax: 814-865-3048.
E-mail: kck@psu.edu
Web Site: ento.psu.edu/facilities/frost
Founded: 1969.
Congressional District: 23
Key Personnel: Cur., Dr. Ke Chung Kim.
Personnel Profile: Full-Time Paid 2; Part-Time Paid 2; Part-Time Volunteers 1; Interns 2.
Governing Authority: university. Parent Institution: The Pennsylvania State University. Tax-exempt.
Specialized Natural History Museum.
Collections: entomology; zoology; biodiversity.
Research Fields: insect systematics; ecology; faunistics; biodiversity survey.
Facilities: 400-vol. library of taxonomy, entomology, monographs & catalogs available for research by special arrangement; separate laboratory operation.
Activities: guided tours; formally organized education programs; permanent & temporary exhibitions; lectures.
Publications: research papers.
Hours & Admission Prices: Mon.-Fri. 9:30-4:30. No charge; donations accepted. ♿
Attendance: 5,000 (estimated)
Membership: Annual $25.

MATSON MUSEUM OF ANTHROPOLOGY, (M), 409 Carpenter Bldg., Pennsylvania State University, University Park, PA 16802-3401. Tel.: 814-865-3853.
Web Site: www.anthro.psu.edu/matson_museum/index.shtml
Key Personnel: Dir., Dr. Clair McHale Milner
Anthropology Museum.
Collections: history of human cultures; cultural & biological differences; photographs.
Facilities: Museum-related items for sale.
Hours & Admission Prices: Fall & Spring: Mon.-Thurs. 9-4, Fri. 9-3; Summer: call for hours. No charge.

PALMER MUSEUM OF ART, THE PENNSYLVANIA STATE UNIVERSITY, (M), Curtin Rd., University Park, PA 16802-2507. Tel.: 814-865-7672. Fax: 814-863-8608.
E-mail: egw4@psu.edu
Web Site: www.palmermuseum.psu.edu
Founded: 1972.
Congressional District: 5
Key Personnel: Dir., Jan Keene Muhlert; Advisory Bd. Chm., Linda Gall; Cur., Dr. Joyce Robinson; Cur. Charles V. Hallman, Dr. Patrick J. McGrady; Cur. American Art, Dr. Leo Mazow; Coord. Membership & Public Rels., Jennifer Lee Cozao; Cur. Education, Dana Carlisle Kletchka; Registrar, Beverly Balger Sutley; Exhibition Designer, Ronald Hand; Administrative Asst., Elizabeth Warner; Exhibition Preparator, Richard Hall; Museum Security & Facility Mgr., Jeremy R. Warner; Museum Store Mgr., Lynne McCormack.
Personnel Profile: Full-Time Paid 12; Part-Time Paid 25; Part-Time Volunteers 84; Interns 5.
Governing Authority: university. Parent Institution: The Pennsylvania State University. Tax-exempt.
Art Museum.
Collections: American & European paintings, drawings, photographs, prints & sculpture; Asian ceramics, painting & prints; limited material in ancient, African & Near Eastern areas; ancient Peruvian ceramics; contemporary European & Japanese studio ceramics.
Major Exhibits: Old Master Drawings, 11/09-1/31/10; I Heard a Voice: The Art of Lesley Dill (T), 1/24/10-4/25/10; Licenc'd to Bark: James Gillray and the Art of Satire, 2/2/10-5/16/10; Italian Old Master Prints from the Permanent Collection, 2/16/10-5/23/10; Prints by Sculptors from the Collection of James and Betty Myford, 6/8/10-9/12/10; A Room of Their Own: The Bloomsbury Artists in American Collections, 7/6/10-9/26/10; Taxing Visions: Financial Episodes in American Painting, 1860-1900 (T), 9/28/10-12/19/10; At the Heart of Progress: Coal, Iron and Steam since 1750 Industrial Imagery from The John P. Eckblad Collection (T), 10/19/10-1/23/11.
Research Fields: Western art from antiquity to the present day; American art.
Facilities: print study room; 150-seat auditorium. Museum-related items for sale.
Activities: guided tours; lectures; temporary & traveling exhibitions; symposia; teachers' workshops; family programs; print & drawing study club.
Publications: catalogs, pamphlets & brochures of exhibitions; triannual newsletter.
Hours & Admission Prices: Tues.-Sat. 10-4:30, Sun. 12-4. No charge; donations accepted. Closed national holidays; Christmas through New Year's Day. ♿
Attendance: 37,504 (accurate)
Membership: Student $10-$34; Individual $35-$59; Family & Household $60-$99; Sustaining $100-$299; Benefactor $300-$599; Sponsor $600-$999; Director's Circle $1,000 & up; Corporate Circle $2,500 & up. Senior Citizens 60 & over 10% discount.

PENN STATE ALL-SPORTS MUSEUM, (M), Beaver Stadium, University Park, PA 16802. Tel.: 814-863-3382.
Founded: 2002.
Key Personnel: Dir., Ken Hickman; Programming & Education, Aimee Brown.
Personnel Profile: Full-Time Paid 3; Part-Time Paid 10; Part-Time Volunteers 50.
Governing Authority: Parent-Institution: The Pennsylvania State University. Tax-exempt.
Sports Museum.
Collections: Penn State's sports history; student-athletes & coaches; photographs; uniforms; trophies; Olympic memorabilia.
Facilities: 30-seat theater.
Hours & Admission Prices: Tues.-Sat. 10-4, Sun. 12-4; call for additional hours. Adults $5, seniors citizens 65 & over, students and children under 14 $3. Closed New Year's Eve & Day; Easter; Memorial Day; Thanksgiving; Christmas Eve & Day. ♿

Upland

THE FRIENDS OF THE CALEB PUSEY HOUSE, INC., 15 Race St., Upland, PA 19015. Mailing Address: P.O. Box 1183, Upland, PA 19015-0183. Tel.: 610-874-5665.
E-mail: calebpuseyhouse@comcast.net
Founded: 1960.
Congressional District: 7
Key Personnel: Pres. (V), Harold R. Peden; Vice Pres., Arthur Hickey; Vice Pres., Ruth Moll.
Personnel Profile: Part-Time Volunteers 27.
Governing Authority: board of directors. Tax-exempt: 501(c)(3).
General Museum: housed in 1683 Caleb Pusey House.
Collections: furniture; architecture; archaeology; herbarium; linens. Historic Houses: 1683 schoolhouse; c.1790 Pennock Log House.
Research Fields: Pusey genealogy.
Facilities: reception area.
Activities: tours; lectures.
Publications: newsletter, The Weathervane.
Hours & Admission Prices: May-Oct. Sat.-Sun. 1-4; groups by special arrangement. No charge; donations accepted. ♿
Attendance: 1,500 (estimated)

Valley Forge

WORLD OF SCOUTING MUSEUM, Rte. 23, Valley Forge, PA 19482. Mailing Address: World of Scouting Museum, Inc., P.O. Box 2226, Valley Forge, PA 19482-2226. Tel.: 610-783-5311.
Web Site: www.worldofscoutingmuseum.org
Founded: 1994.
Key Personnel: Chm. (V), Paul Ware; Cur., Michele D. Vera.
Personnel Profile: Full-Time Paid 1; Part-Time Volunteers 12.
Governing Authority: Tax-exempt.
Scouting Museum.
Collections: scouting memorabilia; photographs; dolls; medals; posters; sashes; certificates; toys; puzzles; uniforms; Air Scouts; Mariner Scouts; equipment; food; handbooks; cookies; Juliette Low, Founder of American Girl Scouts; Dan Beard artwork; games; ephemera; scouting publications.
Hours & Admission Prices: Currently closed.
Attendance: 7,000 (estimated)

Vandergrift

VICTORIAN VANDERGRIFT MUSEUM & HISTORICAL SOCIETY, 184 Sherman Ave., Vandergrift, PA 15690-1136. Tel.: 724-568-1990.
E-mail: staff@vvmhs.com
Web Site: www.vvmhs.com
Key Personnel: Dir., Elizabeth Caporali
Historical Society Museum: housed in the former Sherman School building.
Collections: local history & culture; photographs; personal artifacts; early furnishings.
Hours & Admission Prices: Mon.-Sat. 10-3.

Warren

WARREN COUNTY HISTORICAL SOCIETY, 210 Fourth Ave., Warren, PA 16365-2318. Mailing Address: P.O. Box 427, Warren, PA 16365-0427. Tel.: 814-723-1795.
E-mail: warrenhistory@kinzua.net
Web Site: www.warrenhistory.org
Founded: 1900.
Congressional District: 5
Key Personnel: Mng. Dir., Michelle Gray.
Personnel Profile: Full-Time Paid 2; Part-Time Paid 2; Part-Time Volunteers 90; Interns 2.
Governing Authority: society. Parent Institution: Warren County Historical Society. Subsidiary Institution: Wilder Museum. Tax-exempt: 170(b)(1)(A) & 501(c)(3).
Local History Museum: housed in second empire mansion.
Collections: photographs; paintings; documents; manuscripts; letters; diaries; county records; genealogical records; books; pamphlets; tools & implements; utensils; maps; Victorian furniture.
Research Fields: area history; petroleum history.
Facilities: 2,000-vol. library of Pennsylvania history books available for use on premises; genealogy department; reading room. Books & pamphlets for sale.
Activities: guided tours; lectures; temporary exhibitions.
Publications: periodical, Stepping Stones; Index to Stepping Stones 1955-2006; books, Historic Buildings in Warren County, Vols. 1,2,3,4,5; Of Prescriptions & Playbills, from the diaries of Michael V. Ball, M.D., 1884-86; History & Development of the Petroleum Industry in Warren County, PA; Cavalcade-Warren County's Second Century c.2000; Murder in the Courtroom; Pennsylvania Wilds; Vignettes of Yesteryear Vols. I & II; Images of America Series: Warren.
Hours & Admission Prices: Nov.-March Mon.-Fri. 8:30-4:30; April-Oct. Mon.-Fri. 8:30-4:30, Sat. 9-12; other times by appointment. Adults $1; discounts to AAM & ICOM members; members & children no charge. Closed national holidays. ♿
Attendance: 10,500 (estimated)
Membership: Student $10; Senior 65 & over $15; Individual 18-64 $25; Senior Family (at one address) $25; Family (at one address) $40; Nonprofit Organization $50; Contributing Family (at one address) $75; Patron Family (at one address) $100; Contributing Business $100-$499; Life $500 & up; Patron Business $500-$1,000.

Washington

DAVID BRADFORD HOUSE, 175 S. Main St., Washington, PA 15301-4948. Mailing Address: P.O. Box 537, Washington, PA 15301-0537. Tel.: 724-222-3604.
E-mail: bradfordhouse@verizon.net
Web Site: www.bradfordhouse.org
Founded: 1960.
Congressional District: 22
Key Personnel: Pres., Tripp Kline; Historical Dir., Clay Kilgore; Admin., Steve Dettinger.
Personnel Profile: Part-Time Paid 1; Part-Time Volunteers 10.
Governing Authority: state. Operated by the Bradford House Historical Association for the Pennsylvania Historical & Museum Commission, P.O. Box 1026, Harrisburg, PA 17120. Tax-exempt.
Historic House: housed in c.1788 restored home of a 1794 Whiskey Tax Rebellion leader.
Collections: historic period furnishings; 18th-century plant & herb garden.
Facilities: Museum-related items for sale.
Activities: guided tours; lectures; formally organized education programs for children; demonstrations by guides in Colonial dress.
Publications: newsletter, The Bradford House.
Hours & Admission Prices: April-Dec. Wed. & Fri.-Sat. 11-4, Thurs. 2-7. Adults $5, seniors $4, students 6-18 $3; discounts to AAM & AAA Motor Club members; children under 6 & members no charge.
Attendance: 1,500 (estimated)
Membership: Adults $15; Family $25.

PENNSYLVANIA TROLLEY MUSEUM, 1 Museum Rd., Washington, PA 15301-6133. Tel.: 724-228-9256. Fax: 724-228-9675.
E-mail: ptm@pa-trolley.org
Web Site: www.pa-trolley.org
Founded: 1953.
Congressional District: 20
Key Personnel: Chm. (V) & Pres. (V), William M. Fronczek, Jr., M.D.; Exec. Dir., Scott R. Becker; Sec., Barbara Myers-Ciccone; Treas., Kenneth H. Fraelich; Museum Shop Mgr., Lisa Stout-Bashioum.
Personnel Profile: Full-Time Paid 3; Part-Time Paid 3; Part-Time Volunteers 150; Interns 2.
Governing Authority: nonprofit organization. Parent Institution: Pennsylvania Trolley Museum, Inc., 1 Museum Rd., Washington 15301. Tax-exempt: 501(c)(3).
Railway Museum.
Collections: city & interurban trolley cars, diesel & electric locomotives; railroad cars.
Research Fields: Pennsylvania Electric Railway History.
Facilities: research library collection, periodicals, photo negatives, blueprints; Visitor Education Center; 2 mi. trolley line, trolley car barn; restoration shop; vintage trolley waiting shelters; 28,000 sq. ft. trolley display building; Museum-related items for sale.
Activities: operation of historic trolley cars; car restoration; meetings; lectures; films; tours; archives; education program; guided tours of collections.
Publications: bimonthly news magazine, Trolley Fare; annual report; guidebook of collections.
Hours & Admission Prices: April-May & Sept.-Dec. Mon. & Fri. 10-4, Sat.-Sun. 11-5; Memorial Day-Labor Day Mon.-Fri. 10-4, Sat.-Sun. 11-5. Adults $9, seniors 62 & over $8, children 3-15 $5; children 2 & under no charge. ♿
Attendance: 24,025 (accurate)
Membership: Associate $30; Voting $40; Family $60.

WASHINGTON COUNTY HISTORICAL SOCIETY, LeMoyne House, 49 E. Maiden St., Washington, PA 15301-4941. Tel.: 724-225-6740. Fax: 724-225-8495.
E-mail: info@wchspa.org
Web Site: www.wchspa.org

Founded: 1900.
Congressional District: 20
Key Personnel: Admin., Jim Ross; Pres. Bd., Carol Levy Dolovacky; Administrative Asst., Charlotte Davidson; Research Librarian, Janet Wareham; Coord. Public Rels. & Education, Joyce Mullen; Collections Mgr. & Coord. Education, Clay Kilgore.
Personnel Profile: Full-Time Paid 4; Part-Time Paid 1; Part-Time Volunteers 45; Interns 3.
Governing Authority: nonprofit corporation. Tax-exempt.
Museum #1: Le Moyne House, a national historic landmark of the underground railroad includes historic house, doctor's office & gardens. Museum #2: first crematory in the U.S. listed on National Register of historic places.
Collections: archives; history; Washington County artifacts & memorabilia.
Research Fields: local history, genealogy.
Facilities: library of county history; collection of county history of Washington County.
Activities: guided tours; school programs; workshops; lectures; research service. Annual Events: Christmas Candlelight Tours; Art Show & Sale.
Publications: newsletter; books, Researching Washington County Kit; map, 1817 County Map; engraving, 1896 Bird's Eye View of Washington, PA.
Hours & Admission Prices: Tues.-Fri. 11-4. Adults $5, students $3; discounts to AAA & AAM members; members no charge. Closed holidays.
Attendance: 8,000 (estimated)
Membership: Single $25; Family $45; Sustaining $50; Life $300; Dr. Ausalom Baird Circle $250-$499; Captain David Acheson Circle $500-$999; William Holmes McGuffey Circle $1,000-$4,999; Dr. Francis Julius Lemoyne Circle $5,000 & up.

Washington Crossing

WASHINGTON CROSSING HISTORIC PARK, (M), 1112 River Rd., Washington Crossing, PA 18977-1202. Mailing Address: P.O. Box 103, Washington Crossing, PA 18977-0103. Tel.: 215-493-4076. Fax: 215-493-4820.
Web Site: www.ushistory.org/washingtoncrossing
Founded: 1917.
Congressional District: 8
Key Personnel: Acting Historic Site Admin., Douglas Miller; Museum Educator, Jennifer Phillips April; Museum Shop Mgr., Kathy Pasko.
Personnel Profile: Full-Time Paid 10; Part-Time Paid 4.
Governing Authority: state. Administered by Pennsylvania Historical & Museum Commission, Box 1026, Harrisburg, PA 17120. Tax-exempt.
Historic Site.
Collections: artifacts & paintings; manuscripts. Historic Buildings & Sites: 1702, 1757, 1788 Thompson-Neely; 1757 McKonkey's Ferry Inn; 1776 soldiers' graves; 1840 Thompson's Mill; 1816 Mahlon K. Taylor House.
Research Fields: American Revolution Colonial life & agriculture; Park related history.
Facilities: library of research material available for use by public with appointment. Museum-related items for sale.
Activities: guided tours; lectures; films; gallery talks; drama; study clubs; formally organized education programs for children, adults & undergraduate college students; permanent, temporary & traveling exhibitions; school programs. Annual Event: sheep shearing; Harvest Festival; reenactment of Christmas crossing of the Delaware at 1pm Christmas Day.
Publications: books; park brochure; booklet; pamphlet; painting reproduction folder; guide book, Washington Crossing Historic Park.
Hours & Admission Prices: Tues.-Sat. 9-5, Sun. 12-5. Grounds: daily 9 to dusk. Bowman's Hill Tower: mid-April to Nov. Tues.-Sun. 9:30-4:30. Adults $7, senior citizens 65 and over & groups $6, youth 3-11 $4; discounts to AAM & AAA members; members & children under 3 no charge. Closed New Year's Day; Martin Luther King Jr. Day; Presidents' Day; Columbus Day; Veterans Day; Thanksgiving & day after. ♿
Attendance: 350,000 (estimated)

Waterford

FORT LEBOEUF, 123 S. High St., Waterford, PA 16441. Mailing Address: Dept. of Anthropology, Edinboro University of Pennsylvania, P.O. Box 622, Edinboro, PA 16444-0001. Tel.: 814-732-2575 & 2570. Fax: 814-732-2629.
E-mail: wolynee@edinboro.edu
Web Site: fortleboeuf.edinboro.edu/museum.html
Founded: 1929.
Congressional District: 24
Key Personnel: Property Placement Officer, Robert N. Seiber; Dir., Dr. Renata Wolynec.
Governing Authority: state. Operated by the Dept. of Sociology/Anthropology/Social Work, Edinboro University of Pennsylvania for the Pennsylvania Historical & Museum Commission, Box 1026, Harrisburg, PA. 17120. Tax-exempt.
History Museum: located at the site of a succession of three forts, all named Fort LeBoeuf; built by the French in 1753; rebuilt by the British in 1760; rebuilt by the governor of Pennsylvania in 1795.
Collections: period furniture; artifacts from French occupation; archives; history. Historic Sites: 1753 French Fort; 1760 British Fort; 1795 American Fort.
Research Fields: historic archaeology.
Facilities: 500-vol. library of historical reference books available for research on premises.
Activities: guided tours; lectures; slide show.
Publications: Books, booklets, postcards on Pennsylvania History; brochure, How to Arrange a Tour of the Fort LeBoeuf Museum.
Hours & Admission Prices: Call for hours. No charge.

Watsontown

HISTORIC WARRIOR RUN CHURCH, Intersection Susquehanna Trail & 8th St., Watsontown, PA 17777. Mailing Address: Fort Freeland Heritage Society, P.O. Box 26, Turbotville, PA 17772-0026. Tel.: 570-742-3743.
E-mail: info@freelandfarm.org
Web Site: www.freelandfarm.org/warrior_run_church.php
Founded: 1835.
Congressional District: 17
Key Personnel: Pres., Robert Franks.
Personnel Profile: Full-Time Volunteers 10; Part-Time Volunteers 20.
Governing Authority: state. Operated by The Warrior Run/Fort Freeland Heritage Society for the Pennsylvania Historical & Museum Commission, Bureau of Historic Sites & Museums, Commonwealth Keystone Bldg., 400 North St., Harrisburg, PA 17120-0053. Tax-exempt.
Historic Building & Site: 1835 Country Greek Revival Style Church; Revolutionary War Graveyard.
Collections: church furniture & furnishings; books; records. Graveyard: burials include veterans of Revolutionary War, War 1812, Mexican War & Civil War, 1789-1940.
Research Fields: genealogy.
Facilities: picnic area.
Activities: educational programs. Annual Events: Strawberry Festival; Heritage Days; Christmas Candlelight Service.
Publications: Warrior Run Church Sampler; Reflexions & Images; Preservation of the Past; Tombstones of Historic Warrior Run Church; Fields of Honor.
Hours & Admission Prices: Memorial Day-Labor Day Wed. & Sat.-Sun. 2-5. No charge; donations accepted.
Attendance: 3,000 (estimated)
Membership: Student $1; Annual $10; Life $200.

Wayne

THE FINLEY HOUSE, 113 W. Beech Tree Lane, Wayne, PA 19087-3212. Tel.: 610-688-2668.
Web Site: radnorhistory.org
Founded: 1948.
Congressional District: 5
Key Personnel: Pres. (V), Ted Pollard.
Personnel Profile: Part-Time Volunteers 20; Interns 2.
Governing Authority: society. The Radnor Historical Society. Tax-exempt.
Historical Society Museum: housed in c.1789 Finley House.
Collections: early vehicles; early local photographs; maps; manuscripts; decorative arts.
Research Fields: transportation archives; history.
Facilities: 400-vol. library of books on local history & genealogy available for use on premises or by appointment.
Activities: lectures; permanent & temporary exhibitions; field trips.
Publications: annual magazine, Radnor Historical Society Bulletin.
Hours & Admission Prices: Tues. & Sat. 2-4; other times by appointment. No charge; donations accepted.
Attendance: 400 (estimated)
Membership: Student $5; Individual $15; Family $25; Contributing $50; Patron $100; Benefactor $250.

THE AMERICAN REVOLUTION CENTER, 435 Devon Park Dr., Ste. 801, Wayne, PA 19087-1940. Tel.: 610-975-4948. Fax: 610-225-8420.
E-mail: info@americanrevolutioncenter.org
Web Site: www.americanrevolutioncenter.org
Formerly: National Center for the American Revolution
Founded: 2000.
Key Personnel: Pres. & C.E.O., Bruce Cole; Chm. Bd., H.F. Lensest; Senior Vice Pres., ZeeAnn Mason.
Personnel Profile: Full-Time Paid 2; Part-Time Paid 5.
Governing Authority: society. Tax-exempt: 501(c)(3).
History Museum: located on the site of Valley Forge encampment area.
Collections: Washington memorabilia & artifacts; 18th-century firearms &

accoutrements; decorative arts; archival information including books, manuscripts & documents.
Research Fields: firearms of Revolutionary period.
Hours & Admission Prices: Museum under construction.

Waynesboro

OLLER HOUSE, 138 W. Main St., Waynesboro, PA 17268-1564. Tel.: 717-762-1747.
Web Site: www.waynesborohistory.com
Key Personnel: Mgr., Ken Beam.
Governing Authority: Parent Institution: Waynesboro Historical Society.
Historic House: built in 1892.
Collections: local history & culture; period furnishings; personal artifacts; photographs.
Facilities: library.
Activities: special events.
Hours & Admission Prices: Wed. 1-5, Thurs. & Sat. 10-4, Fri. 10-1; other times by appointment.

RENFREW MUSEUM & PARK, 1010 E. Main St., Waynesboro, PA 17268-2338. Tel.: 717-762-4723. Fax: 717-762-6384.
E-mail: renfrew@innernet.net
Web Site: www.renfrewmuseum.org
Founded: 1973.
Congressional District: 12
Key Personnel: C.E.O., Douglas Tengler; Chm. (V), David Hykes; Admin., Bonnie Iseminger; Supvr. Grounds, John H. Frantz; Museum Shop Mgr., Cheryl Keyser.
Personnel Profile: Full-Time Paid 2; Part-Time Paid 3; Part-Time Volunteers 21.
Governing Authority: municipal. Subsidiary Institution: Renfrew Institute for Cultural & Environmental Studies. Tax-exempt: 170(b)(1)(A).
Decorative Arts Museum: housed in 1812 Pennsylvania German farm house.
Collections: American decorative arts including furniture, furnishings & eight-legged sideboard signed by Aaron Colton of the American Federal period; Windsor chairs; Pennsylvania blanket chests; Chalkware; Canton; John Bell & Bell family pottery; early 19th-century Pennsylvania German farmstead with standing farmhouse, barn, miller's house, tannery & mill sites; Snow Hill archives - a religious off-branch of the Epharata Cloister c.1770; farming tools & household items.
Research Fields: Pennsylvania German culture, historic preservation, colonization & settlement of the Cumberland Valley & Shenandoah regional pottery.
Facilities: library on the decorative arts, historical books, exhibition catalogues; museum studies on historical preservations & periodicals available for use on premises; 107-acre park with picnic area; nature trails; trout stream; changing exhibit gallery; visitors center.
Activities: guided tours; lectures; films; gallery talks; concerts; changing exhibits; sponsored trips; environmental & cultural education programs for school groups; traveling trunk program.
Publications: catalog, Highlights of the Renfrew Collection; quarterly newsletters; special exhibit catalogs; brochures for sites; John Bell catalog & brochure.
Hours & Admission Prices: April-Oct. Tues.-Fri 12-4, Sat.-Sun. 1-4; other times by appointment. Adults $5, seniors $4.50, children 7-12 $3.50; discount to groups; children 6 & under and members no charge. Closed Mother's Day; Memorial Day; Father's Day; Independence Day; Labor Day.
Attendance: 14,500 (estimated)
Membership: Friends of Renfrew: Individual $25; Family $50; Sustaining $150; Renfrew Society $250; Life $2,000.

Waynesburg

GREENE COUNTY HISTORICAL MUSEUM, (M), 918 Rolling Meadows Rd., Waynesburg, PA 15370-3470. Tel.: 724-627-3204. Fax: 724-627-3204.
E-mail: gchsmuseum@windstream.net
Web Site: www.greencountyhistory.com
Founded: 1925.
Congressional District: 50
Key Personnel: Pres., Doug Wilson; Vice Pres., Gretchen Graham; Treas., Jim Weinschenker; Sec., Deborah Wilson; Admin., Bernice Fox.
Personnel Profile: Full-Time Paid 2; Full-Time Volunteers 12; Part-Time Paid 4; Part-Time Volunteers 50.
Governing Authority: society. Parent Institution: Greene County Historical Society. Tax-exempt: 501(c)(3).
Historical Society Museum: housed in 1861 former county home.
Collections: Victorian rooms; archives; archaeology; manuscript collections; Indian artifacts; glassware; pottery.
Research Fields: local history.
Activities: guided tours; permanent & temporary exhibitions; guided tours for groups with reservations. Annual Event: Harvest Festival in October.
Publications: quarterly newsletter; books, Monongahela of Old; Waynesburg-Prosperous & Beautiful; Census of Green County 1800; The Tenmile Country and its Pioneer Families.
Hours & Admission Prices: Tues.-Sat. 10-3, Sun. 1-4. Adults $5, seniors 60 & over $3; discount to AAA members; children under 12 & members no charge. Closed Easter; Thanksgiving; Christmas. ♿
Attendance: 5,000 (estimated)
Membership: Senior $8; Single $10; Couple $15; Family $18; Friend $50; Donor $51-$99.

West Chester

AMERICAN HELICOPTER MUSEUM & EDUCATION CENTER, (M), 1220 American Blvd., West Chester, PA 19380-4268. Tel.: 610-436-9600. Fax: 610-436-8642.
E-mail: info@helicoptermuseum.org
Web Site: www.helicoptermuseum.org
Founded: 1993.
Congressional District: 16
Key Personnel: Pres., Sean Saunders; Chm. Bd., Bob Beggs; Vice Pres., Chuck Schalch; Treas., Chris Nawn.
Personnel Profile: Full-Time Paid 4; Part-Time Paid 2; Part-Time Volunteers 150.
Governing Authority: private; nonprofit. Tax-exempt: 501(c)(3).
Aeronautics Museum.
Collections: concentration on rotary-wing aircraft, autogyros, helicopters & convertaplanes manufactured or operated in the United States.
Facilities: library; archives; 72-seat auditorium; classroom; 14,000 sq. ft. exhibit space. Museum-related items for sale.
Activities: docent program; formal educational programs; guided tours; lectures; rental facilities.
Publications: quarterly newsletter.
Hours & Admission Prices: Wed.-Sat. 10-5, Sun. 12-5. Adults $7, seniors $6, students w/college ID & children 3-18 $5; discounts to AAM members; members no charge. Closed New Year's Day; Christmas. ♿
Attendance: 35,000 (estimated)
Membership: Student & Military $25; Individual $50; Family $75; Friend $100; Sustaining $150; Patron $250; Benefactor $500; President's Circle $1,000.

CHESTER COUNTY HISTORICAL SOCIETY, 225 N. High St., West Chester, PA 19380-2658. Tel.: 610-692-4800. Fax: 610-692-4357.
E-mail: cchs@chestercohistorical.org
Web Site: www.chestercohistorical.org
Founded: 1893.
Congressional District: 16
Key Personnel: Pres. & Dir., Kimberly Hall; Chm. (V), William Latoff; Photo Archivist, Pamela C. Powell; Business Mgr., Ida C. McIntyre; Dir. Collections & Cur., Ellen Endslow; Dir. Education & Public Programs, Beth Twiss Hooting; Dir. Devel., Sachiko Mallach; Librarian, Diane Rofini.
Personnel Profile: Full-Time Paid 10; Part-Time Paid 7; Part-Time Volunteers 280; Interns 6.
Governing Authority: society. Tax-exempt.
History Museum.
Collections: local history & culture; paintings; photographs; sculpture.
Major Exhibits: Samuel Barber: 100 Years, 1/10-10/10; Layers: Unfolding the Stories of Chester County Quilts, 2/10-9/10.
Research Fields: furniture; textiles; costumes; genealogy; local history; preservation.
Facilities: 25,000-vol. library of local history; 80,000 photographs; 70,000 objects & decorative arts all available for study on premises. Collection-related items for sale.
Activities: guided tours; lectures; films; gallery talks; concerts; docent program seminars; field trips; inter-museum loan, permanent & temporary exhibitions; school tours; traveling trunks; hands-on exhibits; history lab.
Publications: biannual newsletter; annual report; quarterly calendar of activities.
Hours & Admission Prices: Museum & Library: Wed.-Sat. 10-5. Museum & Library: adults $5, seniors $4, children $2.50; discounts to AAA, AAM & ICOM members; members no charge. Library: adults $5, seniors $4; discounts to AAA, AAM & ICOM members; members no charge. Closed New Year's Day; Memorial Day; Independence Day; Labor Day; Thanksgiving; Christmas. ♿
Attendance: 20,000 (estimated)
Membership: Senior $40; Individual $45; Family Senior $50; Family $55; Contributor $125; Patron $250; Benefactor $500.

White Mills

DORFLINGER-SUYDAM WILDLIFE SANCTUARY & GLASS MUSEUM, Elizabeth St., White Mills, PA 18473. Mailing Address: P.O. Box 356, White Mills, PA 18473-0356. Tel.: 570-253-1185. Fax: 570-253-5196.
Founded: 1980.
Key Personnel: Exec. Dir., Joan G. Gillner.
Personnel Profile: Full-Time Paid 3; Part-Time Volunteers 100.
Governing Authority: Tax-exempt.
Wildlife Sanctuary & Glass Museum.
Collections: local natural history & culture; Dorflinger glass including over 900 pieces of cut, engraved, etched, gilded & enameled crystal.
Facilities: nature trails.
Activities: educational programs; special events.
Hours & Admission Prices: Sanctuary daily dawn to dusk. Museum: May-Oct. Wed.-Sat. 10-4, Sun. 1-4. Adults $3, seniors 55 & over $2.50; discounts to members.
Attendance: 3,000 (estimated)
Membership: Individual $25; Family $50; Donor $100.

Wilkes-Barre

LUZERNE COUNTY HISTORICAL SOCIETY, (M), 69 S. Franklin St., Wilkes-Barre, PA 18701. Mailing Address: 49 S. Franklin St., Wilkes-Barre, PA 18701-1290. Tel.: 570-823-6244. Fax: 570-823-9011.
E-mail: tonybrooks@luzernehistory.org
Web Site: www.luzernehistory.org
Formerly: Wyoming Historical and Geological Society
Founded: 1858.
Congressional District: 11
Key Personnel: Exec. Dir., Anthony T.P. Brooks; Pres. Bd., Frank E.P. Conyngham; Librarian & Archivist, Amanda Fontenova; Cur., Mary Ruth K. Burke.
Personnel Profile: Full-Time Paid 3; Part-Time Paid 2; Part-Time Volunteers 3; Interns 5.
Governing Authority: nonprofit organization. Branch Museums: 1790 Nathan Denison House, 35 Denison St., Forty Fort, PA; 1803 Swetland Homestead, 885 Wyoming Ave., Wyoming, Pa. Tax-exempt: 501(c)(3).
History Museum.
Collections: archaeology; archives; costumes; geology; Indian artifacts; industry; military; mineralogy; textiles; manuscripts; historic houses.
Major Exhibits: Wilkes-Barre's River Common, 6/10-12/10.
Research Fields: anthracite coal mining; archaeology; geology; genealogy; history of Luzerne County, Pennsylvania.
Facilities: 6,000-vol. library of local history & history of coal industry; reading room.
Activities: formally organized educational programs; permanent & temporary exhibitions.
Publications: books, The Susquehanna Company Papers; Proceedings & Collections; Steamboats on the Susquehanna; Gone But Not Forgotten: Civil War Veterans of Northeastern Pennsylvania; A Story Runs Through It: The Wyoming Valley Levee System; Coloring the Pieces of Luzerne County.
Hours & Admission Prices: Library: Tues.-Fri. 12-4, Sat. 10-4. Non-members $5. Museum: Tues.-Fri. 12-4, Sat. 10-4. No charge; donations accepted.
Attendance: 12,000 (estimated)
Membership: Student $15; Individual $35; Family $50; Patron $100; Business $200; Life $1,000.

SORDONI ART GALLERY, (M), Wilkes University, 150 S. River St., Wilkes-Barre, PA 18766-0001. Tel.: 570-408-4325. Fax: 570-408-7733.
E-mail: brittany.kramer@wilkes.edu
Web Site: wilkes.edu/sordoniartgallery
Founded: 1973.
Congressional District: 11
Key Personnel: Dir., Brittany Kramer DeBalko; Chm. (V), Joel Zitofsky; Preparator, Bruce Lanning.
Personnel Profile: Full-Time Paid 1; Part-Time Paid 8; Interns 1.
Governing Authority: Wilkes University. Tax-exempt.
Art Gallery.
Collections: 19th- & 20th-century American Art.
Research Fields: early 20th-century American & Contemporary Art.
Facilities: 1,600 sq. ft. exhibition space; storage; offices; workrooms.
Activities: guided tours; lectures; gallery talks; formally organized education programs for undergraduate students; loan, temporary & traveling exhibitions; artist-in-residence.
Publications: exhibition catalogs, American Art.
Hours & Admission Prices: Daily 12-4:30. No charge. Closed major holidays. ♿
Attendance: 4,000 (accurate)
Membership: Student $10; Individual $50; Patron $100; Connoisseur $250; Old Master's Circle $500; Collector's Society $1,000 & up.

Williamsport

CHILDREN'S DISCOVERY WORKSHOP, Williamsport YMCA, 343 W. 4th St., Williamsport, PA 17701-6401. Tel.: 570-323-7134.
Web Site: www.williamsportymca.org/cdw/index.html
Children's Museum.
Collections: hands-on exhibits.
Activities: workshops; programs; special events.
Hours & Admission Prices: Call for hours. ♿
Membership: Single Parent $42; Family $54; Corporate $111. (additional adults $12).

PETER HERDIC TRANSPORTATION MUSEUM, 810 Nichols Place, Williamsport, PA 17701. Tel.: 570-601-3455.
Transportation Museum.
Collections: period vehicles including cars, trains, & boats.
Hours & Admission Prices: Tues.-Sat. 10-3; other times by appointment.

* **THE THOMAS T. TABER MUSEUM OF THE LYCOMING COUNTY HISTORICAL SOCIETY, (M),** 858 W. 4th St., Williamsport, PA 17701-5824. Tel.: 570-326-3326. Fax: 570-326-3689.
E-mail: lchsmuseum@verizon.net
Web Site: www.tabermuseum.org
Formerly: Lycoming County Historical Society and Museum
Founded: 1907.
Congressional District: 10
Key Personnel: Dir., Sandra B. Rife; Cur., Scott Sagar; Museum Store Mgr., Anne Persun.
Personnel Profile: Full-Time Paid 3; Part-Time Paid 4; Part-Time Volunteers 90; Interns 3.
Governing Authority: society. Tax-exempt: 501(c)(3).
Regional History Museum.
Collections: American Indian artifacts; archives; 1850-1900 lumber industry; Civil War items; Victorian era period room; blacksmith shop; general store; gristmill; industry; industry trades; military; textiles; farm & home utensils; agriculture; costumes; transportation; music; wildlife; toy train collection; local history & genealogy.
Research Fields: regional archaeology; regional history; 1870-1900 lumber industry.
Facilities: Pamphlets, crafts & museum-related items for sale.
Activities: guided tours; lectures; gallery talks; arts festivals; formally organized education programs for children; family programs; inter-museum loan, permanent & temporary exhibitions.
Publications: bimonthly newsletter; annual Journal; reprints of OP books on local history.
Hours & Admission Prices: May-Oct. Tues.-Fri. 9:30-4, Sat. 11-4, Sun. 1-4; Nov.-April Tues.-Fri. 9:30-4, Sat. 11-4. Adults $5, senior citizens $4, children $2.50; discounts to AAM, ICOM, AARP & AAA members; members no charge. Closed national holidays; Sun. Nov.-April. ♿
Attendance: 13,000 (accurate)
Membership: Individual $35; Family $45; Patron $75; Contributor $100; Business $100-$249; Corporate $250-$500; Benefactor $500; Life $5,000.

Willow Street

1719 HANS HERR HOUSE & MUSEUM, 1849 Hans Herr Dr., Willow Street, PA 17584-9536. Tel.: 717-464-4438.
E-mail: info@hansherr.org
Web Site: www.hansherr.org
Founded: 1974.
Congressional District: 100
Key Personnel: Dir., Becky Gochnauer; Museum Shop Mgr., Linda Harnish; Administrative Asst., Donnalee Mylin.
Personnel Profile: Part-Time Paid 3; Part-Time Volunteers 40.
Governing Authority: Parent Institution: Lancaster Mennonite Historical Society. Tax-exempt: 501(c)(3).
Historic House: 1719 Herr House.
Collections: Mennonite rural life; pre-1750 furnishings; agricultural items.
Research Fields: 1700s Pennsylvania German life; Mennonite history; life in Lancaster County.
Facilities: 2,200 sq. ft. exhibit space; 18th-century garden & orchard.
Activities: guided tours; lectures; organized educational programs. Special Events: candlelight tours at Christmas; 18th-century crafts festival; Fall apple tasting festival.
Publications: quarterly newsletter, Herr House Foundation.
Hours & Admission Prices: April to 1st week Dec. Mon.-Sat. 9-4. Adults $5, children 7-12 $2; discounts to groups of 10 or more. Closed Good Friday; Thanksgiving.

Attendance: 8,200 (estimated)
Membership: Individual $20; Family $30; Donor $50; Partner $75; Supporter $100; Honorary $250.

Womelsdorf

CONRAD WEISER HOMESTEAD AND MEMORIAL PARK, 28 Weiser Lane, Womelsdorf, PA 19567-9768. Tel.: 610-589-2934. Fax: 610-589-9458.
E-mail: info@conradweiserhomestead.org
Web Site: www.conradweiserhomestead.org
Founded: 1928.
Congressional District: 6
Key Personnel: Historic Site Admin., Russell M. Swody; Pres. (V), David G. Sonnen; Groundskeeper, Arnel Greth; Custodial Guide, Mary Fenton.
Personnel Profile: Full-Time Paid 1; Part-Time Paid 2; Part-Time Volunteers 15; Interns 1.
Governing Authority: state. Administered by Pennsylvania Historical & Museum Commission, Commonwealth Keystone Bldg., Plaza Level, 400 North St., Harrisburg, PA 17120. Tax-exempt.
Historic House: 1729-1760 Conrad Weiser homestead.
Collections: period furnishings; artifacts.
Facilities: visitor center; picnic facilities; 26 acre park.
Activities: self-guided tours; craft demonstrations. Annual Events: Charter Day in March; Candlelight Tour in November.
Publications: newsletter.
Hours & Admission Prices: Grounds: dawn to dusk. Homestead: April-Nov. Fri.-Sat. 9-5, Sun. 12-5. Adults 12-64 $5, youth 3-11 $4; discounts to AAM & ICOM members; children under 3 & members no charge. ♿
Attendance: 25,000 (estimated)
Membership: Student $5; Individual $10; Family $20; Sponsor $50; Donor $100. (Special PA Heritage Society Membership package available for $25 extra).

Worcester

PETER WENTZ FARMSTEAD, 2100 Schultz Rd., Worcester, PA 19490. Mailing Address: P.O. Box 240, Worcester, PA 19490-0240. Tel.: 610-584-5104. Fax: 610-584-6860.
E-mail: peterwentzfarmstead@mail.montcopa.org
Web Site: www.montcopa.org
Founded: 1976.
Congressional District: 13
Key Personnel: Pres. (V), Anne Condon; Admin., Dianne M. Cram; Asst. Admin., John Schilling; Farm Mgr., James Nichols; Cur., Morgan McMillan; Educator, Kimberly Boice; Asst. Farm Mgr., Jay Ryan.
Personnel Profile: Full-Time Paid 6; Part-Time Volunteers 190.
Governing Authority: county. Subsidiary Institution: Peter Wentz Farmstead Society. Tax-exempt.
Historic Building & Site: 1758 farmstead belonging to Peter Wentz; used twice by General Washington where he planned the Battle of Germantown & received the word of victory at Saratoga.
Collections: period furniture; decorative arts; costumes; tools; farm implements; working 18th-century farm.
Research Fields: Pennsylvania German history; Revolutionary War; Wentz Family; Schultz Family.
Facilities: research library; classroom. Handmade museum-related items for sale.
Activities: guided tours; lectures; organized education programs for children, adults & undergraduate or graduate college students; docent program; loan & temporary exhibitions; period craft demonstrations; seminars & workshops; intern program for college students; summer day camp (colonial crafts featured) for 3rd, 4th & 5th grades.
Publications: quarterly newsletter, Wentz Post; annual brochures; booklets.
Hours & Admission Prices: Tues.-Sat. 10-4, Sun 1-4. No charge; donations accepted. Closed county holidays. ♿
Attendance: 10,000 (estimated)
Membership: Peter Wentz Farmstead Society, a support group for Farmstead: Student $10; Single Adult $20; Family $30.

Wrightsville

WRIGHTSVILLE HISTORICAL MUSEUM, 309 Locust St., Wrightsville, PA 17368-1221. Tel.: 717-252-1169.
History Museum.
Collections: local history & culture; photographs; period artifacts.
Activities: temporary exhibits.
Hours & Admission Prices: Call for hours. No charge; donations accepted.

Wyalusing

WYALUSING VALLEY MUSEUM, Grovedale Lane, Wyalusing, PA 18853. Mailing Address: P.O. Box 301, Wyalusing, PA 18853-0301. Tel.: 570-746-3979.
E-mail: wyalusingmuseum@frontiernet.net
Web Site: www.wyalusingmuseum.org
Founded: 1980.
Key Personnel: Pres. (V), Mary Skillings; Treas., Karl Peterson; Cur., David G. LaFrance.
Personnel Profile: Part-Time Paid 2.
Governing Authority: Tax-exempt.
History Museum.
Collections: Wyalusing area history; schools; Native Americans; military artifacts; furnishings; personal artifacts.
Facilities: Museum-related items for sale.
Activities: Annual Event: Wine Festival.
Publications: "Local History Gleaned from Articles found in the Wyalusing Rocket-Courier".
Hours & Admission Prices: May-Oct. Sat.-Sun. 12-4; other times by appointment. No charge; donations accepted.
Membership: Individual $10; Household $20; Sponsor $35.

York

POLICE HERITAGE MUSEUM, 54 W. Market St., York, PA 17401-1228. Mailing Address: P.O. Box 1941, York, PA 17405-1941. Tel.: 717-845-2677.
Key Personnel: Chm., John Stine
History Museum.
Collections: law enforcement history & artifacts; photographs; police bicycles & motorcycles; documents; police & prison equipment; badges; patches; personal artifacts; uniforms.
Hours & Admission Prices: April-Oct. Sat. 9-4; group tours by appointment. Adults $3, children 6-12 $1; children under 6 no charge.

USA WEIGHTLIFTING HALL OF FAME, 3300 Board Rd., York, PA 17406-8409. Tel.: 717-767-6481.
Key Personnel: Controller, Dave Kogut
Sports Museum.
Collections: barbells; trophy cups; photographs; barbell mobile; Hall of Fame inductees.
Hours & Admission Prices: Mon.-Sat. 10-5.

YORK COLLEGE GALLERIES, MAC, Wolf Hall, 1 Country Club Rd., York, PA 17403-3643. Tel.: 717-815-1354 & 1528.
Art Gallery.
Collections: works by local & national artists.
Activities: lectures; workshops.
Hours & Admission Prices: Mon.-Tues. & Thurs.-Fri. 10-5, Wed. 10-9, Sat.-Sun. 12-5. No charge. ♿

YORK COUNTY HERITAGE TRUST, AGRICULTURAL AND INDUSTRIAL MUSEUM, 217 W. Princess St., York, PA 17403-2013. Mailing Address: 250 E. Market St., York, PA 17403-2013. Tel.: 717-846-6452. Fax: 717-812-1204.
E-mail: info@yorkheritage.org
Web Site: www.yorkheritage.org
Founded: 1999.
Congressional District: 19
Key Personnel: Dir., Joan Mummert; Dir. Exhibits & Collections, Jennifer Hall; Dir. Education, Scott Royer; Dir. Library & Archives, Lila Fourhman-Shaull; Museum Shop Buyer, Carl Preate.
Personnel Profile: Full-Time Paid 15; Part-Time Paid 6; Part-Time Volunteers 150; Interns 15.
Governing Authority: nonprofit organization. Parent Institution: York County Heritage Trust. Subsidiary Institution: Historical Society Museum, Library & Archives; Fire Museum of York County; Colonial Complex; Bonham House. Tax-exempt: 501(c)(3).
Agriculture & Industrial Museum; 1874-1955 former industrial complex.
Collections: industrial artifacts dating from 19th century to present used in local industries such as wallpaper & wire cloth manufacturing, defense, dentifrices, physical fitness, refrigeration & air conditioning, & automobile manufacturing; agricultural artifacts including a three-story working grist mill.
Research Fields: agriculture & industry.
Facilities: 1,800-vol. library & archives; cafeteria. Museum-related items for sale.
Activities: rental facilities; self-guided & guided tours; permanent & temporary exhibits; education programs for children; docent program; volunteer opportunities.

Publications: quarterly newsletter, The Chronicle; membership newsletter, Trust Talk.
Hours & Admission Prices: Agricultural & Industrial Museum: Tues.-Sat. 10-4. Colonial Complex: Tours Tues.-Sat. 10-4. Historical Society Museum: Tues.-Sat. 10-4. Fire Museum: Sat. 10-4. York County Heritage Sites: adults $10, students $7, children 8-18 $5; discounts for military, AAA, ICOM & AAM members; members no charge. Library $6. Closed New Year's Day; Easter; Memorial Day; Independence Day; Labor Day; Thanksgiving; Christmas. ♿
Attendance: 48,250 (accurate)
Membership: York County Heritage Trust membership: Senior Citizen $35; Individual $40; Senior Couple $45; Family $55.

YORK COUNTY HERITAGE TRUST, FIRE MUSEUM OF YORK COUNTY, 757 W. Market St., York, PA 17401-3650. Mailing Address: 250 E. Market St., York, PA 17403-2013. Tel.: 717-848-1587. Fax: 717-812-1204.
E-mail: info@yorkheritage.org
Web Site: www.yorkheritage.org
Founded: 1973.
Congressional District: 19
Key Personnel: Pres. & CEO, Joan Mummert; Dir. Exhibits & Collections, Jennifer Hall; Dir. Education, Scott Royer; Dir. Library & Archives, Lila Fourhman-Shaull; Museum Shop Buyer, Carl Preate.
Personnel Profile: Full-Time Paid 15; Part-Time Paid 6; Part-Time Volunteers 250; Interns 15.
Governing Authority: nonprofit. Parent Institution: York County Heritage Trust. Subsidiary Institutions: Historical Society Museum; Agricultural and Industrial Museum; Colonial Complex; Bonham House; Murals of York. Tax-exempt: 501(c)(3).
Fire-fighting Museum: housed in 1903-1904 Royal Fire Station #6.
Collections: 1700s-present fire-fighting history in York County.
Facilities: 1,800-vol. library & archives on fire service history; 12,500 sq. ft. exhibit space.
Activities: self-guided & guided tours; volunteer opportunities; permanent & temporary exhibits; education programs.
Publications: quarterly newsletter, The Chronicle.
Hours & Admission Prices: Fire Museum: Sat. 10-4; tours by appointment. Historical Society Museum & Agricultural and Industrial Museum: Tues.-Sat. 10-4. Colonial Complex: Guided Tours Tues.-Sat. 10-4. Bonham House: by appointment. York County Heritage Trust Sites: adults $10, students $7, children 8-18 $5; discounts to groups, seniors, military, AAA, ICOM & AAM members; members no charge. Library $6. Closed New Year's Day; Easter: Memorial Day; Independence Day; Labor Day; Thanksgiving; Christmas. ♿
Attendance: 48,250 (accurate)
Membership: College Students w/ID $30; Senior Citizen 65 & over $35; Individual $40; Senior Couple $45; Family $55; Sustainer $100; Contributor $250; Patron $500; Patriot $1,000.

YORK COUNTY HERITAGE TRUST, HISTORICAL SOCIETY AND LIBRARY/ARCHIVES, (M), 250 E. Market St., York, PA 17403-2013. Tel.: 717-848-1587. Fax: 717-812-1204.
E-mail: info@yorkheritage.org
Web Site: yorkheritage.org
Formerly: The Historical Society of York County
Founded: 1895.
Congressional District: 19
Key Personnel: Pres. & C.E.O., Joan Mummert; Dir. Exhibits & Collections, Jennifer Hall; Dir. Education, Scott Royer; Dir. Library & Archives, Lila Fourhman-Shaull; Museum Shop Buyer, Carl Preate.
Personnel Profile: Full-Time Paid 15; Part-Time Paid 5; Part-Time Volunteers 150; Interns 15.
Governing Authority: nonprofit. Tax-exempt: 501(c)(3).
History Museum.
Collections: costumes; decorative arts; industrial & agricultural machines & products; folk art; historical domestic & cultural artifacts of York Co.; library collections including published manuscripts & photographical materials; genealogy. Historic Houses: 1741 Golden Plough Tavern; 1751 General Gates House; 1812 Log House; 1870s Bonham House; Historical Society Museum & Library; Fire Museum; Agricultural & Industrial Museum.
Research Fields: genealogy; Pennsylvania decorative & folk art; history.
Facilities: 18,000-vol. library; historical society museum; agricultural & industrial museum of York County; Bonham House; colonial complex; Golden Plough Tavern; General Gates House; Barnett Bobb Log House; colonial court house; classroom.
Activities: guided tours; lectures; field trips; gallery talks; formally organized education programs for children; docent program; permanent, temporary & traveling exhibitions; school loan service. Annual Fund Raising Events: Oyster Festival; Celebrity Art & Antique Auction, Brew Fest.
Publications: quarterly newsletter, The Chronicle; membership newsletter, Trust Talk.
Hours & Admission Prices: Historical Society Museum & Library: Tues.-Sat. 9-5. Agricultural & Industrial Museum: adults $10, students $7, senior citizens & children 8-18 $5; discounts for AAA, ICOM & AAM members; members no charge. Colonial Complex: Tues.-Sat. 10-4. Fire Museum: Sat. 10-4. Adults $10, students $7, senior citizens & children 8-18 $5; discounts for AAA, ICOM & AAM members; members no charge. Closed New Year's Day; Easter Monday; Memorial Day; Independence Day; Labor Day; Thanksgiving; Christmas. ♿
Attendance: 48,250 (accurate)
Membership: Individual $35; Couple $40; Family $55; Sustainer $100; Contributor $250; Patron $500; Patriot $1,000.

York Springs

EASTERN MUSEUM OF MOTOR RACING, 100 Baltimore Rd., York Springs, PA 17055. Mailing Address: P.O. Box 688, Mechanicsburg, PA 17055-0688. Tel.: 717-528-8279.
Web Site: www.emmr.org
Founded: 1975.
Congressional District: 19
Personnel Profile: Part-Time Volunteers 50.
General Museum.
Collections: period race cars; photographs; sprint cars; midgets; stock cars; motorcycles; Indy cars; NASCAR; drag racing.
Facilities: research library. Museum-related items for sale.
Activities: special events.
Hours & Admission Prices: April-Dec. Sat.-Sun. 10-4.
Membership: Annual $20.

Zelienople

ZELIENOPLE HISTORICAL SOCIETY, 243 S. Main St., Zelienople, PA 16063-1151. Tel.: 724-452-9457.
E-mail: zhs@zelienoplehistoricalsociety.com
Web Site: www.zelienoplehistoricalsociety.com
Founded: 1975.
Congressional District: 4
Key Personnel: C.E.O., Elizabeth Kelleher; Pres. (V), Margo Hogan; Museum Shop Mgr., Joan Teichart.
Personnel Profile: Full-Time Paid 1; Part-Time Paid 1; Part-Time Volunteers 30.
Governing Authority: nonprofit. Tax-exempt: 501(c)(3).
Historic Houses: Passavant House c.1808 Federal-Georgian brick & frame structure; c.1805 Buhl House.
Collections: early western Pennsylvania living customs; furniture; clothing; cooking; tools; documents; decorative arts; glass; archives; photographs; postal; textiles; rare books; dolls; over 1,000 family letters; genealogy; library of history.
Research Fields: genealogy; religious practices; local history.
Facilities: 1,300-vol. library pertaining to history, genealogy, Goethe, Communal societies & religion.
Activities: guided tours; lectures; arts festivals; theater.
Publications: quarterly newsletter, Zelienople Historical Society Newsletter; brochures; booklets.
Hours & Admission Prices: Tours: June-Sept. Wed. & Sat. 1 & 2:30; groups & other times by appointment. Adults $5, children & students $2.50; discounts to AAA members & groups of 10 or more; members no charge. Office & Library: Mon.-Fri. 9-3. ♿
Attendance: 1,000 (estimated)
Membership: Student $5; Individual $20; Couple $30; Family $35; Individual Life & Corporate $200; Life Couple $250; Life Patron $350 & up.

RHODE ISLAND

(109 listings)

Adamsville

GRAY'S STORE, 4 Main St., Adamsville, RI 02801. Tel.: 401-635-4566.
Congressional District: 1
Key Personnel: Owner, Grayton T. Waite
Historic Building: housed in a general store built by Samuel Church in 1788; also includes first post office (1804).
Collections: local history; period furnishings & artifacts; soda fountain; post office; cigar & tobacco cases.
Hours & Admission Prices: Mon.-Sat. 9-5, Sun. & holidays 12-4. No charge; donations accepted.

Block Island

BLOCK ISLAND HISTORICAL SOCIETY MUSEUM, Old Town Rd., Block Island, RI 02807. Mailing Address: P.O. Box 79, Block Island, RI 02807-0079. Tel.: 401-466-2481.
E-mail: blockhistory@me.com
Web Site: www.blockislandtimes.com/listings/2867912/the-block-island-historical-society
Key Personnel: Exec. Dir., Pamela Gasner; Pres., Dr. Gerald Abbott
Historical Society Museum.
Collections: Block Island history; farming & maritime; period furniture. Historic House: c.1850 farmhouse.
Hours & Admission Prices: Memorial Day to Oct. daily 10-5; other times by appointment. Adults $5, seniors & students $3; members & children under 16 no charge.

Bristol

AUDUBON SOCIETY OF RHODE ISLAND ENVIRONMENTAL EDUCATION CENTER, 1401 Hope St., Bristol, RI 02809-1153. Mailing Address: 12 Sanderson Rd., Smithfield, RI 02917-2606. Tel.: 401-245-7500. Fax: 401-245-9339.
E-mail: jhall@asri.org
Web Site: www.asri.org
Founded: 1897.
Congressional District: 2
Key Personnel: Exec. Dir., Lawrence Taft; Pres., Marc F. Mahoney; Treas., Paul J. Raducha; Sr. Dir. Advancement, Jeffery Hall; Dir., Anne DiMonti; Sr. Dir. Education, Kristen Swanberg; Retail Svcs. Mgr. & Volunteer Coord., Cathy Corey.
Personnel Profile: Full-Time Paid 20; Part-Time Paid 12; Part-Time Volunteers 100; Interns 2.
Governing Authority: private; nonprofit organization. Parent Institution: Audubon Society of Rhode Island. Tax-exempt: 501(c)(3).
Natural History Museum.
Collections: flora, fauna & natural history of Rhode Island; fresh & saltwater aquaria; life-sized models of right whale & harbor seal.
Research Fields: wildlife & habitat change.
Facilities: aquarium; botanical garden; 4,000 sq. ft. exhibit space; 28 acre refuge on Narragansett Bay; 2 classrooms; 100-seat auditorium; nature center; interpretive trails; boardwalk through Red Maple Swamp & Salt Marsh. Museum-related items for sale.
Activities: docent program; formal education programs for children; guided tours; lectures; participatory exhibits; study clubs; touch tank of tidal pool.
Hours & Admission Prices: Memorial Day-Sept. daily 9-5; Oct.-May Mon.-Sat. 9-5, Sun. 12-5. Adults $6, children 4-12 $4; children under 4 & members no charge. ♿
Attendance: 33,000 (accurate)
Membership: Individual $35; Family $45; Family Plus $55; Steward $75; Defender $100; Business $125; Advocate $250; Conservator $500; Benefactor $1,000; Life $3,000.

BLITHEWOLD MANSION, GARDENS & ARBORETUM, 101 Ferry Rd., (Rt. 114), Bristol, RI 02809-2902. Tel.: 401-253-2707. Fax: 401-253-0412.
E-mail: info@blithewold.org
Web Site: www.blithewold.org
Founded: 1976.
Congressional District: 1
Key Personnel: Exec. Dir., Karen Binder; Chm. (V), Arthur Parker; Chm. Emeritus (V), Joan Abrams; Dir. Special Events, Karen Bellavance; Grounds Mgr., Fred Perry; Education Coord, Julie Murphy; Dir. Public Programs & Communications, Cristoff Shay; Cur., Margaret Whitehead; Museum Shop Mgr., Laura Collins.
Personnel Profile: Full-Time Paid 8; Part-Time Paid 17; Part-Time Volunteers 280; Interns 1.
Governing Authority: nonprofit organization. Parent Institution: Blithewold, Inc. Tax-exempt.
Historic Building & Arboretum: 1908 English manor house & summer residence of Augustus Van Wickle.
Collections: 1,500 collection of exotic trees & shrubs; 200 varieties of woody plants; herbaceous garden plants; Van Wickle family furniture & fine art.
Research Fields: plant hardiness testing.
Facilities: 200-vol. library of books on horticultural & garden reference available for research on premises; historic landscape; 33-acre arboretum & flower gardens; 45-room turn-of-the-century mansion; greenhouse. Museum-related items for sale.
Activities: guided tours; lectures; formally organized education programs for adults & undergraduate college students; plant sales; concerts; summer camp. Annual Events: Christmas at Blithwold from late November to early January.
Publications: seasonal newsletter.
Hours & Admission Prices: Mansion: April 11-Oct. 12 Wed.-Sat. 10-4, Sun. 10-3; Nov. 27-Jan. 3 Thurs.-Sat. 1-8, Sun.-Wed. 10-5. Grounds: May 15-Oct. 28 daily 10-4; Oct. 29-May 14 daily 10-5. Grounds: $5. Mansion & Grounds: adults $10, seniors & students $6; discounts to AAA members; children & members no charge. Closed New Year's Eve & Day; Christmas Eve & Day.
Attendance: 32,500 (accurate)
Membership: Individual $37; Family $55; Contributing $100; Business $150; Sponsor $250; Patron $500.

COGGESHALL FARM MUSEUM INC., 1 Colt Dr., Bristol, RI 02809-1019. Mailing Address: P.O. Box 562, Bristol, RI 02809-0562. Tel.: 401-253-9062.
E-mail: coggeshallfarm@verizon.net
Web Site: www.coggeshallfarm.org
Founded: 1968.
Key Personnel: Exec. Dir., George Pare; Pres. (V), Cindy Barber.
Personnel Profile: Full-Time Paid 1; Part-Time Paid 2.
Governing Authority: nonprofit organization. Tax-exempt: 501(c)(3).
Living History Museum.
Collections: cooling house, spring house, 18th-century farming tools, blacksmith shop, farm out buildings, minor breed animals, heirloom vegetable gardens, salt marsh, hayfields & period hand tools.
Research Fields: agriculture & farm life in Rhode Island in the 1790s.
Activities: costumed interpreters; formally organized education programs; docent program; scheduled weekend events year round.
Publications: quarterly newsletter, The Coggeshall Farmer Newsletter.
Hours & Admission Prices: Tues.-Sun. 10-4. Adults $3, children $2; members no charge. Special Events: additional fee. Closed selected holidays. ♿
Attendance: 5,000 (estimated)
Membership: Student & Individual $18; Family $40; Supporting $50; Sustaining $100; Sponsor $250.

HERRESHOFF MARINE MUSEUM/AMERICA'S CUP HALL OF FAME, (M), One Burnside St., Bristol, RI 02809-2003. Mailing Address: P.O. Box 450, Bristol, RI 02809-0450. Tel.: 401-253-5000. Fax: 401-253-6222.
E-mail: l.fisher@herreshoff.org
Web Site: www.herreshoff.org
Founded: 1971.
Congressional District: 2
Key Personnel: Pres., Halsey C. Herreshoff; Chm. (V), Geoff Davis; Exec. Dir., Lawrence A. Fisher; Dir. Devel., Peter Sterrett; Exhibitions & Programs, Jonathan Goff; Cur., John Palmeiri.
Personnel Profile: Full-Time Paid 6; Full-Time Volunteers 2; Part-Time Paid 2; Part-Time Volunteers 60; Interns 1.
Governing Authority: private; nonprofit organization. Subsidiary Institute: Herreshoff Institute & America's Cup Hall of Fame. Tax-exempt: 501(c)(3).
Maritime Museum: located at the site of the former Herreshoff Manufacturing Company.
Collections: 60 sail & power yachts, all built by Herreshoff and many of which were built around 1900; yachts range in size from 8' to 75'; photographs; America's Cup memorabilia.
Facilities: research library covering era of Herreshoff Yacht Building & America's cup.
Activities: N.G. Herreshoff model room.
Publications: newsletters, The Chronicle; Shipshape.
Hours & Admission Prices: April 29-Oct. 31 daily 10-5. Adults $8, senior citizens $7, students $2; children under 12, CAMM & museum members no charge. Closed Independence Day. ♿
Attendance: 15,000 (accurate)
Membership: Individual $35; Family $50; Vigilant $100; Corporate $250; Defender $500; Benefactor $1,000; Reliance Society $1,000 per year for 10 years.

LINDEN PLACE, 500 Hope St., Bristol, RI 02809-1808. Tel.: 401-253-0390. Fax: 401-253-4106.
E-mail: info@lindenplace.org
Web Site: www.lindenplace.org
Key Personnel: Exec. Dir., James Burke Connell; Tour Dir., Joan Doyle Roth; Site Admin., Susan E. Battle
Historic Buildings: housed in an 1810 Federal-style mansion.
Collections: period furnishings; gardens; historic buildings.
Activities: guided tours; special events; summer camps.
Hours & Admission Prices: May 2-Oct. 11 Mon.-Sat. 10-4; other times by appointment. Adults $8, seniors & students $6, children 6-12 $5; discounts to PBS, AAA, & NE Museum members.

MOUNT HOPE FARM, 250 Metacom Ave., Bristol, RI 02809-5180. Mailing Address: P.O. Box 66, Bristol, RI 02809-0066. Tel.: 401-254-1745. Fax: 401-254-1270.
Web Site: www.mounthopefarm.com
Founded: 1998.
Congressional District: 1
Key Personnel: Dir. & Pres. (V), James W. Farley.
Governing Authority: Parent Institution: The Mount Hope Trust in Bristol. Tax-exempt.
Historic Site & Building: housed in Governor Bradford House, c.1745. Listed on the National Register of Historic Places.
Collections: period furnishings; personal artifacts.
Facilities: nature trails; garden.
Activities: rental facilities; retreats; lecture series; education programs.
Hours & Admission Prices: May-Oct. & Dec. Wed.-Sat. 12-4. Admission $6.

Chepachet

GLOCESTER HERITAGE SOCIETY, 1181 Putnam Pike, Chepachet, RI 02814. Mailing Address: P.O. Box 269, Chepachet, RI 02814-0269. Tel.: 401-568-8967.
E-mail: info@glocesterheritagesociety.org
Web Site: www.glocesterheritagesociety.org
Formerly: Job Armstrong Store
Founded: 1967.
Key Personnel: Pres., Edna Kent; Vice Pres., Rose LaVoie.
Governing Authority: Parent Institution: Glocester Heritage Society.
Historic Building: housed in an early 1800s store.
Collections: local history; weaving; quilting; rug hooking.
Research Fields: local history; genealogy.
Facilities: archives; reading room; meeting room. Museum-related items for sale.
Activities: Museum Sponsors: Gala & Silent Auction in spring; Dorr Rebellion Days in June; Heritage Day in September; Peddlar's Faire in November; Candlelight Shopping in December.
Publications: newsletter, Glocester Heritage Society.
Hours & Admission Prices: Thurs. 11-2 by appointment. No charge; donations accepted.
Membership: Senior & Student $10; Single $15; Family $25; Lifetime $300.

Coventry

GENERAL NATHANAEL GREENE HOMESTEAD, 50 Taft St., Coventry, RI 02816-5314. Tel.: 401-821-8630.
Historic House Museum: built in 1770. Listed on the National Register of Historic Places.
Collections: Greene family history & memorabilia; period furniture; photographs; personal artifacts.
Hours & Admission Prices: April-Oct. Wed. & Sat. 10-5, Sun. 1-5; other times by appointment.

PAINE HOUSE, 7 Station St., Coventry, RI 02816. Mailing Address: Western Rhode Island Civic Historical Society, P.O. Box 2, Coventry, RI 02816. Tel.: 401-615-2426.
Governing Authority: Parent Institution: The Western Rhode Island Civic Historical Society.
Historic House Museum.
Collections: local history & culture; personal artifacts; clothing; photographs; quilts; tools; books.
Hours & Admission Prices: May-Sept. Sat. 10-3; other times by appointment. Adults $3, children 6-12 $1.

WESTERN RHODE ISLAND CIVIC HISTORICAL SOCIETY, 7 Station St., Coventry, RI 02816. Mailing Address: 1196 Main St., Coventry, RI 02816-5712. Tel.: 401-385-9997.
E-mail: info@westernrihistory.org
Web Site: westernrihistory.org
Founded: 1945.
Congressional District: 1
Key Personnel: Pres., Norma Smith; Vice Pres., Marilyn Nagy; Sec., Katie McDonald.
Personnel Profile: Part-Time Volunteers 1.
Governing Authority: nonprofit organization. Branch Museum: Paine House, 1 Station St., Washington, RI. Tax-exempt.
Local History Museum.
Collections: costumes; tools; utensils; period furnishings.
Research Fields: history of Western Rhode Island.
Facilities: library of historical books; scrapbooks; old tax books.
Activities: guided tours; permanent exhibitions.
Publications: booklet, The Paine House.
Hours & Admission Prices: May-Dec. Sat. 1-4 by appointment. Adults $3, students & children $1; members no charge.
Attendance: 75 (estimated)
Membership: Individual $10.

Cranston

GOVERNOR SPRAGUE MANSION, 1351 Cranston St., Cranston, RI 02920. Tel.: 401-944-9226; 922-9226.
Web Site: www.cranstonhistoricalsociety.org
Governing Authority: Parent Institution: Cranston Historical Society.
Historic House Museum: housed in the former home of the Sprague family, built in 1790.
Collections: period furnishings; personal artifacts; photographs.
Hours & Admission Prices: Call for hours. Adults 12 & over $10, children under 12 $5.

JOY HOMESTEAD, 156 Scituate Ave., Cranston, RI 02921. Mailing Address: Cranston Historical Society, 1351 Cranston St., Cranston, RI 02920-6721. Tel.: 401-944-9226.
Historic House: housed in the former home of Job Joy; built in 1764. Listed on the National Register of Historic Places.
Collections: local history & culture; period furnishings; personal artifacts; photographs.
Activities: educational programs & activities.
Hours & Admission Prices: Call for hours.

East Greenwich

JAMES MITCHELL VARNUM HOUSE AND MUSEUM, 57 Pierce St., East Greenwich, RI 02818. Mailing Address: 5600 Post Rd., Unit 3, Ste - 150, East Greenwich, RI 02818-3442. Tel.: 401-884-1776.
E-mail: k8bcm@cox.net
Web Site: www.varnumcontinentals.org
Founded: 1939.
Congressional District: 2
Key Personnel: Dir., Col. Bruce C. MacGunnigle; Caretaker, Barlow B. Healy; Cur., Skip Healy.
Personnel Profile: Full-Time Volunteers 2; Part-Time Volunteers 6.
Governing Authority: nonprofit organization. Parent Institution: Varnum Continentals, 6 Main St., East Greenwich, RI 02818. Tax-exempt: 501(c)(3).
Historic House Museum: 1773 home of Major General James Mitchell Varnum.
Collections: eight authentic 18th-century furnished rooms.
Facilities: Museum-related gifts for sale.
Activities: guided tours; permanent exhibitions.
Publications: brochure; book, James Mitchell Varnum 1748-1789: The Man and His Mansion.
Hours & Admission Prices: June-Aug. Sat.-Sun. 10-4; call to confirm hours. Suggested Donations: $5; discounts to AAM & ICOM members. ♿
Attendance: 600 (estimated)
Membership: Annual $35.

NEW ENGLAND WIRELESS & STEAM MUSEUM INC., (M), 1300 Frenchtown Rd., East Greenwich, RI 02818-1309. Mailing Address: 697 Tillinghast Rd., East Greenwich, RI 02818-1424. Tel.: 401-885-0545. Fax: 401-884-0683.
E-mail: newsm@newsm.org
Web Site: www.newsm.org
Founded: 1964.
Congressional District: 2
Key Personnel: Dir., Robert W. Merriam; Chm. (V), Terry K. Jones.
Personnel Profile: Full-Time Volunteers 75.
Governing Authority: nonprofit organization. Tax-exempt: 501(c)(3).
History Museum: listed on the National Register of Historic Places.
Collections: devices from the days of the American Institute of Electrical Engineers (now IEEE) & the American Society of Mechanical Engineers (ASME); electrical communications equipment; stationary steam engines.
Research Fields: electrical & mechanical engineering history.
Facilities: 10,000-vol. non-circulating library on engineering available on premises only; 110-seat auditorium & theater.
Activities: guided tours; lectures; films; hobby workshops; educational courses in electrical & mechanical engineering. Museum Sponsors: Yankee Tune-Up in Summer; Yankee Steam-Up in Fall.
Publications: biannual historical monographs; book, Wireless Communication in the U.S. 1890-1920.
Hours & Admission Prices: Groups by appointment only. Adults $15; discount to groups of 10 or more. ♿
Attendance: 3,000 (estimated)

VARNUM MEMORIAL ARMORY & MILITARY MUSEUM, 6 Main St., East Greenwich, RI 02818-3827. Tel.: 401-884-4110.
E-mail: armory@varnumcontinentals.org
Web Site: www.varnumcontinentals.org
Founded: 1907.
Congressional District: 2
Key Personnel: C.E.O., Col. Bruce C. MacGunnigle; Cur., Capt. Donald Marcum.
Personnel Profile: Part-Time Paid 1; Part-Time Volunteers 6.
Governing Authority: private; nonprofit organization. Branch Museum: Varnum House Museum, 57 Pierce St., East Greenwich. Tax-exempt: 501(c)(3).
Military Museum: 1913 medieval-style armory; headquarters of Varnum Continentals military command dating from 1775, built 1913 in Medieval style & occupied by Varnum Continentals.
Collections: military artifacts; 76th Division artifacts; historical documents from 17th-19th centuries; over 900 WWI & WWII posters; Revolutionary War R.I. train artillery helmet.
Publications: newsletter.
Hours & Admission Prices: By appointment only. No charge; donations accepted.
Attendance: 600 (estimated)
Membership: Annual $35.

East Providence

HUNT HOUSE MUSEUM - EAST PROVIDENCE HISTORICAL SOCIETY, 65 Hunts Mills Rd., East Providence, RI 02916. Mailing Address: P.O. Box 4994, East Providence, RI 02916. Tel.: 401-438-1750.
E-mail: info@ephist.org
Web Site: ephist.org
Founded: 1966.
Key Personnel: Pres. (V), Nancy Moore.
Personnel Profile: Part-Time Volunteers 17.
Governing Authority: Parent Institution: East Providence Historical Society. Tax-exempt.
Historic House Museum.
Collections: local history; period artifacts; Rumford Baking Powder Company history & artifacts; genealogy.
Major Exhibits: 18th Century Christmas at Hunt House, 12/09-1/10; Rumford Collection, 1/10-12/10; Greening of East Providence, 6/10.
Facilities: library.
Publications: monthly, The East Providence Gazette.
Hours & Admission Prices: Summer: 2nd Sun. of month 1-4; other times by appointment. Adults $3; discounts to East Providence residents; members no charge.
Attendance: 700 (estimated)
Membership: Individual $15; Family & Corporate $25; Life $150.

STEAMSHIP HISTORICAL SOCIETY OF AMERICA, 1029 Waterman Ave., East Providence, RI 02914-1314. Tel.: 401-274-0805. Fax: 401-274-0836.
E-mail: info@sshsa.org
Web Site: www.sshsa.org
Founded: 1935.
Congressional District: 2
Key Personnel: Exec. Dir., Matthew C. Schulte; Pres. (V), Robert C. Cleasby; Editor-in-Chief (Steamboat Bill), John H. Shaum, Jr.; Museum Shop Mgr., Susan Ewen; Exec. Asst., Rebecca Torsell; Research Asst., Astrid Drew; Part-time Staff, Jeri Papa; Part-time Staff, Karen Sylvia.
Personnel Profile: Full-Time Paid 2; Full-Time Volunteers 1; Part-Time Paid 3; Part-Time Volunteers 3; Interns 1.
Governing Authority: society. Tax-exempt: 501(c)(3).
Research Library.
Collections: steamship & navigation-related items.
Research Fields: powered shipping & navigation.
Facilities: 10,000-vol. library of books & periodicals; 200,000 photographs in field of powered shipping & navigation; 25,000 postcards; pamphlet & brochure files; ship menus & plans; shipping ephemera.
Activities: marine research, in person & by mail.
Publications: quarterly journal, Steamboat Bill; books, Canadian Coastal and Inland Steam Vessels; Merchant Steam Vessels of the United States; Steamboats on the Muskingum; Steamboats For Rondout; Paddlewheel Inboard; Photographic Portraits of American Ocean Steamships, 1850-1870; booklets, Steam Navigation on the Carolina Sounds and the Chesapeake in 1892; 40th Anniversary.
Hours & Admission Prices: Mon.-Fri. 8:30-4:30. No charge. ♿
Membership: Student $30; Annual $50; Family (per additional person) $2; Contributing $75; Sustaining $100; Benefactor $1,000; Life $2,500.

Exeter

TOMAQUAG INDIAN MEMORIAL MUSEUM, Arcadia Village, 390 Summit Rd., Exeter, RI 02822-1808. Tel.: 401-539-7213 & 491-9063.
Web Site: www.tomaquagmuseum.com
Native American Museum.
Collections: Native American artifacts; Southern New England ash splint baskets; dolls.
Activities: special events.
Hours & Admission Prices: Mon.-Fri. 11-4; other times by appointment. Discounts to groups.

Foster

BORDERS FARM MUSEUM, 33 Balcom Rd., Foster, RI 02825-1321. Tel.: 401-647-4984.
E-mail: farmer@bordersfarm.org
Web Site: www.bordersfarm.org
Key Personnel: Owner, Mary Thomas
Farm Museum.
Collections: farm & agricultural history; farm tools & machinery. Historic Building: 1849 farmhouse.
Facilities: 200 acre farmland.
Activities: educational programs & activities.
Hours & Admission Prices: Daily 8-5.

FOSTER TOWN HOUSE, 181 Howard Hill Rd., Foster, RI 02825-1226. Tel.: 401-392-9200. Fax: 401-702-5010.
Historic House.
Collections: local history; period furnishings; personal artifacts.
Hours & Admission Prices: Summer: Mon.-Thurs. 8:30-5:30.

Jamestown

BEAVERTAIL LIGHTHOUSE MUSEUM, Beavertail State Park, Jamestown, RI 02835. Mailing Address: Beavertail Lighthouse Museum Association, P.O. Box 83, Jamestown, RI 02835-0083. Tel.: 401-423-3270.
E-mail: info@beavertaillight.org
Web Site: www.beavertaillight.org
Founded: 1898.
Lighthouse Museum: the third oldest lighthouse on the Atlantic seacoast.
Collections: lighthouse history; artifacts.
Facilities: Museum-related items for sale.
Activities: panoramic view of Narragansett Bay.
Publications: newsletter.
Hours & Admission Prices: May 24 to mid-June & Sept. to Columbus Day Sat.-Sun. 12-3; June 16 to Labor Day daily 10-4.

JAMESTOWN FIRE DEPARTMENT MEMORIAL MUSEUM, 50 Narragansett Ave., Jamestown, RI 02835-1167. Tel.: 401-423-0062. Fax: 401-423-7278.
E-mail: jamestownfd@msn.com
Web Site: www.jamestownfd.com/museum.htm
Key Personnel: Museum & Web, Kenneth H. Caswell
Fire Fighting Museum.
Collections: period fire fighting equipment; photographs.
Hours & Admission Prices: Call for hours.

JAMESTOWN MUSEUM, 92 Narragansett Ave., Jamestown, RI 02835-1174. Mailing Address: P.O. Box 156, Jamestown, RI 02835-0156. Tel.: 401-423-0784.
Web Site: jamestownhistoricalsociety.org
Founded: 1972.
Congressional District: 1
Key Personnel: Pres. Historical Society, Rosemary Enright.
Personnel Profile: Part-Time Volunteers 50; Interns 1.
Governing Authority: society. Parent Institution: Jamestown Historical Society. Tax-exempt.
Local History Museum: housed in 19th-century schoolhouse.
Collections: history of Jamestown & the old ferry system; Colonial Battery; 18th-century windmill; 18th-century friends meeting house.
Major Exhibits: Our Agricultural Past, 6/10-9/10.
Research Fields: local history; genealogy; architecture.
Activities: temporary exhibitions.
Publications: newsletter; The Jamestown Bridge, 1940-2007: Concept to Demolition.
Hours & Admission Prices: June-Sept. Wed.-Sun. 1-4. No charge; donations accepted. ♿
Attendance: 700 (estimated)
Membership: Single $25; Family $40; Patron $500; 1657 Member $1,000.

SYDNEY L. WRIGHT MUSEUM, Jamestown Philomenian Library, 26 North Rd., Jamestown, RI 02835-1434. Tel.: 401-423-7281.
Web Site: www.jamestownri.com/library/museum.htm
Founded: 1973.
Archaeology Museum.
Collections: Native American artifacts relating to Conanicut Island.
Hours & Admission Prices: Mid-May to mid-June Mon & Tues. 10-9, Wed. 10-5 & 7pm-9pm, Thurs. 12-5 & 7pm-9pm, Fri. & Sat. 10-5; June 15-Sept. 15 Mon. & Tues. 10-9, Wed. 10-5 & 7pm-9pm, Thurs. 12-5 & 7pm-9pm, Fri. 10-5, Sat. 10-2; mid-Sept. to mid-May Mon. & Tues. 10-9, Wed. 10-5 & 7pm-9pm, Thurs. 12-5 & 7pm-9pm, Fri. & Sat. 10-5, Sun. 1-5. ♿

WATSON FARM, 455 North Rd., Jamestown, RI 02835-2238. Mailing Address: 141 Cambridge St., Boston, MA 02114-2702. Tel.: 401-423-0005; 617-227-3956. Fax: 617-227-9204.
Web Site: www.historicnewengland.org
Key Personnel: Pres., Carl Nold; Farm Mgr., Don Minto; Farm Mgr., Heather Minto.
Governing Authority: society; nonprofit organization. Parent Institution: Historic New England, 141 Cambridge St. Boston, MA 02114. Tax-exempt: 501(c)(3).
Historic Farm: c.1796 Watson Farm, 285-acre working farm.
Collections: heritage breed cattle & sheep; hayfields; pastures.
Activities: guided tours; special events & programs; school programs.
Publications: Guide to Historic New England.
Hours & Admission Prices: June-Oct. 15 Tues., Thurs. & Sun. 1-5. Adults $4; discounts to seniors, WGBH, AAA, AAM & ICOM members; Historic New England members no charge. Call for further information.
Attendance: 3,410 (accurate)
Membership: National $35; Individual $45; Household $55; Garden & Landscape $75; Institutional $85; Contributing $100; Historic Homeowner $200; Supporting $250.

Johnston

CLEMENCE-IRONS HOUSE, 38 George Waterman Rd., Johnston, RI 02919. Mailing Address: Historic New England, 141 Cambridge St., Boston, MA 02114-2702. Tel.: 401-295-1030.
Web Site: www.historicnewengland.org
Governing Authority: Parent Institution: Historic New England.
Historic House: built in 1691.
Collections: period furnishings; personal artifacts.
Hours & Admission Prices: Call for hours & appointment. No charge.
Attendance: 41 (accurate)

Kingston

HELME HOUSE GALLERY, 2587 Kingstown Rd., Kingston, RI 02881-1605. Tel.: 401-783-2195.
Art Gallery.
Collections: paintings; photographs; sculpture.
Facilities: Museum-related items for sale.
Activities: rental facilities.
Hours & Admission Prices: Wed.-Sun. 1-5. Closed holidays.

PETTAQUAMSCUTT HISTORICAL SOCIETY, 2636 Kingstown Rd., Kingston, RI 02881-1624. Tel.: 401-783-1328.
E-mail: pettaquamscutt@yahoo.com
Web Site: www.washingtoncountyhistory.org
Founded: 1958.
Congressional District: 2
Key Personnel: Dir., Lori Urso; Pres. (V), Sanford Neuschatz.
Personnel Profile: Full-Time Paid 1; Part-Time Paid 1; Part-Time Volunteers 40.
Governing Authority: nonprofit organization. Tax-exempt: 501(c)(3).
Historical Society Museum: housed in 1858 & 1861 Washington County Jail.
Collections: Civil War artifacts; period furniture; house, shop & farm furnishings; artifacts from late 18th-century to present; local historic manuscripts & printed materials; Ernest Hamlin Baker's mural.
Research Fields: local history; genealogy.
Facilities: 500-vol. local history & genealogy library available for use on site upon request. Museum-related items for sale.
Activities: guided tours; lectures; permanent & temporary exhibitions.
Publications: quarterly newsletter.
Hours & Admission Prices: Tues., Thurs. & Sat. 1-4. Adults $5, students & seniors $3; discounts to AAM members; members and children 12 & under no charge.
Attendance: 2,000 (estimated)
Membership: Individual $20; Family $35; Friend $100; Life 65 & over $1,000.

Kingstown

FAYERWEATHER HOUSE, 1895 Mooresfield Rd., Kingstown, RI 02881-1715. Mailing Address: P.O. Box 222, Wakefield, RI 02880. Tel.: 401-789-9072.
Web Site: www.fayerweatherhouse.8m.net
Historic House Museum: built in 1820. Listed on the National Register of Historic Places.
Collections: family history; period furnishings; personal artifacts; photographs.
Hours & Admission Prices: May-Dec. Tues.-Sat. 10-4. No charge.

Lincoln

ELEAZER ARNOLD HOUSES, 487 Great Rd., Lincoln, RI 02865-1436. Tel.: 401-295-1030.
E-mail: arnoldhouse@historicnewengland.org
Web Site: www.historicnewengland.org
Historic House: built in 1693.
Collections: period furnishings; personal artifacts.
Hours & Admission Prices: Call for hours. Adults $5. June 13, Oct. 4 & 11 and members no charge.

FRIENDS OF HEARTHSIDE, INC., (M), 677 Great Rd., Lincoln, RI 02865-1401. Mailing Address: 757 Great Rd., Lincoln, RI 02865-3820. Tel.: 401-726-0597.
E-mail: kathy.hartley@hearthsidehouse.org
Web Site: www.hearthsidehouse.org
Founded: 2001.
Congressional District: 1
Key Personnel: Chm. (V), Kathryn A. Hartley.
Personnel Profile: Part-Time Volunteers 25; Interns 1.
Governing Authority: Tax-exempt.
Historic House: housed in an 1810 mansion.
Collections: textiles; period furnishings; personal artifacts; blacksmith shop.
Activities: tours; special events; blacksmithing classes.
Publications: email newsletter.
Hours & Admission Prices: Tours: March-Dec. 2nd Sat. of month. No charge; donations accepted.
Attendance: 1,000 (estimated)
Membership: $15-$1,000 & up.

Little Compton

LITTLE COMPTON HISTORICAL SOCIETY, (M), 548 W. Main Rd., Little Compton, RI 02837-1123. Mailing Address: P.O. Box 577, Little Compton, RI 02837-0577. Tel.: 401-635-4035. Fax: 401-635-4035.
E-mail: lchistory@littlecompton.org
Web Site: www.littlecompton.org
Founded: 1937.
Congressional District: 2
Key Personnel: Exec. Dir., Carlton C. Brownell; Mng. Dir., Marjory O'Toole; Pres., Robert Wolter; Admin., Nancy Carignan; Mgr. Collections, Fred Bridge.
Personnel Profile: Part-Time Paid 2; Part-Time Volunteers 50; Interns 1.
Governing Authority: society. Tax-exempt: 170(b)(1)(A).
History Museum: housed in 1850 Wilbor Barn & 1690-1860 Wilbor House.
Collections: built circa 1690, 17th, 18th & 19th century furnishings and artifacts throughout Historic House Museum; outbuildings, which include a carriage house with restored sleighs and coaches; a one-room schoolhouse featuring antique school books, slates, and maps; and a barn which houses, farm tools and equipment, including dairying utensils, vehicles, and looms; a display of Portuguese artifacts, photographs, and documents of Little Compton over the last century; other buildings open to the public include artist Sidney Burleigh's studio, built over the hull of a rescued 19th century catboat and a cookhouse, where food for the Rhode Island Red Chickens was prepared; collections which include Native American artifacts including, stone tools, pottery and baskets; Portuguese artifacts, photographs & documents.
Research Fields: 17th, 18th & 19th century American social history.
Facilities: Friends Meeting House; research facility; exhibition space.
Activities: guided tours; permanent & temporary exhibitions; summer camps; educational programs.
Publications: Notes on Little Compton; Little Compton Families; Little Compton Remembers World War II, Diary of King Philip's War; newsletter, Past Times.
Hours & Admission Prices: late-June to Labor Day Thurs.-Sun 1-5; Sept.-Oct. Sat.-Sun. 1-5; other times by appointment. Adults $5, children $1; discounts to AAM members; reciprocal membership; members & New England Museum Association Members no charge. Call for tour days.
Attendance: 2,600 (estimated)

Membership: Individual $20; Family $30; Contributing $50; Corporate $75; Supporting $100; School Program Sponsor $150.

Middletown

NORMAN BIRD SANCTUARY, 583 Third Beach Rd., Middletown, RI 02842-5738. Tel.: 401-846-2577. Fax: 401-846-2772.
E-mail: rcardeiro@normanbirdsanctuary.org
Web Site: www.normanbirdsanctuary.org
Key Personnel: Exec. Dir., Robert Cardeiro; Dir. Properties, Joseph McLaughlin; Dir. Education, Catherine Arning; Education Coord., Jennifer Klein; Asst. Exec. Dir., Natasha Harrison; Devel. Assoc. & Volunteer Coord., Lesley Muir; Office Mgr., Sarah de Leiris
Bird Sanctuary.
Collections: native birds & plants.
Hours & Admission Prices: Daily 9-5. Trail: adults $5, children 4-13 $2; children under 4 & members no charge. Closed major holidays.

PRESCOTT FARM, 2009 W. Main Rd., Middletown, RI 02842-7963. Tel.: 401-847-6230.
Web Site: www.newportrestoration.org/visit/prescott_farm/
Key Personnel: Exec. Dir., Pieter Roos
History Museum.
Collections: farm history; early American architecture & landscape; period artifacts. Historic Structure: 1812 windmill.
Facilities: nature trails.
Activities: educational programs; rental facilities.
Hours & Admission Prices: June-Sept. Tues.-Sat. 10-3. Guided Tour: adults $5; children under 12 no charge. Grounds: no charge.

SACHUEST POINT NATIONAL WILDLIFE REFUGE, 769 Sachuest Point Rd., Middletown, RI 02842. Mailing Address: 50 Bend Rd., Charlestown, RI 02813-2503. Tel.: 401-847-5511.
Wildlife Refuge.
Collections: over 200 bird species; hands-on exhibits.
Facilities: 242 acre site; visitor center; nature trails; classrooms.
Activities: viewing platforms; fishing; special events.
Hours & Admission Prices: Call for hours.
Attendance: 65,000 (estimated)

WHITEHALL MUSEUM HOUSE, 311 Berkeley Ave., Middletown, RI 02842-5392. Mailing Address: 31 Hunter Ave., Newport, RI 02840-2859. Tel.: 401-846-3116.
Founded: 1900.
Key Personnel: Chm. (V), Nancy P. Bredbeck; Pres. (V), Zulette Catir.
Personnel Profile: Full-Time Volunteers 10; Part-Time Volunteers 14.
Governing Authority: Parent Institution: The National Society of The Colonial Dames of America in the State of RI. Tax-exempt.
Historic House Museum: housed in the former home of Anglican Bishop, George Berkeley; built in 1729.
Collections: period furnishings; herb garden; orchard; books by & about George Berkeley.
Research Fields: philosophy.
Facilities: library.
Activities: Museum Sponsors: Open House in May, October & December; guided tours by philosophers in July and August.
Hours & Admission Prices: July-Aug. Tues.-Sun. 10-4; other times by appointment. Adults $5; members no charge.
Attendance: 534 (accurate)
Membership: Friend of Whitehall $20.

Narragansett

SOUTH COUNTY MUSEUM INC., (M), Strathmore Street, Narragansett, RI 02882. Mailing Address: Box 709, Narragansett, RI 02882-0709. Tel.: 401-783-5400. Fax: 401-783-0506.
E-mail: info@southcountymuseum.org
Web Site: www.southcountymuseum.org
Founded: 1933.
Congressional District: 2
Key Personnel: Pres., Daryl Anne Anderson; Vice Pres., Doris Manganaro; Staff Dir., Jim Crothers; Business Mgr., Carolyn Shea.
Personnel Profile: Part-Time Paid 4; Interns 1.
Governing Authority: nonprofit organization. Tax-exempt.
History Museum.
Collections: rural early America; agriculture; technology; transportation; print shop; blacksmith shop; carpentry shop; household items of Rhode Island rural life 1800-1930; living history farm; maritime; textiles; weaving & cottage industry.
Research Fields: 1800-1930 culture & social history.
Facilities: picnic area.
Activities: educational programs; temporary & permanent exhibits; special events; lectures.
Publications: newsletter, Canonchet Gazette.
Hours & Admission Prices: May-June & Sept.-Oct Fri.-Sat. 10-4, Sun. 12-4; July-Aug. Wed.-Sat. 10-4, Sun. 12-4. Adults $5, seniors $4, children 6-12 $2; discounts to AAM, AAA, NEMA, & AASLH members; children under 6 & members no charge. ♿
Attendance: 1,978 (accurate)
Membership: Individual $25; Family $35; Business $125; Benefactor $100; Life $1,000.

Newport

ARTILLERY COMPANY OF NEWPORT MILITARY MUSEUM, 23 Clarke St., Newport, RI 02840-3023. Mailing Address: P.O. Box 14, Newport, RI 02840-0001. Tel.: 401-846-8488.
E-mail: info@newportartillery.org
Web Site: www.newportartillery.org
Founded: 1959.
Congressional District: 1
Key Personnel: Colonel Commanding, Col. Comm. Robert Edenbach; Exec. Officer, Michael Pine; Operations Officer, Major Steven Colonies; Adjutant & Communications Officer, Joanne Pike; Finance Officer, Pvt. Corinne Edenbach.
Governing Authority: artillery company. Subsidiary Institution: Artillery Company of Newport Foundation. Tax-exempt: 501(c)(3) & 170(b)(1)(A).
Military Museum: housed in c.1836 Armory.
Collections: uniforms & militaria from 125 countries; artillery artifacts include 4 original Paul Revere Cannons.
Research Fields: history of the artillery company & Rhode Island militia.
Activities: guided tours.
Hours & Admission Prices: Sat. 10-4. No charge; donations accepted.
Membership: Annual $45.

ASTORS' BEECHWOOD MANSION - LIVING HISTORY MUSEUM, 580 Bellevue Ave., Newport, RI 02840-4265. Tel.: 401-846-3772. Fax: 401-849-6998.
Web Site: www.astorsbeechwood.com
Formerly: The Astors' Beechwood-Victorian Living History Museum
Founded: 1981.
Congressional District: 1
Key Personnel: Dir., Robert B. Milligan, Jr.; Pres., Sharon L. Toppa; Museum Shop Mgr., Jane Brice.
Personnel Profile: Full-Time Paid 21; Part-Time Paid 20; Part-Time Volunteers 1.
Governing Authority: private corporation. Parent Institution: Historic Newport, L.P.
Living History Museum.
Collections: period furnishings; Victorian era reproductions; reproduction period garments.
Research Fields: anything pertaining to the year 1891 & 1920s; the Astor & Schermerhorn lineage; Titanic related issues & Victoriana.
Facilities: ballroom. Museum-related items for sale.
Activities: formal education programs for adults; guided tours; professional internship for museum theatre actors; murder mysteries; rental facilities. Museum Sponsors: Victorian Christmas Feast; Mrs. Astor's Salon.
Publications: book, Where American Society Began.
Hours & Admission Prices: Feb. to mid-May Fri.-Sun. 10-4; mid-May to early Nov. daily 10-4; early Nov. to Dec. call for hours. Family $45, adults $18, children $8; discounts to groups, ICOM, AAM & AAA members and museum employees.
Attendance: 50,000 (accurate)

BELCOURT CASTLE, 659 Bellevue Ave., Newport, RI 02840-4280. Tel.: 401-849-1566 & 846-0669. Fax: 401-846-5345.
Web Site: www.belcourtcastle.org
Founded: 1957.
Congressional District: 1
Key Personnel: Exec. Dir., Harle H. Tinney.
Personnel Profile: Full-Time Paid 3; Full-Time Volunteers 1; Part-Time Paid 15; Part-Time Volunteers 9; Interns 2.
Governing Authority: private; not-for-profit organization. Tax-exempt: 501(c)(3).
Historic House: 1891-1894 60-room, Louis XII-style Belcourt Castle located in historic Bellevue Ave. district.
Collections: Romanesque, Gothic, Renaissance, Louis XIV & Louis XV and Classic Revival style interiors; European & Oriental royal furniture; 17th- to 19th-century marble, bronze, wood & plaster sculptures; Romanesque through 19th-century fabrics: silks, embroideries, 17th- to 19th-century Oriental rugs; paintings: Riqaud, Kneller & other European artists, 17th to

19th century; 18th- to 19th-century Oriental, Meissen, Dresden, Coalport porcelains; ancient art: small collection of ancient Egyptian & Roman artifacts.
Research Fields: history of the property; investigating provenance of six Nicolas Poussin paintings (unfunded).
Facilities: 2,010-vol. library including 18th to 19th-century steel engravings; special event facility.
Activities: guided tours; candlelight tours; ghost lectures & tours; Sunday afternoon concerts; Christmas teas; rental facilities; weddings & special events. Museum Sponsors: New Year's Eve Ball.
Hours & Admission Prices: Call for hours. Adults $15, senior citizens & college students $10, students 13-18 $7.50, children 6-12 $5; discounts to AAM, AAA & AARP members; members no charge. Closed Thanksgiving; Christmas.
Attendance: 30,000 (estimated)
Membership: Friends of Royal Arts Foundation: Single & Couple $50; Supporter $65; Patron $375; Benefactor $500.

COLONY HOUSE, Washington Square, Newport, RI 02840. Mailing Address: c/o Newport Historical Society, 82 Touro St., Newport, RI 02840-2931. Tel.: 401-846-0813. Fax: 401-846-1853.
Web Site: www.newporthistorical.org
Founded: 1739.
Personnel Profile: Part-Time Paid 3; Interns 5.
Governing Authority: state. Parent Institution: State of Rhode Island. Managed by the Newport Historical Society. Tax-exempt: 501(c)(3).
Historic State House Building: 1739 Colony House.
Collections: antique furnishings.
Hours & Admission Prices: Call for hours. ♿
Attendance: 2,750 (estimated)

EDWARD KING HOUSE, 35 King St., Newport, RI 02840-3595. Tel.: 401-846-7426.
Historic House: former home of China Trade merchant, Edward King; built in c.1845.
Collections: historic house; gardens.
Facilities: banquet facilities.
Activities: tours; rental facilities; weddings; special events.
Hours & Admission Prices: Tours: Mon.-Fri. 9-4; other times by appointment.

FORT ADAMS STATE PARK, 80 Fort Adams Dr., Newport, RI 02840. Mailing Address: Eisenhower House, 1 Lincoln Dr., Newport, RI 02840. Tel.: 401-841-0707. Fax: 401-841-0790.
E-mail: info@fortadams.org
Key Personnel: Exec. Dir., Eric Hertfelder
Park & History Museum.
Collections: local & military history; photographs; period furnishings; personal artifacts.
Facilities: rental facilities. Museum-related items for sale.
Activities: rental facilities; special events; military reenactments; music festivals; classic vehicle shows; guided tours.
Hours & Admission Prices: Memorial Day to Columbus Day 10-4. Adults $10, children 6-17 $5; discounts to groups; children 5 & under no charge.

FRIENDS MEETING HOUSE (QUAKER), 30 Marlborough St., Newport, RI 02840. Tel.: 401-846-0831 (Historical Society).
Historic House: built in 1704
Collections: period furnishings.
Hours & Admission Prices: Call for hours.

INTERNATIONAL TENNIS HALL OF FAME & MUSEUM, 194 Bellevue Ave., Newport, RI 02840-3586. Tel.: 401-849-3990; 800-457-1144. Fax: 401-849-8780 & 851-7920 (Research Center).
E-mail: newport@tennisfame.com
Web Site: www.tennisfame.com
Founded: 1954.
Congressional District: 1
Key Personnel: C.E.O., Mark Stenning; Dir., Douglas Stark; Chm., Christopher E. Clouser; Pres., Tony Trabert; Vice Pres. & Dir. Administration, Nancy Cardoza; Dir. Retail, Leslie Thomas.
Personnel Profile: Full-Time Paid 24; Part-Time Paid 6; Part-Time Volunteers 8; Interns 8.
Governing Authority: nonprofit corporation. Parent Institution: International Tennis Hall of Fame, Inc. Tax-exempt: 501(c)(3).
Sports Museum: housed in the 1880 Newport Casino, site of the first national tennis championships, held in 1881.
Collections: tennis racquets; equipment; trophies; photographs; prints; paintings; sculpture; tennis costume; tennis history; player memorabilia.
Major Exhibits: Monica Seles: Passion and Pride for the Love of the Game, 11/09-5/10.
Research Fields: history of tennis & its players; social history of Newport, the Gilded Age; McKim, Mead & White architecture.
Facilities: 5,000-vol. Information Research Center by appointment only; 13 public access grass courts. Museum-related gifts for sale.
Activities: permanent & temporary exhibitions; concert series; men's professional grass court championship. Museum Sponsors: opening night jazz festival.
Publications: brochures; newsletters.
Hours & Admission Prices: Daily 9:30-5. Family $25, adults $10, seniors, military & college ID $8, children 16 & under $5; discounts to groups, USTA, AAA, ICOM & AAM members; members & children under 5 no charge. Closed Thanksgiving; Christmas. ♿
Attendance: 25,000 (estimated)
Membership: Student $15; Supporter $25; Friend $50; Family $74; Fellow $100; Associate $250; Sponsor $500; Patron $1,000; Sponsoring Patron $2,500; Benefactor $5,000; Leading Benefactor $10,000; Champion $25,000.

MUSEUM OF YACHTING, Fort Adams State Park, 449 Thames St., Newport, RI 02840-6720. Tel.: 401-847-1018. Fax: 401-847-8320.
E-mail: info@museumofyachting.org
Web Site: www.moy.org
Founded: 1983.
Congressional District: 1
Key Personnel: Pres., Terry Nathan; Vice Pres. Mktg., Susan Daly; Facilities Mgr., Per Peterson; Cur., Jay Picotte.
Personnel Profile: Full-Time Paid 3; Part-Time Paid 2; Part-Time Volunteers 100; Interns 1.
Governing Authority: nonprofit organization. Tax-exempt: 501(c)(3).
Yachting Museum: located in Fort Adams State Park.
Collections: history of yachting; small boats; Sailors Hall of Fame; America's Cup history; photographs; trophies; in-water boats.
Research Fields: restoration of old wooden boats; restoration materials, techniques, etc.
Facilities: 3,000-vol. library of sailing history; America's Cup; sailing & boating magazines, available for use by members; 12,000 sq. ft. exhibit space. Gift items for sale.
Activities: formal education programs for adults; experiment with lifting systems; guided tours; lectures; temporary & traveling exhibition. Annual Events: Labor Day weekend, Classic Yacht Regatta; Small Boat Regatta; Unlimited Regatta; Newport 12 Meter Regatta.
Publications: quarterly, Spinnaker.
Hours & Admission Prices: June-Oct. 1 Wed.-Mon. 10-6. Adults $5; discounts to groups; members, students & children under 18 no charge.
Attendance: 8,000 (accurate)
Membership: Crew (Individual) $30; Starboard Watch (Family) $40; Helmsman $50; Watch Captain $100; Navigator $250; Captain $500; Founder $1,000.

NATIONAL MUSEUM OF AMERICAN ILLUSTRATION, (M), Vernon Court, 492 Bellevue Ave., Newport, RI 02840-4127. Tel.: 401-851-8949. Fax: 401-851-8974.
E-mail: art@americanillustration.org
Web Site: www.americanillustration.org
Founded: 1998.
Congressional District: 1
Key Personnel: Dir. & Co-Founder, Judy Goffman Cutler; Chm. & Co-Founder, Laurence S. Cutler; Financial Dir., David Breznicky; Asst. Dir., Zachary W.S. Cutler; Cur., Jennifer P. Greenawalt; Admin. Interiors, Jill Perkins; Dir. External Affairs, Jonathan Trumbull Isham; Public Rels., Dallas Pell; Admin. Exterior, Benjamin Langley, III; Dir. Institutional Devel., Laurence Cutler; Graphic Designer, Catherine Smith.
Personnel Profile: Full-Time Paid 9; Full-Time Volunteers 6; Part-Time Paid 2; Part-Time Volunteers 25; Interns 6.
Governing Authority: private; nonprofit organization. Parent Institution: American Civilization Foundation. Tax-exempt: 501(c)(3).
Art Museum.
Collections: works of illustrators including Norman Rockwell, Maxfield Parrish, N.C. Wyeth, J.C. Leyendecker, Charles Dana Gibson, Jessie Willcox Smith, Howard Pyle, H.C. Christy.
Research Fields: life & works of J.C. Leyendecker, Edith Wharton & Maxfield Parrish; murals by Tiffany studios & James Wall Finn.
Facilities: 4,300-vol. library; 30,000 sq. ft. exhibit space; gardens & park. Museum-related items for sale.
Activities: tours; lectures.
Publications: newsletter, From Time to Time; Guidebook: The Grand Tour; books, Maxfield Parrish & The American Imagists; J.C. Leyendecker; miniature maps.

Hours & Admission Prices: Mon.-Fri. 9-5 or by appointment. Adults $18, senior citizens 60 & over and military with ID $16, groups $15, students with ID $12, children 5-12 $8; AAM, NEMA, & National Arts Club members no charge. Children 5 & under not admitted.
Membership: Friends: Individual $125; Dual $200; Contributing $250; Supporting $500; Founding $750. Fellows: Fellow $1,000; Sponsor $2,500; Contributing $5,000; Supporting $10,000; Founding $25,000.

NAVAL WAR COLLEGE MUSEUM, 686 Cushing Rd., Coasters Harbor Island, Newport, RI 02841-1207. Tel.: 401-841-4052 & 2101. Fax: 401-841-7074.
E-mail: museum@usnwc.edu
Web Site: www.nwc.navy.mil/newportlinks/museum/museum.aspx
Founded: 1978.
Congressional District: 2
Key Personnel: Dir., Prof. John Hattendorf; Dir. Education, John W. Kennedy; Cur., Robert Cembrola; Registrar, John Pentangelo; Sec., Kelly Folger; Museum Shop Mgr., Julia Koster.
Personnel Profile: Full-Time Paid 4; Part-Time Volunteers 8.
Governing Authority: federal-Navy Department. Parent Institution: Naval History and Heritage Command, Washington, DC. Subsidiary Institution: Naval War College. Tax-exempt.
Naval Museum: housed in 1820 Founders Hall, a National Historic Landmark.
Collections: art, artifacts, imprints & prints on the history of naval warfare; naval history & heritage of the Narragansett Bay region.
Research Fields: military history; naval history; naval regional history; Naval War College institutional history.
Facilities: 200-vol. library of books & 10 file drawers of principally imprint (loose) items on Naval warfare, Naval regional history & museum studies.
Activities: guided tours; permanent, temporary & loan exhibitions; staff talks; guest lecturers.
Publications: leaflets; descriptive brochure; exhibit catalogs; National Historic Site (Founders Hall); President's House; museum outdoor displays.
Hours & Admission Prices: June-Sept. Mon.-Fri. 10-4:30, Sat.-Sun. 12-4:30; Oct.-May Mon.-Fri. 10-4:30; by appointment. Adults 18 & over require photo ID. No charge; donations accepted. Closed Federal holidays. ♿
Attendance: 27,674 (accurate)
Membership: Naval War College Foundation, Inc.: Graduate $20; Corporate $500; Associate & Life $1,000.

* **NEWPORT ART MUSEUM & ART ASSOCIATION,** 76 Bellevue Ave., Newport, RI 02840-7411. Tel.: 401-848-8200. Fax: 401-848-8205.
E-mail: info@newportartmuseum.org
Web Site: www.newportartmuseum.org
Founded: 1912.
Congressional District: 1
Key Personnel: Acting Dir., Elizabeth Goddard; Pres., Roderick O'Hanley; Cur., Nancy Whipple Grinnell; Dir. Education, Judy Hambleton.
Personnel Profile: Full-Time Paid 11; Part-Time Paid 17; Part-Time Volunteers 125; Interns 11.
Governing Authority: nonprofit organization. Tax-exempt.
Art Museum.
Collections: permanent collection focuses on Rhode Island & New England artists. Historic House: c.1864 J.N.A. Griswold House.
Major Exhibits: Newport Annual Members' Juried Exhibition, 2/6/10-5/30/10; Airborn: Ovid's Avian Changes: Paintings by Rene Stawicki, 4/3/10-5/30/10; Janet Alling Paintings, 6/12/10-8/15/10; The Japan Craze Art & Craft in Rhode Island, 6/12/10-10/24/10; Net Works, 11/6/10-1/11.
Research Fields: American Art.
Facilities: 7 galleries; art school.
Activities: art classes; summer camps; lecture program; films; concerts; guided tours; temporary exhibitions.
Publications: catalogs; annual report; calendar; newsletter.
Hours & Admission Prices: Memorial Day to Labor Day Tues.-Sat. 10-5, Sun. 12-5; Sept.-May Tues.-Fri. 11-3, Sat. 10-4, Sun. 12-4. Adults $10, senior citizens 65 & over $8, students & military with ID $6; discounts to AAM, AAA, NARM & ICOM members; children 5 & under and members no charge. ♿
Attendance: 30,000 (estimated)
Membership: Student $25; Senior Citizen & Military $35; Individual $45; Senior & Military Household $50; Family/Household $60; Patron $150; Supporting $250.

NEWPORT HISTORICAL SOCIETY & THE MUSEUM OF NEWPORT HISTORY, 127 Thames St., Newport, RI 02840-6627. Mailing Address: 82 Touro St., Newport, RI 02840-2931. Tel.: 401-846-0813 & 841-8770. Fax: 401-846-1853.
E-mail: info@newporthistorical.org
Web Site: newporthistorical.org
Founded: 1854.
Congressional District: 1
Key Personnel: Exec. Dir., Ruth Taylor; Mgr., Kathleen Vanderveer; Pres. (V), Richard I. Burnham; Pres. Emeritus (V), John Salesses; Reference Librarian & Genealogist, Bertram Lippincott, III; Dir. of Education, Ingrid Peters; Administrative & Membership Mgr., Loraine Byrne; Museum Shop Mgr., Ann Arnold.
Personnel Profile: Full-Time Paid 4; Part-Time Paid 10; Part-Time Volunteers 50; Interns 5.
Governing Authority: nonprofit. Tax-exempt: 501(c)(3).
History Museum.
Collections: Newport County & Rhode Island history; computerized survey of Newport Historical Landmark District; town records & documents from earliest days of Newport; 200,000 photographs; family & business records; three centuries worth of manuscripts & letters; paintings; Townsend-Goddard furniture; glass; silver; pewter; tall clocks; textiles; maps; atlases. Historic Houses: c.1697 Wanton-Lyman-Hazard House; c.1699 Great Friends Meeting House; c.1730 Seventh Day Baptist Meeting House; Museum of Newport History at the c.1762 Brick Market.
Research Fields: Newport County & Rhode Island history; architectural history; genealogy; archaeology.
Facilities: 12,000-vol. research library; 17th, 18th & 19th-century manuscripts department; audiovisual programs; tours; lecture series.
Activities: guided & self-guided walking tours; permanent & temporary exhibits; educational programs;
Publications: journal, Newport History; book, Newport: A Short History; book, African Americans in Newport.
Hours & Admission Prices: Newport Historical Society Library & Gallery: Tues.-Fri. 9:30-4:30, Sat. 9:30-12. No charge. Museum of Newport History: Winter: daily 10-5. Summer: Mon.-Sat. 10-6, Sun. 10-5. Suggested Donation: adults $4, children $2; discounts to AAM & ICOM members; members & children under 5 no charge.
Attendance: 30,000 (estimated)
Membership: Student $25; Library & Museum $35; Individual $50; Family $100; Sponsor $250; 1854 Society $1,000.

NEWPORT RESTORATION FOUNDATION, 51 Touro St., Newport, RI 02840-2932. Tel.: 401-849-7300. Fax: 401-849-0125.
Web Site: newportrestoration.org
Founded: 1968.
Key Personnel: Exec. Dir., Pieter N. Roos; Pres. Bd. Trustees, Marian Oates Charles; Dir. Operations, Marlaine Salafia; Cur., A. Bruce MacLeish; Archivist & Preservation Coord., Robert Foley; Visitor Svcs., Barbara Schlubach; Dir. Education & Public Programs, Lisa Dady; Dir. Mktg., Morgan Devlin.
Personnel Profile: Full-Time Paid 32; Part-Time Paid 21; Interns 1.
Governing Authority: private; nonprofit organization. Branch Museums: Rough Point, Newport, RI; Samuel Whitehorne House, Newport, RI; Prescott Farm, Middletown, RI. Tax-exempt.
Historic House Museum.
Collections: 18th & early 19th century houses; European furniture & decorative arts; European fine art; Rhode Island furniture; oriental porcelain; architectural drawings; photographs.
Research Fields: American architecture; vernacular architecture; preservation methods; American furniture.
Facilities: 2,000 sq. ft. exhibit space.
Activities: docent program; formal education programs for adults; guided tours; hobby workshops; temporary exhibitions; training programs for professional museum workers.
Publications: exhibit catalog.
Hours & Admission Prices: Rough Point: mid-April to mid-May Thurs.-Sat. 9:45-1:45; mid-May to early Nov. Tues.-Sat. 9:45-3:45. Adults $25; children 12 & under no charge. Whitehorne House: May-Oct. Thurs.-Mon. 11-3. $10. Adults $6; children 12 & under no charge. Guided Tours: $12. Prescott Farm: June-Sept. Tues.-Sat. 10-3. Adults $5; children 12 & under no charge. Grounds: daily. No charge. ♿

* **THE PRESERVATION SOCIETY OF NEWPORT COUNTY/THE NEWPORT MANSIONS, (M),** 424 Bellevue Ave., Newport, RI 02840-6924. Tel.: 401-847-1000, ext. 100.
E-mail: info@newportmansions.org
Web Site: www.newportmansions.org
Founded: 1945.
Congressional District: 1
Key Personnel: C.E.O., Trudy Coxe; Chm., Pierre duPont Irving; Dir. Mktg. Svcs., John G. Rodman; Academic Programs Dir. & Arch. Historian, John R. Tschirch; Properties Dir., Curt Genga; Chief Cur., Charles J. Moore; Cur., Paul F. Miller; Dir. Special Events, Philip F. Pelletier; Dir. Devel., Caroline Considine; Dir. Museum Experience, John G. Rodman; Dir. Finance, Jim Burress; Conservator, Jeff Moore; Dir. Gardens & Grounds,

Jeff Curtis; Dir. Retail Sales, Cynthia O'Malley; Grant Writer, Melissa Davis; Preservation Architect, William Remsen; Special Projects, Terry Dickinson.
Personnel Profile: Full-Time Paid 103; Part-Time Paid 246; Part-Time Volunteers 125; Interns 5.
Governing Authority: society; nonprofit organization. Tax-exempt: 501(c)(3).
Preservation Project & Historical District: c.1748-1902, group of 11 mansions located within 1-1/2 miles of each other; topiary garden in Portsmouth.
Collections: furniture; furnishings; paintings. Historic Mansions & Museums: Green Animals, Cory's Lane; Portsmouth; 1748 Hunter House, 54 Washington St., a national historic landmark; 1839 Kingscote, Bellevue Ave., a national historic landmark; 1852 Chateau-sur-Mer, Bellevue Ave.; 1892 Marble House, Bellevue Ave.; 1901 The Elms, Bellevue Ave., a national historic landmark; 1895 The Breakers, Ochre Point Ave., a national historic landmark; 1902 Rosecliff, Bellevue Ave; 1895 The Breakers Stable, Coggeshall Ave; 1883 Isaac Bell House, Bellevue Ave., a national historic landmark; 1860 Chepstow, Narragansett Ave.
Research Fields: belle epoch social history; history of architecture & decorative arts.
Activities: guided tours. Museum Sponsors: tours for students of Newport schools; members' tours & lectures; behind the scene tours; walking tours; audio & garden tours; preservation in action tours. Annual Events: The Newport Symposium in Spring; The Newport Student Forum in November; Christmas at The Newport Mansions.
Publications: The Newport Gazette; annual report.
Hours & Admission Prices: Call for hours. $12-$25 per house; special combination tickets; discounts to groups of 20 or more; members no charge.
Attendance: 779,769 (accurate)
Membership: Single $50; Household $90; Steward $250; Patron $500; Benefactor $1,000; President's Circle $5,000.

REDWOOD LIBRARY AND ATHENAEUM, 50 Bellevue Ave., Newport, RI 02840-3292. Tel.: 401-847-0292. Fax: 401-841-5680.
E-mail: redwood@redwoodlibrary.org
Web Site: www.redwoodlibrary.org
Founded: 1747.
Congressional District: 1
Key Personnel: Library Dir., Cheryl V. Helms; Pres. (V), Douglas Riggs.
Personnel Profile: Full-Time Paid 11; Part-Time Paid 13; Part-Time Volunteers 8; Interns 1.
Governing Authority: society. Tax-exempt: 501(c)(3).
Historic Building: c.1750 designed by architect, Peter Harrison.
Collections: paintings by Gilbert Stuart, Charles Bird King, Robert Feke, Rembrandt Peale, Thomas Sully; sculpture; manuscript collections; 18th- & 19th-century material culture collections.
Research Fields: 18th- & 19th-century Americas.
Facilities: 200,000-vol. library of general and special collection books, may be used by researchers.
Activities: guided tours; exhibitions.
Publications: annual report; quarterly booklist; exhibition checklists; occasional publications.
Hours & Admission Prices: Mon.-Wed. & Fri.-Sat. 9:30-5:30, Thurs. 9:30-8, Sun. 1-5; No charge; donations accepted for tours or occasional or specific research. Closed holidays. ♿
Attendance: 18,000 (accurate)
Membership: Youth $25; Individual $70; Household $100.

SAVE THE BAY EXPLORATION CENTER, 175 Memorial Blvd., Newport, RI 02840-3659. Mailing Address: P.O. Box 851, Newport, RI 02840-0010. Tel.: 401-324-6020.
Web Site: www.savebay.org/NetCommunity/Page.aspx?pid=325&srcid=879
Marine Science Learning Center.
Collections: hands-on interactive exhibits.
Hours & Admission Prices: Jan. 16-April 25 & Oct. 3-Dec. 19 Sat. 10-4; call for additional hours; Memorial Day weekend-Labor Day weekend daily 10-4. Adults $5; Save The Bay family members & children 3 and under no charge.

TOURO SYNAGOGUE, 85 Touro St., Newport, RI 02840-2969. Tel.: 401-847-4794.
Key Personnel: Exec. Dir., Steven Sitrin
Historic Building: built in 1763. A National Historic Site.
Collections: Jewish history & culture; religious artifacts; period furnishings; photographs; paintings.
Facilities: Museum-related items for sale.
Activities: tours.
Hours & Admission Prices: By appointment.
Attendance: 30,000 (estimated)

North Kingstown

QUONSET AIR MUSEUM, 488 Eccleston Ave., North Kingstown, RI 02852-7406. Mailing Address: P.O. Box 1571, North Kingston, RI 02852-0629. Tel.: 401-294-9540.
E-mail: info@theqam.org
Web Site: www.theqam.org
Key Personnel: Pres., David Payne
Air Museum.
Collections: Rhode Island's aviation heritage; military history.
Activities: educational programs.
Hours & Admission Prices: June-Sept. daily 10-3; Oct.-May Sat.-Sun. 10-3; other times by appointment. Adults $7, seniors 65 & over $6, children under 12 $3; discounts to groups; military no charge. Closed New Year's Day; Easter; Thanksgiving; Christmas.

SEABEE MUSEUM AND MEMORIAL PARK, 21 Iafrate Way, North Kingstown, RI 02852-1792. Tel.: 401-294-7233.
E-mail: info@seabeemuseum.com
Web Site: www.seabeemuseum.com
Key Personnel: Pres. (V), Nicholas Fisch; Museum Shop Mgr., Robert Schwab.
Governing Authority: Tax-exempt.
Military Museum.
Collections: military artifacts & memorabilia relating to the Seabees.
Hours & Admission Prices: May-Oct. daily 9:30-2; Nov.-April Wed. & Sat.-Sun. 9:30-2; other times by appointment.
Membership: Regular $25; Silver $35; Gold $50; Life $100.

Pawtucket

DAGGETT HOUSE, Slater Memorial Park, Next to Loof Carousel, Pawtucket, RI 02861. Mailing Address: 16 Second St., Pawtucket, RI 02861-3133. Tel.: 401-722-6931.
Key Personnel: Custodian, Joslin A. Brooks.
Governing Authority: Parent Institution: Pawtucket Chapter. Tax-exempt.
Historic House: built 1685. Listed on the National Register of Historic Places.
Collections: period furnishings; family history & personal artifacts; needlework; Civil War; uniforms.
Activities: rental facilities.
Hours & Admission Prices: Call for hours.

* **SLATER MILL,** 67 Roosevelt Ave., Pawtucket, RI 02860-2127. Mailing Address: P.O. Box 696, Pawtucket, RI 02862-0696. Tel.: 401-725-8638. Fax: 401-722-3040.
E-mail: info@slatermill.org
Web Site: www.slatermill.org
Founded: 1921.
Congressional District: 1
Key Personnel: C.E.O. & Exec. Dir., Janice Kissinger; Cur., Andrian Paquette.
Personnel Profile: Full-Time Paid 6; Part-Time Paid 21; Part-Time Volunteers 6.
Governing Authority: nonprofit organization. Parent Institution: Old Slater Mill Association. Tax-exempt.
History Museum of Textile Industry & Arts; Historic site.
Collections: textile machinery & domestic textile implements; machine tools & shop equipment; labor & social history; Artisan's furniture & furnishings; mechanical power generation & transmission equipment Historic Buildings: 1793 old Slater Mill; 1758 Sylvanus Brown House; 1810 Wilkinson Mill; 19th-century machine shop; reconstructed 1820s water wheel & raceway system.
Research Fields: industrial & labor history; technology; waterpower; textiles.
Facilities: 500-vol. library of history & textile books; photograph collection of local industrial sites & textile processes. Museum-related gifts for sale.
Activities: living history portrayals; flexible visiting hours; craft demonstrations; hands-on fibers program for students; fiber arts workshops; special events; membership program; vacation activities for children.
Publications: quarterly newsletter, The Millwright; annual research publications.
Hours & Admission Prices: March-April Sat.-Sun. 11-3; May-Oct. Tues.-Sun. 10-4. Adults $10, senior citizens 65 & over $9, children 6-12 $8; discounts to groups with reservation, AAA, NEMA, AAM & ICOM members; members & children under 6 no charge. ♿
Attendance: 25,000 (estimated)
Membership: Individual $35; Family $50; Contributor $75; Keeper of the Wheel $100; Sponsor $200; Donor $500; Benefactor $1,000. Corporate Contributor $100; Corporate Sponsor $250; Corporate Donor $500; Corporate Patron $1,000.

Peace Dale

MUSEUM OF PRIMITIVE ART AND CULTURE, 1058 Kingstown Rd., Ste. 5, Peace Dale, RI 02879-2487. Tel.: 401-783-5711.
E-mail: mpaac@verizon.net
Web Site: www.primitiveartmuseum.org
Founded: 1892.
Congressional District: 2
Key Personnel: Pres. (V), Virginia Williams.
Personnel Profile: Part-Time Paid 2; Part-Time Volunteers 11.
Governing Authority: private. Tax-exempt.
Anthropology Museum.
Collections: artifacts from New England, North America & other continents.
Research Fields: archaeology; ethnology.
Activities: public education program, including traveling exhibit & lectures at public schools; monthly membership programs; film series; thematic walking & driving tours of the area.
Publications: quarterly newsletter; catalogue, Rhode Island's Prehistoric Past; catalogue, The 19th Century American Collector: A Rhode Island Perspective.
Hours & Admission Prices: Wed. 10-2; other times by appointment. Suggested Donation $1; discounts to AAM, ICOM & NEMA members; members no charge. Closed holidays.
Attendance: 3,000 (estimated)
Membership: Student $5; Individual $20; Family $25; Corporate $35 & up; Contributing $35; Business $50 & up; Sustaining $60; Supporting $100.

Portsmouth

PORTSMOUTH HISTORICAL SOCIETY, (M), 870 E. Main Rd. & Union St., Portsmouth, RI 02871. Mailing Address: P.O. Box 834, Portsmouth, RI 02871-0834. Tel.: 401-683-9178.
E-mail: portsmouthhistorical@yahoo.com
Web Site: www.portsmouthlibrary.org/Portsmouth%20Historical%20Society/index.html
Founded: 1938.
Congressional District: 1
Key Personnel: Pres., Herbert Hall; Cur. & Librarian, Marjorie P. Linhares.
Personnel Profile: Part-Time Volunteers 12.
Governing Authority: society; nonprofit organization.
Local History Museum: housed in 1865 former Portsmouth Christian Union Church. Listed on the National Historic Register.
Collections: farm and home tools; furniture; clothing; hymnals; old toys. Historic Building: 1725 The Southernmost Schoolhouse.
Facilities: 400-vol. library of history books available for use on premises.
Activities: lectures; permanent & temporary exhibits. Museum Sponsors: Yard Sale in September.
Publications: newsletters.
Hours & Admission Prices: Memorial Day-Columbus Day Sun. 2-4; other times by appointment. No charge; donations accepted.
Membership: Individual $10; Family $20.

Providence

ANNMARY BROWN MEMORIAL, 21 Brown St., Providence, RI 02912-9005. Mailing Address: Box A Brown Univ., Providence, RI 02912-0001. Tel.: 401-863-2942.
Web Site: dl.lib.brown.edu/libweb/about/amb
Founded: 1905.
Key Personnel: Head, Business & Facilities, Barbara Schultz; Dir. Special Collections, Samuel Streit.
Personnel Profile: Full-Time Paid 1.
Governing Authority: university. Parent Institution: Brown University Library. Tax-exempt: 103(6).
Art Museum.
Collections: period master paintings; Brown family heirlooms & correspondence; British swords 1700-1900.
Research Fields: American Revolution & Civil War.
Activities: permanent, temporary & traveling exhibitions.
Hours & Admission Prices: Labor Day to Memorial Day Mon.-Fri. 1-5. No charge. Closed national holidays.

BAYARD EWING BUILDING GALLERY, 231 S. Main St., Providence, RI 02903. Tel.: 401-454-6281.
Art Gallery.
Collections: paintings; photographs; sculpture.
Activities: temporary exhibitions; lectures.
Hours & Admission Prices: Call for hours. No charge. ♿

BERT GALLERY, 540 S. Water St., Providence, RI 02903-4322. Tel.: 401-751-2628.
E-mail: info@bertgallery.com
Art Gallery.
Collections: paintings; drawings; woodcuts; sculpture.
Facilities: 1,000 sq. ft. exhibit space; archives. Museum-related items for sale.
Activities: special events.
Hours & Admission Prices: Tues.-Fri. 11-5, Sat. 12-4; other times by appointment.

BETSEY WILLIAMS COTTAGE, Roger Williams Park, Providence, RI 02907. Tel.: 401-785-9457. Fax: 401-461-5146.
Founded: 1871.
Congressional District: 2
Key Personnel: Dir. Roger Williams Park Museum, Renee Gamba; Cur., Marilyn Massaro; Cur. Education, Renee Gamba; Educator, Dawn Valentim.
Personnel Profile: Full-Time Paid 4.
Governing Authority: municipal. Parent Institution: City of Providence, RI. Subsidiary Institution: Parks Department. Tax-exempt.
Historic House: c.1782 Betsey Williams Cottage.
Collections: furniture & furnishings of early 19th century.
Research Fields: history of Roger Williams Park; social history of Providence & Rhode Island; late 18th to early 19th-century rural life in Rhode Island.
Activities: permanent exhibitions; social history programs.
Hours & Admission Prices: House temporarily closed for restoration.

CULINARY ARTS MUSEUM, (M), 315 Harborside Blvd., Providence, RI 02905-5202. Tel.: 401-598-2805. Fax: 401-598-2807.
E-mail: museum@jwu.edu
Web Site: www.culinary.org
Formerly: Culinary Archives & Museum, Johnson & Wales University
Founded: 1989.
Congressional District: 2
Key Personnel: Cur., Richard J.S. Gutman; Mgr. Operations, Stephen Spencer; Mgr. Collections, Erin M. Williams; Events & Program Coord., Kristin Zosa Puleo; Museum Asst., Deborah Pinkham.
Personnel Profile: Full-Time Paid 5; Part-Time Paid 5; Part-Time Volunteers 2; Interns 4.
Governing Authority: private university. Parent Institution: Johnson & Wales University. Tax-exempt.
Culinary & Gastronomy Museum.
Collections: 50,000 cookbooks; 100,000 menus; 80,000 culinary-related postcards; 10,000 culinary pamphlets; tens of thousands of culinary objects; fashion & food prints; silver.
Facilities: library available to public for research; educational facilities.
Activities: lectures & demonstrations; adult education programs; loan, temporary & traveling exhibitions.
Hours & Admission Prices: Tues.-Sun. 10-5; research by appointment only. Adults $7, senior citizens $6, college students $4, children 5-18 $2. Children under 5 no charge. Group rates available. Closed major holidays. ♿
Attendance: 20,000 (accurate)

DAVID WINTON BELL GALLERY, (M), List Art Center, Brown University, 64 College St., Providence, RI 02912-0001. Tel.: 401-863-2932 & 2929. Fax: 401-863-9323.
Web Site: www.brown.edu/bellgallery
Founded: 1971.
Congressional District: 1
Key Personnel: Dir., Jo-Ann Conklin; Prep., Cameron Shaw; Admin., Terrance Abbott.
Personnel Profile: Full-Time Paid 1; Part-Time Paid 20; Interns 2.
Governing Authority: university. Parent Institution: Brown University. Tax-exempt: 501(c)(3).
University Art Gallery.
Collections: 5,000 prints, drawings & photographs from 1500 to present; 200 paintings & sculptures, including works by Olitski, Stella, Motherwell, Bontecou & Caro.
Research Fields: 20th-century art, prints (Old Master to Contemporary).
Facilities: 250-seat auditorium; classrooms; gallery.
Activities: lectures; films; gallery talks; formally organized programs for undergraduate & graduate college students affiliated with Brown University; loan, temporary & traveling exhibitions.
Publications: exhibition catalogues; calendar of events.
Hours & Admission Prices: Sept.-July Mon.-Fri. 11-4, Sat.-Sun. 1-4. No charge; donations accepted. Closed New Year's Day; Memorial Day; Independence Day; Thanksgiving; Christmas. ♿
Attendance: 10,000 (estimated)

GOVERNOR HENRY LIPPITT HOUSE MUSEUM, 199 Hope St., Providence, RI 02906-2136. Mailing Address: 957 N. Main St., Providence, RI 02904-5715. Tel.: 401-453-0688. Fax: 401-453-8221.
E-mail: lippithouse@preserveri.org
Web Site: www.preserveri.org
Founded: 1991.
Key Personnel: C.E.O., Nicholas Brown; Chm. (V), John K. Grosvenor; Exec. Dir., Valerie Talmage; Museum Dir., Theresa Woodmansee; Cur., Sally L. Barker.
Personnel Profile: Full-Time Paid 1; Part-Time Paid 1; Interns 2.
Governing Authority: private; nonprofit organization. Parent Institution: Preserve Rhode Island. Tax-exempt: 501(c)(3).
Historic House: 1865 renaissance-revival style mansion; a National Historic Landmark.
Collections: period furnishings; decorative arts; personal family memorabilia; photographs; documents; woodcarvings; etched & stained glass windows; stenciling; faux marble & wood finishes.
Research Fields: 19th-century paintings; background information on artists; historic fabrics for original furnishings.
Activities: guided tours; lectures; hobby workshops; concerts. Annual Event: Scottish Holiday Fundraiser.
Hours & Admission Prices: May-Oct. Fri. 11-3; other times by appointment. Adults $10, senior citizens, students & children $4; discounts to groups; members no charge. Closed all holidays.
Attendance: 1,000 (estimated)
Membership: Member $35; Contributor $50; Donor $100; Sponsor $500; Patron $750; Benefactor $1,000.

GOVERNOR STEPHEN HOPKINS HOUSE MUSEUM, 15 Hopkins St., Providence, RI 02903. Tel.: 401-421-0694.
Web Site: www.stephenhopkins.org
Founded: 1707.
Key Personnel: Chm. (V), Katherine Barnham; Chm. (V), Alexandra Earle; Pres. (V), Zulette Katir.
Personnel Profile: Part-Time Paid 2; Part-Time Volunteers 15.
Governing Authority: National Society of Colonial Dames of America in the State of Rhode Island. Tax-exempt.
Historic Museum House: 1707 Governor Stephen Hopkins home.
Collections: furnishings; Parterre Garden; Stephen Hopkins furnishings.
Facilities: Postcards & brochures for sale.
Activities: guided tours.
Hours & Admission Prices: May-Oct. Fri.-Sat. 1-4; other times by appointment. No charge; donations accepted.
Attendance: 2,000

HAFFENREFFER MUSEUM OF ANTHROPOLOGY, BROWN UNIVERSITY, (M), 1-21 Prospect St., Providence, RI 02912. Mailing Address: 300 Tower St., Bristol, RI 02809. Tel.: 401-253-8388. Fax: 401-253-1198.
E-mail: haffenreffermuseum@brown.edu
Web Site: www.brown.edu/haffenreffer
Founded: 1956.
Congressional District: 1
Key Personnel: Dir., Shepard Krech, III; Pres., Jeffrey Schrack; Deputy Dir. & Chief Cur., Kevin P. Smith; Cur. Res., Douglas Anderson; Assoc. Cur., Thierry Gentis; Consultant Conservator, Alexandra Allardt; Conservation Asst., Storage Mgr. & Exhibit Preparator, Rip Gerry; Office Mgr., Carol Dutton; Cur. Emerita, Barbara A. Hail.
Personnel Profile: Full-Time Paid 6; Part-Time Paid 2; Part-Time Volunteers 3; Interns 5.
Governing Authority: university. Parent Institution: Brown University, Providence, RI. Satellite Gallery: The Haffenreffer Museum of Anthropology at Manning Hall, Brown University's Central Campus. Tax-exempt: 170(b)(1)(A).
Anthropology Museum.
Collections: American Indian: North, Central & South America, Arctic; African, Pacific, Eastern European, Mid-Eastern, Asian collections; anthropology; archaeology; ethnology.
Research Fields: anthropology; archaeology; ethnology; ethnohistory.
Facilities: 4,000-vol. library of anthropology books available for research on premises.
Activities: lectures; films; gallery talks; formally organized education programs for children, adults, graduate & undergraduate students; permanent & temporary exhibitions; training programs in museology; Friends Association.
Publications: Friends' newsletters; The Cashinahua of Eastern Peru; Burr's Hill: A Seventeenth Century Wampanoag Burial Ground; Hau Kola: The Plains Indian Collection of the Haffenreffer Museum of Anthropology; Traditional Art of Africa; Female Costume of the Sarakatsani; What Cheer! Selections from A Key Into The Language of America; Out of the North: The Subarctic Collection of the Haffenreffer Museum of Anthropology; History on Birchbark: The Art of Tomah Joseph, Passamaquoddy; Passionate Hobby: Rudolf Frederick Haffenreffer & the King Philip Museum; Gifts of Pride & Love: Kiowa and Comanche Cradles; Kayak, Umiak, Canoe; Model Kayaks, Umiaks and Canoes from the North Pacific in Haffenreffer Museum of Anthropology Collections.
Hours & Admission Prices: Manning Hall Gallery: Tues.-Sun. 10-4. No charge; donations accepted. Closed federal holidays; university breaks. ♿
Attendance: 17,000 (estimated)
Membership: Student $15; Individual $25; Dual & Couple $30; Family $35; Contributing $50-$99; Saville Society $100-$249; Giddings Society $250-$499; Mount Hope Society $500-$999; Haffenreffer Society $1,000 & up.

JOHN BROWN HOUSE MUSEUM, 52 Power St., Providence, RI 02906-1012. Mailing Address: 110 Benevolent St., Providence, RI 02906. Tel.: 401-273-7507.
Web Site: www.rihs.org/Museums.html
Congressional District: 1
Key Personnel: Exec. Dir., Bernard Fishman; Bd. Pres. (V), Robert J. Manning; Museum Shop Mgr., Irene Blais.
Personnel Profile: Full-Time Paid 3; Part-Time Paid 4; Part-Time Volunteers 53; Interns 20.
Governing Authority: Parent Institution: Rhode Island Historical Society. Tax-exempt.
Historic House Museum: housed in a three-story Georgian mansion, built in 1788.
Collections: period furnishings & personal artifacts documenting 300 years of Rhode Island's history.
Facilities: Museum-related items for sale.
Publications: Rhode Island History.
Hours & Admission Prices: Museum: Jan. 2-March Fri. & Sat. 10-4; April-Dec. Tues.-Fri. 1-4, Sat. 10-4. Tours: Jan. 2-March Fri. & Sat. 10:30, 12, 1:30 & 3; April-Dec. Tues.-Fri. 1:30 & 3, Sat. 10:30, 12, 1:30 & 3. Adults $8, seniors & students $6, children 7-17 $4; member no charge. Closed New Year's Eve & Day; Independence Day; Thanksgiving & day after; Christmas Eve & Day.
Attendance: 5,817 (accurate)
Membership: Student & Senior $30; Basic $40; Gasper Group $50-$99; May 4th Circle $100-$249; Friends $250 & up; Lifetime $2,000.

JOHN HAY LIBRARY, Brown Univ., 20 Prospect St., Providence, RI 02912. Mailing Address: Box A, Providence, RI 02912-9039. Tel.: 401-863-3723.
Library.
Collections: books; manuscripts; archives; poetry; plays; literature; art; science; history.
Facilities: library.
Activities: research.
Hours & Admission Prices: Academic Year: Mon.-Fri. 9-6, Sun. 1-5; Summer: call for hours.

JOHN NICHOLAS BROWN CENTER FOR PUBLIC HUMANITIES AND CULTURAL HERITAGE, 357 Benefit St., Providence, RI 02903-2929. Mailing Address: Box 1880, Brown University, Providence, RI 02912-1880. Tel.: 401-863-1177. Fax: 401-863-7777.
E-mail: steven_lubar@brown.edu
Web Site: www.brown.edu/jnbc
Founded: 1983.
Congressional District: 1
Key Personnel: Dir., Steven Lubar; Asst. Dir. & Cur., Ron M. Potvin; Assoc. Dir. Programs, Anne Valk; Administrative Coord., Chelsea Shriver.
Personnel Profile: Full-Time Paid 4.
Governing Authority: nonprofit organization. Parent Institution: Brown University. Tax-exempt: 501(c)(3).
Brown University Public Humanities MA Program.
Collections: decorative arts & furniture of America & Europe; historic wallpaper.
Research Fields: public humanities; cultural heritage; oral history; public art; historic house museums.
Facilities: research center.
Activities: fellowship program; lectures; conferences; seminars; professional workshops; special events; permanent exhibitions.
Hours & Admission Prices: Call for information.
Attendance: 1,609 (accurate)

MEETING HOUSE OF THE FIRST BAPTIST CHURCH IN AMERICA, 75 N. Main St., Providence, RI 02903-1307. Tel.: 401-454-3418.
Founded: 1638.
Congressional District: 1
Governing Authority: Tax-exempt.
Historic Building: a National Historic Landmark.
Collections: local history; period furnishings; paintings.

Facilities: library; auditorium. Museum-related items for sale.
Activities: guided & self-guided tours.
Hours & Admission Prices: June to Columbus Day Mon.-Fri. 10-12 & 1-3, Sat. 10-1; Oct.-May Mon.-Fri. 10-12 & 1-3; groups by appointment. Guided Tours: $2 per person. Closed National holidays. ♿

*** MUSEUM OF ART, RHODE ISLAND SCHOOL OF DESIGN, (M),** 224 Benefit St., Providence, RI 02903-2723. Tel.: 401-454-6502. Fax: 401-454-6556. TDD: 800-745-5555.
E-mail: museum@risd.edu
Web Site: www.risd.edu/museum.cfm
Founded: 1877.
Congressional District: 1
Key Personnel: Dir., Hope Alswang; Chm., Peter Weiss; Financial Mgr., Glenn Stinson; Cur. Painting & Sculpture, Maureen O'Brien; Cur. Ancient Art, Gina Borromeo; Cur. Costume & Textiles, Joanne Ingersoll; Cur. Prints, Drawings & Photographs, Jan Howard; Coord. Special Events, Pam Kimel; Cur. Contemporary Art, Judith Tannenbaum; Public Rels., Matt Montgomery; Registrar, Tara Emsley; Mgr. Safety & Security, Philip Lessard.
Personnel Profile: Full-Time Paid 50; Part-Time Paid 20; Part-Time Volunteers 100; Interns 8.
Governing Authority: college; nonprofit organization. Parent Institution: Rhode Island School of Design. Tax-exempt: 501(c)(3).
Art Museum.
Collections: classical art; medieval art; 15th-20th century painting, sculpture & decorative arts; Albert Pilavin Collection of 20th-Century American Art; Nancy Sayles Day Collection of modern Latin American Art; Pendleton House Collection of American furniture, silver, china & decorative arts of the 18th-19th centuries; costume collection; Oriental textiles & art; Lucy Truman Aldrich Collection of 18th-century European porcelain; Abby Aldrich Rockefeller Collection of Japanese prints; contemporary art; Aaron Siskind Center for the Study of Photography.
Facilities: educational facilities. Museum-related items for sale.
Activities: formal education programs for adults, children, undergraduate, & graduate college students; concerts; poetry readings; docent program; videos; guided tours; lectures; loan, temporary & traveling exhibitions; visits to senior centers & children's hospital.
Publications: monthly calendar of events; catalogs.
Hours & Admission Prices: Sept.-July Tues.-Sun. 10-5, 3rd Thurs. of month 10-9. Adults $10, senior citizens 62 & over $7, college students & children 5-18 $3; discounts to AAA, AAM & ICOM members; children under 5 & members no charge. Closed New Year's Day; Independence Day; Thanksgiving; Christmas. ♿
Attendance: 91,857 (accurate)
Membership: Senior Individual $30; Senior Family $35; Individual $40; Family $50; Friend $125; Contributing Friend $250; Supporting Friend $500; Radeke Patron $1,000; Gallery Patron $2,500; Collector's Circle $5,000.

MUSEUM OF NATURAL HISTORY AND PLANETARIUM, Roger Williams Park, Providence, RI 02907. Tel.: 401-785-9457. Fax: 401-461-5146. TDD: 401-751-0203.
E-mail: info@musnathist.com
Web Site: providenceri.com/museum
Formerly: Museum of Natural History, Roger Williams Park
Founded: 1896.
Congressional District: 2
Key Personnel: Dir., Renee Gamba; Cur., Marilyn Massaro; Education Cur., Lily Benedict; Asst. Cur., Michael Kieron; Educator, Sarah Matthews.
Personnel Profile: Full-Time Paid 5; Part-Time Paid 3.
Governing Authority: municipal. Parent Institution: Providence Parks Dept. Subsidiary Institution: Betsey Williams Cottage. Tax-exempt: 501(c)(3).
Natural History Museum.
Collections: regional natural artifacts; Native American & Pacific island anthropology & archaeology.
Research Fields: anthropology; ethnology; folklore; culture history & cultural ecology; natural sciences & education; Native American; Pacific Islands.
Facilities: 125-seat auditorium; planetarium; classroom.
Activities: planetarium shows; educational programs; semi-permanent exhibitions; film & video; lectures; performances; public forums.
Publications: exhibition catalogs; educational materials; cultural guides.
Hours & Admission Prices: Museum: daily 10-5. Adults $2, children under 8 $1. Planetarium Shows: July-Aug. Tues.-Sun. 2 pm; Sept.-June Sat.-Sun. 2 pm. Adults $3, children $2; discounts to AAM & ICOM members. ♿
Attendance: 50,000 (estimated)
Membership: Student $20; Individual $25; Senior Citizens $40; Family $50.

PROVIDENCE ATHENAEUM, 251 Benefit St., Providence, RI 02903-2799. Tel.: 401-421-6970. Fax: 401-421-2860.
E-mail: info@providenceathenaeum.org
Web Site: www.providenceathenaeum.org
Key Personnel: Exec. Dir., Alison Maxell
Historic Building: built in 1753.
Collections: books; works by local artists.
Facilities: library.
Activities: cultural programs; lectures; readings; theatrical presentations; musical performances.
Hours & Admission Prices: June-Aug. Mon.-Thurs. 9-7, Fri. 9-5, Sat. 9-1; Sept.-May Mon.-Thurs. 9-7, Fri.-Sat. 9-5, Sun. 1-5. No charge. Closed New Year's Day; Martin Luther King Jr. Day; Presidents' Day; Easter; Memorial Day; Independence Day; Victory Day; Labor Day; Columbus Day; Veteran's Day; Thanksgiving; Christmas Eve & Day.

PROVIDENCE CHILDREN'S MUSEUM, 100 South St., Providence, RI 02903-4749. Tel.: 401-273-5437 & 5434, ext. 234. Fax: 401-273-1004.
E-mail: provcm@childrenmuseum.org
Web Site: www.childrenmuseum.org
Founded: 1976.
Congressional District: 1
Key Personnel: Exec. Dir., Janice O'Donnell; Business Mgr., Marvin Ronning; Dir. Devel., Jennifer Laurelli; Early Childhood, Mary Scott Hackman; Visitor Svcs. & Volunteer Svcs., Kelly Fenton; Dir. Education, Cathy Saunders; Program & Exhibit Developer, Carly Loeper; Special Events, Kristen Haffenreffer Moran; Museum Shop Mgr., Sua Xiong; Public Rels., Megan Fischer.
Personnel Profile: Full-Time Paid 17; Full-Time Volunteers 9; Part-Time Paid 25; Part-Time Volunteers 100; Interns 15.
Governing Authority: nonprofit organization. Tax-exempt: 501(c)(3).
Children's Museum.
Collections: state & local history; mirrors & lens; water; childhood development; c.1930 marionettes; art for and by children; human skeletal system; bridges & roadways; geometry & building.
Research Fields: child development; subject areas pertinent to exhibits.
Facilities: conference room; classroom; birthday party room; children's garden. Educational items for sale.
Activities: docent & intern program; formally organized educational programs for children; family preservation program in conjunction with social service agencies; scout program; AmeriCorps National Service program; professional development workshops for teachers & childcare providers.
Publications: bimonthly newsletter, Dragon's Tale; annual report; Play With Your Kids! A How To, Why To Guide for Parents.
Hours & Admission Prices: April to Labor Day daily 9-6; Sept.-March Tues.-Sun. 9-6; call for additional hours. Adults $7.50; discounts to groups and AAM, ICOM & NEMA members; first Sun. of the month, members, ACM members, children under one, preschool & elementary school teachers no charge. Closed Thanksgiving; Christmas Eve & Day. ♿
Attendance: 144,684 (accurate)
Membership: Couple $75 (add $10 for each additional family member); Reciprocal for 4 people (add $10 for each additional family member) $125; Library for 4 people $250 half pass, $350 full pass; Corporate for 4 people $1,000.

PROVIDENCE CITY HALL, 25 Dorrance St., Providence, RI 02903-1738. Tel.: 401-421-7740.
Historic Building: built in 1878. Listed on the National Register of Historic Places.
Collections: city & state history and government; photographs; paintings; personal artifacts.
Activities: tours.
Hours & Admission Prices: Tours: Summer: Mon.-Fri. 8:30-4; Winter: Mon.-Fri. 8:30-4:30 by appointment.

THE PROVIDENCE JEWELRY MUSEUM, 4 Edward St., Providence, RI 02904-2404. Tel.: 401-274-0999; 781-3100.
E-mail: info@providencejewelrymuseum.com
Web Site: www.providencejewelrymuseum.com
Jewelry Museum.
Collections: fine & fashion jewelry from the 18th century to the present including match safes, pen & fruit knives, card cases, dresser items.
Hours & Admission Prices: By appointment.

PROVIDENCE PRESERVATION SOCIETY, 21 Meeting St., Providence, RI 02903-1214. Tel.: 401-831-7440. Fax: 401-831-8583.
E-mail: info@ppsri.org
Web Site: www.ppsri.org
Founded: 1956.
Congressional District: 1

Key Personnel: Interim Exec. Dir., Victoria Veh; Coord. Devel., Lauren Goldenberg; Coord. Education, Kathleen McAreavey; Office Admin., John Rogers.
Governing Authority: society. Tax-exempt: 501(c)(3).
Preservation Society: housed in 1772 Shakespeare's Head House & Garden.
Collections: structures.
Research Fields: preservation projects; Providence history, architecture, & planning issues.
Facilities: Brick school house; meeting & lecture room.
Activities: guided tours; lectures; field trips; films; docent training program; consultant bureau services; workshops on use of historic buildings. Museum Sponsors: Festival of Historic Houses in June.
Publications: quarterly newsletter; PPS News; broadsides, A Mile of History: Benefit Street; Providence in 1776; Elmwood, A Victorian Neighborhood; Brown University: A Microcosm of American Architecture; Broadway, A Victorian Boulevard; Downtown Providence: Commerce in Architecture; The Armory District: Harmonious Streetscapes; brochures; The Providence Waterfront; Stained Glass in Providence; PPS/AIA RI Guide to Providence Architecture.
Hours & Admission Prices: Office: Mon.-Fri. 9-5. Closed all major holidays. ♿
Membership: Individual $50; Household $100; Benefactor $250; Leadership $500.

PROVIDENCE PUBLIC LIBRARY, 150 Empire St., Providence, RI 02903-3219. Tel.: 401-455-8000 & 8021.
Key Personnel: Special Collections Librarian, Richard J. Ring
Library.
Collections: books; manuscripts; pamphlets; newspapers; maps; art; period artifacts.
Activities: special events.
Hours & Admission Prices: Mon. & Thurs. 12-8, Tues.-Wed. 10-6, Fri.-Sat. 9-5:30. ♿

RHODE ISLAND BLACK HERITAGE SOCIETY, 55 Eddy St., Providence, RI 02903-1727. Tel.: 401-751-3490. Fax: 401-751-0040.
E-mail: riblackheritagesociety@gmail.com
Web Site: www.providenceri.com/ri_blackheritage
Founded: 1975.
Congressional District: 1
Key Personnel: Pres., Charles C. Newton; Dir., Joaquina Teixeira; Office Mgr., Lee Campinha-Schenck.
Personnel Profile: Full-Time Paid 1.
Governing Authority: nonprofit organization. Tax-exempt: 501(c)(3).
Black Heritage Society Museum.
Collections: Rhode Island Historical documents & art; photographs; Afro-American historical collection; manuscripts.
Research Fields: Afro-Americans in Rhode Island.
Facilities: 2,500-vol. library of Afro-American history available for research by request to institutions; reading room.
Activities: guided tours; lectures; films; concerts; TV programs; formally organized education programs for children; permanent, temporary & traveling exhibitions.
Publications: quarterly newsletter, Rhode Island Black Heritage Society Bulletin; annual, A Selected Scholarly Document.
Hours & Admission Prices: Mon.-Fri. 10:30-3:30; other times by appointment. Special collections research by appointment only; fee charged for searches & archival assistance. No charge; donations accepted. Closed holidays. ♿
Membership: Student & Senior Citizen $15; Individual $25; Family $50.

RHODE ISLAND HISTORICAL PRESERVATION AND HERITAGE COMMISSION, Old State House, 150 Benefit St., Providence, RI 02903-1209. Tel.: 401-222-2678. Fax: 401-222-2968.
E-mail: info@preservation.ri.gov
Web Site: www.preservation.ri.gov/
Formerly: Rhode Island Historical Preservation Commission
Key Personnel: Exec. Dir., Edward F. Sanderson.
Governing Authority: state. Branch Museums: 1901 State House, Providence, RI; 1707-1740 Governor Steven Hopkins House, Providence; Fort Adams State Park, Newport, RI; 1739 Colony House, Newport, RI.
Historical Preservation Commission: housed in 1762 Old State House.
Collections: portraits; furnishings & furniture from the 19th century and primarily from the early 20th century.
Research Fields: historical development; architectural history; archaeology.
Publications: series of historic site & survey reports.
Hours & Admission Prices: Office: Mon.-Fri. 8:30-4:30. No charge.

* **RHODE ISLAND HISTORICAL SOCIETY, (M),** 110 Benevolent St., Providence, RI 02906-3103. Tel.: 401-331-8575. Fax: 401-351-0127.
Web Site: www.rihs.org
Founded: 1822.
Congressional District: 1
Key Personnel: Dir., Bernard P. Fishman; Pres., Robert J. Manning; Vice Pres., William Simmons, Ph.D.; Controller, Charmyne Goodfellow; Deputy Dir. Collections, Kirsten Hammerstrom; Reference Librarian, Lee Teverow; Editor, Hilliard Beller, Ph.D.; Dir. Devel., Marlene Leroy; Dir. Education, Morgan Grefe, Ph.D.
Personnel Profile: Full-Time Paid 18; Part-Time Paid 22; Part-Time Volunteers 140; Interns 8.
Governing Authority: society. Branch Museums: 1786 John Brown House; 1822 Aldrich House; 1874 library; Museum of Work and Culture, Woonsocket. Tax-exempt: 509(a)(1).
Historical Society Museums.
Collections: Rhode Island furniture; works of local artists; historical objects; Chinese porcelain & furniture; dolls & glassware; textiles & clothing; wallpaper; military; Indian artifacts; musical instruments; folk art; silver, domestic & ethnic items; archives; photographs; manuscripts; film & video collections; genealogy. Historic Building: John Brown House, national landmark built in 1786; Aldrich House, national landmark built c.1820.
Research Fields: Rhode Island history; genealogy.
Facilities: 100,000-vol. library of books, 400,000 images, 5,500 manuscript collections; archives; reading room.
Activities: guided tours; lectures; formally organized educational programs; docent program; permanent & temporary exhibitions; films; gallery talks; history exhibits.
Publications: magazine, Rhode Island History; newsletter; The Papers of General Nathanael Greene (13 vols.).
Hours & Admission Prices: Library: Wed.-Fri. 10-5, 2nd Sat. of the month 10-5. Adults $5. John Brown House: Tues.-Sat. 9:30-4:30. Family max. $15, adults $7, students & senior citizens $5.50, children 7-17 $4; members no charge. Museum of Work & Culture: Tues.-Fri. 9:30-4, Sat. 10-5, Sun. 1-5. Adults $6, senior citizens & students $4; discounts groups of 20 or more; children under 10 with adult & RIHS members no charge. Closed New Year's Day; Easter; Independence Day; Thanksgiving; Christmas. ♿
Attendance: 30,000 (accurate)
Membership: Student & Senior $30; Basic $40; Gaspee Group $50-$99; May 4th Circle $100-$249; Friends of Roger Williams $250 & up; Life $2,000.

RHODE ISLAND STATE ARCHIVES, 337 Westminster St., Providence, RI 02903-3302. Tel.: 401-222-2353. Fax: 401-222-3199.
Web Site: www.state.ri.us/archives
Founded: 1647.
Congressional District: 1
Key Personnel: State Archivist, R. Gwenn Stearn.
Governing Authority: state. Affiliated with Secretary of State's Office. Tax-exempt.
State Archives.
Collections: archives; history; legislature; military; manuscripts.
Research Fields: genealogy; military; legislative; state government.
Facilities: library of manuscripts available in office only; reading room.
Hours & Admission Prices: Mon.-Fri. 8:30-4:30. No charge. ♿

ROGER WILLIAMS NATIONAL MEMORIAL, 282 N. Main St., Providence, RI 02903-1240. Tel.: 401-521-7266. Fax: 401-521-7239.
Web Site: www.nps.gov/rowi
Founded: 1965.
Congressional District: 1
Key Personnel: Site Mgr., Jennifer Gonsalves; Supt., Jan Reitsma.
Personnel Profile: Full-Time Paid 5; Part-Time Paid 1; Part-Time Volunteers 3.
Governing Authority: federal. Parent Institution: National Park Service Affiliated with the U.S. Dept. of the Interior. Tax-exempt.
Historic Site.
Collections: exhibits on Roger Williams, the founder of Rhode Island & one of the earliest proponents of religious freedom and democracy in North America; history of Rhode Island.
Research Fields: Roger Williams biography; colonial history.
Facilities: visitor center; 4 acre park.
Activities: talks; slide show; hands-on presentations.
Publications: educational programs brochure; brochure, Roger Williams.
Hours & Admission Prices: Daily 9-4:30. No charge; donations accepted. Closed New Year's Day; Thanksgiving; Christmas. ♿
Attendance: 121,960 (estimated)

ROGER WILLIAMS PARK ZOO, 1000 Elmwood Ave., Providence, RI 02907-3659. Tel.: 401-785-3510 & 941-3910. Fax: 401-941-3988.
E-mail: info@rwpzoo.org
Web Site: www.rogerwilliamsparkzoo.org
Founded: 1872.
Congressional District: 2

Key Personnel: C.E.O., Dir. & Rhode Island Zoological Society, Jack Mulvena; Chm. (V), Cate Roberts; Cur. Education, Shareen Knowlton; Veterinarian, Dr. Michael McBride; Deputy Dir. Animal Care, Tim French.
Personnel Profile: Full-Time Paid 96; Part-Time Paid 50; Part-Time Volunteers 150; Interns 15.
Governing Authority: municipal. Affiliated with the Dept. of Public Parks/Roger Williams Park. Tax-exempt.
Zoo.
Collections: approximately 800 specimens representing over 100 species.
Research Fields: animal behavior; reproductive physiology; invasive plant eradication via beneficial native insects; field conservation.
Facilities: 2,400-vol. library of general animal information; nature conservation center; nature trail; concessions.
Activities: guided tours; informal learning education programs for children; docent program; traveling exhibitions; live animal demonstrations; overnight zoo tours for children; annual special events; conservation lectures; field research.
Publications: membership newsletter, Wild; docent e-newsletter, The Screech Owl; education department newsletter, Wild Adventures; e-newsletter, ZooNews.
Hours & Admission Prices: Daily 9-4. Adults $12, senior citizens 62 & over $8, children 3-12 $6; discounts to AZA members & groups; children under 3 & members no charge. Closed Thanksgiving; Christmas Eve & Day. ♿
Attendance: 520,000 (accurate)
Membership: Individual $49; Family & Grandparent $79; Family Plus $89; Zookeeper $125; Zoo Guardian $250; Director's Circle $500.

Rose Island

ROSE ISLAND LIGHTHOUSE, Rose Island, RI 02840. Mailing Address: Rose Island Lighthouse Foundation, P.O. Box 1419, Newport, RI 02840-0014. Tel.: 401-847-4242. Fax: 401-847-7262.
E-mail: david@roseisland.org
Web Site: www.roseislandlighthouse.org
Key Personnel: Exec. Dir., David McCurdy.
Governing Authority: nonprofit organization. Tax-exempt: 501(c)(3).
Lighthouse Museum: listed on the National Register of Historic Places.
Collections: lighthouse history.
Activities: group tours; scout campovers; meetings. Museum Sponsors: school & youth group programs April to October; seal tours November to April.
Hours & Admission Prices: July to Labor Day daily 10-4; other times by appointment. Island accessible by ferry.

Saunderstown

CASEY FARM, Route 1A, 2325 Boston Neck Rd., Saunderstown, RI 02874. Mailing Address: 141 Cambridge St., Boston, MA 02114-2702. Tel.: 401-295-1030; 617-227-3956. Fax: 401-294-1370; 617-227-9204.
Web Site: www.historicnewengland.org
Founded: 1955.
Congressional District: 2
Key Personnel: Pres., Carl Nold; Farm Mgr., Patrick NcNiff.
Governing Authority: society; nonprofit organization. Parent Institution: Historic New England, 141 Cambridge St. Boston, MA 02114. Tel.: 617-227-3956. Tax-exempt: 501(c)(3).
Historic Homestead: c.1750, homestead still functioning as a working farm.
Collections: barns; out-buildings.
Activities: guided tours; school programs; special events & tours; CSA program. Museum Sponsors: Farmers Market.
Publications: Guide to Historic New England.
Hours & Admission Prices: June 5-Oct. 15 Sat. 9-2. Adult $4; discount to seniors, AAM, ICOM, AAA & WGBH members; Historic New England members no charge. Call for further information.
Attendance: 34,966 (accurate)
Membership: National $35; Individual $45; Household $55; Garden & Landscape $75; Institutional $85; Contributing $100; Historic Homeowner $200; Supporting $250.

THE GILBERT STUART BIRTHPLACE AND MUSEUM, 815 Gilbert Stuart Rd., Saunderstown, RI 02874-2911. Tel.: 401-294-3001. Fax: 401-294-3869.
E-mail: info@gilbertstuartmuseum.org
Web Site: gilbertstuartmuseum.org
Founded: 1930.
Congressional District: 2
Key Personnel: Dir. & Museum Shop Mgr., Margaret O'Connor.
Personnel Profile: Full-Time Paid 2; Part-Time Paid 1; Part-Time Volunteers 65.
Governing Authority: nonprofit organization. Tax-exempt.
Historic House Museum: 1755 birthplace of artist Gilbert Stuart.
Collections: period furnishings. Historic Buildings: 1750 Snuff Mill; 1662 Grist Mill.
Facilities: house museums.
Activities: guided tours; formally organized education programs for children; permanent exhibitions. Museum Sponsors: Herring Run in April.
Publications: Gilbert Stuart Museum Pre and Post Visits Lesson Plans for Teachers.
Hours & Admission Prices: early May to Sept. Mon. & Thurs.-Sat. 11-4, Sun. 12-4. Oct. call for hours. Adults $6, children 6-12 $3; members & children under 6 no charge.
Attendance: 5,400 (estimated)
Membership: Single $30; Family $40.

Smithfield

AUDUBON SOCIETY OF RHODE ISLAND, 12 Sanderson Rd., Smithfield, RI 02917-2600. Tel.: 401-949-5454. Fax: 401-949-5788.
E-mail: audubon@asri.org
Web Site: www.asri.org
Founded: 1897.
Congressional District: 2
Key Personnel: Exec. Dir., Lawrence Taft; Pres. (V), Marc F. Mahoney; Financial Dir., Susan Mansolillo; Cur., Eugenia Marks; Dir. Statewide Education, Denise Fortier; Sr. Dir. Education Programs, Kristen Swanberg; Gift Shop Mgr., Catherine Corey; Publications Asst., Hope Foley.
Personnel Profile: Full-Time Paid 35; Part-Time Paid 15; Part-Time Volunteers 150.
Governing Authority: society; nonprofit organization. Subsidiary Institution: Environmental Education Center, Bristol, RI. Branch Museums: Caratunk Wildlife Refuge, Seekonk, MA; Parker Woodland, Coventry, RI; Eppley Wildlife Sanctuary, Exeter, RI; Kimball Wildlife Refuge, Charlestown, RI; Environmental Education Center, Bristol, RI. Tax-exempt: 501(c)(3).
Nature Conservation Center.
Collections: area natural history; 19th-century art; 19th-century natural history books; Rhode Island bird skins; Rhode Island shells; miscellaneous natural materials & objects.
Research Fields: ecology.
Facilities: 1,075-vol. library of reference, natural history & ecology material; 70-seat auditorium; nature & conservation center; educational facilities. Natural history books, optical equipment & other museum-related items for sale.
Activities: guided tours; lectures; films; study clubs; organized education programs; school loan service. Annual Event: Bird & Wildlife Carving in October.
Publications: quarterly newsletter, Audubon Society of Rhode Island Report.
Hours & Admission Prices: Mon.-Fri. 9-5. No charge; donations accepted for use of trails. Closed New Year's Day; Thanksgiving; Christmas. ♿
Membership: Individual $35; Family $45; Steward $75; Sustaining $100; Associate $250; Benefactor $500.

SMITH-APPLEBY HOUSE, 220 Stillwater Rd., Smithfield, RI 02917-1849. Tel.: 401-231-7363.
E-mail: contact@smithapplebyhouse.org
Web Site: www.smithapplebyhouse.org
Historic House Museum: housed in an 18th century farm house.
Collections: period furnishings; personal artifacts.
Activities: seasonal events.
Hours & Admission Prices: By appointment.

South Kingstown

RHODE ISLAND RAILROAD MUSEUM AT KINGSTON STATION, 1 Railroad Ave., South Kingstown, RI 02982. Mailing Address: P.O. Box 191, West Kingston, RI 02892-0191. Tel.: 401-789-3327.
Railroad Museum.
Collections: railroad history & artifacts; Narragansett Railroad; photographs.
Hours & Admission Prices: Sun. 2-5; other times by appointment.

Tiverton

BUTTERFLY ZOO, 409 Bulgarmarsh Rd., Tiverton, RI 02878. Tel.: 401-849-9519.
Key Personnel: Owner, Marc Schenck
Butterfly Zoo.
Collections: over 30 species of butterflies.
Facilities: Zoo-related items for sale.
Activities: guided & self-guided tours.
Hours & Admission Prices: Memorial Day to Labor Day Mon.-Sat. 11-4, Sun. 12-4. Adults $6, children $4; children under 3 no charge.

CHASE-CORY HOUSES, 3908 Main Rd., Tiverton, RI 02878-4809. Tel.: 401-624-2096.
E-mail: info@tivertonfourcorners.com
Web Site: www.tivertonfourcorners.com
Historic Houses.
Collections: historic buildings; period furnishings.
Activities: special events.
Hours & Admission Prices: By appointment. No charge.

EMILIE RUECKER WILDLIFE REFUGE, Seapowet Ave., Tiverton, RI 02878. Tel.: 401-949-5454.
Wildlife Refuge.
Collections: birds including Great Egrets, Snowy Egrets, & Glossy Ibis.
Facilities: 50 acre site; nature trails.
Activities: hiking; bird watching.
Hours & Admission Prices: Call for hours.

FORT BARTON, Lawton & Highland Aves., Tiverton, RI 02878-4401. Mailing Address: Town Hall, 343 Highland Rd., Tiverton, RI 02878-4499. Tel.: 401-625-6700 & 624-2549.
Key Personnel: Co Chm., Garry Plunkett; Co Chm., Ginger Lacy.
Governing Authority: Parent Institution: Tiverton Open Space and Land Preservation Commission.
History Museum: site was the staging area for the invasion of Aquidneck Island & named after Lt. Col. William Barton. Listed on the National Register of Historic Places.
Collections: Fort Barton history.
Facilities: observation tower.
Activities: nature walks.
Hours & Admission Prices: Call for hours.

Warren

CHARLES W. GREENE MUSEUM, George Hail Free Library, 530 Main St., Warren, RI 02885-4368. Tel.: 401-245-7686.
Web Site: www.georgehail.org/cwgMuseum.htm
History Museum.
Collections: Native American artifacts; domestic artifacts; military artifacts; Warren related artifacts.
Hours & Admission Prices: Museum: Wed. 2-4 or by appointment. Library: Jan.-June & Sept.-Dec. Mon.-Thurs. 10-8, Fri-Sat. 10-5; July-Aug. Mon.-Thurs. 10-8, Fri. 10-5, Sat. 10-3.

FIREMEN'S MUSEUM, 38 Baker St., Warren, RI 02885-3107. Mailing Address: 1 Joyce St., Warren, RI 02885-3238. Tel.: 401-245-7600.
Key Personnel: Dir., Chief Galinelli
Firemen's Museum: housed in the former Narragansett Steam Fire Company Station Number 3.
Collections: fire department history; photographs; equipment; 1802 fire truck.
Hours & Admission Prices: By appointment only. No charge.

TOUISSET MARSH WILDLIFE REFUGE, 107 Touisset Rd., Warren, RI 02885. Mailing Address: 12 Sanderson Rd., Smithfield, RI 02917-2606. Tel.: 508-761-8230.
Web Site: www.asri.org/refuges/touisset-marsh-wildlife.html
Wildlife Refuge.
Collections: wildlife & their habitats; plants; ecology.
Facilities: nature trails.
Activities: hiking; bird watching.
Hours & Admission Prices: Daily dawn-dusk.

Warwick

CLOUDS HILL VICTORIAN HOUSE MUSEUM, 4157 Post Rd., Warwick, RI 02886. Mailing Address: P.O. Box 522, East Greenwich, RI 02818-0522. Tel.: 401-884-9490.
E-mail: office@cloudshill.org
Web Site: www.cloudshill.org
Key Personnel: Dir., Wayne Cabral
Historic House Museum: built in 1872 by William Smith Slater for his daughter, Elizabeth Ives Slater.
Collections: period furnishings; personal artifacts; photographs.
Activities: special events.
Hours & Admission Prices: By appointment. Adults $15, seniors $10; discounts to groups.

JOHN WATERMAN ARNOLD HOUSE, 25 Roger Williams Circle, Warwick, RI 02888. Tel.: 401-467-7647.
Web Site: www.warwickhistoricalsocietyonline.org
Governing Authority: Parent Institution: Warwick Historical Society.
Historic House Museum: built in 1786. Listed on the National Register of Historic Places.
Collections: Waterman family history; period furnishings; personal artifacts; photographs; genealogy.
Hours & Admission Prices: Call for hours.

WARWICK MUSEUM OF ART, Kentish Artillery Armory, 3259 Post Rd., Warwick, RI 02886-7145. Tel.: 401-737-0010. Fax: 401-737-1796.
E-mail: info@warwickmuseum.org
Web Site: www.warwickmuseum.org
Founded: 1976.
Congressional District: 2
Key Personnel: Pres. Bd. Dirs., Michelle Place-Gleason; Program Dir., Patty Martucci.
Personnel Profile: Part-Time Paid 1; Part-Time Volunteers 7; Interns 1.
Governing Authority: nonprofit. Tax-exempt: 501(c)(3).
Art Gallery.
Collections: paintings; photographs; prints; sculpture.
Facilities: 1912 Armory.
Activities: lectures; performance art (10 in series); studio art and craft classes; inter-museum loan & traveling exhibitions. Museum Sponsors: monthly musical performances.
Publications: newsletters; exhibit catalogues.
Hours & Admission Prices: Tues.-Sat. 12-4. No charge; donations accepted. Closed New Year's; Easter; Memorial Day; Independence Day; Labor Day; Rosh Hashanah; Thanksgiving; Christmas. ♿
Attendance: 9,000 (estimated)
Membership: Friend $5; Family $10; Patron $15.

Westerly

BABCOCK-SMITH HOUSE MUSEUM, 124 Granite St., Westerly, RI 02891-2435. Tel.: 401-596-5704.
Web Site: www.babcock-smithhouse.org
Founded: 1972.
Key Personnel: Pres., Jackie Brennan; Chm. (V), John B. Coduri.
Governing Authority: nonprofit organization.
Historic House: housed in an early Georgian-style mansion, built c.1734. Listed on the National Register of Historic Places.
Collections: period furnishings; personal artifacts.
Facilities: Museum-related items for sale.
Hours & Admission Prices: May 24-June & Sept.-Oct. 25 Sat. 2-5; July-Aug. Fri.-Sat. 2-5; other times by appointment. Adults $5, children $1.

WESTERLY PUBLIC LIBRARY, 44 Broad St., Westerly, RI 02891-1856. Tel.: 401-596-2877. Fax: 401-596-5600.
E-mail: ktaylor@westerlylibrary.org
Web Site: www.westerlylibrary.org
Founded: 1894.
Congressional District: 51
Key Personnel: Exec. Dir., Kathryn T. Taylor; Pres., William S. Brown.
Personnel Profile: Full-Time Paid 17; Part-Time Paid 13; Part-Time Volunteers 40.
Governing Authority: board of trustees; nonprofit organization. Parent Institution: Memorial & Library Association of Westerly. Tax-exempt: 501(c)(3).
Art & History Museum: housed in Civil War Memorial building.
Collections: Civil War artifacts; paintings; furniture; minerals; toys; dolls & doll furniture; original art objects; local history & genealogical material.
Facilities: 120,000-vol. library available on premises; archives; 150-seat auditorium; 18-acre Wilcox Park; gallery.
Activities: lectures; gallery talks; concerts; arts festivals; workshops; temporary & traveling exhibitions; school loan & art loan service.
Hours & Admission Prices: June-Sept. Mon.-Wed. 9-8, Thurs.-Fri. 9-6, Sat. 9-4; Oct.-May Sun. 12-4, Mon.-Wed. 9-8, Thurs.-Fri. 9-6, Sat. 9-4. No charge; donations accepted. Closed major holidays. ♿
Attendance: 280,000 (estimated)

Woonsocket

MUSEUM OF WORK & CULTURE, 42 S. Main St., Woonsocket, RI 02895-4274. Tel.: 401-769-9675.
Web Site: www.rihs.org/Museums.html
Governing Authority: Parent Institution: Rhode Island Historical Society.
History Museum.
Collections: interactive exhibits; French Canadians who settled in New England; cultural artifacts.
Hours & Admission Prices: Tues.-Fri. 9:30-4, Sat. 10-5, Sun. 1-4. Adults $7, seniors & students $5; members & children under 10 no charge.

SOUTH CAROLINA

(188 listings)

Abeeville

BURT-STARK MANSION, 400 N. Main St., Abeeville, SC 29620-1706. Mailing Address: P.O. Box 164, Abeeville, SC 29620-0164. Tel.: 864-366-0166.
E-mail: info@burt-stark.com
Web Site: www.burt-stark.com
Historic House: built in 1830s. A National Historic Landmark.
Collections: Stark family's personal artifacts; period furnishings.
Hours & Admission Prices: Feb.-Dec. Fri.-Sat. 1-5; other times by appointment. Adults $10. Closed major holidays.

Aiken

AIKEN CENTER FOR THE ARTS, 122 Laurens St., S.W., Aiken, SC 29801-3888. Tel.: 803-641-9094. Fax: 803-641-2009.
E-mail: acaexecdir@bellsouth.net
Founded: 1972.
Congressional District: 3
Key Personnel: Exec. Dir., Kristin K. Brown; Pres. (V), Dr. Suzanne Ozment; Treas., James Victor; Museum Shop Mgr., Karen Betow.
Personnel Profile: Full-Time Paid 2; Part-Time Paid 4; Part-Time Volunteers 217.
Governing Authority: private; nonprofit organization. Tax-exempt: 501(c)(3).
Art Museum.
Collections: paintings.
Facilities: 8,000 sq. ft. exhibit space; 180-seat theater; educational facilities. Museum-related items for sale.
Activities: rental facilities; formal education programs; special events; concerts; films; guided tours; lectures; participatory & traveling exhibits; theater. Annual Events: Taste of Wine & Art; Antiques in the Heart of Aiken.
Publications: quarterly newsletter, Art Matters.
Hours & Admission Prices: Mon.-Sat. 10-5. No charge. Closed Memorial Day; Independence Day; Labor Day; Thanksgiving; Christmas. ♿
Attendance: 25,000 (estimated)
Membership: Student $25; Individual $50; Family $75; Contributor $150; Patron $350; Benefactor $1,000; Saint & Corporate $2,500.

AIKEN COUNTY HISTORICAL MUSEUM, 433 Newberry St., S.W., Aiken, SC 29801-4844. Tel.: 803-642-2017 & 2015. Fax: 803-642-2016.
E-mail: elevy@aikencountysc.gov
Web Site: www.aikencountysc.gov/tourism/museum
Founded: 1970.
Congressional District: 8
Key Personnel: Dir., Elliott Levy; Asst. Dir. & Educator, Mary White; C.E.O., Owen Clary; Collections Mgr., Brenda Baratto; Museum Shop Mgr., Sally Barrett.
Personnel Profile: Full-Time Paid 3; Part-Time Paid 1; Part-Time Volunteers 85.
Governing Authority: county; nonprofit. Parent Institution: Aiken County. Tax-exempt.
History Museum: 1931 winter colony mansion.
Collections: Aiken County artifacts; archeology collection; industrial, kaolin, textile & nuclear exhibits; restored, non-operational 1930s grist mill; Black history & agriculture. Historic Buildings: 1890 one-room schoolhouse; 1808 furnished log cabin; 1920s miniature circus; winter colony residence.
Research Fields: historical sites; local history.
Facilities: 200-vol. staff research library of historical books; conference room. Museum-related items for sale.
Activities: guided tours; lectures; films; docent program; formally organized education programs for students; permanent & traveling exhibitions.
Publications: quarterly newsletter.
Hours & Admission Prices: Tues.-Sat. 10-5, Sun. 2-5. No charge; donations accepted. Closed national holidays. ♿
Attendance: 20,929 (accurate)
Membership: Individual $10; Family $15; Sponsor $25; Benefactor $50; Patron $100.

AIKEN THOROUGHBRED RACING HALL OF FAME AND MUSEUM, 135 Dupree Place, Aiken, SC 29801. Mailing Address: P.O. Box 1177, Aiken, SC 29802-1177. Tel.: 803-642-7631 & 7650. Fax: 803-642-7639.
E-mail: halloffame@cityofaikensc.gov
Web Site: www.aikenracinghalloffame.com
Founded: 1977.
Congressional District: 81
Key Personnel: C.E.O., Lisa J. Hall.
Personnel Profile: Full-Time Paid 1; Part-Time Volunteers 25.
Governing Authority: nonprofit. Tax-exempt.
Specialized Museum: housed in a restored carriage house.
Collections: Thoroughbred horses; trainers & owners that trained in Aiken.
Facilities: 1,500 sq. ft. exhibit space. Museum-related items for sale.
Activities: loan exhibitions. Museum Sponsors: Induction of Thoroughbreds of Fame into Hall of Fame.
Hours & Admission Prices: June-Aug. Sat.-Sun. 2-5; Sept.-May Tues.-Sun. 2-5. No charge; donations accepted. Closed New Year's Day; Martin Luther King Jr. Day; Good Friday; Easter; Memorial Day; Independence Day; Labor Day; Thanksgiving; Christmas. ♿
Attendance: 20,000 (estimated)

Anderson

ANDERSON COUNTY ARTS CENTER, 405 N. Main St., Anderson, SC 29621-5614. Mailing Address: 110 Federal St., Anderson, SC 29625. Tel.: 864-222-2787. Fax: 864-224-8864.
E-mail: info@andersonartscenter.org
Web Site: www.andersonartscenter.org
Founded: 1972.
Congressional District: 3
Key Personnel: Exec. Dir., Kimberly Spears; Administrative Dir., Annette Buchanan; Pres., Dr. Bob Austin; Dir. Communications, Stacey McAdams.
Personnel Profile: Full-Time Paid 4; Part-Time Paid 1; Part-Time Volunteers 5.
Governing Authority: nonprofit. Tax-exempt: 170(b)(1)(A).
Arts Center: housed in 1908 Carnegie Library Building.
Collections: changing exhibits.
Facilities: classrooms; pottery studio; photography lab; kitchen & banquet facilities.
Activities: lectures; gallery talks; Summer Soiree' festival; rural arts program, changing monthly exhibits, featuring international, national & local artists; workshops; art school classes; musical performances; dance programs; formally organized education programs. Annual Event: Mother-Daughter Christmas Tea.
Publications: art school brochures; monthly invitations; gallery announcements.
Hours & Admission Prices: Jan. 2 to Dec. 22 Mon.-Fri. 9:30-5:30, Sat. open to groups by special request only. No charge; donations accepted. Closed Memorial Day; Labor Day; Thanksgiving & day after; week of Independence Day.
Membership: Individuals $30; Family & Patron $50; Donor $100; Sustaining Donor $250; Benefactor $500.

ANDERSON COUNTY MUSEUM, (M), 202 E. Greenville St., Anderson, SC 29621-5509. Tel.: 864-260-4737. Fax: 864-332-5320.
E-mail: acm@andersoncountysc.org
Web Site: www.andersoncountysc.org/museum.htm
Founded: 1983.
Congressional District: 3
Key Personnel: Exec. Dir., Beverly R. Childs; Cur. Collections, Alison Hinman; Education & Program Coord., Trey Haning; Office Coord., Marian O'Dell.
Personnel Profile: Full-Time Paid 5; Part-Time Volunteers 97; Interns 3.
Governing Authority: nonprofit. Parent Institution: Anderson County. Tax-exempt.
History Museum.
Collections: local history photographs & artifacts.
Research Fields: area & local history.
Facilities: 1500-vol. library of local history material available to the public.
Activities: guided tours; temporary exhibitions; restored harness shop; permanent exhibitions: textile, electricity, religion, military.
Publications: membership newsletter, Musings; volunteer newsletter, Muse News.
Hours & Admission Prices: Tues. 10-7, Wed.-Sat. 10-4; other times upon request. No charge; donations accepted. The Anderson County Reading Room: Thurs. 1-4. ♿
Attendance: 14,200 (accurate)
Membership: Museum Associate $35; Contributor's Circle $50; Sustainer's Society $100; Curator's Club $250; Director's Guild $500; Foundation Fellows $1,000.

Andrews

ANDREWS OLD TOWN HALL MUSEUM, 12 W. Main, Andrews, SC 29510.
Founded: 1980.
Personnel Profile: Part-Time Paid 1.
History Museum.

Collections: railroad memorabilia; photographs; period toys & furniture; pump organ; Victrola; farm shed with tools; early 1900s clothing.
Hours & Admission Prices: Tues. & Thurs. 10-4; other times by appointment. No charge; donations accepted.

Barnwell

BARNWELL COUNTY MUSEUM, 9426 Marlboro Ave., Barnwell, SC 29812. Mailing Address: P.O. Box 422, Barnwell, SC 29812-0422. Tel.: 803-259-1916. Fax: 803-259-1916.
E-mail: barnwell.museum@att.net
Founded: 1978.
Congressional District: 2
Key Personnel: Chm., Anne W. Hagood; Dir., Jerry Morris; Cur., Julia J. Woods.
Personnel Profile: Part-Time Paid 2; Part-Time Volunteers 10.
Governing Authority: county; nonprofit organization. Affiliated with Museum Association & County Council. Tax-exempt.
History Museum.
Collections: papers & books on Barnwell County dating from Revolutionary War times; Tarleton Brown Revolutionary soldier collection; costumes; dolls; implements of plantation farm life; silver; china; photographs; paintings & posters; maps; pottery; Civil War memorabilia; uniforms; medals; clippings; newspapers from World War I to Desert Storm; William Gilmore Simms.
Facilities: Effie Fuller Center gallery.
Activities: guided tours; lectures; gallery talks; concerts; loan, permanent, temporary & traveling exhibitions.
Publications: Memoirs of Tarlton Brown (reprint).
Hours & Admission Prices: Tues.-Thurs. & Sun. 3-5:30. No charge. Closed holidays. ♿
Attendance: 4,500 (estimated)
Membership: Individual $10; Family $25; Friend $50-$249; Benefactor $250 & up.

Beaufort

THE BEAUFORT ARSENAL, 713 Craven St., Beaufort, SC 29902-5571. Mailing Address: P.O. Box 11, Beaufort, SC 29901-0011. Tel.: 843-379-3331. Fax: 843-379-3371.
E-mail: eryan@historicbeaufort.org
Web Site: www.historic-beaufort.org
Formerly: Beaufort Museum at the Arsenal
Founded: 1939.
Congressional District: 2
Key Personnel: Dir. Museums, Elizabeth G. Ryan.
Personnel Profile: Full-Time Paid 3; Part-Time Paid 6; Part-Time Volunteers 90.
Governing Authority: municipality. Parent Institution: Historic Beaufort Foundation. Tax-exempt.
History Museum: built in 1798.
Collections: 1798 Arsenal & 1917 Carnegie Library; history of Beaufort & the Low Country; Native American artifacts; textiles; costumes; household; personal furnishings & accessories; Low Country artwork & photographs.
Research Fields: Beaufort & Low Country history.
Facilities: meeting room. Museum-related items for sale.
Activities: educational programs in galleries; speakers series; slide lecture programs; special events; Summer in the Courtyard.
Publications: newsletter, Museum Muse.
Hours & Admission Prices: Mon.-Tues. & Thurs.-Sat. 10-5. Adults $3; children 6 & under and members no charge. Closed holidays.
Attendance: 12,000 (estimated)
Membership: Student $15; Individual $25; Family $50; Supporter $100; Donor $250; Patron $500; Benefactor $1,000; Sustainer $2,500; Danner $5,000.

THE VERDIER HOUSE, 801 Bay St., Beaufort, SC 29902-5565. Mailing Address: Historic Beaufort Foundation, P.O. Box 11, Beaufort, SC 29901-0011. Tel.: 843-379-3331. Fax: 843-379-3371.
E-mail: eryan@historicbeaufort.org
Web Site: www.historic-beaufort.org
Founded: 1977.
Congressional District: 2
Key Personnel: Dir. Museums, Elizabeth G. Ryan; Exec. Dir., Evan R. Thompson; Exec. Asst., Maxine F. Lutz.
Personnel Profile: Full-Time Paid 4; Part-Time Paid 4; Part-Time Volunteers 60.
Governing Authority: nonprofit organization. Parent Institution: Historic Beaufort Foundation Inc. Tax-exempt: 501(c)(3).
Historic House: housed in the former home of John Mark Verdier; built c.1805.
Collections: 1790-1825 Federal period furnishings & artifacts.
Research Fields: Beaufort style architecture.
Facilities: historic preservation library; meeting space. Museum-related items for sale.
Activities: guided tours; lectures; docent program; preservation of historical buildings & sites in Beaufort County. Museum Sponsors: Lafayette Soiree; Fall Tours in October; Christmas Open House.
Publications: quarterly newsletter, A Guide to Historic Beaufort.
Hours & Admission Prices: Mon.-Sat. 10-3:30; other times by appointment for groups of 10 or more. Verdier House: adults $6, students $4; discounts to South Carolina Federation of Museum members; children under 6 & members no charge. Deere House: $4.
Attendance: 10,000
Membership: Single $25; Family $50; Supporting $100; Donor $250; Patron $500; Benefactor $1,000.

Beech Island

BEECH ISLAND HISTORICAL SOCIETY, 144 Old Jackson Hwy., Beech Island, SC 29842-4568. Tel.: 803-867-3600. Fax: 803-867-3600.
E-mail: bihs@comcast.net
Web Site: www.beech-islandhistory.org
Founded: 1985.
Key Personnel: Pres. (V), Jackie Bartley.
Governing Authority: Tax-exempt.
History & Agricultural Museum.
Collections: Beech Island & agricultural history; personal artifacts.
Activities: special programs & events; monthly meetings; spring house tour.
Publications: newsletter, Four Centuries & More.
Hours & Admission Prices: Wed.-Thurs. 11-1; other times by appointment. No charge; donations accepted. ♿
Attendance: 50 (accurate)
Membership: Single $20; Family $25.

Belton

SOUTH CAROLINA TENNIS HALL OF FAME, 50 N. Main St., Belton, SC 29627. Mailing Address: P.O. Box 843, Belton, SC 29627-0843. Tel.: 864-338-7400. Fax: 864-338-4034.
E-mail: bama7400@aol.com
Web Site: www.beltonsc.com
Founded: 1984.
Congressional District: 6
Key Personnel: C.E.O., Rex Maynard; Chm. (V), David Honeycutt.
Personnel Profile: Part-Time Volunteers 14.
Governing Authority: nonprofit organization. Parent Institution: South Carolina Tennis Patrons Foundation. Tax-exempt: 501(c)(3).
Tennis Museum.
Collections: portraits of inductees; trophies & tennis memorabilia; books; magazines; rackets; oil paintings; mementos.
Research Fields: tennis.
Facilities: 400 sq. ft. exhibit space.
Activities: tours. Museum Sponsors: annual banquet.
Hours & Admission Prices: Wed-Thurs. & Sat. 10-4. No charge; donations accepted. Closed New Year's Day; Independence Day; Labor Day; Thanksgiving; Christmas. ♿
Attendance: 2,500 (estimated)
Membership: Member $25; Friend $50; Patron $100; Sponsor $250; Benefactor $500; Champion $1,000.

Bennettsville

JENNINGS-BROWN HOUSE FEMALE ACADEMY, 123 S. Marlboro St., Bennettsville, SC 29512-4031. Mailing Address: P.O. Box 178, Bennettsville, SC 29512-0178. Tel.: 843-479-5624.
E-mail: marlborough@mecsc.net
Founded: 1967.
Congressional District: 6
Key Personnel: Bd. Pres. Historical Society (V), Marty Rankin; Exec. Dir. Museum, Lucille Carabo.
Personnel Profile: Full-Time Paid 2; Part-Time Volunteers 13.
Governing Authority: county; society. Parent Institution: Marlboro County Historic Preservation Commission. Affiliated with Marlboro County Historical Museum, 123 S. Marlboro St., Bennettsville, SC 29512. Tax-exempt: 501(c)(3).
Historic House: c.1826-27 Jennings-Brown House.
Collections: vintage furnishings and furniture pre-dating 1850.
Facilities: County historical & museum-related items for sale.
Activities: guided tours; traveling exhibitions.
Hours & Admission Prices: Mon.-Thurs. 10-5, Fri. 10-1. Adults $2, students $1.
Attendance: 600 (estimated)
Membership: Adult $10; Couple $15; Family $20; Patron $50-$199; Angel $200 & up.

MARLBORO COUNTY HISTORICAL MUSEUM, 123 S. Marlboro St., Bennettsville, SC 29512-4031. Mailing Address: P.O. Box 178, Bennettsville, SC 29512-0178. Tel.: 843-479-5624.
E-mail: marlborough@mecsc.net
Founded: 1970.
Congressional District: 6
Key Personnel: Pres. (V), Marty Rankin; Dir., Lucille Carabo.
Personnel Profile: Full-Time Paid 2; Part-Time Volunteers 40; Interns 2.
Governing Authority: society. Parent Institution: Marlborough Historical Society. Tax-exempt: 501(c)(3).
Historical & Preservation Society: housed in the former home of Dr. & Mrs. John Frank Kinney; built in 1902.
Collections: pre-1850 southern antiques; local history items from Indians through World War II. Historic Houses: 1826 Jennings Brown House; 1833 Bennettsville Female Academy.
Facilities: Tour booklet, historic site tiles & other history-related items for sale.
Activities: guided tours; lectures; permanent & temporary exhibitions.
Hours & Admission Prices: Mon.-Fri. 10-4. House: adults $2, children $1. Closed major holidays.
Attendance: 2,547 (accurate)
Membership: Individual $10; Couple $15; Family $20; Patron $50-$199; Angel $200 & up.

Bishopville

SOUTH CAROLINA COTTON MUSEUM, (M), 121 W. Cedar Ln., Bishopville, SC 29010-1454. Tel.: 803-484-4497. Fax: 803-484-5203.
E-mail: sccottonmus@ftc-i.net
Web Site: www.sccotton.org
Founded: 1993.
Key Personnel: Exec. Dir., Janson L. Cox; Pres., George Roberts; Business Mgr., Melissa Brundage.
Personnel Profile: Full-Time Paid 1; Full-Time Volunteers 1; Part-Time Paid 3; Part-Time Volunteers 25.
Governing Authority: private; nonprofit organization. Tax-exempt: 501(c)(3).
History Museum.
Collections: economic, social & political impact of cotton in the south.
Research Fields: veterans oral history project, partner with the Library of Congress.
Facilities: meeting room; conference room (both available for rent).
Activities: educational programs; audiovisual programming for groups; Veterans Oral History program as a partner with the Library of Congress.
Publications: monthly newsletter.
Hours & Admission Prices: Mon.-Fri. 10-4:30, Sat. 10-4. Adults $5, senior citizens $3, students $2; discounts to AAM, AAA & ICOM members; active military, members, children 5 & under no charge. ♿
Attendance: 7,350 (accurate)
Membership: Adult $25; Family $35; Business $100 & up; Corporate $1,000.

Blacksburg

KINGS MOUNTAIN NATIONAL MILITARY PARK, 2625 Park Rd., Blacksburg, SC 29702-7325. Tel.: 864-936-7921. Fax: 864-936-9897. TDD: 864-936-7921.
Web Site: www.nps.gov/kimo.htm
Founded: 1931.
Congressional District: 5
Key Personnel: Chief Interpretation & Resource Mgmt., Chris Revels; Bookstore Mgr., Wilma Scoggins.
Personnel Profile: Full-Time Paid 12; Part-Time Paid 5; Part-Time Volunteers 40; Interns 3.
Governing Authority: federal; nonprofit organization. Parent Institution: National Park Service. Tax-exempt.
Military Park Museum.
Collections: military artifacts; 18th-century frontier life.
Research Fields: southern campaign of Revolution & battle of Kings Mountain.
Facilities: 300-vol. library of history of Revolutionary War available for use on premises. Publications for sale.
Activities: movies; permanent & temporary exhibitions.
Hours & Admission Prices: Daily 9-5. No charge; donations accepted. Closed New Year's Day; Thanksgiving; Christmas. ♿
Attendance: 115,000 (accurate)

Blackville

AGRICULTURAL HERITAGE CENTER, Clemson University's Edisto Research and Educ. Ctr., 64 Research Rd., Blackville, SC 29817. Tel.: 803-284-3343. Fax: 803-284-3684.
History Museum.
Collections: local agricultural history; rural life; regional culture & economics; period equipment & artifacts.
Hours & Admission Prices: Call for hours.

Branchville

BRANCHVILLE RAILROAD SHRINE AND MUSEUM, INC., 7504 Freedom Rd., Branchville, SC 29432-2310. Mailing Address: Town of Branchville, P.O. Box 85, Branchville, SC 29432-0085. Tel.: 803-274-8820. Fax: 803-274-8760.
Founded: 1969.
Congressional District: 2
Key Personnel: Pres., Johnny Norris; Vice Pres., Luther Folk.
Governing Authority: nonprofit. Tax-exempt: 501(c)(3).
Transportation Museum: housed in 1877 Branchville Southern Railroad Depot at the site of the first railroad junction of the world.
Collections: railroad artifacts; model trains; historical items used when the town was a railroad center.
Research Fields: railroading.
Facilities: 50-seat restaurant. Gift items for sale.
Activities: guided tours; loan & permanent exhibitions. Museum Sponsors: R.R. Daze Festival in September.
Hours & Admission Prices: Fri.-Sat. 10-2, Sun. 2-5; other times by appointment. No charge; donations accepted. Closed major holidays. ♿
Membership: Individual $5.

Camden

CAMDEN ARCHIVES & MUSEUM, 1314 Broad St., Camden, SC 29020-3535. Tel.: 803-425-6050. Fax: 803-424-4053.
Web Site: www.camdenarchives.org
Founded: 1973.
Congressional District: 5
Key Personnel: Dir., Howard Branham; Chm. (V), Frank Goodale; Assoc. Archivist, Peggy Brakefield; Administrative Asst., Barbara Rogers.
Personnel Profile: Full-Time Paid 1; Part-Time Paid 4; Part-Time Volunteers 3.
Governing Authority: municipal; nonprofit. Parent Institution: City of Camden. Tax-exempt.
Archives & Local History Museum.
Collections: genealogy; archives; local artifacts; memorabilia; sections on American Revolution; Civil War; South Carolina history & biography; The South; local history; collections of South Carolina Society, D.A.R. & South Carolina Chapter, Colonial Dames, 17th-century; manuscripts.
Research Fields: genealogy; local history.
Facilities: 2,800-vol. library available for research on premises only; reading room.
Activities: guided tours; special exhibits.
Publications: brochures.
Hours & Admission Prices: Mon.-Fri. 8-5, 1st & 3rd Sun. of month 1-5. No charge; donations accepted. Closed city holidays. ♿
Attendance: 6,000 (estimated)
Membership: Friends: Individual $25; Family $45; Contributor $100-$249; Patron $250-$499; Benefactor $500 & up.

FINE ARTS CENTER OF KERSHAW COUNTY, INC., 810 Lyttleton St., Camden, SC 29020-4411. Mailing Address: P.O. Box 1498, Camden, SC 29021-8498. Tel.: 803-425-7676. Fax: 803-425-7679.
E-mail: kcobb@fineartscenter.org
Web Site: www.fineartscenter.org
Founded: 1976.
Congressional District: 5
Key Personnel: Exec. Dir., Kristin Cobb; Pres. Bd. Dir., Rose Sheheen; Dir. Facility, Dianne Edwards; Dir. Finance, Daphne Cantey; Dir. Education, Steve LeVan; Dir. Mktg., Jim Litzinger.
Personnel Profile: Full-Time Paid 6; Part-Time Paid 6; Part-Time Volunteers 30.
Governing Authority: nonprofit organization. Tax-exempt: 501(c)(3).
Art Gallery, housed in Bassett Memorial Building.
Collections: Carroll Bassett & sporting art equestrian bronzes; art works; Carroll K. Bassett Memorial Building.
Facilities: 2 galleries; 274-seat auditorium; multi-purpose room; 3 arts education studios for music, visual art & dance.
Activities: lectures; gallery talks; concerts; education programs for children & adults; offerings for all ages in the arts including theatre & visual arts; traveling & permanent exhibits; photography club programs; art association.
Publications: monthly newsletter; season & class brochures.
Hours & Admission Prices: Winter: Mon.-Fri. 12-6, Sat. by appointment. Summer: Mon.-Fri. 9-5, Sat. by appointment. Gallery: no charge; donations accepted. Performance Series: call for admission fee. Closed Easter; Memorial Day; Independence Day; Labor Day; Thanksgiving; Christmas Eve to New Year's Day. ♿
Attendance: 70,000 (accurate)

Membership: Contributor (individual) $35; Supporter $50; Sustainer $150; Advocate $500; Patron $1,000; Benefactor $2,500; Life $10,000.

HISTORIC CAMDEN REVOLUTIONARY WAR SITE, 222 Broad St., Camden, SC 29020. Mailing Address: P.O. Box 710, Camden, SC 29021-0710. Tel.: 803-432-9841. Fax: 803-432-3815.
E-mail: hiscamden@att.net
Web Site: www.historic-camden.net
Founded: 1967.
Congressional District: 5
Key Personnel: Chm., Dwight deLoach; Vice Chm., Wm. Davie Beard; Dir. & Museum Shop Mgr., Joanna Craig.
Personnel Profile: Full-Time Paid 1; Part-Time Paid 5; Part-Time Volunteers 65.
Governing Authority: nonprofit. Parent Institution: Historic Camden Foundation. Tax-exempt: 501(c)(3).
History Museum: housed in reconstructed 1777 Kershaw-Cornwallis House, located on 107 acre archeological park encompassing the colonial to late 18th-century village of Camden.
Collections: archaeological remains from pre-European, colonial & antebellum periods; tools & furnishings from late 18th to the early 19th century.
Research Fields: Indian, colonial & revolutionary periods.
Facilities: 400-vol. library pertaining to Indian, colonial & revolutionary periods; catering service available. Books, local crafts & museum-related items for sale.
Activities: guided tours; lectures; concerts; organized education programs for children & adults; living history demonstrations.
Publications: annual newsletter; calendar of events.
Hours & Admission Prices: Tues.-Sat. 10-5, Sun. 2-5. Guided Tours: Tues.-Fri. 10:30 & 3, Sat. 10:30-4, Sun. 2-4. Adults $5, senior citizens $4, students $3; discounts to Mobil, AAA, AAM & ICOM members; members & children under 6 no charge. Closed major holidays.
Attendance: 22,101 (estimated)
Membership: Senior Citizen $25; Individual $30; Family $40; Contributing $50; Sustaining $100; Leadership $250; Fellow $500; Patron $1,000.

HISTORIC ROBERT MILLS COURTHOUSE, 607 Broad St., Camden, SC 29020-4703. Mailing Address: P.O. Box 605, Camden, SC 29021. Tel.: 800-968-4037; 803-432-2525. Fax: 803-432-4181.
Key Personnel: Exec. Dir., Liz Horton.
Governing Authority: Parent Institution: Kershaw County Chamber of Commerce & Visitors Center.
Historic Building: designed by South Carolina architect, Robert Mills; built in 1827.
Collections: local history & culture; architecture; period furnishings; personal artifacts; photographs.
Activities: guided tours.
Hours & Admission Prices: Mon.-Fri. 9-5, Sat. 10-5, Sun. 1-5. No charge. ♿

KERSHAW COUNTY HISTORICAL SOCIETY, 811 Fair St., Camden, SC 29020-4404. Mailing Address: P.O. Box 501, Camden, SC 29021-0501. Tel.: 803-425-1123.
E-mail: kchistory@camden.net
Web Site: www.kershawcountyhistoricalsociety.org
Founded: 1954.
Congressional District: 5
Key Personnel: Pres., Peggy Ogburn; Dir., Kathleen P. Stahl.
Personnel Profile: Part-Time Paid 1; Part-Time Volunteers 18.
Governing Authority: society; nonprofit organization. Tax-exempt: 501(c)(3).
Historic House: c.1812 home built by man believed to be the first black citizen to purchase his freedom in Kershaw County.
Collections: restored living area of house.
Research Fields: listing of historic battle sites; historic houses in county.
Facilities: Local history books for sale.
Activities: guided tours; organized education programs for adults.
Publications: quarterly newsletter, Update; brochure; books, Historic Camden, Vols. I & II; Camden Homes & Heritage; Decorative Arts in Camden & Kershaw County; Kershaw County Cemetery Survey, Vols. I, II & III; Kershaw County Census, 1800, 1810, 1820, 1830; History and Homes of Liberty Hill, SC; A Guide to Selected Historical Sites in Kershaw County, SC; Kershaw County Legacy I & II; A Guide to Historic Sites in Camden, SC; series of reprints of old pamphlets on county history; Kershaw County State Census of White Population 1839; Kershaw County State Agricultural Census 1868; In the Sunny South: A Winter Colonist's View of Camden, SC & Vicinity in 1901; Battle of Camden, SC; Kershaw County District Business Directory, 1854-1900; Gold Rush Letter from William Lemond, a 49er from Carolina; Kershaw County Confederate Miscellany; Horatio Gates & Battle of Camden; Just Mud Kenshaw County SC Pottery; Wateree River Plantation Rosny from 1815; Genealogy of the McWillie and Cunningham Families; Index for the Genealogy of the McWillie and Cunningham Families.
Hours & Admission Prices: Thurs. 1-5; appointments available. No charge.
Attendance: 150 (estimated)
Membership: Student $10; Senior Citizen $20; Individual $25; Family $35; Business $50; Contributing $75; Sustaining $100; Life $1,000.

NATIONAL STEEPLECHASE MUSEUM, Springdale Race Course, 200 Knights Hill Rd., Camden, SC 29020-2154.
Camden, SC 29020-8008. Tel.: 803-432-6513; 800-780-8117. Fax: 803-432-4062.
E-mail: hopec@nationalsteeplechasemuseum.org
Web Site: www.nationalsteeplechasemuseum.org
Founded: 1998.
Congressional District: 5
Key Personnel: Exec. Dir., Hope Cooper.
Personnel Profile: Full-Time Paid 1; Part-Time Paid 1; Part-Time Volunteers 1.
Governing Authority: Tax-exempt: 501(c)(3).
Steeplechase History Museum.
Collections: history of American steeplechasing; photographs; memorabilia.
Facilities: library; archives.
Activities: interactive exhibits; special events.
Publications: newsletter.
Hours & Admission Prices: Sept.-May Wed.-Sat. 10-4; other times by appointment. No charge; donations accepted. Closed major holidays. ♿
Attendance: 5,000
Membership: Individual $35; Family $50; Supporter $100; Corporate $200; Winner's Circle $500 & up.

Cayce

CAYCE HISTORICAL MUSEUM, City of Cayce Municipal Complex, 1800 12th St., Cayce, SC 29033-2935. Tel.: 803-739-5385. Fax: 803-796-9072.
E-mail: caycemuseum@historysc.com
Key Personnel: Dir., Leo Redmond
History Museum.
Collections: Native American artifacts; period artifacts; furnishings; exhibits relating to the periods of Colonial trade, agricultural development & transportation from the 18th century to the present.
Hours & Admission Prices: Tues.-Fri. 9-4, Sat.-Sun. 2-5. Adults $2, senior citizens & students 13 and over $1, students 12 & under $.50; Sun. no charge. Closed city holidays.

Central

CENTRAL HERITAGE SOCIETY, 416 Church St., Central, SC 29630-9152. Mailing Address: P.O. Box 1162, Central, SC 29630-9152. Tel.: 864-639-2794 & 2156.
History Museum.
Collections: local history & culture; photographs; period furnishings; personal artifacts.
Hours & Admission Prices: Sun. 2-4. Closed holidays.

Charleston

AMERICAN MILITARY MUSEUM, 360 Concord St., Ste. 9, Charleston, SC 29401-6303. Tel.: 843-577-7000. Fax: 843-577-7008.
E-mail: info@americanmilitarymuseum.org
Web Site: www.americanmilitarymuseum.org
Founded: 1987.
Congressional District: 1
Key Personnel: Dir., George E. Meagher; Cur., Michael Lussier; Museum Shop Mgr., Sec. & Treas., Randi Meagher.
Personnel Profile: Full-Time Paid 2; Full-Time Volunteers 3; Part-Time Volunteers 10.
Governing Authority: individual operation. Tax-exempt.
American Military History Museum.
Collections: U.S. military uniforms, insignias, & medals; weapons & personal artifacts; American military history from Revolutionary War to present; military miniatures.
Activities: guided tours. Special events: POW/MIA, Memorial Day, Armed Forces Week.
Hours & Admission Prices: Mon.-Sat. 10-6, Sun. 1-5; school groups by appointment. Adults $7, seniors 55 & over and retired military $5, students 13-18 $3, children 6-12 $2; discounts to groups; active military no charge. Closed Thanksgiving; Christmas. ♿

AVERY RESEARCH CENTER FOR AFRICAN AMERICAN HISTORY & CULTURE, 125 Bull St., College of Charleston, Charleston, SC 29424-0001. Mailing Address: 66 George St., Charleston, SC 29424-0001. Tel.: 843-953-7609; 843-953-7608. Fax: 843-953-7607.
E-mail: mayog@cofu.edu
Web Site: www.cofc.edu/avery
Founded: 1985.
Congressional District: 1
Key Personnel: Interim Dir., Georgette Mayo; Archivist, Sherman Pyatt; Dir. Education & Exhibits, Curtis J. Franks; Dir. Special Projects, Deborah Wright; Mktg. Asst., John Coles; Museum Shop Mgr., Oliver B. Smalls.
Personnel Profile: Full-Time Paid 7; Part-Time Paid 6; Part-Time Volunteers 25; Interns 2.
Governing Authority: college; State of South Carolina. Parent Institution: College of Charleston. Tax-exempt: 501(c)(3).
History Museum & Research Center.
Collections: print materials; photographs; audio & videotape; manuscripts; organizational records related to the history & culture of South Carolina and Low Country African Americans.
Research Fields: African American history; Southern history; folklore; anthropology; linguistics.
Facilities: reference library; reading room; 2 exhibit galleries in historic African American school.
Activities: reference & referral services to scholars, students & the community; public programs.
Publications: quarterly, The Avery Review; biannual newspaper, The Bulletin; quarterly calendar of events.
Hours & Admission Prices: Mon.-Fri. 10-5, Sat. 12-5; group tours by appointment. No charge; donations accepted. Closed university holidays. ♿
Attendance: 8,500 (estimated)
Membership: Student $5; Individual $15; Family & Supporter $25; Sustaining $100; Contributing $300; Patron $500; Benefactor $1,000; Life $5,000 & up.

CALHOUN MANSION, 14-16 Meeting St., Charleston, SC 29401-2706. Tel.: 843-722-8205. Fax: 843-723-1147.
E-mail: cmansion@tmo.blackberry.net
Historic House: former home of George W. Williams, built in 1876.
Collections: local history & culture; period furnishings; decorative painting & lighting.
Facilities: garden. Museum-related items for sale.
Hours & Admission Prices: Tours: March-Nov. daily 11-5; Dec.-Feb. daily 11-4:30. Adults $15.

CHARLES TOWNE LANDING STATE HISTORIC SITE, 1500 Old Towne Rd., Charleston, SC 29407-6099. Tel.: 843-852-4200. Fax: 843-852-4205.
E-mail: ctlandingsp@scprt.com
Web Site: www.charlestownelanding.travel
Founded: 1970.
Key Personnel: Park Mgr. & Retail Mgr., Rob Powell; Asst. Park Mgr., Jayson Sellers; Cur. Animal Forest, Kendle Enter; Maintenance Mgr., Wayne Mazell; Museum Mgr., Patrick Cook.
Personnel Profile: Full-Time Paid 13; Part-Time Paid 6; Part-Time Volunteers 20; Interns 2.
Governing Authority: state. Parent Institution: S.C. Dept. of Parks, Recreation & Tourism, 1205 Pendleton St., Columbia, SC 29201. Tax-exempt: 170(b)(1)(A).
Historic Site: 1670 site of the first permanent European settlement in South Carolina.
Collections: prehistory to plantation era; native animals; crafts. Reproduction Historic Ship: trading ketch 1670 Adventure.
Research Fields: early South Carolina towne life; animal husbandry; agricultural relating to 1670.
Facilities: botanical garden; zoological park; vending area. Museum-related items for sale.
Activities: formally organized education programs for children, adults & undergraduate college students; docent program; training programs for professional museum workers; permanent exhibitions.
Publications: monthly newsletter, Instruc'ns by Friends of CTL.
Hours & Admission Prices: Daily 9-5. Adults $5, seniors & disabled $3.25, children 6-15 $3; discount to groups; children 5 & under no charge. Closed Christmas Eve & Day. ♿
Attendance: 185,000 (accurate)
Membership: Park Pass $50

CHARLESTON LIBRARY SOCIETY, 164 King St., Charleston, SC 29401-2269. Tel.: 843-723-9912. Fax: 843-723-3500.
E-mail: info@charlestonlibrarysociety.org
Web Site: www.charlestonlibrarysociety.org
Founded: 1748.
Congressional District: 1
Key Personnel: Exec. Dir., W. Eric Emerson, Ph.D.
Personnel Profile: Full-Time Paid 5; Part-Time Paid 5.
Governing Authority: society. Tax-exempt: 501(c)(3).
General Library.
Collections: 90,000 books; Charleston newspapers dating from 1732; 18th-century books, pamphlets & periodicals; manuscripts; 1,686 microfilm reels.
Research Fields: South Carolina history; Charleston history; genealogy; military history; S.C. authors.
Facilities: 90,000-vol. library.
Hours & Admission Prices: Mon.-Fri. 9:30-5:30, Sat. 9:30-2. Closed holidays. ♿
Membership: College Student $25; Annual $50.

∗ **THE CHARLESTON MUSEUM, (M),** 360 Meeting St., Charleston, SC 29403-6297. Tel.: 843-722-2996. Fax: 803-722-1784.
E-mail: jbrumgardt@charlestonmuseum.org
Web Site: www.charlestonmuseum.org
Founded: 1773.
Congressional District: 1
Key Personnel: Dir. & C.E.O., Dr. John R. Brumgardt; Bd. Trustees Pres., Dr. John Rashford; Admin. Svcs., Vickie Styles; Asst. Dir., Carl P. Borick; Cur. Natural History, Dr. Albert E. Sanders; Cur. Ornithology, Dr. William Post; Cur. Historical Archaeology, Martha Zierden; Cur. History, J. Grahame Long; Education Coord., Stephanie Thomas; Registrar, Jan Z. Hiester; Archivist, Jennifer E. Scheetz; Admin. Mgr., Susan McKellar; Bldg. Mgr., Robert Gabel; Public Rels. & Events Coord., Rachel Chesser.
Personnel Profile: Full-Time Paid 33; Part-Time Paid 30; Part-Time Volunteers 100.
Governing Authority: nonprofit organization. Branch Museums: Heyward-Washington House, 87 Church St.; Joseph Manigault House, 350 Meeting St; Dill Sanctuary. Tax-exempt: 501(c)(3).
General Museum.
Collections: archaeology & ethnology; natural science; history; decorative arts; major collections' emphasis on Charleston & South Carolina coastal region with comparative material of worldwide scope; regional collections of birds, mammals, fish, reptiles, amphibians, invertebrates, plants, fossils; furniture; silver; textiles; historic archaeology.
Research Fields: whales; historic archaeology; furniture; textiles; silver; ornithology.
Facilities: 20,000-vol. library of books, periodicals, maps, photographs, sheet music, available on inter-library loan & on premises; indoor-outdoor exhibit space; 300-seat auditorium; 75-seat orientation room; classrooms; 30,000 sq. ft. exhibit space in branches. Two National Historic Landmark houses & a wildlife sanctuary. Museum-related items for sale.
Activities: tours; lectures; films; formally organized education programs for children; publications program; docent program; inter-museum loan, permanent & temporary exhibitions.
Publications: quarterly newsletter, Charleston Museum Newsletter; books, Status of South Carolina Birds; Story of Francis Simmons Holmes; Audubon: The Charleston Connection; Charleston Silver; The Story of Sea Island Cotton.
Hours & Admission Prices: Mon.-Sat. 9-5, Sun. 1-5. Adults $10, children $5; discounts to AAM members; museum members no charge; additional charges for other sites. Closed New Year's Day; Easter; Thanksgiving; Christmas. ♿
Attendance: 107,450 (accurate)
Membership: Individual $50; Family $60; Milby Burton Society $125; Business Donor $250; Manigault Society $550; 1773 Society $1,000.

CHILDREN'S MUSEUM OF THE LOWCOUNTRY, 25 Ann St., Charleston, SC 29403-6213. Tel.: 843-853-8962. Fax: 843-853-1042.
E-mail: info@explorecml.org
Web Site: www.explorecml.org
Founded: 2003.
Key Personnel: Dir., Denis R. Chirles.
Personnel Profile: Full-Time Paid 6; Full-Time Volunteers 21; Part-Time Paid 20; Part-Time Volunteers 40; Interns 5.
Children's Museum.
Collections: hands-on exhibits.
Activities: special programs; classes.
Hours & Admission Prices: Tues.-Sat. 10-5, Sun. 1-5. Admission $7; children under one no charge. Closed New Year's Day; Easter; Independence Day; Thanksgiving; Christmas Eve & Day. ♿
Attendance: 103,106 (accurate)
Membership: Grandparent $60; Family $75; Explorer $125; Play $395.

THE CITADEL ARCHIVES & MUSEUM, 171 Moultrie St., Charleston, SC 29409-6141. Tel.: 843-953-6846. Fax: 843-953-6956.
E-mail: yatesj@citadel.edu
Web Site: www.citadel.edu/archivesandmuseum
Founded: 1842.
Congressional District: 1
Key Personnel: Dir. Archives & Museum, Jane M. Yates.
Governing Authority: state. Affiliated with The Citadel, Military College of South Carolina. Tax-exempt: 170(b)(1)(A).
College History Museum.
Collections: cadet uniforms & arms; photographs relating to The Citadel, The Military College of South Carolina.
Research Fields: The Citadel (Institutional).
Facilities: archives open by appointment only.
Activities: tours.
Publications: brochure.
Hours & Admission Prices: Sun.-Fri. 2-5, Sat. 12-5. No charge. Closed college, religious & national holidays. ♿
Attendance: 7,785 (accurate)

CITY HALL COUNCIL CHAMBER GALLERY, Broad & Meeting Sts., Charleston, SC 29401. Mailing Address: 80 Broad St., Charleston, SC 29401-2225. Tel.: 843-724-3799 & 3726. Fax: 843-724-3732.
Founded: 1818.
Congressional District: 1
Key Personnel: C.E.O., Mayor Joseph P. Riley, Jr.
Personnel Profile: Full-Time Paid 1.
Governing Authority: municipal. Parent Institution: City of Charleston. Tax-exempt: 170(b)(1)(A).
Art Gallery: housed in c.1801 1st U.S. Bank Building.
Collections: oil portraits of U.S. Presidents; marble sculptures; period furnishings; Edison light bulbs; council chamber.
Research Fields: local political history.
Facilities: library of municipal government records.
Activities: guided tours; lectures; gallery talks; permanent exhibitions.
Publications: catalogue.
Hours & Admission Prices: Mon.-Fri. 9-5. No charge; donations accepted. Closed major holidays. ♿
Attendance: 20,000 (estimated)

CONFEDERATE MUSEUM, 188 Meeting St., Charleston, SC 29401. Mailing Address: P.O. Box 20997, Charleston, SC 29413-0997. Tel.: 843-723-1541.
Founded: 1898.
Key Personnel: Dir., June Murray Wells.
Personnel Profile: Part-Time Paid 3; Part-Time Volunteers 10.
Governing Authority: Parent Institution: Charleston Chapter, United Daughters of the Confederacy. Tax-exempt.
History Museum.
Collections: Confederate military history; local history & culture; photographs; period artifacts. Historic Building: Market Hall built 1841.
Research Fields: Confederate history & genealogy.
Facilities: library.
Hours & Admission Prices: Tues.-Sat. 11-3:30. Admission $5. Closed major holidays. ♿

* **DRAYTON HALL, (M),** 3380 Ashley River Rd., Hwy. 61, Charleston, SC 29414-7105. Tel.: 843-769-2600. Fax: 843-766-0878.
E-mail: info@draytonhall.org
Web Site: www.draytonhall.org
Founded: 1974.
Congressional District: 1
Key Personnel: Exec. Dir., George W. McDaniel; Exec. Asst., Dawn Brogan; Dir. Finance, Paula Marion; Property Council Chm. (V), Anthony Wood; Supt. Bldgs. & Grounds, John M. Kidder; Group Sales Coord., Debbi Zimmerman; Dir. Mktg., Vera Ford.
Personnel Profile: Full-Time Paid 24; Part-Time Paid 30; Part-Time Volunteers 10; Interns 5.
Governing Authority: nonprofit organization. Property of the National Trust for Historic Preservation 1785 Massachusetts Ave., N.W., Washington, DC 20036. Tax-exempt: 501(c)(3).
Historic House Museum: housed in c.1738-42, Drayton Family Residence.
Collections: Georgian architecture; historic landscape.
Research Fields: Drayton genealogy; 18th & 19th century plantation system; African-American history; historic preservation; architectural history.
Facilities: walking history/nature trails. Museum-related books & gifts for sale.
Activities: guided tours; school programs & special events; lectures.
Publications: newsletter for members; written tour of Drayton Hall (for hearing impaired people; French and German readers).
Hours & Admission Prices: March-Oct. daily 8:30-5; Nov.-Feb. daily 9:30-5. Adults $14, youth 12-18 $8, children 6-11 $6; discounts to AAA members & military; children under 5 & National Trust members no charge. Closed New Year's Day; Thanksgiving; Christmas. ♿
Attendance: 53,000 (accurate)
Membership: Friends of Drayton Hall $40; Joint Membership in the Drayton Hall & National Trust for Historic Preservation $45; Associate $75; Partner $100; Contributor $250; Sustaining $500; Drayton Hall Society $1,000.

* **GIBBES MUSEUM OF ART, (M),** 135 Meeting St., Charleston, SC 29401-2297. Tel.: 843-722-2706. Fax: 843-720-1682.
E-mail: admack@gibbesmuseum.org
Web Site: www.gibbesmuseum.org
Founded: 1858.
Congressional District: 1
Key Personnel: Exec. Dir., Angela D. Mack; Pres., J. Elizabeth Bradham; Dir. Communications, Marla Loftus; Registrar, Zinnia Willits; Museum Sales Mgr., Patsy Nicklas; Operations Mgr., Gregory Jenkins.
Personnel Profile: Full-Time Paid 12; Part-Time Paid 8; Part-Time Volunteers 30; Interns 2.
Governing Authority: nonprofit organization. Parent Institution: Carolina Art Association. Tax-exempt: 501(c)(3).
Art Museum.
Collections: American portraits; prints & miniatures; contemporary art; sculpture; Japanese prints; photography.
Research Fields: Charleston art & architecture; photography.
Facilities: library; exhibition galleries; art studios.
Activities: guided tours; lectures; films; gallery talks; arts festivals; studio classes for children & adults; temporary & permanent exhibitions.
Publications: books, The Miniature Portrait Collection of The Carolina Art Association; catalogue, Selections from Carolina Art Association Collection; tricentennial catalogue, Art in South Carolina 1670 & 1970; Charles Fraser of Charleston; Oystering: A Way of Life; This is Charleston; Alice Ravenel Huger Smith: An Artist, A Place & A Time; In Pursuit of Refinement: Charlestonians Abroad, 1740-1860; Henry Benbridge: Charleston Portrait Painter; Rhythms of Life: The Art of Johnathan Green; Landscape of Slavery: The Plantation in American Art; Landscape of Slavery: The Plantation in American Art.
Hours & Admission Prices: Tues.-Sat. 10-5, Sun. 1-5. Adults $9, seniors, military & students $7, children 6-12 $5; discounts to AAM members; Southeast reciprocal memberships; children under 6 & members no charge. Closed national holidays. ♿
Attendance: 25,000 (estimated)
Membership: Student $30; Individual $45; Family $100.

HALSEY INSTITUTE OF CONTEMPORARY ART AT THE COLLEGE OF CHARLESTON, (M), 54 St. Philip St., Charleston, SC 29424-1413. Mailing Address: 54 St. Philip St., Room 202, Charleston, SC 29424-1413. Tel.: 843-953-5680. Fax: 843-953-7890.
E-mail: sloanm@cofc.edu
Web Site: www.halsey.cofc.edu
Formerly: Halsey Gallery, School of the Arts, College of Charleston
Founded: 1978.
Congressional District: 1
Key Personnel: Dir., Mark Sloan.
Personnel Profile: Full-Time Paid 2; Part-Time Paid 1; Part-Time Volunteers 3; Interns 1.
Governing Authority: college; nonprofit. Parent Institution: College of Charleston. Tax-exempt.
Art Gallery.
Collections: paintings; sculpture.
Major Exhibits: Aldwyth: Work v./work n. (T), 11/09-1/12/10; Call and Response: Africa to America (T), 5/10/10-7/10.
Research Fields: Contemporary art.
Facilities: 125-seat auditorium; classrooms; lecture rooms; studios.
Activities: lectures; formally organized education programs for undergraduates.
Publications: catalogs, Effective Sight: The Paintings of Juan Logan; Self-Made Worlds: Visionary Folk Art Environments; Hung Liu: Washington Town Blues; The Right to Assemble, With Beauty Before Us: The Navajo of Chil Chen Beto; Pop-Luxe: The Language of the Garment; Cheryl Goldsleger: Improvisations; Black Boiled Coffee and the Cacophony of Frogs; Evon Streetman in Retrospect; Appropriate to the Moment: The Paintings of Michael Tyzack; Clifton Peacock's Failure Journal; No Man's Land: Fragile Ecologies and Contemporary Photographs; Alive Inside: The Lure & Lore of the Sideshow; Force of Nature: Site Installations by Ten Japanese Artists; Aldwyth: work v./work n.

Hours & Admission Prices: Sept.-June Mon.-Sat. 11-4. No charge; donations accepted. ♿
Attendance: 7,000 (estimated)
Membership: Conceptualist $10; Minimalist $15; Modernist & Postmodernist $25; Impressionist $50; Expressionist $100; Futurist $250; Going for Baroque $500 & up.

HISTORIC CHARLESTON FOUNDATION, 40 E. Bay, Charleston, SC 29401-2547. Mailing Address: P.O. Box 1120, Charleston, SC 29402-1120. Tel.: 843-723-1623. Fax: 843-577-2067.
E-mail: krobinson@historiccharleston.org
Web Site: historiccharleston.org
Founded: 1947.
Congressional District: 1
Key Personnel: Exec. Dir., Katharine S. Robinson; Dir. Museums & Preservation, Winslow Hastie; Dir. Reproductions, Stephen Hanson; Dir. Communications, Leigh Handal; Dir. Finance, Cynthia Ellis; Dir. Devel., Kathryn Matthew; Dir. Operations, Betty Guerard; Cur., Brandy Culp; Museum Shop Mgr., Rich Gaskalla.
Personnel Profile: Full-Time Paid 24; Part-Time Paid 76; Part-Time Volunteers 500; Interns 6.
Governing Authority: nonprofit organization. Branch Museums: c.1808 Nathaniel Russell House, 51 Meeting St.; c.1818 Aiken-Rhett House, 48 Elizabeth St. Tax-exempt: 501(c)(3).
Foundation Operated House Museums: housed in the Captain James Missroon House; built in 1789.
Collections: fine & decorative arts of the period 1750-1860 with emphasis on Charleston made objects.
Research Fields: preservation of historic houses & buildings; neighborhood revitalization; decorative & fine arts; Charleston social history, African-American history.
Facilities: reproduction shop; preservation center; administrative offices.
Activities: guided & audio tours; lectures; formally organized education programs for docents.
Publications: Grandeur Preserved: The House Museums of Historic Charleston Foundation (2008); occasional technical publications; newsletter, Historic Charleston Foundation; HCF Annual Report.
Hours & Admission Prices: Mon.-Sat. 10-5, Sun. 2-5. $10 per house or combination with Aiken-Rhett House $16, youth 6-16 $5. Private Home Tours: mid-March to mid-April. Adults $45. Closed Thanksgiving; Christmas Eve & Day. ♿
Attendance: 80,000 (accurate)

JOHN RIVERS COMMUNICATIONS MUSEUM, 58 George St., College of Charleston, Charleston, SC 29424-0001. Tel.: 843-953-5810.
E-mail: zenderr@cofc.edu
Web Site: www.cofc.edu/~jrmuseum
Founded: 1989.
Key Personnel: Cur., Rick Zender.
Personnel Profile: Full-Time Paid 1; Part-Time Paid 1; Part-Time Volunteers 1.
Governing Authority: state; public college; nonprofit. Parent Institution: College of Charleston.
Communications Museum: housed in the c.1803 Barnard Elliott House.
Collections: historical artifacts which provide a forum for understanding the scientific & social implications of communications; authentic communications hardware including the pre-1950 phonograph, radio, telegraph and television.
Facilities: 30-seat auditorium.
Activities: documentary film & discussion series; formal education programs for adults & children; guided tours; lectures; school loan service.
Hours & Admission Prices: Mon.-Fri. 12-4 & by appointment. Summer hours vary. No charge; donations accepted. Closed federal, national, state & school holidays.
Attendance: 3,000 (estimated)

MACAULAY MUSEUM OF DENTAL HISTORY, Medical University of South Carolina, 175 Ashley Ave., Charleston, SC 29425-0001. Mailing Address: 175 Ashley Ave., Box 250403, Charleston, SC 29425-0001. Tel.: 843-792-2288. Fax: 843-792-8619.
E-mail: waringhl@musc.edu
Web Site: waring.library.musc.edu
Founded: 1975.
Congressional District: 1
Key Personnel: Cur., Susan Hoffius; Asst. Cur., Kay Carter.
Personnel Profile: Full-Time Paid 4; Part-Time Paid 2.
Governing Authority: state. Parent Institution: Medical University of South Carolina. Tax-exempt.
Dental Museum.
Collections: 6,000 items including early dental chairs, foot powered drills, wooden dental cabinets, dental lathe, old dental X-ray units, itinerant dentists' medicine cases, cases of molds for crowns, dental turn keys, & period dental instruments; manuscripts.
Research Fields: antique dental instruments and equipment of South Carolina dentists.
Facilities: 200-vol. library of medical and dental textbooks of the late 19th and early 20th centuries and books on the history of dentistry available for research on premises.
Activities: guided tours; lectures; permanent exhibitions.
Publications: brochure.
Hours & Admission Prices: Mon.-Fri. 8:30-5; by appointment. No charge; donations accepted. Closed holidays.
Attendance: 250
Membership: Student $5; Regular $20; Contributing $100; Life $1,000.

MAGNOLIA PLANTATION AND GARDENS, 3550 Ashley River Rd., Charleston, SC 29414-7127. Tel.: 843-571-1266. Fax: 843-571-5346.
E-mail: tours@magnoliaplantation.com
Web Site: magnoliaplantation.com
Founded: 1676.
Key Personnel: Dir., F. Preston Wilson; Museum Shop Mgr., Ann McGinnis.
Personnel Profile: Full-Time Paid 40; Part-Time Paid 25; Part-Time Volunteers 18.
Governing Authority: nonprofit. Parent Institution: Magnolia Plantation Corp.
Historic House and Gardens: c.1680s Drayton family home & gardens.
Collections: early natural history & wildlife art; early American furniture.
Research Fields: general horticulture & history.
Facilities: botanical garden; zoological park; 60 acres Audubon swamp garden; nature tours. Art items for sale.
Activities: guided tours.
Publications: brochure; historic book of plantation; art book.
Hours & Admission Prices: Daily 9-5. Plantation: adults $15, children 6-12 $10; discounts to groups, and AAM & ICOM members; children under 6 no charge. House Museum: admission $7; children under 6 no charge. Audubon Swamp Garden: admission $7; children under 6 no charge. Nature Train Tour & Nature Boat Tour $7.
Attendance: 135,500 (estimated)
Membership: Individual $55; Family $75.

MIDDLETON PLACE HOUSE MUSEUM, (M), 4300 Ashley River Rd., Charleston, SC 29414-7206. Tel.: 843-556-6020. Fax: 843-766-4460.
E-mail: ttodd@middletonplace.org
Web Site: middletonplace.org
Founded: 1974.
Key Personnel: Pres., Charles H.P. Duell; Vice Pres. Accounting, Ileen Grange; Vice Pres. Museums, M. Tracey Todd; Archivist, Barbara Doyle; Mgr. Communications, Rani Colbert; Vice Pres. Devel., Libby Skelly; Vice Pres. Mktg., Pat Kennedy; Membership Coord., Sue Braund; Security, Jim Woodle; Museum Shop Mgr., Maria Keneally.
Personnel Profile: Part-Time Volunteers 300.
Governing Authority: public; nonprofit foundation. Parent Institution: Middleton Place Foundation. Subsidiary Institution: Edmondston-Alston House, Charleston, SC. Tax-exempt: 501(c)(3).
Historic House: restored 1755 structure.
Collections: concentration on mid-18th century to present American history; special emphasis on agrarian life of 19th-century Carolina Low Country.
Research Fields: life & work of artist John Izard Middleton, 1785-1849; Henry Middleton, 1770-1846, Minister to Russia (1820-1830); diplomacy; family history; political, cultural & decorative arts influences of period; African-American history & culture; botanical history of gardens & landscape architecture; Arthur Middleton, signer of the Declaration of Independence (1742-1787).
Facilities: 1,000-vol. history library including periodicals & pamphlets; 65-acre garden; 250-seat restaurant. Craft items, folk art, historic reproductions of glassware, furniture & porcelain, books on gardening & estate jewelry and other museum-related items for sale.
Activities: guided tours; lectures; concerts; docent program; participatory exhibits.
Publications: quarterly newsletter, The Notebook.
Hours & Admission Prices: Garden & Plantation Stableyards: daily 9-5. House Museum: Mon. 12-4:30, Tues.-Sun. 10-4:30. House Guided Tour: $10. Garden & Planetarium: adult $25, children 7-15 $5. ♿
Attendance: 100,000 (estimated)
Membership: Couple $100; Multiple $200.

OLD EXCHANGE & PROVOST DUNGEON, 122 E. Bay St., Charleston, SC 29401-2103. Tel.: 843-727-2165; 888-763-0448. Fax: 843-727-2163.
E-mail: oldexchange@infoave.net
Web Site: www.oldexchange.com

Founded: 1976.
Congressional District: 3
Key Personnel: Dir., Tony Youmans; Commission Chm., Mrs. Laura Kennedy LeGrand; Museum Shop Mgr., Suzanne Houser.
Personnel Profile: Full-Time Paid 9; Part-Time Paid 17; Part-Time Volunteers 1.
Governing Authority: state government. Parent Institution: Daughters of American Revolution. Subsidiary Institution: State of South Carolina. Management: City of Charleston, SC. Tax-exempt.
Historic Building: c.1771 The Old Exchange Building, based on its architectural distinction & its role in the formation of the United States, it is historically one of America's significant structures; an exchange & customs house, the building has maintained service to the people politically, socially, economically & educationally.
Collections: colonial artifacts; postal exhibits; civil war art; photographs and history of pirates of the Carolinas.
Facilities: historical tour & educational group destination; banquet facilities. Gift items for sale.
Activities: tours; lectures; organized education programs. Museum Sponsors: Colonial Christmas Program; Halloween Ghostly Guests story-telling presentation; Constitution Week in September.
Hours & Admission Prices: Daily 9-5. Adults $7, children 7-12 & students w/ID $3.50; discounts to AAA & AARP members, seniors, groups, military & students; Friends of the Old Exchange members no charge. Closed major holidays. ♿
Attendance: 56,242 (accurate)
Membership: Students $10; Members $25; $50; $75; $100.

THE OLD SLAVE MART MUSEUM, (M), 6 Chalmers St., Charleston, SC 29401-3005. Tel.: 843-724-3746. Fax: 843-724-3734.
E-mail: vaughn@ci.charleston.sc.us
Key Personnel: Dir., Nichole Green; Dir. Media Rels., Barbara Vaughn; Cur., Elaine Nichols; Archivist, Harlan Greene.
Governing Authority: city.
History Museum: housed in a former slave auction gallery; built in 1859.
Collections: African American history, arts & crafts.
Hours & Admission Prices: Mon.-Sat. 9-5. Closed New Year's Day; Thanksgiving; Christmas.

THE POWDER MAGAZINE, 79 Cumberland St., Charleston, SC 29401-3112. Mailing Address: P.O. Box 22127, Charleston, SC 29413-2127. Tel.: 843-722-9350. Fax: 843-722-3711.
E-mail: powdermag1712@bellsouth.net
Web Site: www.powdermag.org
Founded: 1713.
Congressional District: 1
Key Personnel: Dir., Alan Stello; Chm. (V), Margaret von Werssowetz.
Governing Authority: Parent Institution: National Society of the Colonial Dames of America in the State of South Carolina. Tax-exempt.
History Museum: housed in c. 1713 Powder Magazine.
Collections: artifacts; displays; audio presentations.
Activities: colonial living history; demonstrations; permanent exhibitions.
Publications: The Powder Keg.
Hours & Admission Prices: Mon.-Sat. 10-4, Sun. 1-4. Adults $2, children $1.
Attendance: 12,000 (estimated)

SOUTH CAROLINA AQUARIUM, 100 Aquarium Wharf, Charleston, SC 29401-6300. Tel.: 843-720-1990. Fax: 843-720-3861.
Web Site: www.scaquarium.org
Founded: 2000.
Key Personnel: Cur., Rachel Kalisperis; Education, Whit McMillan; Public Rels., Beth Nathan; Dir. Human Resources, Keisha Legerton.
Personnel Profile: Full-Time Paid 70; Part-Time Volunteers 350; Interns 16.
Governing Authority: private; nonprofit organization. Tax-exempt: 501(c)(3).
Aquarium.
Collections: South Carolina's marine & freshwater animals & plants; aquatic organisms from around the world; videos.
Research Fields: fisheries; shellfish; plankton; marketing & visitor studies; sea turtle rehabilitation.
Facilities: library; aquarium; educational facilities; 75,000 sq. ft. exhibit space; stranded sea turtle rehabilitation hospital. Aquarium-related items for sale.
Activities: docent program; formal education programs; participatory exhibits; rental gallery; teachers training program. Annual Events: Community Appreciation Days in January; members' events; Scuba-do fundraiser.
Publications: quarterly members' magazine, Tributaries.
Hours & Admission Prices: March-Aug. daily 9-5; Sept.-Feb. daily 9-4. Adults $17, senior citizens $16, children 2-11 $10; discounts to groups; children one & under and members no charge. Closed Thanksgiving; Christmas. ♿
Attendance: 427,101 (accurate)
Membership: Individual $50; Dual $65; Individual Plus $75; Grandparent $80; Family $90; Family Plus $135; Friend $250 & up; Associate $500 & up; Patron $1,000 & up; Benefactor $2,500 & up.

SOUTH CAROLINA HISTORICAL SOCIETY, 100 Meeting St., Charleston, SC 29401-2215. Tel.: 843-723-3225. Fax: 843-723-8584.
E-mail: info@schsonline.org
Web Site: www.schsonline.org
Founded: 1855.
Congressional District: 1
Key Personnel: Asst. Dir., John Tucker; C.E.O. & Dir., Faye L. Jensen, Ph.D.; Chm. (V), Thomas S. Tisdale, Jr.; Archivist & Research Consultant, Jane Aldrich; Membership, Stephanie Patterson; Publications, Matt Lockhart; Reference, Mary Jo Fairchild; Programs, Gloria Perla.
Personnel Profile: Full-Time Paid 7; Part-Time Paid 3; Part-Time Volunteers 5; Interns 2.
Governing Authority: nonprofit organization. Tax-exempt: 501(c)(3).
Historical Society Library & Archives: housed in 1822 Robert Mills Building.
Collections: manuscripts; photographs; art; architectural records; maps, plats & monuments; printed material; books; genealogical charts; maritime Civil War research materials & artifacts.
Research Fields: Civil War artifacts; 1700-1900 manuscripts.
Facilities: 40,000-vol. library of books & manuscripts, available to the public; reading room.
Activities: lectures; loan & temporary exhibitions. Society Sponsors: fall plantation tour; annual meeting & house tour; symposia.
Publications: quarterly magazines, South Carolina Historical Magazine; Carologue.
Hours & Admission Prices: Tues.-Fri. 9-4, Sat. 9-2. Adults $5; children & members no charge. Closed federal holidays; New Year's Eve & Day; Christmas Eve, Day & week.
Attendance: 3,500 (estimated)
Membership: Young Carolinians $35; Regular & Libraries $55; Sustainer $100 & up; Business & Corporation $1,000 & up; Sponsor $500; Patron $1,000; Benefactor $2,000 & up.

WARING HISTORICAL LIBRARY, Medical University of South Carolina, 175 Ashley Ave., Charleston, SC 29425-0001. Mailing Address: P.O. Box 250403, Charleston, SC 29425-0001. Tel.: 843-792-2288. Fax: 843-792-8619.
Web Site: waring.library.musc.edu
Founded: 1966.
Congressional District: 1
Key Personnel: Dir., W. Curtis Worthington, Jr., M.D.; Cur., Susan Hoffius; Assoc. Cur., Kay Carter.
Personnel Profile: Full-Time Paid 4; Part-Time Paid 2.
Governing Authority: state. Parent Institution: Medical University of South Carolina. Subsidiary Institution: Health Sciences Library. Tax-exempt.
University Medical Museum & Library: housed in 1894 building designed by architect John Snook.
Collections: medical objects including doctors' saddle bags, medicine chests, amputation kits, electro-therapeutic machines, bleeding instruments, obstetrical specula and forceps; pharmaceutical items; manuscripts; books authored by South Carolinians.
Research Fields: period instruments & equipment of physicians, nurses and pharmacists of South Carolina.
Facilities: 14,000-vol. library of books on the history of the health sciences, particularly medicine; old & new books by South Carolinians available for research.
Activities: guided tours; permanent & temporary exhibitions.
Publications: brochure; newsletter.
Hours & Admission Prices: Mon.-Fri. 8:30-5. No charge; donations accepted. Closed holidays. ♿
Membership: Student $5; Regular $20; Contributing $100; Life $1,000.

Cheraw

CHERAW LYCEUM MUSEUM, 200 Market St., Cheraw, SC 29520-2414. Mailing Address: P.O. Box 219, Cheraw, SC 29520-0219. Tel.: 843-537-8401 & 8425. Fax: 843-537-8407.
Web Site: www.cheraw.com
Founded: 1962.
Congressional District: 5
Key Personnel: C.E.O., J. William Taylor; Treas., Helen D. Funderburk; Cur., Sarah C. Spruill.
Personnel Profile: Part-Time Paid 1; Part-Time Volunteers 2.
Governing Authority: municipal; nonprofit. Parent Institution: Town of Cheraw. Tax-exempt: 501(c)(3).
History Museum: housed in a former court building; built in 1825
Collections: Revolutionary War artifacts; clothing & personal items of early

19th century; Civil War artifacts; products of present industries; Cheraw Indian artifacts & displays; artifacts from steamboat era; 19th-century bank notes & commercial ledgers.
Research Fields: local history; life on Great Pee Dee River; Cheraw Indians; Confederate War; steamboat era; Dizzy Gillespie memorabilia.
Activities: guided tours; arts festivals.
Publications: brochures.
Hours & Admission Prices: Mon.-Fri. 9-5, Sat.-Sun. by appointment. No charge; donations accepted.
Attendance: 4,000 (estimated)

Chester

CHESTER COUNTY HISTORICAL SOCIETY MUSEUM, 107 McAliley St., Chester, SC 29706-1741. Mailing Address: P.O. Box 811, Chester, SC 29706-0811. Tel.: 803-385-2330 & 581-4354.
Founded: 1959.
Congressional District: 6
Key Personnel: Museum Dir., Liz Anderson.
Governing Authority: society; nonprofit organization. Tax-exempt.
Historical Society Museum: housed in 1914 Chester County Jail.
Collections: Gatlin Catawba Indian collection of more than 30,000 artifacts; 1825 Mills' Atlas of South Carolina; portraits of the four former Chester County residents who were signers of the Ordinance of Secession.
Activities: permanent exhibitions.
Publications: quarterly newsletter.
Hours & Admission Prices: Wed. & Fri.-Sat. 10-3, 1st Sun. of month 2-5. Adults $3; members no charge.
Attendance: 300 (estimated)
Membership: Student & Senior $15; Single $20; Family $40.

Clemson

BOB CAMPBELL GEOLOGY MUSEUM, 140 Discovery Lane, Clemson University, Clemson, SC 29634-0001. Tel.: 864-656-4600. Fax: 864-656-4600.
E-mail: bcgm@clemson.edu
Web Site: www.clemson.edu/geomuseum
Founded: 1989.
Key Personnel: Dir., Todd Steadman; Cur., David Cicimurri; Cur. Education, Christian Cicimurri; Museum Shop Mgr., Darlene Evans.
Personnel Profile: Full-Time Paid 3; Part-Time Paid 3; Part-Time Volunteers 12.
Governing Authority: public university; nonprofit. Parent Institution: Clemson University. Tax-exempt.
Geology Museum.
Collections: minerals; gems; fossils; rocks from around the world; meteorites; mining artifacts; fluorescent minerals; skeletal reproduction of saber-toothed cat.
Research Fields: vertebrate paleontology.
Facilities: 1,200-vol. library of geological books, journals & special reports; botanical garden; 2,700 sq. ft. exhibit space; 100 sq. ft. outdoor mining display. Museum-related items for sale.
Activities: guided tours; scout programs by request; after school programs; monthly hikes. Museum Sponsors: Lapidary Arts demonstration in April; Earth Science Week in October; Identification Day.
Publications: semiannual member newsletter, The Geological Record.
Hours & Admission Prices: Garden: daily dawn to dusk. Museum: Wed.-Sat. 10-5, Sun. 1-5. Adults $3, children $2; discounts to SCFM (South Carolina Federation of Museums); museum members, children under 2 & Clemson University students no charge. Closed major holidays & home football games. ♿
Attendance: 8,000 (estimated)
Membership: Individual $35; Family $50; Patron $1,000.

FORT HILL (THE JOHN C. CALHOUN HOUSE), Fort Hill St., Clemson University, Clemson, SC 29634-5615. Mailing Address: Box 345615, Trustee House, Clemson University, Clemson, SC 29634-0001. Tel.: 864-656-2475. Fax: 864-656-1026.
E-mail: hiottw@clemson.edu
Web Site: www.clemson.edu/about/history/properties/fort-hill.html
Founded: 1889.
Congressional District: 3
Key Personnel: Dir., William D. Hiott, Sr
Personnel Profile: Full-Time Paid 2; Part-Time Paid 6; Part-Time Volunteers 10; Interns 18.
Governing Authority: university; society. Parent Institution: Clemson University. Tax-exempt: 501(c)(3).
Historic House Museum: c.1803 home of John C. Calhoun, 1825-1850.
Collections: original furnishings; Flemish & family portraits; personal artifacts; government documents.
Research Fields: American & Clemson history; architecture; decorative arts; horticulture.
Facilities: Museum-related items for sale.
Activities: guided tours; lectures.
Publications: brochure.
Hours & Admission Prices: Mon.-Sat. 10-12 & 1-4:30, Sun. 2-4:30. Suggested Donation: adults $5, senior & student $4, children $2; discounts to groups, AAM & ICOM members. Closed university holidays.
Attendance: 23,583 (accurate)

HANOVER HOUSE, South Carolina Botanical Garden, Perimeter Rd., Clemson University, Clemson, SC 29634-0001. Mailing Address: Box 345615, Historic Properties, Clemson University, Clemson, SC 29634-5615. Tel.: 864-656-2241 & 2475. Fax: 864-656-1026.
E-mail: hiottw@clemson.edu
Web Site: www.clemson.edu/about/history/properties/hanover-house.html
Founded: 1941.
Congressional District: 3
Key Personnel: Dir. & Cur., William D. Hiott, Sr.
Governing Authority: university; society. Parent Institution: Clemson University. Tax-exempt: 501(c)(3).
Historic House Museum: c.1716 Hanover House.
Collections: period furnishings; 18th-19th century artifacts.
Research Fields: early modern Europe; Colonial America; early American Colonial architecture; Huguenots.
Activities: guided tours; lectures.
Publications: Hanover House.
Hours & Admission Prices: Sat. 10-12 & 1-5, Sun. 2-5; groups & other times by appointment. Suggested Donations: adults $5, seniors $4, children $2; discounts for AAM & ICOM members; members no charge. Closed university holidays. ♿

RUDOLPH E. LEE GALLERY, G-50 Lee Hall, Clemson University, Clemson, SC 29634-0001. Mailing Address: P.O. Box 340509, Clemson, SC 29634-0001. Tel.: 864-656-3899. Fax: 864-656-7523.
E-mail: woodwaw@exchange.clemson.edu
Web Site: www.clemson.edu/caah/leegallery
Founded: 1956.
Key Personnel: Pres., James F. Barker; Dir., Denise Woodward-Detrich; Membership, Jennifer Staley; Volunteer Coord., Fleming Markel.
Governing Authority: university. Parent Institution: Clemson University. Tax-exempt.
Art Gallery.
Collections: paintings; graphics; photography; architecture projects.
Facilities: 2,400 sq. ft. exhibit space.
Activities: guided tours; lectures; films; gallery talks; inter-museum loan, permanent, temporary & traveling exhibitions.
Publications: exhibition posters; Clemson National Print and Drawing catalog.
Hours & Admission Prices: Mon.-Thurs. 9-4:30, Sun. 2-5. No charge. Closed university, state & national holidays.

THE SOUTH CAROLINA BOTANICAL GARDEN, 150 Discovery Lane, Clemson University, Clemson, SC 29634-0174. Tel.: 864-656-3405 & 2458. Fax: 864-656-6230.
E-mail: scbg@clemson.edu
Web Site: www.clemson.edu/scbg
Founded: 1961.
Congressional District: 3
Key Personnel: Dir., John W. Kelly; Dir. Education, Lisa Wagner; Creative Awareness & Nature-Based Sculpture Program Facilitator, Ernie Denny; Garden Mgr., James Arnold; Sr. Horticulturist, John Bodiford; Horticulturist, Mac Sprott; Facilities Mgr., Eric Soto; Garden Rentals & Visitor Svcs. Mgr., Judith Gardner.
Personnel Profile: Full-Time Paid 8; Part-Time Paid 8; Part-Time Volunteers 50; Interns 1.
Governing Authority: university. Parent Institution: Clemson University. Tax-exempt.
Botanical Garden: located on part of the original John C. Calhoun Plantation Estate.
Collections: niche gardens; natural woodlands; historic buildings.
Research Fields: plant introductions with USDA; turf grass research plots.
Facilities: botanical garden; classrooms; visitor center; geology museum; cafe.
Activities: guided tours; lectures; formally organized education programs for undergraduate & graduate students; visual & performing arts programs; nature, science & gardening programs; nature walks; cultural festivals; educational series.
Publications: quarterly newsletter, The South Carolina Botanical Garden Quarterly.

Hours & Admission Prices: Daily dawn-dusk. No charge; donations accepted. ♿
Attendance: 100,000 (estimated)
Membership: Contributor $25-$99; Sustaining $100-$249; Associate $250-$499; Patron $500-$999; Benefactor $1,000-$4,999; Fellow $5,000-$9,999; Founder $10,000 & up.

STROM THURMOND INSTITUTE, Clemson University, Silas Pearman Blvd., Clemson, SC 29634-0001. Tel.: 864-656-4700. Fax: 864-656-4780.
E-mail: sti-web@strom.clemson.edu
Web Site: www.strom.clemson.edu
Key Personnel: Dir., Dr. Robert H. Becker.
Governing Authority: nonprofit.
Archive.
Collections: Senator Thurmond's personal papers & memorabilia.
Hours & Admission Prices: Mon.-Fri. 8-4:30. No charge. Closed New Year's Day; Spring break in March; Independence Day; Oct. break; Thanksgiving weekend; Christmas break.

Columbia

COLUMBIA FIRE DEPARTMENT MUSEUM, 1800 Laurel St., Columbia, SC 29201-2627. Tel.: 803-733-8350. Fax: 803-733-8311.
E-mail: cfdjreich@columbiasc.net
Web Site: www.columbiasouthcarolina.com/fire-museum.html
Founded: 1996.
Key Personnel: C.E.O., John D. Jansen, Jr.; Cur., John G. Reich.
Personnel Profile: Full-Time Paid 2.
Governing Authority: municipal government; nonprofit.
Fire-Fighting Museum.
Collections: 1903 metropolitan horse drawn steamer; history of fire service in Columbia, South Carolina.
Research Fields: black history; oral history.
Facilities: 100-vol. library of scrapbooks & yearbooks; classroom.
Publications: committee newsletter published three times annually.
Hours & Admission Prices: Mon.-Fri. 8:30-5, Sat.-Sun. by appointment. No charge; donations accepted. ♿
Attendance: 10,000 (estimated)

* **COLUMBIA MUSEUM OF ART,** 1515 Main St., Columbia, SC 29201. Mailing Address: P.O. Box 2068, Columbia, SC 29202-2068. Tel.: 803-799-2810. Fax: 803-343-2150.
E-mail: ewoodoff@columbiamuseum.org
Web Site: www.columbiamuseum.org
Founded: 1950.
Congressional District: 2
Key Personnel: Exec. Dir., Karen Brosius; Chief Cur., Dr. Todd Herman; Deputy Dir., Joelle Ryan Cook; Dir. Education, Ali Borchardt; Dir. Facility Operations, Michael Roh; Dir. Devel., Scott Nolan; Dir. Mktg. & Communications, Ellen Woodoff; Mgr. Human Resources, Teri Keener Seybt.
Personnel Profile: Full-Time Paid 30; Part-Time Paid 21; Part-Time Volunteers 100; Interns 4.
Governing Authority: nonprofit organization. Tax-exempt: 501(c)(3).
Art Museum.
Collections: European & American fine and decorative arts from the 14th century to present: Samuel H. Kress Collection of Renaissance and Baroque art; painting; prints; sculpture; furniture; ceramics; 19th & 20th century design; photography.
Major Exhibits: Ansel Adams: Masterworks from the Collection of the Turtle Bay Exploration Center, 11/09-1/17/10; Dorothy & Herbert Vogel Collection - 50 Works For 50 States, 11/09-1/17/10; The Chemistry of Color: Contemporary African American Artists, 2/5/10-5/9/10; Innovation and Change: Great Ceramics fro the Ceramics Research Center, 5/27/10-9/5/10.
Research Fields: items pertaining to the collections: European & American fine design & decorative arts; general art.
Facilities: 14,000-vol. library of art history books, journals, and artist files available for on-site research; art studios; 154-seat auditorium; rental facilities. Museum-related items for sale.
Activities: guided tours; training programs; lectures; concerts; films; gallery talks; art classes; family programs.
Publications: collections; annual report; exhibition catalogs.
Hours & Admission Prices: Wed.-Sat. 10-5, 1st Fri. of month 10-8, Sun. 12-5. Adults $10, seniors 65 & over and military $8, students $5; discounts to AAM & ICOM members; children 5 & under, members & Sun. no charge. Closed major holidays. ♿
Attendance: 128,000 (accurate)
Membership: Individual $35; Dual $50; Kids Plus $60; Patron $200; Premier Society $500 & up.

EDVENTURE, INC., 211 Gervais St., Columbia, SC 29201-3067. Mailing Address: P.O. Box 1638, Columbia, SC 29202-1638. Tel.: 803-779-3100. Fax: 803-779-3144.
E-mail: info@edventure.org
Web Site: www.edventure.org
Founded: 1994.
Congressional District: 2
Key Personnel: C.E.O. & Pres., Catherine Wilson Horne; Chm., Michael Borden; Vice Pres. Museum Operations, Julia Kennard; Treas., Britt Borders; Dir. Education, Susan Bonk; Dir. Mktg., Jennifer Suber; Museum Shop Mgr., Julia Kennard.
Personnel Profile: Full-Time Paid 26; Part-Time Paid 40; Part-Time Volunteers 100; Interns 5.
Governing Authority: private; nonprofit organization. Parent Institution: Ed-Venture Inc. Tax-exempt: 501(c)(3).
Children's Museum.
Collections: hands-on learning & discovery; exhibits & programs on health & wellness, communities, communications, environment & international cultures.
Major Exhibits: Team Up! (T), 11/09-1/4/10; Blue Man Group (T), 6/19/10-9/20/10.
Facilities: 67,000 sq. ft. with 8,000 sq. ft. of outdoor exhibits.
Activities: formal education programs for children; traveling exhibitions; school outreach programs.
Publications: bimonthly newsletter.
Hours & Admission Prices: Summer: Mon.-Sat. 9-5, Sun. 12-5; Winter: Tues.-Sat. 9-5, Sun. 12-5. Adults $8.95, children 2-12 $6.95; members no charge. Closed Thanksgiving; Christmas Eve & Day. ♿
Attendance: 200,000 (estimated)
Membership: Weekday $80; Anytime $130; Passport $160; Pal $500-$999; Friend $1,000-$2,499; Patron $5,000-$9,999; Best Friend $2,500-$4,000; Benefactor $10,000 & up. (Add-A-Member $25)

GOVERNOR'S MANSION, 800 Richland St., Columbia, SC 29201-2397. Tel.: 803-737-1710. Fax: 803-737-3860.
E-mail: nbunch@gov.sc.gov
Web Site: www.scgovernorsmansion.org
Founded: 1855.
Key Personnel: C.E.O., Gov. Mark Sanford; Chm. (V), Mary Ross; Cur. & Tour Dir., Nancy B. Bunch; Museum Shop Mgr., Elizabeth Crews.
Personnel Profile: Full-Time Paid 8; Full-Time Volunteers 40; Part-Time Paid 1; Part-Time Volunteers 50.
Governing Authority: state. Governor's Mansion Commission. Tax-exempt.
Historic House: 1855 Governor's Residence.
Collections: furniture; paintings; objects of art which pertain to the history of this state; historical garden. Historic Houses: 1854 The Lace House; 1830 The Caldwell-Boylston House.
Facilities: botanical garden.
Activities: guided tours by appointment; docent program or council; loan, permanent & temporary exhibitions.
Hours & Admission Prices: Tours: summer: Tues.-Wed. 10, 10:30 & 11; winter, spring & fall: Tues.-Thurs. 10, 10:30 & 11. No charge; donations accepted. ♿
Attendance: 12,000 (accurate)

* **HISTORIC COLUMBIA FOUNDATION, (M),** 1601 Richland St., Columbia, SC 29201-2633. Tel.: 803-252-7742, ext. 24. Fax: 803-929-7695.
E-mail: rwaites@historiccolumbia.org
Web Site: www.historiccolumbia.org
Founded: 1961.
Congressional District: 6
Key Personnel: Exec. Dir., Robin Waites; Chmn. (V), Susan Brill; Dir. Cultural Resources, John Sherrer, III; Coord. Visitor & Volunteer Svcs., Ann Posner.
Personnel Profile: Full-Time Paid 12; Part-Time Paid 15; Part-Time Volunteers 200; Interns 2.
Governing Authority: nonprofit organization. Subsidiary Institutions: Mann-Simons Cottage; Woodrow Wilson Family Home; Robert Mills House; Hampton-Preston Mansion; Modjeska Simkins House. Tax-exempt: 501(c)(3).
Historical Society Museum.
Collections: Empire period decorative arts; Wade Hampton family artifacts; Victorian items & decorative arts; Woodrow Wilson material. Historic Houses: Seibels House & Big Apple Club.
Research Fields: local & state history; 19th-century decorative arts; Wade Hampton & Woodrow Wilson families; 19th- & 20th-century architectural history; African-American consumption patterns, 19th-20th century.
Facilities: 11 acres of historical gardens.
Activities: historic house & walking tours; lectures; films; heritage tours; workshops; speaker's bureau; preservation advocacy; rental facility.

Publications: Historic Columbia Foundation News; Richland County's Rural African American School, 1895-1954; Experience Historic Columbia, Main Street Columbia, SC.
Hours & Admission Prices: Robert Mills, Hampton-Preston, Woodrow Wilson & Mann-Simions: Tues.-Sat. 10-4, Sun. 1-5. Houses: $6 each; discounts to AAM, AAA & SEMC members, senior citizens, teachers, students, military; members, Seibels House & Big Apple no charge.
Attendance: 25,000 (estimated)
Membership: Individual $35; Family $50; Friend $100; Woodrow Wilson Society $250; Mamn-Simons Society $500; Hampton-Preston Society $1,000; Seibels Society $2,500; Robert Mills Society $5,000.

THE MUSEUM OF EDUCATION, University of South Carolina, Wardlaw Hall, Greene St., Columbia, SC 29208-0001. Tel.: 803-777-5741.
E-mail: museumofeducation@sc.edu
Web Site: www.ed.sc.edu/MusofEd/index.htm
Key Personnel: Cur., Dr. Craig Kridel
Education Museum.
Collections: exhibitions, publications & programs pertaining to the issues of education.
Hours & Admission Prices: Mon.-Fri. 9-4.

PONDER FINE ARTS GALLERY - BENEDICT COLLEGE, 1600 Harden St., Columbia, SC 29204. Tel.: 803-253-5000.
Art Gallery.
Collections: paintings; photographs; sculpture.
Activities: permanent & temporary exhibits.
Hours & Admission Prices: Mon.-Fri. 10-4. No charge.

RIVERBANKS ZOO & GARDEN, 500 Wildlife Pkwy., Columbia, SC 29210-8093. Mailing Address: P.O. Box 1060, Columbia, SC 29202-1060. Tel.: 803-779-8717. Fax: 803-253-6381.
Web Site: www.riverbanks.org
Founded: 1974.
Congressional District: 6
Key Personnel: Exec. Dir., Palmer E. Krantz, III; Chm., Lloyd S. Liles; Dir. Mktg., Tommy Stringfellow; Financial Dir., George R. Davis; Dir. Animal Collections, Ed Diebold; Retail Sales Mgr., Jason Painter.
Personnel Profile: Full-Time Paid 126; Part-Time Paid 41; Part-Time Volunteers 349; Interns 12.
Governing Authority: nonprofit organization. Parent Institution: Riverbanks Park Commission. Tax-exempt: 501(c)(3).
Zoo & Botanical Garden.
Collections: Specimens: 265 birds; 106 mammals; 326 reptiles; 681 fish; 130 amphibians; Species: 54 birds; 43 mammals; 61 reptiles, 151 fish, 19 amphibians.
Research Fields: reproductive physiology.
Facilities: botanical garden; zoological park; cafeteria. Museum-related items for sale.
Activities: self-guided tours; lectures; concerts; radio programs; formally organized education programs for children & adults.
Publications: 6 issue magazine, Riverbanks.
Hours & Admission Prices: April 4-Oct. 4 Mon.-Fri. 9-5, Sat.-Sun. 9-6; Oct. 5-April 3 daily 9-5. Adults $9.75, military and seniors 62 & over $8.75, children 3-12 $7.25; discount to AZA members; AAZPA & AABGA members, reciprocal zoo societies, children under 3 & members no charge. Closed Thanksgiving; Christmas. ♿
Attendance: 872,000 (accurate)
Membership: Individual $34; Individual Plus $49; Family $59; Family Plus $74; Patron $125; Curators' Circle $250; Director's Circle $500.

* **SOUTH CAROLINA CONFEDERATE RELIC ROOM AND MILITARY MUSEUM, (M),** 301 Gervais St., Columbia, SC 29201-3041. Tel.: 803-737-8095 & 8093. Fax: 803-737-8099.
E-mail: jcassidy@crr.sc.gov
Web Site: www.crr.sc.gov.
Founded: 1896.
Congressional District: 2
Key Personnel: Dir., W. Allen Roberson; Admin. Coord. & Museum Shop Mgr., Shirley D. Schoonover; Cur. Education, William Joe Long; Cur. History, Kristina Dunn Johnson; Registrar, Rachel H. Cockrell; Public Information, Jai Cassidy-Shaiman.
Personnel Profile: Full-Time Paid 7; Part-Time Paid 3; Interns 2.
Governing Authority: state. Tax-exempt.
History Museum.
Collections: Civil War flags; South Carolina uniforms; weapons; archives; 19th-20th century textiles; South Carolina's military history from Revolutionary War to present.
Research Fields: South Carolina history.
Facilities: 5,550-vol. library of historical books, pamphlets & brochures available on the premises.
Activities: guided tours; lectures; permanent & temporary exhibitions.
Publications: e-newsletter, The Regimental Courier.
Hours & Admission Prices: Tues.-Sat. 10-5, 1st Sun. of month 1-5. Adults 18-61 $5, military & seniors $4, youth 13-17 $2; discounts 1st Sun. of month; children 12 & under no charge. Closed most state holidays. ♿
Attendance: 22,000 (accurate)

SOUTH CAROLINA DEPARTMENT OF ARCHIVES & HISTORY, 8301 Parklane Rd., Columbia, SC 29223-4905. Tel.: 803-896-6100. Fax: 803-896-6186.
Web Site: scdah.sc.gov/
Founded: 1905.
Congressional District: 2
Key Personnel: Dir., Rodger E. Stroup, Ph.D.; Chm. (V), A.V. Huff, Jr., Ph.D.; State Archivist & Records Admin., Roy H. Tryon; Dir. Historical Svcs., Elizabeth M. Johnson; Museum Shop Mgr., Dutch Hazewinkel.
Personnel Profile: Full-Time Paid 57; Full-Time Volunteers 1; Part-Time Volunteers 7; Interns 3.
Governing Authority: state.
State Government Historical Agency.
Collections: 27,000 cubic ft. of archival records; 5,000 books and periodicals; 20,000 reels of microfilm; 3,000 item map collection.
Research Fields: history of the state of South Carolina.
Facilities: reading room; meeting rooms; auditorium; multi-purpose classrooms; conservation shop; exhibit gallery.
Activities: temporary exhibitions; curriculum resources development; records management for state & local government; historic markers; national register nominations; historic preservation program; symposium; fundraisers; heritage lecture tours. Museum Sponsors: History Lovers' Market; Annual Statewide Historic Preservation Conference.
Publications: books, Biographical Directory of the House of Representatives; Colonial Records of South Carolina; State Records of South Carolina; brochures; documentary microfilm; popular historical booklets; electronic newsletter.
Hours & Admission Prices: Mon.-Fri. 8:30-5. No charge; donations accepted. Reference Room: closed state holidays. ♿
Attendance: 7,000 (estimated)
Membership: Individual $35; Family $60; Advocate $100; Guardian $250; Ambassador $500; Friend $1,000.

SOUTH CAROLINA DEPARTMENT OF PARKS, RECREATION AND TOURISM, 1205 Pendleton St., Columbia, SC 29201-3756. Tel.: 803-734-0156. Fax: 803-734-1017.
Web Site: www.southcarolinaparks.com
Founded: 1967.
Congressional District: 2
Key Personnel: Exec. Dir., Chad Prosser; Dir. Parks, Phil Gaines; Chief Resource Mgmt., Irvin Pitts; Chief Education & Interpretation, Terry Hurley; Recreation Mgr. & Biology Cur., Stan Hutto.
Personnel Profile: Full-Time Paid 30; Part-Time Paid 15; Part-Time Volunteers 10; Interns 3.
Governing Authority: state. Tax-exempt.
State Park & Museums.
Collections: Historic Houses and Sites: 1832 Rose Hill Plantation Home, Union County; 1756 settler's log dwelling, Richland County; c.1750 Hampton Plantation Home, Charleston County; 1858 Redcliffe Plantation Home, Aiken County. Atalaya, Huntington Beach State Park, Georgetown County: c.1933 Winter Home Archer & Anna Huntington. Historic Sites: Andrew Jackson State Park, Lancaster County: exhibits on country farmlife; Hunting Island Lighthouse Complex, Beaufort: maritime history; Old Dorchester State Park, Dorchester County: 18th century trading and religious settlement, exhibit; Rivers Bridge State Park, Bamberg County: Civil War Battle Site; 1823-50 Landsford Canal State Park, Chester County; 1670 Charles Towne Landing, Charleston County; Kings Mountain State Park, York County: living history farm; Keowee-Toxaway State Park, Pickens County: Cherokee Indian exhibits; Caesar's Head State Park, Greenville County; Hunting Island State Park, Beaufort County; Myrtle Beach State Park, Horry County; Oconee State Park, Oconee County; Poinsett State Park, Midlands-Sumter County.
Research Fields: history; decorative arts; archaeology; folklore; Indian artifacts; industry; marine; transportation; architecture; historic preservation.
Activities: guided tours; lectures; permanent & temporary exhibitions; school programs; organized historical & nature programming.
Publications: brochures; visitors guide.
Hours & Admission Prices: Contact individual park or site for hours & admissions.

SOUTH CAROLINA INSTITUTE OF ARCHAEOLOGY & ANTHROPOLOGY, 1321 Pendleton St., University of South Carolina, Columbia, SC 29208-4103. Tel.: 803-777-8170 & 734-0567. Fax: 803-254-1338.
Web Site: www.cas.sc.edu/sciaa
Founded: 1963.
Congressional District: 2
Key Personnel: Interim Dir., Charles Cobb; State Archaeologist, Jonathan M. Leader; Business Mgr., Susan Lowe; Cur., Sharon L. Pekrul.
Personnel Profile: Full-Time Paid 50; Part-Time Paid 24; Part-Time Volunteers 17; Interns 4.
Governing Authority: state; public college; nonprofit. Parent Institution: State of South Carolina. Subsidiary Institution: The University of South Carolina. Tax-exempt: 170(b)(1)(A).
State Agency; Archaeology & Anthropology Research Institute.
Collections: pre-historic & historic period Native American, African American and Euro American archaeological collections; ethnographic material; fossils & geological samples.
Research Fields: pre-history & history of South Carolina; French & Spanish presence in South Carolina; Civil War & plantation studies; Paleo-Indian studies; maritime studies; protohistoric Indian studies; private artifact collections survey.
Facilities: 29,000-vol. library of archaeology & anthropology reports & reference materials; archaeological site files, field & lab records and maps, photographs & slides; two artifact-processing laboratories; conservation laboratory with waterlogged wood treatment tank; conference room; photographic darkroom; field research station.
Activities: guided tours; lectures; organized education programs for undergraduate & graduate college students affiliated with University of South Carolina. Institution Sponsors: Archaeology Conference; Fall Field Day.
Publications: periodic research reports.
Hours & Admission Prices: Mon.-Fri. 8:30-5. No charge. Closed state holidays. ♿

SOUTH CAROLINA LAW ENFORCEMENT OFFICERS HALL OF FAME, 5400 Broad River Rd., Columbia, SC 29212-3540. Tel.: 803-896-8199. Fax: 803-896-8067.
Web Site: www.scdps.org/hof.asp
Formerly: South Carolina Criminal Justice Hall of Fame
Founded: 1979.
Key Personnel: Admin., Marsha T. Ardila; Administrative Asst., Kitty W. Kelly.
Personnel Profile: Full-Time Paid 3.
Governing Authority: state; nonprofit organization. Parent Institution: Dept. of Public Safety.
Law Museum.
Collections: artifacts related to the history of law enforcement in South Carolina.
Research Fields: historical development of law enforcement in South Carolina.
Facilities: 75-seat auditorium.
Activities: guided tours; permanent & temporary exhibitions.
Publications: brochures on Hall of Fame programs.
Hours & Admission Prices: Mon.-Fri. 8:30-5. No charge. Closed state holidays. ♿
Attendance: 7,000 (accurate)

SOUTH CAROLINA MILITARY MUSEUM, One National Guard Rd., Columbia, SC 29201-4752. Tel.: 803-806-4440. Fax: 803-806-2103.
Founded: 2007.
Congressional District: 5
Key Personnel: Dir. & Cur., Ewell G. Sturgis, Jr.; Chm. (V), Joey R. Preston; Registrar, Joy Maples; Museum Shop Mgr., Edward Y. Hall.
Personnel Profile: Full-Time Paid 2; Part-Time Volunteers 24.
Governing Authority: state; nonprofit. Parent Institution: South Carolina National Guard. Subsidiary Institution: South Carolina Military History Foundation Inc. Tax-exempt.
Military Museum.
Collections: South Carolina militia & National Guard memorabilia artillery.
Activities: guided tours.
Hours & Admission Prices: Tues.-Sat. 10-4, Sun. 1-4. No charge; donations accepted. ♿
Attendance: 6,000 (estimated)

∗ **SOUTH CAROLINA STATE MUSEUM, (M),** 301 Gervais St., Columbia, SC 29201. Tel.: 803-898-4921. Fax: 803-898-4969.
E-mail: publicrelations@scmuseum.org
Web Site: www.southcarolinastatemuseum.org
Founded: 1973.
Congressional District: 2
Key Personnel: Dir., William Calloway; Chm. (V), Gray Culbreath; Mgr. Human Resources, Susan Worthy; Cur. History, Fritz Hamer; Cur. Natural History, Jim Knight; Exhibit Dir., A. Michael Fey; Chief Registrar, Michelle Baker; Dir. Education, Meika Samuel; Cur. Art, Paul Matheny; Museum Shop Mgr., Scottie Ash; Dir. Public Information & Mktg., Tut Underwood.
Personnel Profile: Full-Time Paid 39; Part-Time Paid 36; Part-Time Volunteers 159; Interns 3.
Governing Authority: state. Parent Institution: State of South Carolina. Subsidiary Institution: South Carolina Museum Foundation. Tax-exempt: 170(b)(1)(A).
General Museum: housed in former textile mill building.
Collections: South Carolina history, natural history, art, science & technology.
Major Exhibits: Tangible History: Stoneware from the Holcombe Family Collection, 11/09-1/11; Mesozoic Monsters (T), 11/09-2/10; Deadly Medicine: Creating the Master Race (T), 11/09-2/14/10; From the Pee Dee to the Savannah Endwing Legacies of South Carolina's Fall Line Region, 11/09-3/22/10; Pirates, 3/10-9/10.
Research Fields: South Carolina art; local natural history; South Carolina culture.
Facilities: five changing galleries; 236-seat auditorium; multi-purpose meeting room; science demonstration theater; hands-on discovery center for children; nature program space; one-room schoolhouse; school group orientation room; two educational activity centers; conservation laboratory. Museum-related items for sale.
Activities: long-term, temporary & traveling exhibits; tours; education study visits; inter-museum loan exhibits; science & natural history demonstrations; museum personnel workshops; teacher workshops; facility use program; films; lectures; advisory services to other museums.
Publications: e-newsletter; bulletins; brochures, Common Snakes of South Carolina; magazine, Images.
Hours & Admission Prices: Memorial Day-Labor Day Mon.-Sat. 10-5, Sun. 1-5; Sept.-May Tues.-Sat. 10-5, Sun. 1-5. Adults 13 & over $7, military $6, senior citizens 62 & over $5, children 3-12 $3; discounts to groups of 10 or more, Southeastern Museums Conference & South Carolina Federation of Museums members; members, children under 3 & South Carolina school groups with advance notice no charge. Closed New Year's Day; Easter; Thanksgiving; Christmas Eve & Day. ♿
Attendance: 152,623 (accurate)
Membership: Individual $35; Dual $45; Family & Grandparent $60; Premier $100; Charter Collection $150; Director's Guild $250; Foundation Fellows $500; Trustee's Council $1,000.

∗ **THE UNIVERSITY OF SOUTH CAROLINA MCKISSICK MUSEUM, (M),** 816 Bull St., Columbia, SC 29208-0001. Tel.: 803-777-7251. Fax: 803-777-2829.
E-mail: robertso@mailbox.sc.edu
Web Site: www.cas.sc.edu/mcks/
Founded: 1976.
Congressional District: 2
Key Personnel: Exec. Dir., Lynn Robertson; Chief Cur. Exhibitions, Jason Shaiman; Chief Cur. Research & Folklife, Saddler Taylor; Cur. Temporary Exhibitions, Nathan Stalvey; Cur. Collections, Jill Koverman; Business Mgr., Peggy Nunn; Cur. Faculty, Lana Burgess; Visitor Svcs. Mgr., Ja-Nae Epps.
Personnel Profile: Full-Time Paid 8; Part-Time Paid 10; Part-Time Volunteers 30; Interns 2.
Governing Authority: university. Parent Institution: University of South Carolina. Tax-exempt: 170(b)(1)(A).
University Museum.
Collections: 19th- & 20th-century decorative arts; folk art & material culture of South Carolina and the South; Bernard Baruch silver; gems & minerals.
Major Exhibits: Natural Curiosity: Natural History Study at the University of South Carolina, 1/4/10-12/20/10; Grass Roots: African Origins of an American Art (T), 2/13/10-5/8/10; Spring for Art: Annual Gala Sale Exhibition, 5/22/10-7/31/10; A People of the Land: Low Country Portraits (T), 5/29/10-8/7/10; A Celebration of Barrier Islands: The Art of Mary Edna Fraser (T), 8/14/10-12/18/10.
Research Fields: university history; material & folklife culture of the Southeast; interdisciplinary Southern studies.
Facilities: library; folklife resource center; meeting room; auditorium.
Activities: guided tours; lectures; permanent, temporary & traveling exhibitions; concerts; demonstrations; academic classes; educational programs; workshops; meetings.
Publications: magazine; educator curriculum materials; catalogs; brochures; guides.
Hours & Admission Prices: Mon.-Fri. 8:30-5, Sat. 11-3. No charge; donations accepted. Closed Independence Day; Labor Day; Thanksgiving; Christmas to New Year's Day; University Holidays. ♿
Attendance: 35,000 (estimated)
Membership: Student $10; Individual $25; Dual $35; Household $50; Patron $100-$249; Sponsor $250-$499; Benefactor $500-$999; Director's Circle $1,000.

U.S. ARMY FINANCE CORPS MUSEUM, 4392 Magruder Ave., Columbia, SC 29207. Mailing Address: Commandant, U.S. Army Finance School, 10,000 Hampton Pkwy., Fort Jackson, SC 29207-7050. Tel.: 803-751-3771. Fax: 803-751-1749.
E-mail: atsg-fsa@jackson.army.mil
Founded: 1954.
Key Personnel: Cur., Henry D. Howe, III
Personnel Profile: Full-Time Paid 1.
Governing Authority: federal. Parent Institution: U.S. Army Center of Military History. Tax-exempt.
Military Museum.
Collections: history of the U.S. Army Finance Corps.; American currency from revolutionary war to present; U.S. military currency from Word War II through Vietnam.
Research Fields: military currency.
Activities: guided tours; lectures; traveling exhibitions.
Hours & Admission Prices: Tues.-Fri. 10-4. No charge. Closed federal holidays. ♿
Attendance: 12,000 (accurate)

Conway

HORRY COUNTY MUSEUM, (M), 428 Main St., Conway, SC 29526-4308. Tel.: 843-915-5320. Fax: 843-248-1854.
E-mail: hcgmuseum@horrycounty.org
Web Site: www.horrycountymuseum.org
Founded: 1979.
Congressional District: 6
Key Personnel: Dir., R. Walter Hill, IV; Education Specialist, Carmin F. Samaha.
Personnel Profile: Full-Time Paid 6; Part-Time Paid 1; Part-Time Volunteers 12; Interns 2.
Governing Authority: Parent Institution: Horry County Government.
Anthropology, History & Archaeology Museum.
Collections: material relating to local history, prehistory & natural history of the county.
Research Fields: local history; archaeology; technology; folklore.
Facilities: photographic archives; darkroom.
Activities: guided tours; lectures; hobby workshops; formally organized education programs for children; loan, permanent, temporary & traveling exhibitions; school loan service.
Hours & Admission Prices: Mon.-Sat. 9-5. No charge; donations accepted. Closed county government holidays. ♿
Attendance: 40,000 (estimated)

Darlington

DARLINGTON RACEWAY STOCK CAR MUSEUM, NMPA HALL OF FAME, 1301 Harry Byrd Hwy., Darlington, SC 29532-3517. Mailing Address: P.O. Box 500, Darlington, SC 29540-0500. Tel.: 843-395-8900. Fax: 843-393-3911.
E-mail: jmharris@darlingtonraceway.com
Web Site: www.darlingtonraceway.com
Formerly: NMPA Stock Car Hall of Fame, Joe Weatherly Museum
Founded: 1965.
Congressional District: 6
Key Personnel: Museum Shop Mgr., Vicki Sanders.
Governing Authority: nonprofit organization. Parent Institution: Americrown.
Stock Car Museum.
Collections: stock cars; photos; trophies; engines; stock car racers' Hall of Fame.
Facilities: Racing items for sale.
Activities: track tours.
Hours & Admission Prices: Mon.-Fri. 10-5, Sat. 10-4. Adults $5; children under 12 no charge. ♿
Attendance: 250,000 (estimated)

Dillon

JAMES W. DILLON HOUSE MUSEUM, 1302 W. Main St., Dillon, SC 29536. Mailing Address: Dillon County Historical Society, P.O. Box 1806, Dillon, SC 29536-1806. Tel.: 843-774-9051 & 6122. Fax: 843-774-5521.
Web Site: www.dillonmuseum.com
Founded: 1961.
Congressional District: 6
Key Personnel: Pres., Corky Lane; Resource Mgr., Don Barclay.
Personnel Profile: Part-Time Paid 1; Part-Time Volunteers 18.
Governing Authority: society; nonprofit. Parent Institution: Dillon County Historical Society. Tax-exempt: 501(c)(3).
Historic House.
Collections: period furniture & clothing; archives; 1910 kitchen.
Activities: guided tours.
Publications: brochures.
Hours & Admission Prices: Mon.-Sat. 2-4, Sun. 2-5; other times by appointment. No charge; donations accepted. Closed Easter; Independence Day; Thanksgiving; Christmas. ♿
Attendance: 364 (estimated)

Due West

BOWIE ARTS CENTER, Erskine College, Two Washington St., Due West, SC 29639. Mailing Address: P.O. Box 338, Due West, SC 26939-0338. Tel.: 864-379-8867. Fax: 864-379-2167.
E-mail: jwalker@erskine.edu
Key Personnel: Dir., Jan B. Walker
Art Gallery.
Collections: antique mechanical musical instruments; clocks; decorative arts; glass & porcelain; furnishings from the 19th & early 20th centuries; photographs.
Hours & Admission Prices: July Mon.-Sat. 2-4; Aug.-June Mon.-Thurs. 1-4:30, Sat. & 1st Sun. of the month 2-4; other times by appointment. No charge. Closed major holidays; college breaks.

Eastover

KENSINGTON MANSION, 4001 McCords Ferry Rd./ US 601, Eastover, SC 29044. Mailing Address: P.O. Box 237, Eastover, SC 29044-0237. Tel.: 803-353-0456. Fax: 803-353-0456.
Web Site: www.kensingtonmansion.org
Founded: 1996.
Key Personnel: Dir., Rickie Good; Chm. (V), Will Fowler.
Personnel Profile: Part-Time Paid 3; Part-Time Volunteers 15.
Governing Authority: nonprofit. Partner Institution: International Paper. Tax-exempt: 501(c)(3).
Historic House Museum: 1854 Italianate mansion built by Matthew Richard Singleton.
Collections: Victorian textiles & decorative arts; tools & farm implements.
Activities: Christmas at Kensington.
Publications: quarterly newsletter, Kensington Times.
Hours & Admission Prices: Tours: March-July & Sept.-Dec. Fri.-Sat. 9:30, 11, 1 & 2:30. Adults $5.50, seniors $4.50, children 12-17 $2.50. Closed major holidays.
Attendance: 2,500 (accurate)
Membership: Senior $30; Single 35; Dual $50; Family $65; Patron $100; Executive $500; Benefactor $1,000.

Edgefield

FRESHWATER COAST DISCOVERY CENTER, 405 Main St., Edgefield, SC 29824-1301. Tel.: 803-637-0877.
E-mail: edgefieldDC@scprt.com
Formerly: The Joanne T. Rainsford Heritage Discovery Center
History Museum.
Collections: local history & culture; cotton exhibit; artifacts; photographs.
Hours & Admission Prices: Tues.-Sat. 10-5.

OAKLEY PARK MUSEUM, 300 Columbia Rd., Edgefield, SC 29824-1224. Tel.: 803-637-4027. Fax: 803-637-5182.
E-mail: cjohns15504@bellsouth.net
Formerly: Oakley Park, UDC Shrine
Founded: 1941.
Congressional District: 3
Key Personnel: Pres. (V), Carolyn J. Piekielniak; Museum Shop Mgr., Sally Givens.
Personnel Profile: Full-Time Volunteers 4; Part-Time Volunteers 4; Interns 2.
Governing Authority: nonprofit. Parent Institution: South Carolina Div. of the UDC, Columbia, SC. Tax-exempt.
Historic House: 1835 Oakley Park, where the Red Shirts of South Carolina were organized to ease reconstruction following the Civil War; ancestral home of Gen. Martin W. Gary & Gov. John Gary Evans.
Collections: Civil War memorabilia; period furniture & furnishings; photographs; manuscripts; 1850-1970 letters; quilts; kitchen building; covered well.
Research Fields: Civil War, Edgefield district.
Activities: tours; luncheons; living history program; meetings; weddings; receptions. Museum Sponsors: Civil War encampments.
Hours & Admission Prices: Thurs.-Sat. 10-4; other times by appointment. Adults $5, students $3; discount to senior groups of 20 or more & AAM members with ID; children under 5 no charge. Closed Thanksgiving; Christmas. ♿
Attendance: 4,000 (estimated)
Membership: Individual $5.

TERRY FERRELL'S ANTIQUES & MUSEUM, Turner's Corner Store, 101 Courthouse Square, Edgefield, SC 29824-1362. Tel.: 803-637-4618.
Key Personnel: Owner, Terry Ferrell
History Museum.
Collections: local history & culture; pottery; quilts; glassware.
Hours & Admission Prices: Thurs.-Sat. 10-5; other times by appointment.

WILD TURKEY CENTER AND WINCHESTER MUSEUM, 770 Augusta Rd., Edgefield, SC 29824-1573. Mailing Address: P.O. Box 530, Edgefield, SC 29824-0530. Tel.: 800-THE-NWTF & 637-7626.
Web Site: www.nwtf.org
Wild Turkey History Museum.
Collections: wild turkey history; turkey calls & hunting; habitat management.
Facilities: theater; nature trails. Museum-related items for sale.
Activities: video; tours; school field trips; educational programs. hiking trails; interactive exhibits.
Hours & Admission Prices: Mon.-Fri. 8:30-5, Sat. 10-2. No charge; donations accepted. Closed national holidays.
Attendance: 14,000 (estimated)

Edisto Island

EDISTO ISLAND HISTORIC PRESERVATION SOCIETY MUSEUM, 8123 Chisolm Plantation Rd., Edisto Island, SC 29438-6618. Tel.: 843-869-1954. Fax: 843-869-2754.
E-mail: gsmith@edistomuseum.org
Web Site: www.edistomuseum.org
Founded: 1986.
Congressional District: 6
Key Personnel: C.E.O. & Dir., Gretchen M. Smith; Pres. (V), Pat Neuman.
Personnel Profile: Part-Time Paid 3; Part-Time Volunteers 27; Interns 1.
Governing Authority: private; nonprofit. Tax-exempt: 501(c)(3).
Historical & Preservation Society Museum.
Collections: prehistoric low country to 1920, concentrating on Edisto Island, S.C.
Facilities: 2,500 sq. ft. exhibit space. Museum-related items for sale.
Activities: guided tours; lectures; temporary exhibitions. Museum Sponsors: quarterly meetings with speakers.
Publications: quarterly newsletter, Edisto Echoes; book, Indigo, Gullah & Edisto in 1808.
Hours & Admission Prices: Tues.-Sat. 1-4. Adult $4; discounts to AAM members; members and children 10 & under no charge. ♿
Attendance: 3,500 (estimated)
Membership: Individual $25; Couple $35; Family $45; Toogoodoo Society $100; Russell Creek Society $250; Dauhoo Society $500; Edisto Society $1,000.

Ehrhardt

RIVERS BRIDGE STATE HISTORIC SITE, 325 State Park Rd., Ehrhardt, SC 29081-9157. Tel.: 803-267-3675. Fax: 803-267-3675.
E-mail: riversbridge@scprt.com
Web Site: scprt.com
Key Personnel: Park Mgr., Travis Alderman
Historic Site: battle between the Confederacy & the Union army, Feb. 2-3, 1865. Listed on the National Register of Historic Places.
Collections: Civil War history; military artifacts.
Activities: special programs; rental facilities.
Hours & Admission Prices: Thurs.-Mon. 9-6. No charge; donations accepted. Closed holidays.

Elloree

ELLOREE HERITAGE MUSEUM & CULTURAL CENTER, INC., 2714 Cleveland St., Elloree, SC 29047. Mailing Address: P.O. Box 54, Elloree, SC 29047-0054. Tel.: 803-897-2225. Fax: 803-897-2252.
E-mail: elloreemuseum@ntinet.com
Web Site: www.elloreemuseum.org
History Museum.
Collections: plantation gin house with original gin, cotton press & mechanicals; horse-drawn plows, planters & cultivators; photographs.
Hours & Admission Prices: Wed.-Sat. 10-5. Adults $5, seniors 60 & over $4, children 6-18 $3; discounts to groups; children under 6 no charge.

Florence

FLORENCE MUSEUM OF ART, SCIENCE & HISTORY AND THE FLORENCE RAILROAD MUSEUM, 558 Spruce St., Florence, SC 29501-5152. Tel.: 843-662-3351. Fax: 843-665-9527.
E-mail: flomus@bellsouth.net
Web Site: www.florencemuseum.org
Founded: 1924.
Congressional District: 6
Key Personnel: Exec. Dir., Andrew Russel Stout; C.E.O., Townsend Holt; Cur., Stephen Motte.
Personnel Profile: Full-Time Paid 1; Part-Time Paid 2; Part-Time Volunteers 70; Interns 1.
Governing Authority: quasi-public nonprofit organization. Subsidiary Institution: The Railroad Museum. Tax-exempt: 501(c)(3).
General Museum.
Collections: changing art exhibits; juried competitions; Native American collection; Civil War collection; South Carolina history rooms; Asian Gallery; Greek & Roman artifacts; American Art; railroad cars.
Research Fields: art; history & science.
Activities: lectures; gallery talks; study clubs; inter-museum loans; research; art classes.
Publications: quarterly newsletter, Florence Museum.
Hours & Admission Prices: Tues.-Sat. 10-5, Sun. 2-5. Adults $1; discounts to AAM & SCFM members; members no charge. Tours available for groups by appointment. Closed national holidays.
Attendance: 19,000 (estimated)
Membership: Student over 65 $15; Individual $25; Family, $50; Sponsor $75; Sustaining $100; Donor $250; Patron $500; Benefactor $1,000.

WAR BETWEEN THE STATES MUSEUM, 107 S. Guerry St., Florence, SC 29501-4328. Tel.: 843-669-1266.
Web Site: florenceweb.com/warmuseum.htm
Founded: 1988.
Key Personnel: Dir., Carl Hill, Jr.
Personnel Profile: Full-Time Volunteers 1; Part-Time Volunteers 1.
Governing Authority: bd. of directors.
History Museum.
Collections: Civil War history; photographs; military artifacts; manuscripts.
Facilities: Museum-related items for sale.
Hours & Admission Prices: Wed. & Sat. 10-5. Adults $2, children $1. Closed Christmas.
Attendance: 2,000 (estimated)

Fort Jackson

FORT JACKSON MUSEUM, 4442 Jackson Blvd., Fort Jackson, SC 29207-5100. Mailing Address: 2179 Sumter St., Fort Jackson, SC 29207-6102. Tel.: 803-751-7419. Fax: 803-751-4434.
E-mail: williamsb1@jackson.army.mil
Web Site: www.jackson.army.mil/museum/index.htm
Founded: 1974.
Congressional District: 2
Key Personnel: Cur., Bessie Williams; Museum Specialty, Brandon Wiegand.
Governing Authority: federal. Tax-exempt.
Military Museum.
Collections: military objects of the US Army & history of Fort Jackson, beginning with World War I to present; military objects of U.S. allies & enemies from W.W. I through Desert Storm; local military history including Indian Warriors, the Revolution, War of 1812 Mexican, Civil, & Spanish American War periods, training of individual soldier.
Research Fields: U.S. military history.
Facilities: 1,500-vol. library of military manuals & history sources available for research by special request.
Activities: guided tours; lectures; films; temporary exhibitions.
Hours & Admission Prices: Mon.-Fri. 9-4. No charge; donations accepted. Closed federal holidays. ♿
Attendance: 32,000

U.S. ARMY CHAPLAIN MUSEUM, (M), USACHCS, 10100 Lee Rd., Fort Jackson, SC 29207-7090. Tel.: 803-751-8827 & 8079. Fax: 803-751-8890.
E-mail: marcia.mcmanus@us.army.mil
Web Site: www.usachcs.army.mil
Founded: 1957.
Congressional District: 2
Key Personnel: Dir. & Cur., Marcia McManus; Museum Technician, Tim Taylor.
Personnel Profile: Full-Time Paid 2; Part-Time Volunteers 3.
Governing Authority: federal. Parent Institution: U.S. Army Chaplain Center & School. Subsidiary Institution: U.S. Army Center of Military History. Tax-exempt.
Military History Museum.
Collections: artifacts; photos & documents depicting the U.S. Army Chaplaincy; manuscript collections.
Research Fields: U.S. Army Chaplaincy; religious writings; military uniforms.

Facilities: 4,000-vol. library of theological-military history; archives; photo collections; reading room.
Activities: guided tours; lectures.
Publications: newsletter.
Hours & Admission Prices: Mon.-Fri. 9-4. No charge. Closed federal holidays. ♿
Membership: Chaplain Corps. Regimental Association: Annual $20.

Gaffney

CHEROKEE COUNTY HISTORY AND ARTS MUSEUM, 301 College Dr., Gaffney, SC 29340-3006. Tel.: 864-489-3988. Fax: 864-489-8541.
Key Personnel: Dir., Billy Pennington
History Museum.
Collections: local history & culture; period furnishings; personal artifacts; photographs.
Activities: educational & cultural outreach programs.
Hours & Admission Prices: Wed.-Fri. 10-4, Sat. 2-5. Adults $5, children under 12 $3; month of May no charge.

COWPENS NATIONAL BATTLEFIELD, 4001 Chesnee Hwy., Gaffney, SC 29341. Mailing Address: P.O. Box 308, Chesnee, SC 29323-0308. Tel.: 864-461-2828. Fax: 864-461-7795.
E-mail: cowp_interpretation@nps.gov
Web Site: www.nps.gov/cowp/
Founded: 1933.
Congressional District: 5
Key Personnel: Supt., Tim Stone; Administrative Officer, Michelle Lester; Chief Ranger, Kathy McKay.
Personnel Profile: Full-Time Paid 1; Part-Time Paid 2.
Governing Authority: federal. Affiliated with the Department of Interior, National Park Service, Washington, DC. Tax-exempt.
Military Museum: located on site of 1781 Battle of Cowpens.
Collections: weapons of artillery of Revolutionary period; records of men who fought in the battle. Historic House: 1830 Robert Scruggs House.
Research Fields: American Revolution; Southern Campaign.
Facilities: theater; picnic area with shelter. Books & pamphlets for sale.
Activities: guided tours on request, if staff is available; demonstrations at special events; introductory DVD; fiber optics map. Annual Event: Living History Encampment in January.
Publications: handbook; DVD presentation; books; postcards.
Hours & Admission Prices: Daily 9-5. No charge; donations accepted. Closed New Year's Day; Thanksgiving; Christmas Day. ♿
Attendance: 208,566 (accurate)

WINNIE DAVIS MUSEUM OF HISTORY, Limestone College, 1115 College Dr., Gaffney, SC 29340-3778. Tel.: 864-488-8399. Fax: 864-487-7151.
Web Site: www.limestone.edu
Founded: 1976.
Congressional District: 5
Key Personnel: Librarian, Carolyn T. Hayward.
Governing Authority: college. Parent Institution: Limestone College. Tax-exempt.
College Museum: housed in 1898-1901 Winnie Davis Hall of History, built to house Confederate records.
Collections: college memorabilia; local & South Carolina history; manuscript collections.
Research Fields: local history; Revolutionary War; Civil War.
Hours & Admission Prices: By appointment only. No charge.

Georgetown

GEORGETOWN COUNTY MUSEUM, Georgetown County Historical Society, 632 Prince St., Georgetown, SC 29440-3630. Tel.: 843-545-7020. Fax: 843-545-7020.
E-mail: georgetownmuseum@gmail.com
Web Site: www.georgetowncountymuseum.com
Founded: 2005.
Key Personnel: Dir., Jill Santropietro.
Personnel Profile: Full-Time Paid 1; Part-Time Paid 1; Part-Time Volunteers 8.
Governing Authority: Tax-exempt.
Historical Museum.
Collections: Native Americans; maps; Revolutionary & Civil War artifacts; presidential letters; Low country memorabilia; slavery 19-20th century.
Hours & Admission Prices: Tues.-Fri. 10-5, Sat. 10-3. Adults $4, seniors 64 & over $3; members no charge.
Membership: Individual $25; Family $50; Contributor $100; Silver Sponsor $250; Gold Sponsor $500; Partner $750; Patron $1,000; Benefactor $2,500.

HOPSEWEE PLANTATION, 494 Hopsewee Rd., Georgetown, SC 29440-5598. Tel.: 843-546-7891.
E-mail: mail@hopsewee.com
Web Site: www.hopsewee.com
Founded: 1970.
Congressional District: 6
Key Personnel: Owner, Frank Beattie; Mgr. River Oaks Tea Room, Raejean Beattie; Docent, Jean Efird; Docent, Sara Morrison; Docent, Bessie Keith.
Personnel Profile: Part-Time Paid 7.
Governing Authority: individual operation organized for profit.
Historic House: c.1735-40 birthplace of Thomas Lynch Jr., signer of the Declaration of Independence.
Collections: 18th-19th century furniture & furnishings.
Major Exhibits: Colonial Life In South Carolina (T), 4/10; Georgetown County, 1740-1865, 4/10; First South Carolinians, 5/10.
Activities: guided tours.
Hours & Admission Prices: House & Tea Room: Feb.-Nov. Tues.-Fri. 10-4, Sat. 12-4. Adults $15, children 5-17 $7.50; discounts to AAM members. Grounds: daily $5 per car. Closed Thanksgiving.
Attendance: 5,500 (estimated)

KAMINSKI HOUSE MUSEUM, 1003 Front St., Georgetown, SC 29440-3521. Mailing Address: P.O. Drawer 939, Georgetown, SC 29442. Tel.: 843-546-7706. Fax: 843-527-4871.
E-mail: ckinder@cogsc.com
Web Site: www.kaminskihousemuseum.org
Founded: 1973.
Congressional District: 6
Key Personnel: Dir., Cindy Kinder; Pres. (V), Rene C. King; Museum Shop Mgr., Becky Berry.
Personnel Profile: Full-Time Paid 1; Part-Time Paid 4; Part-Time Volunteers 15; Interns 1.
Governing Authority: municipal government. Parent Institution: City of Georgetown, SC. Tax-exempt: 170(b)(1)(A).
Historic House: 1769 Harold Kaminski House.
Collections: 18th, 19th & 20th-century furniture, glass, silver, china & fine period items.
Research Fields: Social History of House.
Facilities: Museum-related items for sale.
Activities: guided tours; decorative arts lecture series; music series; story telling.
Publications: newsletter, Kaminski House Museum Book.
Hours & Admission Prices: Mon.-Sat. 9-5, Sun. 1-5; tours are conducted on the hour. Adults $7, seniors, AAA & AARP members $5, children 6-12 $3; discounts to AAM, ICOM, SEMC & SCFM members; group tour prices available. Members no charge. Closed New Year's Day; Easter; Thanksgiving; Christmas Eve & Day.
Attendance: 15,000 (accurate)
Membership: Individual $20; Family $35; Commanders Club $100.

THE RICE MUSEUM, Lafayette Park, Front and Screven Sts., 633 Front St., Georgetown, SC 29440. Mailing Address: P.O. Box 902, Georgetown, SC 29442-0902. Tel.: 843-546-7423. Fax: 843-545-9093.
E-mail: thericemuseum@sc.rr.com
Web Site: www.ricemuseum.org
Founded: 1968.
Congressional District: 1
Key Personnel: Dir., James A. Fitch; Chm. (V), Henry Reynolds.
Governing Authority: nonprofit. Parent Institution: Georgetown County Historical Commission. Tax-exempt: 170(b)(1)(3).
History Museum: housed in the 1842 Old Market Building located on the Old Market site.
Collections: rice culture in South Carolina low country. Historic Building: 1845 Clock & Bell Tower.
Facilities: 50-seat auditorium. Rice Cook Book, notepaper & postcards & museum-related items for sale.
Activities: guided tours; lectures; films; changing exhibits.
Publications: Guide to Historic Georgetown County, S.C.; historic Georgetown county leaflets; Pass the Pilau, Please.
Hours & Admission Prices: Mon.-Sat. 10-4:30. Adults $7, seniors $5, students 6-21 $3; discounts to groups; children under 6 no charge. Closed New Year's Day; Thanksgiving; Christmas. ♿
Attendance: 30,000 (estimated)
Membership: Individual $50; Family $100; Contributor $150; Subscriber $250; Patron $500; Benefactor $1,000 & up.

Green Sea

COUNTRY FARM MUSEUM, 1991 Fair Bluff Hwy., Green Sea, SC 29545-4452. Tel.: 843-756-1682.
Farm Museum.
Collections: local history; agriculture; farm machinery & implements; period artifacts & farm toys; hands-on exhibits.
Hours & Admission Prices: Call for hours.

Greenville

BOB JONES UNIVERSITY MUSEUM & GALLERY, INC., 1700 Wade Hampton Blvd., Greenville, SC 29614-0001. Tel.: 864-770-1331. Fax: 864-770-1306.
E-mail: contact@bjumg.org
Web Site: www.bjumg.org
Founded: 1951.
Congressional District: 4
Key Personnel: Dir., Erin Jones; Cur., John Nolan; Dir. Educations, Donnalynn Hess; Registrar, Barbara Sicko; Events Coord., Amy Basinger; Museum Shop Mgr., Kathy May; Dir. Devel., Frank Richards; Grant Specialist, John Elliott.
Personnel Profile: Full-Time Paid 13; Part-Time Paid 3; Part-Time Volunteers 1; Interns 7.
Governing Authority: bd. of trustees. Subsidiary Institution: Museum & Gallery at Heritage Green. Tax-exempt.
Old Masters Museum.
Collections: 14th-19th century European old masters paintings; archaeological & illustrative material relating to the Holy Lands; decorative arts; sculpture; textiles.
Facilities: Museum-related items for sale.
Activities: guided tours for adults and children first grade & above; audio tours; formally organized education programs for educators (private, public & home school); inter-museum loan & permanent exhibitions; performances; interactive learning center.
Publications: catalogues; Bob Jones University Collection of Religious Art; Italian Paintings; John the Baptist and the Baroque Vision; Selected Masterworks from BJU Museum & Gallery; quarterly newsletter, Gallery News; Discovering a Pre-Renaissance Master: Tommaso del Mazza.
Hours & Admission Prices: mid-Jan. to mid-Dec. Tues.-Sun. 2-5. Adults $5, senior citizens $4, students $3; members & children 6-12 no charge. Audio Tour: $5. North American and the Southeastern reciprocal membership programs. Children under 6 not admitted. Closed New Year's Day; Commencement Day; Independence Day; Thanksgiving weekend. Heritage Green: Tues.-Sat. 10-5. Adults $5, senior citizens $4, students $3; members & children 12 & under no charge.
Attendance: 19,823 (accurate)
Membership: Individual $50; Family & Dual $150.

* **GREENVILLE COUNTY MUSEUM OF ART, (M),** 420 College St., Greenville, SC 29601-2099. Tel.: 864-271-7570. Fax: 864-271-7579.
E-mail: info@greenvillemuseum.org
Web Site: www.greenvillemuseum.org
Founded: 1963.
Congressional District: 4
Key Personnel: Dir., Thomas W. Styron; Cur., Martha R. Severens; Comptroller, Jeanne Marsh; Devel. Officer & Museum Shop Mgr., Mary Lawson; Head Collections Mgmt. & Security, Claudia Beckwith; Public Rels., Mary McCarthy.
Personnel Profile: Full-Time Paid 23; Part-Time Paid 8; Part-Time Volunteers 200.
Governing Authority: appointed commission; nonprofit organization. Tax-exempt: 501(c)(3) & 170(b)(1)(A).
Art Museum. American art from the 18th century to present.
Collections: American painting, sculpture & works on paper.
Research Fields: American paintings & sculpture; emphasis on Southern-related art; Andrew Wyeth; Jasper Johns.
Facilities: 76,000 sq. ft. exhibit space; 150-seat film theatre; art studios.
Activities: guided tours; lectures; gallery talks; formally organized education programs for children, adults, undergraduate & graduate college students; docent program; permanent collection of American art; temporary & traveling exhibitions; studio courses for adults & children in painting, drawing, photography, ceramics, printmaking, metal sculpture.
Publications: membership newsletter; brochures; catalogs for exhibitions; Greenville County Museum of Art: The Southern Collection; Andrew Wyeth: America's Painter.
Hours & Admission Prices: Tues.-Wed. & Fri.-Sat. 11-5, Thurs. 11-8, Sun. 1-5. No charge; donations accepted. Closed major holidays. ♿
Attendance: 123,000 (accurate)
Membership: Friend $50; Young Collectors $75; Contributing $100; Sponsor $500; Grand Benefactor $2,500; Director's Circle $5,000; Chairman's Circle $10,000.

GREENVILLE ZOO, 150 Cleveland Park Dr., Greenville, SC 29601-3147. Tel.: 864-467-4300. Fax: 864-467-4314.
E-mail: zooinfo@greenvillesc.gov
Web Site: www.greenvillezoo.com
Key Personnel: Dir., Lee Sims; Exec. Dir. Zoo Friends, Jan Griffin
Zoo.
Collections: 300 animals including large mammals; reptile museum.
Facilities: picnic areas. Museum-related items for sale.
Hours & Admission Prices: Daily 10-4:30. Adults $6, children 3-15 $3; discounts to groups; children under 3 no charge. Closed New Year's Day; Thanksgiving; Christmas. ♿
Attendance: 200,000 (estimated)
Membership: Individual $27; Grandparent $36; Family $42; Family Plus $59; Peacock Society $100.

HOWELL MEMORIAL PLANETARIUM, Bob Jones University, 1700 Wade Hampton Blvd., Bldg. 26, 2nd Fl., Greenville, SC 29614-0001. Tel.: 864-242-5100, ext. 2269.
E-mail: planetarium@bju.edu
Web Site: www.bju.edu/welcome/visit/map/science-building/planetarium.php
Key Personnel: Dir., Dr. Stewart Custer
Planetarium.
Collections: The Spitz Model A2 Star projector.
Activities: school groups; public programs.
Hours & Admission Prices: Sept.-April Sun. 2; other times by appointment. No charge.

ROPER MOUNTAIN SCIENCE CENTER, (M), 402 Roper Mountain Rd., Greenville, SC 29615-4298. Tel.: 864-355-8900. Fax: 864-355-8948.
Web Site: www.ropermountain.org
Founded: 1978.
Key Personnel: C.E.O. & Dir., William Bradshaw; Cur. Planetarium, Charles St. Lucas; Physical Science Cur., Latongia Pepper; Naturalist, Peter DeBoer; Plant Engineer, Charles Head; Office Mgr., Kelli Cox; Health Cur., Kathy Hutchins; Health Programmer, Connie Mathis; Astronomer & Technician, Doug Gegan; Cur. Education, Gregory Cornwell; Computer Specialist/MECC Mgr., Cynthia Childers; Cur. Marine & Earth, Brandis Hartsell; Cur. Natural Science, Tim Taylor.
Personnel Profile: Full-Time Paid 24; Full-Time Volunteers 1; Part-Time Paid 50; Part-Time Volunteers 80; Interns 1.
Governing Authority: public school district. Parent Institution: Greenville County School District. Tax-exempt: 170(b)(1)(A).
Science Center.
Collections: hands-on exhibits; living history farm.
Facilities: arboretum; life science labs; marine lab; observatory; health center; physical science lab; 300-seat auditorium; 170-seat planetarium; computer lab; nature trails; tropical rainforest conservatory.
Activities: summer concerts; teacher courses; summer science camps; formal education lessons for students K-12; science equipment; public observatory viewings; second Saturday events. Annual Event: Starry Friday Nights Programs January to late November.
Publications: newsletter; teacher guides to services.
Hours & Admission Prices: Mon.-Fri. 8:30-5. Nature Trails & Picnic areas only: no charge. 2nd Sat. each month 9-1. Adults $5, senior citizens & children $4; discounts to ASTC members; members no charge. Friday Starry Nights: 7pm to 10pm. Planetarium Shows: 7:30pm, 8:15pm, 8:45pm. Telescope Viewing: 8pm-10pm. ♿
Attendance: 252,626 (accurate)
Membership: Student, Teacher & Senior Citizen $20; Adult $25; Family $45; Sponsor $100; Benefactor $250.

SHOELESS JOE JACKSON MUSEUM AND BASEBALL LIBRARY, 356 Field St., Greenville, SC 29601-3541. Mailing Address: P.O. Box 4755, Greenville, SC 29608-4755. Tel.: 864-235-6280.
E-mail: info@shoelessjoejacksonmuseum.org
Web Site: www.shoelessjoejackson.org
Key Personnel: Pres., Cur. & Publicist, Arlene Marcley
History Museum: housed in the former home of Joe Jackson.
Collections: records, artifacts, photographs & film relating to the life & baseball career of Shoeless Joe Jackson.
Facilities: Museum-related items for sale.
Hours & Admission Prices: Sat. 10-2; other times by appointment. No charge; donations accepted.

SOUTH CAROLINA SCV CONFEDERATE MUSEUM, 15 Boyce Ave., Greenville, SC 29601-3109. Tel.: 864-421-9039.
Web Site: www.confederatemuseum.org
Key Personnel: Dir., V. Michael Couch, Sr.; Chm. (V), Terry L. Rude; Museum Shop Mgr., John Wheeler.
Personnel Profile: Part-Time Volunteers 45.
Governing Authority: Parent Institution: Camp 36, sons of Confederate Veterans, Greenville, SC 29601. Tax-exempt.
History Museum.
Collections: Civil War history; personal artifacts; military equipment; War for Southern Independence artifacts & documents.
Research Fields: genealogy.
Activities: Museum Sponsors: Christmas in Dixie in December.
Publications: quarterly newsletter.
Hours & Admission Prices: Mon. & Wed. 10-3, Fri. 1-9, Sat. 10-5, Sun. 1-5; other times by appointment. No charge; donations accepted. Closed Christmas.
Attendance: 10,000 (estimated)

UPCOUNTRY HISTORY MUSEUM, (M), 540 Buncombe St., Greenville, SC 29601-1906. Tel.: 864-467-3100. Fax: 864-467-3105.
E-mail: info@upcountryhistory.org
Web Site: www.upcountryhistory.org
Founded: 1983.
Congressional District: 4
Key Personnel: Dir., Dawn Deano Hammatt; Chm. (V), Ed Good; Museum Shop Mgr., Kathy Barefoot.
Personnel Profile: Full-Time Paid 7; Part-Time Paid 10; Part-Time Volunteers 50; Interns 4.
Governing Authority: Tax-exempt.
History Museum.
Collections: Upcountry South Carolina history; interactive exhibits; oral histories; photographs.
Research Fields: textile history; WWII; civil rights.
Facilities: 65-seat theatre; classroom; archives. Museum-related items for sale.
Activities: presentations; permanent & temporary exhibits; lectures; living history tours; family programs; school programs; group tours.
Hours & Admission Prices: Tues.-Sat. 10-5, Sun. 1-5. Adults $5; discounts to AAM & ICOM members; members no charge. Closed major holidays. ♿
Attendance: 35,000 (estimated)
Membership: Individual $35; Dual $50; Family $65; Supporting $100; $250; $500; $1,000; $2,500; $5,000; $10,000.

Greenwood

THE MUSEUM, (M), 106 Main St., Greenwood, SC 29646-2763. Tel.: 864-229-7093. Fax: 864-229-9317.
E-mail: themuseum@greenwood.net
Web Site: www.themuseum-greenwood.org
Formerly: The Greenwood Museum
Founded: 1967.
Congressional District: 3
Key Personnel: Exec. Dir., Matthew J. Edwards; Pres. (V), Sandra Johnson; Collections Tech, Clay Barton; Museum Shop Mgr., April Miller.
Personnel Profile: Full-Time Paid 1; Part-Time Paid 3; Part-Time Volunteers 25; Interns 6.
Governing Authority: nonprofit organization. Subsidiary Institution: Railroad Historical Center. Tax-exempt: 501(c)(3) & 170(b)(1)(A).
General Museum.
Collections: general; geology; archaeology; fossils; Indian artifacts; bottles & glass; old kitchen; replicas of doctors office, parlor, country store; 1900 drug store; Thomas A. Edison display, showing replica of first phono made; old photographs; mounted butterflies, birds & moths; shells; firearms; war relics; zoology; animals; animal heads; operational commercial loom; hand loom; c.1910 linotype machine; hand-operated paper cutter; foot-operated job press; book binder press; process from raw bale to finished cloth; full scale replica of Cinderella coach; African collection of Frank Delano; replica of an early century school room; Indian, African & other cultural items.
Facilities: Museum-related items for sale.
Activities: guided tours; formally organized education programs for children; permanent & temporary exhibitions; outreach programs; internships; summer camp; birthday parties; facility rental.
Publications: quarterly bulletin, Museum Newsletter.
Hours & Admission Prices: Museum: Wed.-Sat. 10-5. Railroad History Center: April-Oct. Sat. 10-4. Adults $5, seniors & children $2; discounts to AAM members & groups of 10 or more; members no charge. Closed legal holidays. ♿
Attendance: 6,000 (accurate)
Membership: Student $10; Senior Individual $15; Senior Duo & Individual $25; Family & Supporter $50-$199; Pillar Bronze $200 & over; Pillar Silver $500 & over; Pillar Gold $1,000 & over; Pillar Platinum $1,500 & over.

Greer

GREER HERITAGE MUSEUM, 106 S. Main St., Greer, SC 29651-3430. Tel.: 864-877-3377.
E-mail: greerheritagemuseum@yahoo.com
Key Personnel: Dir. & Cur., Joada Hiatt; Founder, Carm Hudson.
Governing Authority: nonprofit organization.
History Museum housed in the former City Hall.
Collections: local history & culture relating to the city of Greer.
Facilities: library.
Activities: school groups; special events.
Hours & Admission Prices: Fri.-Sat. 10-4; groups of 10 or more by appointment. No charge.

ZENTRUM MUSEUM, 1400 Hwy. 101 S., Greer, SC 29651-6731. Tel.: 864-989-5297 & 6000.
E-mail: greg.bunner@bmwmc.com
Web Site: www.bmwusfactory.com/#/zentrum/1248
BMW History Museum.
Collections: BMW history; racing & touring vehicles; technology & engineering.
Hours & Admission Prices: Mon.-Fri. 9;30-5:30. No charge. Closed New Year's Eve & Day; Good Friday; Memorial Day; Independence Day; Labor Day; Thanksgiving; Christmas Eve, Day & week.

Hampton

HAMPTON COUNTY HISTORICAL SOCIETY MUSEUM, Hwy. 601 S., Hampton, SC 29924. Mailing Address: P.O. Box 202, Hampton, SC 29924-0202. Tel.: 803-943-5484.
Founded: 1979.
Congressional District: 2
Key Personnel: Pres. Hampton County Historical Society, Betty Ruth Crews; Vice Pres., Mary Eleanor Bowers; Chm. (V) & Cur., Marian Platts; Chm. (V) & Cur., Sara Kring; Treas., Christine Peeples; Corresponding Sec., Sarah Jo Withycombe; Recording Sec., Lillian Solomons; Docent, Virginia Sinclair.
Personnel Profile: Part-Time Volunteers 4.
Governing Authority: society; nonprofit organization. Hampton County Historical Society. Tax-exempt.
History Museum: housed in c.1878 Old Jail.
Collections: local history; veterans' of all wars personal artifacts; Prisoners of War artifacts from WWII & Korea; photographs; book & manuscript by Manny Lawton; cemetery records; swords, bayonets & Civil War memorabilia; children's toys & period artifacts; 1878-1930s country store; Civil War & WWII history; black history; early 1800s-1900s women's clothing; genealogy; c.1903 Indian artifacts; Korean, Vietnam, Operation & Desert Storm War memorabilia; natural history room; church records.
Facilities: library of cemetery, church & family records, books & pamphlets available for research on premises; reading & research room; natural history room; children's room.
Activities: guided tours; permanent & temporary exhibitions. Museum Sponsors: Black History month; Women's month; one vet group emphasized every two months.
Publications: brochures; Both Sides of the Swamp; books, Saddle Soldiers; Logging Railroads of S.C.; Railroads and Sawmills; Collector's Illustrated Encyclopedia of the American Revolution; Official Roster of World War II, Vols. 1& 2; Journal of House of Representatives of S.C. c.1785-1786; The Colonial Records of S.C., 1751-1752; The Colonial Records of S.C., 1750-1751; S.C. Historical Magazine; Images of America-Barnwell County, S.C.; The County Officers & Officers of Barnwell County, S.C., 1775-1975; Prisoners of War - WWII & Korea; books, Cultural Values in the Boulhern Sporting Narrative; From the Salkehatchic to the Savannah (A Visual Journey Through Hampton County).
Hours & Admission Prices: Closed for renovations. ♿
Attendance: 1,000 (estimated)
Membership: Adults $15.

Hartsville

CECELIA COKER BELL GALLERY, Coker College, Art Dept., 300 E. College Ave., Hartsville, SC 29550-3742. Tel.: 843-383-8156 & 8150. Fax: 843-383-8048.
E-mail: lmerriman@coker.edu
Web Site: www.coker.edu/art/gallery.html
Founded: 1983.
Key Personnel: Dir., Larry Merriman.

Personnel Profile: Part-Time Paid 1; Interns 2.
Governing Authority: private college.
Art Gallery & Teaching Gallery.
Collections: works by national & international artists.
Facilities: educational facilities; 750 sq. ft. exhibit space.
Activities: guided tours. Annual Events: exhibitions & lectures by visiting artists.
Hours & Admission Prices: Sept. to mid-May Mon.-Fri. 10-4:30. No charge. Closed New Year's Day; Easter; Labor Day; Thanksgiving; Christmas. ♿
Attendance: 4,000 (estimated)

HARTSVILLE MUSEUM, (M), 222 N. Fifth St., Hartsville, SC 29550-4136. Mailing Address: P.O. Box 431, Hartsville, SC 29551-0431. Tel.: 843-383-3005. Fax: 843-383-2477.
E-mail: info@hartsvillemuseum.org
Web Site: www.hartsvillemuseum.org
Founded: 1980.
Congressional District: 6
Key Personnel: C.E.O. & Dir., Kathy M. Dunlap; Chm., Glenn J. Lawhon, Jr.; City Mgr., James Pennington; Museum Shop Mgr., Penny Anthony.
Personnel Profile: Full-Time Paid 2; Part-Time Paid 3; Part-Time Volunteers 21; Interns 4.
Governing Authority: municipal. Parent Institution: City of Hartsville. Tax-exempt.
Local History Museum: housed in restored 1930 U.S. Post Office Building, changing gallery for Arts Programming.
Collections: Eastern Carolina Silver Co. holloware c.1900; iron & wood household objects; historical photos; costumes; documents; papers; ornaments; personal property pertinent to Hartsville & surrounding areas; 1899 locomobile steam car; first car in SC; sculpture courtyard.
Research Fields: local history.
Facilities: conference room.
Activities: guided tours; lectures; loan, permanent & temporary exhibitions.
Publications: booklet, Hartsville's Eastern Carolina Silver Company; Milestones, Hartville's Centennial; book, Recollections of the Major.
Hours & Admission Prices: Mon.-Fri. 10-5, Sat. 10-2. No charge; donations accepted. Closed state holidays. ♿
Attendance: 12,500 (accurate)
Membership: Individual $25; Family $40; Patron $60; Sustainer $100; Business $150; Showcase $250; Heritage $500; "The Mayor" $1,000; Benefactor $3,000.

JACOB KELLEY HOUSE MUSEUM, 2585 Kellytown Rd., Hartsville, SC 29550. Mailing Address: 204 Hewitt St., Darlington, SC 29532-3214. Tel.: 843-332-6401 & 339-9093. Fax: 843-332-8017.
E-mail: DCHC1968@aol.com
Congressional District: 5
Key Personnel: Pres. (V), Jo Ann K. Lee; C.E.O. & Dir., Doris Gandy.
Governing Authority: county; nonprofit. Parent Institution: Darlington County. Subsidiary Institution: Jacob Kelley House Guild. Tax-exempt.
Historic House: 1820 Federal style plantation house used as General Sherman's headquarters during Civil War.
Collections: handcrafted furniture; decorative arts, c.1820-1874.
Activities: guided tours.
Hours & Admission Prices: Feb.-Nov. first Sun. of the month 3-5. No charge; donations accepted.
Membership: Guild $15.

KALMIA GARDENS, 1624 W. Carolina Ave., Hartsville, SC 29550-4906. Tel.: 843-383-8145. Fax: 843-383-8149.
Web Site: www.coker.edu/kalmia
Botanical Garden & Historic House Museum: home of Thomas E. Hart, built in 1820. Listed on the National Register of Historic Places.
Collections: period furnishings; personal artifacts; rhododendrons; camellias; azaleas; wisteria; tea-olives; dogwood; Kalmia latifolia.
Facilities: 35 acre garden.
Hours & Admission Prices: Daily. No charge.

Hilton Head Island

COASTAL DISCOVERY MUSEUM, 100 William Hilton Pkwy., Hilton Head Island, SC 29926-1216. Mailing Address: P.O. Box 23497, Hilton Head Island, SC 29925-3497. Tel.: 843-689-6767. Fax: 843-689-6769.
E-mail: info@coastaldiscovery.org
Web Site: coastaldiscovery.org
Founded: 1985.
Congressional District: 2
Key Personnel: Pres. & C.E.O., Michael J. Marks; Chm. (V), Jim Willard; Vice Pres. Finance & Administration, Jeanette Carlton; Vice Pres. Programs, Natalie Hefter; Mgr. Natural History, Carlos Chacon; Vice Pres. Mktg. & Devel., Robin Swift.
Personnel Profile: Full-Time Paid 5; Full-Time Volunteers 200; Part-Time Paid 2; Part-Time Volunteers 100; Interns 3.
Governing Authority: bd. of trustees; nonprofit. Tax-exempt: 501(c)(3).
General Museum.
Collections: local & North American natural history specimens; South Carolina archaeological materials; historical material relevant to history of the island, Colonial, Plantation, Civil War & current day.
Facilities: lecture hall & classroom; outdoor teaching deck; outdoor natural grounds for land, marsh & water programming; picnic facilities. Museum-related items for sale.
Activities: guided tours; lectures; films; gallery talks; classes; formally organized program for on- & off-site curriculum-based programming for schools.
Publications: newsletter; info-guides.
Hours & Admission Prices: Mon.-Sat. 9-4:30, Sun. 11-3. Museum: $2 donation suggested. Fees for walks, tours & cruises. ♿
Attendance: 96,500 (accurate)
Membership: Individual $35; Family $50; Patron $100.

THE SANDBOX, AN INTERACTIVE CHILDREN'S MUSEUM, 18A Pope Ave., Hilton Head Island, SC 29928-4708. Tel.: 843-842-7645.
E-mail: cpfeffer@thesandbox.org
Web Site: www.thesandbox.org
Founded: 2005.
Key Personnel: Exec. Dir., Carol Pfeffer; Operations Mgr., Caroline Rinehart.
Personnel Profile: Full-Time Paid 1; Part-Time Paid 7; Part-Time Volunteers 1.
Governing Authority: Tax-exempt.
Children's Museum.
Collections: hands-on exhibits.
Activities: special events; birthday parties; rental facilities. Museum Sponsors: Parent's Night Out.
Hours & Admission Prices: April & June-Aug. Mon.-Sat. 10-5; May & Sept.-March Tues.-Sat. 10-5. Admission $6; military, members & children under 2 no charge. Closed Labor Day; Thanksgiving; Christmas. ♿
Attendance: 28,465 (accurate)
Membership: Basic $100; Premier $150; Platinum $200. (additional adult $25)

Hopkins

CONGAREE NATIONAL PARK, 100 National Park Rd., Hopkins, SC 29061-8320. Tel.: 803-776-4396. Fax: 803-783-4241.
Web Site: www.nps.gov/cong
Formerly: Congaree Swamp National Monument
Founded: 1976.
Congressional District: 6
Key Personnel: Mgr. Visitor Center, Fran Rametta; Supt., Tracy Swartout; Chief Resources, Bill Hulslander.
Personnel Profile: Full-Time Paid 12; Part-Time Paid 3; Part-Time Volunteers 100; Interns 2.
Governing Authority: federal. Parent Institution: National Park Service. Tax-exempt.
National Park & Preservation Project: 26,800-acre National Park.
Collections: 5 national Champion trees; 20 state record trees; 86 tree species; loblolly pines; American elms, 17 feet in circumference; bald cypress; 26 feet in circumference; 779 plants; 83 mushrooms; 24 amphibians; 29 reptiles; 44 fish & 200 bird species.
Research Fields: biology; geology; hydrology; ecology.
Facilities: visitor center & headquarters; 20 miles of hiking trail; 16 mile marked canoe trail; 2.5 mile boardwalk loop; self-guided nature trail.
Activities: guided tours; hiking; backpacking; canoeing; birding; photography; fishing; picnicking; primitive camping with permit.
Publications: Official Map & Guide, Official Congaree National Park Map & Guide; Birds of Congaree National Park.
Hours & Admission Prices: Visitor Center: Summer: daily 8:30-7; Winter: daily 8:30-5. No charge; donations accepted. Closed Christmas. ♿
Attendance: 134,000 (accurate)

Johnston

EDGEFIELD COUNTY PEACH MUSEUM, 416 Calhoun St., Johnston, SC 29832-1317. Tel.: 803-275-0010. Fax: 803-275-3586.
History Museum.
Collections: peach history, industry, & production; early pioneers.
Hours & Admission Prices: Mon.-Fri. 8:30-12:30; other times by appointment. Closed holidays.

Kingstree

WILLIAMSBURGH HISTORICAL MUSEUM, 135 Hampton Ave., Kingstree, SC 29556-3423. Tel.: 843-355-3306.
Key Personnel: Dir., Joanne B. Brown
History Museum.
Collections: Historic archives & artifacts; antique china displays; early maps; dug-out canoe.
Hours & Admission Prices: Tues.-Thurs. 10-3. No charge. Closed major holidays.

Lake City

BROWNTOWN MUSEUM, Hwy. 341, Lake City, SC 29560. Mailing Address: 414 Main St., Hemingway, SC 29554-9190. Tel.: 843-558-2355.
Key Personnel: Dir. & Cur., Nell Morris; Pres., Kathy Loyd; Treas., Mona Prosser; Sec., Carol Cockfield.
Governing Authority: nonprofit organization. Parent Institution: Three Rivers Historical Society. Tax-exempt.
Historic Site & Preservation Project.
Collections: cotton gin; corn crib; smokehouse; farm equipment. Historic House: 1845 Brown-Burrows House.
Research Fields: Brown family genealogy; census records; equity rolls; family Bibles; cemeteries; court house records.
Facilities: 44-vol. library.
Activities: guided tours; lectures; organized educational programs for children & adults; annual events.
Publications: quarterly newsletter, The Three Rivers Chronicle.
Hours & Admission Prices: Sat. 9-4, groups by appointment. Adults $5, children $2. ♿
Attendance: 350 (estimated)
Membership: Annual $20.

NATIONAL BEAN MARKET MUSEUM, 111 Henry St., Lake City, SC 29560. Mailing Address: P.O. Box 943, Lake City, SC 29560-0943. Tel.: 843-374-1500.
Historic Building: built in 1936. Listed on the National Register of Historic Places.
Collections: early farm life; local history & culture; pole tobacco barn; agriculture.
Hours & Admission Prices: Mon. & Wed. 8-6, Tues. & Thurs.-Fri. 8-4. No charge. Closed major holidays.

Lancaster

ANDREW JACKSON STATE PARK, 196 Andrew Jackson Park Rd., Lancaster, SC 29720-6404. Tel.: 803-285-3344.
Web Site: southcarolinaparks.com/park-finder/state-park/1797.aspx
Founded: 1954.
Key Personnel: Supt., Kirk Johnson
Park & History Museum: dedicated to Andrew Jackson, the 7th president of the United States.
Collections: Andrew Jackson's life & history; replica 18th-century one-room schoolhouse; statue.
Facilities: amphitheatre; picnic area; nature trails.
Activities: living history programs; camping; fishing; picnicking; rental facilities; concerts; special events. Annual Event: Bluegrass Festival.
Hours & Admission Prices: Park: Summer: daily 9-9; Winter: daily 8-6. Schoolhouse: mid-March to Nov. Sat. 1-5, Sun. 2-5. Museum: Sat.-Sun. 1-5; other times by appointment. Adults $2, seniors $1.25; children 15 & under no charge.

LANCASTER & CHESTER RAILWAY MUSEUM, 512 S. Main St., 2nd Fl., Lancaster, SC 29720-3622. Mailing Address: P.O. Box 1450, Lancaster, SC 29721-1450. Tel.: 803-286-2100 & 2102. Fax: 803-286-4158.
Railway Museum.
Collections: railway history; scale model replica of the railway route; photographs; railway memorabilia.
Hours & Admission Prices: 1st & 3rd Sat of the month 10-4. No charge.

Latta

DILLON COUNTY MUSEUM, 101 S. Marion St., Latta, SC 29565-1558. Mailing Address: Dillon County Historical Society, P.O. Box 1806, Dillon, SC 29536-1806. Tel.: 843-752-9457.
Historic Building: housed in the former office of Dr. Henry Edwards; built in 1925. Listed on the National Register of Historic Places.
Collections: family & local history; Dr. Edwards' dental office; documents; photographs; personal artifacts; period furnishings; cotton & tobacco industries; military artifacts.
Hours & Admission Prices: Daily 2-4; other times by appointment. ♿
Attendance: 1,200

Laurens

THE JAMES DUNKLIN HOUSE, 544 W. Main St., Laurens, SC 29360. Mailing Address: 2009 Lakeview Dr., Laurens, SC 29360-5132. Tel.: 864-984-4735 & 683-2432.
Founded: 1972.
Congressional District: 5
Key Personnel: Pres., James C. Todd, III; Mgr., Shawn Brown.
Governing Authority: nonprofit organization. Affiliated with the Laurens County Landmarks Foundation, 544 W. Main St., Laurens, SC 29360. Tax-exempt: 170(b)(1)(A).
Historic Foundation: housed in 1812 The James Dunklin House. Listed on the National Register of Historic Places.
Collections: furniture.
Activities: guided tours.
Hours & Admission Prices: 1st Sun. of month 2-5; other times by appointment. Adults $2, children 11 & under $1.
Attendance: 300 (accurate)

Lexington

LEXINGTON COUNTY MUSEUM, 231 Fox St., Lexington, SC 29072-2654. Mailing Address: P.O. Box 637, Lexington, SC 29071-0637. Tel.: 803-359-8369. Fax: 803-808-2160.
E-mail: museum@lex-co.com
Founded: 1970.
Congressional District: 2
Key Personnel: Chm. (V), Bill Kiesling; Dir., J.R. Fennell.
Personnel Profile: Full-Time Paid 2; Part-Time Paid 6; Interns 2.
Governing Authority: county. Lexington County Government. Tax-exempt: 170(b)(1)(A).
History Museum.
Collections: Native American artifacts; 18th & 19th century furniture made in Lexington County area; textile collection; manuscript collection; looms; spinning wheels; farm implements including cotton gin, cane press, hand implements. Historic Houses: 1832 John Fox House; 1834 Ernest Hazelius House; 1771 Lawrence Corley Log Cabin; 1772 Henrich Senn Log Cabin; 18th century, Lorick Log Cabin; 1820 lawyer's office; 1850 gin house and barn; 1815, school; 1810 Leaphart Harman House.
Research Fields: local history with emphasis on Swiss & German settlers.
Activities: guided tours; lectures; permanent exhibitions; demonstrations of yarn spinning & cloth weaving.
Publications: brochure.
Hours & Admission Prices: Tues.-Sat. 10-4, Sun. 1-4; last tour 3. Adults $5; members no charge. Closed major holidays.
Attendance: 20,000 (accurate)

Manning

CLARENDON COUNTY ARCHIVES AND HISTORY CENTER, Old Manning Library, N. Brooks St., Manning, SC 29103-3209. Mailing Address: 211 N. Brooks St., Manning, SC 29102-3209. Tel.: 803-435-0328.
History Museum.
Collections: county history & culture; photographs; personal artifacts; maps; manuscripts.
Hours & Admission Prices: Mon.-Fri. 9:30-5, Sat. by appointment.

Marion

MARION COUNTY MUSEUM, 101 Willcox Ave., Marion, SC 29571-2809. Tel.: 843-423-8299.
Key Personnel: Dir., Thomas Gett
Historic Building: housed in a former schoolhouse, c.1886. Listed on the National Register for Historic Sites.
Collections: period furnishings; oriental rugs.
Hours & Admission Prices: Tues.-Fri. 9-12 & 1-5; other times by appointment. No charge.

McClellanville

HAMPTON PLANTATION STATE HISTORIC SITE, 1950 Rutledge Rd., McClellanville, SC 29458-9588. Tel.: 843-546-9361. Fax: 843-527-4995.
E-mail: hampton@scprt.com
Web Site: www.southcarolinaparks.com
Formerly: Hampton Plantation State Park
Founded: 1971.

Congressional District: 1
Key Personnel: Rgnl. Chief, Ray Stevens; Park Mgr., Morgan Baird; Pres. (V), Horry Parker.
Personnel Profile: Full-Time Paid 3; Part-Time Volunteers 1.
Governing Authority: state. Affiliated with South Carolina Dept. of Parks, Recreation & Tourism, Brown Bldg., 1205 Pendleton St., Columbia, SC. 29201. Tel.: 803-758-7507. Tax-exempt.
Historic House: c.1750 Hampton House, former rice plantation.
Collections: local history & culture; photographs; period furnishings; personal artifacts.
Research Fields: rice plantation culture.
Facilities: plantation mansion; gardens.
Activities: guided & self-guided tours; nature trail.
Publications: brochure, Hampton Plantation Visitors Guide.
Hours & Admission Prices: Park: daily 9-6. Mansion: March-Oct. Tues.-Sun. 12-4; Nov.-Feb. Thurs.-Sun. 12-4. Mansion: adults $4, youth 6-15 $3, seniors $2.50. Closed Christmas. ♿
Attendance: 30,000 (accurate)

THE VILLAGE MUSEUM, 401 Pinckney St., McClellanville, SC 29458. Mailing Address: P.O. Box 595, McClellanville, SC 29458. Tel.: 843-887-3030.
E-mail: villagemuseum@tds.net
History Museum.
Collections: local history & culture; early pioneers; Native American artifacts.
Hours & Admission Prices: Thurs.-Sat. 10-5. Adults $3; discounts to groups; members, children & students no charge.

McConnells

HISTORIC BRATTONSVILLE, 1444 Brattonsville Rd., McConnells, SC 29726-8768. Tel.: 803-684-2327. Fax: 803-684-0149.
E-mail: hbratton@chmuseums.org
Web Site: www.chmuseums.org
Founded: 1976.
Congressional District: 5
Key Personnel: Dir., Van Shields; Site Dir., Chuck LeCount; Museum Shop Mgr., Mark Cockerille.
Personnel Profile: Full-Time Paid 15; Part-Time Paid 1; Part-Time Volunteers 200.
Governing Authority: nonprofit organizations. Affiliated with York County Council. Parent Institution: York County Historical Commission. Tax-exempt.
Preservation Project: housed in 1823 federal style mansion located on the site of Huck's Defeat in battle during the Revolutionary War.
Collections: 29 historic structures & programs chronicling Carolina and Piedmont development from the 1750s over 720 acres of a living history village & battlefield. Historic Houses: 1776 Col. William Bratton house; 1823 The Homestead; 1843 Brattonsville Female Seminary.
Research Fields: county records; genealogy; craftsman & occupational data in York County.
Facilities: picnic area.
Activities: guided tours; organized educational programs; festivals. Project Sponsors: Living History Days, Saturdays, March-November.
Publications: book, Historic Brattonsville.
Hours & Admission Prices: Mon.-Sat. 10-5, Sun. 1-5; groups & Christmas tours by appointment. Adults $6, seniors 60 & over $5, youth 4-17 $3; members and children 3 & under no charge. Closed New Year's Day; Thanksgiving; Christmas. ♿
Attendance: 21,920 (accurate)
Membership: Students $20; Senior $25; Individual & Jade Society Individual $35; Senior Family $40; Family & Jade Society Family $50; Grandparents $65; Family 2 Year $90.

McCormick

DORN MILL CENTER, 200 N. Main St., McCormick, SC 29835. Mailing Address: P.O. Box 425, McCormick, SC 29835-0425. Fax: 864-852-6870.
E-mail: dulaney@wctel.net
Web Site: www.mccormickschistory.org
Founded: 1980.
Congressional District: 3
Key Personnel: Chm. (V) & Museum Shop Mgr., Kathy Dulaney.
Personnel Profile: Part-Time Volunteers 6.
Governing Authority: Parent Institution: McCormick Historical Commission. Subsidiary Institution: South Carolina's Governor's Office. Tax-exempt.
Interpretive Center.
Collections: America's agricultural & industrial history; gristmill; cotton gin; weigh station; mill equipment; period artifacts.
Facilities: Museum-related items for sale.
Activities: craft demonstrations.
Hours & Admission Prices: By appointment. No charge; donations accepted. ♿

Moncks Corner

BERKELEY COUNTY MUSEUM & HERITAGE CENTER, 950 Stony Landing Rd., Moncks Corner, SC 29461-2944. Tel.: 843-899-5101. Fax: 843-899-5101.
E-mail: berkmuseum@homesc.com
Formerly: Berkeley Museum, Inc.
Founded: 1992.
Congressional District: 1
Key Personnel: Chm. & Pres. (V), Willard Strong; Mgr., Carolyn Pilgrim.
Personnel Profile: Part-Time Paid 2.
Governing Authority: Tax-exempt.
History Museum. Home of the Little David; birthplace of Francis Marion.
Collections: works of local artists & artisans; replica of CSS David, a semi-submersible torpedo boat.
Facilities: research library.
Activities: Annual Event: Antique Tractor and Engine Show in September.
Publications: newsletter, Historical Society.
Hours & Admission Prices: Tues.-Sat. 9-4:30, Sun. 1-4:30. Adults $3, seniors $2; discounts to groups; children 6 & under no charge. Admission to Old Santee Canal Park includes entry to Berkeley Museum. Closed Easter; Thanksgiving; Christmas. ♿
Attendance: 10,000 (estimated)
Membership: Individual $25; Family $35; Donor $100; Contributor $250; Supporting $500; Benefactor $1,000; Sustaining $2,500; Patron $5,000; Founder $10,000; Chairman's Circle $10,000 & up.

OLD SANTEE CANAL PARK, 900 Stony Landing Rd., Moncks Corner, SC 29461-2944. Tel.: 843-899-5200. Fax: 843-761-7032.
E-mail: parkinfo@santeecooper.com
Web Site: www.oldsanteecanalpark.org
Formerly: Old Santee Canal State Historic Site
Founded: 1991.
Congressional District: 1
Key Personnel: C.E.O., Lonnie N. Carter; Museum Shop Mgr., Cindy Moyer.
Personnel Profile: Full-Time Paid 7; Part-Time Paid 2; Part-Time Volunteers 20; Interns 3.
Governing Authority: state; not-for-profit organization. Parent Institution: Santee Cooper.
Park Museum: located on historic Stony Landing Plantation at southern terminus of the Santee Canal (1800-1850s), the first true canal constructed in the United States.
Collections: Santee Canal & activities of the Stony Landing Plantation; construction of the CSS Little David; natural history of a swamp/wetlands environment.
Activities: monthly events.
Hours & Admission Prices: Daily 9-5. Adults $3, senior citizens over 65 $2; discounts to AAA members; children under 5 no charge. Closed New Year's Day; Easter; Thanksgiving; Christmas Eve & Day. ♿
Attendance: 24,834 (accurate)
Membership: Individual Pass $25; Family Pass $35.

Mount Pleasant

CHARLES PINCKNEY NATIONAL HISTORIC SITE, 1254 Long Point Rd., Mount Pleasant, SC 29464. Mailing Address: 1214 Middle St., Sullivan's Island, SC 29482-9717. Tel.: 843-883-3123. Fax: 843-883-3910.
Web Site: www.nps.gov/chpi
Founded: 1988.
Congressional District: 1
Key Personnel: Supt., Bob Dodson; Chief Ranger, Fran Norton; Cultural Resources Program Mgr., Sandy Pusey; Museum Shop Mgr., Kevin Bates.
Personnel Profile: Full-Time Paid 7; Part-Time Volunteers 6.
Governing Authority: federal government; nonprofit. Parent Institution: National Park Service. Tax-exempt.
Historic Site: located in a c.1828 plantation house.
Collections: emphasis on the life & political career of Charles Pinckney, the U.S. Constitution & plantation life and slavery in early America; archaeological artifacts connected to the Pinckney family occupation, 1754-1817; artifacts connected to Snee Farm plantation during the 17th-20th centuries.
Research Fields: Revolutionary war; U.S. Constitution; slavery; U.S. history to 1825; Gullah.
Facilities: classroom. Museum-related items for sale.
Activities: self-guided tours; video presentation; formally organized education programs for children & adults by reservation; temporary exhibits.
Publications: site brochure; site archaeology bulletin; African Americans at Snee Farm; site bulletin.

Hours & Admission Prices: Daily 9-5. No charge; donations accepted. Closed New Years Day; Thanksgiving; Christmas. ♿
Attendance: 35,000 (accurate)

PATRIOTS POINT NAVAL AND MARITIME MUSEUM, 40 Patriots Point Rd., Mount Pleasant, SC 29464-4377. Tel.: 843-884-2727. Fax: 843-881-4232.
Web Site: www.patriotspoint.org
Founded: 1976.
Congressional District: 1
Key Personnel: Chm., John B. Hagerty; Acting Exec. Dir., Dick Trammell; Dir. Operations, Bob Howard; Dir. Tourism & Business Devel., Dick Trammell; Cur. Museum Collections, E.L. Wimett; Sr. Cur., David A. Clark; Museum Shop Mgr., Samuel Derrick.
Personnel Profile: Full-Time Paid 76; Part-Time Paid 36; Part-Time Volunteers 50.
Governing Authority: state; nonprofit. Affiliated with Patriots Point Development Authority. Tax-exempt: 501(c)(3).
Maritime and Naval Museum: housed in the aircraft carrier USS Yorktown, destroyer USS Laffey, submarine USS Clamagore, Coast Guard cutter Ingham, & located in Charleston Harbor; also houses Congressional Medal of Honor Museum & Carrier Aviation Hall of Fame.
Collections: Navy & Marine Corps aircraft; naval & maritime artifacts; manuscripts.
Research Fields: naval & maritime history.
Facilities: theater; 240-seat auditorium; catering; restaurant. Naval items depicting the five ships for sale.
Activities: films; loan, permanent & temporary exhibitions; concerts; radio programs; scout camping program.
Hours & Admission Prices: Daily 9am to various seasonal closing times. Adults $16, senior citizens & active military $13, children 6-11 $8; discounts to Historic Naval Ships Association; children under 6 no charge. Closed Christmas. ♿
Attendance: 263,000 (accurate)
Membership: Individual $40; Grandparent $75; Family $90; Deluxe Family $125.

Mullins

S.C. TOBACCO MUSEUM, 104 NE Front St., Mullins, SC 29574-2810. Tel.: 800-207-7967; 843-464-8194.
E-mail: cityofmullins@mullinssc.us
Web Site: www.mullinssc.us/sctobaccomuseumindex.html
Founded: 1998.
Congressional District: 6
Key Personnel: Dir., Reginald McDaniel.
Personnel Profile: Full-Time Paid 2; Part-Time Volunteers 2.
Governing Authority: city of Mullins.
History Museum: housed in an historic train depot.
Collections: history of tobacco growing; early farm life; tobacco-related equipment; blacksmith tools; documentary video.
Facilities: research library. Museum-related items for sale.
Activities: research; video; tours.
Hours & Admission Prices: Mon.-Fri. 9-5; groups by appointment. Adults $2, children & seniors $1. Closed holidays. ♿
Attendance: 2,000 (estimated)

Murrells Inlet

* **BROOKGREEN GARDENS, (M),** 1931 Brookgreen Dr., Murrells Inlet, SC 29576. Mailing Address: P.O. Box 3368, Pawleys Island, SC 29585-3368. Tel.: 843-235-6000; 800-849-1931. Fax: 843-235-6039.
E-mail: info@brookgreen.org
Web Site: www.brookgreen.org
Founded: 1931.
Congressional District: 6
Key Personnel: C.E.O. & Pres., Robert Jewell; C.F.O. & Vice Pres. Human Resources & I.T., Alexandra Kempe; Vice Pres. & Cur. of Sculpture, Robin R. Salmon; Vice Pres. Horticulture & Conservation, George Welch; Vice Pres. Devel., Phillip A. Tukey; Vice Pres. Mktg., Helen Benso; Mgr. (V), Kelly Callahan; Museum Shop Mgr., Barbara Harrison.
Personnel Profile: Full-Time Paid 69; Part-Time Paid 34; Part-Time Volunteers 400.
Governing Authority: nonprofit organization. Tax-exempt: 501(c)(3).
Art Museum & Botanical Garden.
Collections: sculpture; botany; native fauna.
Research Fields: American figurative sculpture; maintenance of outdoor sculpture; longleaf pine forest ecosystem.
Facilities: wildlife park; representational American sculpture garden; nature center; cafe. Museum-related items for sale.
Activities: guided tours; temporary & permanent exhibitions; adult education program; day camp (Camp Brookgreen). Annual Events: Cool Summer Evenings in summer; Nights of A Thousand Candles in December.
Publications: biannual, Brookgreen Journal; Catalogue of Sculpture Collection; newsletter, 2 issues per year.
Hours & Admission Prices: June 17-Aug. 14 daily 9:30-7; Aug. 15-June 16 daily 9:30-5. Adults $12, children 6-12 $5; children 5 & under and members no charge. Closed Christmas. ♿
Attendance: 232,000
Membership: Individual $60; Family $90; President's Council $250; Chairman's Council $1,000; Huntington Society $2,500; Atalaya Society $5,000.

Myrtle Beach

THE CHILDREN'S MUSEUM OF SOUTH CAROLINA, (M), 2501 N. Kings Hwy., Myrtle Beach, SC 29577-3054. Tel.: 843-946-9469. Fax: 843-946-7011.
E-mail: contactus@cmsckids.org
Web Site: www.cmsckids.org
Founded: 1993.
Congressional District: 1
Key Personnel: Exec. Dir., Pam Ross; Pres. (V), Brenda Spadoni; Coord. & Museum Shop Mgr., Elaine Fogleman.
Personnel Profile: Full-Time Paid 5; Part-Time Paid 3; Part-Time Volunteers 10.
Governing Authority: private; nonprofit organization. Tax-exempt: 501(c)(3).
Children's Museum.
Collections: hands-on exhibits.
Activities: interactive learning experiences; demonstrations; activities; outreach programs.
Publications: bimonthly newsletter; annual report.
Hours & Admission Prices: Memorial Day weekend-Labor Day weekend Mon.-Sat. 10-4; late May-early Sept. Tues.-Sat. 10-4. Admission $8; discount to groups of 10 or more; ACM members, children under 2 & members no charge. Closed New Year's Day; Memorial Day; Independence Day; Labor Day; Thanksgiving; Christmas Eve & Day. ♿
Attendance: 38,000 (accurate)
Membership: Passports: Summer Fun & Saturday $60; Discovery & Explorer $95; Reciprocal $125.

FRANKLIN G. BURROUGHS-SIMEON B. CHAPIN ART MUSEUM, (M), 3100 S. Ocean Blvd., Myrtle Beach, SC 29577-4858. Tel.: 843-238-2510. Fax: 843-238-2910.
Web Site: myrtlebeachartmuseum.org
Founded: 1989.
Key Personnel: Dir., Patricia Goodwin; Chm., Mary Jo Rogers; Treas., Jim Watson; Museum Shop Mgr., Karen Olson.
Personnel Profile: Full-Time Paid 4; Part-Time Paid 2; Part-Time Volunteers 5; Interns 1.
Governing Authority: private; nonprofit. Tax-exempt: 501(c)(3).
Art Museum.
Collections: regional artists.
Facilities: library.
Activities: formal education programs for adults & children; guided tours; temporary exhibitions.
Publications: quarterly newsletter, Villa Voice.
Hours & Admission Prices: Tues.-Sat. 10-4, Sun. 1-4; call for holiday hours. No charge; donations accepted. ♿
Attendance: 22,000 (estimated)
Membership: Student $15; Individual $50; Family $75; Donor $100; Patron $250; Advocate $500.

MYRTLE BEACH STATE PARK NATURE CENTER, 4401 S. Kings Hwy., Myrtle Beach, SC 29575-4936. Tel.: 843-238-5325 & 0874. Fax: 843-238-9483.
E-mail: awilson@scprt.com
Web Site: www.southcarolinaparks.com
Founded: 1970.
Congressional District: 6
Key Personnel: Naturalist, Ann Malys Wilson.
Personnel Profile: Full-Time Paid 1; Part-Time Paid 2; Part-Time Volunteers 200; Interns 3.
Governing Authority: state; nonprofit.
Nature Center.
Collections: shells; animals, reptiles; natural history.
Research Fields: shells; coastal flora & fauna.
Facilities: 100-vol. library; aquarium; nature center; educational facilities.
Activities: guided tours; lectures; organized educational programs for children, adults & college students; participatory exhibits; hands-on natural history programs & walks; curriculum-related school programs for grades 1-5.

Hours & Admission Prices: June-July Tues.-Sun. 11:30-4:30. Varied hours in off season. Park: adult $4, children 6-15 $1.50; children under 5 no charge. ♿
Attendance: 28,034 (accurate)

SOUTH CAROLINA HALL OF FAME, Myrtle Beach Convention Center, 2101 N. Oak St., Myrtle Beach, SC 29577. Mailing Address: P.O. Box 2115, Myrtle Beach, SC 29578-2115. Tel.: 843-626-7444.
Hall of Fame.
Collections: South Carolina's history & heritage; Hall of Fame inductees.
Hours & Admission Prices: Daily 8:30-5. No charge.

Neeses

NEESES FARM MUSEUM, 6449 Savannah Hwy., Neeses, SC 29107. Mailing Address: P.O. Box 70, Neeses, SC 29107-0070. Tel.: 803-247-5811. Fax: 803-247-5811.
Founded: 1976.
Congressional District: 1
Key Personnel: Chm. (V) & Town Clerk, Sonja Gleaton.
Personnel Profile: Part-Time Volunteers 2.
Governing Authority: municipal. Parent Institution: Town of Neeses. Tax-exempt.
Agriculture Museum.
Collections: period harvest equipment; World War I tools & relics; cotton gin; stone grinder; Edgefield pottery; woodburning cook stove; Farmall tractor; Native American cultural display.
Facilities: picnic shed.
Activities: permanent exhibitions; dancing demonstrations by Pee Dee Indian tour guide by appointment.
Hours & Admission Prices: Closed for renovations until 2011. ♿
Attendance: 500 (estimated)

Newberry

NEWBERRY COUNTY HISTORICAL & SOCIETY MUSEUM, 1503 Nance St., Newberry, SC 29108-2740. Mailing Address: P.O. Box 186, Newberry, SC 29108-0186. Tel.: 803-276-8610.
Web Site: www.newberrycountyhistory.com/museum.html
History Museum.
Collections: artifacts & displays relating to the history of Newberry County. Historic House: Gauntt House, c.1808.
Hours & Admission Prices: 1st & 3rd Sat. of each month 1-4; other times by appointment. No charge; donations accepted.

Ninety Six

NINETY SIX NATIONAL HISTORIC SITE, 1103 Hwy. 248, Ninety Six, SC 29666. Mailing Address: P.O. Box 418, Ninety Six, SC 29666-0418. Tel.: 864-543-4068. Fax: 864-543-2058.
Web Site: www.NPS.gov/NISI
Founded: 1976.
Congressional District: 3
Key Personnel: Cur. & Historian, Eric K. Williams; Park Supt., Tim Stone.
Personnel Profile: Full-Time Paid 1; Part-Time Paid 2; Part-Time Volunteers 15.
Governing Authority: federal. National Park Service, Dept. of the Interior. Tax-exempt.
History Museum & Site: commemorates community & village of the settlement of Ninety Six during the 18th-century & the siege of Ninety Six during the American Revolution interpreting the role of slavery.
Collections: 18th-century Indian artifacts; trade items; tools related to cultivation of flax & building of log cabins; military artifacts; pioneers items; findings of archaeological research. Historic Structure: c.1787 two-story log cabin.
Research Fields: history; archaeology.
Activities: lectures; videos; special events. Museum Sponsors: Living History Events.
Publications: brochure.
Hours & Admission Prices: Visitor Center: daily 9-5. Cabin: open for special occasions & during Living History events. No charge; donations accepted. Closed New Year's Day; Thanksgiving; Christmas. ♿
Attendance: 50,000 (estimated)

North Charleston

NORTH CHARLESTON AND AMERICAN LAFRANCE FIRE MUSEUM AND EDUCATIONAL CENTER, (M), 4975 Centre Pointe Dr., North Charleston, SC 29418-6945. Mailing Address: P.O. Box 190016, North Charleston, SC 29419-9016. Tel.: 843-740-5550.
Founded: 2007.
Key Personnel: Dir., Renee B. Frye.
Personnel Profile: Full-Time Paid 3; Part-Time Paid 10.
Governing Authority: city.
Fire Museum.
Collections: fire fighting history; period fire fighting equipment & trucks; American LaFrance period vehicles; interactive fire & home safety exhibits.
Activities: educational programs.
Hours & Admission Prices: Mon.-Sat. 10-5, Sun. 1-5. Adults 13 & over $6; discounts to groups of 15 or more; children 12 & under no charge. Closed New Year's Day; Thanksgiving & day after; Christmas Eve & Day. ♿
Attendance: 32,000 (estimated)

Orangeburg

I.P. STANBACK MUSEUM & PLANETARIUM, (M), 300 College St., N.E., South Carolina State University, Orangeburg, SC 29117-0001. Mailing Address: Stanback Planetarium & NASA ERC, P.O. Box 7636, South Carolina State Univ., Orangeburg, SC 29117-0001. Tel.: 803-536-7174 & 8711. Fax: 803-536-8309.
E-mail: bmille26@scsu.edu
Web Site: www.scsucrash.blogspot.com
Founded: 1980.
Congressional District: 2
Key Personnel: Pres., Dr. George E. Cooper; Dir., Ellen Zisholtz.
Personnel Profile: Part-Time Paid 5; Interns 1.
Governing Authority: state; nonprofit organization. Parent Institution: South Carolina State University. Tax-exempt: 501(c)(3).
Planetarium & Art Museum.
Collections: contemporary Afro-American art including William H. Johnson, Ellis Wilson, Elton Fax, Romare Bearden; Jacob Lawrence; Lois Jones; bronze statuary from Benin; over 200 pieces from Cameroons & parts of West Africa; 300-400 photographs, Harlem on My Mind Exhibit, including Van Der Zee, Gordon Parks & Susskind.
Research Fields: contemporary Afro-American art; African art.
Facilities: planetarium; education resource center.
Activities: gallery guided tours; formally organized education programs for K-12 students & undergraduate college students; permanent, temporary & traveling exhibitions.
Publications: annual brochure; occasional catalogs for special exhibits.
Hours & Admission Prices: Museum: Mon.-Fri. 9-5. No charge. Planetarium Shows: Tues.-Fri. 4pm. No charge. ♿
Attendance: 30,000 (estimated)
Membership: Students $15; Individual $25; Family $75; Founding $100-$249; Supporting $250-$499; Sustaining $500-$999; Patron's Circle $1,000 & up; Corporate $5,000.

Parris Island

PARRIS ISLAND MUSEUM, (M), Bldg. 111, Panama St., MCRD, Parris Island, SC 29905. Mailing Address: Commanding Gen., ATTN MUS, MCRD ERR, Box 19320, Parris Island, SC 29905-9001. Tel.: 843-228-2951. Fax: 843-228-3065.
E-mail: stephen.wise@usmc.mil
Founded: 1976.
Congressional District: 2
Key Personnel: Dir., Dr. Stephen R. Wise; Pres. (V), Pete Miller; Archaeologist, Dr. Bryon P. Howard; Museum Shop Mgr., Chuck Taliano.
Personnel Profile: Full-Time Paid 7; Part-Time Volunteers 3.
Governing Authority: federal. Parent Institution: Marine Corps History Division. Tax-exempt.
Historic Site & Military Museum: located on the site of c.1566-1587, Spanish settlement, Santa Elena; later the 19th century Port Royal Navy Yard & Marine Corps Recruit Depot.
Collections: ceramics; metal work; uniforms; firearms; archives; photograph collection.
Research Fields: Spanish & French settlements of the Southeast; history of the Port Royal area, Marine Corps history; current recruit training.
Facilities: 200-vol. library pertaining to history of Port Royal & U.S. Marine Corps available for use on the premises.
Activities: guided tours; lectures; films.
Publications: quarterly newsletter; brochure, Driving Tour.

Hours & Admission Prices: Daily 10-4:30. No charge; donations accepted. Closed New Year's Day; Easter; Thanksgiving; Christmas. ♿
Attendance: 108,314 (accurate)
Membership: Student $10; Individual $20; Family $30; Contributor $100; Business Sponsor $100 & up; Sustaining $1,000 or $100 for 10 yrs.

Pendleton

ASHTABULA HISTORIC HOUSE, 2725 Old Greenville Hwy., Pendleton, SC 29670. Mailing Address: Pendleton Historic Foundation, P.O. Box 444, Pendleton, SC 29670-0444. Tel.: 864-646-7249.
E-mail: info@pendletonhistoricfoundation.org
Web Site: www.pendletonhistoricfoundation.org
Founded: 1960.
Congressional District: 3
Key Personnel: Pres. (V), Jackie Reynolds; Treas. (V), Elizabeth Vogt; Sec. (V), Deborah Zungoli; Exec. Dir., Christa Skeen; Museum Shop Mgr., Carole McCullah.
Personnel Profile: Full-Time Volunteers 3; Part-Time Paid 3; Part-Time Volunteers 17.
Governing Authority: private; nonprofit organization. Parent Institution: Pendleton Historic Foundation. Tax-exempt: 501(c)(3).
Historic House: c.1825 2-story Antebellum Plantation House & c.1790 original Brick 2-story House.
Collections: period furnishings; period tools; historic houses.
Research Fields: genealogy 1830-1908.
Activities: guided tours; permanent exhibitions; historical reenactments; first-person interpretive tours; teas & lecture series; docent training programs.
Publications: brochures; quarterly, Pendleton Historic Foundation Newsletter; history books.
Hours & Admission Prices: April-Oct. Tues.-Fri. 1-4, Sun. 1-5; see website for additional holiday hours. Adults $6, children 5-10 $2; children under 5 no charge. ♿
Attendance: 2,856 (accurate)
Membership: Individual $35; Family $50; Patron $100 & up.

PENDLETON DISTRICT AGRICULTURAL MUSEUM, 120 History Lane, Pendleton, SC 29670. Mailing Address: P.O. Box 565, Pendleton, SC 29670-0565. Tel.: 864-646-3782; 800-862-1795. Fax: 864-646-7768.
E-mail: history@pendletondistrict.org
Web Site: www.pendletondistrict.org
Founded: 1976.
Congressional District: 3
Key Personnel: Dir., Vicki B. Fletcher; Chm. (V), Bennie Cunningham; Cur. Collections, Elizabeth Johnson; Coord. Events & Tours, Jo McConnell.
Personnel Profile: Full-Time Paid 3; Part-Time Volunteers 2.
Governing Authority: nonprofit. Parent Institution: Pendleton District Historical, Recreational & Tourism Commission. Tax-exempt: 501(c)(3).
Agricultural Museum.
Collections: local pre-1925 farm tools & equipment.
Activities: guided tours.
Hours & Admission Prices: By appointment only. No charge; donations accepted. ♿
Attendance: 450 (estimated)

PENDLETON DISTRICT HISTORICAL, RECREATIONAL AND TOURISM COMMISSION, (M), 125 E. Queen St., Pendleton, SC 29670-1309. Mailing Address: P.O. Box 565, Pendleton, SC 29670-0565. Tel.: 864-646-3782 & 800-862-1795. Fax: 864-646-7768.
E-mail: pendletontourism@bellsouth.net
Web Site: www.pendleton-district.org
Founded: 1966.
Congressional District: 3
Key Personnel: Chm. (V), Mary Mills; Dir., Vicki B. Fletcher; Cur. Collections, Elizabeth Coker; Events & Tours Coord., Jo McConnell.
Personnel Profile: Full-Time Paid 3; Interns 1.
Governing Authority: county; state. Branch Museum: Agricultural Museum, U.S. 76, Pendleton, SC . Tax-exempt: 170(b)(1)(A).
History Museum.
Collections: 1850 Hunter's Store artifacts; manuscripts; local history library of Anderson, Oconee, Pickens Counties; family genealogies; regional photo collection, 3,000 prints; early farm tools; Civil War military; textile mills records.
Research Fields: general history of Anderson, Oconee, Pickens Counties; family genealogies.
Facilities: 2,000-vol. library of history books available on premises; photostats on request; reading room. Books, arts & crafts, postcards for sale.
Activities: guided tours; lectures; films; arts festivals; formally organized education programs for children and adults; permanent, temporary & traveling exhibitions.
Publications: quarterly newsletter, Friends of the Pendleton District.
Hours & Admission Prices: April-Oct. Mon.-Fri. 9-4:30, Sat. 10-3; Nov.-March Mon.-Fri. 9-4:30. No charge; donations accepted. Closed state holidays. ♿
Attendance: 5,000 (estimated)
Membership: Friends of the Pendleton District $25, $50, $100 & $250.

WOODBURN HISTORIC HOUSE, 130 History Lane, Pendleton, SC 29670-8700. Mailing Address: Pendleton Historic Foundation, P.O. Box 444, Pendleton, SC 29670. Tel.: 864-646-7249.
E-mail: info@pendletonhistoricfoundation.org
Web Site: www.pendletonhistoricfoundation.org
Formerly: Woodburn Plantation
Founded: 1960.
Congressional District: 3
Key Personnel: Pres. (V), Jackie Reynolds; Treas. (V), Elizabeth Vogt; Sec. (V), Deborah Zungoli; Exec. Dir., Christa Skeen; Museum Shop Mgr., Carole McCullan.
Personnel Profile: Full-Time Volunteers 3; Part-Time Paid 3; Part-Time Volunteers 17.
Governing Authority: foundation; nonprofit organization. Parent Institution: Pendleton Historic Foundation. Tax-exempt: 501(c)(3).
Historic House: c.1830 four-story Greek Revival Plantation House.
Collections: period furnishings; old tools. Historic Houses: c.1800 log house; carriage house; c. 1810 log cook house; slave cabin.
Research Fields: genealogy 1830-1908.
Facilities: walking trail.
Activities: guided tours; permanent exhibitions; historical reenactments; first-person interpretive tours; tea & lecture series; children's educational programs & tours; docent training program.
Publications: brochures; quarterly newsletters; history books.
Hours & Admission Prices: April-Oct. Sun. 2-6, Thurs.-Fri. 1-4; other times by appointment. Adults $6, children 5-11 $2.
Attendance: 3,947 (accurate)
Membership: Individual $35; Family $50; Patron $100 & up.

Pickens

HAGOOD-MAULDIN HOUSE AND IRMA MORRIS MUSEUM OF FINE ARTS, 104 N. Lewis St., Pickens, SC 29671-2311. Mailing Address: P.O. Box 775, Pickens, SC 29671-0775. Tel.: 864-898-5963.
Governing Authority: Parent Institution: Pickens County Historical Society.
Art Museum: housed in the former home of attorney James Hagood; built c.1856.
Collections: 17th & 18th century art & furnishings.
Activities: Museum Sponsors: Special Christmas Event in December.
Hours & Admission Prices: April-Dec. 12 3rd Sat. of month 11-4; other times by appointment. Adults $2, students $1. Closed Independence Day; Labor Day; Thanksgiving; Christmas.

PICKENS COUNTY MUSEUM OF ART & HISTORY, (M), 307 Johnson St., Pickens, SC 29671-2463. Tel.: 864-898-5963. Fax: 864-898-5580.
E-mail: picmus@co.pickens.sc.us
Web Site: www.co.pickens.sc.us/culturalcommission
Founded: 1976.
Congressional District: 3
Key Personnel: Exec. Dir., C. Allen Coleman; Chm., Susan Benjamin; Cur., Helen Hockwelt; Mill Site Mgr., Ed L. Bolt; Chief Preparator, Dan M. Brennan; Museum Shop Mgr., Den Keys.
Personnel Profile: Full-Time Paid 5; Part-Time Volunteers 40.
Governing Authority: county government; nonprofit. Parent Institution: Pickens County, SC. Subsidiary Institution: Pickens County Cultural Commission. Tax-exempt.
Art & History Museum.
Collections: regional 20th & 21st century art; art, artifacts & antiquities pertaining to the regional history including Native Americans & settlers; period furnishings; pictures; native plant gardens. Off-site: Hagood Mill Historic Site & Folklife Center; 1845 gristmill & historic park.
Research Fields: regional folklife & history.
Activities: guided tours; lectures; gallery talks; concerts; drama; formally organized education programs; permanent & temporary exhibitions; workshops; classes. Museum Sponsors: Autumn music series; Folklife Festival annual in September; Storytelling Festival in October; Statewide Juried Art Competition in Spring; Youth arts programs; Selugadu: A Native American Celebration in November.
Publications: newsletter, Old Gaol Gazette.
Hours & Admission Prices: Tues.-Wed. & Fri. 9-5, Thurs. 9-7:30, Sat. 9-4:30. No charge; donations accepted. Closed major holidays. ♿
Attendance: 25,000 (estimated)
Membership: Student $10; Senior $20; Individual $29; Family $50; Contributor $100; Director $250; Patron $1,000; Benefactor $2,500.

Ridgeland

PRATT MEMORIAL LIBRARY & WEBEL MUSEUM, 451 E. Wilson St., Ridgeland, SC 29936. Mailing Address: P.O. Box 1540, Ridgeland, SC 29936-2626. Tel.: 843-726-7744. Fax: 843-726-7813.
Key Personnel: Branch Mgr., Marcia Cleland
History Museum & Library.
Collections: 250 rare books on the history of Lowcountry; Indian artifacts from Jasper County; 200 portraits & maps; rice culture dioramas; historical materials on the Revolution & Civil Wars.
Facilities: library.
Hours & Admission Prices: Library: Mon.-Fri. 10:30-5:30. Museum: Mon. 10:30-6, Tues.-Thurs. 10:30-5:30, Fri. 10:30-4:30, Sat. 10-1. No charge. Closed holidays.

Rock Hill

CENTER FOR THE ARTS - DALTON GALLERY, 121 E. Main St., Rock Hill, SC 29730-4539. Mailing Address: P.O. Box 2797, Rock Hill, SC 29732-4797. Tel.: 803-328-2787. Fax: 803-328-2165.
E-mail: arts@yorkcountyarts.org
Web Site: www.yorkcountyarts.org
Key Personnel: Exec. Dir., Debra Heintz
Art Gallery.
Collections: paintings.
Activities: performing arts; classes.
Hours & Admission Prices: 2nd & 4th Sat. 10-2, Sun. 2-4 each month.

* **MUSEUM OF YORK COUNTY, (M),** 4621 Mount Gallant Rd., Rock Hill, SC 29732-9637. Tel.: 803-329-2121. Fax: 803-329-5249.
E-mail: info@chmuseums.org
Web Site: www.chmuseums.org
Founded: 1950.
Congressional District: 5
Key Personnel: Dir., Van W. Shields; Deputy Dir. Mktg. & Visitor Svcs., Jeannie Marion.
Personnel Profile: Full-Time Paid 56; Part-Time Paid 20; Part-Time Volunteers 489; Interns 16.
Governing Authority: county; bd. of trustees. Parent Institution: Culture & Heritage Museums. Tax-exempt: 501(c)(3).
General Museum.
Collections: mounted African hooved mammals; local natural history specimens; mounted North American, animals; cultural materials; ethnological materials from Africa; art by Vernon Grant; regional art; York County history.
Major Exhibits: Turkey Calls: From Function to Art (T), 11/09-4/2/10; Made in Nature, 11/09-4/25/10; Vernon Grant's Wild & Whimsical Animals, 2/27/10-10/10/10; Tinker Tim the Toymaker, 6/5/10-12/10; River Litter Art, 6/5/10-5/11; Vernon Grant's Holiday Images, 11/13/10-1/11.
Research Fields: African animals, astronomy; local natural history; regional historical material culture.
Facilities: picnic facilities; planetarium; auditorium; nature trail; outdoor amphitheatre.
Activities: guided tours; lectures; films; gallery talks; classes; workshops; formally organized education programs for children, adults & undergraduate college students; inter-museum loan, permanent, temporary & traveling exhibitions.
Publications: bimonthly newsletter; posters; brochures; gallery guides; members magazine.
Hours & Admission Prices: Museum: Mon.-Sat. 10-5, Sun. 1-5. Office: Mon.-Fri. 8:30-5:30. Adult $5, senior citizens 60 & over $4, children 4-17 $3; discount to AAM members; members & children 3 and under no charge. Closed New Year's Day; Thanksgiving; Christmas Eve & Day. ♿
Attendance: 60,000 (estimated)
Membership: Senior Citizen $30; Adult $40; Dual $50; Household $65; Sustainer $150; Partner $300; Sponsor $500; Patron $1,000; Benefactor $2,500.

WINTHROP UNIVERSITY GALLERIES, (M), 106 McLaurin Hall, Rock Hill, SC 29733-0001. Tel.: 803-323-2493.
E-mail: derksenk@winthrop.edu
Key Personnel: Dir., Tom Stanley; Asst. Gallery Dir., Karen Derksen
Art Galleries.
Collections: art exhibitions.
Hours & Admission Prices: Mon.-Fri. 9-5. No charge.

Roebuck

WALNUT GROVE PLANTATION, 1200 Otts Shoals Rd., Roebuck, SC 29376-3518. Tel.: 864-576-6546. Fax: 864-576-4058.
E-mail: walnutgrove@spartanburghistory.org
Web Site: www.spartanburghistory.org
Founded: 1961.
Congressional District: 4
Key Personnel: C.E.O. & History Assoc., Jennifer Furrow; Dir., Becky Slayton.
Personnel Profile: Full-Time Paid 1; Part-Time Paid 16; Part-Time Volunteers 2.
Governing Authority: society; nonprofit. Parent Institution: Spartanburg County Historical Association. Tax-exempt: 501(c)(3).
Historic House Museum: c.1765 Walnut Grove Plantation, pre-Revolutionary manor house built on land grant from George III to Charles Moore.
Collections: 1760-1805 furnishings; The Manor House and kitchen; Rocky Springs academy; doctor's office; outbuildings.
Facilities: visitor's center; Pavilion for picnics. Museum-related items for sale.
Activities: guided tours; permanent exhibitions; living history demonstration with reservation. Annual Event: FESTIFALL, weekend living history festival in October.
Publications: booklet, Historic Walnut Grove Plantation 1765; The Drover's Post; Walnut Grove Fun & Learn Book.
Hours & Admission Prices: April-Oct. Tues.-Sat. 11-5, Sun. 2-5; Nov.-March Sat. 11-5, Sun. 2-5; other times by appointment. Adults $6, seniors $5.50, children under 18 $3; discounts to AAA members; members no charge. Closed holidays. ♿
Attendance: 13,000 (accurate)
Membership: Student 18 & under $10; Individual $40; Dual $60; Family $75; Spartan Regiment Society $100 & up; Kate Moore Barry Society $250 & up; Lewis P. Jones Society $500 & up.

Saint Helena Island

YORK W. BAILEY MUSEUM AT PENN CENTER, 110 Martin Luther King, Jr. Dr., Saint Helena Island, SC 29920. Mailing Address: Penn School National Historic Landmark District, P.O. Box 126, Saint Helena Island, SC 29920-0126. Tel.: 843-838-2432. Fax: 843-838-8545.
E-mail: info@penncenter.com
Web Site: www.penncenter.com
Founded: 1971.
Key Personnel: C.E.O. & Dir., Bernie Wright; Chm. (V), Dr. Leo Richardson; Museum Shop Mgr., Rosalyn Browne.
Personnel Profile: Full-Time Paid 1; Part-Time Paid 1; Part-Time Volunteers 7.
Governing Authority: Tax-exempt.
History Museum.
Collections: history of Penn School; Sea Island & African American history; 1863 school bell; photographs.
Research Fields: Reconstruction Era; education of freed slaves.
Facilities: Museum-related items for sale.
Activities: cultural lessons; demonstrations; educational programs. Museum Sponsors: Annual Penn Center Heritage Days Celebration in November.
Publications: membership newsletter.
Hours & Admission Prices: Mon.-Sat. 11-4; other times by appointment. Adults $5, senior citizens $4, children $2; discounts to groups of 10 or more, and AAM & ICOM members. Closed New Year's Day; Independence Day; Labor Day; Thanksgiving; Christmas. ♿
Attendance: 30,000 (estimated)
Membership: Supporting Friends $100-$499; Benefactors $500-$1,999; Leading Friends $2,000-$4,999; Friends for Life $5,000-$10,000.

Saint Matthews

CALHOUN COUNTY MUSEUM & CULTURAL CENTER, (M), 313 Butler St., Saint Matthews, SC 29135-1409. Tel.: 803-874-3964. Fax: 803-874-4790.
E-mail: calmus@oburg.net
Web Site: www.calhouncountymuseumandculturalcenter.org
Founded: 1954.
Congressional District: 93
Key Personnel: Dir., Debbie U. Roland; Chm. & Pres. (V), Martha Emily Shirer; Asst. Dir., Jeff Reid.
Personnel Profile: Full-Time Paid 3.
Governing Authority: county. Tax-exempt.
General Museum.
Collections: archives; costumes; agriculture; archaeology; history; medical; preservation project.
Research Fields: history; genealogy; archaeology; natural history.
Facilities: 450-vol. library of rare books available on premises.
Activities: guided tours; lectures; film series; art exhibits; drama.
Publications: booklet, Brief History of Calhoun County.
Hours & Admission Prices: Tues.-Fri. 9-4; groups of 10 or more & researchers call for appointment. No charge; donations accepted. ♿
Attendance: 7,000 (estimated)

Membership: Friend of Museum: Single $35; Family $55; Patron $100; Corporate $500; Benefactor $1,000 & up.

Saluda

SALUDA COUNTY HISTORICAL SOCIETY MUSEUM AND THEATER, 105 Law Range, Saluda, SC 29138-1701.
Historical Society Museum: listed on the National Register of Historical Places.
Collections: local history & culture; farm tools; liquor still; period scrapbooks; arts & crafts; photographs; personal artifacts. Historic Building: theater, c.1936.
Facilities: theater.
Hours & Admission Prices: Mon.-Fri. 10-4, Sat. 10-1. Closed major holidays.

Seneca

LUNNEY MUSEUM, 211 W. South 1st St., Seneca, SC 29678-3307. Tel.: 864-882-4811.
Key Personnel: Dir., Judy Havice.
Governing Authority: Operated by: Oconee County Museum.
Historic House: housed in a California-style bungalow, built in 1909 by Dr. & Mrs. W.J. Lunney. Listed on the National Register of Historic Places.
Collections: Victorian furniture; personal artifacts; Oconee County history.
Hours & Admission Prices: Thurs.-Sun. 1-5. No charge. Closed major holidays.

THE WORLD OF ENERGY, 7812 Rochester Hwy., Seneca, SC 29672-0752. Tel.: 800-777-1004, ext. 1. Fax: 864-885-4605.
Formerly: World of Energy at Keowee-Toxaway
Founded: 1969.
Congressional District: 3
Key Personnel: Mgr. Community Rels., Sandra Magee.
Personnel Profile: Full-Time Paid 5.
Governing Authority: company. Duke Energy Company.
Science & Technology Center (Energy & Electricity emphasis): overlooking the Oconee Nuclear Station & the nearby lakes Keowee & Jocassee.
Collections: eight participatory energy exhibits; hydro chamber with waterwheel; leaf chamber; coal chamber; fission chamber; model of nuclear reactor; fiber optics display; electronic energy conservation quiz; home energy conservation & recycling exhibit.
Facilities: 120-seat auditorium; classroom; nature trail; picnic shelter; seasonal butterfly garden.
Activities: lectures; films; special events; formally organized education programs; permanent exhibitions; self-guided tours.
Publications: pamphlets, Explore Energy; The Forests & Flowers of Keowee-Toxaway; Catalog of Educational Services; films.
Hours & Admission Prices: Mon.-Fri. 9-5, Sat. 12-5. No charge. Closed holidays. ♿
Attendance: 55,000 (estimated)

Spartanburg

MILLIKEN GALLERY, CONVERSE COLLEGE, 580 E. Main St., Spartanburg, SC 29302-0006. Tel.: 864-596-9214. Fax: 864-596-9606.
E-mail: artdesign@converse.edu
Web Site: www.converse.edu
Founded: 1971.
Congressional District: 3
Key Personnel: Dir., Kathryn Boucher.
Personnel Profile: Part-Time Paid 6; Interns 4.
Governing Authority: college.
College Art Gallery.
Collections: changing exhibitions.
Facilities: Milliken Gallery; Community Outreach Gallery.
Activities: visiting artists; workshops.
Hours & Admission Prices: Sept.-May Mon.-Fri. 9-5, Sun. 2-5. No charge. Closed New Year's Day; school holidays. ♿
Attendance: 1,700

THE SANDOR TESZLER LIBRARY, Wofford College, 429 N. Church St., Spartanburg, SC 29303-3663. Tel.: 864-597-4300. Fax: 864-597-4329.
E-mail: coburnoh@wofford.edu
Web Site: www.wofford.edu/library/
Congressional District: 4
Key Personnel: Dean Library, Oakley H. Coburn.
Governing Authority: college. Wofford College.
Art Gallery & College Museum: located on 1854 campus.
Collections: books; prints; posters; framed paintings & graphics; original & reproduction sculpture.
Facilities: 250,000-vol. library of general liberal arts & rare book collection, private press books, archival & historical & 5,000 vol. art book collection, available for inter-library loan during regular library hours; planetarium; 1,000-seat auditorium; classrooms; 700-seat cafeteria.
Activities: films; arts festivals; formally organized education programs for adults & undergraduate college students; temporary & traveling exhibitions.
Publications: exhibition brochures; catalogs.
Hours & Admission Prices: Sept.-May Mon.-Thurs. 8am to midnight, Fri. 8-7, Sat. 10-5, Sun. 1pm to midnight; Summer: Mon.-Thurs. 8-9, Fri. 8-5; hours vary during school holidays. No charge. ♿
Membership: Friends of the Library: Contributing $15; Sustaining $15-$100; Sponsor $100 & up.

THE SEAY HOUSE, 106 Darby Rd., Spartanburg, SC 29306. Mailing Address: P.O. Box 887, Spartanburg, SC 29304-0887. Tel.: 864-596-3501. Fax: 864-596-2399.
E-mail: seayhouse@spartanburghistory.org
Web Site: www.spartanburghistory.org
Founded: 1974.
Congressional District: 4
Key Personnel: Dir., Becky Slayton.
Personnel Profile: Full-Time Paid 1; Part-Time Paid 1; Part-Time Volunteers 2.
Governing Authority: society; nonprofit organization. Parent Institution: Spartanburg County Historical Association. Tax-exempt: 501(c)(3).
Historic House: c.1890 home.
Collections: c.1890 decorative arts, focus on women's history; Seay family belongings.
Activities: guided tours.
Publications: The Drover's Post.
Hours & Admission Prices: April-Oct. 3rd Sat. of month 11-5; other times by appointment. No charge; donations accepted. Closed holidays. ♿
Attendance: 100 (estimated)
Membership: Student $10; Individual $40; Family $75; Spartan Regiment Society $100; Kate Barry Society $250; Lewis P. Jones Society $500.

SPARTANBURG ART MUSEUM (SAM), 200 E. Saint John St., Spartanburg, SC 29306-5124. Tel.: 864-582-7616. Fax: 864-948-5353. TDD: 864-583-2776.
E-mail: museum@spartanarts.org
Web Site: www.spartanburgartmuseum.org
Formerly: Spartanburg County Museum of Art
Founded: 1969.
Congressional District: 4
Key Personnel: Pres., Brant Bynum; Exec. Dir., Karl Hollander; Assoc. Dir. & Cur., Scott Cunningham; Mktg., Margaret Edmunds; Dir. Art School, Bob LoGrippo.
Personnel Profile: Full-Time Paid 3; Part-Time Paid 5; Part-Time Volunteers 10; Interns 4.
Governing Authority: nonprofit organization. Tax-exempt: 501(c)(3).
Art Museum.
Collections: paintings, graphics & decorative arts by regional, nationally & internationally known artists.
Facilities: 3,000 sq. ft. exhibit space.
Activities: guided tours; lectures; films; traveling exhibitions; Converse College intern program; temporary exhibitions; Art School; C.O.L.O.R.S., a free studio class for inner-city youth; docent programs; art trips; exhibition series. Museum Sponsors: annual meeting; 12-24 art exhibitions annually.
Publications: quarterly art events listing, Art Calendar; membership campaign; special events & exhibits brochures.
Hours & Admission Prices: Tues.-Wed. & Fri.-Sat. 10-5, Thurs. 10-8. Adults $4, seniors & active military $3, studens with college ID $2,50, children 6-18 $2; children 5 & under no charge. Closed New Year's Day; Easter Monday; Memorial Day; Independence Day; Labor Day; Thanksgiving; Christmas Eve & Day. ♿
Attendance: 15,000 (estimated)
Membership: Individual $25; Family $50; Patron $100; Picasso Club $250; Rembrandt Society $500; Michelangelo's Circle $1,000 & up.

SPARTANBURG REGIONAL MUSEUM OF HISTORY, 200 E. St. John St., Spartanburg, SC 29306-5124. Mailing Address: P.O. Box 887, Spartanburg, SC 29304-0887. Tel.: 864-596-3501. Fax: 864-596-2399.
E-mail: regionalmuseum@spartanburghistory.org
Web Site: www.spartanburghistory.org
Formerly: Spartanburg County Regional Museum of History
Founded: 1961.
Congressional District: 4
Key Personnel: Dir., Becky Slayton; Admin., Nannie Jefferies; Collections Mgr., Brad Steinecke.
Personnel Profile: Full-Time Paid 1; Part-Time Volunteers 6; Interns 2.

Governing Authority: society. Parent Institution: Spartanburg County Historical Association. Tax-exempt: 501(c)(3).
Local History Museum.
Collections: Sloan doll collection; photographs throughout Spartanburg in many time periods; quilts; decorative arts.
Facilities: 4,500 sq. ft. exhibit space.
Activities: permanent & temporary exhibitions. Annual Event: Christmas Toys.
Publications: quarterly newsletter, Drover's Post.
Hours & Admission Prices: Tues.-Sat. 10-5. No charge; donations accepted. Closed major holidays. ♿
Attendance: 7,000 (accurate)
Membership: Student $10; Individual $40; Family $75; Spartan Regiment Society $100; Kate Barry Society $250; Lewis P. Jones Society $500.

SPARTANBURG SCIENCE CENTER, 200 E. Saint John St., Spartanburg, SC 29306-5124. Tel.: 864-583-2777. Fax: 864-948-5353.
E-mail: science@spartanarts.org
Web Site: www.spartanarts.org/sciencecenter
Founded: 1978.
Congressional District: 4
Key Personnel: Exec. Dir., John F. Green; Pres. (V), Corinne DeAngelis; Chm. (V), John LeFaure.
Personnel Profile: Full-Time Paid 2; Part-Time Paid 1; Part-Time Volunteers 12; Interns 1.
Governing Authority: nonprofit organization. Tax-exempt: 501(c)(3).
Science Museum & Center.
Collections: skulls; skeletons; fossils; minerals; Indian artifacts; living cold-blooded vertebrates; aquaria; old texts on natural history; 35 mm slide collection of regional flora & fauna and local rocks & minerals; South Carolina wildlife; Thomas Edison; Furman T. Wallace wildlife exhibit; science including astronomy, the human body, insects, plants & pure science.
Research Fields: regional natural history including birds, reptiles & plants.
Facilities: 100-vol. library of books on the sciences & natural history, available for inter-library loan; microscopes; nature center; aquarium; science camp location.
Activities: lectures; films; science summer camps; birthday parties; formally organized education programs for children & adults; permanent & traveling exhibitions; school loan service; Health & Wellness program (preschool); community out reach program; portable planetarium, Starlab, used in local schools; science club.
Publications: biannual newsletter.
Hours & Admission Prices: Mon.-Fri. Adults $4, seniors $3, college students $2.50, children 6-18 $2; children 5 & under and members no charge. ♿
Attendance: 25,000 (accurate)
Membership: Students & Teachers $10; Individual $20; Family $25; Friend $50; Sponsor $100; Supporter $200; Patron $500; Benefactor $1,000.

Sullivan's Island

* **FORT SUMTER NATIONAL MONUMENT,** 1214 Middle St., Sullivan's Island, SC 29482-9748. Tel.: 843-883-3123, ext. 23 (chief ranger); 843-883-3123, ext. 22 (park historian). Fax: 843-883-3910.
E-mail: bill_martin@nps.gov
Web Site: www.nps.gov/fosu
Founded: 1948.
Congressional District: 1
Key Personnel: Superintendent, Bob Dodson; Chief Ranger, Fran Norton; Museum Shop Mgr., Kevin Bates.
Personnel Profile: Full-Time Paid 25; Part-Time Paid 5; Part-Time Volunteers 17; Interns 2.
Governing Authority: federal government. Parent Institution: National Park Service. Tax-exempt: 101(6).
Military Museums: housed in Fort Moultrie Visitor Center & 1829 Fort Sumter.
Collections: artifacts & manuscripts, connected with Fort Sumter & Fort Moultrie; military uniforms; military equipment.
Research Fields: Seacoast Defense; Civil War; Revolutionary War in Charleston; Spanish American War; World War I; World War II.
Facilities: 2,000-vol. library dealing with American Revolution, Civil War & American seacoast defense, available for use under supervision of park employee; reading room; 120-seat auditorium; theater. Museum-related items for sale.
Activities: guided tours; lectures; films; formally organized education programs for children; temporary exhibitions; living history programs.
Publications: park brochures; site bulletins; teacher's guides.
Hours & Admission Prices: Fort Sumter: call for searsonal hours; accessible only by boat. Tour Boat: adults $16, seniors $14.50, children 6-11 $10; children 5 & under no charge. Fort Moultrie: daily 9-5. Families $5, adults $3, seniors 62 & over $1; children 16 & under no charge. Closed New Years Day; Thanksgiving, Christmas. ♿
Attendance: 337,000 (estimated)

Summerville

OLD DORCHESTER STATE HISTORIC SITE, 300 State Park Rd., Summerville, SC 29485-8431. Tel.: 843-873-1740 & 7475 (archaeology lab). Fax: 843-873-1740.
Web Site: www.southcarolinaparks.com
Founded: 1960.
Congressional District: 1
Key Personnel: District Mgr., Larry Duncan; Park Mgr., Ty Houck; Archaeologist, Ashley Chapman.
Personnel Profile: Full-Time Paid 4; Part-Time Volunteers 3; Interns 1.
Governing Authority: state. Affiliated with the South Carolina Dept. of Parks, Recreation & Tourism, Brown Bldg., 1205 Pendleton St., Columbia, SC 29201. Tel.: 803-734-0168. Tax-exempt.
Preservation Project: archaeological site of the colonial Village of Dorchester founded in 1697 by Congregationalists from Massachusetts.
Collections: archaeological remnants of 18th-century village. Historical Buildings: tabby fort 1757-60; Church Tower 1751.
Research Fields: 18th-century trading town of Dorchester.
Facilities: exhibit kiosk.
Activities: educational programs; public excavations 6 days a month & special events offered periodically.
Publications: brochure, Historical Visitors Guide.
Hours & Admission Prices: Daily 9-6. Adult $2, seniors $1.25; children under 15, SC residents 65 & over no charge. ♿
Attendance: 118,300
Membership: Annual Park Passport $40 (for one year, allows any entrance to any South Carolina State Park).

SUMMERVILLE DORCHESTER MUSEUM, 100 E. Doty Ave., Summerville, SC 29483. Mailing Address: P.O. Box 1873, Summerville, SC 29484. Tel.: 843-875-9666.
History Museum: housed in the former Summerville Police Station.
Collections: local history & culture; period furnishings; personal artifacts; photographs.
Activities: lectures.
Hours & Admission Prices: Mon.-Sat. 9-2. Closed Thanksgiving; Christmas.

Sumter

SUMTER COUNTY GALLERY OF ART, 200 Hasel St., Sumter, SC 29150-4506. Mailing Address: Box 1316, Sumter, SC 29151-1316. Tel.: 803-775-0543. Fax: 803-778-2787.
E-mail: director@sumtergallery.com
Web Site: www.sumtergallery.org
Founded: 1970.
Congressional District: 5
Key Personnel: Exec. Dir., Karen Watson; Dir. Art Education, Amanda Cox; Asst. Dir. & Cur., Frank McCauley.
Personnel Profile: Full-Time Paid 3; Part-Time Paid 2; Part-Time Volunteers 10.
Governing Authority: nonprofit organization. Tax-exempt: 501(c)(3).
Art Museum.
Collections: Elizabeth White collection; regional contemporary & traditional art.
Facilities: classrooms. Museum-related items for sale.
Activities: opening receptions; artist lectures; panel discussions; artists-in-residence; summer art camp & scholarship fund; children & adult art classes.
Publications: quarterly newsletters; brochure, Elizabeth White House; general information & membership brochure; monthly gallery guides; art school flyers; exhibition catalogs.
Hours & Admission Prices: Tues.-Sat. 11-5, Sun. 1:30-5. No charge; donations accepted. Closed holidays. ♿
Attendance: 11,000 (estimated)
Membership: Individual & Military $50; Family $75; Patron $100; Bronze $250; Silver $500; Gold $1,000.

THE SUMTER COUNTY MUSEUM, 122 N. Washington St., Sumter, SC 29150-4920. Mailing Address: P.O. Box 1456, Sumter, SC 29151-1456. Tel.: 803-775-0908. Fax: 803-436-5820.
E-mail: krichardson@sumtercountymuseum.org
Web Site: www.sumtercountymuseum.org
Founded: 1976.
Congressional District: 5
Key Personnel: Exec. Dir., Katherine Richardson; Chm. (V), Frank Edwards; Asst. Dir. Finance & Cur. Collections, Rickie Good.
Personnel Profile: Full-Time Paid 3; Part-Time Paid 3; Part-Time Volunteers 40.

Governing Authority: bd. of trustees. Subsidiary Institution: Genealogical & Historical Research Center, 219 W. Liberty St., Sumter. Tel. 803-773-9144. Tax-exempt.
Historic House: Williams-Brice House, a 1916 three story brick house; 1917 Carnegie Public Library building housing historical & genealogical research center.
Collections: area history; early farm & household equipment; textiles; archives, manuscripts, documents, photos.
Research Fields: genealogy; history.
Facilities: meeting rooms; genealogical & research center. Museum-related items for sale.
Activities: guided tours; lectures; temporary & permanent exhibits.
Publications: museum newsletter; historical documents transcribed.
Hours & Admission Prices: Museum: Tues.-Sat. 10-5. Research Center: Tues.-Sat. 10-1 & 2-5. Museum: adults $3, children 6-17 $1. Research Center: $5 per day for non-members. ♿
Attendance: 18,000 (accurate)
Membership: Student $10; Individual $20; Club & Organization $25; Family $35; Business & Patron $50; Distinguished Patron & Corporate Patron $100; Benefactor $250; Distinguished Benefactor $500 & up.

Union

ROSE HILL PLANTATION STATE HISTORIC SITE, 2677 Sardis Rd., Union, SC 29379-7904. Tel.: 864-427-5966. Fax: 864-427-5966.
E-mail: rosehill@scprt.com
Web Site: www.southcarolinaparks.com
Founded: 1960.
Key Personnel: Park Mgr., Casey Connell.
Personnel Profile: Full-Time Paid 2; Part-Time Paid 1; Part-Time Volunteers 2.
Governing Authority: state; not-for-profit organization. Parent Institution: South Carolina Parks; Recreation & Tourism. Subsidiary Institution: State Parks.
State Park: 1828 Rose Hill Plantation, home of South Carolina Governor William Henry Gist.
Collections: 19th-century Southern household & personal items; particular emphasis on artifacts owned by Governor Gist.
Facilities: mansion; kitchen house.
Activities: exhibits; picnicking; hiking; special programs.
Hours & Admission Prices: Mansion: daily 1-4. Adults $4, student $3, South Carolina seniors over 65 $2.50. Park Grounds: daily 9-6. No charge. Closed Thanksgiving, Christmas Eve & Day.
Attendance: 3,500 (estimated)

UNION COUNTY MUSEUM, 127 W. Main St., Union, SC 29379. Mailing Address: P.O. Box 220, Union, SC 29379-0220. Tel.: 864-429-5081.
Governing Authority: Parent Institution: Union County Historical Society.
History Museum.
Collections: local history & culture; photographs; period furnishings; personal artifacts.
Facilities: Museum-related items for sale.
Activities: special events.
Hours & Admission Prices: Tues. & Thurs.-Fri. 9-4, Sat. 2-5; other times by appointment.

Wagener

WAGENER MUSEUM, 12 Short St., Wagener, SC 29164. Mailing Address: P.O. Box 1004, Wagener, SC 29164-1004. Tel.: 803-564-3412 & 3507.
Founded: 1989.
Congressional District: 2
Key Personnel: Chm. (V), Cynthia R. Hardy.
Personnel Profile: Part-Time Paid 1; Part-Time Volunteers 22.
Governing Authority: Parent Institution: Town of Wagener.
History Museum.
Collections: local history & culture; photographs.
Publications: Local History Vol. I 1887-1990; Vol. II 1990-2005.
Hours & Admission Prices: Fri. 8-5, Sat. 10-2, Sun. 2-5; other times by appointment. No charge; donations accepted. Closed national holidays. ♿
Attendance: 90 (estimated)

Walhalla

OCONEE HERITAGE CENTER, 123 Brown Square Dr., Walhalla, SC 29691. Mailing Address: P.O. Box 395, Walhalla, SC 29691. Tel.: 864-638-2224.
E-mail: info@oconeeheritagecenter.org
History Museum.
Collections: county history & culture; personal artifacts; photographs; period furnishings.
Hours & Admission Prices: Tues. & Thurs.-Fri. 12-5, Sat. 10-3; other times by appointment.

PATRIOT'S HALL-OCONEE VETERAN'S MUSEUM, 13 Short St., Walhalla, SC 29691-2229. Mailing Address: P.O. Box 591, Walhalla, SC 29691-0591. Tel.: 864-638-5455 & 944-5112.
Web Site: www.oconeeveteransmuseum.org
Key Personnel: Pres. Bd. (V), Charles Brickett
History Museum: housed in the Old Rock Building; built in 1933.
Collections: artifacts & memorabilia dedicated to Oconee veterans.
Hours & Admission Prices: Sat. 10-3; other times by appointment. No charge.

Walterboro

COLLETON MUSEUM, 239 N. Jeffries Blvd., Walterboro, SC 29488-2907. Tel.: 803-549-2303. Fax: 803-549-7215.
E-mail: museum@colletoncounty.org
Web Site: www.colletoncounty.org
Founded: 1985.
Congressional District: 6
Key Personnel: C.E.O., Dir. & Archivist, Gary Brightwell; Chm. (V) & Education Asst., Elaine Inabinet.
Personnel Profile: Full-Time Paid 2; Part-Time Paid 1; Part-Time Volunteers 20; Interns 2.
Governing Authority: county; nonprofit.
History Museum: housed in c.1855 old jail, a two-story neo-Gothic structure resembling a castle, designed by Edward C. James & Francis P. Lee.
Collections: 19th-century furnishings, personal artifacts & tools; natural history exhibit Animals of the ACE Basin.
Research Fields: history & culture of Colleton County; natural history.
Facilities: 1,200 sq. ft. exhibit space. Books, posters, prints, postcards, jewelry, pewter, educational children's toys, ceramic gifts & other museum-related items for sale.
Activities: guided tours; lectures; docent program; receptions; teachers environmental network; traveling trunks.
Publications: newsletter, Notes From the Old Jail.
Hours & Admission Prices: Tues.-Fri. 10-1 & 2-5, Sat. 12-4. No charge. ♿
Attendance: 7,980 (accurate)
Membership: Student & Senior $20; Individual $30; Family $25; Associate $50; Beaulah Glover Society $100; Walter Family Society $250; Colonel Isaac Hayne Society $500; Sir John Colleton Society $1,000 & up.

SLAVE RELICS MUSEUM, 208 Carn St., Walterboro, SC 29488-3965. Tel.: 843-549-9130.
Web Site: slaverelics.org
History Museum.
Collections: slave-era history & culture; documents; personal artifacts; photographs; period furnishings.
Hours & Admission Prices: Mon.-Thurs. 9:30-5, Sat. 10-3. Adults $6, children $5; discounts to groups.

SOUTH CAROLINA ARTISANS CENTER, 318 Wichman St., Walterboro, SC 29488-2921. Tel.: 843-549-0011. Fax: 843-549-7433.
E-mail: info@scartisanscenter.com
Web Site: scartisanscenter.com
Founded: 1994.
Congressional District: 6
Key Personnel: Pres., Chris Bickley; Exec. Dir., Gale M. Doggette; Treas., Dolly Droze.
Personnel Profile: Full-Time Paid 2; Part-Time Paid 7; Part-Time Volunteers 10.
Governing Authority: private; nonprofit organization. Tax-exempt: 501(c)(3).
Arts & Crafts Museum: housed in a 1910 Victorian cottage in the Hickory Valley Historic District.
Collections: South Carolina fine craft & folk artists; cultural heritage of South Carolina.
Facilities: educational facilities; 4,800 sq. ft. exhibit space. Fine crafts & folk art created by South Carolina residents for sale.
Activities: arts festivals; educational programs for adults & children which include workshops & artist demonstrations; guided tours.
Publications: monthly newsletter.
Hours & Admission Prices: Mon.-Sat. 10-6, Sun. 1-6. No charge. Closed New Year's Day; Easter; Independence Day; Thanksgiving; Christmas. ♿
Attendance: 125,000 (estimated)
Membership: Artist & Student $15; Friend $25; Family $50; Contributor $100; Supporter $250; Patron $500; Corporations & Organizations: Non-Profit $50; Contributor $100; Supporter $250; Patron $500; Fellow $501 & up.

Winnsboro

FAIRFIELD COUNTY MUSEUM, 231 S. Congress St., Winnsboro, SC 29180-1105. Mailing Address: P.O. Box 6, Winnsboro, SC 29180-0006. Tel.: 803-635-9811. Fax: 803-815-9811.
E-mail: fairfieldmus@truvista.net
Web Site: www.fairfieldsc.com/secondary.aspx?pageID=125
Founded: 1963.
Congressional District: 5
Key Personnel: Dir. & Museum Shop Mgr., Pelham Lyles.
Personnel Profile: Full-Time Paid 1; Part-Time Volunteers 2.
Governing Authority: society. Parent Institution: Fairfield County Council. Subsidiary Institution: Friends of the Museum. Tax-exempt.
Historic Building & Site: housed in 1830 Cathcart-Ketchin, 3-story Federal brick structure.
Collections: local living utensils; guns; china; kitchenware; letters; quilts; genealogical data; Indian artifacts; toys; period clothing.
Research Fields: genealogy; local history.
Activities: guided tours; lectures; arts festivals; oral history film project; archaeological field studies; preservation projects; battle reenactments.
Publications: FOTM newsletter.
Hours & Admission Prices: Tues.-Fri. 10-5, Sat. 10-3. No charge.
Attendance: 3,500 (estimated)
Membership: Student $8; Individual $10; Couple $15; Family $20.

THE SOUTH CAROLINA RAILROAD MUSEUM, 110 Industrial Park Rd., Winnsboro, SC 29180-9113. Mailing Address: P.O. Box 7246, Columbia, SC 29202-7246. Tel.: 803-635-4242 & 9893.
E-mail: info@scrm.org
Web Site: www.scrm.org
Founded: 1973.
Key Personnel: Chm. (V), Kelvin Woods; Pres., Richard Freme; Museum Shop Mgr., Rufus Timms.
Personnel Profile: Full-Time Volunteers 6; Part-Time Volunteers 30; Interns 1.
Governing Authority: Tax-exempt.
Railroad Museum.
Collections: historical artifacts & photographs; South Carolina railroad heritage; locomotives; passenger and freight cars; cabooses.
Facilities: Museum-related items for sale.
Activities: train rides; special events.
Hours & Admission Prices: Museum: June -Oct. 1st & 3rd Sat. of month 9-4. Train Rides: adult 12 & over $10, children 1-11 $7; 1st Class $15. ♿
Attendance: 10,000 (accurate)
Membership: Youth $17; Senior $18; Individual $25; Family $35.

Woodruff

HISTORIC PRICE HOUSE, 1200 Oak View Farms Rd., Woodruff, SC 29388-8313. Mailing Address: 1200 Otts Shoals Rd., Roebuck, SC 29376-3518. Tel.: 864-576-6546. Fax: 864-576-4058.
E-mail: pricehouse@spartanburghistory.org
Web Site: www.spartanburghistory.org
Founded: 1972.
Congressional District: 4
Key Personnel: C.E.O. & Exec. Dir., Becky Slayton.
Personnel Profile: Full-Time Paid 1; Part-Time Paid 6; Part-Time Volunteers 2.
Governing Authority: society; nonprofit. Parent Museum: Spartanburg County Historical Association. Tax-exempt: 501(c)(3).
History Museum: housed in c.1795, three story brick structure, once located on 2,000 acres.
Collections: 1790-1820 decorative arts & federal pieces; separate kitchen; double-pen slave cabin.
Activities: guided tours. Annual Event: Taste of the Backcountry Festival in April.
Publications: The Drover's Post.
Hours & Admission Prices: April-Oct. Sat. 11-5, Sun. 2-5; Nov.-March Sun. 2-5. Adults $4, senior citizens $3.50, students under 18 $2.50; discount to groups; children under 6 no charge. Closed holidays.
Attendance: 400 (accurate)
Membership: Student 18 & under $10; Individual $40; Dual $60; Family $75; Spartan Regiment Society $100; Kate Moore Barry Society $250; Lewis P. Jones Society $500.

Yemassee

THE LOWCOUNTRY VISITORS CENTER & MUSEUM, 1 Lowcountry Lane, Yemassee, SC 29945. Mailing Address: P.O. Box 615, Yemassee, SC 29945-0615. Tel.: 843-717-3090; 800-528-6870.
Historic House Museum: housed in the former home of the Frampton family; built in 1868.
Collections: family history; period furnishings & artifacts; photographs.
Facilities: Museum-related items for sale.
Hours & Admission Prices: Daily 9-5:30. No charge. Closed federal & state holidays.

SOUTH DAKOTA

(149 listings)

Aberdeen

DACOTAH PRAIRIE MUSEUM, (M), 21 S. Main St., Aberdeen, SD 57401-4218. Mailing Address: P.O. Box 395, Aberdeen, SD 57402-0395. Tel.: 605-626-7117. Fax: 605-626-4026.
E-mail: dpm@brown.sd.us
Web Site: www.dacotahprairiemuseum.com
Founded: 1964.
Congressional District: 1
Key Personnel: Dir., Sue Gates; Pres. (V), Randy Grismer; Cur. Exhibits, Lora Schaunaman; Cur. Education, Sherri Rawstern.
Personnel Profile: Full-Time Paid 5; Part-Time Paid 1; Part-Time Volunteers 65.
Governing Authority: county. Tax-exempt: 501(c)(3).
General Museum: housed in 1889 bank.
Collections: pioneer artifacts; period rooms; furniture; photographs; natural history; history; Native American artifacts & crafts; archives; art gallery; manuscripts; clothing.
Research Fields: Brown County, SD; railroad history in SD.
Facilities: 500-vol. library of history books available on premises; reading room. Handicrafts, books, notecards & local art for sale.
Activities: guided tours; lectures; gallery talks; formally organized education programs for children; temporary exhibitions; school loan service.
Publications: quarterly, Dacotah Prairie Times; Architectural Records in Brown County Collections.
Hours & Admission Prices: Tues.-Fri. 9-5, Sat.-Sun. 1-4. No charge; donations accepted. Closed national holidays. ♿
Attendance: 76,024 (accurate)
Membership: Student & Senior Citizen $20; Individual $25; Family & Pioneer $50; Collector $125; Curator $250; Benefactor $500; Patron $1,000 & up.

NORTHERN GALLERIES, Northern State University, 1200 S. Jay St., Aberdeen, SD 57401-7198. Tel.: 605-626-7766 & 7762. Fax: 605-626-2263.
E-mail: killianp@northern.edu
Web Site: www.northern.edu/galleries
Key Personnel: Head Art Dept., Peter Killian; Gallery Asst., Scott Cattanach
University Art Gallery.
Collections: contemporary art.
Hours & Admission Prices: Sept.-May Mon.-Fri. 8-4:30.

STORYBOOK LAND, Wylie Park, N. Hwy 281, Aberdeen, SD 57401. Mailing Address: Aberdeen Parks, Recreation and Forestry Department, 225 SE 3rd Ave., Aberdeen, SD 57401-4245. Tel.: 605-626-7015.
Park.
Collections: story book & nursery rhyme sculptures & scenes.
Facilities: theater; visitor center. Museum-related items for sale.
Activities: train rides. Annual Event: Storybook Land Festival in July.
Hours & Admission Prices: mid-April to mid-Oct. daily 10-9. No charge.

WEIN GALLERY, Presentation College, 1500 N. Main St., Aberdeen, SD 57401-1280. Tel.: 605-229-8585.
E-mail: elaine.kling@presentation.edu
Web Site: www.presentation.edu/weingallery
Key Personnel: Dir., Elaine Kling
Art Gallery.
Collections: artwork by local artists.
Hours & Admission Prices: Mon.-Fri. 8-8, Sat. 1-7. No charge.

Armour

DOUGLAS COUNTY MUSEUM COMPLEX, Courthouse Grounds, Armour, SD 57313. Tel.: 605-724-2129.
Founded: 1958.
Congressional District: 2
Key Personnel: Pres. & Cur., Sharon A. Wiese; Dir., Laverne Vanderwerff; Asst. Dir., Dot Hoveng.
Governing Authority: county; society; nonprofit. Parent Institution: Douglas County Historical Society. Tax-exempt.
Historical Society Museum: housed in 1904 County Office Bldg.
Collections: historical items from people of the area: clothing, dishes, farm implements; rock collection; Indian artifacts; photos; records of early

organizations. Historic Buildings: c.1904 County Office Bldg.; c.1886 restored railroad house; one-room country school.
Research Fields: history of Douglas County.
Activities: guided tours; temporary exhibitions. Museum Sponsors: school days in May.
Publications: book, Douglas County-The Little Giant.
Hours & Admission Prices: Tues., Fri. & holidays 1-5; other times by appointment. No charge.
Attendance: 600 (estimated)
Membership: Annual $10.

Belle Fourche

TRI-STATE MUSEUM, (M), 415 5th Ave., Belle Fourche, SD 57717-1435. Tel.: 605-723-1200.
E-mail: tristatemuseum@rushmore.com
Web Site: www.tristatemuseum.com
Key Personnel: Dir., Rochelle Silva; Exhibits Coord., DeEtte Gross; Volunteer Coord., Kim Sjovall
History Museum.
Collections: over 5,000 artifacts; rodeo memorabilia; historical records; antiques; collectibles; fossils.
Hours & Admission Prices: Mon.-Sat. 9-5, Sun. 12-5. No charge; donations accepted.

Box Elder

SOUTH DAKOTA AIR AND SPACE MUSEUM, 2890 Davis Dr., Box Elder, SD 57706. Mailing Address: P.O. Box 871, Ellsworth Air Force Base, Box Elder, SD 57719-0871. Tel.: 605-385-5188.
Web Site: www.ellsworth.af.mil/museum.asp
Military Museum.
Collections: over 25 aircraft including historic bombers, fighters, & utility aircraft; missiles; aviation memorabilia; Aviation Hall of Fame.
Activities: interactive aircraft cockpit; simulators.
Hours & Admission Prices: Daily 8:30-4:30. No charge.

Brookings

BROOKINGS ARTS COUNCIL, 524 Fourth St., Brookings, SD 57006-2045. Tel.: 605-692-4177. Fax: 605-692-8298.
E-mail: artscouncil@brookings.net
Web Site: www.brookingsartscouncil.org
Founded: 1977.
Congressional District: 1
Key Personnel: Pres., Jean Jostad; Dir., Susan Brugger; Gallery Asst., Melanie Kellen.
Governing Authority: nonprofit organization. Tax-exempt.
Cultural Arts Center: housed in 1914 Carnegie Library Building.
Collections: paintings; photographs.
Facilities: 50-vol. library of catalogs available for research on premises; meeting space. Museum-related items for sale.
Activities: theatre performances; dance, poetry & music recitals; visual arts; humanities; formally organized education programs; special public events; lectures; arts workshops; temporary exhibits.
Publications: quarterly newsletter, Brookings Arts Council.
Hours & Admission Prices: Tues.-Sat. 12-5. No charge; donations accepted. Closed national holidays. ♿
Attendance: 12,000 (estimated)
Membership: Student $10; Individual $25-$49; Friend & Family $50-$99; Supporter $100-$199; Patron $200-$499; Benefactor $500 & up.

MCCRORY GARDENS AT SOUTH DAKOTA STATE UNIVERSITY, 6th St. & 22nd Ave., Brookings, SD 57007-0001. Mailing Address: Box 2140A, SNP 201, Brookings, SD 57007-0001. Tel.: 605-688-5136. Fax: 605-688-4713.
E-mail: david.graper@sdstate.edu
Founded: 1964.
Key Personnel: Dir., David F. Graper, Ph.D.; Assoc. Dir., Martin Maca.
Personnel Profile: Full-Time Paid 1.
Governing Authority: Parent Institution: South Dakota State University. Tax-exempt.
Arboretums.
Collections: ornamental plants; trees; shrubs; grasses; flowers; rock garden; prairie garden.
Research Fields: ornamental horticulture.
Activities: children's maze.
Hours & Admission Prices: Dawn to dusk. No charge; donations accepted.
Membership: Individual $25; Family $50; Business $200.

* **SOUTH DAKOTA ART MUSEUM, (M),** Medary Ave. & Harvey Dunn, Brookings, SD 57007-0001. Mailing Address: P.O. Box 2250, Brookings, SD 57007-0001. Tel.: 605-688-5423; 866-805-7590. Fax: 605-688-4445.
E-mail: sdsu.sdam@sdstate.edu
Web Site: www.southdakotaartmuseum.com
Founded: 1969.
Congressional District: 1
Key Personnel: Dir., Lynn Verschoor; Cur. Collections, Lisa Scholten; Cur. Exhibits, John Rychtarik; Museum Shop Mgr., Pam Adler.
Personnel Profile: Full-Time Paid 5; Part-Time Paid 8; Part-Time Volunteers 20.
Governing Authority: state; university. Parent Institution: South Dakota State University. Tax-exempt: 170(b)(1)(A)(iv).
Art Museum.
Collections: state, regional & national art of 19th-20th centuries; Harvey Dunn & Oscar Howe paintings; Native American art; Marghab embroidered linen from Madeira.
Research Fields: South Dakota & Native American art.
Facilities: 2,000-vol. art library available by reservation only; reading room; 150-seat auditorium; multi-purpose room; classroom. Museum-related items for sale.
Activities: guided tours; films; gallery talks; inter-museum loan, permanent, special & touring exhibitions; art in the schools program; kids sensation station for families.
Publications: exhibition catalogues & quarterly, illustrated newsletter.
Hours & Admission Prices: Mon.-Fri. 10-5, Sat. 10-4, Sun. 12-4. No charge; donations accepted. Closed New Year's Day; Thanksgiving; Christmas; state holidays. ♿
Attendance: 100,000 (estimated)
Membership: Individual $30; Family $40.

STATE AGRICULTURAL HERITAGE MUSEUM, (M), South Dakota State University, 925 11th St., Brookings, SD 57007-0001. Mailing Address: SDSU Box 601, Brookings, SD 57007-0001. Tel.: 605-688-6226. Fax: 605-688-6303.
E-mail: sdsu_agmuseum@sdstate.edu
Web Site: www.agmuseum.com
Founded: 1967.
Congressional District: 1
Key Personnel: Pres., Dr. David Chicoine; Dir., Mac R. Harris; Cur., William D. Lee; Cur., Carrie Van Buren; Cur. & Museum Shop Mgr., Michelle Glanzer; Cur., Dawn Stephens.
Personnel Profile: Full-Time Paid 5; Full-Time Volunteers 8; Part-Time Volunteers 4.
Governing Authority: state. Parent Institution: South Dakota State University. Tax-exempt: 170(c).
Agricultural Museum.
Collections: South Dakota history 1860-1950; agriculture & technology publications; photographic archives; ethnography; homesteading; farm machinery; claim shanty; major farm machinery archive.
Research Fields: agricultural history.
Facilities: 2,500-vol. library; archives; 6,500 sq. ft. exhibit space. Gift items for sale.
Activities: docent program; guided tours; lectures; temporary exhibitions; study & work programs for University students.
Hours & Admission Prices: Mon.-Sat. 10-5, Sun. 1-5. No charge; donations accepted. ♿
Attendance: 14,620 (accurate)
Membership: Individual $20; Family $30; Patron $100; Benefactor $250.

Buffalo

BUFFALO HISTORICAL MUSEUM AND ONE-ROOM SCHOOLHOUSE, Hwy. 85, Buffalo, SD 57720. Mailing Address: P.O. Box 63, Buffalo, SD 57720-0063. Tel.: 605-375-3800.
Founded: 1967.
Key Personnel: Pres., Ray Anderson; Cur., Nora Boyer
History Museum.
Collections: local history from the cattle-ranch & homesteading eras; 1914 one-room schoolhouse.
Hours & Admission Prices: Memorial Day to Labor Day Mon.-Fri. 10:30-2:30; other times by appointment. No charge. ♿

Carthage

CAMPBELL ORIGINAL STRAW BALE BUILT MUSEUM, Carthage, SD 57323. Mailing Address: P.O. Box 3, Carthage, SD 57323-0003. Tel.: 605-772-4716 & 4166.
E-mail: dbhurne@alliancecom.net
Web Site: www.strawbalemus.com
History Museum: insulated with home-grown straw.

Collections: historical exhibits.
Hours & Admission Prices: Call for hours.

Chamberlain

AKTA LAKOTA MUSEUM AND CULTURAL CENTER, (M), (I), 1301 N. Main St., Chamberlain, SD 57325-1656. Mailing Address: P.O. Box 89, Chamberlain, SD 57325-0089. Tel.: 605-234-3452 & 3300. Fax: 605-234-3388.
E-mail: aktalakota@stjo.org
Web Site: www.aktalakota.org
Founded: 1991.
Congressional District: 20
Key Personnel: C.E.O., Father Stephen Huffstetter; Dir., Dixie Thompson; Museum Shop Mgr., Vickie Brennan.
Personnel Profile: Full-Time Paid 2; Part-Time Paid 4; Part-Time Volunteers 5.
Governing Authority: Parent Institution: Congregation of the Priests of the Sacred Heart, Inc. of South Dakota. Subsidiary Institution: St. Joseph's Indian School. Tax-exempt.
History Museum: Lakota culture & heritage.
Collections: Native American artifacts; quillwork; beadwork; art collection.
Research Fields: Plains Indians ethnology.
Facilities: library of Native American material & culture; Native American art available for research on premises. Gift items for sale.
Activities: guided tours; permanent & temporary exhibits; gallery talks; workshops; inter-museum loan.
Publications: Children of the Earth.
Hours & Admission Prices: Memorial Day to Labor Day Mon.-Sat. 8-6, Sun. 9-5; Sept.-May Mon.-Fri. 8-5. No charge; donations accepted. Closed legal holidays. ♿
Attendance: 30,000 (accurate)

SOUTH DAKOTA HALL OF FAME, 1480 S. Main, Chamberlain, SD 57325. Mailing Address: P.O. Box 180, Chamberlain, SD 57325-0180. Tel.: 605-734-4216. Fax: 605-734-4216.
E-mail: info@sdhalloffame.com
Web Site: www.sdhalloffame.com
Founded: 1974.
Congressional District: 2
Key Personnel: Chm., Richard Ekstrum; Vice Chm., Glenn Jergenson; Sec. & Treas., Lynne Duling.
Personnel Profile: Full-Time Paid 2; Part-Time Paid 2; Part-Time Volunteers 15.
Governing Authority: nonprofit organization. Tax-exempt: 501(c)(3).
Historic Research Institute & Heritage Center.
Collections: biographical information on persons who were instrumental in building the state of South Dakota; county history books; artwork; artifacts from pioneer & Indian days; South Dakota culture.
Research Fields: personal information on inductees to the hall of fame, biographical memorials & life members.
Facilities: Museum-related items for sale.
Activities: permanent, temporary & traveling exhibitions; scavenger hunt for elementary school children.
Publications: annual, South Dakota Hall of Fame Magazine.
Hours & Admission Prices: Memorial Day to Labor Day Mon.-Fri. 10-5, Sat. 10-4, Sun. 1-4. Winter: Mon.-Fri. 10-5. No charge; donations accepted. Closed state holidays. ♿
Attendance: 4,000 (estimated)
Membership: Family $60; Business $100; Friend; $100-$249; Helper $250-499; Backer $500-$999.

Clark

BEAUVAIS HERITAGE CENTER, Hwy. 212, Clark, SD 57225. Mailing Address: 402 N. Comil St., Clark, SD 57225. Tel.: 605-532-3769. Fax: 605-532-5496.
E-mail: stoker@itctel.com
Web Site: www.clarksd.com/museum
Founded: 1975.
Congressional District: 7
Key Personnel: C.E.O. & Pres. (V), Greg Furness; Business Officer, Ralph Hurlbert; Historian, Ailene Luckhurst; Museum Shop Mgr., Carol Hurlbert.
Personnel Profile: Full-Time Volunteers 10; Part-Time Volunteers 10.
Governing Authority: nonprofit organization. Parent Institution: Clark County Historical Society. Tax-exempt: 170(b)(1)(A).
Cultural & Historical Center.
Collections: memorabilia of 1870-1950; personal artifacts of Gov. Elrod of South Dakota; cup & saucer collection; toys; hand-crafted embroidery crochet; quilts; machinery; area business, family & county records; family & local town histories; military display. Historic Buildings: c.1880 claim shanty; Clark 1910 depot; 1911 church; Heritage school; c.1880 house; headquarters building with displays; basements display of Main St. shops; machinery building.
Research Fields: local & county history.
Facilities: 100-vol. library of county records, township & city records, private business & personal ledgers, old magazines & newspapers, local history videotapes; 900 family history files; county & township history files; available for research with permission from President of Historical Society.
Activities: guided tours; permanent & temporary exhibitions; tours; entertainment. Center Sponsor: Heritage Day in June; Thresing Bee & Tractor displays in August; competitions in August.
Publications: annual newsletter.
Hours & Admission Prices: June-Oct. Wed.-Fri. 1-4; other times by appointment. No charge; donations accepted. ♿
Attendance: 500 (estimated)
Membership: Individual $10; Business $50; Life $200.

Crazy Horse

INDIAN MUSEUM OF NORTH AMERICA AT CRAZY HORSE MEMORIAL, (M), 12151 Avenue of the Chiefs, Crazy Horse, SD 57730-8900. Tel.: 605-673-4681. Fax: 605-673-2185.
E-mail: memorial@crazyhorse.org
Web Site: www.crazyhorsememorial.org
Founded: 1972.
Key Personnel: Dir., Anne Ziolkowski Christensen; C.E.O., Ruth Ziolkowski; Librarian, Janeen Melmer.
Personnel Profile: Full-Time Paid 2; Part-Time Paid 1; Part-Time Volunteers 2.
Governing Authority: nonprofit. Parent Institution: Crazy Horse Memorial, 12151 Avenue of the Chiefs, Crazy Horse, SD 57730-8900. Tax-exempt: 501(c)(3).
American Indian Museum.
Collections: American Indian art; artifacts; mountain carving of Crazy Horse in progress, when completed it will be the world's largest mountain carving at 563' high & 641' long.
Facilities: 14,000-vol. library of books on Indian history; 2 theatres. American Indian made items for sale.
Publications: book, Indian Museum of North America; Crazy Horse Coloring Book; Carving a Dream (History of Crazy Horse Memorial & Korczak).
Hours & Admission Prices: Daily dawn-dusk. Car $27, adults $10; discounts to senior citizens, AAM members, Custer Co. residents, scouts, servicemen in uniform; members, children under 6 & American Indians no charge. ♿
Attendance: 1,000,000 (estimated)
Membership: Crazy Horse Grass Roots Club $41; Korczak's Club $174; Driller's Club $250; Blaster's Club $500; Ruth's Club $1,000; Bronze Club $1,500; Granite Club $2,500; Crazy Horse Circle $5,000; Crazy Horse League $10,000.

Custer

CUSTER COUNTY 1881 COURTHOUSE MUSEUM, (M), 411 Mt. Rushmore Rd., Custer, SD 57730. Mailing Address: P.O. Box 826, Custer, SD 57730-0826. Tel.: 605-673-2443. Fax: 605-673-2443.
E-mail: info@1881courthousemuseum.com
Web Site: www.1881courthousemuseum.com
Founded: 1974.
Key Personnel: Chm. (V), Kathy Larsen; Dir., Sandy Ackman; Museum Shop Mgr., Chuck Cochran.
Personnel Profile: Part-Time Paid 2; Part-Time Volunteers 75.
Governing Authority: society. Parent Institution: Custer County Historical Society, P.O. Box 826, Custer, SD. 57730. Tax-exempt.
Historical Society Museum: housed in 1881 County Court House. Western, pioneer, mining & lumbering.
Collections: rocks; minerals; American Indian collection; period clothing; mining, ranching & lumbering exhibits; Custer 1874 expedition, Illingsworth pictures; mounted animals/birds of area; military uniforms from The Civil War to the present.
Research Fields: county & Black Hills history.
Facilities: library of books of historical value available for research on premises. Books of local history & pioneer information for sale.
Activities: permanent exhibitions.
Publications: Visitors' Brochure.
Hours & Admission Prices: May & Sept. daily 10-4; Memorial Day-Labor Day Mon.-Sat. 9-8, Sun. 1-8. Adults $5, seniors $4, youth 12-18 yrs $1. ♿
Attendance: 6,400 (accurate)
Membership: Custer County Historical Society $10 annual; Lifetime Society $40.

CUSTER STATE PARK, 13329 US Hwy. 16A, Custer, SD 57730-8351. Tel.: 605-255-4464. Fax: 605-255-4460.
E-mail: custerstatepark@state.sd.us
Web Site: www.custerstatepark.info

Founded: 1912.
Congressional District: 32
Key Personnel: Mgr. Southern Black Hills Rgnl., Richard Miller; Naturalist, Julie Brazell; Visitor Svcs. Coord., Craig Pugsley.
Personnel Profile: Full-Time Paid 33; Part-Time Paid 4; Part-Time Volunteers 17; Interns 5.
Governing Authority: state. Parent Institution: South Dakota Department of Game, Fish & Parks, Foss Bldg., 523 E. Capitol, Pierre 57501.
Park & Visitor Center.
Collections: historical & natural history exhibits.
Research Fields: history of programs, park development, culture & nature.
Facilities: visitor's center; hiking trails.
Activities: guided nature hikes; lectures; junior naturalist programs 7-12; gold panning & living history demonstrations; outdoor recreational activities; on-site school field trips; environmental education programs; teacher workshops; special events; permanent exhibits; camping.
Publications: magazine, Tatanka; site bulletins, Prairie Dog; Wildlife; Fisheries and Aquatic Resources; Bats; Charles Badger Clark; Peter Norbeck; Bird Checklist; Wildflower Checklist; brochure, Geocaching; flyer, National Treasure: Book of Secrets.
Hours & Admission Prices: Park: daily. Peter Norbeck Visitor Center: April-Nov. 9-5. Wildlife Station Visitor Center: May-Oct. 10-4. Badger Hole Historical Site: May-Sept. 9-5. Entrance License: $5 per person, $12 vehicles ♿
Attendance: 1,800,000 (estimated)

FOUR MILE OLD WEST TOWN, 11921 W. Hwy. 16, Custer, SD 57730-7114. Tel.: 605-673-3905.
Web Site: www.fourmilesd.com
Formerly: Four Mile Ghost Town
Key Personnel: Dir., Mary Krogman.
Personnel Profile: Full-Time Volunteers 1.
History Museum.
Collections: local history; period furnishings; photographs; postal records. Historic Buildings: town hall; saloon; general store; church; bank; sheriff's office; Dakota Territory Jails; Slat Iron jail cell.
Activities: presentations.
Hours & Admission Prices: Memorial Day to Labor Day daily 8:30-8; Sept. to mid-Oct. daily 8:30-5. Admission $5; discounts to AAM & museum members; children 6 & under no charge. ♿
Attendance: 15,000 (estimated)

JEWEL CAVE NATIONAL MONUMENT, 11149 US Hwy. 16, Bldg. B12, Custer, SD 57730-8166. Tel.: 605-673-8300. Fax: 605-673-8301.
Web Site: www.nps.gov/jeca
Visitor Center and Cave.
Collections: local history; geology.
Activities: cave tours; special events.
Hours & Admission Prices: Visitor Center: May 29-June 13 & Aug. 16-Sept. 12 daily 8:30-5:30; June 14-Aug 15 daily 8:30-7. Scenic Tour: adults 17 & over $8, youth 6-16 & senior citizens $4; children under 5 no charge. Jewel Cave Discovery: adults 16 & over $4; senior citizens & children 15 and under no charge.

NATIONAL MUSEUM OF WOODCARVING, 12111 W. Hwy. 16, Custer, SD 57730. Mailing Address: P.O. Box 747, Custer, SD 57730-0747. Tel.: 605-673-4404. Fax: 605-673-3843.
E-mail: woodcarv@gwtc.net
Web Site: www.blackhills.com/woodcarving
Founded: 1966.
Key Personnel: C.E.O. & Owner, Dale Schaffer; Co-Owner, Gloria Schaffer; Museum Shop Mgr., Lois Massa.
Governing Authority: individual operation.
National Woodcarving Museum: located in the area of the Black Hills where Custer & party found gold in 1874.
Collections: Dr. Niblack (original Disneyland animator) life-work of woodcarvings; over 75 woodcarvers' carvings for sale.
Facilities: snack shop; theater. Gift items for sale.
Activities: self-guided tours; gallery talks; permanent & temporary exhibitions; woodcarving classes thru the summer.
Hours & Admission Prices: May-Oct. 25 daily 9-5. Adults $7.95; discounts to senior citizens & groups. ♿
Attendance: 100,000 (estimated)

De Smet

DE SMET DEPOT MUSEUM, 104 Calumet Ave., N.E., De Smet, SD 57231. Mailing Address: P.O. Drawer 70, De Smet, SD 57231-0007. Tel.: 605-854-3991 & 3731. Fax: 605-854-3731.
Founded: 1965.
Congressional District: 1
Key Personnel: C.E.O. & Mayor, Gary Wolkow; Finance Officer, Eileen Wolkow.
Personnel Profile: Part-Time Paid 1; Part-Time Volunteers 30.
Governing Authority: municipal. Parent Institution: City of De Smet. Tax-exempt.
History Museum: housed in Old Chicago Northwestern Depot & City Bldg.
Collections: pioneer collections; CNW railroad depot.
Activities: tours; pageants.
Publications: brochure
Hours & Admission Prices: June-Aug. Mon.-Sat. 10-5. No charge; donations accepted. ♿
Attendance: 2,500

LAURA INGALLS WILDER MEMORIAL SOCIETY, INC., 105 Olivet, S.E., De Smet, SD 57231. Mailing Address: P.O. Box 426, De Smet, SD 57231-0426. Tel.: 800-880-3383.
E-mail: laura@discoverlaura.org
Web Site: www.discoverlaura.org
General Museum: housed in the original Surveyor's House from Laura's book By the Shores of Silver Lake.
Collections: life & history of Laura Ingalls Wilder.
Facilities: Museum-related items for sale.
Hours & Admission Prices: May & Sept. Mon.-Sat. 9-4; June-Aug. daily 9-5:50, Sun. 10-5:30; Oct.-April Mon.-Fri. 9-4. Adults $8, children 6-12 $4; children 5 & under no charge. ♿

Deadwood

ADAMS MUSEUM & HOUSE, (M), 54 Sherman, Deadwood, SD 57732-1364. Mailing Address: P.O. Box 252, Deadwood, SD 57732-0252. Tel.: 605-578-1714 & 1928. Fax: 605-578-1194.
E-mail: amhdirector@rushmore.com
Web Site: www.adamsmuseumandhouse.org
Founded: 1930.
Congressional District: 31
Key Personnel: Chm. (V), David Wolff; Dir., Mary A. Kopco; Bookkeeper & Office Mgr., April Hoover; Archivist, Carolyn Weber; Cur. Exhibits, Darrel Nelson; Dir. Communications, Rose Speirs; Cur. Adams Museum, Arlette Hansen; Coord. Facilities, Howie Albrecht; Cur. Adams House, Brantley Partin; Educator, Anne Rogers.
Personnel Profile: Full-Time Paid 14; Part-Time Paid 9; Part-Time Volunteers 30.
Governing Authority: bd. of dirs. Subsidiary Institution: Historic Adams House: 22 Van Buren Ave., Deadwood, SD 57732. Tel.: 605-578-3724, Fax: 605-578-3751. Tax-exempt.
History Museum.
Collections: costumes; geology; Native American artifacts; mineralogy; military; paleontology; pioneer room with artifacts; photographs of Deadwood & western personalities; guns; 1879 locomotive; 1834 The Thoen Stone; Russian, Chinese research archives; Victorian & American furniture; mining history.
Major Exhibits: Wild Bill Hickok Collection (T), 11/09-1/11; Risky Business, 11/09-1/11; Building A City, 11/09-1/11.
Research Fields: Deadwood history; Black Hills mining history.
Facilities: Museum-related items for sale.
Activities: permanent & temporary exhibitions; public programs; lectures.
Publications: calendar of historic photographs; Historical Guide to Early Deadwood; Adams Banner Quarterly; The Adams House Revealed.
Hours & Admission Prices: May-Sept. daily 9-5; Oct.-April Tues.-Sat. 10-4. Museum: no charge; donations accepted. Historic Adams House: adults $7; members no charge. Closed winter holidays. ♿
Attendance: 82,500 (estimated)
Membership: Senior $20; Senior Couple $25; Individual $30; Family $40; Calamity Jane $50; Wild Bill $100; Harris Franklin $250; W.E. Adams $500.

DAYS OF '76 MUSEUM, 17 Crescent St., Deadwood, SD 57732-1527. Mailing Address: P.O. Box 391, Deadwood, SD 57732-0391. Tel.: 605-578-2872.
E-mail: info@daysof76.com
Web Site: www.daysof76.com/museum/
Key Personnel: Mgr., Ron Burns
History Museum.
Collections: over 50 horse-drawn vehicles; costumes; archives; photographs; rodeo memorabilia; Native American art & artifacts; early pioneer history.
Activities: group tours.
Hours & Admission Prices: mid-April to mid-Oct. daily 9-5. No charge. ♿

Dell Rapids

DELL RAPIDS SOCIETY FOR HISTORICAL PRESERVATION, 407 E. 4th St., Dell Rapids, SD 57022-1927. Mailing Address: P.O. Box 143, Dell Rapids, SD 57022-0143. Tel.: 605-428-4821.
Key Personnel: Pres., Teri Fiegen; Vice Pres., Dave Chamley
History Museum.
Collections: local history & culture; documents; newspapers; photographs; period artifacts.
Activities: group tours.
Hours & Admission Prices: Memorial Day to Labor Day Tues.-Sat. 1-4. No charge.

LITTLE VILLAGE FARM MUSEUM, 47582 240th St., Dell Rapids, SD 57022-6113. Tel.: 605-428-5979.
Founded: 1995.
Key Personnel: Chm. (V) & Museum Shop Mgr., Joan Redder-Lacey; Pres. (V), James Lacey
Pioneer History Museum.
Collections: pioneer history; historic buildings.
Hours & Admission Prices: April-Oct. daily 8am to early evening by appointment. Adults $5, children $2. ♿
Attendance: 750 (estimated)

Drayton

DRAYTON UNITED METHODIST CHURCH, 203 N. Main St., Drayton, SD 58225-0327. Mailing Address: P.O. Box 327, Drayton, ND 58225-0327. Tel.: 701-454-3880.
Historic Building: housed in a church built in 1905. Listed on the National Register of Historic Places.
Collections: religious artifacts & furnishings; paintings; church history.
Hours & Admission Prices: Tours: by appointment. No charge.

Elk Point

UNION COUNTY HISTORICAL SOCIETY, 124 E. Main, Elk Point, SD 57025. Mailing Address: P.O. Box 552, Elk Point, SD 57025-0552. Tel.: 605-356-3273.
Founded: 1988.
Key Personnel: Pres. (V), Sondra Stickney.
Governing Authority: Tax-exempt.
History Museum.
Collections: Union County history; photographs; personal artifacts; genealogy; Lewis & Clark.
Publications: quarterly newsletter, The Sands of Time.
Hours & Admission Prices: March-Nov. Sat.-Sun. 1-5; other times by appointment. No charge; donations accepted. ♿
Attendance: 285
Membership: Single $20; Family $30; Life $300; Couple Life $500.

Elkton

ELKTON COMMUNITY MUSEUM AND HISTORICAL SOCIETY, 206 Elk St., Community Center, Elkton, SD 57026. Mailing Address: 1976 110th Ave., Elkton, SD 57026-8821. Tel.: 605-542-2451.
Founded: 1989.
Key Personnel: Pres. (V), Beverly Schwing.
Personnel Profile: Full-Time Paid 1.
Governing Authority: Tax-exempt.
History Museum.
Collections: local history & culture; period artifacts; newspapers; photographs; miniature shoes; church history; clothing; genealogy.
Hours & Admission Prices: Mon.-Fri. 9-3. No charge; donations accepted. Closed holidays. ♿
Membership: Individual $5.

Eureka

EUREKA PIONEER MUSEUM OF MCPHERSON COUNTY, INC., 1610 J Ave., Eureka, SD 57437. Mailing Address: P.O. Box 902, Eureka, SD 57437-0902. Tel.: 605-284-2987.
Web Site: www.glpta.org/eurekamuseum.htm
Founded: 1978.
Congressional District: 16
Key Personnel: Chm. (V), Asst. Dir. & Cur., Hulda Opp; Pres., Selma Lapp; Vice Pres., Ron Cooper; Dir., Cur. & Museum Shop Mgr., Edmund Opp; Sec., Carol Schumacher; Treas., Jean Bertsch; Dir. Public Rels., Heidi Morlock.
Personnel Profile: Full-Time Paid 1; Full-Time Volunteers 1; Part-Time Volunteers 11.
Governing Authority: county; nonprofit organization. Tax-exempt.
History Museum with focus on the lives and work of pioneers.
Collections: local memorabilia; antique machinery; manuscripts. Historic Buildings: schoolhouse; sod house; church.
Research Fields: local history.
Facilities: documents & pictures of local nature; reading room.
Activities: guided tours; lectures; arts festivals; study clubs.
Publications: brochure.
Hours & Admission Prices: April 15-Nov. 1 Wed.-Fri. 9-12 & 1-5, Sat.-Sun. 2-5. No charge; donations accepted. ♿
Attendance: 2,500 (estimated)
Membership: Annual $5; Family $10; Contributing $25; Business $30; Sustaining $50; Patron $100.

Faulkton

FAULK COUNTY MUSEUM, 814 Court St., Faulkton, SD 57438-2208. Mailing Address: Faulkton Historical Society, P.O. Box 584, Faulkton, SD 57438-0584. Tel.: 605-598-4285.
Founded: 2005.
Key Personnel: Pres. (V), Jody Moritz; Treas., Joyce Arnold; Cur., Judy Dixon.
Personnel Profile: Part-Time Volunteers 12.
Governing Authority: nonprofit. Parent Institution: Faulk County Historical Society, Inc. Tax-exempt: 501(c)(3).
History Museum.
Collections: Faulk County history & culture; personal artifacts; paintings; photographs.
Major Exhibits: Wedding Dresses 1890-1960, 5/10-8/10.
Activities: formal education programs for children.
Hours & Admission Prices: Summer: Wed. & Fri. 1-4. No charge; donations accepted.
Attendance: 50
Membership: Adult $5.

PICKLER MANSION, 900 8th Ave., Faulkton, SD 57438. Mailing Address: P.O. Box 584, Faulkton, SD 57438-0584. Tel.: 605-598-4285.
E-mail: jody.moritz@k12.sd.us
Web Site: jm008.k12.sd.us/pickler_mansion.htm
Key Personnel: Pres., Jody Moritz; Cur., Judy Dixon.
Governing Authority: Parent Institution: Faulk County Historical Society, Inc. Tax-exempt.
Historic House Museum: home of South Dakota's first U.S. Congressman & his wife, John & Alice Pickler.
Collections: furnishings; personal artifacts.
Hours & Admission Prices: Memorial Day to Labor Day daily 1-5. Adults $5.25.

Flandreau

MOODY COUNTY MUSEUM, 706 E. Pipestone Ave., Flandreau, SD 57028. Mailing Address: P.O. Box 25, Flandreau, SD 57028-0025. Tel.: 605-997-3191.
E-mail: duncana@iw.net
Founded: 1964.
Congressional District: 8
Key Personnel: Dir., Gail Scriver; C.E.O., Anna Duncan; Pres. (V), Dale A. Johnson; Vice Pres., Warren Jackson.
Personnel Profile: Part-Time Paid 1; Part-Time Volunteers 1.
Governing Authority: society. Parent Institution: Moody County Historical Society. Tax-exempt.
History Museum.
Collections: carriage; early dental office; medical exam room; living room; church pulpit; organ; barber shop; pioneer piano; clothing; dolls; bedroom; post office; pictures; tools; rural schoolhouse; Indian artifacts; old photographs; family histories. Historic Buildings: 1881 Milwaukee railroad depot; 1871 Indian River Bend meeting house/church; one-room country schoolhouse.
Research Fields: genealogy.
Activities: guided tours. Museum Sponsors: Fourth of July Festival; monthly brown bag lunch programs Sept.-April; Christmas Tree Festival in December.
Publications: quarterly newsletter, Moody County Pioneer.
Hours & Admission Prices: Mon.-Fri. 10-3; other times by appointment. No charge; donations accepted. Closed New Year's Eve & Day; Memorial Day; Thanksgiving weekend; Christmas Eve & Day. ♿
Attendance: 900 (estimated)
Membership: Individual $20; Family $15; Donor $100; Sponsor $500; Patron $1,000.

Fort Meade

OLD FORT MEADE MUSEUM AND HISTORIC RESEARCH ASSOCIATION, Bldg. 55, Fort Meade, SD 57741. Mailing Address: P.O. Box 164, Fort Meade, SD 57741-0164. Tel.: 605-347-9822.
E-mail: ftmeade@rapidnet.com
Web Site: www.fortmeademuseum.org
Founded: 1964.
Key Personnel: Dir. & Museum Shop Mgr., Charles Rambow; Pres. (V), Peg Aplan; Sec., Marshall Williams.
Personnel Profile: Full-Time Paid 1; Full-Time Volunteers 16; Part-Time Paid 3; Part-Time Volunteers 16; Interns 1.
Governing Authority: private; nonprofit. Tax-exempt.
Military Museum: U.S. Cavalry fort built in 1878 by Seventh Cavalry.
Collections: memorabilia of the units and troopers; chronological history of Old Fort Meade as a military installation from 1878-1944; Custer's 1874 Black Hills expedition; Black Hills Gold Rush; 25th Infantry (Buffalo soldiers); 1935 National Geographic stratosphere balloon flight; C.C.C. camps; German P.O.W.'s; 4th Cavalry horseback maneuvers.
Research Fields: history relating to 1878-1944 military post.
Facilities: Gift items & books for sale.
Activities: tours; self-guided tours; organized education programs for children & adults; Ft. Meade story slide/tape film program; video program; Cavalry Days in June; Re-enactments; living history programs.
Publications: book, The Peace Keeper Post on the Dakota Frontier-1878-1944; videotape; Fort Meade and the Black Hills.
Hours & Admission Prices: May 15th & Sept. 15th 9-5; Memorial Day to Labor Day daily 9-5. Adults $4, groups $3; discounts to AAM members; children under 10, school groups & members no charge.
Attendance: 8,000 (estimated)
Membership: Individual $10; Life $100.

Fort Pierre

VERENDRYE MUSEUM, Deadwood St., Fort Pierre, SD 57532. Mailing Address: PO Box 665, Fort Pierre, SD 57532-0665. Tel.: 605-223-7761.
Key Personnel: Pres. (V), Darby Nutter
History Museum.
Collections: local history; photographs; personal artifacts.
Hours & Admission Prices: Memorial Day to Labor Day daily 9-5; other times by appointment.

Frankfort

FISHER GROVE COUNTRY SCHOOL/FISHER GROVE STATE PARK, 17290 Fishers Lane, Frankfort, SD 57440-6700. Mailing Address: 17268 Fishers Lane, Frankfort, SD 57440-6700. Tel.: 605-472-1212.
Founded: 1884.
Key Personnel: Park Mgr., Charles Jones.
Governing Authority: state. Tax-exempt.
Historic Building: 1884 Deiter School.
Collections: articles from schoolhouse; interpretive display.
Activities: recorded lecture.
Hours & Admission Prices: May-Sept. daily 10-5 by appointment. Park: daily $3 per person, all vehicle occupants $5, seasonal license $23.

Freeman

HERITAGE HALL MUSEUM & ARCHIVES, 748 S. Main St., Freeman, SD 57029-2317. Mailing Address: P.O. Box 693, Freeman, SD 57029-1000. Tel.: 605-925-4237. Fax: 605-925-4271.
E-mail: info@freemanmuseum.org
Web Site: www.freemanmuseum.org
Founded: 1930.
Key Personnel: Pres. (V), Kevin Albrecht; C.E.O., Pam Tieszen; Vice Pres., Jeremy Waltner; Archivist, Duane Schrag; Cur. & Museum Shop Mgr., Russel Waltner.
Personnel Profile: Part-Time Paid 1; Part-Time Volunteers 18.
Governing Authority: 10 community churches. Parent Institution: Freeman Academy. Tax-exempt.
Ethnic Museum.
Collections: German-Russian cultural artifacts; over 450 19th century Plains Indian artifacts; history of pioneer settlers; early life in South Dakota; autos; motorcycles; farm implements; airplane.
Facilities: 1,808-vol. library of South Dakota history, Mennonite history, German Mennonite history, & religious history available for limited inter-library loan & use by the public.
Activities: guided tours; lectures.
Hours & Admission Prices: Memorial Day to Labor Day Tues.-Sat. 11-4:30, Sun. 1-4:30; other times by appointment. Adults $4, students grades 1-12 $2; pre-school no charge. ♿
Attendance: 4,000 (estimated)
Membership: Personnel $100; Business $200; Founding $500.

Garretson

GARRETSON HISTORICAL SOCIETY MUSEUM, 609 Main St., Garretson, SD 57030. Tel.: 605-594-6694.
Historical Society Museum.
Collections: veterans' display; obituary scrapbook; Garretson school & local history; period artifacts; furnishings; photographs.
Hours & Admission Prices: Mon.-Fri. 11-5; other times by appointment.

Geddes

GEDDES HISTORIC DISTRICT VILLAGE, 311 Main St., Geddes, SD 57342-0097. Mailing Address: P.O. Box 97, Geddes, SD 57342-0097. Tel.: 605-337-2501. Fax: 605-337-3535.
E-mail: dufsdfek@midstatesd.net
Founded: 1969.
Congressional District: 1
Key Personnel: C.E.O. & Chm. (V), Ron Dufek; Pres. (V), Irene Merkwan; Sec. & Museum Shop Mgr., Ronald D. Dufek.
Personnel Profile: Full-Time Volunteers 5; Part-Time Volunteers 15.
Governing Authority: nonprofit organization. Tax-exempt: 501(c)(3).
History Museum.
Collections: 1850-1910 period artifacts; desks; maps; photographs; tools; furs; 1910 & 1958 era furniture; partial L&C keel boat replica; pioneer cultural & heritage artifacts; Peter Norbeck documents. Historical Buildings: 1900 Padley Hotel; The Red Oak Bar; 1895 Red, White & Blue Rural Schoolhouse; 1857 Papineau (French Canadian) Trading Post (log cabin); former Gov. Norbeck Boyhood Home; 1804 Lewis & Clark Fur Trader Museum; 1895 Chaims Shanty.
Research Fields: regional & state history.
Facilities: library.
Activities: guided tours. Annual Events: Spring Flea Market & Antique Auction; Peter Norbeck Day in June; Fur Trader Day in August; Fall Flea Market & Antique Auction; Fall Demolition Derby.
Publications: brochures; City of Geddes Profile; book, 100 Year Memories 1900-2000.
Hours & Admission Prices: mid-May to mid-Sept. daily 9-7. No charge; donations accepted. ♿
Attendance: 400 (estimated)
Membership: Annual $10; Business $25; Lifetime $50.

Gettysburg

DAKOTA SUNSET MUSEUM, 205 W. Commercial Ave., Ste. 104, Gettysburg, SD 57442-1103. Tel.: 605-765-9480.
E-mail: dakotasunset@venturecomm.net
Founded: 1984.
Key Personnel: Pres. (V), Bob Potts; Treas., Cur. & Museum Shop Mgr., Kathleen Nagel; Archivist, Eileen Jost.
Personnel Profile: Part-Time Paid 4; Part-Time Volunteers 12.
Governing Authority: private; nonprofit organization. Tax-exempt: 501(c)(3).
History Museum.
Collections: Potter County history from 1880s to 1960s; Medicine Rock, a 40-ton boulder with human footprints & a handprint, sacred to Native Americans; Civil War artifacts; big game animals; home furnishings; period barber shop; carriage barn; country school; blacksmith shop; military artifacts; banking display; medical & dental exhibit; Native American artifacts including a Dentalium shell trade wood dress; general store.
Research Fields: area obituaries.
Facilities: library; 6,000 sq. ft. exhibit space. Museum-related items for sale.
Activities: guided tours; temporary & traveling exhibitions; monthly historical meetings. Annual Event: Summer Flower Show; Christmas Open House.
Publications: newsletter, Dakota Sunset Newsletter.
Hours & Admission Prices: Summer: Mon.-Sat. daily 1-5; Winter: Tues.-Sat. 1-5. No charge; donations accepted. Closed New Year's Day; Easter; Memorial Day; Labor Day; Thanksgiving; Christmas. ♿
Attendance: 1,800 (accurate)
Membership: Adult $5.

Groton

GRANARY MEMORIAL GALLERY, 40161 128th St., Groton, SD 57445-5405. Mailing Address: 11 E. 4th Ave., Groton, SD 57445-2022. Tel.: 605-626-7117.
E-mail: jsieh@nvc.net
Web Site: www.granaryfinearts.org
Founded: 1996.
Key Personnel: Chm. & Pres. (V), John Sieh; Dir., Laura Schaunanman; Museum Shop Mgr., Ben Grote.

Personnel Profile: Full-Time Volunteers 1; Part-Time Paid 1.
Governing Authority: Parent Institution: Dacotah Prairie Museum, 21 S. Main St., Aberdeen, SD 57401. Tax-exempt.
Art Gallery.
Collections: works by local artists.
Activities: Museum Sponsors: All-Dakota High School Exhibition in April.
Hours & Admission Prices: Call for hours. No charge; donations accepted. ♿
Attendance: 3,500 (estimated)
Membership: Individual $25; Family $40; Business $75; Lifetime $500; Lifetime Family $800.

Hermosa

HERMOSA ARTS AND HISTORY MUSEUM, 25 N. Second St., Hermosa, SD 57744. Mailing Address: P.O. Box 175, Hermosa, SD 57744-0175. Tel.: 605-431-0708.
E-mail: hermosamuseum@yahoo.com
Founded: 1999.
Personnel Profile: Part-Time Volunteers 8.
Governing Authority: Parent Institution: Hermosa Arts and History Association, Hermosa, SD.
History Museum: housed in the 1889 Hermosa school.
Collections: local history & culture; photographs; art; Calvin Coolidge; railroad & agricultural memorabilia.
Activities: speakers; book signings; readings. Museum Sponsors: Open House in July & August.
Hours & Admission Prices: By appointment. No charge. ♿

Hill City

BLACK HILLS MUSEUM OF NATURAL HISTORY, (M), 117 Main St., Hill City, SD 57745. Mailing Address: P.O. Box 614, Hill City, SD 57745-0614. Tel.: 605-574-4505. Fax: 605-574-2518.
E-mail: neal@bhmnh.org
Web Site: www.bhmnh.org
Founded: 1990.
Key Personnel: Exec. Dir., Pres. (V) & Cur., Neal L. Larson; Chm. (V), Joe Harris; Treas. & Cur., Robert A. Farrar; Mktg., Deb Casey; Membership & Public Rels., June Zeitner; Museum Shop Mgr., V. Brenda Larson.
Personnel Profile: Full-Time Volunteers 15; Part-Time Paid 1; Part-Time Volunteers 18; Interns 3.
Governing Authority: private; not-for-profit organization. Tax-exempt: 501(c)(3).
Natural History Museum.
Collections: worldwide paleontological specimens; cretaceous ammonites; end of the cretaceous dinosaurs; T-Rex artifacts; invertebrate & vertebrate dinosaur fossils; minerals; meteorites; mining photographs; deeds; Black Hills history.
Research Fields: ammonite locality & stratigraphy; fossil; dinosaur; fishes; mammal & minerals.
Facilities: paleontological library; 4,000 sq. ft. exhibit space; field research station.
Activities: talks & lectures; loan, traveling & temporary exhibitions; school loan service; bi-annual symposium; 1st in 2005 100 years of T-Rex; 2nd in 2007 Dinosaurs of the Hell Creek. Annual Events: Natural History Festival; auction; special dinosaur exhibits.
Hours & Admission Prices: Summer: Mon.-Sat. 9-7, Sun. 10-6; Winter: Mon.-Fri. 9-5, Sat. 10-5. Adults $7.50, children $5. ♿
Attendance: 76,465 (accurate)

Hot Springs

MAMMOTH SITE OF HOT SPRINGS, INC., 1800 Hwy. 18, Bypass, Hot Springs, SD 57747-9604. Mailing Address: P.O. Box 692, Hot Springs, SD 57747-0692. Tel.: 605-745-6017. Fax: 605-745-3038.
E-mail: joem@mammothsite.org
Web Site: www.mammothsite.org
Founded: 1975.
Congressional District: 2
Key Personnel: C.E.O. & Museum Shop Mgr., Joe Muller; Pres. (V), Dr. Frank Ferguson; Vice Pres., Dr. Ken Bowe; Sec., Anna Merrill.
Personnel Profile: Full-Time Paid 13; Part-Time Paid 37; Interns 6.
Governing Authority: nonprofit organization. Tax-exempt: 501(c)(3).
Paleontology Museum.
Collections: mammoth tusks; skulls; bones of mammoth; pleistocene fauna.
Research Fields: paleontology; sedimentology; paleobotany.
Facilities: library of books on paleontology & sedimentology available for research; video presentation. Mammoth site booklets for sale.
Activities: guided tours; lectures; permanent exhibitions.
Publications: booklet, Mammoth Graveyard; book, Mammoth Site of Hot Springs, South Dakota; brochures; Megafauna & Man (1989 Symposium volume); Annotated Bibliography of North American Mammoths 1940-1990.
Hours & Admission Prices: April to mid-May & Sept.-Oct. daily 9-5; mid-May to Aug. daily 8-8; Nov.-March daily 9-3:30. Adults $8, seniors 60 & over $7.50, children 5-12 $6; discounts to AAM & ICOM members; children 4 & under and members no charge. ♿
Attendance: 99,286 (accurate)
Membership: Single $20; Family $35; Donor $50; Contributing $100; Supporting $500; Sustaining $500 & up.

PIONEER HISTORICAL MUSEUM OF SOUTH DAKOTA, 300 N. Chicago St., Hot Springs, SD 57747-1657. Mailing Address: P.O. Box 361, Hot Springs, SD 57747-0361. Tel.: 605-745-5147.
Web Site: www.pioneer-museum.com
Key Personnel: Pres., Jim Bingham
History Museum: built in 1893, used as a school until 1961.
Collections: period furnishings; photographs; sculpture; personal artifacts.
Facilities: Museum-related items for sale.
Activities: tours. Museum Sponsors: Pioneer Days.
Hours & Admission Prices: June-Sept. Mon.-Sat. 9-5. Call for admission prices. ♿

PIONEER MUSEUM IN HOT SPRINGS, 300 N. Chicago Ave., Hot Springs, SD 57747-1657. Mailing Address: Box 361, Hot Springs, SD 57747-0361. Tel.: 605-745-5147.
Formerly: Fall River County Historical Museum
Founded: 1961.
Congressional District: 2
Key Personnel: Pres., Jim Bingham.
Personnel Profile: Full-Time Paid 1; Part-Time Paid 2; Part-Time Volunteers 40.
Governing Authority: society; nonprofit. Parent Institution: Fall River Co. Historical Society. Tax-exempt: 501(c)(3).
Historical Society Museum: housed in 1893 schoolhouse.
Collections: artifacts; furniture; tools; dishes; books & other items showing how pioneers lived; photos; quilts; toys; paintings; photos; medical artifacts; cameras.
Research Fields: local history.
Activities: guided tours; formally organized education programs for children; permanent & temporary exhibitions. Museum Sponsors: Pioneer Days & Benefit Consignment Auction in June.
Publications: books, Fall River County Pioneers Histories; IGLOO: A History of the Black Hills Ordinance Depot.
Hours & Admission Prices: May 15-Oct. 15 Mon.-Sat. 9-5. Adults $5, seniors $4; discounts to families, school groups & bus tours; children 12 & under no charge. ♿
Attendance: 10,000 (accurate)
Membership: Senior $8; Individual $10; Family $15; Business $25; Lifetime $100.

WIND CAVE NATIONAL PARK, Hot Springs, SD 57747. Mailing Address: 26611 U.S. Hwy. 385, Hot Springs, SD 57747-6027. Tel.: 605-745-4600. Fax: 605-745-4207.
E-mail: tom_farrell@nps.gov
Web Site: www.nps.gov/wica/
Founded: 1903.
Congressional District: 2
Key Personnel: Supt., Videl Davila; Cur., Tom Farrell.
Personnel Profile: Full-Time Paid 24; Part-Time Paid 40; Part-Time Volunteers 1; Interns 2.
Governing Authority: federal. Tax-exempt.
Natural History Museum.
Collections: geology; natural history; American Indian artifacts; area history.
Facilities: 1,000-vol. library of natural history books available for use on the premises.
Activities: guided cave tours; lectures; campfire programs.
Hours & Admission Prices: Daily 8-4:30. Cave Tours: Natural Entrance Tour: adults $9, children 6-16 & senior pass holders $4.50. Fair Grounds Tour: adults $9, children 6-16 & senior pass holders $4.50. Garden of Eden Tour: adults $7, children 6-16 $3.50; children under 5 no charge. Museum: no charge. Closed New Year's Day; Thanksgiving; Christmas. ♿
Attendance: 102,000 (estimated)

Howard

MINER COUNTY RURAL LIFE MUSEUM, 127 S. Main St., Howard, SD 57349. Mailing Address: P.O. Box 245, Howard, SD 57349-0245. Tel.: 605-772-4567.
History Museum.

Collections: local history & culture; photographs; personal artifacts.
Activities: group tours.
Hours & Admission Prices: Sun. & Fri. 1-4. ♿
Membership: Miner County Historical Society: Individual $35 ($10 thereafter).

Huron

DAKOTALAND MUSEUM, State Fair Grounds, 1616 1st St., S.W., Huron, SD 57350-1254. Mailing Address: P.O. Box 1254, Huron, SD 57350-1254. Tel.: 605-352-4626.
E-mail: pepper@santel.net
Founded: 1960.
Congressional District: 32
Key Personnel: C.E.O. & Chm. (V), Peggy Gibson; Dir., Charnelle Scheel.
Personnel Profile: Full-Time Paid 1; Part-Time Paid 4; Part-Time Volunteers 6.
Governing Authority: Parent Institution: Dakotaland Museum Board. Subsidiary Institution: Huron City, Beadle County. Tax-exempt.
History Museum.
Collections: pioneer exhibits; American Indian artifacts, including 1,500 arrowheads, beadwork, peacepipes, moccasins, purses, baskets; history; Kauf Natural History Collection including 370 mounted mammals & birds; 1,600 items of clothing dating back to 1860; toys; dolls; furnished bedroom, parlor, physician's office & kitchen including a burled walnut bed & antique organ; hand tools; 1881 corn planter, walking plows & other vintage farm implements; clocks; surrey; radios; model T car; 1914 Monroe automobile; fire engine; glassware; cameras & projectors; baby buggies & cradles; musical instruments; Civil War memorabilia; compressed air locomotive. Historic Houses: 1894 Pyle House; 1870s log cabin.
Research Fields: history books.
Activities: guided tours; permanent & temporary exhibitions.
Publications: brochure.
Hours & Admission Prices: Memorial Day-Labor Day Mon.-Fri. 9-11:30, 1-4 & 6:30-8:30, Sat.-Sun. 1-4 & 6:30-8:30. Dakotaland Museum: family $5; adults $2. Pyle House Museum: daily 1-3:30. Adults 12 & over $1.50. Closed holidays. ♿
Attendance: 1,000 (estimated)

PYLE HOUSE MUSEUM, 376 Idaho Ave., S.E., Huron, SD 57350-2527. Mailing Address: P.O. Box 1254, Huron, SD 57350-1254. Tel.: 605-352-2528.
E-mail: rachelclenden@yahoo.com
Founded: 1985.
Congressional District: 32
Key Personnel: Dir., Rachel Clendenin.
Personnel Profile: Full-Time Paid 1; Part-Time Volunteers 5.
Governing Authority: Parent Institution: Dakota Land Museum/Pyle. Subsidiary Institution: Huron City/Beadle Co. Tax-exempt.
Historic House Museum: housed in the home of Gladys Pyle, the first elected woman U.S. senator, built in 1894.
Collections: period artifacts; furnishings; personal artifacts; original blueprint, architect Dracon 1893-1894.
Hours & Admission Prices: Daily 1-3:30. Adults $1.50; children under 10 no charge. Closed winter holidays.
Attendance: 500 (estimated)

Interior

BADLANDS NATIONAL PARK, Hwy. 240 Loop Off I90, Interior, SD 57750. Mailing Address: 25216 Ben Reifel Rd., P.O. Box 6, Interior, SD 57750-0006. Tel.: 605-433-5361. Fax: 605-433-5404. TDD: 605-433-5361.
Web Site: www.nps.gov/badl
Founded: 1939.
Key Personnel: Chief Resource Education, Judy Olson.
Governing Authority: federal. Affiliated with the U.S. Dept. of the Interior, National Park Service, Washington, DC 20240. Tax-exempt.
Natural History Museum.
Collections: Ben Reifel Visitor Center: life during the Eocene, Oligocene, & Pleistocene periods; films. White River Visitor Center: Sioux Indian artifacts; films.
Research Fields: wildlife: buffalo; prairie dogs; mule deer; Rocky Mountain bighorn; Paleontology; woody draws ecology; grassland ecology problems.
Facilities: visitor centers. Publications for sale.
Activities: Ben Reifel Visitor Center: slide talks; guided nature walks; hikes; night prowls & night sky observation; nature trails; fossil preparation demonstrations; films; touch screens; introductory program.
Publications: booklets, Where Buffalo Roam; Badlands: Its Life and Landscape; Wildflowers of the Northern Plains and Black Hills; This Curious Country; Video: Land of Stone and Light.
Hours & Admission Prices: Ben Reifel Visitor Center: April 15-June 2 daily 8-5; June 3-Oct. 13 daily 8-5; Oct. 14-April 14 daily 8-4. White River Visitor Center: June-Aug. daily 10-4. Badlands National Park: $7 Individual, $15 per car. Closed New Year's Day; Thanksgiving; Christmas. Annual Pass $30. National Park Pass: $80. ♿
Attendance: 906,868 (accurate)

Ipswich

J.W. PARMLEY HISTORICAL HOME SOCIETY, 115 Main St., Ipswich, SD 57451. Mailing Address: P.O. Box 111, Ipswich, SD 57451-0111. Tel.: 605-426-6024 & 6949.
Web Site: www.ipswich-sd.com/calendar.html
Formerly: J.W. Parmley Historical Home Museum
Founded: 1981.
Key Personnel: Dir., Irene Rissman; Pres., Jeff Bergstrasser; Vice Pres., Phyllis M. Merrick; Sec., Candis Kub; Treas., Ray Kub.
Personnel Profile: Full-Time Volunteers 9; Part-Time Volunteers 10.
Governing Authority: board. Additional building at 319 4th St., Ipswich, SD 57451. Tax-exempt.
Historic Building.
Collections: local history; pioneers; early businesses; animal exhibits complied by pioneers; clothing; military; photographs; archives; 1900 business office; 1921 home
Activities: permanent exhibitions, open for special tours. Barbeque at the Land Office in June; Ice Cream Social at the Home in August; Fundraiser in October.
Hours & Admission Prices: Memorial Day to Labor Day Wed., Fri. & Sun. 2-5; other times by appointment. No charge; donations accepted.
Attendance: 500 (accurate)

Kadoka

BADLANDS PETRIFIED GARDENS, Interstate 90, Exit 152, Kadoka, SD 57543. Mailing Address: P.O. Box 27, Kadoka, SD 57543-0027. Tel.: 605-837-2448.
Web Site: www.badlandspetrifiedgardens.com
Founded: 1956.
Key Personnel: Pres. & Deputy Dir., Robert Fugate; Vice Pres., Cathy Fugate; Asst. Dir., Patty Ulman; Business Officer, Floy Fugate; Museum Shop Mgr., Bill Fugate.
Personnel Profile: Full-Time Paid 1; Part-Time Paid 4.
Governing Authority: company organized for profit.
Natural History Museum.
Collections: Badlands petrified wood, logs & stumps; fossil exhibits; agate & minerals; fluorescent mineral displays.
Facilities: Minerals, gemstones, jewelry & gift items for sale.
Activities: tours & permanent exhibitions.
Hours & Admission Prices: mid-April to Nov. 1 daily 7-7. Adults $5, children 6-16 $2.50; tours half price. ♿
Attendance: 15,000 (estimated)

KADOKA DEPOT MUSEUM, S. Main St., Kadoka, SD 57543. Mailing Address: City of Kadoka, Box 58, Kadoka, SD 57543-0058. Tel.: 605-837-2229. Fax: 605-837-1262.
E-mail: kadokacity@wcenet.com
Formerly: Jackson Washabaugh Historical Museum
Founded: 1980.
Key Personnel: City Mayor, Harry Weller; Financial Officer, Patti Ulmen.
Governing Authority: nonprofit; municipal. Kadoka City Council.
Historical Society Museum: housed in 1906 Chicago, Milwaukee, St. Paul Railroad Depot.
Collections: railroad; homestead; bank; school; army & navy photos; local memorabilia.
Research Fields: local memorabilia.
Activities: loan, permanent & temporary exhibitions.
Hours & Admission Prices: June-Labor Day daily 6-8. No charge; donations accepted.
Attendance: 500 (estimated)

Keystone

BIG THUNDER GOLD MINE, 604 Blair, Keystone, SD 57751. Mailing Address: Box 459, Keystone, SD 57751-0459. Tel.: 605-666-4847. Fax: 605-666-4566.
Web Site: www.bigthundermine.com
Founded: 1957.
Congressional District: 1
Key Personnel: C.E.O., Chm. Bd. & Museum Shop Mgr., Sandra McLain.
Personnel Profile: Full-Time Paid 2; Part-Time Paid 21; Part-Time Volunteers 1.
Governing Authority: corporate operation.
Historic Site: 1890s gold mine.

Collections: mining equipment; photographs; 1880's historical equipment; 4,500 sq. ft. gold mill built in 2001.
Facilities: Jewelry and gold panning supplies for sale.
Activities: guided mine tour; gold panning; lectures; prospecting.
Hours & Admission Prices: May-Sept. daily 8-8. Adults $8.75, children 6-12 $5.75; discounts to members, AAM & ICOM members. Gold Panning: $7.75 without tour, $5.75 with tour. ♿
Attendance: 62,000 (accurate)

KEYSTONE AREA HISTORICAL SOCIETY, 410 3rd St., Keystone, SD 57751. Mailing Address: P.O. Box 177, Keystone, SD 57751-0177. Tel.: 605-255-5280. Fax: 605-666-4824.
E-mail: mclainsandra@aol.com
Web Site: www.keystonehistory.com
Founded: 1983.
Congressional District: 1
Key Personnel: Pres., Sandra McLain; Sec. & Museum Shop Mgr., Patty Cofoid; Museum Shop Mgr., Westley Parker; Treas., Carolyn Clifford.
Personnel Profile: Part-Time Paid 1; Part-Time Volunteers 10.
Governing Authority: nonprofit. Tax-exempt: 501(c)(4).
General Museum: housed in c.1900 three-story Victorian frame school house.
Collections: early settlement of the local area & mining camps around Keystone; mining tools & equipment; Victorian period artifacts; Carrie Ingalls & family person artifacts, former residents; Bower Family Band collection; photographs; equipment from Mount Rushmore memorial; rock & gem collection.
Research Fields: mining camps; minerology; local genealogy; historic sites.
Facilities: one-room school. Booklets & prints for sale.
Activities: self-guided walking tours; lectures; films; loan exhibitions; living history one-room school for grades 1-7. Carrie Ingalls Day in August.
Publications: newsletter, Holy Terror Tattler; book, Keystone & Its Colorful Characters.
Hours & Admission Prices: May 15-Sept. 15 Mon.-Sat. 10-3. No charge; donations accepted. ♿
Attendance: 2,000 (accurate)
Membership: Child $1; Adult $5; Charter Single $10; Charter Couple $15.

MOUNT RUSHMORE NATIONAL MEMORIAL, 13000 Hwy. 244, Keystone, SD 57751-0268. Mailing Address: 13000 Hwy. 244, Bldg. 31, Ste. 1, Keystone, SD 57751-0268. Tel.: 605-574-2523. Fax: 605-574-2307.
E-mail: bruce_weisman@nps.gov
Web Site: www.nps.gov/moru/
Founded: 1925.
Key Personnel: Supt., Gerard Baker; Chief Ranger, Mike Pflaum; Chief Interpretation, Judy Olson; Park Cur., Bruce Weisman.
Governing Authority: federal government. Parent Institution: National Park Service, Washington, DC. Tax-exempt.
Park Museum: massive granite sculpture, carved into a mountainside, memorializing the likenesses of four American Presidents; Washington, Jefferson, Theodore Roosevelt & Lincoln.
Collections: 3,500 tools & equipment; 2,000 historic photographs & negatives; 40,000 pieces of archival materials.
Research Fields: background & construction of Mount Rushmore.
Facilities: library of historic papers & journals available for use on premises; 1,300-seat outdoor amphitheater; 5,200 sq. ft. exhibit space; restaurant. Museum-related items & literature for sale.
Activities: lectures; films; summer evening amphitheater program; ranger conducted talks in studio; permanent & temporary exhibits; film loan service.
Publications: brochures in five languages, English, Spanish, French, German & Japanese and braille.
Hours & Admission Prices: Information Center: May-Aug. daily 8am-10pm; Oct.-March daily 8-5. Office: Mon.-Fri. 8-4:30. Sculptor's Studio: May-Sept. daily 9-5. Donations accepted. Parking fee: $10 annual pass; $50 per bus per entry. ♿
Attendance: 2,754,261 (accurate)

NATIONAL PRESIDENTIAL WAX MUSEUM, Hwy. 609 16-A, Keystone, SD 57751. Mailing Address: P.O. Box 238, Keystone, SD 57751-0238. Tel.: 605-666-4455. Fax: 605-666-4455.
Founded: 1970.
Key Personnel: Mgr. Operations & Museum Shop Mgr., Karen Miller.
Governing Authority: company organized for profit.
Wax Museum.
Collections: over 100 life-size wax figures, including all of the U.S. presidents & other famous Americans.
Facilities: Gift items for sale.
Activities: lectures; taped tour.
Publications: brochures.
Hours & Admission Prices: April-May & Sept.-Oct. 9-5; Memorial Day to Labor Day 9-8. Discounts to AAA, active military w/ID.
Attendance: 28,000

RUSHMORE BORGLUM STORY, 342 Winter St., Keystone, SD 57751-2036. Tel.: 605-666-4448. Fax: 605-666-4482.
E-mail: borglum@gwtc.net
Web Site: www.rushmoreborglum.com
History Museum.
Collections: life of Gutzon Borglum's, who at age 60 began carving Mt. Rushmore; paintings, sculptures & personal artifacts.
Facilities: Museum-related items for sale.
Activities: video.
Hours & Admission Prices: May & Sept. to early Oct. call for hours; June-Aug. daily 8-7. ♿

Kimball

SOUTH DAKOTA TRACTOR MUSEUM, 501 S. West St., Kimball, SD 57355. Mailing Address: P.O. Box 418, Kimball, SD 57355-0418. Tel.: 605-778-6513.
E-mail: rbickner@midstatesd.net
Web Site: sdtractormuseum.home.comcast.net
Founded: 2000.
Key Personnel: Pres. (V), Maynard Konechne; Museum Shop Mgr., Dale Stanek.
Personnel Profile: Full-Time Volunteers 31; Part-Time Volunteers 20.
Governing Authority: private; nonprofit organization. Tax-exempt: 501(c)(3).
Agriculture & Antiques Museum.
Collections: South Dakota agriculture; farm machinery; household items. Historic Buildings: 1930s one-room country school; blacksmith shop.
Facilities: library. Museum-related items for sale.
Activities: guided tours; loan, participatory, traveling & temporary exhibitions; broadcast programs; bus tour groups. Annual Events: Independence Day Parade; Desperado Days with Kimball Chamber in July; Homecoming Parade.
Hours & Admission Prices: Memorial Day to Oct. 1 Mon.-Sat. 9-5, Sun. 1-5; Oct.-May by appointment. No charge; donations accepted. ♿
Attendance: 1,730 (accurate)
Membership: Adult $5.

Kyle

OGLALA LAKOTA COLLEGE HISTORICAL CENTER, 3 Mile Creek Rd., Kyle, SD 57752-0310. Mailing Address: P.O. Box 490, Kyle, SD 57752-0490. Tel.: 605-455-6000.
Web Site: www.olc.edu/about/historical_center
Historical Center.
Collections: local history & culture; photographs & artwork from the early 1800s to the Wounded Knee Massacre in 1890.
Hours & Admission Prices: June-Sept. Mon.-Sat. 9-5. No charge.

Lake City

FORT SISSETON HISTORIC STATE PARK, 11907 434th Ave., Lake City, SD 57247-6153. Mailing Address: South Dakota Game Fish and Parks, 523 E. Capitol Ave., Pierre, SD 57501. Tel.: 605-448-5701. Fax: 605-448-5572.
E-mail: fortsisseton@state.sd.us
Founded: 1972.
Congressional District: 1
Key Personnel: Park Mgr., Paul Winckler.
Personnel Profile: Full-Time Paid 2; Part-Time Paid 1; Part-Time Volunteers 1.
Governing Authority: state. Parent Institution: South Dakota Dept. Game, Fish, & Parks. Subsidiary Institution: Div. of Parks & Recreation. Tax-exempt.
Historical Museum: located on site of c.1864 Ft. Wadsworth (Ft. Sisseton).
Collections: Indian artifacts; Civil War weapons & military uniforms; Sam Brown family collection.
Research Fields: Fort Sisseton history.
Facilities: audio-visual room; campground.
Activities: guided tours; films & slides; formally organized education programs for children. Park Sponsors: annual Fort Sisseton Historical Festival in June.
Publications: Fort Sisseton; Chilson's History of Fort Sisseton.
Hours & Admission Prices: Memorial Day-Labor Day daily 10-6; special group tours on request. State Park Entrance Permit required: call for fees. ♿
Attendance: 65,000 (estimated)

Lake Norden

SOUTH DAKOTA AMATEUR BASEBALL HALL OF FAME, 519 Main Ave., Lake Norden, SD 57248. Mailing Address: P.O. Box 80, Lake Norden, SD 57248-0080. Tel.: 605-785-3553. Fax: 605-785-3315.
Founded: 1976.
Key Personnel: Pres., Scott Fiedler; Vice Pres., Jerry Des Lauriers; Exec. Sec. & Cur., Rusty Antonen.
Governing Authority: nonprofit organization. Tax-exempt: 501(c)(3).
Sports Museum.
Collections: pictorial history of amateur baseball in South Dakota; artifacts; equipment; historical documents; Hall of Fame inductees displayed.
Research Fields: amateur baseball in South Dakota.
Activities: concerts; permanent exhibitions.
Hours & Admission Prices: May to Sept. daily 9-7; other times by appointment. No charge; donations accepted. ♿

Lead

BLACK HILLS MINING MUSEUM, 323 W. Main, Lead, SD 57754-1604. Mailing Address: P.O. Box 694, Lead, SD 57754-0694. Tel.: 605-584-1605.
E-mail: bhminmus@mato.com
Web Site: www.mining-museum.blackhills.com
Founded: 1986.
Congressional District: 1
Key Personnel: C.E.O. & Pres., Tom Nelson; Dir., Cyndi Fisher.
Personnel Profile: Full-Time Paid 2; Part-Time Paid 2; Part-Time Volunteers 12.
Governing Authority: nonprofit organization. Tax-exempt: 501(c)(3).
Mining History Museum.
Collections: photographs; historic records from Black Hills mines, 1876-1940s.
Research Fields: Black Hills mining history, 1875-modern times.
Facilities: library available to public for research in facility only; archives; 12,000 sq. ft. exhibit space; 30-seat theater. Museum-related items for sale.
Activities: guided tours; gold panning.
Publications: biannual newsletter, Black Hills Mining Museum; newspaper, The Gold Belt Miner.
Hours & Admission Prices: May 15-Sept. 3 daily 8-5; Sept.-Oct. call for hours. Tours: adults $6, senior citizens & students $5; discounts to groups and AAM & ICOM members; children under 6 & members no charge. ♿
Attendance: 20,000 (estimated)
Membership: Individual & Couple $5; Friend $100; Contributor $250; Donor $500; Sponsor $1,000; Benefactor $2,500; Major Contributor $5,000; Gold Star Contributor $10,000.

HOMESTAKE GOLD MINE VISITOR CENTER, 160 W. Main St., Lead, SD 57754-1362. Tel.: 605-584-3110.
E-mail: hvc@rushmore.com
Web Site: www.homestakevisitorcenter.com
Key Personnel: Dir., Melissa Johnson
Mining History Museum.
Collections: history of mining including hoisting, crushing & milling; open mine pit.
Facilities: Museum-related items for sale.
Activities: guided tour; pan for gold; video.
Hours & Admission Prices: May-Sept. daily 8-6; Oct.-April daily 8-5; groups by appointment. Tours: adults $6, seniors $5.25, students 6-18 $5; children 5 & under no charge.

PRESIDENTS PARK SCULPTURE GARDEN, 11249 Presidents Park Loop, Lead, SD 57754-3846. Mailing Address: 104 S. Galena, Lead, SD 57754-1674. Tel.: 605-584-9925.
Web Site: www.presidentspark.com
Key Personnel: Mgr., Dave Olmstead
History Museum.
Collections: 20 ft. tall sculptures of all 42 Presidents.
Facilities: visitors center; cafe. Museum-related items for sale.
Hours & Admission Prices: Daily 9-6; weather permitting. Adults $8, seniors 60 & over $6.50, children 5-15 $6; discounts to military & groups; children 5 & under no charge. ♿

Lemmon

GRAND RIVER MUSEUM, 114 10th St. W., Lemmon, SD 57638-2202. Tel.: 605-374-3911 & 7574.
E-mail: grmuseum@sdplains.com
Web Site: www.grandrivermuseum.org
Founded: 1998.
Key Personnel: Pres., Stuart T. Schmidt; Dir. & Museum Shop Mgr., Phyllis Schmidt.
Personnel Profile: Part-Time Paid 1; Part-Time Volunteers 5.
Governing Authority: Tax-exempt.
History Museum.
Collections: Grand River area history; animal & plant fossils; Native American people & culture; area ranching.
Facilities: Museum-related items for sale.
Activities: special programs.
Publications: quarterly newsletter.
Hours & Admission Prices: May-Sept. Mon.-Sat. 9-6, Sun. 12-5. No charge; donations accepted. ♿
Attendance: 5,500 (estimated)

PETRIFIED WOOD PARK & MUSEUM, 500 Main St., Lemmon, SD 57638-1523. Tel.: 605-374-3964.
Web Site: www.lemmonsd.com/petrified.html
Key Personnel: Dir., Carolyn Penfield
Geological & Historical Museum.
Collections: artifacts made from petrified wood; sculptures; personal artifacts.
Hours & Admission Prices: Museum: Memorial Day-Labor Day daily 9-5. No charge; donations accepted. ♿

Madison

KARL E. MUNDT HISTORICAL & EDUCATIONAL FOUNDATION, Karl Mundt Library, Dakota State University, Madison, SD 57042. Mailing Address: 820 N. Washington Ave., Madison, SD 57042-0483. Tel.: 605-256-5211.
Web Site: www.departments.dsu.edu/library/archive/archives.htm
Founded: 1963.
Personnel Profile: Full-Time Paid 1; Part-Time Paid 1.
History Museum.
Collections: Senator Mundt's personal & political life; documents; films; photographs; tapes; scrapbooks.
Hours & Admission Prices: Research: Mon.-Fri. 8:30-4. Closed legal holidays. ♿

PRAIRIE VILLAGE, W. Hwy. 34, Madison, SD 57042. Mailing Address: P.O. Box 256, Madison, SD 57042-0256. Tel.: 605-256-3644; 800-693-3644.
Web Site: www.prairievillage.org
Founded: 1966.
Congressional District: 1
Key Personnel: Pres., Lowell DeVries; Vice Pres., George Lee; Museum Shop Mgr., Stan Rauch.
Personnel Profile: Part-Time Paid 6; Part-Time Volunteers 100.
Governing Authority: nonprofit organization. Prairie Historical Society, Inc. Tax-exempt: 501(c)(3).
Village Museum.
Collections: furniture & furnishings; steam tractors & other steam equipment; threshing machines; locomotive; rocks; 3 steam trains. Historic Structures: 1906 church; 1912 Socialist Hall; 1877 claim shanty; 1878 Old Madison Hotel; 1880s country school; jail; print shop; barbershop; dentist office; 1893 steam carousel.
Facilities: library; 350-seat auditorium; classrooms; 50-seat restaurant. Gift items for sale.
Activities: guided tours; annual 6-team; steam train rides. Museum Sponsors: steam & horse threshing at jamboree in August.
Publications: weekly newspaper column, Madison Daily Leader.
Hours & Admission Prices: Village: Mother's Day weekend to Labor Day Mon.-Sat. 10-5, Sun. 11-6. Train Rides: Mother's Day to Sept. 1 Sun. Adults $5; discounts for senior citizens, group tours. Season Pass: $15. ♿
Attendance: 40,000 (estimated)
Membership: 100 hours of volunteer work or $100 contribution.

SMITH-ZIMMERMANN HERITAGE MUSEUM, 221 N.E. 8th St., Madison, SD 57042-1639. Tel.: 605-256-5308.
E-mail: smith.zimmermann@dsu.edu
Web Site: www.smith-zimmermann.dsu.edu
Founded: 1952.
Congressional District: 1
Key Personnel: Pres., Dale Nighbert; Coord., Torrie Ewoldt.
Personnel Profile: Part-Time Volunteers 25.
Governing Authority: Parent Institution: Lake County Historical Society. Tax-exempt.
History Museum.
Collections: pioneer artifacts of eastern South Dakota, specifically Lake County & surrounding area, 1870-1970s; murals depicting pioneer life.
Research Fields: cultural history of eastern South Dakota; genealogical records; pictorial images.
Facilities: period rooms. Books for sale.

Activities: guided tours; changing exhibits; brown-bag programs; educational programs; ethnic cooking programs.
Publications: quarterly newsletter.
Hours & Admission Prices: Tues.-Fri. 1-4:30; other times by appointment. No charge; donations accepted. ♿
Attendance: 5,598 (accurate)
Membership: Family $15.

McLaughlin

MAJOR JAMES MCLAUGHLIN HERITAGE CENTER, Main St., McLaughlin, SD 57642. Mailing Address: P.O. Box 642, McLaughlin, SD 57642-0642. Tel.: 605-823-4590.
Founded: 1989.
Key Personnel: Pres. (V), Sharon Walker; Museum Shop Mgr., Barb Meyer
History Museum.
Collections: local history; agriculture; Native American; Mahto Post Office; country school; James McLaughlin family history; documents.
Hours & Admission Prices: May-Sept. Mon.-Fri. 12-5. No charge.

Midland

MIDLAND PIONEER MUSEUM, Main St., Midland, SD 57552. Mailing Address: 25121 Capa Rd., Midland, SD 57552-3201. Tel.: 605-843-2150.
E-mail: kry@gwtc.net
Web Site: www.gwtc.net/~kry
Founded: 1974.
Key Personnel: C.E.O. & Dir., Janice D. Bierle.
Personnel Profile: Part-Time Paid 1.
History Museum.
Collections: pioneer machinery; period artifacts; photographs.
Hours & Admission Prices: June-Aug. Mon.-Tues. & Fri. 1:30-4; other times by appointment. No charge: donations accepted.

Milbank

GRANT COUNTY HISTORICAL MUSEUM, Third Ave. & Third St., Milbank, SD 57252. Mailing Address: P.O. Box 201, Milbank, SD 57252-0201. Tel.: 605-432-9332.
E-mail: ssteeg65@itctel.com
Web Site: www.grantcountysdhistory.com
Founded: 1970.
Personnel Profile: Part-Time Paid 1.
Governing Authority: Tax-exempt.
Historical Museum. Listed on the National Register of Historic Buildings.
Collections: artifacts from Grant County; photographs; books.
Publications: newsletter.
Hours & Admission Prices: Memorial Day-Labor Day Sun. 2-5; other times by appointment. No charge; donations accepted.
Membership: Student $5; Adult $10; Group & Organization $20; Lifetime $100.

Mission

SICANGU HERITAGE CENTER, Sinte Gleska University, Antelope Lake Campus, Mission, SD 57555. Mailing Address: P.O. Box 675, Mission, SD 57555-0675. Tel.: 605-856-8211.
E-mail: marcella.cash@sintegleska.edu
Web Site: www.sintegleska.edu
Key Personnel: Dir., Marcella Cash; Cur. & Registrar, Keli Herman; Asst. Archivist, Terry Gray.
Governing Authority: bd. of regents. Parent Institution: Sinte Gleska University.
Heritage Center.
Collections: Sicangu culture & history; personal artifacts.
Activities: group tours.
Hours & Admission Prices: Mon.-Fri. 9-4. No charge; donations accepted. Closed SGU holidays.

Mitchell

CARNEGIE RESOURCE CENTER, 119 W. 3rd, Mitchell, SD 57301-3410. Mailing Address: P.O. Box 263, Mitchell, SD 57301-0263. Tel.: 605-996-3209.
Web Site: mitchellcarnegie.org
Formerly: Oscar Howe Art Center & YWCA
Founded: 2006.
Key Personnel: Pres. (V), Lyle W. Swenson.
Personnel Profile: Part-Time Volunteers 15.
Governing Authority: Parent Institution: Mitchell Area Historical Society. Subsidiary Institution: Mitchell Area Genealogical Society. Tax-exempt.
Art Center.
Collections: Corn Palace historical items from 1892-present; dome with Oscar Howe mural; local historical & genealogical materials.
Hours & Admission Prices: Mon.-Sat. 1-5. No charge; donations accepted. Closed holidays.
Membership: Single $10; Family $15.

DAKOTA DISCOVERY MUSEUM, (M), 1300 McGovern Ave., Mitchell, SD 57301-7901. Mailing Address: P.O. Box 1071, Mitchell, SD 57301-7071. Tel.: 605-996-2122. Fax: 605-996-0323.
E-mail: history@dakotadiscovery.com
Web Site: www.dakotadiscovery.com
Formerly: Middle Border Museum & Oscar Howe Art Center
Founded: 1939.
Congressional District: 17
Key Personnel: Exec. Dir., Lori Holmberg; Pres., Jan Henderson; Museum Shop Mgr., Marge Bollack.
Personnel Profile: Full-Time Paid 3; Part-Time Volunteers 54.
Governing Authority: society. Tax-exempt: 501(c)(3). Parent Institution: Friends of the Middle Border, Inc.
Historic Village Museum and Art Center.
Collections: items pertaining to the Middle Border (ND, SD & portions of adjoining states) settlement history exhibits; 1600-1939 era; American Indian artifacts; Charles Hargens Studio & Gallery; LeLand Case Office & Gallery; Oscar Howe, Harvey Dunn, Charles Greener, James Earle Fraser art collections; 4 historical buildings.
Research Fields: early history of ND, SD, NE & surrounding region.
Facilities: five building complex.
Activities: guided tours; lectures; gallery talks; education programs for children & adults; permanent exhibitions; Discovery Land; Children's hands on activities with changing themes. Annual Events: Old Fashion Independence Day in July; Haunted Village in October; Victorian Christmas in December.
Publications: quarterly newsletter; tour guide.
Hours & Admission Prices: May-Sept. Mon.-Sat. 9-6, Sun. 1-4; Oct.-April Mon.-Fri. 10-4, Sat. 1-4. Adults $5, senior citizens $4, children 6-18 $2; discounts to groups & AAA members; members no charge. Closed New Year's Eve & Day; Easter Mon.; Boxing Day; Thanksgiving; Christmas. ♿
Attendance: 6,000 (accurate)
Membership: Individual $25; Individual Premier $35; Family & Grandparent $40; Patron $100.

MITCHELL PREHISTORIC INDIAN VILLAGE, 3200 Indian Village Rd., Mitchell, SD 57301. Tel.: 605-996-5473.
E-mail: info@mitchellindianvillage.org
Web Site: www.mitchellindianvillage.org
Archaeological Site.
Collections: reconstructed earth lodge; exhibits focusing on trade networks, pottery, tools & spear points.
Hours & Admission Prices: April & Oct. Mon.-Fri. 9-4; May & Sept. daily 9-4; Memorial Day weekend-Labor Day daily 8-6. Adults $6, seniors 60 & over $5, children 6-18 $4; children 5 & under no charge.

TELSTAR MUSTANG SHELBY COBRA RESTORATIONS & MUSEUM, 1300-1400 S. Kimball St., Mitchell, SD 57301-4709. Tel.: 605-996-6550.
Web Site: www.telstarmotors.com
Key Personnel: Owner, Jerry Regynski; Owner, Mavis Regynski
Car Museum.
Collections: three Shelby GT 500 Kings of the Roads; two GT 500 428 Super Cobra Jet Drag-Pack convertibles; two Boss 429 engines; 1966 Shelby GT 350 Hertz; 1964 1/2 Mustang convertible; 1965 GT fastback; 1965 Shelby GT 350; 1966 Mustang GT convertible; 1967 Shelby GT 350; 1967 Shelby GT 500; two 1968 Shelby GT 350 convertibles; 1968 Shelby GT 500 convertible; 1968 Shelby GT 500 KR fastback; two 1968 Shelby GT 500 KR convertibles; 1969 Shelby GT 350 fastback; 1970 Boss 302; 1970 Shelby GT 350 fastback.
Hours & Admission Prices: By appointment.

Mobridge

KLEIN MUSEUM, 1820 W. Grand Crossing, W. Hwy. 12, Mobridge, SD 57601-1114. Tel.: 605-845-7243.
E-mail: kleinmuseum@westriv.com
Founded: 1976.
Congressional District: 50
Key Personnel: Chm., Ken Heil; Museum Shop Mgr., Diane Kindt.
Personnel Profile: Full-Time Paid 1; Part-Time Paid 2; Part-Time Volunteers 40.
Governing Authority: nonprofit organization; board of directors. Tax-exempt: 501(c)(3).

General Museum.
Collections: pioneer & Native American artifacts. Historic Buildings: 1920s house; post office; 1920 school; tool shed.
Research Fields: local histories; photographs.
Facilities: Indian pottery & jewelry, books & museum-related items for sale.
Activities: guided tours; permanent & temporary exhibitions.
Publications: folder.
Hours & Admission Prices: April-Oct. Mon. & Wed.-Fri. 9-5, Sat.-Sun. 1-5. Adults $3, students $2; members no charge. ♿
Attendance: 4,000 (estimated)
Membership: Single $17; Family $30; Business $40.

Montrose

PORTER SCULPTURE PARK, 25700 451st Ave., Montrose, SD 57048. Mailing Address: 110 N. Maple, Saint Lawrence, SD 57373. Tel.: 605-853-2266 & 204-0370 (summer).
E-mail: ronporter007@juno.com
Web Site: www.portersculpturepark.com
Founded: 2001.
Key Personnel: Dir., Wayne Porter; Dir., Ron Porter; Dir., Audrey Porter
Sculpture Park.
Collections: over 40 sculptures, including a 60 ft. bull's head sculpture.
Hours & Admission Prices: Memorial Day-Labor Day daily 8-6. Adults $6, children 13-17 $4; discounts to groups.

Murdo

1880 TOWN, I-90 Exit 170, Murdo, SD 57559. Mailing Address: P.O. Box 507, Murdo, SD 57559-0507. Tel.: 605-344-2259.
E-mail: info@1880town.com
Web Site: www.1880town.com
Key Personnel: Mgr., Richard Hollinger
General Museum: built as a movie set but never used for filming.
Collections: period artifacts; Dances with Wolves movie props; 30 buildings.
Hours & Admission Prices: May & Oct. daily 8am to sunset; June-Aug. 6am-9pm; Sept. 7am to sunset. Adults $9, senior citizens $8, teens 13-19 $6, children 6-12 $5; discounts to groups; handicapped & children under 5 no charge.

PIONEER AUTO MUSEUM, 503 E. 5th St., Murdo, SD 57559. Mailing Address: Box 76, Murdo, SD 57559-0076. Tel.: 605-669-2691. Fax: 605-669-3217.
E-mail: pas@pioneerautoshow.com
Web Site: www.pioneerautoshow.com
Founded: 1953.
Key Personnel: C.E.O., Dir. & Cur., Dave Geisler; Deputy Dir. & Cur., John Geisler; Museum Shop Mgr., Janet Miller.
Personnel Profile: Full-Time Paid 1; Part-Time Paid 14.
Governing Authority: company organized for profit.
Transportation Museum & Antique Town: located at the northern head of the Texas Cattle Trail.
Collections: over 200 antique & classic cars; antique motorcycles & a motorcycle room featuring Elvis Presley's motorcycle; bicycles; tractors; farm equipment; buggies & other horse-drawn vehicles; musical instruments; 1906 Case steam engine; costumes; toys & dolls; Zeitner Rocks, Gems & Fossils Collection; circus display; furniture; collectibles. Town Buildings: Jack's Jewelry; Homesteader Claim Shack; Murdo Bank; Blacksmith Shop; Barber Shop; Jail. Historic Buildings: 1906 Milwaukee Railroad Depot & Caboose; 1906 pioneer church; 1806 one-room country school; 1906 general store; butcher's shop; old guns.
Research Fields: automobiles.
Facilities: 50-seat cafeteria. Gifts & museum-related items for sale.
Activities: auctions; sales; Swap Meet.
Hours & Admission Prices: Memorial Day-Labor Day 7-10; Winter: 9-6. Adults $9.50, children 6-13 $4.75; discounts to members, groups, AAM, AAA & ICOM members. Closed New Year's Day; Easter; Thanksgiving; Christmas. ♿
Attendance: 126,000 (estimated)

Newell

NEWELL MUSEUM, 108 3rd St., Newell, SD 57760. Mailing Address: P.O. Box 433, Newell, SD 57760-0433. Tel.: 605-456-1310. Fax: 605-456-2116.
E-mail: newellmuseum@yahoo.com
Web Site: www.sdmuseums.org
Founded: 1983.
Congressional District: 1
Key Personnel: Chm., Larry Vissia; Vice Chm., Rich Ruthford; Treas., Annitta Stolnack; Cur., Linda Velder; Archivist, Lauren Babb; Sec., Sharyl Scott.
Personnel Profile: Full-Time Paid 1; Part-Time Paid 4; Part-Time Volunteers 3; Interns 1.
Governing Authority: municipal government; nonprofit. Parent Institution: City of Newell. Tax-exempt.
History Museum.
Collections: household items; clothing; Native American artifacts & culture; fossils; antique toys & dolls; musical instruments; restored one-room schoolhouse; small barn & buggy; 1890 one-room log cabin; 1911 church.
Research Fields: 1874 Custer expedition; travels of Father DeSmet in Dakota Territory; local pioneer family histories; fur trade history; Orman Dam construction (1903-1912); Gen. George Crook's Horse Meat March after the Battle of Slim Buttes (1876); cattle drives & cowboys; rural schools in Butte County; Lewis & Clark Corp. of Discovery; Murder of Father Arthur Belknap, Lead, SD 1921; Congregational Church History 1907-2006; Newell Methodist Church History 1910-1937; All Trails Lead to Deadwood, Prohibition.
Facilities: library.
Activities: guided tours; participatory & temporary exhibitions. Annual Event: Labor Day Weekend Open House.
Hours & Admission Prices: May 30-Sept. Tues.-Sat. 1-5; other times by appointment. No charge; donations accepted. ♿
Attendance: 670 (accurate)

Oldham

LORIKS PETERSON HERITAGE HOUSE, 108 E. Williams St., Oldham, SD 57051-7216. Mailing Address: RR 1, Box 103, Oldham, SD 57051-7216. Tel.: 605-482-8640.
Web Site: www.sdmuseums.org
Founded: 1975.
Key Personnel: Vice Pres., Patricia Folsland
Historic House Museum.
Collections: period farm machinery; pioneer artifacts; blacksmith equipment.
Hours & Admission Prices: Memorial Day to Labor Day Sun. 1-4; other times by appointment. No charge.

Philip

MINUTEMAN MISSILE NATIONAL HISTORIC SITE, 21280 SD Hwy. 240, Philip, SD 57567-7102. Tel.: 605-433-5552. Fax: 605-433-5558.
Web Site: www.nps.gov/mimi
National Historic Site.
Collections: exhibits pertaining to the Minuteman.
Hours & Admission Prices: Visitor Contact Station: Memorial Day to Labor Day Mon.-Sat. 8-4:30; Sept.-May Mon.-Fri. 8-4:30.

PRAIRIE HOMESTEAD, Exit 131 off Interstate Hwy. 240, Philip, SD 57567-7007. Mailing Address: 21141 Hwy. 240, Philip, SD 57567-7007. Tel.: 605-433-5400.
E-mail: klcrew@gwtc.net
Web Site: www.prairiehomestead.com
Founded: 1962.
Key Personnel: Owner & C.E.O., Keith Crew.
Personnel Profile: Part-Time Paid 13.
Governing Authority: individual operation.
Historic House: 1909 sod dugout, original home of Mr. & Mrs. Ed Brown.
Collections: portion of original furnishings & other furnishings typical of the Sodbusters in the area.
Activities: guided tours.
Publications: books, Homesteading Era Lesson Plan; Prairie Homestead.
Hours & Admission Prices: May-Sept. dawn to dusk. Adults $6.50, seniors $5.50, children $4.50; discount to AAM members; children under 11 accompanied by an adult no charge. ♿
Attendance: 15,000 (estimated)

WEST RIVER MUSEUM SOCIETY, Center Ave., Philip, SD 57567. Mailing Address: P.O. Box 910, Philip, SD 57567-0910. Tel.: 605-859-2525.
Founded: 1965.
Congressional District: 2
Key Personnel: Pres. & C.E.O., Joe Gittings; Deputy Dir., Shirley O'Conner; Sec. & Treas., Kay Ainslie.
Governing Authority: society; nonprofit. Tax-exempt.
Historical Society Museum: housed in 1907 former hotel.
Collections: books; desks; globe maps; pot bellied stove; coal shuttle; teacher's desk; bell; flags. Historic Buildings: 1888 log cabin; rural school.
Facilities: library of pamphlets published history of pioneer rural schools of the area from 1896-1910 available for loan or sale.
Activities: open house on special days.
Publications: pamphlet, Prairie Schools 1896-1910.

Hours & Admission Prices: Open only on special occasions, call for appointment. No charge; donations accepted. ♿
Attendance: 50 (estimated)
Membership: Annual $1.

Piedmont

PETRIFIED FOREST OF THE BLACK HILLS, 8228 Elk Creek Rd., Piedmont, SD 57769-7208. Tel.: 605-787-4560; 877-286-9400. Fax: 605-787-6477.
E-mail: info@elkcreekresort.net
Web Site: www.elkcreekresort.net
Founded: 1929.
Key Personnel: C.E.O., Dir. & Cur., Timothy Ted Scott; Chm. (V) & Museum Shop Mgr., Arvid T. Scott; Gen. Mgr., Tim Scott.
Personnel Profile: Full-Time Paid 5; Part-Time Paid 1.
Governing Authority: private. Tax-exempt.
Natural History Museum.
Collections: cut & polished petrified wood; oligocene animal fossils; minerals.
Facilities: Museum-related items for sale.
Activities: self guided tours with audio stations; trail maps for walking tour; lectures.
Publications: 18 min. (copyright name) video, The Black Hills of South Dakota: Geological Gem of the West.
Hours & Admission Prices: May & Sept. 9-5; June-Aug. 8:30-6. Adults $6.50, senior citizens & youths 13-18 $5, children 6-12 $4; discounts to tour & group buses, AAM & ICOM members; children under 5 no charge. (prices include state sales tax) ♿
Attendance: 10,000 (accurate)

Pierre

SOUTH DAKOTA DISCOVERY CENTER, 805 W. Sioux Ave., Pierre, SD 57501-1858. Tel.: 605-224-8295. Fax: 605-224-2865.
E-mail: kristiemaher@sd-discovery.com
Web Site: www.sd-discovery.com
Founded: 1989.
Congressional District: 1
Key Personnel: C.E.O., Kristie Maher; Pres. (V), Carolyn Perry; Educational Dir., Sue Douglas; Special Programs, Anne Lewis; Museum Shop Mgr., Uncle Matt.
Personnel Profile: Full-Time Paid 2; Part-Time Paid 6; Part-Time Volunteers 30; Interns 3.
Governing Authority: private; nonprofit organization. Tax-exempt: 501(c)(3).
Science Museum.
Collections: hands-on science exhibits.
Major Exhibits: Dinostories (T), 1/10 & 11/10-12/10; Bug's Eye View (T), 4/10-5/30/10; Termespheres (T), 8/10-9/10; Animals as Architects (T), 9/10-10/10; Go Figure! (T), 11/10.
Facilities: classroom; 9,000 sq. ft. exhibit space; planetarium; meeting room; classrooms. Museum-related items for sale.
Activities: participatory exhibits; in-house workshops; teachers workshops; math & science programs; traveling exhibits.
Publications: quarterly program guide; e-news.
Hours & Admission Prices: Memorial Day-Labor Day Mon.-Sat. 10-5, Sun. 1-5. Winter Sun.-Fri. 1-5, Sat. 10-5. Adults $4, children $3; discounts to AAA members & groups; museum & ASTC members no charge. Closed New Year's Day; Good Friday; Easter; Thanksgiving; Christmas Eve & Day. ♿
Attendance: 20,000 (accurate)
Membership: Individual $20; Family or Grandparent & Grandchildren $40; Benefactor $150; Friends of Discovery Center $250 & up.

SOUTH DAKOTA NATIONAL GUARD MUSEUM, 301 E. Dakota Ave., Pierre, SD 57501-3225. Tel.: 605-224-9991.
E-mail: bob.kusser@state.sd.us
Web Site: ngmuseum.sd.gov
Key Personnel: Dir., Bob Kusser; Cur., Seb Axtman.
Governing Authority: nonprofit organization.
Military Museum.
Collections: Civil War, Spanish American War, WWI & WWII, Korean War, Desert Storm, & Bosnian Peace Keeping Mission memorabilia; historical documents; military equipment, records, & relics; A-7-D jet; Sherman tank; armored personnel carrier; 75mm cannon; 105mm Howitzer; anti-aircraft guns; Iraqi Freedom and Enduring Freedom.
Hours & Admission Prices: Mon.-Fri. 9-4; other times by appointment. No charge; donations accepted. ♿
Attendance: 3,000 (accurate)

SOUTH DAKOTA STATE ARCHIVES, 900 Governors Dr., Pierre, SD 57501-2200. Tel.: 605-773-3458 & 3804. Fax: 605-773-6041.
E-mail: Archref@state.sd.us
Web Site: www.sdhistory.org
Founded: 1974.
Congressional District: 1
Key Personnel: State Archivist, Chelle Somsen; Archivist, Virginia Hanson; Archivist, Carol Jennings; Archivist, Matthew Reitzel; Librarian, Marvene Riis; Microfilm Supvr., Kelli Tjeerdsma; Microfilm Asst., Chris Harmon; Research Room Admin., Ken Stewart.
Personnel Profile: Full-Time Paid 8; Part-Time Volunteers 12.
Governing Authority: state. Parent Institution: South Dakota State Historical Society, Pierre, SD 57501. Tax-exempt.
State Archives.
Collections: state agency records; South Dakota local government records; inter-state & federal government records directly related to South Dakota history & culture; photographs; maps; manuscript collections.
Research Fields: South Dakota; Upper Midwest; North Plains; Prairie Culture; High Plains.
Facilities: 15,000-vol. library of South Dakota published documents & reference books, available for research; reading room.
Activities: internships for undergraduate students.
Hours & Admission Prices: Mon.-Fri. & first Sat. of every month 9-4:30. No charge; donations accepted. Closed national & state holidays. ♿
Attendance: 5,200 (accurate)

SOUTH DAKOTA STATE HISTORICAL SOCIETY, 900 Governors Dr., Pierre, SD 57501-2200. Mailing Address: Cultural Heritage Center, 900 Governors Dr., Pierre, SD 57501-2217. Tel.: 605-773-3458. Fax: 605-773-6041.
E-mail: jay.vogt@state.sd.us
Web Site: www.sdhistory.org
Founded: 1901.
Congressional District: 1
Key Personnel: Exec. Dir., Jay D. Vogt; Pres. (V) & Chm. (V), Brad Tennant; Dir. State Historic Preservation Office, Jason Haug; Dir. Museums, Helen B. Louise; Dir. State Archaeological Research Center, Jim Haug; Dir. Research & Publications, Nancy Tystad Koupal; Museum Shop Mgr., Patricia Miller.
Personnel Profile: Full-Time Paid 43; Part-Time Paid 6; Part-Time Volunteers 65; Interns 4.
Governing Authority: state. Parent Institution: State of South Dakota. Programs: State Archives, Pierre; Museum of the South Dakota Historical Society, Pierre; State Historical Preservation Center, Pierre; State Archaeological Research Center, Rapid City; Research & Publishing, Pierre. Tax-exempt.
State Historical Society.
Collections: Native American collection; South Dakota cultural history; library & state archives.
Research Fields: Native American history; South Dakota history.
Facilities: Cultural Heritage Center: rare book library; research room; permanent & changing exhibition galleries, observation gallery; conservation laboratory. Gift items for sale.
Activities: guided tours; permanent, temporary & traveling exhibits; workshops; educational programs; suitcase education kits; history conference.
Publications: quarterly, South Dakota History; newsletter, South Dakota History Notes.
Hours & Admission Prices: Memorial Day to Labor Day Mon.-Sat. 9-6:30, Sun. 1-4:30; Sept.-May Mon.-Sat. 9-4:30, Sun. 1-4:30. Adults $4, senior citizens 60 & over $3; discounts to AAM members; members no charge. Closed New Year's Day; Easter; Thanksgiving; Christmas. ♿
Attendance: 19,899 (accurate)
Membership: Student $30; Individual $35; Family & History-Related Group $45; Foreign $60; Heritage Circle $100 & up.

Pine Ridge

THE HERITAGE CENTER, 100 Mission Dr., Pine Ridge, SD 57770-2100. Tel.: 605-867-5491. Fax: 605-867-1291.
E-mail: heritagecenter@redcloudschool.org
Web Site: www.redcloudschool.org
Founded: 1968.
Congressional District: 1
Key Personnel: Dir., Peter Strong; Pres. (V), Rev. Peter Klink, S.J.; Chm. (V), Norma Tibbitts; Museum Shop Mgr., Myrtle Cedar Face.
Personnel Profile: Full-Time Paid 4; Part-Time Paid 2; Interns 3.
Governing Authority: nonprofit organization. Parent Institution: Red Cloud Indian School, Inc. Tax-exempt: 501(c)(3).
Native American Art Museum: housed in c.1888 Holy Rosary Mission, scene of battle the day after the Wounded Knee Massacre.
Collections: paintings by Native American artists; star quilt collection;

beadwork; quill & pottery collection; Native American print collection; Northwest Coast prints.
Research Fields: Native American art; Lakota artifacts; Lakota culture.
Facilities: 900-vol. library of Native American material & culture, Native American & Western art, available for research on premises only; reading room. Oglala Lakota beadwork & quillwork for sale.
Activities: guided tours; arts festivals; loan, temporary & traveling exhibitions.
Hours & Admission Prices: Mon.-Fri. 9-5. No charge; donations requested. ♿
Attendance: 12,000 (estimated)

Pollock

POLLOCK VISITORS/INTERPRETIVE CENTER, 110 Main St., Pollock, SD 57648. Mailing Address: P.O. Box 43, Pollock, SD 57648-0057. Tel.: 605-889-2450.
Founded: 2002.
Key Personnel: Chm. (V), Delores Kluckman; Museum Shop Mgr., Vina LaFave.
Personnel Profile: Part-Time Paid 1.
Interpretive Center.
Collections: Native American artifacts; historical tools; handmade clocks.
Hours & Admission Prices: Mon.-Tues. & Fri. 9-4, Sat. 1-4. No charge; donations accepted. ♿
Attendance: 750

Rapid City

BEAR COUNTRY U.S.A., 13820 South Hwy. 16, Rapid City, SD 57702-6581. Tel.: 605-343-2290. Fax: 605-341-3206.
E-mail: pabear@bearcountryusa.com
Web Site: www.bearcountryusa.com
Founded: 1972.
Key Personnel: Pres., Kevin Casey; Treas., Sec. & Public Rels., Pauline Casey; Retail Mgr., Shannon Casey-Ballard.
Personnel Profile: Full-Time Paid 10; Part-Time Paid 75.
Governing Authority: company organized for profit.
Zoo. Drive-through Wildlife Park.
Collections: North American wildlife on display.
Research Fields: reproductive physiology of the American black bear.
Facilities: zoological park. Wildlife-related items for sale.
Activities: guided tours; lectures.
Publications: brochure.
Hours & Admission Prices: May & Sept.-Nov. daily 9-4; June-Aug. daily 8-6; groups of 15 or more by appointment. Adults $15, seniors 62 & over $12, children 5-12 $8; discount to groups; children 4 & under no charge. ♿

BLACK HILLS REPTILE GARDENS, INC., Hwy. 16 S., Rapid City, SD 57701. Mailing Address: P.O. Box 620, Rapid City, SD 57709-0620. Tel.: 605-342-5873.
E-mail: getinfo@reptilegardens.com
Web Site: www.reptilegardens.com
Founded: 1937.
Key Personnel: C.E.O., Pres. & Dir., Joe Maierhauser; Gen. Mgr. & Vice Pres., Tom Lang; Cur. & Reptile Project Dir., Ken Earnest; Gift Store Mgr., Jeff Oldham; Public Rels., John Brockelsby.
Personnel Profile: Full-Time Paid 20; Part-Time Paid 75.
Governing Authority: individual operation; S corporation.
Reptile Museum.
Collections: 1,000 specimens of over 200 species of reptiles; herpetology.
Research Fields: breeding rare & endangered reptiles; growth in relation to food on snakes.
Facilities: cafe; arboretum; aviary. Gift items for sale.
Activities: lectures; formally organized education programs for children; permanent exhibitions; lectures; animal shows.
Hours & Admission Prices: April-May & Sept.-Oct. daily 9-4; Memorial Day-Labor Day daily 8-7. Adults $13.50, senior citizen 62 & over $12, children 5-12 $8.50; discount to groups; children 4 & under no charge. ♿
Attendance: 500,000

DAHL ARTS CENTER, (M), 713 Seventh St., Rapid City, SD 57701-3695. Tel.: 605-394-4101. Fax: 605-394-6121.
E-mail: contact@thedahl.org
Web Site: www.thedahl.org
Founded: 1974.
Congressional District: 1
Key Personnel: Exec. Dir., Linda Anderson; Pres. (V), Tim Trithart.
Personnel Profile: Full-Time Paid 8; Part-Time Paid 5; Part-Time Volunteers 50; Interns 2.
Governing Authority: nonprofit organization. Parent Institution: Rapid City Arts Council.
Community Arts Center.
Collections: 200 foot cycloramic oil on canvas mural depicting history of the United States; 140 paintings historically important to Black Hills region; national print collection; early Oscar Howe tempera; contemporary artwork by SD area artists.
Facilities: three classrooms; 240-seat theater; three galleries; mural room; children's gallery; two conference rooms.
Activities: temporary exhibition; gallery talks; guided tours; theater productions; concerts; classes; workshops; films; literary events; community events.
Publications: bimonthly newsletter; exhibition brochures; catalogues.
Hours & Admission Prices: Summer: Tues.-Fri. 12-8, Sat.-Sun. 1-5. Adults $2.50; members no charge. Closed major holidays. ♿
Attendance: 63,000 (estimated)
Membership: Student $15; Senior $20; Individual $35; Household $50; Master $150; Michelangelo $250; Medici $500.

THE JOURNEY MUSEUM, 222 New York St., Rapid City, SD 57701-1199. Tel.: 605-394-6923 & 2249. Fax: 605-394-6940.
E-mail: journey@journeymuseum.org
Web Site: www.journeymuseum.org
Founded: 1997.
Key Personnel: Dir., Ray Summers; Chm. (V), Doyle Estes; Facilities Mgr., Gary Hargens.
Personnel Profile: Full-Time Paid 9; Part-Time Paid 5; Part-Time Volunteers 160; Interns 2.
Governing Authority: Parent Institution: The Museum Alliance of Rapid City. Tax-exempt.
Regional history museum with emphasis on Native Americans & pioneers.
Collections: participating museums and collections include: Museum of Geology, South Dakota School of Mines and Technology; State Archaeological Research Center; Sioux Indian Museum; Minnilusa Pioneer Museum; Duhamel Plains Indians Artifact Collection. Collections tell 2.5 billion years of Black Hills history.
Research Fields: paleontology, geology, archaeology, history, Native American history and culture.
Facilities: Museum-related items for sale.
Activities: interactive exhibits; special shows & events.
Publications: exhibition brochures; quarterly newsletter.
Hours & Admission Prices: Summer: daily 9-5; Winter: Mon.-Sat. 10-5, Sun. 1-5. Adults $7, seniors 62 & over $6, students 11-17 $5; discounts to military, AAA, AAM & ICOM members; children 10 & under and members no charge. ♿
Attendance: 31,896 (estimated)
Membership: Student $15; Individual $25; Family $50; Grand Family $100; Lifetime $1,000.

MINNILUSA PIONEER MUSEUM, 222 New York St., Rapid City, SD 57701-1199. Tel.: 605-394-6099. Fax: 605-394-6940.
E-mail: minnilusa@earthlink.net
Web Site: www.journeymuseum.org
Founded: 1938.
Congressional District: 2
Key Personnel: Dir., Reid L. Riner; Chm. (V), Casey Peterson; Asst., Eileen Howe.
Personnel Profile: Full-Time Paid 1; Part-Time Volunteers 12; Interns 1.
Governing Authority: nonprofit. Parent Institution: Minnilusa Historical Association. Tax-exempt: 501(c)(3).
Historical Society Museum.
Collections: ranching, pioneer life & early fur trade; firearms; mining; transportation; photographs related to western South Dakota & Black Hills; period furniture; household objects & clothing; china; glass; Behrens collection of native bird & animal specimens.
Research Fields: C. Irwin Leedy archives; Valentine T. McGillycuddy papers & collection.
Facilities: 200-vol. library available for research on premises only.
Activities: guided tours; lectures.
Publications: brochure, Minnilusa Pioneer Museum; quarterly newsletter, Minnilusa Pioneer Museum Bulletin; quarterly newsletter, Turtle Times.
Hours & Admission Prices: Daily 9-5. Adults $7, seniors $5, students $4; discount to groups, military & AAA members; members & children under 10 no charge. Closed New Year's Day; Christmas. ♿
Attendance: 40,000 (accurate)

MOTION UNLIMITED MUSEUM & CLASSIC CAR LOT, 6180 S. Hwy. 79, Rapid City, SD 57702-8467. Tel.: 605-348-7373.
E-mail: happymotoring@bluebottle.com
Web Site: www.motionunlimitedmuseum.com
Founded: 1972.

Key Personnel: Owner, Bill Napoli; Owner, Peggy Napoli
Automobile, Motorcycle, & Toy Museum.
Collections: classic cars, pickups, sedans, coups, convertibles & motorcycles; period gas pumps; porcelain, tin & neon signs; posters; photographs; toys; period clothing; over 100 pedal vehicles.
Facilities: Cars & museum-related items for sale.
Hours & Admission Prices: May-Oct. Mon.-Fri. 9-6, Sat. 9-4, Sun. by appointment. Adults $5; discounts to members, AAM & ICOM members; active military and children 12 & under no charge. Closed New Year's Day; Easter; Independence Day; Thanksgiving, Christmas. ♿
Attendance: 1,500 (accurate)

MUSEUM OF GEOLOGY AND PALEONTOLOGY, SOUTH DAKOTA SCHOOL OF MINES AND TECHNOLOGY, 501 E. St. Joseph, Rapid City, SD 57701-3901. Tel.: 605-394-2467. Fax: 605-394-6131.
E-mail: museum@sdsmt.edu
Founded: 1885.
Key Personnel: Pres., Dr. Robert Wharton; Dean, Dr. Duane Hrncir; Exec. Cur., Dr. James Martin; Mgr. Collections, Sally Shelton; Post Doctoral Fellow in Paleontology, Dr. Darrin Pagnac; Program Asst., Heidi Minkler.
Personnel Profile: Full-Time Paid 3; Full-Time Volunteers 1; Part-Time Volunteers 3.
Governing Authority: state. Tax-exempt: 501(c)(3).
Science Museum.
Collections: rocks; minerals; fossil vertebrates; invertebrates; plants; books; archives.
Major Exhibits: 125 Years of Research, 5/10-9/10.
Research Fields: vertebrate paleontology and mineralogy, with a focus on South Dakota and the Black Hills.
Facilities: library; archives. Gift items for sale.
Activities: teaching support for undergraduate & graduate paleontology programs; summer field camps; permanent & temporary exhibitions.
Publications: Dakoterra; Geomuse.
Hours & Admission Prices: Summer: Mon.-Fri. 9-5, Sat. 9-6, Sun. 12-5; Winter: Mon.-Fri. 9-4, Sat. 10-4. No charge; donations accepted. Closed holidays. ♿
Attendance: 23,000 (accurate)

THE OLD SOUTH DAKOTA GOVERNOR'S MANSION, 3777 Anderson Rd., Rapid City, SD 57703-9364. Tel.: 605-393-2344.
E-mail: jeri@sdgovernorsmansion.com
Web Site: www.sdgovernorsmansion.com
Key Personnel: Gen. Mgr., Jeri Deschamp
Historic House: housed in the former home of 16 South Dakota Governors and their families; built in 1936.
Collections: local history & culture; personal artifacts; period furnishings; photographs.
Hours & Admission Prices: Tours: May-Sept. daily 9-6; Oct.-April daily 9-4. Adults $8, senior citizens 55 & over $6; children 10 & under no charge.

SIOUX INDIAN MUSEUM, 222 New York St., Rapid City, SD 57701-1199. Mailing Address: P.O. Box 1504, Rapid City, SD 57709-1504. Tel.: 605-394-2381. Fax: 605-348-6182.
E-mail: montileaux@journeymuseum.org
Web Site: www.journeymuseum.org
Founded: 1939.
Congressional District: 2
Key Personnel: Cur., Paulette Montileaux.
Personnel Profile: Full-Time Paid 2.
Governing Authority: federal. Parent Institution: Indian Arts & Crafts Board, MS 2528-MIB, U.S. Department of the Interior, Washington, DC 20240. Tax-exempt.
Indian Art Museum.
Collections: historic & contemporary arts of the Sioux; Native American arts & crafts; beadwork; quillwork.
Research Fields: contemporary Native American art.
Facilities: Beadwork, jewelry, moccasins, tobacco pouches, quillwork, dance costumes, accessories, headdresses, dolls & paintings.
Activities: guided tours; lectures; gallery talks; permanent & traveling exhibitions; demonstrations; events honoring Native Americans who have achieved fame in literature & performing arts; annual one-person exhibitions.
Publications: exhibition brochures.
Hours & Admission Prices: Memorial Day-Labor Day daily 9-5. Winter: Mon.-Sat. 10-5, Sun. 1-5. Annual $8, adults $7, senior citizens 62 & over $6, students 11-17 $5; discounts to groups of 10 or more; children 10 & under no charge. Closed New Year's Day; Easter; Thanksgiving; Christmas. ♿
Attendance: 45,000 (estimated)

Membership: Student $15; Individual $25; Family $50; Grand Family $100; Lifetime $1,000.

Redfield

REDFIELD'S HISTORIC CHICAGO AND NORTHWESTERN RR DEPOT, 715 3rd St. W., Redfield, SD 57469-1173. Mailing Address: 626 Main St., Redfield, SD 57469-1127. Tel.: 605-472-4566. Fax: 605-472-4567.
E-mail: cnwhistoricrrdepot@redfield.com
Founded: 1914.
Key Personnel: Chm. (V) & Museum Shop Mgr., Kathy Maddox
History Museum: housed in the restored C&NW Depot built in 1914.
Collections: local history; telegraph equipment; railroad memorabilia.
Activities: group tours.
Hours & Admission Prices: May 15-Nov. 1 Thurs.-Sun. 1-5; other times by appointment. No charge; donations accepted. ♿

SPINK COUNTY HISTORICAL SOCIETY, Courthouse Square, 225 E. 8th Ave., Redfield, SD 57469. Tel.: 605-472-0758.
Key Personnel: Treas., Jerry Hansen; Cur., Geri Heim; Cur., Joel Heim
History Museum.
Collections: early pioneer life & history; birds; butterflies; Native American artifacts; farm machinery; military equipment; newspapers photographs.
Hours & Admission Prices: June-Sept. Mon.-Fri. 1-5. No charge; donations accepted. ♿
Membership: Annual $5; Lifetime $50.

Roslyn

INTERNATIONAL VINEGAR MUSEUM, 502 Main St., Roslyn, SD 57261. Mailing Address: P.O. Box 201, Roslyn, SD 57261-0201. Tel.: 605-486-0075.
E-mail: museum@internationalvinegarmuseum.com
Web Site: internationalvinegarmuseum.com
Founded: 1999.
Key Personnel: Chm. (V), Josh Wagner; Museum Shop Mgr., Mary Wagner
Vinegar Museum.
Collections: vinegar from around the world; paper made from vinegar.
Activities: vinegar tasting bar; guided tours. Annual Event: International Vinegar Festival in June.
Hours & Admission Prices: June to Labor Day Thurs.-Sat. 10-6. Adults $2.

Saint Francis

BUECHEL MEMORIAL LAKOTA MUSEUM, St. Francis Mission, 350 S. Oak St. on Rosebud Reservation, Saint Francis, SD 57572. Mailing Address: P.O. Box 499, Saint Francis, SD 57572-0499. Tel.: 605-747-2745. Fax: 605-747-2361.
Web Site: www.sfmission.org/museum
Founded: 1915.
Congressional District: 23
Key Personnel: Dir., Fr. John Hatcher, S.J.
Personnel Profile: Full-Time Paid 2; Part-Time Paid 2; Interns 2.
Governing Authority: church. Affiliated with the St. Francis Indian Mission. Parent Institution: Rosebud Educational Society, Inc. Tax-exempt.
Lakota Indian Museum.
Collections: Rosebud & Pine Ridge Sioux history.
Research Fields: history; ethnology.
Facilities: 190-vol. library of photographs available by request. Indian arts & crafts for sale.
Activities: guided tours.
Publications: books, A Grammar of Lakota; Lakota Dictionary; Bible History in Lakota; Sursoum Corda: Lakota Prayer Book; Photo Album; Lakota Names & Traditional Uses of Native Plants by Sigangu People; Crying for a Vision: A Rosebud Sioux Trilogy.
Hours & Admission Prices: Memorial Day to Labor Day Mon.-Thurs. & Sat. 8-5, Fri. 8-2:30, Sun. 10-4. No charge; donations accepted. Closed holidays.
Attendance: 3,600 (accurate)

Salem

MC COOK COUNTY HISTORICAL SOCIETY AND MUSEUM, 120 W. Norton, Salem, SD 57058. Tel.: 605-425-2340.
E-mail: fat@triotel.net
Web Site: www.sdhistory.org
Founded: 1989.
Key Personnel: Pres. (V) & Museum Shop Mgr., Lou Ella Weber; Treas., Mildred Larson.
Personnel Profile: Part-Time Volunteers 5.

Governing Authority: private; nonprofit organization. Tax-exempt: 501(c)(3).
Antique & History Museum.
Collections: Mc Cook County records; household utensils; office machines; business artifacts; period clothing; school yearbook; local family histories; farming artifacts.
Research Fields: family trees of Mc Cook County residents.
Facilities: library.
Activities: temporary exhibitions. Annual Events: Annual Supper; Christmas Open House; school reunion in July.
Hours & Admission Prices: April-Sept. Fri. 1-5:30; other times by appointment. No charge; donations accepted.
Attendance: 350 (estimated)
Membership: Annual $10.

Scotland

SCOTLAND HERITAGE CHAPEL & MUSEUM, 811 6th St., Scotland, SD 57059. Mailing Address: 351 4th St., Scotland, SD 57059-2112. Tel.: 605-583-4568, 2507 & 4144.
Founded: 1976.
Congressional District: 1
Key Personnel: Pres. (V), Linda Kluthe; Vice Pres., Betty Woehl; Treas., Lori Schmidt; Sec., Carolyn Thaler.
Personnel Profile: Part-Time Volunteers 8.
Governing Authority: nonprofit. Parent Institution: Historical Society. Tax-exempt: 501(c)(3).
Local History Museum: housed in c.1874 Methodist & Siemantal Churches.
Collections: historical artifacts; books; furniture; clothes; household articles; farm tools; implementary & medical supplies; tools; farm machinery; railroad handcar; pencils & pens; local history; family records.
Facilities: 3 buildings.
Activities: guided tours.
Publications: brochure.
Hours & Admission Prices: Summer: holidays & special occasions; other times by appointment. No charge; donations accepted. ♿
Attendance: 25 (estimated)
Membership: Annual $2; Life $25.

Sioux Falls

BATTLESHIP SOUTH DAKOTA MEMORIAL, 12th & Kiwanis, Sioux Falls, SD 57104. Tel.: 605-367-7141 & 7060. Fax: 605-367-8234.
E-mail: ussdakota@aol.com
Founded: 1968.
Congressional District: 1
Key Personnel: Pres., David Witte.
Governing Authority: municipal. Tax-exempt.
Military & Nautical Museum.
Collections: memorabilia of the Battleship U.S.S. South Dakota; silver services; gun barrels; 1/4 scale model of ship; ship's log; bell; books; photographs; mast; anchors; flags.
Facilities: Commemorative coins for sale.
Activities: films; permanent exhibitions; crew member reunion every two years.
Publications: brochure.
Hours & Admission Prices: Memorial Day-Labor Day daily 10-6. No charge.

THE CENTER FOR WESTERN STUDIES, (M), Augustana College, 2121 S. Summit, Sioux Falls, SD 57197-0001. Mailing Address: 2001 S. Summit Ave., Sioux Falls, SD 57197-0001. Tel.: 605-274-4007. Fax: 605-274-4999.
E-mail: cws@augie.edu
Web Site: www.augie.edu/cws/
Founded: 1970.
Congressional District: 1
Key Personnel: Dir. & Dir. Research, Collections & Publications, Dr. Harry F. Thompson; Dir. Outreach & Communication, Timothy M. Hoheisel; Chm. (V), Lynn Aspaas; Sec., Lori Bunjer.
Personnel Profile: Full-Time Paid 4; Part-Time Volunteers 6; Interns 2.
Governing Authority: college. Parent Institution: Augustana College. Tax-exempt.
Cultural, Research & Archival Agency.
Collections: regional artifacts; Norwegian rosemaled furniture; paintings & prints by regional artists; Episcopal Diocese of South Dakota archives; United Church of Christ-South Dakota Conference archives; Stephen Riggs papers; Herbert Krause papers; Augustana college archives; John R. Milton papers; Harold Shunk papers.
Major Exhibits: Marian Henjum (watercolor) & Jon Offutt (blown glass), 3/4/10-5/29/10; JoAnn Bird (Dakota, oil), 6/3/10-8/28/10; Steve Joy (mixed media), 9/2/10-11/27/10.
Research Fields: Dakota (Sioux); South Dakota & Northern Plains history & cultures; Western American literature.
Facilities: 35,000-vol. library of material dealing with the Trans-Mississippi West & the Upper Great Plains region available for use on premises; 22,000 sq. ft. Fantle Bldg. for the Center for Western Studies; manuscript collections; archives.
Activities: conferences on regional themes; annual art show; rotating exhibits; courses & workshops on regional history & historical document editing; forum on public affairs with national & international leaders, Gen. Colin Powell & George Bush; Mikhail Gorbachev; John Major; Barbara Bush; Queen Noor of Jordan; Al Gore; Vicente Fox.
Publications: books, Birding in the Northern Plains; A New South Dakota History; The Northern Pacific Railroad and the Selling of the West; Yanktonai Sioux Water Colors; Sundancing At Rosebud And Pine Ridge; Where The West Begins; The Wind Blows Free; Frederick Manfred: A Bibliography & Publication History; Boy off the Farm; Next Year Will Be Better; What the Tallgrass Says; Prairie Architect; Over a Century of Leadership; South Dakota Territorial and State Governors; The Quartzite Border: Surveying and Marking the North Dakota-South Dakota Boundary, 1891-1892; The Last Contrary; Tomahawk and Cross; An Illustrated History of the Arts in South Dakota; A Noble Calling; Poems and Essays of Herbert Krause; Natural History of the Black Hills and Badlands; Guide to Collections Relating to South Dakota Norwegian-Americans; The Geography of South Dakota; Fort Sisseton; The Lizard Speaks; Essays on the Writings of Frederick Manfred; What It Took: A History of the USGS EROS Data Center; The Family Farmer's Advocate: South Dakota Farmers Union 1914-2000; Soldier, Settler, and Sioux: Fort Ridgely and the Minnesota River Valley, 1853-1967; The Lewis and Clark Expedition: Food, Nutrition and Health; The Lewis and Clark Expedition: Then and Now; Joseph Nicollet and His Map: Exploring the Upper Mississippi River; Sandra Day O'Connor.
Hours & Admission Prices: Mon.-Fri. 8-5, Sat. 10-2. No charge; donations accepted. Closed Independence Day; Christmas. ♿
Attendance: 6,000 (estimated)
Membership: Member $50-$59; Explorer $60-$99; Partner $100-$249; Scout $250-$499; Ranger $500-$999; Business $500 & up; Pioneer $1,000 & up.

EIDE-DALRYMPLE ART GALLERY, Augustana College, 30th St., & Grange Ave., Sioux Falls, SD 57197-0001. Mailing Address: Augustana College, 2001 S. Summit Ave., Sioux Falls, SD 57197-0001. Tel.: 605-274-4609.
Art Gallery.
Collections: works by local & regional artists; European & American prints.
Activities: temporary & permanent exhibits; special events.
Hours & Admission Prices: Mon.-Fri. 10-5, Sat. 12-5. No charge. Closed major holidays.

GREAT PLAINS ZOO & DELBRIDGE MUSEUM OF NATURAL HISTORY, (M), 805 S. Kiwanis Ave., Sioux Falls, SD 57104-3798. Tel.: 605-367-7003. Fax: 605-367-8340.
E-mail: dsimon@gpzoo.org
Web Site: greatzoo.org
Founded: 1957.
Congressional District: 1
Key Personnel: C.E.O. & Pres., Elizabeth Whealy; Vice Pres. Operations, Dan Simon; Dir. Guest Experience, Mark Lindell; Dir. Animal Programs, Jay Tetzloff.
Personnel Profile: Full-Time Paid 34; Part-Time Paid 15; Part-Time Volunteers 73.
Governing Authority: nonprofit organization. Zoological Society of Sioux Falls. Tax-exempt: 501(c)(3).
Zoo & Natural History Museum.
Collections: Henry Brockhouse collection of mounted animals from 1950-1970; mammals; birds; reptiles; insects.
Facilities: 45-acre grounds; concessions. Gift items for sale.
Activities: outreach; summer camps; special events; on-site programs; fund-raisers; childrens zoo; carousel; train rides.
Publications: quarterly membership newsletter; education materials; brochure; map; volunteer newsletter.
Hours & Admission Prices: April-Sept. daily 9-6; Oct.-March daily 10-4. Adults $6.80, seniors $6, youth 3-12 $3.80; children under 3, zoo & museum members no charge. Closed New Year's Day; Thanksgiving; Christmas. ♿
Attendance: 220,000 (accurate)
Membership: Individual & Seniors $27; Family $65; Patron $108.

KIRBY SCIENCE DISCOVERY CENTER AT THE WASHINGTON PAVILION, 301 S. Main Ave., Sioux Falls, SD 57104-6311. Tel.: 605-367-7397, ext. 2307. Fax: 605-731-2397.
E-mail: crossing@washingtonpavilion.org
Web Site: washingtonpavilion.org
Founded: 1999.

Key Personnel: C.E.O., Steve Hoffman; Dir., Chris Rossing; Chm. (V), Jason Crain; Volunteer Coord., Ruth Atkins; Lead Exhibit Technician, Lyle Ehlers; Education Mgr., Nancy VanBeek.
Personnel Profile: Full-Time Paid 7; Part-Time Paid 20; Part-Time Volunteers 50.
Governing Authority: private; nonprofit organization. Parent Institution: Washington Pavilion Management, Inc. Tax-exempt.
Science Technology Center.
Collections: interactive exhibits.
Facilities: large format movie theater.
Activities: interactive exhibits; programs; films.
Publications: bimonthly newsletter, Arts & Science Adventures.
Hours & Admission Prices: Center: Wed.-Thurs. & Sat. 10-5, Fri. 10-8, Sun. 12-5. Theater: Wed.-Thurs. & Sun. 1-4, Fri.-Sat. 11-8. Exhibits: Adults $6.25, seniors $5.25, children $4.25. CineDome: Adults $7, seniors $6.25, children $5.50; ASTC Travel Passport members no charge. Combination Ticket: Adults $10, seniors $8.50, children $7.50; discounts to groups; members no charge. ♿
Attendance: 100,000 (estimated)
Membership: Individual $35; Membership for Two $50; Household $80; Household Plus $135.

MUSEUM OF VISUAL MATERIALS, 500 N. Main Ave., Sioux Falls, SD 57104-5902. Tel.: 605-271-9500. Fax: 605-271-4793.
E-mail: jeremy@sfmvm.com
Web Site: www.sfmvm.com
Key Personnel: Dir., Jeremy Brech
Arts and Crafts Museum.
Collections: over 4,500 books; vinyl records & 8-track tapes; over 80,000 sewing buttons; fabrics; arts & crafts.
Hours & Admission Prices: Mon.-Wed. & Fri.-Sat. 10-4, Thurs. 10-7, Sun. 1-4.

PETTIGREW HOME AND MUSEUM, 131 N. Duluth, Sioux Falls, SD 57104. Mailing Address: 200 W. 6th St., Sioux Falls, SD 57104-6001. Tel.: 605-367-7097.
Key Personnel: Dir., Bill Hoskins; Chm. (V), Julie Brue; Museum Shop Mgr., Tracy Seiner.
Personnel Profile: Full-Time Paid 17; Part-Time Paid 10; Part-Time Volunteers 25; Interns 1.
Governing Authority: Parent Institution: Siouxland Heritage Museums. Tax-exempt.
Historic House Museum: c.1889 home of South Dakota's first senator, Richard Pettigrew.
Collections: photographs; personal artifacts; furnishings.
Major Exhibits: Cabinet of Curiosities: A Look at Sioux Falls First Museum, 1/10-12/10; Speculation and Conflict: The Rise of Sioux Falls, 1/10-12/10; Surveying Dakota, 1/10-12/10.
Activities: video; interactive computer stations.
Publications: newsletter.
Hours & Admission Prices: May-Sept. Mon.-Wed. & Fri.-Sat. 9-5, Thurs. 9-9, Sun. 12-5; Oct.-April daily 12-5. No charge; donations accepted. Closed major holidays. ♿
Attendance: 8,278 (accurate)

SERTOMA BUTTERFLY HOUSE, 4320 Oxbow Ave., Sioux Falls, SD 57106-4110. Tel.: 605-334-9466. Fax: 605-334-9662.
Web Site: www.sertomabutterflyhouse.org
Key Personnel: Exec. Dir., Wendy Lewis
Butterfly House.
Collections: butterflies from around the world.
Hours & Admission Prices: Memorial Day to Labor Day Mon.-Sat. 10-6, Sun. 1-5; Sept.-May Mon.-Sat. 10-4, Sun. 1-4. Adults 19-59 $6, senior citizens 60 & over $4.50, youth 4-18 $4; children 3 & under no charge. Closed Easter; Thanksgiving; Christmas.

SIOUX COUNCIL SCOUT MUSEUM, 800 N. West Ave., Sioux Falls, SD 57104-5720. Tel.: 605-361-2697.
Founded: 2007.
Key Personnel: Chm. (V), Reid Christopherson.
Governing Authority: Parent Institution: Sioux Council BSA. Tax-exempt.
History Museum.
Collections: history of Boy Scouts of America since its founding in 1910; scout uniforms, equipment, & manuals; photographs.
Hours & Admission Prices: Mon.-Fri. 9-6, Sat. 9-3; other times by appointment. No charge. ♿

SIOUX EMPIRE MEDICAL MUSEUM, 1305 W. 18th St., Sioux Falls, SD 57105-0401. Mailing Address: Box 5039, 1305 W. 18th St., Sioux Falls, SD 57117-5039. Tel.: 605-333-6397.
Founded: 1975.
Congressional District: 1
Key Personnel: Chm. History Museum Committee, Thenetta Nield; Co-Chm. (V), Carol Turgeon.
Personnel Profile: Full-Time Volunteers 40.
Governing Authority: nonprofit organization. Sponsored by the Alumni Association of Sioux Valley Hospital School of Nursing, 1305 W. 18th, Sioux Falls, SD 57117. Tax-exempt: 501(c)(3).
Medical Museum.
Collections: 1930 patient's room; orthopaedics; pediatrics; surgery; nursery; X-ray; two dental units; uniformed dolls; photographs of medical staff members; patent medicines.
Facilities: 100-vol. medical library available for use to professionals only.
Activities: guided tours; lectures; permanent & temporary exhibitions.
Hours & Admission Prices: Mon.-Fri. 11-4. No charge; donations accepted. Closed major holidays. ♿
Attendance: 3,500 (accurate)

SIOUXLAND HERITAGE MUSEUMS, (M), 200 W. 6th St., Sioux Falls, SD 57104-6001. Tel.: 605-367-4210, ext. 0. Fax: 605-367-6004.
E-mail: bhoskins@minnehahacounty.org
Web Site: www.siouxlandmuseums.com
Founded: 1926.
Congressional District: 1
Key Personnel: Dir., William J. Hoskins; Chm. (V), Gloria Haule; Pres. (V) & Operations Mgr., Julie Breu; Mktg. Coord., Adam Nelson; Cur. Education, Kevin Gansz; Event Coord., Martha Davidsohn; Cur. Exhibits, April Woodside; Cur. Collections, Lisa Studts; Preparator, William Booker; Accountant & Museum Shop Mgr., Tracy Seiner.
Personnel Profile: Full-Time Paid 17; Part-Time Paid 9; Part-Time Volunteers 71; Interns 2.
Governing Authority: municipal; nonprofit. Parent Institution: Minnehaha County. Branch Museums: 1889 The Pettigrew Home & Museum, 131 N. Duluth, Sioux Falls, SD 57104.; 1889 The Old Courthouse Museum, 200 W. 6th St., Sioux Falls, SD 57104. Tax-exempt.
General Museums: housed in 1889 The Pettigrew Home & Museum; housed in 1890 The Old Courthouse Museum.
Collections: local & regional natural history; Dakota & plains ethnology; local folk arts.
Major Exhibits: Corn: Bushels of Gold, 1/10-12/10; Cruisin' Cuizine: Drive Ins of Sioux Falls, 1/10-12/10; The Art of Architecture, 1/10-12/10; Cabinet of Curiosities: A Look at Sioux Falls First Museum, 1/10-12/10; Speculation & Conflict: The Rise of Sioux Falls, 1/10-12/10.
Research Fields: local history; archaeology; folklife.
Facilities: reference library; archives & photographic archives; permanent & changing exhibitions; auditorium; classroom; inflatable planetarium.
Activities: tours; gallery talks; workshops; conferences; loan kits; formally organized education programs for children & adults; audio-visual shows.
Publications: newsletter, Museums Report.
Hours & Admission Prices: Old Courthouse Museum: Mon.-Wed. & Fri.-Sat. 8-5, Thurs. 8-9, Sun. 12-5. Pettigrew Home and Museum: May-Sept. Mon.-Wed. & Fri.-Sat. 9-5, Thurs, 9-9, Sun. 12-5; Oct.-April daily 12-5. No charge; donations accepted. Closed for major holidays. ♿
Attendance: 72,305 (accurate)
Membership: Individual $15; Family & Couple $25; Patron $50; Corporate $500.

WASHINGTON PAVILION OF ARTS AND SCIENCE, 301 S. Main Ave., Sioux Falls, SD 57104-6311. Tel.: 605-367-7397, ext. 2307. Fax: 605-367-7399.
E-mail: info@washingtonpavilion.org
Web Site: www.washingtonpavilion.org
Formerly: Visual Arts Center at the Washington Pavilion
Founded: 1999.
Key Personnel: Dir., David J. Merhib; Dir., Chris Rossing; Exhibitions & Collections Cur., Howard Spencer; Business Mgr., Paul Groeneveld.
Personnel Profile: Full-Time Paid 4; Part-Time Paid 4; Part-Time Volunteers 150.
Governing Authority: private; nonprofit organization. Parent Institution: Washington Pavilion Management, Inc. Tax-exempt.
Children's Museum.
Collections: paintings; graphics; photographs; sculpture.
Research Fields: regional, national, international art.
Facilities: art library; children's studio; classrooms; CineDome theater. Museum-related items for sale.
Activities: guided tours; gallery talks; hands-on exhibits. Annual Events: Wellness Festival; Outdoor Arts Festival.

Publications: members newsletter, Columns; catalogs.
Hours & Admission Prices: Summer: Mon.-Sat. 10-5, Sun. 12-5; Winter: Tues.-Sat. 10-5, Sun. 12-5. No charge; donations accepted. ♿
Attendance: 41,392 (accurate)
Membership: Individual $35; Membership for Two $50; Household $80; Household Plus $135.

Spearfish

D.C. BOOTH HISTORIC NATIONAL FISH HATCHERY AND ARCHIVE, (M), 423 Hatchery Circle, Spearfish, SD 57783-2643. Tel.: 605-642-7730, ext. 0. Fax: 605-642-2336.
E-mail: dcbooth@fws.gov
Web Site: dcbooth.fws.gov
Formerly: Spearfish Station, Spearfish National Fish Hatchery
Founded: 1896.
Congressional District: 31
Key Personnel: C.E.O., Carlos Martinez; Cur., Randi Smith; Museum Shop Mgr., Eric Davis.
Personnel Profile: Full-Time Paid 4; Part-Time Volunteers 30; Interns 2.
Governing Authority: federal; nonprofit. Parent Institution: U.S. Fish & Wildlife Service. Tax-exempt.
Historic Fisheries Museum: housed in 1899, fish hatchery building on 10-acre historic site on National Register with furnished 1905, superintendent's residence, ponds & raceways; Fish Culture Hall of Fame; underwater trout viewing windows.
Collections: historic fishery & fish culture artifacts; records; photographs; fish car material; U.S. Fish & Wildlife Service history; furnishings.
Research Fields: fish culture; fisheries; U.S. Fish & Wildlife Service history; fish stocking; U.S. Fish Commission, Bureau of Fisheries.
Facilities: research collections; nature trail.
Activities: tours; wildlife observation; live trout feeding.
Publications: semiannual newsletter.
Hours & Admission Prices: Grounds: daily. Fish Car Museum & Booth House & Fish Car: mid-May to mid-Sept. No charge; donations accepted. Group tour charge. ♿
Attendance: 150,000 (estimated)
Membership: Individual $35; Family $50; Business $100 & up.

DOLLS AT HOME MUSEUM, 435 Meier Ave., Spearfish, SD 57783-1977. Mailing Address: P.O. Box 489, Spearfish, SD 57783-0489. Tel.: 605-645-2192.
Founded: 1999.
Key Personnel: Dir. & Pres. (V), Johanna Della Vecchia; Cur. & Museum Shop Mgr., Sonya Albers.
Personnel Profile: Part-Time Volunteers 4.
Governing Authority: private.
Dollhouse Museum.
Collections: dollhouses; modern & antique one-of-a kind items by recognized miniature artists; furniture; antiques & collectibles; over 75 dollhouses & rooms, many with gardens & dioramas; historical Family Tree exhibit detailing history of immigrants to this Black Hills Area.
Facilities: Museum-related items for sale.
Activities: seasonal puppet shows; special birthday parties. Museum Sponsors: Christmas holiday activities.
Hours & Admission Prices: Memorial Day to Labor Day by appointment. Season pass $10, adults $5, children $2.50; members no charge. ♿
Attendance: 500 (estimated)

HIGH PLAINS WESTERN HERITAGE CENTER, 825 Heritage Dr., Spearfish, SD 57783. Mailing Address: P.O. Box 524, Spearfish, SD 57783-0524. Tel.: 605-642-9378.
E-mail: info@westernheritagecenter.com
Web Site: www.westernheritagecenter.com
Key Personnel: Exec. Dir., Peggy Ables
History Museum.
Collections: Western art & artifacts; stagecoach; period kitchen; saddle shop; blacksmith shop; mining; ranching; rodeo; furnished log cabin; rural schoolhouse; period farm equipment.
Facilities: 200-seat theater. Museum-related items for sale.
Activities: special art events; performances.
Hours & Admission Prices: Daily 9-5. Adults 17-61 $7, seniors 62 & over $5, youth 6-16 $3.

Sturgis

BEAR BUTTE STATE PARK VISITORS CENTER, Hwy. 79, Sturgis, SD 57785. Mailing Address: P.O. Box 688, Sturgis, SD 57785-0688. Tel.: 605-347-5240. Fax: 605-347-7627.
Web Site: www.state.sd.us/gfp/sdparks
Founded: 1961.
Congressional District: 2
Key Personnel: Park Mgr., Jim Jandreau; Naturalist, Morri Birkeland.
Personnel Profile: Full-Time Paid 1; Part-Time Paid 5; Part-Time Volunteers 2.
Governing Authority: state. Parent Institution: South Dakota Dept. of Game, Fish & Parks, Foss Bldg., 523 E. Capitol, Pierre, SD 57501-3182. Tel. 605-773-3391. Subsidiary Institution: Dept. of Parks. Tax-exempt.
State Park Visitors Center Museum: located on a Native American traditional religious site.
Collections: Native American clothing & religious artifacts; archaeological site materials; plant displays; geological displays.
Research Fields: Native American Indian religion, anthropology, archaeology & geology.
Activities: guided tours; lectures; gallery talks; formally organized education programs for children & adults; loan, permanent & traveling exhibitions.
Publications: trail guide, Bear Butte Trail Guide; brochure, Bear Butte State Park brochure.
Hours & Admission Prices: Park: 8:30-5:30. Visitors Center: May to mid-Oct. daily 9-5. Car $5, annual sticker $23; those entering for religious activity or those with State Park User Stickers no charge. ♿
Attendance: 15,000

THE ROO RANCH, 11842 US Hwy. 14A, Sturgis, SD 57785-6966. Mailing Address: P.O. Box 587, Deadwood, SD 57732-0587. Tel.: 605-578-1777; 877-578-1777.
E-mail: info@therooranch.com
Web Site: www.rooranch.com
Zoo.
Collections: wildlife includidng 6 species of kangaroos, wallaroos, & wallabies.
Hours & Admission Prices: May-Sept. daily 10-6. Adults 12-61 $10, senior citizens 62 & over and children 3-11 $8.

STURGIS MOTORCYCLE MUSEUM AND HALL OF FAME, (M), 999 Main St., Sturgis, SD 57785-1620. Mailing Address: P.O. Box 602, Sturgis, SD 57785-0602. Tel.: 605-347-2001. Fax: 605-720-0632.
E-mail: christine@sturgismuseum.com
Web Site: www.sturgismuseum.com
Founded: 2001.
Key Personnel: Exec. Dir., Christine Paige Diers; Pres. (V), Dave Davis; Museum Shop Mgr., Arlene Colaiacovo.
Personnel Profile: Full-Time Paid 2; Part-Time Paid 5.
Motorcycle Museum.
Collections: motorcycles; motorcycle memorabilia; racing history; women in motorcycling; photographs; Hall of Fame inductees.
Activities: group tours.
Hours & Admission Prices: Daily call for hours. Adults $5, seniors 65 & over $4; children 12 & under no charge. Closed New Year's Day; Easter; Thanksgiving; Christmas. ♿
Attendance: 26,000 (accurate)

Timber Lake

TIMBER LAKE AND AREA HISTORICAL SOCIETY, Timber Lake, SD 57656. Mailing Address: P.O. Box 181, Timber Lake, SD 57656-0181. Tel.: 605-865-3553 & 3546.
E-mail: info@timberlakehistory.org
Historical Society Museum.
Collections: fossils; traditional Lakota clothing; early reservation Native American items; photographs.
Hours & Admission Prices: By appointment.

Vermillion

AUSTIN-WHITTEMORE HOUSE MUSEUM, 15 Austin Ave., Vermillion, SD 57069-3055. Tel.: 605-624-8266.
E-mail: cleoe@iw.net
Web Site: www.sdhistory.org/soc/Hist_Orgs/clayco.htm
Historic House.
Collections: Victorian furnishings; period artifacts.
Hours & Admission Prices: Memorial Day-Labor Day Mon.-Fri. 10-4:30, Sat.-Sun. by appointment.

* **NATIONAL MUSIC MUSEUM, (M),** Clark & Yale Sts., Vermillion, SD 57069-2390. Mailing Address: 414 E. Clark St., Vermillion, SD 57069-2307. Tel.: 605-677-5306. Fax: 605-677-6995.
E-mail: nmm@usd.edu
Web Site: www.nmmusd.org
Formerly: Shrine To Music Museum
Founded: 1973.

Congressional District: 1
Key Personnel: C.E.O., Dr. Andre P. Larson; Chm. (V), Brad Randall; Conservator, John Koster; Cur., Dr. Margaret Downie Banks; Cur., Dr. Sabine Klaus; Cur., Arian Sheets; Educator, Dr. Deborah Check Reeves; Asst. to the Dir., Barbara Stark; Dir. Visitor Svcs., Vicky Kuklentz.
Personnel Profile: Full-Time Paid 9; Part-Time Paid 6; Part-Time Volunteers 5; Interns 6.
Governing Authority: nonprofit. Affiliated with University of South Dakota. Tax-exempt: 501(c)(3).
Musical Instrument Museum.
Collections: Arne B. Larson collection of American, European & non-Western musical instruments; Wayne Sorenson collection of 19th-century woodwinds; Witten-Rawlins collection of early Italian stringed instruments; bows; tools & documentary source materials; manuscripts; Higbee-Abbott-Zylstra collection of early flutes & recorders; Cecil Leeson saxophone collection & archives; Mazzeo clarinet collection; Utley collection of brass instruments; Bates harmonica collection; William Ludwig II percussion collection.
Research Fields: history of musical instruments.
Facilities: library of music literature available for research on premises by appointment with director; conservation laboratory; concert hall. Postcards, catalogs, posters & recordings for sale.
Activities: guided tours; lectures; gallery talks; concerts; formally organized education programs for undergraduate & graduate students; repairs & restorations; permanent exhibitions; workshops; conferences; self guided audio tours.
Publications: quarterly newsletter; catalogs; recordings.
Hours & Admission Prices: Mon.-Sat. 9-5, Sun. 2-5. No charge; donations requested. Closed New Year's Day; Thanksgiving; Christmas. ♿
Attendance: 279,187 (accurate)
Membership: Member $35; Donor $50; Contributing $100; Sustaining $250; Supporting $500; Life $1,000; Sponsor $5,000; Patron $10,000; Benefactor $25,000.

UNIVERSITY ART GALLERIES, (M), Warren M. Lee Center, University of South Dakota, 414 E. Clark, Vermillion, SD 57069-2307. Tel.: 605-677-3177. Fax: 605-677-5988.
E-mail: eddie.welch@usd.edu
Web Site: www.usd.edu/cfa/cfa.html
Founded: 1976.
Key Personnel: Dir., Edward Welch.
Personnel Profile: Part-Time Paid 3; Part-Time Volunteers 3.
Governing Authority: state; university. Parent Institution: University of South Dakota. Tax-exempt.
Art Gallery.
Collections: art work by contemporary Sioux artist, Oscar Howe; study collection with emphasis on modern & contemporary art on paper; historic art of South Dakota; Asian, African & Native American Art.
Research Fields: South Dakota artists; Northern Plains American Indian art.
Facilities: library.
Activities: lectures; films; gallery talks; loan, permanent, temporary & traveling exhibitions; school loan service.
Publications: exhibition catalogs.
Hours & Admission Prices: Main Gallery: Mon.-Fri. 8-5, Sat.-Sun. 1-5. Oscar Howe Gallery: Mon.-Sat. 1-5. No charge. Closed major holidays. ♿
Attendance: 20,000 (estimated)

W.H. OVER MUSEUM, (M), 1110 Ratingen St., Vermillion, SD 57069. Mailing Address: 414 E. Clark, Vermillion, SD 57069-2307. Tel.: 605-677-5228.
E-mail: whover@usd.edu
Web Site: www.usd.edu/whover
Founded: 1883.
Congressional District: 1
Key Personnel: Pres. Bd., Larry Bradley.
Personnel Profile: Part-Time Paid 2; Part-Time Volunteers 20; Interns 2.
Governing Authority: Parent Institution: Friends of the Museum. Tax-exempt: 501(c)(3).
Natural & Cultural History.
Collections: archeology; geology; natural history; regional history; Plains Indian ethnology; photographs; Stanley J. Morrow collection; David & Elizabeth Clark Memorial collection; contemporary Sioux paintings; Robert Penn.
Research Fields: Dakota & Sioux ethnology; regional & natural history.
Facilities: 4,000-vol. library; classroom. Museum-related items for sale.
Activities: craft classes & craftsmen in residence; tours; traveling exhibits; lecture & film series; school loan exhibits.
Publications: quarterly museum newsletter.
Hours & Admission Prices: Mon.-Sat. 10-4. No charge; donations accepted. Closed major holidays. ♿
Attendance: 19,097 (accurate)
Membership: Student $5; Senior Citizen $8; Individual, Single-Parent Family $10; Family $20; Business & Institute $25; Sustaining $40; Patron $100; Benefactor $250; Life $1,000.

Volga

BROOKINGS COUNTY HISTORICAL SOCIETY MUSEUM, 207 Samara Ave., Volga, SD 57071. Mailing Address: P.O. Box 608, Volga, SD 57071-0608. Tel.: 605-627-9149 & 695-5430.
Founded: 1939.
Key Personnel: C.E.O., Chm. & Pres. (V), Lawrence Barnett; Vice Chm., Harold Christianson; Bd. Member, Barbara Behrend; Sec., Joanne Murphy; Treas., Howard Lee; Bd. Member, Dorothy Husher; Bd. Member, Chuck Cecil; Bd. Member, Donald Kleinjan; Bd. Member, Lyle Strande; Bd. Member, Jerry Leslie; Bd. Member, Deanna Rude; Bd. Member, Ron Ladegaard; Bd. Member, Grace Linn.
Personnel Profile: Part-Time Volunteers 60.
Governing Authority: nonprofit organization. Parent Institution: Brookings County Historical Society, Volga, SD. Tax-exempt.
Local History Museum.
Collections: county history & artifacts. Historic Buildings: 1880 Old Medary School; 1872 Sundet log cabin; early farm equipment building.
Facilities: library of documents, books & periodicals relating to Brookings County history available for use on request.
Activities: guided tours.
Publications: quarterly newsletter, The Window.
Hours & Admission Prices: Memorial Day to Labor Day daily 1-4; appointments available. No charge; donations accepted. ♿
Attendance: 600 (estimated)
Membership: Individual $10; Family $15; Pathfinder $25-$49; Pioneer $50-$99; Homesteader $100 & up.

Wall

WILD WEST HISTORICAL WAX MUSEUM, 601 Main St., Wall, SD 57790. Mailing Address: P.O. Box 441, Wall, SD 57790-0441. Tel.: 605-279-2915.
Wax Museum.
Collections: more than 50 wax figures including James Gang, Wild Bill, Annie Oakley, Sitting Bull & Wyatt Earp.
Hours & Admission Prices: May 1-Oct. 15 daily 8am-9pm. Family $18, adults $4.50, seniors $4, children 13 & under $2.50.

WOUNDED KNEE MUSEUM, (M), Exit 110, Interstate 90, Wall, SD 57790. Mailing Address: 207 10th Ave., P.O. Box 348, Wall, SD 57790-0348. Tel.: 605-279-2573 (seasonal); 970-226-3218 (admin.).
E-mail: info@woundedkneemuseum.org
Web Site: www.woundedkneemuseum.org
Founded: 2001.
History Museum.
Collections: history of the Lakota Indian tribe & the events surrounding the Wounded Knee Massacre; photographs; Native American artifacts.
Facilities: Museum-related items for sale.
Activities: tours.
Hours & Admission Prices: Spring to Oct. 12 daily 8:30-5:30; groups by appointment. Adults $5, senior citizens 60 & over $4; children under 12 no charge. ♿

Watertown

BRAMBLE PARK ZOO, (M), 800 10th St., N.W., Watertown, SD 57201. Mailing Address: P.O. Box 910, Watertown, SD 57201-0910. Tel.: 605-882-6269. Fax: 605-882-5232.
E-mail: dmiller@watertownsd.us
Web Site: brambleparkzoo.com
Founded: 1912.
Key Personnel: C.E.O. & Dir., Dan D. Miller; Pres., Jeanne Flaherty; Treas. City of Watertown (V), Greg Dievsen; Cur., Jim Lloyd; Education, Jaime Stricker; Museum Shop Mgr., Kim Konard.
Personnel Profile: Full-Time Paid 9; Part-Time Paid 12; Part-Time Volunteers 25; Interns 2.
Governing Authority: nonprofit. Tax-exempt: 501(c)(3).
Zoo.
Collections: native South Dakota wildlife, exotic species & selected endangered wildlife; living collection contains 500 specimens representing 130 species & 17 endangered species; 116 specimens of mammals representing 37 species; 215 specimens of birds representing 69 species; 16 reptiles of 10 species & 17 endangered species.
Research Fields: the social interactions of a mixed species exhibit of black lemurs and black & white ruffed lemurs; vaginal swelling and estrus cycling

of female black & white lemurs; captive wildlife management; exotic zoo medicine; zoo education; South Dakota wildlife management.
Facilities: 450-vol. library of books on natural history, captive management, wildlife conservation & animal research; cafeteria. Zoo-related items for sale.
Activities: guided tours; broadcast programs; formal education programs for college students. Annual Events: Water Fest; Kids Day; Animal Enrichment Day; Roots & Shoots Day; Zoo Boo; chili cook-off.
Publications: bimonthly for members, LAZS Newsletter.
Hours & Admission Prices: Summer: daily 9-8. Winter: daily 10-4 (weather permitting). Adults $5.50, children ages 3-12 $3; discounts to AZA members; children under 3 no charge. Closed New Year's Day; Thanksgiving; Christmas. ♿
Attendance: 54,330 (accurate)
Membership: Single & Family $50; Donor $75; Sustaining $150; Life $500; Patron $1,000; Benefactor $5,000.

CODINGTON COUNTY HERITAGE MUSEUM, 27 First Ave., S.E., Watertown, SD 57201-3612. Tel.: 605-886-7335. Fax: 605-882-4383.
E-mail: director@cchsmuseum.org
Web Site: www.cchsmuseum.org
Founded: 1975.
Congressional District: 1
Key Personnel: Exec. Dir., Kevin M. Bailey; Pres. (V), Dr. Bernie Hanson.
Personnel Profile: Full-Time Paid 1; Part-Time Paid 1; Part-Time Volunteers 15.
Governing Authority: society; nonprofit organization. Parent Institution: Codington County Historical Society, Inc. Tax-exempt 501(c)(3).
Local County History Museum: housed in c.1905-06 Carnegie Library Building.
Collections: local history.
Research Fields: local history & prehistory; local Civil War & Spanish American War diaries; local historical cookbooks & recipes; local railroad history; local architectural history; community bands; area homesteaders.
Facilities: meeting room.
Activities: guided tours; lectures; travelling exhibits; research assistance for scholars & family history buffs.
Publications: books. The Civil War Diary of Arthur Calvin Mellette; Maggie: The Civil War Diary of Margaret Wylie Mellette; bimonthly newsletter, The Codington County Courier; Pictorial History of Codington County: 1875-1987; walking & driving tour brochures; bimonthly newsletter, The Codington County Courier.
Hours & Admission Prices: May-Aug. Mon.-Fri. 10-5, Sat. 1-5; Sept.-April Mon.-Fri. 1-5. No charge; donations accepted. Closed holidays.
Attendance: 3,000 (estimated)
Membership: Individual $20; Family $30; Bronze $50; Silver $75; Gold $100; Diamond $250; Platinum $500.

MELLETTE HOUSE, 421 Fifth Ave., N.W., Watertown, SD 57201. Mailing Address: 900 S. Lake Dr., Watertown, SD 57201-5460. Tel.: 605-886-4730.
Founded: 1943.
Congressional District: 1
Key Personnel: Pres. (V), Prudence K. Calvin; Treas. & Sec., Ann Edelman.
Personnel Profile: Part-Time Paid 5; Part-Time Volunteers 15.
Governing Authority: society. Tax-exempt.
Historic House: 1885 Mellette House, home of Arthur Calvin Mellette, first Governor of South Dakota.
Collections: original furnishings; family portraits; heirlooms; Indian collection.
Research Fields: Mellette family history.
Activities: guided tours.
Publications: Arthur's Civil War Diary; Maggie's Civil War Diary; The Mellette's: A Family and a Home.
Hours & Admission Prices: May-Oct. Tues.-Sun. 1-5. No charge; donations accepted.
Attendance: 2,750 (estimated)

REDLIN ART CENTER, 1200 33rd St., S.E., Watertown, SD 57201-7257. Tel.: 605-882-3877. Fax: 605-882-3922.
E-mail: redlinac@redlinart.com
Web Site: www.redlinart.com
Key Personnel: Exec. Dir., Julie Ranum
Art Center.
Collections: over 150 oil paintings by Terry Redlin.
Activities: group tours.
Hours & Admission Prices: Mon.-Fri. 8-5, Sat. 10-4, Sun. 12-4. No charge. ♿

Webster

MUSEUM OF WILDLIFE, SCIENCE & INDUSTRY, 760 W. Hwy. 12, Webster, SD 57274. Mailing Address: P.O. Box 235, Webster, SD 57274-0235. Tel.: 605-345-4751.
E-mail: info@sdmuseum.org
Web Site: www.sdmuseum.org
Key Personnel: Pres., Kurt Gravley; Cur., Betty Schmidt
General Museum.
Collections: culture & heritage of Northeastern South Dakota; period furniture; cars; farm equipment; African big game hunting trophies; 24 buildings.
Hours & Admission Prices: May 15-Oct. 15 Mon.-Sat. 9-5, Sun. 1-5; other times by appointment. No charge; donations accepted.

Wessington Springs

JERAULD COUNTY PIONEER MUSEUM, 105 Main St., Wessington Springs, SD 57382. Mailing Address: P.O. Box 132, Wessington Springs, SD 57382-0132. Tel.: 605-539-9211.
History Museum.
Collections: memorabilia & print information relating to Jerauld County history; artifacts & archives; photographs.
Hours & Admission Prices: Thurs.-Fri. 9:30-12 & 1-4:30; other times by appointment. No charge; donations accepted.

Winner

TRIPP COUNTY HISTORICAL SOCIETY MUSEUM, E. Hwy. 18, Winner, SD 57580. Mailing Address: P.O. Box 287, Winner, SD 57580-0287. Tel.: 605-842-0704.
Historical Society Museum.
Collections: local history & culture; furnishings; photographs; period artifacts.
Hours & Admission Prices: Memorial Day-Labor Day Wed.-Sun. 2-5.

Yankton

BEDE ART GALLERY, Mount Mary College, Art Office, 1105 W. 8th St., Yankton, SD 57078-3725. Tel.: 605-668-1574.
E-mail: dkahle@mtmc.edu
Web Site: www.mtmc.edu
Key Personnel: Dir., David Kahle
Art Gallery.
Collections: student artwork.
Major Exhibits: Mount Marty Student Art Show, 11/29/09-12/11/09; Erica Merchant & Cody Spiegle-Sculpture/Installation, 1/11/10-1/29/10; Judith R. Peterson-Photography/Colour Forms, 2/1/10-2/26/10; Mark Stemwedal-Oil Paintings, 3/1/10-3/26/10; Matthew T. Potts-Black & White Photography, 3/29/10-4/16/10; Mount Marty Student Art Show, 4/19/10-5/7/10.
Hours & Admission Prices: Mon.-Fri. 8-8. No charge.

CRAMER-KENYON HERITAGE HOME, 509 Pine St., Yankton, SD 57078-4036. Tel.: 605-665-7470.
Key Personnel: Pres., Donna Schmidt; Vice Pres., Bonnie Price.
Governing Authority: Tax-exempt.
Historic House Museum: built in 1882 by the Secretary of Dakota Territory.
Collections: 1880s decor; gas & electric chandeliers; oil paintings; period furnishings; art work.
Hours & Admission Prices: Memorial Day to Labor Day daily; other times by appointment. Adults $4, students $2.
Attendance: 600 (estimated)

DAKOTA TERRITORIAL MUSEUM, 610 Summit St., Yankton, SD 57078-3858. Mailing Address: P.O. Box 1033, Yankton, SD 57078-1033. Tel.: 605-665-3898.
E-mail: dtmuseum@iw.net
Web Site: www.dakotaterritorialmuseum.org
Founded: 1961.
Congressional District: 1
Key Personnel: Dir., Crystal Mensch; Pres. (V), Dr. Mal Jameson.
Personnel Profile: Part-Time Volunteers 5; Interns 1.
Governing Authority: society. Parent Institution: Yankton County Historical Society. Tax-exempt: 501(c)(3).
Historical Society Museum.
Collections: Missouri River transportation material; manuscripts; books, photographs & objects pertaining to Dakota territory history; Yankton's role as territorial capital; Plains Indian ethnographic material; 19th-20th century Yankton county history; Max Copper fishing collection. Historic Buildings: c.1900 Gunderson rural schoolhouse; Dakota Territorial council building; c.1890 Great Northern RR depot; Cook blacksmith shop c.1880; 1860 Houden pioneer cabin.

Research Fields: railroad history; Plains Indians; Dakota territory.
Facilities: Art prints & photo prints for sale.
Activities: guided tours; docent program; periodic lecture series.
Hours & Admission Prices: May-Sept. Mon.-Fri. 10-5, Sat.-Sun. 12-4; Oct.-April daily 12-4. No charge; donations accepted. Closed New Year's Eve & Day; Good Friday; Easter; Thanksgiving; Christmas Eve & Day. ♿
Attendance: 5,780 (estimated)
Membership: Individual $25; Family $40; Pioneer $100; Explorer $250; Riverboat Captain $1,000.

GAVINS POINT NATIONAL FISH HATCHERY AND AQUARIUM, 31227 436th Ave., Yankton, SD 57078-6364. Tel.: 605-665-3352. Fax: 605-665-3360.
Founded: 1960.
Congressional District: 1
Key Personnel: Project Leader, Keith McGilvray.
Personnel Profile: Full-Time Paid 7; Part-Time Paid 1; Part-Time Volunteers 5.
Governing Authority: federal. Parent Institution: U.S. Department of the Interior, Washington, DC. Subsidiary Institution: U.S. Fish & Wildlife Service. Tax-exempt.
Aquarium.
Collections: aquatic displays consisting of 40-50 Missouri River Basin fish, reptiles & amphibians.
Activities: guided tours.
Publications: brochure, Gavins Point National Fish Hatchery.
Hours & Admission Prices: Aquarium: April-Oct. daily 10-4. Hatchery: daily 8-4; guided group tours by appointment. No charge; donations accepted. ♿
Attendance: 90,000 (accurate)

TENNESSEE

(195 listings)

Athens

MCMINN COUNTY LIVING HERITAGE MUSEUM, (M), 522 W. Madison Ave., Athens, TN 37303. Mailing Address: P.O. Box 889, Athens, TN 37371-0889. Tel.: 423-745-0329 & 744-8100. Fax: 423-745-0329.
E-mail: livingheritagemuseum@livingheritagemuseum.com
Web Site: www.livingheritagemuseum.com
Founded: 1982.
Congressional District: 2
Key Personnel: Pres., Gerald Martin; Vice Pres., Laura Brown LeNoir; Treas., Tom Biddle; Trustee, Muriel Mayfield; Exec. Dir., Diane Hutsell; Museum Shop Mgr., Robin Muller.
Personnel Profile: Full-Time Paid 3; Full-Time Volunteers 2; Part-Time Paid 3; Part-Time Volunteers 175; Interns 2.
Governing Authority: nonprofit organization. Tax-exempt: 501(c)(3).
History Museum.
Collections: pioneer & Victorian furnishings; decorative arts; needlework; fine art; period costumes; 19th- & early 20th-century quilts; 1880-1930 Burn Industrial Room General Store; 20th-century industrial items; 19th- & 20th-century bisque & china head dolls, toys & clothing; 1850-1935 desks, books & maps; glass ceramics; farming equipment; Indian artifacts; 1820-1900 religious artifacts; 1850-1930 Tennessee Wesleyan College artifacts; 1860-1930 medical, legal & legislative artifacts; war artifacts.
Facilities: 65-vol. library for inter-library loan. Books & related items for sale.
Activities: guided tours; lectures; hobby workshops; organized education programs for children; participatory, loan, temporary & traveling exhibitions. Museum Sponsors: Annual Quilt Show.
Publications: brochure, In Preparation for Life 1840-1940; William E. Nash-His Life; The Heritage Cookbook (2nd printing); Living Legacies-A Guide to Museum Areas & Artifacts.
Hours & Admission Prices: Mon.-Fri. 10-5. Adults $5, senior citizens & students $3; discounts to AAA & AAM members; members no charge. Closed New Year's Day; Easter; Memorial Day; Independence Day; Labor Day; Thanksgiving; Christmas. ♿
Attendance: 22,000 (accurate)
Membership: Student & Senior Citizen $10; Individual $15; Family $35; Life $300; Patron $1,000.

Burns

CUMBERLAND PRESBYTERIAN CHURCH BIRTHPLACE SHRINE, Montgomery Bell State Park, Burns, TN 37029. Mailing Address: 8207 Traditional Place, Cordova, TN 38016-7414. Tel.: 901-276-8602. Fax: 901-272-3913.
E-mail: archives@cumberland.org
Web Site: www.cumberland.org/hfcpc/
Founded: 1810.
Congressional District: 6
Key Personnel: Dir. & C.E.O., Susan Knight Gore; Pres. (V), Gwen McReynolds.
Personnel Profile: Full-Time Paid 1; Part-Time Volunteers 2.
Governing Authority: church. Parent Institution: Cumberland Presbyterian Church, 8207 Traditional Place, Cordova, TN. Tax-exempt: 501(c)(3).
Historic Shrine: located in Montgomery Bell State Park, Dickson, Tennessee.
Collections: c.1800 replica Rev. Samuel McAdow home.
Facilities: 100-seat chapel.
Activities: Sunday morning worship service from June-Sept.; weddings.
Publications: booklets.
Hours & Admission Prices: Daily 8-6. No charge.

Byrdstown

CORDELL HULL BIRTHPLACE & MUSEUM STATE HISTORIC PARK, 1300 Cordell Hill Memorial Dr., Byrdstown, TN 38549-4627. Tel.: 931-864-3247.
E-mail: robin.peeler@state.tn.us
Web Site: www.cordellhullmuseum.com
Founded: 1997.
History Museum: birthplace of Cordell Hull, appointed Secretary of State by President Franklin D. Roosevelt.
Collections: life of Cordell Hull; personal artifacts; photographs;
Facilities: Museum-related items for sale.
Activities: special events & programs. Museum Sponsors: Cordell Hull Folk Festival in September.
Hours & Admission Prices: April-Oct. daily 9-5; Nov.-March daily 9-4. No charge. Call the park for closings. ♿

Camden

TENNESSEE RIVER FRESHWATER PEARL MUSEUM FARM TOUR, Birdsong Resort, Marina & Campground, 255 Marina Rd., Camden, TN 38320-7832. Tel.: 731-584-7880; 800-225-7469 (Tour Bookings). Fax: 731-584-3625.
E-mail: bob@birdsongresort.com
Web Site: www.tennesseeriverpearls.com
Key Personnel: Owner & Tour Guide, Bob Keast
General Museum.
Collections: freshwater pearls & musseling industry.
Hours & Admission Prices: Mon.-Sat. 8-5, Sun. 1-4. Full Tour: adults $49.50. Mini Tour: adults $29.50.

Carthage

SMITH COUNTY HERITAGE MUSEUM, 107 3rd St., Carthage, TN 37030-1472. Mailing Address: P.O. Box 73, Carthage, TN 37030-0073. Tel.: 615-735-1104.
History Museum.
Collections: farming; agriculture; military; education; local churches; architecture; photographs.
Facilities: library. Museum-related items for sale.
Hours & Admission Prices: Wed. & Fri.-Sat. 10-2. No charge.

Castalian Springs

CRAGFONT-HISTORIC CRAGFONT, INC., 200 Cragfont Rd., Castalian Springs, TN 37031-4743. Mailing Address: 1011 Durham Dr., Gallatin, TN 37066-3411. Tel.: 615-452-7070.
Web Site: www.srlab.net/cragfort/
Founded: 1958.
Congressional District: 4
Key Personnel: C.E.O., Mrs. Margaret G. Clark; Chm. Restoration, Mrs. James Gourley; Cur., Mrs. Lowell Fayna; Museum Shop Mgr., Margaret Fayna.
Personnel Profile: Full-Time Paid 2; Part-Time Volunteers 30.
Governing Authority: Tax-exempt: 501(c)(3)
Historic House Museum: c.1798-1802 home of General James Winchester.
Collections: American Federal furnishings; stenciled walls in parlor; period farming tools; archives.
Research Fields: archives.
Facilities: 90-vol. library of original Cragfont books dating from 18th-19th century; restored original flower garden.
Activities: guided tours; lectures; permanent exhibitions.
Publications: descriptive brochure; cookbook; booklets, Cragfont; Haunts, Hauntings & Legends.
Hours & Admission Prices: mid-April to Oct. Tues.-Sat. 10-5, Sun. 1-5; Nov. to mid-April, by appointment. Adults $5, children 6-12 $3; discounts to seniors & groups; members & children under 6 no charge. ♿
Attendance: 5,500 (accurate)
Membership: Individual $15; Family $25.

Chattanooga

CHATTANOOGA AFRICAN MUSEUM/BESSIE SMITH HALL, (M), 200 E. Martin Luther King Blvd., Chattanooga, TN 37403. Mailing Address: P.O. Box 11493, Chattanooga, TN 37401-2493. Tel.: 423-266-8658 & 267-1628. Fax: 423-267-1076.
Web Site: www.caamhistory.org
Founded: 1983.
Congressional District: 3
Key Personnel: Exec. Dir., Rose M. Martin; Pres. (V), Irvin Overton; Membership, Sandra Jones; Education, Carman Davis.
Personnel Profile: Full-Time Paid 5; Part-Time Paid 4; Part-Time Volunteers 19; Interns 2.
Governing Authority: nonprofit organization. Tax-exempt: 501(c)(3).
African-American History Museum.
Collections: African artifacts; recordings; oral history tapes; local artists; VHS tapes of national personalities; photographs of early local prominent citizens; prints by national artists; original clothing from local donors; Bessie Smith collection of local African-American history; oral history tapes (VHS); local history.
Facilities: 10,000-vol. library of fiction & reference books available to the public for research on premises; auditorium. Museum-related items for sale.
Activities: arts festivals; guided tours; lectures; formally organized education programs for children, undergraduate & graduate students; summer art programs featuring crafts, African drumming, dance, music history & museum intern career programs; art fun factory after school program; community outreach program.
Publications: quarterly newsletter, The Heritage; guide to the Chattanooga permanent exhibit; Life Series - Roland Carter, Russell Goode, Black America Series, Chattanooga; workbooks, Chattanooga African American Legacy; Biography & Achievements of the Colored Citizens of Chattanooga in 1904.
Hours & Admission Prices: Mon.-Fri. 10-5, Sat. 12-4. Adults $5, seniors, member adults & students with I.D. $3, children 6-12 $2; discounts to groups, and AAM & NAAM members; children 5 & under no charge. Closed national & legal holidays. ♿
Attendance: 156,000 (accurate)
Membership: Senior & Student $15; Individual $25; Family $50; Family Plus $65; Contributing $100; Organization $250; Corporate $600; Thousandaire $1,000.

CHATTANOOGA HISTORY CENTER, (M), 615 Lindsay St., Ste. 100, Chattanooga, TN 37403-3430. Tel.: 423-265-3247. Fax: 423-266-9280. chattanoogahistorycenter.blogspot.com.
E-mail: dblack@chattanoogahistory.com
Web Site: www.chattanoogahistory.com
Founded: 1978.
Congressional District: 3
Key Personnel: Exec. Dir. & Cur., Dr. Daryl Black; Deputy Dir., Marlene Payne.
Personnel Profile: Full-Time Paid 2; Part-Time Paid 1; Part-Time Volunteers 21; Interns 7.
Governing Authority: nonprofit organization. Tax-exempt: 501(c)(3).
Regional History Museum.
Collections: objects pertaining to 10,000 years of human history in southeastern Tennessee, northern Georgia & northeastern Alabama.
Research Fields: Cherokee, Civil War, mid 20th century business & industry, local environmental changes.
Activities: guided tours; lectures; workshops for children & adults; special events.
Publications: membership newsletter, The Connection.
Hours & Admission Prices: Mon.-Fri. 9-5.
Attendance: 6,033
Membership: Individual $35; Family $50; Collector's Circle $51-$100; Conservator's Circle $101-$250; Curator's Circle $251-$500; Director's Circle $501-$1,000; President's Circle $1,000 & up.

THE CHATTANOOGA NATURE CENTER, 400 Garden Rd., Chattanooga, TN 37419-1807. Tel.: 423-821-1160, ext. 108. Fax: 423-821-1702.
E-mail: tcrawford@chattanature.org
Web Site: www.chattanature.org
Formerly: Tennessee Wildlife Center
Founded: 1978.
Congressional District: 3
Key Personnel: Exec. Dir., Dr. Jean Lomino; Pres. (V), John Mitchum; Dir. Education, Kyle Waggener; Naturalist, Public Program Coord., Susan Russell; Member & Visitor Svcs. Mgr., Diane Morgan; Cur. Wildlife, Tish Gailmard; Asst. Cur. Wildlife, Jenny Nicely; Dir. Devel. & Mktg., Tina Harvey Crawford; Education & Devel. Asst., Corey Hagen; Admin. & Wildlife Asst., Hope Howard.
Personnel Profile: Full-Time Paid 6; Part-Time Paid 5; Part-Time Volunteers 58.
Governing Authority: nonprofit organization. Tax-exempt: 501(c)(3).
Nature Center: located on Lookout Creek on the western side of Lookout Mountain, where the Battle of Lookout Mountain began; now part of species survival program for endangered Red wolves & other animals indigenous to the southeast region.
Collections: wolves; bald eagle; bobcats; raptors; other mammals.
Research Fields: herpetology; botany; wildflower ecology; endangered red wolves.
Facilities: botanical garden; nature & conservation center; reading room; 60-seat auditorium; 1,200 ft. wetland walkway; classrooms. Museum-related items for sale.
Activities: guided tours; lectures; formally organized education programs; permanent, temporary & traveling exhibitions.
Publications: monthly newsletter, Native Ground; wildlife booklet, First Aid & Home Care For Wildlife.
Hours & Admission Prices: April-Oct. Mon.-Sat. 9-5, Sun. 1-5; Nov.-March Mon.-Sat. 9-5. Adults $7, children & senior citizens $4; members no charge. Closed New Year's Day; Easter; Memorial Day; Independence Day; Labor Day; Thanksgiving; Christmas. ♿
Attendance: 61,000 (estimated)
Membership: Student $35; Senior Citizen $40; Individual $45; Family $60; Sponsor $100; Patron $200; Benefactor $500.

CHATTANOOGA ZOO AT WARNER PARK, 1254 E. 3rd St., Chattanooga, TN 37404-2823. Mailing Address: P.O. Box 3204, Chattanooga, TN 37404-0204. Tel.: 423-697-1319. Fax: 423-697-1329.
E-mail: dlongwpz@aol.com
Web Site: www.chattzoo.org
Formerly: Warner Park Zoo
Founded: 1937.
Congressional District: 3
Key Personnel: Dir. & Museum Shop Mgr., Dardenelle Long; Pres. (V), Gary Chazen; C.E.O., Jerry Mitchell.
Personnel Profile: Full-Time Paid 15; Part-Time Paid 9; Part-Time Volunteers 100; Interns 2.
Governing Authority: nonprofit. Parent Institution: City of Chattanooga. Subsidiary Institution: Friends of the Zoo. Tax-exempt.
Zoo.
Collections: animals from around the world.
Activities: summer camp; outreach programs.
Publications: Chatta Zooga.
Hours & Admission Prices: Daily 9-5. Adults $6; discounts to AZA members; members no charge. Closed New Year's Day; Thanksgiving; Christmas. ♿
Attendance: 207,000 (accurate)
Membership: Individual $25; Family & Grandparent $45; Director's Circle $125.

CREATIVE DISCOVERY MUSEUM, (M), 321 Chestnut St., Chattanooga, TN 37402-4902. Mailing Address: P.O. Box 6339, Chattanooga, TN 37401-6339. Tel.: 423-756-2738. Fax: 423-267-9344.
E-mail: info@cdmfun.org
Web Site: www.cdmfun.org
Founded: 1995.
Congressional District: 3
Key Personnel: C.E.O., Henry H. Schulson; Chm. (V), Keith Sanford; Devel., Sharman Sherfey; Education, Jayne Griffin; Public Rels., Sharman Sherfey, CFRE; Bldg. & Exhibit Maintenance, Ken Crider; Visitor Svcs., Carla Parrish; Museum Shop Mgr., Brenda Baskette.
Personnel Profile: Full-Time Paid 21; Part-Time Paid 41; Part-Time Volunteers 144.
Governing Authority: private; nonprofit organization. Tax-exempt: 501(c)(3).
Children's Museum.
Collections: hands-on exhibits.
Major Exhibits: Good For You, 1/10-4/10; Grossology (T), 5/10-8/10; Kids Like You, Kids Like Me (T), 9/10.
Facilities: 26,000 sq. ft. exhibit space; 120-seat auditorium; 25-seat cafe; classroom; art workshop; conservatory. Museum-related items for sale.
Activities: arts festivals; concerts; dance recitals; docent program; films; guided tours; hobby workshops; lectures; rental gallery; theater; participatory & traveling exhibitions; homeschool workshops; birthday program; overnight program; science demonstrations; walk-up art & music lessons.
Publications: quarterly newsletter, GO!; educator's newsletter, Discoveries.
Hours & Admission Prices: March-June 20 Mon.-Sat. 10-5; June 21-Aug. 10 daily 9:30-5:30; Aug. 11-Sept. 1 daily 10-5; Sept. 2-Nov. Mon.-Tues. & Thurs.-Sat. 10-5, Sun. 12-5; Dec.-Feb. Mon.-Tues. & Thurs.-Sat. 10-5. Adults $9.95; members no charge. Closed Thanksgiving; Christmas Eve & Day. ♿
Attendance: 216,931 (accurate)

Membership: My Family $85; My Family Plus 1 $110; Nationwide Family $135.

CRESS GALLERY OF ART, 752 Vine St., Chattanooga, TN 37403. Mailing Address: University of Tennessee at Chattanooga, 615 McCallie Ave., #1305, Chattanooga, TN 37403-2504. Tel.: 423-304-9789 & 425-4600. Fax: 423-425-2101.
E-mail: ruth-grover@utc.edu
Web Site: www.utc.edu/cressgallery
Founded: 1952.
Congressional District: 3
Key Personnel: Dir. & Cur., Ruth Grover.
Personnel Profile: Full-Time Paid 1; Part-Time Paid 3.
Governing Authority: university. Affiliated with University of Tennessee at Chattanooga. Tax-exempt: 501(c)(3).
Art Institute.
Collections: graphics; paintings; sculpture; photographs.
Activities: gallery talks; inter-museum loan, temporary & traveling exhibitions; visiting artist series; annual juried student & senior thesis exhibitions; biennial art faculty exhibition.
Hours & Admission Prices: Sept.-May Mon.-Fri. 9:30-7. No charge. Closed university holidays. ♿
Membership: Friends of the Gallery $50 & up.

DRAGON DREAMS MUSEUM & GIFT SHOP, 6722 E. Brainerd Rd., Chattanooga, TN 37421. Tel.: 423-892-2384.
Web Site: www.dragonvet.com/
Founded: 1990.
Key Personnel: Dir., Barbara Newton; Museum Shop Mgr., Chris Matias.
Personnel Profile: Full-Time Paid 1; Full-Time Volunteers 1.
Dragon Art Museum.
Collections: hand-crafted figurines & furniture; wood, silver, jade, ivory, pewter, porcelain & fabric dragons.
Facilities: Museum-related items for sale.
Activities: special events.
Hours & Admission Prices: Wed.-Sat. 10-6, Sun. 1-6. Adults $10, children $4.50. Closed New Year's Eve & Day; Independence Day; Thanksgiving; Christmas Eve & Day. ♿

HOUSTON MUSEUM OF DECORATIVE ARTS, 201 High St., Chattanooga, TN 37403-1185. Tel.: 423-267-7176.
E-mail: houston@chattanooga.net
Web Site: www.thehoustonmuseum.com
Founded: 1949.
Congressional District: 3
Key Personnel: C.E.O. & Museum Shop Mgr., Amy H. Frierson; Pres., Suzanne S. Caplenor; Coord. Museum Operations, Chevon Mashburn.
Personnel Profile: Full-Time Paid 3; Part-Time Paid 6; Part-Time Volunteers 100.
Governing Authority: nonprofit organization. Tax-exempt: 501(c)(3).
Antique Museum: housed in 1890 building. Decorative Arts Museum.
Collections: early American, French & English glass; Victorian art glass; pressed glass; Tiffany glass; 19th-century decorative arts; colonial through 19th-century furniture; pewter & Mettlach steins; porcelains; dolls; pitcher collection.
Research Fields: glass; pottery; porcelain; furniture; dolls; textiles.
Facilities: library.
Activities: guided tours; lectures; films; gallery talks; TV programs; docent program; permanent exhibitions.
Publications: newssheet.
Hours & Admission Prices: Mon.-Fri. 9:30-4, Sat. 12-4. Adults $9; discount to AAM members; children under 3 & members no charge. Closed major holidays.
Attendance: 10,000 (estimated)
Membership: Student & Senior $25; Individual $35; Family $45; Sponsor $50; Patron $100; Benefactor $250; Grand Benefactor $500; Anna Safley Houston Club $1,000, $2,000 & $5,000.

*** HUNTER MUSEUM OF AMERICAN ART, (M),** 10 Bluff View, Chattanooga, TN 37403-1197. Tel.: 423-267-0968. Fax: 423-267-9844.
E-mail: robkret@huntermuseum.org
Web Site: www.huntermuseum.org
Founded: 1952.
Congressional District: 3
Key Personnel: Dir., Robert A. Kret; Chm. (V), Samuel D. Turner; Chief Cur., Ellen Simak; Cur. Contemporary, Nandini Makrandi; Registrar, Theresa Slowikowski; Exhibits Designer, John Hare; Museum Shop Mgr., Janan Jones.
Personnel Profile: Full-Time Paid 20; Part-Time Paid 36; Part-Time Volunteers 99; Interns 4.
Governing Authority: nonprofit. Tax-exempt: 501(c)(3).
Art Museum: restored antebellum mansion.
Collections: American painting, graphics & sculpture of 18th-20th centuries.
Major Exhibits: The Kennedy's Portrait of a Family (T), 11/29/09-1/24/10; Jellies: Living Art, 11/09-4/12.
Research Fields: American art.
Facilities: 250-vol. library of art books & periodicals; 150-seat auditorium; cafe; studios. Gift items for sale.
Activities: guided tours; lectures; films; gallery talks; permanent, temporary & traveling exhibitions; docent program; workshops; studio classes. Special Events: Spectrum, silent & live auction gala.
Publications: quarterly members magazine; exhibitions catalogs; A Catalogue of the American Collection, Hunter Museum of American Art, Volume I & II.
Hours & Admission Prices: Mon.-Tues. & Fri.-Sat. 10-5, Wed. & Sun. 12-5, Thurs. 10-9. Adults $9.95, seniors $8.95, youth 3-17 $4.95; discounts to AAM & ICOM members; children under 3 & members no charge. North American reciprocal admission. ♿
Attendance: 57,479 (accurate)
Membership: Individual $45; Family $65; Donor $100; Sponsor $350; Chairman's Circle Member $1,000; Chairman's Circle Benefactor $2,500; Chairman's Circle Grand Benefactor $5,000.

NATIONAL MEDAL OF HONOR MUSEUM OF MILITARY HISTORY, Northgate Mall, Hwy. 153, Chattanooga, TN 37403. Mailing Address: P.O. Box 11467, Chattanooga, TN 37401-2467. Tel.: 423-394-0710 & 698-4511.
Web Site: www.mohm.org
Formerly: Medal of Honor Museum
Founded: 1987.
Congressional District: 3
Key Personnel: Dir., Patty Parks; Chm. (V), Dan Saieed.
Personnel Profile: Full-Time Volunteers 9; Part-Time Volunteers 10.
Governing Authority: nonprofit. Tax-exempt.
History & Military Museum.
Collections: uniforms, pre-Civil War to present; weapons, 1776-present; military prints & paintings; medals; badges; Nuremburg collection; Confederate collection; currency collection, 1774-present; helmets; military history library; international marching band recording collection; Medal of Honor citations; photographic archives.
Publications: brochures; newsletter.
Hours & Admission Prices: Mon.-Thurs. 11-5, Fri. 11-6, Sat.-Sun. 1-5. No charge; donations accepted. Closed New Year's Day; Easter; Thanksgiving; Christmas. ♿
Attendance: 12,000 (estimated)

SISKIN MUSEUM OF RELIGIOUS AND CEREMONIAL ART, 1101 Carter St., Chattanooga, TN 37402-5017. Tel.: 423-648-1700. Fax: 423-648-1749.
Founded: 1950.
Congressional District: 3
Key Personnel: Pres., Gerald Jensen; Devel. Officer, Christine Estoye.
Governing Authority: individual operation. Parent Institution: Siskin Memorial Foundation. Tax-exempt: 501(c)(3).
Religious Museum.
Collections: 453 objects of art in silver, ivory, wood, brass & pewter; religious & ceremonial arts; objects pertaining to Judaica & Christian religions; rare books.
Research Fields: religious art & artifacts from Europe & Asia.
Activities: guided tours; lectures; permanent exhibitions.
Hours & Admission Prices: Mon.-Fri. 9-4; other times by appointment. No charge; donations accepted. Closed Christmas Eve-New Year's Day; national holidays. ♿

TENNESSEE AQUARIUM, One Broad St., Chattanooga, TN 37402-1023. Mailing Address: P.O. Box 11048, Chattanooga, TN 37401-2048. Tel.: 800-262-0695; 423-265-0695. Fax: 423-267-3561.
Web Site: www.tennesseeaquarium.org
Founded: 1992.
Congressional District: 3
Key Personnel: Pres., Charles Arant; Retail Sales Mgr., Judy Powell; Public Rels., Thom Benson; Museum Shop Mgr., Laura Kroeger.
Personnel Profile: Full-Time Paid 156; Part-Time Paid 101; Part-Time Volunteers 575; Interns 15.
Governing Authority: Tax-exempt.
Aquarium.
Collections: freshwater & saltwater aquariums.
Facilities: IMAX theater.

Hours & Admission Prices: Daily 10-6. Adults $21.95, children 3-12 $14.95; children under 3 no charge. IMAX Theater: adults $8.50, children 3-12 $6; children under 3 no charge. Combination Ticket: adults $27.95, children 3-12 $19.95; children under 3 no charge. ♿
Attendance: 700,000 (estimated)
Membership: Individual Plus $75; Family $100; Family Plus $135.

TENNESSEE VALLEY RAILROAD MUSEUM INC., 4119 Cromwell Rd., Chattanooga, TN 37421-2164. Tel.: 423-894-8028, ext. 12. Fax: 423-894-8029.
E-mail: info@tvrail.com
Web Site: www.tvrail.com
Founded: 1961.
Congressional District: 3
Key Personnel: Pres., Timothy Andrews; Vice Pres. Mechanical, L. James Miller, III; Sec., Randall Freer; Shop Foreman, George Walker; Museum Shop Mgr., Joyce Soule.
Personnel Profile: Full-Time Paid 7; Full-Time Volunteers 4; Part-Time Paid 10; Part-Time Volunteers 10.
Governing Authority: nonprofit organization. Tax-exempt: 501(c)(3).
Railroad Transportation Museum.
Collections: operating Steam Locomotive 6910, 630, 4501, 610, 509; Pullman car; dining car 3158; c.1929 NC & ST.L. Drovers Caboose; ex-Air Force RSD1 diesel locomotives; ACT 1 experimental electric trains; original tracings from Baldwin Locomotive works; technical books; replica of Union Station; telegraph keys & sounders; artifacts indicative of daily train operations; c.1920-1950 coaches. Historic Buildings: c.1920 East Chattanooga Depot; Grand Junction Depot.
Research Fields: railroad history.
Facilities: cafeteria. Gift items for sale.
Activities: guided tours; daily 6 mile roundtrip ride over historic 1856 railroad through Missionary Ridge tunnel using vintage, restored equipment from the Golden Age of Railroad Travel; lectures; formally organized education programs. Museum Sponsors: steam-pulled excursions 6 times a year.
Publications: quarterly, Smoke and Cinders.
Hours & Admission Prices: mid-March to mid-June & mid-Aug. to Oct. Mon.-Fri. 10-1, Sat.-Sun. 10-5; mid-June to mid-Aug. daily 10-5; Nov. Sat.-Sun. 10-5. Adults $14, children 3-12 $8; discounts to AAA & NRHS members; members no charge. ♿
Attendance: 80,000 (estimated)
Membership: Individual $35, Family $55.

Clarksville

CLARKSVILLE-MONTGOMERY COUNTY MUSEUM DBA CUSTOMS HOUSE MUSEUM & CULTURAL CENTER, (M), 200 S. Second St., Clarksville, TN 37040-3400. Mailing Address: P.O. Box 383, Clarksville, TN 37041-0383. Tel.: 931-648-5780. Fax: 931-553-5179.
E-mail: info@customshousemuseumorg
Web Site: www.customshousemuseum.org
Founded: 1984.
Congressional District: 7
Key Personnel: Chm. Bd., Bill Hoy; Dir., Alan Robison; Chm. (V), Dan Hanley; Asst. Dir., Linda Maki; Pres. Guild, Mary Luther; Cur. Collections, Amy Andersen; Registrar, Amy Lewellen; Exhibit Technician, Randall Spurgeon; Cur. Education, Sue Lewis; Dir. Membership, Harriett Silvey; Public Rels. & Rentals Mgr., Terri Jordan; Museum Shop Mgr., Janie McGregor.
Personnel Profile: Full-Time Paid 8; Part-Time Paid 3; Part-Time Volunteers 2; Interns 1.
Governing Authority: nonprofit organization. Tax-exempt: 501(c)(3).
General Museum: housed in c.1898 Post Office and Customs House.
Collections: photographs; manuscripts; late 19th century horse-drawn vehicles; toys; clothing; art history of tobacco. Memory Lane: fire department, print shop, Mrs. Clarks drapers shop, 1842 log house.
Research Fields: history; genealogy.
Facilities: 400-vol. reference library; newly expanded area to rent for receptions, dinners & meetings; 200-seat fully accessible auditorium. Museum-related items for sale.
Activities: guided tours; lectures; theatrical performances; organized education programs; docent program; loan exhibitions.
Publications: monthly newsletter, Art-N-Facts; books, Edibles from the Archives; Clarksville In The Civil War, A Chronology; Nineteenth Century Heritage; Ordeal by Fire.
Hours & Admission Prices: Tues.-Sat. 10-5, Sun. 1-5. Adults $5, senior citizens $3, college students $2, children 6-18 $1; discounts to AAM, ICOM, TAM, SEMC, AAA & AARP members; members, children 5 and under & Sun. no charge. Closed major holidays. ♿
Attendance: 35,000 (accurate)
Membership: Senior Citizen $15; Senior Citizen Couple $20; Active Military Family $25; Family $30; Patron $50; Contributor $100; Founder $500.

MARGARET FORT TRAHERN GALLERY, College & Eighth Sts., Clarksville, TN 37044-0001. Mailing Address: P.O. Box 4677, Clarksville, TN 37044-0001. Tel.: 931-221-7333. Fax: 931-221-7432.
Web Site: www.apsu.edu/art/gallery/index.html
Founded: 1974.
Congressional District: 7
Key Personnel: Dept. Art, Dixie Webb.
Personnel Profile: Full-Time Paid 1.
Governing Authority: Austin Peay State University. Branch Gallery: Larson Gallery, Harned Hall Building. Tax-exempt: SPA6-B.
University Art Gallery.
Collections: contemporary prints; watercolors; Larson drawing collection; photography.
Activities: temporary & traveling exhibitions; formally organized education programs for adults; biennial & student annual exhibitions; biennial national drawing competition.
Publications: biennial exhibit catalog: Border to Border; exhibit announcement cards.
Hours & Admission Prices: Mon.-Fri. 9-4, Sat. 10-2, Sun. 1-4. No charge. Closed academic holidays. ♿
Attendance: 7,000

Cleveland

MUSEUM CENTER AT 5IVE POINTS, (M), 200 Inman St. E., Cleveland, TN 37311-6039. Tel.: 423-339-5745. Fax: 423-476-7922.
Founded: 1999.
Key Personnel: Exec. Dir., Lisa Simpson Lutts; Museum Shop Mgr., Tracy O'Connell.
Personnel Profile: Full-Time Paid 2; Part-Time Paid 4; Part-Time Volunteers 20.
Governing Authority: Tax-exempt.
History Museum.
Collections: local history & culture; photographs; personal artifacts.
Activities: special events; rental facilities; birthday parties.
Hours & Admission Prices: Tues.-Fri. 10-5, Sat. 10-3. Adults $5; discounts to AAM members; members no charge. ♿
Membership: Individual $25; Family $50; Sponsor $100; Friend $250; Supporter $500; Sustainer $1,000.

RED CLAY STATE HISTORIC PARK, 1140 Red Clay Park Rd., S.W., Cleveland, TN 37311-8386. Tel.: 423-478-0339.
Web Site: www.tennessee.gov/environment/parks/RedClay/
Founded: 1979.
Congressional District: 3
Key Personnel: Park Mgr., Carol Crabtree; Park Ranger, Erin Medley.
Personnel Profile: Full-Time Paid 5; Part-Time Paid 1; Part-Time Volunteers 1.
Governing Authority: state. Parent Institution: TN State Dept. of Environment & Conservation. Tax-exempt.
Historic Site Park: c.1832-38 seat of the Cherokee government & site of eleven general councils national affairs.
Collections: Paleo, Archaic, Mississippian, Woodland & historic period artifacts.
Research Fields: Cherokee removal story c.1832-1838.
Facilities: library of material dealing with Cherokee & American Indian culture, history & natural history available for research on premises; 19th-century Cherokee exhibit & artifact room; reading room; 54-seat auditorium.
Activities: guided tours; lectures; arts festivals; permanent exhibitions.
Hours & Admission Prices: Visitor Center: March-Nov. Sun.-Mon. 1-4:30, Tues.-Sat. 8-4:30; Dec.-Feb. call for hours. Park: March-Nov. daily 8am-sunset; Dec.-Feb. Mon.-Fri. 8-4:15. No charge; donations accepted. Park: closed Christmas. Visitor Center: closed Dec. 22 to New Year's Day. ♿
Attendance: 188,400 (accurate)

Clifton

T.S. STRIBLING MUSEUM, Clifton Library, 300 E. Water St., Clifton, TN 38425. Tel.: 931-676-3188.
E-mail: johnstonw@k12tn.net
Historic Site: housed in the former home of Pulitzer Prize-winning author, T.S. Stribling.
Collections: artifacts & memorabilia of the Stribling family.
Hours & Admission Prices: Tues.-Fri. 11:30-6.

Clinton

MUSEUM OF APPALACHIA, 2819 Andersonville Hwy., Clinton, TN 37716-6756. Mailing Address: P.O. Box 1189, Norris, TN 37828-1189. Tel.: 865-494-7680. Fax: 865-494-8957.
E-mail: museum@museumofappalachia.org

Web Site: www.museumofappalachia.org
Founded: 1967.
Congressional District: 3
Key Personnel: Exec. Dir. & Museum Shop Mgr., Elaine I. Meyer.
Personnel Profile: Full-Time Paid 11; Part-Time Paid 18; Part-Time Volunteers 6.
Governing Authority: Tax-exempt: 501(c)(3).
Appalachian theme; Historic Village and Folk Art Museum: housed in thirty restored pioneer log structures.
Collections: over 200,000 early American & pioneer artifacts. Historic Buildings: Mark Twain family cabin; Cantelever barn; school house; chapel.
Research Fields: culture, heritage, lifestyle of frontier people through study of artifacts; Southern Appalachia mountain region; genealogy.
Facilities: cafe; rental facilities. Crafts, antiques & other museum-related items for sale.
Activities: permanent exhibitions; seasonal Appalachian music; rental facilities. Museum Sponsors: 4th of July Celebration and Anvil Shoot; Student Heritage Day; Girl Scout Day; Tennessee Fall Homecoming; Christmas in Old Appalachia.
Publications: books, Music & Musical Instruments of the Southern Appalachian Mountains; Guns and Gun Making Tools of the Southern Appalachians; Baskets & Basketmakers of Southern Appalachia; A People and Their Quilts; Alex Stewart: Portrait of A Pioneer; The Museum of Appalachia Story. A People and Their Music.
Hours & Admission Prices: Seasonal hours. Adults $15, children 6-12 $5; discounts to senior citizens, groups & AAA members; members no charge.
Attendance: 175,000 (estimated)
Membership: Please call museum for details.

Collierville

BIBLICAL RESOURCE CENTER & MUSEUM, (M), 140 E. Mulberry, Collierville, TN 38017-2675. Tel.: 901-854-9578. Fax: 901-854-9883.
E-mail: info@biblical-museum.org
Web Site: www.biblical-museum.org
Founded: 1995.
Key Personnel: Chm. & C.E.O., Donald E. Bassett; Pres. (V), Larry Papasan; Museum Dir., Nancy W. Bassett; Collections Cur., L. Jacob Shock; Program Dir., Sara Hansen.
Personnel Profile: Full-Time Paid 2; Full-Time Volunteers 1; Part-Time Paid 2; Part-Time Volunteers 4; Interns 1.
Governing Authority: private; nonprofit organization. Tax-exempt: 501(c)(3).
Religious & History Museum.
Collections: biblical, Egyptian & Ancient Near Eastern archaeological artifacts & replicas.
Facilities: 820-vol. library of Biblical reference, ecclesiastical history, educational videos of Bible/Archaeology & Archaeological periodical; educational facilities; 300 sq. ft. exhibit space. Museum-related items for sale.
Activities: formal educational programs for children; guided tours; lectures; school loan service; traveling exhibitions; summer archeological workshop for students; travel programs.
Publications: quarterly newsletter.
Hours & Admission Prices: Tues.-Sat. 10-5. Groups $3 per person; discounts to AAM & ICOM members. Closed major holidays. ♿
Attendance: 10,500 (accurate)
Membership: Individual $25; Family $50.

Columbia

JAMES K. POLK ANCESTRAL HOME, (M), 301 W. 7th St., Columbia, TN 38401-3132. Mailing Address: P.O. Box 741, Columbia, TN 38402-0741. Tel.: 931-388-2354. Fax: 931-388-5971.
E-mail: jameskpolk@bellsouth.net
Web Site: www.jameskpolk.com
Founded: 1924.
Congressional District: 4
Key Personnel: Dir., John C. Holtzapple; Pres. (V), Tiny Jones; Cur. Collections, Thomas E. Price; Museum Shop Mgr., Gayle Davidson.
Personnel Profile: Full-Time Paid 2; Part-Time Paid 8; Part-Time Volunteers 45.
Governing Authority: society. Parent Institution: James K. Polk Memorial Association, Columbia, TN 38402. Tax-exempt: 501(c)(3).
Historic House Museum: 1816 James K. Polk Ancestral Home.
Collections: artifacts & documents that belonged to James K. Polk or relate to his presidency.
Research Fields: James K. Polk's political career; collections.
Facilities: 175-vol. library of books on James K. Polk available for use on premises. Postcards, & books for sale.
Activities: guided tours; permanent & temporary exhibitions; orientation video; outreach programs for area schools & nursing homes; lectures; discussion group; summer history camp.
Publications: brochure, Ancestral Home of James Knox Polk; booklet, A Special House; cookbook, Provisions & Politics.
Hours & Admission Prices: April-Oct. Mon.-Sat. 9-5, Sun. 1-5; Nov.-March Mon.-Sat. 9-4, Sun. 1-5. Adults $7, students 6-18 $4; discounts to groups, AAM members & senior citizens; members no charge. Closed New Year's Day; Thanksgiving; Christmas Eve & Day. ♿
Attendance: 9,945 (accurate)
Membership: Senior Citizen $30; Individual & Family $40.

Cookeville

COOKEVILLE DEPOT MUSEUM, 116 N. Cedar Ave., Cookeville, TN 38501. Mailing Address: Dept. of Leisure Svcs., P.O. Box 998, Cookeville, TN 38503-0998. Tel.: 931-528-8570. Fax: 931-526-1167.
E-mail: depot@cookeville-tn.org
Founded: 1984.
Congressional District: 6
Key Personnel: C.E.O. & Museums Admin., Judy Duke; Pres. (V), Carol Holland.
Personnel Profile: Full-Time Paid 2; Full-Time Volunteers 1; Part-Time Paid 1; Part-Time Volunteers 10.
Governing Authority: municipal government; nonprofit. Parent Institution: City of Cookeville. Subsidiary Institution: Department of Leisure Services. Tax-exempt.
Transportation Museum: built in 1909 by the Tennessee Central Railroad, the Cookeville depot is highlighted by its unique pagoda roof line.
Collections: photographs; memorabilia; artifacts of the Tennessee Central Railroad, particularly in Putnam County; two cabooses are open to visitors; 1913 Baldwin Ten Wheeler steam locomotive, static display.
Publications: biannual, The Highballer.
Hours & Admission Prices: Tues.-Sat. 10-4. No charge; donations accepted. Closed Good Friday; Independence Day; Labor Day; Thanksgiving; Christmas Eve & Day.
Attendance: 10,500 (estimated)
Membership: Family $15; Contributor $30; Sustainer $50; Benefactor $100; Preserver $200; Conductor $500.

Covington

TIPTON COUNTY MUSEUM, VETERAN'S MEMORIAL & NATURE CENTER, 751 Bert Johnston Ave., Covington, TN 38019-2414. Mailing Address: P.O. Box 768, Covington, TN 38019-0768. Tel.: 901-476-0242. Fax: 901-476-0261.
E-mail: afisher@covingtontn.com
Web Site: www.tiptonco.com/museum.htm
Founded: 1998.
Congressional District: 8
Key Personnel: Dir., Alice Fisher; Program Coord., Elizabeth Newman.
Personnel Profile: Full-Time Paid 3.
Governing Authority: private; nonprofit organization. Tax-exempt.
History Museum & Nature Center.
Collections: military history; environmental education; Tipton County residents personal artifacts.
Facilities: 20 acre wildlife area; nature trail; wetlands.
Activities: history exhibits; programs for adults & children.
Publications: newsletter.
Hours & Admission Prices: Tues.-Fri. 9-5, Sat. 9-3. No charge; donations accepted. Closed major holidays. ♿
Attendance: 7,000 (accurate)
Membership: Individual, Senior & Military $20; Family $30; Contributor $50; Philanthropist $100; Benefactor $200; Corporate $500 & up.

Cowan

COWAN RAILROAD MUSEUM, 108 Front St., Cowan, TN 37318-0053. Mailing Address: P.O. Box 53, Cowan, TN 37318-0053. Tel.: 931-967-3078.
Railroad Museum: housed in a former railroad depot, c.1904.
Collections: railroad history & artifacts; photographs; steam locomotive; flat car; caboose; Fairmont motor cars; HO scale model railroads.
Hours & Admission Prices: May-Oct. Thurs.-Sat. 10-4, Sun. 1-4; other times by appointment.

Cross Plains

CROSS PLAINS HERITAGE MUSEUM, LIBRARY & ARCHIVES, 7821 Hwy. 25 E., Cross Plains, TN 37049-4851. Tel.: 615-654-2992.
History Museum.
Collections: local history & culture; photographs; personal artifacts.

Hours & Admission Prices: Tues. & Thurs. 10-4. No charge.

Dover

FORT DONELSON NATIONAL BATTLEFIELD, 120 Fort Donelson Rd., Dover, TN 37058. Mailing Address: P.O. Box 434, Dover, TN 37058-0434. Tel.: 931-232-5706 (Visitor Center) & 5348 (office). Fax: 931-232-6331.
E-mail: fodo_ranger_activities@nps.gob
Web Site: www.nps.gov/fodo
Founded: 1928.
Congressional District: 8
Key Personnel: Supt., Steven A. McCoy; Chief Interpreter & Resource Mgr., Michael Manning.
Governing Authority: federal. A unit of the National Park Service, U.S. Department of the Interior, Washington, DC 20240. Tax-exempt.
National Battlefield Museum.
Collections: Civil War artifacts; archival materials.
Research Fields: Civil War history.
Facilities: library of Civil War books available for use on premises.
Activities: self-guided tours; lectures; films; formally organized education programs for children, adults & undergraduate college students; permanent exhibitions; interpretive demonstrations.
Publications: booklet, Eastern National Parks & Monument Association.
Hours & Admission Prices: Office: Mon.-Fri. 8-4:30. Visitor Center: daily 8-4:30. No charge; donations accepted. Closed Thanksgiving; Christmas. ♿

Ducktown

DUCKTOWN BASIN MUSEUM, 212 Burra Burra St., Ducktown, TN 37326. Mailing Address: P.O. Box 458, Ducktown, TN 37326-0458. Tel.: 423-496-5778.
Key Personnel: Dir., Ken Rush
History Museum: housed on the Burra Burra mine site. Listed on the National Register of Historic Places.
Collections: history of mining & processing operations.
Facilities: Museum-related items for sale.
Hours & Admission Prices: May-Oct. Mon.-Sat. 10-4:30; Nov.-April Mon.-Sat. 9:30-4. Adults $4, seniors $3, children 13-18 $1, children 12 & under $.50. Closed Thanksgiving; Christmas. ♿

Englewood

ENGLEWOOD TEXTILE MUSEUM, 17 S. Niota St., Englewood, TN 37329-3245. Tel.: 423-887-5455.
History Museum.
Collections: textile industry history; life of women in the mills.
Hours & Admission Prices: Mon.-Sat. 10-5. No charge; donations accepted. Closed major holidays.

Farragut

FARRAGUT FOLKLIFE MUSEUM, 11408 Municipal Center Dr., Farragut, TN 37934-2830. Tel.: 865-966-7057. Fax: 865-675-2096.
E-mail: julia.jones@townoffarragut.org
Web Site: www.townoffarragut.org/arts.html
Founded: 1986.
Congressional District: 2
Key Personnel: Museum Coord., Sarah Julia Jones; Public Rels., Chelsea Riemann; Museum Shop Mgr., Donna Hawn.
Personnel Profile: Full-Time Paid 1; Part-Time Volunteers 73.
Governing Authority: municipal. Tax-exempt: 170(b)(1)(A).
History Museum.
Collections: East Tennessee area artifacts; personal artifacts of Admiral David Glasgow Farragut, first Admiral of the U.S. Navy & Civil War hero.
Facilities: 2,000 sq. ft. exhibit space. Museum-related items for sale.
Activities: docent program; guided tours; lectures; special events; open houses. Annual Event: Membership Buffet.
Publications: newsletter, Farragut Folklife Museum Newsletter.
Hours & Admission Prices: Mon.-Fri. 10-4:30. No charge; donations accepted. Closed New Year's week; Martin Luther King Jr. Day; Good Friday; Memorial Day; Independence Day; Labor Day; Thanksgiving & day after; Christmas week. ♿
Attendance: 4,590 (accurate)
Membership: Student $1; Individual $24; Family $36; Business $50; Lifetime $500.

Fayetteville

FAYETTEVILLE LINCOLN COUNTY MUSEUM AND CIVIC CENTER, 521 Main St., S., Fayetteville, TN 37334-3447. Mailing Address: 2270 Lewisburg Hwy., Fayetteville, TN 37334-6449. Tel.: 931-433-2921.
Web Site: www.flcmuseum.com
Key Personnel: Pres., Marie Caldwell; Vice Pres., Danny Bryant; Sec., Jim Harwell, DVM; Treas., Mark Mitchell; Dir., Farris Beasley, DVM; Dir., Eugene Ham; Dir., Ley Jean; Dir., Patty Patrick; Dir., Dusten Stewart; Dir., Kay Ward-Woods; Dir., Delbert Wicks
History Museum.
Collections: James Buchanan Memorial Courtyard; Admiral Frank Kelso; military artifacts; one-room schoolhouse; country store & post office; agricultural tools; Native American; fossils; medical equipment; space & missle command.
Hours & Admission Prices: May-Nov. Thurs.-Sat. 12:30-4:30.

Franklin

CARNTON PLANTATION, (M), 1345 Carnton Lane, Franklin, TN 37064-3259. Tel.: 615-794-0903. Fax: 615-794-6563.
E-mail: info@carnton.org
Web Site: www.carnton.org
Founded: 1977.
Congressional District: 6
Key Personnel: Interim Exec. Dir., Margie Thessin; Asst. Dir., Lisa Patton; Asst. Dir., Eric Jacobson; Staff Historian, James Redford; Coord. Education, Katie Tate; Museum Shop Mgr. & Collections, Joanna Stephens.
Personnel Profile: Full-Time Paid 7; Part-Time Paid 5; Part-Time Volunteers 5.
Governing Authority: private; nonprofit organization. Tax-exempt: 501(c)(3).
Historic Site: 1826 Federal House and Outbuildings.
Collections: furniture, decorative arts & artifacts connected to the McGavock family. Historic Structures: 1826 house including gardens & grounds, slave house, spring house and smokehouse; restored garden.
Research Fields: Civil War; gardens & landscaping; plantation life; slaves; the McGavock family.
Facilities: Civil War-related books & other museum-related items for sale.
Activities: guided tours; lectures; arts festivals; concerts; docent program; education programs for children; volunteer program. Annual Events: Southern Folklife Festival; Anniversary of Battle of Franklin in November; Christmas at Carnton.
Publications: newsletter, Columns.
Hours & Admission Prices: Mon.-Sat. 9-5, Sun. 1-5; last tour at 4. Adults $12, seniors $10, children 6-12 $5; discount to groups of 10 or more; children under 5 no charge.
Attendance: 45,000 (accurate)
Membership: Individual $40; Family $55; Plantation $100; Carnton $250; Carrie McGavock $500; Randal McGavock $1,000.

THE CARTER HOUSE, 1140 Columbia Ave., Franklin, TN 37064-3617. Mailing Address: P.O. Box 555, Franklin, TN 37065-0555. Tel.: 615-791-1861. Fax: 615-794-1327.
E-mail: carterhouse1864@aol.com
Web Site: www.carterhouse1864.com
Congressional District: 6
Key Personnel: Exec. Dir., David Fraley; Cur., Dennis Anderson; Cur., Bobby Hargrove; Office Mgr., Angell Wallace; Gift Shop Mgr., Alan Corry.
Personnel Profile: Full-Time Paid 2; Part-Time Paid 5; Part-Time Volunteers 3.
Governing Authority: state. Tax-exempt.
Historic Site & Museum: housed in the former home of Fountain Branch Carter built in 1830 & located on the site of the Battle of Franklin. Listed on the National Register of Historic Places.
Collections: Civil War artifacts from the Battle of Franklin includes clothing, uniforms, swords & medical sections.
Research Fields: Civil War.
Facilities: library of Civil War material available on the premises. Books, prints & other museum-related items for sale.
Activities: guided tours; film presentation; permanent exhibitions.
Publications: books: Battle of Franklin, Crownover; Carter House-Robinson; The Pillaged Grave of Col. Shy; Recipe Book; brochure; newsletter.
Hours & Admission Prices: Jan. Mon.-Sat. 9-5; Feb. & Oct.-Dec. Mon.-Sat. 9-4, Sun. 1-4; March-Sept. Mon.-Sat. 9-5, Sun. 1-5. Adults $10, seniors 65 & over $9, children 7-14 $6; discounts to military; children 6 & under and members no charge. Closed New Year's Eve & Day; Easter; Independence Day; Thanksgiving; Christmas Eve & Day. ♿
Attendance: 42,000 (estimated)
Membership: Individual $25; Family $40; Gen. Frank Cheatham Society $100; Gen. Patrick Cleburne Society $250; Gen. Jacob Cox Society (Corporate) $500; Captain Tod Carter Society $1,000.

Gallatin

SUMNER COUNTY MUSEUM, 183 W. Main St., Gallatin, TN 37066-3252. Tel.: 615-451-3738. Fax: 651-451-0878.
E-mail: contact@sumnercountymuseum.org
Web Site: www.sumnercountymuseum.org
Key Personnel: Dir., Juanita Frazor; Cur., Allen Haynes
History Museum.
Collections: local history & culture; period artifacts; early pioneer life; Civil War; World War I & II.
Hours & Admission Prices: April-Oct. Wed.-Sat. 1-4:30. Adults $3, children 6-12 $1; children under 6 no charge.

Gatlinburg

ARROWMONT SCHOOL OF ARTS & CRAFTS, 556 Pkwy., Gatlinburg, TN 37738-3202. Mailing Address: P.O. Box 567, Gatlinburg, TN 37738-0567. Tel.: 865-436-5860. Fax: 865-430-4101.
E-mail: info@arrowmont.org
Web Site: www.arrowmont.org
Founded: 1945.
Congressional District: 1
Key Personnel: Dir., David Willard; Chm. Bd. (V), Bob Alcorn; Treas., Julia Clinton; Galleries & Collection, Karen Green; Education, Bill Griffith; Public Rels., Kimberly Newman; Museum Shop Mgr., Angela Wiemken.
Personnel Profile: Full-Time Paid 23; Part-Time Paid 5; Part-Time Volunteers 12; Interns 4.
Governing Authority: private; nonprofit organization. Parent Institution: Pi Beta Phi fraternity. Tax-exempt: 501(c)(3).
Art Gallery.
Collections: arts & crafts from 1950 to present.
Facilities: 5,000-vol. library of art & art making materials; 175-seat auditorium; 175-seat cafeteria; 10 studios; 3,700 sq. ft. exhibit space. Books, supplies & art-related items for sale.
Activities: concerts; formal education programs for adults, children & Univ. of Tennessee students; guided tours; lectures; loan, temporary & traveling exhibitions; mobile vans. Museum Sponsors: resident artist, studio assistant, work study & gallery internship programs.
Publications: quarterly, Arrowmont School of Arts & Crafts Newsletter; quarterly newsletter magazine, The Arrow; Spring & Summer: biannually, Workshop Schedule; Descriptive Poster; electronic newsletter, E-Visions; annual workshop schedule.
Hours & Admission Prices: Mon.-Sat. 8-5. No charge; donations accepted. Closed Christmas to New Year's Day. ♿
Attendance: 4,150 (estimated)

GUINNESS WORLD RECORDS MUSEUM, Baskins Square Mall, 631 Pkwy., Ste. B-11, Gatlinburg, TN 37738-3258. Tel.: 865-436-9100 & 430-7800.
World Record Museum.
Collections: world record feats, facts & record holders; photographs; personal artifacts; movie memorabilia.
Activities: special events.
Hours & Admission Prices: Daily 9am. Adults 12 & over $9.99, children 6-11 $5.99; children 5 & under no charge.

HOLLYWOOD STAR CARS MUSEUM, 914 Pkwy., Gatlinburg, TN 37738-3104. Tel.: 865-430-2200.
Web Site: www.starcarstn.com
Formerly: Star Cars Museum
Key Personnel: Owner, Charles Moore
Car Museum.
Collections: cars from Hollywood movies & TV shows of the last 50 years.
Hours & Admission Prices: Daily 9am to 10pm. Adult $11.99, children 6-12 $6.99 children under 6 no charge.

SALT AND PEPPER SHAKER MUSEUM, 527 Cherry St., Gatlinburg, TN 37738-4706. Tel.: 888-778-1802; 865-430-5515.
Web Site: www.thesaltandpeppershakermuseum.com
Key Personnel: Owner, Andrea Ludden; Owner, Rolf Ludden
General Museum.
Collections: over 20,000 salt & pepper shakers from around the world; pepper mills.
Facilities: Museum-related items for sale.
Hours & Admission Prices: Daily 10-4. Adults $3; children 12 & under no charge.

SUGARLANDS VISITOR CENTER, Great Smoky Mountains National Park, 107 Park Headquarters Rd., Gatlinburg, TN 37738-4102. Tel.: 865-436-1291 & 1200. Fax: 865-436-1220.
E-mail: GRSM_smokies_information@nps.gov
Web Site: www.nps.gov/grsm
Founded: 1961.
Congressional District: 1
Key Personnel: Supt., Mike Tollefson; District Supvr., Tyrone Brandyburg; Visitor Center Supvr., Tim Cruise.
Personnel Profile: Full-Time Paid 3; Part-Time Paid 2; Part-Time Volunteers 50; Interns 1.
Governing Authority: federal. Parent Institution: National Park Service. Tax-exempt.
Park Museum.
Collections: herbarium & insect specimens; bird & mammal skins; wet specimens (amphibians & reptiles); art collection; photographs of park habitats; freeze-dried specimens of birds & smaller mammals, mounted larger specimens; plant specimens & plastic reproductions of reptiles, amphibians & fungi & plants; herbarium.
Research Fields: natural & cultural history.
Facilities: 5,000-vol. library of general reference books available for use by permission on premises only; 150-seat auditorium. Postcards, slides, film & natural history books for sale.
Activities: permanent exhibitions; general orientation film about the park.
Publications: varied scientific reports.
Hours & Admission Prices: Jan.-Feb & Dec. daily 8-4:30; March & Nov. daily 8-5; April-May & Sept.-Oct. daily 8-6; June-Aug. daily 8-7. No charge; donations accepted. Closed Christmas. ♿
Attendance: 874,393 (accurate)

Germantown

THE P.T. BOAT MUSEUM & LIBRARY, 1384 Cordova Rd., Ste. 2, Germantown, TN 38138-2219. Mailing Address: P.O. Box 38070, Germantown, TN 38183-0070. Tel.: 901-755-8440. Fax: 901-751-0522.
E-mail: ptboats@ptboats.org
Web Site: www.ptboats.org
Founded: 1946.
Congressional District: 10
Key Personnel: C.E.O. & Treas., Alyce N. Guthrie; Pres. (V), Charles B. Jones; P.T. Boat Cur., Don Shannon; Administrative Asst., Allyson Bethune; Museum Shop Mgr., Rick Bethune.
Personnel Profile: Full-Time Paid 2; Part-Time Paid 1; Part-Time Volunteers 1.
Governing Authority: private; nonprofit organization. P.T. Boats, Inc. Tax-exempt: 501(c)(3).
Maritime, Naval Museum: located at Battleship Cove.
Collections: World War II P.T. boats; one-man Japanese suicide demolition boat; books, diaries, insignias, memorabilia of 43 operating squadrons of World War II P.T. boats; U.S. mosquito fleet; tenders; bases; films; archives; 10,000 photographs; plans.
Research Fields: World War II P.T. boat operations; bases; tender ships.
Facilities: 1,000-vol. library. Books & museum-related items for sale.
Activities: lectures; films; restoration; research; photographic services. Museum Sponsors: reunions & regional meetings.
Publications: semiannual newsmagazine; books, The U.S. Mosquito Fleet; Early Elco P.T. Boats; P.T. Squadrons, Bases, Tenders ALL HANDS.
Hours & Admission Prices: Battle Ship Cove: Spring to May 23 daily 9-4:30; Summer daily 9-5. Adults $14, children 6-12 $8, seniors $12; members & military in uniform no charge. Germantown Headquarters: Mon.-Fri. 8-4. Closed New Year's Eve & Day; Independence Day; Reunion week; Thanksgiving; Christmas week.
Attendance: 100,000 (estimated)
Membership: Veteran of P.T. Any Amount; Non-Veteran of P.T. $25; Overseas $49; Citation $500; Bronze Medal of Honor $1,000; Silver Medal of Honor $5,000; Gold Medal of Honor $10,000.

Goodlettsville

MANSKER'S STATION & BOWEN PLANTATION HOUSE, 705 Caldwell Lane, Moss Wright Park, Goodlettsville, TN 37072. Tel.: 615-859-3678.
History Museum: housed in the former home of Captain William Bowen, c.1787. Mansker's Station: reconstructed 1779 fort.
Collections: House: period furnishings. Fort: 18th century pioneer life.
Activities: demonstrations; living history encampments.
Hours & Admission Prices: Tues.-Sat. 9-12 & 1-5.

Grand Junction

NATIONAL BIRD DOG MUSEUM, 505 Hwy. 57, Grand Junction, TN 38039-6059. Mailing Address: P.O. Box 774, Grand Junction, TN 38039-0774. Tel.: 731-764-2058. Fax: 731-764-3004.
Web Site: www.birddogfoundation.com
Founded: 1989.
Key Personnel: Exec. Dir., David Smith; Sec., Barbara Sweeney; Education Coord. & Librarian, Lucy Cogbill
General Museum.
Collections: pointing dog & retriever breeds history; art; paintings; photography; memorabilia; hunting; field trial activities; shooting sports; early history of the National Field Trials.
Facilities: library. Museum-related items for sale.
Activities: special events; meetings.
Hours & Admission Prices: Tues.-Fri. 9-2, Sat. 10-4, Sun. 1-4. No charge; donations accepted. ♿
Membership: Youth Supporter $10; Benefactor $50; Life Benefactor & Corporate $500; Life Patron & Patron Memorial $1,200; Founder $5,000.

Granville

GRANVILLE MUSEUM, INC., Clover St., Granville, TN 38564. Mailing Address: P.O. Box 26, Granville, TN 38564-0026. Tel.: 931-653-4511. Fax: 615-443-7117.
Web Site: www.granvillemuseum.com
Founded: 1999.
Key Personnel: Dir., Randall Clemons; Treas., Suzanne Stafford; Cur., Patsy Yates; Archivist, Anna Moffitt; Museum Shop Mgr., Joe Moore.
Personnel Profile: Part-Time Volunteers 19.
Governing Authority: private; nonprofit organization. Tax-exempt: 501(c)(3).
History Museum.
Collections: business; military; schools; sports; music; church; family; river; clothing; early 1900s home; 1880 general store.
Facilities: restaurant. Museum-related items for sale.
Publications: biannual newsletter.
Hours & Admission Prices: Wed.-Sat. 12-3; other times by appointment. No charge; donations accepted.
Attendance: 8,500 (estimated)
Membership: Friends $25.

Gray

EAST TENNESSEE STATE UNIVERSITY AND GENERAL SHALE BRICK NATURAL HISTORY MUSEUM AND GRAY FOSSIL SITE, (M), 1212 Suncrest Dr., Gray, TN 37615-4114. Mailing Address: P.O. Box 9221, Gray, TN 37615-9221. Tel.: 423-439-3659; 866-202-6223.
E-mail: info@grayfossilmuseum.com
Web Site: www.grayfossilmuseum.com
Founded: 2007.
Congressional District: 1
Key Personnel: Dir., Jeanne L. Zavada.
Personnel Profile: Full-Time Paid 9; Part-Time Volunteers 100; Interns 3.
Governing Authority: Parent Institution: East Tennessee State University. Tax-exempt.
Natural History Museum.
Collections: fossils from alligators, camels, sloth, elephant, rhino, tapirs & peccary.
Major Exhibits: Dinosaur Revolution (T), 1/16/10-5/16/10; Tusks! (T), 5/29/10-9/6/10.
Research Fields: paleontology; sedimentology; geomatics; geomorphology; geology; paleoecology.
Hours & Admission Prices: Daily 8:30-5. Gray Fossil Site Walk-in Tour: adults 5, seniors 65 & over $4, children 5-12 $3. All access Pass: adults $10, seniors 65 & over $9, children 5-12 $7. Closed New Year's Day; Thanksgiving; Christmas. ♿
Attendance: 90,426 (accurate)

Greeneville

ANDREW JOHNSON NATIONAL HISTORIC SITE, 101 N. College St., Greeneville, TN 37743-5607. Mailing Address: 121 Monument Ave., Greeneville, TN 37743-5552. Tel.: 423-638-3551 (Visitor Center) & 639-3711 (Admin.). Fax: 423-638-9194 (Visitor Center) & 798-0754 (Admin.).
Web Site: www.nps.gov/anjo/
Founded: 1942.
Congressional District: 1
Key Personnel: Supt., Lizzie Watts; Chief Operations, Jim Small; Museum Shop Mgr., Daniel Luther.
Personnel Profile: Full-Time Paid 8; Part-Time Paid 3; Part-Time Volunteers 1.
Governing Authority: federal. Parent Institution: U.S. Dept. of the Interior, National Park Service, Southeast Region, Appalachian Cluster, Atlanta Federal Center, 1924 Building, 100 Alabama St., S.W., Atlanta, GA 30303. Tax-exempt.
History Museum and Historic Houses.
Collections: artifacts of the Johnson period, c.1820s-1875. Historic Houses: 1830s-1851 Johnson House; 1830s-1840s Andrew Johnson Tailor Shop; 1851-1875 Andrew Johnson Homestead.
Research Fields: history.
Facilities: 550-vol. park library available on premises; visitor center; tailor shop complex; early 1830s-1851 house; 1851-1875 homestead; Andrew Johnson National Cemetery. Books & other museum-related items for sale.
Activities: ranger guided tours; self-guided tours; Video interpretive film at visitor center; film: Andrew Johnson Defender of the Constitution; film loan service; off-site programs upon request. Special Events: Wreath Laying at AJ Cemetery; Memorial Service at AJ Cemetery; Junior Ranger program.
Publications: park folder, Andrew Johnson National Historic Site; Impeachment Folder; Cemetery Folder; Andrew Johnson and His Slaves Folder; Junior Ranger Program.
Hours & Admission Prices: Site: daily 9-5. House Tours: 9:30, 10:30, 11:30, 1:30, 2:30, 3:30, 4:30 (tickets available at Visitor Center). Closed New Year's Day; Thanksgiving; Christmas. ♿
Attendance: 48,553 (accurate)

DOAK HOUSE MUSEUM, Tusculum College, Greeneville, TN 37743. Mailing Address: Tusculum College, P.O. Box 5026, Greeneville, TN 37743-0001. Tel.: 423-636-8554 & 7348. Fax: 423-638-7166.
E-mail: clucas@tusculum.edu
Web Site: www.doakhouse.tusculum.edu
Founded: 1980.
Congressional District: 1
Key Personnel: Dir., George Collins; Assoc. Dir. & Cur., Cindy L. Lucas.
Personnel Profile: Full-Time Paid 2; Part-Time Paid 1; Part-Time Volunteers 24.
Governing Authority: college. Tax-exempt: 501(c)(3).
College Museum; located in home of Samuel W. Doak, founder of Tusculum College. Listed on the National Register of Historic Places.
Collections: college-related artifacts; East Tennessee education artifacts & documents; period furniture.
Hours & Admission Prices: Mon.-Fri. 9-5; other times by appointment. Adults $2, children $1; discounts to AAM members. Closed New Year's Day; Good Friday; Memorial Day; Independence Day; Labor Day; Thanksgiving Day & day after; last week in Dec. & first week in Jan.
Attendance: 6,509 (accurate)

NATHANAEL GREENE MUSEUM, 101 W. McKee St., Greeneville, TN 37743-4813. Tel.: 423-636-1558.
E-mail: director@nathanaelgreenemuseum.com
Web Site: nathanaelgreenemuseum.com
Heritage Museum.
Collections: local history & heritage; photographs; personal artifacts; early furnishings.
Hours & Admission Prices: Tues.-Sat. 10-4; other times by appointment. No charge; donations accepted.

PRESIDENT ANDREW JOHNSON MUSEUM AND LIBRARY, Tusculum College, Greeneville, TN 37743. Mailing Address: Tusculum College, P.O. Box 5026, Greeneville, TN 37743-0001. Tel.: 423-636-7348. Fax: 423-638-7166.
E-mail: gcollins@tusculum.edu
Web Site: www.ajmuseum.tusculum.edu
Founded: 1993.
Congressional District: 1
Key Personnel: Dir., George Collins; Museum Asst., Kathy Cuff.
Personnel Profile: Full-Time Paid 2; Part-Time Volunteers 9.
Governing Authority: private college; nonprofit. Tax-exempt: 501(c)(3)
Presidential Library: housed in 1841 college building. Listed on the National Register of Historic Places.
Collections: political memorabilia; music sheets; manuscripts; Johnson family possessions; books; pamphlets; maps; photographs; newspapers; printed & written media related to the growth, development & history of Tusculum College; college artifacts.
Hours & Admission Prices: Mon.-Fri. 9-5. No charge. Closed New Year's Day; Good Friday; Memorial Day; Independence Day; Labor Day; Thanksgiving & the day after; last week of Dec. & first week in Jan. ♿
Attendance: 2,800 (accurate)

Halls

THE VETERANS' MUSEUM, 100 Veterans' Dr., Halls, TN 38040-1342. Tel.: 731-836-7400.
Web Site: www.dyaab.us
Founded: 1997.
Congressional District: 8
Key Personnel: Dir., Chm. & Pres. (V), Patricia M. Higdon; Cur., Bernard M. Higdon; Administrative Asst. & Museum Shop Mgr., Lisa Godsey.
Personnel Profile: Full-Time Paid 1; Part-Time Volunteers 5.
Governing Authority: Parent Institution: The Dyersburg Army Air Base Memorial Assoc., Inc. Tax-exempt.
Military History Museum.
Collections: WWI & II, Korea, Vietnam, & Desert Storm memorabilia; military vehicles; photographs; documents; diaries; personal & official letters; murals; personal artifacts; microfilm.
Research Fields: WWII history.
Facilities: library.
Activities: tours; special programs. Museum Sponsors: Armed Forces Day in November; Christmas Music in December.
Publications: members' newsletter.
Hours & Admission Prices: Sat.-Tues. 2-5. No charge; donations accepted. ♿
Attendance: 4,000 (accurate)
Membership: Individual $50.

Harrogate

ABRAHAM LINCOLN LIBRARY & MUSEUM, LINCOLN MEMORIAL UNIVERSITY, (M), 6965 Cumberland Gap Pkwy., Harrogate, TN 37752. Mailing Address: P.O. Box 2006, Harrogate, TN 37752. Tel.: 423-869-6235. Fax: 423-869-6350.
E-mail: thomas.mackie@lmunet.edu
Web Site: lmunet.edu/museum
Founded: 1897.
Congressional District: 4
Key Personnel: Dir., Thomas Mackie; Cur. & Asst. Dir., Steven Wilson; Education Coord., Program & Tourism Dir., Carol Campbell; Museum Archivist, Michelle Ganz; Guest Svcs., Jonathan Smallwood; Admin. Asst., Barbara Garman.
Personnel Profile: Full-Time Paid 5; Part-Time Paid 1; Part-Time Volunteers 5.
Governing Authority: board of advisors. Parent Institution: Lincoln Memorial University. Tax-exempt: 501(c)(3).
History Museum.
Collections: Abraham Lincoln & Civil War materials: 30,000 artifacts; books; manuscripts; statuary; engravings; sheet music; pamphlets.
Major Exhibits: Abraham Lincoln and the Presidents (T), 11/09-8/10.
Research Fields: Abraham Lincoln; the field of Lincolniana; Civil War music, politics & military aspects of war.
Facilities: library; workshops; reading room; 140-seat auditorium & theater.
Activities: guided tours; permanent exhibitions; student training programs.
Publications: The Lincoln Herald; Lincoln Letters.
Hours & Admission Prices: Mon.-Fri. 10-5, Sat. 12-5, Sun. 1-5. Adults $5, senior citizens $3.50, children 6-12 $3; discounts to groups, AAA & AAM members; children under 6 no charge. Closed New Year's Day; Easter; Thanksgiving; Christmas.
Attendance: 13,500 (accurate)

Hendersonville

HISTORIC ROCK CASTLE, 139 Rock Castle Lane, Hendersonville, TN 37075-4522. Tel.: 615-824-0502; 866-949-0502. Fax: 615-824-3342.
E-mail: rkcastle@bellsouth.net
Web Site: www.historicrockcastle.com
Founded: 1981.
Congressional District: 6
Key Personnel: Pres. (V), Kenneth Hoppes.
Personnel Profile: Full-Time Paid 1; Part-Time Paid 3; Part-Time Volunteers 30.
Historic House Museum.
Collections: local history & culture; period furnishings; photographs.
Facilities: Museum-related items for sale.
Activities: rental facilities; special events. Museum Sponsors: Colonial Fair in the Fall.
Hours & Admission Prices: Call for hours.
Membership: Individual & Family $50; Surveyor $100; Patron $500; General's Club $1,000; Daniel Smith Society $2,500 & up.

Henning

ALEX HALEY HOME AND MUSEUM, 200 S. Church St., Henning, TN 38041-7201. Tel.: 731-738-2240.
Key Personnel: Dir., Baris Douglas
Historic House Museum: housed in the boyhood home of author & Pulitzer Prize winner, Alex Haley. Listed on the National Register of Historic Places.
Collections: period furnishings; personal artifacts.
Hours & Admission Prices: Tues.-Sat. 10-5, Sun. 1-5.

FORT PILLOW STATE HISTORIC PARK, 3122 Park Rd., Henning, TN 38041-5210. Tel.: 731-738-5581 & 5731. Fax: 731-738-9117.
Web Site: www.state.tn.us/environment/parks/FortPillow/index.shtml
History Museum.
Collections: Civil War artifacts; local history & culture; photographs.
Facilities: nature trails.
Activities: video; guided tours; educational programs.
Hours & Admission Prices: Park: daily 8am to sunset. Museum: daily 8-11:30 & 12:30-4. No charge. Closed Thanksgiving; Christmas Eve & Day.

Hermitage

THE HERMITAGE: HOME OF PRESIDENT ANDREW JACKSON, 4580 Rachel's Lane, Hermitage, TN 37076-1331. Tel.: 615-889-2941. Fax: 615-889-9909.
E-mail: info@thehermitage.com
Web Site: www.thehermitage.com
Founded: 1889.
Congressional District: 5
Key Personnel: Regent, Martha Cooper; Chief Cur. & Dir. Museum Svcs., Marsha A. Mullin; Archaeologist, Daniel Brock; Dir. Finance, Carolyn Faulkenberry; Dir. Mktg., Paula Hankins; Guest Svcs., Tonoa Foster-Freeman; Exec. Asst. & Membership, Jane Maggard.
Personnel Profile: Full-Time Paid 40; Part-Time Paid 40; Interns 9.
Governing Authority: nonprofit organization. Parent Institution: Ladies' Hermitage Assn.; trust deed from state of TN. Tax-exempt: 501(c)(3).
Historic House.
Collections: archaeological; architectural; horticultural; gardens & grounds; furnishings; costumes; manuscripts; family possessions; carriages. Historic Buildings: 1804 log cabin; 1821-1836 Hermitage mansion & outbuildings; 1836 Tulip Grove mansion; 1823; Old Hermitage church; 1833 President's Tomb.
Research Fields: Andrew Jackson & his family; 19th-century horticulture & gardens; slave life.
Facilities: library; 120-seat restaurant; meeting & party facilities; visitor center. Books & museum-related items for sale.
Activities: Hermitage Mansion restoration; orientation film; temporary exhibitions; tour; school & adult education programs; archaeology programs.
Publications: guidebook.
Hours & Admission Prices: April-Oct. 15 daily 8:30-5; Oct. 16-March daily 9-4:30. Adults $17, senior citizens $14, students 13-18 $11, children 6-12 $7; discounts to groups, AAA, AAM & ICOM members; children 5 & under and members no charge. Closed Thanksgiving; Christmas. ♿
Attendance: 235,603 (accurate)
Membership: Student & Teacher $20; Senior $40; Individual $45; Dual $50; Family $60; Congressman's Circle $125; Senator's Circle $500; General's Circle $1,000.

Hohenwald

MERIWETHER LEWIS NATIONAL MONUMENT, 189 Meriwether Lewis Park, Hohenwald, TN 38462-5591. Mailing Address: National Park Service, Natchez Trace Pkwy., 2680 Natchez Trace Pkwy., Tupelo, MS 38804. Tel.: 800-305-7417. Fax: 662-680-4034.
Web Site: www.nps.gov/natr
Founded: 1936.
Congressional District: 3
Key Personnel: U.S. Ranger, Terry Kelly; District Ranger, Dave Hajdik.
Personnel Profile: Full-Time Paid 5; Part-Time Volunteers 2.
Governing Authority: federal. Affiliated with National Park Service, Natchez Trace Pkwy., 2680 Natchez Trace Pkwy., Tupelo, MS 38804. Tax-exempt.
Historic Site Museum: 1809 death & burial site of Meriwether Lewis.
Collections: pertaining to Lewis' life & death, 1774-1809, Lewis' grave & monument.
Facilities: 34 campground & picnic areas.
Activities: Annual Event: Craft Fair in October.
Hours & Admission Prices: Daily 8-5. No charge.
Attendance: 9,000 (estimated)

Humboldt

WEST TENNESSEE REGIONAL ART CENTER, 1200 Main St., Humboldt, TN 38343-3339. Mailing Address: P.O. Box 951, Humboldt, TN 38343-0951. Tel.: 731-784-1787. Fax: 901-784-1573.
Web Site: www.wtrac.tn.org
Founded: 1994.
Congressional District: 8
Key Personnel: Chm. Bd., Charles Guy; Treas, Carolyn Barnett; Cur., Bill Hickerson.
Personnel Profile: Full-Time Paid 1; Part-Time Volunteers 12.
Governing Authority: Tax-exempt.
Art Center.
Collections: fine arts.
Hours & Admission Prices: Mon.-Fri. 9-4:30, Sat.-Sun. group tours by appointment. Upstairs Gallery: $2; Downstairs Gallery: no charge. Closed holidays. ♿
Attendance: 10,000 (estimated)

Hurricane Mills

COAL MINER'S DAUGHTER MUSEUM, 1877 Hurricane Mills Rd., Hurricane Mills, TN 37078. Tel.: 931-296-1840.
Web Site: www.lorettalynn.com
History Museum.
Collections: Loretta Lynn's career including memorabilia & awards; photographs; personal artifacts.
Hours & Admission Prices: Daily 9-5. Museum: no charge. Home Tours: adults $12, children 6-12 $6.

Jackson

CASEY JONES HOME AND RAILROAD MUSEUM, Casey Jones Village, 30 Casey Lane, Jackson, TN 38305. Mailing Address: P.O. Box 11597, Jackson, TN 38308-0126. Tel.: 731-668-1222. Fax: 731-664-7782.
E-mail: casey@caseyjones.com
Web Site: www.caseyjonesvillage.com
Founded: 1956.
Congressional District: 7
Key Personnel: Dir., J. Lawrence Taylor; Historian, Norma Taylor.
Personnel Profile: Full-Time Paid 2; Part-Time Paid 1.
Governing Authority: municipal. Parent Institution: Old Country Store Inc.
Railroad Museum: housed in c.1900 home of Casey Jones.
Collections: house & furnishings; steam locomotive engine; old railroad passes; timetables; telegraph instruments; lanterns; steam whistles.
Research Fields: life & home of Casey Jones; items pertaining to the steam era.
Facilities: Railroad items & stamps for sale.
Hours & Admission Prices: Jan.-Feb. daily 9-5; March-Dec. daily 9-8. Adults $6.50, seniors $5.50, children 6-12 $4; discounts to groups & AAA members; children under 6 no charge. Closed Easter; Thanksgiving; Christmas.
Attendance: 50,000 (estimated)

INTERNATIONAL ROCK-A-BILLY HALL OF FAME MUSEUM, 105 N. Church St., Jackson, TN 38301-6213. Tel.: 731-427-6262.
Web Site: www.rockabilly.org
History Museum.
Collections: artifacts & memorabilia relating to early rock & roll hillbilly music.
Hours & Admission Prices: Mon.-Fri. 10-4, Sat. 10-2.

N.C. & ST. L. DEPOT & RAILROAD MUSEUM, 582 S. Royal St., Jackson, TN 38301-7308. Tel.: 731-425-8223.
Historic Building: built in 1907. Listed on the National Register of Historic Places.
Collections: railroad & depot history; railroad artifacts & memorabilia; photographs; model replica; paintings.
Activities: special events; permanent & temporary exhibits; birthday parties.
Hours & Admission Prices: Mon.-Sat. 10-3. No charge.

Jefferson City

GLENMORE MANSION, 1280 N. Chucky Pike, Jefferson City, TN 37760-4926. Mailing Address: P.O. Box 403, Jefferson City, TN 37760-0403.
Key Personnel: Pres. (V), Helen T. Gray.
Governing Authority: nonprofit organization. Parent Institution: Association for the Preservation of TN Antiquities. Tax-exempt.
Historic House: built in 1868. Listed on the National Register of Historic Places.
Collections: period furnishings; personal artifacts; photographs.
Activities: rental facilities; educational programs.
Publications: biannual newsletter.
Hours & Admission Prices: May-Oct. Sat.-Sun. 1-5. Adults $5, children under 12 $3; other times by appointment.
Membership: Junior $10; Individual $25.

Johnson City

* **CARROLL REECE MUSEUM, (M),** Gilbreath Dr., East Tennessee State University, Johnson City, TN 37614. Mailing Address: P.O. Box 70660, ETSU, Johnson City, TN 37614-1701. Tel.: 423-439-4392. Fax: 423-439-4283.
E-mail: burchete@etsu.edu
Web Site: www.etsu.edu/reece
Founded: 1965.
Congressional District: 1
Key Personnel: Dir., Theresa Burchett-Anderson; Pres. ETSU, Dr. Paul Stanton.
Personnel Profile: Full-Time Paid 2; Part-Time Volunteers 2; Interns 1.
Governing Authority: university. Parent Institution: East Tennessee State University. Tax-exempt: 501(c)(3).
History & Art Museum.
Collections: 18th-19th century East Tennessee history & contemporary regional art; paintings; graphics; history; textiles; Tennessee crafts; costumes; folklore; B. Carroll Reece Memorial collection; printing.
Research Fields: paintings; graphics; history; textiles; Tennessee crafts; costumes; printing; musical instruments.
Activities: self guided tours; lectures; gallery talks; concerts; formally organized education programs for children & adults; inter-museum loan, permanent, temporary & traveling exhibitions.
Publications: catalogs; quarterly newsletter; exhibit brochures; calendar.
Hours & Admission Prices: Tues.-Wed. & Fri. 9-4, Thurs. 9-7. Suggested Donation: $3. Closed major holidays. ♿
Attendance: 10,000 (estimated)

HANDS ON! REGIONAL MUSEUM, 315 E. Main St., Johnson City, TN 37601-5700. Tel.: 423-928-6508 & 6509. Fax: 423-928-6915.
E-mail: handson@handsonmuseum.org
Web Site: www.handsonmuseum.org
Founded: 1986.
Congressional District: 1
Key Personnel: Exec. Dir., Trish Patterson; Mktg. & Membership, Kristine Amerine Carter; Finance Mgr., Kay Hobbs; Education, Prog & Science Lab Mgr., April Bunch; Exhibits & Outreach Coord., Franci Sloan; Reservations, Karen Deckard.
Personnel Profile: Full-Time Paid 7; Part-Time Paid 15; Part-Time Volunteers 100; Interns 1.
Governing Authority: nonprofit organization. Tax-exempt: 501(c)(3).
Children's Museum.
Collections: ark animals.
Facilities: aquarium; 27,000 sq. ft. exhibit space; educational exhibits. Museum-related items for sale.
Activities: organized education programs for children; participatory & traveling exhibitions; Tennessee curriculum school programs; night rentals; birthday parties; sleepovers. Museum Sponsors: Festival of Trees; Museum-in-a-Box outreach program; Summer Learning vacation program.
Publications: quarterly newsletter, Handprints; annual report.
Hours & Admission Prices: June-Aug. Mon.-Fri. 9-5, Sat. 10-5, Sun. 1-5; Sept.-May Tues.-Fri. 9-5, Sat. 10-5, Sun. 1-5. Adults $8; discounts to groups & ASTC members; members & children under 3 no charge. Closed New Year's Day; Martin Luther King Jr. Day; Easter; Memorial Day; Independence Day; Labor Day; Thanksgiving; Christmas Eve & Day.
Attendance: 70,013 (accurate)
Membership: Individual $30; Grandparent $50; Family $60; Joint Parent/Grandparent $95; Friend $100; Associate $250; Sponsor $500; Principal $1,000; Benefactor $2,500; Sustainer $5,000; Guarantor $10,000; Presidential $20,000 and up.

MUSEUM AT MOUNTAIN HOME - EAST TENNESSEE STATE UNIVERSITY, Dept. Learning Resources, Johnson City, TN 37614-1710. Mailing Address: P.O. Box 70693, Johnson City, TN 37614-1710. Tel.: 423-439-8069. Fax: 423-439-7025.
Founded: 1994.
Congressional District: 1
Key Personnel: Pres. (V), Janet Fisher.
Personnel Profile: Part-Time Paid 1; Part-Time Volunteers 3.
Governing Authority: Tax-exempt.
Medical & Military Museum.
Collections: medical & military artifacts.

Hours & Admission Prices: Tues. & Thurs. 9-11, Wed. 1:30-3:30. No charge; donations accepted. Closed holidays. ♿

SLOCUMB GALLERIES, Ball Hall, Dept. of Art & Design, ETSU, Johnson City, TN 37614. Mailing Address: Box 70708 ETSU, Johnson City, TN 37614-1710. Tel.: 423-483-3179. Fax: 423-439-4393.
E-mail: contrera@etsu.edu
Web Site: art.etsu.edu/slocumb
Founded: 1965.
Congressional District: 1
Key Personnel: Dir., Karlota I. Contreras-Koterbay.
Personnel Profile: Full-Time Paid 1; Interns 5.
Governing Authority: university. Parent Institution: East Tennessee State University. Subsidiary Institution: Dept. of Art & Design. Tax-exempt.
Art Gallery.
Collections: diverse art media.
Activities: BFA/MFA graduate shows; artist's talks; lectures; traveling show; invited artists exhibit; national art competition; loan & temporary exhibition.
Publications: catalogs; e-newsletter; posters; art essays.
Hours & Admission Prices: Mon.-Fri. 8:30-4. No charge. Closed university holidays. ♿
Attendance: 5,000 (estimated)

TIPTON-HAYNES STATE HISTORIC SITE, (M), 2620 S. Roan St., Johnson City, TN 37601-7585. Mailing Address: P.O. Box 225, Johnson City, TN 37605-0225. Tel.: 423-926-3631.
E-mail: tiptonhaynes@embarqmail.com
Web Site: tipton-haynes.org
Founded: 1965.
Congressional District: 1
Key Personnel: C.E.O., Penny McLaughlin; Chm. (V), Mark Edmonds.
Personnel Profile: Full-Time Paid 1; Full-Time Volunteers 2; Part-Time Paid 1; Part-Time Volunteers 202.
Governing Authority: state. Affiliated with Tennessee Historical Commission, 2941 Lebanon Rd., Nashville, TN 37243-0442. Tax-exempt: 501(c)(3).
Historic Home: c.1850 Tipton & Haynes House.
Collections: agriculture; history; outdoor museum; folklore. Historic Buildings: c.1850 Haynes home & law office; George Hayne home (slave); c.1784 barn, corn crib, spring house, smokehouse, still house & pig pen.
Research Fields: families of Col. John Tipton & Landon Carter Haynes.
Facilities: Museum-related items for sale.
Activities: guided tours; permanent exhibitions; summer history enrichment program, grades 1-6. Annual Events: Andre Michaux Day in Spring; Sorghum Festival in September; Stories from the Pumpkin Patch in October; Visions of Christmas re-enactment in December.
Publications: handbook for tour guides; quarterly newsletter; brochures of site.
Hours & Admission Prices: April-Nov. Tues.-Sat. 9-4; Dec.-March call for hours. Adults $4, students $2; discount AAA members, school & scout groups; members no charge. Closed New Year's Eve & Day; Thanksgiving & day after; Christmas week. ♿
Attendance: 9,000 (estimated)
Membership: Student $20; Individual $25; Family $35; Supporting $50; Sustaining $100; Benefactor $250; Grand Benefactor $500; Philanthropist $1,000.

Jonesborough

JONESBOROUGH-WASHINGTON COUNTY HISTORY MUSEUM, (M), 117 Boone St., Historic Jonesborough Visitors Center, Jonesborough, TN 37659. Mailing Address: 212 E. Sabin Dr., Jonesborough, TN 37659-1306. Tel.: 423-753-9580. Fax: 423-753-5281.
E-mail: dmontanti@heritageall.org
Web Site: www.heritageall.org
Founded: 1982.
Congressional District: 1
Key Personnel: Museum Dir., Deborah Montanti.
Personnel Profile: Full-Time Paid 1; Part-Time Paid 2; Part-Time Volunteers 17.
Governing Authority: nonprofit. Parent Institution: Heritage Alliance. Tax-exempt: 501(c)(3).
History Museum.
Collections: local artifacts from 1770-present; prehistoric artifacts; history of Jonesborough-Washington County, Tennessee's first town & county; restored 1886 one-room school building.
Research Fields: Jonesborough & Washington County; history; historic preservation; architectural; An 1886 One-Room Schoolhouse Teacher's Resource and Curriculum Guide.
Facilities: 500-vol. library of local history, museum methodology, historic preservation available for use on premises during normal business hours; reading room; display area; community room & auditorium available for use in visitor's center.
Activities: permanent & temporary exhibitions; guided tours of historic district; school tours; suitcase exhibits which travel to schools; scout programs; craft programs in summer; teacher in-service programs; films; lectures; heritage education program in one-room school.
Hours & Admission Prices: Mon.-Fri. 9-5, Sat.-Sun. 10-5. Adults $2, senior citizens $1.50, children under 18 $1; discounts to AAM members; members no charge. ♿
Attendance: 5,735 (accurate)
Membership: Student $10; Individual $15; Family $20; Donor $50; Contributing $100; Benefactor $500.

Kingsport

NETHERLAND INN HOUSE MUSEUM & BOATYARD COMPLEX, 2144 Netherland Inn Rd., Kingsport, TN 37660-3052. Mailing Address: P.O. Box 293, Kingsport, TN 37660. Tel.: 423-335-5552.
E-mail: jgibson@naxs.net
Web Site: netherlandinn.com
Founded: 1966.
Congressional District: 1
Key Personnel: C.E.O. & Steering Committee Chm., Mrs. Dennis Phillips; Museum Dir., Furnishings Maintenance Chm. & Catalog Dept. Chm., Mrs. Jane Gibson; Guide Chm., Annette Pannell; Museum Shop Mgr., Mrs. Lib Findley.
Personnel Profile: Part-Time Paid 2; Part-Time Volunteers 110.
Governing Authority: private; nonprofit association. Parent Institution: Netherland Inn/Exchange Place Association, Inc., Box 293, Kingsport. Tax-exempt: 501(c)(3).
Historic House Museum: housed in 1802-1818, 13-room Netherland Inn with 3 log outbuildings; 3-story Inn with 2-story kitchen wing; 1773 2-story Boone Log Cabin Children's Museum; 1790 log Ross Ordinary used 1878 as Old Schoolhouse; 1830s two story log Visitor's Center-Museum shop.
Collections: late 18th- & early 19th-century period furnishings; costumes; documents; manuscript collection; guns; musical instruments; toys; farm equipment; tools; cooking utensils; flatboat replica; stagecoach; railroading items; forts; antique dolls; antique furniture; wagons; period kitchen; wellhouse; historical monuments. Historic Structures: 1773-1775 two-story Log Cabin Children's Museum; 1795 Ross Ordinary; over 300 period costumes; 16 rooms with 18th- & 19th-century furnishings.
Research Fields: families, land transactions, history of area; furnishings, uses in connection with restorations.
Facilities: boat yard riverfront park; gardens; monuments.
Activities: guided tours; school tours; lectures; slide tape programs; temporary & permanent exhibits; crafts; manuscript collections; children's museum teaching activities; boat yard riverfront park. Special Events: guest lecturers re: history & cultures; English High Tea in May; Wine & Cheese Party in June; Fun Inn the Sun in July; Old Time Fiddlers & Blue Grass Festival in August; East Tenn. Country Scottish Dancers in October; Concert on the Green; hearth-side cooking demonstrations; annual 1818 Netherland Inn Assoc. Christmas Party in December; banquet; walking & windshield tours of historic districts.
Publications: quarterly newsletter, Newsletter of Netherland Inn Assn.; brochures; Netherland Family Genealogy; Netherland Inn & Boat Yard Booklet; Netherland Inn Cookbook; historical map of the Long Island of the Holston; History of Early Kingsport, Prehistory to 1900; Kingsport Heritage: The Early Years 1700-1900; Lithograph, Birth of Kingsport; The Netherland Inn Chronicles.
Hours & Admission Prices: Guided Tours: May-Oct. Sat.-Sun. 2-4; groups & other times by appointment. Adults $4, children 6 & under $1; discount to groups; Tourism Bureau & museum members no charge. Additional fee for some special events. ♿
Attendance: 9,000 (estimated)
Membership: Individuals: Student $5; Individual $25; Family $40; Patron $100; Benefactor $500; Life $5,000. Corporate & Professional: Club $50; Patron $100; Benefactor $500.

Kingston

ROANE COUNTY MUSEUM OF HISTORY & ART, 119 Court St., Kingston, TN 37763-2810. Mailing Address: P.O. Box 738, Kingston, TN 37763-0738. Tel.: 865-376-9211.
Web Site: www.roanetnheritage.com
Key Personnel: Dir., Darlene Trent
Art & History Museum: housed in former antebellum courthouse.
Collections: Roane County & Tennessee history.
Facilities: library.
Hours & Admission Prices: Mon.-Fri. 9-4. No charge.

Knoxville

BECK CULTURAL EXCHANGE CENTER, INC., 1927 Dandridge Ave., Knoxville, TN 37915-1909. Tel.: 865-524-8461. Fax: 865-524-8462.
E-mail: beckcenter@beckcenter.net
Web Site: www.beckcenter.net
Founded: 1975.
Congressional District: 2
Key Personnel: Exec. Dir. & C.E.O., Avon William Rollins, Sr.; 1st Vice Pres., Ms. Carol Scott; 2nd Vice Pres., Arnold Cohen; Pres., James "Jim" Ware; Archivist, Timothy Vasser; Administrative Asst., Andre Canty.
Personnel Profile: Full-Time Paid 5; Part-Time Paid 2; Part-Time Volunteers 40.
Governing Authority: nonprofit. Tax-exempt: 501(c)(3).
History Museum, Cultural Center & Local Black History.
Collections: books written by local Black authors; Black weekly newspapers; works of art by local artists; oral histories; biographies; manuscripts; phonograph records & photographs; Federal Judge William A. Hastle collection.
Major Exhibits: Martin Luther King Jr., 1/10-2/7/10; School Desegregation in East Tennessee, 2/10-3/10; Review of E. Tennessee's Black Communities, 4/10-6/10; Urban Renewal/Negro Removal, 7/10-9/10; Local Art, 10/10-11/10.
Research Fields: local Black history; state & national history.
Facilities: library of books on Black history available for research on premises; reading room; video room; classrooms.
Activities: guided tours; lectures; permanent & temporary exhibitions.
Publications: quarterly newsletter, Historically Speaking; books, Tales From Back Then; Down Memory Lane; Blacks in Knoxville-The First 100 Years, 1791-1891; Two Hundred Years of Black Culture In Knoxville, Tennessee 1791-1991; historic calendars; And There Was Light! 120 Year History of Knoxville College.
Hours & Admission Prices: Tues.-Sat. 10-6. No charge; donations accepted. Closed holidays. ♿
Attendance: 70,000 (accurate)
Membership: Student $20; Individual $25; Family $50; Organization $200; Sustaining $250; Sponsor $100; Patron $500; Corporate $1,000; Corporate Gold $5,000; Corporate Platinum $10,000.

BLOUNT MANSION, (M), 200 W. Hill Ave., Knoxville, TN 37902-1812. Mailing Address: P.O. Box 1703, Knoxville, TN 37901-1703. Tel.: 865-525-2375; 888-654-0016 (toll free). Fax: 865-546-5315.
E-mail: blountmansion@hotmail.com
Web Site: www.blountmansion.org
Founded: 1926.
Congressional District: 2
Key Personnel: C.E.O., Billye J. Chabot.
Personnel Profile: Full-Time Paid 3; Part-Time Paid 4; Part-Time Volunteers 45.
Governing Authority: nonprofit organization. Parent Institution: Blount Mansion Association. Branch Museum: 1818, Craighead-Jackson House, 1000 State St. Tax-exempt: 501(c)(3).
Historic House Museum: 1792 home & office of William Blount, governor of the Territory of the United States South of the River Ohio (Southwest Territory).
Collections: late 18th-century decorative arts.
Facilities: 18th-century garden; visitors center with exhibit gallery, audio visual program & 1818 Craighead Jackson House.
Activities: guided tours; docent program; permanent & temporary exhibitions; monthly lecture series; educational programs for school groups.
Hours & Admission Prices: Jan.-March Mon.-Fri. 9:30-5; April-Dec. Mon.-Sat. 9:30-5; other times by appointment. Adults $7, senior citizens, and CAA & AAA members $6, children 6-17 $4; discounts to groups; children under 5 and AAM, ICOM, AASLH members no charge.
Attendance: 10,100 (accurate)
Membership: Senior $25; Single $35; Family $50; Patron $100; Delegate $250; Federalist $500; Governor's Cabinet $1,000.

CONFEDERATE MEMORIAL HALL-BLEAK HOUSE, 3148 Kingston Pike, S.W., Knoxville, TN 37919-4627. Tel.: 865-522-2371.
E-mail: bleakhouseevents@yahoo.com
Web Site: www.knoxvillecmh.org
Founded: 1959.
Congressional District: 2
Key Personnel: Pres., Namuni Young.
Personnel Profile: Part-Time Volunteers 25.
Governing Authority: nonprofit organization. Affiliated with United Daughters of the Confederacy, Tennessee Division, Nashville, TN 37221. Tax-exempt: 501(c)(3).
General Museum: housed in 1858 Bleak House.
Collections: Confederate history; furniture & relics of Civil War period; archives; botany; costumes.
Research Fields: Civil War; reference: war records of confederate soldiers; records of confederate cemeteries; battles of Civil War; Generals.
Facilities: 1,000-vol. library of books available for use by permission of Executive Board; reading room. Confederacy memorabilia & postcards for sale.
Activities: guided tours; programs; civic & historical meetings, weddings, receptions, teas, political rallies, documentaries & videos.
Publications: brochure.
Hours & Admission Prices: March-Dec. Wed.-Fri. 1-4; other times by appointment, school & bus tours by appointment. Adults $5, senior citizens $4, students $3, children 7-12 $1.50.
Attendance: 1,300 (estimated)

CRESCENT BEND/THE ARMSTRONG-LOCKETT HOUSE AND THE WILLIAM P. TOMS MEMORIAL GARDENS, 2728 Kingston Pike, Knoxville, TN 37919-4600. Tel.: 865-637-3163 & 544-3000. Fax: 865-637-1709.
E-mail: rbrett@tds.net
Web Site: www.kornet.org/cresbend
Founded: 1975.
Key Personnel: Chm., Ron Grimm.
Governing Authority: foundation. The Toms Foundation. Tax-exempt.
Decorative Arts Museum: housed in 1834 Armstrong-Lockett House.
Collections: c.1720-1820 American and English furniture; paintings; mirrors; 1610-1820 English silver collection.
Facilities: library of books on English silver, American furniture & decorative arts.
Activities: guided tours; lectures.
Hours & Admission Prices: March-Dec. Tues.-Sat. 10-4, Sun. 1-4. Adults $7, students $5; discounts to AAA members & groups of 20 or more; children under 12 no charge. Closed major holidays.
Attendance: 9,250 (accurate)

DISCOVERY CENTER (EAST TENNESSEE DISCOVERY CENTER), 516 N. Beaman St., Chilhowee Park, Knoxville, TN 37914-4410. Mailing Address: P.O. Box 6204, Knoxville, TN 37914-0204. Tel.: 865-594-1494. Fax: 865-594-1469.
E-mail: etdc@comcast.net
Web Site: www.etdiscovery.org
Founded: 1960.
Congressional District: 2
Key Personnel: Chm. (V), Joe Johnson; Exec. Dir., Margaret Maddox; Education Facilitator & Museum Shop Mgr., Christy Lewis; Administrative Asst., Karen Sullivan; Planetarium Facilitator, Charles Ferguson.
Personnel Profile: Full-Time Paid 4; Part-Time Paid 11; Part-Time Volunteers 10.
Governing Authority: nonprofit organization. Tax-exempt: 501(c)(3).
Science Museum & Planetarium.
Collections: physical, life & earth sciences; astronomy.
Facilities: 30 ft. hyperhemisphere dome in the planetarium; insect zoo; eight tank aquaria; health and science education classrooms. Museum-related items for sale.
Activities: guided tours; lectures; films; gallery talks; hobby workshops; formally organized education programs for children; permanent, temporary & traveling exhibitions.
Publications: pamphlets; newsletters; program guides.
Hours & Admission Prices: Mon.-Fri. 9-5, Sat. 10-5. Adults $4, senior citizens & children 5 and over $3, children 3-4 $2; discounts to AAM & AAA members; museum & ASTC members and children under 3 no charge. ♿
Attendance: 57,000 (accurate)
Membership: Student $15; Individual $25; Family $50; Supporter $100; Friend $250; Patron $500.

EAST TENNESSEE HISTORICAL SOCIETY, 601 S. Gay St., Knoxville, TN 37902-1604. Mailing Address: P.O. Box 1629, Knoxville, TN 37901-1629. Tel.: 865-215-8824. Fax: 865-215-8819.
E-mail: eths@east-tennessee-history.org
Web Site: www.easttnhistory.org
Founded: 1834.
Congressional District: 2
Key Personnel: Dir., Cherel Henderson; Chm. (V), Jack E. Williams; Cur. Education, Lisa Oakley; Cur. Collections, Michele MacDonald; Cur. Exhibits, Adam Alfrey; Dir. Devel., Lisa Belleman; TAH Grant Mgr., William Hardy; Museum Shop Mgr., Diane Bohannon; Office Mgr., Stephanie Hankins.
Personnel Profile: Full-Time Paid 6; Full-Time Volunteers 1; Part-Time Paid 4; Part-Time Volunteers 50.
Governing Authority: private; nonprofit organization. Tax-exempt: 501(c)(3).

Historical Society Museum: housed in the Old Custom House, which was built between 1870-1874.
Collections: concentration on East Tennessee history from mid-1700s to late 20th century.
Major Exhibits: The Life & Work of W. Russell Briscoe, 11/09-2/7/10; East Tennessee Fringe: Recent Photography by Don Dudenbostel, 3/1/10-5/9/10; FGS & Civil War Exhibitions, 5/3/10-10/3/10; Bagels and Barbecue, 10/10-12/10.
Activities: lecture series; school programming; special events; permanent exhibits.
Publications: annual scholarly journal, Journal of East Tennessee History; triannual genealogy publication, Tennessee Ancestors; quarterly newsletter, Newsline.
Hours & Admission Prices: Mon.-Fri. 9-4, Sat. 10-4, Sun. 1-5. Adults $5, senior citizens $4; members and children 16 & under no charge. Closed New Year's Day; Thanksgiving; Christmas Eve & Day. ♿
Attendance: 93,931 (accurate)
Membership: Student $20; Affiliate $25; Nonprofit Institutional $35; Individual $35; Family $45; Contributing $75; Sustaining $125; Patron $250; Benefactor $500; Grand Benefactor $1,000.

EWING GALLERY - UNIVERSITY OF TENNESSEE, Art & Architecture Bldg., 1715 Volunteer Blvd., Knoxville, TN 37996-2410. Tel.: 865-974-3199.
Web Site: www.ewing-gallery.utk.edu
Key Personnel: Dir., Sam Yates
Art & Architecture Museum.
Collections: art & architecture history & current trends; drawings; photographs.
Activities: workshops; lectures; films; research.
Hours & Admission Prices: Mon. & Thurs. 10-8, Tues.-Wed. & Fri. 10-5, Sun. 1-4. Closed national holidays.

* **FRANK H. MCCLUNG MUSEUM, (M),** University of Tennessee, 1327 Circle Park Dr., Knoxville, TN 37996-0001. Tel.: 865-974-2144. Fax: 865-974-3827.
E-mail: museum@utk.edu
Web Site: mcclungmuseum.utk.edu
Founded: 1961.
Congressional District: 2
Key Personnel: Dir., Dr. Jefferson Chapman; Cur., Elaine A. Evans; Cur. Paleoethnobotany, Dr. Gary Crites; Cur. Archaeology, Dr. Lynne Sullivan; Cur. Malacology, Gerald Dinkins; Registrar, Robert Pennington; Photographer, Lindsay Kromer; Exhibits Coord., Steve Long; Exhibit Preparator, Chris Weddig; Museum Educator, Deborah Woodiel; Museum Shop Mgr., Vera Bremseth.
Personnel Profile: Full-Time Paid 12; Part-Time Paid 8; Part-Time Volunteers 90; Interns 3.
Governing Authority: university. Parent Institution: The University of Tennessee. Tax-exempt: 170(b)(1)(A).
General Museum.
Collections: Lewis-Kneberg collection of Tennessee archaeology; archaeological collections from Tennessee reservoirs; Eleanor Deane Audigier art collection; historical & natural science materials; ancient Egyptian; ethnological collections; paleoethnobotanical collection; fresh water mussel collection; ornithological lithographs; vertebrate paleontology.
Major Exhibits: 2,000 Years of Chinese Art, 2/10-5/10; Shells: Gems of the Sea, 6/10-8/10; Painted Metaphors: Pottery & Politics of the Ancient Maya (T), 9/10-12/10.
Research Fields: Tennessee archaeology; zooarchaeology; malacology; paleoethnobotany; vertebrate paleontology.
Facilities: 6,000-vol. library of archaeological journals, newsletters, museum catalogs & reference material available for use on premises; reading room; 260-seat auditorium.
Activities: guided tours; inter-museum loan, permanent, temporary & traveling exhibitions; lectures.
Publications: exhibit catalogues; books on regional archaeology; monthly bulletin; research notes.
Hours & Admission Prices: Mon.-Sat. 9-5, Sun. 1-5. No charge; donations accepted. Closed New Year's Day; Easter; Memorial Day; Independence Day; Labor Day; Thanksgiving; Christmas Eve & Day. ♿
Attendance: 41,213 (accurate)
Membership: University $15; Individual & Family $30; Contributing $50; Sustaining $100; Supporting $250; Patron $500; Benefactor $1,000; Grand Benefactor $2,500.

GOVERNOR JOHN SEVIER MEMORIAL ASSOCIATION, 1220 W. Gov. John Sevier Hwy., Knoxville, TN 37920. Tel.: 865-573-5508. Fax: 865-573-9768.
E-mail: marblesprings@hotmail.com
Web Site: www.discoveret.org/jsma/
Founded: 1941.
Congressional District: 2
Key Personnel: C.E.O., Tracy Caskey; Chm. & Pres. (V), Jim Buckenmyer.
Personnel Profile: Full-Time Paid 1; Part-Time Volunteers 10.
Governing Authority: state. Parent Institution: State of Tennessee. Affiliated with Tennessee Historical Commission, State Library & Archives Bldg., Nashville, TN 37219. Tax-exempt.
Historic House: 1783-1815 Marble Springs plantation home of Tennessee's first governor, John Sevier.
Collections: agriculture; pioneer furniture & artifacts; focus on frontier history and pioneer way of life, 1780-1815; influence of Sevier on early history of the settlements in North Carolina, State of Franklin, territory south of the River Ohio & Tennessee. Historic Buildings: c.1783-1815 smokehouse & barn with several farm animals; loomhouse; springhouse; Sevier Main house, kitchen; Trading Post & Tavern.
Research Fields: Gov. John Sevier & his family records; pioneer life.
Facilities: Gift items for sale.
Activities: living history tours. Museum Sponsors: Colonial Workshop Demonstration in April; Statehood Celebration in June; John Sevier Memorial Shoot in June; John Sevier Days in September; Fall Festival in October; Candlelight Tours in December.
Publications: books.
Hours & Admission Prices: Tues.-Sun. 10-5. Living History Tours: adults $4; members & children under 10 no charge. Closed Easter; Independence Day; Thanksgiving; Christmas.
Attendance: 3,886 (estimated)
Membership: Individual $25; Family $45; Contributing $75; Sustaining $100; Governor Sevier Followers $500; Life $1,000.

THE KNOXVILLE BOTANICAL GARDENS AND ARBORETUM, 2743 Wimpole Ave., Knoxville, TN 37914-5958. Tel.: 865-862-8717. Fax: 865-862-8721.
E-mail: info@knoxgarden.org
Web Site: knoxgarden.org
Key Personnel: Dir., Steve Seifreid; Admin. & Special Events Coord., Danielle Velez; Garden Mgr., Brian Campbell
Botanical Garden & Arboretum.
Collections: Knoxville's cultural & horticultural history; gardens; arboretum; bird sanctuary; Civil War; Native American.
Facilities: 44-acre site; amphitheater.
Activities: plays; concerts; festivals; special events.
Hours & Admission Prices: Daily sunrise-sunset. No charge.

* **KNOXVILLE MUSEUM OF ART, (M),** 1050 World's Fair Park Dr., Knoxville, TN 37916-1653. Tel.: 865-525-6101, ext. 0 & ext. 256. Fax: 865-546-3635.
E-mail: info@kmaonline.org
Web Site: www.knoxart.org
Founded: 1961.
Congressional District: 2
Key Personnel: Chm. (V), Greg Hall; Exec. Dir., David L. Butler; Cur., Stephen C. Wicks; Devel. Assoc., Krishna Adams; Assoc. Cur. Education K-12, Rosalind Martin; Dir. Finance, Joyce Jones; Alive After Five Coord., Michael Gill; Security Chief, Frank Vallone; Dir. Devel., Donna Dempster; Dir. Mktg., Angela Thomas; Asst. Dir. Devel., Margo Carpenter; Dir. Administration & Visitor Svcs., Shirley Brown; Coord. Fundraising Events, Sharon Hudson; Museum Shop Mgr., Susan Creswell; Curatorial Asst., Clark Gillespie; Assoc. Cur. Education & Adult Programs, Chris Molinski; Asst. Security Chief, Jim Mullins.
Personnel Profile: Full-Time Paid 12; Part-Time Paid 18; Part-Time Volunteers 285; Interns 4.
Governing Authority: nonprofit organization. Tax-exempt: 501(c)(3).
Art Museum: housed in an Edward Larrabee Barnes-designed facility.
Collections: 20th & 21st century art; regional art & fine craft.
Major Exhibits: Devorah Sperber: Threads of Perception (T), 11/09-1/10; Anne Wilson: Wind/Rewind/Weave, 1/10-4/10; Uncertain Terrain, 4/10-8/10; A Sense of Place: Southern Photographs by Baldwin Lee, Walker Evans, & Eudora Welty, 5/10-8/10; Contemporary Focus, 9/10-11/10.
Research Fields: east Tennessee region - contemporary art.
Facilities: 2,497-vol. library of art books & slides available by request.
Activities: docent & audio guided tours; lectures; concerts; arts festivals; school, youth, family programs; outreach programs; docent program; visitor

service representatives; inter-museum loan, permanent, temporary & traveling exhibitions; exploratory gallery; teacher professional development programs; youth & adult art classes.
Publications: biannual, Canvas; exhibition catalogues with scholarly essays for emerging artist series; educator's learning guides.
Hours & Admission Prices: Tues.-Sat. 10-8, Sun. 1-4. No charge; donations accepted. Closed New Year's Day; Martin Luther King Jr. Day; Easter; Memorial Day; Independence Day; Labor Day; Thanksgiving; Christmas. ♿
Attendance: 59,041 (accurate)
Membership: Student $20; Senior $35; KMA Guild $35 & $40; Individual $40; Senior Couple $55; Family $60; Associate $125; Fellow $250; Curator's Circle $500; Corporate $500 & up; Director's Circle $1,000; Benefactor $2,500-$4,999; Sustaining $5,000-$9,999; Masters $10,000-$24,999; Grand Masters $25,000-$49,999; Chairman's Club $50,000 & up.

KNOXVILLE ZOOLOGICAL GARDENS, 3500 Knoxville Zoo Dr., Knoxville, TN 37914. Mailing Address: P.O. Box 6040, Knoxville, TN 37914-0040. Tel.: 865-637-5331, ext. 300. Fax: 865-637-1943.
Web Site: www.knoxville-zoo.org
Founded: 1948.
Congressional District: 2
Key Personnel: Exec. Dir., Jim Vlna; Bd. Chm., David Moon; Dir. Animal Collection, Lisa New; Dir. Education, Kevin Hils; Dir. Guest Svcs., Marie Vlna; Dir. Herpetology, Bern Tryon; Dir. Operations, Keith Montgomery; Dir. Mktg., Alison Swank.
Personnel Profile: Full-Time Paid 108; Part-Time Paid 103; Part-Time Volunteers 200; Interns 53.
Governing Authority: nonprofit organization. Tax-exempt: 501(c)(3).
Zoo.
Collections: large mammals; reptiles & birds; red pandas; white rhinos; African elephants; Chinese alligators; American black bears; chimpanzees; giraffe; gorillas.
Research Fields: biology; zoology.
Facilities: 1,700-vol. library of animal reference used by employees on premises only; 53 acres zoological park. Zoo related items for sale.
Activities: docent program; permanent & traveling exhibitions; SSP programs; tram ride; elephant demonstration; camel ride; special events; keeper chats; animal encounters.
Publications: zoo map; 4 times a year, membership news magazine.
Hours & Admission Prices: Winter: daily 10-4:30; Summer: daily 9:30-6. Adults $16.95, senior citizens 65 & up and children 2-12 $12.95; discount to groups; children under 2, members & AZA members no charge. Closed Christmas. ♿
Attendance: 430,088 (accurate)
Membership: Grandparent & Individual $60; One Parent Family $65; Two Parent Family $75; Supporting $125; Sponsoring $250; Patron $500; Honor Society $1,000.

MABRY-HAZEN HOUSE, 1711 Dandridge Ave., Knoxville, TN 37915-1905. Tel.: 865-522-8661. Fax: 865-522-8471.
E-mail: mabryhazenhouse@gmail.com
Web Site: mabryhazen.com
Founded: 1992.
Congressional District: 2
Key Personnel: Exec. Dir., Calvin Chappelle.
Personnel Profile: Full-Time Paid 1.
Governing Authority: private; nonprofit organization. Parent Institution: The Hazen Historical Museum Foundation, Inc. Tax-exempt.
Historic House: an 1858 Italianate Fourover Four Home, built by Joseph Alexander Mabry; used by the South and then the North, in the Civil War.
Collections: 3,000 original artifacts collected by the Mabry-Hazen families over 130 years as occupants of the house; glass; ceramics; painting; furniture; books; papers; photographs; letters.
Research Fields: genealogy of Mabry-Hazen families; history of Knoxville 1858-1987.
Facilities: 1,600-vol. library of textbooks (1858-1987), novels, letters, manuscripts & resource books on decorative arts and museology; botanical garden; 4,500 sq. ft. exhibit space; 60-seat theater. Publications for sale.
Activities: concerts; docent program; films; formal education programs for children & adults; guided tours; lectures. Annual Events: Victorian Christmas; Open Gardens-Dogwood Arts Festival; Teas in spring & fall.
Publications: The Seduction of Miss Evelyn Hazen.
Hours & Admission Prices: Wed.-Fri. 11-5, Sat. 10-3; other times by appointment. Adults $5, senior citizens $4.50, students K-12 $2.50; tours $4 per person; discounts to AAA members. Closed New Year's Day; Independence Day; Thanksgiving; Christmas. ♿
Attendance: 2,000 (estimated)
Membership: Student $15; Individual $35; Family $50; Contributing $100; Sustaining $500; Patron $1,000.

RAMSEY HOUSE PLANTATION, 2614 Thorngrove Pike, Knoxville, TN 37914-9704. Tel.: 865-546-0745. Fax: 865-546-1851. TDD: 856-546-0745.
E-mail: info@ramseyhouse.org
Web Site: www.ramseyhouse.org
Founded: 1952.
Congressional District: 2
Key Personnel: Pres. Bd. Dir., Janet Oakes; Dir., Sandra Gammon.
Personnel Profile: Full-Time Paid 1; Part-Time Paid 2; Part-Time Volunteers 25.
Governing Authority: nonprofit organization. Parent Institution: Association for the Preservation of Tennessee Antiquities, Belle Meade Mansion, Leake Ave., Nashville, TN 37205. Subsidiary Institution: Knoxville Chapter, Association for the Preservation of Tennessee Antiquities. Tax-exempt: 501(c)(3).
Historical House Museum: c.1796-97 Ramsey House, formerly Swan Pond, restored; Heirloom Gardens.
Collections: furnishings of the period c.1797-1820; 18th-century textiles.
Major Exhibits: Covering History: Quilts and Coverlets of Ramsey House, 7/10-8/10.
Research Fields: authentic restoration of house and furnishings; Ramsey family; reconstruction of farm buildings; restoration of gardens; costumes of period & history of textiles.
Facilities: 50-vol. library of historical, religious, legal and medical books. Booklets, postcards, books & magazines for sale.
Activities: guided tours; special events; lectures; children's education program; permanent exhibitions.
Publications: brochures, Ramsey House; Lebanon In-the-Fork; Research Resume for Ramsey Period Dress; Presbyterian Church; quarterly newsletter; education guide.
Hours & Admission Prices: Tues.-Sat. 10-4, Sun. 12-4. Adults $7, children 6-12 $5; discounts to seniors, AAA & National Trust members; Museums of Knoxville & Tennessee, Association of Museums members & children under 6 no charge. Closed major holidays. ♿
Attendance: 11,382 (accurate)
Membership: Friend of Ramsey House $25; Individual $30; Family $50; Contributing $75; Sustaining $100; Patron $250; Col. Ramsey's Circle $500; Swan Pond $1,000; Corporate $1,000.

Lexington

BEECH RIVER CULTURAL CENTER & MUSEUM, 26 S. Broad St., Lexington, TN 38351-2002. Tel.: 731-967-0306.
History Museum.
Collections: Henderson County history & culture; geology; early settlers; wars; personal artifacts.
Hours & Admission Prices: March 2-Dec. Wed. & Fri.-Sat. 10-3. No charge; donations accepted.

Lookout Mountain

BATTLES FOR CHATTANOOGA MUSEUM, 1110 E. Brow Rd., Lookout Mountain, TN 37350-1016.
E-mail: battle@seerockcity.com
Web Site: www.battlesforchattanooga.com
History Museum.
Collections: Civil War history; weapons; miniature battle presentations.
Facilities: Museum-related items for sale.
Hours & Admission Prices: Summer: 9-6; Winter: daily 10-5. Adults $8, children 5-12 $6; children 4 & under no charge. ♿

CRAVENS HOUSE, Point Park Visitor Center, IN 148 Scenic Hwy., Lookout Mountain, TN 37350. Tel.: 423-821-7786. Fax: 423-825-5129.
Congressional District: 3
Key Personnel: Acting Park Supt., Eric Smith; Chief Ranger, Sam Weddle; District Interpreter, Anton J. Heinlein.
Personnel Profile: Full-Time Paid 6; Part-Time Paid 5; Part-Time Volunteers 3.
Governing Authority: federal. Dept. of the Interior, National Park Service. Parent Institution: Chickamauga & Chattanooga National Military Park. Tax-exempt.
Historic House: 1866 Cravens House, Post-Civil War home.
Collections: furniture dating from 1830 through 1890s.
Activities: guided tours.
Publications: brochures, Park and Cravens House.
Hours & Admission Prices: mid-June to mid-Aug. Fri.-Sun. 9-4:30. No charge; donations accepted. Closed Christmas.
Attendance: 2,000 (accurate)

Lynchburg

TENNESSEE WALKING HORSE MUSEUM, 183 Main St., Lynchburg, TN 37352-8300. Mailing Address: P.O. Box 1010, Shelbyville, TN 37160. Tel.: 931-759-5747.
History Museum.
Collections: walking horse history; hands-on exhibits; photographs; breed registry; World Grand Champions; care & training; saddles; videos.
Activities: Annual Event: Tennessee Walking Horse National Celebration in August.
Hours & Admission Prices: Tues.-Sat. 10-12 & 1-4. No charge. Closed major holidays.

Martin

J. HOUSTON GORDON MUSEUM, 10 Wayne Fisher Dr., The University of Tennessee at Martin, Martin, TN 38238-0001. Tel.: 731-881-7094. Fax: 731-881-7074.
E-mail: museum@utm.edu
Formerly: University Museum
Founded: 1981.
Congressional District: 8
Key Personnel: Dir., Richard Saunders.
Personnel Profile: Part-Time Paid 1.
Governing Authority: university; nonprofit. Parent Institution: The University of Tennessee. Tax-exempt.
General University Museum.
Collections: rotating & traveling exhibits.
Facilities: 600 sq. ft. exhibit space.
Publications: brochure.
Hours & Admission Prices: Mon.-Fri. 8-4:30. No charge. Closed university holidays. ♿
Attendance: 1,000 (estimated)

Maryville

SAM HOUSTON MEMORIAL ASSOCIATION, (M), 3650 Old Sam Houston School Rd., Maryville, TN 37804-5644. Tel.: 865-983-1550.
E-mail: samhoustonsch@aol.com
Web Site: samhoustonhistoricschoolhouse.org
Formerly: Sam Houston Historical Schoolhouse
Founded: 1965.
Congressional District: 2
Key Personnel: Pres., Enoch B. Simerly; Vice Pres., Clara Peals; Treas., Karen Blow; Museum Shop Mgr., Mary Lynne Bell.
Personnel Profile: Full-Time Paid 1; Part-Time Volunteers 10.
Governing Authority: state. Parent Institution: Sam Houston Memorial Association. Tax-exempt.
Park Museum.
Collections: early school and pioneer artifacts; genealogy of Houston family. Historic Building: 1794 Log School.
Research Fields: Sam Houston's youth.
Facilities: picnic area; enclosed pavilion with kitchen. Museum-related items for sale.
Activities: Annual Events: Sam's Birthday Celebration in March; Pioneer Encampment in June; Fall Festival; Colonial Encampment in October; Christmas Open House in December.
Publications: book, Sam Houston, The Man; Sam Houston, Man of Destiny; Sam Houston, Man of Mystery; Sam Houston Schoolhouse Cookbook; local history books; Cherokee culture and characters; local cookbooks.
Hours & Admission Prices: Feb.-Dec. Tues.-Sat. 10-5, Sun. 1-5. Adults $1; members & children under 10 no charge. Closed New Year's Day; Easter; Thanksgiving; Christmas week. ♿
Attendance: 8,000 (estimated)
Membership: Individual $10; Family $15; Contributing $25; Life $200.

McKenzie

GORDON BROWNING MUSEUM & GENEALOGICAL LIBRARY, 640 Main St. N., McKenzie, TN 38201-1720. Tel.: 731-352-3510. Fax: 731-352-3456.
Founded: 1971.
Congressional District: 7
Key Personnel: Dir., Jere R. Cox; Pres., James E. Choate.
Personnel Profile: Full-Time Volunteers 1; Part-Time Volunteers 2.
Governing Authority: Parent Institution: Carroll County Historical Society. Tax-exempt: 501(c)(3).
History Museum.
Collections: local history & culture; photographs; documents; WWI, WWII, Korean uniforms, flags & artifacts; Civil War artifacts.
Hours & Admission Prices: Mon.-Tues. & Thurs.-Fri. 9-4. No charge. Closed New Year's Day; Independence Day; Labor Day; Thanksgiving; Christmas.

McMinnville

SOUTHERN MUSEUM & GALLERIES OF PHOTOGRAPHY, 210 E. Main St., McMinnville, TN 37110-2508. Tel.: 931-507-8102.
E-mail: artgallery@multipro.com
Art Gallery.
Collections: photographs.
Hours & Admission Prices: Wed. & Fri.-Sat. 10-4.

Memphis

ART MUSEUM OF THE UNIVERSITY OF MEMPHIS, (M), 3750 Norriswood Ave., CFA Bldg., Memphis, TN 38152-0001. Mailing Address: 142 Communication/Fine Arts Bldg., Memphis, TN 38152-0001. Tel.: 901-678-2224. Fax: 901-678-5118.
E-mail: artmuseum@memphis.edu
Web Site: www.amum.org
Founded: 1981.
Congressional District: 9
Key Personnel: Dir., Leslie Luebbers; Asst. Dir. & Registrar, Lisa F. Abitz; Chm. (V), Stanley E. Stevens, Jr.; Cur. Asst., Anita Huggins; Museum Asst., Angela Taylor.
Personnel Profile: Full-Time Paid 4; Part-Time Paid 1; Part-Time Volunteers 1; Interns 3.
Governing Authority: university. Parent Institution: The University of Memphis. Subsidiary Institution: Friends of the Art Museum. Parallel Institution: Institute of Egyptian Art & Archaeology. Tax-exempt.
Fine Arts Museum.
Collections: Egyptian collection: antiquities 3500 BC-700 AD: mummies, religious & funerary items; jewelry.
Major Exhibits: 27th Annual Juried Student Exhibition, 1/30/10-2/10; Allegories of Strife: The Diptychs of Alison Weld, 1990-2005, 3/6/10-4/17/10; MFA Thesis Exhibition, 4/24/10-6/19/10; Paul R. Williams: The Power of Example (T), 7/6/10-11/13/10; MFA Thesis Exhibition, 11/20-10-1/8/11.
Research Fields: Egyptian art & archaeology, history of art.
Facilities: 6,000-vol. Egyptian library.
Activities: temporary & traveling exhibitions; guided tours; lectures; museum study classes; internship; musical programs Institute of Egyptian Art & Archaeology symposia; I.E.A.A. Arts in School program; interdisciplinary colloquia & proceedings.
Publications: triannual newsletter, AM Edition; brochures; symposia papers; exhibition catalogs; collection catalogs; proceedings; educators guide to collections.
Hours & Admission Prices: Mon.-Sat. 9-5. Suggested Donation: $2. ♿
Attendance: 8,464 (accurate)
Membership: Student $20 (single & dual); Faculty $40 (single & dual); Good Friend $50 (single & dual); Close Friend $150 (single & dual); Best Friend $500 (single & dual); Corporate Friend $1,000-$5,000.

BELZ MUSEUM OF ASIAN & JUDAIC ART, 119 S. Main St., Memphis, TN 38103-3647. Tel.: 901-523-ARTS.
E-mail: info@belzmuseum.org
Web Site: www.belzmuseum.org
Key Personnel: Dir., Nancy Knight; Guest Svcs. Admin., Melanie Miller; Research Assoc., Daniel Graubman; Research Asst., Michelle D. Williams
Art Museum.
Collections: Asian art pertaining to China's Quing Dynasty, including works in jade & ivory; Chinese puppets; historic & literal pieces relating to Judaism.
Hours & Admission Prices: Tues.-Fri. 10-5:30, Sat.-Sun. 12-5. Adults $6, seniors $5, students $4. Closed New Year's Day; Easter; Independence Day; Thanksgiving; Christmas.

C.H. NASH MUSEUM AT CHUCALISSA, 1987 Indian Village Dr., Memphis, TN 38109-3005. Tel.: 901-785-3160. Fax: 901-785-0519.
E-mail: chucalissa@memphis.edu
Web Site: www.chucalissa.memphis.edu
Founded: 1958.
Congressional District: 9
Key Personnel: Dir., Dr. Robert Connolly; Administrative Assoc., Alex Hutson; Museum Shop Mgr., Sonny Bell.
Personnel Profile: Full-Time Paid 4; Part-Time Paid 2; Interns 3.
Governing Authority: Parent Institution: University of Memphis, 38152. Tax-exempt.
Archaeology Museum: S.E. Native American, Choctaw & Pre-historic Native Mississippian culture.
Collections: archaeological research collections from sites in western Tennessee & adjacent areas; Chert reference collection from various geological formations in Midsouth; ceramic type collection from region & projective point type collection from region.
Research Fields: archaeology of Midsouth.

Facilities: 2,000-vol. library of archaeology; geology; laboratory; Mississippian Temple Mound Complex; 100-seat auditorium; dioramas.
Activities: guided tours; formally organized education programs for all ages; permanent & temporary exhibitions; Native American arts; special events with Native American games & dances; hands-on archaeology lab exhibit.
Publications: tour guide; occasional papers.
Hours & Admission Prices: Tues.-Sat. 9-5, Sun. 1-5. Adults $5, children & senior citizens $3; discounts to AAA, groups of 10 or more, Get Away from Memphis members, University of Memphis faculty & students; members no charge. No admittance after 4:30. ♿
Attendance: 10,000 (accurate)
Membership: Students & Seniors $15; Individual $25; Family $40; Patron $100; Donor $200; President's Circle $500; Sinti Circle $1,000.

THE CHILDREN'S MUSEUM OF MEMPHIS, 2525 Central Ave., Memphis, TN 38104-5926. Tel.: 901-458-2678. Fax: 901-458-4033.
E-mail: children@cmom.com
Web Site: www.cmom.com
Founded: 1987.
Congressional District: 9
Key Personnel: C.E.O., Richard Hackett; Pres., Margaret Fraser; C.F.O., Jenny Reid; Dir. Education, Amanda LaMountain; Membership & Devel. Mgr., Debbie Wilkins; Group Programs, Keosha Williams; Dir. Public Rels. & Mktg., Randy McKeel; Mgr. Visitor Svcs., Brad Laney; Dir. Operations, Cliff Drake; Program Mgr., Loni Wellman; Dir. Volunteer Svcs., Felicia Jones.
Personnel Profile: Full-Time Paid 11; Part-Time Paid 11; Part-Time Volunteers 75; Interns 5.
Governing Authority: nonprofit organization. Tax-exempt: 501(c)(3).
Children's Museum.
Collections: interactive, hands-on, discovery museum with exhibit galleries, concentrating on a different theme including: Cityscape (kid-size city); Going Places (flight & distribution); WaterWORKS! (the Mississippi River and hydrology); Art Smart (visual & performing arts).
Major Exhibits: Building Brainstorm (T), 11/09-1/10; Run, Jump, Fly: Adventures in Action (T), 1/10-5/10; Shipwrecks (T), 5/10-9/10; Come to Gullah, 9/10-1/11.
Facilities: 20,000 sq. ft. exhibit space; classrooms; 200-seat auditorium; cafe; 2 birthday party rooms. Exhibition-related items for sale.
Activities: organized education programs for children; participatory & traveling exhibitions; annual special events.
Publications: bimonthly newsletter, Sparks!; biannual newsletter, Learning Journeys.
Hours & Admission Prices: Mon.-Sat. 9-5, Sun. 12-5. Admission $9; discounts to ACM members; members no charge. Closed Easter; Thanksgiving; Christmas. ♿
Attendance: 158,544 (accurate)
Membership: Basic (2 people) $70; Family I (4 people) $90; Family II (6 people) $105; Supporter $150; Sponsor $300; Benefactor $500; Patron $1,000.

CLOUGH-HANSON GALLERY, RHODES COLLEGE, 2000 N. Parkway, Memphis, TN 38112-1690. Tel.: 901-843-3442. Fax: 901-843-3727.
Web Site: www.rhodes.edu/academics/5264.asp
Founded: 1970.
Congressional District: 9
Key Personnel: Dir., Hamlett Dobbins.
Personnel Profile: Part-Time Paid 1; Interns 4.
Governing Authority: private; college. Tax-exempt: 501(c)(3).
College Art Gallery.
Collections: Edward Curtis photographs; Asian woodcut prints; porcelain; fabrics & other objects; regional painting & sculpture; 20th-century prints.
Activities: lectures; temporary & traveling exhibitions. Annual Event: World AIDS Day Event.
Publications: annual exhibition catalog.
Hours & Admission Prices: Tues.-Sat. 11-5. No charge. Closed Martin Luther King Jr. Day; spring break; Good Friday; Easter; Memorial Day; Labor Day; fall break; Thanksgiving; Christmas. ♿
Attendance: 2,300 (estimated)

THE COTTON MUSEUM AT THE MEMPHIS COTTON EXCHANGE, 65 Union Ave., Memphis, TN 38103-5196. Tel.: 901-531-7826. Fax: 901-531-7827.
Web Site: www.memphiscottonmuseum.org
Key Personnel: Operations Mgr., Carol Perel
Textile Museum.
Collections: artifacts & memorabilia relating to the cotton industry.
Hours & Admission Prices: Mon.-Sat. 10-5, Sun. 12-5. Adults $6, seniors $5.50, students $5, children 6-12 $4; children under 6 no charge.

* **DIXON GALLERY AND GARDENS, (M),** 4339 Park Ave., Memphis, TN 38117-4698. Tel.: 901-761-5250. Fax: 901-682-0943.
E-mail: ntrenthem@dixon.org
Web Site: www.dixon.org
Founded: 1976.
Congressional District: 9
Key Personnel: Chm., R. Brad Martin; Dir., Kevin Sharp; Asst. Dir., Marilyn R. Cheeseman; Dir. Horticulture & Horticulturist Mgr., Dale Skaggs; Registrar, Neil O'Brien; Dir. Devel., Susan Johnson; Assoc. Cur. Education, Margarita Palmer; Comptroller, Gail Hopper; Museum Shop Mgr., Nancy Robertson.
Personnel Profile: Full-Time Paid 28; Part-Time Paid 12; Part-Time Volunteers 175; Interns 6.
Governing Authority: nonprofit organization. Tax-exempt: 501(c)(3).
Art Museum.
Collections: 18th, 19th & early 20th-century paintings, prints & sculpture with emphasis on French & American Impressionists & Post-Impressionists, includes works of Bonnard, Boudin, Braque, Butler, Cals, Carpeaux, Carrier-Beleuse, Cassatt, Cezanne, Chagall, Corot, Cox, Cross, Daubigny, Degas, Dufy, Fantin-Latour, Forain, Gauguin, Grandjean, Guigou, Guillaumin, Harpignies, Jacques, Jongkind, LaTouche, Legros, Lepine, Luce, Marquet, Mathey, Matisse, Monet, Morisot, Munch, Noufflard, Oberteuffer, Piette, Pissarro, Prendergast, Raeburn, Raffaelli, Renoir, Reynolds, Rouart, Sargent, Signac, Sisley, Toulouse-Lautrec, Tucker, Utrillo, Walker & Vuillard; European porcelain; Stout collection of 18th-century German porcelain; Adler collection of European & American Pewter; Hooker collection of 18-19th century English porcelain; 17 acres of gardens.
Major Exhibits: Monet to Matisse: French Masterworks from the Dixon Permanent Collection, 1/31/10-4/4/10; Memphis Flower Show: Anything But Clear, 4/15/10-4/18/10; Anything But Clear: Contemporary Glass from the Habatat Gallery, Chicago, 4/15/10-5/13/10; Quiet Spirit Skillful Hands: The Graphic Work of Claire Leighton (T), 6/27/10-9/18/10; Richmond Barthe: His Life In Art (T), 10/3/10-1/2/11; Objects of Wonder: Four Centuries of Still-Life from the Norton Museum of Art, 10/17/10-1/9/11.
Research Fields: Impressionist period; 18th-century European porcelain, particularly German & English.
Facilities: 3,000-vol. library by appointment; 6,800 sq. ft. exhibit space; 17 acres of gardens; 250-seat auditorium.
Activities: guided tours; random access audio tour; lectures; gallery talks; films; performing arts programs; symposiums; docent program; museum sponsored foreign tours; art history, museology & horticulture internships; inter-museum, permanent, & temporary exhibitions; rental facilities.
Publications: quarterly newsletter; catalogues: Mary Cassatt and The American Impressionists; Impressionists in 1877; Henri-Joseph Harpignies; Henriette Amiard Oberteuffer and George Oberteuffer; Joseph Mallord William Turner; Homage to Camille Pissarro; The Last Years 1890-1903; The Genius of Van Gogh; An International Episode: Millet, Monet and their North American Counterparts; An Assemblage of Decorative Arts; A View of Tennessee Silversmiths; Marc Chagall-Selected Works, 1911-1981; Sources of the Modern Vision: A Selection of French Paintings from the Phillips Collection; Milton Avery's Mexico; ceramics, The Chinese Legacy; Vital Diversity: Japanese Paintings and Ceramics of the Edo Period; The Impressionist Vision; The Passion of Rodin: Sculpture from the B. Gerald Cantor collection; From Arcadia to Barbizon: A Journey in French Landscape Painting; Toulouse-Lautrec: The Guardsmark Collection; Odilon Redon: The Ian Woodner Family Collection; Louis XV and Madame de Pompadour: A Love Affair with Style; The Lamps of Tiffany; Highlights from the Egon and Hildegard Neustadt Collection; Jean-Louis Forain: The Impressionist Years; The Dixon Gallery & Gardens Permanent Collection Catalogue; Celebrate America: 19th Century Paintings from the Manoogian Collection; Visualizing the Blues: Images of the American South; The Call of the Wild: Sporting Art in the Mississippi Flyway; Regional Dialect: American Scene Paintings from the John and Susan Horseman Collection.
Hours & Admission Prices: Tues.-Fri. 10-4, Sat. 10-5, Sun. 1-5. Adults $7, seniors 65 & over and students 18 & over $5, children 7-17 $3; discounts to AAM members and groups of 10 or more; Sat. 10am-12pm, members and children 6 & under no charge. Closed New Year's Day; Independence Day; Thanksgiving; Christmas. ♿
Attendance: 48,180 (accurate)
Membership: Individual $45; Dual & Family $60-$124; Sponsor $125-$249; Young At Art $150-$249; Donor $250-$499; Cosmopolitans $300 per couple; Patron $500-$999; Sustainer $1,000-$1,499; Contributor $1,500-$2,499; Supporter $2,500-$4,999; Benefactor $5,000 & up; Life $25,000.

FIRE MUSEUM OF MEMPHIS, 118 Adams Ave., Memphis, TN 38103-2012. Tel.: 901-320-5658. Fax: 901-529-8422.
E-mail: brier@firemuseum.com
Web Site: www.firemuseum.com
Founded: 1993.
Congressional District: 9

Key Personnel: Exec. Dir., Brier Smith Turner; Chm. (V), Thomas O'Malley.
Personnel Profile: Full-Time Paid 6; Part-Time Paid 2.
Governing Authority: private; nonprofit. Tax-exempt: 501(c)(3).
Fire-Fighting Museum: housed in 1910 Fire Engine House No. 1, which served as a fire station until 1973 and is listed on the National Register of Historic Places.
Collections: concentration on historic fire apparatus, fire-fighting tools, equipment & apparel; photographs; film; books; examples of modern technology & fire prevention materials.
Research Fields: history of fire fighting in Memphis & surrounding area; fire prevention and safety education.
Facilities: library on fire history & service; educational facilities; 30-seat theater; facilities available for private parties with advanced arrangements. Fire memorabilia & home safety items for sale.
Activities: films; formal education programs for children; participatory & temporary exhibitions.
Publications: quarterly newsletter.
Hours & Admission Prices: Mon.-Sat. 9-5. Adults $6, children 3-12 $5, seniors over 60 & military $4; discount to groups; members, children 2 & under no charge. ♿
Attendance: 33,000 (accurate)
Membership: Family $50; Corporate $5,000.

GIBSON GUITAR FACTORY, 145 Lt. George W. Lee Ave., Memphis, TN 38103. Tel.: 901-544-7998, ext. 4080.
E-mail: thelounge@gibson.com
Web Site: www.gibson.com
Guitar Factory.
Collections: guitar-making process.
Hours & Admission Prices: Tours: Mon.-Sat. 11, 12, 1, 2, 3 & 4, Sun. 12, 1, 2, 3 & 4. Adults $10.

GRACELAND, 3764 Elvis Presley Blvd., Memphis, TN 38116-4198. Mailing Address: P.O. Box 16508, Memphis, TN 38186-0508. Tel.: 901-332-3322. Fax: 901-344-3116. TDD: 901-344-3146.
E-mail: gracelandtours@elvis.com
Web Site: www.elvis.com
Founded: 1982.
Congressional District: 8
Key Personnel: C.E.O. & Pres., Jack Soden; Gen. Mgr. & Vice Pres., Regina Gambill; Vice Pres. Entertainment & Music Publishing, Gary Hovey; Dir. Licensing, Carol Butler; Dir. Merchandising, Danny Hiltenbrand; Archives Mgr., Angela Marchese.
Personnel Profile: Full-Time Paid 250; Part-Time Paid 250.
Governing Authority: corporation. Parent Institution: CKX, Inc., 650 Madison Ave., 16th Fl., New York, NY 10022. Subsidiary Institution: Elvis Presley Enterprises, Inc.
Historic Home & Music Museum: housed in 1939 mansion occupied by singer/entertainer Elvis Presley from 1957 until his death in 1977.
Collections: clothing; costumes; jewelry; guitars; gold records & awards; photographs; personal mementoes; furnishings; automobiles; jet planes; personal books & papers; pianos; twentieth century music & popular culture.
Research Fields: Elvis Presley.
Facilities: mansion & 14-acre estate; wedding chapel in the woods; Elvis Presley's Heartbreak Hotel. Visitor Center Complex: automobile museum; Lisa Marie/Jetstar Airplanes exhibit; 100-seat theater; two restaurants; ticket office; shuttle staging area; rentable indoor activity facility available. Gift items for sale.
Activities: audio tours. Annual Events: Elvis Presley Birthday Celebration in January; Elvis Week in August; Christmas at Graceland in December.
Publications: brochures; pamphlets; quarterly newsletter.
Hours & Admission Prices: Grounds: March-Oct. Mon.-Sat. 9-5, Sun. 10-4; Nov. daily 10-4; Dec.-Feb. Wed.-Mon. 10-4. Mansion: March-May Mon.-Sat. 9-5, Sun. 10-4; June-Aug. Mon.-Sat. 9-5, Sun. 9-4; Sept.-Oct. Mon.-Sat. 9-5, Sun. 10-4; Nov. daily 10-4; Dec.-Feb. Wed.-Mon. 10-4. Mansion: adults $28, students and seniors 62 & over $25.20, children 7-12 $12; children 6 & under no charge. Platinum Tour: adults $33, students and seniors 62 & over $29.70, children 7-12 $15; children 6 & under no charge. Closed New Year's Day; Thanksgiving; Christmas. ♿
Attendance: 650,000 (estimated)

LICHTERMAN NATURE CENTER, 5992 Quince Rd., Memphis, TN 38119-7257. Tel.: 901-767-7322. Fax: 901-682-3050.
E-mail: andy.williams@memphistn.gov
Web Site: www.memphismuseums.org
Founded: 1983.
Key Personnel: Mgr., Andy Williams; Program Mgr., Barbara Moses; Museum Shop Mgr., Steven Swift.
Personnel Profile: Full-Time Paid 10; Part-Time Paid 25; Part-Time Volunteers 25; Interns 1.
Governing Authority: municipal. Parent Institution: City of Memphis. Subsidiary Institution: Memphis Museums, Inc. Tax-exempt: 501(c)(3).
Environmental Education Center.
Collections: 65-acres of forest, meadow and lake habitats; natural history materials & artifacts.
Facilities: visitors center; special events pavilion & lawn; demonstration gardens & greenhouse; trails; boardwalks. Museum-related items for sale.
Activities: guided tours; lectures; organized education programs for children, college students & adults; participatory exhibits; demonstrations of raising wild flowers. Museum Sponsors: family field trips; National Wildlife Week Celebration.
Publications: Museumscope.
Hours & Admission Prices: Tues.-Thurs. 9-4, Fri.-Sat. 9-5. Adults $6, senior citizen $5.50, children 3-12 $4.50; children under 3 no charge. Closed New Year's Day; Thanksgiving; Christmas Eve & Day. ♿
Attendance: 40,000 (estimated)
Membership: Individual $50; Family $75; IMAX Club $100.

MAGEVNEY HOUSE, 198 Adams Ave., Memphis, TN 38103. Mailing Address: 3050 Central Ave, Memphis, TN 38111-3316. Tel.: 901-320-6326. Fax: 901-320-6391.
Web Site: www.memphismuseums.org
Founded: 1941.
Congressional District: 8
Key Personnel: Asst. Mgr., Jorja Frazier.
Personnel Profile: Part-Time Paid 1.
Governing Authority: municipal. Parent Institution: Pink Palace Family of Museums. Subsidiary Institution: Memphis Museum, Inc. Tax-exempt: 501(c)(3).
Historic House: c.1836 Magevney House.
Collections: period furniture.
Research Fields: historical investigation of Memphis pertaining to the home & its occupants.
Activities: guided tours; organized education programs for children; docent program; kitchen garden tours.
Hours & Admission Prices: Temporarily closed.
Attendance: 1,584 (accurate)

MALLORY-NEELY HOUSE, 652 Adams Ave., Memphis, TN 38105. Mailing Address: 3050 Central Ave., Memphis, TN 38111-3316. Tel.: 901-320-6370. Fax: 901-320-6391.
Web Site: www.memphismuseums.org
Founded: 1973.
Congressional District: 9
Governing Authority: municipal. Parent Institution: Pink Palace Family of Museums. Tax-exempt: 501(c)(3).
Historic House.
Collections: original furnishings of the Victorian period through the 1960s.
Research Fields: extensive research into structure of home for preservation purposes; historical investigation of Memphis pertaining to home & occupants.
Facilities: classroom. Gift items for sale.
Activities: docent programs; formal education programs; guided tours. Museum Sponsors: seasonal exhibits.
Hours & Admission Prices: Temporarily closed. Call for more information.

MEMPHIS BELLE MEMORIAL ASSOCIATION, 5118 Park Ave., Ste. 110, Memphis, TN 38117-5710. Mailing Address: P.O. Box 1942, Memphis, TN 38101-1942. Fax: 901-767-4612.
E-mail: doctorhar@aol.com
Web Site: www.memphisbelle.com
Formerly: Memphis Bell B17 Flying Fortress
Founded: 1967.
Key Personnel: Pres., George Burns.
Personnel Profile: Part-Time Volunteers 38.
Governing Authority: Memphis Belle Memorial Association & U.S. Air Force Museum.
Military Museum.
Collections: B-17 aircraft.
Hours & Admission Prices: Summer daily. Island admission prices vary.

MEMPHIS BOTANIC GARDEN, GOLDSMITH CIVIC GARDEN CENTER, 750 Cherry Rd., Memphis, TN 38117-4699. Tel.: 901-576-4100. Fax: 901-682-1561.
E-mail: jamerbro@memphis.magibox.net
Web Site: www.memphisbotanicgarden.com
Founded: 1964.
Congressional District: 9

Key Personnel: Exec. Dir., Huey Holden; Bd. Pres., William B. Dunavant, III; Education & Admissions, Jim R. Browne; Dir. Devel., Margaret Frazier; Membership Coord., Felicia Thompson; Museum Shop Mgr., Michelle Darby; Youth Dir., Mary Helen Butler; Horticulturist, Ronnie McCarty.
Personnel Profile: Full-Time Paid 28; Part-Time Paid 8; Part-Time Volunteers 350.
Governing Authority: City of Memphis. Parent Institution: Memphis Park Commission. Subsidiary Institution: Memphis Botanic Garden Foundation. Tax-exempt: 501(c)(3).
Botanic Garden: home of the Goldsmith Civic Garden Center.
Collections: Goldsmith Civic Garden Center; Rose Garden; Tennessee Bicentennial Iris Garden; Fonville Four Seasons Garden; Wild Flower Woodland; Michie Magnolia Trail; Orchid House Azalea & Dogwood Trail; Charlotte Sawyer Memorial Daffodil Trail; Japanese Garden of Tranquility; W.C. Paul Arboretum; Conifer Collection; Little Garden Club Sensory Garden; Perennial Trial Garden; herb collection; open meadow; cactus collection; organic garden; sculpture garden; Audubon Lake & Pavilion; water garden; Daylily collection; Little Garden Club Orientation Theater; Hardin Hall.
Research Fields: plant material.
Facilities: 2,000-vol. library of books on plants available for research on premises only; botanic garden; reading room; 250-seat auditorium; classroom; art gallery; visitor center. Gift items for sale.
Activities: guided tours; lectures; films; study clubs; hobby workshops; organized education programs for children, adults & undergraduate college students affiliated with University of Memphis; docent program; participatory & temporary exhibitions. Center Sponsors: art exhibits; plant shows; outdoor concerts.
Publications: magazine, The Dirt; brochures; curriculum guide; educational catalog.
Hours & Admission Prices: March 9-Nov. 1 Mon.-Sat. 9-6, Sun. 11-6; Nov. 2-March 8 Mon.-Sat. 9-4:30, Sun. 11-4:30. Adults $5, seniors 62 & over $4, children 3-12 $3; discounts to groups, and AHS & AABGA Reciprocal Gardens members; children under 2, members & Tues. after 12pm no charge. ♿
Attendance: 130,000 (accurate)
Membership: Individual Plus One $35; Family & Grandparents $45-$74; Sustaining $75-$124; Contributing $125-$249; Photography $150; Donor $250-$499; Patron $500-$999; Benefactor $1,000 & up.

*** MEMPHIS BROOKS MUSEUM OF ART, (M),** 1934 Poplar Ave., Overton Park, Memphis, TN 38104-2765. Tel.: 901-544-6200. Fax: 901-725-4071.
E-mail: brooks@brooksmuseum.org
Web Site: www.brooksmuseum.org
Founded: 1916.
Congressional District: 9
Key Personnel: Dir., Cameron Kitchin; Asst. Dir., Rick Bartemus; Chief Cur., Marina Pacini; Assoc. Cur., Stanton Thomas; Cur. Education, Karleen Gardner; Assoc. Cur. Education, Kathy Dumlao; Collections Mgr., Kip Peterson; Assoc. Registrar, Marilyn Masler; Dir. Devel., Diane Jalfon; Devel. Assoc., Kiley Robinette; Dir. Mktg., Claudia Towell; Art Dir., Heather Klein; Museum Shop Mgr., Mimi Atkinson; Public Rels. & Public Events Mgr., Elisabeth Callihan.
Personnel Profile: Full-Time Paid 46; Part-Time Paid 37; Part-Time Volunteers 100; Interns 5.
Governing Authority: nonprofit corp. Parent Institution: Memphis Brooks Museum of Art, Inc. Tax-exempt: 501(c)(3) & 170(b)(1)(A).
Fine Arts Museum.
Collections: Kress collection of Italian, Medieval, Renaissance & Baroque paintings & sculpture; 16th-19th century Northern European paintings & sculpture; 17th & 18th century English portraits & landscapes; 19th & 20th-century American paintings & sculpture; French Impressionists; 5,000 prints; porcelain; glass; furniture; artists books.
Major Exhibits: Venice in the Age of Canaletts (T), 2/14/10-5/9/10; Who Shot Rock & Roll (T), 6/26/10-9/26/10; William Christenberry: Photographs, 1961-2000 (T), 10/15/10-2/9/11.
Research Fields: pertaining to permanent collection.
Facilities: 8,000-vol. art reference library; 273-seat auditorium; orientation theatre; restaurant. Museum-related items for sale.
Activities: guided tours; lectures; films; demonstrations; student art activity area; musical events; gallery talks; docent program inter-museum loan, permanent, temporary & traveling exhibitions; outreach school program.
Publications: members' magazine; exhibition catalogues; interpretative exhibition; general museum brochures.
Hours & Admission Prices: Wed. & Fri. 10-4, Thurs. 10-8, Sat. 10-5, Sun. 11:30-5. Adults $7, seniors $6, students $3; discounts to AAM and ICOM members & scheduled groups; children under 6 & members no charge. Closed New Year's Day; Independence Day; Thanksgiving; Christmas. ♿
Attendance: 100,000 (accurate)
Membership: Individual $50; Dual $65; Family $75; Advocate $150; Fellow $300; Benefactor $500; Patron $1,000; Masterpiece Circle $2,500; Moss Society $5,000.

MEMPHIS COLLEGE OF ART, 1930 Poplar Ave., Overton Park, Memphis, TN 38104-2756. Tel.: 901-272-5100; 800-727-1088. Fax: 901-272-5104.
E-mail: info@mca.edu
Web Site: www.mca.edu
Founded: 1936.
Congressional District: 9
Key Personnel: C.F.O., Sherry Yelvington; Pres., Jeffrey D. Nesin; Chm. (V), Gary Backaus; Registrar, Monica Haynes; Dir. Public Rels., Michelle Byrd.
Personnel Profile: Full-Time Paid 49; Part-Time Paid 24.
Governing Authority: college. Tax-exempt: 501(c)(3).
Art College.
Collections: Jacob Marks Memorial Collection; works of college graduates.
Major Exhibits: Those Who Do: Mid-South Regional Art Teachers Exhibition, 1/4/10-1/29/10; Local Flavors: Seven Regional Artists, 2/20/10-4/11/10; BFA Exhibition, 4/19/10-5/15/10.
Facilities: 16,000-vol. library of visual art books available for inter-library loan for teachers & graduate students on premises; 342-seat auditorium; classrooms. Art material for sale.
Activities: guided tours; lectures; films; arts festivals; organized education programs for children, adults & undergraduate college students; temporary exhibitions.
Publications: occasional catalogs; newsletter.
Hours & Admission Prices: Mon.-Fri. 8-5, Sat. 9-4, Sun. 12-4. No charge. Closed holidays. ♿
Attendance: 15,000 (estimated)
Membership: Individual $40; Family $50; Associate $100; Benefactor $250; President's Circle $500; Chairman's Circle $1,000; Trustees Circle $2,500; The Academy Society $5,000.

MEMPHIS ROCK 'N' SOUL MUSEUM, 191 Beale St., Ste. 100, Memphis, TN 38103-3715. Tel.: 901-205-2533. Fax: 901-205-2534.
E-mail: info@memphisrocknsoul.org
Web Site: www.memphisrocknsoul.org
Founded: 2000.
Key Personnel: Exec. Dir., John Doyle; Chm. (V), Kevin Kane; Museum Shop Mgr., Pam Hetsel.
Personnel Profile: Full-Time Paid 4; Part-Time Paid 8; Part-Time Volunteers 3.
Music History Museum.
Collections: rock & soul music history; musical instruments; musicians.
Activities: rental facilities.
Hours & Admission Prices: Daily 10-7. Adults $10, youth 5-17 $7; discounts to AAA, AARP, & military. Closed New Year's Day; Thanksgiving; Christmas Eve & Day. ♿

MEMPHIS ZOO, 2000 Prentiss Place, Memphis, TN 38112-5033. Tel.: 901-276-(WILD). Fax: 901-725-9305.
E-mail: zooinfo@memphiszoo.org
Web Site: www.memphiszoo.org
Founded: 1906.
Congressional District: 9
Key Personnel: Pres. & C.E.O., Dr. Charles A. Brady; Dir. Operations, Wayne Carlisle; Cur. Mammals, Matt Thompson; Cur. Birds, Herb Roberts; Museum Shop Mgr., Conne Bellett; Cur. Reptiles, Steve Reichling.
Personnel Profile: Full-Time Paid 159; Part-Time Paid 50; Part-Time Volunteers 25; Interns 5.
Governing Authority: managed by society; city-owned. Parent Institution: Memphis Park Commission. Tax-exempt.
Zoo.
Collections: live animals.
Research Fields: animal behavior; captive behavior.
Facilities: library; aquarium; education center; classroom.
Activities: special events; children & family programs; field trips; school programs.
Publications: bimonthly magazine, Exzooberance.
Hours & Admission Prices: March-Oct. daily 9-5; Nov.-Feb. daily 9-4; last admission 1 hour before closing. Adults 12-59 $13, senior citizens 60 & over $12, children 2-11 $8; children under 2 & zoo members no charge. Closed Thanksgiving; Christmas Eve & Day. ♿
Attendance: 1,066,000 (estimated)
Membership: Individual $60; Dual $70; Family & Grandparent $79; Contributing $165; Associate $300; Patron $500.

MISSISSIPPI RIVER MUSEUM AT MUD ISLAND RIVER PARK, 125 N. Front St., Memphis, TN 38103-1713. Mailing Address: 101 N. Island Dr., Memphis, TN 38103. Tel.: 901-576-7241; 800-507-6507. Fax: 901-576-6666.
E-mail: trey@mudisland.com
Web Site: www.mudisland.com
Founded: 1978.
Congressional District: 9
Key Personnel: General Mgr., Trey Giuntini; Museum Mgr., Alisa Bradley.
Personnel Profile: Full-Time Paid 2; Part-Time Paid 25.
Governing Authority: Parent Institution: Riverfront Development Corp. Tax-exempt.
History Museum Complex.
Collections: full size reconstruction of riverboat & Civil War gunboat with period furnishings; artifacts & archival relating to prehistoric & historic Indians, settlement & boat development; Civil War on the Mississippi River; Delta Music from Blues to Rock-n-Roll; boat models & engines; river engineering; natural history & sciences; related art collection; outdoor exhibition: five-block-long scale model of river focusing on cultural & natural history of the lower Mississippi River.
Facilities: aquarium; outdoor scale model of river; 5,000-seat outdoor theater; 4 eating facilities; 105-seat theater. Museum-related items for sale.
Activities: guided tours; lectures; films; gallery talks; concerts; formally organized education programs for children & adults; permanent & temporary exhibitions; rental facilities.
Hours & Admission Prices: April 11 to May & Sept.-Oct. Tues.-Sun. 10-5; Memorial Day-Labor Day Tues.-Sun. 10-6. Adults $8, senior $6, children 5-11 $5; discounts to groups; children 4 & under no charge. ♿
Attendance: 97,000 (estimated)

* **NATIONAL CIVIL RIGHTS MUSEUM AT THE LORRAINE MOTEL, (M),** 450 Mulberry St., Memphis, TN 38103-4214. Tel.: 901-521-9699. Fax: 901-521-9740.
E-mail: contact@civilrightsmuseum.org
Web Site: www.civilrightsmuseum.org
Founded: 1991.
Congressional District: 9
Key Personnel: Chm. (V), Dr. Benjamin Hooks; Chm. Exec. Committee, Mr. J.R. Hyde; Exec. Dir., Beverly Robertson.
Governing Authority: private; nonprofit organization. Tax-exempt: 501(c)(3).
History Museum: located at the Lorraine Motel, site of the assassination of Dr. Martin Luther King Jr.
Collections: artifacts that document civil rights activities & associated segregationist activity chiefly from 1619-2000; books; organizational pamphlets; photographs; original correspondence; paintings; clothing; art works; film; video.
Facilities: 40,000 sq. ft. exhibit space.
Activities: Museum Sponsors: Freedom Award; King Holiday.
Publications: Movement Newsletter; annual report.
Hours & Admission Prices: June-Aug. Mon. & Wed.-Sat. 9-6, Sun. 1-6; Sept.-May Mon. & Wed.-Sat. 9-5, Sun. 1-5. Adults $12, senior citizens & students $10, children 4-12 $8.50; discounts to military, AAA, AAM & AARP members; members no charge. Closed New Year's Day; Thanksgiving & Christmas. ♿
Attendance: 160,000 (accurate)
Membership: Individual $30; Family $60; Advocate $150.

NATIONAL ORNAMENTAL METAL MUSEUM, 374 Metal Museum Dr., Memphis, TN 38106-1514. Tel.: 901-774-6380. Fax: 901-774-6382.
E-mail: info@metalmuseum.org
Web Site: www.metalmuseum.org
Founded: 1976.
Congressional District: 96
Key Personnel: Dir., Carissa Hussong; Pres. (V), Rob Keeler; C.O.O., Charles Ferryman; Registrar, Leila Hamdan; Museum Shop Mgr., Nancy Jackson; Studio Mgr., James Masterson.
Personnel Profile: Full-Time Paid 9; Part-Time Paid 4; Part-Time Volunteers 200; Interns 2.
Governing Authority: nonprofit organization. Tax-exempt: 501(c)(3).
Metal Museum: historic & contemporary decorative & fine art metalwork.
Collections: decorative metalwork; sculpture; jewelry; tools; hollowware; architectural forged & cast iron; drawings; videos; slides.
Major Exhibits: Remake/Remodel, 11/09-1/10; Different Tempers (T), 2/10-3/10; South African Studio Jewelry (T), 4/10-5/10; Iron 2010 (T), 5/10-8/10; Master Metalsmith, 9/10-11/10.
Research Fields: ironwork; decorative ironwork; restoration of ferrous & non-ferrous objects; historic & contemporary ferrous & non-ferrous metalwork.
Facilities: 20,000-vol. library & slide collection; teaching & demonstration building; 3.2 acres of grounds & sculpture garden; 2,800 sq. ft. exhibit space. Handcrafted jewelry, ironwork, books & other items for sale.
Activities: guided tours; lectures; organized programs for children & adults; training programs for professional museum workers; loan, temporary & traveling exhibitions; classes & workshops for beginners & professional metalsmiths; metal conservation & restoration services available to public & private collectors. Museum Sponsors: Repair Days.
Publications: quarterly newsletter; exhibition catalogues.
Hours & Admission Prices: Tues.-Sat. 10-5, Sun. 12-5. Adults $5, senior citizens $4, students $3; discounts to Tenn. Association of Museum members, employees of other museums, AAM & AAA members; members & children under 5 no charge. Closed Christmas Eve through New Year's Day; Easter; Independence Day; Thanksgiving; during exhibit changes. ♿
Attendance: 38,000 (estimated)
Membership: Student & Senior $35; Individual $40; Dual & Family $55; Supporting Friend $100; Donor $250; Silver Corporate/Individual $500; Gold Corporate/Individual $1,000.

* **PINK PALACE FAMILY OF MUSEUMS,** 3050 Central Ave., Memphis, TN 38111-3399. Tel.: 901-320-6320 & 6398. Fax: 901-320-6391.
Web Site: www.memphismuseums.org
Formerly: Memphis Pink Palace Museum & Sharpe Planetarium and IMAX Theater
Founded: 1928.
Congressional District: 9
Key Personnel: Dir., Stephen J. Pike; Pres., John W. Straton; Admin. Program Affairs, Wesley Creel; Mgr. Collections, Louella Weaver; Mgr. Exhibits & Graphic Svcs., Steve Masler; Mgr. Education, Alice A. "Alex" Eilers; Crew Training Intl. IMAX Theater, Tony Hardy; Business Affairs Mgr., Nancy H. Albonetti; Admin. Public Affairs, Richard Pugh; Mgr. Lichterman Nature Center, Andy Williams.
Personnel Profile: Full-Time Paid 62; Part-Time Paid 133; Part-Time Volunteers 360; Interns 4.
Governing Authority: municipal. Headquarters: Pink Palace Family of Museums. Parent Institution: City of Memphis. Subsidiary Institution: Memphis Museums, Inc.; Lichterman Nature Center; Mallory/Neely House; Magevney House; Coon Creek Science Center. Tax-exempt: 501(c)(3).
General, Natural History, Science & Cultural History Museum.
Collections: artifacts, specimens & documents relating to the cultural & natural history of Memphis & the mid southern region; African American artifacts.
Major Exhibits: Chocolate, 1/30/10-4/25/10; Moving Stories, 2/5/10-5/1/11; Bagels & BBQ: The Jewish Experience in Tennessee, 2/6/10-4/11/10; Surviving: The Body of Evidence, Summer 2010.
Facilities: 2,500-vol. library of history & natural science available for inter-library loan & on premises; planetarium; snack area; classrooms; teaching laboratories; 240-seat IMAX theater; 200-seat science theater. Museum-related items for sale.
Activities: films; hobby workshops; TV programs; formally organized education programs for children & adults; docent program or council; permanent, temporary & traveling exhibitions; school loan service; planetarium shows; IMAX shows.
Publications: bimonthly newsletter, Museumscope; biannual, Adventures; tri-annual, Quest; book, Memphis, 1800-1900, Vols. I-III; booklet, From Saddlebags to Science: A Century of Healthcare in Memphis, 1830-1930; occasional papers, Nonconnah Creek Mastodon Report; Magevney House Archaeological Investigation Report.
Hours & Admission Prices: Mon.-Sat. 9-5, Sun. 12-5. Adults $8.75, senior citizens $8.25, children $6.25; discounts to ASTC & AAM members; Tues. 1-4, children under 3 & members no charge. Planetarium: adults $4.50, senior citizens & children $4. IMAX: adults $8, senior citizens $7.25, children $6.25; discounts for exhibit & planetarium packages. Closed New Year's Day; Thanksgiving; Christmas Eve & Day. ♿
Attendance: 546,853 (accurate)
Membership: Individual $50; Family $75; IMAX Club $100; Palace Guard $175; Benefactor $250; Advocate $500; Director's Circle $1,000.

SLAVE HAVEN UNDERGROUND RAILROAD MUSEUM (BURKLE ESTATE), 826 N. Second St., Memphis, TN 38107-2302. Mailing Address: P.O. Box 3142, Memphis, TN 38173-0142. Tel.: 901-527-3427.
Historic House: former home of Jacob Burkle, built in 1849.
Collections: memorabilia from the Underground Railroad.
Hours & Admission Prices: Summer: Mon.-Sat. 10-4; Winter: Wed.-Sat. 10-4. Tours: adults $6, students 4-17 $4.

STAX MUSEUM OF AMERICAN SOUL MUSIC, 926 E. McLemore Ave., Memphis, TN 38106-3338. Tel.: 901-946-2535. Fax: 901-507-1463.
Web Site: www.staxmuseum.com
Founded: 2003.
Key Personnel: Interim C.E.O., Deanie Parker; Pres. (V), Howard Robertson;

Senior Mgr. Operations, Susan Green; Vice Pres. Finance, Duke Herenton; Public Rels., Tim Sampson; Museum Shop Mgr., Steve Walker.
Personnel Profile: Full-Time Paid 3; Part-Time Paid 7; Part-Time Volunteers 10; Interns 3.
Governing Authority: private; nonprofit organization. Parent Institution: Soulsville, 870 McLemore Ave., Memphis, TN 38106. Tax-exempt: 501(c)(3).
Soul Music Museum.
Collections: over 2,000 cultural artifacts; photographs; sound recordings; musical & recording equipment; stage costumes; advertising; albums.
Research Fields: oral histories; local artists & community members.
Facilities: 60-seat theater. Museum-related items for sale.
Activities: concerts; formal education programs for children; lectures; loan & traveling exhibitions; theater; rental facility. Annual Events: fundraisers; Black History Month; Black Music History Month.
Hours & Admission Prices: April-Oct. Mon.-Sat. 10-5, Sun. 1-5; Nov.-March Tues.-Sat. 10-5, Sun. 1-5. Adults $12, senior citizens, students & military $11, children $9; discounts to groups & AAA members; members no charge. Closed New Year's Day; Easter; Thanksgiving; Christmas. ♿
Attendance: 42,422 (accurate)
Membership: $50, $100, $250, $500.

WONDERS: MEMPHIS INTERNATIONAL CULTURAL SERIES, 119 S. Main St., Ste. 500, Memphis, TN 38103-3659.
Founded: 1985.
Key Personnel: Pres. & C.E.O., Richard C. Hackett; Deputy Dir. & C.O.O., Glen A. Campbell; Chm. (V), Diane Rudner; Dir. Cur. & Educational Programs, Steve Masler; Dir. Sales & Mktg., Twyla Dixon; C.F.O., Ted Ferris; Sales Mgr., Joyce Ann Parker.
Personnel Profile: Full-Time Paid 7; Part-Time Paid 60; Part-Time Volunteers 2,000.
Governing Authority: municipal government. Parent Institution: The City of Memphis. Tax-exempt: 501(c)(3).
Exhibit Space.
Facilities: 22,000 sq. ft. exhibit space; 150-seat restaurant; 100-seat theatre. Books & items pertaining to current exhibitions for sale.
Activities: loan exhibitions; lectures; organized education programs for children; docent program.
Publications: catalogues for each touring exhibition.
Hours & Admission Prices: April-Oct. daily 9-7. Adults $12, senior citizens 60 & over $11, youth 5-12 $5, school groups $3. ♿
Attendance: 635,000 (accurate)

WOODRUFF-FONTAINE HOUSE MUSEUM, 680 Adams Ave., Memphis, TN 38105-4902. Tel.: 901-526-1469. Fax: 901-526-4531.
E-mail: wfhouse@bellsouth.net
Web Site: www.woodruff-fontaine.com
Historic House: French Victorian mansion built in 1870 along "Millionaires Row."
Collections: period artifacts.
Hours & Admission Prices: Wed.-Sun. 12-4. Closed holidays.

Morristown

CROCKETT TAVERN MUSEUM, 2002 Morningside Dr., Morristown, TN 37814-5461. Tel.: 423-587-9900.
E-mail: crockett@discoveret.org
Web Site: www.discoveret.org/crockett
Founded: 1958.
Congressional District: 4
Key Personnel: Pres. (V) Hamblen County Chapter A.P.T.A. & Museum Shop Mgr., Sally A. Baker.
Personnel Profile: Part-Time Paid 1; Part-Time Volunteers 1.
Governing Authority: nonprofit organization. Affiliated with the Assoc. for the Preservation of Tennessee Antiquities, Belle Meade Mansion, Harding Rd. at Leake Ave., Nashville, TN 37205. Tax-exempt: 170(b)(1)(A).
History Museum: housed in 1794 replica of boyhood home of David Crockett.
Collections: furniture; pioneer utensils; historical articles used by early pioneers.
Facilities: Crockett books, prints, buttons, pioneer-related & other museum-related items for sale.
Activities: guided tours; permanent exhibitions. Museum Sponsors: Davy Crockett Birthday Party in August.
Publications: newsletter for Hamblen County Chapter APTA members, Trailblazer.
Hours & Admission Prices: May-Oct. Tues.-Sat. 11-5. Adults $5, students 5-18 $1; discount to groups & AAA members; members, children under 5, APTA members, and school & group trip chaperones no charge.
Attendance: 1,500 (estimated)
Membership: Sustaining $20.

ROSE CENTER MUSEUM, 442 W. 2nd N. St., Morristown, TN 37814-4026. Mailing Address: P.O. Box 1976, Morristown, TN 37816-1976. Tel.: 423-581-4330. Fax: 423-581-4307.
E-mail: postmaster@rosecenter.org
Web Site: www.rosecenter.org
Founded: 1976.
Congressional District: 1
Key Personnel: Dir., Robert Lydick; Pres. (V), Vicki Porter; Administrative Asst., Patty Gracey.
Personnel Profile: Full-Time Paid 3; Part-Time Paid 2; Part-Time Volunteers 50.
Governing Authority: nonprofit organization. Tax-exempt.
Civic Art & Cultural Center: housed in 1892 former high school.
Collections: early Morristown photographs; Murrell airplane & its history; local Civil War era artifacts & photos; Morristown College artifacts, documents & photos.
Facilities: auditorium; classrooms.
Activities: dance recitals; arts festivals; hobby workshops; formally organized education programs for children & adults; temporary exhibits.
Publications: monthly newsletter; quarterly arts calendar.
Hours & Admission Prices: Mon.-Fri. 9:30-5, Sat. 9-1. No charge; donations accepted. Closed New Year's Day; Martin Luther King Day; Memorial Day; Independence Day; Labor Day; Thanksgiving; Christmas. ♿
Attendance: 65,000 (estimated)
Membership: Individual $30; Family $45; Contributor $75; Sustaining $125; Life $1,000.

Murfreesboro

BALDWIN PHOTOGRAPHIC GALLERY, Learning Resources Center, Murfreesboro, TN 37132-0001. Mailing Address: MTSU, Box 305, Murfreesboro, TN 37132-0001. Tel.: 615-898-2085 & 5628 (Off. of Secy.). Fax: 615-898-5682.
E-mail: tjimison@mtsu.edu
Founded: 1961.
Congressional District: 6
Key Personnel: Cur., Tom Jimison; Archivist, Valerie Menard.
Personnel Profile: Full-Time Paid 1; Part-Time Paid 1; Part-Time Volunteers 10; Interns 1.
Governing Authority: public university; nonprofit organization. Tax-exempt.
Photography Art Museum.
Collections: contemporary photography of past 20 years.
Facilities: photograph archive.
Activities: lectures; traveling exhibitions.
Publications: monthly, show announcements; posters.
Hours & Admission Prices: mid-Jan. to June & Sept. to mid-Dec. Mon.-Fri. 8-4:30, Sat. 9-11:45, Sun. 6pm-10pm; July-Aug. by appointment. No charge. Closed Labor Day. ♿
Attendance: 30,000 (estimated)

DISCOVERY CENTER AT MURFREE SPRING, 502 S.E. Broad St., Murfreesboro, TN 37130-4237. Tel.: 615-890-2300.
E-mail: info@discoverycenteronline.org
Web Site: www.discoverycenteronline.org
Key Personnel: Exec. Dir., Billie Little; Dir. Mktg. & Public Rels., Ann Mapp
Children's Museum.
Collections: hands-on exhibits.
Facilities: restaurant. Museum-related items for sale.
Activities: special events; educational programs; school groups; community outreach; school break camps.
Hours & Admission Prices: Mon.-Sat. 10-5, Sun. 1-5. Admission $5; children under 2 & members no charge. Closed major holidays. ♿

OAKLANDS HISTORIC HOUSE MUSEUM, 900 N. Maney Ave., Murfreesboro, TN 37130-2955. Mailing Address: P.O. Box 432, Murfreesboro, TN 37133-0432. Tel.: 615-893-0022. Fax: 615-893-0513.
E-mail: info@oaklandsmuseum.org
Web Site: www.oaklandsmuseum.org
Founded: 1959.
Congressional District: 6
Key Personnel: Exec. Dir., James W. Manning, Jr.; Pres., Kirby McNabb; Dir. Education, Mary Beth Nevills; Museum Shop Mgr., Lebby Vantine.
Personnel Profile: Full-Time Paid 2; Part-Time Paid 7; Part-Time Volunteers 15.
Governing Authority: nonprofit organization. Parent Institution: Oaklands Association Inc. Tax-exempt: 501(c)(3).
Historic House: 1818-1865 cotton plantation.
Collections: period furnishings; military; textiles; medical.
Research Fields: history of Maney family & Oaklands; Victorian history of life & times in Tennessee.

Facilities: nature trail; picnic areas; visitor center. Museum-related items for sale.
Activities: guided tours; lectures; arts festivals; docent program; temporary exhibitions; educational program; wetlands program.
Publications: books, The Oaklands Cookbook; Hearthstones; DVD, The History of Oaklands.
Hours & Admission Prices: Tues.-Sat. 10-4, Sun. 1-4; last tour starts at 3. Adults $7, senior citizens, college students with ID, military & AAA members $6, college students & children 6-17 $5; discounts to AAM & ICOM members and groups of 10 or more; members no charge. Closed New Year's Day; Easter; Christmas. ♿
Attendance: 5,824 (accurate)
Membership: Student $20; Contributor $30-$49; Sponsor $50-$99; Patron $100-$499; Grand Patron $500-$999; Benefactor $1,000 & up.

STONES RIVER NATIONAL BATTLEFIELD, 3501 Old Nashville Hwy., Murfreesboro, TN 37129-8621. Tel.: 615-893-9501. Fax: 615-893-9508. TDD: 615-893-9501.
E-mail: stri_information@nps.gov
Web Site: www.nps.gov/stri
Founded: 1927.
Congressional District: 6
Key Personnel: C.E.O. & Supt., Stuart Johnson; Park Ranger & Museum Mgr., James B. Lewis; Museum Shop Mgr., Amber Brosbol.
Personnel Profile: Full-Time Paid 11; Part-Time Paid 6; Part-Time Volunteers 280; Interns 4.
Governing Authority: federal. Parent Institution: National Park Service, U.S. Department of Interior, Interior Building, Washington, DC 20240. Tax-exempt.
Park & Military Museum: adjacent to Stones River National Cemetery.
Collections: Civil War items pertaining to the battle of Stones River; manuscripts.
Research Fields: Battle of Stones River.
Facilities: 1,000-vol. library, including 128 vols. of official records & state troop rosters, available for use on premises; no reading room. Museum-related items for sale.
Activities: lectures; films; formally organized education programs for children & adults; permanent exhibitions. Museum Sponsors: Living History demonstrations during summer months.
Publications: brochure, Stones River; area map.
Hours & Admission Prices: Daily 8-5. No charge; donations accepted. Closed Thanksgiving; Christmas. ♿
Attendance: 192,355 (accurate)
Membership: Friends of Stones River National Battlefield $5.

Nashville

ADVENTURE SCIENCE CENTER, 800 Fort Negley Blvd., Nashville, TN 37203-4833. Tel.: 615-862-5160. Fax: 615-862-5178.
Web Site: www.adventuresci.com
Formerly: Cumberland Science Museum
Founded: 1944.
Congressional District: 5
Key Personnel: C.E.O. & Pres., Susan B. Duvenhage; Chm. (V), Edward Lang; Exhibits & Collections Mgr., Herschell Parker; Dir. Operations, Tina Brown; Dir. Education, Jeri Hasselbring; Bldg. Supt., Dan Slayden; Dir. Planetarium, Kris McCall; Museum Shop Mgr., Polly DuBose; Dir. Devel., Rae Hummell.
Personnel Profile: Full-Time Paid 36; Part-Time Paid 90; Part-Time Volunteers 150.
Governing Authority: Tax-exempt.
Science Center.
Collections: geology; science; technology; human health; hands-on exhibits.
Research Fields: informal education in contemporary science.
Facilities: 44,000 sq. ft. exhibit space; 166-seat planetarium; classrooms; theater.
Activities: lectures; demonstrations; science camps; planetarium programs; field trips; camp-ins; educational programs; public programs.
Publications: newsletters.
Hours & Admission Prices: Mon.-Sat. 10-5, Sun. 12:30-5:30. Adults $11, seniors, military, college students & youth 3-12 $9; discounts to ASTC members; members no charge. Planetarium Shows: $6 non-members, $4 members. Closed Thanksgiving; Christmas. ♿
Attendance: 264,576 (accurate)
Membership: Individual $55; Single Parent Family $65; Grandparent $85; Family $90; Family Deluxe $145.

ASSOCIATION FOR THE PRESERVATION OF TENNESSEE ANTIQUITIES, 110 Leake Ave., Nashville, TN 37205-3706. Tel.: 615-352-8247. Fax: 615-352-8247.
E-mail: apta1951@bellsouth.net
Web Site: www.theapta.org
Founded: 1951.
Congressional District: 5
Key Personnel: Exec. Dir., Martha Sloan; Pres., Robert Notestine, III
Personnel Profile: Part-Time Paid 1; Part-Time Volunteers 40.
Governing Authority: nonprofit organization. Branch Museums: The Athenaeum, 808 Athenaeum Place, Columbia, TN 38401; Belle Meade Plantation, 5025 Harding Rd., Nashville, TN 37205; The Buchanan Log House, 2910 Elm Hill Pike, Nashville, TN 37214; Rachel H.K. Burrow Museum & Historic Post Office, Arlington, TN 38002; Crockett Tavern-Museum, 2002 Morningside Dr., Morristown, TN 37814; Glenmore, 1280 N. Chuckey Pike, Jefferson City, TN 37760; The Little Courthouse, E. Market St., Bolivar, TN 38008; The Pillars, Washington St., Bolivar, TN 38008; Ramsey House, 2614 Thorngrove Pike, Knoxville, TN 37914; Woodruff-Fontaine House & Lee Memorial House, 680-690 Adams, Memphis, TN 38102. Tax-exempt.
Historic Preservation Society: housed in c.1853 Belle Meade Plantation garden house.
Collections: costumes; decorative items; Civil War memorabilia; ante-bellum, Victorian & early American furniture, books, textiles & fans.
Research Fields: historic preservation; Tennessee history.
Activities: guided tours; lectures; films; formally organized education programs for children & adults; permanent & temporary exhibitions.
Publications: biannual newsletter; advertising brochure.
Hours & Admission Prices: Call or write for information & details on chapter house museums. Members no charge. Closed New Year's Day; Thanksgiving; Christmas.
Membership: Individual $25; Family $40. Each chapter has different membership dues.

BELLE MEADE PLANTATION, 5025 Harding Rd., Nashville, TN 37205-2810. Tel.: 615-356-0501 & 800-270-3991. Fax: 615-356-2336.
E-mail: info@bellemeadeplantation.com
Web Site: www.bellemeadeplantation.com
Founded: 1953.
Congressional District: 5
Key Personnel: Pres., Alton W. Kelley; Museum Shop Mgr., Joanne Floyd.
Personnel Profile: Full-Time Paid 20; Part-Time Paid 10; Part-Time Volunteers 30; Interns 1.
Governing Authority: nonprofit organization. Parent Institution: Association For The Preservation of Tennessee Antiquities, 110 Leake Ave., Nashville, TN 37205. Tel.: 615-352-8247. Tax-exempt.
Historic House: 1820 Belle Meade Mansion.
Collections: costumes; period furniture; Civil War memorabilia; antebellum, Victorian & Early American furniture & books; carriages. Historic Structures: c.1790 log cabin; 1840 garden house; 1840 smoke house; 1840 mausoleum; 1853 Greek Revival mansion; 1884 creamery; c.1890 child's playhouse; c.1893 carriage house & stables; 1830s slave cabin; chicken coop.
Research Fields: lineage of thoroughbred studs & mares.
Facilities: visitor center; restaurant; education building; theatre; 30 acre historic site. Museum-related items for sale.
Activities: guided tours; lectures; films; organized education programs for children & adults; permanent & temporary exhibitions.
Publications: brochure; Widows, Weepers & Wakes - Mourning in Middle Tennessee; Purging Pestilence - Dealing with Disease in the 19th Century; Belle Meade Bloodlines; Belle Meade Plantation.
Hours & Admission Prices: Mon.-Sat. 9-5, Sun. 11-5. Adults 13-64 $15, senior citizens 65 & over $13, children 6-18 $7; discount to groups; children 5 & under and members no charge. Closed New Year's Day; Easter; Thanksgiving; Christmas. ♿
Attendance: 135,000 (accurate)
Membership: Individual $40; Family $60; Contributing $125; Patron $250; Bonnie Scotland $1,000.

BELMONT MANSION ASSOCIATION, 1900 Belmont Blvd., Nashville, TN 37212-3758. Tel.: 615-460-5459. Fax: 615-460-5688.
E-mail: belmontmansion@mail.belmont.edu
Web Site: www.belmontmansion.com
Founded: 1972.
Historic House Museum.
Collections: period furnishings; personal artifacts.
Activities: Behind-the-Scenes tours. Annual Events: Twilight Party; Adelicia's Birthday; Appraisal Fair; Christmas Lunch & Dinner.
Publications: quarterly newsletter, A View from the Monte.
Hours & Admission Prices: Mon.-Sat. 10-4, Sun. 1-4; groups by appointment. Adults $10, seniors 60 & over $9, children 6-12 $3; discounts to AAA members & groups of 15 or more; members no charge. Closed New Year's Day; Independence Day; Thanksgiving; Christmas.
Attendance: 20,000 (estimated)

Membership: Senior $20; Individual $25; Family $30; Patron $50; Grand Patron $100; Benefactor $500; Life $1,500.

∗ CHEEKWOOD BOTANICAL GARDEN & MUSEUM OF ART, (M), 1200 Forrest Park Dr., Nashville, TN 37205-4242. Tel.: 615-353-6964. Fax: 615-353-0919.
Web Site: www.cheekwood.org
Founded: 1960.
Congressional District: 6
Key Personnel: C.E.O. & Pres., Jack Becker, Ph.D.; Chm. (V), Dr. Paul Sternberg, Jr.; Dir. Finance & Operations, Becket Moore; Dir. Exhibitions & Programs, Allison Reid; Cur. Art, Jochen Wierich, Ph.D.; Registrar, Kaye Crouch.
Personnel Profile: Full-Time Paid 53; Part-Time Paid 52; Part-Time Volunteers 100.
Governing Authority: nonprofit organization.
Art Museum & Botanical Garden.
Collections: Museum: 19th & 20th-century American art featuring works by The Eight; sculpture by William Edmondson; contemporary outdoor sculpture; Worcester porcelain; American & European silver. Matilda Geddings Gray Foundation collection of Faberge. Botanical Garden: native southeast; bromellia; crape myrtle; dogwoods; ferns; magnolias; redbuds; roses; boxwoods; herbs; daffodils; trillium; iris; daylilies.
Major Exhibits: The Scholastic Art Competition, 1/31/10-2/21/10; Abstract Visions: 20th Century Art, 3/13/10-5/3/10; Temporary Contemporary Series, 3/13/10-6/13/10; The American Impressionists in the Garden (T), 3/13/10-9/6/10; Video Installation Galleries, 3/13/10-9/12/10; Chihuly at Cheekwood, 5/25/10-10/10/10; Temporary Contemporary Series, 6/26/10-9/12/10; Collecting for Tomorrow: Recent Acquisitions, 10/9/10-1/2/11; Temporary Contemporary Series, 10/9/10-1/2/11; Video Installation Galleries, 10/9/10-1/2/11.
Research Fields: William Edmondson; Worchester porcelain.
Facilities: 9,000-vol. library of botany & fine arts available for inter-library loan & for use on premises; nature center; learning center; 1mile sculpture trail; auditorium; classrooms; tea room. Botanic art, museum-related items for sale.
Activities: guided tours; lectures; gallery talks; formally organized education programs; docent program; permanent, temporary & traveling exhibitions; monthly contemporary series; audio tours.
Publications: quarterly calendar; newsletter; catalogues; brochures; posters; exhibition catalogues.
Hours & Admission Prices: Tues.-Sat. 9:30-4:30, Sun. 11-4:30. Adults $10, senior citizens $8, students $5; discounts to groups, AAM, AABGA & AAA members; members & children under 5 no charge. Closed New Year's Day; 2nd Sat. June; Thanksgiving; Christmas Day. ♿
Attendance: 175,000 (estimated)
Membership: Student $30; Educator $35; Individual (Day Pass) $40; Senior Family $50; Individual (Full Benefits) $55; Educator Family $60; Family $75; Supporting $135; Pineapple Society $300; Boxwood $600; Benefactor $1,250; Founder $2,500; Cheekwood Round Table $5,000; Cheekwood Cornerstone $10,000; Bryant Fleming Circle $25,000.

∗ COUNTRY MUSIC HALL OF FAME AND MUSEUM, COUNTRY MUSIC FOUNDATION, (M), 222 5th Ave., S., Nashville, TN 37203-4206. Tel.: 615-416-2001; 800-852-6437 (group reservations & special events). Fax: 615-255-2245.
E-mail: info@countrymusichalloffame.com
Web Site: www.countrymusichalloffame.com
Founded: 1964.
Congressional District: 5
Key Personnel: C.E.O., Kyle Young; Chm. (V), E.W. (Bud) Wendell; Pres. (V), Vince Gill; Asst. to Dir., Rachel Neetmarl; Vice Pres. Finance & Operations, Nina Hammontree; Vice Pres. Museum Svcs., Lauren Bufferd; Vice Pres. Devel. & Mktg., Karen Fleming; Vice Pres. Public Rels., Liz Thiels, Sr.; Museum Shop Mgr., Lisa Lane.
Personnel Profile: Full-Time Paid 50; Part-Time Paid 17; Part-Time Volunteers 170; Interns 12.
Governing Authority: nonprofit organization. Owned & operated by Country Music Foundation, Inc. Branch Museum: Studio B, Roy Acuff Place & Music Sq. W., Nashville, TN 37203; Hatch Show Print. Tax-exempt: 501(c)(3).
Country Music Museum & Historic Recording Studio and Historic Woodblock Print Shop.
Collections: musical instruments & memorabilia associated with the development of country music; sight & sound exhibits; costumes; more than 200,000 sound recordings; videos, films & photographs; print collection of books, periodicals, songbooks, sheet music, manuscripts, newspaper & magazine clippings, artist biographies & publicity materials; biographical exhibits.
Research Fields: history of country, traditional, folk & American music.
Facilities: research library; 40,000 sq. ft. exhibit space; artifact & photograph storage vaults; reading room; audio restoration lab; 3 gallery theaters; 250-seat acoustically sound theater; Hatch Show Print, a historic woodblock print shop; Studio B. Prints, books, tapes, crafts & country music related items for sale.
Activities: films; permanent & temporary exhibitions; oral history program; education department; outreach school programs & kits; museum available for private use after hours, call 1-800-852-6437 & ask for special events.
Publications: triannual, Journal of Country Music; The Official Country Calendar; Bill Monroe & His Blue Grass Boys; Truth is Stranger than Publicity; Country Music Legends in the Hall of Fame; Sing Your Heart Out, Country Boy; Country: The Music and the Musicians; The Explosion of American Music: BMI's 50th Anniversary; Bob Wills: Hubbin' It.; Ramblin' Rose: The Life and Career of Rose Maddox; A Good Natured Riot: The Birth of the Grand Ole Opry by Charles Wolfe; True Adventures with the King of Bluegrass-Jimmy Martin by Tom Piazza. Various anthologies & television specials: Hank Williams: Just Me & My Guitar, The First Recordings, Rare Demos; Jim Reeves: Live at the Opry; Mark O'Connor: The Championship Years; Jerry & Tammy Sullivan: A Joyful Noise; Raise Your Window: A Cajun Music Anthology; Webb Pierce: King of the Honky-Tonk; Jean Shepard: Honky-Tonk Heroine; Johnny Paycheck: The Real Mr. Heartache, The Little Darlin' Years. Major Label Collaborations: Gene Autry: Columbia Historic Edition; Roy Rogers: Columbia Historic Edition; Elvis Presley: Elvis in Nashville, Known Only To Him; Jim Reeves: Welcome to My World; Patsy Cline: The Patsy Cline Collection, Live at the Opry, Live, Volume II; Heartaches by the Number; Singing in the Saddle: The History of the Singing Cowboy; Finding Her Voice: Women In Country Music.
Hours & Admission Prices: Jan.-Feb. Wed.-Mon. 9-5; March-Dec. daily 9-5. Adults $19.99, seniors 60 & over $17.99, children 6-12 $11.99; discounts to AAA, AAM, Military & Students; children 5 & under and members no charge. Closed New Year's Day; Thanksgiving; Christmas. ♿
Attendance: 293,975 (accurate)
Membership: Children $10; Adult $25.

CULTURAL MUSEUM, 1008 19th Ave. S., Nashville, TN 37212-2126. Tel.: 615-340-7481 & 7500. Fax: 615-340-7551.
E-mail: museum@scarrittbennett.org
Web Site: www.scarrittbennett.org
Formerly: Hartzler-Towner Multicultural Museum
Founded: 1992.
Congressional District: 5
Key Personnel: Pres., Sharon Howell; Cur., Adriana Larios.
Personnel Profile: Part-Time Paid 2.
Governing Authority: nonprofit. Parent Institution: Scarritt-Bennett Center. Tax-exempt: 501(c)(3).
Anthropology Museum: housed on a campus of collegiate gothic-style buildings, c.1923.
Collections: 10,000 anthropological (ethnographic) artifacts from diverse, worldwide cultures, especially from Asia, Africa & The Americas.
Facilities: 3,000 sq. ft. exhibit space.
Activities: multicultural education programs for children; permanent exhibitions of our own collections.
Hours & Admission Prices: Mon.-Fri. 9-5, Sat.-Sun. 9-2. No charge. ♿
Attendance: 600 (estimated)

DISCIPLES OF CHRIST HISTORICAL SOCIETY, 1101 19th Ave. S., Nashville, TN 37212-2196. Tel.: 615-327-1444; 866-834-7563 (Toll Free). Fax: 615-327-1445.
E-mail: mail@discipleshistory.org
Web Site: www.discipleshistory.org
Founded: 1941.
Congressional District: 5
Key Personnel: Pres., Glenn T. Carson; Vice Pres. Information Svcs., Sara Harwell; Cur., Elaine Philpott; Cur., Sharman Hartson.
Personnel Profile: Full-Time Paid 4; Part-Time Paid 5; Part-Time Volunteers 3; Interns 1.
Governing Authority: society; board of trustees. Parent Institution: Christian Church (Disciples of Christ). Tax-exempt: 170(b)(1)(A).
Religious Museum.
Collections: historical artifacts & art objects pertaining to the religious heritage, backgrounds, origins, development & general history of the Disciples of Christ, Christian Churches, Churches of Christ & related groups.
Major Exhibits: Communion, 11/09-10/10.
Research Fields: history of the Disciples of Christ, Christian Churches, Churches of Christ & related groups.
Facilities: 34,000-vol. library & archives of resources related to three church bodies, available for member use & inter-library loan.
Activities: guided tours; lectures; permanent & temporary exhibitions.
Publications: quarterly magazine, Discipliana; books.

Hours & Admission Prices: Mon.-Fri. 9-4. No charge. Closed national holidays. ♿
Attendance: 1,000 (estimated)
Membership: Individual $100; Friends of President $250; The Millennial Group $1,000; The Unity Circle $2,500.

THE FISK UNIVERSITY GALLERIES, Fisk University, 1000 17th Ave., N., Nashville, TN 37208-3051. Tel.: 615-329-8720 & 8500. Fax: 615-329-8544.
E-mail: galleries@fisk.edu
Web Site: www.fisk.edu/gallery/
Founded: 1949.
Congressional District: 5
Key Personnel: C.E.O., Dr. Carolyn Reid-Wallace; Chm. (V), Mr. Virgis W. Colbert; Chm. Art Committee, Aaronetta Pierce; Archivist, Beth Howse; Public Rels., Angela Bevens; Administrative Asst., Tabitha Williams.
Personnel Profile: Full-Time Paid 2; Part-Time Volunteers 20.
Governing Authority: university. Parent Institution: Fisk University. Branch Museums: Carl Van Vechten Gallery; Aaron Douglas Gallery. Tax-exempt: 501(c)(3).
Art Gallery & Museum: art galleries housed in 1888 Neo-Romanesque building & university library building.
Collections: Afro-American paintings, sculpture & graphics; photography; the Contemporary & Classical African Collection; the Cyrus Baldridge Collection of Drawings; the Alfred Stieglitz Collection; the Winold Reiss Collection; the Carl Van Vechten Collection of Photographs; the James Collection of African-American Folk Art.
Research Fields: African and Afro-American art.
Facilities: 4,500-vol. library of materials pertaining to art available for use on premises; classroom. Art & museum-related items for sale.
Activities: self-guided tours; lectures; films; gallery talks; annual arts festival; inter-museum loan; traveling & temporary exhibitions; docent program.
Publications: catalogs; exhibition brochures; calendar of events; newsletter, Fisk Art Report.
Hours & Admission Prices: Summer Tues.-Fri. 10-5; Sept.-June Mon.-Fri. 10-5. No charge, donations accepted. ♿
Attendance: 42,000 (accurate)
Membership: Augusta Savage $50-$99; Pearl Creswell $100-$249; Carl Van Vechten $250-$499; Georgia O'Keefe $500-$999; Tanner Art League $1,000 & up.

FORT NASHBOROUGH, 170 1st Ave., N., Nashville, TN 37201-1924. Mailing Address: Centennial Park Office, Nashville, TN 37201. Tel.: 615-862-8400. Fax: 615-862-5493.
E-mail: jackie.jones@nashville.gov
Web Site: www.nashville.gov/parks
Founded: 1780.
Congressional District: 5
Key Personnel: Dir., Roy E. Wilson.
Governing Authority: city. Parent Institution: Metro Board of Parks & Recreation. Tax-exempt.
Historic Building/Site Museum: 1780 site of Fort Nashborough, first settlement in Nashville.
Collections: five log cabin reproductions.
Research Fields: historical.
Activities: self-guided with directional signage.
Hours & Admission Prices: Daily 9-5. No charge. Closed legal holidays. ♿

* **FRIST CENTER FOR THE VISUAL ARTS, (M), (I),** 919 Broadway, Nashville, TN 37203-3822. Tel.: 615-244-3340. Fax: 615-244-3339.
E-mail: mail@fristcenter.org
Web Site: www.fristcenter.org
Founded: 2001.
Congressional District: 5
Key Personnel: C.E.O., Susan Edwards; Devel., Ashley Howell; Chm. & Pres., William R. Frist; Education, Anne Henderson; Public Rels., Ellen Pryor; Treas., Dwight McWhorter; Registrar, Amie Geremia; Cur., Mark Scala; Security, Paul Cotter; Retail Mgr., Suzy Herron.
Personnel Profile: Full-Time Paid 71; Part-Time Paid 12; Part-Time Volunteers 300.
Governing Authority: private; nonprofit organization. Tax-exempt: 501(c)(3).
Art Museum.
Collections: works by local, regional & national artists.
Major Exhibits: Heroes: Mortals and Myths in Ancient Greece (T), 1/29/10-4/25/10; Masterpieces of European Painting from Museo de Arte (T), 2/19/10-5/16/10; U-ram Choe, 2/19/10-5/16/10; Dale Chihuly Glass, 5/14/10-1/2/11; Golden Age of Couture: Paris and London, 1947-1957 (T), 6/18/10-9/12/10; Tokihiro Sato, 6/18/10-9/12/10; The Birth of Impressionism: Masterpiece from the Musee d'Orsay (T), 10/15/10-1/30/11.
Facilities: 406-vol. library; 225-seat auditorium; 120-seat restaurant; 20,000 sq. ft. exhibit space. Museum-related items for sale.
Activities: formal education programs; guided tours; lectures; traveling exhibitions; family day programs.
Publications: quarterly newsletter, Members Gallery.
Hours & Admission Prices: Mon.-Wed. & Sat. 10-5:30, Thurs.-Fri. 10-9, Sun. 1-5:30. Adults $8.50, senior citizens & military $7.50, students $6.50; discounts to groups, AAM & ICOM members; members and children 18 & under no charge. Additional pricing for special exhibitions. Closed New Years Day; Thanksgiving; Christmas. ♿
Attendance: 205,333 (accurate)
Membership: Teacher & College Student $25; Senior $35; Individual & Dual Senior $45; Dual $60; Family $65; Friend $100; Patron $250; Benefactor $500; Director's Circle $1,000; President's Circle $2,500; Rembrandt's Circle $5,000; Picasso Circle $10,000.

LANE MOTOR MUSEUM, 702 Murfreesboro Pike, Nashville, TN 37210-4522. Tel.: 615-742-7445.
Web Site: www.lanemotormuseum.org
Key Personnel: Dir., Jeff Lane
Transportation Museum.
Collections: 150 unique cars & motorcycles dating from the 1920s to the present.
Hours & Admission Prices: Thurs.-Mon. 10-5. Adults 18-64 $7, seniors 65 & over $5, youth 6-17 $2; children under 5 no charge. Closed New Year's Day; Thanksgiving; Christmas.

MUSIC VALLEY WAX MUSEUM, 2515 McGavock Pike, Nashville, TN 37214-1203. Tel.: 615-884-7876 & 883-3612.
Wax Museum.
Collections: over 50 wax figures.
Hours & Admission Prices: Memorial Day to Labor Day daily 8am-10pm; Sept.-May daily 9-5. Adults $9, seniors $6; children 14 & under no charge. Closed New Year's Day; Thanksgiving; Christmas.

NASHVILLE ZOO AT GRASSMERE, 3777 Nolensville Rd., Nashville, TN 37211-3324. Tel.: 615-833-1534. Fax: 615-333-0728.
E-mail: pr@nashvillezoo.org
Web Site: www.nashvillezoo.org
Founded: 1990.
Congressional District: 5
Key Personnel: Dir., Rick Schwartz; Chm. (V), Jennifer Frist; Admin., Beth Murdock.
Personnel Profile: Full-Time Paid 84; Full-Time Volunteers 125; Part-Time Paid 17.
Governing Authority: Parent Institution: Nashville Zoo. Tax-exempt.
Zoological Park.
Collections: live animals; historic home & farm.
Research Fields: animal care & behavior; conservation studies.
Facilities: 28,300 sq. ft. Croft Center; 200-acre park; cafe. Museum-related items for sale.
Publications: Zoo View.
Hours & Admission Prices: March 15-Oct. 14 daily 9-6; Oct. 15-March 14 daily 9-4. Adults $14, seniors $12, children 2-12 $9; discounts to groups; members & children under 2 no charge. ♿
Attendance: 529,828 (accurate)
Membership: Senior & Student $40; Individual $50; Grandparent $70; Family $85; Safari Set $135; Keepers Circle $275; Curator's Club $550; Claws, Paws & Jaws Society $1,000.

THE PARTHENON, (M), Centennial Park, West End at 25th Ave., N., Nashville, TN 37203. Mailing Address: P.O. Box 196340, Nashville, TN 37219-6340. Tel.: 615-862-8431. Fax: 615-880-2265.
E-mail: info@parthenon.org
Web Site: www.parthenon.org
Founded: 1897.
Congressional District: 5
Key Personnel: Dir., Wesley M. Paine; Facilities Mgr., Lauren Buffer; Museum Shop Mgr., Timothy Cartmell.
Personnel Profile: Full-Time Paid 11; Part-Time Paid 1; Part-Time Volunteers 40; Interns 3.
Governing Authority: municipal. Parent Institution: Metropolitan Board of Parks & Recreation. Tax-exempt.
Art Museum: housed in exact reproduction of Athenian Parthenon.
Collections: 1850-1925, James M. Cowan collection of paintings; pre-Columbian art from Mexico; contemporary art; 42-ft. replica of Athena Parthenos statue.
Facilities: Museum-related items for sale.

Activities: guided tours by reservation only; rotating art shows; permanent, temporary & traveling exhibitions.
Publications: quarterly newsletter, The Agora; catalogue, The Cowan Collection; A Tale of Two Parthenons; Winslow Homer: An American Genius at the Parthenon.
Hours & Admission Prices: June-Aug. Tues.-Sat. 9-4:30, Sun. 12:30-4:30; Sept.-May Tues.-Sat. 9-4:30; Summer: call for hours; groups by appointment. Adults $6, seniors 62 & over and children 4-17 $3.50; discounts to AAM members; members & children under 4 no charge. Closed New Year's Day; Thanksgiving; Christmas. ♿
Attendance: 138,500 (accurate)
Membership: Senior & Student $15; Individual $25; Family $50; Hero $100-$749; Champion $750-$1,499; Niki $1,500-$2,999; Olympian $3,000 & up.

THE PUBLIC LIBRARY OF NASHVILLE AND DAVIDSON COUNTY, Nashville Room, Special Collections Div., 615 Church St., Nashville, TN 37219-2314. Tel.: 615-862-5782. Fax: 615-862-5838.
E-mail: aimee.james@nashville.gov
Web Site: www.library.nashville.org
Founded: 1887.
Congressional District: 5
Key Personnel: Dir., Donna Nicely; Mgr. Nashville Rm., Aimee B. James, C.A.
Personnel Profile: Full-Time Paid 12; Part-Time Volunteers 35; Interns 1.
Governing Authority: municipal. Parent Institution: Nashville Public Library. Tax-exempt: 170(b)(1)(A).
Local History Library.
Collections: community culture & history; over 28,000 books; ephemera; photographs; maps; architectural drawings; manuscripts; oral histories for the Civil Rights Oral History Project & the Veterans History Project; The Nashville Banner newspaper archives.
Research Fields: history of Nashville & Davidson County; collection of Nashville authors; genealogy; image collection; Banner newspaper collection; civil rights.
Facilities: library pertaining to Nashville & Tennessee history.
Activities: guided tours; permanent & temporary exhibitions.
Hours & Admission Prices: Mon.-Fri. 9-6, Sat. 9-5, Sun. 2-5. No charge. Closed national holidays. ♿
Attendance: 52,140 (accurate)

SOUTHERN BAPTIST HISTORICAL LIBRARY AND ARCHIVES, 901 Commerce St., Ste. 400, Nashville, TN 37203-3628. Tel.: 615-244-0344. Fax: 615-782-4821.
E-mail: bill@sbhla.org
Web Site: www.sbhla.org
Founded: 1951.
Congressional District: 5
Key Personnel: Dir. Library & Archives, Bill Sumners; Accountant, Debbie Keen; Librarian, Joy DuBose; Archivist, Taffey Hall; Asst. Librarian, Jean Forbis.
Personnel Profile: Full-Time Paid 5; Full-Time Volunteers 1; Part-Time Paid 3.
Governing Authority: denominational group. Affiliated with Southern Baptist Convention, 901 Commerce St., Nashville, TN. 37203. Tax-exempt.
Religious Museum.
Collections: artifacts & archival materials related to Baptist history; manuscripts.
Research Fields: Baptist history.
Facilities: 32,000-vol. library of books, periodicals, denominational annuals, audio-visuals; microfilm collection of Baptist materials from Eastern Europe, Soviet Union, Baptist Missionary Society Archives, London, England, 1792-1914, available for use on premises; reading room.
Activities: guided tours; temporary exhibitions.
Hours & Admission Prices: Mon.-Fri. 9-4; other times by appointment. No charge. Closed national holidays. ♿
Attendance: 1,100 (estimated)

TENNESSEE AGRICULTURAL MUSEUM, Ellington Agricultural Center, Nashville, TN 37204. Tel.: 615-837-5197.
E-mail: tennessee.agricultural.museum@tn.gov
Web Site: tnagmuseum.org
Personnel Profile: Full-Time Paid 2; Part-Time Paid 1; Part-Time Volunteers 110.
Governing Authority: Parent Institution: State of Tennessee, Tennessee Dept. of Agriculture.
Agriculture Museum: housed in a former horse barn which was once part of the Brentwood Hall estate of financier Rogers Caldwell.
Collections: home & farm artifacts; prints; textiles; woodworking artifacts; wagons; garden.
Facilities: garden; nature trail.
Activities: summer Saturdays; Pioneer Journey traveling trunk; adult classes; demonstrations; educational programs. Annual Events: Historic Rural Life Festival in May; Music & Molasses Arts & Crafts Festival in October.
Publications: children's activity book, Through the Garden Gate.
Hours & Admission Prices: Mon.-Fri. 9-4; groups by appointment. Museum: no charge; donations accepted. Special Events: call for admission prices. Closed state holidays. ♿
Attendance: 29,961 (accurate)
Membership: Individual $15; Family $30; Life $200.

TENNESSEE CENTRAL RAILWAY MUSEUM, 220 Willow St., Nashville, TN 37210-2159. Tel.: 615-244-9001. Fax: 615-244-2120.
E-mail: hultman@bellsouth.net
Web Site: www.tcry.org
Founded: 1990.
Congressional District: 5
Key Personnel: C.E.O & Pres. (V), Terry L. Bebout; Treas., J. Allen Hicks; Cur. & Archivist, Charles Owens; Devel., George Gilbert; Public Rels., Robert E. Hultman; Museum Shop Mgr., Eddie Justice.
Personnel Profile: Full-Time Volunteers 60; Part-Time Paid 1; Part-Time Volunteers 50.
Governing Authority: private; nonprofit organization. Tax-exempt: 501(c)(3).
Railroad Museum.
Collections: rolling stock, passenger rolling stock; historic pieces relating to the TC RY, Nashville, Chattanooga & St. Louis Ry, and L&N RR; RR paper & hardware concentration in southeastern US railways.
Research Fields: various freight cars bought & operated by L&N RR & the NC&StL RY.
Facilities: 500-vol. library of books on railroad history; 700 sq. ft. exhibit space. Museum-related items for sale.
Activities: formal education programs for children; guided tours; hobby workshops; lectures; loan exhibitions; excursion trains. Museum Sponsors: Trains of Christmas; Model Train Shows in the Middle Tennessee; Day Out with Thomas the Tank Engine.
Publications: newsletter published 10 times annually, The Order Board.
Hours & Admission Prices: Tues., Thurs. & Sat. 9-3; hours vary when trains is in operation or when train shows are scheduled. No charge; donations accepted.
Attendance: 42,000 (estimated)
Membership: Regular $30; Household & Family $35.

TENNESSEE HISTORICAL COMMISSION, 2941 Lebanon Rd., Nashville, TN 37243-0442. Tel.: 615-532-1550. Fax: 615-532-1549.
E-mail: patrick.mcIntyre@tn.gov
Web Site: www.state.tn.us/environment/hist
Founded: 1919.
Congressional District: 5
Key Personnel: Exec. Dir., Patrick McIntyre; Chm. (V), Norman J. Hill; Asst. Dir. State Programs, Linda T. Wynn; Fiscal Officer, Doyal Vaughan; Deputy State Historic Preservation Officer, Richard G. Tune; Historic Preservation Specialist, James Jones; Historic Preservation Supvr., Steve Rogers; Historic Preservation Specialist, Joe Garrison; Historic Preservation Specialist, Claudette Stager; Historic Preservation Specialist, Louis Jackson; Military Sites Preservation Specialist, Fred Prouty; Historic Preservation Specialist, Brian Beadles; Sec., Angela Staggs.
Personnel Profile: Full-Time Paid 15.
Governing Authority: state. Tax-exempt.
State Historic Preservation Agency.
Collections: period furnishings; personal artifacts; photographs.
Facilities: 200-300-vol. library of history, architecture, archaeology, historic preservation & folklore available for research.
Activities: lectures; formally organized education programs for undergraduate & graduate college students affiliated with historic preservation internship; operate all state-owned historic sites under an agreement with local clubs & organizations; administer programs of The National Historic Preservation Act; operates historical markers program.
Publications: periodical, The Courier; catalog, Tennessee Historical Markers; magazine, Guide to Civil War in Tennessee; Houston & Crocket: Heroes of Tennessee & Texas; Biographical Directory of the Tennessee General Assembly Vols. 1-6; Messages of the Governors of Tennessee Vols. 1-10.
Hours & Admission Prices: Mon.-Fri. 8-4:30 by appointment. No charge. Closed holidays. ♿

TENNESSEE HISTORICAL SOCIETY, Ground Fl., War Memorial Bldg., Nashville, TN 37243. Tel.: 615-741-8934. Fax: 615-741-8937.
E-mail: tnhissoc@tennesseehistory.org
Web Site: www.tennesseehistory.org
Founded: 1849.
Congressional District: 5

Key Personnel: Exec. Dir., Ann Toplovich; Pres. (V), William P. Morrelli; Dir. Membership & Prog., Kelly Wilkerson.
Personnel Profile: Full-Time Paid 6; Full-Time Volunteers 2; Part-Time Paid 2.
Governing Authority: society. Tax-exempt.
History Museum: membership organization with collections housed in Tennessee State Museum & Tennessee State Library & Archives. No independent museum or library.
Collections: paintings; manuscripts, artifacts; books.
Research Fields: Tennessee history.
Facilities: library; reading room; archives.
Activities: guided tours; permanent & temporary exhibitions.
Publications: magazine, Tennessee Historical Quarterly; monthly newsletter, News in Tennessee History; quarterly newsletter.
Hours & Admission Prices: Mon.-Fri. 8-4:30. No charge; donations accepted. Closed national holidays. ♿
Membership: Individual $35; Family & Institutions $45; Canada $55; Other $65; Sustaining $75; Bicentennial Club $100; John Haywood Society $250.

* **TENNESSEE STATE MUSEUM, (M),** 505 Deaderick St., Nashville, TN 37243-1402. Tel.: 615-741-2692. Fax: 615-741-7231.
E-mail: museuminfo@trimuseum.org
Web Site: tnmuseum.org; www.tn4me.org
Founded: 1937.
Congressional District: 5
Key Personnel: Exec. Dir., Lois S. Riggins-Ezzell; Dir. Collections, Dan E. Pomeroy; Dir. Exhibits Fabrication, Stephen Cox; Dir. Administration, Mary Jane Crockett-Green; Dir. External Affairs, Leigh Hendry; Dir. Public Programs, Paulette Fox; Dir. Capitol Projects, Patricia Rasbury; Registrar, Bob White; Media Contact, Mary Skinner; Museum Shop Mgr., Sunshine Thompson.
Personnel Profile: Full-Time Paid 50; Part-Time Volunteers 20.
Governing Authority: state. Parent Institution: TN Arts Commission. Branch Museum: Tennessee State Museum Military Branch, 7th & Union, Nashville 37243-1120. Tax-exempt: 170(b)(1)(A).
History Museum.
Collections: military memorabilia from 1780-present; historic paintings of prominent Tennesseans; fine arts collections of contemporary artists; historic materials reflecting the history and culture of the state; objects related to famous personalities; early 19th-century Tennessee-made silver, firearms, furniture, quilts.
Major Exhibits: 50th Anniversary Nashville Sit-ins, 2/10.
Research Fields: History Art Museum.
Facilities: 5,000-vol. library of book on general history available for inter-library loan on request. Museum-related items for sale.
Activities: lectures; gallery talks; docent program or council; loan, temporary & traveling exhibitions; school loan service.
Publications: quarterly newsletter.
Hours & Admission Prices: Tues.-Sat. 10-5, Sun. 1-5. No charge; donations accepted. Closed New Year's Day; Easter; Thanksgiving; Christmas.
Attendance: 150,000 (estimated)
Membership: Teacher $25; Individual $30; Dual $40; Family $50; Contributing $100; Sustaining $500; John Sevier Member $1,000.

TRAVELLERS REST PLANTATION & MUSEUM, 636 Farrell Pkwy., Nashville, TN 37220-1218. Tel.: 615-832-8197. Fax: 615-832-8169.
E-mail: director@travellersrestplantation.org
Web Site: www.travellersrestplantation.org
Formerly: Travellers Rest Historic House Museum, Inc.
Founded: 1954.
Congressional District: 5
Key Personnel: Interim Exec. Dir., Candace Page; Dir. Education, Tonya Staggs; Cur., Brian Allison.
Personnel Profile: Full-Time Paid 5; Part-Time Paid 1; Part-Time Volunteers 10.
Governing Authority: society. Parent Institution: National Society of the Colonial Dames of America in TN. Tax-exempt.
Historic House Museum: housed in 1799 home of Judge John Overton.
Collections: federal & early empire decorative arts; Civil War Nashville artifacts; Travellers Rest Arabian horse artifacts & archival materials; historic Nashville; Tennessee Society of Colonial Dame; historic houses.
Research Fields: Historic Nashville; Civil War; Arabian horses; early Tennessee decorative arts; African-American history.
Facilities: 800-vol. library that includes books, photographs, & archival materials related to historic Nashville; education barn available for special events & rentals; 11-acre grounds. Gift items for sale.
Activities: guided tours; permanent & temporary exhibitions. Special Events: Celtic Music Festival in June; Restoration Fair in September; 19th Century Trades Day in October; Civil War Symposium in November; Holiday Tours in December.
Publications: site book, Civil War DVD; Arabian Horse DVD; book, Judge John Overton.
Hours & Admission Prices: Mon.-Sat. 10-4, Sun. 1-4. Adults $10, seniors $8, students $5, children 6-12 $3; discounts to groups, AAA, AAM & ICOM members; children under 6 & members no charge. Closed New Year's Day, Thanksgiving; Christmas. ♿
Attendance: 15,000 (estimated)

UPPER ROOM CHAPEL MUSEUM, 1908 Grand Ave., Nashville, TN 37212-2188. Mailing Address: P.O. Box 340004, Nashville, TN 37203-0004. Tel.: 615-340-7206. Fax: 615-340-7293.
E-mail: chapel-museum@upperroom.org
Web Site: www.upperroom.org
Founded: 1953.
Congressional District: 5
Key Personnel: Editor & Publisher, Stephen Bryant; Dir., Cur. & Museum Shop Mgr., Kathryn A. Kimball.
Personnel Profile: Full-Time Paid 3; Part-Time Paid 6.
Governing Authority: Parent Institution: United Methodist Church. Tax-exempt.
Religious Museum.
Collections: art objects having religious significance.
Research Fields: church history & music to selected groups.
Facilities: 13,000-vol. library of books & manuscripts on family devotion, worship, meditation, prayers & Methodist history available for inter-library loan; 200-seat chapel; reading room. Museum-related items for sale.
Activities: guided tours; permanent & temporary exhibitions.
Publications: daily devotional guide, The Upper Room; Weavings; Alive Now; Pockets; DevoZine.
Hours & Admission Prices: Mon.-Fri. 8-4:30. No charge; donations accepted. Closed major holidays. ♿
Attendance: 10,250 (estimated)

VANDERBILT UNIVERSITY FINE ARTS GALLERY, 1214 21st Ave. S., Nashville, TN 37203. Mailing Address: PMB 0273, 230 Appleton Place, Nashville, TN 37203-5721. Tel.: 615-322-0605 & 343-1704. Fax: 615-343-1382.
Web Site: www.vanderbilt.edu/gallery
Founded: 1961.
Congressional District: 5
Key Personnel: Dir., Joseph S. Mella.
Personnel Profile: Full-Time Paid 2; Part-Time Paid 5; Part-Time Volunteers 2.
Governing Authority: university. Affiliated with Vanderbilt University. Tax-exempt.
Art Gallery: housed in renovated 1927 building designed by McLain, Mead & White.
Collections: Vanderbilt art collection of paintings, sculpture & graphics; Harold P. Stern collection of Asian art; Samuel H. Kress study collection of Renaissance paintings; Anna C. Hoyt collection of old masters & modern prints; ceramics; contemporary works on paper & multiples.
Facilities: visual resources.
Activities: lectures; inter-museum loan; temporary & traveling exhibitions.
Publications: exhibition catalogues.
Hours & Admission Prices: School Year: Mon.-Fri. 12-4, Sat.-Sun. 1-5; Summer: Tues.-Fri. 12-4, Sat. 1-5. No charge. Closed school holidays. ♿
Attendance: 5,000 (estimated)

WATKINS INSTITUTE - BROWNLEE O. CURRY JR. GALLERY, 2298 Rosa L. Parks Blvd., Nashville, TN 37228-1306. Tel.: 615-383-4848. Fax: 615-383-4849.
E-mail: jryan@watkins.edu
Web Site: watkins.edu
Founded: 1885.
Congressional District: 5
Key Personnel: Pres., Ellen Meyer; Gallery Dir., Jack Ryan; Dir. Art School, Terry Thacker.
Governing Authority: board of trustees; nonprofit organization. Tax-exempt: 501(c)(3).
Art Gallery with Art School.
Collections: Tennessee All-State Art Collection of paintings, graphics & sculpture; 50 etchings by Nahum Tschacbasov; paintings from Childe Hassam Fund; seven Elihu Vedder paintings; nine antique hand colored prints of classical interiors & artifacts.
Facilities: studio classrooms for commercial & fine arts.
Activities: lectures; formally organized education programs for children & adults; inter-museum loan, permanent & traveling exhibitions. Museum Sponsors: Annual Arts Festival; Student Art Show; Tennessee All-State purchase award show; Faculty Art Show.
Publications: school catalogs & brochures; annual all-state exhibition catalog.

Hours & Admission Prices: Mon.-Fri. 9-8, Sat. 10-4, Sun. 2-4. No charge. Closed New Year's Day; Independence Day; Labor Day; Thanksgiving; Christmas. ♿

WILLIE NELSON & FRIENDS GENERAL STORE & MUSEUM, 2613 McGavock Pike, Nashville, TN 37214-1215. Tel.: 615-885-1515.
Country Music Stars Museum.
Collections: Willie Nelson & other country music stars' memorabilia; personal artifacts; photographs.
Facilities: Museum-related items for sale.
Activities: special events.
Hours & Admission Prices: Mon.-Thurs. 9-7, Fri.-Sat. 9-8, Sun. 9-6.

Oak Ridge

AMERICAN MUSEUM OF SCIENCE & ENERGY, (M), 300 S. Tulane Ave., Oak Ridge, TN 37830-6700. Tel.: 865-576-3200. Fax: 865-576-6024.
E-mail: jcomish@amse.org
Web Site: www.amse.org
Founded: 1949.
Congressional District: 3
Key Personnel: Exec. Dir., James R. Comish; Deputy Dir., Kenneth Mayes; Information Officer, Lissa Clarke; Volunteer Coord., Glenda Bingham; Exhibits Design, Jerry King; Facilities Mgr., Rex Haun; Museum Coord., Ann Armstrong; Museum Discovery Shop Mgr., Caroline Baker.
Personnel Profile: Full-Time Paid 15; Part-Time Paid 9; Part-Time Volunteers 36; Interns 1.
Governing Authority: federal. Operated by Enterprise Advisory Services, Inc. Parent Institution: Oak Ridge National Laboratory-operated by U.T. Battelle. Subsidiary Institution: U.T. Battelle. Tax-exempt: 501(c)(3).
Science & Technology Museum.
Collections: World of the Atom; Y-12 & National Defense; Earth's Energy Resources; The Oak Ridge Story; AMSE Lab-Hands-On Science; history of the Manhattan Project.
Facilities: 312-seat auditorium; two 50-seat demonstration areas; laboratory classroom; picnic area. Educational & gift items for sale.
Activities: self-guided tours; lectures; demonstrations; films; traveling & permanent exhibitions; tours of Oak Ridge Manhattan Project sites; nature walks; internet experiences; outreach to schools.
Hours & Admission Prices: Mon.-Sat. 9-5, Sun. 1-5. Adults 18-64 $5, seniors 65 & over $4, children 6-17 $3; ASTC Passport members, members & children under 6 no charge. Closed New Year's Day; Thanksgiving; Christmas. ♿
Attendance: 126,000 (accurate)
Membership: Individual $25; Grandparent $30; Family $35; Family & Friends $75; The Sunday Punch Club $150; The U-235 Club $235.

CHILDREN'S MUSEUM OF OAK RIDGE, INC., (M), 461 W. Outer Dr., Oak Ridge, TN 37830-3700. Tel.: 865-482-1074. Fax: 865-481-4889.
E-mail: chmor@bellsouth.net
Web Site: www.childrensmuseumofoakridge.org
Founded: 1973.
Congressional District: 3
Key Personnel: Exec. Dir., Mary Ann Damos; Pres. Bd. Trustees, Larry Burkholder; Designer, Peg Heddleson; Business Mgr., Dawn Van Eek; Dir. Education, Joyce Gralak; Deputy Dir., Carroll Welch; Collections Mgr., Kay Palmateer.
Personnel Profile: Full-Time Paid 5; Full-Time Volunteers 2; Part-Time Paid 4; Part-Time Volunteers 40.
Governing Authority: nonprofit organization. Tax-exempt: 501(c)(3).
Children's Museum.
Collections: Appalachian primitives; Japanese Kokeski Dolls; foreign dolls; Liberian artifacts; Appalachian folk art; coal mining artifacts; Cherokee Indian artifacts; costumes; natural history; early Oak Ridge artifacts; doll house; life-size birdroom; Brazilian Rainforest; model trains; history of Oak Ridge & the Manhattan Project.
Research Fields: Appalachian life.
Facilities: 1,000-vol. library of books; 500 tapes, video cassettes & video center, slides & photographs on Appalachian history; reading room; 1,000-seat auditorium; theater; classrooms. Local handcrafts, exhibit-related items for sale.
Activities: guided tours; lectures; films; gallery talks; concerts; arts festivals; drama; hobby workshops; TV & radio programs; formally organized education programs for children, adults & undergraduate college students; docent program; loan, permanent, temporary & traveling exhibitions.
Publications: books, Encyclopedia of East Tennessee; These Are Our Voices-The Story of Oak Ridge 1942-1970; quarterly newsletter, Children's Museum Newsletter; teachers manual, When Grandma Was a Girl; Ridges & Valleys, Vols. I & II; Andreson County: A Pictorial History; Oak Ridge & Me - From Youth to Maturity.
Hours & Admission Prices: June-Aug. Mon.-Fri. 9-5, Sat. 10-4, Sun. 1-4; Sept.-May Tues.-Fri. 9-5, Sat. 10-4, Sun. 1-4. Adults $7, senior citizens $6, children 3 & over $5; discounts to groups; children under 3 & members no charge. Closed Independence Day; Thanksgiving; Christmas.
Attendance: 150,000 (estimated)

OAK RIDGE ART CENTER, 201 Badger Ave., Oak Ridge, TN 37830-6216. Mailing Address: P.O. Box 7005, Oak Ridge, TN 37831-3305. Tel.: 865-482-1441. Fax: 865-482-1441 (call first).
E-mail: cre8tivtn@cs.com
Web Site: oakridgeartcenter.org
Founded: 1952.
Congressional District: 3
Key Personnel: Dir., Leah Marcum-Estes; Pres. (V), Lawrence Metcalf.
Personnel Profile: Full-Time Paid 1; Part-Time Paid 2.
Governing Authority: nonprofit organization. Tax-exempt: 501(c)(3).
Art Center.
Collections: Gomez Collection of post-World War II art; primitive to contemporary art.
Facilities: library; painting & drawing studios; ceramics studio.
Activities: guided tours; lectures; films; concerts; arts festivals; broadcast programs; organized education programs for children, adults & undergraduate college students affiliated with Roane State Community College; temporary & loan exhibitions; docent program. Center Sponsors: Hot Pots & Cool Art in summer; Spring Tea in April.
Publications: monthly newsletter; monthly arts calendar.
Hours & Admission Prices: Tues.-Fri. 9-5, Sat.-Mon. 1-4. No charge; donations accepted. Closed major holidays. ♿
Attendance: 50,000 (estimated)
Membership: Retired Individual $25; Individual & Retired Family $35; Family $45; Friend $50; Patron $100; Sponsor $250; Benefactor $350; Corporate $500; Life $1,000.

UNIVERSITY OF TENNESSEE ARBORETUM, 901 S. Illinois Ave., Oak Ridge, TN 37830-8032. Tel.: 865-483-3571. Fax: 865-483-3572.
E-mail: utforest@utk.edu
Web Site: forestry.tennessee.edu/arboretum
Founded: 1964.
Congressional District: 3
Key Personnel: C.E.O. & Dir., Richard M. Evans; Sec., Lynne Lucas.
Personnel Profile: Part-Time Volunteers 5; Interns 4.
Governing Authority: university. Parent Institution: University of Tennessee. Tax-exempt.
Arboretum.
Collections: forestry; horticulture.
Research Fields: forest tree breeding & adaptation; shade tree & visual screening research; urban forestry; tree physiology.
Facilities: visitor center; greenhouse.
Activities: self-guided tours.
Publications: biannual, University of Tennessee Arboretum Society Bulletin; trail guides; nature pamphlets.
Hours & Admission Prices: Daily 8am-Sunset. Office: Mon.-Fri. 8-4:30. No charge; donations accepted. Closed national holidays.
Attendance: 35,000 (estimated)
Membership: Student $15; Individual $30; Family $45; Society Friend $100; Patron $500; Corporate $1,000.

Paris

PARIS-HENRY COUNTY HERITAGE CENTER, (M), 614 N. Poplar St., Paris, TN 38242-3440. Mailing Address: P.O. Box 822, Paris, TN 38242-0822. Tel.: 731-642-1030. Fax: 731-642-1096.
Web Site: www.phchc.com
Founded: 1989.
Congressional District: 8
Key Personnel: Dir., Norma B. Steele; Chm. (V), Gerry Scholes; Treas., Vicki Muzzall.
Personnel Profile: Full-Time Paid 1; Part-Time Volunteers 30.
Governing Authority: private; nonprofit organization. Tax-exempt: 501(c)(3).
History Museum.
Collections: history of Henry County & the city of Paris; Camp Tyson, WWII.
Major Exhibits: Black History, 1/10-2/10; Boy Scouts Happy 100th Birthday, 2/10-3/10; Scarecrows, 10/10.
Research Fields: Civil War; E.W. Grove; Gilded Age, Paris, TN.
Facilities: library; 832 sq. ft. exhibit space. Museum-related items for sale.
Activities: docent program; guided tours; lectures; temporary exhibitions. Annual Events: Grapes & Gourmet; Fish Fry in April.
Publications: biannual newsletter, Inkwell.
Hours & Admission Prices: Tues.-Fri. 10-4, Sat. 10-2. No charge; donations accepted. Closed New Year's Day; Thanksgiving; Christmas. ♿

Attendance: 4,161 (estimated)
Membership: Cavitt Place Friend $25; Legacy $50; Century $100; Historian $250; Sponsor $500; Heritage $1,000.

Parsons

PARSONS AND GREATER AREA MUSEUM, (M), 535 Tennessee Ave., Municipal Bldg., Parsons, TN 38363. Mailing Address: P.O. Box 128, Parsons, TN 38363-0128. Tel.: 731-847-6358. Fax: 731-847-9272.
Founded: 2007.
Key Personnel: Treas., Judy Daugherty
History Museum.
Collections: area history & culture; Native American; railroad artifacts; minerals & fossils; farming; schools; churches.
Facilities: library.
Activities: school programs.
Hours & Admission Prices: Mon.-Fri. 10-4:30, Sat. 10 am-12 pm. No charge.

Pigeon Forge

DINOSAUR WALK MUSEUM, 106 Showplace Blvd., Pigeon Forge, TN 37863-4977. Tel.: 865-428-4003.
E-mail: info@dinosaurwalkmuseum.com
Web Site: www.dinowalk.com
Dinosaur Museum.
Collections: over 50 life-sized dinosaurs; reptiles.
Facilities: Museum-related items for sale.
Activities: video presentations; Discovery Dig; special programs; educational events.
Hours & Admission Prices: Daily 9-5. Adults 12 & over $9.95, children 4-11 $3.95; children 3 & under no charge. Closed Christmas.

ELVIS PRESLEY MUSEUM, 2638 Parkway, Pigeon Forge, TN 37863-3246. Tel.: 865-428-2001.
Web Site: www.elvispresleymuseum.com
Key Personnel: Contact, Grace Savern
History Museum.
Collections: Elvis' life, family history, & memorabilia; personal artifacts; 1973 Lincoln Continental limousine; 1967 honeymoon Cadillac; jewelry.
Facilities: theatre. Museum-related items for sale.
Activities: live performances by tribute performers; videos.
Hours & Admission Prices: Call for hours. Adults $17, seniors 65 & over and students $15, children 6-11 $12. Closed Thanksgiving; Christmas.

Piney Flats

* **ROCKY MOUNT MUSEUM, (M),** 200 Hyder Hill Rd., Piney Flats, TN 37686-4630. Mailing Address: P.O. Box 160, Piney Flats, TN 37686-0160. Tel.: 423-538-7396. Fax: 423-538-1086.
E-mail: info@rockymountmuseum.com
Web Site: www.rockymountmuseum.com
Founded: 1958.
Congressional District: 1
Key Personnel: C.E.O. & Exec. Dir., Gary Walrath; Pres. (V), David Tipton; Exec. Asst., Ms. Reda Greene; Museum Shop Mgr., Delores Miller.
Personnel Profile: Full-Time Paid 3; Part-Time Paid 16; Part-Time Volunteers 60.
Governing Authority: state; nonprofit organization. Affiliated with State of Tennessee & Rocky Mount Historical Association. Tax-exempt: 501(c)(3).
Historic Site: 1790-92 original U.S. Territorial Capitol of Southwest Territory; c.1770-1772 log house; separate kitchen; weaving cabin; smokehouse; blacksmith's shop; slave cabin; farm area, including garden & crops of 1791 period & animals.
Collections: furniture & furnishings of log house including kitchen, servants' quarters; barn; artifacts; textile collection; separate museum of overmountain history; manuscripts.
Research Fields: early history of Southwest Territory; early agricultural history.
Facilities: historical library available for use on premises; conference center; rental facilities.
Activities: guided tours; first person living history interpretation; changing & permanent exhibitions; public & educational programming; adult education series; rental facilities.
Publications: occasional publications; bimonthly newsletter.
Hours & Admission Prices: Jan.-Feb. by appointment only; Office: Mon.-Fri 9-5; March to mid-Dec. Living History Tours: Tues.-Sat. 11-5. Adults $6, seniors $5, children (6-17) $4; discounts to groups, AAM, AAA & AARP members. Closed Thanksgiving. ♿
Attendance: 26,500 (estimated)
Membership: Individual $25; Family $35; Contributing $50; Small Business & Patron $100; Corporate $200; Supporting Donor $250; Corporate Sponsor, Fellow Donor & Foundation Member $500; Corporate Patron, Sustaining Donor & Foundation Sponsor $1,000; Corporate Partner $2,500; Foundation Partner $5,000.

Pinson

PINSON MOUNDS STATE ARCHAEOLOGICAL AREA, 460 Ozier Rd., Pinson, TN 38366-9626. Tel.: 731-988-5614. Fax: 901-424-3909.
Web Site: www.tennessee.gov/environment/parks/pinsonmounds
Founded: 1980.
Congressional District: 7
Key Personnel: Park Mgr., Tim Poole; Park Ranger, Wes Williams.
Governing Authority: state. Managed by the Tennessee Dept. of Environment and Conservation, Div. of Parks and Recreation, 401 Church St., Nashville, TN 37243. Tel. 615-532-0001.
Archaeological Site: Middle Woodland Period ceremonial site, with mounds & earthworks.
Collections: artifacts from on-site fieldwork; regional & site specific prehistory.
Research Fields: Native American cultures; archaeology, with emphasis on the mid-south.
Facilities: 617-vol. library of archaeology research material, site reports, ethnographic, popular, museological, available for research on premises only; field research station; separate lab operation; 80-seat theater; on-site housing for research students. Museum-related items for sale.
Activities: guided tours; lectures; films; video programs.
Publications: booklet, Dept. of Conservation, Div. of Archaeology, Research Series.
Hours & Admission Prices: March-Nov. Mon.-Sat. 8-4:30, Sun. 1-5; Dec.-Feb. Mon.-Fri. 8-4:30, Sun. 1-4:30. No charge. Closed state winter holidays. ♿
Attendance: 110,000 (estimated)

Rogersville

TENNESSEE NEWSPAPER & PRINTING MUSEUM, 415 S. Depot St., Rogersville, TN 37857-3331. Tel.: 423-272-1961. Fax: 423-272-1961.
History Museum: housed in a restored 1890 Southern Railway depot. Listed on the National Register of Historic Places.
Collections: newspaper & printing industries; local history; period machinery & equipment; newspapers.
Hours & Admission Prices: Daily 10-4 by appointment. No charge; donations accepted.

Rugby

HISTORIC RUGBY, 5517 State Hwy. 52, Rugby, TN 37733. Mailing Address: P.O. Box 8, Rugby, TN 37733-0008. Tel.: 423-628-2441. Fax: 423-628-2266.
E-mail: historicrugby@highland.net
Web Site: www.historicrugby.org
Founded: 1966.
Congressional District: 12
Key Personnel: Exec. Dir., Cheryl Cribbet; Pres., Greg Reed; Asst. Exec. Dir., Cathy Hannaway; Dir. Properties, John Gilliat; Museum Shop Mgr., Rita Elliott.
Personnel Profile: Full-Time Paid 18; Part-Time Paid 10; Part-Time Volunteers 3.
Governing Authority: society; nonprofit organization. Tax-exempt: 501(c)(3); 170(b)(1)(A).
Historic Site.
Collections: preservation project; archives; manuscript collections. Historic Buildings: 1884 Kingstone Lisle; 1882 Thomas Hughes Library; 1884 Percy Cottage reconstruction; 1887 Christ Church, Episcopal; 1907 Rugby Public School; 1880 Pioneer Cottage; 1880 Newbury House Inn; 1881 Rugby Commissary Reconstruction; 1880 Board of Aid reconstruction.
Research Fields: regional culture, Victorian arts, crafts & music, 19th century British culture.
Facilities: 7,000-vol. library of books on Victorian literature available for use on premises by appointment; craft commissary; lodging in historic homes; restaurant. Books for sale.
Activities: guided tours; lectures; concerts. Museum Sponsors: annual pilgrimage, spring music festival & craft festival, Christmas at Rugby, year round workshops, stage presentations.
Publications: biannual newsletter, The Rugbeian; books, Rugby Recipes; Distant Eden-A Rugby History; Images of America Historic Rugby.
Hours & Admission Prices: Jan. by appointment; Winter: Mon.-Sat. 9:30-4:30; Sun. 12-5:30; Summer call for extended hours. Adults $7, senior citizens $6, students $3; discount to groups; members no charge. Closed New Year's Day; Thanksgiving; Christmas Eve & Day. ♿
Attendance: 60,000 (estimated)
Membership: Individual $25; Family & Sustaining $40.

Rutherford

DAVID CROCKETT CABIN, 219 N. Trenton St., Rutherford, TN 38369. Mailing Address: 945 S. Trenton, Rutherford, TN 38369-9670. Tel.: 731-665-7253.
E-mail: jobne@msn.com
Web Site: www.davycrockettcabin.org
Founded: 1954.
Congressional District: 8
Key Personnel: Pres. & Treas. (V), Joe Bone; Chm. (V), Hobert Walker.
Personnel Profile: Part-Time Paid 2; Part-Time Volunteers 6.
Governing Authority: society. The David Crockett board of directors. Parent Institution: town of Rutherford. Subsidiary Institution: Rutherford Lions Club. Tax-exempt.
Historic Building: 1800s David Crockett Cabin.
Collections: period furniture; grave of David Crockett's mother; Davy's letters to his family.
Activities: guided tours; permanent exhibitions. Museum Sponsors: Davy Crockett Parade in October.
Publications: postcards; brochures; book, The Fabulous Davy Crockett.
Hours & Admission Prices: Memorial Day to Labor Day Tues.-Sat. 9-5, Sun. 1-4:30; Sept.-May Tues.-Sat. 9-5; other times by appointment. Family $5, adults $2, children over 6 $1; discounts to students & seniors groups; under 6 no charge.
Attendance: 1,500 (estimated)

Savannah

CHERRY MANSION, 265 Main St., Savannah, TN 38372. Tel.: 731-607-1208.
Historic House: built in 1830, former home of W.H. Cherry & headquarters for General U.S. Grant in 1862.
Collections: period furnishings.
Hours & Admission Prices: Call for hours. Tours: adults $10, students $5.

TENNESSEE RIVER MUSEUM, 495 Main St., Savannah, TN 38372-2062. Tel.: 800-552-3866; 731-925-8181. Fax: 731-925-6987.
Key Personnel: Tourism Dir., Rachel Baker
History Museum.
Collections: local history & culture; photographs; personal artifacts; period furnishings.
Hours & Admission Prices: Mon.-Sat. 9-5, Sun. 1-5. Adults $3; children 18 & under no charge.

Sevierville

NATIONAL KNIFE MUSEUM, INC., 2320 Winfield Dunn Pkwy., Sevierville, TN 37876-0557. Mailing Address: P.O. Box 4430, Sevierville, TN 37864. Tel.: 865-453-5871, ext. 259.
E-mail: nkmuskw@gmail.com
Web Site: www.nkcaknife.org
Founded: 1981.
Key Personnel: Pres., Perry Miller; Vice Pres., David Mullins; Cur., Peter N. Cohan; Staff, Una Gillespie; Staff, Audrey Kelley.
Personnel Profile: Full-Time Volunteers 1; Part-Time Paid 2; Part-Time Volunteers 3.
Governing Authority: private; nonprofit organization. Tax-exempt: 501(c)(3).
Knife and Cutlery Museum.
Collections: knives, knife & sword memorabilia: fruit, glass cake, period, commemorative & Rambo knife collections; pocket cutlery 1,500 CE to present; daggers; stone artifacts; scalpels; exhibition knives 1860s-1920s; custom knives 1930s-present.
Research Fields: cutlery history; metallurgy; human culture & the knife's importance.
Facilities: 650-vol. library; 4,400 sq. ft. exhibit space.
Activities: docent program; formal education programs; self-guided tours; special events celebrating knives; youth programs; training programs for professional workers; demonstrations.
Hours & Admission Prices: Daily 10-9. No charge; donations requested. ♿
Attendance: 40,000 (accurate)
Membership: Friends of National Knife Museum: $30, $100; $500 & up.

SEVIER COUNTY HERITAGE MUSEUM, 167 E. Bruce St., Sevierville, TN 37862-3501. Tel.: 865-453-4058.
History Museum: housed in the former post office. Listed on the National Register of Historic Places.
Collections: local history & culture; period artifacts; early furnishings; photographs.
Activities: lectures; classes.
Hours & Admission Prices: Mon.-Fri. 12-5, Sat. 12-3. No charge.

TENNESSEE MUSEUM OF AVIATION, (M), 135 Air Museum Way, Sevierville, TN 37862-8703. Mailing Address: P.O. Box 5587, 37864, TN Tel.: 865-908-0171 & 0760. Fax: 865-908-8421.
E-mail: rmelton1@earthlink.net
Web Site: www.tnairmuseum.com
Founded: 2000.
Congressional District: 1
Key Personnel: Pres., C.E.O. & Chm. (V), R. Neal Melton; Membership Coord. & Education, Sandra Layman; Cur. & Archivist, Tom Walker; Museum Shop Mgr., Lana Johnson; Volunteer, Rhonda Melton.
Personnel Profile: Full-Time Paid 4; Full-Time Volunteers 2; Part-Time Paid 2; Part-Time Volunteers 20.
Governing Authority: private; nonprofit organization. Tax-exempt: 501(c)(3).
Aviation Museum: state's official Aviation Hall of Fame.
Collections: aviation history from early flight to modern times; Tennessee aviation history; WWII combat aircraft; uniforms.
Research Fields: WWII aviation; WWI aviation; women's service in WWII military; WWII homefront efforts; uniform identification.
Facilities: library; 15,000 sq. ft. exhibit space; hangar area available for dinners or receptions. Museum-related items for sale.
Activities: docent program; guided tours; temporary & traveling exhibitions; theater; lecture series; story telling. Annual Events: Fly-Ins; Tennessee Aviation Hall of Fame Induction.
Hours & Admission Prices: Mon.-Sat. 10-6, Sun. 1-6. Adults $12.75, senior citizens $9.75, children 6-12 $6.75; discounts to AAM & ICOM members; members and children 5 & under no charge. ♿
Attendance: 50,000 (estimated)
Membership: Military & Veteran Silver $20; Student & Senior $25; Individual $35; Military & Veteran Gold $40; Couple $50; Family $65; Echelon $250-$499; Wings $500-$999; TN Aviation Historical Society $1,000-$9,999; Life $10,000 & up.

Sewanee

UNIVERSITY ART GALLERY, UNIVERSITY OF THE SOUTH, Guerry Hall, Georgia Ave., Sewanee, TN 37383-0001. Mailing Address: 735 University Ave., Sewanee, TN 37383-1000. Tel.: 931-598-1223. Fax: 931-598-3335.
E-mail: sjmaclar@sewanee.edu
Web Site: www.sewanee.edu/gallery
Founded: 1965.
Congressional District: 4
Key Personnel: Gallery Dir., Shelley MacLaren.
Personnel Profile: Full-Time Paid 1; Part-Time Paid 10.
Governing Authority: university. Parent Institution: The University of the South. Tax-exempt: 501(c)(3).
University Art Gallery.
Collections: works of contemporary art.
Major Exhibits: Caroline Allison, 2/19/10-4/11/10; Sewanee Senior Art Majors, 4/20/10-5/8/10.
Activities: guided tours; lectures; films; gallery talks; formally organized education programs for undergraduate college & graduate students; loan, permanent, temporary exhibitions.
Publications: bulletin; two annual catalogues.
Hours & Admission Prices: Tues.-Fri. 10-5, Sat.-Sun. 12-4. No charge; donations accepted. Closed university holidays. ♿
Attendance: 6,000 (estimated)

Shiloh

SHILOH NATIONAL MILITARY PARK & CEMETERY, 1055 Pittsburg Landing Rd., Shiloh, TN 38376-4331. Tel.: 731-689-5696. Fax: 731-689-5450.
E-mail: shil_administration@nps.gov
Web Site: www.nps.gov/shil
Founded: 1894.
Congressional District: 6
Key Personnel: Chief Interpretation & Resource Mgmt., Stacy D. Allen; Supt., Haywood S. Harrell.
Personnel Profile: Full-Time Paid 26; Part-Time Paid 6; Part-Time Volunteers 1.
Governing Authority: federal. Affiliated with U.S. National Park Services, U.S. Department of the Interior, Washington, DC 20240.
Military Museum.
Collections: history; military; manuscript collections; Indian artifacts. Historic Building: pre-Civil War war cabin.
Research Fields: Civil War history.
Facilities: 1,500-vol. library of Civil War source books & documents available for use on premises; historic battlefield. Historical publications for sale.
Activities: guided tours; lectures; films; permanent exhibitions; demonstrations.

Publications: Park folder & driving tour guide.
Hours & Admission Prices: Daily 8-5. Family $5, adults $3. Closed Christmas. ♿
Attendance: 115,000 (estimated)

Smithville

APPALACHIAN CENTER FOR CRAFT, 1560 Craft Center Dr., Smithville, TN 37166-7352. Tel.: 615-597-6801. Fax: 615-597-6803.
E-mail: craftcenter@tntech.edu
Web Site: www.tntech.edu/craftcenter
Founded: 1979.
Key Personnel: Dir., Ward Doubet; Gallery Mgr., Gail S. Looper; Pres. (V), Karla Clarke.
Personnel Profile: Full-Time Paid 1; Part-Time Paid 4; Interns 1.
Governing Authority: state government & public university. Parent Institution: Tennessee Tech University. Tax-exempt.
General Museum.
Collections: over 25 exhibitions annually of contemporary & traditional fine craft.
Facilities: Museum-related items for sale.
Activities: Bachelor of Fine Arts degree & craft certificate programs; craft workshops. Annual Events: Holiday Festival; Annual Celebration of Craft Silent Auction in April.
Publications: annual exhibition calendar; workshop catalog; academic brochures.
Hours & Admission Prices: Daily 9-5. No charge; donations accepted. Closed New Year's Day; Easter; Thanksgiving; Christmas to New Year's Eve. ♿
Attendance: 150,000 (estimated)

Smyrna

SAM DAVIS HOME, 1399 Sam Davis Rd., Smyrna, TN 37167-2744. Tel.: 615-459-2341.
Key Personnel: Exec. Dir., Anita Teague
Historic House Museum.
Collections: period furnishings; personal artifacts.
Activities: special events.
Hours & Admission Prices: June-Aug. Mon.-Sat. 9-5, Sun. 1-5; Sept.-May Mon.-Sat. 10-4, Sun. 1-4. Museum & House: adults $8.50, seniors $6.50, children $3. Museum: adults $5, seniors $4, children 6-12 $1.50; children under 6 no charge.

Springfield

MUSEUM OF BEVERAGE CONTAINERS & ADVERTISING, 3052 Old New Cut Rd., Springfield, TN 37172-5716. Tel.: 615-859-5236 & 382-9299. Fax: 615-382-8905.
History Museum.
Collections: period bottles & cans; signs; trays; glasses; steins; coasters; matchbook covers; bottle caps.
Hours & Admission Prices: By appointment. No charge; donations accepted.

ROBERTSON COUNTY HISTORY MUSEUM, 124 Sixth Ave. W., Springfield, TN 37172-2405. Mailing Address: P.O. Box 1022, Springfield, TN 37172-1022. Tel.: 615-382-7173.
Founded: 1993.
Congressional District: 6
Personnel Profile: Full-Time Paid 1; Part-Time Volunteers 24.
Governing Authority: Parent Institution: Robertson County Historical Society. Tax-exempt.
History Museum: housed in the former U.S. Post Office.
Collections: county history including tobacco & whiskey trades; photographs.
Publications: quarterly newsletter.
Hours & Admission Prices: Wed.-Fri. 10-4, Sat. by appointment. Adults $4, seniors $2, students $1; discounts to groups; members no charge. Closed most holidays. ♿
Membership: Individual $15; Household $25.

Stanton

HATCHIE NATIONAL WILDLIFE REFUGE, 6772 Hwy. 76 S., Stanton, TN 38069-3648. Tel.: 731-772-0501. Fax: 731-772-7839.
E-mail: hatchie@fws.gov
Web Site: www.fws.gov/hatchie
Key Personnel: Refuge Mgr., Michael Chouinard
Wildlife Refuge.
Collections: waterfowl.
Hours & Admission Prices: Call for hours.

Sweetwater

THE LOST SEA, 140 Lost Sea Rd., Sweetwater, TN 37874-6724. Tel.: 423-337-6616.
Natural History Museum: a Registered National Landmark.
Collections: underground lake; caverns; 18th century village; local history; Native American artifacts; photographs.
Activities: cave tours.
Hours & Admission Prices: March-April & Sept.-Oct. daily 9-6; May-June & Aug. daily 9-7; July daily 9-8; Nov.-Feb. daily 9-5. Adults $15.95, children 5-12 $7.45; discounts to groups or 20 or more by appointment.

SWEETWATER HERITAGE MUSEUM, North & High Sts., Sweetwater, TN 37874. Mailing Address: P.O. Box 143, Etowah, TN 37331.
History Museum.
Collections: local history & culture; photographs; period furnishings; personal artifacts.
Hours & Admission Prices: March-Oct. Wed. & Sat.-Sun. 2-4.

Tellico Plains

CHARLES HALL MUSEUM, 229 Cherohala Skyway, Tellico Plains, TN 37385-5500. Tel.: 423-253-6767.
Founded: 2003.
Congressional District: 2
Personnel Profile: Full-Time Volunteers 1.
History Museum.
Collections: local history & culture; photographs; personal artifacts; early furnishings; over 200 guns; telephones; coins.
Facilities: Museum-related items for sale.
Hours & Admission Prices: Daily. No charge. ♿
Attendance: 30,000 (estimated)

Townsend

CADES COVE VISITOR CENTER AND OPEN-AIR MUSEUM, Great Smoky Mountains National Park, 10042 Campgrounds Dr., Townsend, TN 37882-5004. Mailing Address: Great Smoky Mountains National Park, 107 Park Headquarters Rd., Gatlinburg, TN 37738-4102. Tel.: 877-444-6777. Fax: 865-436-1220.
E-mail: grsm_smokies_information@nps.gov
Web Site: www.nps.gov/grsm
Founded: 1951.
Key Personnel: Chief Resource Education, Cathleen Cook.
Governing Authority: federal. Tax-exempt.
Preservation Project: Cable Mill Area & other historic structures typical of Southern Appalachia at turn of the 20th century.
Collections: water powered grist mill; historic house.
Facilities: visitor center; nature trail. Postcards, slides & books for sale.
Activities: permanent exhibitions; self-guided auto tour & nature trail; demonstrations of pioneer crafts.
Publications: booklet, Cades Cove Auto Tour.
Hours & Admission Prices: Museum: daily dawn to dusk. Visitor Center: Feb. & Nov. daily 9-5; March & Sept.-Oct. daily 9-6; April-Aug. daily 9-7; Dec.-Jan. daily 9-4:30. No charge. ♿
Attendance: 1,000,000

GREAT SMOKY MOUNTAINS HERITAGE CENTER, (M), 123 Cromwell Dr., Townsend, TN 37882-4323. Mailing Address: P.O. Box 268, Townsend, TN 37882-0268. Tel.: 865-448-0044. Fax: 865-448-6975.
Web Site: www.gsmheritagecenter.org
Founded: 2006.
Congressional District: 2
Key Personnel: Dir., Robert Patterson; Pres. (V), Richard Way; Treas., Bob Sullivan; Admin. Asst., Pam Hanby; Cur., Katherine Prince; Exhibit Technician, Bob Hood; Dir. Mktg., Nancy Williams; Museum Shop Mgr., Don Alexander.
Personnel Profile: Full-Time Paid 5; Part-Time Paid 3; Part-Time Volunteers 120; Interns 3.
Governing Authority: private; nonprofit organization. Tax-exempt: 501(c)(3).
History Museum.
Collections: East Tennessee mountain history & culture; transportation; Native American artifacts; horse-drawn vehicles; 8 historic buildings & furnishings; textiles; tools; archaeological artifacts.
Facilities: 100-vol. library; 100-seat auditorium; educational facilities; 500-seat amphitheater. Museum-related items for sale.
Activities: concerts; docent program; films; guided tours; hobby workshops; lectures; participatory exhibits; theater; broadcast programs. Annual Events: Heritage Happenings Fund-raiser; Winter Heritage Festival; Spring Heritage Festival; Sunset Music Series; Blue Ribbon Country Fair; Christmas Memories.

Publications: quarterly newsletter, Mountain Echoes; book, Flavors of Our Heritage Cookbook; video, Peace of Ground.
Hours & Admission Prices: Tues.-Sat. 10-5, Sun. 1-5. Adults $6, senior citizens & students $4; discounts to groups of 8 or more, AAM & ICOM members; children under 6 no charge. Closed New Year's Day; Easter; Thanksgiving; Christmas Eve & Day. ♿
Attendance: 25,000 (accurate)
Membership: Individual $15; Family $25; Patron $50; Contributor $100.

Tullahoma

BEECHCRAFT HERITAGE MUSEUM, 570 Old Shelbyville Hwy., Tullahoma, TN 37388-4703. Mailing Address: P.O. Box 550, Tullahoma, TN 37388-0550. Tel.: 931-455-1974. Fax: 931-455-1994.
E-mail: info@beechcraftheritagemuseum.org
Web Site: beechcraftheritagemuseum.org
Aviation Museum.
Collections: period Beechcraft airplanes & memorabilia.
Hours & Admission Prices: Tues.-Sat. 8:30-4:30. Adults $10, children 12-17 $5; children 11 & under no charge.

FLOYD AND MARGARET MITCHELL MUSEUM, South Jackson Civic Center, 404 S. Jackson St., Tullahoma, TN 37388. Mailing Address: P.O. Box 326, Tullahoma, TN 37388-0326. Tel.: 931-455-5321.
E-mail: sojack@lighttube.net
Web Site: southjackson.org/museum.html
Key Personnel: Chm., Blossom Merryman
History Museum.
Collections: local history, business & culture; photographs; personal artifacts; period furnishings; Native American; military memorabilia.
Hours & Admission Prices: 1st Sun. of month 2-4; other times by appointment.

Union City

DIXIE GUN WORKS' OLD CAR MUSEUM, 1412 W. Reelfoot Ave., Union City, TN 38261-5508. Tel.: 731-885-0561. Fax: 731-885-0440.
E-mail: dixiegun@earthlink.net
Web Site: www.dixiegunworks.com
Founded: 1954.
Congressional District: 7
Key Personnel: Vice Pres., Hunter M.F. Kirkland.
Personnel Profile: Full-Time Paid 26.
Governing Authority: private; nonprofit. Parent Institution: Dixie Gun Works.
Automobile Museum.
Collections: American period automotives; 16th to 19th-century firearms.
Facilities: 15,000 sq. ft. exhibit space. Museum-related items for sale.
Hours & Admission Prices: Mon.-Fri. 8-5, Sat. 8-12. Adults $2, senior citizens & children $1. Closed New Year's Day; Memorial Day; Independence Day; Labor Day; Thanksgiving; Christmas.
Attendance: 3,000 (estimated)

OBION COUNTY MUSEUM, (M), 1004 Edwards St., Union City, TN 38261-5316. Tel.: 731-885-6774.
Key Personnel: Chm. (V), Larry Mink; Museum Shop Mgr., Polly Putman.
Personnel Profile: Part-Time Volunteers 15.
History Museum.
Collections: local history & cultural heritage; photographs.
Hours & Admission Prices: Sat.-Sun. 1-4; other times by appointment. Adults $2, children $1; members no charge. ♿
Attendance: 1,788 (accurate)
Membership: Individual $30; Family $50; Business $100; Heritage Circle $500.

Vonore

FORT LOUDOUN STATE HISTORIC PARK, 338 Fort Loudoun Rd., Vonore, TN 37885-2704. Tel.: 423-884-6217. Fax: 423-884-2287.
Park Museum.
Collections: local history; 18th century British fort replica; Tellico Blockhouse ruins.
Facilities: nature trails.
Activities: reenactments; hiking. Annual Event: 18th Century Trade Faire in September.
Hours & Admission Prices: Call for hours.

THE SEQUOYAH BIRTHPLACE MUSEUM, 576 Hwy. 360, Vonore, TN 37885-2816. Mailing Address: P.O. Box 69, Vonore, TN 37885-0069. Tel.: 423-884-6246. Fax: 423-884-2102.
E-mail: seqmus@tds.net
Web Site: www.sequoyahmuseum.org
Cultural History Museum.
Collections: Cherokee Indian writing system; culture & history.
Facilities: Museum-related items for sale.
Activities: special events; workshops; school programs.
Hours & Admission Prices: Mon.-Sat. 9-5, Sun. 12-5. Closed New Year's Day; Thanksgiving; Christmas.

VONORE HERITAGE MUSEUM, 619 Church St., Vonore, TN 37885-2324. Tel.: 423-884-2989.
Founded: 1996.
Key Personnel: Chm. (V), Kathleen Miller; Pres. (V), Violet K. Wolfe; Museum Shop Mgr., Paul Graves
History Museum.
Collections: local history & culture; farm tools & equipment; household artifacts; photographs.
Hours & Admission Prices: Wed. & Sat. 1-3; other times by appointment. No charge; donations accepted. Closed Thanksgiving; Christmas. ♿
Attendance: 1,025 (accurate)

Waverly

WORLD O' TOOLS MUSEUM, 2431 Hwy. 13 S., Waverly, TN 37185-2930. Tel.: 931-296-3218.
E-mail: hunterp@usit.net
Founded: 1973.
Congressional District: 6
Key Personnel: Owner & Cur., Hunter M. Pilkinton.
Governing Authority: individual operation; nonprofit.
Hobby Museum.
Collections: 25,000 early wood & metal working craft tools; pictures; statuettes; advertising memorabilia; books; catalogs.
Research Fields: early tools.
Facilities: 5,000-vol. library of reference books, trade catalogs & magazines on tools & their uses available with approval on premises; reading room.
Activities: guided tours; lectures; permanent exhibitions.
Publications: brochure.
Hours & Admission Prices: By appointment. No charge; donations accepted. ♿
Attendance: 500 (estimated)

Winchester

FRANKLIN COUNTY OLD JAIL MUSEUM, 400 Dinah Shore Blvd., Winchester, TN 37398-1421. Mailing Address: 7895 Sewanee Hwy., Cowan, TN 37318-3706. Tel.: 931-967-0524.
Founded: 1973.
Congressional District: 4
Key Personnel: C.E.O., Pres. (V) Chm. Old Jail Museum Commission, Mrs. Nancy Hall; Hostess, Mrs. Ruth McNutt; Treas., Harry Fanning; Sec., Kathy Howse.
Personnel Profile: Full-Time Volunteers 8; Part-Time Volunteers 15.
Governing Authority: society; nonprofit. Parent Institution: Old Jail Museum Commission. Tax-exempt.
History of Franklin County.
Collections: history of Franklin County; tools; pictures; household articles; records.
Research Fields: local history; Normandy Invasion during World War II.
Facilities: Books, prints by local artists, and museum-related items for sale.
Activities: guided tours; slide program for schools.
Publications: newspaper.
Hours & Admission Prices: April-Nov. 14 Tues.-Sat. 10-4. Adults $1, youth & children under 12 $.50; discounts for senior citizens; special rates for groups.
Attendance: 450 (estimated)

TEXAS

(518 listings)

Abilene

ABILENE ZOOLOGICAL GARDENS, 2070 Zoo Lane, Abilene, TX 79602-1996. Tel.: 325-676-6085. Fax: 325-676-6084.
E-mail: abilene.zoo@abilenetx.com
Web Site: www.abilenetx.com/zoo
Founded: 1965.
Congressional District: 17
Key Personnel: Exec. Dir., W.K. Baker, Jr.; Cur. Education, Joy Harsh; Gift Shop Mgr., Linda Pape.
Personnel Profile: Full-Time Paid 20; Part-Time Paid 10; Part-Time Volunteers 2.

Governing Authority: municipal; nonprofit organization. Affiliated with Abilene Zoological Society. Tax-exempt: 501(c)(3).
Zoo.
Collections: mammals; birds; reptiles; amphibians; invertebrates; native plants.
Research Fields: captive reproduction; artificial incubation behavior; maps; Attwater's prairie chicken introduction project.
Facilities: 1,000-vol. library of books available for use in zoo society office only. Animal-related items for sale.
Activities: guided tours; lectures; TV & radio programs; educational programs.
Publications: quarterly newsletter, Pronghorn Press; video, Habitat Restoration.
Hours & Admission Prices: Memorial Day to Labor Day Thurs. 9-9, Fri.-Wed. 9-5; Sept.-May daily 9-5. Adults $4, seniors 60 & over $3, children 3-12 $2; discounts to groups, AZS & AZA members; members & children under 3 no charge. Closed New Year's Day; Thanksgiving; Christmas. ♿
Attendance: 152,693 (accurate)
Membership: Individual $30; Family $45; Circle of Life $75; Species Protector $100; Caregiver $15 additional to any level.

* **THE GRACE MUSEUM, (M),** 102 Cypress St., Abilene, TX 79601-5817. Mailing Address: P.O. Box 33, Abilene, TX 79604-0033. Tel.: 325-673-4587. Fax: 325-675-5993.
E-mail: info@thegracemuseum.org
Web Site: www.thegracemuseum.org
Founded: 1937.
Congressional District: 17
Key Personnel: Chm., Brian Etchison; Exec. Dir., Francine Carraro, Ph.D.
Personnel Profile: Full-Time Paid 10; Part-Time Paid 6; Part-Time Volunteers 123; Interns 2.
Governing Authority: nonprofit organization. Tax-exempt: 501(c)(3).
Art, History & Children's Participatory Museums.
Collections: 20th-century American art with emphasis on printmaking from 1930s & 40s; modern graphics; Texas regional art; Abilene history 1900-45; Texas & Pacific Railway Co.
Major Exhibits: John James Audubon: Artist and Naturalist (T), 2/3/10-5/7/10; Beverly Penn, 10/10-1/8/11.
Research Fields: early Texas artists; Abilene history; Texas & Pacific Railway.
Facilities: restored 1909 hotel; classrooms; rental space; staff & volunteer offices; restored lobby & ballroom; galleries; courtyard; rooftop terrace.
Activities: tours; lectures; films; gallery talks; annual state competition; volunteer & docent program; temporary & traveling exhibitions; school loan service.
Publications: newsletter; annual report; brochures; catalogs.
Hours & Admission Prices: Tues.-Wed. & Fri.-Sat. 10-5, Thurs. 10-8. Adults $6, seniors, students & military $4, children 4-12 $3; discounts to AAM & ICOM members; children 3 & under, members & Thurs. 5-8 no charge. ♿
Attendance: 70,678 (accurate)
Membership: Friend $50; Supporter $75; Associate $100; Advocate $200; Patron $300; Sustainer $600; Benefactor $1,200; Champion $2,400.

NATIONAL CENTER FOR CHILDREN'S ILLUSTRATED LITERATURE, (M), 102 Cedar, Abilene, TX 79601-5718. Tel.: 325-673-4586. Fax: 325-673-0085.
E-mail: info@nccil.org
Web Site: www.nccil.org
Founded: 1997.
Congressional District: 19
Key Personnel: Exec. Dir., Sarah Mulkey; Chm. (V), Rebecca McMurray.
Personnel Profile: Full-Time Paid 1; Part-Time Paid 3; Part-Time Volunteers 8.
Governing Authority: Tax-exempt.
Art Museum.
Collections: original illustrations in children's literature.
Major Exhibits: Bravo! Chris Raschka (T), 11/09-2/10; World of William Joyce (T), 2/10-4/10; Golden Kite Awards (T), 7/10-9/10; Art of Brian Selznick (T), 10/10-2/11.
Hours & Admission Prices: Center: Tues.-Sat. 10-4. Artwalk: 2nd Thurs. each month 5:30-8. No charge; donations accepted. ♿
Attendance: 18,000 (estimated)
Membership: Gallery Circle $50; Author's Circle $100; Collector's Circle $250; Illustrator's Circle $500; Artists Circle $1,000.

Addison

CAVANAUGH FLIGHT MUSEUM, (M), 4572 Claire Chennault, (at Addison Airport), Addison, TX 75001. Tel.: 972-380-8800. Fax: 972-248-0907.
Web Site: www.cavanaughflightmuseum.com
Key Personnel: Dir., Doug Jeanes; Gift Shop Mgr., Christy Bonds
History Museum.
Collections: period aircraft.
Hours & Admission Prices: Mon.-Sat. 9-5, Sun. 11-5. Adults $8, seniors 55 & over, military and student with ID $7, children 6-12 $4; children under 6 no charge. Closed New Year's Day; Thanksgiving; Christmas Day.

MARY KAY MUSEUM, 16251 Dallas Pkwy., Addison, TX 75001. Tel.: 972-687-5720.
Governing Authority: Manufacturing Facility: 1330 Regal Row, Dallas, TX.
Company Museum.
Collections: life & history of Mary Kay Ash and her company; awards; portraits; company product line; personal artifacts; photographs; clothing; sculpture; news articles.
Facilities: restaurant; theater.
Hours & Admission Prices: Mon.-Fri. 9-4:30. Guided Museum Tours: Mon.-Fri. 10 & 2 by appointment. Manufacturing Tour: Mon. 2pm, Tues.-Thurs. 10:30am & 2pm by appointment. No charge. Closed major holidays.

Albany

* **THE OLD JAIL ART CENTER, (M),** 201 S. Second St., Albany, TX 76430-2503. Tel.: 325-762-2269. Fax: 325-762-2260.
E-mail: info@theoldjailartcenter.org
Web Site: www.theoldjailartcenter.org
Founded: 1977.
Congressional District: 17
Key Personnel: Chm. (V), Glenn A. Picquet; Registrar, Rebecca Bridges; Preparator, Pat Kelly; Treas., Steve Waller; Dir. Education, Kathryn Mitchell; Archivist & Librarian, Molly Sauder; Office Mgr., Dorothy Walker.
Personnel Profile: Full-Time Paid 9; Part-Time Paid 1; Part-Time Volunteers 80.
Governing Authority: nonprofit organization. Tax-exempt: 501(c)(3).
Art Museum: housed in c.1877 stone two-storied, Victorian classic-style jail building.
Collections: 19th, 20th & 21st century American & European paintings, drawings, prints, & sculpture; Asian collections featuring Chinese terra cotta tomb figures; pre-Columbian collection; local history archives, local heritage room & memorabilia collection.
Research Fields: contemporary artists; local history.
Facilities: 2,500-vol. library pertaining to contemporary art, art history, world art & regional history available for inter-library loan & public use; 7,328 sq. ft. exhibition space; The Stasney Center for Education; 3,500 sq. ft. enclosed sculpture yard. Books on art & local history for sale.
Activities: guided tours; lectures; concerts; theatre; facilities rental Gallery; organized educational programs; docent program; loan, temporary & traveling exhibitions.
Publications: newsletter (published 3 times per year), The Old Jail Art Center.
Hours & Admission Prices: Tues.-Sat. 10-5, Sun. 2-5. No charge; donations accepted. Closed holidays. ♿
Attendance: 11,029 (accurate)
Membership: Associate Member $12.50; Member $25; Contributor $50; Friend $100; Patron $250; Sustainer $500; Founders Circle $1,000 & up.

Aledo

THE LIVING WORD NATIONAL BIBLE MUSEUM, 3909 Snow Creek Dr., Aledo, TX 76008-3593. Tel.: 817-244-4504 & 845-3761. Fax: 817-244-4504.
E-mail: johnhellstern@charter.net
Web Site: webpages.charter.net/johnellstern/
Founded: 1991.
Key Personnel: C.E.O., Dr. John R. Hellstern; Chm. (V), Dr. Donald L. Brake, Sr.; Museum Shop Mgr., Jean Hellstern.
Personnel Profile: Full-Time Paid 1; Part-Time Paid 1; Part-Time Volunteers 20.
Governing Authority: private; nonprofit organization. Tax-exempt: 501(c)(3).
Bible Museum.
Collections: ancient bibles & scrolls; full-scale Gutenberg press; video clips on the Dead Sea Scrolls; audio recordings; film; papyrus from 1st to 6th centuries; Israeli pottery; manuscripts in Latin, Arabic, Coptic, Hebrew & Greek from the 12th to 17th centuries; 15th-century early printed bibles; English bible from 1536-1611; Ethiopian Book of Psalms; Latin Vulgate manuscript bibles; French Book of Hours of 1460; Gutenberg Page, 1452.
Facilities: 2,000 sq. ft. exhibit space; 41-seat theater. Museum-related items for sale.
Activities: guided tours; lectures; participatory exhibits; theater.
Hours & Admission Prices: Mon.-Sat. 9-8, Sun. 1:15-3. No charge; donations accepted. ♿
Attendance: 20,000 (estimated)
Membership: William Tyndale $120; Myles Coverdale $300; John Wycliffe $600; King James $1,200.

Alice

SOUTH TEXAS MUSEUM, 66 S. Wright St., Alice, TX 78332-4904. Mailing Address: P.O. Box 3232, Alice, TX 78333-3232. Tel.: 512-668-8891.
E-mail: stmuseum@sbcglobal.net
Founded: 1975.
Congressional District: 20
Key Personnel: Chm., Bren Ball; Vice Chm., Marin Perez; Sec., Virginia Bedgood.
Personnel Profile: Full-Time Paid 1.
Governing Authority: nonprofit organization. Tax-exempt: 501(c)(3).
History Museum: housed in c.1940 headquarters for the McGill Brothers ranching operations; Texas historic landmark.
Collections: firearms; Civil War items; farm & ranch tools; saddles; antique furniture; clothing; barbed wire collection; photographs; family histories; typewriters.
Research Fields: local history.
Facilities: 186-vol. Civil War library.
Activities: guided tours; lectures; study clubs; organized educational programs.
Publications: brochure; STM newsletter.
Hours & Admission Prices: Mon.-Fri. 10-12 & 1-5, Sat. 9-1; other times by appointment. No charge; donations accepted. Closed Easter; Memorial Day; Independence Day; Labor Day; Thanksgiving; Christmas.
Attendance: 1,200 (estimated)
Membership: Student $5; Individual $20; Family $35; Business $50; Contributor $100; Sponsor $250; Patron $500.

Alpine

HALLIE'S HALL OF FAME MUSEUM, 430 HC 65, Alpine, TX 79830-9752. Tel.: 432-376-2244.
E-mail: info@stillwellstore.com
Web Site: stillwellstore.com/hall-of-fame
History Museum.
Collections: mementos & relics from the late Hallie Stillwell's ranch.
Hours & Admission Prices: Call for hours.

LAST FRONTIER MUSEUM, Antelope Lodge, 2310 W. Hwy. 90, Alpine, TX 79830-4106. Tel.: 432-837-2451.
Mineralogy Museum.
Collections: rocks, gems & minerals of the region.
Hours & Admission Prices: Daily 9-9.

MUSEUM OF THE BIG BEND, (M), Sul Ross State University, Alpine, TX 79832-0001. Mailing Address: C-101, Alpine, TX 79832-0001. Tel.: 432-837-8143. Fax: 432-837-8901.
E-mail: ejackson@sulross.edu
Web Site: www.sulross.edu/~museum/
Founded: 1926.
Congressional District: 21
Key Personnel: Dir. & C.E.O., Larry Francell; Cur., Matt Walter; Cur. & Collections Mgr., Mary Bridges; Asst. to Dir., Liz Jackson.
Personnel Profile: Full-Time Paid 4; Part-Time Paid 5; Part-Time Volunteers 25.
Governing Authority: Sul Ross State University. Tax-exempt: 501(c)(3).
Regional History Museum.
Collections: late 19th- & early 20th-century historical materials; archaeological artifacts from paleo-man to modern ethnology; regional art; archival collections in ranching, mining & business; 19th-century photographs of west Texas; rare books; Texana & Big Bend region special books.
Research Fields: regional photographic history of Anglo- & Mexican-American settlement; historical & archaeological collections.
Facilities: 2,000-vol. library pertaining to American material culture & museum science, available for research use; primary materials, such as archaeological field notes & historical documents, available for use to professional researchers. Museum-related items & books for sale.
Activities: guided tours; university class tours; education programs for children, undergraduate & graduate college students; temporary exhibitions.
Publications: booklets; newsletter.
Hours & Admission Prices: Tues.-Sat. 9-5, Sun. 1-5. No charge; donations accepted. ♿
Attendance: 18,000 (estimated)

Alto

CADDO MOUNDS STATE HISTORIC SITE, 1649 State Hwy. 21 W., Alto, TX 75925-5739. Tel.: 936-858-3218. Fax: 936-858-3227.
E-mail: jennifer.price-toole@thc.state.tx.us
Web Site: www.thc.state.tx.us
Formerly: Caddoan Mounds State Historic Site
Founded: 1982.
Congressional District: 1
Key Personnel: Site Mgr., Jennifer L. Price-Toole.
Personnel Profile: Full-Time Paid 5.
Governing Authority: Parent Institution: Texas Historical Commission, P.O. Box 12276, Capitol Station, Austin, TX, 78711. Tax-exempt.
State Historic Site: located on a Caddo Village and Ceremonial Grounds, 750-1400 A.D.
Collections: artifacts & archaeological findings associated with early Caddo culture excavated at the site.
Research Fields: Caddo archaeology.
Facilities: library of archaeological reports, theses, dissertations and related anthropological material available for research on premises only; materials for teachers & youth group leaders; 3/4 mile interpretive trail with 3 examples of prehistoric mounds, borrow pit.
Activities: guided tours; audiovisual shows; permanent exhibitions; scout & youth workshops; mock dig; cooking on a hot rock; pottery making; atlatl throw. Museum Sponsors: Caddo Culture Day; Texas Historical Commission; Caddo Nation.
Publications: pamphlet; book, Caddo Mounds: Temples and Tombs of an Ancient People.
Hours & Admission Prices: Tues.-Sun. 8:30-4:30. Adults $2, senior citizens 65 & over $1; children 12 & under no charge. Closed New Year's Eve & Day; Thanksgiving; Christmas Eve & Day. ♿
Attendance: 50,000

Alvin

ALVIN HISTORICAL MUSEUM, 300 W. Sealy, Alvin, TX 77511. Tel.: 281-331-4469.
Governing Authority: Parent Institution: Alvin Museum Society.
History Museum.
Collections: local history & culture; photographs; period artifacts.
Facilities: Museum-related items for sale.
Hours & Admission Prices: Thurs.-Fri. & 1st Sat. of month 11-3. Adults $3; children under 12 no charge. Closed holidays.

MARGUERITE ROGERS HOUSE MUSEUM, 113 E. Dumble, Alvin, TX 77511. Mailing Address: Alvin Museum Society, P.O. Box 1902, Alvin, TX 77512-1902. Tel.: 281-585-2803.
Governing Authority: Parent Institution: Alvin Museum Society.
Historic House: built early 1900s.
Collections: local history & culture; period furnishings; photographs.
Hours & Admission Prices: Tours: Thurs.-Fri. & 1st Sat. of month 11-3. Adults $3; children under 12 no charge. Closed holidays.

NOLAN RYAN CENTER, 2925 S. Bypass 35, Alvin, TX 77511. Tel.: 281-388-1134. Fax: 281-388-1135.
Sports History Museum.
Collections: Nolan Ryan's life & career; photographs; personal artifacts; baseball memorabilia; broadcast audio.
Facilities: theater.
Activities: interactive pitch-catch exhibit; videos.
Hours & Admission Prices: Mon.-Sat. 9-4. Adults $5, students & seniors $2.50; discounts to groups; children under 6 no charge.

Amarillo

* **AMARILLO MUSEUM OF ART, (M),** 2200 S. Van Buren, Amarillo, TX 79109-2407. Mailing Address: P.O. Box 447, Amarillo, TX 79178-0001. Tel.: 806-371-5050. Fax: 806-373-9235.
E-mail: amoa@actx.edu
Web Site: www.amarilloart.org
Founded: 1972.
Congressional District: 67
Key Personnel: Exec. Dir. & Chief Cur., Graziella Marchicelli, Ph.D.; Pres. Bd. Trustees, Scott Howard; Deputy Dir., Kim Mahan; Asst. Cur. Education, Charlie Vaughan; Dir. Devel., Kay Kennedy.
Personnel Profile: Full-Time Paid 3; Part-Time Paid 9.
Governing Authority: nonprofit organization. Tax-exempt: 501(c)(3).
Art Museum.
Collections: 20th-century American paintings; prints; drawings; photographs; sculpture; Asian art; Southeast Asian art & sculpture; Japanese prints; Middle Eastern textiles.
Major Exhibits: An Uncommon Dream The Amarillo High School Collection of 19th & 20th Century Art, 1/31/10-4/11/10; Amarillo College/WTAMU Student Faculty Exhibit, 4/16/10-5/2/10; Panhandle Student Show, 5/7/10-5/23/10; Art of the Music Poster of the 60's & 70's (T), 6/18/10-9/19/10; Leo Jensen: Total Pop Art, 10/8/10-1/16/11.
Research Fields: American art history; contemporary art; photography; Asian & Southeast Asian art.

Facilities: library; sculpture courtyard; classrooms.
Activities: guided tours; lectures; films; gallery talks; formally organized educational programs; docent program; inter-museum loan, temporary & traveling exhibitions; scholarships for talented children who cannot afford to attend.
Publications: quarterly newsletter; exhibit catalogues; gallery guides for adults & children; posters.
Hours & Admission Prices: Tues.-Wed. & Fri. 10-5, Thurs. 10-9, Sat.-Sun. 1-5. No charge; donations accepted. Closed major national holidays. ♿
Membership: Family $50; Contributor $150; Patron $250; Sponsor $500; Benefactor $1,000.

AMERICAN QUARTER HORSE HALL OF FAME & MUSEUM, (M), 2601 I-40 E, Amarillo, TX 79104-3405. Tel.: 806-376-5181. Fax: 806-376-1005.
E-mail: museum@aqha.org
Web Site: www.aqhhalloffame.com
Formerly: American Quarter Horse Heritage Center & Museum
Founded: 1991.
Congressional District: 13
Key Personnel: C.E.O., Bill Brewer; Dir., Ross Middleton; Pres. (V), Kew Mumy; Treas., Trent Taylor; Dir. Devel., Chris Sitz; Senior Mgr. Retail Sales, Robin Blanchard; Archivist, Gene Storlie; Cur. Collections, Crystal Phares; Mgr. Education Programs, Ande Ragsdale.
Personnel Profile: Full-Time Paid 17; Part-Time Paid 4; Interns 1.
Governing Authority: Parent Institution: American Quarter Horse Assoc. Tax-exempt: 501(c)(3).
Equine Hall of Fame & Museum.
Collections: equine items relating to all aspects of the American Quarter Horse; ranching; racing; rodeo; American Quarter Horse Association registry.
Facilities: 5,000-vol. library of equine & historical works; educational facilities; 18,000 sq. ft. exhibit space; 85-seat theatre. Museum-related items for sale.
Activities: films; formal education programs; lectures; participatory & temporary exhibitions.
Hours & Admission Prices: Memorial Day-Labor Day Mon.-Sat. 9-5, Sun. 12-5. Adults $6, senior citizens $5, children 6-18 $2; discounts for groups of 15 or more, AAM & ICOM members; AQHA, AQYA members & children under 6 no charge. Closed New Year's Day; Easter; Thanksgiving; Christmas Eve & Day. ♿
Attendance: 35,000 (accurate)
Membership: Annual $35.

DON HARRINGTON DISCOVERY CENTER, 1200 Streit Dr., Amarillo, TX 79106-1759. Tel.: 806-355-9547, ext. 24. Fax: 806-355-5703.
E-mail: joeh@dhdc.org
Web Site: www.dhdc.org
Founded: 1968.
Congressional District: 18
Key Personnel: Bd. Pres. (V), Mary Emeny; Exec. Dir., Joe Hastings; Assoc. Dir., Chip Lindsey; Planetarium Coord., Aaron Guzman; Dir. Devel., Liz Bentley; Dir. Education, Mandi Ried; Museum Shop Mgr., Kim May.
Personnel Profile: Full-Time Paid 9; Part-Time Paid 20; Part-Time Volunteers 20.
Governing Authority: nonprofit organization. Parent Institution: Foundation For Health & Science Education, Inc. Tax-exempt: 501(c)(3); 170(b)(1)(A).
Science Museum & Planetarium.
Collections: hands-on exhibits; helium monument.
Facilities: 95-seat Digistar 3 digital theater; 45,000 sq. ft. exhibit space; 24 projector multi-image system.
Activities: public & curriculum coordinated presentations in health, astronomy, physical & earth science.
Publications: Discoveries Newsletter of Science Education & Events.
Hours & Admission Prices: Summer: Mon.-Sat. 9:30-4:30, Sun. 12-4:30; Winter: Tues.-Sat. 9:30-4:30, Sun. 12-4:30. Adults $5.50; discounts to ASTC members; members and children 2 & under no charge. ♿
Attendance: 65,000 (accurate)
Membership: Individual Plus Guest $35; Family $55; Grandparents $55; Family Plus $75.

TEXAS PHARMACY MUSEUM, (M), Texas Tech School of Pharmacy, 1300 S Coulter St., Amarillo, TX 79106-1712. Tel.: 806-356-4000, ext. 268. Fax: 806-356-4017.
E-mail: paul.katz@ttuhsc.edu
Web Site: www.ttuhsc.edu/sop/prospective/visitors/museum.aspx
Founded: 1998.
Congressional District: 13
Key Personnel: Dir. (V), Dean Arthur Nelson, R.Ph., Ph.D.; Cur., Paul Katz, Ph.D.
Personnel Profile: Part-Time Paid 2.
Governing Authority: nonprofit; public college. Tax-exempt: 501(c)(3).
Pharmacy Museum.
Collections: history of pharmacy in Texas, the U.S. & Western Europe; early 20th century pharmacy; tools; pharmacy products & delivery systems; pharmacy art; Texas practitioners; books; containers; furniture; laboratory glassware; medical items; show globes; mortars & pestles.
Facilities: 500-vol. library; 3,000 sq. ft. exhibit space; 250-seat auditorium.
Activities: guided tours; lectures; graduate course; temporary exhibitions.
Hours & Admission Prices: Mon.-Fri. 1-5. No charge. Closed New Year's Eve & Day; Martin Luther King Jr. Day; Memorial Day; Independence Day; Labor Day; Thanksgiving; Christmas Eve & Day. ♿
Attendance: 420 (accurate)

WILDCAT BLUFF NATURE CENTER, 2301 N. Soncy Rd., Amarillo, TX 79124-5766. Mailing Address: P.O. Box 52132, Amarillo, TX 79159-2132. Tel.: 806-352-6007. Fax: 806-352-2274.
Founded: 1992.
Nature Center.
Collections: reptiles; birds; mammals; invertebrates.
Facilities: nature trails.
Activities: special events.
Hours & Admission Prices: Tues.-Sat. 9-5. Adults $3, children & seniors $2; children under 3 no charge. Closed holidays.
Membership: Student $20; Teacher & Senior $25; Individual $35; Grandparent $40; Family $50; Friend $100; Supporter $250; Sustaining $500; Benefactor Lifetime $1,000.

Angleton

BRAZORIA COUNTY HISTORICAL MUSEUM, (M), 100 E. Cedar, Angleton, TX 77515-4602. Tel.: 979-864-1208. Fax: 979-864-1217.
E-mail: bchm@bchm.org
Web Site: www.bchm.org
Founded: 1983.
Congressional District: 22
Key Personnel: Dir., Jackie Haynes; Pres., Morris Paschall.
Personnel Profile: Full-Time Paid 8.
Governing Authority: county. Tax-exempt: 501(c)(3).
History Museum: housed in 1897 Brazoria County Courthouse.
Collections: Brazoria County history from prehistoric to modern times; historical & archaeological materials; archives; photographs.
Major Exhibits: Jasper Texas: The Healing of a Community in Crisis (T), 2/10; Literary East Texas (T), 3/10; Voices (T), 10/10.
Facilities: library; 4,437 sq. ft. exhibit space.
Activities: guided tours; lectures; films; organized education programs for children; docent program; temporary exhibition; summer concerts featuring Zydeco & other music.
Publications: monthly newsletter.
Hours & Admission Prices: Mon.-Fri. 9-5, Sat. 9-3. No charge; donations accepted. Closed major holidays. ♿
Attendance: 20,000 (estimated)
Membership: Student & Senior $30; Family $50; General $100; Commander $250; Presidential $500; Corporate $1,000.

Archer City

ARCHER COUNTY MUSEUM, N. Sycamore St., Archer City, TX 76351. Mailing Address: 2627 Loftin Rd., Windthorst, TX 76389-4641. Tel.: 940-423-6426 & 574-2502.
Founded: 1974.
Key Personnel: Cur., Jack Loftin.
Governing Authority: county. Tax-exempt.
General Museum: housed in 1910 Old County Jail.
Collections: barbed wire; bridle bits; spurs; blacksmith tools; prehistoric lizard fossils/fossil bones; art & western paintings; old clothing; farm machinery; vehicles; grinding implements; Indian artifacts; early pictures & newspapers; surrey; hack oil field equipment & trucks; Archer County artifacts.
Activities: permanent exhibitions.
Hours & Admission Prices: May-Nov. Sat. 9-5, Sun. 1-5; other times by appointment. No charge; donations accepted.
Attendance: 500 (estimated)

Arlington

ARLINGTON MUSEUM OF ART, 201 W. Main St., Arlington, TX 76010. Mailing Address: P.O. Box 114, Arlington, TX 76004-0114. Tel.: 817-275-4600. Fax: 817-860-4800.
E-mail: ama@arlingtonmuseum.org
Web Site: www.arlingtonmuseum.org
Founded: 1987.

Congressional District: 24
Key Personnel: Pres. & Chm. (V), Walter Virden; Sec., Lynda Freeman.
Personnel Profile: Part-Time Paid 1; Part-Time Volunteers 25; Interns 5.
Governing Authority: private; nonprofit organization. Tax-exempt.
Art Museum & Gallery: located in a former 1950s storefront building on Main St. in downtown Arlington.
Collections: works by emerging and established artists.
Facilities: browsing library; 20,000 sq. ft. exhibit space.
Activities: guided tours; lectures; workshops; educational programs. Annual Events: Art Auction; Youth Encounters; Haunted House; summer art camp.
Publications: biannual newsletter, AMA news; Artivities, workbook for children; exhibition catalogues.
Hours & Admission Prices: Wed.-Fri. 1-5, Sat. 10-5, Sun. 12-5. No charge; donations accepted. Closed New Year's Day; Independence Day; Thanksgiving; Christmas. ♿
Attendance: 18,000 (estimated)
Membership: Individual $15; Household $50; Associates $100; Partners $240; Director's Circle $1,000 & up; Twenty-First Century $2,100; Sponsor $5,000.

THE GALLERY AT UTA, 502 S. Cooper St., Fine Arts Bldg., Arlington, TX 76019-0001. Mailing Address: Box 19089, Arlington, TX 76019-0001. Tel.: 817-272-3143 & 5658. Fax: 817-272-2805.
E-mail: bhuerta@uta.edu
Web Site: www.uta.edu/gallery
Formerly: CRCA: The Gallery at UTA
Founded: 1976.
Congressional District: 24
Key Personnel: Dir., Benito Huerta; Asst. Dir., Patricia Healy.
Personnel Profile: Part-Time Paid 7.
Governing Authority: university. Parent Institution: University of Texas at Arlington. Tax-exempt.
Art Museum.
Collections: monthly exhibitions.
Research Fields: contemporary art.
Facilities: 4,000 sq. ft. gallery.
Activities: traveling & loan exhibitions; video & film series; artist residencies & lectures.
Publications: exhibition announcements & brochures; posters.
Hours & Admission Prices: Mon.-Fri. 10-5, Sat. 12-5. No charge. Closed school holidays. ♿
Attendance: 7,400 (accurate)

INTERNATIONAL BOWLING MUSEUM AND HALL OF FAME, (M), 621 Six Flags Dr., Arlington, TX 76011-6305. Tel.: 817-385-8210.
Web Site: www.bowlingmuseum.com
Key Personnel: Chm. (V), Patrick Ciniello; Cur., James M. Baltz.
Personnel Profile: Full-Time Paid 1.
Governing Authority: nonprofit. Tax-exempt: 501(c)(3).
Sports Museum.
Collections: 18th to 20th-century historical artifacts; equipment; uniforms; graphics; trophies; home to St. Louis Cardinals Hall of Fame Museum.
Research Fields: history of bowling, women's sports, international sports & American social history.
Facilities: research library; theater.
Activities: films; permanent exhibitions; old time bowling alley re-creation; math programs for school children; guided instructional tours.
Publications: brochures; quarterly newsletter; periodic news releases and news photos.
Hours & Admission Prices: Closed until Jan. 2010. ♿

RIVER LEGACY LIVING SCIENCE CENTER, 703 N.W. Green Oaks Blvd., Arlington, TX 76006-2404. Tel.: 817-860-6752. Fax: 817-860-1595.
E-mail: phyllis@riverlegacy.org
Web Site: www.riverlegacy.org
Founded: 1996.
Congressional District: 6
Key Personnel: Exec. Dir., Phyllis Snider; Pres. (V), Steve Cavender; Financial Dir., Bob Murday; Museum Shop Mgr., Sylvia Greene.
Personnel Profile: Full-Time Paid 12; Part-Time Paid 6; Part-Time Volunteers 140.
Governing Authority: private; nonprofit organization. Parent Institution: River Legacy Foundation. Tax-exempt.
Science Museum.
Collections: live animals; preserved animals; botany; archaeology; geology.
Facilities: library of material on Nature Education & Natural Science; botanical garden; classrooms; 3,000 sq. ft. exhibit space; 1,300 acres of natural habitat; nature center. Museum-related gifts for sale.
Activities: docent program; films; formal education programs for children & college students; self-guided tours; professional development workshops; lectures; study clubs; participatory, temporary & traveling exhibitions; nature study programs for preschool age through adult.
Publications: biannual newsletter, River Legacy Parks.
Hours & Admission Prices: Tues.-Sat. 9-5. No charge; donations accepted. Closed New Year's Day; Easter; Independence Day; Thanksgiving; Christmas Eve & Day. ♿
Attendance: 75,000 (estimated)

Athens

EAST TEXAS ARBORETUM & BOTAINICAL SOCIETY, 1601 Patterson Rd., Athens, TX 75751. Mailing Address: P.O. Box 2231, Athens, TX 75751-7231. Tel.: 903-675-5630. Fax: 903-675-1618.
E-mail: etabs@mycvc.net
Governing Authority: nonprofit organization. Tax-exempt: 501(c)(3).
History Museum.
Collections: Gardens: plants; flowers; trees. House: period furnishings; personal artifacts. Historic House: Wofford House, c.1800.
Facilities: 100 acre site; nature trails.
Activities: rental facilities; special events; hiking.
Publications: newsletter.
Hours & Admission Prices: Spring & Summer: daily 7:30-7:30; Fall & Winter: daily 8-6. Suggested Donations: adults 12 & over $2; members no charge.

HENDERSON COUNTY HISTORICAL SOCIETY MUSEUM, 217 N. Prairieville, Athens, TX 75751-2042. Mailing Address: P.O. Box 943, Athens, TX 75751-0943. Tel.: 903-677-3611.
Historical Society Museum.
Collections: local history & culture; Native Indian artifacts; dinosaur bones; military; scout memorabilia; period furnishings.
Facilities: library.
Activities: guided tours; docent program; lectures.
Publications: quarterly newsletter.
Hours & Admission Prices: Fri.-Sat. 10-3. No charge; donations accepted.

Austin

ARTHOUSE, (M), The Jones Center, 700 Congress Ave., Austin, TX 78701-3217. Tel.: 512-453-5312. Fax: 512-459-4830.
E-mail: info@arthousetexas.org
Web Site: www.arthousetexas.org
Formerly: Texas Fine Arts Association
Founded: 1911.
Congressional District: 10
Key Personnel: Exec. Dir., Sue Graze; Pres. (V), Julie Thornton; Devel., Melissa Berry; Devel., Jennifer Gardner; Education, Erin Gentry; Public Rels., Virginia Jones; Cur., Elizabeth Dunbar; Coord. Membership, Ben Slade; Exhibition Coord., Kirk Nickel; Coord. Capital Campaign, Caitlin Sweeney; Preparator, Nathan Green.
Personnel Profile: Full-Time Paid 6; Part-Time Paid 6; Part-Time Volunteers 2; Interns 3.
Governing Authority: private; nonprofit organization. Tax-exempt: 501(c)(3).
Art Museum.
Collections: works by contemporary artists.
Activities: contemporary art exhibitions; educational programs for teens; guided tours; lectures; screenings; commission new art work; annual fundraisers; off-site programming. Museum Sponsors: Arthouse Texas Prize.
Publications: exhibition catalogs; member e-newsletter.
Hours & Admission Prices: Closed for renovation until fall 2010. Tues.-Wed. & Fri. 11-7, Thurs. 11-9, Sat. 10-5, Sun. 1-5. No charge; donations accepted. Closed New Year's Day; Independence Day; Thanksgiving; Christmas Eve & Day. ♿
Attendance: 25,000 (estimated)
Membership: Student $15; Supporter $40; Patron $100; Benefactor $250; Sustainer $500; Collectors Circle $1,500; Center Circle $5,000.

AUSTIN CHILDREN'S MUSEUM, 201 Colorado St., Austin, TX 78701-3922. Tel.: 512-472-2499. Fax: 512-472-2495.
E-mail: ppaine@austinkids.org
Web Site: www.austinkids.org
Founded: 1983.
Congressional District: 10
Key Personnel: Exec. Dir., Mike Nellis.
Personnel Profile: Full-Time Paid 26; Part-Time Paid 35; Part-Time Volunteers 1,500; Interns 12.
Governing Authority: nonprofit organization. Tax-exempt: 501(c)(3).
Children's Museum.
Collections: hands on exhibits.
Major Exhibits: Air Fair, 1/30/10-5/22/10; Big Game, 5/29/10.

Research Fields: parent & child relations; cognition & learning; science literacy.
Facilities: 12,500 sq. ft. exhibit space. Educational & cultural items for sale.
Activities: storytime; group tours; gingerbread workshops; birthday parties; facility rental. Museum Sponsors: Engineering Saturday; Science Sunday; Community Night.
Publications: quarterly newsletter.
Hours & Admission Prices: Tues. & Thurs.-Sat. 10-5, Wed. 10-8, Sun. 12-5. Adults & children over 2 $6.50, children under 2 $4:50; Wed. by donation; Sun. 4-5 no charge. ASTC & ACM reciprocal memberships. Closed all major holidays. ♿
Attendance: 200,000 (accurate)
Membership: Basic $75; Premier $125

AUSTIN HISTORY CENTER, 810 Guadalupe St., Austin, TX 78701. Mailing Address: P.O. Box 2287, Austin, TX 78768-2287. Tel.: 512-974-7400. Fax: 512-974-7483.
E-mail: ahc_reference@ci.austin.tx.us
Web Site: www.cityofaustin.org/library/ahc
Founded: 1955.
Congressional District: 10
Key Personnel: Mgr., Mike Miller.
Personnel Profile: Full-Time Paid 13; Part-Time Paid 1; Part-Time Volunteers 35; Interns 10.
Governing Authority: municipal government. Parent Institution: Austin Public Library. Tax-exempt.
Archives & Library: housed in 1933 Austin library building. A Texas Historic Landmark.
Collections: local history books; photographs; maps; ephemera; newspapers; archives; drawings; Austin & Travis County history.
Major Exhibits: Not a Museum: The Austin History Center-Your Story, Your Archive, 11/09-1/10; The Great Depression & New Deal in Austin, 2/10-7/10; Mexican American Firsts: Trailblazers of Austin and Travis County (T), 8/10-1/11.
Research Fields: Austin & Travis County.
Facilities: 60,000-vol. library of local history books; vertical files; photographs; archives, available for use by public; meeting rooms; photography lab; 1,000 sq. ft. exhibit space.
Activities: temporary exhibitions; author events; public programs. Annual Event: Archives Clinic in October.
Hours & Admission Prices: Tues.-Sat. 10-6, Sun. 12-6. No charge; donations accepted. ♿

AUSTIN MUSEUM OF ART - DOWNTOWN, 823 Congress Ave., Austin, TX 78701-2405. Mailing Address: 823 Congress Ave., Ste. 100, Austin, TX 78701-2435. Tel.: 512-495-9224. Fax: 512-495-9029.
E-mail: info@amoa.org
Web Site: www.amoa.org
Founded: 1961.
Congressional District: 10
Key Personnel: Pres. & Chm. (V), Bettye H. Nowlin; Treas., Clay Cary; Exec. Dir. & Chief Cur., Dana Friis-Hansen; Sr. Dir. Education, Judith Sims; Registrar, Cassandra Smith; Sr. Dir. Devel., Tom Jackson; Dir. Facilities & Operations, Bill Nichols; Dir. Finance & Operations, Curt Shinaberry; Museum Shop Mgr., Justin Hearne.
Personnel Profile: Full-Time Paid 17; Part-Time Paid 14; Part-Time Volunteers 1,470; Interns 15.
Governing Authority: nonprofit organization. Branch Museum: Austin Museum of Art - Laguna Gloria, 3809 W. 35th St., Austin, TX 78703. Tel.: 512-458-8191. Tax-exempt: 501(c)(3).
Art Museum.
Collections: modern & contemporary art; paintings; sculpture; photography; prints; drawings; video; multimedia installations.
Major Exhibits: David Bates, 11/21/09-1/10; American Letterpress: Hatch Prints, 2/13/10-5/9/10; Chris Jordan: Running the Numbers, 5/22/10-8/15/10.
Research Fields: 20th century & contemporary art.
Facilities: Downtown: art galleries. Museum-related items for sale. Laguna Gloria: historic home & gardens; sculpture grounds; The Art School with classrooms & ceramic studio.
Activities: changing exhibitions; art classes for children & adults; docent tours; lectures; performances; films; concerts; hands-on interactive space for schools & families. Fund Raisers: Art Ball (annual gala & art auction); La Dolce Vita (annual wine tasting & art auction); Austin Fine Arts Festival.
Publications: e-newsletter.
Hours & Admission Prices: Downtown: Tues.-Wed. & Fri. 10-5, Thurs. 10-8, Sat. 10-6, Sun. 12-5. Adults $5, students & seniors $4; discounts to AAM, ICOM, AICA, TAM & AMP members and Tues.; children under 12 & members no charge. 1st Sat. of month pay what you wish. Laguna Gloria: Grounds Mon.-Sat. 9-5, Sun. 11-5. Villa daily 11-4. Suggested donation $3. Closed holidays. ♿
Attendance: 275,510 (accurate)
Membership: Individual $30; Household $60; Associate $150; Advocate $250; Collector's Forum $500; Director's Circle of Fellows $1,000; Director's Circle of Patrons $2,500; Director's Circle of Benefactor's $5,000.

AUSTIN NATURE & SCIENCE CENTER, 301 Nature Center Dr., Austin, TX 78746-5775. Tel.: 512-327-8181. Fax: 512-327-8745.
Web Site: www.cityofaustin.org/ansc
Founded: 1960.
Congressional District: 10
Key Personnel: Dir., Kathy Maddox.
Personnel Profile: Full-Time Paid 12; Part-Time Paid 40; Part-Time Volunteers 700.
Governing Authority: municipal. City of Austin, Parks & Recreation Dept. Branch Facilities: Austin Nature Center, 301 Nature Center Dr., Austin, TX. 78746.
Nature Center.
Collections: native Texas mammals, fish, birds, reptiles & insects; microscope tables & exhibits, touch-table; participatory exhibits; Small Wonders of animal adaptations; Eco-Detective hands on trail; The Nature of Austin.
Research Fields: wildlife rehabilitation; ornithology; native plants; butterflies.
Facilities: Austin Nature Center: 80-acres of trails & exhibits; natural science library; activity rooms; visitor pavilion; Living Systems Building; Wildlife & Exhibit Building; Trailhouse Natural Gardens; headquarters of Heritage Conservation. Books, equipment, posters & other museum-related items for sale.
Activities: preschool classes; family nature series; environmental education programs; Wildlife Rehabilitation; bird walks; plant hikes; nature photography; wildlife volunteers; Austin Wilderness Institute; caving; canoeing; backpacking; wildflower forays; night hikes; school tours & classroom programs; rocks & fossils hikes; field trips to Wild Basin Wilderness, Bee Creek Preserve, Westcave Nature Preserve; Clean-The-Scene Hikes; Austin Guide To: Down To Earth City Living; Deep Eddy Community Gardens; organic gardening classes & workshops; extensive school & teacher workshops.
Publications: Teachers Resource Guide; Natural Selections; Naturalist's Workshop Trading Counter.
Hours & Admission Prices: Austin Nature Center: Mon.-Sat. 9-5, Sun. 12-5. No charge; donations accepted. Closed Independence Day; Thanksgiving; Christmas. ♿
Attendance: 250,000 (accurate)
Membership: Kids' and Critters' Club: Individual $25; Family $35; Small Business $50; Corporate $100.

BG JOHN C.L. SCRIBNER TEXAS MILITARY FORCES MUSEUM, 2200 W. 35th St., Austin, TX 78703-1222. Mailing Address: P.O. Box 5218, Austin, TX 78763-5218. Tel.: 512-782-5659. Fax: 512-782-6750.
E-mail: museum@tx.ngb.army.mil
Web Site: www.texasmilitaryforcesmuseum.org
Founded: 1992.
Congressional District: 10
Key Personnel: Dir., Jeff Hunt; Deputy Dir. & Registrar, Lisa Sharik; Pres., Col. (Ret.) Albert Lloyd; Vice Chm., Richard Gruetzner; Cur. Exhibits, Edward Zapedea; Budget Analyst, Gene Emmons.
Personnel Profile: Full-Time Paid 5; Full-Time Volunteers 5; Part-Time Volunteers 95; Interns 2.
Governing Authority: Parent Institution: Texas Adjutant General's Dept., P.O. Box 5218, Austin, TX 78763-5218. Tax-exempt: 501(c)(3).
Military Museum: housed at historic Camp Mabry.
Collections: personal artifacts; photographs; paintings; military history of Texas from 1823 to present; vehicles; equipment; uniforms; weapons.
Research Fields: history of Texas military forces from 1823 to present including Texas Revolution, Republic of Texas, Civil War, Indian Wars, Texas Rangers, Spanish American War, WWI, WWII, Cold War, Korean War, State Missions, Global War on Terror.
Facilities: 20,000-vol. library of military history books; classroom; field research station. Museum-related items for sale.
Activities: docent program; guided tours; temporary exhibitions; training programs for professional museum workers; symposia series. Annual Events: American Heroes Celebration - Army & Air Guard displays & reenactments; Close Assault 1944 Living History Demonstrations.
Publications: quarterly newsletter, Texas Military Forces Museum; outdoor display guide; Historical Camp Mabey Walking Tour.
Hours & Admission Prices: Wed.-Sun. 10-4. Photo ID required for entry. No charge; donations accepted. Closed New Year's Day; Thanksgiving; Christmas Eve, Day & day after. ♿
Attendance: 14,603 (accurate)
Membership: Annual $20; Life $250.

* **BLANTON MUSEUM OF ART, (M),** 200 E. Martin Luther King, Austin, TX 78701. Mailing Address: 1 University Station D1303, Austin, TX 78712-0338. Tel.: 512-471-7324. Fax: 512-471-7023.
E-mail: info@blantonmuseum.org
Web Site: www.blantonmuseum.org
Founded: 1963.
Congressional District: 10
Key Personnel: Dir., Ned Rifkin; Assoc. Dir., Ann Wilso; Dir. Devel., Simone Wicha; Membership Coord., Kim Theel; Registrar, Sue Ellen Jeffers; Cur. Prints & Drawings, European Painting, Jonathan Bober; Cur. American Art & Dir. Curatorial Affairs, Annette DiMeo Carlozzi; Interim Cur. Latina American Art, Ursula Davila-Villa; Business Officer, Stacey Cilek; Public Affairs Officer, Kathleen Brady; Project Coord., Tom Flowers.
Personnel Profile: Full-Time Paid 50; Part-Time Paid 14; Part-Time Volunteers 80; Interns 6.
Governing Authority: state. Parent Institution: The University of Texas at Austin. Tax-exempt: 501(c)(3).
Art Museum.
Collections: antiquities; Renaissance & Baroque art (Suida-Manning Collection); 19th century American art (Michener Collection); contemporary Latin American art; prints & drawings from the 15th-21st centuries.
Research Fields: Renaissance & Baroque art; 20th-century American art; contemporary Latin American art; prints & drawings.
Facilities: 300-seat auditorium; cafe; garden. Museum-related items for sale.
Activities: concerts; docent program; guided tours; lectures; films; gallery talks; formally organized education programs for children & college students; loan, temporary & traveling exhibitions; training programs for professional museum workers.
Publications: calendar of exhibitions; catalogues; newsletter.
Hours & Admission Prices: Tues.-Fri. 10-5, 3rd Thurs. of month 10-9, Sat. 11-5, Sun. 1-5. Adults $7, seniors $5, youth & college students $3; discounts to AAM members; members and children 12 & under no charge. ♿
Attendance: 170,000 (accurate)
Membership: Individual $45; Dual $60; Family $75; Sustaining $110; Founding $300.

BOB BULLOCK TEXAS STATE HISTORY MUSEUM, (M), 1800 N. Congress Ave., Austin, TX 78701-1342. Mailing Address: P.O. Box 12874, Austin, TX 78711-2874. Tel.: 512-936-8746. Fax: 512-936-4699.
E-mail: contactus@thestoryoftexas.com
Web Site: www.thestoryoftexas.com
Key Personnel: Dir., Nashid Madyun.
Governing Authority: Parent Institution: City of Austin Parks and Recreation Dept., Cultural Affairs Division.
History Museum.
Collections: interactive exhibits; sculpture; Texas history & culture.
Facilities: theater; cafe. Museum-related items for sale.
Activities: educational programs.
Hours & Admission Prices: Mon.-Sat. 9-6, Sun. 12-6. Adults $7, seniors, military, & college students $6, children 5-18 $4; members and children 4 & under no charge. Closed New Year's Day; Easter; Thanksgiving; Christmas Eve & Day.

CAPITOL VISITORS CENTER, A DIVISION OF THE STATE PRESERVATION BOARD, 112 E. Eleventh St., Austin, TX 78701-2403. Mailing Address: P.O. Box 13286, Austin, TX 78711-3286. Tel.: 512-305-8400. Fax: 512-305-8401.
E-mail: cvc.cvc@tspb.state.tx.us
Web Site: www.texascapitolvisitorscenter.com
Founded: 1994.
Congressional District: 21
Key Personnel: Capitol Cur., Ali James; Program Supvr., Kyle Schlafer; Tour Coord., Elizabeth Garzore; Museum Shop Mgr., Shawn Goodnight.
Personnel Profile: Full-Time Paid 4; Part-Time Paid 3.
Governing Authority: state government. Parent Institution: Texas State Preservation Board. Tax-exempt.
Visitors Center: housed in the c.1856 Old General Land Office Building, designed by German architect C.C. Stremme. Oldest state office building in Texas.
Collections: multimedia presentations on the Texas Capitol & Texas history.
Major Exhibits: Cattle Queens, 11/09-2/10; From the Ashes, 3/10-7/10; Texas Elections, 8/10-11/10; From Design to Decoration, 11/10-1/11.
Research Fields: land history; Texas State Capitol.
Activities: guided tours; interactive exhibits.
Hours & Admission Prices: Mon.-Sat. 9-5, Sun. 12-5. No charge; donations accepted. Closed New Year's Day; Easter; Thanksgiving; Christmas Eve & Day. ♿
Attendance: 123,799 (accurate)

CENTER FOR AMERICAN HISTORY, Sid Richardson Hall, Unit 2, Univ. of Texas at Austin, Austin, TX 78712-0335. Mailing Address: Sid Richardson Hall 2.101, 1 University Station D1100, Austin, TX 78712-0335. Tel.: 512-495-4515. Fax: 512-495-4542.
E-mail: cahref@uts.cc.utexas.edu
Web Site: www.cah.utexas.edu
Congressional District: 10
Key Personnel: Dir., Dr. Don Carleton; Assoc. Dir., Alison Beck; Assoc. Dir., Brenda Gunn; Assoc. Dir. Congressional Collections, Dr. Patrick Cox; Asst. Dir. Winedale, Erin Purdy; Cur. Exhibits, Lynn Bell.
Personnel Profile: Full-Time Paid 50; Part-Time Paid 31; Part-Time Volunteers 10; Interns 3.
Governing Authority: public university; nonprofit. Parent Institution: University of Texas at Austin. Subsidiary Institutions: Sam Rayburn Library and Museum, P.O. Box 309, Bonham, TX 75418; Winedale, P.O. Box 11, Round Top, TX 78954; John Nance Garner Museum, 333 N. Park, Uvalde, TX 78801. Tax-exempt.
History Museum.
Collections: special collections & programs relating to the history of Texas, the South, Rocky Mountain West and select national areas.
Publications: Center for American History Newsletter.
Hours & Admission Prices: Center: Mon.-Sat. 9-5. Rayburn: Mon.-Fri. 10-5, Sat. 1-5, Sun. 2-5. Winedale: call 979-278-3530 for hours. No charge. Closed university holidays (center); New Year's Day; Independence Day; Labor Day; Thanksgiving; Christmas (Rayburn). ♿
Attendance: 39,000 (estimated)

ELISABET NEY MUSEUM, 304 E. 44th St., Austin, TX 78751-3813. Tel.: 512-458-2255. Fax: 512-453-0638.
E-mail: enm@ci.austin.tx.us
Web Site: www.elisabetneymuseum.org
Founded: 1911.
Congressional District: 10
Key Personnel: Dir. & Cur., Mary Collins Blackmon.
Personnel Profile: Full-Time Paid 2; Part-Time Paid 2; Part-Time Volunteers 15.
Governing Authority: City of Austin, Texas. Tax-exempt: 501(c)(1).
Historic Site & Interpretive Center.
Collections: Elisabet Ney's portraits in marble & plaster & personal artifacts, letters & memorabilia, housed & displayed in her former Austin, Texas studio.
Research Fields: portrait sculpture; 19th-century art history; Texas cultural history; women's studies; women artists.
Facilities: restored studio/museum; classroom annex.
Activities: guided tours; lectures; concerts; educational & public programming.
Hours & Admission Prices: Wed.-Sat. 10-5, Sun. 12-5. No charge.
Attendance: 13,000 (accurate)

THE FRENCH LEGATION MUSEUM, (M), 802 San Marcos St., Austin, TX 78702-2647. Tel.: 512-472-8180. Fax: 512-472-9547.
E-mail: director@frenchlegationmuseum.org
Web Site: www.frenchlegationmuseum.org
Founded: 1956.
Congressional District: 10
Key Personnel: Chm., Gayla Lawson; Dir., Stephanie Jarvis.
Personnel Profile: Full-Time Paid 2; Part-Time Paid 4; Part-Time Volunteers 15.
Governing Authority: Daughters of the Republic of Texas, Inc. Tax-exempt.
Historic Building Museum: 1841 French Legation, built by the first French Charge d'affaires to Texas during the Republic of Texas.
Collections: period French & early American furnishings; artifacts reflecting life in early days of Republic of Texas, c.1836-1846.
Facilities: meeting room. Museum-related items for sale.
Activities: guided tours; concerts; weddings; seasonal events; children's summer camp.
Publications: books, The French Legation in Austin, Volumes I & II; A History of the French Legation in Texas.
Hours & Admission Prices: Tues.-Sun. 1-5. Adult $5, senior citizen $3, students & teachers $2; discounts to groups, Texas Assoc. of Museums, Daughters of the Republic of Texas, AAA & AAM members; children under 5 no charge. Closed holidays. ♿
Attendance: 10,000 (estimated)
Membership: Bronze $25-$99; Silver $100-$249; Gold $250-$499; Platinum $500 & up.

GEORGE WASHINGTON CARVER MUSEUM & CULTURAL CENTER, 1165 Angelina St., Austin, TX 78702-2034. Tel.: 512-974-4926. Fax: 512-974-3699.
E-mail: carver.museum@ci.austin.tx.us
Web Site: www.carvermuseum.org

Governing Authority: Parent Institution: Parks and Recreation Dept.
African American History Museum.
Collections: African-American history, culture, & art.
Activities: special events; school programs.
Hours & Admission Prices: Mon. & Fri. 9:30-6, Tues.-Thurs. 9:30-8, Sat. 1-5. No charge. ♿

GOODWILL COMPUTER MUSEUM, (M), 1015 Norwood Park Blvd., Austin, TX 78753-6608.
E-mail: museum@austingoodwill.org
Web Site: www.goodwillcomputermuseum.org
Founded: 2005.
Personnel Profile: Part-Time Paid 1; Part-Time Volunteers 8.
Governing Authority: Parent Institution: Goodwill Industries of Central Texas. Tax-exempt.
Computer Museum.
Collections: computing history; period artifacts; documentation; marketing materials; restored & functional early computers; hands-on exhibits; recycled computer art; early computer hardware & software.
Research Fields: legacy data recovery.
Facilities: 1,200 sq. ft. exhibit space; laboratories.
Activities: hands-on interactive displays; functional legacy computer hardware; early computer games.
Publications: quarterly newsletter, Binary.
Hours & Admission Prices: Mon.-Fri. 9-3. No charge. ♿
Attendance: 3,000 (estimated)
Membership: Student & Senior $25; Individual $50; Family $100; Supporting $250; Champion $500.

HARRY RANSOM CENTER AT THE UNIVERSITY OF TEXAS AT AUSTIN, 21st & Guadalupe, Austin, TX 78705. Mailing Address: P.O. Box 7219, Austin, TX 78713-7219. Tel.: 512-471-8944. Fax: 512-471-9646.
E-mail: webmail@hrc.vtexas.edu
Web Site: www.hrc.utexas.edu
Founded: 1957.
Congressional District: 10
Key Personnel: Dir., Dr. Thomas F. Staley; Exec. Assoc. Dir., Mary Beth Bigger; Cur. Photography, David Coleman; Librarian, Dr. Richard W. Oram; Cur. Art, Peter Mears.
Personnel Profile: Full-Time Paid 110; Part-Time Volunteers 25.
Governing Authority: university; nonprofit. Parent Institution: University of Texas at Austin. Tax-exempt: 501(c)(3).
Humanities Research Library.
Collections: Gutenberg bible c.1455; first photograph c.1826; film archives of David O. Selznick & Robert DeNiro; paintings by Frida Kahlo & Diego River; manuscripts of James Joyce, Ernest Hemingway, T.S. Eliot, D.H. Lawrence, Isaac Bashen's Singer, Tennessee Williams, & Norman Mailer.
Major Exhibits: Making Movies, 2/10-8/10.
Research Fields: 20th-21st century American, British & anglophone literature, manuscripts & books; 20th-21st century photography; 20th-21st century French literature & culture; art; performing arts; film.
Facilities: library; archives; educational facilities.
Activities: guided tours; lectures; temporary exhibits; docent program; graduate student internship program; post-doctoral research fellowship award program.
Publications: newsletter & books for an imprint series.
Hours & Admission Prices: Library Reading Room: Mon.-Fri. 9-5, Sat. 9-12. Exhibits: Tues.-Wed. & Fri. 10-5, Thurs. 10-7, Sat.-Sun. 12-5. No charge. Closed university holidays. ♿
Attendance: 80,000 (accurate)
Membership: Individual $50; Dual $100; Alliance $250; Guild $500; Director's Society $1,000.

LADY BIRD JOHNSON WILDFLOWER CENTER, 4801 La Crosse Ave., Austin, TX 78739-1702. Tel.: 512-232-0100. Fax: 512-232-0156.
Web Site: www.wildflower.org
Founded: 1982.
Key Personnel: Pres., Deacon Turner; Founder, Lady Bird Johnson; Founder, Helen Hayes; Exec. Dir., Susan K. Rieff; Dir. Communications, Saralee Tiede; Dir. Plant Conservation, Flo Oxley; Dir. Finance & Operations, Richard Tomhave; Dir. Product Mktg., Joseph Hammer; Dir. Landscape Restoration, Steve Windhager, Ph.D.; Dir. Devel., Justin Michalka; Dir. Gardens, Andrea DeLong-Amaya; Museum Shop Mgr., Joe Hammer.
Personnel Profile: Full-Time Paid 50; Part-Time Paid 13; Part-Time Volunteers 400; Interns 5.
Governing Authority: not for profit organization. Parent Institution: University of Texas at Austin. Tax-exempt: 501(c)(3).
Botanical Garden & Nature Center.
Collections: plants from the Southwest U.S. & northern Mexico; 25,000 images of North American native plants.
Research Fields: urban ecological engineering; restoration; ecology; native plant propagation.
Facilities: 1,800-vol. library on native plants of temperate North America; 232-seat auditorium; visitors gallery; cafe; children's Little House; home comparison gardens; 23 theme gardens; nature center. Museum-related items for sale.
Activities: guided tours; lectures; workshops; traveling exhibitions; education programs for children & adults; docent program; internship programs for college students. Annual Events: Wildflower Days; spring & fall plant sales; Luminations Winter Festival; Goblins in the Garden; Artisans Festival; Holiday Shopping Event.
Publications: monthly newsletter; quarterly magazine, Wildflower; quarterly calendar of events.
Hours & Admission Prices: Center: April-May daily 9-5:30; June-March Tues.-Sun. 9-5:30. Cafe: Tues.-Sat. 9-4, Sun. 11-4. Adults $7, students & senior citizens over 60 $6, children 5 & over $3; discounts to AAM members; children 4 & under and members no charge. Closed New Year's Day; Independence Day; Thanksgiving; Christmas Eve, Day & week. ♿
Attendance: 100,000 (accurate)
Membership: Students & Seniors $30; Students & Seniors Dual $38; Individual $40; Dual $50; Family $65; Supporting $100; Contributor $250; Sustaining $500; Champion $1,000; Sunflower Society $1,500.

LYNDON BAINES JOHNSON LIBRARY AND MUSEUM, 2313 Red River St., Austin, TX 78705-5737. Tel.: 512-721-0200. Fax: 512-721-0171 & 0170.
E-mail: johnson.library@nara.gov
Web Site: www.lbjlib.utexas.edu
Founded: 1971.
Congressional District: 10
Key Personnel: Dir., Mark Updegrove; Museum Cur., Sandor Cohen; Registrar, Michael McDonald; Asst. Registrar, Renee Gravois; Volunteer Coord., Judy Davidson-Englert; Museum Shop Mgr., Carol K. Johnson.
Personnel Profile: Full-Time Paid 38; Part-Time Paid 16; Part-Time Volunteers 135.
Governing Authority: federal. Parent Institution: National Archives & Records Admin., Washington, DC 20408. Tax-exempt: 170(b)(1)(A).
Presidential Library.
Collections: personal papers; government records; still photographs; motion picture films; audio & video tapes; sound recordings; head of state gifts; gifts from private citizens; political campaign items; personal & family memorabilia.
Major Exhibits: School House to the White House: The Education of the Presidents (T), 11/09-2/10.
Research Fields: 1960s; life, times, career & administration of the 36th President of the United States.
Facilities: 15,000-vol. library; 3,900 serials; auditoriums & conference rooms; manuscript reading room; photography & video laboratory. Museum-related items for sale.
Activities: guided tours; lectures; films; permanent, temporary & traveling exhibitions; organized educational programs for children, adults, undergraduate & graduate college students; docent program; symposiums.
Publications: exhibition catalogues; list of holdings; bibliography; books, The Rand & The Post, History of the Town and Village of Painted and Erwin; general information brochures.
Hours & Admission Prices: Daily 9-5. No charge; donations accepted. Closed Christmas. ♿
Attendance: 183,000 (estimated)
Membership: Senior Citizen $50; Individual $65; Sustaining $200.

MEXIC-ARTE MUSEUM, 419 Congress, Austin, TX 78701-3619. Mailing Address: P.O. Box 2273, Austin, TX 78768-2273. Tel.: 512-480-9373. Fax: 512-480-8626.
E-mail: info@mexic-artemuseum.org
Web Site: www.mexic-artemuseum.org
Founded: 1984.
Congressional District: 10
Key Personnel: C.E.O., Sylvia Orozco; Pres. (V), Lulu Flores; Dir. Public Rels., Alexandra M. Landeros; Museum Shop Mgr., Angela Hicks.
Personnel Profile: Full-Time Paid 9; Full-Time Volunteers 5; Part-Time Paid 5; Part-Time Volunteers 10; Interns 7.
Governing Authority: private; nonprofit organization. Tax-exempt: 501(c)(3).
Art Museum; focus on Mexican & Latin American culture.
Collections: concentration on 20th-century Mexican art; prints from the workshop of Popular Graphics; Jose Guadalupe Posada prints; photographs by Agustin Casasola of the Mexican Revolution; masks from Guerrero; photographs documenting Mexican-American history in Austin.
Major Exhibits: Imagining Mexico: Expressions in Popular Culture, 1/10-4/10;

Ruben Herrera: Master Artist & Teacher, 5/10-7/10; Independence & Revolution: Artists Imagining Mexico, 9/10-11/10; Dia de los Muertos, 10/10-12/10.
Facilities: 3000-vol. library.
Publications: newsletter; catalogues for major exhibits.
Hours & Admission Prices: Mon.-Thurs. 10-6, Fri.-Sat. 10-5, Sun 12-5. Adults $5; discounts to AAM members; Sun. & members no charge. Closed major holidays. ♿
Attendance: 50,000 (estimated)
Membership: $35 & up.

NEILL-COCHRAN HOUSE MUSEUM, 2310 San Gabriel St., Austin, TX 78705-5014. Tel.: 512-478-2335. Fax: 512-478-1865.
E-mail: info@nchmuseum.org
Web Site: www.nchmuseum.org
Founded: 1962.
Congressional District: 10
Key Personnel: Dir., Cecille Marcato; Coord. Projects, Amy Hollister.
Personnel Profile: Full-Time Paid 3; Part-Time Volunteers 30.
Governing Authority: NSCDA in Texas. Tax-exempt.
Historic House: 1855 Neill-Cochran House.
Collections: furniture & furnishings of the period 1855-1910.
Major Exhibits: Constancy & Change, 11/09-12/10.
Facilities: 200-vol. library of genealogical books & material available for research by permission.
Activities: guided tours; speaker series; docent course; temporary exhibitions.
Publications: members newsletter, Among Friends.
Hours & Admission Prices: Tues.-Sat. 2-5. Adults $5; discounts to AAA members, Time Travelers & school groups; members no charge. Closed New Year's Eve & Day; Easter; Thanksgiving; Christmas Eve & Day. ♿
Attendance: 2,500 (accurate)
Membership: Student $20; House Society $35; Hill Society $50; Neill Society $100; Cochran Society $500; Abner Cook Society $1,000; Museum Society $1,500; Bluebonnet Circle $2,000.

O. HENRY MUSEUM, 409 E. 5th St., Austin, TX 78701-3705. Tel.: 512-472-1903. Fax: 512-472-7102.
E-mail: ohenrymuseum@ci.austin.tx.us
Web Site: www.ohenrymuseum.org
Founded: 1934.
Congressional District: 10
Key Personnel: Cur., Valerie Bennett.
Personnel Profile: Full-Time Paid 1; Part-Time Paid 1; Part-Time Volunteers 10.
Governing Authority: municipal. Parent Institution: Austin Parks and Recreation Dept. Tax-exempt.
Historic House Museum: 1891 home of O. Henry.
Collections: furnishings; memorabilia; documents; letters; photographs.
Activities: guided tours; permanent exhibitions; special events; writing classes; historical & literary outreach. Museum Sponsors: Pun-Off.
Publications: newsletter, Pun-Intended.
Hours & Admission Prices: Wed.-Sun. 12-5. No charge; donations accepted. Closed New Year's Day; Independence Day; Labor Day; Thanksgiving; Christmas.
Attendance: 15,000 (estimated)
Membership: Student & Seniors $15; Individual $20; Family $25; Benefactor & Sponsor $100, $500, $1,000.

REPUBLIC OF TEXAS MUSEUM, (M), 510 E. Anderson Lane, Austin, TX 78752-1218. Tel.: 512-339-1997. Fax: 512-339-1998.
E-mail: museum@drtmuseum.org
Web Site: www.drt-inc.org
Founded: 1895.
Governing Authority: nonprofit organization.
History Museum.
Collections: Republic of Texas history & culture; photographs.
Facilities: library. Museum-related items for sale.
Activities: lectures; special events; educational programs.
Hours & Admission Prices: Mon.-Fri. 10-4. Adults $2, seniors $1.50, children & students $1. ♿

TEXAS ASSOCIATION OF MUSEUMS, (M), 3939 Bee Caves, Bldg. A, Ste. 1B, Austin, TX 78746-6431. Tel.: 512-328-6812. Fax: 512-327-9775.
E-mail: admin@texasmuseums.org
Web Site: www.texasmuseums.org
Founded: 1960.
Congressional District: 10
Key Personnel: Exec. Dir., Ruth Ann Rugg; Office Mgr., Joy Barnett; Program Assoc., Sandy Sage.
Personnel Profile: Full-Time Paid 3.
Governing Authority: nonprofit organization. Tax-exempt: 501(c)(3).
State Museum Association.
Activities: training programs for professional museum workers; workshops. Association Sponsors: annual conference.
Publications: quarterly newsletter, Museline; books, Museum Forms Book; Action Plan: Multicultural Initiatives in Texas Museums; A Window to Texas Museums: Resource Sharing Directory.
Hours & Admission Prices: Call for hours.
Membership: Student $30; Individual & Contributing $50; Sustaining $100; Business $100-$500; Supporting $250; Patron $500; Benefactor $1,000. Institutional $100-$1,000.

TEXAS GOVERNOR'S MANSION, 1010 Colorado, Austin, TX 78701-2334. Tel.: 512-463-5518 & 5516. Fax: 512-463-1850.
E-mail: admin@txfgm.org
Web Site: www.txfgm.org
Founded: 1856.
Key Personnel: Admin., Ellen Read.
Governing Authority: state government; nonprofit.
Historic House & Site: designated as a National Historic Landmark in 1975.
Collections: furnishings; American Federal & Empire periods; furniture & decorative arts.
Publications: video, Texas Governor's Mansion.
Hours & Admission Prices: Temporarily closed for restoration. ♿

TEXAS HISTORICAL COMMISSION, 1511 Colorado, Austin, TX 78701-1664. Mailing Address: P.O. Box 12276, Austin, TX 78711-2276. Tel.: 512-463-5853. Fax: 512-463-5750.
E-mail: thc@thc.state.tx.us
Web Site: www.thc.state.tx.us
Founded: 1953.
Congressional District: 5
Key Personnel: Chm. Commission, Jon Hansen; Exec. Dir., Mark Wolfe; Archaeology Div., Jim Bruseth; Architecture Div., Stan Graves; Staff Svcs. Div., Penny Black; Mktg. & Communications Div., Heather McBride; History Programs Div., Bratten Thomason; Historic Sites Div., Donna Williams.
Personnel Profile: Full-Time Paid 220.
Governing Authority: state. Branch Museum: Sam Rayburn House Museum, Bonham, TX. Tax-exempt: 501(c)(3).
State Agency.
Collections: Historic Houses: 1854, Carrington-Covert House; 1883, Gethsemane Church; Sam Rayburn House Museum; 1854, Carrington-Covert House (Austin); 1883, Gethsemane Lutheran Church (THC Library, Austin); 1916, Sam Rayburn House Museum (Bonham).
Research Fields: preservation of historic landmarks; architecture; archaeology; historic sites; cultural resource management; museum management & services; field work data processing.
Facilities: 1,500-vol. library on Texas history, museology, management, preservation, archaeology, conservation, for use on premises.
Activities: lectures; administration of historic preservation programs for state; workshops; conferences.
Publications: bimonthly newsletter, Medallion; biennial reports; heritage tourism brochures.
Hours & Admission Prices: Call for hours. ♿

TEXAS MUSIC MUSEUM, 1109 E. 11th St., Austin, TX 78761. Mailing Address: P.O. Box 16467, Austin, TX 78761-6467. Tel.: 512-472-8891 & 471-0520. Fax: 512-471-9600.
E-mail: cshorkey@mail.utexas.edu
Web Site: www.texasmusicmuseum.org
Founded: 1984.
Congressional District: 10
Key Personnel: Pres. (V), Dr. Clayton Shorkey; Vice Pres., Sharon Herfurth; Sec., Eve Falcon-Korems; Treas., Joyce Davids Christianson.
Personnel Profile: Part-Time Volunteers 30.
Governing Authority: private; nonprofit organization. Tax-exempt.
Music Museum.
Collections: music instrument-makers; recording & reproduction devices; music art, education, publishing & mechanical devices; artifacts; achievements & memorabilia pertaining to the composition, performance, reproduction & promotion of musical arts in Texas.
Research Fields: musical heritage of Texas.
Facilities: 100-vol. library of Texas music books.
Activities: educational & recreational programs; meetings; performances; rental gallery; traveling exhibitions.
Hours & Admission Prices: Mon.-Fri. 8-5. No charge; donations accepted. ♿
Attendance: 10,000 (estimated)

TEXAS NATURAL SCIENCE CENTER, (M), 2400 Trinity, Austin, TX 78705-5730. Tel.: 512-471-1604. Fax: 512-471-4794.
E-mail: tmmweb@uts.cc.utexas.edu
Web Site: www.texasmemorialmuseum.org
Formerly: Texas Memorial Museum
Founded: 1936.
Congressional District: 10
Key Personnel: Dir., Edward C. Theriot; Dir. Museum Operations, Margaret Fischer; Dir. External Affairs, Susan Romberg; Accountant, Sara Gray; Museum Educator, Christina Ramsey Cid; Webmaster, Sharon Ruether; Artist, John Maisano; Museum Shop Mgr., Louise Meeks; LAN Mgr., Melissa Winans; Security, Paul Wood; Cur. Ichthyology, Dean A. Hendrickson; Cur. Entomology, John Abbott; Cur. Arthropods, James R. Reddell; Cur. Herpetology, David C. Cannatella; Asst. Cur. Herpetology, Travis LaDuc; Dir. Vertebrate Paleontology Lab, Timothy Rowe; Professor Emeritus, Vertebrate Paleontology Lab, Wann Langston; Professor Emeritus, Vertebrate Paleontology, Ernest Lundelius; Preparator, Vertebrate Paleontology Lab, Robert Rainey; Collection Coord., Non-Vertebrate Paleontology Collection, Ann Molineux; Collections Mgr. Ichthyology, Jessica Rosales; Sr. Paleontology Educator, Pamela Owen; Paleontology Educator, Laura Naski.
Personnel Profile: Full-Time Paid 18; Part-Time Paid 14; Part-Time Volunteers 23; Interns 2.
Governing Authority: state. Parent Institution: University of Texas at Austin. Tax-exempt: 170(b)(1)(A).
Natural Science Museum.
Collections: geology; mineralogy; meteorites; tektites; vertebrate & invertebrate paleontology; paleobotany; vertebrate zoology; marine invertebrate zoology; entomology; arachnology.
Research Fields: paleontology; geology; vertebrate & invertebrate zoology; entomology; ichthyology; herpetology.
Facilities: reference library of scientific materials; exhibits; Vertebrate Paleontology Laboratory; Texas Natural History Laboratory; Ecological & Systematic Survey of Texas Arthropods; Texas Archives for Geological Research; research space. Museum-related items for sale.
Activities: permanent & temporary exhibitions; offsite exhibits; guided tours; collections care and maintenance; inter-museum loans; teacher training. Museum Studies courses in collaboration with the Univ. of Texas at Austin; research & publications; self-guided tours; weekend special events & activities; Museum Express.
Publications: quarterly newsletter, Collection Notes.
Hours & Admission Prices: Mon.-Fri. 9-5, Sat. 10-5, Sun. 1-5. No charge; donations accepted. Closed New Year's Day; Easter; Independence Day; Thanksgiving; Christmas. ♿
Attendance: 80,952 (accurate)
Membership: Individual $40; Family $75; Naturalist $125; Super Naturalist $250; Explorer $500; Visionary $1,000; Director's Circle $5,000 & up.

TEXAS PARKS AND WILDLIFE DEPARTMENT, 4200 Smith School Rd., Austin, TX 78744-3292. Tel.: 512-389-4800 & 800-792-1112.
Web Site: www.tpwd.state.tx.us
Founded: 1963.
Congressional District: 10
Key Personnel: Exec. Dir., Carter Smith; Dir. State Parks, Walt Dabney; Dir. Cultural Resources Mgmt., Michael Strutt; Dir. Interpretation & Exhibits Program, Phil Hewitt; Chief Cur., Joanne Avant; Dir. Natural Resources Management, David Riskind.
Governing Authority: state. Historic Sites: 116 parks all located within Texas. Tax-exempt.
Texas Parks & Wildlife Agency: administers over 130 state parks, recreation areas, historical parks, historic sites, historic structures & natural areas.
Collections: decorative arts; period furnishings; personal articles of early Texas settlers & statesmen; World War I & II military materials as they relate to the Battleship Texas; archaeological material culture; pictographs; petroglyphs; paleontological; natural history; living history reenactments; landscaping; mechanical systems; architecture; farming; ranching; agriculture; 19th-century transportation, railroad & stagecoach; 19th-century frontier military history; clothing & textile; photographs; department division collection.
Research Fields: natural history; threatened & endangered species; archaeology; decorative arts; military history; Texas & Civil War history; Texas Revolution; World Wars I & II; 19th-century costume & textile history; state, regional, county & local history; Civilian Conservation Corps in Texas.
Facilities: picnic areas; camping; hiking trails; visitor centers; interpretive centers; inn lodgings; amphitheaters.
Activities: guided tours; self-guided tours; lectures; films; audiovisual programs; permanent, temporary & traveling exhibitions; education programs; volunteer & docent training.
Publications: brochures; maps; trail guides; pamphlets; books; newsletters; department monthly magazine; six hunting, fishing & non-game stamps issued annually.
Hours & Admission Prices: Headquarters: Mon.-Fri. 8-5, call sites for hours. Historic Sites: adults $1-$5, children 6-12 $.50; children under 6 no charge; annual park entrance permit $50. ♿
Membership: Various friends, volunteers and other support groups attached to each particular park.

TEXAS STATE LIBRARY & ARCHIVES COMMISSION, 1201 Brazos St., Austin, TX 78701-1938. Mailing Address: Box 12927, Austin, TX 78711-2927. Tel.: 512-463-5460. Fax: 512-463-5436.
E-mail: info@tsl.state.tx.us
Web Site: www.tsl.state.tx.us
Founded: 1839.
Key Personnel: Dir. & Librarian, Peggy D. Rudd; Asst. State Librarian, Edward Seidenberg.
Governing Authority: state. Tax-exempt: 501(c)(3).
History Museum.
Collections: documents; artifacts; firearms; archives; manuscripts; photographs.
Research Fields: Texas history.
Facilities: 35,000-vol. library of Texana & general reference books available for research on premises; reading room.
Activities: permanent exhibitions.
Hours & Admission Prices: Library: Mon.-Fri. 8-5. Genealogy Section: Mon.-Fri. 8-5. Sam Houston Center: Mon.-Fri. 8-5, Sat. 9-4. No charge. Closed major holidays. ♿
Attendance: 5,000

UMLAUF SCULPTURE GARDEN & MUSEUM, (M), 605 Robert E. Lee Rd., Austin, TX 78704-1453. Tel.: 512-445-5582. Fax: 512-445-5583.
E-mail: info@umlaufsculpture.org
Web Site: www.umlaufsculpture.org
Founded: 1991.
Congressional District: 10
Key Personnel: Dir., Ms. Nelie Plourde.
Personnel Profile: Full-Time Paid 2; Part-Time Paid 3; Part-Time Volunteers 85; Interns 2.
Governing Authority: private; nonprofit organization. Tax-exempt: 501(c)(3).
Sculpture Museum.
Collections: over 130 sculptures by Charles Umlauf; bronze castings; marble carvings; drawings; paintings; mediums used by Umlauf include exotic woods, stone, aluminum, pewter, cast stone, stoneware, terra cotta.
Research Fields: sculptor Charles Umlauf; locating Umlauf sculptures in public placements across the U.S. (in conjunction with Save Outdoor Sculpture); developing museum programs for special needs visitors; developing interactive workbooks about sculpture for school children visiting the museum & self-guided tour kits for families.
Facilities: library available for scholarly research; archives; xeriscape garden; touch tours of outdoor sculptures; 3,500 sq. ft. exhibit space. Museum-related items for sale.
Activities: guided tours; lectures; sculpture demonstrations; poetry readings; dance recitals; formal education programs for children; docent program; training programs for professional museum workers; arts festivals; temporary exhibits; museum video captioned for hearing-impaired visitors; Touch Tours available for vision-impaired visitors. Annual Events: Museum's Birthday Celebration in June.
Publications: biannual museum newsletter, Garden Grapevine; monthly volunteers newsletter, Volunteer View; interactive workbooks about sculpture for school children; self-guided tour kits for families.
Hours & Admission Prices: Wed.-Fri. 10-4:30, Sat.-Sun.1-4:30; groups of 20 or more by appointment. Adults $3.50, senior citizens $2.50, students $1; discounts for AAM & Texas Association Museum members; members & children under 6 no charge. Closed New Year's Eve & Day; Independence Day; Thanksgiving; Christmas Eve & Day. ♿
Attendance: 27,000 (accurate)
Membership: Terra Cotta $50; Bronze $100; Marble $500; Onyx $1,000; Gold $5,000.

Baird

CALLAHAN COUNTY PIONEER MUSEUM, 100 W. 4th, B-1, Baird, TX 79504-5305. Tel.: 325-854-5875. Fax: 325-854-5841.
E-mail: sonia.walker@callahancounty.org
Founded: 1940.
Congressional District: 87
Key Personnel: C.E.O., Lucibel Manion; Cur., Sonia Walker.
Personnel Profile: Part-Time Paid 1.

Governing Authority: nonprofit organization. Parent Institution: Wednesday Club.
History Museum.
Collections: local pioneer articles.
Hours & Admission Prices: Mon.-Fri. 1-5. No charge. Closed major holidays. ♿
Attendance: 324 (accurate)

Bandera

FRONTIER TIMES MUSEUM, (M), 510 13th St., Bandera, TX 78003. Mailing Address: P.O. Box 1918, Bandera, TX 78003-1918. Tel.: 830-796-3864.
Web Site: www.frontiertimesmuseum.com
Founded: 1933.
Congressional District: 21
Key Personnel: Pres., Johnny Boyle; Vice Pres., George Sharman; Treas., Florida Barnes; Sec., Theresa Helbert; Museum Shop Mgr. & Historian, Patsy Muller.
Personnel Profile: Full-Time Paid 1; Part-Time Paid 2; Part-Time Volunteers 17.
Governing Authority: nonprofit organization. Tax-exempt: 501(c)(3).
Historic Building.
Collections: emphasizing the Old West & Texas' early pioneer and ranching days; Western art; folk art; historical photographs; music boxes; artifacts from around the world; international bell collection.
Facilities: Museum-related items for sale.
Activities: Annual Event: Living History - Cowboys on Main Street. Annual Event: National Day of the Cowboy.
Publications: annual membership letter.
Hours & Admission Prices: Mon.-Sat. 10-4:30. Adults $5, seniors $3, students 6-18 $2; discounts to groups upon approval; children under 6 & members no charge. Closed Easter; Thanksgiving; Christmas. ♿
Attendance: 10,000 (accurate)
Membership: Student $10; Individual $25; Family $50; Business $100.

Bay City

MATAGORDA COUNTY MUSEUM, (M), 2100 Ave. F, Bay City, TX 77414-0851. Tel.: 979-245-7502. Fax: 979-245-1233.
E-mail: mcma@matagordamuseum.com
Web Site: www.matagordamuseum.com
Founded: 1965.
Congressional District: 14
Key Personnel: Exec. Dir., Sarah Higgins; Asst. Dir., Barbara Smith.
Personnel Profile: Part-Time Paid 5; Part-Time Volunteers 40.
Governing Authority: nonprofit organization. Parent Institution: Matagorda County Museum Assn. Tax-exempt: 501(c)(3).
Historical Society Museum: housed in c.1917 federal post office building.
Collections: Matagorda County history from the time of the Karankawa Indians; Stephen F. Austin colonization; Republic of Texas; Civil War; cattle ranching into the 20th century; LaBelle shipwreck.
Facilities: 150-vol. library on Texas History; 87 annuals dating back to 1910; probate records & marriage records (1837-1900), available for public use; 8,000 sq. ft. exhibit space. Note cards & postcards for sale.
Activities: guided tours; lectures; docent program; formal education programs for children; rental gallery; temporary & traveling exhibitions; dinner theatre. Museum Sponsors: Annual Christmas Tour; Historical Summer Camp - children's museum.
Publications: quarterly newsletter, Matagorda County Musings.
Hours & Admission Prices: Wed.-Sun. 1-5. Adults $4, seniors $3, children $2; discounts to AAM, ICOM, TAM & SETMA members; members & children under 2 no charge. Closed New Year's Day; Memorial Day; Good Friday; Labor Day; Thanksgiving; Christmas. ♿
Attendance: 10,500 (accurate)
Membership: Individual $20; Family $30; Friend $50; Donor $100; Sponsor $250; Patron $500; Benefactor $1,000.

Baytown

BAYTOWN HISTORICAL MUSEUM, 220 W. Defee St., Baytown, TX 77520-4010. Tel.: 281-427-8768.
History Museum.
Collections: local history & culture; early pioneer life; period artifacts; photographs.
Hours & Admission Prices: Tues.-Sat. 10-2. No charge.

BAYTOWN NATURE CENTER, 6813 Bayway Dr., Baytown, TX 77520. Tel.: 281-932-1972.
Governing Authority: nonprofit organization.
Nature Center.
Collections: wildlife including over 300 species of birds; butterfly garden.
Facilities: visitor center; children's discovery center.
Hours & Admission Prices: Daily sunrise to sunset. Adults $3; children 12 & under no charge.

EDDIE V. GRAY WETLANDS CENTER, 1724 Market St., Baytown, TX 77520. Tel.: 281-420-7128.
Governing Authority: city.
Nature Center.
Collections: local history; alligators; turtles; fish; butterflies; mounted animals; photographs; aquariums; terrariums.
Facilities: 9,000 sq. ft. exhibit space.
Activities: hands-on exhibits; educational programs.
Hours & Admission Prices: Mon.-Fri. 9-4, Sat. 10-4; groups by appointment. Closed holidays.

Beaumont

* **ART MUSEUM OF SOUTHEAST TEXAS, (M),** 500 Main St., Beaumont, TX 77701-3213. Mailing Address: P.O. Box 3703, Beaumont, TX 77704-3703. Tel.: 409-832-3432. Fax: 409-832-8508.
E-mail: info@amset.org
Web Site: www.amset.org
Founded: 1950.
Congressional District: 5
Key Personnel: Exec. Dir., Lynn P. Castle; Cur. Exhibitions & Collections, Sarah Hamilton; Pres., Judy Black; Administrator Finance & Personnel, Patricia Siebert; Registrar, Paula Rodriguez; Public Rels., Melissa Tilley; Asst. to Dir., Elizabeth Gorris; Cur. Education, Sandra Laurette; Museum Shop Mgr., Kathy Boudreaux.
Personnel Profile: Full-Time Paid 7; Part-Time Paid 9; Part-Time Volunteers 165.
Governing Authority: nonprofit corporation. Tax-exempt: 501(c)(3).
Art Museum.
Collections: 19th-21st century American painting, sculpture, photography & folk art.
Research Fields: 20th-21st century American art; 20th-21st century Texas & American self-taught art.
Facilities: 1,500-vol. library of books on art & 6,000 slides available for research; 120-seat auditorium; restaurant; classrooms. Museum-related items for sale.
Activities: guided tours; travel tours; lectures; films; gallery talks; mobile outreach program; public children's computer lab; docent program for teens & adults; summer art camp; after school programs; Headstart; high school art contest. Museum Sponsors: Family Arts Day.
Publications: exhibition catalogues; gallery handouts; quarterly newsletter; posters.
Hours & Admission Prices: Mon.-Fri. 9-5, Sat. 10-5, Sun. 12-5. No charge; donations accepted. Closed New Year's Eve & Day; Easter; Independence Day; Thanksgiving; Christmas Eve & Day. ♿
Attendance: 36,000 (accurate)
Membership: Individual $30; Family $35; Friend $100; Fellow $200; Patron $500; President's Club $1,000; Sustainer $2,500; Business $250-$10,000.

THE ART STUDIO, INC., 720 Franklin St., Beaumont, TX 77701-4424. Tel.: 409-838-5393. Fax: 409-838-4695.
E-mail: artstudio@artstudio.org
Web Site: www.artstudio.org
Founded: 1983.
Congressional District: 9
Key Personnel: C.E.O., Dir. & Public Rels., Greg Busceme; Chm. (V), Stephan Malick; Devel. & Membership, Tim Postlewait; Administrative Asst., Cathy Atkinson; Museum Shop Mgr., Monica Hay.
Personnel Profile: Full-Time Paid 1; Full-Time Volunteers 3; Part-Time Paid 1; Part-Time Volunteers 16; Interns 5.
Governing Authority: nonprofit organization. Tax-exempt: 501(c)(3).
Art Gallery with Exhibit Area.
Collections: Bob Willis Memorial Ceramic Collection & Memorial Art Library.
Facilities: classrooms; 14,000 sq. ft. exhibit space; studios. Art by local artists for sale.
Activities: guided tours; lectures; hobby workshops; organized educational programs; at risk youth outreach; participatory exhibits.
Publications: monthly alternative press open to artists, writers & musicians, Issue.
Hours & Admission Prices: Tues.-Sat. 10-6; other times by appointment. No charge; donations accepted. ♿
Attendance: 5,000 (estimated)
Membership: Artist & Student $20; Family & Group $35; Friend & Business $50; Sustaining $100; Patron $250; Angel $500; Life $5,000.

BABE DIDRIKSON ZAHARIAS MUSEUM, 1750 E IH-10, Beaumont, TX 77704. Mailing Address: P.O. Box 3827, Beaumont, TX 77704-3827. Tel.: 409-833-4622. Fax: 409-880-3750.
E-mail: klewis@ci.beaumont.tx.us
Web Site: www.babedidriksonzaharias.org
Founded: 1976.
Key Personnel: Cur., Karen Lewis.
Personnel Profile: Part-Time Paid 4; Part-Time Volunteers 1.
Governing Authority: municipal government; nonprofit. Tax-exempt.
Sports Museum.
Collections: sports trophies; golf clubs & bags; newspaper clippings; photographs; Olympic medals & videotape relating to Babe Didrikson Zaharias.
Hours & Admission Prices: Daily 9-5. No charge; donations accepted. Closed Christmas. ♿
Attendance: 7,000 (estimated)

BEAUMONT ART LEAGUE, 2675 Gulf St., Fairgrounds, Beaumont, TX 77703-4417. Tel.: 409-833-4179.
E-mail: beaumontartleague@yahoo.com
Founded: 1943.
Congressional District: 9
Key Personnel: Pres., Sue Bard; Dir., Dana Dorman.
Personnel Profile: Part-Time Paid 1; Part-Time Volunteers 50.
Governing Authority: nonprofit organization. Tax-exempt: 501(c)(3).
Art Museum & Gallery.
Collections: works by local & national artists; paintings; drawings; prints; photographs; sculpture.
Facilities: classroom; 4,757 sq. ft. exhibit space. Art work for sale.
Activities: educational programs; participatory exhibits; workshops.
Publications: monthly newsletter, Beaumont Art League; class schedule; exhibit invitations.
Hours & Admission Prices: Tues.-Fri. 10-4, Sat. 10-2 & by appointment. No charge; donations accepted. Closed New Year's Day; Independence Day; Thanksgiving; Christmas. ♿
Attendance: 2,000 (estimated)
Membership: Student $20; Individual $35; Family $45; Friend $50; Patron $100; Benefactor $500; Lifetime $1,000.

BEAUMONT BOTANICAL GARDENS, 6088 Babe Zaharias Dr., Beaumont, TX 77705-6747. Tel.: 409-842-3135. Fax: 409-840-6456.
E-mail: myver@aol.com
Web Site: www.beaumontbotanicalgardens.com
Formerly: Beaumont Council of Garden Clubs-Beaumont Garden Center
Founded: 1971.
Congressional District: 9
Key Personnel: Chair, Dr. Elizabeth Gibbs; Treas. & Education, Randy Hammerling; Devel. & Membership, Frankie Pletzer.
Personnel Profile: Full-Time Paid 3; Full-Time Volunteers 1; Part-Time Paid 1; Part-Time Volunteers 12.
Governing Authority: nonprofit organization. Tax-exempt: 501(c)(3).
Botanical Garden.
Collections: horticultural specimens of ferns, shrubs, annuals, perennials, & bulbs; rose garden with 260 bushes; Japanese Garden. Warren Loose Conservatory: tropical plants including bromeliads, ferns, palms, citrus.
Facilities: 1500-vol. library of material on horticulture, native plants, artistic design of flowers & landscape design available to the public; 250-seat auditorium; 10-acre botanical garden; nature & conservation center.
Activities: guided tours; lectures; films; study clubs; organized educational programs; docent program; flower shows. Museum Sponsors: Annual Spring Garden Tour.
Publications: quarterly newsletter, Take Time to Smell the Flowers; brochures.
Hours & Admission Prices: Daily 7:30 a.m.-dusk; guided tours by appointment. No charge; donations accepted. Warren Loose Conservatory: Wed.-Fri. 10-2, Sat. 10-5, Sun. 1-5. Adults $3, seniors $2, children 6-12 $1. ♿
Attendance: 33,000 (estimated)
Membership: $10-$20 per club according to number of members.

BROWN-SCURLOCK GALLERIES, 2675 Gulf St., Beaumont, TX 77703-4417. Tel.: 409-833-4179.
Governing Authority: Operated by Beaumont Art League.
Art Gallery.
Collections: paintings; photographs; sculpture.
Activities: art classes.
Hours & Admission Prices: Tues.-Fri. 10-4, Sat. 10-2.

DISHMAN ART MUSEUM, (M), 1030 E. Lavaca, Beaumont, TX 77705. Mailing Address: P.O. Box 10027, Beaumont, TX 77710-0027. Tel.: 409-880-8959. Fax: 409-880-1799.
E-mail: dishman_art@hal.lamar.edu
Web Site: www.lamar.edu
Founded: 1983.
Congressional District: 9
Key Personnel: Dir., Dr. Fu-Chia-Wen Lien; Museum Asst., Alicia Hargreaves.
Personnel Profile: Full-Time Paid 2; Part-Time Paid 1; Part-Time Volunteers 2; Interns 2.
Governing Authority: public university. Parent Institution: Lamar University. Tax-exempt.
Art Museum.
Collections: African & New Guinea masks & shields; 140 19th-century paintings; 250 19th-century porcelains; contemporary paintings & prints.
Research Fields: 19th-century academic European & American paintings.
Facilities: 500-vol. library of 19th-century & modern books; 3,000 sq. ft. exhibit space.
Activities: arts festivals; lectures. Annual Events: fundraiser ball; artist in residence.
Publications: catalogues to selected exhibitions.
Hours & Admission Prices: Mon.-Fri. 8-5. No charge; donations accepted. Closed New Year's Day; Good Friday; Memorial Day; Labor Day; Thanksgiving & day after; Christmas. ♿
Attendance: 4,000 (estimated)

EDISON MUSEUM, 350 Pine St., Beaumont, TX 77701-2437. Tel.: 409-981-3089. Fax: 409-838-2361.
E-mail: info@edisonmuseum.org
Web Site: www.edisonmuseum.org
Formerly: Edison Plaza Museum
Founded: 1980.
Congressional District: 9
Key Personnel: C.E.O. & Dir., Mellissa Bijoux; Chm. (V), Michael Barnhill.
Personnel Profile: Full-Time Paid 1; Part-Time Paid 1; Part-Time Volunteers 4.
Governing Authority: private; not-for-profit organization. Parent Institution: Entergy/Texas. Tax-exempt.
History Museum: housed in the Travis Street substation; the first substation to distribute electric power in Southeast Texas.
Collections: focus is on inventions & innovations of Thomas A. Edison.
Activities: Edison Junior Inventor Program.
Publications: A Teacher's Guide To The Edison Plaza Museum; The Inventor Bulletin Series.
Hours & Admission Prices: Mon.-Fri. 9-5. No charge; donations accepted. Closed major holidays. ♿
Attendance: 3,380 (accurate)

FIRE MUSEUM OF TEXAS, 400 Walnut at Mulberry, Beaumont, TX 77701. Mailing Address: P.O. Box 3827, Beaumont, TX 77704-3827. Tel.: 409-880-3927. Fax: 409-880-3914.
E-mail: firemuseum@ci.beaumont.tx.us
Web Site: www.firemuseumoftexas.org
Founded: 1986.
Congressional District: 9
Key Personnel: Exec. Dir., Carol Gary; Fire Chief, Anne Huff; Pres. Association (V), Allison Golias.
Personnel Profile: Full-Time Paid 1; Part-Time Volunteers 24; Interns 1.
Governing Authority: municipal; City of Beaumont Fire Dept. Tax-exempt: 501(c)(3).
Firefighting Museum: 1927 Beaumont Fire Department Firehouse; Texas Historical Landmark; Spanish Renaissance Revival.
Collections: firefighting services in Texas; hands-on fire safety; photographs & patches; fire alarm systems; international firefighting memorabilia; fire pumpers: 1856 Hand Drawn Tub pumper; 1909 American La France aerial ladder; 1917 American La France piston pumper; 1926 American La France rotary pumper.
Research Fields: history of fire service in Beaumont & in Texas; fire alarm systems; fire prevention education.
Facilities: 100-vol. library available for research by permission only; theater; kitchen facilities; fire safety activity center. Fire service related items for sale.
Activities: guided tours; fire prevention education programs; docent program; children's hands-on fire safety activity center; fire safety summer camps; annual car show; fire safety special events.
Publications: brochure; annual report; biannual newsletter.
Hours & Admission Prices: Mon.-Fri. 8-4:30, Sat.-Sun. by appointment. No charge; donations accepted. Closed New Year's Day; Martin Luther King Jr. Day; Good Friday; Memorial Day; Independence Day; Labor Day; Thanksgiving & day after; Christmas. ♿
Attendance: 22,837 (accurate)
Membership: Junior Firefighter 12 & under $5; Firefighter $15; Individual $20; Family $35; Driver $50; Captain $100; District Chief $250; Asst. Fire Chief $500; Fire Chief $1,000.

JOHN JAY FRENCH HOUSE, BEAUMONT HERITAGE SOCIETY, (M), 3025 French Rd., Beaumont, TX 77706-7920. Tel.: 409-898-0348. Fax: 409-898-8487.
E-mail: jjfrench@sbcglobal.net
Web Site: beaumontheritage.org
Founded: 1968.
Congressional District: 9
Key Personnel: Pres. (V), Allison Golias; Exec. Dir., Darlene Chodzinski; Financial Dir., John Quigley.
Personnel Profile: Full-Time Paid 1; Part-Time Paid 4; Part-Time Volunteers 18.
Governing Authority: nonprofit organization. Parent Institution: Beaumont Heritage Society. Tax-exempt: 501(c)(3).
Historic House Museum: c.1845 Greek Revival house, John Jay French home.
Collections: mid-1840s decorative arts; pre-Civil War era furnishing & accessories; blacksmith shop; semi-detached kitchen.
Research Fields: Beaumont history; decorative arts & crafts.
Facilities: 425-vol. research library; 680 sq. ft. exhibit space. Museum-related items for sale.
Activities: guided tours; lectures; docent training program; formal education program for children & undergraduate or graduate college students. Museum Sponsors: Christmas Candlelight Tour; Tex Fest; ethnic food fair; heritage dinner.
Publications: quarterly newsletter.
Hours & Admission Prices: Tues.-Sat. 10-4; group tours by appointment; school tours mornings Feb.-April. Adults $3, senior citizens $2; students $1. Closed major holidays. ♿
Attendance: 12,000 (estimated)
Membership: Scholar & Student $10; Pioneer $35; Frontiersman $75; Blacksmith $100; Landowner $200; Business $250-$1000; French Town Settler $1,500.

* **MCFADDIN-WARD HOUSE, (M),** Visitor Center, 1906 Calder Ave., Beaumont, TX 77701-1517. Mailing Address: 725 Third St., Beaumont, TX 77701-1629. Tel.: 409-832-1906 & 2134. Fax: 409-832-3483.
E-mail: arlene@mcfaddin-ward.org
Web Site: www.mcfaddin-ward.org
Founded: 1983.
Congressional District: 9
Key Personnel: Dir., Matthew L. White; Cur. Interpretation & Education, Judy Linsley; Educator, Becky Fertitta; Cur. Collections, Allen Lea; Buildings & Grounds Supvr., Felix McFarland.
Personnel Profile: Full-Time Paid 13; Part-Time Paid 6; Part-Time Volunteers 130; Interns 1.
Governing Authority: nonprofit. Tax-exempt: 501(c)(3).
Historic House: 1906 Beaux Arts Colonial house built by early Texas oil & ranching family.
Collections: American factory-made furniture; arts & crafts; furniture & decorative arts; original 19th & 20th-century family furnishings including English & American silver, ceramics, glass, oriental rugs, paintings.
Research Fields: local & southeast Texas history; 20th-century furniture; English & American silver; ceramics; glass; oriental rugs.
Facilities: historic house; carriage house; administrative office house (1903 restored exterior); visitor center.
Activities: guided tours; educational programs; special events; seasonal interpretations.
Publications: quarterly newsletter; annual report; exhibit catalog; historical conference proceedings.
Hours & Admission Prices: Tues.-Sat. 10-4, Sun. 1-4. McFaddin-Ward House: children under 8 not admitted. Carriage House: Sat. 10-3, Sun. 1-3; open to all ages. Adults $3; discount to AAM members; members no charge. Closed major holidays. ♿
Attendance: 8,858 (accurate)
Membership: Individual $5.

SPINDLETOP/GLADYS CITY BOOMTOWN MUSEUM, 5550 University Dr., Beaumont, TX 77705. Mailing Address: P.O. Box 10070, Beaumont, TX 77710-0070. Tel.: 409-835-0823. Fax: 409-832-1782.
E-mail: christy.marino@lamar.edu
Web Site: www.spindletop.org
Founded: 1975.
Congressional District: 9
Key Personnel: Cur., Christy Marino.
Personnel Profile: Full-Time Paid 1; Part-Time Paid 4; Part-Time Volunteers 10.
Governing Authority: state; nonprofit. Parent Institution: Lamar University. Tax-exempt: 501(c)(3).
Recreation of Oil Boomtown: located at the site of the Spindletop oilfield, the first major oilfield in the U.S., discovered in 1901.
Collections: oilfield machinery & tools; paper goods; household items; furniture; textiles; glass items; photographs; books.
Research Fields: Spindletop oil field history; oral history collection.
Facilities: 15-building complex.
Activities: guided tours; educational programs; research.
Hours & Admission Prices: Tues.-Sat. 10-5, Sun. 1-5. Adults $3, senior citizens $2, children $1; school groups by appointment; no charge. Closed all major holidays. ♿
Attendance: 25,000 (estimated)

TEXAS ENERGY MUSEUM, 600 Main St., Beaumont, TX 77701-3305. Tel.: 409-833-5100. Fax: 409-833-4282.
E-mail: ryan@texasenergymuseum.org
Web Site: www.texasenergymuseum.org
Founded: 1987.
Congressional District: 9
Key Personnel: Dir. & C.E.O., D. Ryan Smith; Pres. (V), Pat Avery; Museum Shop Mgr., Raphaella Cortello.
Personnel Profile: Full-Time Paid 3; Part-Time Paid 2; Part-Time Volunteers 20.
Governing Authority: not-for-profit organization. Tax-exempt: 501(c)(3).
Industry History Museum.
Collections: petroleum geology & technology; history of the petroleum industry especially relating to southeast Texas.
Research Fields: history, economics & technology of the world wide oil & gas industry, with emphasis on the U.S., Mexico & Canada; astronomy; chemistry; physics; geology; paleontology; oceanography.
Facilities: aquarium; educational facilities; 16,000 sq. ft. exhibit space. Museum-related items for sale.
Activities: docent program; guided tours; lectures; temporary exhibitions; children's programs.
Publications: brochures.
Hours & Admission Prices: Tues.-Sat. 9-5, Sun. 1-5. Adults $2, senior citizens & children 6-12 $1; discounts to AAM & ICOM members; Lamar University students with valid I.D. & Texas Assoc. of Museums members no charge. ♿
Attendance: 16,000 (accurate)

TYRRELL HISTORICAL LIBRARY, 695 Pearl St., Beaumont, TX 77701. Tel.: 409-833-2759.
Historical Library: housed in a former Baptist Church; built in 1903. Listed on the National Register of Historic Places.
Collections: books; genealogy; paintings.
Facilities: library of Texas history books.
Activities: research.
Hours & Admission Prices: Tues. 8:30-8, Wed.-Sat. 8:30-5:30.

Beeville

BEEVILLE ART MUSEUM, (M), 401 E. Fannin, Beeville, TX 78102-3515. Tel.: 361-358-8615. Fax: 361-358-0413.
Key Personnel: Dir., Tracy Bell Saucier.
Governing Authority: Tax-exempt: 501(c)(3).
Art Museum.
Collections: works by local artists.
Facilities: library.
Activities: educational programs; summer art camps; workshops.
Hours & Admission Prices: Mon.-Fri. 9-5, Sat. 10-2. No charge.

Belton

BELL COUNTY MUSEUM, (M), 201 N. Main St., Belton, TX 76513-3160. Mailing Address: P.O. Box 1381, Belton, TX 76513-5381. Tel.: 254-933-5243. Fax: 254-933-5756.
E-mail: museum@co.bell.tx.us
Web Site: www.bellcountymuseum.org
Founded: 1975.
Congressional District: 11
Key Personnel: Dir., Stephanie Turnham; Chm., Jeannette Kelley; Cur., Cynthia Evans.
Personnel Profile: Full-Time Paid 4; Full-Time Volunteers 1; Part-Time Volunteers 30; Interns 2.
Governing Authority: county. Parent Institution: Bell County. Subsidiary Institution: Bell County Museum Association, Inc. Tax-exempt: 170(b)(1)(A).
History Museum: housed in c.1904 Carnegie Library Building.
Collections: local history items; Governor Miriam A. (Ma) Ferguson collection.
Major Exhibits: Meet The Fergusons, 11/09-3/3/10; 1968 in America, 4/6/10-5/25/10.

Research Fields: Bell County & central Texas regional history.
Facilities: 3,000 sq. ft. exhibit space.
Activities: theater; organized educational programs; tours.
Publications: bimonthly newsletter.
Hours & Admission Prices: Tues.-Sat. 12-5. No charge; donations accepted. ♿
Attendance: 7,500 (estimated)
Membership: Friend $25; Family $50; Patron $100; Partner $250; Benefactor $500; Associate $1,000 & up.

Benjamin

WICHITA - BRAZOS MUSEUM & CULTURAL CENTER, 200 E. Hayes St., Benjamin, TX 79505. Mailing Address: Box 104, Benjamin, TX 79505-0104. Tel.: 940-459-2229. Fax: 940-459-2229.
E-mail: kchc@srcaccess.net
Web Site: www.knoxcountytexas.com
Formerly: Knox County Museum
Founded: 1966.
Congressional District: 13
Key Personnel: C.E.O. & Chm. (V), Mary Jane Young; Experienced Works, Rosa Laverne Whisenhunt; Experienced Works, F. Janette Kilgore.
Personnel Profile: Part-Time Volunteers 26.
Governing Authority: county; nonprofit. Parent Institution: Friends of Knox County Historical Commission. Tax-exempt.
History Museum.
Collections: photographs & books relating to life in Knox County from prehistoric period to early 20th-century; pioneer artifacts; Civil War items; family histories; Knox County Veterans Memorial listing over 2,000 area veterans.
Research Fields: Knox County & region prehistoric to present, emphasis on 1860-1945; family history file; the great southern buffalo herd hunt of 1870s.
Publications: survey of cemetery; compiling genealogical history of Knox County families 1800-present; book, Knox County Historical Cookbook; Knox County annual calendar.
Hours & Admission Prices: Tues.-Fri. 8-5. No charge; donations accepted. Closed legal holidays. ♿
Attendance: 500 (estimated)

Big Bend National Park

BIG BEND NATIONAL PARK, Science and Resource Management Center, 266 Tecolote Dr., Big Bend National Park, TX 79834. Mailing Address: Science and Resource Management Center, P.O. Box 129, Big Bend National Park, TX 79834-0129. Tel.: 432-477-1151. Fax: 432-477-1153.
E-mail: kate_hogue@nps.gov
Web Site: www.nps.gov/bibe
Founded: 1950.
Congressional District: 21
Key Personnel: Cur., Kate Hogue; Chief, Science & Resource Management, Phil Wilson.
Personnel Profile: Part-Time Paid 1.
Governing Authority: federal. Parent Institution: U.S. Dept. of the Interior, National Park Service. Tax-exempt.
National Park Visitor Centers.
Collections: herbarium; insects; herpetology; archaeological; historical; paleontological; geological; period photographs; archives.
Research Fields: biological; archaeological; archives.
Facilities: 1,500-vol. library of books about local, human & natural history available for use on premises; archives. Books, slides & posters for sale.
Activities: guided tours; formally organized education programs; illustrated programs.
Publications: orientation brochures; park brochures; site bulletins; park newspaper.
Hours & Admission Prices: Daily 8-5. Annual Pass $40; autos $20 per week; bicycles, motorcycles & bus passengers $10 per week; Golden Age Passports: U.S. citizens 62 & over $10. ♿
Attendance: 360,000 (accurate)
Membership: Big Bend Natural History Association: Regular $25; Associate $50; Life $250; Corporate $500; Benefactor $1,000.

Big Spring

HANGAR 25 AIR MUSEUM, (M), 1911 Apron Dr., Big Spring, TX 79720-7807. Mailing Address: P.O. Box 2925, Big Spring, TX 79721-2925. Tel.: 432-264-1999. Fax: 432-466-0316.
E-mail: hangar25@crcom.net
Web Site: www.hangar25airmuseum.com
Founded: 1999.
Key Personnel: Pres. Bd., Emma Bogard; Admin., Meghan Fernandez Bias.
Governing Authority: Tax-exempt: 501(c)(3).
Military History Museum.
Collections: military aviation history; aircraft; uniforms; photographs; newspapers.
Facilities: 14,000 sq. ft. exhibit space.
Activities: research.
Publications: newsletter.
Hours & Admission Prices: Tues.-Fri. 8-4, Sat. 9-3. No charge; donations accepted. ♿
Attendance: 3,500 (estimated)
Membership: Student $15; Individual $30; Family $60; Sponsor $100; Supporting $250; Patron $500; Founder $1,000.

HERITAGE MUSEUM & POTTON HOUSE, 510 Scurry, Big Spring, TX 79720-2736. Tel.: 432-267-8255. Fax: 432-267-9998 (call first).
E-mail: heritagemus@gmail.com
Web Site: www.bigspringmuseum.com
Founded: 1971.
Congressional District: 17
Key Personnel: Pres., Katie Cathey; Dir., Nancy Raney; Cur., Tammy Schrecengost.
Personnel Profile: Full-Time Paid 3; Full-Time Volunteers 23; Part-Time Paid 3; Part-Time Volunteers 4.
Governing Authority: nonprofit. Subsidiary Institution: Potton House. Tax-exempt.
Historic Museum.
Collections: paintings by Harvey W. Caylor; early artifacts of the area; pioneer settlement; cattle industry railroad; ranching, farm & industry items; photographs; clothing; prehistoric cultures; architecture.
Research Fields: local & county history.
Facilities: 150-vol. library of local & ranching history available to the public.
Activities: guided tours; films; docent program; school loan service; lectures; historical & modern slideshow with sound tape narration; gallery talks; formally organized educational programs; temporary & traveling exhibitions.
Publications: quarterly newsletter; books, Howard County Historian; Gettin' Started: Howard County's First 25 Years; H.W. Caylor: Frontier Artist; Howard County In The Making.
Hours & Admission Prices: Tues.-Fri. 8:30-4, Sat. 10-4. Adults $2, students & seniors $1; members no charge. Closed national holidays. ♿
Attendance: 15,000 (accurate)
Membership: Individual $15; Sustaining $20; Sponsor $30; Patron $50; Endowment $100; Benefactor $500.

Boerne

AGRICULTURAL HERITAGE MUSEUM, 102 City Park Rd., Boerne, TX 78006. Mailing Address: P.O. Box 1076, Boerne, TX 78006-1076. Tel.: 830-249-6007. Fax: 269-857-2464.
E-mail: info@agmuseum.org
Web Site: www.agmuseum.org
Founded: 1986.
Congressional District: 21
Key Personnel: Dir. & Pres., Craig Davis; Vice Pres., Paul Thomas; Treas., John Barteau.
Personnel Profile: Full-Time Volunteers 12; Part-Time Volunteers 45.
Governing Authority: nonprofit. Tax-exempt: 501(c)(3).
Agriculture Museum.
Collections: articles relating to outdoor ranching and farming life in Texas Hill country & south Texas; steam-powered blacksmith shop; woodworking shop.
Facilities: 20-vol. library of agricultural material available to the public; 5 acres of exhibit space.
Activities: guided tours; organized education programs for children; traveling exhibitions. Museum Sponsors: Antique Tractor Show; Chuckwagon Cookoff; Fall Festival.
Publications: biannual newsletter.
Hours & Admission Prices: late Jan. to late Nov. Sat. 10-4; other times by appointment. No charge; donations accepted. Closed major holidays. ♿
Attendance: 4,000 (estimated)

KUHLMANN KING HISTORICAL HOUSE AND MUSEUM, 402 E. Blanco, Boerne, TX 78006-2008. Mailing Address: P.O. Box 178, Boerne, TX 78006-0178. Tel.: 830-249-7277.
Web Site: www.nootsweb.com/~txkendal
Formerly: Boerne Area Historical Preservation Society
Founded: 1970.
Congressional District: 21
Key Personnel: Pres., Colonel Bettie Edmonds; Chm. & Vice Pres., Emmeline Whitworth; Treas., Louise Davis.
Personnel Profile: Part-Time Volunteers 20.

Governing Authority: nonprofit organization. Parent Institution: City of Boerne. Tax-exempt.
Historic House: c.1880, Kuhlmann-King Family Home. Historical Landmark.
Collections: telephone operator's switchboard; period telephones; Ad Toepperwein sharp shooter; early Ebensberger Mortuary tools; Boerne Village Band (1860-2007); family photographs & histories; pioneer kitchen; 1614 Low German bible; historic structures.
Research Fields: family history; Boerne area & Kendall County History.
Facilities: Museum-related items for sale.
Activities: tours; Dickens on Main; permanent & temporary exhibits.
Publications: books, Gone But Not Forgotten; Vols. I & II; Cemetery Surveys; Kuhlman-King House Museum & Archives; self-guided tour of Boerne Cemetery; Journey to Boerne.
Hours & Admission Prices: Appointment only. No charge; donations accepted. ♿
Attendance: 1,500 (estimated)
Membership: Individual $15; Couple $20; Booster $50; Support $100; Business $250.

Bonham

FANNIN COUNTY MUSEUM OF HISTORY, 1 N. Main St., Bonham, TX 75418-4345. Tel.: 903-583-8042 & 5558.
History Museum: housed in the former Texas and Pacific Railway Depot; c.1900. Listed on the National Register of Historic Places.
Collections: local history & culture; railroad memorabilia & artifacts; fossils; Native American artifacts; period clothing; telephone switchboard; personal artifacts; photographs.
Hours & Admission Prices: April-Sept. 1 Tues.-Sat. 10-4; Sept. 2-March Tues.-Sat. 12-4. No charge; donations accepted.

FORT INGLISH, Hwy. 56 & Chinner St., Bonham, TX 75418. Mailing Address: P.O. Box 395, Bonham, TX 75418-0395. Tel.: 903-583-3943.
Founded: 1976.
Congressional District: 4
Key Personnel: Pres. (V), Wayne Moore; Chm. (V), Tom Thornton; Museum Shop Mgr., Mildred Welch.
Personnel Profile: Full-Time Volunteers 1; Part-Time Volunteers 20.
Governing Authority: private; nonprofit. Tax-exempt: 501(c)(3).
History Museum: housed in a replica of log fort used as protection against Indians, 1837-1843.
Collections: concentration on northeast Texas history, 1837-1850; period artifacts & furniture. Historic Buildings: blacksmith shop; general store; one-room cabin; school & church; 1830s log cabin.
Facilities: educational facilities; 1,800 sq. ft. exhibit space. Museum-related items for sale.
Activities: volunteers (tour available by appointment only): dress in period attire; recite the history of Northeast Texas; perform daily chores & crafts of frontier life; informal education programs for children; self-guided & guided tours; lye soap made on premises.
Publications: annual newsletter, Fort Inglish Courier.
Hours & Admission Prices: April-Sept. 1 Tues.-Sat. 10-4; groups by appointment. No charge; donations accepted. ♿
Attendance: 3,500 (accurate)
Membership: Single $20; Family $25; Benefactor $26-$249; Life $250.

SAM RAYBURN HOUSE MUSEUM, 890 W. Hwy. 56, Bonham, TX 75418. Mailing Address: P.O. Box 308, Bonham, TX 75418-0308. Tel.: 903-583-5558. Fax: 903-640-0800.
Web Site: www.thc.state.tx.us/samrayhouse/srhoefault.html
Founded: 1975.
Congressional District: 4
Key Personnel: Dir., Carole Stanton; Cur., Anne Carlson.
Personnel Profile: Full-Time Paid 4; Part-Time Volunteers 2.
Governing Authority: state. Operated by the Texas Historical Commission, P.O. Box 12276, Austin, TX. 78711. Tax-exempt.
Historic House: 1916 two-story frame farmhouse with Colonial Revival facade, built by Sam Rayburn.
Collections: personal belongings & household furnishings of Sam Rayburn; vehicles owned by Sam Rayburn.
Research Fields: U.S. Government, particularly the office of the Speaker of the House of Representatives; local history; the functioning of the U.S. Congress & the electoral process; history of Sam Rayburn.
Facilities: Books & gifts for sale.
Activities: guided tours; lectures; community workshops; docent program.
Publications: quarterly newsletter.
Hours & Admission Prices: Tues.-Sun. 9-5. Adults $3, students $2, seniors 65 & over $1; discounts to groups of 8 or more. Closed federal & state holidays. ♿
Attendance: 7,500 (accurate)
Membership: Adult $10; Family $20; Corporate $50; Contributor $100; Patron $500; Founder $1,000.

THE SAM RAYBURN LIBRARY AND MUSEUM, A DIVISION OF THE DOLPH BRISCOE CENTER FOR AMERICAN HISTORY, 800 W. Sam Rayburn Dr., Bonham, TX 75418-4103. Mailing Address: P.O. Box 309, Bonham, TX 75418-0309. Tel.: 903-583-2455. Fax: 903-583-7394.
Web Site: www.cah.utexas.edu
Founded: 1957.
Congressional District: 4
Key Personnel: Assoc. Dir., Dr. Patrick Cox; Consultant & Dir. Emeritus, H.G. Dulaney.
Personnel Profile: Full-Time Paid 2.
Governing Authority: board of trustees. Affiliated with the University of Texas at Austin. Tax-exempt: 501(c)(3).
Research Library.
Collections: paintings; memorabilia; Sam Rayburn's personal papers on microfilm; American history & government books; reproduction of seals; replica of Speaker's official office in the Capitol Building with original furniture.
Research Fields: history & government.
Facilities: library & reading room; film room.
Activities: guided tours; films.
Publications: newsletter; book, Speak, Mr. Speaker; cartoon book, Impressions of Mr. Sam: A Cartoon Profile.
Hours & Admission Prices: Mon.-Fri. 9-5, Sat. 1-5. No charge. Closed all major holidays. ♿
Attendance: 10,000

Borger

HUTCHINSON COUNTY MUSEUM, (M), 618 N. Main, Borger, TX 79007-3529. Tel.: 806-273-0130. Fax: 806-273-0128.
E-mail: hcmuseum@cableone.net
Web Site: www.hutchinsoncountymuseum.org
Founded: 1977.
Congressional District: 18
Key Personnel: Museum Dir., Edward Benz; Chm., Randy Hatfield; Administrative Asst., Lynn Hopkins; Museum Shop Mgr., Judy Mihm.
Personnel Profile: Full-Time Paid 3; Full-Time Volunteers 25; Part-Time Paid 2; Part-Time Volunteers 25.
Governing Authority: county. Parent Institution: Hutchinson County Historical Commission. Tax-exempt.
History Museum: housed in 1927 Grand Hardware, early store, located in 1926 Oil Boom Town.
Collections: local history of the county from prehistoric times to the present, emphasizing the Oil Boom of 1926 & adobe walls, 1874. Artifacts from the oil industry.
Research Fields: early history of the county.
Facilities: archive; library; reading room.
Activities: guided tours; lectures; films; formally organized educational programs; permanent exhibitions.
Publications: book, Hutchinson County History; Hutchinson County Museum: 1977-1997; Hutchinson County, A Pictorial Legacy, 2003.
Hours & Admission Prices: Memorial Day-Labor Day Mon.-Fri. 9-5, Sat. 11-4:30. No charge; donations accepted. Closed Easter; Thanksgiving; Christmas & legal holidays. ♿
Attendance: 6,189 (accurate)

Breckenridge

SWENSON MEMORIAL MUSEUM OF STEPHENS COUNTY, 116 W. Walker, Breckenridge, TX 76424-3530. Mailing Address: P.O. Box 350, Breckenridge, TX 76424-0350. Tel.: 254-559-8471.
Founded: 1970.
Congressional District: 17
Key Personnel: Dir. & Exhibits, Freda Mitchell; Business Officer, David Duggan; Sec., Margaret Ables; Chm. Bd., Burrell McKelvain.
Personnel Profile: Full-Time Paid 1; Part-Time Paid 2; Part-Time Volunteers 2.
Governing Authority: nonprofit organization. Subsidiary Institution: J.D. Sandefer Oil Annex. Tax-exempt: 501(c)(3).
History Museum: housed in 1920 bank building.
Collections: farming; business; ranching; furniture & furnishings; oil equipment; photographs & memorabilia of oil boom times in county; J.D. Sandefer Oil Annex; school, doctor & lawyers offices.
Research Fields: petroleum history of North Central Texas.
Facilities: 300-vol. library of history & museum-related material available for research; reading room.
Activities: guided tours; lectures; gallery talks; school loan service; temporary & permanent exhibitions.
Publications: brochures.

Hours & Admission Prices: Tues.-Sat. 10-12, 1-5. No charge: donations accepted. Closed Independence Day; Thanksgiving; Christmas. ♿
Attendance: 1,200 (accurate)

Brenham

TEXAS BAPTIST HISTORICAL CENTER MUSEUM, 10405 FM 50, Brenham, TX 77833-6424.
Founded: 1965.
Congressional District: 14
Key Personnel: Dir. & Cur., D.H. Strickland.
Personnel Profile: Full-Time Paid 1; Part-Time Volunteers 1.
Governing Authority: church. Parent Institution: Baptist General Convention of Texas, 333 N. Washington, Dallas, TX 75246-1798. Tax-exempt: 170(b)(1)(A).
History Museum: housed in 1839 church, the original home of Baylor University.
Collections: artifacts of Sam Houston & family; items from Baylor University; furniture; church artifacts; manuscripts.
Research Fields: local early Texas history.
Facilities: 200-vol. library of books on early Texas & Texas Baptist history available for loan on premises; reading room.
Activities: guided tours; lectures; films; temporary exhibits.
Publications: brochures.
Hours & Admission Prices: Tues.-Sat. 9-4. No charge; donations accepted. Closed New Year's Day; Easter; Independence Day; Christmas. ♿
Attendance: 10,000

Brooks Air Force Base

EDWARD H. WHITE II MEMORIAL MUSEUM, 311 ABG/MU, 8008 Inner Circle Dr., Brooks Air Force Base, TX 78235-5329. Tel.: 210-536-2203. Fax: 210-536-3224.
E-mail: museum@platinum.brooks.af.mil
Web Site: www.brooks.af.mil/ABG/mh/general/html
Founded: 1966.
Congressional District: 23
Key Personnel: Dir., Lt. Col. Ulysses S. Rhodes, Jr.; Museum Shop Mgr., Mrs. Shelia Klein.
Personnel Profile: Full-Time Paid 1; Part-Time Volunteers 2.
Governing Authority: federal. Parent Institution: U.S. Air Force; Air Force Museum/CCC Wright-Patterson AFB, OH. 45433. Tax-exempt.
Aeronautics and Space Medicine Museum: housed in 1918 Hangar 9, only remaining World War I hangar in the U.S.; USAF Aero-Medical Evacuation Annex building.
Collections: aviation medical training devices & artifacts; flight nursing & air evacuation artifacts & memorabilia; space material dealing with the development of manned space flight.
Research Fields: aviation; aviation & space medicine.
Facilities: hangar; USAF Aeromedical EVAC annex building.
Activities: guided tours; lectures.
Publications: book, 75 Years of Brooks AFB, 1917-1992.
Hours & Admission Prices: Mon.-Fri. 8-3. No charge. Closed major holidays. ♿
Attendance: 16,000 (estimated)
Membership: Brooks Heritage Foundation: International, Armed Services & Associate $10; Member $25; Sponsor $50; Patron $100; Corporate & Founder $250.

Brownsville

BROWNSVILLE MUSEUM OF FINE ART, (M), 660 E. Ringgold St., Brownsville, TX 78520. Tel.: 956-542-0941. Fax: 956-542-6931.
Web Site: www.brownsvillemfa.org
Formerly: Brownsville Art League
Founded: 1935.
Congressional District: 27
Key Personnel: Exec. Dir., Barry T. Horn; Pres. (V), Eddie Knebel; Administrative Dir. & Show Dir., Tencha Sloss; Cur., Jennifer Cahn, Ph.D.; Accountant, Deyanira Ramirez; Education Coord., Linda W. Marin.
Personnel Profile: Full-Time Paid 5; Part-Time Paid 2; Part-Time Volunteers 30; Interns 2.
Governing Authority: nonprofit organization. Tax-exempt: 501(c)(3).
Art Museum.
Collections: fine art including oil paintings; watercolors; collages; prints; sculpture; acrylics; pastels; pencil.
Research Fields: late 19th-20th Century south Texas & north Mexico artists.
Facilities: library; reading room; classrooms; kitchen; rental facility.
Activities: lectures; gallery talks; arts festivals; workshops; formally organized education programs for adults; inter-museum, permanent, temporary & traveling exhibitions.
Hours & Admission Prices: Tues. & Thurs.-Sat. 10-4, Wed. 10-8. Adults $5, children 6-12, students, & seniors over 65 $3; discounts to groups; members, Wed. after 5pm and children under 6 no charge. Closed New Year's Day; Good Friday; Easter; Memorial Day; Independence Day; Veterans Day; Thanksgiving; Christmas. ♿
Attendance: 16,000 (accurate)
Membership: Seasonal, Student, & Friends $60; Family $75; Active $120; Family Active $150.

GLADYS PORTER ZOO, 500 Ringgold St., Brownsville, TX 78520-7998. Tel.: 956-546-7187 & 2177. Fax: 956-541-4940.
E-mail: admin@gpz.org
Web Site: www.gpz.org
Founded: 1971.
Congressional District: 27
Key Personnel: C.E.O., Dr. Don D. Farst; Deputy Dir., Dr. Patrick M. Burchfield; Chm. (V), Mary Lou Ryan Ray; Comptroller, Oralia Berlanga; Gen. Cur., Greeley A. Stones; Veterinarian, Thomas W. DeMaar, DVM; Dir. Public Rels. & Mktg., Cynthia Garza Galvan; Sales Shop Mgr., Debbie Kerr.
Personnel Profile: Full-Time Paid 84; Part-Time Paid 45; Part-Time Volunteers 70; Interns 4.
Governing Authority: nonprofit organization. Parent Institution: Valley Zoological Society. Tax-exempt: 501(c)(3).
Botanical Gardens & Zoo with Aquarium.
Collections: 345 animal species & 1,557 animal specimens; 150 plant species & over 2,000 specimens.
Research Fields: animal health; reproduction & behavior.
Facilities: 900-vol. library of zoology, ecology, botany, veterinary medicine, available for research on premises; botanical garden; aquarium; classrooms; snack shops. Museum-related items for sale.
Activities: guided tours; lectures; TV & radio programs; formally organized educational program; docent program or council.
Publications: newsletter, Gladys Porter Zoo News.
Hours & Admission Prices: Summer: Mon.-Fri. 9-6, Sat.-Sun. 9-6:30; Winter: daily 9-5. Adults $9, seniors 65 & over $7.50, children 2-13 $6; discounts to groups of 10 or more, AARP & AZA members; members no charge. ♿
Attendance: 344,154 (accurate)
Membership: Individual $35; Individual Plus $50; Family $55; Family Plus $70; Supporting $200; Sustaining $500; Patron $1,000; Life $5,000.

Brownwood

MARTIN & FRANCES LEHNIS RAILROAD MUSEUM, (M), 700 E. Adams, Brownwood, TX 76801-7002. Mailing Address: P.O. Box 1389, Brownwood, TX 76804-1389. Tel.: 325-643-6376.
E-mail: mirving@ci.brownwood.tx.us
Web Site: www.ci.brownwood.tx.us/lrm
Founded: 2007.
Key Personnel: Dir., Mary Lynn Irving; Chm. (V) & Pres. (V), Jack Lamkin; Museum Shop Mgr., Joan Lamkin.
Personnel Profile: Full-Time Paid 1; Full-Time Volunteers 1; Part-Time Paid 1; Part-Time Volunteers 2.
Governing Authority: city. Tax-exempt.
Transportation Museum.
Collections: railroad history; railcars; railway china; lanterns; photographs.
Hours & Admission Prices: Tues.-Sat. 10-4. Adults $3, seniors $2.50, children 5 & over $2; discounts to members, AAM & ICOM members, TAM, senior citizens, & active military. Closed holidays. ♿
Attendance: 3,500 (accurate)
Membership: $25; $50; $100; $250; $500; $1,000.

Bryan

BRAZOS VALLEY MUSEUM OF NATURAL HISTORY, 3232 Briarcrest Dr., Bryan, TX 77802-3015. Tel.: 979-776-2195. Fax: 979-774-0252.
E-mail: dcowman@brazosvalleymuseum.org
Web Site: www.brazosvalleymuseum.org
Founded: 1961.
Congressional District: 8
Key Personnel: Exec. Dir., Dr. Deborah F. Cowman; Pres. Bd. Trustees, Jacque Flagg; Education Coord., Assoc. Dir. & Museum Shop Mgr., Maria Lazo; Cur. Collections & Exhibits, Elisabeth Manning.
Personnel Profile: Full-Time Paid 3; Part-Time Paid 3; Part-Time Volunteers 40; Interns 6.
Governing Authority: nonprofit organization. Tax-exempt: 501(c)(3).
Natural History Museum.
Collections: paleontology, vertebrate & invertebrate; anthropology; archaeology; geology & mineralogy; mammalogy; ornithology; paleobotany; botany; entomology; Gulf Coast & Caribbean malacology; local history; cultural history.

Research Fields: archaeology; history.
Facilities: library; discovery room; nature lab; classrooms; nature trail; live animal & insect observatory; gem & mineral room; wildflower garden; prehistoric lithic industries of Texas; Wildscape with demonstration wetlands, yaupon thicket, prairie & post oak Savanna; local history exhibits. Museum-related items for sale.
Activities: guided tours of current major exhibits & discovery room; lectures; formally organized education programs; permanent & temporary exhibitions; school loan service; discovery kits; summer nature camp; cultural & environmental tours; cooperative agreements with Department of Anthropology, History Department, and Texas Cooperative Wildlife Collections (Wildlife & Fisheries Science, Texas A & M University).
Publications: biannual newsletter.
Hours & Admission Prices: Mon.-Sat. 10-5. Adults $5, seniors & students $4; members and children 3 & under accompanied by parent no charge. Prices and hours change with major exhibits. Closed New Year's Day; Easter; Memorial Day; Thanksgiving; Christmas. ♿
Attendance: 30,000 (estimated)
Membership: College Student & Seniors Citizen $30; Individual $50; Dual $75; Family $100; Sponsor $150; Contributor $250; Benefactor $500; President's Circle $1,000.

THE CHILDREN'S MUSEUM OF THE BRAZOS VALLEY, 111 E. 27th St., Bryan, TX 77803-6947. Tel.: 979-779-5437. Fax: 979-775-4908.
Web Site: www.mymuseum.com
Key Personnel: Pres., Dave Stevenson; Dir. Devel., Rebecca Christopher
Children's Museum.
Collections: hands-on interactive exhibits.
Facilities: Museum-related items for sale.
Activities: parties; school programs; festivals.
Hours & Admission Prices: Mon.-Sat. 10-5. Adults & children $4, senior citizens $3; children under one no charge. Parking: no charge.

Buffalo Gap

BUFFALO GAP HISTORIC VILLAGE, 133 N. William, Buffalo Gap, TX 79508. Mailing Address: P.O. Box 818, Buffalo Gap, TX 79508-0818. Tel.: 325-572-3365.
Founded: 1956.
Living History Museum.
Collections: history & heritage of the Texas frontier; period artifacts; personal artifacts.
Facilities: Museum-related items for sale.
Activities: special events; demonstrations; rental facilities.
Hours & Admission Prices: Memorial Day to Labor Day Mon.-Sat. 10-6, Sun. 12-6. Adults $7, seniors & military $6, students $4; discount to AAA & AAM members & tour groups; members & children under 5 no charge. Closed New Year's Day; Thanksgiving; Christmas.
Attendance: 15,000 (accurate)
Membership: Family $35.

Burnet

FORT CROGHAN MUSEUM, 703 Buchanan Dr., Burnet, TX 78611. Mailing Address: P.O. Box 74, Burnet, TX 78611-0074. Tel.: 512-756-8281.
E-mail: info@fortcroghan.org
Web Site: www.fortcroghan.org
Founded: 1957.
Key Personnel: Chm. (V), Paul Shell; Museum Dir., Mildred Williams.
Personnel Profile: Part-Time Paid 1; Part-Time Volunteers 20.
Governing Authority: Parent Institution: Burnet County Heritage Society. Tax-exempt.
History Museum: located on the site of 1849 Fort Croghan.
Collections: stone & log cabins from the 1850s & 1860s; Old Fort building; blacksmith's shop; 5 pioneer cabins; farm implements; historic displays.
Research Fields: county & regional history.
Activities: Museum Sponsors: Annual Fort Croghan Day 2nd Saturday in October; Christmas at Fort Croghan 2nd Saturday in December.
Publications: leaflets, History of Fort Croghan & Museum; Burnet County Cemetery Records; Burnet County History, vols. I & II.
Hours & Admission Prices: April-Aug. Thurs.-Sat. 10-5. No charge; donations requested. ♿
Attendance: 2,000 (estimated)
Membership: Annual $5.

Burton

BURTON COTTON GIN & MUSEUM, (M), 307 N. Main, Burton, TX 77835. Mailing Address: P.O. Box 98, Burton, TX 77835-0098. Tel.: 979-289-3378.
Founded: 1989.
Key Personnel: Dir., Linda Russell; Chm. (V), Steve Finn.
Personnel Profile: Full-Time Paid 2; Part-Time Volunteers 15.
History Museum.
Collections: operational cotton gin; local history & culture; machines; tools; engines; vehicles.
Activities: guided tours.
Hours & Admission Prices: Museum: Tues.-Sat. 10-4. Gin Tours: Tues.-Sat. 10 & 2. Museum: No charge. Gin Tours: adults $6, students 8-18 $4; discounts to groups of 10 or more, AAM & ICOM members. Closed major holidays. ♿

Caldwell

BURLESON COUNTY HISTORICAL MUSEUM, Burleson County Courthouse, Caldwell, TX 77836. Mailing Address: P.O. Box 127, Caldwell, TX 77836-0127. Tel.: 979-567-7196.
E-mail: burlesoncohissoc@aol.com
Founded: 1968.
Congressional District: 10
Key Personnel: Chm. Burleson County Historical Commission, Tammy Kubecka.
Governing Authority: county. Parent Institution: Burleson County. Tax-exempt.
Local History Museum.
Collections: Fort Tenoxtitlan artifacts; photographs; manuscript collections; country store exhibit; early settler's artifacts; Indian artifacts; exhibits on plantation days & ranching in Burleson County; antique toys & children's furniture; c.1860-1890s.
Research Fields: history of Burleson County & its relation to Texas history.
Activities: guided tours; permanent & temporary exhibitions. Annual Events: Heritage Week in March; Archaeology Awareness Week in October.
Publications: facsimile reprint, Reminiscences of Burleson County, Texas; book, Treasured Recipes of Burleson County; book, Astride the Old San Antonio Road, A History of Burleson county.
Hours & Admission Prices: Fri. 2-4:30; other times by appointment. No charge; donations accepted. ♿

Cameron

MILAM COUNTY HISTORICAL MUSEUM & ANNEX, 201 E. Main, Cameron, TX 76520-4275. Mailing Address: P.O. Box 966, Cameron, TX 76520-0966. Tel.: 254-697-4770 & 8963. Fax: 254-697-4770.
E-mail: milamco@vvm.com
Web Site: cameron-tx.com
Founded: 1977.
Congressional District: 11
Key Personnel: Pres., Barbara Hajovsky; Vice Pres., Margia Barkemeyer; Dir., Charles King.
Personnel Profile: Full-Time Paid 1.
Governing Authority: nonprofit organization. Annex: 102 E. Main, Cameron, TX 76520. Tax-exempt. 501(c)(3).
History Museum: housed in 1895 Milam County Jail & Annex Building.
Collections: original Sam Houston & Benjamin Bryant documents; Civil War letters & documents; Spanish mission artifacts; WWI & II artifacts; clothing; household items; guns; dolls; farm tools; furniture; photographs; handcrafts.
Activities: guided tours; permanent & temporary loan exhibits.
Publications: The Milam County Courthouse; And then Came the People; Milam County - Birthplace of a Region; Spanish Missions of Milan County; Matchless Milam.
Hours & Admission Prices: Tues.-Sat. annex 8-12, jail 1-5. No charge; donations accepted. ♿
Attendance: 4,500 (estimated)
Membership: Basic $30; Supporter $40; Active & Institutional $50; Participating $100; Sustaining & Corporate $200.

Canadian

RIVER VALLEY PIONEER MUSEUM, 118 N. 2nd St., Canadian, TX 79014-2202. Mailing Address: P.O. Box 1201, Canadian, TX 79014-1201. Tel.: 806-323-6548. Fax: 806-232-8993.
History Museum.
Collections: local history & culture; photographs; Native American artifacts; archaeological; ranching.
Facilities: Museum-related items for sale.
Activities: rental facilities; educational programs.
Hours & Admission Prices: Tues.-Fri. 9-12 & 1-4, Sun. 2-4. No charge; donations accepted. ♿

Canyon

* **PANHANDLE-PLAINS HISTORICAL MUSEUM, (M),** 2503 Fourth Ave., Canyon, TX 79015-4183. Mailing Address: WTAMU, Box 60967, Canyon, TX 79016-0001. Tel.: 806-651-2244. Fax: 806-651-2250.
E-mail: museum@pphm.wtamu.edu
Web Site: www.panhandleplains.org
Founded: 1921.
Congressional District: 13
Key Personnel: Dir., Guy C. Vanderpool; Auxiliary Chm., Jane Stephens; Pres. (V), Alice Hyde; Conservation Center Dir., Richard Trela; Dir. Mktg., Linda Moreland; Cur. Art, Michael R. Grauer; Dir. Education, Mary Ann Ruelas; Asst. Archaeologist, Rolla Shaller; Cur. History, Dr. William E. Green; Asst. History Cur., Susan Denney; Cur. Archaeology, Dr. Jeff Indeck; Asst. Archivist & Librarian, Betty Bustos; Exhibits Supervisor, Kenny Schneider; Registrar, Mary Moore; Programs Coord., Amy David; Museum Shop Mgr., Tammy St. Pierre.
Personnel Profile: Full-Time Paid 27; Part-Time Paid 24; Part-Time Volunteers 10.
Governing Authority: state. Parent Institution: West Texas A&M University. Subsidiary Institution: Panhandle Plains Historical Society. Tax-exempt: 501(c)(3) & 170(b)(1)(A).
History Museum.
Collections: geology; Plains Indian ethnology; paleontology; manuscripts; 150,000 photographs; transportation; anthropology; archaeology; cattle industry; pioneer life; agriculture; art; clothing and textiles; firearms; science & technology; furniture; restored T-Anchor Ranch.
Research Fields: general Texas & Southwestern History; ranching history, westward expansion; history of windmills; Southwest Indians.
Facilities: 10,000-vol. library & archive on history of Texas & the Southwest. Museum-related items for sale.
Activities: guided tours; lectures; educational programs for schools; regional museum clinics; permanent & temporary exhibits.
Publications: journal, Panhandle-Plains Historical Review; newsletter, PPHM News.
Hours & Admission Prices: Summer: Mon.-Sat. 9-6; Winter: Mon.-Sat. 9-5, Sun. 1-6. Adults $10, senior citizens 65 & over $9, children 4-12 $5; discounts to groups; members & children under 4 no charge. Closed New Year's Day; Thanksgiving; Christmas Eve & Day. ♿
Attendance: 75,000 (estimated)
Membership: Friend $50; Family $75; Contributor $100; Supporter $250; Patron $500; Goodnight Circle $1,000.

Carrollton

A. W. PERRY HOMESTEAD MUSEUM, 1509 N. Perry Rd., Carrollton, TX 75006-6122. Mailing Address: P.O. Box 110535, Carrollton, TX 75011-0535. Tel.: 972-466-6380.
Web Site: cityofcarrollton.com/museum
Founded: 1976.
Key Personnel: Dir., Toyia Pointer.
Personnel Profile: Full-Time Paid 1; Part-Time Paid 1; Part-Time Volunteers 6.
Governing Authority: city. Tax-exempt.
Historic House: housed in the former home of A.W. Perry; built in 1857, rebuilt in 1909 by his son using some of the lumber from the original house.
Collections: Perry family history & culture; early pioneer life; period artifacts & furnishings; photographs.
Activities: group tours; rental facilities; special events; research; birthday parties; classes. Annual Events: Silent Film Series; Mother's Day Concert; Old Fashioned Christmas.
Publications: newsletter, The Homestead.
Hours & Admission Prices: Wed.-Sat. 10-12 & 1-5. No charge. ♿
Attendance: 2,900 (estimated)

Center

SHELBY COUNTY MUSEUM, 230 Pecan St., Center, TX 75935-3649. Mailing Address: P.O. Box 1542, Center, TX 75935-1542. Tel.: 936-598-3613.
E-mail: shelbymuseum@sbcglobal.net
Web Site: www.shelbycountytexashistory.org
Governing Authority: Parent Institution: Shelby County Historical Society. Tax-exempt: 501(c)(3).
History Museum: housed in c.1900 Weaver-Oates House built by E.H. Barron.
Collections: personal artifacts; period furnishings; photographs.
Facilities: library.
Activities: research.
Hours & Admission Prices: Mon.-Fri. 12-4; other times by appointment. No charge; donations accepted.

Chappell Hill

CHAPPELL HILL HISTORICAL SOCIETY MUSEUM, (M), 9220 Poplar St., Chappell Hill, TX 77426-6312. Tel.: 979-836-6033. Fax: 979-836-7438.
E-mail: chmuseum@chappellhillmuseum.org
Web Site: www.chappellhillmuseum.org
Founded: 1964.
Congressional District: 14
Key Personnel: Administrative Dir., Ladonna Vest.
Personnel Profile: Part-Time Paid 1; Part-Time Volunteers 35.
Governing Authority: society; nonprofit. Parent Institution: Chappell Hill Historical Society. Tax-exempt.
General Museum.
Collections: confederate, early Texas history of Chappell Hill; archives; farm implements; documents of early families; early carpenters tools; Johnnie Swearingen folk art; photographs.
Research Fields: local history; genealogy.
Facilities: 150-seat auditorium; 3,200 sq. ft. exhibit space.
Activities: guided tours; permanent exhibitions; special exhibits. Annual Events: Bluebonnet Festival in Spring; Scarecrow Festival in Fall.
Publications: monthly newsletter; annual, Chappell Hill Historical Review.
Hours & Admission Prices: Wed.-Sat. 10-4, Sun. 1-4. Scheduled Tours: groups $2 person with $30 minimum. Closed New Year's Eve & Day; Independence Day; Thanksgiving; Christmas Eve & Day. ♿
Attendance: 3,500 (accurate)
Membership: Society: Individual $20; Family $30; Patron & Patron Business $50; Sustaining & Sustaining Business $100; Life $500.

Childress

CHILDRESS COUNTY HERITAGE MUSEUM, 210 3rd St., N.W., Childress, TX 79201-4540. Tel.: 940-937-2261. Fax: 940-937-0144.
E-mail: childressmuseum@sbcglobal.net
Web Site: www.biz.childresstexas.net/childressmuseum.com
Founded: 1976.
Congressional District: 13
Key Personnel: Exec. Dir., Chm. & Pres., JoAnn De La Cruz; Pres. (V), Richard Chambless; Dir. Public Rels. & Registrar, Laura Jones.
Personnel Profile: Full-Time Paid 1; Part-Time Paid 2; Part-Time Volunteers 1; Interns 1.
Governing Authority: county; nonprofit organization. Branch Museum: Antique Transportation Museum. Tax-exempt: 501(c)(3).
History Museum.
Collections: history of the area from Paleolithic era to present; Republic of Texas; Texas under Six Flags; ranching; farming; pioneering; rocks & minerals; autos; scale model train; linotype. Historic Buildings: late 1800s one room house; one room school.
Activities: slide programs to school & other organizations; local history program for 2nd, 3rd & 7th grades. Museum Sponsors: District History Fair for 6-12th graders; School Tours K-8th grade; Youth Explorer Days.
Hours & Admission Prices: Mon.-Fri. 10-12 & 1-5, Sat.-Sun. by appointment. No charge; donations accepted. Closed national holidays. ♿
Attendance: 7,000 (estimated)
Membership: Single $35; Family $50; Business $100; Group $200; Life $1,500.

Cleburne

LAYLAND MUSEUM, (M), 201 N. Caddo, Cleburne, TX 76031-4903. Tel.: 817-645-0940. Fax: 817-641-4161.
E-mail: museum@cleburne.net
Founded: 1964.
Congressional District: 6
Key Personnel: Dir., Julie P. Baker; Administrative Asst. & Museum Shop Mgr., Dianne Kidd; Cur. Collections, Ben Hammons.
Personnel Profile: Full-Time Paid 2; Part-Time Paid 4; Part-Time Volunteers 4.
Governing Authority: municipal government. Parent Institution: City of Cleburne, 10 N. Robinson, Cleburne 76031. Tax-exempt.
History Museum: housed in 1905 Carnegie Library building.
Collections: Native American & American domestic artifacts; Marchbanks confederate uniform; Kit Carson Saddle; household furnishings; clothing; firearms; manuscripts; documents; photographs; street train; Santa Fe caboose.
Research Fields: American home life; shelter; foodways; crafts; leisure activities; county history.
Facilities: research library; 130-seat theatre. Gift items for sale.
Activities: formally organized educational programs; performance & lecture series; gallery talks; craft demonstration; school loan trunks; heritage tours; festival events; traveling exhibitions.
Publications: books, Civil War Veterans Buried in Cleburne Cemetery; Civil

War Veterans of Johnson County; Johnson County Marriages 1892-1919; The History of Cleburne & Johnson County; Cherished Recipes.
Hours & Admission Prices: Mon.-Fri. 9-12 & 1-5, second & fourth Sat. of each month 10-4. No charge; donations accepted. Closed national holidays. ♿
Attendance: 8,000 (accurate)
Membership: $15; $25; $50; $100; $500; $1,000; $2,500.

Clifton

BOSQUE MUSEUM, (M), 301 S. Ave. O, Clifton, TX 76634. Mailing Address: P.O. Box 345, Clifton, TX 76634-0345. Tel.: 254-675-3845. Fax: 254-675-8801.
E-mail: info@bosquemuseum.org
Founded: 1924.
Congressional District: 17
Key Personnel: Dir., George W. Larson, Ph.D.; Chm., Tom Henderson; Devel., Willene Pack; Public Rels., Trudy Sheffield; Treas., Kenneth Van Tassel; Cur., Bernie Dutton; Archivist, Patricia Seavolt.
Personnel Profile: Full-Time Paid 2; Part-Time Paid 3; Part-Time Volunteers 4.
Governing Authority: private; nonprofit organization. Tax-exempt: 501(c)(3).
History Museum.
Collections: Bosque County history; Texas & Norwegian immigration; lithic; paleoamerican.
Research Fields: Lithic Indian occupation in Bosque County.
Facilities: 2,800-vol. library. Museum-related items for sale.
Activities: guided tours; lectures; school loan service; temporary & traveling exhibitions. Annual Events: Community Festivals: Octoberfest; Norwegian Christmas; Archaeology Lecture & Program.
Publications: quarterly newsletter, Museum Musings; book, The Horn Shelter; book, Juana.
Hours & Admission Prices: Tues.-Sat. 10-5. No charge; donations accepted. Closed New Year's Day; Independence Day; Thanksgiving; Christmas. ♿
Attendance: 6,600 (accurate)
Membership: Individual $50; Patron $150; Benefactor $360; Friends $1,000; Angel's $5,000 & up.

Clute

BRAZOSPORT MUSEUM OF NATURAL SCIENCE, (M), 400 College Blvd., Clute, TX 77531-4778. Tel.: 979-265-7831. Fax: 979-265-6022.
E-mail: bmns@bcfas.org
Web Site: bmns.org
Founded: 1962.
Congressional District: 6
Key Personnel: C.E.O. & Pres. (V), Wayne Humbird; Museum Shop Mgr., Freida White.
Personnel Profile: Full-Time Volunteers 1; Part-Time Volunteers 43.
Governing Authority: board of trustees; nonprofit organization. Tax-exempt.
Natural Science Museum.
Collections: archaeology; botany; geology; malacology; marine; mineralogy; paleontology; zoology. A.P. Beutel Hall of Minerals; Bryan Cooney Hall of Fossils; Mildred Tate Hall of Malacology; Raymond Walley Hall of Archaeology: Hall of Wildlife; Children's Hall.
Research Fields: malacology; archaeology.
Facilities: 2,000-vol. library of natural science; aquarium; nature center; classrooms. Shells, rocks & fossils for sale.
Activities: guided tours; lectures; films; study clubs; workshops; formally organized educational programs; inter-museum loan, permanent, & temporary exhibitions. Affiliated Groups: Brazosport Archaeological Society; Brazosport Birders; Brazosport Birders & Naturalists; Sea Shell Searchers of Brazoria County. Special Events: Discovery Week; Annual Open House.
Publications: booklet; annual report.
Hours & Admission Prices: Tues.-Sat. 10-5, Sun. 2-5. No charge; donations accepted. ♿
Attendance: 14,021 (accurate)
Membership: Individual $10; Family $20; Patron $50; Benefactor $100; Sustaining $250; Life $1,000.

College Station

THE GEORGE BUSH PRESIDENTIAL LIBRARY AND MUSEUM, (M), 1000 George Bush Dr. W., College Station, TX 77845-3906. Tel.: 979-691-4000. Fax: 979-691-4050. TTY: 979-691-4091.
Web Site: bushlibrary.tamu.edu
Founded: 1997.
Congressional District: 31
Key Personnel: Dir., Warren L. Finch; Asst. Dir. & Cur., Patricia Burchfield; Administrative Officer, Karen Gonzalez; Education, Dr. Shirley Hammond; Supervisory Archivist, Dr. Robert Holzweiss; Public Rels., Brian Blake; Registrar, Weldon Svoboda; Volunteer Coord., Sharon Merrill; Museum Shop Mgr., Joyce Cain; Security, James Mullins.
Personnel Profile: Full-Time Paid 30; Part-Time Paid 1; Part-Time Volunteers 200; Interns 8.
Governing Authority: federal government. Parent Institution: National Archives and Records Admin., Washington, D.C. 20408. Tax-exempt: 170(b)(1)(A).
Presidential Library.
Collections: personal papers; government records; photographs; film; video tapes; head of state gifts; gifts from private citizens; political campaign items; personal & family memorabilia; 80,000 artifacts.
Major Exhibits: The Culture of Wine, 11/09-8/22/10.
Research Fields: life, times, career & admin. of the 41st President of the U.S.
Facilities: library & archives; 600-seat auditorium; educational facilities; 21,000 sq. ft. exhibit space; 146-seat large screen theater; manuscript reference room. Museum-related items for sale.
Activities: concerts; docent program; films; formal education programs for children, adults & Texas A&M University students; guided tours; loan, traveling & temporary exhibitions; lectures. Annual Events: Easter Egg Roll; Holidays in the Rotunda; Independence Day Celebration.
Hours & Admission Prices: Mon.-Sat. 9:30-5, Sun. 12-5. Adults $7, seniors $6, children 6-17 $3; discounts to groups & military; members and children 5 & under no charge. Closed New Year's Day; Thanksgiving; Christmas. ♿
Attendance: 138,252 (accurate)
Membership: Associates $50; Associate Patron $100; Associates Sponsor $500; Senior Associates $1,000; Presidents Club $10,000.

J. WAYNE STARK UNIVERSITY CENTER GALLERIES, (M), Mem. Student Ctr., Rm. 193, College Station, TX 77844. Mailing Address: 4229 TAMU, College Station, TX 77843-0001. Tel.: 979-845-6081 & 8501. Fax: 979-862-3381.
E-mail: uart@stark.tamu.edu
Web Site: stark.tamu.edu
Founded: 1992.
Congressional District: 8
Key Personnel: Dir., Catherine A. Hastedt; Collections Mgr., Nicole Y. Dupre; Admin. Sec., Beverly Wagner.
Personnel Profile: Full-Time Paid 3; Part-Time Paid 8; Part-Time Volunteers 40.
Governing Authority: state; university. Parent Institution: Texas A&M University. Tax-exempt: 170(b)(1)(A).
University Art Gallery.
Collections: works by Texas artists of the 20th century including E.M. (Buck) Schiwetz, Michael Frary, Russell Waterhouse, Dorothy Hood, Charles Schorre, John Alexander, David Caton.
Facilities: 3 galleries.
Activities: guided tours; lectures; films; gallery talks; docent program; permanent & traveling exhibitions.
Publications: exhibit catalogues.
Hours & Admission Prices: Tues.-Fri. 9-8, Sat.-Sun. 12-6. No charge. Closed university holidays. ♿
Attendance: 51,549 (accurate)

MSC FORSYTH CENTER GALLERIES, TEXAS A&M UNIVERSITY, (M), Joe Routt Blvd., College Station, TX 77843-0001. Mailing Address: 1237 Tamu, College Station, TX 77843-0001. Tel.: 979-845-9251. Fax: 979-845-5117.
E-mail: ncurtis@msc.tamu.edu
Web Site: forsyth.tamu.edu
Founded: 1989.
Congressional District: 8
Key Personnel: Dir., Nan Curtis; Program Coord., Myiesha Gordon; Mgr. Collections, Nicole Dupre; Asst. to Dir., Estela Feagin; Registrar & Cur., Cory Arcak.
Personnel Profile: Full-Time Paid 4; Part-Time Paid 8; Part-Time Volunteers 30; Interns 1.
Governing Authority: Texas A&M University. Tax-exempt: 501(c)(3).
Art Museum
Collections: 19th-century English Cameo glass; 19th- & early 20th-century American art glass; 1850-1950 American paintings; 20th century quilts; Guatemalan textiles; early 20th-century French Cameo glass; American rich cut glass from the American Cut Glass Association; late 19th-century American Wooten cabinet secretary.
Research Fields: American painting & art glass; English cameo glass.
Facilities: 2,100 sq. ft. exhibit space.
Activities: guided tours; lectures; films; docent program; international glass tours; student art committee; visual arts gallery; loan & traveling exhibitions.
Publications: exhibit catalogues, A Texas Paperweight Celebration; A Rich and Lasting Beauty: Masterpieces from the American Cut Glass Association National Collection.
Hours & Admission Prices: Mon.-Fri. 9-8, Sat.-Sun. 12-6; call to confirm

hours. No charge; donations accepted. Closed Independence Day; Thanksgiving Day; week of Christmas to New Year's Day. ♿
Attendance: 25,000 (estimated)

Colorado City

HEART OF WEST TEXAS MUSEUM, 340 E. 3rd St., Colorado City, TX 79512-6408. Tel.: 325-728-8285. Fax: 325-728-8944.
E-mail: ccmuseum@wtxs.net
Web Site: www.coloradocity.net/MuseumHeartOfWestTexas
Founded: 1960.
Congressional District: 17
Key Personnel: C.E.O., Chm. & Pres., Jay McCollum; Dir., Shirley Scott.
Personnel Profile: Full-Time Paid 1.
Governing Authority: municipal. Parent Institution: City of Colorado City, Texas. Tax-exempt.
History Museum.
Collections: paleontology; pioneer memorabilia; photographs of early settlers and scenes; old coaches; period artifacts; china; bison antiquities replica; Columbian mammoth exhibit.
Activities: guided tours.
Publications: guide book showing historical markers.
Hours & Admission Prices: Tues.-Fri. 10-5, Sat. 10-2. No charge; donations accepted. ♿
Attendance: 2,000 (accurate)
Membership: Student $5; Single $15; Family $25.

Comstock

SEMINOLE CANYON STATE PARK AND HISTORIC SITE, U.S. Hwy. 90 W., Comstock, TX 78837. Mailing Address: P.O. Box 820, U.S. Hwy. 90 West, Park Rd. 67, Comstock, TX 78837-0820. Tel.: 432-292-4464. Fax: 432-292-4596.
Web Site: www.tpwd.state.tx.us
Formerly: Seminole Canyon State Historical Park
Founded: 1980.
Congressional District: 19
Key Personnel: C.E.O., Carter Smith; Supt., Randy Rosales; Chm. Commission, Peter M. Holt; Chief Cur., Billie Foster.
Personnel Profile: Full-Time Paid 5; Part-Time Paid 1; Part-Time Volunteers 30.
Governing Authority: state. Parent Institution: Texas Parks & Wildlife Dept., 4200 Smith School Rd., Austin, TX 78744. Tel. 512-479-4882. Tax-exempt.
Park & Archaeology Site: located in canyon is Fate Bell Shelter containing 4,000-year old pictographs & some of the oldest cave dwellings in North America.
Collections: prehistoric artifacts; 19th-century railroad artifacts; items relating to modern ranching; Native American Indian paintings; cave dwellings.
Facilities: shelters, picnic area; camping facilities; hiking trails; visitor center.
Activities: guided rock art tours; lectures; permanent exhibitions.
Publications: brochures.
Hours & Admission Prices: Daily 8-4:45. Adults over 12 $3; children under 12 no charge. Rock Art Tour: June-Aug. Wed.-Sun. 10 a.m.; Sept.-May Wed.-Sun. 10 & 3. Admission over 8 $5, children under 8 no charge. ♿
Attendance: 44,694 (accurate)
Membership: Texas State Parks Pass $60.

Corpus Christi

ART MUSEUM OF SOUTH TEXAS, (M), 1902 N. Shoreline, Corpus Christi, TX 78401-1164. Tel.: 361-825-3500. Fax: 361-825-3520.
E-mail: artmuseum@tamucc.edu
Web Site: artmuseumofsouthtexas.org
Founded: 1943.
Key Personnel: Dir., Joseph B. Schenk; Asst. Dir., Marilyn Ramey; Assoc. Cur. & Registrar, Michelle Locke; Cur. Education, Linda Rodriguez; Assoc. Cur., Deborah Fullerton; Mktg., Cindy Anderson.
Governing Authority: nonprofit organization. Affiliated with Corpus Christi Art Foundation. Tax-exempt: 501(c)(3).
Art Museum.
Collections: paintings; drawings; sculpture; graphics; photographs.
Facilities: 2,500-vol. library of art books available by request; 231-seat auditorium; classrooms. Gift items for sale.
Activities: temporary & traveling exhibitions; guided tours; lectures; films; gallery talks; concerts; formally organized education programs; docent program or council.
Publications: exhibition catalogs.
Hours & Admission Prices: Tues.-Sat. 10-5, Sun. 1-5. Adults $6; discounts to AAM members; members no charge. Closed New Year's Day; Thanksgiving; Christmas. ♿
Membership: Student $15; Individual $40; Couple $50; Family $60; Supporting $100; Associate Patron $250; Patron $500; Donor Benefactor $1,000; Foundation Circle $3,000.

* **CORPUS CHRISTI MUSEUM OF SCIENCE AND HISTORY, (M),** 1900 N. Chaparral, Corpus Christi, TX 78401-1114. Tel.: 361-826-4667. Fax: 361-884-7392.
Web Site: www.ccmuseum.com
Founded: 1957.
Congressional District: 14
Key Personnel: C.E.O. & Dir., Richard R. Stryker, Jr.; Chm. (V), Kathy Juneau; Pres. (V), Jim Moloney; Cur., Donald P. Zuris; Exhibit Designer, Roy Garrett; Educator, Sandra Linderman; Museum Shop Mgr., Lori Bryant.
Personnel Profile: Full-Time Paid 18; Part-Time Paid 7; Part-Time Volunteers 35.
Governing Authority: municipal. Parent Institution: City of Corpus Christi. Tax-exempt: 170(b)(1)(A)(v).
General Museum.
Collections: history; marine science; earth science; marine & terrestrial archaeology; Texas mollusks; South Texas plants; Columbus replica ships.
Research Fields: local history; natural history; South Texas Native American cultures; marine archaeology.
Facilities: 10,000-vol. library available by appointment; 175-seat auditorium; classrooms. Museum-related items for sale.
Activities: permanent exhibits; educational programs; lectures.
Publications: Occasional Papers: Berangers Discovery of Aransas Pass; History of Nueces County; Museums & the Student; Museums & the Teacher; Papermaking at Home; Almanac for the Year 1980; The Boll Weevil Comes to Texas; Fires & Hard Times; Minerals Around Corpus Christi Bay.
Hours & Admission Prices: Tues.-Sat. 10-5, Sun. 12-5. Adults $11.50, seniors & military $9, children $6; discounts AAM members; members no charge. Closed New Year's Day; Thanksgiving; Christmas. ♿
Attendance: 65,475 (accurate)
Membership: Student $30; Individual $40; Senior Family $50; Family $60; Contributor $12; Supporter $500; Benefactor $1,000 & up; Corporate $2,500.

PADRE ISLAND NATIONAL SEASHORE, 20301 Park Rd. 22, Corpus Christi, TX 78418. Mailing Address: P.O. Box 181300, Corpus Christi, TX 78480-1300. Tel.: 361-949-8173, ext. 223. Fax: 361-949-8023.
E-mail: jose_escoto@nps.gov
Web Site: www.nps.gov/pais
Founded: 1962.
Congressional District: 14 & 15
Key Personnel: Supt., Joe Escoto.
Personnel Profile: Full-Time Paid 1.
Governing Authority: federal. Parent Institution: Dept. of the Interior, National Park Service, Washington, DC. Tax-exempt.
National Park Visitor Center & Museum.
Collections: shells; fulgurite; insect; seashells; herbarium; archaeology; archives, photographs; oral history; artifacts from 1554 Spanish shipwrecks; Spanish coins.
Research Fields: natural history; archaeology.
Facilities: library of material dealing with the natural & cultural resources of the island available for use on premises with advance notice required.
Activities: scheduled programs year round.
Publications: orientation brochures; natural history publications; SPMA publication on the park; site bulletins on Flora, Fauna and cultural history.
Hours & Admission Prices: Headquarters: Mon.-Fri. 8-4:30. Museum: June-Aug. daily 8:30-6; Sept.-May daily 8:30-4:30. Visitors Center & Museum no charge. Parking fee $10, Annual Pass $20. ♿
Attendance: 60,888 (accurate)

TEXAS STATE MUSEUM OF ASIAN CULTURES & EDUCATIONAL CENTER, 1809 N. Champarral St., Corpus Christi, TX 78401-1111. Tel.: 361-882-2641. Fax: 361-882-5718.
E-mail: asianculturesmuseum@sbcglobal.net
Web Site: www.asianculturesmuseum.org
Founded: 1973.
Congressional District: 27
Key Personnel: Dir., Catherine Lacroix; Pres. Bd., Richard L. Bowers.
Personnel Profile: Full-Time Paid 2; Part-Time Paid 2; Part-Time Volunteers 7.
Governing Authority: nonprofit organization. Parent Institution: Billie Trimble Chandler Art Foundation, Inc. Tax-exempt: 501(c)(3).
Cultural Museum.
Collections: decorative arts of Japan, China, India & Korea, including Hakata dolls; porcelains; metalware; cloisonne; lacquerware; Buddhist & Hindu images; clothing; costumes; oriental fan.
Research Fields: Japanese, Chinese, Indian, Korean & Philippine culture, & religion, art.

Facilities: 600-vol. library of books plus magazines, pamphlets available for research on premises only; reading room; classrooms. Oriental curios for sale.
Activities: lectures; art & culture festivals; hobby workshops; formally organized education programs; guided tours by appointment. Museum Sponsors: Ladies Auxiliary.
Publications: quarterly newsletter.
Hours & Admission Prices: Tues.-Sat. 10-5. Adults $6, children $4, children under 12 $3; discounts to AAM members; members no charge. Closed New Year's Day; Easter; Thanksgiving; Christmas. ♿
Attendance: 15,000 (estimated)
Membership: Student & Senior Citizen $15; Individual $25; Family $50; Supporting $100; Sustaining $500; Patron $1,000; Benefactor $5,000.

USS LEXINGTON MUSEUM ON THE BAY, 2914 N. Shoreline Blvd., Corpus Christi, TX 78402-1116. Mailing Address: P.O. Box 23076, Corpus Christi, TX 78403-3076. Tel.: 800-ladylex. Fax: 361-883-8361.
Web Site: www.usslexington.com
Founded: 1991.
Congressional District: 27
Key Personnel: Exec. Dir., Frank Montesano; Operations, Security & Exhibits Dir., M. Charles Reustle; Historian Curatorial Research & Registrar, Judith Whipple; Public Rels., Sandi McNorton; Museum Shop Mgr., Maria Robles.
Personnel Profile: Full-Time Paid 56; Part-Time Paid 11; Part-Time Volunteers 75.
Governing Authority: private; nonprofit organization. Tax-exempt: 501(c)(3).
Naval Military Museum: housed in the USS Lexington Aircraft Carrier.
Collections: armed services (all branches with specialty toward U.S. Navy); aircraft; machinery; guns.
Research Fields: World War II, all areas of Navy & other military; exhibits on all phases of military; crew; ship.
Facilities: 150-seat cafeteria; educational facilities. USS Lexington & Navy-related items for sale.
Activities: arts festivals; concerts; dance recitals; docent program; films; formal education programs for children; guided tours; participatory & temporary exhibitions.
Publications: bimonthly newsletter, The Catapult.
Hours & Admission Prices: Daily 9-5. Adults $12.95, military & senior citizens $10.95, children 4-12 $7.95; members no charge. Closed Thanksgiving; Christmas. ♿
Attendance: 340,000 (estimated)
Membership: Student $20; Individual $35; Couple $50; Family $65; Senior & Military $5 discount; Commander $125; Captain $250; Admiral $500.

Corsicana

NAVARRO COUNTY HISTORICAL SOCIETY, PIONEER VILLAGE, 912 W. Park Ave., Corsicana, TX 75110-2931. Tel.: 903-654-4846. Fax: 903-654-4983.
Founded: 1958.
Congressional District: 6
Key Personnel: Exec. Dir. Navarro County Historical Society, Dir. Pioneer Village & Cur., Bobbie Young; Pres. (V), Eddie Peyehouse.
Personnel Profile: Full-Time Paid 1; Part-Time Paid 1.
Governing Authority: municipal; county; society. Parent Institution: Navarro County Historical Society. Tax-exempt.
Village Museum: eight log buildings constructed in Navarro County during 1838-1865, moved to City Park & restored.
Collections: period furnishings; newspapers; tools; cooking utensils; early country music from Texas; agriculture; archaeology; archives; period county artifacts; manuscripts; costumes; ethnology; folklore; general history; Native American artifacts. Historic Buildings: blacksmith shop; 1838 Indian trading post; 1846 pioneer kitchen; 1851 general store; 1854 frontier home; 1860 slave quarters; 1865 the old barn; 1890 blacksmith shop; tack shed; Redden House; carriage house; McKie Playhouse; Peace Officers Museum; Sam Roberts Museum; Lefty Frizzell Museum; Carriage House, houses a surrey with fringed top, 4-wheeled buckboards, 2-wheeled cart & 1930 tractor; Hall of Fame.
Research Fields: general history; genealogy.
Facilities: archives of research books & documents available for use by public.
Activities: guided tours; lectures; permanent exhibitions.
Publications: annual book, Scroll; books, Navarro County Histories Vols. 1-5; The Women of Navarro County, Navarro County History Vol. 6; 1996 Sesquicentennial Year, Moments in Time Vol. 7.
Hours & Admission Prices: Mon.-Fri. 8-5, Sat. 9-5, Sun. 1-5; call for holiday hours. Adults $3, college students & children 4-18 $1. ♿
Attendance: 2,620 (accurate)
Membership: Navarro County Historical Society: Individual $10; Family $15; Sustaining $120.

PEARCE COLLECTIONS MUSEUM, (M), 3100 W. Collin St., Corsicana, TX 75110-3904. Tel.: 903-875-7642; 800-988-5317. Fax: 903-875-7593.
E-mail: archives@navarrocollege.edu
Web Site: www.pearcecollections.us
Founded: 1996.
Congressional District: 6
Key Personnel: C.E.O., Education & Cur., Julie Holcomb, Ed.D.; Chm. (V), Terry Jacobson; Museum Shop Mgr., Pat Granger.
Personnel Profile: Full-Time Paid 2; Part-Time Paid 2; Part-Time Volunteers 30; Interns 1.
Governing Authority: public college. Subsidiary Institutions: Navarro College Foundation, Corsicana, TX; Navarro College, Corsicana, TX. Tax-exempt: 501(c)(3).
History Museum.
Collections: artifacts; photographs; memorabilia; ephemera; graphic materials; American Western art; history of Navarro College, Navarro County & U.S. Civil War.
Facilities: 500-vol. library of Civil War & American Western Art books; 200-seat auditorium; educational facilities; 15,000 sq. ft. exhibit space; planetarium; 42-seat theater. Museum-related items for sale.
Activities: arts festival; docent program; films; formal education programs; guided tours; lectures. Annual Events: art lectures; Civil War lectures; artist-in-residence program.
Hours & Admission Prices: Pearce Collections: Mon.-Fri. 11-4, Sat. 12-4. Cook Education Center: Mon.-Fri. 10-5, Sat. 12-4. Adults $8, seniors $6, children 3-18 & students $4; discounts to groups. ♿
Attendance: 8,000 (estimated)
Membership: Individual $35; Family $60; Patron $150.

Cotulla

BRUSH COUNTRY MUSEUM, 201 S. Stewart, Cotulla, TX 78014-3070. Mailing Address: P.O. Box 369, Cotulla, TX 78014-0369. Tel.: 830-879-2429.
Web Site: www.historicdistrict.com/museum
Founded: 1982.
Congressional District: 28
Key Personnel: Chm. (V), James C. Barbour; Treas., Nora Mae Tyler; Cur., Nita Gierisch; Cur., Elizabeth Seidel.
Personnel Profile: Part-Time Paid 1; Part-Time Volunteers 3.
Governing Authority: county; nonprofit. Tax-exempt.
History Museum.
Collections: photographs; artifacts; history of La Salle County & the Brush Country of South Texas.
Activities: guided tours.
Hours & Admission Prices: Tues. & Thurs. 10-12 & 2-4, Wed. & Fri.-Sat. 1-4. No charge; donations accepted. Closed New Year's Day; Independence Day; Thanksgiving; Christmas. ♿
Attendance: 495 (accurate)
Membership: Individual $15; Family $25; Pioneer Family $50.

Crane

MUSEUM OF THE DESERT SOUTHWEST, 409 S. Gaston, Crane, TX 79731-2621. Tel.: 432-558-2311.
History Museum.
Collections: Native American, cowboy & Horsehead Crossing artifacts; Castle Gap fossils; petroleum industry.
Hours & Admission Prices: May-Sept. Sat. 9-12 & 1-5, Sun.-Fri. 1-4; Oct.-April Mon.-Fri. 1-4.

Cresson

PATE MUSEUM OF TRANSPORTATION, 18501 Hwy. 377, Cresson, TX 76035. Mailing Address: 1227 W. Magnolia Ave., Suite 420, Fort Worth, TX 76104-4400. Tel.: 817-922-9504(office); 396-4305 (museum). Fax: 817-922-9536.
Founded: 1969.
Congressional District: 16
Key Personnel: Pres., Sebert L. Pate.
Governing Authority: nonprofit organization. Parent Institution: Pate Foundation, Inc. Tax-exempt: 170(b)(1)(A).
Transportation Museum.
Collections: period and classic autos; aircraft; railroad artifacts; space exhibits.
Research Fields: transportation history.
Facilities: 1,500-vol. library of books & magazines on transportation available for inter-library loan or use on the premises; reading room.
Publications: brochures.
Hours & Admission Prices: Tues.-Sat. 10-5, Sun. 12-5. No charge; donations accepted. Closed holidays. ♿
Attendance: 15,000 (estimated)

Crosbyton

CROSBY COUNTY PIONEER MEMORIAL MUSEUM, (M), 101 W. Main, (intersection U.S. 82 & F.M. 651), Crosbyton, TX 79322-2252. Tel.: 806-675-2331.
E-mail: ccpmm@door.net
Web Site: www.crosbycountymuseum.com
Founded: 1958.
Congressional District: 17
Key Personnel: C.E.O., Gary Mitchell; Dir., Verna Anne Wheeler; Administrative Asst., Lynn Dybendall.
Personnel Profile: Full-Time Paid 2; Full-Time Volunteers 1; Part-Time Paid 2; Part-Time Volunteers 18; Interns 2.
Governing Authority: nonprofit; municipal. Parent Institution: City of Crosbyton, TX. Tax-exempt.
Local History Museum: partially housed in replica of Hank Smith rock house, original structure in 1876-77.
Collections: agriculture; home & family artifacts; Texas plains area artifacts; Native American artifacts; cowboy memorabilia; archives; cultural materials from prehistoric Plains Indians to 20th-century pioneers.
Research Fields: pioneer & oral histories; educational history of West Texas & Crosby County; community history of Crosby County; archaeological research; prehistoric Plains Indians to 20th-century pioneers; village & city development; agrarian society & technological advancements.
Facilities: library of early editions on education & history; archival research on people & places of Crosby County & West Texas available on premises; 500-seat auditorium; meeting room. Historical publications, maps & gifts for sale.
Activities: guided tours; lectures; films; gallery talks; arts festivals; drama; study clubs; hobby workshops; formally organized educational programs; permanent & temporary exhibitions; school loan service; cooperative education program.
Publications: bulletins; brochures; cards; historical maps; books, A History of Crosby County 1876-1977, Sun Rising on the West, Rock House Kitchen, Crosby County Cemetery Survey; A History of Black Families, Crosby County 1921-2001; Estacado Cradle of Culture & Civilization on the Staked Plains of Texas; Teachers Hand Book, Grades 2-5.
Hours & Admission Prices: Jan. to mid-Dec. Tues.-Sat. 9-12 & 1-5. No charge; donations accepted. Closed national holidays. ♿
Attendance: 12,403 (accurate)
Membership: Heritage Association: Annual $15.

Cuero

DEWITT COUNTY HISTORICAL MUSEUM, 312 E. Broadway, Cuero, TX 77954-2806. Tel.: 361-275-6322.
Web Site: www.cuero.org
Founded: 1973.
Congressional District: 14
Key Personnel: Chm. (V), Patsy Goebel; Dir., Verna Smith.
Personnel Profile: Full-Time Paid 1; Part-Time Paid 1.
Governing Authority: society. Affiliated with DeWitt County Historical Commission. Tax-exempt: 509(A).
Local History Museum: housed in 1886 Bates-Sheppard Home.
Collections: furnishings; traveling exhibits.
Research Fields: DeWitt County history.
Facilities: two-story house; dog trot log cabin.
Activities: tours; special group tours; preview parties; research. Annual Event: Wildflowers of Texas in April.
Hours & Admission Prices: Thurs.-Fri. 9-12 & 1-5, Sun. 2-5. No charge; donations accepted. ♿
Attendance: 3,000 (estimated)
Membership: Student $2; Individual $10; Family $15; Sustaining $35; Corporate $100; Life $150.

Dalhart

DALLAM-HARTLEY XIT MUSEUM, 108 E. 5th St., Dalhart, TX 79022. Mailing Address: P.O. Box 730, Dalhart, TX 79022-0730. Tel.: 806-244-5390. Fax: 806-244-3031.
E-mail: xitmusm@xit.net
Web Site: xitmuseum.com
Founded: 1975.
Congressional District: 13
Key Personnel: Dir. & Cur., Nicky Olson; Pres., Sylvia Renick.
Personnel Profile: Full-Time Paid 1; Part-Time Paid 1; Part-Time Volunteers 2.
Governing Authority: nonprofit organization. Parent Institution: Dallam-Hartley Counties Historical Assn., Inc. Tax-exempt.
Historical Society Museum: housed in a terra-cotta brick building.
Collections: memorabilia from Dallam & Hartley Counties & the XIT Ranch history; art gallery with changing exhibits.
Research Fields: Dallam, Hartley Counties, & Dalhart history.
Activities: guided tours; concerts; arts festivals; study clubs; permanent & temporary exhibitions. Museum Sponsors: Open House during the XIT Reunion & Rodeo held yearly in August; four artist receptions per year.
Hours & Admission Prices: Tues.-Sat. 9-5. No charge; donations accepted. ♿
Attendance: 5,000 (accurate)
Membership: Annual Individual $35; Contributor $100; Supporter $250; Patron $500; Benefactor $1,000; Founder $5,000.

Dallas

AFRICAN AMERICAN MUSEUM, 3536 Grand Ave., Dallas, TX 75210-1005. Mailing Address: P.O. Box 150157, Dallas, TX 75315-0157. Tel.: 214-565-9026; 877-852-3292 (toll free). Fax: 214-421-8204.
Web Site: www.aamdallas.org
Founded: 1974.
Congressional District: 5
Key Personnel: Pres. Bd. Trustees, Dr. Harry Robinson, Jr.; Asst. Dir. Admin., Betty Cunningham; Dir. Devel., Jane Jones; Cur., Phillip Collins; Museum Shop Mgr., Mark Proctor.
Personnel Profile: Full-Time Paid 15; Part-Time Paid 2; Interns 3.
Governing Authority: nonprofit organization. Parent Institution: Foundation for African-American Art. Tax-exempt: 501(c)(3).
African American Culture Museum.
Collections: African American fine art & folk art; Texas Black History; Texas Black Women's Archives.
Research Fields: Black history in Texas; folk art.
Facilities: 1,500-vol. library of books; 100-seat auditorium; classrooms; courtyard; cafeteria.
Activities: lectures; organized educational program; docent program; loan, temporary & traveling exhibitions. Museum Sponsors: history conference; literary conference; history fair.
Publications: quarterly newsletter.
Hours & Admission Prices: Tues.-Fri. 12-5, Sat. 10-5, Sun. 1-5. No charge; donations accepted. Closed New Year's Day; Independence Day; Thanksgiving Day; Christmas. ♿
Attendance: 201,000 (estimated)
Membership: Student & Senior Citizen $15; Individual $25; Family $35; Friend $50; Patron $100; Associate $500; Benefactor $1,000 & up.

BIBLICAL ARTS CENTER, 7500 Park Lane, Dallas, TX 75225-2025. Mailing Address: P.O. Box 12727, Dallas, TX 75225-0727. Tel.: 214-691-4662. Fax: 214-691-4752.
E-mail: frontdesk@biblicalarts.org
Web Site: www.biblicalarts.org
Founded: 1966.
Congressional District: 5
Key Personnel: Co Dir., R.J. Machacek; Co Dir., Scott Peck; Asst. Dir., Dr. Val Robinson.
Personnel Profile: Full-Time Paid 4; Part-Time Paid 6.
Governing Authority: nonprofit organization. Parent Institution: Miracle at Pentecost Foundation. Tax-exempt: 501(c)(3).
Religious Art Museum.
Collections: 16th century to present art in mediums including performing arts pertaining to the Bible.
Facilities: multi-purpose auditorium; theater.
Activities: docent program; lectures; permanent & traveling exhibitions; formally organized education courses; performing arts programs.
Publications: books, Creation of a Masterpiece.
Hours & Admission Prices: Mon.-Sat. 10-5, Sun. 1-5. Galleries: no charge; donations accepted. Program: adults $7; senior citizens & children 6-18 $6. Closed New Year's Day; Thanksgiving; Christmas Eve & Day. ♿
Attendance: 70,000 (accurate)
Membership: Individual & Basic $35; Family $75.

CHILDREN'S AQUARIUM AT FAIR PARK, 1462 1st Ave., Dallas, TX 75210-1010. Mailing Address: P.O. Box 150113, Dallas, TX 75315-0113. Tel.: 214-670-8443 (info) & 8453. Fax: 214-670-8452.
E-mail: info@dalzoo.org
Web Site: www.dallas-zoo.com
Formerly: The Dallas Aquarium at Fair Park
Founded: 1936.
Congressional District: 5
Key Personnel: C.E.O. & Dir., Greggory Hudson; Cur., Brian J. Potvin; Supvr., Barrett Christie; Senior Aquarist, Charles Yancey; Aquarist, Martin Conricote; Aquarist, Eric Julius; Deputy Dir. Operations, Doug Dykman.
Personnel Profile: Full-Time Paid 11; Part-Time Paid 2; Part-Time Volunteers 26; Interns 1.
Governing Authority: municipal. Parent Institution: Dallas Zoo. Tax-exempt.
Aquarium.

Collections: freshwater & marine fish; reptiles; amphibians; invertebrates.
Research Fields: desert fish; Edwards Aquifer endemics; reproductive studies; husbandry research; seahorse & elasmobranch conservation; unionid biology & conservation.
Facilities: shell exhibit; educational building.
Activities: guided tours; lectures; formally organized education programs for children; daily keeper presentations to the general public; touch tank & dive presentations on weekends.
Publications: Paradigm; Zookeeper; Tracks & Facts; The Wildlife Saver.
Hours & Admission Prices: Closed for renovations until 2010. ♿
Attendance: 180,000 (estimated)
Membership: Individual $40; Individual Plus $50; Family $55; Family Plus $75; Sustaining $125; Patron $250; Sponsor $500.

DALLAS ARBORETUM & BOTANICAL GARDEN, 8525 Garland Rd., Dallas, TX 75218-4335. Mailing Address: 8617 Garland Rd., Dallas, TX 75218-3914. Tel.: 214-515-6500. Fax: 214-324-9801.
Web Site: www.dallasarboretum.org
Founded: 1974.
Key Personnel: Pres., Mary Brinegar; Vice Pres. Gardens, Dave Forehand; Vice Pres. Public Rels., Chris Emrich; Mgr., Alexandra Wall-Gilmore.
Personnel Profile: Full-Time Paid 50; Part-Time Paid 10; Part-Time Volunteers 300; Interns 6.
Governing Authority: board of directors; nonprofit organization. Parent Institution: Dallas Arboretum & Botanical Garden Society. Tax-exempt.
Arboretum & Botanical Garden.
Collections: plant materials.
Research Fields: horticulture; botany; ecology.
Facilities: botanical garden; reading room. Museum-related items for sale.
Activities: guided tours; lectures; concerts; festivals; study clubs; hobby workshops; TV & radio programs; formally organized education programs for children, adults, undergraduate & graduate students; docent program or council; permanent & temporary exhibitions; volunteer groups.
Publications: bimonthly newsletter, The Dallas Arboretum; plant information handouts.
Hours & Admission Prices: Daily 9-5. Adults $10, seniors 65 & over $9, children 3-12 $7; members no charge. Parking $7. Closed New Year's Day; Thanksgiving; Christmas. ♿
Attendance: 300,000 (accurate)
Membership: Individual $45; Family $75; Family plus $85; Sustaining $150; Fellows $350; Patrons $650; Friends $1,000 & up.

DALLAS CONTEMPORARY, (M), 2801 Swiss Ave., Dallas, TX 75204-5925. Tel.: 214-821-2522. Fax: 214-821-9103.
E-mail: info@thecontemporary.net
Web Site: www.dallascontemporary.org
Founded: 1981.
Congressional District: 30
Key Personnel: Dir. & Cur., Joan Davidow; Pres., Guicho Pons; Mgr. Operations, Holly Torres; Coord. Events, Andrea Gage; Education, Diane Sikes; Membership, Jennifer Stark; Exhibitions, Megan Goetz; Campaign Mgr., Cassandra Porter.
Personnel Profile: Full-Time Paid 8; Part-Time Paid 1; Interns 10.
Governing Authority: nonprofit. Tax-exempt: 501(c)(3).
Contemporary Art Museum.
Collections: contemporary art.
Research Fields: contemporary Texas art in a global context; Texas artists; opportunities for artists.
Facilities: library & information center; sculpture garden.
Activities: art talks; studio classes; workshops on collecting art, resource & information center for artists. Annual Events: Membership Show; Mix! Series of artists with diverse ethnic backgrounds; Auction, Legends, Luncheon in May.
Publications: biannual newsletter; exhibition brochures.
Hours & Admission Prices: Tues.-Sat. 10-5. No charge; donations accepted. Closed major holidays. ♿
Attendance: 30,000 (estimated)
Membership: Minimalist $50; Realist $100; Surrealist $250; Collectors $500-$1,000; Patrons $2,500; Private & Corporate $1,500-$10,000.

DALLAS FIREFIGHTER'S MUSEUM, INC., 3801 Parry Ave., Dallas, TX 75226-1753. Tel.: 214-821-1500.
Web Site: www.dallasfiremuseum.com
Founded: 1972.
Key Personnel: Pres. (V), Stuart Grant; Vice Pres., Rett Blankenship.
Personnel Profile: Part-Time Paid 3.
Governing Authority: nonprofit organization. Tax-exempt.
Firefighter's Museum.
Collections: period fire trucks including an 1884 horse-drawn steam pumper & 1936 ladder truck; firefighting history; extinguishers; helmets; suits; uniforms; photographs.
Facilities: Museum-related items for sale.
Activities: fire & life safety.
Publications: 2008 calendar.
Hours & Admission Prices: Wed.-Sat. 9-4. Adults $4, children $2; members no charge. Closed New Year's Day; Thanksgiving; Christmas.
Attendance: 3,500 (estimated)
Membership: Individual $24; Lifetime $500.

* **DALLAS HERITAGE VILLAGE AT OLD CITY PARK, (M),** 1515 S. Harwood St., Dallas, TX 75215. Tel.: 214-421-5141. Fax: 214-428-6351.
E-mail: gnsmith@oldcitypark.org
Web Site: www.dallasheritagevillage.org
Formerly: Old City Park: The Historical Village of Dallas
Founded: 1966.
Congressional District: 5
Key Personnel: Exec. Dir. & Pres., Gary N. Smith; Dir. Facilities, Steven Santos; Chm. (V), Sharon Wooldridge; Chief Cur., Hal Simon; Lead Interpreter, 1860s Living Farmstead, Kelly Kring; Dir. Devel., Nancy Farina; Vice Pres. Museum Svcs., Andrea Brown; Program Mgr., Melissa Pryor; Business Mgr., Mary Keil; Membership Coord., Clay Oehlschlaeger; Dir. Sales, Michelle Davis; Tour Mgr. & Museum Shop Mgr., Barbara Judkins.
Personnel Profile: Full-Time Paid 12; Part-Time Paid 17; Part-Time Volunteers 300.
Governing Authority: private. Parent Institution: Dallas County Heritage Society. Tax-exempt: 501(c)(3).
Village Museum.
Collections: 38 historic structures from the period c.1840-1910; 19th-century material culture & decorative arts with emphasis on North Central Texas.
Research Fields: north central Texas; Dallas; American decorative arts; crafts.
Facilities: library. Museum-related items for sale.
Activities: interpretive programs; outreach programs; lectures; films; docent program; orientation program; craft demonstrations; permanent & temporary exhibitions; weddings in the church & bandstand. Museum Sponsors: 3 major special events.
Publications: membership newsletter, Heritage News; newsletter for volunteers, Gazette.
Hours & Admission Prices: Tues.-Sat. 10-4, Sun. 12-4. Adults $7, seniors $5, children 3-12 $4; discounts to AAM & ICOM members; museum professionals & members no charge. Closed New Year's Day; Memorial Day; Thanksgiving; Christmas. ♿
Attendance: 70,000 (estimated)
Membership: Scout $60; Family $75; Settler $125; Pioneer $300; Jr. Curator's Circle $550; Trailblazer $600; Curator's Circle $1,250; Corporate levels also available.

DALLAS HISTORICAL SOCIETY, Hall of State, Fair Park, 3939 Grand Ave., Dallas, TX 75210. Mailing Address: P.O. Box 150038, Dallas, TX 75315-0038. Tel.: 214-421-4500. Fax: 214-421-7500.
E-mail: nora@dallashistory.org
Web Site: www.dallashistory.org
Founded: 1922.
Congressional District: 5
Key Personnel: Exec. Dir., Jack Bunning; Chm. (V), Diane Bumpus.
Personnel Profile: Full-Time Paid 6; Part-Time Paid 2; Part-Time Volunteers 60; Interns 4.
Governing Authority: society; nonprofit. Tax-exempt: 501(c)(3).
History Museum.
Collections: artifacts, books, archive materials relating to southwestern & U.S. history; manuscript collections; costume collections.
Major Exhibits: Bonnie and Clyde, Fall 2010.
Research Fields: American, Texas & Dallas history.
Facilities: 14,000-vol. library & 3,000,000 pages of archives on Southwestern U.S. available for use on premises; reading room; 400-seat auditorium; G.B. Dealey Research Library; Hall of State Reception Room.
Activities: guided tours; formally organized education programs for kindergarten through adult; docent program; lectures; gallery talks; hobby workshops; training programs; loan, permanent & temporary exhibitions; Hall of State available for special events.
Publications: monthly newsletter, Dallas Historical Society Register; books, Dallas Rediscovered; When Dallas Becomes a City; semi-annual historical journal, Legacies.
Hours & Admission Prices: Tues.-Sat. 9-5, Sun. 1-5. No charge; donations accepted. Closed New Year's Day; Thanksgiving; Christmas. ♿
Attendance: 209,165 (estimated)
Membership: Individual & Family $50; Biographer $100; Collector $250; Fellow $1,250.

DALLAS HOLOCAUST MUSEUM/CENTER FOR EDUCATION & TOLERANCE, 211 N. Record St., Ste. 100, Dallas, TX 75202-3361. Tel.: 214-741-7500, ext. 105. Fax: 214-747-2270.
E-mail: info@dallasholocaustmuseum.org
Web Site: www.dallasholocaustmuseum.org
Formerly: Dallas Holocaust Memorial Center
Founded: 1984.
Congressional District: 3
Key Personnel: Exec. Dir., Elliott Dlin; Pres., James M. Hogue; Dir. Education & Programming, Kathy Chapman; Dir. Devel., Stephanie Bohan Gandy; Administrative Asst., Marsha Friedman; Volunteer & Tour Coord., Hope Levine; Bookkeeper & Weekend Mgr., Ginger Evans; Archivist, Jennifer Moore.
Personnel Profile: Full-Time Paid 6; Part-Time Paid 2; Part-Time Volunteers 75; Interns 2.
Governing Authority: not-for-profit organization. Tax-exempt: 501(c)(3).
History Museum.
Collections: photographs & artifacts from the Holocaust & Jewish life in Europe before the Holocaust.
Facilities: 3,500-vol. library on the Holocaust & anti-Semitism; 135-seat auditorium; 2,500 sq. ft. exhibit space.
Activities: docent program; films; guided tours; lectures; school loan service; teachers training seminar.
Publications: triannual, Dallas Holocaust Museum Newsletter.
Hours & Admission Prices: Mon.-Fri. 10-5, Sat.-Sun. 11-5. Adults $6, students, seniors, active military & groups of 15 or more $4. Closed New Year's Day; Easter; Rosh Hashanah; Independence Day; Yom Kippur; Thanksgiving; Christmas Eve & Day. ♿
Attendance: 50,000 (estimated)
Membership: Friend $36; Associate $54; Supporter $108; Patron $250; Outreach Partners $500; Guardians of Memory $1,000; Teachers of Tolerance $2,500; Defenders of Honor $5,000; Liberators from Indifference $7,500; Keepers of the Eternal Flame $10,000 & up.

* **DALLAS MUSEUM OF ART, (M),** 1717 N. Harwood St., Dallas, TX 75201-2398. Tel.: 214-922-1200. Fax: 214-922-1350.
E-mail: JConner@DallasMuseumofArt.org
Web Site: www.DallasMuseumofArt.org
Founded: 1903.
Congressional District: 5
Key Personnel: Pres. Bd. Trustees, John Eagle; Chm. Bd. Trustees, Deedie Ponce Rose; Dir., Bonnie Pitman; Sr. Cur. Arts of Africa, the Pacific & the Americas, Dr. Roslyn A. Walker; Cur. Arts of the Americas & the Pacific, Carol Robbins; Cur. Decorative Arts & Design, Kevin W. Tucker; Cur. Contemporary Art, Charles Wylie; Dir. Exhibitions & Publications, Tamara Wooton-Bonner; Dir. Collections Management, Gabriela Truly; Dir. Education, Gail Davitt; Dir. Libraries & Imaging Svcs., Jacqueline Allen; Dir. Mktg. & Communications, Judy Conner; Public Rels., Jill Bernstein; Museum Shop Mgr., Janet Stieve; Dir. Human Resources, Pamela Autry.
Personnel Profile: Full-Time Paid 209; Part-Time Paid 38; Part-Time Volunteers 900; Interns 6.
Governing Authority: nonprofit organization. Tax-exempt: 501(c)(3).
Art Museum.
Collections: European, American & Latin American painting, sculpture & decorative arts and design; contemporary international art; ancient Mediterranean art; Asian art; Indonesian & Oceanic art; African art; pre-Columbian art.
Facilities: 50,000-vol. library of art books & reference material available on premises; reading room; 350-seat auditorium; 2 restaurants. Museum-related items for sale.
Activities: guided tours; lectures; films; family programs; gallery talks; concerts; late night events; formally organized educational programs; docent program; training programs for professional museum workers; inter-museum loan, permanent, temporary, traveling & participatory exhibitions, live literary program. Museum Sponsors: annual Awards to Artists program.
Publications: member magazine; exhibition catalogues & brochures; collection catalogues; annual report.
Hours & Admission Prices: Tues.-Wed. & Fri.-Sun. 11-5, Thurs. 11-9. Adults $10, senior citizens $7, students $5; discount to AAM members; Thurs. after 5, 1st Tues. of month, members and children under 12 no charge. Special exhibition admission varies. Closed New Year's Day; Thanksgiving; Christmas. ♿
Attendance: 700,000 (accurate)
Membership: Member $75; Sustainer $125; Friend $250; Advocate $500; Junior Associates Circle $625; Contributor $1,000; Associates Circle $2,000; Patrons Circle $5,000; Fellows Circle $10,000; Leaders Circle $15,000; Benefactors Circle $25,000; Director's Circle $50,000; President's Circle $100,000; Chairman's Circle $250,000.

THE DALLAS WORLD AQUARIUM, 1801 N. Griffin St., Dallas, TX 75202-1503. Tel.: 214-720-2224.
E-mail: info@dwazoo.com
Web Site: www.dwazoo.com/aquarian.html
Aquarium.
Collections: Aquarium: marine life from around the world. Rainforest: flora & fauna.
Facilities: restaurants. Museum-related items for sale.
Hours & Admission Prices: Daily 10-5. Adults $18.95, seniors 60 & over $14.95, children 3-12 $10.95; children 2 & under no charge. Closed Thanksgiving; Christmas.

DALLAS ZOO, 650 S. R.L. Thornton Freeway, Dallas, TX 75203-3013. Tel.: 214-670-5656. Fax: 214-670-7450.
E-mail: info@dalzoo.org
Web Site: www.dallaszoo.com
Founded: 1888.
Congressional District: 24
Key Personnel: Dir. Zoo, Richard W. Buickerood; Pres. Dallas Zoological Society, Michael Meadows; Deputy Dir. Animal Management, Chuck Siegel; Cur. Birds, Chris Brown; Business Mgr., Kerry Rhines; Cur. Mammals, Ken Kaemmerer; Cur. Mammals, Todd Bowsher; Staff Veterinarian, Dr. Tom Alvarado; Volunteer Coord., Sherri Reneau; Deputy Dir. Operations, Doug Dykman; Cur. Research & Education, Dr. Cynthia Bennett; Facility Mgr., Jeff Rash.
Personnel Profile: Full-Time Paid 236; Part-Time Paid 16; Part-Time Volunteers 500; Interns 2.
Governing Authority: municipal. Parent Institution: City of Dallas/Parks Department. Subsidiary Institution: Dallas Zoological Society. Tax-exempt.
Zoo.
Collections: mammals; birds; reptiles; amphibians.
Research Fields: reproductive physiology; animal behavior.
Facilities: 2,000-vol. library of zoology & natural history available for reference & research on premises; 100 seat auditorium.
Activities: guided & self-guided tours; lectures; formally organized education programs for children; docent program or council; zooniversity classes; permanent exhibitions.
Publications: Adopt-an-Animal newsletter; members' newsletter; annual report.
Hours & Admission Prices: Daily 9-5. Adults $12, senior citizens 65 & over and children 3-11 $9; members & children under 3 no charge. Parking: $5. Closed Christmas. ♿
Attendance: 576,300 (accurate)
Membership: Individual $30; Family $40; Family Plus $60; Company Member $250; Corporate Council Leopard $2,500; Corporate Council Lion $5,000; Corporate Council Elephant $10,000.

FRONTIERS OF FLIGHT MUSEUM, 6911 Lemmon Ave., Dallas, TX 75209-3603. Tel.: 214-350-3600 & 1651. Fax: 214-351-0101.
E-mail: info@flightmuseum.com
Web Site: www.flightmuseum.com
Founded: 1988.
Congressional District: 5
Key Personnel: C.E.O. & Pres. (V), J. Jan Collmer; Chm., Senator Kay Bailey Hutchison; Pres. (V), Ray Woodland; Exec. Dir., Dan Hamilton; Cur., Chris Woodul; Financial Dir., Sam Montgomery; Devel. & Education, Dr. Sharon Spalding; Vice Pres. Advancement, Ilene Stern; Vice Pres. Programs, Bruce Bleakley; Gift Shop Mgr., Brenda Magee; Asst. to Exec. Dir., Anne Marie Evans.
Personnel Profile: Full-Time Paid 10; Full-Time Volunteers 5; Part-Time Paid 4; Part-Time Volunteers 150.
Governing Authority: nonprofit organization. Affiliated with the History of Aviation Collection/University of Texas at Dallas. Tax-exempt: 501(c)(3).
Aeronautical History Museum.
Collections: aviation history from pre-Wright brothers through modern space age; photos; models; Admiral Charles E. Rosendahl's lighter than air collection; World War I & II artifacts & exhibits; Admiral Richard E. Byrd's Antarctic expedition collection; business & commercial aviation exhibits; one-of-a-kind artifacts. Historic Aircraft: Sopwith Pup; Temple Monoplane, Glasflugel Sailplane; F16B No. 2; Gossamer Penguin; F-105F; T-33A; F4 WST.
Research Fields: lighter than air; commercial aviation; aircraft production & aviation training in Texas.
Facilities: 90-seat auditorium & theater; 3,600 sq. ft. exhibit space. Gift items for sale.
Activities: guided tours; lectures; organized educational programs; docent program. Annual Event: George E. Haddaway Award Gala in May.
Publications: quarterly newsletter; tour guide; education brochures; volunteer newsletter; joint North Texas Aviation Museum brochure.
Hours & Admission Prices: Mon.-Sat. 10-5, Sun. 1-5. Adults $8, seniors 65 &

over $6, children 3-17 $5; discounts to groups, AAM, ICOM & TAM members; students & members no charge. Closed New Year's Eve & Day; Easter; Memorial Day; Independence Day; Labor Day; Thanksgiving; Christmas. ♿
Attendance: 100,000 (accurate)
Membership: Individual $50; Family $75; Patron $100; Sustaining $500. Corporate: $1,000; $2,500; $5,000.

INTERNATIONAL MUSEUM OF CULTURES, 7500 W. Camp Wisdom Rd., Dallas, TX 75236-5629. Tel.: 972-708-7537. Fax: 972-708-7341.
E-mail: mfkamm@internationalmuseumofcultures.org
Web Site: www.internationalmuseumofcultures.org
Founded: 1974.
Congressional District: 6
Key Personnel: C.E.O., Mary Fae Kamm; Chm. (V), Dr. Kevin Fegan; Chm.-Elect, Florentino Ramirez.
Personnel Profile: Full-Time Paid 2; Full-Time Volunteers 2; Part-Time Paid 3; Part-Time Volunteers 24; Interns 3.
Governing Authority: nonprofit organization. Tax-exempt: 501(c)(3).
Anthropology Museum.
Collections: ethnographic collections from South America, Papua New Guinea, Africa, Southeast Asia, East Asia, Mexico, Native American.
Research Fields: Cultural & Social Anthropology; Theoretical & Applied Linguistics.
Facilities: 15,000-vol. library of books on anthropology, linguistics & literacy available for use on premises; field research stations.
Activities: Film and lecture series on cultures of the world.
Publications: Museum of Cultures Publications Series (23 volumes).
Hours & Admission Prices: Mon.-Fri. 10-4. Scheduled Tours: adults $4, seniors & children $3; discounts to AAM members; members no charge. ♿
Attendance: 12,000 (accurate)
Membership: Student $20; Regular $40; Family $50; Sustaining Hero $100; Supporting Hero $500; Authentic Hero $1,000.

JUANITA J. CRAFT CIVIL RIGHTS HOUSE, 2618 Warren Ave., Dallas, TX 75215-2911. Tel.: 214-670-8637.
Historic House Museum: housed in the former home of civil rights organizer, Juanita J. Craft; visited here by President Lyndon Johnson & Martin Luther King Jr. to discuss the future of the civil rights movement.
Collections: local history & culture; period furnishings; personal artifacts; photographs.
Hours & Admission Prices: Mon.-Fri. 9-5:30 by appointment.

MEADOWS MUSEUM, (M), Southern Methodist University, 5900 Bishop Blvd., Dallas, TX 75205. Tel.: 214-768-2516. Fax: 214-768-1688.
E-mail: info@meadowsmuseumdallas.org
Web Site: www.meadowsmuseumdallas.org
Founded: 1965.
Congressional District: 3
Key Personnel: Dir., Mark A. Roglan; Deputy Dir., Elizabeth Hunt Blanc; Dir. Education, M. Carmen Smith; Financial Officer, Roni Arifin; Collections Mgr. & Cur. of Exhibitions, Bridget Marx; Mgr. Membership, Catherine Baetz; Mgr. Operations, Charles Guijarro; Security Mgr., Brenda Laury.
Personnel Profile: Full-Time Paid 20; Part-Time Paid 10; Part-Time Volunteers 75; Interns 5.
Governing Authority: university. Parent Institution: Southern Methodist University. Tax-exempt.
Art Museum.
Collections: 10th-21st century Spanish art by painters El Greco, Velazquez, Ribera, Murillo, Goya, Miro & Picasso; Renaissance altarpieces; Baroque canvases; rococo oil sketches; polychrome wood sculptures; impressionist landscapes; modernist abstractions; graphic works of Goya; 20th century sculptures.
Research Fields: Spanish art history.
Facilities: 1,000-vol. library of books & periodicals on history of Spanish art available on request; reading room; works on paper research room; restaurant; special event halls; auditorium. Museum-related items for sale.
Activities: guided tours; gallery talks; concerts; lecture series; film programs; formally organized education programs for undergraduate & graduate students affiliated with Southern Methodist University; members' exhibition previews.
Publications: newsletter; exhibition catalogues.
Hours & Admission Prices: Tues.-Wed. & Fri.-Sat. 10-5, Thurs. 10-8, Sun. 12-5. Adults $8; members, children under 12, SMU faculty, staff, students & staff members of other museums no charge. Closed New Year's Day; Easter; Thanksgiving; Christmas Eve & Day. ♿
Attendance: 69,000 (accurate)
Membership: Goya Friend $60; El Greco Circle $150; Velazquez Court $300; Ribera Patron $500; Murilla Benefactor $1,000; Fortuny Angel $2,500. Corporate memberships vary.

MUSEUM OF GEOMETRIC & MADI ART, (M), 3109 Carlisle, Dallas, TX 75204-1194. Tel.: 214-855-7802. Fax: 214-855-5479.
E-mail: dorothy@madimuseumdallas.org
Web Site: www.madimuseumdallas.org
Formerly: MADI Museum
Founded: 2003.
Congressional District: 30
Key Personnel: C.E.O. (V) & Cur., Dorothy Masterson; Chm. & Pres. (V), William P. Irwin; Treas., Bo Irwin; Dir. Education & Museum Shop Mgr., Patricia Canning; Dir. Membership & Registrar, MaryAnne Preston; Public Rels., Keith Nix.
Personnel Profile: Full-Time Volunteers 1; Part-Time Paid 5; Part-Time Volunteers 3; Interns 1.
Governing Authority: private; nonprofit organization. Tax-exempt: 501(c)(3).
Art Museum.
Collections: works by founder Carmelo Arden Quin, Rothfuss, Kosice, Herbin, Blaszko, Vardanega, Carreno, Guevara; artists from South & North America, Japan, France, Italy, Hungary, & other European countries.
Major Exhibits: Small Geometric Works, 12/4/09-2/10; Pamela Nelson & Heather Marcus, 3/5/10-5/30/10; Local Student Art Show, 6/4/10-8/29/10; Italian Geometric Artists, 9/3/10-11/8/10.
Facilities: Museum-related items for sale.
Activities: docent program; guided tours; lectures; participatory exhibits; printmaking & collage classes.
Publications: Biography of Carmelo Arden Quin; show catalogues.
Hours & Admission Prices: Tues.-Wed. & Fri.-Sat. 11-5, Thurs. 11-7, Sun. 1-5. No charge; donations accepted. Closed New Year's Day; Thanksgiving; Christmas. ♿
Attendance: 3,316 (accurate)
Membership: Student $25; Basic $50; Family $100; Sponsor $250; Patron $500; Benefactor $1,000; Angel $2,500.

MUSEUM OF NATURE & SCIENCE, 1318 S. 2nd Ave., 3535 Grand Ave. & 1620 1st Ave., Dallas, TX 75210. Mailing Address: P.O. Box 151469, Dallas, TX 75315-1469. Tel.: 214-428-5555. Fax: 214-428-4356.
E-mail: info@natureandscience.org
Web Site: www.natureandscience.org
Formerly: Southwest Museum of Science and Technology, The Science Place & TI Founders IMAX Theater, the Dallas Children's Museum
Founded: 2006.
Congressional District: 30
Key Personnel: C.E.O., Nicole Small; Chm., Frank-Paul King; C.F.O., Sally Pietsch; Dir. Finance, Nadine Chaffin; Dir. Mktg., Beth Hook; Dir. Exhibits, Paul Vinson; Dir. Operations, Harley Cozewith; Mgr. Volunteers, Susan Meyer; Dir. Education, Steve Hinkley; Cur. Earth Science, Dr. Anthony Fiorillo; Public Programs Coord., Stacey Bucklin; Dir. Individual & Foundation Giving, Patricia J. Broyles; Dir. Corporate Giving, Megan Harrison; Dir. Membership, Murphey Harmon.
Personnel Profile: Full-Time Paid 48; Part-Time Paid 61; Part-Time Volunteers 602.
Governing Authority: nonprofit organization. Tax-exempt: 501(c)(3) & 170(b)(1)(A).
Natural History, Science & Technology Museum.
Collections: over 6,600 scientific bird specimens; 14,000 malacology specimens; 3,300 rocks & minerals; 3,300 mammal specimens; 34,700 paleontology specimens.
Major Exhibits: Water: H2O=Life (T), 5/28/10-8/22/10.
Research Fields: vertebrate paleontology.
Facilities: library; 175-seat auditorium; 323-seat IMAX dome theater; 40-seat planetarium; classrooms; food court. Museum-related items for sale.
Activities: lectures; films; gallery talks; demonstrations; formally-organized educational programs; training programs for museum workers; teacher training; seasonal workshops; museum school; electric theater; school programs (onsite & outreach); after school programs; planetarium shows; day camps; family festival events; birthday parties; sleepovers; scouting adventures; parent-and-child drop-in programs.
Publications: seasonal newsletter, Explorations; teacher's guide; brochures; fliers.
Hours & Admission Prices: Mon.-Sat. 10-5, Sun. 12-5. General admission: adults $9.50, senior citizens 62 & over, students 19 & over with ID, & youth 12-18 $8, child 3-11 $6; discounts to groups; members no charge. Planetarium: $3.50 per person; discounts to members. IMAX: adults $7, senior citizens, students & children $6; discounts to members. Special exhibitions may have additional cost. Closed New Year's Day; Thanksgiving; Christmas. ♿
Attendance: 500,000 (estimated)

Membership: Student $40; Individual $60; Family $90; Family Plus $150; Bailey Society $200; Inventor $250; Naturalist $500; Explorer $1,000.

MUSEUM OF THE AMERICAN RAILROAD, (M), 1105 Washington St., Fair Park, Dallas, TX 75210. Mailing Address: P.O. Box 153259, Dallas, TX 75315-3259. Tel.: 214-428-0101 & 0102. Fax: 214-426-1937.
E-mail: info@dallasrailwaymuseum.com
Web Site: www.dallasrailwaymuseum.com
Formerly: Age of Steam Railroad Museum
Founded: 1963.
Key Personnel: C.E.O., Robert LaPrelle; Chm., Robert Willis; Vice Chair, Jack Maxson; Dir. Public Programs, Kelly Murphy; Dir. Education, Garl Latham; Dir. Devel., Melissa Smith.
Personnel Profile: Full-Time Paid 3; Part-Time Paid 1; Part-Time Volunteers 55; Interns 1.
Governing Authority: society. Tax-exempt: 501(c)(3).
Railroad Museum.
Collections: 36 pieces of rolling stock including 4 steam locomotives, 7 diesel locomotives, 1 electric locomotive, 17 passenger cars, & 6 freight cars; books; archives; photographs. Historic Railroad Buildings: 1901 Dallas Depot; 1905 Santa Fe Railway Interlocking Tower.
Research Fields: history of U.S. railroads.
Facilities: Museum-related items for sale.
Activities: lectures; films; permanent & traveling exhibitions.
Publications: bimonthly newsletter, The Clearance Card; brochure, The Age of Steam Exhibit; book, Iron Horses of the Santa Fe Trail.
Hours & Admission Prices: Museum: Wed.-Sun. 10-5. State Fair: Oct. daily 10-6. Adults $5, children under 13 $2.50; discounts to AAM members; members no charge.
Attendance: 46,000 (accurate)
Membership: Trainman $30; Family $40; Station Master $60; Engineer $100; Conductor $500; Railroad Magnate $1,000.

NASHER SCULPTURE CENTER, (M), 2001 Flora St., Dallas, TX 75201-2336. Tel.: 214-242-5100. Fax: 214-242-5155.
Web Site: www.nashersculpturecenter.org
Founded: 2003.
Congressional District: 30
Key Personnel: Dir., Jeremy Strick; Devel., Jane Offenbach; Education, Stephen Ross; Public Rels., Kristen Gibbins; C.F.O., John McBride; Registrar, Jennifer Ritchie; Cur., Jed Morse; Museum Shop Mgr., Dana Mullins; Security, Mike Jensen.
Personnel Profile: Full-Time Paid 23; Part-Time Paid 21; Part-Time Volunteers 40; Interns 3.
Governing Authority: private; nonprofit organization. Tax-exempt: 501(c)(3).
Art Museum & Sculpture Garden.
Collections: Raymond and Patsy Nasher collection of modern & contemporary sculpture from 19th-century to present.
Facilities: 3,000-vol. library of sculpture books; 10,000 sq. ft. exhibit space; 100-seat restaurant; classrooms; 200-seat theater. Museum-related items for sale.
Activities: arts festivals; concerts; dance recitals; docent program; films; formal education programs; guided tours; lectures; loan, temporary & traveling exhibitions.
Publications: quarterly members newsletter.
Hours & Admission Prices: Tues.-Wed. & Fri.-Sun. 11-5, Thurs. 11-9. Adults $10, senior citizens $7, students $5; children under 12 & members no charge. Closed Independence Day; Thanksgiving; Christmas.
Attendance: 250,000
Membership: Giacometti $75; Moore $125; Calder $500; Miro $1,000; Brancusi $2,500; Matisse $5,000; Rodin $10,000.

* **THE SIXTH FLOOR MUSEUM AT DEALEY PLAZA, (M),** 411 Elm St., Dallas, TX 75202-3301. Tel.: 214-747-6660; 888-485-4854. Fax: 214-747-6662.
E-mail: jfk@jfk.org
Web Site: www.jfk.org
Founded: 1989.
Congressional District: 30
Key Personnel: Exec. Dir., Nicola Longford; Chm. Bd. Dir., Jill Johnson; Dir. Communications, Deborah Marine; Dir. Operations, Stephen Truly; Dir. Collections, Megan Bryant; Dir. Finance, John Sadeghi; Cur., Gary Mack; Cur. Education, Sharron Conrad.
Personnel Profile: Full-Time Paid 27; Part-Time Paid 5; Interns 1.
Governing Authority: private; nonprofit organization. Parent Institution: Dallas County Historical Foundation. Tax-exempt.
History Museum & Historical Site: the former Texas School Book Depository.
Collections: photographs; film & video footage; documents; period artifacts; oral histories related to the assassination & legacy of President John F. Kennedy.
Major Exhibits: A Photographer's Story: Bob Jackson and the Kennedy Assassination, 12/10.
Research Fields: Kennedy assassination & investigations; 1960s Dallas history & culture; presidential history.
Facilities: visitor center; rental facilities; reading room; cafe. Museum-related items for sale.
Activities: audio guide in 7 languages; cell phone tour; education programs for children & adults; public programs; permanent & temporary exhibitions; special events.
Publications: guide book, Dealey Plaza National Historic Landmark; DVD, Films from The Sixth Floor; brochures; student gallery guides.
Hours & Admission Prices: Mon. 12-6, Tues.-Sun. 10-6. Adults $13.50, senior citizens 65 & over and youth 6-18 $12.50, children 5 & under $3.50 with audio; discounts to groups; TAM, AAM members, children 5 & under no charge without audio. Audio Tour: available in 7 languages included in admission. Closed Thanksgiving; Christmas. ♿
Attendance: 333,000 (accurate)

TEXAS DISCOVERY GARDENS, Fair Park, 3601 Martin Luther King Blvd., Dallas, TX 75210. Mailing Address: P.O. Box 152537, Dallas, TX 75315-2537. Tel.: 214-428-7476. Fax: 214-428-5338.
E-mail: tdg@texasdiscoverygardens.org
Web Site: www.texasdiscoverygardens.org
Formerly: Dallas Horticulture Center
Founded: 1941.
Congressional District: 5
Key Personnel: Exec. Dir., Melissa Martin; Chm. (V), Barbara Hunt Crow.
Personnel Profile: Full-Time Paid 10; Part-Time Paid 7; Interns 3.
Governing Authority: nonprofit organization. Tax-exempt: 501(c)(3).
Arboretum & Botanical Garden Museum, Conservatory & Horticultural Resource Center; c.1936 National Historic Landmark.
Collections: gardens including native plants; water features & outdoor sculpture; live butterflies; insectarium.
Facilities: 7 1/2-acre grounds; botanical garden; visitor center; butterfly house.
Activities: seminars; lectures & workshops; education programs for children; permanent & temporary exhibitions; seasonal events & festivals; community resource for public & private events, performing arts groups, weddings & conferences; garden tours.
Publications: quarterly newsletter.
Hours & Admission Prices: Tues.-Sat. 10-5, Sun. 1-5. Adults $3, seniors $2, children 3-11 $1.50; members, children under 3 & Tues. no charge. Closed federal holidays. ♿
Attendance: 180,000 (estimated)
Membership: Students, Teachers, and Seniors 60 & over $40; Individual $60; Dual $80; Family $90; Friends $150; Patron $300; Benefactor $600; Sustaining $1,200.

TEXAS FIRE MUSEUM, City of Dallas Fire Dept. Maintenance Facility, 2600 Chalk Hill Rd., Dallas, TX 75212-4506. Tel.: 214-267-1867.
Governing Authority: nonprofit organization. Tax-exempt: 501(c)(3).
Fire Museum.
Collections: fire service history; period fire equipment & trucks; personal artifacts; photographs.
Facilities: restaurant. Museum-related items for sale.
Publications: monthly newsletter.
Hours & Admission Prices: Thurs.-Sat. 10-2. No charge. ♿

THE TRAMMELL & MARGARET CROW COLLECTION OF ASIAN ART, 2010 Flora St., Dallas, TX 75201-2335. Tel.: 214-979-6430. Fax: 214-979-6439.
E-mail: marketing@crowcollection.org
Web Site: www.crowcollection.org
Founded: 1998.
Key Personnel: Dir., Amy L. Hofland; Asst. Dir., Jennifer Parker; Pres. (V), Trammell S. Crow; Museum Shop Mgr., Corrie Martin; Membership & Special Events Coord., Jennifer Thomas; Education Coord., Krystal Read; Registrar & Junior Cur., Mr. Shi'Yuau Yuan; Dir. Exhibitions, Dimitris Skliris; Dir. Education, Neil Sreenan; Business Mgr., Cory Beth Lifto; Conservator, Csilla Felker-Dennis.
Personnel Profile: Full-Time Paid 8; Part-Time Paid 7; Part-Time Volunteers 45; Interns 6.
Governing Authority: private; nonprofit organization. Tax-exempt.
Art Museum.
Collections: arts from Japan, China, Cambodia, India, Thailand, Myanmar & Tibet.
Facilities: 100-vol. library of Asian art & culture; 9,000 sq. ft. exhibit space. Museum-related items for sale.

Activities: arts festivals; concerts; dance recitals; docent program; guided tours; lectures; temporary exhibitions; theater.
Hours & Admission Prices: Tues.-Sat. 10-9. No charge; donations accepted. Closed New Year's Day, Independence Day; Thanksgiving; Christmas. ♿
Attendance: 51,235 (accurate)
Membership: Teacher & Student $30; Individual & Jade Individual $50; Family & Dual $65; Jade Dual/Couple $75; Pearl Circle $125; Bamboo Circle $250; Lotus Circle $500; Peony Circle $1,000; Bronze Circle $2,500; Ivory Circle $5,000; Crystal Circle $7,500; Imperial Circle $10,000.

THE WOMEN'S MUSEUM: AN INSTITUTE FOR THE FUTURE, 3800 Parry Ave., Dallas, TX 75226-1752. Tel.: 214-915-0860. Fax: 214-915-0870.
E-mail: info@thewomensmuseum.org
Web Site: www.thewomensmuseum.org
Founded: 2000.
Congressional District: 30
Key Personnel: C.E.O., Wanda R. Brice; Dir. Devel., Fran Lobpries; Mgr. Exhibits, Maury Ford; Mgr. Events, Shana Hamilton; Mgr. Mktg., Haley Curry; Mgr. Programs, Denita Powell-Malvern.
Personnel Profile: Full-Time Paid 10; Part-Time Paid 11; Interns 6.
Governing Authority: private; nonprofit. Tax-exempt: 501(c)(3).
Women's American History Museum.
Collections: paper; books; buttons; posters; garments; personal artifacts relating to women's history.
Research Fields: women's history.
Facilities: 172-seat auditorium; 17,000 sq. ft. exhibit space; 50-seat cafeteria; 32 station computer lab. Museum-related items for sale.
Activities: interactive exhibits; docent program; films; guided tours; lectures; loan exhibitions; technology training in computer lab; film series.
Publications: quarterly newsletter; monthly e-newsletter.
Hours & Admission Prices: Tues.-Sun. 12-5. Adults $5, senior citizens & students $4, children 5-12 $3; discounts to groups, Texas Association of Museums & Smithsonian affiliates; children under 5 & members no charge. Closed major holidays. ♿
Attendance: 219,000 (accurate)
Membership: Individual $50; Dual $60; Family $70; Smithsonian Affiliate $100; Mentor $500; Director's Inner Circle & Leadership Council $1,000.

Decatur

WISE COUNTY HERITAGE MUSEUM, 1602 S. Trinity, Decatur, TX 76234-2717. Mailing Address: P.O. Box 427, Decatur, TX 76234-0427. Tel.: 940-627-5586.
E-mail: wisemuseum@embarqmail.com
Web Site: www.wisehistory.com
Founded: 1967.
Congressional District: 13
Key Personnel: C.E.O., Treas. & Chm. Wise County Historical Commission, Rosalie Gregg; Pres., Kerry Clower; Vice Pres., Exhibits Chm. & Museum Shop Mgr., Bettye Jane Dodds; Sec. & Trustee, Sally Pegues; Trustee, Sue Tackel; Trustee, Franklin Blank.
Personnel Profile: Part-Time Paid 1; Part-Time Volunteers 4.
Governing Authority: society. Parent Institution: Wise County Historical Society, Inc. Tax-exempt: 501(c)(3).
Local History Museum.
Collections: historical artifacts; manuscripts; genealogy.
Research Fields: genealogy; family histories.
Facilities: over 2,000-vol. library of material on county history & newspaper abstracts available for use on premises; reading room; 300 seat auditorium; exhibit rooms; newspapers on microfilm; Wise County census records. Cemetery, census, birth, marriage records. Material on Tennessee, Virginia & other states. A room dedicated to members of the Lost Battalion (Prisoners of War of the Japanese during WWII); dedication to the survivors of the USS Houston CA-30 & members of armed forces of England, Australia & Holland who were also POW's. Members of the 131st Field Artillery & the USS Houston CA-30. Gift items, plaques, cards, pictures & books pertaining to Wise County for sale.
Activities: guided tours; films; drama; hobby workshops; permanent & temporary exhibitions; weddings. Museum Sponsors: Fundraising Events; Wise County Fine Arts Festival October to December.
Publications: monthly newsletters; History of Wise County, A Link With The Past Vol. I; Vol. II; Vol. III; Pioneer History reprint; History of Rhome, TX; memoirs by former World War II POWs of the Lost Battalion who spent 3-1/2 years building the railroad that led to the bridge over the River Kwai.
Hours & Admission Prices: Mon.-Sat. 10-3. Adults $1, children under 12 & school groups through high school $.50; members no charge. Closed major holidays. ♿
Attendance: 7,000 (estimated)
Membership: Individual $10; Husband & Wife $15; Life Time $150.

Del Rio

WHITEHEAD MEMORIAL MUSEUM, (M), 1308 S. Main St., Del Rio, TX 78840-5998. Tel.: 830-774-7568. Fax: 830-774-7568.
E-mail: whiteheadmuseum@bizstx.rr.com
Web Site: www.whitehead-museum.com
Founded: 1962.
Congressional District: 23
Key Personnel: C.E.O. & Museum Shop Mgr, Lee Lincoln; Pres. (V), Mike Parker.
Personnel Profile: Full-Time Paid 3; Part-Time Paid 1; Part-Time Volunteers 8.
Governing Authority: municipal. Tax-exempt.
Historical Museum.
Collections: 2-1/2 acre site with over 14 historical & replica buildings including the 1870 Perry Store; Black Seminole Indian Scouts exhibit; graves of Judge Roy Bean & son Sam; Jersey Lily Saloon replica; pioneer log cabin; a folk art exhibit, the Cadena Nativity.
Research Fields: Dr. John Brinkley; Judge Roy Bean; Seminole Negro Indian Scouts; U-2 Spy Plane (USAF); genealogy, railroad; Val Verde County; Buffalo Soldier; Texas Rock Art; Lower Percos River.
Facilities: visitor center. Museum-related gifts for sale.
Activities: guided tours.
Publications: brochures
Hours & Admission Prices: Tues.-Sat. 9-4:30, Sun. 1-5, guided tours by appointment. Adults $5, seniors $4, youths 13-18 $3, children 6-12 $2; discount to AAM, ICOM & TAM members; members no charge. ♿
Attendance: 11,000 (estimated)
Membership: Single $15; Family $25; Corporate $50; Contributing $75; Sustaining $100 & up.

Denison

EISENHOWER BIRTHPLACE STATE HISTORIC SITE, 609 S. Lamar Ave., Denison, TX 75021-4821. Tel.: 903-465-8908. Fax: 903-465-8988.
Web Site: www.visiteisenhowerbirthplace.com
Founded: 1946.
Congressional District: 4
Key Personnel: Site Mgr., Robin Gilliam.
Personnel Profile: Full-Time Paid 3; Part-Time Paid 3; Part-Time Volunteers 12.
Governing Authority: state. Parent Institution: Texas Historical Commission. Tax-exempt.
Historic House: 1881 house where Dwight D. Eisenhower was born.
Collections: 1890 period furnishings; political campaign memorabilia.
Facilities: visitor center; covered pavilion; education center; meeting & community room. Museum-related items for sale.
Activities: guided tours; permanent exhibitions.
Publications: brochure.
Hours & Admission Prices: Tues.-Sat. 9-5, Sun. 1-5; last tour 4pm. Adults $3, children 12-18 $2; discounts for AAM & ICOM members; children under 12 & members no charge. Closed New Year's Day; Thanksgiving; Christmas Eve & Day. ♿
Attendance: 15,000 (estimated)

Denton

BAYLESS-SELBY HOUSE MUSEUM, 317 W. Mulberry St., Denton, TX 76201-6062. Tel.: 940-349-2865. Fax: 940-349-2851.
E-mail: managerbsh@dentoncounty.com
Web Site: www.dentoncounty.com/bsh
Founded: 2001.
Key Personnel: Mgr., Robyn L. Lee
Historic House Museum.
Collections: Victorian period artifacts & furnishings.
Activities: lectures.
Hours & Admission Prices: Tues.-Sat. 10-12 & 1-3; groups by appointment. Group Tours: $1 per person. ♿

COURTHOUSE-ON-THE-SQUARE MUSEUM, 110 W. Hickory, Denton, TX 76201-4116. Tel.: 940-349-2850. Fax: 940-349-2851.
Key Personnel: Exec. Dir., Dr. Georgia Kemp Caraway; Cur. Collections, Kim McCoig Cupit; Dir. Education & Tourism, Sara Dee; Museum Specialist, Dr. Kathryn R. Lynass
History Museum: housed in the former county courthouse; built in 1896. Listed on the National Register of Historic Places.
Collections: local history & culture; African American & Hispanic heritage; dolls; farming; weapons; period furnishings; personal artifacts.
Activities: lectures; special events.
Hours & Admission Prices: Mon.-Fri. 10-4:30, Sat. 11-3. Group Tours: $1 per person. Closed holidays & holiday weekends. ♿

DAR MUSEUM FIRST LADIES OF TEXAS HISTORIC COSTUMES COLLECTION, Texas Woman's University, Administration Conference Tower, 2nd Fl., Denton, TX 76204. Mailing Address: P.O. Box 425379, Denton, TX 76204-5379. Tel.: 940-898-3644. Fax: 940-898-3386.
Web Site: www.twu.edu
Founded: 1940.
Congressional District: 26
Key Personnel: Dir. Conference Svcs., David Sweeten.
Governing Authority: Parent Institution: Texas Woman's University. Subsidiary Institution: Dept. of Family Sciences.
Costume Museum.
Collections: Inaugural Ball gowns of Texas first ladies, including wives of the presidents of the Republic of Texas & the governors of the State; gowns worn by the wives of Vice President John Nance Garner, President Dwight D. Eisenhower & President Lyndon B. Johnson.
Activities: tours by appointment.
Publications: descriptive booklet of the collection; Texas' First Ladies Historical Costume Collection.
Hours & Admission Prices: Mon.-Fri. 8-5; groups by appointment only. No charge. Closed national holidays; university holidays. ♿

DENTON COUNTY AFRICAN AMERICAN MUSEUM, 317 W. Mulberry St., Denton, TX 76201-6062. Tel.: 940-349-2865. Fax: 940-349-2851.
E-mail: managerbsh@dentoncounty.com
Web Site: www.dentoncounty.com/dcaam
Founded: 2008.
Key Personnel: Mgr., Robyn L. Lee
African American History Museum.
Collections: photographs; texts; personal artifacts; period furnishings.
Activities: group tours.
Hours & Admission Prices: Tues.-Sat. 10-12 & 1-3; groups by appointment. Groups: $1 per person. Closed holidays. ♿

HANGAR 10 FLYING MUSEUM, 1945 Matt Wright Lane, Denton Municipal Airport, Denton, TX 76207-4537. Tel.: 940-565-1945.
Governing Authority: nonprofit organization. Tax-exempt: 501(c)(3).
Aviation History Museum.
Collections: civil & military aircraft; aviation history; military memorabilia; personal artifacts.
Hours & Admission Prices: Mon.-Sat. 8:30-3; other times by appointment. No charge; donations accepted.

TEXAS WOMAN'S UNIVERSITY ART GALLERIES, 1200 Frame St., Visual Arts Bldg., corner Oakland & Texas, Denton, TX 76204. Mailing Address: Box 425469, TWU Station, Denton, TX 76204-5469. Tel.: 940-898-2530 & 2533. Fax: 940-898-2496.
E-mail: visualarts@twu.edu
Web Site: www.twu.edu
Founded: 1901.
Congressional District: 26
Key Personnel: Chm. Visual Art Dept., John Weinkein.
Governing Authority: state; university. Affiliated with Texas Woman's University.
Art Museum.
Collections: paintings; photographs; sculpture.
Activities: guided tours; lectures; films; gallery talks; formally organized education programs for children, adults, undergraduate and graduate students; temporary exhibitions; student thesis exhibition show.
Hours & Admission Prices: Mon.-Fri. 8-5. No charge. Closed national holidays. ♿

UNIVERSITY OF NORTH TEXAS ART GALLERY, School of Visual Arts, 1201 W. Mulberry, Denton, TX 76203. Mailing Address: P.O. Box 305100, Denton, TX 76203-5100. Tel.: 940-565-4005 & 4001. Fax: 940-565-4717.
E-mail: gallery@unt.edu
Web Site: www.art.unt.edu
Founded: 1972.
Congressional District: 26
Key Personnel: Dir., Tracee W. Robertson; Asst. Dir., Victoria Estrada-Berg; Dean School Visual Arts, Dr. Robert Milnes; Exhibition Designer, Brian Wheeler.
Personnel Profile: Full-Time Paid 2; Part-Time Paid 9; Part-Time Volunteers 5.
Governing Authority: university; nonprofit. Parent Institution: Univ. of North Texas. Subsidiary Institutions: Cora Stafford Gallery; Lightwell Gallery (both have same mailing address as above); UNT Artspace FW; Design Gallery. Tax-exempt.
Art Gallery.
Collections: 20th century contemporary art most of which is by former students & faculty. Visual art: painting; ceramics; prints; graphics; sculpture. A significant portion of the collection was donated by patrons & artists (such as DeKooning & Motherwell).
Research Fields: internships available in Museum/Gallery studies.
Facilities: 3,150 sq. ft. exhibit space.
Activities: formally organized education programs for undergraduates & graduates; over 700 works in the permanent collection available for loan to faculty & staff; temporary, loan & traveling exhibitions. Museum Sponsors: annual juried competition; MFA Exhibition for graduates.
Publications: exhibition catalogues.
Hours & Admission Prices: Mon.-Tues. 12-8, Wed.-Sat. 12-5. Call for summer hours. No charge; donations accepted. Closed between semesters; spring break. ♿
Attendance: 8,000 (accurate)

Dripping Springs

HARBOR RANCH, U.S. 290 W., Dripping Springs, TX 78620. Mailing Address: 1200 Belmont Pkwy., Austin, TX 78703-1414. Tel.: 512-469-0716. Fax: 512-494-8574.
Formerly: Galloping Road Compound & Poker Alley; Harbor Ranch
Founded: 1950.
Congressional District: 14
Key Personnel: Owner & C.E.O., Harriet Rutland.
Governing Authority: individual operation. Branch Museum: Harbor Ranch, US 290, Dripping Springs, TX 78620.
Historic House Museum.
Collections: Texas-made furniture; farm tools; period artifacts. Historic Buildings: bunkhouse; barns.
Activities: guided tours; study clubs.
Hours & Admission Prices: By appointment only. No charge.
Attendance: 100 (estimated)

Dublin

DUBLIN DR PEPPER BOTTLING COMPANY MUSEUM, 105 E. Elm, Dublin, TX 76446-2309. Mailing Address: 221 S. Patrick St., Dublin, TX 76446-2347. Tel.: 254-445-4210. Fax: 254-445-4677.
Founded: 1995.
Key Personnel: Museum Shop Mgr., Lori Dodd
Company Museum.
Collections: company history, bottling, marketing & advertising; photographs; catalogs.
Activities: guided tours.
Hours & Admission Prices: Memorial Day to Labor Day daily 10-5; Sept.-May Tues.-Sun. 10-5. Adults $2.50, senior citizens & children 6-12 $2; children 5 & under no charge. ♿
Attendance: 65,000 (estimated)

Dumas

MOORE COUNTY ART ASSOCIATION, The Art Center, 1810 S. Dumas Ave., Dumas, TX 79029-6002. Tel.: 806-935-5312. Fax: 806-934-4447.
E-mail: fineart54@valornet.com
Web Site: www.dumasmuseumandartcenter.org
Founded: 1954.
Key Personnel: C.E.O. Procurement & Pres., Carolyn Stallwitz; Dir. & Museum Shop Mgr., Marti Christman; Cur. Finance, Business Officer & Memorials, Glynda Pflug; Vice Pres., Ralph Bynum; Cur. Catalogue, Jaimye Pool.
Personnel Profile: Full-Time Paid 1; Part-Time Paid 2; Part-Time Volunteers 2.
Governing Authority: nonprofit organization. Subsidiary Institution: Moore County Texas. Tax-exempt: 170(b)(1)(A).
Art Center.
Collections: paintings; photographs; prints; sculpture.
Research Fields: local history.
Activities: guided tours; loan, permanent & temporary exhibitions; school tours.
Publications: brochure.
Hours & Admission Prices: Mon.-Sat. 10-5. No charge; donations accepted. Closed Thanksgiving; Christmas. ♿
Attendance: 6,600 (accurate)
Membership: Individual $10; Family $20; Patron $50; Friend $75 & up; Benefactor $500.

MOORE COUNTY HISTORICAL MUSEUM, (M), Window on the Plains, 1820 S. Dumas Ave., Dumas, TX 79029-6002. Tel.: 806-935-3113. Fax: 806-934-3621.
E-mail: dumasmuseum@windstream.net
Web Site: www.dumasmuseumandartcenter.org
Founded: 1976.

Congressional District: 31
Key Personnel: C.E.O. Procurement & Pres., Kurt Stallwitz; Dir. & Museum Shop Mgr., Terri George; Pres., Scott Higgingbotham; Cur. Finance, Business Officer & Memorials, Glynda Pflug.
Personnel Profile: Full-Time Paid 1; Part-Time Paid 1; Part-Time Volunteers 35.
Governing Authority: nonprofit organization. Subsidiary Institution: Moore County Texas. Tax-exempt: 170(b)(1)(A).
History and Wildlife Museum.
Collections: local wild life; historical items; Indian artifacts; local photographs; oral tapes; newspapers; archives.
Research Fields: local history.
Activities: guided tours; loan, permanent & temporary exhibitions; school tours.
Publications: brochures concentrating on Texas & Dumas.
Hours & Admission Prices: Mon.-Sat. 10-5. No charge; donations accepted. Closed Thanksgiving; Christmas. ♿
Attendance: 6,209 (accurate)
Membership: Individual $10; Family $15; Patron $25; Friend $100; Benefactor $500.

Eagle Lake

PRAIRIE EDGE MUSEUM, 408 E. Main St., Eagle Lake, TX 77434-2534. Tel.: 979-234-7442.
History Museum.
Collections: area natural & cultural history; plant & animal life; Native American artifacts; early pioneers; military.
Activities: educational programs; presentations; celebrations.
Hours & Admission Prices: Mon.-Fri. 8:30-12:30, Sat.-Sun. 2-5.

Edinburg

MUSEUM OF SOUTH TEXAS HISTORY, (M), 200 N. Closner Blvd., Edinburg, TX 78541-3554. Tel.: 956-383-6911. Fax: 956-381-8518.
E-mail: info@mosthistory.org
Web Site: www.mosthistory.org
Formerly: Hidalgo County Historical Museum
Founded: 1967.
Congressional District: 15
Key Personnel: Exec. Dir., Shan Rankin; Chm. Bd. Trustees, Barbara Guerra; Accounting, Alma Vargas; Devel., Lynne Beeching; Registrar, Lisa Adam; Coord. Education, Judy McClelland; Programming Officer, Melissa Tijerina; Public Rels., Joel A. Garza; Cur. Archives & Collections, Barbara Stokes; Receptionist, Sandra Luna; Sr. Cur., Tom A. Fort; IT Specialist & Archives Asst., Steve Lomas; Maintenance, Nazario Reyna; Bldg. Supvr., Joe Hernandez.
Personnel Profile: Full-Time Paid 13; Part-Time Volunteers 25; Interns 40.
Governing Authority: nonprofit organization. Tax-exempt: 501(c)(3).
History Museum: partly housed in 1910 County Jail.
Collections: history & culture of the Rio Grande Valley, South Texas (south of the Nueces River) & northeastern Mexico region; clothing, books, photographs, furniture, machinery, weapons from prehistoric Indian era to 1900's; folklife; Spanish colonial settlement era; ranching; law enforcement; early agriculture; jail's original hanging room & trap door; archival documentation.
Research Fields: architecture; customs & traditions of Rio Grande Valley; Spanish settlement, colonization & early ranch life, genealogy; early agriculture, ranching, transportation, settlement.
Facilities: library; archives relating to the lower Rio Grande Valley, available for research or sale; 10,000 sq. ft. exhibit areas. Museum-related gift items & books for sale.
Activities: guided tours with advance notice (bilingual available); video presentations; docent & volunteer programs; permanent & temporary exhibitions; educational & community service programs.
Publications: books, Folk Life & Folklore of the Mexican Border; Wild Horse Desert: The Heritage of South Texas; Rio Grande Heritage: A Pictorial History; Heritage Cookbook: A Round-up of Wild & Regional Foods; Mesquite Country: Taste & Traditions from the Tip of Texas (regional recipes & history); quarterly newsletter; annual report; Jewel of the Rio Grande (a history of the Museum); The Heritage Sampler: selections from the rich & colorful history of the Rio Grande Valley; Borderlands: The Heritage of the Lower Rio Grande through the Art of Jose Cisneros; Museum of South Texas History.
Hours & Admission Prices: Tues.-Sat. 10-5. Adults $5.50, senior citizens 62 & over and military $4.50, students $4, children 4-12 $3; children 3 & under and members no charge. Closed New Year's Eve & Day; Easter; Memorial Day; Independence Day; Labor Day; Thanksgiving; Christmas Eve & Day. ♿
Attendance: 50,000 (accurate)
Membership: Student $10; Individual $35; Family $50; Sustainer $75; Contributor $100 & up; Benefactor $250; Patron $500; Heritage Associate Contributor $1,000; Heritage Assoc. Patron $2,500; Heritage Council $5,000; Chairman's Circle $10,000.

Edna

TEXANA MUSEUM AND LIBRARY ASSOCIATION, 403 N. Wells, Edna, TX 77957-2730. Tel.: 361-782-5431.
Founded: 1967.
Congressional District: 14
Key Personnel: C.E.O. & Pres. (V), Mary Sayles.
Personnel Profile: Part-Time Paid 1; Part-Time Volunteers 3.
Governing Authority: nonprofit organization. Tax-exempt: 501(c)(3).
History Museum.
Collections: historical artifacts; documents.
Research Fields: local history.
Facilities: 400-vol. library of historical subject matter available for research on site; reading room.
Activities: guided tours.
Hours & Admission Prices: Wed.-Fri. 1-5. No charge; donations accepted. Closed holidays. ♿
Attendance: 1,200 (estimated)
Membership: Individual $5; Family $10; Friend $25; Patron $100; Corporate $250; Benefactor $500.

El Campo

EL CAMPO MUSEUM OF NATURAL HISTORY, 2350 N. Mechanic, El Campo, TX 77437-2343. Mailing Address: P.O. Box 23, El Campo, TX 77437-0023. Tel.: 979-543-6885. Fax: 979-543-5788.
Web Site: www.elcampomuseum.com
Formerly: El Campo Museum of Art, History and Natural Science
Founded: 1978.
Congressional District: 14
Key Personnel: Dir. & Museum Shop Mgr., Cheri McGuirk.
Personnel Profile: Full-Time Paid 1; Part-Time Paid 1; Part-Time Volunteers 30.
Governing Authority: nonprofit organization. Tax-exempt: 501(c)(3).
Natural History Museum.
Collections: wildlife dioramas; seashells; clowns; childrens hands-on exhibits.
Research Fields: animal specimens; local history.
Activities: guided tours; permanent, temporary & traveling exhibitions; interactive computers.
Publications: booklets & brochures, El Campo Museum.
Hours & Admission Prices: Tues.-Fri. 10-12 & 1-5, Sat. 10-3. No charge; donations accepted. Closed major holidays. ♿
Attendance: 7,000 (estimated)
Membership: Individual $20; Family $30; Nonprofit & Business $75; Patron $125; Explorer $250; Collector $500.

El Paso

CASASOLA MUSEUM, 619 Prospect St., El Paso, TX 79902-3745. Mailing Address: P.O. Box 922, Sunland Park, TX 88063-0922. Tel.: 505-312-0257.
Art & History Museum.
Collections: history & culture; paintings; photographs.
Activities: educational programs.
Hours & Admission Prices: Daily 10-5.

CENTENNIAL MUSEUM AND CHIHUAHUAN DESERT GARDENS, Corner of University and Wiggins Rd., El Paso, TX 79968-0001. Mailing Address: 500 W. University Ave., El Paso, TX 79968-8900. Tel.: 915-747-5565. Fax: 915-747-5411.
E-mail: museum@utep.edu
Web Site: www.utep.edu/museum/
Founded: 1936.
Congressional District: 16
Key Personnel: Dir., Dr. Marshall Carter Tripp; Cur. Collections & Exhibits, Scott Cutler; Dir. Laboratory of Environmental Biology, Dr. Art Harris; Administrative Asst. & Museum Shop Mgr., Kaye Mullins; Cur. Botanical, Wynn Anderson.
Personnel Profile: Full-Time Paid 4; Part-Time Paid 2; Part-Time Volunteers 16; Interns 4.
Governing Authority: state. Parent Institution: University of Texas at El Paso, West University Ave. Tax-exempt: 170(b)(1)(A).
Natural History Museum.
Collections: natural & human history; archaeology; botany; geology; paleontology; mineralogy; ethnology; anthropology; fauna of the El Paso area; chihuhuan desert gardens.
Research Fields: archaeology; ethnology; geology; history; paleontology.
Facilities: Museum-related items & books for sale.

Activities: guided tours; lectures; films; permanent & temporary exhibitions; youth classes; adult workshops.
Hours & Admission Prices: Tues.-Sat. 10-4:30. No charge; donations accepted. Closed New Year's Day; Easter; Thanksgiving; Christmas; university holidays. ♿
Attendance: 15,000 (estimated)

CHAMIZAL NATIONAL MEMORIAL, 800 S. San Marcial, El Paso, TX 79905-4123. Tel.: 915-532-7273. Fax: 915-532-7240.
Web Site: www.nps.gov/cham
Founded: 1967.
Congressional District: 16
Key Personnel: Supt., Rick Harris; Chief Ranger, Jerry Flood; Facilities Mgr., Ray Moore; Administrative Officer, Connie Hufford; Creative Dir., Paul Roney; Education & Interpretation, Michael Groomer.
Governing Authority: federal. Parent Institution: National Park Service, Dept. of Interior, Washington, DC 20008. Tax-exempt.
Park Museum: located on land acquired from Mexico through 1963 Treaty.
Collections: history; art; ethnology.
Research Fields: modern & historic cultures of Western Hemisphere; border history.
Facilities: 1,000-vol. library of history & cultural management; 7,500-seat informal amphitheater; 503-seat theater; 55-acre urban park.
Activities: lectures; films; gallery talks; concerts; dance recitals; arts festivals; folk festivals; drama; inter-museum loan & permanent exhibitions. Museum Sponsors: Classic Spanish Drama Festival in March; Border Folk Festival in September; urban programs in Spanish; programs imported from Mexico, Latin American & Europe.
Publications: orientation brochures.
Hours & Admission Prices: Grounds: daily 5am-10pm. Office: Tues.-Sat. 8-5. No charge. Call for theater information & pricing. Closed national holidays. ♿
Attendance: 226,353

EL PASO FIREFIGHTERS MUSEUM, 8600 Montana Ave., El Paso, TX 79925-1214. Tel.: 915-771-1000.
Fire-Fighting Museum.
Collections: firefighting equipment including a 1930 American La France Fire Engine & an 1898 American Fire Engine Company "Steamer."
Hours & Admission Prices: Mon.-Fri. 8-5. No charge.

EL PASO HOLOCAUST MUSEUM & STUDY CENTER, (M), 715 N. Oregon, El Paso, TX 79902-3911. Tel.: 915-351-0048. Fax: 915-351-0908.
E-mail: info@elpasoholocaustmuseum.org
Web Site: elpasoholocaustmuseum.org
Founded: 1992.
Congressional District: 16
Key Personnel: Pres. (V), Ann Schaechner; Treas., Dona Scurry.
Personnel Profile: Full-Time Paid 2; Part-Time Volunteers 30.
Governing Authority: private; nonprofit organization. Tax-exempt: 501(c)(3).
History Museum.
Collections: artifacts; dramatic displays; pictures; posters; authentic history of Europe during the Nazi era.
Facilities: library of children & adult books on WWII & Holocaust.
Activities: docent program; films; guided tours; lectures; traveling exhibitions. Annual Event: Fundraising Dinner Commemoration of the Holocaust.
Publications: quarterly in house, El Paso Holocaust Museum & Study Center.
Hours & Admission Prices: Tues.-Fri. 9-4, Sat.-Sun. 1-5. No charge; donations accepted. Closed New Year's Day; Easter; Labor Day; Rosh Hashanah; Yom Kippur; Christmas. ♿
Attendance: 5,000 (estimated)
Membership: Student $18; Individual $35; Family $50; Bronze $100; Silver $250; Gold $500; Silver $1,000.

EL PASO MUSEUM OF ARCHAEOLOGY, 4301 Transmountain Rd., El Paso, TX 79924-3753. Tel.: 915-755-4332. Fax: 915-759-6824.
Founded: 1977.
Congressional District: 16
Key Personnel: Dir., Marc Thompson; Cur. Education, Marilyn Guida.
Personnel Profile: Full-Time Paid 3; Part-Time Paid 1; Part-Time Volunteers 18; Interns 1.
Governing Authority: municipal. Parent Institution: Museum and Cultural Affairs Department, One Arts Festival Plaza, El Paso, TX 79901. Tax-exempt: 170(b)(1)(A).
Anthropology Museum & Nature Center.
Collections: prehistoric artifacts of the American southwest & northern Mexico; ceramics; textiles; stone tools; American Indian southwest arts & crafts; pottery; basketry.
Research Fields: archaeology & ethnology of the American southwest & northern Mexico.
Facilities: 400-vol. library on southwest anthropology & archaeology available for research only; 100-vols. educational materials; 60-seat auditorium; temporary exhibit space. Museum-related items for sale.
Activities: guided tours; traveling exhibitions; docent program; field trips; workshops. Annual Event: Texas Archaeology Awareness Week.
Publications: Jornada Mogollon Conference publication; Mimbres Twins: Icons of Pueblo Ideology; Prehistoric Indians of the El Paso Area.
Hours & Admission Prices: Tues.-Sat. 9-5, Sun 12-5. No charge; donations accepted. Closed New Year's Day; Martin Luther King Jr. Day; Memorial Day; Independence Day; Labor Day; Thanksgiving & day after; Christmas. ♿
Attendance: 37,000 (accurate)
Membership: Student $15; Senior & Military Individual $20; Individual $25; Military Family $35; Family $40; Supporter's Circle $100-$500; Donor's Circle & Corporate Circle $1,000 & up.

*** EL PASO MUSEUM OF ART, (M), (I),** One Arts Festival Plaza, El Paso, TX 79901-1135. Tel.: 915-532-1707. Fax: 915-532-1010.
Web Site: www.elpasoartmuseum.org
Founded: 1930.
Congressional District: 16
Key Personnel: Dir., Michael Tomor, Ph.D.; Cur., Christian Gerstheimer; Accountant, Polly Perez; Asst. Cur. Education, Ben Fyffe; EPMA Foundation Chair, Jack Maxon; Operations Supvr., Jesus Salgado; Events Coord., Lilia Fierro; Head Devel., Jeffrey Romney; Preparator, Nick Munoz; Registrar, Michelle Villa; Publicist, Kimberly McCarden; Museum Shop Mgr., Armando Vargas.
Personnel Profile: Full-Time Paid 31; Part-Time Paid 1; Part-Time Volunteers 125.
Governing Authority: municipal; nonprofit organization. Parent Institution: City of El Paso. Subsidiary Institution: El Paso Museum of Archaeology at Wilderness Park; El Paso Museum of History. Tax-exempt: 501(c)(3).
Art Museum.
Collections: Samuel H. Kress collection of 13th- to 18th-century European painting & sculpture; 18th- to 21st centuries American art; 20th-century paintings of the Taos & Santa Fe schools; 18th- to 19th-centuries Mexican colonial art; 17th- to 20th-centuries Mexican Retablo painting; Contemporary Art from Texas, New Mexico and the U.S-Mexican border.
Research Fields: pertaining to collections.
Facilities: 2,000-vol. library of art reference books, an affiliate site of National Gallery Extension Programs, available for use by request; 200-seat auditorium; classrooms. Museum-related items for sale.
Activities: guided tours; lectures; films; gallery talks; arts festivals; formally organized educational programs; adult & teen docent program; permanent, temporary & traveling exhibitions.
Publications: quarterly newsletter; exhibition catalogs.
Hours & Admission Prices: Tues.-Wed. & Fri.-Sat. 9-5, Thurs. 9-9, Sun. 12-5. No charge; donations accepted. Closed New Year's Day; Martin Luther King Jr. Day; Memorial Day; Independence Day; Labor Day; Thanksgiving; Christmas. ♿
Attendance: 100,000 (estimated)
Membership: Student & Senior Citizen $15; Individual $25; Military Family $45; Family $50; Contributor $100; Supporter $250; Collector's Circle $500; Sponsor $1,000; Donors Circle $2,500; Patron $5,000; Benefactor $10,000.

EL PASO MUSEUM OF HISTORY, 510 N. Santa Fe St., El Paso, TX 79901-1145.
E-mail: cityhistorymuseum@elpasotexas.gov
Web Site: www.elpasotexas.gov/history
Founded: 1974.
Congressional District: 16
Key Personnel: Dir., Julia H. Bussinger; Sr. Cur., Barbara J. Angus; Dir. Devel., Jim Murphy.
Personnel Profile: Full-Time Paid 12; Part-Time Volunteers 10.
Governing Authority: municipal. Parent Institution: History Museums Dept., City of El Paso, El Paso, TX 79901. Tax-exempt.
History Museum.
Collections: guns; horse gear; historical clothing; photographs; cavalry gear; items pertaining to history of El Paso; leatherworking & bottle collections.
Research Fields: El Paso regional history.
Activities: guided tours; docent program; permanent & traveling exhibitions; organized education programs.
Hours & Admission Prices: Tues.-Wed. & Fri.-Sat. 10-5, Thurs. 9-9, Sun. 12-5. No charge; donations accepted. Closed city holidays. ♿
Attendance: 31,542 (accurate)
Membership: Student, Senior & Military $20; Individual $25; Family $50;

Advocate $250; Corporate & Provider $1,000; Supporter $2,500; Champion $5,000; Patron $10,000; Benefactor $20,000.

EL PASO ZOO, 4001 E. Paisano, El Paso, TX 79905-4223. Tel.: 915-521-1850. Fax: 915-521-1857.
E-mail: elpasozoo@elpasotexas.gov
Web Site: www.elpasozoo.org
Founded: 1941.
Congressional District: 16
Key Personnel: Dir., Steve Marshall; Park Operations, Scott Gilliland; Gen. Cur., John Kiseda; Veterinarian, Victoria Milne, DVM; Education Cur., Rick LoBello; Mktg. Coord., Liz Kern; Security Coord., Eduardo Armendariz; Office Mgr., Rose M. Greenough; Exec. Dir. Zoological Society, Kathleen Mason.
Personnel Profile: Full-Time Paid 89; Part-Time Paid 2; Part-Time Volunteers 60; Interns 2.
Governing Authority: municipal; nonprofit organization. Parent Institution: City of El Paso. Tax-exempt: 501(c)(3).
Zoo.
Collections: zoological exhibits; animal skull collection; conservation biofacts; original art; cultural artifacts.
Research Fields: animal behavior, physiology & medical.
Facilities: library of animal-oriented, biology, zoology, behavior & captive management books available for research on premises only. Animal-related items for sale.
Activities: daily programs & presentations; formal & informal education programs; special events.
Hours & Admission Prices: Winter: daily 9:30-4; Summer: Mon.-Fri. 9:30-4, Sat.-Sun. 9:30-5. Adults $5, seniors 63 & over $4, children 3-12 $3; discounts to AZA & reciprocating zoo members; children 2 & under and members no charge. Closed New Year's Day; Thanksgiving; Christmas. ♿
Attendance: 285,971 (accurate)
Membership: Spider Monkey $30; Sun Bear $40; Paraje Pals $45; Wolf Pack $50; Prime-Mates $50; Tiger Team $65; Critter Club $100; Safari Society $1,500.

INSIGHTS-EL PASO SCIENCE MUSEUM, 505 N. Santa Fe, El Paso, TX 79901-1144. Tel.: 915-534-0000, ext. 0. Fax: 915-532-7416.
E-mail: insightsepmuseum@elp.rr.com
Web Site: www.insightselpaso.org
Founded: 1979.
Congressional District: 16
Key Personnel: Exec. Dir, Mandy Chew.
Personnel Profile: Full-Time Paid 8; Part-Time Paid 11; Part-Time Volunteers 5; Interns 1.
Governing Authority: nonprofit organization. Tax-exempt: 501(c)(3).
Science Center.
Collections: participatory science exhibits on perception & energy; microcomputers; human anatomy.
Facilities: exhibits; observatory; science classes; adult computer classes. Science oriented gifts for sale. Museum Sponsors: science camps in summer.
Activities: formally organized education programs for children; loan & permanent exhibitions; sight, smell, touch & hearing exhibits; energy exhibits; mobile unit programming in community; formally organized community education program; rooftop observatory for Friday evening observing 8-10pm, weather permitting.
Publications: membership newsletter, The Insights Insider.
Hours & Admission Prices: Tues.-Sat. 10-5, Sun. 12-5. Adults $6, seniors 62 & over, military & students $5, children 4-11 $4; discounts to groups, AAM & ICOM members; ASTC members, children under 3 & members no charge. Closed major holidays. ♿
Attendance: 75,000 (accurate)

INTERNATIONAL MUSEUM OF ART, 1211 Montana Ave., El Paso, TX 79902-5511. Tel.: 915-543-6747.
Web Site: www.internationalmuseumofart.net
Art Museum: housed in the Turney Home.
Collections: Asian & African art; Mexican Revolution collection including replicas of Pancho Villa's death mask & a Mexican casita.
Activities: permanent & temporary exhibits.
Hours & Admission Prices: Thurs.-Sun. 1-5.

MAGOFFIN HOME STATE HISTORIC SITE, 1120 Magoffin Ave., El Paso, TX 79901. Tel.: 915-533-5147. Fax: 915-544-4398.
E-mail: leslie.bergloff@thc.state.tx.us
Web Site: www.thc.state.tx.us
Founded: 1976.
Congressional District: 16
Key Personnel: Site Dir., Leslie Bergloff; Dir. THC Historic Sites, Donna Williams.
Personnel Profile: Full-Time Paid 5; Part-Time Paid 1.
Governing Authority: state. Parent Institution: Texas Historical Commission, P.O. Box 12276, Austin, TX 78711-2276. Tel. 512-463-6100. Tax-exempt.
Historic House Museum: 1875 territorial adobe house built by pioneer, businessman, and civic leader Joseph Magoffin. Listed on the National Register of Historic Places.
Collections: household furnishings; memorabilia & documents of the Magoffin family; Southwestern decorative arts.
Research Fields: historical architecture; Southwest borderland history; El Paso & Texas history; military history; 19th & 20th century social & cultural history; family history; decorative arts.
Activities: guided tour; special events; outreach programs.
Publications: THC Interpretive Guide.
Hours & Admission Prices: Tues.-Sun. 9-5; tours on the hour; last tour begins at 4pm; school tours by appointment. Adults $3; discounts to groups of 10 or more; children 12 & under no charge. Closed New Year's Eve & Day; Martin Luther King Jr. Day; Presidents Day; Memorial Day; Thanksgiving; Christmas Eve & Day. ♿
Attendance: 10,000 (accurate)

THE NATIONAL BORDER PATROL MUSEUM AND MEMORIAL LIBRARY, 4315 Transmountain Rd., El Paso, TX 79924-3753. Tel.: 915-759-6060. Fax: 915-759-0992.
E-mail: nbpm@borderpatrolmuseum.com
Web Site: www.borderpatrolmuseum.com
Founded: 1985.
Key Personnel: Pres. (V), David Ham; Cur., Brenda Tisdale; Museum Shop Mgr., Kristi Rasura.
Personnel Profile: Full-Time Paid 2; Part-Time Paid 2; Part-Time Volunteers 6.
Governing Authority: nonprofit. Tax-exempt.
U.S. Border Patrol History Museum.
Collections: uniforms; weapons; vehicles; USBP Line of Duty memorial; Newton/Azrak memorial; Anthony L. Oneto memorial; sculpture.
Facilities: Gift items for sale. (museum members receive 10% discount)
Publications: brochures; flyers; gift shop catalogues; historical photos; books, Tales of the Rio Grande; Recuerdos; No Flag for My Coffin.
Hours & Admission Prices: Tues.-Sat. 9-5. No charge; donations accepted. Tours welcomed; guided tours must be scheduled in advance. Closed major holidays. ♿
Attendance: 23,326 (accurate)
Membership: Individual $35.

RAILROAD & TRANSPORTATION MUSEUM OF EL PASO, 400 W. San Antonio Ave., El Paso, TX 79901. Tel.: 915-422-3420.
Web Site: www.elpasorails.org
Railroad Museum.
Collections: railroad artifacts & memorabilia including a restored 4-4-0 classic American 1857 locomotive.
Hours & Admission Prices: Tues.-Sat. 11-5, Sun. 1-5. No charge; donations accepted.

STANLEE & GERALD RUBIN CENTER FOR THE VISUAL ARTS, UNIVERSITY OF TEXAS, EL PASO, (M), Dawson Dr. at Sun Bowl Dr., El Paso, TX 79902. Mailing Address: 500 W. University Ave., El Paso, TX 79968-8900. Fax: 915-747-6067.
Web Site: www.utep.edu/artsculture/
Founded: 2004.
Key Personnel: Dir., Kate Bonansinga; Asst. Dir., Kerry Doyle; Registrar & Preparator, Daniel Szwaczkowski.
Personnel Profile: Full-Time Paid 4; Interns 4.
Governing Authority: private; university. Parent Institution: University of Texas at El Paso. Tax-exempt.
Art Museum.
Collections: contemporary fine art & design.
Major Exhibits: Up Against the Wall: Posters of Social Change (T), 4/10-8/10; Seasons: Ceramic Sculpture of Sun Koo Yuh (T), 4/10-8/10; Tremor: New Media Art from Mexico, 9/10-12/10.
Research Fields: contemporary art.
Facilities: 3,500 sq. ft. exhibit space.
Activities: films; formal education programs for undergraduate or graduate University of Texas at El Paso students; guided tours; lectures; loans, participatory & traveling exhibitions; young curators' program; "Talk Back" program for high school students; family programs; art making workshops.
Publications: exhibition catalogues.
Hours & Admission Prices: Tues.-Wed. & Fri. 10-5, Thurs. 10-7, Sat. 12-5. No charge. Closed New Year's Eve & Day; Thanksgiving; Christmas Eve. ♿
Attendance: 11,000 (estimated)

Membership: Student $25; Individual $50; Family $60.

Emory

A.C. MCMILLAN AFRICAN AMERICAN MUSEUM, 149 Texas St., Emory, TX 75440. Mailing Address: P.O. Box 1046, Emory, TX 75440-1046. Tel.: 903-474-0083. Fax: 214-398-4277.
Founded: 2000.
Key Personnel: Dir., Gwen McMillian Lowe
History Museum.
Collections: African American history & art; slavery; photographs; personal artifacts; dolls of color; African American postage stamps; Buffalo Soldiers; Jim Crow images; Negro baseball leagues.
Facilities: library. Museum-related items for sale.
Activities: summer day camp; classes; group tours.
Hours & Admission Prices: Thurs.-Sat. 10-4. No charge.

Fairfield

BRADLEY HOUSE RESTORATION FOUNDATION, 318 Moody St., Fairfield, TX 75840-3034. Mailing Address: P.O. Box 1405, Fairfield, TX 75840-0026. Tel.: 903-389-2945.
E-mail: pattate@ezmailbox.net
Founded: 1967.
Congressional District: 2
Key Personnel: Chm. (V), Patricia Tate; Treas., Kathryn Davis.
Governing Authority: society. Tax-exempt.
Historic House: 1860 Moody-Bradley House, birthplace of W.L. Moody, Jr. who established Moody Foundation.
Collections: period furnishings.
Facilities: Texas place mats, publications, historical plates & bazaar items for sale.
Activities: guided tours; films; drama about Mr. Moody; arts festivals; study clubs; hobby workshops.
Publications: brochure.
Hours & Admission Prices: first Sun. in May 11:30-2:30; other times by appointment. Adults $.50, children $.25; members & school children no charge. ♿
Attendance: 200

FREESTONE COUNTY HISTORICAL MUSEUM, 302 E. Main St., Fairfield, TX 75840-1530. Mailing Address: P.O. Box 524, Fairfield, TX 75840-0009. Tel.: 903-389-3738.
Web Site: www.fairfieldtx.com
Founded: 1967.
Congressional District: 6
Key Personnel: Pres. (V), Jason Long; Cur., Molly Fryer.
Personnel Profile: Part-Time Paid 1; Part-Time Volunteers 1.
Governing Authority: county. Parent Institution: Freestone County. Tax-exempt: 501(c)(3).
Local History & Telephone Museum: housed in 1879 old jail.
Collections: historical items pertaining to Freestone County; manuscripts. Historic Houses: 1845 Carter Log House; 1852 Watson Log House; 1930's Assembly of God Country Church; telephone museum.
Activities: tours.
Hours & Admission Prices: Wed. & Fri.-Sat. 9-4; other times by appointment. Adults $3; children under 12 no charge. ♿
Attendance: 4,000 (accurate)
Membership: Individual $10; Family $20.

Falfurrias

THE HERITAGE MUSEUM AT FALFURRIAS, INC., 415 N. St. Mary's St., Falfurrias, TX 78355. Mailing Address: P.O. Box 86, Falfurrias, TX 78355-0086. Tel.: 361-325-2907.
Web Site: www.heritagemuseum-falfurrias.com
Founded: 1965.
Congressional District: 15
Key Personnel: Pres. Bd. (V), Lourdes Trevino-Cantu; Museum Shop Mgr., Ramiro Rodriguez.
Personnel Profile: Part-Time Paid 2; Part-Time Volunteers 2.
Governing Authority: nonprofit organization: Brooks County Historical Commission. Tax-exempt.
History Museum.
Collections: Texas Ranger Room; Dryden photo negative collection; farm equipment; Falfurrias creamery collection; local history pictures; arrowheads & Native American bow; Veterans Memorial display.
Research Fields: area history; archaeology; genealogy; Texas Ranger History; 50-year span photo negative collection of area people & events, reprinting by museum for small fee.
Facilities: Texas Ranger room; archives.
Activities: lectures; demonstrations; tours by appointment. Annual Event: Tribute to Trejano Music Legends in March; Native American Powwow in November.
Publications: books, Don Pedrito Jarmillio, Faith Healer of Los Almos; Falfurrias; Political Brooks County Elected Officials; Brooks Co. Diamond Jubilee.
Hours & Admission Prices: Tues.-Fri. 9-4, Sat. 9-1. No charge; donations accepted. ♿
Attendance: 1,000 (estimated)
Membership: Active $5; Sustaining $10; Life & Memorials $50; Gold Star $100.

Farmers Branch

FARMERS BRANCH HISTORICAL PARK, 2540 Farmers Branch Lane, Farmers Branch, TX 75234-6214. Mailing Address: P.O. Box 819010, Farmers Branch, TX 75381-9010. Tel.: 972-406-0184. Fax: 972-247-3939.
E-mail: historicalpark@farmersbranch.info
Web Site: www.farmersbranch.info
Founded: 1986.
Congressional District: 26
Key Personnel: Dir. Parks & Recreation, Jeff Fuller; Park Supt., Derrick Birdsall; Cur., Jamie Rigsby; Museum Educator, Barbara Judkins; Museum Shop Mgr., Kim Chapman.
Personnel Profile: Full-Time Paid 5; Part-Time Paid 2; Part-Time Volunteers 50.
Governing Authority: municipal; nonprofit. Parent Institution: City of Farmers Branch. Tax-exempt.
Historical Park & Archives.
Collections: books, photographs, artifacts & archival material documenting the history of Texas with an emphasis on Peters Colony & Farmers Branch; Paleo Indian artifacts. Historic Houses: 1937 Dodson House (home of Farmers Branch's first mayor; Texas Historic Landmark); 1900 one-room school; 1891 church; 1885 Queen Anne Victorian cottage; 1876 depot; 1856 Gilbert house (oldest structure on original foundation in Dallas County & National Register of Historic Places & Landmarks); 1840's log homestead & barns; 1930's Marathon gas station replica; 1936 cab-over-engine Ford truck; 1840s replica of The Peters Colony Land Grant Office.
Facilities: 500-vol. library of research books; archives housing diaries, photographs & documents of local history material.
Activities: guided tours; lectures; concerts; festivals; archeology fair; organized education programs for children; docent program; school loan service; archival research. Museum Sponsors: Star Parties.
Publications: quarterly newsletter; book: Once Upon A Time in Farmers Branch, in conjunction with 3rd grade educational curriculum; book, Farmers Branch, Texas: A Pictorial History, 1842-1996.
Hours & Admission Prices: Mon.-Fri. 8-6, Sat.-Sun. 12-6. Tours: by reservation. No charge; donations accepted. Closed New Year's Day, Easter, Thanksgiving & Christmas. ♿
Attendance: 50,000 (estimated)

Floydada

FLOYD COUNTY HISTORICAL MUSEUM, 105 E. Missouri St., Floydada, TX 79235. Mailing Address: P.O. Box 304, Floydada, TX 79235-0304. Tel.: 806-983-2415.
Founded: 1971.
History Museum.
Collections: local history & genealogy; early pioneers; Thomas Montgomery ranch house replica; photographs.
Facilities: library; history & genealogy center.
Publications: annual newsletter, Muse Briefs.
Hours & Admission Prices: Mon.-Fri. 1-5; other times by appointment. No charge; donations accepted. ♿
Attendance: 1,000
Membership: Adult $5; Family $10; Contributing $25; Life $500.

Fort Bliss

U.S. ARMY AIR DEFENSE ARTILLERY MUSEUM & FORT BLISS MUSEUM, Marshall Rd., Bldg. 1735, Fort Bliss, TX 79916. Tel.: 915-568-5412. Fax: 915-568-7166.
E-mail: rossd@emhio.bliss.army.mil
Web Site: www.bliss.army.mil/museum/fort_bliss_museum.htm
Founded: 1975.
Congressional District: 16
Key Personnel: Dir., Peter Poessiger; Cur., Jennifer Nielsen; Cur. & Registrar, Mary Ann Neubert; Museum Shop Mgr., Bonnie Heincy.
Governing Authority: federal. Parent Institution: U.S. Army Museums Div. Subsidiary Institution: U.S. Army Air Defense Artillery Association. Tax-exempt: 501(c)(3).

Military Museum.
Collections: weaponry, uniforms, insignia, vehicles, radars, search lights, archival holdings, books, documents, photographs, ephemera, associated with the history of the Air Defense Artillery.
Research Fields: military history.
Facilities: 1,000-vol. library of books on military history, primarily related to the Antiaircraft & Air Defense branch of the army, available for research on premises or by prearranged inter-museum loan; reading room; theater; classrooms; main gallery; orientation gallery. Museum-related items for sale.
Activities: formally organized education programs for adults & undergraduate college students affiliated with University of Texas at El Paso; permanent & traveling exhibitions.
Publications: book, Reasons Why II; book, Pocket History of Air Defense Artillery.
Hours & Admission Prices: Mon.-Sat. 9-4:30. No charge. Closed federal holidays. ♿
Attendance: 60,000 (accurate)

Fort Davis

CHIHUAHUAN DESERT RESEARCH INSTITUTE, Visitor Center, 4 mi. S. of Fort Davis on Hwy. 118, Fort Davis, TX 79734. Mailing Address: P.O. Box 905, Fort Davis, TX 79734-0010. Tel.: 432-364-2499. Fax: 432-364-2686.
Web Site: www.cdri.org
Founded: 1973.
Key Personnel: Exec. Dir., Dr. Cathryn A. Hoyt; Pres. (V), Rob L. Dunagan; Museum Shop Mgr., Melissa Brady.
Personnel Profile: Full-Time Paid 3; Part-Time Paid 4; Part-Time Volunteers 50; Interns 1.
Governing Authority: nonprofit organization. Tax-exempt: 501(c)(3).
Arboretum & Visitor Center.
Collections: trees, shrubs, cacti & succulents native to Chihuahuan Desert Region of the U.S. & Mexico.
Research Fields: natural science research in the Chihuahuan Desert Region.
Facilities: 22,000-vol. library of books, reprints & journals; botanical garden; outdoor classroom pavilion; greenhouse facilities; nature & conservation center; nature trails. Native plants, books & gift items for sale.
Activities: guided tours; lectures; films; organized education programs.
Publications: semi-annual magazine, The Chihuahuan Desert Discovery.
Hours & Admission Prices: Mon.-Sat. 9-5. Adults $5, seniors 65 & over $4; children under 12 & members no charge. ♿
Attendance: 8,000 (estimated)
Membership: Student & Senior over 65 $25; Individual $35; Family $50.

FORT DAVIS NATIONAL HISTORIC SITE, Lt. Flipper Dr., Fort Davis, TX 79734-0015. Mailing Address: P.O. Box 1379, Fort Davis, TX 79734-0015. Tel.: 432-426-3224, ext. 25 (Historian Office). Fax: 432-426-3122.
E-mail: FODA_Superintendent@nps.gov
Web Site: www.nps.gov/foda
Founded: 1961.
Congressional District: 16
Key Personnel: Historian, Mary L. Williams; Chief Interpretation, John Heiner; Coord. Volunteers, Donna Smith; Museum Shop Mgr., Patricia Hartnett.
Personnel Profile: Full-Time Paid 13; Part-Time Paid 5; Part-Time Volunteers 200.
Governing Authority: federal. Parent Institution: National Park Service; Dept. of Interior. Tax-exempt.
Military Museum: located on the site of 1854-1891 Fort Davis.
Collections: late 19th-century military & civilian artifacts including weapons, photographs, & regimental records; manuscripts; restored commanding officer's quarters; lieutenant's quarters; enlisted men's barracks; officer's kitchen; servant's quarters; commissary; late 19th century medical instruments.
Research Fields: American frontier military history; frontier Indian wars; Buffalo Soldier regiments.
Facilities: 2,500-vol. library including 150 reels of microfilm, 155 rare books & manuscript material on military history available for use on premises; reading room; 48-seat auditorium. Books, postcards, historic maps, records & tapes of military music for sale.
Activities: 14-minute video program; 18 minute recording of a Dress Retreat Parade; Bugle Calls; self guiding tours of restored & refurnished buildings and grounds; education programs for grades K-12. Special Events: costumed interpreters in summer.
Hours & Admission Prices: Daily 8-5; research by appointment. Adults 16 & over $3; children 15 & under, Golden Age, Golden Eagle, Golden Access Passport, & National Parks Pass holders no charge. Closed New Year's Day; Martin Luther King Jr. Day; Presidents' Day; Thanksgiving; Christmas. ♿
Attendance: 50,000 (accurate)

Fort Hood

1ST CAVALRY DIVISION MUSEUM, (M), Bldg. 2218, 56th & 761 Tank Bn. Ave., Fort Hood, TX 76544-0187. Mailing Address: P.O. Box 5187, Fort Hood, TX 76544-0187. Tel.: 254-287-3626 & 532-2075 (Gift Shop). Fax: 254-287-6423 & 532-6490 (Gift Shop).
E-mail: steven.c.draper@us.army.mil
Web Site: www.hood.army.mil/1stcavdiv/1cdmuseum/index
Founded: 1971.
Congressional District: 11
Key Personnel: Dir., Cur. & Chm. (V), Steven C. Draper; Museum Foundation, Terry Maddox; Deputy & Exhibit Specialist, Jack Dugan; Collections Specialist, Amber Hills; Museum Shop Mgr., Michelle Wolf.
Personnel Profile: Full-Time Paid 5; Part-Time Volunteers 15.
Governing Authority: federal. Parent Institution: 1st Cavalry Division, U.S. Army and Army Center of Military History. Tax-exempt: 501(c)(3).
Military Museum.
Collections: military artifacts of 1st Cavalry Division & its regiments from 1855 to present.
Research Fields: history of 1st Cavalry Division; regimental & unit histories of the division; U.S. Cavalry.
Facilities: research library; archives. Museum-related items for sale.
Activities: permanent & temporary exhibits; guided tours; films; off site programs; living history demonstrations; children's programs.
Publications: History of the 1st Cavalry Division; Vehicles Park Guide; Children's Treasure Hunt; Museum Fact Sheets; Reference Guide.
Hours & Admission Prices: Mon.-Fri. 9-4, Sat. 10-4, Sun. 12-4. No charge; donations accepted. Closed New Year's Day; Easter; Thanksgiving; Christmas. ♿
Attendance: 50,000 (accurate)

4TH INFANTRY DIVISION MUSEUM, Bldg. 418, 761st Tank Bn. Ave. & 27th St., Fort Hood, TX 76544. Mailing Address: P.O. Box 5917, Fort Hood, TX 76544-0917. Tel.: 254-287-8811. Fax: 254-287-3833.
E-mail: ceilia.m.stratton@us.army.mil
Founded: 1949.
Congressional District: 11
Key Personnel: Dir. & Cur., Ceilia M. Stratton; Museum Shop Mgr., Sherry MacWillie.
Personnel Profile: Full-Time Paid 5; Part-Time Volunteers 5.
Governing Authority: federal. Admin. by Dept. of Army (111 Corps & Fort Hood). Tax-exempt: 501(c)(3) & 170(b)(1)(A).
Military Museum.
Collections: military & related material of the 4th Infantry Division, the United States Army & opposing forces from World War I until present; approx. 60 military vehicles exhibited; tank destroyers; III Corps, Camp/Fort Hood.
Research Fields: history of the 4th Infantry Division from 1918 until present day; military material culture with emphasis on the 20th century, especially armored warfare.
Facilities: reference library, archives & study collections available to researchers, advance notice recommended; audio-visuals. Museum-related items for sale.
Activities: self-guided tours; special guided tours upon request; audiovisual programs; lectures; classes.
Publications: condensed history of Division guide brochure; Brief History of the 4th Infantry Division.
Hours & Admission Prices: Mon.-Fri. 9-4, Sat. 10-4, Sun. 12-4. No charge. Closed New Year's; Thanksgiving; Christmas. ♿
Attendance: 51,000 (estimated)

Fort McKavett

FORT MCKAVETT STATE HISTORICAL SITE, FM 864, Fort McKavett, TX 76841. Mailing Address: P.O. Box 68, Fort McKavett, TX 76841. Tel.: 325-396-2358. Fax: 325-396-2818.
E-mail: ft-mckavett@thc.state.tx.us
Web Site: www.tpwd.state.tx.us
Founded: 1968.
Congressional District: 21
Key Personnel: Supt., Michael A. Garza; Office Mgr., Genevieve Hough; Park Ranger IV, Alfredo Munoz; Maintenance Asst., Ken Lester.
Personnel Profile: Full-Time Paid 4.
Governing Authority: Parent Institution: Texas Historical Commission.
Historic Site & Military Museum: 1852-1883 Fort McKavett, home to four Buffalo solder regiments.
Collections: 1852-59 & 1868-83 artifacts & interpretive materials associated with military occupation; late 19th-century civilian occupation; 18 restored structures & 9 ruins surrounding two parade areas.
Research Fields: late 19th century frontier military history; minority groups.
Facilities: research library; picnic area. Museum-related items for sale.
Activities: research library; in-house living history interpretation: uniforms and

equipment demonstrations of 1870s-1880s infantry & cavalry; permanent exhibits; self-guided or guided tours; audiovisual room.
Publications: brochure; newsletter; booklet, walking guide.
Hours & Admission Prices: Daily 9-5. Adults $3, students $1; discounts to groups; children 12 & under no charge. Closed Christmas. ♿
Attendance: 10,500 (estimated)
Membership: $5-$25.

Fort Sam Houston

FORT SAM HOUSTON MUSEUM, (M), 1210 Stanley Rd., Fort Sam Houston, TX 78234-7501. Mailing Address: 2250 Stanley Rd., Ste. 36, Fort Sam Houston, TX 78234-6111. Tel.: 210-221-1886 & 0019. Fax: 210-221-1311.
E-mail: john.manguso@amedd.army.mil
Web Site: ameddregiment.amedd.army.mil/fshmuse/fshmuse/htm
Formerly: Fort Sam Houston Military Museum
Founded: 1967.
Congressional District: 20
Key Personnel: Dir., John M. Manguso; Cur., Jacqueline B. Davis; Museum Specialist, Martin L. Callahan; Animal Caretaker, Adam Quintero.
Personnel Profile: Full-Time Paid 3; Part-Time Volunteers 5.
Governing Authority: federal. Parent Institution: U.S. Army Medical Dept. Center and School. Tax-exempt.
Military Historical Museum: located on Fort Sam Houston National Historic Landmark.
Collections: army uniforms; equipment; accoutrements; weapons from 1835 to present; military vehicles & artillery; photographs; personal papers; memorabilia; microfilmed historical records of Ft. Sam Houston.
Research Fields: history of Fort Sam Houston; history of US Army in San Antonio; army operations in Texas since 1845; Army life of soldiers & families.
Facilities: 5,000-vol. library of military history, technical publications on types of military equipment & uniforms, available for research with approval of curator on premises; 30 seat auditorium.
Activities: guided tours; permanent, temporary & travelling exhibits; audiovisual programs; formal & informal educational programs. Museum Sponsors: Historic Neighborhood Awareness Program.
Publications: Pocket Guide to Historic Sam Houston; Surrounded by History; Pocket Guide to the New Post; Pocket Guide to the Cavalry & Light Artillery Post; Fort Sam Houston and the Korean War; Pocket Guide to the Staff Post; Hospitals at Fort Sam Houston; Fort Sam Houston: National Historic Landmark (tour map).
Hours & Admission Prices: Wed.-Sun. 10-4. No charge; donations accepted. Closed New Year's Day; Thanksgiving; Christmas; Sun. before Mon. holidays. ♿
Attendance: 30,000 (estimated)

* **U.S. ARMY MEDICAL DEPARTMENT MUSEUM, (M),** 2310 Stanley Rd., Bldg. 1046, Fort Sam Houston, TX 78234-2636. Mailing Address: P.O. Box 340 244, Fort Sam Houston, TX 78234. Tel.: 210-221-6358. Fax: 210-221-6781.
E-mail: thomas.mcmasters@amedd.army.mil
Web Site: www.ameddmuseumfoundation.com
Founded: 1955.
Congressional District: 20
Key Personnel: Dir., Thomas O. McMasters, (Ret.); C.E.O., M.G. Patrick Sculley, (Ret.); Pres. (V), Col. Jesse Brewer, (Ret.); Registrar, Maria Forte; Cur. & Archivist, Scott Schoner; Museum Tech., Charles Franson; Gift Shop Mgr., Cheryl Musket; Museum Specialist, Paula Assgry.
Personnel Profile: Full-Time Paid 5; Part-Time Paid 1; Part-Time Volunteers 30.
Governing Authority: federal; nonprofit. Parent Institution: U.S. Army Medical Dept. Center & School. Subsidiary Institution: AMEDD Museum Foundation, Inc. Tax-exempt: 501(c)(3).
Military Medical Museum.
Collections: Army medical equipment; uniforms; Army medical insignia; military ambulances; POW material; unit colors; artwork; archives.
Research Fields: 1775 to present, Army medical department.
Facilities: 50-seat auditorium & theater; 11,000 sq. ft. exhibit hall & outdoor exhibits; memorial garden; activity room; memorial plaza; hospital train ambulance car; combat medic memorial. Books, prints, jewelry & other gift items for sale.
Activities: guided tours; lectures; films.
Publications: monthly newsletter.
Hours & Admission Prices: Tues.-Sat. 10-4. No charge. Closed federal holidays. ♿
Attendance: 35,718 (accurate)

Fort Stockton

ANNIE RIGGS MEMORIAL MUSEUM, 301 S. Main St., Fort Stockton, TX 79735-7209. Tel.: 432-336-2167. Fax: 432-336-7529.
Founded: 1955.
Congressional District: 21
Key Personnel: Dir. & Cur., Martha King.
Personnel Profile: Full-Time Paid 1; Part-Time Paid 4; Part-Time Volunteers 3.
Governing Authority: nonprofit organization. Parent Institution: Fort Stockton Historical Society. Subsidiary Institution: Historic Fort Stockton. Tax-exempt.
General Museum: housed in 1899 Riggs Hotel.
Collections: historic textiles; Native American artifacts; cowboy & ranch implements; geologic specimens; religious items; kitchen utensils; area archaeology.
Research Fields: history of Pecos County.
Facilities: historical library.
Activities: tours; special events; summer concert series.
Publications: newsletter.
Hours & Admission Prices: Summer: July-Aug. Mon.-Sat. 9-7; Winter: Sept.-June Mon.-Sat. 9-5, Sun. 1-6. Adults $3, seniors 65 & over $2.50, children 2-12 $2. Closed New Year's Day; Easter; Thanksgiving; Christmas Eve, Day & day after. ♿
Attendance: 6,400 (accurate)
Membership: Individual $15; Family $20; Business $60; Lifetime $1,000.

HISTORIC FORT STOCKTON, 301 E. Third, Fort Stockton, TX 79735-5702. Tel.: 432-336-2400; 432-336-2167. Fax: 432-336-0575.
Founded: 1990.
Congressional District: 21
Key Personnel: Cur., Martha King.
Personnel Profile: Full-Time Paid 1; Part-Time Paid 3; Part-Time Volunteers 20.
Governing Authority: society; nonprofit. Parent Institution: City of Fort Stockton. Tax-exempt.
Historic Site & Military Museum: 1867-1886 frontier fort during Indian Wars; includes original Guardhouse & 3 Officers' Quarters; reconstructed kitchens & two Enlisted Barracks; listed on National Register of Historic Places.
Collections: military & supporting contractors directly relating to Fort Stockton, 1867-1886; uniforms; weapons; archaeological artifacts; archives.
Research Fields: Fort Stockton, TX (military post); Indian Wars; frontier forts; Indians of West Texas, 1850-1900; trails & routes through West Texas.
Facilities: 65-vol. library on Fort Stockton, Indian Wars & local history; 1,600 sq. ft. exhibit space; 30-seat theater; multi-purpose classrooms. Museum-related items for sale.
Activities: guided tours; films; lectures; educational programs; docent program; living history interpreters. Annual Events: Living History Days; Christmas at Old Fort Stockton; recognition reception for EMT & firefighters.
Publications: Fort Stockton Historical Society Newsletter.
Hours & Admission Prices: July-Aug. Mon.-Sat. 9-7; Sept.-June Mon.-Sat. 9-5. Adults $3, senior citizens $2.50, children 6-12 $2; discounts to groups; TAM & AAM members and children under 6 no charge. Closed New Year's Day; Easter; Thanksgiving; Christmas. ♿
Attendance: 12,000 (estimated)
Membership: Individual $10; Family $15; Sponsor $50 & up.

Fort Worth

AMERICAN AIRLINES C.R. SMITH MUSEUM, 4601 Hwy. 360 at FAA Road, Fort Worth, TX 76155. Mailing Address: P.O. Box 619617, GSWFA MD808, Dallas-Fort Worth Airport, TX 75261-9617. Tel.: 817-967-1560. Fax: 817-967-5737.
Web Site: www.crsmithmuseum.org
Founded: 1993.
Key Personnel: Exec. Dir., Jay Luippold; Assoc. Dir. & Chief Cur., Jeffrey D. Johns; Cur. Education, Bobbye Jo Coke; Admin., Gloria Randles; Membership & Advertising, Latanne Steel; Museum Shop Mgr., Barbara Gotcher; Technician, Robin Hopper.
Personnel Profile: Full-Time Paid 7; Part-Time Paid 2; Part-Time Volunteers 64.
Governing Authority: private; nonprofit organization. Tax-exempt.
Company Museum.
Collections: American Airlines history; corporation acquired airlines; general aviation history; life of C.R. Smith, early C.E.O. of American Airlines.
Research Fields: early airlines in the United States; individuals who help make up the American Airline's family.
Facilities: 500-vol. library on aviation; theater. Gift items for sale.
Activities: educational programs; Eagle Aviation Academy; films; guided & self- guided tours.
Publications: biannual newsletter.
Hours & Admission Prices: Tues.-Sat. 10-6; see website for extended holiday

hours. Adults $4, seniors 55 & over $2; AMR corporation employees & members no charge. ♿
Attendance: 50,000 (accurate)
Membership: Annual $25; Family Annual $50; Lifetime-Gold $250; Lifetime Flagship $500; Lifetime-Platinum $1,000.

*** AMON CARTER MUSEUM, (M),** 3501 Camp Bowie Blvd., Fort Worth, TX 76107-2695. Tel.: 817-738-1933. Fax: 817-989-5099.
E-mail: tracygreene@cartermuseum.org
Web Site: www.cartermuseum.org
Founded: 1961.
Congressional District: 12
Key Personnel: Pres (V), Ruth Carter Stevenson; Dir., Ron Tyler; C.F.O., Randy Ray; Exec. Asst. to Dir., Trish Williamson; C.O.O., Lori Eklund; Dir. Devel., Carol Noel; Accounting Mgr., Tricia Pentecost; Sr. Cur. Prints & Drawings, Jane Myers; Sr. Cur. Photographs, John Rohrbach; Sr. Cur. Western Paintings & Sculpture, Rick Stewart; Asst. Cur. Photographs, Jessica May; Asst. Cur. Paintings & Sculpture, Shirley Reece-Hughes; Public Information Officer, Tracy Greene; Dir. Publications, Will Gillham; Dir. Exhibitions & Collections Admin., Wendy Haynes; Registrar, Melissa Thompson; Human Resources Mgr., Kathy Goodale; Facilities Mgr., Alfred Walker; Dir. Security, Shannon Locke; Cur. Paintings & Sculpture, Rebecca Lawton; Head of Education, Stacy Fuller; Retail Mgr., Amy Rasor; Dir. Library, Sam Duncan.
Personnel Profile: Full-Time Paid 77; Part-Time Paid 33; Part-Time Volunteers 214; Interns 10.
Governing Authority: nonprofit organization. Tax-exempt: 501(c)(3).
Art Museum.
Collections: American painting; sculpture; works on paper; Carter collection of Remington & Russell works; over 250,000 photographic prints & negatives.
Major Exhibits: Views and Visions: Prints of the American West, 11/09-1/10; American Moderns on Paper: Masterworks from the Wadsworth Atheneum Museum, 2/10-5/10; American Modern: Abbott, Evans, Bourke-White, 10/10-1/11.
Research Fields: American art & history.
Facilities: 40,000-vol. library of North American history, art & photography available for inter-library loan to institutions & for individual researchers on premises by appointment; Regional Reference Center for Archives of American Art, Smithsonian Institution with 7,500 microfilm reels; 160-seat theatre; microfilm archive of 19th-century American newspapers & illustrated periodicals; reading room. Books, art reproductions, cards & slides for sale.
Activities: guided tours; docent program; inter-museum loan, temporary & traveling exhibitions; lectures; films; video programs.
Publications: books on American art & cultural history; biannual program of events & exhibitions.
Hours & Admission Prices: Tues.-Wed. & Fri.-Sat. 10-5, Thurs. 10-8, Sun. 12-5. No charge; donations accepted. Closed major holidays. ♿
Attendance: 103,546 (accurate)
Membership: Individual $50; Dual & Family $100; Sustainer $250; Patron $500; Director's Council $1,000; President's Council $3,000; Trustees' Council $5,000; Founder's Circle $10,000. Corporate Leaders Society: Director's Circle $1,000; President's Circle $2,500; Trustees' Circle $5,000; Founder's Circle $10,000; Leaders' Circle $25,000; Silver Leaders' Circle $50,000; Gold Leaders' Circle $75,000. TheGallery (young professionals): Individual $125; Dual & Family $200.

CATTLE RAISERS MUSEUM, 1301 W. Seventh St., Fort Worth, TX 76102-2604. Mailing Address: P.O. Box 868, Fort Worth, TX 76101-0868. Tel.: 817-332-8551. Fax: 817-336-2470.
E-mail: ksmith@cowgirl.net
Web Site: www.cattleraisersmuseum.org
Founded: 1981.
Congressional District: 12
Key Personnel: Pres. (V), Bradford S. Barnes; Assoc. Dir., Kim Smith.
Personnel Profile: Full-Time Paid 2; Part-Time Volunteers 15.
Governing Authority: nonprofit organization. Parent Institution: Texas & Southwestern Cattle Raisers Foundation. Tax-exempt.
History Museum.
Collections: history of the cattle industry in Texas; cowboy & ranching artifacts; photographs; murals; life-size longhorns; breed wall; audio-visual hands-on exhibit.
Research Fields: cattle & ranching industry.
Facilities: 1,000-vol. library for use in premises.
Activities: educational & outreach programs; special exhibits.
Publications: magazine, The Cattleman.
Hours & Admission Prices: Temporarily closed. Will reopen in a new location in 2009. ♿
Attendance: 20,000 (estimated)

FORT WORTH BOTANIC GARDEN, 3220 Botanic Garden Blvd., Fort Worth, TX 76107-3420. Tel.: 817-871-7686 & 7680. Fax: 817-871-7638.
E-mail: steve.huddleston@fortworthgov.org
Web Site: www.fwbg.org
Founded: 1934.
Congressional District: 12
Key Personnel: Dir., Henry Painter; Receptionist, Dolores Santos.
Personnel Profile: Full-Time Paid 40; Part-Time Paid 3; Part-Time Volunteers 821.
Governing Authority: municipal. Parent Institution: City of Fort Worth, TX. Tax-exempt.
Botanical Garden.
Collections: roses; miniature roses; iris; orchids; begonias; native plants; tropical plants under glass; ficus collection; perennials; cactus; succulents; shrubs; trees.
Facilities: 5,000-vol. library of botany books available for use by holders of library cards; garden center; 241-seat lecture hall; rental facilities; boardwalk; conservatory; greenhouses; Japanese garden; restaurant. Gift-related items for sale.
Activities: education programs offering tours for school children & scout groups; takeout programs for nursing homes; annual fall & spring festival in Japanese garden; workshops for teachers; spring & fall workshops; summer garden clubs for children; plant sales; lectures; annual 1k, 5k & 10k run; summer concert series.
Publications: booklet, Japanese Garden; members bimonthly newsletter, The Redbud.
Hours & Admission Prices: Garden: daily 8 am-dusk. No charge. Japanese Garden: April-Oct. daily 9-7; Nov.-March daily 10-5. Adults $4 weekdays & $4.50 weekends, children 4-12 $3; discounts to seniors; members & children under 4 no charge. Conservatory: April-Oct. Mon.-Sat. 10-6, Sun. 1-6; Nov.-March Mon.-Sat. 10-4, Sun. 1-4. Adults $1, seniors & children 4-12 $.50; members no charge. Garden Center & Japanese Garden closed Christmas. ♿
Attendance: 700,000 (estimated)
Membership: Individual $35; Mr. & Mrs. $50; Family $60; Contributing $20-$99; Friend $100; Life $500; Benefactor $1,000.

*** FORT WORTH MUSEUM OF SCIENCE AND HISTORY, (M),** 1600 Gendy St., Fort Worth, TX 76107-4062. Tel.: 817-255-9300, ext. 0. Fax: 817-732-7635.
E-mail: webmaster@fwmsh.org
Web Site: www.fortworthmuseum.org
Founded: 1941.
Congressional District: 12
Key Personnel: Pres., Van A. Romans; Sr. Vice Pres. Education, Kit Goolsby; Sr. Vice Pres. Devel. & Mktg., Carl G. Hamm, CFRE; Exec. Vice Pres. Innovation., Colleen Blair; Exec. Vice Pres. Finance & Admin., Tom Mitchell, CPA; Exec. Vice Pres. Programs, Charles H. Walter; Vice Pres. Community Rels., Gretchen Denny; Vice Pres. Operations, Amy M. Duncan; Cur. Science., Dr. Aaron Pan; Cur. History, Dr. Gene Allen Smith; Dir. Bldg. Svcs., Rick Aguirre; Dir. Public Affairs, Becky E. Adamietz; Asst. Cur. Science, Leishawn Spotted Bear; Asst. Cur. History, Renee Tucker; Archivist/Research Librarian, Christina Hardman; Chm. (V), BobLansford.
Personnel Profile: Full-Time Paid 85; Part-Time Paid 224; Part-Time Volunteers 30; Interns 6.
Governing Authority: nonprofit organization. Tax-exempt: 501(c)(3).
General Museum.
Collections: botany; entomology; malacology; ethnology; herpetology; zoology; anthropology; mammology; mineralogy; meteoritics; paleontology; local history; western history; Fort Worth Stock Show collection.
Facilities: 6,000-vol. library; planetarium; Omni IMAX theatre; educational facilities; laboratories. Museum-related items for sale.
Activities: interactive exhibitions; 4-D theater; 3-D theater; museum school for preschool learning; demonstrations; lectures; films workshops; distance learning; training programs for educators; permanent & temporary exhibitions; school loan service; fossil digs & research.
Publications: newsletter, Stories.
Hours & Admission Prices: Daily 10-5. Adults $14, seniors 60 & over & children 3-12 $10; discounts to ASTC, TAM, AAM & ICOM members and groups; children under 3 & members no charge. Omni Theater: adults $7, children 3-12 & seniors $6; discounts to FWMSH Discovery members; FWMSH Discover Plus members no charge. Combination tickets available. Closed Thanksgiving; Christmas Eve & Day. ♿
Attendance: 792,581 (accurate)
Membership: Basic 2 $65; Basic 5 $85; Basic 8 $145; MAX 2 $115; MAX 5 $185; MAX 8 $245.

FORT WORTH NATURE CENTER AND REFUGE, 9601 Fossil Ridge Rd., Fort Worth, TX 76135-9148. Tel.: 817-392-7410. Fax: 817-392-7415.
Web Site: www.fwnaturecenter.org
Founded: 1964.
Congressional District: 12
Governing Authority: city. Tax-exempt.
Nature Center & Refuge.
Collections: wildlife & their habitats; native flora & fauna.
Facilities: interpretive center.
Hours & Admission Prices: Summer: Mon.-Fri. 8-7, Sat.-Sun. 7-7; Winter: daily 8-5. Adult $4, seniors 65 & over $3, children 3-17 $2; children under 3 no charge. Closed Thanksgiving; Christmas. ♿
Attendance: 37,730 (accurate)
Membership: Individual $45; Family $75.

FORT WORTH ZOOLOGICAL ASSOCIATION, INC., 1989 Colonial Pkwy., Fort Worth, TX 76110-6640. Tel.: 817-759-7500 & 7555. Fax: 817-759-7501.
E-mail: awilson@fortworthzoo.com
Web Site: www.fortworthzoo.org
Formerly: Fort Worth Zoological Park
Founded: 1909.
Congressional District: 12
Key Personnel: C.E.O., Michael Fouraker; C.F.O., Scott Wilcox; Co-Chm., Mrs. Lee M. Bass; Co-Chm., Mrs. Charles Moncrief; Pres. (V), Ardon Moore; Communications Dir., Alexis Wilson; Dir. Operations, Kelley Allred; Conservation & Animal Programs Dir., Tarren Wagener; Veterinarian, Nancy Lung; Bird Cur., Katie Unger; Mammal Cur., Ron Surratt; Dir. Education, David Walker.
Personnel Profile: Full-Time Paid 100; Part-Time Paid 200; Part-Time Volunteers 50; Interns 2.
Governing Authority: municipal. Parent Institution: city of Fort Worth. Management contracted to Fort Worth Zoological Assoc. Tax-exempt.
Zoo.
Collections: aviary; herpetarium; African diorama; zoo geographic exhibits; Asian Falls; World of Primates; Raptor Canyon; Texas exhibit; wildlife art gallery; African savannah; penguins.
Research Fields: animal behavior; field conservation; International Rhino Foundation.
Facilities: Zoo-related gifts for sale.
Activities: formally organized education programs for children & families.
Publications: quarterly magazine, Roar!
Hours & Admission Prices: Daily 10-5; extended hours seasonally. Adults $10.50, children 3-12 $8, senior citizens 65 & over $7; group rates available; Wed. half price; children under 3 & members no charge. Parking $5. ♿
Attendance: 1,000,000 (estimated)
Membership: First Child $25; Second Child $20; Additional Child $15; First Adult $55; Second Adult $40; Additional Adult $50.

KIMBELL ART MUSEUM, 3333 Camp Bowie Blvd., Fort Worth, TX 76107-2792. Tel.: 817-332-8451. Fax: 817-877-1264.
E-mail: info@kimbellmuseum.org
Web Site: www.kimbellart.org
Founded: 1972.
Congressional District: 12
Key Personnel: Dir., Eric McCauley Lee; Pres., Mrs. Ben J. Fortson; Deputy Dir., Malcolm Warner; Cur. European Art & Head of Academic Svcs., Nancy E. Edwards; Cur. Asian & Non-Western Art, Jennifer Casler Price; Assoc. Cur. European Art, C. D. Dickerson; Chief Conservator of Paintings, Claire M. Barry; Mgr. Publications & Public Access, Wendy Gottlieb; Cur. Architecture & Archivist, Patricia C. Loud; Dir. Finance & Admin., Susan R. Drake; Librarian, Chia-Chun Shih; Registrar, Patricia Decoster; Mgr. Membership, Robert McAn; Head Mktg. & Public Rels., Jessica Brandrup; Buffet Mgr., Shelby Schafer; Mgr. Operations, Larry Eubank; Mgr. Security, David McMillan.
Personnel Profile: Full-Time Paid 72; Part-Time Paid 70; Part-Time Volunteers 74; Interns 6.
Governing Authority: nonprofit organization. Parent Institution: Kimbell Art Foundation. Tax-exempt: 501(c)(3).
Art Museum.
Collections: western European paintings; sculpture from antiquity to 20th-century; pre-Columbian artifacts; Asian sculpture, screens, scrolls & ceramics; African sculpture; books & periodicals.
Major Exhibits: Private Collection, Texas: European Masterpieces from Texas Homes, Past & Present, 11/22/09-3/21/10.
Research Fields: pertaining to collection.
Facilities: library; reading room; 180-seat auditorium; restaurant. Scholarly & popular art books, catalogs, children's books for sale.
Activities: guided tours; gallery talks; lectures; symposia; formally organized education programs for children, adults, undergraduate & graduate college students; family programs; studio workshops; teacher training; docent program; inter-museum loan; permanent & temporary exhibitions.
Publications: Light is the Theme: Louis I. Kahn & the Kimbell Art Museum; The Great Age of Japanese Buddhist Sculpture A.D. 600-1300; J. B. Oudry, 1686-1755; Henri Matisse: Sculptor/Painter; Bernardo Cavallino of Naples, 1616-1656; Spanish Still Life in the Golden Age, 1600-1650; Durer to Delacroix: Great Master Drawings from Stockholm; The Blood of Kings: Dynasty and Ritual in Maya Art; Giuseppe Maria Crespi and the Emergence of Genre Painting in Italy; Kimbell Art Museum Address Book; Kimbell Cookbook; In Pursuit of Quality, The Kimbell Art Museum: An Illustrated History of the Art and Architecture; Poussin, The Early Years in Rome: The Origins of French Classicism; The Loves of the Gods: Mythological Painting from Watteau to David; Jacopo Bassano; Giambattista Tiepolo: Master of the Oil Sketch; Ludovico Carracci; Tomb Treasures from China: The Buried Art of Ancient Xi'an; The Path to Enlightenment: Masterpieces of Buddhist Sculpture from the National Museum of Asian Arts/Musee Guimet, Paris; Monet and the Mediterranean; Matisse and Picasso: A Gentle Rivalry; Giovanni Battista Moroni: Portraitist; Mondrian, 1892-1914: The Path to Abstraction; Kimbell Art Museum: Handbook of the Collection; Stubbs and the Horse; Gaugin and Impressionism; The Art of the Goldsmith in Late Fifteenth-Century Germany: The Kimbell Virgin and Her Bishop; The Mirror and the Mask: Portraiture in the Age of Picasso; Picturing the Bible: The Earliest Christian Art; Reconstructing the Renaissance: Saint James Freeing Hermogenes by Fra Angelico; A Nativity from Naples: Presepio Sculpture in the 18th Century.
Hours & Admission Prices: Tues.-Thurs. & Sat. 10-5, Fri. 12-8, Sun. 12-5. Special exhibition charge only. Closed New Year's Day; Independence Day; Thanksgiving; Christmas. ♿
Attendance: 260,000 (estimated)
Membership: Subscriber $40; Individual Patron $65; Dual & Family Patron $100; Sustaining Patron $300; Director's Circle $600; Collector's Circle $5,000; Benefactor's Circle $10,000.

LOG CABIN VILLAGE, (M), 2100 Log Cabin Village Lane, Fort Worth, TX 76109-1000. Tel.: 817-392-5881.
E-mail: director@logcabinvillage.org
Web Site: logcabinvillage.org
Founded: 1966.
Congressional District: 12
Key Personnel: Museum Dir., Kelli L. Pickard; Museum Cur., Ivette Ray; Museum Educator, Rena Lawrence; Clerk, David Clark; Clerk, Fred Gersch; Clerk, Mike Garrett; Clerk, Marilyn Tonn; Maintenance, Steven Suarez.
Personnel Profile: Full-Time Paid 4; Part-Time Paid 11; Part-Time Volunteers 25.
Governing Authority: municipal. Parent Institution: Parks & Community Services Dept., City of Fort Worth, 1000 Throckmorton, 76102. Tax-exempt: 501(c)(3).
Village Museum.
Collections: 19th-century log structures, furniture, quilts & other artifacts & reproductions related to Texas pioneers; original & copies of documents relating to pioneer families; original & copies of photographs. Historic Buildings: 1848 Isaac Parker Cabin; 1853 John Baptist Tompkins Cabin; 1855 Isaac Seela Cabin; 1853 Harry A. Foster Log House; 1850 Hartsford Howard Cabin; 1853 Thomas J. Shaw Cabin converted into operating grist mill; a reproduction blacksmith shop; 1870's Marine School; 1860s Reynolds Smokehouse.
Research Fields: history; genealogical.
Activities: formally organized education programs for children; pioneer craft & grist mill demonstrations; permanent & temporary exhibitions.
Publications: booklets, Log Cabin Village: A History & Guide.
Hours & Admission Prices: Tues.-Fri. 9-4, Sat.-Sun. 1-5; groups by appointment. Adult $3.50, senior citizens & youth $3; discounts to AAM & Texas Association of Museums members; members no charge. History Programs $2-$5. ♿
Attendance: 29,033 (accurate)
Membership: Student $10; Individual $25; Family $45; Pioneer $100; Settler $250; Merchant $500; Lifetime $1,000.

* **MODERN ART MUSEUM OF FORT WORTH,** 3200 Darnell St., Fort Worth, TX 76107-2872. Tel.: 817-738-9215. Fax: 817-735-1161.
E-mail: info@themodern.org
Web Site: www.themodern.org
Founded: 1892.
Congressional District: 12
Key Personnel: Dir., Dr. Marla Price; Chief Cur., Michael Auping; Controller, Jo Garwood; Dir. Membership & Special Events, Suzanne Woo; Cur. Education, Terri Thornton; Bookstore Mgr., Mary Beth Ebert; Head Design & Installation, Tony Wright; Cur., Andrea Karnes; Registrar, Rick Floyd;

Public Rels. Mgr., Kendal Smith Lake; Editor, Stefanie Ball-Piwetz; Supvr. Security, Mark Evans; Computer Systems Mgr., Jim Colegrove; Curatorial Administrative Asst., Susan Colegrove; Accounting, Karen Seidler; Human Resources Mgr., Sally McCracken; Tour & Docent Coord., Leslie Murrell; Asst. Special Events, Tina Gorski.
Personnel Profile: Full-Time Paid 57; Part-Time Paid 24; Part-Time Volunteers 110; Interns 3.
Governing Authority: nonprofit corporation. Operated by Fort Worth Art Association. Tax-exempt: 501(c)(3).
Art Museum.
Collections: Post World War II international art in all media.
Major Exhibits: Andy Warhol: The Last Decade (T), 2/10-5/10.
Research Fields: post 1940 modern & contemporary art.
Facilities: print study.
Activities: special exhibitions; lectures; films; gallery talks; guided tours; inter-museum loan; education programs; art camp.
Publications: biannual illustrated calendar for members; exhibition catalogs; posters; special mailings; exhibition brochures & cards.
Hours & Admission Prices: Adults $10; members no charge. Closed holidays. ♿
Attendance: 180,000 (estimated)
Membership: Basic $65; Associate $125; Sustainer $200; Contributor $500; Patron $1,000; President's Circle $5,000.

NATIONAL COWGIRL MUSEUM AND HALL OF FAME, 1720 Gendy St., Fort Worth, TX 76107-4064. Tel.: 817-336-4475. Fax: 817-336-2470.
Web Site: www.cowgirl.net
Founded: 1975.
Congressional District: 6 & 12
Key Personnel: Exec. Dir., Pat Riley; Assoc. Dir., Kim Smith; Dir. Finance, Barbara Mounts; Cur. & Collections Mgr., Tricia Taylor Dixon; Dir. Education, Diana Vela, Ph.D.; Devel., Emmy Lou Prescott; Coord. Membership, Wendy Morton; Museum Shop Mgr., Amy Moorhouse.
Personnel Profile: Full-Time Paid 14; Part-Time Paid 4; Part-Time Volunteers 40; Interns 2.
Governing Authority: nonprofit organization. Tax-exempt: 501(c)(3).
Research Center: emphasis on all aspects of Western American women.
Collections: costumes; western attire; cowgirl & western photos; saddles; ropes; trophies; western art; pop culture.
Major Exhibits: Georgia O'Keeffe & the Far Away: Nature & Image, 2/10-9/10; Heart of the West Art Exhibition, 10/1/10-10/24/10; 101 Ranch: The Real Wild West, 11/10-5/11.
Research Fields: western, pioneer & rodeo women; contribution of women to Western U.S. history.
Facilities: library; research center; auditorium. Museum-related items for sale.
Activities: temporary & traveling exhibits; research; rental gallery. Annual Event: Honoree Induction Luncheon.
Publications: books; brochures; newsletter.
Hours & Admission Prices: Mon.-Sat. 9-5, Sun. 12-5. Adults $8, seniors 60 & over & children 3-12 $7; children 2 & under and members no charge. Closed New Year's Day; Thanksgiving; Christmas Eve & Day. ♿
Attendance: 82,543 (accurate)
Membership: Youth (under 18) $25; 2 People $50; Family $100; Rodeo Cowgirl $300; Cowgirl Legend $500; Hall of Fame $1,000; Silver Spur $2,500; Golden Spur $5,000; Platinum $10,000.

NATIONAL MULTICULTURAL WESTERN HERITAGE MUSEUM, 3400 Mount Vernon Ave., Fort Worth, TX 76103-2525. Mailing Address: 2401 Scott Ave., Fort Worth, TX 76103-2228. Tel.: 817-534-8801. Fax: 817-534-6277.
Web Site: www.cowboysofcolor.org
Formerly: National Cowboys of Color Museum and Hall of Fame
Founded: 2001.
Congressional District: 26
Key Personnel: Exec. Dir., Gloria R. Austin; Chm. (V) & Pres. (V), Eric Peterson; Museum Shop Mgr., Rich Robinson.
Personnel Profile: Full-Time Paid 1; Part-Time Paid 1.
Governing Authority: Tax-exempt.
History Museum.
Collections: African American, Hispanic American, Native American, & European American pioneers; western culture; photographs; Tuskegee Airmen; Buffalo Soldiers; Hall of Fame inductees.
Research Fields: Western heritage.
Activities: programs; workshops; storytelling. Museum Sponsors: Western Heritage Symposium; Hall of Fame Induction Ceremony.
Publications: e-newsletter, Western Round-Up.
Hours & Admission Prices: Wed.-Sat. 11-6. Adults $6, senior citizens $4, students $3; members and children 5 & under no charge. ♿
Attendance: 19,000 (estimated)
Membership: Student $20; Senior Individual $25; Educator $40; Individual & Senior Family $50; Family $75; Rancher $250; Buckaroo $500; Lifetime Individual $750; Wrangler $1,000; Foreman $2,500; Partner $5,000.

OSCAR E. MONNIG METEORITE GALLERY - TEXAS CHRISTIAN UNIVERSITY, Sid Richardson Science Bldg., 250 W. Bowie St., Fort Worth, TX 76129. Mailing Address: P.O. Box 298830, Fort Worth, TX 76129. Tel.: 817-257-6277. Fax: 817-257-7789.
Key Personnel: Dir., Teresa Moss; Cur., Dr. Arthur Ehlmann
Geology Museum.
Collections: over 1,000 meteorites; hands-on exhibits.
Activities: hands-on exhibits; special events.
Hours & Admission Prices: Tues.-Fri. 1-4, Sat. 9-4; groups by appointment. No charge. Closed university holidays.

OSCAR E. MONNING METEORITE GALLERY, Texas Christian University, Sid Richarson Science Bldg., 2950 W. Bowie, Fort Worth, TX 76109. Mailing Address: Box 298830, Fort Worth, TX 76129-0001. Tel.: 817-257-6277. Fax: 817-257-7789.
E-mail: t.moss@tcu.edu
Web Site: www.monningmuseum.tcu.edu
Key Personnel: Dir., Teresa Moss; Cur., Dr. Arthur Ehlmann
Meteorite Gallery.
Collections: hands-on exhibits pertaining to meteorites.
Hours & Admission Prices: Tues.-Fri. 1-4, Sat. 9-4. No charge.

SID RICHARDSON MUSEUM, (M), 309 Main St., Fort Worth, TX 76102-4006. Tel.: 888-332-6554. Fax: 817-332-8671.
E-mail: info@sidrichardsonmuseum.org
Web Site: www.sidrichardsonmuseum.org
Formerly: Sid Richardson Collection of Western Art
Founded: 1982.
Congressional District: 12
Key Personnel: Dir., Jan Scott; Asst. Dir., Monica Herman; Dir. Gallery Programs, Mary Burke; Dir. Education Outreach, Rebecca Martin.
Personnel Profile: Full-Time Paid 7; Part-Time Paid 8; Part-Time Volunteers 16; Interns 2.
Governing Authority: nonprofit organization. Parent Institution: Sid W. Richardson Foundation. Tax-exempt: 501(c)(3).
Art Museum.
Collections: works by Western artists including paintings by Frederic Remington & Charles M. Russell.
Facilities: Museum-related items for sale.
Activities: educational program & guided tours by appointment.
Publications: brochure; gallery guides; museum catalog.
Hours & Admission Prices: Mon.-Thurs. 9-5, Fri.-Sat. 9-8, Sun. 12-5. No charge. Closed holidays. ♿
Attendance: 40,000 (estimated)

STOCKYARDS MUSEUM, 131 E. Exchange Ave., Ste. 113, Fort Worth, TX 76164-8213. Tel.: 817-625-5087. Fax: 817-625-5083.
Governing Authority: Parent Institution: North Fort Worth Historical Society. Tax-exempt: 501(c)(3).
History Museum.
Collections: local history; photographs; railroading; cattle industry; wagon trail.
Facilities: 2,300 sq. ft. exhibit space. Museum-related items for sale.
Hours & Admission Prices: Mon.-Sat. 10-5. No charge; donations accepted. ♿

TEXAS CIVIL WAR MUSEUM, (M), 760 Jim Wright Freeway N., Fort Worth, TX 76108-1222. Tel.: 817-246-2323. Fax: 817-246-3951.
Web Site: texascivilwarmuseum.com
Founded: 2006.
Key Personnel: Pres. & Cur., Ray Richey; Exec. Dir., Esther Froelich Sims; Cur., Judy Richey.
Personnel Profile: Full-Time Paid 1; Part-Time Volunteers 4.
Governing Authority: nonprofit organization. Tax-exempt.
History Museum.
Collections: Civil War artifacts; over 60 flags; firearms; uniforms; period clothing; Victorian era dresses.
Hours & Admission Prices: Tues.-Sat. 9-5. Adults $6, students 7-12 $3; discounts to AAM members, groups & active military; children under 6 no charge. Closed New Year's Day; Independence Day; Thanksgiving; Christmas Eve & Day.
Attendance: 20,000 (estimated)

TEXAS COWBOY HALL OF FAME, 128 E. Exchange Ave., Fort Worth, TX 76164-8210. Tel.: 817-626-7131. Fax: 817-626-7171.
E-mail: info@texascowboyhalloffame.com
Web Site: www.texascowboyhalloffame.com
Key Personnel: Exec. Asst., Julie Buswold
History Museum.

Collections: cowboy history; Texas men & women of rodeo and cutting; photographs; videos; Sterquell wagons.
Facilities: Museum-related items for sale.
Activities: rental facilities.
Hours & Admission Prices: Mon.-Thurs. 10-6, Fri.-Sat. 10-7, Sun. 12-6. Family Package (2 adults, 4 children 5-12): $15, adults 18-59 $5, seniors 60 & over & students 13-17 with valid college ID $4, children 5-12 $3; military with ID & children 4 & under no charge; discounts to groups. Closed Christmas.

UNIVERSITY ART GALLERY, TEXAS CHRISTIAN UNIVERSITY, University Dr. & Cantey, Fort Worth, TX 76129-0001. Mailing Address: Department of Art, P.O. Box 298000, Fort Worth, TX 76129-0001. Tel.: 817-257-7643. Fax: 817-257-7399.
E-mail: r.watson@tcu.edu
Web Site: www.artanddesign.tcu.edu/
Formerly: Moody Exhibition Hall, Texas Christian University
Founded: 1874.
Congressional District: 12
Key Personnel: Dir. & Chm., Ronald Watson.
Governing Authority: private university; nonprofit organization. Tax-exempt: 501(c)(3).
University Art Gallery.
Collections: works on paper by traditional as well as contemporary artists.
Activities: lectures; education programs for adults, undergraduate & graduate students.
Hours & Admission Prices: Academic Year: Mon. 11-6, Tues.-Fri. 11-4, Sat.-Sun. 1-4. No charge; donations accepted. Closed Easter; Christmas. ♿
Attendance: 4,100 (accurate)

VINTAGE FLYING MUSEUM, Meacham International Airport, 505 N.W. 38th St., Hangar 33 S., Fort Worth, TX 76106. Mailing Address: P.O. Box 820099, Fort Worth, TX 76182-0099. Tel.: 817-624-1935. Fax: 817-624-2840.
Web Site: www.vintageflyingmuseum.org
Formerly: B.C. Vintage Flying Machines
Founded: 1980.
Key Personnel: C.E.O./Dir., W.D. Hospers, Col. MC, USA, (Ret.)
Personnel Profile: Full-Time Volunteers 2; Part-Time Volunteers 20.
Governing Authority: Tax-exempt: 501(c)(3).
Military Aircraft Museum.
Collections: WWII memorabilia & artifacts; aircraft models; 1930s & 1940s aircraft.
Activities: workshops; summer camps; educational programs; local B-17 rides.
Publications: newsletter, Wingtips.
Hours & Admission Prices: Sat. 10-5, Sun. 12-5, Mon.-Fri. by appointment. Adults $8, children 13-17 & seniors $5, children 6-12 $3; children under 6 no charge. ♿
Attendance: 12,000
Membership: Individual $36; Family $45; Life$1,000.

Fredericksburg

GILLESPIE COUNTY HISTORICAL SOCIETY, 312 W. San Antonio St., Fredericksburg, TX 78624-3760. Tel.: 830-997-2835. Fax: 830-997-3891.
E-mail: vickibeasley@austin.rr.com
Web Site: www.pioneermuseum.com
Founded: 1935.
Key Personnel: Exec. Dir., Paul Camfield; Pres., Trudy Hutton; Administrative Sec., Sharon Buford; Museum Shop Mgr., M.J. Barbre.
Personnel Profile: Full-Time Paid 3; Part-Time Paid 9; Part-Time Volunteers 300.
Governing Authority: private; nonprofit organization. Subsidiary Institutions: Pioneer Museum, Fredericksburg, TX; Vereins Kirche Museum, Fredericksburg, TX; Fort Martin Scott, 2.5 miles East of Fredericksburg, TX on Hwy. 290 E. Tax-exempt: 501(c)(3).
Historical Society.
Collections: Pioneer Museum: 9 historic period furnished buildings; native plant gardens. Vereins Kirche Museum: artifacts pertaining to the immigration & settlement of Germans from 1846 to early 1900s.
Research Fields: agricultural history; German immigrant history; social history of Texas Hill Country 1846 to present; frontier fort history.
Facilities: 100-vol. library of various historical books; botanical garden; 10,000 sq. ft. exhibit space; 228-seat auditorium; field research station. Museum-related items for sale.
Activities: guided tours; lectures. Annual Events: Fort: Texas Rangers encampment in April; Intertribal POW WOW in May; Founders Day Festival in May; Texan Thanksgiving Living History event; Christmas Candlelight Tour in December; Stars of Texas Preservation Awards Luncheon in December.
Publications: quarterly newsletter, Der Trompeter.
Hours & Admission Prices: Office: Mon.-Fri. 9-5. Pioneer Museum: Mon.-Sat. 10-5, Sun. 1-5. Vereins Kirche Museum: Mon.-Sat. 10-4, Sun. 1-4. Adults $5, students 6-17 $3; children 5 & under no charge. Fort Martin Scott: Tues.-Sun. 10-5. No charge. Closed New Year's Day; Easter; Thanksgiving; Christmas Eve & Day.
Attendance: 22,000 (estimated)
Membership: Individual $25; Family $40; Company $75; Founders Club $125.

NATIONAL MUSEUM OF THE PACIFIC WAR, (M), 340 E. Main St., Fredericksburg, TX 78624-4612. Tel.: 830-997-4379, ext. 225. Fax: 830-997-8220.
Web Site: www.nimitz-museum.org
Founded: 1967.
Congressional District: 21
Key Personnel: Museum Dir., Joe Cavanaugh; Exec. Dir., Charles Grojean; Asst. Dir., Pat Vaughan; Program Dir., Helen McDonald; Museum Shop Mgr., Carol Sattler.
Personnel Profile: Full-Time Paid 14; Part-Time Paid 3; Part-Time Volunteers 115.
Governing Authority: state. Parent Institution: Texas Parks & Wildlife Department, Austin, TX. Tax-exempt.
History Museum: housed in 1850 Nimitz Hotel, a famous hostelry until about the turn of the century.
Collections: Pacific World War II related artifacts including uniforms, personal equipment, weapons, flags & souvenirs; Admiral Nimitz, Nimitz Hotel & Fredericksburg-related artifacts; archives collection with manuscripts, war diaries, correspondences, photos, scrapbooks, ephemera; macro collection along history walk of the Pacific War, including two American & two Japanese aircraft, Japanese & American tanks, Half-Track, DUKW, naval & land based artillery of both sides; 5 traveling exhibits available for loan; prints & posters developed for Symposia Series.
Research Fields: historic Fredericksburg; career of Admiral Nimitz; World War II in the Pacific.
Facilities: research library on Admiral Nimitz & the war in the Pacific open by appointment; 100-seat auditorium; 23,000 sq. ft. exhibit space, 3.5 acre outdoor exhibit; George Bush Gallery.
Activities: living history programs; annual Pacific War Symposium; guided tours; lectures; illustrated talks by advance arrangements; temporary & permanent exhibitions; educational programs.
Publications: book; Tarawa, The Story of a Battle; books & booklets relating to life & career of Admiral Nimitz & World War II in the Pacific; Attack on Pearl Harbor by Two Who Were There; Day of Infamy; The Cactus Air Force; The Cruise of the Lanikai; A Guide to the National Museum of the Pacific War.
Hours & Admission Prices: Daily 9-5. Adults $7, students $4; discounts to TAM & AAM members; children under 6 & members no charge. Closed Thanksgiving; Christmas. ♿
Attendance: 120,000 (accurate)
Membership: Shipmate $20; Advisor $50; Skipper $100; Patron $250; Admiral's Circle $500; Benefactor $1,000.

PIONEER MUSEUM AND VEREINS KIRCHE, 309 W. Main St., Fredericksburg, TX 78624-3711. Mailing Address: 312 W. San Antonio St., Fredericksburg, TX 78624-3760. Tel.: 830-997-2835. Fax: 830-997-3891.
E-mail: sbuford@pioneermuseum.com
Web Site: www.pioneermuseum.com
Founded: 1936.
Congressional District: 21
Key Personnel: Pres. Gillespie County Historical Society (V), Brent Waldoch; Pres. (V), Janet Lindemann; Dir., Paul Camfield; Administrative Asst., Sharon Buford; Lead Interpreter Pioneer Museum, Evelyn Stork; Lead Interpreter Vereins Kirche, Eugenia Peterman; Museum Shop Mgr., M.J. Barbre.
Personnel Profile: Full-Time Paid 3; Part-Time Paid 13; Part-Time Volunteers 2.
Governing Authority: society. Parent Institution: Gillespie County Historical Society. Vereins Kirche Museum, Center of Marktplatz, Fredericksburg, TX. Tax-exempt: 501(c)(3).
History Museum, House & Sites.
Collections: Historic Houses: c.1935 Vereins Kirche; c.1849-87 Kammlah Family Home & outbuildings; c.1878-1959 Fassel-Roeder House; c.1904 Weber Sunday House; c.1880 Walton Smith Cabin; c.1880 Schandua House; c. late 1920s White Oak School House; over 1,000 objects relating to the domestic life, commerce, ranching & farming of Gillespie county; Ty Cox tool collection, over 850 19th & early 20th-century tools; over 300 pieces of archival material associated; archives collection with manuscripts, photographs & oral history; early settlement of Fredericksburg & Gillespie county & subsequent chronicle of daily life in the county; Vereins Kirche Museum (1935) replica of original built in 1847.

Research Fields: German immigration to Texas Hill Country, daily life in Gillespie county from 1846 onward.
Facilities: archives located in the Society Historical Center, 2 acre Pioneer Museum Complex; covered wagon shed; old Methodist Church Sanctuary. Museum-related items for sale.
Activities: daily guided tours; special German meal & tour for groups; school tours. Annual Events: Christmas candlelight tour of homes; founders day celebration & lectures.
Publications: quarterly newsletter; brochures; books: Gillespie County A View of Its Past, Pioneers in God's Hills, Vol. II.
Hours & Admission Prices: Pioneer Museum: Mon.-Sat. 10-5, Sun. 1-5. Admission 12 & over $4; children under 11 no charge. Vereins Kirche Museum: Mon.-Sat. 10-4, Sun. 1-4. Admission 12 & over $1; children under 12 no charge; group rates available. ♿
Attendance: 30,000 (estimated)
Membership: Individual $25; Family $40; Company & Business $75; Founder's Club $125.

Frisco

THE FRISCO HERITAGE MUSEUM, (M), 6455 Page St., Frisco, TX 75034-3486. Tel.: 972-292-5665.
Founded: 2008.
Governing Authority: Parent Institution: Frisco Public LIbrary.
History Museum.
Collections: rare artifacts & photographs depicting Frisco's past.
Hours & Admission Prices: Wed.-Sat. 10-5, Sun. 1-5. Family $8, adults $4, children 5-11 $2; children 4 & under no charge. ♿
Attendance: 11,530 (accurate)

Fritch

LAKE MEREDITH AQUATIC AND WILDLIFE MUSEUM, 101 N. Robey, Fritch, TX 79036. Mailing Address: P.O. Box 758, Fritch, TX 79036-0758. Tel.: 806-857-2458. Fax: 806-857-3229.
Web Site: www.geocities.com/lakemeredithmuseum
Founded: 1976.
Congressional District: 13
Key Personnel: Dir. & Museum Shop Mgr., Renee Laney; Chm. (V), Walt Poling; Pres. (V), Wes Phillips.
Personnel Profile: Full-Time Paid 1; Part-Time Paid 2; Part-Time Volunteers 3.
Governing Authority: municipal; nonprofit organization. Parent Institution: City of Fritch. Tax-exempt: 501(c)(3).
Natural History Museum.
Collections: vegetation & wildlife by LaNelle Poling; Playa Lake.
Facilities: 2 aquariums. Museum-related items for sale.
Activities: guided tours; lectures; films; traveling exhibitions; school loan service; special programs for children.
Publications: brochure; monthly newsletter.
Hours & Admission Prices: Mon.-Sat. 10-5. No charge; donations accepted. Closed New Year's Day; Thanksgiving; Christmas. ♿
Attendance: 6,500 (estimated)
Membership: Membership Fee $5 & up.

Gainesville

MORTON MUSEUM OF COOKE COUNTY, 210 S. Dixon St., Gainesville, TX 76240-4719. Mailing Address: P.O. Box 150, Gainesville, TX 76241-0150. Tel.: 940-668-8900. Fax: 940-668-0533.
E-mail: mortonmuseum@att.net
Web Site: www.mortonmuseum.org
Founded: 1968.
Congressional District: 17
Key Personnel: Museum Coord., Cathy Farquhar; CCHS Pres., Harriett Dickson; Chm. (V), Jayleane Smith; Museum Shop Mgr., Shelly Kuehn.
Personnel Profile: Full-Time Paid 2; Part-Time Paid 1; Part-Time Volunteers 1.
Governing Authority: society. Affiliated with Cooke County Heritage Society, Inc. Tax-exempt: 501(c)(3).
Historic Building, Historic Site & History Museum: housed in 1884 fire station, city hall & jail.
Collections: preservation project; Cooke County, Texas artifacts & manuscripts.
Research Fields: county history.
Facilities: 100-vol. library of books on history of Cooke County available for use on premises. Books & museum-related items for sale.
Activities: guided tours; formally organized educational programs; temporary & traveling exhibitions.
Publications: booklet, Texas: Cooke County, Its People, Productions & Resources, 1888; newsletter, Heritage Highlights; books, Early Days in Cooke County, 1848-1873; Cooke County Texas-Where the South & the West Meet; History of Cooke County-A Pictorial Essay; Gainesville and Cooke County-A Pictorial History (in Images of American Series).
Hours & Admission Prices: Tues.-Fri. 10-5, Sat. 2-5; other times by special arrangement. No charge; donations accepted. Closed major holidays. ♿
Attendance: 5,000 (estimated)
Membership: Individual $15; Family $25; Contributing $50-$99; Business $100; Lifetime $500; Lifetime Benefactor %501-$999; Lifetime Patron $1,000 & up.

Galveston

ASHTON VILLA & THE HERITAGE VISITOR CENTER, 2328 Broadway, Galveston, TX 77550-4642. Tel.: 409-762-3933. Fax: 409-762-1904.
E-mail: foundation@galvestonhistory.org
Web Site: www.galvestonhistory.org
Founded: 1974.
Congressional District: 9
Key Personnel: C.E.O., Dwayne Jones; Chm. (V), Merri Edwards; Pres. (V), Raymond Lewis; Museum Shop Mgr., Brandon Ragen.
Personnel Profile: Full-Time Paid 3; Part-Time Paid 8.
Governing Authority: municipal; historic foundation. Parent Institution: Galveston Historical Foundation, 502 20 St., Galveston, TX 77550. Tax-exempt.
Historic House: 1859 Ashton Villa, home of James Moreau Brown, an early Galveston community leader.
Collections: furnishings; paintings; art objects; textiles.
Research Fields: decorative arts; textiles; photographs; postcards.
Facilities: ballroom available. Museum-related items for sale.
Activities: guided tours; docent programs & exhibits. Foundation Sponsors: Christmas events.
Publications: brochure, Ashton; book, The History of Ashton Villa.
Hours & Admission Prices: Mon.-Sat. 10-4, Sun. 12-4. Adults $7, students 6-18 $6; children under 5 & members no charge. Closed Thanksgiving; Christmas Eve & Day. ♿
Attendance: 15,000 (estimated)
Membership: Senior Citizen 65 & over and Students $20; Individual $35; Family (1 household & its children under 19) $45.

THE BISHOP'S PALACE, 1402 Broadway, Galveston, TX 77550-2014. Mailing Address: 502 20th St., Galveston, TX 77550-2014. Tel.: 409-762-2475. Fax: 409-762-1801.
Founded: 1886.
Congressional District: 9
Key Personnel: Cur., Archbishop Daniel diNardo; Exec. Dir., Rev. William D. Bartniski.
Personnel Profile: Part-Time Paid 10; Part-Time Volunteers 2.
Governing Authority: Catholic Diocese of Galveston-Houston. Tax-exempt.
Historic Building: 1886 Walter Gresham Home/Bishop's Palace.
Collections: Victorian furniture.
Facilities: Postcards, brochures & gift items for sale.
Activities: guided tours.
Publications: flyers; newspapers; magazines.
Hours & Admission Prices: Call for hours & admission prices.
Attendance: 40,124 (accurate)

GALVESTON ARTS CENTER, (M), 2127 Strand, Galveston, TX 77550-1632. Tel.: 409-763-2403. Fax: 409-763-0531.
E-mail: information@galvestonartscenter.org
Web Site: www.galvestonartscenter.org
Founded: 1987.
Congressional District: 14
Key Personnel: Exec. Dir., Alexandra L. Irvine; Pres. (V), Tim Beeton; Cur., Clint Willour; Museum Shop Mgr., Janice Broussard; Administrative Dir., Robin Cushman.
Personnel Profile: Full-Time Paid 3; Part-Time Paid 1; Part-Time Volunteers 40; Interns 1.
Governing Authority: private; nonprofit organization. Tax-exempt: 501(c)(3).
Contemporary Art Museum: housed in the 1878 First National Bank building located in the Strand Historic District.
Collections: works by artists from around the state.
Publications: Catalogue for Al Souza: Addenda, 2006; The Art Guys Go Public, 2007.
Hours & Admission Prices: Closed until early 2010. ♿
Attendance: 53,000 (estimated)
Membership: Student & Senior Citizen $25; Individual $40; Household $75; Patron $100; Arts Sponsor $250.

GALVESTON COUNTY HISTORICAL MUSEUM, Shearn Moody Plaza Bldg., Ste. 4157, 123 25th St., Galveston, TX 77550-1494. Tel.: 409-766-2340.
E-mail: jodi.wright-gidley@galvestonhistory.org
Web Site: www.galvestonhistory.org

Founded: 1972.
Congressional District: 9
Key Personnel: Exec. Dir., Dwayne Jones; Dir., Jodi Wright-Gidley.
Personnel Profile: Full-Time Paid 2; Part-Time Paid 3; Part-Time Volunteers 50.
Governing Authority: A joint project of Galveston Historical Foundation, private nonprofit foundation & Galveston Co. Commissioners Court, county governing agency. Tax-exempt: 501(c)(3).
History Museum: housed in 1919 City National Bank.
Collections: photographs; clothing; Galveston county history; lighthouse lens; Edison film of 1900 storm.
Research Fields: county history; 1900 Hurricane; Texas City Disaster; State Historical maker records; local & regional architecture.
Facilities: research library; 2,400 sq. ft. exhibit space.
Activities: guided tours; lectures; films; interpretive events; formal education programs for children; temporary exhibitions.
Hours & Admission Prices: Temporarily closed. ♿
Attendance: 15,000 (estimated)
Membership: Full time Student $25; Senior $25; Senior Couple $45; Individual $40; Family $55; Patron $100; Benefactor $250; Menard Society $1,000.

GALVESTON HISTORICAL FOUNDATION, INC., 502 20th St., Galveston, TX 77550-1661. Tel.: 409-765-7834. Fax: 409-765-7851.
Web Site: www.galvestonhistory.org
Founded: 1871.
Congressional District: 9
Key Personnel: C.E.O., Dwayne Jones; Chm., Raymond Lewis.
Personnel Profile: Full-Time Paid 30; Part-Time Paid 45; Part-Time Volunteers 2,000.
Governing Authority: foundation. Subsidiary Institutions: 1859 Ashton Villa; 1859 St. Joseph Church; 1839 Samuel May Williams House; Texas Seaport Museum, home of the 1877 barque Elissa; Galveston County Historical Museum; Great Storm Theater; Heritage Visitors Center; 1838 Michele B. Menard House. Tax-exempt.
Preservation Project.
Collections: furnishings & memorabilia; maritime artifacts.
Research Fields: immigration through port of Galveston. 19th century social & religious history.
Facilities: 1859 Ashton Villa; 1839 William's House; Texas Seaport Museum-ELISSA; Galveston County Historical Museum; 1838 Menard House; 1880 Garten Verein Pavilion; 1859 St. Joseph's Church; 1861 Custom House.
Activities: guided tours; formally organized education programs for children; docent program; permanent & temporary exhibitions; special events; historic homes tour. Museum Sponsors: Victorian street festival.
Publications: quarterly newsletter, attractions & special events brochures.
Hours & Admission Prices: Call for hours. No charge; donations accepted. ♿
Attendance: 600,000 (accurate)
Membership: Personal: Student $20; Individual $35; Family $45; Sustaining $65; Patron $100; Benefactor $250; Good Fellow $500; Life Member $1,500. Corporate: Business $100; Sponsor $250; Leader $500; Pacesetter $1,000.

GALVESTON RAILROAD MUSEUM, 25th at Strand, Galveston, TX 77550. Mailing Address: 2602 Santa Fe Place, Galveston, TX 77550-1493. Tel.: 409-765-5700. Fax: 409-765-5744.
E-mail: galvrrmuseum@sbcglobal.net
Web Site: www.galvestonrrmuseum.com
Founded: 1983.
Congressional District: 14
Key Personnel: Exec. Dir., Morris S. Gould; Chm. (V), Dr. John E. Bertini; Dir. Mktg. & Coord. Events, Sandi Cobb; Museum Shop Mgr., Betty Morris.
Governing Authority: Tax-exempt.
Railroad Museum.
Collections: steam & diesel engines; HO scale trains; passenger cars; O scale layout; HO scale layout.
Facilities: Museum-related items for sale.
Activities: birthday parties; rental facilities; special events; locomotive & caboose rides. Museum Sponsors: Easter Egg Hunt & Brunch in April; Model Train Show in May; Independence Day Parade; Hobo Night in October; Santa Train in December.
Publications: newsletter.
Hours & Admission Prices: May-Sept. 10-5; Oct.-April 10-4. Adults $7, senior citizens 65 & over $6, children 4-12 $5; discounts to groups. Train Rides: Sat. 11-1. Closed New Year's Day; Thanksgiving; Christmas Eve & Day. ♿

JOHN SYDNOR'S 1847 POWHATAN HOUSE, 3427 Avenue O, Galveston, TX 77550-6734. Mailing Address: 20 Colony Park Circle, Galveston, TX 77551-1738. Tel.: 409-763-0077. Fax: 979-234-7131.
E-mail: evangelinewhorton@yahoo.com
Founded: 1938.
Congressional District: 17
Key Personnel: C.E.O., Pres. & Chm. (V), Kay Rose.
Personnel Profile: Part-Time Volunteers 20.
Governing Authority: nonprofit organization. Parent Institution: Galveston Garden Club, Inc. Subsidiary Institution: Powhatan House Headquarters. Tax-exempt: 501(c)(3).
Historic Building & Site: c.1847 home of pioneer businessman & the first Mayor of Galveston; originally built for use as 24-room family dwelling and guest house. Listed on the National Register of Historic Places.
Collections: furnishings of antebellum & Victorian period; artifacts; personal papers; letters; Civil War battle account; documents; photographs; primary research journals; research & architectural documents of Charles Ladd & Caroline Willis Ladd's relocated in 1895.
Research Fields: gardening & horticulture; life and times of the Sydnor Family.
Facilities: 350-vol. library of books on gardening & flower arranging; documents & published material about John S. Sydnor, available for study & reference on the premises.
Activities: self-guided tours; lectures; formally organized education programs; docent program; permanent exhibitions. Annual Events: 20th Annual Powhatan Pansy Potpourri in November; 19th Caladium Bulb Sales in March.
Publications: fact sheets; brochure; supplementary materials; monthly newsletter, Broadside.
Hours & Admission Prices: Closed for restoration until 2010.
Attendance: 2,000 (estimated)
Membership: Individual $30.

LONE STAR FLIGHT MUSEUM/TEXAS AVIATION HALL OF FAME, 2002 Terminal Dr., Galveston, TX 77554-9279. Mailing Address: P.O. Box 3099, Galveston, TX 77552-0099. Tel.: 409-740-7722. Fax: 409-740-7612.
Web Site: www.lsfm.org
Founded: 1986.
Congressional District: 9
Key Personnel: Dir., Larry Gregory; Cur., Elizabeth French; Educator, Beth Tragus; Museum Shop Mgr., Deb Kolojaco.
Personnel Profile: Full-Time Paid 12; Part-Time Paid 2; Part-Time Volunteers 100; Interns 2.
Governing Authority: nonprofit organization. Tax-exempt: 501(c)(3).
Aeronautics Museum.
Collections: history of aviation; 40 vintage military & civilian aircraft from 1930s-1970s, most in flying condition or undergoing restoration; history of aviation in Texas.
Research Fields: military & civilian Texas aviation.
Facilities: 102,000 sq. ft. exhibit hangars.
Activities: Warbird rides: B-17, B-25, T6, Stearman. Annual Events: Two-Day Airshow in April; Texas Aviation Hall of Fame Induction Gala & Flyday in November.
Publications: quarterly newsletter.
Hours & Admission Prices: Daily 9-5. Adults $8, senior citizens & children 5-17 $5; tour rates available; discounts to AARP members; Texas Assoc. of Museum members, children 4 & under and members no charge. Closed Thanksgiving; Christmas. ♿
Attendance: 75,000 (estimated)
Membership: Student $48; Family $75; Crewmember $125; Participating $150; Contributing $250; Supporting $500; Sustaining $1,000; Life $3,500.

THE MOODY MANSION MUSEUM, 2618 Broadway, Galveston, TX 77550-4427. Tel.: 409-762-7668. Fax: 409-762-7055.
E-mail: k.guernsey@northenendowment.org
Web Site: www.moodymansion.org
Founded: 1991.
Congressional District: 9
Key Personnel: Pres., Edward L. Protz; Dir. Endowment, Betty Massey; Security & Maintenance, Mary Hoehne; Visitor Operations & Museum Shop Mgr., Karen Guernsey.
Personnel Profile: Full-Time Paid 6; Part-Time Paid 20.

Governing Authority: Parent Institution: Center for Twentieth Century Texas Studies. Tax-exempt.
Historic House Museum: built between 1893 & 1895 31-room mansion.
Collections: late 19th & early 20th-century architecture, decorative arts, social & local history; furniture; ceramics; glass; costume & textiles; photographs; Moody family possessions.
Research Fields: early 20th-century decorative arts & material culture; social, cultural, political & business history of Galveston, Texas & U.S. from 1820-1980.
Facilities: 1,500-vol. archive of books on decorative arts, material culture and U.S. & Texas history.
Activities: guided tours; seasonal special events; evenings & lectures.
Publications: newsletter; brochure; booklet.
Hours & Admission Prices: Winter: Mon.-Sat. 10-3, Sun. 12-3; Summer: Mon.-Sat. 10-4, Sun. 12-4. Adults $7, senior citizens $5, students $3.50, children 6-18 $3; discount to AAM & TAM members; children under 6 no charge. Closed New Year's Day; Easter; Thanksgiving; Christmas.
Attendance: 31,000 (estimated)

OCEAN STAR OFFSHORE DRILLING RIG & MUSEUM, (M), 20th St. at Harborside Dr., 2002 Wharf C, Galveston, TX 77553-2040. Mailing Address: 200 N. Dairy Ashford Rd., #6220, Houston, TX 77079-1101. Tel.: 281-679-8040; 409-766-7827. Fax: 281-544-2441.
E-mail: osmuseum@aol.com
Web Site: www.oceanstaroec.com
Founded: 1997.
Key Personnel: Exec. Dir., Sandra Mourton; Account Mgr., Don Staples; Dir. Operations, Lisa Lisinicchia; Museum Shop Mgr., Margi Peterson.
Personnel Profile: Full-Time Paid 6; Part-Time Paid 11; Part-Time Volunteers 4.
Governing Authority: private; nonprofit organization. Tax-exempt: 501(c)(3).
Science & Technology Museum.
Collections: offshore energy: drilling equipment, geology, seismic, production, well servicing & completions; science technology; safety, construction & transportation relating to offshore drilling; videos; rigs; platforms; vessels; environmental exhibit.
Research Fields: pioneers & history of industry.
Facilities: aquarium; 32-seat classroom; 36-seat theater. Museum-related items for sale.
Activities: formal education programs; guided tours; school loan service; scout overnight programs; summer camps; family days.
Publications: quarterly newsletter, The Star.
Hours & Admission Prices: Call for hours. Adults $8. ♿
Attendance: 36,000 (accurate)

ROSENBERG LIBRARY, (M), 2310 Sealy Ave., Galveston, TX 77550-2296. Tel.: 409-763-8854, ext. 125. Fax: 409-763-0275. TDD: 409-763-8854.
E-mail: eclark@rosenberg-library.org
Web Site: www.rosenberg-library.org
Founded: 1904.
Congressional District: 9
Key Personnel: Pres. (V), Mrs. Jan Coggeshall; C.E.O. & Exec. Dir., John Augelli; Head Special Collections, Casey Edward Greene; Collections Mgr., Nikkie Ferre.
Personnel Profile: Full-Time Paid 20; Part-Time Volunteers 1.
Governing Authority: nonprofit organization. Tax-exempt: 401(6)(c).
General Museum & Library.
Collections: Galveston & Texas history; personal artifacts; maritime history; American Indian artifacts; clothing & textiles; regional artwork: Grace Spaulding John, Paul R. Schumann; Boyer Gonzales, Sr., Julius Stockfleth; Jean Scrimgeour Morgan.
Research Fields: Galveston & Texas history, archives; regional art.
Facilities: 1,864,000-vol. library of books, documents, manuscripts, maps & special collections related to history of Texas & Southwest available for use on premises; reading room.
Activities: self-guided tours; lectures; loan program; rotating exhibits.
Publications: books, Henry Rosenberg, 1824-1893; Samuel May Williams, 1795-1858 Biography & Calendar to Samuel May Williams Papers; Mier Expedition Diary; The Diary of Millie Gray, 1832-1840; Julius Stockfleth, Gulf Coast Marine & Landscape Painter; manuscript sources in the Rosenberg Library, a selective guide; Cartographic Sources from the Rosenberg Library; Through A Night of Horrors: Voices from the 1900 Storm; With Bold Strokes: Boyer Gonzales, 1864-1934.
Hours & Admission Prices: Tues.-Sat. 9-6. No charge; donations accepted. Closed national holidays. ♿
Attendance: 351,755
Membership: Friends of Rosenberg Library: Student $10; Individual $15; Family $25; Sustainer $50 & up; Business & Organization $100.

TEXAS SEAPORT MUSEUM, Pier 21, No. 8, Galveston, TX 77550. Tel.: 409-763-1877. Fax: 409-763-3037.
E-mail: elissa@galvestonhistory.org
Web Site: www.tsm-elissa.org
Founded: 1982.
Congressional District: 9
Key Personnel: Interim Dir., John Moran; C.E.O., Marsh Davis; Chm. (V), Geoff Mills; Coord. Education, Christine Hayes; Museum Shop Mgr., Tery Alexander.
Personnel Profile: Full-Time Paid 8; Part-Time Paid 10; Part-Time Volunteers 175.
Governing Authority: private; not-for-profit organization. Parent Institution: Galveston Historical Foundation. Tax-exempt: 501(c)(3).
Maritime Museum.
Collections: artifacts, cultural manifestations and exhibits of skills which demonstrate the nature of maritime commerce of Texas and the Gulf Coast. Historic Ship: 1877 iron barque Elissa.
Facilities: 8,000 sq. ft. museum space; 4,000 sq. ft. workshop & sail loft.
Activities: sail training program on board National Historic Landmark, 1877 tall ship Elissa.
Publications: newsletter, Elissa Log.
Hours & Admission Prices: Daily 10-5. Adults $8, students & children 6-18 $6; discounts to AAM members; members, children 5 & under and GHF members no charge. Closed Thanksgiving; Christmas. ♿
Attendance: 55,000 (estimated)
Membership: Senior Citizen (65 & over) & Student $20; Family (1 household & its children 19 & under) $45; Sustaining $65; Patron $100; all fees are annual.

George West

GRACE ARMANTROUT MUSEUM, Hwy. 281 S., George West, TX 78022. Mailing Address: P.O. Box 248, George West, TX 78022-0248. Tel.: 361-449-3325. Fax: 361-449-3295.
E-mail: armant@the-i.net
Web Site: www.the-i.net/~armant
Key Personnel: Dir., Mary R. Johnson
History Museum.
Collections: local history; personal artifacts; 1860-1940 furniture; period firearms; china & glassware; paintings; period farm & ranch equipment; 850 paving bricks engraved with the names of those who have lived in Live Oak County; train caboose.
Facilities: Museum-related items for sale.
Activities: community field trips; student programs; classroom trunk shows; summer activities; arts & crafts; calligraphy. Museum Sponsors: Winter Bridge Tournament; Spring Barbecue.
Hours & Admission Prices: Wed.-Fri. & Sun. 1-5, Sat. 12-4. No charge; donations accepted.

Gilmer

FLIGHT OF THE PHOENIX AVIATION MUSEUM, Hangar One, Gilmer, TX 75644. Mailing Address: P.O. Box 610, Gilmer, TX 75644-0610. Tel.: 903-843-2457. Fax: 903-843-3123.
Aviation Museum.
Collections: military aircraft & equipment.
Hours & Admission Prices: Call for hours.

HISTORIC UPSHUR MUSEUM, 119 Simpson St., Gilmer, TX 75644-2231. Tel.: 903-843-5483. Fax: 903-843-5483.
History Museum.
Collections: local history; photographs; period furniture; military uniforms; costumes; pottery.
Facilities: Museum-related items for sale.
Activities: docent programs; lectures; workshops.
Hours & Admission Prices: Tues.-Sat. 10:30-4. No charge; donations accepted.

LITERARY MUSEUM, 917 Madelaine St., Gilmer, TX 75644-3047. Tel.: 903-843-2282. Fax: 903-845-2155.
History Museum.
Collections: memorabilia pertaining to Presidents, British Royalty, American & British authors and characters; photographs; paintings; manuscripts; busts of American & British writers; dolls.
Facilities: library.
Hours & Admission Prices: By appointment.

Glen Rose

BARNARD'S MILL & ART MUSEUM, 307 S.W. Barnard St., Glen Rose, TX 76043. Mailing Address: P.O. Box 2537, Glen Rose, TX 76043-2537. Tel.: 254-897-7494.
Founded: 1989.
Key Personnel: Dir., Richard H. Moore; Chm. (V), S.C. Coconaur; Treas., David B. Morrow; Cur., Hollis Taylor.
Personnel Profile: Part-Time Paid 2.
Governing Authority: nonprofit. Parent Institution: Somervell History Foundation. Tax-exempt: 501(c)(3).
Art & History Museums: housed in historic Barnard's Mill built in 1860. Listed on the National Register of Historic Places.
Collections: 200 paintings, bronzes & etchings, works of artist Amy Miears Jackson, Lester Hughes, Jack Bryant, Robert Summers, Adolph Dehn, Bryon Fullerton, Morris Henry Hobbs, Frederik Taubes, Harding Black, Sherry Jo Horton, Bill Chappell, Jim Powell & Robert Wood; Marchman collection; period furnishings; local history & culture.
Facilities: library of instructional art & antique books.
Activities: guided tours; formal education program for college students affiliated with Tarleton State University.
Hours & Admission Prices: Sat. 10-5, Sun. 1-5; guided tours by appointment. No charge; donations accepted. Closed Christmas Eve & Day. ♿
Attendance: 650 (estimated)

CREATION EVIDENCE MUSEUM, 3102 FM 205, Glen Rose, TX 76043-0309. Mailing Address: P.O. Box 309, Glen Rose, TX 76043-0309. Tel.: 254-897-3200. Fax: 254-897-3100.
E-mail: creation@creationevidence.org
Web Site: www.creationevidence.org
Key Personnel: Founder & Dir., Carl Baugh
Science Museum.
Collections: archaeology; geology; paleontology.
Hours & Admission Prices: Tues.-Sat. 10-4. Admission $2; discounts to families.

DINOSAUR VALLEY STATE PARK, off FM 205 on Park Rd. 59, Glen Rose, TX 76043. Mailing Address: P.O. Box 396, Glen Rose, TX 76043-0396. Tel.: 254-897-4588; 800-792-1112.
Web Site: www.tpwd.state.tx.us
Founded: 1969.
Key Personnel: Supt., Billy P. Baker.
Personnel Profile: Full-Time Paid 6; Part-Time Paid 3; Part-Time Volunteers 3; Interns 1.
Governing Authority: state. Parent Institution: Texas Parks & Wildlife Dept., 4200 Smith School Rd., Austin. Tax-exempt.
Paleontological Site.
Collections: dinosaur tracks from the Cretaceous period; life-size dinosaur statues; dinosaur models.
Facilities: 1,523-acre park.
Hours & Admission Prices: Daily 8am-10pm. Adults $5, Texas resident seniors 65 & over $3; children under 13 no charge. ♿
Attendance: 400,000 (estimated)

DINOSAUR WORLD, 1058 Park Rd. 59, Glen Rose, TX 76043. Tel.: 254-898-1526. Fax: 254-898-1782.
Natural History Museum.
Collections: over 150 life size dinosaur; dinosaur eggs; raptor claws.
Facilities: theatre; picnic area. Museum-related items for sale.
Activities: classes; educational programs; fossil dig; outreach programs; birthday parties.
Hours & Admission Prices: Daily 9-6. Adults $12.75, seniors over 60 $10.75, children 3-12 $10.75; discounts to groups & military dependents; active military no charge. Closed Thanksgiving; Christmas.

FOSSIL RIM WILDLIFE CENTER, 2155 County Rd. 2008, Glen Rose, TX 76043. Mailing Address: P.O. Box 2189, Glen Rose, TX 76043-2189. Tel.: 254-897-2960. Fax: 254-897-3785.
E-mail: visitor-services@fossilrim.org
Web Site: www.fossilrim.org
Founded: 1974.
Congressional District: 17
Key Personnel: C.E.O. & Exec. Dir., Dr. Patrick Condy; Chm. (V), Dr. Joel Thierstein; C.F.O., Pam Adams; Dir. Mktg. & Public Rels., Chris Payne; Volunteer & Docent Coord., Jan Bussey.
Personnel Profile: Full-Time Paid 60; Full-Time Volunteers 1; Part-Time Paid 15; Part-Time Volunteers 70; Interns 15.
Governing Authority: nonprofit. Parent Institution: Earth Promise dba Fossil Rim Wildlife Center. Tax-exempt: 501(c)(3).
Wildlife Conservation Center.
Collections: ecological facts; lifestyle conservation issues; local, national and international endangered species issues; nature & wildlife awareness.
Research Fields: social behavior, metapopulation structure, genetic variability, reproductive studies, etc. of endangered species as it applies to conservation medicine & conservation issues.
Facilities: 400-vol. library of conservation & wildlife books; 100-seat auditorium; restaurant; picnic areas; classroom; 1,300 sq. ft. exhibit space; nature center; field research station; wilderness camping. Gift & nature items for sale.
Activities: guided tours; lectures; organized education programs for children, adults & undergraduate or graduate students; special overnight conservation activities for schools and scout groups; internship programs in conservation medicine, education and animal care.
Publications: scientific research papers; monthly email newsletter to members.
Hours & Admission Prices: Daily 8:30am to two hours before sunset. Adults $18.95, seniors 62 & over $14.95, children 3-11 $12.95; discounts to groups; members and children 3 & under no charge. Closed Thanksgiving; Christmas Eve & Day. ♿
Attendance: 135,000 (accurate)
Membership: Senior $40; Adult $72; Dual Senior $75; Dual $90; Family $120.

SOMERVELL COUNTY HISTORICAL MUSEUM, Elm & Vernon Sts., Glen Rose, TX 76043. Mailing Address: Box 669, Glen Rose, TX 76043-0669. Tel.: 254-898-0640.
Founded: 1966.
Congressional District: 17
Key Personnel: C.E.O., Mary Lee Lilly; Chm. (V) & Museum Shop Mgr., Jean King.
Personnel Profile: Full-Time Volunteers 1; Part-Time Volunteers 9.
Governing Authority: society. Parent Institution: Somervell Historical Society. Tax-exempt: 501(c)(3).
Historical Society Museum.
Collections: agriculture; archaeology; archives; geology; Indian artifacts; dinosaur foot tracks; fossils displays from local River Paluxy Whiskey Still; early settlers artifacts.
Facilities: Museum-related items for sale.
Activities: permanent exhibitions.
Publications: city & county map.
Hours & Admission Prices: Mon.-Tues. by appointment, Wed.-Sat. 11-4, call to confirm. No charge; donations accepted. ♿
Attendance: 5,000 (estimated)
Membership: Individual $10; Contributing $15; Sustaining $50; Life $100.

Goliad

GOLIAD STATE PARK, 108 Park Rd. 6, Goliad, TX 77963-3206. Tel.: 361-645-3405. Fax: 361-645-8538.
E-mail: brenda.justice@tpwd.state.tx.us
Web Site: www.tpwd.state.tx.us
Founded: 1931.
Congressional District: 15
Key Personnel: Exec. Dir., Carter Smith; Supt., Brenda Justice; Chm. Commission, Peter Holt; Dir. Parks, Walt Dabney; Education Devel., Beth Ellis.
Personnel Profile: Full-Time Paid 13; Part-Time Paid 3; Part-Time Volunteers 3.
Governing Authority: state. Parent Institution: Texas Parks & Wildlife Dept. 4200 Smith School Rd., Austin, TX 78744. Tel. 512-479-4800. Tax-exempt.
Historic Sites: 1749-1830 sites of Spanish mission Espiritu Santo de Zuniga.
Collections: archaeological artifacts; Spanish Colonial & early Texas items & memorabilia. Historic Sites: ruins of mid to late 18th-century Mission Nuestra Senora del Rosario; 1829 birthplace of Gen. Ignacio Zaragoza.
Research Fields: Spanish Colonial history.
Facilities: history & nature trails; picnic area; camping facilities.
Activities: guided tours; formally organized education programs for children; permanent exhibitions; demonstrations; crafts workshops; living history programs. Museum Sponsors: two spring concerts; Spanish Tracks & Trails; Christmas concert.
Publications: various natural & cultural resource topics.
Hours & Admission Prices: Daily 8-5. Adults $3. Closed Christmas. ♿
Attendance: 150,000 (estimated)
Membership: One Cardholder $60; Two Cardholders $75.

PRESIDIO LA BAHIA, Refugio Hwy., 1 mile south of Goliad on Hwy. 183, Goliad, TX 77963. Mailing Address: P.O. Box 57, Goliad, TX 77963-0057. Tel.: 512-645-3752. Fax: 512-645-1706.
E-mail: presidiolabahia@goliad.net
Web Site: www.presidiolabahia.org
Founded: 1966.

Key Personnel: Dir., Newton M. Warzecha.
Personnel Profile: Full-Time Paid 1; Part-Time Paid 2; Part-Time Volunteers 25.
Governing Authority: church. Parent Institution: Diocese of Victoria. Tax-exempt.
Historic Site Museum: Spanish Fort on lower San Antonio River, part of the 1772 Presidio Line, scene of Goliad Massacre.
Collections: artifacts showing 9 levels of civilization; artifacts of habitation, including pre-colonial, Spanish, Mexican & Texan era.
Research Fields: pre-Columbian, Spanish, colonial & Mexican cultural materials; military specimens; Spanish, Colonial architecture, archaeology & documents.
Facilities: archives & library; living history programs.
Activities: tours.
Publications: book, Presidio La Bahia.
Hours & Admission Prices: Daily 9-5. Adults $3, senior citizens $2.50, children 5-11 $1; members no charge. Closed New Year's Day; Easter; Thanksgiving; Christmas. ♿
Attendance: 27,000 (accurate)
Membership: Individual $25; Family $50; Supporting $150; Caballero $250; Empresario $500; Alcalde $1,000.

Gonzales

GONZALES MEMORIAL MUSEUM, 414 Smith, Gonzales, TX 78629. Mailing Address: P.O. Box 547, Gonzales, TX 78629-0547. Tel.: 830-672-6350. Fax: 830-672-2813.
E-mail: curator@cityofgonzales.org
Web Site: www.cityofgonzales.org
Founded: 1936.
Congressional District: 14
Key Personnel: Chm. (V), Kay Bakken; Dir. Economic Devel., Carolyn Gibson; Cur., Oliver Davis.
Personnel Profile: Full-Time Paid 1; Part-Time Volunteers 10.
Governing Authority: city. Tax-exempt.
History Museum.
Collections: original documents & relics dating to 1660 dealing with Texas, Mexico & the Great Southwest; manuscripts; cannon used in the frist battle in Texas' fight for independence from Mexico; George Washigton Davis' journal.
Activities: guided tours; inter-museum loan & permanent exhibitions.
Hours & Admission Prices: Tues.-Sat. 10-5, Sun. 1-5. No charge; donations accepted. Closed Christmas. ♿
Attendance: 7,000 (accurate)

Grapevine

GRAPEVINE HISTORICAL MUSEUM, 705 S. Main St., Grapevine, TX 76051-5351. Mailing Address: Grapevine Historical Society, P.O. Box 995, Grapevine, TX 76099-0995. Tel.: 817-481-3774.
Founded: 1973.
History Museum.
Collections: local history & culture; photographs; personal artifacts; period furnishings; archaeological artifacts.
Hours & Admission Prices: Mon.-Sat. 9-5, Sun. 1-5. No charge; donations accepted.
Attendance: 33,000

Greenville

AUDIE MURPHY/AMERICAN COTTON MUSEUM, INC, (M), 600 I-30, E., Greenville, TX 75401. Mailing Address: P.O. Box 347, Greenville, TX 75403-0347. Tel.: 903-450-4502. Fax: 903-454-1990.
E-mail: amacm@att.net
Web Site: www.cottonmuseum.com
Founded: 1987.
Congressional District: 1
Key Personnel: Pres. & C.E.O., Susan Lanning; Chm. (V), Steve Ramsey.
Personnel Profile: Full-Time Paid 2; Part-Time Paid 1; Part-Time Volunteers 32.
Governing Authority: board of trustees. Tax-exempt.
Cotton & History Museum.
Collections: regional history; National cotton production; memorabilia from Audie Murphy's military service & movie career; military history; 10 ft. bronze statue of Audie Murphy.
Research Fields: Cotton industry & history; Greenville & Hunt county; military history.
Facilities: library; archives.
Activities: guided tours; monthly speaker; educational programs; family fun day programs; summer camp. Annual Events: Cotton History Conference; Audie Murphy Days; Easter After Dark; Hidden Treasures; Military Gun Show.
Publications: brochure; monthly newsletter, The Compress; annual report.
Hours & Admission Prices: Tues.-Sat. 10-5. Adults $5, senior citizens $3; students $1; discounts to AAM & ICOM members; active military & members no charge. Closed major holidays. ♿
Attendance: 7,197 (accurate)
Membership: Senior Citizen $15; Individual $30; Family & Small Business $60; Contributing $100; Sustaining $250; Sponsor $500; Benefactor $1,000; Lifetime $2,500.

Harlingen

RIO GRANDE VALLEY MUSEUM, 2425 Boxwood at Raintree, Harlingen, TX 78550. Tel.: 956-430-8500. Fax: 956-427-8806.
E-mail: rgvmuse@hiline.net
Web Site: hiline.net/rgvmuse
Founded: 1967.
Congressional District: 15
Key Personnel: Dir., Linn Keller.
Personnel Profile: Full-Time Paid 2; Part-Time Paid 5; Part-Time Volunteers 2.
Governing Authority: municipal; nonprofit. Branch Museums: New Museum; Historical Museum; Lon C. Hill Home; Paso Real Stagecoach Inn; Harlingen Hospital Museum. Tax-exempt.
History Museum.
Collections: Valley history including Republic of Texas; natural history; period clothing, furniture & household objects; period archives of Civil War & other conflicts. Historic Buildings: c.1850 Paso Real Stage Coach Inn, c.1923 Harlingen Hospital, home of city founder.
Research Fields: historical events of Rio Grande Valley.
Facilities: auditorium & video facilities.
Activities: guided tours; lectures; permanent & temporary exhibitions.
Hours & Admission Prices: Wed.-Sat. 10-4, Sun. 1-4. Adults $2, senior citizens & children $1. Closed Easter; Independence Day; Labor Day; Thanksgiving; Christmas. ♿
Attendance: 15,500 (estimated)
Membership: Personal $15; Family $25; Patron $50; Benefactor $100.

Henderson

THE DEPOT MUSEUM COMPLEX, 514 N. High St., Henderson, TX 75652-5912. Tel.: 903-657-4303. Fax: 903-657-2679.
E-mail: depot@depotmuseum.com
Web Site: www.depotmuseum.com
Founded: 1979.
Congressional District: 1
Key Personnel: Chm. (V), Jim White; Dir., Vickie Armstrong.
Personnel Profile: Full-Time Paid 1; Part-Time Paid 2; Part-Time Volunteers 35.
Governing Authority: county; nonprofit. Parent Institution: Rusk County. Subsidiary Institution: Rusk County Historical Commission. Tax-exempt: 501(c)(3).
History Museum.
Collections: costumes; tools; photographs; rural southern; communication artifacts; local, state, pre-historic & modern artifacts. Historic Structures: 1901 Depot; 1841 log cabin; 1908 outhouse; c.1880 doctor's office; 1884 dog trot home; syrup mill; printing shop; saw mill; steam drilling rig; country store; oil derrick & pumping jack; c.1920 cotton gin.
Research Fields: 1830-1970 Texas life; culture, lifestyle, social institution & folk arts of Rusk County.
Facilities: archives; 7,900 sq. ft. exhibit space; 45-seat theater. Genealogical books & other museum-related items for sale.
Activities: guided tours; organized educational programs; participatory exhibits. Museum Sponsors: Heritage Folkart Day for children; Grandparent's Day in July; Heritage Syrup Festival, syrup making demo plus other folkarts in November.
Publications: monthly newsletter, The Telegram.
Hours & Admission Prices: Mon.-Fri. 9-12 & 1-5, Sat. 9-1. Adults $3, seniors $2, children $1; discounts to AAM & Texas Museum Association members, bus tours & groups; members no charge. Closed state & federal holidays. ♿
Attendance: 17,486 (accurate)
Membership: Individual $10; Family $15; Club $25; Friend $50; Patron $100; Benefactor $300; Life $1,000.

HOWARD-DICKINSON HOUSE MUSEUM, 501 S. Main St., Henderson, TX 75654-3544. Mailing Address: P.O. Box 2434, Henderson, TX 75653-2434. Tel.: 903-657-5528 & 7405. Fax: 903-657-9283.
Founded: 1964.
Congressional District: 9
Key Personnel: Pres., Cyndi Walker; Treas., Louise Slover.
Personnel Profile: Part-Time Volunteers 6.
Governing Authority: nonprofit. Rusk County Heritage Association. Tax-exempt: 501(c)(3).

Historic House Museum: 1855 restored Howard-Dickinson House with 1905 frame-wing authentically restored & furnished.
Collections: furnishings; historical books; papers; paintings; manuscript collections; clothing; linens; lace; dolls; china; glass; silver.
Research Fields: local history; genealogy.
Facilities: 240-vol. library of medical books, genealogy, history, cookbooks, fiction, poetry & biography available for use on premises; reading room.
Activities: guided group & school tours by appointment; facilities available for rent.
Publications: brochures; Howard-Dickinson House Cook Book.
Hours & Admission Prices: By appointment only. Adults $5, children $1. Closed major holidays. ♿
Attendance: 1,479

Hereford

DEAF SMITH COUNTY MUSEUM, 400 Sampson, Hereford, TX 79045. Mailing Address: P.O. Box 1007, Hereford, TX 79045-1007. Tel.: 806-363-7070.
E-mail: deafsmithmuseum@wtrt.net
Web Site: www.deafsmithcountymuseum.org
Founded: 1966.
Congressional District: 19
Key Personnel: Exec. Dir., Paula Edwards.
Personnel Profile: Full-Time Paid 2; Part-Time Volunteers 25.
Governing Authority: county. Tax-exempt.
History Museum: housed in 1927 Catholic schoolhouse; former site of St. Anthony's Catholic school by official Texas historical marker; 1909 Victorian Home, 508 W. Third, Hereford, TX; entered on National Register of Historic Places.
Collections: 1905 household items; ranching gear; 1898 dug-out; Santa Fe caboose; early farm machinery; jail cells from first county seat, La Plata; windmill; general store; fashions; textiles; historic chapel.
Facilities: 100-vol. library of school books of late 1800s; novels; magazines; 1900s music study magazines & song books available for use by special arrangement.
Activities: guided tours; lectures; arts festivals; docent program or council; permanent & temporary exhibitions.
Publications: newsletter, The Deaf Smithsonian.
Hours & Admission Prices: Mon.-Fri. 10-12 & 1-5, Sat. 10-12 & 1-3; Sun. by appointment only. No charge; donations accepted. Closed major holidays.
Attendance: 3,750 (estimated)
Membership: Through Deaf Smith County Historical Society: Adult $15; Business $25; Life $250.

Hidalgo

OLD HIDALGO PUMPHOUSE, 902 S. Second St., Hidalgo, TX 78557-2703. Tel.: 956-843-8686. Fax: 956-843-6519.
E-mail: pump_house@sbcglobal.net
Web Site: www.hidalgotexas.com
Formerly: Hidalgo Pumphouse Heritage and Discovery Park
Founded: 1999.
Congressional District: 25
Key Personnel: Dir., Irma D. Duran; Administrative Asst., Viola Arismendez.
Personnel Profile: Full-Time Paid 2; Part-Time Paid 1; Part-Time Volunteers 3.
Governing Authority: municipal; nonprofit. Tax-exempt.
Agriculture Museum: housed in a restored pumphouse which operated from 1909 to 1983 pumping water from the Rio Grande for agricultural irrigation.
Collections: two 1911-1912 Worthington 60-inch pumps driven by two double action, double expansion Hamilton-Corliss steam engines; 1948 Worthington diesel engine & pump; 1952 Ingersoll-Rand diesel engine & pump.
Research Fields: history of steam power in the industrial revolution & the machine age.
Facilities: 7,500 sq. ft. exhibit space; nature center; New World Birding Center satellite. Museum-related items for sale.
Activities: guided group tours; participatory exhibits.
Hours & Admission Prices: Mon.-Fri. 10-5, Sun. 1-5. Adults $3, senior citizens $2, children & students $1. Closed national holidays. ♿
Attendance: 3,000 (estimated)
Membership: Oiler $25-$49; Pipefitter $50-$99; Fireman $100-$499; Steam Engine $500-$999; Super Heated Steam $1,000 & up.

Hillsboro

HILL COUNTY CELL BLOCK MUSEUM, 200 N. Waco St., Hillsboro, TX 76645-2140. Mailing Address: P.O. Box 555, Hillsboro, TX 76645-0555. Tel.: 254-582-8912.
Governing Authority: nonprofit organization.
History Museum: housed in the former county jail & sheriff's family home; built in 1893. Listed on the National Register of Historic Places.
Collections: local history & culture; period furnishings; personal artifacts; photographs.
Hours & Admission Prices: April-Oct. Sat. 10-4; other times by appointment. No charge; donations accepted.
Membership: General $15; Club $20; Business $30.

TEXAS HERITAGE MUSEUM, (M), 112 Lamar Dr., Hillsboro, TX 76645-2711. Tel.: 254-659-7750. Fax: 254-580-9529.
E-mail: jversluis@hillcollege.edu
Web Site: www.hillcollege.edu
Founded: 1963.
Congressional District: 6
Key Personnel: Dir., John Versluis.
Personnel Profile: Full-Time Paid 2; Part-Time Paid 2.
Governing Authority: college. Parent Institution: Hill College. Subsidiary Institution: History Center. Tax-exempt.
Military History Museum.
Collections: Hood's Texas Brigade; Civil War & WWI & WWII military guns; artifacts; manuscripts; Audie Murphy memorabilia.
Research Fields: Texas military history; weaponry history; World War II history; military history of Texas; War between the States.
Facilities: 7,000-vol. library of books on military history of the United States and of Texas.
Activities: self-guided tours of exhibit; research facilities for Civil War soldiers & units. Museum Sponsors: Annual History Symposium.
Publications: scholarly monographs.
Hours & Admission Prices: Memorial Day to Labor Day Mon.-Thurs. 8-4:30, Fri. 8-4, Sat. 10-5; Sept.-May Mon.-Thurs. 8-4:30, Fri. 8-4. No charge; donations accepted. Closed national holidays. ♿
Attendance: 6,800 (accurate)
Membership: Individual $25; Family $35; Business $50; Patron $100; Benefactor $250.

Houston

ART LEAGUE OF HOUSTON, 1953 Montrose Blvd., Houston, TX 77006-1243. Tel.: 713-523-9530. Fax: 713-523-4053.
E-mail: alh@artleaguehouston.org
Web Site: www.artleaguehouston.org
Founded: 1948.
Congressional District: 18
Key Personnel: Exec. Dir., Vanessa Perez McCalla; Pres., Mike Rudelson.
Personnel Profile: Full-Time Paid 3; Part-Time Paid 1; Part-Time Volunteers 100; Interns 2.
Governing Authority: nonprofit. Tax-exempt: 501(c)(3).
Art Gallery.
Collections: various forms of art media.
Research Fields: Art Registry of Texas; Art League's Visual Arts.
Facilities: classrooms; studios; slide file; bulletin board.
Activities: lectures; workshops; formally organized educational programs; traveling exhibitions; temporary juried exhibits; selection of Texas artist of the year.
Publications: bimonthly newsletter; monthly E-Newsletter.
Hours & Admission Prices: Mon.-Fri. 9-5, Sat. 11-5. No charge, donations accepted. Closed national holidays. ♿
Attendance: 10,000 (estimated)
Membership: Artist $25; Individual $35; Family $60; Patron $100-$499; Benefactor $500-$999.

BAYOU BEND COLLECTION AND GARDENS, 1 Westcott at Memorial Dr., Houston, TX 77007. Mailing Address: P.O. Box 6826, Houston, TX 77265-6826. Tel.: 713-639-7750. Fax: 713-639-7770.
E-mail: bayoubend@mfah.org
Web Site: www.mfah.org/bayoubend
Founded: 1957.
Congressional District: 7
Key Personnel: Chm., Mrs. Lacy Crain; Dir., Bonnie Campbell; Cur. Collections, Michael K. Brown; Cur. Education, Kathleen B. O'Connor; Conservator, Steven Pine; Cur. Gardens, Bart Brechter.
Personnel Profile: Full-Time Paid 32; Part-Time Paid 8; Part-Time Volunteers 291; Interns 1.
Governing Authority: nonprofit organization. Parent Institution: Museum of Fine Arts, Houston. Tax-exempt: 501(c)(3).
Historic House & Site.
Collections: c.1620-1876 American decorative arts; American paintings; c.1700-1840 English ceramics; gardens; historic house.
Research Fields: decorative arts; paintings; American history & culture.
Facilities: 14 acres of gardens.
Activities: guided & self-guided tours; audio tours of house & gardens; lectures; family & adult programs; formally organized education programs

for children, undergraduate college students, schools & teachers; docent programs; permanent exhibitions.
Publications: books, America's Treasures at Bayou Bend: Celebrating Fifty Years; Bayou Bend Gardens; Bayou Bend Intelligencer; exhibition catalogues; collection brochures.
Hours & Admission Prices: House: Tues.-Fri. 10-11:30 & 1-2:45 (90 min. docent-guided tours) by reservation, Sat. 10-11am (90 min. docent-guided tours) by reservation, 1-4 (60 min. self-guided audio tours), Sun. 1-4 (60 min. self-guided audio tour). Self-Guided Garden Audio Tours: Tues.-Sat. 10-5, Sun. 1-5. House & Garden: adults $10, senior citizens & students $8, children 10-17 $5; discounts to AAA & MFAH members; children 9 & under during audio tours no charge. Gardens: $3; children 9 & under no charge. Family Day: Sept.-May 3rd Sun. of month 1-5. No charge. ♿
Attendance: 67,000 (estimated)
Membership: Friend $100; Patron $500; Founder $1,500; Fellow $2,500; Gallery $5,000; Director's Circle $10,000 & up.

BLAFFER GALLERY, THE ART MUSEUM OF THE UNIVERSITY OF HOUSTON, (M), 120 Fine Arts Bldg., Houston, TX 77204-0001. Tel.: 713-743-9521. Fax: 713-743-9525.
Web Site: www.blaffergallery.org
Founded: 1973.
Congressional District: 18
Key Personnel: Acting Dir. & Deputy Dir., David L. Vollmer; Chm., Russell Sherrill; Devel., Susan Conaway; Public Rels., Jeffrey Bowen; Registrar, Young Min Chung; Administrator, Karen Zicterman; Preparator, Kelly Bennett; Cur. Education, Katherine Veneman; Cur. University Collections, Michael Guidry; Asst. Cur. Education, Katy Lopez.
Personnel Profile: Full-Time Paid 10; Part-Time Paid 30; Interns 2.
Governing Authority: public university; nonprofit. Parent Institution: University of Houston. Tax-exempt: 501(c)(3).
Art Gallery.
Collections: Blaffer Gallery is a non-collecting institution that presents a series of changing exhibitions which focus on art of the past 100 years.
Facilities: 7,500 sq. ft. exhibit space.
Activities: docent program; formal educational programs; guided tours; lectures; traveling exhibitions; tours in foreign languages; young artist apprenticeship workshops & program; brown bag gallery tours; contemporary salon; summer arts program.
Publications: triannual newsletter, Blaffer; exhibition catalogs; education kits.
Hours & Admission Prices: Tues.-Sat. 10-5. No charge; donations accepted. Closed university holidays. ♿
Attendance: 45,000 (accurate)
Membership: Community Partner $35; Supporting Partner $100; Leading Partner $250; Founding Partner $500; Visionary Partner $1,000; Corporate or Director's Partners $2,500; Corporate or Director's Circle Partner $5,000.

BUFFALO SOLDIERS NATIONAL MUSEUM, 1834 Southmore, Houston, TX 77004-5947. Tel.: 713-942-8920. Fax: 713-942-8912.
E-mail: matthews@buffalosoldiermuseum.com
Web Site: www.buffalosoldiermuseum.com
Military Museum.
Collections: American military history from 1770 to 2000; photographs.
Activities: outreach programs; lectures; youth drill team; summer high school ROTC internship program.
Hours & Admission Prices: Mon.-Fri. 10-5, Sat. 10-4. Groups of 10 or more $2 per person.

THE CHILDREN'S MUSEUM OF HOUSTON, (M), 1500 Binz, Houston, TX 77004-7112. Tel.: 713-535-7200. Fax: 713-522-5747.
E-mail: info@cmhouston.org
Web Site: www.cmhouston.org
Founded: 1980.
Congressional District: 18
Key Personnel: Exec. Dir., Tammie Kahn; Pres. Bd., Mike Plank; Controller, Lila Soussan; Dir. Finance, Richard Daigneault; Asst. Dir. Devel., Alison Griffith; Dir. Education, Cheryl McCallum; Dir. Exhibits Devel., Keith Ostfeld; Receptionist, Sonia Trevino; Museum Admin., Lori Gunningham; Volunteer & Member Events Coord., Jennifer Belt; Gallery Mgr., Eric Lock; Dir. Facilities, Pete Lancaster; Dir. Public Rels., Shannon Gilliam; Dir. Business Devel., Alexandra Vasquez; Box Office Supvr., Yedidah Rose; Retail Operations Mgr., Connie Schnupp; Traveling Exhibit Coord., Sharon Smallwood; Public Rels. Assoc., Henry Yao; Arts Educator, Bunmi Gaidi; Reservations Coord., Lydia Dungus.
Personnel Profile: Full-Time Paid 64; Part-Time Paid 120; Interns 3.
Governing Authority: nonprofit organization. Tax-exempt: 501(c)(3).
Children's Museum.
Collections: participatory exhibits & programs in art, science, cultures, technology & environment.
Major Exhibits: Dragons & Fairies (T), 11/09-9/12/10; Cool Moves, 11/09-1/24/10; Ashley Bryan (T), 1/14/10-3/28/10; Building Brainstorm (T), 1/30/10-5/23/10; Universal Language of People, 4/1/10-7/25/10; Secrets of Circles (T), 5/29/10-9/19/10; Campaign for Achievement, 6/29/10-11/7/10; Yalalag, 9/18/10-2/6/12; Children of Hangzhou (T), 9/25/10-1/23/11; Seasons of Sharing, 11/13/10-1/9/11.
Research Fields: evaluations.
Facilities: Museum-related items for sale.
Activities: guided tours; rotating exhibits; special events; kids committee; junior volunteer program; museum guild; birthday parties; overnights; performances; demonstrations; teacher & parent workshops and lectures; outreach programs; parent resource library.
Publications: newsletter, Calendar of Events; newsletter, In-Touch; exhibit catalogues; hands-on activity guides.
Hours & Admission Prices: Memorial Day to Labor Day Mon.-Wed. & Fri.-Sat. 10-6, Thurs. 10-8, Sun. 12-6; Sept.-May Tues.-Wed. & Fri.-Sat. 10-6, Thurs. 10-8, Sun. 12-6. Adults $7, senior citizens 65 & over $6; discounts to military with ID, YMCA, ASTC & AAM members; children under 1, members & Thurs. nights no charge. Closed New Year's Day; Easter; Thanksgiving; Christmas. ♿
Attendance: 620,000 (accurate)
Membership: Family I $75; Family Plus $95; Patron Family $150;Explorer $150; Junior Sponsor $250; Benefactor & Discoverer $500; Caryakid & Inventor $1,000.

* **CONTEMPORARY ARTS MUSEUM HOUSTON, (M),** 5216 Montrose Blvd., Houston, TX 77006-6547. Tel.: 713-284-8250. Fax: 713-284-8275.
Web Site: www.camh.org
Founded: 1948.
Congressional District: 7
Key Personnel: Asst. Dir., Michael Reed; Chm. (V), Edward R. Allen, III; Pres. (V), Sissy Kempner; Sr. Cur., Toby Kamps; Cur., Valerie Cassel Oliver; Dir. Education, Public Programs & Cur., Paula Newton; Museum Shop Mgr., Sue Pruden; Registrar, Tim Barkley.
Personnel Profile: Full-Time Paid 19; Part-Time Paid 40; Interns 3.
Governing Authority: nonprofit organization. Tax-exempt: 501(c)(3).
Art Museum.
Collections: contemporary works of art.
Major Exhibits: Matthew Day Jackson: The Immeasurable Distance (T), 11/09-1/17/10; Benjamin Patterson: Born in the State of Flux/US, 11/6/09-1/30/10; Perspectives 168: Anna Krachey, Jessica Malios, & Adam Schreiber, 11/6/09-2/7/10; Barkley L. Hendricks: Birth of the Cool (T), 1/10-4/18/10; Perspectives 169: Odili Donald Odita, 2/12/10-5/2/10; Perspectives 170: Cruz Ortiz, 5/7/10-7/11/10; Hand + Made, 5/15/10-7/25/10.
Research Fields: contemporary art.
Facilities: education resource center. Museum-related items for sale.
Activities: lectures; gallery talks; school programs; audio tours; family activities; children's workshops; tours with information guides; temporary exhibitions.
Publications: exhibition catalogs; Gallery Notes; Young People's Guides.
Hours & Admission Prices: Tues.-Wed. & Sat. 10-5, Thurs. 10-9, Sun. 12-5. No charge; donations accepted. Closed New Year's Day; Thanksgiving; Christmas. ♿
Attendance: 67,006 (accurate)
Membership: Artist, Student & Senior Citizen $35; Individual $50; Household $100; Partner $150; Sponsor $250; Advocate $500; Fellow $1,000.

CY TWOMBLY GALLERY, 1501 Branard St., Houston, TX 77006. Mailing Address: 1511 Branard, Houston, TX 77006-4721. Tel.: 713-525-9400 & 9450. Fax: 713-525-9444.
E-mail: info@menil.org
Web Site: www.menil.org
Founded: 1995.
Key Personnel: Dir., Josef Helfstein.
Governing Authority: Tax-exempt.
Art Gallery.
Collections: Cy Twombly's contemporary abstract expressionism art work.
Hours & Admission Prices: Wed.-Sun. 11-7. No charge. ♿
Attendance: 30,000 (accurate)

* **THE HERITAGE SOCIETY, (M),** 1100 Bagby St., Houston, TX 77002-2504. Tel.: 713-655-1912, ext. 114. Fax: 713-655-9249.
E-mail: info@heritagesociety.org
Web Site: www.heritagesociety.org
Founded: 1954.
Congressional District: 18
Key Personnel: C.E.O. & Exec. Dir., Alice Collette; Chm. Bd. & Pres. (V),

William Hill; Dir. Communications, Debbie Duty; Dir. Finance, Peggy Horn; Cur. Collections, Wallace Saage; Registrar, Ginger Berni.
Personnel Profile: Full-Time Paid 7; Part-Time Volunteers 618; Interns 3.
Governing Authority: nonprofit organization; board of directors. Tax-exempt: 501(c)(3).
History Museum & Historic House Site.
Collections: Historic Structures: 1823 Old Place cabin; 1847 Kellum Noble house; 1850 Nichols-Rice Cherry house; 1868 Pillot house; 1868 San Felipe German Cottage; 1870 Jack Yates early African-American home; 1891 St. John rural church; 1905 Staiti house; 1860 Fourth Ward Cottage.
Major Exhibits: Hidden Treasures from THS Collections, 11/09-1/3/10; Houston Professional Baseball, 1/12/10-4/4/10; Fotofest, 3/12/10-4/25/10; Images of Valor: US Latinos & Latinas of WWII, Spring 2010 (T); Forgotten Gateway: Coming to America Through Galveston Island, Summer & Fall 2010 (T).
Research Fields: Houston history; decorative arts.
Facilities: library & archives; 6,000 sq. ft. museum gallery; tea room. Museum-related items for sale.
Activities: guided tours; slide presentations; educational trips, lectures & programs; outreach programs; museum exhibits. Museum Sponsors: Candlelight Christmas tour; annual ball.
Publications: quarterly, Panorama.
Hours & Admission Prices: Tues.-Sat. 10-4, Sun. 1-4. Historical House Tour: Tues.-Sat. 10, 11:30, 1 & 2:30, Sun. 1 & 2:30. Adults $8, senior citizens $6; discounts to members, AAM, ICOM, AAA & TAM members; children 18 & under and members no charge. Closed major holidays. ♿
Attendance: 232,677 (accurate)
Membership: Individual $50; Family $60; Sustaining $100; Patron $250; Sponsor $500; Corporate $1,250.

HOLOCAUST MUSEUM HOUSTON, (M), 5401 Caroline St., Houston, TX 77004-6804. Tel.: 713-942-8000, ext. 100. Fax: 713-942-7953.
E-mail: info@hmh.org
Web Site: www.hmh.org
Founded: 1996.
Congressional District: 18
Key Personnel: C.E.O., Susan Myers; Chm. (V), Michael Goldberg; Financial Dir. & Museum Shop Mgr., Deana Hyma; Cur. Permanent Exhibit, Marci Dallas; Devel., Steven Lightfoot; Education, Mary Lee Webeck; Public Rels., Ira D. Perry; Security, Capt. Johnny Bone.
Personnel Profile: Full-Time Paid 21; Part-Time Paid 1; Part-Time Volunteers 225; Interns 5.
Governing Authority: private; nonprofit organization. Tax-exempt.
History Museum.
Collections: books; diaries; photographs; film reels; maps; documents; personal items; prison uniforms; bricks from Auschwitz & the Warsaw ghetto.
Facilities: 6,000-vol. library of history books; 11,768 sq. ft. exhibit space; 102-seat theater; 2 classrooms. Museum-related items for sale.
Activities: docent program; films; formal education programs for children; guided tours; lectures; participatory exhibits; theater. Annual Events: Guardian of the Human Spirit Award; LBJ Moral Courage Award.
Publications: quarterly newsletter; emazz newsletter.
Hours & Admission Prices: Mon.-Fri. 9-5, Sat.-Sun. 12-5. No charge; donations accepted. Closed New Year's Day; 1st day of Rosh Hashana; Yom Kippur; Thanksgiving; Christmas. ♿
Attendance: 150,000 (accurate)
Membership: Student & Educator $18; Individual $36; Family $54; Bronze $100; Silver $250; Gold $500; Platinum $1,000.

HOUSTON CENTER FOR CONTEMPORARY CRAFT, 4848 Main St., Houston, TX 77002-9718. Tel.: 713-529-4848.
E-mail: mheadrick@crafthouston.org
Web Site: www.crafthouston.org
Founded: 2001.
Key Personnel: Exec. Dir., Julie Farr; Pres. Bd., David Pesikoff; Cur. Fine Craft, Gwynne Rukenbrod; Dir. Communication, Mary Headrick; Facility & Operation Mgr., Randall Dorn; Artist-in-Residence & Volunteer Coord., Jason Kishell; Retail Mgr., Suzanne Sippel.
Personnel Profile: Full-Time Paid 6; Part-Time Paid 7; Part-Time Volunteers 11.
Governing Authority: nonprofit organization. Tax-exempt.
Craft Museum.
Collections: works using craft media including fiber, metal, glass, clay & wood.
Facilities: Museum-related items for sale.
Activities: outreach to over 15,000 students; workshops.
Hours & Admission Prices: Tues.-Sat. 10-5, Sun. 12-5. No charge; donations accepted. Closed New Year's Day; Thanksgiving; Christmas.
Attendance: 20,000 (accurate)
Membership: $40; $75; $150; $250.

HOUSTON CENTER FOR PHOTOGRAPHY, (M), 1441 W. Alabama, Houston, TX 77006-4103. Tel.: 713-529-4755. Fax: 713-529-9248.
E-mail: info@hcponline.org
Key Personnel: Exec. Dir., Madeline Yale
Art Gallery.
Collections: photographs.
Facilities: facility rental.
Activities: temporary exhibits; special events; educational programs; workshops.
Hours & Admission Prices: Wed. & Fri. 11-5, Thurs. 11-9, Sat.-Sun. 12-6. No charge; donations accepted. Closed New Year's Day; Thanksgiving; Christmas. ♿

HOUSTON FIRE MUSEUM, 2403 Milam St., Houston, TX 77006-2359. Tel.: 713-524-2526. Fax: 713-520-7566.
E-mail: hfmi@houstonfiremuseum.org
Web Site: www.houstonfiremuseum.org
Founded: 1982.
Congressional District: 18
Key Personnel: Dir., Angela Rayne; Pres. (V), Tom McDonald.
Personnel Profile: Full-Time Paid 4; Part-Time Paid 2; Part-Time Volunteers 50.
Governing Authority: municipal; nonprofit. Tax-exempt: 501(c)(3).
Fire-Fighting Museum: housed in 1899 Fire Station No. 7, active until 1969.
Collections: fire-fighting tools & equipment; fire trucks; badges; photographs; fire department artifacts.
Research Fields: Houston Fire Dept.; fire-fighting.
Facilities: 200-vol. library of fire service history material available to the public; classrooms. Gift items for sale.
Activities: self-guided tours; participatory & loan exhibitions. Museum Sponsors: annual parade & festival; special events.
Publications: quarterly newsletter, The Leather Bucket.
Hours & Admission Prices: Tues.-Sat. 10-4. Adults $3, senior citizens & children $2; discounts to AAM, ICOM & Texas Assoc. of Museums members; members no charge. Closed holidays.
Attendance: 18,379 (accurate)
Membership: Firefighter $15; Individual $30; Family $40; Patron $100; Life $500 & up.

HOUSTON MARITIME MUSEUM, 2204 Dorrington, Houston, TX 77030-3210. Tel.: 713-666-1910. Fax: 713-838-8557.
Founded: 2000.
Key Personnel: Dir., John A. Kendall; Chm. (V), Phil Dunn.
Governing Authority: nonprofit organization. Tax-exempt: 501(c)(3).
Maritime Museum.
Collections: maritime history, artifacts, & navigation instruments; ship models; Merchant Marine veterans; books.
Facilities: library. Museum-related items for sale.
Hours & Admission Prices: Tues.-Sat. 9-4:30. Adults $5, children 11 & under $3. Closed New Year's Day; Thanksgiving; Christmas. ♿
Membership: Student $10; Single $50; Family $100; Contributing $200; Benefactor $500; Chairman's Club $1,000.

* **HOUSTON MUSEUM OF NATURAL SCIENCE,** One Hermann Circle Dr., Houston, TX 77030-1749. Tel.: 713-639-4629. Fax: 713-523-4125. TDD: 713-639-4687.
Web Site: www.hmns.org
Founded: 1909.
Congressional District: 18
Key Personnel: C.E.O. & Pres., Joel A. Bartsch; Chm. (V), Fox Benton, III; C.F.O., Stephen Sachnik; Vice Pres. Devel. & Membership, Barbara Hawthorn; Vice Pres. Mktg. & Communications, Latha Thomas; Vice Pres. Astronomy & Physics, Dr. Carolyn Sumners; Vice Pres. Collections, Lisa Rebori; Vice Pres. Exhibits, Hayden Valdes; Dir. Horticulture, Eddie Holik; Vice Pres. IMAX Operations & Production, Charlotte Brohi; Cur. Anthropology, Dr. Dirk Van Tuerenhout; Cur. Vertebrate Zoology, Dr. Dan Brooks; Dir. Youth Education, Nicole Temple.
Personnel Profile: Full-Time Paid 82; Part-Time Paid 90; Part-Time Volunteers 475; Interns 7.
Governing Authority: nonprofit corporation. Subsidiary Institution: George Observatory. Tax-exempt: 501(c)(3).
Natural Science Museum.
Collections: natural science; anthropology (pre-Columbian & Native American emphasis); astronomy; gems & minerals; entomology; malacology; paleontology; vertebrate zoology; Texas wildlife; space & petroleum technology.
Research Fields: malacology; mineralogy.
Facilities: 400-seat IMAX theatre; 232-seat planetarium; 400-seat auditorium;

Challenger Learning Center; butterfly center; classrooms; off-site observatory. Gift items for sale.
Activities: guided tours; lectures; films; formally organized educational programs; docent program or council; permanent & temporary exhibitions.
Publications: quarterly newsletter, Museum News; monthly calendar listings; annual report; brochures.
Hours & Admission Prices: Oct. 19-Dec. 18 Mon. & Wed.-Sun. 9-5, Tues. 9-8; Dec. 19-Jan. 3 Mon. & Wed.-Sun. 9-6, Tues. 9-8; call for additional hours. Museum Exhibits: adults $15, children 3-11, college students with ID & seniors $10; members no charge. IMAX: adults $11, children 3-11, college students with ID & seniors $9, members $6. Butterfly Center: adults $8, children 3-11, college students with ID & seniors $7, members $4. Planetarium: adults $8, children 3-11, college students with ID & seniors $4, members $3. Closed Thanksgiving; Christmas. ♿
Attendance: 2,700,000 (accurate)
Membership: Individual $50; Family $75; Voyager $150; Discoverer $250; Benefactor $500; President's Circle $1,200.

HOUSTON POLICE MUSEUM, 17000 Aldine Westfield Rd., Houston, TX 77073-5102. Tel.: 281-230-2353. Fax: 281-230-2314.
E-mail: hpdmuseum@cityofhouston.net
Web Site: www.houstontx.gov/police/museum/museum.htm
Founded: 1981.
Key Personnel: Dir., James Chapman.
Governing Authority: city. Houston Police Dept. Tax-exempt: 170(b)(1)(A).
Police History Museum: located at the Houston Police Academy.
Collections: 1841-present day items pertaining to the history of the Police Dept.; helicopter; motorcycles; cars; uniforms; guns; photographs; material relating to the development of the department & famous cases.
Research Fields: Houston city history; Houston Police Dept.
Facilities: 600-vol. library pertaining to law enforcement available for research by appointment only; classrooms; 200-seat auditorium.
Activities: guided tours; lectures; films; gallery talks; formally organized education programs; permanent & temporary exhibitions.
Hours & Admission Prices: Mon.-Fri. 8-3; guided tours by appointment. No charge. Closed city holidays.

HOUSTON ZOO, INC., 1513 N. MacGregor, Houston, TX 77030-1603. Tel.: 713-533-6500. Fax: 713-533-6755.
E-mail: bhill@houstonzoo.org
Web Site: www.houstonzoo.org
Formerly: Houston Zoological Gardens
Founded: 1922.
Congressional District: 18
Key Personnel: Pres. & C.E.O., Deborah Cannon; Dir., Rick Barongi; Vice Pres. Animal Operations, Sharon Joseph; Vice Pres. Operations, Joe Kalla; Vice Pres. Advancement, Deborah Lackey; Vice Pres. Mktg., David Brady; C.F.O., Leslie Forestier; Cur. Children's Zoo, Tinker Boyd; Cur. Birds, Hannah Bailey; Cur. Herpetology, Stan Mays; Cur. Aquarium, George Brandy; Cur. Primates, Hollie Colahan; Cur. Large Mammals, Daryl Hoffman; Cur. Natural Encounters, Beth Schaefer; Public Rels., Brian Hill; Dir. Veterinary Svcs., Joe Flanagan; Museum Shop Mgr., Sharla McCulley.
Personnel Profile: Full-Time Paid 270; Part-Time Paid 25; Part-Time Volunteers 381; Interns 2.
Governing Authority: municipal. Tax-exempt: 501(c)(3).
Zoo.
Collections: 800 species; 4,500 animals.
Research Fields: conservation programs; captive breeding & management of endangered species; field research & conservation; behavioral enrichment programs.
Facilities: children's zoo; education center; aquarium; restaurants. Gift items for sale.
Activities: formally organized educational programs; volunteer programs; lectures; tours; classes; camps; kits to loan; overnight programs; outreach van & programs; speakers' bureau.
Publications: bimonthly members' newsletter, WildLife; course catalogs.
Hours & Admission Prices: March 8-Nov. 1 daily 9-7; Nov. 2-March 7 daily 9-6. Adults 12-64 $10, senior citizens 65 & over and children 2-11 $6; children under 2 & members no charge. Closed Christmas. ♿
Attendance: 1,700,000 (accurate)
Membership: Individual $55; Family $80; Family Plus & Grandparent $90; Supporting $130; Sustaining $250; Conservator $500.

JOHN P. MCGOVERN MUSEUM OF HEALTH & MEDICAL SCIENCE, (M), 1515 Hermann Dr., Houston, TX 77004-7126. Tel.: 713-942-7054. Fax: 713-526-1434.
E-mail: info@thehealthmuseum.org
Web Site: www.thehealthmuseum.org
Formerly: Museum of Health & Medical Science
Founded: 1969.
Congressional District: 25
Key Personnel: Pres. & C.E.O., Jon Iszard; Chm., Margaret Guerriero; Vice Chm., Denton Cooley, M.D.; Vice Pres. Devel., Suzanne Gschwind; Vice Pres. Exhibits & Business Devel., Phil Lindsey; Vice Pres. Mktg. & Communications, Anna Hawley; Dir. Exhibits, Brian Mancuso; Vice Pres. Education, Becky Seabrook; Dir. Operations, Leila Hall; Dir. Accounting, Sharon Campbell; Bd. Sec. & Admin. Mgr., Cindy Viaud.
Personnel Profile: Full-Time Paid 24; Part-Time Paid 12; Part-Time Volunteers 400; Interns 10.
Governing Authority: Tax-exempt.
Health Museum.
Collections: health and science of the human body; interactive exhibits.
Major Exhibits: Animation (T), 5/10-9/10.
Facilities: 4D theater; learning center.
Activities: programs & classes for school-aged children, but are accessible to adults; traveling exhibits; homeschool classes; scouts; spring & summer camps.
Publications: member newsletter, Muse News; annual report.
Hours & Admission Prices: Mon.-Sat. 9-5. Adults $8, senior citizens & children 3-12 $6; members & families Thurs. 2-5 no charge. Closed Thanksgiving; Christmas. ♿
Attendance: 141,000 (accurate)
Membership: Professional Circle $35; Plus One $45; Family $60; Family Plus $70; Associate $125; Contributing $250; Sustaining $500; Director's Circle $1,000; President's Circle $2,500; Chairman's Circle $5,000.

THE MENIL COLLECTION, (M), 1515 Sul Ross, Houston, TX 77006. Mailing Address: 1511 Branard St., Houston, TX 77006-4721. Tel.: 713-525-9400. Fax: 713-525-9444.
E-mail: info@menil.org
Web Site: www.menil.org
Founded: 1987.
Key Personnel: Chm., Louisa Stude Sarofim; Pres., Harry Pinson; Dir., Josef Helfenstein; C.F.O., Tom Madonna; Dir. Advancement, Aline Wilson; Cur. Modern & Contemporary Art, Franklin Sirmans; Assoc. Cur. Collections, Kristina Van Dyke; Chief Conservator, Brad Epley; Dir. Public Affairs, Vance Muse; Coord. Special Events, Elsian Cozens; Coord. Membership, Marta Galicki; Registrar, Anne Adams; Dir. Programs, Karl Kilian; Security, Steve McConathy; Museum Shop Mgr., Patrick Phipps.
Personnel Profile: Full-Time Paid 103; Part-Time Paid 2.
Governing Authority: nonprofit. Branch Museums: The Rothko Chapel, Byzantine Fresco Chapel Museum, Richmond Hall; Cy Twombly Gallery, 1501 Branard St., Houston. Tax-exempt: 501(c)(3).
Art Museum.
Collections: Paleolithic & antiquities; Byzantine & Medieval art; indigenous arts of Africa, Oceania & the Pacific Northwest; modern & contemporary art; Andy Warhol; Pablo Picasso; Henri Matisse; Fernand Leger; Robert Rauschenberg; Barnett Newman; Mark Rothko; Jasper Johns; Michael Heizer; Elsworth Kelly. Cy Twombly Gallery: paintings, sculpture & works on paper by American painter Cy Twombly.
Major Exhibits: Maurizio Cattelan, 2/12/10-8/15/10; Leaps into the Void: Documents of Noveau Realist Performance, 3/19/10-8/8/10; Steve Wolfe on Paper (T), 4/2/10-10/31/10; Ancestors of the Lake: Art from Lake Sentani and Humboldt Bay, 9/24/10-1/16/11; Kurt Schwitters: Colors and Collage, 10/22/10-1/30/11; Vija Clemins, 11/12/10-4/10/11.
Research Fields: 20th-century; Rene Magritte Catalogue Raisonne; conservation; Byzantine; Image of the Black in Western Art.
Facilities: 20,000-vol. library.
Activities: loan, temporary & traveling exhibitions.
Publications: exhibition catalogues; collection monographs.
Hours & Admission Prices: Wed.-Sun. 11-7. No charge. Closed Martin Luther King Jr. Day; Easter; Memorial Day; Independence Day; Labor Day; Thanksgiving; Christmas. ♿
Attendance: 120,000 (accurate)
Membership: Student $25; $100; $250; $500; $1,000; $5,000; $10,000.

MICHAEL E. DEBAKEY LIBRARY AND MUSEUM, Baylor College of Medicine, One Baylor Plaza, DeBakey Center for Biomedical Education & Research, Houston, TX 77030-3411. Tel.: 713-798-4710 & 6194.
Key Personnel: Cur., JoAnn Pospisil
Medical Museum.
Collections: Dr. DeBakey's life & career including instruments, inventions, awards, papers, photographs, & video displays; Baylor history; medical advances.
Facilities: library.
Hours & Admission Prices: Closed until late 2009/early 2010.

MUSEUM OF AMERICAN ARCHITECTURE AND DECORATIVE ARTS, (M), Houston Baptist Univ., 7502 Fondren Rd., Houston, TX 77074-3204. Tel.: 281-649-3311.
Web Site: www.hbu.edu
Founded: 1964.
Key Personnel: Dir., Lynn Miller; Cur. Bible in America Museum, Dr. Diana Severance.
Personnel Profile: Full-Time Paid 1.
Governing Authority: college. Affiliated with Houston Baptist University. Branch Museum: Dunham Family (BIA) Museum. Tel.: 281-649-3287. Tax-exempt: 501(c)(3).
Social History & Doll Museum.
Collections: Schissler miniature furniture; household goods & decorative arts of the ethnic groups who established the Republic of Texas; the doll collection of Theo Redwood Blank; pre-Columbian art; African art.
Research Fields: dolls, history of decorative arts, tools & photographs of early Texas architecture.
Facilities: 150-vol. reference and research library available for use in reading room.
Activities: guided tours; lectures; films; permanent, temporary & traveling exhibitions. Museum Sponsors: special events in summer; Christmas exhibit.
Publications: books, Days of Colonial Texas; Native Houstonian.
Hours & Admission Prices: Museum of American Architecture and Decorative Arts: Mon.-Sat. 10-4; special tours by appointment. Bible In America Museum: Tues. 10-4, Thurs. 11-4, 2nd Sat. of month 12-5. Closed Easter; Independence Day; Thanksgiving; Christmas vacation; university holidays. ♿
Attendance: 3,000 (estimated)

* **THE MUSEUM OF FINE ARTS, HOUSTON, (M), (I),** 1001 Bissonnet, Houston, TX 77005-1896. Mailing Address: P.O. Box 6826, Houston, TX 77265-6826. Tel.: 713-639-7300. Fax: 713-639-7784. TDD: 713-639-7390.
E-mail: visitorservices@mfah.org
Web Site: www.mfah.org
Founded: 1900.
Congressional District: 18
Key Personnel: Dir., Peter C. Marzio; Chm., Cornelia C. Long; Guild Pres., Kathy Shaw; Dir. Glassell School of Art, Joseph Havel; Assoc. Dir. Administration, Willard Holmes; Assoc. Dir. Investment & Finance, Gwendolyn H. Goffe; Assoc. Dir. Devel., Amy Purvis; Cur. Prints & Drawings and 20th-Century Art, Barry Walker; Cur. Renaissance, Baroque Painting & Sculpture, The Blaffer Collection, James Clifton; Audrey Jones Beck Cur. European Art, Edgar Peters Bowron; Cur. Modern & Contemporary Art, Alison de Lima Greene; Gus & Lyndall Wortham Cur. Photography, Anne Wilkes Tucker; Dir. Rienzi, Katherine S. Howe; Dir. Bayou Bend, Bonnie Campbell; Cur. Bayou Bend Collection, Michael K. Brown; Cur. Film & Video, Marian Luntz; The Wortham Cur. of Latin American Art & Dir. Intl. Center for the Arts of the Americas (ICAA), Mari Carmen Ramirez; Cur. American Painting & Sculpture, Emily Neff; Cur. The Glassell Collections, Frances Marzio; Cur. Modern & Contemporary Decorative Arts and Design, Cindi Strauss; Cur. Asian Art, Christine Starkman; Junior School Dean, Norma Dolcater; Dir. Communications & Mktg., Mary Haus; Mgr. Docent Program, Danielle Stephens; Mgr. Preparations, Michael Kennaugh; Mgr. Preparations, Richard Hinson; Librarian, Margaret Culbertson; Registrar, Julia Bakke; Chief Technology Officer, Shemor Bar-Tal; Controller, Marchell King; Curatorial Admin., Karen Vetter; Dir. Conservation, Wynne Phelan; Dir. Publications, Diane Lovejoy; Dir. Human Resources, Sheila Armsworth; Dir. Retail Operations, Patricia Smith; Photographic Svcs. Mgr., Marty Stein; Staff Photographer, Thomas DuBrock; Coord. Volunteer Svcs., Joi Maria Probus; Museum Shop Mgr., Suzanne Harrison.
Personnel Profile: Full-Time Paid 495; Part-Time Paid 97; Part-Time Volunteers 1,100; Interns 14.
Governing Authority: nonprofit organization. Branch Museums: Rienzi, 1406 Kirby Dr., Houston, TX 77019; The Glassell School of Art, 5101 W. Montrose Blvd., Houston, TX 77006-6534; Bayou Bend Collection & Gardens, 1 Westcott St., Houston, TX 77007. Tax-exempt: 501(c)(3).
Art Museum.
Collections: European & American paintings; decorative arts; sculpture; graphics; pre-Columbian art & archaeology; photography; antiquities; American Indian art; African & Oceanic art; Far Eastern art; textiles & costumes; prints & drawings.
Research Fields: European painting & sculpture; 20th-century art; decorative arts; photography; Far Eastern art; art of the Americas, Africa & Oceania; Renaissance art; textiles & costumes; prints & drawings; Latin American art.
Facilities: 90,000-vol. art library; archives; auditorium; cafe; sculpture garden. Museum-related items for sale.
Activities: guided tours; lectures; films; gallery talks; concerts; formally organized education programs; docent program or council; inter-museum, permanent, temporary & traveling exhibitions; outreach programs & exhibitions.
Publications: exhibition catalogues; bimonthly magazine, MFAH Calendar; quarterly magazine, MFAH Today; educational materials for adults & children.
Hours & Admission Prices: Mon. holidays & Tues.-Wed. 10-5, Thurs. 10-9, Fri.-Sat. 10-7, Sun. 12:15-7. Adults $7, students, seniors & children 6-18 $3.50; discounts to AAM & ICOM members; children with library cards Sat.-Sun., members & Thurs. no charge. Closed Thanksgiving; Christmas. ♿
Attendance: 2,643,901 (accurate)
Membership: Student $40; Individual $50; Dual $65; Family $85; Patron $150; Supporting $275; Sponsor $550; Benefactor $1,200.

THE MUSEUM OF PRINTING HISTORY, 1324 W. Clay, Houston, TX 77019-4036. Tel.: 713-522-4652. Fax: 713-522-5694.
E-mail: akasman@printingmuseum.org
Web Site: www.printingmuseum.org
Founded: 1983.
Key Personnel: Exec. Dir., Ann Kasman; Chm. Bd., George Kronman; Cur., Amanda Stevenson; Museum Asst., Rose Watts; Administrative Asst. & Museum Shop Mgr., Delores Young; Custodian, George Torres.
Personnel Profile: Full-Time Paid 6; Part-Time Volunteers 14; Interns 1.
Governing Authority: private; nonprofit organization. Tax-exempt: 501(c)(3) and 509(a)(1).
History & Art Museum.
Collections: history of communication beginning with writing on clay tablets to modern day newspapers; period workshops & bookbinding filled with period tools & machines; Bible & Bible leaves; great master printers & early printing; lithography from its beginnings through the Belle Epoch (Talouse-Lautrec) & beyond; the Great Books of the World; history of graphic communication, arts & design; paper making facility.
Research Fields: history of books and printing.
Facilities: library; 20,000 sq. ft. exhibit space; 67-seat theater. Museum-related items for sale.
Activities: docent program; guided tours; hobby workshops; lectures; rental gallery; temporary & traveling exhibitions. Annual Events: Dickens Print Shop; gala.
Publications: quarterly newsletter, The Printed Word.
Hours & Admission Prices: Tues.-Sat. 10-5. Guided group tours: adults $4, students $2. Closed New Year's Day; Memorial Day; Independence Day; Labor Day; Thanksgiving; Christmas Eve & Day. ♿
Attendance: 18,000 (estimated)
Membership: Student & Senior Citizens $20; Individual $35; Family $60; Sponsor $250; Patron $500; Gutenberg Society $1,000.

THE MUSEUM OF SOUTHERN HISTORY, Cultural Arts Center, Houston Baptist Univ., 7502 Fondren Rd., Houston, TX 77074-3298. Tel.: 281-649-3997. Fax: 281-649-3993.
E-mail: ssnoddy@hbu.edu
Web Site: www.hbu.edu
Founded: 1978.
Congressional District: 22
Key Personnel: Administrative Asst., Suzie Snoddy; Cur. Collections, Erin Price; Mktg., Martha Morrow; Mktg. Advancement, Charles Bacarisse.
Personnel Profile: Full-Time Paid 3; Part-Time Paid 1; Part-Time Volunteers 6.
Governing Authority: private; nonprofit. Parent Institution: Houston Baptist University. Tax-exempt: 501(c)(3).
Regional History Museum.
Collections: US colonial era to 1950 southern history; Civil War artifacts, 1861-1865; weapons; uniforms; letters from soldiers; prints; paintings; furniture; clothing & medical supplies; The Terry's Texas Rangers; War of the Rebellion official records; southern historical society papers; early periodicals; books; original sharecropper's furnished cabin.
Research Fields: Texas & Confederates.
Facilities: 884-vol. library. Books, t-shirts, ties, charms, pictures, prints, posters, caps, dolls & toy soldiers for sale.
Activities: guided tours; lecture program; special exhibits. Museum Sponsors: Old South Ball; southern hospitality luncheon.
Publications: newsletter published thrice annually; brochures.
Hours & Admission Prices: Tues.-Sat. 10-4. Adults $5, senior citizens $4, children 6-12 $3; discounts to AAM members; members no charge. Closed major holidays. ♿
Attendance: 7,500 (accurate)
Membership: Individual $35; Family $50; Life $1,000; Corporate $2,500.

MUSICAL BOX SOCIETY INTERNATIONAL, 1102 Heights Blvd., Houston, TX 77008-6916. Tel.: 713-869-3332. Fax: 713-880-9771.
E-mail: biesboehck@mindspring.com
Web Site: www.mbsi.org
Founded: 1949.
Key Personnel: Pres. (V), Ralph Schack; Chm. (V), Alan J. Bies.
Personnel Profile: Part-Time Volunteers 25.
Governing Authority: private; nonprofit organization. Branch Museum: Lockwood Mathews Mansion, 295 West Ave., Norwalk, CT 06850. Tel: 203-838-1434. Tax-exempt.
Musical Instruments Museum.
Collections: mechanical musical instruments (music boxes, reproducing pianos, orchestrions, organettes, automata, etc.), primarily 1840-1925.
Activities: permanent & temporary exhibits; occasional talks; Sun. tours by Musical Box Society docents.
Publications: Journal of Mechanical Music; MBSI News bulletin; occasional books on mechanical music.
Hours & Admission Prices: Lockwood Mathews Mansion: Tues.-Fri. 11-2, Sun. 1-3. Charlotte Museum of History: Tues.-Fri. 10-5, Sat.-Sun. 2-5.
Attendance: 55,000 (estimated)
Membership: U.S. Resident $50; Non-U.S. Resident $75

NATIONAL MUSEUM OF FUNERAL HISTORY, 415 Barren Springs Dr., Houston, TX 77090-5918. Tel.: 281-876-3063. Fax: 281-876-4403.
E-mail: info@nmfh.org
Web Site: www.nmfh.org
Founded: 1992.
Key Personnel: Dir., Bob Boetticher.
Personnel Profile: Full-Time Paid 1.
Governing Authority: nonprofit. Tax-exempt: 501(c)(3).
History Museum.
Collections: concentration on funeral-related artifacts & memorabilia, from mid-19th century through mid-20th century America, documenting the history of American funeral customs.
Hours & Admission Prices: Mon.-Fri. 10-4, Sat.-Sun. 12-4. Adults $6, veterans & senior citizens $5, children 3-12 $3; discount to groups, children under 3 no charge. Closed New Year's Day; Thanksgiving; Christmas. ♿
Attendance: 5,000 (accurate)

1940 AIR TERMINAL MUSEUM, William P. Hobby Airport, 8325 Travelair Rd., Houston, TX 77061-4716. Tel.: 713-454-1940. Fax: 713-454-1930.
Key Personnel: C.E.O., Drew Coats.
Personnel Profile: Full-Time Paid 1.
Governing Authority: Tax-exempt.
Aviation History Museum.
Collections: aviation history & memorabilia; period aircraft.
Facilities: library; theater. Museum-related items for sale.
Activities: educational outreach program; rental facilities.
Publications: quarterly newsletter.
Hours & Admission Prices: Tues.-Sat. 10-5, Sun. 1-5. Adults $5, children $2; member adults, military, law enforcement, firefighters, & their families no charge.
Membership: Observation Deck $75; Barnstormer $194; Travelair $500; Clipper $940; Starliner $1,940; Texanaire $5,000.

ROBERT A. VINES ENVIRONMENTAL SCIENCE CENTER, 8856 Westview Dr., Houston, TX 77055-4705. Tel.: 713-365-4175. Fax: 713-365-4178.
Web Site: www.springbranchisd.com
Key Personnel: Dir., Dee Goldberg.
Governing Authority: public school district; nonprofit. Tax-exempt.
Natural Science Museum.
Collections: natural history of Houston, Texas region.
Hours & Admission Prices: June-Aug. Mon.-Thurs. 8:30-4:30; Sept.-May Mon.-Fri. 8:30-4:30. No charge; donations accepted. Closed Memorial Day; Independence Day; Labor Day; Thanksgiving; spring break; two weeks during Christmas break. ♿
Attendance: 5,000 (estimated)

ROTHKO CHAPEL, 1409 Sul Ross, Houston, TX 77006-4829. Tel.: 713-524-9839. Fax: 713-524-7461.
E-mail: info@rothkochapel.org
Web Site: www.rothkochapel.org
Founded: 1971.
Key Personnel: Dir., Emilee Whitehurst; Chm. (V), Gayle Ross DeGeurin.
Personnel Profile: Full-Time Paid 6; Part-Time Paid 5.
Governing Authority: Tax-exempt.
Religious, Art & Architecture Museum.
Collections: 14 panels painted by Mark Rothko.
Hours & Admission Prices: Daily 10-6; groups by appointment. No charge; donations accepted. ♿
Attendance: 57,000 (accurate)

SPACE CENTER HOUSTON, 1601 NASA Pkwy., Houston, TX 77058-3199. Tel.: 281-244-2100. Fax: 281-283-7724. TDD: 713-283-7730.
Web Site: www.spacecenter.org
Founded: 1992.
Congressional District: 25
Key Personnel: C.E.O. & Pres., Richard Allen; Chm. (V), Joel B. Walker; Museum Shop Mgr., Sharon Glenn.
Personnel Profile: Full-Time Paid 148; Part-Time Paid 74; Part-Time Volunteers 25.
Governing Authority: nonprofit organization. Parent Institution: Manned Space Flight Education Foundation, Inc. Tax-exempt.
Space Museum.
Collections: artifacts & exhibits pertaining to America's manned space program.
Facilities: mission simulation & training facility; rocket park; mission control center; IMAX theater; cafeteria. Museum-related items for sale.
Activities: guided tours; mission control center briefings; films; lectures; formally organized education programs for children.
Hours & Admission Prices: Winter: Mon.-Fri. 10-5, Sat.-Sun. & holidays 10-6. Summer: daily 9-7. Adults $19.95, seniors $18.95, children 4-11 $15.95; children under 4 no charge. Closed Christmas. ♿
Attendance: 850,000 (accurate)
Membership: Annual Member $29.95; Annual Family $59.95.

Huntsville

H.E.A.R.T.S. VETERANS MUSEUM OF TEXAS, 2 Financial Plaza, Ste. 220, Huntsville, TX 77340-3554. Mailing Address: P.O. Box 6060, Huntsville, TX 77342-6060. Tel.: 936-295-5959. Fax: 936-295-0714.
E-mail: info@heartsmuseum.com
Web Site: www.heartsmuseum.com
Founded: 2000.
Key Personnel: Dir., Charlotte Oleinik; Chm. (V), Richie Harris; Treas., Tom Oleinik; Museum Shop Mgr., Reva Bishop.
Personnel Profile: Full-Time Paid 1; Part-Time Paid 1; Part-Time Volunteers 200.
Governing Authority: private; nonprofit organization. Tax-exempt: 501(c)(3).
Military History Museum.
Collections: military history & artifacts; photographs; women in the military; war timelines.
Facilities: library. Museum-related items for sale.
Activities: guided tours; temporary exhibitions.
Hours & Admission Prices: Tues.-Sat. 10-5. No charge; donations accepted. Closed Thanksgiving; Christmas. ♿
Attendance: 200 (estimated)

* **SAM HOUSTON MEMORIAL MUSEUM, (M),** 1836 Sam Houston Ave., Huntsville, TX 77341-0001. Mailing Address: Box 2057, SHSU, Huntsville, TX 77341-2057. Tel.: 936-294-1832 & 1831. Fax: 936-294-3670.
E-mail: SMM_PBN@shsu.edu
Web Site: www.samhouston.memorial.museum
Founded: 1927.
Congressional District: 2
Key Personnel: Dir., Patrick B. Nolan; Cur. Collections, Mac Woodward; Cur. Education, Michael Sproat; Cur. Exhibits, Casey Roon; Interpreter, Helen Belcher; Interpreter, Elizabeth Barry; Interpreter, Rebecca Lewis; Registrar, Sandra Rogers; Coord. Mktg. & Museum Shop Mgr., Megan Buro; Administrative Asst., JoAnn Purvis.
Personnel Profile: Full-Time Paid 10; Part-Time Paid 5; Part-Time Volunteers 25; Interns 1.
Governing Authority: university. Parent Institution: Sam Houston State University; State of Texas. Tax-exempt.
History Museum: 15-acre historical site.
Collections: personal possessions of General Houston, his family, Mexican President, Santa Ana; objects related to Texas history, two homes; law office; period kitchen; blacksmith shop; park & pond.
Research Fields: Texas history; genealogy.
Facilities: education center; memorial museum. Gifts & books for sale.
Activities: guided tours; lectures; formally organized educational programs.
Publications: books: Braving the Storm, The Houstons at Home, Woodland Home.
Hours & Admission Prices: Tues.-Sat. 9-4:30, Sun. 12-4:30. Adults $4, children 6-17 $2; discounts to AAM & ICOM members; members no charge. Closed New Year's Day; Thanksgiving; Christmas. ♿
Attendance: 46,267 (accurate)

Membership: Individual $35; Family $50; Contributing $100; Supporting $250; Sustaining $500.

TEXAS PRISON MUSEUM, 491 State Hwy. 75 N., Huntsville, TX 77320-1119.
Web Site: www.txprisonmuseum.org
Founded: 1989.
Prison Museum.
Collections: history of the Texas penal system from 1848 to present; photographs; electric chair; contraband; prison hardware; prison uniform.
Activities: rental facility; special events.
Hours & Admission Prices: Mon.-Sat. 10-5, Sun. 12-5. Adults $4, seniors $3, children 6-17 $2; children under 6 no charge.

Iraan

IRAAN MUSEUM, 1000 Park Side St., Iraan, TX 79744. Mailing Address: P.O. Box 95, Iraan, TX 79744-0095. Tel.: 432-639-2522.
Founded: 1965.
Congressional District: 21
Key Personnel: Chm. (V), Cur. & Museum Shop Mgr., Morine Collett; Asst. Cur., Tammie Williford; Pres. Bd., Jean Owens.
Personnel Profile: Full-Time Paid 1; Part-Time Paid 2; Part-Time Volunteers 1.
Governing Authority: city. Tax-exempt.
Archaeological & Historic Museum: located on what was once the San Antonio-San Diego Stage Line.
Collections: stone tools & weapons; period Spanish artifacts; ranchlife & cattle trails displays; relics from military forts & stage coach stations; cretaceous fossils; minerals; cores from oil wells; steel oil derrick with shopmade wellhead; Lufkin wooden walking beam pumping unit, 1927 American pumping unit; Red Line pumping unit; print shop; linotype; Iraan newspaper; tack room; surgery table; 1926 fire extinguishers; hospital equipment; desks; books; photo record; year books; military photos, WWII; 112 ft. windtower blade; flagtail & mule deer; redtail squirrels. Museum Park: over 60 species of native & migratory birds;
Research Fields: local Indian archaeology; fossils; oil; ranching; military.
Activities: Iraan Archaeology Society field trips to archaeological & historical sites; programs; recording & cataloging artifacts and sites. Museum Sponsors: Southwestern Federation Archaeological Symposium in April; Texas Archaeological Society Archaeological Awareness Month in October.
Publications: annual bulletin, Southwestern Federation of Archaeological Societies; Rock Art photos; Iraan Archeological Society monthly newsletter.
Hours & Admission Prices: Feb.-Dec. Thurs.-Sun. 1-5; groups & other times by appointment. No charge. ♿
Attendance: 800 (estimated)
Membership: Iraan Archaeological Society: Individual $10; Family $12.

Irving

IRVING ARTS CENTER, (M), 3333 N. MacArthur Blvd., Ste. 300, Irving, TX 75062-4497. Tel.: 972-252-7558. Fax: 972-570-4962.
E-mail: minman@cityofirving.org
Web Site: www.irvingartscenter.com
Founded: 1990.
Congressional District: 30
Key Personnel: Exec. Dir., Richard E. Huff; Chm. Bd., Lorraine Taylor; Asst. Dir., Rosemary Meng; Asst. Dir., Kass Prince; Gallery Dir. & Cur., Marcie J. Inman; Public Rels. Specialist, Jennifer Wilson.
Personnel Profile: Full-Time Paid 23; Part-Time Paid 6; Interns 5.
Governing Authority: municipal; nonprofit organization. Parent Institution: City of Irving. Tax-exempt.
Art Museum & Center.
Collections: Sculpture Garden: works by Jesus Bautista Moroles & Michael Manjarris.
Facilities: 8,000 sq. ft. exhibit space; classrooms; studios; 2 theaters; 2 rehearsal halls; 2 acre sculpture garden; visual & performing arts center.
Activities: concerts; dance recitals; docent program; formal education programs for children; guided tours; lectures; traveling & participatory exhibits; theater; musical theater
Publications: quarterly newsletter, Calendar of Events; exhibition brochures & catalogues.
Hours & Admission Prices: Mon.-Wed. & Fri. 9-5, Thurs. 9-8, Sat. 10-5, Sun. 1-5. No charge. Closed New Year's Day; Thanksgiving; Christmas. ♿
Attendance: 48,000 (estimated)
Membership: Student $10; Artist & Senior Citizen $30; Individual $40; Senior Citizen & Spouse $40; Smithsonian Affiliate & Family $75; Patron $125; Connoisseur $250; Benefactor $500; Director's Circle $1,000.

IRVING HERITAGE HOUSE, 303 S. O'Connor, Irving, TX 75060-2949. Tel.: 972-252-3838.
Historic House Museum: housed in the former home of C.P. Schultz, co-founder of Irving; built in 1912. A Texas State Historical Landmark.
Collections: Schyulze family & local history; life & works of author Washington Irving; period furnishings; photographs; personal artifacts.
Hours & Admission Prices: March-Dec. 1st Sun. of month 3-5. No charge; donations accepted.

NATIONAL SCOUTING MUSEUM, (M), 1329 West Walnut Hill Lane, Irving, TX 75038-3027. Tel.: 800-303-3047; 972-580-2100. Fax: 972-580-2020.
E-mail: nsmuseum@scouting.org
Web Site: nationalscoutingmuseum.org
Founded: 1959.
Key Personnel: Exec. Dir., Janice Babineaux.
Personnel Profile: Full-Time Paid 8; Part-Time Paid 4; Part-Time Volunteers 30.
Governing Authority: nonprofit organization. Parent Institution: Boy Scouts of America. Tax-exempt: 501(c)(3).
Scouting Museum.
Collections: over 500,000 items & artifacts; objects related to the history of the Boy Scouts of America & other youth & scouting organizations, including equipment & records of founders Baden-Powell, West, Beard & Seton; original Norman Rockwell paintings of scouting; Norman Rockwell scouting theme collection of original works of art.
Research Fields: history; scouting; youth organizations.
Facilities: 50,000 sq. ft. exhibit space; rental space. Museum-related items for sale.
Activities: virtual reality adventures; hands on learning experiences; school programs & tours; special public programs; interactive exhibits.
Publications: newsletter, Bridges & Trails; museum guide.
Hours & Admission Prices: Mon.-Sat. 10-5, Sun. 1-5. Adults $8, seniors $7, children $6, Scout $5; discounts to AAM members; members & children under 4 no charge. ♿
Attendance: 25,129 (accurate)
Membership: Individual $50; Family $100; Contributing $150; Supporting $200; Sustaining $250; Sponsor $500; Patron $1,000; Benefactor $5,000.

Jacksboro

FORT RICHARDSON STATE HISTORICAL PARK, 228 Park Rd. 61, Jacksboro, TX 76458. Tel.: 940-567-3506. Fax: 940-567-5488.
Web Site: www.tpwd.state.tx.us
Founded: 1968.
Key Personnel: C.E.O. & Exec. Dir., Carter Smith; Park Supt., Robert Frie; Dir. Public Lands, Walt Dabney; Dir. Interpretation & Exhibits, Glenn Barnett.
Personnel Profile: Full-Time Paid 7; Part-Time Paid 3.
Governing Authority: state. Subsidiary Institution: Texas Parks and Wildlife Dept. Tax-exempt.
Park Museum: located on the site of 1867 Old Cavalry Fort.
Collections: items pertaining to Fort Richardson, Jack County & Lost Battalion.
Facilities: Interpretive Visitor Center.
Activities: tours; Fort Richardson Days, Annual Living History event in April.
Hours & Admission Prices: Call for hours. Adults $3, seniors $2; children under 12 no charge. Closed Christmas. ♿
Attendance: 65,000 (accurate)

Jefferson

EXCELSIOR HOUSE, 211 W. Austin St., Jefferson, TX 75657-2245. Tel.: 903-665-2513; 800-490-7270. Fax: 903-665-9389.
E-mail: jgoulds@aol.com
Web Site: www.theexcelsiorhouse.com
Founded: 1850.
Congressional District: 1
Key Personnel: Pres., Karl Frederickson.
Governing Authority: board of directors of Jessie Allen Wise Garden Club.
Historic Hotel.
Collections: period furnishings.
Facilities: overnight guest ballroom & banquet facilities available.
Activities: guided tours.
Publications: Excelsior House Cookbook.
Hours & Admission Prices: Daily 7-9. Adults $4; children under 10 no charge. Closed Christmas Eve & Day.

JEFFERSON HISTORICAL SOCIETY AND MUSEUM, 223 W. Austin, Jefferson, TX 75657-2253. Tel.: 903-665-2775.
E-mail: jeffersonmuseum@yahoo.com
Web Site: www.jeffersonhistoricalmuseum.com
Founded: 1948.
Congressional District: 1
Key Personnel: Admin., David Sinclair.
Personnel Profile: Part-Time Paid 2; Part-Time Volunteers 6.
Governing Authority: society. Tax-exempt.
Historical Society Museum: housed in 1888 building.
Collections: Civil War artifacts; dolls; glass; medical items; paintings; farm implements; costumes; period furniture; bibles; Republic of Texas documents & money; manuscripts.
Facilities: 500-vol. library of genealogy & history books available for use on the premises; reading room.
Activities: guided tours for groups; permanent exhibitions.
Hours & Admission Prices: Daily 9:30-4:30. Adults 19-61 $4.50, senior over 62 $4, youth 13-18 $3, children 6-12 $1.50; discounts to student groups; pre-school children no charge. Closed New Year's Eve; Easter; Thanksgiving; Christmas Eve & Day.
Attendance: 19,500 (estimated)
Membership: Individual $7.50; Family $15; Life $75; Sustaining $200; Patron $300; Benefactor $1,000.

Johnson City

LYNDON B. JOHNSON NATIONAL HISTORICAL PARK, 100 Ladybird Lane, Johnson City, TX 78636. Mailing Address: P.O. Box 329, Johnson City, TX 78636-0329. Tel.: 830-868-7128. Fax: 830-868-0810 & 7863.
E-mail: lyjo_superintendent@nps.gov
Web Site: www.nps.gov/lyjo
Founded: 1969.
Congressional District: 11 & 21
Key Personnel: Supt., Russ Whitlock; Cur., Virginia Kilby; Public Affairs Specialist, Sherry Justus; Volunteer Coord., Elizabeth Lindig.
Personnel Profile: Full-Time Paid 52; Part-Time Paid 18; Part-Time Volunteers 55.
Governing Authority: federal. Parent Institution: National Park Service, Dept. of Interior. Tax-exempt.
Historic Site and Museum: 1901 Lyndon B. Johnson boyhood home, Johnson City, restored 1973-1974; 1867 Johnson Settlement, Johnson City, restored 1972-1974; 1888 Lyndon B. Johnson Birthplace, Stonewall, reconstructed 1964; Johnson Family Cemetery; 1894 Johnson Ranch, Stonewall.
Collections: furnishings; farm & ranch equipment; historic automobiles & vehicles; Lyndon B. Johnson & Lady Bird Johnson memorabilia & personal effects reflecting their lives in the hill country.
Research Fields: Texas settlement & ranching; life & presidency of Lyndon B. Johnson; collections management; care of living history site; pre-arranged graduate research projects related to contemporary material culture.
Facilities: materials relating to President Lyndon B. Johnson & Texas hill country life available for research in park library & archives; in-depth studies can be arranged with the Curator.
Activities: tours; bus tours of LBJ Ranch; lectures; permanent exhibitions.
Publications: orientation brochures; newsletters, LBJ National Historical Park, LBJ State Park & LBJ Country.
Hours & Admission Prices: Visitor Center: daily 8:45-5. Johnson City Unit: daily 9-5. No charge. Ranch Unit: daily 10-4. Minimal charge. Closed New Year's Day; Thanksgiving; Christmas. ♿
Attendance: 76,000 (accurate)

Junction

KIMBLE COUNTY HISTORICAL MUSEUM, 101 N. 4th St., Junction, TX 76849-4705. Mailing Address: P.O. Box 271, Junction, TX 76849-0271. Tel.: 325-446-4219. Fax: 325-446-2871.
E-mail: fwyatt30@yahoo.com
Web Site: www.junctiontexas.net/museum.htm
Founded: 1966.
Congressional District: 21
Key Personnel: Cur., Frederica Wyatt.
Personnel Profile: Full-Time Volunteers 2; Part-Time Volunteers 3.
Governing Authority: county.
History Museum.
Collections: farm & ranch tools; household items; guns; photographs; clothing.
Hours & Admission Prices: Mon.-Fri. 2-5; other times by appointment. No charge; donations accepted. Closed major holidays.
Attendance: 3,000 (estimated)

Katy

KATY VETERANS MEMORIAL MUSEUM, (M), 6206 George Bush Dr., Katy, TX 77493-1806. Tel.: 281-391-8387.
Military History & Memorial Museum.
Collections: war memorabilia; photographs; personal artifacts.
Hours & Admission Prices: Call for hours.

Kerrville

THE HILL COUNTRY MUSEUM, 226 Earl Garrett St., Kerrville, TX 78028-5305. Tel.: 830-896-8633.
Founded: 1983.
Congressional District: 21
Key Personnel: Pres. (V), Josephine S. Parker; Dir., Griffiths Carnes.
Personnel Profile: Full-Time Paid 1; Part-Time Paid 1; Part-Time Volunteers 50.
Governing Authority: private; nonprofit organization. Parent Institution: Hill Country Preservation Society. Tax-exempt: 501(c)(3).
Historic House: 1870s home of Capt. Charles Schreiner.
Collections: local history of Hill Country from 1850s to 1930s with special interest in Kerrville & Kerr County.
Hours & Admission Prices: Mon.-Sat. 10-4:30. Adults $5, children 6-18 $2; discounts to schools & tour groups; children under 6 no charge. Closed holidays.
Attendance: 10,600 (estimated)
Membership: Family $25; Sustaining $50; Patron $100; Benefactor $500 & up.

L.D. "BRINK" BRINKMAN FOUNDATION, (M), 444 Sidney Baker St. S., Kerrville, TX 78028-5919. Tel.: 830-257-2000. Fax: 830-257-2030.
Founded: 1985.
Congressional District: 21
Key Personnel: C.E.O. & Dir., L.D. Brinkman; Dir., Pam Stone; Dir., Charles C. Thomas.
Personnel Profile: Part-Time Volunteers 5.
Governing Authority: nonprofit. Tax-exempt: 501(c)(3).
Art Foundation: housed in LDB Corporation's headquarters.
Collections: Western art.
Activities: guided tours by appointment only.
Hours & Admission Prices: Mon.-Fri. 9-12. No charge. Closed major national holidays.
Attendance: 900 (estimated)

THE MUSEUM OF WESTERN ART, (M), 1550 Bandera Hwy., Kerrville, TX 78028-9547. Mailing Address: P.O. Box 294300, Kerrville, TX 78029-4300. Tel.: 830-896-2553, ext. 228. Fax: 830-896-4408.
E-mail: richard.assunto@americanwesternart.org
Web Site: www.americanwesternart.org
Formerly: National Center for American Western Art
Founded: 1983.
Congressional District: 21
Key Personnel: Chm., Bill Sims; Exec. Dir., Jack Steele; Pres., Bob Schmerbeck; Western Art Academy, Lynette Waldon; Publicity Coord., Diana Comer; Museum Shop Mgr., Tansy James; Librarian, Nan Stover; Office Coord., Sarah Cowen.
Personnel Profile: Full-Time Paid 6; Part-Time Paid 6; Part-Time Volunteers 80.
Governing Authority: nonprofit organization. Tax-exempt: 501(c)(3).
Art Museum.
Collections: paintings; drawings; sculpture.
Research Fields: written & photographic records.
Facilities: 2,500-vol. library pertaining to range cattle industry & Western American realistic art available for research by appointment on premises only; 80-seat auditorium. Prints, books, cards & other museum-related items for sale.
Activities: education programs for youth & adults; guided tours; lectures; gallery talks; loan & permanent exhibitions; art workshops for young professional artists; history workshop.
Publications: quarterly newsletter; pamphlets; book, Visions West; exhibit catalogs.
Hours & Admission Prices: Tues.-Sat. 9-5, Sun. 1-5. Adults $7, senior citizens 65 & over $6, children 9-17 $5; discounts to groups and AAM & ICOM members; children 8 & under and members no charge. Closed New Year's Day; Easter; Memorial Day; Labor Day; Thanksgiving; Christmas. ♿
Attendance: 30,000 (estimated)
Membership: Student $15; Cowboy $30; Settler $50; Wrangler $100; Rangerider $250; Wagonmaster $500; Sustaining $1,000.

RIVERSIDE NATURE CENTER, 150 Francisco Lemos, Kerrville, TX 78028-5211. Tel.: 830-257-4837. Fax: 830-257-4837.
E-mail: office@riversidenaturecenter.org
Web Site: www.riversidenaturecenter.org
Founded: 1989.
Congressional District: 21
Key Personnel: Exec. Dir., Cass Keen; Pres., Gloria Olsen; Museum Shop Mgr., Ann Laughlin.
Personnel Profile: Part-Time Paid 2; Part-Time Volunteers 50; Interns 1.
Governing Authority: private; nonprofit organization. Tax-exempt.
Herbarium.
Collections: flora & fauna of the upper Guadalupe River watershed & Texas Hill Country.
Research Fields: coordinating information for a watershed map; collect data on flora & fauna species.
Facilities: library; botanical garden; nature center; educational facilities. Field guides, arts & crafts reflecting natural diversity of Hill Country & museum-related items for sale.
Activities: guided tours; lectures; formal educational programs; participatory exhibits. Museum Sponsors: Earth Day Celebration; Down By the Riverside Festival.
Publications: quarterly newsletter; trail guide.
Hours & Admission Prices: Tree Trail: daily dawn to dusk. Visitor's Center: Mon-Fri. 9-4, Sat.-Sun. 10-3. No charge; donations accepted. ♿
Attendance: 6,500 (estimated)
Membership: Individual $25-$34; Family $35-$49; Friend $50-$99; Supporter $100-$249; Sustaining $250-$499; Benefactor $500-$999; Patron $1,000 & up.

Kilgore

EAST TEXAS OIL MUSEUM AT KILGORE COLLEGE, Hwy. 259 at Ross St., Kilgore, TX 75662. Tel.: 903-983-8295. Fax: 903-983-8659.
E-mail: info@easttexasoilmuseum.com
Web Site: www.easttexasoilmuseum.com
Founded: 1980.
Congressional District: 1
Key Personnel: Dir., Joe L. White.
Personnel Profile: Full-Time Paid 3; Part-Time Paid 2; Part-Time Volunteers 40.
Governing Authority: college; not-for-profit. Parent Institution: Kilgore College. Tax-exempt: 501(c)(3).
Oil Museum.
Collections: 1920s-1930s in East Texas when East Texas Oil Field was discovered & developed, largest oil field in the world at that time.
Hours & Admission Prices: Jan. 2-March & Oct.-Dec. 19 Tues.-Sat. 9-4, Sun. 2-5; Dec. 20-Dec. 30 call for hours; April-Sept. Tues.-Sat. 9-5, Sun. 2-5. Adults $6, children 3-11 $4. Closed New Year's Eve & Day; Easter; Thanksgiving; Christmas. ♿
Attendance: 50,000 (accurate)

Kingsville

JOHN E. CONNER MUSEUM, Texas A&M University-Kingsville, 905 W. Santa Gertrudis, Kingsville, TX 78363. Mailing Address: P.O. Box 2172, Station 1, Kingsville, TX 78363-8321. Tel.: 361-593-2810. Fax: 361-593-2112.
Founded: 1925.
Congressional District: 27
Key Personnel: Dir., Hal Ham; Cur., Jonathan Plant; Educator, Brenda Canizalez; Administrative Asst., Cynthia F. Villalon.
Personnel Profile: Full-Time Paid 4; Part-Time Paid 3; Part-Time Volunteers 15.
Governing Authority: university. Parent Institution: Texas A&M University-Kingsville. Tax-exempt.
General Museum.
Collections: south Texas & University history; Farm & Ranching tools & equipment; Native American & Mexican American cultural materials; south Texas & Meso American archaeology; south Texas natural history; geology; Graves Peeler mounted trophy specimens.
Research Fields: local, regional & natural history.
Facilities: Texana books for sale.
Activities: guided tours; field trips; lectures; films; videotapes; hobby workshops; formally organized education programs for children, graduate & undergraduate students affiliated with Texas A&M University - Kingsville; volunteer training programs; permanent, temporary & traveling exhibitions; school loan service; docent outreach programs on subjects related to the museum for local & area schools.
Publications: loose-leaf guide for docents, Las Manos; quarterly newsletter; handbook, South Texas Wildflowers: Collection I; color brochure; exhibit catalog, El Rancho in South Texas; natural history video, The Living Mosaic.
Hours & Admission Prices: Mon.-Sat. 9-5. No charge; donations accepted. Closed university holidays. ♿
Attendance: 20,000 (estimated)
Membership: Individual $15; Family $25; Participating $100; Sustaining $500; Patron $1,000; Life $2,000.

Kountze

BIG THICKET NATIONAL PRESERVE, 6044 FM 420, Kountze, TX 77625-7841. Tel.: 409-951-6700. Fax: 409-951-6717.
E-mail: leslie.dubey@nps.gov
Web Site: www.nps.gov/bith/
Founded: 1974.
Congressional District: 2
Key Personnel: C.E.O. & Supt., Todd Brindle; Chief Div. Interpretation, Leslie Dubey; Museum Shop Mgr., Cindy Reed.
Personnel Profile: Full-Time Paid 36; Full-Time Volunteers 34; Part-Time Paid 2; Part-Time Volunteers 10; Interns 2.
Governing Authority: federal. Parent Institution: National Park Service, Dept. of the Interior. Tax-exempt.
Biological Preserve.
Collections: natural history; herbarium; skulls & skins; insects; cultural history; pioneer artifacts. Visitor Center: plant communities; interactive dioramas; ecology of the Big Thicket film.
Research Fields: biological.
Facilities: library available for use on premises; visitor center; nature trails. Museum-related items for sale.
Activities: self-guided trails; guided hikes; environmental education program; Jr. Ranger program.
Publications: pamphlets; checklists.
Hours & Admission Prices: Visitor Center: daily 9-5. Headquarters: Mon.-Fri. 8-4:30. No charge; donations accepted. ♿
Attendance: 115,000 (estimated)

La Grange

FAYETTE HERITAGE MUSEUM & ARCHIVES, 855 S. Jefferson, La Grange, TX 78945-3230. Tel.: 979-968-6418. Fax: 979-968-5357.
E-mail: library@cityoflg.com
Founded: 1978.
Congressional District: 14
Key Personnel: Dir. & Museum Shop Mgr., Kathy Carter.
Personnel Profile: Full-Time Paid 3; Part-Time Volunteers 3.
Governing Authority: municipal; nonprofit. Parent Institution: City of LaGrange. Tax-exempt.
History Museum.
Collections: local history items; photos; newspapers; maps; school, business, organization & personal papers.
Research Fields: local history.
Facilities: 500-vol. library available to the public; meeting room. Books for sale.
Activities: participatory & temporary exhibitions.
Hours & Admission Prices: Tues.-Fri. 10-5, Sat. 10-1, Sun. 1-5. No charge. Closed major holidays. ♿
Attendance: 2,500 (estimated)

NATHANIEL W. FAISON HOME AND MUSEUM, 822 S. Jefferson St., State Hwy. 77, La Grange, TX 78945. Mailing Address: 259 N. Main St., La Grange, TX 78945-2233. Tel.: 979-968-9416 & 5756.
E-mail: mariewatts@cvtv.net
Web Site: www.faisonhouse.org
Founded: 1960.
Congressional District: 14
Key Personnel: Arnold Romberg Suzy Romberg.
Personnel Profile: Part-Time Volunteers 12.
Governing Authority: nonprofit organization. Affiliated with the La Grange Garden Club. Tax-exempt.
Historic House: 1840-1855 Nathaniel W. Faison Home.
Collections: paintings; history of Texas; original furniture; documents.
Facilities: senior citizen AARP community center; movie theatre; garden club; ballrooms & bowling alley.
Activities: guided tours; permanent exhibitions; educational programs & scholarships for children in the community. Annual Event: Christmas Open House in December.
Publications: brochure.
Hours & Admission Prices: 2nd Sat. of month 10-4; tours by appointment. Admission $3; children 11 & under no charge.
Attendance: 400 (estimated)

Membership: Active Members $10; Associate Members $25.

La Porte

BATTLESHIP TEXAS STATE HISTORIC SITE, 3527 Battleground Rd., La Porte, TX 77571-9773. Tel.: 281-479-2431, ext. 236 & 248. Fax: 281-479-4197.
Web Site: www.tpwd.state.tx.us/park/battlesh
Formerly: Battleship Texas State Historical Park
Founded: 1948.
Congressional District: 25
Key Personnel: Dir., Andy Smith; Pres. (V), Don Fischer; Cur., Angela McCleaf; Mgr. Collections, Janice Sniker; Museum Shop Mgr., Jerry Moak.
Personnel Profile: Full-Time Paid 20; Part-Time Volunteers 51; Interns 3.
Governing Authority: state. Parent Institution: Texas Parks & Wildlife Dept. Tax-exempt.
Historic Warship.
Collections: photos, documents, furnishings, & artifacts relating to operation & history of the Battleship TEXAS, only surviving World War I era DREADNOUGHT; veteran of Vera Cruz Incident (1914), World War I (1917-18) & World War II (1941-45).
Research Fields: material pertaining to USS Texas (BB00) & (BB35) with some material relating to other U.S. Naval forces 1914-1945.
Facilities: battleship.
Activities: self-guided tour; guided hard hat tours. Museum Sponsors: Living History Program in February; Veterans Art & Essay Contest in November; Santa's Swingin 40's Christmas in December.
Publications: The Dreadnought quarterly; weekly e-newsletter, Battle Report.
Hours & Admission Prices: Daily 10-5; guided tours by appointment. Adults $10, seniors $4, student 6-18 $3; children under 6 no charge. Closed Thanksgiving; Christmas.
Attendance: 111,000 (estimated)

SAN JACINTO MUSEUM OF HISTORY ASSOCIATION, (M), One Monument Circle, La Porte, TX 77571-9585. Tel.: 281-479-2421. Fax: 281-479-2428.
E-mail: sjm@sanjacinto-museum.org
Web Site: sanjacinto-museum.org
Founded: 1938.
Congressional District: 8
Key Personnel: C.O.O. & Pres., Larry Spasic.
Personnel Profile: Full-Time Paid 14; Part-Time Paid 3.
Governing Authority: nonprofit organization. Tax-exempt: 501(c)(3).
Historic Building: 1939 San Jacinto Monument.
Collections: history of region & Texas; artifacts; manuscripts; documents; visual arts.
Facilities: 25,000-vol. library of history books, newspapers & periodicals available for use by appointment only; 162-seat theater & audio-visual production. Texas history books, postcards, slides & museum-related items for sale.
Activities: permanent, temporary & traveling exhibitions.
Publications: occasional monographs; quarterly newsletter.
Hours & Admission Prices: Daily 9-6. No charge. AV show: adults $4.50, children under 12 $3.50. Closed Thanksgiving; Christmas Eve & Day. ♿
Attendance: 450,000
Membership: Student & Senior Citizen $20; Individual $40; Dual $60; Freedom $120; Independence $500; Monument $1,000; Sam Houston & Corporate $3,000.

Lackland Air Force Base

HISTORY AND TRADITIONS MUSEUM, 37 TRW/MU, Bldg. 5206, 2051 George Ave., Lackland Air Force Base, TX 78236-5218. Tel.: 210-671-3055. Fax: 210-671-0347.
Founded: 1956.
Congressional District: 20
Key Personnel: Museum Dir., Fernando Cortez; Museum Specialist, Belinda Riojas.
Personnel Profile: Full-Time Paid 2; Part-Time Volunteers 3.
Governing Authority: federal.
Military Museum.
Collections: rare aeronautical equipment; 40 static aircraft painted to represent noted pilots & squadrons; engines, weapons & memorabilia dating back from WWI up until the present.
Research Fields: aviation & aerospace history.
Facilities: library of books, periodicals, photographs, news clippings.
Activities: guided tours; films; educational programs.
Publications: museum brochure.
Hours & Admission Prices: Mon.-Fri. 9-4:30. No charge; donation accepted. Closed federal holidays.
Attendance: 30,000 (accurate)

Lake Jackson

LAKE JACKSON HISTORICAL MUSEUM, (M), 249 Circle Way, Lake Jackson, TX 77566-5232. Mailing Address: P.O. Box 242, Lake Jackson, TX 77566-0242. Tel.: 979-297-1570. Fax: 979-285-0043.
Web Site: lakejacksonmuseum.org
Founded: 1981.
Key Personnel: Dir., Jennifer Caulkins; Pres., Gayle Driskill; Treas., Harry Sargent; Museum Shop Mgr., Angela Villarreal.
Personnel Profile: Full-Time Paid 2; Part-Time Paid 1; Part-Time Volunteers 45.
Governing Authority: private; nonprofit organization. Tax-exempt: 501(c)(3).
History Museum.
Collections: history of Lake Jackson; art; clothing; textiles; documents; photographs; audio & video; newspapers.
Facilities: 24-seat auditorium; 15,000 sq. ft. exhibit space. Museum-related items for sale.
Activities: docent program; formal education programs; guided tours; lectures; temporary & traveling exhibitions; theater; oral history programs.
Publications: quarterly newsletter, "The Lake Jackson Historian".
Hours & Admission Prices: Tues.-Sat. 10-4, Sun. 1-4. No charge. ♿
Attendance: 6,000 (accurate)
Membership: Student & Individual Senior $20; Senior Family $35; Family $40; Nonprofits $50; Business $100; Life $500; Patron $1,000; Benefactor $5,000.

Lamesa

DAL-PASO MUSEUM, 310 S. First St., Lamesa, TX 79331. Mailing Address: P.O. Box 1445, Lamesa, TX 79331-1445. Tel.: 806-872-5007. Fax: 806-872-2181.
Founded: 1988.
Congressional District: 19
Key Personnel: C.E.O., Wayne C. Smith, Ed.D.; Pres., Walter Buckel; Museum Shop Mgr., Lorraine Johnson.
Personnel Profile: Part-Time Paid 1.
Governing Authority: municipal; county. Parent Institution: Lamesa-Dawson County Museum Association. Tax-exempt: 501(c)(3).
General Museum: housed in 1925 restored Dal Paso Hotel.
Collections: general & historical interest to local viewers.
Research Fields: local history.
Activities: guided tours.
Hours & Admission Prices: June to Labor Day Tues.-Sat. 2-5. Winter: Tues. & Sat. 2-5. No charge. ♿
Attendance: 1,000 (estimated)

Langtry

JUDGE ROY BEAN VISITOR CENTER, Hwy. 90, W., Loop 25, Langtry, TX 78871. Mailing Address: P.O. Box 160, Langtry, TX 78871-0160. Tel.: 800-452-9292. Fax: 915-291-3366.
E-mail: lytic@dot.state.tx.us
Web Site: www.dot.state.tx.us
Founded: 1939.
Congressional District: 21
Key Personnel: Supvr., Kenneth R. Fatheree.
Personnel Profile: Full-Time Paid 6.
Governing Authority: state. Tax-exempt.
Historic Building Museum: c.1896 Judge Roy Bean Saloon.
Collections: relics pertaining to Judge Roy Bean, Law West of the Pecos.
Research Fields: history concerning Roy Bean.
Facilities: botanical garden.
Hours & Admission Prices: Daily 8-5. No charge. Closed New Year's Day; Easter; Thanksgiving; Christmas Eve & Day. ♿
Attendance: 70,000 (estimated)

Laredo

IMAGINARIUM OF SOUTH TEXAS, 5300 San Dario, Ste. 505, Mall del Norte, Laredo, TX 78041-3000. Tel.: 956-728-0404. Fax: 956-725-7776.
E-mail: info@imaginariumstx.org
Web Site: www.imaginariumstx.org
Formerly: Laredo Childrens Museum
Founded: 1991.
Key Personnel: Dir., Melissa Cigarroa.
Personnel Profile: Full-Time Paid 2; Full-Time Volunteers 2; Part-Time Paid 3; Part-Time Volunteers 100; Interns 3.
Governing Authority: nonprofit organization. Parent Institution: Laredo Children's Museum, Inc. Tax-exempt: 501(c)(3).
Children's Museum: housed in c.1900 Fort McIntosh chapel & guardhouse.
Collections: Mayan Temple; dinosaur dig; grocery store; construction zone; toddler space; dream workshop; science.

Facilities: 4,000 sq. ft. exhibit space; train car.
Activities: formal education programs for undergraduate or graduate students affiliated with Laredo Junior College & Laredo State Univ.; mobile vans; participatory & traveling exhibitions; theatre; seasonal camps; community workshops; teacher-training workshops.
Publications: quarterly, Laredo Children's Museum Newsletter.
Hours & Admission Prices: Wed.-Thurs. 10-7, Fri.-Sat. 10-8, Sun. 12-6. Children $3, adults $2; members no charge. Closed New Year's Day; Easter; Thanksgiving; Chirstmas Eve & Day. ♿
Attendance: 20,000 (estimated)
Membership: Student $35; Bright Choice $50; Texans $75; Passport $100; Lone Star $250; Rio Grande $500.

LAREDO CENTER FOR THE ARTS, 500 San Agustin, Laredo, TX 78040-8103. Tel.: 956-725-1715. Fax: 956-725-1741.
E-mail: info@laredoartcenter.org
Web Site: www.laredoartcenter.org
Key Personnel: Exec. Dir., Norma Saldana-Lopez; Chm., Celinda Gonzalez
Art Museum.
Collections: works by local & international artists.
Activities: workshops.
Publications: quarterly newsletters.
Hours & Admission Prices: Summer: Tues.-Fri. 11-6, Sat. 10-5; Winter: Tues.-Fri. 9-5, Sat. 10-5.

League City

WEST BAY COMMON SCHOOL CHILDREN'S MUSEUM, 210 N. Kansas Ave., League City, TX 77573-2466. Tel.: 281-554-2994.
E-mail: catharin@orbitworld.net
Web Site: www.oneroomschoolhouse.org/
Key Personnel: Dir., Catharin Lewis.
Governing Authority: Parent: League City Historical Society.
Children's Museum.
Collections: hands-on history learning environment.
Hours & Admission Prices: Mon.-Thurs. 9-4, Fri. 9-1; other times by appointment. Admission $4.

Liberty

SAM HOUSTON REGIONAL LIBRARY & RESEARCH CENTER, 650 FM 1011, Liberty, TX 77575-6841. Mailing Address: P.O. Box 310, Liberty, TX 77575-0310. Tel.: 936-336-8821.
E-mail: samhoustoncenter@tsl.state.tx.us
Web Site: www.tsl.state.tx.us
Founded: 1977.
Congressional District: 2
Key Personnel: Dir., Robert L. Schaadt; Librarian, Darlene Mott; Museum Cur., Lisa Meisch.
Personnel Profile: Full-Time Paid 5; Full-Time Volunteers 2; Part-Time Paid 1; Part-Time Volunteers 2.
Governing Authority: nonprofit; state. Parent Institution: Texas State Library & Archives Commission. Tax-exempt: 501(c)(3).
Regional Museum & Archives.
Collections: Southeast Texas history; Indian artifacts; household goods; glass; archives; Civil War items; photographs. Historic House: 1848 Gillard-Duncan House; Gov. Price Daniel House; Sam Houston artifacts; 1883 Norman House; 1898 Episcopal Church.
Research Fields: pre-historic to modern times history of southeast Texas; General Sam Houston.
Facilities: 12,182-vol. library of Texana & Southeast Texas history and local government records; educational facilities; 11,000 sq. ft. exhibit space.
Activities: guided tours; lectures; radio programs; Friend's meeting; workshops.
Hours & Admission Prices: Mon.-Fri. 8-5, Sat. 9-4; other times by appointment. No charge; donations accepted. Closed major holidays. ♿
Attendance: 6,178 (accurate)

Livingston

POLK COUNTY MEMORIAL MUSEUM, 514 W. Mill St., Livingston, TX 77351-3231. Tel.: 936-327-8192. Fax: 936-327-8192.
E-mail: museum@livingston.net
Web Site: www.livingston.net/museum
Founded: 1963.
Congressional District: 2
Key Personnel: C.E.O., Josh David; Chm. (V), J.D. Coogler.
Personnel Profile: Full-Time Paid 2; Part-Time Paid 1; Part-Time Volunteers 35.
Governing Authority: nonprofit organization. Parent Institution: Polk County Historical Commission. Tax-exempt.
History Museum.
Collections: Polk County history; agriculture; archaeology; archives; folklore; glass; Indian artifacts; geological exhibits; textiles; military; numismatic; manuscript collections.
Major Exhibits: June Brides, 5/10-7/10.
Research Fields: local history.
Facilities: archives; tapes; microfilm; reference books available for use on premises; reading room.
Activities: guided tours; lectures; films; formally organized education programs for children; permanent & temporary exhibitions.
Publications: Civil War: There Never Were Such Men Before; Peebles; Polk County Pictorial History; Cemeteries in Polk County; The History of Polk County; Torched - Fire of 1902.
Hours & Admission Prices: Mon.-Fri. 9-5. No charge; donations accepted. ♿
Attendance: 4,500 (accurate)

Longview

GREGG COUNTY HISTORICAL MUSEUM, 214 N. Fredonia St., Longview, TX 75601-7222. Mailing Address: P.O. Box 3342, Longview, TX 75606-3342. Tel.: 903-753-5840. Fax: 903-753-5854.
E-mail: neina@gregghistorical.org
Web Site: gregghistorical.org
Founded: 1983.
Congressional District: 7
Key Personnel: Exec. Dir., Neina Kennedy; Pres. (V), Walter Northcutt; Records Mgr. & Coord., Glenda Wood.
Personnel Profile: Full-Time Paid 1; Part-Time Paid 1; Part-Time Volunteers 65; Interns 1.
Governing Authority: nonprofit organization; society. Parent Institutions: The Gregg County Historical Foundation & Gregg County Historical & Genealogical Society. Tax-exempt: 501(c)(3).
County Museum: housed in 1910 brick Everett bank building.
Collections: artifacts, memorabilia & photographs illustrating the development of Gregg County from 1870-1930; exhibits progress chronologically from early settler's subsistence farming, to commercial agriculture to the growth of cities in early 1900s; theme rooms & areas: barn; railroad depot; dentist office; parlor; bedroom; general mercantile store; log cabin interior; newspaper presses; military collection; manuscript collections; Texas architecture; Caddo Indians.
Research Fields: genealogy; local history; county history; Texas architecture.
Facilities: library of books & archives pertaining to local & county history available for research on premises only; reading room; meeting room; classroom. Museum-related items for sale.
Activities: guided tours; lectures; demonstrations; study clubs; organized education programs for children; volunteer program; docent organization; permanent exhibits; oral history program.
Publications: Gregg County Historical Museum Newsletter; activity books for children; books, Home Grown: How We Grew; Did You Know; Guide to Gregg County's Historical Markers; Traditions of the Land: The History of Gregg County, Texas.
Hours & Admission Prices: Tues.-Sat. 10-4. Adults $2, children under 18 & senior citizens $1; discount to groups, AAA members; members no charge; Texas Association of Museums reciprocal admissions program. Closed major holidays.
Attendance: 12,000 (estimated)
Membership: Senior over 64 $25; Individual $40; Family $75; Contributing $100; Sustaining $250; Sponsor $500; Benefactor $1,000 & up.

LONGVIEW MUSEUM OF FINE ARTS, 215 E. Tyler St., Longview, TX 75601-7219. Mailing Address: P.O. Box 3484, Longview, TX 75606-3484. Tel.: 903-753-8103. Fax: 903-753-8217.
E-mail: fineart@lmfa.org
Web Site: www.lmfa.org
Founded: 1958.
Congressional District: 4
Key Personnel: Dir., Renee Hawkins; Guild Pres. & Dir. Education, Niki Blaske; Pres. (V), Tiffany Jehorek; Events Coord., Stephanie Peters; Registrar, Paula Davis.
Personnel Profile: Full-Time Paid 3; Part-Time Paid 1; Part-Time Volunteers 18; Interns 1.
Governing Authority: nonprofit organization. Tax-exempt: 501(c)(3).
Art Museum.
Collections: paintings; sculpture; graphics; photographs.
Facilities: 2,500-vol. library of catalogs, art reference works, periodicals & photographs; educational facilities; sculpture garden.
Activities: guided tours; lectures; films; formally organized education programs; docent program; inter-museum loan, temporary & traveling exhibitions.
Publications: quarterly newsletter; annual reports; gallery guides; brochures; checklists.

Hours & Admission Prices: Tues.-Fri. 10-4, Sat. 12-4. No charge; donations accepted. Closed national holidays. ♿
Attendance: 16,000 (estimated)
Membership: Student $10; Individual $25; General $50; Contributor $100; Advocate $250; Supporter $500; Patron $1,000; Sustainer $2,500; Benefactor $5,000.

Lubbock

AMERICAN MUSEUM OF AGRICULTURE, 1501 Canyon Lake Dr., Lubbock, TX 79403-4911. Mailing Address: P.O. Box 505, Lubbock, TX 79408-0505. Tel.: 806-239-5796. Fax: 806-775-1357.
Key Personnel: Dir., Lacee Fraze.
Governing Authority: Tax-exempt.
Agriculture Museum.
Collections: agricultural history; farm equipment; tractors; farming.
Hours & Admission Prices: Wed.-Sat. 10-5.

BUDDY HOLLY CENTER, (M), 1801 Crickets Ave., Lubbock, TX 79401-5128. Tel.: 806-775-3560. Fax: 806-767-0732.
E-mail: info@buddyhollycenter.org
Web Site: www.buddyhollycenter.org
Key Personnel: Dir., Brooke Allison.
Personnel Profile: Full-Time Paid 7; Part-Time Paid 4.
Governing Authority: Parent Institution: City of Lubbock. Tax-exempt.
History Museum.
Collections: life & music of Buddy Holly; clothing; photographs; recording contracts; personal artifacts; Texas Musicians Hall of Fame; artists & musicians of West Texas.
Facilities: Museum-related items for sale.
Activities: special events.
Hours & Admission Prices: Tues.-Fri. 10-6, Sat. 11-6; groups by appointment. Adults $5, senior citizens 55 & over $3, students $2; discounts to groups of 20 or more; members & children under 12 no charge.

* **MUSEUM OF TEXAS TECH UNIVERSITY, (I),** 3301 4th St., Lubbock, TX 79403-4613. Mailing Address: P.O. Box 43191, Lubbock, TX 79409-3191. Tel.: 806-742-2442. Fax: 806-742-1136.
E-mail: museum.texastech@ttu.edu
Web Site: www.museum.ttu.edu
Founded: 1929.
Congressional District: 19
Key Personnel: Exec. Dir., Gary Edson; Pres., Dr. Jon Whitmore; Chancellor, Dr. David Smith; Assoc. Dir. Operations & Programs, David Dean; Registrar, Nicola Ladkin; Cur. Anthropology, Dr. Eileen Johnson; Cur. Ethnology & Textiles, Mei Campbell; Cur. & Dir. Natural Science Research Lab., Dr. Robert Baker; Cur. Paleontology, Dr. Sankar Chatterjee; Cur. Education, Dr. Lee Brodie; Cur. History, Henry B. Crawford; Cur. Art, Dr. Peter S. Briggs; Business Mgr., Jamie Looney; Museum Shop Mgr., Mary M. Hooper; Head Guard, Sharon R. Williams; Administrative Asst., Claudia Cory.
Personnel Profile: Full-Time Paid 62; Full-Time Volunteers 1; Part-Time Paid 32; Part-Time Volunteers 50; Interns 2.
Governing Authority: state; university. Parent Institution: Texas Tech University. Supporting Organization: Museum of TTU Association. Tax-exempt: 170(b)(l)(iii).
General Museum.
Collections: art; clothing; textiles; historical furnishings & artifacts; ethnology; anthropology; mammology; paleontology; geology; ornithology; frozen tissues.
Research Fields: mammalogy; anthropology; paleontology; history; historical architecture; historical textiles; earth sciences; invertebrates; vital tissues.
Facilities: 10,000-vol. library; planetarium; archeological site; research labs. Museum-related items for sale.
Activities: Master of Arts Museum Science Program; Master of Science in Heritage Management; planetarium programs; school tours programs; docent guild; guided tours; gallery talks; films; symposia; permanent, temporary & traveling exhibits.
Publications: quarterlies by support organizations; museum journal; occasional papers; special publications; newsletter, MuseNews.
Hours & Admission Prices: Tues.-Wed. & Fri.-Sat. 10-5, Thurs. 10-8:30, Sun. 1-5. Main building: no charge; donations accepted. Planetarium: adults $2, students & seniors $1, children $.50; children 5 & under no charge. Closed New Year's Eve & Day; Martin Luther King Jr. Day; Memorial Day; Independence Day; Thanksgiving; Christmas Eve & Day. ♿
Attendance: 166,043 (accurate)
Membership: Museum of TTU Association: Student $10; Educator $25; Individual $35; Family $40; Museum League $75; Patron $150; Benefactor $250; Director's Circle $500.

SCIENCE SPECTRUM, 2579 S. Loop 289 #250, Lubbock, TX 79423-1400. Tel.: 806-745-2525. Fax: 806-745-1115.
E-mail: sandy@sciencespectrum.org
Web Site: www.sciencespectrum.org
Founded: 1986.
Congressional District: 19
Key Personnel: Dir., Cassandra L. Henry; Museum Shop Mgr., Kay Dudley.
Personnel Profile: Full-Time Paid 8; Part-Time Paid 25; Part-Time Volunteers 8; Interns 1.
Governing Authority: private; nonprofit organization. Tax-exempt: 501(c)(3).
Science Museum.
Collections: hands-on displays of science, focusing on physical science, health, aquariums, economics & space flight; Kidspace, children's museum area.
Major Exhibits: Prehistoric Beasts: The Ice Age (T), 3/5/10-6/5/10.
Hours & Admission Prices: Mon.-Fri. 10-5, Sat. 10-6, Sun. 1-5. Museum: adults $7.50, senior citizens 60 & over and children 3-12 $6; discounts to groups; members no charge. Omni Theater: adults $8, senior citizens 60 & over and children 3-12 $6.50; members $6; discounts to groups. Combination tickets available. Closed Thanksgiving; Christmas. ♿
Attendance: 200,000 (accurate)
Membership: Explorer (up to 5 people) $100 ($15 each additional); Discoverer (up to 2 people) $60; LIfe $1,000.

SILENT WINGS MUSEUM, (M), 6202 N. Interstate 27, Lubbock, TX 79403-7523. Tel.: 806-775-2047. Fax: 806-775-3337.
E-mail: egrigsby@mail.ci.lubbock.tx.us
Web Site: www.silentwingsmuseum.com
Formerly: Military Glider Pilots Association, Silent Wings Museum
Founded: 1979.
Key Personnel: Dir., Brooke Allison; Asst. Dir., Eddy Grigsby; Cur., Shelly Crittendon; Museum Shop Mgr., David Seitz.
Personnel Profile: Full-Time Paid 6; Full-Time Volunteers 1; Part-Time Paid 5; Part-Time Volunteers 8; Interns 2.
Governing Authority: Parent Institution: City of Lubbock. Tax-exempt.
Military Museum.
Collections: military history; historical aviation memorabilia; World War II gliders & airborne forces, 1940-1946.
Research Fields: military aviation history.
Facilities: 500-vol. library of fiction & non-fiction on action of World War II airborne forces; theater. Videos, books and unit & organization pins of airborne units for sale.
Activities: children's workshops; family activities.
Publications: quarterly newsletter, Museum News.
Hours & Admission Prices: Tues.-Sat. 10-5, Sun. 1-5. Adults $5; members, WWII glider pilots & spouses, and military personnel in uniform no charge. ♿
Attendance: 10,000 (accurate)
Membership: Bronze Wings $35; Silver Wings $50; Gold Wings $100 Corporate $1,000-$5,000.

Lufkin

ELLEN TROUT ZOO, 402 Zoo Circle, Lufkin, TX 75904-1345. Tel.: 936-633-0399. Fax: 936-633-0311.
E-mail: gordon@ellentroutzoo.com
Web Site: www.ellentroutzoo.com
Founded: 1967.
Congressional District: 2
Key Personnel: Zoo Dir., Gordon B. Henley, Jr.; Pres., Ted Fajen; Gen. Cur., Celia K. Falzone; Dir. Educational Svcs., Charlotte Henley; Staff Veterinarian, Mike Nance, D.V.M; Museum Shop Mgr., Rita Cambiano.
Personnel Profile: Full-Time Paid 22; Part-Time Paid 2; Part-Time Volunteers 15; Interns 1.
Governing Authority: municipal. Parent Institution: City of Lufkin, TX. Tax-exempt.
Zoo.
Collections: variety of vertebrate animals, including amphibians, reptiles, birds & mammals.
Facilities: 2,000-vol. library of zoological & related books, available for research by special request; zoological park; classrooms.
Activities: guided tours; lectures; films; TV & radio programs; formally organized education programs for children; docent program and council; permanent exhibitions; mobile vans; in-school programs.
Publications: book, Wildlife on Wheels; teacher training manual, Zookeeper Training; employee manual, Docent Handbook.
Hours & Admission Prices: Daily 9-5. Adults $5; members, AZA, members & zoo reciprocity list no charge. ♿
Attendance: 180,000
Membership: Individual $25; Family & Grandparent $40; Tiger $100; Giraffe $200; Corporate $250; Hippopotamus $500; White Rhino $2,000.

THE MUSEUM OF EAST TEXAS, 503 N. Second St., Lufkin, TX 75901-3013. Tel.: 936-639-4434. Fax: 936-639-4435.
Founded: 1975.
Congressional District: 2
Key Personnel: Exec. Dir., J.P. McDonald; Pres., Rebecca Chance; Pres. Museum Guild, Debbie Alexander; Cur. Education, Laura Hudgins; Administrative Asst., Claudine Lovejoy; Museum Shop Mgr., Eloise Havard.
Personnel Profile: Full-Time Paid 4; Part-Time Paid 3; Part-Time Volunteers 3.
Governing Authority: nonprofit organization. Tax-exempt: 501(c)(3).
Museum of Art & History.
Collections: regional history artifacts through the present; fine arts collection of American, European & regional artists; changing national, regional & international art & history exhibits.
Research Fields: local human history; regional art.
Facilities: 2,000-vol. library of books on art & regional history; photo archives; 14,000 sq. ft. exhibit space; 200-seat auditorium; public gardens; rental space. Museum-related items for sale.
Activities: guided tours; lectures; docent programs; program series; school tours; traveling exhibits.
Publications: quarterly newsletter; annual report; exhibits catalog; collections catalogs.
Hours & Admission Prices: Tues.-Fri. 10-5, Sat.-Sun. 1-5. No charge; donations accepted. Closed major holidays. ♿
Attendance: 18,093 (accurate)
Membership: Individual $25; Family $50; Contributor $100; Sponsor $150; Sustainer $250; Patron $500; Guarantor $1,000; Benefactor $5,000; Life Member $10,000.

TEXAS FORESTRY MUSEUM, 1905 Atkinson Dr., Lufkin, TX 75901-2505. Tel.: 936-632-9535 & 633-6248. Fax: 936-632-9543.
E-mail: info@treetexas.com
Web Site: www.treetexas.com
Founded: 1972.
Congressional District: 2
Key Personnel: Dir., Ginger Trotter; Pres., Mike Jones; Sec. & Treas., R.H. Hufford.
Personnel Profile: Full-Time Paid 3; Part-Time Paid 1; Part-Time Volunteers 200.
Governing Authority: private; nonprofit organization. Tax-exempt.
Forestry Museum.
Collections: logging equipment; tools; logging train; chain saws; fire lookout tower; photographs; paper industry. Historic Building: logging town Railroad Depot.
Research Fields: photographs.
Facilities: woodland trail. Gift items for sale.
Activities: guided tours; slide program for civic clubs & organizations.
Publications: brochure; membership quarterly, Crosscut.
Hours & Admission Prices: Mon.-Sat. 10-5, Sun.1-5 & by appointment. No charge; donations accepted. Closed New Year's Eve & Day; Easter; Thanksgiving; Christmas Eve & Day. ♿
Attendance: 8,000 (estimated)
Membership: Individual $25, $40, $60, $100, $500; Life $1,000; Corporate $100, $250, $500, $1,000.

Luling

CENTRAL TEXAS OIL PATCH MUSEUM, 421 E. Davis St., Luling, TX 78648-2316. Mailing Address: P.O. Box 1002, Luling, TX 78648-1002. Tel.: 830-875-1922.
History Museum.
Collections: local oil producing methods, equipment & workers; photographs; period artifacts; cultural history.
Hours & Admission Prices: Mon.-Fri. 9-5.

Marfa

CHINATI FOUNDATION, One Cavalry Row, Marfa, TX 79843. Mailing Address: P.O. Box 1135, Marfa, TX 79843-1135. Tel.: 432-729-4362. Fax: 432-729-4597.
E-mail: information@chinati.org
Web Site: www.chinati.org
Founded: 1986.
Congressional District: 23
Key Personnel: Dir., Marianne Stockebrand; Pres., Arlene Dayton; Museum Shop Mgr., Sandra Hinojos.
Personnel Profile: Full-Time Paid 11; Part-Time Paid 4; Part-Time Volunteers 50; Interns 19.
Governing Authority: public; nonprofit. Tax-exempt: 501(c)(3).
Art Museum: housed in c.1919 & 1938 buildings of former Fort D.A. Russell.
Collections: installations by contemporary artists including Donald Judd, Carl Andre, Ingolfur Arnarsson, John Chamberlain, Dan Flavin, Roni Horn, Ilya Kabakov, Richard Long, Claes Oldenburg; Coosje Van Bruggen, David Rabinowitch, & John Wesley.
Facilities: educational facilities; reading room; studio & exhibition space for artists in residence.
Activities: children's summer art classes; lectures & symposia. Annual Event: Open House Celebration.
Publications: annual newsletter; symposia books.
Hours & Admission Prices: Guided Tours: Wed.-Sun. 10am & 2pm by appointment. Adults $10, students & senior citizens $5; discounts to AAM & ICOM members; members no charge. ♿
Attendance: 15,000 (estimated)
Membership: Student & Senior Citizen $50; Individual & Family $100; Supporting $250-$500; Sustaining $1,000-$2,500; Friend $5,000.

MARFA AND PRESIDIO COUNTY MUSEUM, 110 W. San Antonio St., Marfa, TX 79843. Mailing Address: P.O. Box 538, Marfa, TX 79843-0538. Tel.: 432-729-4140.
Web Site: www.marfamuseum.org
History Museum.
Collections: fossils; Jumano & Native American tools; early ranching; rural life; military history; photographs.
Hours & Admission Prices: Mon.-Sat. 2-5. No charge; donations accepted.
Attendance: 1,200
Membership: Individual $10; Family $25.

Marshall

HARRISON COUNTY HISTORICAL MUSEUM, (M), 707 N. Washington, Marshall, TX 75670. Mailing Address: P.O. Box 1987, Marshall, TX 75671-1987. Tel.: 903-938-2680. Fax: 903-927-2534.
E-mail: info@harrisoncountymuseum.org
Web Site: www.harrisoncountymuseum.org
Formerly: Old Courthouse Museum/Harrison County Historical Museum
Founded: 1965.
Congressional District: 1
Key Personnel: C.E.O., Carol Fletcher; Chm. (V), Alice Barron; Pres., Garrett Boersma; Sec., Anne Yappen; Dir., Robert Bailey; Museum Shop Mgr., Gwen Nolan Warren.
Personnel Profile: Full-Time Paid 1; Part-Time Paid 1; Part-Time Volunteers 4.
Governing Authority: society. Parent Institution: Harrison County Historical Society. Tax-exempt: 170(b)(1)(A).
Historical Museum: housed in 1896 hotel located in the Ginocchio Historic District.
Collections: portraits; paintings; porcelains; jewelry; silverware; manuscripts; photographs; costumes; hand-painted china; cut & pressed glass; time pieces; Doctors' Room; Dentist's Office; photographs; Edison Room; 400 B.C.-1982 ceramics; 1890-1910 talking machines; c.1900 Edison recording machine; 1919-1935 radios; 1780s-1900s ethnic group heritage, including sport uniforms; string & wind instruments; folios; songbooks; needlecraft implements & specimens; pioneer implements; local industries; transportation & communications; mementoes of the Elks, Odd Fellows, Woodmen of the World & Masons; religious; politics; military; celebrities; school pictures; old text books; toys; flags; history; genealogy; Caddo Lake memorabilia; dolls; miniature soldiers & knights.
Research Fields: genealogy; local history; Civil War records.
Facilities: 2,000-vol. library of books on history, genealogy, art gallery & biography available for use on premises; children's room. Postcards & publications for sale.
Activities: tours; permanent exhibitions.
Publications: monthly newsletter.
Hours & Admission Prices: Tues.-Fri. 10-4, Sat. 10-1. Adults & students $2; children under 6 no charge. Closed New Year's Day; Independence Day; Labor Day; Thanksgiving; Christmas Eve & Day. ♿
Attendance: 11,000 (estimated)
Membership: Individual $25; Family $35; Sustaining $50; Patron $100; Benefactor $250; Corporation $500; Individual Life $1,000.

MICHELSON MUSEUM OF ART, (M), 216 N. Bolivar, Marshall, TX 75670-3307. Mailing Address: P.O. Box 8290, Marshall, TX 75671-8290. Tel.: 903-935-9480. Fax: 903-935-1974.
E-mail: leomich@shreve.net
Web Site: www.michelsonmuseum.org
Founded: 1985.
Congressional District: 1
Key Personnel: Dir., Susan Spears; C.E.O., Gayle Weinberg; Dir. Education, Bonnie Strauss; Pres. (V), Keith Feille.
Personnel Profile: Full-Time Paid 4; Part-Time Paid 1; Part-Time Volunteers 80.
Governing Authority: nonprofit organization. Tax-exempt: 501(c)(3).
Art Museum.

Collections: 1887-1978 Russian-American works of Leo Michelson, including 100 oil paintings, 1,000 drawings, watercolors, lithographs, etchings with documentation; Kronenberg collection including works by Milton Avery, David Burliuk, Henri Matisse, Abraham Walkowitz, John Edward Costigan; Ramona & Jay Ward collection of African masks & artifacts; works by Milton Avery, Joseph Stella, Ralston Crawford, & Byron Browne.
Facilities: 5,000 sq. ft. exhibit space.
Activities: guided tours; docent program; loan, temporary & traveling exhibitions.
Publications: newsletters.
Hours & Admission Prices: Tues.-Fri. 12-5, Sat.-Sun. 1-4. No charge; donations accepted. Closed Easter; Independence Day; Thanksgiving; Christmas. ♿
Attendance: 8,000 (estimated)
Membership: Student & Senior $15; Fellow $25; Supporter $50; Sustainer $100; Donor $200; Sponsor $500; Founder $1,000; Patron $2,500; Corporate $500-$2,500; Life $5,000; Benefactor $10,000.

Mason

MASON COUNTY MUSEUM, 321 Moody St., Mason, TX 76856. Tel.: 325-347-6681.
Founded: 1965.
Congressional District: 21
Key Personnel: Pres. (V), Weldon Whittaker; Vice Pres., Mike Innis; Chm., Judy Schoenfeld; Treas., Marjorie Tinsley.
Governing Authority: society. Parent Institution: Mason County Historical Society.
Local History Museum: housed in 1876 school building.
Collections: local history & culture; photographs; period artifacts.
Activities: guided tours.
Hours & Admission Prices: Thurs.-Sat. 10-4.

McAllen

* **INTERNATIONAL MUSEUM OF ART AND SCIENCE, (M),** 1900 Nolana, McAllen, TX 78504-4199. Tel.: 956-682-1564, ext. 104. Fax: 956-686-1813.
E-mail: srosenkrantz@imasonline.org
Web Site: www.imasonline.org
Formerly: McAllen International Museum
Founded: 1967.
Congressional District: 15
Key Personnel: Exec. Dir., Serena M. Rosenkrantz; Devel. Officer, Eva Paschal; Pres., Dr. John Gerling; Dir. Education, Jerry Durham; Cur., Maria Elena Macias; Museum Shop Mgr., Mattie Chavero; Dir Mktg., Mike Perez.
Personnel Profile: Full-Time Paid 20; Full-Time Volunteers 1; Part-Time Paid 10; Interns 2.
Governing Authority: nonprofit organization. Tax-exempt.
Arts & Sciences Museum.
Collections: science; geology; paleontology; fine & contemporary art; Mexican folk art.
Facilities: 2,000-vol. reference library available on the premises; classrooms; meeting rooms. Museum-related items for sale.
Activities: guided tours; lectures; films; gallery talks; docent program; permanent & traveling exhibitions; class program.
Publications: quarterly newsletter; annual report; brochures; postcards.
Hours & Admission Prices: Tues.-Wed. & Fri.-Sat. 9-5, Thurs. 9-8, Sun. 1-5. Adults $7, seniors & students $5, children 4-12 $3; children 3 & under and members no charge. Closed holidays. ♿
Attendance: 110,000 (estimated)
Membership: Individual $35; Family & Associate $50; Maestro $100; Visionary $250; Patron $500; Benefactor $1,000 & up.

MCALLEN HERITAGE CENTER, (M), 301 S. Main St., McAllen, TX 78501-4806. Tel.: 956-687-1904.
Key Personnel: Dir., Karen Gebhardt Fort
History Museum.
Collections: antique wheelchair; 19th century maps of the Rio Grande Valley; historic items; photographs; books.
Hours & Admission Prices: Mon.-Fri. 1-5.

McCamey

MENDOZA TRAIL MUSEUM, Hwy. 67 E., McCamey, TX 79752. Mailing Address: P.O. Box 1409, McCamey, TX 79752-1409. Tel.: 432-652-3192.
History Museum.
Collections: Native American artifacts; fossils; oil boom memorabilia; period furniture.
Hours & Admission Prices: By appointment only.

McKinney

CHESTNUT SQUARE - HERITAGE GUILD OF COLLIN COUNTY, (M), 315 S. Chestnut St., McKinney, TX 75069-5607. Mailing Address: P.O. Box 583, McKinney, TX 75070-8139. Tel.: 972-562-8790. Fax: 972-562-8790.
Web Site: www.chestnutsquare.org
Founded: 1973.
Congressional District: 3
Key Personnel: Dir., Cindy Johnson; Chm. (V), Tim Baker; Museum Shop Mgr., Laurie Tirmenstein.
Personnel Profile: Full-Time Volunteers 3; Part-Time Paid 3; Part-Time Volunteers 50; Interns 1.
History Museum.
Collections: area history & culture; five house; general store; chapel; stage coach inn; period furnishings.
Activities: special events; rental facilities. Museum Sponsors: Living History Days.
Hours & Admission Prices: Tues., Thurs. & Sat. 11. Tours: adults $5, children under 12 $3. ♿
Attendance: 15,000 (estimated)

COLLIN COUNTY FARM MUSEUM, 7117 County Rd. 166, McKinney, TX 75070. Mailing Address: 300 E. Virginia, McKinney, TX 75069-4325. Tel.: 972-542-9457. Fax: 972-542-4594.
E-mail: curator@northtexashistorycenter.org
Web Site: www.co.collin.tx.us
Founded: 1976.
Key Personnel: Exec. Dir., Victoria Day; Cur., Bryan Lean; Cur. Education, Sarah Hatcher.
Personnel Profile: Full-Time Paid 1; Part-Time Paid 1; Part-Time Volunteers 50.
Governing Authority: county. Parent Institution: Collin County Government. Subsidiary Institution: Farm Museum Foundation of Collin County, Inc. Tax-exempt.
Farm Museum.
Collections: agricultural tools & machinery; kitchen & household furnishings; 2 farmhouses.
Research Fields: agricultural heritage of Collin County from earliest settlement through 1940.
Facilities: 200-vol. library of farming & local history; granary; windmill.
Activities: docent program; formal educational programs; guided tours; hobby workshops; loan, participatory & traveling exhibitions; school loan service; children's day camps.
Publications: quarterly newsletter, Collin County Farm Museum News.
Hours & Admission Prices: March-June & Sept.-Dec. Sat.-Sun. 12-4; other times by appointment. Admission $1. Closed major holidays. ♿
Attendance: 3,000 (estimated)

HEARD-CRAIG HOUSE, 205 W. Hunt St., McKinney, TX 75069. Tel.: 972-569-6909.
E-mail: bjohnson@heardcraig.org
Historic House Museum: built in 1900.
Collections: family history, heirlooms, art, furnishings & personal artifacts.
Activities: educational progams; special events.
Hours & Admission Prices: Tues. & Thurs. 2pm, Sat. 1, 2, 3. Adults $5, children $3; other times by appointment.

HEARD NATURAL SCIENCE MUSEUM & WILDLIFE SANCTUARY, 1 Nature Place, McKinney, TX 75069-8840. Tel.: 972-562-5566. Fax: 972-548-9119.
E-mail: info@heardmuseum.org
Web Site: www.heardmuseum.org
Founded: 1967.
Congressional District: 4
Key Personnel: Dir., Sy Shahid.
Personnel Profile: Full-Time Paid 16; Part-Time Paid 8; Part-Time Volunteers 150.
Governing Authority: nonprofit organization. Tax-exempt: 501(c)(3).
Natural Science Museum & Wildlife Sanctuary.
Collections: malachology; insects; herpetology; ornithology; mammalogy; rocks & minerals; fossils; anthropology; nature prints.
Major Exhibits: Dinosaurs Alive, 11/09-1/10.
Research Fields: ornithology; prairie ecology; environmental assessments; wetlands.
Facilities: nature center; 289 acre wildlife sanctuary; classrooms; 2-acre native plant garden; science technology center. Museum-related items for sale.
Activities: lectures; formally organized educational programs; docent program; nature trails guided & self-guided; handicap trail; travel tours; summer camps; permanent & temporary exhibits; museum ancillary groups: hobby beekeepers, Prairie & Timbers Audubon Club, Heard Nature Photographers

Club; Collin County Archeological Society; Collin County Chapter of the Native Plant Society of TX.
Publications: bimonthly email newsletter.
Hours & Admission Prices: Mon.-Sat. 9-5, Sun. 1-5. Adults $8, children 3-12 $5; discounts to AAM & ASTC members; members no charge. Closed New Year's Day; Thanksgiving; Christmas Day. ♿
Attendance: 100,000 (estimated)
Membership: Seniors, Student, Active Military & Educator $40; Individual $60; Family $75; Road Runner $150; Bobcat $500; Red-Tailed Hawk $1,500; Golden Eagle $2,500.

NORTH TEXAS HISTORY CENTER, 300 E. Virginia St., McKinney, TX 75069-4325. Tel.: 972-542-9457, ext. 100. Fax: 972-542-4594.
E-mail: grouptours@northtexashistorycenter.org
Web Site: www.northtexashistorycenter.org
Formerly: Collin County Historical Society, Inc. & History Museum
Founded: 1957.
Congressional District: 4
Key Personnel: Exec. Dir., Bicke Day; Pres. (V), Claude Frazier; Dir. Devel., Janis Cable; Cur. Education, Sarah Hatcher; Asst. Cur. Education, Kate O'Donnell; Cur. Collections, Bryan Lean.
Personnel Profile: Full-Time Paid 5; Part-Time Paid 3; Part-Time Volunteers 15; Interns 3.
Governing Authority: private; nonprofit organization. Subsidiary Museum: Collin County Farm Museum, 7117 County Rd. 166, McKinney, TX 75071. Tax-exempt: 501(c)(3).
History Museum.
Collections: Collin County & North Texas history.
Research Fields: Collin County; North Texas; Civil War in Texas.
Facilities: 800-vol. library; educational facilities; 5,500 exhibit space. Museum-related items for sale.
Activities: docent program; lectures; traveling trunk K-1st grade; education programs for grades 2-5.
Publications: quarterly newsletter, Collin County History; books.
Hours & Admission Prices: Mon.-Sat. 11-4; other times by appointment. Families $8, adults $4, children & seniors $2; members no charge. Closed New Year's Day; Easter; Thanksgiving; Christmas.
Attendance: 10,000 (estimated)
Membership: Individual $25; Couple $50; Family $60; Enthusiast $100; Supporter $250; Devotee $500; Benefactor $1,000; Patron $2,500. Corporate Partner $100-$2,500.

McLean

MCLEAN-ALANREED AREA MUSEUM, 116 Main St., McLean, TX 79057. Mailing Address: P.O. Box 354, McLean, TX 79057-0354. Tel.: 806-779-2731.
Founded: 1969.
Congressional District: 31
Key Personnel: Chm. (V), Delbert Trew; Treas., Lynn D. Reeves; Cur., Dorothy McKee; Devel. & Membership, Zelda McClellan.
Personnel Profile: Full-Time Paid 1; Part-Time Paid 1.
Governing Authority: nonprofit. Tax-exempt: 501(c)(3).
Historical Society Museum.
Collections: pioneer costumes; western exhibits including saddles, ranch tools, plows & Indian artifacts; photographs; vet supplies; documents; firetruck; Model T car; barber shop, doctor's office, POW camp (World War II) display; German POW camp display.
Facilities: library; 5,500 sq. ft. exhibit space.
Activities: guided tours; study clubs.
Hours & Admission Prices: Tues.-Sat. 10-4. No charge; donation accepted. Closed major holidays. ♿
Attendance: 1,800 (accurate)
Membership: Individual $5; Supporting $100; Patron $500.

Mesquite

FLORENCE RANCH HOMESTEAD, (M), 1424 Barnes Bridge Rd., Mesquite, TX 75150-4206. Mailing Address: P.O. Box 850137, Mesquite, TX 75185-0137. Tel.: 972-216-6468. Fax: 972-329-8340.
E-mail: corr@ci.mesquite.tx.us
Web Site: historicmesquite.org
Founded: 1987.
Congressional District: 3
Key Personnel: Exec. Dir., Charlene Orr; Chm. (V), Kelly Baird; Museum Shop Mgr., Becky Allen.
Personnel Profile: Full-Time Paid 1; Part-Time Paid 2; Part-Time Volunteers 5.
Governing Authority: Historic Mesquite, Inc. Tax-exempt.
Historic Site.
Collections: artifacts from 1880-1920. Historic Buildings: Ranch House; Homestead.
Facilities: Museum-related items for sale.
Hours & Admission Prices: Tues. & Thurs.-Fri. 12-4, Wed. 1-5, 2nd Sat of month 10-1; other times by appointment. No charge; donations accepted. ♿
Attendance: 1,100 (estimated)
Membership: Student $15; Pioneer $25; Settler $50; Homesteader $100; Frontiersman $250; Trailblazer $500.

Miami

ROBERTS COUNTY MUSEUM, 120 E. Commercial, Miami, TX 79059. Mailing Address: P.O. Box 306, Miami, TX 79059-0306. Tel.: 806-868-3291. Fax: 806-868-3381.
E-mail: robertscomuseum@amaonline.net
Web Site: robertscountymuseum.org
Founded: 1979.
Congressional District: 31
Key Personnel: Exec. Dir., Cecil Gill.
Personnel Profile: Full-Time Paid 1; Part-Time Volunteers 15.
Governing Authority: county. Tax-exempt.
Historic Building & Museum: housed in c.1888 Santa Fe Depot.
Collections: East Room: photographs; medical toys; school memorabilia; American War artifacts. West Room: cattle brands; barbed wire; period tools & supplies from covered wagons. Ferguson Room: animals native to Roberts County in their natural habitat; typical pioneer home with period clothing, furnishings & paintings; general store; railroad displays; quilts & handwork; wedding dresses. Payne Memorial Barn: blacksmith shop; tin shop; buggies; saddles; chuck wagon. Dugout & farm equipment. Paleontology & Native American Room: 1920 silk screen prints by Kiowa and other artists; 1200 pottery, rugs, baskets & blankets of the Southwestern Indian tribes; fossils & skeletal remains of the Clovis culture; Mead collection of rocks, minerals & arrowheads; Pioneer Miami 1900-1910.
Facilities: 208-vol. library pertaining to county history available for research on premises only. Books pertaining to Texas history-local & statewide available for check-out. Books & museum-related items for sale.
Activities: guided tours; permanent & temporary exhibitions.
Publications: brochures; books, Roberts County History Book I and II; Miami Mammoth Kill Site.
Hours & Admission Prices: Tues.-Fri. 10-5, Sat.-Sun. call for hours. No charge; donations accepted. Closed New Year's Day; Memorial Day; Independence Day; Labor Day; Veterans Day; Thanksgiving; Christmas. ♿
Attendance: 3,000 (accurate)

Midland

* **CAF AIRPOWER MUSEUM, (M),** 9600 Wright Dr., Midland, TX 79711. Mailing Address: P.O. Box 62000, Midland, TX 79711-2000. Tel.: 432-567-3010. Fax: 432-567-3047.
E-mail: visitorinfo@aahm.org
Web Site: www.airpowermuseum.org
Formerly: American Airpower Heritage Museum, Inc. & Commemorative Air Force Headquarters
Founded: 1957.
Key Personnel: Exec. Dir., Tami O'Bannion; Bd. Pres., Gordon Stevenson; Dir. Devel. & Public Rels., Jennifer Borlinghaus; Interpretive Dir., Jeff Wood; Librarian, Dot Britton; Museum Shop Mgr., Leah Block; Gift Shop Asst., Pat Moore; Dir. Publications, Emily Broome; Dir. Preservation, Annelorre Robertson; Patron Svcs. Specialist, Darrell Sanders; Dir. Education, Clay Francell.
Personnel Profile: Full-Time Paid 6; Part-Time Paid 3; Part-Time Volunteers 50; Interns 2.
Governing Authority: nonprofit organization. Affiliated with The Commemorative Air Force. Tax-exempt: 501(c)(3).
World War II, Military Aviation Museum.
Collections: U.S. & foreign combat aircraft of World War II; weapons; uniforms & equipment; photographs; memorabilia of the era c.1939-1945.
Research Fields: World War II combat aircraft; militaria.
Facilities: 60,000 sq. ft. hangar with restored aircraft; 14,000 sq. ft. exhibit hall; oral history department; historical research library & archives available for use on premises by appointment. Museum-related gift items for sale.
Activities: guided tours; lectures; docent program; films; permanent, traveling & loan exhibitions; outreach programs; actively collecting World War II oral histories; aviation cadet academy for 10-18 year olds.
Publications: The Co-Pilot Communique; Dispatch.
Hours & Admission Prices: Tues.-Sat. 9-5. Adults $10, senior citizens & teens 13-18 $9, children 6-12 $7, school groups $2; discounts to groups, AAA, AAM, CAA, TAM & National Historical Society members; children under 6 & members no charge. Closed New Year's Eve & Day; Thanksgiving; Christmas Eve & Day. ♿
Attendance: 37,283 (accurate)

Membership: Co-Pilot Club: Active $55; Family $75; Patron $150; Sustaining $250; Corporate $1,000; Benefactor $1,500; Lifetime $2,500.

THE GEORGE W. BUSH CHILDHOOD HOME, 1412 W. Ohio Ave., Midland, TX 79701. Mailing Address: P.O. Box 8586, Midland, TX 79708-8586. Tel.: 432-685-1112; 866-684-4380. Fax: 432-684-7012.
E-mail: gwbhome@bushchildhoodhome.org
Web Site: www.bushchildhoodhome.org
Key Personnel: Exec. Dir., Paul St. Hilaire
Historic Home: housed in the childhood home of former President George W. Bush.
Collections: furnishings from 1952-1956; photographs; Bush family artifacts & memorabilia.
Hours & Admission Prices: Tues.-Sat. 10-5, Sun. 2-5. Adults $5. Closed New Year's Day; Thanksgiving; Christmas. ♿

MCCORMICK GALLERY, Midland College, Allison Fine Arts Bldg., 3600 N. Garfield, Midland, TX 79705. Tel.: 432-685-4770.
E-mail: mccormickgallery@midland.edu
Web Site: www.midland.edu/mccormick
Founded: 1978.
Congressional District: 11
Key Personnel: Dir., J. Don Wallace.
Personnel Profile: Part-Time Paid 1; Part-Time Volunteers 8.
Governing Authority: Parent Institution: Midland College. Tax-exempt.
Art Gallery.
Collections: paintings; photography; ceramics; sculpture.
Hours & Admission Prices: Mon.-Thurs. 8am-10pm, Fri. 8-5, Sat. 10-5, Sun. 1-5. No charge. Closed holidays. ♿
Attendance: 2,500 (accurate)

MIDLAND COUNTY HISTORICAL MUSEUM, 301 W. Missouri, Midland, TX 79701-5108. Mailing Address: 2102 Community Lane, Midland, TX 79701-4018. Tel.: 915-682-2931 & 688-8947.
Founded: 1930.
Congressional District: 19
Key Personnel: Pres. Midland County Historical Society (V), Mrs. Nancy R. McKinley.
Personnel Profile: Part-Time Volunteers 2.
Governing Authority: county. Tax-exempt: 501(c)(3).
General Museum.
Collections: archives; archaeology; manuscripts; glass; original pictures of Midland; early obituary files; geology; Indian artifacts; medicine; history. Historic House: 1899 Taylor Brown-Sarah Dorsey Home.
Research Fields: archives; archaeology; Indian artifacts; history.
Facilities: Midland County history & classified news clipping file on all phases of Midland County growth available for use on premises.
Activities: guided tours; lectures; permanent & temporary exhibitions.
Publications: weekly newspaper article, Historical Markers.
Hours & Admission Prices: Wed. & Fri. 2-5. No charge, donations accepted. Closed New Year's Day; Independence Day; Labor Day; Thanksgiving; Christmas. ♿
Attendance: 1,000 (estimated)
Membership: Historical Society: Regular $10; Patron $25; Life $100.

* **MUSEUM OF THE SOUTHWEST, (M),** 1705 W. Missouri Ave., Midland, TX 79701-6516. Tel.: 432-683-2882. Fax: 432-684-9151.
E-mail: tjones@museumsw.org
Web Site: www.museumsw.org
Founded: 1965.
Congressional District: 21
Key Personnel: Dir., Thomas Jones; Pres. Bd. Trustees, Greg Dove; Dir. Devel., Cathy Burgess; Dir. Mktg., Jean Hoelscher; Dir. Planetarium, Gene Hardy; Asst. Registrar, Chris Lovett; Chief Security, Pamela J. Vaughn; Complex Mgr., Metta Preas; Cur. Children's Museum, Karen Winkler; Cur. Collections & Exhibitions, James Lovett; Adjunct Cur. Art Education, Debbie Hedrick.
Personnel Profile: Full-Time Paid 10; Part-Time Paid 8; Part-Time Volunteers 100.
Governing Authority: nonprofit. Tax-exempt: 501(c)(3).
Regional Art, Children's Museum & Planetarium.
Collections: southwestern art, anthropology; archaeology; Margaret & C.E. Bud Bissell archaeological collection of West Texas; Fred T. & Novadean Hogan Taos Founders Collection; contemporary & historic southwestern art with emphasis on Texas & New Mexico; the Barrett Collection of contemporary Texas art; Audubon's Texas animals, Karl Bodmer collection; Native American; Retablo; sculpture garden.
Major Exhibits: The Nature of Holography (T), 1/10; Nashville Portraits: Photographs by Jim McGuire (T), 1/10-3/10; New York September 11 by Magnum Photographers (T), 4/2/10-5/10; Nature of the Beast by John Banovich, 8/19/10-10/17/10; Contemporary Artists Series (T), 3/10-11/10.
Research Fields: art of the American & Southwest.
Facilities: planetarium; multi-purpose room.
Activities: arts & crafts festival; docent program; lectures; workshops; temporary & traveling exhibitions; planetarium programs; lawn concerts; art classes; meet the artists receptions; cultural travel; Midland City Limits; speakers bureau; traveling trunks. Museum Sponsors: Christmas at the mansion.
Publications: quarterly newsletter; gallery materials.
Hours & Admission Prices: Museum: Tues.-Sat. 10-5, Sun. 2-5. Planetarium: call for hours. Art Museum: no charge. Children's Museum: admission $3; discounts to AAM & ICOM members; children under one & Sun. no charge. Closed major holidays. ♿
Attendance: 90,000 (estimated)
Membership: Individual $40; Family $60; Family Plus $125; Supporter $250; Patron $500; President's Club $1,200; Corporate $250 & up.

NITA STEWART HALEY MEMORIAL LIBRARY & J. EVETTS HALEY HISTORY CENTER, 1805 W. Indiana, Midland, TX 79701-6949. Tel.: 432-682-5785. Fax: 432-685-3512.
E-mail: haley-mail@att.net
Web Site: www.haleylibrary.com
Founded: 1976.
Congressional District: 21
Key Personnel: Chm. (V), Jeff Haley; Chm., Brian McLaughlin; Office Staff & Archivist, Jim Bradshaw; Office Staff, Glenna Gifford; Dir., Pat McDaniel; Librarian, Nancy Jordan.
Personnel Profile: Full-Time Paid 2; Part-Time Paid 3.
Governing Authority: nonprofit organization. Tax-exempt: 501(c)(3).
Research Library & History Center.
Collections: Western art; photography collection; glassware; archives; tack; western gear; Indian baskets & blankets; maps; books; interviews pertaining to early range cattle history & frontier settlement; bronzes by Ed Fraughton, Glenna Goodacre, Veryl Goodnight, Buck McCain, Joe Beeler & others; paintings by Robert Lockheed, Charlie Dye & other masters of the West.
Research Fields: cattle industry in southwestern & western U.S., Canada, Mexico & South America; Indians; Texas Rangers; county histories; education; religion; politics; agriculture; horses.
Facilities: 30,000-vol. research library pertaining to the Southwest. Books, art prints, postcards & other related items for sale.
Activities: guided tours; organized educational programs for adults, undergraduate & graduate college students affiliated with the Univ. of Texas of the Permian Basin; docent program; participatory, temporary & traveling exhibitions. Museum Sponsors: Annual Art Show & Sale in March. Library: 3 art fundraiser shows a year.
Publications: quarterly newsletter, The Haley Library Newsletter.
Hours & Admission Prices: Mon.-Fri. 9-5. No charge; donations accepted. Closed New Year's Day; Memorial Day; Independence Day; Labor Day; Thanksgiving; Christmas Eve & Day. ♿
Attendance: 2,000 (estimated)
Membership: Old Maude $35; Abilene Couple $60; XIT Cowboy $100; Jeff Milton Ranger $250; Alamo Mission Bell $500; Charles Goodnight Traildriver $1,000; J. Evetts Haley History Center Benefactor $5,000.

THE PETROLEUM MUSEUM, (M), 1500 Interstate 20 West, Midland, TX 79701-2041. Tel.: 432-683-4403. Fax: 432-683-4509.
E-mail: info@petroleummuseum.org
Web Site: www.petroleummuseum.org
Founded: 1967.
Congressional District: 19
Key Personnel: Pres. (V), Roy Williamson; Exec. Dir., Kathy Shannon; Dir. Education, Brenda Rathjen; Dir. Archives, Leslie Meyer; Museum Shop Mgr., Fifi Sanchez.
Personnel Profile: Full-Time Paid 10; Part-Time Paid 5; Part-Time Volunteers 200.
Governing Authority: nonprofit corporation. Tax-exempt: 501(c)(3).
History & Technology Museum.
Collections: original paintings showing historical & oil industry subjects; period oil industry machinery; geology; paleontology; technology relating to petroleum; photos & documents relating to West Texas oil fields; 14 original paintings by two-time Prix de West Gold Medal Awardee, Tom Lovell; 7 Chaparral race cars by designer & racer Jim Hall.
Research Fields: regional petroleum industry & social history.
Facilities: 10,000-vol. library of books; 230,000 image photo collection; 250-seat auditorium. Petroleum & museum-related items for sale.
Activities: guided tours; films; docent program; permanent & temporary exhibitions; field trips; classes.
Publications: books, Oil In West Texas And New Mexico; Permian: A

Continuing Saga; Tom Lovell, Storyteller With a Brush; Chaparral, Can Am & Prototype Race Cars.
Hours & Admission Prices: Mon.-Sat. 10-5, Sun. 2-5. Adults $8, senior citizens & students 12-17 $6, children 6-11 $5; discounts to Texas Hwy. Travel Passports, AAM & AAA members; children under 6 & members no charge. Closed New Year's Day Thanksgiving; Christmas Eve & Day. ♿
Attendance: 35,000 (estimated)
Membership: Senior $20; Individual $35; Family $50; Friend $100-$149; Associate $250-$499; Supporter $500-$999; Patron $1,000-$2,499; Sustaining $2,500-$4,999; Benefactor $5,000-$9,999; Underwriter $10,000-$20,000; Director $20,000 & up.

Z. TAYLOR BROWN-SARAH DORSEY HOUSE, 213 N. Weatherford, Midland, TX 79701. Mailing Address: 2102 Community Lane, Midland, TX 79701-4018. Tel.: 432-682-2931.
Founded: 1899.
Congressional District: 21
Key Personnel: Pres. Midland County Hist. Society, Mrs. John P. McKinley.
Personnel Profile: Part-Time Volunteers 6.
Governing Authority: society; nonprofit. Parent Institution: Midland County Historical Society. Tax-exempt: 501(c)(3).
Historic House: housed in c.1899 Z. Taylor Brown House.
Collections: furniture & furnishings; historical artifacts.
Activities: guided tours; lectures; films; colored slide programs.
Hours & Admission Prices: By special appointment for groups. No charge; donations accepted.
Attendance: 800 (estimated)
Membership: Individual $10; Sponsor $25; Benefactor $100.

Mingus

W.K. GORDON CENTER FOR INDUSTRIAL HISTORY OF TEXAS, (M), 65258 I-20, Mingus, TX 76463. Mailing Address: P.O. Box 218, Mingus, TX 76463-0218. Tel.: 254-968-1886. Fax: 254-968-1903.
Web Site: www.tarleton.edu/~gordoncenter/index.html
Founded: 2002.
Congressional District: 31
Key Personnel: Dir., Dr. T. Lindsay Baker; Cur., LeAnna Biles Schooley.
Personnel Profile: Full-Time Paid 2; Part-Time Paid 4.
Governing Authority: public university. Parent Institution: Tarleton State University, Stephenville, TX. Tax-exempt: 501(c)(3).
Industrial Museum.
Collections: Texas industrial history with emphasis on Thurber and the Texas & Pacific Coal Company.
Research Fields: Texas & Pacific Coal Company; Thurber & it's residents; Thurber brick.
Facilities: library; 7,200 sq. ft. exhibit space; 40-seat theater. Museum-related items for sale.
Activities: concerts; formal education programs; lectures; rental gallery; temporary exhibitions; theater.
Hours & Admission Prices: Tues.-Sat. 10-4, Sun. 1-4. Adults $4, children $2; discounts to groups. Closed New Year's Day; Easter; Thanksgiving; Christmas; university holidays. ♿
Attendance: 3,000 (estimated)

Mission

MISSION HISTORICAL MUSEUM, (M), 1201 E. 8th St., Mission, TX 78572-5812. Tel.: 956-580-8646.
Key Personnel: Dir., Adela Ortega.
Governing Authority: nonprofit organization.
History Museum.
Collections: local history & culture; period clothing & furniture; photographs; sports memorabilia; military artifacts.
Hours & Admission Prices: Mon.-Fri. 10-4. Adults $2, seniors $1.50, children 6-18 $1; children under 6 no charge.

Monahans

MILLION BARREL MUSEUM, 400 Museum Blvd., Monahans, TX 79756. Tel.: 432-943-8401.
E-mail: millionbarrel_museum@monahans.org
Web Site: www.monahans.org/new/chamber/museums.html
History Museum.
Collections: oil storage tank; original Monahans jail; period caboose; eclipse windmill; early farm equipment. Historic House: Holman House.
Hours & Admission Prices: Call for hours.

Mount Pleasant

MODERN WESTERN MUSEUM, 2747 Old Paris Rd., Mount Pleasant, TX 75455-2098. Tel.: 903-572-9416.
E-mail: llmu@suddenlink.net
General Museum.
Collections: old west heroes & villains; cavalry memorabilia; Texas history; Colt, black powder pistols; Winchester rifles; John Wayne memorabilia; photographs.
Activities: school field trips; group tours.
Hours & Admission Prices: Tues.-Sat. Adults $2, students $1.

Mount Vernon

FRANKLIN COUNTY HISTORICAL MUSEUM, 201 S. Kaufman, Mount Vernon, TX 75457. Mailing Address: 111 Kaufman St., P.O. Box 289, Mount Vernon, TX 75457-0289. Tel.: 903-537-4760.
Web Site: www.mt-vernon.com/~chbrewer/museum.htm
History Museum.
Collections: area history; butterflies; bird eggs; violins; wood carvings; Indian artifacts; dental equipment.
Hours & Admission Prices: Office: Tues. & Thurs. 10-4. Museum: by appointment. No charge; donations accepted.

Nacogdoches

DURST-TAYLOR HISTORIC HOUSE AND GARDENS, 304 North St., Nacogdoches, TX 75961-5002. Mailing Address: City of Nacogdoches, Historic Sites Dept., P.O. Box 635030, Nacogdoches, TX 75963-5030. Tel.: 936-560-4443. Fax: 936-560-4448.
Web Site: www.ci.nacogdoches.tx.us
Founded: 2006.
Congressional District: 2
Key Personnel: Mgr. Historic Sites, Brian W. Bray; Cur. Collections & Education, Jessica Wood.
Personnel Profile: Full-Time Paid 2; Part-Time Paid 2; Part-Time Volunteers 2.
Governing Authority: municipal; nonprofit. Tax-exempt: 501(c)(3).
Historic House Museum: former home of Bennet Blake, delegate to the 1875 Constitutional Convention and later to Thomas J. Rusk, a signer of the Texas Declaration of Independence; built c.1830s. Listed on the National Register of Historic Sites.
Collections: local history; period furnishings; photographs; personal artifacts; blacksmith shop; smokehouse; gardens.
Facilities: visitors center; gardens.
Activities: guided tours. Annual Event: Sugar Cane Syrup Making.
Hours & Admission Prices: Tues.-Sat. 10-4. No charge; donations accepted. Closed major holidays.
Attendance: 1,200 (estimated)

STERNE-HOYA HOUSE MUSEUM AND LIBRARY, 211 S. Lanana St., Nacogdoches, TX 75961-5148. Mailing Address: City of Nacogdoches, Historic Sites Dept., P.O. Box 635030, Nacogdoches, TX 75963-5030. Tel.: 936-560-5426. Fax: 936-569-9813.
E-mail: brayb@ci.nacogdoches.tx.us
Web Site: ci.nacogdoches.tx.us
Founded: 1959.
Congressional District: 2
Key Personnel: Historic Sites Mgr., Brian W. Bray; Cur. Collections, Jessica Wood.
Personnel Profile: Full-Time Paid 2; Part-Time Paid 2; Part-Time Volunteers 2; Interns 2.
Governing Authority: municipal. Parent Institution: City of Nacogdoches. Tax-exempt.
History Museum: housed in Adolphus Sterne Home.
Collections: Texas artifacts; furniture; household fixtures.
Facilities: 5,000-vol. library of Texas history books available for use on premises.
Activities: historical tours.
Hours & Admission Prices: Mon. group tours only, Tues.-Sat. 10-4. No charge; donations accepted. Closed national holidays. ♿
Attendance: 4,894 (accurate)

STONE FORT MUSEUM, (M), 1808 Alumni Dr., N., Nacogdoches, TX 75962-0001. Mailing Address: P.O. Box 6075, SFASU, Nacogdoches, TX 75962-0001. Tel.: 936-468-2408. Fax: 936-468-7084.
E-mail: cspears@sfasu.edu
Founded: 1936.
Congressional District: 2
Key Personnel: Dir., Carolyn Spears; Pres. University, Dr. Baker Patillo; Chm. University Bd., Joe Max Green.
Personnel Profile: Part-Time Volunteers 8; Interns 1.

Governing Authority: state. Parent Institution: Stephen F. Austin State University. Tax-exempt: 501(c)(3).
Local History Museum: housed in 1936 reconstruction of 1780s structure.
Collections: East Texas artifacts dating prior to 20th-century.
Research Fields: 19th-century technology; Spanish & Mexican periods in East Texas.
Activities: guided tours; permanent & temporary exhibitions.
Hours & Admission Prices: Tues.-Sat. 9-5, Sun. 1-5. No charge; donations accepted. Closed national & university holidays. ♿
Attendance: 8,200 (estimated)
Membership: Student $5-$34; Individual $35; Contributor $50; Patron $100; Sponsor $250; Bronze $1,000; Gold $2,500; Diamond $5,000.

New Braunfels

MCKENNA CHILDREN'S MUSEUM, 801 W. San Antonio St., New Braunfels, TX 78130-5503. Tel.: 830-606-9525. Fax: 830-606-9535.
E-mail: ajewell@mckenna.org
Web Site: www.mckennakids.org
Formerly: The Children's Museum in New Braunfels
Founded: 1986.
Congressional District: 28
Key Personnel: C.E.O., Tim Brierty; Dir., Alice Jewell.
Personnel Profile: Full-Time Paid 4; Part-Time Paid 2; Part-Time Volunteers 10.
Governing Authority: nonprofit. Parent Institution: McKenna. Tax-exempt.
Children's Museum.
Collections: hands-on exhibits.
Facilities: 18,000 sq. ft. exhibit space.
Activities: art, science, cooking, garden & health programming.
Publications: quarterly newsletter.
Hours & Admission Prices: Memorial Day to Labor Day Mon.-Sat. 10-5, Sun. 12-5; Sept.-May Tues.-Sat. 10-5, Sun. 12-5. Adults: Memorial Day to Labor Day $7.50; Labor Day to Memorial Day $5.50; members no charge. Closed New Year's Day; Easter; Memorial Day; Independence Day; Labor Day; Thanksgiving; Christmas. ♿
Attendance: 60,000
Membership: Spass Family $125; Spiel Meister $165.

NEW BRAUNFELS CONSERVATION SOCIETY, 1300 Church Hill Dr., New Braunfels, TX 78130-3205. Tel.: 210-629-2943.
E-mail: nbcs@axs4u.net
Web Site: www.nbconservation.org
Founded: 1964.
Congressional District: 21
Key Personnel: Dir., Martha Rehler; Pres., Barron Schlameus; Treas., JoBeth Oestreich; Security, Josef Campos.
Personnel Profile: Part-Time Paid 1; Part-Time Volunteers 30.
Governing Authority: private; nonprofit organization. Tax-exempt: 501(c)(3).
Historical & Preservation Society: located on 3 sites-Conservation Plaza (13 buildings & Rose Conservatory over three and a half acres), Lindheimer Home, Buckhorn Barber Shop & Museum.
Collections: handmade furniture; household items, c.1845-1900s. Conservation Plaza: 19 restored structures.
Facilities: botanical garden. Museum-related items for sale.
Activities: guided tours; lectures; rental gallery; participatory & temporary exhibitions. Annual Events: two membership appreciation dinners; Gartenfest & Historic Home Tour in March; Kaffee Haus-Conservation Plaza in November; Elderhostels.
Publications: monthly (except summer) newsletter; brochure.
Hours & Admission Prices: Lindheimer Haus: by appointment. Wurstfest daily 2-5. Adults $2.50, students $.50; discounts to AAM members. Buckhorn Barber Shop & Museum: by appointment. Antique Rose Conservatory & Conservation Plaza: Tues.-Fri. 10-2:30, Sat.-Sun. 2-5. Closed Thanksgiving; Christmas-New Years.
Attendance: 4,000 (estimated)
Membership: Active $15; Patron $25; Family $30.

NEW BRAUNFELS MUSEUM OF ART & MUSIC, 1259 Gruene Rd., New Braunfels, TX 78130-3003.
Founded: 1991.
Key Personnel: C.E.O. & Dir., Charles R. Gallagher; Devel., Cassey Parkey; Education, Ruth Sullivan; Pres. (V), Charles Teeter; Public Rels., Janelle Berger; Treas., Debbie Voorhees; Registrar, Tony Lyle; Cur., Craig Hillis; Museum Shop Mgr., Nancy Webb.
Personnel Profile: Full-Time Paid 5; Full-Time Volunteers 2; Part-Time Paid 5; Part-Time Volunteers 10; Interns 2.
Governing Authority: private; nonprofit organization. Tax-exempt: 501(c)(3).
Music History Museum.
Collections: photographs; oral histories; recordings; film documentaries; visual art; folk art; music & crafts in Texas.
Research Fields: Texas musicology; oral histories of living Texas artists.
Facilities: lab; 299-seat restaurant; 15,000 sq. ft. exhibit space. Museum-related items for sale.
Activities: concerts; dance recitals; docent program; formal education programs. Annual Events: 4th Annual Music & Arts Festival; Lone Star Arts Award.
Hours & Admission Prices: Temporarily closed.

SOPHIENBURG MUSEUM & ARCHIVES INC., (M), 401 W. Coll St., New Braunfels, TX 78130-5618. Tel.: 830-629-1572. Fax: 830-629-3906.
Web Site: www.sophienburg.com
Founded: 1926.
Congressional District: 21
Personnel Profile: Part-Time Paid 8; Part-Time Volunteers 160; Interns 1.
Governing Authority: society. Affiliated with Sophienburg Museum & Archives. Tax-exempt.
History Museum: housed in fieldstone veneer building on site of the headquarters of original German colony founded in 1845 in Republic of Texas.
Collections: local history; German immigration & settlement in Texas 1840 to present; manuscript materials; genealogy records; photographs; German & local artifacts; tools & equipment; guns & armament.
Research Fields: TX history; genealogy; German Immigration; photographs.
Facilities: library; archives.
Activities: educational services; guided tours. Museum Sponsors: Fourth of July Celebration; Weihnachtsmarkt, German Christmas Market in November; traditional visit of St. Nicholas in December.
Publications: cookbook, Guten Appetit; New Braunfels Comal County, Texas: A Pictorial History; The New Braunfels Sesquicentennial Minutes; It's Fair Time - History of the Comal County Fair, Kindermaskenball - Past and Present; War Between the States Participants from Comal County, Texas.
Hours & Admission Prices: Tues.-Sat. 10-4. Museum: adults $5, students $1; AAM members & museum members no charge. Archives: adults & students $10. Closed New Year's Eve & Day; Good Friday; Independence Day; Thanksgiving; Christmas Eve & Day. ♿
Attendance: 5,600 (accurate)
Membership: Individual $30; Family $50; Business $100.

Newcastle

FORT BELKNAP MUSEUM AND ARCHIVES, INC., Farm to Market Rd., 2 mi. south of Newcastle, Newcastle, TX 76372. Mailing Address: P.O. Box 444, Graham, TX 76450-0444. Tel.: 940-846-3222.
Founded: 1851.
Congressional District: 17
Key Personnel: C.E.O., Dr. Harry Hewitt.
Governing Authority: county. Affiliated with Texas Wesleyan College. Tax-exempt: 501(c)(3).
History & Military Museum.
Collections: archives; Indian artifacts; preservation project; photographs. Historic Houses: 1853, Corn House; officer's quarters; magazine; army barracks #1, #2 and #4; c.1854 commissary; household items from 1850s-1890s.
Research Fields: Texas history & government; frontier & Indian history; 19th-century military; frontier biography; genealogy; archaeology.
Facilities: 2,000-vol. library of rare books. Publications, curios and postcards for sale.
Activities: guided tours; lectures; films; arts festivals; study clubs; inter-museum loan & permanent exhibitions; rental space available.
Publications: annual books, Fort Belknap Society Yearbook; Fort Belknap Genealogical Association Bulletin.
Hours & Admission Prices: Museum: Mon.-Tues. & Thurs.-Sat. 9-12 & 1:30-5, Sun. 1-5. No charge; donations accepted. Archives: Sat. 8:30-5:30. Adults $10. ♿
Attendance: 30,000 (estimated)
Membership: Individual $5; Sustaining $25; Life $100.

Odessa

* **THE ELLEN NOEL ART MUSEUM OF THE PERMIAN BASIN, (M),** 2909 East University Blvd., Odessa, TX 79762-7960. Mailing Address: P.O. Box 13928, Odessa, TX 79768-3928. Tel.: 432-550-9696. Fax: 432-550-9226.
E-mail: marilyn@noelartmuseum.org
Web Site: noelartmuseum.org
Founded: 1985.
Congressional District: 19
Key Personnel: Exec. Dir., Marilyn Bassinger; Pres. Bd., Barbara Davis.
Personnel Profile: Full-Time Paid 5; Part-Time Paid 4; Part-Time Volunteers 125.

Governing Authority: nonprofit organization. Tax-exempt: 501(c)(3).
Art Museum.
Collections: temporary exhibitions of art.
Facilities: art classrooms; sensory & sculpture garden.
Activities: guided tours; lectures; films; concerts; study clubs; hobby workshops; organized education programs; docent program; traveling exhibitions; art classes; outreach programs; summer art camp.
Publications: quarterly newsletter; exhibit catalogs.
Hours & Admission Prices: Tues.-Sat. 10-5, Sun. 2-5. No charge; donations accepted. Closed national holidays. ♿
Attendance: 22,000 (accurate)
Membership: Friend $50; Household $100; Patron $250; Connoisseur $500-$1,000.

THE ODESSA METEOR CRATER AND MUSEUM, 620 N. Grant Ave., Ste. 1204, Odessa, TX 79761-4549. Tel.: 432-381-0946.
Web Site: www.netwest.com/virtdomains/meteorcrater/About.htm
Geology Museum.
Collections: meteorites; tektites; meteorite impact products; videos.
Hours & Admission Prices: Museum: Sat. 10-5, Sun. 1-5. Crater Tours: daily 9-6.

THE PRESIDENTIAL MUSEUM AND LEADERSHIP LIBRARY, 4919 E. University Blvd., Odessa, TX 79762-8144. Tel.: 432-363-7737. Fax: 432-366-6133.
E-mail: nancy.alison@yahoo.com
Web Site: www.presidentialmuseum.org
Founded: 1964.
Congressional District: 23
Key Personnel: Admin., Lettie M. England; Pres., Juan Alcantar.
Personnel Profile: Full-Time Paid 1; Part-Time Paid 1; Part-Time Volunteers 10.
Governing Authority: Tax-exempt: 501(c)(3).
History Museum.
Collections: 6,000 books, journals & papers pertaining to the presidency; photographs; campaign memorabilia; posters; buttons; letters; personal artifacts from presidents & first ladies.
Research Fields: presidential campaigns; political parties; U.S. history.
Facilities: 6,000-vol. library; meeting room.
Activities: guided tours; lectures; docent program or council; inter-museum loan, permanent, temporary & traveling exhibitions; workshops; film festivals & demonstrations.
Publications: newsletter.
Hours & Admission Prices: Tues.-Sat. 10-5. Adults $8, senior citizens & students K-12 $5; discounts to AAA members; children under 6, military with ID, & members no charge ♿
Attendance: 5,210 (accurate)
Membership: Student $10; Individual $25; Family: $40; Ambassador $100; Cabinet $250; President's Circle $500. Business & Corporate: Supporter $500; Patron $1,000; Benefactor $2,500; Advocate $5,000 & up.

Orange

HERITAGE HOUSE OF ORANGE COUNTY ASSOCIATION INC., 905 W. Division, Orange, TX 77630-6959. Tel.: 409-886-5385. Fax: 409-886-0917.
E-mail: hhmuseum@exp.net
Web Site: www.heritagehouseoforange.org
Founded: 1977.
Congressional District: 19
Key Personnel: Pres. & Dir., Joyce Atkins; Chm., Linda Garrett.
Personnel Profile: Full-Time Paid 1; Part-Time Volunteers 30.
Governing Authority: nonprofit organization. Branch Museums: Heritage House Museum, 905 W. Division, Orange, TX 77630; Heritage History Museum of Orange County, 110 Border St., Orange, TX 77630. Tax-exempt: 501(c)(3).
Historic House & History Museum: housed in 1902 turn-of-the-century house.
Collections: Orange County History from early Indian settlements to present day; period rooms; medical instruments; archival & photographic images; costumes & textiles; decorative arts; historic furnishings.
Research Fields: Orange County history; artifacts.
Facilities: library.
Activities: guided tours; lectures; organized education programs for children; docent program; training programs for professional museum workers; participatory, loan & temporary exhibitions.
Publications: quarterly newsletter, Nostalgic News.
Hours & Admission Prices: Temporarily closed. ♿
Attendance: 1,800 (estimated)
Membership: Regular & Civic Clubs $25; Patron $35; Benefactor $50; Sustaining & Corporate $100.

STARK MUSEUM OF ART, (M), 712 Green Ave., Orange, TX 77630-5721. Tel.: 409-886-2787. Fax: 409-883-6361.
E-mail: starkmuseum@starkmuseum.org
Web Site: www.starkmuseum.org
Founded: 1974.
Congressional District: 2
Key Personnel: C.E.O., Nelda C. and H. J. Lutcher Stark Foundation, Walter G. Riedel, III; Dir., Dr. Sarah E. Boehme; Registrar, Allison H. Evans; Mgr. Collections & Exhibitions, Terri Fox; Chief Security, Tom Parks; Coord. Museum Svcs., Mary Vesty; Librarian, Jenniffer Hudson Connors; Dir. Education & Programs, Sue Harris; Photographer, Tom Eckert; Museum Shop Mgr., Sue Denosowicz.
Personnel Profile: Full-Time Paid 19; Part-Time Paid 18; Part-Time Volunteers 14.
Governing Authority: nonprofit organization. Parent Institution: Nelda C. and H.J. Lutcher Stark Foundation. Tax-exempt: 501(c)(3).
Art Museum.
Collections: Western American art including Paul Kane collection; Taos Society of Artists; American Indian art; porcelain & crystal.
Research Fields: relating to the collections.
Facilities: 2,500-vol. library related to areas of collections. Books, catalogues, posters & postcards for sale.
Activities: guided tours; gallery talks.
Publications: catalogues; The Western Collection; Taos Portfolio; The American & British Birds of Dorothy Doughty; The Steuben Glass Collection; A Mirror Unto Nature; The Art and Life of W. Herbert Dunton, 1878-1936; First Artistic Traditions; A Guide to the Galleries.
Hours & Admission Prices: Tues.-Sat. 10-5. No charge. Closed New Year's Day; Easter; Independence Day; Thanksgiving; Christmas. ♿
Attendance: 14,040 (accurate)

THE W.H. STARK HOUSE, 610 W. Main Ave., Orange, TX 77630-5704. Mailing Address: P.O. Drawer 909, Orange, TX 77631-0909. Tel.: 409-883-0871. Fax: 409-883-3530.
E-mail: info@whstarkhouse.org
Web Site: www.whstarkhouse.org
Founded: 1981.
Congressional District: 2
Key Personnel: C.E.O., Walter Riedel, III; Dir., Patricia L. Herrington.
Personnel Profile: Full-Time Paid 4; Part-Time Paid 22.
Governing Authority: owned & operated by the Nelda C. & H.J. Lutcher Stark Foundation. Tax-exempt: 501(c)(3).
Historic House: 1894 Victorian Home of William H. Stark & Miriam Lutcher Stark.
Collections: original furniture; rugs; family portraits; lace curtains; silver; ceramics; glass; oriental rugs.
Activities: guided tours.
Publications: video tour.
Hours & Admission Prices: Tues.-Sat. 10-3. Adults $5, students & seniors 65 & over $2; children under 10 not admitted.
Attendance: 2,900 (accurate)

Ozona

CROCKETT COUNTY MUSEUM, 408 11th St., Ozona, TX 76943. Mailing Address: P.O. Box 1444, Ozona, TX 76943-1444. Tel.: 325-392-2837. Fax: 325-392-5654.
Founded: 1939.
Congressional District: 67
Key Personnel: Dir., Patsy White; Pres. (V), Jan Van Schoubrouek; Museum Coord., Camille Dammon; Aide, Roberta Schoenhals.
Personnel Profile: Full-Time Paid 1; Full-Time Volunteers 1; Part-Time Paid 2; Part-Time Volunteers 20.
Governing Authority: society; nonprofit organization. Parent Institution: Crockett County Historical Society. Tax-exempt: 170(b)(1)(A).
History Museum.
Collections: prehistoric & historic Indian tools, weapons, & artifacts; geological specimens of the county; county wildflowers & plants; memorabilia of early ranchers, ranching industry & brands; photographs of early pioneers; guns; furniture.
Facilities: library of county history available on premises; reading room.
Activities: Museum Sponsors: Shrimp Fest.
Publications: brochure on museum & county; books: A History of Crockett County (handout brochure); An Activity Book on Crockett County & Ozona (children); video: This Rugged Land Called Crockett County; 1991 Centennial Pageant.
Hours & Admission Prices: Mon.-Fri. 9-5, Sat. 10-3. Adults $2. Closed New Year's Day; Thanksgiving; Christmas; county holidays. ♿
Attendance: 2,459 (accurate)
Membership: Individual $20; Family $25.

Pampa

WHITE DEER LAND MUSEUM, 112-116 S. Cuyler, Pampa, TX 79065. Mailing Address: P.O. Box 1556, Pampa, TX 79066-1556. Tel.: 806-669-8041. Fax: 806-669-8030.
E-mail: wdlmuseum@graycch.com
Web Site: www.museuminpampa.org
Founded: 1970.
Congressional District: 31
Key Personnel: Cur., Ann Davidson; Asst. Cur., Deborah Chambers.
Personnel Profile: Full-Time Paid 2; Part-Time Paid 2; Part-Time Volunteers 6.
Governing Authority: county. Tax-exempt.
General Museum: housed in 1916 White Deer Land Co. Building.
Collections: Rolla J. Sailor arrowheads; David F. Barry limited edition photographs; furniture; clothing; documents; manuscripts; toys; dolls; musical instruments; carriages; farm machinery; military items; wood carvings; replica of first wood-derrick oil well on White Deer lands; replica of first Gray County court house; maps; chapel furnished with items from early day churches of Pampa; Red River War artifacts 1874-1875.
Research Fields: history.
Facilities: library of M.K. Brown Range Life Series of ranch life in the Southwest & complete company records of White Deer Land Company available for use on premises.
Activities: guided tours; special programs for civic clubs, study clubs, scout troops elementary & secondary school classes; permanent & temporary exhibits & demonstrations.
Publications: brochure; books, Personal Diary of GCT, History of Pampa Post Office, For the Reason We Climb Mountains, Red River Expedition, White Deer Land Museum History Wall, Gray County History Book, The Log House on White Deer Creek, History of M.K. Brown, History of C.P. Buckler, History of T.D. Hobart, White Deer Land Building.
Hours & Admission Prices: Winter: Tues.-Sun. 1:30-4; Summer: Tues.-Fri. 10-4, Sat.-Sun. 1-4; group tours by appointment. No charge; donations accepted. Closed national holidays. ♿
Attendance: 2,000 (accurate)

Panhandle

CARSON COUNTY SQUARE HOUSE MUSEUM, (M), TX Hwy. 207 @ Fifth St., Panhandle, TX 79068. Mailing Address: P.O. Box 276, Panhandle, TX 79068-0276. Tel.: 806-537-3524. Fax: 806-537-5628.
E-mail: shm@squarehousemuseum.org
Web Site: www.squarehousemuseum.org
Founded: 1965.
Congressional District: 18
Key Personnel: Exec. Dir. & C.E.O., Viola Moore; Chm. (V), Kenneth Cox; Educator, Holly Hicks; Registrar, Carla Martinez; Administrative Asst., Bobbie Smith; Museum Shop Mgr., Nita Ramming.
Personnel Profile: Full-Time Paid 4; Part-Time Paid 2; Part-Time Volunteers 37.
Governing Authority: board of trustees. Tax-exempt: 501(c)(3).
General Museum: located at the former terminus of the Santa Fe railroad.
Collections: agriculture; archaeology; archives; paintings; costumes; manuscripts; entomology; ethnology; folklore; glass; Indian artifacts; military, music; paleontology; transportation; period artifacts; furniture; guns. Historic Structures: mid-1880 Square House; caboose; reconstructed pioneer dugout; windmill; relocated 1912 community church; full-sized activity-specific diorama.
Research Fields: local & regional (Texas Panhandle) prehistory, history, natural history & art.
Facilities: research library of Texana books; photographic archives. Museum-related books & items for sale.
Activities: guided tours; lectures; films; study clubs; hobby workshops; formally organized educational programs; docent program; permanent & temporary exhibitions; school loan service; bus tours to archaeological & historic sites; 29 historic videos may be viewed at the museum or loaned to organizations or individuals.
Publications: 4-vol. book, A Time To Purpose; coloring book, Land of Coronado; poems, Voices of the Square House; cookbook, The Square House Cook Book.
Hours & Admission Prices: Mon.-Sat. 9-5, Sun. 1-5. No charge; donations accepted. Closed New Year's Day; Easter; Thanksgiving; Christmas Day. ♿
Attendance: 18,957 (accurate)

Paris

HAYDEN MUSEUM OF AMERICAN ART, 930 Cardinal Lane, Paris, TX 75460-6522. Tel.: 903-785-1925. Fax: 903-784-7631.
Founded: 1992.
Key Personnel: Dir. & Pres. (V), William deG. Hayden, M.D.
American Art Museum.
Collections: history of American art from folk art to modern & contemporary; paintings; decorative arts; prints; photographs; sculpture.
Facilities: library.
Activities: seminar; lectures.
Hours & Admission Prices: By appointment. No charge.
Attendance: 2,500 (estimated)

SAM BELL MAXEY HOUSE STATE HISTORIC SITE, 812 S. Church St., Paris, TX 75460-7112. Tel.: 903-785-5716. Fax: 903-785-6716.
E-mail: sam-bell-maxey@thc.state.tx.us
Web Site: www.visitsbmh.com
Congressional District: 1
Personnel Profile: Full-Time Paid 5; Part-Time Volunteers 15.
Governing Authority: state. Parent Institution: Texas Historical Commission, Austin, TX 78744. Tel. 512-479-4882. Tax-exempt.
Historic House Museum: 1868 High Victorian Italianate style home belonging to Civil War Confederate Gen. & U.S. Senator, Sam Bell Maxey.
Collections: household furnishings; 1830-1950 clothing, textiles & memorabilia of the Sam Bell Maxey family; manuscript & music collections.
Research Fields: 19th-century decorative arts; Texas & Civil War history; career of U.S. Senator, Sam Bell Maxey.
Facilities: 3,000-vol. library of books, programs and documents pertaining to Texas history and 19th & early 20th-century material culture available for qualified research by appointment.
Activities: guided tours; lectures; formally organized education programs for children & undergraduate students.
Publications: visitors guide.
Hours & Admission Prices: Guided Tours: daily 9-4; groups of 8 or more by appointment. Adults $3; discounts to students, seniors over 65 & groups of 8 or more; members no charge. Closed New Year's Eve & Day; Thanksgiving; Christmas Eve & Day. ♿
Attendance: 2,000 (estimated)

Pasadena

ARMAND BAYOU NATURE CENTER, 8500 Bay Area Blvd., Pasadena, TX 77507. Mailing Address: P.O. Box 58828, Houston, TX 77258-8828. Tel.: 281-474-2551. Fax: 281-474-2552.
E-mail: abnc@abnc.org
Web Site: www.abnc.org
Founded: 1974.
Congressional District: 25
Key Personnel: Pres. Bd. Trustees (V), James Callan; Exec. Dir., Tom Kartrude; Museum Shop Mgr., Barbara Baxter.
Personnel Profile: Full-Time Paid 6; Part-Time Paid 6; Part-Time Volunteers 185.
Governing Authority: nonprofit organization. Tax-exempt: 501(c)(3).
Nature Center & Preserve: located on 2,500 acres of tallgrass prairie, forest and bayou including a demonstration turn-of-century farm, also includes several prehistoric archeological sites.
Collections: prairie, bayou & woodland preserves; native animal (birds, mammals, reptiles, amphibians, fish) study skins and specimens; early 1900's farmhouse; farm implements; furnishings.
Research Fields: Texas Upper Coast flora & fauna; prairie restoration & management; marsh restoration & management; local water shed water quality.
Facilities: 2,800 sq. ft. exhibit space; 100-seat auditorium; indoor classrooms. Gift items for sale.
Activities: guided tours; lectures; organized educational programs; docent program; participatory exhibits. Annual Events: Fall Festival; Creepy Crawlers; Second Saturdays at ABNC.
Publications: quarterly membership newsletter, Along the Bayou; volunteer monthly, The Bayou Foliage.
Hours & Admission Prices: Tues.-Sat. 9-5, Sun. 12-5. Adults $3, children 5-17 & seniors over 61 $1; discounts to groups; children under 5 & members no charge. ♿
Attendance: 30,830 (accurate)
Membership: Seniors $40; Individual $45; Family $55.

Pecos

WEST OF THE PECOS MUSEUM, (M), First at Cedar (U.S. 285), Pecos, TX 79772. Mailing Address: Box 1784, Pecos, TX 79772-1784. Tel.: 432-445-5076. Fax: 432-445-3149.
E-mail: wpmuseum@nwol.net
Web Site: www.westofthepecosmuseum.com
Founded: 1962.
Congressional District: 23
Key Personnel: Pres. (V), Bill Oglesby; Dir., Debra Thomas; Cur., Dorinda Millan.

Personnel Profile: Full-Time Paid 4; Part-Time Paid 2; Part-Time Volunteers 50.
Governing Authority: board of trustees; nonprofit organization. Tax-exempt.
History Museum: housed in 1896 two-story red sandstone saloon & c.1904 three-story concrete block Orient Hotel.
Collections: local history memorabilia; saloon; railroad & telegraph memorabilia; western ranch life; school room; bridal suite; barber & beauty room; local pictures & history; Indian artifacts; horse-drawn wagons; chuck wagons; water wagon.
Research Fields: local history.
Facilities: courtyard; park.
Activities: self-guided tours; educational & cultural activities & exhibits. Museum Sponsors: Friends of the Museum; Old Timer's Reunion, Student Art Festival; Kid's Programs; Presidents exhibit in February; Art Show & Sale in July & October; Fall Fair; History Trivia Contest; Living Christmas Tree exhibit.
Publications: brochure (English & Spanish); cookbooks; local history books & brochures; newsletters.
Hours & Admission Prices: June-Aug. Mon.-Sat. 9-5, Sun. 1-4; Sept.-May Tues.-Sat. 9-5. Adults $4, senior citizens & tours $3, children 6-18 $1; discounts to AAM members; members, children under 6, tour bus driver & guides no charge. Closed Christmas week. ♿
Attendance: 10,000 (accurate)
Membership: Friends of the Museum: Individual $25; Family $50; Associate $100; Sponsor $250; Supporter $500; Partner $1,000.

Perryton

MUSEUM OF THE PLAINS, 1200 N. Main, Perryton, TX 79070-2314. Tel.: 806-435-6400.
E-mail: motp@ptsi.net
Web Site: www.museumoftheplains.com
History Museum.
Collections: lives of settlers in the 1800s; period bottles; natural history; religion.
Facilities: Museum-related items for sale.
Hours & Admission Prices: Mon.-Fri. 9-5, Sat. 10-5, Sun. 1-5. No charge; donations accepted. Closed New Year's Day; Thanksgiving; Christmas.

Pharr

OLD CLOCK MUSEUM, 929 E. Preston St., Pharr, TX 78577-5013. Tel.: 956-787-1923.
Founded: 1968.
Key Personnel: Mgr., Gene Shawn.
Governing Authority: individual operation; nonprofit.
Horological Museum.
Collections: clocks.
Research Fields: horological.
Facilities: 60-vol. library of historical books and catalogs on old clocks & watches and their makers available for use on premises. Postcards for sale.
Activities: private tours.
Hours & Admission Prices: Mon.-Fri. 1-5. Adults $1.

Pittsburg

NORTHEAST TEXAS RURAL HERITAGE MUSEUM, 204 W. Marshall, Pittsburg, TX 75686-1312. Mailing Address: P.O. Box 157, Pittsburg, TX 75686-0157. Tel.: 903-856-1200. Fax: 903-856-5045.
E-mail: campcountymuseum@aol.com
Web Site: www.pittsburgtxmuseum.com
Founded: 1989.
Congressional District: 4
Key Personnel: Pres., Glen Gatlin; Treas. (V), Bob Turner; Cur., Glenda Brogiotti.
Personnel Profile: Full-Time Paid 1; Part-Time Paid 3; Part-Time Volunteers 18.
Governing Authority: private; nonprofit organization. Tax-exempt: 501(c)(3).
History Museum.
Collections: history of Northeast Texas rural life & inhabitants from prehistoric times to 1950s. Historic Buildings: 1901 farmstead, barn, outhouse, smokehouse, blacksmith shop, general store; 1900 Cotton Belt Depot & annex with caboose; Ezekiel Airship.
Facilities: garden. Museum-related items for sale.
Activities: docent program; films; formal education programs for children; guided tours; lectures; loan, participatory, temporary & traveling exhibitions; rental gallery. Annual Events: Fantasy Ball; Samuel Morse Day; Star Party; Black History Celebration.
Publications: quarterly newsletter, Museum News.
Hours & Admission Prices: Thurs.-Sat. 10-4. Adults $4, senior citizens $3, students $2; discount to student groups & AAM members; members no charge. Closed New Year's Eve & Day; Christmas Eve & Day. ♿

Attendance: 2,741 (accurate)
Membership: Senior & Student $10; Individual $25; Family $50; Century Club $100; Supporter $250; Sponsor $500; Benefactor $1,000.

Plains

TSA MO GA MEMORIAL MUSEUM, 1109 Ave. H, Plains, TX 79355. Mailing Address: P.O. Box 718, Plains, TX 79355-0718. Tel.: 806-456-8855.
Founded: 1959.
Congressional District: 19
Key Personnel: Dir., Mrs. P.W. St. Romain.
Personnel Profile: Part-Time Volunteers 4.
Governing Authority: nonprofit organization. Parent Institution: Tsa Mo Ga Club. Tax-exempt.
Local History Museum.
Collections: pioneer & Civil War articles; two room bonus shack; early cowboy artifacts; local history.
Research Fields: pioneer items; local history.
Activities: guided tours. Museum Sponsors: Old Settler's Days in August.
Hours & Admission Prices: By appointment. No charge.
Attendance: 18 (estimated)

Plainview

MUSEUM OF THE LLANO ESTACADO, Wayland University, J.E. & L.E. Mabee Rgnl. Heritage Ctr., Plainview, TX 79072. Mailing Address: 1900 W. 7th St., #299, Plainview, TX 79072-6900. Tel.: 806-291-3660. Fax: 806-291-1982.
E-mail: watsonr@wbu.edu
Web Site: www.wbu.edu
Founded: 1976.
Congressional District: 19
Key Personnel: Dir., Rodney Watson; Administrative Asst., Elva Hipolito.
Personnel Profile: Full-Time Paid 2; Part-Time Paid 2; Part-Time Volunteers 6.
Governing Authority: university. Parent Institution: Wayland University. Tax-exempt.
General Museum.
Collections: geological, archaeological development of the Llano Estacado region; natural history & history.
Research Fields: the Llano Estacado Region.
Facilities: 110-seat auditorium; seminar room.
Activities: lectures; traveling exhibits; programs to schools & other museums; guided tours; films; special lectureships & exhibits; courses in museum-related arts.
Publications: audio-visual programs; occasional reports of activities.
Hours & Admission Prices: April-Nov. Mon.-Thurs. 9-5, Fri. 9-4, Sat.-Sun. 1-5; Dec.-March Mon.-Thurs. 9-5, Fri. 9-4. No charge; donations accepted. Closed college holidays. ♿
Attendance: 6,200 (accurate)
Membership: Students $5; Regular $10; Family $15; Organizational & Commercial $25; Associate $50; Participating $100; Sustaining $200; Sponsor $250; Benefactor $500; Patron $750; Founder $1,000.

Plano

* **HERITAGE FARMSTEAD MUSEUM, (M),** 1900 W. 15th St., Plano, TX 75075-7329. Tel.: 972-881-0140. Fax: 972-422-6481.
E-mail: administration@heritgefarmstead.org
Web Site: www.heritage.farmstead.museum
Founded: 1986.
Congressional District: 3
Key Personnel: Exec. Dir., Hal Simon; Dir. Children's Programs & Education, Lynda Morley; Cur., Doug Hawes; Cur. Exhibits, Lolisa Laenger; Office Mgr., Mary Marks; Dir. Education, Kathy Strobel; Mktg. & Publicity, Angie Carroll; Facilities Mgr., Kelly Kring; Business Mgr., Michelle Prengle; Education Asst., Tracy Gardner.
Personnel Profile: Full-Time Paid 3; Part-Time Paid 6; Part-Time Volunteers 200.
Governing Authority: nonprofit organization. Tax-exempt: 501(c)(3).
Historic House: 1891 Victorian farmhouse located on a 4-acre historic site.
Collections: one-room 1897 schoolhouse; period furnishings from late 19th century; farm implements (1890-1940); textiles; photographs; toys; games; windmill, barns, cisterns, smokehouse, old-fashioned flower, herb & vegetable gardens & farm animals.
Research Fields: Texas; Collin County; Blackland Prairie; pioneer farm life.
Facilities: grounds available for rental; party barn. Crafts & other museum-related items for sale.
Activities: concerts; docent program; formally organized educational program; guided tours; lectures; participatory & temporary exhibits. Annual Events: Fall Family Day; Texas Women's Day; Lantern Light Tours; Heritage Scout Day: Spring Festival.

Publications: quarterly newsletter, Heritage Today; books, One Room Schools of Collin County, Texas, Hunter's New Adventure.
Hours & Admission Prices: Grounds: daily 9-4:30. Tours: Tues.-Sun. 1:30. Self Guided Tours: adults $2; discounts to AAM members. Guided Tours: adults $5, senior citizens 66 & over and children 3-18 $3.50; discounts to AAM members. Closed holidays. ♿
Attendance: 32,612 (accurate)
Membership: Individual $35; Family $65; Patron $125; Partner $300; Preservation $500; Corporate $1,000.

INTERURBAN RAILWAY MUSEUM, 901 E. 15th St., Plano, TX 75074-5807. Mailing Address: P.O. Box 861810, Plano, TX 75086-1800. Tel.: 972-941-2117. Fax: 972-941-2656.
E-mail: planoconservancy@earthlink.net
Web Site: www.interurbanplano.org
Formerly: Interurban Railway Station Museum
Transportation Museum.
Collections: electric rail & interurban transportation; working model O gauge.
Hours & Admission Prices: Mon.-Fri. 10-2, Sat. 1-5. No charge; donations accepted. ♿
Attendance: 20,000
Membership: Individual $5-$250; Business $75-$1,000.

JC PENNEY ARCHIVES AND HISTORICAL MUSEUM, 6501 Legacy Dr., Plano, TX 75024-3698. Mailing Address: P.O. Box 10001, Dallas, TX 75301-0001. Tel.: 972-431-7926. Fax: 972-431-7896.
Company History Museum.
Collections: company history; 20th-century American clothes & artifacts; period records; photographs; company newspapers & catalogues; recreated first JC Penney store.
Hours & Admission Prices: Mon.-Fri. 8-5. No charge.

Pleasanton

LONGHORN MUSEUM, 1959 Hwy. 97 E., Pleasanton, TX 78064-6500. Tel.: 830-569-6313.
Web Site: www.pleasantontx.org/museum.html
Founded: 1976.
Key Personnel: Dir., Donna Rice; Asst., Valerie Purgason.
Personnel Profile: Full-Time Paid 2; Full-Time Volunteers 1; Part-Time Paid 1.
Governing Authority: nonprofit. Tax-exempt.
History Museum.
Collections: local history & culture; ranching; personal artifacts; farming & industry.
Hours & Admission Prices: Mon.-Sat. 8-5; groups by appointment. No charge; donations accepted. Closed New Year's Day; Easter; Memorial Day; Independence Day; Labor Day; Thanksgiving; Christmas; Saturdays before Monday holidays. ♿
Attendance: 2,500 (estimated)

Port Arthur

MUSEUM OF THE GULF COAST, (M), 700 Procter St., Port Arthur, TX 77640-6521. Tel.: 409-982-7000. Fax: 409-982-9614.
E-mail: Shannon.Harris@lamarpa.edu
Web Site: www.museumofthegulfcoast.org
Founded: 1964.
Congressional District: 9
Key Personnel: Pres. (V), Dr. Sam Monroe; Dir., Shannon Harris; Education Coord., Carol Boethcher; Treas., Betty Herlin; Museum Shop Mgr., Peggy Arrant.
Personnel Profile: Full-Time Paid 4; Part-Time Paid 7; Part-Time Volunteers 25.
Governing Authority: society. Parent Institution: Port Arthur Historical Society, 1953 Lakeshore, Port Arthur, TX 77640. Subsidiary Institution: Lamar State College, Port Arthur, TX. Tax-exempt: 501(c)(3).
Regional History Museum.
Collections: flora & fauna of the Gulf Coast area; geology; Paleo-Indian artifacts from McFadden Beach; social & cultural materials from the Port Arthur region; decorative arts; pop culture memorabilia.
Research Fields: Sabine Pass Battle 1863.
Facilities: music hall.
Activities: guided tours; enviro-kids summer camp; arts express after school program; lectures; workshops; school loan service. Museum Sponsors: fund-raising musicals.
Publications: newsletter, Mosquito Bytes.
Hours & Admission Prices: Mon.-Sat. 9-5, Sun. 1-5. Adults $4, senior citizens over 62 & college students $3, students 4-18 $2; discounts to groups over 20; children 3 & under and members no charge. Closed New Year's Eve afternoon & Day; Easter; Independence Day; Thanksgiving; Christmas Eve & Day. ♿
Attendance: 15,000 (accurate)
Membership: General $20-$1,000.

Port Lavaca

CALHOUN COUNTY MUSEUM, (M), 301 S. Ann St., Port Lavaca, TX 77979-4205. Tel.: 361-553-4689. Fax: 361-553-4689.
E-mail: director@calhouncountymuseum.org
Web Site: www.calhouncountymuseum.org
Founded: 1964.
Congressional District: 14
Key Personnel: Dir., George Ann Cormier.
Personnel Profile: Full-Time Paid 1; Part-Time Paid 1.
Governing Authority: county; nonprofit. Tax-exempt.
History Museum.
Collections: lens from the Matagorda Island Lighthouse; Calhoun County history.
Research Fields: photographs of Indianola, Port Lavaca, Seadrift, Point Comfort, Port O'Connor, Olivia; French influence in Calhoun County & LaSalle; natural history of area.
Activities: guided tours; temporary exhibitions.
Hours & Admission Prices: Tues.-Wed. 10:30-4:30, Thurs.-Fri. 10:30-5, Sat. 10-3. No charge; donations accepted. Closed county holidays.
Attendance: 1,785 (accurate)

Presidio

FORT LEATON STATE HISTORICAL SITE, 17000 EFM 170, Presidio, TX 79845. Mailing Address: P.O. Box 2439, Presidio, TX 79845-2439. Tel.: 432-229-3613. Fax: 432-229-4814.
Web Site: www.tpwd.state.tx.us
Founded: 1977.
Congressional District: 21
Key Personnel: C.E.O., Robert Cook; Chm. Commission, Peter M. Holt; Dir. Parks, Walt Dabney.
Personnel Profile: Full-Time Paid 4; Part-Time Paid 1; Part-Time Volunteers 8; Interns 2.
Governing Authority: state. Parent Institution: Texas Parks & Wildlife Dept., 4200 Smith School Rd., Austin, TX 78744. Tel. 512-479-4882. Tax-exempt.
Historic Building & Museum: 1848 private 40-room adobe fortress built by Indian trader Benjamin Leaton, located on old Indianola-San Antonio-Chihuahua Trail & overlooking the Rio Grande.
Collections: 16th to late 19th-century artifacts & interpretive materials covering the history of La Junta de los Rios now known as the Presidio-Ojinaga region.
Facilities: picnic sites.
Activities: guided tours; films; permanent exhibitions.
Publications: brochure.
Hours & Admission Prices: Daily 8-4:30. Adults $3; children under 12 no charge. Closed Christmas.
Attendance: 3,600 (accurate)
Membership: Friends Group $15-$250.

Pyote

RATTLESNAKE BOMBER BASE MUSEUM, 10th & Ward, Pyote, TX 79777. Mailing Address: P.O. Box 120, Pyote, TX 79777-0120. Tel.: 432-943-2187.
Military Museum.
Collections: area history; military artifacts & memorabilia.
Hours & Admission Prices: Sat. 9-6, Sun. 2-6.

Quitman

LIGHT CRUST DOUGHBOYS HALL OF FAME & MUSEUM - GOVERNOR JIM HOGG CITY PARK, 100 Gov. Hogg Pkwy., Quitman, TX 75783. Mailing Address: P.O. Box 767, Quitman, TX 75783-0767. Tel.: 903-763-2701. Fax: 903-763-2764.
E-mail: info@quitmanheritage.org
Web Site: quitmanheritage.org
Formerly: Governor Hogg Shrine State Park
Founded: 2005.
Key Personnel: Exec. Dir. & Museum Mgr., Rebecca Barrett; Chm. (V) & Pres., Gordon Stone; Vice Pres., Jo An Coker; Treas., Barry Carlson.
Personnel Profile: Full-Time Paid 1; Part-Time Paid 1; Part-Time Volunteers 10.
Governing Authority: state. Parent Institution: Texas Parks & Wildlife Dept., 4200 Smith School Road, Austin, TX 78744, 512-389-4889. Subsidiary Institution: City of Quitman. Tax-exempt.
Historic Houses: 1869 Stinson Home; honeymoon cottage of Governor Hogg.
Collections: history items of Wood County & northeast Texas; period furnishings; Light Crust Doughboys collection; Gov. W. Lee (Pappy) O'Daniel.

Facilities: playground; picnic areas; Pony Truss Bridge on Nature Trail.
Activities: self-guided & guided tours; half mile nature & hiking trail. Park Sponsors: Western Swing Festival in May; Old Settlers Reunion in August.
Publications: quarterly newsletter, Quitman Heritage Foundation.
Hours & Admission Prices: Mon.-Sat. 9-4. Adults $3. Closed New Year's Day; Thanksgiving; Christmas Eve & Day. ♿
Attendance: 5,000 (estimated)
Membership: Quitman Heritage Foundation: Friend $30; Family $100; Supporter $250; Patron $500; Lifetime $1,000.

Ralls

RALLS HISTORICAL MUSEUM, 801 Main St., Ralls, TX 79357. Mailing Address: P.O. Box 384, Ralls, TX 79357-0384. Tel.: 806-253-2425.
E-mail: rallshistoricalmuseum@windstream.net
Founded: 1970.
Congressional District: 84
Key Personnel: Dir., Donna Harris; Pres. (V), Dale Sedgwick; Treas., Brenda Valentine; Registrar, Jeanette Wilson.
Personnel Profile: Full-Time Paid 1.
Governing Authority: nonprofit organization. Tax-exempt: 501(c)(3).
General Museum: housed in 1918 First National Bank.
Collections: art objects; history; archaeology; science; natural history; ethnology; military.
Research Fields: history.
Activities: guided tours; permanent & temporary exhibitions. Museum Sponsors: Pioneer Family Days, quilt shows, doll shows.
Hours & Admission Prices: Tues.-Fri. 10-12 & 1-3. No charge; donations accepted.
Attendance: 474 (accurate)
Membership: Student $1; Family $5; Contributor $10-$25; Life $100; Sustaining $250; Benefactor $500.

Rankin

RANKIN MUSEUM, 100 W. First, Rankin, TX 79778. Mailing Address: P.O. Box 82, Rankin, TX 79778-0082. Tel.: 915-693-2758 & 2422. Fax: 915-693-2303.
E-mail: jcpg@yahoo.com
Web Site: www.rootsweb.com/~txupton/
Founded: 1974.
Congressional District: 21
Key Personnel: Pres. (V), Judy Greer.
Personnel Profile: Part-Time Paid 1.
Governing Authority: nonprofit organization. Parent Institution: Rankin Museum Association. Tax-exempt.
Local History Museum.
Collections: costumes; geology; glass; machinery; brands; restored 1940 firetruck, fully operative; photographs.
Research Fields: geology; local history; genealogy.
Facilities: library of local period ledgers.
Activities: visits from school groups; exhibits by local artists; planned programs for local organizations & school; building used for special functions.
Publications: articles in local newspaper; occasional write-ups in area publications.
Hours & Admission Prices: Thurs.-Fri. 2-5, Sat. 1-5; other times by appointment. No charge; donations accepted. ♿
Attendance: 1,000 (estimated)
Membership: Annual $1; Life $50.

Refugio

REFUGIO COUNTY MUSEUM, (M), 102 W. West St., Refugio, TX 78377-2433. Tel.: 361-526-5555.
E-mail: brefugiomuseum@aol.com
Founded: 1983.
Key Personnel: C.E.O. & Pres. (V), Bart Wales; Chm. (V), Maxine H. Reilly.
Personnel Profile: Full-Time Paid 1; Part-Time Paid 2.
Governing Authority: society; nonprofit. Parent Institution: Refugio County Historical Society. Tax-exempt: 501(c)(3).
Local History Museum.
Collections: history & culture of Refugio County; period artifacts; medical artifacts; nostalgia items.
Research Fields: local history; genealogy.
Facilities: 520-vol. library, including 5,000 newspapers; 1,500 sq. ft. exhibit space. Local history books, cookbooks & other items of local interest for sale.
Activities: guided tours; lectures; films; organized educational programs; participatory, loan & temporary exhibitions.
Publications: newsletter.
Hours & Admission Prices: Tues.-Fri. 12-4, Sat. 1-5. No charge; donations accepted. Closed major holidays. ♿
Attendance: 2,500
Membership: Individual $10.

Richardson

THE NATIONAL MUSEUM OF COMMUNICATIONS, 2001 Plymouth Rock, Richardson, TX 75081-3946. Tel.: 972-690-3636; 214-616-6562. Fax: 972-889-2329.
E-mail: billbragg@mail.com
Web Site: www.yesterdayusa.com
Founded: 1979.
Congressional District: 4
Key Personnel: Founder & Exec. Cur., William J. Bragg; Chm. Bd. (V), Kim Bragg; C.E.O., Walden Hughes; Chief Engineer, Roger Wenzel; Tour Dir., Don Richards; Museum Shop Mgr., Mike Handy.
Personnel Profile: Full-Time Paid 5; Part-Time Paid 5; Part-Time Volunteers 3.
Governing Authority: nonprofit organization. Tax-exempt: 501(c)(3).
Communications Museum.
Collections: vintage radio equipment; master control console from Voice of America in Washington, D.C.; vintage phonographs; radio & television sets; radio station transmitter, including audio control console, turntables & microphones; record-cutting lathe; replica of 1960s television studio; first type of color TV camera; Walter Cronkite's microphone; Thomas Edison's microscope; Edison mimeograph; wax cylinder dictating machines; records; news tapes; technical journals; linotype machine; rare books; photography & motion picture film equipment; working amateur radio station; period telegraph keys & telephones.
Facilities: 60,000-vol. library of books, films, video tapes, wire recordings, pictures, phonograph records for research; 65-seat auditorium; educational facilities.
Activities: guided tours; films; vintage TV & radio programs.
Publications: newsletter, The Transcription.
Hours & Admission Prices: Call for information on hours. Adults $9.95, senior citizens 65 & over $7.95; discounts to AAM & ICOM members. ♿
Attendance: 70,000 (estimated)

Richmond

* **FORT BEND COUNTY MUSEUM ASSOCIATION, (M),** 500 Houston, Richmond, TX 77469-3522. Mailing Address: P.O. Drawer 460, Richmond, TX 77406-0460. Tel.: 281-342-6478 & 1256. Fax: 281-342-3782.
E-mail: cjones@fortbendmuseum.org
Web Site: www.fortbendmuseum.org
Founded: 1967.
Congressional District: 22
Key Personnel: Dir., Candace Jones; Pres. (V), Pat Hebert; Museum Shop Mgr., Jerry Hoover.
Personnel Profile: Full-Time Paid 34; Part-Time Paid 45; Part-Time Volunteers 230.
Governing Authority: society. Subsidiary Institution: George Ranch Historical Park. Tax-exempt: 501(c)(3).
Local History Museum.
Collections: settlement of Stephen F. Austin's colony; agriculture; crafts; industry; furniture; clothes; manuscripts; documents; photographs; livestock and artifacts of history of George Ranch, 1824-1950. Historic Buildings: 1883 John M. Moore Mansion; 1901 Railroad Station; 1856 Alexander McNabb House; 1840 Jane Long House; 1896 County Jail; 1890s Kochn-Reed Home.
Research Fields: 1821-1836 culture and material culture of Austin's colony; county history; biographies of local leaders.
Facilities: auditorium; 150-vol. library of books about area and local leaders available for research by appointment only. Books, original sketches and postcards for sale.
Activities: guided tours; lectures; films; docent program; living history demonstration; spinning & weaving demonstrations; permanent & temporary exhibitions.
Publications: book, Sowell's History of Fort Bend County; cookbook, Czech Cookbook; book, Wharton's History of Fort Bend County.
Hours & Admission Prices: Ranch: Tues.-Sat. 9-5. Adults $9, children $4. Museum: Mon.-Fri. 9-5, Sat. 10-5, Sun. 1-5. Adults $5, senior citizens $2.50, children $2; discounts to AAM members; members no charge. Closed New Year's Day; Easter; Independence Day; Thanksgiving & Day after; Christmas. ♿
Attendance: 91,265 (accurate)
Membership: Individual & Family $50; Sustaining $100; Corporate $1,000.

Rockport

FULTON MANSION STATE HISTORIC SITE, 317 Fulton Beach Rd., Rockport, TX 78382. Mailing Address: P.O. Box 1859, Fulton, TX 78358-1859. Tel.: 361-729-0386, ext. 26. Fax: 361-729-6581.
E-mail: fulton-mansion@thc.state.tx.us
Web Site: www.thc.state.tx.us
Founded: 1983.
Congressional District: 18
Key Personnel: C.E.O., Texas Parks & Wildlife Dept., Robert Cook; Pres. (V), Frances Symank; Dir., Diana Kirby; Asst. Dir., Dr. Marsha Hendrix; Educator, Pearlie Bushong.
Personnel Profile: Full-Time Paid 5; Part-Time Paid 3; Part-Time Volunteers 40.
Historic House Museum: c.1877 French Second Empire style Mansion.
Collections: period furniture; middle to late 19th-century decorative arts.
Research Fields: 19th-century decorative arts; material culture; landscaping & mechanical systems; ranching.
Facilities: 2.3 acres of grounds; maintenance complex.
Activities: guided tours; lectures; study clubs; docent program; formally organized educational programs; permanent & temporary exhibitions.
Publications: brochures; cookbook; newsletters.
Hours & Admission Prices: Tues.-Sat. 10-3, Sun. 1-3; groups of 10 or more by appointment. Adults $6, students with ID $2. Closed New Year's Day; Thanksgiving; Christmas. ♿
Attendance: 20,100 (accurate)
Membership: Individual $25; Family $50; Supporting $100; Corporate $250; Sustaining $500.

* **TEXAS MARITIME MUSEUM, (M),** 1202 Navigation Cir., Rockport, TX 78382-2773. Tel.: 361-729-1271 & 6644; 866-729-2469. Fax: 361-729-9938.
E-mail: klrd@pelicancoast.net
Web Site: www.texasmaritimemuseum.org
Founded: 1980.
Congressional District: 14
Key Personnel: Pres., Ken Craven; C.E.O., Kathy Roberts-Douglass; Museum Shop Mgr., Sally Reynolds.
Personnel Profile: Full-Time Paid 4; Part-Time Paid 4; Part-Time Volunteers 56.
Governing Authority: nonprofit. Tax-exempt: 501(c)(3).
Texas Maritime Museum.
Collections: nautical equipment; commercial fishing equipment; ship & small boat building tools; photographs.
Facilities: 1,201-vol. library of maritime & nautical material; 3,000 sq. ft. exhibit space.
Activities: organized activities for children; temporary exhibits; educational programs for children; tours for Elder Hostel groups; River Barge tours.
Publications: quarterly newsletter, The Log Line.
Hours & Admission Prices: Tues.-Sat. 10-4, Sun. 1-4. Adults $6, seniors $5, children 6-12 $3; discounts for group, AAM & ICOM members w/ID & groups of 10 or more with 2 weeks notice; children 5 & under and members no charge. Closed New Year's; Easter; Memorial Day; Thanksgiving; Christmas Day. ♿
Attendance: 16,232 (accurate)
Membership: Individual $25; Family $35; Sponsor $100; Benefactor $500.

Rosanky

CENTRAL TEXAS MUSEUM OF AUTOMOTIVE HISTORY, 2502 Hwy. 304, Rosanky, TX 78953. Tel.: 512-237-2635. Fax: 512-754-2405.
E-mail: dburdick@thermon.com
Web Site: www.ctmah.org
Founded: 1982.
Congressional District: 10
Key Personnel: Dir., Richard L. Burdick; Financial Dir., P. Kenneth Pitzer; Cur. & Museum Shop Mgr., Kurt McCowan; Restoration, Ray Terry.
Personnel Profile: Full-Time Paid 2; Part-Time Paid 1.
Governing Authority: private; nonprofit. Tax-exempt: 501(c)(3).
Transportation Museum.
Collections: emphasis on restoration & preservation of early automobiles, accessories and other related items.
Facilities: library. Furniture, accessories & museum-related items for sale.
Hours & Admission Prices: April-Sept. Wed.-Sat. 10-5, Sun. 1:30-5; Oct.-March Fri.-Sat. 10-5, Sun. 1:30-5. Adults $5, children 6-12 $2.50; discount to groups. Closed Christmas.

Round Top

BRISCOE CENTER FOR AMERICAN HISTORY-WINEDALE HISTORICAL CENTER, UNIVERSITY OF TEXAS AT AUSTIN, 3738 FM Road 2714, Round Top, TX 78954. Mailing Address: P.O. Box 11, Round Top, TX 78954-0011. Tel.: 979-278-3530. Fax: 979-278-3531.
E-mail: winedale@austin.utexas.edu
Web Site: www.cah.utexas.edu
Formerly: Winedale, Center for American History, University of Texas at Austin
Founded: 1966.
Congressional District: 25
Key Personnel: Dir., Dr. Don Carleton; Administrative Coord., Barbara B. White; Office Mgr., Beth Stewart.
Personnel Profile: Full-Time Paid 6; Part-Time Paid 8; Part-Time Volunteers 4.
Governing Authority: state. Parent Institution: University of Texas at Austin. Tax-exempt.
Historic House.
Collections: decorative arts, folk art, furniture, tools & agricultural implements pertaining to German settlement of Texas; historic houses complete with c.1850s furnishings. Historic Buildings: Lewis Wagner House (1848); McGregor-Grimm House.
Research Fields: Texas-German cultural history; agricultural history; American social history; cabinetmaking; textiles; slavery in central Texas.
Facilities: 24-person dorm & dining facility; classrooms; interpretive center; visitor's center; conference facility; outdoor pavilion.
Activities: guided tours; lectures; workshops; permanent & temporary exhibits; plays; museum & library seminars. Museum Sponsors: American History Symposium; Shakespeare Festival; Christmas at Winedale-19th Century Folklife Reenactment.
Publications: quarterly newsletter, Quid Nunc; occasional papers; catalogs.
Hours & Admission Prices: Mon.-Fri. 8-5. Tours: by appointment. Closed holidays. ♿
Attendance: 5,600 (estimated)
Membership: Student $10; Contributing $25; Associate $50; Sustaining $100; Patron $250; Life Member $1,000.

FESTIVAL-INSTITUTE, JAMES DICK FOUNDATION, 248 Jaster Rd., Round Top, TX 78954-5445. Mailing Address: P.O. Box 89, Round Top, TX 78954-0089. Tel.: 979-249-3129. Fax: 409-249-5078.
E-mail: lamarl@festivalhill.org
Web Site: www.festivalhill.org
Founded: 1971.
Congressional District: 15
Key Personnel: Founder, Dir. & Pres., James Dick; Dir. Museum & Library Collections, Lamar Lentz; Treas., Richard R. Royall; Information Officer, Alain Declert.
Personnel Profile: Full-Time Paid 9; Full-Time Volunteers 2; Part-Time Paid 7; Part-Time Volunteers 58; Interns 2.
Governing Authority: public; nonprofit. Tax-exempt: 501(c)(3) & 170(b)(1)(A).
Architecture & Art Museum: historic restorations include 1883 Edythe Bates Old Chapel; 1884 William Lockhart Clayton House; 1902 C.A. Menke House.
Collections: art; architecture; furniture; paintings; ceramics; glass; textiles; photographs; prints; metalworks; musical instruments; recordings; music; Festival Concert Hall with period rooms: David W. Guion museum room; Anders Gustav Fredrik & Josephine Oxehufwud Swedish museum room; Winfrey Toscanini collection; James and June Painter art collection.
Research Fields: architecture and decorative arts of the 19th & early 20th century; 19th-century Texas history; American and European art; 16th-century Northern Renaissance art; 16th-20th century Swedish Art & Decorative Arts; garden history; British Country House Guides; Country House Art Catalogues, 1750-1950; music.
Facilities: 14,000-vol. library of music, art, architecture, decorative arts, garden and landscape history, Texas history; 20,000 historic recordings; 1,000-seat auditorium; herb garden; educational facilities; conference facility. Compact discs, T-shirts, books, prints & note cards for sale.
Activities: concerts; films; formal educational programs; guided tours; lectures; permanent & temporary exhibitions; forums; walking tours.
Publications: exhibition catalogues.
Hours & Admission Prices: Mon.-Sat. by appointment. Tours: $5 per person; self-guided tours of grounds during day; discounts to AAM members. Closed Thanksgiving; Christmas. ♿
Attendance: 34,000 (estimated)
Membership: Contributor $35; Friend $150; Patron $500; Sponsor $1,000; Guarantor $5,000.

Salado

CENTRAL TEXAS AREA MUSEUM, INC., 423 S. Main St., Salado, TX 76571. Mailing Address: Box 36, Salado, TX 76571-0036. Tel.: 254-947-5232. Fax: 254-947-5232.
E-mail: office@ctam-salado.org
Web Site: www.ctam-salado.org
Founded: 1958.
Key Personnel: Pres., Scott Fletcher; 1st Vice Pres., Robert Rangel; 2nd Vice Pres., Beth Rangel; Librarian, Joy Dunaway; Librarian, Bob Dunaway; Historian, Crystal Calbreath; Museum Shop Mgr., Mary Mendez.
Personnel Profile: Full-Time Paid 1.
Governing Authority: nonprofit. Subsidiary Institution: Wee Scots Shop. Tax-exempt: 501(c)(3).
General Museum: housed in an early Central Texas store building.
Collections: genealogy; history; archives; Scottish folklore; Central Texas artifacts; Tonkawa artifacts; period artifacts.
Research Fields: central Texas history; Scottish heritage & other ethnic cultures.
Facilities: library of material on history with emphasis on Central Texas, including fine arts, genealogy, Scottish history & lore; auditorium. Books, Scottish merchandise, fine bone china, pressed and cut glass.
Activities: monthly programs; readers & writers roundtable ethnic shows. Museum Sponsors: Salado Scottish Games & Competitions.
Hours & Admission Prices: Tues.-Sat. 10-5. No charge; donations accepted.
Membership: Individual $15; Husband/Wife & Family with children under 18 $25; Sustaining $40; Benefactor $100; Life $400; Corporations $1,000.

Salt Flat

GUADALUPE MOUNTAINS NATIONAL PARK, 400 Pine Canyon Dr., Salt Flat, TX 79847-4755. Tel.: 915-828-3251. Fax: 915-828-3269. TDD: 915-828-3251.
E-mail: gumo_superintendent@nps.gov
Web Site: www.nps.gov/gumo
Founded: 1972.
Congressional District: 16
Key Personnel: Chief Resource Mgmt., Janice Wobbenhorst.
Governing Authority: federal. Parent Institution: National Park Service, Dept. of the Interior. Tax-exempt.
National Park Museum.
Collections: natural history; local history; archaeology; historic sites.
Research Fields: geology; biology; history; archaeology.
Facilities: visitor centers; campground; back-country trails.
Activities: campfire programs; special walks; hikes; self-guiding nature trails.
Publications: brochure, The Guadalupes; Wilderness: The Guadalupe Mountains.
Hours & Admission Prices: Summer: daily 8-6. Winter: daily 8-4:30. No charge; donations accepted. ♿
Attendance: 76,000 (accurate)

San Angelo

FORT CONCHO NATIONAL HISTORIC LANDMARK, (M), 630 S. Oakes St., San Angelo, TX 76903-7013. Tel.: 325-481-2646 & 657-4444. Fax: 325-657-4540.
Web Site: fortconcho.com
Founded: 1928.
Congressional District: 11
Key Personnel: Dir., Robert Bluthardt; Chm. (V), Lee Pucicitt; Pres., Bill Shaw; Librarian & Archivist, Evelyn Lemons; Dir. Education, Chris Morgan; Special Events, Carol Cummings; Mng. & Visitor Svcs., Cory Robinson.
Personnel Profile: Full-Time Paid 12; Part-Time Paid 2; Part-Time Volunteers 250; Interns 1.
Governing Authority: municipal. Parent Institution: City of San Angelo. Cooperates with Angelo State University & San Angelo Independent School District. Tax-exempt.
Historic Landmark.
Collections: costumes; furniture; military artifacts; historic photographs; historic buildings.
Research Fields: Southern Plains Indians; military history of Plains Indian Wars; frontier settlement after 1864; San Angelo and West Texas history, 1870-1930.
Facilities: 4,000-vol. library; meeting space; activities space. Postcards & museum-related items for sale.
Activities: guided tours; lectures; educational programs; permanent, temporary & traveling exhibitions; festivals; frontier school; craft demonstrations; living history programs; concerts; holiday celebrations; summer children's programs; teacher training workshops.
Publications: quarterly newsletter, The Guidon; Fort Concho Museum Press publications.
Hours & Admission Prices: Mon.-Sat. 9-5, Sun. 1-5. Adults $3; discounts for senior citizens, military, groups, Texas Forts Trail, AAA & TAM members; members & children under 6 no charge. Closed New Year's Day; Thanksgiving; Christmas Day. ♿
Attendance: 75,000 (accurate)
Membership: Lieutenant $35; Captain $75; Major $100; Lt. Colonel $150; Colonel $250; Brigadier General $500; Major General $1,000; Lt. General $2,500; General $5,000.

RAILWAY MUSEUM OF SAN ANGELO, 703 S. Chadbourne, San Angelo, TX 76903-6931. Tel.: 325-486-2140.
Web Site: www.railwaymuseumsanangelo.homestead.com
Key Personnel: Pres., Nolan Mears
Railway Museum: housed in the 1909 Orient-Santa Fe Depot built by the KCM&O.
Collections: trains; train memorabilia.
Activities: Model Railroad Club. Annual Events: Santa's Santa Fe Christmas.
Hours & Admission Prices: Sat. 10-4.

* **SAN ANGELO MUSEUM OF FINE ARTS, (M),** One Love St., San Angelo, TX 76903-6911. Tel.: 325-653-3333. Fax: 325-658-6800.
E-mail: museum@samfa.org
Web Site: www.samfa.org
Founded: 1981.
Congressional District: 11
Key Personnel: Dir., Howard Taylor; Pres., Jan Duncan; Exec. Asst., Gracie Fernandez; Collections Mgr., Karen Zimmerly; Preparator, John Mattson; Bookkeeper, Martha McCloskey; Educator, Lillian Lewis; Weekend Supvr., Sylvia Grimaldo; Museum Shop Mgr., Betty Connally; Receptionist, Karen Leigh.
Personnel Profile: Full-Time Paid 6; Part-Time Paid 20; Part-Time Volunteers 40; Interns 3.
Governing Authority: nonprofit. Tax-exempt: 501(c)(3).
Art Museum.
Collections: the work of Texas artists from 1945; ceramic arts emphasizing work created since 1945; American painting and sculptures; Mexican & Mexican-American art; European, Oriental & African.
Research Fields: West Texas art & cultural history, late 20th-century crafts, design & architecture.
Facilities: sculpture garden; education center. Museum-related items for sale.
Activities: guided tours; lectures; concerts; films; organized educational programs; docent program; changing exhibitions.
Publications: newsletter; exhibit catalogues; gallery guides.
Hours & Admission Prices: Tues.-Sat. 10-4, Sun. 1-4. Adults $2, senior citizens and children 12 & under $1; discounts to groups of 10 or more, Texas Assoc. of Museums, AAM & ICOM members; members, local school groups & military no charge. Closed national holidays. ♿
Attendance: 60,000 (estimated)
Membership: Individuals $10; Families $20.

San Antonio

THE ALAMEDA NATIONAL CENTER FOR LATINO ARTS AND CULTURE, 101 S. Santa Rosa, San Antonio, TX 78207-4509. Tel.: 210-299-4300. Fax: 210-299-4340.
E-mail: info@thealameda.org
Web Site: www.thealameda.org
Latino Arts & Culture.
Collections: Latino arts & cultural heritage
Activities: performance; educational programs.
Hours & Admission Prices: Tues. & Thurs.-Sat. 10-6, Wed. 10-8, Sun. 12-6. Adults $4, seniors 55 & over, military and educators $3, students & children 4-11 $2; discounts to groups; children under 3 no charge. Closed New Year's Day; Easter; Battle of Flowers; Memorial Day; Independence Day; Thanksgiving; Christmas.

THE ALAMO, 300 Alamo Plaza, San Antonio, TX 78205-2606. Mailing Address: P.O. Box 2599, San Antonio, TX 78299-2599. Tel.: 210-225-1391. Fax: 210-354-3602.
E-mail: dstewart@thealamo.org
Web Site: www.thealamo.org
Founded: 1905.
Congressional District: 20
Key Personnel: C.E.O., David Stewart; Pres. Gen. (V), Madge Roberts; Alamo Committee Chm. (V), Diane MacDiarmid; Historian & Cur., Dr. Bruce Winders; Museum Shop Mgr., Barbara Langford.
Personnel Profile: Full-Time Paid 80; Part-Time Paid 6; Part-Time Volunteers 10.

Governing Authority: nonprofit organization. Parent Institution: Daughters of the Republic of Texas, Inc. Tax-exempt: 501(c)(3).
Historic Site & Complex: 1836 Mission San Antonio De Valero, site of the Battle of the Alamo.
Collections: rifles; pistols; cannon; knives; spurs; jewelry; glass; ceramics; documents; paintings; dioramas; utilitarian objects; textiles; furniture; clothing from the Texas Revolution & the Republic of Texas periods. Historic Structure: 18th-century Long Barrack & Alamo chapel.
Research Fields: Republic of Texas; Texas Revolution; genealogy; archeology; illustration; textbooks; publications; conservation preservation.
Facilities: botanical garden; 9,700 sq. ft. exhibit space; video system. Museum-related items for sale.
Activities: guided tours; lectures; films; organized education programs for children; temporary exhibitions. Museum Sponsors: Texas Independence; Pilgrimage to the Alamo; Fall at the Alamo.
Publications: book, The Long Barrack; The Wall of History
Hours & Admission Prices: Mon.-Sat. 9-5:30, Sun. 10-5:30. No charge; donations accepted. Closed Christmas Eve & Day. ♿
Attendance: 2,479,329 (accurate)

ARTPACE SAN ANTONIO, (M), 445 N. Main Ave., San Antonio, TX 78205-1441. Tel.: 210-212-4900. Fax: 210-212-4990.
E-mail: info@artpace.org
Web Site: www.artpace.org
Founded: 1995.
Congressional District: 20
Key Personnel: Exec. Dir., Matthew J.W. Drutt; Grants, Trisha Tanner; Devel., Mary Heathcott; Public Rels., Celina Bustamante Emery; Education, Kendra Curry; C.F.O., Tricia Peebles; Studio Dir., Riley Robinson; Archivist, Kimberly Aubuchon; Membership, Matt Johns.
Personnel Profile: Full-Time Paid 16; Part-Time Paid 6; Part-Time Volunteers 161; Interns 18.
Governing Authority: nonprofit organization. Tax-exempt: 501(c)(3).
Art Museum.
Collections: contemporary art.
Major Exhibits: HSR 10.1, 1/10-5/10; Windowworks 10.1, 1/10-5/10; IAIR 10.1, 3/10-5/10; HSR 10.2, 5/10-9/10; Windowworks 10.2, 5/10-9/10; IAIR 10.2, 7/10-9/10; Windowworks 10.3, 9/10-11/10; HSR 10.3, 9/10-1/11; IAIR 10.3, 11/10-1/11; Holiday Window, 12/10.
Facilities: library; educational facilities; 7,000 sq. ft. exhibit space. Museum-related items for sale.
Activities: arts festival; films; formal education programs; guided tours; lectures; participatory exhibits; teacher workshops & professional artists; summer art camps; international artist-in-residence program. Annual Events: Chalk It Up.
Publications: magazine, "Artpace"; annual exhibition catalogue.
Hours & Admission Prices: Wed.-Sun. 12-5; other times by appointment. No charge; donations accepted. Closed New Year's Day; Fiesta Day; Easter; Independence Day; Thanksgiving; Christmas Eve & Day. ♿
Attendance: 118,296 (estimated)
Membership: Student, Educator, Artist & Senior $25; Individual $40; Dual & Household $75; Associate $150; Connector $250; Supporter $500; Patron $750. Corporate: Enthusiast $1,000-$2,499; Executive $2,500-$4,999; Advocate $5,000-$9,999; Catalyst $10,000-$14,999; Leader $15,000-$24,999; Partner $25,000 & up.

BLUE STAR CONTEMPORARY ART CENTER, 116 Blue Star, San Antonio, TX 78204-1713. Tel.: 210-227-6960. Fax: 210-229-9412.
Web Site: www.bluestarart.org
Founded: 1986.
Congressional District: 20
Key Personnel: Exec. Dir. & Pres., Bill FitzGibbons; Chm. (V), Ed Valdespino; Asst. Dir. & Dir. Education, Roland Mazuca; Exec. Asst. & Office Mgr., Karen Branson; Exhibitions & Program Mgr., Zinnia Salcedo; Grant Writer, Libby Tilley; Asst. Preparator, Tommy Gregory; IT Specialist, Kyle Olson.
Personnel Profile: Full-Time Paid 4; Part-Time Paid 3; Part-Time Volunteers 10; Interns 12.
Governing Authority: private; nonprofit organization. Parent Institution: Contemporary Art for San Antonio. Tax-exempt: 501(c)(3).
Contemporary Art Museum
Collections: contemporary art by Alex Rubio, James Surls, Vincent Valdez, Jesus Morales, Dan Borris, Ricardo Legorreta & Graciela Hurbide.
Facilities: 13,000 sq. ft. exhibit space. Museum-related items for sale.
Activities: arts festivals; concerts; formal education programs for all ages; lectures; loan, participatory & traveling exhibitions; rental gallery.
Publications: quarterly newsletter.
Hours & Admission Prices: Gallery: Wed.-Sun. 12-6. Office: Mon.-Fri. 9-6. No charge; donations accepted. Closed New Year's Day; Martin Luther King Jr. Day; Memorial Day; Independence Day; Labor Day; Thanksgiving & day after; Christmas Eve & Day. ♿
Attendance: 125,000 (estimated)
Membership: Artist $25; Artist Family $35; Bluestar $40; Bluestar Family $60; Contemporaries $250; Contemporaries Family $350; Society de Cien $1,000.

BUCKHORN SALOON & MUSEUM, 318 E. Houston St., San Antonio, TX 78205-1816. Tel.: 210-247-4000. Fax: 210-247-4020.
E-mail: sales@buckhornmuseum.com
Web Site: www.buckhornmuseum.com
Founded: 1881.
Congressional District: 20
Key Personnel: Dir., Dave George.
Governing Authority: county. Parent Institution: Gunnison County Pioneer & Historical Society. Subsidiary Institution: Pioneer Museum.
Natural History Museum; Texas - San Antonio historic house site.
Collections: wildlife; marine; birds; cowboy collectables & gear; cowboy art; Texas History Wax Museum. Historic House: Texas History Hall.
Facilities: 38,000 sq. ft. exhibit space; banquet hall.
Activities: guided tours; lectures.
Publications: brochures & footnotes of the Buckhorn.
Hours & Admission Prices: Memorial Day to Labor Day daily 10-6; Sept.-May daily 10-5. Adults $10.99, seniors $9.99, children 4-11 $7.99. Children 3 & under no charge. Closed Thanksgiving; Christmas. ♿
Attendance: 200,000

CASA NAVARRO STATE HISTORICAL PARK, 228 S. Laredo St., San Antonio, TX 78207-4544. Tel.: 210-226-4801. Fax: 210-226-4801.
E-mail: casa-navarro@thc.state.tx.us
Web Site: www.thc.state.tx.us/hsites/hs_navarro.aspx?site=navarro
Founded: 1964.
Congressional District: 20
Key Personnel: Site Mgr., Jose Zapata; Chief Cur., Laura DeNormandie-Bass.
Personnel Profile: Full-Time Paid 2.
Governing Authority: state. Parent Institution: Texas Historical Commission, P.O. Box 12276, Austin, TX 78711-2276. Tel. 512-463-6100.
Historic Site & House Museum: c.1850 home site of Texas patriot, Jose Antonio Navarro.
Collections: period furnishings; early Texas decorative arts; items pertaining to the lifestyle of a Tejano family of San Antonio.
Research Fields: career of Jose Antonio Navarro; Southwestern, Spanish Colonial & Mexican history.
Facilities: Publications for sale.
Activities: guided tours.
Publications: pamphlet.
Hours & Admission Prices: Tues.-Sun. 9-4. Adults $2; children 12 & under no charge. ♿
Attendance: 4,277 (accurate)

GUINNESS WORLD RECORDS MUSEUM, 329 Alamo Plaza, San Antonio, TX 78205-2667. Tel.: 210-226-2828.
World Records Museum.
Collections: world record facts, feats & record holders; photographs; personal artifacts; movie memorabilia.
Hours & Admission Prices: Sun.-Thurs. 10-10, Fri.-Sat. 10 am-12 am. Adults 13 & over $15.95, children 4-12 $8.95.

INSTITUTE OF TEXAN CULTURES, (M), 851 E. Durango Blvd., San Antonio, TX 78205-3296. Mailing Address: 801 S. Bowie, San Antonio, TX 78205-3296. Tel.: 210-458-2300. Fax: 210-458-2380.
E-mail: itcweb@utsa.edu
Web Site: www.texancultures.com
Founded: 1968.
Congressional District: 21
Key Personnel: Exec. Dir., Tim Gette; Dir. Production, Matt Solorio; Dir. Texas Folklife Festival, Jo Ann Andera; Dir. Volunteer Programs, Mary Ellen Smith; Dir. Admin. & Budgets, Pat Gamez-Bryant.
Personnel Profile: Part-Time Volunteers 350.
Governing Authority: state; university. Parent Institution: University of Texas at San Antonio. Tax-exempt.
Educational center for the history & diverse cultures of Texas.
Collections: 3.5 million historical photographs.
Research Fields: humanities; ethnic history; history; folklore; multicultural studies.
Facilities: 6,500-vol. non-circulating research library available to the public; 200-seat auditorium; conference center with AV capabilities.
Activities: guided tours; lectures; gallery talks; cultural festivals; formally

organized education programs for children, adults, undergraduate & graduate college students; docent program; inter-museum loan, permanent, temporary & traveling exhibitions; outreach program to the state. Museum Sponsors: Texas Folklife Festival.

Publications: pamphlet series, The Texians and Texans; books, The Melting Pot; Texans One and All; The Texas Rangers: Images & Incidents; The Swedish Texans; With Domingo Leal In San Antonio; The Irish Texans; Journey To Pleasant Hill: The Civil War Letters of Capt. E.P. Petty; Reflections on Texas, A Teacher's Guide To The Institute of Texan Cultures; Vaquero: Genesis of the Texas Cowboy; The Hungarian Texans; The German Texans; The Polish Texans; Exploration in Texas Ancient and Otherwise, With Thoughts on the Nature of Evidence; The Japanese Texans, The English Texans; Echoes of the Past: The Cowboy Poetry of Melvin Whipple; Texans: A Story of Texan Cultures for Young People; The Irish Texans.

Hours & Admission Prices: Tues.-Sat. 10-5, Sun. 12-5. Adults $8, seniors over 65 $7, military & children 3-11 $6; discounts for AAM members, tours & school groups; children under 2 & members no charge. Closed New Year's Day; Easter; Thanksgiving; Christmas. ♿

Attendance: 200,000 (estimated)

Membership: Educator $25; Senior 65 & over $35; Individual $50; Family $75.

THE MAGIC LANTERN CASTLE MUSEUM, (M), 1419 Austin Hwy., San Antonio, TX 78209-4337. Tel.: 210-805-0011. Fax: 210-822-1226.

E-mail: castle@magiclanterns.org

Web Site: www.magiclanterns.org

Founded: 1991.

Key Personnel: C.E.O. & Cur., Jack Judson.

Personnel Profile: Full-Time Volunteers 2; Part-Time Paid 6; Part-Time Volunteers 2.

Governing Authority: private sole ownership; nonprofit.

Audiovisual slide & Film Museum.

Collections: concentration on magic lanterns from 1700s into the 20th-century; glass slides, prints, books, accessories & related paraphernalia; worldwide scientific instruments for optical projection.

Research Fields: history of the magic lantern throughout the world.

Facilities: library; 50-seat auditorium; 4,000 sq. ft. exhibit space; 1,000 sq. ft. research area.

Activities: guided tours; lectures; demonstrations.

Hours & Admission Prices: by appointment, request or invitation. No charge. Closed state & national holidays.

Attendance: 2,000 (estimated)

* **MCNAY ART MUSEUM, (M),** 6000 N. New Braunfels Ave., San Antonio, TX 78209-4618. Mailing Address: P.O. Box 6069, San Antonio, TX 78209-0069. Tel.: 210-824-5368. Fax: 210-824-0218.

E-mail: info@mcnayart.org

Web Site: www.mcnayart.org

Formerly: Marion Koogler McNay Art Museum

Founded: 1950.

Congressional District: 21

Key Personnel: Dir., William J. Chiego; Pres., Mrs. J. R. Hurd; Chief Cur., Cur. Art after 1945, Rene Paul Barilleaux; Cur. Education, Rose M. Glennon; Chief Devel. Officer, Colleen Kelly; Head Librarian, Ann Jones; C.O.O. & Controller, Bryan Dome; Cur. Prints & Drawings, Lyle Williams; Cur. Tobin Collection of Theatre Arts, Jody Blake; Collections Mgr. & Exhibitions Coord., Heather Lammers; Mgr. Bldg. & Grounds, Robert Sanderson; Museum Store Mgr., Janet Goddard; Security & Visitor Svcs. Mgr., James Jones.

Personnel Profile: Full-Time Paid 74; Part-Time Paid 16; Part-Time Volunteers 250; Interns 2.

Governing Authority: nonprofit organization. Tax-exempt: 501(c)(3).

Fine Arts Museum.

Collections: modern art; 19th- to 20th-century European & American paintings; graphic arts & sculpture; arts and crafts of New Mexico; Medieval & Rennaisance art; theatre arts collection of books, sketches, paintings & maquettes relating to the opera, ballet & musical stage.

Major Exhibits: An Impressionist Sensibility: The Halff Collection, 2/3/10-5/9/10; Truth Beauty: Pictorialism and the Photograph as Art, 1845-1945 (T), 2/3/10-5/9/10; Ellen Phelan: Theme and Variations, 1972-2010 (T), 6/9/10-9/5/10; Landscapes from the Age of Impressionism, 10/6/10-1/2/11.

Research Fields: painting; sculpture; graphics; theatre arts.

Facilities: 30,000-vol. library of art reference material; 226-seat lecture hall; auditorium; learning centers; sculpture garden; teacher resource center.

Activities: lectures; films; gallery talks; concerts; seminars; teacher workshops.

Publications: annual report; exhibition catalogs; members magazine, Impressions.

Hours & Admission Prices: Tues.-Wed. & Fri. 10-4, Thurs. 10-9, Sat. 10-5, Sun. 12-5. Adults $8; students, seniors 65 & over, & active military $5; discount to AAM members; children 12 & under and members no charge. Closed New Year's Day; Independence Day; Thanksgiving; Christmas. ♿

Attendance: 125,500 (estimated)

Membership: Individual $45; Family/Dual $75; Supporting $150; Contributing $250; Sustaining $500; Patron $750; Associate $1,500; Sponsor $2,500; Benefactor $5,000; Philanthropist $10,000; Director's Circle $25,000.

PIONEERS, TRAIL DRIVERS AND TEXAS RANGERS MEMORIAL MUSEUM, 3805 Broadway, San Antonio, TX 78209-6309. Mailing Address: P.O. Box 6869, San Antonio, TX 78209-0869. Tel.: 210-822-9011.

E-mail: gccarnes@ktc.com

Founded: 1936.

Congressional District: 20

Key Personnel: Pres. (V), Pat Halpin; Sec., Peg Gerhardt; Museum Shop Mgr., Peggy Coleman.

Personnel Profile: Full-Time Paid 3; Full-Time Volunteers 2; Part-Time Volunteers 20.

Governing Authority: nonprofit. Parent Institution: Texas Pioneers, Old Trail Drivers & Former Texas Rangers. Tax-exempt.

History Museum.

Collections: photographs & relics that depict life in early Texas (1830-1900); artifacts & gun collections belonging to former Texas Rangers; saddles, branding irons, items used during trail drives and clothing, pioneer furniture & household items; early 1800s-present, Texas Ranger history.

Research Fields: history of former rangers, pioneers & cattle drivers of Texas.

Facilities: Museum-related items & books of Texas history for sale.

Activities: guided tours; permanent exhibitions.

Hours & Admission Prices: May-Aug. Mon.-Sat. 10-5, Sun. 12-5; Sept.-April Mon.-Thurs. 11-4, Fri.-Sat. 10-4, Sun. 12-4. Adults $5, senior citizens $3, children 6-12 $1; discounts to AAM & ICOM members & groups; members & children under 6 no charge. Closed New Year's Day; Thanksgiving; Christmas. ♿

Attendance: 24,000 (estimated)

Membership: Annual $25.

SAN ANTONIO ART LEAGUE MUSEUM, 130 King William St., San Antonio, TX 78204-1311. Tel.: 210-223-1140.

E-mail: saalm@att.net

Web Site: www.saalm.org

Founded: 1912.

Key Personnel: Chm. (V), Helen Fey

Art Museum.

Collections: paintings; graphic art; photography; ceramics; sculpture; drawings; silverware; furniture; fabric; wall hangings.

Activities: lectures.

Hours & Admission Prices: Tues.-Sat. 10-2. No charge; donations accepted. ♿

Attendance: 500

Membership: Individual $35; Family $50; Supporting $100 & above; Sustaining $250 & above; Patron $500 & above.

SAN ANTONIO BOTANICAL GARDEN, 555 Funston Place, San Antonio, TX 78209-6631. Tel.: 210-207-3250. Fax: 210-207-3274. TDD: 210-207-3255.

Web Site: www.sabot.org

Founded: 1977.

Key Personnel: Bd. Chm. (V), Claire Alexander; Dir., Bob Brackman; Museum Shop Mgr., Cynthia Reed.

Personnel Profile: Full-Time Paid 28; Part-Time Paid 2; Part-Time Volunteers 100; Interns 1.

Governing Authority: municipal. Parent Institution: City of San Antonio, TX. Subsidiary Institution: San Antonio Botanical Center Society. Tax-exempt: 501(c)(3).

Botanical Garden.

Collections: woody & herbaceous native plant material from the regions of East Texas, South Texas, & Edwards Plateau; neo-tropical flora in the Lucile Halsell Conservatory. Historic Buildings: 1840 Schumacher House; 1860 East Texas log cabin; 1896 Sullivan carriage house & stables.

Major Exhibits: Play Houses & Forts, 7/10-10/10.

Research Fields: endangered plant species of Texas.

Facilities: Horticultural books & other botanical items for sale.

Activities: guided tours; lectures; concerts; children's garden; summer children's courses; docent program.

Publications: quarterly newsletter.

Hours & Admission Prices: Daily 9-5. Adults $7, senior citizens, students & military $5, children 3-13 $4; discount to groups; AHS members & members no charge. Closed New Year's Day; Thanksgiving; Christmas. ♿

Attendance: 100,000 (estimated)

Membership: Individual $45; Family $60; Esperanza $100; Ceniza $250; Mountain Laurel $500; Wisteria $1,000.

SAN ANTONIO CHILDREN'S MUSEUM, 305 E. Houston St., San Antonio, TX 78205-1802. Tel.: 210-212-4453. Fax: 210-242-1313.
E-mail: lupita@sakids.org
Web Site: www.sakids.org
Founded: 1995.
Key Personnel: Exec. Dir., Chris Sinick; Pres., Patricia Wilson.
Personnel Profile: Full-Time Paid 20; Part-Time Paid 6; Part-Time Volunteers 100.
Governing Authority: private; nonprofit organization. Tax-exempt: 501(c)(3).
Children's Museum.
Collections: hands-on exhibits.
Hours & Admission Prices: Feb.-May Mon.-Fri. 9-4, Sat. 9-6, Sun. 12-4; Sept.-Jan. Tues.-Fri. 9-4, Sat. 9-6, Sun. 12-4. Adults $7; children under 2 & members no charge. Closed Good Friday; Easter; Battle of Flowers Parade; Independence Day; Thanksgiving; Christmas Eve & Day. ♿
Attendance: 144,000 (accurate)
Membership: Family & Grandparent $60; Extended Family $75; Family Sharing $85; ACM Reciprocal $100.

SAN ANTONIO CONSERVATION SOCIETY, 107 King William St., San Antonio, TX 78204-1312. Tel.: 210-224-6163. Fax: 210-224-6168.
E-mail: conserve@saconservation.org
Web Site: www.saconservation.org
Founded: 1924.
Congressional District: 20
Key Personnel: Exec. Dir., Bruce MacDougal; Pres., Marcie Ince; Administrative Asst., Glory Bohne.
Personnel Profile: Full-Time Paid 18; Part-Time Paid 3.
Governing Authority: society. Branch Museum: 1876 Steves Homestead, 509 King William St., San Antonio, Tx. Tel: 210-225-5924. Tax-exempt: 501(c)(3).
Historic House Museums: Wulff House (library only; no tours); 1840-1860 Yturri-Edmunds Historic Site; 1876 Steves Homestead House Museum.
Collections: Steves Homestead: decorative arts; Victorian period furniture; family memorabilia & treasures. Yturri-Edmunds: family memorabilia; photos; local history, preservation & restoration projects.
Research Fields: local history; preservation & restoration projects; architectural history.
Facilities: 3,000-vol. library of books pertaining to history & preservation; slide collection available for research.
Activities: guided tours; permanent & temporary exhibitions; food festivals; historic preservation seminars; speakers bureau.
Publications: monthly, San Antonio Conservation Society Newsletter; brochures, King William Walking Tour; Texas Star Trail; Steves Homestead.
Hours & Admission Prices: Yturri Edmunds: tours by appointment only. Steves Homestead: daily 10-4:15. Adults $6, seniors & groups $4, students & military $3; children under 12 no charge. Closed most major holidays. ♿
Attendance: 11,000 (accurate)
Membership: Associate & Active $25.

SAN ANTONIO MISSIONS NATIONAL HISTORICAL PARK, Visitor Center, 6701 San Jose Dr., San Antonio, TX 78210. Mailing Address: 2202 Roosevelt Ave., San Antonio, TX 78210-4919. Tel.: 210-534-8833. Fax: 210-534-1106.
E-mail: saan_administration@nps.gov
Web Site: www.nps.gov/saan
Founded: 1978.
Congressional District: 28
Key Personnel: Park Supt., Stephen Whitesell.
Personnel Profile: Full-Time Paid 45; Part-Time Volunteers 120.
Governing Authority: federal. National Park Service, Dept. of Interior. Washington, DC. Tax-exempt.
National Historic Park: comprised of the following four Spanish missions: 1720 San Jose Y San Miguel de Aguayo; 1731 La Purisima Concepcion; 1731 San Juan Capistrano; 1731 San Francisco de la Espada.
Collections: anthropology; archaeology; archives; Indian artifacts; Spanish Colonial collections; technology.
Research Fields: Spanish Colonial history & architecture; building stabilization & preservation.
Facilities: visitor center.
Activities: self-guided tours; teacher's guide; temporary & permanent exhibitions; ranger programs; film.
Publications: San Antonio Missions National Historical Park Brochure (English & Spanish).
Hours & Admission Prices: Daily 9-5. No charge; donations accepted. Closed New Year's Day; Thanksgiving; Christmas. ♿
Attendance: 1,400,000 (estimated)

∗ **SAN ANTONIO MUSEUM OF ART, (M),** 200 W. Jones Ave., San Antonio, TX 78215-1406. Tel.: 210-978-8100 & 8111. Fax: 210-978-8182.
E-mail: info@samuseum.org
Web Site: www.samuseum.org
Founded: 1981.
Congressional District: 1
Key Personnel: Dir. of Adminstration & Finance, Polly Vidaurri; Deputy Dir., Emily Jones; Dir. & Cur. Latin American Art, Dr. Marion Oettinger, Jr.; Chm. Bd., Karen Hixon; Dir. Operations, Dan Walton; Registrar, Karen Baker; AT&T Dir. Education, Olga Sample Davis; Communications Mgr., Leigh Baldwin; Museum Shop Mgr., Arleen West; Dir. Exhibits, Tim Foerster.
Personnel Profile: Full-Time Paid 43; Full-Time Volunteers 2; Part-Time Paid 14; Part-Time Volunteers 85; Interns 10.
Governing Authority: nonprofit organization. Tax-exempt: 501(c)(3).
Art Museum: housed in restored turn-of-the-century Lone Star Brewing Company.
Collections: American & contemporary art; American painting, sculpture, glass from 18th-, 19th- & 20th-centuries; Ancient Egyptian, Greek & Roman art; period glass; Asian art; contemporary Latin American art; 17th- to 20th-century European paintings & works on paper; Irish silver; Islamic art; Latin American folk art; Oceanic art; 20th-century photography; pre-columbian art; Spanish Colonial art; Texas furniture, paintings & decorative arts.
Research Fields: Latin American art; Asian art; Ancient Egyptian, Greek & Roman antiquities; American & Contemporary art.
Facilities: 188-seat auditorium. Museum-related items for sale.
Activities: guided tours; lectures; films; gallery talks; concerts; formally organized education programs for children & adults; docent program & council; loan, temporary, permanent & traveling exhibitions; annual endowed symposia.
Publications: exhibition catalogs; quarterly calendar & newsletter; teacher resource guides; special collection catalogues.
Hours & Admission Prices: Sun. 12-6, Tues. 10-9, Wed.-Sat. 10-5. Closed New Year's Day; Easter; Fiesta Friday; Thanksgiving; Christmas. ♿
Attendance: 67,238 (accurate)
Membership: Senior Citizen 65 & over $35; Individual $45; Friends Support Group $50; Senior Family 65 & over $60; Family $75; Sponsor $125; Connoisseur $150; Associate $250; Arte-preneur Support Group $300; Patron $500; Society $1,000; Benefactor $5,000; Leader $10,000; Philanthropist $25,000. Corporate Levels: Corporate Society $1,000; Corporate Patron $2,500; Corporate Benefactor $5,000; Corporate Leader $10,000; Corporate Circle $25,000 & up.

SAN ANTONIO ZOOLOGICAL SOCIETY, 3903 N. Saint Mary's St., San Antonio, TX 78212-3173. Tel.: 210-734-7184. Fax: 210-734-7291.
E-mail: information@sazoo-aq.org
Web Site: www.sazoo-aq.org
Founded: 1914.
Congressional District: 20
Key Personnel: Exec. Dir., J. Stephen McCusker; Pres. (V), Joe N. Haynes; Visitor Svcs. Mgr., Ron Kipp.
Personnel Profile: Full-Time Paid 180; Part-Time Paid 15; Part-Time Volunteers 225; Interns 3.
Governing Authority: society. Parent Institution: San Antonio Zoological Society. Tax-exempt: 501(c)(3).
Zoo.
Collections: birds; mammals; reptiles; aquarium.
Research Fields: animal reproduction; behavioral research.
Facilities: 547-vol. library of technical & general reference material relating to zoos & zoo operation available for use on premises; education center. Publications & gifts for sale.
Activities: guided tours; filmstrip programs; summer programs; elephant behavioral training demonstration; keeper connections presentations.
Publications: quarterly news magazine, News From the Zoo.
Hours & Admission Prices: Summer: daily 9-6. Winter: daily 9-5. Adults $9, senior citizens 62 & over and children 3-11 $7; discount to school groups & members of reciprocal zoos; members no charge. ♿
Attendance: 900,000 (estimated)
Membership: Add One $20; Senior Citizen Individual $30; Individual & Senior Citizen Couple $40; Family & Individual Plus One $60; Family Plus One $80; Contributing $100; Benefactor $250; Patron $500; Zoo Master $1,000.

SOUTHWEST SCHOOL OF ART & CRAFT, 300 Augusta St., San Antonio, TX 78205-1216. Tel.: 210-224-1848. Fax: 210-224-9337.
E-mail: information@swschool.org
Web Site: www.swschool.org
Founded: 1965.

Key Personnel: Dir., Paula Owen; Assoc. Cur., Kathy Armstrong; Museum Shop Mgr., Clare Watters.
Personnel Profile: Full-Time Paid 32; Part-Time Paid 120; Part-Time Volunteers 300; Interns 2.
Governing Authority: nonprofit organization. Tax-exempt: 501(c)(3).
Contemporary Art Center & History Museum.
Collections: changing exhibitions; various artistic media.
Major Exhibits: Vincent Valdez, 2/11/10-4/11/10; The Miniature Worlds of Bruce Metcalf (T), 2/11/10-4/11/10; Eden Revisited: The Ceramic Art of Kart Weisser (T), 4/29/10-6/27/10; Kent Rush, 9/23/10-11/28/10.
Research Fields: studio arts.
Facilities: educational & studio facilities; 100-seat restaurant; 3,500 sq. ft. exhibition space.
Activities: guided tours; lectures; arts festivals; organized educational programs; classes; rental facilities.
Publications: brochures; invitations; catalogues.
Hours & Admission Prices: Exhibitions: Mon.-Sat. 9-5. Museum Shop: Mon.-Sat. 10-5. No charge; donations accepted. Closed major holidays. ♿
Attendance: 250,000 (estimated)
Membership: Individual $45; Family $75; Patron $150.

SPANISH GOVERNOR'S PALACE, 105 Plaza de Armas, San Antonio, TX 78205-2412. Tel.: 210-224-0601. Fax: 210-223-5562.
E-mail: charlotte.boord@sanantonio.gov
Web Site: www.sanantoniocvb.com/things/attract.htm
Founded: 1749.
Key Personnel: Dir. Downtown Operations, Paula X. Stallcup; Asst Dir. Downtown Operations, Colleen Swain; Museum Asst., Charlotte Boord.
Personnel Profile: Full-Time Paid 3.
Governing Authority: municipal. Parent Institution: City of San Antonio. Subsidiary Institution: Dept. of Downtown Operations. Tax-exempt.
Historic Building: 1722 Spanish Governor's Palace.
Collections: Spanish culture; history; paintings; decorative arts; agriculture; graphics; sculpture; interpretation.
Facilities: botanical garden. Postcards & historical literature for sale.
Activities: self-guided tours.
Publications: brochure.
Hours & Admission Prices: Tues.-Sat. 9-5, Sun. 10-5. Adults $2, seniors 60 & over, military & groups of 10 or more $1.50, children 7-13 $1; discounts to AAM & ICOM members; children under 7 no charge. Closed New Year's Day; Easter; Battle of Flowers Parade Friday; Thanksgiving; Christmas. ♿

STEVES HOMESTEAD, 509 King William St., San Antonio, TX 78204-1411. Tel.: 210-225-5924 & 227-9160. Fax: 210-223-9014.
E-mail: dchenoweth@saconservation.org
Web Site: www.saconservation.org/tours/steves.htm
Founded: 1924.
Congressional District: 20
Key Personnel: Pres., Rollette Schreckenghost; Exec. Dir., Bruce MacDougal; Administrative Asst., Glory Bohne; House Museum Mgr., Diana Chenoweth.
Personnel Profile: Full-Time Paid 2; Part-Time Paid 4; Part-Time Volunteers 10.
Governing Authority: society. Parent Institution: San Antonio Conservation Society Foundation, 107 King William St., San Antonio, TX 78204. Branch Museum: 1840-60 Yturri-Edmunds Historic Site, 128 Mission Rd., 210-534-8237. Tax-exempt: 501(c)(3).
History Museum.
Collections: local history; preservation & restoration projects; photos; Victorian period furniture; decorative arts. Historic Houses: 1876 Steves Homestead; Wulff House (library only; no tours); 1840-1860 Yturri-Edmunds Historic Site.
Research Fields: local history; preservation & restoration projects; architectural history.
Facilities: 3,000-vol. library of books pertaining to history & preservation; visitor center. San Antonio Conservation Society Office: slide collection available for research.
Activities: guided tours; permanent & temporary exhibitions; food festivals; historic preservation seminars; speakers bureau.
Publications: monthly, San Antonio Conservation Newsletter; brochures; King William Walking Tour; Texas Star Trail; Steve Homestead brochure.
Hours & Admission Prices: Steves Homestead: daily 10-4:15; last tour 3:30. Adults $6, seniors & groups $5, students & military $4; children under 12 & members no charge. Wulff House: no tours; research library only. Mon.-Thurs. 10-3. Call for information for other sites. Yturri-Edmunds by appointment only. Closed most major holidays.
Attendance: 10,154 (accurate)
Membership: Associate & Active (voting) $25.

TEXAS TRANSPORTATION MUSEUM, 11731 Wetmore Rd., San Antonio, TX 78247-3606. Tel.: 210-490-3554.
E-mail: hugh@txtransportationmuseum.org
Web Site: www.txtransportationmuseum.org
Founded: 1964.
Key Personnel: Dir. & Museum Shop Mgr., Hugh Hemphill; Chm. (V), Pat Halpin.
Personnel Profile: Full-Time Paid 1; Part-Time Paid 1; Part-Time Volunteers 200.
Governing Authority: Tax-exempt: 501(c)(3).
Transportation Museum.
Collections: area transportation history; model railroads; automobiles; trucks; horse carriages.
Activities: train rides; fire truck rides.
Publications: The Dust Collector.
Hours & Admission Prices: Thurs.-Fri. 9-3, Sat.-Sun. 10-5. Adults $8, children under 12 $5; discounts to military & senior citizens. ♿
Attendance: 10,000 (accurate)
Membership: Annual $35.

THE UNIVERSITY OF TEXAS AT SAN ANTONIO, ART GALLERY, 6900 N. Loop 1604, W., San Antonio, TX 78249-1130. Tel.: 210-458-4352. Fax: 210-458-4356.
Web Site: altamira.arts.utsa.edu
Founded: 1982.
Congressional District: 21
Key Personnel: Dir., Scott Scherer.
Personnel Profile: Full-Time Paid 1.
Governing Authority: university. Tax-exempt.
University Art Gallery.
Collections: changing exhibits; portfolios of Elliott Erwitt & Manuel Alvarez Bravo.
Research Fields: contemporary regional & national art.
Facilities: security storage; preparation & photography area; fabrication shop.
Activities: guided tours; lectures; films; practicum in Gallery work; participatory, loan, temporary & traveling exhibitions.
Publications: catalogues, Texans Past and Present; The Soul of Mexico; Catherine Lee Catalogue; Biennial Faculty Exhibition; Aberrations; Mapping.
Hours & Admission Prices: Sept.-May Mon.-Fri. 10-4, Sun. 1-4. No charge; donations accepted. Closed university holidays. ♿
Attendance: 3,000 (estimated)

* **WITTE MUSEUM, (M),** 3801 Broadway, San Antonio, TX 78209-6396. Tel.: 210-357-1900 & 1910. Fax: 210-357-1882.
E-mail: witte@wittemuseum.org
Web Site: www.wittemuseum.org
Founded: 1926.
Congressional District: 9
Key Personnel: Pres., Marise McDermott; Dir., Mimi Quintanilla; Dir. Devel., Nancy Hunt; Dir. Mktg. & Public Rels., Jim Dalglish; Dir. Admin. Svcs., Bea Abercrombie; Cur., Michael Haynes, Ph.D.; Cur. Archives & Registrar, Rebecca Huffstutler; Exhibits Mgr., John Edmundson; Dir. Guest Rels., Ralph Voight.
Personnel Profile: Full-Time Paid 34; Part-Time Paid 45; Part-Time Volunteers 103; Interns 8.
Governing Authority: nonprofit organization. Tax-exempt: 501(c)(3).
History Museum: located in Brackenridge Park.
Collections: Texana items; Texas paintings; textiles & costumes; wildlife & ecology exhibits & dioramas; Southwest Indian artifacts; dinosaurs; participatory exhibits; Texas stone artifacts; Filipino artifacts; historical photographs; Lower Pecos archaeology; Central Plains Indian artifacts; cowboy & western artifacts; Hertzberg Circus collection; firearms. Historic Houses: 1753 Ruiz House; 1835 Navarro House; 1840 Twohig House; two reconstructed log cabins; H-E-B Science Treehouse.
Research Fields: anthropology; basketry; archaeology of the lower Pecos; history: Texas art & decorative arts, costumes & textiles.
Facilities: library of historical photographs & 2,200 slides all pertaining to Texas & natural history, archaeology, decorative, primitive & Texas art available for research on premise by appointment only; 300-seat auditorium; H.E.B. Science Treehouse; native plant garden. Gift items for sale.
Activities: lectures; theatre; permanent & temporary exhibitions; Museum-School programs for children, adults & families; concerts; live science demonstrations.
Publications: books, Mary Bonner: Impressions of a Printmaker; San Antonio Was; Touring Texas: Through the Eyes of an Artists; Ancient Texans: Rock Art & Lifeways Along the Lower Pecos; Snakes of Bexar County; Art for History's Sake: The Texas Collection of the Witte Museum; Prehistoric Basketry of the Lower Pecos, Texas; Patterns With Potential; Tischlermeister Jahn; Iwonski in Texas, Painter and Citizen.

Hours & Admission Prices: Mon. & Wed.-Sat. 10-5, Tues. 10-8, Sun. 12-5. Adults $7, senior citizens 65 & over $6, children 4-11 $5; discounts to groups, Texas Assoc. of Museums, ASTC, AASLH, AAM & ICOM members; children 3 & under, members & Tues. 3-8 no charge. Closed Thanksgiving; Christmas. ♿
Attendance: 200,000 (accurate)
Membership: Individual $35; Senior Family $55; Family $60; Inventor $125; Explorer $250; Navigator $500; Quillin Society Sustainer $1,000; Quillin Society Benefactor $5,000; Quillin Society Diamond Circle of Giving $7,500.

WOODEN NICKEL HISTORICAL MUSEUM, 345 Austin Rd., San Antonio, TX 78209-6933. Tel.: 210-829-1291. Fax: 210-832-8965.
E-mail: museum@wooden-nickel.net
Web Site: www.wooden-nickel.net
Founded: 1998.
Key Personnel: C.E.O., Herb Hornung.
Personnel Profile: Part-Time Volunteers 2.
Governing Authority: private; not for profit.
General Museum.
Collections: wooden nickels 1931-present; printing plates; printing equipment.
Facilities: 2,000 sq. ft. exhibit space. Museum-related items for sale.
Hours & Admission Prices: Mon.-Fri. 9-5, Sat. by appointment. No charge.
Attendance: 400 (estimated)

San Elizario

LOS PORTALES MUSEUM & INFORMATION CENTER, 1521 San Elizario Rd., San Elizario, TX 78949. Tel.: 915-851-1682.
History Museum.
Collections: artifacts & memorabilia pertaining to San Elizario.
Hours & Admission Prices: Tues.-Sat. 10-2, Sun. 12-4. No charge.

San Marcos

CALABOOSE AFRICAN AMERICAN HISTORY MUSEUM, 200 W. Martin Luther King Jr. Dr., San Marcos, TX 78666-5522. Mailing Address: 1421 W. Hopkins St., San Marcos, TX 78666-4120. Tel.: 512-393-8421.
Web Site: www.sanmarcosarts.com/calaboose.htm
Key Personnel: Dir., Mrs. Johnnie Armstead
History Museum.
Collections: local black history; Buffalo soldiers; period artifacts.
Hours & Admission Prices: Sat. 1-5; other times by appointment. Suggested Donation: $3.

CASETA: CENTER FOR THE ADVANCEMENT OF EARLY TEXAS ART, Texas State University-San Marcos, 601 University Dr., JC Kellam 150, San Marcos, TX 78666-4684. Tel.: 512-245-1986. Fax: 512-245-1980.
E-mail: cd26@txstate.edu
Web Site: www.caseta.org
Key Personnel: Exec. Dir., Olivia Thompson; Chm., Robert Summers
Art Museum.
Collections: works by Texas artists including paintings; sculpture & watercolor; art history.
Hours & Admission Prices: Call for hours.

LBJ MUSEUM OF SAN MARCOS, 131 N. Guadalupe, San Marcos, TX 78666-5606. Mailing Address: P.O. Box 3, San Marcos, TX 78667-0003. Tel.: 512-353-3300.
Web Site: www.lbjmuseum.com/contactus.htm
Founded: 1997.
Congressional District: 14
Key Personnel: Pres. (V), Pat Murdock.
Personnel Profile: Full-Time Paid 1.
Governing Authority: Tax-exempt.
History Museum.
Collections: LBJ-related campaign memorabilia; presidential buttons; personal artifacts; sample voting machine; hats; photographs; manuscripts; periodicals; audiovisual materials.
Facilities: library; archives.
Activities: school programs; internships; research; rental facilities; special events; presentations.
Publications: LBJ Connection.
Hours & Admission Prices: Thurs.-Fri. & Sun. 1-5, Sat. 10-5. No charge; donations accepted. ♿
Membership: Sponsor $100; Educator $250; Senatorial $1,000; Presidential $10,000.

Sanderson

TERRELL COUNTY MEMORIAL MUSEUM, 203 E. Mansfield St., Sanderson, TX 79848. Mailing Address: P.O. Box 702, Sanderson, TX 79848-0702. Tel.: 432-345-2936.
Web Site: www.sandersontx.info/pages/thingstodo/museum.html
Key Personnel: Caretaker, Maria Galvan
History Museum: former home of the Lemmons family.
Collections: railroad memorabilia; period costumes; cowboy & ranching relics; tools; pioneer furnishings; Terrell County history books.
Hours & Admission Prices: Mon.-Fri. 10-12 & 1-3.

Schulenburg

STANZEL MODEL AIRCRAFT MUSEUM, 311 Baumgarten St., Schulenburg, TX 78956-2101. Mailing Address: P.O. Box 6, Schulenburg, TX 78956-0006. Tel.: 979-743-6559. Fax: 979-743-2525.
E-mail: museum@stanzelmuseum.org
Web Site: www.stanzelmuseum.org
Founded: 1999.
Key Personnel: Pres., Robert Stanzel; Vice Pres., Theodore Stanzel; Museum Mgr., Archivist & Museum Shop Mgr., Eugenia Reeves.
Personnel Profile: Part-Time Paid 7.
Governing Authority: private; nonprofit organization. Tax-exempt: 501(c)(3).
Aircraft Museum.
Collections: history of flight; model aircraft; videos; photographs; furnishings; personal artifacts; farmhouse.
Facilities: nature center; theater; farmhouse & garden. Museum-related items for sale.
Activities: guided tours. Annual Event: Air Show.
Hours & Admission Prices: Mon., Wed. & Fri.-Sat. 10:30-4:30, Sun. 1:30-4:30. Adults $2, senior citizens $1; school groups & children under 12 no charge. Closed New Year's Day; Martin Luther King Jr. Day; Presidents' Day; Good Friday; Mother's Day; Memorial Day; Independence Day; Labor Day; Veterans Day; Thanksgiving; Christmas Eve & Day. ♿
Attendance: 4,099 (accurate)

Seabrook

BAY AREA MUSEUM, 5000 Nasa Rd. I, Seabrook, TX 77586. Mailing Address: P.O. Box 58348, Webster, TX 77598-8348. Tel.: 281-326-5950. Fax: 281-326-5950.
Founded: 1984.
Congressional District: 25
Key Personnel: Pres., Peggy Clause; Dir., Joy Smitherman.
Governing Authority: nonprofit. Parent Institution: Lunar Rendezvous, Inc. Tax-exempt.
General Museum: housed in the church which Buzz Aldrin celebrated communion from the surface of the moon in 1969.
Collections: history of the area from late 19th century to the development of NASA; from Arrowheads to astronauts.
Research Fields: local history.
Activities: lectures; loan & temporary exhibitions.
Publications: quarterly newsletter.
Hours & Admission Prices: Sun.-Fri. 1-5, Sat. 10-4. No charge; donations accepted. Closed federal holidays. ♿
Membership: Family $35; Sustaining $50.

Seagraves

SEAGRAVES-LOOP MUSEUM AND ART CENTER INC., Seagraves-Loop Div., 201 Main, Seagraves, TX 79359. Mailing Address: Box 1387, Seagraves, TX 79359-1387. Tel.: 806-546-2810. Fax: 806-546-2810.
Founded: 1974.
Congressional District: 19
Key Personnel: C.E.O., Dan Calfee; Dir., Treas. & Museum Shop Mgr., Leslie McConal; Sec., Penny Hayes.
Personnel Profile: Full-Time Paid 1; Part-Time Paid 1; Part-Time Volunteers 3.
Governing Authority: county government. Tax-exempt: 501(c)(3).
Historic Building: built in 1926, survived a town fire.
Collections: barbed wire collections; Indian artifacts; early settlers artifacts; Santa Fe depot with caboose; military exhibit; restored 1937 fire truck.
Research Fields: local history; art; collections.
Activities: Museum Sponsors: arts & craft show; spring harvest festival; school tours in May.
Hours & Admission Prices: Mon.-Fri. 9-12 & 1-5. No charge; donations accepted. ♿
Membership: Student $1; Individual $5; Family $10; Associate $25; Contributing $50; Sustaining $100; Life $500.

Seguin

FIEDLER MEMORIAL MUSEUM, Texas Lutheran University, Seguin, TX 78155. Tel.: 830-372-8038. Fax: 830-372-8188.
Web Site: www.txlutheran.edu
Founded: 1973.
Congressional District: 23
Key Personnel: Dir., Evelyn Fiedler Streng.
Governing Authority: college & individual; nonprofit. Texas Lutheran University, Seguin, TX. Tax-exempt.
Geology Museum.
Collections: rocks, minerals & fossils; New Guinea artifacts; Native American artifacts; geological & geographic slides.
Research Fields: geology.
Facilities: outdoor rock display; open-space classroom; learning center.
Activities: guided tours; lectures; informally organized education programs for children; permanent exhibitions.
Publications: Study Guides to Displays; Rock Walk Guide.
Hours & Admission Prices: Mon.-Fri. 1-5; other times by appointment. No charge. Closed school holidays. ♿

LOS NOGALES MUSEUM, 415 S. River, Seguin, TX 78155. Mailing Address: P.O. Box 245, Seguin, TX 78156-0245. Tel.: 830-379-3257. Fax: 830-379-4685.
Founded: 1952.
Congressional District: 25
Key Personnel: Dir. & Museum Shop Mgr., Greg Ander; Pres. (V), Cristen Ledbetter.
Governing Authority: society. Affiliated with Seguin Conservation Society, P.O. Box 245, Seguin, TX 78155. Tax-exempt: 501(c)(3).
Conservation Society Museum: housed in 1849 building.
Collections: historical items; books; court minutes; early photos; doll house; log cabin; adobe building; calaboose. Historic House: 1894 Queen Anne home; first church built in Seguin as a church.
Research Fields: genealogy.
Activities: guided tours; programs pertaining to history of Seguin.
Publications: County History.
Hours & Admission Prices: May-Oct. Sun. 2-5; other times by appointment. No charge; donations accepted.
Attendance: 2,000
Membership: Individual $15; Family $25; Business $50.

Sherman

C.S. ROBERTS HOUSE MUSEUM, 915 S. Crockett, Sherman, TX 75090. Mailing Address: P.O. Box 159, Sherman, TX 75091-1059. Tel.: 903-893-4067.
Historic House Museum: built in 1896.
Collections: local & family history; period furnishings; personal artifacts.
Activities: rental facilities; lectures; special events; traveling trunk program.
Hours & Admission Prices: Sun. 1-4; other times by appointment. Adults 17 & over $5, senior citizens 55 & over $3, children 11-16 $2; children under 10 no charge.

RED RIVER HISTORICAL MUSEUM, (M), 301 S. Walnut, Sherman, TX 75090-7152. Tel.: 903-893-7623. Fax: 903-892-4303.
Web Site: www.texoma.net/rrhms
Founded: 1976.
Congressional District: 4
Key Personnel: Dir., Marcia K. Rolbiecki.
Personnel Profile: Full-Time Paid 2; Part-Time Paid 2; Part-Time Volunteers 1; Interns 1.
Governing Authority: private; nonprofit organization. Tax-exempt: 501(c)(3).
History Museum: housed in 1914 Andrew Carnegie Library building.
Collections: local & area historic photographs & memorabilia.
Facilities: library. Museum-related items for sale.
Activities: lectures; films; guided tours; hobby workshops; temporary exhibitions. Annual Events: fundraiser in January & July; Arts Festival in September; History Saturday; Craft Saturday.
Publications: newsletter, The Sentinal.
Hours & Admission Prices: Tues.-Sat. 10-4. No charge; donations accepted. Closed Thanksgiving; Christmas.
Attendance: 3,000 (accurate)
Membership: Individual $25; Family $50; Sustainer $100; Sponsor $250; Patron $500; Benefactor $1,000.

Shiner

EDWIN WOLTERS MEMORIAL MUSEUM, 306 S. Ave. I, Shiner, TX 77984. Mailing Address: P.O. Box 308, Shiner, TX 77984-0308. Tel.: 512-594-3774 & 3362. Fax: 512-594-3566.
Founded: 1963.
Key Personnel: Cur., Bernard Siegel, Jr.
Personnel Profile: Full-Time Paid 1; Part-Time Paid 1.
Governing Authority: municipal. Tax-exempt.
General Museum: housed in 1900 home of Edwin Wolters, founder of museum.
Collections: local history; industry; Indian artifacts; archaeology; costumes; botany; dolls; period furniture.
Facilities: old country store.
Activities: guided tours; permanent & temporary exhibitions; displays for children.
Hours & Admission Prices: Mon.-Fri. 8-5, 2nd & 4th Sun. 2-5; groups by appointment. No charge; donations accepted. ♿
Attendance: 741 (accurate)

Sinton

WELDER WILDLIFE FOUNDATION & REFUGE, 10620 Hwy. 77 N., Sinton, TX 78387. Mailing Address: P.O. Box 1400, Sinton, TX 78387-1400. Tel.: 361-364-2643. Fax: 361-364-2650.
E-mail: welderfoundation@welderwildlife.org
Web Site: www.welderwildlife.org
Founded: 1954.
Key Personnel: Dir., Dr. Terry L. Blankenship; Asst. Dir., Dr. Selma N. Glasscock.
Personnel Profile: Full-Time Paid 7; Part-Time Paid 2; Interns 1.
Wildlife Refuge.
Collections: reptiles & amphibians; wildlife paintings; 2,000 bird skins; 500 mammal skins; 300 mounted birds.
Research Fields: wildlife management.
Activities: educational workshops & classes; college courses; training programs for professional teachers; research.
Publications: biennial reports; books.
Hours & Admission Prices: Thurs. 3pm. No charge; donations accepted.
Attendance: 2,500 (accurate)

Slaton

TEXAS AIR MUSEUM, FM 400, Slaton, TX 79364. Mailing Address: P.O. Box 667, Slaton, TX 79364-4192. Tel.: 806-796-7618.
Web Site: www.slaton.tx.us
Founded: 1986.
Congressional District: 27
Key Personnel: C.E.O., Mike Delano; Chm. (V), Malcolm Laing; Bd. Member & Treas., Kristin Snow; Museum Shop Mgr., Steve Oldham.
Personnel Profile: Full-Time Volunteers 2; Part-Time Volunteers 25.
Governing Authority: private; nonprofit organization. Parent Institution: Texas Air Museum, Inc. Subsidiary Institution: TAM Stinson & South Plains Chapter. Tax-exempt.
Aeronautics Museum.
Collections: concentration on aircraft used for warfare, commerce & agriculture, 1904-present; emphasis on aircraft used in WWI & II, Korea, WASPS-Women Military Pilots of WWII & Vietnam.
Research Fields: WWII Axis aircraft & support equipment; female pilots in U.S. aviation.
Facilities: library of books, videos & other printed materials available to public on premises; 22,000 sq. ft. exhibit space; air strip. Museum-related items for sale.
Activities: films; guided tours; lectures; loan & temporary exhibitions; school loan service.
Publications: quarterly newsletter, Airspeed.
Hours & Admission Prices: Sat. 9-4. Adults $5, senior citizens $4, youth 12-16 $3, children 11 & under $2; discounts for groups, AAM & ICOM members; members no charge. Closed New Year's Day; Thanksgiving; Christmas. ♿
Attendance: 6,324 (accurate)
Membership: Annual $40; Individual $250; Corporate $2,000.

Snyder

* **SCURRY COUNTY MUSEUM, (M),** Western Texas College, 6200 College Ave., Snyder, TX 79549-6105. Tel.: 325-573-6107. Fax: 325-573-9321.
E-mail: scm@snydertex.com
Web Site: www.scurrycountymuseum.org
Founded: 1970.

Congressional District: 17
Key Personnel: Dir., Charlene Akers; Pres. (V), Frank Miller; Cur., Shirley Leftwich.
Personnel Profile: Full-Time Paid 1; Full-Time Volunteers 42; Part-Time Paid 2; Part-Time Volunteers 42.
Governing Authority: Parent Institution: Scurry County Museum Association. Tax-exempt: 501(c)(3).
History Museum.
Collections: archives; farming & ranching equipment; frontier furnishings; county records; contemporary prints; Victorian lamps; costumes; local history memorabilia; oil production tools & equipment.
Research Fields: local & regional history.
Facilities: library of law & medical books & county records dating from 19th century to 1960; meeting facilities; classrooms. Museum-related items for sale.
Activities: guided tours; lectures; films; gallery talks; arts festivals; docent program; permanent & temporary exhibitions. Museum Sponsors: Christmas special.
Publications: quarterly newsletter.
Hours & Admission Prices: Summer: Mon.-Thurs. 9-5; other times by appointment; Sept.-June Mon.-Thurs. 9-5, Fri. 9-4. No charge; donations accepted. ♿
Attendance: 4,462 (accurate)
Membership: Individual $20; Family $35; Patron $75; Business & Club $100; Sustaining Patron $250; Benefactor $500; Sustaining Benefactor $1,000.

Sonora

SUTTON COUNTY HISTORICAL SOCIETY - MIERS HOME MUSEUM, CAUTHORN MEMORIAL DEPOT, 307 Oak St., Sonora, TX 76950-2647. Mailing Address: P.O. Box 885, Sonora, TX 76950-0885. Tel.: 325-387-5084.
E-mail: schs@sonoratx.net
Founded: 1968.
Key Personnel: Pres. (V), Rose Mary Whitehead Jones; Vice Pres., Marvin F. Sharley; Sec., Jo-Ann E. Palmer; Treas., JoAnn Hernandez.
Personnel Profile: Full-Time Volunteers 3; Part-Time Volunteers 10.
Governing Authority: society. Tax exempt.
History Museum.
Collections: local & area history; furniture 1890s-1950s; period photographs; 100 years of The Devils River News; sheriff's office photos & archives; branding irons of county; period ranching artifacts. Historic Buildings: 1890 Miers Home Period Museum; 1928 West Texas Utility Building; 1930s Old Santa Fe Depot; John & Mildred Cauthorn Memorial Bldg.
Research Fields: Sutton County History Book 1887-1977; family histories.
Facilities: archives.
Activities: guided tours; full orchestra fundraiser. Annual Event: Sutton County Days in August.
Publications: books: The True Story of Will Carver, Sutton County 1889-1890; Bad Old Days In and Around Sutton County 1889-1939; Sutton County Marriage Records 1890-1940; John Eatons Tales of Wild Bill Taylor; Johnny Ward Cowboy.
Hours & Admission Prices: Tues. & Thurs. 9-12:30, Sat. 8-12. No charge; donations accepted.
Attendance: 234 (accurate)
Membership: Individual $10; Group $25.

Spring

PEARL FINCHER MUSEUM OF FINE ARTS, 6815 Cypresswood Dr., Spring, TX 77379-7705. Tel.: 281-376-6322. Fax: 281-376-2944.
Art Museum.
Collections: paintings; drawings; sculpture.
Facilities: rental facilities.
Activities: special events; educational programs; summer camp; workshops; art competitions.
Hours & Admission Prices: Tues.-Wed. & Sat. 10-5, Thurs. 10-8, Fri. 10-6, Sun. 12-5. Suggested Donation: $5 per person.

Stanton

MARTIN COUNTY HISTORICAL MUSEUM, 207 E. Broadway, Stanton, TX 79782. Mailing Address: P.O. Box 929, Stanton, TX 79782-0929. Tel.: 432-756-2722.
E-mail: mcmuseum@crcom.net
Founded: 1978.
Congressional District: 17
Key Personnel: Dir., Shelly Daly; Pres., Steve Stalling.
Personnel Profile: Full-Time Paid 1; Part-Time Volunteers 15.
Governing Authority: board of trustees; nonprofit organization. Tax-exempt.
County History Museum: includes old jail & Connell House.
Collections: history of Martin County; prehistoric & Native American artifacts; early settlers; railroad; Catholic heritage; farming, ranching & oil production; schools, churches; wedding dresses & fashions; military display; barbed wire collection; cowboy regalia; blacksmith shop; archives; old jail; Cannell house.
Facilities: library of Martin County history; Martin County citizens' genealogy; Texas history; Texas county histories; Permian Basin history; U.S. & world history; reading room. Art, books & other gift items for sale.
Activities: permanent & temporary exhibitions; Jr. Historian Clubs; special Memorial Day services; Veterans' History program.
Publications: quarterly newsletter.
Hours & Admission Prices: Mon.-Fri. 9-5:30; other times by appointment. No charge; donations accepted. Closed major holidays. ♿
Attendance: 1,000 (estimated)
Membership: Individual $15; Couple $25; Commercial $50; Patron $100; Benefactor & Special Gifts $500 & up.

Stephenville

STEPHENVILLE MUSEUM, 525 E. Washington, Stephenville, TX 76401-4439. Mailing Address: P.O. Box 899, Buffalo Gap, TX 79508-0899. Tel.: 254-965-5880.
E-mail: llohr@our-town.com
Formerly: Stephenville Historical House Museum
Founded: 1965.
Congressional District: 17
Key Personnel: Pres., Betty Heath; Treas., Ben Baty.
Personnel Profile: Part-Time Paid 2; Part-Time Volunteers 20.
Governing Authority: municipal. Parent Institution: City of Stephenville. Tax-exempt.
General Museum: housed in 1869 Berry House; blacksmith shop.
Collections: pressed glass; rocks; early day tools; period furnishings for a house of the late 19th century; children's toys; barbed wire; photographs. Historic Sites, Buildings & homestead cabin: 1858 homestead log cabin; 1899 Gothic church; 1870 dogtrot log cabin; 19th-century church; carriage house; 1861 log corncrib; 1890 two-room schoolhouse; Tarleton house (important to local university).
Research Fields: local history.
Facilities: church; school; 1870 ranch house; log cabins; blacksmith shop.
Activities: guided tours by arrangement.
Hours & Admission Prices: Fri.-Sun. 2-5. No charge; donations accepted.
Attendance: 5,000 (estimated)

Sulphur Springs

SOUTHWEST DAIRY MUSEUM, 1210 Houston, Sulphur Springs, TX 75482-2310. Mailing Address: Southwest Dairy Farmers, P.O. Box 936, Sulphur Springs, TX 75483. Tel.: 903-439-6455. Fax: 903-439-1125.
Founded: 1982.
Congressional District: 4
Key Personnel: Gen. Mgr., James Hill; Pres. (V), David DeJong.
Personnel Profile: Full-Time Paid 26; Part-Time Paid 1.
Governing Authority: Tax-exempt.
Dairy Museum.
Collections: dairy industry history; period artifacts; documents; hands-on exhibits.
Activities: hands-on exhibits.
Hours & Admission Prices: Museum: Mon.-Fri. 9-4. Office: Mon.-Fri. 8-5. No charge; donations accepted. ♿

Sweetwater

CITY COUNTY PIONEER MUSEUM, 610 E. Third, Sweetwater, TX 79556-4643. Tel.: 325-235-8547.
Founded: 1968.
Congressional District: 5
Key Personnel: Dir., Mrs. Franzas Cupp; Chm. (V), Kent Boalright; Mgr., Beverly Puckett.
Personnel Profile: Part-Time Paid 3; Part-Time Volunteers 8.
Governing Authority: municipal; county. Tax-exempt.
Local History Museum.
Collections: furniture; documents; artifacts; china; glassware; period gowns; ranch & farm equipment; saddles; photos; historic house.
Research Fields: local history.
Activities: guided tours; lectures; special exhibits; monthly bake sales; public school trunk shows; group & individual tours. Annual Events: quilt show in August; Christmas exhibit.
Hours & Admission Prices: Tues.-Sat. 1-5; other times by appointment. No charge; donations accepted. Closed holidays. ♿
Attendance: 3,500 (estimated)

Teague

BURLINGTON-ROCK ISLAND RAILROAD AND HISTORICAL MUSEUM, 208 S. 3rd Ave., Teague, TX 75860-1645. Mailing Address: P.O. Box 604, Teague, TX 75860-0604. Tel.: 254-739-2145.
Web Site: therailroadmuseum.com
Founded: 1969.
Congressional District: 2
Key Personnel: Pres., Benny Walker; Financial Dir., Billy McSpadden; Cur. Emeritus, Dorothy McVey; Museum Shop Mgr., Mrs. Marie McSpadden.
Personnel Profile: Full-Time Volunteers 20; Part-Time Volunteers 20.
Governing Authority: nonprofit. Parent Institution: City of Teague, TX. Tax-exempt: 501(c)(3).
History Museum: housed in 1906 former Trinity & Brazos Valley Railway Depot, listed on National Register of Historic Places.
Collections: railroad memorabilia including 1925 Baldwin locomotive; 1928 fire engine; grist mill; loom; farming implements; dishes & cooking utensils; clothing; Indian artifacts; printing press; military items; Boy Scout memorabilia; medical; local history; two-room log house built in early 1850s; family history records; model trains; veterans memorabilia.
Research Fields: local & county historical research; genealogical research for the Teague Family Research Center; transportation & railroad history.
Facilities: Cookbooks, pins, postcards, railroad spikes, lanterns & other related items for sale.
Activities: guided tours; study clubs; loan, permanent & temporary exhibitions.
Publications: History of Freestone County, Texas.
Hours & Admission Prices: Sat.-Sun. 1-5; group tours by appointment. Adults $2, children $1; discounts to groups; members & school group tours no charge. Closed New Year's Eve & Day; Easter; Christmas. ♿
Attendance: 2,000 (estimated)
Membership: Individual $5; Family $10.

Temple

CZECH HERITAGE MUSEUM & GENEALOGY CENTER, 119 W. French, Temple, TX 76501. Mailing Address: P.O. Box 434, Temple, TX 76503-0434. Tel.: 254-899-2935. Fax: 254-774-7447.
E-mail: ssandiwicker@aol.com
Web Site: www.chmgc.com
Formerly: SPJST Library Archives & Museum
Founded: 1971.
Congressional District: 11
Key Personnel: Exec. Dir., Sandi Wicker; Chm. (V), Jerry B. Milan; Cur., Melba Foreman.
Personnel Profile: Full-Time Paid 1.
Governing Authority: society. Parent Institution: SPJST. Tax-exempt.
Library & Museum of Czech History, Culture & Genealogy.
Collections: artifacts & articles of early pioneer Czech-Texas settlers; housewares; musical instruments; agricultural implements; medical displays; pioneer kitchen; blacksmith shop; military displays; log replica of the first Czech Home built in Texas.
Research Fields: habits & living modes of Czech-Texas pioneers; history of the SPJST dating back to 1897.
Facilities: more than 22,000-vol. library mostly in the Czech language available for interlibrary loan & on premises.
Activities: guided tours; lectures; film strips; study clubs; inter-museum loan.
Publications: brochure, Vestnik Society Paper.
Hours & Admission Prices: Daily 8-12 & 1-5. No charge; donations accepted. Closed holidays. ♿
Attendance: 2,195 (estimated)

RAILROAD AND HERITAGE MUSEUM INC., (M), 315 W Ave. B, Temple, TX 76501-4226. Tel.: 254-298-5172. Fax: 254-298-5171.
E-mail: museum@rrhm.org
Web Site: www.rrhm.org
Formerly: Railroad Pioneer Museum
Founded: 1973.
Congressional District: 44
Key Personnel: Dir., Judith A. Covington; Chm. (V), David Krauss; Vice Chm., Tony Hennes.
Personnel Profile: Full-Time Paid 5; Part-Time Paid 1; Part-Time Volunteers 75.
Governing Authority: board of directors. Tax-exempt.
Transportation & History Museum.
Collections: railroad & pioneer items; documents; photographs; furniture; 1910 restored train station; clothing; tools; archives; steam engine & three cabooses; World War II Troop Sleeper; ATSF 2301 diesel locomotive; 1917 Pullman Sleeper.
Research Fields: railroad; pioneer history; local history.
Facilities: library; archives.
Activities: tours; educational programs.
Publications: newsletter, RRHM.
Hours & Admission Prices: Tues.-Sat. 10-4. Adults $4, senior citizens & military $3, children $2; discounts to AAM members; children under 5 no charge. ♿
Attendance: 20,000 (accurate)
Membership: Individual $25; Family $50; Sustaining $100; Sponsor $250; Patron $500; Benefactor $1,000.

Texarkana

ACE OF CLUBS HOUSE, 420 Pine St., Texarkana, TX 75501-5513. Mailing Address: P.O. Box 2343, Texarkana, TX 75504-2343. Tel.: 903-793-4831. Fax: 903-793-7108.
E-mail: texarkanamuseums@cableone.net
Web Site: www.texarkanamuseums.org
Founded: 1985.
Congressional District: 1
Key Personnel: Exec. Dir., Ina McDowell; Pres., Brent Stewart; Cur., Jamie Simmons; Cur. Draughon-Moore Collection, Melissa Nesbitt.
Personnel Profile: Full-Time Paid 1; Part-Time Paid 1; Part-Time Volunteers 15.
Governing Authority: society; nonprofit. Parent Institution: Texarkana Museums System. Tax-exempt: 501(c)(3).
Historic House: 1885 Italianate house in form of rectangle with three octagonal bays, club shape & surrounded by dry moat.
Collections: furnishings; personal artifacts; recreational artifacts, 1885-1950.
Research Fields: late 19th-century architecture & decorative arts; regional social history 1885-1950.
Facilities: 2,500-vol. library of reference materials; media room with video, film & slide facilities. Gift items for sale.
Activities: guided tours; lectures; workshops; organized educational programs; docent program; training programs for professional museum workers; temporary exhibitions; school loan service; summer programs; Spring lecture series. Museum Sponsors: Christmas Open House.
Publications: monthly volunteer newsletter; quarterly membership newsletter, Artifacts.
Hours & Admission Prices: Tues.-Sat. 10-4 (last tour begins at 3). Adults $6, seniors $5, children 5 & up $4; discounts for groups & AAA members; children 4 & under and members no charge. Closed national holidays. ♿
Attendance: 3,225 (accurate)
Membership: Student $20; Individual $50; Family $75.

* **TEXARKANA MUSEUMS SYSTEM, (M),** 219 N. State Line Ave., Texarkana, TX 75501-5606. Mailing Address: P.O. Box 2343, Texarkana, TX 75504-2343. Tel.: 903-793-4831. Fax: 903-793-7108.
E-mail: texarkanamuseums@cableone.net
Web Site: www.texarkanamuseums.org
Founded: 1971.
Congressional District: 1
Key Personnel: Exec. Dir., Melanie Doud; Cur. Draughon-Moore House, Melissa Nesbitt; Cur., Jamie Simmons; Office Mgr., Bettie Blackmon.
Personnel Profile: Full-Time Paid 7; Part-Time Paid 2; Part-Time Volunteers 30; Interns 1.
Governing Authority: nonprofit organization. Parent Institution: Texarkana Museums System. Branch Museum: Discovery Place; The Ace of Clubs House; The Texarkana Museum of Regional History. Tax-exempt: 501(c)(3).
History & Science Museum.
Collections: historical development of area; Caddo people; regional history; 11,000 photographs.
Research Fields: pertaining to collections.
Facilities: 2,500-vol. library of medical, genealogical & history books; archives; 50-seat theater; classrooms.
Activities: guided tours; lectures; films; docent program or council; permanent, temporary & traveling exhibitions; school loan service; classroom lectures in schools; annual arts & crafts festival; summer program for students. Museum Sponsors: programs in community centers.
Publications: quarterly newsletter, Artifacts.
Hours & Admission Prices: Tues.-Sat. 10-4. Admission varies for each site; discounts for AAM, TAM & AMA members. Closed legal holidays. ♿
Attendance: 17,500 (accurate)
Membership: Student $10; Individual $50; Family $75; Patron $100; Contributing $250; Sustaining $500; Landmark $5,000; Corporate $10,000.

Texas City

TEXAS CITY MUSEUM, (M), 409 Sixth St. N., Texas City, TX 77590-7854. Tel.: 409-643-5799. Fax: 409-949-9972.
E-mail: tcmuseum@prodigy.net
Web Site: www.texas-city-tx.org
Founded: 1991.

Key Personnel: Coord., Linda Turner.
Personnel Profile: Full-Time Paid 1; Part-Time Paid 1; Part-Time Volunteers 6.
Governing Authority: private; nonprofit organization. Tax-exempt: 501(c)(3).
History Museum.
Collections: concentration on the Mainland area of Galveston County from the 1900s-present with special emphasis on the history of Texas City & the local refineries; 1947 Texas City explosion film.
Activities: children's discovery area.
Hours & Admission Prices: Tues.-Sat. 10-4. Adults $3, seniors $2, students $1; members & children under 6 no charge. Closed Easter; Thanksgiving; Christmas Eve & Day. ♿
Attendance: 7,000 (estimated)

Tomball

TOMBALL COMMUNITY MUSEUM CENTER, 510 N. Pine St., Tomball, TX 77375-4400. Mailing Address: P.O. Box 457, Tomball, TX 77377-0457. Tel.: 281-444-2449.
Founded: 1961.
Congressional District: 4
Key Personnel: Dir., Jean Alexander; Pres., Charles Hall; Treas., Mary McCoy; Sec., Lessie Upchurch.
Personnel Profile: Part-Time Paid 1; Part-Time Volunteers 6.
Governing Authority: society. Affiliated with Spring Creek County Historical Association. Tax-exempt.
Historic House: 1860 Griffin Memorial House.
Collections: 19th-century decorative art collection; pioneer country doctor's office; 1800s cotton gin; farming implements & domestic artifacts to depict the rural & cultural heritage of Northwest Harris county; 1905 Trinity Evangelical Lutheran Church; c.1800 log house & corn crib; c.1866 German Pioneer farmhouse; 1940 Oil Camp House; 1920 country schoolhouse; Esther Bubley photographs taken in Tomball in 1945.
Activities: guided educational tours for adults, school & Scout groups; lectures on topics of historical interest; Candlelight Tour; pioneer heritage day; permanent exhibitions.
Publications: Sept.-May newsletter.
Hours & Admission Prices: Thurs. 10-2, Sun. 2-4; groups by appointment. Donations: $2 per person.
Attendance: 9,000 (estimated)
Membership: Individual $15; Family $25.

Tulia

SWISHER COUNTY ARCHIVES AND MUSEUM ASSOCIATION, 127 S.W. Second, Tulia, TX 79088-2700. Mailing Address: P.O. Box 445, Tulia, TX 79088-0445. Tel.: 806-995-2819.
E-mail: pioneer042001@yahoo.com
Founded: 1965.
Congressional District: 13
Key Personnel: Pres., Jo Venhaus; Dir., Alan Glasscock; Treas., Joe Cowan.
Personnel Profile: Full-Time Paid 1; Part-Time Volunteers 3.
Governing Authority: nonprofit organization. Tax-exempt.
History Museum & Archives: housed in community building.
Collections: local memorabilia; furniture; clothing; photographs; farm equipment; stagecoach; needle art; Indian artifacts; blacksmith; J.O. Bass; Quanah Parker; woodworking tools; dolls of the world; seashells; Swisher County memorabilia.
Research Fields: quilts; blacksmith; early history of Swisher County.
Facilities: 200-vol. library of publications dealing with Swisher County, cemetery & genealogy records, available for use on premises.
Activities: guided tours; permanent exhibitions; educational.
Hours & Admission Prices: Tues.-Sat. 10-4; other times by appointment. No charge; donations accepted. ♿
Attendance: 6,228 (accurate)
Membership: Individual $10.

Tyler

CALDWELL ZOO, 2203 W. Martin Luther King, Tyler, TX 75702-2954. Mailing Address: P.O. Box 4785, Tyler, TX 75712-4785. Tel.: 903-593-0121. Fax: 903-595-5083.
E-mail: info@caldwellzoo.org
Web Site: www.caldwellzoo.org
Founded: 1953.
Key Personnel: C.E.O., Dr. Michael McArthur; Exec. Dir., Hayes Caldwell; Asst. Dir. & Gen. Cur., Scott Maddox; Dir. Visitor Svcs., Mike Tucker; Gift Shop Mgr., Kim Ables.
Personnel Profile: Full-Time Paid 80; Part-Time Paid 4.
Governing Authority: Parent Institution: Caldwell Foundation. Tax-exempt.
Zoo.
Collections: North American, South American & East African species; 2,000 animals, including 250 species, covering 85 acres.
Hours & Admission Prices: March to Labor Day daily 9-5; Sept.-Feb. daily 9-4. Adults $8.50, senior citizens $7.25, children $5; children under 2 no charge. Closed New Year's Day; Thanksgiving; Christmas. ♿
Attendance: 600,000 (estimated)

DISCOVERY SCIENCE PLACE, (M), 308 N. Broadway Ave., Tyler, TX 75702-5711. Tel.: 903-533-8011.
E-mail: michael@discoveryscienceplace.org
Web Site: www.discoveryscienceplace.org
Founded: 1993.
Key Personnel: C.E.O., Michael Shanklin, ED; Dir. Devel., Leslie Watson; Dir. Mktg. & Public Rels., Val Williamson; Dir. Education, Kris Parks; Dir. Special Initiatives, Lucinda Presley; Museum Shop Mgr., Fred Powell.
Personnel Profile: Full-Time Paid 10; Part-Time Paid 8; Part-Time Volunteers 4.
Governing Authority: nonprofit.
Children's Museum.
Collections: hands-on exhibits.
Hours & Admission Prices: Mon.-Sat. 9-5, Sun. 1-5. Admission $6; discounts to AAM members & groups of 14 or more with reservations; children 2 & under and members no charge. Closed New Year's Day; Easter; Memorial Day; Independence Day; Labor Day; Thanksgiving; Christmas.
Attendance: 60,000 (estimated)
Membership: Annual $50-$100.

GOODMAN MUSEUM, 624 N. Broadway, Tyler, TX 75702-5344. Tel.: 903-531-1286.
E-mail: gmuseum@tylertexas.com
Founded: 1962.
Congressional District: 4
Key Personnel: Cur., Patricia J. Heaton.
Personnel Profile: Full-Time Paid 1.
Governing Authority: municipal & nonprofit organization. Operated by City of Tyler, Parks & Recreation Dept., P.O. Box 2039, Tyler, TX 75710. Tax-exempt.
Historic House: 1859 4-room cottage remodeled in 1880 into 2-story Texas Colonial by Dr. William J. Goodman, remodeled in 1924 into a Greek Revival Mansion by Dr. Goodman's daughter, Sallie Goodman LeGrand.
Collections: house furnishings of the Goodmans; cradles; china imported from England & France.
Activities: guided tours; lectures; loan, permanent & temporary exhibitions.
Publications: brochure.
Hours & Admission Prices: Tues.-Sat. 10-4. No charge; donations accepted. Closed New Year's; Memorial Day; Independence Day; Thanksgiving; Christmas. ♿
Attendance: 6,000 (estimated)

HISTORIC AVIATION MEMORIAL MUSEUM, (M), Tyler Pounds Airport, 150 Airport Dr., Tyler, TX 75704. Mailing Address: 150 Airport Dr., Box 2-7, Tyler, TX 75704-6600. Tel.: 903-526-1945.
Key Personnel: Cur., Mike Burke; Pres., Carolyn Verver; Museum Shop Mgr., Dave Verver.
Personnel Profile: Full-Time Paid 1; Part-Time Paid 2; Part-Time Volunteers 50.
Governing Authority: nonprofit organization. Tax-exempt.
Aviation Museum.
Collections: aircraft; aviation artifacts.
Facilities: library. Museum-related items for sale.
Hours & Admission Prices: Tues.-Sat. 10-5, Sun. 1-5. Adults $5, teens 13-18 $3; discounts to senior citizens; active military & members no charge. ♿
Attendance: 6,000 (accurate)
Membership: Individual $40; Family $75; Life $400.

SMITH COUNTY HISTORICAL SOCIETY, 125 S. College Ave., Tyler, TX 75702-7216. Tel.: 903-592-5993. Fax: 903-526-0924.
E-mail: info@smithcountyhistoricalsociety.org
Web Site: www.smithcountyhistoricalsociety.org
Founded: 1959.
Congressional District: 4
Key Personnel: Pres., Robert Reed; Vice Pres., Randal B. Gilbert.
Personnel Profile: Full-Time Volunteers 1; Part-Time Paid 1; Part-Time Volunteers 15; Interns 1.
Governing Authority: nonprofit organization. Tax-exempt: 501(c)(3).
History Museum: housed in c.1905 Carnegie Library.
Collections: Smith County history; Native American items; Civil War items; Gilded Age; clothing; 1930s kitchenware; World War I & II uniforms; Camp Fannin; WWII training camp; Camp Ford Confederate Training Camp & Union Prisoner of War Camp; audiovisual & film; decorative arts; textiles; murals of Smith County History; late 19th-century furnishings;

games & toys; wireless telegraphic equipment; typewriters; writing implements; period toys; business & institutional documents; newspapers; photographs.
Research Fields: Smith County & east Texas history; Smith County history.
Facilities: 1,500-vol. library; archives; 111-seat auditorium.
Activities: guided tours; docent program; educational programs for school children; monthly society programs; outreach programs to schools & retirement homes; films.
Publications: monthly newsletter; biannual, Chronicles of Smith County, Texas; brochure; Camp Ford lithograph; books, The History of Smith County; Born In Dixie; Uncovering Camp Ford - Archaeological Interpretations of a Confederate Prisoner-of-War Camp in East Texas, a Chronological History of Smith County, Texas; Never in Doubt, a History of Delta Drilling Company.
Hours & Admission Prices: Tues.-Sat. 10-4; other times by appointment. No charge; donations accepted. ♿
Attendance: 3,600 (estimated)
Membership: Student $7.50; Individual $25; Family $35; Sustaining $50; Patron $100; Life $500; Life Patron $750; Benefactor $1,000.

* **TYLER MUSEUM OF ART,** 1300 S. Mahon Ave., Tyler, TX 75701-3438. Tel.: 903-595-1001. Fax: 903-595-1055.
E-mail: info@tylermuseum.org
Web Site: www.tylermuseum.org
Founded: 1969.
Congressional District: 4
Key Personnel: Pres., Betty Summers; Dir., Kimberley Bush Tomio; Exhibitions Asst., Kyle Harper; Accounting & Human Resources, Ida Beene; Facility Mgr., Robert Owen; Head Education, Kentaro Tomio; Public Rels. & Mktg. Coord., Zoe Kerr; Dir. Devel., Amy Lively; Mgr. Special Events & Programs, Caroline King Wylie; Collections Mgr., Katie Powell; Museum Shop Mgr., Jane Hansen.
Personnel Profile: Full-Time Paid 10; Part-Time Paid 10; Part-Time Volunteers 27; Interns 3.
Governing Authority: nonprofit organization. Tax-exempt: 501(c)(3).
Art Museum.
Collections: fine art from 19th-century to present; Harry Worthman Archive collection; early & contemporary Texas art; Dan and Laura Boeckman Collection of Contemporary Mexican Art.
Research Fields: general fine arts; early Texas art; Mexican folk art; 19th century American art.
Facilities: 1,500-vol. library of art surveys & periodicals available upon request on premises; classrooms; cafe. Museum-related items for sale.
Activities: guided tours; lectures; gallery talks; formally organized education programs for children, adults & college students; temporary & traveling exhibitions.
Publications: exhibition catalogs; members magazine, Preview.
Hours & Admission Prices: Admissions fee for special exhibits. Closed national holidays. ♿
Attendance: 25,000 (accurate)
Membership: Student: $10; Educator $25; Individual $50; Individual Plus & Family $75; Supporter $100; Sustainer $300; Guarantor $500; Patron $1,000; Benefactor $1,500; Corporate $1,500, $2,500 & $5,000; Director's Circle $5,000; Collector's Circle $10,000 & up.

TYLER ROSE MUSEUM, 420 Rose Park Dr., Tyler, TX 75702-6859. Tel.: 903-597-3130. Fax: 903-597-3031.
E-mail: info@texasrosefestival.com
Key Personnel: Exec. Dir. & Cur., Jennifer Gaston
Rose Museum.
Collections: over 40,000 rose bushes & 500 varieties of roses.
Facilities: Museum-related items for sale.
Hours & Admission Prices: Mon.-Fri. 9-4:30, Sat. 10-4:30, Sun. 1:30-4:30. Adults $3.50, children 3-11 $2.
Attendance: 100,000

Uvalde

JOHN NANCE GARNER MUSEUM, 333 N. Park St., Uvalde, TX 78801-4658. Tel.: 830-278-5018. Fax: 830-279-0512.
E-mail: bbhadley@austin.utexas.edu
Web Site: www.cah.utexas.edu
Formerly: Garner Memorial Museum
Founded: 1952.
Congressional District: 23
Key Personnel: C.E.O., Dr. Don Carleton; Dir., Dr. Patrick Cox.
Personnel Profile: Full-Time Paid 2.
Governing Authority: Parent Institution: University of Texas at Austin. Subsidiary Institution: Center for American History. Tax-exempt.
Historic House: 1920 Home of Vice President John N. Garner.
Collections: photographs; political material; furniture, clothing & other items pertaining to the life & career of John Nance Garner.
Research Fields: life, career & political achievements of John Nance Garner.
Activities: permanent & temporary exhibitions.
Hours & Admission Prices: Closed for renovation.
Attendance: 3,500 (accurate)

Van Horn

CLARK HOTEL MUSEUM, (M), 112 W. Broadway, Van Horn, TX 79855-0112. Mailing Address: Box 231, Van Horn, TX 79855-0231. Tel.: 432-283-8028.
E-mail: oldwest@windstream.net
Formerly: Culberson County Historical Museum
Founded: 1975.
Congressional District: 16
Key Personnel: C.E.O., Chm., Dir. & Cur., Robert Stuckey; Sec., Ellen Lipsey.
Personnel Profile: Full-Time Volunteers 1; Part-Time Volunteers 15; Interns 6.
Governing Authority: Parent Institution: Culbertson County Historical Society. Tax-exempt: 501(c)(3).
General Museum: housed in 1906 two-story adobe & cement block, Clark Hotel Building.
Collections: Indian artifacts; pioneer articles; costumes; local art; photographs; old furniture; antique bar; rocks & fossils; mineral & mine exhibit.
Research Fields: local history.
Facilities: 200-vol. library of history books available for research on premises; reading room.
Activities: guided tours; lectures; films; docent program or council; permanent exhibitions.
Publications: brochure.
Hours & Admission Prices: No charge; donations accepted. ♿
Attendance: 1,200 (estimated)
Membership: Individual $10; Family $25; Sustaining $50; Contributing $100; Memorial $500 & up.

Vernon

RED RIVER VALLEY MUSEUM, (M), 4600 College Dr., Vernon, TX 76384-4052. Mailing Address: P.O. Box 2004, Vernon, TX 76385-2004. Tel.: 940-553-1848. Fax: 940-553-1849.
E-mail: director@redrivervalleymuseum.org
Web Site: www.redrivervalleymuseum.org
Founded: 1963.
Congressional District: 13
Key Personnel: Exec. Dir., Mary Ann McCuistion; Pres. (V), Katheryne Johnson; Pres. Bd. Dir., John Wright; Asst. Dir., Karen Jones.
Personnel Profile: Part-Time Paid 4; Part-Time Volunteers 25.
Governing Authority: nonprofit organization. Tax-exempt: 501(c)(3).
History, Science & Fine Arts Museum.
Collections: J. Henry Ray Indian artifacts; early Wilbarger Co. history; Electra Waggone Bigg studio exhibit; original sculptor's models of bronzes by Electra Waggoner Biggs; Wm. A. Bond Big Game collection; Adrian Martinez mural; Texas ranching history; Great Western Cattle Trail; Jack Teagarden; Gideon dollhouses.
Facilities: Commemorative coins, local history book, pamphlets & museum-related items for sale.
Activities: guided tours; loan, permanent & traveling exhibitions; videos; educational trunk shows.
Hours & Admission Prices: Tues.-Sun. 1-5; other times by appointment. No charge; donations accepted. Closed some major holidays. ♿
Attendance: 8,000 (estimated)
Membership: Active$15; Associate $20.

Victoria

MCNAMARA HOUSE MUSEUM, (M), 502 N. Liberty, Victoria, TX 77901-6534. Tel.: 361-575-8227. Fax: 361-575-8228.
E-mail: vrma@victoriaregionalmuseum.com
Web Site: www.victoriaregionalmuseum.com/mcnamara/
Founded: 1959.
Congressional District: 14
Key Personnel: Exec. Dir., Denise Roussel; Admin. Asst., Teresa Giles; Gallery Attendant, Aileen Cruz.
Personnel Profile: Full-Time Paid 2; Part-Time Paid 2; Part-Time Volunteers 21.
Governing Authority: nonprofit organization. Parent Institution: Victoria Regional Museum Association. Subsidiary Institution: Nave Museum, 306 W. Commercial St., Victoria, TX 77901. Tax-exempt: 501(c)(3).
Historic House.
Collections: Victorian era furniture, textiles, decorative arts & documents.
Research Fields: social history.

Facilities: educational facilities.
Activities: guided tours; lectures; films; concerts; organized educational programs; docent program; participatory, loan & temporary exhibitions.
Publications: VRMA Newsletter.
Hours & Admission Prices: Tues.-Sun. 1-5. Adults $2, children & students $1; members no charge. Closed New Year's Eve & Day; Easter; Thanksgiving; Christmas Eve & Day. ♿
Attendance: 3,500 (estimated)
Membership: Student $30; Family $40; Sponsor $125; Friend $250; Patron $500; Benefactor $1,000.

MUSEUM OF THE COASTAL BEND, (M), The Victoria College, 2200 E. Red River, Victoria, TX 77901-4442. Tel.: 361-582-2511. Fax: 361-582-2437.
Founded: 2003.
Key Personnel: Dir., Sue Prudhomme; Chm. (V), Amy Mundy; Museum Shop Mgr., Cheryl Beran.
Personnel Profile: Full-Time Paid 2; Part-Time Paid 4; Part-Time Volunteers 30.
Governing Authority: Parent Institution: The Victoria College. Tax-exempt.
Cultural History Museum.
Collections: local history & culture; maritime artifacts; ranching industry.
Major Exhibits: Victoria: Where TX History Began, 3/10-12/10.
Research Fields: archaeology.
Hours & Admission Prices: Tues.-Sat. 10-4. Adults $3.50, senior citizens $2.50, students $2; members & children under 4 no charge. Closed major holidays. ♿

NAVE MUSEUM, 306 W. Commercial, Victoria, TX 77901-6602. Mailing Address: 502 N. Liberty, Victoria, TX 77901-6534. Tel.: 361-575-8227. Fax: 361-575-8228.
E-mail: vrma@victoriaregionalmuseum.com
Web Site: www.victoriaregionalmuseum.com
Founded: 1976.
Congressional District: 14
Key Personnel: Pres., Jim Wearden; Administrative Asst., Teresa Giles; Museum Shop Mgr., Virginia Kisalus.
Personnel Profile: Full-Time Paid 2; Part-Time Paid 2; Part-Time Volunteers 30.
Governing Authority: nonprofit organization. Parent Institution: Victoria Regional Museum Assoc., 502 N. Liberty, Victoria, TX 77901. Subsidiary Institution: McNamara House Museum. Tax-exempt: 501(c)(3).
Art Museum.
Collections: early 20th century paintings by Royston Nave.
Facilities: educational facilities.
Activities: guided tours; lectures; films; concerts; organized educational programs; docent program; participatory, loan & temporary exhibitions.
Publications: VRMA Newsletter.
Hours & Admission Prices: Tues.-Sun. 1-5. Adults $2; members no charge. Closed New Year's Eve & Day; Easter; Thanksgiving; Christmas Eve & Day. ♿
Attendance: 8,000 (estimated)
Membership: Student $30; Friend $40; Advocate $75; Sponsor $125; Collectors Society $250; Patron $500; Benefactor $1,000.

THE TEXAS ZOO, 110 Memorial Dr., Victoria, TX 77901-6334. Tel.: 361-573-7681. Fax: 361-576-1094.
E-mail: texas200@texaszoo.org
Web Site: www.texaszoo.org
Founded: 1976.
Congressional District: 14
Key Personnel: Bd. Pres., Doug Hotle; Dir. Education & Outreach, Jennifer DiSilvestro; Museum Shop Mgr., P.J. Dilbeck; Dir. Operations & Maintenance, Eddie Overby.
Personnel Profile: Full-Time Paid 10; Part-Time Paid 2; Part-Time Volunteers 30.
Governing Authority: South Texas Zoological Society. Tax-exempt: 501(c)(3).
Zoo.
Collections: wildlife indigenous to Texas; animals from around the world; natural history displays; dinosaur bones & teeth; modern day birds & eggs; endangered Texans Caboose; animal kingdom exhibits.
Facilities: educational station; animal kingdom building; concession stand. Museum-related items for sale.
Activities: programs; teacher in-service training; hobby workshops; formally organized educational programs; docent program; permanent exhibitions; family playroom. Museum Sponsors: Zoo Fest; Auction/Dinner; Annual Easter Egg Hunt; Annual Amateur Animal Photo Contest; Boo at the Zoo; Wildlights; summer camps; Annual Pow Wow; Annual Earth Day.
Publications: quarterly newsletter, View From the Zoo.
Hours & Admission Prices: Memorial Day to Labor Day daily 9-6; Sept.-May daily 9-5. Adults $5, children 3-12 $4, seniors 65 & over $3.50; discounts to AZA members; members & children 2 & under no charge. Closed Thanksgiving; Christmas Eve & Day. ♿
Attendance: 50,000 (estimated)
Membership: South Texas Zoological Society: Individual $30; Senior Citizen $40; Family Plus $55; Patron $110; Benefactor $250; Corporate $500 & up; Life $1,000 & up.

Waco

ARMSTRONG BROWNING LIBRARY, Baylor University, Eighth & Speight Sts., Waco, TX 76706. Mailing Address: One Bear Place, #97152, Waco, TX 76798-7152. Tel.: 254-710-3566. Fax: 254-710-3552.
E-mail: avery_sharp@baylor.edu
Web Site: www.browninglibrary.org
Founded: 1918.
Congressional District: 11
Key Personnel: Interim Dir. & Cur. Manuscripts, Rita Patteson; Cur. Books & Printed Materials, Cynthia Burgess; Research Librarian & Museum Coord., Avery T. Sharp; Public Rels. & Facilities Supvr., Kathryn Brogdon.
Personnel Profile: Full-Time Paid 6; Part-Time Paid 4.
Governing Authority: university. Parent Institution: Baylor University, Waco, TX. Tax-exempt.
Library of Browningiana.
Collections: items pertaining to Robert & Elizabeth Barrett Browning & the Victorian Age, including original letters, manuscripts, books, periodical articles, pamphlets & other publications; personal artifacts.
Research Fields: Robert & Elizabeth Barrett Browning; the Victorian Age.
Facilities: 26,000-vol. library available for use on premises only; reading rooms. Publications of the library, paperweights, slides, postcards & souvenir items for sale.
Activities: guided tours; lectures; films; permanent & temporary exhibitions. Library Sponsors: annual Pied Piper Tours for 5th grade students.
Publications: annual periodical, Studies in Browning & His Circle; semiannual newsletter, Armstrong Browning Library Newsletter; periodical, Baylor Browning Interests; books, Browning's Old Schoolfellow - The Artistic Relationship Between Two Robert Brownings; The Browning Collections: A Reconstruction with other memorabilia; The Letters of Elizabeth Barrett Browning to Mary Russell Mitford, 1836-1854; Armstrong Browning Library; More Than Friend: The Letters of Robert Browning to Katharine de Kay Bronson; Robert Browning's Flowers; Elizabeth Barrett Browning at The Mercy of Her Publishers; descriptive catalogs, Meeting the Brownings; Browning Music; Robert Browning-A Telescopic View, 1812-1889; Elizabeth Barrett Browning: Life in a New Rhythm.
Hours & Admission Prices: Mon.-Fri. 9-5, Sat. 9-12. No charge; donations accepted. Closed University holidays. ♿
Attendance: 25,368 (accurate)
Membership: Individual $50; Life $1,000.

* **ART CENTER WACO, (M),** 1300 College Dr., Waco, TX 76708-1401. Tel.: 254-752-4371. Fax: 254-752-3506.
E-mail: info@artcenterwaco.org
Web Site: www.artcenterwaco.org
Founded: 1972.
Congressional District: 11
Key Personnel: Exec. Dir., Mark Arnold; Education Coord., Shirley Atwood.
Personnel Profile: Full-Time Paid 3; Full-Time Volunteers 1; Part-Time Paid 4; Part-Time Volunteers 200; Interns 1.
Governing Authority: nonprofit corporation. Tax-exempt: 501(c)(3) & 170(b)(1)(A).
Art Center.
Collections: Historic House: 1924 William Cameron summer house.
Facilities: library; studio classrooms; courtyard. Museum-related items for sale.
Activities: guided tours; lectures; films; education programs; traveling exhibitions; weekend programs for children.
Publications: catalogs; newsletter.
Hours & Admission Prices: Tues.-Sat. 10-5, Sun. 1-5. Suggested Donation: adults $2, educator & children 5-12 $1. Closed New Year's Day; Martin Luther King Jr. Day; Memorial Day; Independence Day; Labor Day; Thanksgiving; Christmas. ♿
Attendance: 120,000 (estimated)
Membership: Educator's & Seniors $25; Individual $35; Family $75; Patron $150; Sustainer $300; Guarantor $750; Benefactor $1,000.

CAMERON PARK ZOO, 1701 N. 4th St., Waco, TX 76707-2463. Tel.: 254-750-8400. Fax: 254-754-8430.
E-mail: jimf@ci.waco.tx.us
Web Site: www.cameronparkzoo.com

Founded: 1955.
Congressional District: 11
Key Personnel: Zoo Dir., Jim Fleshman; Pres., K. Paul Holt; Gen. Cur., Johnny Binder; Cur. Exhibits & Programs, Terri Cox; Membership Svcs. & Museum Shop Mgr., Frances Gonce; Membership Mgr., Diane Jordon; Cur. Education, Connie Kassner; Office Mgr., Laney Van Antwerp; Mktg. Mgr., Duane McGregor.
Personnel Profile: Full-Time Paid 56; Part-Time Paid 17; Part-Time Volunteers 35.
Governing Authority: municipal. Parent Institution: City of Waco. Subsidiary Institution: Cameron Park Zoological Society. Tax-exempt: 501(c)(3).
General Museum.
Collections: mammals; birds; reptiles; fish; amphibians; plants.
Research Fields: animal breeding; conservation projects in Caribbean, Africa & Texas.
Facilities: 200-vol. library of magazines, reference books & books on management of zoo animals available for research on premises only. Zoo-related items for sale.
Activities: guided tours; lectures; films; formally organized educational programs; docent program or council.
Publications: quarterly magazine, Zoo News; bimonthly newsletter.
Hours & Admission Prices: Mon.-Sat. 9-5, Sun. 11-5. Adults $7, children $5; discount to groups; members & AZA members no charge. Closed New Year's Day; Thanksgiving; Christmas. ♿
Attendance: 240,384 (accurate)
Membership: Individual $25; Family $60; Patron $150; Business $175 & up.

DR PEPPER MUSEUM AND FREE ENTERPRISE INSTITUTE, 300 S. 5th, Waco, TX 76701-2115. Tel.: 254-757-1025. Fax: 254-757-2221.
E-mail: dp-info@drpeppermuseum.com
Web Site: www.drpeppermuseum.com
Founded: 1989.
Key Personnel: Dir., Jack N. McKinney; Mgr. Programs, Brian Henson; Dir. Exhibition & Collections, Jessica Harris; Communication Coord., Jennie Sheppard.
Personnel Profile: Full-Time Paid 7; Part-Time Paid 12; Part-Time Volunteers 39; Interns 1.
Governing Authority: private; nonprofit. Subsidiary Institution: DP Museum Enterprise, Inc., a for-profit company. Tax-exempt: 501(c)(3).
History Museum; housed in a 3-story, 18,000 sq. ft. 1906 building, which was the home of Dr Pepper. Structure is of architectural significance to Waco, reflecting the popularity of Richardsonian Romanesque architecture in Texas.
Collections: soft drink industry; machinery; advertising; from fountain to factory; Dr Pepper artifacts; historical & current soft drinks brands.
Research Fields: developing a new definition of soft drinks to meet current market developments; Waco tornado research; Big Red; international soft drink advertising & brands.
Facilities: 50-vol. bound magazine library for use on premises; printed advertising art; photos; personal & industry files; 6,000 sq. ft. exhibit space; classroom; operational historic soda fountain. Museum-related items for sale.
Activities: films; formal education programs for children; guided tours; lectures; temporary exhibitions; training programs for museum workers & junior high school & high school students.
Publications: quarterly newsletter, Bottlecaps; brochure, Soda Pop.
Hours & Admission Prices: Summer: Mon.-Sat. 10-5, Sun. 12-5; Sept.-June Mon.-Sat. 10-4, Sun. 12-4. Adults $6, senior citizens $4, students $3; discount to groups with reservations; preschool children, AAM members, Texas Association of Museums & members no charge. Closed New Year's Day; Thanksgiving; Christmas. ♿
Attendance: 58,089 (accurate)
Membership: Jr. Pepper $5; Student $10; Sr. Pepper $15; Individual $25; Family $40.

THE EARLE-HARRISON HOUSE AND GARDENS ON 5TH STREET, 1901 N. 5th St., Waco, TX 76708-3603. Tel.: 254-753-2032.
E-mail: earleharrisonpapegardens@gmail.com
Web Site: www.earleharrison.com
Founded: 1956.
Congressional District: 11
Key Personnel: C.E.O., Stanley A. Latham; Chm. (V), Holt Getterman; Pres. (V), Mrs. Beverly Fallon.
Personnel Profile: Full-Time Paid 3; Part-Time Paid 5.
Governing Authority: private; nonprofit. Parent Institution: The G.H. Pape Foundation, Waco, TX. Tax-exempt: 501(c)(3).
Historic House: 1858-1859 Greek Revival antebellum house.
Collections: Earle & Harrison family heirlooms; pieces from the Victorian period c.1850-1900.
Activities: docent program; guided tours. Annual Events: Gardening on 5th Street; Christmas Season at the Earle-Harrison House.
Publications: The Columns.
Hours & Admission Prices: By appointment. Admission $5; discounts to AAM members; children under 12 & members no charge. Closed New Year's Eve & Day; Good Friday; Easter weekend; Memorial Day; Independence Day; Labor Day; Thanksgiving; Christmas Eve & Day. ♿
Attendance: 19,100 (accurate)
Membership: Garden Sprout $5; Family Sprout, Student & Senior Citizens $10; Individual $30; Friends of the Earles and Harrisons $50; Dr. Earle $100; The Column Society $250.

* **HISTORIC WACO FOUNDATION, (M),** 810 S. Fourth St., Waco, TX 76706-1036. Tel.: 254-753-5166. Fax: 254-714-1242.
E-mail: hwf@hot.rr.com
Web Site: www.historicwaco.org
Founded: 1967.
Congressional District: 11
Key Personnel: Exec. Dir., Donald B. Davis; Administrative Asst., Deborah Vardiman.
Personnel Profile: Full-Time Paid 2; Part-Time Paid 2; Part-Time Volunteers 65.
Governing Authority: society. Branch Museums: 1858 Earle-Napier-Kinnard House, 814 S. 4th St.; 1872, East Terrace, 100 Mill St.; 1868 Fort House, 503 S. Fourth St.; 1866 McCulloch House, 407 Columbus Ave. Tax-exempt.
Historic Foundation & Historic Houses.
Collections: period furnishings & clothing.
Research Fields: Old Waco.
Facilities: 60-seat lecture hall.
Activities: guided tours; lectures; docent program; permanent exhibitions; two major fundraising events.
Publications: semiannual, Waco Heritage & History; bimonthly newsletter.
Hours & Admission Prices: Earle-Napier-Kinnard: Sat.-Sun. 2-5. East Terrace Tues.-Fri. 11-3, Sat.-Sun. 2-5. McCulloch House & Fort House Sat.-Sun. 2-5. Adults $3, seniors $2.50, students $2, children over 5 $1; discounts to AAM members & visiting more than one house; children under 5 & members no charge. ♿
Attendance: 20,292 (accurate)
Membership: Student $15; General $35; Contributor $50; Sponsor $100; Sustainer $250; Patron $500; Benefactor $1,000.

MASONIC GRAND LODGE LIBRARY AND MUSEUM OF TEXAS, 715 Columbus, Waco, TX 76701-1349. Mailing Address: P.O. Box 446, Waco, TX 76703-0446. Tel.: 254-753-7395. Fax: 254-753-2944.
E-mail: gs@grandlodgeoftexas.org
Web Site: grandlodgeoftexas.org
Founded: 1936.
Congressional District: 11
Key Personnel: C.E.O., Jack Hightower; Cur. & Librarian, Barbara Mechell.
Governing Authority: bd. dirs. Tax-exempt: 501(c)(3).
History Museum: Educational Masonic Library.
Collections: history & biography of Masons & Texas; bibliographical & general reference tools; Masonic artifacts including jewels, symbolic tools, aprons, gavels, tilers, swords, Bibles, certificates.
Research Fields: Texas; Masonic.
Facilities: 33,491-vol. library of Masonic & Texas materials available for research on premises; reading room.
Activities: permanent exhibits.
Hours & Admission Prices: Jan. 3-Dec. 22 Mon.-Fri. 8:30-4. No charge; donations accepted. Closed national holidays. ♿
Attendance: 10,000
Membership: Supporting $25; Sam Houston Hall of Fame $1,000; Patron $5,000.

MAYBORN MUSEUM COMPLEX, (M), 1300 S. University Parks Dr., Baylor University, Waco, TX 76706-1221. Mailing Address: One Bear Place #97154, Baylor Univ., Waco, TX 76798-7154. Tel.: 254-710-1110. Fax: 254-710-1173.
Web Site: www.baylor.edu/mayborn/
Formerly: Strecker Museum Complex
Founded: 1893.
Congressional District: 11
Key Personnel: Dir., Dr. Ellie Caston; Asst. Dir. Visitor Experience, Lesa Bush; Mgr. Museum Operations, Patricia Pack; Asst. Dir. Promotions & Events, Mark Smith; Asst. Dir. Facilities & Collections, Tom Haddad; Collections Mgr., Anita Benedict; Dir. Community Rels., Sarah Levine; Assoc. Prof., Interim Chm. Museum Studies & Dir. Academic Programs, Dr. Ken Hafertepe.
Personnel Profile: Full-Time Paid 28; Part-Time Paid 11; Part-Time Volunteers 200.

Governing Authority: Parent Institution: Baylor University. Tax-exempt: 501(c)(3).
Natural Science & History Museum.
Collections: natural science & cultural history; science; zoology; herpetology; archaeology; anthropology; entomology; paleontology; botany; geology; mineralogy; interactive themed rooms; historic village 1880-1910.
Research Fields: archaeology; herpetology; natural history; zoology; 1880-1910 rural central Texas towns.
Facilities: 143,000 sq. ft. exhibit space; nature pathway.
Activities: guided tours; lectures; formally organized education programs for children; museum studies program leading to M.A. degree; volunteer program; inter-museum loan & permanent exhibitions.
Publications: monthly e-newsletter; Mammoths in Waco: Exploring the Mystery.
Hours & Admission Prices: Mon.-Wed. & Fri.-Sat. 10-5, Thurs. 10-8, Sun. 1-5. Adults $6, seniors 65 & over $5, children 18 months to 12 yrs. $4; discounts to AAM members. Closed New Year's Day; Easter weekend; Thanksgiving; Christmas Day. ♿
Attendance: 94,944 (accurate)
Membership: Individual $30; Family $75; Contributing $100; Sustaining $250; Patron $500; Benefactor $1,000.

TEXAS RANGER HALL OF FAME AND MUSEUM, 100 Texas Ranger Trail, Waco, TX 76706-1209. Mailing Address: P.O. Box 2570, Waco, TX 76702-2570. Tel.: 254-750-8631. Fax: 254-750-8629.
E-mail: info@texasranger.org
Web Site: www.texasranger.org
Founded: 1968.
Congressional District: 11
Key Personnel: Dir., Byron A. Johnson; Chm. (V), Joe Hinton; Museum Shop Mgr., Lisa Daniel.
Personnel Profile: Full-Time Paid 13; Part-Time Paid 4; Part-Time Volunteers 4.
Governing Authority: municipal. Parent Institution: State of Texas, City of Waco. Tax-exempt.
Western History Museum: specializing in Texas Ranger History.
Collections: Texas Ranger artifacts including arms, saddles, badges, Colt & Winchester firearms; Western cattle range; photographs; historical papers; oral history; Western history, paintings, sculpture & costumes.
Research Fields: Texas frontier history items; Texas Colonial items; Texas law enforcement; American west; Mexico.
Facilities: 2,200-vol. library; multimedia show area; banquet facility; education facility. Museum-related items for sale.
Activities: guided tours; lectures; special events.
Publications: online journal, Dispatch.
Hours & Admission Prices: Daily 9-5; guided tours by appointment. Adults $6, children 6-12 $3; discounts to groups, & law enforcement personnel; children 5 & under no charge. Closed New Year's Day; Thanksgiving; Christmas. ♿
Attendance: 80,000 (accurate)
Membership: Circle Star $35; Silver Star $55; Gold Star $250 ($55 annual renewal); Corporate Club $500, 1,500, $2,500, & $5,000; Captain's Circle $5,000; 3rd Century Club $10,000.

TEXAS SPORTS HALL OF FAME, 1108 S. University Parks Dr., Waco, TX 76706-1223. Tel.: 254-756-1633; 800-567-9561. Fax: 254-756-2384.
E-mail: phyllis.trice@tshof.org
Web Site: www.tshof.org
Founded: 1989.
Congressional District: 11
Key Personnel: Exec. Dir., Steve Fallon; Pres. (V), Lee Fischer; Cur. & Museum Shop Mgr., Jay Black; Operations Mgr., Sales & Mktg. Coord., Phyllis Trice.
Personnel Profile: Full-Time Paid 3; Part-Time Paid 5; Part-Time Volunteers 1.
Governing Authority: private; nonprofit.
Sports Museum.
Collections: personal artifacts & memorabilia related to Texas high school, college & professional sports figures.
Facilities: library of books, magazines, programs, media guides & photographs; 11,000 sq. ft. exhibit space; 50-seat theater. Sports-related items for sale.
Activities: films; guided tours; loan exhibitions; broadcast programs. Annual Event: induction ceremonies.
Publications: quarterly newsletter, The Scoreboard.
Hours & Admission Prices: Mon.-Sat. 9-5, Sun. 12-5. Adults $6, seniors 60 & over $5, students & children over 5 $3; discounts to groups of 10 or more; active military & children under 6 no charge. Closed New Year's Day; Easter; Thanksgiving; Christmas. ♿
Attendance: 30,000 (accurate)
Membership: Student $20; Individual $30; Family $50; Patron $100; Supporting $250; Sustaining $500; Corporate $1,000 & up.

Washington

BARRINGTON LIVING HISTORY FARM, Washington-on-the-Brazos State Historic Site, 23100 Barrington Lane, Washington, TX 77880. Mailing Address: P.O. Box 305, Washington, TX 77880-0305. Tel.: 936-878-2213 & 2214. Fax: 936-878-2810.
Web Site: www.birthplaceoftexas.com
Founded: 1936.
Congressional District: 10
Key Personnel: Complex Mgr., Tom Scaggs; Site Mgr., Bill Irwin; Museum Shop Mgr., Diana Evans.
Personnel Profile: Full-Time Paid 15; Part-Time Paid 5; Part-Time Volunteers 20; Interns 1.
Governing Authority: state. Parent Institution: Texas Parks & Wildlife Dept., 4200 Smith School Rd., Austin, TX 78744. Tax-exempt.
Historic House: 1844-57 Barrington, home of Anson Jones, fourth & last president of the Republic of Texas; house was moved to Washington State Park, site of the signing of the Texas Declaration of Independence.
Collections: Anson Jones family personal artifacts; home furnishings from 1840-1860.
Research Fields: Republic of Texas, 1836-1846; Texas agriculture 1840-1860.
Facilities: reconstructed Anson Jones Farm, Barrington.
Activities: site tours; living history demonstrations & special events.
Hours & Admission Prices: Farm: daily 10-4:30. Park: daily 8am to sundown. Adults $4, students any age $2. ♿
Attendance: 265,000 (estimated)

* **STAR OF THE REPUBLIC MUSEUM, (M),** 23200 Park Rd. 12, Washington, TX 77880. Mailing Address: P.O. Box 317, Washington, TX 77880-0317. Tel.: 936-878-2461. Fax: 936-878-2462.
E-mail: star@blinn.edu
Web Site: www.starmuseum.org
Founded: 1970.
Congressional District: 14
Key Personnel: Dir., Houston McGaugh; Cur. Collections, Dr. Shawn Carlson; Cur. Education, Anne McGaugh; Public Program Coord., Jodi Jungman; Administrative Asst., Effie Wellmann.
Personnel Profile: Full-Time Paid 6; Part-Time Paid 7; Part-Time Volunteers 10; Interns 1.
Governing Authority: college; Blinn College, Brenham, TX. Tax-exempt.
History Museum: located on the site of the signing of the Texas Declaration of Independence, twice the capital of the Republic of Texas.
Collections: cultural, social, economic & political history of pre-1850 Texas.
Research Fields: The Republic of Texas 1836-1846.
Facilities: library; theater.
Activities: temporary exhibitions; group presentations; school educational programs; audiovisual interpretive programs; Texas Independence Day celebration.
Publications: quarterly newsletter; exhibition catalogs.
Hours & Admission Prices: Daily 10-5. Family $15, Adults $5, students $3; discounts to AAM, ICOM & Texas Assoc. of Museums members. Closed Thanksgiving; Christmas Eve, Day & week. ♿
Attendance: 35,000 (accurate)

Waxahachie

ELLIS COUNTY MUSEUM, INC., 201 S. College, Waxahachie, TX 75165-3711. Mailing Address: P.O. Box 706, Waxahachie, TX 75168-0706. Tel.: 972-937-0681.
E-mail: ecmuseum@sbcglobal.net
Web Site: www.rootsweb.ancestry.com/~txecm
Founded: 1967.
Congressional District: 6
Key Personnel: Dir. & Cur., Shannon Simpson; Pres. (V), David Smith.
Personnel Profile: Full-Time Paid 1; Part-Time Paid 1; Part-Time Volunteers 200.
Governing Authority: nonprofit. Tax-exempt: 501(c)(3).
History Museum: housed in 1889 Masonic Lodge Hall Bldg.
Collections: relics; photographs; manuscripts; period furniture & furnishings.
Research Fields: local & county history.
Facilities: Arts & crafts, Gingerbread Trail items & other museum-related items for sale.
Activities: Annual Event: Gingerbread Trail Home Tour.
Publications: quarterly newsletter; book: Ellis County, A Photohistory, 1993; booklet: Ellis County Courthouse, 1995.
Hours & Admission Prices: Mon.-Sat. 10-5, Sun.1-5. No charge; donations accepted.
Attendance: 9,000 (accurate)

Membership: Individual $15; Family $25; Patron $100; Sponsor $200; Advocate $500; Benefactor $1,000; Organization & Business $50-$100.

Weatherford

DOSS HERITAGE AND CULTURE CENTER, 1400 Texas Dr., Weatherford, TX 76086. Mailing Address: P.O. Box 215, Weatherford, TX 76086-0215. Tel.: 817-599-6168. Fax: 817-599-6193.
Key Personnel: Exec. Dir., John E. Scovil
History Museum.
Collections: local history & culture; period furnishings; personal artifacts; photographs; Native American artifacts; tools.
Activities: hands-on exhibits.
Hours & Admission Prices: Tues.-Sat. 10-5, Sun. 1-5. Adults $3, senior citizens & students $2.

THE NATIONAL VIETNAM WAR MUSEUM, 12685 Mineral Wells Hwy., Weatherford, TX 76088. Mailing Address: P.O. Box 146, Weatherford, TX 76088. Tel.: 940-664-3918.
E-mail: info@nationalvnwarmuseum.org
Web Site: nationalvnwarmuseum.org
Key Personnel: Dir., Gerald Brazell; Devel., Charles Bogle; Treas., Jim Messinger.
Personnel Profile: Part-Time Volunteers 32.
Governing Authority: private; nonprofit organization.
Military Museum.
Collections: Vietnam era artifacts; personal artifacts; photographs; military weapons & uniforms.
Activities: guided tours; loan exhibitions.
Publications: newsletter.
Hours & Admission Prices: Memorial Gardens: daily dawn to dusk. Visitor Center: opening early 2010. No charge; donations accepted.
Attendance: 15,000 (accurate)

Wellington

COLLINGSWORTH COUNTY MUSEUM, 824 East Ave., Wellington, TX 79095. Mailing Address: P.O. Box 495, Wellington, TX 79095-0495. Tel.: 806-447-5327.
E-mail: collingsworthmuseum@windstream.net
Web Site: www.collingsworthcountymuseum.org
Founded: 1971.
Key Personnel: Chm. (V), Bettye Baumgardner; Vice Pres. & Dir., W. Doris Stallings.
Governing Authority: Branch Museums: The Pruden Building & Sullivan Buildings. Tax-exempt.
History Museums.
Collections: Tyler House: agricultural & ranching artifacts. Pruden Building: works by local artists. Sullivan Buildings: historical artifacts; schoolroom; Templeton Law Office; soda fountain; Mothuskek square piano; military artifacts; quilts.
Hours & Admission Prices: Mon.-Fri. 9-5; other times by appointment. No charge; donations accepted. ♿
Attendance: 1,262 (accurate)
Membership: Individual $10; Angel $100; Patron $1,000.

Weslaco

FRONTERA AUDUBON SOCIETY, 1101 S. Texas Blvd., Weslaco, TX 78596-7001. Tel.: 956-968-3275. Fax: 956-968-1388.
E-mail: frontera@fronteraaudubon.org
Web Site: www.fronteraaudubon.org
Founded: 1974.
Congressional District: 15
Key Personnel: C.E.O., Dr. Rey Ramirez.
Personnel Profile: Full-Time Paid 4; Part-Time Paid 1; Part-Time Volunteers 5.
Governing Authority: Tax-exempt.
Wildlife Refuge.
Collections: agricultural developments; human influences; organic orchard; historical homestead.
Hours & Admission Prices: Sun.-Fri. 8-4, Sat. 7-7. Adults $2.50, children 12 & under $1; members no charge. ♿
Attendance: 2,351 (accurate)
Membership: Individual $20; Family $25; Group $35; Black-bellied Whistling-Duck $50; Kiskadee $70; Buff-bellied Hummingbird $100; Chachalaca $250; Altamira Oriole $500; Life $1,000.

LOWER RIO GRANDE VALLEY NATURE CENTER, 301 S. Border Ave., Weslaco, TX 78596-5815. Mailing Address: P.O. Box 8125, Weslaco, TX 78599-8125. Tel.: 956-969-2475. Fax: 956-969-9915.
E-mail: info@valleynaturecenter.org
Web Site: www.valleynaturecenter.org
Founded: 1984.
Key Personnel: Exec. Dir., Martin Hagne; Pres., Mark Gibbs; Office Mgr., Cindy Flores; Dir. Education, Allie Zamora; Dir. Education Asst., Susan Hoehne; Park Technician, Marissa Latigo; Park Tech Asst., Paul Garza.
Personnel Profile: Full-Time Paid 7; Part-Time Paid 2.
Governing Authority: Subsidiary Institution: Rio Grande Valley Bird Observatory. Tax-exempt.
Nature Center.
Collections: Nature Center: species of Rio Grande Valley of Texas including flora & fauna; shells of the Gulf; birds' nests; butterflies; reptiles; insects; mammals; native woods; hand-carved birds & small collection of wildlife photography and paintings. Exhibit Hall & Theater/meeting room: connected to 5 1/2 acre nature park with signs identifying trees & native plants; migrating & resident birds; native lizards & tortoises; butterfly garden.
Research Fields: cultivation of native plant species.
Facilities: library; 6 acres nature preserve; visitors center; meeting room. Museum-related items for sale.
Activities: nature trails; learning activities. Annual Events: Spring Fest in February; Dragonfly Days in May.
Publications: monthly newsletter; Lower Rio Grande Valley bird checklist; wildlife brochure series.
Hours & Admission Prices: Tues.-Fri. 9-5, Sat. 8-5, Sun. 1-5. Adults $3, seniors 55 & over $2.50, children $1; members no charge.
Attendance: 10,000 (accurate)
Membership: Student $15; Individual $25; Family $35.

WESLACO MUSEUM, 500 S. Texas, Weslaco, TX 78596-6202. Mailing Address: P.O. Box 8062, Weslaco, TX 78599-8062. Tel.: 956-968-9142. Fax: 956-447-0955.
E-mail: director@weslacomuseum.org
Web Site: texasescapes.net
Formerly: Weslaco Bicultural Museum
Founded: 1971.
Congressional District: 15
Key Personnel: Dir., Luis Contreras; Pres. (V), Benita Valadez.
Personnel Profile: Full-Time Paid 2; Full-Time Volunteers 60; Part-Time Paid 1; Part-Time Volunteers 15; Interns 2.
Governing Authority: private; nonprofit organization. Parent Institution: City of Weslaeo. Tax-exempt: 501(c)(3).
History Museum.
Collections: early 20th century local & border history artifacts & archives; photographs.
Research Fields: local history.
Facilities: 150-vol. library; 2,500 sq. ft. exhibit space.
Activities: guided tours; docent program; lectures; formal education programs for University of Texas-Pan American students; loan, traveling & temporary exhibitions; study clubs; cultural & art programs; historical programs.
Publications: quarterly newsletter; Images of America Series (through Arcadia Publishing).
Hours & Admission Prices: Tues.-Sat. 10-4. Adults $3, seniors $2, students $1; children 5 & under no charge. Closed New Year's Day; Good Friday; Memorial Day; Independence Day; Labor Day; Thanksgiving; Christmas. ♿
Attendance: 5,000 (accurate)
Membership: Regular $15; Associate $25; Sustaining $50; Sponsor $100; Patron $500; Founders $1,000.

West Columbia

VARNER-HOGG PLANTATION STATE HISTORIC SITE, 1702 N. 13th St., West Columbia, TX 77486. Mailing Address: P.O. Box 696, West Columbia, TX 77486-0696. Tel.: 979-345-4656. Fax: 979-345-4412.
Web Site: www.thc.state.tx.us
Founded: 1958.
Congressional District: 22
Key Personnel: Exec. Dir. THC, Mark Wolfe; Site Mgr., Sue Miller.
Personnel Profile: Full-Time Paid 7; Part-Time Paid 1; Part-Time Volunteers 25.
Governing Authority: state. Parent Institution: Texas Historical Commission, P.O. Box 12276., Austin, TX 78711-2276. Tax-exempt.
State Historic Site.
Collections: decorative arts; agriculture; archaeology; mementos relating to Gov. James Stephen Hogg & early events in Texas history; furniture from 1850's-1860's; Texian campaignware & other china; cemetery; sugar mill equipment; barn; slavequarter. Historic Building: c.1835 mansion.
Research Fields: history; furniture; decorative arts; Texas-made furniture.

Facilities: picnic area. Museum-related items for sale.
Activities: guided house tours; permanent exhibitions; grounds tour; folkway programs.
Publications: site leaflet, Interpretive Guide.
Hours & Admission Prices: Tues.-Sun. 8-5. Tours: Tues.-Sun. 10-3. Site: $1 entrance fee. Mansion: adults $6, students & children over 5 $2. Closed New Year's Day; Easter; Thanksgiving; Christmas Eve & Day.
Attendance: 5,000 (estimated)

Wharton

WHARTON COUNTY HISTORICAL MUSEUM, 3615 N. Richmond Rd., Wharton, TX 77488-2022. Mailing Address: P.O. Box 349, Wharton, TX 77488-0349. Tel.: 979-532-2600. Fax: 979-532-0871.
E-mail: wchm@awesomenet.net
Web Site: www.whartoncountymuseum.org
Founded: 1979.
Congressional District: 14
Key Personnel: C.E.O. & Museum Shop Mgr., Marvin Albrecht; Pres. (V), Linda Joy Stovall.
Personnel Profile: Full-Time Paid 3; Part-Time Paid 2; Part-Time Volunteers 32.
Governing Authority: nonprofit organization. Tax-exempt: 501(c)(3).
History Museum: housed in former Marshall & Lillie A. Johnson residence.
Collections: over 6,000 historic photos of Wharton County; land grants & maps dating from 1824-1830; listing of doctors of Wharton County; medical equipment; silver, china, quilts, dressing apparel & furniture; sulphur mine exhibit; handmade dolls; military records, service decorations, clippings & photos; Shanghai Pierce Ranch exhibit; business journals; city & county record books; Indian artifacts; military Post West Bernard artifacts; barbed wire; telephone company switchboard; sports, including Hall of Famers; two Medal of Honor recipients exhibits: M/Sgt Roy P. Benavidez (Army) & SFC Johnnie D. Hutchins (Navy); Dan Rather shotgun house; pulitzer prize & Emmy award winning author & playwrite Horton Foote exhibit; Marshall Johnson's big game trophy room.
Research Fields: local history.
Activities: guided tours; formally organized education programs for children; docent program or council; training programs; temporary exhibitions.
Publications: newsletter; newspapers; brochures.
Hours & Admission Prices: Mon.-Fri. 9:30-4:30, Sat.-Sun. 1-5; appointments available in evenings for special groups. No charge; donations accepted. ♿
Attendance: 6,000 (estimated)
Membership: Associate $25; Friend $50; Supporter $100; Patron $250; Sponsor $500; Benefactor $1,000.

White Settlement

WHITE SETTLEMENT HISTORICAL MUSEUM, 8320 Hanon Dr., White Settlement, TX 76108-2317. Tel.: 817-246-9719.
E-mail: hanontx@lycos.com
Web Site: www.wsmuseum.com
Founded: 1991.
Congressional District: 12
Key Personnel: Mgr., Carol L. Davis.
Personnel Profile: Part-Time Paid 1; Part-Time Volunteers 8.
Governing Authority: Tax-exempt.
History Museum.
Collections: local history & culture; photographs; period artifacts & documents; 1940s windmill; farm milk shed; 1927 Farmall tractor; WWI horse & mule drinking trough; farm equipment; blacksmith tools; B-36 Peacemaker/7th Bomb Wing room. Historic Buildings: 1864 Allen log cabin; 1940s playhouse.
Research Fields: local history & genealogy.
Facilities: library.
Activities: special events. Museum Sponsors: White Settlement Days.
Publications: Memories of Liberator Village.
Hours & Admission Prices: Tues.-Sat. 10-3. No charge; donations accepted. Closed New Year's Day; Independence Day; Thanksgiving; Christmas. ♿
Attendance: 1,200 (estimated)

Wichita Falls

KELL HOUSE MUSEUM, 900 Bluff St., Wichita Falls, TX 76301-3203. Tel.: 940-723-2712. Fax: 940-723-6592.
E-mail: kellhouse@sbcglobal.net
Web Site: www.wichitaheritage.org
Founded: 1981.
Congressional District: 13
Key Personnel: Exec. Dir., Delores Culley; Chm. (V), Monica Morris; Pres. (V), Mike Wheat; Cur., Stacie Crosetto Flood.
Personnel Profile: Full-Time Paid 2; Part-Time Paid 1; Part-Time Volunteers 50.
Governing Authority: nonprofit organization. Parent Institution: Wichita County Heritage Society. Tax-exempt: 501(c)(3).
Historic House: 1909 home of Frank Kell.
Collections: Wichita Falls history from 1900-1980; furniture; decorative arts; fabrics; costumes; documents; photographs.
Research Fields: local history.
Facilities: 4,800 sq. ft. exhibit space; gardens.
Activities: guided tours; organized education programs for children; docent program; temporary exhibitions. Annual Events: Mother/Daughter Garden Tea in May; July 4th celebration; Santa House.
Publications: quarterly newsletter.
Hours & Admission Prices: Tues.-Fri. 10-3, Sat.-Sun. 2-4. Adults $5, seniors & military $4, children & students $1; members no charge. Closed major holidays.
Attendance: 6,500 (estimated)
Membership: Heritage $50; Preservation $100; Conservation $250; Restoration $500; Revitalization $1,000.

KEMP CENTER FOR THE ARTS, 1300 Lamar, Wichita Falls, TX 76301-7031. Tel.: 940-767-2787. Fax: 940-767-3956.
E-mail: info@kempcenter.org
Web Site: www.kempcenter.org
Formerly: Arts Council Wichita Falls Area
Founded: 1995.
Key Personnel: Exec. Dir., Carlana Fitch; Pres. (V), Bob Thompson; Gallery Mgr., Janie Hotchkiss.
Personnel Profile: Full-Time Paid 4; Part-Time Paid 3.
Governing Authority: Tax-exempt.
Community Art Center.
Collections: works by regional artists.
Facilities: 250-seat performance hall; sculpture garden. Museum-related items for sale.
Activities: classes; temporary exhibitions. Museum Sponsors: Arts Festival; 3 Performing Arts Series; Home & Garden Festival.
Publications: quarterly newsletter; annual sculpture catalogue.
Hours & Admission Prices: Mon.-Fri. 9-5. No charge; donations accepted. Closed New Year's Day; Good Friday; Memorial Day; Independence Day; Labor Day; Thanksgiving; Christmas. ♿
Attendance: 32,000 (estimated)
Membership: Individual $40; Family $75; Performer $100; Collector $250; Director $500; Benefactor $1,000.

MUSEUM OF NORTH TEXAS HISTORY, (M), 720 Indiana, Wichita Falls, TX 76301-6512. Mailing Address: P.O. Box 1619, Wichita Falls, TX 76307-1619. Tel.: 940-322-7628.
Web Site: www.month-ntx.org
Founded: 2000.
Congressional District: 13
Key Personnel: Dir., Lita Watson; Pres. (V), Douglas James.
Personnel Profile: Full-Time Paid 1; Part-Time Paid 1; Part-Time Volunteers 10.
Governing Authority: Branch Museum: Call Field Army Air Base, 4515 Jacksboro Hwy. (Kickapoo Airport), Wichita Falls, TX. Tax-exempt.
History Museum.
Collections: North Texas history; photographs; military; petroleum; over 500 western hats.
Activities: school tours; temporary & permanent exhibits.
Hours & Admission Prices: Tues.-Fri. 10-12 & 1-4, Sat. 10-2; other times by appointment. No charge; donations accepted. Closed all major holidays. ♿
Attendance: 4,500 (accurate)
Membership: Individual $35; Family $50; Business & Contributor $100; Patron $150; Pioneer $250; Benefactor $500; Historian $1,000.

WICHITA FALLS MUSEUM AND ART CENTER, Two Eureka Cir., Wichita Falls, TX 76308-2998. Tel.: 940-692-0923. Fax: 940-696-5358.
E-mail: cohndrennan@mwsu.edu
Web Site: www.mwsu.edu/wfma
Founded: 1964.
Congressional District: 13
Key Personnel: Pres. (V), Dale Brock; Dir., Cohn Drennan; Mgr. Facility and Interactive Exhibits, Jeff Desborough; Cur. Collections & Exhibits, Danny Bills.
Personnel Profile: Full-Time Paid 2; Part-Time Paid 4; Part-Time Volunteers 4.
Governing Authority: nonprofit. Tax-exempt: 501(c)(3).
General Museum; planetarium; laser; children's galleries.
Collections: contemporary American prints; art galleries.
Research Fields: local & regional history.
Facilities: 1,500-vol. library of art & exhibit reference books available by

request and on the premises; planetarium; 250-seat auditorium; classrooms; hands on science gallery; discovery room.
Activities: guided tours; lectures; films; gallery talks; arts festivals; formally organized educational programs; docent program or council; inter-museum, temporary & traveling exhibitions; school loan service; Museum School-Humanities curriculum for ages 3-17.
Publications: Muse News Quarterly.
Hours & Admission Prices: Tues.-Fri. 9:30-4:30, 1st Thurs. of month 9:30-7:30, Sat. 10-4:30. Adults $4, children $3; discounts to AAM & ASTC members; members no charge. Closed holidays. ♿
Attendance: 50,000 (estimated)
Membership: Individual $30; Family $45; Grandparents Plan $55; Associate $100; Friend $150; Contributor $250; Patron $500; Benefactor $1,000.

Wimberley

OLD WEST MUSEUM, 333 Wayside Dr., Wimberley, TX 78676-5117. Tel.: 512-847-3338.
E-mail: cowboymuseum@earthlink.net
Web Site: cowboymuseum.net
Formerly: Cowboy Museum
Founded: 1956.
Key Personnel: Owner & Cur., Jack N. Glover; Co-Owner, Cherie Glover.
Governing Authority: individual operation.
General Museum.
Collections: Indian artifacts; agriculture; history; early farming; anthropology; paintings; sculpture; graphics; archaeology; folklore; medical; military; natural history; oil field.
Research Fields: pertaining to collections.
Facilities: 500-vol. library of Indian & frontier books available for use on premises. Antiques, Indian artifacts, ranch items, original art & arrow heads for sale.
Activities: guided tours; lectures; formally organized education programs for children, adults, undergraduate & graduate college students; permanent & traveling exhibitions.
Publications: monthly magazine, International Barbwire Gazette; books, Barbwire Bible, VI; Sex Life of American Indian; Glovers Illustrated Letters.
Hours & Admission Prices: Daily 9-5. No charge. ♿
Attendance: 2,500 (estimated)

PIONEER TOWN, 333 Wayside Dr., Wimberley, TX 78676-5117. Tel.: 512-847-3289. Fax: 512-847-6705.
Founded: 1956.
Congressional District: 10
Key Personnel: Sec. & Treas., John D. White.
Personnel Profile: Full-Time Volunteers 1; Part-Time Paid 4.
Governing Authority: individual operation. Parent Institution: Pioneer Museum of Western Art.
Village Museum: authentic reproduction of c.1880 old West Town.
Collections: artifacts of the Old West; complete Frederic Remington sculpture museum of all 22 sculptures; Russell bronze sculptures; sculpture & metal art of the West. Historic House: 1861 Texas style log cabin.
Research Fields: culture of the Old West; bronze sculptures.
Facilities: 500-vol. library of Old West, history, material of people & places of the Old West available for use on premises.
Activities: tours by appointment.
Publications: newsletters; brochures; catalogs; books, Frederic Remington 1861-1909: He Knew the Horse, What's A Bronze.
Hours & Admission Prices: by appointment. No charge; donations accepted.
Attendance: 35,000 (estimated)

Wink

ROY ORBISON MUSEUM, Texas 115, Wink, TX 79789. Mailing Address: P.O. Box 621, Wink, TX 79789-0621. Tel.: 432-527-3622.
Key Personnel: Cur., Dorothy Wolf
History Museum.
Collections: artifacts & memorabilia from Roy Orbison's childhood & music career.
Activities: Museum Sponsors: Annual Festival.
Hours & Admission Prices: By appointment only. No charge; donations accepted.

Woodville

ALLAN SHIVERS MUSEUM, 302 N. Charlton, Woodville, TX 75979-4806. Tel.: 409-283-3709. Fax: 409-283-5258.
E-mail: rbunch75979@yahoo.com
Founded: 1963.
Congressional District: 2
Key Personnel: Pres. (V), Mrs. L.G. Burton; Dir. Library & Museum, Rosemary Bunch.
Personnel Profile: Part-Time Paid 4; Part-Time Volunteers 1.
Governing Authority: county. Tax-exempt.
Historic House Museum: 1881 restored building.
Collections: period furnishings; mementos of the family of Allan Shivers, governor of Texas, including documents, photographs, inaugural ballgowns.
Research Fields: state history.
Facilities: 1,500-vol. library of historical & political books available for use on premises.
Activities: guided tours; films; permanent exhibitions.
Hours & Admission Prices: Mon.-Fri. 9-4:30, Sat. 10-1:30. Adults $3, seniors $2, schoolchildren $1; preschool no charge. Closed major holidays. ♿
Attendance: 5,101 (accurate)

HERITAGE VILLAGE MUSEUM, 157 PR 6000, Woodville, TX 75979. Mailing Address: P.O. Box 888, Woodville, TX 75979-0888. Tel.: 409-283-2272; 800-323-0389. Fax: 409-283-2194.
E-mail: hvillage@eastex.net
Web Site: www.heritage-village.org
Key Personnel: Dir. & Museum Shop Mgr., Ofeira Gazzaway; Pres., Elizabeth Toliver.
Personnel Profile: Part-Time Paid 5.
Governing Authority: private; nonprofit organization. Tax-exempt: 501(c)(3).
Pioneer Village Museum.
Collections: 1840-1900 early East Texas Pioneer farming village including 36 buildings; costumes; tools.
Research Fields: Whitmeyer Research & Genealogy Library.
Activities: skills demonstrations.
Hours & Admission Prices: Daily 9-5. Adults $4, senior citizens $3, students $2; members no charge. Closed major holidays. ♿
Attendance: 15,000 (estimated)
Membership: Individual $15; Family $25; Business $50.

Woodway

CARLEEN BRIGHT ARBORETUM, 9001 Bosque Blvd., Woodway, TX 76712-3486. Tel.: 254-399-9204. Fax: 254-399-9216.
E-mail: kobric@woodway-texas.com
Web Site: www.woodway-texas.com/lev1.cfm/9
Key Personnel: Mgr., Karen O'bric
Arboretum.
Collections: trees; plants.
Facilities: nature trail.
Activities: rental facility.
Hours & Admission Prices: Daily 8am to dark.

Yorktown

YORKTOWN HISTORICAL MUSEUM, 144 W. Main St., Yorktown, TX 78164. Mailing Address: P.O. Box 1284, Yorktown, TX 78164-1284. Tel.: 361-564-2345. Fax: 361-938-5403.
Founded: 1978.
Congressional District: 15
Key Personnel: Pres., Irene Wulf; Vice Pres., Shirley Mueller; Treas., Beverly Bruns; Sec., Laura Burrows.
Personnel Profile: Part-Time Volunteers 45.
Governing Authority: Parent Institution: Yorktown Historical Society. Tax-exempt: 501(c)(3).
Historical & Preservation Society: housed in 1876 C. Eckhardt & Sons Store.
Collections: period furnishings; clothing; musical instruments; documents; pictures; books; archeological dig findings; Indian arrowheads; early tools & farm implements; school memorabilia.
Research Fields: history & artifacts of the City of Yorktown.
Facilities: 50-seat auditorium. Museum-related items for sale.
Activities: guided tours; lectures; films; wildflower & historic cemetery tours; handwork & art displays.
Publications: book, Yorktown, TX, It's History, l848-l989; postcards; revised book, 1848-1998 Yorktown Texas - 150 Year Anniversary.
Hours & Admission Prices: Thurs.-Sat. 10-2. No charge; donations accepted. ♿
Attendance: 700 (accurate)
Membership: Individual $5; Family $10; Business $25; Life $100.

UTAH

(120 listings)

Alpine

ALPINE ART CENTER, 450 S. Alpine Hwy., Alpine, UT 84004-1508. Tel.: 801-763-7173. Fax: 801-763-9799.
Key Personnel: Event Dir., Steve Streadbeck
Art Center.
Collections: paintings; sculpture.
Hours & Admission Prices: Art Center: Mon.-Fri. 10-5. Sculpture Park & Gardens: daily.

American Fork

TIMPANOGOS CAVE NATIONAL MONUMENT, R.R. 3, American Fork, UT 84003-9803. Mailing Address: R.R. 3, P.O. Box 200, American Fork, UT 84003-9803. Tel.: 801-756-5238. Fax: 801-756-5661.
Web Site: www.nps.gov/tica/index.htm
Founded: 1922.
Congressional District: 3
Key Personnel: Supt., Denis Davis.
Governing Authority: federal. Parent Institution: U.S. Dept. of the Interior, National Park Service.
Park Museum.
Collections: photographs; geological, botanical & paleontological items; historical artifacts.
Research Fields: speleogenesis; speleomorphology; cave biology, hydrology & hydrochemistry; Timpanogos Cave history.
Facilities: archive & curatorial storage area; library with natural history books & articles related to the monument & displays in the visitor center.
Activities: temporary exhibitions & special interpretive programs dealing with the history of the monument.
Publications: trail guide; book, Timpanogos Cave: Window Into the Earth; Park brochure.
Hours & Admission Prices: May to Labor Day daily 7-5:30; Fall Mon.-Fri. 8-5, last hike 3, Sat.-Sun. 8-5, last hike 3:30, call to confirm last hike times. No charge for use of facilities. ♿
Attendance: 12 (accurate)

Blanding

THE DINOSAUR MUSEUM, 754 S. 200 W., Blanding, UT 84511-3909. Tel.: 435-678-3454.
E-mail: dinos@dinosaur-museum.org
Web Site: www.dinosaur-museum.org
Founded: 1992.
Dinosaur History Museum.
Collections: paleontology; dinosaur history; skeletons; fossilized skin, eggs & footprints; sculptures.
Facilities: theater.
Activities: tours; movies.
Hours & Admission Prices: April 15-Oct. 15 Mon.-Sat. 9-5. Adults $2.50, senior citizens $1.50, children $1; discounts to groups of 10 or more; members no charge. ♿
Membership: Individual $20; Family $25.

EDGE OF THE CEDARS STATE PARK MUSEUM, 660 West, 400 N., Blanding, UT 84511-0788. Tel.: 435-678-2238. Fax: 435-678-3348.
E-mail: edgeofthecedars@utah.gov
Web Site: parks.state.ut.us/parks/www1/edge.htm
Founded: 1978.
Congressional District: 3
Key Personnel: Museum Dir., Teri Paul; Museum Shop Mgr., Kathrina Perkins; Cur. Collections, Deborah Westfall; Maintenance & Historic Replication, Andrew Goodwin; Cur. Education, Rebecca Stoneman.
Personnel Profile: Full-Time Paid 5; Part-Time Paid 3; Part-Time Volunteers 4; Interns 1.
Governing Authority: state. Parent Institution: State of Utah Div. of Parks & Recreation, P.O. Box 146001, Salt Lake City, UT 84114-6001. Tax-exempt.
Native American Cultural Museum: site of ancestral Puebloan village occupied A.D. 700-1220.
Collections: prehistoric Paleoindian, Archaic, & Ancestral Puebloan artifacts; Navajo & Ute artifacts; Navajo oral histories; paintings; photographs; sculptures; textiles.
Research Fields: anthropology; ethnology.
Facilities: 2,100-vol. library of archaeology and Indian culture; 4,200 sq. ft. exhibit area; labs; 50-seat indoor auditorium; 100-seat outdoor amphitheater & Indian dance plaza; visitor information center. Museum-related items for sale.
Activities: archaeology & Native American craft workshops & programs; self-guided & guided tours; lectures; permanent & temporary exhibitions.
Publications: Spirit Windows: Native American Rock Art of Southeastern Utah.
Hours & Admission Prices: mid-April to mid-Sept. daily 9-6; mid-Sept. to mid-April daily 9-5. Adults $5; discounts to Fun Tag members 65 & over; children no charge. Closed New Year's Day; Thanksgiving; Christmas. ♿
Attendance: 19,777 (accurate)

HUCK'S MUSEUM AND TRADING POST, 1243 S. Main St., Blanding, UT 84511-3204. Tel.: 435-678-2329.
Founded: 1976.
History Museum.
Collections: Native American culture & history; pottery; beads; arrowheads.
Hours & Admission Prices: Daily 8-5. Adults $3, children $2.

Boulder

ANASAZI STATE PARK MUSEUM, (M), 460 N. Hwy. 12, Boulder, UT 84716. Mailing Address: P.O. Box 1429, Boulder, UT 84716-1429. Tel.: 435-335-7308. Fax: 435-335-7352.
E-mail: nrdpr.ansp@state.ut.us
Web Site: www.stateparks.utah.gov/parks/anasazi
Founded: 1970.
Congressional District: 1
Key Personnel: Park Supt., Mike Nelson; Div. Dir., Mary Tullis; Cur., Bill Latady; Cur., Don Montoya; Museum Shop Mgr., Brenda Woolsey.
Personnel Profile: Full-Time Paid 3; Part-Time Paid 1; Part-Time Volunteers 1.
Governing Authority: state. Utah State Div. of Parks & Recreation, 1636 W. North Temple, Salt Lake City, UT. 84116.
Historic Site: 1050-1200 A.D., excavated Anasazi Indian Village.
Collections: artifacts representative of the Kayenta Anasazi culture during the period 1050-1200 A.D.; replica of Coombs Village.
Research Fields: the Coombs site; primitive technology manufacture methods.
Facilities: Publications & museum-related items for sale.
Activities: guided tours; lectures; films.
Hours & Admission Prices: Memorial Day-Labor Day daily 8-6; Sept.-May daily 9-5. Admission: $3 per person; $5 per car; discount to groups; children under 6 & senior citizens from State of Utah no charge. Closed New Year's Day; Thanksgiving; Christmas. ♿
Attendance: 35,000 (accurate)

Bountiful

BOUNTIFUL/DAVIS ART CENTER, 745 S. Main St., Bountiful, UT 84010-6326. Tel.: 801-292-0367. Fax: 801-292-7298.
E-mail: info@bdac.org
Web Site: www.bdac.org
Founded: 1974.
Congressional District: 1
Key Personnel: Exec. Dir. & Museum Shop Mgr., Emma J. Dugal; Chm. (V), Aida Mattingley.
Personnel Profile: Full-Time Paid 2; Part-Time Paid 1; Part-Time Volunteers 25.
Governing Authority: Tax-exempt.
Art Center.
Collections: paintings; drawings; sculpture; photography; printmaking.
Activities: education programs.
Hours & Admission Prices: Mon. 5pm-9pm, Tues.-Fri. 10-6, Sat. 2-5. No charge. Closed holidays.
Attendance: 15,000 (estimated)
Membership: Bronze $35-$499; Silver $500-$4,999; Gold over $5,000 (annual), $10,000 (lifetime member)

BOUNTIFUL HISTORICAL MUSEUM, 845 S. Main St., Ste. B5, Bountiful, UT 84010-6482. Tel.: 801-296-2060.
Web Site: www.bountifulutah.gov/HistoricalCommission/A_index01.html
History Museum.
Collections: local history & culture; period artifacts.
Hours & Admission Prices: Wed. 2-4, Sat. 1-3.

Brigham City

BRIGHAM CITY MUSEUM-GALLERY, 24 N. 300 W., Brigham City, UT 84302-2030. Mailing Address: P.O. Box 583, Brigham City, UT 84302-0583. Tel.: 435-723-6769. Fax: 435-723-6769.
Web Site: www.brighamcity.utah.gov
Founded: 1970.
Congressional District: 1
Key Personnel: C.E.O. & Dir., Larry Douglass; Dir. Research, Mary Alice Hobbs.

Personnel Profile: Full-Time Paid 1; Part-Time Paid 2.
Governing Authority: municipal government. Parent Institution: Brigham City Corporation. Tax-exempt.
Art Gallery & History Museum: collections focus on the Mormon Communitarian Society in Brigham City 1865-1881.
Collections: local & state art; 1855-1900 furniture, furnishings, guns, tools, documents relating to the history of Brigham City; 1900-1960 photographs & documents.
Research Fields: local artists; economic, political & folk history of Brigham City and Box Elder county.
Activities: lectures; films.
Publications: brochures; Historic Tour of Brigham City; Polygamy in Lorenzo Show's Brigham City: An Architectural Tour; Mayors of Brigham City.
Hours & Admission Prices: Tues.-Fri. 11-6, Sat. 1-5. No charge. ♿
Attendance: 10,000 (estimated)

GOLDEN SPIKE NATIONAL HISTORIC SITE, Hwy. 83, Brigham City, UT 84302-0897. Mailing Address: P.O. Box 897, Brigham City, UT 84302-0897. Tel.: 435-471-2209, ext. 29. Fax: 435-471-2341.
E-mail: gosp_interpretation@nps.gov
Web Site: www.nps.gov/gosp
Founded: 1965.
Congressional District: 1
Key Personnel: Supt., Leslie Crossland; Chief Operations, Tammy Benson; Museum Shop Mgr., Julie Mann-Cherry.
Personnel Profile: Full-Time Paid 8; Part-Time Paid 5; Part-Time Volunteers 15.
Governing Authority: federal. U.S. Dept. of the Interior, National Park Service.
National Historic Site: first transcontinental railroad was completed here on May 10, 1869.
Collections: materials relating to the railroad, railroad construction, & railroad workers; manuscript collection.
Research Fields: first transcontinental railroad; the effects of the railroad on the development of the West & America; Promontory Summit, Utah.
Facilities: Publications for sale.
Activities: self-guided auto tours; tours; interpretive talks; films; Big Fill Walk; locomotive runs.
Publications: Promontory Trail; Golden Spike handbook; Golden Spike brochure.
Hours & Admission Prices: Daily 9-5. Federal Interagency passes honored. Closed New Year's Day; Thanksgiving; Christmas. ♿
Attendance: 47,500 (accurate)
Membership: Western National Parks Association $25.

Bryce

BRYCE CANYON NATIONAL PARK VISITOR CENTER, Bryce Canyon National Park, Bryce, UT 84764. Mailing Address: P.O. Box 640201, Bryce, UT 84764-0201. Tel.: 435-834-5322. Fax: 435-834-4102. TDD: 435-834-5322.
E-mail: brca_reception_area@nps.gov
Web Site: www.nps.gov/brca
Founded: 1959.
Congressional District: 1
Key Personnel: Supt., Eddie Lopez; Chm. (V), Dan Ng; Museum Shop Mgr., Gayle Pollock.
Personnel Profile: Full-Time Paid 52; Part-Time Volunteers 60; Interns 4.
Governing Authority: federal. Parent Institution: U.S. Dept. of Interior, National Park Service, Washington, DC. Subsidiary Institution: Bryce Canyon Natural History Association. Tax-exempt.
Natural History Museum.
Collections: geology; herbarium; mammal skins; American Indian artifacts; insects; birds; fauna & flora.
Research Fields: Utah prairie dog; peregrine falcon; baseline inventories.
Facilities: library of natural history; 120-seat auditorium. Publications & post cards for sale.
Activities: guided tours; interpretive talks; films; permanent exhibitions.
Publications: A Kid's Guide to Bryce Canyon; A Natural History Guide to Bryce Canyon National Park; Queen's Garden at Sunrise Point Guide; Bryce Canyon National Park; Bryce Canyon Auto & Hiking Guide; Bryce Canyon Discovery; Shadows of Time: The Geology of Bryce Canyon National Park; Wildflowers of Southwestern Utah.
Hours & Admission Prices: Visitors Center: April & Oct. daily 8-6; May-Sept. daily 8-8; Nov.-March daily 8-4:30. Park: daily. Park: $12 per individual hiking or biking; $25 per car. Visitors Center: closed Thanksgiving; Christmas. ♿
Attendance: 1,600,000 (estimated)

PAUNSAUGUNT WILDLIFE MUSEUM, 1945 W. Utah State Hwy. 12, Bryce, UT 84764. Mailing Address: P.O. Box 640049, Bryce, UT 84764-0049. Tel.: 435-834-5555.
E-mail: terri@brycecanyonmuseum.com
Web Site: www.brycecanyonmuseum.com
Founded: 1995.
Key Personnel: Owner & Cur., Robert Driedonks; Owner & Cur., Terri Driedonks
History Museum.
Collections: over 800 animals in a natural setting; Native American artifacts; butterflies; birds of prey; bugs; ocean fish; seashells; endangered Utah prairie dogs; early Western artifacts.
Facilities: Museum-related items for sale.
Activities: hand feed deer.
Hours & Admission Prices: April-Nov. 15 daily 9-9. Adults $8, children 6-12 $5; children under 3 no charge. ♿

Castle Dale

EMERY COUNTY PIONEER MUSEUM, 64 E. 100 N., Castle Dale, UT 84513. Mailing Address: P.O. Box 1088, Castle Dale, UT 84513. Tel.: 435-381-5154.
Key Personnel: Dir., Margaret Keller
Pioneer Museum.
Collections: pioneer life & history; farm equipment; period clothing; personal artifacts; photographs; local outlaws.
Hours & Admission Prices: Mon.-Fri. 10-4, Sat. 12-4.Donations Accepted

MUSEUM OF SAN RAFAEL, 64 N. 100 E., Castle Dale, UT 84513. Mailing Address: P.O. Box 1088, Castle Dale, UT 84513-1088. Tel.: 435-381-5252.
Web Site: www.museumsanrafael.org
Key Personnel: Dir., Margaret Kelley
History Museum.
Collections: dinosaurs; early Americans; pioneer settlers; taxidermy; archaeological artifacts.
Hours & Admission Prices: Mon.-Fri. 10-4, Sat. 12-4. No charge.

Cedar City

BRAITHWAITE FINE ARTS GALLERY, Southern Utah University, Cedar City, UT 84720-2470. Mailing Address: Southern Utah University, 351 W. Center St., Cedar City, UT 84720-2470. Tel.: 435-586-5432. Fax: 435-865-8012.
E-mail: museums@suu.edu
Web Site: www.suu.edu/pva/artgallery
Founded: 1976.
Congressional District: 1
Key Personnel: Dir., Reece Summers.
Personnel Profile: Full-Time Paid 1; Part-Time Paid 4.
Governing Authority: college. Parent Institution: Southern Utah University, Cedar City, UT 84720. Tax-exempt: 501(c)(3).
College Art Gallery.
Collections: 19th- & 20th-century American art.
Activities: guided tours; illustrated lectures; art films; gallery talks; formally organized education programs; temporary & traveling exhibitions.
Hours & Admission Prices: Tues.-Sat. 12-7. No charge; donations accepted. Closed major holidays; academic breaks. ♿
Attendance: 10,000 (estimated)
Membership: Individual $50; Sponsor $250; Patron $500.

CEDAR BREAKS NATIONAL MONUMENT, 2390 W. Hwy. 56, Ste. 11, Cedar City, UT 84720-4151. Tel.: 435-586-9451. Fax: 435-586-3813.
Web Site: www.nps/cebr
Founded: 1933.
Congressional District: 1
Key Personnel: Supt., Paul Roelandt; Museum Shop Mgr., Lyman Hafen; Chief Park Ranger, Danica Bloom.
Personnel Profile: Full-Time Paid 1; Part-Time Paid 6; Part-Time Volunteers 1; Interns 1.
Governing Authority: federal. Parent Institution: U.S. Dept. of Interior, National Park Service. Tax-exempt.
Park Museum.
Collections: flora; fauna; geology specimens.
Research Fields: geology; flora.
Facilities: visitor center; viewing terrace.
Activities: guided tours; lectures.
Publications: books; guides; pamphlets; brochures; maps.
Hours & Admission Prices: late May to mid-Oct. daily 8-6. $3 per person; $4 per car. ♿
Attendance: 60,000 (estimated)

FRONTIER HOMESTEAD STATE PARK & MUSEUM, 635 N. Main, Cedar City, UT 84721-6179. Tel.: 435-586-9290.
E-mail: ironmission@utah.gov
Web Site: www.stateparks.utah.gov
Formerly: Iron Mission State Park & Museum
Founded: 1973.
Congressional District: 8
Key Personnel: Park Manager, Todd Prince; Cur., Ryan Paul; Historic Replicator, Ray Warner.
Personnel Profile: Full-Time Paid 3; Part-Time Paid 2; Interns 2.
Governing Authority: state. Utah State Div. of Parks & Recreation, 1594 W. North Temple, Ste. 116, Box 146001, Salt Lake City, UT 84114-6001. Tax-exempt.
Pioneer History Museum.
Collections: Gronway Parry collection; horse drawn vehicle; early pioneer displays.
Research Fields: Iron County history; 1851-1924 agrarian history.
Facilities: library.
Activities: guided tours; lectures; artist in residence.
Hours & Admission Prices: Mon.-Sat. 9-5. Adults $3; children under 6 no charge. Closed New Year's Day; Thanksgiving; Christmas. ♿
Attendance: 20,000 (estimated)
Membership: Individual $25; Foundation $500 & up.

Coalville

SUMMIT COUNTY HISTORICAL MUSEUM, 60 N. Main St., Coalville, UT 84017-9809. Mailing Address: P.O. Box 128, Coalville, UT 84017-0128. Tel.: 435-336-3200 & 3015.
History Museum.
Collections: local history & culture; photographs; period furnishings; personal artifacts.
Activities: research; guided tours.
Hours & Admission Prices: Daily 8-5; other times by appointment.

Delta

GREAT BASIN HISTORICAL SOCIETY & MUSEUM, 328 W. 100 N., Delta, UT 84624. Mailing Address: P.O. Box 550, Delta, UT 84624-0550. Tel.: 435-864-5013. Fax: 435-864-2446.
E-mail: greatbasin@hubwest.com
Founded: 1988.
Key Personnel: Dir. & Pres., Owen Neilsen; Treas. & Devel., Linda Neilsen; Cur. & Sec., Sindy McMichael.
Personnel Profile: Part-Time Paid 1; Part-Time Volunteers 17; Interns 1.
Governing Authority: private; nonprofit organization. Tax-exempt: 501(c)(3).
Historical Society Museum.
Collections: geological specimens; photographs; personal artifacts; tools & implements for geology.
Hours & Admission Prices: Mon.-Sat. 10-4, call for additional hours. No charge; donations accepted.
Attendance: 3,100 (accurate)
Membership: Individual & Family $10; Institutional $50; Contributing $100; Life $500.

Ephraim

CENTRAL UTAH ART CENTER, 86 N. Main, Ephraim, UT 84627-1133. Tel.: 435-283-5110.
E-mail: art@cuartcenter.org
Web Site: www.cuartcenter.org
Key Personnel: Dir., Jared Latimer
Art Center.
Collections: works by local & national artists.
Activities: workshops.
Hours & Admission Prices: Tues.-Fri. 11-6, Sat. 11-4.

SNOW COLLEGE ART GALLERY, 150 E. College Ave., Ephraim, UT 84627-1550. Tel.: 435-283-7416.
E-mail: adam.larsen@snow.edu
Web Site: www.snow.edu/art/gallery/index.html
Key Personnel: Dir., Adam Larsen
Art Gallery.
Collections: works by student & faculty.
Hours & Admission Prices: Mon.-Fri. 9-5; other times by appointment.

Eureka

TINTIC MINING MUSEUM, Main St., Eureka, UT 84628. Mailing Address: P.O. Box 218, Eureka, UT 84628-0218. Tel.: 435-433-6915 (Festival info). Fax: 435-433-6891.
Founded: 1974.
Congressional District: 2
Key Personnel: C.E.O., Dir. & Registrar, J. L. McNulty; Chm. (V), Deborah Treloar; Asst. Dir., E.C. McNulty; Museum Shop Mgr., Joan Morris.
Personnel Profile: Full-Time Volunteers 4; Part-Time Volunteers 5.
Governing Authority: nonprofit organization. Parent Institution: Utah State Historical Society, 300 Rio Grande, Salt Lake City, UT 84101. Tax-exempt: 501(c)(3).
Mining Museum: housed in 1899 Eureka City Hall.
Collections: mining artifacts; complete mineral display; photos of the area. Historic Building: 1924 Union Pacific Railroad Depot.
Research Fields: mines.
Facilities: library of Eureka Reporter newspapers from 1902 to 1942, available for use on premises; history room.
Activities: self-guided tours. Museum Sponsors: Tintic Silver Festival.
Hours & Admission Prices: May-Sept. Sat.-Sun. 3-5; other times by appointment. No charge; donations accepted. ♿
Attendance: 1,500
Membership: Annual $5; Lifetime Individual $35; Lifetime Couple $50.

Fairfield

CAMP FLOYD/STAGECOACH INN STATE PARK, 18035 W. 1540 N., Fairfield, UT 84013-9612. Tel.: 801-768-8932. Fax: 801-768-2794.
E-mail: marktrotter@utah.gov
Web Site: www.stateparks.utah.gov/parks/camp-floyd
Founded: 1964.
Key Personnel: Park Supt., Mark A. Trotter.
Personnel Profile: Full-Time Paid 2; Part-Time Paid 3; Part-Time Volunteers 3; Interns 1.
Governing Authority: state. Parent Institution: Utah State Parks, 1636 W. North Temple, Salt Lake City, UT 84116.
Historic Site: 1858 site of Camp Floyd, former army camp of Utah.
Collections: local history & culture; period artifacts.
Activities: guided tours; lectures.
Hours & Admission Prices: Mon.-Sat. 9-5. Family $6, adults $2; children 5 & under no charge. Closed New Year's Day; Thanksgiving; Christmas. ♿
Attendance: 16,000 (accurate)

Fairview

FAIRVIEW MUSEUM OF HISTORY & ART, 85 N. 100 E., Fairview, UT 84629. Mailing Address: P.O. Box 157, Fairview, UT 84629-0157. Tel.: 435-427-9216.
E-mail: fvmuseum@cut.net
Web Site: www.sanpete.com
Founded: 1966.
Congressional District: 3
Key Personnel: Pres. (V), Jerry Nelson; Dir., Ron Staker.
Personnel Profile: Part-Time Paid 1; Part-Time Volunteers 17.
Governing Authority: nonprofit; board of trustees. Tax-exempt.
General Museum & Pioneer Park.
Collections: pioneer relics & histories; Indian artifacts; miniature carvings; arts & crafts; Indian bead & leather art; engines; historic farm machines & vehicles; Columbian mammoth; statuary by Avard T. Fairbanks; geology & rocks; paintings & prints; local school children's artwork.
Research Fields: Indian & pioneer histories; geology.
Facilities: garden.
Activities: guided tours.
Hours & Admission Prices: Summer: Mon.-Sat. 10-6, Sun. 2-6. Winter: Mon.-Sat. 10-5, Sun. 2-5. No charge; donations accepted. ♿
Attendance: 20,000 (accurate)
Membership: Contributing $25; Supporting $50; Sustaining $100; Sponsor $250; Patron $500; Benefactor $1,000.

Farmington

PIONEER VILLAGE, 375 N. Lagoon Lane, Farmington, UT 84025-2502. Mailing Address: P.O. Box 696, Farmington, UT 84025-0696. Tel.: 801-451-8050. Fax: 801-451-8015.
Founded: 1954.
Congressional District: 1
Key Personnel: Dir., Peter Freed; Deputy Dir., Howard Freed.
Personnel Profile: Full-Time Paid 5; Part-Time Paid 30.
Governing Authority: nonprofit organization. Lagoon Corp., Box N, Farmington, UT 84025.

History Museum.
Collections: carriages; guns; Indian artifacts; pioneer artifacts; toys; coins & silver. Historic Buildings: log & stone buildings; stores; homes.
Facilities: 700-vol. library; restaurant. Museum-related items for sale.
Activities: temporary & permanent exhibits.
Hours & Admission Prices: April-May & Sept.-Oct. Sat.-Sun. 10-7; June-Aug. daily 10-8. Admission $10; seniors no charge. ♿
Attendance: 500,000 (accurate)

S & S SHORTLINE TRAIN PARK & MUSEUM, 575 N. 1525 W., Farmington, UT 84025-2615. Tel.: 801-451-0222.
Web Site: www.sssrr.ssshortlineleasing.com/index.html
Railroad Museum.
Collections: railroad artifacts & memorabilia.
Hours & Admission Prices: May-June & Aug.-Sept. 1st Sat. of month 10-6; July 2nd Sat. of month 10-6.

Fillmore

TERRITORIAL STATEHOUSE STATE PARK & MUSEUM, 50 W. Capitol Ave., Fillmore, UT 84631-5556. Tel.: 435-743-5316. Fax: 435-743-4723.
Founded: 1930.
Key Personnel: Park Mgr. & Cur., Carl Camp.
Personnel Profile: Full-Time Paid 1; Part-Time Paid 2; Part-Time Volunteers 15.
Governing Authority: state. Utah State Division of Parks & Recreation, 1636 W. North Temple, Salt Lake City, 84116. Tax-exempt.
Regional History Museum: housed in Utah's first territorial Capitol 1855-1858.
Collections: pioneer furniture, tools, pictures, handicrafts; Indian artifacts; music; cotton; pioneer farm implements; paintings; sculpture; costumes; decorative arts. Historic Buildings: 1867 rock schoolhouse; 1870 log cabin.
Facilities: 100-vol. library of books pertaining to history of people & localities, schoolbooks, personal histories, ancestor photographs, Bibles of several countries & songbooks available for research on premises. Cards & brochures for sale.
Activities: guided tours; lectures; hands-on activities. Museum Sponsors: pioneer dances; Arts & Living History Festival; Old Fashioned Christmas program.
Hours & Admission Prices: Mon.-Sat. 9-5; other times by appointment. Admission 12 & over $2, children 6-11 $1; children under 6 no charge. Closed New Year's Day; Thanksgiving; Christmas. ♿
Attendance: 45,000 (estimated)

Fort Douglas

FORT DOUGLAS MILITARY MUSEUM, 32 Potter St., Fort Douglas, UT 84113-5046. Tel.: 801-581-1710 & 1251. Fax: 801-581-9846.
E-mail: admin@fortdouglas.org
Web Site: www.fortdouglas.org
Founded: 1974.
Congressional District: 2
Key Personnel: C.E.O., Robert S. Voyles; Pres. (V), Dave Gunn; Dir., Robert S. Voyles; Cur. Collections, Ephriam D. Dickson, III; Museum Shop Mgr., Su Richards.
Personnel Profile: Full-Time Paid 1; Part-Time Paid 4; Part-Time Volunteers 14.
Governing Authority: state. Parent Institution: Utah National Guard, Box 1776, Draper, UT 84020-1776. Tax-exempt.
Military Museum: housed in 1875 Quartermaster Victorian Infantry Barracks Building, located in Fort Douglas, founded in 1862 by California Volunteers to protect the Overland Mail & Telegraph lines.
Collections: military uniforms, accoutrements, memorabilia, documents; insignia of the Army 1857-present; military equipage of Navy, Marines, Air Corps and Coast Guard from 1860 to present; military vehicles; tanks; artillery pieces.
Research Fields: military history of Utah, the Utah National Guard & militia.
Facilities: 1,500-vol. library of military history of Utah and Fort Douglas and the history of military in Utah, available for use on premises; reading room. Books of military history for sale.
Activities: guided tours; lectures; films; gallery talks; study clubs; permanent & temporary exhibitions; 3rd California Infantry Fife, Drum and Bugle Corp. available for community events & museum activities.
Publications: monographs, Col. Patrick Edward Connor, Stephen Douglas, Utah's Navy Ships, and Utah & the Air Force Connection; Battle of Bear River; U.S. Army Pioneers; The Black Soldier in Utah; Opening of Uintah Indian Reservation; Prisoners at Fort Douglas; Patrick Edward Connor, A Closer Look; The Daily Union Vedette; Who Really Was Bonneville?
Hours & Admission Prices: Tues.-Sat. 12-5. No charge; donations accepted. Closed federal holidays weekends. ♿
Attendance: 6,000 (accurate)

Membership: Individual $20; Life $300.

Fort Duchesne

CULTURAL RIGHTS AND PROTECTION DEPARTMENT/UTE INDIAN TRIBE, Hwy. 40, Fort Duchesne, UT 84026. Mailing Address: Box 190, Fort Duchesne, UT 84026-0190. Tel.: 435-722-5141. Fax: 435-722-2083.
Web Site: www.utetribe.com
Founded: 1976.
Congressional District: 3
Key Personnel: Dir., Betsy Chapoose.
Governing Authority: tribal. Tax-exempt.
Indian Museum: located on site related to the era of U.S. Cavalry and Old Fort Duchesne.
Collections: Indian-produced artwork in various media; old books from nearby military fort; Indian artifacts.
Research Fields: early Western American history; Ute history; archaeological; personal interviews with elderly to document verbal Indian history.
Facilities: 160-vol. library of books & research papers on Indian & early Western American history available for use on premises, or by request to research staff; reading room.
Activities: lectures.
Publications: book, A History of the Northern Ute People.
Hours & Admission Prices: Mon.-Thurs. 8-4:30.

Grantsville

DONNER-REED PIONEER MUSEUM, 90 N. Cooley, Grantsville, UT 84029. Tel.: 435-884-0824 & 3411.
Web Site: www.donner-reed-museum.org
History Museum.
Collections: local history & culture; period furnishings; personal artifacts; photographs.
Hours & Admission Prices: By appointment.

UTAH FIREFIGHTERS MUSEUM, 444 S. Quirk, Grantsville, UT 84029-9456. Mailing Address: P.O. Box 1128, Grantsville, UT 84029-1128. Tel.: 435-884-3376.
Fire Museum.
Collections: firefighting history; period fire trucks & equipment; personal artifacts; photographs.
Hours & Admission Prices: Fri.-Sat. 11-3; other times by appointment.

Green River

JOHN WESLEY POWELL MUSEUM, 1765 E. Main St., Green River, UT 84525. Mailing Address: P.O. Box 620, Green River, UT 84525-0620. Tel.: 435-564-3427.
Web Site: www.jwprhm.com
Governing Authority: Tax-exempt.
River History Museum.
Collections: works by local & regional artists; southern Utah history; riverboats; Native Americans; mountain men; explorers; River Rafter's Hall of Fame.
Facilities: 200-seat auditorium. Museum-related items for sale.
Hours & Admission Prices: Summer: daily 8-7; Winter: Tues.-Sat. 9-5. Groups 10 & over $30, family $8, adult $4, children 3-12 $1; children 2 & under and locals with guests no charge. Closed New Year's Day; Thanksgiving; Christmas. ♿
Attendance: 30,000

Helper

WESTERN MINING + RAILROAD MUSEUM, 296 S. Main St., Helper, UT 84526. Mailing Address: P.O. Box 221, Helper, UT 84526-0221. Tel.: 435-472-3009.
E-mail: helpermuseum@helpercity.net
Web Site: www.wmrrm.org
Founded: 1963.
Key Personnel: Dir. & Museum Shop Mgr., Stephanie Fitzsimons; Chm. (V), Pat Kokal.
Personnel Profile: Part-Time Paid 2; Part-Time Volunteers 8.
Governing Authority: Parent Institution: Helper City. Tax-exempt.
History Museum: housed in the Old Helper Hotel, built c.1913.
Collections: railroad, mining & cultural history; photographs; coal mining tools & equipment; railroad office & artifacts.
Facilities: Museum-related items for sale.
Activities: special events.
Hours & Admission Prices: May-Sept. Mon.-Sat. 10-5; Oct.-April Tues.-Sat. 11-4. No charge; donations accepted.

Attendance: 9,357 (accurate)

Hill Air Force Base

HILL AEROSPACE MUSEUM, 7961 Wardleigh Rd., Hill Air Force Base, UT 84056-5842. Tel.: 801-777-6868 & 6818. Fax: 801-777-6386.
Web Site: www.hill.af.mil/library/museum/index.asp
Founded: 1985.
Key Personnel: Dir., Scott Wirz; Chm. (V), Marc Reynolds; Museum Shop Mgr., Lorrie Slade.
Personnel Profile: Full-Time Paid 5; Part-Time Volunteers 100; Interns 1.
Governing Authority: federal; nonprofit. Parent Institution: Hill Air Force Base, USAF. Tax-exempt: 501(c)(3).
Aerospace Museum.
Collections: aircraft from 1918 to present; WWII chapel & barracks.
Research Fields: Hill AFB history; USAF technology.
Activities: education programs.
Publications: foundation newsletter, Volunteer Gazette.
Hours & Admission Prices: Daily 9-4:30. No charge; donations accepted. Closed New Year's Day; Thanksgiving; Christmas. ♿
Attendance: 165,000 (accurate)

Hurricane

HURRICANE VALLEY HERITAGE PARK MUSEUM, 35 W. State, Hurricane, UT 84737-1961. Mailing Address: P.O. Box 91, Hurricane, UT 84737-0091. Tel.: 435-635-3245. Fax: 435-635-4696.
E-mail: hurricanemuseum@hotmail.com
Web Site: www.hurricane-pioneer.org
Founded: 1989.
Key Personnel: C.E.O. & Pres. (V), Gregory Lawton; Treas., Verna Hinton; Cur., Phyllis Lawton; Education, Stella Shamo; Registrar, Lee Beaty.
Personnel Profile: Full-Time Paid 1; Full-Time Volunteers 2; Part-Time Paid 3; Part-Time Volunteers 6.
Governing Authority: private; nonprofit organization. Tax-exempt: 501(c)(3).
General Museum.
Collections: local pioneer & Indian culture artifacts; pioneer homes; photographs; dolls; tools; family histories; history of town military men. Buildings: 2 homes; barn; blacksmith shop.
Research Fields: pioneer homes, activities, pictures & personal histories.
Facilities: library; 60-seat auditorium; 2,000 sq. ft. exhibit space. Museum-related items for sale.
Activities: arts festival; concerts; films; guided tours; lectures. Museum Sponsors: Outdoor Historical Pageant.
Publications: History of Homes of Hurricane.
Hours & Admission Prices: Mon.-Sat. 9-5. No charge; donations accepted. Closed New Year's Day; Thanksgiving; Christmas. ♿
Attendance: 10,000 (estimated)
Membership: Individual $10; Family $20; Business $50; Patron $500.

Hyrum

HYRUM CITY MUSEUM, 83 W. Main St., Hyrum, UT 84319-1297. Tel.: 435-245-0208.
Key Personnel: Cur, Jeff McBride
History Museum.
Collections: dinosaur bones; Egyptian artifacts; 19th century tools; minerals & rocks; pioneer artifacts; Mormon memorabilia; photographs.
Hours & Admission Prices: Tues., Thurs. & Sat. 3-5. No charge.

Kanab

KANAB HERITAGE MUSEUM & JUNIPER FINE ARTS GALLERY, 13 S. 100 E., Kanab, UT 84741. Mailing Address: City Office, 76 N. Main, Kanab, UT 84741. Tel.: 435-644-3966.
Personnel Profile: Part-Time Paid 1.
History Museum & Art Gallery.
Collections: local history & culture; period furnishings; photographs; personal artifacts; works by local artists.
Hours & Admission Prices: Summer: Mon.-Fri. 1-5. No charge; donations accepted.

Kaysville

KAYSVILLE LECONTE STEWART GALLERY OF ART, 44 N. Main, Kaysville, UT 84037-1949. Tel.: 801-544-2826. Fax: 801-544-5646.
E-mail: admin@kaysvillecity.com
Art Gallery.
Collections: works by LeConte Stewart.
Hours & Admission Prices: Call for hours.

Layton

HERITAGE MUSEUM OF LAYTON, 403 N. Wasatch Dr., Layton, UT 84041-3238. Tel.: 801-336-3930.
Web Site: www.laytoncity.org/public/museum/default.aspx
Founded: 1980.
Personnel Profile: Full-Time Paid 1; Part-Time Volunteers 20.
Governing Authority: Parent Institution: Layton City Corporation.
History Museum.
Collections: local history & culture; photographs; personal artifacts; documents; industry; Native American artifacts; newspapers.
Publications: Heritage Horizon, Spring & Fall.
Hours & Admission Prices: Tues.-Fri. 11-6, Sat. 1-5. No charge. Closed holidays.
Attendance: 6,500 (accurate)

Lehi

JOHN HUTCHINGS MUSEUM OF NATURAL HISTORY, 55 N. Center St., Lehi, UT 84043-1826. Tel.: 801-768-7180.
Web Site: www.hutchingsmuseum.org
Founded: 1955.
Congressional District: 1
Key Personnel: Dir., Ben Woodruff; Chm. Bd., Esther Sumsion.
Personnel Profile: Full-Time Paid 1; Part-Time Paid 6; Part-Time Volunteers 9.
Governing Authority: non-profit organization. Parent Institution: John Hutchings Museum of Natural History Board of Directors and Lehi City Corp. Tax-exempt: 501(c)(3).
Natural History Museum.
Collections: rocks; minerals; fossils; shells; birds; eggs; pioneer tools & household items; Native American weapons; tools; baskets; guns; Porter Rockwell; Johnston's army; 19th century pharmaceuticals & inventions.
Research Fields: archaeology; geology; biology.
Facilities: library.
Activities: guided tours; lectures; workshops; summer camps; permanent & changing exhibitions; inter-museum loan; special events. Museum Sponsors: Easter Event in Spring; Pre-History Week in May; Round Up Week in June; Museum Day in September; Family Week in November; Gifts of Nature in December.
Publications: e-mail bulletin.
Hours & Admission Prices: Tues.-Sat. 11-5. Adults $4, senior citizens, children & students $3; discount to groups; children under 2 no charge. Closed national holidays. ♿
Attendance: 13,820 (accurate)
Membership: Individual $30; Family $60.

NORTH AMERICAN MUSEUM OF ANCIENT LIFE, 2929 Thanksgiving Way, Lehi, UT 84043-3740. Tel.: 801-766-5000.
Web Site: www.thanksgivingpoint.com/visit/museum_of_ancient_life/about.html
Paleontology Museum.
Collections: local history; mounted dinosaurs; fossils; skeletons; hands-on exhibits.
Facilities: cafe. Museum-related items for sale.
Activities: educational programs; field trips.
Hours & Admission Prices: Mon.-Sat. 10-8. Exhibits: adults $10, senior citizens 65 & over and children 3-12 $8. Exhibits & Movie: adults $15, senior citizens 65 & over and children 3-12 $12. Closed Thanksgiving; Christmas.

Logan

INTERMOUNTAIN HERBARIUM, UTAH STATE UNIVERSITY, Dept. of Biology, Utah State Univ., Logan, UT 84322-0001. Mailing Address: 5305 Old Main Hill, Utah State University, Logan, UT 84322-5305. Tel.: 435-797-0061 & 1584. Fax: 435-797-1575.
E-mail: mary@biology.usu.edu
Web Site: herbarium.usu.edu/
Founded: 1931.
Key Personnel: Dir., Dr. Mary E. Barkworth.
Personnel Profile: Full-Time Paid 2; Part-Time Paid 2; Part-Time Volunteers 2.
Governing Authority: state; university. Parent Institution: Utah State University. Subsidiary Institution: Dept. of Biology.
Herbarium.
Collections: 249,000 specimens: mostly vascular plants of the Intermountain Region, some mosses, fungi & lichens; seeds; photographic slides.
Research Fields: flora of the inter-mountain region; North American grasses; plant systematics; fungal systematics.
Facilities: 2,000-vol. library of plant taxonomy books available for use on premises; reading room.

Activities: research; inter-museum loan & exchanges; temporary exhibitions; teaching.
Hours & Admission Prices: Mon.-Fri. 8-5. No charge; donations accepted. Closed state & national holidays.
Attendance: 300 (accurate)

* **NORA ECCLES HARRISON MUSEUM OF ART, (M),** Utah State University, 650 N. 1100 E., Logan, UT 84322-0001. Mailing Address: 4020 Old Main Hill, Logan, UT 84322-4020. Tel.: 435-797-0163. Fax: 435-797-3423.
E-mail: rachel.hamm@usu.edu
Web Site: www.artmuseum.usu.edu
Founded: 1982.
Congressional District: 1
Key Personnel: C.E.O. & Dir., Victoria Rowe Berry; Business Mgr., Rachel Hamm; Registrar, Casey Allen; Cur. Education, Nadra E. Haffar; Asst. Cur. Programs, Deborah Banerjee; Dir. Arts Bridge, Laurie Baefsky.
Personnel Profile: Full-Time Paid 6; Part-Time Paid 2; Part-Time Volunteers 3.
Governing Authority: university. Parent Institution: Utah State University. Tax-exempt: 170(b)(1)(A).
Art Museum.
Collections: 20th- & 21st-century West coast American paintings, sculpture & drawings; 20th- & 21st-century West coast ceramic vessels; Native American arts representing Pueblo, Hopi & Navajo tribes; Vogel Collection: 50 Works for 50 States.
Research Fields: related to collections.
Facilities: temporary & permanent exhibition galleries.
Activities: guided tours; lectures; participatory, permanent & temporary exhibitions; docent tours.
Publications: exhibition brochures; catalogues.
Hours & Admission Prices: Tues.-Sat. 11-4. Suggested Donations: adults $3; members no charge. Closed holidays. ♿
Attendance: 29,000 (accurate)
Membership: Student & Senior Citizen $10; Individual $20; Family $35; Contributor $50-$99; Patron $100-$199; Associate $200-$249; Benefactor $250-$499; President's Circle $500 & up.

STOKES NATURE CENTER, 2696 E. Hwy. 89, Logan, UT 84323. Mailing Address: P.O. Box 4204, Logan, UT 84323-4204. Tel.: 435-755-3239. Fax: 435-755-6586.
E-mail: nature@logannature.org
Web Site: www.logannature.org
Key Personnel: Exec. Dir., Holly Strand
Nature Center.
Collections: natural science & history.
Activities: school groups; science programs.
Hours & Admission Prices: Tues.-Fri. & 2nd Sat. of month 10-4; call to confirm.

UTAH STATE UNIVERSITY'S MUSEUM OF ANTHROPOLOGY, (M), 730 Old Main Hill, Logan, UT 84322-0730. Tel.: 435-797-7545. Fax: 435-797-1240.
E-mail: anthro.museum@usu.edu
Web Site: www.usu.edu/anthro/museum
Founded: 1963.
Key Personnel: Dir., Dr. Bonnie Pitblado; Cur., Mary Kay Gabriel.
Personnel Profile: Full-Time Paid 1; Part-Time Paid 11; Part-Time Volunteers 6; Interns 6.
Governing Authority: public university. Tax-exempt: 170(b)(1)(A).
Anthropology Museum.
Collections: archaeological includes the Great Basin, Ancestral Puebloan people, Mayan civilization, and Petra Jordon; ethnographic includes Africa, India, the west coast from California to Alaska, Polynesia, New Zealand, & Peru; Native American artifacts.
Facilities: 1,600 sq. ft. exhibit space.
Activities: docent program; formal education programs; guided tours; school loan service; community programs. Museum Sponsors: biannual Archaeology Merit Badge sessions for BSA in Cache Valley.
Hours & Admission Prices: Mon.-Fri. 8-5, Sat. 10-4. No charge; donations accepted. Closed university holidays; federal holidays. ♿
Attendance: 7,000 (estimated)

WILLOW PARK ZOO, 419 W. 700 S., Logan, UT 84321-5599. Mailing Address: P.O. Box 527, Logan, UT 84323-0527. Tel.: 435-716-9265. Fax: 435-716-9254.
E-mail: dharvey@loganutah.org
Web Site: www.loganutah.org/parks_and_rec/willow_park/index.cfm
Founded: 1970.
Key Personnel: Supt., Rod Wilhelm.
Personnel Profile: Full-Time Paid 4; Part-Time Paid 8; Part-Time Volunteers 4; Interns 1.
Governing Authority: Parent Institution: city of Logan. Tax-exempt.
Zoo.
Collections: over 100 species of birds; 12 species of mammals; fish; turtles.
Hours & Admission Prices: Daily 9am to sunset. Adults $1, children 12 & under $.50; AZA & museum members no charge. Closed New Year's Day; Thanksgiving; Christmas.
Membership: Individual $25; Individual Plus One $30; Family & Grandparents $40; Family & Friends Circle $50.

Magna

MAGNA ETHNIC AND MINING MUSEUM, 8980 W. 2700 S., Magna, UT 84044-1149. Mailing Address: P.O. Box 324, Magna, UT 84044-0324. Tel.: 801-250-5656.
Mining Museum.
Collections: local history & culture; mining industry; photographs.
Hours & Admission Prices: Call for hours.

Midvale

MIDVALE HISTORICAL SOCIETY MUSEUM, 7699 S. Main St., Midvale, UT 84047-7107. Tel.: 801-569-8040.
Historical Society Museum.
Collections: local history & culture; photographs; period artifacts; early pioneers; mining; transportation.
Hours & Admission Prices: Mon.-Wed. & Fri.-Sat. 12-4. No charge.

Moab

ARCHES NATIONAL PARK VISITOR CENTER, N. Hwy. 191, Moab, UT 84532. Mailing Address: P.O. Box 907, Moab, UT 84532-0907. Tel.: 435-259-8161. Fax: 435-719-2305. TDD: 435-719-2319.
E-mail: archinfo@nps.gov
Web Site: www.nps.gov/arch
Congressional District: 3
Key Personnel: Park Ranger, Nancy Holman.
Personnel Profile: Full-Time Paid 5; Full-Time Volunteers 4; Part-Time Paid 3; Part-Time Volunteers 2.
Governing Authority: federal. Parent Institution: National Park Service. Tax-exempt.
Natural History Museum.
Collections: herbarium; geology; botany; archaeology; entomology. Historic House: 1906 Wolfe Cabin.
Facilities: picnic area; campsite.
Activities: guided tours; organized education programs.
Publications: Visitor's Guide to Arches National Park.
Hours & Admission Prices: April-Oct. daily 7:30-6:30; Nov.-March daily 8-4:30. Admission: $5 per person for self walk-in, $10 per vehicle (7-day pass), Annual $25. Closed Christmas. ♿
Attendance: 733,000 (accurate)

DAN O'LAURIE MUSEUM OF MOAB, (M), 118 E. Center St., Moab, UT 84532-2430. Tel.: 435-259-7985.
E-mail: moabmuseum@frontiernet.net
Web Site: www.moab-utah.com/danolaurie/museum.html
Formerly: Dan O'Laurie Canyon Country Museum
Founded: 1958.
Congressional District: 3
Key Personnel: Dir., Travis Shawk; Chm. (V), Jim Tharp.
Personnel Profile: Part-Time Paid 2; Part-Time Volunteers 10.
Governing Authority: county; nonprofit. Parent Institution: Southeast Utah Society of Arts & Sciences. Tax-exempt.
General Museum.
Collections: archaeology; geology; early Moab history.
Research Fields: archaeology; oral history.
Activities: permanent, traveling & temporary exhibits.
Publications: Canyon Legacy.
Hours & Admission Prices: Summer: Mon.-Fri. 10-6, Sat.-Sun. 12-6; Winter: Mon.-Fri. 10-3, Sat.-Sun. 12-5. Family $7, adult $3; members no charge. Closed New Year's Eve & Day; Independence Day; Labor Day; Thanksgiving; Christmas. ♿
Attendance: 7,000 (accurate)
Membership: Contributing $25; Sustaining $50; Donor $100; Associate $500; Patron $1,000.

DEAD HORSE POINT STATE PARK, Hwy. 313, Moab, UT 84532. Mailing Address: P.O. Box 609, Moab, UT 84532-0609. Tel.: 435-259-2614. Fax: 435-259-2615.
E-mail: parkcomment@utah.gov
Web Site: www.stateparks.utah.gov
Founded: 1959.
Key Personnel: Park Mgr., Megan Blackwelder; Asst. Mgr., Crystal Carpenter.
Governing Authority: state. Parent Institution: State of Utah, Div. of Parks & Recreation, 1636 W. North Temple, Salt Lake City, UT. 84116. Tax-exempt.
State Park Visitor Center.
Collections: anthropology; arboretum; archaeology; ethnology; folklore; geology; history; Indian artifacts; mineralogy; natural history; zoology.
Facilities: visitor center.
Activities: guided walks; campfire programs; junior ranger program.
Hours & Admission Prices: Visitor Center: mid-March to mid-Sept. 8-6; mid-Sept. to mid-March 8-5. Park: daily. Daytime: $10 per car; Camping: $20 per night; call for campground reservations. Visitor Center: closed New Year's Day; Thanksgiving; Christmas. ♿
Attendance: 240,000

HOLE N" THE ROCK, 11037 S. Hwy. 191, Moab, UT 84532-3969. Tel.: 435-686-2250.
Web Site: www.theholeintherock.com
Historic Home: housed in the home, carved out of rock by Albert and Gladys Christenson.
Collections: family history; personal artifacts; furnishings; paintings; sculpture.
Facilities: Museum-related items for sale.
Hours & Admission Prices: Daily 9-5. Tours: adults $5, children 5-10 $3.50; children under 5 no charge.

MOAB MUSEUM OF FILM & WESTERN HERITAGE, Red Cliffs Lodge, Mile Post 14., Hwy. 128, Moab, UT 84532-9618. Tel.: 435-259-2002; 866-812-2002. Fax: 435-259-5050.
Web Site: www.redcliffslodge.com/museum
History & Film Museum.
Collections: early cowboy ranching & local movie memorabilia.
Hours & Admission Prices: Call for hours.

Monticello

FRONTIER MUSEUM, 216 S. Main, Monticello, UT 84535. Mailing Address: P.O. Box 305, Monticello, UT 84535-0305. Tel.: 435-587-3401.
Web Site: www.utahscanyoncountry.com/en/entities/226/
History Museum.
Collections: local history & culture; early pioneers; vintage clothing; household items; early telephones; period artifacts; remains from the Home of Truth.
Hours & Admission Prices: Call for hours.

Mount Carmel

THUNDERBIRD FOUNDATION FOR THE ARTS, 2002 State St., Mount Carmel, UT 84755. Mailing Address: P.O. Box 5555, Mount Carmel, UT 84755-5555. Tel.: 435-648-2653.
Web Site: www.maynarddixon.com
Founded: 2001.
Congressional District: 2
Key Personnel: Dir., Susan Bingham; Chm. (V), Paul Bingham; Pres. (V), Daniel Shea; Treas., Emily Hollingshead; Devel., Bruce Bell; Admin., Irene Shack Von Brockdorff; Security, Eric Esplin.
Personnel Profile: Full-Time Paid 1; Full-Time Volunteers 2; Part-Time Paid 4; Part-Time Volunteers 4.
Governing Authority: private; nonprofit organization. Tax-exempt: 501(c)(3).
Art Museum: housed in the summer home of American painter, Maynard Dixon.
Collections: Maynard Dixon's works, furnishings & personal artifacts; Robert Henri illustration; photographs by Jack Hellers & Father Bernard Hubard.
Facilities: 100-seat theater; 4,500 sq. ft. exhibit space. Museum-related items for sale.
Activities: formal education programs for adults. Annual Event: Maynard Dixon Country Invitational August to September.
Publications: quarterly newsletter.
Hours & Admission Prices: March-Oct. daily 10-4; other times by appointment. Guided Tour $20, Self-guided Tour $10. ♿
Attendance: 3,000 (estimated)
Membership: Friends $100; Dual $175; Contributing $500; Sponsor $1,000; Supporting $5,000; Founding $10,000.

Mount Pleasant

MT. PLEASANT PIONEER MUSEUM, 150 S. State St., Mount Pleasant, UT 84647. Tel.: 435-462-2456. Fax: 435-462-2581.
Historic House Museum.
Collections: local history & culture; photographs; period furnishings.
Hours & Admission Prices: Mon.-Tues. 10-2, Wed.-Sat. 10-6.

Ogden

ECCLES COMMUNITY ARTS CENTER, 2580 Jefferson, Ogden, UT 84401-2411. Tel.: 801-392-6935. Fax: 801-392-5295.
E-mail: eccles@ogden4arts.org
Web Site: www.ogden4arts.org
Founded: 1957.
Congressional District: 1
Key Personnel: C.E.O., Sandra H. Havas; Chm., David Trimble; Museum Shop Mgr., Arlene Muller.
Personnel Profile: Full-Time Paid 3; Part-Time Paid 2; Part-Time Volunteers 20.
Governing Authority: nonprofit organization. Tax-exempt: 501(c)(3).
Art Center: housed in c.1893 David Eccles Home.
Collections: work of local artists.
Facilities: library of art & art-related literature available for use by the Ogden community; classrooms. Gift-related items for sale.
Activities: guided tours; lectures; gallery talks; piano recitals; temporary exhibitions.
Publications: quarterly newsletter, class schedule.
Hours & Admission Prices: Mon.-Fri. 9-5, Sat. 9-3. No charge; donations accepted. Closed national holidays. ♿
Attendance: 30,000 (estimated)
Membership: Friend $25; Organization $30; Donor $50; Sponsor $100; Corporate $200; Special $500; Life $1,000.

FORT BUENAVENTURA, 2450 A Ave., Ogden, UT 84401. Mailing Address: 1181 N. Fairgrounds, Ogden, UT 84404-3100. Tel.: 801-399-8099.
Web Site: www.co.weber.ut.us/parks/fortb
Founded: 1980.
Key Personnel: Park Mgr., Tim Maycock.
Personnel Profile: Full-Time Paid 1; Part-Time Paid 3.
Governing Authority: state. Parent Institution: Weber County Corp., 2380 Washington Blvd., Ogden, UT 84401. Tax-exempt: 170 (b)(1)(A).
Historic Site: housed in an 1846 fort & 1874 Browning home.
Collections: stockade; cabins.
Hours & Admission Prices: Easter to Oct. daily 8-8. Admission $2 per person with education program, $1 per person without education program; discounts to family & school groups; children under 5 no charge. Season Pass: family $100, individual $30. ♿
Attendance: 14,700 (estimated)

MUSEUM OF NATURAL SCIENCE, Weber State University, 3848 Harrison Blvd., Ogden, UT 84408-2509. Tel.: 801-626-6160.
E-mail: sohlhorst@weber.edu
Web Site: www.community.weber.edu/sciencemuseum
Founded: 1969.
Key Personnel: Dir., Sharon Ohlhorst
Natural Science Museum.
Collections: exploration; native cultures; geoscience; animal world; planet world; physical world.
Hours & Admission Prices: Mon.-Fri. 8-5. No changes.
Attendance: 18,000 (estimated)

OGDEN NATURE CENTER, 966 W. 12th St., Ogden, UT 84404-5410. Tel.: 801-621-7595. Fax: 801-621-1867.
E-mail: info@ogdennaturecenter.org
Web Site: www.ogdennaturecenter.org
Founded: 1970.
Key Personnel: Dir., Mary McKinley; Chm. (V), Nicole Okazaki; Museum Shop Mgr., Linda Page.
Personnel Profile: Full-Time Paid 8; Part-Time Paid 8; Part-Time Volunteers 600; Interns 1.
Governing Authority: Tax-exempt.
Nature Center.
Collections: wildlife; natural history; treehouses.
Facilities: 152-acre nature preserve; walking trails; observation tower. Museum-related items for sale.
Activities: school programs; workshops; summer camps; classses; special events; summer concerts. Annual Events: Annual Birdhouse Competition;

Earth Day; Fly With The Flock 5K Fun Run/Walk; Sunshine Breakfast; Creatures of the Night; Holiday Gift Shop Open House.
Publications: biannual newsletter, The Nature Log.
Hours & Admission Prices: Mon.-Fri. 9-5, Sat. 9-4. Adults 12-64 $4, seniors 65 & over $3, children 2-11 $2; members no charge. Closed major holidays.
Attendance: 36,000 (accurate)
Membership: Student $15 & up; Individual $30-$44; Family $45-$99; Grandparents $45-$99; Discovery Club $100-$249; Trails Alliance $250-$499; Preservation Grove $1,000-$4,999; Lifetime $5,000 & up.

OGDEN UNION STATION MUSEUMS, (M), 25th & Wall Ave., Union Station, Ogden, UT 84401. Mailing Address: 2501 Wall Ave., Ogden, UT 84401-1359. Tel.: 801-393-9886. Fax: 801-621-0230.
Web Site: www.theunionstation.org
Founded: 1975.
Congressional District: 1
Key Personnel: C.E.O., Jack McDonald; Chm. (V), Bill Asay; Exec. Dir., Roberta Beverly; Museum & Volunteer Mgr., Keri Wilde; Museum Shop Mgr., Sandi Schwager.
Personnel Profile: Full-Time Paid 2; Part-Time Paid 2; Part-Time Volunteers 100.
Governing Authority: Parent Institution: Union Station Foundation. Tax-exempt.
History Museum: housed in 1924 Ogden Union Depot.
Collections: inventor's models & prototypes of Browning firearms, including milling machine, lathes, handtools, furniture & memorabilia; railroad artifacts including a steam-powered rotary snowplow, #6916 locomotive & wooden caboose, a derrick from Union Pacific, SP GP-9 locomotive, SP caboose; Moonglow observation car from 1947 Train of Tomorrow; photographs; Kimball-Browning vintage cars including 9 classic automobiles; 1,200 sq. ft. HO scale model railroad; VP gas turbine; art; replicas of Jupiter.
Research Fields: railroad; geology of Great Basin; American automobiles.
Facilities: reading room; 600-seat auditorium; theater; classrooms;. Museum-related items for sale.
Activities: guided tours; films; gallery talks; concerts; dance recitals; drama; formally organized education programs; docent program; temporary & permanent exhibitions.
Publications: newsletter, All Aboard Annual
Hours & Admission Prices: Mon.-Sat. 10-5. Adults $5, seniors $4, children 2-12 $3; discounts to groups with reservations, AAM & AAA members. Closed New Year's Day; Thanksgiving; Christmas Eve & Day. ♿
Attendance: 49,428 (accurate)
Membership: Family $40; Contributing $50; Sustaining $100; Corporate & Professional $150; Patron $500.

OGDEN'S GEORGE S. ECCLES DINOSAUR PARK, 1544 E. Park Blvd., Ogden, UT 84401-0803. Tel.: 801-393-3466. Fax: 801-399-0895.
E-mail: dinotemp@ci.ogden.ut.us
Web Site: www.dinosaurpark.org
Founded: 1993.
Key Personnel: Dir., Kevin Ireland.
Governing Authority: George S. Eccles Dinosaur Park and the Elizabeth Dee Shaw Stewart Dinosaur Museum.
Dinosaur Park & Museum.
Collections: Museum: hands-on exhibits; paleontology. Outdoor Park: full size dinosaur replicas in natural settings.
Facilities: lecture hall; paleontology lab. Museum-related items for sale.
Activities: special events; children's sand pit; lectures; birthday parties.
Hours & Admission Prices: Memorial Day to Labor Day Mon.-Sat. 10-8, Sun. 12-6; Sept.-May Mon.-Sat. 10-6. Adults $7, senior citizens 62 & over and students $6, children 2-12 $5; discounts to groups of 15 or more; children one & under no charge. Closed New Year's Eve & Day; Thanksgiving & day after; Christmas Eve & Day. ♿
Attendance: 117,000 (accurate)
Membership: Individual $25; Double $35; Family & Grandparent $50; Family Plus $60.

OTT PLANETARIUM, Weber State University, 3750 Harrison Blvd., Ogden, UT 84408-0001. Mailing Address: 2508 University Circle, Ogden, UT 84408-2508. Tel.: 801-626-6871.
E-mail: planetarium@weber.edu
Web Site: community.weber.edu/planetarium
Key Personnel: Interim Dir., Dr. Stacy Palen
Planetarium.
Collections: space science.
Hours & Admission Prices: Call or see website for hours & admission prices.

TREEHOUSE CHILDREN'S MUSEUM, 347 22nd St., Ogden, UT 84401-1415. Tel.: 801-394-9663.
E-mail: treehouse@treehousemuseum.org
Web Site: www.treehousemuseum.org
Founded: 1992.
Key Personnel: Dir., Lynne Goodwin.
Personnel Profile: Full-Time Paid 7; Part-Time Paid 18; Part-Time Volunteers 100; Interns 2.
Governing Authority: nonprofit organization. Tax-exempt.
Children's Museum.
Collections: hands-on exhibits.
Facilities: theater.
Activities: special programs; birthday parties; facility rental.
Hours & Admission Prices: Mon. 10-4, Tues.-Thurs. 10-6, Fri.-Sat. 10-3. Children $5, adults 16 & over $4; discounts to scheduled groups; members no charge. Closed New Year's Day; Independence Day; Thanksgiving; Christmas. ♿
Attendance: 169,621 (accurate)
Membership: One Child & 2 Adults $40; 2 Children & 2 Adults $75; 3 or more Children & 2 Adults $85; Donor I $150; Donor II $250; Donor III $500; Treehouse Pals $501-$999; Best Buddies $1,000-$9,999; Childhood Friends $10,000-$49,999; Champions of Children $50,000-$99,999; Angels $100,000 & up.

WEBER STATE UNIVERSITY ART GALLERY, Art Dept., 2001 University Cir., Ogden, UT 84408-0001. Tel.: 801-626-7689. Fax: 801-626-6976.
Founded: 1960.
Key Personnel: Gallery Dir., Monica Del Bosque; Outreach Coord., Brandee Johnsen.
Personnel Profile: Full-Time Paid 2.
Governing Authority: university. Parent Institution: Weber State University. Tax-exempt.
Art Gallery.
Collections: contemporary prints, photos, drawings & ceramics.
Activities: films; formal education programs for undergraduate & graduate college students; lectures.
Hours & Admission Prices: Mon.-Fri. 11-5, 1st Fri. of month 11-9, Sat. 12-5. No charge. ♿

Orem

WOODBURY ART MUSEUM, 575 E. University Pkwy., #250, Orem, UT 84097-7400. Tel.: 801-863-6200.
E-mail: vincema@uvu.edu
Web Site: www.uvu.edu/museum
Key Personnel: Dir., Marcus Alan Vincent; Registrar, Robin DeSpain; Graphic Designer, Vegor Pedersen; Asst. Registrar & Preparator, Dyami Sorensen; Museum Asst., Meghan Weimer
Art Museum.
Collections: artwork.
Hours & Admission Prices: Mon.-Fri. 11-7. No charge.

Park City

KIMBALL ART CENTER, 638 Park Ave., Park City, UT 84060-5106. Mailing Address: P.O. Box 1478, Park City, UT 84060-1478. Tel.: 435-649-8882. Fax: 435-649-8889.
Founded: 1976.
Key Personnel: Chm. (V), Laurie Eastwood.
Personnel Profile: Full-Time Paid 3; Part-Time Paid 9; Part-Time Volunteers 200.
Governing Authority: Tax-exempt.
Art Center.
Collections: works by regional & national artists.
Activities: education program; art events; temporary exhibits. Museum Sponsors: Park City Kimball Arts Festival.
Hours & Admission Prices: Mon.-Fri. 10-5, Sat.-Sun. 12-5. No charge. ♿
Membership: Individual $50; Family $95.

PARK CITY MUSEUM, (M), 528 Main St., Park City, UT 84060. Mailing Address: P.O. Box 555, Park City, UT 84060-0555. Tel.: 435-649-7457. Fax: 435-649-7384.
E-mail: museum@parkcityhistory.org
Web Site: www.parkcityhistory.org
Formerly: Park City Historical Society & Museum
Founded: 1984.
Congressional District: 2
Key Personnel: Dir., Sandra Morrison.
Personnel Profile: Full-Time Paid 4; Full-Time Volunteers 1; Part-Time Volunteers 150.

Governing Authority: nonprofit organization. Tax-exempt.
History Museum: housed three floors, including original city hall & library buildings.
Collections: historic artifacts of Western Summit County from 1860s-present; photos.
Major Exhibits: New Harmonies (Smithsonian on Main Street), 4/10/10-5/25/10.
Research Fields: early mining history; fires; railroads; early settlers; early businesses; history of skiing in the area; immigration; 2002 Winter Olympic Games; Sundance Film Festival.
Facilities: research library.
Activities: guided walking tours; videos; temporary exhibitions of own collections; docent-led tours of museums; outreach school programs; family backpacks; lecture series; living history seasonal events.
Publications: quarterly newsletter; cemetery tour brochure; self-guided walking tour; a photographic collection, Portraits of Park City by Pop Jenks; newspaper articles, Way We Were.
Hours & Admission Prices: Mon.-Sat. 10-7, Sun. 12-6. Adults $8, children $5. Closed Thanksgiving; Christmas. ♿
Attendance: 73,505 (accurate)
Membership: Senior & Student $15; Individual $25; Senior Couple $30; Family $50; Silver Donor $100-$499; Bonanza $500-$999; Motherlode $1,000.

Parowan

PAROWAN OLD ROCK CHURCH MUSEUM, 90 S. Main, Parowan, UT 84761. Mailing Address: P.O. Box 576, Parowan, UT 84761-0576. Tel.: 435-477-3549.
Historic Church: housed in a church built by hand by early pioneers in 1865.
Collections: local history & culture; photographs; music boxes; swords; period clothing & furnishings; books; dolls.
Hours & Admission Prices: Memorial Day to Labor Day Mon.-Sat. 1-5; other times by appointment. No charge.

Payson

HISTORIC PETEETNEET MUSEUM, CULTURAL ARTS AND SOCIAL CENTER, 10 N. 600 E., Payson, UT 84651-2359. Mailing Address: P.O. Box 603, Payson, UT 84651-0603. Tel.: 801-465-5265. Fax: 801-465-9427.
Historic Building: housed in a Victorian school building built in 1901.
Collections: local history & culture; early pioneer artifacts; history of writing; period clothing; paintings; sculptures; blacksmith shop.
Hours & Admission Prices: Mon.-Fri. 10-4. No charge.

Price

COLLEGE OF EASTERN UTAH ART GALLERY, GALLERY EAST, 451 E. 400 North, Price, UT 84501-2699. Tel.: 435-613-5241. Fax: 435-613-4102.
E-mail: robert.degroff@ceu.edu
Web Site: www.ceu.edu
Founded: 1937.
Congressional District: 1
Key Personnel: Dir., Nole Carmack.
Governing Authority: college. Tax-exempt.
Art Gallery.
Collections: paintings; sculpture; photographs.
Facilities: 25,000-vol. reference library available for use within the state.
Activities: guided tours; lectures; gallery talks; arts festivals; formally organized education programs; traveling & temporary exhibits.
Hours & Admission Prices: mid-Sept. to May Mon.-Fri. 9-5; call for special arrangements. No charge. Closed major holidays. ♿
Attendance: 10,000 (estimated)

* **COLLEGE OF EASTERN UTAH PREHISTORIC MUSEUM, (M),** 155 E. Main St., Price, UT 84501-3033. Mailing Address: 451 E. 400, N., Price, UT 84501-2699. Tel.: 435-613-5060; 800-817-9949. Fax: 435-637-2514.
E-mail: reese.barrick@ceu.edu
Web Site: museum.ceu.edu
Founded: 1961.
Congressional District: 3
Key Personnel: Dir. & Cur. Paleontology, Dr. Reese Barrick; Dir. Collections & Research, Jeff Bartlett.
Personnel Profile: Full-Time Paid 6; Part-Time Paid 11; Part-Time Volunteers 32.
Governing Authority: state. Parent Institution: College of Eastern Utah. Tax-exempt.
Anthropology, Paleontology & Geology Museum.
Collections: dinosaurs; minerals; fossils of Utah; American Indian artifacts; paleontology; geology.
Research Fields: paleontology, Jurassic & Cretaceous dinosaurs; archaeology, Fremont Indians, proto-historic period.
Facilities: classroom; children's area. Museum-related items for sale.
Activities: guided tours; lectures; gallery talks; permanent & temporary exhibitions; school loan service.
Publications: newsletter, Raptor Review.
Hours & Admission Prices: April-Sept. daily 9-6; Oct.-March Mon.-Sat. 9-5. Family $15, adult $5, seniors $4, children 2-12 $2; members no charge. ♿
Attendance: 40,000 (accurate)
Membership: Individual $30; Saber Tooth $100; Utahraptor $500; Eolambia $1,000; Mammoth $5,000; Allosaur $10,000; Tyrannosaurus $25,000.

Provo

BRIGHAM YOUNG UNIVERSITY MUSEUM OF ART, (M), N. Campus Dr., Provo, UT 84602-1400. Mailing Address: 492 MOA, N. Campus Dr., Provo, UT 84602-1400. Tel.: 801-422-8287. Fax: 801-422-0527.
E-mail: moa@byu.edu
Web Site: moa.byu.edu
Founded: 1993.
Congressional District: 3
Key Personnel: Dir., Dr. Campbell B. Gray; Assoc. Dir., Ed Lind; Cur., Paul Anderson; Cur., Dawn Pheysey; Cur., Dr. Marian Wardle; Cur., Diana Turnbow; Exhibition Design, Jeff Barney; Educator, Campus, Rita Wright; Education Research, Dr. Herman du Toit; Head Cur., Dr. Cheryll May; Educator K-12, Lynda Palma; Cur., Jeff Lambson; Mgr. Exhibition Fabrication, John Adams; Head Security, Randy O'Hara; Museum Shop Mgr., Bethany Kramer; Cafe Mgr., Rebecca Armstrong; Exec. Asst., Hannah Diamond; Registrar, Emily Poulsen; Mktg. & Communications Mgr., Christopher Wilson; Designer, Brian Bird; Custodial Supvr., Suzanne Barney; Grounds Supvr., Steven Roylance; Business Mgr., Braden Burgon; Event Scheduler, Edie Zambrano.
Personnel Profile: Full-Time Paid 31; Full-Time Volunteers 1; Part-Time Paid 80; Part-Time Volunteers 210; Interns 5.
Governing Authority: college. Parent Institution: Brigham Young University. Tax-exempt: 501(c)(3).
Art Museum.
Collections: 19th- & 20th-century American collection representing the Hudson River School, American Impressionism, California Regionalism, Ashcan School & Western including such artists as John Singer Sargent, Daniel Ridgway Knight, Francis David Millet, J. Alden Weir, Mahonri M. Young, Minerva Teichert & Maynard Dixon; American photography; 19th- & 20th-century Utah artists including C.C.A Christensen, John W. Clawson, Edwin Evans, J.B. Fairbanks. Rose Hartwell, J.T. Harwood, B.F. Larsen, Lee Greene Richards, John Hafen, Cyrus Dallin; 19th- & 20th-century religious work; European and American prints & drawings.
Major Exhibits: Types and Shadows: Informations of Divinity, 11/09-3/13/10; Mirror Mirror: Contemporary Portraits and the Fugitive Self, 11/09-5/8/10; The First 100 Years: Collecting Art at BYU, 12/3/09-9/25/10.
Research Fields: American art; photography; Baroque & Renaissance prints; religious art; musicology.
Facilities: family interactive center; print study room; auditorium; 2 lecture rooms.
Activities: lectures; gallery talks; formally organized education programs for undergraduate & graduate students; docent program; loan, inter-museum loan, permanent, temporary & traveling exhibitions; continuing education for adults; academic support for university classes; symposia; children's programs and activities.
Publications: catalogues, J. Alden Weir, An American Printmaker, The American Image 1830-1940: Selections from the Museum's Collection; New Directions in Mormon Art; Cipriano de Rore's Venus Motet; 150 Years of American Painting, 1794-1944; Rembrandt; Rembrandt?; Sacred Images: A Vision of Native American Rock Art; A Song of Joys: The Biography of Mahonri Mackintosh Young; Escape to Reality: The Western World of Maynard Dixon; American Women Modernists: The Legacy of Robert Henri, 1910-1945 (co-published with Rutgers University Press); Beholding Salvation: The Life of Christ in Words and Art; Minerva Teichert: Pageants in Paint.
Hours & Admission Prices: Mon.-Wed. & Fri. 10-6, Thurs. 10-9, Sat. 12-5. No charge; donations accepted. Closed Independence Day; Thanksgiving; Christmas Eve & Day. ♿
Attendance: 327,000 (accurate)
Membership: Students & Seniors $30; Museum Passport $50; Silver Passport $100; Gold Passport $300; Platinum Passport $1,000; Corporate according to employee number.

BRIGHAM YOUNG UNIVERSITY MUSEUM OF PALEONTOLOGY, (M), 1683 N. Canyon Rd., Provo, UT 84602. Mailing Address: 140 ESM, BYU, P.O. Box 23300, Provo, UT 84602-3300. Tel.: 801-422-3939. Fax: 801-378-7919.
E-mail: rod_scheetz@byu.edu
Web Site: cpms.byu.edu/esm/
Formerly: Brigham Young University Earth Science Museum
Founded: 1987.
Congressional District: 3
Key Personnel: C.E.O. Brigham Young Univ., Gordon B. Hinckley; Pres. Brigham Young Univ., Cecil O. Samuelson; Cur., Rod Scheetz, Ph.D.; Vertebrate Paleontologist, Brooks Britt, Ph.D.
Personnel Profile: Full-Time Paid 1; Part-Time Paid 12; Part-Time Volunteers 4; Interns 2.
Governing Authority: private university; not-for-profit. Parent Institution: Latter Day Saints Church. Subsidiary Institution: Brigham Young Univ. Tax-exempt.
Paleontology Museum.
Collections: fossils from most geologic periods; research collections of dinosaurs & other vertebrates, especially from Jurassic and early Cretaceous Periods.
Research Fields: Tertiary period mammals from the U.S. & Mexico; Mesozoic period dinosaurs of Utah, Colorado & surrounding states.
Facilities: 250-vol. library of books on vertebrate paleontology; 4,500 papers on vertebrate paleontology, available for inter-library loan; educational facilities; 3,600 sq. ft. exhibit space.
Activities: docent program; films; formal education programs for undergraduate or graduate students; guided tours; lectures; loan, temporary & traveling exhibitions; school loan service.
Publications: BYU Geology Studies.
Hours & Admission Prices: Mon.-Fri. 9-5. No charge; donations accepted. Closed state holidays. ♿
Attendance: 25,000 (estimated)

THE CRANDALL HISTORICAL PRINTING MUSEUM, 275 E. Center St., Provo, UT 84606-3133. Tel.: 801-377-7777. Fax: 801-374-3333.
E-mail: lou_crandall@yahoo.com
Web Site: crandallprintingmuseum.org
Founded: 1996.
Congressional District: 3
Key Personnel: Dir. & Pres. (V), Louis E. Crandall; Chm. (V), Dann W. Hone; Chief Docent & Museum Shop Mgr., Wally Saling; Technical Dir., Dr. Thomas Hinckley.
Personnel Profile: Full-Time Paid 1; Full-Time Volunteers 4; Part-Time Volunteers 3; Interns 1.
Governing Authority: Tax-exempt.
Writing & Printing History Museum.
Collections: writing & printing history; type casting; printing; bookbinding; paper making; wood block prints; Gutenberg Press; period & replica documents; early English common press; Acorn press; linotype machine; 19th century book binding equipment; monotype machine; 20th century presses.
Major Exhibits: Hall of American History, 7/2/10-7/5/10; Colonial Days at America's Freedom Festival in Provo, 7/2/10-7/5/10.
Activities: Museum Sponsors: Utah Printer's Hall of Fame Recognition Banquet in April.
Publications: quarterly newsletter, The Printed Word.
Hours & Admission Prices: Mon.-Fri. 9-2. $3 per person to groups with minimum of 15. Closed major holidays.

* **MONTE L. BEAN LIFE SCIENCE MUSEUM, (M),** 290 MLBM Bldg., Brigham Young University, Provo, UT 84602. Tel.: 801-422-5052. Fax: 801-422-0093.
E-mail: secretary@museum.byu.edu
Web Site: mlbean.byu.edu/
Founded: 1978.
Key Personnel: Dir., Larry L. St. Clair; Assoc. Dir., Dr. Jack Sites; Asst. Dir., Marta Adair; Museum Shop Mgr., Patty Jones.
Personnel Profile: Full-Time Paid 9; Full-Time Volunteers 3; Part-Time Paid 38; Part-Time Volunteers 6.
Governing Authority: university. Parent Institution: Brigham Young University. Subsidiary Institution: The Lytle Nature Preserve (an off-site preserve managed by the museum located in Utah's Mojave Desert in the southwest corner of the state. Tax-exempt.
Life Science Museum.
Collections: herbarium; entomology; herpetology; shells; ichthyology; ornithology; mammalogy.
Research Fields: pertaining to collections.
Facilities: Museum-related items for sale.
Activities: guided tours; lectures; films; formally organized education programs for children and undergraduate college students; temporary & permanent exhibitions.
Publications: quarterly scientific journal, Western North American Naturalist.
Hours & Admission Prices: Mon.-Fri. 10-9, Sat. 10-5. No charge. Closed New Year's Day; Thanksgiving; Christmas. ♿
Attendance: 210,000 (estimated)
Membership: Student $10; Regular $15; Family $25; School & Society $50; Business & Corporation $100; Donor $500.

MUSEUM OF PEOPLES AND CULTURES, (M), BYU, 700 N. 100 E., Allen Bldg., Provo, UT 84602. Mailing Address: 105 Allen-BYU, Provo, UT 84602. Tel.: 801-422-0020. Fax: 801-422-0026.
E-mail: mpc_programs@byu.edu
Web Site: mpc.byu.edu
Founded: 1946.
Congressional District: 3
Key Personnel: Interim Dir., Paul Stavast; Cur. Education, Kari Nelson.
Personnel Profile: Full-Time Paid 1; Part-Time Paid 14; Part-Time Volunteers 8; Interns 3.
Governing Authority: church affiliated. Parent Institution: Brigham Young University. Tax-exempt.
Anthropology and Ethnology Museum.
Collections: archaeology & ethnology.
Research Fields: Mesoamerica; Southwest; Polynesia; Great Basin; Andean cultures.
Facilities: 2,500-vol. library; field research station; laboratory; classroom.
Activities: guided tours; temporary exhibits; instruction in museum practices through BYU Dept. of Anthropology; research; outreach education programs.
Publications: Publications in Archaeology; Museum of Peoples and Cultures Occasional Papers; Popular Series.
Hours & Admission Prices: Mon.-Fri. 9-5. No charge; donations accepted. Closed New Year's Day; Presidents' Day; Civil Rights Day; Memorial Day; Independence Day; Labor Day; Thanksgiving; Christmas. ♿
Attendance: 16,000 (accurate)

Roy

ROY HISTORICAL MUSEUM, 5550 S. 1700 W., Roy, UT 84067. Mailing Address: P.O. Box 614, Roy, UT 84067-0614. Tel.: 801-776-3626.
Founded: 1985.
Key Personnel: Chm. (V), Faye Field; Museum Shop Mgr., Jean P. George
History Museum.
Collections: local history & culture; photographs; period artifacts; early furnishings; coins; paintings; clothing.
Activities: special events.
Hours & Admission Prices: Mon.-Sat. 10-5. No charge. ♿
Attendance: 8,500 (accurate)
Membership: Individual $15; Couple $25.

Saint George

BRIGHAM YOUNG'S WINTER HOME, 67 West 200 North, Saint George, UT 84770. Mailing Address: St. George Visitor's Center, 490 S. 300 E., Saint George, UT 84770-3665. Tel.: 435-673-5181.
E-mail: vcsgeorge@ldschurch.org
Web Site: www.stgeorgetemplevisitorcenter.org/byounghome.html
Founded: 1975.
Congressional District: 2
Key Personnel: Dir. Exhibits & Visitors' Centers, LDS Church, Tom Peterson; Cur. Exhibits & Historic Sites, Don Enders; Cur. Art & Artifacts, Richard G. Oman; Registrar, T. Michael Smith.
Personnel Profile: Full-Time Paid 1; Full-Time Volunteers 10.
Governing Authority: church. Parent Institution: LDS Church, 50 East North Temple, Salt Lake City, UT 84150. Tax-exempt.
Historic House: 1869-70 Brigham Young Winter Home.
Collections: household furnishings & other items typical of the West in the 1870s, some belonging to Brigham Young.
Facilities: botanical garden.
Activities: guided tours.
Publications: brochure.
Hours & Admission Prices: Winter: daily 9-5. Summer: daily 9-7. No charge.
Attendance: 39,746 (accurate)

ROSENBRUCH WILDLIFE MUSEUM, (M), 1835 Convention Center Dr., Saint George, UT 84790-5842. Tel.: 435-656-0033 & 986-6697. Fax: 435-986-6694.
E-mail: angieh@rosenbruch.org
Web Site: www.rosenbruch.org
Founded: 2001.

Key Personnel: Exec. Dir. Museum & Foundation, Angie Rosenbruch-Hammer; Pres. (V), Jimmie C. Rosenbruch; Cur., Dustin Hammer; Dir. Mktg., Noel McDaniel.
Personnel Profile: Full-Time Paid 4; Part-Time Paid 8; Part-Time Volunteers 5.
Governing Authority: private; nonprofit organization. Tax-exempt: 501(c)(3).
Wildlife Museum.
Collections: over 400 species of animals from Africa, Asia, the South Pacific, Europe & North America; insects; wildlife art.
Facilities: 180-seat auditorium; 30,000 sq. ft. exhibit space. Museum-related items for sale.
Activities: films; guest speakers; guided tours; lectures; temporary & traveling exhibitions; theater.
Publications: newsletter.
Hours & Admission Prices: Mon. 10-8, Tues.-Sat. 10-6. Adults $8, senior citizens $6, children 3-12 $4; discounts to Utah Museum Assoc. members. Annual Pass available. Closed New Year's Day; Thanksgiving; Christmas. ♿
Attendance: 40,500 (accurate)

ST. GEORGE ART MUSEUM, (M), 47 E. 200 N., Saint George, UT 84770-2843. Tel.: 435-627-4525.
E-mail: museum@sgcity.org
Web Site: www.sgartmuseum.org
Founded: 1997.
Congressional District: 2
Key Personnel: Dir., Deborah Reeder; Chm. (V), Carol Lakin; Museum Shop Mgr., Valerie Sullivan.
Personnel Profile: Full-Time Paid 1; Part-Time Paid 5.
Governing Authority: Parent Institution: St. George City. Tax-exempt.
Art Museum.
Collections: works by artists of the West primarily from Utah.
Major Exhibits: Visions of Zion - All Media [0096] The Best of Zion from Kanab to Ivins, Cedar to Mesquite, 11/09-1/16/10; A Portrait of St. George & Surrounds, 1/30/10-4/3/10; Upside Down by Kathy Cieslewicz, 4/17/10-7/10/10; Capturing the Southwest by Willie Holdman; Retrospective by Armado Pena, 7/24/10-10/16/10; Into the Mystery by Robert Perkins; Beyond the Literal: Berryhill, Logan, Meadows, Weiler-Brown; Royden Card, 10/30/10-1/8/11.
Facilities: Museum-related items for sale.
Activities: school & adult tours by appointment; adult study center; care for your art center; family discovery center. Museum Sponsors: art conversations 3rd Thursday.
Publications: catalog, A Century of Sanctuary: The Art of Zion National Park.
Hours & Admission Prices: Mon.-Sat. 10-5. Adults $3, children 3-11 $1; discounts to AAM & ICOM members; museum professionals, children under 3 & members no charge. ♿
Attendance: 7,000 (accurate)
Membership: Student $15; Individual $35; Family $50; Supporting $75-$1,000; Corporate $3,000 & up.

ST. GEORGE DINOSAUR DISCOVERY SITE AT JOHNSON FARM, 2180 E. Riverside, Saint George, UT 84790-2483. Tel.: 435-574-3466. Fax: 435-627-0340.
Web Site: www.sgcity.org/dinotrax/indexmain.php
Key Personnel: Cur., Andrew R. C. Milner; Coord., Anneli M. Sequra
Paleontology Museum.
Collections: dinosaur fossil replicas; dinosaur tracks; fossil fish; plants.
Hours & Admission Prices: Mon.-Sat. 10-6. Adults $3, children 4-11 $2; children under 4 no charge.

Salt Lake City

BEEHIVE HOUSE, 67 E. South Temple, Salt Lake City, UT 84150-9719. Tel.: 801-240-2681. Fax: 801-240-2695. TDD: 801-240-2672.
Founded: 1961.
Key Personnel: Dir., Mr. McLea.
Personnel Profile: Full-Time Volunteers 6.
Governing Authority: church. Parent Institution: Latter-Day Saints Church, 50 E. North Temple, Salt Lake City, UT 84150. Tax-exempt.
Historic House: 1854-1877 Brigham Young's residence & office.
Collections: 1850-1870s household furnishings.
Activities: tours.
Publications: brochure.
Hours & Admission Prices: June-Aug. Mon.-Fri. 9:30-6:30; Sept.-May Mon.-Sat. 9:30-4:30, Sun. 10-1. No charge. Closed New Year's Day; Thanksgiving; Christmas.
Attendance: 200,000 (estimated)

CHASE HOME MUSEUM OF UTAH FOLK ARTS, center of Liberty Park (approx. 600 E. 1100 S.), Salt Lake City, UT 84105. Mailing Address: c/o Utah Arts Council, 617 E. South Temple, Salt Lake City, UT 84102-1101. Tel.: 801-533-5760. Fax: 801-533-4202. TDD: 800-346-4128.
E-mail: cedison@utah.gov
Web Site: www.folkartsmuseum.net
Founded: 1986.
Congressional District: 1
Key Personnel: Dir., Carol Edison; Folk Arts Coord., Craig Miller.
Personnel Profile: Full-Time Paid 2; Part-Time Paid 3; Part-Time Volunteers 1; Interns 1.
Governing Authority: state government. Parent Institution: Utah Arts Council. Tax-exempt: state agency.
Folk Arts Museum: 1853 two-story adobe structure built by Isaac Chase and Mormon leader Brigham Young, sold to city in 1880, renovated in 2000.
Collections: folk & ethnic art by Utah residents; quilts; saddles; Indian beadwork; needlework; rugs; woodcarving; horse tack; Indian basketry; cultural communities featured include Anglo pioneer, Native American (Goshute, Paiute, Shoshone, Ute & Navajo), Tongan, Hispanic & ranching. Ethnographical; textiles.
Research Fields: cultural communities of Utah including Anglo pioneer, Native American (Goshute, Paiute, Shoshone, Ute & Navajo), Tongan, Hispanic & ranching.
Activities: guided tours on request; archive of photographs & sound recordings; concerts. Annual Events: concerts in July & August.
Publications: booklet, Hecho en Utah (Made in Utah); recording, Listening In: Utah Storytelling; Willow Stories: Contemporary Navajo Baskets; Social Dance in the Mormon West; calendar, Annual Utah Traditions.
Hours & Admission Prices: Spring & Fall Sat.-Sun. 12-5; Memorial Day-Labor Day: Mon.-Thurs. 12-5, Fri.-Sun. 2-7. No charge. ♿
Attendance: 15,000 (estimated)

CLARK PLANETARIUM, 110 S. 400 W., Salt Lake City, UT 84101-1145. Tel.: 801-456-7827, ext. 0. Fax: 801-456-4928.
Web Site: www.clarkplanetarium.org
Formerly: Hansen Planetarium
Founded: 1965.
Congressional District: 2
Key Personnel: C.E.O. & Dir., Seth Jarvis; Museum Shop Mgr., Mike Sheehan.
Personnel Profile: Full-Time Paid 24; Part-Time Paid 65.
Governing Authority: Salt Lake County. Tax-exempt.
Planetarium, Space Science Museum.
Collections: meteorites; space technology; Apollo 15 Moon rock; large scale model solar system; moonscape; marsscape; George Rhoades' kinetic rolling ball sculpture; Foucault pendulum; 75-inch earth globe.
Facilities: classroom; 217-seat theatre; 3-D IMAX theater. Books, executive toys & educational instruments for sale.
Activities: star programs; guided tours; lectures; science demonstrations; films; gallery talks; arts festivals; drama; study clubs; hobby workshops; TV & radio programs; formerly organized education programs for children & adults; permanent & temporary exhibitions; traveling science demonstration service.
Hours & Admission Prices: Mon.-Wed. 10:30-8, Thurs. 10:30-9, Fri.-Sat. 10:30-11, Sun. 10:30-6. Star Show: adults $8, children 12 & under $6; discounts to shows before 5pm; ASTC reciprocal admission; members no charge. Call 801-456-7827 for current showtimes & prices. ♿
Attendance: 350,000 (accurate)
Membership: Duo $49; Family $99; Super Family $149.

CLASSIC CARS INTERNATIONAL, 355 W. 700 South St., Salt Lake City, UT 84101-2609. Tel.: 801-322-5509; 582-6883 & 560-5171. Fax: 801-322-5509.
E-mail: classiccarsintl@hotmail.com
Web Site: www.classiccarmuseumsales.com
Founded: 1975.
Key Personnel: C.E.O., Stacy Williams.
Personnel Profile: Full-Time Paid 1; Full-Time Volunteers 2; Part-Time Paid 1.
Governing Authority: private; nonprofit organization.
Automobile Museum.
Collections: over 300 restored automobiles 1907-1970.
Hours & Admission Prices: Mon.-Sat. 9-4; Sun. by appointment. Adults $6, senior citizens & students $4; discounts to AAA, AAM & ICOM members. Closed Christmas to New Year's. ♿
Attendance: 1,000 (estimated)

DAUGHTERS OF UTAH PIONEERS PIONEER MEMORIAL MUSEUM & INTERNATIONAL SOCIETY DAUGHTERS OF UTAH PIONEERS, 300 N. Main St., Salt Lake City, UT 84103-1699. Tel.: 801-532-6479, ext. 201. Fax: 801-532-4436.
E-mail: info@dupinternational.org
Web Site: www.dupinternational.org
Founded: 1901.
Key Personnel: C.E.O. & Pres., Bette F. Barton; 1st Vice Pres., Maurine P. Smith; Sec., Cheryl R. Searle; Custodian Museum Artifacts, Joellen Dillard; Museum Shop Mgr., Irleen Eddington.
Personnel Profile: Full-Time Paid 1; Full-Time Volunteers 100; Part-Time Paid 5; Part-Time Volunteers 125.
Governing Authority: society. Tax-exempt.
Pioneer History Museum.
Collections: pioneer vehicles; crafts; art; relics of the Utah pioneer period, 1847-1900; manuscript collections.
Research Fields: Utah pioneer history.
Facilities: auditorium. Museum-related items for sale.
Activities: permanent exhibitions; VCR program.
Publications: pamphlets; books, An Enduring Legacy; Our Pioneer Heritage; Chronicles of Courage; reproduction cards; Pioneer Pathways; Museum Memories.
Hours & Admission Prices: June-Aug. Mon.-Sat. 9-5, Sun. 1-5; Sept.-May Mon.-Sat. 9-5. No charge; donations accepted. Closed national holidays. ♿
Attendance: 36,263 (accurate)
Membership: Annual $10.

DISCOVERY GATEWAY CHILDREN'S MUSEUM, 444 W. 100 S., Salt Lake City, UT 84101-1195. Tel.: 801-456-KIDS (5437). Fax: 801-456-5440.
Web Site: www.discoverygateway.org
Formerly: The Children's Museum of Utah
Founded: 1979.
Congressional District: 2
Key Personnel: Exec. Dir., Maria Farrington; Chm. (V), Steven Suite; Dir. Mktg. & Communications, Lindsie Smith; Dir. Administration, Victoria Bernier.
Personnel Profile: Full-Time Paid 30; Part-Time Paid 35; Part-Time Volunteers 75; Interns 1.
Governing Authority: private; nonprofit organization. Tax-exempt: 501(c)(3).
Children's Museum & Discovery Center.
Collections: participatory exhibits emphasizing science & technology; cultural artifacts; dolls; toys.
Activities: hands-on discovery center for children. Annual Events: Spring Concert; Great Pumpkin Party; Harvest Festival.
Publications: quarterly newsletter; monthly calendar of events.
Hours & Admission Prices: Mon.-Thurs. 10-6, Fri.-Sat. 10-8, Sun. 12-6. Admission $8.50; discounts to ASTC members; members no charge. Closed Easter; Thanksgiving; Christmas. ♿
Attendance: 305,000 (estimated)
Membership: Basic $115; Family Connection $150; Family Inspiration $250; VIP Support $500; Child Lifetime $1,000.

FINCH LANE GALLERY, 54 Finch Lane, Salt Lake City, UT 84102-1809. Tel.: 801-596-5000.
Key Personnel: Dir., Nancy Bosskoff
Art Gallery.
Collections: mixed media; photography; paintings.
Hours & Admission Prices: Mon.-Fri. 9-5. No charge. Closed holidays; between scheduled exhibits.

HELLENIC CULTURAL MUSEUM, 279 S. 300 W., Salt Lake City, UT 84101-1703. Tel.: 801-328-9681.
E-mail: billrek@gmail.com
Founded: 1986.
Greek Heritage Museum.
Collections: Utah's Greek heritage & history; personal artifacts; clothing; costumes; photographs.
Facilities: Museum-related items for sale.
Activities: video; special events.
Hours & Admission Prices: Wed. 9-12, Sun. after church services; groups of 30 or more by appointment.

MUSEUM OF CHURCH HISTORY AND ART, 45 N. West Temple St., Salt Lake City, UT 84150-9718. Tel.: 801-240-4615. Fax: 801-240-5342.
Web Site: www.lds.org/churchhistory/museum
Founded: 1869.
Congressional District: 2
Key Personnel: Mng. Dir., Steven L. Olsen; Mgr. Exhibits, Ray K. Halls; Senior Cur. Art, Richard G. Oman; Senior Cur. Historic Sites, Donald L. Enders; Senior Product Devel., Robert O. Davis; Senior Product Devel., Kirk B. Henrichsen; Senior Historic Sites Researcher, Mark L. Staker; Historic Sites Researcher, T. Michael Smith; Historic Sites Researcher, Emily Utt; Historic Sites Researcher, Gary Boatright; Sr. Registrar, Carrie Snow; Registrar, Gloria Scovill; Registrar, Jennifer Hadley; Mgr. Historic Sites, Jennifer L. Lund; Product Devel., Dean Soderquist; Product Devel., Craig Rohde; Conservator, James L. Raines; Conservator, Larry Montgomery; Museum Store Mgr., Annette Burdette; Senior Sec., Karen Westenskow.
Personnel Profile: Full-Time Paid 18; Part-Time Paid 3; Part-Time Volunteers 325; Interns 5.
Governing Authority: Parent Institution: The Church of Jesus Christ of Latter-day Saints. Tax-exempt: 501(c)(3).
History & Art Museum.
Collections: art & artifacts emphasizing the history & culture of The Church of Jesus Christ of Latter-day Saints from the 1820s-present; fine art; folk art; native arts; furniture; costumes; decorative arts; tools; crafts; historical memorabilia.
Research Fields: LDS Church history, historic sites; art; artists.
Facilities: 2,000-vol. library pertaining to the history, art & artifacts of The Church of Jesus Christ of Latter-day Saints; 180-seat auditorium. Books, art reproductions & other related items for sale.
Activities: guided tours; lectures; films; theater; organized education programs for children & adults; docent program; temporary exhibitions of your own collections; gallery talks; School Outreach Programs.
Publications: exhibit catalogues; brochures; fine art prints; posters; postcards; slides; notecards.
Hours & Admission Prices: Mon.-Fri. 9-9, Sat.-Sun. 10-7, holidays 9-5. No charge. Closed New Year's Day; Easter; Thanksgiving; Christmas Eve & Day. ♿
Attendance: 209,261 (accurate)

PRICE FAMILY HOLOCAUST MEMORIAL, I.J. and Jeanne Wagner Jewish Community Center, 2 N. Medical Dr., Salt Lake City, UT 84113-1101. Tel.: 801-581-0098. Fax: 801-581-0718.
Web Site: www.slcjcc.org
History Museum.
Collections: Holocaust history; Jewish life before the war; Nazi regime; Diaspora.
Hours & Admission Prices: Call for hours. No charge. ♿

RED BUTTE GARDEN & ARBORETUM, University of Utah, 300 Wakara Way, Salt Lake City, UT 84108. Tel.: 801-581-0556. Fax: 801-585-6491.
E-mail: information@redbutte.utah.edu
Web Site: www.redbuttegarden.org
Founded: 1961.
Congressional District: 1
Key Personnel: Exec. Dir., Gregory Lee; Chm. (V), Tony Rampton; Dir. Devel., Chris Agnello; Volunteer Coord., Marianne Zenger; Mktg. & Public Rels., Bryn Ramjoue; Visitor Svcs. Dir. & Museum Shop Mgr., Derrek Hanson; Horticulture Education Dir., Patrick Newman; Museum Shop Mgr., Dianne Crosby.
Personnel Profile: Full-Time Paid 25; Part-Time Paid 22; Part-Time Volunteers 200; Interns 2.
Governing Authority: university. Parent Institution: University of Utah. Tax-exempt: 501(c)(3).
Botanical Garden: 150 acres at mouth of Red Butte Canyon, 25 acres of which are formal gardens; 4 miles of hiking trails. Arboretum: 1,500 acres with over 9,000 specimens of trees & shrubs from around the world.
Collections: hybrid oak grove; conifers; day lily garden; Dyke's Award iris collection; ornamental grasses; sage brush; penstemon; lilacs; crabapples; woody shrubs; aquatic plants & perennial display; medicinal, herbs & fragrant plant display; natural riparian area; 18 endangered species.
Research Fields: oak hybridizing; urban tree evaluation; cultivation of endangered plant species; Great Basin & Intermountain regional representative for center for plant conservation activity.
Facilities: visitor center; classroom; 60,000 sq. ft. children's garden; 3,000-seat public amphitheater; 25 acres of botanical gardens; four miles of mountain trails. Museum-related items for sale.
Activities: guided tours; lectures; temporary exhibitions; botany & horticulture classes; workshops; field trips; concerts; plant sales; theatre; children's programs.
Publications: quarterly newsletter; quarterly catalog of courses & events; Self Guided Tree Tour; State Arboretum of Utah Pub. #1, Oak Hybridization at the University of Utah 1982; periodic papers; nature interpretation trail guides.
Hours & Admission Prices: May-Sept. daily 9-9; Oct.-April Tues.-Sun. 10-5; call for hours on concert days. Adults $6, students & seniors $4; AHS

reciprocal garden program; children under 3 & members no charge. Closed New Year's Eve & Day; Thanksgiving; Christmas Eve, Day & week. ♿
Attendance: 160,000 (accurate)
Membership: Individual $30; Duo $40; Family & Circle of Friends $55; Contributor $100; Sponsor $250 & up; Patron Club $1,000-$2,499; Director's Club $2,500 & up. Corporate & Garden Club memberships, call 801-585-5658 for information.

SALT LAKE ART CENTER, (M), 20 S. West Temple, Salt Lake City, UT 84101-1406. Tel.: 801-328-4201. Fax: 801-322-4323.
E-mail: saras@slartcenter.org
Web Site: www.slartcenter.org
Founded: 1931.
Congressional District: 2
Key Personnel: Exec. Dir., Heather Ferrell; Pres. (V), Erik A. Christiansen; Controller, Erin M. Call; Dir. Devel., John B. Wither; Cur. Exhibits, Jay Heuman; Finance & Operations Admin., Sara South; Dir. Communications, Marlow Hoffman; Devel. Mgr., Patti Hanson; Visitor Svcs. Mgr., Kate Ithurralde; Co-Dir. Art Center School, Rodger Newbold; Co-Dir. Art Center School, Steve Fredrick.
Personnel Profile: Full-Time Paid 8; Part-Time Paid 4; Part-Time Volunteers 18; Interns 4.
Governing Authority: nonprofit. Tax-exempt: 501(c)(3).
Art Museum & Center.
Collections: paintings; photographs.
Major Exhibits: Tilman Crane's Jordan River Photographs, 11/09-1/23/10; Displacement: The Three Gorges Dam and Contemporary Chinese Art (T), 11/21/09-2/27/10; ISC 2009 Outstanding Student Achievement, 3/13/10-5/29/10.
Research Fields: contemporary art; contemporary Utah art.
Facilities: auditorium; classrooms. Books & periodicals for sale.
Activities: guided tours; changing exhibition programs; art workshops; performing arts; films; formally organized education programs & art classes for children & adults; lecture series.
Publications: quarterly newsletter; monthly calendar; exhibition catalogs.
Hours & Admission Prices: Tues.-Thurs. & Sat. 11-6, Fri. 11-9. No charge; donations accepted. Closed holidays. ♿
Attendance: 18,000 (estimated)
Membership: Student, Educator & Senior $20; Working Artist $30; Individual $35; Companion $50; Enthusiast $100; Advocate $250; Friends of Contemporary Art $500; Director's Circle $1,000.

THIS IS THE PLACE HERITAGE PARK, 2601 E. Sunnyside Ave., Salt Lake City, UT 84108-1453. Tel.: 801-582-1847. Fax: 801-583-1869.
Web Site: www.thisistheplace.org
Founded: 1947.
Congressional District: 2
Key Personnel: C.E.O. & Pres., Paul Williams; Chm. (V), Randon Wilson; Exec. Dir., Matt Dahl; Vice Pres. Finance, Wayne Lee; Vice Pres. Mktg., Russ Wood; Vice Pres. Operations, Cameron Witson; Cur. Education, Cathy Quinton; Financial Mgr., Carolyn Kimball; Village Coord., Michael Bennett; Mktg. Mgr., Andrew Lambert; Volunteer Coord., Sharon Camp; Receptionist, Arline Ockey; Bldg. & Grounds Supt., Jim Bonham; Administrative Asst., Margaret Yeates; Farm Mgr., Joe Todd.
Governing Authority: state. Parent Institution: Utah State Div. of Parks and Recreation, 1636 W. North Temple, Salt Lake City, UT 84116. Tax-exempt.
Park Visitor Center, Monument & Living History Museum.
Collections: site of This Is The Place Monument; Brigham Young's Forest Farm House & Old Deseret, a pioneer village depicting the culture & heritage of Utah's pre-railroad (1869) era; Pony Express monument; Journey's End monument.
Research Fields: Utah social history; mid-19th century furnishing patterns.
Facilities: Visitor Center; historic homes; picnic area.
Activities: self-guided tours; educational events; special holiday events; living history programs. Annual Event: Pioneer Christmas Tour.
Hours & Admission Prices: Visitor Center & This Is The Place Monument: Mon.-Sat. 9-5. Old Deseret Village: Memorial Day-Labor Day Mon.-Sat. 11-5. Adults $8, seniors & children 3-11 $6. Closed New Year's Day; Thanksgiving; Christmas. ♿
Attendance: 400,000 (estimated)
Membership: Subject to change.

TRACY AVIARY, 589 E. 1300 S., Salt Lake City, UT 84105-1111. Tel.: 801-596-8500. Fax: 801-596-7325.
E-mail: info@tracyaviary.org
Web Site: www.tracyaviary.org
Founded: 1938.
Key Personnel: C.E.O. & Exec. Dir., Tim Brown; Chm. (V), Davis Mullholand.
Personnel Profile: Full-Time Paid 18; Part-Time Paid 4; Part-Time Volunteers 50; Interns 3.
Governing Authority: municipal. Parent Institution: Friends of Tracy Aviary. Tax-exempt.
Aviary.
Collections: birds from throughout the world.
Facilities: zoological park.
Activities: guided tours; bird shows; classes; camps; interactive Parrot Encounter exhibit.
Publications: quarterly newsletter, The Birds Eye View.
Hours & Admission Prices: April 10-Oct. 19 9-6; Oct. 20-April 9 9-4:30; Adults $5, students & seniors $4, children $3; discount to groups; members & children under 3 no charge. Closed Christmas Day. ♿
Attendance: 70,000 (estimated)
Membership: Student $15; Individual $20; Family $35.

* **UTAH MUSEUM OF FINE ARTS, (M),** Marcia and John Price Museum Bldg., University of Utah, 410 Campus Center Dr., Salt Lake City, UT 84112-0360. Tel.: 801-581-7332. Fax: 801-585-5198.
E-mail: umfa.publicrelations@utah.edu
Web Site: www.umfa.utah.edu
Founded: 1951.
Congressional District: 2
Key Personnel: Interim Dir., Gretchen Dietrich; Dir. Finance & Operations, George Lindsey; Dir. Collections & Exhibits, David Carroll; Dir. Public Programs & Cur. Education, Virginia Catherall; Visitor Svcs., Anne Linscott; Assoc. Registrar, Steven Eichner; Preparator & Chief Exhibit Designer, David Hardy; Volunteer Coord., Amy Edwards; Cur. Education, Megan Hallett; Museum Svcs. Coord., Jenny Woods; Dir. Security, Ann Penman-Morgan; Exhibition Designer, Sarah Palmer; Cafe Mgr., Luke Folger.
Personnel Profile: Full-Time Paid 20; Part-Time Paid 32; Part-Time Volunteers 163; Interns 6.
Governing Authority: state; university. Parent Institution: University of Utah, 204 Park Building. Tax-exempt.
Art Museum.
Collections: 19th-century American paintings; 18th-century French decorative art & tapestries; 17th-18th century English furniture; European art from the 14th-20th century; contemporary graphic works; Egyptian antiquities; objects from Buddhist cultures; Italian Renaissance furniture; African, pre-Columbian & Indonesian art; Chinese porcelains; Japanese screens; Utah art; sculpture court; The Val A. Browing Memorial Collection of 500 Years of European Masterworks; The Marriner S. Eccles Collection of Masterworks.
Research Fields: African art.
Facilities: 500-vol. library of reference books; 248-seat auditorium.
Activities: guided tours; lectures; films; gallery talks; concerts; formally organized education programs for public school children & undergraduate college students; inter-museum loan, permanent, temporary & traveling exhibitions; Museum on the Road; Teacher Resource Center; Museum Experiences for Senior Citizens; docent program or council.
Publications: Exhibition catalogues: Albert Tissandier: Drawings of Nature and Industry in the United States; American Women at Work: Prints by Women Artists of the Nineteen Thirties; The Big Print; The Bungalow Lifestyle and the Arts & Crafts Movement in the Intermountain West; Earl Jones; George Dibble Drawings; Images of the Great Salt Lake; In Support of the Arts in Utah: An Eccles Family Tradition; J. George Midgley 1882-1979: Utah Photographer; Lee Green Richards; Paging Through Medieval Lives. Exhibition brochures: Innovation and Tradition in Japanese Woodblock Prints; Photography by Jim Frankoski: The Restoration of the Cathedral of the Madeleine; Prints by the Nabis: Vuillard and His Contemporaries; Utah Art from the Permanent Collection: An Exhibition Honoring the Utah Statehood Centennial 1896-1996. American Art: Challenging Traditional Interpretations; Enlightened by Peace, Amsterdam Inspires the Arts: A Painted Allegory by Domenicus Van Wijnen (1661-ca. 1700); The Marriner S. Eccles Collection of Masterworks; The Utah Museum of Fine Arts: Selected Works; The Val A. Browning Memorial Collection of 500 Years of European Masterworks; The Val A. Browning Collection: A Selection of Old Master Paintings.
Hours & Admission Prices: Tues. & Thurs.-Fri. 10-5, Wed. 10-8, Sat.-Sun. 11-5. Adults $7, youth 6-18 & seniors $5; discounts to AAM & ICOM members; members & University of Utah students, staff & faculty no charge. Closed major holidays. ♿
Attendance: 109,920 (estimated)
Membership: Student $15; Senior $30; Individual $40; Duo $50; Family $65; Patron $100. Friends of the Art Museum: Grand Patron & Young Benefactor $250; Benefactor $500; Connoisseur's Circle $1,000; Collector's Circle $2,500; Director's Circle $5,000.

*** UTAH MUSEUM OF NATURAL HISTORY, (M),** University of Utah, 1390 E. Presidents Circle, Salt Lake City, UT 84112-1102. Tel.: 801-581-6927. Fax: 801-585-3684.
E-mail: sgeorge@umnh.utah.edu
Web Site: www.umnh.utah.edu
Founded: 1963.
Congressional District: 2
Key Personnel: Dir., Sarah B. George; Assoc. Dir. Community Rels., Ann Hanniball; Chief Cur., Duncan Metcalfe; Dir. School Programs, Madlyn Runburg; Dir. Public Programs, Becky Menlove; Dir. Mktg., Janet Frasier; Mgr. Public Rels., Patti Carpenter; Dir. Devel., Chris Eisenburg; Cur. Paleontology, Randall Irmis; Cur. Vertebrates, Eric Rickart; Cur. Herbarium, Mitchell Power; Operations Mgr. & Museum Shop Mgr., Tony Millet.
Personnel Profile: Full-Time Paid 45; Part-Time Paid 54; Part-Time Volunteers 200; Interns 10.
Governing Authority: university. Parent Institution: University of Utah. Tax-exempt: 501(c)(3) & 170(b)(A).
Natural History Museum.
Collections: Utah geology; Jurassic & Cretaceous dinosaurs; Great Basin & Colorado Plateau ethnology & archaeology; Norton Hall of Minerals; mammal dioramas; fossil mammals; Garrett herbarium; research collections of biology, geology, paleontology & anthropology.
Research Fields: mammalian systematics; dinosaur systematics; plant & mammal biogeography; textile analysis; human foraging ecology; Fremont archaeology; plant paleoecology.
Facilities: classrooms; education wing. Books & native arts for sale.
Activities: guided tours; lectures; formally organized education programs for children & adults; docent program; teacher in-service workshops; permanent, temporary & traveling exhibitions; school outreach programs; Junior Science Academy; statewide exhibit & education outreach; at-risk youth program; Natural History Now.
Publications: quarterly newsletter; adults/children education course listing, Adventures.
Hours & Admission Prices: Mon.-Sat. 9:30-5:30, Sun. & holidays 12-5. Adults $6, senior citizens & children $3.50; discounts to AAM & ASTC members; University of Utah students, faculty, staff, members & children under 3 no charge. Closed New Year's Day; Easter; Independence Day; Pioneer Day; Thanksgiving; Christmas. ♿
Attendance: 75,500 (accurate)
Membership: Individual $25; Duo $35; Family $55; Explorer $100; Adventurer $250; Patron $500.

UTAH STATE HISTORICAL SOCIETY, 300 Rio Grande St., Salt Lake City, UT 84101-1182. Tel.: 801-533-3500. Fax: 801-533-3503. TDD: 801-533-3502.
E-mail: ushs@history.utah.gov
Web Site: www.history.utah.gov
Founded: 1897.
Congressional District: 8
Key Personnel: Dir., Philip Notarianni; Chm. (V), Michael Homer; Public History & Publications, Kent Powell; Administrative Sec., Lynette Lloyd; Public Formation, Kristen Rogers; Historian, Craig Fuller; Cur. Education & Membership Office Tech., Bonnie Rogers; State Archaeologist, Kevin Jones; Asst. State Archaeologist, Ron Rood; Archaeologist, Arie Leeflang; Archaeology Asst., Renae Weder; Grants Mgr., Debbie Dahl; Collections Coord., Doug Misner; Photo & Map Librarian, Susan Whetstone; Regulation Assistance, Janice Reed Campbell; Historic Preservation Coord., Barbara Murphy; Historical Architect, Don Hartley; Information Svcs., Greg Walz; Budget & Accounting Officer, Londi Rowley; Accounting Tech., Jinnie Edgar; Public Info. Spec., Alicia Aldrich; Information Center, Melissa Ferguson; Preservation Program Sec., Chris Hansen; GIS Mgr., Kristen Jensen; Information Center, Louis Lott; Cemetery Documentation Project, Tania Tully; State Historic Preservation Officer, Wilson Martin; Preservation Specialist, Cory Jensen; Preservation Specialist, Nelson Knight.
Personnel Profile: Full-Time Paid 37; Part-Time Paid 5; Part-Time Volunteers 40; Interns 2.
Governing Authority: state. Tax-exempt.
Historical Society Museum.
Collections: furnishings; historic prints; photographs; drawings; paintings; artifacts of 20th-century Utah; period artifacts; porcelain glass; object d'art collection; specimens; maps; books.
Research Fields: Utah, Western, Mormon & related history; archaeological & paleontological research.
Facilities: 23,000-vol. library of books, 20,000 pamphlets, 30,000 maps, 300,000 photographs & manuscripts available for use on premises. Publications for sale.
Activities: self-guided tours; docent tours; lectures; films; temporary & traveling exhibitions.
Publications: journal, Utah Historical Quarterly; books on Utah history; annual, Utah Preservation; annual, Beehive History; bimonthly, Utah State Historical Society Newsletter.
Hours & Admission Prices: Building: Mon.-Fri. 8-5, Sat. 10-3. Library: Mon.-Fri. 10-5, Sat. 10-2. No charge; donations accepted. Closed national & state holidays. ♿
Attendance: 75,000 (estimated)
Membership: Student & Senior Citizen $15; Individual $20; Institution & Contributing $25; Sustaining $35; Patron $50; Business $100.

UTAH'S HOGLE ZOO, 2600 E. Sunnyside Ave., Salt Lake City, UT 84108-1454. Tel.: 801-582-1631. Fax: 801-584-1770.
E-mail: hoglezoo@xmission.com
Web Site: www.hoglezoo.org
Founded: 1931.
Congressional District: 2
Key Personnel: Dir., Craig Dinsmore; Asst. Dir., Kimberly Davidson; Asst. Dir., Jerry Good; Cur. Education, Chris Schmitz; Museum Shop Mgr., Hillary McClellan.
Personnel Profile: Full-Time Paid 104; Part-Time Paid 150; Part-Time Volunteers 215.
Governing Authority: society. Parent Institution: Utah Zoological Society. Tax-exempt: 170(b)(1)(A).
Zoo.
Collections: general animal collection.
Research Fields: snake venom research; captive breeding.
Facilities: 1,107-vol. library of animal life & natural history available for inter-zoo loan & for use on premises; picnic areas. Animal-related items for sale.
Activities: guided tours; lectures; films; broadcast programs; formally organized education programs for children, adults & undergraduate college students; docent program or council; animal walk and talks; exhibit interpretation by Eco-explorer staff; seasonal Bird Show and Discovery Theater Animal Show. Zoo Sponsors: in-school lectures with animals.
Publications: biannual newsletter, Safari.
Hours & Admission Prices: Summer: daily 9-5; Winter: daily 9-4. Adults $8, children 3-12 & senior citizens $6; children under 2 & educational groups no charge. Carousel Ride $2, Train Ride $1. Closed New Year's Day; Christmas. ♿
Attendance: 847,831 (accurate)
Membership: Individual $40; Couple & Single Parent $50; Family & Grandparent $65; Family Plus & Grandparent Plus $75; Zoo Booster $100; Keeper's Circle $250; Curator Circle $500; Director's Den $1,000.

WHEELER HISTORIC FARM, 6351 South 900 E., Salt Lake City, UT 84121-2438. Tel.: 801-264-2241. Fax: 801-264-2213.
E-mail: wheeler1@slco.org
Web Site: www.wheelerfarm.com
Founded: 1976.
Congressional District: 2
Key Personnel: Dir. & Tours Coord., Vickie Rodman; Chm. & Pres. (V), Susan Lind; Cur. Agriculture, John Peterson; Tours Coord., Julie Zyzh.
Personnel Profile: Full-Time Paid 3; Part-Time Paid 30; Part-Time Volunteers 20.
Governing Authority: county; nonprofit. Parent Institution: Salt Lake County. Tax-exempt: 170(b)(1)(A).
Preservation Project: 1898 Wheeler Farm House, representing the initial statehood period & typical of Utah agriculture in 1898.
Collections: agricultural, dairy & ice industry collections maintained as living history; family life of the period; photographs. Historic Buildings: c.1870 granary, of adobe construction; barn; ice house.
Research Fields: community, agricultural & economic history relating to Utah dairy farms; ice industry; Settlement Salt Lake Valley.
Facilities: classrooms; operative ice ponds & icehouse dairy; milk house; multipurpose building. Reproductions of historic clothing, household goods & farm items for sale.
Activities: guided tours; lectures; films; docent program; wagon rides; nature walks; demonstrations.
Hours & Admission Prices: March-Oct. Mon.-Fri. 9:30-5; Nov.-Feb. 1-5:30. Museum: no charge. Wagon Rides: $1.50. House Tours $.50. ♿
Attendance: 395,735 (accurate)

Sandy

HILL GALLERY & SCULPTURE PARK, Canyon Ridge Center, 9045 S. 1300 E., Sandy, UT 84094-3134. Tel.: 801-562-9242.
Web Site: www.danhillsculpture.com/sculpturepark.phtml
Gallery and Sculpture Park.
Collections: works by local & regional artists; life-size outdoor sculptures;

carvings; paintings; giclee prints; photographs; kaleidoscopes; lamps; baskets; cards; books.
Hours & Admission Prices: Tues.-Fri. 12-5; other times by appointment.

LIVING PLANET AQUARIUM, 725 E. 10600 S., Sandy, UT 84094-4409. Tel.: 801-355-3474.
E-mail: info@thelivingplanet.com
Web Site: www.thelivingplanet.com
Aquarium.
Collections: marine life including endangered & threatened species.
Facilities: cafe.
Activities: children's programs.
Hours & Admission Prices: Summer: Fri.-Sat. 10-8, Sun.-Thurs. 10-7; Winter: Fri.-Sat. 11-7, Sun.-Thurs. 11-6. Adults $8, seniors, military & students $7, children $6; children 2 & under no charge.

SANDY MUSEUM, 8744 S. 150 E., Sandy, UT 84070-1404. Tel.: 801-566-0878. Fax: 801-566-9608.
Founded: 1987.
Congressional District: 2
Key Personnel: Dir., Joyce Skidmore.
Personnel Profile: Full-Time Paid 1; Part-Time Volunteers 4.
Governing Authority: private; nonprofit organization. Tax-exempt: 501(c)(3).
History Museum: built 1890.
Collections: local history & culture.
Major Exhibits: Living Gardens Spring 2010-Fall 2010.
Facilities: library; classroom. Museum-related items for sale.
Activities: films; formal education programs for children; guided tours; lectures.
Publications: monthly newsletter, The Sandy Museum Bell.
Hours & Admission Prices: Tues.-Thurs. & Sat. 1-5; other times by appointment. No charge; donations accepted. Closed Independence Day; Thanksgiving; Christmas Eve & Day. ♿
Attendance: 750
Membership: Individual $25.

Santa Clara

JACOB HAMBLIN HOME, 3325 Hamlin Dr., Santa Clara, UT 84770. Mailing Address: Visitor's Center, 490 S. 300 East, Saint George, UT 84770-3665. Tel.: 435-673-5181. Fax: 435-652-9589.
E-mail: vcsgeorge@ldschurch.org
Founded: 1975.
Congressional District: 2
Key Personnel: Cur. Exhibits & Historic Sites, Don Enders; Cur. Art & Artifacts, Richard G. Oman; Registrar, T. Michael Smith.
Personnel Profile: Full-Time Paid 1; Part-Time Volunteers 10.
Governing Authority: church. LDS Church, 50 East North Temple, Salt Lake City, UT. 84150. Tax-exempt.
Historic House: 1862-64 Jacob Hamblin Home, church leader & pioneer of the area.
Collections: household furnishings typical of a pioneer home in the 1860s, some belonging to Jacob Hamblin & his family.
Activities: guided tours.
Publications: brochure.
Hours & Admission Prices: Winter: daily 9-5; Summer: daily 9-7. No charge. ♿
Attendance: 22,592 (accurate)

Sevier

FREMONT INDIAN STATE PARK AND MUSEUM, 3820 W. Clear Creek Canyon Rd., Sevier, UT 84766-6058. Tel.: 435-527-4631.
Web Site: stateparks.utah.gov/stateparks/parks/fremont/
Park Museum.
Collections: local history & culture; photographs; period artifacts.
Hours & Admission Prices: Visitor Center & Museum: summer daily 9-6, winter daily 9-5. Closed New Year's Day; Thanksgiving; Christmas.

Springdale

ZION HUMAN HISTORY MUSEUM, Zion National Park, Springdale, UT 84767-1099. Tel.: 435-772-3256. Fax: 435-772-3426.
E-mail: zion_park_information@nps.gov
Web Site: www.nps.gov/zion
Formerly: Zion National Park Museum
Founded: 1919.
Congressional District: 1
Key Personnel: Chief Park Naturalist, Ron Terry; Supt., Jock Whitworth; Cur., Leslie Courtright; Zion Natural History Assoc., Lyman Hafen.
Personnel Profile: Full-Time Paid 2; Part-Time Volunteers 2.
Governing Authority: federal. Parent Institution: U.S. Dept. of the Interior National Park Service.
Natural History and Human History Museum.
Collections: archaeological objects c.6500 B.C. - 1900 A.D. related to Archaic, Ancestral Puebloan, Southern Paiute & Mormon cultures; historic objects of the Euro-American settlement of Zion Canyon; excavation equipment; tools; construction projects of 1920s & 1930s; archival materials of park's administrative history & resource management; herbarium; zoological; geological; paleontological; photographs c.1910 to present.
Research Fields: various aspects of park ecology.
Facilities: 2,700-vol. library of history; natural history; geology; Indian books available for inter-library loan & for use on premises. Books, slides, postcards & maps for sale.
Activities: Zion National Park: guided hikes; lectures; films; permanent exhibitions. Museum Sponsors: Junior Ranger Program; Zion Nature Center for children ages 6-12 Memorial Day to Labor Day.
Publications: maps; Geological Cross Section of the Cedar Breaks-Zion-Grand Canyon Region; books, Canyon Overlook Trail Guide; Zion National Park; The Sculpturing of Zion; Zion Album; The Outstanding Wonder-Zion Canyon's Cable Mountain Draw Works; Why the North Star Stands Still; Zion, The Story Behind The Scenery; Discover Zion; Posters, Temples & Towers of the Virgin; color slides.
Hours & Admission Prices: Archives: by appointment. Human History Museum & Visitor Center: Winter: daily 8-6; Summer: daily 8-7. Park entrance fee $25 per vehicle, bicyclist or pedestrian $12. Special fees for commercial bus tours: Golden Eagle, Golden Angel & Golden Access passes accepted. Shuttle bus through Zion National Park & Springdale, Utah no charge. ♿
Attendance: 2,500,000 (estimated)
Membership: Zion Natural History Assoc. $15.

Springville

SPRINGVILLE MUSEUM OF ART, (M), 126 E. 400 S., Springville, UT 84663-1953. Tel.: 801-489-2727. Fax: 801-489-2739.
E-mail: vswanson@smofa.org
Web Site: www.smofa.org
Founded: 1903.
Congressional District: 3
Key Personnel: Dir., Dr. Vern G. Swanson; Pres. (V), David Cook; Assoc. Dir., Natalie Petersen; Asst. Dir., Dr. Virgil Jacobsen; Pres. (V), Debbie Balzotti; Pres. (V), Ron Forbeck; Pres. (V), Sharee Forbeck.
Personnel Profile: Full-Time Paid 5; Full-Time Volunteers 105; Part-Time Paid 9; Part-Time Volunteers 5; Interns 5.
Governing Authority: Art Assoc. board of directors, nonprofit organization. Parent Institution: Springville City. Tax-exempt: 501(c)(3).
State Museum of Utah Art.
Collections: 1,900-piece permanent collection of 19th- to 20th-century Utah art; collection of Cyrus E. Dallin, sculptor; John Hafen, painter, specializing in Utah art history; 20th-century American Realist paintings & sculpture; 20th century Soviet Socialist Realist paintings.
Major Exhibits: Images of Workers from The Soviet Era, 1/5/10-2/1/10; 38th Annual All-State High Schools of Utah Show, 2/24/10-3/27/10; 86th Annual Spring Salon, 4/24/10-7/3/10; 37th Annual Quilt Show, 7/17/10-9/4/10; The Technology Sublime: Trains, Planes, Boats & Automobiles, 7/17/10-9/4/10; Utah Women Artists Exhibition (AAUW), 9/11/10-10/16/10; 25th Annual Religious Spiritual Art of UT, 10/30/10-12/28/10; 25th Annual Christmas Lamb Show, 11/10-12/10.
Research Fields: history of Utah art; 20th-century American Realist painting & Soviet Socialist Realism.
Facilities: library; classrooms; reception area; courtyard.
Activities: guided tours; lectures; gallery talks; concerts; arts festivals; intern program; docent program or council; permanent & traveling exhibitions; art workshops; films.
Publications: catalogs; exhibitions catalogs; books, biography of Cyrus E. Dallin; The History of Utah Art Through the Springville Museum's Collection.
Hours & Admission Prices: Tues. & Thurs.-Sat. 10-5, Wed. 10-9, Sun. 3-6. No charge; donations accepted. Closed holidays. ♿
Attendance: 110,000 (estimated)
Membership: Individual $20; Family $30; Sustaining $100; Patron $250; Friend $500; Benefactor $1,000.

Stansbury Park

BENSON GRIST MILL, 325 State Rd. 138, Stansbury Park, UT 84074. Tel.: 435-882-7678.
E-mail: bensonmill@trilobyte.net
Founded: 1854.
Congressional District: 3

Key Personnel: Dir., Mark McKendrick.
Personnel Profile: Full-Time Paid 1; Part-Time Paid 11.
Governing Authority: Parent Institution: Tooele County Parks & Recreation. Tax-exempt.
History Museum: listed on the National Register of Historic Sites.
Collections: 150 year old mill; area history.
Hours & Admission Prices: May-Oct. Mon.-Sat. 10-4. No charge; donations accepted. ♿
Attendance: 12,000 (estimated)

Syracuse

SYRACUSE MUSEUM & CULTURAL CENTER, 1891 W. 1700 S., Syracuse, UT 84075. Mailing Address: 300 Rio Grande, Salt Lake City, UT 84101-1106. Tel.: 801-825-3633.
Web Site: www.syracuseut.com/page.php/publicamenities-museum/museum.html
History Museum.
Collections: Syracuse history & culture; period furnishings; photographs.
Activities: special events.
Hours & Admission Prices: Tues.-Thurs. 2-5, Fri. 1-4.

Tooele

OQUIRRH MOUNTAIN MINING MUSEUM, 47 S. Maine, Tooele, UT 84074-2148. Tel.: 435-843-4000.
Mining Museum.
Collections: local mining history & operations; mines; Gold Rush era.
Hours & Admission Prices: Call for hours. No charge.

TOOELE PIONEER MUSEUM, 47 E. Vine St., Tooele, UT 84074-2133. Tel.: 435-843-0771 & 882-1092.
E-mail: pioneer@wirelessbeehive.com
Web Site: tooelepioneermuseum.com
Founded: 2001.
Key Personnel: Dir. & Chm. (V), James Bevan; Museum Shop Mgr., Russell Hammond.
Governing Authority: Tax-exempt.
History Museum.
Collections: local history & culture; photographs; period furnishings; personal artifacts.
Hours & Admission Prices: May-Sept. 25 Mon. 6pm-8pm, Tues., Fri.-Sat. & holidays 10-4; Sept. 26-April Mon. 6pm-8pm, Tues. & Sat. 10-4; other times by appointment. No charge; donations accepted. ♿
Attendance: 1,146 (accurate)

TOOELE VALLEY RAILROAD MUSEUM, 35 N. Broadway, Tooele, UT 84074. Mailing Address: 90 N. Main St., Tooele, UT 84074-2139. Tel.: 435-882-2836. Fax: 435-643-7888.
Web Site: www.tooelecity.org/citydepartments/railroadmuseum.asp
Founded: 1980.
Key Personnel: Chm., Larry Deppe, Ph.D.; Dir. & Chm. (V), Jean Mogus; Pres., Bruce Grim.
Personnel Profile: Part-Time Paid 1; Part-Time Volunteers 7.
Governing Authority: Parent Institution: Tooele City Corp. Tax-exempt.
History Museum.
Collections: railroad, mining, & smelting history; photographs; medical artifcts; rolling stock; simulated mine; school photographs; military artifacts.
Hours & Admission Prices: Memorial Day to Labor Day Tues.-Sat. 1-4. No charge; donations accepted. Closed Independence Day. ♿
Attendance: 3,000 (accurate)

UTAH STATE FIREFIGHTERS MUSEUM, Deseret Peak Complex, 2930 W. Hwy. 112, Tooele, UT 84074. Tel.: 435-843-4040.
Web Site: www.deseretpeakcomplex.com/files/venues/dpfire.htm
Fire-Fighting Museum.
Collections: fire-fighting artifacts & memorabilia including over 50 fire engines from different eras & locations throughout Utah.
Hours & Admission Prices: Call for hours.

Torrey

CAPITOL REEF NATIONAL PARK VISITOR CENTER, Capitol Reef National Park, Torrey, UT 84775. Mailing Address: Capitol Reef National Park, HC 70 Box 15, Torrey, UT 84775. Tel.: 435-425-3791, ext. 111 & 146. Fax: 435-425-3026.
E-mail: tom_o_clark@nps.gov
Web Site: www.nps.gov/care
Founded: 1968.
Congressional District: 1 & 2
Key Personnel: C.E.O., Albert J. Hendricks; Chief Interpreter, Riley Mitchell; Collections Mgr., Tom O. Clark; Museum Shop Mgr. & National History Dir., Shirley Torgerson.
Personnel Profile: Part-Time Paid 1.
Governing Authority: federal. National Park Service. Tax-exempt.
Natural History & Native American Ethnology Museum.
Collections: archaeology; geology; history; natural history; Fremont Indian culture; paleontology, Mormon history. Historic Building: 1890s, Old Fruita Schoolhouse.
Facilities: picnic area; camp grounds; nature center. Books for sale.
Activities: guided tours; amphitheater programs; junior ranger; junior geologist.
Publications: Geologic Cross Section; Geologic Map of Park; Geology of Capitol Reef; History of Fruita; Plant Ecology of Park; Dwellers of the Rainbow.
Hours & Admission Prices: Summer: daily 8-6; Winter: daily 8-4:30. Park: $4 per vehicle; museum, Golden Eagle & Golden Age/Access cardholders no charge. ♿
Attendance: 750,000 (estimated)

Tremonton

NORTH BOX ELDER COUNTY MUSEUM, 150 S. Tremont St., Tremonton, UT 84337-1636. Tel.: 435-257-3371.
History Museum.
Collections: period furnishings; general store; post office; barber; blacksmith shop.
Hours & Admission Prices: Mon.-Fri. 1-5; other times by appointment. No charge. Closed major holidays.

Vernal

UTAH FIELD HOUSE OF NATURAL HISTORY STATE PARK, 496 E. Main St., Vernal, UT 84078-2610. Tel.: 435-789-3799. Fax: 435-789-4883.
Web Site: www.stateparks.utah.gov
Founded: 1948.
Key Personnel: Park Mgr., Steven D. Sroka; Cur. Education, Mary Beth Bennis-Smith; Cur. Collections, Heather Finlayson; Museum Maintenance, Craig Gerber; Retail Sales Mgr., Colleen Lawson.
Personnel Profile: Full-Time Paid 5; Part-Time Paid 3; Part-Time Volunteers 3.
Governing Authority: state. Parent Institution: Utah State Div. of Parks & Recreation, 1636 W. North Temple, Salt Lake City, UT 84116. Tax-exempt: 501(c)(3).
Natural History Museum.
Collections: geology; fossils; archaeology; natural history of the Uinta Basin; 18 lifesize prehistoric replicas in garden setting.
Research Fields: geology; paleontology.
Facilities: Postcards, books, dinosaur models & souvenirs for sale.
Activities: lectures; tours; State Information Center.
Hours & Admission Prices: Mon.-Sat. 9-5. Adults $6, children 6-12 $3; children under 6 no charge. Closed New Years; Thanksgiving; Christmas. ♿
Attendance: 45,000 (accurate)

WESTERN HERITAGE MUSEUM, 328 East 200 S., Vernal, UT 84078-3220. Tel.: 435-789-7399. Fax: 435-789-9798.
E-mail: whm@co.uintah.ut.us
Web Site: www.co.uintah.ut.us/museum/whMuseum.php
Founded: 1991.
Congressional District: 2
Governing Authority: county. Tax-exempt.
History Museum.
Collections: early settlers, Fremont & Ute Indian artifacts; blacksmith display; barbershop; country store; 1890-1900 ladies fashions; one-room schoolhouse; Gilsonite exhibit; early rifles; saddles; tack & leather; First Ladies of the White House dolls.
Hours & Admission Prices: Memorial Day to Labor Day Mon.-Fri. 9-6, Sat. 10-4; Sept.-May Mon.-Fri. 9-5, Sat. 10-2. No charge; donations accepted. Closed New Year's; Human Rights Day; President's Day; Memorial Day; Independence Day; Pioneer Day; Labor Day; Columbus Day; Veteran's Day; Thanksgiving; Christmas. ♿

Wellsville

AMERICAN WEST HERITAGE CENTER, 4025 S. Hwy., 89-91, Wellsville, UT 84339. Tel.: 435-245-6050; 800-225-3378. Fax: 435-245-6052.
E-mail: info@awhc.org
Web Site: www.awhc.org
Formerly: Ronald V. Jensen Living Historical Farm
Founded: 1979.
Congressional District: 1

Key Personnel: Exec. Dir., Steve Delong; Chm. (V), Gary Anderson; Cur., Reece Summers; Program Admin., Lorraine Bowen.
Personnel Profile: Full-Time Paid 3; Part-Time Paid 12; Part-Time Volunteers 80; Interns 6.
Governing Authority: university. Parent Institution: American West Heritage Foundation. Subsidiary Institution: Utah State University. Branch Museum: Jensen Historical Farm. Tax-exempt.
Living Historical Farm: 1917 farm based on operations of Scandinavian & British emigrants influenced by extension programs of Utah Agricultural College.
Collections: 1917 farm with outbuildings; implements of the period; work horses; dairy cows; sheep; hogs; poultry; crops; pioneer setting of 1850; Native American Shoshone encampment 1835; Mountaineer 1830; 1895 print shop; 1880 woodworking shop.
Research Fields: rural life in Utah, World War I era; lifeways from 1820-1920, including Native cultures, Mountain Men, Pioneers.
Facilities: library; Farm: 40 acres of irrigated fields; workshops; classroom; picnic shelter; pond; hay fields; welcome center; livery stable.
Activities: demonstrations of early 20th-century farm practice & life; recreation of family farm life in Utah 1917. Museum Sponsors: over 15 special events during year.
Publications: quarterly newsletter, Hay Derrick.
Hours & Admission Prices: Jan.-May & Sept.-Oct. Mon.-Fri. 10-4; Memorial Day-Labor Day Tues.-Sat. 10-4. Adults $7, senior citizens & students $6, children $5; discounts to members. Closed New Year's Eve & Day; Christmas Eve, Day & week. ♿
Attendance: 60,000 (accurate)
Membership: Individual $25; Family $50.

Wendover

BONNEVILLE SPEEDWAY MUSEUM, 1000 E. Wendover Blvd., Wendover, UT 84083. Tel.: 435-665-7721.
Racing Museum.
Collections: speed racing memorabilia & films.
Hours & Admission Prices: June-Nov. daily 10-6. Adults $6, children $1.

VERMONT

(160 listings)

Addison

CHIMNEY POINT STATE HISTORIC SITE, 7305 VT Rte. 125, Addison, VT 05491-8751. Tel.: 802-759-2412. Fax: 802-759-2547.
E-mail: chimneypoint@historicvermont.org
Web Site: www.historicvermont.org/chimneypoint
Founded: 1968.
Congressional District: 1
Key Personnel: Historic Site Operations Chief, John P. Dumville; Site Admin., Elsa Gilbertson.
Personnel Profile: Full-Time Paid 1; Part-Time Paid 1.
Governing Authority: state. Parent Institution: State of Vermont, Div. for Historic Preservation, National Life Bldg., Drawer 20, Montpelier, VT 05620-0501. Tax-exempt.
Historic Building: late 18th-century tavern.
Collections: furnishings; memorabilia; historic structures; Native American artifacts; archaeological; French colonial history.
Research Fields: Native Americans in Vermont, French settlement of Champlain Valley; early Champlain Valley history.
Facilities: visitors' center. Museum-related items for sale.
Activities: temporary exhibits; school program; Northeastern Open Atlatl Championship; special events.
Publications: guide.
Hours & Admission Prices: late-May to Columbus Day Wed.-Sun. 9:30-5:30. Adults $3, children 15 and under & senior citizens $1; discounts to AAM members & museum professionals; school groups & children under 15 accompanied by adult no charge. ♿
Attendance: 2,300 (accurate)

Arlington

NORMAN ROCKWELL EXHIBITION, 3772 VT Rte. 7-A, Arlington, VT 05250. Mailing Address: P.O. Box 510, Arlington, VT 05250-0510. Tel.: 802-375-6423.
Key Personnel: Owner, Joy Hinrichsen
Art Museum.
Collections: works by Norman Rockwell while living in Arlington from 1939-1953 including Satuday Evening Post covers, illustrations, & prints.
Hours & Admission Prices: May-Oct. daily 9-5; Nov.-April Fri.-Mon. 9-5.

Barnet

BARNET HISTORICAL SOCIETY, 802 Warden Rd., Barnet, VT 05821-9555. Tel.: 802-633-2325.
Founded: 1967.
Key Personnel: Pres., David Warden; Vice Pres., Dylan Ford; Treas., John Fairchild; Sec., Lorna Fogg.
Personnel Profile: Part-Time Volunteers 6.
Governing Authority: society. Tax-exempt.
Historical Society Museum: housed in c.1790 Goodwille House.
Collections: early pictures of the area; household & farm equipment; store ledgers; Roy Brothers Croquet factory.
Research Fields: local history.
Activities: guided tours by appointment; temporary exhibitions.
Hours & Admission Prices: July-Sept. 10-4; tours by appointment. ♿
Attendance: 200 (estimated)
Membership: Contributing $10.

Barre

STUDIO PLACE ARTS, 201 N. Main St., Barre, VT 05641-4125. Tel.: 802-479-7069.
Key Personnel: Exec. Dir., Sue Higby
Art Gallery.
Collections: paintings; photographs; sculpture.
Activities: art classes; temporary & permanent exhibits; workshops; lectures.
Hours & Admission Prices: Call for hours. No charge.

Barton

CRYSTAL LAKE FALLS HISTORICAL ASSOCIATION, 97 Water St., Barton, VT 05822. Mailing Address: 536 Breezy Hill Rd., Barton, VT 05822-8641. Tel.: 802-525-3703.
E-mail: jfbrown259@adelphia.net
Founded: 1984.
Key Personnel: Pres., Earle Randall; Vice Pres., Richard Douse; Treas., Bill May.
Personnel Profile: Part-Time Volunteers 15.
Governing Authority: private; nonprofit organization. Tax-exempt: 501(c)(3).
Historical and Industrial Museum: housed in a c.1820 structure.
Collections: artifacts from education in Barton; Barton's industries.
Research Fields: Barton's history, industries & education.
Facilities: 30-vol. library of books & memorabilia on Gov. Emerson; 600 sq. ft. exhibit space. Museum-related items for sale.
Activities: video; guided tours; lectures; talks & story telling to school children. Annual Event: Open House in June.
Publications: biannual newsletter.
Hours & Admission Prices: June-Aug. Sun. 1-4; other times by appointment. No charge; donations accepted.
Attendance: 186 (accurate)
Membership: Student $.50; Adult $5; Lifetime $100.

Bellows Falls

ADAMS OLD STONE GRIST MILL, Mill St., Bellows Falls, VT 05101. Mailing Address: 47 Atkinson, Bellows Falls, VT 05101-1675. Tel.: 802-463-3734.
Founded: 1965.
Key Personnel: Pres. Historical Society, Dennis Ladd.
Governing Authority: nonprofit. Operated by the Bellows Falls Historical Society. Tax-exempt.
Historical Society Museum.
Collections: 19th-century milling equipment; locally manufactured machinery; farming implements; railroad items; documents & records; household furnishings. Historic Structure: 1831 gristmill (160th year anniversary).
Activities: guided tours; permanent exhibitions.
Hours & Admission Prices: June-Oct. Sat.-Sun. 1-4; other times by appointment. No charge; donations accepted.
Attendance: 340

ROCKINGHAM FREE PUBLIC LIBRARY AND MUSEUM, 65 Westminster St., Bellows Falls, VT 05101-1555. Tel.: 802-463-4270.
E-mail: rockingham@dol.state.vt.us
Web Site: www.rockingham.lib.vt.us
Founded: 1909.
Key Personnel: Dir., Celina Houlne.
Personnel Profile: Full-Time Paid 4; Part-Time Paid 5.
Governing Authority: municipal. Tax-exempt.
History Museum.
Collections: photographs; Civil War artifacts; local histories; local newspapers; machinery manufactured in town; articles owned by local citizens from 1700 to 1900; stereopticon views & viewers.

Facilities: 47,000-vol. library including children's books, available for interlibrary loan; reading room.
Activities: temporary exhibitions; genealogy research; local history events.
Hours & Admission Prices: Mon.-Wed. 10-7, Thurs.-Fri. 10-5:30, Sat. 10-2; other times by appointment. No charge. Closed legal holidays. ♿
Attendance: 386 (accurate)

Belmont

MOUNT HOLLY COMMUNITY HISTORICAL MUSEUM, Tarbelville Rd., Belmont, VT 05730. Mailing Address: P.O. Box 17, Belmont, VT 05730-0017. Tel.: 802-259-2460.
Web Site: www.mounthollyvtmuseum.org
Formerly: Community Historical Museum of Mount Holly
Founded: 1968.
Congressional District: 4
Key Personnel: Chm. (V), Dennis Devereux; Vice Chm., Lory Doolittle; Sec., Maggie Blane; Treas., Linda Nexon; Cur., Robin Eatmon.
Personnel Profile: Part-Time Volunteers 18.
Governing Authority: nonprofit organization. Tax-exempt.
General & Historical Society Museum: housed in 1834 blacksmith shop.
Collections: quilts; clothing; old farm tools; early records; apothecary bottles; blacksmith equipment; local photographs; early records; cemetery records; local history; post office.
Research Fields: local history.
Activities: permanent & temporary exhibitions; demonstrations of crafts; lectures; dinners with guest speakers.
Publications: books, Mount Holly, Its Early Days: History of Mt. Holly; annual newsletter.
Hours & Admission Prices: July-Aug. Sat.-Sun. 2-4. No charge; donations accepted. ♿
Attendance: 550 (estimated)
Membership: Individual $10; Family $25; Patron $50; Sustaining $100; Life $500.

Bennington

BENNINGTON CENTER FOR THE NATURAL & CULTURAL ARTS, 44 Gypsy Lane at VT Rte. 9, Bennington, VT 05201-9692. Mailing Address: P.O. Box 260, Bennington, VT 05201-0260. Tel.: 802-442-7158.
E-mail: shirley@benningtoncenterforthearts.org
Web Site: www.benningtoncenterforthearts.org/index.html
Key Personnel: Dir., Shirley Hutchins
Art, Nature & Culture Center.
Collections: Native American artifacts; Navajo weavings; Navajo, Hopi & Zuni jewelry; pottery; sculptures; paintings.
Hours & Admission Prices: Call for hours. Adults $8, seniors & students $7; children under 12 no charge.

* **THE BENNINGTON MUSEUM, (M),** 75 Main St., Bennington, VT 05201-2885. Tel.: 802-447-1571. Fax: 802-442-8305.
E-mail: info@benningtonmuseum.org
Web Site: www.benningtonmuseum.org
Founded: 1852.
Key Personnel: Exec. Dir., Stephen Perkins; Chm. Bd., Don Miller; Cur., Jamie Franklin; Dir. Public Programs, Deana Flanders; Devel. Assoc., Joy Danila; Public Rels., Susan Strano; Collections Mgr., Callie Stewart; Visitor Svcs., Karen Harrington.
Personnel Profile: Full-Time Paid 13; Part-Time Paid 18; Part-Time Volunteers 128; Interns 2.
Governing Authority: nonprofit corporation. Tax-exempt: 501(c) (3).
Art, Decorative Arts & History Museum.
Collections: regional painting & sculpture; New England early Vermont furniture; Bennington pottery-Rockingham, Flint Enamel & Parian pottery ware; early American glass; American silver & Vermont coins; regional historical materials; c.1920 Bennington made Martin-WASP touring car; flags; costumes & uniforms; dolls; toys; paintings & memorabilia of Grandma Moses. Historic Building: 1838 Grandma Moses Schoolhouse.
Major Exhibits: State of Craft, 5/10-11/10.
Research Fields: Bennington pottery; Bennington regional history; New England painting & furniture; Vermont silver; Grandma Moses.
Facilities: 5,002-vol. library of genealogy books, records & related materials available for use on premises; reading room. Museum-related reproductions & Vermont-made items for sale.
Activities: guided tours; lectures; permanent, temporary & traveling exhibitions; workshops; school out-reach.
Publications: annual report, The Bennington Museum Notes. exhibition catalogues; Highlights from the Bennington Museum; Norton Stoneware & American Redware, The Bennington Museum Collection; The Best The Country Affords: Vermont Furniture, 1765-1858.
Hours & Admission Prices: Thurs.-Tues. 10-5. Adults $9, senior citizen & students $8, groups of 10 or more $6:50 per person; discounts to AAM & ICOM members; members & children under 18 no charge. Closed New Year's Day; Thanksgiving Day; Christmas. ♿
Attendance: 34,820 (accurate)
Membership: Individual $40; Family $60; Contributing $100; Sustaining $200; Friend $300; Patron $500; Benefactor $1,000; Director's Circle $1,500; Corporate $100-$1,500.

THE BURGHDORF GALLERY AT SOUTHERN VERMONT COLLEGE, 982 Mansion Dr., Bennington, VT 05201-9269. Tel.: 802-447-6316. Fax: 802-447-4695.
E-mail: gwinter@svc.edu
Formerly: Southern Vermont College Art Gallery
Founded: 1979.
Key Personnel: Dir., Greg Winterhalter.
Governing Authority: college. Parent Institution: Southern Vermont College, Monument Ave., Bennington, VT 05201. Tax-exempt: 501(c)(3).
College Art Gallery: housed in 1910 Everett Estate, built in the style of a 14th century English-Norman castle. Listed on the National Register of Historic Places.
Collections: photo collection of 1910 Everett Mansion construction.
Activities: temporary exhibits.
Hours & Admission Prices: Mon.-Fri. 9-3. No charge; donations accepted. Closed major holidays. ♿
Attendance: 5,000

HAWKINS HOUSE, 262 N. St., Bennington, VT 05201-1828. Tel.: 802-447-0488; 800-442-6463. Fax: 802-447-0488.
Web Site: www.hawkinshouse.net
Key Personnel: Pres., Liz Ganger; Co-Owner, Jonah Spivak
Art Museum.
Collections: works by over 450 artisans & artists.
Facilities: Museum-related items for sale.
Hours & Admission Prices: Jan.-June Mon.-Sat. 10-5:30, Sun. 12-5:30; July-Dec. Mon.-Sat. 10-6, Sun. 11-5:30.

SUZANNE LEMBERG USDAN GALLERY, Bennington College, 1 College Dr., Bennington, VT 05201-6003. Tel.: 802-442-5401.
Art Gallery.
Collections: works by professional artists, college faculty, graduate students & graduating seniors.
Activities: lectures; workshops.
Hours & Admission Prices: March-June & Sept.-Dec. Tues.-Sat. 1-5. No charge.

VERMONT COVERED BRIDGE MUSEUM, 44 Gypsy Lane, Bennington, VT 05201-9692. Mailing Address: P.O. Box 260, Bennington, VT 05201-0260. Tel.: 802-442-7158.
Web Site: www.benningtoncenterforthearts.org/CBMHome.htm
History Museum.
Collections: covered bridge history; truss designs; transportation history; portal styles; photographs; paintings; tools.
Hours & Admission Prices: Mon. & Wed.-Sun. 10-5. Familes $20, adults $9, students & seniors $8; children under 12 no charge.

Bethel

BETHEL HISTORICAL SOCIETY, Church St., Bethel, VT 05032. Mailing Address: 1398 Brink Hill Rd., Bethel, VT 05032. Tel.: 802-234-9413.
Historical Society Museum: housed in the Brick Church on the green; built in 1816.
Collections: local history & culture; photographs; paintings; period artifacts.
Hours & Admission Prices: July-Aug. Sun. 2-5.

Bradford

BRADFORD HISTORICAL SOCIETY INC., Town Hall, Main St., Bradford, VT 05033. Mailing Address: 67 Summer St., Bradford, VT 05033-9142. Tel.: 802-222-4011 & 4423.
E-mail: lccoffin@charter.net
Founded: 1959.
Key Personnel: Pres., Lawrence Coffin; Vice Pres., Wayne Kenyon; Sec., Jeanette Nordham; Treas., Diane Smarro; Cur., Karen DeRosa.
Personnel Profile: Part-Time Volunteers 8.
Governing Authority: board of directors; nonprofit. Tax-exempt.
Historical Society Museum: housed in 1894 Woods School.
Collections: Civil War artifacts; items manufactured in Bradford; photographs; scrapbooks; store signs; china; 19th-century costumes; jewelry; furniture; cemetery survey; town & school reports; Admiral Charles Clark memorabilia; James Wilson, manufacturer of first world globe produced in USA, 1810.

Research Fields: genealogical.
Facilities: 300-vol. library of town reports, histories, Vermont history & folklore. Notepaper, prints, medals & commemorative items for sale.
Activities: guided tours; lectures; films; formally organized education programs; permanent, temporary & loan exhibitions.
Publications: annual newsletter.
Hours & Admission Prices: Fri. 2-4; other times by appointment. No charge; donations accepted. Closed holidays. ♿
Attendance: 300 (estimated)
Membership: Individual $5; Family $10; Contributing $25; Life $100.

Brattleboro

BRATTLEBORO HISTORICAL SOCIETY, Municipal Center, 230 Main St., Brattleboro, VT 05301. Mailing Address: P.O. Box 6392, Brattleboro, VT 05302-6392. Tel.: 802-258-4957.
E-mail: histsoc@sover.net
Web Site: www.brattleborohistoricalsociety.org
Founded: 1982.
Historical Society Museum.
Collections: local history & culture; photographs; period artifacts.
Activities: research.
Hours & Admission Prices: Thurs. 1-4, Sat. 10 to noon; other times by appointment.
Membership: Individual $15; Family $25; Contributing $50.

BRATTLEBORO MUSEUM & ART CENTER, 10 Vernon St., Brattleboro, VT 05301-3390. Tel.: 802-257-0124. Fax: 802-258-9182.
E-mail: info@brattleboromuseum.org
Web Site: www.brattleboromuseum.org
Founded: 1972.
Congressional District: 4
Key Personnel: Dir., Danny Lichtenfeld; Pres. Bd, Betsy Gentile; Gallery Mgr., Margaret Shipman.
Personnel Profile: Full-Time Paid 2; Part-Time Paid 3; Part-Time Volunteers 130; Interns 4.
Governing Authority: private; nonprofit. Tax-exempt: 501(c)(3).
Visual Art Center: housed in 1915 former Union Railroad Station.
Collections: changing visual arts exhibitions; art of our times.
Facilities: Museum-related items for sale.
Activities: school programs; lectures; performance workshops; temporary visual art exhibitions based on annual theme; public openings; family events.
Publications: exhibition brochures; catalogues; posters; newsletters.
Hours & Admission Prices: April-Feb. Thurs.-Mon. 11-5. Adults $6, senior citizens $4, students $3; discounts to AAM, Vermont Museum & Gallery Alliance and New England Museum Association members; children 5 & under and members no charge. Closed New Year's Day; Independence Day; Thanksgiving; Christmas. ♿
Attendance: 23,421 (estimated)
Membership: Senior $30; Individual $40; Family & Dual $70; Donor $125; Sustaining $300; Patron $500; Benefactor $1,000.

ESTEY ORGAN MUSEUM, 108 Birge St., Brattleboro, VT 05301-6460. Tel.: 802-246-8366.
Web Site: www.esteyorganmuseum.org
Founded: 2002.
Governing Authority: nonprofit organization. Tax-exempt: 501(c)(3).
Organ Museum.
Collections: company history; reed, pipe & electronic organs; photographs; Estey tools, advertising, & catalogs; personal artifacts.
Activities: workshops; lectures; special events.
Hours & Admission Prices: Sat. 1-4. Admission $3; members no charge.
Membership: Student & Senior $15; Individual $25; Family $35; Business $50.

Bristol

BRISTOL HISTORICAL SOCIETY MUSEUM, Howden Hall Community Center, 19 West St., Bristol, VT 05443-1227. Tel.: 802-453-3429 & 2888.
E-mail: lscoffin@guavt.net
Key Personnel: Pres., Sylvia Coffin; Vice Pres., Gerald Heffernan
Historical Society Museum.
Collections: local history; photographs; maps; postcards; newspapers.
Hours & Admission Prices: June 15-Oct. 15 Mon.-Fri. 10-4 by appointment. No charge; donations accepted.

Brookfield Center

HISTORICAL SOCIETY OF BROOKFIELD-MARVIN NEWTON HOUSE, 1133 Ridge Rd., Brookfield Center, VT 05036. Mailing Address: P.O. Box 447, Brookfield, VT 05036-0447. Tel.: 802-276-3959 & 3497. Fax: 802-276-3023.
Web Site: brookfieldhistoricalsociety.wordpress.com
Founded: 1935.
Key Personnel: Pres., Michael Dempsey; Treas., Mary Waldo; Trustee, Linda Runnion; Trustee, Gary Lord; Trustee & News Editor, Greg Sauer; Trustee, Bonnie Fallon; Trustee, Joanna Boden Weber; Cur., Jacalin Wilder; Historian & Genealogist, Elinor Gray.
Personnel Profile: Part-Time Volunteers 15.
Governing Authority: society. Tax-exempt.
Historic House: 1835, Marvin Newton house.
Collections: 19th-century furnishings & artifacts.
Activities: guided tours; inter-museum loan & permanent exhibitions.
Publications: newsletter; annual pictorial calendar.
Hours & Admission Prices: July-Aug. Sun. 2-5; other times by appointment. Adults $2.
Attendance: 135 (estimated)
Membership: Individual annual $15; Family annual $25; Individual life $150; Family life $250.

Brownington

ORLEANS COUNTY HISTORICAL SOCIETY & THE OLD STONE HOUSE MUSEUM, 109 Old Stone House Rd., Brownington, VT 05860-4420. Tel.: 802-754-2022.
E-mail: information@oldstonehousemuseum.org
Web Site: oldstonehousemuseum.org
Founded: 1916.
Congressional District: 1
Key Personnel: Dir., Peggy Day Gibson; Chm. (V), Dr. George Linton; Museum Shop Mgr., Linda Child.
Personnel Profile: Full-Time Paid 1; Part-Time Paid 5; Part-Time Volunteers 25; Interns 1.
Governing Authority: society. Parent Institution: Orleans County Historical Society, Inc., Brownington, VT. Tax-exempt: 501(c)(3).
Local History Museum: housed in 1836 Old Stone House built by Rev. Alexander Twilight, originally used as school dormitory.
Collections: period furniture; school texts & reference material on Orleans County history; paintings; early farm; household & military artifacts; Vermont imprints.
Research Fields: Orleans County history.
Facilities: 2,000-vol. library of local and state history; old textbooks; newspaper collection from 1860 available for research on premises by arrangement with librarian; reading room.
Activities: guided tours; permanent exhibitions; educational programs; classes in traditional skills.
Publications: quarterly bulletin; books.
Hours & Admission Prices: May 15-Oct. 15 Wed.-Sun. 11-5. Adults $6, Orleans county residents $5, students $3; discount to groups, NEMA & VMGA members, Orleans County residents & AAA members; members no charge. ♿
Attendance: 3,000 (estimated)
Membership: Individual $15; Family $25; Contributing $35; Sustaining $50; Life $150.

Brownsville

WEST WINDSOR HISTORICAL SOCIETY, Rte. 44, Brownsville, VT 05037. Mailing Address: P.O. Box 12, Brownsville, VT 05037-0012. Tel.: 802-436-2262.
E-mail: pdugdale@valley.net
Key Personnel: Chm., Pat Dugdale
Historical Society Museum.
Collections: local history & culture; photographs; personal artifacts.
Hours & Admission Prices: May-Oct. Wed. 9-11:30 am; other times by appointment. No charge.

Burlington

ECHO LAKE AQUARIUM AND SCIENCE CENTER/LEAHY CENTER FOR LAKE CHAMPLAIN, One College St., Leahy Center for Lake Champlain, Burlington, VT 05401-5215. Tel.: 802-864-1848, ext. 125; 877-ECHOFUN. Fax: 802-864-6832.
E-mail: info@echovermont.org
Web Site: www.echovermont.org
Founded: 1995.
Key Personnel: Chm. (V), Jane Clifford; Exec. Dir., Phelan R. Fretz; Dir.

Mktg. & Communications, Steven Leibman; Dir. New Product Devel., Julie Silverman, M.A.T.; Dir. Finance, Chris Miller, Ph.D., CPA; Dir. Animal Care & Facilities Mgmt., Steve Smith; Treas., Larry Walsh.
Personnel Profile: Full-Time Paid 22; Part-Time Paid 6; Part-Time Volunteers 200; Interns 30.
Governing Authority: private; nonprofit organization. Tax-exempt: 501(c)(3).
Lake Aquarium & Science Center
Collections: history, ecology & culture of the Lake Champlain basin; hands on interactive exhibits; live aquatic animals.
Facilities: library; educational facilities; aquarium; laboratory; resource room. Museum-related items for sale.
Activities: formal education programs; guided tours; lectures; participatory exhibits; demonstrations; outreach programs; environmental monitoring classes; kit rental.
Publications: educational program flyer.
Hours & Admission Prices: Daily 10-5. Adult $9.50, seniors 60 & over and college students with ID $8.50, children 3-17 $7.50; discount to ASTC members; children under 3 & members no charge. Closed Thanksgiving; Christmas Eve & Day. ♿
Attendance: 153,000 (accurate)
Membership: Child $18; Senior & Student $24; Adult $27.

ETHAN ALLEN HOMESTEAD MUSEUM & HISTORIC SITE, 1 Ethan Allen Homestead, Burlington, VT 05408-1141. Tel.: 802-865-4556. Fax: 802-865-0661.
E-mail: info@ethanallenhomestead.org
Web Site: www.ethanallenhomestead.org
Founded: 1988.
Key Personnel: Exec. Dir., Daniel O'Neil; Pres. (V), Roger Marshall.
Personnel Profile: Full-Time Paid 1; Part-Time Volunteers 53; Interns 1.
Governing Authority: Parent Institution: Ethan Allen Homestead Foundation. Tax-exempt.
Historic Site.
Collections: life of Ethan Allen; Native American artifacts; local history; gardens.
Facilities: interpretive center. Museum-related items for sale.
Activities: children's programs; educational programs; live demonstrations; reenactments; family events.
Hours & Admission Prices: May-Oct. Thurs.-Mon. 10-4; groups by appointment. Adults $7 nonresident, $5 VT resident, seniors $5, children 6-12 $3; children under 6 & members no charge.
Attendance: 4,000 (estimated)

THE FIREHOUSE GALLERY, 135 Church St., Firehouse Center for the Visual Arts, Ground Fl., Burlington, VT 05401-8415. Mailing Address: Burlington City Arts, 149 Church St., Burlington, VT 05401. Tel.: 802-865-7166. Fax: 802-865-5839.
Web Site: www.burlingtoncityarts.com/firehousegallery
Key Personnel: Exec. Dir., Doreen Kraft; Cur., Chris Thompson
Art Museum.
Collections: painting; sculpture; photography.
Hours & Admission Prices: Mon.-Sat. 9-5, Sun. 12-5. ♿

FRANCIS COLBURN GALLERY, University of Vermont, Dept. of Art & Art History, Williams Hall, 72 University Pl., Burlington, VT 05405-0168. Tel.: 802-656-2014. Fax: 802-656-2064.
E-mail: artdept@uvm.edu
Web Site: www.uvm.edu/~artdept
Founded: 1975.
Key Personnel: Administrative Asst., Simone Blaise.
Governing Authority: university.
University Art Gallery: housed in 1896 campus building.
Collections: various forms of art media exhibited by students, faculty & visiting artists.
Activities: lectures; films; gallery talks; formally organized education programs for undergraduate college students; loan & temporary exhibitions.
Publications: exhibition announcements.
Hours & Admission Prices: Sept.-May Mon.-Fri. 9-4:30. No charge. ♿

FROG HOLLOW GALLERIES, 85 Church St., Burlington, VT 05401-4420. Tel.: 802-863-6458. Fax: 802-860-6506.
Web Site: www.froghollow.org
Governing Authority: nonprofit organization. Tax-exempt: 501(c)(3).
Art Gallery.
Collections: works by Vermont artists.
Activities: art & craft classes for students.
Hours & Admission Prices: Mon.-Wed. 10-6, Thurs.-Sat. 10-8, Sun. 11-6.

PERKINS GEOLOGY MUSEUM AT THE UNIVERSITY OF VERMONT, Delehanty Hall - Trinity Campus, 180 colchester Ave., Burlington, VT 05405-1758. Tel.: 802-656-8694.
Geology Museum.
Collections: geological artifacts; rocks; fossils; hands-on exhibits.
Activities: hands-on exhibits; educational programs.
Hours & Admission Prices: Academic Year: Mon.-Fri. 9-6, Sat.-Sun. 11-6; Summer call for hours. No charge. ♿

* **ROBERT HULL FLEMING MUSEUM, (M),** Univ. of Vermont, 61 Colchester Ave., Burlington, VT 05405-0001. Tel.: 802-656-0750. Fax: 802-656-8059.
E-mail: fleming@uvm.edu
Web Site: www.flemingmuseum.org
Founded: 1931.
Key Personnel: Dir., Janie Cohen; Cur., Aimee Marcereau DeGalan; Education & Public Programs Cur., Christina Fearon; Public Rels. & Mktg. Mgr., Chris Dissinger; Mgr. Collections & Exhibitions, Margaret Tamulonis; Exhibition Designer & Preparator, Perry Price; Financial Mgr., Stephanie Glock; Museum Shop Mgr., Kristen Kilbashian.
Personnel Profile: Full-Time Paid 8; Part-Time Paid 2.
Governing Authority: university. Parent Institution: University of Vermont. Tax-exempt.
Art & Anthropology Museum.
Collections: American & European paintings; sculpture, prints & drawings, medieval to modern; African, Oceanic, Asian, pre-Columbian, ancient; decorative arts; costumes; textiles; anthropological & archeological artifacts; Native American.
Major Exhibits: Views and Re-Views: Soviet Political Posters and Cartoons, Spring 2010 (T); Andrew Raftery, Fall 2010.
Research Fields: pertaining to collections & exhibitions.
Facilities: 2,000-vol. library on art history; on-premises research; reading room; classrooms; auditorium; seminar study room. Museum-related items for sale.
Activities: guided tours; lectures; gallery talks; concerts; arts festivals; permanent, temporary & traveling exhibitions; school services program; community outreach; public programs; films; symposia; workshops.
Publications: Seasonal Calendars; exhibition catalogs; brochures; posters.
Hours & Admission Prices: May to Labor Day. Tues.-Fri. 12-4, Sat.-Sun. 1-5; Sept.-April Tues. & Thurs.-Fri. 9-4, Wed. 9-8. Adults $5, seniors & students $3; discounts to AAM members; members no charge. Closed major holidays. ♿
Attendance: 25,000 (estimated)
Membership: Individual $30; Family & Dual $45; Contributing $100; Patron $250; Benefactor $500; Director's Circle $1,000; $5 reduced rate for artists, educators, and seniors.

Cabot

CABOT CREAMERY VISITORS CENTER, 2878 Main St., Cabot, VT 05647. Tel.: 802-229-9361; 800-837-4261. Fax: 802-371-1200.
E-mail: vctr@cabotcheese.coop
Web Site: www.cabot.cheese.coop
Company History Museum.
Collections: Cabot Creamery history; cheese-making process; video; Vermont agricultural history.
Facilities: visitor center. Museum-related items for sale.
Activities: factory tours; food tastings; video.
Hours & Admission Prices: Jan. Mon.-Sat. 10-4; June-Oct. daily 9-5; Nov.-May Mon.-Sat. 9-4. Adults $2; children under 12 no charge.

CABOT HISTORICAL SOCIETY, 193 McKinistry, Cabot, VT 05647-9755. Mailing Address: P.O. Box 275, Cabot, VT 05647-0275. Tel.: 802-563-2547.
E-mail: bonniesd@together.net
Web Site: cabothistory.org
Founded: 1966.
Key Personnel: Pres., Bonnie S. Dannenberg; Cur., Eric Ginette.
Governing Authority: nonprofit. Tax-exempt: 501(c)(3).
Historical & Preservation Society: housed in 1845 schoolhouse in Cabot Village.
Collections: artifacts; pictures; documents; manuscripts.
Research Fields: local history.
Facilities: 25-vol. library of newspapers & account books available for research by permission of society officers. Local maps, church history & other museum-related items for sale.
Activities: guided tours; lectures; permanent & temporary exhibitions.
Hours & Admission Prices: Special local holidays & by appointment. No charge; donations accepted.
Attendance: 500 (estimated)

Membership: General $1.

Castleton

CASTLETON HISTORICAL SOCIETY, The Higley Homestead, 407 Main St., Castleton, VT 05735-0219. Mailing Address: P.O. Box 219, Castleton, VT 05735-0219. Tel.: 802-468-5105.
Founded: 1947.
Key Personnel: Pres. (V) & Museum Shop Mgr., Holly Hitchcock.
Personnel Profile: Part-Time Volunteers 10.
Governing Authority: private; nonprofit organization. Tax-exempt: 501(c)(3).
Village Museum: main office housed in 1811 Federal-style Georgian house, The Higley Homestead, listed on National Register of Historic Places.
Collections: decorative arts; furnishings; personal artifacts.
Activities: guided tours; temporary exhibits.
Publications: book, Castleton Looking Back; Castleton Scenes of Yesterday.
Hours & Admission Prices: May-Dec. by appointment. No charge; donations accepted. ♿
Attendance: 150 (estimated)
Membership: Adult $8.

CHRISTINE PRICE GALLERY, Castleton State College, Castleton, VT 05735. Tel.: 802-468-5611. Fax: 802-468-1440.
E-mail: william.ramage@castleton.edu
Art Gallery.
Collections: paintings; photographs; sculpture; drawings.
Activities: temporary exhibitions.
Hours & Admission Prices: Academic Year: Mon.-Fri. 9-5.

Cavendish

CAVENDISH HISTORICAL SOCIETY MUSEUM, Main St., Rte. 131, Cavendish, VT 05142. Mailing Address: P.O. Box 472, Cavendish, VT 05142-9647. Tel.: 802-226-7807.
E-mail: margoc@tds.net
Web Site: cavendishhistory.org
Key Personnel: Coord., Margo Caulfield
Historical Society Museum: housed in a former 19th-century town hall.
Collections: period history & culture; photographs; farm equipment & tools; household utensils; costumes; textiles;
Hours & Admission Prices: late June to mid-Oct. Sun. 2-4; other times by appointment. No charge.

Chester

CHESTER ART GUILD, The Green, Main St., Chester, VT 05143. Mailing Address: P.O. Box 154, Chester, VT 05143-0154. Tel.: 802-875-3767.
E-mail: dorisingram@mymailstation.com
Founded: 1960.
Key Personnel: Pres. & Chm. (V), Doris Ingram; Treas., Molly Ferris; Membership Coord., Dale O'Brien; Public Rels., Nancy Ball.
Personnel Profile: Full-Time Volunteers 70; Part-Time Volunteers 70.
Governing Authority: volunteer group. Tax-exempt.
Art Association Gallery: restored former elementary school.
Collections: paintings by local artists.
Facilities: library relating to artists & art history; 800 sq. ft. exhibit space; classrooms & studio. All exhibited items for sale, except permanent collection.
Activities: lectures; workshops; educational programs; two high school scholarships for Governor's Institute on Art summer school at Castleton State College; demonstrations; outdoor shows; theme shows; college scholarship; classes. Annual Events: Holiday Sale.
Publications: quarterly members newsletter, Argus.
Hours & Admission Prices: mid-June to mid-Oct. Fri. & Sun. 1-4, Sat. 9-4. Art Gallery: June-Oct. Fri. & Sun. 1-4, Sat. 9-4. Studio Group: Tues.-Sat. 9-12. No charge; donations accepted. ♿
Attendance: 2,400 (estimated)
Membership: Student $2; Patron $6; Artist & Corporate or Sustaining $20; Family $35; Life $200.

Colchester

MCCARTHY ARTS CENTER GALLERY, Saint Michael's College, One Winooski Park, Colchester, VT 05439-0001. Tel.: 802-654-2246.
Web Site: www.smcvt.edu/academics/finearts
Art Gallery.
Collections: paintings; contemporary graphics.
Hours & Admission Prices: Mon.-Fri. 9-5. No charge.

Concord

CONCORD HISTORICAL SOCIETY MUSEUM, Concord Town Hall, Concord, VT 05824. Mailing Address: P.O. Box 195, Concord, VT 08524-0195.
Key Personnel: Pres. (V), Kathleen Fisher
Historical Society Museum.
Collections: replica of local doctor's office & smoking room; period post office; schoolroom; furnishings; tools; clothing; toys.
Publications: quarterly newsletter, Concord Historical Society; Concord "Then and Now."
Hours & Admission Prices: Sept. last Sat.-Sun.; other times by appointment. No charge; donations accepted.

Cuttingsville

SHREWSBURY HISTORICAL SOCIETY, 5419 Rte. 103, Cuttingsville, VT 05738. Tel.: 802-492-3324.
Web Site: shrewsburyhistoricalsociety.com
Historical Society Museum.
Collections: local history & culture; photographs; period furnishings; costumes; books; toys; videos.
Hours & Admission Prices: July-Oct. Sun. 1-3. No charge.

Dorset

DORSET HISTORICAL SOCIETY, Rte. 30 at Kent Hill Rd., Dorset, VT 05251. Mailing Address: P.O. Box 52, Dorset, VT 05251-0052. Tel.: 802-867-0331. Fax: 802-867-0412.
Founded: 1963.
Key Personnel: Chm. (V) & Pres. (V), Richard Hittle.
Personnel Profile: Part-Time Paid 2; Part-Time Volunteers 15.
Historical Society Museum: housed in Bley House.
Collections: local history; genealogy; farm & household artifacts; photographs; pottery; paintings; decorative arts.
Major Exhibits: The Artistry and Collection of Jessica H. Bone, 1/1/10-5/30/10.
Research Fields: family histories.
Facilities: genealogical library.
Activities: lectures; programs.
Publications: quarterly newsletter; Dorset In The Shadow of the Marble Mountain; Quabbin to Dorset; Walking Tour - Driving Tour.
Hours & Admission Prices: April 15-Oct. 15 Wed. 10-12, Thurs.-Sat. 10-2; Oct. 16-April 14 Wed. & Fri.-Sat. 10-12; other times by appointment. Closed Christmas. ♿
Attendance: 640 (accurate)
Membership: Regular $35; Supporter $50; Sustaining $100; Patron $250; Benefactor $500.

East Calais

NDAKINNA CULTURAL CENTER & MUSEUM, 34 Moscow Woods Rd., East Calais, VT 05650. Mailing Address: P.O. Box 7, East Calais, VT 05650-0007. Tel.: 802-456-8884.
Native American Museum.
Collections: Native American culture, heritage & history; photographs; personal artifacts; Abenaki baskets; clothing; ceremonial dress; beads; dream catchers.
Facilities: Museum-related items for sale.
Activities: classes; workshops.
Hours & Admission Prices: Jan.-March Sat. 9-4, Sun. 12-4; April-Dec. 24 Wed.-Fri. 12-5, Sat. 9-3. No charge; donations accepted.

East Poultney

POULTNEY HISTORICAL SOCIETY MUSEUM, The Green, East Poultney, VT 05741. Mailing Address: P.O. Box 605, ., East Poultney, VT 05741-0605. Tel.: 802-287-5252.
E-mail: info@poultneyhistoricalsociety.org
Web Site: poultneyhistoricalsociety.org
Founded: 1935.
Key Personnel: Pres., Richard Hanson.
Personnel Profile: Part-Time Volunteers 12.
Governing Authority: nonprofit. Affiliated with the Poultney Historical Society, Inc. Tax-exempt.
Antiques Museum: housed in 1800 Old Blacksmith Shop & Melodeon Factory; 1791 brick schoolhouse; 1895 Victorian schoolhouse.
Collections: early Poultney history; costumes; farm & home implements; archives; cemetery records; town records; Horace Greeley items; melodeons; artifacts.
Research Fields: local history; genealogy.

Activities: guided tours; formally organized education programs for children; permanent exhibitions.
Hours & Admission Prices: Memorial Day to Labor Day Sun. 1-4; other times by appointment. No charge; donations accepted.
Attendance: 350 (estimated)
Membership: Patron $5; Family $8; Contributing $25; Life $100.

Fairfield

PRESIDENT CHESTER A. ARTHUR HISTORIC SITE, 4588 Chester Arthur Road, Fairfield, VT 05455. Mailing Address: Historic Preservation, National Life Building, 2nd Fl., Montpelier, VT 05633-0001. Tel.: 802-828-3051. Fax: 802-828-3206.
E-mail: john.dumville@state.vt.us
Web Site: www.historicvermont.org/arthur
Founded: 1953.
Key Personnel: Historic Sites Operations Chief, John P. Dumville.
Personnel Profile: Full-Time Paid 1; Part-Time Paid 1.
Governing Authority: state. Parent Institution: State of Vermont. Subsidiary Institution: Division for Historic Preservation, Pavilion Building, Montpelier 05602. Tax-exempt.
Historic Houses: c.1830 Chester A. Arthur birthplace; 1820 Brick Church.
Collections: memorabilia. Historic Building: c.1820 Old Brick Church.
Facilities: picnic area.
Activities: permanent exhibitions.
Publications: brochures, Birthplace of Chester A. Arthur; Guide to Historic Sites In Vermont.
Hours & Admission Prices: June to mid-Oct. Wed.-Sun. 11-5. Adults $2. ♿
Attendance: 3,000 (estimated)

Ferrisburgh

ROKEBY MUSEUM, (M), 4334 Rte. 7, Ferrisburgh, VT 05456-9779. Tel.: 802-877-3406. Fax: 802-877-3406.
E-mail: rokeby@comcast.net
Web Site: www.rokeby.org
Formerly: Rokeby (Ancestral Estate of Rowland Evans Robinson)
Founded: 1962.
Key Personnel: Pres. (V), JoAnne C. LaBerge; Dir., Jane Williamson.
Personnel Profile: Part-Time Paid 3; Part-Time Volunteers 10.
Governing Authority: nonprofit organization. Tax-exempt.
Historic House: c.1784 Rokeby.
Collections: 18th & 19th century Vermont furnishings; writings of Rowland Robinson; underground railroad station; local history, folklore; photographs; art collections; letters; Indian artifacts & spiritualism; manuscript collections; agricultural implements.
Research Fields: local & state history; social history; 18th- & 19th-century literature; 19th- & 20th-century agriculture; abolition Quakers.
Facilities: 3,000-vol. library of the family available for use by appointment; reading room.
Activities: guided tours; permanent exhibitions; special events.
Publications: newsletter, Rokeby Messenger.
Hours & Admission Prices: May-Oct. Thurs.-Sun. Tours: 11, 12:30 & 2. Adults $6, seniors & students $4, children under 13 $2; discounts to groups & Vermont museum employees; members no charge. ♿
Attendance: 2,400 (accurate)
Membership: Individual $25; Family $40; Life $500.

Glover

BREAD & PUPPET MUSEUM, 753 Heights Rd., Rte. 122, Glover, VT 05839-9637. Tel.: 802-525-6972 & 3031. Fax: 802-525-3618.
E-mail: breadpup@together.net
Web Site: www.breadandpuppet.org
Founded: 1975.
Key Personnel: Dir., Peter Schumann; Sec. & Museum Shop Mgr., Elka Schumann.
Personnel Profile: Part-Time Paid 1; Part-Time Volunteers 2.
Governing Authority: individual operation; nonprofit organization. Parent Institution: Bread & Puppet Theater. Tax-exempt: 170(b)(1)(A).
Puppet Theater & Museum: housed in a 100 year old barn.
Collections: Peter Schumann works; puppets of all sizes; masks; banners; reliefs; paintings; graphics; stages; posters & literature on Bread & Puppet Theater; theater artifacts.
Research Fields: puppetry; theater; masks; street theater; pageants.
Facilities: library of printed matter concerning the works of the Bread & Puppet theater.
Activities: guided tours.
Publications: Bread and Puppet Museum. Please write to us for our annual mail order catalog of publications, posters, postcards & videos.
Hours & Admission Prices: June-Nov. 1 daily 10-6; other times by appointment. No charge; donations accepted.
Attendance: 20,000 (estimated)

Grafton

GRAFTON HISTORICAL SOCIETY, 147 Main St., Grafton, VT 05146. Mailing Address: P.O. Box 202, Grafton, VT 05146-0202. Tel.: 802-843-2489 & 1010.
E-mail: grafhist@sover.net
Web Site: www.graftonhistory.org
Founded: 1962.
Key Personnel: Pres., Dick Desrochers; Cur. & Chm. (V), Elisha Prouty; Sec., Linda Hughs.
Personnel Profile: Part-Time Paid 1; Part-Time Volunteers 45.
Governing Authority: nonprofit organization. Tax-exempt: 501(c)(3).
Local History Museum.
Collections: Grafton history; photographs; soapstone; writing accessories; furniture; tools; textiles.
Major Exhibits: Families, 5/10-10/10.
Research Fields: genealogy; local history.
Activities: permanent exhibitions; special exhibits of historical interest; lectures on Vermont & local history.
Publications: book, $5 and a Jug of Rum, a history of Grafton, Vermont 1754-2000; booklets, 125 Years with the Grafton Cornet Band; Barrett Store & Customers, 1816-1830; Innkeeping in Grafton 100 Years Ago; map, The First Map of Grafton 1764; Releasing Rebecca, An Exploration of Life, Death and Gravestone Art in Early Vermont; History of Grafton; Life of a Vermont Farmer; The Grafton Quilt Coloring Book; Grafton's Founding Century 1754-2004.
Hours & Admission Prices: Memorial Day to Columbus Day daily 10-4; Oct.-May Mon. & Fri. 10-4; other times by appointment. Adults $3.
Attendance: 1,700 (accurate)
Membership: Individual $10; Household $25; Sustaining $50; Household Sustaining $75; Patron $200; Household Patron $300.

THE NATURE MUSEUM AT GRAFTON, 186 Townshend Rd., Grafton, VT 05146. Mailing Address: P.O. Box 38, Grafton, VT 05146-0038. Tel.: 802-843-2111. Fax: 802-843-1164.
E-mail: info@nature-museum.org
Web Site: www.nature-museum.org
Founded: 1989.
Key Personnel: Pres. (V), Laurie Danforth; Exec. Dir., Lillian Willis; Treas., Will Danforth; Museum Shop Mgr., Sue Nostrand; Dir. Education & Cur., Betsy Stacey.
Personnel Profile: Full-Time Paid 2; Part-Time Paid 4; Part-Time Volunteers 10; Interns 1.
Governing Authority: private; nonprofit organization. Tax-exempt: 501(c)(3).
Natural History Museum.
Collections: emphasis on the mammals, birds & geology of New England.
Facilities: educational facilities; 2,000 sq. ft. exhibit space; nature trails; wildlife gardens. Museum-related items for sale.
Activities: educational programs; guided tours; lectures; participatory exhibits; nature trails; wild life gardens; outreach school programs.
Publications: biannual, The TNM Journal; quarterly calendar & newsletter.
Hours & Admission Prices: Sat. 10-4, Sun. 1-4; other times by appointment. Call for additional hours. Adults $4, seniors $3, children 3-12 $2; discounts to VMGA members; members no charge. Closed major holidays.
Attendance: 4,550 (accurate)
Membership: Individual $20; Family $30; Supporting $50; Sustaining $100; Patron $250.

Grand Isle

GRAND ISLE HISTORICAL SOCIETY, U.S. Rte. 2, Grand Isle, VT 05458. Mailing Address: P.O. Box 23, Grand Isle, VT 05458-0023. Tel.: 802-372-4058.
Historical Society Museum.
Collections: local history & culture; photographs; furniture; clothing; period furnishings. Historic Buildings: c.1784 Hyde Log Cabin; Block Schoolhouse built in 1814.
Hours & Admission Prices: Memorial Day to Columbus Day Thurs.-Mon. 11-5. Adults $2; children under 14 no charge. ♿

Graniteville

ROCK OF AGES VISITOR CENTER, 558 Graniteville Rd., Graniteville, VT 05654. Mailing Address: P.O. Box 482, Barre, VT 05641-0482. Tel.: 802-476-3119. Fax: 802-476-2110.
Founded: 1885.
Key Personnel: Dir., Todd Paton
Granite Industry Museum.

Collections: granite manufacturing history; photographs; granite artifacts & sculptures.
Facilities: theatre. Museum-related items for sale.
Activities: granite quarry demonstrations; video; outdoor granite bowling; make your own stone gift.
Hours & Admission Prices: Visitors Center: mid-May to mid-Sept. Mon.-Sat. 9-5; mid-Sept. to Oct. daily 9-5. Quarry Tours: Memorial Day to mid-Sept. Mon.-Sat. 9:15-3:35; mid-Sept. to mid-Oct. daily 9:15-3:35. Closed Independence Day.

Guilford

GUILFORD HISTORICAL SOCIETY, Guilford Center Rd., Guilford, VT 05301. Tel.: 802-257-0147 & 254-5910.
E-mail: pulpitfm@myfairpoint.net
Founded: 1973.
Key Personnel: Pres. (V), Adelaide W. Minoti; Cur., Ann Bonneville
Historical Society Museum: housed in the Town Hall building; built in 1822.
Collections: local history & culture; photographs; tools; household artifacts.
Facilities: Museum-related items for sale.
Activities: special events.
Hours & Admission Prices: June-Sept. Tues.-Sat. 10-2.

Hartland

HARTLAND HISTORICAL SOCIETY, Rte. 12, Hartland, VT 05048. Mailing Address: P.O. Box 297, Hartland, VT 05048-0297. Tel.: 802-436-1703.
E-mail: info@hartlandhistory.org
Web Site: www.hartlandhistory.org
Key Personnel: Pres., Carol Mowry
Historical Society Museum
Collections: local history & culture; photographs; letters; diaries; church records; uniforms; period furnishings.
Hours & Admission Prices: Mon. 1-4, Fri. 9-11am; other times by appointment. No charge.

Holland

HOLLAND HISTORICAL SOCIETY MUSEUM, INC., Gore Rd., Holland, VT 05830. Mailing Address: 591 Page Hill Rd., Derby Line, VT 05830-8838. Tel.: 802-895-2917.
Founded: 1972.
Congressional District: 17
Key Personnel: Dir., Ernest Judd; Dir., Martha Judd; Dir., Albert Hauver; Dir., Laurel Mosher; Pres., Penelope Tice; Vice Pres., Melody Ricard; Treas., Evelyn Page; Sec., Bea Nelson.
Personnel Profile: Part-Time Volunteers 8.
Governing Authority: nonprofit organization. Tax-exempt: 170(b)(1)(A).
Historical Society Museum: housed in c.1848 Congregational Church, birth town of Horace Tabor, the Silver king of Colorado.
Collections: period artifacts; pews; lecterns; local history artifacts; tools; 19th-century paintings & portraits; maps; organs; horse shed replica.
Activities: permanent & temporary exhibitions; dinners; meetings. Museum Sponsors: Open House by appointment; Annual Old Home Day in August; Old Timer's Day in September.
Publications: newsletter, annual activity & financial report.
Hours & Admission Prices: Call for hours. No charge; donations accepted.
Attendance: 175 (estimated)
Membership: Annual $5; Life $100.

Hubbardton

HUBBARDTON BATTLEFIELD MUSEUM, 5696 Monument Hill Rd., Hubbardton, VT 05749. Mailing Address: Historic Preservation, National Life Building, 2nd Fl., Montpelier, VT 05620-0001. Tel.: 802-759-2412 & 828-3051. Fax: 802-828-3206.
E-mail: john.dumville@state.vt.us
Web Site: www.historicvermont.org/hubbardton
Founded: 1948.
Key Personnel: Historic Sites Operations Chief, John P. Dumville; Site Admin., Elsa Gilbertson.
Personnel Profile: Full-Time Paid 1; Part-Time Paid 2.
Governing Authority: state. Parent Institution: State of Vermont, Div. for Historic Preservation, National Life Bldg., Drawer 20, Montpelier 05620. Tax-exempt.
State Historic Site: Hubbardton Battlefield.
Collections: military; Revolutionary War.
Research Fields: Revolutionary War in Vermont & environs.
Facilities: visitor's center.
Activities: reenactment program.
Publications: brochure; books, The Battle of Hubbardton; The American Rebels Stem the Tide.
Hours & Admission Prices: mid-May to mid-Oct. Wed.-Sun. 11-5. Adults $2; registered school groups & children under 14 no charge. ♿
Attendance: 5,000 (estimated)

Huntington

BIRDS OF VERMONT MUSEUM, 900 Sherman Hollow Rd., Huntington, VT 05462-9420. Tel.: 802-434-2167.
E-mail: museum@birdsofvermont.org
Web Site: www.birdsofvermont.org
Founded: 1987.
Key Personnel: Dir., Erin Talmage; Chm. (V), Shirley Johnson.
Governing Authority: private; nonprofit organization.
Woodcarving Museum.
Collections: over 480 life-size carved birds representing 255 species; butterfly garden.
Research Fields: field ornithology.
Facilities: picnic area; walking trails.
Activities: school field trips; nature walks; carving classes; special programs & events.
Publications: quarterly newsletter, Chip Notes.
Hours & Admission Prices: May-Oct. daily 10-4; Nov.-April by appointment. Adults $6, seniors $5, children 3-17 $3; discounts to VT Public TV, AAA, VMGA members; members no charge. ♿
Attendance: 4,500 (accurate)
Membership: Individual $25; Family $40; Contributing $50; Supporting $100; Sponsor $250; Patron $500; Spear Society $1,000.

Isle La Motte

ISLE LA MOTTE HISTORICAL SOCIETY, 283 School St., Isle La Motte, VT 05463-9808. Mailing Address: P.O. Box 18, Isle La Motte, VT 05463-0018. Tel.: 802-928-3077.
E-mail: gloilm@yahoo.com
Founded: 1925.
Key Personnel: Pres., Robert McEwen; Vice Pres., Mary Jane Tiedgen; Treas., Lilian Masters; Cur., Gloria McEwen; Sec., Marty Dale.
Personnel Profile: Part-Time Volunteers 12.
Governing Authority: society. Tax-exempt: 501(c)(3).
Local History Museum.
Collections: 18th to 19th-century artifacts; Indian culture. Historic Buildings: 19th-century blacksmith shop; 19-century stone schoolhouse; 19th century log/slab house.
Research Fields: genealogy.
Publications: annual newsletter; History of Isle Le Motte, VT; 75th Anniversary Booklet of Isle Le Motte Historical Society; History of Isle La Motte.
Hours & Admission Prices: July-Aug. Sat. 1-4, or by appointment. No charge, donations accepted.
Attendance: 500 (estimated)
Membership: Student $5; Adult $10; Couple $15; Family $20; Lifetime $100.

Jacksonville

WHITINGHAM HISTORICAL MUSEUM, 669 Reed Hill Rd., Jacksonville, VT 05342-9733. Mailing Address: P.O. Box 125, Jacksonville, VT 05342-0125. Tel.: 802-368-2448.
Founded: 1973.
Congressional District: 1
Key Personnel: Pres., Stella Stevens; Sec., Corrinne Boyd.
Personnel Profile: Part-Time Volunteers 20.
Governing Authority: nonprofit organization. Affiliated with Whitingham Historical Society, Jacksonville, VT 05342. Tax-exempt: 501(c)(3).
History Museum.
Collections: local costumes; tools; historical papers; photographs; textiles.
Activities: guided tours; lectures; formally organized education programs for children; school group programs.
Publications: annual newsletter, Sadawga Springs.
Hours & Admission Prices: June-Oct. Sun. 2-4; school groups & other times by appointment. No charge; donations accepted. ♿
Attendance: 375 (estimated)
Membership: Individual $7; Family $10; Life $75.

Jeffersonville

BRYAN MEMORIAL GALLERY, 180 Main St., Jeffersonville, VT 05464. Mailing Address: P.O. Box 340, Jeffersonville, VT 05464-0340. Tel.: 802-644-5100. Fax: 802-644-8342.
E-mail: info@bryangallery.org
Web Site: www.bryangallery.org

Key Personnel: Exec. Dir., Mickey Myers
Art Gallery.
Collections: paintings.
Activities: workshops; educational programs.
Hours & Admission Prices: Jan. 19-March Fri.-Sat. 10-4; other times by appointment; April 17-May 25 & Nov.-Dec. Thurs.-Sun. 10-4; May 25-Oct. daily 10-5.

BRYAN MEMORIAL GALLERY, 180 Main St., Jeffersonville, VT 05464. Mailing Address: P.O. Box 340, Jeffersonville, VT 05464-0340. Tel.: 802-644-5100. Fax: 802-644-8342.
E-mail: info@bryangallery.org
Art Gallery.
Collections: paintings; photographs.
Activities: workshops; educational programs.
Hours & Admission Prices: Jan. 19-March Fri.-Sat. 10-4; April 17-May 25 & Nov.-Dec. Thurs.-Sun. 10-4; May 26-Oct. daily 10-5; other times by appointment.

Jericho

EMILE A. GRUPPE GALLERY, 22 Barber Farm Rd., Jericho, VT 05465-9795. Tel.: 802-899-3211.
Art Gallery: housed in an 1860s English Sheep barn at the home of Emile's daughter, Emilie Gruppe Alexander & her husband.
Collections: paintings; photographs.
Hours & Admission Prices: Thurs.-Sun. 10-3; other times by appointment.

JERICHO HISTORICAL SOCIETY, 4A Red Mill Dr., Jericho, VT 05465. Mailing Address: P.O. Box 35, Jericho, VT 05465-0035. Tel.: 802-899-3225.
Web Site: jerichohistoricalsociety.org
Founded: 1971.
Congressional District: 1
Key Personnel: Pres. (V), Ann Squires; Archives Chm., Wayne Howe; Sales Shop Mgr., Gail Prior.
Governing Authority: society; nonprofit. Tax-exempt: 501(c)(3).
Historical Society Museum: housed in 1885 Chittenden Mills, five-story building once used as a grist mill.
Collections: 150 photographs & slides made from Wilson Bentley's original glass photographic plates along with many articles by & about Bentley; films; early photographs & memorabilia; Chitterden Mills historical material; roller milling process; period industrial artifacts. Historic Building: 1859 Mill House.
Research Fields: journals; accounts; Bentley archives; milling information.
Facilities: Locally made crafts, jewelry, china, glass & stationery for sale.
Activities: films; school loan service; temporary & loan exhibitions.
Publications: books, Old Mill Coloring Book; Old Mill Cook Book; Local Town History; History of Jericho, Vol. I (reprint) & Vol. II.
Hours & Admission Prices: Jan.-March Wed. & Sat. 10-5, Sun. 11:30-4; April-Dec. Mon.-Sat. 10-5, Sun. 11:30-4. Call to confirm hours. No charge; donations accepted. Closed Easter; Independence Day; Thanksgiving; Christmas. ♿
Attendance: 14,000 (estimated)
Membership: Active $10; Family & Business $15; Supporting $25; Benefactor $50; Life $100.

Johnson

JULIAN SCOTT MEMORIAL GALLERY, Johnson State College, Dibden Center, 337 College Hill, Johnson, VT 06565. Tel.: 800-635-2356.
Key Personnel: Dir., Leila Bandar
Art Gallery.
Collections: paintings; drawings; sculptures.
Hours & Admission Prices: Summer: Tues.-Fri. 12-6, Sat. 12-4; Winter: call for hours.

Lincoln

LINCOLN HISTORICAL SOCIETY, 88 Quaker St., Lincoln, VT 05443-9253. Tel.: 802-453-2807.
Founded: 1986.
Key Personnel: Pres., Eleanor Menzer; Vice Pres., Eleanor Thompson; Treas., Larry Masterson.
Personnel Profile: Part-Time Paid 1; Part-Time Volunteers 6.
Historical Society Museum.
Collections: local history. Historic Buildings: 18th-century farmhouse; 19th-century barn.
Activities: Museum Sponsors: Pumpkin-Carving Contest in October.
Hours & Admission Prices: Memorial Day to mid-Oct. 2nd & 4th Sun. 1-5; other times by appointment. No charge; donations accepted.

Ludlow

BLACK RIVER ACADEMY MUSEUM, (M), High St., Ludlow, VT 05149. Mailing Address: P.O. Box 73, Ludlow, VT 05149-0073. Tel.: 802-228-5050. Fax: 802-228-7444.
E-mail: glbrehm@tds.net
Web Site: bramvt.org
Founded: 1972.
Congressional District: 1
Key Personnel: Pres. (V), Susan Pollender; Dir., Georgia Brehm.
Personnel Profile: Part-Time Paid 2; Part-Time Volunteers 8.
Governing Authority: society; nonprofit. Parent Institution: Black River Historical Society, Inc. Tax-exempt.
Historical Society Museum: housed in Black River Academy, from which Pres. Calvin Coolidge, 30th president, graduated in 1890.
Collections: paintings; portraits; photographs; economic, cultural, political & domestic area history.
Research Fields: local history.
Facilities: library of educational, political & historical material, available for use on premises.
Activities: concerts; lectures; performances; permanent & changing exhibitions.
Publications: History of Ludlow; The History of Black River Academy; Ludlow Village Walking Tour.
Hours & Admission Prices: June to Labor Day Tues.-Sat. 12-4; Sept. to Columbus Day Sat.-Sun. 12-4. Adults $2; children under 2 no charge.
Attendance: 1,100
Membership: Single $25; Dual $45; $100; $500; $1,000.

Lyndon Center

SHORES MEMORIAL MUSEUM, 202 Center St., Lyndon Center, VT 05850. Mailing Address: P.O. Box 85, Lyndon Center, VT 05850-0085.
Web Site: www.shoresmuseum.org
Key Personnel: Cur., Chris Raymond.
Governing Authority: city. Parent Institution: Lyndon Historical Society.
History Museum: housed in 1896 Queen Anne style home built by James Shores.
Collections: wooden plates & bowls; a mortar & pestle; wire basket for collecting eggs; long-handled bedwarmer; sadiron for pressing clothes; photographs; period organs; sheet music; musical instruments; trophies; period clothing; war memorabilia; dolls.
Activities: tours; living history classes; research.
Hours & Admission Prices: By appointment. Donations requested.

Lyndonville

QUIMBY GALLERY, 1001 College Rd., Lyndonville, VT 05851. Mailing Address: P.O. Box 919, Lyndonville, VT 05851. Tel.: 802-626-6487.
E-mail: barclay.tucker@lyndonstate.edu
Governing Authority: Parent Institution: Lyndon State College.
Art Gallery.
Collections: works by contemporary artists.
Activities: art shows.
Hours & Admission Prices: Academic Year: Mon.-Fri. 8-4. No charge.

Manchester

* **THE AMERICAN MUSEUM OF FLY FISHING, (M),** 4070 Main St., Manchester, VT 05254. Mailing Address: P.O. Box 42, Manchester, VT 05254-0042. Tel.: 802-362-3300. Fax: 802-362-3308.
E-mail: ccomar@amff.com
Web Site: www.amff.com
Founded: 1968.
Congressional District: 1
Key Personnel: Chm., Dave Walsh; Pres. (V), George Gibson; Exec. Dir., Cathi Comar; Deputy Dir., Yoshi Akiyama; Events Coord., Kim Murphy; Project & Admin. Coord., Sarah Moore; Art Dir., Sara Wilcox; Editor, Kathleen Achor.
Personnel Profile: Full-Time Paid 4; Part-Time Paid 1; Part-Time Volunteers 3.
Governing Authority: nonprofit organization. Tax-exempt: 501(c)(3).
Sports Museum.
Collections: reels; fly rods; flies; fly boxes; paintings; memorabilia; rare books.
Research Fields: sporting & conservation history; belles lettres.
Facilities: 7,000-vol. library. Museum-related items for sale.
Activities: inter-museum loan; permanent & temporary exhibitions; tours; seminars; demonstrations. Annual Events: Fly Fishing Festival; Ice Cream Social; Art Auction.
Publications: quarterly, The American Fly Fisher; books, American Fly Fishing: A History, A Treasury of Reels: The Fishing Reel Collection of the American Museum of Fly Fishing; prints; exhibition catalog.

Hours & Admission Prices: June-Oct. Tues.-Sun. 10-4; Nov.-May Tues.-Sat. 10-4 Adults $5, children $3; discounts to AAM & VMGA members; members no charge. Closed major holidays. ♿
Attendance: 2,731 (accurate)
Membership: Associate $50; Benefactor $100; Business $250; Sponsor $500; Friends $1,000.

HILDENE, THE LINCOLN FAMILY HOME, 1005 Hildene Rd., Manchester, VT 05254. Mailing Address: P.O. Box 377, Manchester, VT 05254-0377. Tel.: 802-362-1788; 800-578-1788. Fax: 802-362-1564.
E-mail: info@hildene.org
Web Site: www.hildene.org
Founded: 1978.
Congressional District: 1
Key Personnel: Chm. (V), Michael Powers; Exec. Dir., Seth B. Bongartz; Dir. Education, Diane Newton; Deputy Dir., Laine Akiyama; Volunteer Coord., Paula Maynard; Cur., Brian L. Knight; Accountant, Ann Dailey; Farm Mgr., Peggy Galloup; Grounds Maintenance, Cary Lewis; Buildings Maintenance, T.J. Lillie; Dir. Private Functions, Sheila Burks; Museum Shop Mgr., Carol Korzelius.
Personnel Profile: Full-Time Paid 16; Part-Time Paid 9; Part-Time Volunteers 340; Interns 2.
Governing Authority: nonprofit organization. Parent Institution: Friends of Hildene, Inc. Tax-exempt: 501(c)(3).
Historic House: 1905 Robert Todd Lincoln Home.
Collections: Lincoln family history; furniture; President Lincoln .
Major Exhibits: Abraham Lincoln, The 2nd Inaugural and the American Ideal, 11/09-11/11.
Research Fields: Lincoln family; President Lincoln; Civil War; Captains of Industry; Gilded Age.
Facilities: 2,500-vol. library of Lincoln's family, general reading material available for research by arrangement; nature center; welcome center. Lincoln-related items & Vermont items for sale.
Activities: tours; lectures; concerts; docent program; working farm; observatory; walking trails; picnicking; cross country skiing; permanent & temporary exhibitions. Museum Sponsors: crafts fairs; antique festivals; Holiday Open Houses; Symposia; lecture series.
Publications: newsletter, News From Historic Hildene; calendar; book, No Braver Deeds; 4 Marys and A Jessie; Robert Todd Lincoln: A Man In His Own Right; Mary, Wife of Lincoln; Mr. Lincoln's Gift.
Hours & Admission Prices: June-Oct. daily 9:30-4:30; Nov.-May Thurs.-Mon. 11-3. Adults $12.50, children 6-14 $5, pre-reserved group tours $10 per person. Grounds (no tour): adults $5, children 6-14 $3; discounts to VT Museum, Gallery Alliance, VMGA, AAM & AAA members; children under 6 & members no charge. Closed Easter; Thanksgiving; Christmas. ♿
Attendance: 35,000 (estimated)
Membership: Individual $50; Family $80; Sustaining $150; Associate $500; Preservation Society $1,000; Life $5,000.

MANCHESTER HISTORICAL SOCIETY, 48 West Rd., Manchester, VT 05254. Mailing Address: P.O. Box 363, Manchester, VT 05254-0363. Tel.: 802-362-3708.
Founded: 1898.
Governing Authority: Tax-exempt.
Historical Society Museum.
Collections: local history & culture; photographs.
Hours & Admission Prices: Thurs. 1-3; other times by appointment.

SOUTHERN VERMONT ART CENTER, West Rd., Manchester, VT 05254. Mailing Address: P.O. Box 617, Manchester, VT 05254-0617. Tel.: 802-362-1405. Fax: 802-362-3279.
E-mail: info@svac.org
Web Site: www.svac.org
Founded: 1929.
Congressional District: 1
Key Personnel: Exec. Dir., Christopher Madkour; Business Mgr., Melissa G. Klick; Chm. (V), Stan Stroup.
Personnel Profile: Full-Time Paid 8; Full-Time Volunteers 1; Part-Time Paid 3; Part-Time Volunteers 300; Interns 4.
Governing Authority: nonprofit. Tax-exempt.
Art Center, museum & performing arts.
Collections: paintings; sculpture; graphics; photographs.
Research Fields: New England artists.
Facilities: 1,000-vol. library of art books; music; films available in members' room; botany trail; nature walks.
Activities: lectures; films; gallery talks; summer art classes; music festival; temporary & traveling exhibitions; school loan service; international art tours; docent tours; Artists in the Schools program.
Publications: annual catalog, Festival of the Arts; brochures, Calendar of Events; Summer Study Programs; SVA Music Festival.
Hours & Admission Prices: Tues.-Sat. 10-5, Sun. 12-5. Adults $8, students 3; children under 13 & members no charge. Special exhibits $10. ♿
Attendance: 35,000 (accurate)
Membership: Individual $55; Artist & Family $75; Donor $150-$499; Patron $500-$999; Benefactor $1,000-$2,999; Collectors Guild $3,000-$4,999; Lucioni Circle $5,000 & up.

Marlboro

MARLBORO HISTORICAL SOCIETY, 364 South Rd., Marlboro, VT 05344. Mailing Address: P.O. Box 242, Marlboro, VT 05344-0242. Tel.: 802-464-0329.
E-mail: forrest810@gmail.com
Web Site: www.marlboro.vt.us
Founded: 1958.
Key Personnel: Pres., Forrest Holzapfel; Vice Pres., Donald Sherefkin; Sec., Barbara Parker; Treas., Richard Lewontin; Clerk, Augusta Bartlett.
Personnel Profile: Part-Time Paid 2; Part-Time Volunteers 10.
Governing Authority: society. Tax-exempt.
Local History Museum, Historical & Preservation Society: housed in 1814 Rev. Ephraim Holland Newton House & 1895 Houghton Schoolhouse.
Collections: household items; farm implements; furniture; crockery. Historic House: 1895 Houghton Schoolhouse.
Research Fields: local genealogy.
Facilities: library of books available for research on premises; reading room.
Activities: guided tours; demonstrations of crafts; lectures; concerts; herb sale; quilt display; walks to historic sites & buildings.
Publications: local newsletter.
Hours & Admission Prices: June-Labor Day Sat. 2-5; for private research appointment call 802-254-2172. No charge; donations accepted.
Attendance: 100 (estimated)
Membership: Individual $5; Family $8.

Middlebury

HENRY SHELDON MUSEUM OF VERMONT HISTORY, (M), One Park St., Middlebury, VT 05753-1101. Tel.: 802-388-2117. Fax: 802-388-2112.
E-mail: info@henrysheldonmuseum.org
Web Site: henrysheldonmuseum.org
Founded: 1882.
Congressional District: 1
Key Personnel: Pres. (V), Cy Tall; Exec. Dir., Jan Albers; Assoc. Dir., Mary Ward Manley; Education Coord., Susan Peden; Mgr. Collections, Mary Towle-Hilt; Museum Shop Mgr., Roberta Anderson; Research Center Librarian, Orson Kingsley; Bookkeeper, Rachael Gosselin.
Personnel Profile: Part-Time Paid 8; Part-Time Volunteers 140; Interns 4.
Governing Authority: nonprofit organization. Tax-exempt: 501(c)(3).
History Museum: housed in 1829 Judd-Harris House.
Collections: 30,000 letters; manuscript collections; 1,200 photographs; Middlebury newspapers 1801 to present; 19th-century Vermont furniture: pianos, clocks, portraits, china, pewter, kitchen utensils, tools & toys; musical instruments; Vermont portraits & landscapes; 1888 Barn; cabinet of curiosities.
Research Fields: state & local history.
Facilities: research center. Museum-related items for sale.
Activities: guided tours; permanent & temporary exhibitions; lectures; concerts; art exhibits; workshops; school program.
Publications: quarterly newsletter; annual report; A Walking History of Middlebury.
Hours & Admission Prices: Tues.-Sat. 10-5. Families $12, adults $5, senior citizens $4.50; discounts to NEMA, Vermont Museum & Gallery Alliance members; children 18 & under, students with ID and members no charge. Closed New Year's Day; Independence Day; Thanksgiving; Christmas. ♿
Attendance: 10,000 (estimated)
Membership: Student $10; Individual $30; Dual Family $45; Friend $75; Supporter $125; Patron $500; Benefactor $1,000 & up.

* **MIDDLEBURY COLLEGE MUSEUM OF ART, (M),** Mahaney Center for the Arts, Middlebury, VT 05753-6177. Tel.: 802-443-5235 & 5007. Fax: 802-443-2069.
Web Site: museum.middlebury.edu
Founded: 1968.
Key Personnel: Dir., Richard H. Saunders; Head Cur., Emmie Donadio; Chm. Friends of Art, Nancy Ewen; Exhibit Designer, Kenneth Pohlman; Registrar, Margaret Wallace; Cur. Education, Sandra Olivo; Admin. Operations Mgr., Douglas Perkins; Event & Program Coord., Andrea Solomon; Museum Preparator, John Houskeeper; Museum Preparator, Christine Fraioli; Cur. Asian Art, Colin Mackenzie; Bookstore & Receptionist Coord., Mikki Lane.

Personnel Profile: Full-Time Paid 7; Part-Time Paid 4; Interns 5.
Governing Authority: college. Parent Institution: Middlebury College. Tax-exempt.
Art Museum.
Collections: prints; drawings; paintings; sculpture; photographs.
Research Fields: 19th-century sculpture.
Facilities: 5,200 sq. ft. exhibit space.
Activities: public lectures & gallery talks; programs for students of Middlebury College & local school groups; permanent & traveling exhibitions.
Publications: newsletter; brochures; exhibition catalogues; annual report.
Hours & Admission Prices: Sept. to mid-Aug. Tues.-Fri. 10-5, Sat.-Sun. 12-5. No charge. Closed New Year's Eve & Day; Christmas Day & week. ♿
Attendance: 18,446 (accurate)
Membership: Student $15; Individual $30; Family & Couple $50; Contributor $100; Sponsor $250; Patron $500.

VERMONT FOLKLIFE CENTER, 88 Main St., Middlebury, VT 05753-1425. Tel.: 802-388-4964. Fax: 802-388-1844.
E-mail: info@vermontfolklifecenter.org
Web Site: www.vermontfolklifecenter.org
Founded: 1983.
Key Personnel: Exec. Dir., Brent Bjorkman; Chm. (V), Bill Schubart; Dir. Education, Gregory Sharrow; Operations Mgr., Sarah Stahl.
Personnel Profile: Full-Time Paid 4; Part-Time Paid 2.
Governing Authority: private; nonprofit organization. Tax-exempt: 501(c)(3).
Folk Art Center & Archive.
Collections: 4,000 taped interviews on the heritage & traditions of Vermont from settlement in the 18th-century to present; historic & contemporary photographs related to Vermont folklife; written documents, including family histories, diaries & letters; contemporary folk art.
Research Fields: agricultural, ethnic & maritime heritage.
Facilities: media resource center; 600 sq. ft. exhibit space. Books & audio tapes for sale.
Activities: traveling exhibitions; special workshops & demonstrations. Annual Event: Holiday Showcase of traditional crafts.
Publications: newsletter twice annually; Visit'N (yearbook of oral history); exhibit catalogues; educational manuals.
Hours & Admission Prices: Gallery & Shop: Mon.-Sat. 10-5, Sun. 11-4. Archive & Research Center: Mon.-Fri. 10-4. No charge; donations accepted. Closed Christmas through New Year's week. ♿
Attendance: 3,000 (estimated)
Membership: Individual $35; Family $50; Supporter $100; Patron $250; Benefactor $500; Founder $1,000.

VERMONT SOAPWORKS DISCOUNT FACTORY OUTLET AND SOAP MUSEUM, 616 Exchange St., Middlebury, VT 05753-1181. Tel.: 802-388-4302; 866-762-7482 (toll free). Fax: 802-388-7471.
E-mail: info@vtsoap.com
Web Site: www.vermontsoap.com
Founded: 1992.
Key Personnel: Gen. Mgr., Hilde Whalley.
Personnel Profile: Full-Time Paid 25; Part-Time Paid 2.
Soap Museum.
Collections: history of soap; soap products; period washing machine.
Facilities: Museum-related items for sale.
Activities: soap making demonstrations; children's programs; special events.
Hours & Admission Prices: Summer: Mon.-Fri. 9-5, Sat.-Sun. 10-4; Winter: Mon.-Fri. 9-5, Sat. 10-4. No charge. ♿
Attendance: 10,000 (estimated)

Milton

MILTON HISTORICAL MUSEUM, 13 School St., Milton, VT 05468. Mailing Address: Box 2, Milton, VT 05468-0002. Tel.: 802-893-1604.
E-mail: miltonhistorical@yahoo.com
Formerly: Milton Museum
Founded: 1979.
Key Personnel: Museum Dir., Jane Fitzgerald; Pres. (V) Milton Historical Society, Jim Ballard.
Governing Authority: society. Parent Institution: Milton Historical Society. Tax-exempt: 501(c)(3).
Local History Museum.
Collections: wedding gowns of early Milton brides; doctor's chair & medical bag; maps; old gazetteers; pictures; tools; mantle clock; kitchen items; Indian artifacts; bicentennial quilt; furniture; books; Native American artifacts.
Research Fields: Milton history.
Facilities: 300-vol. library of books including Walton's Register & history of early Milton & Vermont available for research on premises.
Activities: guided tours; loan, permanent & temporary exhibitions.
Publications: annual newsletter; Town Reports; Historic Timeline & Population Graph (1878-2000); 200 years pictorial exhibit & documentation.
Hours & Admission Prices: April-Oct. 1st & 3rd Sat.-Sun. 1-4. Other times by appointment, please call 802-893-2340. No charge; donations accepted. ♿
Attendance: 750 (accurate)
Membership: Students $1; Single $5; Couple & Family $7.50.

Montpelier

T.W. WOOD GALLERY & ARTS CENTER, 36 College St., Vermont College, Montpelier, VT 05602-3145. Mailing Address: 36 College St., College Hall, Montpelier, VT 05602-3145. Tel.: 802-828-8743. Fax: 802-828-8645.
E-mail: info@twwoodgallery.org
Web Site: twwoodgallery.org
Founded: 1891.
Key Personnel: C.E.O., Joyce Mandevile; Bd. Trustees Pres. (V), John Landy.
Personnel Profile: Part-Time Paid 2; Part-Time Volunteers 60; Interns 2.
Governing Authority: nonprofit organization. Tax-exempt.
Art Gallery.
Collections: 438 oils, drawings & watercolors by Thomas Waterman Wood, & his contemporaries including A.H. Wyant, A.B. Durard, J.G. Brown, DeHass; American artists of the 1920s & 30s; 60 works in WPA collection.
Research Fields: T.W. Wood; WPA art & artists.
Activities: films; loan, permanent & changing exhibitions; lectures; art classes; exhibition workshop.
Publications: booklet, Thomas Waterman Wood PNA.
Hours & Admission Prices: Tues.-Sun. 12-4. No charge; donations accepted. Closed major holidays. ♿
Attendance: 7,000 (accurate)
Membership: Individual $35; Family $50; Contributor $100 & up; Sustainer $250 & up; Benefactor $500 & up.

USS MONTPELIER MUSEUM, 39 Main St., 2nd Fl., Montpelier, VT 05602-3064. Tel.: 802-223-9502.
Web Site: www.montpelier-vt.org/ussmontpelier
Key Personnel: Co Dir., Jeanette Quinn; Co Dir., George Walker
Naval History Museum.
Collections: Naval history of ships named Montpelier & their crews; photographs; documents.
Hours & Admission Prices: Call for hours.

VERMONT HISTORICAL SOCIETY MUSEUM, (M), 109 State St., Montpelier, VT 05609-0002. Tel.: 802-828-2291. Fax: 802-828-1415.
E-mail: museum@state.vt.us
Web Site: www.vermonthistory.org
Founded: 1838.
Key Personnel: Exec. Dir., Mark Hudson; Pres. (V), Sarah Dopp; Registrar, Mary Labate Rogstad; Cur., Jacqueline Calder; Librarian, Paul Carnahan; Asst. Librarian, Marjorie Strong.
Personnel Profile: Full-Time Paid 13; Part-Time Paid 7.
Governing Authority: society. Parent Institution: Vermont Historical Society. Library: Vermont History Center, 60 Washington St., Barre, VT 05641-4209. Tel.: 802-479-8500. Tax-exempt: 501(c)(3).
History Museum.
Collections: state history from 1600 to present; pewter; tools; furniture; glass; costumes; paintings; textiles; film; fine & decorative arts; manuscripts.
Research Fields: Vermont history; New England genealogy.
Facilities: 40,000-vol. library of genealogy, Vermont & New England history books available for inter-library loan & use on premises; reading room; 5,000 sq. ft. exhibit space. Museum-related items for sale.
Activities: school tours; lectures; workshops; family programming.
Publications: biannual journal, Vermont History; books; quarterly newsletter, History Connections; exhibition catalogs; teacher guides & curricular aids.
Hours & Admission Prices: Museum: May-Oct. Tues.-Sat. 10-4, Sun. 12-4; Nov.-April Tues.-Sat. 10-4. Library: Tues.-Fri. 9-4:30, 2nd Sat. each month 9-4. Adults $5; discounts to AAM & ICOM members; members no charge. Closed major holidays. ♿
Attendance: 18,000 (estimated)
Membership: Senior & Institutional $35; Individual $40; Household $50.

THE VERMONT STATE HOUSE, 115 State St., Montpelier, VT 05633-0004. Tel.: 802-828-2231. Fax: 802-828-2424.
Web Site: www.leg.state.vt.us
Founded: 1808.
Key Personnel: Cur., David Schutz; Chief Security, Leslie R. Dimick.
Personnel Profile: Full-Time Paid 2; Part-Time Paid 1; Part-Time Volunteers 115.
Governing Authority: state government; nonprofit. Tax-exempt: 501(c)(3).
Historic Building.

Collections: period furnishings; paintings; sculpture; decorative arts; costumes; textiles.
Facilities: 200-seat cafeteria; 175 sq. ft. exhibit space. Vermont products & state house items for sale.
Activities: concerts; docent program; guided tours; lectures; temporary exhibitions of our own collection; broadcast programs.
Publications: biannual newsletter, Friends Proceedings; tour brochure; history guidebook.
Hours & Admission Prices: Mon.-Fri. 8-4. Tours: July to mid-Oct. Mon.-Fri. 10-3:30, Sat. 11-2:30; mid-Oct. to June Mon.-Fri. 9-3; other times by appointment. No charge; donations accepted. Closed state & federal holidays.
Attendance: 100,000 (estimated)
Membership: Individual & Family $30; Gold Dome $50; Cedar Creek $100; Supreme Court $300; Governor's Cabinet $500; Ammi Young $1,000. Corporate Support $100 & up.

Morrisville

NOYES HOUSE MUSEUM, 122 Lower Main St., Morrisville, VT 05661. Mailing Address: Morristown Historical Society, P.O. Box 1299, Morrisville, VT 05661-1299. Tel.: 802-888-7617.
Founded: 1952.
Key Personnel: Dir., Scott A. McLaughlin; Pres. (V), Bill Lizotte.
Personnel Profile: Part-Time Paid 2.
Governing Authority: Parent Institution: Morristown Historical Society. Tax-exempt.
Historic House Museum: built in the early 19th-century by the Safford family.
Collections: local & regional history; photographs; furnishings; toys; household & farm tools; quilts; costumes; military artifacts; carriage barn.
Research Fields: local history; archives; collections.
Activities: guided tours; lectures; family events. Annual Event: Open House.
Publications: newsletter.
Hours & Admission Prices: June to mid-Oct. Wed.-Sat. 1-5; groups by appointment. No charge; donations accepted. ♿
Attendance: 500 (estimated)
Membership: Individual $15; Family $25; Business $50; Life $250.

Moscow

LITTLE RIVER HOTGLASS STUDIO & GALLERY, 593 Moscow Rd., Moscow, VT 05662. Mailing Address: P.O. Box 1504, Stowe, VT 05672-1504. Tel.: 802-253-0889. Fax: 802-253-4128.
Art Gallery.
Collections: blown glass sculptures.
Activities: glass blowing demonstrations.
Hours & Admission Prices: Wed.-Mon. 10-5.

Newfane

HISTORICAL SOCIETY OF WINDHAM COUNTY, Rte. 30, Newfane, VT 05345. Mailing Address: P.O. Box 246, Newfane, VT 05345-0246. Tel.: 802-365-4148.
E-mail: histwind@sover.net
Web Site: www.sover.net/~histwind
Historical Society Museum.
Collections: local history & culture; photographs; personal artifacts; period furnishings; portraits; folk art; Civil War artifacts; West River Railroad.
Activities: educational programs.
Publications: quarterly newsletter.
Hours & Admission Prices: late May to late Oct. Wed.-Sun. 12-5. No charge; donations accepted.

North Bennington

HISTORIC PARK-MCCULLOUGH, One Park St., North Bennington, VT 05257. Mailing Address: P.O. Box 388, North Bennington, VT 05257-0388. Tel.: 802-442-5441. Fax: 802-442-5442.
E-mail: info@parkmccullough.org
Web Site: www.parkmccullough.org
Founded: 1968.
Congressional District: 1
Key Personnel: Exec. Dir., Patricia Gordon Michael; Deputy Dir., Mark Sekora; Pres. (V), Eunice Schleif; Mgr. Programs & Events, Hope A. Heinzman; Bookkeeper, Kathy Eastman; Groundskeeper, John Briggs.
Personnel Profile: Full-Time Paid 3; Part-Time Paid 3; Part-Time Volunteers 35; Interns 2.
Governing Authority: nonprofit organization. Parent Institution: Park-McCullough House Assoc. Tax-exempt: 501(c)(3).
Historic House Museum: housed in 1865 Second Empire mansion built for Trenor & Laura Hall Park which was also the home of two Vermont Governors.
Collections: books; furniture; carriages; art; papers; documents; Victorian artifacts & clothes; Chinese porcelain; photographic library including works of Carlton Watkins; Album prints of Yosemite.
Research Fields: genealogy of family; 19th-century technology; Vermont history; costumes; California history: 1850s & 1860s; carriage barn; New York City history; photography.
Facilities: library of family books available on premises for research by qualified people with references; children's playhouse; Victorian garden; carriage house; fountain; stable; fishpond.
Activities: guided tours; lectures; films; gallery talks; concerts; study clubs; formally organized educational programs; temporary exhibitions; Open Garden Days; tours & programming related to the museum's formal gardens; rental facilities.
Publications: booklets; monthly calendar; newsletter; The Park-McCullough House Historic House & Museum guide book; book, Within One's Memory.
Hours & Admission Prices: Hourly Tours: mid-May to Oct. daily 9-5. Adults $10, senior citizens $9, students $7; discounts to groups, AAM, VMGA, AAA & NEMA members; children under 12 & members no charge. ♿
Attendance: 6,500 (estimated)
Membership: Senior Citizen & Student $25; Individual $40; Family & Dual $60; Supporting $100; Sustaining $250; President's Circle $500; Corporate $1,000.

North Danville

DANVILLE HISTORICAL SOCIETY, North Danville School, North Danville, VT 05828. Mailing Address: P.O. Box 45, Danville, VT 05828. Tel.: 802-684-3857.
Key Personnel: Pres., Mary Pryor
Library & Archives.
Collections: books; local history.
Hours & Admission Prices: Mon., Wed. & Fri. 2-4; other times by appointment.

North Troy

MISSISQUOI VALLEY HISTORICAL SOCIETY, Main St., North Troy, VT 05859. Mailing Address: P.O. Box 237, North Troy, VT 05859-0237. Tel.: 802-988-2397.
E-mail: missisco@hotmail.com
Founded: 1976.
Key Personnel: Pres. (V), Nancy L. Allen; Vice Pres., John Starr; Treas., Roy Barnett.
Governing Authority: society; nonprofit. Tax-exempt.
Historical Society Museum: housed in 1883 former St. Augustine Church.
Collections: general store memorabilia; photographs; household utensils; textiles; tools; cobblers tools; 19th century furniture; saw mill; medical instruments.
Facilities: 75-vol. library of local records & old school books available for research on premises.
Activities: rotating & loan exhibitions.
Publications: book, Memories of the Early Days in the Town of Troy.
Hours & Admission Prices: Memorial Day to Labor Day Sun. 1-3. No charge; donations accepted. ♿
Attendance: 50
Membership: Individual $2.50; Family $5; Life $25.

Northfield

SULLIVAN MUSEUM AND HISTORY CENTER, (M), 158 Harmon Dr., Northfield, VT 05663-1000. Tel.: 802-485-2183. Fax: 802-485-2749.
E-mail: numuseum@norwich.edu
Web Site: www.norwich.edu/museum
Formerly: Norwich University Museum
Founded: 1819.
Congressional District: 1
Key Personnel: Dir., Marilyn C. Solvay; Cur., Erin Doane; University Historian, Gary T. Lord.
Personnel Profile: Full-Time Paid 2; Part-Time Paid 4; Part-Time Volunteers 3.
Governing Authority: university. Affiliated with Norwich University. Tax-exempt: 501(c)(3).
University Museum.
Collections: history of Norwich exhibits; personal memorabilia of founder Alden Partridge; achievements of alumni such as: Adm. George Dewey, Gen. Alonzo Jackman, Gen. Grenville Dodge, builder of the Union-Pacific railroad; Norwich uniforms; flags; weapons; military accoutrements; 19th & 20th-century academic paraphernalia.
Research Fields: military history; Norwich history.
Facilities: archives.
Activities: permanent & temporary exhibitions; research.
Hours & Admission Prices: Mon.-Fri. 9-4; other times by appointment. No charge. Closed university holidays. ♿

Attendance: 6,100 (accurate)
Membership: Student $5; Individual $25; Patron $100; Sponsor $500; Founder's $1,000.

Norwich

MONTSHIRE MUSEUM OF SCIENCE, INC., 1 Montshire Rd., Norwich, VT 05055-9334. Tel.: 802-649-2200. Fax: 802-649-3637.
E-mail: montshire@montshire.org
Web Site: www.montshire.org
Founded: 1975.
Key Personnel: Dir., David Goudy; Chm. (V), Jennifer Williams; Dir. Education, Greg DeFrancis; Dir. Mktg. & Communications, Beth Krusi; Dir. Devel., Jennifer Rickards; Museum Shop Mgr., Barbara Mathewson.
Personnel Profile: Full-Time Paid 16; Part-Time Paid 10; Part-Time Volunteers 560; Interns 4.
Governing Authority: nonprofit organization. Tax-exempt: 501(c)(3).
Science Museum.
Collections: interactive science exhibits.
Facilities: classroom; nature area.
Activities: lectures; workshops; organized educational programs; docent program; intern & work-study programs; public issues programs & forums; special events; permanent & temporary exhibits on physical & natural sciences.
Publications: quarterly newsletter; e-newsletter.
Hours & Admission Prices: Daily 10-5. Adults $10, children 2-17 $8; members & children under 2 no charge. Closed New Year's Day; Thanksgiving; Christmas. ♿
Attendance: 151,000 (accurate)
Membership: 2 Person $75; 4 Person $90; 6 Person $105.

NORWICH HISTORICAL SOCIETY, 277 Main St., Norwich, VT 05055. Mailing Address: P.O. Box 1680, Norwich, VT 05055-1680. Tel.: 802-649-0124.
E-mail: NHS@tpk.net
Web Site: www.norwichhistory.org
Founded: 1951.
Key Personnel: Pres., Nancy Hoggson; Vice Pres., Melinda Stricker; Treas., Mike Woods; Museum Shop Mgr., Martha Howard.
Personnel Profile: Part-Time Paid 1; Part-Time Volunteers 14.
Governing Authority: private; not-for-profit organization. Tax-exempt.
Historical Society Museum: located in Lewis House. Listed on the National Register of Historic Places.
Collections: artifacts dating from 1769 to present; textiles; documents; photographs; maps; tools; samplers; costumes.
Facilities: library; 500 sq. ft. exhibit space.
Activities: lectures; temporary exhibitions; broadcast programs.
Publications: newsletter, Norwich Historical Society.
Hours & Admission Prices: Memorial Day to Oct. Wed. 10-4, Sat. 10am to noon; other times by appointment. No charge; donations accepted. ♿
Attendance: 500 (estimated)
Membership: Individual $1-$250.

Old Bennington

BENNINGTON BATTLE MONUMENT, 15 Monument Cir., Old Bennington, VT 05201-2134. Mailing Address: Historic Preservation, National Life Bldg., 2nd Fl., Montpelier, VT 05620-0001. Tel.: 802-828-3051. Fax: 802-447-0550 (call first).
E-mail: john.dumville@state.vt.us
Web Site: www.historicvermont.org/bennington
Founded: 1891.
Key Personnel: Historic Sites Operations Chief, John P. Dumville; Site Admin., Marylou Chicote.
Personnel Profile: Full-Time Paid 1; Part-Time Paid 7.
Governing Authority: state. Parent Institution: State of Vermont. Subsidiary Institution: Div. for Historic Preservation, Montpelier 05602. Tax-exempt.
State Historic Site: located near the site of the Bennington Battle of the Revolutionary War.
Collections: diorama depicting Bennington Battle of the Revolutionary War; General Burgoyne's camp kettle.
Facilities: observation room.
Activities: guided tours; permanent exhibitions.
Publications: brochure, A Guide to Historic Sites in Vermont; Bennington Battle Monument.
Hours & Admission Prices: April-Oct. daily 9-5. Adults $2, children $.50; registered school groups no charge. ♿
Attendance: 50,000 (estimated)

Orwell

MOUNT INDEPENDENCE HISTORIC SITE, Mount Independence Rd., Orwell, VT 05760. Mailing Address: Historic Preservation, National Life Building, 2nd Fl., Montpelier, VT 05620-0001. Tel.: 802-828-3051. Fax: 802-828-3206.
E-mail: john.dumville@state.vt.us
Web Site: www.historicvermont.org/mountindependence
Founded: 1950.
Key Personnel: Operations Chief, John P. Dumville; Site Admin., Elsa Gilbertson.
Personnel Profile: Full-Time Paid 1; Part-Time Paid 1.
Governing Authority: state. Parent Institution: State of Vermont., Division for Historic Preservation, Pavilion Building, Montpelier 05602. Tax-exempt.
Historic Site: site of major Revolutionary War fort.
Collections: archaeological items from site.
Research Fields: Revolutionary War; Archaeological Field Schools.
Facilities: trails.
Activities: self guided tours.
Publications: brochure, A Guide To Historic Sites In Vermont & Mount Independence; booklet, Mount for Dependence; book, Mount Independence and the American Revolution, 1776-1777.
Hours & Admission Prices: mid-May to mid-Oct. daily 9:30-5:30. Adults & children 15 & over $5; children 14 & under no charge. ♿
Attendance: 8,000 (accurate)

Peacham

PEACHAM HISTORICAL ASSOCIATION, 643 Bayley-Hazen Rd., Peacham, VT 05862. Mailing Address: P.O. Box 101, Peacham, VT 05862-0101. Tel.: 802-592-3571.
Founded: 1916.
Key Personnel: Pres. (V), Jutta Scott.
Personnel Profile: Part-Time Volunteers 12.
Governing Authority: Tax-exempt.
Historical Society Museum.
Collections: period artifacts; tools; paintings; photographs; maps; furniture; costumes; quilts; manuscripts.
Research Fields: Vermont history; Civil War; Caledonia County grammar school, Peacham Academy.
Activities: ghost walk.
Publications: Peacham Patriot; Peacham Anthology; Historic Homes of Peacham.
Hours & Admission Prices: June 3-Oct. 7 Sun.-Mon. 2-4; other times by appointment. No charge; donations accepted. ♿
Attendance: 400 (estimated)
Membership: Senior $5; Individual $10; Family $15; Family Life $250.

Pittsford

NEW ENGLAND MAPLE MUSEUM, U.S. Rte. 7, Pittsford, VT 05763. Mailing Address: P.O. Box 1615, Rutland, VT 05701-1615. Tel.: 802-483-9414. Fax: 802-775-1650.
E-mail: info@maplemuseum.com
Web Site: www.maplemuseum.com
Founded: 1977.
Key Personnel: Pres., Thomas H. Olson; Dir. & Museum Shop Mgr., Dona A. Olson.
Governing Authority: corporation.
History Museum.
Collections: maple sugaring artifacts; wooden sap buckets; period sugar tubs; maple sugaring paintings by Vermont artists.
Facilities: theater. Maple products & Vermont crafts for sale.
Activities: lectures; permanent exhibitions.
Hours & Admission Prices: mid-March to Dec. daily 8:30-5:30. Adults $2.50, tours & children 12 and under $.75; discounts to members, AAM & ICOM members. ♿
Attendance: 35,000

PITTSFORD HISTORICAL SOCIETY MUSEUM, U.S. Rte. 7 #3399, Pittsford, VT 05763. Mailing Address: P.O. Box 423, Pittsford, VT 05763-9774. Tel.: 802-483-2040.
E-mail: peggy.armitage@gmail.com
Web Site: www.pittsfordhistorical.com
Founded: 1960.
Congressional District: 1
Key Personnel: Pres. (V), Robert W. Welch; Cur., Anne Pelkey.
Personnel Profile: Part-Time Volunteers 20.
Governing Authority: private; nonprofit organization. Parent Institution: Pittsford Historical Society, Inc. Tax-exempt.
Historical Society Museum: located in Eaton Hall, former Masonic Hall.

Collections: concentration on the history of Pittsford from the mid-1700s to present.
Research Fields: vital statistics of local people; genealogies of Pittsford residents.
Facilities: Printed material for sale.
Activities: formal education program for adults & children; guided tours; permanent & temporary exhibitions.
Publications: Pittsford's Second Century, 1872-1997; postcards; pamphlet, Gleanings; Around Pittsford.
Hours & Admission Prices: April-June Tues 9-4; July-Oct. Tues. 9-4, Sun. 1-4. No charge; donations accepted. ♿
Attendance: 275 (accurate)
Membership: Student $10; Individual $15; Family $20; Sponsor $50; Life $200.

Plymouth

THE CALVIN COOLIDGE MEMORIAL FOUNDATION, INC., 43 Messer Hill Rd., Plymouth, VT 05056. Mailing Address: Box 97, Plymouth, VT 05056-0097. Tel.: 802-672-3389. Fax: 260-572-3389.
E-mail: info@calvin-coolidge.org
Web Site: www.calvin-coolidge.org
Founded: 1960.
Key Personnel: Exec. Dir., Len Vignola; Pres., Robert P. Kirby.
Personnel Profile: Full-Time Paid 3; Full-Time Volunteers 22; Part-Time Paid 2; Part-Time Volunteers 30.
Governing Authority: nonprofit executive committee. Parent Institution: The Calvin Coolidge Memorial Foundation. Tax-exempt: 501(c)(3).
Historic Foundation.
Collections: items relating to Coolidge Era & Plymouth history; books; newspapers; magazines; photographs; postcards; philatelic envelopes; Coolidge ephemera, memorabilia & materials. Historic Structure: 1840 Union Christian Church.
Research Fields: Coolidge Era; oral history of Plymouth.
Facilities: 275-vol. general reference library; 2,000 sq. ft. exhibit space. Coolidge books & memorabilia items for sale.
Activities: lectures; films; organized educational programs; loan & temporary exhibitions. Museum Sponsors: Presidential Birth Celebration; Foundation Annual Meeting.
Publications: periodic newsletter, Plymouth Notch Newsletter; annual booklet, The Real Calvin Coolidge; books, The Autobiography of Calvin Coolidge; Meet Calvin Coolidge; Homestead Inaugural; Calvin Coolidge's Unique Vermont Inauguration; Coolidge & the Historians; Calvin Coolidge, Jr.; Growing Up in Plymouth, Notch, Vermont, 1872-1895; Calvin Coolidge Meets Charles Garman; Return to These Hills: Calvin Coolidge in Vermont; From Plymouth Notch to President; A Plymouth Album; Calvin Coolidge Memorial Foundation; photographs; records; stationery; medals; Ephemera; Philatelic Commemoratives.
Hours & Admission Prices: Mon.-Fri. 9-4. No charge; donations accepted. Closed federal holidays except Independence Day. ♿
Attendance: 70,000 (estimated)
Membership: Individual $35; Family $50; Contributing $100; Supporting $250; Sustaining $500; Benefactor $1,000 & up.

Plymouth Notch

CALVIN COOLIDGE HISTORIC SITE, 3780 Rte. 100A, Plymouth Notch, VT 05056. Mailing Address: Historic Preservation, National Life Bldg., 2nd Fl., Montpelier, VT 05620-0001. Tel.: 802-828-3051& 672-3773. Fax: 802-828-3206.
E-mail: john.dumville@state.vt.us
Web Site: www.historicvermont.org/coolidge
Founded: 1947.
Key Personnel: Historic Sites Operations Chief, John P. Dumville; Site Admin., William Jenney.
Personnel Profile: Full-Time Paid 1; Part-Time Paid 15; Interns 2.
Governing Authority: Parent Institution: State of Vermont, Division for Historic Preservation, National Life Bldg., Drawer 20 Montpelier 05620. Tax-exempt.
Historic House Museum: Calvin Coolidge birthplace & homestead.
Collections: furnishings used on Aug. 23, 1923, the night Calvin Coolidge was sworn in by his father as President of the United States; Coolidge general store; photographs; Presidential memorabilia; Wilder barn with agricultural exhibits; Plymouth Notch Village.
Research Fields: President Calvin Coolidge era.
Facilities: visitors center; Wilder House Restaurant.
Activities: permanent exhibitions; self-guided tours.
Publications: brochure Plymouth Notch; booklet, Coolidge Homestead.
Hours & Admission Prices: mid-May to mid-Oct. daily 9:30-5:30. Adults over 13 $7.50; registered school groups no charge. ♿
Attendance: 40,000 (estimated)

Pownal

MUSEUM OF BLACK WWII HISTORY, 179 Oak Hill School Rd., Pownal, VT 05261. Tel.: 802-823-5519.
Founded: 2006.
Key Personnel: Founder & Cur., Bruce Bird
History Museum.
Collections: African American military history; photographs; personal artifacts.
Hours & Admission Prices: Feb. 5 to late Nov. Thurs.-Mon. 10-5; other times by appointment. Adults $5, veterans, seniors over 65 & students $3.
Attendance: 350 (estimated)

Proctor

VERMONT MARBLE MUSEUM, 52 Main St., Proctor, VT 05765-1177. Mailing Address: P.O. Box 607, 52 Main St., Proctor, VT 05765-0607. Tel.: 802-459-2300; 800-427-1396. Fax: 802-459-2948.
E-mail: info@vermont-marble.com
Web Site: www.vermont-marble.com
Founded: 1933.
Key Personnel: C.E.O., Marsha Hemm; Mgr., Robert Pye; Museum Shop Mgr., Cathy Miglorle.
Governing Authority: private; profit.
Mining & Geology Museum.
Collections: sculpture; photographs; rocks; minerals.
Facilities: 70-seat theater; cafe. Marble-related items for sale.
Hours & Admission Prices: mid-May to Oct. daily 9-5:30. Adults $7, senior citizens $5, teens 15-18 $4, groups $3.50 per person; children 12 & under with parent no charge. ♿
Attendance: 45,000 (estimated)

WILSON CASTLE, W. Proctor Rd., Proctor, VT 05765. Mailing Address: P.O. Box 290, Center Rutland, VT 05736-0290. Tel.: 802-773-3284. Fax: 802-773-3284.
E-mail: wilsoncastle@aol.com
Web Site: www.wilsoncastle.com
Founded: 1961.
Key Personnel: Dir., Denise Davine; Entertaiment Dir., Rusty Trombley.
Governing Authority: nonprofit organization; Wilson Family Foundation.
Historic Building: 1867 Wilson Castle, Victorian Building.
Collections: European & Oriental objects d'art; stained glass; furniture; period artifacts.
Facilities: Gift items for sale.
Activities: guided tours; lectures; concerts; permanent & temporary exhibitions.
Publications: brochure.
Hours & Admission Prices: late-May to late Oct. daily 9-6; last tour at 5:30. Adults $9.50, children 6-12 $5.50; discounts to AAA, AAM & ICOM members; children 5 & under no charge. ♿
Attendance: 75,000

Putney

PUTNEY HISTORICAL SOCIETY, Putney Town Hall, Rte. 5, Putney, VT 05346. Mailing Address: c/o Putney Town Hall, P.O. Box 233, Putney, VT 05346-0233. Tel.: 802-387-5862.
E-mail: info@putneyhistory.us
Web Site: www.putneyhistory.us
Founded: 1959.
Congressional District: Vermont
Key Personnel: Cur., Laura Heller; Cur., Elaine Dixon.
Governing Authority: nonprofit organization. Tax-exempt.
History Museum: housed in 1871 Town Hall.
Collections: artifacts relating to the town; Indian artifacts; photographs; costumes; memorabilia of John Humphrey Noyes.
Research Fields: genealogy; John Humphrey Noyes & Perfectionists; local Native American culture.
Facilities: 50-vol. library of Vermont and Putney history, available for use on premises; reading room.
Activities: lectures; changing exhibits.
Publications: newsletter; brochures.
Hours & Admission Prices: June-Aug. Tues. & Sat. 10-2; other times by appointment. No charge; donations accepted. ♿
Attendance: 250 (estimated)
Membership: Senior $5; Individual $15; Sustaining $25; Benefactor $50; Patron $100.

Quechee

VERMONT INSTITUTE OF NATURAL SCIENCE, 6565 Woodstock Rd., Rte. 4, Quechee, VT 05059. Mailing Address: P.O. Box 1281, Quechee, VT 05059. Tel.: 802-359-5000. Fax: 802-359-5001.
E-mail: info@vinsweb.org
Web Site: www.vinsweb.org
Founded: 1972.
Key Personnel: Pres., John Dolan; Mgr. Nature Center Programs, Chris Collier; Museum Shop Mgr., Kathy Thompson.
Personnel Profile: Full-Time Paid 30; Part-Time Paid 5; Part-Time Volunteers 42; Interns 5.
Governing Authority: Tax-exempt: 501(c)(3).
Natural Science Museum.
Collections: native Vermont raptors representing 20 species including hawks; owls; eagles; falcons.
Facilities: walking trails; classroom. Museum-related items for sale.
Activities: educational programs; walking trails.
Hours & Admission Prices: May-Oct. daily 10-5; Nov.-April Wed.-Sun. 10-4. Adults $10, seniors 65 & over $9, youth 3-18 $8; children under 2 & members no charge. Closed New Year's Day; Thanksgiving; Christmas.
Attendance: 35,000
Membership: Individual $60.

Randolph

RANDOLPH HISTORICAL SOCIETY, INC., Salisbury St., Randolph, VT 05060. Mailing Address: 9 Pleasant St., #304, Randolph Center, VT 05060-1148. Tel.: 802-728-6677.
E-mail: hatchasse@earthlink.net
Founded: 1960.
Key Personnel: C.E.O., Laurence Leonard; Cur. & Museum Shop Mgr., Harriet Chase; Cur., Ron Samford.
Personnel Profile: Part-Time Volunteers 6.
Governing Authority: society; nonprofit organization. Tax-exempt: 170(b)(1)(A).
History Museum.
Collections: 1890 drug store & soda fountain; photo studio; period rooms; barber shop; early farm & home tools; costumes; pipe organ; early musical instruments; photographs; manuscripts; military artifacts; school books; Raleigh bottles; printing artifacts.
Research Fields: local history.
Facilities: research room; genealogical file.
Activities: permanent & temporary exhibitions; films; lectures. Annual Event: Independence Day Celebration.
Publications: books, Potash & Pine; Rustic Rhymes; Randolph Historical Sketches; Jonathan Carpenters Journal - the diary of a Revolutionary soldier and pioneer of VT. in conjunction with Greenhills books; Randolph's Beginnings; The 27 Flood; Randolph VT 1777-1927.
Hours & Admission Prices: May-Oct. 3rd Sun. of month 2-4; other times by appointment. No charge; donations accepted.
Attendance: 550 (estimated)
Membership: Individual $10; Family $15; Business $50; Patron $75.

Reading

READING HISTORICAL SOCIETY, Main St., Rte. 106, Reading, VT 05062. Mailing Address: P.O. Box 252, Reading, VT 05062-0252. Tel.: 802-674-2649.
Founded: 1953.
Key Personnel: Pres., Jonathan Springer; Trustee, Howard Sanderson, Jr.; Treas., Esther Allen.
Governing Authority: executive committee. Tax-exempt.
General Museum.
Collections: history; military; medical; music; manuscripts; textiles. Historic House: Felchville Village.
Facilities: 100-vol. library of books, photographs, town reports, school registers, maps; reading room.
Activities: permanent & temporary exhibitions.
Hours & Admission Prices: By appointment only. No charge; donations accepted.
Membership: Senior $5; Regular $10; Family $15; Sustaining $100; Life $200.

Readsboro

READSBORO HISTORICAL SOCIETY, Main St., Readsboro, VT 05350. Mailing Address: 152 Glen Ave., Readsboro, VT 05350-9798. Tel.: 802-423-5432.
Founded: 1972.
Key Personnel: Pres. (V), Betty Bolognani; Vice Pres., Eunice Crowell; Treas., Priscilla Margola; Sec., Priscilla Thayer.
Personnel Profile: Part-Time Volunteers 12.
Governing Authority: society; nonprofit. Tax-exempt.
Historical Society Museum: housed in 1840 frame structured church.
Collections: day books of the area dating back to the 1700s; 19th- & 20th-century photographs; period artifacts; spinning wheels; quilts; fireman's hose wheel; 19th-century costumes; c.1900 infant clothes.
Research Fields: historical sites.
Facilities: Museum-related items for sale.
Activities: lectures; films; hobby workshops; permanent & temporary exhibitions.
Publications: Down Thru the Years; computer CDs of photos of Early Readsboro; over 40 interview tapes of older residents.
Hours & Admission Prices: June-Oct. Sun. 1-3; other times by appointment. No charge; donations accepted.
Attendance: 100 (accurate)
Membership: Individual $3; Family $5; Lifetime $25.

Richmond

OLD ROUND CHURCH - RICHMOND HISTORICAL SOCIETY, 25 Round Church Rd., Richmond, VT 05477. Mailing Address: P.O. Box 453, Richmond, VT 05477-0453. Tel.: 802-434-3654.
E-mail: rhs@oldroundchurch.com
Web Site: www.oldroundchurch.com
Governing Authority: Tax-exempt: 501(c)(3).
Historic Building: housed in a 16-sided church built in 1812. A National Historic Landmark.
Collections: local history & culture; church history; religious artifacts; photographs.
Activities: summer concerts; weddings; community programs.
Hours & Admission Prices: Summer & Fall daily 10-4.

Royalton

ROYALTON HISTORICAL SOCIETY, 4184 Rte. 14, Royalton, VT 05068-5084. Tel.: 802-828-3051. Fax: 802-828-3206.
E-mail: john.dumville@state.vt.us
Founded: 1967.
Key Personnel: Pres., John P. Dumville; Asst. Dir., Ralph Eddy; Business Officer & Publications Dir., Helen Dumville.
Personnel Profile: Part-Time Volunteers 6.
Governing Authority: society. Tax-exempt.
Historical Society Museum: housed in 1840 Royalton Town House located on Town Common.
Collections: photographs, manuscripts, printed matter, furniture, clothing & general artifacts. Historic Building: 1844 Royalton Center School; 1840 Town House; 1836 Episcopal Church.
Research Fields: local history.
Facilities: 200-vol. library of Royalton & Vermont history, available for use on premises; reading room; 300-seat auditorium.
Activities: guided tours; lectures; school loan service; permanent & temporary exhibits.
Publications: book, Royalton Vermont.
Hours & Admission Prices: Summer by appointment. No charge; donations accepted.
Attendance: 1,000 (estimated)
Membership: Individual $2; Life $100.

Rutland

NORMAN ROCKWELL MUSEUM OF VERMONT, 654 Rte. 4 E., Rutland, VT 05701. Tel.: 877-773-6095 (toll free). Fax: 802-775-2440.
E-mail: sales@normanrockwellvt.com
Web Site: www.normanrockwellvt.com
Key Personnel: Mgr., Rachel Lynes-Bells
Art Museum.
Collections: Norman Rockwell's art, prints & posters; magazine covers; advertisements; calendars; books.
Facilities: Museum-related items for sale.
Hours & Admission Prices: Daily 9-4. Adults $5.50, seniors 62 & above $5, children $2.50; discount to AAA members & groups 10 and over.

RUTLAND AREA ART ASSOCIATION D/B/A CHAFFEE ART CENTER, 16 S. Main St., Rutland, VT 05701-4136. Mailing Address: P.O. Box 1447, Rutland, VT 05701-1447. Tel.: 802-775-0356. Fax: 802-775-6242.
E-mail: mary@chaffeeartcenter.org
Web Site: www.chaffeeartcenter.org
Formerly: Chaffee Center for the Visual Arts
Founded: 1961.
Key Personnel: Pres., Patricia Hunter; Vice Pres., Patricia A. Cuddy; Exec. Dir., Mary Mitiguy; Pres. (V), James Reddy.

Personnel Profile: Full-Time Paid 1; Part-Time Paid 1.
Governing Authority: Tax-exempt.
Art Center.
Collections: works by Vermont artists.
Major Exhibits: Art in Action, 5/16/10-5/31/10; Hand 2 Hand (T), 8/10.
Hours & Admission Prices: Tues.-Sat. 10-5, Sun. 12-4. No charge; donations accepted.
Membership: Regular & Artist $50.

RUTLAND HISTORICAL SOCIETY, 96 Center St., Rutland, VT 05701-4023. Tel.: 802-775-2006.
Web Site: rutlandhistory.com
Founded: 1969.
Key Personnel: Chm. (V), Lloyd Davis; Pres. (V), Chuck Piotrowski.
Personnel Profile: Part-Time Volunteers 30.
Governing Authority: Tax-exempt.
Historical Society: housed in the former Nickwackett Firehouse, built in 1860.
Collections: local history; manuscripts; documents; books; photographs; costumes.
Publications: quarterly magazine.
Hours & Admission Prices: Mon. 6-9pm, Sat. 1-4pm; other times by appointment. No charge. ♿
Membership: Student & Senior $8; Regular $10; Contributing $20; Sponsor $50; Life $200.

Saint Albans

ST. ALBANS HISTORICAL MUSEUM, 9 Church St., Saint Albans, VT 05478-1675. Mailing Address: P.O. Box 722, Saint Albans, VT 05478-0722. Tel.: 802-527-7933.
E-mail: stamuseum.history@myfairport.net
Web Site: www.stamuseum.com
Founded: 1971.
Key Personnel: Dir., A J McDonald; Pres. (V), Warren C. Hamm; Treas., Michael Thibault; Museum Shop Mgr., Betty Anderson.
Personnel Profile: Full-Time Paid 1; Part-Time Paid 1; Part-Time Volunteers 50.
Governing Authority: nonprofit organization. Parent Institution: St. Albans Historical Society. Tax-exempt: 501(c)(3).
Historical Society Museum: housed in 1861 three-story brick Franklin County Grammar School.
Collections: Saint Albans Raid Data; historical reference books; photographs; china & glass; maps; paintings; gowns; country doctor's office; furniture; jewelry; quilts; linens; laces; paintings; Central Vermont railway articles; military items; sports equipment; toys; dolls; craft items; X-ray collection; made-to-scale historic diorama northwest corner of Vermont; St. Albans & Champlain Valley history.
Research Fields: Vermont & local history.
Facilities: library & reference room.
Activities: guided tours; meetings; history classes.
Publications: newsletter; local history pamphlets.
Hours & Admission Prices: May 15-Oct. 15 Tues.-Sat. 1-4; other times by appointment. Adults $5; children 6-14 $2; members & children under 6 no charge. ♿
Attendance: 1,200 (accurate)
Membership: St. Albans Historical Society: Individual $35; Family $40; Life $1,000.

STAART GALLERY, 42 S. Main St., Saint Albans, VT 05478-2202. Tel.: 802-524-5700.
Art Gallery.
Collections: works by Vermont artists including paintings; photography.
Activities: receptions; classes; special events.
Hours & Admission Prices: Tues.-Sat. 12-6.

Saint Johnsbury

* **FAIRBANKS MUSEUM AND PLANETARIUM, (M),** 1302 Main St., Saint Johnsbury, VT 05819-2224. Tel.: 802-748-2372. Fax: 802-748-1893.
E-mail: info@fairbanksmuseum.org
Web Site: www.fairbanksmuseum.org
Founded: 1889.
Key Personnel: C.E.O., Charles C. Browne; Chm. (V), Arthur S. Brooks; Museum Shop Mgr., Betsy Millmann.
Personnel Profile: Full-Time Paid 7; Part-Time Paid 14; Part-Time Volunteers 140; Interns 16.
Governing Authority: private; nonprofit organization. Tax-exempt: 501(c)(3).
General Museum & Planetarium.
Collections: 2,600 mounted birds & mammals; regional toys, tools, furniture, agriculture & industrial equipment; North American, Far Eastern, Middle Eastern, Polynesian & African ethnology; sculpture; herbarium; regional photographs; maps; newspapers; documents; weather records & natural history records.
Research Fields: Vermont's natural environments & history; historic preservation; science & history education; weather forecasting.
Facilities: 2,500-vol. library of reference books; archives center; garden; planetarium; NOAA & FAA weather stations; meeting rooms; classrooms.
Activities: lectures; daily weather & information broadcasts; special exhibitions; formally organized education programs for children & adults; field trips.
Publications: e-newsletter; information sheets; brochures; Annual Report.
Hours & Admission Prices: Museum: May-Sept. Mon.-Sat. 9-5, Sun. 1-5; Oct.-April Tues.-Sat. 9-5. Adults $6, senior citizens & children 5-17 $4; discounts to groups; members no charge. Planetarium: July-Aug. daily 11 & 1:30; Sept.-June Sat.-Sun. 1:30; other times by appointment. $3 per person; discounts to groups, AAM, VMGA, ASTC & NEMA members. Closed New Year's Day; Easter; Thanksgiving; Christmas. ♿
Attendance: 65,000 (accurate)
Membership: Individuals $35; Family $55; Sustaining $100; Friends of the Museum $100 & up.

MAPLE GROVE MUSEUM AND FACTORY, 1052 Portland St., Saint Johnsbury, VT 05819-2041. Tel.: 802-748-5141.
E-mail: maple@maplegrove.com
Web Site: www.maplegrove.com
Historic Building: housed in a former sugarhouse.
Collections: period & modern sugaring equipment.
Hours & Admission Prices: Tours: Mon.-Fri. 8-2. Gift Shop: Jan.-May Mon.-Fri. 8-5; June-Dec. Mon.-Fri. 8-5, Sat.-Sun. 9-5. Tours: adults 12 & over $1; children under 12 no charge.

NORTHEAST KINGDOM ARTISANS GUILD, 430 Railroad St., #2, Saint Johnsbury, VT 05819-1727. Tel.: 802-748-0158.
Art Gallery.
Collections: handmade crafts & fine art including baskets, clay, fiber, glass, metal, paper, & wood; prints; watercolors; oils; photographs.
Facilities: Museum-related items for sale.
Activities: temporary exhibits.
Hours & Admission Prices: Mon.-Sat. 10:30-5:30.

ST. JOHNSBURY ATHENAEUM, 1171 Main St., Saint Johnsbury, VT 05819-2289. Tel.: 802-748-8291. Fax: 802-748-8086.
E-mail: inform@stjathenaeum.org
Web Site: www.stjathenaeum.org
Founded: 1873.
Congressional District: 3
Key Personnel: Exec. Dir., Irwin Gelber; Chm. (V), Ron Steen; Library Dir., Lisa Von Kann.
Personnel Profile: Full-Time Paid 4; Part-Time Paid 9; Part-Time Volunteers 50; Interns 1.
Governing Authority: nonprofit organization. Tax-exempt: 501(c)(3).
Art Museum and National Historic Landmark.
Collections: 100 works of art, primarily 19th-century American; paintings & sculpture reflect collectors' tastes 1865-1890; Hudson River school landscapes.
Facilities: 45,000-vol. public library collection; reading room.
Activities: poetry readings; school tours; interpretive art lectures; arts & humanities programs.
Publications: catalogue.
Hours & Admission Prices: Mon.-Fri. 10-5:30, Sat. 9:30-5. Art Gallery: adults $5; members no charge. Closed national holidays. ♿
Attendance: 70,000 (estimated)
Membership: Basic $15.20.

STEPHEN HUNECK GALLERY AT DOG MOUNTAIN, 143 Parks Rd., Saint Johnsbury, VT 05819-8907. Tel.: 800-449-2580; 802-748-2700. Fax: 802-748-3075.
E-mail: info@dogmt.com
Web Site: www.dogmt.com
Art Gallery.
Collections: sculptures; paintings; photographs.
Hours & Admission Prices: Mon.-Sat. 10-5, Sun. 11-4.

Saxtons River

SAXTONS RIVER HISTORICAL SOCIETY, Main St., Saxtons River, VT 05154. Mailing Address: P.O. Box 18, Saxtons River, VT 05154-0018. Tel.: 802-869-2566.
Historical Society Museum: housed in the former Congregational Church, built in 1836.

Collections: local history & culture; photographs; toys; farm implements & tools; period furnishings; genealogical records.
Hours & Admission Prices: Summer: Sun. 2-4:30; other times by appointment. No charge.

Shaftsbury

ROBERT FROST STONE HOUSE MUSEUM, 121 Historic Rte. 7A, Shaftsbury, VT 05262. Tel.: 802-447-6200.
E-mail: ffriends@sover.net
Web Site: www.frostfriends.org
Founded: 2002.
Historic House Museum: housed in the former home of American poet, Robert Frost.
Collections: Frost's life & works; personal artifacts.
Hours & Admission Prices: Oct. daily 10-5; Nov. Tues.-Sun.11-4 by appointment. Adults $5, students under 18 $2.50; children under 6 no charge.

SHAFTSBURY HISTORICAL SOCIETY, 3542 VT Rte. 7A, Shaftsbury, VT 05262. Mailing Address: P.O. Box 401, Shaftsbury, VT 05262-0401. Tel.: 802-375-6376.
E-mail: gronning@sover.net
Founded: 1967.
Congressional District: 1
Key Personnel: Pres. (V), Norman D. Gronning; Vice Pres., Angie Abbatello; Vice Pres., Robert Millington; Treas., David Curtis; Sec., Ruth Levin.
Personnel Profile: Part-Time Paid 1; Part-Time Volunteers 30.
Governing Authority: nonprofit organization. Tax-exempt: 170(b)(1)(A).
Historical Society Museum: housed in 1846 Meeting House, oldest Baptist Church in Vermont.
Collections: tools & furnishings; historical documents; decorative arts; crafts; costumes; industries; clothing; records & artifacts of early settlers; manuscripts; Bibles.
Research Fields: genealogy; local buildings; cemeteries & early gravestones; 19th-century economic & social history.
Facilities: 300-vol. library of old books, diaries & newspapers available for use by request; 3,000 historical & genealogical documents; 200-seat auditorium. Museum-related items for sale.
Activities: guided tours; lectures; temporary exhibitions.
Publications: pamphlets, Shaftsbury Historic House Tour; Introduction to the Shaftsbury Historical Society Museum; Shaftsbury Historical Map. Books, Ordinary Heroes-The Story of Shaftsbury; Shaftsbury Gravestone Records; History of the Baptist Church in Shaftsbury, Vermont.
Hours & Admission Prices: June 15-Oct. 15 Mon., Wed. & Fri. 1-4, Sat.-Sun. 2-4. No charge; donations accepted.
Attendance: 200 (estimated)
Membership: Student $2; Adult $5; Family $10; Associate $25; Patron $100.

Shelburne

FURCHGOTT SOURDIFFE GALLERY, 86 Falls Rd., Shelburne, VT 05482-6208. Tel.: 802-985-3848.
Art Gallery.
Collections: paintings; pottery.
Hours & Admission Prices: Tues.-Fri. 9:30-5:30, Sat. 10-5.

NATIONAL MUSEUM OF THE MORGAN HORSE, (M), 122 Bostwick Rd., Shelburne, VT 05482-4417. Mailing Address: P.O. Box 700, Shelburne, VT 05482-0700. Tel.: 802-985-8665. Fax: 802-985-5242.
E-mail: morgans@together.net
Web Site: morganmuseum.org
Founded: 1988.
Congressional District: 1
Personnel Profile: Part-Time Paid 1; Part-Time Volunteers 4.
Governing Authority: private; nonprofit organization. Parent Institution: American Morgan Horse Institute. Tax-exempt: 501(c)(3).
Equine Museum.
Collections: concentration on the Morgan breed of horses & associated people from mid-18th century to present; photographs, paintings, ephemera & items related to equine world.
Research Fields: Morgan horse; equine; civilian military use of horses, including transportation, agricultural & warfare.
Facilities: 700-vol. library of various equine titles; 1,100 sq. ft. exhibit space & archive. Museum-related items for sale.
Activities: self-guided tours; rotating exhibits featuring items from the archive; occasional solo exhibits by contemporary artists; occasional live horse demonstrations.
Publications: quarterly newsletter.
Hours & Admission Prices: Tues.-Fri. 10-3, Sat. 11-3. Adults $2; No charge; donations accepted. Closed major holidays. ♿
Attendance: 4,500 (estimated)
Membership: Contributor $25-$99; Supporter $100-$499; Sponsor $500-$999; Patron $1,000 & up.

SHELBURNE MUSEUM, INC., 5555 Shelburne Rd., Shelburne, VT 05482-7491. Mailing Address: P.O. Box 10, Shelburne, VT 05482-0010. Tel.: 802-985-3346. Fax: 802-985-2331.
E-mail: info@shelburnemuseum.org
Web Site: www.shelburnemuseum.org
Founded: 1947.
Congressional District: 1
Key Personnel: Chm., James Pizzagalli; Co Vice Chm., Peter Martin; Co Vice Chm., Caroline Almy Gerry; Dir., Stephan F.F. Jost; Dir. Devel., Deborah Shenk; Assoc. Dir. Devel., Sam Ankerson; Dir. Finance & Admin., Lois Nial; Dir. Preservation & Conservation, Richard Kerschner; Dir. Bldgs., Chip Stolen; Dir. Protection Svcs., Stephen Dixon; Merchandising Mgr., Lee Wheeler; Mktg. & Public Rels. Mgr., Leslie Wright; Sr. Cur., Jean Burks; Dir. Grounds & Gardens, Rick Peters.
Personnel Profile: Full-Time Paid 51; Part-Time Paid 103; Part-Time Volunteers 160; Interns 10.
Governing Authority: nonprofit. Tax-exempt: 501(c)(3).
Art & Design Museum.
Collections: 38 historic buildings; American folk art; objects of everyday life; tools; horse-drawn vehicles; toys; decorative arts; circus collection; dolls; flower, herb & heritage vegetable gardens; orchard; arboreta; American paintings; European impressionist paintings.
Research Fields: American folk art; decorative art; textiles; horsedrawn vehicles; Vermont history, early American life.
Facilities: 5,000-vol. library; archives; cafeteria; family activity center. Museum store with publications, photos, prints & reproductions for sale.
Activities: lectures; tours; gallery talks; children's programs; special events; annual symposium; workshops.
Publications: catalogs; newsletters; calendars; annual report; occasional publications.
Hours & Admission Prices: mid-May to Oct. daily 10-5. ♿
Attendance: 103,913 (accurate)
Membership: Student & VT teacher $30; Individual $45; Dual $65; Family $75; Sustaining $250; Patron $500; Benefactor $1,000.

Shoreham

SHOREHAM HISTORICAL SOCIETY, Rte. 22-A, Old Stone Schoolhouse, Shoreham, VT 05770. Mailing Address: P.O. Box 235, Shoreham, VT 05770-0235. Tel.: 802-897-2572.
Key Personnel: Pres., Dale Birdsill; Cur., Ginny Spadaccini
Historical Society Museum.
Collections: Shoreham history & culture; photographs; documents; arrowheads; genealogy; sleighs.
Hours & Admission Prices: By appointment. No charge.

South Hero

SOUTH HERO BICENTENNIAL MUSEUM, Rte. 2, South Hero, VT 05486. Mailing Address: 19 Phelps Lane, South Hero, VT 05486-4802. Tel.: 802-372-5259.
E-mail: lmjshvt@aol.com
Founded: 1974.
Key Personnel: Chm. (V), Cur. & Pres. (V), Barbara Winch.
Personnel Profile: Part-Time Volunteers 5.
Governing Authority: nonprofit. Tax-exempt.
Local History Museum.
Collections: bibles; local historic pieces.
Activities: loan, permanent & temporary exhibitions; hobby workshops; arts & crafts exhibits & demonstrations.
Hours & Admission Prices: June-Aug. Mon. & Thurs. 1:30-3:30. No charge.
Attendance: 75 (estimated)

Springfield

EUREKA SCHOOL HOUSE, 470 Charlestown Rd., Rte. 11, Springfield, VT 05156. Mailing Address: Historic Preservation, National Life Building, 2nd Fl., Montpelier, VT 05620-0001. Tel.: 802-828-3051. Fax: 802-828-3206.
E-mail: john.dumville@state.vt.us
Web Site: www.historicvermont.org
Founded: 1968.
Key Personnel: Historic Sites Operations Chief, John P. Dumville; Site Admin., William Jenney.
Personnel Profile: Part-Time Paid 1.
Governing Authority: state. Parent Institution: State of Vermont, Division for Historic Preservation, Pavilion Building, Montpelier, VT 05602. Tax-exempt.

Historic Buildings: 1785 Eureka School House; Lattice Truss Covered Bridge.
Collections: period furnishings; memorabilia; historic structures.
Facilities: schoolhouse; covered bridge.
Publications: A Guide to Historic Sites in Vermont; brochure, Eureka School-house.
Hours & Admission Prices: mid-May to mid-Oct. daily 9-5. No charge; donations accepted. ♿
Attendance: 3,000 (estimated)

JAMES HARTNESS-RUSSELL PORTER ASTRONOMY MUSEUM, 30 Orchard St., Springfield, VT 05156-2612. Tel.: 800-732-4789; 802-885-2115.
Astronomy Museum.
Collections: astronomy history & instruments; paintings; drawings; Porter Garden Telescope; Cassegrain and Coude telescopes; photographs; Hartness sundial.
Activities: guided tours.
Hours & Admission Prices: Call for hours.

SPRINGFIELD ART & HISTORICAL SOCIETY - MILLER ART CENTER, 9 Elm Hill, Springfield, VT 05156-0313. Mailing Address: P.O. Box 313, Springfield, VT 05156-0313. Tel.: 802-885-2415.
E-mail: info@millerartcenter.com
Web Site: www.millerartcenter.com
Founded: 1956.
Key Personnel: Dir., Jessica Yager; Bd. Pres., John Swanson.
Personnel Profile: Part-Time Paid 1; Part-Time Volunteers 10.
Governing Authority: society. Parent Institution: Springfield Art & Historical Society. Tax-exempt: 501(c)(3).
Art Museum: housed in 1865 house last occupied by Edward W. Miller & family.
Collections: Richard Lee pewter; machine tool industry photos; Vermont novelty works; dolls; carriages; toys; primitive portraits; Bennington pottery; local artist collections; textile (costumes); archives.
Facilities: historical records available for inter-library loan & on premises; classrooms. Handcrafts & paintings for sale.
Activities: guided tours; lectures; gallery talks; arts festivals; hobby workshops; formally organized education programs; permanent, temporary & traveling exhibitions.
Publications: annual calendar of events; brochure; quarterly newsletter; workshops announcements.
Hours & Admission Prices: Thurs.-Fri. 11-5, Sat. 11-4. No charge; donations accepted. ♿
Attendance: 1,500 (estimated)
Membership: Individual $20; Family $35; Sponsor $50; Corporate $100.

Stannard

STANNARD HISTORICAL SOCIETY, Old Methodist Church, Stannard Mountain Rd., Stannard, VT 05842. Mailing Address: 92 Old Pasture Rd., Greensboro Bend, VT 05842-2100. Tel.: 802-533-2561.
Key Personnel: Pres., Jan Lewandoski
Historical Society Museum: housed in an 1888 church. Listed on the National Register of Historic Sites.
Collections: religious artifacts; period furnishings.
Activities: Museum Sponsors: Old Home Day in August.
Hours & Admission Prices: By appointment.

Stowe

CLARKE GALLERIES, 51 S. Main St., Stowe, VT 05672. Mailing Address: P.O. Box 777, Stowe, VT 05672-0777. Tel.: 917-454-8779.
Art Gallery.
Collections: American & European paintings and sculpture from 1800s to present; photographs; prints.
Hours & Admission Prices: Call for hours.

GREEN MOUNTAIN FINE ART GALLERY, 64 S. Main St., Stowe, VT 05672. Mailing Address: P.O. Box 1384, Stowe, VT 05672-1384. Tel.: 802-253-1818. Fax: 802-253-6837.
Art Gallery.
Collections: watercolors; oils; pastels; prints; mixed media; photography.
Hours & Admission Prices: Wed.-Mon. 10-6.

HELEN DAY ART CENTER, 5 School St., Stowe, VT 05672. Mailing Address: P.O. Box 411, Stowe, VT 05672-0411. Tel.: 802-253-8358. Fax: 802-253-2703.
E-mail: mail@helenday.com
Web Site: www.helenday.com
Founded: 1981.
Key Personnel: Exec. Dir., Nathan Suter; Chm. (V), Shap Smith; Vice Chm., Simone Rueschemeyer; Education & Facilities Coord., Kiersten Williams; Exhibits Dir., Odin Cathcart.
Personnel Profile: Full-Time Paid 3; Part-Time Paid 3; Part-Time Volunteers 350.
Governing Authority: nonprofit organization. Tax-exempt: 501(c)(3).
Art Center: housed in 1863 Greek Revival Building used as a school for 100 years.
Collections: paintings; sculpture.
Facilities: Exhibit-related items for sale.
Activities: guided tours; lectures; films; concerts; arts festivals; organized education programs; docent program; participatory & loan exhibitions; public programs.
Publications: seasonal newsletter; exhibit brochures.
Hours & Admission Prices: Wed.-Sun. 12-5 & by appointment. Adults $5, senior citizens & students $3; VMGA, AAM & ICOM members & children no charge. Closed New Year's Day; President's Day; Easter; Memorial Day; Independence Day; Thanksgiving; Christmas. ♿
Attendance: 20,000
Membership: Single $30; Family & Dual $45; Corporate $125.

ROBERT PAUL GALLERY, 394 Mountain Rd., Stowe, VT 05672. Mailing Address: P.O. Box 1413, Stowe, VT 05672-1413. Tel.: 800-873-3791.
Art Gallery.
Collections: paintings; sculpture; photography.
Hours & Admission Prices: Mon.-Sat. 10-6, Sun. 10-5.

STOWE HISTORICAL SOCIETY MUSEUM, Akeley Memorial Bldg., Main St., Stowe, VT 05672. Mailing Address: P.O. Box 730, Stowe, VT 05672-0730. Tel.: 802-253-8428.
Web Site: www.gostowe.com
Historical Society Museum.
Collections: local history & culture; photographs; Civil War artifacts; personal artifacts.
Activities: educational programs; research.
Hours & Admission Prices: Tues.-Fri. 10-12; other times by appointment. No charge; donations accepted.

VERMONT SKI MUSEUM, The Perkins Bldg., One S. Main St., Stowe, VT 05672. Mailing Address: The Perkins Bldg., P.O. Box 1511, Stowe, VT 05672-1511. Tel.: 802-253-9911. Fax: 802-253-2616.
E-mail: info@vermontskimuseum.org
Web Site: www.vermontskimuseum.org
Founded: 1988.
Key Personnel: Dir. & Cur., Meredith Scott; Pres. (V), Lynne Bertram; Museum Shop Mgr., Susi Clark.
Personnel Profile: Full-Time Paid 2; Part-Time Paid 1; Part-Time Volunteers 1; Interns 2.
Governing Authority: Tax-exempt.
History Museum.
Collections: Vermont's ski history; period clothing; equipment; ski lifts 1934 to present; personal artifacts; Vermont racing history; snowboarding; films; Hall of Fame.
Facilities: library & archives by appointment. Museum-related items for sale.
Activities: tours; films. Annual Events: Vermont Ski Museum Hall of Fame Induction; Vermont Antique Ski Race; Stowe Mountain Film Festival.
Publications: quarterly newsletter.
Hours & Admission Prices: June-Oct. 30 & Dec.-March Wed.-Mon. 12-5. Suggested Donations: family $5, individual $3; discounts to groups; members no charge. ♿
Attendance: 12,000 (estimated)
Membership: Senior & Student $25; Individual $45; Family $60; Curator $100; Patron $500; Benefactor $1000.

WEST BRANCH GALLERY & SCULPTURE PARK, 17 Towne Farm Lane, Stowe, VT 05672-4138. Mailing Address: P.O. Box 250, Stowe, VT 05672-0250. Tel.: 802-253-8943.
Art Gallery.
Collections: paintings; sculpture; photographs.
Hours & Admission Prices: Wed.-Sun. 11-6; other times by appointment.

Strafford

JUSTIN SMITH MORRILL HOMESTEAD, 214 Justin Morrill Memorial Hwy., Strafford, VT 05072. Mailing Address: Historic Preservation, National Life Bldg., 2nd Fl., Montpelier, VT 05620-0001. Tel.: 802-828-3051. Fax: 802-828-3206.
E-mail: john.dumville@state.vt.us
Web Site: www.historicvermont.org/morrill
Founded: 1969.

Key Personnel: Historic Site Operations Chief, John P. Dumville.
Personnel Profile: Full-Time Paid 1; Part-Time Paid 7.
Governing Authority: state. Parent Institution: State of Vermont, Division for Historic Preservation, National Life Bldg., Drawer 20, Montpelier 05620-0501. Tax-exempt.
Historic House Museum: c.1849 Justin Smith Morrill Homestead, Gothic Revival Homestead with seven Agricultural Buildings.
Collections: original furnishings & memorabilia; historic structures.
Research Fields: period landscape, land grant colleges.
Publications: A Guide to Historic Sites in Vermont; brochure, The Justin Smith Morrill Homestead.
Hours & Admission Prices: mid-May to mid-Oct. Wed.-Sun. 9:30-5:30. Adults $2; registered school groups no charge. ♿
Attendance: 2,000 (estimated)

Swanton

ABENAKI TRIBAL MUSEUM & CULTURAL CENTER, 100 Grand Ave., Swanton, VT 05488-1424. Tel.: 802-868-2559.
Web Site: www.abenakination.org/museums
Native American Museum.
Collections: Abenaki history, culture & life; personal artifacts; clothing; photographs.
Hours & Admission Prices: Call for hours.

Thetford

THETFORD HISTORICAL SOCIETY LIBRARY AND MUSEUM, Bicentennial Bldg., 16 Library Rd., Thetford, VT 05074. Mailing Address: P.O. Box 33, Thetford, VT 05074-0033. Tel.: 802-785-2068.
E-mail: info@www.thefordhistoricalsociety.org
Founded: 1943.
Key Personnel: Pres. (V) & Librarian, Charles Latham; Asst. Dir., Martha Howard.
Personnel Profile: Part-Time Paid 1; Part-Time Volunteers 12.
Governing Authority: society. Tax-exempt.
Library & Agriculture Museum.
Collections: Clara Siprell photographs; library; portraits; furniture; tools; agricultural implements.
Research Fields: town history; genealogy; agricultural history; town industry.
Facilities: library of books, pamphlets, pictures & advertisements relating to local history, genealogy, tools & agriculture available for research by permission of curator.
Activities: permanent & temporary exhibitions; program for local elementary school students & students at Thetford Academy; special exhibits at Thetford Hill on Fair Day.
Publications: books, History & Folklore of Post Mills; Short History of Thetford; Beloved Village; The Mills & Villages of Thetford, VT; The Life of Asa Burton; bicentennial map of Thetford; Green Mountain Copper.
Hours & Admission Prices: Library: Mon. & Thurs. 2-4, Tues. 10-12. Barn Museum: Aug. Sun. 2-5. No charge; donations accepted.
Attendance: 300 (estimated)
Membership: Individual $3; Family $5; Sustaining $10; Honorary $25.

Vergennes

BIXBY MEMORIAL LIBRARY, 258 Main St., Vergennes, VT 05491-1056. Tel.: 802-877-2211. Fax: 802-877-2411.
E-mail: bixby_verg@vals.state.vt.us
Web Site: www.bixbylibrary.org
Key Personnel: Dir. & Librarian, Rachel Plant; Bd. Chm., Kitty Oxholm; Asst. Librarian, Linda Braginton; Librarian's Asst., Carolyn Tallen
Library & History Museum.
Collections: books; Native American artifacts; paintings by Vermont artists; maps; documents; manuscripts; Vermont stamps & covers.
Facilities: library & archives.
Activities: Annual Event: Summer Art Show.
Hours & Admission Prices: Mon. 12:30-8, Tues. & Fri. 12:30-5, Wed. & Thurs. 10-5, Sat. 10-2.

THE LAKE CHAMPLAIN MARITIME MUSEUM, 4472 Basin Harbor Rd., Vergennes, VT 05491-9192. Tel.: 802-475-2022. Fax: 802-475-2953.
E-mail: info@lcmm.org
Web Site: lcmm.org
Founded: 1985.
Key Personnel: Exec. Dir., Arthur B. Cohn; Basin Harbor Site Mgr. & Nautical Archaeologist, Adam Kane; Dir. Devel., Helena VanVoorst; Dir. Conservation, Chris Sabick; Dir. Exhibits & Collections, Eloise Beil; Dir. Boatbuilding & Outdoor Education, Nick Patch.
Personnel Profile: Full-Time Paid 14; Full-Time Volunteers 1; Part-Time Paid 29; Part-Time Volunteers 10; Interns 5.
Governing Authority: private; not-for-profit organization. Subsidiary Institution: Maritime Research Institute. Tax-exempt: 501(c)(3).
Maritime & Nautical Archaeology Museum.
Collections: pre-17th century to mid-20th century artifacts, reflecting the lake's colonial through commercial periods; Native American artifacts; full-size working replica vessel from Revolutionary War, 54-ft. square-rigged Philadelphia II; replica 1862 class sailing canal boat. Historic Buildings: c.1818 stone schoolhouse; c.1920 Adirondack-style camp; Westport Winch House.
Research Fields: nautical archaeology; historic shipwrecks of Lake Champlain; effects of non-native nuisance species, specifically the zebra mussel; history of Lake Champlain Basin.
Facilities: Nathan R. Owen education center (with research library); conservation laboratory & collections storage facility; nautical archaeology center; 12,000 sq. ft. exhibit space; working boat shop; forge & blacksmithing teaching suite; Gateway visitor center. Museum-related items for sale.
Activities: guided & self-guided tours; maritime skills workshops; lectures; films; education programs for adults, children & Univ. of Vermont, Middlebury College and Texas A&M college students; docent program; participatory & traveling exhibits. Special Events: Small Boat Show; lake cruises; Kids Maritime Festival; Rabble in Arms.
Publications: biannual newsletter, The LCMM News; technical reports.
Hours & Admission Prices: June 17-Oct. 15 daily 10-5. Adults $10, senior citizens $9, students 5-17 $6; discounts to AAM, AAA & VT museum & Gallery Alliance members; Council of American Maritime Museums, children under 5 & members no charge. ♿
Attendance: 24,856 (accurate)
Membership: Student $20; Single $30; Dual $40; Family $50; Family Plus 4 $60; Family Plus 8 $125; Family Plus $500; Friend of Museum $1,000.

Vernon

VERNON HISTORIANS, INC., Vernon Historical Museum, 4201 Fort Bridgman Rd., Vernon, VT 05354. Mailing Address: P.O. Box 282, Vernon, VT 05354-0282. Tel.: 802-257-0292.
Founded: 1968.
Key Personnel: Pres., Paul Miller.
Personnel Profile: Part-Time Volunteers 20.
Governing Authority: nonprofit organization. Branch Museum: Pond Road Chapel, 634 Pond Rd., Vernon, VT 05354. Tax-exempt: 501(c)(3).
Historical Museum & Chapel.
Collections: books, bibles, postcards, photographs and diaries of early pioneers of the town; school desks; school-related material; early kitchen utensils; farm tools; costumes; manuscripts. Historic Buildings: 1860 Pond Road Chapel; 1848 Red Brick School House.
Research Fields: local history.
Facilities: library of Bibles and Vermont history books available by permission.
Activities: guided tours; lectures; films; drama; formally organized education programs; permanent exhibitions.
Publications: occasional newsletter.
Hours & Admission Prices: Museum: June-Sept. Sun. 2-4. Pond Road Chapel: by appointment. No charge; donations accepted.
Attendance: 200 (estimated)
Membership: Junior (under 18) $1; Adult $5; Sustaining $10; Institutional $25; Life $100.

Waitsfield

GENERAL WAIT HOUSE, 4061 Main St., Waitsfield, VT 05673. Mailing Address: P.O. Box 816, Waitsfield, VT 05673-0816. Tel.: 802-496-3733 & 2027. Fax: 802-496-3733.
Web Site: www.waitsfieldhistoricalsociety.com
Founded: 1970.
Key Personnel: Pres., Jean Sherman; Vice Pres., Peter Laskowsky; Sec. & Treas., Sandra Reilly; Archivist & Cur., Judy Dodds.
Personnel Profile: Part-Time Volunteers 20.
Governing Authority: board. Parent Institution: Waitsfield Historical Society. Tax-exempt.
Historic Site: original home of General Wait c.1790.
Collections: local history & culture; personal artifacts; period furnishings; photographs.
Research Fields: Vermont history.
Facilities: visitor's center; garden; restored parlor & hall.
Activities: barn tours; historic home walking tours; temporary exhibitions.
Publications: quarterly newsletter.
Hours & Admission Prices: Daily 9-5. No charge; donations accepted. ♿
Attendance: 1,500 (estimated)
Membership: General Wait House Membership $15, $25 & $50.

Waterbury

GREEN MOUNTAIN COFFEE VISITOR CENTER, 1 Rotarian Place, Waterbury, VT 05676-1582. Tel.: 877-879-2326.
Visitor Center: housed in an 1867 Amtrak station.
Collections: company history; process of growing, roasting, & packaging coffee.
Facilities: cafe. Museum-related items for sale.
Activities: self-guided tours.
Hours & Admission Prices: Memorial Day to Labor Day daily 7-7; Winter: daily 7-6; groups by appointment. Suggested Donation: $1. Closed New Year's Day; Thanksgiving; Christmas.

Waterbury Center

GREEN MOUNTAIN CLUB, INC., 4711 Waterbury Stowe Rd., Waterbury Center, VT 05677-8325. Tel.: 802-244-7037. Fax: 802-244-5867.
E-mail: gmc@greenmountainclub.org
Web Site: greenmountainclub.org
Founded: 1910.
Key Personnel: Exec. Dir., Ben Rose; Pres. (V), Richard Windish; Dir. Devel., Shawn Keeley, Jr.; Dir. Finance, Arthur Goldsweig.
Personnel Profile: Full-Time Paid 8; Part-Time Paid 3; Part-Time Volunteers 800; Interns 4.
Governing Authority: private; nonprofit organization. Tax-exempt: 501(c)(3).
History Museum.
Collections: historical photographs, artifacts & documents relating to the Green Mountain Club (formed in 1910), Vermont's Long Trail hiking trail and hiking in Vermont & the northeast.
Facilities: 100-vol. library relating to hiking & outdoor activity information; 150-seat auditorium; hiking & nature trails. Gift items for sale.
Activities: lectures. Annual Events: meeting of members; James P. Taylor Series-educational & participation events; workshops; conferences.
Publications: quarterly newsletter, Long Trail News; guidebooks; maps; history books.
Hours & Admission Prices: Memorial Day-Oct. Mon.-Fri. 9-5, Sat.-Sun. 8-4; Nov.-May Mon.-Sat. 10-5. No charge; donations accepted. Closed federal holidays; Christmas Eve.
Attendance: 5,000 (estimated)
Membership: Limited Income $22; Adult $40; Family $50; Business & Corporation $150; Life $1,000.

Weathersfield

REVEREND DAN FOSTER HOUSE, MUSEUM OF THE WEATHERSFIELD HISTORICAL SOCIETY, 2656 Weathersfield Center Rd., Weathersfield, VT 05156. Mailing Address: P.O. Box 126, Perkinsville, VT 05151-0126. Tel.: 802-263-5230. Fax: 802-263-9263.
E-mail: ellen.clattenburg@dresden.us
Founded: 1951.
Key Personnel: Pres., Allison Roth; Vice Pres., Virginia Wimberg; Cur., Ellen F. Clattenburg.
Personnel Profile: Part-Time Volunteers 5.
Governing Authority: society. Parent Institution: Weathersfield Historical Society. Tax-exempt: 501(c)(3).
Local History Museum.
Collections: 1787 barn replica; local artifacts: costumes; furniture; pictures; Civil War items; old cobbler's tools; early American farm tools; blacksmith shop; genealogic & photographic records; quilts; coverlets; musical instruments; post office equipment; photographs; ephemera.
Research Fields: local history; genealogy of Weathersfield inhabitants.
Facilities: 500-vol. library of historical books & Bibles with family records; catalogued collection of photographs.
Activities: guided tours; temporary exhibitions; various programs.
Publications: triannual newsletter; annual report; books, Weathersfield History Vols. I & II; The Weathersfield Burying Grounds; The Inhabitants of Weathersfield (reissued 1990); The Life of Consul William Jarvis; The Warren Family & Weathersfield, VT; three videos: A Lot of Water Over The Dam - the removal of lower Perkinsville in 1959 to make way for a flood control dam; The Weathersfield Meeting House Rebuilt - 1985-87 following a devastating fire in August of 1985; A Crash Course in the history of Weathersfield; Weathersfield Historical Society cookbook, Spider Bread, Cider Pie & Rhubarb Wine 2001.
Hours & Admission Prices: June-Oct. by appointment. No charge; donations accepted.
Attendance: 200 (estimated)
Membership: Regular $7.50; Family $15; Contributing $25; Sustaining $50; Life $150.

West Addison

DAR JOHN STRONG MANSION MUSEUM, 6656 VT Rte. 17 W., West Addison, VT 05491-8893. Tel.: 802-759-2309.
Web Site: www.northshirecomputer.com/VTDAR
Founded: 1934.
Key Personnel: Cur., Maureen Labenski.
Personnel Profile: Part-Time Volunteers 30.
Governing Authority: society. Parent Institution: Vermont Society, Daughters of the American Revolution. Tax-exempt.
Historic House.
Collections: period furniture, 1790-1860; art; textiles; decorative artifacts; household implements.
Facilities: 30-vol. collection of genealogy books available for reference on premises.
Activities: educational events & speakers.
Publications: brochure.
Hours & Admission Prices: Memorial Day weekend to Labor Day weekend. Sat.-Sun. 10-5. Family $10, adults $5, seniors & students $3; discount to groups, AAM, ICOM & VMGA members; members no charge. ♿
Attendance: 500 (accurate)

West Halifax

HALIFAX HISTORICAL SOCIETY MUSEUM, Branch Rd., West Halifax, VT 05358. Mailing Address: P.O. Box 94, West Halifax, VT 05358. Tel.: 802-368-7490.
Historical Society Museum: housed in a 2-room schoolhouse.
Collections: local history & culture; period furnishings; clothing; quilts; photographs.
Activities: demonstrations.
Hours & Admission Prices: Summer: Sat. 2-4; other times by appointment. No charge.

West Marlboro

SOUTHERN VERMONT NATURAL HISTORY MUSEUM, Hogback Mt. Overlook, Vermont Rte. 9, West Marlboro, VT Mailing Address: 7599 VT Rte. 9, Wilmington, VT 05363. Tel.: 802-464-0048.
E-mail: museum@sover.net
Web Site: www.vermontmuseum.org
Founded: 1962.
Congressional District: 1
Key Personnel: Chm. (V), John North; Pres. (V) & Exec. Dir., Edward C. Metcalfe.
Personnel Profile: Full-Time Paid 2; Full-Time Volunteers 2; Part-Time Paid 2; Part-Time Volunteers 6; Interns 1.
Governing Authority: private; nonprofit organization. Tax-exempt: 501(c)(3).
Natural History Museum.
Collections: natural history of the northeast U.S.
Facilities: aquarium; nature & conservation center. Museum-related items for sale.
Publications: quarterly newsletter, Wildlife Notes.
Hours & Admission Prices: Memorial Day-Columbus Day daily 10-5; extended foliage season hours; Winter call for hours. Adults 13 & over $5, senior citizens $3, children 5-12 $2; children under 5, NEMA, UMGA, SPNHC, AAM & ICOM members no charge. Closed Thanksgiving; Christmas Day. ♿
Attendance: 15,000 (estimated)
Membership: Student $10; Individual $15; Family $25; Supporting $50; Sustaining $100; Benefactor $500.

West Rutland

CARVING STUDIO & SCULPTURE CENTER, 636 Marble St., West Rutland, VT 05777. Mailing Address: P.O. Box 495, West Rutland, VT 05777-0495. Tel.: 802-438-2097. Fax: 802-438-2020.
E-mail: info@carvingstudio.org
Web Site: www.carvingstudio.org
Sculpture Center.
Collections: sculptures.
Facilities: sculpture garden.
Activities: workshops; temporary & permanent exhibitions; special events.
Hours & Admission Prices: Call for hours.

Westminster

WESTMINSTER HISTORICAL SOCIETY, Main St., Westminster, VT 05158. Mailing Address: P.O. Box 2, Westminster, VT 05158-0002.
Founded: 1966.
Key Personnel: C.E.O. & Pres. (V), Virginia Lisai; Vice Pres., Pat Haas; Sec. & Treas., Linda Fawcett; Dir., Karen Larsen.

Personnel Profile: Part-Time Volunteers 20.
Governing Authority: nonprofit. Tax-exempt.
Historical Society Museum: housed in c.1890 Old Town Hall.
Collections: history.
Research Fields: genealogy; history of the Abenaque Machine Works, 1893-1930.
Activities: permanent exhibitions.
Publications: book, Abenaque Machine Works; Vignettes of Westminster, Vermont; Around Bellows Falls.
Hours & Admission Prices: July-Sept. Sun. 2-4. No charge.
Attendance: 100 (estimated)
Membership: Individual $5; Couple $10; Business $25; Life $100.

Weston

FARRAR-MANSUR HOUSE & OLD MILL MUSEUM, Main St., Weston, VT 05161. Mailing Address: P.O. Box 247, Weston, VT 05161-0247. Tel.: 802-824-5294. Fax: 802-824-5294, ext. 51.
Founded: 1933.
Key Personnel: Pres. (V) Weston Historical Society, Robert Brandt; Dir., Jean Lindman.
Personnel Profile: Part-Time Paid 1; Part-Time Volunteers 7; Interns 1.
Governing Authority: society. Parent Institution: The Weston Community Association. Affiliated with The Weston Historical Society. Tax-exempt.
Historic House Museum.
Collections: local period artifacts; murals; dolls; portraits; family bibles; school & church records; 19th-century house furnishings; period mill tools; 19th-century band wagon, uniforms & instruments; 18th-19th century New England Village life; guns; pianos; melodeons; loom; spinning wheels; niddy noddies. Historic Buildings: 1785 grist mill; 1797 house.
Facilities: library of local history & genealogy books available for use on premises. Museum-related items for sale.
Activities: guided tours; permanent & temporary exhibitions; school groups; programs. Museum Sponsors: Open Houses; Hearth Cooking Candlelight Dinners.
Publications: newsletter.
Hours & Admission Prices: Call for hours. Admission by voluntary contributions.
Attendance: 900 (estimated)
Membership: Individual $10; Family $25; Supporting $50; Sustaining $50; Associate $75; Friends of Farrar-Mansur $100 & up.

White River Junction

THE MAIN STREET MUSEUM, 58 Bridge St., White River Junction, VT 05001-7040. Tel.: 802-356-2776.
Web Site: www.mainstreetmuseum.org/wiki
Founded: 1992.
Key Personnel: Dir., David Fairbanks Ford; Pres. (V), Bunny Harvey; Museum Shop Mgr., Christopher W. Comperry.
Personnel Profile: Full-Time Volunteers 1; Part-Time Volunteers 4; Interns 5.
Governing Authority: nonprofit organization. Tax-exempt: 501(c)(3).
General Museum.
Collections: local history & culture; photographs; sculptures; paintings; natural history.
Major Exhibits: Invasive and Non-Invasive Species of White River Junction (T), 1/10-12/10; Tiny Shoes & More Tiny Shoes, 1/10-12/10; Relics from the Life & Works of Alexander Pushkin (T), 1/10-12/10; Around the World With The Main Street Museum (T), 1/10-12/10; The Connecticut River Monster (T), 1/10-12/10; Tramp & Hobo Symposium (T), 1/10-12/10; Teeth & More Teeth, 1/10-12/10; Workaday World of White River Junction, 1/10-12/10; Flocked Items & Unidentified Mammals, 1/10-12/10; The Heather Collection; Journals & Bling (T), 1/10-12/10.
Research Fields: flora; fauna; rocks; generations.
Activities: music; movies; films; lectures.
Publications: The Electric Organ.
Hours & Admission Prices: Thurs.-Sun. 1-6. Suggested Donation: $3-$5; discounts to groups; members no charge. ♿
Attendance: 5,000 (accurate)
Membership: Individual $35.

NEW ENGLAND TRANSPORTATION INSTITUTE AND MUSEUM, 100 Railroad Row, White River Junction, VT 05001. Tel.: 802-291-9838.
E-mail: info@netransportation.org
Transportation Museum.
Collections: transportation history; railroad, river, & air transportation; equipment; period artifacts; photographs.
Activities: educational programs.
Hours & Admission Prices: Jan.-May Tues.-Fri. 9-1; Memorial Day to Labor Day Tues.-Sun. 10-5; other times by appointment.

Williamstown

WEATHERED BARN DOLL MUSEUM, 452 George Rd., Williamstown, VT 05679-9403. Tel.: 802-433-6077.
Doll Museum.
Collections: over 5,000 dolls.
Hours & Admission Prices: May-Dec. call for hours.

Windsor

AMERICAN PRECISION MUSEUM, 196 Main St., Windsor, VT 05089-1312. Mailing Address: P.O. Box 679, Windsor, VT 05089-0679. Tel.: 802-674-5781. Fax: 802-674-2524.
E-mail: info@americanprecision.org
Web Site: www.americanprecision.org
Founded: 1966.
Congressional District: 1
Key Personnel: C.E.O., Ann Lawless; Chm. (V), Gilbert Whittemore.
Personnel Profile: Full-Time Paid 3; Part-Time Paid 3; Part-Time Volunteers 15; Interns 5.
Governing Authority: nonprofit organization. Tax-exempt: 501(c)(3).
Industrial History Museum: housed in 1846 Robbins & Lawrence Armory. National Historic Landmark.
Collections: machine tools; gun-making machines; wood-working machines; metal-working machinery; hand tools; firearms; models; typewriters.
Activities: permanent & temporary exhibitions; special programs; traveling education kits for schools.
Publications: newsletter, Tools & Technology.
Hours & Admission Prices: Memorial Day-Oct. daily 10-5. Family $18, adults $6, students $4; discounts to groups & VMGA members; members no charge. ♿
Attendance: 5,000 (accurate)
Membership: Individual $35; Dual & Family $55; Associate $100; Patron $250; Steward $500; Benefactor $1,000.

CORNISH COLONY MUSEUM, 147 Main St., Windsor, VT 05089-1338. Mailing Address: P. O. Box 63, Windsor, VT 05089-0063. Tel.: 802-674-6008. Fax: 802-674-6011.
Founded: 1998.
Key Personnel: Dir., Donna Van Fleet; Pres. (V), Robert Dean; Museum Shop Mgr., Tom Cole.
Personnel Profile: Full-Time Paid 3; Part-Time Volunteers 3.
Governing Authority: Tax-exempt.
Art Museum.
Collections: works by Maxfield Parrish, local artists, sculptors, writers, architects & landscape designers.
Major Exhibits: Cornish Colony 125th Anniversary, 5/10-10/10.
Publications: exhibit catalogs.
Hours & Admission Prices: Tues.-Sun. Adults $6; discount to AAM members; members no charge. ♿
Attendance: 4,000 (estimated)
Membership: Individual $30; Family $60; Sponsors $125-$10,000.

OLD CONSTITUTION HOUSE, 16 N. Main St., Windsor, VT 05089-1307. Mailing Address: Historic Preservation, National Life Building, 2nd Fl., Montpelier, VT 05620-0001. Tel.: 802-672-3773. Fax: 802-828-3206.
E-mail: john.dumville@state.vt.us
Web Site: www.historicvermont.org/constitution
Founded: 1961.
Key Personnel: Historic Sites Operations Chief, John P. Dumville; Site Admin., William Jenney.
Personnel Profile: Full-Time Paid 1; Part-Time Paid 1.
Governing Authority: state. Parent Institution: State of Vermont, Division for Historic Preservation, Pavilion Bldg., Montpelier, VT 05602. Tax-exempt.
Historic House Museum: 1777 Old Constitution House.
Collections: Colonial & Civil War periods; pottery; furniture.
Research Fields: Republic of Vermont (1777-1791), Vermont constitution.
Activities: permanent exhibitions.
Publications: brochure; guide.
Hours & Admission Prices: mid-May to mid-Oct. daily 10-5. Adults $1; registered school groups no charge. ♿
Attendance: 2,000 (estimated)

Winooski

HERITAGE WINOOSKI MILL MUSEUM, Champlain Mill, Winooski, VT 05404. Mailing Address: Saint Michael's College, P.O. Box 181, Colchester, VT 05439. Tel.: 802-655-9744.
History Museum.
Collections: mill history, machinery & equipment; photographs; period artifacts; tools.

Activities: educational programs; school tours; internship program; teachers' workshops; lectures.
Hours & Admission Prices: Mon.-Sat. 10-7, Sun. 12-5. No charge. ♿

MCCARTHY GALLERY, McCarthy Arts Center, St. Michael's College, Winooski, VT 05404. Tel.: 802-654-2246.
Art Gallery.
Collections: paintings; photographs; sculpture.
Hours & Admission Prices: Mon.-Fri. 3-5 & 7:30-9:30, Sat.-Sun. 1-5.

Woodstock

BILLINGS FARM & MUSEUM, (M), 53-02 River Rd., Woodstock, VT 05091. Mailing Address: P.O. Box 489, Woodstock, VT 05091-0489. Tel.: 802-457-2355. Fax: 802-457-4663.
E-mail: info@billingsfarm.org
Web Site: www.billingsfarm.org
Founded: 1976.
Congressional District: 1
Key Personnel: Pres., David A. Donath; Vice Pres., Darlyne S. Franzen; Dir. Education & Interpretation, David A. Miles; Farm Mgr., B.J. Hanfield; Admin. Officer, Marian E. Koetsier; Dir. Program Devel., Corwin Sharp; Cur. Exhibits, Robert G. Benz; Collections Mgr., Rebecca A. Helland; Facilities Mgr., David V. Ferrero; Museum Asst., Megan Campbell; Public Rels. Coord., Susan Plump; Sec., Marjorie Wakefield; Asst. Farm Mgr., Shawn Yeatts; Farm Worker, Michael Binkett; Farm Worker, Keith Tiff; Teamster, Sarah Littlefield.
Personnel Profile: Full-Time Paid 15; Part-Time Paid 35; Part-Time Volunteers 25.
Governing Authority: nonprofit organization. Parent Institution: Woodstock Foundation, Inc. Tax-exempt: 501(c)(3).
History Museum & 320 acre dairy farm: 1890 restored & furnished farm house, creamery & ice house.
Collections: 16,000 objects relating to agriculture & folklife in east-central Vermont during the late 19th century. Historic Buildings: 1890 farm house; 19th-century farm barns.
Major Exhibits: 24th Annual Quilt Exhibition, 7/31/10-9/26/10.
Research Fields: agriculture & rural life in east-central Vermont during the late 19th century; The roles of George Perkins Marsh, Frederick Billings, and Laurance S. Rockefeller as conservationists.
Facilities: 7,500-vol. library including archives, photos & microforms for research use; visitor center; classroom; 100-seat theatre; 230-acre dairy farm. Local crafts, books & products for sale.
Activities: special events; year-round educational program; volunteer program; special activities; temporary exhibitions; daily livestock & agricultural programs.
Publications: education brochures; visitor guides; book, The Vermont Farm Year; annual report.
Hours & Admission Prices: May-Oct. daily 10-5; Nov.-Feb. Sat.-Sun. 10-3:30, call for additional hours. Adults $11, seniors $10, children 5-15 $6, children 3-4 $3; discounts to AAM & ICOM members; members & children 2 & under no charge. ♿
Attendance: 52,716 (accurate)
Membership: Individual $30; Family $50; Friend $100; Supporter $175; Subscriber $250; Sustaining $500; Benefactor $1,000.

WOODSTOCK HISTORICAL SOCIETY, INC., 26 Elm St., Woodstock, VT 05091-1024. Tel.: 802-457-1822. Fax: 802-457-2811.
E-mail: info@woodstockhistorical.org
Web Site: www.woodstockhistorical.org
Founded: 1943.
Key Personnel: Dir., Jack Anderson; Chm., Chuck Wise; Guide Admin., Gina Moore; Coord. Education, Jennie Shurtleff.
Personnel Profile: Full-Time Paid 1; Part-Time Paid 10; Part-Time Volunteers 4.
Governing Authority: board of trustees; nonprofit organization. Tax-exempt: 501(c)(3).
History Museum: housed in 1807 Federal style house with brick gables, designed by Nathaniel Smith.
Collections: portraits; John Taylor Arms etchings; 1740-1900 furniture; toys; dolls; doll houses; silver & glass; costumes; artisan & craft tools; winter sports equipment; Woodstock's Royal charter; manuscripts, photographs, & business records relating to Woodstock & environs. Historic Building: 1807 Dana House.
Research Fields: Woodstock history & genealogy.
Facilities: 800-vol. research library of local history, biography of local residents, local imprints, genealogical reference, books & papers of the Dana family; 50-seat auditorium.
Activities: lectures; temporary & permanent exhibitions; education program for children.
Publications: Walking Guide to the Village of Woodstock; The Long Light of Those Days: Recollections of a Vermont Village at Mid-century; The Hills Were Full of Dairy Farmers: Memories of Farming in the Region of Woodstock, VT; Woodstock's Heritage - A Brief History of the Shire Town.
Hours & Admission Prices: Office: Mon.-Fri. 9-5. Library: Wed.-Fri. 9:30-4. Dana House: May-Oct. Wed.-Sun. 11-4; other times by appointment. Adults $5; discounts to VMGA, AAA, AAM & NEMA members; members and youth 16 & under no charge. ♿
Attendance: 4,450 (accurate)
Membership: Student & Senior $15; Individual $25; Family $35; Contributing $75; Subscribing $150; Sustaining $250; Patron $500.

VIRGINIA

(377 listings)

Abingdon

HISTORICAL SOCIETY OF WASHINGTON COUNTY, VIRGINIA, 306 Depot Square, Abingdon, VA 24210-3102. Mailing Address: P.O. Box 484, Abingdon, VA 24212-0484. Tel.: 276-623-8337.
E-mail: office@hswcv.org
Web Site: hswcv.org
Key Personnel: Pres. (V), Joella J. Barbour; Vice Pres., Eleanor Grasselli; Treas., Mike Shaffer; Recording Sec., Doris Wells; Corresponding Sec., Ina Stephenson-Marbury; Membership, Riley Clark; Local History, Joella Barbour; Bulletin Editor, Eleanor Grasselli; Newsletter Editor, Greg McMillian; Database Mgr., Jack Niemann; Photo Digitization, Jane Oakes; Library Mgr., Melissa Watson.
Personnel Profile: Full-Time Paid 1.
Historical Society Library.
Collections: local history pertaining to Washington County & Abingdon; genealogy files; photographs.
Research Fields: genealogy; local history.
Facilities: library; archives.
Activities: educational programs. Museum Sponsors: Virginia Highlands Festival activities; tour of local homes in December.
Publications: newsletters; HSWC Bulletin.
Hours & Admission Prices: Jan. 15-March & Dec. 1-Dec. 15 Mon.-Fri. 10-4; April-Nov. Mon.-Fri. 10-4 & 1st and 3rd Sat. 11-4. No charge; donations accepted.

* **WILLIAM KING MUSEUM CENTER FOR ART AND CULTURAL HERITAGE, (M),** 415 Academy Dr., Abingdon, VA 24210-2617. Mailing Address: P.O. Box 2256, Abingdon, VA 24212-2256. Tel.: 276-628-5005. Fax: 276-628-3922.
Web Site: www.williamkingmuseum.org
Formerly: William King Regional Arts Center
Founded: 1979.
Congressional District: 9
Key Personnel: Exec. Dir., Lemont Dobson; Pres. Bd. (V), Ben Jennings; Vice Pres., Steve Morris; Treas., Steve Givens; Sec., Rhonda Hurt; Deputy Dir., Kathy Lowdermilk; Cur. Fine Art, Adam Justice; Chief Admin., Deb Kerr; Devel. Officer, Emily Woolwine; Museum Shop Mgr., Nancy Harte.
Personnel Profile: Full-Time Paid 8; Part-Time Paid 3; Part-Time Volunteers 25; Interns 2.
Governing Authority: private; nonprofit organization. Tax-exempt: 501(c)(3).
Art Museum: housed in 1913 school building.
Collections: decorative arts.
Major Exhibits: From These Hills, 11/09-2/10; Matisse, Picasso, and Art in Paris (T), 12/09-2/10.
Facilities: classrooms; 7,500 sq. ft. exhibit space. Museum-related items for sale.
Activities: guided tours; lectures; exhibition receptions; community family days; facility rental; adult & children's educational programs; resident studio artists.
Publications: gallery guides; exhibition catalogs & posters; reception announcement cards; annual reports; program calendars.
Hours & Admission Prices: Tues. 10-9, Wed.-Sat. 10-5, Sun. 1-5. Suggested Donation: $5; members no charge. Closed New Year's Eve & Day; Easter; Memorial Day; Independence Day; Labor Day; Thanksgiving; Christmas Eve & Day. ♿
Attendance: 40,000 (accurate)
Membership: Individual $50; Family $100; Silver Palette $150; Gold Palette $300; Academy $500; William King Society $1,000.

Alexandria

ALEXANDRIA ARCHAEOLOGY MUSEUM, 105 N. Union St., No. 327, Alexandria, VA 22314-3217. Tel.: 703-838-4399. Fax: 703-838-6491.
E-mail: archaeology@alexandriava.gov
Web Site: www.alexandriaarchaeology.org
Founded: 1977.
Congressional District: 8
Key Personnel: Dir., Dr. Pamela J. Cressey; Asst. Dir., Dr. Steven J. Shephard; Asst. Dir., Barbara H. Magid; Preservation Archaeologist, Francine Bromberg; Education Coord., Ruth Reeder; Sec., Jennifer Barker.
Personnel Profile: Full-Time Paid 3; Part-Time Paid 3; Part-Time Volunteers 102.
Governing Authority: municipal. Parent Institution: City of Alexandria. Subsidiary Institution: Office of Historic Alexandria. Tax-exempt: 501(c)(3).
Archaeology Museum.
Collections: 18th- & 19th-century artifacts from archaeological digs in Alexandria; field notes; photographs; research files associated with collections; prehistoric stone tools.
Research Fields: urban archaeological research; historic neighborhoods; Alexandria waterfront local history.
Facilities: 300-vol. library pertaining to local history, archaeology & antiques; research laboratory.
Activities: guided tours; lectures; interpreter program; organized education program for undergraduate or graduate college students affiliated with George Washington University; temporary exhibitions; volunteer program; video of sites; museum & outreach programs for elementary school children; family programs in the museum & on site; Alexandria Archaeology Institute for adults.
Publications: brochure has 43 listings including, Geographical Methods in Urban Preservation Planning, Historical Methods in Urban Preservation Planning; The Volunteer in Alexandria Archaeology; A Field Manual for Alexandria Archaeology; A Laboratory Manual for Alexandria Archaeology; A Guide to the Alexandria Archaeological Research Museum; the Potter's Art: Salt-glazed Stoneware of 19th-Century Alexandria; papers, Approaches to Preserving a City's Past, The Alexandria Waterfront Forum: Birth & ReBirth 1730-1983, Alexandria Antiquity 1984, Across the Fence, But a World Apart; Archaeologists at Work: A Teacher's Guide to Classroom Archaeology; catalogue, Artifacts, Advertisements & Archaeology; monthly newsletter, Alexandria Archaeology Volunteer News; Alexandria, Virginia; Walking with Washington; Walk and Bike the Alexandria Heritage Trail.
Hours & Admission Prices: Tues.-Fri. 10-3, Sat. 10-5, Sun. 1-5. No charge; donations accepted. ♿
Attendance: 29,570 (accurate)
Membership: Friends of Alexandria Archaeology: Individual $20; Family & Group $25; Sponsor $50; Benefactor $100; Corporate $500.

ALEXANDRIA BLACK HISTORY MUSEUM, (M), 902 Wythe St., Alexandria, VA 22314-1839. Tel.: 703-838-4356. Fax: 703-706-3999.
E-mail: blackhistory@alexandriava.gov
Web Site: www.alexblackhistory.org
Formerly: Alexandria Black History Resource Center
Founded: 1983.
Congressional District: 8
Key Personnel: Dir., Louis Hicks; Asst. Dir & Cur., Audrey P. Davis; Cur., Lillian Patterson; Sec., Jewel Plummer.
Personnel Profile: Full-Time Paid 2; Full-Time Volunteers 2; Part-Time Paid 2; Part-Time Volunteers 50; Interns 6.
Governing Authority: municipal. Parent Institution: Office of Historic Alexandria. Tax-exempt: 501(c)(3).
History Museum: located in former public library.
Collections: photographs; documents.
Research Fields: local African-American history.
Activities: lectures; slide presentations; workshops; walking tours.
Publications: book, Black Word Find.
Hours & Admission Prices: Tues.-Sat. 10-4. Admission $2. Closed New Year's Day; Martin Luther King Jr. Day; Easter; Independence Day; Thanksgiving; Christmas. ♿
Attendance: 10,300 (estimated)
Membership: Alexandria Society for the Preservation of Black Heritage $20.

ALEXANDRIA LIBRARY - LOCAL HISTORY & SPECIAL COLLECTIONS, 717 Queen St., Alexandria, VA 22314-2420. Tel.: 703-838-4577. Fax: 703-706-3912.
Library.
Collections: local history & culture; photographs; genealogy; books; microfilm; manuscripts.
Facilities: library.
Activities: research; special events.
Hours & Admission Prices: Mon.-Thurs. 9-9, Fri. 9-6, Sat. 9-5.

* **CARLYLE HOUSE HISTORIC PARK, (M),** 121 N. Fairfax St., Alexandria, VA 22314-3229. Tel.: 703-549-2997. Fax: 703-549-5738.
E-mail: carlyle@NVRPA.org
Web Site: www.carlylehouse.org
Founded: 1976.
Congressional District: 8
Key Personnel: Dir., Jim Bartlinski; Cur. Education, Heather Dunn; Cur., Sarah Coster.
Personnel Profile: Full-Time Paid 3; Part-Time Paid 14; Part-Time Volunteers 95.
Governing Authority: nonprofit organization. Operated by the Northern Virginia Regional Park Authority, 5400 Ox Rd., Fairfax Station, VA 22039. Tax-exempt: 501(c)(3).
Historic House: 1753 Carlyle House, Georgian Palladian style, used by General Braddock as headquarters for planning early campaigns of French & Indian War.
Collections: 18th-century decorative arts; archaeological collection.
Research Fields: local history; archaeology; furnishings.
Facilities: classroom.
Activities: guided tours; formally organized education programs; docent program; special events.
Publications: brochures; book, Who Built Alexandria Architects in Alexandria, 1750-1900; Colo. John Carlyle, Gent. 1720-1780.
Hours & Admission Prices: Tues.-Sat. 10-4, Sun. 12-4. Adults $5, children 11-17 $3; discount to AAM members; members & children 10 & under no charge. Closed New Year's Day; Thanksgiving; Christmas Eve & Day. ♿
Attendance: 22,000 (accurate)
Membership: Member $25; Contributor $50; Patron $100; Benefactor $500; Braddock Society $1,000.

COLLINGWOOD LIBRARY AND MUSEUM ON AMERICANISM, 8301 E. Boulevard Dr., Alexandria, VA 22308-1399. Tel.: 703-765-1652. Fax: 703-765-8213.
E-mail: curator@collingwoodlibrary.com
Web Site: collingwoodlibrary.com
Founded: 1977.
Congressional District: 8
Key Personnel: Pres., Frank Harris; Treas., Bill Williamson; Sec., John Mayers.
Personnel Profile: Part-Time Paid 2.
Governing Authority: nonprofit organization. Tax-exempt: 501(c)(3).
American History Museum: housed in 1785 structure used as overseer's house for George Washington's River Farm.
Collections: Indian artifacts; coins, china; state & colonial flags; Revolutionary War items; militaria; replicas of historic documents & artifacts.
Research Fields: local history; military; Masonic.
Facilities: 7,000-vol. library pertaining to American history for public use; 19,000 microfiche.
Activities: guided tours; lectures; loan exhibitions.
Publications: quarterly newsletter.
Hours & Admission Prices: Mon. & Wed.-Sat. 10-4, Sun. 1-4. No charge; donations accepted. ♿
Attendance: 9,000

* **FORT WARD MUSEUM AND HISTORIC SITE, (M),** 4301 W. Braddock Rd., Alexandria, VA 22304-1007. Tel.: 703-838-4848. Fax: 703-671-7350.
E-mail: fort.ward@alexandriava.gov
Web Site: oha.alexandriava.gov/fortward/
Founded: 1964.
Congressional District: 8
Key Personnel: Dir., Susan G. Cumbey; Cur., Walton H. Owen.
Personnel Profile: Full-Time Paid 2; Part-Time Paid 3; Part-Time Volunteers 15.
Governing Authority: municipal. Parent Institution: City of Alexandria. Subsidiary Institution: Office of Historic Alexandria. Tax-exempt: 501(c)(3).
Military Museum: located on the site of 1861-65 Fort Ward, built to protect Washington DC during the Civil War.
Collections: Civil War artifacts; library collection; historic site: preserved Union Fort featuring restored Northwest Bastion.
Research Fields: The Civil War; mid-19th-century American military, local & social history.
Facilities: 2,000-vol. library on Civil War available for research on premises; reading room; park setting. Museum-related items for sale.
Activities: guided tours; lectures; permanent & temporary exhibitions; outreach program: Life During the Civil War; interpretive programs.
Publications: newsletter; site & exhibition brochures.
Hours & Admission Prices: Museum: April-Oct. Tues.-Sat. 9-5, Sun. 12-5; Nov.-March Tues.-Sat. 10-5, Sun. 12-5. Park: daily 9-sunset. No charge; donations accepted. Closed New Year's Day; Thanksgiving; Christmas. ♿

Attendance: 34,000 (estimated)
Membership: Individual $10; Organization $25; Supporting $35.

FRANK LLOYD WRIGHT'S POPE-LEIGHEY HOUSE, 9000 Richmond Hwy., Alexandria, VA 22309. Mailing Address: P.O. Box 15097, Alexandria, VA 22309-0097. Tel.: 703-780-4000. Fax: 703-780-8509.
E-mail: woodlawn@nthp.org
Web Site: www.popeleighey1940.org
Founded: 1964.
Congressional District: 10
Key Personnel: Council Chm., Cindy Conner; Exec. Dir., Laurie Ossman; Site Admin., Stacey Hawkins.
Personnel Profile: Full-Time Paid 3; Part-Time Paid 45; Part-Time Volunteers 50.
Governing Authority: nonprofit. Property of the National Trust for Historic Preservation, 1785 Massachusetts Ave., N.W., Washington, DC 20036. Tax-exempt: 501(c)(3).
Historic House: 1940 Frank Lloyd Wright Usonian house, located on the grounds of Woodlawn.
Collections: Frank Lloyd Wright furniture & furnishings.
Research Fields: works of Frank Lloyd Wright.
Facilities: 1,250 sq. ft. exhibit space; nature trails; wildflower landscape. Books & museum related items for sale.
Activities: guided tours; lectures; formally organized educational programs; Tech Tours first Sunday of every month; book club tours.
Hours & Admission Prices: March-Dec. Thurs.-Sun. 10-4. Adults $8.50, children K-12 $3. Combination with Woodlawn: adult $15, children grades K-12 $5; discounts to military & AIA members; National Trust members & Friends of Pope-Leighey House no charge. Closed New Year's Day; Thanksgiving; Christmas.
Attendance: 42,000
Membership: Friend $30; Family $40; Contributing $50; Sustaining $100; Supporting $500; Pope-Leighey Forum $1,000 & up.

FRIENDSHIP FIREHOUSE, 107 S. Alfred St., Alexandria, VA 22314-3001. Tel.: 703-838-3891 & 4994. Fax: 703-838-4997.
E-mail: lyceum@alexandriava.gov
Web Site: www.friendshipfirehouse.org
Founded: 1993.
Congressional District: 8
Key Personnel: Museum Aide, Michael Carter.
Personnel Profile: Part-Time Paid 1.
Governing Authority: municipal; nonprofit. Parent Institution: City of Alexandria, VA. Subsidiary Institution: Office of Historic Alexandria. Tax-exempt.
Firehouse Museum: housed in c.1855 Italianate-style brick building which has a first-floor engine room for storing apparatus & a second-floor meeting room for social & ceremonial activities.
Collections: history of Friendship Fire Company & local firefighting history; firefighting apparatus, equipment, & uniforms; letters; photographs; period furnishings.
Research Fields: history of Friendship Fire Company & other local firefighting history.
Facilities: 500 sq. ft. exhibit space.
Activities: Museum Sponsors: Birthday Party/Public Safety Festival in August.
Hours & Admission Prices: Fri.-Sat. 10-4, Sun. 1-4. Adults $2; discounts to AAM & ICOM members. Closed New Year's Day; Thanksgiving; Christmas. ♿
Attendance: 3,935 (accurate)
Membership: Friendship Veterans Fire Engine Association $30.

* **GADSBY'S TAVERN MUSEUM, (M),** 134 N. Royal St., Alexandria, VA 22314-3226. Tel.: 703-838-4242. Fax: 703-838-4270.
E-mail: gadsbys.tavern@alexandriava.gov
Web Site: gadsbystavern.org
Founded: 1976.
Congressional District: 8
Key Personnel: Dir., Gretchen M. Bulova; Asst. Dir., Lizabeth Williams; Cur. Collections, Callie Stapp; Cur. Education, Michele Longo; Museum Shop Mgr., Sue Walker.
Personnel Profile: Full-Time Paid 2; Part-Time Paid 14; Part-Time Volunteers 150; Interns 1.
Governing Authority: municipal. Parent Institution: City of Alexandria, VA. Subsidiary Institution: Office of Historic Alexandria. Tax-exempt: 501(c)(3).
Historic Buildings: c.1785 tavern; 1792 Federal style City Hotel.
Collections: 18th- & early 19th-century furnishings; decorative arts.
Research Fields: late 18th- & early 19th-century furnishings & decorative arts; taverns & travel accommodations, 1770-1810.
Facilities: library; research room; restaurant.
Activities: guided tours; seminars; workshops; concerts; special exhibits & events; private rentals available.
Publications: brochure; history pamphlet; interpretive bulletins; Furnishings Plan Book.
Hours & Admission Prices: April-Oct. Sun.-Mon. 1-5, Tues.-Sat. 10-5; Nov.-March Wed.-Sat. 11-4, Sun. 1-4. Adults $4, children 11-17 $2; discounts to groups, AAM, ICOM & AAA members & Gadsby's Tavern Restaurant patrons; children 10 & under with adult no charge. Closed major holidays.
Attendance: 24,270 (accurate)
Membership: Gadsby's Tavern Museum Society: Student $15; Individual $25; Family $35; Merchant $50; Patron $100; Lifetime $1,000.

GEORGE WASHINGTON MASONIC MEMORIAL, 101 Callahan Dr., Alexandria, VA 22301-2751. Tel.: 703-683-2007. Fax: 703-519-9270.
E-mail: gseghers@gwmemorial.org
Web Site: www.gwmemorial.org
Founded: 1910.
Congressional District: 10
Key Personnel: Exec. Dir., George D. Seghers; Dir. Collections, Mark A. Tabbert; Museum Shop Mgr., Radka Maurova.
Personnel Profile: Full-Time Paid 8; Part-Time Paid 26; Part-Time Volunteers 1; Interns 1.
Governing Authority: nonprofit organization. Tax-exempt: 501(c)(3).
History Museum.
Collections: 18th- & early 19th-century Washington related artifacts; furniture; paintings; books; ceramics; glass; prints & manuscripts; Masonic regalia.
Research Fields: George Washington & his family; Masonic affiliations of Washington & his associates.
Facilities: 20,000-vol library; archive collection; auditorium; observation deck; 36-acre site including Fort Ellsworth.
Activities: guided tours; permanent & temporary exhibitions.
Publications: quarterly newsletter; annual report.
Hours & Admission Prices: Daily 10-4. No charge; donations accepted. Closed New Year's Day; Veterans Day; Memorial Day; Independence Day; Labor Day; Thanksgiving; Christmas. ♿
Attendance: 51,400 (accurate)
Membership: Silver Craftsman $100; Gold Master $250; Platinum Presidential $500; 21st Century $1,000; Millennium Architect $5,000; Millennium Master Architect $10,000; Millennium Builder $25,000; Millennium Master Builder $50,000; Millennium Grand Master Builder $100,000.

GUM SPRINGS MUSEUM & CULTURAL CENTER, 8100 Fordson Rd., Alexandria, VA 22306-3128. Tel.: 703-799-1198.
Web Site: www.gshsfcva.org/gshs05.htm
Key Personnel: Pres., Ron Chase
History Museum.
Collections: history of the Gum Springs community; photographs of Gum Springs' residents & founding families.
Hours & Admission Prices: Mon. & Wed.-Fri. 6pm-8pm, Tues. & Sat. 1-3.

JEROME "BUDDIE" FORD NATURE CENTER, 5750 Sanger Ave., Alexandria, VA 22311-5602. Tel.: 703-838-4829; 746-5559.
E-mail: mark.kelly@alexandriava.gov
Web Site: alexandriava.gov/recreation/info/default.aspx?id=12362
Founded: 1979.
Key Personnel: Dir., Mark S. Kelly.
Personnel Profile: Full-Time Paid 2; Part-Time Paid 3; Part-Time Volunteers 2; Interns 1.
Governing Authority: municipal. Parent Institution: City of Alexandria, Dept. of Recreation & Parks. Tax-exempt.
Nature Center.
Collections: nature displays; aquariums; live animals; prehistoric Native Americans; rocks; minerals; fossils.
Research Fields: natural history.
Facilities: 250-vol. natural history library available for use on premises; nature & conservation center.
Activities: formally organized environmental education programs; interpretive tours of the park; lectures; films; nature day camp.
Publications: monthly calendar of events, Nature News; self-guiding trail brochure; fliers of special events.
Hours & Admission Prices: Wed.-Sat. 10-5, Sun. 1-5. No charge; donations accepted. Closed holidays. ♿
Attendance: 23,500 (accurate)

LEE-FENDALL HOUSE MUSEUM AND GARDEN, 614 Oronoco St., Alexandria, VA 22314-2308. Tel.: 703-548-1789. Fax: 703-548-0931.
E-mail: contact@leefendallhouse.org
Web Site: www.leefendallhouse.org

Founded: 1974.
Congressional District: 8
Key Personnel: Exec. Dir., Tracy Sullivan; Financial Officer, Philip Slattery.
Personnel Profile: Full-Time Paid 1; Part-Time Paid 5; Part-Time Volunteers 25; Interns 2.
Governing Authority: nonprofit organization. Parent Institution: Virginia Trust for Historic Preservation. Tax-exempt: 501(c)(3).
Historic House: 1785 Lee-Fendall House, Lee family home & former home of labor leader John L. Lewis, located in Alexandria's Old Town Historic District.
Collections: Lee family heirlooms; 18th- & 19th-century decorative arts.
Research Fields: Lee family history; Alexandria history; John L. Lewis; social history of the Victorian period.
Facilities: award-winning garden.
Activities: guided tours; education program for children; docent program; intern program; available to rent for meetings or parties; temporary & permanent exhibitions.
Publications: brochure; newsletters.
Hours & Admission Prices: Feb. to mid-Dec. Wed.-Sat. 10-3, Sun. 1-3. Adults $5, students $3; discounts to AAM & ICOM members; children 11 & under no charge. Closed major holidays; private events.
Attendance: 9,500 (accurate)
Membership: Individual $35; Family $50; Contributor $100; Supporter $250; Patron $500; Lee-Fendall Society $1,000.

* **THE LYCEUM, ALEXANDRIA'S HISTORY MUSEUM, (M),** 201 S. Washington St., Alexandria, VA 22314-3697. Tel.: 703-838-4994. Fax: 703-838-4997.
E-mail: lyceum@alexandriava.gov
Web Site: www.alexandriahistory.org
Founded: 1974.
Congressional District: 8
Key Personnel: Dir., James C. Mackay; Asst. Dir., Kristin B. Lloyd; Facilities Coord., Bob Schurk; Visitor Svcs., Pamela Budde.
Personnel Profile: Full-Time Paid 3; Part-Time Paid 10; Part-Time Volunteers 40.
Governing Authority: municipal. Parent Institution: City of Alexandria, VA. Administered by the Office of Historic Alexandria. Tax-exempt: 501(c)(3).
History Museum: housed in 1839 The Lyceum.
Collections: 18th-, 19th- & 20th-century artifacts relating to Alexandria & northern Virginia.
Research Fields: Alexandria history; Lyceum history; Northern Virginia history; Benjamin Hallowell.
Facilities: lecture hall; meeting room. Museum-related items for sale.
Activities: education programs for elementary students; older adult tour programs; special events; changing exhibits; docent programs; concerts; summer group programs; history camp.
Publications: newsletter, The Alexandria Observer; Guide to Historic Alexandria; 3 Centuries of Alexandria Silver.
Hours & Admission Prices: Mon.-Sat. 10-5, Sun. 1-5. Adults $2; discounts to AAM & ICOM members. Closed New Year's Day; Thanksgiving; Christmas. ♿
Attendance: 32,186 (accurate)
Membership: The Lyceum Company: Individual $20; Family & Couple $30; Patron $100; Sponsor $500; Benefactor $1,000.

NATIONAL INVENTORS HALL OF FAME AND MUSEUM, 600 Dulany St., Madison Bldg., W #1C65, Alexandria, VA 22314-5790. Tel.: 571-272-0095. Fax: 571-273-0340.
Web Site: www.uspto.gov
Formerly: U.S. Patent and Trademark Office - Museum
Founded: 1995.
Key Personnel: C.E.O., Richard Maulsby; Cur., Ruth Ann Nyblod.
Personnel Profile: Full-Time Paid 1; Part-Time Volunteers 6; Interns 1.
Governing Authority: federal; nonprofit organization.
U.S. Patent and Trademark Museum.
Collections: history of the patent & trademark systems; patent models of future inventions from 1840-1893; tribute to women & minority inventors.
Activities: guided tours; lectures; temporary exhibitions.
Hours & Admission Prices: Mon.-Fri. 9-5, Sat. 12-5. No charge. Closed federal holidays.
Attendance: 8,000 (estimated)

THE NORTHERN VIRGINIA FINE ARTS ASSOCIATION AT THE ATHENAEUM, 201 Prince St., Alexandria, VA 22314-3313. Tel.: 703-548-0035. Fax: 703-548-0456.
E-mail: admin@nvfaa.org
Web Site: www.nvfaa.org
Founded: 1961.
Congressional District: 8
Key Personnel: Exec. Dir., Leigh Donlan; Pres., Harry E. Mahon.
Personnel Profile: Full-Time Paid 1; Full-Time Volunteers 1; Part-Time Paid 1; Part-Time Volunteers 68; Interns 1.
Governing Authority: nonprofit; a Virginia corp. Tax-exempt: 501(c)(3).
Art Gallery: housed in 1851, restored Greek Revival Building.
Collections: paintings; photographs; prints; sculpture.
Research Fields: American artists and their impact on the times in which they work.
Facilities: lecture area; walled sculpture garden.
Activities: art exhibits; lectures; annual juried show; dance classes for children and adults. Small professional ballet company.
Publications: newsletter; calendar; brochures pertaining to exhibits.
Hours & Admission Prices: Thurs.-Fri. & Sun. 12-4, Sat. 1-4. Lecture & performance fees discounted for members. Closed major holidays.
Attendance: 41,000 (estimated)
Membership: Individual, Student & Senior $25; Family $35; Sponsor $100; Patron $500; Benefactor $1,000.

OFFICE OF HISTORIC ALEXANDRIA, (M), 220 N. Washington St., Alexandria, VA 22314-2521. Tel.: 703-838-4554. Fax: 703-838-6451.
Web Site: oha.alexandriava.gov/contactus
Founded: 1978.
Congressional District: 8
Key Personnel: Dir. Office of Historic Alexandria & Dir. Friendship Firehouse, J. Lance Mallamo; Dir. The Lyceum, James Mackay; Dir. Gadsby's Tavern Museum, Gretchen M. Bulova; Dir. Alexandria Archaeology, Dr. Pamela J. Cressey; Dir. Black History Museum, Louis Hicks.
Personnel Profile: Full-Time Paid 20; Part-Time Paid 70; Part-Time Volunteers 800; Interns 10.
Governing Authority: municipal. Branch Museums: Alexandria Archaeology; Archives & Records Management; Black History Resource Center; Fort Ward Museum; Friendship Firehouse; Gadsby's Tavern Museum; The Lyceum; Torpedo Factory Art Center. Tax-exempt: 501(c)(3).
Historical Agency.
Collections: local history.
Research Fields: urban history.
Activities: guided tours; lectures; annual seminar on historic preservation; docent program; organized educational programs for children, adults & undergraduate or graduate college students affiliated with George Washington University; loan, temporary & traveling exhibitions; volunteer program.
Publications: Historic Alexandria Quarterly.
Hours & Admission Prices: For times & admissions see individual listings. ♿
Attendance: 1,000,000 (estimated)

RAMSAY HOUSE VISITORS CENTER, 221 King St., Alexandria, VA 22314-3209. Tel.: 703-838-4200. Fax: 703-838-4683. TDD: 703-838-6494.
Web Site: visitalexandriava.com/
Founded: 1962.
Congressional District: 8
Key Personnel: Pres. & C.E.O., Stephanie Brown; Mgr., Renee Cardone.
Personnel Profile: Full-Time Paid 9; Part-Time Paid 10; Part-Time Volunteers 3.
Governing Authority: municipal. Administered by the Alexandria Convention & Visitor's Center. Parent Institution: City of Alexandria. Tax-exempt: 501(c)(3).
Historic House & Visitor Center: c.1724 home of William Ramsay, First Lord Mayor, first postmaster.
Collections: local history & culture; period artifacts; photographs.
Facilities: historical material on Alexandria & Scottish events available for research to travel writers & others promoting the city; visitor information; botanical garden. Gift items for sale.
Publications: book, Occupied City: Portrait of Civil War Alexandria, Virginia; calendar of events; restaurant, shops & hotel guides; group tour manual; meeting planner guide.
Hours & Admission Prices: Daily 9-8. No charge; donations accepted. Closed New Year's Day; Thanksgiving; Christmas. ♿
Attendance: 194,256

STABLER-LEADBEATER APOTHECARY MUSEUM, 105-107 S. Fairfax St., Alexandria, VA 22314. Tel.: 703-838-3852. Fax: 703-838-3837.
E-mail: aptohecary.museum@alexandriava.gov
Web Site: www.apothecarymuseum.org
Founded: 1939.
Congressional District: 8
Personnel Profile: Full-Time Paid 1; Part-Time Paid 6; Part-Time Volunteers 12; Interns 1.
Governing Authority: Parent Institution: City of Alexandria. Tax-exempt.
Pharmaceutical Museum: housed in 1796 drugstore building.

Collections: pharmaceutical equipment; apothecary bottles; pharmaceutical artifacts.
Facilities: Museum-related items for sale.
Activities: guided tours; permanent exhibitions.
Hours & Admission Prices: April-Oct. Sun.-Mon. 1-5, Tues.-Sat. 10-5; Nov.-March Wed.-Sat. 11-4, Sun. 1-4. Adults $5, children 5-12 $3; discounts to AAM members; members no charge. Closed Thanksgiving; Christmas.
Attendance: 10,000 (estimated)

TORPEDO FACTORY ART CENTER, 105 N. Union St., Alexandria, VA 22314-3217. Tel.: 703-838-4565, ext. 1. Fax: 888-882-7695.
E-mail: rjohnson@torpedofactory.org
Web Site: www.torpedofactory.org
Founded: 1974.
Congressional District: 8
Key Personnel: Dir. Facilities, Richard Johnson.
Personnel Profile: Full-Time Paid 6; Part-Time Paid 1; Part-Time Volunteers 3; Interns 3.
Art Center: housed in World War II torpedo factory.
Collections: history of the torpedo factory; U.S. Navy loaned torpedoes; art collection; ceramics.
Facilities: educational facilities. Museum-related items for sale.
Activities: special exhibits; artist-led tours; city archaeology program; 82 studios open to public to watch artists at work; art school.
Publications: Torpedo Factory Art Center Visitor's Guide; photo brochure; Art League schedule of classes.
Hours & Admission Prices: Thurs.10-9, Fri.-Wed. 10-6. No charge. Closed New Year's Day; Easter; Independence Day; Thanksgiving; Christmas. ♿
Attendance: 500,000 (accurate)

WOODLAWN, 9000 Richmond Hwy., Alexandria, VA 22309. Mailing Address: P.O. Box 15097, Alexandria, VA 22309. Tel.: 703-780-4000. Fax: 703-780-8509.
E-mail: woodlawn@nthp.org
Web Site: www.woodlawn1805.org
Founded: 1951.
Congressional District: 10
Key Personnel: Chm. Property Council, Cindy Conner; Exec. Dir., Dr. Laurie Ossman; Special Events & Weddings, Stacey Hawkins.
Personnel Profile: Full-Time Paid 3; Part-Time Paid 75; Part-Time Volunteers 50.
Governing Authority: nonprofit organization. Parent Institution: National Trust for Historic Preservation, 1785 Massachusetts Ave., N.W. Washington, DC 20036. Tax-exempt: 501(c)(3).
Historic House: 1800-1805 Woodlawn Home of Maj. Lawrence & Eleanor Parke Custis Lewis, nephew and granddaughter of George & Martha Washington.
Collections: 19th-century decorative arts; furniture; paintings; china; glassware; needlework; textiles; Washington family memorabilia.
Research Fields: Civil War; Quaker community; slavery; archaeology.
Facilities: library; archives; reconstructed gardens; nature trails; select rooms and grounds available for rental. Books & museum-related items for sale.
Activities: special high teas; guided tours; lectures; programs. Museum Sponsors: Washington's Birthday celebration; annual Needlework Exhibit.
Hours & Admission Prices: Thurs.-Sun. 10-4. Adults $8.50; discounts to children 6-18 & military; National Trust members & children under 6 no charge. Closed New Year's Day; Thanksgiving; Christmas.
Attendance: 58,000 (accurate)
Membership: Individual $30; Family $40; Contributing $50; Sustaining $100; Supporting $500; Woodlawn Assembly $1,000.

Altavista

AVOCA MUSEUM, 1514 Main St., Altavista, VA 24517-1161. Tel.: 434-369-1076. Fax: 434-369-1077 (call first).
E-mail: avocamuseums@embarqmail.com
Web Site: www.avocamuseum.org
Founded: 1922.
Congressional District: 5
Key Personnel: Dir., Frank Murray.
Governing Authority: Parent Institution: Avoca Historical Society.
History Museum.
Collections: local history & culture; personal artifacts; historical artifacts; arrowheads; period pieces; photographs.
Hours & Admission Prices: mid-April to Oct. Thurs.-Sat. 11-3, Sun. 1:30-4:30; call to confirm hours. Adults $5, seniors $4, children under 18 $2; children under 6 & members no charge.

Amherst

AMHERST COUNTY MUSEUM & HISTORICAL SOCIETY, 154 S. Main St., Amherst, VA 24521. Mailing Address: P.O. Box 741, Amherst, VA 24521-0741. Tel.: 434-946-9068.
E-mail: achmuseum@aol.com
Web Site: www.amherstcountymuseum.org/
Founded: 1973.
Congressional District: 6
Key Personnel: Pres., Leona Wilkins; Dir., Holly Mills.
Personnel Profile: Full-Time Paid 1; Part-Time Paid 1; Part-Time Volunteers 20.
Governing Authority: nonprofit organization. Tax-exempt.
County History Museum: housed in 1910 Georgian Revival house; reconstructed one-room schoolhouse.
Collections: aspects of former Amherst life-styles; maps & books.
Research Fields: Amherst County; central Virginia; family history & genealogy.
Facilities: 400-vol. library on family histories; Amherst County; Virginia; Civil War; U.S. Census, available for research.
Activities: guided tours; docent program; permanent & temporary exhibitions.
Publications: bimonthly newsletter, Newsletter of ACHM; brochure.
Hours & Admission Prices: Tues.-Sat. 10-12 & 1-5. No charge; donations accepted. Closed major holidays. ♿
Attendance: 1,300 (accurate)
Membership: Student $5; Senior $10; Active & Couple $15; Business $50; Corporate $100.

Appomattox

APPOMATTOX COURT HOUSE NATIONAL HISTORICAL PARK, VA Rte. 24, Appomattox, VA 24522. Mailing Address: P.O. Box 218, Appomattox, VA 24522-0218. Tel.: 434-352-8987, ext. 26. Fax: 434-352-8330.
E-mail: joe_williams@nps.gov
Web Site: www.nps.gov/apco
Founded: 1940.
Congressional District: 5
Key Personnel: Supt., H. Reed Johnson; Historian, Patrick Schroeder; Chief Museum Svcs., Joe Williams.
Personnel Profile: Full-Time Paid 14; Part-Time Volunteers 3.
Governing Authority: federal. Affiliated with the National Park Service, Interior Building, Washington, DC. Tax-exempt.
Historic Village Museum: located on the site where General Lee surrendered to General Grant to end the Civil War.
Collections: furnishings; Civil War objects. Historic Buildings: 1846 The Courthouse; 1848 The McLean House; Meeks General Store; The Woodson Law Office; 1819 Clover Hill Tavern; The County Jail; The Jones Law Office; The Peers House; The Mariah Wright House; The Isbell House.
Research Fields: Civil War.
Facilities: 2,000-vol. library on the Civil War available for use on the premises by appointment; 72-seat auditorium. Civil War publications for sale.
Activities: guided tours; films; formally organized education programs for children; permanent exhibitions. Museum Sponsors: living history program.
Publications: book, Appomattox Court House.
Hours & Admission Prices: Daily 8:30-5. Call for admission prices. Closed New Year's Day; Thanksgiving; Christmas. ♿
Attendance: 200,000 (accurate)

Arlington

ARLINGTON ARTS CENTER, 3550 Wilson Blvd., Arlington, VA 22201-2348. Tel.: 703-248-6800. Fax: 703-248-6849.
E-mail: information@arlingtonartscenter.org
Web Site: www.arlingtonartscenter.org
Founded: 1976.
Congressional District: 10
Key Personnel: Exec. Dir., Claire Huschle; Pres. (V), Martha Foster; Dir. Education, Penelope Nunes; Dir. Exhibitions, Jeffry Cudlin; Cur. Educator, Gerry Rogers.
Personnel Profile: Full-Time Paid 4; Part-Time Paid 1; Part-Time Volunteers 10; Interns 2.
Governing Authority: nonprofit organization. Tax-exempt: 501(c)(3).
Art Center: housed in 1910 Matthew F. Maury School.
Collections: visual arts.
Major Exhibits: Juried Photo Exhibition, 11/20/09-1/16/10; Transhuman Conditions, 1/29/10-4/3/10; Winter/Spring Solos, 4/16/10-6/5/10; Comic Art Show, 6/18/10-8/21/10; Fall Solos, 9/10/10-11/6/10; Juried Photo Show, 11/19/10-1/15/11.
Facilities: 1,550 sq. ft. exhibit space; program & education room; one acre outdoor park.

Activities: lectures; panel discussions; art classes for children & adulst; solo & group, juried & curated exhibitions; workshops; resident artist program.
Publications: newsletter, Programs; exhibition announcements & checklists; occasional catalogs; brochures.
Hours & Admission Prices: Tues.-Sat. 11-5. No charge; donations accepted. ♿
Attendance: 30,000 (estimated)
Membership: Student, Senior Citizen, & Artist $35; Individual $50; Family $60; Studio Circle $100; Curator's Circle $250; Director's Circle $500; Collector's Circle $1,000; Gallerist's Circle $2,000; Patron's Circle $5,000; Benefactor's Circle $10,000.

ARLINGTON HISTORICAL SOCIETY, (M), 1805 S. Arlington Ridge Rd., Arlington, VA 22202-1628. Mailing Address: P.O. Box 100402, Arlington, VA 22210-3402. Tel.: 703-892-4204.
E-mail: info@arlingtonhistoricalsociety.org
Web Site: www.arlingtonhistoricalsociety.org
Founded: 1956.
Congressional District: 8
Key Personnel: Pres. (V), Jennifer Sale Crane; Acquisitions & Collections Mgmt., Linda Y. Gouaze.
Personnel Profile: Part-Time Volunteers 35.
Governing Authority: Subsidiary Institution: Darlington Historical Museum, 1805 S. Arlington Ridge Rd., Arlington, VA 22202; Ball-Sellers House, 5620 S. Third St., Arlington, VA 22204. Tax-exempt.
Local History Museum.
Collections: local history artifacts from English exploration period to present. Historic Buildings: Hume School built in 1891; Ball-Sellers log cabin built mid-18th century.
Research Fields: local Arlington history.
Facilities: Publications for sale.
Activities: five Society meetings annually; guest lecturers; Arlington Reunion - 4 sessions per season: group oral history - neighborhood area discussions; permanent & temporary exhibitions; annual banquet; special events; receptions for local & regional authors. Museum Sponsors: County Fair booth.
Publications: annual, The Arlington Historical Magazine; quarterly newsletter; Arlington County, Virginia: A History; Washington & Old Dominion Railroad (reprint); periodic leaflets for society & museum collections.
Hours & Admission Prices: Museum: Sat.-Sun. 1-4; other times by appointment. Ball-Sellers: April-Oct. 1-4. No charge; donations accepted.
Attendance: 1,000 (estimated)
Membership: Adult $25; Family $30; Sponsor $50; Donor $100; Life $400.

ARLINGTON HOUSE, THE ROBERT E. LEE MEMORIAL, Arlington National Cemetery, Arlington, VA 22211. Mailing Address: National Park Service-George Washington Memorial Pkwy., Turkey Run Park, McLean, VA 22101. Tel.: 703-235-1530. Fax: 703-235-1546.
E-mail: gwmp-arlingtonhouse@nps.gov
Web Site: www.nps.gov/arho
Founded: 1925.
Congressional District: 2
Key Personnel: Rgnl. Dir., Margaret O'Dell; Acting Cur., Maria Capozzi; Field Park Supt., Dottie Marshall; Site Mgr., Kendell Thompson; Volunteer Coord., Delphine Gross.
Personnel Profile: Full-Time Paid 11; Part-Time Paid 10; Part-Time Volunteers 15.
Governing Authority: federal. Parent Institution: National Park Service, 18th between D & C, Washington, DC 20240. Subsidiary Institution: Dept. of Interior. Tax-exempt.
Historic House Museum: residence of Gen. Robert E. Lee, built by George Washington Parke Custis, foster son of George Washington, restored to 1861 appearance as a national memorial to General Lee.
Collections: decorative arts; archives; music; manuscripts; 18th & 19th-century furnishings; furnishings & memorabilia of the Robert E. Lee & G.W.P. Custis families; museum exhibit on R.E. Lee's life with artifacts. Historic Buildings: house & two slave quarters.
Research Fields: life & activities of R.E. Lee & family members; furnishings; gardens; Arlington House structural history & restoration; slave life.
Facilities: 600-vol. library of history related to R.E. Lee & George Washington Parke Custis available for use by appointment with curator. Books, slides & postcards for sale.
Activities: self-guided & guided tours; formally organized education programs for grades K-12 by appointment only; volunteer program; permanent & temporary exhibitions; applied history internship program; flower garden.
Publications: pamphlet, Arlington House; historic handbook, Arlington House.
Hours & Admission Prices: By appointment during renovations. ♿
Attendance: 500,000 (accurate)

BLUEMONT HISTORICAL RAILROAD JUNCTION, Bluemont Junction Park, 601 N. Manchester St., Arlington, VA 22203-1081. Tel.: 703-525-0294.
Web Site: geocities.com/yosemite/trails/9401/railroad.html#cabooses
Founded: 1992.
Congressional District: 8
Key Personnel: Ranger, Sedgewick Moss; Ranger Coord., Lynne Everly.
Personnel Profile: Part-Time Paid 1; Part-Time Volunteers 3.
Governing Authority: county government; nonprofit. Parent Institution: Arlington County Dept. of Parks & Recreation. Tax-exempt: 170(b)(1)(A).
Transportation Museum: housed in former Southern Railway Caboose X-441, built in 1972, on the W&OD trail.
Collections: history of W&OD, RF&P and trolley line area communities; photographs & artifacts of local rail history.
Activities: guided tours.
Hours & Admission Prices: May-Sept. Sat. & holidays 10-6, Sun. 1-5. No charge; donations accepted.
Attendance: 5,000 (estimated)

DEA MUSEUM & VISITORS CENTER, (M), 700 Army Navy Dr., Arlington, VA 22202-4222. Tel.: 202-307-3463. Fax: 202-307-8956.
Web Site: www.deamuseum.org
Founded: 1999.
Key Personnel: Dir., Sean T. Fearns; Pres. (V), William Alden; Museum Shop Mgr., Jim Lumsden.
Personnel Profile: Full-Time Paid 4; Part-Time Paid 2; Part-Time Volunteers 12; Interns 2.
Governing Authority: Parent Institution: Drug Enforcement Administration (DEA). Subsidiary Institution: DEA Educational Foundation. Tax-exempt.
History Museum.
Collections: history of drug, drug addiction & drug enforcement in the U.S.
Activities: school & group programs; outreach programs.
Hours & Admission Prices: Tues.-Fri. 10-4; groups by appointment. No charge. ♿

GULF BRANCH NATURE CENTER, 3608 N. Military Rd., Arlington, VA 22207-4830. Tel.: 703-228-3403.
Web Site: www.arlingtonva.us
Key Personnel: Dir., Denise Chauvette
Nature Center.
Collections: hands-on exhibits; restored log cabin; live animals.
Facilities: 20-seat classroom.
Activities: environmental education programs.
Hours & Admission Prices: Sun. 1-5, Wed.-Sat. 10-5. No charge.

LONG BRANCH NATURE CENTER, 625 S. Carlin Springs Rd., Arlington, VA 22204-1000. Tel.: 703-228-6535. Fax: 703-845-2654.
E-mail: aabugattas@arlingtonva.us
Key Personnel: Acting Dir., Alonso Abugattas
Nature Center.
Collections: native plants; gardens; live animals.
Facilities: 17 acres; 40-seat classroom; gardens; nature center; trails; amphitheater.
Hours & Admission Prices: Sun. 1-5, Tues.-Sat. 10-5. No charge. ♿

THE NATURE CONSERVANCY, 4245 N. Fairfax Dr., Ste. 100, Arlington, VA 22203-1606. Tel.: 703-841-5300. Fax: 703-841-1283.
Web Site: www.nature.org
Founded: 1951.
Key Personnel: Pres. & C.E.O., Mark R. Tercek; Coord., Maria Fisher.
Governing Authority: nonprofit organization. Tax-exempt: 501(c)(3).
Conservation Area: educational & passive recreational opportunities on largest private nature preserve system in country.
Collections: national data bank on rare & endangered species.
Research Fields: rare & endangered plant & animal species.
Facilities: nature conservation center.
Activities: annual events.
Publications: magazine, Nature Conservancy.
Hours & Admission Prices: Mon.-Fri. 9-5. No charge; donations accepted. Closed federal holidays.
Attendance: 200,500 (estimated)
Membership: Individual $25-$1,000; Corporate $1,000.

Ashland

FLIPPO GALLERY, Randolph-Macon College, Pace-Armistead Hall, 211 N. Center St., Ashland, VA 23005. Tel.: 804-752-7200.
Key Personnel: Cur., Katie Shaw
Art Gallery: housed in Pace-Armistead Hall c.1876, listed on the National Register of Historic Places.

Collections: student & faculty artwork; exhibits by national & state artists.
Hours & Admission Prices: Mon.-Fri. 10-4, Sat.-Sun. by appointment.

Bastian

WOLF CREEK INDIAN VILLAGE & MUSEUM, (M), 6394 N. Scenic Hwy., Bastian, VA 24314-5202. Tel.: 276-688-3438. Fax: 276-688-2496.
E-mail: info@indianvillage.org
Web Site: indianvillage.org
Founded: 1996.
Congressional District: 9
Key Personnel: Co Dir. WCIV, Penny Plummer; Co Dir. WCIV, Denise A. Smith; Pres. EDA (V), David Dillow.
Personnel Profile: Full-Time Paid 4; Part-Time Paid 4; Part-Time Volunteers 12.
Governing Authority: Parent Institution: Economic Development Authority. Tax-exempt.
American Indian History Museum.
Collections: Eastern Woodland Indian history; personal artifacts.
Major Exhibits: Rebirth of the Ancient Village: Rebuilding Wolf Creek Indian Village, 1/10-12/10.
Research Fields: eastern Woodland Indians; Bland County VA history.
Facilities: archives; nature trails; picnic area. Museum-related items for sale.
Activities: tours; special events; demonstrations; local history programs.
Publications: Wolf Creek Times.
Hours & Admission Prices: Tues.-Sat. 10-5. Adults $10, children 5-16 $6; discounts to AAA, AAM, & ICOM members & groups of 10 or more; children under 5 no charge. Closed Thanksgiving; Christmas Eve & Day. ♿
Attendance: 30,000 (estimated)
Membership: Annual $10; Lifetime $150.

Beaverdam

SCOTCHTOWN, 16120 Chiswell Lane, Beaverdam, VA 23015-1726. Tel.: 804-227-3500. Fax: 804-227-3559.
E-mail: scotchtown@apva.org
Web Site: www.apva.org/scotchtown
Founded: 1958.
Congressional District: 1
Key Personnel: Site Mgr., Ann Reid.
Personnel Profile: Part-Time Paid 11; Part-Time Volunteers 8; Interns 1.
Governing Authority: nonprofit organization. Parent Institution: The Association for the Preservation of Virginia Antiquities, 2300 E. Grace St., Richmond, VA 23223. Tax-exempt.
Historic House Museum: housed in home of Patrick Henry 1771-1778; childhood home of Dolly Madison.
Collections: 18th-century furnishings; Henry Map table.
Research Fields: Henry Patrick.
Facilities: Stationery, handmade & museum-related items for sale.
Activities: guided tours.
Hours & Admission Prices: March-Dec. Fri.-Sat. 10-5, Sun. 1-5; other times by appointment. Adults $8, seniors $6, students $4; discount to groups & AAA members. Closed Easter; Christmas Eve & Day.
Attendance: 4,500 (estimated)
Membership: Adults $20; Family $30.

Bedford

BEDFORD MUSEUM AND GENEALOGICAL LIBRARY, (M), 201 E. Main St., Bedford, VA 24523-2012. Tel.: 540-586-4520.
E-mail: bccm-info@bedfordvamuseum.org
Web Site: www.bedfordvamuseum.org
Formerly: Bedford City/County Museum
Founded: 1932.
Congressional District: 5
Key Personnel: Dir., Doug Cooper; Chm. (V) & Cur., Annie Pollard; Aide, Ruth Farrar; Museum Shop Mgr., Shirley Wheeler.
Personnel Profile: Part-Time Paid 4; Part-Time Volunteers 75.
Governing Authority: nonprofit organization. Tax-exempt: 501(c)(3).
History Museum & Historic Building: c.1895 three-story Masonic building.
Collections: Indian relics; tools & implements; Revolutionary War artifacts; Civil War artifacts; clothing; military uniforms; household articles; furniture; linens; photographs; 19th-century general store.
Major Exhibits: History of Radio, 1/10-12/10.
Research Fields: Indian life; Revolutionary War; Civil War; genealogy records of local families; local history.
Facilities: 1,000-vol. library pertaining to genealogy & local history.
Activities: guided tours; lectures; films; organized education programs for adults; participatory, loan & temporary exhibitions; school loan service; genealogy classes.
Publications: newsletter, Museum Report.
Hours & Admission Prices: June-Sept. Mon.-Sat. 10-5. No charge; donations accepted. ♿
Attendance: 8,725 (accurate)
Membership: Donor $10; Annual Patron $25; Sustaining Patron $50; Annual Patron $100; Building Facility Patron $500; Benefactor $1,000.

PEAKS OF OTTER VISITOR CENTER, 85919 Blue Ridge Pkwy., Bedford, VA 24523-3795. Tel.: 540-586-4357. Fax: 540-586-9445.
Web Site: www.nps.gov/blri
Key Personnel: District Ranger, Paulette Mullinox; Interpretive Specialist, Randy Sutton; Park Ranger, Bobby Miller.
Governing Authority: federal. Affiliated with National Park Service, Blue Ridge Pkwy., 700 Northwestern Bank Bldg., Asheville, NC. 28807. Tax-exempt.
Natural History & Cultural Museum.
Collections: Indian era rural farm life; 1920s cultural & natural history items & artifacts.
Facilities: visitors center.
Activities: guided walks & tours; evening programs; living history demonstrations.
Hours & Admission Prices: late April to May Fri.-Tues. 9-5; Memorial Day to Oct. daily 9-5. No charge.

Berryville

CLARKE COUNTY HISTORICAL ASSOCIATION, INC., 32 E. Main St., Berryville, VA 22611-1338. Mailing Address: P.O. Box 306, Berryville, VA 22611-0306. Tel.: 540-955-2600. Fax: 540-955-0285.
E-mail: ccha@visuallink.com
Web Site: www.clarkehistory.org
Founded: 1939.
Congressional District: 7
Key Personnel: Pres. (V), Roger Chavez; Exec. Dir., Jennifer Lee; Treas., Susi Bailey; Archivist, Mary T. Morris.
Personnel Profile: Full-Time Paid 2; Part-Time Paid 1; Part-Time Volunteers 60.
Governing Authority: society. Branch Museum: Burwell-Morgan Mill. Tax-exempt: 501(c)(3).
Historical Society Museum: housed in 19th century home.
Collections: Clarke Co. archives; photographs; portrait photos; early Fairfax land grants; newspapers; Civil War artifacts; costumes. Historic Building: 1785 Burwell-Morgan Mill.
Research Fields: lands & families, 1738-present.
Facilities: 1,000-vol. library of local history books, available for use by public; 1,000 sq. ft. exhibit space. Society publications for sale.
Activities: organized educational programs; temporary exhibitions.
Publications: biannual historical journal, Clarke Co. Proceedings; quarterly newsletter.
Hours & Admission Prices: Museum: call for hours. Archives: Mon.-Fri. 10-5. Museum: no charge; donations accepted. Archives: Adults $5; members & locals no charge. Closed Fri. before Christmas to Jan. 2. ♿
Attendance: 500 (estimated)
Membership: Individual $25; Family $50; Life $500.

Big Stone Gap

HARRY W. MEADOR, JR. COAL MUSEUM, East Third and Shawnee Ave., Big Stone Gap, VA 24219. Mailing Address: 505 E. 5th St. S., Big Stone Gap, VA 24219-3050. Tel.: 276-523-9209.
Web Site: www.bigstonegap.org/attract/coal.htm
Coal Mining Museum.
Collections: exhibits & objects collected by the late Harry W. Meador.
Hours & Admission Prices: Wed.-Sat. 10-5, Sun. 1-5; other times by appointment. No charge.

SOUTHWEST VIRGINIA MUSEUM HISTORICAL STATE PARK, 10 W. 1st St. N., Big Stone Gap, VA 24219-2528. Mailing Address: Box 742, Big Stone Gap, VA 24219-0742. Tel.: 276-523-1322. Fax: 276-523-6616.
E-mail: swvamuseum@dcr.state.va.us
Web Site: www.dcr.state.va.us/parks/swvamus.htm
Founded: 1948.
Congressional District: 9
Key Personnel: Dir., Sharon B. Ewing.
Personnel Profile: Full-Time Paid 3; Part-Time Paid 11; Part-Time Volunteers 7.
Governing Authority: state. Parent Institution: Commonwealth of Virginia. Subsidiary Institution: Div. of State Parks. Tax-exempt.
State Park & Historic House: 1888-95 Ayers Mansion.
Collections: early history & pioneer period of Southwest Virginia through the industrial development, coal boom & preceding years; Victorian furnishings.

Facilities: rental facilities. Museum-related items for sale.
Activities: guided tours with prior reservations; permanent & temporary exhibitions; interpretive programs; children's & school programs; monthly programs; workshops.
Publications: General Museum; General State Park; brochures, Museum Self Guided Grounds, Victorian Parlor.
Hours & Admission Prices: March-May & Sept.-Dec. Tues.-Thurs. 10-4, Fri. 9-4, Sat. 10-5, Sun. 1-5; Memorial Day-Labor Day Mon.-Thurs. 10-4, Fri. 9-4, Sat. 10-5, Sun. 1-5. Adults $3, children $2; discounts to groups, AAM & ICOM members. Closed Thanksgiving; Christmas.
Attendance: 19,984 (accurate)
Membership: Child $3; Adult $5; Family $15.

Blacksburg

HISTORIC SMITHFIELD, 1000 Smithfield Plantation Rd., Blacksburg, VA 24060. Tel.: 540-231-3947. Fax: 540-231-3006.
E-mail: info@smithfieldplantation.org
Web Site: smithfieldplantation.org
Formerly: Smithfield Plantation
Founded: 1964.
Congressional District: 9
Key Personnel: Dir. Bd., Carol McAlister; Administrative Dir., Lori Tolliver-Jones; Museum Shop Mgr., Diane Hoover.
Personnel Profile: Full-Time Paid 2; Part-Time Paid 4; Part-Time Volunteers 120; Interns 3.
Governing Authority: society; nonprofit. Parent Institution: Association for the Preservation of Virginia Antiquities, 204 W. Franklin St., Richmond, VA 23220. Tax-exempt.
Historic House: 1774 Smithfield Plantation built by Revolutionary War hero, William Preston & later the home of three Virginia Governors.
Collections: furnishings from the Colonial & Federal periods. Historic Building: 1774 house.
Research Fields: local history; slave life at Smithfield; plantation crops.
Facilities: historic gardens; orchard.
Activities: children's activities; junior interpreter program; adult group tours; school tours; guest speakers; children's summer history camps; monthly guild meetings. Museum Sponsors: Opening Day; Juneteenth - A Commemoration of Slaves Lives at Smithfield in June; Independence Day Celebration; Holidays at Smithfield in December.
Publications: newsletter; Smithfield Review.
Hours & Admission Prices: April to 1st weekend in Dec. Mon.-Tues. & Thurs.-Sat. 10-5, Sun. 1-5; special tours by appointment. Adults $7, students $4, children 5-11 $3; discounts to Time Traveler (VA state program), AAA members & groups; APVA members no charge.
Attendance: 5,500 (estimated)
Membership: Association for the Preservation of Virginia Antiquities: Individual $40; Mr. & Mrs. $50; Family $60.

MUSEUM OF GEOSCIENCES, Virginia Tech MC0420, 2062 Derring Hall, Blacksburg, VA 24061-0001. Tel.: 540-231-6894. Fax: 540-231-3386.
E-mail: llyn@vt.edu
Web Site: www.outreach.geos.vt.edu/museum
Formerly: Museum of the Geological Sciences
Founded: 1969.
Congressional District: 9
Key Personnel: Coord., Llyn Sharp.
Personnel Profile: Part-Time Paid 3; Part-Time Volunteers 3; Interns 1.
Governing Authority: university. Parent Institution: Dept. of Geosciences, Virginia Tech. Tax-exempt.
Geology & Mineralogy Museum.
Collections: Dr. C.A. Michael gems & minerals; Dr. A.A. Kirk cut gemstones; paleontology; D. Murray minerals from Australia & Tsumeb Namibia; J. Hearn collection.
Research Fields: minerals & crystallography.
Facilities: 30,000-vol. library of geology books, available for inter-library loan; laboratory; classrooms.
Activities: tours; lectures; permanent & temporary exhibits; teacher workshops; educational material loans.
Hours & Admission Prices: Mon.-Fri. 8-5; call to confirm. No charge; donations accepted. Closed New Year's Eve & Day; Independence Day; Thanksgiving; Christmas Eve & Day; university breaks. ♿
Attendance: 6,000 (accurate)

PERSPECTIVE GALLERY, Virginia Technological Institute, 225 Squires Student Center, Blacksburg, VA 24061-0001. Tel.: 540-231-4053. Fax: 540-231-5430.
E-mail: tartaro@vt.edu
Web Site: www.uusa.vt.edu/artgallery/
Key Personnel: Art Dir., Mary Tartaro
Art Gallery.
Collections: works by local, regional, national & international artists.
Hours & Admission Prices: Tues.-Thurs. 10-5, Fri. 12-7, Sat. 12-5. No charge.

Boyce

ORLAND E. WHITE ARBORETUM, Blandy Experimental Farm, 400 Blandy Farm Lane, Boyce, VA 22620-2117. Tel.: 540-837-1758. Fax: 540-837-1523.
E-mail: blandy@virginia.edu
Web Site: www.virginia.edu/~blandy
Founded: 1927.
Congressional District: 7
Key Personnel: Dir., Dr. David E. Carr; Cur., Dr. T'ai H. Roulston; Dir., Foundation of State Arboretum, Vic Arthur; Pres., Foundation of State Arboretum, Thomas Dunning; Arborist, Robert D. Arnold; Public Rels. Coord., Tim Farmer; Dir. Education, Candace Lutzow-Felling; Dir. Pub. Programs, Dr. Steven B. Carroll; Landscape Architect, Nancy Takahashi; Bldg. Supt., Dennis Heflin.
Personnel Profile: Full-Time Paid 19; Part-Time Paid 8; Part-Time Volunteers 180; Interns 1.
Governing Authority: university. Parent Institution: University of Virginia, Charlottesville. Subsidiary Institution: Blandy Experimental Farm. Tax-exempt.
Arboretum.
Collections: Buxus types; Quercus species & hybrids; Pinus species conifers of Northern hemisphere; 1,000 species of plants.
Research Fields: environmental sciences; biology; pollination; plant ecology & conservation; plant-herbivore interactions.
Facilities: library; meeting facilities for small groups; greenhouses; laboratories; herbarium.
Activities: adult education classes; accredited university classes; horticultural fair; tours; lectures; educational programs for school groups.
Publications: newsletter, Arbor-Vitae; Guide to the Natural Forms of Boxwood; calendar, Education Programs/Spring & Fall; brochure; trail guides
Hours & Admission Prices: Daily sunrise-sunset; tours by appointment. Office: Mon.-Fri. 9-4. No charge; donations accepted.
Attendance: 100,000 (estimated)
Membership: Individual $35; Family, Nonprofit & Business $50; Sustainer $150; Benefactor $300; Individual Life $600; Dual & Spousal Life $1,000; Corporate $1,500.

Bridgewater

REUEL B. PRITCHETT MUSEUM, (M), Bridgewater College, 402 E. College St., Bridgewater, VA 22812. Mailing Address: 402 E. College St., Bridgewater, VA 22812-1511. Tel.: 540-828-5462 & 5457. Fax: 540-828-5482.
E-mail: dharter@bridgewater.edu
Web Site: www.bridgewater.edu
Founded: 1954.
Congressional District: 9
Key Personnel: Dir. Library & Museum, Andrew Pearson; Cur., Dale Harter.
Personnel Profile: Full-Time Paid 1.
Governing Authority: board of trustees. Parent Institution: Bridgewater College, Bridgewater, VA 22812. Tax-exempt: 501(c)(3).
College Museum.
Collections: rare books & Bibles; coin & currency; bottles & jugs; weaving looms, spinning wheels & accessories; tools; folk items from the Philippines, India, Africa & China; guns; glass, pottery & chinaware.
Major Exhibits: Musical Heritage of Bridgewater College, 11/09-5/10.
Activities: guided tours; formally organized education programs for undergraduate college students affiliated with Bridgewater College & for area middle, high, public & private school students; permanent exhibits.
Hours & Admission Prices: Mon.-Fri. 1-4:30; other times by appointment. No charge; donations accepted. Closed holidays. ♿
Attendance: 500 (estimated)

Brookneal

RED HILL-PATRICK HENRY NATIONAL MEMORIAL, 1250 Red Hill Rd., Brookneal, VA 24528-3302. Tel.: 434-376-2044. Fax: 434-376-2647.
E-mail: redhill@redhill.org
Web Site: www.redhill.org
Founded: 1944.
Congressional District: 5
Key Personnel: Acting Exec. Vice Pres., Karen Gorham; Pres. (V), Gene Dixon, Jr.; Admin., Karen Gorham.
Personnel Profile: Full-Time Paid 5; Full-Time Volunteers 2; Part-Time Paid 5; Part-Time Volunteers 45.
Governing Authority: private. Patrick Henry Memorial Foundation, Inc. Tax-exempt.

Historic Site: Last home & burial place of Patrick Henry.
Collections: Rothermel painting of Patrick Henry's Stamp Act speech; 18th century furnishings; Patrick Henry artifacts & furniture; jewelry & musical instruments of Patrick Henry & his family; 18th & 19th-century law books, paintings & engravings; land grants.
Research Fields: Red Hill plantation; career & works of Patrick Henry; genealogy of Patrick Henry & his descendants.
Facilities: library containing law books of Patrick Henry & William Wirt Henry and files of Dr. Robert D. Meade, the author of 2 volumes of Patrick Henry history, available for use on premises; reading room; picnic area. Museum-related items for sale.
Activities: guided tours; temporary & permanent exhibitions; videotape showings; slide lectures; educational tours; living history demonstrations. Museum Sponsors: July 4th celebration; annual Christmas by Candlelight program; Governor Henry Lecture Series.
Publications: quarterly newsletter, Elvira Henry's Cooking Book; Proceedings of the Virginia Convention of 1775; Patrick Henry, The Last Years 1789-1799; Patrick Henry: Economic, Domestic and Political Life in Eighteenth Century Virginia; Patrick Henry: Prophet of the Revolution; Patrick Henry's Thoughts on Life, Liberty (or Death) and the Pursuit of Happiness; Patrick Henry Essays; Patrick Henry and Thomas Jefferson; Patrick Henry's Virginia.
Hours & Admission Prices: April-Oct. Mon.-Sat. 9-5, Sun. 1-5; Nov.-March Tues.-Sat. 9-4, Sun. 1-4, Mon. by appointment. Adults $6, students $2; discounts to groups & VA Assoc. members. Closed New Year's Day; Thanksgiving; Christmas. ♿
Attendance: 9,289 (accurate)
Membership: Student & Teacher $10; Individual $25; Family $35; Burgess $100; Orator $250; Governor $500; Patriot $1,000.

Cape Charles

CAPE CHARLES MUSEUM AND WELCOME CENTER, 814 Randolph Ave., Cape Charles, VA 23310. Mailing Address: The Cape Charles Historical Society, P.O. Box 11, Cape Charles, VA 23310-0011. Tel.: 757-331-1008.
Founded: 1986.
Congressional District: 2
Key Personnel: Chm. & Pres. (V), Marion Naar; Museum Shop Mgr., Linda Schulz.
Personnel Profile: Part-Time Paid 2; Part-Time Volunteers 10.
Governing Authority: Tax-exempt.
History Museum.
Collections: Cape Charles history; Native American artifacts; photographs; railroad & steamer artifacts; 18th century Arlington mansion artifacts; Chesapeake Bay impact crater, bridge-tunnel.
Facilities: research archives. Eastern Shore history, travel books & postcards for sale.
Activities: fundraisers. Museum Sponsors: Spring Shrimp Boil; Fall Oyster Roast & Live Band.
Hours & Admission Prices: April-Nov. Mon.-Fri. 10-2, Sat. 10-5, Sun. 1-5. No charge; donations accepted. ♿
Attendance: 2,358 (accurate)
Membership: Single $20; Household $25; Business $35.

Chantilly

WALNEY VISITOR CENTER-AT ELLANOR C. LAWRENCE PARK, 5040 Walney Rd., Chantilly, VA 20151-2306. Tel.: 703-631-0013. Fax: 703-631-8319.
Web Site: www.fairfaxcounty.gov/parks
Founded: 1971.
Congressional District: 10
Key Personnel: Park Mgr. & Naturalist, Leon Nawojchik; Asst. Park Mgr. & Historian, John Shafer.
Personnel Profile: Full-Time Paid 5; Part-Time Paid 8; Part-Time Volunteers 75; Interns 1.
Governing Authority: county; nonprofit. Parent Institution: Fairfax County Park Authority. Tax-exempt.
Visitor Center: housed in 1780 structure, located on 650-acre park.
Collections: 19th-century local history & natural history; stone barn & ice house ruins; reconstructed smoke house.
Research Fields: local history; natural & cultural resource inventory; cultural & natural history.
Facilities: classroom; 19th-century gristmill available for rental; demonstration agricultural field with gardens. Books, clay pipes & native-oriented objects for sale.
Activities: guided tours; lectures; films; concerts; organized interpretive programs for children & adults; docent program; temporary exhibitions of your own collections; live animal displays.
Publications: brochures; newsletters; quarterly calendar of events.
Hours & Admission Prices: Jan.-Feb. Wed.-Mon. 12-5; March-Dec. Mon. & Wed.-Fri. 9-5, Sat.-Sun. 12-5. No charge; donations accepted. Closed New Year's Day; Thanksgiving; Christmas. ♿
Attendance: 34,550 (accurate)

Charles City

BERKELEY PLANTATION, 12602 Harrison Landing Rd., Charles City, VA 23030-3339. Tel.: 804-829-6018; 888-466-6018. Fax: 804-829-6757.
Web Site: www.berkeleyplantation.com
Founded: 1619.
Congressional District: 1
Key Personnel: Owner & Operator, Malcolm E. Jamieson.
Personnel Profile: Full-Time Paid 2; Part-Time Paid 10.
Governing Authority: individual operation.
Historic House: 1726 Berkeley Plantation.
Collections: period artifacts; Indian relics; Civil War relics.
Facilities: Brass, glass, pottery, china, relics, wood articles for sale.
Activities: guided tours; slide presentation; gardens.
Publications: Berkeley Brochure, The Army of the Potomac at Berkeley Plantation.
Hours & Admission Prices: Tours daily 9-5. Adults $11, students 13-16 $7.50, children 6-12 $6; discounts to groups, senior citizens, military & AAA members. Closed Thanksgiving; Christmas.

NORTH BEND PLANTATION, 12200 Weyanoke Rd., Charles City, VA 23030. Tel.: 804-829-5176.
Historic House Museum: built in 1801. Listed on the National Register of Historic Places.
Collections: local history & culture; period furnishings; personal artifacts; photographs. Historic Buildings: 1819 smoke house; 1819 daily house; 1819 ice house.
Hours & Admission Prices: Daily 9-5.

SHERWOOD FOREST PLANTATION, (M), 14501 John Tyler Memorial Hwy., Charles City, VA 23030. Mailing Address: P.O. Box 8, Charles City, VA 23030-0008. Tel.: 804-829-5377. Fax: 804-829-2947.
E-mail: ktyler@sherwoodforest.org
Web Site: www.sherwoodforest.org
Founded: 1975.
Key Personnel: Dir., Harrison R. Tyler; Pres. (V), Frances P.B. Tyler
Historic House: c.1730, home of Pres. John Tyler.
Collections: original furniture, silver, china of Pres. Tyler; George Moreland; G.P.A. Healy, Scarboro, Edouart & Sully paintings; original furniture used in the White House; Virginia & Southern furniture; 19th century Oriental rug collection; milk house; smoke house; garden house; slave house; 19th century Overseer's House; 1660-1848 kitchen, laundry & wine house; longest frame house in U.S. (300 ft.); 80 trees (36 varieties not indigenous to America), including many more than 250 years old; 25 acres of landscaped lawn & trees; 11 original plantation buildings (1660-1846).
Research Fields: history of John Tyler & authentication of his belongings; history of Charles City County, VA.
Facilities: meeting room; private rentals available. Museum-related items for sale.
Activities: Annual Events: birthday celebration for President John Tyler in March; Historic Garden Week in April; Christmas activities.
Publications: James River Plantation Cookbook; Virginia Presidential Homes Cookbook.
Hours & Admission Prices: Grounds: daily 9-5. Adults $10; children under 15 no charge. House Tours: by appointment. Adults $35. Closed Thanksgiving; Christmas. ♿
Attendance: 5,000 (estimated)

SHIRLEY PLANTATION, 501 Shirley Plantation Rd., Charles City, VA 23030-2907. Tel.: 804-829-5121. Fax: 804-829-6322.
E-mail: info@shirleyplantation.com
Web Site: www.shirleyplantation.com
Founded: 1952.
Congressional District: 3
Key Personnel: Dir., Janet Appel.
Personnel Profile: Full-Time Paid 3; Part-Time Paid 14.
Governing Authority: individual operation.
Historic Site: Virginia's first plantation, 1613.
Collections: 17th- to 19th-century furniture includes items by craftsmen Robert Walker & John Seldon; 17th- to 18th-century portraits by Sir Godfrey Kneller, Charles Bridges & John Wollaston; 18th-century crested English silver collection; Queen Anne style house c.1723 with carved woodwork & three story square flying staircase; kitchen; laundry; tool barn; icehouse; stable; smoke house; pump house; root cellar; corn crib; dovecote; Historic House: Great House; 6 generations of family portraits.

Research Fields: history of the Hill & Carter families; 18th-century Queen Anne architecture; southern agriculture (1613-present); collection of Carter papers including rare books, letters, journals, pictures, drawings housed in the Rockefeller Library in Colonial Williamsburg, Virginia; black history; Civil War; Robert E. Lee.
Facilities: Museum-related items for sale.
Activities: guided tours; hands-on activities. Annual Events: Historic Garden Week in April; The Christmas activities.
Hours & Admission Prices: Daily 9-5. Adults $11, senior 60 & over $10, youth 6-18 $7.50; discounts to AAA, groups of 20 or more, & military w/ID; children under 6 no charge. Closed Thanksgiving; Christmas.
Attendance: 50,000 (accurate)

Charlottesville

ALBEMARLE CHARLOTTESVILLE HISTORICAL SOCIETY, McIntire Bldg., 200 Second St., NE, Charlottesville, VA 22902-5245. Tel.: 434-296-1492. Fax: 434-296-4576.
E-mail: info@albemarlehistory.org
Web Site: albemarlehistory.org
Formerly: The Albemarle County Historical Society
Founded: 1940.
Key Personnel: Pres., Steven G. Meeks; Librarian, Margaret M. O'Bryant; Communications & Collections Mgr., Keri Matthews.
Governing Authority: Tax-exempt: 501(c)(3).
Historical Society Museum.
Collections: over 1,500 artifacts pertaining to Charlottesville & Albemarle County; photographs; manuscripts; books.
Research Fields: central Virginia.
Facilities: research library.
Activities: walking tours; spirit walk; quarterly meetings.
Publications: annual magazine, Albemarle County History; quarterly bulletin.
Hours & Admission Prices: Library: Mon.-Fri. 9-5, Sat. 10-1. No charge; donations accepted. Closed holidays. ♿
Membership: Single $35; Family $50.

ASH LAWN-HIGHLAND, 1000 James Monroe Pkwy., Charlottesville, VA 22902-7505. Tel.: 434-293-8000. Fax: 434-979-9181.
E-mail: info@al-h.us
Web Site: ashlawnhighland.org
Founded: 1930.
Congressional District: 7
Key Personnel: Exec. Dir., Carolyn C. Holmes; Consultant, David B. Voelkel; Summer Festival Gen. Mgr., Judy Walker; Museum Shop Mgr., Barbara Hensley; Accountant, Marie Edwards; Office Mgr., Baylor Reinhart.
Personnel Profile: Full-Time Paid 5; Part-Time Paid 55; Part-Time Volunteers 100; Interns 6.
Governing Authority: college. Parent Institution: College of William & Mary, Williamsburg, VA 23187. Tax-exempt.
Historic House: 1799 Ash Lawn-Highland house built by James Monroe with 535-acre working plantation.
Collections: Monroe American & French furnishings & period artifacts 1799-1823; garden pavilion. Historic Buildings: Monroe House & outbuildings.
Major Exhibits: Seated in Style: Monroe Chairs, 11/09-1/10.
Research Fields: American history; American & European decorative arts.
Facilities: picnic area; mountain trails; ornamental & kitchen gardens. Gifts, handicrafts, herbs & reproductions for sale.
Activities: guided tours; lectures; concerts; summer festival of operas, plays, chamber music & family entertainment; craft demonstrations; hands-on educational workshops. Museum Sponsors: Monroe Farm Tour for children K-2; Spring Festival of Virginia Wines.
Publications: booklet, Ash Lawn-Highland, Home of James Monroe; coloring book, Ash Lawn; Elizabeth Kortright Monroe; Monroe & the Constitution; Monroe Family Recipes; Monroe USA; Monroe On...; Monroe Portraits; Monroe & Music; The Religion of the Founding Fathers; Life of James Monroe; The Presidency of James Monroe, 1817-1825.
Hours & Admission Prices: March-Oct. daily 9-6; Nov.-Feb. daily 10-5. Adults $10, children 6-11 $5; discounts to groups, AAM, ICOM & AAA members; members no charge. Closed New Year's Day; Thanksgiving; Christmas. ♿
Attendance: 68,000 (accurate)
Membership: Supporter $100; Sponsor $250; Patron $500; Sustainer $1,000; Investor $2,500; Benefactor $5,000; Advocate $10,000 & up.

KLUGE-RUHE ABORIGINAL ART COLLECTION, UVA, 400 Worrell Dr., Pantops, Peter Jefferson Pl., Charlottesville, VA 22911-8691. Tel.: 434-244-0234. Fax: 434-244-0235.
E-mail: kluge-ruhe@virginia.edu
Web Site: www.virginia.edu/kluge-ruhe
Founded: 1998.
Key Personnel: Dir. & Cur., Margo Smith; Assoc. Cur., Dominique Cocuzza; Adjunct Cur., Howard Morphy.
Personnel Profile: Full-Time Paid 2; Part-Time Paid 1; Part-Time Volunteers 10; Interns 2.
Governing Authority: Parent Institution: University of Virginia.
Art & Culture Museum.
Collections: Australian Aboriginal art.
Facilities: library.
Activities: temporary exhibits; lectures; education programs.
Publications: newsletter.
Hours & Admission Prices: Tues.-Sat. 10-4, Sun. 1-5. Guided Tour: Sat. 10:30. No charge. ♿

LEANDER J. MCCORMICK OBSERVATORY, Dept. of Astronomy, 530 McCormick Rd., The University of Virginia, Charlottesville, VA 22904. Mailing Address: P.O. Box 400325, Charlottesville, VA 22904-4325. Tel.: 434-924-7494. Fax: 434-924-3104. TDD: 434-982-4327.
E-mail: dept@mail.astro.virginia.edu
Web Site: www.astro.virginia.edu
Founded: 1885.
Congressional District: 5
Key Personnel: Dir., Ed Murphy.
Personnel Profile: Full-Time Paid 1; Part-Time Paid 2; Part-Time Volunteers 5.
Governing Authority: university. Parent Institution: University of Virginia. Subsidiary Institution: Department of Astronomy. Tax-exempt.
Observatory.
Collections: photographic archive; 26-inch Alvan Clark refracting telescope.
Research Fields: astrometry of nearby stars & planets.
Facilities: 45-seat auditorium; classrooms.
Activities: guided tours; organized education programs for undergraduate or graduate college students affiliated with the Univ. of Virginia.
Hours & Admission Prices: April-Oct. 1st & 3rd Fri. each month 9pm-11pm; Nov.-March 1st & 3rd Fri. each month 7pm-9pm. No charge.
Attendance: 4,000 (estimated)
Membership: Individual $35; Family $60; Stone Fellow $100; Mitchell Contributor $250; Alden Benefactor $500; Fredrick Assoc. $1,000; McCormick Trustee $2,500.

MCGUFFEY ART CENTER, 201 Second St., N.W., Charlottesville, VA 22902-5012. Tel.: 434-295-7973. Fax: 434-295-0322.
E-mail: mcguffey@mcguffeyartcenter.com
Web Site: www.mcguffeyartcenter.com
Art Center.
Collections: photographs; sculpture; paintings.
Facilities: Museum-related items for sale.
Activities: art, dance & theater classes.
Hours & Admission Prices: Tues.-Sat. 10-6, Sun. 1-5. No charge. Closed New Year's Day; Independence Day; Thanksgiving; Christmas.

MICHIE TAVERN CA. 1784, 683 Thomas Jefferson Pkwy., Rt. 53, Charlottesville, VA 22902-7145. Tel.: 434-977-1234. Fax: 434-296-7203.
E-mail: info@michietavern.com
Web Site: www.michietavern.com
Founded: 1928.
Congressional District: 5
Key Personnel: Gen. Mgr., Gregory L. MacDonald; Asst. Mgr., Sam Morris; Cur., Cynthia Conte; Museum Shop Mgr., Wendy Pugh.
Governing Authority: individual operation.
Historic Tavern: housed in c.1784 structure, relocated to present site in 1927 at the height of the Colonial Revival era; grist mill c.1797, Piney River Cabin c.1790, Sowell House c. 1820; 1784 tavern; 1822 rural Virginia house.
Collections: 18th- to 19th-century Southern furniture & artifacts.
Facilities: Period items for sale.
Activities: guided tours. Museum Sponsors: living history from April to October.
Publications: book, Cooking Treasures of the Past.
Hours & Admission Prices: Daily 9-5. Adults $9, senior citizens $8, children 6-11 $4.50; children under 6 & members no charge. Closed New Year's Day; Christmas. ♿

MONTICELLO, HOME OF THOMAS JEFFERSON, THOMAS JEFFERSON FOUNDATION, INC., 931 Thomas Jefferson Pkwy., Charlottesville, VA 22902-7148. Mailing Address: P.O. Box 316, Charlottesville, VA 22902-0316. Tel.: 434-984-9822. Fax: 434-977-7751.
E-mail: publicaffairs@monticello.org
Web Site: www.monticello.org
Formerly: Thomas Jefferson Memorial Foundation
Founded: 1923.
Congressional District: 5
Key Personnel: Pres., Leslie Green Bowman; Exec. Vice Pres., Ann H. Taylor;

Vice Pres & C.F.O., Victoria Jones; Vice Pres. Museum Programs & Cur., Susan R. Stein; Dir. Communications, Wayne Mogielnicki; Dir. Restoration, William L. Beiswanger; Dir. Grounds, Peter J. Hatch; Dir. Archaeology, Fraser D. Neiman, Ph.D.; Dir. Center for Historic Plants, Peggy L. Cornett; Dir. Education, Robin H. Gabriel; Dir. Buildings, John R. Houghton; Dir. Visitor Operations, Glen A. Slosson; Dir. Museum Sales, Sharon McElroy; Controller, Tracy Lovelady.
Personnel Profile: Full-Time Paid 130; Part-Time Paid 130; Part-Time Volunteers 2; Interns 4.
Governing Authority: private. Parent Institution: Thomas Jefferson Foundation, Inc. Tax-exempt: 501(c)(3).
Historic House Museum and Plantation: 1769-1826 Monticello, designed by Thomas Jefferson.
Collections: Jeffersonian furniture; memorabilia; art objects; manuscripts; books & personal items; slavery artifacts.
Research Fields: fine arts of the Colonial & early National Periods; Thomas Jefferson's personal life; slavery & plantation life.
Facilities: botanical garden; center for historic plants; visitor center; research center. Books, reproduction items, curios, china and silver for sale.
Activities: guided tours; permanent & temporary exhibitions; educational programs.
Publications: brochures; guidebook; publications related to Thomas Jefferson.
Hours & Admission Prices: March-Oct. daily 8-5; Nov.-Feb. daily 9-4:30. Adults $15-$20, children 6-11 $8; discounts to groups; children under 6 no charge. Closed Christmas. ♿
Attendance: 450,112 (accurate)

THE ROTUNDA, UNIVERSITY OF VIRGINIA, 1826 University Ave., Charlottesville, VA 22904-0305. Mailing Address: P.O. Box 400305, Charlottesville, VA 22904-4305. Tel.: 434-924-7969 & 1019. Fax: 434-924-3817.
E-mail: rotunda@virginia.edu
Web Site: www.virginia.edu/~urelat/Tours/rotunda/rotunda.html
Founded: 1819.
Key Personnel: C.E.O., Leonard Sandridge; Admin., Leslie M. Comstock; Pres., John T. Casteen.
Personnel Profile: Full-Time Paid 1; Part-Time Paid 12; Part-Time Volunteers 9.
Governing Authority: university. Parent Institution: University of Virginia. Tax-exempt.
Historic Buildings: site of Thomas Jefferson's original academical village, which includes the Rotunda, pavilions, student rooms & the lawn (1817-1826).
Collections: the founding of the University & its architectural history; prints & engravings of the grounds, early 19th-century American furniture.
Facilities: 50-vol. library pertaining to Thomas Jefferson & history of University of Virginia.
Activities: guided tours.
Hours & Admission Prices: mid-Jan. to mid-Dec. daily 9-4:45. Historical Tours: daily 10, 11, 2, 3, 4. No charge. ♿
Attendance: 135,000 (accurate)

SECOND STREET GALLERY, 115 Second St., S.E., Charlottesville, VA 22902-5270. Tel.: 434-977-7284. Fax: 434-979-9793.
E-mail: ssg@secondstreetgallery.org
Web Site: www.secondstreetgallery.org
Founded: 1973.
Congressional District: 7
Key Personnel: Exec. Dir., Rebecca K. Schoenthal; Chm., Steve Taylor; Pres. (V), Steve Delgado; Membership & Devel. Assoc., Amanda Currie Jones; Mgr. Operations & Outreach Coord., Andrew Greeley.
Personnel Profile: Full-Time Paid 3; Part-Time Volunteers 30; Interns 3.
Governing Authority: nonprofit organization. Tax-exempt.
Contemporary Art Gallery.
Collections: contemporary art in all media.
Facilities: 1,880 sq. ft. exhibit space.
Activities: guided tours; lectures; workshops.
Publications: exhibition catalogues; brochures.
Hours & Admission Prices: Tues.-Sat. 11-6. Suggested Donation: $3. ♿
Attendance: 15,000 (estimated)
Membership: Individual $35; Friend $100; Patron $250; Benefactor $500.

* **UNIVERSITY OF VIRGINIA ART MUSEUM, (M),** 155 Rugby Rd., Charlottesville, VA 22903-2427. Mailing Address: P.O. Box 400119, Charlottesville, VA 22904-4119. Tel.: 434-924-3592. Fax: 434-924-6321.
E-mail: bab8sa@virginia.edu
Web Site: www.virginia.edu/artmuseum
Formerly: Bayly Art Museum of the University of Virginia
Founded: 1935.
Congressional District: 7
Key Personnel: Dir., Bruce Boucher; Chm. (V), Terry Lockhart; Pres. (V), Jo Rowan; Admin., David Chennault; Cur., Andrea Douglas; Mgr. Collections, Jean Collier; Dir. Annual Giving, Kathy Douglas; Mgr. Exhibitions, Ana Marie Liddell.
Personnel Profile: Full-Time Paid 10; Part-Time Paid 9; Part-Time Volunteers 130; Interns 5.
Governing Authority: university. Parent Institution: University of Virginia. Tax-exempt.
Art Museum.
Collections: 15th-20th-century American & European paintings, sculpture & works on paper; ancient art; pre-Columbian art; Asian art; African sculpture; American Indian art; contemporary American art; photography.
Activities: inter-museum loan, permanent, temporary & traveling exhibitions; guided tours.
Publications: newsletter; exhibition catalogs; annual reports.
Hours & Admission Prices: Tues.-Sun. 12-5. No charge; donations accepted. Closed Thanksgiving; Christmas. ♿
Attendance: 28,089 (accurate)
Membership: Senior 65 & over and UVA Faculty & Staff $40; Basic $75; Sponsor $200; Patron $500; Benefactor $1,000; Curator's Circle $2,500; Director's Circle $5,000.

THE VIRGINIA DISCOVERY MUSEUM, (M), 524 E. Main St., East End of the Downtown Mall, Charlottesville, VA 22902. Mailing Address: P.O. Box 1128, Charlottesville, VA 22902-1128. Tel.: 434-977-1025. Fax: 434-977-9681.
E-mail: vadm@vadm.org
Web Site: www.vadm.org
Founded: 1981.
Congressional District: 5
Key Personnel: C.E.O., Peppy G. Linden; Co Chm. Bd. (V), Elizabeth Chew; Co Chm. Bd. (V), Galloway Beck; Pres. (V), Andrea Ayres; Exhibit Coord., Mike Clark; Volunteer Coord., Margie Rein; Business Mgr., Louise Trudel.
Personnel Profile: Full-Time Paid 6; Part-Time Paid 4; Part-Time Volunteers 132; Interns 1.
Governing Authority: nonprofit organization. Tax-exempt: 501(c)(3).
Children's Museum.
Collections: 400 brass animals; puppets; Nigerian collection; Pueblo collection; participatory exhibits, including 200-year old loghouse, playscape, Virginia Faces.
Major Exhibits: Freedom of Expression, 11/09-1/10/10; Illumination Station: Light, Lasers, Lenses, 1/16/10-5/9/10; It's Easy Being Green!, 5/15/10-9/12/10; Ancient Egypt, 9/18/10-1/16/11.
Facilities: educational facilities.
Activities: educational programs; school tours; camps; special events; portable planetarium (Starlab).
Publications: bimonthly program calendar; annual report; field trip brochure.
Hours & Admission Prices: Tues.-Sat. 10-5, Sun. 1-5. Admission $4; discounts to AAA members & groups; first Sun. of month, ASTC, ACM & museum members no charge. Closed major holidays. ♿
Attendance: 57,722 (accurate)
Membership: Individual $50; Grandparent $60; Family/Basic $75; Family/Explorer $125.

Chase City

MACCALLUM MORE MUSEUM AND GARDENS, (M), 603 Hudgins St., Chase City, VA 23924-1237. Mailing Address: P.O. Box 104, Chase City, VA 23924-0104. Tel.: 434-372-0502. Fax: 434-372-3483.
E-mail: mmmg@verizon.net
Web Site: www.mmmg.org
Founded: 1991.
Congressional District: 5
Key Personnel: Exec. Dir., Liz Lowrance; Pres. (V), Diana Ramsey; Treas., Dr. Earle Moore; Public Rels., Joe Epps.
Personnel Profile: Full-Time Paid 1; Part-Time Paid 2; Part-Time Volunteers 25.
Governing Authority: private; nonprofit organization. Tax-exempt: 501(c)(3).
General Museum & Botanical Garden.
Collections: Arthur Robertson Indian artifact exhibit dating from 9500 BC to 1600 AD; artifacts in garden from around the world: 1st-century Roman bust, 13th-century Italian wellhead, Spanish cloister, eight fountains; Mecklenberg Hotel memorabilia, known for its curative waters; Thyne Institute, an African American boarding and day school established in Chase City in 1876; herb, rose, all white & all pink gardens; native plants; backyard wildlife habitat.
Facilities: arboretum; birding & wildlife trail; Botanical Gardens. Garden, environmental, museum & nature items for sale.
Activities: guided tours; concerts; seasonal workshops; monthly garden lectures. Museum Sponsors: Native American Day; Archaeology Day; Herb

Festival; Spring Concert; Melodies In The Garden; Fall Fundraiser; Christmas Bazaar; Museum & Gardens Gala; New Year's Eve Gala.
Publications: brochure with map, points of interest, and brief history.
Hours & Admission Prices: Museum, Office & Gift Shop: Mon.-Fri. 10-5, Sat. 10-1. Gardens: daily 10-5. Gardens: $2 donation (unguided). Museum: adults $3.50, senior citizens $3, children under 12 $2.50; discounts to AAM & ICOM members; members no charge. ♿
Attendance: 6,500 (estimated)
Membership: Individual $25; Family $35; Friend $50-$99; Patron $100-$499; Sponsor $500-$999; Corporate $1,000 & up.

Chesapeake

CHESAPEAKE PLANETARIUM, 312 Cedar Rd., Chesapeake, VA 23322-5514. Mailing Address: P.O. Box 16496, Chesapeake, VA 23328-6496. Tel.: 757-547-0336 & 0153.
E-mail: hittrja@cps.k12.va.us
Founded: 1963.
Key Personnel: C.E.O., Dr. Robert J. Hitt.
Governing Authority: public school district. Tax-exempt.
Planetarium & Space Science Museum.
Collections: astronomy; space science.
Research Fields: meteor showers; solar eclipses; sun spot activity.
Activities: lectures; films; formally organized education programs; permanent & traveling exhibitions; telescope available for observing on clear nights after programs.
Publications: monthly newsletter, Astronomy News.
Hours & Admission Prices: Winter: Mon.-Wed. & Fri. 10:30-4:30, Thurs. 10:30-4:30 & 8 p.m.; June & Aug. Thurs. 8pm or by appointment. Group lectures or demonstrations $45; Chesapeake school groups no charge. ♿
Attendance: 40,000 (estimated)

PORTLOCK GALLERIES AT SONO, 3815 Bainbridge Blvd., Chesapeake, VA 23324-1607. Tel.: 727-502-4901.
E-mail: nbenson@cityofchesapeake.net
Web Site: www.portlockgalleries.com
Founded: 2005.
Key Personnel: Gallery Dir., Nicole Benson.
Governing Authority; city.
Art Gallery: housed in a 1908 four-room schoolhouse.
Collections: art exhibitions.
Hours & Admission Prices: Tues.-Fri. 10-5, Sat.-Sun. 12-4. No charge. Closed holidays. ♿

Chesterfield

CHESTERFIELD COUNTY MUSEUM COMPLEX, 6813 Mimms Loop, Chesterfield, VA 23832. Mailing Address: P.O. Box 40, Chesterfield, VA 23832-0040. Tel.: 804-768-7311. Fax: 804-751-4131.
E-mail: rushh@chesterfield.gov
Web Site: www.chesterfield.gov
Formerly: Chesterfield Historical Society of Virginia
Founded: 1961.
Congressional District: 3
Key Personnel: Mgr. Historic Sites, Holly Rush; Historic Sites Specialist, Bryan Truzzie; Site Coord., Tamara Evans.
Personnel Profile: Full-Time Paid 2; Part-Time Paid 3; Part-Time Volunteers 30; Interns 2.
Governing Authority: Parent Institution: Chesterfield Historical Society of Virginia.
Museum Complex.
Collections: replica 1750 Courthouse; photographs; stone implements used by the Appomattox & Monocan Indians; Sir Thomas Dale's portrait; 18th-century kitchen, household & farm tools; 1749 Commission of Peace; coal mine artifacts; Sidney King painting; fossils; Civil War weapons, household items, uniforms; period loom; archaeological artifacts recovered from the site of the 1732 Ware Bottom Church, built by Captain Thomas Jefferson, grandfather of Pres. Jefferson. Historic Structures: 1892 Jail; 1828 Court Green clerk's office; monuments to imprisoned Baptist ministers & Chesterfield's Confederate soldiers; 1822 Federal period Magnolia Grange house; 1817 federal period Castlewood plantation house containing local history & genealogy research library.
Research Fields: local history & genealogy.
Facilities: 45-seat auditorium; research library.
Activities: guided tours; organized education programs for children; docent program. Museum Sponsors: Celebrate Chesterfield Lecture Series.
Hours & Admission Prices: Tues.-Fri. 10-4, Sat. 10-2. Magnolia Grange: adults $4, seniors $3, students $2; members no charge. County Museum: no charge. ♿
Attendance: 6,614 (accurate)
Membership: Senior $15; Individual $20; Household $30; Sustaining $100.

Chincoteague

THE OYSTER AND MARITIME MUSEUM OF CHINCOTEAGUE, (M), 7125 Maddox Blvd., Chincoteague, VA 23336. Mailing Address: P.O. Box 352, Chincoteague, VA 23336-0352. Tel.: 757-336-6117.
Founded: 1966.
Congressional District: 1
Key Personnel: Admin., Sheila Faith; Dir., Officer & Pres. (V), James Bott; Officer, Kelly Conklin; Officer, Ellen Richardson.
Personnel Profile: Full-Time Paid 1; Part-Time Paid 2; Part-Time Volunteers 3.
Governing Authority: nonprofit organization. Tax-exempt: 170(b)(1)(A).
Natural Science Museum.
Collections: fossils; seashells; Indian artifacts; shellfish farming implements; diorama of oyster industry; first order Fresnel Lens from Assateague Lighthouse; boat models; local history.
Facilities: 100-vol. library of material on marine biology & zoology available on premises; aquarium; local video about the island.
Activities: self tour; films.
Hours & Admission Prices: Spring & Fall Fri. & Sun. 12-5, Sat. 10-7; Summer: Mon.-Thurs. 10-6, Fri.-Sat. 10-7, Sun. 12-5. Adults $4. ♿
Attendance: 13,000 (accurate)

Christiansburg

MONTGOMERY MUSEUM & LEWIS MILLER REGIONAL ART CENTER, (M), 300 S. Pepper St., Christiansburg, VA 24073-3537. Tel.: 540-382-5644.
E-mail: info@montgomerymuseum.org
Web Site: www.montgomerymuseum.org
Founded: 1983.
Congressional District: 9
Key Personnel: Exec. Dir., Sue Farrar; Pres., Sherry Wyatt; Vice Pres., Mary Ann Hinshel Wood; Treas., Bob Poff.
Personnel Profile: Part-Time Paid 1; Part-Time Volunteers 40.
Governing Authority: nonprofit organization. Tax-exempt: 501(c)(3).
Historic House: 1850 Presbyterian Manse.
Collections: photographs; genealogical; New River Valley artifacts; Civil War items; prehistoric Indian artifacts; local history items; archaeological site artifacts; art work of regional historic artifacts, local artists; history books containing area histories.
Major Exhibits: Growing Up in Montgomery County, 11/09-5/10; Those Who Serve Patriotism, 5/10-11/10.
Research Fields: genealogy & local history.
Facilities: archaeology lab; community room; gazebo; picnic area. Museum-related items for sale.
Activities: guided tours; arts festivals; docent program; participatory, loan & temporary exhibitions. Annual Events: Benefit Dinner; Wilderness Trail Festival; Candlelight Dinner; Country Home Tour; Heritage Day.
Publications: booklet, self-guided tour of Christiansburg; quarterly newsletter; book, The Montgomery County Story 1776-1957.
Hours & Admission Prices: Tues.-Sat. 10:30-4:30. Tour groups: adults $2, children under 12 $1; members no charge. ♿
Attendance: 3,500 (estimated)
Membership: Individual Student $10; Individual $20; Family Member (including spouse & children under 18) $30; Associate & Business $75; Friend $150; Patron $500.

Clarksville

OCCONEECHEE STATE PARK, 1192 Occoneechee Park Rd., Clarksville, VA 23927-2946. Tel.: 434-374-2210.
E-mail: occoneechee@dcr.virginia.gov
Web Site: www.dcr.virginia.gov/state_parks/occ.shtml
Key Personnel: Dir., Joseph H. Maroon
Native American History Museum.
Collections: Native American history; personal artifacts.
Facilities: nature trails. Museum-related items for sale.
Hours & Admission Prices: Parking: Mon.-Fri. $2, Sat.-Sun. $3. ♿

PRESTWOULD FOUNDATION, 429 Prestwould Dr., Clarksville, VA 23927. Mailing Address: P.O. Box 872, Clarksville, VA 23927-0872. Tel.: 434-374-8672. Fax: 434-374-3060.
Founded: 1963.
Congressional District: 5
Key Personnel: C.E.O., Dr. Julian D. Hudson.
Personnel Profile: Full-Time Paid 1.
Governing Authority: nonprofit organization. Tax-exempt: 501(c)(3).
Local History Museum: house built in 1795 Prestwould House.
Collections: archives; costumes; original furniture; original French scenic wallpaper; manuscripts.
Facilities: 1,000-vol. library of Lady Jean Skipwith, housed at Prestwould; Colonial gardens.

Activities: guided tours; temporary exhibitions.
Publications: Life by the Roaring Roanoke.
Hours & Admission Prices: April 15-Oct. Thurs.-Sat. 12:30-3:30, Sun. 1:30-3:30. Adults $10, seniors over 65 $8, children 6-12 $4; discounts to groups of 15 or more. Grounds only $4.
Attendance: 3,000
Membership: Individual $40; Family $50; Summer House Society $100-$499; Garden Club $500-$999; Manor House Society $1,000 & up.

Clifton Forge

ALLEGHENY HIGHLANDS ARTS & CRAFTS CENTER, INC., 439 E. Ridgeway St., Clifton Forge, VA 24422-1326. Mailing Address: P.O. Box 273, Clifton Forge, VA 24422-0273. Tel.: 540-862-4447.
E-mail: info@HighlandsArtsandCrafts.com
Web Site: highlandsartsandcrafts.com
Founded: 1984.
Congressional District: 6
Key Personnel: Exec. Dir., Nancy Newhard-Farrar; Pres. (V), Carolyn O. Conner; Museum Shop Mgr., Madelyn Miller.
Personnel Profile: Full-Time Paid 1; Full-Time Volunteers 5; Part-Time Paid 1; Part-Time Volunteers 90.
Governing Authority: nonprofit organization. Tax-exempt: 501(c)(3).
Arts & Crafts Center: housed in early 1900s building.
Collections: works produced by Highlands & other regional artists & crafts people.
Facilities: Art & crafts work for sale.
Activities: temporary exhibitions; classes; off site visual arts residency at area high schools; workshops.
Publications: bimonthly, Volunteer Voice; triannual newsletter, Center News.
Hours & Admission Prices: Jan.-April Tues.-Sat. 10-4:30; May-Dec. Mon.-Sat. 10-4:30; groups by appointment. No charge; donations accepted. Closed Thanksgiving; Christmas Eve & Day. ♿
Attendance: 13,928 (accurate)
Membership: Student $8; Individual $20; Family $30.

Clintwood

RALPH STANLEY MUSEUM, (M), Clintwood, VA 24228. Mailing Address: P.O. Box 945, Clintwood, VA 24228-0945. Tel.: 276-926-8550 & 5591. Fax: 276-926-8693.
E-mail: pam@ralphstanleymuseum.com
Web Site: www.ralphstanleymuseum.com
Key Personnel: Interim Dir., Pam Morris
History Museum.
Collections: memorabilia from the life & career of Ralph Stanley; audio-visual displays; photographs.
Hours & Admission Prices: April 2-Dec. 24 Tues.-Sat. 10-4, Sun. 1-5; Dec. 25-April 1 Wed.-Sat. 10-4, Sun. 1-5. Adults $7.50, students, seniors 55 and over & Dickenson, Wise, Buchanan County residents $5; children 12 & under no charge. Closed New Year's; Memorial Day; Thanksgiving; Christmas.

Colonial Beach

GEORGE WASHINGTON BIRTHPLACE NATIONAL MONUMENT, 1732 Popes Creek Rd., Colonial Beach, VA 22443-5115. Tel.: 804-224-1732. Fax: 804-224-2142.
Web Site: www.nps.gov/gewa
Founded: 1930.
Congressional District: 1
Key Personnel: Supt., Lucy Lawless; Museum Shop Mgr., Rijk Morane.
Governing Authority: federal. Parent Institution: U.S. National Park Service, Northeast Regional Office, U.S. Customs House, 200 Chestnut St., Fifth Floor, Philadelphia, PA 19106. Tax-exempt.
Historic Site: birthplace of George Washington, 1730-1750.
Collections: Washington family colonial history, 1657-1730; colonial furnishings; living farm.
Research Fields: Washington family history; colonial tidewater plantation life; lands owned by John Washington.
Facilities: plantation grounds owned by Augustine Washington, George's father; foundation of the house in which Washington was born; Washington family burial ground which contains the remains of Washington's father, grandfather & great grandfather; picnic area; visitor center; nature trail; slave quarters exhibit; Wayside exhibits; Memorial house & colonial kitchen with artifacts, living history demonstrations & historic animal varieties. Postcards & publications for sale.
Activities: guided tours; lectures; orientation film; colonial craft demonstrations; living colonial farm.
Publications: book, Popes Creek Plantation.
Hours & Admission Prices: Daily 9-5. Adults over 16 $4; discounts to Golden Age & Golden Eagle pass holders; children under 15 no charge. Closed New Year's Day; Thanksgiving; Christmas. ♿
Attendance: 131,000 (accurate)

Colonial Heights

VIOLET BANK MUSEUM, 303 Virginia Ave., Colonial Heights, VA 23834. Tel.: 804-520-9395.
E-mail: woodburnr@colonial-heights.com
Web Site: www.colonial-heights.com
Founded: 1968.
Personnel Profile: Full-Time Paid 1; Part-Time Paid 1; Part-Time Volunteers 1.
Governing Authority: Tax-exempt.
History Museum: housed in a manor house, built in 1815. Former headquarters of Gen. Robert E. Lee.
Collections: Civil War artifacts; period furniture from 1815-1873; textiles & ceramics.
Major Exhibits: Faces of War - Photographic Portraits of the Civil War, 11/09-11/1/10; As We Sit: An Exploration of Sargent's Supper Party, 11/09-12/10; Putting the Arm in Armies, 11/09-2/11.
Hours & Admission Prices: Tues.-Sat. 10-5, Sun. 1-6. No charge; donations accepted.

Courtland

RAWLS MUSEUM ARTS, (M), 22376 Linden St., Courtland, VA 23837-1143. Tel.: 757-653-0754. Fax: 757-653-0341.
E-mail: leighanne@rawlsart.com
Web Site: www.rawlsarts.com
Founded: 1958.
Congressional District: 4
Key Personnel: Pres. Bd., Pat Hartman; Exec. Dir., Leigh Anne Chambers.
Personnel Profile: Full-Time Paid 1; Part-Time Paid 2; Part-Time Volunteers 24; Interns 1.
Governing Authority: nonprofit organization. Tax-exempt: 501(c)(3); 170(b)(1)(A).
Art Museum & Visual Arts Center.
Collections: contemporary regional painting; glass; Indian artifacts; seashells.
Facilities: Museum-related items for sale.
Activities: concerts; arts festivals; organized educational programs; loan & temporary exhibitions; lectures.
Publications: newsletter; flyers; RMA Happenings.
Hours & Admission Prices: Tues. & Sat.-Sun. 1-5, Wed.-Fri. 10-5. No charge; donations accepted. ♿
Attendance: 6,749 (estimated)
Membership: Student $12; Individual $30; Family $42; Patron $50; Corporate $250; Sustaining $500.

Critz

REYNOLDS HOMESTEAD, 463 Homestead Lane, Critz, VA 24082-3044. Tel.: 276-694-7181. Fax: 276-694-7183.
E-mail: kdunkley@vt.edu
Web Site: www.reynoldshomestead.vt.edu
Founded: 1970.
Congressional District: 5
Key Personnel: Dir., Dr. Kay Dunkley; Administrative Asst., Michele Faircloth; Program Coord., Lisa Martin; Asst. Program Coord., Traci Petty; Historical Svcs. Asst., Beth Ford; Coord. Bldgs. & Grounds, Douglas Turner.
Personnel Profile: Full-Time Paid 3; Part-Time Paid 5; Part-Time Volunteers 10.
Governing Authority: state. Parent Institution: Virginia Tech. Tax-exempt.
Historic House: 1843 boyhood home of R.J. Reynolds, founder of Reynolds Tobacco.
Collections: furnishings of Reynolds' family; 19th-century furnishings; c.1840 rosewood grand piano made by Henry Gaehle; Victorian furniture; photograph album; paintings; silver.
Activities: guided tours; lectures; concerts; arts festivals; theater; study clubs; hobby workshops; organized educational programs; docent program; organized non-credit programs for children & adults throughout the region; participatory exhibits.
Publications: brochure; semiannual calendar of events.
Hours & Admission Prices: April-Oct. Sat.-Sun. 1-4. Adults $3, students $2. Closed New Year's Day; Thanksgiving; Christmas. ♿
Attendance: 1,500 (estimated)

Culpeper

THE MUSEUM OF CULPEPER HISTORY, (M), 803 S. Main St., Culpeper, VA 22701-3213. Mailing Address: P.O. Box 951, Culpeper, VA 22701-0951. Tel.: 540-829-1749. Fax: 540-829-9698.
E-mail: director@culpepermuseum.com
Web Site: www.culpepermuseum.com
Formerly: Culpeper Cavalry Museum
Founded: 1975.
Key Personnel: Bd. Pres., C. Ed. Higgins; Exec. Dir., Lee Langston-Harrison; Museum Coord., Linda B. Montgomery.
Personnel Profile: Full-Time Paid 1; Part-Time Paid 2; Part-Time Volunteers 35; Interns 2.
Governing Authority: nonprofit organization. Tax-exempt: 501(c)(3).
History Museum.
Collections: fossils; 215 million year old dinosaur tracks; Native American artifacts; American Revolution & Civil War artifacts; art; ethnography; photos; prints; textiles; commercial memorabilia. Historic Building: Burgandine House c.1750s.
Research Fields: local history.
Facilities: archives. Museum-related items for sale.
Activities: guided tours; educational programs; monthly special events; permanent & temporary exhibits. Annual Events: Remembrance Days; Downtown Holiday Open House; History Alfresco; Holiday Tour of Homes.
Publications: educational booklets; newsletter; web site.
Hours & Admission Prices: Feb.-Dec. Mon.-Sat. 10-5, Sun. 1-5; tours by appointment. Adults $3; discounts to AAM, AARP, VAM & AAA members; children, members, and town & county residents no charge. ♿
Attendance: 15,000 (accurate)
Membership: Minutemen $50-$199; Colonials $200-$599; Explorers $600-$999; Heritage $1,000-$4,999; Council $5,000 & up.

Danville

DANVILLE MUSEUM OF FINE ARTS & HISTORY, (M), 975 Main St., Danville, VA 24541-1822. Tel.: 434-793-5644. Fax: 804-799-6145.
E-mail: artandhistory@danvillemuseum.org
Web Site: danvillemuseum.org
Founded: 1974.
Congressional District: 5
Key Personnel: Exec. Dir., Lynne Bjarnesen; Pres. (V), Jack Neal, Jr.; Education Coord., Patsi Compton; Office Mgr., Gerry Scearce; Visitor Svcs., Sarah Latham; Museum Shop Mgr., Tim Stowe.
Personnel Profile: Full-Time Paid 2; Part-Time Paid 10; Part-Time Volunteers 100.
Governing Authority: nonprofit organization. Tax-exempt.
Art & History Museum: located in the Sutherlin Mansion where confederate President Jefferson Davis stayed when the confederacy fled Richmond in 1865 and issued the last proclamation of the confederacy.
Collections: paintings; prints; Victorian furnishing, textiles; American costumes; historic documents & artifacts pertaining to the history of Danville.
Research Fields: biographies of area citizens who have achieved national or international prominence; collection items; contemporary art; local architecture; local history.
Facilities: meeting rooms; auditorium; art studios; classroom.
Activities: art classes; camps; lecture series; changing exhibitions; annual juried art show; history workshops; Civil War history camp. Museum Sponsors: Art on the Lawn; Victorian Holiday; May Day.
Publications: quarterly newsletter; Last Capitol of the Confederacy.
Hours & Admission Prices: Tues.-Fri. 10-5, Sat.-Sun. 2-5. Adults $5, senior citizens 55 & over and students $4; children 6 & under and members no charge. ♿
Attendance: 14,264 (accurate)
Membership: Individual $35; Family $65; Sponsor $100; Patron $250-$999; Benefactor $1,000; Corporate $1,000-$5,000.

DANVILLE SCIENCE CENTER, 677 Craghead St., Danville, VA 24541-1503. Tel.: 434-791-5160. Fax: 434-791-5168.
E-mail: dscstaff@smv.org
Web Site: www.dsc.smv.org
Founded: 1995.
Congressional District: 5
Key Personnel: Chm. Trustees, Robert O. Satterfield; Pres. DSC, Inc. Directors, Margie E. Wilkinson; Exec. Dir., Jeff Liverman; Asst. Dir., Sonya Wolen; Education Coord., Robin H. Bailey; Exec. Dir. DSC, Inc., Deborah L. Anderson.
Personnel Profile: Full-Time Paid 4; Part-Time Paid 5; Part-Time Volunteers 125.
Governing Authority: state. Parent Institution: Science Museum of Virginia. Tax-exempt.
Science Museum.
Collections: astronomy; physics; chemistry; rocks & minerals; computers; zoology.
Research Fields: science education in a museum environment; environmental studies.
Facilities: early childhood learning center; seasonal butterfly greenhouse; classrooms; ZOOM zone; Outdoor River lab. Museum-related items for sale.
Activities: outreach & StarLab programs; education programs for pre-K through high school level; science lectures & events; exhibit hall demonstrations; hands-on exhibits.
Publications: annual report; quarterly newsletter for members; group visit planning guide; program brochures.
Hours & Admission Prices: Tues.-Sat. & holiday Mon. 9:30-5, Sun. 1-5. Adults $6, seniors & youth 4-12 $5; discounts to groups, AAA & military; members, ASTC members and children 3 & under no charge. Closed Thanksgiving; Christmas. ♿
Attendance: 20,000 (estimated)
Membership: Individual $25; Family $40; Associate $100; Contributor $250; Benefactor $500; Sustainer $1,000. Volunteer -25 hours of volunteer service annually-free.

TANK MUSEUM, (M), 3401 U.S. Hwy. 29B, Danville, VA 24540-1429. Tel.: 434-836-5323. Fax: 434-836-3532.
E-mail: aaftank@gamewood.net
Web Site: www.aaftankmuseum.com
Founded: 1981.
Personnel Profile: Full-Time Paid 2; Full-Time Volunteers 2; Part-Time Paid 3.
Governing Authority: Tax-exempt: 501(c)(3).
Military Museum.
Collections: military history; tanks; cavalry artifacts.
Hours & Admission Prices: Mon.-Sat. 10-4. Adults $10; members no charge. Closed Thanksgiving; Christmas.
Attendance: 22,000 (accurate)
Membership: Individual $25; Family $50; Associate $80.

Dayton

HARRISONBURG-ROCKINGHAM HISTORICAL SOCIETY, 382 High St., Dayton, VA 22821. Mailing Address: P.O. Box 716, Dayton, VA 22821-0716. Tel.: 540-879-2616 & 2681. Fax: 540-879-2616.
E-mail: museum@heritagecenter.com
Web Site: www.heritagecenter.com
Formerly: Shenandoah Valley Folk Art and Heritage Center
Founded: 1895.
Congressional District: 6
Key Personnel: Pres. (V) & C.E.O., Dale MacAllister; Admin., Mary Nelson.
Personnel Profile: Full-Time Paid 1; Part-Time Paid 3; Part-Time Volunteers 35.
Governing Authority: nonprofit organization. Parent Institution: Harrisonburg-Rockingham Historical Society. Tax-exempt.
Historical Society Museum.
Collections: local folklore; folk art of the Society; electric map of Stonewall Jackson's Valley campaign; music exhibitions; archives; Civil War items; photographs; costumes; glass; ceramics; firearms; Shenandoah Valley history, 1700s-present.
Research Fields: genealogical; old homes; wills & deeds; history pertaining to Harrisonburg, Rockingham Co. & Shenandoah Valley.
Facilities: approx. 800-vol. library of local history books; reading room. Gift items for sale.
Activities: slide shows; speakers; permanent & temporary exhibitions; genealogical research; community activities.
Publications: quarterly newsletter, The Rockingham Recorder.
Hours & Admission Prices: Mon.-Sat. 10-4. Adults $5, children 5-18 $1; members no charge. ♿
Attendance: 7,493 (accurate)
Membership: Individual & Family $25; Friends of Society $50-$99; Associate $100-$249; Patron $250-499; Sponsor $500 & up.

Deltaville

DELTAVILLE MARITIME MUSEUM & HOLLY POINT NATURE PARK, 287 Jackson Creek Rd., Deltaville, VA 23043. Mailing Address: P.O. Box 466, Deltaville, VA 23043-0466. Tel.: 804-776-7200.
E-mail: museumpark@oonl.com
Web Site: deltavilleva.com/museumpark
Founded: 2002.
Congressional District: 1
Key Personnel: Chm. (V), Bob Kates; Dir., Dick Urban.
Personnel Profile: Full-Time Paid 3; Full-Time Volunteers 5; Part-Time Paid 2; Part-Time Volunteers 200; Interns 2.

Governing Authority: Parent Institution: Deltaville Community Assoc. Tax-exempt.
Maritime Museum.
Collections: Deltaville's history & culture; photographs; restored period boats; ship models.
Facilities: library.
Activities: special events. Museum Sponsors: Family Boat Building Week; Historical Reenactments; Art Show.
Hours & Admission Prices: Call for hours. Adults $5; members no charge. ♿
Attendance: 12,000 (accurate)
Membership: Student $5; Individual $15; Family $25; Sustaining $100; Patron $250; Sponsor $500; Benefactor $1,000.

Duffield

NATURAL TUNNEL STATE PARK - COVE RIDGE CENTER, 1420 Natural Tunnel Pkwy., Duffield, VA 24244-3672. Tel.: 276-940-2674 & 2696. Fax: 276-940-2029.
E-mail: naturaltunnel@dcr.virginia.gov
Web Site: www.naturaltunnel.info
State Park.
Collections: local history & culture.
Facilities: nature trails; visitor center. Museum-related items for sale.
Activities: guided tours; hiking; educational programs.
Hours & Admission Prices: Visitor Center: March-May & mid-Sept.-Oct. Sat.-Sun. 10-4; Memorial Day-Labor Day Mon.-Fri. 10-5, Sat.-Sun. 10-6.

Dumfries

WEEMS-BOTTS MUSEUM, (M), 3944 Cameron St., Dumfries, VA 22026. Mailing Address: P.O. Box 26, Dumfries, VA 22026-0026. Tel.: 703-221-2218. Fax: 703-221-2218.
E-mail: weemsbotts@msn.com
Web Site: historicdumfries.com/weemsbotts.html
Founded: 1974.
Congressional District: 11
Key Personnel: Pres., Mike Cecere; Cur., Tammy Messick; Volunteer Coord., Claudia Smith; Treas., Stephanie Bradley.
Personnel Profile: Part-Time Paid 4; Part-Time Volunteers 20.
Governing Authority: society. Parent Institution: Historic Dumfries Virginia, Inc. Tax-exempt: 501(c)(3).
Historic House.
Collections: Colonial history; Colonial tobacco farming; Civil War items; period furniture; original documents; artifacts.
Research Fields: early Colonial history; genealogical research of Colonial period.
Facilities: 200-vol. library pertaining to Colonial history of Dumfries & surrounding area; research facility; reception center. Books for sale.
Activities: guided tours; lectures; docent program; temporary exhibitions; school outreach program. Museum Sponsors: Children's Colonial Camp; Charter Day Celebration; 18th-Century Tavern Night; Cherry Jubilee.
Publications: book, Records of Dettingen Parish; bimonthly, Newsletter of Historic Dumfries, VA Inc.; educational curriculum packet issued to Prince William County schools; coloring/activity book.
Hours & Admission Prices: Jan. 16-May 15 & Labor Day-Dec. 12 Wed.-Sat. 10-4, Sun. 12-4; May 16-Sept. Wed.-Sun. 10-4. Adults $3, senior citizens, children 6-16 & adult group 10 or more $2 each, youth groups 10 or more $1.50 each; discounts to AAM & ICOM members; children under 6, AAM & area Virginia museum members no charge. Closed New Year's Day; Easter; Thanksgiving; Christmas. ♿
Attendance: 4,000 (estimated)
Membership: Student & Senior Citizen $10; Individual $15; Family $30.

Fairfax

* **FAIRFAX COUNTY PARK AUTHORITY, RESOURCE MANAGEMENT DIVISION, (M),** 12055 Government Center Pkwy., #927, Fairfax, VA 22035-1118. Tel.: 703-324-8702. Fax: 703-324-3996.
Web Site: www.fairfaxcounty.gov/parks
Founded: 1972.
Congressional District: 10
Key Personnel: Div. Dir., Cindy Walsh; Mgr. Cultural Resources Protection, Liz Crowell; Mgr. Colvin Run Mill, Mike Henry; Mgr. Sully, Carol McDonnell; Site Operations Branch Mgr., Todd Brown; Mgr. Green Spring Gardens, Mary Olien; Mgr. Ellanor C. Lawrence Park, Leon Nawojchik; Mgr. Huntley Meadows Park, Kevin Munroe; Mgr. Hidden Oaks Nature Center, Michael McDonnell; Mgr. Hidden Pond Nature Center, Jim Pomeroy; Mgr. Riverbend, Marty Smith.
Personnel Profile: Full-Time Paid 95; Part-Time Paid 93; Part-Time Volunteers 700; Interns 10.
Governing Authority: county board of supervisors. Parent Institution: Fairfax County Government. Subsidiary Institution: Fairfax County Park Authority Board. Tax-exempt.
Historic Sites & House Museums.
Collections: period furniture & domestic furnishings; decorative arts; agricultural machinery; tools; country store merchandise. Historic Buildings: 1760 Green Spring; 1794 Sully Plantation; 1780 Walney; 1811 Colvin Run Mill; 1815 Colvin Run Mill Millers House; 1750 Cabells Mill; 1820 Cabells Mill House; 1823 Dranesville Tavern. Historic Sites: 1902 Clark House; Ash Grove 1792; Lahey Lost Valley 1760; Green Spring Farm; Frying Pan Farm; Dranesville Tavern; Freedom Hill Fort; Walney; Middlegate; Hunter House; Wakefield Chapel; Sully; c.1820 Huntley House. Heritage Resource Sites: Lanes Mill; Summers Cemetery; Frying Pan Baptist Meeting House; Mt. Air; Union Mills; Ox Hill Battlefield.
Research Fields: pertaining to collections; historic preservation easements; historic sites; natural & cultural resource management.
Facilities: Books & reproductions for sale.
Activities: lectures; films; concerts; arts festivals; interpretive programs; preservation easement program; formally organized educational programs; docent program; Museum Sponsors: handicapped interpretation; training program in historic crafts; archaeological services; preservation consulting services.
Publications: books: Sully, Biography of a House; Sully, An Architectural Study; History of Fairfax County; Historic District Publications; Huntley, A Study for Preservation; Dranesville Tavern; Colvin Run Mill; A History Program for Fairfax County; Green Spring Farm; brochures; Michael Straight on Green Spring Farm; Stories from Floris; Resources.
Hours & Admission Prices: Call for hours. Grounds: no charge. Closed New Year's Day; Thanksgiving; Christmas. ♿
Attendance: 403,939 (accurate)

FAIRFAX MUSEUM & VISITOR CENTER, 10209 Main St., Fairfax, VA 22030-2403. Tel.: 703-385-8414 & 8415. Fax: 703-385-8692.
E-mail: sgray@fairfaxva.gov
Web Site: www.fairfaxva.gov
Founded: 1992.
Congressional District: 11
Key Personnel: Cur. & Visitor Svcs. Mgr., Susan Inskeep Gray.
Personnel Profile: Full-Time Paid 2; Part-Time Paid 3; Part-Time Volunteers 40.
Governing Authority: nonprofit organization. Parent Institution: City of Fairfax. Tax-exempt.
History Museum & Historic Site: housed in 1873 historic Fairfax elementary school, the first brick public school in Fairfax County.
Collections: personal & archaeological artifacts; photographs.
Research Fields: history & educational system of northern Virginia & City of Fairfax; Civil War history; Fairfax County Courthouse.
Facilities: 2,000 sq. ft. exhibit space. Educational books & museum-related items for sale.
Activities: guided tours. Annual Event: Civil War weekend.
Hours & Admission Prices: Daily 9-5. No charge; donations accepted. Closed New Year's Day; Easter; Thanksgiving; Christmas Eve & Day. ♿
Attendance: 10,200 (accurate)
Membership: Individual, Family & Nonprofit Organizations $25; Profit Organizations $50.

NATIONAL FIREARMS MUSEUM, (M), 11250 Waples Mill Rd., Fairfax, VA 22030-7400. Tel.: 703-267-1620. Fax: 703-267-3913.
E-mail: nfmstaff@nrahq.org
Web Site: www.nrahq.org
Founded: 1871.
Congressional District: 11
Key Personnel: Pres., John Sigler; Exec. Vice Pres., Wayne LaPierre; Museum Dir., Jim Supica; Museum Cur., Doug Wicklund; Museum Cur., Phil Schreier; Program Asst., Kimberley Robbins; Museum Shop Mgr., Benjamin Van Scoyoc.
Personnel Profile: Full-Time Paid 7; Part-Time Paid 4; Part-Time Volunteers 15.
Governing Authority: Parent Institution: National Rifle Association. Associate Institution: The NRA Foundation. Tax-exempt: 501(c)(3).
Firearms Museum focus on American society from 1350 to present.
Collections: over 4,500 firearms including period & modern; over 2,500 non-firearm artifacts.
Research Fields: history of firearms development.
Facilities: library; laboratory.
Activities: self-guided tours; permanent & traveling exhibitions.
Publications: National Firearms Museum Brochures; Five Hundred Years of North American Freedom & Liberty; Firearms, Freedom, and the American Experience: The National Firearms Museum Exhibit Guide.
Hours & Admission Prices: Sun.-Fri. 9:30-5, Sat. 9:30-7. No charge; donations accepted. Closed some holidays. ♿

Attendance: 30,000 (accurate)

Falls Church

CHERRY HILL FARMHOUSE & BARN, 312 Park Ave., Falls Church, VA 22046-3301. Tel.: 703-248-5171. Fax: 703-536-8150.
E-mail: recreation@fallschurchva.gov
Web Site: www.fallschurchva.gov
Historic Site: listed on the National Register of Historic Places, built in 1845.
Collections: 19th century furniture, tools, & farming; period farm implements. Historic Building: 1856 timber barn.
Hours & Admission Prices: April-Oct. Sat. 10-1; Nov.-March Mon.-Thurs. 10-3. No charge; donations accepted. ♿
Membership: 2 Years: $20; Lifetime $200.

Farmville

LONGWOOD CENTER FOR THE VISUAL ARTS, (M), 129 N. Main St., Farmville, VA 23901-1305. Tel.: 434-395-2206. Fax: 434-392-6441. TDD: 800-828-1120.
Web Site: www.longwood.edu/lcva/
Founded: 1971.
Congressional District: 5
Key Personnel: Dir., K. Johnson Bowles; Chm. (V), Heyn Kjerulf.
Personnel Profile: Full-Time Paid 4; Part-Time Paid 6; Part-Time Volunteers 8; Interns 3.
Governing Authority: college. Parent Institution: Longwood University. Tax-exempt: 501(c)(3).
College Art Museum.
Collections: 19th-century American art; African & Chinese art; contemporary Virginia artists collection; regional crafts.
Facilities: activity room; education classroom.
Activities: lectures; gallery talks; formally organized education programs; loan, permanent & traveling exhibitions; community art school.
Publications: exhibit catalogs; exhibition gallery handouts.
Hours & Admission Prices: Galleries: Mon.-Sat. 11-5. Administrative: Mon.-Fri. 8:30-5. No charge; donations accepted. Closed college holidays; Thanksgiving; Christmas. ♿
Attendance: 35,000 (accurate)
Membership: Friend $1-$99; Advocate $100-$249; Fellow $250-$499; Collector $500-$749; Connoisseur $750-$1,249; Benefactor $1,250-$2,499; Champion $2,500-$4,999; Patron $5,000 & up.

ROBERT RUSSA MOTON MUSEUM, (M), 900 Griffin Blvd., Farmville, VA 23901-2236. Mailing Address: P.O. Box 908, Farmville, VA 23901. Tel.: 434-315-8775. Fax: 434-392-8568.
History Museum.
Collections: Civil Rights & U.S. history; photographs; period furnishings.
Facilities: Museum-related items for sale.
Hours & Admission Prices: By appointment. No charge.

Ferrum

BLUE RIDGE INSTITUTE AND MUSEUM, 20 Museum Dr., Ferrum College, Ferrum, VA 24088. Mailing Address: P.O. Box 1000, Ferrum, VA 24088-9001. Tel.: 540-365-4412. Fax: 540-365-4419.
E-mail: bri@ferrum.edu
Web Site: www.blueridgeinstitute.org
Founded: 1971.
Congressional District: 5
Key Personnel: Dir., J. Roderick Moore; Office Mgr., Jenny Rorrer; Asst. Dir., Vaughan Webb; Head Interpreter, Rebecca Austin; Archivist, Andrew Pauly; Special Projects, Amanda Hedrick.
Personnel Profile: Full-Time Paid 4; Part-Time Paid 7; Interns 1.
Governing Authority: college. Parent Institution: Ferrum College, Ferrum, VA 24088. Tax-exempt: 501(c)(3).
History Museum.
Collections: items from the Blue Ridge Mountains from the late 18th century to the present; farm tools & implements; textiles; furniture. Historic Building: 1800 German Farm.
Research Fields: folklore & folklife; music; crafts; regional history & folkways.
Facilities: 1,500-vol. library on folklore & folklife, available for research; field research station; classrooms.
Activities: guided tours; lectures; concerts; festivals; TV & radio programs; formally organized education programs for children; training program for professional museum workers; temporary exhibitions; research.
Publications: BRI records, Virginia Traditions Series BRI001-BRI010.
Hours & Admission Prices: BRI Museum & Blue Ridge Heritage Archive: daily 10-4. Closed holidays. Farm Museum: May-Aug. Sat. 10-5, Sun. 1-5. Farm tour $5, special tours, senior citizens & children 6-15 $4; discount to ICOM, AAM & VA Assoc. of Museums members; children under 6 no charge. ♿
Attendance: 15,000 (estimated)

Fincastle

BOTETOURT COUNTY HISTORICAL SOCIETY, 1 W. Main St., Fincastle, VA 24090-3006. Mailing Address: P.O. Box 468, Fincastle, VA 24090-0468. Tel.: 540-473-8394.
E-mail: info@bothistsoc.org
Web Site: www.co.botetourt.va.us/about/history.php
Key Personnel: Pres., John W. Rader, Jr.
Historical Society Museum.
Collections: personal artifacts; period furniture; photographs.
Facilities: Museum-related items for sale.
Publications: quarterly newsletter.
Hours & Admission Prices: Mon.-Sat. 10-2, Sun. 2-4.

Forest

THOMAS JEFFERSON'S POPLAR FOREST, 1008 Poplar Forest Dr., Forest, VA 24551. Mailing Address: P.O. Box 419, Forest, VA 24551-0419. Tel.: 434-525-1806. Fax: 434-525-7252.
Web Site: www.poplarforest.org
Founded: 1983.
Congressional District: 5
Key Personnel: Pres., Lynn A. Beebe; Dir. Finance & Administration, Sherri M. Goodwin; Chm., Judith Schultz; Dir. Mktg. & Public Rels., Anna M. Bentson; Dir. Interpretation, Octavia Starbuck; Mgr. Visitor Svcs., Dianne Kinney; Dir. Archaeology & Landscapes, Jack Gary; Assoc. Archaeologist, Eric Proebsting; Dir. Architectural Restoration, Travis C. McDonald; Dir. Information Technology, Jackie Almond; Dir. Maintenance, Emile deKeyser; Museum Shop Mgr., Suzan Bryan.
Personnel Profile: Full-Time Paid 18; Full-Time Volunteers 1; Part-Time Paid 18; Part-Time Volunteers 137.
Governing Authority: nonprofit organization. Parent Institution: The Corporation for Jefferson's Poplar Forest. Tax-exempt: 501(c)(3).
Historic House: 1806 octagon house Thomas Jefferson designed & used as his personal retreat; architectural restoration in progress.
Collections: Jefferson Letters.
Research Fields: history of Poplar Forest & Jefferson's life at his retreat; archaeological research focusing on Jefferson, slavery & landscape.
Facilities: Museum shop with books & items related to Thomas Jefferson & 19th-century plantation life for sale.
Activities: guided tours; docent program; archaeology & restoration field schools; school programs; concerts; family programming; hands on activities for children & adults; democracy broadcasts to schools; circulating curriculum kits. Museum Sponsors: Independence Day Celebration; Annual Conversations with Thomas Jefferson.
Publications: spring & fall newsletters; brochures; visitor's guide.
Hours & Admission Prices: April-Nov. Wed.-Mon. 10-4; group tours by appointment. Adults $10, senior citizens $9; students 12-18 $5, children 6-11 $2; discount to groups & AAA members; children under 5 no charge.
Attendance: 22,473 (accurate)
Membership: Individual $50.

Fort Defiance

THE AUGUSTA MILITARY ACADEMY MUSEUM, 1640 Lee Hwy., Fort Defiance, VA 24437. Mailing Address: P.O. Box 100, Fort Defiance, VA 24437-0100. Tel.: 540-248-3007. Fax: 540-248-4533.
E-mail: amaalumnihouse@aol.com
Web Site: www.amaalumni.org
Founded: 2000.
Key Personnel: Exec. Dir., Tina Shafer.
Personnel Profile: Full-Time Paid 1; Part-Time Volunteers 4.
Military History Museum: housed in Alumni House, built in the 1870s.
Collections: period furnishings; recreation of a cadet barracks room; uniforms; period military school artifacts.
Activities: Annual Event: Alumni Reunion.
Publications: quarterly, The Bayonet.
Hours & Admission Prices: Tues.-Sun. 10-4; other times by appointment. No charge. Closed major holidays. ♿
Attendance: 2,000 (estimated)

Fort Eustis

U.S. ARMY TRANSPORTATION MUSEUM, 300 Washington Blvd., Besson Hall, Fort Eustis, VA 23604-5260. Tel.: 757-878-1115 & 1182. Fax: 757-878-5656.
E-mail: david.hanselman@us.army.mil
Web Site: www.transchool.eustis.army.mil/museum/museum.html
Founded: 1959.
Congressional District: 1
Key Personnel: Dir., David S. Hanselman; Pres., Col. James Rockey, (Ret.); Cur., Marc W. Sammis; Asst. Cur., James E. Atwater; Museum Shop Mgr., Trish Wright.
Personnel Profile: Full-Time Paid 5; Part-Time Paid 1; Part-Time Volunteers 2.
Governing Authority: federal. Parent Institution: Dept. Army, Army Transportation Center. Tax-exempt.
Military Transportation Museum.
Collections: transportation; military.
Research Fields: transportation; military.
Facilities: archives includes official army documents, studies & histories dealing with the history & development of army transportation available for research by written request; auditorium. Museum-related items for sale.
Activities: film series; permanent & temporary exhibitions.
Publications: Red Book, listing of retired Transportation Corps personnel; museum brochure; marine, rail, aircraft & cargo-handling display guide pamphlets; Transportation Corps-An Illustrated History; Memorializations on Fort Eustis & Fort Story, VA.
Hours & Admission Prices: Tues.-Sun. 9-4:40. No charge; donations accepted. Closed federal holidays; Easter. ♿
Attendance: 78,000 (accurate)
Membership: $100; $500; $1,000; $5,000; $10,000; $25,000.

Fort Lee

* **THE UNITED STATES ARMY QUARTERMASTER MUSEUM, (M),** Bldg. 5218, A Ave., Fort Lee, VA 23801-1601. Mailing Address: Quartermaster Museum, USA Quartermaster Ctr., 1201 22nd St., Fort Lee, VA 23801-1601. Tel.: 804-734-4203. Fax: 804-734-4359.
Web Site: www.qmmuseum.lee.army.mil
Founded: 1957.
Congressional District: 4
Key Personnel: Dir., Tim O'Gorman; Cur., Luther D. Hanson; Exhibits Technician, Patrick Fisher; Cur. Education, Selena McColley; Office Svcs. Asst., Susan Tatum; Museum Shop Mgr., Paulette Crocker.
Personnel Profile: Full-Time Paid 4; Part-Time Volunteers 23; Interns 1.
Governing Authority: federal. Parent Institution: U.S. Army Quartermaster Center & School. Tax-exempt.
Military & History Museum.
Collections: uniforms; flags; insignia; equestrian equipment; weapons; historical military dioramas; paintings; photographs; personal artifacts; clothing; furnishings.
Research Fields: U.S. Army uniforms; quartermaster equipment; unit insignia; Quartermaster history; military manuals, publications & photos.
Facilities: research library by appointment; 100-seat auditorium. Museum-related items for sale.
Activities: inter-museum loan, permanent & temporary exhibitions; guided tours; training programs.
Publications: pamphlet; brochure, QM Museum.
Hours & Admission Prices: Tues.-Fri. 10-5, Sat.-Sun. & holidays 11-5. No charge; donations accepted. Closed New Year's; Thanksgiving; Christmas. ♿
Attendance: 45,000 (estimated)

U.S. ARMY WOMEN'S MUSEUM, (M), 2100 A Ave., Fort Lee, VA 23801-2100. Tel.: 804-734-4327. Fax: 804-734-4337.
E-mail: leeeawmweb@conus.army.mil
Web Site: www.awm.lee.army.mil
Founded: 1955.
Congressional District: 4
Key Personnel: Pres. Bd., Lt. Col. Pat Siegel; Dir., Judith Matteson.
Personnel Profile: Full-Time Paid 3; Part-Time Paid 1; Part-Time Volunteers 10.
Governing Authority: federal. Parent Institution: Center of Military History. Subsidiary Institution: U.S. Army's Women's Museum Foundation. Tax-exempt.
Military History Museum.
Collections: history, tradition & development of the WAAC/ WAC, army women of today and beyond to include the Army Nurse Corps and the Women Air Service Pilots (WASPs); military uniforms; war art; costumes; music; archival material; flags; guidons; books; pamphlets; photographs pertaining to the WAAC/WAC & women in the Army.
Research Fields: women in the Army.
Facilities: 410-vol. library of books, videos & albums relating to U.S. Women's Army Corps available for use on premises with consent of curator; research area; mini-theatre.
Activities: student intern program; guided tours; lectures; films; permanent, temporary & loan exhibitions. Annual Events: essay contest; living history program; Christmas Open House.
Publications: brochure, History of Women in the Army; biannual newsletter, Army Women's Museum Foundation Newsletter.
Hours & Admission Prices: Tues.-Fri. 10-5, Sat.-Sun. 11-5; other times by appointment. No charge; donations accepted. Closed New Year's Day; Thanksgiving; Christmas. ♿
Attendance: 70,000 (estimated)

Fort Monroe

CASEMATE MUSEUM, (M), 20 Bernard Rd., Fort Monroe, VA 23651-1004. Mailing Address: P.O. Box 51341, Fort Monroe, VA 23651-0341. Tel.: 757-788-3391. Fax: 757-788-3886.
E-mail: paul.morando@us.army.mil
Web Site: www.monroe.army.mil/monroe/sites/installation/museum/casemate_museum.aspx/
Founded: 1951.
Congressional District: 1
Key Personnel: Dir., Paul Morando; Pres. Foundation (V), LTC (Ret.) Robert Martin; Coord., Carol Hanson; Museum Specialist, Claire Samuelson; Exhibit Specialist, Charles T. Payne; Museum Technician, David J. Johnson; Museum Shop Mgr., Rosalinda Watson.
Personnel Profile: Full-Time Paid 5; Part-Time Paid 7; Part-Time Volunteers 25.
Governing Authority: U.S. Army. Parent Institution: U.S. Army Center of Military History. Tax-exempt.
Military Museum: built in 1826 casemates in Fort Monroe, VA.
Collections: restored cell where Jefferson Davis was imprisoned in 1865; models; dioramas; documents on the Monitor & Merrimack; documents, pictures & artifacts on Jefferson Davis, Grant, Poe, Black Hawk, Robert E. Lee; prints, painting, relics of Fort Monroe history, Civil War; military; U.S. Army Coast Artillery Museum.
Research Fields: history of Fort Monroe, VA; Civil War in southeast Virginia; Coast Artillery.
Facilities: 4,000-vol. research library on the history of Fort Monroe & Civil War & Coast Artillery. Postcards, historical pamphlets, books, models & prints for sale.
Activities: guided tours; lectures; gallery talks; audiovisual program; permanent exhibitions; monthly military film series.
Publications: pamphlets, Tales of Old Fort Monroe, Nos. 1-15; Dr. Craven & the Captivity of Jefferson Davis; Harrison Phoebus: From Farm to Fortune; Annual History of Fort Monroe; Controversial Ben Butler; The Shackling of Jefferson Davis; Fort Wool; Highlights of Black History at Fort Monroe; museum guidebook.
Hours & Admission Prices: Daily 10:30-4:30. No charge; donations accepted. Closed New Year's Day; Thanksgiving; Christmas. ♿
Attendance: 32,835 (accurate)
Membership: Member $12-$34; Donor $35-$99; Patron $100-$499; Participating Patron $500-$999; Contributing Patron $1,000-$4,999; Sustaining Patron $5,000-$9,999; Distinguished Patron $10,000-$24,999; Gallery Patron $25,000 & up.

Fort Myer

THE OLD GUARD MUSEUM, Fort Myer, VA 22211-1199. Mailing Address: Arog-ogm, 201 Jackson St., Fort Myer, VA 22211-1199. Tel.: 703-696-6670. Fax: 703-696-4256.
E-mail: kirk.heflin@fmmc.army.mil
Founded: 1962.
Key Personnel: Dir., Kirk Heflin; Exhibit Specialist, John Manes.
Personnel Profile: Full-Time Paid 3.
Governing Authority: federal government. Parent Institution: U.S. Army. Subsidiary Institution: U.S. Army Museum System. Tax-exempt.
Military Museum: housed in late 19th-century building originally used as barracks.
Collections: military uniforms & weapons; accoutrements of the 3rd INF Regiment 1784-present.
Research Fields: history of the 3rd U.S. Infantry; history of Military District of Washington; history, traditions & values of the U.S. Army.
Facilities: 600-vol. library pertaining to United States Army history; professional development of soldiers. Gift items for sale.
Activities: guided tours; films.
Hours & Admission Prices: Temporarily closed for relocation.
Attendance: 8,000 (estimated)

Fredericksburg

CENTRAL RAPPAHANNOCK HERITAGE CENTER, 900 Barton St., Unit 111, Fredericksburg, VA 22401-5784. Tel.: 540-373-3704.
E-mail: crhc@verizon.net
Web Site: www.crhcarchives.org
Founded: 1997.
Key Personnel: Dir., O. Clinton Jones, III
Governing Authority: Tax-exempt.
History Museum.
Collections: area history; documents; archives.
Hours & Admission Prices: Tues.-Thurs. 10-4, 1st Sat. of each month 9-12; other times by appointment. No charge; donations accepted. ♿

CIVIL WAR LIFE - THE SOLDIER'S MUSEUM, (M), 4712 Southpoint Pkwy., Fredericksburg, VA 22407-2657. Tel.: 540-834-1859. Fax: 540-834-1859.
E-mail: civilwarlife@yahoo.com
Web Site: civilwar-life.com/index.htm
Founded: 2000.
Congressional District: 1
Key Personnel: Cur., Terry Thomann; Chm. (V), Horace McCaskill; Gift Shop Mgr., Jane Thomann.
Personnel Profile: Full-Time Paid 2; Part-Time Paid 2.
Governing Authority: Parent Institution: National Civil War Foundation. Tax-exempt.
Military Museum.
Collections: Civil war life, weapons, equipment & personal artifacts; photographs.
Research Fields: Civil War veterans; flag passions of the Confederate South.
Facilities: 300-vol. library; 20-seat auditorium; 2,000 sq. ft. exhibit space; 20-seat theater. Museum-related items for sale.
Activities: films; guided tours; lectures.
Hours & Admission Prices: Call for hours. Museum: adults $5, children 7-16 $2.50; discounts to active military, seniors & AAM members. 3-D Theater: $3. Combo: adult $7, child $4.50. Closed Thanksgiving; Christmas. ♿
Attendance: 10,000 (accurate)

FREDERICKSBURG & SPOTSYLVANIA NATIONAL MILITARY PARK, 120 Chatham Lane, Fredericksburg, VA 22405-2508. Tel.: 540-371-0802; 373-6122 (visitor's center). Fax: 540-371-1907.
Web Site: www.nps.gov/ffrsp
Founded: 1927.
Congressional District: 1 & 3
Key Personnel: Supt., Russell P. Smith; Chief Historian, Robert K. Krick; Staff Historian, Donald C. Pfanz.
Governing Authority: federal. Affiliated with National Park Service, Washington, DC. Branch Museums: Chancellorsville Visitor Center, Chancellor; Fredericksburg Battlefield Visitor Center, Fredericksburg; Jackson Shrine, Guinea.
Military Park Museum: located on the site of the Battlefields of Fredericksburg, Chancellorsville, Wilderness & Spotsylvania.
Collections: military artifacts; manuscripts. Historic Houses: pre-Civil War Innis House; 1771 Chatham; 1790 Ellwood; 1844 Salem Church; 1828 Chandler office.
Research Fields: Civil War military history.
Facilities: 5,000-vol. library of books on the Civil War available by permission; 100-seat auditorium. Civil War books for sale.
Activities: guided tours; lectures; films; permanent & temporary exhibitions.
Publications: brochures; pamphlets on Civil War events.
Hours & Admission Prices: Fredericksburg Battlefield Visitor Center, Chancellorsville Visitor Center: Mon.-Fri 9-5, Sat.-Sun. 9-6. Chatham Manor: daily 9-4:30. Jackson Shrine: daily 9-5. Adults $3; children 16 & under no charge. Closed New Year's Day; Christmas. ♿
Attendance: 230,000 (accurate)

*** FREDERICKSBURG AREA MUSEUM & CULTURAL CENTER, INC., (M),** 1001 Princess Anne St., Fredericksburg, VA 22401. Mailing Address: P.O. Box 922, Fredericksburg, VA 22404-0922. Tel.: 540-371-3037. Fax: 540-371-1001.
E-mail: famoffice@earthlink.net
Web Site: www.famcc.org
Founded: 1985.
Congressional District: 7
Key Personnel: Dir., Pres. & C.E.O., Christa Stabler; Pres. Emeritus, Edwin W. Watson; Sr. Vice Pres. & Cur. Collections, Mary H. Dellinger; Chm. (V), Patricia Jones Lynch; Dir. Special Events, Mitzi Saffos; Education Coord., Paula V. Gorsuch; Shop Mgr., Nancy Guerin; Asst. Cur., Christopher Uebelhor; Coord. Membership, Lindsay McIntee.
Personnel Profile: Full-Time Paid 9; Part-Time Paid 10; Part-Time Volunteers 22; Interns 3.
Governing Authority: nonprofit organization. Tax-exempt: 501(c)3.
History Museum.
Collections: Native American artifacts; Civil War items; decorative arts; glass; ceramic; photographs; furniture; silver. Historic Buildings: c.1816 town hall & market house; 1927 bank.
Research Fields: Fredericksburg history & culture.
Activities: guided tours; lectures; films; concerts; organized education programs for adults, children, undergraduate & graduate college students affiliated with Mary Washington College-Center for Historic Preservation; participatory & temporary exhibitions.
Publications: quarterly newsletter.
Hours & Admission Prices: March-Nov. Mon.-Sat. 10-5, Sun. 1-5; Dec.-Feb. Mon.-Sat. 10-4, Sun. 1-4. Adults $7, students $2; discounts to AAA & AARP members; members & children under 6 no charge. Closed New Year's Day; Thanksgiving; Christmas. ♿
Attendance: 22,900 (accurate)
Membership: Individual $35; Family $45; Benefactor $100; Town Hall Council $250; General Lafayette Circle $500; General Washington Circle $1,000.

*** GARI MELCHERS HOME AND STUDIO, (M),** 224 Washington St., Fredericksburg, VA 22405-2360. Tel.: 540-654-1015. Fax: 540-654-1785.
E-mail: belmont@umw.edu
Web Site: www.garimelchers.org
Formerly: Belmont, The Gari Melchers Estate and Memorial Gallery
Founded: 1975.
Congressional District: 7
Key Personnel: Dir., David S. Berreth; Cur., Joanna D. Catron; Museum Shop Mgr., Susan Taylor-Schran; Coord. Education, Michelle Dolby; Grounds Preservation Supvr., Beate Jensen; Coord. Special Events, Betsy Labar.
Personnel Profile: Full-Time Paid 6; Part-Time Paid 26.
Governing Authority: state. Parent Institution: University of Mary Washington. Tax-exempt.
Art Museum: housed in 18th-century Belmont, the home & studio of the American artist Gari Melchers, 1860-1932.
Collections: 1871-1932 paintings & sketches by Gari Melchers; European antiquities; china & furnishings; 17th-20th century European & American paintings; correspondence of Mr. & Mrs. Gari Melchers.
Major Exhibits: Picturing Health: Norman Rockwell & The Art Of Illustration (T), 10/31/09-1/31/10.
Research Fields: art of Gari Melchers.
Facilities: orientation theatre; 200-seat public event room; formal gardens; walking trails; visitor's center. Museum-related items for sale.
Activities: guided tours; lectures; gallery talks; docent program; school-age aesthetics program; education programs & internships for undergraduate college students affiliated with University of Mary Washington; permanent & temporary exhibitions; rentals for weddings & receptions.
Publications: quarterly newsletter; brochures; catalogues, True & Clear: The Story of Gari Melchers; True & Clear: The Gift of Belmont.
Hours & Admission Prices: Daily 10-5. Adults $10, adult groups, seniors & AAA members $9, children 6-18 $5; discounts to AAM & museum members; other museum staffs, volunteers, students, faculty & staff of University of Mary Washington no charge. Closed New Year's Eve & Day; Thanksgiving; Christmas Eve & Day. ♿
Attendance: 18,000 (accurate)
Membership: Friends of Belmont: Individual $45; Household $65; Artisan $150; Supporter $250; Patron $500; Donor & Business Partner $1,000.

THE GEORGE WASHINGTON FOUNDATION, HISTORIC KENMORE & WASHINGTON'S FERRY FARM, 1201 Washington Ave., Fredericksburg, VA 22401-3747. Tel.: 540-373-3381. Fax: 540-371-6066.
E-mail: mailroom@kenmore.org
Web Site: www.kenmore.org
Formerly: George Washington's Fredericksburg Foundation
Founded: 1922.
Congressional District: 1
Key Personnel: Pres., William E. Garner; Chm. Bd. Trustees, Joanne G. Hall; Vice Chm., Joseph D. Logan, III
Personnel Profile: Full-Time Paid 21; Part-Time Paid 27; Part-Time Volunteers 150; Interns 3.
Governing Authority: board of trustees. Parent Institution: The George Washington Foundation. Tax-exempt.
Historic Houses: Kenmore, the 18th century home of Revolutionary War patriot Fielding Lewis and his wife, Betty, sister of George Washington. Ferry Farm: George Washington's boyhood home from 6 to 20 years old.
Collections: 18th-century decorative & fine arts; ornamental plaster ceilings & overmantels; archaeological artifacts.
Facilities: gardens.
Activities: guided house tours; hands-on educational programs; special events.
Publications: semiannual newsletter.

Hours & Admission Prices: March-Oct. daily 10-5; Nov.-Dec. daily 10-4. Kenmore: adults $8, seniors 60 & over $7, children 6-17 $4; discounts to groups, students 17 & over, trolley passengers, Time Travelers, AAA, DAR members & active military; children under 6 no charge. Ferry Farm: adults $5, seniors 60 & over $4, children 6-17 $3; discounts to groups, students 17 & over, trolley passengers, Time Travelers, AAA, DAR members & active military; children under 6 no charge. Closed New Year's Eve & Day; Thanksgiving; Christmas Eve & Day. ♿
Attendance: 33,688 (accurate)

HUGH MERCER APOTHECARY SHOP, 1020 Caroline St., Fredericksburg, VA 22401-3814. Mailing Address: 1200 Charles St., Fredericksburg, VA 22401. Tel.: 540-373-3362. Fax: 540-373-1569.
Web Site: www.apva.org
Founded: 1761.
Congressional District: 7
Key Personnel: Dir., Gail G. Braxton; Mgr., Genevieve Bugay.
Personnel Profile: Part-Time Paid 10.
Governing Authority: nonprofit corporation. Parent Institution: The Association for the Preservation of Virginia Antiquities, 204 W. Franklin St., Richmond, VA 23222-5091. Tax-exempt.
Historic Building: 1761 Hugh Mercer Apothecary Shop.
Collections: pharmaceutical implements; medical implements; historic papers.
Activities: guided tours.
Hours & Admission Prices: Call for hours. Adults $5, children $2; discount to members, AAA members, military families & groups; active military & APVA members no charge. Closed New Year's Eve & Day; Thanksgiving; Christmas Eve & Day.
Attendance: 18,500 (accurate)
Membership: Student & Teacher $25; Associate $30-$40; Individual $40; Individual Plus One $50; Family $60; Century $100; Sponsor $250; Benefactor $500.

JAMES MONROE MUSEUM AND MEMORIAL LIBRARY, (M), 908 Charles St., Fredericksburg, VA 22401-5801. Tel.: 540-654-1043. Fax: 540-654-1106. TTY: 800-828-1120.
E-mail: jmmuseum@umw.edu
Web Site: umw.edu/jamesmonroemuseum
Founded: 1927.
Congressional District: 1
Key Personnel: Dir., John N. Pearce; Asst. Dir. & Cur., Meghan Budinger; Membership & Events Coord., Adele Uphaus; Office Mgr., Cathleen Romine.
Personnel Profile: Full-Time Paid 2; Part-Time Paid 17; Part-Time Volunteers 4; Interns 4.
Governing Authority: state; nonprofit organization, administered by University of Mary Washington. Tax-exempt.
Presidential Historical Museum & Library.
Collections: personal furnishings; jewelry; possessions of President & Mrs. James Monroe; manuscripts; rare books; U.S. presidential collection; 27,000 historic documents, prints, maps, manuscripts & family papers.
Research Fields: life of James Monroe; Virginia families; U.S. presidents; foreign policy; 18th- & 19th-century American history; papers & books of James Monroe.
Facilities: 10,000-vol. library of Monroe's life & times available by appointment only. Museum-related items for sale.
Activities: guided tours; internship education programs for undergraduate college students; permanent exhibitions; changing annual & temporary exhibits; scholarly & special events. Museum Sponsors: annual James Monroe Lecture; Monroe Birthday Celebration; Christmas with the Monroes; Welsh Festival.
Publications: catalogues: The Library of James Monroe, Images of a President: Portraits of James Monroe (1992); brochure; catalogue, A Presidential Legacy, by Lee Langston-Harrison; jointly produced publications.
Hours & Admission Prices: March-Nov. Mon.-Sat. 10-5, Sun. 1-5; Dec.-Feb. daily 10-4. Adults $5, students & children $1; discounts to senior citizens, groups, AAM, AAA, ICOM, VAM & Timeless Ticket to Fredericksburg members; MW college students & museum members no charge. Closed New Year's Eve & Day; Thanksgiving; Christmas Eve & Day.
Attendance: 10,000 (estimated)
Membership: The Friends of James Monroe Museum: Individual $25; Couples & Households $35; Representatives $50; Senators $100; Diplomats $500; Presidential $1,000 & up.

MARY WASHINGTON HOUSE, 1200 Charles St., Fredericksburg, VA 22401-3706. Tel.: 540-373-1569. Fax: 540-373-1569.
E-mail: mwhouse@preservationvirginia.org
Web Site: www.preservationvirginia.org
Founded: 1772.
Congressional District: 7
Key Personnel: Dir. & C.E.O., Gail G. Braxton; Mgr. & Administrative Asst., Myra Wiggins; Museum Shop Mgr., Robin Medsker.
Personnel Profile: Part-Time Paid 15; Part-Time Volunteers 30.
Governing Authority: nonprofit organization. Parent Institution: Association for the Preservation of Virginia Antiquities, 204 W. Franklin St., Richmond, VA 23220-5091. Tax-exempt.
History Museum: 1772-1789 home of Mary Ball Washington.
Collections: 18th-century furnishings.
Research Fields: pertaining to collections.
Facilities: Museum-related items for sale.
Activities: guided tours of house & gardens.
Publications: brochure.
Hours & Admission Prices: Call for hours. Adults $5, children $2; discounts to AAA members, military families, and groups of 10 & over; active military & APVA members no charge. Closed New Year's Eve & Day; Thanksgiving; Christmas Eve & Day.
Attendance: 18,000 (estimated)
Membership: APVA: Student & Teacher $25; Individual $40; Individual Plus One $50; Family $60; Century $100; Sponsor $250; Benefactor $500.

RISING SUN TAVERN, 1304 Caroline St., Fredericksburg, VA 22401-3704. Mailing Address: 1200 Charles St., Fredericksburg, VA 22401. Tel.: 540-371-1494. Fax: 540-373-1569.
Web Site: www.apva.org
Founded: 1760.
Congressional District: 7
Key Personnel: Dir., Gail G. Braxton; Mgr., Jo Atkins.
Personnel Profile: Part-Time Paid 12.
Governing Authority: nonprofit organization. Association for the Preservation of Virginia Antiquities, 204 W. Franklin St., Richmond, VA 23220-5091. Tax-exempt.
Historic House Museum: c.1760 built by Charles Washington as his home; later used as tavern.
Collections: American and English pewter; 18th-century furniture, instruments & music; Tap Room.
Facilities: Museum-related items for sale.
Activities: guided tours.
Publications: brochure.
Hours & Admission Prices: Call for hours. Adults $5, children $2; discounts to AAA members, military families & groups of 10 or more; active military & APVA members no charge. Closed New Year's Eve & Day; Thanksgiving; Christmas Eve & Day.
Attendance: 20,000 (accurate)
Membership: Students & Teacher $25; Associate $30-$40; Individual $40; Individual Plus One $50; Family $60; Century $100; Sponsor $250; Benefactor $500.

ST. JAMES' HOUSE, 1300 Charles St., Fredericksburg, VA 22401-3708. Mailing Address: 1200 Charles St., Fredericksburg, VA 22401. Tel.: 540-373-1569. Fax: 540-373-1569.
Web Site: www.apva.org
Founded: 1760.
Congressional District: 7
Key Personnel: Dir., Gail G. Braxton; Resident Mgr., Elizabeth Butler.
Personnel Profile: Part-Time Volunteers 12.
Governing Authority: nonprofit society. Association for the Preservation of Virginia Antiquities, 204 W. Franklin St., Richmond, VA 23220-5091. Tax-exempt.
Historic House: c.1770 home of Hon. James Mercer.
Collections: private collection of the donors, William H. Tolerton and Daniel J. Breslin.
Activities: guided tours during Garden Week in April & October and by appointment.
Publications: brochure.
Hours & Admission Prices: Garden Week: April & 1st week Oct.; other times by appointment. Adults $3, children 6-18 $1; discount to groups; APVA members no charge.
Attendance: 300 (estimated)
Membership: Student & Teacher $25; Individual $40; Individual Plus One $50; Family $60; Century $100; Sponsor $250; Benefactor $500.

UNIVERSITY OF MARY WASHINGTON GALLERIES, (M), College Ave. at Seacobeck St., Fredericksburg, VA 22401-5358. Tel.: 540-654-1013. Fax: 540-654-1171. TDD: 540-654-1104.
E-mail: gallery@umw.edu
Web Site: galleries.umw.edu
Formerly: Mary Washington College Galleries
Founded: 1956.

Congressional District: 7
Key Personnel: Dir., Anne Timpano; Asst. Cur. & Registrar, Laura Tenekjian; Coord. Visitors Svcs., Megan Parry Byrnes; Office Mgr., Angela Whitley.
Personnel Profile: Full-Time Paid 1; Part-Time Paid 3; Interns 20.
Governing Authority: nonprofit. Parent Institution: University of Mary Washington.
College Art Galleries.
Collections: 19th & 20th-century European & American art; Asian art.
Major Exhibits: Adjunct Faculty Show, 1/15/10-2/9/10; Mid-Atlantic New Painting 2010, 1/22/10-2/26/10; Senior Exhibitions, 2/13/10-2/19/10; Senior Exhibitions, 3/13/10-3/19/10; Ladies First: Women in the Permanent Collection, 3/19/10-4/23/10; Annual Juried Student Show, 4/3/10-4/16/10.
Research Fields: American Art; 20th century art; contemporary art.
Activities: museum certificate program for undergraduate students; guided tours; lectures by visiting speakers.
Publications: exhibition catalogs; members newsletter.
Hours & Admission Prices: Museum: Mon., Wed. & Fri. 10-4, Sat.-Sun. 1-4 during college session only. Office: Mon.-Fri. 8-5. No charge. Closed New Year's Day; Thanksgiving; Christmas; university holidays & breaks. ♿
Attendance: 7,000 (accurate)
Membership: Student $5; Individual $25; Family $50; Contributor $125; Patron $500; Ridderhof Martin Society $1,000.

Front Royal

WARREN RIFLES CONFEDERATE MUSEUM, 95 Chester St., Front Royal, VA 22630-3368. Mailing Address: P.O. Box 1304, Front Royal, VA 22630-0027. Tel.: 540-636-6982 & 660-0941.
E-mail: wrcmm@embarqmail.com
Founded: 1959.
Congressional District: 7
Key Personnel: Dir. & Chm. (V), Suzanne Silek; Museum Shop Mgr., Esther Knight.
Personnel Profile: Full-Time Paid 1; Full-Time Volunteers 2; Part-Time Paid 2; Part-Time Volunteers 8.
Governing Authority: society. Parent Institution: Chapter 934, United Daughters of the Confederacy. Tax-exempt.
History & Military Museum: located on one of oldest streets in Front Royal.
Collections: relics of the War between the States including guns, uniforms, flags, swords, cutlasses, bayonets; letters & other signed documents, including a signed photograph of Belle Boyd; rare books; chromolithographs & engravings; furniture & furnishings of the period.
Research Fields: the War between the States.
Facilities: 500-vol. library of history books, available for use by appointment. Books & other items relating to U.S. history for sale.
Activities: guided tours; permanent collections.
Publications: brochures.
Hours & Admission Prices: mid-April to Nov. Mon.-Sat. 9-4, Sun. 12-4; other times by appointment. Groups: call for admission prices; discounts to members, AAA, AAM & AARP members; students no charge. ♿
Attendance: 1,000 (estimated)

Galax

JEFF MATTHEWS MEMORIAL MUSEUM, 606 W. Stuart Dr., Galax, VA 24333-2718. Tel.: 276-236-7874.
E-mail: info@jeffmatthewsmuseum.org
Web Site: www.jeffmatthewsmuseum.org
Founded: 1974.
Congressional District: 27
Key Personnel: Chm. (V), Bobby Thomson, Jr.; Cur., Tony Burcham.
Personnel Profile: Part-Time Paid 2.
Governing Authority: municipal. Parent Institution: City of Galax. Tax-exempt. 170(b)(1)(A).
History Museum.
Collections: over 10,000 Indian artifacts; 1,000 knives; tools; over 50 animal trophies; rugs of North America; receipts maps; land grants; two reconstructed 19th century log cabins with period furnishings; Miss America display; over 100 African artifacts; pictures of local Civil War veterans; 1860s covered wagon. Historic Building: 1834 Log Cabin.
Facilities: 8,000 sq. ft. exhibit space.
Activities: guided tours.
Publications: brochure.
Hours & Admission Prices: Wed.-Sat. 11-4; other times by appointment. No charge; donations accepted. Closed New Year's Day; Easter; Thanksgiving; Christmas. ♿
Attendance: 4,253 (accurate)
Membership: Annual $10.

Glen Allen

THE CULTURAL ARTS CENTER AT GLEN ALLEN, 2880 Mountain Rd., Glen Allen, VA 23060-2121. Mailing Address: P.O. Box 1249, Glen Allen, VA 23060-1249. Tel.: 804-261-2787.
E-mail: info@artsglenallen.com
Web Site: www.artsglenallen.com
Key Personnel: Pres., K. Alferio; Performing Arts Mgr. & Technical Dir., Richard Koch; Visual Arts Mgr., Lauren Hall; Dir. Devel., Ann R. Payes; Dir. Mktg. & Public Rels., Anita Waters
Cultural Arts Center.
Collections: art exhibitions.
Hours & Admission Prices: Call for hours.

Gloucester

GLOUCESTER MUSEUM OF HISTORY, 6539 Main St., Gloucester, VA 23061. Mailing Address: P.O. Box 5, White Marsh, VA 23183-0005. Tel.: 804-693-1234. Fax: 804-693-1234.
E-mail: bdeal@gloucesterva.info
Web Site: www.gloucesterva.info/museum/historyhome.htm
Key Personnel: Dir., Betty Jean Deal.
Personnel Profile: Part-Time Paid 2; Part-Time Volunteers 30.
History Museum: built ca 1770.
Collections: local history & culture; photographs; period furnishings.
Major Exhibits: African American History, 2/10; Daffodil Exhibit, 3/10-4/10; Military Appreciation Exhibit, 5/10; "The Good Old Days", 6/10-9/10; Archaeology Exhibit, 10/10-11/10; Holiday Exhibit, 12/10.
Hours & Admission Prices: Mon.-Sat. 10-3; tours by appointment. No charge; donations accepted. Closed holidays.
Attendance: 3,000 (accurate)
Membership: Friends of Museum $10.

ROSEWELL RUINS, 5113 Old Rosewell Lane, Gloucester, VA 23061. Mailing Address: P.O. Box 1456, Gloucester, VA 23061. Tel.: 804-693-2585.
Governing Authority: Parent Institution: Rosewell Foundation. Tax-exempt: 501(c)(3).
Historic House Museum: the ruins of the Page family mansion; built in 1725.
Collections: Page family life & history; mansion ruins.
Facilities: visitor center. Museum-related items for sale.
Activities: educational programs.
Hours & Admission Prices: Summer: Mon.-Sat. 10-4, Sun. 1-4; Winter: call for hours; groups by appointment. Adults $4, children 6-12 $2; discount to Student Time Travelers; children 5 & under no charge.

WARNER HALL GRAVEYARD, 4750 Warner Hall Rd, Gloucester, VA 23061-4507. Tel.: 804-648-1889.
E-mail: apva@apva.org
Web Site: www.apva.org/warnergraveyard
Congressional District: 1
Key Personnel: Exec. Dir., Elizabeth Kostelny.
Governing Authority: nonprofit society. Parent Institution: Association for the Preservation of Virginia Antiquities, 2300 E. Grace St., Richmond, VA 23223. Tax-exempt.
Historic Site: graveyard containing the tombs of the Warner & Lewis Families; including that of Augustine Warner, the first Warner to settle in Gloucester County & the forefather of George Washington.
Collections: tombstones of the Colonial period.
Research Fields: genealogy; history.
Hours & Admission Prices: Daily dawn to dusk. No charge. ♿
Attendance: 500 (estimated)

Gloucester County

WALTER REED BIRTHPLACE, At the corner of Hwy. 614 & 616, Gloucester County, VA 23061. Mailing Address: P.O. Box 160, Gloucester, VA 23061-0160. Tel.: 804-693-3663.
E-mail: ccbzanoni@aol.com
Founded: 1927.
Congressional District: 1
Key Personnel: Chm. (V), Ceci Brown.
Personnel Profile: Full-Time Volunteers 1; Part-Time Paid 1; Part-Time Volunteers 5.
Governing Authority: nonprofit society. Parent Institution: Assoc. for Preservation of Virginia Antiquities (APVA), 2300 E. Grace St., Richmond, VA 23223. Tax-exempt: 501(c)(3).
Historic House: three-room frame house, the birthplace of Walter Reed, September, 1851, a Major in the U.S. Army & the surgeon who is known as the conqueror of yellow fever.
Collections: period furniture; mid-19th century lifestyle.

Research Fields: history; architecture.
Activities: Annual Events: Historic Garden Week in April; Mother Day in May; Anniversary of his birth in September.
Publications: brochure on facility.
Hours & Admission Prices: May-Oct. by appointment. Suggested Donation: adults $5; APVA members, children under 17 & members no charge.
Attendance: 1,000 (estimated)
Membership: Student $15; Annual $25; Sustaining & Benefactor $500; Life $1,000.

Gloucester Point

VIRGINIA INSTITUTE OF MARINE SCIENCE, Rte. 1208, Greate Rd., Gloucester Point, VA 23062. Mailing Address: P.O. Box 1346, Gloucester Point, VA 23062-1346. Tel.: 804-684-7000 & 7285. Fax: 804-684-7097.
E-mail: jmusick@vims.edu
Web Site: www.vims.edu
Founded: 1969.
Congressional District: 1
Key Personnel: Dean & Dir., John Wells; Chief Administrative Officer, Jennifer LaTour; Dir. Communications, Dave Malmquist; Dir. Library, Carl Coughlin; Bibliographic Svcs. Librarian, Marilyn Lewis; Cur., Paul Gerdes.
Governing Authority: college. College of William & Mary, Williamsburg, VA 23185. Tax-exempt.
Marine Research Institute: located on Colonial Village archaeological site.
Collections: 100,000 specimens of preserved fishes; marine fishes from Nova Scotia to Florida; deep sea fishes; deep-sea sharks; Appalachian freshwater fishes; scientific Ichthyology collection.
Research Fields: systematics & ecology of fishes & herps.
Facilities: 29,000-vol. library of bound journals & books on marine science, available for inter-library loan; aquarium; field research station; 100-seat auditorium; classrooms.
Activities: formally organized education programs for graduate students affiliated with William & Mary College; systematic fish collections for scientific study.
Publications: VIMS special scientific reports series.
Hours & Admission Prices: Mon.-Fri. 9-4:30. Open to qualified professional scientists. No charge. ♿

Goldvein

THE GOLD MINING CAMP MUSEUM, 14421 Gold Dust Pkwy., Goldvein, VA 22720. Mailing Address: P.O. Box 219, Goldvein, VA 22720-0219. Tel.: 540-752-5330. Fax: 540-752-5325.
E-mail: southparks@fauquiercounty.gov
Web Site: www.goldvein.com/visitors.html
History Museum.
Collections: artifacts, photographs & painting relating to gold mining.
Hours & Admission Prices: Tues.-Wed. & Fri.-Sat. 9:30-5. Closed New Year's Day; Thanksgiving; Christmas.

Goochland

GOOCHLAND COUNTY MUSEUM & HISTORICAL CENTER, 2875 River Rd. W., Rte. 6, Goochland, VA 23063. Mailing Address: P.O. Box 602, Goochland, VA 23063-0602. Tel.: 804-556-3966. Fax: 804-556-3966. TDD: 804-556-5300.
E-mail: goochlandhistory@verizon.net
Web Site: www.goochlandhistory.org
Founded: 1968.
Congressional District: 3
Key Personnel: Pres. (V), Peter Rippe; Dir., Phyllis Silber.
Personnel Profile: Part-Time Paid 2; Part-Time Volunteers 25; Interns 1.
Governing Authority: society. Goochland County Historical Society. Tax-exempt: 501(c)(3).
Local History Center: housed in 1836 old jail.
Collections: archives; folklore; archaeology; artifacts; maps; documents; medical instruments.
Research Fields: pre-history-Indians; histories of Goochland medicine, schools & churches; genealogy.
Facilities: workroom; library.
Activities: lectures; oral history; scholarship program with schools. Annual Event: tour historic houses in October.
Publications: annual magazine; newsletter; books.
Hours & Admission Prices: Historical Center: Winter Wed.-Fri. 10-3; Spring & Summer Tues.-Fri. 10-3. Jail Museum: by appointment. No charge; donations accepted. Closed legal holidays. ♿
Attendance: 500 (accurate)
Membership: Library & Institution $15; Friends $25; Supporting & Business $50; Courthouse $50-99; Gold Mine $100-$249; Byrd Creek $250-$499; James River $500 & up.

Gordonsville

CIVIL WAR MUSEUM AT THE EXCHANGE HOTEL, 400 S. Main St., Gordonsville, VA 22942. Mailing Address: P.O. Box 542, Gordonsville, VA 22942-0542. Tel.: 540-832-2944.
Web Site: www.hgiexchange.org
Founded: 1971.
Congressional District: 7
Key Personnel: Tour Guide, M. Lynn Compton; Tour Guide, Sarah Lowe; Tour Guide, Kathleen Chapman.
Personnel Profile: Part-Time Paid 3; Part-Time Volunteers 2.
Governing Authority: nonprofit organization. Parent Institution: Historic Gordonsville, Inc. Tax-exempt: 501(c)(3).
Civil War Museum: built in 1860 railroad hotel used as a Confederate receiving hospital during the Civil War.
Collections: Civil War uniforms, weapons & other items; period artifacts from hotel; medical instruments & equipment; railroad memorabilia; research library.
Facilities: 30-vol. library of material relating to the town of Gordonsville & Civil War as it pertains to the hotel available to the public. Museum-related items for sale.
Activities: guided tours; organized educational programs; loan exhibitions. Museum Sponsors: Medical & Military Living History, spring & fall; Christmas Open House.
Publications: quarterly newsletter.
Hours & Admission Prices: April-Dec. 15 Mon.-Tues. & Thurs.-Sat. 10-4, Sun. 1-4. Adults $6, senior citizens $5, children 6-15 $3; members & children under 6 no charge.
Attendance: 4,400 (accurate)
Membership: Senior Citizen $15; Individual $25; Family $40.

Gwynn's Island

GWYNN'S ISLAND MUSEUM, Old Ferry Rd., Gwynn's Island, VA 23066. Tel.: 804-725-7949.
Web Site: www.gwynnsislandmuseum.org
History Museum.
Collections: local history & culture; period furnishings; early clothing; photographs; weapons; uniforms; school room.
Hours & Admission Prices: April-Oct. Fri.-Sun. 1-5; other times by appointment. No charge; donations accepted.

Hampden-Sydney

THE ESTHER THOMAS ATKINSON MUSEUM, College Rd., Hampden-Sydney, VA 23943. Mailing Address: P.O. Box 745, Hampden-Sydney, VA 23943-0745. Tel.: 434-223-6134 & 6000. Fax: 434-223-6344.
E-mail: away@hsc.edu
Web Site: www.hsc.edu/museum/
Founded: 1968.
Congressional District: 5
Key Personnel: Chm. Advisory Bd., Daniel M. Hawks; Dir. & Cur., Angela Way; Vice Chm., J. Sheppard Haw, III; Cur., Mrs. Lorie Mastemaker; Vice Pres. Administration of College, Dr. Paul S. Baker; Sec. Museum Bd., John L. Brinkley.
Personnel Profile: Full-Time Paid 1; Part-Time Volunteers 20.
Governing Authority: college; nonprofit. Parent Institution: Hampden-Sydney College. Tax-exempt: 501(c)(3).
College Museum.
Collections: Hampden-Sydney college history from 18th century-present; Draper camera.
Research Fields: museum collections.
Activities: guided tours; lectures; temporary exhibitions; workshops; special events.
Publications: newsletter; museum brochure; personalized brick brochure.
Hours & Admission Prices: Summer: Wed. & Fri. 12:30-4:30; Academic Year: Tues.-Fri. 12:30-5; other times by appointment. No charge; donations accepted. Closed school holidays. ♿
Attendance: 3,100 (estimated)
Membership: Contributor up to $199; 1775 Club $200-$499; Preservation Circle $500-$999; Curator's Circle $1,000-$2,499; Spencer Patron Society $2,500-$4,999; Bowman Heritage Society $5,000-$9,999; Atkinson Leadership Society $10,000 & up; Sponsorship $500-$15,000.

Hampton

AIR POWER PARK & MUSEUM, 413 W. Mercury Blvd., Hampton, VA 23666-4313. Tel.: 804-727-1163.
Founded: 1964.
Congressional District: 1
Key Personnel: Cur. & Dir., Jim Wilson.

Governing Authority: municipal government. Tax-exempt.
Military Aircraft Museum.
Collections: model aircraft; rockets; missiles; exhibits emphasizing history of military aviation in Hampton Roads area. Historic Aircraft: F-86L Sabrejet; F-89-J Scorpion; F-100 D Supersabre; F-101 B Voodoo; F-105-D Thunderchief; two T-33A Thunderbirds; P-1127 Kestrel; RF4C Phantom 2.
Research Fields: history of aviation in Hampton Roads area.
Facilities: 200-vol. library of aircraft, rocket & missile books, available for use by public; 50-seat auditorium; 3,500 sq. ft. exhibit space; picnic area. Gift items for sale.
Activities: guided tours on request; participatory, loan & temporary exhibitions.
Hours & Admission Prices: Daily 9-4:30. No charge; donations accepted. Closed New Year's Day; Thanksgiving; Christmas. ♿
Attendance: 52,000 (accurate)

CHARLES H. TAYLOR ARTS CENTER, 4205 Victoria Blvd., Hampton, VA 23669-4243. Tel.: 757-727-1490. Fax: 757-727-1167.
E-mail: artscom@hampton.gov
Web Site: www.hamptonarts.net
Founded: 1989.
Congressional District: 2
Key Personnel: Dir., Michael P. Curry; Gallery Mgr., James Warwick Jones; Chm. (V), Jim Thompson.
Personnel Profile: Full-Time Paid 5; Part-Time Paid 7; Part-Time Volunteers 100.
Governing Authority: municipal government. Tax-exempt: 170(b)(1)(A).
Arts Commission.
Collections: regional & national artists.
Activities: guided tours; lectures; films; performing arts productions & festivals; hobby workshops; organized education programs; docent program; loan exhibitions.
Publications: bimonthly Diversions magazine, includes calendar; monthly Calls for Entries.
Hours & Admission Prices: Tues.-Fri. 10-6, Sat.-Sun. 1-5. No charge; donations accepted. Closed New Year's Day; Presidents' Day; Memorial Day; Independence Day; Labor Day; Thanksgiving; Christmas; city holidays. ♿
Attendance: 10,348 (accurate)
Membership: Artists Organization $25.

HAMPTON HISTORY MUSEUM, (M), 120 Old Hampton Lane, Hampton, VA 23669-4096. Tel.: 757-727-1610. Fax: 757-727-6712.
E-mail: gdrummond@hampton.gov
Web Site: www.hampton1610.com
Founded: 2003.
Congressional District: 2
Key Personnel: Operations Mgr. & Grants Admin., Gaynell Drummond; Museum Assn. Pres., Tim Smith; Museum Assn. Treas., Robert Allsbrook; Museum Educator & Public Rels., Winette Jeffery; Registrar, Bethany Austin; Cur., Michael Cobb; Museum Shop Mgr., Vivian Tanzer; Administrative Asst., Gloria Jones.
Personnel Profile: Full-Time Paid 3; Part-Time Paid 5; Part-Time Volunteers 20; Interns 1.
Governing Authority: municipal government. Parent Institution: City of Hampton. Tax-exempt.
History Museum.
Collections: area history from 1607 to present.
Major Exhibits: The Old Point Comfort Resort, 11/09-1/10/10; Cheney Photographs of Hampton, 11/09-7/31/11; Hampton: Yesterday and Today, 3/5/10-8/31/10.
Research Fields: American history including settlement, colonial, revolution, antebellum, Civil War, modern, Native American, African American, women, military, & maritime.
Facilities: 7,000 sq. ft. exhibit space; rental hall. Museum-related items for sale.
Activities: docent program; formal education programs; guided tours; lectures; loan, participatory, traveling & temporary exhibitions; rental gallery; lecture series.
Publications: quarterly newsletter.
Hours & Admission Prices: Mon.-Sat. 10-5, Sun. 1-5. Adults $5, senior citizens, students & children $4; discount to groups & AAM members; members no charge. Closed New Year's Day; Thanksgiving; Christmas. ♿
Membership: Student $10; Individual $20; Couple $30; Family $50; Kecoughtan Society $100-$299; Fort Algernon Society $300-$499; Elizabeth City Society $500-$999; Port Hampton Society $1,000 & up.

HAMPTON UNIVERSITY MUSEUM, Hampton University, Hampton, VA 23668-0001. Tel.: 757-727-5308. Fax: 757-727-5170.
E-mail: museumeducation@hamptonu.edu
Web Site: museum.hamptonu.edu
Founded: 1868.
Congressional District: 1
Key Personnel: C.E.O., William R. Harvey; Dir., Vernon S. Courtney; Cur. Collections, Vanessa Thaxton-Ward; Office Mgr., Brenda Carpenter; Visitor Svcs., Robert Jondreau; Editor International Review of African American Art, Juliette Harris; Asst. to the Archivist, Donzella Maupin; Archivist Staff, Cynthia Poston; Archivist Staff, Andreese Scott.
Personnel Profile: Full-Time Paid 8; Part-Time Paid 1; Part-Time Volunteers 100.
Governing Authority: university. Parent Institution: Hampton University. Tax-exempt: 501(c)(3).
General Museum.
Collections: traditional African, Asian, Oceanic & American Indian art; 19th- & 20th-century African American art; contemporary African art; Hampton University history.
Research Fields: African, North American Indian & African American Art.
Facilities: 1,000-vol. library of books on traditional art & ethnology available for use upon request.
Activities: guided tours; lectures; gallery talks; formally organized education programs for children; permanent, temporary & traveling exhibitions.
Publications: books, To Lead & to Serve: American Indian Education at Hampton Institute 1878-1923; Five Decades: John Biggers & the Hampton Tradition in the Arts; The Frederick Douglass & Harriet Tubman Series of 1938-40; Magazine: The International Review of African American Art; book, A Taste for the Beautiful: Zairian Art from the Hampton University Museum; The Murals of John Thomas Biggers: American Muralist, African American Artist; Elizabeth Catlett: Works On Paper 1944-1992.
Hours & Admission Prices: Mon.-Fri. 8-5, Sat. 12-4. No charge; donations accepted. Closed national holidays; campus holidays. ♿
Attendance: 30,000 (estimated)
Membership: Student & Senior Citizen $15; Individual $25; Dual $30; Family $40; Organization $60; Contributor $100; Supporting $250; Sustaining $500; Benefactor $1,000.

ST. JOHN'S CHURCH AND PARISH MUSEUM, 100 W. Queens Way, Hampton, VA 23669-4014. Tel.: 757-722-2567. Fax: 757-722-0641.
E-mail: office@stjohnshampton.org
Web Site: www.stjohnshampton.org
Founded: 1976.
Congressional District: 1
Key Personnel: Parish Historian & Cur., Beverly F. Gundry.
Personnel Profile: Part-Time Volunteers 8.
Governing Authority: church. Parent Institution: Diocese of Southern VA. Tax-exempt.
Historic Buildings: c.1728 church, fourth site of worship in Elizabeth City Parish, established in 1610, the oldest parish in continuous existence in the English-settled United States. Museum housed in 1889, Parish Hall. Two 17th century sites are owned by the church & contain exhibits of interest; gravestones & pictorial displays.
Collections: 16th to 18th-century prayer books & bible; artifacts from the 1623-4 church site; ceramics; photographs & illustrations; memorabilia.
Research Fields: parish history & archaeological research.
Activities: guided tours.
Publications: Cemetery Inscriptions.
Hours & Admission Prices: Mon.-Fri. 9-3:30, Sat. 9-12. No charge; donations accepted. Closed holidays. ♿
Attendance: 1,969 (estimated)

VIRGINIA AIR & SPACE CENTER, 600 Settlers Landing Rd., Hampton, VA 23669-4033. Tel.: 757-727-0900. Fax: 757-727-0898.
E-mail: tbridgford@vasc.org
Web Site: www.vasc.org
Formerly: Virginia Air and Space Center and Hampton Roads History Center
Founded: 1991.
Congressional District: 1
Key Personnel: C.E.O., Todd C. Bridgford; Pres. (V), Jean M. Yokum; Dir. Education, Richard Byles; Dir. Administrative Svcs., Jenny Kelly; Cur. & Dir. of Exhibits & Collections, Allen Hoilman; Deputy Dir., Kim Hinson; Museum Shop Mgr., Danielle Price.
Personnel Profile: Full-Time Paid 30; Part-Time Paid 60; Part-Time Volunteers 174; Interns 3.
Governing Authority: nonprofit organization. Tax-exempt: 501(c)(3).
Air, space, science & technology museum.
Collections: aerospace accomplishments in the region; military & civilian aircraft; research aircraft; NASA spacecraft & other space artifacts.
Major Exhibits: Animal Grossology (T), 2/10-9/10.

Research Fields: aerospace history; math & science education techniques; visitor studies.
Facilities: 600-vol. library of aerospace material; 300-seat IMAX 3D theatre; educational facilities; 50,000 sq. ft. exhibit space; cafe. Museum-related items for sale.
Activities: docent program; films; formal education programs for children; guided tours; loan, temporary, traveling & participatory exhibits; rental gallery; IMAX 3D theatre.
Publications: quarterly newsletter, CenterLine.
Hours & Admission Prices: Jan. 4-March 15 & Sept. 14-Dec. 14 Tues.-Sat. 10-5, Sun. 12-5, call for additional winter hours; Summer: Mon.-Wed. 10-5, Thurs.-Sun. 10-7. Exhibits: adults $9.50, senior citizens $8.50, children $7.50. Exhibits & IMAX: adults $15, senior citizens $14, children $12. IMAX: adults $8, senior citizens $7, children $6.75; discounts for military, NASA, AAM, AAA, & ASTC members, military & NASA; members no charge for exhibits. Closed Thanksgiving; Christmas. ♿
Attendance: 412,815 (accurate)
Membership: Commuter $65; First Class $95; Gold Preferred $120; Executive $275; Million Miler $500; Corporate $1,000.

Hanover

HANOVER HISTORICAL SOCIETY MUSEUM - OLD JAIL, Hwy. 301, Court Green, Hanover, VA 23069. Mailing Address: 8516 E. Patrick Henry Rd., Ashland, VA 23005-7417. Tel.: 804-537-5815.
Founded: 1967.
Congressional District: 7
Key Personnel: C.E.O., Anne Cross; Book Chm., Mrs. W.C. Wickham; Chm. (V), Lois Wickham.
Personnel Profile: Full-Time Volunteers 2; Part-Time Volunteers 2.
Governing Authority: society. Parent Institution: Hanover Historical Society. Tax-exempt.
Historical Society Museum.
Collections: local historical material; 1860 school maps; portraits. Historic Buildings: 1835 county jail; 1735 courthouse; 1727 tavern.
Research Fields: pre-1865 homes & buildings.
Activities: lectures; permanent & temporary exhibitions; tours by appointment. Museum Sponsors: Old Hanover Day.
Publications: Hanover in Retrospect; Hanover Historical Society Bulletin; books, History of Hanover County; Old Homes of Hanover County Virginia; Portraits in Courthouse; Names on Confederate Monument; A Child's History of Hanover; Bulletin Vol. I.; Hanover County Graveyards Vol. I & II; biannual members bulletin.
Hours & Admission Prices: By appointment. No charge; donations accepted.
Attendance: 8,042 (estimated)
Membership: Annual $10; Life $100.

Hardy

BOOKER T. WASHINGTON NATIONAL MONUMENT, 12130 Booker T. Washington Hwy., Hardy, VA 24101-3968. Tel.: 540-721-2094. Fax: 540-721-8311 & 5128.
Web Site: www.nps.gov/bowa
Founded: 1956.
Congressional District: 5
Key Personnel: C.E.O., Carla Whitfield; Bookstore Mgr., L. Betsy G. Haynes; Volunteer Coord., Timothy Sims.
Personnel Profile: Full-Time Paid 10; Part-Time Paid 2; Part-Time Volunteers 15; Interns 1.
Governing Authority: federal. Parent Institution: Department of the Interior, National Park Service, Washington, DC. Tax-exempt.
National Monument: located on the site of Burroughs Plantation, birthplace & early home of Booker T. Washington.
Collections: plantation equipment & furniture; blacksmith tools; archaeological artifacts.
Research Fields: period crops & clothing; life & influence of Booker T. Washington.
Facilities: 1,000-vol. library of books on agriculture, biographical, slavery, Black history; living history farm; 48-seat auditorium; 90-seat multipurpose room & exhibition hall; 1.5 mile National Recreation Trail. Postcards, videos & books for sale.
Activities: guided tours; lectures; slide presentation; living history programs; special events.
Publications: brochures; Rack Cards.
Hours & Admission Prices: Daily 9-5. No charge; donations accepted. Closed New Year's Day; Thanksgiving; Christmas. ♿
Attendance: 20,000 (estimated)

Harrisonburg

D. RALPH HOSTETTER MUSEUM OF NATURAL HISTORY, Eastern Mennonite University, 1200 Park Rd., Harrisonburg, VA 22802-2462. Tel.: 540-432-4400 & 4000. Fax: 540-432-4488.
E-mail: dossc@emu.edu
Web Site: http://www.emu.edu/sciencecenter
Founded: 1968.
Congressional District: 7
Key Personnel: Museum Educator, Christine C. Hill; Educational Dir., Maureen Gallon; Cur., James Yoder.
Personnel Profile: Part-Time Paid 4.
Governing Authority: college. Parent Institution: Eastern Mennonite University. Tax-exempt.
Natural History Museum.
Collections: geology; mineralogy; zoology; anthropology; paleontology; fluorescent specimens.
Activities: guided tours; permanent exhibitions; study programs for elementary, high school, & college groups.
Publications: yearly brochure.
Hours & Admission Prices: Sun. 2-5 during academic year. Groups of 15 or less $30, over 15 $2. For appointments call 540-432-4400 9-12 & 1-4. ♿
Attendance: 6,000 (accurate)

JOHN C. WELLS PLANETARIUM, James Madison University, c/o Physics Dept., Harrisonburg, VA 22807-0001. Mailing Address: James Madison University, Miller Hall Rm 102, MSC-4502, Harrisonburg, VA 22807-0001. Tel.: 540-568-2312. Fax: 540-568-2800.
Web Site: www.jmu.edu/planetarium
Founded: 1975.
Congressional District: 6
Key Personnel: Dir., William R. Alexander.
Personnel Profile: Full-Time Paid 1.
Governing Authority: state. Commonwealth of Virginia. Parent Institution: James Madison University. Tax-exempt.
Planetarium.
Collections: meteorites; 6 Meade telescopes; Chronos Star projector; Digistar 3.
Facilities: planetarium theater.
Activities: public programs; special groups; public observations; school groups.
Hours & Admission Prices: See website. No charge; donations accepted. ♿
Attendance: 3,057 (estimated)

SAWHILL GALLERY, JAMES MADISON UNIVERSITY, Main & Grace Sts., Duke Hall, Rm. 101, Harrisonburg, VA 22807-0001. Mailing Address: MSC 7101, Duke Hall, Rm. 101, Harrisonburg, VA 22807-0001. Tel.: 540-568-6407. Fax: 540-568-5862.
E-mail: freebugl@jmu.edu
Founded: 1967.
Congressional District: 6
Key Personnel: Dir., Gary L. Freeburg.
Personnel Profile: Full-Time Paid 1; Part-Time Paid 3; Interns 12.
Governing Authority: university. Affiliated with Art Department, James Madison University. Tax-exempt.
Art Gallery.
Collections: Ernest Staples Collection; Indonesian works; Sawhill collection; pre-classical & classical items; modern works of art.
Activities: temporary exhibitions.
Hours & Admission Prices: Academic Year Mon.-Fri. 10-5, Sat. 12-5; Summer: call for hours. No charge. Closed university holidays. ♿
Attendance: 10,000 (estimated)

VIRGINIA QUILT MUSEUM, (M), 301 S. Main St., Harrisonburg, VA 22801-2606. Tel.: 540-433-3818. Fax: 540-433-3818.
Founded: 1992.
Congressional District: 26
Governing Authority: bd of directors; nonprofit organization.
Quilt Museum.
Collections: early & contemporary quilts; quilting; sewing machines.
Major Exhibits: Virginia Quilt Museum, Celebrating 15 Years, 2/10-12/10.
Facilities: Museum-related items for sale.
Activities: classes; programs.
Publications: quarterly newsletter.
Hours & Admission Prices: Feb.-Dec. Tues.-Sat. 10-4. Adults $5, students 12-18 $3, youth 5-11 $2; children under 5 no charge. Closed major holidays. ♿
Attendance: 5,962 (accurate)
Membership: Basic $25; Contributor $50; Patron & Guild $100; Sponsor $250.

Heathsville

NORTHERN NECK FARM MUSEUM, 12705 Northumberland Hwy., Heathsville, VA 22473. Mailing Address: P.O. Box 365, Heathsville, VA 22473-0365. Tel.: 804-443-1118.
Farm Museum.
Collections: agricultural history; farming equipment & tools; photographs.
Activities: school groups; educational programs; special events.
Hours & Admission Prices: May-Oct. Sat.-Sun.

Herndon

KIDWELL FARM AT FRYING PAN PARK, 2709 W. Ox Rd., Herndon, VA 20171-3807. Tel.: 703-437-9101.
Web Site: www.fairfaxcounty.gov/parks/fpp/kidwell.htm
Living History Museum: depicting a family dairy farm from 1920-1950.
Collections: period farm equipment; dairy; smokehouse; corn cribs; equipment sheds; chicken house.
Facilities: Museum-related items for sale.
Activities: special events; educational programs. Museum Sponsors: hayrides March to November.
Hours & Admission Prices: Park: daily dawn to dusk. Farm: daily 9-5.

Hood

ROARING TWENTIES ANTIQUE CAR MUSEUM, Rte. 230, W., Hood, VA 22723. Mailing Address: 1445 Wolftown-Hood Rd., Hood, VA 22723-9802. Tel.: 540-948-6290. Fax: 540-948-6290.
E-mail: info@roaring-twenties.com
Web Site: www.roaring-twenties.com
Founded: 1967.
Congressional District: 7
Key Personnel: C.E.O. & Owner, Clarissa Dudley; Cur. & Museum Shop Mgr., Martha Dudley.
Governing Authority: private.
Transportation Museum.
Collections: classic cars of 1920s & 1930s with emphasis on rare body styles & models.
Facilities: Museum-related items for sale.
Hours & Admission Prices: daylight hours by appointment. Adults & students $10, children 6-12 $3; discounts to AAM, ICOM, AACA, Car Club members & groups of 2 or more; children under 6 no charge.
Attendance: 225 (estimated)

Independence

GRAYSON CROSSROADS MUSEUM AND CULTURAL EXHIBITS, 107 E. Main St., Independence, VA 24348. Mailing Address: P.O. Box 336, Independence, VA 24348-0336. Tel.: 276-773-3711.
Founded: 1994.
Congressional District: 9
Key Personnel: Bd. Pres., Laura Bryant.
Personnel Profile: Part-Time Paid 1; Part-Time Volunteers 4.
Governing Authority: Parent Institution: 1908 Courthouse Foundation. Tax-exempt.
Local History Museum: housed in the former county courthouse, 1908.
Collections: Grayson County history & culture; period artifacts; photographs; furnishings; personal artifacts.
Facilities: Museum-related items for sale.
Activities: music jams. Museum Sponsors: Mountain Foliage Festival in October; Christmas Parade.
Hours & Admission Prices: Mon.-Fri. 10-5, Sat. 10-4. No charge; donations accepted. Closed holidays. ♿
Attendance: 3,000 (estimated)

Irvington

FOUNDATION FOR HISTORIC CHRIST CHURCH, INC., (M), State Rtes. 646 & 709, Irvington, VA 22480. Mailing Address: P.O. Box 24, Irvington, VA 22480-0024. Tel.: 804-438-6855. Fax: 804-438-5186.
E-mail: fhcc@crosslink.net
Web Site: www.christchurch1735.org
Founded: 1958.
Congressional District: 1
Key Personnel: Exec. Dir., Camille E. Bennett; Pres. (V), Rev. Hugh C. White, III; Office Mgr., Trish Geeson.
Personnel Profile: Full-Time Paid 3; Part-Time Volunteers 260.
Governing Authority: nonprofit organization. Tax-exempt: 501(c)(3).
Historic Foundation: housed in c.1735 Christ Church.
Collections: original & transcriptions or copies of original documents, maps, photos & related materials concerning the church & social history of its people in Lancaster County; historic archaeological artifacts & support materials portraying colonial life.
Research Fields: social history of church & its builder Robert King Carter & archaeological research into the site surrounding the church; historic architecture; political & economic history of the colonial county, parish & population.
Facilities: 200-vol. library on Colonial history, genealogy & social life available for use on premises; 16-seat theater; community meeting facility.
Activities: guided tours; docent program; video; programs for school children; permanent exhibitions; continuing education; cultural events.
Publications: books, Historic Structure Report (1994); Christ Church Parish Vestry Book, 1739-1786 & 1832-1869; Christ Church, Lancaster County, Virginia (2001); Robert King Carter, Builder of Christ Church (2001); People in Profile, Christ Church Parish, 1720-1750 (2002); Landholders & Landholdings, Christ Church Parish (2004); activity book, Discover History at Historic Christ Church.
Hours & Admission Prices: Historic Christ Church: April-Nov. Mon.-Fri. 8:30-4:30, Sat. 10-4, Sun. 2-5; Dec.-March Mon.-Fri. 8:30-4:30. Carter Reception Center: April-Nov. Mon.-Sat. 10-4, Sun. 2-5; other times by appointment. Adults $5, senior citizens $4; discounts to groups. Closed New Year's Eve & Day; Thanksgiving & day after; Christmas Eve & Day. ♿
Attendance: 12,200 (estimated)
Membership: Student & Teacher $10; Individual $20; Family $40; Associates $100; Patron $250; Guardians $500; 1735 Society $1,000.

STEAMBOAT ERA MUSEUM, (M), 156 King Carter Dr., Irvington, VA 22480. Mailing Address: P.O. Box 132, Irvington, VA 22480-0132. Tel.: 804-438-6888. Fax: 804-438-6598.
E-mail: director@steamboatmuseum.org
Web Site: www.steamboateramuseum.org
Congressional District: 1
Key Personnel: Exec. Dir., Terri Thaxton; Pres. (V), Richard T. Wilson, III; Museum Shop Mgr., Jennifer Britt.
Personnel Profile: Full-Time Paid 1; Part-Time Volunteers 50.
Governing Authority: Tax-exempt.
Steamboat Museum.
Collections: steamboat history & artifacts; Chesapeake Bay; film; oral histories; photographs.
Hours & Admission Prices: Thurs.-Sat. 10-4, Sun. 1-4; other times by appointment. No charge; donations accepted. ♿
Membership: Upperdeck $30; Cabin $50; Stateroom $125; Captain's Table $250; Wheelhouse $500; Commodore $1,000.

Isle of Wight

BOYKIN'S TAVERN MUSEUM, 17130 Monument Cir., Isle of Wight, VA 23397. Tel.: 757-365-9771.
Historic Building: built in 1762. Listed on the National Register of Historic Places.
Collections: local history & culture; photographs; period artifacts.
Activities: special events.
Hours & Admission Prices: Feb. 4 to late Dec. Thurs.-Sat. 11-4, Sun. 1-5. Closed Easter; Thanksgiving; Christmas Eve, Day & week.

Jamestown

HISTORIC JAMESTOWNE, 1365 Colonial Pkwy., Jamestown, VA 23081. Tel.: 757-229-0412. Fax: 757-564-3844.
E-mail: info@historicjamestowne.org
Web Site: www.historicjamestowne.org
Formerly: Jamestown National Historic Site
Founded: 1607.
Congressional District: 1
Key Personnel: Exec. Dir. Preservation Virginia, Elizabeth Kostelny; Dir. Research & Interpretation, Preservation Virginia, Dr. William Kelso; Dir. Administration & Operations, Preservation Virginia, Ann Berry; Supt., CNHP, Dan Smith; Cur. Archaeology, Preservation Virginia, Beverly Straube; Information Officer, CNHP, Michael Litterst; Mktg. & Public Rels., Preservation Virginia, Tina Calhoun; Site Mgr., CNHP, James Perry; Program Coord, Preservation Virginia, Tom Patton; Retail Mgr., Preservation Virginia, Jack McCartney.
Personnel Profile: Full-Time Paid 28; Part-Time Paid 18; Part-Time Volunteers 90.
Governing Authority: nonprofit society. Joint venture of Preservation Virginia and Colonial National Historic Park, National Park Service. Tax-exempt.
Historic Site & Preservation Project: first permanent English settlement in America.
Collections: interpretive markers; monuments; memorials; 17th-century artifacts. Historic Buildings: 17th century church tower; 1907 memorial church.

Research Fields: 17th-century Virginia history; the remains of 1607 fort.
Facilities: visitors center; restaurant.
Activities: archaeological excavations; tours.
Publications: Jamestown Rediscovery Monographs; Jamestown: The Buried Truth; The Jamestown Archaeological Assessment; The Archaearium: Rediscovering Jamestown 1607-1699; Historic Jamestowne Guidebook.
Hours & Admission Prices: Daily 8:30-4:30. Adults $10; children under 15, Preservation Virginia & National Park Service members no charge. Closed New Year's Day; Thanksgiving; Christmas. ♿
Attendance: 266,752 (accurate)

Kilmarnock

KILMARNOCK MUSEUM, 76 N. Main St., Kilmarnock, VA 22482. Tel.: 804-436-9100.
History Museum.
Collections: local history, business, commerce, & culture; photographs; period furnishings; personal artifacts.
Hours & Admission Prices: Thurs.-Sat. 11-3.

King George

KING GEORGE MUSEUM AND RESEARCH CENTER, 9483 Kings Hwy., King George County Courthouse, King George, VA 22485. Mailing Address: P.O. Box 424, King George, VA 22485-0424. Tel.: 540-775-9477.
Web Site: www.kghistory.org
Governing Authority: Parent Institution: King George County Historical Society.
Historical Society Museum.
Collections: local history, heritage, & culture; photographs; genealogy; period artifacts.
Facilities: library.
Activities: educational programs; hands-on activities for children; research.
Hours & Admission Prices: March-Oct. Thurs. & Sat. 10-2; Nov.-Feb. Sat. 10-2; other times by appointment. Closed New Year's Eve & Day; Easter; Memorial Day; Independence Day; Labor Day; Thanksgiving weekend; Christmas Eve, Day & week.

King William

KING WILLIAM HISTORICAL MUSEUM, 227 Horse Landing Rd., King William, VA 23086. Mailing Address: P.O. Box 233, King William, VA 23086-0233. Tel.: 804-769-9619.
Web Site: www.kingwilliamcounty.us
History Museum.
Collections: county history & culture; African American, Colonial & Native American artifacts; murals; photographs; period artifacts.
Hours & Admission Prices: Sat.-Sun. 1-5; other times by appointment.

PAMUNKEY INDIAN MUSEUM, 175 Lay Landing Rd., King William, VA 23086-2126. Tel.: 804-843-4792.
Web Site: www.pamunkey.net/museum.html
Key Personnel: Mgr., Joyce Krigsvold
American Indian Museum.
Collections: life & culture of Pamunkey Indians.
Facilities: Museum-related items for sale.
Hours & Admission Prices: Tues.-Sat. 10-4, Sun. 1-4. Adults $2.50, seniors $1.75, children 6-12 $1.25; children under 6 no charge.

Kinsale

KINSALE FOUNDATION AND MUSEUM, 449 Kinsale Rd., Kinsale, VA 22488. Mailing Address: P.O. Box 307, Kinsale, VA 22488-0307. Tel.: 804-472-3001.
History Museum.
Collections: local history & culture; photographs; period artifacts.
Facilities: Museum-related items for sale.
Hours & Admission Prices: May-Sept. Fri.-Sat. 10-5, Sun. 2-5; Oct.-April Fri.-Sat. 10-5. No charge.

Lancaster

MARY BALL WASHINGTON MUSEUM & LIBRARY, INC., (M), 8346 Mary Ball Rd., Lancaster, VA 22503. Mailing Address: Box 97, Lancaster, VA 22503-0097. Tel.: 804-462-7280. Fax: 804-462-6107.
Web Site: www.MBWM.org
Founded: 1958.
Congressional District: 1
Key Personnel: Mgr., Valencia Keeve; C.E.O., Karen Hart; Pres. (V), C. Jeffers Schmidt.
Personnel Profile: Full-Time Paid 1; Part-Time Paid 1; Part-Time Volunteers 40.
Governing Authority: nonprofit organization. Tax-exempt: 501(c)(3).
Local History Museum.
Collections: 18th-20th century artifacts pertaining to Virginia's Northern Neck region including textiles; furniture; paintings; family & regional memorabilia; oral histories; folklife relics; Civil War artifacts; archives; genealogical & family research center; genealogy. Historic Buildings: 1821 jail; 1797 clerks office; 1830 Lancaster House.
Research Fields: local history; Virginia genealogy; regional folk culture; regional historic architecture.
Facilities: 6,000-vol. library.
Activities: permanent & temporary exhibitions; historic site surveys; oral history; public & membership programs; Virginia standards of learning based school programs.
Publications: newsletter; 1850 Census of Lancaster County, Abstracts of Wills of Lancaster County WB-1796-1839, Millenbeck Report; Abstracts of Wills of Lancaster County WB 29 & 30, 1840-1925; Queenstown, Early Port Town of Lancaster County; The Thomas Carters of Lancaster, Virginia; James Gordon & His Family of Lancaster; Ball Family Outline; 1860 Census, Lancaster County, Virginia; Where the River Meets the Bay; Civil War Roster, Lancaster County, 1860-1864; Land Between Waters; occasional paper series, "Echoes of Yesteryear".
Hours & Admission Prices: Museum: Wed.-Fri. 10-4, Sat. by appointment; other times by appointment. Adults $2; members no charge. Library: Tues.-Fri. 10-4, Sat. 10-2; other times by appointment. Research: $5. Closed major holidays.
Attendance: 6,000 (estimated)
Membership: Individual $25; Family & Household $50; Sustaining $100; MBWM Friends $500; Mary Ball Society $1,000.

Lawrenceville

BRUNSWICK COUNTY MUSEUM, 228 N. Main St., Lawrenceville, VA 23868-1823. Mailing Address: P.O. Box 837, Lawrenceville, VA 23868. Tel.: 434-848-6773; 866-783-9768 (Toll Free). Fax: 434-848-8553.
History Museum.
Collections: county's history & culture; Native American artifacts; Gov. Albertis Harrison; period dolls & clothing; furnishings.
Activities: special events.
Hours & Admission Prices: Tues. & Thurs. 10:30-1, Sat. 1:30-4; other times by appointment.

Leesburg

THE GEORGE C. MARSHALL INTERNATIONAL CENTER AT DODONA MANOR, 217 Edwards Ferry Rd., Leesburg, VA 20176-2305. Tel.: 703-777-1880 & 1301. Fax: 703-777-1889.
E-mail: dodona@georgecmarshall.org
Web Site: www.georgecmarshall.org
Founded: 2005.
Congressional District: 10
Key Personnel: Operations Mgr., Richard Rohrer; Pres. (V), Fred Morefield; Tours & Events Coord., Janet Vandervaart; Docent Coord., Pat Black.
Personnel Profile: Full-Time Paid 4; Part-Time Paid 2; Part-Time Volunteers 50.
Historic House Museum: housed in the former residence of General & Mrs. George C. Marshall. A National Historic Landmark.
Collections: period furnishings; personal artifacts; photographs.
Hours & Admission Prices: June-Aug. 1-5; Sept.-May Sat. 10-5, Sun. 1-5; groups by appointment. Adults $10; seniors & groups $8; students with ID & children 9-17 $5.
Attendance: 4,000 (estimated)
Membership: Thank You George Marshall $35-$50; Friend of George Marshall $75-$125; Friend of Dodona Manor $200-$300; Special Friend of Dodona Manor $500; George and Katherine Marshall Society $2,000; Marshall Legady Trust $5,000; Marshall Legady Trust Laureate $10,000.

LOUDOUN MUSEUM, INC., 16 Loudoun St., S.W., Leesburg, VA 20175-2907. Tel.: 703-777-7427. Fax: 703-777-8873.
E-mail: info@loudounmuseum.org
Web Site: www.loudounmuseum.org
Founded: 1967.
Congressional District: 10
Key Personnel: Pres. (V), Elizabeth Whiting; Cur., Pam Stewart; Dir. Administration, Beth Friedmann.
Personnel Profile: Full-Time Paid 2; Part-Time Paid 2; Part-Time Volunteers 15; Interns 3.
Governing Authority: nonprofit organization. Tax-exempt.
Local History Museum: housed in mid-19th century buildings.

Collections: life in the county from prehistory-present; historic documents; manuscripts; decorative arts; costumes; flat textiles; photographs; furniture; tools.
Research Fields: local history; Civil War history.
Facilities: library of reference books & materials on county history available for study on premises. Books for sale.
Activities: lectures; tours; permanent & temporary exhibitions; school programs; special events; audiovisual program on county history.
Publications: book, Legends of Loudoun, A Walk Around Leesburg; quarterly newsletter, The Heritage Review; The Lure of Loudoun.
Hours & Admission Prices: Sun. 1-5, Mon. & Wed.-Sat. 10-5, Tues. by appointment. Adults $3, seniors, teachers & students $1; children under 4, military & members no charge. Closed New Year's Day; Thanksgiving; Christmas Eve & Day. ♿
Attendance: 35,500 (estimated)
Membership: Teacher, Student & Senior Citizen $25; Individual $30; Family $40; Sustainer $100; Patron $250; Benefactor $500; Corporate $1,000.

MORVEN PARK, (M), 17263 Southern Planter Lane, Leesburg, VA 20176-7131. Mailing Address: P.O. Box 6228, Leesburg, VA 20178-7433. Tel.: 703-777-6034. Fax: 703-771-9211.
E-mail: tgillespie@morvenpark.org
Web Site: www.morvenpark.com
Founded: 1955.
Congressional District: 10
Key Personnel: C.E.O. & Exec. Dir., William F. O'Keefe; Chm., Jill Gruver; Dir. Historical Operations, Tracy J. Gillespie; Dir. Education, Richard T. Gillespie; Mgr. Collections, Aimee Summers.
Personnel Profile: Full-Time Paid 5; Part-Time Paid 11; Part-Time Volunteers 2.
Governing Authority: nonprofit organization. Parent Institution: Westmoreland Davis Memorial Foundation. Tax-exempt: 501(c)(3).
Historic House Museum.
Collections: preservation project; carriage & fox hunting museum; history; agriculture; 16th-century tapestries from Flanders; early 20th-century lifestyle & political history.
Research Fields: agriculture; early 20th-century Virginia political history.
Facilities: 3,000-vol. library of sports, economics, agriculture & Virginia government available on premises with prior appointment; nature trails.
Activities: guided tours; lectures; programs; permanent exhibitions; formally & informally organized education programs for special groups & general public; education programs for schools.
Publications: thematic brochures of Morven Park's history & inhabitants.
Hours & Admission Prices: April-Nov. Fri.-Mon. & other times by appointment. Adults $7. ♿
Attendance: 8,000 (estimated)

OATLANDS, 20850 Oatlands Plantation Lane, Leesburg, VA 20175-6572. Tel.: 703-777-3174. Fax: 703-777-4427.
E-mail: oatlands@erols.com
Web Site: www.oatlands.org
Founded: 1965.
Congressional District: 10
Key Personnel: Exec. Dir. & Historian, David Y. Boyce; Chm. (V), Tina Gulland; Museum Shop Mgr., Carolyn Barnett.
Personnel Profile: Full-Time Paid 11; Part-Time Paid 24; Part-Time Volunteers 80; Interns 1.
Governing Authority: Parent Institution: National Trust for Historic Preservation, 1785 Massachusetts Ave., N.W., Washington, DC 20036. Subsidiary Institution: Oatlands Plantation. Tax-exempt: 501(c)(3).
Historic House Museum: 1804 Oatlands mansion with English walled garden, built by George Carter; a portico with Corinthian capitals, carved by Henry Farnham, was added in 1827.
Collections: 18th- to 20th-century decorative arts.
Research Fields: decorative arts.
Facilities: dependencies; formal gardens; carriage house. Museum-related items for sale.
Activities: exhibits.
Publications: quarterly newsletter.
Hours & Admission Prices: Mon.-Sat. 10-4:30, Sun. 1-4:30. Adults $10, senior citizens $7, children under 12 $1; discounts to groups, National Trust for Historic Preservation members & friends of Oatlands; members no charge. ♿
Attendance: 39,772 (accurate)
Membership: Single $50; Contributor $100; Supporter $250; Donor $500; Carter-Eustis $1,000; Corporate $2,500.

Lexington

GEORGE C. MARSHALL MUSEUM, (M), 1600 VMI Parade Ground, Lexington, VA 24450. Mailing Address: P.O. Drawer 1600, Lexington, VA 24450-1600. Tel.: 540-463-7103, ext. 125. Fax: 540-464-5229.
E-mail: collections@marshallfoundation.org
Web Site: www.marshallfoundation.org
Formerly: George C. Marshall Research Foundation
Founded: 1953.
Congressional District: 6
Key Personnel: Pres., Brian D. Shaw; Vice Pres. & Dir. Programs, Robert B. James; Dir. Admin., Carol E. Wheeler; Assoc. Editor, Marshall Papers, Sharon Stevens; Dir. Library & Archives, Paul B. Barron.
Personnel Profile: Full-Time Paid 16; Part-Time Paid 10; Part-Time Volunteers 10; Interns 8.
Governing Authority: nonprofit organization. Parent Institution: George C. Marshall Foundation. Tax-exempt: 501(c)(3).
Library and History Museum.
Collections: artifacts of the life & times of Army General George C. Marshall; Marshall papers & other related collections; archives.
Research Fields: 20th-century American military history & diplomatic history; World War I & II.
Facilities: 25,000-vol. library of 20th-century American military history & diplomatic history of World War I & II and the Korean Conflict.
Activities: educational programs for student & adult groups by appointment. Museum Sponsors: Living Traditions: The VMI Parade, weekly Sept.-May; George C. Marshall Lecture Series.
Publications: bulletin, Topics; book, The China Mission; Marshall Biography; Papers of George Catlett Marshall-Vols. I, II, III, IV & V; book, The George C. Marshall Interviews and Reminiscences for Forrest C. Pogue.
Hours & Admission Prices: Daily 9-5. Adults $5, senior citizens $3, students $2; discounts to groups & AAM members; children & active military no charge. ♿
Attendance: 18,000 (estimated)

LEE CHAPEL & MUSEUM, (M), Washington & Lee University, Lexington, VA 24450-2116. Mailing Address: 11 University Place, Lexington, VA 24450-2116. Tel.: 540-458-8768. Fax: 540-458-5804.
E-mail: ldonald@wlu.edu
Web Site: leechapel.wlu.edu
Founded: 1928.
Congressional District: 6
Key Personnel: Mgr., Linda Donald; Administrative Asst., Pat Larew; Museum Shop Mgr., Gloria Gorlin; Museum Shop Mgr., Margaret Samdahl.
Personnel Profile: Full-Time Paid 2; Part-Time Paid 20.
Governing Authority: private university; nonprofit. Parent Institution: Washington & Lee University. Tax-exempt: 501(c)(3).
History Museum: housed in 1868 historic building constructed under the direction of R.E. Lee.
Collections: university history with emphasis on its namesakes; Washington, Custis & Lee portraits; Lee family artifacts & memorabilia; statue of Lee by Edward Valentine; statue chamber; Lee family crypt; Lee's office.
Major Exhibits: Robert E. Lee: Lasting Ties to West Point, 11/09-5/10.
Facilities: 525-seat auditorium. Museum-related items for sale.
Activities: school & guided tours; permanent exhibitions; lectures.
Hours & Admission Prices: April-Oct. Mon.-Sat. 9-5, Sun. 1-5; Nov.-March Mon.-Sat. 9-4, Sun.1-4; call to verify. Suggested Donation: adults $5, children under 12 $3. Closed New Year's Eve & Day; Easter; Independence Day; Thanksgiving & weekend after; Christmas Eve, Day & week; university holidays. ♿
Attendance: 43,994 (accurate)

THE REEVES CENTER, WASHINGTON AND LEE UNIVERSITY, Lexington, VA 24450. Tel.: 540-458-8744 & 8476. Fax: 540-458-8741.
E-mail: pgrover@wlu.edu
Founded: 1982.
Congressional District: 6
Key Personnel: Dir., Peter Dun Grover.
Personnel Profile: Full-Time Paid 4; Part-Time Volunteers 2; Interns 6.
Governing Authority: private; nonprofit university. Parent Institution: Washington and Lee University. Tax-exempt: 501(c)(3).
Art Museum: housed in two buildings - 1840 Greek Revival house on the front campus & a Palladian-style pavilion with two galleries.
Collections: Chinese ceramics, 2nd to 19th-centuries; European ceramics, 17th-to 19th-centuries; paintings, 17th- to 19th-centuries; Japanese tearoom with tea utensils, scrolls & chabaria containers.
Research Fields: Chinese export porcelain; English & European ceramics; 19th-century American art; decorative arts.
Facilities: 900-vol. library on ceramics, art history, decorative arts & history available to the public on site; seminar room; lecture hall; 3,500 sq. ft. exhibit space.

Activities: formal education programs for university students; guided tours; lectures; loan, temporary & traveling exhibitions.
Publications: catalogs; books, Chinese Export Porcelain in the Reeves Center Collections at Washington & Lee University; A Fragile Union: The Story of Louise Herreshoff.
Hours & Admission Prices: Mon.-Fri. 9-4:30, Sat.-Sun. by appointment. No charge. Closed Memorial Day; Independence Day; Thanksgiving; Christmas to New Year's. ♿
Attendance: 5,000 (estimated)

ROCKBRIDGE HISTORICAL SOCIETY, 101 E. Washington St., Lexington, VA 24450. Mailing Address: P.O. Box 1409, Lexington, VA 24450-1409. Tel.: 540-464-1058.
E-mail: rochist@hotmail.com
Web Site: rockhist.org
Founded: 1939.
Congressional District: 6
Key Personnel: Exec. Dir., George W. Warren, IV; Pres. (V), Dr. Charles A. Bodie.
Personnel Profile: Full-Time Paid 1; Part-Time Volunteers 31; Interns 3.
Governing Authority: society. Tax-exempt: 501(c)(3).
General Museum: housed in c.1844 Campbell House, a 3-story brick home.
Collections: books; documents; journals; photographs; works of art; tools; furnishings; furniture relating to history of Rockbridge County with associated artifacts.
Research Fields: local architecture; local history; genealogy.
Facilities: 600-vol. library of family papers, clippings, local newspapers located at the library of Washington-Lee University.
Activities: interpretative presentations; bimonthly meetings. Museum Sponsors: Traditional Folklife Festival; Victorian Christmas Open House; Ice Cream Social.
Publications: bimonthly newsletter; Roads of Rockbridge; RHS Proceedings.
Hours & Admission Prices: mid-April to mid-Oct. Mon.-Sat. 10-4, Sun. 12-4; mid-Oct. to mid-April Mon.-Sat. 10-1, Sun. 1-4. No charge; donations accepted. Closed New Year's Eve & Day; Christmas Eve, Day & week. ♿
Attendance: 5,800 (accurate)
Membership: Student $10; Individual $20; Family $30; Corporate $50.

STANIAR GALLERY, Wilson Hall, 100 Glasgow St., Washington & Lee University, Lexington, VA 24450-2116. Tel.: 540-458-8861 & 8860. Fax: 540-458-8112.
E-mail: archerc@wlu.edu
Web Site: www.wlu.edu
Formerly: Dupont Gallery
Founded: 2006.
Congressional District: 6
Key Personnel: Dir., Clover Archer Lyle.
Personnel Profile: Full-Time Paid 1; Interns 1.
Governing Authority: college. Parent Institution: Washington and Lee University. Tax-exempt: 501(c)(3).
University Art Gallery.
Collections: non-collecting contemporary art gallery.
Major Exhibits: Louviere & Vanessa: Persistence of Vision, 1/4/10-2/11/10; Beyond Text and Image: The Book as Art, 2/25/10-4/2/10; Constructs (T), 4/19/10-5/14/10.
Activities: lectures; panel discussions; cross-disciplinary symposia; visiting artists' workshops that link the gallery & the university's curriculum.
Publications: exhibition catalogs for selected exhibitions.
Hours & Admission Prices: Sept.-May Mon.-Fri. 9-5. No charge. ♿

STONEWALL JACKSON HOUSE, (M), 8 E. Washington St., Lexington, VA 24450-2529. Tel.: 540-463-2552. Fax: 540-463-4088.
E-mail: director@stonewalljackson.org
Web Site: www.stonewalljackson.org
Founded: 1954.
Congressional District: 6
Key Personnel: Exec. Dir., Michael Anne Lynn; Pres. (V), George H. Roberts, Jr.; Cur., Heidi Wing Sheldon.
Personnel Profile: Full-Time Paid 4; Part-Time Paid 15; Part-Time Volunteers 60; Interns 1.
Governing Authority: nonprofit organization. Parent Institution: Stonewall Jackson Foundation, 8 E. Washington St., Lexington, VA 24450. Tax-exempt: 501(c)(3).
Historic House Museum: 1859-1861 Stonewall Jackson Home.
Collections: furniture & furnishings owned by T. J. Jackson & his family; period furniture appropriate to 1851-1861 small town life; manuscripts.
Research Fields: life & times of Gen. Thomas J. Jackson; Civil War; ante-bellum Virginia; social history.
Facilities: restored gardens. Museum-related items for sale.
Activities: guided tours; lectures; formally organized education programs for children; permanent & temporary exhibitions; biennial symposium on Stonewall Jackson; summer fellowships for graduate students.
Publications: books, Stonewall Jackson & the Virginia Military Institute: The Lexington Years; Stonewall Jackson in Lexington: The Christian Soldier.
Hours & Admission Prices: Summer: Mon.-Sat. 9-5, Sun. 1-5; Winter call for hours. Adults $6, children 18 & under $3; discounts to groups, and AAM, VAM & SEMC members. Closed New Year's Day; Easter; Thanksgiving; Christmas.
Attendance: 20,709 (accurate)

* **VIRGINIA MILITARY INSTITUTE MUSEUM, (M),** Virginia Military Institute, Jackson Memorial Hall, Lexington, VA 24450-2194. Tel.: 540-464-7334. Fax: 540-464-7112. TDD: 540-464-7616.
E-mail: gibsonke@vmi.edu
Web Site: www.vmi.edu/museum
Founded: 1856.
Congressional District: 9
Key Personnel: Exec. Dir., Keith E. Gibson; Registrar, Barbara J. Blakey; Museum Shop Mgr., Betty E. Skillman.
Personnel Profile: Full-Time Paid 3; Part-Time Paid 4; Part-Time Volunteers 4.
Governing Authority: university. Parent Institution: Virginia Military Institute. Branch Museum: ROTC Building, Kilbourne Hall. Tax-exempt.
Military, National Historic District and General Museum: located on Virginia Military Institute campus.
Collections: artifacts, drawings, paintings and photographs relating to the history of VMI and its immediate vicinity; memorabilia of alumni & faculty; military uniforms & equipment.
Research Fields: history of VMI, alumni, faculty and vicinity.
Facilities: 350-vol. library of books available for use on premises; auditorium. Postcards, prints & books for sale.
Activities: guided tours; lectures; films; inter-museum loan, permanent & temporary exhibitions.
Publications: booklet, They Were Heard From VMI Alumni in the Civil War.
Hours & Admission Prices: Daily 9-5. No charge; donations accepted. Closed New Year's Eve, Day & day after; Thanksgiving; Christmas Eve, Day & week. ♿
Attendance: 40,000 (accurate)

Lorton

POHICK EPISCOPAL CHURCH, 9301 Richmond Hwy., Lorton, VA 22079-1519. Tel.: 703-339-6572. Fax: 703-339-9884.
E-mail: troknya@pohick.org
Web Site: www.pohick.org
Founded: 1774.
Key Personnel: Rector, Rev. Donald D. Binder.
Personnel Profile: Full-Time Paid 5; Part-Time Paid 3; Part-Time Volunteers 6; Interns 1.
Governing Authority: The Episcopal Church, Diocese of Virginia. Tax-exempt.
Active Church: housed in 1774 parish church of George Washington & George Mason.
Collections: interior box pews; two baptismal fonts; c.1968 pipe organ made of 880 pipes, 13 stops & 17 ranks; Vestry book, containing records from 1732-1985; 1761 Big Prayer Book; 1796 2-vol. Bible; c.1737 Lee plate & cup of hammered silver; chalice; silver bread box & cruets; silver ewer; 2 silver communion chalices; one of the baptismal fonts was originally a mortar (late Saxon-early Norman).
Activities: guided tours; concerts; study clubs; organized educational programs; docent program; regular church programs.
Publications: book, Minutes of the Vestry, Truro Parish 1732-1785; brochure; book of genealogical records.
Hours & Admission Prices: Mon.-Sat. 9-4:30, Sun. 8-4:30. No charge. ♿

Louisa

LOUISA COUNTY HISTORICAL SOCIETY, 214 Fredericksburg Ave., Louisa, VA 23093-6531. Mailing Address: P.O. Box 1172, Louisa, VA 23093-1172. Tel.: 540-967-5975.
E-mail: louisahistory@verizon.net
Web Site: www.louisahistory.org
Founded: 1966.
Congressional District: 7
Key Personnel: Pres. (V), Jack Manzari.
Governing Authority: society. Tax-exempt.
Historical Society Museum: housed in 1868 jail.
Collections: Louisa County history from prehistoric to modern times.
Facilities: 100-vol. library of local & Virginia history, available to the public.
Publications: biannual, Louisa County Historical Magazine; quarterly newsletter.

Hours & Admission Prices: Jail Museum: April-Sept. Fri.-Sat. 10am-12pm. Sargeant Museum: Mon.-Sat. 10-4, call to confirm. No charge; donations accepted.
Attendance: 200 (estimated)
Membership: Individual $27; Family $32; Supporting $50; Sustaining $200; Life $350; Benefactor $1,000.

Lovettsville

LOVETTSVILLE HISTORICAL SOCIETY MUSEUM, 4 E. Pennsylvania Ave., Lovettsville, VA 20180. Mailing Address: P.O. Box 5, Lovettsville, VA 20180-0005. Tel.: 540-822-5499.
E-mail: harrison@lovettsvillemuseum.com
Web Site: lovettsvillemuseum.com
Historical Society Museum.
Collections: Lovettsville history & heritage; genealogy.
Facilities: Books for sale.
Hours & Admission Prices: May-Dec. Sat. 1-4; other times by appointment.

Luray

SHENANDOAH NATIONAL PARK, 3655 U.S. Hwy. 211 E., Luray, VA 22835-4702. Tel.: 540-999-3500. Fax: 540-999-3601.
E-mail: reed_engle@nps.gov
Web Site: www.nps.gov/shen
Founded: 1935.
Congressional District: 7
Key Personnel: Supt., Martha Bogle.
Governing Authority: federal. National Park Service, Interior Building, Washington, DC. Visitors Centers: Dickey Ridge, Front Royal, VA., 22630. Byrd Visitor Center. Tax-exempt.
Park Museum & Visitor Center.
Collections: history; herbarium; geology; archives.
Facilities: 1,600-vol. library of books pertaining to area history. Books, maps, guides, pictures, colored slides for sale.
Activities: guided hikes; movies; evening programs; environmental education study areas.
Publications: booklets; books; maps; Everything Was Wonderful: A Pictorial History of the Civilian Conservation Corps. in Shenandoah National Park.
Hours & Admission Prices: Park: daily 24 hours. $10 per car, camping $14-17 per night per site. Byrd Visitor Center & Dickey Ridge Visitor Center: April-Nov. daily 9-5. ♿
Attendance: 1,900,000
Membership: Shenandoah Natural History Association: Student $8; Individual $20; Family $25; Supporting $50; Corporate $500.

Lynchburg

AMAZEMENT SQUARE, THE RIGHTMIRE CHILDREN'S MUSEUM, 27 Ninth St., Lynchburg, VA 24504-1422. Tel.: 434-845-1888. Fax: 434-845-5221.
E-mail: visitus@amazementsquare.com
Web Site: www.amazementsquare.org
Founded: 1993.
Key Personnel: Pres. & C.E.O., Mort Sajadian, Ph.D.; Chm. (V), Thomas C. Jividen; Treas., Thomas Pettyjohn, Jr.; Vice Pres. Devel., Melissa Zadell; Vice Pres. Operations, Tabitha Abbott; Exhibit Fabricator, John Kastner; Museum Shop Mgr., Emily Gibbs.
Personnel Profile: Full-Time Paid 12; Part-Time Paid 23; Part-Time Volunteers 63; Interns 2.
Governing Authority: private; nonprofit organization. Tax-exempt: 501(c)(3).
Children's Museum.
Collections: hands-on exhibits; paintings; multicultural dolls.
Major Exhibits: Celebrating Differences: Access for All, 11/09-5/10; Flights of Fancy, 1/10-12/10.
Research Fields: Everyone is Special Partnership with the Laurel Regional School studying the impact & use of multisensory environments and adaptive technology on severely handicapped children.
Facilities: library; educational facilities; 18,000 sq. ft. exhibit space; education center; 600-seat outdoor theater. Museum-related items for sale.
Activities: arts festivals; docent program; films; formal education programs for children; guided tours; loan, participatory & traveling exhibitions; theater; mentoring programs; outreach programs to underserved communities. Annual Events: Ugly Bug Ball; Gathering of Goddesses; Amazing Mile Children's Run.
Publications: quarterly newsletter; comic book series, Amazing Adventures of Scorpy Bug.
Hours & Admission Prices: Memorial Day to Labor Day Sun.-Mon. 1-5, Tues.-Sat. 10-5; Sept.-May Tues.-Sat. 10-5, Sun. 1-5. Family Fun Night: second & fourth Sat. of month 5-8. Admission $7; discounts to groups; members & children under 2 no charge. ♿
Attendance: 92,517 (accurate)
Membership: Teacher $60-$105; Fantastic $75-$120; Super $140; Amazing $250; Grand $325.

THE ANNE SPENCER MEMORIAL FOUNDATION, INC., 1313 Pierce St., Lynchburg, VA 24501-1935. Tel.: 434-845-1313.
Founded: 1977.
Congressional District: 6
Key Personnel: Chm., Hugh R. Jones; Chm. Tours, Liz Lovern.
Personnel Profile: Part-Time Volunteers 15.
Governing Authority: nonprofit organization. Tax-exempt.
Historic House & Garden: housed in the former home of poet, Anne Spencer; built in 1903. Listed on the National Register of Historic Places.
Collections: photographs; Victorian furnishings; writings of Anne Spencer; book; stained glass window; African head; statue of Minerva; flowers & shrubs.
Research Fields: Victorian era.
Facilities: 300-vol. library. Museum-related items for sale.
Activities: guided tours; films.
Hours & Admission Prices: By appointment only. Adults $5, seniors $4, college students $3, children under 12 $2.
Attendance: 1,000 (estimated)
Membership: Membership by donation.

DAURA GALLERY, (M), Lynchburg College, 1501 Lakeside Dr., Lynchburg, VA 24501-3199. Tel.: 434-544-8343 & 8349. Fax: 804-544-8277.
E-mail: rothermel@lynchburg.edu
Web Site: www.lynchburg.edu/daura
Founded: 1974.
Congressional District: 6
Key Personnel: Dir., Barbara Rothermel; Asst. Dir., Steve Riffee.
Personnel Profile: Full-Time Paid 2; Part-Time Paid 2; Part-Time Volunteers 6; Interns 3.
Governing Authority: private college; nonprofit. Parent Institution: Lynchburg College. Tax-exempt.
Art Gallery.
Collections: 2,000 pieces including 20th-century American and European artists; art of Catalan-American Modernist Pierre Daura.
Research Fields: museum studies.
Facilities: library.
Activities: guided tours by appointment; temporary exhibitions; rotating exhibitions of various artists.
Publications: newsletter; exhibition catalogs; brochures.
Hours & Admission Prices: Aug.-May Mon.-Fri. 9-4, Sun. call for hours; June-July by appointment. No charge; donations accepted. Closed college holidays; New Year's Day; Thanksgiving; Christmas. ♿
Attendance: 6,000 (estimated)
Membership: Individual $25; Family $50; Patron $100; Curator's Circle $250; Virginia Davis Society $500; Georgia Morgan Society $1,000; Pierre & Louis Daura Society $2,500 & up.

LEGACY MUSEUM OF AFRICAN-AMERICAN HISTORY, 403 Monroe St., Lynchburg, VA 24504-2808. Mailing Address: P.O. Box 308, Lynchburg, VA 24505-0308. Tel.: 434-845-3455. Fax: 434-845-9809.
E-mail: legacymuseum@ntelos.net
Web Site: www.legacymuseum.org
Key Personnel: Museum Admin., Cheryl Robinson
History Museum.
Collections: local African American history & culture.
Activities: exhibit-related programs; special events.
Hours & Admission Prices: Wed.-Sat. 12-4, Sun. 2-4; other times by appointment. Adults $5, seniors $3, youth $2; children under 6 no charge. Closed major holidays. ♿

LYNCHBURG MUSEUM SYSTEM, (M), 901 Court St., Lynchburg, VA 24504-1603. Mailing Address: P.O. Box 529, Lynchburg, VA 24505-0529. Tel.: 434-455-6226. Fax: 804-528-0162.
Web Site: www.lynchburgmuseum.org
Founded: 1976.
Congressional District: 6
Key Personnel: Dir., Douglas K. Harvey; Pres. (V) & Museum Shop Mgr., Laura Crumbley.
Personnel Profile: Full-Time Paid 4; Part-Time Paid 7; Part-Time Volunteers 55.
Governing Authority: municipal. Parent Institution: City of Lynchburg, Virginia. Tax-exempt.
History Museum.
Collections: furniture; costumes; art exhibit; photographs; machinery; decorative arts. Historic Buildings: 1855 Old Court House; 1815 Point of Honor.

Research Fields: Lynchburg history.
Activities: volunteer programs; tours; permanent exhibits; living history program. Museum Sponsors: Fall Festival in October; Christmas Open House; Garden Day tour.
Publications: quarterly, MuseNews.
Hours & Admission Prices: Mon.-Sat. 10-4, Sun. 12-4. Historic House: adults $6. Museum: adults $6; AAM members no charge. Closed New Year's Day; Thanksgiving; Christmas Eve & Day.
Attendance: 11,071 (accurate)

MAIER MUSEUM OF ART, RANDOLPH COLLEGE, (M), One Quinlan St., Lynchburg, VA 24503-1519. Mailing Address: 2500 Rivermont Ave., Lynchburg, VA 24503-1526. Tel.: 434-947-8136 & 8000. Fax: 434-947-8726.
E-mail: museum@randolphcollege.edu
Web Site: maiermuseum.org
Formerly: Maier Museum of Art, Randolph-Macon Woman's College
Founded: 1920.
Congressional District: 6
Key Personnel: Interim Dir., Martha Kjeseth Johnson; Registrar, Deborah Spanich; Office Mgr., Sarah Bare.
Personnel Profile: Part-Time Paid 3; Part-Time Volunteers 60.
Governing Authority: college. Parent Institution: Randolph College. Tax-exempt: 501(c)(3).
Art.
Collections: American paintings; works on paper; photographs.
Research Fields: 19th, 20th & 21st century American art.
Activities: inter-museum loans, permanent & temporary exhibitions; docent program; public lectures; gallery tours; museum education programs.
Publications: catalogue of the Collection; brochure; exhibition catalogues; members newsletter; online collection catalog.
Hours & Admission Prices: late April to late Aug. Wed.-Sun. 1-4; late Aug. to late April Tues.-Sun. 1-5. No charge; donations accepted. Closed academic holidays, New Year's; Easter; Independence Day; Thanksgiving; Christmas.
Attendance: 7,200 (estimated)
Membership: Special $35; Individual $45; Family & Household $65; Friend $100; Patron $250; Sponsor $500; Mary Frances Williams Society $1,000; Benefactor $2,500; Maier Circle $5,000.

MUSEUM OF EARTH AND LIFE HISTORY, Liberty University Library, 1971 University Blvd., Lynchburg, VA 24502. Tel.: 434-582-2228.
Web Site: www.liberty.edu
Founded: 1985.
Congressional District: 6
Key Personnel: Dir., David A. DeWitt, Ph.D.
Governing Authority: Parent Institution: Liberty University. Tax-exempt.
Natural History Museum.
Collections: natural history.
Hours & Admission Prices: Mon.-Tues. & Thurs.-Fri. 8-8, Wed. 8-4, Sat. 9-6, Sun. 1-4. No charge.

OLD CITY CEMETERY MUSEUM & ARBORETUM, (M), 401 Taylor St., Lynchburg, VA 24501-1245. Tel.: 434-847-1465.
E-mail: occ@gravegarden.org
Web Site: www.gravegarden.org
Founded: 1806.
Congressional District: 6
Key Personnel: Dir., D. Bruce Christian; Pres. (V), R. Chambliss Light, Jr.
Personnel Profile: Full-Time Paid 2; Part-Time Paid 3; Part-Time Volunteers 130.
Governing Authority: Parent Institution: Southern Memorial Association. Tax-exempt.
Historic Landmark: listed on the National Register of Historic Places.
Collections: local history & culture; mourning customs; hand tools; grave-markers; gravestone carvers; railroad history.
Major Exhibits: Diuguid Undertakers of Lynchburg, 1817-1950, 1/10-12/10.
Activities: programs; guided tours; events; museums & chapel equipped with push-button audio.
Publications: books, Free Blacks of Lynchburg, Virginia 1805-1865; Food to Die For, A Book of Funeral Food, Tips and Tales.
Hours & Admission Prices: Cemetery: daily dawn to dusk. Visitor Center & Victorian Mourning Exhibit: daily 11-3. No charge; donations accepted. Guided Tours: call for admission prices.
Attendance: 25,000 (estimated)

POINT OF HONOR, 112 Cabell St., Lynchburg, VA 24504-1211. Mailing Address: Lynchburg Museum System, P.O. Box 529, Lynchburg, VA 24505-0529. Tel.: 434-455-6226. Fax: 434-528-0162.
Web Site: www.pointofhonor.org
Founded: 1976.
Congressional District: 6
Key Personnel: Admin., Douglas K. Harvey; Pres. (V), James K. Dill; Museum Shop Mgr., Laura Crumbley.
Personnel Profile: Full-Time Paid 4; Part-Time Paid 7; Part-Time Volunteers 45.
Governing Authority: municipal. Parent Institution: Point of Honor, Inc.; Subsidiary Institution: Lynchburg Museum System. Tax-exempt: 501(c)(3).
Historic House: home of Dr. George Cabell, physician to Patrick Henry.
Collections: furnishings, accessories & decorative arts reflecting the lifestyle of the 1800-1830 period.
Research Fields: Federal period Virginia furnishings & decorative arts; Genealogical investigation of the former owners of Point of Honor.
Facilities: meeting facility. Museum-related items for sale.
Activities: guided tours; lectures; organized education programs for children; docent program.
Hours & Admission Prices: Mon.-Sat. 10-4, Sun. 12-4. Adults $6, seniors 60 & over $5, youth 6-17 $3; discounts to AAM members; children under 6 no charge. Closed New Year's Day; Thanksgiving; Christmas Eve & Day.
Attendance: 5,992 (accurate)

SOUTH RIVER MEETING HOUSE, 5810 Fort Ave., Lynchburg, VA 24502-1928. Tel.: 434-239-2548. Fax: 434-239-6071.
Web Site: qmpc.org/contents/meetinghousehistory.shtml
Founded: 1757.
Congressional District: 6
Key Personnel: Dir., Diane Baldwin.
Personnel Profile: Part-Time Volunteers 7.
Governing Authority: church. Parent Institution: Quaker Memorial Presbyterian Church. Tax-exempt: 501(c)(3); 170(b)(1)(A); 509(a)(1).
Historic Site: a restored Society of Friends meeting house, c.1791. Listed on the National Register of Historic Places.
Collections: photographs; artifacts from 1864 Civil War battle; documents relating to history of Quakers & Meeting House; Quaker cemetery.
Research Fields: local Quaker history.
Facilities: 25-vol. library of books on Quaker history, spirituality & genealogy housed in adjacent Quaker Memorial Presbyterian Church.
Activities: guided tours; lectures; organized educational programs; interpreter; training programs.
Publications: brochures; book, Lynchburg's Pioneer Quakers & Their Meeting House.
Hours & Admission Prices: Mon.-Fri. 9-3; guided tours by appointment. No charge; donations accepted. Closed major holidays. ♿
Attendance: 350

Machipongo

EASTERN SHORE OF VIRGINIA BARRIER ISLANDS CENTER, 7295 Young St., Machipongo, VA 23405. Mailing Address: P.O. Box 206, Machipongo, VA 23405-0206. Tel.: 757-678-5550; 888-678-5572. Fax: 888-315-8780.
E-mail: barrierislandscenter@live.com
Web Site: www.barrierislandscenter.com/navigation.html
History Museum.
Collections: Virginia's Barrier Island history & culture; maritime artifacts.
Facilities: Museum-related items for sale.
Activities: lectures; classes; special events.
Hours & Admission Prices: June to Labor Day Tues.-Sat. 10-4, Sun. 1-5; Sept.-May Tues.-Sat. 10-4.

Manassas

MANASSAS MUSEUM SYSTEM, (M), 9101 Prince William St., Manassas, VA 20110-5615. Tel.: 703-368-1873. Fax: 703-257-8406. TDD: 703-257-8255.
Web Site: www.manassasmuseum.org
Founded: 1973.
Congressional District: 8
Key Personnel: C.E.O., John Verrill; Chm. (V), Suzanne Parker; Museum Shop Mgr., Jane Riley.
Personnel Profile: Full-Time Paid 8; Part-Time Paid 5; Part-Time Volunteers 95.
Governing Authority: municipal government; nonprofit. Parent Institution: City of Manassas, 9101 Prince William St., Manassas, VA 20110. Branch Sites: The Manassas Museum; The Hopkins Candy Factory; Mayfield Fort; Manassas Train Depot; Manassas Industrial School/Jennie Dean Memorial; Liberia Plantation; Cannon Branch Fort; Speiden Carper House. Tax-exempt: 170(b)(1)(A).
History Museum.

Collections: photographs; local & regional industrial, commercial, personal & household collections including buildings and their archaeological materials.
Research Fields: Civil War; local history; African-American history; historical architecture; modern life.
Activities: guided tours; living history programs; school programs; discovery room; changing exhibitions. Museum Sponsors: museum trunk outreach.
Publications: monthly newsletters, Word from the Junction; volunteer bulletin.
Hours & Admission Prices: Daily dawn-dusk. Adults $5, children under 18 $2; discount to senior citizens, AAM & AAA members and groups; members no charge. Closed New Year's Day; Thanksgiving; Christmas. ♿
Attendance: 45,000 (estimated)
Membership: Student & Senior Citizen $20; Individual $30; Family $40; Sustainer $50; Patron & Corporate $100 & up.

* **MANASSAS NATIONAL BATTLEFIELD PARK,** 6511 Sudley Rd., (Rt. 234), Manassas, VA 20109-2358. Tel.: 703-361-1339. Fax: 703-361-7106. TDD: 703-361-7075.
E-mail: mana_superintendent@nps.gov
Web Site: www.nps.gov/mana
Founded: 1940.
Congressional District: 10
Key Personnel: Supt., Edward W. Clark; Chm. (V), Henry Elliott; Acting Chief Interpretation, Ray Brown; Collection Mgr., James Burgess; Chief Ranger, Bud Walsh; Museum Shop Mgr., Larry Swanson.
Personnel Profile: Full-Time Paid 28; Part-Time Paid 2; Part-Time Volunteers 511; Interns 3.
Governing Authority: federal. Parent Institution: U.S. Dept. of Interior. Subsidiary Institution: National Park Service. Tax-exempt.
Park Museum & Visitor Center
Collections: historic artifacts & documentary materials relating to first & second Battles of Manassas; archaeological & architectural materials associated with the civilian & military occupation of the battlefield. Historic House: 1848 Stone house, L. Dogan house.
Research Fields: American Civil War.
Facilities: 2,000-vol. reference library of military history books & manuscripts open to researchers Mon.-Fri. by appointment only.
Activities: guided & self-guided tours; orientation film; battle map program; permanent & temporary exhibits; living history demonstrations.
Publications: folders; maps; site bulletins.
Hours & Admission Prices: Daily 8:30-5. Adults 16 & over $3; children & disabled no charge. Closed Thanksgiving; Christmas. ♿
Attendance: 595,471 (accurate)

Marion

SMYTH COUNTY MUSEUM, (M), 105 E. Strother St., Marion, VA 24354-2707. Mailing Address: P.O. Box 710, Marion, VA 24354-0710. Tel.: 276-783-7286.
Founded: 1961.
Congressional District: 9
Key Personnel: Pres. (V), Brenda Gwyn.
Personnel Profile: Part-Time Volunteers 12.
Governing Authority: society. Parent Institution: Smyth County Historical & Museum Society, Inc. Headquarters for Smyth County Museum: Staley/Collins House, 109 W. Strother St., Marion, VA 24354, Tel.: 540-783-7286; Wed. & Thurs. 10-3. Tax-exempt: 170(b)(1)(A).
General Museum: housed in 1838 schoolhouse.
Collections: artifacts pertaining to women's & men's culture; weaving; pictorial history of county; 1861-65 Civil War artifacts; period medical items from Southwestern State Hospital; country store; 1908 Marion High School.
Research Fields: local history; genealogy; costumes; archaeology.
Facilities: library & archives of over 3,000 newspaper, books & journals.
Activities: lectures; research.
Publications: Historical Gossip.
Hours & Admission Prices: Fri.-Sat. 10-4. No charge; donations accepted. ♿
Attendance: 3,500
Membership: Students $5; Individual $10; Family $20; Contributor $25; Sponsor $50; Patron $100; Benefactor $500; Sustaining $1,000.

Martinsville

* **PIEDMONT ARTS ASSOCIATION,** 215 Starling Ave., Martinsville, VA 24112-3832. Tel.: 276-632-3221. Fax: 276-638-3963.
E-mail: joewilliams@piedmontarts.org
Web Site: www.piedmontarts.org
Founded: 1961.
Congressional District: 5
Key Personnel: Interim Exec. Dir., Joe Williams; Mgr. Finance, Nancy Plygon; Pres., Thurman Echols; Vice Pres., Harrison Toms; Administrative Asst., Barbara Bradshaw; Dir. Exhibitions, Tina Sell; Coord. Education, Heidi Pinkston; Dir. Programs, Barbara Parker; Maintenance, Nat Cooper.
Personnel Profile: Full-Time Paid 6; Part-Time Paid 9; Part-Time Volunteers 432.
Governing Authority: nonprofit organization. Tax-exempt.
Arts Center: housed in c.1900 M.R. Schottland Estate.
Collections: works by national & regional artists and craftsmen.
Facilities: art studios; public meeting rooms; classroom/studio. Craft-items for sale.
Activities: guided tours; lectures; films; concerts; arts festivals; organized educational programs for children; docent program; loan & temporary exhibitions.
Publications: quarterly newsletter; annual report; brochure; exhibition catalogs.
Hours & Admission Prices: Tues.-Fri. 10-5, Sat. 10-3, Sun. 1:30-4:30. No charge; donations accepted. Closed holidays. ♿
Attendance: 36,000 (estimated)
Membership: Senior Citizen & Student $25; Single $35; Family $45; Patron $150; Major Patron $250; Sustaining Patron $500; Benefactor $1,000.

* **VIRGINIA MUSEUM OF NATURAL HISTORY, (M),** 21 Starling Ave., Martinsville, VA 24112-2921. Tel.: 276-634-4141. Fax: 276-634-4199. TDD: 276-634-4149.
E-mail: information@vmnh.virginia.gov
Web Site: www.vmnh.net
Founded: 1984.
Congressional District: 5
Key Personnel: Chm. Bd. Trustees, Pamela A. Armstrong; Pres. VMNH Foundation, David Sweet; Interim Exec. Dir., Gloria Niblett; Dir. Devel., Debra J. Lewis; Dir. Education & Public Programs, Dennis A. Casey, Ph.D.; Dir. Mktg. & External Affairs, Ryan L. Barber; Dir. Research & Collections, Cur. Earth Sciences, James S. Beard, Ph.D.; Cur. Archaeology, Elizabeth A. Moore, Ph.D.; Cur. Mammalogy, Nancy D. Moncrief, Ph.D.; Cur. Marine Biology, Judith E. Winston, Ph.D.; Visitor Svcs. Mgr., Diane Clark.
Personnel Profile: Full-Time Paid 42; Part-Time Paid 25; Part-Time Volunteers 200.
Governing Authority: Parent Institution: Commonwealth of Virginia of Natural Resources.
Natural History Museum.
Collections: Mesozoic & Cenozoic vertebrate & plant fossils; Virginia archaeology; rocks & minerals; mounted Virginia vertebrates; insects; marine invertebrates; invertebrate fossils; bryozoans.
Major Exhibits: Clues to the Past: Archaeology in Virginia, 11/09-7/10; Treasures from the Triassic, 1/10-9/10; Eyes on Earth (T), 10/10-1/11.
Research Fields: invertebrate biology; invertebrate paleontology; earth sciences; vertebrate paleontology; mammalogy; conservation of natural history specimens; bryology; archaeology.
Facilities: research library; lecture hall; educational facilities; laboratories; high-definition theater; coffee shop. Museum-related items for sale.
Activities: guided tours; lectures; films; field trips; hobby workshops; organized education programs; docent program; temporary exhibitions.
Publications: scientific publications, including Memoirs of the Virginia Museum of Natural History; Jeffersonia; Myriapodologica.
Hours & Admission Prices: Mon.-Sat. 9-5:30, Sun. 12-5:30; groups by appointment. Adults $9, seniors 60 & over and college students $7, children 3-18 $5; children under 3 & members no charge. Closed New Year's Day; Thanksgiving; Christmas. ♿
Attendance: 43,905 (accurate)
Membership: Individual $40; Family & Grandparent $55; Smithsonian $100; Dogwood $250; Cardinal $500; Tiger Swallowtail $1,000.

Mason Neck

* **GUNSTON HALL PLANTATION, (M),** 10709 Gunston Rd., Mason Neck, VA 22079-3901. Tel.: 703-550-9220. Fax: 703-550-9480. TDD: 703-550-9220 (V/TDD).
E-mail: Historic@GunstonHall.org
Web Site: www.gunstonhall.org
Founded: 1932.
Congressional District: 8
Key Personnel: Dir., David L. Leese; First Regent (V), Mrs. Wiley G. Raab; Cur., Caroline Relley; Devel. Coord., Susan Blankenship; Museum Educator, Denise McHugh; Administrative Asst., Lena McAllister; Education Asst., Frank Varker; Librarian & Archivist, Mionele Lee; Docent Chm., Shawn Zurlo; Archaeologist, David Shonyo; Museum Shop Mgr., Karen E. Bazzle.
Personnel Profile: Full-Time Paid 15; Part-Time Paid 35; Part-Time Volunteers 85; Interns 3.
Governing Authority: state. Parent Institution: Commonwealth of Virginia. Subsidiary Institution: The National Society of The Colonial Dames of America. Tax-exempt.

Historic House: 1755 Gunston Hall, plantation home of George Mason.
Collections: furniture & fine arts of the 18th century; rare books; decorative arts; archives; manuscripts; plantation tools.
Research Fields: 18th-century life styles, room use, George Mason.
Facilities: 5,000-vol. library of decorative arts & history books & 1,500-vol. rare book library available for use by appointment; 200-seat auditorium; nature trail; Mason Family grave yard; meeting room; Boxwood gardens; picnic area. Museum-related items for sale.
Activities: guided tours; lectures; docent programs; special events; permanent & temporary exhibitions; active archaeological site; active farmyard.
Publications: semi-annual Gunston Hall Newsletter; special events programs flyers; brochures; books, Enchanted Ground; George Mason's Gunston Hall; The Five George Masons; George Mason, Gentleman Revolutionary; It's A Great Day: The Story of Rusty, The Gunston Hall Fox; videotape, George Mason & The Bill of Rights.
Hours & Admission Prices: Daily 9:30-5. Adults $9, senior citizens 60 & over $8, children 6-18 $4; discount to AAM members; members and children under 6 no charge. Closed New Year's Day; Thanksgiving; Christmas. ♿
Attendance: 46,733 (accurate)
Membership: Individual $25; Family $35; Sponsor $50; Patron $100; Sustaining $250; Benefactor $500; Guardian $1,000 & up.

Mathews

TOMPKINS COTTAGE, 27 Brickbat Rd., Mathews, VA 23109. Mailing Address: P.O. Box 855, Mathews, VA 23109-0855. Tel.: 804-725-4229.
Governing Authority: Parent Institution: Mathews County Historical Society.
Historic House: housed in a former mercantile store owned by Christopher Tompkins, father of Captain Sally Tompkins, the first female commissioned officer in the U.S. military; built in 1815.
Collections: local history & culture; photographs; personal artifacts; early furnishings.
Facilities: Museum-related items for sale.
Hours & Admission Prices: Spring & Summer Fri.-Sat. 11-2. No charge; donations accepted.

McDowell

HIGHLAND COUNTY MUSEUM AND HERITAGE CENTER, 161 Mansion House Rd., McDowell, VA 24458. Mailing Address: P.O. Box 63, McDowell, VA 24458-0063. Tel.: 540-396-4478. Fax: 540-396-4478.
E-mail: highlandhist@mgwnet.com
Founded: 2005.
Congressional District: 6
Key Personnel: Exec. Dir., Crysta Stanton; Chm., Lorraine White; Vice Chm., Sarah Samples; Treas., James Blagg.
Personnel Profile: Full-Time Paid 1; Part-Time Paid 1; Part-Time Volunteers 7.
Governing Authority: private; nonprofit organization. Parent Institution: Highland Historical Society, McDowell, VA 24458. Tax-exempt: 501(c)(3).
History Museum: housed in an 1851 former hospital used during the Civil War which later became a hotel & stagecoach stop on the Staunton to Parkersburg Turnpike.
Collections: Battle of McDowell; local artifacts; period furnishings; Virginia history; Highland County.
Facilities: educational center; 100 sq. ft. exhibit space. Museum-related items for sale.
Activities: docent program; films; lectures; genealogy classes; related special events.
Publications: quarterly newsletter.
Hours & Admission Prices: Fri.-Sat. 11-4, Sun. 1-4. No charge; donations accepted.
Attendance: 1,200 (estimated)
Membership: Individual $15; Family & Business $25; Life $250.

McLean

NATIONAL PARK SERVICE-GREAT FALLS PARK, 9200 Old Dominion Dr., McLean, VA 22102-1019. Mailing Address: Great Falls Park c/o GWMP/Turkey Run Park, McLean, VA 22101. Tel.: 703-285-2966. Fax: 703-285-2223. TDD: 703-285-2966.
Web Site: www.nps.gov/gwmp/grfa
Founded: 1966.
Congressional District: 10
Key Personnel: Park Supt., Dottie Marshall; Site Mgr., Walter McDowney; Ranger Supvr., Joseph Burns; Museum Shop Mgr., Kevin Butler.
Personnel Profile: Full-Time Paid 16; Part-Time Volunteers 6.
Governing Authority: federal; nonprofit. Tax-exempt.
Park Museum: site of the 1785 Patowmack Canal developed by George Washington.
Collections: artifacts & exhibits emphasizing the Patowmack Canal.
Facilities: 100-seat auditorium; nature & conservation center; snack shop; picnic area. Books pertaining to canal history & natural sciences for sale.
Activities: guided tours; films; organized educational programs. Museum Sponsors: Patowmack Canal Festival.
Hours & Admission Prices: Mon.-Fri. 10-5, Sat.-Sun. 10-6; seasonal hours vary. $5 per vehicle, $3 per person; discounts to seniors 62 & over and disabled. Annual passes available. ♿
Attendance: 500,000 (estimated)

Middleburg

THE NATIONAL SPORTING LIBRARY, (M), 102 Plains Rd., Middleburg, VA 20118. Mailing Address: P.O. Box 1335, Middleburg, VA 20118-1335. Tel.: 540-687-6542. Fax: 540-687-8540.
Web Site: www.nsl.org
Founded: 1954.
Congressional District: 8
Key Personnel: Pres. & CEO, Nancy H. Parsons; Asst. to Pres., Karen Halver; Cur. Fine Arts, F. Turner Reuter, Jr.; Office Mgr., Judy Sheehan; Librarian, Lisa Campbell; Dir. Communications & Research, Elizabeth Tobey, Ph.D.; Bookkeeper, Mary Deppa; CPA, Melanie Fuller; Curatorial Asst., Brenda Elliot
Sporting Library & Art Museum.
Collections: 15,000 books on horse & field sports; scrapbooks; photographs; papers; audio visual materials; art work by Paul Brown, Edward Troye, Alvan Fisher, Frank Voss, Henry Alken, John Ferneley, George Stubbs, J.F. Herring Sr. and many others.
Hours & Admission Prices: Tues.-Fri. 10-4. Sat. 1-4. Closed Christmas Day & day after; New Year's Day. ♿

Middletown

BELLE GROVE PLANTATION, (M), 336 Belle Grove Rd., Middletown, VA 22645. Mailing Address: P.O. Box 537, Middletown, VA 22645-0537. Tel.: 540-869-2028. Fax: 540-869-9638.
E-mail: info@bellegrove.org
Web Site: www.bellegrove.org
Founded: 1964.
Congressional District: 10
Key Personnel: Exec. Dir., Elizabeth McClung; Program & Devel. Asst., Sarah Ainsworth; Administrative Asst., Betsey Anderson; Supt. Bldgs. & Grounds, Dennis Campbell; Bookkeeper, Renee Maines; Pres. Belle Grove, Inc. (V), Phillips Griffin, II; Museum Shop Mgr., Kelly DeTample; Visitor Svcs. Clerk, Sally Humphrey; Housekeeper, Dorothy Fletcher.
Personnel Profile: Full-Time Paid 5; Part-Time Paid 5; Part-Time Volunteers 80; Interns 3.
Governing Authority: nonprofit organization. Operated by Belle Grove, Inc. Property of National Trust for Historic Preservation, 1785 Massachusetts Ave., N.W., Washington, D.C. 20036. Parent Institution: National Trust for Historic Preservation. Subsidiary Institution: Belle Grove, Inc. Tax-exempt: 501(c)(3).
Historic House: 1794 Belle Grove home of Revolutionary War officer Maj. Isaac Hite, Jr., brother-in-law of President James Madison, & 1864 Civil War headquarters of Gen. Philip Sheridan, Civil War Battle of Cedar Creek was fought on Belle Grove's grounds. Thomas Jefferson assisted on design.
Collections: decorative arts; architecture; Shenandoah Valley furniture.
Research Fields: local history; rural folk cultures.
Facilities: library of local, architectural, crafts & agricultural history books; barn; demonstration garden; heritage apple orchard. Museum-related items for sale.
Activities: guided tours; school programs; special events; lectures.
Publications: calendar of events; newsletter; guidebook; Hite family letters; Hite and Bowman Cemetery Guides; cookbook, Belle Grove; book, The Women of Belle Grove.
Hours & Admission Prices: April-Oct. Mon.-Sat. 10-4 (last tour 3:15), Sun. 1-5 (last tour 4:15); Nov.-Dec. call for hours. Adults $8, senior citizens $7, students 6-12 $4; discounts to AAA, Mobile Travel, NTHP, AAM, ICOM & Belle Grove members, & groups; members no charge. Closed Easter; Memorial Day; Independence Day; Labor Day; Columbus Day.
Attendance: 25,000 (estimated)
Membership: Belle Grove, Inc.: Individual $35; Family $40. National Trust for Historic Preservation: Individual $40; Family $50. Combination: Hite Society $100; Hunnewell Society $250; President's Society $500; Heritage Society $1,000; Madison Society $2,500.

Millwood

BURWELL-MORGAN MILL, 15 Tannery Lane, Millwood, VA 22646. Mailing Address: P.O. Box 306, Berryville, VA 22611-0306. Tel.: 540-837-1799. Fax: 540-955-0285.
E-mail: ccha@visuallink.com
Web Site: www.clarkehistory.org/themill.htm
Founded: 1964.

Congressional District: 7
Key Personnel: Pres. (V), Don Cady; Exec. Dir., Jennifer Lee; Archivist, Mary Morris.
Personnel Profile: Full-Time Paid 2; Part-Time Volunteers 30.
Governing Authority: society. Parent Institution: Clarke County Historical Assoc. Tel.: 540-955-2600. Tax-exempt: 501(c)(3).
History Museum: 1782-85, operating, water-powered Merchant Grist & Flour Mill.
Collections: wooden water wheel and gear train; grinding stones; 1784 wooden mill equipment; iron gudgeon bearings; spindle shafts; colonial kitchen equipment; farm tools. Historic Building: 1840 Miller's House.
Research Fields: mill design and techniques; 18th century financial records.
Facilities: Mill products for sale.
Activities: guided tours; operation of mill; permanent exhibitions; art shows; antique shows; special tours for school children.
Publications: quarterly newsletter, CCHA.
Hours & Admission Prices: May-Nov. Sat. 10-5, Sun. 12-5. No charge.
Attendance: 10,000 (estimated)
Membership: Individual $25; Family $50; Corporate $100; Life $500.

Mineral

NORTH ANNA NUCLEAR INFORMATION CENTER, Rte. 700, 1022 Haley Dr., Mineral, VA 23117. Mailing Address: 1022 Haley Dr., Mineral, VA 23117-4527. Tel.: 804-771-3200 & 540-894-2029. Fax: 540-894-0379.
E-mail: mike.duffey@dom.com
Web Site: www.dom.com
Founded: 1973.
Congressional District: 7
Key Personnel: Information Representative, Debbie Seay; Coord., Michael Duffey.
Personnel Profile: Full-Time Paid 2.
Governing Authority: profit-making organization. Parent Institution: Dominion. Subsidiary Institution: Dominion Resources Services.
Nuclear Energy Museum.
Collections: narrated & animated exhibits describing how electricity is generated by nuclear fuel.
Facilities: North Anna Power Station; two 100-seat auditoriums; 32-seat theater.
Activities: self-guided tours; lectures; films; organized education programs for children, adults & undergraduate college students.
Publications: booklet, Vepco & Nuclear Power, Now & For the Future; brochure, North Anna Nuclear Information Center.
Hours & Admission Prices: Mon.-Fri. 9-4. No charge. Closed major holidays. ♿
Attendance: 3,058 (accurate)

Monterey

HIGHLAND MAPLE MUSEUM, U.S. 220 S., Monterey, VA 24465. Mailing Address: P.O. Box 223, Monterey, VA 24465-0223. Tel.: 540-468-2550. Fax: 540-468-2551.
Founded: 1983.
Congressional District: 6
Key Personnel: C.E.O., Carolyn Pohowsky.
Personnel Profile: Part-Time Volunteers 2.
Governing Authority: nonprofit organization. Parent Institution: Highland County Chamber of Commerce. Tax-exempt.
Agriculture Museum.
Collections: old & new tools; exhibits demonstrating techniques of maple syrup & sugar production from Indian times to present.
Facilities: 600 sq. ft. exhibit space.
Hours & Admission Prices: Open 24 hours. No charge; donations accepted. ♿
Attendance: 3,000 (estimated)

Montpelier Station

JAMES MADISON'S MONTPELIER - THE MONTPELIER FOUNDATION, 11395 Constitution Hwy., Montpelier Station, VA 22957. Mailing Address: P.O. Box 911, Orange, VA 22960-0551. Tel.: 540-672-2728, ext. 100. Fax: 540-672-0411.
E-mail: education@montpelier.org
Web Site: www.montpelier.org
Founded: 1984.
Congressional District: 7
Key Personnel: Pres. & Exec. Dir., Michael C. Quinn; Montpelier Foundation Chm. (V), Joe Grills; Vice Pres. Devel., Kimberly Skelly; Vice Pres. Museum Programs, Lynne Hastings; Dir. Communications, Peggy Vaughn; Dir. Archaeology, Dr. Matthew Reeves; Dir. Finance & Administration, Sherida Hawthorne; Dir. Facilities, Doug Arnold; Acting Cur., Allison Deeds; Horticulturist, Sandy Mudrinich; Exec. Sec., Pat Mahanes; Exec. Dir. Center for the Constitution, Sean O'Brien; Dir. Special Events, Phyllis Johnson; Dir. Restoration, John Jeanes; Student Education Coord., Christian Cotz.
Personnel Profile: Full-Time Paid 80; Part-Time Paid 80; Part-Time Volunteers 50; Interns 5.
Governing Authority: nonprofit. Parent Institution: National Trust for Historic Preservation, 1785 Massachusetts Ave., N.W. Washington, DC 20036. Subsidiary Institution: The Montpelier Foundation. Tax-exempt: 501(c)(3).
Historic House: lifelong home of President James Madison (1751-1836); 20th century home of William DuPont family.
Collections: furnishings & memorabilia of the Madison & duPont families; photographs; extensive grounds including gardens, formal gardens, J. Madison Landmark Forest walking trails, race track, train station & post office.
Research Fields: archaeology; architecture; Madison archival research; African American history; Civil War history.
Facilities: visitor center; theater; cafe; archaeology lab; Landmark Forest Trail; Civil War encampment site and trail; Gilmore Cabin; Annie du Pont formal garden. Gift items for sale.
Activities: audio tour; guided tours; orientation film. Museum Sponsors: Dolly's Kitchen Outdoor Cooking Demonstration; Hands on Restoration Tent April to October.
Publications: newsletter, Discovering Montpelier; monograph, Building A President's House; souvenir guidebook; commemorative copy of the Constitution.
Hours & Admission Prices: House: April-Oct. daily 9-5, Nov.-March daily 9-4. Adults $14, children 6-14 & National Trust members $7; children under 6 & Friends of Montpelier no charge. Closed Thanksgiving; Christmas. ♿
Attendance: 90,000 (estimated)
Membership: Friends of Montpelier: Family $50; Mount Pleasant Circle $100-$249; Blue Ridge Circle $250-$499; Colonnade Circle $500-$999; Portico Circle $1,000-$2,499; Dolley Madison Society $2,500-$4,999. Madison Cabinet: Delegates Council $5,000-$9,999; Congressional Council $10,000-$14,999; Secretary of State's Council $15,000-$24,999; President's Council $25,000 & up.

Montross

ARMSTEAD TASKER JOHNSON HIGH SCHOOL MUSEUM, 18849 King's Hwy., Montross, VA 22520. Tel.: 804-493-7070.
History Museum: housed in the first high school in the Northern Neck for African American students.
Collections: local history & culture; period furnishings; photographs; memorabilia.
Hours & Admission Prices: Call for hours.

WESTMORELAND COUNTY MUSEUM AND LIBRARY, INC., 43 Court Square, Montross, VA 22520. Mailing Address: P.O. Box 247, Montross, VA 22520-0247. Tel.: 804-493-8440. Fax: 804-493-1312.
E-mail: wcmuseum@verizon.net
Web Site: www.westmoreland-county.org
Founded: 1939.
Congressional District: 1
Personnel Profile: Part-Time Paid 3.
History Museum.
Collections: local history & culture; paintings; photographs; period artifacts; furnishings; archaeological artifacts.
Hours & Admission Prices: Mon.-Sat. 10-4. No charge; donations accepted. Closed county holidays.
Membership: Individual $25; Family/Joint $45; Patriot $100.

Morattico

MORATTICO WATERFRONT MUSEUM, Morattico Rd., Morattico, VA 22523. Mailing Address: P.O. Box 80, Morattico, VA 22523-0080. Tel.: 804-462-0532.
Governing Authority: Tax-exempt: 501(c)(3).
History Museum: housed in the former Morattico General Store; built in 1901.
Collections: local history & culture; period furnishings; personal artifacts; photographs.
Hours & Admission Prices: May-Oct. Sat. 12-4, Sun. 1-4.

Mount Vernon

MOUNT VERNON: GEORGE WASHINGTON'S ESTATE & GARDENS, (M), South End of George Washington Memorial Pkwy., Mount Vernon, VA 22309. Mailing Address: George Washington's Mount Vernon, P.O. Box 110, Mount Vernon, VA 22121-0110. Tel.: 703-780-2000. Fax: 703-799-8654. TDD: 703-799-8121.
E-mail: info@mountvernon.org
Web Site: visit.mountvernon.org

Founded: 1853.
Congressional District: 11
Key Personnel: Regent, Ansley Boyce; Exec. Dir., James C. Rees; C.F.O., Barton Groh; Assoc. Dir. Education, Ann Bay; Assoc. Dir. Preservation, Dr. Dennis Pogue; Assoc. Dir. Public Affairs, Emily Coleman Dibella; Assoc. Dir. Devel., Julie Carter; Assoc. Dir. Collections, Carol Borchert Cadon; Dir. Operations & Mgmt., Joe Sliger; Dir. Security, Debora Brooke; Dir. Retail, Julia Mosley; Dir. Human Resources, Megan Dunn; Dir. Horticulture, Dean Norton; Mount Vernon Inn Mgr., William H. Robertson; Librarian, Joan Stahl.
Personnel Profile: Full-Time Paid 188; Part-Time Paid 418; Part-Time Volunteers 400.
Governing Authority: nonprofit organization. Subsidiary Institution Mount Vernon Inn, Inc.; Ford Orientation Center; Donald W. Reynolds Museum and Education Center. Tax-exempt: 170(b)(1)(a).
Historic Plantation: 1735-1799 Mount Vernon, home of George Washington.
Collections: decorative arts; graphic arts; textiles; archaeology; fine arts; research & study collections; Washington memorabilia; furnishings; manuscripts; books; boxwood gardens; reconstructed greenhouse; kitchen building with larder; stable; coach house; wash house; storehouses; spinning house; slaves quarters; cobbler shops; smoke house; tombs of George & Martha Washington; pioneer farm site; reconstruction of 16-sided threshing barn & slave cabin; 18th century working farm; hands-on history children's area.
Major Exhibits: Discover The Real George Washington: New Views from Mount Vernon (T), 1/10-12/10.
Research Fields: life & times of George Washington, his family & associates; history of Mount Vernon Estate from time of original patent to present, architectural development, horticulture, agriculture & household furnishings of the period of George Washington's ownership.
Facilities: 12,000-vol. general library available by appointment on premises; restaurant. Publications and museum-related items for sale.
Activities: in-school programs; garden tour; slave life tour; children's activities; films; permanent & temporary exhibitions; sightseeing cruises. Special Events: Colonial Days; public wreath-laying at tomb; Slave Memorial Commemoration; gardening days; Candlelight Tours; Wine Festivals; Spring Garden Party; George Washington's Birthday Celebration; Independence Day Celebration; 18th Century Craft Fair; Fall Harvest Family Days; Christmas at Mount Vernon.
Publications: annual periodical, Annual Report; semi-annual newsletter, Mount Vernon: Yesterday, Today & Tomorrow; handbook; specialized publications of the collections; photographic reproductions of paintings, prints & maps.
Hours & Admission Prices: March & Sept.-Oct. daily 9-5; April-Aug. daily 8-5; Nov.-Feb. 9-4. Adults $15, senior citizens $14, children 6-11, students & youth groups grades 1-12 $7; discount to groups of 20 or more; scouting groups in uniform no charge Nov. to 3rd Sun. in Feb. Annual Pass $25. ♿
Attendance: 1,154,781 (accurate)
Membership: Palladian Society $50-$99; Piazza Society $100-$249; Colonnade Society $250-$499; Cupola $500-$999; Regent's Circle Silver: $1,000-$2,499; Regent's Circle Gold $2,500-$4,999; Mount Vernon One Hundred $5,000 & up; Washington Council $10,000 & up.

Natural Bridge

NATURAL BRIDGE WAX MUSEUM, 70 W. Faulkner Hwy., Natural Bridge, VA 24578. Mailing Address: P.O. Box 85, Natural Bridge, VA 24578-0085. Tel.: 540-291-2426. Fax: 540-291-3785.
E-mail: thebridge@naturalbridgeva.com
Web Site: www.naturalbridgeva.com
Founded: 1978.
Congressional District: 4
Key Personnel: Dir., John McFerren; Museum Shop Mgr., Sherry Crawford.
Personnel Profile: Full-Time Paid 4; Part-Time Paid 5.
Governing Authority: Parent Institution: Dorfman Museums, Inc. Tax-exempt.
Wax Museum.
Collections: wax figures including Native Americans, explorers, & presidents; scenes of Virginia and Natural Bridge history.
Hours & Admission Prices: March-Nov. daily 10-6; Dec.-Feb. Sat.-Sun. 10-6. Adult $10, children $6. ♿
Attendance: 65,000 (estimated)

NATURAL BRIDGE ZOOLOGICAL PARK, Rte. 11, Natural Bridge, VA 24578. Mailing Address: P.O. Box 88, Natural Bridge, VA 24578-0088. Tel.: 540-291-2420. Fax: 540-291-1891.
E-mail: naturalbridgezoo@hotmail.com
Web Site: www.naturalbridgezoo.net
Founded: 1972.
Zoo.
Collections: zoological.
Facilities: Museum-related items for sale.
Activities: elephant rides; petting zoo; photos with baby animals.
Hours & Admission Prices: March 15-May 22 daily 9-6; May 23-Sept. 7 Mon.-Fri. 10-5, Sat.-Sun. 9-7; Sept. 8-Oct. Mon.-Fri. 10-5, Sat.-Sun. 9-6; Nov. 1-Nov. 25 daily 10-5; Nov. 27-Nov. 29 daily 10-4; call to confirm. Adults $12, senior citizens $10, children 3-12 $8; children 2 & under no charge.

New Market

NEW MARKET BATTLEFIELD STATE HISTORICAL PARK, 8895 George Collins Dr., New Market, VA 22844. Mailing Address: P.O. Box 1864, New Market, VA 22844-1864. Tel.: 540-740-3101; 866-515-1864 (toll free). Fax: 540-740-3033. TDD: 703-464-7616.
E-mail: nmbshp@vmi.edu
Web Site: www.vmi.edu/newmarket
Founded: 1967.
Congressional District: 7
Key Personnel: Exec. Dir., Keith E. Gibson; Dir., Scott H. Harris; Visitor Svcs. Supvr., Judith Drury; Supvr. Historical Interpretation, Troy D. Marshall; Coord., Stacey Nacew; Office Mgr., Brittney Phillips.
Personnel Profile: Full-Time Paid 7; Part-Time Paid 11; Part-Time Volunteers 17.
Governing Authority: college. Parent Institution: Virginia Military Institute, Lexington, VA 24450. Tax-exempt.
Military History Museum: located on the site of the 1864 Battle of New Market.
Collections: Civil War artifacts; Historic House; (1830-1865) Bushong House & period farm collections.
Research Fields: Shenandoah Valley 1855-1870.
Facilities: 300-vol. library on secondary historical reference works available upon request for use on premises. Museum-related items for sale.
Activities: guided tours; Emmy Award-winning film; interpretive exhibits; self-guided battlefield tour.
Publications: magazine reprint, Battle of New Market.
Hours & Admission Prices: Daily 9-5. Adults $10, seniors $9, children 6-12 $6; discounts to groups, seniors, Military & AAM members. Closed New Year's Day; Thanksgiving; Christmas Eve and Day. ♿
Attendance: 41,258 (accurate)

Newbern

WILDERNESS ROAD REGIONAL MUSEUM, State Rt. 611, 5240 Wilderness Rd., Newbern, VA 24126. Mailing Address: P.O. Box 373, Newbern, VA 24126-0373. Tel.: 540-674-4835.
E-mail: wrrm@psknet.com
Founded: 1980.
Congressional District: 9
Key Personnel: C.E.O. & Chm. (V), Philip D. Jordan; Dir. & Museum Shop Mgr., Ann S. Bailey; Librarian, Betty Allen; Treas., Barbara Duncan; Dir. Public Rels., Lloyd Mathews; Administrative Asst., Mary C. Williams; Maintenance, Jimmy Johnson.
Personnel Profile: Part-Time Paid 5; Part-Time Volunteers 25.
Governing Authority: nonprofit organizations. Parent Institution: New River Historical Society. Tax-exempt: 501(c)(3); 170(b)(1)(A).
Historical Society Museum: housed in c.1810 2-story frame/log building located in Old Newbern National Historic District.
Collections: regional history of New River Valley from 1810-1875; dolls & quilts; archives of local history, Civil War items; photographs; farm & hand tools; buggy.
Research Fields: genealogy; local history.
Facilities: 700-vol. library of Virginiana & local historical publications available to the public; classrooms. Museum-related items for sale.
Activities: guided tours; arts festivals; organized educational programs; docent program; participatory & temporary exhibitions. Museum Sponsors: Civil War reenactments; 3 buffet dinners per year; Fall Festival of Arts & Crafts; genealogy workshop in May; Heritage quilt show & sale; annual used book sale; Deck the Halls open house; 2 yard sales.
Publications: annual Journal, N.R.H.S.; quarterly newsletter, Benchmarks.
Hours & Admission Prices: Mon.-Sat. 10:30-4:30. Adults $3, children 6-12 $1.50; discounts to AAA members; members no charge. Closed New Year's Day; Easter; Mother's Day; Labor Day; Thanksgiving; Christmas. ♿
Attendance: 20,000 (estimated)

Newport News

ENDVIEW PLANTATION, 362 Yorktown Rd., Newport News, VA 23603-1017. Tel.: 757-887-1862. Fax: 757-888-3869.
E-mail: endview@nngov.com
Web Site: www.endview.org
Historic House Museum: plantation built c.1769.
Collections: plantation history; Civil War artifacts; American culture & history; period furnishings; photographs.

Activities: educational programs.
Hours & Admission Prices: Jan.-March Mon. & Thurs.-Sat. 10-4, Sun. 1-5; April-Dec. Mon. & Wed.-Sat. 10-4, Sun. 1-5. Adults $6, seniors 62 & over $5, children 7-18 $4; discounts to groups; children under 7 no charge.

GOLF MUSEUM, (M), 1500 Country Club Rd., Newport News, VA 23606-2840. Mailing Address: James River Country Club, 1500 Country Club Rd., Newport News, VA 23606. Tel.: 757-595-3327. Fax: 757-596-4807.
Founded: 1932.
Congressional District: 1
Key Personnel: Dir., William S. Aargette; Cur., Leroy E. Thompson.
Personnel Profile: Full-Time Volunteers 1; Part-Time Volunteers 9.
Governing Authority: board of trustees; nonprofit. Tax-exempt.
Sports Museum.
Collections: international golf history; golf clubs; balls; tees; books; engravings; paintings; photographs; silver; medals; tools; 16th-20th century golf artifacts; first printed reference to golf 1566; Bobby Jones' club (Brassie) used in achieving his 1930 Grand Slam.
Facilities: 1,000-vol. library available to researchers only.
Activities: guided tours; loan exhibitions.
Hours & Admission Prices: By appointment. No charge. Closed holidays.
Attendance: 1,000 (estimated)

JAMES A. FIELDS HOUSE, 617 27th St., Newport News, VA 23607. Tel.: 757-245-1991.
Historic House Museum: housed in the former home & law office of James A. Fields. Listed on the National Register of Historic Places.
Collections: local history & culture; period furnishings; personal artifacts; photographs.
Hours & Admission Prices: Tues.-Sat. 11-4. Admission $3.

LEE HALL MANSION, 163 Yorktown Rd., Newport News, VA 23603-1127. Tel.: 757-888-3371. Fax: 757-888-3373.
E-mail: bgutierr@ci.newport-news.va.us
Web Site: www.leehall.org
Key Personnel: Site Coord., Braxton Gutierrez.
Governing Authority: Parent Institution: the City of Newport News, Department of Parks and Recreation, Historical Services Division.
Historic House Museum: housed in the former home of Richard Decauter Lee, built in 1859.
Collections: period artifacts & furnishings; weaponry.
Facilities: Museum-related items for sale.
Activities: special programs; lectures.
Hours & Admission Prices: Jan.-March Mon. & Thurs.-Sat. 10-4, Sun. 1-5; April-Dec. Mon. & Wed.-Sat. 10-4, Sun. 1-5. Adults $6, senior citizens $5, children 7-18 $4; children under 7 no charge. Closed New Year's Day; Easter; Thanksgiving; Christmas. ♿

* **THE MARINERS' MUSEUM, (M),** 100 Museum Dr., Newport News, VA 23606-3759. Tel.: 757-596-2222; 800-581-7245. Fax: 757-591-7311.
E-mail: info@marinersmuseum.org
Web Site: www.marinersmuseum.org
Founded: 1930.
Congressional District: 1
Key Personnel: Pres. & C.E.O., Timothy J. Sullivan; Chm., John R. Lawson, II; Exec. Vice Pres. & C.O.O., William B. Cogar; Vice Pres. Human Resources, Noreen Becci; Vice Pres. Museum Collections, Anna Holloway; Chief Cur., Lyles Forbes; Chief Conservator, Marcie Renner; Museum Shop Mgr. & Dir. Visitor Svcs., Florence Brown.
Personnel Profile: Full-Time Paid 83; Part-Time Paid 23; Part-Time Volunteers 178; Interns 10.
Governing Authority: nonprofit organization. Tax-exempt: 501(c)(3).
International & National Maritime History Museum.
Collections: Age of Exploration Gallery; Crabtree miniature ships; Chesapeake Bay Gallery; International Small Craft Center; navigational instruments; ship equipment; whaling & fishing equipment; naval armament; sailors' handiwork; figureheads; lighthouse & lifesaving equipment; maritime decorative arts; prints, paintings & drawings of maritime subject matter; archives; industrial history; folklore; Chris-Craft archives; rare books; journals; Haviland collection of maritime photographs, information, and news clippings; USS Monitor Center exhibition & conservation laboratory; Titanic exhibit and artifacts.
Major Exhibits: Building Better Ships, 11/09-2/10; A to Z: Pieces from the Collection, 6/10.
Research Fields: regional, national & international maritime & naval history; history of technology; Civil War ironclads; small craft; maritime art.
Facilities: 1,750,000-vol. research library & archives; 80,000 sq. ft. exhibit space; 27-seat lecture room; 50-seat orientation theater; 2 classrooms; cafe; 550 acre park with lake & 5 mile walking trail; picnic area; scenic Lion's Bridge by the James River. Museum-related items for sale.
Activities: guided tours; lectures; gallery talks, costumed interpreters; formal education programs for children, adults & college students; permanent & temporary exhibitions; symposia; Civil War programming; boatbuilding; paddleboats; concerts; internet video classes.
Publications: annual; books; monographs; brochures; quarterly newsletter.
Hours & Admission Prices: Mon.-Sat. 10-5, Sun. 12-5. Adults $14, students $8; discounts to senior citizens 65 & older, active duty military, AAA, AAM, ICOM & CAMM members; members, children 5 & under no charge. Closed Thanksgiving; Christmas. ♿
Attendance: 80,000 (estimated)
Membership: Student & Senior Individual $35; Individual & National Associate $45; Senior Couple $55; Family $75; Contributor $125; Donor $250; Sponsor $500; Ferguson Society $1,000; Huntington Society $2,500; Lancaster Eagle Society $5,000; Leif Eriksson Society $10,000.

THE NEWSOME HOUSE MUSEUM & CULTURAL CENTER, 2803 Oak Ave., Newport News, VA 23607-3713. Tel.: 757-247-2360. Fax: 757-928-6754.
E-mail: ddavis@nngov.com
Web Site: www.newsomehouse.org
Founded: 1991.
Congressional District: 3
Key Personnel: Historic Site Mgr., Mary Kayaselcuk.
Personnel Profile: Full-Time Paid 2; Part-Time Paid 1; Part-Time Volunteers 5.
Governing Authority: municipal government; nonprofit. City of Newport News. Parent Institution: Virginia War Museum. Tax-exempt: 501(c)(3).
Historic House: built in 1899 The Newsome House is a modified Queen Anne structure, which was home to the Joseph Thomas Newsome family from 1906-1977.
Collections: personal papers of the Newsome family; local African-American history & culture; folkart of Anderson Johnson.
Research Fields: local African-American history.
Facilities: 500-vol. library on Black history & the books and papers of the Newsome family; meeting rooms; 1,500 sq. ft. exhibit space; banquet facilities; grounds available for picnics or musical programs. Lithographs for sale.
Activities: formal education programs for adults & children; internships; guided tours; workshops; lectures; temporary exhibits. Museum Sponsors: art exhibits & demonstrations; workshops on genealogy & Black history. Annual Events: Holiday Open House; A Newsome House Christmas.
Publications: book; A Life in Newport News: An Oral History of Inettie Banks Edwards; Huntington High School: Symbol of Community Hope and Unity.
Hours & Admission Prices: Mon. & Wed.-Sat. 10-4, Sun. 1-5. Suggested Donation: adults $2. Closed New Year's Day; Easter; Thanksgiving; Christmas Eve & Day. ♿
Attendance: 5,000 (estimated)
Membership: Friends of the Newsome House: Student $5; Individual $10; Family $20; Patron $50; Lifetime $100; Organization $250; Sponsor $1,000.

* **PENINSULA FINE ARTS CENTER, (M),** 101 Museum Dr., Newport News, VA 23606-3758. Tel.: 757-596-8175. Fax: 757-596-0807.
E-mail: info@pfac-va.org
Web Site: www.pfac-va.org
Founded: 1962.
Congressional District: 1
Key Personnel: Exec. Dir., Luci Cochran; Pres. & Chm. (v), Keith Vander Vennet; Dir. Programs, Michael Preble; Staff Accountant & Personnel Mgr., Lynn Evans; Dir. Mktg., Michael McGrann; Mgr. Exhibitions & Facilities, Fred Rich; Museum Shop Mgr., Jo Harding.
Personnel Profile: Full-Time Paid 9; Part-Time Paid 4; Part-Time Volunteers 214; Interns 2.
Governing Authority: nonprofit organization. Affiliate of Virginia Museum of Fine Arts. Tax-exempt: 501(c)(3).
Arts Center.
Collections: temporary exhibitions during the year.
Research Fields: contemporary American art.
Facilities: studios; video gallery; sculpture courtyard. Museum-related items for sale.
Activities: guided tours; public programs; arts festivals; organized educational experiences; loan & traveling exhibitions.
Publications: newsletter; class schedules; exhibition catalogs.
Hours & Admission Prices: Wed. & Fri.-Sat. 10-5, Tues. & Thurs. 10-8, Sun. 1-5. Adults $6.50, children 6-12 $4; discounts to students, seniors & military; members & children under 6 no charge. Call for special exhibition charges. Closed New Year's Day; Thanksgiving Day; Christmas Day. ♿
Attendance: 40,000 (estimated)
Membership: Student & Senior Citizen $25; Individual $35; Family $50.

* **VIRGINIA LIVING MUSEUM,** 524 J. Clyde Morris Blvd., Newport News, VA 23601-1999. Tel.: 757-595-1900. Fax: 757-599-4897. TDD: 757-595-1900.
E-mail: webmaster@thevlm.org
Web Site: www.thevlm.org
Founded: 1964.
Congressional District: 1
Key Personnel: Exec. Dir., Page Hayhurst; Deputy Dir., Fred Farris; Pres. (V), Conway Sheild, III; Curatorial Dir., George K. Mathews, Jr.; Dir. Devel., Carolyn Cuthrell; Dir. Education, Chris Lewis; Dir. Finance & I.T., Dave Osman; Dir. Mktg., Virginia Gabriele; Dir. Volunteer Svcs., Shandran J. Thornburgh; Museum Shop Mgr., Sarah Wilcox.
Personnel Profile: Full-Time Paid 39; Part-Time Paid 55; Part-Time Volunteers 350.
Governing Authority: nonprofit organization. Tax-exempt: 501(c)(3).
Specialized Natural Center.
Collections: live native animals, plants, birds, insects, mammals, reptiles, amphibians, marine & freshwater animals; rocks, minerals, fossils, botanical specimens.
Major Exhibits: Megaledon: Largest Shark That Ever Lived (T), 11/09-1/10/10; Beguiled by the Wild: The Art of Charley Harper, 2/6/10-4/11/10; Dinosaurs!, 5/29/10-9/6/10; Amazing Butterflies! (T), 5/28/10-9/5/11.
Facilities: library; marine & freshwater aquariums; aviary; planetarium; observatory; discovery center; nature trail & boardwalk; classrooms.
Activities: lectures; films; hobby workshops; formally organized educational programs; docent program; permanent & temporary exhibitions; interpretive exhibits; classrooms; nature trail; behind the scenes tours.
Publications: quarterly newsletter, Paws & Reflect; annual report, Teachers Guide; program brochures; promotional brochure.
Hours & Admission Prices: Summer: daily 9-5; Winter: Mon.-Sat. 9-5, Sun. 12-5. Museum: adults $15, children 3-12 $12; members & children under 3 no charge. Museum & Planetarium: adults $19, children 3-12 $16; discounts for senior citizens, groups & ASTC members; members no charge. Closed New Year's Day; Thanksgiving; Christmas Eve & Day. ♿
Attendance: 236,098 (accurate)
Membership: Individual $40; Couple $65; Family & Grandparents with 3 Guests $85; Family with 3 Guests & Grandparents with 6 Guests $110.

THE VIRGINIA WAR MUSEUM, 9285 Warwick Blvd., Huntington Park, Newport News, VA 23607-1537. Tel.: 757-247-8523. Fax: 757-247-8627.
E-mail: info@warmuseum.org
Web Site: www.warmuseum.org
Founded: 1924.
Congressional District: 1
Key Personnel: Cur., G. Richard Hoffeditz; Registrar, Jerry Coggeshall; Public Rels. & Museum Shop Mgr., Colin Romanick.
Personnel Profile: Full-Time Paid 9; Full-Time Volunteers 2; Part-Time Paid 3; Part-Time Volunteers 12; Interns 3.
Governing Authority: municipal. Parent Institution: Newport News. Subsidiary Institution: Newsome House; Lee Hall Mansion, Newport News, VA; Endview Plantation, Newport News, VA. Tax-exempt: 501(c)(3).
Military Museum.
Collections: weapons; uniforms; posters; prints; vehicles; tanks; insignia; artillery & accoutrements relating to United States military involvement from 1775 to present.
Research Fields: Military-United States & European.
Facilities: 20,000-vol. library on military, historical & photographic files available for research; 120-seat theater; educational facilities. Museum-related items for sale.
Activities: films; lectures; historical groups; permanent & temporary exhibitions; docent program; formal education programs; theater; broadcast programs. Annual Events: Military Vehicle Show; Toy Soldier Show; Tuskegee Airmen; Peal Harbor Day Ceremony.
Publications: quarterly newsletter, Dufflebag.
Hours & Admission Prices: Mon.-Sat. 9-5, Sun. 1-5. Adults $6, military & senior citizens $5, children 6-15 & students $4; discounts to AAA members; members no charge. Closed New Year's Day; Christmas Eve & Day. ♿
Attendance: 50,000 (estimated)
Membership: Student $10; Individual $20; Family $35; Supporter $100-$499; Patron $500-$999; Lifetime $1,000.

Norfolk

AFRICAN ART GALLERY, Norfolk State University, Presidential Pkwy., Norfolk, VA 23504-8050. Tel.: 757-823-2002. Fax: 757-823-2005.
Web Site: www.nsu.edu/archives/gallery
Formerly: Lois E. Woods Museum
Key Personnel: Dir., Dr. Tommy L. Bogger; Asst. Dir., Annette Montgomery; Exec. Coord., Grace A. Lee.
Personnel Profile: Full-Time Paid 2; Part-Time Volunteers 2.
Governing Authority: Parent Institution: Norfolk State University. Tax-exempt.
African Art Gallery.
Collections: African art; African-American art & memorabilia.
Publications: gallery brochure.
Hours & Admission Prices: Mon.-Fri. 9-5. No charge; donations accepted. Closed holidays. ♿
Attendance: 1,300 (estimated)

BARON & ELLIN GORDON ART GALLERIES, OLD DOMINION UNIVERSITY, 4509 Monarch Way, Norfolk, VA 23529-0001. Mailing Address: 9000 Batten Arts and Letters, Norfolk, VA 23529-0001. Tel.: 757-683-6271. Fax: 757-683-6776.
E-mail: fbayersd@odu.edu
Web Site: al.odu.edu/art/gallery/about.shtml
Founded: 1971.
Congressional District: 2
Key Personnel: Asst. Dean & Dir., Frederick S. Bayersdorfer; Cur., Ramona Austin.
Personnel Profile: Full-Time Paid 2; Part-Time Paid 3; Part-Time Volunteers 8; Interns 1.
Governing Authority: public university; nonprofit. Parent Institution: Old Dominion University. Subsidiary Institution: College of Arts & Letters. Tax-exempt.
University Art Gallery
Collections: American self-taught art; contemporary art; paintings; prints; sculpture.
Research Fields: self-taught American art.
Activities: lectures; workshops.
Publications: newsletter; posters; invitations; catalogs.
Hours & Admission Prices: Jan. 7-Dec. 19 Tues.-Sat. 11-5, Sun. 1-5. No charge. ♿
Attendance: 7,432 (accurate)

* **CHRYSLER MUSEUM OF ART, (M),** 245 W. Olney Rd., Norfolk, VA 23510-1587. Tel.: 757-664-6200. Fax: 757-664-6201.
E-mail: museum@chrysler.org
Web Site: www.chrysler.org
Founded: 1933.
Congressional District: 2
Key Personnel: Pres. & Dir., William J. Hennessey; Dir. Finance & C.F.O., Dana Fuqua; Chm. Bd., Dixie Wolf; Public Rels. Dir., Richard Salzberg; Dir. Education & Public Programs, Scott L. Howe; Chief Cur. & Acting Cur. American and Contemporary Art, Jefferson Harrison; Cur. Glass, Kelly Conway; Cur. Photography, Brooks Johnson; Deputy Dir. Operations, Catherine Jordan Wass; Museum Shop Mgr., Linda Foster.
Personnel Profile: Full-Time Paid 75; Part-Time Paid 36; Part-Time Volunteers 250; Interns 10.
Governing Authority: private. Tax-exempt: 501(c)(3). Branch Museum: The Norfolk History Museum & Moses Myers House.
Art Museum.
Collections: arts from Egypt, Greece, Rome, Near East, Middle East, Far East, Africa, Orient, pre-Columbian America; Italian, French, Dutch, Flemish, English, German, American paintings & sculptures of all periods; ancient to modern glass from Asia, Africa, Europe, Sandwich, Tiffany, Galle, New England; American, English, French, Italian, German furniture; Ricau Collection; decorative arts; textiles; costumes; jewelry; photographs; silver; china; artifacts. Historic Houses: 1792 Moses Myers House; Norfolk History Museum at the Willoughby-Baylor House, c.1794.
Facilities: 80,000-vol. library of art reference books; 375-seat theatre; restaurant. Museum-related items for sale.
Activities: guided tours; lectures; films; gallery talks; concerts; docent program; formally organized education programs for families & school groups; permanent & temporary exhibitions; art travel program. Museum Sponsors: Annual Juried Student Gallery Exhibition.
Publications: quarterly program & exhibition schedules; bimonthly calendar of events.
Hours & Admission Prices: Museum: Wed. 10-9; Thurs.-Sat. 10-5; Sun. 12-5. Adults $7, seniors & military $5; discounts to AAM & AAA members; children 5 & under, students, members and Wed. no charge. Closed New Year's Day; Independence Day; Thanksgiving; Christmas. ♿
Attendance: 150,000 (accurate)
Membership: Student $25; Senior, Teacher & Military $45; Individual $55; Senior, Teacher & Military Household $65; Household $75; Associate $150; Friend $250; Patron $500; Director's Circle $1,000; Masterpiece Society $2,500 & up.

GENERAL DOUGLAS MACARTHUR MEMORIAL, MacArthur Sq., Norfolk, VA 23510-2382. Tel.: 757-441-2965. Fax: 757-441-5389.
E-mail: macarthurmemorial@norfolk.gov
Web Site: www.macarthurmemorial.org
Founded: 1964.

Congressional District: 2
Key Personnel: Dir., William J. Davis; Administrative Asst., Janice S. Dudley; Archivist, James W. Zobel; Cur., Charles R. Knight; Museum Shop Mgr., Mitzi N. Van Horn.
Personnel Profile: Full-Time Paid 10; Part-Time Paid 5; Part-Time Volunteers 7.
Governing Authority: municipal. Parent Institution: City of Norfolk, VA. Tax-exempt: 501(c)(3).
Military Museum: housed in 1850 courthouse building.
Collections: history; personal papers & mementoes.
Research Fields: life of Gen. MacArthur; military history of World War I, World War II, & Korean War; the occupation of Japan; 1898-1945 history of the Philippines; 1914-1960 American military & diplomatic history.
Facilities: 5,700-vol. personal library of Gen. MacArthur, including official & personal papers, photographs available for use on premises under supervision only; working archive of 2.5 million documents; 150-seat theater. Gen. MacArthur & MacArthur Memorial items for sale.
Activities: lectures; film; temporary, permanent & loan exhibitions; training programs for professional museum workers.
Publications: brochure, quarterly newsletter, General Douglas MacArthur Memorial; The MacArthur Report.
Hours & Admission Prices: Mon.-Sat. 10-5, Sun. 11-5. No charge; donations accepted. Closed New Year's Day; Thanksgiving; Christmas. ♿
Attendance: 37,712 (accurate)
Membership: National Member: $25; $50; $75. Corporate Member: $250; $500. Five Star Member: $100. MacArthur One Thousand Member: $1,000.

* **HAMPTON ROADS NAVAL MUSEUM, (M),** One Waterside Dr., Ste. 248, Norfolk, VA 23510-1607. Tel.: 757-322-2987 & 444-8971. Fax: 757-445-1867.
E-mail: elizabeth.poulliot@navy.mil
Web Site: www.hrnm.navy.mil
Founded: 1979.
Congressional District: 2
Key Personnel: Foundation Exec. Dir., Capt. Thomas H. Smith, USN (Ret.); Dir., Elizabeth A. Poulliot; Foundation Pres., RADM Charles J. Beers, Jr., USN (Ret.); Public Rels., Susanne Greene; Cur., Joseph M. Judge; Volunteer Coord., Tom M. Dandes; Exhibits Specialist, Marta E. Nelson; Events Coord. & Educator, Katherine Renfrew; Architectural Historian, Michael V. Taylor; Museum Technician, Ofelia B. Elbo; Newsletter Editor, Gordon B. Calhoun; Officer in Charge, BMC Dawn Greene; LPO/Educator, AW2 (AW/NAC/IUSS) Erin Hendrick; Ceremony Coord., EM3 Melanie McFarland; Museum Shop Mgr., Andrea D. Condon-Auen.
Personnel Profile: Full-Time Paid 15; Part-Time Paid 13; Part-Time Volunteers 73; Interns 2.
Governing Authority: federal government. Parent Institution: Naval Historical Center. Tax-exempt.
Naval History Museum: housed on the second floor of NAUTICUS.
Collections: naval artifacts & artworks; ship & aircraft models, weaponry, electric maps; underwater artifacts; period photographs; naval artwork; ship memorabilia; naval uniforms. Historic battleship USS Wisconsin: WWII era, Iowa class battleship; artifacts; photographs; audiovisual history of ship; historic ship, maritime & military history.
Research Fields: naval history of Hampton Roads region.
Facilities: 3,000-vol. library.
Activities: tours; lectures; slide presentations; videos; docent training; school & community outreach programs; off-site exhibits; interpretive docents in period reproduction uniforms; interpreter vignettes; travelling programs; speakers' bureau.
Publications: pamphlets; newsletter.
Hours & Admission Prices: Memorial Day to Labor Day daily 10-5; Sept.-May Tues.-Sat. 10-5, Sun. 12-5. No charge; donations accepted. Closed Thanksgiving; Christmas Eve & Day. ♿
Attendance: 224,000 (estimated)
Membership: Shipmate $35; Plankowner $125; Corporate $350.

HERMITAGE MUSEUM AND GARDENS, (M), 7637 North Shore Rd., Norfolk, VA 23505-1730. Tel.: 757-423-2052. Fax: 757-423-2410.
E-mail: info@thfm.org
Web Site: www.thfm.org
Founded: 1937.
Congressional District: 2
Key Personnel: Pres. Bd. Trustees, Maxwell Dale; Exec. Dir., Melanie L. Mathewes; Mgr. Public Programs, Kate Gebler; Mgr. Tour & Events, Beth Usry; Cur. Gardens, Yolima Carr; Site Coord., Tom Allan; Mktg. Mgr., Matt Serino.
Personnel Profile: Full-Time Paid 7; Part-Time Paid 8; Part-Time Volunteers 30; Interns 2.
Governing Authority: nonprofit organization. Tax-exempt: 501(c)(3).
Art Museum.
Collections: paintings, sculpture & decorative arts from Western & Oriental cultures; family papers & photographs.
Activities: guided tours; lectures; permanent exhibitions; facility rental. Museum Sponsors: art scholarships.
Publications: quarterly newsletter, Hermitage Press.
Hours & Admission Prices: Mon.-Tues. & Fri.-Sat. 10-5, Sun. 1-5. Adults $5, college students w/ID $3, children 6-18 $2; discounts to AAM, SERM & NARM members; children under 6, active military & members no charge. Closed New Year's Day; Memorial Day; Independence Day; Labor Day; Thanksgiving; Christmas. ♿
Attendance: 39,425 (accurate)
Membership: Seniors, Students & Military $15; Individual $25; Household & Grandparent $50; Donor $100; Benefactor $250.

HUNTER HOUSE VICTORIAN MUSEUM, 240 W. Freemason St., Norfolk, VA 23510-1221. Tel.: 757-623-9814.
E-mail: thequeen1894@hunterhousemuseum.org
Web Site: www.hunterhousemuseum.org
Historic House Museum.
Collections: decorative arts; furnishings; paintings.
Facilities: Museum-related items for sale.
Activities: educational programs; tours; special events.
Hours & Admission Prices: April-Dec. Wed.-Sat. 10:30-3:30, Sun. 12:30-3:30; other times by appointment. Adults $5, senior citizens $4, children $1.

MOSES MYERS HOUSE, 323 E. Freemason St., Norfolk, VA 23510. Mailing Address: Chrysler Museum of Art, 245 W. Olney Rd., Norfolk, VA 23510-1587. Tel.: 757-441-1526. Fax: 757-333-1089.
E-mail: jchristiansen@chrysler.org
Web Site: www.chrysler.org
Founded: 1951.
Congressional District: 2
Key Personnel: Dir., Dr. William Hennessey; Historic House Mgr., John Christiansen.
Personnel Profile: Full-Time Paid 2; Part-Time Paid 10; Part-Time Volunteers 50; Interns 1.
Governing Authority: private nonprofit. Parent Institution: Chrysler Museum of Art, 245 W. Olney Rd., Norfolk. Tax-exempt: 501(c)(3).
Historic House: c.1792 late Georgian, early Federal brick 2-story townhouse.
Collections: American & English furniture; glass; silver; china; textiles; costumes; copper implements; working kitchen; Jewish culture & history.
Research Fields: local history, Jewish history; American, French & English decorative arts; maritime commerce; architecture.
Activities: Jewish programs; guided tours; lectures; films; concerts; study clubs; hobby workshops; organized education programs; docent program; garden programs.
Publications: brochures; workbooks; educational materials.
Hours & Admission Prices: Wed.-Sat. 10-4, Sun. 12-4. No charge; donations accepted. Closed New Year's Day; Independence Day; Thanksgiving; Christmas.
Attendance: 7,500 (accurate)
Membership: Individual $15; Dual & Family $25.

NAUTICUS, One Waterside Dr., Norfolk, VA 23510-1737. Tel.: 757-664-1000; 800-664-1080. Fax: 757-623-1287.
Web Site: www.nauticus.org
Formerly: Nauticus, The National Maritime Center
Founded: 1994.
Congressional District: 2
Key Personnel: Acting Dir., John Rhamstine; Chm. (V), Robert T. Taylor; Dir. Finance, Yvonne Eberflus; Dir. Education, Jennifer Petro; Deputy Dir. Education & Research, Rolf Johnson; Dir. Mktg. & Public Rels., Shelia Harrison; Enterprise Controller, Raymond McEvoy; Museum Shop Mgr., Liz Etheridge; Dir. Visitor Svcs., Christine Arrasate.
Personnel Profile: Full-Time Paid 35; Full-Time Volunteers 55; Part-Time Paid 30; Interns 8.
Governing Authority: municipal. Parent Institution: City of Norfolk (municipal). Subsidiary Institution: National Maritime Center Foundation. Tax-exempt: 501(c)(3).
Maritime Museum.
Collections: computer & video interactives; commerce & military-related displays; USS Wisconsin & related exhibits; exotic aquaria; aquatic animals; exotic aquaria; Hampton Roads Naval Museum
Facilities: Hampton Roads Naval Museum; USS Wisconsin. Museum-related items for sale.
Activities: arts festivals; concerts; films; formal educational programs; guided tours; lectures; rental gallery; theater; traveling exhibitions; hands-on exhibits including computer & video interactives; touch pools; shark petting.

Publications: quarterly newsletter, Signals; annual report.
Hours & Admission Prices: Memorial Day to Labor Day daily 9-5; Sept.-May Tues.-Sat. 10-5, Sun. 12-5. Adults $10.95, senior citizens $9.95, children 4-12 $8.50; discount to AAA members, active military & groups; members and children 3 & under no charge. Closed New Year's Day; Thanksgiving; Christmas. ♿
Attendance: 320,000 (accurate)
Membership: Senior 55 & over, Student & Teacher $20; Individual $30; Individual Plus One $40; Grandparents $50; Family $60; Family Plus $100; Schooner & Family Silver $250; Brigantine & Family Gold $500. Corporate Silver $500; Corporate Gold $1,000; Corporate Platinum $2,000.

* **NORFOLK BOTANICAL GARDEN,** 6700 Azalea Garden Rd., Norfolk, VA 23518-5337. Tel.: 757-441-5830, ext. 324. Fax: 757-853-8294.
E-mail: don.buma@nbgs.org
Web Site: www.norfolkbotanicalgarden.org
Founded: 1938.
Congressional District: 2
Key Personnel: Exec. Dir., Donald R. Buma; Pres., William C. Eisenbeiss; Dir. Visitor Svcs. & Special Events, Marcia Riley; Dir. Horticulture, Brian O'Neil; Dir. Science, Tim Motley; Dir. Education, Donna Krabill; Dir. Donor Rels., Cathy Fitzgerald; Dir. Finance, Douglas A. Ward; Museum Shop Mgr., Lynn Clark.
Personnel Profile: Full-Time Paid 45; Part-Time Paid 55; Part-Time Volunteers 865; Interns 2.
Governing Authority: society; nonprofit. Parent Institution: Norfolk Botanical Garden Society. Tax-exempt.
Botanical Garden.
Collections: azaleas; rhododendrons; camellias; holly; roses; crapemyrtle; conifers; general; sculpture; VA native plants; hydrangea.
Research Fields: designated a National Camellia collection by the North American Association of Botanical Gardens & Arboreta.
Facilities: 1,910-vol. library of horticulture available for use on premises; reading room; 200-seat auditorium; classrooms; restaurant.
Activities: guided tours; narrated boat & train tours; lectures; hobby workshops; formally organized educational programs; temporary exhibitions. Museum Sponsors: Garden Lights in November & December.
Publications: quarterly, Norfolk Botanical Garden Society Newsletter; quarterly members publication, Bloom; quarterly educational programs publication, Grow.
Hours & Admission Prices: Gardens: April-Oct. 15 daily 9-7; Oct. 16-March daily 9-5. Buildings: Mon.-Fri. 8:30-5, Sat.-Sun. 10-5. Adults $7, seniors & military $6, children 3-18 $5; discounts to groups & AAA members; children under 3 & members no charge. Closed New Year's Day; Thanksgiving; Christmas. ♿
Attendance: 263,000 (accurate)
Membership: Individual $45; Family $75; Azalea Level $125; Camellia Level $300.

NORFOLK HISTORICAL SOCIETY, 810 Front St., Norfolk, VA 23510. Mailing Address: P.O. Box 6367, Norfolk, VA 23508-0367. Tel.: 757-640-1720.
E-mail: info@norfolkhistorical.org
Web Site: www.norfolkhistorical.org
Founded: 1965.
Congressional District: 2
Key Personnel: Pres. (V), Louis Guy.
Personnel Profile: Part-Time Volunteers 25.
Governing Authority: board of directors. Tax-exempt: 501(c)(3).
Historic Site: 1810 fort.
Collections: history.
Research Fields: history of Norfolk & Hampton Roads area.
Facilities: 600-vol. library of books pertaining to the history of Norfolk & surrounding areas available for research on premises.
Activities: reenactment of War of 1812; Civil War; lecture series.
Publications: book, Norfolk Highlights, 1584-1881; quarterly newsletter, Norfolk Historical Society Courier.
Hours & Admission Prices: Call for hours. No charge; donations accepted.
Attendance: 500 (estimated)
Membership: Students $10; Individual $25; Family $35; Supporter $50; Contributor $100; Grand Old Sentinel $200.

NORFOLK HISTORY MUSEUM, 601 E. Freemason St., Norfolk, VA 23510-2404. Mailing Address: Chrysler Museum of Art, 245 W. Olney Rd., Norfolk, VA 23510-1587. Tel.: 757-441-1526. Fax: 757-333-1089.
E-mail: jchristiansen@chrysler.org
Web Site: www.chrysler.org
Formerly: Willoughby-Baylor House
Founded: 1962.
Congressional District: 2
Key Personnel: Dir., Dr. William Hennessey; Historic House Mgr., John Christiansen.
Personnel Profile: Full-Time Paid 2; Part-Time Paid 10; Part-Time Volunteers 5; Interns 1.
Governing Authority: municipal. Parent Institution: The Chrysler Museum, 245 W. Olney Rd., Norfolk. Tax-exempt: 501(c)(3).
History Museum: housed in former home of Captain William Willoughby.
Collections: Norfolk history.
Research Fields: local history.
Activities: guided tours; lectures; films; concerts; study clubs; hobby workshops; organized education programs; docent program; gardening.
Publications: brochures.
Hours & Admission Prices: Wed.-Sat. 10-4, Sun. 12-4. No charge; donations accepted. Closed New Year's Day; Independence Day; Thanksgiving; Christmas.
Attendance: 4,000 (accurate)
Membership: Individual $15; Dual & Family $25.

OHEF SHOLOM TEMPLE ARCHIVES, (M), 530 Raleigh Ave., Norfolk, VA 23507-2199. Tel.: 757-625-4295. Fax: 757-625-2775.
E-mail: archives@ohefsholom.org
Web Site: www.ohefsholom.org
Founded: 1992.
Congressional District: 2
Key Personnel: Chm. (V), Mark Friedman; Admin., Lynn Evans.
Personnel Profile: Part-Time Paid 1; Part-Time Volunteers 5.
Governing Authority: Parent Institution: Ohef Sholom Temple. Tax-exempt.
Religious Museum.
Collections: history of congregation & local Jewry; photographs; documents; 24 4x5 framed panels.
Research Fields: Norfolk Jewry.
Hours & Admission Prices: Mon.-Fri. 9-5. No charge; donations accepted. ♿
Attendance: 2,000 (estimated)

PRETLOW PLANETARIUM, Old Dominion University, Alfriend Hall, 5115 Hampton Blvd., Norfolk, VA 23529-0001. Tel.: 757-683-4619.
E-mail: ddepaor@odu.edu
Web Site: sci.odu.edu/physics/about/pretlow.shtml
Key Personnel: Dir., Dr. Declan DePaor
Planetarium.
Collections: space science.
Activities: shows.
Hours & Admission Prices: Call for hours; groups by appointment.

VIRGINIA ZOOLOGICAL PARK, 3500 Granby St., Norfolk, VA 23504-1329. Tel.: 757-441-5227 & 2374. Fax: 757-441-5408.
E-mail: virginiazoo@norfolk.gov
Web Site: www.virginiazoo.org
Founded: 1902.
Congressional District: 2
Key Personnel: Pres. (V), Larry Brett; Zoo Supt., Gary D. Ochsenbein; Exec. Dir., Greg Bockheim; Supvr. Animal Svcs., Louise L. Hill; Asst. Supvr. Animal Svcs., Craig Pelke; Asst. Supvr. Animal Svcs., Joseph M. Roman; Horticulture Cur., Mark Schneider; Supvr. Maintenance, Charles E. Ryan; Administrative Asst., Stacey Connolly.
Personnel Profile: Full-Time Paid 55; Part-Time Paid 24; Part-Time Volunteers 30; Interns 2.
Governing Authority: municipal. Parent Institution: City of Norfolk, Executive Dept., 1101 City Hall Ave., 810 Union St., Norfolk, VA. 23510. Subsidiary Institution: Virginia Zoological Society. Tax-exempt.
Zoology Museum.
Collections: zoological & botanical specimens.
Research Fields: reptile veterinary medicine & reproduction; photo biology of captive reptiles.
Facilities: 150-vol. library of books, primarily zoological, zoo biology, horticulture available for research by students of zoo biology on premises; zoological park. Gift items for sale.
Activities: guided tours; docent program; permanent exhibitions; school loan service.
Publications: quarterly newsletter, Virginia Zoo Review.
Hours & Admission Prices: Daily 10-5. Adults $7, senior citizens 62 & over $6, children 2-11 $5; children under 2 no charge. Closed New Year's Day; Thanksgiving; Christmas. ♿
Attendance: 285,000 (estimated)
Membership: Individual $35; Military Family $40; Zoo for Two $45; Family $55; Family Plus $65; Family & Guests $100; Zookeeper $250; Curator $500; Leadership Society: $1,000 & up.

Occoquan

HISTORIC OCCOQUAN, INC., 413 Mill St., Occoquan, VA 22125. Mailing Address: P.O. Box 65, Occoquan, VA 22125-0065. Tel.: 703-491-7525.
Founded: 1969.
Congressional District: 8
Personnel Profile: Part-Time Paid 5.
Governing Authority: county; nonprofit. Tax-exempt: 501(c)(3).
General Museum: housed in 1768 Miller's Cottage of Grist Mill.
Collections: Indian lore; Civil War history; old costumes & clothing; household items; farm items; toys; miscellaneous items.
Facilities: limited library available to the public; 250 sq. ft. exhibit space; restaurant. China cups, pitchers, post cards & other items for sale.
Activities: guided tours; films; docent program; temporary exhibitions.
Publications: monthly newsletter.
Hours & Admission Prices: Daily 11-4. No charge. Closed New Year's; Thanksgiving; Christmas. ♿
Attendance: 9,300 (estimated)
Membership: Annual $15.

Onancock

KER PLACE, (M), 69 Market St., Onancock, VA 23417-4223. Mailing Address: P.O. Box 179, Onancock, VA 23417-0179. Tel.: 757-787-8012. Fax: 757-787-4271.
E-mail: kerplace@verizon.net
Web Site: kerrplace.org
Founded: 1957.
Congressional District: 1
Key Personnel: Exec. Dir., Peter Holland; Pres., Susan Stinson; Treas., Ridgway Dunton; Membership Sec., Judy Jacobs.
Personnel Profile: Full-Time Paid 1; Part-Time Paid 3; Part-Time Volunteers 30.
Governing Authority: society. Parent Institution: Eastern Shore of Virginia Historical Society, Inc. Tax-exempt.
Historical Society Museum: housed in c.1799 federal period 2-story building.
Collections: 1760-1875 furniture; glass & china; area reference books; c.1782 uniforms & furnishings of Gen. John Cropper; 17th-18th century portraits; local history; paintings.
Research Fields: Eastern shore history.
Facilities: 500-vol. library.
Activities: guided tours.
Publications: newsletter.
Hours & Admission Prices: April-Nov. Tues.-Sat. 11-4. Adults $5, students $2; discounts to AAM members & groups; members no charge. Closed national holidays.
Attendance: 1,000 (estimated)
Membership: Student, Teacher, Researcher $5; Individual $30; Family $50; Friends of the Historical Society $100; Sustaining $250; Patron $500; Benefactor $1,000.

Orange

THE ARTS CENTER IN ORANGE, 129 E. Main St., Orange, VA 22960. Mailing Address: P.O. Box 13, Orange, VA 22960-0011. Tel.: 540-672-7311.
E-mail: theartsorange@aol.com
Web Site: www.artscenterorange.org
Key Personnel: Exec. Dir., Laura Thompson; Pres., Ed Harvey
Art Museum.
Collections: works by emerging artists.
Facilities: Museum-related items for sale.
Activities: classes.
Hours & Admission Prices: Mon.-Sat. 10-5.

THE JAMES MADISON MUSEUM, 129 Caroline St., Orange, VA 22960-1532. Tel.: 540-672-1776. Fax: 540-672-0231.
E-mail: info@jamesmadisonmus.org
Web Site: www.jamesmadisonmus.org
Founded: 1976.
Congressional District: 7
Key Personnel: Pres., Helen Marie Taylor; Museum Shop Mgr. & Asst. Admin., Marguerite Anders.
Personnel Profile: Full-Time Paid 2; Part-Time Paid 1; Part-Time Volunteers 25; Interns 1.
Governing Authority: nonprofit organization. Parent Institution: The James Madison Memorial Foundation. Tax-exempt: 501(c)(3).
History Museum.
Collections: James & Dolley P. Madison artifacts; Orange County rural culture; 18th-20th century agriculture; cube house; transportation.
Research Fields: James Madison; Orange County; agriculture; the Constitution.
Facilities: Books & items dealing with James Madison, agriculture & local history for sale.
Activities: loan, permanent & temporary exhibitions; workshops & programs related to exhibits.
Publications: quarterly newsletter.
Hours & Admission Prices: Mon.-Fri. 9-5, Sat. 10-5, Sun. 1-5. Adults $5, senior citizens over 60 $3; discounts to Time Travelers, AAM, AAA, VAM, & ICOM members; students, members & children under 6 no charge. ♿
Attendance: 4,500 (accurate)
Membership: Student & Teacher $15; Individual $25; Family $35; Friend $100; Sustainer $250; Contributor $500; Patron $1,000; Benefactor $5,000.

Palmyra

THE FLUVANNA COUNTY HISTORICAL SOCIETY OLD STONE JAIL MUSEUM, Court Square, Palmyra, VA 22963. Mailing Address: P.O. Box 8, Palmyra, VA 22963-0008. Tel.: 434-589-7910. Fax: 434-589-7910 (call first).
E-mail: info@fluvannahistory.org
Web Site: www.fluvannahistory.org
Founded: 1964.
Key Personnel: Pres., Marvin Moss; Dir., Judith Mickelson.
Personnel Profile: Full-Time Paid 1; Part-Time Volunteers 58; Interns 2.
Governing Authority: nonprofit society. Parent Institution: Fluvanna County Historical Society. Branch Museum: Holland Page Place Museum. Tax-exempt.
Historical Society Museum.
Collections: firearms from Revolutionary War-WWI; uniforms from War of 1812-WW I; 19th- & early 20th-century textiles; 19th-century furniture, glassware & prints; books; photographs; household & farm items. Historic Buildings: 1828 stone jail; c.1865 log cabin, Holland Page Place.
Research Fields: genealogy; local history.
Facilities: Museum-related items for sale.
Activities: guided tours; organized educational programs; docent program; temporary exhibitions.
Publications: Fluvanna County Historical Society History; semiannual newsletters.
Hours & Admission Prices: Archives: Tues.-Thurs. 1-4. Museum: June-Oct. Wed. & Sat. 1-4, Sun. 2-5; other times by appointment. Donations Suggested.
Attendance: 500 (estimated)
Membership: Family $25; Sustaining $50; Life $300.

Parksley

EASTERN SHORE RAILROAD MUSEUM, 18468 Dunne Ave., Parksley, VA 23421. Mailing Address: P.O. Box 135, Parksley, VA 23421. Tel.: 757-665-7245.
Historic Buildings: housed in a former railroad station.
Collections: local history; railroad artifacts; tools.
Hours & Admission Prices: April-Oct. Mon.-Sat. 10-4, Sun. 1-4; Nov.-March Thurs.-Tues. 10-4. Adults $2; children under 12 no charge. Closed New Year's Day; Thanksgiving; Christmas.

Petersburg

ARCHIBALD GRAHAM MCILWAINE HOUSE, 425 Cockade Alley, Petersburg, VA 23803-4556.
Founded: 1984.
Congressional District: 3
Personnel Profile: Full-Time Paid 1; Part-Time Paid 43; Interns 2.
Historic House Museum.
Collections: 19th-century architecture.
Hours & Admission Prices: Closed for renovations. ♿

BLANDFORD CHURCH & RECEPTION CTR. (THE PETERSBURG MUSEUMS), 321 S. Crater Rd., Petersburg, VA 23803-3213. Mailing Address: Petersburg Museums, 15 W. Bank St., Petersburg, VA 23803-3213. Tel.: 804-733-2400. Fax: 804-863-0837.
E-mail: blandfordchurch@mindspring.com
Web Site: www.petersburg-va.org/tourism/blanford.htm
Founded: 1972.
Congressional District: 3
Key Personnel: Site Coord., Martha Atkinson; Cur. Collections, Laura Willoughby.
Personnel Profile: Full-Time Paid 5; Part-Time Paid 30; Interns 1.
Governing Authority: municipal. Parent Institution: City of Petersburg, VA. Tax-exempt.
Historic Building: 1735 Colonial Church of Bristol Parish, located in Blandford Cemetery, containing graves of 30,000 Confederate soldiers.

Collections: Tiffany stained-glass windows donated by the Confederate states, Maryland & Missouri, The Ladies Memorial Association of Petersburg & Tiffany.
Research Fields: Church, Colonial, Tiffany & Confederate history.
Facilities: Museum-related items for sale.
Activities: guided tours; lectures. Annual Events: Confederate Memorial Day in June; Cemetery Halloween tour in October.
Publications: pamphlets, Walking Tour of Blandford Cemetery; Old Blandford Church; Blandford Cemetery, Death and Life at Petersburg, Virginia.
Hours & Admission Prices: Jan.-March Mon. & Wed.-Sat. 10-5, Sun. 1-5; April-Sept. Mon.-Sat. 10-5, Sun. 1-5; Oct.-March Tues.-Sat. 10-5, Sun. 1-5. Adults $5, senior citizens, active duty military & children 7-12 $4; discounts to AAM & ICOM members. Closed New Year's Day; Thanksgiving; Christmas Eve & Day. ♿
Attendance: 10,000 (estimated)

CENTRE HILL MUSEUM (THE PETERSBURG MUSEUMS), 1 Centre Hill Ave., Petersburg, VA 23803-3213. Mailing Address: Petersburg Museums, 15 W. Bank St., Petersburg, VA 23803-3213. Tel.: 804-733-2401. Fax: 804-863-0837.
E-mail: petgcurator@earthlink.net
Web Site: www.petersburg-va.org/tourism.cntrhill.htm
Founded: 1976.
Congressional District: 3
Key Personnel: Cur., Laura Willoughby; Site Coord., Ann L. Brown.
Personnel Profile: Full-Time Paid 5; Part-Time Paid 34.
Governing Authority: municipal government. Parent Institution: City of Petersburg. Part of Petersburg Museum System. Tax-exempt.
Historic House: c.1823 Centre Hill Mansion.
Collections: Federal, Greek revival & colonial revival architecture; period furnishings; architecture; decorative arts; archives & historic photographs relating to the history City of Petersburg.
Research Fields: 19th-century decorative arts & architecture; repository for archival & photographic material related to Petersburg's history.
Facilities: 500-vol. library emphasizing Petersburg history & decorative arts. Museum-related items for sale.
Activities: guided tours; lectures; temporary exhibitions; research by appointment only.
Hours & Admission Prices: Adults $5, Block Ticket to 3 Museums: Adults $11; discounts to seniors, children, military, AAM & ICOM members; Petersburg residents no charge. Closed New Year's Day; Thanksgiving; Christmas Eve & Day.
Attendance: 4,000 (estimated)

FARMERS BANK (THE PETERSBURG MUSEUMS), 19 Bollingbrook St., Petersburg, VA 23803-4548. Mailing Address: 15 W. Bank St., Petersburg, VA 23803. Tel.: 804-733-2400. Fax: 804-863-0837 & 861-0883.
Web Site: www.petersburg-va.org
Founded: 1974.
Congressional District: 3
Key Personnel: Dir., Kevin Kirby; Site. Coord., George Bass.
Personnel Profile: Full-Time Paid 5; Part-Time Paid 42.
Governing Authority: municipal, City of Petersburg. Parent Institution: Association for the Preservation of Virginia Antiquities, Fort Henry Branch. Tax-exempt.
Bank Museum.
Collections: pre-Civil War banking; furnishings used in banks of the period; how bank notes were made; gold storage area.
Research Fields: banking history; general Petersburg.
Activities: tours.
Hours & Admission Prices: Sat. 10am-12pm. Adults $5, senior citizens, active duty military & children 7-12 $4; block tickets available; discounts to AAM & ICOM members. Closed New Year's Day; Thanksgiving; Christmas Eve & Day.

PAMPLIN HISTORICAL PARK AND THE NATIONAL MUSEUM OF THE CIVIL WAR SOLDIER, (M), 6125 Boydton Plank Rd., Petersburg, VA 23803-7494. Tel.: 804-861-2408. Fax: 804-861-2820.
E-mail: generalmailbox@pamplinpark.org
Web Site: www.pamplinpark.org
Founded: 1994.
Congressional District: 4
Key Personnel: Pres. & C.E.O., A. Wilson Greene; Exec. Vice Pres. & C.O.O., Patrick A. Olienyk; Museum Shop Mgr., Jim Glenn.
Personnel Profile: Full-Time Paid 49; Part-Time Paid 23; Part-Time Volunteers 4.
Governing Authority: private; nonprofit. Parent Institution: Pamplin Foundation, Portland, OR. Tax-exempt: 501(c)(3).
Military History Museum: Park includes The National Museum of the Civil War Soldier; Tudor Hall Plantation & Field Quarter; The Banks House; re-created Military Encampment; Battlefield Center; The Breakthrough Battlefield, a National Historic Landmark; Civil War Adventure Camp; Hart Farm.
Collections: Civil War military artifacts with emphasis on enlisted soldiers; Antebellum furnishings, decorative arts, agricultural tools & equipment; kitchen/slave quarter; four historic houses; battlefield with earthworks.
Research Fields: Petersburg Campaign of 1864-65 & the Breakthrough of April 2, 1865; life of the Civil War soldier; life on antebellum Virginia plantations.
Facilities: cafe; banquet facilities; 100-seat education center. Museum-related items for sale.
Activities: formal educational programs; guided tours; living history demonstrations; children's day camps; annual historical symposium; overnight programs; special events.
Publications: park guide, Pamplin Historical Park & the National Museum of the Civil War Soldier; Duty Called Me Here: The Soldier Comrades of the National Museum of the Civil War Soldier; Tudor Hall: The Boisseau Family Farm.
Hours & Admission Prices: mid-June to mid-Aug. daily 9-6; mid-Aug. to mid-June daily 9-5. Adults $15, seniors 65 & over and military with ID $13.50, children 6-12 $9; discounts to schools & groups; members & children under 6 no charge. Closed New Year's Day; Thanksgiving; Christmas. ♿
Membership: Individual $42.65; Family $100; Pamplin Society $500.

PETERSBURG AREA ART LEAGUE, 7 E. Old St., Petersburg, VA 23803-4558. Tel.: 804-861-4611.
E-mail: info@paalart.com
Web Site: www.paalart.org
Founded: 1932.
Key Personnel: Pres. (V), Ellen Ende; Membership & Corresponding Sec., Walt Smith.
Personnel Profile: Full-Time Paid 1; Part-Time Paid 3.
Governing Authority: nonprofit. Parent Institution: Virginia Museum of Fine Arts.
Art Gallery: housed in c.1700 granary where Indians came to trade goods.
Collections: various forms of rotating art of local artists.
Activities: lectures; workshops; organized educational programs; participatory & temporary exhibitions. Annual Events: Poplar Lawn Art Festival; Trees of Christmas; fund-raisers.
Publications: newsletter.
Hours & Admission Prices: Tues.-Fri. 12-6, Sat. 10-4. No charge; donations accepted. Closed major holidays. ♿
Attendance: 4,300
Membership: Student $15; Single $30; Family & Joint $40; Patron $50-$99; Sponsor $100-$499; Corporate Sponsor $250 & up; Benefactor $500 & up.

PETERSBURG NATIONAL BATTLEFIELD, 1539 Hickory Hill Rd., Petersburg, VA 23803-4721. Tel.: 804-732-3531. Fax: 804-732-3615.
Web Site: www.nps.gov/pete
Founded: 1926.
Congressional District: 5
Key Personnel: Historian, James H. Blankenship, Jr.
Governing Authority: federal. Parent Institution: National Park Service, U.S. Dept. of Interior. Branch Locations: Grant's Headquarter's at City Point, 1001 Pecan Ave., Hopewell, VA. Tel.: 804-458-9504; Five Forks Battlefield, 9840 Courhouse Rd., Dinwiddie, VA. Tel.: 804-469-4093; Eastern Front, 5001 Siege Rd., Petersburg, VA. Tel.: 804-732-3531; Poplar Grove National Cemetery, 8005 Vaughan Rd., Petersburg, VA. Tax-exempt.
Military Museum: located on Petersburg Battlefield.
Collections: military history of campaign for Petersburg; artillery; maps.
Research Fields: Petersburg Campaign; Civil War.
Facilities: 2,000-vol. library by appointment only. Historical publications, postcards & other museum-related items for sale.
Activities: guided tours; lectures; films; permanent exhibits; 17-minute map presentation on Civil War Siege of Petersburg.
Publications: folder, Petersburg; 5 site bulletins: City Point; Poplar Grove National Cemetery; Five Forks Battlefield; African Americans at Petersburg; African-Americans on Lee's Retreat, April 1865.
Hours & Admission Prices: Daily 9-5. Vehicle $5, adults $3; children under 16 no charge. Closed New Year's Day; Thanksgiving; Christmas. ♿

PETERSBURG REGIONAL ART CENTER, 132 N. Sycamore St., Petersburg, VA 23803-3245. Tel.: 804-733-8200.
E-mail: djacobs306@aol.com
Web Site: www.pracarts.com
Formerly: Shockoe Bottom Arts Center
Founded: 1993.

Key Personnel: Co Founder SBAC, Rusty Davis; Co Founder SBAC, Deanna Thomas
Art Center.
Collections: works by local artists.
Hours & Admission Prices: Wed.-Sat. 10-4. No charge. ♿
Membership: Individual $50.

SIEGE MUSEUM (THE PETERSBURG MUSEUMS), (M), 15 W. Bank St., Petersburg, VA 23803-3213. Tel.: 804-733-2403. Fax: 804-863-0837.
E-mail: petgcurator@earthlink.net
Web Site: www.petersburg-va.org/tourism/siege.htm
Founded: 1976.
Congressional District: 3
Key Personnel: Dir. Tourism, Kevin Kirby; Cur. Collections, Laura Willoughby.
Personnel Profile: Full-Time Paid 2; Part-Time Paid 35; Interns 2.
Governing Authority: municipal. Parent Institution: City of Petersburg. Subsidiary Institution: Petersburg Museum System. Tax-exempt.
Historic Building: 1839 Wheat Grain Exchange Building.
Collections: Civil War artifacts & household items; Siege of Petersburg; film.
Research Fields: Civil War in Petersburg; Petersburg history.
Facilities: theater.
Activities: guided tours; children's scavenger hunt.
Hours & Admission Prices: Jan.-March Tues. 1-5, Wed.-Sat. 10-5, Sun. 1-5; April-Sept. Mon.-Sat. 10-5, Sun. 1-5; Oct.-Dec. Tues.-Sat. 10-5, Sun. 1-5. Adults $5; discounts to seniors, children, military, AAM & ICOM members; Petersburg residents no charge. Closed New Year's Day; Thanksgiving; Christmas Eve & Day. ♿
Attendance: 6,000 (estimated)

Pocahontas

POCAHONTAS MINE & MUSEUM, 11 Centre St., Pocahontas, VA 24635. Mailing Address: P.O. Box 128, Pocahontas, VA 24635-0128. Tel.: 276-945-2134 & 9522. Fax: 276-945-9904.
E-mail: pocahontas@comcast.net
History Museum: designated as a national historic landmark.
Collections: coal mining history.
Hours & Admission Prices: April to Oct. Mon.-Sat. 10-5, Sun. 1-5. Adults $7, children 6-12 $4.50; discounts to AAA members & groups; children under 6 no charge.

Portsmouth

CHILDREN'S MUSEUM OF VIRGINIA, 420 High St., Portsmouth, VA 23704. Mailing Address: 521 Middle St., Portsmouth, VA 23704-3708. Tel.: 757-393-5258.
Founded: 1980.
Governing Authority: Tax-exempt.
Children's Museum.
Collections: hands-on exhibits.
Hours & Admission Prices: Tues.-Sat. 9-5, Sun. 11-5. Admission $5; children under 2 no charge.

COURTHOUSE GALLERIES ART MUSEUM, 420 High St., Portsmouth, VA 23704. Tel.: 757-393-8543; 800-767-8782.
Web Site: www.courthousegalleries.com
Key Personnel: Cur., Gayle Paul
Art Museum.
Collections: paintings; sculpture.
Facilities: Museum-related items for sale.
Activities: lectures; classes; workshops; performances.
Hours & Admission Prices: Memorial Day to Labor Day Tues.-Sat. 10-5, Sun. 1-5; Winter: Wed.-Sat. 10-5, Sun. 1-5.

THE HILL HOUSE, 221 North St., Portsmouth, VA 23704. Tel.: 757-393-0241.
Historic House Museum.
Collections: Hill family history; period furnishings; personal artifacts; photographs.
Hours & Admission Prices: April-Dec. Wed. 12:30-4:30, Sat.-Sun. 1-5.

PORTSMOUTH HISTORICAL ASSOCIATION, 221 North St., Portsmouth, VA 23704-2601. Tel.: 757-393-0241.
Founded: 1957.
Congressional District: 3
Key Personnel: C.E.O. & Pres. (V), Alice C. Hanes; 1st Vice Pres., Marshall W. Butt, Jr.; 2nd Vice Pres., Ms. Macon Williams.
Personnel Profile: Part-Time Volunteers 20.
Historical House: c.1830 Hill House.
Collections: original period furnishings.
Activities: guided tours.
Hours & Admission Prices: April-Dec. Sat.-Sun. 1-5; tour groups by appointment at other times. Adults $3, children 6-12 $1; children under 6 with adult & members with dues card no charge.
Attendance: 601 (accurate)
Membership: Individual $5.

PORTSMOUTH MUSEUM OF MILITARY HISTORY INC., 701 Court St., Portsmouth, VA 23704-3625. Tel.: 757-393-2773. Fax: 757-393-2883.
Formerly: Museum of Military History
Founded: 1998.
Key Personnel: C.E.O. & Pres., Dale Davis.
Personnel Profile: Part-Time Paid 3; Part-Time Volunteers 2.
Governing Authority: private; nonprofit organization.
Military Museum.
Collections: military war artifacts.
Publications: The Victory Garden.
Hours & Admission Prices: Winter: Sat. 10-5, Sun. 1-5; Summer: Tues.-Sat. 10-5, Sun. 1-5. Adults $5, members $3; discounts to AAM members. ♿
Attendance: 900 (estimated)

PORTSMOUTH MUSEUMS, (M), 521 Middle St., Portsmouth, VA 23704-3622. Tel.: 757-393-8983. Fax: 757-393-5228.
E-mail: perryn@portsmouthva.gov
Web Site: www.portsmouthva.gov
Founded: 1980.
Congressional District: 4
Key Personnel: Dir., Nancy Perry; Site Mgr. Children's Museum of Virginia, Al Schweizer; Courthouse Galleries Cur., Gayle Paul; Naval Shipyards & Lightship Museum Cur., Corey Thornton; Education Coord., Christine Matyseck; Exhibit Specialist, Pat Jensen; Volunteer Coord., Barbara Pickett; Volunteer Coord., Stephen Grunett.
Personnel Profile: Full-Time Paid 26; Part-Time Paid 16; Part-Time Volunteers 60; Interns 1.
Governing Authority: municipal. City of Portsmouth, 801 Crawford St., Portsmouth, VA 23704-3266. Tel.: 757-393-8641. Branch Museums: Courthouse Galleries, High & Court St., Portsmouth, VA 23704-3266. Tel.: 757-393-8543; Children's Museum of Virginia (housed in Andalo's Clubhouse, a satellite location during renovations), 420 High St., Portsmouth, VA 23704-3266. Tel.: 757-393-5258; Portsmouth Naval Shipyard Museum, 2 High St. Portsmouth, VA 23704-3266. Tel.: 757-393-8591; The Lightship Portsmouth Museum, Foot of London at Water St., Portsmouth, VA 23704-3266. Tel.: 757-393-8741. Tax-exempt.
General Museum.
Collections: Courthouse Galleries, no permanent collections, all exhibits are traveling or created. Children's Museum of Virginia, educational & participatory exhibits concentrating on science, art & the humanities. Lancaster Antique Toy & Train collection of more than 10,000 objects, and Planetarium. Naval Shipyard Museum, history of the Naval Shipyard & Portsmouth, models, uniforms, flags, arms, maps, military, research library. Lightship Portsmouth, restored & furnished c.1915 Coast Guard Lightship.
Major Exhibits: Cancer Art, 1/17/10-2/21/10; 2010 Outdoor Sculpture, 2/5/10-10/10/10; Annual Portfolio: Tidewater Art Alliance, 3/5/10-4/25/10; Fairy Tale Art: Illustrations from Children's Books, 5/7/10-7/11/10; Inspired Forms: A Retrospective of Ceramic Art by J. Howard Johnson, 7/23/10-10/10/10; Winter Wonderland: The Coleman Collection, 11/20/10-12/10.
Research Fields: The Lightship Portsmouth: lightship service. Portsmouth Naval Shipyard Museum: naval & local history.
Facilities: Courthouse Galleries: gift items for sale. Portsmouth Naval Shipyard Museum: 5,000-vol. library of naval & local history available for research by appointment. Gift items for sale.
Activities: Courthouse Galleries, traveling exhibitions; concerts; lectures; workshops; youth art programs. Children's Museum of Virginia, out-reach & education programs; workshops; teacher training; special events; boy scout & girl scout programs; camps. Naval Shipyard Museum: lectures; family programs.
Publications: quarterly newsletters.
Hours & Admission Prices: Courthouse Galleries: Tues.-Sat. 9-5, Sun. 11-5. Admission $3. Children's Museum of Virginia (temporary satellite location at Andalo's Clubhouse: Tues.-Sat. 9-5, Sun. 11-5. Portsmouth Naval Shipyard Museum: Mon.-Sat. 10-5, Sun. 1-5. Lightship Museum: Memorial Day to Labor Day Mon.-Sat. 10-5, Sun. 1-5; Sept.-May Sat. 10-5, Sun. 1-5. Admission $3; discounts to AAM, VAM & ICOM members; members no charge. Combination tickets available.
Attendance: 173,164 (accurate)
Membership: Student & Senior Citizen $25; Individual $30; Grandparent & Senior Couple $45; Family $55; Sponsor $100; Patron $250; Director's Circle $500; Contributor $1,000.

VIRGINIA SPORTS HALL OF FAME, 206 High St., Portsmouth, VA 23704-3720. Mailing Address: P.O. Box 370, Portsmouth, VA 23705-0370. Tel.: 757-393-8031. Fax: 757-393-8288.
E-mail: info@vshfm.com
Web Site: www.vshfm.com
Founded: 1972.
Congressional District: 4
Key Personnel: Pres., Eddie Webb; Chm., David Tynch; Dir. Mktg., Sales & Event Planning, Steve Givens; Administrative Coord., Donna Swain; Museum Shop Mgr., Elizabeth Goodwin.
Personnel Profile: Full-Time Paid 7; Part-Time Paid 16; Part-Time Volunteers 5; Interns 3.
Governing Authority: nonprofit organization. Tax-exempt: 501(c)(3).
Sports Museum: located in Historic Olde Towne Portsmouth.
Collections: historical & contemporary Virginia sports figures.
Research Fields: Virginia sportsmen & sportswomen.
Facilities: 17,000 sq. ft. exhibit space.
Activities: guided tours; films; children's programs; video game tournaments; health fairs. Museum Sponsors: annual Induction Banquet. Celebrity golf tournament.
Publications: annual banquet program; magazine, The Press Box.
Hours & Admission Prices: Summer: Mon.-Sat. 10-5, Sun. 1-5; Sept.-May Mon.-Fri. 10-2, Sat. 10-5, Sun. 1-5. Adults $7; members no charge. Closed New Year's Day; Thanksgiving; Christmas. ♿
Attendance: 70,000 (estimated)
Membership: Individual $30; Small College & Small Business $100; University $200; Corporate $250.

Pulaski

FINE ARTS CENTER FOR NEW RIVER VALLEY, 21 W. Main St., Pulaski, VA 24301-5015. Mailing Address: P.O. Box 309, Pulaski, VA 24301-0309. Tel.: 540-980-7363. Fax: 540-980-7363.
E-mail: info@facnrv.org
Web Site: www.facnrv.org
Founded: 1978.
Congressional District: 9
Key Personnel: Dir., Judy C. Ison; Pres. (V), Gary Hancock; Asst., Rhonda Hodge.
Personnel Profile: Full-Time Paid 2; Part-Time Volunteers 20; Interns 2.
Governing Authority: nonprofit. Tax-exempt: 501(c)(3)
Art Museum: housed in 1898 Victorian Commercial structure.
Collections: eclectic & contemporary works by local & regional artists.
Research Fields: area artists.
Facilities: 150-vol. library of visual & performing arts for public use; educational facilities; catering service available; meeting facilities. Paintings, pottery, weaving, basketry & other related items for sale.
Activities: guided tours; lectures; concerts; dance recitals; arts festivals; theater; hobby workshops; organized education programs; docent program; participatory, loan, temporary & traveling exhibitions; performance sponsorship.
Publications: monthly newsletter, Centerpiece.
Hours & Admission Prices: Mon.-Fri. 10-5, Sat. 11-3. No charge; donations accepted. Closed federal holidays. ♿
Attendance: 20,000 (estimated)
Membership: Student $10; Individual $15; Family $25; Patron $75; Sponsor $125; Sustaining $500. Business Memberships: Business Sponsor $150; Sustaining Corporation $550; Corporate Benefactor $1,000.

Radford

GLENCOE MUSEUM, 600 Unruh Dr., Radford, VA 24141-1501. Mailing Address: P.O. Box 3339, Radford, VA 24143-3339. Tel.: 540-731-5031.
E-mail: info@glencoemuseum.org
Web Site: www.glencoemuseum.org
Founded: 1998.
Congressional District: 9
Key Personnel: Dir., John W. Barksdale; Chm. (V), Annyce Levy.
Personnel Profile: Part-Time Paid 1; Part-Time Volunteers 30; Interns 1.
Governing Authority: Parent Institution: Radford Heritage Foundation. Tax-exempt.
History Museum: housed in c.1870 home built by Gen. Gabriel Colvin Wharton.
Collections: period furnishings; decorative arts; photographs; historical documents.
Research Fields: local & regional history.
Activities: special events; educational programs; temporary exhibitions; summer history camp; Glencoe lecture series. Museum Sponsors: Radford Heritage Days.
Hours & Admission Prices: Tues.-Sat. 10-4, Sun. 1-4. No charge; donations accepted. Closed national holidays. ♿
Attendance: 2,271 (accurate)
Membership: Individual $25; Family $50; Sustaining $100; Patron $500; Leadership Giving $1,000.

RADFORD UNIVERSITY ART MUSEUM, (M), 200 Powell Hall, Radford, VA 24142. Mailing Address: P.O. Box 6965, Radford, VA 24142-6965. Tel.: 540-831-5754. Fax: 540-831-6799.
E-mail: ruartmuseum@radford.edu
Web Site: rumuseum.asp.radford.edu
Founded: 1985.
Congressional District: 9
Key Personnel: Chief Cur., Steve Arbury; Cur., Jim Knipe; Cur., Halide Salam; Registrar, Kim Cochran.
Personnel Profile: Full-Time Paid 1; Part-Time Paid 2; Part-Time Volunteers 10.
Governing Authority: Parent Institution: Radford University. Tax-exempt.
University Art Museum.
Collections: late 20th-century painting & sculpture; ancillary collections of Nigerian & Huichol art from Mexico.
Research Fields: contemporary art.
Facilities: 2,000 sq. ft. exhibit space; 16,000 sq. ft. sculpture court; sculpture collection placed throughout campus; satellite galleries; art repository.
Activities: national, regional & international artists; loan exhibitions; lectures & symposia in conjunction with exhibitions; public sculpture.
Publications: brochures; catalogs; Selections from the Permanent Collection; Dorothy Gillespie; Ibram Lassaw; Adolf Dehu.
Hours & Admission Prices: May-July Mon.-Fri. 10-4, Sat.-Sun. 12-4; Sept.-April Mon.-Fri. 10-5, Sat.-Sun. 12-4. No charge. Closed national holidays & school vacations. ♿
Attendance: 17,400 (accurate)
Membership: Associate $100-$249; Patron $250-$499; Sponsor $500-$999; Benefactor $1,000 & up.

Reedville

REEDVILLE FISHERMEN'S MUSEUM, (M), 504 Main St., Reedville, VA 22539-4401. Mailing Address: P.O. Box 306, Reedville, VA 22539-0306. Tel.: 804-453-6529. Fax: 804-453-7159.
E-mail: office@rfmuseum.org
Web Site: www.rfmuseum.org
Founded: 1986.
Congressional District: 1
Key Personnel: Dir., Katrina P. Lawrimore; Pres. (V), Maureen Gillmer; Museum Shop Mgr., Jane Kimball; Office Mgr., Karen Rogers.
Personnel Profile: Full-Time Paid 1; Part-Time Paid 2; Part-Time Volunteers 277.
Governing Authority: Parent Institute: Greater Reedville Association, Inc. Tax-exempt.
Regional Maritime Museum.
Collections: tools & equipment related to commercial and recreational fishing, crabbing & oyster industries; photographs. Historic Buildings: The William Walker House built in the 1870's and furnished as a typical waterman's home of the early 1900's; The Covington Building: fishing industry, watermen's culture of Chesapeake Bay; regional history of the Northern Neck of Virginia; The Pendleton Building: boat & model making shops; The Butler House: museum offices, library & archives; in the water are displayed the Claud W. Somers, a 42-foot skipjack built in 1911 and the Elva C., a 55-foot traditional workboat built in 1922.
Major Exhibits: A Fishing Expedition, 5/31/10-10/10.
Research Fields: Menhaden fisheries; maritime history; lower Chesapeake Bay.
Facilities: library & archives documenting the Menhaden fishing industry 1870 century to the present day.
Activities: lecture series on topics related to life on the lower Chesapeake Bay; craft workshops for children & adults; boat building & model making classes; apprenticeship opportunities; monthly meetings of groups interested in wooden boats, photography, quilting and fly fishing; educational cruises aboard the restored buy boat and skipjack. Annual Events; Antique & Classic Boat Show in September; Old fashioned Independence day celebration in July; Oyster Roast in November; Christmas on Cockrell's Creek in December.
Publications: quarterly newsletter, Starry Banner.
Hours & Admission Prices: March-April Sat.-Sun. 10:30-4:30; May-Oct. daily 10:30-4:30; Nov.-Jan. Fri.-Mon. 10-30-4:30. Adults $5, senior citizens over 60 $3; discounts to CAMM members; children under 12 & members no charge. ♿
Attendance: 12,842 (accurate)
Membership: Student $15; Individual $25; Family $35; Sustaining $100; Patron $250; Sponsor $500.

Reston

THE GREATER RESTON ARTS CENTER (GRACE), 12001 Market St., Ste. 103, Reston, VA 20190-6244. Tel.: 703-471-9242. Fax: 703-471-0952.
E-mail: info@restonarts.rog
Web Site: www.restonarts.org
Founded: 1974.
Congressional District: 8
Key Personnel: Pres. & C.E.O., John Alciati; Exhibitions Dir., Joanne Bauer.
Personnel Profile: Full-Time Paid 4; Part-Time Paid 1; Part-Time Volunteers 10.
Governing Authority: nonprofit organization. Tax-exempt: 501(c)(3).
Civic Art & Cultural Center.
Collections: works of contemporary artists.
Research Fields: contemporary visual art.
Facilities: Handmade contemporary crafts for sale.
Activities: lectures; gallery talks; lectures; children's workshops; docent program; Art-In-the-Schools program. Special Event: Northern Virginia Fine Arts Festival.
Publications: triannual newsletter, Visions.
Hours & Admission Prices: Tues.-Sat. 11-5. No charge. Closed New Year's Day; Easter; Christmas. ♿
Attendance: 20,000
Membership: Individual $25; Artist $40; Family $45; Friend $100; Sustainer $250; Patron $500; Benefactor $1,000 & up.

RESTON MUSEUM, 1639 Washington Plaza, Reston, VA 20190-4305. Mailing Address: P.O. Box 2803, Reston, VA 20195-0803. Tel.: 703-709-7700.
E-mail: restonmuseum@gmail.com
Web Site: www.restonmuseum.org
Founded: 1997.
Congressional District: 8
Key Personnel: Chm. (V), Lynn Lilienthal; Pres. (V), Vicky Wingert; Museum Shop Mgr., Arja Sahramaa.
Personnel Profile: Part-Time Paid 1; Part-Time Volunteers 22; Interns 1.
Governing Authority: Tax-exempt.
History Museum.
Collections: Reston history.
Facilities: Museum-related items for sale.
Activities: walking tours; children's workshops.
Hours & Admission Prices: Tues.-Sun. 12-5, Sat. 10-5. No charge; donations accepted.
Attendance: 6,347 (accurate)
Membership: Senior & Student $15; Individual $25; Household $40; Patron $100; Benefactor $500.

Richmond

AGECROFT HALL, 4305 Sulgrave Rd., Richmond, VA 23221-3256. Tel.: 804-353-4241. Fax: 804-353-2151.
Web Site: www.agecrofthall.com
Founded: 1967.
Congressional District: 3
Key Personnel: Exec. Dir., Richard W. Moxley; Pres. (V), Evans B. Brasfield; Business Officer & Museum Shop Mgr., Sieglinde F. Nix; Cur. Education, Jill Pesesky; Mgr. Tour Svcs., Jennifer Paton.
Personnel Profile: Full-Time Paid 7; Part-Time Paid 20; Part-Time Volunteers 2.
Governing Authority: nonprofit organization. Tax-exempt.
Historic House: 15th-century English Country Manor House disassembled in 1926, brought over & rebuilt; formerly located at Lancashire, England.
Collections: 16th- & 17th-century English furnishings & paintings; textiles; armor; musical instruments.
Research Fields: 16th- & early 17th-century English country life & related pursuits.
Facilities: herb garden; knot garden; formal gardens & Tradescant garden.
Activities: guided tours; children's programs; living history presentations; lectures, theatrical & musical presentations.
Publications: online newsletter.
Hours & Admission Prices: Tues.-Sat. 10-4, Sun. 12:30-5. Adults $8, senior citizens $7, students $5; discounts to AAA & active military. Closed legal holidays. ♿
Attendance: 17,979 (accurate)

THE AMERICAN CIVIL WAR CENTER AT HISTORIC TREDEGAR, (M), 490 Tredegar St., Richmond, VA 23219-4328. Tel.: 804-780-1865. Fax: 804-780-0264.
E-mail: info@tredegar.org
Web Site: www.tredegar.org
Formerly: Tredegar National Civil War Center Foundation
Key Personnel: Pres., Christy S. Coleman; Vice Pres. Operations, Adam Scher; Dir. Mktg. & Pub. Rels., Anedra Bourne; Chief Administrative Officer, Mimi Daniel; Cur., Jennifer A Gaudio; Dir. Devel., Celia Luxmoore; Mgr. Devel., Cindy Holma; Dir. Education, Mark Howell; Museum Shop Mgr., Keith Nelson
History Museum.
Collections: Civil War history; period artifacts; photographs; hands-on exhibits.
Activities: educational programs; teacher development workshops; guest historian lecturers; website training; Civil War history programs; monographs.
Hours & Admission Prices: Daily 9-5. Adults $8, students & seniors $6, children 7-12 $2; children 6 & under no charge. Closed New Year's Day; Thanksgiving; Christmas. ♿
Membership: Student & Senior $30; Senior Plus One $45; Individual $40; Individual Plus One $55; Family $65.

ANDERSON GALLERY, SCHOOL OF THE ARTS, VIRGINIA COMMONWEALTH UNIVERSITY, (M), 907 1/2 W. Franklin St., Richmond, VA 23284-2514. Mailing Address: Anderson Gallery/VCU, 907 1/2 W. Franklin St., P.O. Box 842514, Richmond, VA 23284-2514. Tel.: 804-828-1522. Fax: 804-828-8585. TDD: 804-367-0100.
Web Site: www.vcu.edu/arts/gallery
Founded: 1969.
Congressional District: 3
Key Personnel: Dir., Ashley Kistler; Gallery Mgr., Leon Roper; Gallery Coord., Traci Horne Flores; Gallery Assoc., Michael Lease.
Personnel Profile: Full-Time Paid 2; Part-Time Paid 13; Part-Time Volunteers 29; Interns 6.
Governing Authority: Parent Institution: Virginia Commonwealth University. Subsidiary Institution: School of the Arts. Tax-exempt: 170(b)(1)(A).
University Museum.
Collections: prints; photographs; contemporary painting & sculpture; folk art; Mayan contemporary textiles.
Research Fields: European & American graphic arts; photography; contemporary art.
Facilities: study collection of visual materials available by special arrangement. Books & art related items for sale.
Activities: lectures; films; gallery talks; training programs for professional museum workers; inter-museum loan, temporary & traveling exhibitions.
Publications: catalogs; posters; limited edition graphics.
Hours & Admission Prices: June-Aug. Tues.-Sat. 12-5; Sept.-May Tues.-Fri. 10-5, Sat.-Sun. 1-5. No charge. Closed state & university holidays.
Attendance: 30,000 (accurate)

APVA PRESERVATION VIRGINIA, 204 W. Franklin St., Richmond, VA 23220-5012. Tel.: 804-648-1889. Fax: 804-775-0802.
Web Site: www.apva.org
Formerly: Association for the Preservation of Virginia Antiquities
Founded: 1889.
Congressional District: 3
Key Personnel: Exec. Dir., Elizabeth Kostelny; Dir. Membership, Betty Fuccella; Publications Editor & Admin. Asst., Catherine A. Long; Pres., John Guy; Dir. Preservation Svcs., Louis J. Malon; Controller, Cheryl Greenday; Cur. Collections, Catherine E. Dean; Mgr. Programs, Terry Graham; Mgr. Revolving Fund, Sarah Cooleen; Museum Shop Mgr., Carrie Wiggins.
Personnel Profile: Full-Time Paid 31; Part-Time Paid 150; Part-Time Volunteers 200; Interns 2.
Governing Authority: society; nonprofit organization. House Sites: 1760 Rising Sun Tavern, Fredericksburg; early 18th century Scotchtown, home of Patrick Henry; 1774 Smithfield Plantation, Blacksburg; c.1772 Mary Washington House, Fredericksburg; c.1760 Smith's Fort Plantation, near Surry Courthouse; 1607 Historic Jamestowne; 1790 John Marshall House, Richmond; 1817 Farmers Bank, Petersburg; 1665 Bacon's Castle, Surry; mid-18th century, Hugh Mercer Apothecary Shop, Fredericksburg; 1800 Walter Reed Birthplace, Gloucester County; 1750 Isle of Wight Courthouse, Smithfield; c.1760 Old Tobacco Warehouse, Urbanna; 1791 Cape Henry Lighthouse, Virginia Beach; 1775 Old Stone House (Edgar Allen Poe Museum), Richmond; late 18th-century St. James Cottage, Fredericksburg; 1782 Debtor's Prison, Accomac; 1731-1814 Eastville Courthouse Buildings; 18th-century Holly Brook, Eastville. Tax-exempt: 501(c)(3).
Historic Building & Site; Preservation Project.
Collections: 17th- to 19th-century furniture; decorative arts; textiles; metals; ceramics; glass; fine arts; photographs; archaeology.
Research Fields: architecture; period furnishings & decorative arts; 17th-century history; preservation technology; archaeology.
Activities: guided tours; lectures; participatory, permanent, temporary & loan exhibitions; education programs; concerts; docent program. Annual Events: Preservation Conference & Preservation Workshops; VA's Most Endangered Sites: VA Preservation Awards; Revolving Fund.

Publications: biannual, Journal; annual, Ventures; publications relating to sites.
Hours & Admission Prices: For hours & admission prices of House Museums see separate listings or web site.
Attendance: 400,000 (estimated)
Membership: Student & Teacher $25; Individual $40; Plus One $50; Family $60; Century $100; Sponsor $250; The Virginia Company $300; Benefactor $500. Out-of-State: Individual Associate $30; Individual Associate Plus One $35; Family Associate $40; Organizational $50.

BETH AHABAH MUSEUM & ARCHIVES, (M), 1109 W. Franklin St., Richmond, VA 23220-3700. Tel.: 804-353-2668. Fax: 804-358-3451.
E-mail: bama@bethahabah.org
Web Site: www.bethahabah.org
Founded: 1977.
Key Personnel: Exec. Dir., David Farris; Docent & Administrative Asst., Dorothy Heffron; Admin., Bonnie Eisenman.
Personnel Profile: Part-Time Paid 3; Part-Time Volunteers 3; Interns 2.
Governing Authority: religious institution. Parent Institution: Cong. Beth Ahabah. Tax-exempt.
Jewish History Museum.
Collections: records & items concerning KK Beth Shalome, Cong. Beth Ahabah & the Richmond Jewish Community.
Research Fields: Jewish genealogy & history.
Facilities: library pertaining to Judaic genealogy & history. Museum-related items for sale.
Activities: guided tours; lectures; organized educational programs; docent program; participatory, loan & temporary exhibitions.
Publications: monthly inclusion, Temple Bulletin; News from the Archives; quarterly scholarly publication, Generations.
Hours & Admission Prices: Sun.-Thurs. 10-3; call to confirm. No charge; donations accepted. Closed Jewish & national holidays. ♿
Attendance: 1,500 (accurate)
Membership: Support $25-$79; Friend $80-$149; Donor $150-$499; Sponsor $500-$999; Patron $1,000 & up.

BLACK HISTORY MUSEUM & CULTURAL CENTER OF VIRGINIA, (M), 00 Clay St., Richmond, VA 23219. Mailing Address: P.O. Box 61052, Richmond, VA 23261. Tel.: 804-780-9093. Fax: 804-780-9107.
E-mail: information.bhm@gmail.com
Web Site: www.blackhistorymuseum.org
Founded: 1981.
Key Personnel: Dir., Dr. Maureen Elgersman Lee.
Governing Authority: bd. of trustees. Tax-exempt.
History Museum.
Collections: lives & accomplishments of Blacks in Virginia; documents; limited editions; prints; art & photographs; written records.
Major Exhibits: Take Our Stand (T), 2/10-5/10.
Facilities: Museum-related items for sale.
Hours & Admission Prices: Tues.-Sat. 10-5. Adults $5, seniors & students $4, children 12 & under $3; members no charge. Closed New Year's Eve & Day; Easter; Memorial Day; Labor Day; Thanksgiving & day after; Christmas Eve & Day.

CHILDREN'S MUSEUM OF RICHMOND, (M), 2626 W. Broad St., Richmond, VA 23220-1904. Tel.: 804-474-7000 & CMOR. Fax: 804-474-7099.
E-mail: info@c-mor.org
Web Site: www.c-mor.org
Founded: 1977.
Congressional District: 9
Key Personnel: Dir., Karen Coltrane; Chm., Brian Pitney; Treas., Paul Van De Putte; Museum Shop Mgr., Jennifer Boyle.
Personnel Profile: Full-Time Paid 15; Part-Time Paid 65; Part-Time Volunteers 145; Interns 8.
Governing Authority: nonprofit organization; board directors. Tax-exempt: 501(c)(3).
Children's Museum.
Collections: replica of Virginia limestone cave.
Facilities: celebration center; children's pavilion; performing arts area; art studio; resource center.
Activities: performances; organized education programs for children, participatory, hands-on exhibits focused on art, humanities, & special events; outreach field trips; backyard outdoor experience; birthday parties.
Publications: annual report; bimonthly email newsletter.
Hours & Admission Prices: Mon.-Sat. 9:30-5, Sun. 12-5. Adults & children $8, seniors $7; discounts to groups, AYM, VAM & AAM members and after 4pm; museum members & children under one no charge. Closed New Year's Day; Easter; Thanksgiving; Christmas. ♿
Attendance: 225,000 (accurate)
Membership: Family & Grandparent $100; Family Advantage $200; Patron $350.

EDGAR ALLAN POE MUSEUM, (M), 1914-16 E. Main St., Richmond, VA 23223-6964. Tel.: 804-648-5523. Fax: 804-648-8729.
E-mail: info@poemuseum.org
Web Site: www.poemuseum.org
Founded: 1922.
Congressional District: 3
Key Personnel: Pres. (V), Harry Poe; Treas., Edward D. Campbell, Jr.; Exec. Dir., Katarina Spears.
Personnel Profile: Part-Time Paid 4; Part-Time Volunteers 8.
Governing Authority: literary foundation. Parent Institution: Poe Foundation. Tax-exempt: 170(b)(1)(A).
Literary Museum: c.1737-1740 Old Stone House.
Collections: family ephemera; personal artifacts; Poe books & furnishings; manuscripts; memorabilia; illustrations; model of Old Richmond prior to 1849.
Research Fields: 19th-century American literature; Edgar Allan Poe; history of Richmond.
Facilities: 1,000-vol. library of Poe-related items & manuscripts available for research on premises by appointment. Gift items for sale.
Activities: guided tours; lectures; readings; performances; school programs. Museum Sponsors: Poe's Birthday Party in January.
Publications: magazine, The Poe Messenger; newsletter, Evermore; book, The Incredible Mr. Poe: Comic Book Adaptations of the Works of E.A. Poe, 1943-2007.
Hours & Admission Prices: Tues.-Sat. 10-5, Sun. 11-5; tours on the hour. Adults $6, senior citizens 60 & over and students 8 & over $5; discounts to AAA members; AAM members, children under 8 & members no charge. Group tours available, call 804-648-5523. Closed New Year's Day; Christmas Day.
Attendance: 17,000 (estimated)
Membership: Student & Teacher $15; Individual $25; Family $35; Contributing $100; Benefactor $250.

ELEGBA FOLKLORE SOCIETY'S CULTURAL CENTER, 101 E. Broad St., Richmond, VA 23219-1733. Tel.: 804-644-3900. Fax: 804-644-3919.
E-mail: story1@efsinc.org
Web Site: www.efsinc.org
Founded: 1990.
Key Personnel: Found Pres. & Artistic Dir., Janine Beil.
Governing Authority: nonprofit organization. Tax-exempt.
Art Museum.
Collections: paintings; sculpture; drawings; dolls; multicultural crafts.
Hours & Admission Prices: Mon.-Fri. 10-6, Sat. 12-4; other times by appointment. No charge; donations accepted.

FOLK ART SOCIETY OF AMERICA, (M), 1904 Byrd Ave., #312, Richmond, VA 23230-3029. Mailing Address: P.O. Box 17041, Richmond, VA 23226-7041. Tel.: 804-285-4532.
E-mail: fasa@folkart.org
Web Site: www.folkart.org
Founded: 1987.
Key Personnel: Pres. (V), Ann Oppenhimer; Financial Dir., William Oppenhimer; Administrative Asst., Rosemary Seltzer.
Personnel Profile: Full-Time Volunteers 1; Part-Time Paid 1; Part-Time Volunteers 6.
Governing Authority: private; nonprofit. Tax-exempt: 501(c)(3).
Folk Art Museum.
Collections: field of folk, outsider & self-taught art; slide library; videos; photographs; archival materials.
Research Fields: folk & self-taught art with emphasis on late 20th-century contemporary American.
Facilities: library.
Activities: lectures. Annual Event: symposium conference.
Publications: three times annual journal, Folk Art Messenger.
Hours & Admission Prices: Sept.-July open by appointment only. No charge. ♿
Attendance: 300 (estimated)
Membership: Individual $35; Family $50; Foreign & Patron $60; Contributor $100; Bronze Star $250; Silver Star $500; Gold Star $1,000.

GRAND LODGE AF&AM LIBRARY, MUSEUM AND HISTORICAL FOUNDATION - ALLEN E. ROBERTS MASONIC LIBRARY AND MUSEUM, 4115 Nine Mile Rd., Richmond, VA 23223-4926. Tel.: 804-222-3110.
E-mail: library@grandlodgeofvirginia.org
Web Site: www.grandlodgeofvirginia.org/library1.htm
Founded: 1778.

Personnel Profile: Part-Time Paid 1; Part-Time Volunteers 2.
Governing Authority: Parent Institution: Grand Lodge AF&AM of Virginia. Tax-exempt: 501(c)(3).
Fraternal Museum & Freemasonry.
Collections: Virginia Masonic history; portraits; Grand Lodge commemorative & local Lodge artifacts; furniture; textiles; glassware; tokens; jewelry.
Research Fields: history of freemasonry in Virginia.
Facilities: library.
Publications: The Virginia Masonic Herald.
Hours & Admission Prices: Mon., Wed. & Fri. 9-12:30 & 1:30-4. No charge; donations accepted. Closed Presidents' Day; Easter Mon.; Memorial Day; Labor Day; Thanksgiving; Christmas.
Attendance: 300

HENRICO COUNTY HISTORIC PRESERVATION & MUSEUM SERVICES, 8600 Dixon Powers Dr., Richmond, VA 23228-2735. Mailing Address: P.O. Box 27032, Richmond, VA 23273. Tel.: 804-501-5736 & 7275. Fax: 804-501-5284.
E-mail: gre26@co.henrico.va.us
Web Site: www.co.henrico.va.us/rec
Founded: 1977.
Congressional District: 7
Key Personnel: History Supvr., Christopher M. Gregson; Cur., Kimberly Sicola; Asst. Cur., Alyson Rhodes-Murphy; Site Mgr., Anna Truong; Asst. Site Mgr., Linda Eikmeier.
Personnel Profile: Full-Time Paid 6; Part-Time Paid 3; Part-Time Volunteers 50; Interns 4.
Governing Authority: county. Parent Institution: Henrico County. Tax-exempt.
History Museum: housed in c.1810 Meadow Farm, depicting mid-19th century rural life in southeastern Virginia.
Collections: c.1772-1960 furniture, textiles, decorative arts, kitchen equipment, porcelain, glassware, flat & hollow silverware; costumes; paintings; prints; photographs; military paraphernalia, including camping equipment, insignias, arms & cavalry equipment; agricultural tools & equipment; medical tools, books & manuscripts; family papers; archival material; contemporary folk art; local school photographs; school books, desks & supplies from 19th & early 20th century. Historic Buildings: Deep Run School, 1902 two room schoolhouse; Spring Park, 1890 Springhouse; Walkerton, 1820s Inn; c.1925 Courtney Road service station.
Research Fields: agriculture; material culture & socio-economics of southeastern Virginia in the 19th century; local history of people, places & events; local architectural history; 19th-20th century folk art.
Facilities: 1,000-vol. library of 19th-century books on medicine, history, health, housekeeping, schoolbooks & fiction available for scholarly research on premises; orientation center. Gift items for sale.
Activities: education programs for children, adults, undergraduate & graduate college students; docent program; loan, permanent & traveling exhibitions; military reenactments; special holiday events.
Publications: guidebook, Manuscript Collection of the Sheppard Family of Meadow Farm; calendar of events; semiannual newsletter; exhibit flyers; brochures; event posters.
Hours & Admission Prices: March to mid-Dec. Tues.-Sun. 12-4. No charge. ♿
Attendance: 60,000 (estimated)

THE JOHN MARSHALL HOUSE, 818 E. Marshall St., Richmond, VA 23219-1917. Tel.: 804-648-7998. Fax: 804-648-5880.
E-mail: johnmarshallhouse@preservationvirginia.org
Web Site: www.preservationvirginia
Founded: 1911.
Congressional District: 3
Key Personnel: Exec. Dir. APVA, Elizabeth Kostelny; Cur., Catherine Dean; Coord. Education, Jennifer Hurst; Museum Shop Buyer, Kerry Mann.
Personnel Profile: Part-Time Paid 12; Interns 1.
Governing Authority: nonprofit society. Parent Institution: Preservation Virginia, 204 W. Franklin St., Richmond, VA 23220. Tax-exempt.
Historic Site & Historic House: 1790 home of U.S. Chief Justice John Marshall & only surviving 18th-century brick Federal house in Richmond.
Collections: furnishings associated with the Chief Justice; 18th to early 19th-century glass; textiles; porcelain; paintings; silver; musical instruments; writing implements; Chief Justice John Marshall's judicial robe.
Research Fields: John Marshall & 18th-century politics & architecture; Richmond city history, the law, social life in the 18th & early 19th century.
Facilities: Museum-related items for sale.
Activities: guided tours; special events.
Publications: newsletter, Preservation Virginia.
Hours & Admission Prices: Visit website for hours.
Attendance: 4,000 (accurate)
Membership: Student & Teacher $25; Individual $40; Individual Plus One & Group $50; Family $60; Century $100; Sponsor $250; Benefactor $500.

LEWIS GINTER BOTANICAL GARDEN, 1800 Lakeside Ave., Richmond, VA 23228-4700. Tel.: 804-262-9887. Fax: 804-262-9934.
E-mail: frankr@lewisginter.org
Web Site: www.lewisginter.org
Founded: 1984.
Congressional District: 3
Key Personnel: Exec. Dir., Frank L. Robinson; Chm. (V), Kitten Clarke; Pres. (V), William H. King, Jr.; Asst. Dir., Shane Tippet; Business Mgr., Freda M. Lushbaugh; Mgr. Horticulture, Neil Beasley; Dir. Devel., Jennifer Little; Mgr. Education, Randee Humphrey; Mgr. Public Rels., Beth Monroe; Gift Shop Mgr., Martha Anne Ellis.
Personnel Profile: Full-Time Paid 45; Full-Time Volunteers 130; Part-Time Paid 45; Part-Time Volunteers 220; Interns 3.
Governing Authority: nonprofit organization. Tax-exempt: 501(c)(3).
Botanical Garden & Historic House: c.1888.
Collections: Lora & Claiborne Robins Tea House; Henry M. Flagler perennial garden; Grace Arents garden; Martha & Reed West Island garden; Lucy Payne Minor Memorial Garden; The Asian Valley; Cottage Garden; Children's garden; seasonal annuals; aquatic plants; rhododendron & azalea collections; Conservatory: exotic & unusual plants from around the world.
Research Fields: introduction of new & superior plants to zones 7 & 8.
Facilities: 3,500-vol. library on horticulture & gardening, available for use by the public; classroom; herbarium; 80 acres of grounds; Henry M. Flagler Perennial Garden, 3 acres; Lucy Payne Minor Memorial Garden; Children's Garden; Lora & Clairborne Robins Tea House; Grace Arents Garden; visitor center. Education & Library Complex: education center; classroom; laboratory; conference center; auditorium; meeting areas. Books & items related to the garden & gardening for sale.
Activities: guided tours; lectures; concerts; arts festivals; rental gallery; organized educational programs. Garden Sponsors: plant sales; major symposia; Daffodil Show; Charles F. Gillette Forum on landscape design & history; Mother's Day Concert; Gardenfest of Lights, a holiday illumination.
Publications: Garden Times; annual report.
Hours & Admission Prices: June Tues. 9-9, Wed.-Mon. 9-5; July-Aug. Tues. & Thurs. 9-9, Wed.-Mon. 9-5; Sept. Thurs. 9-9, Fri.-Wed. 9-5; Oct.-May daily 9-5. Adults $10, seniors $9, children 3-12 $6; children under 3 & members no charge. Closed New Year's Day; Thanksgiving; Christmas Eve & Day. ♿
Attendance: 175,000 (accurate)
Membership: Teacher & Student $35; Senior Citizen $40; Individual $50; Dual $60; Family $70; Contributing $125; Supporting $250; Sponsoring $500.

THE LIBRARY OF VIRGINIA, (M), 800 E. Broad St., Richmond, VA 23219-8000. Tel.: 804-692-3535. Fax: 804-692-3556. TTY: 804-692-3976.
Web Site: www.lva.virginia.gov
Founded: 1823.
Congressional District: 3
Key Personnel: State Librarian, Sandra G. Treadway; Financial Dir., Ann Harris; Public Rels., Janice M. Hathcock; Archivist, Conley L. Edwards, III; Library Devel. & Networking, Elizabeth Lewis; Education & Outreach Svcs., Gregg Kimball; Research & Information Svcs., Suzy Szasz Palmer; Collection Management Svcs., John D. Metz.
Personnel Profile: Full-Time Paid 173; Part-Time Paid 42; Part-Time Volunteers 21.
Governing Authority: state government agency. Tax-exempt.
State Library & Archives.
Collections: books; maps; personal papers; Virginiana; genealogy records; newspapers; local & state government records; deeds; governors' papers; photographs; Virginia portraiture; prints; broadsides; paintings; music sheets.
Major Exhibits: The Land We Live In, The Land We Left: Virginia's People, 1/10-8/10; Succession or Union, 9/10-7/11.
Research Fields: Virginia history; colonial records; genealogy.
Facilities: library; archives; 100 sq. ft. exhibit space.
Activities: guided tours; lectures; participatory exhibits.
Publications: quarterly, Broadside; LVA e-newsletter.
Hours & Admission Prices: Mon.-Sat. 9-5. No charge; donations accepted. Closed most state holidays. ♿
Attendance: 159,382 (estimated)

MAGGIE L. WALKER NATIONAL HISTORIC SITE, 600 N. 2nd St., Richmond, VA 23219. Mailing Address: 3215 E. Broad St., Richmond, VA 23223-7517. Tel.: 804-771-2017. Fax: 804-771-2226.
E-mail: cynthia_macleod@nps.gov
Web Site: www.nps.gov/malw/
Founded: 1978.
Congressional District: 3
Key Personnel: Supt., David R. Ruth; Chief Interpreter, Mike Andrus; Cur.,

Klydie Thomas; Supvr. Park Rangers, Eola Dance; Park Guide, Janet Blanchard; Park Guide, John Donoghue.
Personnel Profile: Full-Time Paid 5; Part-Time Paid 1; Part-Time Volunteers 10.
Governing Authority: federal. Parent Institution: National Park Service. Tax-exempt.
Historic House: Victorian-Italianate home of Maggie Lena Walker, first woman founder & president of an African American bank, newspaper editor & African-American community leader; African-American & women's history.
Collections: period furniture, clothing; personal items of Maggie Lena Walker; family photos; furnishings & memorabilia.
Research Fields: Maggie L. Walker.
Facilities: 50-vol. library pertaining to Black history for use on premises only.
Activities: guided tours.
Publications: brochure; curriculum guide for classroom study.
Hours & Admission Prices: March-Oct. Mon.-Sat. 9-5; Nov.-Feb. Mon.-Sat. 9-4:30. No charge; donations accepted. Closed New Year's Day; Thanksgiving; Christmas. ♿
Attendance: 12,000 (accurate)

MAYMONT, 1700 Hampton St., Richmond, VA 23220-6899. Tel.: 804-358-7166, ext. 310. Fax: 804-358-9994.
E-mail: info@maymont.org
Web Site: www.maymont.org
Founded: 1925.
Congressional District: 3
Key Personnel: Exec. Dir., Norman O. Burns, II; Assoc. Exec. Dir., C. Fred Murray; Pres. (V), Amy McDaniel Williams; Dir. Historical Collections & Programs, Dale C. Wheary; Dir. Nature Center, Henry Bireline; Mgr. Zoology, Debbie Rea; Carriage Collections Mgr., Armistead Wellford; Mgr. Historical Programs, Carol Harris; Special Program Coord., Nancy Lowden; Rental Coord., Rebekah Davis; Dir. Finance, Ron Thompson; Administrative Dir., Ann Voss; Mgr. Environmental Education, Kate Jarrell; Dir. Devel., Carol Akin; Dir. Public Rels. & Mktg., Cathie Rosenberg; Asst. Dir. Public Rels., Carla Murray; Mgr. Historical Collections, Kathy Garrett Cox; Mgr. Horticulture, Peggy M. Singlemann; Dir. Special Events, Kim Pauley.
Personnel Profile: Full-Time Paid 54; Part-Time Paid 35; Part-Time Volunteers 470; Interns 4.
Governing Authority: nonprofit organization. Property & facilities owned by City of Richmond. Tax-exempt: 501(c)(3).
Historic House & Gardens: housed in c.1890s estate of James H. Dooley.
Collections: turn-of-the-century furniture & decorative arts; 19th-century carriages; 150 species of native Virginia live animals; 200 species of trees & shrubs.
Major Exhibits: From Morning to Night: Domestic Service in the Gilded Age South (T), 11/09-12/11.
Research Fields: late Victorian & gilded age history; decorative arts & architecture landscape history & preservation.
Facilities: 26,000 sq. ft. Nature & Visitor Center; Japanese garden; Italian garden; zoological park; children's farm; historic house; arboretum; aquarium. Museum-related items for sale.
Activities: guided tours; lectures; films; concerts; workshops; formal historical & environmental educational programs for children; carriage rides; docent program; permanent exhibitions; annual special events.
Publications: photographic essay, Maymont; quarterly newsletter; events programs; guide to school programs.
Hours & Admission Prices: Maymont House: Tues.-Sun. 12-5. Suggested Donation: $5. Robins Nature Center & Grounds: daily 10-5. Exhibits: Tues.-Sun. 12-5. Suggested Donation $4. Children's Farm Barn: Tues.-Sun. 12-5. Tram: Tues.-Sun. 12-5. Adults $3, children $2; members no charge. Carriage Rides: Sun. 12-4. Closed New Year's Day; Thanksgiving; Christmas. ♿
Attendance: 500,000 (estimated)
Membership: Senior & Student $35; Individual $45; Family Senior $50; Family $60.

THE MUSEUM OF THE CONFEDERACY, (M), 1201 E. Clay St., Richmond, VA 23219-1615. Tel.: 804-649-1861. Fax: 804-644-7150.
Web Site: www.moc.org
Founded: 1896.
Congressional District: 3
Key Personnel: Pres. & C.E.O., S. Waite Rawls, III; Chm. (V), Carleton Moffatt; Vice Pres. Advancement, Otis C. Crowther, Jr.; Cur., Robert Hancock; Cur. & Registrar, Melinda Gales; Dir. Museum Operations, Eric D. App; Historian, Dr. John M. Coski; Dir. Mktg. & Public Rels., Vickie Yates; Membership & Annual Giving, Diane Willard; Museum Shop Mgr., Tim Edgell.
Personnel Profile: Full-Time Paid 21; Part-Time Paid 23; Part-Time Volunteers 10.
Governing Authority: nonprofit organization. Parent Institution: Confederate Memorial Literary Society. Branch Museum: 1817-18 White House of the Confederacy. Tax-exempt: 501(c)(3).
History Museum: historic site.
Collections: artifacts & documents pertaining to the Confederate States of America; southern history; the Confederate & Civil War years; the White House of the Confederacy; decorative arts; prints; photographs; Confederate militaria: flags, uniforms, weapons; Jefferson Davis Collection; Confederate bonds & currency; imprints.
Research Fields: Civil War; Confederate States of America; southern history.
Facilities: Brockenbrough Library. Gifts & books for sale.
Activities: tours; school tours; bus tours; permanent, temporary & traveling exhibitions; education program; lecture & film series; book awards; living history programs; outreach programs.
Publications: The Museum of the Confederacy Journal; occasional catalogues; checklists; books; magazine, The Museum of the Confederacy.
Hours & Admission Prices: Museum: Mon.-Sat. 10-5, Sun. 12-5. White House: March-Dec. Mon.-Sat. 10-5, Sun. 12-5. Combination Ticket $11. White House or Museum $8; discounts for seniors, & AAA members; AAM members & members no charge. Closed New Year's Day; Thanksgiving; Christmas. ♿
Attendance: 48,000 (estimated)
Membership: Senior Citizen & Outside Richmond Region Individual $30; Senior Citizen Couple $35; Outside Richmond Region Family $40; Richmond Metro Individual $50; Richmond Metro Family $60; Sustaining $100; Patron $500; 1896 Society $1,896.

OLD DOMINION RAILWAY MUSEUM, 102 Hull St., Richmond, VA 23224-4240. Mailing Address: P.O. Box 8583, Richmond, VA 23226-0583. Tel.: 804-233-6237.
Web Site: www.odcnrhs.org
Founded: 1990.
Congressional District: 3
Key Personnel: C.E.O., Pres. (V) & Registrar, Bill Todd; Chm. (V), Bob Dickinson; Chm. (V), Robert Stevens; Archivist, Calvin Boles; Devel., Giles F. Scott, Jr.
Personnel Profile: Full-Time Volunteers 40; Part-Time Volunteers 45.
Governing Authority: private; nonprofit organization. Parent Institution: Old Dominion Chapter, NRHS, P.O. Box 8583, Richmond, VA 23226. Tax-exempt: 501(c)(3).
Railroad History Museum: housed at site of 1915-1957 Southern Railway depot.
Collections: railroading history in Central Virginia; steam, caboose, passenger & freight equipment; locomotives & rolling stock from first half of 20th century; railroad company archives, especially the Seaboard Air Line, Richmond Fredericksburg & Potomac, and Richmond electric streetcar lines; photographs.
Research Fields: Hull Street Station (Richmond, VA) & environs.
Facilities: 500-vol. library including railroad company account books, law books, journals & manuals; 250 sq. ft. exhibit space. Museum-related items for sale.
Activities: formal education programs for children; guided tours; lectures; loan & temporary exhibitions; railroad excursions. Annual Events: Children's Day; annual picnic.
Publications: monthly newsletter, Highball.
Hours & Admission Prices: Sat. 11-4, Sun. 1-4. No charge; donations accepted. Closed Christmas Eve & Day.
Attendance: 2,000 (accurate)
Membership: Adult $36; Family $41.

RICHMOND NATIONAL BATTLEFIELD PARK, Chimborazo Medical Museum, 3215 E. Broad St., Richmond, VA 23223-7517. Tel.: 804-226-1981, ext. 3. Fax: 804-771-8522.
Web Site: www.nps.gov/rich
Founded: 1936.
Congressional District: 7
Key Personnel: Supt., Dave Ruth; Chief Interpretation, Mike Andrus; Chief Ranger, Timothy Mauch; Cur., Klydie Thomas.
Governing Authority: federal. Parent Institution: National Park Service, Dept. of Interior, Washington, DC 20240. Visitor Centers: Civil War Visitor Center at Tredegar Iron Works, 470 Tredegar St., Richmond, VA; Cold Harbor Battlefield Visitor Center: 5515 Anderson-Wright Dr.; Fort Harrison Visitor Center, 8621 Battlefield Park Rd., Richmond, VA; Glendale/Malvern Hill Battlefield Visitor Center, 8301 Willis Church Rd. Tax-exempt: 170(b)(1)(A).
Civil War Military Museum.
Collections: military artifacts; Civil War history; medical equipment & hospital life. Historic Houses & Sites: 1835 Watt House, Gaines' Mill

battlefield; 1800 Garthright House, Cold Harbor & Malvern Hill battlefields; 1720s Shelton House, Totopotomy Creek Battlefield.
Research Fields: African-American Civil War history; Civil War medicine; Richmond history; historic preservation.
Facilities: 600-vol. library of Civil War books available for use by special permission from the superintendent. Civil War manuscript material relative to Richmond; publications, postcards, slides, prints for sale.
Activities: self-guided tours & trails; lectures; films; formally organized education programs for children; living history programs.
Publications: pamphlets; folders & handbooks about the battles for Richmond.
Hours & Admission Prices: Tredgar Iron Works, Cold Harbor Visitor Center, & Chimborazo Medical Museum: daily 9-5. Glendale/Malvern Hill Visitor Center & Fort Harrison Visitor Center: seasonal. No charge; donations accepted. Closed New Year's Day; Thanksgiving; Christmas. ♿
Attendance: 245,504

ST. JOHN'S EPISCOPAL CHURCH, 2401 E. Broad St., Richmond, VA 23223-7128. Tel.: 804-648-5015. Fax: 804-649-0878.
E-mail: kpeninger@saintjohns.cc
Web Site: www.historicstjohnschurch.org
Founded: 1920.
Congressional District: 3
Key Personnel: Exec. Dir., Kay Peninger; Pres., Neill Goff; Treas., Everett Melton; Museum Shop Mgr., Trudy Russell.
Personnel Profile: Full-Time Paid 1; Part-Time Paid 21.
Governing Authority: church; nonprofit organization. Tax-exempt: 170(b)(1)(A).
Historic Building & Site: 1741 church, location of the 2nd Virginia Convention where Patrick Henry addressed the Convention-1775 with his famous, Give me liberty or give me death speech; first cemetery in Richmond.
Collections: items pertaining to the church's 250 year history, including three-decker pulpit, rector's reading desk, mid-18th century chandeliers, Lotto rug, early 18th-century marble font, 1730-1773 manuscript of colonial vestry-book, 1700 Prayer-Book, a gift from King George VI.
Research Fields: church history.
Facilities: Items pertaining to the Revolution, Patrick Henry & Richmond history for sale.
Activities: guided tours. Museum Sponsors: reenactment of the 2nd Virginia Convention from May to September.
Hours & Admission Prices: Mon.-Sat. 10-3:30, Sun. 1-3:30. Adults $6, senior citizens 62 & over $5, students $4; discounts to groups of 10 or more; children under 7 no charge. Closed New Year's Eve & Day; Easter; Thanksgiving; Christmas Eve & Day. ♿
Attendance: 40,000 (accurate)

* **SCIENCE MUSEUM OF VIRGINIA,** 2500 W. Broad St., Richmond, VA 23220-2057. Tel.: 804-864-1400; 800-659-1727. Fax: 804-864-1560.
E-mail: smvfeedback@smv.org
Web Site: www.smv.org
Founded: 1970.
Congressional District: 3
Key Personnel: Chm., James H. Starkey; Pres. FDN Directors, John C. Ivins, Jr., Esq.; Dir. & C.E.O., Richard C. Conti; Dir. Science, Education, Eugene Maurakis, Ph.D.; Museum Shop Mgr., Jennifer Morehead.
Personnel Profile: Full-Time Paid 66; Part-Time Paid 55; Part-Time Volunteers 1,100; Interns 10.
Governing Authority: state. Parent Institution: Commonwealth of Virginia. Subsidiary Institutions: Danville Science Center; Virginia Aviation Museum; SciencePort. Tax-exempt.
Science Museum.
Collections: rocks & minerals; astronomy; computers; aircraft; aviation; physics; chemistry; technology; zoology; submarine; life sciences.
Major Exhibits: Maps: Tools for Adventure (T), 1/10-9/10.
Research Fields: science education in a museum environment; exhibit development through formative evaluation; environmental studies.
Facilities: large format films & planetarium shows in 250-seat Ethyl IMAX(R) DOME Theater; computer lab; stepped theater; 120-seat lecture hall; classrooms; railroad cars; birthday caboose; submarine; outdoor park; amphitheaters. Museum-related items for sale.
Activities: hands-on science exhibits; outreach van programs; education programs for Pre-K through high school levels; distance learning & university science courses & collaborations; science lectures & seminars; science events; exhibit hall demonstrations; live theatrical performances.
Publications: annual report; quarterly newsletter for members; group visit planning guide; program brochures; educator newsletters.
Hours & Admission Prices: Memorial Day to Sept. Mon.-Thurs. 9:30-5, Fri.-Sat. 9:30-7, Sun 11:30-5; Winter: Mon.-Sat. 9:30-5, Sun. 11:30-5. Exhibits only: adults 13-59 $10, senior citizens 60 & over and youth 4-12 $9.50; members no charge. IMAX(R)DOME Film only: admission $8.50. Exhibit & Film: adults 13-59 $15, senior citizens 60 & over and youth 4-12 $14, members $7.50; discounts to AAA & ASTC members; children 3 & under no charge. ♿
Attendance: 396,905 (accurate)
Membership: Franklin $50; Curie $60; Edison $95; Mendel $115.

1708 GALLERY, 319 W. Broad St., Richmond, VA 23220-4218. Mailing Address: P.O. Box 12520, Richmond, VA 23241-0520. Tel.: 804-643-1708. Fax: 804-643-7839.
E-mail: info@1708gallery.org
Web Site: 1708gallery.com
Key Personnel: Exec. Dir., Tatjana Beylotte; Museum Shop Mgr., Jolene Giandomenico
Art Gallery.
Collections: works by local & regional artists.
Hours & Admission Prices: Tues.-Fri. 11-5, Sat. 1-5; other times by appointment.

UNIVERSITY OF RICHMOND MUSEUMS, (M), Richmond, VA 23173-. Tel.: 804-289-8276. Fax: 804-287-1894.
E-mail: museums@richmond.edu
Web Site: museums.richmond.edu
Formerly: Marsh Art Gallery, University of Richmond
Founded: 1830.
Congressional District: 3
Key Personnel: Exec. Dir., Richard Waller; Deputy Dir. & Cur. Exhibitions, Elizabeth Schlatter; Museum Preparator, Stephen Duggins; Museum Preparator, Henley Guild; Cur. Museum Programs, Heather Campbell; Cur. Museum Collections, Matthew Houle; Administrative Specialist, Joan Maitre; Asst. Collections Mgr., David Hershey.
Personnel Profile: Full-Time Paid 8; Part-Time Paid 18; Part-Time Volunteers 4; Interns 2.
Governing Authority: nonprofit. Parent Institution: University of Richmond. Branch Museums: Joel & Lila Harnett Museum of Art, 1968; Joel & Lila Harnett Print Study Center, 2001; Lora Robins Gallery of Design from Nature, 1977. Tax-exempt: 501(c)(3).
University Museums.
Collections: Joel & Lila Harnett Museum of Art: all media fine arts; Joel & Lila Harnett Print Study Center: Renaissance prints to present; I. Webb Surratt, Jr. print collection; Lora Robins Gallery of Design from Nature: minerals; gems; shells; fossils; ancient Greek & Roman through Byzantine gold, silver & bronze coins; Carver collection of Chinese ceramics; cultural artifacts; decorative arts.
Major Exhibits: John Cage: Zen Ox-Herding Pictures (T), 11/09-4/10; Traces of Time: Fossils from the Collection, 11/09-6/10; Slightly Unbalanced (T), 1/10-3/10; Rincon Falls, Trinidad: A Print Series by Chris Ofili, 1/10-6/10; Going to the Dogs: Victorian Staffordshire Pottery from the Collection, 2/10-9/10; Surface Tension: Pottery, Texture and Rhythm in Art from the Collection, 3/10-5/10; Woman vs Image: Museum Studies Seminar Exhibition, 4/10-6/10; Visions from the Other Side: Paintings and Drawings by Nikolas Rerikh, 8/10-10/10; 2010 Harnett Biennial of American Prints, 10/10-12/10.
Research Fields: modern & contemporary art; historical fine arts; printmaking; photography; decorative arts; Asian art; geology; minerology; earth & natural sciences.
Facilities: sculpture courtyard; print study center; publications for sale.
Activities: guided tours; lectures; traveling & temporary exhibits; films; gallery talks; videos; workshops; symposia; concerts; formal education programs for undergraduate & graduate students; internships.
Publications: exhibition catalogues; brochures; posters.
Hours & Admission Prices: Joel and Lila Harnett Museum of Art: mid-Aug. to April Tues.-Sun. 1-5; May-June Wed.-Fri. 1-4. Lora Robins Gallery of Design from Nature: Tues.-Fri. 11-5, Sat.-Sun. 1-5. Joel & Lila Harnett Print Study Center: mid-Sept. to midf-April Wed.-Sat. 1-5 & by appointment. No charge. Closed spring break; fall break; Thanksgiving week; Easter weekend; semester breaks. ♿
Attendance: 8,956 (accurate)

* **VALENTINE RICHMOND HISTORY CENTER,** 1015 E. Clay St., Richmond, VA 23219-1527. Tel.: 804-649-0711. Fax: 804-643-3510.
E-mail: info@richmondhistorycenter.com
Web Site: www.richmondhistorycenter.com
Formerly: Valentine Museum/Richmond History Center
Founded: 1892.
Congressional District: 3
Key Personnel: Chm., James W. Klaus; Vice Chm., Pamela J. Royal, M.D.; Dir., William J. Martin; Dir. Finance, Thomas Yeatman; Dir. Educ., Pat Armbrust; Dir. Public Rels., Lesley Bruno; Dir. Operations, Ken Myers; Dir. Devel., Liz Musselman; Dir. Collections & Interpretation, Suzanne

Savery; Dir. Archives, Meghan Glass Hughes; Registrar, Jackie Mullins; Dir. Tours, Linda Krinsky; Museum Shop Mgr., Jane Seaman.
Personnel Profile: Full-Time Paid 17; Part-Time Paid 30; Part-Time Volunteers 75; Interns 10.
Governing Authority: private; nonprofit organization. Tax-exempt: 501(c)(3).
Urban History Museum.
Collections: neo-classical wall paintings; sculpture studio of E.V. Valentine; costumes, 1600-present; flat textiles; laces; quilts; coverlets; embroideries; decorative arts relating to Richmond history; portraits; landscapes; tools and industrial artifacts; items relating to minority history; 19th-century toys; photographs; manuscripts; prints on Richmond & Virginia history. Historic Building: Wickam house (1812).
Major Exhibits: Waste Not Want Not: Richmond During the 1920s & 1930s, 11/09-9/10.
Research Fields: American urban history; American social history; historic preservation; costumes; decorative arts; photographs.
Facilities: research library of books, pamphlets, manuscripts & photographs on Richmond available by appointment; reading room; conference & reception areas; kitchen; 19th-century formal garden; cafe. Books & museum-related items for sale.
Activities: self-guided tours of museum; guided tours of historic house; lectures; formally organized educational programs; inter-museum loan; temporary & traveling exhibitions; museum intern program; minority intern program; guided walking & bus tours; special events.
Publications: quarterly newsletter; exhibition catalogs; monographs.
Hours & Admission Prices: Tues.-Sat. 10-5, Sun. 12-5. Adults $8, senior citizens 55 & over, students, children 4-18 and groups of 10 or more $7; children under 4 & members no charge. Court End Passport $10. Closed New Year's Day; Thanksgiving; Christmas Eve & Day. ♿
Attendance: 39,112 (accurate)
Membership: Senior, Teacher & Student $25; Young Professional $30; Individual $45; Dual & Family $60; Participating $150; Sustainer $250; Sponsor $500; Associate $1,000; Trustees' Council $2,500; Founder's Circle $5,000.

VIRGINIA ASSOCIATION OF MUSEUMS, (M), 200 South Third St., Richmond, VA 23219-3700. Tel.: 804-788-5821. Fax: 804-788-5826.
E-mail: mcarlock@vamuseums.org
Web Site: vamuseums.org
Founded: 1968.
Congressional District: 3
Key Personnel: Dir., Margo Carlock; Pres. (V), John Verrill.
Personnel Profile: Full-Time Paid 3; Part-Time Paid 2; Part-Time Volunteers 2.
Governing Authority: private; nonprofit association. Tax-exempt.
State Association: service organization to museum professionals throughout Virginia.
Facilities: reference library for members & job board.
Activities: training programs for professional museum workers. Annual Events: VAM Annual Conference (workshops, keynote addresses, concurrent sessions, exhibit hall; workshop series.
Publications: VAM Quarterly Newsletter; Directory of Virginia Museums; VAM membership directory; VAM admissions guide.
Hours & Admission Prices: Mon.-Fri. 9-5. ♿
Membership: Student & Faculty $20; Staff (of member institution) $25; Individual $40; Business Affiliate $50; Business Individual $100; Patron & Business Member $150; Business Sponsor $500; Business Patron $1,000; Corporate Sponsor $2,000.

VIRGINIA BAPTIST HISTORICAL SOCIETY, Boatwright Library, University of Richmond, Richmond, VA 23173-0001. Mailing Address: P.O. Box 34, University of Richmond, Richmond, VA 23173-0001. Tel.: 804-289-8434. Fax: 804-289-8953.
Web Site: www.baptistheritage.org
Founded: 1876.
Congressional District: 3
Key Personnel: C.E.O., Fred Anderson; Pres. (V), Dennis E. Sacrey.
Personnel Profile: Full-Time Paid 2; Part-Time Paid 2; Part-Time Volunteers 8.
Governing Authority: society. Tax-exempt: 501(c)(3).
Historical Society Museum.
Collections: Virginia Baptist history; University of Richmond archives.
Research Fields: Virginia Baptist history; University of Richmond archives.
Facilities: 20,000-vol. library pertaining to Virginia Baptist history available to the public.
Activities: guided tours; lectures; organized education programs for adults, children, undergraduate & graduate college students; temporary & traveling exhibitions.
Publications: annual journal, Virginia Baptist Register.
Hours & Admission Prices: Mon.-Fri. 9-12 & 1-4:30. No charge; donations accepted. Closed legal holidays.
Attendance: 5,000 (estimated)
Membership: Individual $25; Family $35; Institute $50.

VIRGINIA CENTER FOR ARCHITECTURE, (M), 2501 Monument Ave., Richmond, VA 23220-2618. Tel.: 804-644-3041. Fax: 804-643-4607.
Web Site: www.virginiaarchitecture.org
Key Personnel: C.E.O., Ginger Bower; Dir. Programs, Margaret Yarbrough
Architecture Museum.
Collections: architecture history & design.
Hours & Admission Prices: Tues.-Fri. 10-5, Sat.-Sun. 1-5; groups by appointment. Suggested Donation: $5. ♿

VIRGINIA DEPARTMENT OF CONSERVATION AND RECREATION, 203 Governors' St., Richmond, VA 23219-2049. Tel.: 804-786-1712. Fax: 804-786-9294. TDD: 804-786-2121.
E-mail: pco@dcr.virginia.gov
Web Site: dcr.virginia.gov
Founded: 1926.
Key Personnel: Parks Dir., Joe Elton; Operations Dir., Nancy Healthman.
Governing Authority: state. Tax-exempt.
State Parks & Historic Sites.
Collections: botany; entomology; geology; herbarium; herpetology. Historic Sites: 1700s Chippokes Plantation, Surry County; 1800s Sailor's Creek Battlefield Park & House, Amelia & Prince Edward Counties; 1800s Shot Tower, Wythe County; 1700s George Washington's Grist Mill, Alexandria; 1800s Southwest Virginia Museum, Big Stone Gap.
Research Fields: botany; entomology; geology; herbarium; herpetology.
Facilities: 150-vol. library of natural history books; visitor & nature center interpretive displays.
Activities: guided tours; lectures; films; interpretive & environmental education activities.
Publications: brochure; annual bulletin.
Hours & Admission Prices: Call for hours & admission fees, information differs for separate locations. ♿

VIRGINIA DEPARTMENT OF HISTORIC RESOURCES, 2801 Kensington Ave., Richmond, VA 23221-2470. Tel.: 804-367-2323. Fax: 804-367-2391. TDD: 804-367-2386.
E-mail: dee.deroche@dhr.virginia.gov
Web Site: www.dhr.state.va.us
Founded: 1966.
Congressional District: 7
Key Personnel: Dir., Kathleen Kilpatrick; Deputy Dir. Policy & Planning, Catherine Slusser; Deputy Dir. Community Svcs. Div., Robert A. Carter; State Archaeologist, Michael B. Barber; Chief Cur., Dee DeRoche; Conservator, Caitlin O'Grady.
Personnel Profile: Full-Time Paid 46; Part-Time Paid 2; Interns 5.
Governing Authority: state. Parent Institution: Commonwealth of Virginia, Secretariat of Natural Resources. Regional Preservation Offices: Capital Region, 2801 Kensington Ave., Richmond, VA 23221; Roanoke Region, 1030 Penmar Ave., S.E., Roanoke, VA 24013; Tidewater Region, 14415 Old Courthouse Way, 2nd Fl., Newport News, VA 23608; Northern Region, 5357 Main St., P.O. Box 519, Stephens City, VA 22655. Tax-exempt.
Preservation Agency.
Collections: archaeology; architecture; history.
Research Fields: history & architecture of Virginia; archaeology.
Facilities: 5,377-vol. library of books & publications pertaining to Virginia history, architecture & archaeology available upon written application; field research station; curation center for archaeology collections.
Activities: workshops providing technical assistance; preservation planning conferences.
Publications: annual journal, Notes on Virginia; books, Virginia Landmarks Register; Preserving a Legacy; brochures pertaining to agency & Open-Space Easements in Virginia; A Guide to Historic Highway Markers in Virginia; publications: Archaeological Bibliographies; Research Report Series; Handbook and Resource Guide for owners of Virginia's historic houses.
Hours & Admission Prices: Mon.-Fri. 8:15-5. No charge. Closed state holidays. ♿
Attendance: 2,000 (estimated)

* **VIRGINIA HISTORICAL SOCIETY, (M),** 428 North Blvd., Richmond, VA 23220-3307. Mailing Address: P.O. Box 7311, Richmond, VA 23221-0311. Tel.: 804-358-4901. Fax: 804-342-9647.
E-mail: jguild@vahistorical.org
Web Site: www.vahistorical.org
Founded: 1831.
Congressional District: 7
Key Personnel: Chm., J. Stewart Bryan, III; Vice Chm., W. Taylor Reveley, III; Pres. & C.E.O., Dr. Paul A. Levengood; Exec. Vice Pres. & C.O.O., Robert F. Strohm; Cur. Art, William Rasmussen; Vice Pres. Advancement, Pamela

R. Seay; Devel. Grants Officer, Carol Anne Baker; Media Rels. Specialist, Jennifer M. Guild; Dir. Museums, James C. Kelly; Dir. Publications & Scholarship, Nelson Lankford; Dir. Library Svcs., Frances Pollard; Dir. Manuscripts & Archives, E. Lee Shepard; Asst. Dir. Education Svcs., Bill Obrochta; Mgr. Virginia House, Tracey Bryan; Dir. Retail Operations, Doris Delk; Volunteer Coord., Dana Fariss.

Personnel Profile: Full-Time Paid 77; Part-Time Paid 33; Part-Time Volunteers 94; Interns 5.

Governing Authority: society, nonprofit organization. Tax-exempt: 501(c)(3) & 170(b)(1)(A).

Virginia History Museum: Virginia House.

Collections: 10,000,000 manuscripts; 150,000 books (15,000 rare books); over 5,000 maps; 1,200 newspapers; 300 serials; over 4,000 pieces of sheet music; over 1,000 paintings; 200,000 photographs; textiles; silver; furniture; weaponry.

Major Exhibits: The Portent: John Brown's Raid in American Memory, 11/09-4/11/10; Heads and Tales, 1/30/10-12/30/10; Memories of World War II: Photographs from the National Archives, 5/24/10-8/1/10; Organized Labor in Virginia, 9/4/10-12/30/10.

Research Fields: Virginia history; Colonial American history; Civil War history; English history.

Facilities: 125,000-vol. library for genealogical & historical research; lecture hall; 25,500 sq. ft. exhibit space. Museum-related items for sale.

Activities: lectures; educational programs & outreach; temporary, permanent & traveling exhibits; membership function; films.

Publications: Virginia Magazine of History and Biography; History Notes.

Hours & Admission Prices: Tues.-Sat. 10-5, Sun. 1-5. Adults $5; discount to AAA members; members no charge. Closed New Year's Eve & Day; Easter; Independence Day; Thanksgiving; Christmas Eve & Day. ♿

Attendance: 60,000 (estimated)

Membership: Student, Teacher & Military $32; Senior over 65 $42; Individual $45; Senior Couple over 65, Individual Plus One & Military Family $55; Family $62.

VIRGINIA HOLOCAUST MUSEUM, 2000 E. Cary St., Richmond, VA 23223-7032. Tel.: 804-257-5400. Fax: 804-257-4314.

Web Site: www.va-holocaust.com

Founded: 1997.

Congressional District: 3

Key Personnel: Dir. & Pres. (V), Jay M. Ipson; Chm., Marcus M. Weinstein; Asst. to Dir., Leigh Weeden; Registrar, Timothy Hensley; Cur. & Archivist, Dianna Gabay; Security, Frank Seldes.

Personnel Profile: Full-Time Paid 12; Full-Time Volunteers 5; Part-Time Paid 4; Part-Time Volunteers 20; Interns 8.

Governing Authority: private; nonprofit organization. Tax-exempt: 501(c)(3).

History Museum.

Collections: European & Nazi wartime memorabilia; Holocaust history; personal artifacts.

Research Fields: survivors & liberators of the Holocaust.

Facilities: research library; educational facilities; 10,000 sq. ft. exhibit space; 300-seat theater. Museum-related items for sale.

Activities: special events; tours; film series; lectures; docent program; formal education programs; guided tours; rental gallery; theater. Annual Events: Annual Gala; Historic Passover Seder.

Publications: quarterly newsletter, De Malyene.

Hours & Admission Prices: Mon.-Fri. 9-5, Sat.-Sun. 11-5; groups of 10 or more by appointment. No charge. Closed New Year's Day; First Day of Rosh Hashana; Yom Kippur; Thanksgiving; Christmas. ♿

Attendance: 37,000 (accurate)

Membership: Young Friends $20; Individual $25; Family $50; Supports $100; Educator $250; Witness $500.

* **VIRGINIA MUSEUM OF FINE ARTS, (M), (I),** 200 N. Boulevard, Richmond, VA 23220-4007. Tel.: 804-340-1400 & 1401; 800-943-8632. Fax: 804-340-1548. TDD: 804-340-1401.

E-mail: contact@vmfa.museum

Web Site: www.vmfa.museum

Founded: 1934.

Congressional District: 3

Key Personnel: Dir. & C.E.O., Alexander Nyerges; Pres., Pamela Reynolds; Pres. Virginia Museum of Fine Arts Foundation, Birch Douglas; C.O.O., Carol Amato; Foundation Vice Pres. Finance & Admin., David B. Bradley; Mgr. Major Gifts & Planned Giving, Kate Merlino Haydon; Donor Rels. Mgr., Chasity Miller; VMFA Fund Mgr., Marcia Collier; Dir. Membership, Jenna Mosman; Corp. Gifts Mgr., Elizabeth Lowsley-Williams; Sr. Assoc. Dir. Architecture & Design and Cur. African Art, Richard B. Woodward; Deputy Dir. Exhibitions, Robin Nicholson; Coord. Exhibitions Planning, Aiesha Halstead

E. Rhodes and Leona B. Carpenter Cur. South Asian & Islamic Art, Head Dept. of Asian Art and Curatorial Chm. Dr. Joseph M. Dye, III; E. Rhodes and Leona B. Carpenter Cur. East Asian Art, Li Jian; Cur. Ancient Art, Dr. Peter Schertz; Assoc. Cur. American Art, Dr. Elizabeth O'Leary; Cochrane Cur. American Art, Dr. Sylvia Yount; Assoc. Cur. South Asian & Islamic Art, John Henry Rice; Paul Mellon Cur. & Head Dept. of European Art, Dr. Mitchell Merling; Sydney and Frances Lewis Family Cur. Modern & Contemporary Art, John Ravenal; Asst. Cur. American Decorative Art, Dr. Susan J. Rawles; Curatorial Fellow Modern & Contemporary Art, Emily Smith; Asst. Cur. Ancient American Art, Dr. Lee Anne Hurt; Sydney and Frances Lewis Family Cur. Decorative Arts from 1890 to Present, Barry Shifman; Mgr. Photographic Resources, Howell Perkins; Chief Conservator & Deputy Dir. Collections Management, Stephen Bonadies; Conservator Paintings, Carol Sawyer; Conservator Sculpture & Decorative Arts, Kathy Gillis; Fine Arts Librarian & Head Publications Dept., Dr. Suzanne Freeman; Registrar, Elizabeth H. Hancock; Deputy Dir. Education & Statewide Partnerships, Sandy Rusak; Coord. Educational Resource Room, Bob Johns; Coord. E&O Administration, Coord. Fellowship Programs & Internships, Lee Schultz; The Thomas C. Gordon Jr. Dir. Studio School, Mary Holland; Assoc. Dir. Education & Statewide Partnerships, Della Watkins; Mgr. Human Resources, Randy Webne; Dir. Community Affairs, Carmen F. Foster; Head Special Events & Food Svcs., Cathy Turner; Council Pres., Tina Stoneburner; Mgr. VMFA Shop, Barbara Lenhardt; Chief Communications Officer, Suzanne D. Hall; Head Budgeting, Procurement & Information Technology, David Barbour; Head Statewide Partnerships, Susan Ferrell; Head Risk Management & Protective Svcs., Kenton Towner; Deputy Dir. Sales & Mktg., Alexis Vaughn.

Personnel Profile: Full-Time Paid 171; Part-Time Paid 125; Part-Time Volunteers 853; Interns 31.

Governing Authority: state. State of Virginia. Tax-exempt: 501(c)(3).

Art Museum.

Collections: ancient Egyptian, Greek, Etruscan, Roman, Byzantine, European medieval; ancient American; African; Chinese, Japanese, Korean, Indian, Tibetan & Nepalese art; American painting, sculpture & decorative arts; European decorative arts, works on paper & old master paintings; the Lillian Thomas Pratt collection of Faberge; Mellon collection of British sporting art, French Impressionist & Post-Impressionist art; the Sydney & Frances Lewis collection of modern & contemporary art; art nouveau; arts & crafts; art deco; modern decorative arts; the Jerome & Rita Gans collection of English silver.

Major Exhibits: American Art from the McGlothlin Collection, 5/10-7/10; Matisse, Picasso, and Modern Art in Paris (T), 5/10-7/10; Tiffany: Color and Light (T), 5/10-8/10; Jun Kaneko, 7/10-2/11; Darkroom: Photography and New Medium in South Africa: 1950-Present (T), 8/10-10/10; Sally Mann, 12/10-2/11.

Facilities: 70,000-vol. art reference library; reading room; sculpture garden; restaurants; center for education and outreach; classrooms; banquet facilities; lecture hall; theater; studio school. Museum-related items for sale.

Activities: docent guided tours; teachers workshops; in-services; summer teachers' institute; performance art programs; lectures; films; gallery talks; concerts; dance, music recitals; arts festivals; education programs for children, adults, students; docent program; participatory, permanent, loan, temporary & traveling exhibitions; studio art & art history classes; school loan service; statewide outreach exhibitions & programs.

Publications: magazine, My VMFA; monthly e-newsletters; annual report; African Art: Virginia Museum of Fine Arts Collection, The Making of Virginia Architecture; Selections from the Virginia Museum of Fine Arts; Modern & Contemporary Art at the Virginia Museum of Fine Arts; The Jerome and Rita Gans Collection of English Silver; Art of Late Roman & Byzantium in the Virginia Museum of Fine Arts; British Sporting Paintings: The Paul Mellon Collection in the Virginia Museum of Fine Arts; Designed to Sell: Turn-of-the-Century American Posters; Video Series: Five African Art Facts; Tangible Spirits With Alison Saar; Women's Work: Urban Bush Women; An American's Dream: Jack Warner on Collecting American Art; Faberge: Shopping, Collecting, Remembering; Impressionist Paintings; What Color is Black...; The Fine Art of Life; Tigers and Sails and ABC Tales; Faberge: Virginia Museum of Fine Arts Collection; French Paintings: the Collection of Mr. & Mrs. Paul Mellon in the Virginia Museum of Fine Arts; Late 19th and Early 20th Century Decorative Arts: The Sydney & Frances Lewis Collection in the Virginia Museum of Fine Arts; German Expressionist Art: The Ludwig & Rosy Fischer Collection; Old-Russian Enamels; Three Masters of Landscape: Fragonard, Robert, Boucher; Champion Animals: Sculptures by Herbert Haseltine; American Dreams: Paintings & Decorative Arts from the Warner Collection; Ancient Art: Virginia Museum of Fine Arts; Selections: Virginia Museum of Fine Arts; Tigers and Sails and ABC Tales; Robert Lazzarini; James McNeil Whistler: Uneasy Pieces; William Blake: The Book of Job; The Arts of India; Outer and Inner Space: Pipolotti Rist, Shirin Neshat, Jane & Louise Wilson and the History of Video Art; Capturing Beauty: American Impressionist and Realist Paintings from the McGlothlin Collection; Rule Britannia! Art, Royalty &

Power in the Age of Jamestown; Great British Watercolors from the Paul Mellon Collection; A Noble Feast: English Silver from the Jerome & Rita Gans Collection.
Hours & Admission Prices: Call for hours. No charge. Closed New Year's Day; Independence Day; Thanksgiving; Christmas. ♿
Attendance: 82,960 (accurate)
Membership: Student $15; State & National Individual (outside metro area) and Statewide Partners $25; Teacher $30; Senior $35; State & National Dual and Metropolitan Individual $40; Senior Dual $50; Metropolitan Dual & Family $60; Contributor $100; Supporter $250; Curator's Circle $500; Patron $1,000.

* **VIRGINIA WAR MEMORIAL, (M),** 621 S. Belvidere St., Richmond, VA 23220-6504. Tel.: 804-786-2060.
Web Site: www.vawarmemorial.org
Founded: 1956.
Key Personnel: Exec. Dir., Jon C. Hatfield; Education Specialist, Candice L. Shelton; Museum Shop Mgr., Rachael Snyder.
Governing Authority: Parent Institution: State of Virginia. Tax-exempt.
Military Memorial.
Collections: Shrine of Memory includes names of 11,634 veterans killed in action from WWII to Persian Gulf War.
Facilities: 200-seat auditorium.
Activities: educational programs; group tours; student seminars; monthly patriotic events.
Publications: newsletter.
Hours & Admission Prices: Shrine of Memory: daily. Visitor Center: daily 9-4. No charge; donations accepted. ♿
Attendance: 22,000 (accurate)

* **WILTON HOUSE MUSEUM, (M),** 215 S. Wilton Rd., Richmond, VA 23226-2212. Tel.: 804-282-5936. Fax: 804-288-9805.
E-mail: wiltonmuseum@comcast.net
Web Site: www.wiltonhousemuseum.org
Founded: 1934.
Congressional District: 2
Key Personnel: Dir., Dana Hand Evans; Pres., Carrie Weedon; Chm., Joan Moody; Exec. Sec., Marianne Zwicker; Office Mgr., Elizabeth Gosack-Fleming; Museum Shop Mgr., Elizabeth Richardson.
Personnel Profile: Full-Time Paid 2; Full-Time Volunteers 1; Part-Time Paid 10; Part-Time Volunteers 60; Interns 3.
Governing Authority: society. Parent Institution: National Society of the Colonial Dames of America in the Commonwealth of Virginia. Tax-exempt: 501(c)(3).
Historic House: 1753 Georgian brick mansion, home of William Randolph, III & moved to present James River location in 1935.
Collections: fully paneled interior; period furniture; Randolph family portraits; archives; 18th & 19th-century decorative arts.
Research Fields: Virginia genealogy; architecture; furniture; 18th century social & material culture history.
Facilities: meeting room; lecture hall.
Activities: guided tours; permanent & temporary exhibitions; meeting room; school tours with costumed docents; musical performance. Museum Sponsors: Garden Week; lecture series.
Publications: Wilton; Lafayette at Camp Wilton on the James.
Hours & Admission Prices: Tues.-Fri. 10-1, Sat. 10-4:30, Sun. 1:30-4:30; group tours by appointment. Adults $10, seniors $8, students $6; discounts to groups, AAA, VAM & AAM members; Colonial Dames & children under 6 no charge. Closed national holidays.
Attendance: 3,500 (accurate)
Membership: Friends of Wilton: Individual & Foot Soldier $25; Individual & Patriot $50; Family & VA Company $100; Signer $250; Historic Founder $500.

Richmond International Airport

VIRGINIA AVIATION MUSEUM, 5701 Huntsman Rd., Richmond International Airport, VA 23250-2416. Tel.: 804-236-3620 & 3622. Fax: 804-236-3623.
E-mail: mboehme@smv.org
Web Site: www.vam.smv.org
Founded: 1987.
Congressional District: 3
Key Personnel: Pres. FDN Directors, Debbie Trainer; Exec. Dir., Michael P. Boehme; Asst. Dir. & Cur., David Hahn; Asst. Dir. Operations, Kimberly W. Leigh; Dir. Mktg. & Public Affairs, Rick McKeel; Exec. Dir. SMV Foundation, Julia Carr; Museum Shop Mgr., Jennifer Morehead.
Personnel Profile: Full-Time Paid 3; Part-Time Paid 6; Part-Time Volunteers 45.
Governing Authority: state. Parent Institution: Science Museum of Virginia. Tax-exempt.
Aviation Museum.
Collections: aircraft; aviation; WWII memorabilia.
Research Fields: aviation history relating to Virginia's rich aviation heritage.
Facilities: large video projection in 65-seat J.D. Benn Theater; aircraft renovation facility; Neilson J. November Observation deck; Kid's Ready Room. Museum-related items for sale.
Activities: hands-on exhibits; education program for preschoolers through 12th grade; model railroad show-Wings and Rails; wind tunnel & forces of flight demonstrations; flight simulators; SR-71 Forum; Wright Brothers Symposium.
Publications: annual report (included within SMV); quarterly newsletter for members (included within SMV); group visit planning guide; program brochures.
Hours & Admission Prices: Tues.-Sat. 9:30-5, Sun. 12-5; call for additional hours. Adults $6, seniors 60 & over and youth 4-12 $5; discounts to groups, active military, ASTC & VAHS members; children 3 & under and SMV members no charge. Closed Thanksgiving; Christmas Eve & Day. ♿
Attendance: 24,000 (estimated)
Membership: Single $55; Family $85; Subscriber $100; Pilot $180; Senior Pilot $500; Command Pilot $750. Volunteer-100 hours of volunteer service annually-no charge.

Roanoke

CATHOLIC HISTORICAL SOCIETY OF THE ROANOKE VALLEY, 400 Campbell Ave., S.W., Roanoke, VA 24016-3627. Tel.: 540-982-0152. Fax: 540-982-0152.
Founded: 1983.
Congressional District: 6
Key Personnel: Pres. (V), John Wagner; Museum Shop Mgr., Loretta Jolley.
Personnel Profile: Part-Time Volunteers 16.
Governing Authority: society; nonprofit organization. Tax-exempt: 501(c)(3).
History Museum.
Collections: religious articles; photographs; Roanoke Valley religious historical data.
Research Fields: Local religious & education history; Diocese of Richmond.
Facilities: 300-vol. library of religious material available to the public. Museum-related items for sale.
Activities: research; guided tours; permanent & temporary exhibitions.
Publications: quarterly newsletter.
Hours & Admission Prices: Tues. 10-2; other times by appointment. No charge; donations accepted. ♿
Attendance: 500 (estimated)
Membership: Individual $15; Family $20; Patron $30; Sponsor $50; Benefactor $100.

ELEANOR D. WILSON MUSEUM, HOLLINS UNIVERSITY, (M), Richard Wetherill Visual Arts Center, 8009 Fishburn Dr., Roanoke, VA 24020-1679. Mailing Address: P.O. Box 9769, Roanoke, VA 24020-1679. Tel.: 540-362-6532. Fax: 540-362-6694.
E-mail: amoorefield@hollins.edu
Web Site: www.hollins.edu/museum
Founded: 1964.
Key Personnel: Dir., Amy G. Moorefield; Exhibition & Program Coord., Laura Jane Ramsburg; Preparator & Collections, Janet Carty; Museum Coord., Karyn McAden.
Personnel Profile: Full-Time Paid 2; Part-Time Paid 13; Part-Time Volunteers 6; Interns 5.
Governing Authority: Parent Institution: Hollins University. Tax-exempt.
Art Museum.
Collections: modern & contemporary paintings, photographs & prints.
Major Exhibits: Fiona Ross: Walking the Parallels to Terminus, 1/10; When Janey Comes Marching Home: Portraits of Women Combat Veterans (T), 2/10-4/10; Stanley Lewis: 2010 Artist in Residence, 2/10-4/10; Senior Majors Exhibition, 5/10; Reunion 2010, 5/10-6/10.
Facilities: 2,700 sq. ft. exhibit space; 3 inter-connected galleries.
Activities: artists talks; lectures; workshops & demonstrations; exhibitions.
Publications: triannual newsletters; exhibition catalogues.
Hours & Admission Prices: Tues.-Fri. 10-4, Sat. 1-5. No charge; donations accepted. Closed university breaks. ♿
Attendance: 11,500 (accurate)
Membership: Friend $40; Supporter $100; Patron $250; Program Circle $1,000; Collector's Circle $2,000; Director's Circle $3,000.

HARRISON MUSEUM OF AFRICAN-AMERICAN CULTURE, 523 Harrison Ave., N.W., Roanoke, VA 24016-1740. Tel.: 540-345-4818.
E-mail: asbolden@harrisonmuseum.org
Web Site: www.harrisonmuseum.org
Key Personnel: Exec. Dir., Aletha Bolden; Exec. Asst., Donna Davis

History Museum.
Collections: African-American history; photographs; African & contemporary art.
Facilities: Museum-related items for sale.
Activities: lectures. Museum Sponsors: Henry Street Heritage Festival in September.
Hours & Admission Prices: Tues.-Sat. 1-5. No charge; donations accepted.

HISTORY MUSEUM OF WESTERN VIRGINIA, (M), One Market Square, Roanoke, VA 24011-1429. Mailing Address: Box 1904, Roanoke, VA 24008-1904. Tel.: 540-342-5770 & 5724. Fax: 540-224-1256.
E-mail: info.hswv@cox.net
Web Site: history-museum.org
Formerly: History Museum and Historical Society of Western Virginia
Founded: 1957.
Congressional District: 6
Key Personnel: Pres., W. Tucker Lemon; C.E.O., Jeanne Bollendorf; Coord. Visitor Svcs., Holly Guerin.
Personnel Profile: Full-Time Paid 4; Part-Time Paid 4; Part-Time Volunteers 90; Interns 2.
Governing Authority: society; nonprofit organization. Parent Institution: Historical Society of Western Virginia. Tax-exempt: 501(c)(3).
History Museum.
Collections: archival & oral history repository; archeology; excavational railroad collection.
Research Fields: southwest Virginia history; oral history; genealogy.
Facilities: research library; 9,000 sq. ft. exhibit space.
Activities: guided tours; lectures; educational programs for children; historic bus tours.
Publications: monthly newsletter; books, Tour Games; Colonel William Fleming of Botetourt; Roanoke 1740-1982; The Journal of History Museum and Historical Society of Western Virginia; Iron Horses in the Valley; William Flemming, Patriot; The Visits of Lewis and Clark to Fincastle, Virginia; various historic maps; Notable Women West of the Blue Ridge; History of Roanoke; Charles Johnston's Frontier Adventure.
Hours & Admission Prices: Tues.-Fri. 10-4, Sat. 10-5, Sun. 1-5. Adults $3, children & senior citizens over 60 $2; discounts to AAM members & groups over 10; members & children under 6 no charge. Closed New Year's; Martin Luther King Jr. Day; Memorial Day; Independence Day; Labor Day; Thanksgiving; Christmas. ♿
Attendance: 22,100 (accurate)
Membership: Senior $40; Individual $45; Family Senior $50; Family $55; Friend $51-$149; Associate $150-$249; Patron $250-$499; Sponsor $500-$999; Benefactor $1,000-$2,499; Angel $2,500 & up.

MILL MOUNTAIN ZOO, Pkwy. Spur Rd., Roanoke, VA 24034. Mailing Address: P.O. Box 13484, Roanoke, VA 24034-3484. Tel.: 540-343-3241. Fax: 540-343-8111.
E-mail: info@mmzoo.org
Web Site: www.mmzoo.org
Key Personnel: Exec. Dir., Sean Greene; Administration Mgr., Michaela Pace-Wilson
Zoo.
Collections: 39 species; 135 animals.
Facilities: train. Museum-related items for sale.
Hours & Admission Prices: Daily 10-5. Adults $7.12, children 3-11 $4.75; children 2 & under no charge. Closed Christmas. ♿

O. WINSTON LINK MUSEUM, 101 Shenandoah Ave., Roanoke, VA 24016-2044. Tel.: 540-982-5465. Fax: 540-982-5683.
Web Site: www.linkmuseum.org
Founded: 2004.
Key Personnel: Dir., Kimberly Parker; Interim Chm. (V), Tucker Lemon; Pres. (V), David Helmer; Exec. Dir., Jeanne M. Bollendorf; Education & Vol. Coord., Leah Gardner; Treas., Ron Sink; Devel. Officer, Monica Johnson; Security, Jack Stilton; Museum Shop Mgr., Jennifer Miller.
Personnel Profile: Full-Time Paid 4; Part-Time Paid 1; Part-Time Volunteers 90.
Governing Authority: private; nonprofit organization. Parent Institution: Historical Society of Western VA, Roanoke, VA. Tax-exempt: 501(c)(3).
Photography Museum.
Collections: photographs; film; camera & lighting equipment; period artifacts.
Research Fields: Raymond Loewy.
Facilities: 75-seat auditorium; 17,000 sq. ft. exhibit space; 75-seat theater. Museum-related items for sale.
Activities: docent program; films; formal education programs; guided tours; hobby workshops; lectures; loan, temporary & traveling exhibitions. Annual Events: Celebration at the Station: Santa by Rail; Annual Norfolk Southern Calendar exhibit; Haunted Museum.
Publications: quarterly newsletter, Link News.
Hours & Admission Prices: Jan.-Feb. Mon.-Sat. 10-5, Sun. 12-5; March-Dec. daily 10-5. Adults $5, senior citizens $4.50, children $4; discounts to groups; members no charge. Closed New Year's Day; Easter; Thanksgiving; Christmas. ♿
Attendance: 18,679 (accurate)
Membership: Individual $30; Family $60; Photographer $90; Conductor $160; Engineer $250.

* **SCIENCE MUSEUM OF WESTERN VIRGINIA,** One Market Sq., Roanoke, VA 24011-1429. Tel.: 540-342-5710. Fax: 540-224-1240.
E-mail: frontdesk1@smwv.org
Web Site: www.smwv.org
Founded: 1970.
Congressional District: 6
Key Personnel: Exec. Dir., Nancy McCrickard; Dir. Operations, Betsy Williams; Asst. Dir. Education, Brenda Brown.
Personnel Profile: Full-Time Paid 11; Part-Time Paid 11; Part-Time Volunteers 82.
Governing Authority: nonprofit organization. Tax-exempt: 501(c)(3).
Science Museum.
Collections: pertaining to earth science, health, energy, natural history & physical science.
Facilities: 30,000 sq. ft. exhibit space; educational facilities; laboratory; lecture hall; 140-seat planetarium; Starlab program outreach; Mega Dome Theatre. Science items for sale.
Activities: guided tours; lectures; films; planetarium shows; formally organized educational programs; loan & permanent exhibits.
Publications: quarterly newsletter; curriculum guides; educator newsletter; member newsletter, Science News for Schools.
Hours & Admission Prices: Tues.-Sat. 10-5, Sun. 1-5. Exhibits & Planetarium: adults $8, senior citizens 60 & over $7, children 3-12 $6; discounts to ASTC members; children under 2 & members no charge. Closed New Year's Day; Easter; Independence Day; Thanksgiving; Christmas. ♿
Attendance: 150,000 (estimated)
Membership: Youth $20; Individual $35; Dual, Family & Grandparent $55.

* **TAUBMAN MUSEUM OF ART, (M),** 110 Salem Ave., S.E., Roanoke, VA 24011-1410. Tel.: 540-342-5760. Fax: 540-342-5798.
E-mail: info@taubmanmuseum.org
Web Site: taubmanmuseum.org
Formerly: Art Museum of Western Virginia
Founded: 1951.
Congressional District: 6
Key Personnel: Exec. Dir., David Mickenberg; Pres. Bd. Trustees, John B. Williamson III; Deputy Dir. Operations, Jim Beckner; Deputy Dir. Museum Affairs, Lisa Martin; Deputy Dir. Art, David Brown; Deputy Dir. Education, Scott Crawford.
Personnel Profile: Full-Time Paid 33; Part-Time Paid 8; Part-Time Volunteers 305; Interns 20.
Governing Authority: nonprofit organization. Tax-exempt: 501(c)(3).
Art Museum.
Collections: 19th-century to present American paintings; photography; sculpture; prints & drawings; contemporary folk art; International art; Japanese prints, graphic & decorative arts.
Research Fields: regional art, general fine arts, 19th- & 20th-century American art, outsider folk art; Thomas Eakins & His Circle.
Facilities: 2,600-vol. library; auditorium, theatre, cafe. Museum-related items for sale.
Activities: guided tours; lectures; gallery talks; concerts; arts festivals; education programs for children, adults, undergraduate & graduate college students; inter-museum loan, permanent, temporary & traveling exhibitions. Museum Sponsors: outreach education programs across region.
Publications: biannual newsletter; Docent Guild newsletter; annual report; exhibition catalogs; monthly volunteer and membership newsletters.
Hours & Admission Prices: Tues.-Wed. & Fri.-Sat. 10-5, Thurs. 10-7, Sun. 12-5. Adults $10.50, seniors $9, students w/ID $8.50, children 5-12 $5.50; discounts to groups; members and children 3 & under no charge. Closed holidays. ♿
Attendance: 110,000 (accurate)
Membership: Student $35; Individual $45; Family $70; Friend $100; Sustainer $250; Patron $500; Benefactor $1,000.

VIRGINIA MUSEUM OF TRANSPORTATION, INC., (M), 303 Norfolk Ave., S.W., Roanoke, VA 24016-3620. Tel.: 540-342-5670. Fax: 540-342-6898.
E-mail: info@vmt.org
Web Site: www.vmt.org
Founded: 1963.

Congressional District: 6
Key Personnel: Pres., Tom Cox; Dir. Administration & Exec. Asst. to Dir., Steve Murray; Dir. Retail & Volunteers, Phillip Staten; Office Mgr., William Thompson; Dir. Retail & Museum Svcs., Jerry Dillon; Museum Shop Mgr., Grace Helmer.
Personnel Profile: Full-Time Paid 5; Part-Time Paid 5; Part-Time Volunteers 32.
Governing Authority: private; nonprofit organization. Tax-exempt.
Transportation Museum.
Collections: transportation equipment, vintage cars & carriages, locomotives & railcars, aviation pieces; interactive & historical exhibits; model layouts.
Research Fields: all models of transportation; technology.
Facilities: historic railroad freight depot & railroad yard.
Activities: guided tours; workshops; outreach programs; camps; permanent exhibitions; revolving displays; annual special events.
Publications: quarterly newsletter.
Hours & Admission Prices: Mon.-Sat. 10-5, Sun. 1-5. Adults $8, senior citizens $7, children 3-11 $6; discounts to AAA members; children under 3 & members no charge. Closed New Year's Eve & Day; Easter, Thanksgiving; Christmas Eve & Day. ♿
Attendance: 65,000 (estimated)
Membership: Educator $20; Individual $30; Grandparents $40; Family $50; Navigator $100 & up.

Salem

THE SALEM MUSEUM, (M), 801 E. Main St., Salem, VA 24153-4312. Tel.: 540-389-6760.
E-mail: info@salemmuseum.org
Web Site: www.salemmuseum.org
Founded: 1992.
Congressional District: 6
Key Personnel: Dir., John D. Long; Pres., W. Frank Chapman, Jr.
Personnel Profile: Full-Time Paid 1; Part-Time Paid 2; Part-Time Volunteers 50; Interns 2.
Governing Authority: private; nonprofit organization. Parent Institution: Salem Historical Society. Tax-exempt.
History Museum: located in the c.1845 Williams-Brown House-Store.
Collections: concentration on history from prehistoric-modern in the Roanoke Valley of Virginia; emphasis on Salem; long term exhibits on the Civil War; Victorian Parlour; African American history; works by local artist, Walter Biggs.
Research Fields: local structures; pictorial history; Native American Settlements in the area; local history.
Facilities: 2,500 sq. ft. exhibit space; herb and kitchen garden. Museum-related items for sale.
Activities: internship program; guided tours; lectures; temporary & traveling exhibitions; weekend programs for children. Annual Events: Olde Salem Days Open House in September; Ghost Walk in October; Holiday Homes Tour in December.
Publications: monthly newsletter; seasonal historical newspaper featuring walking tour; occasional transcription & reproductions of local history documents; pictorial history.
Hours & Admission Prices: Tues.-Fri. 10-4, Sat. 12-5. No charge; donations accepted. Closed New Year's weekend; Independence Day; Thanksgiving; Christmas.
Attendance: 7,000 (estimated)
Membership: Individual $30; Family $45; Sustaining $120; Associate $275; Life $600.

Saltville

MUSEUM OF THE MIDDLE APPALACHIANS, (M), 123 Palmer Ave., Saltville, VA 24370. Mailing Address: P.O. Box 910, Saltville, VA 24370-0910. Tel.: 276-496-3633. Fax: 276-496-7033.
E-mail: info@museum-mid-app.org
Web Site: www.museum-mid-app.org
Founded: 1998.
Congressional District: 9
Key Personnel: Foundation Pres., Jim Glanville; Friends Pres. (V), Marnie Maule; Treas., Carl Rickman; Devel., Christine Helton; Mgr., Harry Haynes; Coord., Janice Orr; Museum Shop Mgr., Harry Haynes.
Personnel Profile: Full-Time Paid 1; Full-Time Volunteers 1; Part-Time Paid 1; Part-Time Volunteers 20.
Governing Authority: private; nonprofit organization. Parent Institution: The Saltville Foundation, 123 Palmer Ave., P.O. Box 910, Saltville, VA 24370. Tax-exempt: 501(c)(3).
Natural History Museum.
Collections: natural & cultural heritage; rocks; minerals; fossils; maps; Woodland Indians; Civil War artifacts; Ice Age fossils; photographs.
Research Fields: Ice Age paleontological digs; Civil War fortifications.
Facilities: library; educational facilities; field research station; 7,500 sq. ft. exhibit space; classroom; conference room. Museum-related items for sale.
Activities: lectures; temporary exhibitions; school & scout programs. Annual Events: Woolly Day; Kids Ice Age Dig.
Publications: quarterly newsletter.
Hours & Admission Prices: Mon.-Sat. 10-4, Sun. 1-4. Adults $3, senior citizens & children 6-12 $2, senior & student groups $1; members & children under 6 no charge. Closed New Year's Day; Easter; Thanksgiving; Christmas. ♿
Attendance: 12,000 (accurate)
Membership: Senior & Student $10 & up; Individual $15 & up; Family $35 & up; Sustaining $100 & up; Century $1,000 & up.

Scottsville

SCOTTSVILLE MUSEUM, 290 Main St., Scottsville, VA 24590. Mailing Address: 290 Main St., P.O. Box 101, Scottsville, VA 24590-0101. Tel.: 434-286-2247.
E-mail: smuseum@avenue.org
Founded: 1970.
History Museum.
Collections: town history; James River transportation; the Civil War; Native American artifacts; school life; clothing; toys; furniture; photographs.
Facilities: theater.
Activities: group tours.
Hours & Admission Prices: April-Oct. Sat. 10-5, Sun. 1-5; other times by appointment. No charge; donations accepted.

Smithfield

ISLE OF WIGHT COURTHOUSE, 130 Main St., Smithfield, VA 23430-1323. Mailing Address: 204 W. Franklin St., Richmond, VA 23220-5012. Tel.: 804-357-3502. Fax: 804-775-0802.
Web Site: www.apva.org/isleofwight
Founded: 1750.
Congressional District: 4
Key Personnel: Exec. Dir., Elizabeth Kostelny; Pres. (V), John H. Guy, IV; Chm. (V), Tom Mayes; Dir. Properties, Louis Malon.
Personnel Profile: Part-Time Paid 2; Part-Time Volunteers 2.
Governing Authority: nonprofit. Parent Institution: APVA Preservation Virginia, 204 W. Franklin St., Richmond, VA 23220.
Historic Building: 1750 restored Court House.
Collections: local history & culture; paintings; perid furnishings.
Hours & Admission Prices: Feb. Fri.-Sat. 10-4, Sun. 1-4; March-Dec. Tues.-Thurs. & Sun. 1-4, Fri.-Sat. 10-4. No charge. Closed Thanksgiving; Christmas.
Attendance: 5,000 (estimated)

SCHOOLHOUSE MUSEUM, 516 Main St., Smithfield, VA 23430. Mailing Address: P.O. Box 1113, Smithfield, VA 23431. Tel.: 757-365-4789.
Historic Building: housed in a former one-room schoolhouse built to educate county African American children.
Collections: local history & culture; period furnishings.
Hours & Admission Prices: Call for hours.

South Boston

SOUTH BOSTON-HALIFAX COUNTY MUSEUM OF FINE ARTS & HISTORY, (M), 1540 Wilborn Ave., South Boston, VA 24592-2400. Mailing Address: P.O. Box 383, South Boston, VA 24592-0383. Tel.: 434-572-9200. Fax: 434-572-8996.
E-mail: sbhcm@halifax.com
Web Site: sbhcmuseum.org
Founded: 1981.
Congressional District: 5
Key Personnel: Pres., Katherine Shortt; Vice Pres., Shirla Hudson; Dir., Beth Redd; Treas., Jane Jones; Sec., Louise Sheppard.
Personnel Profile: Full-Time Paid 1; Part-Time Paid 2; Part-Time Volunteers 60.
Governing Authority: nonprofit organization. Tax-exempt: 501(c)(3).
History Museum.
Collections: artifacts from South Boston, Halifax County & Southside Virginia.
Facilities: library; 20,000 sq. ft. exhibit space; premises available for rental. Museum-related items for sale.
Activities: guided tours; films; concerts; temporary & traveling exhibitions; lectures.
Publications: annual, Museum Newsletter; quarterly newsletter; museum flyer; books, Civil War Letters; Black History in Halifax County; Black Schools in Halifax County 1940s; National Tobacco Festivals 1935-1941; Historic Delights Cookbook; Virginia Born Presidents.

Hours & Admission Prices: Wed.-Sat. 10-4, Sun. 2-4:30. No charge; donations accepted. Closed New Year's Day; Thanksgiving; Christmas. ♿
Attendance: 10,000 (accurate)
Membership: Student & Senior Citizen $10; Individual $15; Family $25; Contributive $30; "100 Plus" Club $100 and up; Roundtable Partners $250; Inner Circle Partners $500.

Spotsylvania

SPOTSYLVANIA HISTORICAL ASSOCIATION AND MUSEUM, 8956 Courthouse Rd., Spotsylvania, VA 22553. Mailing Address: P.O. Box 64, Spotsylvania, VA 22553-0064. Tel.: 540-507-7112.
Founded: 1962.
Congressional District: 8
Key Personnel: Cur., Dir & Treas., Caroline L. Bradley; Pres., John E. Pruitt, Jr.; Vice Pres., Stephen P. Lampert.
Personnel Profile: Part-Time Paid 4.
Governing Authority: state. nonprofit organization. Operated by the Spotsylvania Historical Association, Inc. Tax-exempt: 170(b)(1)(A).
General Museum.
Collections: Indian relics; early Colonial artifacts; china; tools; pottery; dolls; maps; genealogies and manuscripts; diaries; Civil War artifacts; weapons; pharmaceutical collection; books. Historic Building: 1856 church.
Research Fields: local history; archaeology; military; Revolutionary and Civil War; genealogy.
Facilities: 2,500-vol. library of books, diaries and old maps of county available for use on premises. Commemorative coins & museum-related items for sale.
Activities: organized educational programs; permanent & temporary exhibitions.
Publications: manuscript, Court Houses of Spotsylvania County; books, Patriots 1775-1781; A History of Early Spotsylvania; booklets, Church Histories; Histories of Old Homes.
Hours & Admission Prices: Mon.-Sat. 9-5. No charge; donations accepted. Closed New Year's Day; Thanksgiving; Christmas Eve & Day.
Attendance: 3,000 (estimated)
Membership: Individual & Family $15; Life $100.

Staunton

AUGUSTA COUNTY HISTORICAL SOCIETY, 20 S. New St., 3rd Fl., Staunton, VA 24401. Mailing Address: P.O. Box 686, Staunton, VA 24402-0686. Tel.: 540-248-4151.
E-mail: augustachs@ntelos.net
Web Site: www.augustacountyhs.org
Historical Society Museum.
Collections: county history & culture; manuscripts; books.
Hours & Admission Prices: Tues. & Thurs.-Fri. 9-12; other times by appointment.

* **FRONTIER CULTURE MUSEUM,** 1290 Richmond Rd., Staunton, VA 24401-4976. Mailing Address: P.O. Box 810, Staunton, VA 24402-0810. Tel.: 540-332-7850. Fax: 540-332-9989. TDD: 540-332-7850.
E-mail: info@fcmv.virginia.gov
Web Site: www.frontier.virginia.gov
Founded: 1982.
Congressional District: 6
Key Personnel: Chm. Public Bd. (V), Gail Nardi; Chm. Private Bd., Maricia Capps; Exec. Dir., G. John Avoli.
Personnel Profile: Full-Time Paid 39; Part-Time Paid 50; Part-Time Volunteers 55; Interns 6.
Governing Authority: state. Parent Institution: Commonwealth of Virginia. Subsidiary Institution: Secretariat of Education. Tax-exempt: 501(c)(3).
Outdoor Living History Museum.
Collections: German, Scotch-Irish, English, American, West African/IBO folklife & culture; reconstructed 17th- to 19th-century farms & buildings; study collections; furniture & other related furnishings; textile-weaving; agricultural tools; domestic craft; trade materials & equipment; archives; ledgers; family papers.
Research Fields: European cultures from Ireland, England, Germany & America; immigration to America & Virginia; 18th & 19th century agricultural, social & economic life; West Africa/Ibo culture.
Facilities: 4,000-vol. library pertaining to European & Virginian history, agriculture & architecture; research & educational facilities; 120 & 60 seat theater & lecture rooms. Museum-related items for sale.
Activities: living history demonstrations; outreach programs; guided tours; organized education programs; participatory exhibits; workshops; lecture series; special events. Museum Sponsors: traditional Oktoberfest; traditional holiday tours.
Publications: quarterly newsletter, News From The Frontier; annual calendar of events; museum guidebook.
Hours & Admission Prices: mid-March to Nov. daily 9-5; Dec. to mid-March daily 10-4; group & educational tours available. Adults $10, children 6-12 $6; discounts to AAM members; children under 6 & members no charge. Closed New Year's Day; Thanksgiving; Christmas. ♿
Attendance: 78,000 (accurate)
Membership: Student $20; Individual $30; Family or Grandparent $50; Contributor $100; Associate $250; Corporate Patron $500; Benefactor $1,000.

MARY BALDWIN COLLEGE/HUNT GALLERY, Market & Vine, Staunton, VA 24401. Mailing Address: Dept. of Art & Art History, Deming Hall, Mary Baldwin College, Staunton, VA 24401-3610. Tel.: 540-887-7196. Fax: 540-887-7139.
E-mail: pryan@mbc.edu
Web Site: www.mbc.edu/college/events/huntgallery.asp
Founded: 1842.
Key Personnel: Dir., Paul Ryan.
Personnel Profile: Interns 2.
Governing Authority: college; Mary Baldwin College. Tax-exempt.
College Art Gallery & Museum.
Collections: 20th-century contemporary paintings, drawings, prints & photographs; contemporary works by regional artists & national artists connected to the college.
Activities: lectures; formal education programs for adults; participatory & loan exhibitions.
Publications: exhibition catalogs.
Hours & Admission Prices: Sept.-May Mon.-Fri. 9-5. No charge. ♿
Attendance: 1,200 (estimated)

STAUNTON AUGUSTA ART CENTER, 20 S. New St., Staunton, VA 24401-4308. Tel.: 540-885-2028. Fax: 540-885-6000.
E-mail: info@saartcenter.org
Web Site: www.saartcenter.org
Founded: 1961.
Congressional District: 6
Key Personnel: Exec. Dir., Beth Hodge; Pres. (V), Phillip Nolley; Administrative Asst., Lynn Morell.
Personnel Profile: Full-Time Paid 2; Part-Time Volunteers 100; Interns 3.
Governing Authority: nonprofit organization. Parent Institution: Virginia Museum of Fine Art. Tax-exempt: 501(c)(3).
Art Association: housed in 19th-century pump house which once supplied water for the city of Staunton.
Collections: paintings; sculpture; photographs.
Activities: gallery talks; lectures; films; educational programs; workshops; annual outdoor art show. Museum Sponsors: summer studio art camp for children ages 4-15; Art for All Ages, an outreach program for area seniors; Outside the Line, program exploring issues of mental health & art.
Publications: biennial newsletter.
Hours & Admission Prices: Mon.-Fri. 10-5, Sat. 10-4, Sun. 1-4. No charge; donations accepted. Closed major holidays; between exhibitions. ♿
Attendance: 14,000 (estimated)
Membership: Individual $35; Family $50; Pumphouse Club $51-$99; The Gallery $100-$249; Impressionist Society $250-$499; Renaissance Circle $500-$999; Ruth Owen Patron of the Arts $1,000 & up.

* **WOODROW WILSON PRESIDENTIAL LIBRARY, (M),** 20 N. Coalter St., Staunton, VA 24401-4332. Mailing Address: P.O. Box 24, Staunton, VA 24402-0024. Tel.: 540-885-0897. Fax: 540-886-9874.
E-mail: info@woodrowwilson.org
Web Site: www.woodrowwilson.org
Formerly: Woodrow Wilson Birthplace & Museum
Founded: 1938.
Congressional District: 6
Key Personnel: Exec. Dir., Don W. Wilson, Ph.D.; Chm. (V), Dr. A. Stanley Link, Jr.; Dir. Administration & Finance, Janet E. Campbell; Dir. Education, Joel Hodson; Dir. Library & Archives, Peggy Dillard; Dir. Devel., Nancy McIntyre; Museum Shop Mgr., Virginia M. Engleman.
Personnel Profile: Full-Time Paid 11; Part-Time Paid 14; Part-Time Volunteers 205; Interns 24.
Governing Authority: nonprofit organization. Tax-exempt: 501(c)(3).
Historic House: 1846 former Presbyterian Manse & birthplace of Woodrow Wilson, 28th President of the U.S.
Collections: decorative arts; furnishings; costumes; uniforms; textiles; musical instruments; paintings, graphics; photographs; sculpture; manuscripts; rare books; his accomplishments as author, scholar, university president, governor & statesman. Historic Houses: 1880 Emily P. Smith Administration Bldg.; 1856 Dolores Lescure Center (Museum).
Research Fields: relating to collections & the life & times of President Woodrow Wilson, 1856-1924.

Facilities: 8,000-vol. research library; education center; carriage house; meeting rooms. Museum-related items for sale.
Activities: guided tours; films; lectures; gallery talks; on-site programs for school groups K-8; packet program for school groups 9-12; summer internships & informal educational programs for undergraduate college students; semester internships at graduate level in museology; permanent & temporary exhibitions; inter museum loans.
Publications: quarterly newsletter; interpretive brochures; pamphlets; books.
Hours & Admission Prices: Daily 9-5. Adults $12, groups of 10 or more $8, children 6-12 $3; discounts to school groups, AAM, ICOM & AAA members; members & children under 6 no charge. Closed New Year's Day; Easter; Thanksgiving; Christmas Eve & Day. ♿
Attendance: 20,000
Membership: Associates $50-$99; Diplomats $100-$199; Ambassadors $200-$499; Statesmen $500-$999; Cabinet Members $1,000 (5 Years); Oval Office $2,000 (5 Years); Benefactors $5,000 (5 Years); Fellows $10,000 (5 Years); Founders $20,000 (5 Years).

Steeles Tavern

CYRUS H. MCCORMICK MEMORIAL MUSEUM, 128 McCormick Farm Circle, Steeles Tavern, VA 24476. Mailing Address: P.O. Box 100, Steeles Tavern, VA 24476-0100. Tel.: 540-377-2255. Fax: 540-377-5850.
E-mail: dafiske@vt.edu
Web Site: www.vaes.vt.edu/steeles/history.html
Founded: 1956.
Congressional District: 6
Key Personnel: Supt., David A. Fiske.
Governing Authority: university. Affiliated with Virginia Polytechnic Institute.
History Museum.
Collections: agriculture; McCormick reaper; c.1800 grist mill; replicas of first & subsequent reapers and mowing machines.
Facilities: picnic grounds.
Activities: permanent exhibitions.
Hours & Admission Prices: Daily 8-5. No charge. ♿
Attendance: 8,000 (estimated)

Stephens City

NEWTOWN HISTORY CENTER, (M), 5408 Main St., Stephens City, VA 22655-2829. Mailing Address: P.O. Box 143, Stephens City, VA 22655-0143. Tel.: 540-869-1700. Fax: 540-869-0400.
E-mail: info@newtownhistorycenter.org
Web Site: newtownhistorycenter.org
Formerly: Historic Stephensburg Museums
Founded: 1990.
Congressional District: 10
Key Personnel: Pres. (V), Linden A. Fravel; Dir. & Cur., Byron C. Smith; Treas., Julia S. Davidson; Mgr. Collections & Programs, Wayne A. Eldred.
Personnel Profile: Full-Time Paid 2; Part-Time Volunteers 11.
Governing Authority: private; nonprofit organization. Parent Institution: Stone House Foundation. Tax-exempt: 501(c)(3).
History Museum.
Collections: lower Shenandoah Valley history for prehistoric to modern times; history of Stephens City, VA from early settlement to Civil War.
Research Fields: freight wagons of the Shenandoah Valley; local African American history.
Facilities: 260-vol. library; classrooms; 3,416 sq. ft. exhibit space. Museum-related items for sale.
Activities: lectures; guided tours; study clubs. Annual Event: Newtown Heritage Festival.
Publications: quarterly newsletter, Museum Musings.
Hours & Admission Prices: June-Aug. Tues.-Sat. 10-4, Sun. 1-5; Sept.-Nov. Wed.-Sat. 10-4, Sun. 1-5; Dec.-May by appointment. Adults $2, students & children over 6 $1; discount to families; members no charge. Closed New Year's Day; Martin Luther King Jr. Day; Presidents' Day; Good Friday; Labor Day; Columbus Day; Thanksgiving & day after; Christmas Eve & Day .
Attendance: 1,460 (accurate)
Membership: Individual $10; Family $25; Contributing $55; Supporting $100; Sustaining $200; Patron $500.

Sterling

HERITAGE FARM MUSEUM OF LOUDOUN COUNTY, (M), 21668 Heritage Farm Lane, Sterling, VA 20164-9207. Tel.: 571-258-3800. Fax: 571-258-3801.
E-mail: mary.novotny@loudoun.gov
Web Site: www.heritagefarmmuseum.org
Founded: 1999.
Congressional District: 10
Key Personnel: Pres. (V), Su Webb; Mgr., Mary Novotny; Cur., Katherine Jones.
Personnel Profile: Full-Time Paid 4; Full-Time Volunteers 4; Part-Time Volunteers 172; Interns 3.
Governing Authority: private; nonprofit organization. Parent Institution: County of Loudoun. Subsidiary Institution: Loudoun Heritage Farm Museum, Inc.; Parks Recreation & Community Svcs. Tax-exempt: 501(c)(3).
Agriculture Museum.
Collections: agricultural implements & machinery; livestock; gardening; horticulture; early 20th century general store items.
Major Exhibits: Kitchesn on the Farm, 1/10-12/10; Maps of Loudoun, 1/10-12/10.
Research Fields: agriculture; history of Loudoun County.
Facilities: 200-vol. library; 7,500 sq. ft. exhibit space; classroom; 30-seat theater. Museum-related items for sale.
Activities: docent program; formal education programs for children & Northern Virginia Community College students; hobby workshops; livestock interactive animal programming; guided tours; loan, temporary & participatory exhibits; theater.
Publications: quarterly newsletter, The Windmill.
Hours & Admission Prices: Tues.-Sat. 10-5, Sun. 12-5. Adults $5, senior citizens $4, children $3; discount to groups, AAM & ACHFAM members. Closed New Year's; Christmas. ♿
Attendance: 16,400 (accurate)
Membership: Student $15; Individual $25; Family $50; Thresher $250; Sower $500; Reaper $1,000; Harvester $5,000.

Strasburg

CRYSTAL CAVERNS AT HUPP'S HILL HISTORIC PARK, 33231 Old Valley Pike, Strasburg, VA 22657-3715. Tel.: 540-465-5884.
E-mail: wayside@shentel.net
Web Site: www.crystalcavernsofva.com
Founded: 1998.
Key Personnel: C.E.O., Babs B. Funkhouser; Pres. (V), Ami Aronson.
Personnel Profile: Full-Time Paid 1; Part-Time Paid 3.
Governing Authority: public; nonprofit foundation. Parent Institution: Wayside Foundation, Strasburg, VA. Tax-exempt: 501(c)(3).
Geology Museum: housed in the first discovered cave in Virginia.
Collections: historical cavern artifacts; calcite crystals; cave drawings from Archaic Indian culture (on cave ceiling).
Research Fields: endangered species of amphipods & bats; historical use of caves.
Facilities: nature center; 200 sq. ft. exhibit space; walking trail. Museum-related items for sale.
Activities: formal education programs for children; guided tours; lantern tours. Museum Sponsors: living history events.
Publications: quarterly newsletter, By The Wayside.
Hours & Admission Prices: Daily 11-4. Adults $10, senior citizens, students, government, military, police, fire & rescue with ID; children $8; discounts to AAM & ICOM members. Closed New Year's Eve & Day; Easter; Thanksgiving; Christmas Eve & Day.
Attendance: 8,000 (estimated)

STONEWALL JACKSON MUSEUM AT HUPP'S HILL HISTORIC PARK, 33229 Old Valley Pike, Strasburg, VA 22657-3715. Tel.: 540-465-5884.
E-mail: wayside@shentel.net
Web Site: www.stonewalljacksonmuseum.org
Founded: 1991.
Key Personnel: C.E.O., Babs B. Funkhouser; Pres. (V), Ami Aronson.
Personnel Profile: Full-Time Paid 1; Part-Time Paid 3; Part-Time Volunteers 5.
Governing Authority: public; nonprofit foundation. Parent Institution: Wayside Foundation, Strasburg, VA. Tax-exempt: 501(c)(3).
History Museum.
Collections: Civil War artifacts from 1862-1864 Shenandoah Valley Campaigns; military & civilian artifacts; hands-on reproductions; children's hands-on room; 1864 infantry & artillery trenches.
Research Fields: military & civilian life during the Civil War; Black & Indian soldiers during the Civil War.
Facilities: 250-vol. library; 4,000 sq. ft. exhibit space; nature center. Museum-related items for sale.
Activities: formal education programs for children; guided tours; lectures; participatory exhibits; school loan service; living history events; children's participatory camp.
Publications: quarterly newsletter, By The Wayside.
Hours & Admission Prices: Daily 10-5. Adults $5, seniors, students, government, military, police, fire & rescue with ID & children $4; discounts to AAM & ICOM members; members no charge. Closed New Year's Day; Easter Sunday; Thanksgiving Day; Christmas Eve & Day. ♿
Attendance: 8,000 (estimated)

Membership: Senior Citizen $10; Individual $15; Family $20.

STRASBURG MUSEUM, 440 E. King St., Strasburg, VA 22657-2433. Mailing Address: P.O. Box 333, Strasburg, VA 22657-0333. Tel.: 540-465-3175 & 3728.
E-mail: gastick@shentel.net
Web Site: csonner.net/museum.htm
Founded: 1970.
Congressional District: 7
Key Personnel: Pres., Gloria Stickley; Sec., John Adamson; Treas., Pat Clem; Museum Shop Mgr., Marguerite Hammock.
Personnel Profile: Part-Time Volunteers 75.
Governing Authority: nonprofit. Tax-exempt.
History Museum: housed in 1891 pottery factory.
Collections: local history; Shenandoah Valley agriculture & crafts; Strasburg pottery 1830-1910.
Facilities: Local craft items & history books for sale.
Activities: workshops; tours.
Publications: books, The Story of Strasburg, Virginia; A Strasburg Potter's Daughter; Strasburg Community Memories: A Pictorial Display in the Strasburg Museum.
Hours & Admission Prices: May-Oct. daily 10-4. Adults $3; members no charge. ♿
Attendance: 3,500 (estimated)
Membership: Individual $3; Family $7.50; Sustaining $20; Life $100.

Stratford

STRATFORD HALL, ROBERT E. LEE MEMORIAL ASSOCIATION, INC., 483 Great House Rd., Stratford, VA 22558-0001. Tel.: 804-493-8038. Fax: 804-493-0333.
E-mail: info@stratfordhall.org
Web Site: www.stratfordhall.org
Formerly: Stratford, Robert E. Lee Memorial Association, Inc.
Founded: 1929.
Congressional District: 1
Key Personnel: Exec. Dir., Paul C. Reber; Pres. (V), Carol B. Price; Asst. Exec. Dir., Jerome J. Jarecki; Dir. Research & Library Collections, Judith S. Hynson; Dir. Education, Kenneth M. McFarland; Dir. Mktg., Jim Schepmoes; Cur., Gretchen Goodell; Plantation Store Mgr., Janet Branson.
Personnel Profile: Full-Time Paid 30; Part-Time Paid 63; Part-Time Volunteers 20; Interns 6.
Governing Authority: nonprofit organization. Tax-exempt: 501(c)(3).
Historic Site & General Museum: housed in 1738 Stratford Hall with operating plantation.
Collections: 18th- & 19th-century decorative arts; furniture, silver, ceramics, textiles, portraits & prints; archaeology artifacts; rare books & manuscripts; archives.
Research Fields: American history; 18th-century life.
Facilities: 8,000-vol. library of Virginiana available for research only; visitor center with museum; introductory & interactive videos; plantation store; seven original & eight reconstructed plantation buildings; operating grist mill; gardens; dining room.
Activities: guided tours; lectures; mill demonstrations; films; inter-museum loan, permanent & temporary exhibitions; elementary & secondary educational programs; seminars; conferences; archaeology field school; nature trails.
Publications: handbook; archaeology book; Paul Buchanan: Stratford Hall and other Architectural Studies; Robert E. Lee: Commemorative Essays on the Bicentennial of His Birth.
Hours & Admission Prices: Daily 9:30-4. Dining Room: Tues.-Sat. 11-3. Adults $10, senior citizens 60 & over, AAA members, groups of 20 or more, servicemen with valid ID $9, children 6-11 $5; discounts to the National Trust for Historical Preservation members & AAM members; children under 6, friends of Stratford members & Virginia Assoc. of Museum members no charge. Closed New Year's Eve & Day; Thanksgiving; Christmas Eve & Day. ♿
Attendance: 31,277 (accurate)
Membership: Friends of Stratford, various categories starting at $35.

Suffolk

RIDDICK'S FOLLY HOUSE MUSEUM, 510 N. Main St., Suffolk, VA 23434. Tel.: 757-934-0822. Fax: 757-934-0822.
E-mail: rfcurator@verizon.net
Web Site: www.riddicksfolly.org
Founded: 1978.
Congressional District: 4
Key Personnel: Pres., James E. Butler, III; Cur. & Museum Shop Mgr., Edward L. King; Cur., Lee King.
Personnel Profile: Part-Time Paid 1; Part-Time Volunteers 35.
Governing Authority: nonprofit. Tax-exempt: 501(c)(3).
Historic House Museum: built in 1837 Greek revival home of the Riddick family which was commandeered by the Union army as a headquarters during the occupation of Suffolk.
Collections: Riddick family items; Suffolk history; Empire period furniture & decorative arts; Gov. Mills E. Godwin, Jr. memorabilia; Civil War artifacts.
Research Fields: Riddick family history; Suffolk history; 19th century American south.
Facilities: 1,165 sq. ft. exhibit space; multipurpose room. Books, artwork by local artists & craftsmen, brass reproductions & other items for sale.
Activities: guided tours; lectures; organized educational programs; temporary & traveling exhibitions; changing exhibits in art & history.
Publications: quarterly newsletter.
Hours & Admission Prices: Wed.-Fri. 10-5, Sat. 10-4, Sun. 1-5; groups by appointment. Adults $4, seniors 55 & over and active military $3, children 3-12 $2. Closed New Year's Day; Easter; Independence Day; Thanksgiving; Christmas. ♿
Attendance: 4,000 (estimated)
Membership: Student $10; Individual $15; Family $25; Associate $50; Sustainer $100; Patron $250; Fellow $500.

THE SUFFOLK MUSEUM, 118 Bosley Ave., Suffolk, VA 23434-5755. Tel.: 757-514-7284. Fax: 757-538-0833.
E-mail: nkinzinger@city.suffolk.va.us
Founded: 1986.
Congressional District: 4
Key Personnel: Dir., Nancy Kinzinger.
Personnel Profile: Full-Time Paid 1; Full-Time Volunteers 2; Part-Time Paid 2; Part-Time Volunteers 5; Interns 1.
Governing Authority: municipal; nonprofit. Parent Institution: City of Suffolk. Tax-exempt: 501(c)(3).
Art Museum.
Collections: paintings; sculpture; photographs.
Research Fields: related to exhibitions.
Facilities: 3,000 sq. ft. exhibit space; educational studio room.
Activities: guided tours; lectures; concerts; theater; hobby workshops; organized education programs; participatory, loan & traveling exhibitions; demonstrations; classes.
Publications: quarterly newsletter; monthly exhibition program.
Hours & Admission Prices: Tues.-Sat. 10-5, Sun. 1-5. No charge. Closed New Year's Day; Lee-Jackson-King Day; Washington's Birthday; Easter; Memorial Day; Independence Day; Labor Day; Veterans Day; Thanksgiving; Christmas. ♿
Attendance: 18,000 (accurate)

SUFFOLK SEABOARD STATION RAILROAD MUSEUM, 326 N. Main St., Suffolk, VA 23434. Mailing Address: P.O. Box 1255, Suffolk, VA 23439-1255. Tel.: 757-923-4750. Fax: 757-923-4751.
Historic Building: housed in a former railroad station; built in 1885.
Collections: local history; railroad memorabilia; HO-scale model; caboose.
Facilities: Museum-related items for sale.
Hours & Admission Prices: Thurs.-Sat. 10-4, Sun. 1-4.

Surry

CHIPPOKES FARM & FORESTRY MUSEUM, (M), 868 Plantation Rd., Surry, VA 23883-2406. Tel.: 757-294-3439. Fax: 757-294-3550.
Founded: 1990.
Congressional District: 4
Key Personnel: Pres. (V), Sen. Frederick M. Quayle; Exec. Dir., Linda Guntharp; Museum Shop Mgr., Sarah Cosby.
Personnel Profile: Full-Time Paid 2; Part-Time Paid 6.
Governing Authority: nonprofit organization. Parent Institution: Chippokes Plantation Farm Foundation. Tax-exempt: 170(b)(1)(A).
Farm & Forestry Museum: housed in series of buildings, two of which are historically significant, at Chippokes Plantation State Park.
Collections: period farm & forestry equipment; tools; housewares.
Major Exhibits: Steam & Gas Engine Festival, 6/5/10-6/6/10.
Activities: guided tours; steam & gas engine show.
Publications: annual newsletter, Plantation Quarterly; calendar of events.
Hours & Admission Prices: April-Oct. Mon. & Wed.-Fri. 10-3, Sat. 10-5, Sun. 12-5. No charge. Fee for special events. ♿
Attendance: 8,408 (accurate)

SMITH'S FORT PLANTATION, 217 Smith's Fort Lane, Rte. 31 (halfway between Jamestown Ferry & Surry C.H.), Surry, VA 23883. Mailing Address: Box 240, Surry, VA 23883-0240. Tel.: 757-294-3872. TDD: 757-294-3872.
Web Site: www.apva.org/smithsfort
Founded: 1925.

Congressional District: 4
Key Personnel: C.E.O., Elizabeth Kostelny; Dir., A. Kent Harrell; Mgr., Thomas Forehand.
Personnel Profile: Part-Time Paid 4.
Governing Authority: nonprofit organization. Parent Institution: Association for the Preservation of Virginia Antiquities, Cole Diggs House, 204 W. Franklin St., Richmond, VA 23220-5091. Tel. 804-648-1889. Tax-exempt.
Historic House Museum: 17th-century fort site; earthworks remain of fort started in 1609 by Capt. John Smith; property a dower gift in 1614 from Powhatan to John Rolfe & Pocahontas; 18th-century brick dwelling a Faulcon family property 1754-1835.
Collections: Indian artifacts; 17th- to 18th-century furnishings; formal boxwood garden.
Research Fields: 17th- to 18th-century colonial Virginia history.
Facilities: picnic.
Activities: guided tours.
Hours & Admission Prices: March & Nov. Sat.-Sun. 12-5; April-Oct. Wed.-Sun. 12-5. Adults $8, AAA members $7, senior citizens $6, students $5, groups $4; children under 6 & APVA members no charge.
Attendance: 3,000 (estimated)
Membership: Individual $40; Family $60; Contributor $100; Sponsor $250; Benefactor $500.

SURRY NUCLEAR INFORMATION CENTER, 5570 Hog Island Rd., Surry, VA 23883. Tel.: 757-357-5410. Fax: 757-357-4711.
Web Site: www.dom.com
Science Museum.
Collections: hands-on exhibits on energy, electricity, & nuclear power.
Hours & Admission Prices: Mon.-Fri. 9-4. Closed major holidays.

Surry County

BACON'S CASTLE, 465 Bacon's Castle Trail, Surry County, VA 23883-2213. Mailing Address: A.P.V.A. 204 W. Franklin St., Richmond, VA 23220. Tel.: 757-357-5976; 804-648-1889. Fax: 804-775-0802.
Web Site: www.apva.org/baconscastle
Founded: 1665.
Congressional District: 4
Key Personnel: Exec. Dir., Elizabeth Kostelny; Pres. (V), John H. Guy, IV; Dir. Properties, Louis J. Macon; Cur., Catherine E. Dean; Museum Shop Mgr., Dorothy Somerset.
Personnel Profile: Part-Time Paid 7.
Governing Authority: nonprofit corporation. APVA Preservation Virginia, 204 W. Franklin St., Richmond, VA 23220. Tax-exempt 501(c)(3).
Historic Site & Historic House: 1665 Jacobean manor house used by Nathaniel Bacon's troops as a fortress during the rebellion against Royal Governor William Berkeley in 1676.
Collections: 17th- to 18th-century American & English decorative arts; restored 17th-century garden.
Research Fields: 17th- to 19th-century political, social & economic history; historical archaeology; horticultural history.
Publications: Bacon's Castle.
Hours & Admission Prices: March & Nov. Sat.-Sun. 12-5; April-Oct. Wed.-Sun. 12-5. Adults $8, seniors $7, students $5; children under 6 & APVA members no charge. Closed Independence Day.
Attendance: 5,188 (accurate)
Membership: Teacher & Student $25; Associate Individual Out-of-State $30; Associate Plus One $35; Individual In-State & Family Associate $40; Orgnizational & Plus One $50; Family $60.

Sweet Briar

SWEET BRIAR COLLEGE ART COLLECTION AND GALLERIES, (M), Sweet Briar College, Sweet Briar, VA 24595. Mailing Address: Pannell 208, Sweet Briar College, Sweet Briar, VA 24595. Tel.: 434-381-6248. Fax: 434-381-6489.
E-mail: klawson@sbc.edu
Web Site: www.artgallery.sbc.edu/
Founded: 1901.
Congressional District: 6
Key Personnel: Dir., Karol A. Lawson, Ph.D.; Chm. (V), Wendy C. Weiler; Registrarial Asst., Nancy McDearmon.
Personnel Profile: Full-Time Paid 1; Part-Time Paid 15; Part-Time Volunteers 25; Interns 5.
Governing Authority: college. Parent Institution: Sweet Briar College. Tax-exempt: 501(c)(3).
College Art Gallery.
Collections: 13th to 20th-century European & American paintings, drawings & prints; 18th & 19th-century Japanese prints; works by contemporary women.
Research Fields: 13th to 20th-century European & American art.
Facilities: 3 galleries; main exhibition space located in 1906 historic landmark building.
Activities: lectures; tours; children's classes; special exhibitions.
Publications: catalogues; annual newsletter of the Friends of Art, Visions.
Hours & Admission Prices: Sept.-May Mon.-Thurs. 10-5, Fri. 10-2, Sun. 1-4; Summer by appointment. No charge; donations accepted. Closed college breaks; reading days; exams. ♿
Attendance: 8,000 (accurate)
Membership: Friends of Art: Student $10; Regular $25; Family $50; Contributor $100; Sponsor $250; Benefactor $500; Patron $1,000.

SWEET BRIAR MUSEUM, Sweet Briar College, Boxwood Alumnae House, Sweet Briar, VA 24595. Mailing Address: P.O. Box F, Sweet Briar, VA 24595-1056. Tel.: 434-381-6246 & 6207. Fax: 434-381-6132.
E-mail: museum@sbc.edu
Web Site: www.museum.sbc.edu
Founded: 1980.
Congressional District: 6
Key Personnel: Dir., Christian Carr.
Personnel Profile: Full-Time Paid 1; Part-Time Paid 8; Interns 4.
Governing Authority: college; nonprofit organization. Parent Institution: Sweet Briar College. Tax-exempt.
College History Museum: housed in 19th-century National Register Tuscan revival Villa. Various collections housed in: Farm Tool Museum & Alumnae House, all located on Sweet Briar campus.
Collections: alumnae memorabilia, including class rings, china, photos; founding family items, including 19th-century clothing, furniture, jewelry, silver, lace, decorative arts & photos; college memorabilia; over 200 19th & 20th-century plantation farm tools housed in remaining slave cabin.
Research Fields: 19th-century decorative arts; history of plantation & college.
Facilities: 300-vol. library containing year books, alumnae publications & magazines for use on premises; President's mansion.
Activities: guided tours; lectures; organized education programs for undergraduate or graduate college students; temporary exhibitions; walking tours of Sweet Briar Arboretum & President's House.
Publications: brochures; flyers on farm tools; booklets on college history.
Hours & Admission Prices: Academic Year: Mon.-Fri. 10-5, call to confirm. No charge; donations accepted. ♿
Attendance: 5,000 (estimated)

Tangier Island

TANGIER HISTORY MUSEUM & INTERPRETIVE CULTURAL CENTER, 16215 Main Ridge, Tangier Island, VA 23440. Mailing Address: P.O. Box 182, Tangier, VA 23440-0182. Tel.: 302-234-1660.
Web Site: tangierhistorymuseum.org
Founded: 2008.
Key Personnel: Dir., Neil S. Kaye, M.D.; Museum Shop Mgr., Susan Kaye
History Museum.
Collections: island history & culture; photographs; period furnishings; personal artifacts.
Facilities: nature trails.
Hours & Admission Prices: Call for hours. No charge; donations accepted. ♿
Attendance: 15,000 (accurate)

Tappahannock

ESSEX COUNTY MUSEUM & HISTORICAL SOCIETY, 218 Water Lane, Tappahannock, VA 22560. Mailing Address: P.O. Box 404, Tappahannock, VA 22560-0404. Tel.: 804-443-4690.
E-mail: info@ccmhs.org
Web Site: www.essexmuseum.org
Founded: 1996.
Key Personnel: Pres., Priscilla Vaughen
Historical Society Museum.
Collections: County history & culture; personal artifacts; war memorabilia; photographs; Native American.
Hours & Admission Prices: Mon. & Thurs.-Sat. 10-3, Sun. 1-3.

Tazewell

HISTORIC CRAB ORCHARD MUSEUM & PIONEER PARK, INC., (M), Rts.19 & 460 at Crab Orchard Rd., 3663 Crab Orchard Rd., Tazewell, VA 24651-9200. Tel.: 276-988-6755. Fax: 276-988-9400.
E-mail: info@craborchardmuseum.com
Web Site: www.craborchardmuseum.com
Founded: 1978.
Congressional District: 9
Key Personnel: C.E.O. & Dir., Charlotte G. Whitted; Chm. (V), Martha Hurst; Dir. Museum Programs, I. Joan Yates; Museum Shop Mgr., Cindy Ringstaff; Cur., Cortney A. Honaker.

Personnel Profile: Full-Time Paid 5; Part-Time Paid 5; Part-Time Volunteers 180.
Governing Authority: nonprofit organization. Tax-exempt: 501(c)(3).
Historic Houses & Site: located on Big Crab Orchard Archaeological & Historic Site.
Collections: paleo, archaic, & woodland Indian artifacts; manuscripts; 19th-century log structures; furnishings; farming implements; blacksmith, cobbler, cooper & weavers' tools; clothing; Revolutionary & Civil War military equipment; medical instruments; horse-powered equipment; barn; period hand-woven textiles.
Research Fields: history & genealogy.
Facilities: 800-vol. library pertaining to local & regional history, reference on archaeological & genealogical resources, available for research on premises. Books, crafts & other museum-related items for sale.
Activities: guided tours; lectures; films; gallery talks; holiday festivals; reading room; formally organized educational programs; permanent & temporary exhibitions; living history outreach to school classes. Museum Sponsors: Skirmish at Jeffersonville Civil War reenactment; Tazewell County Old Time & Bluegrass Fiddler's Convention; Independence Day Celebration; Christmas on the Frontier.
Publications: quarterly newsletter, The Pisgah Pathfinder.
Hours & Admission Prices: Jan.-March Mon.-Fri. 9-5; April-May & Sept.-Dec. Mon.-Sat. 9-5; Memorial Day to Labor Day Mon.-Sat. 9-5, Sun. 1-5. Adults $4, senior citizens over 60 $3, children 6-12 $2; discounts to AAM, AAA, AARP & Time Travelers members; children under 6 & members no charge. Closed New Year's Day; Thanksgiving; Christmas. ♿
Attendance: 20,000 (accurate)
Membership: Students & Senior Citizens $25; Family $60; Sustaining $100; Patron $500; Benefactor $1,000.

The Plains

AFRO AMERICAN HISTORICAL ASSOCIATION OF FAUQUIER COUNTY, 4243 Loudoun Ave., The Plains, VA 20198-0340. Mailing Address: P.O. Box 340, The Plains, VA 20198-0340. Tel.: 540-253-7488. Fax: 540-253-5126.
E-mail: info@aahafauquier
Web Site: aahafauquier.org
Founded: 1992.
Key Personnel: Pres., Karen Hughes White; Vice Pres., Karen King Lavore.
Governing Authority: bd. of directors. Tax-exempt.
History Museum.
Collections: African American history; personal artifacts.
Publications: semiannual newsletters.
Hours & Admission Prices: Tues.-Wed. 10-3; other times by appointment. No charge; donations accepted. Closed holidays. ♿
Attendance: 2,188 (accurate)
Membership: Individual $25; Family $40; Nonprofit $50; Corporation $250; Lifetime $500.

Triangle

NATIONAL MUSEUM OF THE MARINE CORPS, 18900 Jefferson Davis Hwy., Triangle, VA 22172-1938. Tel.: 877-653-1775. Fax: 703-432-0029.
E-mail: info@usmcmuseum.org
Web Site: www.usmcmuseum.org
Founded: 2006.
Congressional District: 1
Key Personnel: Dir., Lin Ezell; Mgr. Visitor Svcs., Patrick Mooney.
Personnel Profile: Full-Time Paid 48; Part-Time Volunteers 205; Interns 12.
Governing Authority: Tax-exempt.
Military Museum.
Collections: military artifacts including WWII, Korean War & Vietnam; combat art.
Major Exhibits: In Plane View (T), 10/1/10-1/13/11.
Research Fields: military & US history; Marine Corps history.
Activities: hands-on activities; programs; classes. Museum Sponsors: Monthly Family Day.
Hours & Admission Prices: Daily 9-5. No charge; donations accepted. Closed Christmas. ♿
Attendance: 507,652 (accurate)

PRINCE WILLIAM FOREST PARK VISITOR CENTER, 18100 Park Headquarters Rd., Triangle, VA 22172-1644. Tel.: 703-221-7181 & 4706. Fax: 703-221-3258. TDD: 703-221-7181.
E-mail: prwi_info@nps.gov
Web Site: www.nps.gov/prwi
Founded: 1936.
Congressional District: 1, 10 & 11
Key Personnel: Asst. Supt., George Liffert; Chief Interpretation, Laura Cohen.
Personnel Profile: Full-Time Paid 1; Part-Time Paid 3; Part-Time Volunteers 3; Interns 1.
Governing Authority: federal. U.S. Dept. of Interior National Park Service. Tax-exempt.
Park Museum.
Collections: zoological, botanical & geological specimens; cultural history artifacts; 2000 BC-1940 AD archeological artifacts; photographs; maps; archival papers.
Research Fields: Civilian Conservation Corps 1933-1942; World War II U.S. Army Office of Strategic Services, 1942-1945; Cabin Branch Pyrite Mine 1889-1920.
Facilities: auditorium. Books for sale.
Activities: organized education programs; interpretive programs & walks; docent program; participatory exhibits.
Publications: park map.
Hours & Admission Prices: Daily 9-5. Seven Day Pass: $5 per vehicle, $3 per person; children under 16 & permanently disabled or blind persons no charge. Closed New Year's Day; Thanksgiving; Christmas. ♿
Attendance: 30,000
Membership: Daily & Weekly Pass $5; Annual Pass $20; National Parks Pass $50.

Vienna

MEADOWLARK BOTANICAL GARDENS, 9750 Meadowlark Gardens Ct., Vienna, VA 22182. Tel.: 703-255-3631.
Botanical Gardens.
Collections: native plants & wildflowers; cherry trees; irises; peonies.
Facilities: 96 acres; nature trails.
Activities: educational programs; workshops; concerts; tours.
Hours & Admission Prices: March & Oct. daily 10-6; April & Sept. daily 10-7; May daily 10-7:30; June-Aug. daily 10-8; Nov.-Feb. daily 10-5. Closed New Year's Day; Thanksgiving; Christmas.

Virginia Beach

ADAM THOROUGHGOOD HOUSE, 1636 Parish Rd., Virginia Beach, VA 23455-4401. Mailing Address: Francis Land House, 3131 Virginia Beach Blvd., Virginia Beach, VA 23452-6923. Tel.: 757-460-7588.
E-mail: mreed@vbgov.com
Founded: 1961.
Congressional District: 2
Key Personnel: Admin., Mark A. Reed.
Personnel Profile: Part-Time Paid 8; Part-Time Volunteers 10.
Governing Authority: municipal. Parent Institution: City of Virginia Beach, VA-Dept. of Museums and Cultural Arts, 717 General Booth Blvd., Virginia Beach, VA 23451. Tax-exempt: 501(c)(3).
Historic House: c.1680 Southern modified hall & parlor, one & one-half story brick structure located on the Grand Patent of 1636 which is part of the original land grant given to Adam Thoroughgood.
Collections: late 17th & early 18th century English artifacts including furniture, ceramics & pewter.
Research Fields: local history; American, French & English decorative arts.
Facilities: 17th-century garden. Museum-related items for sale.
Activities: guided tours; lectures; concerts; hobby workshops; organized education programs; docent program.
Publications: brochures.
Hours & Admission Prices: Closed for renovations until 2010.
Attendance: 6,899 (accurate)

ATLANTIC WILDFOWL HERITAGE MUSEUM, 1113 Atlantic Ave., Virginia Beach, VA 23451-3503. Tel.: 757-437-8432. Fax: 757-437-9055.
E-mail: atlanticwildfowl@rcn.com
Web Site: www.awhm.org
Founded: 1995.
Key Personnel: Dir., Thomas P. Beatty; Chm. (V), Herbert Verhaagen; Museum Shop Mgr., Ann Smith.
Personnel Profile: Full-Time Paid 2; Part-Time Volunteers 15.
Governing Authority: private; nonprofit. Parent Institution: Back Bay Wildfowl Guild, Inc. Tax-exempt: 501(c)(3).
Wildfowl Museum: located in an 1895 three-story beach house on the Atlantic Ocean; an example of Queen Anne architecture.
Collections: concentration on waterfowl of the Atlantic Flyway; special emphasis on turn-of-the-century decoys; hunting paraphernalia; carving; boatbuilding demonstrations.
Research Fields: ecohistory of Back Bay & Currituck Sound; gunning clubs of the region.
Facilities: library; educational facilities. Museum-related items for sale.
Activities: docent program; formal education programs for adults; guided

tours; hobby workshops; lectures; participatory exhibits; school loan service. Annual Events: Mid-Atlantic Wildfowl & Wildlife Festival; Back Bay Birding Club.
Hours & Admission Prices: Memorial Day-Oct. 1 Mon.-Sat. 10-5, Sun. 12-5; Oct. 2-May Tues.-Sat. 10-5, Sun. 12-5. No charge; donations accepted. Closed New Year's Day; Thanksgiving; Christmas. ♿
Attendance: 15,000 (accurate)
Membership: Individual $25; Family $35.

BACK BAY NATIONAL WILDLIFE REFUGE, 4005 Sandpiper Rd., Virginia Beach, VA 23456-4325. Tel.: 757-721-2412. Fax: 757-721-6141.
Wildlife Refuge.
Collections: wildlife & their habitats including ducks, snow geese, loggerhead sea turtles, piping plovers, peregrine falcons, & bald eagles.
Facilities: 9,000 acre refuge; nature trails.
Activities: educational programs.
Hours & Admission Prices: Refuge: daily dawn to dusk. Visitor Center: April-Nov. Mon.-Fri. 8-4, Sat.-Sun. 9-4; Dec.-March Mon.-Fri. 8-4, Sun. 9-4.

CAPE HENRY LIGHTHOUSE, 583 Atlantic Ave., Fort Story, Virginia Beach, VA 23459-1048. Mailing Address: 204 W. Franklin St., Richmond, VA 23220-5012. Tel.: 757-422-9421.
E-mail: oldcapehenry@aol.com
Web Site: www.apva.org/capehenry
Founded: 1791.
Congressional District: 2
Key Personnel: Exec. Dir. APVA, Elizabeth Kostelny; Pres. (V), John H. Guy, IV; Dir. Properties, Louis J. Malon; Site Coord., John Starling.
Personnel Profile: Full-Time Paid 1; Part-Time Paid 8; Part-Time Volunteers 10.
Governing Authority: nonprofit society. Parent Institution: APVA Preservation Virginia, 204 W. Franklin St., Richmond, VA. 23220.
Historic Building: 1791 first commissioned public works building in the United States, built near the monument marking the first landing of the Jamestown colonists.
Collections: local history; historic building.
Facilities: Museum-related items for sale.
Hours & Admission Prices: March 16-Oct. daily 10-5; Nov.-March 15 daily 10-4. Adults $4, children 3-12 $2; members & children under 3 no charge. Closed New Year's Eve & Day; Thanksgiving; Christmas Eve, Day & week after.
Attendance: 63,073 (accurate)
Membership: Teacher & Student $25; Out of State $30-$40; Individual $40; Plus One & Organization $50; Family $60; Century $100; Sponsor $250; Benefactor $500.

CONTEMPORARY ART CENTER OF VIRGINIA, (M), 2200 Parks Ave., Virginia Beach, VA 23451-4062. Tel.: 757-425-0000, ext. 0. Fax: 757-425-8186.
E-mail: kate@cacv.org
Web Site: www.cacv.org
Founded: 1952.
Congressional District: 2
Key Personnel: Dir., Debra C. Gray; Chm. Bd. Trustees, Randy Sutton; Exec. Asst., Jody Rose; Dir. Exhibitions & Education, Ragan Cole-Cunningham; Dir. Facilities Mktg., Irene Tavenner; Dir. Security, Louis Cross; Mgr. Accounting, Elaine Allen; Curatorial Asst., Monee Bengston; Dir. Operations, Kate Pittman; Dir. Devel., Amy Walton; Mgr. Gallery & Youth Programs, Holly Ackiss; Assoc. Cur. Education, Alison Byrne; Public Rels. Assoc., Erika Guess; Assoc. Cur., Heather Hakimzadeh; Devel. Assoc., Margie Donovan.
Personnel Profile: Full-Time Paid 19; Part-Time Paid 28; Part-Time Volunteers 445; Interns 2.
Governing Authority: private; nonprofit organization. Tax-exempt: 501(c)(3).
Art Museum, Center & School.
Collections: rotating traveling exhibitions.
Research Fields: contemporary art.
Facilities: classrooms; studios; auditorium.
Activities: lectures; gallery talks; arts festivals; formally organized educational programs; loan, permanent & traveling exhibitions; film festivals; performing arts.
Publications: quarterly newsletter; catalogues.
Hours & Admission Prices: Tues.-Fri. 10-5, Sat. 10-4, Sun. 12-4. Adults $7, seniors & military $5; discounts to AAM, ICOM & VAM members; members & children under 18 no charge. Closed New Year's Day; Thanksgiving; Christmas. ♿
Attendance: 517,000 (estimated)
Membership: Student, Senior, Military & Teacher $30; Individual $50; Student, Senior, Military & Teacher Household $55; Standard Household $65; Associate $125; Patron $250; Donor $500; Collector's Circle $1,250; Chairman's Circle $2,500.

FIRST LANDING STATE PARK, 2500 Shore Dr., Virginia Beach, VA 23451-1415. Tel.: 757-412-2320. Fax: 757-412-2315.
E-mail: firstlanding@dcr.virginia.gov
Web Site: www.virginiastateparks.gov
Founded: 1936.
Congressional District: 2
Key Personnel: District Mgr., Fred Hazelwood, IV; Park Mgr., Bruce Widener; District Program Specialist, Staci R. Martin; Chief Ranger & Interpreter, James Young; Volunteer Coord., Pam Kern.
Personnel Profile: Full-Time Paid 10; Part-Time Paid 35; Part-Time Volunteers 1,200; Interns 1.
Governing Authority: state. Parent Institution: Commonwealth of Virginia. Branch of First Landing State Park. Tel.: 757-412-2320. Tax-exempt.
Park Museum.
Collections: local Indian artifacts; leatherback sea turtle; great blue heron; brown pelican; osprey; great horned owl; screech owl; cormorants; Bald Cypress knees exhibit; children's touch table; first landing of English colonists on their way to Jamestown; Chesapeake Bay marine environment.
Facilities: 150-vol. library of reference books available in interpretive services office under supervision of park interpreter; slide programs; nature & conservation center; theater. Interpretive book sales area.
Activities: guided tours; lectures; films.
Publications: pamphlet, Bald Cypress Nature Trail; Birds of First Landing State Park; Checklists of Species.
Hours & Admission Prices: April-Nov. daily 9-4. No charge. Parking: Mon.-Fri. $4, Sat.-Sun. $5. Annual parking passes available. ♿
Attendance: 1,600,000 (estimated)

FRANCIS LAND HOUSE HISTORIC SITE, (M), 3131 Virginia Beach Blvd., Virginia Beach, VA 23452-6923. Tel.: 757-385-5100 & 5104.
E-mail: mreed@vbgov.com
Web Site: www.vbgov.com
Founded: 1986.
Congressional District: 2
Key Personnel: Chm. (V) Admin., Mark Reed; Museum Educator II, Nora Jean Corillo; Museum Educator II, Starr D. Donlon.
Personnel Profile: Full-Time Paid 4; Part-Time Paid 3; Part-Time Volunteers 85.
Governing Authority: municipal. City of Virginia Beach, 717 General Booth Blvd., Virginia Beach, VA 23451. Subsidiary Institution: Dept. of Museums and Cultural Arts. Tax-exempt.
Historic Site & House: late 18th-early 19th century brick plantation home of gentry-class planters, built by later generation of Land family.
Collections: period furnishings.
Research Fields: Land family; 18th century history of Virginia Beach; material culture of gentry class plantation; agricultural methods; slavery & African-American history.
Facilities: meeting rooms; wedding & banquet facilities available; herb garden; 18th century vegetable garden; park & trail. Museum-related items for sale.
Activities: guided tours; lectures; concerts; organized educational programs; docent programs; training programs for professional museum workers; participatory exhibits; textile programs including flax growing & processing. Museum Sponsors: 12th Night interpretive program in January.
Publications: brochure; quarterly newsletter, The Francis Land House.
Hours & Admission Prices: Tues.-Sat. 9-5, Sun. 11-5. Adults $5, senior citizens $4, students 6 & over $3; discounts to groups, AAM & VAM members; members no charge. Closed most major holidays. ♿
Attendance: 13,807 (accurate)
Membership: Individual $15; Family $20; Contributing $25; Sustaining $50; Patron $100; Corporate $250; Life $500.

LYNNHAVEN HOUSE, 4405 Wishart Rd., Virginia Beach, VA 23455. Mailing Address: 4401 Wishart Rd., Virginia Beach, VA 23455-5524. Tel.: 757-431-4000.
E-mail: apva@apva.org
Web Site: www.apva.org
Founded: 1976.
Congressional District: 2
Key Personnel: C.E.O. (APVA), Elizabeth Kostelny; Chm. (V), William Chitty; APVA & Chm. Finance Committee (V), David Sparks; Chm. (V), Rosemary Wilson; Admin., Shirley S. Bueche; Museum Shop Mgr., Peggie Everett.
Personnel Profile: Part-Time Paid 3; Part-Time Volunteers 35.
Governing Authority: nonprofit society. Parent Institution: Association for the

Preservation of Virginia Antiquities, 204 W. Franklin St., Richmond, VA 23220-5091. Subsidiary Institution: Southeastern Branch. Tax-exempt.
Historic House: preserved c.1725 brick dwelling, that is an example of early 18th-century eastern Virginia vernacular architecture.
Collections: household furnishings.
Facilities: graveyard; herb garden; colonial garden; 3 flower beds indigenous to the time & area. Museum-related items for sale.
Activities: tours; school programs, on-site & at schools; special school tours; craft & skill demonstrations; music programs; Civil War encampments; 2 colonial experiences-hands on camps for kids; 2 drama camps. Museum Sponsors: Revolutionary encampment in May; medieval days in September; Craft Show in November; Christmas open house in December.
Publications: brochure, Lynnhaven House; docent handbook; schedule of annual special events.
Hours & Admission Prices: May-Oct. Tues.-Sat. 10-4, Sun. 12-4; extended hours for special events. Adults $4, seniors $3, children 6-18 $2; discount to groups & Time Travelers; children under 5 & APVA members no charge.
Attendance: 3,510 (accurate)
Membership: Teacher & Student $25; Assoc. Individual $30; Assoc. Individual Plus One $35; Individual & Assoc. Family $40; Individual Plus One $50; Family $60; Century $100; Sponsor $250; Benefactor $500.

MILITARY AVIATION MUSEUM, 1341 Princess Anne Rd., Virginia Beach, VA 23457-1542. Tel.: 757-721-7767. Fax: 757-497-8083.
Web Site: www.militaryaviationmuseum.org
Founded: 2006.
Key Personnel: Dir., David Hunt.
Personnel Profile: Full-Time Paid 2.
Governing Authority: Tax-exempt.
Military Aviation Museum.
Collections: World War II warbirds; World War I aircraft replicas.
Research Fields: historical aviation.
Activities: monthly special events; guest speakers; flight demonstrations. Annual Event: Air Show in May.
Publications: quarterly members newsletter.
Hours & Admission Prices: Daily 9-5. Adults $10; discounts to active military & groups; WWII veterans & members no charge. Closed Thanksgiving; Christmas. ♿
Attendance: 10,000 (estimated)
Membership: Individual $50; Family $80.

VIRGINIA AQUARIUM & MARINE SCIENCE CENTER, 717 General Booth Blvd., Virginia Beach, VA 23451-4811. Tel.: 757-385-FISH (24 hour recording) & 385-7777 (office). Fax: 757-437-4976.
E-mail: fish@virginiaaquarium.com
Web Site: www.virginiaaquarium.com
Founded: 1986.
Congressional District: 2
Key Personnel: C.E.O., Lynn Clements; Pres. Virginia Aquarium Foundation, Dorcas Helfant-Browning; Deputy Dir., Stanley Burchfield; Controller, Donna Ellis; Dir. Devel., Russell Turner; Dir. Research & Conservation, Mark Swingle; Dir. Education, Chris Witherspoon; Dir. Exhibits, Maylon White; Dir. Retail Operations, Ruth Ann Steenburgh; Dir. Mktg., Linda Candler; Public Rels. Mgr., Joan Barns; Volunteer Resources Mgr., Kathleen Reed.
Personnel Profile: Full-Time Paid 76; Part-Time Paid 45; Part-Time Volunteers 916; Interns 15.
Governing Authority: city; nonprofit organization. Tax-exempt: 501(c)(3).
Marine Science Center & Aquarium.
Collections: 800,000 gallons of aquariums; 360 interactive exhibits; 12,000 live animals & their habitats representing over 700 species; two touch pools.
Research Fields: sea turtle conservation; marine animal strandings & rehabilitation.
Facilities: 1/3 mile nature trail; Virginia native gardens; aviary with 30 species; 300-seat 3D IMAX theater; classrooms; 800,000 gallons of aquariums; 88-seat interactive theater; restaurant; traveling ocean in motion truck. Aquarium-related items for sale.
Activities: K-12 curriculum-based school program; daily floor programs including fish feedings, lectures, field trips & craft programs for adults & children; touch pool; interactive exhibits; ocean collection & coastal explorer pontoon boat trips; traveling ocean in motion truck; whale & dolphin watching; teacher in-services; graduate & undergraduate courses; volunteer program; marine animal stranding program; changing exhibits; harbor seal splash encounter program; harbor seal & sea turtles behind the scenes programs.
Publications: bimonthly members newsletter, SeaBrowser; quarterly volunteer newsletter, Owls Creek Gazette; quarterly newsletter from the Virginia Aquarium Stranding Response Program, Strandlines; marine science information pamphlets; K-12 curriculum packages; educational resource guide; program brochures.
Hours & Admission Prices: Memorial Day to Labor Day daily 9-6; Sept.-May daily 9-5. Aquarium: adults $17, senior citizens 62 & over $16, children 3-11 $12. IMAX Film: adults $8.50, senior citizens $8, children $7.50. Aquarium & IMAX Film: adults $23, senior citizens $22, children 3-11 $18; discounts to groups, active duty military & aquarium members; children 2 & under no charge. Closed Thanksgiving; Christmas. ♿
Attendance: 622,000 (estimated)
Membership: Otter $75; Crab $100; Hedgehog $150; Stingray $275; Seal $500.

VIRGINIA BEACH MARITIME MUSEUM, INC./THE OLD COAST GUARD STATION, (M), 24th St. & Atlantic Ave., Virginia Beach, VA 23451. Mailing Address: P.O. Box 1035, Virginia Beach, VA 23451-0035. Tel.: 757-422-1587. Fax: 757-491-8609.
E-mail: FTylerVB2@aol.com
Web Site: www.oldcoastguardstation.com
Founded: 1981.
Congressional District: 2
Key Personnel: Exec. Dir., Fielding L. Tyler; Pres. Bd. Directors, Kimberly Goold; Pres. (V), Bill Mereno; Admin. Dir. & Museum Store Mgr., Julie J. Pouliot; Dir. Education, Volunteers & Programs, Kathryn A. Fisher.
Personnel Profile: Full-Time Paid 3; Part-Time Paid 3; Part-Time Volunteers 60.
Governing Authority: nonprofit organization. Tax-exempt: 501(c)(3).
Maritime Museum: housed in 1903 former United States Life-Saving & Coast Guard Station.
Collections: ship models; photographs; maritime artifacts; audiovisual programs; uniforms.
Research Fields: shipwrecks off Virginia Coast; personal histories of the Surfmen; history of U.S. Life-saving Service & Coast Guard in Virginia.
Facilities: 500-vol. library pertaining to United States Life-Saving Service & Coast Guard history & related maritime topics available to researchers on premises. Nautical items, books, art, jewelry, children's corner, and nautical reproductions for sale.
Activities: guided tours; lectures; films; organized educational programs; docent program; participatory, loan, temporary & traveling exhibitions; special events. Museum Sponsors: Family Fun Day in April, June, July, & August; Beach Art Partners in April.
Publications: quarterly newsletter, The Keeper.
Hours & Admission Prices: Memorial Day to Sept. Mon.-Sat. 10-5, Sun. 12-5; Oct.-May Tues.-Sat. 10-5, Sun. 10-5. Adults $4, senior citizens & military $3, children 6-18 $2; discounts to AAM members; museum members & children under 6 no charge. Closed New Year's Eve & Day; Thanksgiving; Christmas.
Attendance: 16,000 (estimated)
Membership: Senior Citizen $15; Individual $25; Family $35; Associate $50; Sponsor $100; Friend $250; Patron $500; Benefactor $1,000.

Wallops Island

NASA WALLOPS VISITOR CENTER, Bldg. J-17, Rte. 175, Wallops Island, VA 23337. Tel.: 757-824-2298.
Science Museum.
Collections: space science; solar system; photographs.
Facilities: theater.
Hours & Admission Prices: March-June & Sept.-Nov. Thurs.-Mon. 10-4; July to Labor Day daily 10-4; Dec.-Feb. Mon.-Fri. 10-4. No charge. Closed New Year's Day; Martin Luther King Jr. Day; President's Day; Columbus Day; Veterans Day; Thanksgiving; Christmas.

Warm Springs

BATH COUNTY HISTORICAL SOCIETY, Courthouse Hill Rd., Warm Springs, VA 24484. Mailing Address: P.O. Box 212, Warm Springs, VA 24484-0212. Tel.: 540-839-2543. Fax: 540-839-2566.
E-mail: bathcountyhistory@tds.net
Web Site: www.bathcountyhistory.org
Founded: 1969.
Congressional District: 6
Key Personnel: Exec. Dir., A. Keene Byrd; Docent, Betsy B. Byrd; Pres. (V), Nell Carpenter; Vice Pres., Michael Wildasin.
Personnel Profile: Full-Time Paid 1.
Governing Authority: Tax-exempt: 501(c)(3).
Historical Society Museum.
Collections: Bath County history & culture from 1745 to present; photographs; clothing; historic buildings.
Hours & Admission Prices: Spring, Summer & Fall Wed.-Sat. 10-4; Winter: Fri.-Sat. 10-4. No charge; donations accepted. Researchers: $5 per day; residents & members no charge. ♿

Membership: Educators & Seniors $15; Individual $25; Professional $50.

Warrenton

BRENTMOOR: THE SPILMAN-MOSBY HOUSE, The John Singleton Mosby Museum Foundation, 33 N. Calhoun St., Warrenton, VA 20188. Mailing Address: John Singleton Mosby Museum Foundation, P.O. Box 146, Warrenton, VA 20188-0146. Tel.: 540-351-1600. Fax: 540-351-1648.
Historic House Museum: housed in the former home of Judge Edward Spilman, Judge James Keith, Colonel John Singleton Mosby, & U.S. Senator Eppa Hunton; 1859-1902. Listed on the National Register of Historic Places.
Collections: local history & culture; personal artifacts; photographs; period furnishings.
Facilities: Museum-related items for sale.
Activities: special events.
Hours & Admission Prices: Mon.-Fri. 9-5.

THE OLD JAIL MUSEUM, 10 Ashby St. Courthouse Sq., Warrenton, VA 20186. Mailing Address: P.O. Box 675, Warrenton, VA 20188-0675. Tel.: 540-347-5525.
E-mail: oldjailmuseum@erols.com
Web Site: www.fauquierhistory.org
Founded: 1964.
Congressional District: 10
Key Personnel: Dir., Frances Allshouse; Pres. (V), Richard Gookin.
Personnel Profile: Full-Time Paid 1; Full-Time Volunteers 2; Part-Time Paid 3; Part-Time Volunteers 5; Interns 2.
Governing Authority: society; nonprofit. Parent Institution: Fauquier Historical Society. Tax-exempt.
Local History Museum: housed in two buildings, 1808 jail and 1823 jail, the town's only existing jail until 1965.
Collections: Fauquier County history & Northern Virginia history; local artifacts; Civil War, World War I & II items; documents; photographs; kitchen items.
Facilities: limited library of materials available to the public for use on premises.
Activities: guided & self-guided tours; lectures; docent program; Time Travelers program participant.
Publications: biannual newsletter, News & Notes.
Hours & Admission Prices: Tues.-Sun. 10-4. No charge; donations accepted. Closed New Year's Day; Thanksgiving; Christmas.
Attendance: 9,145 (accurate)
Membership: Student $10; Basic $25; Family $35; Patron & Nonprofit $50; Sponsor $100; Corporate $100.

Warsaw

RICHMOND COUNTY MUSEUM, 5874 Richmond Rd., Warsaw, VA 22572. Mailing Address: P.O. Box 884, Warsaw, VA 22572. Tel.: 804-333-3607.
History Museum: housed in a two-story brick county jail; built in 1872.
Collections: county history & culture; early artifacts; photographs; personal artifacts.
Activities: educational programs.
Hours & Admission Prices: Feb. to mid-Dec. Wed.-Sat. 11-3; other times by appointment. No charge. Closed holidays.

Waverly

MILES B. CARPENTER MUSEUM, 201 Hunter St., Waverly, VA 23890-2631. Tel.: 804-834-2151 & 3327.
Founded: 1986.
Congressional District: 4
Key Personnel: Pres. (V) & Cur., Shirley S. Yancey; Financial Dir., Letha Olson; Archivist, Frances B. Gray; Devel. & Mktg., Thelma Wyatt; Sec., Beverly P. Hartz.
Governing Authority: nonprofit organization. Tax-exempt: 501(c)(3).
Folk Art Museum, Peanut & Wood Products Museums.
Collections: Miles Carpenter art & memorabilia; history of peanuts; peanut farm machinery; history of area timber operations.
Major Exhibits: Wood Carvings, 12/09-1/10; Black History, 2/10; Student Art-School Students, 3/10-4/10; Creations by Miles, 5/10-6/10; Oil Paintings, 7/10-8/10; Nimble Fingers (Quilting), 9/10-10/10; Harvest Time, 11/10; Ancestral Toys, 12/10.
Research Fields: folk art; peanuts.
Facilities: 185-vol. library; educational facilities; 2,689 sq. ft. exhibit space.
Activities: guided tours; lectures; films; concerts; arts festivals; theatre; formal education programs; docent program; temporary exhibitions of new artists. Annual Events: Cherry Blossom Time in March; Folk Art Festival in May; Peanut Harvest Time in November. ancestral toys December to January.
Publications: Cutting the Mustard.
Hours & Admission Prices: Thurs.-Mon. 2-5. No charge; donations accepted. ♿
Attendance: 6,000 (accurate)

Waynesboro

HUMPBACK ROCKS MOUNTAIN FARM & VISITOR CENTER, Blue Ridge Pkwy., Mile Post 5.9, Waynesboro, VA 24483. Mailing Address: 133 Whetstone Ridge Rd., Vesuvius, VA 24483-2113. Tel.: 540-377-2377 (Montebello Ranger Station). Fax: 540-377-6758.
Web Site: www.nps.gov/blri
Founded: 1939.
Congressional District: 6
Key Personnel: District Ranger, Bruce Bytnar; Interpretive Specialist, Randy Sutton; Supt. Blue Ridge Pkwy., Phil Francis; Admin. Tech., Susan Bryant.
Governing Authority: federal. Parent Institution: National Park Service, Dept. of Interior, Blue Ridge Pkwy., 200 Northwestern Bank Bldg., Asheville, NC 28807. Tax-exempt.
Park Museum: 1880-1900 pioneer mountain farm.
Collections: mountain life.
Research Fields: oral history; Southern Appalachian rural life.
Facilities: library pertaining to natural & cultural history. Museum-related items for sale.
Activities: participatory exhibits; living history cultural demonstrations.
Publications: general, natural & cultural history of Southern Appalachians.
Hours & Admission Prices: late April to Nov. 1 daily 9-5. No charge. ♿
Attendance: 150,000

P. BUCKLEY MOSS MUSEUM, 150 P. Buckley Moss Dr., Waynesboro, VA 22980. Tel.: 540-949-6476; 800-343-8643.
E-mail: mossmuseum@aol.com
Web Site: pbuckleymoss.com
Founded: 1989.
Key Personnel: Dir., Corrado Gabellieri; Pres., Jake Henderson; Museum Shop Mgr., Jo Cowherd.
Personnel Profile: Full-Time Paid 3; Part-Time Paid 20.
Governing Authority: Parent Institution: P. Buckley Moss Galleries Ltd.
Art Museum.
Collections: works by P. Buckley Moss.
Hours & Admission Prices: Summer: Mon.-Sat. 10-6, Sun. 12:30-5:30. Winter: call for hours. No charge. Closed holidays. ♿
Attendance: 19,056 (accurate)

West Point

CHELSEA PLANTATION, 874 Chelsea Plantation Lane, West Point, VA 23181. Tel.: 804-843-2386.
Historic House Museum; built in 1709.
Collections: local history; period furnishings; personal artifacts; photographs.
Hours & Admission Prices: Thurs.-Sun. 10-4:30; other times by appointment.

MATTAPONI INDIAN MUSEUM, 1271 Mattaponi Reservation Cir., West Point, VA 23181. Mailing Address: P.O. Box 255, West Point, VA 23181-0255. Tel.: 804-769-2229 & 2194.
Key Personnel: Dir., Gertrude Custalow
Native American Museum.
Collections: Mattaponi Indian life, culture & history; period artifacts.
Hours & Admission Prices: Sat.-Sun. 2-5. Admission $2.

Williamsburg

ABBY ALDRICH ROCKEFELLER FOLK ART MUSEUM, 326 W. Francis St., Williamsburg, VA 23185. Mailing Address: P.O. Box 1776, Williamsburg, VA 23187-1776. Tel.: 757-220-7554. Fax: 757-565-8804.
E-mail: museums@cwf.org
Web Site: www.colonialwilliamsburg.org/history/museums
Founded: 1957.
Congressional District: 1
Key Personnel: C.E.O. & Chm., Colin Campbell; Vice Pres. Collections & Museums, Ron Hurst; Dir., Richard Hadley; Cur., Barbara Luck; Museum Shop Mgr., Joanna Heitz; Education & Programs, Christina Westenberger; Exhibits Mgr., Jan Gilliam; Dir. Exhibitions, Richard Hadley.
Personnel Profile: Full-Time Paid 7; Part-Time Paid 3; Part-Time Volunteers 50.
Governing Authority: nonprofit organization. Parent Institution: Colonial Williamsburg Foundation. Tax-exempt: 501(c)(3) & 170(b)(1)(A).
Art Museum.
Collections: paintings; sculpture; drawings.
Major Exhibits: Seeing Stars in American Bedcovers, 1/10-4/10; Sidewalks to

Rooftops: Outdoor Folk Art, 1/10-12/10; We the People: Three Centuries of American Folk Portraits, 1/10-12/10; Exciting Expressions: Painted Furniture, 1/10-12/10; Conserving the Carolina Room, 1/10-12/10; Inspiration and Ingenuity: American Stoneware, 1/10-12/10; Down on the Farm: A Family-Fun Art Adventure, 1/10-12/10; Cross Rhythms: Folk Musical Instruments, 1/10-12/10; Material Witnesses: Quilts and Their Makers, 5/29/10-6/12.
Research Fields: American folk art.
Facilities: 242-seat auditorium; cafe.
Activities: live, musical, interactive, family & educational programs; tours.
Publications: Colonial Williamsburg; The Journal of the Colonial Williamsburg Foundation.
Hours & Admission Prices: Daily call for hours. Admission by Colonial Williamsburg Museum Ticket or other Colonial Williamsburg Pass. ♿
Attendance: 217,756 (accurate)

BASSETT HALL, 522 E. Francis St., Williamsburg, VA 23185-4207. Mailing Address: c/o Colonial Williamsburg Foundation, P.O. Box 1776, Williamsburg, VA 23187-1776. Tel.: 757-220-7453. Fax: 757-220-7173.
E-mail: museums@cwf.org
Web Site: www.colonialwilliamsburg.org/history/museums
Founded: 1979.
Congressional District: 1
Key Personnel: C.E.O. & Chm., Colin Campbell; Dir., Richard Hadley; Vice Pres. Museums & Collections, Ron Hurst.
Personnel Profile: Full-Time Paid 4; Part-Time Paid 3.
Governing Authority: nonprofit organization. Affiliated with the Colonial Williamsburg Foundation, Goodwin Bldg., Williamsburg 23187. Tel.: 804-229-1000. Tax-exempt: 501(c)(3).
Historic House Museum & Grounds: built in c.1753, purchased in 1800 by Burwell Bassett, nephew of Martha Washington, and acquired by the Rockefellers in the 1920s.
Collections: furnishings from the 1930s belonging to Mr. & Mrs. John D. Rockefeller, Jr.; American folk art; ceramics; textiles; decorative arts; garden; nature trails. Historic Structures: 18th-century house, kitchen outbuilding, dairy & smokehouse.
Research Fields: American folk art; decorative arts; history of the property & the individuals associated with it.
Facilities: orientation video; 585-acre site; garden; two self-guided nature trails.
Activities: guided tours; interactive family art programs; character interpreters.
Publications: guidebook, Bassett Hall: The Williamsburg Home of Mr. & Mrs. John D. Rockefeller, Jr.
Hours & Admission Prices: Wed.-Thurs. & Sat. call for hours. Admission by Colonial Williamsburg Museum Ticket or other Colonial Williamsburg Pass. ♿
Attendance: 34,006 (accurate)

* **COLONIAL WILLIAMSBURG, (M),** 134 N. Henry St., Williamsburg, VA 23185-4138. Mailing Address: P.O. Box 1776, Williamsburg, VA 23187-1776. Tel.: 757-229-1000 & 220-7286. Fax: 757-220-7702. TDD: 757-221-8939.
E-mail: mcottrill@cwf.org
Web Site: www.colonialwilliamsburg.org
Founded: 1926.
Congressional District: 1
Key Personnel: C.E.O. & Pres., Colin G. Campbell; Pres. Colonial Williamsburg Hospitality Group, John Hallowell; Sr. Vice Pres., Robert Taylor; Vice Pres. Collections & Museums, Ronald L. Hurst; Vice Pres. Research, James Horn; Vice Pres. Devel., Glenn Williams; Vice Pres. Sec. & Gen., John S. Bacon; Vice Pres. Products, Jim Easton.
Personnel Profile: Full-Time Paid 1,893; Part-Time Volunteers 900; Interns 2.
Governing Authority: nonprofit organization. Administered by The Colonial Williamsburg Foundation. Tax-exempt: 501(c)(3).
Art & History Museum District: an on-site preservation of the former capital of Virginia colony.
Collections: archaeology; archives; manuscripts; paintings; sculpture; graphics; decorative arts; costumes; folk art; history; military; music; textiles; transportation. Historic Buildings: over 400 buildings from 1693-1837.
Research Fields: 17th- & 18th-century social, cultural, architectural & decorative arts history of Tidewater, Virginia area.
Facilities: 55,000-vol. library of 17th- & 18th-century Virginia, Colonial & United States history; archival materials available for inter-library loan & research by special arrangement; 450-seat auditorium; theater; classrooms; restaurants. Reproduction & museum-related items for sale.
Activities: guided tours; lectures; films; gallery talks; concerts; drama; TV & radio programs; formally organized education programs for children, adults & undergraduate college students; permanent & temporary exhibitions. Foundation Sponsors: special weekend & monthly activities.
Publications: books; films; filmstrips; videotapes; recordings; CD's.
Hours & Admission Prices: Visitor Center: daily 8:45-5:45. Basic Ticket: adults $36, children 6-14 $18. Freedom Pass (annual): adults $49, children $24.50 (holders eligible for discount on evening programs). DeWitt Wallace Museum or Abby Aldrich Rockefeller Folk Art Museum: adults $9.95, children 6-17 $4.95. Annual Museums Pass to all three museums: adults $19.95, children $9.95; discounts to military, AAM & ICOM members & staff from other museums. ♿
Attendance: 780,000 (accurate)

DEWITT WALLACE DECORATIVE ARTS MUSEUM, 326 W. Francis St., Williamsburg, VA 23185. Mailing Address: P.O. Box 1776, Williamsburg, VA 23187-1776. Tel.: 757-220-7554. Fax: 757-565-8804.
E-mail: museums@cwf.org
Web Site: www.colonialwilliamsburg.org/history/museums
Founded: 1985.
Congressional District: 1
Key Personnel: C.E.O., Colin Campbell; Dir., Richard Hadley; Education, Patricia Balderson; Exhibition Design & Production, Richard J. Hadley; Exhibition Planning, Jan Gilliam; Vice Pres. Collections & Museum, Ron Hurst; Exhibition Conservation, Patty Silence; Registrar, Enice Glosson; Security, Barbara Banks; Programs, Mary Cottrill; Museum Shop Mgr., Joanna Heitz.
Personnel Profile: Full-Time Paid 13; Part-Time Paid 13; Part-Time Volunteers 61; Interns 2.
Governing Authority: private; nonprofit organization. Subsidiary Museum: Colonial Williamsburg Foundation, Williamsburg, VA. Tax-exempt.
Decorative Arts Museum.
Collections: British & American decorative arts from 1600-1830; furniture; metals; ceramics; glass; paintings; prints; maps; textiles.
Major Exhibits: Quilted Fashions, 1/10-8/10; Pounds, Pence and Pistarens: Coins and Currency in Colonial America, 1/10-12/10; Artistry and Ingenuity: Kitchen Equipment, 1/10-12/10; Revolution in Taste: An 18th-Century Array of Ceramic and Metal Tablewares, 1/10-12/10; Treasure Quest: Eighteenth-Century Silver and Their Collectors, 1/10-12/10; Identifying Ceramics: The Who, What and Ware, 1/10-12/10; Lock, Stock, and Barrel: Firearms, 1/10-12/10; Masterworks: Highlights of the Colonial Williamsburg Collections, 1/10-12/10; Declarations of Independence: Copies to Celebrate it's 50th Anniversary, 1/10-12/10; Pottery with a Past: Stoneware in Early America, 1/10-1/2/11.
Research Fields: decorative arts from 1600-1830.
Facilities: 240-seat auditorium; 62-seat cafeteria; 27,200 sq. ft. exhibit space. Museum-related items for sale.
Activities: musical concerts; docent program; formal education programs; guided tours; lectures; loan, temporary & traveling exhibitions; family programs.
Publications: Colonial Williamsburg; The Journal of the Colonial Williamsburg Foundation.
Hours & Admission Prices: Daily call for hours. Admission by Colonial Williamsburg Museum Ticket or other Colonial Williamsburg Pass. ♿
Attendance: 217,756 (accurate)

* **JAMESTOWN SETTLEMENT, YORKTOWN VICTORY CENTER, THE JAMESTOWN-YORKTOWN FOUNDATION, (M),** Rte. 31 S., Williamsburg, VA 23185. Mailing Address: P.O. Box 1607, Williamsburg, VA 23187-1607. Tel.: 757-253-4838 & 4840. Fax: 757-253-5299. TDD: 757-253-5110.
E-mail: laura.bailey@jyf.virginia.gov
Web Site: www.historyisfun.org
Founded: 1957.
Congressional District: 1
Key Personnel: Exec. Dir., Philip G. Emerson; Exec. Asst. to Bd., Laura W. Bailey; Deputy Exec. Dir. Administration, J. Jeffrey Lunsford; Sr. Dir. Museum Operations & Education, Joseph A. Gutierrez, Jr.; Sr. Dir. Mktg. & Retail Operations, Susan K. Bak; Dir. Museum Education Svcs., James S. Holloway; Dir. Outreach & Special Svcs., Pamela J. Pettengell; Curatorial Svcs. Mgr., Dr. Thomas E. Davidson; Human Resources Mgr., Debra P. Jarvis; Sr. Retail Operations Mgr., Gary T. Joyner; Chief Devel. Officer, Carter S. Sonders.
Personnel Profile: Full-Time Paid 190; Part-Time Paid 300; Part-Time Volunteers 1,000; Interns 20.
Governing Authority: state. Parent Institution: Commonwealth of Virginia. Subsidiary Institution: Jamestown-Yorktown Foundation, Inc. Tax-exempt.
History Museum.
Collections: 17th- to 18th-century Virginia archaeology; prehistoric Indian artifacts; 16th- to 18th-century English & American artifacts; military, medical objects, navigational instruments, domestic & decorative arts relating to the settling of Jamestown, the War of Independence & siege of Yorktown.
Major Exhibits: Werowocomoco: Seat of Power, 5/15/10-11/15/10.
Research Fields: 17th-century Jamestown & Virginia Indian history; colonial

history & culture; American Revolutionary War period; history of the town of York & Yorktown's sunken fleet.
Facilities: library, museum galleries & outdoor living history areas including recreation of a fort, Powhatan Indian village, Riverfront Discovery Area & 3 ships; Revolutionary War encampment; 1780s farmsite; theater & film at each museum. Museum-related gifts for sale.
Activities: guided tours for school groups; living-history demonstrations; crafts program; special programs; films for schools; outreach programs for schools.
Publications: Education Planner; Jamestown-Yorktown Foundation Facts/Annual Highlights; brochure, Special Programs; Group Tour Planner; periodical newsletter, Dispatch; brochures, Jamestown Settlement and Yorktown Victory Center; Jamestown Settlement Ships; Jamestown Settlement and Yorktown Victory Center Museum Guide; brochure, Commemoration Highlights; America's 400th Anniversary - Jamestown 2007 Steering Committee Report.
Hours & Admission Prices: Jamestown Settlement: June 15-Aug. 15 daily 9-6; Aug. 16-June 14 daily 9-5. Adults $14, children 6-12 $6.50. Yorktown Victory Center: June 15-Aug. 15 daily 9-6; Aug. 16-June 14 daily 9-5. Adults $9.50, children 6-12 $5.25. Combination: adults $19.25, children $9.25; discounts to groups & AAM members; museum members no charge. American Heritage Annual Pass: adults $35, children 6-12 $17.50; children 5 & under no charge. Closed New Year's Day; Christmas. ♿
Attendance: 692,086 (accurate)

* **MUSCARELLE MUSEUM OF ART, (M),** Lamberson Hall, College of William and Mary, 603 Jamestown Rd., Rm. 1, Williamsburg, VA 23185. Mailing Address: Lamberson Hall, College of William and Mary, P.O. Box 8795, Williamsburg, VA 23187-8795. Tel.: 757-221-2710. Fax: 757-221-2711.
Web Site: www.wm.edu/muscarelle
Founded: 1982.
Congressional District: 1
Key Personnel: Chm., Julian Fore; Dir., Aaron H. De Groft, Ph.D.; Asst. Dir. & Cur., Odilia Bonebakker; Asst. to Dir., Cindy Lucas; Registrar, Melissa M. Parris; Cur. Education, Amy Gorman, Ph.D.; Exhibitions & Operations Mgr., Kevin Gillian; Special Projects Admin., Ursula McLaughlin-Miller; Membership Mgr., Bronwen Watts.
Personnel Profile: Full-Time Paid 10; Part-Time Paid 3; Part-Time Volunteers 95; Interns 15.
Governing Authority: Parent Institution: College of William and Mary, Williamsburg, VA 23185. Tax-exempt.
Art Museum.
Collections: 16th- to 20th-century Western paintings, works on paper, sculpture & Asian, African, Islamic & American Contemporary art; Native American pottery; German expressionism.
Research Fields: 16th- to 20th-century European & American art.
Facilities: permanent & temporary exhibition galleries. Museum-related items for sale.
Activities: lectures; gallery talks; guided tours; docent program; school programs; loan, permanent & temporary exhibitions.
Publications: exhibition catalogs; bulletin.
Hours & Admission Prices: Tues.-Fri. 10-5, Sat.-Sun. 12-4. Special Exhibitions: adults $5; members no charge. Closed all major holidays; New Year's Eve & Day; Christmas Eve, Day & week. ♿
Attendance: 60,000 (estimated)
Membership: University Membership $40; Affiliate $75; Subscriber $125; Contributor $250; Supporter $500; Patron $1,000; Sustainer $2,500; Benefactor $5,000; Lamberson Circle $10,000; Muscarelle Circle $25,000.

PRESIDENTIAL PET MUSEUM, 211 Water Country Pkwy., Williamsburg, VA 23185-5827. Tel.: 757-259-1121; 800-588-4327.
E-mail: enewman@presidentspark.org
Web Site: www.presidentialpetmuseum.com
Founded: 2004.
Congressional District: 1
Key Personnel: C.E.O., Chm. & Pres., E. Haley Newman; Devel., Ginger Martus; Treas., Christie Applequist.
Governing Authority: Parent Institution: Presidential Pet Museum Assoc. Tax-exempt.
Presidential Pet Museum.
Collections: memorabilia & artifacts related to U.S. Presidents and their pets.
Facilities: 100-vol. library. Gift items for sale.
Activities: temporary exhibitions. Annual Events: Dog Show; Open House; Pet Expo.
Publications: newsletter.
Hours & Admission Prices: Jan 2-March 7 Tues.-Sun. 10-4; March 8-May 24 & Sept. 8-Dec. Tues.-Sun. 10-5; May 25-Sept. 7 Tues.-Sun. 9-7. Admission $12.75. Closed New Year's Day, Thanksgiving & Christmas. ♿
Attendance: 58,000 (accurate)

Membership: Founder $100 & up.

PRESIDENTS PARK, 211 Water Country Pkwy., Williamsburg, VA 23185-5827. Tel.: 757-259-1121; 800-588-4327.
Web Site: www.presidentspark.org
Founded: 2004.
Congressional District: 1
Key Personnel: C.E.O., Chm. & Pres., E. Haley Newman
History Museum.
Collections: United States history; 42 Presidential statues; 43 Presidential histories; personal artifacts.
Facilities: cafe. Museum-related items for sale.
Activities: tours.
Hours & Admission Prices: Jan 2-March 7 daily 10-4; March 8-May 24 & Sept. 8-Dec. daily 10-5; May 25-Sept. 7 daily 9-7. Admission $12.75. Closed New Year's Day, Thanksgiving & Christmas. ♿

THIS CENTURY ART GALLERY, 219 N. Boundary St., Williamsburg, VA 23185-3610. Mailing Address: P.O. Box 388, Williamsburg, VA 23187-0388. Tel.: 757-229-4949. Fax: 757-258-5624.
E-mail: thiscenturyartgallery@verizon.net
Web Site: www.thiscenturyartgallery.org
Formerly: The Twentieth Century Gallery
Founded: 1959.
Congressional District: 1
Key Personnel: Pres. (V), Michael Kirby; Vice Pres., Robert Zolad; Artistic Dir., Darrell Craig; Business Mgr., Charlene Zolad.
Personnel Profile: Part-Time Paid 2; Part-Time Volunteers 100.
Governing Authority: nonprofit organization. Parent Institution: Twentieth Century Art Gallery. Tax-exempt: 501(c)(3).
Art Gallery.
Collections: arts & crafts of contemporary artists.
Facilities: Arts & crafts for sale.
Activities: lectures; workshops; organized educational programs; participatory exhibits; monthly exhibits; mobile vans.
Publications: annual brochure; quarterly newsletter.
Hours & Admission Prices: Tues.-Sun. 11-5. No charge; donations accepted. Closed Thanksgiving; Christmas. ♿
Attendance: 4,800 (estimated)
Membership: Student $10; Individual $35; Family $50; Friends $100-$249; Sustainer $250-$499; Patron $500-$999; Benefactor $1,000 & up.

Winchester

SHENANDOAH VALLEY DISCOVERY MUSEUM, (M), 54 S. Loudoun St., Winchester, VA 22601-4720. Mailing Address: P.O. Box 239, Winchester, VA 22604-0239. Tel.: 540-722-2020. Fax: 540-722-2189.
E-mail: nwilson@discoverymuseum.net
Web Site: www.discoverymuseum.net
Founded: 1993.
Key Personnel: Exec. Dir., Margaret McKee; Chm., Phil Glaize; Dir. Programs, Jan Kirby; Dir. Mktg. & Devel., Niki Wilson; Business & Operations, Peggy Doerwaldt; Dir. Capital Campaign, Dee Dee Barbour; Gallery Mgr., Mark Lawson; Paleontologist, Geb Bennett; Dir. Exhibits, Martha Wolfe; Volunteer Coord. & Museum Shop Mgr., Sarah Gemmell.
Personnel Profile: Full-Time Paid 7; Part-Time Paid 3; Part-Time Volunteers 10.
Governing Authority: Tax-exempt.
Children's Discovery Museum.
Collections: fossils; dinosaurs; hands-on science, technology, culture, art & humanity exhibits.
Research Fields: paleontology in Hell Creek, Montana.
Activities: Museum Sponsors: Visiting Artist Series.
Publications: quarterly, Bright Ideas; biannual, Friends of Hell Creek.
Hours & Admission Prices: Mon.-Sat. 9-5, Sun. 1-5. Adults $6; discounts to ASTC, ACM, & AAA members; members no charge. Closed Federal holidays. ♿
Attendance: 39,805 (accurate)
Membership: Individual $25; Grandparent $65; Family $100; ACM Reciprocal $150.

WINCHESTER-FREDERICK COUNTY HISTORICAL SOCIETY, INC., 1340 S. Pleasant Valley Rd., Winchester, VA 22601-4447. Tel.: 540-662-6550. Fax: 540-662-6991.
E-mail: wfchs@verizon.net
Web Site: www.winchesterhistory.org
Founded: 1930.
Congressional District: 7
Key Personnel: Pres. & Dir., George R. Schember.
Personnel Profile: Full-Time Paid 1; Part-Time Paid 15; Part-Time Volunteers 5.

Governing Authority: society. Tax-exempt: 501(c)(3).
History Museum Complex.
Collections: furniture; artifacts; Civil War relics; manuscripts; early surveying instruments. Historic Houses: 1755-1756 George Washington's office; 1754 Abrams Delight; 1861-1862 Stonewall Jackson headquarters.
Research Fields: Civil War; Washington 1748-1758.
Facilities: Museum-related items for sale.
Activities: guided tours; meetings. Museum Sponsors: Washington's Birthday Celebration; Candlelight tour in December.
Publications: books, Men & Events of the Revolution; Civil War Battles in Winchester & Frederick County, VA. 1861-1865; Images of the Past; 1748-1758 George Washington & Winchester; What I Know About Winchester 1800-1891; Winchester-Frederick County Historical Society Journal, Vols. IV-XX.
Hours & Admission Prices: April-Oct. daily 10-4, Sun. 12-4. Abrams's Delight & Stonewall Jackson's Headquarters: adults $5, senior citizens $4.50, children $2.50. George Washington's Office: adults $5, children $1.75. Block Tickets: adults $12; members & children under 6 no charge.
Attendance: 16,000 (accurate)
Membership: Individual $30; Couple $40; Patron $100; Life Individual $500; Life Couple $700.

Wise

WISE COUNTY HISTORICAL SOCIETY, Wise County Courthouse, Rm 250, Wise, VA 24293. Mailing Address: P.O. Box 368, Wise, VA 24293-0368. Tel.: 276-328-6451 & 6569.
E-mail: wchs_133@yahoo.com
Web Site: www.wisevahistoricalsoc.org
Key Personnel: Pres. (V), William C. Gobble; Vice Pres., Denver J. Osborne; Treas., Wanda Rose; Sec., Dorothy Witt; Archivist, Fannie Steele
Historical Society.
Collections: over 5,000 items including books, manuscripts, old marriage records & photographs.
Hours & Admission Prices: Mon.-Thurs. 9-4, Fri. 9-12.

Woodstock

WOODSTOCK MUSEUM OF SHENANDOAH COUNTY, INC., 104 S. Muhlenberg St., Woodstock, VA 22664. Mailing Address: P.O. Box 741, Woodstock, VA 22664-0741. Tel.: 540-459-5518.
E-mail: info@thewoodstockmuseum.org
Web Site: thewoodstockmuseum.org/
Founded: 1969.
Congressional District: 7
Key Personnel: Pres., Robert Lowerre.
Personnel Profile: Part-Time Volunteers 20.
Governing Authority: nonprofit organization. Tax-exempt: 501(c)(3).
Local History Museum.
Collections: local history; manuscripts.
Research Fields: genealogy.
Facilities: archives room.
Activities: guided tours; lectures; permanent exhibitions.
Publications: books, Yesterday in Woodstock According to Fred Painter; Glimpses of the Past in the Shenandoah Valley; Early Woodstock.
Hours & Admission Prices: May-Oct. Thurs.-Sat. 12-4. No charge; donations accepted.
Attendance: 305 (accurate)
Membership: Single $25; Family $40; Business Supporter $50; Business Sponsor $100; Life $250.

Wytheville

THE EDITH BOLLING WILSON BIRTHPLACE, 145 E. Main St., Wytheville, VA 24382-2319. Tel.: 276-223-3484 & 228-8474. Fax: 276-228-5987.
Web Site: www.edithbollingwilson.org
Key Personnel: Dir., Leslie King.
Governing Authority: Parent Institution: The Edith Bolling Wilson Birthplace Foundation.
Historic House Museum: housed in the birthplace of First Lady Edith Bolling Wilson, the second wife of the 28th President of the United States, Woodrow Wilson.
Collections: life & history of Edith Bolling Wilson, her family & President Wilson; furniture; books; letters; paintings; photographs; personal artifacts; presidential artifacts.
Activities: Annual Event: Edith Bolling Wilson Birthday Celebration in October.
Hours & Admission Prices: Tues.-Sat. 10-5. No charge; donations accepted. Closed Thanksgiving; Christmas. ♿

ROCK HOUSE MUSEUM, (M), 205 Tazwell St., Wytheville, VA 24382-2313. Mailing Address: P.O. Drawer 533, Wytheville, VA 24382. Tel.: 276-223-3330. Fax: 276-223-3455.
E-mail: museum@wytheville.org
Web Site: museums.wytheville.org/museums.htm
Founded: 1970.
Congressional District: 9
Key Personnel: Museum Dir., Francis Emerson.
Personnel Profile: Full-Time Paid 1; Part-Time Paid 3; Part-Time Volunteers 30.
Governing Authority: nonprofit. Parent Institution: City of Wytheville Tax-exempt.
Historic House: 1823 home of Dr. John Haller, the first resident physician of Wytheville.
Collections: furniture; artifacts; memorabilia of Wytheville.
Research Fields: genealogy.
Facilities: library.
Activities: guided tours. Museum Sponsors: Christmas Open House.
Publications: quarterly newsletter, Wythe County Historical Review; brochure.
Hours & Admission Prices: April-Oct. Mon.-Fri. & 3rd Sat. of month 10-4, 1st Sun. of month 1-5; Nov.-March Mon.-Fri. & 3rd Sat. of month 10-4. One House: adults $4, children $2; children 5 & under no charge. Two Houses: adults $6, children 6-12 $3; children 5 & under no charge.
Attendance: 3,000 (estimated)
Membership: Individual $20; Family $35; Contributing $50; Life $300.

THE THOMAS J. BOYD, 295 Tazwell St., Wytheville, VA 24382. Mailing Address: P.O. Drawer 533, Wytheville, VA 24382-0533. Tel.: 540-223-3330. Fax: 540-223-3315.
E-mail: museums@wytheville.org/museums.htm
Web Site: museumswytheville.org/museums.htm
Key Personnel: Museum Dir., Frances Emerson.
Personnel Profile: Full-Time Paid 1; Part-Time Paid 3; Part-Time Volunteers 30.
Governing Authority: municipal. Town of Wytheville.
General History Museum.
Collections: children's museum; town's 1st fire truck; farming & mining equipment; Civil War exhibit.
Hours & Admission Prices: April-Oct. Mon.-Fri. & 3rd Sat. of month 10-4, 1st Sun. of month 1-5; Nov.-March Mon.-Fri. & 3rd Sat. of month 10-4. One House: adults $4, children $2; children 5 & under no charge. Two Houses: adults $6, children 6-12 $3; children 5 & under no charge.
Attendance: 3,000 (estimated)
Membership: Individual $20; Family $35; Sustaining $50; Life $300.

Yorktown

COLONIAL NATIONAL HISTORICAL PARK: JAMESTOWN & YORKTOWN, Colonial Pkwy. & Rte. 238, Yorktown, VA 23690. Mailing Address: P.O. Box 210, Yorktown, VA 23690. Tel.: 757-898-2416. Fax: 757-898-6346.
E-mail: colo_interpretation@nps.gov
Web Site: www.nps.gov/colo/
Founded: 1930.
Congressional District: 1
Key Personnel: Supt., P. Daniel Smith; Chief Historian, Karen Rehm; Cur. Jamestown, James Perry; Cur. Yorktown, David Riggs; Museum Shop Mgr., Brenda Cummins.
Personnel Profile: Full-Time Paid 82; Part-Time Paid 3; Part-Time Volunteers 150; Interns 4.
Governing Authority: federal. Parent Institution: National Park Service; U.S. Dept. of Interior, Washington DC 20240. Tax-exempt.
Historical Park: 1607-1781, first permanent English settlement at Jamestown Island & last major battle of American Revolution at Yorktown, VA.
Collections: 17th & 18th-century arms & artifacts on display at the Jamestown Museum & Yorktown Visitor Center; 18th-century Moore House & Nelson House.
Research Fields: 1607-1781 colonial American history.
Facilities: library of 17th & 18th century Virginia history; visitor centers; theaters. Books & museum-related items for sale.
Activities: guided tours; permanent exhibitions; informational & interpretive programs. Museum Sponsors: glass blowing demonstration at Glasshouse.
Publications: interpretive folders; handbooks, Jamestown & Yorktown.
Hours & Admission Prices: Yorktown: daily 9-5. Jamestown: daily 8:30-4:30. Yorktown & Jamestown: adult $10; children 16 & under no charge. Senior Interagency, Access Interagency & America The Beautiful passes honored. Closed New Year's Day; Thanksgiving; Christmas. ♿
Attendance: 3,100,000 (estimated)

GALLERY ON THE YORK - YORKTOWN ARTS FOUNDATION, 7907 George Washington Memorial Hwy., Yorktown, VA 23692-4857. Tel.: 757-898-3076.
Web Site: www.galleryontheyork.com
Formerly: On the Hill Cultural Arts Center
Founded: 1976.
Key Personnel: Chm. & Pres. (V), Gary Hess; Gallery Mgr., Brian Lobarr; Museum Shop Mgr., Helen C. Hughes.
Personnel Profile: Full-Time Volunteers 1; Part-Time Volunteers 25.
Governing Authority: nonprofit organization. Parent Institution: Yorktown Arts Foundation. Tax-exempt: 501(c)(3).
Art Center & Gallery.
Collections: original art & crafts by Virginia & North Carolina artists; pottery; crafts.
Facilities: educational facilities.
Activities: guided tours; lectures; films; concerts; arts festivals; organized educational programs; participatory & temporary exhibitions. Museum Sponsors: four juried art shows; Small Works; Fall Family Festival; photographic show, Aperture.
Publications: quarterly newsletter; program brochure.
Hours & Admission Prices: Tues.-Sat. 10-5, Sun. 1-4. No charge; donations accepted. Closed New Year's Day; Mother's Day; Thanksgiving; Christmas. ♿
Attendance: 8,000 (estimated)
Membership: Patrons & Nonparticipating Artists $35; Participating Artist $50.

WATERMEN'S MUSEUM, 309 Water St., Yorktown, VA 23690. Mailing Address: P.O. Box 519, Yorktown, VA 23690-0519. Tel.: 757-887-2641. Fax: 757-888-2089.
E-mail: admin@watermens.hrcoxmail.com
Web Site: watermens.org
Founded: 1980.
Congressional District: 1
Key Personnel: Pres., John Hanna; Mng. Dir., David Niebuhr; Vice Pres., Dick Lane; Sec., Jim Smith; Treas., Fred Malvin; Founder, Marian Hornsby Bowditch; Coord. Education, Kathryn Hanna; Public Rels., Jim Baumgardner; Asst. To Dir., Linda Myers; Museum Shop Mgr., Joan Karafa; Gift Shop Mgr., Tina McManus.
Personnel Profile: Full-Time Paid 1; Part-Time Paid 5; Part-Time Volunteers 100.
Governing Authority: nonprofit organization. Tax-exempt: 501(c)(3).
Seafood Industry Museum: housed in 1935 Colonial Revival house & outbuildings.
Collections: Watermen who fish the Chesapeake Bay, their work & history.
Research Fields: Virginia watermen's tools & experiences.
Facilities: children's museum, Minnows & Mates; outdoor wharf; pier; carriage house.
Activities: guided tours; lectures; arts festivals; organized educational programs; docent program; participatory & temporary exhibitions. Museum Sponsors: On-The-Water education program.
Publications: quarterly newsletter, The Ship's Log.
Hours & Admission Prices: April to late Nov. Tues.-Sat. 10-5, Sun. 1-5; late Nov. to March Sat. 10-5, Sun. 1-5. Adults $4, students $1; discounts for pre-arranged groups of 20 or more; members no charge. ♿
Attendance: 7,572 (accurate)
Membership: Deckhand $30; Mates $50; Patent Tonger $125; Captain $250; Marian J Crew $500; Marian Hornsby Bowditch Society $1,000.

YORK COUNTY HISTORICAL MUSEUM, (M), 301 Main St., Yorktown, VA 23692-5431. Mailing Address: P.O. Box 2431, Yorktown, VA 23692-5431. Tel.: 757-890-3508.
E-mail: meredith@yorkcounty.gov
History Museum.
Collections: local history & culture; Native American tools; Revolutionary & Civil War artifacts; USS Yorktown.
Hours & Admission Prices: Tues.-Sat. 10-3:30, Sun. 1-3:30.

WASHINGTON

(251 listings)

Aberdeen

ABERDEEN MUSEUM OF HISTORY, 111 E. Third St., Aberdeen, WA 98520-4002. Tel.: 360-533-1976.
E-mail: museum@aberdeen-museum.org
Web Site: www.aberdeen-museum.org
History Museum.
Collections: native cultures & artifacts; Pacific Northwest maritime documents; Grays Harbor history; WA state history; blacksmith shop; period fire engine; general store; photographs.
Facilities: Museum-related items for sale.
Hours & Admission Prices: Tues.-Sat. 10-5, Sun. 12-4. Suggested Donations: adults $2, students & seniors $1.

Anacortes

ANACORTES MUSEUM, (M), 1305 8th, Anacortes, WA 98221-1833. Tel.: 360-293-1915. Fax: 360-293-1929.
E-mail: coa.museum@cityofanacortes.org
Web Site: museum.cityofanacortes.org
Founded: 1957.
Key Personnel: Dir., Steve Oakley; Registrar, Evelyn Adams; Educator, Terry Slotemaker; Cur. Collections, Judy Hakins; Cur. Maritime History, Vernon Lauridsen.
Personnel Profile: Full-Time Paid 1; Part-Time Paid 10; Part-Time Volunteers 3.
Governing Authority: municipal. Parent Institution: City of Anacortes. Tax-exempt: 501(c)(3).
History Museum: housed in 1910 Carnegie Library Building.
Collections: clothing of early Anacortes; pictures; photos; tools; ledgers; school books; military; furniture; glass; medical & dental instruments; musical instruments; artifacts, photos, documents related to history of Anacortes, Fidalgo & Guemes Islands; records of early Salmon Cannery. Historic Ship: W.T. Preston, 1939 sternwheel snagboat, National Historic Landmark.
Research Fields: history of Anacortes, & Fidalgo & Guemes Islands.
Facilities: research library. Museum-related items for sale.
Publications: books, Fidalgo Fishing; Exploration of Whidbey, Fidalgo and Guemes Islands; From Logs to Lumber; The Geology of Fidalgo Island.
Hours & Admission Prices: Gallery: Mon.-Tues. & Thurs.-Sat. 10-4, Sun. 1-4. No charge; donations accepted. Vessel: March-May & Sept.-Oct. Sat. 10-4, Sun. 11-4; June-Aug. Mon.-Sat. 10-4, Sun. 11-4. Adults $3, seniors 65 & over $2, children 8-16 $1; children under 8 no charge. Closed New Year's Day; Easter; Thanksgiving; Christmas Eve & Day. ♿
Attendance: 5,000 (estimated)
Membership: Student & Senior $10; Individual $20; Family $35; Business & Organization $50; Sponsor $250.

Anderson Island

ANDERSON ISLAND HISTORICAL SOCIETY, 9306 Otso Point Rd., Anderson Island, WA 98303-9653.
Web Site: www.andersonislandhs.com
Founded: 1975.
Congressional District: 9
Key Personnel: Pres. (V), Ed Stephenson; Museum Shop Mgr., Jeanne Ditmore.
Governing Authority: bd. of directors. Tax-exempt.
Historical Society Museum.
Collections: local history & culture; personal artifacts; furnishings; quilts.
Publications: newsletter.
Hours & Admission Prices: Call for hours. No charge; donations accepted.
Attendance: 5,000 (estimated)
Membership: Household $15; Supporting $30; Sustaining $100.

Arlington

STILLAGUAMISH VALLEY PIONEER MUSEUM, 20722 67th Ave., N.E., Arlington, WA 98223. Tel.: 360-435-7289.
History Museum.
Collections: local history & culture; photographs; personal artifacts; period furnishings; logging; dairy industry; military; railroad; sports; medical; education; music.
Activities: special events.
Hours & Admission Prices: March-Oct. Wed. & Sat.-Sun. 1-4; other times by appointment. Adults $5, children 12 & under $2. Closed Easter; Mother's Day; Father's Day; Independence Day.

Ashford

MT. RAINIER NATIONAL PARK, Tahoma Woods, Star Rte., Ashford, WA 98304. Mailing Address: 55210 238th Ave. E., Ashford, WA 98304. Tel.: 360-569-2211, ext. 3314. Fax: 360-569-2187.
Web Site: www.nps.gov/mora/
Founded: 1928.
Congressional District: 8
Key Personnel: Supt., Dave Uberuaga.
Personnel Profile: Full-Time Paid 1; Part-Time Paid 6; Part-Time Volunteers 4.
Governing Authority: federal. Parent Institution: U.S. Dept. of Interior, National Park Service, Washington, DC 20240.
Natural History Museum.

Collections: zoology; geology; botany; history; Indian artifacts. Historic Building: 1888 Longmire cabin.
Research Fields: geology; zoology; hydrology; glaciology; botany; history; park management; artifacts concerning Mount Rainier National Park.
Facilities: 3,000-vol. library of books on natural history, conservation, ecology, history of park; campgrounds.
Activities: guided tours; lectures; films; interpretive programs for children & adults; permanent exhibits.
Publications: park newspaper & guide to seasonal activities & facilities, Tahoma; park-related publications, Northwest Interpretive Association; catalog.
Hours & Admission Prices: Longmire Museum: June-Sept. daily 9-5; Oct.-May 9-4. Paradise Visitor Center: May-Oct. daily 9-6; Oct.-April Sat.-Sun. 10-5. Ohanapecosh Visitor Center: Memorial Day to mid-Oct. daily 9-6. Sunrise Visitor Center: July to early Sept. daily 9-6. Park: $15 per automobile, $5 per person, good for seven days. Annual Pass: $30. ♿
Attendance: 2,000,000 (accurate)

Auburn

NEELY MANSION, 12303 Auburn-Black Diamond Rd., Auburn, WA 98071-0658. Mailing Address: P.O. Box 738, Auburn, WA 98071-0738. Tel.: 253-833-9404.
Web Site: www.neelymansion.org
Governing Authority: Tax-exempt: 501(c)(3).
Historic House Museum: built in 1891 by Aaron & David Neely.
Collections: period furnishings; personal artifacts.
Activities: rental facilities.
Hours & Admission Prices: Summer: Sat. 1-4; other times by appointment. Donation: $1.

WHITE RIVER VALLEY MUSEUM, 918 H St., S.E., Auburn Community Campus, Auburn, WA 98002-6112. Tel.: 253-288-7433. Fax: 253-931-3098.
Web Site: www.wrvmuseum.org
Founded: 1959.
Congressional District: 8
Key Personnel: C.E.O., Patricia Cosgrove; Chm. (V), Ronnie Beyersdorf.
Personnel Profile: Full-Time Paid 2; Part-Time Paid 6; Part-Time Volunteers 80.
Governing Authority: partnership between municipal government & private nonprofit organization. Tax-exempt: 501(c)(3).
Historical Museum.
Collections: interactive exhibits; life of Native Americans & settlers from 1855-1920; history of Auburn, Washington with emphasis on railroading & farming. Historic Building: Mary Olson Farm, c.1879.
Research Fields: Japanese-American regional history; railroading social history.
Facilities: 1,300-vol. library of rare & local history books, scrapbooks & railroad manuals; 4,500 sq. ft. exhibit space; 50-seat auditorium; botanical garden. Museum-related items for sale.
Activities: docent program; guided tours; school loan service; loan, participatory, traveling & temporary exhibitions.
Publications: quarterly newsletter, White River Journal.
Hours & Admission Prices: Jan. 5-Dec. 20 Wed.-Sun. 12-4 by appointment for group tours & research. Adults $2, seniors & children $1; Wed. no charge. ♿
Attendance: 15,000 (accurate)
Membership: Steward $10; Brakeman $35; Switchman $50; Engineer $100; Conductor $250; Train Master $500.

Bainbridge Island

BAINBRIDGE ISLAND HISTORICAL MUSEUM, (M), 215 Ericksen Ave., N.E., Bainbridge Island, WA 98110-1855. Tel.: 206-842-2773. Fax: 206-842-0914.
Governing Authority: nonprofit organization. Tax-exempt: 501(c)(3).
Historical Society Museum.
Collections: Bainbridge Island history & culture; photographs.
Facilities: library. Museum-related items for sale.
Activities: school programs; research; special events.
Hours & Admission Prices: Summer: Sun.-Mon. & Wed.-Fri. 1-4, Sat. 10-1; Winter: Wed.-Mon. 1-4. Closed New Year's Day; Easter; Thanksgiving; Christmas.
Membership: Basic $20.

THE BLOEDEL RESERVE, 7571 NE Dolphin Dr., Bainbridge Island, WA 98110-1097. Tel.: 206-842-7631. Fax: 206-842-8970.
E-mail: email@bloedelreserve.org
Web Site: www.bloedelreserve.org
Wildlife Refuge.
Collections: native birds & plants.
Hours & Admission Prices: Wed.-Sun. 10-4. Adults $10, seniors 65 & over $8, children 5-12 $6, college/university horticulture, botany class groups & youth clubs $4.

Bellevue

BELLEVUE ARTS MUSEUM, 510 Bellevue Way, N.E., Bellevue, WA 98004-5014. Tel.: 425-519-0770. Fax: 425-637-1799.
E-mail: info@bellevuearts.org
Web Site: www.bellevuearts.org
Founded: 1975.
Congressional District: 8
Key Personnel: Exec. Dir. & C.E.O., Mark Crawford; Dir. Curatorial Affairs, Michael Monroe; Deputy Dir., Renate Raymond; Bd. Pres., Susan Edelheit; Docent Pres., Miriam Charney; C.F.O., Marguerite Stanley; Cur., Stefano Catalani; Mktg. & Public Rels. Dir., Tanja Baumann; Museum Shop Mgr., Jessica Glover.
Personnel Profile: Full-Time Paid 19; Part-Time Paid 18; Part-Time Volunteers 320; Interns 10.
Governing Authority: nonprofit organization. Tax-exempt: 501(c)(3).
Art Museum.
Collections: contemporary art; craft; design.
Major Exhibits: Beth Levine: Frist Lady of Shoes (T), 2/18/10-6/6/10; Lisa Gralnick: The Gold Standard (T), 3/25/10-8/8/10; Eyes for Glass, The Joyce and John Price Collection, 3/25/10-8/8/10; The Art of Discovery: Celebrating 50 Years of Inspiring Young Minds, 6/22/10-9/19/10; Arline Fisch: Creatures from the Deep, 6/22/10-10/11/10; Ginny Ruffner: Aesthetic Engineering - The Imagination Cycle, 10/5/10-2/6/11.
Research Fields: related to exhibitions.
Facilities: art studio.
Activities: guided tours in seven languages; lectures; children's education program; docent program; volunteer program; temporary & traveling exhibitions. Museum Sponsors: Bellevue Arts Museum ArtsFair; Bellevue Arts Museum KidsFair.
Publications: catalogues, Michael Peterson: Evolution/Revolution; The Book Borrowers; Tip Toland: Melt, The Figure in Clay; A Tapestry of Memories: The Art of Dinh Q. Le; Dim Sum at the On-On Tea Room: The Jewelry of Ron Ho.
Hours & Admission Prices: Mon.-Thurs. 11-5, Fri. 11-8, Sat.-Sun. 12-5. Adults $9, students & senior citizens $7; discounts to AAM members; children under 6 & members no charge. Closed New Year's Day; Martin Luther King Jr, Day; Presidents' Day; Easter; Memorial Day; Labor Day; Thanksgiving; Christmas. ♿
Attendance: 50,000 (estimated)
Membership: Student $25; Senior & Teacher $30; Individual $50; National Friend & Dual Senior $55; Family $75; Patron $175; Supporting $250; Benefactor $500; Bronze Circle $1,000; Silver Circle $2,500; Gold Circle $5,000; Platinum Circle $10,000.

THE BELLEVUE BOTANICAL GARDEN, 12001 Main St., Bellevue, WA 98005-3522. Tel.: 425-452-2750.
E-mail: nkortes@bellevuewa.gov
Web Site: www.bellevuebotanical.org
Founded: 1992.
Botanical Garden.
Collections: 53 acres of display gardens, woodlands, meadows & wetlands.
Hours & Admission Prices: Garden: daily dawn to dusk. Visitor Center: daily 9-4. No charge; donations accepted.

EASTSIDE HERITAGE CENTER, 2102 Bellevue Way, S.E., Bellevue, WA 98004. Mailing Address: P.O. Box 40535, Bellevue, WA 98015-4535. Tel.: 425-450-1049. Fax: 425-450-1050.
E-mail: director@eastsideheritagecenter.org
Web Site: eastsideheritagecenter.org
Founded: 1965.
Congressional District: 1
Key Personnel: Bd. Pres., Ross McIvor; Dir., Heather Trescases; Education Coord., Jane Morton; Archivist, Megan Carlisle.
Personnel Profile: Full-Time Paid 1; Part-Time Paid 3; Part-Time Volunteers 15; Interns 2.
Governing Authority: nonprofit organization. Tax-exempt: 501(c)(3).
Historical Society Museum.
Collections: artifacts & archival material of the region dating from the 1850s; manuscripts; lumbering; costumes; room furnishings; fixtures; photographs.
Research Fields: local history.
Facilities: 200-vol. library of general reading books, school books, school records & photographs available for research. Museum Sponsors: annual strawberry festival. Books for sale.
Activities: guided tours; outreach loan program of historic photos & artifacts;

permanent & temporary exhibitions; outreach loan program of slides & videos and hands-on loan boxes.
Publications: quarterly newsletter; books: Our Town Redmond, Willowmoor, The Story of Marymoor Park; Collected Memoirs of the Central School, Kirkland; Bellevue: Its First 100 Years; Eastside Historic Coloring Book; Bellevue Timeline; Lake Washington: The East Side; Culinary History of a Pacific Northwest Town: Bellevue, Washington; Generations: Kemper Freeman, Jr. and the Freeman Family.
Hours & Admission Prices: Winters House at 2102 Bellevue Way S.E. open Mon.-Fri. 10-4, Sat. 10-2. No charge; donations accepted. ♿
Attendance: 10,040 (accurate)
Membership: Student $15; Individual $25; Family $40; Contributor & Organization $100; Sponsor & Steward $250; Benefactor $1,000.

KIDSQUEST CHILDREN'S MUSEUM, 4091 Factoria Mall, S.E., Bellevue, WA 98006-6125. Mailing Address: P.O. Box 5637, Bellevue, WA 98006-0137. Tel.: 425-637-8100.
E-mail: info@kidsquestmuseum.org
Web Site: www.kidsquestmuseum.org
Formerly: iQuest Children's Museum
Founded: 1997.
Congressional District: 8
Key Personnel: Exec. Dir., Putter Bert; Co Chm. (V), Dale King; Co Chm. (V), Molly Lambright; Dir. Education & Exhibits, Stacy Winegardner.
Personnel Profile: Full-Time Paid 11; Part-Time Paid 11; Part-Time Volunteers 65.
Governing Authority: private; nonprofit organization. Tax-exempt: 501(c)(3).
Children's Museum.
Collections: hands-on exploration of the arts, sciences, culture & life experiences.
Research Fields: Early Childhood Learning.
Facilities: 6,000 sq. ft. exhibit space.
Activities: education programs; workshops; day camps; science clubs.
Publications: newsletter, KidsQuest Quarterly.
Hours & Admission Prices: Call for hours. Adults $7.50; discounts to ACM & NWAYM members; members no charge. ♿
Attendance: 147,912 (accurate)
Membership: Family Fun $85; Family Fun Flex $100; Family Fun Deluxe $125; Family Fun Patron $250.

ROSALIE WHYEL MUSEUM OF DOLL ART, 1116 108th Ave., N.E., Bellevue, WA 98004-4321. Tel.: 425-455-1116. Fax: 425-455-4793.
E-mail: dollart@dollart.com
Web Site: www.dollart.com
Founded: 1989.
Congressional District: 1
Key Personnel: Pres. (V) & Dir., Rosalie Whyel; Treas., George Whyel; Cur., Jill Gorman; Accountant, Cristina Bloomquist.
Personnel Profile: Full-Time Paid 7; Part-Time Paid 4; Part-Time Volunteers 27.
Governing Authority: individual operation. Parent Institution: Doll Art, Inc.
Doll Museum.
Collections: history of dolls from pre-historic to contemporary artists dolls; accessories; toys; games; books; photographs; costumes; history of toys & toymakers; history of costume; miniatures.
Major Exhibits: Mint In Box - Dolls and Toys, 11/09-2/21/10; Terri Lee and Family, 2/27/10-5/16/10; The World Embellished - Lace!, 5/22/10-10/17/10.
Research Fields: history of the doll; doll makers; body styles; fashions; toys; toy makers.
Facilities: library of doll research & identification; meeting facilities; 8,000 sq. ft. exhibit space; English garden. Dolls, books & related items for sale.
Activities: docent program; formal and informal education programs for children & adults; guided tours; hobby workshops; lectures; loan, temporary & participatory exhibitions; study clubs; broadcast programs.
Publications: quarterly newsletter; gallery guides & classroom materials; The Rosalie Whyel Museum of Doll Art; Opening Our Doors to You: A Pictorial Review; The Rose Unfolds: Rarities of the Rosalie Whyel Museum of Doll Art; The Heart of the Tree: Early Wooden Dolls to the 1850s.
Hours & Admission Prices: Mon.-Sat. 10-5, Sun. 1-5. Adults $8, seniors $7, children & students 5-17 $5; children under 5 & members no charge. ♿
Attendance: 25,000 (estimated)
Membership: Child $25; Annual Pass $30; Adult & Annual Family Pass $50.

Bellingham

AMERICAN MUSEUM OF RADIO AND ELECTRICITY, 1312 Bay St., Bellingham, WA 98225-4322. Tel.: 360-738-3886. Fax: 360-733-2532.
E-mail: lynne@amre.us
Web Site: www.amre.us
Founded: 1996.
Congressional District: 2
Key Personnel: Exec. Dir., Lynne Sherwood Parker; Chm. (V), Craig Cole; Pres. (V), John Jenkins; Pres. (V), Jonathan Winter; Treas., Paul Tholfsen.
Personnel Profile: Full-Time Paid 1; Full-Time Volunteers 3; Part-Time Paid 3; Part-Time Volunteers 20; Interns 1.
Governing Authority: private; nonprofit organization. Tax-exempt: 501(c)(3).
Science Museum.
Collections: history of radio & electricity from 1600s-1950s; radio, telegraph equipment; electrical apparatus; books; analog radio content; static electric machines; early television; over 10,000 vacuum tubes.
Major Exhibits: Static Lab, 11/09-12/10; Theramin, 11/09-12/10.
Facilities: 12,000 sq. ft. exhibit space. Museum-related items for sale.
Activities: permanent & temporary exhibits; workshops; education programs; lectures; performances.
Publications: newsletter, Currents.
Hours & Admission Prices: Wed.-Sat. 11-4; other times by appointment. Adults $5, children 12 & under $2; discounts to AAM & ICOM members; members no charge. Closed national holidays. ♿
Attendance: 12,000 (estimated)
Membership: Individual $35; Family $80; Contributing $125; Supporting $250; Sustaining $500; Associate $1,000.

BELLINGHAM RAILWAY MUSEUM, 1320 Commercial St., Bellingham, WA 98225. Tel.: 360-393-7540.
Web Site: www.bellinghamrailwaymuseum.com
Founded: 2003.
Key Personnel: Dir., Fred Dodds; Pres. (V), John D. Stephens
Railway Museum.
Collections: railrway history; railroad artifacts; lanterns; period railroad equipment; tools; photographs; Lionel trains.
Major Exhibits: Microsoft Train Simulator, 1/10-12/10.
Hours & Admission Prices: Tues. & Thurs.-Sat. 12-5; other times by appointment. Adults $4, children 2-16 $1; Fri. & children under 2 no charge. Closed Thanksgiving; Christmas. ♿
Attendance: 7,000

HERITAGE FLIGHT MUSEUM, 2000 W. Bakerview Rd., Bellingham, WA 98226-7686. Tel.: 360-733-4422. Fax: 360-733-4423.
Military Aircraft Museum.
Collections: period military aircraft.
Activities: special events & programs.
Hours & Admission Prices: Call for hours.

VIKING UNION GALLERY, Western Washington University, Bellingham, WA 98225-5996. Mailing Address: VU Gallery, 516 High St., Bellingham, WA 98225-5946. Tel.: 360-650-6534.
E-mail: asp.vu.gallery@wwu.edu
Web Site: gallery.as.wwu.edu
Founded: 1950.
Congressional District: 2
Key Personnel: Coord., Cory Budden; Asst. Coord., Allie Paul.
Personnel Profile: Part-Time Paid 2.
Governing Authority: university. Western Washington University. Parent Institution: Associated Students of WWU. Tax-exempt.
University Art Gallery.
Collections: student art collection of paintings, drawings & lithographs.
Activities: lectures; gallery talks; temporary exhibitions; visiting artists.
Hours & Admission Prices: Mon.-Fri. 10-5; members no charge. No charge. Closed national holidays. ♿
Attendance: 10,000 (estimated)

WESTERN GALLERY, WESTERN WASHINGTON UNIVERSITY, (M), Fine Arts Complex, Bellingham, WA 98225-9068. Tel.: 360-650-3900 & 3963. Fax: 360-650-6878.
E-mail: sarah.clarklangager@wwu.edu
Web Site: www.westerngallery.wwu.edu
Founded: 1950.
Congressional District: 40
Key Personnel: Dir. & C.E.O., Sarah Clark-Langager, Ph.D.; Museum Preservation Specialist II, Paul Brower.
Personnel Profile: Full-Time Paid 1; Part-Time Paid 1; Interns 10.
Governing Authority: university. Parent Institution: Western Washington University. Tax-exempt: 501(c)(3).
University Art Gallery.
Collections: 20th century prints & drawings; study collection of chairs by 20th century international designers; outdoor sculpture.
Research Fields: contemporary art & sculpture.
Facilities: 4,500 sq. ft. exhibit gallery.
Activities: films; formal education programs for undergraduate & graduate

students; guided tours; temporary, loan & traveling exhibitions; lectures; gallery talks; arts festivals.
Publications: exhibition catalogues if organized by Western Gallery; audiophone tour & catalogues of Outdoor Sculpture Collection; brochures.
Hours & Admission Prices: Academic Year: Mon.-Tues. & Thurs.-Fri. 10-4, Wed. 10-8, Sat. 12-4. No charge; donations accepted. ♿
Attendance: 55,000 (estimated)
Membership: Friends of Gallery: Individual $25; Family $50; Supporting $100; Sponsor $500; Patron $1,000 & up.

* **WHATCOM MUSEUM OF HISTORY AND ART, (M),** 121 Prospect St., Bellingham, WA 98225-4497. Tel.: 360-778-8930. Fax: 360-778-8931.
E-mail: museuminfo@cob.org
Web Site: www.whatcommuseum.org
Founded: 1940.
Congressional District: 2
Key Personnel: Dir., Patricia Leach; Pres. (V), Cheric Walker; Education Asst., Mary Jo Maute; Photo Research, Jeff Jewell; Designer, Scott Wallin; Accountant, Judy Frost; Education Coord., Richard Vanderway; Collections Mgr., Jan Olson.
Personnel Profile: Full-Time Paid 20; Part-Time Paid 23; Part-Time Volunteers 300; Interns 10.
Governing Authority: municipal. Parent Institution: City of Bellingham. Subsidiary Institution: Whatcom Museum Society. Tax-exempt: 501(c)(3).
Art, History & Children's Museum: housed in three buildings including the 1892 Old City Hall.
Collections: Northwest coast Indian ethnology; American art; Darius Kinsey photo collection; Wilbur Sandison photo collection; H.C. Hanson naval architecture; American Folk Art & Americana.
Research Fields: historical on a regional basis; photography; contemporary art.
Facilities: photo archives with research & reproduction services. Museum-related items for sale.
Activities: permanent & temporary exhibitions; guided tours; lectures; national & international art & history tours; films; gallery talks; concerts; formally organized education programs for children; inter-museum loan; museum outreach program.
Publications: books, The Tree Project; John Cole Paintings; Dale Gottlieb; An Enduring Legacy: Women Painters of Washington, 1930-2005; Northwest Designer Craftsmen at 50; annual reports.
Hours & Admission Prices: Tues.-Sun. 12-5. No charge; donations accepted. Admission for Children's Museum. Closed most holidays. ♿
Attendance: 106,001 (accurate)
Membership: Student & Senior $30; Individual $40; Grandparents $55; Family $65; Friend $100; Contributor $250; Patron $500; Benefactor $1,000; Community Partner $2,500 & up.

Beverly

WANAPUM DAM HERITAGE CENTER, 15655 Wanapum Village Lane, S.W., Beverly, WA 99321-9705. Mailing Address: P.O. Box 878, Ephrata, WA 98823-0878. Tel.: 509-754-5088, ext. 2571. Fax: 509-766-2522 & 5020.
Founded: 1966.
Key Personnel: Cultural Resources Supvr., Leon Hoepner; Museum Dir., Angela Buck.
Personnel Profile: Full-Time Paid 3; Part-Time Paid 2.
Governing Authority: board of commissioners. Parent Institution: Public Utility District of Grant County. Tax-exempt.
General Museum.
Collections: Native American artifacts; dioramas; archaeology; photos.
Research Fields: local history & archaeology.
Activities: guided tours.
Hours & Admission Prices: Mon.-Fri. 8:30-4:30, Sat.-Sun. 9-5. No charge. ♿
Attendance: 13,780 (accurate)

Bingen

GORGE HERITAGE MUSEUM, 202 E. Humboldt, Bingen, WA 98605. Mailing Address: P.O. Box 394, Bingen, WA 98605-0394. Tel.: 509-493-3228.
E-mail: ghm@gorge.net
Web Site: community.gorge.net/ghmuseum/About.htm
Historic Building Museum: housed in the former Bingen Congregational Church; c.1912.
Collections: local history & culture; Native American artifacts; clothing; household items; tools; medical & surgical equipment; documents; newspapers.
Hours & Admission Prices: May 23-Oct. Thurs.-Sun. 11:30-4:30; other times by appointment. Adults $5; members no charge.

Black Diamond

BLACK DIAMOND MUSEUM, 32626 Railroad Ave., Black Diamond, WA 98010. Mailing Address: P.O. Box 232, Black Diamond, WA 98010-0232. Tel.: 360-886-2142.
E-mail: museum@blackdiamondmuseum.org
Web Site: www.blackdiamondmuseum.org
Key Personnel: Pres., Keith Watson; Vice Pres., Don Malgari.
Governing Authority: nonprofit organization. Tax Exempt: 501 (c)(3)
Historic Building Museum: housed in the former train depot.
Collections: local history; period artifacts; photographs.
Hours & Admission Prices: Summer: Thurs. 9-4, Sat.-Sun. 12-4; Winter: Thurs. 9-4, Sat.-Sun. 12-3.

Bremerton

KITSAP COUNTY HISTORICAL SOCIETY MUSEUM, 280 4th St., Bremerton, WA 98337-1813. Tel.: 360-479-6226. Fax: 360-415-9294.
E-mail: khsinfo@kitsaphistory.org
Web Site: www.kitsaphistory.org
Founded: 1948.
Congressional District: 1 & 6
Key Personnel: Exec. Asst., Prudence McCabe; Cur., Jane Roth Williams; Pres. (V), Paul Middents; Vice. Pres., Mark Williamson; Museum Shop Mgr., Virginia McBride.
Personnel Profile: Full-Time Paid 1; Full-Time Volunteers 3; Part-Time Paid 2; Part-Time Volunteers 90.
Governing Authority: society. Parent Institution: Kitsap County Historical Society. Tax-exempt: 501(c)(3).
History Museum: housed in 1949 bank building.
Collections: hands-on exhibits depict the history of Kitsap County including logging, natural history, Native Americans, agriculture, naval history, the Mosquito fleet & the Homefront of WWII.
Research Fields: Kitsap County; Native Americans; government housing projects; county records; county government & services; Edward & Asahel Curtis; Navy.
Facilities: library of Northwest history books & diaries available for use on premises; archives available for use by appointment. Books pertaining to local area for sale.
Activities: guided tours; lectures; gallery talks; slides; permanent & temporary exhibitions; classes; special events.
Publications: local history books, Poulsbo; Port Madison; Little City by the Sea; Port Blakely: The Community Capt. Renton Built; Fair Winds of Change: Navy Yard History; newsletter.
Hours & Admission Prices: Tues.- Sat. 10-5, 1st Fri. of month 10-8. Suggested Donations: adults $2, children 7-17 $1; discounts to AAM, AASLH & WMA members & members; children under 7 no charge. Closed holidays. ♿
Attendance: 6,000 (accurate)
Membership: Seniors & Students $20; Individual $30; Family $40; Sustaining $100.

PUGET SOUND NAVY MUSEUM, 251 First St., Bremerton, WA 98337-5612. Tel.: 360-627-2270. Fax: 360-627-2273.
E-mail: lindy.dosher@navy.mil
Formerly: Bremerton Naval Museum
Founded: 1954.
Congressional District: 23
Key Personnel: Dir., William Galvani; Deputy Dir., Lindy Dosher; Cur., Danelle Feddes; Mgr. Collections, Heather Mygatt; Mgr. Collections, Kathrine Young; Mgr. Collections, Heather Guindon.
Personnel Profile: Full-Time Paid 3; Part-Time Volunteers 30; Interns 1.
Governing Authority: municipal. Parent Institution: Navy Museum Northwest. Tax-exempt: 501(c)(3).
Naval History Museum.
Collections: Puget Sound naval history from 1840s to present; Puget Sound Naval Shipyard; paintings; photographs.
Research Fields: Puget Sound; US Navy; Puget Sound Naval Shipyard.
Facilities: library. Museum-related items for sale.
Activities: self-guided tours; children's activities; permanent & temporary exhibitions.
Hours & Admission Prices: Mon.-Sat. 10-4, Sun. 1-4. No charge; donations accepted. Closed New Year's Day; Easter; Thanksgiving; Christmas. ♿
Attendance: 13,000 (estimated)
Membership: Student $10; Individual $25; Family & Club $35; Business $50; Life $500-$5,000.

USS TURNER JOY MUSEUM SHIP, 300 Washington Beach Ave., Bremerton, WA 98337-5668. Tel.: 360-792-2457.
Military Ship Museum: housed on a Navy destroyer from the Vietnam War.

Collections: Navy & ship history; Navy men & women memorial; military artifacts; photographs; personal artifacts.
Facilities: Museum-related items for sale.
Activities: overnight program; guided tours.
Hours & Admission Prices: May-Sept. daily 10-5; Oct.-April Fri.-Sun. 10-4. Adults $10, seniors 62 & over $8, children 5-12 $6; children under 5 no charge. Closed New Year's Day; Thanksgiving; Christmas.

Brewster

FORT OKANOGAN INTERPRETIVE CENTER, 14379 Hwy. 17, Brewster, WA 98812. Mailing Address: Alta Lake State Park, 1 B Otto Rd., Pateros, WA 98846-9618. Tel.: 509-923-2473. Fax: 509-923-2980.
Web Site: www.parks.wa.gov
Founded: 1962.
Key Personnel: Dir., Rex Derr; Park Mgr., Sharon Soelter.
Personnel Profile: Full-Time Volunteers 2; Part-Time Volunteers 2.
Governing Authority: state. Parent Institution: Alta Lake State Park. Affiliated with the Washington State Parks and Recreation Commission, 7150 Cleanwater Lane, Olympia, WA 98504. Tax-exempt.
Historic Building & Site: history of fur trade & Indian Interpretive Center.
Collections: Indian & pioneer items: basketry; weapons.
Activities: permanent exhibitions.
Publications: books.
Hours & Admission Prices: May 14-Aug. Wed.-Sun. 9-5; other times by appointment only. No charge; donations accepted. ♿
Attendance: 9,000 (estimated)

Buckley

FOOTHILLS HISTORICAL SOCIETY & MUSEUM, 128 River Ave., Buckley, WA 98321. Mailing Address: P.O. Box 530, Buckley, WA 98321-0530. Tel.: 360-829-1291.
Historical Society Museum.
Collections: local history & culture; photographs; period artifacts.
Hours & Admission Prices: Winter: Wed.-Thurs. 12-4, Sun. 11-4; Summer: Wed.-Thurs. 12-4, Sun. 1-4.

Cashmere

CASHMERE PIONEER VILLAGE & MUSEUM, 600 Cotlets Way, Cashmere, WA 98815-1602. Mailing Address: P.O. Box 22, Cashmere, WA 98815-0022. Tel.: 509-782-3230. Fax: 509-782-3219.
E-mail: pioneer49@verizon.net
Web Site: cashmeremuseum.org
Formerly: Chelan County Historical Museum
Founded: 1956.
Congressional District: 4
Key Personnel: Co Mgr. & Museum Shop Mgr., Kari Bohnstedt; Co Mgr., Patricia Lynd; Pres. & Trustee, Dean Rainey; Vice Pres. & Trustee, Jim Wann; Caretaker, Fred Harvey.
Personnel Profile: Part-Time Paid 3; Part-Time Volunteers 54.
Governing Authority: nonprofit organization. Parent Institution: Chelan County Historical Society. Tax-exempt: 501(c)(3).
History Museum & Village.
Collections: history of Central Washington from earliest inhabitants to present; Native American artifacts; natural history; Tonk paintings; memorial plaques; pioneer artifacts; Graham paintings; mineralogy; Great Northern passenger car; Great Northern wooden caboose; 1921 Toro Model B dumptruck; 1891 waterwheel; Meso-American artifacts from Colima & Michoacan Mexico 600-800 A.D. Historic Buildings: 1872 Horan cabin; 1889 log school; 1856-1863 log mission; 1879 Assay office; 1889 blacksmith shop; 1888 Richardson Cabin; 1872 post office: 1890 doctor & dentist office; 1886 Buckhorn Saloon; geology; 1891 Weythman Cabin; 1896 general store; 1895 barber shop; 1898 Mission Hotel; c.1885 millinery shop; c.1885 jail; 1895 depot; 1896 print shop.
Research Fields: archaeology.
Facilities: picnic pavilion; gardens. Books, crafts & other items for sale.
Activities: guided tours & lectures by appointment; permanent & temporary exhibitions; treasure hunt for children. Museum Sponsors: Apple Days in October.
Publications: quarterly news bulletin, Cashmere Museum News.
Hours & Admission Prices: March-Nov 1. daily 9:30-4:30. Adults $5, seniors 62 and over & students over 12 $4 children 6-12 $3; children under 5 & members no charge. School Tours: adults $4.50, students 6-12 $2.50. Closed Easter. ♿
Attendance: 11,000 (accurate)
Membership: Junior & Senior $20; Individual $25; Family $40; Pioneer $125; Curator $250; Village Builder $500; Museum Builder $1,000.

Castle Rock

MOUNT ST. HELENS VISITOR CENTER AT SILVER LAKE, 3029 Spirit Lake Hwy., Castle Rock, WA 98611-8706. Tel.: 360-274-0962.
Visitor Center.
Collections: Mount St. Helen's history.
Hours & Admission Prices: Summer: daily 9-5. Adults $3. Closed New Year's; Thanksgiving; Christmas.

Cathlamet

WAHKIAKUM COUNTY HISTORICAL MUSEUM, 65 River St. & Division, Cathlamet, WA 98612. Mailing Address: P.O. Box 541, Cathlamet, WA 98612-0541. Tel.: 360-795-3954.
Founded: 1956.
Congressional District: 19B, 10A
Key Personnel: Chm. (V), Richard Nikkila; Cur., Kari Kandoll.
Personnel Profile: Full-Time Volunteers 1; Part-Time Paid 1; Part-Time Volunteers 10.
Governing Authority: society.
Natural History Museum & Historic Site: housed in the former homestead of Judge William Strong, the first Territorial Judge in the Oregon Territory.
Collections: history of the Pacific Northwest; pioneer items of the lower Columbia River; Indian artifacts; early logging; early Americana; fishing.
Activities: guided tours; formally organized education programs for children.
Publications: biannual newsletter.
Hours & Admission Prices: June-Sept. Tues.-Sun. 11-4; Oct.-May Thurs.-Sun. 1-4. Adults $3, seniors $1.50. Closed New Year's Day; Thanksgiving; Christmas.
Attendance: 1,000 (estimated)
Membership: Individual $20; Couple $30; Family $35.

Chehalis

LEWIS COUNTY HISTORICAL MUSEUM, (M), 599 N.W. Front Way, Chehalis, WA 98532-2048. Tel.: 360-748-0831. Fax: 360-740-5646.
E-mail: lchm@lewiscountymuseum.org
Web Site: www.lewiscountymuseum.org
Founded: 1965.
Congressional District: 3
Key Personnel: Pres. (V), Kathy Gavin; Exec. Dir., Debbie Knapp; Museum Shop Mgr., Dee Cairns.
Personnel Profile: Full-Time Paid 1; Full-Time Volunteers 2; Part-Time Paid 1; Part-Time Volunteers 10.
Governing Authority: county; society. Parent Institution: Lewis Co. Historical Society. Tax-exempt: 170(b)(1)(A) & 501(c)(3).
Local History Museum.
Collections: general county historical artifacts; Lewis County history archives; over 20,000 indexed photographs; Chehalis Indian artifacts; manuscripts; 400 oral history cassette tapes.
Major Exhibits: Two Rivers, 3/10.
Research Fields: genealogy; cemeteries; Chehalis Indians; schools & churches; pioneer's histories; obituary file of county residents; Cowlitz Indians.
Facilities: 1,600-vol. research library on local & state history; Indian archive collection; census & cemetery records.
Activities: guided tours.
Publications: Postmarked Washington; Lewis & Cowlitz Counties; Territorial Marriages; 1871 Census; quarterly, The Historian; books, 1989 Centennial Cookbook; Lewis County Pictorial History.
Hours & Admission Prices: Tues.-Sat. 10-5. Adults $4; discounts to AAM members; members no charge. Closed major holidays. ♿
Attendance: 5,836 (accurate)
Membership: Student & Senior $13; Individual $18; Family $30; Sustaining $50; Supporting $150; Fellow $250; Patron $500.

VETERANS MEMORIAL MUSEUM, 100 S. W. Veterans Way, Chehalis, WA 98532-1100. Tel.: 360-740-8875.
E-mail: vmm@compprime.com
Web Site: www.veteransmuseum.org
Founded: 1995.
Congressional District: 20
Key Personnel: Dir., Lee T. Grimes; Pres. (V), Ernest Graichen.
Personnel Profile: Full-Time Paid 2; Part-Time Volunteers 35.
Military Museum.
Collections: Armed Forces veterans; uniforms; personal artifacts; photographs; military equipment.
Facilities: banquet facilities.
Activities: special events; rental facilities.
Publications: quarterly, Veterans Museum News.

Hours & Admission Prices: Call for hours. Adults $5, children 6-18 $3; members no charge. ♿
Attendance: 20,000 (accurate)
Membership: Students $10; Veterans & Seniors $20; Adults $25; Business & Organization $100.

Chinook

FORT COLUMBIA HOUSE MUSEUM, Fort Columbia State Park, Hwy. 101, Chinook, WA 98614. Mailing Address: P.O. Box 488, Ilwaco, WA 98624-0488. Tel.: 360-777-8221. Fax: 360-642-4216.
E-mail: lcic@parks.wa.gov
Founded: 1954.
Congressional District: 5
Key Personnel: Park Mgr., Larry Chapman; Cur., Donella Lucero.
Governing Authority: Administered by Washington State Parks & Recreation Commission, 7150 Clean Water Lane, Olympia, WA 98504.
Historic House: 1902 Commanding Officer's house at Fort Columbia State Park.
Collections: period furniture & appliances.
Hours & Admission Prices: May 27-Sept. 30 daily 10-5. No charge; donations appreciated.

FORT COLUMBIA INTERPRETIVE CENTER, Off Hwy. 101, Chinook, WA 98624. Mailing Address: Fort Columbia State Park, P.O. Box 488, Ilwaco, WA 98624-0488. Tel.: 360-777-8221 & 642-3078. Fax: 360-642-4216.
E-mail: lcic@parks.wa.gov
Formerly: Fort Columbia State Park
Founded: 1954.
Key Personnel: Park Mgr., Evan Roberts.
Governing Authority: state. Affiliated with the Washington State Parks & Recreation Commission, 7150 Clean Water Lane, Olympia, WA 98504.
Military History Museum: housed in restored artillery barracks located on a segment of Lewis & Clark Trail, former coastal fortification, important Columbia River navigation point.
Collections: Native American & pioneer artifacts; shipwreck materials; dioramas; coastal defense; maritime; local history; historic house.
Research Fields: coastal defense.
Facilities: library.
Activities: permanent & temporary exhibitions. Museum Sponsors: Living History Events.
Hours & Admission Prices: July-Sept. 15 daily 10-5. No charge; donations accepted.
Attendance: 10,000 (accurate)

Clarkston

VALLEY ART CENTER, INC., 842-6th St., Clarkston, WA 99403-2013. Tel.: 509-758-8331.
E-mail: valleyarts@clarkston.com
Founded: 1968.
Congressional District: 9
Key Personnel: Pres. Bd. Directors, Judy Wayne; Museum Shop Mgr., H. Craig Whitcomb.
Personnel Profile: Full-Time Volunteers 1; Part-Time Volunteers 10.
Governing Authority: nonprofit organization. Tax-exempt: 501(c)(3).
Art Center.
Collections: historical & Indian art; graphic art; sculpture.
Facilities: library of art books & publications available for inter-library loan.
Activities: guided tours; lectures; gallery talks; arts festivals; hobby workshops; formally organized education programs for children & adults; temporary exhibitions; traveling community art show; affiliated with Walla Walla, Washington, Community College for accredited art classes; antique shows; mobile art workshop. Annual Events: Pacific Northwest Heritage Art Exhibit; summer art show; benefit gallery.
Publications: quarterly events calendar, Artist's Registry.
Hours & Admission Prices: Jan. 2 to Dec. 23 Tues.-Sat. 9-4; other times for tours by appointment. No charge; donations accepted. ♿
Attendance: 6,800 (estimated)
Membership: Associate $50; Patron $75; Supporting $100.

Cle Elum

CLE ELUM TELEPHONE MUSEUM, 221 E. 1st St., Cle Elum, WA 98922-1103. Mailing Address: P.O. Box 462, South Cle Elum, WA 98943-0462. Tel.: 509-674-5939.
E-mail: maryp@cleelum.com
Web Site: www.nkcmuseums.org/PhoneMuseum.html
Founded: 1967.
Congressional District: 13
Key Personnel: Pres., Bonnie Hawk.
Personnel Profile: Part-Time Volunteers 41.
Governing Authority: state; nonprofit organization. Parent Institution: Cle Elum Historical Society. Subsidiary: Telephone Museum. Tax-exempt.
Communications Museum: housed in a former Bell Telephone building.
Collections: history of the phone; telephone parts; old & new phones; old manually used board; miner's equipment; history & pictures of area.
Facilities: Commemorative plates, tote bags & tiles for sale.
Activities: hands-on dial system for children.
Publications: brochure.
Hours & Admission Prices: Memorial Day-Labor Day Sat.-Sun. 12-4 by appointment. Suggested Donation: $1 per person.
Attendance: 500 (estimated)
Membership: Senior & Student $10; Individual $15; Family $25; Business & Corporate $50.

NKCHS NORTHERN KITTITAS COUNTY HISTORICAL SOCIETY, 302 W. Third St., Cle Elum, WA 98922-1026. Mailing Address: P.O. Box 462, South Cle Elum, WA 98943-0462. Tel.: 509-674-9766.
E-mail: maryp@cleelum.com
Web Site: www.nkcmuseums.org
Formerly: Carpenter Home Museum and Gallery
Founded: 1989.
Congressional District: 13
Key Personnel: Chm. (V) & Treas., Mary Pittis; Pres. (V), Bonnie Hawk.
Personnel Profile: Full-Time Volunteers 2; Part-Time Volunteers 20.
Governing Authority: state; nonprofit organization. Parent Institution: Northern Kittitas County Historical Society (NKCHS). Subsidiary Institution: High Country Artists. Tax-exempt.
Carpenter Museum: housed in 1914 home, with ballroom & a special maid's room with a private stairway.
Collections: Tiffany lamps; period furniture; pictures; acid cut backlights; pioneer artifacts; ethnic heritage costumes of miners & farmers who settled the upper county; display of 1st bank office, 1904 state bank; display of Pech Point school room.
Facilities: Tote bags, cards, stationery & museum-related items for sale.
Activities: tours; art shows. Annual Events: Queen's Tea, Independence Day; Christmas In Cle Elum Open House.
Publications: brochures; flyers.
Hours & Admission Prices: Fri.-Sun. & some holidays 12-4; groups by appointment. No charge; donations requested.
Attendance: 800 (estimated)
Membership: Student & Senior $10; Individual $15; Family $25; Business & Corporate $50.

Coulee City

DRY FALLS INTERPRETIVE CENTER, Sun Lakes State Park, 34875 Park Lake Rd., N.E., Coulee City, WA 99115-9607. Tel.: 509-632-5583 & 5214. Fax: 509-632-5971.
E-mail: dry.falls@parks.wa.gov
Web Site: www.parks.wa.gov
Founded: 1965.
Key Personnel: Park Mgr., Denis Felton; Asst. Park Mgr., John Ashley; Chief Interpretive Svcs., Steve Wang.
Governing Authority: state. Affiliated with the Washington State Parks and Recreation Commission, 9150 Cleanwater Lane, Olympia, WA 98504.
Natural Science Museum.
Collections: local geological events; archaeological investigations; anthropology; ethnology; Indian artifacts.
Activities: permanent exhibitions.
Hours & Admission Prices: May-Sept. daily 9-5; Oct.-April Mon., Wed. & Fri. 9-4. other times by appointment only. Donation: $1.
Attendance: 22,000

Coupeville

ADMIRALTY HEAD LIGHTHOUSE, 1280 Engle Rd., Coupeville, WA 98239. Mailing Address: P.O. Box 5000, Coupeville, WA 98239-5000. Tel.: 360-240-5584. Fax: 360-678-4120.
E-mail: admiraltyheadlighthouse@gmail.com
Web Site: admiraltyhead.wsu.edu
Formerly: Fort Casey Interpretive Center
Founded: 1903.
Congressional District: 10
Key Personnel: Chief Interpretive Svcs., Steve Wang; Park Mgr., Ken Hageman; Ranger II, Brett Bayne.
Governing Authority: state. Affiliated with the Washington State Parks & Recreation Commission.
Military/Lighthouse Museum: housed in late 1890s masonry lighthouse located within the former boundaries of Fort Casey, an Endicott period coastal fortification.

Collections: coast artillery artifacts & memorabilia including two 10 inch disappearing cannons; artifacts affiliated with natural history, sea life & park history.
Activities: permanent exhibitions.
Hours & Admission Prices: March Sat.-Sun. 11-5; April Fri.-Sun. 11-5; May Thurs.-Mon. 11-5; June-Sept. daily 11-5; Oct. Fri.-Sun. 11-5; Halloween-Christmas Fri.-Sun. 11-4. No charge; donations accepted. Parking: $5 per vehicle.
Attendance: 42,000
Membership: Individual $25; Family $50; Supporting $100; Lifetime $500; Corporate $1,000.

ISLAND COUNTY HISTORICAL SOCIETY MUSEUM, (M), 908 N.W. Alexander St., Coupeville, WA 98239. Mailing Address: P.O. Box 305, Coupeville, WA 98239-0305. Tel.: 360-678-3310. Fax: 360-678-1702.
E-mail: ichscpvl@whidbey.net
Web Site: www.islandhistory.org
Founded: 1949.
Congressional District: 10
Key Personnel: Exec. Dir., Richard Castellano; Pres. (V), Rick Walti; Education Asst., Gordon Grant; Archival Librarian, Janet Enzmann; Admissions, Mary Ann Burke.
Personnel Profile: Full-Time Paid 1; Part-Time Paid 3; Part-Time Volunteers 65; Interns 6.
Governing Authority: nonprofit. Parent Institution: Island County Historical Society. Tax-exempt: 501(c)(3).
Local History Museum: located in the historic town of Coupeville, founded in 1853.
Collections: Indian artifacts; sea captains; Pioneer Families; military history in Island County.
Research Fields: local and county history.
Facilities: 100-vol. library of general reference material available on special request; meeting room. Admirality Head Lighthouse; Town of Coupeville; Island Country; Methodist Church; Ebey's National Reserve. Stationery and books for sale.
Activities: guided tours; formally organized education programs; permanent & temporary collections.
Publications: quarterly newsletter; books, A History of Whidbey's Island; A Particular Friend, Penn's Cove, Sails, Steamships & Sea Captains.
Hours & Admission Prices: May-Sept. Wed.-Mon. 10-5; Oct.-April Fri.-Mon. 10-4. Family $6, adults $3, military, students & senior citizens $2.50; children under 5 & members no charge. ♿
Attendance: 12,000 (estimated)
Membership: Student $15; Individual $30; Dual Senior $35; Dual Adult $45; Family $50; Associate $90; NW Partner $120; Corporate $200.

Davenport

FORT SPOKANE VISITOR CENTER: NPS (NATIONAL PARK SERVICE), 44150 District Office Lane N., Davenport, WA 99122-9338. Tel.: 509-725-2715 & 633-3830. Fax: 509-633-3834.
Web Site: www.nps.gov/laro
Founded: 1965.
Congressional District: 5
Key Personnel: Chief of Interpretational Education, Jerald Weaver.
Governing Authority: federal. Parent Institution: National Park Service, U.S. Dept. of the Interior, Washington, DC.
Military Museum: housed in 1892 guardhouse located on the site of Fort Spokane, former army reservation 1880-99 & Indian agency headquarters, school & hospital 1899-1929.
Collections: originals & machine copies of historic documents & photographs relating to Fort Spokane between 1880-1929; uniforms; anthropology; archaeology; Indian artifacts. Historic Buildings: 1883 quartermaster stable; 1888 powder magazine; 1889 reservoir house; 1892 guardhouse.
Facilities: library of manuscripts & documents from Fort Spokane during the army period 1880-1900 & Colville Indian Agency period 1900-1929, limited availability for inter-library loan; auditorium. Books & booklets on natural science & history for sale.
Activities: guided tours; lectures; films; permanent exhibitions.
Publications: book, Sentinel of Silence-History of Ft. Spokane; historical photos.
Hours & Admission Prices: Memorial Day to Labor Day call for hours. No charge. ♿
Attendance: 5,000 (accurate)

LINCOLN COUNTY HISTORICAL MUSEUM, 7th & Park, Davenport, WA 99122. Mailing Address: P.O. Box 585, Davenport, WA 99122-0585. Tel.: 509-725-6711.
Founded: 1972.
Congressional District: 5
Key Personnel: Pres. (V), John Coley; Treas., Nancy Ellis; Dir. Visitors Information Center & Sec., Tannis Jeschke.
Personnel Profile: Full-Time Paid 1; Part-Time Volunteers 3.
Governing Authority: nonprofit organization. Parent Institution: Lincoln County Historical Society. Tax-exempt: 600.437.715
General Museum: located on the site of an early Indian campsite along Cottonwood Springs Crossroads for early pioneer trails.
Collections: early agricultural tools & equipment, combine harvester, 1899 Case steam engine; photographic history; cameras; printing tools & equipment; quilts; costumes; furniture; guns; Indian artifacts; dolls; archival history; permanent & rotating displays; fire engines; railroad material.
Facilities: 50-vol. limited desk library pertaining to the history of the area & genealogical studies. Museum-related items for sale.
Activities: Pioneer Day Living History, third weekend in July.
Publications: quarterly newsletter, Lincoln County Historical Society.
Hours & Admission Prices: May 1 to Sept. 30 Mon.-Sat. 9-5. No charge; donations accepted.
Attendance: 1,500 (estimated)
Membership: Individual $15; Family $20; Commercial $25; Life $200; Patron $500; Benefactor $1,000 & up.

Dayton

DAYTON HISTORICAL DEPOT SOCIETY, 222 E. Commercial, Dayton, WA 99328-1313. Mailing Address: P.O. Box 316, Dayton, WA 99328-0316. Tel.: 509-382-2026. Fax: 509-382-2640.
Web Site: daytonhistoricdepot.org
Founded: 1974.
Congressional District: 5
Key Personnel: Pres. (V) & Museum Shop Mgr., Mary Laughery; Mgr., Mary Byrd; Treas., Eric Johnson.
Personnel Profile: Full-Time Paid 1; Part-Time Volunteers 30.
Governing Authority: society. Tax-exempt.
Historical Society Museum: housed in 1881 railroad depot.
Collections: depot memorabilia; picture; clothes; furniture.
Research Fields: Columbia County pioneer history.
Facilities: historic railroad depot.
Activities: guided tours; arts festivals; temporary exhibitions. Society Sponsors: Victorian Christmas.
Publications: Columbia County & Dayton Washington Visitor Information Guide.
Hours & Admission Prices: Summer: Wed.-Sat. 10-12 & 1-5, Sun.1-4; Winter: Wed.-Sat. 11-12 & 1-4. Adults $5; members no charge. Closed holidays. ♿
Attendance: 3,650 (accurate)
Membership: Annual $15; Couples $25; Life Member $300.

DuPont

DUPONT HISTORICAL SOCIETY, 207 Barksdale Ave., DuPont, WA 98327-9001. Tel.: 253-964-2399 & 3492. Fax: 253-964-3554.
E-mail: info@dupontmuseum.com
Web Site: www.dupontmuseum.com
Formerly: Dupont Historical Museum
Founded: 1976.
Congressional District: 2
Key Personnel: Pres. (V), Lee McDonald; Treas., Joe Babb; Museum Mgr., Johanna Jones.
Personnel Profile: Full-Time Volunteers 1; Part-Time Volunteers 14.
Governing Authority: municipal; nonprofit. Tax-exempt.
Historical Society Museum: housed in 1910 building constructed by DuPont Co. as part of a company town.
Collections: photographs, site of 1833 Ft. Nisqually; site of Nisqually Mission 1839-1842 (first US settlers in Western Washington); site of Wilkes Observatory 1841; site of 1843 Ft. Nisqually; maps & artifacts of Hudson Bay Co.; photos, artifacts of DuPont, the Company Town & DuPont Explosive Manufacturing Co., 1906-1976.
Research Fields: Hudson Bay in 1830 & DuPont in 1906; Nisqually Methodist Episcopal Mission 1839-41.
Activities: guided tours; lectures; films; celebration of first 4th of July west of Missouri River with personnel and Wilkes personnel participating.
Publications: DuPont-The Story of a Company Town.
Hours & Admission Prices: Wed., Fri. & Sun. 1-4, Thurs. 11-4 or by appointment. No charge; donations accepted. Closed holidays. ♿
Attendance: 1,000 (estimated)

Eatonville

NORTHWEST TREK WILDLIFE PARK, 11610 Trek Dr. E., Eatonville, WA 98328-9502. Tel.: 360-832-6117. Fax: 360-832-6118.
E-mail: whitney.dalbalcon@pdza.org
Web Site: www.nwtrek.org

Founded: 1975.
Congressional District: 6
Key Personnel: Dir., Gary Geddes; Public Rels., Cherilyn Williams; Deputy Dir., David Ellis; Museum Shop Mgr., Donna Powell.
Personnel Profile: Full-Time Paid 25; Part-Time Paid 50; Part-Time Volunteers 90; Interns 8.
Governing Authority: municipal. Parent Institution: Metropolitan Park Tacoma. Tax-exempt: 170(b)(1)(A).
Wildlife Park.
Collections: native North American species.
Facilities: food service available. Gift items for sale.
Activities: guided tours; films; organized education programs for children; docent program; meeting room rentals.
Publications: brochure, Northwest Trek Wildlife Park; quarterly membership newsletter, Trek Tracks.
Hours & Admission Prices: March-Oct. daily 9:30; Nov.-Feb. Fri.-Sun. 9:30. Adults 13-64 $15, senior citizens 65 & over $13.50, youth 5-12 $10, tots 3-4 $7; discounts for Pierce County residents & military personnel; children under 3 & members no charge. Seasonal hours, please call or check website for special times. Closed Thanksgiving; Christmas. ♿
Attendance: 182,000 (accurate)
Membership: One + One $55; Household & Grandparent $85; Deluxe Household $100; Sponsor $195; Patron $260,

PIONEER FARM MUSEUM AND OHOP INDIAN VILLAGE, 7716 Ohop Valley Rd. E., Eatonville, WA 98328-9342. Tel.: 360-832-6300. Fax: 360-832-4533.
E-mail: pioneer@mashell.com
Web Site: www.pioneerfarmmuseum.org
Founded: 1975.
Congressional District: 2
Key Personnel: Bd. Pres. (V), Ed Kettman; Office Mgr., Nora Cady; Sec. & Treas., Lori Ramsey; Museum Shop Mgr., Valerie Sivertson.
Personnel Profile: Part-Time Paid 13; Part-Time Volunteers 2.
Governing Authority: nonprofit organization. Tax-exempt: 501(c)(3).
History Museum: hands-on living history c.1880 farm.
Collections: hands-on guided pioneer experience includes 6 buildings in a farm setting: 1887 trading post, 1888 two-story cabin, interpreters cabin, pole barn with animals & hay loft, working blacksmith shop, working wood work shop; 1892 replica of one room schoolhouse.
Activities: hands on living history guided tour, grind grain, churn butter, card wool, scrub clothing, curl hair, milking, pet farm animals, spud logs, jump in hay; hands on tour of the traditional Native American lifestyles of the Northwest; Pioneer Farm, pioneer folklore & crafts, program, schoolhouse lesson; nature trail walk; overnight Pioneer Living Experience; Native American Season tour, Indian lore & craft program; Co-Salish overnight program.
Hours & Admission Prices: Public Tours: March-May & Sept. to mid-Nov. Sat.-Sun. 11-4; Father's Day-Labor Day daily 11-4. Group Tours: mid-March to Thanksgiving by reservation only. Adults $7.50, children $6.50; discounts to AAA members. Native American Seasons Tour: Father's Day to Labor Day Fri.-Sun. 1 & 2:30. Adults $7, children $6. ♿
Attendance: 26,000 (estimated)
Membership: Senior 61 & over $20; Individual $25; Family $75; Lifetime $1,000.

Edmonds

EDMONDS ART FESTIVAL MUSEUM, Frances Anderson Center, 700 Main St., Edmonds, WA 98020-3032. Mailing Address: Edmonds Arts Festival Foundation, P.O. Box 699, Edmonds, WA 98020-0699. Tel.: 425-771-1984.
E-mail: hardarmc@verizon.net
Web Site: www.eaffoundation.org
Founded: 1979.
Congressional District: 2
Key Personnel: Pres., Terry Vehrs; Cur., Darlene McLelland.
Personnel Profile: Part-Time Paid 1.
Governing Authority: nonprofit organization. Subsidiary Institution: Edmonds Arts Festival. Tax-exempt: 501(c)(3).
Art Museum: located in Frances Anderson Center.
Collections: various forms of art media.
Activities: arts festival; organized education programs for undergraduate or graduate college students affiliated with Edmonds Community College; temporary & traveling exhibitions.
Hours & Admission Prices: Mon.-Fri. 9-9, Sat. 10-4. No charge. Closed federal holidays. ♿
Attendance: 250,000 (estimated)
Membership: Annual $2; Patron $60; Business $50; Sustaining $125; Life Patron $500.

EDMONDS SOUTH SNOHOMISH COUNTY HISTORICAL SOCIETY, INC., 118 Fifth Ave., N., Edmonds, WA 98020-3145. Mailing Address: P.O. Box 52, Edmonds, WA 98020-0052. Tel.: 425-774-0900. Fax: 425-774-6507.
E-mail: jonisein@yahoo.com
Web Site: www.historicedmonds.org
Founded: 1973.
Congressional District: 1
Key Personnel: Dir., Joni L. Sein; Pres. (V), Fred Bell.
Personnel Profile: Part-Time Paid 2; Part-Time Volunteers 100.
Governing Authority: society; nonprofit organization. Tax-exempt: 501(c)(3).
Historical Society Museum: housed in 1910 Carnegie Library.
Collections: business, industrial & domestic artifacts relating to the settlement & history of Edmonds & south Snohomish County; archival documents; photographs; permanent exhibit on history of Edmonds including working shingle mill diorama & historic hotel room; Victorian parlor; 1910 town scene diorama; maritime gallery.
Research Fields: local history.
Activities: guided tours; special events; permanent & temporary exhibitions.
Publications: quarterly newsletter.
Hours & Admission Prices: Wed.-Sun. 1-4. Suggested Donation: adults $2, students $1. Closed holidays. ♿
Attendance: 4,700 (estimated)
Membership: Individual $20; Family $30; Business $50; Sustaining $100; Benefactor $300.

Ellensburg

CWU ANTHROPOLOGY DEPARTMENT, 400 E. University Way, Ellensburg, WA 98926-7591. Tel.: 509-963-3201. Fax: 509-963-3215.
E-mail: anthro@cwu.edu
Web Site: www.cwu.edu/~anthro/dept
Founded: 1972.
Congressional District: 4
Personnel Profile: Full-Time Paid 1.
Governing Authority: state. Affiliated with Central Washington University. Tax-exempt.
University Anthropology Museum.
Collections: ethnographic materials from New Guinea, Mexico, Western Plateau, San Blas Islands, Panama, Africa, Southwest & Northwest Coast U.S.
Research Fields: archaeology; ethnology.
Facilities: classrooms; research labs.
Activities: temporary exhibitions, some training opportunities.
Hours & Admission Prices: Mon.-Fri. 8-5 by appointment only. No charge. ♿

CLYMER MUSEUM OF ART, 416 N. Pearl St., Ellensburg, WA 98926-3112. Tel.: 509-962-6416. Fax: 509-962-6424.
E-mail: clymermuseum@charter.net
Web Site: www.clymermuseum.org
Founded: 1988.
Congressional District: 13
Key Personnel: Dir., Mia Merendino.
Personnel Profile: Full-Time Paid 1; Part-Time Paid 3; Part-Time Volunteers 36; Interns 2.
Governing Authority: nonprofit organization. Tax-exempt.
Art Museum: honoring John F. Clymer housed in 1901 building in historic downtown Ellensburg.
Collections: works of John Clymer.
Facilities: 7,100 sq. ft. exhibit space. Gift items for sale.
Activities: docent programs; formal education programs for adults & children; guided tours; lectures; loan exhibitions; broadcast programs.
Publications: newsletter.
Hours & Admission Prices: Mon.-Fri. 10-5, Sat. 10-4, Sun. 12-4. No charge; donations accepted. Closed major holidays. ♿
Attendance: 40,000 (accurate)
Membership: Individual $35; Family $50; friend $75; Associate $100; Patron $250; Premier $500; Benefactor $1,000 & up.

KITTITAS COUNTY HISTORICAL MUSEUM, 114 E. Third Ave., Ellensburg, WA 98926-3346. Tel.: 509-925-3778.
Founded: 1963.
Key Personnel: Dir., Lori Foulke.
Personnel Profile: Full-Time Paid 2; Part-Time Volunteers 4.
Governing Authority: Parent Institution: Kittitas County Historical Society. Tax-exempt.
History Museum.
Collections: Kittitas County history & culture; household furnishings; decorative arts; clothing & textiles; Native American bags & baskets; archives;

photographs; early businesses; ranching; farming; geological specimens; automobiles; dolls.
Facilities: over 7,000 sq. ft. exhibit space.
Activities: school tours; lunch & lecture series; permanent & temporary exhibits.
Hours & Admission Prices: Mon.-Sat. 10-4. No charge; donations accepted. ♿
Attendance: 5,563 (accurate)
Membership: Student & Senior $10; Individual $15; Family $25; Supporter $50 & up; Contributor $100 & up; Patron $250 & up; Benefactor $500 & up.

OLMSTEAD PLACE STATE PARK, 921 N. Ferguson Rd., Ellensburg, WA 98926-8109. Tel.: 509-925-1943. Fax: 509-925-1955.
E-mail: olmstead.place@parks.wa.gov
Web Site: www.parks.gov
Founded: 1968.
Congressional District: 13
Key Personnel: Park Ranger, Brandon Holkstra.
Personnel Profile: Full-Time Paid 1; Full-Time Volunteers 1; Part-Time Volunteers 5.
Governing Authority: state. Parent Institution: Washington State Parks & Recreation Commission. Tax-exempt.
Historic Site: 160-acre 1875 homestead.
Collections: agricultural equipment.
Research Fields: agricultural history.
Facilities: 100-vol. library pertaining to agricultural; 1875 log cabin; 1908 farmhouse; 19th-century Seaton Schoolhouse; barns & outbuildings; hiking trail; picnic & play areas.
Activities: guided tours; participatory exhibits.
Publications: brochures: Olmstead Place, Altapes Creek Trail; coloring book: Olmstead Place; Seaton Cabin Schoolhouse.
Hours & Admission Prices: Summer: 6:30am to dusk; Winter: 8am to dusk. No charge; donations accepted.
Attendance: 43,000
Membership: Friend $10 or 4 hours of labor; Supporting Friend $100 or 40 hours of labor; Life Friend $1,000 or 400 hours of labor.

Enumclaw

ENUMCLAW PLATEAU HISTORICAL SOCIETY, 1087 Marion St., Enumclaw, WA 98022. Mailing Address: P.O. Box 1087, Enumclaw, WA 98022-1087.
Founded: 2005.
Key Personnel: Dir. & Pres. (V), Ronald Tyler; Treas., Robert Stygar.
Personnel Profile: Part-Time Volunteers 10.
Governing Authority: private; nonprofit organization. Tax-exempt: 501(c)(3).
Historical Society Museum: housed in a former Masonic Hall, c.1909.
Collections: local history from mid-1800s to present; personal artifacts; furnishings; photographs; family records; obituaries, weddings, anniversary & business history catalogs from 1935 to present.
Research Fields: photographs of local homes & sites from 1950s to present.
Facilities: library; 200 sq. ft. exhibit space.
Activities: Annual Events: History Award Dinner; Holiday Bazaar.
Publications: biannual newsletter, Links.
Hours & Admission Prices: Thurs. & Sun. 1-4. No charge; donations accepted. Closed most holidays. ♿
Attendance: 600 (accurate)
Membership: Senior & Student $5, Individual $15; Household $20; Business $30; Patron $100; Life $200.

Ephrata

GRANT COUNTY HISTORICAL MUSEUM, 742 Basin St., N.W., Ephrata, WA 98823-1635. Mailing Address: P.O. Box 1141, Ephrata, WA 98823-1141. Tel.: 509-754-3334. Fax: 509-754-2148.
E-mail: grantcomuseum@mail.com
Founded: 1951.
Congressional District: 13
Key Personnel: Pres. (V), Robert Mack; Dir., Pat Witham.
Personnel Profile: Full-Time Paid 3; Part-Time Paid 1; Part-Time Volunteers 12.
Governing Authority: board of directors & county commissioners; nonprofit organization. Parent Institution: Grant County Historical Society. Tax-exempt.
Local History Museum: 36 building village.
Collections: early history of county; furnishings; early cattleman's equipment; pioneer village & homestead with fixtures & furniture; replica of Grant County Fire Hall; clothing; archives; early dishes & utensils used by settlers; farm machinery; photographs; oral histories; documents; pictorial history of Grand Coulee Dam, 1933-completion. Historic Buildings: St. Rose of Lima Catholic church; land office; replica of Wilson Creek State Bank; livery stable; Line Cabin; Marlin (Krupp) jail; 1902 homestead; one-room schoolhouse; saloon; dress shop; barber shop; newspaper office; blacksmith shop; country store; line cabin; millinery shop; Justice of the Peace; country store; camera shop; old time doctor's & dentist's office; pharmacy; Grant County Journal; 1971 Burlington Northern Caboose.
Research Fields: history of Grant County; pioneer settlers; early county schools; Grand Coulee Dam.
Facilities: interpretive center; picnic area. Museum-related items for sale.
Activities: pre-arranged tours; permanent & temporary exhibitions. Museum Sponsors: living museum during Sage & Sun Festival in June; Pioneer Day in September; Old Time Political Rally in fall on election years.
Publications: quarterly newsletter; oral history compilation, Memories of Grant County, Washington.
Hours & Admission Prices: May-Sept. Mon.-Tues. & Thurs.-Sat. 10-5, Sun. 1-4; tours by appointment. Adults $3.50, students 5-15 $2.50; children under 5 no charge. ♿
Attendance: 7,500 (estimated)
Membership: Student $5; Individual $10; Family $25; Caliche $100; Basalt $500; Granite $1,000.

Everett

FLYING HERITAGE COLLECTION, 3407 109th St., S.W., Everett, WA 98204-1351. Tel.: 206-342-4242. Fax: 206-342-4235.
Web Site: www.flyingheritage.com
Key Personnel: Exec. Dir., Adrian Hunt; Museum Shop Mgr., Liz Davidson
Military Aviation History.
Collections: aviation history; combat aircraft & artifacts.
Activities: special events.
Hours & Admission Prices: Memorial Day to Labor Day daily 10-5; Sept.-May Tues.-Sun. 10-5. Adults $12, military & seniors $10, youth 6-15 $8; discounts to groups of 15 or more; children 5 & under no charge. ♿

IMAGINE CHILDREN'S MUSEUM, 1502 Wall St., Everett, WA 98201-4008. Tel.: 425-258-1006. Fax: 425-258-5406.
E-mail: info@imaginecm.org
Web Site: www.imaginecm.org
Key Personnel: Exec. Dir., Nancy Johnson; Museum Shop Mgr., Julie Vogel.
Personnel Profile: Part-Time Volunteers 3.
Governing Authority: nonprofit organization. Tax-exempt: 501(c)(3).
Children's Museum.
Collections: hands-on exhibits.
Activities: special events; parties; meetings.
Hours & Admission Prices: Tues.-Wed. & Sat. 10-4, Thurs.-Fri. 10-5:30, Sun. 11-5. Admission $7; discounts Thurs. 3:30-5:30; children one & under no charge. Closed New Year's Day; Easter; Memorial Day; Labor Day; Thanksgiving; Christmas.

RUSSELL DAY GALLERY, Everett Community College, Parks Student Union Bldg., Rm. 219, 2000 Tower St., Everett, WA 98201-1352. Tel.: 425-388-9036.
E-mail: slepper@everettcc.edu
Web Site: www.everettcc.edu/russelldaygallery
Key Personnel: Dir., Sandra Lepper
Art Gallery.
Collections: artwork.
Hours & Admission Prices: Mon.-Wed. 8am-7pm, Thurs.-Fri. 8-4.

SNOHOMISH COUNTY MUSEUM OF HISTORY, 3001 Oakes Ave., Everett, WA 98201-3657. Tel.: 425-345-7349.
E-mail: b.georgeathome@comcast.net
Web Site: snocomuseum.org
Key Personnel: Exec. Dir., Barbara George
History Museum.
Collections: local history & culture; period furnishings; personal artifacts; photographs.
Activities: educational programs.
Hours & Admission Prices: Call for hours.

Federal Way

PACIFIC RIM BONSAI COLLECTION, 33663 Weyerhaeuser Way S., Federal Way, WA 98001-9620. Mailing Address: P.O. Box 9777, Federal Way, WA 98063-9777. Tel.: 253-924-5206; 800-525-5400, ext. 5206. Fax: 253-924-3837.
E-mail: david.degroot@weyerhaeuser.com
Web Site: www.weyerhaeuser.com/bonsai
Founded: 1989.
Key Personnel: Cur., David De Groot.

Personnel Profile: Full-Time Paid 2; Part-Time Paid 2; Part-Time Volunteers 20.
Governing Authority: Parent Institution: Weyerhaeuser Company.
Conservatory.
Collections: over 60 bonsai trees from Canada, China, Japan, Korea, Taiwan & the U.S.
Activities: special events.
Hours & Admission Prices: Temporarily closed. ♿
Attendance: 32,000 (accurate)

RHODODENDRON SPECIES BOTANICAL GARDEN, 2525 S. 336th St., Federal Way, WA 98003-7825. Mailing Address: P.O. Box 3798, Federal Way, WA 98063-3798. Tel.: 253-838-4646 & 927-6960. Fax: 253-838-4686.
E-mail: rsf@rhodygarden.org
Web Site: www.rhodygarden.org
Founded: 1964.
Congressional District: 30
Key Personnel: Exec. Dir & Cur., Steve Hootman; Museum Shop Mgr., Tammi Finnick.
Personnel Profile: Full-Time Paid 5; Part-Time Paid 3; Part-Time Volunteers 80; Interns 3.
Governing Authority: nonprofit organization. Tax-exempt: 501(c)(3).
Botanical Garden.
Collections: plants; species rhododendron.
Research Fields: species rhododendron.
Facilities: reference library of books, pamphlets, maps, vertical files on the genus rhododendron & other horticultural subjects available for research on site; slide library; botanical garden; reading room; 22-acre display garden. Museum-related items for sale.
Activities: guided tours; lectures; slide programs; docent program or council; permanent exhibitions; traveling display.
Publications: books, Rhododendrons of China; The Rhododendron Species, Volume I, Lepidotes; RSF newsletter.
Hours & Admission Prices: March-Sept. Fri.-Wed. 10-4; Oct.-Feb. Sat.-Wed. 11-4. Adults $5, seniors & students $3; discounts to groups; Weyerhaeuser employees, members, school groups & children under 12 no charge. ♿
Attendance: 13,848 (accurate)
Membership: Student $15; Individual $35; Family $50; Supporting $100; Sustaining $250; Patron $500; Garden Society $1,000.

Fife

FIFE HISTORY MUSEUM, 2820 54th Ave. E., Fife, WA 98424-2140. Tel.: 253-896-4710.
E-mail: fifehistorymuseum@gmail.com
Founded: 2001.
Key Personnel: Pres. (V), Louise Hospenthal.
Personnel Profile: Part-Time Volunteers 11.
Governing Authority: nonprofit organization. Tax-exempt: 501(c)(3).
History Museum: housed in the former home of Louis Dacca, a member of the original Fife City Council.
Collections: local history & culture; period furnishings; personal artifacts; photographs.
Hours & Admission Prices: Wed. & Sat. 11:30-4:30, Fri. 9-4:30; other times by appointment. No charge; donations accepted. ♿
Attendance: 1,000 (estimated)
Membership: Student $10; Senior $15; Individual $20; Family $35; Patron & Business $100; Corporate 250 Plus Employees $250.

Forks

FORKS TIMBER MUSEUM, 1421 S. Forks Ave., Forks, WA 98331-9383. Mailing Address: P.O. Box 873, Forks, WA 98331-0873. Tel.: 360-374-9663.
Key Personnel: Mgr., Sherrill Fouts
Logging History Museum.
Collections: local history; loggers; logging tools; photographs; personal artifacts; period furnishings.
Facilities: nature trails; garden.
Activities: hiking; tours.
Hours & Admission Prices: Summer: Mon.-Sat. 9-5; Winter: by appointment.

Fort Lewis

FORT LEWIS MILITARY MUSEUM, Constitution Ave. & Main St., Bldg. 4320, Fort Lewis, WA 98433-5000. Mailing Address: P.O. Box 331001, Fort Lewis, WA 98433-1001. Tel.: 253-967-7208. Fax: 253-966-3029.
E-mail: lewisdptmsmuseum@conus.army.mil
Web Site: www.lewis.army.mil/dptms/pomfi/museum.htm
Founded: 1970.
Key Personnel: Dir. & Cur., Greg Hagge; Museum Shop Mgr., Col. Ian Larson.
Personnel Profile: Full-Time Paid 3; Full-Time Volunteers 2.
Governing Authority: Dept. of the Army. Tax-exempt.
Military Museum.
Collections: uniforms, equipment, weapons, photographs, books related to the military history of the Northwest from Lewis & Clark to present day; military vehicles.
Research Fields: military organizational histories; Fort Lewis; Northwest military.
Facilities: artillery. Museum-related gifts for sale.
Activities: guided tours; historical society.
Publications: brochures; quarterly journal, The Banner.
Hours & Admission Prices: Wed.-Sun. 12-4. No charge. Closed legal holidays. ♿
Attendance: 58,000 (estimated)
Membership: Single $10; Family $15; Sustaining Single & Family $25; Life $100; Silver Life $500; Gold Life $1,000 & up.

Fox Island

FOX ISLAND HISTORICAL SOCIETY, 1017 Ninth Ave., Fox Island, WA 98333. Mailing Address: P.O. Box 242, Fox Island, WA 98333-0242. Tel.: 253-549-2835.
E-mail: museum@foxisland.net
Web Site: foxisland.net/historical.htm
Founded: 1895.
Congressional District: 6
Key Personnel: Pres. & Acting Dir., Marie Weis; Treas., Vera Hackett.
Personnel Profile: Part-Time Volunteers 30.
Governing Authority: nonprofit organization. Parent Institution: Washington State Historical Society. Tax-exempt: 501(c)(3).
Historical Society Museum.
Collections: 3,000 artifacts pertaining to life on Fox Island & in Washington State; 500 pulley blocks; household goods; farm equipment; albums; photographs; textiles; Indian baskets; local history scrapbooks.
Research Fields: local history.
Facilities: 250-vol. library pertaining to Fox Island, State & natural history; auditorium. Books, local maps, postcards & other gift items for sale.
Activities: guided tours; organized education programs for children; docent program; participatory, loan, temporary & traveling exhibitions.
Publications: books: A History of Fox Island; Island in the Sound; Fox Island; Echoes of Yesterday.
Hours & Admission Prices: Wed. & Sat.-Sun. 1-4. No charge; donations accepted. Closed New Year's Day; Easter; Christmas. ♿
Attendance: 600 (estimated)
Membership: Senior $5; Individual $10; Family $20.

Friday Harbor

ISLAND MUSEUM OF ART, WESTCOTT BAY INSTITUTE, 314 Spring St., Friday Harbor, WA 98250. Mailing Address: P.O. Box 339, Friday Harbor, WA 98250-0339. Tel.: 360-370-5050. Fax: 360-370-5805.
E-mail: info@wbay.org
Web Site: www.wbay.org
Founded: 2000.
Key Personnel: Exec. Dir., Victoria Compton; Pres. (V), Arnold Klaus; Treas., Beth Nicholson.
Personnel Profile: Full-Time Paid 1; Part-Time Paid 1; Part-Time Volunteers 30; Interns 3.
Governing Authority: private; nonprofit organization. Tax-exempt: 501(c)(3).
Art Museum.
Collections: works of art by Northwest & West Coast artists.
Facilities: 800 sq. ft. exhibit space; 19 acre sculpture park. Museum-related items for sale.
Activities: arts festivals; dance recitals; docent program; formal education programs; student internships; temporary exhibitions. Annual Events: 2 Festivals
Publications: annual newsletter.
Hours & Admission Prices: Island Museum of Art: March 10-April & Oct.-Dec. 22 Tues.-Sat. 11-5; May-Sept. Tues.-Sun. 11-5. Sculpture Park: daily dawn to dusk. Museum: no charge; donations accepted. Park: admission $5; children no charge. ♿
Attendance: 20,000 (estimated)
Membership: Individual $30; Family $50; Donor $100; Sponsor $250; Patron $500; Benefactor $1,000.

SAN JUAN HISTORICAL SOCIETY, 405 Price St., Friday Harbor, WA 98250. Mailing Address: P.O. Box 441, Friday Harbor, WA 98250-0441. Tel.: 360-378-3949. Fax: 360-378-3949 (call first).
Web Site: www.sjmuseum.org
Founded: 1961.

Congressional District: 40
Key Personnel: Pres., Mary Jean Cahail; Exec. Dir., Kevin Loftus; Treas., Dave Hylton.
Personnel Profile: Part-Time Paid 1; Part-Time Volunteers 80; Interns 1.
Governing Authority: society. Tax-exempt: 501(c)(3).
Historical Society Museum: housed in turn-of-the-century farmhouse.
Collections: San Juan Island history; Native American baskets. Historic Buildings: town jail; log cabin; farmhouse; barn; carriage house; milk house; root cellar.
Activities: guided tours; organized education programs for adults & children; public events; lectures.
Publications: quarterly newsletter.
Hours & Admission Prices: April & Oct. Sat. 10-4; June-Sept. Wed.-Sat. 10-4, Sun. 1-4; Nov.-March by appointment only. Suggested Donation: adults $5; members no charge.
Attendance: 6,500 (estimated)
Membership: Seniors 60 & over $10; Individual $15; Business & Family $25; Sponsor $50; Benefactor $100.

SAN JUAN ISLAND NATIONAL HISTORICAL PARK, 650 Mullis St., Ste. 100, Friday Harbor, WA 98250-7951. Mailing Address: P.O. Box 429, Friday Harbor, WA 98250-0429. Tel.: 360-378-2240 & 2902. Fax: 360-378-2615.
E-mail: sajh_interpretation@nps.gov
Web Site: www.nps.gov/sajh
Founded: 1966.
Congressional District: 2
Key Personnel: Supt., Peter Dederich; Chief Ranger, John Sherman.
Personnel Profile: Full-Time Paid 8; Full-Time Volunteers 8; Part-Time Paid 4.
Governing Authority: federal. Parent Institution: National Park Service. Tax-exempt.
Park Museum: area includes American & English camps. Joint occupation of San Juan Island by British & Americans occurred until the final settlement of the water boundary dispute & the Pig War in 1872.
Collections: artifacts associated with the Pig War, 1859-72; U.S. Army & British Royal Marines. Historic Buildings: Restored 1860 Block House, 1859 earthwork, Barracks & Commissary; Officers' Quarters at American Camp.
Research Fields: pertaining to collections.
Facilities: 200-vol. library of diplomatic, Pacific Northwest & military history 1846-1872 & environmental material available for use on premises.
Activities: guided & self guided tours; AV program; summer weekend interpretive programs; special events; Jackle's Lagoon Guided Walk.
Publications: brochures, A Historic Guided Walk: American Camp, A Historic Guided Walk: English Camp.
Hours & Admission Prices: March 15-May 24 & Oct.-Nov. 1 daily 8:30-4:30; May 31-Sept. 4 daily 8:30-5; Sept. 5-Sept. 30 Tues.-Wed. 8:30-4, Thurs.-Mon. 8:30-5; Nov.-March 14 Wed.-Sun. No charge. Closed federal holidays in winter. ♿
Attendance: 274,000 (estimated)

THE WHALE MUSEUM, 62 1st St. N., Friday Harbor, WA 98250. Mailing Address: P.O. Box 945, Friday Harbor, WA 98250-0945. Tel.: 360-378-4710; 800-946-7227, ext. 30. Fax: 360-378-5790.
E-mail: info@whalemuseum.org
Web Site: www.whalemuseum.org
Founded: 1979.
Congressional District: 2
Key Personnel: Dir., Jenny L. Atkinson; Bd. Pres., Dr. Val Veirs; Assoc. Dir., Mary Blevins; Collections Cur., Amy Traxler; Education Cur., Cindy Hansen; Museum Shop Mgr., Sue Vulgares.
Personnel Profile: Full-Time Paid 5; Part-Time Paid 6; Part-Time Volunteers 25; Interns 3.
Governing Authority: society; nonprofit. Tax-exempt: 501(c)(3).
Natural History Museum.
Collections: interpretive graphics; life-size models; skeletons; biological specimens; ethnographical artifacts related to cetaceans; current research on resident orcas; wild whales.
Research Fields: natural history of the marine environment, with special emphasis on cetaceans, physiology & demographics of resident orcas, & human impacts on cetaceans.
Facilities: library of books & scientific reprints on natural history, ecology, communications, physiology, bioacoustics, general biology of marine mammals, museology available for research by request; exhibit hall; field research station; 50-seat auditorium. Books, original art, prints & other museum-related items for sale.
Activities: guided tours; lectures; films; gallery talks; concerts; formally organized education programs for children, adults & college students; permanent & temporary loans and traveling exhibits.
Publications: Cetus biannual newsletter; field guides; scientific papers; educational teaching packages.
Hours & Admission Prices: Feb.-May & Oct. daily 10-5; June-Sept. daily 9-6; Winter: call for hours. Adults $6, senior citizens $5, college student & children $3; children under 5 & members no charge. Closed New Year's Day; Thanksgiving; Christmas.
Attendance: 25,000 (accurate)
Membership: Individual $25; Individual Plus Adoption $35; Family $40; Business $50 & up; Supporter $100; Contributor $250; Patron $500; Benefactor $1,000; Steward $2,500 & up.

Gig Harbor

HARBOR HISTORY MUSEUM, 4218 Harborview Dr., Gig Harbor, WA 98332. Mailing Address: P.O. Box 744, Gig Harbor, WA 98335-0744. Tel.: 253-858-6722. Fax: 253-853-4211.
E-mail: info@harborhistorymuseum.org
Web Site: www.harborhistorymuseum.org
Formerly: Gig Harbor Peninsula History Museum
Founded: 1963.
Congressional District: 6
Key Personnel: Exec. Dir., Jennifer Kilmer; Pres. Bd. Dirs. (V), Walter H. Smith; Treas., Mark Caviness; Cur. Exhibitions & Collections, Victoria Gehl-Blackwell.
Personnel Profile: Full-Time Paid 3; Part-Time Paid 2; Part-Time Volunteers 60.
Governing Authority: articles of incorporation/board of trustees; nonprofit. Tax-exempt: 501(c)(3).
Historical Society Museum.
Collections: Gig Harbor & local peninsulas social & occupational history; fishing; logging; farming; school records; personal archives; photographs; local biographies.
Research Fields: personal biographies; local history.
Facilities: permanent & temporary exhibitions; research room. Museum-related items for sale.
Activities: films; organized education programs for children & adults; history cruise. Museum Sponsors: Heritage Row.
Publications: membership newsletter; Gig Harbor History Walk; An Excellent Little Bay - A History of Gig Harbor.
Hours & Admission Prices: Museum: currently closed. Research: by appointment. ♿
Attendance: 2,611 (accurate)
Membership: Senior $35; Senior Family $50; Friend $50; Family $60; Supporting $100; Sustaining $200; Patron $500; Benefactor $1,000.

Goldendale

GOLDENDALE OBSERVATORY, 1602 Observatory Dr., Goldendale, WA 98620-3315. Tel.: 509-773-3141. Fax: 509-773-6929.
E-mail: goldendale.observatory@parks.wa.gov
Web Site: www.perr.com/gosp.html
Founded: 1973.
Key Personnel: Dir., Rex Derr; Museum Shop Mgr., Steve R. Stout.
Personnel Profile: Full-Time Paid 1; Part-Time Paid 1; Part-Time Volunteers 3.
Governing Authority: state. Affiliated with Washington State Parks & Recreation Commission, 7150 Cleanwater Dr., Olympia, WA 98504.
Observatory.
Collections: astronomical displays; telescopes.
Facilities: telescopes available for use by public.
Activities: slide shows; demonstrations; view astronomical objects through a telescope.
Hours & Admission Prices: April-Sept. Wed.-Sun. 2-5 & 8-midnight; Oct.-March Fri.-Sun. 2-5 & 7-10. No charge; donations accepted. ♿
Attendance: 22,581 (estimated)

KLICKITAT COUNTY HISTORICAL SOCIETY, 127 W. Broadway, Goldendale, WA 98620. Mailing Address: P.O. Box 86, Goldendale, WA 98620-0086. Tel.: 509-773-4303.
Founded: 1958.
Congressional District: 4
Key Personnel: C.E.O. & Pres. (V), Bonnie Beeks; Sec., Mary Evans Childs; Treas. & Museum Shop Mgr., Marilyn Enwards; Museum Shop Mgr., Terry Durgan.
Personnel Profile: Full-Time Paid 1; Part-Time Paid 1; Part-Time Volunteers 20.
Governing Authority: society; board of directors. Tax-exempt: 501(c)(3).
History Museum: housed in 1903 W.B. Presby Mansion.
Collections: agriculture; clothing; glass; 1900 period house & furnishings; 126 coffee mills; turn-of-the-century school display; linens; photographs; newspaper & advertising copperplate page set up stereotype castings; toys; dolls; velocipede; printshop; cameras; period school documents; books; period

dental chair & x-ray; late 18th- and early 19th-century woodworking tools; record cylinders & records; pianola & player piano; military memorabilia including WWI & WWII.

Research Fields: county history; genealogy; cemeteries; early abstracts & surveys of county.

Activities: guided tours; permanent & temporary exhibitions. Museum Sponsors: Heritage Barn Tour in September; Quilt Show; Christmas Concert.

Publications: books, They Worked Hard; Citizens of the Century; Goldendale 1904; The White Salmon Valley; The Goldens of Goldendale; Klickitat County Death and Birth Records; 1860, 1870 and 1880 Census of Klickitat County, Washington; Blockhouse Bicentennial; Poems from a Saddle Bag; The Nichols - Sheppard Steam Engine; The Joys of Yesterday Can be Found In The Memories of Today; leaflets: Sam Hill, Stonehenge and Maryhill Town; The Story of Maryhill Museum; The Life of Samual Hill; Stonehenge; Who Were the Guests at the Central Hotel; The Old Red House; Andrew J. Bolon: U.S. Indian Agent; Winthrop B. Presby; annual magazine, Klickitat Heritage; The History of Klickitat County.

Hours & Admission Prices: April 15-Oct. 16 daily 9-5; other times by appointment. Adults $4.50, students 6-12 & school tours $1; discount to groups; members no charge. ♿

Attendance: 2,534 (accurate)

Membership: Students $10; Individual $15; Couple $20; Family $25; Sustaining & Small Business $30; Patron $50; Sponsor $100.

* **MARYHILL MUSEUM OF ART, (M),** 35 Maryhill Museum Dr., Goldendale, WA 98620-4601. Tel.: 509-773-3733. Fax: 509-773-6138.

E-mail: maryhill@maryhillmuseum.org

Web Site: www.maryhillmuseum.org

Founded: 1923.

Congressional District: 4

Key Personnel: C.E.O. & Dir., Colleen Schafroth; Pres. (V), Jim Foster; Dir. Devel., Tim Copeland; Cur. Exhibits, Lee Musgrave; Cur. Education, Carrie Clark-Peck; Adjunct Cur. Native American Collections, Mary Schlick; Collections Mgr. & Registrar, Betty Long; Facilities & Retail Mgr., Patricia Perry; Operations & Finance Mgr., Leslie Wetherell.

Personnel Profile: Full-Time Paid 8; Part-Time Paid 5; Part-Time Volunteers 90.

Governing Authority: nonprofit organization. Tax-exempt: 501(c)(3).

Art Museum: housed in a European, beaux-arts style concrete mansion; built in 1914. Listed on the National Register of Historic Places.

Collections: Rodin watercolors & sculptures; North American Native American art & cultural materials; rare & modern chess sets; Queen Marie of Roumania royal furnishings; European & American paintings, sculpture & decorative arts; 1945 French fashion mannequins & theatre sets; history of Sam Hill, founder, Russian icons; 15,000 photographs; Stonehenge monument.

Research Fields: Sam Hill documents, including Good Roads Movement; Pacific Northwest history; Loie Fuller papers; materials & papers of Queen Marie of Romania; icons; Native American cultures.

Facilities: 1,500 vol. fine & native arts library available for use on premises by appointment; 26 acre park; cafe; 5,300 acres of ranchlands; educational resource room. Museum-related gifts for sale.

Activities: self-guided tours; special tours by appointment; lecture series; seminars; symposia; youth & adult art appreciation classes; performing arts events; teacher institutes; permanent, temporary, off-site regional & traveling exhibitions.

Publications: book, Maryhill Museum of Art; books & publications on the collections.

Hours & Admission Prices: mid-March to mid-Nov. daily 9-5. Adults $7, senior citizens 65 & over $6, children 6-16 $2; discounts to AAM, ICOM & WMC members; county weekends no charge. ♿

Attendance: 42,997 (accurate)

Membership: Individual $35; Family $50; Sponsor $100; Patron $250; Sustaining $500; Sam Hill Society: Associate $1,000; Friend $1,750; Fellow $2,500; Director's Circle $5,000.

Granite Falls

GRANITE FALLS HISTORICAL MUSEUM, 109 E. Union St., Granite Falls, WA 98252. Mailing Address: P.O. Box 1414, Granite Falls, WA 98252-1414. Tel.: 360-691-2603.

History Museum.

Collections: local history & culture; logging; railroad; mining mills; transportation; schools; business; fashion; personal artifacts; period furnishings; photographs.

Activities: special events.

Hours & Admission Prices: Sun. 12-5; other times by appointment.

Greenbank

MEERKERK RHODODENDRON GARDENS, 3531 Meerkerk Lane, Greenbank, WA 98253. Mailing Address: P.O. Box 154, Greenbank, WA 98253-0154. Tel.: 360-678-1912.

Garden.

Collections: plants; trees; flowers.

Facilities: nature trails. Museum-related items for sale.

Activities: educational programs; guided tours; youth programs.

Hours & Admission Prices: March 15-Sept. 15 daily 9-4; Sept. 16-March 14 Wed.-Sun. 9-4. Adults $8; children under 16 no charge.

ROB SCHOUTEN GALLERY, Greenbank Farm, C103, 765 Wonn Rd., Greenbank, WA 98253. Tel.: 360-222-3070.

Art Gallery.

Collections: works by Rob Schouten including oil paintings, etchings, & Giclee prints; works by other artists include paintings, drawings, printmaking, & sculpture.

Hours & Admission Prices: Summer: daily 10-5; Winter: daily 11-4.

Greenwater

CATHERINE MONTGOMERY INTERPRETIVE CENTER, Federation Forest State Park, 49201 Hwy. 410, Greenwater, WA 98022-8015. Tel.: 360-663-2207. Fax: 360-663-0172.

Web Site: www.parks.wa.gov

Founded: 1949.

Congressional District: 8

Key Personnel: Park Mgr., Eric Lewis; Chief Interpretive Svcs., Steve Wang.

Personnel Profile: Full-Time Paid 1; Part-Time Paid 2; Part-Time Volunteers 2; Interns 1.

Governing Authority: state. Parent Institution: The Washington State Parks & Recreation Commission, 7150 Clean Water Lane, Olympia, WA 98504.

Nature Center.

Collections: specimens located in natural settings surrounding the interpretive center.

Facilities: interpretive center; trails; picnic area; hiking trails.

Activities: guided tours; permanent exhibitions.

Hours & Admission Prices: April Sat.-Sun. 9-4; May-Sept. Wed.-Sun. 9-4; other times by appointment. No charge; donations accepted. ♿

Attendance: 75,000 (estimated)

Hoquiam

POLSON MUSEUM, (M), 1611 Riverside Ave., Hoquiam, WA 98550-2739. Mailing Address: P.O. Box 432, Hoquiam, WA 98550-0432. Tel.: 360-533-5862.

E-mail: jbl@polsonmuseum.org

Web Site: www.polsonmuseum.org

Founded: 1976.

Congressional District: 6

Key Personnel: Dir., John Larson; Pres. (V), Norm Callaghan.

Personnel Profile: Full-Time Paid 1; Part-Time Paid 1; Part-Time Volunteers 25.

Governing Authority: nonprofit organization. Tax-exempt: 501(c)(3).

Park & Museum: 1924 mansion located on 1884 homestead site of timber pioneer Alex Polson.

Collections: Grays Harbor history including photographs, maps & written materials; logging & sawmill artifacts; sports; houseware items; dolls; military items; fraternal organizations.

Research Fields: 1845-1915 genealogical study of the area.

Facilities: library pertaining local history & biographies; railroad camp. Books, art work, & gift items for sale.

Activities: guided tours.

Publications: quarterly bulletin, Polson Museum News.

Hours & Admission Prices: April-Dec. 23 Wed.-Sat. 11-4, Sun. 12-4; Dec. 27-March Sat.-Sun. 12-4. Families $10, adults $4, students $2, children $1; discounts to AASLH members; AAM members & members no charge.

Attendance: 4,000 (estimated)

Membership: Senior Citizen & Student $15; Individual $20; Couple $30; Family $40; Sustaining $60 & up.

Ilwaco

COLUMBIA PACIFIC HERITAGE MUSEUM, 115 S.E. Lake St., Ilwaco, WA 98624. Mailing Address: P.O. Box 153, Ilwaco, WA 98624-0153. Tel.: 360-642-3446. Fax: 360-642-4615.

E-mail: info@columbiapacificheritagemuseum.org

Web Site: columbiapacificheritagemuseum.org

Formerly: Ilwaco Heritage Museum

Founded: 1983.

Congressional District: 19
Key Personnel: Exec. Dir., Betsy Millard; Chm. Bd. & Pres. (V), Karla Nelson; Librarian, Carol Bell; Collections Mgr., Barbara Minard; Museum Shop Mgr., Stacey Pierro.
Personnel Profile: Part-Time Paid 6; Part-Time Volunteers 30; Interns 1.
Governing Authority: nonprofit organization. Parent Institution: Ilwaco Heritage Foundation. Tax-exempt: 501(c)(3).
History Museum.
Collections: southwest Washington history from prehistoric to modern times; Lewis & Clark's expedition stay in Nov. 1805; Chinook culture; pioneer household items & tools; railroad depot; train car.
Research Fields: history; regional Native American culture.
Facilities: Museum-related items for sale.
Activities: temporary exhibitions. Annual Events: Railroad Days Festival in July; Cranberrian Festival in October; Ocian in View Lecture Series in November.
Publications: quarterly newsletter; historical shipwreck map; books, Coast Country; They Remembered I, II, III, IV.
Hours & Admission Prices: Mon.-Sat. 10-4, Sun. 12-4. Adults $5, seniors $4, youths 12-17 $2.50; Thurs. & members no charge. Closed Thanksgiving; Christmas. ♿
Attendance: 8,000 (accurate)
Membership: Individual $20; Family $30; Contributing $50; Supporting $100; Patron $250; Sustaining $500.

LEWIS & CLARK INTERPRETIVE CENTER, Cape Disappointment State Park, Ilwaco, WA 98624. Mailing Address: P.O. Box 488, Ilwaco, WA 98624-0488. Tel.: 360-642-3029. Fax: 360-642-4216.
E-mail: lcic@parks.wa.gov
Web Site: www.capedisappointment.org
Founded: 1976.
Key Personnel: Mgr., Aaron Webster.
Personnel Profile: Full-Time Paid 2; Part-Time Volunteers 24.
Governing Authority: state. Affiliated with Washington State Parks & Recreation Commission, 7150 Clean Water Lane, Olympia, WA 98504.
Interpretive Center.
Collections: Lewis & Clark related items; coast artillery items; Coast Guard & lighthouse artifacts.
Research Fields: Lewis & Clark; coast artillery.
Activities: self-guided tour; permanent exhibits.
Hours & Admission Prices: Daily 10-5. Adults $5, children $2.50. Closed Thanksgiving; Christmas. ♿
Attendance: 48,000 (estimated)

Issaquah

ISSAQUAH HISTORY MUSEUM, 165 S.E. Andrews & 50 Rainier Blvd. N., Issaquah, WA 98027. Mailing Address: P.O. Box 695, Issaquah, WA 98027-0026. Tel.: 425-392-3500. Fax: 425-392-4236.
E-mail: info@issaquahhistory.org
Web Site: www.issaquahhistory.org
Formerly: Gilman Town Hall Museum
Founded: 1972.
Congressional District: 8
Key Personnel: Pres., Mary Scott; Dir., Erica S. Maniez; Volunteer Coord., Karen Klein; Mgr. Collections, Julie Hunter.
Personnel Profile: Part-Time Paid 3; Part-Time Volunteers 25; Interns 3.
Governing Authority: municipal; society; nonprofit. Parent Institution: Issaquah Historical Society. Tax-exempt: 501(c)(3).
Historical Society/Gilman Town Hall Museum & Train Depot.
Collections: artifacts; memorabilia. Historic Structures: 1889 Town Hall; 1889 Train Depot; 1914 Town Jail.
Research Fields: historical.
Facilities: 200-vol. library for public use; educational facilities. Books & other museum-related items for sale.
Activities: guided tours; lectures; slides; organized education programs for children; participatory, loan & temporary exhibitions; school loan service.
Publications: quarterly newsletter; Preserving the Stories of Issaquah; King County Lumber Index; Images of America: Issaquah, WA.
Hours & Admission Prices: Depot: Fri.-Sun. 11-3. Town Hall: Thurs.-Sat. 11-3. Adults $2, children $1; members no charge. Closed holidays & holiday weekends. ♿
Attendance: 7,000 (accurate)
Membership: Student & Senior Citizen $10; Senior Family $15 Individual $20; Family $25; Corporate $50.

Kelso

COWLITZ COUNTY HISTORICAL MUSEUM, 405 Allen St., Kelso, WA 98626-4103. Tel.: 360-577-3119. Fax: 360-423-9987.
E-mail: freeced@co.cowlitz.wa.us
Web Site: www.co.cowlitz.wa.us/museum
Founded: 1953.
Congressional District: 3
Key Personnel: Pres. (V), Maila Cadd; Exec. Dir., David W. Freece; Cur., Bill Watson; Education Coord., Danielle Robbins; Administrative Asst., Jim Elliott.
Personnel Profile: Full-Time Paid 1; Part-Time Paid 3; Part-Time Volunteers 25.
Governing Authority: nonprofit. Parent Institution: Cowlitz County and Cowlitz County Historical Society. Tax-exempt: 501(c)(3).
History Museum.
Collections: community histories; tools of pioneer logging industry; photographs; manuscripts; books; ceramics; glass; textiles; Indian artifacts; doll collection; costumes; World War I & World War II collections; city planning archives; toys; waterfowl decoys; Historic Building: 1884, Ben Beighle cabin.
Research Fields: local history; genealogy; biography; Northern Pacific Railroad; river transportation.
Facilities: 1,000-vol. library of reference material available for use on premises; manuscripts, photographs & archival materials. Museum-related items for sale.
Activities: guided tours; training programs for museum interns; permanent & temporary exhibitions; lectures; workshops.
Publications: magazine, Cowlitz Historical Quarterly; quarterly newsletter; books, They Came to Six Rivers: The Story of Cowlitz County; Cowlitz County: Then and Now.
Hours & Admission Prices: Tues.-Sat. 10-4. No charge; donations accepted. Closed holidays. ♿
Attendance: 12,000 (estimated)
Membership: Individual $35; Family $40; Contributing $75; Benefactor & Business $150-$499; Sponsor $500-$999; Life $1,500 & up.

Kennewick

EAST BENTON COUNTY HISTORICAL MUSEUM, 205 Keewaydin Dr., Kennewick, WA 99336-0602. Tel.: 509-582-7704.
E-mail: ebchs@verizon.net
Web Site: ebchs.org
History Museum.
Collections: local history & culture; Native American petroglyphs; pioneer farm equipment & tools; photographs; personal artifacts; period furnishings; agriculture.
Activities: educational programs.
Hours & Admission Prices: Tues.-Sat. 12-4. Adults $4, seniors $2, children 5-17 $1; active military no charge. ♿
Membership: Single $25; Family $35.

Kent

HYDROPLANE & RACEBOAT MUSEUM, 5917 S. 196th St., Kent, WA 98032-2132. Tel.: 206-764-9453. Fax: 206-766-9620.
E-mail: ddw@thunderboats.org
Web Site: www.thunderboats.org/
Key Personnel: Dir., David D. Williams; Museum Shop Mgr., Glenn Raymond.
Personnel Profile: Full-Time Paid 2; Part-Time Paid 1; Part-Time Volunteers 20.
Sport Museum.
Collections: hydroplanes including boats that have won 17 Gold Cups; hydroplane racing history; books, magazines, race programs, newspaper, photos, trophies, & memorabilia; hydroplane racing videos from 1940s to present.
Facilities: Museum-related items for sale.
Activities: Annual Event: Gala Dinner & Auction in August.
Hours & Admission Prices: Tues. & Thurs. 10-8, Wed. & Fri.-Sat. 10-4. Adults $10, seniors & students $5; discounts to groups; members no charge. Closed holidays. ♿
Membership: Limited $50; General $100; Premium $200; Benefactor $500; Lifetime $2,500.

KENT HISTORICAL SOCIETY MUSEUM, 855 E. Smith St., Kent, WA 98030-4623. Tel.: 253-854-4330.
Web Site: www.kenthistoricalmuseum.org/index.html
Key Personnel: Dir., Linda Wagner; Cur., Allison Jurgens
Historical Society Museum.
Collections: artifacts; historic books; historic public & personal documents; newspaper archive; photograph archive; map archive; e-media archive; reference books.
Hours & Admission Prices: Wed.-Sat. 12-4. No charge; donations accepted.

Keyport

NAVAL UNDERSEA MUSEUM, 1 Garnett Way, Keyport, WA 98345-7600. Mailing Address: Navy Region Northwest, 1103 Hunley Rd., Silverdale, WA 98315-1103. Tel.: 360-396-4148.
Web Site: www.navalunderseamuseum.org
Military Museum.
Collections: Navy history, scinece & operations; torpedoes; weapons; mine; hands-on exhibits; submarine technology; diving suits; submarine battle flags.
Activities: educational programs; concerts; lectures; hands-on exhibits; videos.
Hours & Admission Prices: June-Sept. daily 10-4, Oct.-May Wed.-Mon. 10-4. No charge. Closed New Year's Day; Easter; Thanksgiving; Christmas.
Attendance: 47,366 (accurate)

Kirkland

KIRKLAND ARTS CENTER, 620 Market St., Kirkland, WA 98033-5421. Tel.: 425-822-7161. Fax: 425-889-2963.
E-mail: support@kirklandartscenter.org
Web Site: www.kirklandartscenter.org
Founded: 1962.
Key Personnel: Exec. Dir., Christopher Shainin.
Personnel Profile: Full-Time Paid 4; Part-Time Paid 4.
Art Museum.
Collections: paintings; sculpture; ceramics; prints.
Activities: classes.
Hours & Admission Prices: Mon.-Fri. 11-6, Sat. 11-5. No charge; donations accepted. Closed national holidays.
Membership: Adult $500 & up.

La Conner

LA CONNER QUILT & TEXTILE MUSEUM, (M), 703 S. 2nd St., La Conner, WA 98257. Mailing Address: P.O. Box 1270, La Conner, WA 98257-1270. Tel.: 360-466-4288. Fax: 360-466-1051.
E-mail: info@laconnerquilts.com
Web Site: laconnerquilts.com
Founded: 1996.
Key Personnel: Dir., Liz Theaker; Pres. (V), Susan Wells Hall.
Personnel Profile: Full-Time Paid 1; Part-Time Paid 1.
Governing Authority: nonprofit organization. Tax-exempt.
Quilt & Textile Museum: housed in a Victorian mansion built in 1891.
Collections: national & international quilts with a focus on works from the Pacific Northwest.
Activities: monthly textile enrichment series; special events. Annual Events: Autumn Quilt Fest; Arts Alive in November.
Publications: quarterly newsletter.
Hours & Admission Prices: Jan. 17-March & May-Dec. Wed.-Sun. 11-5; April daily 10-5. Adults $5; members no charge. Closed Thanksgiving; Christmas. ♿
Attendance: 7,200 (estimated)
Membership: Individual $30; Family $40; Sponsor $100; Patron $500.

MUSEUM OF NORTHWEST ART, 121 S. First St., La Conner, WA 98257. Mailing Address: P.O. Box 969, La Conner, WA 98257-0969. Tel.: 360-466-4446, ext. 109. Fax: 360-466-7431.
E-mail: gmrobinson@comcast.net
Web Site: www.museumofnwart.org
Founded: 1981.
Congressional District: 40
Key Personnel: C.E.O. & Pres. (V), Stephen Lindstrom; Exec. Dir., Gregory Robinson; Cur., Kathleen Moles; Museum Shop Mgr., Jacque Chase.
Personnel Profile: Full-Time Paid 5; Part-Time Paid 4; Part-Time Volunteers 140.
Governing Authority: nonprofit organization. Tax-exempt: 501(c)(3).
Art Museum.
Collections: Pacific Northwest regional art, early 20th century to present.
Research Fields: Pacific Northwest Art.
Facilities: library; 12,000 sq. ft. exhibit space. Gift items for sale.
Activities: permanent collection; guided tours; lectures; arts festivals; organized education programs for adults & children; loan & temporary exhibitions.
Publications: quarterly newsletter; exhibition books.
Hours & Admission Prices: Daily 10-5. Adults $5, seniors $4, student $2; members & youth under 12 no charge. Closed Thanksgiving; Christmas Eve & Day. ♿
Attendance: 14,291 (accurate)
Membership: Student $15; Individual $35; Family & Small Business $50; Donor $100; Sponsor $250; Patron $500; Benefactor $1,000.

SKAGIT COUNTY HISTORICAL MUSEUM, 501 S. 4th St., La Conner, WA 98257-0818. Mailing Address: P.O. Box 818, La Conner, WA 98257-0818. Tel.: 360-466-3365. Fax: 360-466-1611.
E-mail: museum@co.skagit.wa.us
Web Site: www.skagitcounty.net/museum
Founded: 1959.
Congressional District: 2
Key Personnel: Dir., Karen Marshall; Pres. (V), Cindy Ritchie; Cur. Education, Janet Oakley; Registrar & Cur., Patricia A. Doran; Librarian, Mari C. Anderson-Densmore; Public Rels. Coord. & Museum Shop Mgr., Janet Saunders; Maintenance & Security, Bob Skeele; Business Mgr., Lynn Albright.
Personnel Profile: Full-Time Paid 1; Part-Time Paid 7; Part-Time Volunteers 30.
Governing Authority: Parent Institution: Skagit County Historical Society. Subsidiary Institution: Skagit County. Tax-exempt: 501(c)(3).
History Museum.
Collections: library; archives; manuscripts; oral history; photographs; general artifact collections documenting local history topics: recreation; entertainment; art; domestic life; clothing; ethnicity; politics; communication; transportation; commerce; industry; agriculture.
Research Fields: Skagit county history.
Facilities: 1,500-vol. research library & 15,000 photographs available for use by appointment; long-term, temporary, traveling & hands-on exhibitions; video theater; historic Rosario School. Books & other museum-related items for sale.
Activities: guided tours; lectures; workshops; educational programs for children; long-term, temporary, traveling & hands-on exhibitions; video programs; outreach programs for children & adults. Museum Sponsors: Heritage Award; special events; Treaty Day Celebration; Rosario School Picnic.
Publications: books, Skagit County History (5 volumes); Chechacos All; Indians of Skagit County; Skagit Memories; Sternwheelers & the Skagit River; Skagit Settlers; Skagit County Grows Up, 1917-1941; Last Frontier in the North Cascades; Harvesting the Light: Images of Contemporary Skagit Farm Life, 2007; self-guided walking tour of La Conner; quarterly newsletter; brochures.
Hours & Admission Prices: Tues.-Sun. 11-5. Family $8, adults $4, seniors & children 6-12 $3; discounts to AAM & ICOM members; historical society members and children 5 & under no charge. ♿
Attendance: 10,000 (estimated)

Lacey

LACEY MUSEUM, 829 1/2 Lacey St., S.E., Lacey, WA 98503. Tel.: 360-438-0209.
Key Personnel: Cur., Amber Raney
History Museum.
Collections: community history from the Oregon Trail days to the present.
Hours & Admission Prices: Thurs.-Fri. 11-3, Sat. 9-5; other times by appointment. No charge; donations accepted.

Lakewood

HISTORIC FORT STEILACOOM, 9601 Steilacoom Blvd. S.W. (on Western State Hospital grounds), Lakewood, WA 98498-7213. Mailing Address: P.O. Box 88447, Steilacoom, WA 98388-0447. Tel.: 253-582-5838.
E-mail: hrhjoe1@comcast.net
Web Site: www.historicfortsteilacoom.com
Founded: 1983.
Congressional District: 9
Key Personnel: Pres. (V), C. Gideon Pete; Treas., Kenneth A. Morgan; Dir. & Sec., Joseph W. Lewis.
Personnel Profile: Part-Time Volunteers 16.
Governing Authority: nonprofit organization. Tax-exempt: 501(c)(3).
Historic Site: four original buildings remaining on the site of Fort Steilacoom.
Collections: artifacts; recreated furnishings.
Research Fields: Pierce County history; military history (1849-1868).
Facilities: meeting rooms; interpretive center. Gift items for sale.
Activities: guided tours; lecture series; docent program; events relating to local history; living history.
Publications: Historic Fort Steilacoom newsletter; brochure; tour guide.
Hours & Admission Prices: Jan.-April & Oct.-Nov. first Sun. of month 1-4; May-Sept. Sun. 1-4. No charge; donations accepted.
Membership: Senior Citizen & Student $15; Individual $20; Family $35; Patron $100; Life $300.

Activities: history & art exhibits; cultural events; art workshops; school program; family activities.
Publications: quarterly newsletter; quarterly activity schedule.
Hours & Admission Prices: Tues.-Sat. 11-5. No charge. Closed major holidays. ♿
Attendance: 13,000 (estimated)
Membership: Senior & Student $20; Individual $30; Family $40; Associate $55; Booster $100; Sponsor $250; Patron $500; Benefactor $1,000.

Mukilteo

FUTURE OF FLIGHT AVIATION CENTER & BOEING TOUR, 8415 Paine Field Blvd., Mukilteo, WA 98275-3239. Tel.: 425-438-8100. Fax: 425-265-9808.
Web Site: www.futureofflightfoundation.org
Founded: 2005.
Congressional District: 1
Key Personnel: Dir., Barry Smith; Pres. (V), Dan Ralkonen; Museum Shop Mgr., Peter Bro.
Personnel Profile: Full-Time Paid 10; Part-Time Paid 20; Part-Time Volunteers 24; Interns 10.
Aviation Center.
Collections: aviation history; airplanes; innovations in aviation; photographs; videos.
Major Exhibits: Regional Airlines, 11/09-3/10.
Facilities: 240-seat theater; 125-seat restaurant; strato deck. Museum-related items for sale.
Activities: design your own airplane; hands-on exhibits; assembly plant tour; rental facilities; educational program for middle school students.
Publications: foundation newsletter.
Hours & Admission Prices: Daily 8:30-5:30. Adults $15, senior citizens 65 & over and active military $14, children 15 & under $8. Closed Thanksgiving; Christmas. ♿
Attendance: 180,000 (accurate)

MUKILTEO LIGHT STATION & INTERPRETIVE CENTER, 608 Front St., Mukilteo, WA 98275. Tel.: 425-513-9602.
Light Station Museum.
Collections: local history & culture; documents; photographs; papers; personal artifacts.
Facilities: Museum-related items for sale.
Activities: guided tours; special events; rental facilities.
Hours & Admission Prices: Grounds: daily. Lighthouse & Center: April-Sept. Sat.-Sun. & holidays 12-5; other times by appointment. No charge.

Neah Bay

MAKAH CULTURAL AND RESEARCH CENTER, 1880 Bayview Ave., Neah Bay, WA 98357. Mailing Address: P.O. Box 160, Neah Bay, WA 98357. Tel.: 360-645-2711. Fax: 360-645-2656.
Native American History Museum.
Collections: Native American history, culture, & artifacts; photographs; dug-out canoes; whaling; sealing; fishing; basketry; tools.
Facilities: Museum-related items for sale.
Activities: educational programs.
Hours & Admission Prices: Daily. Adults $5, students & seniors $4; discounts to groups.

Nine Mile Falls

SPOKANE HOUSE INTERPRETIVE CENTER, 9711 W. Charles, Nine Mile Falls, WA 99026-8648. Tel.: 509-465-5064 & 466-4747. Fax: 509-465-5571.
E-mail: riverside@parks.wa.gov
Web Site: www.riversidestatepark.org
Founded: 1950.
Congressional District: 6
Key Personnel: Chief Interpretive Svcs., Steve Wang; Agency Dir., Rex Derr; Park Mgr., Rene Wiley.
Personnel Profile: Part-Time Paid 1; Part-Time Volunteers 5.
Governing Authority: state. Parent Institution: Riverside State Park. Affiliated with the Washington State Parks & Recreation Commission, 7150 Clean Water Ln., Olympia, WA 98504.
Historic Site Museum: 1810, trading post used as a fur trading post & operated at various times by British, Canadian & American interests.
Collections: archaeological investigations; American Indian culture & artifacts; Tribes of the Plateau.
Activities: permanent exhibitions.
Publications: brochure.
Hours & Admission Prices: Memorial Day to Labor Day Sat.-Sun. 10-4. No charge; donations accepted. ♿
Attendance: 7,000 (accurate)

North Bend

SNOQUALMIE VALLEY HISTORICAL MUSEUM, 320 Bendigo Blvd., S., North Bend, WA 98045-8260. Mailing Address: P.O. Box 179, North Bend, WA 98045-0179. Tel.: 425-888-3200. Fax: 425-888-3200.
E-mail: snovalmuseum@isomedia.com
Web Site: www.snoqualmievalleymuseum.org
Founded: 1960.
Congressional District: 8
Key Personnel: Pres. (V), Kris Kirby; Treas., Gardiner Vinnedge; Correspondent Sec., Vicki Bettes.
Governing Authority: Parent Institution: Snoqualmie Valley Historical Society. Tax-exempt.
Local Historical Museum.
Collections: local pioneer artifacts and photographs; local Indian and N. W. artifacts and history; photographic collection of Valley; pioneer diaries; manuscript collection. Historic Structures: 1912 vintage parlor; farm shed with vintage implements of agriculture, transportation & industry; early logging diorama.
Research Fields: local area history; valley forts; Snoqualmie Pass Wagon Road.
Facilities: history library available by appointment; early school texts; medical books available on premises or by appointment. Local historical books, booklets, map & tour guide brochure of Valley historic sites & other museum-related items for sale.
Activities: guided tours; lectures; docent program; informal education tours; mythology of Southern Puget Sound; slide programs.
Publications: books, A History of the Snoqualmie Valley; Fall City in the Valley of the Moon; booklet, Forts of the Snoqualmie Valley; brochure; historic tour guide; quarterly newsletter.
Hours & Admission Prices: April-Oct. Thurs.-Sun. 1-5; other times by appointment. Suggested Donation $1. Closed national holidays. ♿
Attendance: 4,000
Membership: Junior $2; Single $10; Family $15; Sustaining $20; Group & Business $30; Life $100; Business Life $250.

Olympia

BIGELOW HOUSE MUSEUM, 918 Glass Ave., N.E., Olympia, WA 98506-3976. Mailing Address: P.O. Box 1821, Olympia, WA 98507-1821. Tel.: 360-753-1215.
E-mail: staff@bigelowhouse.org
Web Site: www.bigelowhouse.org
Founded: 1992.
Congressional District: 3
Key Personnel: Pres. (V), Roger Easton.
Personnel Profile: Part-Time Volunteers 25.
Governing Authority: nonprofit organization. Administered by Bigelow House Preservation Association. Tax-exempt.
Historic House Museum: ca. 1860 Bigelow House.
Collections: 19th-century furnishings; books; photographs; domestic arts.
Research Fields: Social, political & domestic history of Washington Territory.
Activities: guided tours; lectures.
Publications: book, Stories of the Oregon Trail; Workingman's Hill: History of an Olympia Neighborhood.
Hours & Admission Prices: May-Oct. Sat.-Sun. 12-4; other times by appointment. Adults $3, children 18 & under $1; discounts to Life Balance Program members; members no charge. ♿
Attendance: 930 (accurate)
Membership: Family $35; Pioneer $75; Territorial $150; Third Century $300; Lifetime $1,859.

EVERGREEN GALLERY, (M), The Evergreen State College, 2700 Evergreen Pkwy., N.W., Olympia, WA 98505-0001. Tel.: 360-867-5125. Fax: 360-867-6794.
E-mail: gallery@evergreen.edu
Web Site: www.evergreen.edu/gallery
Founded: 1970.
Congressional District: 3
Key Personnel: Dir., Ann Friedman.
Personnel Profile: Part-Time Paid 1.
Governing Authority: college. Affiliated with The Evergreen State College. Tax-exempt.
College Art Gallery.
Collections: Pacific Northwest photography & printmaking; West Coast functional & sculptural ceramics; Chicano posters; black & white photography.
Facilities: gallery.
Activities: artist talks & workshops; loan, temporary & traveling exhibitions.

Hours & Admission Prices: Oct.-May Mon.-Thurs. 12-4. No charge. Closed national holidays. ♿

HANDS ON CHILDREN'S MUSEUM, 106 11th Ave., S.W., Olympia, WA 98501-2201. Tel.: 360-956-0818, ext. 0. Fax: 360-754-8626.
E-mail: hocm@hocm.org
Web Site: www.hocm.org
Founded: 1987.
Congressional District: 3
Key Personnel: C.E.O. & Dir., Patty Belmonte; Pres. (V), Sam Armour; Financial Dir., Daryl Fourtner; Museum Shop Mgr., Kathy Irwin.
Personnel Profile: Full-Time Paid 23; Part-Time Paid 20; Part-Time Volunteers 1,000; Interns 2.
Governing Authority: private; nonprofit organization. Tax-exempt: 501(c)(3).
Children's Museum.
Collections: hands-on exhibits.
Facilities: 11,000 sq. ft. exhibit space; four workshop and birthday party rooms. Museum-related items for sale.
Activities: art & science workshops; guest artists, performers & scientists; field trips; guided tours; participatory exhibits; parents' night out; campouts; birthday parties; toddler time; preschool, summer & spring break camps.
Publications: quarterly newsletter, Applause.
Hours & Admission Prices: Mon.-Sat. 10-5, Sun. 12-5. Adults $7.95; members & first Fri. of month 5-9 no charge. Closed New Year's Day; Easter; Independence Day; Thanksgiving; Christmas. ♿
Attendance: 106,000 (accurate)
Membership: One Plus One, Military & Grandparent $70; Family $90; Extended Family $120; Deluxe Extended Family $150; Corporate $250-$1,000.

OLYMPIC FLIGHT MUSEUM, 7637 A Old Hwy. 99, S.E., Olympia, WA 98501-5728. Tel.: 360-705-3925. Fax: 360-236-9839.
E-mail: info@olympicflightmuseum.com
Web Site: www.olympicflightmuseum.com/
Founded: 1998.
Key Personnel: Pres. & Founder, Brian Reynolds.
Governing Authority: nonprofit organization. Tax-exempt.
Aviation History Museum.
Collections: aviation history; World War II artifacts & memorabilia; lithographs; paintings; inert weapon systems; aircraft models; WWII, Korean, & Vietnam era aircraft.
Facilities: rental facility. Gift items for sale.
Activities: special events; lectures; tours; rental facility; meetings. Annual Event: Olympic Air Show in June.
Publications: newsletter, Flight Line.
Hours & Admission Prices: Tues.-Sun. 11-5. Adults $7, children 7-12 $5; discounts to AAA members; members and children 6 & under no charge. Closed Thanksgiving; Christmas. ♿
Attendance: 20,000 (accurate)
Membership: Family $60.

WASHINGTON STATE CAPITAL MUSEUM AND OUTREACH CENTER, 211 21st Ave., S.W., Olympia, WA 98501-2811. Tel.: 360-753-2580. Fax: 360-586-8322.
E-mail: srohrer@wshs.wa.gov
Web Site: www.washingtonhistory.org/scmoc/
Founded: 1941.
Congressional District: 3
Key Personnel: Cur. Education, Susan Rohrer; Administrative Asst., Chris Nicandri; Preservation & Museum Specialist, Mark Vessey; Coord. Women's History Consortium, Shanna Stevenson.
Personnel Profile: Full-Time Paid 5; Part-Time Volunteers 10; Interns 2.
Governing Authority: Parent Institution: Washington State Historical Society. Subsidiary Institution: Capital Museum Foundation. Tax-exempt: 501(c)(3).
History Museum: housed in Lord Mansion, c.1923.
Collections: history & culture of Washington; Native American artifacts; living botanical collection; garden.
Activities: tours; lectures; formally organized education program for children & adults; school loan service; technical assistance to heritage organizations statewide; Women's History Consortium; Heritage Resource Center. Museum Sponsors: National History Day.
Hours & Admission Prices: Wed.-Sat. 11-3. Family $5, adults $2, senior citizens $1.75, children $1; discounts to AAM members; members no charge. Closed state holidays. ♿
Attendance: 12,000 (estimated)
Membership: refer to Washington State Historical Society information.

Orcas Island

ORCAS ISLAND HISTORICAL MUSEUM, 181 N. Beach Rd., Orcas Island, WA 98245. Mailing Address: P.O. Box 134, Eastsound, WA 98245-0134. Tel.: 360-376-4849. Fax: 360-376-4869.
E-mail: orcasmuseum@rockisland.com
Web Site: orcasmuseum.org
Founded: 1950.
Congressional District: 42
Key Personnel: Administrative Asst., Heather Wallace.
Personnel Profile: Part-Time Paid 1; Part-Time Volunteers 25.
Governing Authority: society. Parent Institution: Orcas Island Historical Society. Tax-exempt: 501(c)(3).
General Museum: housed in six original homestead cabins built between the 1880s & 1890s.
Collections: Native American artifacts; history of the islands first peoples, Lummi & Samish Nations; woodworking & farming implements; objects associated with early industries such as fruit farming; objects utilized by early homesteaders; homestead grants; local historical photos; various types of early records & documents.
Research Fields: family genealogies; aspects of Orcas Island History: fruit farming, homesteading, Native Americans from this area, lime kilns/production, water transportation, ferry history, communication, farming.
Activities: guided tours available by request; lectures; permanent exhibitions. Museum Sponsors: Historical Parade in July; Historical Day Fair in July.
Publications: quarterly newsletter, The Orcas Islander.
Hours & Admission Prices: Memorial Day to Sept. Tues.-Thurs. & Sat.-Sun. 10-3, Fri. 1-6; other times for groups by appointment. Family $10, adults $3, seniors & students $2, children 6-12 $.50; discounts for AAM & ICOM members; museum members & children under 6 no charge.
Attendance: 3,250 (accurate)
Membership: Senior 65 & up & Student $10; Individual $15; Family & Business $25; Sponsor $50; Benefactor $100.

Pasco

CHILDREN'S MUSEUM OF THE THREE RIVERS, Broadmoor Square Mall, 5220 Outlet Dr., Pasco, WA 99301-8969. Tel.: 509-543-7866.
E-mail: trcmuseum@yahoo.com
Web Site: www.childrensmuseumtr.org
Governing Authority: nonprofit organization. Tax-exempt: 501(c)(3).
Children's Museum.
Collections: hands-on exhibits.
Activities: birthday parties; classes; field trips.
Hours & Admission Prices: Wed.-Fri. 10-5, Sat. 12-5. Admission $3; discounts to groups of 18 or more. Closed major holidays. ♿
Attendance: 17,500 (estimated)
Membership: Basic $25; Family $50; Supporting $75; Patron $100.

FRANKLIN COUNTY HISTORICAL MUSEUM, 305 N. 4th Ave., Pasco, WA 99301-5324. Tel.: 509-547-3714. Fax: 509-545-2168.
Founded: 1982.
Congressional District: 8
Key Personnel: Pres., Anne Hayden; Treas., Hazel Hanson; Museum Shop Mgr., Gracie Cooper; Admin., Sherel Webb.
Personnel Profile: Part-Time Paid 5; Part-Time Volunteers 18.
Governing Authority: nonprofit organization. Parent Institution: Franklin County Historical Society. Tax-exempt: 501(c)(3).
Historical Society Museum: housed in 1911 Andrew Carnegie library building.
Collections: Franklin County history; Indian culture; railroad history; homesteading; agriculture; river transportation; aviation.
Facilities: Gift items & historical publications available for sale.
Activities: organized educational programs; guided tours; lectures; films; docent program.
Publications: monthly newsletter, Franklin Express; quarterly historical publication, Franklin Flyer.
Hours & Admission Prices: Tues.-Sat. 12-4. No charge; donations accepted. Society members 10% off gift shop purchases. Closed national holidays. ♿
Attendance: 6,280 (accurate)
Membership: Library & School $7.50; Individual $20; Couple $30; Business $50 & up; Lifetime $500.

SACAJAWEA INTERPRETIVE CENTER, Sacajawea State Park, 2503 Sacajawea Park Rd., Pasco, WA 99301-6413. Tel.: 509-545-2361.
Web Site: www.park.wa.gov
Founded: 1940.
Key Personnel: Chief Interpretive Svcs., Steve Wang; Park Mgr., Read Obern.
Governing Authority: state. Affiliated with the Washington State Parks &

Recreation Commission, 7150 Cleanwater Lane, Ky-11, Olympia, WA 98504. Tax-exempt.
Interpretive Center.
Collections: c.7000 B.C. to early 19th-century stone & bone tools of Columbia Plateau Indians; displays honoring Lewis & Clark Expedition; material culture of area Indians.
Research Fields: Indians of S.E. Washington; Lewis & Clark; NPRR town of Ainsworth, 1878-1886.
Facilities: picnic area; swimming area; boating facilities.
Activities: permanent exhibitions; interpretive & school programs; tours.
Publications: brochures; reading lists; educational packets.
Hours & Admission Prices: April-Nov. 1 daily 10-5. ♿
Attendance: 650 (estimated)

WASHINGTON STATE RAILROADS HISTORICAL SOCIETY MUSEUM, 122 N. Tacoma Ave., Pasco, WA 99301. Mailing Address: P.O. Box 552, Pasco, WA 99301-0552. Tel.: 509-543-4159.
Historical Society Museum.
Collections: railroad history & artifacts; photographs; steam locomotives.
Facilities: Museum-related items for sale.
Hours & Admission Prices: Fri. 12-4, Sat. 9-3. Adults $2, teens & seniors $1; children & members no charge.

Port Angeles

CLALLAM COUNTY HISTORICAL SOCIETY, Museum at the Carnegie, 207 S. Lincoln St., Port Angeles, WA 98362. Mailing Address: P.O. Box 1327, Port Angeles, WA 98362-0244. Tel.: 360-452-2662. Fax: 360-452-2662.
E-mail: artifact@olypen.com
Web Site: clallamhistoricalsociety.com
Formerly: The Museum of Clallam Historical Society
Founded: 1948.
Congressional District: 3
Key Personnel: Pres. (V), John Norton, Sr.; Exec. Dir., Kathryn M. Monds.
Personnel Profile: Full-Time Paid 1; Part-Time Volunteers 70.
Governing Authority: society; nonprofit. Affiliated with the Clallam County Historical Society, Port Angeles, WA 98362. Administrative Center, Research & Genealogy Libraries, 931-933 West 9th, Port Angeles, WA 98363. Tax-exempt: 501(c)(3).
History Museum.
Collections: period furniture; photographs; artifacts; history. Historic Building: 1888, Beaumont Cabin.
Research Fields: local history; oral taping; genealogy.
Facilities: 6,590-vol. library.
Activities: workshops; organized education programs; lectures; guided tours; training programs for volunteer museum workers; docent program; temporary exhibitions.
Publications: quarterly bulletin, Strait News; brochures; pamphlets.
Hours & Admission Prices: Wed.-Sat. 1-4. Suggested donation: Family $5, adults $2. ♿
Attendance: 8,000 (estimated)
Membership: Senior Citizen $25; Individual $30; Family $35; Clubs & Service Clubs $50; Business & Sponsor $100; Patron $250; Sustaining Patron $500; Benefactor $1,000.

FEIRO MARINE LIFE CENTER, 315 N. Lincoln St., Port Angeles, WA 98362. Mailing Address: P.O. Box 625, Port Angeles, WA 98362-0112. Tel.: 360-417-6254.
E-mail: feirolab@dypen.com
Formerly: Arthur D. Feiro Marine Life Center c/o Peninsula College
Founded: 1981.
Key Personnel: Chm. (V), Orville Campbell; Coord., Robert Campbell; Administrative & Education Coord., Deborah Moriarty; Education, Burton Foote.
Personnel Profile: Part-Time Paid 2; Part-Time Volunteers 30; Interns 2.
Governing Authority: private college; nonprofit. Tax-exempt: 501(c)(3).
Marine Life Center.
Collections: local Pacific Northwest marine life; plankton & jellyfish; giant pacific octopus; vertebrate; invertebrate; fossils.
Research Fields: marine baseline water conditions.
Facilities: aquarium; 1,800 sq. ft. exhibit space. Museum-related items for sale.
Activities: docent program; films; formal education programs; guided tours; temporary exhibitions.
Hours & Admission Prices: Memorial Day to Labor Day daily 10-5; Sept.-May Sat.-Sun. 12-4; other times by appointment. Adults $3, senior citizens $2, youth 4-17 $1; children 3 & under no charge. ♿
Attendance: 12,000 (accurate)

OLYMPIC NATIONAL PARK VISITOR CENTER, 3002 Mt. Angeles Rd., Port Angeles, WA 98362-6775. Tel.: 360-565-3130 & 3000. Fax: 360-565-3147.
E-mail: kathy_steichen@nps.gov
Web Site: www.nps.gov/olym
Founded: 1957.
Congressional District: 5
Key Personnel: Supt., Karen Gustin; Chief Park Interpreter, Kathy Steichen; Museum Shop Mgr., Margaret Baker.
Personnel Profile: Full-Time Paid 1; Part-Time Paid 3; Part-Time Volunteers 8; Interns 4.
Governing Authority: federal. Parent Institution: National Park Service, Washington, DC. Tax-exempt: 501(c)(3).
Visitor Center for National Park.
Collections: Historic House: 1880 Beaumont Cabin.
Facilities: 1,800-vol. library of books on natural history, history & anthropology available for use on premises. Books, maps, slides & postcards for sale.
Activities: lectures; films; formally organized education programs for children & adults; permanent exhibitions; Northwest Indian culture demonstrations of crafts in summer.
Publications: books; information handouts.
Hours & Admission Prices: Oct.-April Thurs.-Mon. 10-4; Summer: daily. No charge. ♿
Attendance: 160,000 (accurate)

PORT ANGELES FINE ARTS CENTER & WEBSTER'S WOODS ART PARK, 1203 E. Lauridsen Blvd., Port Angeles, WA 98362-6630. Tel.: 360-457-3532 & 417-4590. Fax: 360-457-3532.
E-mail: pafac@olypen.com
Web Site: www.pafac.org
Founded: 1986.
Congressional District: 2
Key Personnel: C.E.O., Jake Seniuk; Chm. (V), Darlene Ryan; Pres., Jean Heessels-Petit; Cur. Education & Asst., Barbara Slavik.
Personnel Profile: Full-Time Paid 3; Part-Time Paid 1; Part-Time Volunteers 50; Interns 1.
Governing Authority: municipal government; nonprofit. Parent Institution: City of Port Angeles. Subsidiary Institution: PAFAC Foundation. Tax-exempt: 501(c)(3).
Art Museum.
Collections: paintings & drawings from donor Esther Webster; Northwestern artists; sculpture garden.
Activities: lectures; readings; performances.
Publications: bimonthly newsletter, On Center.
Hours & Admission Prices: Thurs.-Sun. 11-5. No charge. Closed New Year's Eve & Day; Independence Day; Thanksgiving; Christmas Eve & Day. ♿
Attendance: 18,000 (estimated)
Membership: Friend $35-$49; Good Friend $50-$99; Close Friend $100-$499; Esteemed Friend $500-$999; Sustaining Friend $1,000 & up.

Port Gamble

PORT GAMBLE HISTORIC MUSEUM, 32400 Rainier Ave., N.E., Port Gamble, WA 98364. Mailing Address: P.O. Box 85, Port Gamble, WA 98364-0085. Tel.: 360-297-8074. Fax: 360-297-7455.
E-mail: ssmith@orminc.com
Web Site: www.portgamble.com
Founded: 1976.
Congressional District: 23
Key Personnel: C.E.O., Dave Nunes; Cur. & Museum Shop Mgr., Shana Smith.
Personnel Profile: Full-Time Paid 1; Part-Time Paid 3.
Governing Authority: Parent Institution: Pope Resources. Subsidiary Institution: Olympic Property Group.
History Museum; housed in 1853 Port Gamble General Store.
Collections: founding family memorabilia; maritime; sales office; manuscripts; artifacts. Historic Buildings: 1853 U.S. Post Office; 1872 Masonic Temple; 1859 Thompson House; 1879 St. Paul's Episcopal Church; 1887 Walker-Ames House; 1870 M.S. Drew House.
Research Fields: corporate & family history.
Facilities: library of books on corporate archives available for research by request, reviewed on individual basis. Forest industry historical books for sale.
Activities: permanent & temporary exhibitions.
Publications: booklet, Port Gamble Historic Museum; brochure, Welcome to Historic Port Gamble; book, Pope Resources, Rooted in the Past, Growing in the Future.
Hours & Admission Prices: May-Oct. daily 9:30-5; Nov.-April Fri.-Sun. 9:30-5. Adults $4, students & senior citizens $2; children 5 & under no charge. ♿
Attendance: 7,800 (accurate)

Port Townsend

JEFFERSON COUNTY HISTORICAL SOCIETY MUSEUM, (M), 540 Water St., Port Townsend, WA 98368-5725. Tel.: 360-385-1003. Fax: 360-385-1042.
E-mail: jchsmuseum@olympus.net
Web Site: www.jchsmuseum.org
Founded: 1951.
Congressional District: 3
Key Personnel: Pres. (V), Victoria Davis; Dir., William Tennent; Museum Coord., Phyllis Snyder; Archivist, Marsha Moratti.
Personnel Profile: Full-Time Paid 2; Part-Time Paid 5; Part-Time Volunteers 200.
Governing Authority: (scope); nonprofit organization. Parent Institution: Jefferson County Historical Society. Subsidiary Institution: Research Center, 13694 Airport Cutoff Rd., Port Townsend, WA 98368. Tax-exempt: 501(c)(3).
Historical Museum: housed in 1892 City Hall focusing on Jefferson County history & prehistory (Native American & European).
Collections: local memorabilia; maritime heritage; Victorian Era & early Pioneer exhibits; Victorian furniture & clothing; Indian & Alaskan baskets & artifacts; 20,000 photographs; sailing ships; bound volumes of Port Townsend Leaders; family histories; reference books on preservation & restoration; hearse from 1886-1912; ship rudder of sunken 1880 ship; old police court; jail; old fire hall; 1890 Parlor & bedroom; button collection; buildings & pioneers; maps; deeds; genealogy. Historic Buildings: 1889 Fire Bell Tower; Rothschild House 1868.
Research Fields: census records; voting records; school records; family histories; property records; maritime records; military records; local newspapers from 1860.
Activities: permanent & temporary exhibits; lecture series; local preservation projects; docent program; awards program.
Publications: quarterly newsletter.
Hours & Admission Prices: Daily 11-4; special tours available. Adults $4, children under 12 $1; members no charge. Closed New Year's Day; Thanksgiving; Christmas. ♿
Attendance: 20,000 (estimated)
Membership: Student & Senior $20; Individual $30; Family $40; Patron $100; Sponsor $250; Sustaining $1,000.

KELLY ART DECO LIGHT MUSEUM, (M), Vintage Hardware, 2000 Sims Way, Port Townsend, WA 98368-2229. Tel.: 360-379-9030.
Web Site: www.thedecomuseum.com
Founded: 2004.
Key Personnel: Dir., Chm., Pres. & Founder, Ken Kelly
Decorative Art Museum.
Collections: over 400 fixtures including hanging chandeliers, wall sconces & table lights from the Great Depression.
Research Fields: how the Great Depression changed lighting companies in the 30s; mktg. & product devel.; artistic companies that were lost during the depression.
Hours & Admission Prices: Daily 10-5. No charge.

PORT TOWNSEND AERO MUSEUM, 105 Airport Rd., Port Townsend, WA 98368. Mailing Address: P.O. Box 101, Chimacum, WA 98325-0101. Tel.: 360-379-5244.
Web Site: www.ptaeromuseum.com
Founded: 2001.
Key Personnel: Dir., G. F. Thuotte.
Personnel Profile: Full-Time Paid 1; Full-Time Volunteers 2; Part-Time Volunteers 12; Interns 15.
Governing Authority: tax-exempt.
Aviation Museum.
Collections: over 30 aircraft; 100 pieces of aviation art; aviation photographs; 200 aircraft models.
Activities: special events.
Hours & Admission Prices: Wed.-Sun. 9-4; groups by appointment. Adults $10; members no charge. Closed Thanksgiving & Christmas ♿
Membership: Individual $35; Family $50; Supporter $250; Sponsor $500; Lifetime $1,000; Visionary $5,000.

PORT TOWNSEND MARINE SCIENCE CENTER, Fort Worden State Park, 532 Battery Way, Port Townsend, WA 98368-3431. Tel.: 360-385-5582. Fax: 360-385-7248.
E-mail: info@ptmsc.org
Web Site: www.ptmsc.org
Founded: 1983.
Congressional District: 24
Key Personnel: Dir., Anne Murphy.
Personnel Profile: Full-Time Paid 3; Part-Time Paid 5; Part-Time Volunteers 80; Interns 2.
Governing Authority: nonprofit organization. Parent Institution: Port Township Marine Science Society. Tax-exempt: 501(c)(3).
Marine & Natural History Museum: housed at c.1900 Fort Worden.
Collections: live exhibits of local marine animals in touch tanks & glass aquariums; microscopes for viewing plankton; wall exhibits on other aspects of marine science; underwater video camera for viewing sealife; daily interpretive programs; natural history of Puget Sound; fossilized ancestors of local animals; sands from around the world; geological formation of Washington.
Research Fields: water quality.
Facilities: 400-vol. library of books, field guides, reference books, scientific studies, periodicals & videotapes available to the public; aquarium; 50-seat theater.
Activities: guided tours; lectures; films; organized education programs for adults & children; docent program; participatory exhibits, touchtables; summer camps. Museum Sponsors: cruises to National Wildlife Refuge in spring, summer & fall.
Publications: newsletter, Octopress.
Hours & Admission Prices: Summer, Spring & Fall: Two Exhibits. Adults $5, youth $3; members no charge. Winter: One Exhibit. Adults $3, youth $2; members no charge. ♿
Attendance: 18,500 (accurate)
Membership: Student $15; Individual $25; Family $35; Patron $50; Friend $75; Sustaining $100; Business $125; Octopress Sponsor $250; Benefactor $500; Sponsor $1,000.

PUGET SOUND COAST ARTILLERY MUSEUM AT FORT WORDEN, Bldg. 201, Fort Worden State Park, Port Townsend, WA 98368. Mailing Address: 200 Battery Way, Port Townsend, WA 98368-3621. Tel.: 360-385-0373.
E-mail: artymus@olypen.com
Web Site: www.fortworden.org
Founded: 1976.
Congressional District: 6
Key Personnel: Pres., Alfred Chiswell; Vice Pres., Ron Novak; Treas. & Museum Shop Mgr., Joanne Fritz; Park Mgr., Kate Burke.
Personnel Profile: Full-Time Volunteers 1; Part-Time Volunteers 11.
Governing Authority: nonprofit. Tax-exempt: 501(c)(3).
Military Museum: housed in 1904, Enlisted Barracks, Bldg. 201 of the Harbor Defense of Puget Sound.
Collections: artifacts of seacoast artillery; 1890-1944 harbor defenses; personal artifacts; papers; photos; military rifle collection from 26 countries.
Research Fields: coast artillery, harbor defense of Puget Sound & the United States.
Facilities: 700-vol. library of military related books, service manuals, official orders, private correspondence, related photographs available for research with permission from director-librarian on premises; theater.
Activities: guided tours; lectures; permanent & temporary exhibitions.
Publications: Fort Worden Guide.
Hours & Admission Prices: July-Aug. Sun.-Thurs. 11-4, Fri.-Sat. 10-5; Sept.-June daily 11-4. Adults $3, children $2; active military no charge. ♿
Attendance: 11,982 (accurate)
Membership: Individual $15; Family $25; Patron $100.

ROTHSCHILD HOUSE STATE PARK, Franklin St., Port Townsend, WA 98368. Mailing Address: Fort Worden State Park, 200 Battery Way, Port Townsend, WA 98368-3621. Tel.: 360-385-1003 & 344-4400. Fax: 360-385-7248.
E-mail: kate.burke@parks.wa.gov
Web Site: www.fortworden.org
Founded: 1959.
Congressional District: 6
Key Personnel: Park Mgr. Fort Worden, Kate Burke; Museum Mgr., Phyllis Snyder.
Personnel Profile: Full-Time Paid 1; Part-Time Paid 2; Part-Time Volunteers 2.
Governing Authority: state. Parent Institution: Fort Worden State Park. Subsidiary Institution: Jefferson County Historical Society. Tax-exempt.
Historic House Museum: 1868 Rothschild House, built by the merchant D.C.H. Rothschild.
Collections: furnished 19th-century home; Rothschild family artifacts
Activities: guided tours; permanent exhibitions.
Publications: brochure.
Hours & Admission Prices: May-Sept. daily 11-4. Adults $4, children $1; discounts to JCHS members.
Attendance: 3,225 (accurate)

Poulsbo

POULSBO MARINE SCIENCE CENTER, 18743 Front St., N.E., Poulsbo, WA 98370. Mailing Address: P.O. Box 408, Keyport, WA 98345-0408. Tel.: 360-598-4460.
E-mail: info@poulsbomsc.org
Web Site: www.poulsbomsc.org
Key Personnel: Dir. Aquarium, Patrick Mus; Dir. Education, Dr. Susan Crawford
Science Center.
Collections: hands-on exhibits; aquariums.
Facilities: library; aquariums.
Activities: educational programs; videos.
Hours & Admission Prices: Thurs.-Sun. 11-4.

SUQUAMISH MUSEUM, (M), 15838 Sandy Hook Rd., Poulsbo, WA 98370-7867. Mailing Address: P.O. Box 498, Suquamish, WA 98392-0498. Tel.: 360-598-3311, ext. 422 & 394-8496. Fax: 360-598-6295.
E-mail: mjones@suquamish.nsn.us
Web Site: www.suquamish.nsn.us
Founded: 1983.
Congressional District: 1
Key Personnel: Tribal Chm., Leonard Forsman; Tribal Council Sec., Linda Holt; Dir., Marilyn Jones; Cur., Charles Sigo.
Personnel Profile: Full-Time Paid 4; Part-Time Volunteers 1.
Governing Authority: nonprofit organization. Parent Institution: Suquamish Tribal Cultural Center. Tax-exempt: 501(c)(3).
Native American Museum: located on the Port Madison Indian Reservation.
Collections: traditional culture of the Suquamish Tribe & other Puget Sound Tribes; 1792-present photographs & artifacts, including basketry, carvings, tools, mats, bowls, spoons & fishing gear.
Research Fields: history of federal Indian policy in respect to land & education; Indian Treaty Rights protection; traditional & contemporary religion; traditional uses of natural resources by Indians; basketry techniques.
Facilities: 120-vol. library pertaining to Puget Sound Indian history; 40-seat auditorium; 75-seat restaurant; educational facilities; 3,000 sq. ft. exhibit space; field research station; 500 capacity gym. Beadwork, jewelry, posters & other museum-related items for sale.
Activities: guided tours; lectures; films; arts festivals; rental gallery; participatory, loan & traveling exhibitions; organized education programs for college students. Museum Sponsors: Native American Art Fair; Chief Seattle Days Celebration.
Publications: exhibit catalogue, The Eyes of Chief Seattle; quarterly newsletter.
Hours & Admission Prices: May-Sept. daily 10-5; Oct.-April Fri.-Sun. 11-4. Adults $4, senior citizens 55 & over $3, children 12 & under $2; discounts to AAA, AAM & Friends of Suquamish Museum members. Closed New Year's Day; Easter; Thanksgiving & day after; Christmas. ♿
Attendance: 10,000 (estimated)
Membership: Individual $15; Family $25; Sustaining $50; Supporting $100; Patron $500; Benefactor $1,000.

SUQUAMISH MUSEUM, 15838 Sandy Hook Rd., Poulsbo, WA 98392. Mailing Address: P.O. Box 498, Suquamish, WA 98392-0498. Tel.: 360-394-8496.
Key Personnel: Dir., Marilyn Jones
Native American History Museum.
Collections: Suquamish culture & history; personal artifacts; paintings.
Facilities: Museum-related items for sale.
Hours & Admission Prices: May-Sept. daily 10-5; Oct.-April Fri.-Sun. 11-4. Adults $4, seniors 55 & over $3, children 12 & under $2; discounts to AAA members & military with ID at gift shop.
Membership: Individual $15; Family $25; Sustaining $50; Supporting $100.

Prosser

BENTON COUNTY HISTORICAL MUSEUM, 1000 Paterson Rd. (located in the city park), Prosser, WA 99350. Mailing Address: P.O. Box 1407, Prosser, WA 99350-0800. Tel.: 509-786-3842 & 1267.
Founded: 1968.
Congressional District: 4
Key Personnel: Pres. (V), Dick Sampson; Cur., Frankie Wallace.
Personnel Profile: Part-Time Paid 1; Part-Time Volunteers 10.
Governing Authority: society; nonprofit organization. Parent Institution: Benton County Museum and Historical Society, Inc. Tax-exempt.
General Museum.
Collections: early Americana; Indian artifacts; natural history; guns; dolls; china; handwork; cavern crystals; corals & sea shells; oral histories; Homestead Shack; The Parlor; Farm Room, replica 1890 Holt Combine; hand-carved work horses in action; replica carousel with calliope music; doll house; general store; 1843-1920 gown collection; 1867 Chickering piano, playable; NASA's space items to moon & back.
Facilities: 5,000 sq. ft. exhibit space.
Activities: tours by appointment.
Publications: brochures.
Hours & Admission Prices: Tues.-Sat. 11-4, Sun. call for hours. Adults $2, children $1; students no charge. Closed New Year's Day; Easter; Thanksgiving; Christmas. ♿
Attendance: 2,400 (estimated)
Membership: Annual $10; Life Supporting $100; Silver Historian $250; Golden Pioneer $500.

Pullman

CHARLES R. CONNER MUSEUM, Washington State University, Pullman, WA 99164-0001. Tel.: 509-335-3515. Fax: 509-335-3184.
E-mail: connermuseum@wsu.edu
Web Site: sbs.wsu.edu/connermuseum
Founded: 1894.
Congressional District: 5
Key Personnel: Dir., Larry Hufford; Cur., Dr. Kelly M. Cassidy.
Personnel Profile: Full-Time Paid 2; Part-Time Paid 2; Interns 2.
Governing Authority: state. Parent Institution: Washington State University. Tax-exempt: 501(c)(3).
Zoology Museum; Natural History Museum.
Collections: herpetology; ornithology; mammalogy.
Research Fields: systematics; ecology; zoogeography of vertebrate animals.
Facilities: 500-vol. library.
Activities: permanent exhibitions; research collections; school outreach.
Hours & Admission Prices: Daily 8-5. No charge; donations accepted. ♿
Attendance: 23,000 (estimated)

MUSEUM OF ANTHROPOLOGY, Department of Anthropology, Washington State University, Pullman, WA 99164-0001. Tel.: 509-335-3441. Fax: 509-335-3999.
E-mail: collinsm@wsu.edu
Founded: 1966.
Congressional District: 5
Key Personnel: Dir., Mary Collins.
Personnel Profile: Full-Time Paid 2; Part-Time Volunteers 10.
Governing Authority: university. Parent Institution: Washington State University.
Anthropology Museum.
Collections: archaeological & ethnographic collections from Western North America, South America, Africa, Asia & Oceana; basketry from Western U.S.; material from China, S. America, W. Africa & New Guinea.
Activities: guided tours; permanent & temporary exhibitions.
Hours & Admission Prices: Sept.-April Mon.-Fri. 10-4. No charge; donations accepted. Closed school holidays & vacations. ♿
Attendance: 4,000 (estimated)

MUSEUM OF ART, (M), Washington State University, Pullman, WA 99164-0001. Mailing Address: P.O. Box 647460, Pullman, WA 99164-7460. Tel.: 509-335-1910. Fax: 509-335-1908.
E-mail: artmuse@wsu.edu
Web Site: www.wsu.edu/artmuse
Founded: 1973.
Congressional District: 5
Key Personnel: Dir., Chris Bruce; Asst. Dir., Anna-Maria Shannon; Program Coord., Tonya Murray; Cur., Keith Wells; Media Coord., Camille Rigby.
Personnel Profile: Full-Time Paid 5; Part-Time Paid 11; Part-Time Volunteers 13; Interns 2.
Governing Authority: university. Parent Institution: Washington State University. Tax-exempt: 115-(A).
University Art Museum.
Collections: late 19th-century to contemporary American & European paintings & graphics.
Research Fields: 19th- & 20th-century American & European art, with emphasis on contemporary & regional collections.
Facilities: library; classrooms; 145-seat auditorium; conference room.
Activities: temporary exhibitions; guided tours; lectures; films; gallery talks; education programs for undergraduate & graduate students; art workshops for children.
Publications: posters; catalogues include A Temporary Possession: The Human Image in 20th-Century Photography; Artist & Place: American Landscape Painting 1860-1914; Wendell Brazeau: 1910-1974; Diverse Directions: The Fiber Arts; Goya: Los Disparates; George Inness: Evening Landscape, 1863; Laisner; Norman Lundin; Recent Acquisitions - Ancient Art, the J. Paul Getty Museum; Rodin: The Maryhill Collection; Six From California;

Margaret Tomkins; Works on Paper: American Art 1945-1975; Mel Katz Works 1971-1978; A Partial View: Young Photographers in the Northwest; Drawings 1900-1945: A Survey of American Works, 1979; Swords of the Samurai; Contemporary Metals: Focus on Idea; Noritake Art Deco Porcelains; Fabric Traditions of Indonesia; Gaylen Hansen: The Paintings of a Decade, 1975-1985; books, Extending the Artist's Hand: Contemporary Sculpture from the Walla Walla Foundry; Roy Lichtenstein Prints 1956-1997: From the Collections of Jordan D. Schnitzer and His Family Foundation; Art & Context: The 1950's and 60's; Gaylen Hansen: Three Decades of Paintings; Sherry Markovitz: Shimmer.
Hours & Admission Prices: July-Aug. Tues.-Sat. 12-4; Sept.-June Mon.-Wed. & Fri.-Sat. 10-4, Thurs.10-7. No charge; donations accepted. Closed during semester breaks & between exhibition installations. ♿
Attendance: 30,000 (estimated)
Membership: Student $15; Individual $35; Family $50; Associate $100; Patron $250; Sustaining $500; President's Associate $1,000; Silver PA $2,500; Crimson PA $5,000; Platinum PA $10,000.

Puyallup

EZRA MEEKER MANSION, 312 Spring St., Puyallup, WA 98372-3268. Mailing Address: P.O. Box 103, Puyallup, WA 98371-0011. Tel.: 253-848-1770.
Web Site: www.meekermansion.org
Founded: 1970.
Congressional District: 9
Key Personnel: Historian, Andy Anderson; Museum Shop Mgr., Dan Stats.
Personnel Profile: Part-Time Paid 2.
Governing Authority: society; nonprofit organization. Parent Institution: Ezra Meeker Historical Society. Tax-exempt: 501(c)(3).
Historic House Museum: 1890 Ezra Meeker Home, a Victorian mansion located at end of the Oregon Trail.
Collections: furnishings of the period; the books & writings of Ezra Meeker; textiles; clothing; art displays.
Research Fields: pioneers of the area in print & photos.
Facilities: library of books written by Ezra Meeker available for research with the approval of the board for use on premises; antique rose garden; available for weddings.
Activities: guided tours; lectures. Museum Sponsors: Victorian Teas in May; Meeker Days in June; sourdough pancake breakfast; cider squeeze; doll house show; Christmas at the Mansion in December; Country Crafters Sale.
Publications: book, Ezra Meeker; Bentley's Tale of the Oregon Trail; The Ox Team or the Old Oregon Trail; Uncle Ezra's Short Stories for Children; Ezra Meeker a Brief Resume of His Life & Adventures.
Hours & Admission Prices: March to mid-Dec. Wed.-Sun. 12-4; other times for special events. Adults $4, senior citizens & students $3, children $2; members no charge. Closed Easter; Thanksgiving. ♿
Attendance: 10,000 (accurate)
Membership: Individual $15; Family $25; Donor $40; Business $50; Supporting $100; Lifetime $1,000.

THE FRED OLDFIELD WESTERN HERITAGE & ART CENTER, 110 9th S.W., Puyallup, WA 98371. Mailing Address: P.O. Box 1539, Puyallup, WA 98371-0216. Tel.: 253-752-9708; 866-445-9175 (Toll Free). Fax: 253-752-9708.
Founded: 2002.
Heritage Center.
Collections: Western art; American West history & heritage; paintings; sketches; American Indian baskets & artifacts.
Activities: classes; tours; special events; educational programs; seminars.
Hours & Admission Prices: Sat. 12-4; other times by appointment. ♿

PAUL H. KARSHNER MEMORIAL MUSEUM, 309 Fourth St., N.E., Puyallup, WA 98372-3062. Tel.: 253-841-8748. Fax: 253-840-8951.
E-mail: curator@karshnermuseum.org
Web Site: www.karshnermuseum.org
Founded: 1930.
Congressional District: 2
Key Personnel: Admin., Bob Livingston; Cur., Beth Bestrom.
Personnel Profile: Full-Time Paid 1; Part-Time Paid 2.
Governing Authority: public school district. Parent Institution: Puyallup School District. Tax-exempt.
Children's History Museum: housed in c.1920 school building.
Collections: Indian artifacts; geology; paleontology; entomology; natural science; trade items, American pioneer clothing, utensils, tools & artifacts.
Facilities: 500-vol. library of historical, religious & text books available for use by arrangement.
Activities: guided tours; lectures; formally organized education programs for children; permanent & temporary exhibitions. Museum Sponsors: Family Days.
Publications: annual booklet.
Hours & Admission Prices: Labor Day to mid-June Mon.-Fri. 9-3. No charge; donations accepted. Closed national holidays. Open for Family Day first Sat. of the month 10-2. Adults $1, family $4. ♿
Attendance: 12,000 (estimated)
Membership: Friends of the Karshner Museum $8.

Quilcene

QUILCENE HISTORICAL MUSEUM, 151 E. Columbia St., Quilcene, WA 98376. Mailing Address: P.O. Box 574, Quilcene, WA 98376-0574. Tel.: 360-765-4848.
Founded: 1991.
Congressional District: 6
Key Personnel: Chm. (V), Mari Phillips; Museum Shop Mgr., Claire French.
Personnel Profile: Part-Time Volunteers 12.
Governing Authority: Tax-exempt.
History Museum.
Collections: local history & culture; period artifacts, photographs; country store; early 1900s kitchen; millinery shop; early 1900s school; toys; business; logging; early pioneers; clubs & organizations.
Publications: Quilcene Cooks: Past and Present; Quilcene's Heritage: Looking Back; Dub of South Burlap; Timber Country Revisited; Brinnon: A Scrapbook of History; King of the Sea World; Home Cookin'...from Quilcene and other Northwest Kitchens; Discover Historic Washington State.
Hours & Admission Prices: mid-April to mid-Sept. Fri.-Mon. 1-5. No charge; donations accepted. ♿
Attendance: 2,100 (estimated)
Membership: Individual $10; Family $15; Service Group $25; Business $50; Lifetime $150; Couple Lifetime $200.

Raymond

THE NORTHWEST CARRIAGE MUSEUM, 314 Alder St., Raymond, WA 98577-2434. Tel.: 360-942-4150.
E-mail: nwcarriages@willapabay.org
Web Site: www.nwcarriagemuseum.org
Founded: 2002.
Key Personnel: Museum Shop Mgr., Amy Dennis.
Governing Authority: Tax-exempt.
Transportation Museum.
Collections: over 20 horse drawn carriages, buggies & sleighs from the late 19th century.
Hours & Admission Prices: April-Sept. Wed.-Sat. 10-4, Sun. 12-4; Oct.-March Wed.-Sat. 10-4. Adults $3; members no charge. ♿
Membership: Individual $25; Family $30; Business $50.

WILLAPA SEAPORT MUSEUM, 310 Alder St., Raymond, WA 98577-2434. Tel.: 360-942-4149.
Web Site: willapaseaportmuseum.org
Seaport Museum.
Collections: Willapa Bay history; marine artifacts; logging industry; shipbuilding; life saving service; Spruce Division (WWI); Native Americans; lightships; lighthouses.
Hours & Admission Prices: Wed. - Sat. 12-4. Families $5, adults $3, military, veterans & seniors $2, high school students $1, elementary students $.50; teachers no charge.

Renton

RENTON HISTORICAL SOCIETY AND MUSEUM, (M), 235 Mill Ave. S., Renton, WA 98057-2133. Tel.: 425-255-2330. Fax: 425-255-1570.
E-mail: info@rentonhistory.org
Web Site: www.rentonhistory.org
Founded: 1966.
Congressional District: 11
Key Personnel: Dir., Elizabeth P. Stewart; Pres., Laura Clawson; Treas., Phyllis Hunt; Collection Mgr., Sarah Iles; Volunteer Coord., Dorota Rahn.
Personnel Profile: Full-Time Paid 2; Part-Time Paid 3; Part-Time Volunteers 60.
Governing Authority: nonprofit. Parent Institution: City of Renton. Tax-exempt: 501(c)(3).
Historic Fire Station: 1942 art deco building.
Collections: more than 13,000 photographs; clothing; newspapers; cultural artifacts; coal mining artifacts; home furnishings; turn-of-the-century coal car & logging equipment; vintage neon movie theater sign.
Research Fields: local history.
Facilities: 500-vol. library for public use. Books & gift items for sale.
Activities: guided tours; lectures; organized education programs for children,

adults, undergraduate & graduate college students; docent program; loan, temporary & traveling exhibitions.
Publications: newsletter, Renton Historical Quarterly.
Hours & Admission Prices: Tues.-Sat. 10-4. Adults: non-city residents $3, city residents $2, children ages 8-16 $1; discounts to AAM & ICOM members; members no charge. ♿
Attendance: 4,000 (accurate)
Membership: Student & Senior $12; Individual & Senior Couple $20; Family $30; Patron & Benefactor $100; Life $500.

Republic

STONEROSE INTERPRETIVE CENTER, 15-1 N. Kean St., Republic, WA 99166. Mailing Address: P.O. Box 987, Republic, WA 99166-0987. Tel.: 509-775-2295.
Web Site: www.stonerosefossil.org
Key Personnel: Dir., Kathryn Brown
Geology Museum.
Collections: Pacific Northwest's geological & biological history; fossils.
Activities: dig for fossils.
Hours & Admission Prices: May & Sept.-Oct. 27 Wed.-Sun. 8-5; Memorial Day to Labor Day daily 8-5. Site Admission Sticker: adults $5, children 6-18 & senior citizens 62 & over $3; children under 6 & members no charge.

Richland

COLUMBIA RIVER EXHIBITION OF HISTORY, SCIENCE AND TECHNOLOGY, 95 Lee Blvd., Richland, WA 99352-4222. Mailing Address: P.O. Box 1890, Richland, WA 99352-6490. Tel.: 509-943-9000. Fax: 509-943-1770.
E-mail: crehstmuseum@crehst.org
Web Site: www.crehst.org
Founded: 1963.
Congressional District: 4
Key Personnel: Exec. Dir., Ellen Low; Cur., Connie Estep.
Personnel Profile: Full-Time Paid 4; Part-Time Paid 5; Part-Time Volunteers 50.
Governing Authority: private foundation. Parent Institution: Environmental Science & Technology Foundation; under Contract to U.S. Dept. of Energy. Tax-exempt.
History & Science Museum.
Collections: nuclear & alternate energy sources with hands-on exhibits, emphasizing Hanford programs; atomic marbles & nuclear waste storage & clean-up display; history of the mid-Columbia Basin & the Hanford Atomic site.
Research Fields: broad range of environmental sciences & historical exhibits.
Facilities: 50-seat auditorium. Atomic marbles, collection of Hanford-related books and videos & other museum-related items for sale.
Activities: guided tours; lectures; films & videos; formally organized education programs for children & adults.
Publications: video, Termination Winds; cookbook, history & photos, In the Shadow of Rattlesnake Mountain.
Hours & Admission Prices: Mon.-Sat. 10-5, Sun. 12-5. Adults $4, seniors & youth $3; ASTC & CREHST members, members & children 6 & under no charge. Closed New Year's Day; Thanksgiving; Christmas. ♿
Attendance: 13,000 (estimated)
Membership: Senior & Educator $22; Individual $25; Family & Grand Family $40; Museum Donor $100; Museum Patron $250-$999; Gold Circle Benefactor $1,000. Business & Corporate: Business Donor $100; Business Patron $250-$999; Business Benefactor $1,000; Corporate Partner $2,500-$4,900; Gold Sponsor $5,000; Platinum Sponsor $10,000.

HANFORD REACH NATIONAL MONUMENT HERITAGE & VISITOR CENTER (THE REACH), (M), 710 George Washington, Ste. BB, Richland, WA 99352-4209. Mailing Address: P.O. Box 1160, Richland, WA 99352-1160. Tel.: 509-943-4100. Fax: 509-943-4133.
Web Site: visitthereach.org/contact.php
Key Personnel: Exec. Dir., Kimberly Camp
History Museum.
Collections: geological; ecological; cultural history.
Hours & Admission Prices: Opening 2011. Call for information.

Seattle

* **BURKE MUSEUM OF NATURAL HISTORY AND CULTURE, (M),** University of Washington Campus, 17th Ave. N.E. & N.E. 45th St., Seattle, WA 98195-0001. Mailing Address: Univ. of Washington, Box 353010, Seattle, WA 98195-0001. Tel.: 206-543-5590. Fax: 206-685-3039.
E-mail: recept@u.washington.edu
Web Site: www.burkemuseum.org
Founded: 1885.
Congressional District: 7
Key Personnel: Exec. Dir., Dr. Julie K. Stein; Acting Interim Admin., Leslie Jones; Dir. Education, Diane Quinn; Assoc. Dir. Exhibits & Institutional Planning, Erin Younger; Dir. External Communications, MaryAnn Barron; Registrar, Hollye Keister; Cur. Archaeology, Dr. Peter Lape; Cur. Herbarium & Assoc. Dir. Research, Dr. Richard Olmstead; Cur. Invertebrate Paleontology, Dr. Elizabeth Nesbitt; Cur. Native American Art, Dr. Robin K. Wright; Cur. Vertebrate Paleontology, Christian Sidor; Cur. Paleobotany, Caroline Stromberg; Cur. Native American Ethnology, Deana Dartt-Newton; Cur. Fishes, Ted Pietsch; Museum Shop Mgr., Lee Mueller.
Personnel Profile: Full-Time Paid 60; Full-Time Volunteers 1; Part-Time Paid 40; Part-Time Volunteers 96.
Governing Authority: state; university. Parent Institution: University of Washington. Subsidiary Institution: Burke Museum Association. Tax-exempt: 501(c)(3).
Anthropology & Natural History Museum.
Collections: Pacific Rim anthropology; Northwest Coast native art; paleontology; mineralogy; geology; zoology; entomology; mammalogy; ornithology; malacology; botany; ichthyology; genetic resources; herbarium; lepidoptera.
Major Exhibits: Fossil Starfish, 11/20/09-8/30/10; Cruisin the Fossil Freeway, 12/19/09-5/10; Evolution Evidence, 12/19/09-5/10; International Conservation Photography, 6/19/10-9/6/10; Weaving Heritage: Textile Masterpieces, 9/25/10-2/27/11.
Research Fields: paleontology; geology; zoology; anthropology including archaeology; botany; genetics.
Facilities: classroom; events room; cafe. Museum-related items for sale.
Activities: temporary exhibits; docent guided tours; K-12 group tours & traveling study collections; lectures & gallery talks.
Publications: research reports; member's newsletter; exhibit-related publications.
Hours & Admission Prices: Call for hours. Adults $9.50, senior citizens $7.50, students and youth 5 & over $6; discounts to AAA, WMA, AAM & ICOM members; members & 1st Thurs. of month no charge. Closed New Year's Day; Independence Day; Thanksgiving; Christmas. ♿
Attendance: 109,000 (accurate)
Membership: Student $10; Senior Citizen $20; Individual $30; Dual Senior $35; UW Family $36; Family $55; Cascade Associate $100; Northwest Partner $250; Pacific Patron $500; Director's Circle $1,000.

CARL S. ENGLISH BOTANICAL GARDENS, 3015 N.W. 54th St., Seattle, WA 98107-4213. Tel.: 206-789-2622, ext. 230. Fax: 206-782-3192.
Web Site: www.nws.usace.army.mil
Botanical Gardens.
Collections: over 500 species & 1,500 varieties of plants from around the world.
Facilities: 7 acres.
Hours & Admission Prices: Grounds: daily 7am-9pm. Visitor Center: May-Sept. daily 10-6; Oct.-April Thurs.-Mon. 10-4. No charge.

CENTER FOR WOODEN BOATS, (M), 1010 Valley St., Seattle, WA 98109-4444. Tel.: 206-382-2628. Fax: 206-382-2699.
E-mail: cwb@cwb.org
Web Site: www.cwb.org
Founded: 1978.
Congressional District: 1
Key Personnel: Pres., Alex Bennet; Founding Dir., Dick Wagner; Exec. Dir., Elizabeth Davis; Business Mgr., Katy Mathias; Business Asst., Laurie Leak; Events & Operations Mgr., Eldon Tam; Lead Boatwright, Heron Scott; Boat Sales Mgr. & Instructor, Patrick Gould; Waterfront Programs Mgr., Jake Beattie; Coord. Youth Field Trip, Tom Baltzell; Livery Mgr., Dock Master & Youth Sailing, Zach Carver; Boatwright & Workshop Coord., Edel O'Connor; Curriculum, Courtney Bartlett; Custodian, Bud Ricketts; Shipwright in Residence, Geoff Braden; Operations Asst., Sarah Salter; Sailing Instructor, Julia Makowski; Sail Now! Coord., Vern Velez.
Personnel Profile: Full-Time Paid 11; Full-Time Volunteers 1; Part-Time Paid 5; Part-Time Volunteers 690; Interns 2.
Governing Authority: nonprofit organization. Tax-exempt: 501(c)(3).
Operational Maritime Museum.
Collections: traditional small craft, up to 35 ft. in length; historic photos; models of small craft; tools.
Research Fields: historic small craft of the world.
Facilities: 1,500-vol. library pertaining to maritime history; construction of voyages of small craft; technical information on wood & woodworking tools & techniques available to the public; working boatshop; botanical garden. Museum-related items for sale.
Activities: guided tours lectures; films; rowing, paddle a canoe; regattas; steam-bend a boat's rib; cast an oarlock; forge the hank for a foresail; splice

a line; loft a hull; organized education programs for adults & children; various activities for members.
Publications: bimonthly newsletter, Shavings; monographs on historic small craft.
Hours & Admission Prices: March 21 to May & Sept.-Nov. 1 daily 10-6; Memorial Day to Labor Day daily 10-8; Nov. 2 to March 20 Tues.-Sun. 10-5. Fees for use of boats & maritime skills workshops. Closed Thanksgiving; Christmas. ♿
Attendance: 60,000 (estimated)
Membership: Senior Citizen & Student $15; Individual $35; Household $50; Contributing $100; Benefactor $250; Sustaining $500; Captain's Circle $1,000.

CENTER ON CONTEMPORARY ART, 6413 Seaview Ave., N.W., Seattle, WA 98107-2666. Tel.: 206-728-1980. Fax: 206-728-1980.
E-mail: info@cocaseattle.org
Web Site: www.cocaseattle.org
Founded: 1981.
Congressional District: 7
Key Personnel: Pres., Ray Freeman; Vice Pres. & Chm., Danilo Bonilla; Dir. Talent & Mktg., Lauren Collins.
Personnel Profile: Full-Time Volunteers 1; Part-Time Volunteers 65; Interns 2.
Governing Authority: private; nonprofit organization. Congressional District: WA 7th District. Tax-exempt: 501(c)(3).
Art Museum.
Collections: contemporary art; performance art; multimedia & multidisciplinary programs.
Facilities: 4,000 sq. ft. exhibit space. Museum-related items for sale.
Activities: concerts; films; guided tours; lectures; participatory exhibits; members meetings. Annual Events: Northwest Annual: Juried Show; 24 House Painting Marathon & Auction; COCA Holiday Store; Seafair Ball & Art Invitational.
Publications: biannual newsletter, COCA Newsletter.
Hours & Admission Prices: Mon.-Fri. 10-5. No charge; donations accepted. Closed Independence Day; Thanksgiving; Christmas. ♿
Attendance: 15,000 (estimated)
Membership: Artist, Student & Senior Citizens $30; Individual $40; Couple $65; Family $100; Small Business $125; Donor $500; Millennium $1,000.

THE CHILDREN'S MUSEUM, SEATTLE, 305 Harrison St., Seattle, WA 98109-4623. Tel.: 206-441-1768. Fax: 206-448-0910.
E-mail: info@thechildrensmuseum.org
Web Site: www.thechildrensmuseum.org
Founded: 1981.
Congressional District: 7
Key Personnel: C.E.O., K.C. Gauldine; Chm. (V), Tom Gerlach; Exec. Dir., Donna Marie Bertrand; Museum Shop Mgr., Kristin Weswig.
Personnel Profile: Full-Time Paid 25; Full-Time Volunteers 5; Part-Time Paid 10; Interns 2.
Governing Authority: nonprofit organization. Tax-exempt: 501(c)(3).
Children's Museum.
Collections: hands-on exhibits, including a child-sized neighborhood; infant-toddler discovery area; multicultural exhibits; drop-in art center.
Facilities: Museum-related items for sale.
Activities: interactive programs for children from birth to 10 years old.
Publications: quarterly newsletter, Kidzette; monthly e-newsletter.
Hours & Admission Prices: Mon.-Fri. 10-5, Sat.-Sun. 10-6. Admission $7.50, seniors $6.50; discounts to groups of 10 or more, AAM, ICOM & AAA members; children under one no charge. Closed New Year's Day; Labor Day weekend; Thanksgiving; Christmas. ♿
Attendance: 232,000 (accurate)
Membership: Teacher $45; Grandparent $55; Family $75.

DES MOINES HISTORICAL SOCIETY MUSEUM, 730 S. 225th St., Seattle, WA 98198-6824. Mailing Address: P.O. Box 98055, Des Moines, WA 98198-0055. Tel.: 206-824-5226.
Governing Authority: nonprofit organization. Tax-exempt: 501(c)(3).
History Museum.
Collections: local history & culture; photographs; personal artifacts; period furnishings.
Hours & Admission Prices: Memorial Day to Labor Day Sat. 1-4; other times by appointment. No charge; donations accepted.

EXPERIENCE MUSIC PROJECT/SCIENCE FICTION MUSEUM, (M), 325 5th Ave. N., Seattle, WA 98109-4630. Mailing Address: 330 6th Ave. N, Ste. 200, Seattle, WA 98109-4613. Tel.: 206-770-2700. Fax: 206-770-2727.
E-mail: experience@empsfm.org
Web Site: www.empsfm.org
Founded: 1999.
Congressional District: 7
Key Personnel: C.E.O. & Dir., Christina Orr-Cahall; C.F.O., Traci Carman; Dir. Curatorial Affairs, EMP, Jasen Emmons; Deputy Dir. External Rels. & Devel., Patty Isacson Sabee; Dir. Education, Margie Maynard; Dir. Public Programming, Sam Vance.
Personnel Profile: Full-Time Paid 100; Full-Time Volunteers 8; Part-Time Paid 9; Part-Time Volunteers 66; Interns 9.
Governing Authority: private; nonprofit organization. Parent Institution: Experience Learning Community. Tax-exempt: 501(c)(3).
Musical Instruments & Science Fiction Museum.
Collections: Jimi Hendrix, instruments; Northwest music; roots of rock 'n' roll, hip-hop, punk, reggae; film; video; photography.
Major Exhibits: Taking Airm: Unforgettable Rock 'n' Roll Photographs Selected by Graham Nash (T), 2/10-9/10; Nirvana & The Northwest Underground: 1982-1992, 7/10.
Research Fields: American pop music; blues; music videos; science fiction; fantasy; horror; film; audio oral histories.
Facilities: digital library; lounge; 2 learning labs; digital lab; 140,000 sq. ft. exhibit space; 191-seat theater; sound lab. Gift items for sale.
Activities: guided tours; lectures; concerts; films; formal education programs; family programs; permanent, temporary & traveling exhibitions; public programs. Annual Events: Founders Award: Science Fiction Hall of Fame Induction Ceremony; Science Fiction & Fantasy Short Film Festival; Pop Conference; Jazz in January; Sound Off!; Experience: The Band.
Publications: exhibition catalogues; quarterly member publication, IMPRINT.
Hours & Admission Prices: Memorial Day to Labor Day daily 10-7; Sept.-May daily 10-5. Adults $15, senior citizens 65 & over, military, students & children 5-17 $12; discounts to AAM members; members and children 4 & under no charge. Closed Thanksgiving; Christmas. ♿
Attendance: 500,000 (accurate)
Membership: Traveler $40; Senior $45; Individual $50; Dual Senior $60; Dual $65; Family $75; Contributing $150; Supporting $250; Sustaining $500; Friend $1,000; Associate $2,500; Director $5,000; Investor $10,000; Benefactor $20,000.

* **FRYE ART MUSEUM, (M),** 704 Terry Ave., Seattle, WA 98104-2019. Tel.: 206-622-9250. Fax: 206-223-1707.
E-mail: info@fryemuseum.org
Web Site: www.fryemuseum.org
Founded: 1952.
Congressional District: 1
Key Personnel: Exec. Dir., Midge Bowman; Pres., David Buck; Deputy Dir., Jill Rullkoetter; Collections Mgr. & Registrar, Donna Kovalenko; Chief Cur., Robin Held; Museum Exhibitions Designer, Shane Montgomery; Museum Designer, Charla Reid; C.F.O., Donna DiFiore; Administration Coord., Roxanne Hadfield; Museum Shop Mgr., Karla Glanzman.
Personnel Profile: Full-Time Paid 22; Part-Time Paid 34; Part-Time Volunteers 40; Interns 3.
Governing Authority: nonprofit foundation. Tax-exempt: 501(c)(3).
Art Museum.
Collections: 19th- & 20th-century European & American paintings; contemporary figurative & representational paintings.
Facilities: 3,000-vol. library; 12,000 sq. ft. exhibit space; art studio; 142-seat auditorium; restaurant. Museum-related items for sale.
Activities: guided tours; gallery talks; lectures; concerts; workshops; classes for adults & children; traveling exhibitions.
Publications: quarterly bulletin, FRYE; 4 exhibition catalogs annually.
Hours & Admission Prices: Tues.-Wed. & Fri.-Sat. 10-5, Thurs. 10-8, Sun. 12-5. No charge; donations accepted. Closed New Year's Day; Independence Day; Thanksgiving; Christmas. ♿
Attendance: 100,000 (estimated)
Membership: Student $25; Senior $30; Working Artist & Teacher $40; Dual Senior $45; Individual $50; Dual & Family $75; Supporter $150; Contributor $300; Patron $500; Frye Art Circle $1,000; Corporate $2,500; Frye Leadership Circle $5,000.

GEORGETOWN POWERPLANT MUSEUM, 6605 13th Ave. S., Seattle, WA 98108. Tel.: 206-763-2542.
Steam Power Plant Museum: built in 1906.
Collections: power plant history, machinery, & equipment; photographs; miniature steam locomotives; a Calliophone; period fire engine.
Activities: plant tours; special events.
Hours & Admission Prices: Call for hours.

* **HENRY ART GALLERY, (M),** 15th Ave. N.E. & N.E. 41st St., University of Washington, Seattle, WA 98195-0001. Mailing Address: U.W. Box 351410, Seattle, WA 98195-0001. Tel.: 206-543-2280 & 2281. Fax: 206-685-3123.
E-mail: info@henryart.org
Web Site: www.henryart.org

Founded: 1927.
Congressional District: 1
Key Personnel: Dir., Sylvia Wolf; Pres. (V), Natalie Angelillo; Chm. (V), John Behnke; Chief Cur., Elizabeth Brown; Assoc. Dir. Communications & Outreach, Betsey Brock; Cur. Collections, Judy Sourakli; Exhibitions Mgr., Paul Cabarga; Head Preparator, Jim Rittimann; Dir. Devel., Robyn Macintire; Admin., Gina Glascock-Broze; Dir. Finance, Anne Walsh; Graphic Designer, Gabriel Stromberg; Visitor Svcs. & Tour Coord., Maria Reyna; Visitor Svcs. Coord. & Security Supvr., Eric Carson; Operations Mgr., Owen Santos.
Personnel Profile: Full-Time Paid 31; Part-Time Paid 17; Part-Time Volunteers 200; Interns 5.
Governing Authority: Parent Institution: University of Washington. Subsidiary Institution: Henry Gallery Association. Tax-exempt.
Art Museum.
Collections: 19th- to 20th-century American & European landscape paintings; paintings, prints, drawings & photographs; Japanese mingei ceramics; textiles & costumes from 131 countries, concentrated on handwoven techniques; mid-19th century American & European dress.
Research Fields: 19th- & 20th-century American art history; contemporary art criticism; costume & textile history, design & techniques.
Facilities: print study room.
Activities: lectures & symposia; collection research; community art services.
Publications: Art Into Life: Russian Constructivism 1914-1932; Myth of the West; Through Their Own Eyes: The Personal Portfolios of Edward Weston & Ansel Adams; Ann Hamilton: Sao Paulo & Seattle; James Turrell: Sensing Space; Gary Hill; After Art: Rethinking 150 Years of Photography; An Historical Anecdote About Fashion: Josiah McElheny; What it Meant to be Modern: Seattle Art at mid-Century; Shifting Ground: Transformed Views of the American Landscape; Short Stories on Photography: The Joseph and Elaine Monsen Photography Collection at the Henry Art Gallery; WOW, (The Work of the Work); Maya Lin: Systematic Landscapes.
Hours & Admission Prices: Thurs.-Fri. 11-9, Sat.-Sun. 11-4, Wed. by appointment. Adults $10, senior citizens 65 & over $6; discounts to AAM, AAA & ICOM members; members, students & children no charge. Closed New Year's Day; Independence Day; Thanksgiving; Christmas Eve & Day. ♿
Attendance: 71,646 (accurate)
Membership: Student $25; Senior $30; Individual $45; Dual Senior $50; Family $65; Sustaining $125; Henry Contemporaries $250-$999; Patron's Circle $1,000-$2,999; Director's Circle $3,000-$4,999; Chairman's Circle $5,000-$9,999; Artist's Circle $10, 000 & up.

HIRAM M. CHITTENDEN LOCKS VISITOR CENTER, 3015 N.W. 54th St., Seattle, WA 98107-4213. Tel.: 206-783-7059.
History Museum.
Collections: history & operation of the ship canal & locks; gardens; fish ladders; Army Corps of Engineers.
Facilities: botanical gardens. Museum-related items for sale.
Activities: fish-viewing; locks raising & lowering boats.
Hours & Admission Prices: May-Sept. daily 10-6; Oct.-April Thurs.-Mon. 10-4.

KLONDIKE GOLD RUSH NATIONAL HISTORICAL PARK, 319 Second Ave. S., Seattle, WA 98104-2618. Tel.: 206-220-4240. Fax: 206-381-0664.
E-mail: klse_Ranger_Activities@nps.gov
Web Site: www.nps.gov/klse
Founded: 1979.
Congressional District: 7
Key Personnel: Supt., Karen Beppler-Dorn; Volunteer Coord., Sean O'Meara.
Personnel Profile: Full-Time Paid 7; Part-Time Paid 1; Part-Time Volunteers 9.
Governing Authority: federal. Parent Institution: National Park Service, Washington, DC. Tax-exempt.
Housed in a historic building in Seattle's Pioneer Square Historical District.
Collections: 1897-1898 artifacts from the Klondike stampede; equipment replicas & historic artifacts related to the gold rush.
Research Fields: historical Seattle as it related to Klondike Gold Rush.
Facilities: 70-seat auditorium.
Activities: guided tours; gold panning demonstrations; films; permanent & temporary exhibitions.
Publications: brochure.
Hours & Admission Prices: Daily 9-5. No charge; donations accepted. Closed New Year's Day; Thanksgiving; Christmas. ♿
Attendance: 70,000 (estimated)

LOG HOUSE MUSEUM, 3003 61st Ave., S.W., Seattle, WA 98116-2810. Tel.: 206-338-5293.
E-mail: loghousemuseum@comcast.net
Web Site: www.loghousemuseum.org/
Founded: 1997.
Key Personnel: Dir., Andrea Mercado; Pres., Judy Bently; Pres. (V), Larry Carpenter; Museum Shop Mgr., Sarah Frederick.
Personnel Profile: Part-Time Paid 2; Part-Time Volunteers 32.
Governing Authority: Parent Institution: Southwest Seattle Historical Society. Tax-exempt.
History Museum: log house; built in 1903.
Collections: history of the Duwamish Peninsula & west Seattle; photographs; archives.
Facilities: library; gardens. Museum-related items for sale.
Activities: heritage education trunk kits; school tour presentations; teen docent program; speaker series; heritage tours & walks.
Publications: newsletter, Footprints in the Sands of Time; All Aboard for the Luna Park; Memories of Southwest Seattle Businesses; Tell Me A Story: A Memory Book for Youth From the Log House Museum; West Seattle Memories - Alki.
Hours & Admission Prices: Thurs.-Sun. 12-4. Suggested Donation: adults $3, children $1. Closed holidays. ♿
Attendance: 2,500 (estimated)
Membership: Senior & Student $15; Individual & Nonprofit $20; Family $35.

MUSEUM OF COMMUNICATIONS, 7000 E. Marginal Way S., Seattle, WA 98108-3411. Mailing Address: P.O. Box 81103, Seattle, WA 98108-1103. Tel.: 206-767-3012.
E-mail: qwest541@qwest.net
Web Site: www.museumofcommunications.org
Formerly: Vintage Telephone Museum
Founded: 1985.
Key Personnel: Dir., Don Ostrand.
Personnel Profile: Part-Time Volunteers 15.
Governing Authority: Tax-exempt.
Communications Museum.
Collections: telephone history; Alexander Graham Bell's first communications device to modern technology; telephone directories from 1900 to present.
Research Fields: genealogy.
Hours & Admission Prices: Tues. 8:30-2; other times by appointment. No charge; donations accepted. ♿

* **THE MUSEUM OF FLIGHT, (M),** 9404 E. Marginal Way S., Seattle, WA 98108-4097. Tel.: 206-764-5700 (Admin.) & 5720 (Visitor Information). Fax: 206-764-5707.
E-mail: info@museumofflight.org
Web Site: www.museumofflight.org
Founded: 1964.
Congressional District: 7
Key Personnel: Pres. & C.E.O., Bonnie J. Dunbar, Ph.D.; Vice Pres. & C.O.O., Laurie B. Haag; Vice Pres. & C.F.O., Edward Waale; Vice Pres. Devel., Caren M. Handleman, Ed.D.; Chm. (V), J. Kevin Callaghan; Sr. Cur., Dan Hagedorn; Dir. Education, Seth Margolis; Dir. Exhibits, Chris Mailander; Dir. Sales, Rich Rime; Dir. Aircraft Collections, Tom Cathcart; Controller, Lynda King; Museum Mgr., Jeffrey Frignoca; Museum Shop Mgr., Mary Christensen; Dir. Facilities, Clark Miller.
Personnel Profile: Full-Time Paid 105; Part-Time Paid 40; Part-Time Volunteers 800.
Governing Authority: nonprofit organization. Tax-exempt: 501(c)(3).
Aeronautics & Space Museum: c.1910 the first aircraft manufacturing facility in the region
Collections: over 125 historic aircraft; thousands of smaller artifacts including aircraft parts, garments, flight test instruments & model aircraft; space flight artifacts.
Major Exhibits: In Search of Amelia Earhart, 11/09-4/10.
Research Fields: aviation & space industry history in the United States; history of fighter aviation in WWI & WWII.
Facilities: library of textbooks, technical, popular & historical books & publications; 268-seat auditorium; educational facilities; aircraft restoration center; outdoor aircraft gallery; 178,000 sq. ft. exhibit space. Books, model aircraft & other related items for sale.
Activities: guided tours; lectures; films; rental gallery; organized educational programs for children; docent program; participatory, loan & temporary exhibitions; outreach to schools taking mini-museum; special aerospace events; fly-ins of historic aircraft; Challenger Learning Center missions.
Publications: bimonthly newsletter, Aloft; books, monographs.
Hours & Admission Prices: Daily 10-5; first Thurs. each month 10-9. Adults $14, seniors $13, children $7.50; discount to groups, AAM & ICOM members; members no charge. Closed Thanksgiving; Christmas. ♿
Attendance: 469,000 (estimated)
Membership: Navigator Solo $50; Aviator Family $75; Captain Family $100; Flight Leader Family $250; Barnstormer Family $500; Barnstormer Gold Family $1,000.

*** MUSEUM OF HISTORY & INDUSTRY (MOHAI), (M),** 2700 24th Ave., E., Seattle, WA 98112-2099. Tel.: 206-324-1126. Fax: 206-324-1346.
E-mail: information@seattlehistory.org
Web Site: www.seattlehistory.org
Founded: 1914.
Congressional District: 7
Key Personnel: Co Pres. Bd., Maggie Walker; Co Pres. Bd., Jerry Vandenberg; Dir., Leonard Garfield; Deputy Dir., Martha Aldridge; Librarian, Carolyn Marr; Historian, Dr. Lorraine McConaghy; Registrar, Kristin Halunen; Mgr. Collections, Betsy Bruemmer; Mgr. Public Programs, Helen Diujak; Mgr. Education, Martha Lindsey; Cur. Photography, Howard Giske; Cur. Textiles & Asst. Librarian, Mary Montgomery.
Personnel Profile: Full-Time Paid 32; Part-Time Paid 11; Part-Time Volunteers 130; Interns 5.
Governing Authority: Historical Society of Seattle & King County. Tax-exempt: 501(c)(3).
History & Industry Museum.
Collections: 800,000 items including mid-19th to 20th-century costumes; more than 2,000,000 photographs recording the history of the Pacific Northwest; textiles; decorative arts; furniture; silver; china; glassware; handmade items; folk art; paintings; tools & equipment related to communications & local industries: maritime, fishing, agriculture, logging, mining; recreation items: toys, musical instruments & sports; vintage vehicles: boats, airplanes & cable cars.
Research Fields: history of Seattle & Puget Sound Region from 1850 including pioneering, settlement, westward movement & activities & events thereof; preservation of photograph collection.
Facilities: Sophie Frye Bass Library of Northwest Americana contains books, photographs, films, videotapes; sound recordings; manuscripts; ephemeral materials; holdings of the Puget Sound Maritime Historical Society & Black Heritage Society of Washington State; 375-seat auditorium; meeting room. Books, notecards, toys, games, jewelry & other museum-related items for sale.
Activities: guided tours; lectures; workshops; rental gallery; formally organized education programs for children; docent programs; permanent & temporary exhibitions.
Publications: MOHAI newsletter, Old News.
Hours & Admission Prices: Daily 10-5, 1st Thurs. of month 10-8. Adults $8, seniors 62 & over, students and military w/ID $7, youth 5-17 $6; discounts to AAM & AAA members; children 4 & under, members and 1st Thurs. of month no charge. Closed Thanksgiving; Christmas. ♿
Attendance: 62,857 (accurate)
Membership: Seniors 62 & over, Students and Teachers $10 discount for any membership level; Individual $45; Dual $55; Family $65; Friend $100-$249; Patron $250-$499; Benefactor $500-$999; Heritage Guild $1,000.

NORDIC HERITAGE MUSEUM, (M), 3014 N.W. 67th St., Seattle, WA 98117-6215. Tel.: 206-789-5707. Fax: 206-789-3271.
E-mail: nordic@nordicmuseum.org
Web Site: www.nordicmuseum.org
Founded: 1979.
Congressional District: 5
Key Personnel: Dir. & C.E.O., Eric Nelson; Pres., Allan Osberg; Treas., Pirkko Borland; Cur. Collections, Lisa Hill-Festa; Devel. Officer, Gordon Strand; Administrative Asst., Sharmon Maguire; Education Coord., Alison Church.
Personnel Profile: Full-Time Paid 8; Full-Time Volunteers 1; Part-Time Paid 6; Part-Time Volunteers 175; Interns 2.
Governing Authority: nonprofit organization. Tax-exempt: 501(c)(3).
Heritage Museum: housed in 1907 Daniel Webster School.
Collections: folk costumes; textiles; woodcarvings; logging, fishing & mining equipment; furniture & household items; art by Nordic American artists.
Research Fields: Nordic immigration & settlement.
Facilities: 12,000-vol. library of Nordic language books; 150-seat auditorium; classrooms; 31,000 sq. ft. exhibit space; meeting rooms. Gift items for sale.
Activities: guided tours; language classes; folk art classes; lectures; films; concerts; arts festivals; study clubs; hobby workshops; organized education programs for children & adults; docent program; loan, temporary, & traveling exhibitions. Special Events: Christmas Crafts Fair; Summer Crafts/Music & Dance Festival; oral history project; annual summer camp for children.
Publications: bimonthly newsletter, Nordic News; Nordic Heritage Museum Historical Journal; Tasty Traditions; Voices of Ballard: Immigrant Stories from the Vanishing Generation.
Hours & Admission Prices: Tues.-Sat. 10-4, Sun. 12-4. Adults $6, senior citizens $5, children K-12 $4; discounts to AAA, WACH, AAM, ICOM & Scandinavian-American members; members & children under 5 no charge. Closed New Year's Eve & Day; Thanksgiving; Christmas Eve & Day. ♿
Attendance: 55,000 (estimated)
Membership: Senior $20; Individual $30; Senior Couple $35; Family $50; Organization $50/$100; Sustaining $100; Patron & Corporate $250; President's Club $750.

NORTH SEATTLE COMMUNITY COLLEGE ART GALLERY, 9600 College Way N., Instructional Bldg. Rm. 1322, Seattle, WA 98103-3599. Tel.: 206-528-4557.
E-mail: banderson@sccd.ctc.edu
Web Site: www.northseattle.edu/services/art.htm
Key Personnel: Coord. & Cur., Brenda Anderson
Art Gallery.
Collections: works by local & regional artists.
Activities: workshops; special events; art group meetings.
Hours & Admission Prices: During Exhibitions: Mon.-Tues. & Fri. 11-3, Wed.-Thurs. 11-3 & 6-8.

NORTHWEST AFRICAN AMERICAN MUSEUM, (M), 2300 S. Massachusetts St., Seattle, WA 98144-3821. Tel.: 206-518-6000. Fax: 206-518-5665.
E-mail: info@naamnw.org
Web Site: www.naamnw.org
Founded: 2007.
Congressional District: 37
Key Personnel: Exec. Dir., Barbara Earl Thomas
African American Museum.
Collections: African American history & culture; photographs; art; personal artifacts.
Facilities: cafe. Museum-related items for sale.
Activities: educational programs; school groups; facility rental.
Hours & Admission Prices: Wed. & Fri. 11-4:30, Thurs. 11-7, Sat. 11-4, Sun. 12-4. Adults $6, students & seniors $4; members, 1st Thurs. of month, and children 5 & under no charge. Closed New Year's Eve, Day & day after; Independence Day; Thanksgiving & weekend after; Christmas Eve, Day & week. ♿

ODYSSEY MARITIME DISCOVERY CENTER, 2205 Alaskan Way, Pier 66, Seattle, WA 98121-1604. Tel.: 206-374-4000. Fax: 206-374-4002.
E-mail: info@ody.org
Founded: 1998.
Congressional District: 7
Key Personnel: Pres. (V), Paul E. Stevens; Education Mgr., Cassandra Sandkam; Media Contact, Leigh Barer.
Personnel Profile: Full-Time Paid 5; Part-Time Paid 3; Part-Time Volunteers 22.
Governing Authority: private; nonprofit organization. Tax-exempt: 501(c)(3).
Maritime Museum.
Collections: maritime history & heritage; hands-on exhibits; photographs.
Research Fields: visitor studies; museum education; museum governance.
Facilities: educational facilities; 20,000 sq. ft. exhibit space; waterfront sitting. Maritime-related items for sale.
Activities: docent program; participatory exhibits; hands-on exhibits.
Publications: quarterly newsletter, Voyages.
Hours & Admission Prices: Wed.-Thurs. 10-3, Fri. 10-4, Sat.-Sun. 11-5. Call 206-374-4000 for additional hours. Adults $7, senior citizens & students $5, children 2-4 $2; discounts for military, groups & AAM members; children under 2 & members no charge. Closed New Year's Day; Thanksgiving; Christmas. ♿
Attendance: 40,135 (accurate)
Membership: Individual $30; Family $60; Silver $100; Gold $200; Platinum $350; Lifetime $10,000. Admiral's Club: Petty Officer $250; Mater Chief $500; Lieutenant $1,000; Commander $2,500; Captain $5,000; Commodore $10,000.

OLYMPIC SCULPTURE PARK, 2901 Western Ave., Seattle, WA 98121-1025. Mailing Address: 1300 First Ave., Seattle, WA 98101-2003. Tel.: 206-654-3100 & 332-1377. TDD: 206-344-5267.
E-mail: webmaster@seattleartmuseum.org
Web Site: www.seattleartmuseum.org/visit/osp
Sculpture Park Museum.
Collections: classic, modern & contemporary sculptures; native plants.
Facilities: 9 acre park; visitors pavilion.
Activities: temporary exhibits; educational programs.
Hours & Admission Prices: Sculpture Park: April-Oct. daily 6 am-10 pm; Nov.-March daily 7-6. Pavilion: May to Labor Day Tues.-Sun. 10-5; Sept.-April Tues.-Sun. 10-4. No charge. Closed New Year's Eve & Day; Labor Day; Thanksgiving; Christmas Eve & Day.

PACIFIC SCIENCE CENTER, (M), 200 2nd Ave. N., Seattle, WA 98109-4895. Tel.: 206-443-2001. Fax: 206-443-3631. TDD: 206-443-2887.
Web Site: pacificsciencecenter.org
Founded: 1962.
Congressional District: 36
Key Personnel: C.E.O. & Pres., R. Bryce Seidl; Chm., Scott Armstrong; Chm. (V), Colin Moseley; Vice Pres. Public Programs & Visitor Svcs., Diane Carlson; Vice Pres. Develop., Erik Pihl; Sr. Vice Pres. Strategic Programs, Dennis Schatz.
Personnel Profile: Full-Time Paid 136; Part-Time Paid 269; Part-Time Volunteers 132.
Governing Authority: nonprofit organization. Tax-exempt: 501(c)(3).
Science & Technology Museum.
Collections: astronomy; space sciences; anthropology; biology; geology; historical models; health sciences; life sciences; robotics; computer applications.
Facilities: classrooms; 400-seat IMAX theater; 350-seat IMAX theater; 300-person laser theater; planetarium; 50,000 sq. ft. exhibit space; restaurant; live animal area; rental facilities. Museum-related items for sale.
Activities: participatory exhibits; science demonstrations; film series; science enrichment classes for adults & children; lectures; field trips; in-school traveling education program; intern & volunteer programs; summer camps.
Publications: bimonthly newsletter, Discover Pacific Science Center; weekly e-newsletter.
Hours & Admission Prices: Daily 10 am. Exhibits & IMAX: adults $18, seniors $16, youth 6-15 $13, children 3-5 $11. Exhibits: adults $14, senior citizens 65 & over $12, youth 6-15 $9, children 3-5 $7; members no charge. IMAX: adults $9, seniors $12, youth $9. Closed Thanksgiving; Christmas. ♿
Attendance: 1,000,000 (accurate)
Membership: Nickel $45; Copper $60; Silver $80; Gold $100; Platinum $250; Titanium $500.

SEATTLE AQUARIUM, 1483 Alaskan Way, Pier 59, Seattle, WA 98101-2015. Tel.: 206-386-4300. Fax: 206-386-4328.
E-mail: aquarium.programs@seattle.gov
Web Site: www.seattleaquarium.org
Founded: 1977.
Congressional District: 1
Key Personnel: Dir., John Braden; Mgr. Mktg., Tim Kuniholm; Strategic Advisor, Alfredo Verzosa; Volunteer & Guest Svcs., Sue Donohue Smith; Cur. Education, Kathy Sider; Cur. Life Sciences, C.J. Casson; Mgr. Operations & Exhibits, Robert Anderson.
Personnel Profile: Full-Time Paid 60; Part-Time Paid 16; Part-Time Volunteers 625.
Governing Authority: municipal. Parent Institution: City of Seattle Parks and Recreation, 100 Dexter Ave. N., Seattle, WA 98109. Tax-exempt.
Aquarium and Marine Museum: located on downtown waterfront.
Collections: live collection of fishes, invertebrates, marine mammals & birds; from local saltwater environment & fresh, saltwater habitats over the world; environmental exhibits on Puget Sound.
Research Fields: biological fields relating to marine life; educational research on teacher use of field trip sites.
Facilities: library; classrooms.
Activities: self-guided tours for school groups; lectures; films; formally organized education programs for children & adults; outdoor trips; teacher workshops; special events.
Publications: quarterly newsletter, seasonal brochures, annual school program brochures.
Hours & Admission Prices: Daily 9:30-5. Adults $16, youth 4-12 $10.50; children 3 & under, members and AAM, ICOM & AZA members no charge. Closed one day in June for fundraiser. ♿
Attendance: 820,000 (accurate)
Membership: Individual $65; Family $80; Family Plus $95.

* **SEATTLE ART MUSEUM, (M),** 1300 First Ave., Seattle, WA 98101-2003. Tel.: 206-654-3100. Fax: 206-654-3135. TDD: 206-654-3137.
E-mail: webmaster@seattleartmuseum.org
Web Site: www.seattleartmuseum.org
Founded: 1933.
Congressional District: 1
Key Personnel: Dir. The Illsley Ball Nordstrom, Mimi Gardner Gates; Chm. Bd., Stan Savage; Pres. Bd., Christine Nicolov; Deputy Dir. Finance & Operations, Robert Cundall; Controller, Nancy Zwieback; Cur. Art of Africa & Oceania, Pamela McClusky; Jon & Mary Shirley Cur. Modern & Contemporary Art, Michael Darling; The Ruth J. Nutt, Cur. Decorative Arts, Julie Emerson; Deputy Dir. Art & Cur. European Painting, Chiyo Ishikawa; The Kayla Skinner Dir. Education & Public Programs, Sandra Jackson-Dumont; Senior Registrar, Lauren Mellon; Volunteer Mgr., Kathleen Maki; Dir. Exhibition Design & Museum Svcs., Michael McCafferty; Conservator, Nicholas Dorman; Head of Mktg., Susan Bartlett; Mgr. Exhibitions & Cur. Publications, Zora Hutlova-Foy; Cur. Native American Art, Barbara Brotherton; Corporate & Foundation Rels. Officer, Jeannine Foucher; Facilities Mktg. Mgr., John Ferguson; Dir. Public Rels., Cara Egan; Foundation Rels. Mgr., Laura Hopkins; Senior Deputy Dir., Maryann Jordan; Mgr. Community Rels., Davita Ingram; Librarian, Traci Timmons; Dir. Facilities, Brandon Weathers; Mgr. Retail Operations, Brad Bigelow; Head Human Resources, M. Therese Ortega.
Personnel Profile: Full-Time Paid 180; Part-Time Paid 106; Part-Time Volunteers 500; Interns 4.
Governing Authority: nonprofit. Subsidiary Institution: Seattle Asian Art Museum; Olympic Sculpture Park. Tax-exempt: 501(c)(3).
Art Museum.
Collections: Chinese, Japanese, Korean, Indian & South East Asian art; Chinese jades; Katherine White Collections of African Art; ancient American & Oceanic art; Northwest Coast; modern & contemporary European & American paintings, sculpture, prints & photography; European & American decorative arts; Near Eastern, Egyptian, Greek, Roman, Medieval, Renaissance & Baroque paintings; numismatics; textiles.
Research Fields:
Facilities: library; slide library; 70,000 sq. ft. exhibit space; auditorium & lecture hall (each with assistive listening devices); restaurant. Museum-related items for sale.
Activities: guided tours; lectures; films; gallery talks; demonstrations; tea ceremonies; workshops; concerts; formally organized education programs; outreach programs to children & adults; CD-ROM Audio Gallery Guide; interactive multimedia computer kiosk on permanent collection; curriculum packets & workshops for teachers; inter-museum loans; permanent, temporary & traveling exhibitions; docent tours; special preview events.
Publications: annual report; members newsletter & program guides; permanent collection catalogs; exhibition catalogs; brochures; gallery guides (many in large type).
Hours & Admission Prices: Museum: Tues.-Wed. & Sat.-Sun. 10-5, Thurs.-Fri. 10-9. Suggested Admissions: adults $13, seniors 62 & over $10; students & children 13-17 $7; discounts to AAM, ICOM, AAA & Entertainment members; members, children 12 & under and 1st Thurs. of month no charge. Closed New Year's Eve & Day; Columbus Day; Thanksgiving; Christmas Eve & Day. ♿
Attendance: 500,000 (estimated)
Membership: Student $30; Senior Citizen $35; Individual $60; Dual $75; Family $85; Patron $200; Friend $300; Fellow $600; Ambassador $1,000.

SEATTLE ASIAN ART MUSEUM, 1400 E. Prospect, Volunteer Park, Seattle, WA 98112-3303. Tel.: 206-654-3100. Fax: 206-654-3191. TDD: 206-344-5267.
E-mail: webmaster@seattleartmuseum.org
Web Site: www.seattleartmuseum.org
Founded: 1933.
Congressional District: 1
Key Personnel: Dir. The llsley Ball Nordstrom, Derrick Cartwright; Chm. Bd., Jon Shirley; Pres. Bd., Susan Brotman; Librarian, Traci Timmons; Maintenance Supvr., Jim Haarsager; Foster Foundation Asst. Cur. Chinese Art, Josh Yiu.
Personnel Profile: Full-Time Paid 162; Full-Time Volunteers 512; Part-Time Paid 30; Interns 6.
Governing Authority: private; nonprofit organization. Parent Institution: Seattle Art Museum. Tax-exempt: 501(c)(3).
Art Museum.
Collections: Japanese, Korean, Indian, Southeast Asian & Chinese art.
Research Fields:
Facilities: 3,500-vol. library of books on the arts & sciences of Asia; auditorium; activities room; art storage; teacher resource center. Asian-related merchandise including art books, cards & jewelry for sale.
Activities: guided tours; lectures; films; gallery talks; demonstrations; workshops; concerts; formally organized education programs for adults, families, senior citizens, children & undergraduate college students, teachers & members; outreach programs for children & adults; curriculum packets & workshops for teachers; inter-museum loan, permanent, temporary & traveling exhibitions; docent tours; special preview events.
Publications: annual report; member newsletter/program guides; permanent collection & exhibition catalogs; brochures; gallery guides (many in large type).
Hours & Admission Prices: Summer: Tues.-Wed. & Fri.-Sun. 10-5, Thurs. 10-9; Winter: Wed. & Fri.-Sun. 10-5, Thurs. 10-9. Suggested: adults $7 students, youth 13-17 & seniors $5; discounts to AAM & ICOM members; members no charge. Closed New Year's Eve & Day; Labor Day; Thanksgiving; Christmas Eve & Day. ♿
Attendance: 74,878 (accurate)
Membership: Student & Senior $30; Individual $55; Dual $70; Family $75; Patron $175; Friend $250; Fellow $550; Ambassadors Circle $1,000;

Stewards Circle $2,500; Curators Circle $5,000; Benefactors Circle $10,000; Directors Circle $15,000; Presidents Circle $25,000; Chairmans Circle $50,000.

SEATTLE MUSEUM OF THE MYSTERIES, 623 Broadway E., Seattle, WA 98102-5025. Tel.: 206-328-6499.
Paranormal Science Museum.
Collections: UFO & ghost history; Bigfoot casts; photographs; movie memorabilia.
Facilities: library.
Activities: ghost tour; lectures; ghost poker; special events.
Hours & Admission Prices: Thurs. 1-8:30, Sat. 12-10, Sun. 1-6:30. Lock-in: Sat. 10 pm to midnight. Suggested Donation: adults $2, youth 9-17 $1; children 8 & under no charge. Lock-in: adults $5, youth 8-16 $3.

SHORELINE HISTORICAL MUSEUM, (M), 749 N. 175th, Seattle, WA 98133-4801. Mailing Address: P.O. Box 55594, Shoreline, WA 98155-0594. Tel.: 206-542-7111.
E-mail: shorelinehistorical@juno.com
Web Site: shorelinehistoricalmuseum.org
Founded: 1976.
Congressional District: 1
Key Personnel: Exec. Dir. & C.E.O., Victoria Stiles; Chm. (V), Henry Reed.
Personnel Profile: Full-Time Paid 1; Part-Time Paid 1; Part-Time Volunteers 70; Interns 3.
Governing Authority: board of trustees. Tax-exempt: 501(c)(3), 170(b)(1)(A).
Historical Museum: housed in 1912 Ronald School Building, the oldest standing school in the district.
Collections: Shoreline, Lake Forest Park, north Seattle, northwest King County history; period home & business memorabilia; schoolroom; photographs; blacksmith shop; early Richmond Beach post office; country store & farmyard; Playland Amusement Park.
Research Fields: oral histories of area pioneers; written accounts; maps; books; tools; household items; pictures; early art & crafts; archival photography; church & school histories; businesses; historic locations; descriptions.
Facilities: classrooms; meeting rooms; multipurpose room.
Activities: guided tours; lectures; films; antique show; docent program or council; loan, permanent, temporary & traveling exhibitions; internships (volunteer); pioneer luncheon.
Publications: quarterly newsletter; books, Shoreline Memories; Shoreline or Steamers, Stumps and Strawberries; Growing Up with Lake Forest Park, vols. 1; Country Store Nevermore; Broadview Memories; Once Upon a Time in Playland; Judge James T. Ronald Memoir.
Hours & Admission Prices: Tues.-Sat. 10-4. No charge; donations accepted. Closed New Year's Day; Independence Day; Thanksgiving; Christmas. ♿
Attendance: 8,000 (estimated)
Membership: Individual $15; Family $25; Business $50; Life $1,000.

SWEDISH FINN HISTORICAL SOCIETY ARCHIVES AND LIBRARY, 1920 Dexter Ave. N., Seattle, WA 98109-2718. Tel.: 206-706-0738. Fax: 206-782-5813.
Historical Society Museum.
Collections: Swedish-Finn culture, tradition & history; photographs; books.
Facilities: library; archives.
Activities: research.
Hours & Admission Prices: Mon. & Thurs. 9:30-12:30, 1st Sat. of month 12-4.

UNIVERSITY OF WASHINGTON BOTANIC GARDEN, 2300 Arboretum Dr. E., Seattle, WA 98112-2300. Mailing Address: Box 354115, Seattle, WA 98195-4115. Tel.: 206-543-8616 & 8800. Fax: 206-685-2692.
E-mail: uwbg@u.washington.edu
Web Site: www.uwbotanicgardens.org
Formerly: Washington Park Arboretum
Founded: 1934.
Congressional District: 1
Key Personnel: C.E.O., Dr. David J. Mabberley; Pres. Arboretum Foundation, John Johnston; Chm. (V), Susan Black; Mgr., Fred Hoyt; Lead Gardener, David Zuckerman; Registrar & Recorder, Randall Hitchin; Chm. (V) & Education Cur., Elizabeth Louden; City Seattle Liaison, Dept. Parks & Recreation, Don Harris; Buyer, Lynn Garvey; Books, Pat Ratmussen; Exec. Dir. Arboretum Foundation, Deborah Andrews; Arborist, Lou Stubecki; Museum Shop Mgr., Mary Ellen Mulder.
Personnel Profile: Full-Time Paid 17; Part-Time Paid 22; Part-Time Volunteers 250; Interns 7.
Governing Authority: municipal; nonprofit organization. Parent Institution: University of Washington, City of Seattle. Tax-exempt: 170(b)(1)(A).
Arboretum & Botanical Garden.
Collections: 230-acres containing approximately 4,400 taxa of woody plants. Historic Houses: 1936 Stone Cottage; 1936 Dawson Plan (Olmsted Brothers).
Research Fields: horticultural taxonomy; woody plant introduction & testing; plant conservation; urban ecology & forestry; horticultural education; habitat restoration.
Facilities: visitor center; lecture room; outdoor classrooms; greenhouse; reading room. Museum-related items for sale.
Activities: guided tours; lectures; films; formally organized education programs for adults; docent program; slide programs; primary school programs; primary school programs (saplings); family programs; tours. Arboretum Sponsors: Branching Out (inner city); summer day camp.
Publications: quarterly magazine & journal, Volunteer News Washington Arboretum Bulletin; Arboreta Foundation Newsletter; Center for Urban Horticulture: CUH Presents; Pro Hort.
Hours & Admission Prices: Arboretum: daily sunrise-sunset. No charge. Visitors' Center: Mon.-Fri. 10-4, Sat.-Sun. 12-4. Japanese Garden $5. Closed New Year's Day; Thanksgiving; Christmas.
Attendance: 400,000 (estimated)
Membership: Arboretum Foundation Annual $25.

WING LUKE ASIAN MUSEUM, 719 S. King St., Seattle, WA 98104-3035. Tel.: 206-623-5124. Fax: 206-623-4559.
E-mail: folks@wingluke.org
Web Site: www.wingluke.org
Founded: 1967.
Congressional District: 7
Key Personnel: Dir., Ron Chew; C.E.O., Beth Takekawa; Public Rels. Mgr., Joann Natalia Aquino; Education Coord., Russel Bareng; Program Coord., Vivian Chan; Exhibit Planner, Joshua Heim; Deputy Program Dir., Cassie Chinn; Membership Assoc., Claire Cho; Visitor Svcs. Coord., Cesar Cueva; Collections Mgr., Robert Fisher; Dir. Donor Devel., Mary Ann Harper; TeensWAY Coord., Ammara Hun; Dir. Business Devel., Ray Ishii; Education Asst., Islanda Khau; Devel. Assoc., Adam Lee; Accounting Asst., Tommy Lee; Senior Program Mgr., Charlene Mano; Dir. Fund Devel., Lena Park; Exhibits Coord., George Quibuyen; Capital Campaign Mgr., Joy Shigaki.
Personnel Profile: Full-Time Paid 14; Part-Time Paid 7; Part-Time Volunteers 90; Interns 18.
Governing Authority: nonprofit organization. Tax-exempt: 501(c)(3).
Asian Pacific American History, Art & Culture Museum.
Collections: Asian-American and Asian history, art & culture.
Research Fields: early Asians & Pacific islanders in the Pacific Northwest; northwest Asian-American history.
Facilities: 500-vol. library of material pertaining to the collection & research fields available on premises; community & social service use & sponsorship.
Activities: guided tours; lectures; formally organized education programs for adults & children; inter-museum loan & traveling exhibitions; video documentaries; film & discussion series; readings.
Publications: quarterly membership newsletter; books, Executive Order 9066: 50 Years Before & 50 Years After, Reflections of Seattle's Chinese-Americans: The First 100 Years, They Painted from Their Hearts: Pioneer Asian-American Artists, Beyond the Rock Garden: Craft Form for a New World; Divided Destiny: A History of Japanese Americans in Seattle; P.I. (Made in America): Filipino American Artists in the Pacific Northwest; CD: A Bridge Home.
Hours & Admission Prices: Tues.-Sun. 10-5, 1st Thurs & 3rd Sat. of month 10-8. Adults $8, seniors & students $6, children 5-12 $5; discounts to AAM & ICOM members; 1st Thurs. & 3rd Sat. of month, members & children under 5 no charge. Closed New Year's Day; Independence Day; Thanksgiving; Christmas Eve & Day. ♿
Attendance: 244,000 (accurate)
Membership: Senior Citizen & Student $20; Individual $30; Friends & Family $50; Donor $100; Patron $200; Benefactor $500; President's Club $1,000.

WOODLAND PARK ZOO, 5500 Phinney Ave. N., Seattle, WA 98103-5897. Mailing Address: 601 N. 59th St., Seattle, WA 98103-5858. Tel.: 206-548-2500. Fax: 206-548-1536. TTY: 206-548-2599.
E-mail: webkeeper@zoo.org
Web Site: www.zoo.org
Formerly: Woodland Park Zoological Gardens
Founded: 1900.
Congressional District: 32
Key Personnel: Pres. & C.E.O., Deborah B. Jensen, Ph.D.; Vice Pres. Devel., David Wu; Dir. Guest Svcs., Jodie Levey; Dir. Human Resources, Damian King; Dir. Mktg., Jim Bennett; Deputy Dir., Bruce Bohmke; Gen. Cur., Nancy Hawkes; Acting Dir. Animal Health, Kelly Helmick, D.V.M.; Dir. Education, Stephanie Stowell; Dir. Conservation, Lisa Dabek; Zoo Store Mgr., Terry Blumer.
Personnel Profile: Full-Time Paid 235; Full-Time Volunteers 700; Part-Time Paid 37.

Governing Authority: Woodland Park Zoological Society, 601 N. 59th St., Seattle, WA 98103. Tax-exempt.
Zoo.
Collections: birds; mammals; reptiles; amphibians; insects; exotic & native fauna & flora.
Research Fields: reproduction; psychology & behavior.
Facilities: zoological gardens.
Activities: guided tours; lectures; docent program; zoo education classes for general public; inter-museum loan, permanent & traveling exhibitions; educational self-guided tours.
Publications: self-guided tour brochures; books; zoo activity & teacher packets; member magazine.
Hours & Admission Prices: May-Sept. daily 9:30-6; Oct.-April daily 9:30-4. Summer: adults $16.50, children 3-12 $11; children 2 & under no charge. Winter: adults $11, children 3-12 $8; children 2 & under no charge. Closed Christmas. ♿
Attendance: 1,128,020 (accurate)
Membership: Wolf One (Individual) $50; Lion's Liar (2 adults) $80; Gorilla Troop (1adult & kids) $85; Wolf Pack (2 adults & kids) $110; Elephant Herd (family & flex guest) $150. Discounts online.

Sedro-Woolley

SEDRO-WOOLLEY MUSEUM, 725 Murdock St., Sedro-Woolley, WA 98284-1450. Tel.: 360-855-2390.
Web Site: sedrowoolleymuseum.org
Founded: 1991.
Congressional District: 39
Key Personnel: Pres. (V) & Museum Shop Mgr., Carolyn Freeman; Vice Pres., Dale Robertson.
Personnel Profile: Full-Time Volunteers 12; Part-Time Volunteers 35.
Governing Authority: nonprofit organization. Tax-exempt.
History Museum.
Collections: local history & culture; photographs; personal artifacts; logging; agricultural equipment.
Activities: Museum Sponsors: Founders' Day in September; Holiday Home Tour in December.
Publications: quarterly newsletter.
Hours & Admission Prices: Wed.-Thurs. 12-4, Sat. 9-4, Sun. 1:30-4:30; other times by appointment. Suggested Donation: adults $1.50, seniors & children $1; members no charge. ♿
Attendance: 3,750 (accurate)
Membership: Senior $7; Individual $12; Couple $15; Family $25; Business & Organization $35.

Sequim

DUNGENESS RIVER AUDUBON CENTER AT RAILROAD BRIDGE PARK, 2151 Hendrickson Rd., Sequim, WA 98382. Mailing Address: P.O. Box 2450, Sequim, WA 98382-2450. Tel.: 360-681-4076. Fax: 360-681-8060.
E-mail: rivercenter@olympus.net
Web Site: www.dungenessrivercenter.org
Formerly: Dungeness River Audubon Center
Key Personnel: Dir., Bob Boekelheide
Audubon Center.
Collections: Olympic Peninsula; Dungeness River & watershed; local wildlife; native plants & trees.
Facilities: nature trail.
Activities: educational & interpretive programs; bird walks.
Hours & Admission Prices: Tues.-Sat. 10-4, Sun. 12-4. No charge; donations accepted. ♿
Attendance: 21,500 (accurate)

MUSEUM AND ARTS CENTER IN THE SEQUIM DUNGENESS VALLEY, 175 W. Cedar, Sequim, WA 98382-3318. Tel.: 360-683-8110. Fax: 360-681-2325.
E-mail: info@museumandartscenter.org
Web Site: www.museumandartscenter.org
Founded: 1977.
Congressional District: 6
Key Personnel: Exec. Dir. & Registrar, Katherine Vollenweider; Pres. (V), Layton Carr; Volunteer Coord., Renne Brock-Richmond; Museum Shop Mgr., Ilene Voltaire.
Personnel Profile: Full-Time Paid 1; Full-Time Volunteers 2; Part-Time Paid 3; Part-Time Volunteers 150; Interns 1.
Governing Authority: private; nonprofit organization. Parent Institution: Museum & Arts Center. Tax-exempt: 501(c)(3).
General Museum.
Collections: Sequim area artifacts & photographs; archives; dairy farming tools & equipment; Manis Mastodon specimens.
Research Fields: pioneer genealogy; video histories of local historic sites & people; medicine; midwives; farming; local Native American-S'Klallam Tribal artifacts; morticians; mastodon & mammoth bones, tusks & teeth; pioneer artifacts, logging & dairy implements; regional photographic archive; dairy industry artifacts & records; textiles with emphasis on clothing; timber industry; Manis Mastodon; John Cowan collection; local school district history.
Facilities: Whatton research library for local genealogical and historical research; photo archives of historical photos; photo lab.
Activities: North Olympic Peninsula history class; traveling exhibits to schools; Seniors Making Art classes; Art-iculate(R) art classes. Museum Sponsors: Community Independence Day Picnic; Elegant Flea Show & Fundraiser; Holiday Tea at Historic Dungeness School; First Friday Sequim Art Walk.
Publications: quarterly newsletter.
Hours & Admission Prices: Tues.-Sat. 10-3:30. No charge; donations accepted. Closed holidays. ♿
Attendance: 4,000 (estimated)
Membership: Individual $20; Family $30.

Shaw Island

SHAW ISLAND LIBRARY & HISTORICAL SOCIETY, Blind Bay Rd., Shaw Island, WA 98286. Mailing Address: P.O. Box 844, Shaw Island, WA 98286-0844. Tel.: 360-468-4068.
E-mail: rkg@rockisland.com
Web Site: www.shawislanders.org/others/library/library.htm
Founded: 1966.
Congressional District: 2
Key Personnel: Pres., Jennifer Swanson; Cur., Alex McCloud; Historian, Sheri Christiansen; Head Librarian, Jeb Nichols.
Governing Authority:: society. Tax-exempt: 501(c)(3).
Local History Museum: housed in c.1870 one room log cabin.
Collections: items of local historic interest.
Activities: permanent exhibitions.
Hours & Admission Prices: Tues. 2-4, Thurs. 11-1, Sat. 10-12 & 2-4; other times by appointment. No charge.
Membership: Individual $1; Life $25.

Snohomish

BLACKMAN HOUSE MUSEUM, 118 Ave. B, Snohomish, WA 98290. Mailing Address: P.O. Box 174, Snohomish, WA 98291-0174. Tel.: 360-568-5235.
Web Site: www.snohomishhistoricalsociety.org
Founded: 1969.
Congressional District: 2
Key Personnel: Pres. (V), Warner Blake; Archivist, Middy Ruthruff.
Personnel Profile: Part-Time Paid 2; Part-Time Volunteers 14.
Governing Authority: society; nonprofit. Parent Institution: Snohomish Historical Society. Tax-exempt.
Historical Society Museum: 1878 Blackman House, home of town's first mayor.
Collections: furniture & furnishings of the late 1800s; logging tools & artifacts; period clothing; photographs.
Research Fields: early town history.
Facilities: library of early community photography & printed matter available for research by private arrangement. Museum-related items for sale.
Activities: guided tours; temporary exhibitions. Museum Sponsors: annual Tour of Historic Homes; Holiday Parlor Tours of Historic Homes.
Publications: books, River Reflections-History of Snohomish from 1859 to 1910; River Reflections 1910-1959; Early Snohomish.
Hours & Admission Prices: April to mid-Dec. Sat.-Sun. 11-3. Donation requested. Closed Mother's Day.
Attendance: 1,000 (estimated)
Membership: Individual $10; Family $12; Business $25; Honorary over age 75.

Snoqualmie

NORTHWEST RAILWAY MUSEUM, (M), 38625 S.E. King St., Snoqualmie, WA 98065. Mailing Address: P.O. Box 459, Snoqualmie, WA 98065-0459. Tel.: 425-888-3030, ext. 201. Fax: 425-888-9311.
E-mail: director@trainmuseum.org
Web Site: www.trainmuseum.org
Founded: 1957.
Congressional District: 8
Key Personnel: Exec. Dir., Richard R. Anderson; Chm. (V) & Pres. (V), Susan Hankins; Vice Pres., Dennis Snook; Sec., Carol Waters; Treas., Jon Beveridge; Museum Shop Mgr., James Sackey.
Personnel Profile: Full-Time Paid 5; Part-Time Paid 3; Part-Time Volunteers 137.

Governing Authority: volunteer nonprofit organization. Tax-exempt: 501(c)(3).
Railroad Museum & Historic Building: c.1890 railroad depot.
Collections: railway vehicles including steam & diesel locomotives, passenger coaches & freight cars, rotary snow plow, cranes, observation cars, maintenance-of-way equipment, kitchen car; logging railway artifacts.
Major Exhibits: Wellington Remembered, 2/10-12/10.
Research Fields: maintenance & restoration of steam & diesel locomotives.
Facilities: picnic area. Books & other railway-related items for sale.
Activities: permanent exhibitions; diesel passenger train ride; charter service available; school field trip program; self guided walking tour.
Publications: bimonthly newsletter, Sounder; bimonthly children's newsletter, Jr. Sounder.
Hours & Admission Prices: Memorial Day to Labor Day daily 10-5. No charge. Railway Excursion: April-Oct. Sat.-Sun., occasional weekdays & holidays. Adults $11, seniors 62 & over $10, children 3-12 $8; discounts to groups & AAM members; children under 3 no charge. ♿
Attendance: 85,757 (accurate)
Membership: Cecil the Diesel Club (children 3-10) $30; Individual $35; Family $50; Business $75; Patron $125; Benefactor $250.

South Bend

PACIFIC COUNTY HISTORICAL MUSEUM, 1008 W. Robert Bush Dr., South Bend, WA 98586-0039. Mailing Address: P.O. Box P, South Bend, WA 98586-0039. Tel.: 360-875-5224. Fax: 360-875-5224 (call first).
E-mail: museum@willapabay.org
Web Site: www.pacificcohistory.org
Founded: 1970.
Congressional District: 3
Key Personnel: Pres. (V), Steve Rogers; Mgr., Karla Webber.
Personnel Profile: Full-Time Paid 1; Part-Time Volunteers 8.
Governing Authority: nonprofit organization. Parent Institution: Pacific County Historical Society. Tax-exempt: 501(c)(3).
Local History Museum.
Collections: Indian artifacts & relics; records; documents; photographs; relics of pioneers; school records & photos; census records; manuscripts; archives.
Research Fields: ethnic groups; industries; local history; maritime facts & lore.
Facilities: 600-vol. library of printed books; census records; school teaching records; business cash books; diaries; letters; scrapbooks; land office records available for research by appointment or special request; reading room. Books of Pacific Northwest history for sale.
Activities: guided tours; temporary exhibitions.
Publications: quarterly magazine, The Sou'wester.
Hours & Admission Prices: Daily 11-4. No charge; donations accepted. Closed Thanksgiving; Christmas. ♿
Attendance: 3,750 (estimated)
Membership: Single $25; Family $35; Contributing $50; Corporate $100; Benefactor $200; Grantor $300; Steward $500; Sponsor $1,000 & up.

South Cle Elum

DEPOT MUSEUM/CASCADE RAIL FOUNDATION, 801 Milwaukee Rd., South Cle Elum, WA 98943. Mailing Address: P.O. Box 462, South Cle Elum, WA 98943-0462. Tel.: 509-674-5939. Fax: 509-674-1708.
E-mail: maryp@cleelum.com
Web Site: www.milwelectric.org
Founded: 2006.
Congressional District: 4
Key Personnel: Pres. (V), Bruce Reason; Vice Pres., David Newcomb; Treas., Mary Pittis; Education, Mark Borleske; Public Rels., Donovan Gray.
Personnel Profile: Full-Time Volunteers 9; Part-Time Volunteers 2.
Governing Authority: private; nonprofit organization. Tax-exempt: 501(c)(3).
Railroad Museum.
Collections: railroad artifacts; photographs; Milwaukee board's western expansion from 1906-1980.
Research Fields: 1946 Milwaukee caboose rehabilitation; original drawings & photographs.
Facilities: 2,000 sq. ft. exhibit space; 49-seat restaurant; interpretive trail. Museum-related items for sale.
Activities: Annual Events: Depot Days in June; Brewfest in July. Museum Sponsors: Milwaukee Modelers Meet in October.
Hours & Admission Prices: May-Oct. Sat.-Sun. 12-4. No charge; donations accepted.
Attendance: 317 (accurate)
Membership: Gandy Dancer $35; Telegrapher $50; Engineer $75; Conductor $100; Dispatcher $250; Roadmaster $500; Trainmaster $750; Superintendent's Club $1,000; President's Club $2,500.

Spokane

CORBIN ART CENTER, 507 W. 7th Ave., Spokane, WA 99204-2709. Mailing Address: 808 W. Spokane Falls Blvd., 5th Fl. City Hall, Spokane, WA 99201-3301. Tel.: 509-625-6677.
E-mail: spokaneparks@spokanecity.org
Web Site: www.spokaneparks.org/recreation/CAC.htm
Key Personnel: Dir., Gary Lawton.
Governing Authority: Parent Institution: City of Spokane Parks and Recreation Department.
Art Gallery: housed in D.C. Corbin house, built in 1898. Listed on the National Register of Historic Places.
Collections: paintings.
Activities: fine arts & crafts classes.
Hours & Admission Prices: Mon.-Thurs. 9-4. No charge.

JOHN A. FINCH ARBORETUM, 3404 W. Woodland Blvd., Spokane, WA 99224-2240. Mailing Address: Park Operations, 810 N. Stone St., Spokane, WA 99202. Tel.: 509-363-5455. Fax: 509-363-5454.
Web Site: www.spokanecity.org/parks
Founded: 1947.
Key Personnel: Park Div. Mgr., Tony Madunich.
Personnel Profile: Full-Time Paid 1; Part-Time Paid 4.
Governing Authority: municipal. Affiliated with City of Spokane Park Board, 4th Fl., Municipal Bldg., W. 808 Spokane Falls Blvd., Spokane, WA. 99201.
Arboretum.
Collections: 65-acres of trees & shrubs.
Facilities: 600-vol. library of plant books; reading room.
Activities: Arbor Day & Fall Leaf Festival.
Hours & Admission Prices: Mon.-Fri. 7:30-12 & 1-4. No charge; donations accepted.

JUNDT ART MUSEUM, 502 E. Boone Ave., Spokane, WA 99258-0001. Tel.: 509-313-6611. Fax: 509-313-5525.
E-mail: patnode@calvin.gonzaga.edu
Web Site: www.gonzaga.edu
Founded: 1995.
Congressional District: 5
Key Personnel: Dir. & Cur., J. Scott Patnode; Asst. Cur. Education, Karen Kaiser; Program Coord., Anita Martello.
Personnel Profile: Full-Time Paid 3; Part-Time Volunteers 23; Interns 6.
Governing Authority: university. Parent Institution: Gonzaga University. Tax-exempt.
Art Museum/Center.
Collections: student prints; Old Master's prints; photography prints; contemporary prints; Auguste Rodin sculptures; Chihuly glass installation.
Research Fields: printmaking survey.
Facilities: 118-seat auditorium; print study room.
Activities: lectures; gallery talks.
Hours & Admission Prices: Winter: Mon.-Fri. 10-4, Sat. 12-4; Summer: call for hours. No charge. Closed university holidays. ♿
Attendance: 25,000

MOBIUS KIDS, 808 W. Main, Lower Level, Spokane, WA 99201. Tel.: 509-624-5437. Fax: 509-624-6453.
E-mail: info@mobiusspokane.org
Web Site: www.mobiusspokane.org
Formerly: Children's Museum of Spokane
Founded: 1995.
Congressional District: 5
Key Personnel: Dir., Marty Gonzales; Pres., Neil Worrall; Event & Volunteer Coord., Karen Hudson.
Personnel Profile: Full-Time Paid 2; Part-Time Paid 7; Part-Time Volunteers 150; Interns 5.
Governing Authority: private; nonprofit organization. Tax-exempt: 501(c)(3).
Children's Museum.
Collections: hands-on exhibits.
Publications: newsletter, Mobius Matters.
Hours & Admission Prices: Mon.-Sat. 10-5, Sun. 11-5. Adults $5.75, seniors & military $4.75; members & children under 1 no charge. Closed New Year's Day; Easter; Thanksgiving; Christmas. ♿
Attendance: 60,000 (estimated)
Membership: Supporting $12; Grandparent $60; Family $65; Premier $199; Corporate $1,000.

* **NORTHWEST MUSEUM OF ARTS & CULTURE (EASTERN WASHINGTON STATE HISTORICAL SOCIETY), (M),** W. 2316 First Ave., Spokane, WA 99201-5906. Tel.: 509-456-3931. Fax: 509-363-5303.
E-mail: ronr@northwestmuseum.org
Web Site: www.northwestmuseum.org

Formerly: Eastern Washington State Historical Society, Cheney Cowles Museum
Founded: 1916.
Congressional District: 5
Key Personnel: Bd. Pres., David Brukardt; Exec. Dir., Ron Rector; Dir. Center for Plateau Cultural Studies, Michael Holloman; Cur. History, Marsha Rooney; C.F.O., John Drexel; Volunteer Coord., David Brum; Cur. Education, Kris Major; Membership Coord. & Facility Rentals, Gina Harris; Cur. Art, Ben Mitchell; Museum Operations Mgr., Laura Thayer; Registrar, Val Wahl; Museum Support Operations, Lori Bertis.
Personnel Profile: Full-Time Paid 35; Part-Time Paid 19; Part-Time Volunteers 300.
Governing Authority: state society. Parent Institution: Washington State. Subsidiary Institution: Art @ Work Gallery. Tax-exempt: 501(c)(3).
General Museum.
Collections: American Indian cultural materials representing all Tribes of North America; regional history of Spokane, WA & the Inland NW region of WA, ID & MT; contemporary & historical art with concentration on the Inland N.W.; photographs. Historic House. Historic Building: 1898 Campbell house.
Major Exhibits: Living Legacy: The American Indian Collection, 11/09-7/10; Spokane Timeline: Personal Voices, 11/09-12/10; Plateau Indian Celebrations, 11/09-2/10; Art & People: The Spokane Art Center and the Great Depression, 11/09-4/10; Jumpin' with the Big Band, 12/09-4/10; The Arts & Crafts Movement in the Pacific Northwest (T), 3/10-6/10; Atzlan alla (Beyond Borders): The Art of Ruben Trejo, 5/10-9/10; Harold Balazs, 7/10-10/10; Women's Votes, Women's Voices (T), 10/10-6/11.
Research Fields: regional history; ethnology & art.
Facilities: 12,000-vol. reference library of inland Northwest history & the American Indian; manuscripts, archives, 200,000 historical photographs, oral history materials restricted to library use; 180-seat auditorium; 5 exhibition galleries; audio-visual center. Books & other museum-related items for sale.
Activities: cultural guided tours; changing art, history & American Indian exhibitions; docent program; films; loan & temporary exhibitions; lectures; films; concerts; organized educational programs for elementary through graduate college levels; traveling art & history exhibits; internships by arrangement with colleges in area; rental gallery. Annual Events: ArtFest; Works From The Heart; American Indian Friendship Dance; Antique Appraisal Days; Mother's Day Historic Neighborhood Tour; Campbell House Holidays; Family MACFests October to March.
Publications: Campbell House: Age of Elegance; American Firearms; Changing Frontier; Cornhusk Bags of the Plateau Indians; Viewing the Past, an Interpretive Guide; Spokane's Historic Architecture; Guide to the Cutter Collection; A Guide to the Manuscript Collections in the Eastern Washington State Historical Society; Frank Palmer, Scenic Photographer; Lewis & Clark High School: The Hart Years; exhibition catalogues; Enchanted Visions: The Taos Society of Artists & Ancient Cultures.
Hours & Admission Prices: Wed.-Sat. 10-6. Adults $7, students & seniors $5; discount to National Trust for Historic Preservation members; reciprocal with NARM & Time Travelers; first Fri. of month 5-8pm by donation; members & children 5 & under no charge. Closed major holidays. ♿
Attendance: 100,000 (estimated)
Membership: Student & Senior $25; Individual $35; Dual Senior & Student $40; Dual $50; Family, Household & Grand Family $75; MAC Smithsonian Affiliate $150; Patron $500; Sustainer $1,000.

SPOKANE ARTS COMMISSION-CHASE GALLERY, Spokane City Hall, 808 W. Spokane Falls Blvd., Spokane, WA 99201-3301. Tel.: 509-625-6050.
E-mail: arts@spokanecity.org
Web Site: www.spokanearts.org/chase.aspx
Founded: 1984.
Congressional District: 3
Key Personnel: Dir., Karen Mobley.
Personnel Profile: Full-Time Paid 1; Interns 2.
Governing Authority: Parent Institution: City of Spokane.
Art Gallery.
Collections: works by local & regional artists.
Activities: evening artists receptions.
Hours & Admission Prices: Mon.-Fri. 8-5. No charge. ♿

SPOKANE FALLS COMMUNITY COLLEGE FINE ART GALLERY, Fine Arts Bldg., Bldg. 6, 3410 W. Fort George Wright Dr., Spokane, WA 99224-5288. Tel.: 509-533-3710. Fax: 509-533-3484.
E-mail: tomo@spokanefalls.edu
College Art Gallery.
Collections: works by regional, national & international artists.
Activities: workshop. Museum Sponsors: Visiting Artist Lecture Series.
Hours & Admission Prices: Sept.-May Mon.-Fri. 8-4, Sat. 11-2. No charge. Closed college holidays & breaks.

Stanwood

STANWOOD AREA HISTORY MUSEUM & D. O. PEARSON HOUSE MUSEUM, 27108 102nd Ave., N.W., Stanwood, WA 98292. Mailing Address: P.O. Box 69, Stanwood, WA 98292-0069. Tel.: 360-629-6110.
Web Site: www.sahs-fncc.org
History Museum.
Collections: local history & culture; period furnishings; personal artifacts; photographs. Historic Buildings: Pearson House c.1890; Tolin House 1880s.
Major Exhibits: Berries Farms & Dairies, 11/09-9/12.
Hours & Admission Prices: Wed., Fri. & Sun. 1-4. No charge; donations accepted. ♿

Steilacoom

STEILACOOM HISTORICAL MUSEUM ASSOCIATION, Rainier & Main, Steilacoom, WA 98388. Mailing Address: P.O. Box 88016, Steilacoom, WA 98388-0016. Tel.: 253-584-4133.
E-mail: steilacoomhistorical@gmail.com
Web Site: www.steilacoomhistorical.org
Founded: 1970.
Congressional District: 6
Key Personnel: Pres. (V), Randi Slatten; Past Pres. (V), Joan Shalikashvili; Cur., Joan Curtis; Museum Shop Mgr., Marianne Bull.
Personnel Profile: Part-Time Volunteers 1.
Governing Authority: society. Branch Museums: Nathaniel Orr Home & Pioneer Orchard, Steilacoom, WA; Bair Drug & Hardware Store, 1617 Lafayette St., Steilacoom, WA. Tax-exempt: 501(c)(3).
Local History.
Collections: Steilacoom history & early pioneer memorabilia.
Research Fields: local history.
Facilities: 500-vol. library of books from first chartered library in the state; research library for local & regional history; restaurant; living museum. Notepaper, books, calendars & brochures of local interest for sale.
Activities: guided tours; programs of local interest; fund raising activities; school tours; the preservation of the Steilacoom Historical District.
Publications: quarterly magazine, Steilacoom Historical Museum Quarterly; book, Town on the Sound: Stories of Steilacoom.
Hours & Admission Prices: Spring-Fall Sat.-Sun. 12-4. Suggested Donation: $2. ♿
Attendance: 4,800 (estimated)
Membership: Individual Senior Citizen $25; Individual $30; Senior Family $35; Family $50; Friend of History $51 & up; Patron of History $100 & up; Benefactor of History $350 & up.

Stevenson

COLUMBIA GORGE INTERPRETIVE CENTER MUSEUM, 990 S.W. Rock Creek Dr., Stevenson, WA 98648. Mailing Address: P.O. Box 396, Stevenson, WA 98648-0396. Tel.: 509-427-8211. Fax: 509-427-7429.
E-mail: info@columbiagorge.org
Web Site: www.columbiagorge.org
Founded: 1959.
Congressional District: 17
Key Personnel: Dir., Sharon Tiffany; Chm. & Pres. (V), Ken Cole; Museum Shop Mgr., Tina Bartley.
Personnel Profile: Full-Time Paid 4; Full-Time Volunteers 1; Part-Time Paid 5; Part-Time Volunteers 25.
Governing Authority: society. Parent Institution: Skamania County Historical Society. Tax-exempt.
Local History Museum.
Collections: Indian artifacts; pioneer artifacts; Rosary Collection; Corliss steam engine; logging artifacts; 1917 Curtiss JN-4 biplane.
Research Fields: local history via oral interviews.
Facilities: 11,000 sq. ft. exhibit space.
Activities: lectures; guided tours with advanced notice.
Publications: newsletter, Explorations.
Hours & Admission Prices: Daily 10-5. Adults $7, students & senior citizens $6, children 6-12 $5; discounts to AAM, ICOM, AAA members, media & tourism industry members; county residents on 1st Sat. of month, members, children 5 & under, and during the anniversary celebration no charge. Closed New Year's Day; Thanksgiving; Christmas. ♿
Attendance: 19,542 (accurate)
Membership: Student & Senior 60 & over $15; Individual $25; Family $35; Sustaining $50; Supporting $100; Sponsor $500; Benefactor $1,000; Explorer $2,000; Guardian $2,500.

Sunnyside

SUNNYSIDE HISTORICAL MUSEUM, 704 S. 4th St., Sunnyside, WA 98944-2162. Mailing Address: Box 782, Sunnyside, WA 98944-0782. Tel.: 509-837-6010 & 2105.
E-mail: ssmuseum@bentonrea.com
Founded: 1972.
Congressional District: 4
Key Personnel: Pres., John Saras; Vice Pres. & Cur., Don Wade.
Personnel Profile: Part-Time Volunteers 10.
Governing Authority: nonprofit organization. Tax-exempt.
Early Pioneer Museum.
Collections: pioneer kitchen; dining room; living room; quilts; costumes; period glassware & toys; paintings; painted mural; carvings; early irrigation; period photographs; mounted animals. Historic Structure: 1859 Snipes cabin.
Activities: guided tours.
Hours & Admission Prices: Thurs.-Sun. 1-4. No charge; donations accepted. ♿
Attendance: 1,000 (estimated)
Membership: Individual $5.

Tacoma

CAMP 6 LOGGING MUSEUM, Point Defiance Park, North End of Pearl St., Tacoma, WA 98407. Mailing Address: P.O. Box 340, Tacoma, WA 98401-0340. Tel.: 253-752-0047.
E-mail: camp6museum@harbornet.com
Web Site: www.camp-6-museum.org/c6.html
Founded: 1964.
Congressional District: 27
Key Personnel: Dir., Don Olson, P.E.; Gen. Mgr., Rick Bacon.
Personnel Profile: Full-Time Volunteers 1; Part-Time Volunteers 23.
Governing Authority: nonprofit. Parent Institution: Tacoma Chapter, National Railway Historical Society Inc. Tax-exempt: 501(c)(3).
Logging & Lumber Museum Complex: buildings, cars & operational logging railroad from logging camps.
Collections: logging related artifacts; Kapowsin bunkhouses; Quinalt camp cars; restored steam locomotive; eight steam-powered logging machines; 1887 Dolbeer donkey; 1929 Ledgerwood tower sledder.
Research Fields: economic & cultural development of Pacific Northwest.
Facilities: Books, post cards, clothes & railroad related items for sale.
Activities: guided tours; films; tourist railroads.
Publications: informational & guidance brochure.
Hours & Admission Prices: Museum: April-May Wed.-Sun. 10-4; Memorial Day-Sept. Wed.-Fri. 10-4, Sat.-Sun. 10-6. No charge. Grounds: daily sunrise-sunset. Loggins Train Ride: April-May Sat.-Sun. 12-4; Memorial Day-Sept. Sat.-Sun. 12-6. Train: adults 13-54 $4, senior citizens 55-99 $3, children 3-12 $2.50; senior citizens over 99 & children under 3 no charge. Santa Train: 1st three weekends in Dec. 10-4. Admission $1. ♿
Attendance: 30,000 (estimated)

CHILDREN'S MUSEUM OF TACOMA, 936 Broadway, Tacoma, WA 98402-4405. Tel.: 253-627-6031. Fax: 253-627-2436.
E-mail: tandrews@childrensmuseumoftacoma.org
Web Site: www.childrensmuseumoftacoma.org
Founded: 1985.
Key Personnel: Exec. Dir., Tanya Andrews; Pres. Bd., Joanne Bamford; Dir. Education, Debbie Kray; Assoc. Dir., Sara Inveen; Mgr. Experience, Deean Marsh; Mgr. Research & Assessment, Kimberly McKenney; Mgr. Devel., Jennifer Schlatter; Museum Coord., Alysia Jines.
Personnel Profile: Full-Time Paid 6; Part-Time Paid 8.
Governing Authority: nonprofit organization.
Children's Museum.
Collections: hands-on exhibits.
Activities: education programs; parties; camps; workshops.
Publications: Play Times; exhibit parent play guides.
Hours & Admission Prices: Mon.-Sat. 10-5, Sun. 12-5. Members only: Mon.-Sat. 9am-10pm. Admission $6; 1st Fri. of month, members & children under one no charge. Closed New Year's Day; Easter; Independence Day; Labor Day; Thanksgiving; Christmas Eve & Day. ♿
Attendance: 42,000 (estimated)
Membership: Military $55; Grandparents & Me $65; Play-Full $75; Little Travelers $100; Gift of Play $250.

FORT NISQUALLY LIVING HISTORY MUSEUM, 5400 N. Pearl St., #11, Tacoma, WA 98407-3224. Tel.: 253-591-5339. Fax: 253-759-6184.
E-mail: fortnisqually@tacomaparks.com
Web Site: www.fortnisqually.org
Formerly: Fort Nisqually Historic Site
Founded: 1937.
Congressional District: 6
Key Personnel: Chm. (V), Glen Sutt; Cur. Education, J. Michael McGuire; Cur., Bill Rhind; Museum Shop Mgr., Jill Stephenson; Education Specialist, Lane Sample; Special Projects, Peggy Barchi.
Personnel Profile: Full-Time Paid 3; Part-Time Paid 10; Part-Time Volunteers 100.
Governing Authority: municipal. Parent Institution: Metropolitan Park District. Subsidiary Institution: Fort Nisqually Foundation. Tax-exempt.
Historic Site & History Museum Complex.
Collections: blueprints; maps; charts; photographs; Hudson's Bay Company trade goods; agricultural & farming implements; reference material; Puget Sound artifacts; 7 building replicas of Old Fort Nisqually. Historic Structures: c.1854 Gentlemen's Dwelling House; c.1850 & 1851granary, storehouse; replica of c.1884 Blacksmith Shop, Trade Store, kitchen; c.1855 laborer's dwelling; two c.1850 defensive bastions.
Research Fields: physical structures; ethnic cultures in fur trade era of Washington.
Facilities: reference books on the northwest fur trade & related maps, charts & documents. Museum-related items & replicas for sale.
Activities: special events; school & public group tours; docent training program.
Publications: quarterly journal, Occurrences; brochure, Self-Guided Tour of Fort Nisqually; informational pamphlet.
Hours & Admission Prices: April-May Wed.-Sun. 11-5; June-Aug. daily 11-5; Sept.-March Wed.-Sun. 11-4. Adults $6, children $3; discounts to AAM & AAA members; members no charge. Closed New Year's Day; Thanksgiving; Christmas. ♿
Attendance: 30,000 (accurate)
Membership: Engage (Individual) $25; Master (Family) $35; Clerk $50; Trader $100; Factor $250; Governor $1,000.

FOSS WATERWAY SEAPORT, 705 Dock St., Tacoma, WA 98402-4625. Tel.: 253-272-2750. Fax: 253-272-3023.
E-mail: info@fosswaterwayseaport.org
Web Site: www.fosswaterwayseaport.org
Formerly: Working Waterfront Maritime Museum
Key Personnel: Exec. Dir., Tom Cashman
Maritime Museum.
Collections: maritime crafts & skills.
Activities: demonstrations; educational programs.
Hours & Admission Prices: Mon.-Fri. 10-5, Sat.-Sun. 12-5. Adults $6, senior citizens 62 & over, students, and military $3; members no charge. Closed New Year's Day; Easter; Independence Day; Memorial Day; Thanksgiving; Christmas.
Membership: Family $50.

HAROLD E. LEMAY MUSEUM, 325 152nd St. E., Tacoma, WA 98445-1214. Mailing Address: P.O. Box 1117, Tacoma, WA 98401-1117. Tel.: 253-779-8490. Fax: 253-779-8499.
Web Site: www.lemaymuseum.org
Transportation Museum.
Collections: automobiles; motorcycles; trucks.
Activities: Museum Sponsors: Annual Car Show in August.
Hours & Admission Prices: Tues.-Sun. 10-5; tours by appointment. Admission to museum is by guided tour only; members no charge. Closed major holidays.

JAMES R. SLATER MUSEUM OF NATURAL HISTORY, University of Puget Sound Cmb-1088, Tacoma, WA 98416-0001. Tel.: 253-879-2798.
E-mail: pwimberger@ups.edu
Web Site: www.ups.edu/slatermuseum.xm1
Formerly: Puget Sound Museum
Founded: 1926.
Congressional District: 6
Key Personnel: Dir., Dr. Peter Wimberger; Mgr. Collections, Dr. Gary Shugart; Dir. Emeritus, Dr. Dennis R. Paulson.
Personnel Profile: Full-Time Paid 1; Part-Time Paid 1.
Governing Authority: University of Puget Sound. Tax-exempt.
Natural History Museum.
Collections: Northwest flora & fauna, including approximately 30,000 mammal skins & skulls; 18,000 bird skins & skeletons; 4,400 bird wings; 4,600 sets of bird eggs; 8,500 reptiles & amphibians; 9,000 plants on herbarium sheets; 2,000 invertebrates; 1,200 bird nests.
Research Fields: mammalogy; ornithology; herpetology; marine invertebrate zoology; botany.
Facilities: 1,600-vol. library of books, monographs & journals, reprints & articles available for use on premises.

Activities: guided tours; acquisition, preparation & maintenance of research collections for visiting scientists & students; undergraduate teaching; exhibit programs.
Publications: Slater Museum of Natural History Occasional Papers.
Hours & Admission Prices: Mon.-Fri. 9-5; groups by appointment. No charge. Closed holidays. ♿

JOB CARR CABIN MUSEUM, 2350 N. 30th St., Tacoma, WA 98403-3323. Mailing Address: P.O. Box 7609, Tacoma, WA 98417-0609. Tel.: 253-627-5405.
E-mail: mdeck@jobcarrmuseum.org
Web Site: www.jobcarrmuseum.org
Founded: 2000.
Key Personnel: Dir., Margie Deck
History Museum: housed in a replica of Job Carr's home built in 1865. He was Tacoma's first settler, Postmaster and Mayor.
Collections: period furnishings.
Research Fields: Tacoma history; Oregon Trail.
Activities: educational programs; special events; Traveling Trunk education program.
Publications: Eureka Times.
Hours & Admission Prices: Jan. by appointment; Feb.-May Wed.-Sat. 1-4; Summer: Wed.-Sat. 12-4.
Membership: Student $12; Senior $15; Individual $20; Family & Nonprofit $35; Small Business $75; Corporate $125.

KITTREDGE GALLERY, UNIVERSITY OF PUGET SOUND ART DEPT., 1500 N. Warner St., CMB 1072, Tacoma, WA 98416-0005. Tel.: 253-879-3701. Fax: 253-879-3500.
Web Site: www.pugetsound.edu/kittredge
Founded: 1950.
Congressional District: 6
Personnel Profile: Part-Time Paid 1.
Governing Authority: university; not-for-profit. Parent Institution: University of Puget Sound. Tax-exempt.
Art Gallery.
Collections: Abby Williams Hill paintings & drawings; contemporary American ceramics; contemporary northwest art.
Facilities: 2,100 sq. ft. exhibit space.
Activities: lectures; temporary exhibitions.
Hours & Admission Prices: Sept. to mid-May Mon.-Fri. 10-5, Sat. 12-5. No charge. Closed holidays; semester breaks. ♿
Attendance: 1,500 (estimated)

MCCHORD AIR MUSEUM, Airforce Base, 100 Main St., Tacoma, WA 98438-1114. Mailing Address: McChord Air Museum Foundation, P.O. Box 4205, Tacoma, WA 98438-0205. Tel.: 253-982-2419. Fax: 253-982-9560.
E-mail: raymond.jordan@mcchord.af.mil
Web Site: www.mcchordmuseum.org
Key Personnel: Vice Pres., Ernie White, II; Pres. (V), Herb Mellor; Museum Shop Mgr., Ed Baker.
Personnel Profile: Full-Time Volunteers 1; Part-Time Volunteers 60.
Governing Authority: private; nonprofit organization. Parent Institution: McChord Airforce Base. Tax-exempt.
Military Museum.
Collections: history of the Air Force units associated with McChord.
Publications: quarterly, The Rip Chord.
Hours & Admission Prices: Wed.-Sat. 12-4; military ID required for entry. No charge.
Attendance: 5,000 (accurate)
Membership: Student & Airman $5; Regular $20; Silver Wing Contributor $50-$499; Silver Wing Patron $500-$999; Silver Wing Benefactor $1,000 & up.

MUSEUM OF GLASS, (M), 1801 Dock St., Tacoma, WA 98402-3217. Tel.: 253-284-4750 & 4719; 866-4MUSEUM. Fax: 253-396-1769.
E-mail: info@museumofglass.org
Web Site: www.museumofglass.org
Founded: 1995.
Congressional District: 9
Key Personnel: C.E.O., Timothy Close; Chm. (V), Randall P. Lert; Museum Shop Mgr., Tom Findlay.
Personnel Profile: Full-Time Paid 33; Part-Time Paid 25; Part-Time Volunteers 35; Interns 6.
Governing Authority: private; nonprofit organization. Tax-exempt: 501(c)(3).
Art Museum.
Collections: contemporary works of art in glass.
Major Exhibits: Preston Singletary: Echoes, Fire and Shadows (T), 11/09-9/10; Kids Design Glass (T), 11/09-2/11.
Facilities: cafe; 200-theater; 11,000 sq. ft. exhibit space. Museum-related items for sale.
Activities: docent led tours; dramatic performances; conversations with artists.
Publications: quarterly newsletter, Fuse.
Hours & Admission Prices: Adults $12; discounts to AAM members; members no charge. ♿
Attendance: 178,000 (accurate)
Membership: Student $30; Senior $35; Educator $40; Individual $50; Dual & Family $75; Supporting $150; Contributing $250; Patron $500; Investor $1,000.

PACIFIC LUTHERAN UNIVERSITY GALLERY, Dept. of Art, Ingram Hall, Tacoma, WA 98447-0001. Tel.: 253-535-7150. Fax: 253-536-5063.
E-mail: soac@plu.edu
Web Site: www.plu.edu/~soac/
Key Personnel: Prof. Heather Mathews.
Governing Authority: Parent Institution: Pacific Lutheran University.
University Art Gallery.
Collections: works by contemporary artists.
Hours & Admission Prices: Mon.-Fri. 9-4. No charge.

POINT DEFIANCE ZOO & AQUARIUM, 5400 N. Pearl St., Tacoma, WA 98407-3224. Tel.: 253-591-5337 & 404-3631. Fax: 253-591-5448.
E-mail: pdzacomments@tacomaparks.com
Web Site: www.pdza.org
Founded: 1905.
Congressional District: 6
Key Personnel: Dir., Gary Geddes; Pres. (V) Zoo Society, Clark D'Elia; Exec. Dir. Zoo Society, Kathleen Olson; Deputy Dir., John Houck; Dir. Devel., Brent Mason; Mktg. Mgr., Jean Jackman; Museum Shop Mgr., Donna Powell; Gen. Cur., Dr. Karen Goodrowe Beck; Veterinarian, Dr. Holly Reed; Cur. Education, Carla Collerre.
Personnel Profile: Full-Time Paid 68; Part-Time Paid 60; Part-Time Volunteers 160; Interns 5.
Governing Authority: municipal. Parent Institution: Metro Parks Tacoma.
Zoo & Aquarium.
Collections: Pacific Rim zoo & aquarium.
Publications: member newsletter, Zoopoints.
Hours & Admission Prices: Jan.-April 25 & Sept. 29-Dec. daily 9:30-4; April 26-May 23 & Sept. 2-Sept. 28 daily 9:30-5; May 24-Sept. 1 daily 9:30-6. Adults $11, senior citizens $10, students 5-12 $9, children 3-4 $5; discounts to groups, AAA members & Pierce county residents; children under 3 no charge. Closed Thanksgiving; Christmas. ♿
Attendance: 500,000 (accurate)
Membership: One Plus One $35; Family & Grandparent $49; Sponsor $125; Patron $175; Benefactor $295.

SHANAMAN SPORTS MUSEUM, 2727 E. "D" St. (Tacoma Dome), Tacoma, WA 98421-1216. Mailing Address: 9908-63rd Ave. Ct. E., Puyallup, WA 98373-1170. Tel.: 253-627-5857.
Founded: 1994.
Key Personnel: Pres., Marc Blau
Sports Museum.
Collections: sports history; personal artifacts of recreational, amateur, & professional athletes, coaches & teams; photographs; sports officials, broadcasters & sportswriters.
Hours & Admission Prices: During sporting events & trade shows; other times by appointment. No charge when attending sporting event.

* **TACOMA ART MUSEUM,** 1701 Pacific Ave., Tacoma, WA 98402-3214. Tel.: 253-272-4258, ext. 3035. Fax: 253-627-1898.
E-mail: info@tacomaartmuseum.org
Web Site: www.tacomaartmuseum.org
Founded: 1935.
Congressional District: 6
Key Personnel: Pres. (V), Janine Terrano; Dir., Stephanie A. Stebich; Deputy Dir., Cameron Fellows; Dir. Devel., Kara Hefley; Dir. Education & Audience Devel., Paula McArdle; Dir. Curatorial Admin., Rock Hushka; Museum Shop Mgr., Kristie Worthey.
Personnel Profile: Full-Time Paid 30; Part-Time Paid 22; Part-Time Volunteers 129; Interns 4.
Governing Authority: nonprofit organization. Tax-exempt: 501(c)(3) & 170(b)(1)(A).
Art Museum.
Collections: emphasis on northwest art of the modern period (1800-present): American Eight, Pacific Northwest; Dale Chihuly Retrospective Installation; 19th-century European paintings; Japanese Ukiyo-e prints.
Major Exhibits: Joe Fedderson: Vital Signs (T), 11/09-1/10; A Concise History

of Northwest Art, 11/09-6/10; The Movement of Impressionism, 11/09-10/10; Speaking Parts, 11/09-11/10.
Research Fields: exhibitions; Northwest art.
Facilities: 6,000-vol. library of art volumes available for use on premises; reading room; 25,000 sq. ft. exhibit space; 200-seat event space.
Activities: guided tours; lectures; films; gallery talks; concerts; ongoing art making opportunities that complement formally organized education programs for children, adults, undergraduate & graduate college students; docent program; inter-museum loan, permanent & temporary exhibitions.
Publications: quarterly bulletins; exhibition catalogs; gallery guides.
Hours & Admission Prices: Summer: Tues.-Sat. 10-5, Sun. 12-5; Winter: Wed.-Sun. 10-5. Adults $9, student, military and seniors 65 & over $8; discounts to families, AAM & staff of other museums; third Thurs. of the month, members, and children 5 & under no charge. Closed New Year's Day; Martin Luther King Jr. Day; Thanksgiving; Christmas. ♿
Attendance: 76,000 (accurate)
Membership: Educator, Senior, Student & Military $30; Individual $50; Family & Friends $75; Gallery $125; Studio $200; Collector $500; Patron's Circle $1,000 & up.

TACOMA HISTORICAL SOCIETY, 747 Broadway, Tacoma, WA 98402-3709. Mailing Address: P.O. Box 1865, Tacoma, WA 98401-1865. Tel.: 253-472-3738.
Founded: 1990.
Congressional District: 6
Key Personnel: Dir., Mary Bowlby.
Personnel Profile: Part-Time Paid 1; Part-Time Volunteers 130.
Governing Authority: Tax-exempt: 501(c)(3).
Historical Society Museum.
Collections: local history & culture; photographs; personal artifacts; period furnishings.
Facilities: Museum-related items for sale.
Activities: special events; historic homes tour; lecture series.
Publications: newsletter; Herbert Hunt, History of Tacoma, 2003.
Hours & Admission Prices: Wed.-Sat. 12-5. Admission by donation; discounts to WMA members.
Attendance: 1,500
Membership: Individual $25; Family $35; Corporate $150 & up.

TACOMA PUBLIC LIBRARY/THOMAS HANDFORTH GALLERY, 1102 Tacoma Ave., S., Tacoma, WA 98402-2098. Tel.: 253-591-5666. Fax: 253-591-5470.
E-mail: ddomkoski@tpl.lib.wa.us
Web Site: www.tpl.lib.wa.us
Founded: 1886.
Congressional District: 6
Key Personnel: Acting Dir. Library, Susan Odencrantz; Asst. Dir. Management Svcs., Darrell Matz; Mgr. Special Collections, Gary Reese; Community Rels. Officer, David Domkoski.
Governing Authority: municipal government. Tax-exempt: 170(b)(1)(A).
Public Library & Art Gallery: housed in 1903 Carnegie Building.
Collections: Thomas Handforth prints & sketches; photographic prints & negatives; World War I posters; Asahel Curtis, Edward S. Curtis, Turner Richards & Verna Haffer photo collections; rare book room; 1.2 million photographs; 36,000-vol. Pacific Northwest Americana; 30,000 maps; 15,000-vol. genealogy & local history books.
Facilities: 600,000-vol. library.
Activities: guided tours; lectures; films; study clubs; organized education programs for children & adults; participatory & temporary exhibitions; rotating exhibits of Pacific N.W. artists & craftspeople.
Publications: quarterly newsletters, Handforth Gallery Preview.
Hours & Admission Prices: Mon.-Thurs. 9-9, Fri.-Sat. 9-6. No charge. ♿
Attendance: 1,600,000

THE KARPELES MANUSCRIPT MUSEUM, 407 S. "G" St., Tacoma, WA 98405-4711. Tel.: 253-383-2575.
E-mail: kmuseumtaq@aol.com
Key Personnel: Dir., Thomas M. Jutilla
History Museum.
Collections: original papers of historic importance.
Hours & Admission Prices: Tues.-Sun. 10-4.

W.W. SEYMOUR BOTANICAL CONSERVATORY, 316 S. G St., Tacoma, WA 98405-4733. Tel.: 253-591-5330. Fax: 253-627-2192.
E-mail: wwseymour@tacomaparks.com
Web Site: www.metroparkstacoma.org
Founded: 1908.
Congressional District: 6
Key Personnel: C.E.O., Jack Wilson; Museum Shop Mgr., Horticulture & Conservatory Supvr., Marina Becker; Museum Shop Mgr., Theresa Atkinson-Betz; Horticulture Supvr., Mary Anderson.
Personnel Profile: Full-Time Paid 1; Part-Time Paid 1; Part-Time Volunteers 10.
Governing Authority: municipal. Parent Institution: Metropolitan Park District of Tacoma.
Botanical Garden: museum housed in Victorian styled conservatory with twelve-sided central dome containing two side wings & an entry wing.
Collections: over 200 species of exotic tropical plants including ornamental figs, tropical fruit trees, Bird of Paradise, bromeliads & orchids. Flower displays change monthly: spring bulbs, azaleas, Easter lilies, summer annuals, flowering houseplants, chrysanthemums, a Halloween pumpkin patch & Christmas poinsettias.
Facilities: botanical garden.
Activities: guided tours; organized education programs.
Publications: brochure, Seymour Botanical Conservatory; quarterly newsletter, Botanical Prints.
Hours & Admission Prices: Tues.-Sun. 10-4:30. No charge; donations accepted. Closed New Year's; Thanksgiving; Christmas. ♿
Attendance: 78,000
Membership: Senior Citizen $15; Member $25; Friend $50; Benefactor $100

WASHINGTON STATE HISTORICAL SOCIETY, 1911 Pacific Ave., Tacoma, WA 98402-3109. Tel.: 888-238-4373; 253-272-3500. Fax: 253-272-9518.
E-mail: dnicandri@wshs.wa.gov
Web Site: www.washingtonhistory.org
Founded: 1891.
Congressional District: 6
Key Personnel: Dir., David L. Nicandri; Pres., Daniel K Grimm; Dir. Museum Svcs., Patricia Tobiason; Dir. Support Svcs., Mark Sylvester; Dir. Outreach Svcs., Garry Schalliol; Head Collections, Lynette Miller; Head Special Collections, Edward V. Nolan; Asst. Librarian Manuscripts, Joy Werlink; Publications, Christina DuBois; C.F.O., Christopher Lee; Head Exhibits, Redmond J. Barnett; Mktg. & Devel. Mgr., Brenda Hanan; Membership Svcs., Tasha Holland; Head State Capital Museum, Susan Rohrer; Coord. Public Rels., Kimberly Adams; Head Education, Stephanie Lile; Natl. History Day Asst., Mark Vessey; Exhibits Designer, SueSan Chan; Volunteer Coord., Magda Nieves; Cur., Maria Pascualy; Coord. School Programs, Gwen Perkins; Supvr. Admissions, Amy Coggins; Info Tech Mgr., Tamara Georgick; Asst. Dir. Human Resources & Admin., Misty Reese; Registrar & Digital Assets Mgr., Fred Poyner, IV
Personnel Profile: Full-Time Paid 33; Part-Time Paid 34; Part-Time Volunteers 136; Interns 12.
Governing Authority: state. Subsidiary Institutions: State Capital Museum & Center for Columbia River History. Tax-exempt: 509(a) & 501(c)(3).
History Museum.
Collections: Pacific Northwest history, paintings, furnishings, textiles & ethnology; rare books; 450,000 photographs, 300 manuscripts; maps, pamphlets & ephemera; over 1,000 microfilm.
Major Exhibits: Icons of Washington, 11/11/09-7/3/10; Giants in the Mountains: The Search for Sasquatch, 1/23/10-6/27/10; Arts & Crafts Movemnet in the Pacific Northwest (T), 8/7/10-11/28/10.
Research Fields: Washington state & Pacific Northwest history.
Facilities: 12,000-vol. library of Pacific Northwest reference books; 106,000 sq. ft. Washington State history museum; outdoor amphitheatre; research center; reading room; cafe. Museum-related items for sale.
Activities: lectures; films & special events promoting exhibits; inter-museum loan, permanent & temporary exhibitions; formal education programs for elementary & high school students; internships for college students; group tours.
Publications: quarterly, Columbia, The Magazine of Northwest History.
Hours & Admission Prices: Call for hours. Adults $8; discounts to AAM & ICOM members; members & museum professionals with business card no charge. Closed major holidays. ♿
Attendance: 101,053 (accurate)
Membership: Subscription & Student $35; Senior $40; Individual & Dual Senior $45; Dual $50; Family $65; Sustaining $125; Business $300; Patron $500; Benefactor $1,000.

* **WASHINGTON STATE HISTORY MUSEUM, (M),** 1911 Pacific Ave., Tacoma, WA 98402. Tel.: 253-272-3500. Fax: 253-272-9518.
Founded: 1891.
Key Personnel: Dir., David L. Nicandri; Pres. (V), Daniel K. Grimm.
Personnel Profile: Full-Time Paid 28; Part-Time Paid 34; Part-Time Volunteers 140.
Governing Authority: Parent Institution: WA State Historical Society. Tax-exempt.
History Museum.

Collections: local & state history; culture; photographs; personal artifacts; hands-on exhibits.
Major Exhibits: Icons of Washington, 11/09-6/10.
Facilities: cafe.
Activities: storytelling; rental facilities; special events; educational programs; hands-on exhibits. Museum Sponsors: Native Arts Festival.
Publications: magazine, Columbia.
Hours & Admission Prices: Tues.-Fri. 10-4, Sat.-Sun. 10-6. Adults $8, seniors 60 & over $7, students 6-17 $6; discounts to groups; members and children 5 & under no charge. Closed Memorial Day; Independence Day; Labor Day; Thanksgiving; Christmas. ♿
Attendance: 80,000 (accurate)
Membership: Subscription $35; Individual $45; Dual $50; Family $65; Sustaining $125.

Tenino

TENINO DEPOT MUSEUM, 399 W. Park, Tenino, WA 98589. Mailing Address: P.O. Box 339, Tenino, WA 98589-0339. Tel.: 360-264-4321.
Founded: 1974.
Congressional District: 3
Personnel Profile: Part-Time Volunteers 10.
Governing Authority: nonprofit organization. Parent Institution: South Thurston County Historical Society. Tax-exempt: 501(c)(3).
Local History Museum.
Collections: pioneer days-present; doctor's office; school room; artifacts; Tenino wooden money; wooden money printing press; sandstone display & tools; railroad room.
Activities: guided tours; temporary exhibitions. Museum Sponsors: Wooden Money Printed in July; Annual Dinner in October; Biannual Appraisal Fair.
Publications: newsletter.
Hours & Admission Prices: mid-April to mid-Oct. Sat.-Sun. 12-4. No charge; donations accepted. ♿
Attendance: 1,800 (estimated)
Membership: Individual $10; Family $25; Life $100.

Toppenish

NORTHERN PACIFIC RAILWAY MUSEUM, 10 Asotin Ave., Toppenish, WA 98948-1300. Mailing Address: P.O. Box 889, Toppenish, WA 98948-0889. Tel.: 509-930-7210 (Director).
E-mail: lamarenter@aol.com
Web Site: www.nprymuseum.org
Formerly: Yakima Valley Rail & Steam Museum
Founded: 1989.
Congressional District: 4
Key Personnel: Museum Dir., Cur. & Archivist, Larry Rice; Pres., Dennis Lee; Financial Dir. & Treas., Ken Severson; Gift Shop Mgr., Roger O'Dell; Gift Shop Mgr., Mary O'Dell.
Personnel Profile: Part-Time Volunteers 8.
Governing Authority: private; nonprofit organization. A division of The Yakima Valley Rail & Steam Museum Association. Tax-exempt: 501(c)(3).
Railway Museum.
Collections: railroad artifacts; 2 steam locomotives. Historic Building: c.1911 depot.
Facilities: 30-vol. library of railroad maintenance reference books; 51,560 sq. ft. exhibit space. Museum-related items for sale.
Activities: guided tours; caboose rides; engineer classes for diesel & steam. Annual Events: Railroad Days in June; Railroad and Western Art Show in August; Hobo Days in September.
Publications: newsletter every 4 months, The Orderboard.
Hours & Admission Prices: May-Oct. Tues.-Fri. 10-4, Sun. 11-4. Adults $5, children 12 & under $3; discount to groups & Pacific Historical Association members; members no charge. ♿
Attendance: 4,700 (accurate)
Membership: Student & Senior $30; Annual Dues $40; Family (Husband & Wife) $50; Life $500.

TOPPENISH MUSEUM, One S. Elm, Toppenish, WA 98948-1574. Tel.: 509-865-4510. Fax: 509-865-3864.
Founded: 1975.
Congressional District: 4
Key Personnel: Chm. (V), Marian Ross; Museum Shop Mgr., Doris Cook.
Personnel Profile: Full-Time Volunteers 1; Part-Time Paid 2; Part-Time Volunteers 12.
Governing Authority: municipal. Dept. of the City of Toppenish, WA. Tax-exempt.
History Museum: housed in 1923 first Agency Building for the Yakima Indian Nation.
Collections: period artifacts; Indian baskets; regional contemporary arts & crafts.
Research Fields: local history.
Facilities: 18,500-vol. Toppenish Public Library located on lower floor.
Activities: gallery talks; permanent & traveling exhibitions.
Publications: quarterly newsletter; reprints of local history.
Hours & Admission Prices: Mon.-Thurs. 1-4; other times by appointment. Adults $1.50, children $.50; each local household no charge.

YAKAMA NATION MUSEUM, 100 Spiel-yi Loop, Toppenish, WA 98948. Mailing Address: P.O. Box 151, Toppenish, WA 98948-0151. Tel.: 509-865-2800. Fax: 509-865-5749.
E-mail: pamela@yakama.com
Web Site: www.yakamamuseum.com
Founded: 1980.
Congressional District: 15
Key Personnel: Tribal Chm., Lavina Washines; Tribal Admin., Carroll Palmer; Mgr., Pamela K. Fabela; Cur. & Registrar, Marilyn Malatare; Photograph Collection, Liz Antelope; Registrar & Webmaster, Heather Hull.
Personnel Profile: Full-Time Paid 3.
Governing Authority: tribe; nonprofit organization. Tax-exempt: 501(c)(3).
Tribal Museum: located on the Yakima Indian Reservation.
Collections: Northwest Native American artifacts; items collected by Nipo Strongheart (1891-1966) during his career as a Hollywood movie consultant; Northwestern Plateau artifacts including buckskin & beaded shirts, pipes, spoons, baskets, fishing nets, mats, bags.
Research Fields: oral interviews.
Facilities: library; restaurant; theater. Handcrafted items for sale.
Activities: Klickitat basketry; Yakama beadwork, woodcarving & buckskin work by artists & craftspeople; lectures. Annual events: Treaty Day Celebration commemorating the June 9 signing of the Yakama Nation & United States treaty; Yakama Nation Film Festival; Tiin Ma Gathering & Tribal Jam.
Publications: booklets, Mother Nature's Lesson; Time Ball; brochure, Art of the Yakama Nation; Promotion of Yakama art & craft.
Hours & Admission Prices: Mon.-Fri. 8-5, Sat.-Sun. 9-5. Adults $5, college students, senior citizens, active military, & children 11-18 $3, children 10 & under $1. Guided Tours: $25. ♿
Attendance: 70,000 (estimated)

Union Gap

CENTRAL WASHINGTON AGRICULTURAL MUSEUM, 4508 Main St., Union Gap, WA 98903-2138. Tel.: 509-457-8735.
Founded: 1979.
Congressional District: 4
Key Personnel: Pres. (V), Wally Moen; Vice Pres., Nick Schultz; Treas., Dick Drew; Sec., Kathy Schultz; Sec., Marty Humphrey.
Personnel Profile: Full-Time Volunteers 1; Part-Time Volunteers 42.
Governing Authority: city; board of directors; nonprofit. Tax-exempt.
Agricultural Museum.
Collections: plows; discs; cultivators; sprayers; hay equipment; dusters; steam engines; choppers; beet harvest equipment; planters; various period farm equipment; tractors; cold storage compressor; portable hop-picking machinery; pea picker; horse drawn machinery; hand tools; blacksmith shop; saw mill; apple picking line; log cabin; working windmill; railroad box car; trappers cabin.
Activities: Annual Events: Truck Show in May; Tractor Pull in June; Farm Expo in August; Central WA Fair.
Publications: quarterly newsletter.
Hours & Admission Prices: April-Oct. Tues. 9-3, Wed.-Sat. 9-5, Sun. 1-4; Nov.-March Tues. 9-3, Thurs.-Sun. 1-4. No charge; donations accepted. Closed New Year's Day; Thanksgiving; Christmas. ♿
Attendance: 8,500 (estimated)
Membership: Individual $15; Family $25; Sponsor $30-$40; Supporting $50-$99; Patron $100-$499; Benefactor $500 & up.

Vancouver

THE ARCHER GALLERY, Clark College, Penguin Student Union Building, 1933 Fort Vancouver Way, Vancouver, WA 98663-3501. Tel.: 360-992-2246. Fax: 360-992-2888.
E-mail: mhirsch@clark.edu
Web Site: www.clark.edu
Founded: 1978.
Key Personnel: Dir., Marjorie Hirsch.
Personnel Profile: Part-Time Paid 1.
Governing Authority: college; Parent Institution: Clark College. Tax-exempt.
Art Gallery.
Collections: paintings; photographs; sculpture.
Activities: lectures; films.
Hours & Admission Prices: Tues.-Thurs. 10-7, Fri. 10-4, Sat. 1-5. No charge; donations accepted. ♿

Attendance: 5,000 (estimated)

CLARK COUNTY HISTORICAL SOCIETY & MUSEUM, (M), 1511 Main St., Vancouver, WA 98660-2945. Mailing Address: P.O. Box 61916, Vancouver, WA 98666. Tel.: 360-993-5679. Fax: 360-993-5683.
E-mail: cchm@pacifier.com
Web Site: www.cchmuseum.org
Founded: 1917.
Congressional District: 3
Key Personnel: Exec. Dir., Susan M.G. Tissot; Bd. Chm. & Pres., Joan Dengerink.
Personnel Profile: Full-Time Paid 1; Full-Time Volunteers 5; Part-Time Paid 3; Part-Time Volunteers 10.
Governing Authority: nonprofit organization. Parent Institution: Clark County Historical Society of Clark County, WA. Tax-exempt: 501(c)(3).
General Museum.
Collections: Northwest history from pre-historic settlement to present including Native American exhibits; pre-native culture ceramics; railway equipment; Hudson Bay Company & textiles; household items; agriculture; oral history collection; archives; photographs; historical research library; Grant House collection.
Research Fields: Northwest & local history.
Facilities: 3,800-vol. library of letters, diaries, ledgers & books pertaining to local & Pacific Northwest history; reading room; classroom; archives.
Activities: guided tours; lectures; permanent & traveling exhibitions; seasonal walking tours; adult education classes; Mr. Carnegies Grand Tour of Washington. Annual Event: Harvest Fun Day.
Publications: annual book, Clark County History; four times a year newsletter, It's History; Naming Clark County; Darkness Next Door; Woven History; 12 Days in Clark County.
Hours & Admission Prices: Tues.-Sat. 11-4, 1st Thurs. of month call for additional hours. Adults $4, seniors & students $3, children 6-18 $2; discounts to WMA, AAM & ICOM members; members and children 5 & under no charge. Closed major holidays. ♿
Attendance: 15,000 (estimated)
Membership: Basic Membership: Student $25; Individual $40; Family $60; Friend of the Museum $100; Business $250; Historian $500; President's Circle $1,000.

FORT VANCOUVER NATIONAL HISTORIC SITE, 612 E. Reserve St., Vancouver, WA 98661-3897. Tel.: 360-816-6200. Fax: 360-816-6363.
E-mail: FOVA_superintendent@nps.gov
Web Site: www.nps.gov/fova
Founded: 1948.
Congressional District: 3
Key Personnel: Park Supt., Tracy Fortmann; Cur. Park, Tessa Langford; Chief Ranger, Greg Shine; Museum Shop Mgr., Corrie Hausman.
Personnel Profile: Full-Time Volunteers 100.
Governing Authority: federal. Parent Institution: National Park Service. Tax-exempt.
Historic Site: site of Old Fort Vancouver, administrative headquarters & supply depot for the Hudson's Bay Company 1829-1860.
Collections: archaeology; military; fur trade; agriculture; manufacturing; ceramic spodeware.
Research Fields: Hudson's Bay Company in the Pacific Northwest; U.S. Army until 1945 in the Pacific Northwest.
Facilities: 1,400-vol. library on fur trade & early military history in the Pacific Northwest.
Activities: guided tours; lectures; films; formally organized education programs for children; permanent & temporary exhibitions.
Publications: Fort Vancouver Handbook.
Hours & Admission Prices: March-Oct. daily 9-5; Nov.-Feb. daily 9-4. Entrance fee: $3 per person, $5 per family. Closed Thanksgiving; Christmas Eve & Day. ♿
Attendance: 800,000 (estimated)

PEARSON AIR MUSEUM, (M), 1115 E. 5th St., Vancouver, WA 98661-3802. Tel.: 360-694-7026. Fax: 360-694-0824.
E-mail: bill.alley@fortvan.org
Web Site: www.pearsonairmuseum.org
Founded: 1987.
Congressional District: 17
Key Personnel: Dir. & Cur., Bill Alley; Tourism Mgr., Eliza Lane; Museum Store Mgr., Deborah Bessette.
Personnel Profile: Full-Time Paid 3; Part-Time Paid 2; Part-Time Volunteers 35.
Governing Authority: private; nonprofit organization. Parent Institution: Vancouver National Historic Trust. Tax-exempt: 501(c)(3).
Aeronautics Museum: located on the site of 1905 Pearson Field; a pre-WWII army air corps field.
Collections: period furnishings; historic flyable aircraft; photos; relics; art work; models; videos; 3 historic buildings c.1904.
Facilities: 20,000 sq. ft. exhibit space. Aviation-related items for sale.
Activities: Annual Events: annual summer dance; annual open cockpit day; Al Coupe summer camp.
Publications: newsletter, Fort Vancouver Times.
Hours & Admission Prices: Wed.-Sat. 10-5. Family $22, Adults $7, senior citizens & active military $5, students 6-17 $3; pre-schoolers & members no charge. Tour rates available. Closed New Year's Day; Christmas. ♿
Attendance: 60,000 (estimated)
Membership: Junior Flyer $5; Flyer $35; Co-Pilots $55; Squadron Family $75; Crew Chief $100; Barnstormer $250; Flying Ace $500; Aviator $1,000; Wing Commander.

Vantage

GINKGO PETRIFIED FOREST STATE PARK, Interstate 90, Exit 136, Vantage, WA 98950. Mailing Address: P.O. Box 1203, Vantage, WA 98950-1203. Tel.: 509-856-2700. Fax: 509-856-2294.
Web Site: parks.wa.gov
Founded: 1936.
Key Personnel: Dir., Cleve Pinnix; Area Mgr., Jim Mitchell; Chief Interpretive Svcs., Steve Wang.
Personnel Profile: Part-Time Paid 2.
Governing Authority: state: Affiliated with Washington State Parks & Recreation Commission, 7150 Clear Water Lane, Olympia, WA. 98504.
State Park Museum.
Collections: Frank Bobo petrified wood collection; Professor George Beck's collections.
Facilities: 7,470-acre park; interpretive trails and center.
Activities: tours; permanent exhibitions.
Hours & Admission Prices: Summer: daily 6:30am to dusk. Winter: Sat.-Sun. 8am to dusk. Suggested Donation $1.
Attendance: 35,000 (accurate)

Vashon

VASHON MAURY ISLAND HERITAGE ASSOCIATION, 10105 S.W. Bank Rd., Vashon, WA 98070-4645. Mailing Address: P.O. Box 723, Vashon, WA 98070-0723. Tel.: 206-463-7808.
E-mail: admin@vashonheritage.org
Web Site: www.vashonhistory.org
Founded: 1975.
Congressional District: 30
Key Personnel: Pres., Bob Fetterley; Vice Pres., Laurie Tucker; Treas., Steve Church; Sec., Jean Findlay; Corresponding Sec., Barbara Steen; Museum Shop Mgr., Yvonne Kuperberg.
Personnel Profile: Part-Time Volunteers 30.
Governing Authority: nonprofit organization. Tax-exempt: 501(c)(3).
History Museum.
Collections: 1877 pre-settlement artifacts; industry; agriculture.
Research Fields: local history.
Facilities: 40-vol. library pertaining to Vashon & Maury Island history.
Activities: lectures; films; organized education programs for children. Museum Sponsors: slide shows; Vashon Festival.
Publications: quarterly newsletter.
Hours & Admission Prices: Wed.-Sun. 1-4. No charge; donations accepted. ♿
Attendance: 1,833 (accurate)
Membership: Senior Citizen & Student $15; Individual $20; Family $50; Supporting $75; Patron $100; Life $500; Benefactor $1,000 & up.

Walla Walla

FORT WALLA WALLA MUSEUM, (M), 755 Myra Rd., Walla Walla, WA 99362-8035. Tel.: 509-525-7703. Fax: 509-525-7798.
E-mail: info@fortwallawallamuseum.org
Web Site: fortwallawallamuseum.org
Founded: 1968.
Congressional District: 5
Key Personnel: Exec. Dir., James Payne; Pres. (V), Barbara Stubblefield; Bookkeeper, Carolyn Burdine; Collection Mgr., Laura Schulz; Operations Mgr., Don Locati; Communications Mgr., Paul Franzmann; Tour Coord., Bill Lake; Mgr. Bldgs. & Grounds, James Klees.
Personnel Profile: Full-Time Paid 5; Part-Time Paid 4; Part-Time Volunteers 300; Interns 2.
Governing Authority: nonprofit organization. Parent Institution: Fort Walla Walla Museum, Walla Walla Valley Historical Society. Tax-exempt: 501(c)(3).
Pioneer Settlement & Agricultural Museum: housed on the 1858 military reservation of Old Ft. Walla Walla. General history.

Collections: wooden combine hitched to 33 fiberglass mules surrounded by wheat harvest mural; 34,000 historical artifacts. Historic Buildings: 1859 Ransom Clark cabin; 1868 Union schoolhouse; c.1888 Babcock railway depot; block house; barber shop; 1903 Prescott Jail; horse era agriculture; pioneer & military artifacts; 40,000 historical artifacts.
Facilities: 22 buildings on 15 acres.
Activities: guided tours; lectures; permanent & rotating exhibitions.
Publications: bimonthly newsletter, The Dispatch.
Hours & Admission Prices: April-Oct. daily 10-5; tours by appointment. Adults $7, senior citizens & students $6, children 6-12 $3; discounts to AAA members & Time Travelers; members and children 5 & under no charge. ♿
Attendance: 25,100 (accurate)
Membership: Student & Senior $25; Individual $30; Family $40; Fort Walla Walla $100; Pioneer $250; Explorer $500; Life $1,000.

KIRKMAN HOUSE MUSEUM, 214 N. Colville St., Walla Walla, WA 99362-1917. Tel.: 509-529-4373.
Web Site: www.kirkmanhousemuseum.org
Key Personnel: Kirsten R. Schober.
Personnel Profile: Full-Time Paid 2.
Governing Authority: Tax-exempt.
Historic House Museum: built in 1874. Listed on the National Register of Historic Places.
Collections: period furnishings; personal artifacts.
Hours & Admission Prices: Wed.-Sat. 10-4, Sun. 1-4. No charge; donations accepted.

SHEEHAN GALLERY AT WHITMAN COLLEGE, Olin Hall, 814 Isaacs, Walla Walla, WA 99362. Mailing Address: 345 Boyer Ave., Walla Walla, WA 99362-2083. Tel.: 509-527-5249. Fax: 509-527-5039.
E-mail: forbesdm@whitman.edu
Web Site: www.whitman.edu/sheehan/sheehan_mission.html
Founded: 1972.
Congressional District: 16
Key Personnel: Interim Dir., Dawn Forbes; Pres. Whitman College, Thomas E. Cronin; Pres. Bd. Trustees, Charles E. Anderson; Dean Faculty, Patrick Keef, Ph.D.; Treas., Peter Harvey; Collections & Exhibitions Mgr., Kynde Kiefel.
Personnel Profile: Full-Time Paid 1; Part-Time Paid 1; Part-Time Volunteers 12; Interns 10.
Governing Authority: college; nonprofit. Parent Institution: Whitman College. Tax-exempt: 501(c)(3).
Art Museum/Center.
Collections: Thomas Potter Davis/Seafirst Bank Asian art; Floyd Whittington ceramics; Pacific Northwest paintings & prints.
Research Fields: contemporary art; Asian art & art history; Buddhist art; 20th-century German art; Pacific Northwest modern & contemporary art.
Facilities: 2,400 sq. ft. exhibit space.
Activities: 6 exhibits per year; guided tours; lectures; films.
Publications: exhibition notices; posters; catalogues; Chinese Ceramics in the Thomas Davis/Seafirst Bank Collection; Paths to Enlightenment: Buddhist Art in the Davis/Seafirst Collection; The Doll Theater; Bunraku Puppets in the Davis/Seafirst Collection; Schwarzweiss: The Revival of the Print in Germany; Palm Leaves & Postcards; Material Culture & its Representation in Colonial Ceylon; Thomas O'Day: wake 1/wake 2; We the People: Satiric Prints; Contemporary English Crafts; Piranesi's Careri: Sources of Invention; Auto as Icon (With George Eastman house); The Japanese Artist's Book: Wood block Impressions from the 17th-20th Centuries; George Tsutakawa & Morris Graves; Wendall Brazeau, 1910-1974.
Hours & Admission Prices: Sept.-May Tues.-Fri. 12-5, Sat.-Sun. 12-4. No charge; donations accepted. Closed spring breaks; Christmas. ♿
Attendance: 12,000 (estimated)

WHITMAN MISSION NATIONAL HISTORIC SITE, 328 Whitman Mission Rd., Walla Walla, WA 99362-7299. Tel.: 509-522-6360. Fax: 509-522-6355. TDD: 509-522-6357.
E-mail: terry_darby@nps.gov
Web Site: www.nps.gov/whmi
Founded: 1936.
Congressional District: 5
Key Personnel: Supt., Francis Darby; Supervisory Park Ranger, Roger Trick.
Personnel Profile: Full-Time Paid 8; Part-Time Paid 2; Part-Time Volunteers 5.
Governing Authority: federal. Affiliated with National Park Service, Interior Building, Washington, DC. Tax-exempt.
Park Museum.
Collections: various exhibits dealing with history of Whitman & missionary era in Pacific Northwest.
Research Fields: Oregon territory mission stations.
Facilities: 1200-vol. library of books relating to the Whitman story available for inter-library loan & for use on premises; self-guiding trail; visitor center; auditorium. Printed matter, maps & cultural craft kits for sale.
Activities: lectures; films; formally organized education programs for children, adults & undergraduate college students; permanent & temporary exhibitions; cultural demonstrations.
Publications: handbook & minifolder, Whitman Mission.
Hours & Admission Prices: Fall, Winter, Spring daily 8-4:30; Summer daily 8-6. Adults $3; youths under 17 & seniors over 62 no charge. Annual Park Pass: $10; National Pass $80. Closed New Year's Day; Thanksgiving; Christmas. ♿
Attendance: 70,000 (accurate)
Membership: Annual: Park Pass $10; National Pass $50.

Washougal

TWO RIVERS HERITAGE MUSEUM, 1 Durgan St., Washougal, WA 98671. Mailing Address: P.O. Box 204, Washougal, WA 98671-0204. Tel.: 360-835-8742.
Web Site: www.historyfish.net/tworiversheritagemuseum
Founded: 1978.
Key Personnel: Dir., Betty Ramsey.
Personnel Profile: Part-Time Volunteers 45.
Governing Authority: Parent Institution: Camas Washougal Historical Society. Tax-exempt.
History Museum.
Collections: local history; over 8,000 photographs & 250 oral histories; land records & local families histories; Native American artifacts & period baskets; art; memorabilia; books, local craft items & keepsakes; early wagons; logging; physicians; mining; musical instruments; dolls; toy
Research Fields: family histories; area town & communities.
Facilities: Museum-related items for sale.
Activities: quarterly society members meetings.
Publications: quarterly newsletter.
Hours & Admission Prices: Tues.-Sat. 11-3. Families $8, adults $3, seniors 60 & over $2, students $1; discounts to AAA members; children under 5 no charge. ♿
Membership: Single $15; Family $25.

Wenatchee

ROBERT GRAVES GALLERY, Wenatchee Valley College, 1300 5th St., Wenatchee, WA 98801-1741. Tel.: 509-682-6776.
E-mail: gallery76@wvc.edu
Web Site: www.wvc.edu
Formerly: Gallery '76
Founded: 1976.
Congressional District: 4
Key Personnel: Pres. (V) & Acting Coord., John Crew.
Personnel Profile: Full-Time Volunteers 1; Part-Time Volunteers 35.
Governing Authority: nonprofit organization. Tax-exempt.
Art Gallery.
Collections: paintings; drawings; sculpture.
Activities: guided tours; lectures; docent program; organized education programs for undergraduate college students affiliated with Wenatchee Valley College; loan & traveling exhibitions.
Publications: Gallery 76 News.
Hours & Admission Prices: Mon.-Fri. 9-1, Sat. 11-3; other times by appointment. No charge; donations accepted. Closed holidays. ♿
Attendance: 4,500 (accurate)
Membership: Student $10; Senior $20; Individual $25; Family $35; Supporting $50; Patron $100; Benefactor & Exhibit Sponsor $500.

ROCKY REACH DAM, 5000 97A, Wenatchee, WA 98801-2011. Mailing Address: P.O. Box 1231, Wenatchee, WA 98807-1231. Tel.: 509-663-7522 & 661-4960, ext. 4960. Fax: 509-661-8149.
E-mail: debbie.gallaher@chelanpud.org
Web Site: www.chelanpud.org
Founded: 1963.
Congressional District: 4
Key Personnel: C.E.O., Rich Riazzi; Museum Shop Mgr., Debbie Gallaher.
Personnel Profile: Full-Time Paid 5; Part-Time Paid 6; Part-Time Volunteers 3.
Governing Authority: county. Parent Institution: Public Utility District #1 of Chelan County.
General Interpretive Museum.
Collections: paintings; graphics; Indian artifacts; Gallery of the Columbia; Gallery of Electricity; electrical antiques; Thomas Edison artifacts.
Research Fields: interpretive local geology; prehistory; history; electrical.
Facilities: fish viewing room; theater; picnic area; gardens; snack bar. Gifts for sale.

Activities: self-guided tours; guided tours during summer or when personnel available; films; permanent & temporary exhibitions; art, craft & hobby displays.
Publications: brochures.
Hours & Admission Prices: mid-March to Oct. daily 9-4. No charge. ♿
Attendance: 60,000 (accurate)

WENATCHEE VALLEY MUSEUM AND CULTURAL CENTER, (M), 127 S. Mission, Wenatchee, WA 98801-3039. Tel.: 509-888-6240. Fax: 509-888-6256.
E-mail: info@wvmcc.org
Web Site: www.wvmcc.org
Formerly: North Central Washington Museum
Founded: 1939.
Key Personnel: Dir., Brenda Abney; Pres. (V), Grace Lynch; Cur., Mark Behler; Exhibits, Bill Rietveldt; Public Rels., Chris Rader; Education, Michelle Loudon; Historic Preservation, Kris Bassett; Museum Shop Mgr., Carol Hoffman; Sec., Pauline Sweeney; Receptionist, Michelle Lorrain.
Personnel Profile: Full-Time Paid 7; Part-Time Paid 3; Part-Time Volunteers 150; Interns 3.
Governing Authority: municipal; nonprofit organization. Tax-exempt: 501(c)(3).
General Museum.
Collections: North Central Washington artifacts & memorabilia: pioneer & farm equipment; archaeological collections; printing paraphernalia; archival & manuscript holdings; fruit industry exhibit; fine arts. Operating Exhibits: Theater Pipe Organ; Print Shop; Great Northern Railroad Model; 1920's Vintage Apple Packing Warehouse; Apple Theater, AV Multiscreen Presentations, Celebration.
Research Fields: regional Native American information; regional history; development of fruit industry; Great Northern Railroad; hydroelectric dams & irrigation; genealogy; heritage reference.
Facilities: genealogy library; archives & reference center; two theaters; auditorium; interpretive center; meeting rooms. Museum-related items for sale.
Activities: guided tours; traveling, permanent & temporary exhibits; school programs; demonstrations; lecture series; pipe organ programs; concert & silent movie; hands-on activities; bus tours; exhibit receptions; catering facilities.
Publications: quarterly newsletter; Walking Tour of Wenatchee; quarterly magazine, The Confluence.
Hours & Admission Prices: Tues.-Sat. 10-4. Adults $5, seniors & students $4, children 5-12 $2; members & children under 5 no charge. Closed major holidays. ♿
Attendance: 32,523 (accurate)
Membership: Senior & Student $25; Individual $30; Senior Couple $40; Family $45; Friend $100; Patron $250; Director's Circle $500 & up.

West Seattle

SOUTH SEATTLE COMMUNITY COLLEGE ART GALLERY, South Seattle Community College, Jerry Brockey Student Center, West Seattle, WA 98106. Mailing Address: 6000 16th Ave., S.W., Seattle, WA 98106-1499. Tel.: 206-764-5337 & 5308.
E-mail: rrhodes@sccd.ctc.edu
Web Site: studentlife.southseattle.edu/art.html
Key Personnel: Gallery Coord., Renee Rhodes
Art Gallery.
Collections: paintings.
Activities: Museum Sponsors: student & community art shows.
Hours & Admission Prices: Aug.-May Mon.-Wed. 10-6, Thurs.-Fri. 10-5. No charge. Closed school holidays & breaks.

Westport

WESTPORT MARITIME MUSEUM, 2201 Westhaven Dr., Westport, WA 98595. Mailing Address: P.O. Box 1074, Westport, WA 98595-1074. Tel.: 360-268-0078. Fax: 360-268-1288.
E-mail: westport.maritime@comcast.net
Web Site: westportwa.com/museum
Founded: 1985.
Congressional District: 3
Key Personnel: Exec. Dir., Rex Paul Martin; Pres. (V), Peggy Coverdale; Treas., Ina Rowley; Museum Shop Mgr., Kathy Ruchty.
Personnel Profile: Full-Time Paid 1; Part-Time Paid 3; Part-Time Volunteers 90.
Governing Authority: private; nonprofit organization. Parent Institution: Westport-South Beach Historical Society, P.O. Box 1074, Westport, WA 98595. Tax-exempt: 501(c)(3).
Maritime Museum.
Collections: Fresnel lens, 1st order & 3rd order; whale skeletons; local history; local Coast Guard history; local industries, fishing, logging, cranberry growing & ship building.
Research Fields: life in a maritime community; local logging camps; evolution of navigational aids.
Facilities: children's discovery room; 3,000 sq. ft. exhibit space; 90-seat auditorium; lighthouse. Museum-related items for sale.
Activities: docent program; guided tours; lectures; fireside chats; guest speakers. Annual Events: Run 4 The Light; Holiday tour of Historic Homes; Haunted Light Station Tour; Naughty But Nice List; Old Fashioned Independence Day; Santa by the Sea; Annual Arts Festival; Community Appreciation Day.
Publications: monthly newsletter, Foghorn.
Hours & Admission Prices: April-Sept. daily 10-4; Oct.-March Fri.-Mon. 12-4. Museum: adults $4, children 5-15 $2. Lighthouse: Feb.-Nov. Admission $4.
Attendance: 16,661 (accurate)
Membership: Individual $15; Family $30; Business $50; Patron $75; Benefactor $100; Corporate $500-$5,000.

White Swan

FORT SIMCOE STATE PARK, 5150 Fort Simcoe Rd., White Swan, WA 98952-9745. Tel.: 509-874-2372. Fax: 509-874-2351.
Formerly: Fort Simcoe Interpretive Center
Key Personnel: Dir., Cleve Pinnix; Chief Interpretive Svcs., Steve Wang; Park Mgr. Fort Simcoe State Park, Jim Mitchell.
Governing Authority: state. Affiliated with Washington State Parks & Recreation Commission, 7150 Clean Water Lane, Olympia, WA 98504.
Military Museum: housed in 1856-59 military outpost.
Collections: materials related to life at the fort; military & Indian exhibits & artifacts.
Activities: permanent exhibitions.
Hours & Admission Prices: Summer: 6:30am to dusk; Sept. 29-March 20 8am to dusk. No charge.

Winlock

JOHN R. JACKSON HOUSE, Lewis & Clark State Park, Winlock, WA 98596. Mailing Address: 4583 Jackson Hwy., Winlock, WA 98596-9646. Tel.: 360-864-2643.
Founded: 1915.
Key Personnel: Dir., Rex Derr; Chief Interpretive Svcs., Steve Wang.
Governing Authority: state. Affiliated with Washington State Parks & Recreation Commission, 7150 Clean Water Lane, Olympia, WA 98504. Tax-exempt.
Historic House Museum: 1850 John R. Jackson Home.
Collections: owner's books and possessions.
Activities: guided tours; lectures.
Publications: brochure.
Hours & Admission Prices: House: April-Sept. 8am to dusk; tours by appointment. No charge; donations accepted. ♿

Winthrop

SHAFER HISTORICAL MUSEUM, 285 Castle Ave., Winthrop, WA 98862. Mailing Address: P.O. Box 46, Winthrop, WA 98862-0046. Tel.: 509-996-2712.
E-mail: staff@shafermuseum.com
Web Site: shafermuseum.com
Founded: 1974.
Congressional District: 5
Governing Authority: Parent Institution: Okanogan County Historical Society. Tax-exempt.
Historic Buildings: listed in the National Register of Historical Places.
Collections: pioneer artifacts; mining equipment; period farm equipment & cars; photographs; historic buildings.
Facilities: Museum-related items for sale.
Hours & Admission Prices: Memorial Day to Labor Day Thurs.-Mon. 10-5. Adults $2; members no charge.
Attendance: 6,000 (estimated)
Membership: Individual $25.

Yacolt

POMEROY LIVING HISTORY FARM, 20902 N.E. Lucia Falls Rd., Yacolt, WA 98675-3100. Tel.: 360-686-3537. Fax: 360-686-8111.
E-mail: staff@pomeroyfarm.org
Web Site: www.pomeroyfarm.org
Founded: 1989.
Congressional District: 3
Key Personnel: C.E.O., Bob Brink; Pres. (V), Jane Brink.
Personnel Profile: Part-Time Paid 5; Part-Time Volunteers 130.

Governing Authority: private; nonprofit organization. Tax-exempt: 501(c)(3).
Farm Museum.
Collections: Pomeroy family collection, 1920s-present, including antique farm machinery; pre-electrical farm life in S.W. Washington.
Facilities: 350-vol. library of books; 17-seat tea room. Museum-related items for sale.
Activities: docent program. Annual Events: Herb Festival in May; Quilt Festival in August; Pumpkin Festival in October.
Publications: quarterly newsletter, Down on the Farm.
Hours & Admission Prices: 1st full weekend June-Sept. Sat. 10-5, Sun. 1-5. Adults $6, children 3-11 $4; members and children 2 & under no charge. ♿
Attendance: 12,103 (accurate)
Membership: Friend up to $49; Contributing Friend $50-$99; Supporter $100-$249; Sustaining $250-$499; Sponsor $500-$999; Benefactor $1,000-$4,999; Visionary $5,000 & up.

Yakima

LARSON MUSEUM AND GALLERY, S. 16th Ave. and Nob Hill Blvd., Yakima Valley Community College, Yakima, WA 98902. Mailing Address: P.O. Box 22520, Yakima, WA 98907-2520. Tel.: 509-574-4875. Fax: 509-574-6826. TDD: 509-574-4600.
E-mail: gallery@yvcc.edu
Web Site: www.larsongallery.org
Founded: 1949.
Congressional District: 4
Key Personnel: Chm. (V) & Asst. Dir., Denise Olsen; Dir., Cheryl H. Hahn.
Personnel Profile: Full-Time Paid 1; Part-Time Paid 4; Part-Time Volunteers 20.
Governing Authority: nonprofit organization. Parent Institution: Yakima Valley Community College. Tax-exempt: 501(c)(3).
Art Gallery.
Collections: fine arts, ethnic arts & annual juried art.
Activities: guided tours; arts workshops; organized education programs for children; participatory exhibits. Museum Sponsors: summer workshops in June & July.
Publications: newsletter; annual catalogue, Central Washington Artists Exhibition.
Hours & Admission Prices: Sept.-July 14 Tues.-Sat. 10-5. No charge, donations accepted. ♿
Attendance: 15,000 (estimated)
Membership: Student & Senior $20; Supporter $40; Contributor $65; Family $70; Donor $120; Patron $275; Benefactor $500; Advocate $1,000.

PEGGY LEWIS GALLERY, 5000 W. Lincoln Ave., Yakima, WA 98908-2657. Tel.: 509-966-0930. Fax: 509-966-0934.
E-mail: info@alliedartsyakima.org
Web Site: www.alliedartsyakima.org
Formerly: Allied Arts Council of Yakima Valley Gallery
Founded: 1965.
Congressional District: 14
Key Personnel: Exec. Dir., Jessica Moskwa; Office Mgr., Clay Maer; Coord. Mktg., Lindsey Merrell.
Personnel Profile: Full-Time Paid 3; Part-Time Volunteers 19; Interns 2.
Governing Authority: nonprofit.
Art Museum.
Collections: photographs; paintings.
Activities: summer camps; special events; classes; rental facilities.
Publications: quarterly newsletter, Art Scope.
Hours & Admission Prices: Mon.-Fri. 9-5. No charge.

YAKIMA AREA ARBORETUM & BOTANICAL GARDEN, 1401 Arboretum Dr., Yakima, WA 98901-8513. Tel.: 509-248-7337. Fax: 509-248-8197.
E-mail: info@ahtrees.org
Web Site: www.ahtrees.org
Founded: 1967.
Key Personnel: Co.-Exec. Dir., Colleen Adams-Schuppe; Co.-Exec. Dir., Jheri Ketcham; Groundkeeper, Jeff Neal; Care Taker, Joy Howell; Care Taker, Bob Howell; Office Asst., Chrystal Gentry.
Personnel Profile: Full-Time Paid 2; Part-Time Paid 1; Part-Time Volunteers 1.
Governing Authority: Board of Directors.
Arboretum & Botanical Garden.
Collections: native & exotic species of woody plants; trees; shrubs.
Facilities: display garden. Museum-related items for sale.
Activities: educational classes. Annual Events: arbor festivals; garden tour; luminaria.
Hours & Admission Prices: Daily dawn to dusk. Visitor Center: Tues.-Sun. 9-4. No charge.

* **YAKIMA VALLEY MUSEUM AND HISTORICAL ASSOCIATION, (M),** 2105 Tieton Dr., Yakima, WA 98902-3766. Tel.: 509-248-0747. Fax: 509-453-4890.
E-mail: info@yakimavalleymuseum.org
Web Site: www.yakimavalleymuseum.org
Founded: 1952.
Congressional District: 4
Key Personnel: C.E.O. & Dir., John A. Baule; Pres. (V), Stephen Muehleck; Cur. Collections, Michael Siebol; Cur. Exhibits & Programs, Andrew Granitto; Cur. Education, Katharyne Sample; Mktg. & Fund Devel., David Lynx; Museum Shop Mgr., Deborah Vlcek.
Personnel Profile: Full-Time Paid 4; Part-Time Paid 5; Part-Time Volunteers 73; Interns 2.
Governing Authority: nonprofit organization. Subsidiary Institution: H. M. Gilbert Homeplace. Tax-exempt: 501(c)(3).
Historical Museum.
Collections: archival repository; horse-drawn vehicles; Native American artifacts; textile & costume collections; household furnishings; agricultural artifacts; mineral collections; personal accessories; irrigation artifacts; The Children's Underground, a hands-on center focusing on natural & human history of the area; operating 1930's Art Deco ice cream soda fountain.
Major Exhibits: Women's Voices/Women's Votes (T), 2/10-6/10; Bicycle Eclectic (T), 7/10-10/10; Heels: 100 Years of Women's Shoes, 9/10-12/10.
Research Fields: Yakima Valley & central Washington history.
Facilities: Museum-related gifts & books for sale.
Activities: guided tours; lectures; college classes & seminars; music & cultural programs.
Publications: quarterly newsletter; books; report to membership.
Hours & Admission Prices: Tues.-Sun. 11-5. Families $12, adults $5, students & senior citizens $2.50; discounts to AASLH, AAA, ICOM & AAM members; members & children under 6 no charge. Children's Underground: Wed.-Sun 11-5. ♿
Attendance: 27,000 (estimated)
Membership: Individual $30; Family $40; Sponsor $75; Supporting $100; Patron $300; Benefactor $500.

WEST VIRGINIA

(114 listings)

Ansted

CONTENTMENT, Rte. 60, Ansted, WV 25812. Mailing Address: HC 66 Box 94B, Hico, WV 25854-7468.
Personnel Profile: Full-Time Volunteers 1.
Historic House Museum: housed in the former home of Civil War Col. George Imboden.
Collections: period furnishings; personal artifacts; 3 historic buildings.
Activities: school tours; special events.
Hours & Admission Prices: June-Aug. Mon.-Sat. 10-4.

Arthurdale

ARTHURDALE HERITAGE, INC., (M), Q & A Rds., Arthurdale, WV 26520. Mailing Address: P.O. Box 850, Arthurdale, WV 26520-0850. Tel.: 304-864-3959. Fax: 304-864-4602.
E-mail: ahi@arthurdaleheritage.org
Web Site: www.arthurdaleheritage.org
Founded: 1985.
Congressional District: 1
Key Personnel: Dir., Theresa Marthey; Pres. (V), Rick Rodenheaver; Museum Shop Mgr., Loretta Davis; Museum Shop Mgr., Donna Summers.
Personnel Profile: Part-Time Paid 2; Part-Time Volunteers 50.
Governing Authority: private; nonprofit. Tax-exempt: 501(c)(3).
Historic Site: housed in several buildings constructed in 1930s when Arthurdale became the first New Deal homestead.
Collections: structures; tools & equipment; artisan crafts. Historic House: working 1930s homestead.
Research Fields: 1930s New Deal homestead communities; Arthurdale oral history, 1947-present.
Facilities: library; archives; 800 sq. ft. exhibit space.
Activities: guided tours; concerts; temporary exhibits; blacksmith & other craft demonstrations. Annual Events: New Deal Festival in July; Traditional Crafts in July; Old Fashioned Ice Cream Social; parade.
Publications: quarterly, The Newsletter of Arthurdale Heritage; quarterly newsletter, Restoring Yesterday for Tomorrow.
Hours & Admission Prices: May-Oct. Tues.-Sun. 12-4; Nov.-April Tues.-Fri. 12-4; other times by appointment. Adults $5; discounts to members. ♿
Attendance: 5,000 (estimated)
Membership: Individual $15; Household $25; Business $50.

Beckley

RALEIGH COUNTY VETERANS MUSEUM, 1557 Harper Rd., Beckley, WV 25801-3307. Mailing Address: P.O. Box 3165, Beckley, WV 25801-1945. Tel.: 304-253-1775.
Web Site: rcvm.org
Veterans Museum.
Collections: military history from Revolutionary War to present; photographs.
Hours & Admission Prices: April-Oct. Fri.-Sat. 1-7, Sun. 1-5; other times by appointment. Adults $2, children 12 & under $.50.

WILDWOOD HOUSE MUSEUM, 121 Laurel Ter., Beckley, WV 25801-4217. Mailing Address: P.O. Box 2514, Beckley, WV 25802-2514. Tel.: 304-252-8614.
Historic House: housed in the former home of General Alfred Beckley; built in 1836. Listed on the National Register of Historic Places.
Collections: Beckley family history; period furnishings; personal artifacts.
Hours & Admission Prices: April-Nov. Sat.-Sun. 10-6 Adults $5.

YOUTH MUSEUM OF SOUTHERN WEST VIRGINIA, 509 Ewart Ave., Beckley, WV 25802. Mailing Address: P.O. Box 2514, Beckley, WV 25802-2514. Tel.: 304-252-3730. Fax: 304-252-3764.
E-mail: sparker@beckleymine.com
Web Site: beckleymine.com
Founded: 1977.
Congressional District: 3
Key Personnel: Exec. Dir. & C.E.O., Sandi Parker; Museum Coord., Leslie Baker; Administrative Coord., Donna Clark Totten.
Personnel Profile: Full-Time Paid 2; Part-Time Paid 4; Part-Time Volunteers 2.
Governing Authority: The city of Beckley.
Youth Museum.
Collections: used to interpret Appalachian heritage in the Mountain Homestead.
Major Exhibits: Chagall for Children (T), 2/10-8/26/10; Kids Create Art (T), 3/10-6/10.
Research Fields: developing hands-on science curriculum.
Facilities: 120-vol. library; educational facilities; 1,500 sq. ft. exhibit space; planetarium; 200-seat amphitheater. Museum-related items for sale.
Activities: arts festivals; concerts; films; guided tours; lectures; participatory & traveling exhibitions. Annual Events: Tailgate Halloween; Appalachian Heritage Day; Christmas in the Homestead.
Publications: quarterly newsletter, Museum News.
Hours & Admission Prices: April-Nov. 1 daily 10-6; Nov. 2-March Tues.-Sat. 10-5. Call for rate schedule. Closed New Year's Day; Christmas. ♿
Attendance: 50,000 (estimated)
Membership: Individual $15; Couple $25; Family $35; Sponsor $50; Community $100; WV $250; Patron $500.

Benwood

CASTLE HALLOWEEN MUSEUM AND SHOP, 577 Boggs Run Rd., Benwood, WV 26031-1050. Tel.: 304-233-1031.
Web Site: www.castlehalloween.com
Key Personnel: Owner, Pamela Apkarian-Russell
Halloween Museum.
Collections: Halloween-related artifacts; arcade machines; costumes; paintings; toys; postcards.
Hours & Admission Prices: Call for hours.

Berkeley Springs

MUSEUM OF THE BERKELEY SPRINGS, Berkeley Springs, WV 25411. Mailing Address: P.O. Box 99, Berkeley Springs, WV 25411-0099. Tel.: 800-447-8797.
E-mail: history@museumoftheberkeleysprings
Founded: 1984.
Congressional District: 2
Key Personnel: Pres., David Milburn; Vice Pres., Betty Lou Harmison; Treas., Susan Winkeler-Milburn; Exec. Dir. & Museum Shop Mgr., Tamme Marggraf.
Personnel Profile: Part-Time Paid 4; Part-Time Volunteers 1.
Governing Authority: private; nonprofit organization. Tax-exempt: 501(c)(3).
History Museum: housed in the c.1820 Roman Bath building in Berkeley Springs State Park.
Collections: local history associated with the mineral springs at Berkeley Springs, the town & county.
Facilities: 1,250 sq. ft. exhibit space. Museum-related items for sale.
Activities: guided tours.
Publications: annual newsletter; pamphlets.
Hours & Admission Prices: Feb.-Dec. Sat.-Sun. 11-4; call for additional hours. No charge; donations accepted. ♿
Attendance: 8,476 (accurate)
Membership: Individual $15; Family $25; Trustee $100.

Bethany

HISTORIC BETHANY - ALEXANDER CAMPBELL MANSION, Bethany College, Rte. 67 E., Bethany, WV 26032. Mailing Address: PO Box 478, Bethany, WV 26032-0478. Tel.: 304-829-4258. Fax: 304-829-4258.
E-mail: historic@bethanywv.edu
Founded: 1840.
Key Personnel: C.E.O., Dr. G.T. Smith; Cur., Felicity Ruggiero.
Personnel Profile: Full-Time Paid 1; Full-Time Volunteers 6; Part-Time Paid 4; Part-Time Volunteers 10.
Governing Authority: Parent Institution: Bethany College; nonprofit. Tax-exempt.
Historic Mansion: housed in the former home of Bethany College founder, Alexander Campbell; built c.1794. Listed on the National Register of Historic Places.
Collections: Alexander Campbell family house items; Campbell books & papers; Upper Ohio Valley collection; historic buildings.
Research Fields: Campbell & his relationship to early U.S. history; Thomas Barclay & family; early U.S. history.
Facilities: 210,000-vol. general resource materials & special collections library available for inter-library loan; educational facilities. Museum-related items for sale.
Activities: guided tours. Annual Event: Children's Heritage Day.
Publications: quarterly, newsletter, The Campbell Light.
Hours & Admission Prices: April-Oct. Tues.-Fri. 10-12 & 1-4; other times by appointment. Adults $4, youth 1-12 grade $2; discounts to AAM & AAA members. Closed holidays. ♿
Attendance: 3,500 (estimated)

Beverly

RANDOLPH COUNTY MUSEUM (AT BEVERLY), Main St., Beverly, WV 26253. Mailing Address: P.O. Box 1164, Elkins, WV 26241-1164. Tel.: 304-636-0841.
E-mail: dlrice@citynet.net
Founded: 1924.
Congressional District: 2
Key Personnel: C.E.O. (V) & Pres. (V), Randy Allan; Acting Cur. & Archivist, Donald Rice.
Personnel Profile: Part-Time Volunteers 4.
Governing Authority: private; nonprofit organization. Parent Institution: Randolph County Historical Society. Tax-exempt: 501(c)(3).
History Museum: housed in the Blackman-Bosworth Store building.
Collections: 200 years of Randolph County history.
Research Fields: Rich Mountain Civil War Battlefield; Beverly town & Randolph County history; genealogy.
Facilities: 1,600 sq. ft. exhibit space. Books for sale.
Activities: formal education programs for children; guided tours; lectures; temporary exhibitions; special events. Annual Event: Beverly Historic Days.
Publications: books; journals.
Hours & Admission Prices: Museum: mid-May to mid-Oct. Fri.-Sat. 12-4; other times by appointment. Donations requested.
Attendance: 700 (estimated)
Membership: Society: Children $2; Seniors $10; Adult $20.

Bluefield

BUDDY'S COUNTRY STORE & MUSEUM, Old Rte. 52, Bluefield, WV 24701. Mailing Address: Box 534, Bluefield, WV 24701-9254. Tel.: 304-589-5659.
History Museum.
Collections: local history; coal camp house replica; period artifacts & memorabilia; photographs.
Hours & Admission Prices: May-Sept. by appointment. No charge.

THE SCIENCE CENTER OF WEST VIRGINIA, 500 Bland St., Bluefield, WV 24701-4257. Tel.: 304-325-8855. Fax: 304-324-0513.
Web Site: www.sciencecenterwv.com
Founded: 1994.
Congressional District: 3
Key Personnel: Chm. (V) & Pres. (V), Patty Wilkinson; Dir., Thomas Willmiten; Museum Shop Mgr. & Administrative Asst., Pam R. Lester.
Personnel Profile: Full-Time Paid 2; Part-Time Paid 6; Part-Time Volunteers 4.
Governing Authority: nonprofit organization. Parent Institution: Alliance for the Arts, Ltd. Tax-exempt.
Science Center/Museum.
Collections: interactive science exhibits.

Hours & Admission Prices: June-Aug. Tues.-Sat. 10-5; Sept.-May Tues.-Thurs. 9-3, Sat. 10-4. Adults $5; discounts to groups & ASTC members; children under 2 & members no charge. Closed holidays. ♿
Attendance: 20,000 (estimated)
Membership: Individual $45; Family $65; Supporters $100; Benefactors $1,000.

Ceredo

RAMSDELL HOUSE, 1108 B St., Ceredo, WV 25507. Mailing Address: P.O. Box 446, Ceredo, WV 25507-0446. Tel.: 304-453-2482.
Historic House: housed in the home of Union Capt. Z.D. Ramsdell; built in 1858.
Collections: Civil War records & memorabilia; period artifacts.
Activities: school tours; special events.
Hours & Admission Prices: By appointment. ♿

Charles Town

JEFFERSON COUNTY MUSEUM, 200 E. Washington St., Charles Town, WV 25414-1006. Tel.: 304-725-8628.
E-mail: curator@jeffctywvmuseum.org
Web Site: www.jeffctywvmuseum.org
Founded: 1965.
Key Personnel: Cur., Susan Collins.
Personnel Profile: Interns 1.
Governing Authority: Parent Institution: Old Charles Town Library, Inc. Subsidiary Institution: Old Charles Town Library. Tax-exempt.
History Museum.
Collections: area history; personal artifacts; Native American to WWII artifacts; Civil War uniforms, silver & china, photographs, dolls & toys.
Activities: research; tours. Annual Event: Antiques Appraisal Fair.
Publications: brochure; postcards; book, Chew's Battery of Stuart's Horse Artillery.
Hours & Admission Prices: mid-March to mid-Dec. Tues.-Sat. 11-4. Adults $3; members and children 18 & under no charge.
Attendance: 1,500 (estimated)
Membership: Annual $10.

Charleston

* **CLAY CENTER FOR ARTS & SCIENCES WEST VIRGINIA, (M),** One Clay Sq., Charleston, WV 25301-2424. Tel.: 304-561-3552. Fax: 304-561-3598.
E-mail: info@avampatodiscoverymuseum.org
Web Site: www.theclaycenter.org
Formerly: Avampato Discovery Museum
Founded: 1961.
Congressional District: 3
Key Personnel: Chm., Melvin Jones; C.E.O. & Pres., Judith Wellington; C.F.O., Rebecca Gillespie; Dir. Exhibits & Art Cur., Barbara Racker; Dir. Art & Science Education, Lewis Ferguson; Dir. Mktg. & Communications, Traci West-McCombs; Dir. Performing Arts, Lakin Cook; Museum Shop Mgr., Megan Douglas.
Personnel Profile: Full-Time Paid 51; Part-Time Paid 10; Part-Time Volunteers 175.
Governing Authority: private; nonprofit organization. Tax-exempt: 501(c)(3).
Performing & Visual Arts & Science Museum.
Collections: 19th- & 20th-century American painting; sculpture; works on paper.
Research Fields: American art.
Facilities: GEMS teacher training center; large format theater; planetarium; cafe; classrooms; 2 performance halls.
Activities: guided tours; lectures; films; educational programs in galleries; workshops; exhibitions; classes; special events; demonstrations; performances.
Publications: quarterly newsletter.
Hours & Admission Prices: Wed.-Sat. 10-5, Sun. 12-5; groups by appointment. Adults $7, senior citizens, teachers & children $5.50; discounts to groups & AAM members; museum members, children under 3 & ASTC members no charge. Closed national holidays. ♿
Attendance: 180,000 (accurate)
Membership: Individual Plus $55; Family $75; Film Lovers $100; Contributor $125; Art Enthusiasts $150; Supporter $300; Patron $600; Bronze $1,000; Silver $1,500; Gold $2,500; Platinum $5,000.

CRAIK-PATTON HOUSE, 2809 Kanawha Blvd. E., Charleston, WV 25311-1727. Tel.: 304-925-5341.
Web Site: www.craik-patton.com
Historic House Museum: built by James Craik in 1834; owned by George Smith Patton, a leader in the Confederate Army & grandfather of General George S. Patton.
Collections: southern West Virginia history & culture; period furnishings; gardens.
Facilities: picnic area.
Activities: rental facilities.
Hours & Admission Prices: mid-April to Sept. Tues.-Thurs. 10-4; other times by appointment. Adults $3.

WEST VIRGINIA STATE MUSEUM, (M), 1900 Kanawha Blvd., E., Charleston, WV 25305-0009. Tel.: 304-558-0220. Fax: 304-558-2779. TDD: 304-558-3562.
E-mail: charles.morris@wvculture.org
Web Site: www.wvculture.org
Founded: 1894.
Congressional District: 3
Key Personnel: Commissioner, Randall Reid-Smith; Dir. West Virginia State Museum, Adam Hodges; Dir. Archives & History, Joe Geiger; Coord. Exhibits, Betty Gay; Coord. Exhibits, Emily Ritchie; Dir. Historic Preservation, Susan Pierce; Dir. Collections & Exhibitions, Charles Morris; Editor-Goldenseal, John Lilly; Dir. West Virginia Independence Hall, Melissa Brown; Dir. Grave Creek Mound Historic Site, Susan Yoho; Cur., James Mitchell.
Personnel Profile: Full-Time Paid 80; Part-Time Paid 3; Part-Time Volunteers 75.
Governing Authority: state. Parent Institution: State of West Virginia, WV Div. of Culture & History. Tax-exempt.
Cultural Center; History Museum.
Collections: history & culture of West Virginia; archaeological artifacts; historic costumes & textiles; settlement & Civil War artifacts; firearms & edged weapons; early industrial tools & products; WV. Regimental flags; 19th century household goods & furnishings; fine arts; historic & contemporary WV folk arts & crafts; television newsfilm; WV travel & documentary films; numismatic & philatelic collections; archival collections of manuscripts, public documents, state & county records, photographs; Boyd Stutler Civil War collection; C.O. Ericksen coin & currency collection.
Research Fields: West Virginia history; state & regional genealogy; colonial America; Civil War; regional military history; Appalachian culture.
Facilities: historical research library; public library; theater; technical shop; video studio; art exhibit areas; meeting & conference rooms.
Activities: tours; arts festivals highlighting traditional music, arts & crafts, jazz, dance & theater; conferences on historic preservation, literary arts & arts management; marketing programs include WV. Juried Exhibition & Performing Arts showcase; concerts; films; recitals; theatrical productions; outreach programs & Arts & Humanities & Historic Preservation grants programs; oral interviews.
Publications: quarterly, checklist of State Publications; quarterly, Folklife Magazine; annual, Grants Brochure; annual, West Virginia History; periodic Elderberry books and records.
Hours & Admission Prices: Tues.-Sat. 9-5, Sun. 12-5. No charge. Closed Christmas; most holidays. ♿
Attendance: 182,000 (accurate)

Clifftop

WEST VIRGINIA CAMP WASHINGTON-CARVER, Rte. 41 S., Clifftop, WV 25831. Mailing Address: HC 35, Box 5, Clifftop, WV 25831-9001. Tel.: 304-438-3005. Fax: 304-438-3006.
E-mail: campwashingtoncarver@wvculture.org
Web Site: www.wvculture.org/sites/carver.html
Founded: 1979.
Key Personnel: Facility Mgr., George Sheaves.
Personnel Profile: Full-Time Paid 3.
Governing Authority: state. Parent Institution: West Virginia Dept. of Culture and History, Cultural Center, Capitol Complex, Charleston, WV 25305. Tax-exempt.
Historic Site: Park Museum/Visitor Center; camp built as first 4-H Camp for blacks in U.S.
Collections: Historic Building: 1939-1940 chestnut building designed by J.R. Strock & built by the WPA.
Research Fields: history of Camp Washington-Carver.
Facilities: 5,500 sq. ft. open free space; 4 indoor exhibition spaces; indoor & outdoor performance areas.
Activities: changing exhibitions; performances; craft demonstrations.
Hours & Admission Prices: June-Oct. Mon.-Fri. call for appointment. No charge. ♿
Attendance: 10,000 (estimated)

Elizabeth

BEAUCHAMP NEWMAN MUSEUM, Court St., Elizabeth, WV 26143. Mailing Address: P.O. Box 621, Elizabeth, WV 26143-0621. Tel.: 304-275-6534.
Founded: 1950.
Key Personnel: Regent (V), Edwina Ott; Cur., Jean Dailey
Historic House.
Collections: furniture; costumes; domestic artifacts.
Activities: guided tours.
Hours & Admission Prices: By appointment. No charge; donations accepted.

Elkins

DARBY'S PREHISTORIC AND EARLY PIONEER'S ART MUSEUM, 100 Campus Dr., Davis and Elkins College, Elkins, WV 26241-3971. Tel.: 304-637-1341. Fax: 304-637-1238.
E-mail: morganw@elkins.edu
Web Site: www.davisandelkins.edu
History Museum.
Collections: early pioneer history & culture; period clothing; personal artifacts.
Activities: school tours.
Hours & Admission Prices: Mon.-Fri. 8-4:30; other times by appointment. ♿

Fairmont

MARION COUNTY HISTORICAL SOCIETY MUSEUM, 210 Adams St., Fairmont, WV 26554-2826. Mailing Address: P.O. Box 1636, Fairmont, WV 26555-1636. Tel.: 304-367-5398.
E-mail: marionhistorical@yahoo.org
Web Site: www.marionhistorical.org
Founded: 1986.
Key Personnel: Pres. (V), Dora Kay Grubb.
Personnel Profile: Part-Time Paid 2; Part-Time Volunteers 1.
Governing Authority: Parent Institution: Marion County Historical Society, Inc. Tax-exempt.
Historical Society Museum: housed in the Marion County Sheriffs' home from 1913-1985. Listed on the National Historic Register of Landmarks.
Collections: county history & culture; period artifacts; documents; historical papers.
Facilities: Books & pamphlets for sale.
Activities: school tours. Museum Sponsors: Founders' Month; WV's Birthday Historic Home Tour; Julie Pierpont Day in May.
Publications: quarterly newsletter.
Hours & Admission Prices: Memorial Day to Labor Day Mon.-Sat. 10-2; Sept.-May Mon.-Fri. 10-2; other times by appointment. No charge.
Attendance: 2,000
Membership: Individual $10; Family $15.

PRICKETTS FORT, Rte. 3, Fairmont, WV 26554-9470. Mailing Address: Box 407, Fairmont, WV 26554-9470. Tel.: 304-363-3030. Fax: 304-363-3857.
E-mail: director@prickettsfort.org
Web Site: www.prickettsfort.org
Founded: 1976.
Congressional District: 1
Key Personnel: C.E.O., Melissa May; Chm., Ray Richardson.
Personnel Profile: Full-Time Paid 3; Part-Time Paid 7; Part-Time Volunteers 50; Interns 2.
Governing Authority: not-for-profit organization. Parent Institution: Pricketts Fort Memorial Foundation. Tax-exempt.
Historic Site & House: c.1859 Job Prickett House & 18th century civilian refuge fort.
Collections: artifacts of the late 18th & 19th centuries.
Facilities: 500-vol. library; 400-seat theater. Museum-related items for sale.
Activities: guided tours; concerts; education programs for children; participatory exhibits; theater; docent program; training program for professional museum workers; School of the Longhunter; reenactments.
Publications: quarterly newsletter, Gatepost; catalogues.
Hours & Admission Prices: Mid-April to May & Sept.-Oct. Wed.-Sat. 10-5, Sun. 12-5; Memorial Day to Labor Day Mon.-Sat. 10-5, Sun. 12-5. Adults $6, senior citizens $5, children $3; discounts to Frontiers to Mountaineers, tour groups, AAA & CAA members; members no charge. ♿
Attendance: 13,652 (accurate)
Membership: Individual $25; Family $35; Sustaining $75.

French Creek

WEST VIRGINIA STATE WILDLIFE CENTER, Rte. 20 S., French Creek, WV 26218. Mailing Address: P.O. Box 38, French Creek, WV 26218-0038. Tel.: 304-924-6211. Fax: 304-924-6781.
E-mail: robsilvester@wvdnr.gov
Web Site: www.dnr.state.wv.us/wvwildlife/wildlifectr.htm
Founded: 1923.
Congressional District: 13
Key Personnel: Dir. WV Div. Natural Resources, Frank Jezioro; Biologist, Robert A. Silvester; Museum Shop Mgr., Joann Kruk.
Personnel Profile: Full-Time Paid 5; Part-Time Paid 6.
Governing Authority: state. Parent Institution: WV Div. of Natural Resources, 1800 Washington St., East Charleston, WV 25305.
Zoo.
Collections: animals & birds native to West Virginia.
Research Fields: wildlife.
Facilities: natural environmental enclosures.
Activities: guided tours; movies; special events.
Publications: descriptive brochure.
Hours & Admission Prices: Adults $3, children 3-15 $1.50; discounts to groups & Golden Mountaineer members; children under 3 no charge. Annual passes also available. ♿
Attendance: 75,000 (estimated)
Membership: Individual $10; Family $25; Friends & Family $40.

Grafton

ANNA JARVIS BIRTHPLACE MUSEUM, Rte. 119/250 S., Grafton, WV 26354. Mailing Address: Rte. 2, Box 352, Grafton, WV 26354-9643. Tel.: 304-265-5549.
Founded: 1994.
Key Personnel: Pres. (V), Tom Dadisman; Museum Shop Mgr., Olive Dadisman.
Personnel Profile: Part-Time Volunteers 3.
Historic House Museum: housed in the birthplace of Anna Jarvis, the founder of Mother's Day.
Collections: family history; personal artifacts; period furnishings; photographs.
Hours & Admission Prices: April-Dec. Tues.-Sun. 10-4. Adults $5; discounts to AAM & ICOM members; children under 12 no charge. ♿

INTERNATIONAL MOTHERS DAY SHRINE AND MUSEUM, 11 E. Main St., Grafton, WV 26354-1322. Mailing Address: P.O. Box 513, Grafton, WV 26354-0513. Tel.: 304-265-1589.
E-mail: info@mothersdayshrine.com
Web Site: www.mothersdayshrine.com/
Historic Church: built in 1873. Listed on the National Register of Historic Places.
Collections: religious artifacts.
Facilities: Museum-related items for sale.
Activities: weddings; tour groups; rental facility.
Hours & Admission Prices: April 15-Oct. 15 Fri.-Sat. 10-4, Sun. 12-4; groups & other times by appointment. No charge; donations accepted. Closed holidays.

Hamlin

MUD RIVER MUSEUM, 315 Main St., Hamlin, WV 25523-1413. Tel.: 304-824-2186. Fax: 304-824-5178.
Key Personnel: Dir., Dan Kebles
Science Museum.
Collections: earth science.
Hours & Admission Prices: By appointment.

Harpers Ferry

THE APPALACHIAN TRAIL CONSERVANCY, 799 Washington St., Harpers Ferry, WV 25425-6587. Mailing Address: P.O. Box 807, Harpers Ferry, WV 25425-0807. Tel.: 304-535-6331. Fax: 304-535-2667.
E-mail: info@appalachiantrail.org
Web Site: www.appalachiantrail.org
Founded: 1925.
Congressional District: 2
Key Personnel: Exec. Dir., David N. Startzell; Chm. (V), Bob Almand; Treas., Kennard Honick; Dir. Devel., Royce Gibson; Foundation & Corp. Rels. Mgr., Amy McCormick; Gift Shop Mgr., Laurie Potteiger.
Personnel Profile: Full-Time Paid 40; Part-Time Paid 6; Part-Time Volunteers 15.
Governing Authority: nonprofit organization. Tax-exempt: 501(c)(3).
Appalachian Trail Maintenance Association: housed in 1892 building.

Collections: natural resources & historical development of the volunteer-maintained Appalachian trail, including original maps & planning documents; library & memorabilia of regional planner E. Benton MacKay; archives of the Appalachian Trail Conference; photographs; publications.
Research Fields: state-by-state inventories of rare, threatened & endangered species within 500 ft. of the 2,160 mile Appalachian Trail; legislative history of the Appalachian National Scenic Trail & public & private cooperative management of it.
Facilities: 1,275-vol. library; 400 sq. ft. exhibit space; archival research area. Trail related items for sale.
Activities: loan & temporary exhibitions.
Publications: 6-times yearly "A.T. Journeys"; quarterly publication, The E-Register.
Hours & Admission Prices: Daily 9-5. No charge; donations accepted. Closed New Year's Day; Washington's Birthday; Columbus Day; Thanksgiving & day after; Christmas. ♿
Attendance: 29,000 (estimated)
Membership: Senior Citizen, Student or Affiliated Club (Individual) $25; Individual Adult $30; Supporting Organization $100; Individual Life & Corporate $600; Couple Life $900.

HARPERS FERRY CENTER, (M), Interp. Design Ctr., 67 Mather Place, Harpers Ferry, WV 25425-0050. Mailing Address: P.O. Box 50, Charles town, WV 25425-0050. Tel.: 304-535-6262. Fax: 304-535-6492.
E-mail: david_nathanson@nps.gov
Web Site: www.nps.gov/hfc
Founded: 1970.
Congressional District: 2
Key Personnel: Chief Exhibits, Mary Herber; Chief Audio-Visual Arts, Brian Jones; Registrar, Alice Newton; Chief Historic Furnishing, John Brucksch; Chief Conservation, Martin Burke; Chief Wayside Exhibits, Phil Musselwhite; Chief Publications, Melissa Cronyn.
Governing Authority: federal. Parent Institution: U.S. National Park Service. Tax-exempt.
Museum Development & Support Facility.
Collections: archives; artifacts; 1,500,000 historic images; 1872-1991 National Park Service Uniforms series.
Research Fields: conservation; historic furnishings; audio-visual technology; NPS history; historic preservation.
Facilities: 35,000-vol. library of American history, material culture, decorative arts, museology, military art & science; historic preservation facilities; conservation laboratories; exhibit mounting shop.
Activities: traveling exhibitions; audiovisuals; media development.
Publications: informational folders for the 370 NPS sites; handbooks; posters; Index to The Courier: Newsmagazine of the National Park Service; National Park Service Uniforms & Equipment Series; disk, Guide to the Trade Catalog Collection.
Hours & Admission Prices: Daily 8-5. Park Pass: vehicle $6, individual $4. Closed New Year's Day; Thanksgiving; Christmas.

* **HARPERS FERRY NATIONAL HISTORICAL PARK, (M),** Fillmore St., Harpers Ferry, WV 25425. Mailing Address: P.O. Box 65, Harpers Ferry, WV 25425-0065. Tel.: 304-535-6224. Fax: 304-535-6244.
Web Site: www.nps.gov/hafe/home.htm
Founded: 1944.
Congressional District: 2
Key Personnel: Rgnl. Dir., Margaret O'Dell; Supt., Rebecca L. Harriett; Chief Ranger, Jeffrie Woods; Cultural Resources Mgr., Dennis Frye; Museum Shop Mgr., Deborah Piscitelli; Lands Management Asst., Andrew Lee; Education Specialist, Catherine Bragaw; Visitor Svcs., Todd P.H. Bolton; Volunteers & Outreach, Jessica Liptak.
Personnel Profile: Full-Time Paid 99; Part-Time Paid 9; Part-Time Volunteers 769.
Governing Authority: federal. Parent Institution: National Park Service, U.S. Dept. of Interior, Washington, DC 20240.
National Historic Park: approx. 56 restored buildings & Civil War fortifications.
Collections: artifacts specific to historical period; Harpers Ferry Arms; John Brown; Civil War; 19th-century African American education; 19th-century water-powered technology. Historic Buildings: 1775 Harper House; 1858 Master Armorer's House; 1826 Stagecoach Inn; exhibits pertaining to Storer College, Archeology, Restoration and Industry, Wetlands & Jefferson Rock.
Research Fields: John Brown raid; Civil War; industry; social; transportation; African American history; 19th-century America.
Facilities: 2,000-vol. research library specific to John Brown, Civil War, African American history and the industrial/transportation and social history of Harpers Ferry; visitor center. Gift items for sale.
Activities: Special tours offered daily Memorial Day-Labor Day on John Brown's Raid, Civil War, Stonewall's Brilliant Victory, C&O Canal Walk, Harpers Ferry Marsh Walk, Voices from Harpers Ferry and the Guns of Harper's Ferry. Seasonally scheduled Living History Exhibits & Interpretation. Education programs for schools throughout the year with reservations. Harpers Ferry Historical Association Sponsors: Elderhostel programs. Hiking & walking trails include Virginius Island Trail, Hamilton St., Jefferson Rock Trail, Maryland Heights Trail and intersecting at Harpers Ferry are the Appalachian Trail and the C&O Canal.
Hours & Admission Prices: Summer: daily 8-6; Winter: daily 8-5. $5 per car or $3 per person 17-62 (7 day pass); seniors, children 16 & under no charge. $20 family yearly pass available. NPS Golden Eagle, Golden Age & Golden Access pass available and honored. ♿
Attendance: 350,000 (estimated)
Membership: Family $20.

JOHN BROWN WAX MUSEUM INC., 168 High St., Harpers Ferry, WV 25425. Mailing Address: P.O. Box 806, Harpers Ferry, WV 25425-0806. Tel.: 304-535-6342.
Web Site: www.johnbrownwaxmuseum.com
Formerly: National Historical John Brown Wax Museum
Founded: 1964.
Congressional District: 16
Governing Authority: private corporation.
Wax Museum: housed in c.1820 historic town building.
Collections: wax figures & scenes; authentic costumes.
Research Fields: John Brown's life from boyhood to gallows.
Hours & Admission Prices: mid-March to mid-Dec. daily 9-5; call for additional hours. Adults $7, senior citizens 60 & up $6, child 6-12 $5; discounts to groups of 10 or more; children under 6 no charge.

Helvetia

HELVETIA MUSEUM, General Delivery, Helvetia, WV 26224-9999. Mailing Address: P.O. Box 42, Helvetia, WV 26224-0042. Tel.: 304-924-6435.
Founded: 1969.
Congressional District: 12
Key Personnel: Pres., David H. Sutton; Mgr., Eleanor F. Mailloux; Museum Shop Mgr., Margie Daetwyler.
Governing Authority: society. Affiliated with the Historical Society of Helvetia. Tax-exempt.
Historical & Preservation Society: housed in 1871 Betler Cabin.
Collections: Swiss immigration to West Virginia memorabilia; agricultural tools used in Helvetia; furniture of Swiss design.
Research Fields: Swiss immigration to West Virginia.
Activities: guided tours by appointment; gallery talks; permanent exhibitions.
Hours & Admission Prices: May-Sept. Sat.-Sun. 12-4; other times by special arrangement. No charge; donations accepted. ♿
Attendance: 500 (estimated)
Membership: Annual $2; Life $20.

Hillsboro

PEARL S. BUCK BIRTHPLACE FOUNDATION, Rte. 219 N., Hillsboro, WV 24946. Mailing Address: P.O. Box 126, Hillsboro, WV 24946-0126. Tel.: 304-653-4430.
Web Site: www.pearlsbuckbirthplace.com
Founded: 1974.
Congressional District: 2
Key Personnel: Pres. (V), Rose Anderson; Mgr., Anita Withrow.
Personnel Profile: Full-Time Paid 2; Part-Time Paid 1.
Governing Authority: nonprofit. Tax-exempt: 501(c)(3).
Historic House Museum: Sydenstricker house was Pearl S. Buck's fathers' childhood home; Stulting House, built by Pearl S. Buck's maternal ancestors & birthplace of Pearl S. Buck.
Collections: memorabilia of Pearl S. Buck; original family furniture in restored rooms; original manuscripts of Pearl S. Buck, housed at West Virginia Wesleyan College, available by appointment only. Historic Building: restored 19th century barn & machinery.
Research Fields: genealogical research into Pearl S. Buck ancestry.
Facilities: Pearl S. Buck books & West Virginia crafts for sale.
Activities: guided tours. Museum Sponsors: Pearl S. Buck Birthday celebration; Author's Day Ceremony.
Hours & Admission Prices: May-Oct. Mon.-Sat. 9-4:30. Adults $6, senior citizens $5, students $1; children under 6 no charge. Closed New Year's Day; Thanksgiving; Christmas. ♿
Attendance: 1,993 (accurate)
Membership: Individual $5; Sustaining $10; Organizational $15; Supporting $25; Contributing $50; Donor $100; Patron $500; Life $1,000.

Hinton

CAMPBELL FLANNAGAN MURRELL HOUSE, 422 Summer St., Hinton, WV 25951-2221. Mailing Address: P.O. Box 1504, Hinton, WV 25951-1504. Tel.: 304-466-1401.
Key Personnel: Pres., Dwight Emrich
Historic House Museum: built in 1875. Listed on the National Register of Historic Places.
Collections: local history & culture; period furnishings; personal artifacts.
Hours & Admission Prices: Call for hours.

HINTON RAILROAD MUSEUM, 206 Temple St., Hinton, WV 25951-2331. Tel.: 304-466-5420. Fax: 304-466-5420.
Key Personnel: Dir., Dorothy Jean Boley
Railroad Museum.
Collections: C&O Railway history; photographs; tools; books; uniforms.
Facilities: Museum-related items for sale.
Activities: school tours; special events.
Hours & Admission Prices: Summer: Mon.-Sat. 10-4. Winter: Mon.-Sat. 10-2. No charge; donations accepted. ♿

VETERANS MEMORIAL MUSEUM, 419 Ballengee St., Hinton, WV 25951. Mailing Address: P.O. Box 694, Hinton, WV 25951-0694. Tel.: 304-466-4443.
Military History Museum.
Collections: military & war history; uniforms; military vehicles; General MacArthur's footlocker; photographs; personal artifacts.
Hours & Admission Prices: May-Nov. Fri.-Sat. 12-4; other times by appointment.

Huntington

BENJY'S HARLEY-DAVIDSON, 408 4th St., Huntington, WV 25701-1315. Tel.: 304-523-1340. Fax: 304-523-5474.
E-mail: info@benjyshd.com
Motorcycle Museum.
Collections: motorcycles from 1916 to present.
Facilities: diner. Museum-related items for sale.
Activities: tours.
Hours & Admission Prices: Mon.-Thurs. 10-6, Fri. 10-9, Sat. 10-2:30. No charge.

COLLIS P. HUNTINGTON RAILROAD HISTORICAL SOCIETY, INC., 1323 8th Ave., Huntington, WV 25701-2919. Mailing Address: P.O. Box 393, Huntington, WV 25708-0393. Tel.: 866-639-7487; 304-523-0364. Fax: 304-523-0366.
E-mail: newrivertrain@aol.com
Web Site: www.newrivertrain.com
Formerly: Huntington Railroad Museum
Founded: 1959.
Key Personnel: Exec. & Trip Dir., Donald R. Maxwell; Pres., Stephen W. Ferrell; Pres., Walter Cavender; Archivist, Thomas Lambert; Museum Shop Mgr., Karol Cavender.
Personnel Profile: Full-Time Paid 1; Part-Time Paid 1; Part-Time Volunteers 30.
Governing Authority: private; nonprofit organization. Parent Institution: National Railway Historical Society. Indoor: 1323 8th Ave., Huntington, WV 25701. Tax-exempt: 501(c)(3).
Transportation Museum.
Collections: Chesapeake & Ohio 1949 steam locomotive & 1950 caboose; 1960s CSX diesel locomotive cab; 1920s working pump handcar on track; lifesaver caboose; over 600 books on railroads; videos; railroad artifacts.
Facilities: 600-vol. library of railroad books; 250-vol. video & DVD library.
Activities: guided tours; operating Garden G gauge railroad; railroad excursions. Museum Sponsors: Tri-state Railroad Show in March; Model Railroad Show in April; New River Train Excursions in October.
Publications: newsletter, Gondola Gazette.
Hours & Admission Prices: Open on call all year for groups & out of town visitors. No charge; donations accepted.
Attendance: 6,800 (estimated)
Membership: Students $26; Individual $53; Family $62.

GEOLOGY MUSEUM, Marshall University, One John Marshall Dr., Huntington, WV 25755. Mailing Address: Dept. of Geology, 176 Science Bldg., Huntington, WV 25755-0001. Tel.: 304-696-6720. Fax: 304-696-3243.
Founded: 1837.
Key Personnel: Geology Dept., Dr. Ronald L. Martino; Chm., Dr. Dewey D. Sanderson; Geology Dept., Dr. William Niemann; Geology Dept., Dr. Aley El-Shazly.
Governing Authority: university. Parent Institution: Marshall University.
Geology Museum.
Collections: geology; minerals; rocks & fossils.
Activities: guided tours by appointment; permanent exhibitions.
Hours & Admission Prices: Mon.-Fri. 8-4:30. No charge. Closed university holidays. ♿

HERITAGE FARM MUSEUM & VILLAGE, 3350 Harvey Rd., Huntington, WV 25704-9112. Tel.: 304-522-1244. Fax: 304-523-6115.
E-mail: hfmv@comcast.net
Web Site: www.heritagefarmmuseum.com
Founded: 2002.
Congressional District: 3
Key Personnel: Chm. (V), A. Michael Perry; Pres. (V), Henriella Perry
History Museum.
Collections: farm history; personal artifacts; period furnishings; 15 restored buildings; period farm equipment; 1917 Model T; steam engines; 1908 electric truck; 1910 Sears Hi Wheeler.
Facilities: Museum-related items for sale.
Activities: tours; corporate retreats; educational outings; special events; petting zoo parties; weddings; bed & breakfast inns.
Hours & Admission Prices: March-Nov. Mon.-Sat. 10-3. Guided Tours: adults 13-64 $8, senior citizens 65 & over $7, children 3-12 $6; discounts to groups of 15 or more; children 2 & under no charge. Closed holidays. ♿
Attendance: 5,000 (estimated)

* **HUNTINGTON MUSEUM OF ART, INC., (M),** 2033 McCoy Rd., Huntington, WV 25701-4999. Tel.: 304-529-2701. Fax: 304-529-7447.
Web Site: www.hmoa.org
Founded: 1947.
Congressional District: 4
Key Personnel: Pres. Bd. Trustees, Brandon Roisman; Exec. Dir., Margaret Mary Layne; Dir. Finance, Billie Marie Karnes; Dir. Library, Chris Hatten; Sr. Cur., Jenine Culligan; Dir. Education, Katherine Cox; Dir. Public Rels., John Gillispie; Dir. Horticulture, Mike Beck, Ph.D.; Exec. Asst., Judy Clark; Dir. Devel., Carolyn Bagby; Dir. Facilities, Matt Matney; Appeals & Events Admin., Sandra Stone; Museum Shop Mgr., Patsy Lansaw.
Personnel Profile: Full-Time Paid 24; Full-Time Volunteers 3; Part-Time Paid 9; Part-Time Volunteers 600; Interns 3.
Governing Authority: nonprofit organization. Tax-exempt: 501(c)(3).
Art Museum & Conservatory Gardens: includes 50 acres of woodlands & the C. Fred Edwards Conservatory.
Collections: 19th- & 20th-century American & European paintings, drawings, prints & sculpture; Appalachian folk art; American decorative arts & furniture; Ohio River Valley glass; American & European studio glass & art glass; Herman P. Dean firearms; English Georgian silver; Near Eastern decorative arts & furniture; Islamic prayer rugs; pre-Columbian pottery & artifacts; British Portraits; antique firearms; landscape sculpture; children's gallery.
Facilities: 20,000-vol. art research library; 3,000 sq. ft. plant conservatory; reading room; 1 1/2 miles of marked nature trails; 300-seat auditorium; open air stage.
Activities: guided & audio tours; lectures; films; gallery talks; concerts; arts festivals; drama; formally organized education programs for children & adults; docent program or council; inter-museum loan, permanent & temporary exhibitions.
Publications: member's magazine; exhibition catalogues; collection catalogues.
Hours & Admission Prices: Tues. 10-9, Wed.-Sat. 10-5, Sun. 12-5. Special Exhibitions: adults $5; discounts to SEMC & AAM members; members no charge. Closed New Year's Day; Independence Day; Thanksgiving; Christmas. ♿
Attendance: 45,448 (accurate)
Membership: Friend $25-$49; Donor $50-$99; Contributing $100-$249; Sponsor $250-$499; Benefactor $500-$999. Presidents Club: Bronze Door $1,000-$1,499; Silver Door $1,500-$2,499; Emerald Door $2,500-$3,749; Gold Door $3,750-$4,999; Platinum Door $5,000-$9,999; Diamond Door $10,000 & up.

MADIE CARROLL HOUSE, 234 Guyan St., Huntington, WV 25702-1526. Mailing Address: P.O. Box 3266, Huntington, WV 25702-0266. Tel.: 304-736-1655.
E-mail: info@madiecarrollhouse.com
Web Site: www.madiecarrollhouse.org
Key Personnel: Pres., Richard Pettit; Vice Pres., Johnny Nance; Recording Sec., Karen N. Nance; Cur., Dovie Dunn
Historic House Museum: built c.1810.
Collections: period furnishing; personal artifacts.
Activities: special events.
Hours & Admission Prices: By appointment & special events.

MUSEUM OF RADIO & TECHNOLOGY, INC., 1640 Florence Ave., Huntington, WV 25701-4546. Tel.: 304-525-8890.
Web Site: www.mrtwv.org
Founded: 1992.
Key Personnel: Pres. (V) & Registrar, Lloyd E. McIntyre, II; Vice Pres., Randall Brown; Sec. & Treas., Bill Reich; Bd. Member, Dave Bond; Archivist & Museum Shop Mgr., Geoffrey Bourne; Education, Fred Crews; Public Rels., Garry Ritchie; Public Rels., Jack Woodrum.
Personnel Profile: Full-Time Volunteers 2; Part-Time Volunteers 28.
Governing Authority: private; nonprofit organization. Tax-exempt: 501(c)(3).
Technology Museum: housed in c.1931 school building.
Collections: working amateur radio station & communications display; radio & related artifacts; A.C. Gilbert toys; recreation of a 1920s radio store & shop; West Virginia Broadcasters Hall of Fame.
Facilities: library; 250-seat auditorium; classrooms & lab; 250-seat large screen theater; 10,000 sq. ft. exhibit space. Museum-related items for sale.
Activities: docent program; films; formal education programs for adults; guided tours; hobby workshops; lectures; participatory & temporary exhibitions; training programs for professional museum workers; community activities. Annual Events: auctions; banquets.
Publications: bimonthly newsletter, Radio Museum News.
Hours & Admission Prices: Jan.-April call for hours; May-Dec. Fri.-Sat. 10-4, Sun. 1-4. No charge; donations accepted. ♿
Attendance: 5,000 (estimated)
Membership: Institutional $25.

Hurricane

MUSEUM IN THE COMMUNITY, 3 Valley Park Dr., Hurricane, WV 25526-9032. Mailing Address: P.O. Box 423, Hurricane, WV 25526-0423. Tel.: 304-562-0484. Fax: 304-562-9537.
E-mail: info@museuminthecommunity.org
Founded: 1983.
Congressional District: 3
Key Personnel: Exec. Dir., Kelli S. Burns; Pres. (V), John E. Arthur; Treas., John A. Hall; Dir. Administration, Jacqueline Wright; Exhibitions & Program Asst./Teen Bd. Advisor, Gregg Oxley.
Personnel Profile: Full-Time Paid 3; Part-Time Paid 1; Part-Time Volunteers 50.
Governing Authority: nonprofit organization. Tax-exempt.
Art Center.
Collections: paintings; photographs; sculpture.
Research Fields:
Facilities: 7,800 sq. ft. exhibit space; performance space; classroom; kitchen; multi-purpose room; gardens.
Activities: concerts; docent program; films; formal education programs for adults & children; guided tours; hobby workshops; lectures; loan, participatory & traveling exhibitions; theatre performances.
Publications: quarterly newsletter; education packets; exhibit brochures; membership brochure; exhibit invitations.
Hours & Admission Prices: Tues.-Wed. & Fri. 10-5, Thurs.-Sat. 10-7, Sun. 12-4. No charge; donations accepted. Closed New Year's Day; Easter; Memorial Day; Labor Day; Thanksgiving; Christmas. ♿
Attendance: 45,000 (accurate)
Membership: Student & Senior $15; Individual $25; Family $40; Friend $75; Sustaining $150; Patron $250; Benefactor $500. Corporate Level: Bronze $250; Silver $350; Gold $500.

Lewisburg

CARNEGIE HALL MUSEUM, 105 Church St., Lewisburg, WV 24901-1303. Tel.: 304-645-7917. Fax: 304-645-5228.
E-mail: info@carnegiehallwv.com
Web Site: www.carnegiehallwv.com
Key Personnel: Exec. Dir., Susan Adkins; Artistic Dir., Lynn Creamer
Art Museum.
Collections: works by local & regional artists.
Facilities: Museum-related items for sale.
Activities: temporary exhibits.
Hours & Admission Prices: Mon.-Fri. 9-4:30, Sat. 10-1. No charge. ♿

GREENBRIER MILITARY SCHOOL MEMORIAL MUSEUM, 400 N. Lee St., Lewisburg, WV 24901-1128. Mailing Address: P.O. Box 922, Lewisburg, WV 24901-0922. Tel.: 304-645-3247.
Web Site: www.gmsaa.org
Founded: 1982.
Congressional District: 3
Key Personnel: Cur., Mary Essig-Beatty.
Personnel Profile: Part-Time Paid 1; Part-Time Volunteers 1.
Governing Authority: Tax-exempt.
Historical Museum.
Collections: school memorabilia & artifacts from 1812-1972.
Hours & Admission Prices: Mon.-Fri. No charge. Closed holidays. ♿
Attendance: 450 (estimated)

NORTH HOUSE MUSEUM, (M), 301 W. Washington St., Lewisburg, WV 24901-1324. Tel.: 304-645-3398. Fax: 304-645-5201.
E-mail: tammy@greenbrierhistorical.org
Web Site: www.greenbrierhistorical.org
Founded: 1963.
Congressional District: 3
Key Personnel: Pres., John B. Arbuckle, Jr.; C.E.O., Tammy Shifflett; Treas., Jason Ream; Archivist, James Talbert; Museum Shop Mgr., Linda Babcock.
Personnel Profile: Full-Time Paid 1; Part-Time Paid 3; Part-Time Volunteers 30.
Governing Authority: nonprofit organization. Parent Institution: Greenbier Historical Society, Lewisburg, WV 24901. Tax-exempt: 501(c)(3).
Historic Home Museum: built in 1820.
Collections: Civil War & Indian artifacts; textiles; early tools; 18th- & 19th-century antiques; artifacts & vehicles, including Civil War; Greenbrier County artifacts.
Facilities: library storing archival area with genealogy records, books & records.
Activities: guided tours; educational program; group museum tour with tea; group historic homes tour; greenbrier homes tour.
Publications: quarterly, Appalachian Springs; annual journal, Journal of the Greenbier Historical Society.
Hours & Admission Prices: Mon.-Sat. 10-4. Adults $5, seniors $4.50, students $2; archives visit $2; members and children under 6 no charge. Closed New Year's Day; Thanksgiving; Christmas. ♿
Attendance: 5,000 (estimated)
Membership: Junior $10; Adult $20; Business & Family $30; Life $400.

Logan

MUSEUM IN THE PARK, Chief Logan State Park, 376 Little Buffalo Creek Rd., Logan, WV 25601. Tel.: 304-792-7229.
Web Site: www.chiefloganstatepark.com/activities.html
Park Museum.
Collections: local & regional history; photographs; early coal mining & railroad industries; period sewing machine; sewing implements.
Hours & Admission Prices: Wed.-Sat. 10-6, Sun. 1-6.

Lost Creek

WATTERS SMITH MEMORIAL STATE PARK, Duck Creek Rd., Lost Creek, WV 26385. Mailing Address: P.O. Box 296, Lost Creek, WV 26385-0296. Tel.: 304-745-3081. Fax: 304-745-3631.
Web Site: www.watterssmithstatepark.com
Founded: 1964.
Congressional District: 3
Key Personnel: Supt., Larry A. Jones.
Personnel Profile: Full-Time Paid 2; Interns 10.
Governing Authority: state. Owned by WV Dept. of Commerce, Div. of Parks & Recreation, 1800 Washington St., E., Charleston, WV 25305. Tel.: 304-558-2764. Tax-exempt.
Historic House & State Park: located on site of 1876 Watters Smith Farm.
Collections: farm machinery; farm utensils; household tools & utensils; letters; bills; documents; buggies; manuscripts; historic house.
Facilities: visitor center; activity building; hiking trails; picnic area. Gift items for sale.
Activities: permanent exhibitions.
Hours & Admission Prices: Memorial Day-Labor Day daily 11-7. No charge; donations accepted. ♿

Lost River

LOST RIVER MUSEUM, Harper Barn, Rte. 259, Lost River, WV 26810. Mailing Address: P.O. Box 26, Lost River, WV 26810-0026. Tel.: 304-897-7242.
History Museum.
Collections: local history & culture; period furnishings; personal artifacts; early tools; photographs.
Hours & Admission Prices: Call for hours.

Madison

BITUMINOUS COAL HERITAGE FOUNDATION MUSEUM, 347 Main St., Madison, WV 25130-1221. Tel.: 304-369-5180 & 9118. Fax: 304-369-9130.
E-mail: boonedevcorp@yahoo.com

Web Site: wvcoalmuseum.org
Key Personnel: Pres., Joy Underwood; Sec. & Treas., Larry V. Lodato
History Museum.
Collections: southern WV coal fields; miner's tools; photographs; oral histories; company records; state mining history.
Hours & Admission Prices: Mon.-Fri. 12-4.
Membership: Individual $15; Business & Professional $100; Corporate $250.

Marlinton

POCAHONTAS COUNTY MUSEUM, Seneca Trail, Marlinton, WV 24954. Mailing Address: 810 Second Ave., Marlinton, WV 24954-1091. Tel.: 304-799-4369. Fax: 304-799-6466.
Founded: 1962.
Congressional District: 3
Key Personnel: Pres. (V), Mary Lou Dilley; Librarian & Historian, William P. McNeel; Museum Shop Mgr., Jane P. Sharp.
Personnel Profile: Part-Time Paid 1; Part-Time Volunteers 5.
Governing Authority: nonprofit organization. Affiliated with Pocahontas County Historical Society, Inc.
Local History & Historical Society Museum: housed in the Frank & Anna Hunter Home.
Collections: history of Pocahontas County & surrounding area from the time of the Indians to present; historic photo collection; archives. Historic House: 1840s log cabin.
Research Fields: Pocahontas County History.
Facilities: 1,000-vol. local history library; reading rooms. West Virginia local crafts & books by West Virginian authors for sale.
Activities: school tours; meetings with programs on local history; art exhibits.
Publications: annual newsletter to members.
Hours & Admission Prices: Memorial Day-Labor Day Mon.-Sat. & holidays 11-5, Sun. 1-5. Adults $2, students 12-17 $1; discounts to groups; members & children under 12 no charge.
Attendance: 741 (accurate)
Membership: Regular $5; Sustaining $10.

Martinsburg

THE ARTS CENTRE, INC., 300 W. King St., Martinsburg, WV 25401-3202. Tel.: 304-263-0224. Fax: 304-263-0857.
Web Site: www.theartcentre.org
Key Personnel: Pres., Mary Lewis; Prog. Coord., Justis Saradji
Art Museum.
Collections: works by local artists & craftsmen.
Activities: lectures; demonstrations; art classes.
Hours & Admission Prices: Call for hours.

BERKELEY COUNTY HISTORICAL SOCIETY, 126 E. Race St., Martinsburg, WV 25401-4310. Tel.: 304-267-4713.
Historical Society Museum.
Collections: local history & culture; photographs; period furnishings.
Activities: research.
Hours & Admission Prices: Call for hours.

GENERAL ADAM STEPHEN HOUSE, 309 E. John St., Martinsburg, WV 25402. Mailing Address: General Adam Stephen Memorial Association, P.O. Box 1496, Martinsburg, WV 25402-1496. Tel.: 304-267-4434.
Web Site: www.orgsites.com/wv/adam-stephen
Founded: 1959.
Congressional District: 2
Key Personnel: Pres. (V), Martin Keesecker; Cur., Keith E. Hammersla.
Personnel Profile: Part-Time Paid 1; Part-Time Volunteers 12.
Governing Authority: municipal. Tax-exempt: 501(c)(3).
Historic House: 1772-1789 Gen. Adam Stephen House.
Collections: period furniture.
Research Fields: Major Gen. Adam Stephen.
Facilities: library of letters, documents, pictures & maps available for use by appointment.
Activities: guided tours; lectures; temporary exhibitions.
Publications: booklets, General Adam Stephen, Founder; The Adam Stephen Memorial Project; single sheet, General Adam Stephen & His Home.
Hours & Admission Prices: May-Oct. Sat.-Sun. 2-5; other times by appointment. No charge; donations accepted. ♿
Attendance: 2,500 (estimated)
Membership: Individual $3.

Mathias

LOST RIVER STATE PARK, 321 Park Dr., Mathias, WV 26812-8088. Tel.: 304-897-5372. Fax: 304-897-5325.
E-mail: lostriver@wvdnr.gov
Web Site: www.lostriversp.com
Founded: 1968.
Congressional District: 2
Key Personnel: Park Supt., Dorenda Taylor; Asst. Supt., Mike Foster.
Governing Authority: state. Affiliated with West Virginia Dept. of Commerce, Div. of Parks & Recreation, 1800 Washington St. E., Charleston, WV 25305. Tel.: 304-348-2764.
Park Museum & Historic House: housed in 1800 Lee Cabin Museum, summer home of Henry (Light-Horse Harry) Lee, Revolutionary War general & father of Robert E. Lee.
Collections: old documents; clothing; tools.
Facilities: hiking trails; swimming pool; riding stables; game courts; recreational buildings; picnic area; lodgings; restaurant. Gift items for sale.
Activities: guided tours. Park Sponsors: Heritage Weekend in September.
Hours & Admission Prices: Memorial Day-Labor Day Sat. 10-4, Sun.12-6. Office: Mon.-Fri. 8-4, Sat.-Sun. 10-3; other times by appointment. No charge.

Middlebourne

TYLER COUNTY HERITAGE & HISTORICAL SOCIETY, Dodd St., Middlebourne, WV 26149. Mailing Address: P.O. Box 317, Middlebourne, WV 26149-0317. Tel.: 304-758-2100 & 4288.
E-mail: tchandhs@verizon.net
Founded: 1994.
Key Personnel: Pres. (V), Ruth Moore.
Governing Authority: Tax-exempt.
Historic Building: housed in the former Tyler County High School; built in 1908.
Collections: Tyler County heritage; personal artifacts; documents; tools; military; genealogical books.
Facilities: Museum-related items for sale.
Publications: Heritage Windows; History of Tyler County Vol. 1 & 2; birth records; death records; marriage records; census records.
Hours & Admission Prices: May-Oct. Sun., Tues. & Thurs. 1-4; tours by appointment. No charge; donations accepted. ♿
Membership: Individual $10; Life $150.

Mineral Wells

NEW ERA ONE-ROOM SCHOOL - LIVING HERITAGE MUSEUM, 1838 Elizabeth Pike, Mineral Wells, WV 26150. Mailing Address: P.O. Box 340, Mineral Wells, WV 26150-0340. Tel.: 304-863-3583.
E-mail: lcarroll@access.k12.wv.us
Web Site: www.neweraoneroomschool.com
Governing Authority: Tax-exempt.
History Museum: housed in one-room school built in 1884.
Collections: period furnishings; pot-bellied stove; desks; photographs.
Activities: school tours.
Hours & Admission Prices: May-Oct. Tues. 1-3; other times by appointment.

Morgantown

COOK-HAYMAN PHARMACY MUSEUM, 1132 Health Sciences North, 1st Fl., Morgantown, WV 26506. Mailing Address: P.O. Box 9500, Morgantown, WV 26506-9500. Tel.: 304-293-7806.
Pharmacy Museum.
Collections: pharmacy history; pharmacists' period equipment; medicines; books.
Hours & Admission Prices: By appointment. ♿

CORE ARBORETUM, Monongahela Blvd., Rte. 7, WVU Evansdale Campus, Morgantown, WV 26506. Mailing Address: Dept. of Bio., P.O. Box 6057, Morgantown, WV 26506-6057. Tel.: 304-293-5201, ext. 31547. Fax: 304-293-6363.
E-mail: jweems@wvu.edu
Web Site: www.wvu.edu/biology/facility/arboretum.html
Founded: 1948.
Congressional District: 2
Key Personnel: Arboretum Specialist, Jonathan Weems.
Personnel Profile: Full-Time Paid 1; Part-Time Volunteers 3.
Governing Authority: state. Parent Institution: West Virginia Dept. of Biology. Tax-exempt: 501(c)(3).
Arboretum & Botanical Gardens.
Collections: botany.
Research Fields: botany; dendrology; plant ecology; population biology; native flora & ecosystems.

Facilities: 91-acres; 3.5 miles of woodland trails; woody plants labeled; interpretive signs; small amphitheater.
Activities: lectures; guided tours by appointment; special wildflower tours in April; birdwalks in April & May.
Publications: brochures available on site; checklist of birds.
Hours & Admission Prices: Daily dawn-dusk. No charge; donations accepted.
Attendance: 30,000 (estimated)

MONONGALIA ARTS CENTER, 107 High St., Morgantown, WV 26505-5412. Mailing Address: P.O. Box 239, Morgantown, WV 26507-0239. Tel.: 304-292-3325. Fax: 304-292-3326.
E-mail: info@monartscenter.com
Web Site: www.monartscenter.com
Founded: 1976.
Key Personnel: Exec. Dir., Ro Brooks; Museum Lobby Mgr., Danny Gibbons.
Personnel Profile: Full-Time Paid 2; Full-Time Volunteers 1; Part-Time Paid 2; Part-Time Volunteers 50.
Governing Authority: Tax-exempt.
Arts & Culture Center.
Collections: paintings.
Facilities: theater; 2 galleries.
Activities: classes; community theater; art outreach.
Hours & Admission Prices: Mon.-Fri. 11-7, Sat. 11-4, Sun. by appointment. Closed major holidays. ♿
Membership: Student & Senior $20; Individual $30; Family $50; Friend $75; Sustaining $100; Patron $250; Corporate $250 & up; Angel $500; Benefactor $1,000 & up.

MORGANTOWN HISTORY MUSEUM, 145 Clay St., Morgantown, WV 26501. Tel.: 304-319-1800.
E-mail: morgantownmuseum@yahoo.com
Web Site: www.morgantownhistorymuseum.org
Founded: 2005.
Congressional District: 1
Key Personnel: Chm. (V), Pamela A. Ball.
Personnel Profile: Part-Time Paid 1; Part-Time Volunteers 12.
Governing Authority: municipal.
History Museum.
Collections: local history, culture & industry; paintings; photographs; tools; glass.
Major Exhibits: Monongahela River Exhibit, 4/10-5/10; Morgantown Ethnic Diversity and Neighborhoods, 6/10-7/10; Sterling Faucet Exhibit, 6/10-7/10; Mason-Dixon Exhibit, 9/10-10/10.
Research Fields: history of Sterling Faucet Company & glass companies; development of Morgantown and Monongahela County.
Facilities: 2,400 sq. ft. exhibit space.
Activities: guided tours; films; formal education programs for adults & children; lectures.
Publications: biannual newsletter, Museum News.
Hours & Admission Prices: Tues.-Sat. 10-4. No charge; donations accepted. Closed New Year's Day; Memorial Day; Independence Day; Veterans Day; Thanksgiving; Christmas.
Attendance: 1,000

ROYCE J. & CAROLINE B. WATTS MUSEUM, 377 Mineral Resources Bldg., Morgantown, WV 26506-6070. Mailing Address: West Virginia University, Box 6070, Morgantown, WV 26506-6070. Tel.: 304-293-5695, ext. 2102. Fax: 304-293-5708.
Web Site: www.cemr.wvu.edu
Formerly: Comer Museum
Founded: 1990.
Congressional District: 2
Key Personnel: Dir., Royce J. Watts.
Personnel Profile: Full-Time Paid 1; Part-Time Paid 1.
Governing Authority: public college; nonprofit. Parent Institution: West Virginia University. Tax-exempt: 501(c)(3).
Mining Museum.
Collections: concentration on West Virginia with special emphasis on the coal, oil & natural gas industries & the social, technological & historical aspects of these industries.
Research Fields: history & development of coal miner's safety hat; history of mine lighting.
Facilities: classrooms; labs; amphitheater; 500 sq. ft. exhibit space; 300-seat auditorium.
Activities: guided tours; formal education programs for children; loan, temporary & traveling exhibits. Annual Events: Coal Mining Cultural Heritage Day.
Hours & Admission Prices: Tues.-Fri. call for hours; other times by appointment. No charge. Closed Martin Luther King Jr. Day; spring break; Easter; Labor Day; Thanksgiving; Christmas break. ♿
Attendance: 2,000 (estimated)

WEST VIRGINIA UNIVERSITY-MESAROS GALLERIES, Creative Arts Center, Evansdale Campus, West Virginia University, Douglas O. Blaney Lobby, Morgantown, WV 26506-6111. Mailing Address: P.O. Box 6111, Div. of Art, Morgantown, WV 26506-6111. Tel.: 304-293-4841, ext. 3210. Fax: 304-293-5731.
E-mail: bob.bridges@mail.wvu.edu
Web Site: artanddesign.wvu.edu/mesaros_galleries
Founded: 1968.
Congressional District: 1
Key Personnel: Dean & Dir., Bernard Schultz; Chm., Paul Krainik; Cur., Robert Bridges.
Personnel Profile: Full-Time Paid 1; Part-Time Paid 12.
Governing Authority: public university. Parent Institution: West Virginia University. Tax-exempt.
College Art Gallery.
Collections: paintings; photographs; sculpture.
Facilities: classrooms; studios; 200-seat auditorium; 2,200 sq. ft. exhibit space.
Activities: guided tours; lectures; formal education programs for undergraduate & graduate students in Art History & Studio Art. Annual Event: Visiting Artists Lecture Series.
Hours & Admission Prices: Mon.-Sat. 12-9:30. No charge. Closed university holidays. ♿
Attendance: 20,000 (accurate)

Moundsville

FOSTORIA GLASS MUSEUM, 511 Tomlinson Ave., Moundsville, WV 26041. Mailing Address: P.O. Box 826, Moundsville, WV 26041-0826. Tel.: 304-845-9188. Fax: 304-845-9188.
E-mail: fostoriaglassmuseum@verizon.net
Web Site: www.fostoriaglass.org
Founded: 1991.
Key Personnel: Dir. & Pres. (V), Jim Davis; Chm. & Museum Shop Mgr., Ralph C. Clark.
Personnel Profile: Part-Time Paid 1; Part-Time Volunteers 1.
Governing Authority: Parent Institution: Fostoria Glass Society of America.
Glass Museum.
Collections: Fostoria glass; history of glass making.
Hours & Admission Prices: March-Nov. Wed.-Sat. 1-4. Closed holidays. ♿
Attendance: 1,000 (estimated)
Membership: Individual $25.

GRAVE CREEK MOUND ARCHAEOLOGICAL COMPLEX, 801 Jefferson Ave., Moundsville, WV 26041-2241. Mailing Address: P.O. Box 527, Moundsville, WV 26041-0527. Tel.: 304-843-4128. Fax: 304-843-4131.
E-mail: grave.creek@wvculture.org
Web Site: www.wvculture.org
Formerly: Grave Creek Mound Historic Site
Founded: 1978.
Congressional District: 1
Key Personnel: Mgr., David E. Rotenizer.
Personnel Profile: Full-Time Paid 7; Part-Time Volunteers 3.
Governing Authority: Parent Institution: West Virginia Div. of Culture & History. Tax-exempt.
Adena Culture Mound, Interpretive Museum, & State Cultural Facility.
Collections: West Virginia archaeology. Historic Site: 250-150 B.C. Mammoth Grave Creek Mound.
Facilities: 150-seat auditorium; 7 acre grounds; activity room.
Activities: permanent exhibitions; monthly art exhibits; cultural events; educational & other related programs. Annual Events: Archaeology Month Promotion; Student Art Show.
Hours & Admission Prices: Museum: Mon.-Sat. 9-5, Sun. 12-5. Mound & Gift Shop: Mon.-Sat. 9-4:30, Sun. 12-4:30. No charge; donations accepted. Closed holidays. ♿
Attendance: 30,000 (accurate)

THE OFFICIAL MARX TOY MUSEUM, 915 2nd St., Moundsville, WV 26041-1422. Tel.: 304-845-6022.
Web Site: www.marxtoymuseum.com
Founded: 2001.
Key Personnel: Owner, Francis Turner.
Personnel Profile: Part-Time Paid 2.
Toy Museum.
Collections: history of Marx toys; toys from 1920s to 1980s.
Facilities: Museum-related items for sale.

Activities: special events.
Hours & Admission Prices: April-Dec. Tues.-Sat. 11-5; other times by appointment. Adults $8.50, seniors $7.50, students $5; discounts to groups; children under 6 no charge.

WEST VIRGINIA PENITENTIARY, 818 Jefferson Ave., Moundsville, WV 26041-2235. Tel.: 304-845-6200. Fax: 304-843-4146.
E-mail: pat@wvpentours.com
Web Site: www.wvpentours.com
Key Personnel: Pres. (V), Sid Grisell; Dir., Paul Kirby; Museum Shop Mgr., Tom Stiles.
Governing Authority: Tax-exempt: 501(c)(3).
Penitentiary Museum.
Collections: penitentiary history; Justice System; Deathhouse.
Facilities: Museum-related items for sale.
Activities: guided tours; night tours. Museum Sponsors: Elizabethtown Festival in May; Ghost Hunts; Dungeon of Horrors.
Hours & Admission Prices: April-Nov. Tues.-Sun. 11-4. Closed holidays.
Attendance: 30,000 (accurate)

Mullens

TWIN FALLS STATE PARK & MUSEUM, Hwy. Rt. 97, Mullens, WV 25882. Mailing Address: P.O. Box 667, Mullens, WV 25882-0667. Tel.: 304-294-4000. Fax: 304-294-5000.
E-mail: twinfallsinfo@wvstateparks.com
Web Site: www.twinfallsresort.com
Founded: 1976.
Key Personnel: Supt., A. Scott Durham.
Governing Authority: society. Affiliated with the Wyoming County Women's Club, Box 706, Pineville, WV. 24874. Tax-exempt.
State Park & Historic House: 1920 Old Severt Home, now housing Wyoming County Museum.
Collections: furniture; household items; tools; books; clothing & artifacts of a local & general historical interest.
Activities: guided tours.
Publications: brochure.
Hours & Admission Prices: Memorial Day-Labor Day daily 10-6. No charge; donations accepted.

New Cumberland

HANCOCK COUNTY HISTORICAL MUSEUM, 1008 Ridge Ave., New Cumberland, WV 26047-9501. Mailing Address: P.O. Box 672, New Cumberland, WV 26047-0672. Tel.: 304-387-0354 & 564-4800. Fax: 304-387-1427.
E-mail: kellerjfonf@hotmail.com
Key Personnel: Exec. Dir., Janet Keller
Historic House Museum: housed in the Victorian home of Oliver Sheridan Marshall, past president of the WV State Senate; built in 1887.
Collections: period furnishings; personal artifacts.
Activities: rental facilities; tours.
Hours & Admission Prices: Sun. 12:30-4; other times by appointment. No charge; donations accepted.

Nitro

NITRO WORLD WAR I BOOMTOWN MUSEUM, 302 21st St., Nitro, WV 25143-1738. Mailing Address: P.O. Box 308, Nitro, WV 25143-0308. Tel.: 304-759-0200.
E-mail: nitrowarmuseum@yahoo.com
Web Site: nitrowarmuseum.com
Military Museum.
Collections: military memorabilia; Nitro bungalow living room replica; historical artifacts.
Hours & Admission Prices: Fri. 10-4, Sat. 9-12.

Parkersburg

THE BLENNERHASSETT MUSEUM OF REGIONAL HISTORY, 137 Juliana St., Parkersburg, WV 26101-5331. Tel.: 304-420-4800.
Web Site: www.blennerhassettislandstatepark.com/museum.html
Founded: 1983.
History Museum.
Collections: period Indian tools; jewelry; weapons; household items; oil paintings; early clothing; guns; military artifacts; furniture; farm implements.
Hours & Admission Prices: Call for hours. ♿

OIL & GAS MUSEUM, 119 Third St., Parkersburg, WV 26101-5310. Mailing Address: P.O. Box 1685, Parkersburg, WV 26102-1685. Tel.: 304-485-5446 & 428-8015.
Web Site: oilandgasmuseum.com
Founded: 1989.
Key Personnel: Dir., David L. McKain.
Governing Authority: Parent Institution: Oil, Gas & Industrial History Assoc. Tax-exempt.
History Museum.
Collections: oil & gas industry; general industry; Civil War; West Virginia & Parkersburg history; gas engine history; photographs; furniture; military history & artifacts; industrial artifacts; videos.
Facilities: visitors center.
Publications: newsletter.
Hours & Admission Prices: Mon.-Fri. 11-4, Sat. 11-5, Sun. 12-5. Adults $3, children $1.
Attendance: 4,000 (estimated)
Membership: Annual $15.

PARKERSBURG ART CENTER, 725 Market St., Parkersburg, WV 26101-4628. Tel.: 304-485-3859. Fax: 304-485-3850.
E-mail: info@parkersburgartcenter.org
Web Site: parkersburgartcenter.org
Formerly: The Cultural Center of Fine Arts
Founded: 1938.
Congressional District: 1
Key Personnel: Exec. Dir., Abby Hayhurst; Pres. Bd. (V), Sam Winans; Chm. (V), Kelley Cartwright; Dir. Education & Membership, Marcia Ritchie; Museum Shop Mgr., Carol Bidstrup.
Personnel Profile: Full-Time Paid 4; Part-Time Paid 2; Part-Time Volunteers 30; Interns 1.
Governing Authority: private; nonprofit organization. Tax-exempt: 501(c)(3).
Arts Center.
Collections: rotating exhibits; all style of work both 2-3 dimensional; American Realism collection; traveling exhibits.
Facilities: library of books and magazines pertaining to art; reading room; classrooms; video library-artists, art history. Paintings & crafts by local artists for sale.
Activities: guided tours; lectures; films; gallery talks; art festivals; hobby workshops; formally organized education programs for children and adults; inter-museum & temporary exhibitions; school loan service; photography & print, painting & drawing competitions.
Publications: monthly newsletter; exhibition catalogs & brochures.
Hours & Admission Prices: Wed.-Sat. 10-5, Sun. 1-5; groups by appointment. Donations: adults $2; discounts for AAM members; members no charge. Closed national holidays. ♿
Attendance: 18,000 (estimated)
Membership: Senior Citizen & Student $35; Individual $60; Family $75; Sustaining $150; Patron $1,000; Corporate $1,500; Benefactor $2,500; Life $10,000.

SUMNERITE AFRICAN AMERICAN HISTORY MUSEUM, 1016 Avery St., Parkersburg, WV 26101-4727. Mailing Address: P.O. Box 4426, Parkersburg, WV 26104-4426. Tel.: 304-485-1152 & 422-0985.
African American History Museum.
Collections: African American history & culture; photographs; art; period artifacts.
Hours & Admission Prices: By appointment.

VETERANS MUSEUM OF MID-OHIO VALLEY, 1829 7th St., Parkersburg, WV 26101-4250. Tel.: 304-420-0332 & 0337.
E-mail: veteransmuseum@hotmail.com
Web Site: veteransmuseumofmidohiovalley.com
Founded: 2002.
Key Personnel: Dir., Gary Farris; Pres. (V), Darrell Nutter.
Personnel Profile: Full-Time Paid 1; Part-Time Paid 1; Part-Time Volunteers 3.
Governing Authority: board of directors.
Veterans Museum.
Collections: military history; veterans' memorabilia; personal artifacts.
Facilities: library. Museum -related items for sale.
Activities: school tours; docent program; reunion headquarters; model building classes; medal replacement program for veterans.
Publications: monthly newsletter.
Hours & Admission Prices: Mon.-Sat. 9-5, Sun. by appointment. Suggested Donation: adults $5, children $3; school groups & members no charge. Closed New Year's Day; Christmas. ♿
Attendance: 350 (accurate)
Membership: Annual $20; Lifetime $150.

Pence Springs

GRAHAM HOUSE, Rte 3 & 12 at Lowell, Pence Springs, WV 24962. Mailing Address: P.O. Box 218, Pence Springs, WV 24962-0218. Tel.: 304-466-3321 & 716-6430.
E-mail: jbowling@wildblue.com
Governing Authority: Parent Institution: Graham House Preservation Society.
Historic House Museum: housed in the 2 story log home of Colonel James Graham; built in 1770.
Collections: period furnishings; personal artifacts.
Facilities: Museum-related items for sale.
Activities: school tours; special events. Museum Sponsors: Heritage Craft Festival in October.
Hours & Admission Prices: Memorial Day to Labor Day Fri.-Sat. 11-5, Sun. 1-5; Sept.-May Sat. 11-5, Sun. 1-5. Adults $2, children $.50. ♿

Pennsboro

OLD STONE HOUSE MUSEUM, 310 Myles Ave., Pennsboro, WV 26415-1329. Tel.: 304-643-2738.
Key Personnel: Pres., David Scott.
Governing Authority: Parent Institution: Ritchie County Historical Society.
Historic House Museum: built c.1810. Listed on the National Register of Historic Places.
Collections: local history & culture; photographs; personal artifacts; period furnishings.
Facilities: genealogy library.
Hours & Admission Prices: By appointment.

Petersburg

TOP KICK'S MILITARY MUSEUM, Rte. 55, Petersburg, WV 26847. Mailing Address: P.O. Box 152, Petersburg, WV 26847-0152. Tel.: 304-257-1392.
Military Museum.
Collections: military history, vehicles, equipment, & uniforms; photographs; personal artifacts.
Hours & Admission Prices: Mon.-Sat. 9 am to dusk, Sun. 12 to dusk. Donation requested.

Philippi

ADALAND MANSION AND HISTORIC BARN, Rte. 3 Berryburg, Philippi, WV 26416. Mailing Address: P.O. Box 74, Philippi, WV 26416-0074. Tel.: 304-457-1587 & 2415. Fax: 304-457-2703.
Web Site: adaland.org
Founded: 1999.
Congressional District: 1
Key Personnel: Chm. (V) & Museum Shop Mgr., Ann Serafin; Pres. (V), Okey F. Gallien, Jr.
Personnel Profile: Full-Time Paid 1; Full-Time Volunteers 2; Part-Time Paid 4; Part-Time Volunteers 3.
Governing Authority: Tax-exempt.
Historic House Museum: housed in the former home of an early county sheriff & bank president. Listed on the National Register of Historic Places.
Collections: period furnishings; personal artifacts; photographs; law office; tools; equipment. Historic Building: 1850 barn.
Activities: demonstrations; special events; school tours.
Hours & Admission Prices: Call for hours. Adults $10; discounts to AAA, AAM & ICOM members. ♿
Attendance: 5,000 (accurate)

BARBOUR COUNTY HISTORICAL SOCIETY MUSEUM, 200 N. Main St., Philippi, WV 26416-1100. Tel.: 304-457-4846 & 3349 (Toll Free).
Founded: 1985.
Governing Authority: bd. of directors. Tax-exempt.
Historical Society Museum: housed in a renovated railway station.
Collections: Barbour County history & culture; Civil War memorabilia; Philippi covered bridges; Philippi mummies; J.W. Myers dynasty; B&O railroad.
Research Fields: genealogy; Civil War history.
Hours & Admission Prices: May-Oct. Mon.-Sat. 11-4, Sun. 1-4; other times by appointment.
Attendance: 4,000 (accurate)
Membership: Annual $5; Lifetime $50.

ONE ROOM CAMPBELL SCHOOL, Alderson Broaddus College, Philippi, WV 26416. Mailing Address: P.O. Box 2125, Philippi, WV 26416-6125. Tel.: 304-457-5180. Fax: 304-457-6239.
Historic Building: c.1865.
Collections: local history & culture; period furnishings; early 20th century learning materials.
Hours & Admission Prices: Call for hours.

Point Pleasant

POINT PLEASANT RIVER MUSEUM, 28 Main St., Point Pleasant, WV 25550-1026. Mailing Address: P.O. Box 412, Point Pleasant, WV 25550-0412. Tel.: 304-674-0144.
E-mail: museum@pprivermuseum.com
Web Site: www.pprivermuseum.com/
Key Personnel: Dir., Jack Fowler; Pres., Don Waldie
History Museum.
Collections: local history & culture; period furnishings; personal artifacts; photographs.
Hours & Admission Prices: Tues.-Fri. 10-3, Sat. 11-4, Sun. 1-5. Adults $4, children $1; Life members no charge.

TU-ENDIE-WEI STATE PARK, 1 Main St., Point Pleasant, WV 25550-1025. Mailing Address: P.O. Box 486, Point Pleasant, WV 25550-0486. Tel.: 304-675-0869. Fax: 304-674-6162.
Web Site: www.tu-endie-weistatepark.com
Formerly: Point Pleasant Battle Monument State Park
Founded: 1901.
Congressional District: 3
Key Personnel: Park Supt., Doug Wiant.
Personnel Profile: Full-Time Paid 1; Part-Time Paid 5.
Governing Authority: state. Owned by the state of West Virginia; operated by Dept. of Commerce with collections belonging to the D.A.R. Chapter from Point Pleasant Area. Tax-exempt.
Historic House & Site: 1796, The Mansion House, built by Walter Newman, first hand-hewn log house built in Kanawha Valley, where the first battle of the Revolution was fought.
Collections: heirlooms, relics; large square piano; authentic four poster beds; monument commemorating the first battle of the Revolutionary War; Chief Cornstalk.
Activities: guided tours.
Hours & Admission Prices: May-Oct. Mon.-Sat. 10-4:30, Sun. 1-4:30; tour groups by appointment. No charge; donations accepted. ♿
Attendance: 40,000

WEST VIRGINIA STATE FARM MUSEUM, 1458 Fairground Rd., Point Pleasant, WV 25550-3421. Tel.: 304-675-5737. Fax: 304-675-5430.
E-mail: wvsfm@wvfarmmuseum.org
Web Site: www.wvfarmmuseum.org
Founded: 1974.
Key Personnel: Acting Dir., Lloyd Akers; Financial Dir. & Treas., Dennis Brumfield.
Personnel Profile: Full-Time Paid 2; Part-Time Paid 2; Part-Time Volunteers 40.
Governing Authority: private; nonprofit organization. Tax-exempt.
Agriculture Museum & Historic Village: over 31 buildings; largest historical farm museum east of the Mississippi River.
Collections: houses & buildings built in early 1800s; period artifacts; period tractor & steam engines.
Facilities: restaurant. Local arts & crafts and museum-related items for sale.
Activities: guided tours; docent program; formal education programs for children & adults; festivals. Annual Events: Steam & Gas Engine Show in May; Country Fall Festival in October; Christmas Light Show in December.
Hours & Admission Prices: April-Nov. 15 Tues.-Sat. 9-5, Sun. 1-5. No charge; donations accepted. Closed major holidays. ♿
Attendance: 100,000 (accurate)
Membership: Annual $2; Lifetime $25.

Princeton

PRINCETON RAILROAD MUSEUM, 99 Mercer St., Princeton, WV 24740. Tel.: 304-487-5060.
Railroad Museum.
Collections: railroading history; railroad art & artifacts; photographs; over 100 lanterns.
Hours & Admission Prices: May-Aug. Tues.-Sat. 1-5, Sun. 2-5; Sept.-April Fri.-Sat. 10-2, Sun. 2-5. Adults $5, children 10 & under $2; children 3 & under no charge.

THOSE WHO SERVED WAR MUSEUM, 1500 W. Main St., Princeton, WV 24740-2627. Tel.: 304-487-3670.
Key Personnel: Pres., Tony Whitlow; Sec. & Treas., Bill Blankenship
Military History Museum.
Collections: military history & artifacts; photographs; uniforms; Civil War;

Revolutionary War; WWI & WWII; Korean War; Vietnam; Desert Storm; Spanish-American War.
Hours & Admission Prices: Mon.-Fri. 10-4. No charge; donations accepted.

Ravenswood

WASHINGTON'S LANDS MUSEUM & SAYRE LOG HOUSE, Old Lock Bldg. #22, Riverfront Park, Ravenswood, WV 26164. Mailing Address: Jackson County Historical Society, Box 22, Ripley, WV 25271. Tel.: 304-273-2621 & 372-5343.
Founded: 1970.
Congressional District: 3
Key Personnel: Pres., Jackson County Historical Society, Bill Mullins; Sec., Jackson County Historical Society, Maxine Landfried.
Personnel Profile: Part-Time Paid 2; Part-Time Volunteers 10.
Governing Authority: society. Parent Institution: Jackson County Historical Society. Tax-exempt.
Historical Society Museum: located on site of Ravenswood Land, once owned by George Washington.
Collections: local tools; clothing; old photos; Indian artifacts. Historic Building: 1870 house.
Facilities: Society publications & gift items for sale.
Activities: guided tours; permanent exhibitions.
Hours & Admission Prices: May-Oct. Sat.-Sun. 1-5. No charge; donations accepted.
Attendance: 2,393 (accurate)

Rowlesburg

ROWLESBURG AREA HISTORICAL SOCIETY, Buffalo St., Rowlesburg, WV 26425. Mailing Address: P.O. Box 605, Rowlesburg, WV 26425-0605. Tel.: 304-454-9303.
Historical Society Museum.
Collections: local history & culture; photographs; personal artifacts; tools.
Hours & Admission Prices: By appointment. No charge.

Saint Albans

C & O DEPOT MUSEUM, 406 Fourth Ave., Saint Albans, WV 25177. Mailing Address: 69 Central Ave., Saint Albans, WV 25177-2411. Tel.: 304-727-4439.
Railroad Depot Museum: housed in the Chesapeake & Ohio Railroad Depot.
Collections: railroad history & artifacts; photographs.
Facilities: Museum-related items for sale.
Hours & Admission Prices: By appointment only.

MORGAN'S KITCHEN PLANTATION MUSEUM, Rte. 60 MacCorkle Ave., Saint Albans, WV 25177. Mailing Address: 404 4th Ave., Saint Albans, WV 25177-2829. Tel.: 304-727-2654.
Founded: 1972.
Key Personnel: Pres. (V), Bill Dean
Plantation Museum: built in 1846.
Collections: kitchen artifacts; utensils; period artifacts.
Activities: school tours.
Hours & Admission Prices: Memorial Day to Labor Day Sun. 2-4; other times by appointment. No charge.
Membership: Individual $7; Family $10.

Scarbro

WHIPPLE COMPANY STORE & APPALACHIAN HERITAGE EDUCATIONAL MUSEUM, 7485 Okey L. Patterson Rd., Scarbro, WV 25917. Mailing Address: P.O. Box 150, Scarbro, WV 25917-0150. Tel.: 304-465-0331.
E-mail: whipple@whipplecompanystore.com
Web Site: www.whipplecompanystore.com
Company History Museum.
Collections: artifacts & memorabilia pertaining to the West Virginia Coal Mining family.
Hours & Admission Prices: May-Oct. Wed.-Mon. 11-6. Tours: adults $6; children 4 & under no charge.

Shepherdstown

HISTORIC SHEPHERDSTOWN MUSEUM, (M), 129 E. German St., Shepherdstown, WV 25443. Mailing Address: P.O. Box 1786, Sheperdstown, WV 25443-1786. Tel.: 304-876-0910. Fax: 304-876-0910.
E-mail: hsc86@citlink.net
Web Site: www.historicshepherdstown.com
Founded: 1983.
Congressional District: 2
Key Personnel: Pres., John Griffith; Museum Shop Mgr., Cynthia C. Schott.
Personnel Profile: Full-Time Paid 1; Part-Time Volunteers 2; Interns 1.
Governing Authority: private; nonprofit organization. Parent Institution: Historic Shepherdstown Commission. Tax-exempt.
Historic Building: housed in the 1786 Entler Hotel.
Collections: concentration on West Virginia-Jefferson County history with emphasis on town of Shepherdstown; model of Rumsey steam boat.
Publications: Shepherdstown Vol. I, II, & III; Walking Tour of Shepherdstown.
Hours & Admission Prices: April-Oct. Sat. 11-5, Sun. 1-4. No charge; donations accepted.
Attendance: 2,200 (accurate)
Membership: Individual & Family $25-$49; Sustaining $50-$99; Sponsor $100-$249; Patron $250-$499; Benefactor $500-$999; Preservation $1,000 & up.

Shinnston

BICE-FERGUSON MEMORIAL MUSEUM, 400 Pike St., Shinnston, WV 26431-1406. Mailing Address: 40 Main St., Shinnston, WV 26431-1199. Tel.: 304-592-1942. Fax: 304-592-1597.
Web Site: shinnstonwv.com
Founded: 2006.
Congressional District: 1
Key Personnel: Dir., Maxine Weser.
Personnel Profile: Part-Time Paid 1.
History Museum.
Collections: telephones; telephone memorabilia from 1890-1960; period furnishings.
Activities: history programming.
Hours & Admission Prices: April-Dec. Fri.-Sun. 2-6. No charge; donations accepted. Closed holidays. ♿
Attendance: 500 (accurate)
Membership: Individual $15; Family $30.

South Charleston

SOUTH CHARLESTON MUSEUM, 311 D St., South Charleston, WV 25303-3105. Mailing Address: 311 D St., South Charleston, WV 25303-3105. Tel.: 304-744-9711. Fax: 304-720-3769.
E-mail: SCMuseum@yahoo.com
Founded: 1989.
Congressional District: 2
Key Personnel: Chm. (V), Lura Watkins; Sec., Peggy Thompson; Treas., Bill Breese; Asst. Treas., Phyllis Wehrmana.
Personnel Profile: Part-Time Paid 1; Part-Time Volunteers 10.
Governing Authority: private; nonprofit organization. Parent Institution: South Charleston Museum Foundation. Tax-exempt: 501(c)(3).
History Museum.
Collections: history of Kanawha Valley, South Charleston Mound, historic Midland Trail; films on West Virginia; Belgian glass artifacts.
Research Fields: Native American heritage in South Charleston & the surrounding area; Belgian heritage in South Charleston & West Virginia.
Facilities: research archives; 300-seat theater; 400 sq. ft. exhibit space.
Activities: docent program; guided tours; lectures; loan, temporary exhibitions; storytelling; demonstrations. Museum Sponsors: Film Festivals; Belgian Heritage Festival; monthly WV Film Series.
Publications: book, History of South Charleston.
Hours & Admission Prices: Mon.-Sat. 10-5; groups by appointment. Archives by appointment. Adults $4; discounts to members & AAM members. Closed major holidays. ♿
Attendance: 5,000 (estimated)
Membership: Individual $10; Family $25; Friend $50. Corporate & Club: Sustaining $100; Patron $250; Benefactor $500 & up.

Summersville

CARNIFEX FERRY BATTLEFIELD STATE PARK & MUSEUM, 1194 Carnifex Ferry Rd., Summersville, WV 26651-4911. Tel.: 304-872-0825; 800-225-5982. Fax: 304-872-3820.
E-mail: carnifexferry@wvdnr.gov
Web Site: www.carnifexferrybattlefieldstatepark.com
Congressional District: 3
Key Personnel: Supt., Samuel Cowell.
Personnel Profile: Full-Time Paid 2; Part-Time Paid 4.
Governing Authority: state. West Virginia Dept. of Commerce, Labor & Environmental Resources, West Virginia Commerce Division Tourism & Parks, Charleston, WV 25305. Tel. 304-348-2764. Tax-exempt.
State Park & History Museum: housed in c.1855 frame house, built by Henry Patterson.
Collections: Civil War relics, memorabilia, utensils & implements of that era.

Facilities: picnic area.
Activities: Museum Sponsors: Battle Reenactment in September.
Hours & Admission Prices: Memorial Day weekend-Labor Day Sat.-Sun. 10-5. No charge.

Terra Alta

HISTORY HOUSE - PRESTON COUNTY HISTORICAL SOCIETY, 109 E. Washington Ave., Terra Alta, WV 26764-1203. Mailing Address: 100 Richfield Lane, Terra Alta, WV 26764. Tel.: 304-379-6612.
Founded: 1958.
Key Personnel: Pres. (V), Dave Thomas; Vice Pres. & Cur., Edna Britton.
Governing Authority: Tax-exempt.
Historical Society Museum.
Collections: county history; period furnishings; photographs; Bucklew collection; historic house.
Activities: school tours.
Publications: semiannual, Now...and Long Ago; 1979 Preston County History.
Hours & Admission Prices: June-Sept. Sun.; other times by appointment. No charge; donations accepted.
Membership: Annual $7.

RECKART'S MILL, 17 Reckart Mill Rd., RR 2, Terra Alta, WV 26764. Tel.: 304-789-2225.
Historic Building: grist mill powered by a 20 ft. Filz water wheel; built in 1865.
Collections: mill history; French millstones.
Facilities: Museum-related items for sale.
Activities: school tours; special events.
Hours & Admission Prices: April-Oct. Sun.-Thurs. by appointment; Fri.-Sat. 10-4. ♿

Wellsburg

BROOKE COUNTY HISTORICAL MUSEUM, 600 Main St., Wellsburg, WV 26070-1727. Tel.: 304-737-0506 & 0240.
History Museum: housed in Miller's Tavern and Inn built in 1797.
Collections: Brooke County history from 1797 to present; business & industry; early education; pioneer life.
Hours & Admission Prices: April-Oct. Fri. & Sun. 1-5; other times by appointment. No charge. ♿

BROOKE COUNTY PUBLIC LIBRARY MUSEUM BRANCH, 945 Main St., Wellsburg, WV 26070. Tel.: 304-737-1551. Fax: 304-737-1010.
E-mail: bcpl@lycos.com
Web Site: wellsburg.lib.wv.us
Founded: 2002.
Congressional District: 1
Key Personnel: Pres. & Dir., John Cole; Chm., David Hubbard; Devel. & Public Rels., George Wallace; Education, Kimberly Harless; Treas., Edward Jackfert; Registrar, Doris Tennant; Cur., Mary Kay Wallace; Security, Jeff Cionni; Archivist, Jane Kraina; Museum Shop Mgr., Dorothy Craig.
Personnel Profile: Part-Time Paid 2; Part-Time Volunteers 2; Interns 1.
Governing Authority: public; nonprofit. Parent Institution: Brooke County Public Library, Wellsburg, WV. Tax-exempt: 501(c)(3).
History Museum.
Collections: WWII history including Defenders of the Philippines 1941-1945; military artifacts; photographs; personal artifacts; medals; ribbons; citations; books; audiotapes; prints; maps; videos.
Research Fields: Japanese atrocities; slave laborers; hell ships; Bataan Death March; Philippine scouts; residual effects of captivity as a POW; compensation by Japanese companies who benefited by slave labor.
Facilities: 32,305-vol. library; 1,000 sq. ft. exhibit space; field research station; 60-seat theater. Museum-related items for sale.
Activities: films; formal education programs for adults, children, and undergraduate & graduate college students of Franciscan University of Steubenville, OH; lectures; theater. Annual Events: POW Recognition Day; Memorial Day; Veterans Day; End of WWII in August.
Publications: quarterly magazine, The QUAN.
Hours & Admission Prices: Mon.-Thurs. 10-7, Fri.-Sat. 10-5. No charge; donations accepted. Closed New Year's Day; Easter; Thanksgiving; Christmas. ♿
Attendance: 635 (accurate)

Weston

JACKSON'S MILL HISTORIC AREA, WVU Jackson's Mill State 4-H Conference Center, 160 WVU Jackson Mill Rd., Weston, WV 26452-8011. Tel.: 800-287-8206, ext. 121. Fax: 304-269-3409.
E-mail: jacksons.mill@mail.wvu.edu
Web Site: www.jacksonsmill.wvu.edu
Founded: 1968.
Congressional District: 3
Key Personnel: C.E.O., Terry Patterson; Heritage Program Specialist, Dean Hardman.
Personnel Profile: Full-Time Paid 2; Part-Time Paid 3; Part-Time Volunteers 10.
Governing Authority: university. Affiliated with West Virginia University. Tax-exempt.
Historic Building.
Collections: agricultural tools & artifacts; grist & saw milling equipment; blacksmith shop. Historic Buildings: 1796 Blaker's Mill (grinding wheat & corn); c.1800 Mary Conrad Cabin; c.1700 McWhorter Cabin; c.1800 Jackson's Mill.
Facilities: Museum-related items for sale.
Activities: guided tours; permanent exhibitions.
Hours & Admission Prices: April-May & Sept.-Oct. Thurs.-Sun. 10-5; Memorial Day-Labor Day Tues.-Sun. 10-5. Call for admission prices. ♿
Attendance: 60,000 (estimated)
Membership: Jackson's Mill Heritage Foundation $10.

THE MOUNTAINEER MILITARY MUSEUM, 345 Center Ave., Weston, WV 26452-2030. Tel.: 304-472-3943; 800-296-7329.
Military Museum: housed in the historic Colored School of Weston.
Collections: military history; personal artifacts; photographs.
Hours & Admission Prices: Sat. 10-5; other times by appointment.

MUSEUM OF AMERICAN GLASS IN WEST VIRGINIA, 230 Main Ave., Weston, WV 26452. Mailing Address: P.O. Box 574, Weston, WV 26452-0574. Tel.: 304-269-5006. Fax: 304-269-5006.
E-mail: wvmuseumofglass@aol.com
Web Site: wvmag.bglances.com
Founded: 1991.
Key Personnel: C.E.O., Dean Six; Pres. (V), Noel J. Pletcher.
Personnel Profile: Part-Time Paid 1.
Governing Authority: Tax-exempt.
Glass Museum.
Collections: history of glass, tools, machines, glass factories & workers, 1900-1940.
Facilities: Museum-related items for sale.
Activities: special events.
Publications: magazine, All About Glass.
Hours & Admission Prices: Mon.-Tues. & Thurs.-Sat. 12-4. No charge.
Membership: Annual $25; Supporting $35; Sustaining $50; Patron $100; Benefactor $500.

Wheeling

CHILDREN'S MUSEUM OF THE OHIO VALLEY, 1000 Main St., Wheeling, WV 26003. Tel.: 304-214-5437. Fax: 304-214-5437.
Founded: 2000.
Key Personnel: Dir. Museum Operations, Melissa Adams; Pres., Liz Hofreuter-Londini
Children's Museum.
Collections: hands-on interactive exhibits; science; art; literature; history.
Hours & Admission Prices: Wed.-Sat. 10-5, Sun.-Tues. groups only by appointment. Child $4, adult $2; discounts to groups of 10 or more.
Membership: Family $20; Family Plus $25; Annual Family $75; Annual Family Plus $90; Annual Reciprocal $100.

THE ECKHART HOUSE, 810 Main St., Wheeling, WV 26003-2530. Tel.: 888-700-0118; 304-232-5439.
E-mail: gfigaretti@gmail.com
Web Site: www.eckharthouse.com
Historic House Museum: housed in the former home of banker, George W. Eckhart, Jr.; built in 1892. Listed on the National Register of Historic Places.
Collections: local history; period furnishings.
Facilities: Museum-related items for sale.
Activities: guided tours. Museum Sponsors: Parlor Teas.
Hours & Admission Prices: Tours: Wed.-Sat. 1-4. Parlor Teas: by appointment. Tours: $3.50 per person. Teas: $15 per person.

KRUGER STREET TOY & TRAIN MUSEUM, 144 Kruger St., Wheeling, WV 26003-5158. Tel.: 304-242-8133; 877-242-8133 (Toll Free). Fax: 304-242-1925.
E-mail: museum@toyandtrain.com
Web Site: www.toyandtrain.com
Founded: 1998.
Congressional District: 1

Key Personnel: C.E.O., Pres. & Cur., Allan R. Miller; Museum Shop Mgr., Melody Clovis.
Personnel Profile: Full-Time Paid 3; Part-Time Paid 8; Interns 1.
Governing Authority: Parent Institution: The Eibel Corporation.
Toy Museum: housed in a Victorian-era schoolhouse.
Collections: research & development; materials related to toy manufacturer; drawings; prototypes; mock-ups; display units; factory samples; toys; trains; restored railroad caboose.
Facilities: rental facilities. Museum-related items for sale.
Activities: tours; interactive exhibits; student programs; scout badge programs; meetings; birthday parties. Annual Events: 5th Annual West Virginia Mego Meet in June; 11th Annual Marx Toy & Train Collectors National Convention in June.
Publications: newsletter, to museum members.
Hours & Admission Prices: Jan.-May Sat.-Sun. 9-5; Memorial Day to Dec. daily 9-5. Adults $9, senior citizens 65 & over $7.50, children 6-18 $5; discounts to AAA & active military; children under 6 & members no charge. Closed New Year's Day, Easter, Thanksgiving, Christmas. ♿
Attendance: 20,000 (estimated)
Membership: Individual $15; Family $40.

* **THE MUSEUMS OF OGLEBAY INSTITUTE - MANSION MUSEUM & GLASS MUSEUM, (M),** The Burton Center, Rte. 88, Oglebay Resort, Wheeling, WV 26003. Mailing Address: 1330 National Rd., Wheeling, WV 26003-5706. Tel.: 304-242-7272. Fax: 304-242-7287.
Web Site: www.oionline.com
Founded: 1930.
Congressional District: 1
Key Personnel: Dir., Christin L. Stein; Pres., Kathleen McDermott; Chm. (V), Richard Carter; Asst. Dir., Mary Coffman; Cur., Megan Clark; Cur. Glass, Holly McCluskey.
Personnel Profile: Full-Time Paid 4; Part-Time Paid 10; Part-Time Volunteers 90; Interns 2.
Governing Authority: nonprofit organization. Parent Institution: Oglebay Institute. Tax-exempt: 501(c)(3).
Decorative Arts & History Museum: housed in 1846 brick farm house renovated to be a mansion at the turn of the century.
Collections: Wheeling and Midwestern glass; Anglo-American china; Wheeling china, 1839-1912; period rooms, 1740-1850; decorative arts; history; manuscripts.
Major Exhibits: Vision to Legacy: 80 Years of Oglebay Institute, 4/10-10/10.
Research Fields: local history; glass; ceramics; decorative arts; pottery.
Facilities: 750-vol. library of local history & decorative arts books by appointment; 75-seat public programming area. Museum publications for sale.
Activities: guided tours; lectures; gallery talks; formally organized education programs for children & adults; permanent & temporary exhibitions.
Publications: Wheeling Glass (1829-1939) Collection of the Oglebay Institute Glass Museum.
Hours & Admission Prices: Feb.-March Sat.-Sun. 10-5; April-Oct. daily 10-5; Nov.-Dec. daily call for extended hours. One Museum: adults $6; Two Museums: adults $9; discounts to AAM members; Oglebay Institute members and children 12 & under no charge. Closed New Year's Day; Thanksgiving; Christmas. ♿
Attendance: 39,011 (accurate)
Membership: Individual $35; Dual $50; Family $75; Friend $100; Patron $250.

OGLEBAY'S GOOD ZOO, Oglebay Park, Rte. 88 N., Wheeling, WV 26003-9361. Tel.: 304-243-4027. Fax: 304-243-4110.
E-mail: pmiller@oglebay-resort.com
Web Site: www.oglebay-resort.com/goodzoo/
Founded: 1977.
Congressional District: 23
Key Personnel: C.E.O., Douglas Dalby; Dir., Penny Miller; Cur. Education, Vickie Markey; Animal Mgr., Joe Greathouse; Dir. Theater, Steve Mitch; Gift Shop Mgr., Jill Neumann.
Personnel Profile: Full-Time Paid 20; Part-Time Volunteers 100; Interns 10.
Governing Authority: nonprofit organization. Parent Institution: The Wheeling Park Commission, Oglebay Park, Wheeling, WV 26003. Tax-exempt.
Zoo.
Collections: goats, bears, river otters, waterfowl, fish, snakes, fruit bats, monkeys, ocelot; red pandas; bald eagles; African Wild Dogs.
Research Fields: Raptor rehabilitation-Isis.
Facilities: library of books on animals & planetariums, available for research on premises; zoological park; aquarium; planetarium; 133-seat auditorium; theater; refreshment stands. Zoo-related items for sale.
Activities: films; docent program; special events; camps; Master Naturalist Program; education programs for pre-school to elder hostel groups; scout programs.
Publications: newsletter, Good Zoo News.
Hours & Admission Prices: Daily 11-4. Adults $7, children 3-12 $5.50; children 2 & under and members no charge. ♿
Attendance: 124,575 (accurate)
Membership: Individual $35; Family & Grandparent $52; Grandparents Plus & Family Plus $71; Sustaining $85; Patron $100; Lifetime $1,000.

POINT OVERLOOK MUSEUM, 989 Grandview St., Wheeling, WV 26003-3048. Tel.: 304-232-3010.
Tourist Center & Museum.
Collections: local history & culture; photographs; videos.
Hours & Admission Prices: Daily 10-3. Adults $3, senior $2; children 12 & under no charge.

SCHRADER ENVIRONMENTAL EDUCATION CENTER, The Burton Center, Wheeling, WV 26003. Tel.: 304-242-6855. Fax: 304-242-5197.
E-mail: ejanelsins@oionline.com
Web Site: www.oionline.com
Founded: 1930.
Key Personnel: Dir., Eriks Janelsins; Museum Shop Mgr., Jane Link.
Personnel Profile: Full-Time Paid 6; Part-Time Paid 20.
Governing Authority: Parent Institution: Oglebay Institute.
Natural History Museum.
Collections: interactive & natural history exhibits; butterfly garden.
Research Fields: herpetology; astacology.
Facilities: nature trail; observatory.
Activities: school tours; special events.
Hours & Admission Prices: April-Oct. Mon.-Sat. 9:30-5, Sun. 12-5; Nov.-March daily 12-5. ♿
Attendance: 45,000

WEST VIRGINIA INDEPENDENCE HALL, 1528 Market St., Wheeling, WV 26003-3532. Tel.: 304-238-1300. Fax: 304-238-1302.
E-mail: melissa.brown@wvculture.org
Web Site: www.wvculture.org
Founded: 1964.
Congressional District: 1
Key Personnel: Dir., Melissa Brown.
Personnel Profile: Full-Time Paid 3; Part-Time Paid 3.
Governing Authority: state. West Virginia Div. of Culture & History, Cultural Center, Capitol Complex, Charleston, WV 25305. Tax-exempt.
History Museum & Historic Site.
Collections: artifacts; documents & portraits from 1861-1863, Wheeling & Statehood Conventions; 1863, Statehood Movement; furnishings of Governor's office & anterooms; architectural artifacts & historic preservation records; Civil War battle flags.
Facilities: theater; meeting rooms; courtroom.
Activities: guided & self-guided tours; films; changing exhibitions; performances.
Publications: Goldenseal: West Virginia Traditional Life.
Hours & Admission Prices: Mon.-Sat. 10-4; groups of 10 or more by appointment. No charge; donations accepted. Closed major holidays. ♿
Attendance: 6,000 (estimated)

WEST VIRGINIA NORTHERN COMMUNITY COLLEGE ALUMNI ASSOCIATION MUSEUM, 1704 Market St., Wheeling, WV 26003-3643. Tel.: 304-233-5900, ext. 8817. Fax: 304-232-0965.
E-mail: alumni@northern.wvnet.edu
Web Site: www.wvnorthern.edu
Founded: 1984.
Key Personnel: Pres., Darryl Ruth; Sec. & Treas., Joan Weiskircher.
Personnel Profile: Full-Time Paid 1; Full-Time Volunteers 2; Part-Time Volunteers 8.
Governing Authority: private; nonprofit.
History Museum: two of four collections are located in historic landmark buildings listed in the national register.
Collections: concentration on artifacts as they relate to former inhabitants of the historic landmarks or to the history of the community; glass collection is located in the former headquarters of a glass company & on another campus where glass was produced; railroad collection is in a former passenger station; local history of Wheeling and Northern Panhandle, Panhandle of WV.
Research Fields: train engine photographs; train & other railroad photos, B&ORR history, engine history & other railroad history.
Facilities: 75-vol. library of railroad history; 200-seat auditorium; educational facilities.
Activities: guided tours; loan, temporary & traveling exhibitions; training programs for professional museum workers. Museum Sponsors: three openings per year.
Publications: semiannual newsletter, WVNCC Alumni Association Museum; annual brochures.

Hours & Admission Prices: Fall, Winter & Spring: Mon.-Fri. 9-8; Summer: Mon.-Fri. 9-4 with some exceptions. No charge; donations accepted. Closed New Year's Day & day after; Martin Luther King Jr. Day; week before Easter; Memorial Day; Independence Day; Labor Day; Thanksgiving. Closed New Year's Eve, Day & day after; Christmas Eve, Day & week. ♿
Attendance: 92,000 (accurate)
Membership: Museum Friend $20.

WYMER'S GENERAL STORE MUSEUM AT THE ARTISAN CENTER AT HERITAGE SQUARE, 1400 Main St., Wheeling, WV 26003-2824. Mailing Address: 1330 National Rd., Wheeling, WV 26003-5706. Tel.: 304-232-1810.
Web Site: www.artisancenter.com
History Museum.
Collections: Wheeling history; general store representing the 1800s.
Facilities: Museum-related items for sale.
Activities: pump organ & Victrola demonstrations; art shows; craft demonstrations; special events; school tours.
Hours & Admission Prices: Mon.-Thurs. 11-7, Fri.-Sat. 11-9, Sun. by appointment. ♿

White Sulphur Springs

PRESIDENT'S COTTAGE MUSEUM-THE GREENBRIER, 300 W. Main St., White Sulphur Springs, WV 24986-2414. Tel.: 304-536-1110, ext. 7314 & 7198. Fax: 304-536-7854.
E-mail: the_greenbrier@greenbrier.com
Web Site: www.greenbrier.com
Founded: 1932.
Key Personnel: Cur., Dr. Robert S. Conte.
Personnel Profile: Full-Time Paid 1; Part-Time Paid 2.
Governing Authority: CSX Hotels Corporation, White Sulphur Springs.
History Museum: housed in 1835-1858 summer cottage used as the vacation home & resort of Presidents Van Buren, Tyler, Pierce, Fillmore & Buchanan.
Collections: photographs; letters; official correspondence; furnishings typical of that era; memorabilia housed in adjacent archives; paintings; prints; material documenting the 200-year history of the Greenbrier resorts.
Activities: guided tours; lectures.
Publications: The History of the Greenbrier: America's Resort.
Hours & Admission Prices: April-Nov. Mon.-Sat. 10-5, Sun. 10-3; other times by appointment. No charge.
Attendance: 15,000 (estimated)

Williamson

WILLIAMSON AREA RAILROAD MUSEUM, INC., 100 Prichard St., Williamson, WV 25661. Mailing Address: P.O. Box 466, Williamson, WV 25661-0466. Tel.: 304-235-0105. Fax: 304-235-4910.
Web Site: williamsonrailroadmuseum.com
Key Personnel: Pres. (V), R. Doyle Van Meter, II
Railroad Museum.
Collections: N & W memorabilia; model train; railroad artifacts.
Facilities: library.
Hours & Admission Prices: Fri.-Sat. 10-4.No charge; donations accepted.
Membership: Student $15; Senior Citizen $25; Individual $35.

Williamstown

FENTON GLASS MUSEUM, 420 Caroline Ave., Williamstown, WV 26187-1121. Tel.: 304-375-7772; 800-319-7793. Fax: 304-375-6459.
E-mail: museum@fentongiftshop.com
Web Site: www.fentongiftshop.com/museum.asp
Founded: 1977.
Key Personnel: Pres., George Fenton; Museum Shop Mgr., Charles Mayer.
Governing Authority: private business. Parent Institution: Fenton Gift Shops Inc.
Company Museum.
Collections: art glass made by glass companies in the upper Ohio Valley from Parkersburg, West Virginia to Steubenville, Ohio during the years from 1880 to 1980; history of Fenton Art Glass; a movie showing the manufacture of this glass and special factory tours of The Fenton Art Glass Co. production process; historical information on the glass industry is available.
Research Fields: the glass industry; Fenton Art Glass Co.
Facilities: library; archives of records & files of National Association of Manufacturers of Pressed & Blown Glassware covering 1887-1965; 65-seat theater. Museum-related items for sale.
Activities: guided tours; lectures; films.
Hours & Admission Prices: June-Aug. Mon.-Fri. 8-7, Sat. 8-5, Sun. 12-5; Sept.-Dec. Mon.-Fri. 8-6, Sat. 8-5, Sun. 12-5. No charge. Closed New Year's Day; Easter; Thanksgiving; Christmas. ♿
Attendance: 50,000 (accurate)

WISCONSIN

(256 listings)

Antigo

LANGLADE COUNTY HISTORICAL SOCIETY MUSEUM, 404 Superior St., Antigo, WI 54409-1855. Tel.: 715-627-4464.
E-mail: lchs@dwave.net
Web Site: langladehistory.com
Founded: 1929.
Congressional District: 8
Key Personnel: C.E.O., Dir. & Pres. (V), Joe Hermolin; Treas., Glenn Bugni; Museum Shop Mgr., Mary Kay Wolf.
Personnel Profile: Full-Time Paid 1; Part-Time Paid 1; Part-Time Volunteers 18.
Governing Authority: state. Parent Institution: Langlade County Historical Society, Inc. Tax-exempt.
Historic Building & Museum.
Collections: farm and logging tools; domestic implements & furnishings; newspaper files; World War I memorabilia; medical & musical equipment; 440 locomotive & caboose. Historic House: c.1878 Deleglise cabin.
Research Fields: genealogy.
Activities: guided tours; permanent exhibitions; lectures.
Publications: semi-annual newsletter.
Hours & Admission Prices: Wed.-Sat. 9:30-3:30; other times by appointment. No charge; donations accepted.
Attendance: 16,000 (estimated)
Membership: Junior $3; Individual $25; Family $30; Business $100; Life $250.

Appleton

APPLETON ART CENTER, 111 W. College Ave., Appleton, WI 54911-5781. Tel.: 920-733-4089. Fax: 920-733-4149.
E-mail: info@appletonartcenter.org
Web Site: www.appletonartcenter.org
Founded: 1960.
Congressional District: 8
Key Personnel: Exec. Dir., Timothy Riley; Pres. (V), William Gibson, Jr.; Dir. Membership, Marie Marschke; Mgr. Education, Lori Lemke; Gallery Attendant, Lori Schoenberger; Gallery Attendant, Stephanie Tsoris; Gallery Attendant, Kari Witthuhn-Henning.
Personnel Profile: Full-Time Paid 3; Part-Time Paid 3; Part-Time Volunteers 50; Interns 1.
Governing Authority: private; nonprofit. Tax-exempt: 501(c)(3).
Art Museum.
Collections: visual arts exhibitions.
Research Fields: art history; contemporary artwork.
Facilities: educational facilities.
Activities: guided tours; education programs; arts festivals; participatory exhibits. Annual Event: Art in the Park.
Hours & Admission Prices: Mon.-Fri. 9-5, Sat. 10-4; tours by appointment. Suggested Donation: adults $6, students & seniors $4; members and children 10 & under no charge. Closed New Year's Day; Easter weekend; Memorial Day; Independence Day; Labor Day; Thanksgiving; Christmas. ♿
Attendance: 100,000 (estimated)
Membership: Student $25; Individual $45; Family & Artist $50; Apprentice $100-$249; Artisan $250-$499; Academy $500-$999; Guild $1,000-$2,499; Master $2,500-$4,999; Patron $5,000 & up.

THE BUILDING FOR KIDS, 100 W. College Ave., Appleton, WI 54911-5735. Tel.: 920-734-3226.
E-mail: contact@buildingforkids.org
Web Site: www.thebuildingforkids.org
Formerly: Fox Cities Children's Museum
Key Personnel: Exec. Dir., Dorrie Hipschman; Mgr. Operations, Julie Runnfeldt
Children's Museum.
Collections: hands-on exhibits.
Activities: birthday parties; classes; overnights; special events.
Hours & Admission Prices: Tues.-Fri. 9-5, Sat. 10-5, Sun. 12-5. Admission $7; children under one & members no charge. Closed New Year's Day; Easter; Memorial Day; Independence Day; Labor Day; Thanksgiving; Christmas. ♿

HEARTHSTONE HISTORIC HOUSE MUSEUM, (M), 625 W. Prospect Ave., Appleton, WI 54911-6042. Tel.: 920-730-8204. Fax: 920-730-8266.
E-mail: heartheducator@att.net
Web Site: www.hearthstonemuseum.org
Founded: 1986.
Congressional District: 8
Key Personnel: Pres. (V), Mary Strange; Financial Dir., Brian Hoefs; Dir. Programs, Andrea Malnar; Maintenance & Housekeeping, Lynn DeWall.
Personnel Profile: Full-Time Paid 2; Part-Time Paid 1; Part-Time Volunteers 75.
Governing Authority: nonprofit. Tax-exempt: 501(c)(3).
Historic House Museum: first residence in the world to be lighted from a central hydroelectric power plant using the Edison system in 1882.
Collections: late 19th-century furnishings, decorative arts, fine arts & utilitarian items; original Edison light fixtures & switches; items related to early history of electrical lighting.
Research Fields: late 19th-century social & cultural history with an emphasis on the Fox River Valley and effects of residential electricity; decorative arts; art; architecture; restoration & conservation.
Facilities: research library; house restoration resource.
Activities: guided tours; lectures; organized education programs for children, adults, undergraduate or graduate college students; volunteer program; participatory & temporary exhibitions.
Publications: quarterly newsletter, Upstairs & Downstairs; bimonthly volunteer newsletter.
Hours & Admission Prices: Tues.-Fri. 10-3:30, Sat. 11-3:30; daily group tours; special evening hours during Victorian Christmas exhibition. Adults $5, students & children $2.50; discounts to groups, Time Travelers, AASLH, AAM, ICOM, & AAA members; members no charge. Christmas Exhibition: adults $6, children $3. Closed holidays.
Attendance: 5,040 (accurate)
Membership: Bricks & Mortar $30; Electric $50; Family $100; Hearthstone 1882 $250; Community Treasure $500; Heritage $1,000; Landmark $2,500; Legacy $5,000; Futures $10,000; Sustainers $25,000 & up.

THE HISTORY MUSEUM AT THE CASTLE, (M), 330 E. College Ave., Appleton, WI 54911-5715. Tel.: 920-733-8445. Fax: 920-733-8636.
E-mail: terry@myhistorymuseum.org
Web Site: www.myhistorymuseum.org
Formerly: Outagamie Museum
Founded: 1872.
Congressional District: 8
Key Personnel: Exec. Dir., Terry Bergen; Pres. (V), Janet Wullner-Faiss Cloak; Dir. Interpretive Programs & Cur. Collections, Matthew Carpenter.
Personnel Profile: Full-Time Paid 6; Part-Time Paid 4; Part-Time Volunteers 240; Interns 2.
Governing Authority: Outagamie County Historical Society, Inc. Branch Museums: Grignon Mansion, 1313 Augustine St., Kaukauna, WI 54130. Tax-exempt: 501(c)(3).
Regional History Museum.
Collections: local history collections documenting the social, industrial, agricultural & political history of Wisconsin's Fox River Valley; famous & infamous locals including escape artist, Harry Houdini & Senator Joseph McCarthy and Pulitzer Prize winning author, Edna Ferber.
Research Fields: regional history; local history.
Facilities: library; archives; theater.
Activities: annual meetings; temporary exhibits; educational programs; school tours; slide shows; lecture series; papermaking demonstration; educational programs; genealogy classes; theater.
Publications: quarterly newsletter, History Today; quarterly newsletter.
Hours & Admission Prices: June-Aug. Mon.-Sat. 10-4, Sun. 12-4; Sept.-May Tues.-Sat. 10-4, Sun. 12-4. Family $12, adults $5, seniors $4, children 5-17 $2.50; discounts to AAA, AAM & ICOM members; members no charge. ♿
Attendance: 19,019 (accurate)
Membership: Senior Citizen & Student $15; Individual $25; Family $50; Professional $75; Benefactor $150; Life $1,000.

PAPER DISCOVERY CENTER, (M), 425 W. Water St., Appleton, WI 54911-6058. Tel.: 920-380-7491. Fax: 920-731-2704.
Web Site: www.paperdiscoverycenter.org
Founded: 2005.
Congressional District: 8
Key Personnel: Exec. Dir., Dave Lee; Chm. (V), Harry Spiegelberg; Treas. (V), William H. Geenen; Mng. Dir. & Coord. Education, Barbara Sauer; Educator, Dave Lee.
Personnel Profile: Full-Time Paid 3; Part-Time Volunteers 22; Interns 1.
Governing Authority: private; nonprofit organization. Parent Institution: Paper Industry International Hall of Fame, Inc., Appleton, WI. Tax-exempt: 501(c)(3).
Paper Museum.
Collections: paper industry history; Atlas Mill history.
Facilities: 50-vol. library; educational facilities; 45- seat theater. Museum-related items for sale.
Activities: formal education programs for children; guided tours; hobby workshops; temporary exhibitions.
Publications: monthly newsletter, All Things Paper.
Hours & Admission Prices: Mon.-Sat. 10-4. Adults $5, seniors $4, students $3; discounts to families; members no charge. Closed holidays. ♿
Attendance: 7,000 (accurate)
Membership: Individual $45; Family $65; Friend $100; Partner $250; Benefactor $500; Patron $1,000.

WRISTON ART CENTER GALLERIES, Lawrence Univ., 613 E. College Ave., Appleton, WI 54912-0599. Mailing Address: P.O. Box 599, Appleton, WI 54912-0599. Tel.: 920-832-6890. Fax: 920-832-7362.
E-mail: frank.c.lewis@lawrence.edu
Web Site: www.lawrence.edu/dept/wriston
Founded: 1989.
Congressional District: 8
Key Personnel: Dir. Exhibitions & Cur. Collections, Frank C. Lewis; Collections Mgr., Leslie Walfish.
Personnel Profile: Full-Time Paid 2; Part-Time Paid 10; Interns 5.
Governing Authority: college; nonprofit organization. Parent Institution: Lawrence University. Tax-exempt.
Art Gallery.
Collections: 19th & 20th-century paintings & prints; La Vera Pohl collection of German Expressionist art; Japanese prints & drawings; Greek & Roman coins.
Research Fields: catalogue of Ottilia Beurger's collection of Greek & Roman coins; catalogue of The La Vera Pohl Collection of German Expressionist Art.
Facilities: print study room.
Activities: films; formal education program for undergraduates & graduates; lectures; loan, temporary & traveling exhibitions.
Hours & Admission Prices: Oct.-May Tues.-Fri. 10-4, Sat.-Sun. 12-4; call for hours during summer. No charge. Closed Memorial Day; Independence Day; Thanksgiving weekend. ♿
Attendance: 7,472 (accurate)

Ashland

ASHLAND HISTORICAL SOCIETY MUSEUM, 509 W. Main, Ashland, WI 54806-1513. Tel.: 715-682-4911.
E-mail: ashlandhistory@centurytel.net
Web Site: ashlandhistory.com
Founded: 1954.
Congressional District: 7
Key Personnel: Pres. (V) & Museum Shop Mgr., Alice Nelson; Cur., Sharon Manthei.
Personnel Profile: Part-Time Paid 2; Part-Time Volunteers 25.
Governing Authority: under management of Ashland Historical Society. Tax-exempt: 501(c)(3).
General Museum.
Collections: costumes; history; military; transportation; Ashland history.
Research Fields: genealogy; local history.
Facilities: research library.
Activities: temporary exhibitions.
Publications: Garland City Gazette, newsletter of Ashland Historical Society.
Hours & Admission Prices: June to mid-Sept. Mon.-Fri. 10-4, Sat. 10-2; mid-Sept. to May Mon.-Fri. 10-4. No charge; donations accepted. Closed major holidays. ♿
Attendance: 400 (estimated)
Membership: Senior Citizens over 62 $5; Individual $8; Family $15; Organization & Business $50.

Ashwaubenon

ASHWAUBENON HISTORICAL SOCIETY, 737 Cormier Rd., Ashwaubenon, WI 54304-4825. Tel.: 920-429-2863.
Web Site: www.ashwaubenonhistoricalsociety.com
Governing Authority: Tax-exempt: 501(c)(3).
Historical Society Museum.
Collections: local history & culture; photographs.
Hours & Admission Prices: April-Dec. Wed. & Sat. 1-4.

Baileys Harbor

THE RIDGES SANCTUARY, INC., 8270 Hwy. 57, Baileys Harbor, WI 54202. Mailing Address: Box 152, Baileys Harbor, WI 54202-0152. Tel.: 920-839-2802 & 1101. Fax: 920-839-2234.
E-mail: info@ridgessanctuary.org

Web Site: www.ridgessanctuary.org
Founded: 1937.
Congressional District: 8
Key Personnel: Exec. Dir., Steve Leonard; Asst. Dir. & Naturalist, Karen Newbern; Pres., Ed Pentecoste.
Personnel Profile: Full-Time Paid 4; Part-Time Paid 1; Part-Time Volunteers 150.
Governing Authority: nonprofit organization; board of directors. Tax-exempt: 501(c)(3).
Nature Center: in 1873 log building. Sanctuary consisting of 1440-acres of wooded bogs, sandy ridges, swales & Lake Michigan beaches. Baileys Harbor Range lights built in 1869.
Collections: 475 species of vascular plants in local area, including local mosses, lichens, & liverworts; 48 collection boxes housing moths, butterflies, wildflower sanctuary & other insects native to area.
Research Fields: entomology; phenology of butterflies & moths, including information of life cycle; Ram's head ladyslipper Orchid study; bird breeding.
Facilities: 550-vol. library pertaining to natural history & plant study; boardwalk system; educational facilities; nature center. Bird houses & other museum-related items for sale.
Activities: guided tours; walking trail; lectures; organized educational programs for children & adults; participatory & temporary exhibitions.
Publications: quarterly newsletter, Ridges News; trail guide; History of the Ridges.
Hours & Admission Prices: Nature Center: May to mid-Oct. Mon.-Sat. 9-4, Sun. 11-3. Sanctuary: daily dawn to dusk.
Attendance: 17,500 (estimated)
Membership: Adult $40; Family $65; Ridges Sustainer $125; Sanctuary Steward $250; Ridges Advocate $500; Life $1,000.

Balsam Lake

POLK COUNTY MUSEUM, 120 Main St., Balsam Lake, WI 54810. Mailing Address: P.O. Box 41, Balsam Lake, WI 54810-0041. Tel.: 715-483-3979 & 9269.
E-mail: darose@centurytel.net
Web Site: www.co.polk.wi.us/history
Founded: 1960.
Congressional District: 3
Key Personnel: C.E.O. & Dir., Rosalie Kittleson; Pres. (V), Darrell Kittleson.
Personnel Profile: Full-Time Volunteers 20; Part-Time Paid 1; Part-Time Volunteers 37; Interns 1.
Governing Authority: county; nonprofit organization. Subsidiary Institution: St. Croix Falls Historical Society. Branch Museums: Polk County Red School House, St. Croix Falls-Fairgrounds; Rural Life Museum, Balsam Lake; Polk County Museum. Tax-exempt.
General Museum.
Collections: area history; art & craft exhibits. Historic Building: 1899 courthouse.
Research Fields: county history.
Facilities: 800-vol. historical library available for use on premises.
Activities: guided tours; lectures; films; formally organized education programs for adults & children.
Publications: books, Polk County Memories; Polk County's First Written History 1876; Building of the Dam at St. Croix Falls; Polk County Postal History & Directory.
Hours & Admission Prices: Daily 12-4. Adults $3, students 12-18 $1; children under 12 with adult no charge. Call for tour reservations. ♿
Attendance: 2,500 (accurate)
Membership: Individual $15; Life $100.

Baraboo

CIRCUS WORLD MUSEUM, 550 Water St., Baraboo, WI 53913-2578. Tel.: 608-356-8341. Fax: 608-356-1800.
E-mail: ringmaster@circusworldmuseum.com
Web Site: www.circusworldmuseum.com
Founded: 1959.
Congressional District: 2
Key Personnel: Chm. (V), Renee Boldt; Exec. Dir., Stephen Freese; Museum Shop Mgr., Susan Topham.
Personnel Profile: Full-Time Paid 7; Part-Time Paid 15; Part-Time Volunteers 50.
Governing Authority: nonprofit organization. Parent Institution: Wisconsin Historical Society, 816 State St., Madison, WI 53706. Tax-exempt: 501(c)(3).
Circus Museum: site of 1884-1918 original winter quarters of Ringling Bros. Circus.
Collections: circus artifacts; circus wagons; railroad cars; archives; route books; programs; negatives; lithographs; couriers; heralds; business records.
Research Fields: circus & wild west.
Facilities: library & research center with books available for inter-museum loan.
Activities: guided tours; films; interactive programs; live circus performances including period circus music concerts, side shows & demonstrations; parades; circus dining department; calliope concerts; unloading of circus train; travelling displays; magic shows. Annual Event: produce circus at annual Wisconsin State Fair.
Hours & Admission Prices: Summer: daily 9-6; Fall & Spring: daily 10-4; Winter: Nov.-April 17 Mon.-Fri. 10-4. Summer: adults $14.95, senior citizens $12.95, children 5-11 $7.95; discount to groups; children under 5 & members no charge. Fall, Winter & Spring: adults $7, seniors $6, children 5-11 $3.50; children under 5 & members no charge. Library & Research Center: call for hours. Closed New Year's Day; Easter; Thanksgiving; Christmas. ♿
Attendance: 71,109 (accurate)
Membership: Individual $30; Annual Dual (2 people) $45; Annual Family $60.

INTERNATIONAL CRANE FOUNDATION, E. 11376 Shady Lane Rd., Baraboo, WI 53913-0447. Mailing Address: P.O. Box 447, Baraboo, WI 53913-0447. Tel.: 608-356-9462, ext. 118. Fax: 608-356-9465.
E-mail: cranes@savingcranes.org
Web Site: www.savingcranes.org
Founded: 1973.
Congressional District: 2
Key Personnel: Chair Emeritus (V), Mary E. Wickhem; Chm. Bd., Joseph Branch; Vice Chm. Bd. & Co-Founder, George Archibald; C.E.O. & Pres., James Hook; Treas., Richard Fox; Cur. Birds, Sharon Reilly; Field Ecologist, Jeb Barzen; Gift Shop Mgr., Barbara Allard Bluske.
Personnel Profile: Full-Time Paid 31; Part-Time Paid 10; Part-Time Volunteers 35; Interns 15.
Governing Authority: nonprofit organization. Tax-exempt: 501(c)(3).
Aviary & Ornithology Museum.
Collections: 140 cranes of 15 species; crane related artifacts from all over the world; research library, restored prairie.
Research Fields: cranes, their captive propagation, general maintenance, behavior; restoration of marsh, prairie & savanna.
Facilities: research library; 2,000 papers on cranes & related materials, available for research on premises with permission of the deputy director; nature center; field research station; 120-seat auditorium; zoo; trails. Museum-related items for sale.
Activities: guided tours; lectures; films; formally organized education programs for children, adults, undergraduate & graduate college students; docent program or council.
Publications: quarterly newsletter, The ICF Bugle; booklet, Cranes, Cranes, Cranes; books, Crane Research around the World; Reflections; Proceedings of the 1980 International Crane Workshop; Proceedings of the 1983 International Crane Workshop.
Hours & Admission Prices: April 15-Oct. daily 9-5. Guided Tours: April-May & Sept.-Oct. Sat.-Sun. 10, 1 & 3; Memorial Day to Labor Day daily 10, 1 & 3. Adults $9.50, senior citizens 62 & over and students $8, children 6-17 $5; children 5 & under and members no charge. ♿
Attendance: 26,475 (accurate)
Membership: Student & Senior $25; Individual $35; Family & Foreign $50; Associate $100; Sustaining $250; Sponsor $500; Patron $1,000; Benefactor $2,000.

SAUK COUNTY HISTORICAL SOCIETY AND MUSEUM, 531 4th Ave., Baraboo, WI 53913-2034. Mailing Address: P.O. Box 651, Baraboo, WI 53913-0651. Tel.: 608-356-1001.
E-mail: history@saukcountyhistory.org
Web Site: www.saukcountyhistory.org
Founded: 1906.
Congressional District: 2
Key Personnel: Exec. Dir., Orris Smith; Pres., Paul Wolter; Staff Asst., Mary Farrell Stieve; Cur., Sue Teska.
Personnel Profile: Full-Time Paid 2; Part-Time Paid 1; Part-Time Volunteers 8.
Governing Authority: nonprofit organization. Branch Museums: Man Mound Park & Yellow Thunder Monument & Park. Tax-exempt: 501(c)(3).
General Museum.
Collections: artifacts & photos from pioneer days to present; Indian exhibits; circus mementoes & displays; archaeological & geological materials; guns; quilts; textiles; toys; china.
Research Fields: county history; genealogy.
Facilities: 1,050-vol. library pertaining to local history available for use upon request.

Activities: guided tours; annual meeting, Museum Sponsors: annual banquet; annual social; tour of historic homes.
Publications: newsletter, Sauk Trails; Early Baraboo & Sauk County histories.
Hours & Admission Prices: Tues.-Sat. 12-4:30. No charge; donations accepted. Closed major holidays. ♿
Attendance: 2,000 (estimated)
Membership: Individual $20; Family $35; Friend $50; Sponsor $100; Patron $250 and up; Benefactor $500 and up.

Bayfield

APOSTLES ISLANDS NATIONAL LAKESHORE, 415 Washington Ave., Bayfield, WI 54814-4809. Tel.: 715-779-7007 & 3397. Fax: 715-779-3049.
E-mail: susan_mackreth@nps.gov
Web Site: www.nps.gov/apis
Founded: 1970.
Congressional District: 7
Key Personnel: Supt., Robert J. Krumenaker; Chief of Resource Education, Myra Dec.
Governing Authority: federal. Parent Institution: U.S. Dept. of the Interior, National Park Service. Tax-exempt.
Maritime Museum.
Collections: lighthouse artifacts & objects; collection of objects & artifacts, as well as buildings & docks from small family commercial fishing operations; insect collection; furs & study skins; artifacts from logging camps & brown stone quarries. Historic Building: 1920s Hokenson Fishery, including artifacts from the Lake Superior fishing industry & the Twilite, early 1900s fishing boat.
Research Fields: natural & cultural history of northern Wisconsin.
Facilities: 1,000-vol. library on the natural & cultural history of northern Wisconsin; nature & conservation center; 50-seat auditorium; slide & photo file on the Apostle Islands. National Park Service publications for sale.
Activities: guided tours; films; slide programs.
Publications: annual newspaper, Around the Archipelago; brochure, Apostle Islands National Lakeshore; monographs/brochures relating to natural & cultural history themes of area.
Hours & Admission Prices: Visitor Center: Memorial Day-Labor Day daily 8-6; Sept. to mid-Oct. daily 8-5; mid-Oct. to May Mon.-Fri. 8-4:30. Fishery Tours: mid-June to Labor Day. No charge; donations accepted. Visitor's Center closed New Year's Day; Thanksgiving; Christmas. ♿

Beaver Dam

DODGE COUNTY HISTORICAL SOCIETY MUSEUM, 105 Park Ave., Beaver Dam, WI 53916-2107. Tel.: 920-887-1266.
E-mail: dchs@powercom.net
Web Site: www2.powercom.net/~dchs
Formerly: Williams Free Library
Founded: 1938.
Congressional District: 9
Key Personnel: Cur., Mary Beth Jacobson; Pres. (V), Glen Link.
Personnel Profile: Part-Time Paid 2.
Governing Authority: nonprofit organization. Parent Institution: Dodge County Historical Society. Tax-exempt: 170(b)(A).
General Museum.
Collections: arrowheads; replica of one-room schoolhouse; Celebrity Wall-Our Community Goes to War display from Civil War to present; Monarch ranges; 1903 Rambler.
Research Fields: Dodge County history; Native American; natural history; genealogy; Monarch Range Co.
Activities: guided tours; school group tours; slide presentation; permanent & temporary exhibits.
Publications: quarterly newsletter.
Hours & Admission Prices: Tues.-Sat. 1-4; tours by appointment. No charge; donations accepted. Closed holidays.
Attendance: 1,800 (estimated)
Membership: Student $1; Household $20; Affiliate $50-$99; Patron $100-$249; Sustaining $250-$499; Heritage $500 & up.

SEIPPEL HOMESTEAD AND CENTER FOR THE ARTS, 1605 N. Spring St., Beaver Dam, WI 53916-1103. Mailing Address: P.O. Box 442, Beaver Dam, WI 53916-0442. Tel.: 920-885-3635 & 887-8593.
E-mail: bdaaa@charterinternet.com
Web Site: www.bdaaa.org
Key Personnel: Exec. Dir., Karla R. Jensen; Pres. (V), Julie Flemming; Museum Shop Mgr., Betty Singer.
Governing Authority: Tax-exempt.
Art Museum.
Collections: oil paintings.
Major Exhibits: Brotherhood of Art, 1/10-2/10; Area High School Art Show, 3/10-4/10; Wildlife & Nature Exhibit, 8/10-10/10; Holiday Gift Gallery, 11/10-12/10.
Facilities: Museum-related items for sale.
Activities: Museum Sponsors: Youth Art monthly; Youth Art Camp in June; Special Needs Youth Art Camp in June.
Hours & Admission Prices: Wed.-Sun. 1-4. No charge.

Beloit

THE ANGEL MUSEUM, 656 Pleasant St., Beloit, WI 53511-6242. Mailing Address: P.O. Box 816, Beloit, WI 53512-0816. Tel.: 608-362-9099.
E-mail: admin@angelmuseum.com
Web Site: www.angelmuseum.com
Founded: 1998.
Governing Authority: city; nonprofit organization.
Historic Site: built in 1914; formerly St. Paul's Catholic Church. Listed on the Register for Historical Landmarks.
Collections: over 12,000 angel artifacts made of over 100 different materials from 50 different countries.
Facilities: gardens. Museum-related items for sale.
Activities: group tours; special events; facility rental.
Hours & Admission Prices: March-Dec. Tues.-Sat. 10-4. Call for admission prices. ♿
Attendance: 17,000 (estimated)
Membership: Call museum.

BELOIT FINE ARTS INCUBATOR, 520 E. Grand Ave., Beloit, WI 53511-6314. Tel.: 608-313-9083.
E-mail: bfaiwi@yahoo.com
Web Site: beloitfineartsincubator.com
Key Personnel: Bd. Pres., Dean Folts; Bd. Vice Pres., Jerry Sveum
Art Gallery.
Collections: works by resident & regional artists.
Activities: traveling exhibits; classes.
Hours & Admission Prices: Mon.-Fri. 10-2.

BELOIT HISTORICAL SOCIETY, 845 Hackett St., Beloit, WI 53511-5227. Tel.: 608-365-7835. Fax: 608-365-5999.
E-mail: pkerr@beloithistoricalsociety.com
Web Site: www.beloithistoricalsociety.com
Formerly: Hanchett Bartlett Homestead
Founded: 1910.
Congressional District: 1
Key Personnel: Dir., Paul K. Kerr; Pres. (V), William Yoss; Business Mgr., Scott Reichard; Volunteer Coord., Loretta Hatch.
Personnel Profile: Full-Time Paid 2; Part-Time Paid 3; Part-Time Volunteers 100; Interns 1.
Governing Authority: Beloit Historical Society. Affiliated with State Historical Society of Wisconsin. Branch Museum: Hanchett-Bartlett Homestead, 2149 St. Lawrence Ave., Beloit, WI 53511. Tax-exempt: 501(c)(3).
Historic Site & History Museum: housed in 1857 restored homestead.
Collections: period furnishings; Stone barn & smokehouse; 1857 district 12 rural schoolhouse.
Research Fields: Beloit area individuals, architecture, businesses, industries, social & political history.
Activities: guided tours; lectures; formally organized education programs for children & adults; Hall of Fame for area leaders; Heritage Days; school group tours.
Publications: monthly newsletter, Lincoln in Beloit; Pioneer Beloit; Confluence.
Hours & Admission Prices: Hanchett-Bartlett Homestead: June-Oct. Sat.-Sun. 1-4. Office: Tues.-Fri. 12-4. Adults $3, seniors & children 12-18 $2; discounts to Heritage Rock County Consortium members; children under 12 & members no charge. ♿
Attendance: 8,500 (estimated)
Membership: Individual $20; Family $25.

* **LOGAN MUSEUM OF ANTHROPOLOGY, (M),** 700 College St., Beloit, WI 53511-5509. Tel.: 608-363-2677 & 2119. Fax: 608-363-7144.
Web Site: www.beloit.edu/logan
Founded: 1893.
Congressional District: 1
Key Personnel: Dir., William Green; Cur. Exhibits & Education, Dan Bartlett; Cur. Collections, Nicolette Meister; Museum Shop Mgr., Becky Moffett.
Personnel Profile: Full-Time Paid 2; Part-Time Paid 10; Interns 1.
Governing Authority: Parent Institution: Beloit College. Tax-exempt: 170(b)(1)(A).
Anthropology Museum.
Collections: American Indian, North, Meso & South American archaeology &

ethnology; European & North African Paleolithic; Asian & New Guinea ethnology. Historic Building: 1869 Civil War Memorial Hall.
Research Fields: archeology & ethnology of Latin America, North America; ethnology of Latin America, Africa, North America, New Guinea; European Paleolithic.
Facilities: visible storage of collections, laboratories, classrooms.
Activities: guided tours; lectures; films; gallery talks; cultural resource projects; study clubs; education programs for adults & undergraduate college students; inter-museum loan, permanent & temporary exhibitions; school programs.
Publications: monographs, Occasional Contributions to Anthropology; guides; Logan Museum Bulletin.
Hours & Admission Prices: Tues.-Sun. 11-4. No charge; donations accepted. Closed college holidays. ♿
Attendance: 5,000 (accurate)

WRIGHT MUSEUM OF ART, BELOIT COLLEGE, (M), 700 College St., Beloit, WI 53511-5595. Tel.: 608-363-2095. Fax: 608-363-2248.
E-mail: museum@beloit.edu
Web Site: www.beloit.edu/wright/
Founded: 1892.
Congressional District: 1
Key Personnel: Dir., Joy Beckman; Collections Mgr., Craig Hadley; Asst. & Museum Shop Mgr., Becky Moffett.
Personnel Profile: Full-Time Paid 2; Part-Time Paid 1.
Governing Authority: Parent Institution: Beloit College. Tax-exempt: 170(b)(1)(A).
Art Museum.
Collections: European & American paintings; works on paper; historic & contemporary photography; sculpture; Asian textiles, ceramics & other arts.
Research Fields: American & European art; works on paper; Asian art; photography.
Facilities: auditorium; classrooms.
Activities: guided tours; lectures; films; gallery talks; concerts; arts festivals; drama; formally organized education programs for undergraduate college students; inter-museum loan, semi-permanent, temporary & traveling exhibitions; children's art classes; children & adult programs.
Publications: exhibitions catalogs; posters.
Hours & Admission Prices: Tues.-Sun. 11-4. No charge; donations accepted. Closed college holidays. ♿
Attendance: 20,000 (estimated)
Membership: Friends of the Beloit College Museums Memberships $10-$500.

Berlin

BERLIN AREA HISTORICAL SOCIETY MUSEUM OF LOCAL HISTORY, 111 S. Adams Ave., Berlin, WI 54923-2023. Mailing Address: P.O Box 83, Berlin, WI 54923-0083. Tel.: 920-361-1274 & 2460.
E-mail: lerdmann@centurytel.net
Founded: 1962.
Congressional District: 6
Key Personnel: Pres., David Olson; Cur., Dan Freimark.
Governing Authority: nonprofit organization. Affiliated with Berlin Historical Society. Tax-exempt.
Historic Building: 1868 Clark School, one room schoolhouse.
Collections: local school history; 3 historic buildings.
Facilities: 100-vol. library of old school books available for use by special arrangement with curator.
Activities: permanent exhibitions.
Hours & Admission Prices: June to Labor Day 2nd & 4th Sun. 1-4; other times by appointment. No charge; donations accepted.
Attendance: 275 (estimated)
Membership: Individual $10; Family $15.

Black River Falls

JACKSON COUNTY HISTORICAL SOCIETY, 13 S. 1st St. & 321 Main St., Black River Falls, WI 54615-0037. Mailing Address: P.O. Box 37, Black River Falls, WI 54615-0037. Tel.: 715-284-5314.
Web Site: www.blackriverfalls.com
Founded: 1916.
Congressional District: 7
Key Personnel: Pres. (V), Eugene Gutknecht; Vice Pres., Jerry Johnson; Museum Dir. & Treas., Gary Morris; Sec. & Cur. Ho Chunk Photos, Mildred Evenson; Cur. Ho Chunk Artifacts, Leona McKee; Cur. Clothing & Artifacts, Gloria Curran; Cur. Manuscripts, Clarice Phillips; Cur. Photos, Jo Anne Dougherty.
Personnel Profile: Full-Time Volunteers 12; Part-Time Volunteers 20.
Governing Authority: board of directors of society. Tax-exempt.
Historical Society Museum: housed in 1885 former Van Schaick Photograph Gallery, and in former 1915 Carnegie Library.
Collections: costumes; tools; school artifacts; collection of photographs 1880-1920; furniture; dairy & logging artifacts; kitchen & household items; manuscripts; dentist office; Victorian bedroom; Americana Music room; musicians of the area.
Research Fields: history of owner-operators of businesses in Black River Falls; identification of Winnebago Indian photos & artifacts; genealogies; flood of 1911.
Facilities: meeting room; work room.
Activities: guided tours; lectures; films; gallery talks; permanent & temporary exhibitions.
Publications: Jackson County-A History.
Hours & Admission Prices: Fri.-Sat. 10-3; other times by appointment only. No charge; donations accepted.
Attendance: 790 (accurate)
Membership: Individual $6; Family $8; Life $50.

Blue Mounds

CAVE OF THE MOUNDS -NATIONAL NATURAL LANDMARK, 2975 Cave of the Mounds Rd., Blue Mounds, WI 53517-0148. Mailing Address: P.O. Box 148, Blue Mounds, WI 53517-0148. Tel.: 608-437-3038.
Founded: 1939.
Natural History Museum.
Collections: local history; cave formations; fossils; rocks; geology.
Facilities: Museum-related items for sale.
Activities: guided tours.
Hours & Admission Prices: Call for hours. Adults $14, children 4-12 $7; children 3 & under no charge.

LITTLE NORWAY, INC., 3576 Hwy. JG N., Blue Mounds, WI 53517. Tel.: 608-437-8211. Fax: 608-437-7827.
E-mail: info@littlenorway.com
Web Site: www.littlenorway.com
Founded: 1926.
Congressional District: 2
Key Personnel: Pres., Scott Winner; Sec. & Treas., John D. Winner.
Governing Authority: individual operation.
Historic Site Museum: housed in 1856 Norwegian pioneer homestead built by Austin Haugen.
Collections: original farmstead buildings; Norwegian & pioneer artifacts. Historic Building: 1893 replica of 12th-century Norwegian Christian Church.
Facilities: Museum-related items & items of Scandinavian origin for sale.
Activities: guided tours.
Hours & Admission Prices: May-June & Sept.-Oct. daily 9-5; July-Aug. daily 9-7. Adults $12, senior citizens $11, groups of 20 or more $10, children 5-12 $5; children under 5 no charge.
Attendance: 38,500

Cable

CABLE NATURAL HISTORY MUSEUM, (M), 13470 County Hwy. M, Cable, WI 54821. Mailing Address: P.O. Box 416, Cable, WI 54821-0416. Tel.: 715-798-3890. Fax: 715-798-3828.
E-mail: info@cablemuseum.org
Web Site: cablemuseum.org
Founded: 1968.
Congressional District: 7
Key Personnel: Chm. (V), Ronald G. Anderson; Exec. Dir., Michelle L. Gostomski, C.F.R.E.; Dir. Education, Sue Benson; Administrative Asst., Colleen Jossart; Naturalist, Cully Shelton; Coord. Events, Sheila Applen; Administrative Dir., Deb Malesevich; Bookkeeper, Diane Cooper; Museum Shop Mgr., Glen Laedtke; Museum Shop Mgr., Claire Laedtke.
Personnel Profile: Full-Time Paid 3; Part-Time Paid 4; Part-Time Volunteers 100.
Governing Authority: nonprofit organization. Tax-exempt: 501(c)(3).
Natural History Museum.
Collections: natural history items.
Major Exhibits: Brain Teasers 2 (T), 11/09-1/10.
Facilities: trail system; outdoor classroom.
Activities: lectures; organized education programs for children; workshops for children & adults; school outreach programs; field trips; annual scholarship; travel programs.
Publications: bimonthly newsletter, Museum Messenger.
Hours & Admission Prices: Tues.-Sat. 10-4. No charge; donations accepted. ♿
Attendance: 25,000 (estimated)
Membership: Cricket up to $49; Pink Ladyslipper $50-$99; Green Frog $100-$249; Butterfly $250-$499; Bluebird $500-$999; Wood Duck $1,000-$2,499; Dragonfly $2,500-$4,999; Common Loon $5,000 & up.

Cambridge

CAMBRIDGE HISTORIC MUSEUM, 213 South St., Cambridge, WI 53523-9617. Mailing Address: P.O. Box 214, Cambridge, WI 53523-0214. Tel.: 608-423-3327.
E-mail: koplin1@msn.com
Web Site: www.cambridgehistoricmuseum.org
Key Personnel: Dir., Nancy Koplin; Pres. (V), Eileen M. Scott.
Personnel Profile: Full-Time Volunteers 1.
Governing Authority: Tax-exempt.
Historic Building: housed in the former Cambridge school building built in 1906.
Collections: school history; Far East & African artifacts; farm equipment; photographs; personal artifacts.
Publications: newsletter.
Hours & Admission Prices: May-Oct. Tues.-Sat. 10-3; other times by appointment. No charge; donations accepted. Closed holidays.
Membership: Senior $15; Individual $20; Family $35; Organization $200.

Cameron

BARRON COUNTY HISTORICAL SOCIETY'S PIONEER VILLAGE MUSEUM, 1 1/2 mile west of Cameron on Museum Rd., Cameron, WI 54822. Mailing Address: P.O. Box 242, Cameron, WI 54822-0242. Tel.: 715-458-2080.
Web Site: www.barroncountymuseum.com
Founded: 1960.
Congressional District: 75
Key Personnel: Pres. (V), Harold Thorson; Mgr. & Museum Shop Mgr., Pat Knapp.
Personnel Profile: Full-Time Paid 1; Part-Time Paid 1; Part-Time Volunteers 150.
Governing Authority: nonprofit organization. Affiliated with State Historical Society. Tax-exempt.
state and local history.
Collections: agricultural, logging & household items; American Indian artifacts; books & manuscripts; dental, medical & veterinary tools; barbershop; depot; farmstead; dentists office; general store; post office; doctor's office; meeting house; filling station; town hall; Jerome Hall Display Bldg.; blacksmith shop; newspaper & printing office; law office; woodwork shop; leather shop-shoe & harness; cheese factory; saloon; period restored outboard motors; 1920 boat used by lumber baron, F.D. Stout; fishing equipment; 1958 Edsel; 1908 International Auto Wagon; 1934 Chevrolet; 1926 Pontiac; 1921 Ford. Historic Buildings: 1906 Joliet Schoolhouse; 1908 Ebenezer Lutheran Church; 1890 Hedin log house & contents; 1900 stone jail.
Activities: guided tours; formally organized education programs for children. Museum Sponsors: Antique Quilt & Needlework Show in July; Heritage Days in July; Civil War Encampment; Voyagers Encampment - Life of Fur Traders in August; Bluegrass Festival; 50's Day Car Show; Great American Magic Road Show; Vintage Baseball - featuring the Milwaukee Cream Citys.
Publications: quarterly, Pioneer Village Gazette.
Hours & Admission Prices: June-Labor Day Thurs.-Sun. 1-5. Adults $5, children 12 & under $3; children under 5 no charge. ♿
Attendance: 5,000 (estimated)
Membership: Single $8; Couple $12; Contributing $25; Supporting $50; Benefactor $100.

Camp Douglas

WISCONSIN NATIONAL GUARD MUSEUM, 101 Independence Dr., Volk Field, Camp Douglas, WI 54618. Tel.: 608-427-1280. Fax: 608-427-1399.
E-mail: eric.lent@dva.state.wi.us
Founded: 1984.
Congressional District: 6
Key Personnel: Cur., Eric Lent.
Personnel Profile: Full-Time Paid 5; Full-Time Volunteers 2; Part-Time Paid 1; Part-Time Volunteers 20.
Governing Authority: state. Parent Institution: State of Wisconsin; Wisconsin Dept. of Veterans' Affairs; Wisconsin Veterans' Museums. Tax-exempt.
Military Museum: housed in 1896 rustic lodge made of white pine logs.
Collections: artifacts & archival materials relative to the history of the men & women of the Wisconsin National Guard from pre-Civil War times to present; general military items that help to describe the changes in warfare & weapons.
Research Fields: ongoing investigations to support exhibit work & programs.
Facilities: 2,500 sq. ft. exhibit space; outdoor aircraft & military equipment static displays.
Activities: slide programs; guided tours; lectures; loan exhibitions; observe air operations on Volk Field. Museum Sponsors: Volk Field fly-in & open house in even number years. Annual Events: Veterans Day Winebago Pow-Wow.
Publications: newsletter published 3 times annually, Volunteer; occasional information & guides, Panorama.
Hours & Admission Prices: Wed.-Sat. 9-4, Sun. 10-2; call to confirm hours. No charge; donations accepted. Closed New Year's Day; Easter; Thanksgiving; Christmas. ♿
Attendance: 8,500 (estimated)
Membership: Associate $10; Bronze Friends $25; Silver Friends $50; Gold Friends $75; Platinum Friends & Organizational $100; Corporate $1,000.

Campbellsport

HENRY S. REUSS ICE AGE VISITOR CENTER, DNR, Kettle Moraine State Forest - Northern Unit, N2875 Hwy. 67, Campbellsport, WI 53010. Mailing Address: N1765 Hwy. G, Campbellsport, WI 53010-3303. Tel.: 920-533-8322; 262-626-2116. Fax: 262-626-2117.
E-mail: jackie.scharfenberg@wisconsin.gov
Web Site: www.dnr.state.wi.us
Founded: 1980.
Congressional District: 6
Key Personnel: Supt., Jerry Leiterman; Forest Naturalist, Jackie Scharfenberg; Museum Shop Mgr., Sue Lawn.
Personnel Profile: Full-Time Paid 1; Part-Time Paid 5; Part-Time Volunteers 235.
Governing Authority: state. Dept. of Natural Resources, Box 7921, Madison, WI 53707. Affiliated area of National Park Service. Tax-exempt.
Park & Geology Museum.
Collections: glacial geology; films.
Research Fields: glacial geology; forest & aquatic ecosystems.
Facilities: films.
Activities: guided tours; interpretive programs.
Publications: brochures; film, Night of the Sun.
Hours & Admission Prices: April-Oct. Mon.-Fri. 8:30-4, Sat.-Sun. 9:30-5; Nov.-March call for hours. No charge; donations accepted. Closed Thanksgiving; Christmas. ♿
Attendance: 28,000 (estimated)

Cassville

STONEFIELD HISTORIC SITE, 12195 County Rd. V V, Cassville, WI 53806. Mailing Address: P.O. Box 125, Cassville, WI 53806-0125. Tel.: 608-725-5210. Fax: 608-725-5919.
Web Site: www.wisconsinhistory.org/stonefield
Founded: 1952.
Congressional District: 3
Key Personnel: Dir., Allen Schroeder.
Personnel Profile: Full-Time Paid 2; Part-Time Paid 10; Part-Time Volunteers 25.
Governing Authority: state. Parent Institution: State Historical Society of Wisconsin, 816 State St., Madison, WI 53706.
State Agricultural Museum: housed on re-created 1890 village open air museum & historic site, situated on 2,000-acre 1868 agricultural estate of Wisconsin's first state governor, Nelson Dewey.
Collections: agricultural & trades tools; professional, commercial & domestic artifacts.
Facilities: six historic buildings, reconstructed village (33 buildings) & contemporary museum.
Activities: guided tours; special events.
Publications: Guide to Stonefield.
Hours & Admission Prices: Memorial Day-early Oct. daily 10-4. Adults $8, senior citizens $6.75, members & children 5-17 $4; discount to groups; children under 5 no charge.
Attendance: 7,200 (accurate)
Membership: Senior Citizen $22.50; Individual & Senior Citizen Family $27.50; Institutional $30; Family $32.50; Supporting $100; Sustaining $250; Patron $500; Life $1,000.

Cedarburg

GENERAL STORE MUSEUM, W61 N480 Washington Ave., Cedarburg, WI 53012-2426. Tel.: 262-375-3676.
E-mail: cccenter@ameritech.net
Web Site: www.cedarburgculturalcenter.org
Governing Authority: Parent Institution: Cedarburg Cultural Center.
History Museum: housed in a restored 1860's era frame building.
Collections: The Roger C. Christensen Collection of antique packaging & advertising art; photographs.
Hours & Admission Prices: Call for hours.

KUHEFUSS HOUSE MUSEUM, W63 N627 Washington Ave., Cedarburg, WI 53012-1945. Mailing Address: P.O. Box 84, W62 N546 Washington Ave., Cedarburg, WI 53012-0084. Tel.: 262-375-3676.
E-mail: cccenter@ameritech.net
Web Site: www.cedarburgculturalcenter.org
Governing Authority: Parent Institution: Cedarburg Cultural Center.
Historic House.
Collections: family photographs & memorabilia.
Hours & Admission Prices: Call for hours.

WISCONSIN FINE ARTS ASSOCIATION, INC., W62N718 Riveredge Dr., Cedarburg, WI 53012-1337. Tel.: 262-377-8230.
E-mail: ozaukeeartcenter@chorus.net
Formerly: Ozaukee Art Center
Founded: 1971.
Congressional District: 9
Key Personnel: C.E.O., Chm. & Pres., Lon Horton; Dir., Paul Yank.
Governing Authority: nonprofit organization. Parent Institution: Wisconsin Fine Arts Association, Inc. Tax-exempt.
Art Gallery: housed in 1843 Cedarburg brewery.
Collections: paintings; sculpture; prints; ceramics; jewelry; glass.
Facilities: fine arts printing department; photography galleries; darkroom; figure drawing studio. Art for sale.
Activities: guided tours; arts festivals; lectures; classes; formally organized education programs for adults & children.
Publications: monthly newsletter.
Hours & Admission Prices: Wed.-Sun. 1-4. No charge; donations accepted. Closed national holidays. ♿
Attendance: 10,000 (estimated)
Membership: Student $12; Senior Citizens $15; Individual $22; Family $30; 1% Club-Family $100; 5% Sustainer $500-$999; 10% Patron $1,000 & up.

WISCONSIN MUSEUM OF QUILTS & FIBER ART, N50 W5050 Portland Rd., Cedarburg, WI 53012-2158. Mailing Address: P.O. Box 562, Cedarburg, WI 53012-0562. Tel.: 262-546-0300.
E-mail: info@wiquiltmuseum.com
Web Site: www.wiquiltmuseum.com
Founded: 2001.
History Museum.
Collections: artwork & quilts of mid-western artists.
Publications: biannual newsletter.
Hours & Admission Prices: Wed.-Sat. 11-3, Sun. 1-4; call to confirm. Adults $2; members no charge.

Chilton

CALUMET COUNTY HISTORICAL SOCIETY, INC., 928 Wieting Ct., Chilton, WI 53014. Tel.: 920-849-4042.
Founded: 1963.
Congressional District: 6
Key Personnel: Pres., Terry Friederichs; Vice Pres., Chuck Schuknecht; Treas., Karen Gerhartz; Historian & Sec., Doris Zarling.
Personnel Profile: Part-Time Volunteers 4.
Governing Authority: nonprofit organization. Tax-exempt.
Farm Museum.
Collections: agriculture; general.
Activities: guided tours; permanent & temporary exhibitions.
Hours & Admission Prices: June-Aug. Sun. 1-4; other times by appointment. No charge; donations accepted. ♿
Attendance: 200 (estimated)
Membership: Senior 65 & over $5; Individual $10; Family $15; Corporate $25; Lifetime $100.

Chippewa Falls

CHIPPEWA FALLS MUSEUM OF INDUSTRY AND TECHNOLOGY, (M), 21 E. Grand Ave., Chippewa Falls, WI 54729-2560. Mailing Address: P.O. Box 711, Chippewa Falls, WI 54729-0711. Tel.: 715-720-9206. Fax: 715-720-9206.
E-mail: cfmit@charter.net
Web Site: www.cfmit.org
Key Personnel: Dir., Rebecca Lorberter
Industry & Technology Museum.
Collections: local history of manufacturing & processing industries; photographs.
Hours & Admission Prices: Tues.-Fri. 11-4, Sat. 10-4; other times by appointment. Adults 13 & over $3, children under 13 $1; members no charge. Closed Independence Day; Thanksgiving; Christmas.
Membership: Homesteader $30; Explorer $100; Voyageur $250; Pathfinder $500; Heritage $1,000. Business Level: Bronze $100; Silver $250; Gold $500; Platinum $1,000; Patron $2,500.

Clear Lake

CLEAR LAKE AREA HISTORICAL MUSEUM, 450 Fifth Ave., Clear Lake, WI 54005. Mailing Address: P.O. Box 242, Clear Lake, WI 54005-0242. Tel.: 715-263-3050 & 2042.
Founded: 1977.
Congressional District: 10
Key Personnel: Pres. (V) & Cur., Charles T. Clark; Vice Pres., Tim Wyss; Treas. & Sec., Ardeth Clark.
Governing Authority: nonprofit organization. Tax-exempt: 501(c)(3).
Historical Society Museum: housed in 1912 Old Brick Elementary School.
Collections: Clear Lake area from 1875 to present; Sen. Gaylord Nelson Room; Baseball Hall of Famer Burleigh Grimes exhibits; films from Gaylord Nelson's career & Burleigh Grimes.
Research Fields: local history.
Facilities: library; reading room; TVs & VCRs; 16mm movies. Specialty items for sale.
Activities: tours; permanent exhibitions.
Publications: brochure; monthly newsletter, Clear Lake Museum Chronicle.
Hours & Admission Prices: Memorial Day to Labor Day Tues. & Fri. 11-4, Sun. 1:30-4:30; other times by appointment. No charge; donations accepted.
Attendance: 1,200
Membership: Individual $25.

Clintonville

FOUR WHEEL DRIVE FOUNDATION, Foot of E. 11th St., Clintonville, WI 54929. Mailing Address: 105 E. 12th St., Clintonville, WI 54929-1518. Tel.: 715-823-2141, ext. 1209. Fax: 715-823-5768.
Founded: 1948.
Key Personnel: Pres., James M. Green.
Governing Authority: nonprofit organization. Parent Institution: FWD Corporation. Tax-exempt.
Company Museum: housed in 1906, Zachow-Besserdick Machine Shop.
Collections: racing and passenger cars; trucks; fire engines; vintage vehicles; World War I ammunition carriers; 1911, passenger car; 1942, FWD/Eliason motor toboggan.
Activities: guided tours.
Hours & Admission Prices: By appointment only. No charge; donations accepted. ♿
Attendance: 500

Coon Valley

NORSKEDALEN NATURE & HERITAGE CENTER, N455 O. Ophus Rd., Coon Valley, WI 54623. Mailing Address: P.O. Box 235, Coon Valley, WI 54623-0235. Tel.: 608-452-3424.
E-mail: info@norskedalen.org
Web Site: www.norskedalen.org
Founded: 1977.
Key Personnel: Business Mgr., Tammy Potaracke.
Governing Authority: Tax-exempt.
Nature & Heritage Center.
Collections: hands-on nature exhibits; local natural & cultural heritage history. Historic Building: 1800s log homestead.
Facilities: nature trails. Museum-related items for sale.
Activities: special events; classes; educational programs; guided tours.
Hours & Admission Prices: Thrune Visitors' Center: May-Oct. Mon.-Fri. 9-6, Sat. 9-5, Sun. 12-5; Nov.-April Mon.-Fri. 8-4, 1st & 3rd Sat. 9-12, Sun. 12-4. Farm: June-Aug. Mon.-Fri. 12-6, Sat. 10-5, Sun. 12-5. Adults $5, children K-12 $2; discounts to groups of 10 or more. Closed New Year's Day; Thanksgiving; Christmas. ♿

Crandon

FOREST COUNTY POTAWATOMI CULTURAL CENTER AND MUSEUM, (M), 5460 Everybody's Rd., Crandon, WI 54520. Mailing Address: P.O. Box 340, Crandon, WI 54520-0340. Tel.: 800-960-5479.
Web Site: www.potawatomimuseum.com
Key Personnel: Dir., Mike Alloway, Sr.; Tribal Librarian, Kim Wensaut
Cultural Center & Museum.
Collections: Potawatomi life & culture; area history; photographs.
Facilities: Museum-related items for sale.
Hours & Admission Prices: Mon.-Fri. 9-4, Sat. by appointment. Adults $3, children 5-12 & senior citizens over 55 $1; discounts to groups; children under 5 no charge.

Danbury

FORTS FOLLE AVOINE HISTORIC PARK, 8500 County Rd. U, Danbury, WI 54830-9351. Tel.: 715-866-8890. Fax: 715-866-8081.
E-mail: fahp@centurytel.net
Web Site: www.theforts.org
Founded: 1945.
Congressional District: 7
Key Personnel: Dir., Steve Wierschem; Pres., Dianne Gravesen; Museum Shop Mgr., Sue Long.
Personnel Profile: Full-Time Paid 2; Part-Time Paid 1; Part-Time Volunteers 317.
Governing Authority: county; society. Parent Institution: Burnett County Historical Society. Tax-exempt.
Fur Trade Museum.
Collections: 18th & 19th-century material relating to North American fur trade; Native American culture of Woodlands, Ojibwe; blacksmith shop; fur trade post; log country school.
Major Exhibits: A Sense of Place, 11/09-1/11.
Research Fields: archaeology; fur trade; county history.
Facilities: library; visitors center.
Activities: historic site tours. Museum Sponsors: Fur Trade Rendezvous; BBQ Fest; Yellow River Echoes - Living History Event, 1802-1805; Christmas at the Fort.
Publications: The Power of Sand; Cecilia; Voices from Our Past; newsletter 3 times a year.
Hours & Admission Prices: Memorial Day to Labor Day Wed.-Sun. 10-4; Sept. Sat.-Sun. 10-4. Adults $7, children under 13 $5; children 5 & under and members no charge. ♿
Attendance: 12,000 (estimated)
Membership: Paddler $25; Trader $50; Explorer $100; Voyageur $500.

De Pere

ONEIDA NATION MUSEUM, (M), W892 County Trunk EE, De Pere, WI 54115. Mailing Address: P.O. Box 365, Oneida, WI 54155-0365. Tel.: 920-869-2768. Fax: 920-869-2959.
Web Site: museum.oneidanation.org
Founded: 1979.
Congressional District: 8
Key Personnel: Dir., Rita Lara; Asst. Dir., Sara Summers; Area Mgr., Dr. Carol Cornelius; Administrative Asst., Susan Peterson.
Personnel Profile: Full-Time Paid 6.
Governing Authority: Indian Nation; Oneida Business Committee. Parent Institution: Oneida Tribe of Indians of Wisconsin. Tax-exempt.
History & Cultural Museum: located on site of original Wisconsin reservation land.
Collections: Oneida Nation and Iroquois Confederacy exhibits; Oneida & Iroquois history, culture & arts; Indian artifacts; tools; clothing; photographs; pre-Columbian to present history; formation of the League of the Iroquois; men's, women's & children's roles in society; Civil War artifacts; lace; dolls; quillwork; moose hair work; weapons; toys; medicines.
Research Fields: tribal history; genealogy; oral histories of Oneida elders; photographic collections; Oneida & Iroquois culture; regional research center: University of Wisconsin-Green Bay; State Historical Society.
Facilities: nature trail; medicinal garden; vegetable garden; picnic area. Local artwork & greeting cards, books & souvenirs for sale.
Activities: guided tours; workshops; lectures; gallery talks; hobby workshops; formally organized education programs; loan, permanent, temporary & participatory exhibitions; off-site hands-on program; annual cultural festival.
Publications: newsletter; brochure.
Hours & Admission Prices: Feb.-May & Sept.-Dec. Tues.-Fri. 9-5; June-Aug. Tues.-Sat. 9-5; group tours by appointment. Adults $2, children $1; discounts to AAM members; Oneida Tribal members & employees no charge. Closed most major holidays. ♿
Attendance: 8,138 (accurate)

WHITE PILLARS MUSEUM, DE PERE HISTORICAL SOCIETY, 403 N. Broadway, De Pere, WI 54115-2511. Tel.: 920-336-3877.
E-mail: info@deperehistoricalsociety.org
Web Site: www.deperehistoricalsociety.org
Founded: 1970.
Congressional District: 8
Key Personnel: Pres. (V), Tom Walsh.
Personnel Profile: Part-Time Paid 1; Part-Time Volunteers 15.
Governing Authority: nonprofit organization. Tax-exempt: 501(c)(3).
Local History Museum: housed in 1836 Greek Revival bank building.
Collections: archives; artifacts; local history; photographs dating back to 1870; funeral cards; city maps; yearbooks; tax records.
Research Fields: city & local history.
Facilities: library containing city & school records from 1857.
Activities: lectures; video presentations; picture shows.
Publications: newsletter.
Hours & Admission Prices: Mon.-Fri. 12-4, other times by appointment. No charge; donations accepted. Closed holidays. ♿
Attendance: 1,553 (accurate)
Membership: Sponsor $20; Benefactor $50; Patron $100; Founder $250; Millennium $500 & up.

Delafield

HAWKS INN HISTORICAL SOCIETY, INC., 426 Wells St., Delafield, WI 53018-1419. Mailing Address: P.O. Box 180104, Delafield, WI 53018-0104. Tel.: 262-646-4794.
Web Site: www.hawksinn.org
Founded: 1960.
Congressional District: 9
Key Personnel: Pres. (V), Mary Daniel; Museum Shop Mgr., Ruth Brehmer.
Personnel Profile: Part-Time Volunteers 25.
Governing Authority: Hawks Inn Historical Society, Inc. Affiliated with the Wisconsin State Historical Society. Tax-exempt.
Historic Building Museum: 1846, restored stage coach inn.
Collections: 1846-1865; furnishings; historical artifacts from the early settlement period.
Research Fields: crafts & furniture of the 1800's; cooking & kitchen use; history of settlement period 1830-present; genealogical research of pioneer settlers of the Township Delafield & surrounding area.
Facilities: visitors' center which includes a multi purpose room for seminars, educational displays, meetings and other functions; galley for group catering. Museum-related items for sale.
Activities: guided tours; lectures; study clubs; docent program; program of developing craft programs based on daily activities of 1846-1863 pioneer Wisconsin.
Publications: quarterly newsletter, Hawks Inn Newsletter.
Hours & Admission Prices: May-Oct. Sat. 1-4; tours by appointment. No charge, donations accepted. ♿
Attendance: 1,250 (estimated)
Membership: Individual $15; Family $25; Business $50; Contributing $100; Patron $500.

ST. JOHN'S NORTHWESTERN MILITARY ACADEMY ARCHIVES & MUSEUM, 1101 N. Genesee St., Delafield, WI 53018-1411. Tel.: 262-646-7220. Fax: 262-646-7222.
E-mail: advancement@sjnma.org
Web Site: www.sjnma.org
Founded: 1984.
Congressional District: 9th
Key Personnel: Supvr., Margaret H. Koller; Archivist, Lynette Ahlgren.
Personnel Profile: Part-Time Paid 1.
Governing Authority: private secondary school; nonprofit. Tax-exempt.
History Museum: housed in 1884 military school.
Collections: academy artifacts, photographs, publications, uniforms, sabers; student items.
Facilities: 600-vol. library of yearbooks & catalogs; over 10,000 photographs; 845 books from Fred C. Best collection of Military Science & History; 1,400 sq. ft. exhibit space.
Activities: guided tours; lectures.
Publications: quarterly magazine, The Beacon.
Hours & Admission Prices: By appointment. No charge; donations accepted.

Dodgeville

IOWA COUNTY HISTORICAL SOCIETY MUSEUM, 1301 N. Bequette St., Dodgeville, WI 53533. Tel.: 608-935-7694.
E-mail: ichistory@mhtc.net
Web Site: iowacountyhistoricalsociety.org
Founded: 1976.
Congressional District: 51
Personnel Profile: Part-Time Paid 1; Part-Time Volunteers 6.
Historical Society Museum.
Collections: local history & culture; photographs; period artifacts.
Research Fields: genealogy.
Publications: quarterly newsletter.
Hours & Admission Prices: Mon.-Fri. 1-4; other times by appointment.
Membership: Individual $10; Couple $15; Historian $25; Master Historian $50.

Eagle

OLD WORLD WISCONSIN, S103 W37890 Hwy. 67, Eagle, WI 53119-2004. Mailing Address: 123 E. Main St., Eagle, WI 53119-2004. Tel.: 262-594-6300. Fax: 262-594-6342.
E-mail: oww@wisconsinhistory.org
Web Site: www.oldworldwisconsin.org
Founded: 1976.
Congressional District: 9
Key Personnel: Dir., Dawn St. George; Cur. Research, Martin Perkins; Cur. Interpretation, Jennifer Van Haaften; Museum Shop Mgr. & Visitor Svcs., Kathleen Reilly; Volunteer Coord., Ruth Burczyk.
Personnel Profile: Full-Time Paid 11; Part-Time Paid 200; Part-Time Volunteers 500.
Governing Authority: state. Parent Institution: The State Historical Society of Wisconsin, 816 State St., Madison, WI 53706. Tax-exempt.
Ethnic Museum & Historic Village.
Collections: over 65 original buildings built by 19th & early 20th-century immigrants; relocated, restored & arranged in 10 ethnic farmsteads & 1870s rural village.
Research Fields: 19th- & early 20th-century Wisconsin & American history with emphasis on immigration, architecture & social institutions; folkways; rural history.
Facilities: dining facilities in restored barn; picnic areas. Gifts items for sale.
Activities: orientation film; special events & exhibitions; living history interpretation; heirloom gardens; 19th-century farms; adult & children's workshops; shuttle tram transport; audio tour guides.
Publications: four booklets on Black, Danish, Finnish, German & Norwegian immigration & settlement in Wisconsin; book, Old World Wisconsin: America's Heartland, A Guide to Our Past.
Hours & Admission Prices: Spring: May 1-June 8 Mon.-Fri. 10-3, Sat. 10-5, Summer: June 9-June 30 Mon.-Fri. 10-4, Sat. 10-5, Sun. 12-5, July 1-Sept. 3 Mon.-Sat. 10-5, Sun. 12-5, Fall: Sept.4-Oct. 31 Mon.-Fri. 10-3, Sat. 10-5, Sun. 12-5. Adults $16, senior citizens 65 & over and students $14, children 5-17 $9; discounts to groups & members; children under 5 no charge. ♿
Attendance: 100,000 (estimated)
Membership: Individual $30; Individual & Guest or Family $50; Family & Guest $65; Sustainer $125; Sponsor $350; Patron $500; Benefactor $1,000.

Eagle River

NORTHWOODS CHILDREN'S MUSEUM, 346 W. Division St., Eagle River, WI 54521. Mailing Address: P.O. Box 216, Eagle River, WI 54521-0216. Tel.: 715-479-4623. Fax: 715-479-3289.
E-mail: ncm.er@verizon.net
Web Site: www.northwoodschildrensmuseum.com
Founded: 1998.
Key Personnel: Dir., Ron Nelson; Museum Shop Mgr., Rouleen Gartner.
Personnel Profile: Full-Time Paid 4; Part-Time Volunteers 50.
Children's Museum.
Collections: hands-on exhibits.
Facilities: Museum-related items for sale.
Activities: special events; birthday parties; programs; art & craft workshops.
Publications: newsletters.
Hours & Admission Prices: Memorial Day to Labor Day Mon.-Sat. 10-5, Sun. 12-5; Sept.-May Tues.-Fri. 10-3, Sat. 10-5, Sun. 12-5. Admission $6 per person; ACM reciprocal membership; members no charge. Closed New Year's Eve & Day; Easter; Mother's Day; Independence Day; Labor Day; Thanksgiving; Christmas Eve & Day. ♿
Attendance: 25,000 (estimated)
Membership: Basic $70; Plus $100.

East Troy

EAST TROY ELECTRIC RAILROAD MUSEUM, 2002 Church St., East Troy, WI 53120-1302. Mailing Address: P.O. Box 943, East Troy, WI 53120-0943. Tel.: 262-642-3263. Fax: 262-642-3197.
E-mail: info@easttroyrr.org
Web Site: www.easttroyrr.org
Formerly: Wisconsin Trolley Museum, Inc.
Founded: 1975.
Key Personnel: Pres. (V), Richard Cecil; Exec. Dir. Operations, Chris Lanning.
Personnel Profile: Full-Time Paid 1; Part-Time Volunteers 35.
Governing Authority: nonprofit. Tax-exempt.
Transportation Museum.
Collections: trolley cars; electric railway cars.
Facilities: Museum-related items for sale.
Activities: slide show; demonstration train rides; 10-mile train ride; dinner rides.
Publications: newsletter, Trolley Gazette.
Hours & Admission Prices: May to Oct. Wed.-Sun. 10-5; June-Aug. Wed.-Fri. 10-2; Sept. Fri. 10-2. Adults $12.50, seniors $10.50, children $8; children under 3 no charge.
Attendance: 18,000 (estimated)
Membership: Individual $35; Family $60 (annual).

Eau Claire

* **CHIPPEWA VALLEY MUSEUM, INC., (M),** 1204 Carson Park Dr., Eau Claire, WI 54703. Mailing Address: P.O. Box 1204, Eau Claire, WI 54702-1204. Tel.: 715-834-7871. Fax: 715-834-6624.
E-mail: info@cvmuseum.com
Web Site: www.cvmuseum.com
Founded: 1966.
Congressional District: 3
Key Personnel: C.E.O. & Dir., Susan M. McLeod; Pres. (V), Marty Fisher-Blakeley; Librarian, Eldbjorg Tobin; Education, Karen DeMars; Cur., Carrie Ronnander; Volunteer Coord., Mary Fandel; Researcher, Melissa Holmen; Facilities Mgr., Donalynn Hayden; Asst. Cur. & Office Mgr., Kathie Roy; Editor, Frank Smoot; B[illegible]ess Mgr., Dorie Boetcher; Coord. Community Programs, Liz Fisher.
Personnel Profile: Full-Time Paid 8; P[illegible]ime Paid 4; Part-Time Volunteers 279; Interns 1.
Governing Authority: private; nonprofit organization. Tax-exempt: 501(c)(3).
Regional Historical Museum.
Collections: historical artifacts of the Chippewa Valley; manuscripts; oral histories; photographs. Historic Buildings: 1860 Lars Anderson log house; 1882 Sunnyview school; 1871-1906 Schlegelmilch house.
Research Fields: history of Chippewa Valley; Wisconsin Indian history; Hmong history; farm & rural life.
Facilities: library & archives; ice cream parlor. Museum-related items for sale.
Activities: guided tours; curriculum-related programs; mini-classes; children's activities; teacher institutes; traveling exhibits. Museum Sponsors: Fourth of July celebration.
Publications: quarterly newsletter; book, Paths of the People: The Ojibwe in the Chippewa Valley; Settlement & Survival: Building Towns in the Chippewa Valley, 1850-1925; Hmong in America: Journey from a Secret War; Farm Life: A Century of Change for Farm Families & Their Neighbors; Farm Crossing: The Amazing Adventures of Addie & Zachery; Ralph Owen's Eau Claire: The Character of a City, 1884-1909; Ralph Owen's Eau Claire: The City Grows Up, 1920-1960.
Hours & Admission Prices: Memorial Day-Labor Day Sat. 10-5, Sun. 1-5; Sept.-May Tues.-Sun. 1-5. Adults $4, children under 18 $2; discounts to AAM, ICOM & AASLH members; children under 2, members & Tues. 5-8 no charge. Closed New Year's Day; Thanksgiving; Christmas Eve & Day. ♿
Attendance: 32,815 (accurate)
Membership: Regular $30; Sustaining $60; Associate $80; Heritage Club $150; Pathfinder $250; Carson Club $500; Ingram Society $1,000.

FOSTER GALLERY, UNIVERSITY OF WISCONSIN-EAU CLAIRE, 121 Water St., Eau Claire, WI 54702-4004. Mailing Address: Foster Gallery/UWEC, 105 Garfield Ave., Eau Claire, WI 54702-4004. Tel.: 715-836-2328 & 3277. Fax: 715-8[illegible]6-4882.
E-mail: wagenetk@uwec.edu
Web Site: www.uwec.edu
Founded: 1970.
Congressional District: 3
Key Personnel: Dir., Thomas K[illegible]nancial Dir., Christos Theo.
Personnel Profile: Full-Time Pa[illegible]ne Paid 8; Part-Time Volunteers 30; Interns 1.
Governing Authority: university, [illegible] organization. Parent Institution: University of Wisconsin-Eau C[illegible]x-exempt.
University Gallery.
Collections: photographs; paintings.
Activities: formal education programs for undergraduate & graduate college students affiliated with UW-Eau Claire; lectures; loan, participatory & traveling exhibitions.
Publications: posters & brochures for each exhibit.
Hours & Admission Prices: Mon.-Wed. & Fri. 10-4:30, Thurs. 10-4:30 & 6pm-8pm, Sat.-Sun. 1-4:30. No charge. Closed academic holidays. ♿
Attendance: 9,520 (accurate)

PAUL BUNYAN LOGGING CAMP MUSEUM, 1110 Carson Park Dr., Eau Claire, WI 54703. Mailing Address: P.O. Box 221, Eau Claire, WI 54702-0221. Tel.: 715-835-6200. Fax: 715-835-6293.
Web Site: www.paulbunyancamp.org
Founded: 1934.
Congressional District: 3
Key Personnel: Pres., Gordon Wall; Vice Pres., Sam Retallick; Exec. Dir. & Museum Shop Mgr., Diana Peterson; Sec. & Treas., Edward Wells.
Personnel Profile: Part-Time Paid 7; Part-Time Volunteers 45.

Governing Authority: bd. of directors. Tax-exempt.
Logging & Lumbering Museum.
Collections: 1890s logging camp including blacksmith shop, barn, cook shanty, bunkhouse, filer's shanty, foreman's office, wanigan, & heavy equipment shed.
Research Fields: logging & lumbering.
Facilities: interactive children's room; interpretive center. Museum-related items for sale.
Activities: guided tours; permanent exhibitions; tall tales room for children.
Publications: brochures for children & adults; booklet.
Hours & Admission Prices: May-Sept. daily 10-4:30. Adults $4, children 4-17 $2; discounts AAA members, WI teachers, & Big Brothers & Sisters. Closed Easter. ♿
Attendance: 12,000 (accurate)
Membership: Annual $30.

Edgerton

ALBION ACADEMY HISTORICAL MUSEUM, 605 Campus Lane, Edgerton, WI 53534. Mailing Address: 1423 E. Rd. 5, Edgerton, WI 53534-8760. Tel.: 608-884-3896 & 6598.
Founded: 1959.
Congressional District: 2
Key Personnel: Chm. & Pres. (V), Robert Babcock; Treas., Rosemarie Burdick; Sec., Lucille Bartz.
Personnel Profile: Part-Time Volunteers 18.
Governing Authority: nonprofit society. Parent Institution: Wisconsin State Historical Society. Tax-exempt.
Historical Society Museum: located on site of 1853, rebuilt Albion Academy, first coeducational institution of higher learning in the state of Wisconsin.
Collections: 1880s furniture; Academy books & records; school equipment; clothing; refurbished school bell; taxidermy artifacts. Historic Building: c.1860s one-room school.
Facilities: library; 100-seat auditorium; picnic grounds.
Activities: guided tours.
Publications: book, History of Albion Academy.
Hours & Admission Prices: June-Aug. Sun. 1-4. No charge; donations accepted.
Attendance: 267 (accurate)
Membership: Individual $10; Life $50.

Egg Harbor

CHIEF OSHKOSH NATIVE AMERICAN ARTS, 7631 Egg Harbor Rd., Egg Harbor, WI 54209-9548. Tel.: 920-868-3240.
Founded: 1975.
Congressional District: 8
Key Personnel: Dir., Coleen Bins.
Governing Authority: Affiliated with the Door County Chamber of Commerce, P.O. Box 219, Sturgeon Bay, WI 54235. Tel.: 414-743-4456.
Native American Art Gallery.
Collections: artwork produced by Native American artists.
Hours & Admission Prices: Memorial Day to Labor Day daily 10-5; Sept. to Dec. call for hours. Closed most holidays. No charge; donations accepted.

CUPOLA HOUSE, 7836 Hwy. 42, Egg Harbor, WI 54209-9564. Tel.: 800-871-1871. Fax: 920-868-1710.
E-mail: cupolahouse@itol.com
Web Site: www.cupolahouse.com
Founded: 1871.
Key Personnel: C.E.O., Gloria Hansen.
Personnel Profile: Full-Time Paid 1; Part-Time Paid 4.
Governing Authority: Affiliated with the Door County Chamber of Commerce, Box 219, Sturgeon Bay, WI. 54235. Tel.: 414-743-4456.
Historic House: 1871 house built by Levi Thorp, located on the Door County Peninsula.
Collections: period furnishings & furniture; pottery; Amish quilts; collectibles.
Facilities: ice-cream parlor; restaurant; art gallery. Gifts & collectibles for sale.
Activities: artist receptions; art shows. Annual Events: Amish Quilt Show; Pumpkin Patch Festival.
Publications: brochure.
Hours & Admission Prices: Daily 10-6. No charge; donations accepted
Attendance: 100,000 (estimated)

Elkhorn

WEBSTER HOUSE MUSEUM, 9 E. Rockwell, Elkhorn, WI 53121-1728. Mailing Address: P.O. Box 273, Elkhorn, WI 53121-0273. Tel.: 262-723-4248.
E-mail: walcohistory@elknet.net
Web Site: walcohistory.org
Founded: 1955.
Congressional District: 1
Key Personnel: Pres. & C.E.O., Philip G. Strong; Dir. Education, Marilynn Coogan; Museum Shop Mgr., Betty Cassagranda.
Personnel Profile: Full-Time Volunteers 6; Part-Time Volunteers 40.
Governing Authority: county; society. Parent Institution: Walworth County Historical Society. Tax-exempt.
Historic House: 1830s Webster House.
Collections: children's museum; costumes; music of composer, Joseph P. Webster; history; Indian artifacts; mounted bird collection; general; agriculture. Historic Buildings: 1889 one-room schoolhouse; 1892 Sharon Town Hall; 1850s carriage barn of John W. Boyd; Doris M. Reinke Resource Center.
Research Fields: Walworth county genealogy; history.
Facilities: 1,500-vol. library of history books, photographs, atlases & maps available for use on premises; resource center; genealogies; reading room.
Activities: guided tours; lectures; permanent exhibitions; educational program for 4th & 5th graders, Morning in a One-Room School, by reservation only.
Publications: monthly newsletter; annual pamphlets, Story of Sweet Bye and Bye; Walworth County History; Without Firing A Shot; school day essay collections, Treasured Moments; Golden Memories; North Walworth County History; audio tape, Sweet Bye and Bye; postcards; booklets; video, Webster House Museum; tape; Sweet By & By & Lorena.
Hours & Admission Prices: May to mid-Oct. Wed.-Sat. 1-5. Adults $5, student & children 6-12 $2; discounts to groups, AAM, AARP, AAA members, senior citizens & Walworth County Residents; children under 6 & members no charge. ♿
Attendance: 7,000 (estimated)
Membership: Junior $5; Single $15; Family $20; Contributing $25; Patron $50.

Ellison Bay

NEWPORT STATE PARK, 475 Cty. Hwy. NP, Ellison Bay, WI 54210. Tel.: 920-854-2500. Fax: 920-854-1914.
Web Site: www.dcty.com/newport/nws.html
Key Personnel: Supt., Michelle M. Hefty.
Personnel Profile: Full-Time Paid 2; Part-Time Paid 6.
Governing Authority: state. Affiliated with the Door County Chamber of Commerce, Box 219, Sturgeon Bay, WI 54235. Tel. 414-743-4456. Tax-exempt.
State Park: located on the Door County Peninsula.
Collections: rocks & minerals; photographs; birds & mammal (taxidermy).
Facilities: 28-mile hiking trails; 16 backpack campsites; sand beach; picnic areas; 23-mile cross-country ski trails; 6 mile snowshoe trail.
Activities: interpretive programs & hikes.
Hours & Admission Prices: Daily 6am-11pm. Call for entrance & camping fees. ♿

Ephraim

EPHRAIM HISTORICAL FOUNDATION, 3060 Anderson Lane, Ephraim, WI 54211. Mailing Address: P.O. Box 165, Ephraim, WI 54211-0165. Tel.: 920-854-9688. Fax: 920-854-7232.
E-mail: info@ephraim.org
Web Site: ephraim.org
Founded: 1949.
Congressional District: 8
Key Personnel: Dir., Sally Jacobson; Pres. (V), Mardi Glenn; Dir. Program & Mktg., Kelli C. Torpey.
Personnel Profile: Full-Time Paid 2; Part-Time Paid 5; Part-Time Volunteers 65; Interns 1.
Governing Authority: Parent Institution: The Ephraim Historical Foundation, Inc. Branch Museums: The Thomas Goodletson House; Pioneer School House; Anderson Store Museum; Anderson Barn Museum. Tax-exempt.
Historic House: c.1853, one of the first permanent buildings built on the Door County Peninsula.
Collections: 1853 restored home with period furnishings; original 1880 schoolhouse with period furnishings & costumes; 1850s log cabin with period furnishings; 1880s barn with Door County art exhibit & general local history & photo exhibits; 1857 general store with original fixtures.
Research Fields: Ephraim & Door county history.
Facilities: archives.
Activities: guided walking tours; Sunday night sing-alongs; child's play stories & crafts; MP3 tours; school tours; children's programming. Museum Sponsors: Historical Programs & Presentations in July.
Publications: quarterly newsletter; walking tour guide; cookbook, Amazing Grazing; books, Door County Letters; Did the Eagle Get You, Dr. Moss?; Images of America - Ephraim; Horseshoe Island - The Folda Years.
Hours & Admission Prices: late June to Labor Day Tues.-Sat. 11-4; Sept. to mid-Oct. Fri.-Sat. 11-4. Adults $5, students 6-18 $3; children under 6 & members no charge. Closed Independence Day; Labor Day. ♿

Attendance: 6,400 (estimated)
Membership: Regular $50-$74; Contributing $75-$99; Supporting $100-$249; Sustaining $250-$499; Patron $500-$999; Founder's Circle $1,000 & up.

Fifield

OLD TOWN HALL MUSEUM, W7213 Pine St., Fifield, WI 54524-0156. Mailing Address: Box 156, Fifield, WI 54524-0156. Tel.: 715-339-2254.
E-mail: matrojak@pctcnet.net
Web Site: www.pricecountyhistoricalsociety.com
Founded: 1969.
Congressional District: 7
Key Personnel: Pres. (V), Therese Trojak; Chm. (V), Larry Wollner.
Personnel Profile: Part-Time Volunteers 20.
Governing Authority: society. Parent Institution: Price County Historical Society. Affiliated with State Historical Society, 816 State St., Madison, WI 83706. Tax-exempt.
History Museum: housed in 1894 Old Town Hall.
Collections: artifacts of the logging era; Price County history; model living room & kitchen; one room school.
Facilities: stage. Crafts, books & museum-related items for sale.
Activities: lectures; demonstrations; school tours.
Publications: brochure; newsletter; books on local history.
Hours & Admission Prices: June to Labor Day Fri. & Sun. 1-5. No charge; donations accepted. ♿
Attendance: 714 (accurate)
Membership: Single $7; Family $9; Contributing $12; Sustaining $17; Life $150.

Fish Creek

EAGLE BLUFF LIGHTHOUSE, Peninsula State Park, Fish Creek, WI 54212. Mailing Address: P.O. Box 218, Bailey's Harbor, WI 54202-9165. Tel.: 920-839-2377.
E-mail: info@eaglebluffighthouse.org
Web Site: www.eaglebluffighthouse.org
Founded: 1964.
Congressional District: 8
Key Personnel: C.E.O., Wayne A. Lemburg.
Personnel Profile: Part-Time Paid 21.
Governing Authority: society. Parent Institution: Door County Historical Society. Tax-exempt.
Historic House: 1868 Eagle Bluff Lighthouse located on the Door County Peninsula.
Collections: maritime & period furnishings.
Hours & Admission Prices: Memorial Weekend to 3rd week in Oct. daily 10-4. Adults $4, children 6-18 $1; children under 5 no charge.
Attendance: 24,793 (accurate)

PENINSULA STATE PARK, Hwy. 42, Fish Creek, WI 54212-9696. Mailing Address: 9462 Shore Rd., Fish Creek, WI 54212-9696. Tel.: 920-854-5976 & 868-3258. Fax: 920-868-1931.
E-mail: thomas.blackwood@wisconsin.gov
Key Personnel: Supt., Tom Blackwood.
Governing Authority: state. Affiliated with the Door County Historical Society, Sturgeon Bay, WI. 54235.
State Park: located on the Door County Peninsula.
Collections: geological, botanical & wildlife exhibits. Historic Structure: Eagle Lighthouse (see separate listing).
Facilities: picnic areas; concession stand; 467 campsites; lookout tower; amphitheater.
Activities: nature center; self guided nature & hiking trails; exercise trail; guided hikes; tennis; tours. Museum Sponsors: musical performances July-Aug.
Publications: brochure, Peninsula State Park.
Hours & Admission Prices: Daily 6am-11pm; call for reservations. Phone for entrance fees & camping fees, camping reservations in writing on state forms accepted Jan.-Sept. Nature Center: Memorial Day to Labor Day daily 10-2; Sept.-May call for hours.

Fond du Lac

GALLOWAY HOUSE AND VILLAGE - BLAKELY MUSEUM, 336 Old Pioneer Rd., Fond du Lac, WI 54935-6126. Mailing Address: P.O. Box 1284, Fond du Lac, WI 54936-1284. Tel.: 920-922-0991.
E-mail: fchs@dotnet.com
Web Site: www.fdl.com/history
Founded: 1948.
Congressional District: 6
Key Personnel: Pres., Sally Albertz; Gen. Mgr., Bob Kuhnz; Chief Cur., Jim Glassel; Vice Pres., Sue Williams; Sec., Donald Kenyon; Treas., Chris Steinert; Membership Chm., Jim Bothe; Cur., William J. Weinshrott; Tour Chm., Carol Henke; Museum Shop Mgr., Dolores Mick.
Personnel Profile: Full-Time Volunteers 50; Part-Time Paid 5; Part-Time Volunteers 225; Interns 1.
Governing Authority: nonprofit organization; society. Owned & operated by Fond du Lac County Historical Society. Branch Museum: Blakely Museum. Tax-exempt: 501(c)(3).
Historic Village & General Museums: c.1868 Victorian mansion, Galloway House & 1982 Blakely Museum.
Collections: Victorian household items; flower gardens; furniture; clothing; artifacts from log cabin times to late 1800s; Indian & Eskimo artifacts; pioneer tools; guns; items from American wars; early industrial tools & machines; paintings; prints; photographs; mounted animals; Susan Colman collection. Historic Buildings: mid & late 1800s village, one-room school; church; courthouse & law office; print shop; toy shop; general store; post office; blacksmith shop; photo shop; railroad depot; grist mill; carpenter shop; leather shop; carriage house; dress shop; quarry locomotive & stone car; railroad depot & caboose; fire house; gazebo; log cabin; drug store doctor's office; bank; town hall; barn; machine shop; farm machinery; 30 historic buildings.
Research Fields: Fond du Lac County.
Facilities: research library on Fond du Lac County. Gifts, old fashioned candy & museum-related items for sale.
Activities: guided tours; permanent exhibitions. Museum Sponsors: Ice Cream Social; Wisconsin 3rd Infantry Regiment (Civil War); WWI dough boys; Halloween & Christmas at Galloway House; Farm & Antique Machinery - Harvest Barn Dance.
Publications: brochures & pamphlets; Fond du Lac County History Video & accompanying Book; newsletter;
Hours & Admission Prices: Memorial Day-Labor Day daily; Sept. 15-Oct. 31 Sat.-Sun. 10-5. Adults $10, seniors & students 13-17 $9, children 5-12 $6; children under 4 no charge; members no charge. ♿
Attendance: 7,000 (estimated)
Membership: Senior Citizen $10; Individual $15; Family $25.

WISCONSIN AVIATION MUSEUM INC., (M), FDL County Airport, Fond du Lac, WI 54935. Mailing Address: 89 N. Pioneer Rd., Fond du Lac, WI 54935-9401. Tel.: 920-924-9998. Fax: 920-921-3186.
Founded: 1999.
Congressional District: 6
Key Personnel: Dir., John Zorn.
Governing Authority: bd of directors. Tax-exempt: 501(c)(3).
Aviation Museum.
Collections: aircraft; aviation memorabilia; military vehicles.
Activities: seminars; educational programs.
Hours & Admission Prices: Call for information.
Membership: Annual $50; Family $100; Lifetime $500.

Fort Atkinson

HOARD HISTORICAL MUSEUM AND NATIONAL DAIRY SHRINE'S VISITORS CENTER, 401 Whitewater Ave., Fort Atkinson, WI 53538-2255. Tel.: 920-563-7769. Fax: 920-568-3203.
E-mail: oberle@hoardmuseum.org
Web Site: www.hoardmuseum.org
Founded: 1933.
Congressional District: 9
Key Personnel: Pres. (V), Sally Koehler; Dir., Kori Oberle; Cur., Karen O'Connor; Volunteer Coord., Tammy Doellstedt; Maintenance, Greg Misfeldt; Accountant, Linda Winn.
Personnel Profile: Full-Time Paid 2; Part-Time Paid 3; Part-Time Volunteers 115; Interns 1.
Governing Authority: municipal; society. Parent Institution: Fort Atkinson Historical Society. Tax-exempt: 170(b)(1)(A).
Local History Museum: housed in 1864 Hoard House.
Collections: history of Jefferson County, Wisconsin; Wisconsin archaeology; U.S. dairy history; early tools & crafts; quilts; dolls; local artwork; decorative arts; Civil War artifacts; National Dairy Shrine exhibit; books; archives. Historic Buildings: 1841 Dwight Foster House; 1867 Frank W. Hoard House.
Research Fields: local Native American history; Black Hawk War; local history & genealogy; Civil War.
Facilities: 3,500-vol. library; archives; reading room.
Activities: guided tours; bus tours; lectures; gallery talks; permanent & temporary exhibitions; Lincoln Era Library & Exhibit; audio walking tour of historic downtown Fort Atkinson; ten o'clock scholar program for 5th graders; fourth grade history essay exhibition. Museum Sponsors: local annual art shows; Ice Cream Social in July; Christmas Open House.
Publications: quarterly newsletter; maps; annual programs; book, The Mounds of Koshkonong; 3-vol. set on the Black Hawk War, Hunting A Shadow, The Battle of Wisconsin Heights, The Battle of Bad Axe.

Hours & Admission Prices: Memorial Day-Labor Day Tues.-Sat. 9:30-4:30, Sun. 11-3; Sept.-May Tues.-Sat. 9:30-3:30. No charge. ♿
Attendance: 14,500 (estimated)
Membership: Individual $20; Family $35; Sponsor $100; Patron $250; Benefactor $500 & up.

Fox Lake

FOX LAKE HISTORICAL MUSEUM, INC., 211 Cordelia St. & S. College Ave., Fox Lake, WI 53933. Mailing Address: P.O. Box 493, Fox Lake, WI 53933-0493. Tel.: 920-296-0254.
E-mail: frankdesigns@powerweb.net
Founded: 1970.
Congressional District: 2
Key Personnel: C.E.O. & Pres. (V), Scott Frank; Museum Shop Mgr., Jim Clark.
Personnel Profile: Part-Time Volunteers 9.
Governing Authority: nonprofit. Parent Institution: City of Fox Lake. Tax-exempt: 170(b)(1)(A).
Railroad Museum.
Collections: Fox Lake & railroad depot history; baggage wagons; time tables; railroad lanterns; miniature display depicting railroad loop; Elmwood Island Indians archaeological exhibit; period kitchen; working blacksmith shop; Fairbanks motorized hand car.
Research Fields: Main Street, Fox Lake.
Facilities: picnic area.
Activities: tours; permanent exhibitions.
Publications: brochures; newsletters.
Hours & Admission Prices: June-Oct. 1st & 3rd Sun. 1-4; other times by appointment. No charge; donations accepted. ♿
Attendance: 250 (estimated)
Membership: Junior $1; Individual & Senior Citizens $3; Family $5; Business $10; Industry $25.

Genesee Depot

TEN CHIMNEYS FOUNDATION, S43 W31575 Depot Rd., Genesee Depot, WI 53127. Mailing Address: P.O. Box 225, Genesee Depot, WI 53127-0225. Tel.: 262-968-4110. Fax: 262-968-4267.
Web Site: www.tenchimneys.org
Founded: 1996.
Key Personnel: Pres., Sean Malone; Chm. Bd., Randy Bryant; Devel., Amanda Shilling; Programs, Kristine Weir-Martell; Mktg., Courtney Kihslinger; Accounting, Elsa Knysak; Cur., Keith MacKay; Devel. & Pro. Asst., Mark Neufang; Volunteer Mgr., Becci Terrill; Museum Store Mgr., Richard Quick.
Personnel Profile: Full-Time Paid 9; Part-Time Paid 1; Part-Time Volunteers 270; Interns 3.
Governing Authority: private; nonprofit organization. Tax-exempt: 501(c)(3).
Historic House: housed in the estate of theatre legends, Alfred Lunt and Lynn Fontanne. Listed on the National Registry of Historic Places.
Collections: personal artifacts; cultural, historic, & artistic materials; historic buildings & furnishings.
Facilities: 2,400-vol. library. Museum-related items for sale.
Activities: docent program; guided tours; lectures; temporary exhibitions; play readings; lectures. Annual Event: Music in the Drawing Room.
Publications: seasonal newsletter, Cast Notes.
Hours & Admission Prices: Tours: May to mid-Nov. Tues.-Sat. reservations recommended. Office: Mon.-Fri. 9-5. Adults $28-$35; children under 12 not admitted. Closed New Year's Eve & Day; Easter; Memorial Day; Independence Day; Labor Day; Thanksgiving & day after; Christmas. ♿
Attendance: 12,000 (estimated)
Membership: Grand Entrance in the Arrival Hall $50; Brunch w/Helen Hayes in the Garden Terrace $250; Game of Hearts w/Larry Olivier in the Library $500; Chat w/Kate Hepburn in the Flirtation Room $1,500; Song w/Noel Coward in the Drawing Room $5,000; Dinner w/Lynn and Alfred in the Dining Room and Lunt-Fontanne Society Member $10,000.

Gills Rock

DOOR COUNTY MARITIME MUSEUM (AT GILLS ROCK), 12724 Wisconsin Bay Rd., Gills Rock, WI 54210-9796. Mailing Address: 120 N. Madison Ave., Sturgeon Bay, WI 54235-3416. Tel.: 920-854-1844 & 743-5958. Fax: 920-743-9483.
E-mail: info@dcmm.org
Web Site: www.dcmm.org
Founded: 1969.
Congressional District: 8
Key Personnel: Exec. Dir., Brian Kelsey; Pres. (V), Dan Austad; Vice Pres. (V), Jeff Weborg; Treas., Pete Horton; Volunteer Coord., Kay Reiche; Museum Shop Mgr., Jan Johnson.
Personnel Profile: Full-Time Paid 5; Part-Time Paid 6; Part-Time Volunteers 2.
Governing Authority: Parent Institution: Sturgeon Bay; registered with State Historical Society. Branch Museum: Sturgeon Bay Maritime Museum (see separate listing); Cana Island Lighthouse & Grounds. Tax-exempt.
Maritime Museum & Historic Site: including shipbuilding history & artifacts located on the Door County Peninsula at Sturgeon Bay; Cana Island, restored historic site.
Collections: artifacts of sailing, Coast Guard & commercial fishing; collection of artifacts & history of the shipbuilding industry. Three shipyards in Sturgeon Bay; Cana Island lighthouse.
Research Fields: shipbuilding & commercial fishing industries.
Facilities: alternate access to island via natural stone causeway (pedestrians only). Museum-related items for sale.
Activities: Annual Events: Door County Lighthouse Walk in May; Door County Maritime Museum Festival in August.
Publications: book on history of the shipbuilding industry in Sturgeon Bay; quarterly newsletter.
Hours & Admission Prices: Fishing Industry Museum: Memorial Day to mid-Oct. daily 10-5. Family $10.50, adults $4.50, children $1.50; discount to groups. ♿
Attendance: 5,000 (estimated)
Membership: Individual $35; Family $45.

Gordon

GORDON-WASCOTT HISTORICAL MUSEUM, 9672 E. County Rd. Y, Gordon, WI 54838. Tel.: 715-376-4249.
Key Personnel: Pres. (V), David D. Benson; Museum Shop Mgr., Pat Finstad
Historical Society Museum.
Collections: local history & culture; photographs.
Hours & Admission Prices: Memorial Day-Labor Day Fri.-Mon. 10-4.

Green Bay

GREEN BAY BOTANICAL GARDEN, 2600 Larsen Rd., Green Bay, WI 54303-4841. Tel.: 920-490-9457. Fax: 920-490-9461.
E-mail: info@gbbg.org
Web Site: www.gbbg.org/index.htm
Key Personnel: Exec. Dir., Susan Garot; Dir. Horticulture, Mark A. Konlock
Botanical Garden.
Collections: plants; flowers; trees.
Facilities: library; 47-acres. Museum-related items for sale.
Activities: educational programs.
Hours & Admission Prices: May-Oct. daily 9-8; Nov.-April Mon.-Fri. 9-4. Adults 13 & over $7, children 5-12 $2; discounts to seniors & AAA members; members and children 4 & under no charge. Closed New Year's Day; Thanksgiving; Christmas. ♿

GREEN BAY PACKERS HALL OF FAME, 1265 Lombardi Ave., Green Bay, WI 54304-3997. Mailing Address: P.O. Box 10628, Green Bay, WI 54307-0628. Tel.: 920-569-7512. Fax: 920-569-7122.
Web Site: www.packers.com
Founded: 1969.
Congressional District: 8
Key Personnel: Pres. Hall of Fame, Inc. (V), Mike Gage; Hall of Fame & Stadium Tour Mgr., Krissy Zegers.
Personnel Profile: Full-Time Paid 3; Part-Time Paid 14.
Governing Authority: nonprofit organization. Parent Institution: Green Bay Packers. Tax-exempt: 501(c)(3).
Sports Museum.
Collections: sports memorabilia of Green Bay Packers from beginning to present.
Facilities: 8 theaters. Green Bay Packer gift items for sale in Pro Shop & Extra Points stores.
Activities: self-guided tours; films; permanent & temporary exhibitions.
Publications: promotional brochure; exhibit guide.
Hours & Admission Prices: Mon.-Sat. 9-6, Sun. 10-5; hours vary on home game days. Adults $10, senior citizens $8, children 6-11 $5; discount to groups. Closed Easter; Thanksgiving; Christmas. ♿
Attendance: 100,000 (estimated)

HAZELWOOD HISTORIC HOME MUSEUM, 1008 S. Monroe Ave., Green Bay, WI 54301-3206. Tel.: 920-437-1840.
Founded: 1995.
Personnel Profile: Part-Time Paid 1.
Governing Authority: Parent Institution: Brown County Historical Society. Tax-exempt.
Historic House Museum: built in 1837.
Collections: period furnishings; photographs.
Hours & Admission Prices: May Sat.-Sun. 12-4; June-Aug. Thurs.-Sun. 12-4. Adults $4; members no charge.

Attendance: 1,500 (estimated)
Membership: Single $25; Family $35-$50; Partner $100-$199; Provider $200-$499; Benefactor $500-$999; Founder's Circle $1,000 & up.

HERITAGE HILL STATE HISTORICAL PARK, 2640 S. Webster Ave., Green Bay, WI 54301-2997. Tel.: 920-448-5150, ext. 118. Fax: 920-448-5147.
E-mail: charleshhsp@tds.net
Web Site: www.heritagehillgb.org
Founded: 1976.
Congressional District: 8th
Key Personnel: Dir., Kristen Paquet; Site Supvr., Debbie Ashmann; Program Coord., Sally Enlow; Chief Cur., Randy Klemm; Cur. Collections, Jack Moga; Supvr. Education, Daniel Liedtke; Preservation Specialist, Nick Backhaus; Museum Shop Mgr., Pat Buckmaster.
Personnel Profile: Full-Time Paid 7; Part-Time Paid 30.
Governing Authority: nonprofit organization. Parent Institution: Heritage Hill corporation under lease agreement with the Wisconsin Dept. of Natural Resources. Tax-exempt: 170(b)(1)(A), 509(a)(1) & 501(c)(3).
Village & Park Museum: located on the site of 1820s Camp Smith, former army outpost.
Collections: Historic Buildings & Furnishings: Franklin Hose Co.; Y.M.C.A. library; 1897 Dewitt blacksmith shop; 1835 Baird law office; 1800-1820 cabin; 1912 Allouez town hall; 1817 cotton house; 1700 Tank College; 1851 Moravian church; 1905 Belgian farmstead; 1902 cheese factory; Franklin Hose Company;
Research Fields: area history relating to the museum's time periods & historic structures.
Facilities: Local history books & period reproductions for sale.
Activities: living history outdoor museum using first & third person interpretation; crafts programs; scenario reenactment of daily activities of the past; formally organized education programs for children.
Hours & Admission Prices: May 4-Sept. 1 Tues.-Sat. 10-4:30, Sun. 12-4:30; Sept. Sat. 10-4:30, Sun. 12-4:30; Oct.-May Mon.-Fri. 10-4:30. Adults $8, senior citizens $7, children 5-17 $6; discount to AAA members; children 4 & under no charge. ♿
Attendance: 36,000 (accurate)
Membership: Heritage Pass $60; Cotton Club $150.

LAWTON GALLERY, UNIVERSITY OF WISCONSIN-GREEN BAY, (M), 2420 Nicolet Dr. (TH 331), Green Bay, WI 54311-7003. Tel.: 920-465-2916. Fax: 920-465-2890.
E-mail: perkinss@uwgb.edu
Web Site: www.uwgb.edu/lawton
Key Personnel: Cur. Art, Stephen Perkins, Ph.D.; Asst. Cur., Natalie Vann; Administrative Asst., Denise Olson
Art Gallery.
Collections: student artwork.
Hours & Admission Prices: Jan.-May & Sept.-Dec. Tues.-Sat. 10-3.

NATIONAL RAILROAD MUSEUM, 2285 S. Broadway, Green Bay, WI 54304-4832. Tel.: 920-437-7623, ext. 10. Fax: 920-437-1291.
E-mail: staff@nationalrrmuseum.org
Web Site: www.nationalrrmuseum.org
Founded: 1956.
Congressional District: 8
Key Personnel: Pres. Bd. Dir., Paul Koch; Exec. Dir., Michael E. Telzrow; Mgr. Operations, Bob Lettenberger; Cur., Daniel Liedtke; C.F.O., Robert Bloedorn; Dir. Education, Jacqueline D. Frank; Museum Shop Mgr., Joan Yskes.
Personnel Profile: Full-Time Paid 10; Full-Time Volunteers 25; Part-Time Paid 10; Part-Time Volunteers 200; Interns 2.
Governing Authority: nonprofit organization. Tax-exempt: 501(c)(3).
Railroad Museum.
Collections: 20 steam & diesel-electric locomotives; 50 examples of rolling stock dating to 1890; Eisenhower equipment; railroad related papers, photographs & artifacts; 19th century maps.
Research Fields: mid-19th century development of railroads in the Midwest.
Facilities: library; archives; 25 acres including a 42,000 sq. ft. train pavilion; 36,000 sq. ft. exhibit center; 95-seat theater. Museum-related items for sale.
Activities: guided tours; lectures; films; permanent & temporary exhibitions; school programs.
Publications: quarterly newsletter, Rail Lines; collection catalog.
Hours & Admission Prices: Jan.-April Tues.-Sat. 9-5, Sun. 11-5; May-Dec. Mon.-Sat. 9-5, Sun. 11-5. Adults $9, senior citizens $8, children 4-12 $6.50; discounts to AAA members; children 3 & under no charge. Closed New Year's Day; Easter; Thanksgiving; Christmas Eve & Day. ♿
Attendance: 75,000 (accurate)
Membership: Individual $35; Family $50; Deluxe $175; Lifetime $1,200.

* **NEVILLE PUBLIC MUSEUM OF BROWN COUNTY, (M),** 210 Museum Place, Green Bay, WI 54303-2780. Tel.: 920-448-4460. Fax: 920-448-4458.
E-mail: bc_museum@co.brown.wi.us
Web Site: www.nevillepublicmuseum.org
Founded: 1915.
Congressional District: 8
Key Personnel: Dir., Eugene Umberger; Chm. (V), Kramer Rock; Pres. NPM Foundation, Becky McKee; Cur. Education, Matt Welter; Cur. Science, John Jacobs; Cur. Art, Marilyn Stasiak; Cur. Collections, Louise Pfotenhauer; Cur. Exhibits, Dennis Grignon; AV Technician, Larry LaMalfa; Recorder, Jeanine Mead.
Personnel Profile: Full-Time Paid 14; Part-Time Paid 1; Part-Time Volunteers 145; Interns 10.
Governing Authority: county. Tax-exempt.
General Museum.
Collections: history items; natural history; anthropology; archaeology; glass; mineralogy; geology; costumes; paintings; sculpture; decorative arts; military; numismatic; historic negatives & photographs; manuscripts; anatomical mannequin; TV news film.
Major Exhibits: Spiders!, 11/14/09-5/23/10; Whatever Happened to...Operation Area Arts, 1/30-10-4/5/10; Here Comes the Bride: Weddings in America (T), 4/24/10-8/29/10; Hatching the Past: Dinosaur Eggs & Babies (T), 6/5/10-5/22/11; Dichos: Words to Live, Love and Laugh By in Latin America (T), 9/10-10/5/10; Through the Needle's Eye and America the Beautiful, The National Tapestry of the Embroiders' Guild of America (T), 10/23/10-2/13/11.
Facilities: 6,000-vol. library; meeting rooms; 132-seat theater. Gift items for sale.
Activities: guided tours; lectures; films; gallery talks; study clubs; formally organized education programs; observe artists at work; inter-museum loan, permanent, temporary & traveling exhibitions; teacher in-service workshops; docent program; TV & radio programs; field trips.
Publications: brochures; newsletters; e-newsletter, 'N Touch; biennial report; special events mailings.
Hours & Admission Prices: Sun. 12-5, Mon.-Tues. & Fri.-Sat. 9-5, Wed.-Thurs. 9-8. Adult $4, children 6-15 $2; discounts to AAM members and school & youth groups; Thurs. 6-8 pm, members and children 5 & under no charge. Closed New Year's Day; Thanksgiving; Christmas. ♿
Attendance: 64,508 (accurate)
Membership: Individual $30; Family $50; Pioneer $100; Explorer $250; Adventurer $500.

Greenbush

WADE HOUSE HISTORIC SITE, W7824 Center St., Greenbush, WI 53026. Mailing Address: P.O. Box 34, Greenbush, WI 53026-0034. Tel.: 920-526-3271. Fax: 920-526-3626.
E-mail: wadehouse@wisconsinhistory.org
Web Site: www.wadehouse.org
Formerly: Wade House Stagecoach Inn & Wesley Jung Carriage Museum State Historic Site
Founded: 1953.
Congressional District: 6
Key Personnel: Dir., David Simmons; Cur. Education, Jeffrey Murray; Maintenance Supvr., Ron Biskobing; Museum Shop Mgr., Jenni Laning.
Personnel Profile: Full-Time Paid 4; Part-Time Paid 29; Part-Time Volunteers 150.
Governing Authority: state. Parent Institution: Wisconsin Historical Society, 816 State St., Madison, 53706. Tax-exempt.
Historic Site & Transportation Museum.
Collections: over 100 horse & hand-drawn vehicles of late 19th & early 20th century; 3-story Greek revival Stagecoach Inn; 2-story Greek revival home; blacksmith shop; Muley sawmill.
Research Fields: historic horse drawn transportation; carriage manufacturing industry; Yankee town builders; farming & agricultural practices; historic foodways; saw milling.
Facilities: picnic area; hiking trails; cafe. Museum-related items for sale.
Activities: guided and self-guided tours; summer day camp programs for children; historic foodway & dinner programs for adults; period games and amusements; candle-making. Special events throughout the season.
Publications: Education Plan; video, Site History.
Hours & Admission Prices: May 12-Oct. 19 daily 10-5. Adults $11, students & seniors $9.25, children & SHSW member $5.50; discounts to groups, AAM & ICOM members and local museum professionals & docents. ♿
Attendance: 23,057 (accurate)
Membership: Individual $35; Individual & Guest $60; Family $60; Patron $100.

Greenfield

GREENFIELD HISTORICAL SOCIETY, 5601 W. Layton Ave., Greenfield, WI 53220. Mailing Address: W208 S6833 High Bluff Dr., Muskego, WI 53150-9681. Tel.: 262-679-5016.
E-mail: bodamer@live.com
Web Site: www.web.me.com/greenfieldwihs
Founded: 1965.
Congressional District: 4
Key Personnel: Pres., Robert Roesler; Vice Pres., Anita Bodamer; Treas., Jean Spouder.
Personnel Profile: Part-Time Volunteers 20.
Governing Authority: nonprofit organization. Parent Institution: Wisconsin Historical Society. Tax-exempt: 501(c)(3).
Historical Society Museum.
Collections: tools; housewares; clothes; furniture & other items pertaining to early history of City of Greenfield. Historic Structures: 1836 log cabin; 1856 Cream City Brick Home.
Facilities: park shelter.
Activities: guided tours.
Publications: newsletter; book, History of Greenfield 1841-1976; CD, Images From the Town of Greenfield, 1845-1945.
Hours & Admission Prices: Open during major events occurring at the civic facility. No charge; donations accepted.
Attendance: 200 (estimated)
Membership: Family $10; Business $25.

Hales Corners

BOERNER BOTANICAL GARDENS, 9400 Boerner Dr., Hales Corners, WI 53130-2273. Tel.: 414-525-5650 & 5601. Fax: 414-525-5610.
E-mail: shirley.dommerwalczak@milwcnty.com
Web Site: www.boernerbotanicalgardens.org
Founded: 1939.
Key Personnel: Exec. Dir., Ellen Hayward; Pres., Lee A. Riordan.
Governing Authority: Parent Institution: Milwaukee County. Tax-exempt.
Botanical Gardens.
Collections: over 500 varieties of roses; herbs; annuals; shrubs; daylilies; peonies; sculptures.
Facilities: 40 acres of formal gardens; cafe. Museum-related items for sale.
Activities: group tours.
Publications: newsletter.
Hours & Admission Prices: Garden: May-Sept. daily 8 to sunset; late April & early Nov. call for hours. Education & Visitor Center: May-Sept. daily 8-7; Oct.-April Mon.-Fri. 8-4. Adults $4.50, seniors 60 & over $3.50, disabled $3, children 6-17 $2.50. ♿

Hartford

WISCONSIN AUTOMOTIVE MUSEUM, 147 N. Rural St., Hartford, WI 53027-1407. Tel.: 262-673-7999.
E-mail: info@wisconsinautomuseum.com
Web Site: www.wisconsinautomuseum.com
Formerly: Hartford Heritage Auto Museum
Founded: 1982.
Congressional District: 9
Key Personnel: Dir., Dale W. Anderson; Pres. (V), Alan Egelseer.
Personnel Profile: Full-Time Paid 1; Part-Time Paid 7; Part-Time Volunteers 50.
Governing Authority: nonprofit organization. Tax-exempt: 501(c)(3).
Transportation Museum.
Collections: 1906-1931 Kissel Motor Car Company automobiles; other vintage cars, trucks, fire engines, and auto-related memorabilia; outboard motors & period engines.
Research Fields: Kissel Motor Car Company.
Facilities: 165-vol. library of auto repair manuals; 78,000 sq. ft. exhibit space. Auto-related items for sale.
Activities: guided tours; concerts. Annual Events: Old Car Show; Spring Concert: annual meeting Kissel Kar Klub International.
Publications: newsletter, Kissel Kar Klub.
Hours & Admission Prices: May-Sept. Mon.-Sat. 10-5, Sun. 12-5; Oct.-April Wed.-Sat. 10-5, Sun. 12-5. Adults $8, seniors over 62 & students $7, children 8-16 $6; discounts to groups & AAM members; children under 8 no charge. Closed New Year's Day; Easter; Thanksgiving; Christmas. ♿
Attendance: 10,000 (estimated)

Hayward

NATIONAL FRESH WATER FISHING HALL OF FAME, 10630 Hall of Fame Dr., Hayward, WI 54843. Mailing Address: P.O. Box 690, Hall of Fame Dr., Hayward, WI 54843-0690. Tel.: 715-634-4440. Fax: 715-634-4440.
E-mail: fishhall@chegnet.net
Web Site: www.freshwater-fishing.org
Founded: 1960.
Congressional District: 7
Key Personnel: Founder, Bob Kutz; Pres., Bill Beckwith; Dir., Emmett A. Brown, Jr.; Business Officer & Sales Shop Mgr., Kathy Polich.
Personnel Profile: Full-Time Paid 3; Part-Time Paid 3.
Governing Authority: nonprofit organization. Tax-exempt: 501(c)(3).
Freshwater & Marine Museum.
Collections: 450 classic outboard motors; 400 mounted fish; 1,000 reels; 5,000 lures; 300 rods; accessories.
Research Fields: fishing records; dated artifacts; world enshrinement for achievement.
Facilities: library of catalogues & books pertaining to fresh water fishing, conservation, history & development, available for research by visit to library by appointment; reading room; cafeteria. Insignia articles & other museum-related items for sale.
Activities: self-guided group tours; periodic seminars & clinics.
Publications: annual book, World Records on Fresh Water Fish; quarterly magazine, Splash.
Hours & Admission Prices: mid-April to Nov. 1 daily 9:30-4:30; Nov. 2 to mid-April office only. Adults $6.50, seniors $6, children 10-17 $3.75, children under 10 $2.75; discounts to tour groups; members no charge. Closed Christmas to New Year's Day. ♿
Attendance: 40,000 (estimated)
Membership: Clubs & Business $50-$100; Life $300.

Hilbert

MAIN STREET ART WORKS, 627 E. Main St., Hilbert, WI 54129. Mailing Address: P.O. Box 77, Hilbert, WI 54129-0077. Tel.: 920-853-7348.
Web Site: www.mainstreetartworks.com
Art Gallery.
Collections: works by local & regional artists including prints, photography, & paintings.
Activities: demonstrations.
Hours & Admission Prices: Fri. 11-7, Sat.-Sun. 11-4; other times by appointment.

Hillsboro

HILLSBORO AREA HISTORICAL SOCIETY, Maple St. - City Park, Hillsboro, WI 54634. Mailing Address: 715 Salsbery Cir., Unit 2, Hillsboro, WI 54634-4305. Tel.: 608-489-3192.
Founded: 1958.
Congressional District: 3
Key Personnel: C.E.O. & Pres. (V), Betty Havlik; Sec., Arlene Schiefelbein; Treas., Nancy Hotek.
Personnel Profile: Part-Time Volunteers 30.
Governing Authority: society. Affiliated with Wisconsin State Historical Society, Madison. Tax-exempt: 501(c)(3).
General Museum.
Collections: photographs; local history items; memorabilia; one-room schoolhouse replica. Historic Building: 1853 log cabin.
Research Fields: local history.
Activities: quilting scrapbook; meetings; guided tours.
Publications: Civil War Letters of Private Eno; The Lucky Kickapoo; Rockton; West Lima; Trippville; Greenwood.
Hours & Admission Prices: June-Labor Day Sun. 1-4; other times by appointment. No charge; donations accepted.
Attendance: 325 (accurate)
Membership: Individual $5; Family $10.

Horicon

SATTERLEE CLARK HOUSE, 322 Winter St., Horicon, WI 53032-1035. Mailing Address: Box 65, Horicon, WI 53032-0065. Tel.: 414-485-2011 & 4028.
Founded: 1972.
Congressional District: 2
Key Personnel: Pres., Geri Pyrek; Vice Pres., Tom K. Jahnke; Sec., Margaret A. Drewa; Treas., Sally Jahnke.
Personnel Profile: Part-Time Volunteers 6.
Governing Authority: society; nonprofit organization. Parent Institution: Wisconsin Historical Society. Tax-exempt: 501(c)(3).

Historical Society Museum: housed in c.1863, Satterlee Clark Home.
Collections: period furnishings; Indian artifacts; blacksmith shop & forge; restored wooden working loom; old black iron cookware; red wing pottery; country schoolhouse.
Research Fields: genealogy.
Facilities: library of books, newspapers & microfilm pertaining to local history available for use by appointment; botanical garden.
Activities: guided tours; films; reading room; temporary exhibitions; map. Annual Event: Old Fashioned Christmas.
Publications: brochure, A Walking Tour of Historic Buildings.
Hours & Admission Prices: May-Oct. 4th Sun. of month 1-4; Dec. 1st Sun. of month 1-4; other times by appointment. No charge; donations accepted.
Attendance: 300 (estimated)
Membership: Active $5; Associate $10; Contributing $25; Sustaining $50; Patron $100.

Hudson

THE OCTAGON HOUSE, 1004 Third St., Hudson, WI 54016-1219. Tel.: 715-386-2654.
E-mail: octagonhousemuseum@juno.com
Founded: 1948.
Congressional District: 3
Key Personnel: Pres. (V), Dolores Taavola; Treas., Dorothy Wilson; Dir., Heidi Rushmann; Vice Pres., Opal Rong; Sec., LaVonne McCombie.
Personnel Profile: Part-Time Paid 1; Part-Time Volunteers 56; Interns 2.
Governing Authority: nonprofit society. Parent Institution: St. Croix County Historical Society. Tax-exempt: 170(b)(1)(A).
Victorian Museum: housed in 1855 Octagonal House; carriage house & garden house.
Collections: furniture; books; doll collection; tools; clothing; c.1800 miscellaneous items from St. Croix homes; carriage house; Garden House: 19th century blacksmith shop, country store, summer kitchen.
Research Fields: local & county-wide history; genealogies of county residents.
Facilities: 600-vol. library of county history, novels, Bibles & other reference books available for study on premises.
Activities: lectures; training program for museum guides; tours of St. Croix Valley; tapings of old settlers of county; house tour for groups of 30 or more; city tours; tea tours; cemetery tour. Annual Events: Theatre in the garden July & August; Christmas Tour of Homes in November; Lite-up Night in December.
Publications: pamphlets, Westward to the St. Croix; Hudson in the Early Days; Historical Map of St. Croix County; The Life of a Boy in the Middle West; Hudson, 1900-1909, a Rail-River Town; History of the Octagon House Family; 50 Years on Petticoat Lane, Historic Hudson Revisited.
Hours & Admission Prices: May-Aug. Wed.-Sat. 12-4:30, Sun. 2-4:30; Sept.-Oct. & Dec. Sat. 12-4:30, Sun. 2-4:30. Adults $7, teens $3, children $2; discounts to AAA members. Closed national holidays.
Attendance: 3,000 (estimated)
Membership: Individual $10; Family $15.

Hurley

IRON COUNTY HISTORICAL MUSEUM, 303 Iron St., Hurley, WI 54534-1356. Tel.: 715-561-2244.
E-mail: genec@chartermi.net
Web Site: www.hurleywi.com/historymuseum1.aspx
Formerly: Old Iron County Courthouse Museum
Founded: 1976.
Congressional District: 7
Key Personnel: C.E.O., Chm., Pres. (V) & Museum Shop Mgr., Gene Cisewski; Treas., Minerva Stefani; Sec., Helen Zuvich.
Personnel Profile: Full-Time Volunteers 20; Part-Time Volunteers 20; Interns 2.
Governing Authority: society; nonprofit. Parent Institution: Wisconsin State Historical Society. Tax-exempt: 501(c)(3).
General Museum: housed in 1893 Old Iron County Courthouse.
Collections: mining, farm, lumbering & household artifacts; textiles; period clothing & home furnishings; picture gallery; microfilm collection of county newspapers.
Research Fields: mining.
Facilities: library available for use on premises only; 200-seat auditorium. Hand-crafted & other museum-related items for sale.
Activities: guided tours; permanent exhibitions; ancient carpet weaving demonstrations.
Publications: brochures.
Hours & Admission Prices: Mon., Wed. & Fri.-Sat. 10-2; other times by appointment. No charge; donations accepted. Closed holidays. ♿
Attendance: 5,200 (estimated)
Membership: Individual $5; Family $10; Business & Clubs $25; Life $175.

Janesville

THE LINCOLN-TALLMAN RESTORATIONS, 440 N. Jackson St., Janesville, WI 53548. Mailing Address: P.O. Box 8096, Janesville, WI 53547-8096. Tel.: 608-752-4519 & 756-4509; 800-577-1859. Fax: 608-741-9596.
E-mail: jvanhaaften@rchs.us
Web Site: www.rchs.us
Founded: 1951.
Congressional District: 1
Key Personnel: C.E.O., Joel Van Haaften; Administrative Asst., Joyce Dodge; Collections Mgr., Laurel Fant.
Personnel Profile: Full-Time Paid 1; Part-Time Paid 7; Part-Time Volunteers 300; Interns 1.
Governing Authority: nonprofit organization. Parent Institution: The Rock County Historical Society. Tax-exempt: 501(c)(3).
Historic House.
Collections: 19th-century decorative arts & furnishings; Tallman family furnishings & personal artifacts; Tallman ethnological collection. Historic Buildings: 1842 Stone House; 1855-57 The Tallman House; 1855-57 Tallman Horse Barn.
Research Fields: 19th-century life & customs.
Facilities: Museum-related items for sale.
Activities: guided tours; docent program; permanent & temporary exhibits; special events; children's educational programs; historic reenactments pertaining to Tallman family events.
Publications: information circulars; annual report; Preservation Ordinances in Action: Rock County; A Good & Caring Woman: The Life & Times of Nellie Tallman; There Stands Old Rock, County, Wisconsin & the War to Preserve the Union; The Recorder, quarterly newsletter.
Hours & Admission Prices: June-Sept. daily 9-4; Nov. 20-Dec. holiday tours daily. Adults $8, senior citizens $7.50, students 6-18 $4; discounts to groups, Time Travelers, AAA, AAM & ICOM members; members no charge. Closed all major holidays. ♿
Attendance: 4,480 (accurate)
Membership: Student $5; Senior Individual $15; Individual $25; Household $45; Patron $100; Benefactor $250; Corporate $500; Life $1,000.

ROCK COUNTY HISTORICAL SOCIETY, (M), 426 N. Jackson St., Janesville, WI 53548. Mailing Address: P.O. Box 8096, Janesville, WI 53547-8096. Tel.: 608-756-4509 & 800-577-1859. Fax: 608-741-9596.
E-mail: rchs@rchs.us
Founded: 1948.
Congressional District: 1
Key Personnel: C.E.O. & Exec. Dir., Madge B. Murphy; Pres. (V), Pat Thom; Administrative Asst., Joyce Dodge; Collections Mgr., Melissa deBie.
Personnel Profile: Full-Time Paid 2; Full-Time Volunteers 1; Part-Time Paid 1; Part-Time Volunteers 300; Interns 1.
Governing Authority: nonprofit organization. Branch Museum: 1853, Frances Willard Schoolhouse, 4-H Fairgrounds; The Lincoln-Tallman Restorations: 1855-1857, Tallman House & Horse Barn; Helen Jeffris Wood Museum Center 1910, 426 N. Jackson St.; 1842, Stone House, 440 N. Jackson, Janesville, WI. Tax-exempt: 501(c)(3).
Historical Society Museum.
Collections: local history; 19th-century decorative arts & furnishings; social history & vehicles; manuscript & iconographic collections.
Research Fields: Rock County & Wisconsin history.
Facilities: 3,000-vol. library of material on Rock County & Wisconsin available for use on premises; meeting room; two galleries. Historic publications & other museum-related items for sale.
Activities: guided tours; lectures; concerts; arts festival; formally organized education programs for children; docent program; permanent & temporary exhibitions; school loan service.
Publications: irregular booklets & guides; information circulars; annual report; Preservation Ordinances in Action: Rock County; A Good & Caring Woman: The Life & Times of Nellie Tallman; There Stands Old Rock, Rock County, Wisconsin and the War to Preserve the Union; The Recorder, quarterly newsletter.
Hours & Admission Prices: Archives: Wed.-Thurs. 9-3, Fri. 12-3 & by appointment. Museum: daily 9-4. Lincoln-Tallman House: Adults $8, members & seniors $7.50, children $4; discounts to Time Travelers, Beloit Historical Society, Milton Historical Society, AAA, AAM & AASLH members. ♿
Attendance: 16,000 (estimated)
Membership: Student $5; Senior Individual $15; Individual $25; Household $45; Patron $100; Benefactor $250; Corporate $500; Life $1,000.

Jefferson

AZTALAN MUSEUM, N. 6264 Hwy. Q, Jefferson, WI 53549. Mailing Address: P.O. Box 122, Lake Mills, WI 53551-0122. Tel.: 920-648-4362; 8575 (off season).
Founded: 1941.
Congressional District: 9
Key Personnel: Bd. Member (V) & Sec., Dr. Cheryl D. Peterson; Pres. (V), Michael Ayers; Cur., Steve Steigerwald; Museum Shop Mgr., Bob Conlin; Museum Shop Mgr., Deb Conlin.
Personnel Profile: Full-Time Volunteers 2; Part-Time Volunteers 40.
Governing Authority: society. Parent Institution: Lake Mills - Aztalan Historical Society, Inc. Tax-exempt.
General Museum.
Collections: American Indian artifacts; history; archaeology; Hansen Granary Tool Collection. Historic Buildings: 1852 Aztalan Baptist Church; 1843 Pettey cabin; 1849 Bornell Cabin; 1867 Zickert house; 1850s Mamre Church (log cabin construction, built by Moravians); 1918 Aztalan one room school.
Facilities: library of manuscripts, letters, maps, newspapers, books, & magazines pertaining to local history available to researchers at public library at Lake Mills. Society publications & other museum-related items for sale.
Activities: Museum Sponsors: Aztalan Day in July.
Publications: leaflets, The Aztalan Story; The Pioneer Aztalan Story; booklet, The Ancient Aztalan Story; annual program.
Hours & Admission Prices: mid May to Sept. Thurs.-Sun. 12-4. Adults $3, children 6-17 $1; discounts to groups; members & children under 6 no charge.
Attendance: 6,000 (estimated)
Membership: Individual $10; Life $100.

Kaukauna

CHARLES A. GRIGNON MANSION, 1313 Augustine St., Kaukauna, WI 54130-1613. Mailing Address: 330 E. College Ave., Appleton, WI 54911-5715. Tel.: 920-735-9370. Fax: 920-733-8636.
E-mail: ochs@myhistorymuseum.org
Web Site: www.myhistorymuseum.org
Founded: 1837.
Congressional District: 8
Key Personnel: C.E.O., Terry Bergen; Pres. (V), Ed Bush.
Personnel Profile: Part-Time Volunteers 30.
Governing Authority: society. Parent Institution: Outagamie County Historical Society, Inc. Subsidiary Institutions: Outagamie Museum and Houdini Historical Center, 330 E. College Ave.; The History Museum, 330 E. College Ave., Appleton, WI 54911. Tax-exempt: 501(c)(3).
Historic House: 1837 Charles A. Grignon Mansion.
Collections: Greek revival home furnished in pre-Civil War era photographs, furnishings, decorative & fine arts; books.
Research Fields: mid-19th century rural life; fur trade era.
Facilities: Museum-related items for sale.
Activities: guided thematic tours.
Publications: quarterly, History Today.
Hours & Admission Prices: By appointment only to groups of ten or more. Closed major holidays.
Attendance: 6,000 (accurate)

Kenosha

DINOSAUR DISCOVERY MUSEUM, 5608 Tenth Ave., Kenosha, WI 53140-4007. Mailing Address: 5500 First Ave., Kenosha, WI 53140-3778. Tel.: 262-653-4450. Fax: 262-653-4445.
E-mail: ptouhey@kenosha.org
Web Site: kenosha.org/dinosaurdiscovery
Founded: 2006.
Congressional District: 1
Key Personnel: Dir., Paula Touhey; Pres. (V), Loren Keating; Vice Pres., Leo Chiappetta; Coord. Devel., Peggy Gregorski; Sr. Cur. Education, Nancy Mathews; Cur. Education, Chris DeSantis; Cur. Exhibits, Rachel Klees Andersen; Sr. Cur. Collections & Exhibits, Dan Joyce; Cur. Collections, Gina Radandt; Office Mgr., Rita Myers.
Personnel Profile: Part-Time Paid 7; Part-Time Volunteers 25; Interns 2.
Governing Authority: municipal; nonprofit. Parent Institution: Kenosha Public Museum, Kenosha, WI. Tax-exempt: 170(b)(1)(A).
Dinosaur Museum.
Collections: life-sized carnivore dinosaur replicas; hands-on dinosaur & fossil exhibits.
Research Fields: evolutionary link between meat-eating therapods & modern birds.
Facilities: classroom; lab; 5,000 sq. ft. exhibit space; field research station. Museum-related items for sale.
Activities: volunteer program; formal education program; temporary exhibitions; hands-on activities.
Publications: bimonthly newsletter, Friends of the Museum News.
Hours & Admission Prices: Tues.-Sun. 12-5. No charge; donations accepted. Closed New Year's Eve & Day; Martin Luther King Jr. Day; Good Friday; Memorial Day; Independence Day; Labor Day; Thanksgiving; Christmas Eve & Day. ♿
Attendance: 17,200 (accurate)
Membership: Individual $15; Family $25; Patron $50; Sponsor $100; Life $500; Benefactor $1,000.

KENOSHA COUNTY HISTORICAL SOCIETY AND MUSEUM, INC., (M), 220 51st Place, Kenosha, WI 53140-2909. Tel.: 262-654-5770, ext. 102. Fax: 262-654-1730.
E-mail: kchs@kenoshahistorycenter.org
Web Site: www.kenoshahistorycenter.org
Founded: 1878.
Congressional District: 1
Key Personnel: Pres. (V), P. Mike Maki; Exec. Dir., Tom Schleif; Collections Mgr., Cynthia J. Nelson; Dir. Operations & Museum Shop Mgr., Don Shepard; Bookkeeper, Kim Chiodo.
Personnel Profile: Full-Time Paid 2; Part-Time Paid 4; Part-Time Volunteers 65.
Governing Authority: private; nonprofit corporation. Tax-exempt: 501(c)(3).
Local History Museum.
Collections: manuscripts; toys & dolls; American decorative arts; folk art & portraits; Kenosha automotive manufacturing; general historic objects relating to Kenosha county.
Research Fields: city & county of Kenosha; southeastern Wisconsin; school curriculum development.
Facilities: 2,000-vol. library of local, state & U.S. history books & bound volumes of newspapers available for use on premises; 5,000 photographic images; reading room. Booklets for sale.
Activities: guided tours; permanent & temporary exhibitions; educational materials & kits; programs.
Publications: quarterly newsletter; occasional books & pamphlets; History in the Making.
Hours & Admission Prices: Tues.-Fri. 10-4:30, Sat. 10-4, Sun. 12-4. Archives: Wed.-Fri. 2-4:30. Suggested Donation: Adults $1, children $.50. Closed holidays. ♿
Attendance: 16,000 (accurate)
Membership: Senior $15; Individual $20; Family, Club & Corporate $30; Homesteader $100; Settler $250; Lighthouse Keeper $500; Rambler $1,000; Ambassador $5,000.

* **KENOSHA PUBLIC MUSEUM, (M),** 5500 1st Ave., Kenosha, WI 53140-3778. Tel.: 262-653-4140. Fax: 262-653-4437.
E-mail: ptouhey@kenosha.org
Web Site: kenosha.org/museum
Founded: 1933.
Congressional District: 1
Key Personnel: Dir., Paula Touhey; Pres. (V), Loren Keating; Chm. (V), Leo Chiappetta; Sr. Cur. Exhibits & Collections, Dan Joyce; Sr. Cur. Education, Nancy Mathews; Cur. Exhibits, Rachel Klees Anderson; Cur. Collections, Gina Radandt; Devel. Coord., Peggy Gregorski; Office & Museum Shop Mgr., Rita Myers; Coord. Operations, Ken Ade.
Personnel Profile: Full-Time Paid 11; Part-Time Paid 14; Part-Time Volunteers 150; Interns 4.
Governing Authority: municipal. Subsidiary Institutions: Dinosaur Discovery Museum; Civil War Museum. Tax-exempt: 170(b)(1)(A).
Natural History & Art Museum.
Collections: Asian art & ivory carvings, Ethnographic Collections (Native American, Oceania, African); zoology; botany; geology; anthropology; archaeology; study collections; mammals of the world: mammoths & excavation exhibits; local, national & international art.
Research Fields: archaeology; anthropology; geology; megafauna research; mammoths; Paleo-Indian; museum education.
Facilities: 4,000-vol. library on art, cultural & natural history available on premises; 200-seat auditorium. Museum-related items for sale.
Activities: tours for groups; lectures; films; formally organized education programs for children & adults; outreach loan service; temporary & permanent exhibitions.
Publications: FOM newsletter; pamphlet, The Lorado Z. Taft Dioramas; Early Wisconsin Pottery; quarterly program schedule; Peter V. Bianchi: The Art of Science.
Hours & Admission Prices: Sun.-Mon. 12-5, Tues.-Sat. 9-5. No charge; donations accepted. Closed New Year's Eve & Day; Martin Luther King Jr. Day; Good Friday; Memorial Day; Independence Day; Labor Day; Thanksgiving; Christmas Eve & Day. ♿
Attendance: 113,500 (accurate)

Membership: Annual $15; Family $25; Associate & Corporation $50; Patron $100; Life $500; Benefactor $1,000.

Kewaunee

KEWAUNEE COUNTY HISTORICAL JAIL MUSEUM, Court House Sq., Kewaunee, WI 54216. Mailing Address: 613 Dodge St., Kewaunee, WI 54216-1322. Tel.: 920-388-7176 & 3858.
Web Site: www.rootsweb.com/~wikchs
Founded: 1970.
Congressional District: 8
Key Personnel: Pres. (V), Thomas Schuller; Vice Pres., Jerry Abitz; Treas., Joe Blazei; Sec., Julie Bloor.
Personnel Profile: Part-Time Volunteers 50.
Governing Authority: society. Affiliated with Wisconsin State Historical Society. Tax-exempt: 170(B)(1)(A).
General Museum: housed in 1876 sheriff's residence & adjoining dungeon type jail cells.
Collections: furnished living room, bedroom, sheriff's office; tool shed; manuscripts; Indian artifacts; early settlers artifacts; U.S.S. Pueblo display & replica; war mementos; silver; children's toys; writings by old settlers; wood carvings including one of Custer's Last Stand.
Research Fields: on our collections.
Activities: guided tours for schools & organizations on request; permanent & temporary exhibitions; annual fund drive.
Publications: quarterly newsletter to members; books on Kewaunee County History; audio & VHS tapes.
Hours & Admission Prices: Memorial Day-Labor Day daily 12-4. Suggested Donation: adults $2, students $1.
Attendance: 356 (accurate)

King

WISCONSIN VETERANS MUSEUM-KING, Wisconsin Veterans Home, Hwy. QQ, King, WI 54946. Mailing Address: 30 W. Mifflin St., Madison, WI 53703-2589. Tel.: 608-267-7207; 715-258-1486 & 5586. Fax: 608-264-7615; 715-258-5736.
Web Site: museum.dva.state.wi.us
Founded: 1935.
Congressional District: 6
Key Personnel: C.E.O., John Scocos; Chm., Mack E. Hughes; Chm. (V), John Driscoll; Acting Dir., Tony Cappozzo; Cur. Exhibitions & Collections Mgr., Jeff Kollatin; Museum Operations Mgr., Lynnette M. Wolfe; Registrar, Kristine Zickuhr; Cur., William Brewster; Acting Museum Shop Mgr., Crystal Pierce.
Personnel Profile: Full-Time Paid 12; Full-Time Volunteers 6; Part-Time Paid 15; Part-Time Volunteers 6; Interns 2.
Governing Authority: state. Parent Institution: Wisconsin Dept. Veterans Affairs. Affiliated Museum: Wisconsin Veterans Museum-Madison. Tax-exempt.
Military History Museum.
Collections: Civil War & World War II artifacts and displays including exhibits relating to Korean & Vietnam Wars; uniforms; arms; equipment.
Research Fields: Wars; military, veteran history.
Activities: permanent & temporary exhibitions.
Publications: brochures, Wisconsin in the World Wars; When America Fought Its Costliest War, Wisconsin Served in the Front Rank; Wisconsin at War.
Hours & Admission Prices: Mon.-Fri. 8-4, Sat.-Sun. 8-11 & 1-4. No charge. ♿
Attendance: 8,000 (estimated)

La Crosse

HIXON HOUSE, 429 N. 7th St., La Crosse, WI 54601-3301. Mailing Address: La Crosse County Historical Society, P.O. Box 1272, La Crosse, WI 54602-1272. Tel.: 608-782-1980. Fax: 608-793-1359.
E-mail: lchs@centurytel.net
Web Site: lchsweb.org
Founded: 1898.
Congressional District: 3
Key Personnel: C.E.O., Dr. Carl R. Miller; Pres. (V) & Chm. (V), Dr. Erik Gundersen; Cur., Nisse Taunt; Museum Shop Mgr., Lori Strom; Admin., Michelle Logan.
Personnel Profile: Full-Time Paid 2; Full-Time Volunteers 1; Part-Time Paid 9; Part-Time Volunteers 32.
Governing Authority: society. Parent Institution: La Crosse Historical Society. Tax-exempt: 501(c)(3).
Period Home: housed in c.1859 Hixon House.
Collections: artifacts that reflect life in La Crosse between 1860-1910; historical sketches; personal family collection reflecting upper class 19th century life style; furniture; paintings; fabrics & textiles; imported & domestic glassware & china.
Research Fields: local history.
Facilities: historic house. Museum-related items for sale.
Activities: guided tours; permanent & temporary exhibits; Christmas tours.
Publications: newsletter, Past, Present & Future; reprints of local histories.
Hours & Admission Prices: Memorial Day to Labor Day daily 11-5, group tours by appointment. Adults $8.50, children 12 & under $4.50; discounts to senior citizens & groups. ♿
Attendance: 8,000 (estimated)
Membership: Individual $35; Family $50; Century $125; Business $200; Patron $250; Benefactor $500; Heritage $1,000; Fellows Club $5,000.

PUMP HOUSE REGIONAL ARTS CENTER, 119 King St., La Crosse, WI 54601-4080. Tel.: 608-785-1434. Fax: 608-785-1432.
E-mail: info@thepumphouse.org
Web Site: www.thepumphouse.org
Founded: 1977.
Congressional District: 30
Key Personnel: Exec. Dir., Toni Asher; Pres. (V), Deb Stover.
Personnel Profile: Full-Time Paid 1; Part-Time Paid 2; Part-Time Volunteers 10; Interns 1.
Governing Authority: not-for-profit organization. Tax-exempt: 501(c)(3).
Arts Center: housed in 1880 brick Romanesque revival water pumping building listed on National Register of Historical Buildings.
Collections: Midwestern art of regional artists & craftspersons Historical photographs.
Research Fields:
Facilities: 2,000 sq. ft. exhibit space; 4 galleries.
Activities: workshops & classes for all ages; docent led tours; performing arts events.
Publications: quarterly newsletter, Revue Arts.
Hours & Admission Prices: Tues.- Fri. noon-5, Sat.10-4. No charge; donations accepted. Closed New Year's Day; Memorial Day; Independence Day; Labor Day; Thanksgiving; Christmas. ♿
Attendance: 12,000 (estimated)
Membership: Student $20; Individual $30; Household $40; Sustaining $75; Patron $125; Arts Angel $250; Director $500; Benefactor $1,000.

RIVERSIDE MUSEUM, (M), 410 E. Veterans Memorial Dr., La Crosse, WI 54601-4490. Mailing Address: P.O. Box 1272, La Crosse, WI 54602-1272. Tel.: 608-782-1980. Fax: 608-793-1359.
E-mail: lchs@centurytel.net
Web Site: lchsweb.org
Founded: 1990.
Congressional District: 3
Key Personnel: C.E.O. & Dir., Carl R. Miller; Pres. (V), Dr. Erik Gundersen; Museum Coord., Lori Strom; Admin., Michelle Logan.
Personnel Profile: Full-Time Paid 2; Full-Time Volunteers 1; Part-Time Paid 9; Part-Time Volunteers 32.
Governing Authority: private; nonprofit. Parent Institution: La Crosse County Historical Society. Tax-exempt: 501(c)(3).
History Museum: housed in an old fish hatchery building. Listed on the National Register of Historic Sites.
Collections: concentration on area history, from prehistoric to modern times with special emphasis on importance of river system.
Research Fields: riverboat travel.
Facilities: 2,000 sq. ft. exhibit space; 35-seat theater.
Activities: films; participatory exhibits. Annual Event: War Eagle Days-commemoration the sinking of the riverboat in 1870.
Publications: bimonthly newsletter, Past, Present and Future.
Hours & Admission Prices: Memorial Day-Labor Day daily 10-5; tours by appointment. Families $5, adults $2, children $1. ♿
Attendance: 12,000 (accurate)
Membership: Individual $35; Family $50; Century $125; Business $200; Patron $250; Sustaining $500; Heritage $1,000; Fellows Club $5,000.

SWARTHOUT MEMORIAL MUSEUM, 112 S. 9th St., La Crosse, WI 54601-4111. Mailing Address: La Crosse County Historical Society, P.O. Box 1272, La Crosse, WI 54602-1272. Tel.: 608-782-1980. Fax: 608-793-1359.
E-mail: lchs@centurytel.net
Web Site: lchsweb.org
Founded: 1898.
Congressional District: 3
Key Personnel: C.E.O. & Dir., Dr. Carl Miller; Pres. (V), Dr. Erik Gundersen; Museum Coord., Lori Strom; Admin., Michelle Logan.
Personnel Profile: Full-Time Paid 2; Full-Time Volunteers 1; Part-Time Paid 9; Part-Time Volunteers 32.
Governing Authority: nonprofit organization. Parent Institution: La Crosse

County Historical Society, Inc., P.O. Box 1272, La Crosse, WI. 54602. Tel.: 608-782-1980. Tax-exempt.
Historical Society Museum.
Collections: Hixon collection representing 19th century lifestyle; Mississippi River community; lumbering; brewing; period costumes; photographs; textiles; decorative arts; local documents.
Research Fields: transportation; clothing; local history; brewing industry; lumbering; river lore.
Facilities: research library. Local histories & other museum related items for sale.
Activities: permanent, changing & traveling exhibits; traveling guided tours; heritage tour of city, La Crosse.
Publications: society newsletter, Past, Present and Future; reprints of local histories.
Hours & Admission Prices: Tues.-Fri. 10-5, Sat.-Sun. 1-5. Adults $1, students $.50, children no charge. ♿
Attendance: 15,000 (estimated)
Membership: Individual $35; Family $50; Century $125; Business $200; Patron $250; Sustaining $500; Heritage $1,000; Fellows Club $5,000.

La Pointe

MADELINE ISLAND MUSEUM, Woods Ave. & Main St., La Pointe, WI 54850. Mailing Address: P.O. Box 9, La Pointe, WI 54850-0009. Tel.: 715-747-2415. Fax: 715-747-6985.
E-mail: madeline@wisconsinhistory.org
Web Site: www.madelineislandmuseum.org
Founded: 1958.
Congressional District: 7
Key Personnel: Dir. Div. Historic Sites, Alicia L. Goehring; Site Dir., Steven R. Cotherman; Cur., Sheree Peterson; Supt. Bldgs. & Grounds, Tim Eldred; Museum Shop Mgr., Marcia Coleman.
Personnel Profile: Full-Time Paid 2; Part-Time Paid 8.
Governing Authority: state. Parent Institution: Wisconsin Historical Society, 816 State St., Madison 53706. Tax-exempt.
Historic Site & Museum.
Collections: area history; artifacts reflecting the exploration & settlement of the Apostle Islands, including Native American history; French & English exploration & fur trade; 19th-century industries including fishing, lumbering, shipping & mining; ephemera; photographs; cultural history of Madeline Island from 19th century to present.
Major Exhibits: Traditions and Transformation: Ojibwe Art, Then and Now, 6/10-10/10.
Research Fields: 17th- & 18th-century exploration of Apostle Islands; Madeline Island Settlement; fur trade; lake & forest industries; Lake Superior history; Ojibwa cultural history.
Facilities: 5,200 sq. ft. exhibit space.
Activities: permanent exhibitions; formally organized educational programs for children; tours; island history video.
Publications: brochure, Madeline Island and the Chequamegon Region; A 50th Anniversary Commemorative Guidebook to the Madeline Island Museum.
Hours & Admission Prices: Memorial Day weekend to 1st weekend in Oct. daily 10-5. Family $17, adults $6, senior citizens $5, children & members $3; discounts to AAM & ICOM members & groups. ♿
Attendance: 15,037 (accurate)
Membership: State Historical Society of Wisconsin: Senior Citizen $25; Individual & Senior Couple $30; Family & Institution $35; Supporting $100; Sustaining $250; Patron $500; Life $1,000.

Lac du Flambeau

OJIBWE MUSEUM AND CULTURAL CENTER, (M), 603 Peace Pipe Rd., Lac du Flambeau, WI 54538. Mailing Address: P.O. Box 804, Lac du Flambeau, WI 54538. Tel.: 715-588-3333. Fax: 715-588-2355.
E-mail: ojibwemuseum@yahoo.com
Founded: 1989.
Key Personnel: Dir., Teresa Mitchell.
Personnel Profile: Full-Time Paid 1; Part-Time Volunteers 2.
Governing Authority: Parent Institution: Lac du Flambeau Tribe.
Native American History Museum.
Collections: Ojibwe culture & History; canoes; traditional clothing; French fur trading post.
Facilities: Museum-related items for sale.
Activities: workshops; special events.
Hours & Admission Prices: Summer: Mon.-Fri. 10-4, Sat. call for hours; Winter: Mon.-Fri. 10-4. Adults $4, seniors & children $3; discounts to AAA members. Closed holidays. ♿
Attendance: 2,500 (estimated)

Ladysmith

RUSK COUNTY HISTORICAL SOCIETY, Rusk County Fairgrounds, Hwy. 8, Ladysmith, WI 54848. Mailing Address: 408 Phillips Ave. E., Ladysmith, WI 54848-2333. Tel.: 715-532-5615.
E-mail: jplatteter@yahoo.com
Web Site: www.ruskcounty.org
Founded: 1961.
Congressional District: 7
Key Personnel: Pres., Henry Golat; Vice Pres., Lynn Kaiser; Treas., Melanie Meyer; Sec., Mary Lou Bisson; Cur., Janet Platteter; Chm. Genealogy Dept., Joyce Tomczak Molla Clark.
Personnel Profile: Full-Time Volunteers 10; Part-Time Volunteers 5.
Governing Authority: society. Branch Museums: 1895 Apollonia Church, Bruce, WI; 1900's Little Red School House, Ladysmith. Tax-exempt.
Historical Museum.
Collections: local historical artifacts & archives; Gates County courthouse artifacts; logging; machinery; horse drawn machinery; 306 straight razors & related barbering items; logstamp hammers; rail display; 1912 teaching. Historic Buildings: c.1900 Little Red School House; information building from Flambeau Mine; old Glen Flora jail; state of the art log cabin; teacher's cabin.
Facilities: 300-vol. library of old school books available for research on premises. Cookbooks, booklets of recollections by area residents for sale.
Activities: childrens classes; obituary research. Museum Sponsors: Heritage Day; Log Cabin Day in June.
Publications: maps of Rusk County; books, History of Rusk County; History of Rural Schools of Rusk County; Glen Flora Pioneers; My Time in the Army; Glen Flora; Dear Tales of Cloverland; Birth of Gates Co.; In Cub Chains; Volcanogenic Massive Sulfide Deposits in Northern Wisconsin; Travels with Sophie; book, Rusk County Centennial.
Hours & Admission Prices: Memorial Day-Labor Day, Sat.-Sun. 12:30-4:30. No charge; donations accepted. ♿
Attendance: 2,067 (estimated)
Membership: Junior $.50; Annual $2; Life $15.

Lake Geneva

GENEVA LAKE MUSEUM, 255 Mill St., Lake Geneva, WI 53147-1927. Tel.: 262-248-6060.
E-mail: staff@genevalakemuseum.org
Web Site: www.genevalakemuseum.org
Founded: 1984.
Key Personnel: Pres. (V), Vern Magee.
Personnel Profile: Part-Time Paid 3; Part-Time Volunteers 30.
Governing Authority: Tax-exempt: 501(c)(3).
History Museum: located in the 1929 Wisconsin Power and Light Building.
Collections: farm implements; facades of historic Lake Geneva homes; log structure with Potawatomi Indian arrowheads & tools; furnishings; blacksmith shop with iron anvils & ice cutting tools; fire engine house with c.1890 hose wagon; Spring house for cooling milk; telephone switchboard; 1920's dental work station; general store; Chicago & northwestern railway memorabilia; Frank Lloyd Wright's Hotel Geneva artifacts.
Publications: newsletter.
Hours & Admission Prices: March-April & Nov.-Dec. Fri.-Sat. 10-4, Sun. 12-3; May-Oct. Mon. & Thurs.-Sat. 10-4, Sun. 12-3. Adults $6, seniors & students with ID $5; children 11 & under and members with ID no charge. ♿
Membership: Seniors $10; Individual $15; Supporting $35; Patron $50; Benefactor $100.

Lake Tomahawk

LAKE TOMAHAWK HISTORICAL SOCIETY, 7247 Kelly Dr., Lake Tomahawk, WI 54539. Mailing Address: P.O. Box 325, Lake Tomahawk, WI 54539-0325. Tel.: 715-277-3123 & 2261. Fax: 715-277-3123.
E-mail: lkhbowen@newnorth.net
Formerly: Northland Historical Society, Inc.
Founded: 1957.
Congressional District: 7
Key Personnel: Pres. (V), Linda Kay Houghton-Bowen; Vice Pres., Fred Hills; Treas., Andrew J. Bowen; Sec., Beverly Fagan.
Governing Authority: nonprofit organization. Tax-exempt: 170(b)(1)(A).
Historical Society Museum.
Collections: early costumes; pictures; maps; books; artifacts from settlers & Indians.
Research Fields: historical sites; buildings; travel routes of Indians, voyageurs, loggers & settlers.
Facilities: 500-vol. library of books on early logging, settlers, ethnic, sites & early maps available for research on premises only; 100-seat auditorium.

Activities: guided tours; lectures; films; formally organized education programs for adults; loan, permanent & temporary exhibitions; program meetings. Museum Sponsors: Northwoods Fall Conference in September.
Publications: The Deacon's Bench.
Hours & Admission Prices: Memorial Day to Labor Day Sat. 1-3; other times by appointment. No charge; donations accepted. ♿
Attendance: 150 (estimated)
Membership: Junior $2.50; Individual $10; Family $20; Contributing $25; Ebert Club $100 & up.

Laona

CAMP FIVE MUSEUM FOUNDATION, INC., (M), 5480 Connor Farm Rd., Laona, WI 54541-9201. Mailing Address: P.O. Box 5, Laona, WI 54541-0005. Tel.: 715-674-3414. Fax: 715-674-7400.
E-mail: info@lumberjacksteamtrain.com
Web Site: www.lumberjacksteamtrain.com
Founded: 1969.
Congressional District: 8
Key Personnel: Pres. (V), Mrs. Edward J. Dellin; Dir. Education, Sara W. Connor.
Personnel Profile: Full-Time Paid 1; Part-Time Paid 40; Part-Time Volunteers 3.
Governing Authority: nonprofit. Subsidiary Institution: Laona & Northern Railway. Tax-exempt.
Logging Museum & Ecology Complex: operates Laona & Northern Railway's Lumberjack Special steam train.
Collections: early farm tools; logging tools including pointer boats; early tractors; ice rutters; waterwagons; railroad artifacts; Native American artifacts; surveying instruments; woodworking implements; lumber company tokens-money; tree display; harness shop; depot; active blacksmith shop; early logging artifacts; 1916 Vulcan steam engine; 1920 coaches & cabooses; 1900 cracker barrel store.
Facilities: early logging history; nature center with northern Wisconsin wildlife diorama; arboretum; audio-visual orientation center for historic lumber camp operations; steam engine video; 1900 cracker barrel store; operating blacksmith shop; petting corral; picnic area; snack bar. Museum-related items for sale.
Activities: steam train video; permanent logging, harness & blacksmith shop, steam train video exhibitions; audio-visual presentations; Green Treasure forest tour; hayrack & pontoon boat rides; petting corral.
Publications: coloring books; brochures; Forests for All: The Economics of Conservation, video & accompanying textbook for grades 3-12.
Hours & Admission Prices: mid-June to late Aug. Mon.-Sat. Trains at 11, 12, 1 & 2 to Camp Five Logging Museum Complex. Adults $19, children 4-12 $8; discounts to members, groups, AAA, AAM & ICOM members, seniors & active military duty; children under 3 no charge. Hayrack & Pontoon Ride: adults $5, children $3. ♿
Attendance: 11,022 (accurate)

Madison

* **CHAZEN MUSEUM OF ART, (M),** 800 University Ave., Madison, WI 53706-1479. Tel.: 608-263-2246. Fax: 608-263-8188.
Web Site: chazen.wisc.edu
Formerly: Elvehjem Museum of Art
Founded: 1962.
Congressional District: 2
Key Personnel: Dir., Dr. Russell Panczenko; Registrar, Andrea Selbig; Registrar, Ann Sinfield; Preparator, Steve Johanowicz; Asst. Dir. Admin., Brian Thompson; Asst. Dir. External Affairs, Mary Carr Lee; Editor, Susan Day; Cur. Paintings, Sculpture & Decorative Arts, Maria Saffiotti Dale; Cur. Education, Anne Lambert; Cur., Prints & Drawings, Andrew Stevens; Museum Shop Mgr., Ann Dwyer; Exhibitions Coord., Mary Ann Fitzgerald; Exhibition Designer & Chief Preparator, Jerl Richmond.
Personnel Profile: Full-Time Paid 15; Full-Time Volunteers 3; Part-Time Paid 25; Part-Time Volunteers 105; Interns 2.
Governing Authority: university. Parent Institution: University of Wisconsin at Madison.
Art Museum.
Collections: paintings; prints; drawings; sculpture; decorative arts; archaeology; Watson Collection of Indian miniatures; Van Vleck Collection of Japanese Prints; Hall Collection of European Medals; Davies Collection of Russian icons, Russian & Soviet paintings.
Research Fields: pertaining to collections.
Facilities: 100,000-vol. library of art books available for inter-library loan & for loan by permission of librarian; reading room; 4 auditoriums; classrooms. Art objects, books, catalogs & other museum-related items for sale.
Activities: guided tours; lectures; gallery talks; concerts; docent program; formally organized education programs for undergraduate & graduate students affiliated with the University of Wisconsin & adults; permanent, temporary & traveling exhibitions.
Publications: biannual bulletin; bimonthly calendar; catalogs of major exhibitions; semiannual newsletter.
Hours & Admission Prices: Tues.-Fri. 9-5, Sat.-Sun. 11-5. No charge; donations accepted. Closed New Year's Day; Thanksgiving; Christmas Eve & Day. ♿
Attendance: 65,000 (accurate)
Membership: Student & Senior Citizen $25; Individual $35; Senior Couple $40; Family $50; Patron $75; Founder $125; Associate $250; Fellow $500; Director's Circle $1,000.

HELEN LOUISE ALLEN TEXTILE COLLECTION, (M), 1300 Linden Dr., Univ. of Wisconsin, Madison, WI 53706-1524. Tel.: 608-262-1162. Fax: 608-265-5099.
E-mail: hlatc@mail.sohe.wisc.edu
Web Site: sohe.wisc.edu/depts/hlatc
Founded: 1968.
Congressional District: 2
Key Personnel: Cur., Maya Lea; Asst. Cur., Diana Zlatanovski; Gallery Coord., Jody Clowes.
Personnel Profile: Full-Time Paid 2; Part-Time Paid 5; Part-Time Volunteers 5.
Governing Authority: university. Parent Institution: University of Wisconsin. Tax-exempt: 170(b)(1)(A).
Textile & Costume Collection.
Collections: 13,000 textiles including ethnographic textiles & costumes; European & American home furnishings & apparel fabrics.
Research Fields: cultural anthropology; textile history, design, interior design & textile science.
Facilities: 10,000-vol. research library; 2,450 sq. ft. gallery.
Activities: lectures; tours & educational programs; temporary exhibitions.
Publications: website blog; annual newsletter; exhibition catalogues; collection monographs.
Hours & Admission Prices: Closed for relocation. ♿
Membership: Friend $50; Sustainer $100; Patron $250; Benefactor $500.

HENRY VILAS PARK ZOO, 702 S. Randall Ave., Madison, WI 53715-1600. Tel.: 608-266-4733. Fax: 608-266-5923.
E-mail: zoo@co.dane.wi.us
Web Site: www.vilaszoo.org
Founded: 1911.
Key Personnel: Dir., Jim Hubing.
Personnel Profile: Full-Time Paid 17; Part-Time Paid 1; Interns 8.
Governing Authority: municipal; county. Dane County. Tax-exempt.
Zoo.
Collections: general zoological park; children's zoo.
Facilities: concessions. Gift items for sale.
Activities: permanent exhibitions.
Hours & Admission Prices: Buildings: daily 10-4. Grounds: June-Labor Day daily 9:30-8; Sept.-May daily 9:30-5. No charge. Closed New Year's Eve & Day; Martin Luther King Jr. Day; Thanksgiving; Christmas Eve & Day. ♿
Attendance: 700,000 (estimated)
Membership: Student $10; Senior Citizen $15; Single $20; Family $25; Sustaining $50; Patron $100.

MADISON CHILDREN'S MUSEUM, 100 State St., Madison, WI 53703-2573. Tel.: 608-256-6445; 268-1231. Fax: 608-256-3226.
Web Site: www.madisonchildrensmuseum.org
Founded: 1980.
Congressional District: 1
Key Personnel: Exec. Dir., Ruth G. Shelly; Exhibit Dir., Brenda Baker; Visitor Svcs. Supvr., Jennifer Neuls.
Personnel Profile: Full-Time Paid 19; Part-Time Paid 12; Part-Time Volunteers 604; Interns 5.
Governing Authority: nonprofit organization. Tax-exempt: 501(c)(3).
Children's Museum.
Collections: interactive exhibits with arts, science & humanities themes.
Research Fields: education.
Facilities: 9,034 sq. ft. exhibit. Museum-related items for sale.
Activities: hands-on exhibits & programs for children ages birth to 8; outreach programs to area schools & community groups; in-depth collaboration with university schools & other groups.
Publications: quarterly newsletter.
Hours & Admission Prices: Mon.-Fri. 9-4, Sat. 9-5, Sun. 12-5. Admission $5, seniors 55 & over $4; discounts to groups; 1st Sun. of month & children under one no charge. Closed some national holidays. ♿
Attendance: 77,437 (accurate)
Membership: Grandparent Investigator $45; Investigator $50; Grandparent Inventor $60; Inventor $65; Innovator $100.

* **MADISON MUSEUM OF CONTEMPORARY ART, (M),** 227 State St., Madison, WI 53703-2214. Tel.: 608-257-0158. Fax: 608-257-5722.
E-mail: info@mmoca.org
Web Site: www.mmoca.org
Formerly: Madison Art Center
Founded: 1901.
Congressional District: 2
Key Personnel: Pres., Jesse Ishikawa; Dir., Stephen Fleischman; Cur. Exhibitions, Jane Simon; Cur. Collections, Richard H. Axsom; Cur. Education, Sheri Castelnuovo; Business Mgr., Michael Paggie; Dir. Devel., Nicole Allen; Registrar, Marilyn Sohi; Dir. Public Information, Katie Kazan; Dir. Retail Operations, Leslie Genszler; Asst. Gallery Shop Mgr., Laurie Saager; Assoc. Dir., Exec. Affairs, Jennifer Holmes; Accountant, Judy Schwickerath; Supvr. Technical Svcs., Mark Verstegen.
Personnel Profile: Full-Time Paid 17; Full-Time Volunteers 1; Part-Time Paid 20; Part-Time Volunteers 50; Interns 4.
Governing Authority: nonprofit organization. Tax-exempt: 501(c)(3).
Art Museum.
Collections: contemporary art; Rudolph E. Langer Collection; American paintings, sculpture & prints; photography; Japanese, Mexican & European artworks; works on paper.
Major Exhibits: "Signs of the Times: Robert Ruuschenberg's America", 11/09-1/3/10; "Wisconsin Triennial", 5/21/10-8/15/10; "Rob and Christian Clayton: Inside Out", 9/11/10-12/20/10.
Research Fields: pertaining to permanent collections.
Activities: rotating exhibitions; guided tours; films; lectures; inter-museum loans; docent programs; community & school outreach programs; family resources & events; teacher resources; interactive website. Museum Sponsors: New Media & Performance Art; Art Fair on the Square; Arts Ball; bus trips to neighboring museums.
Publications: newsletter; exhibitions catalogues & brochures.
Hours & Admission Prices: Tues.-Thurs. 12-5, Fri. 12-8, Sat. 10-8, Sun. 12-5. No charge; donations accepted. Closed major holidays. ♿
Attendance: 150,000 (estimated)
Membership: Senior Citizen & Student $30; Individual $40; Household $60; Supporting $125; Langer Society & Business Council $250 & up.

OLBRICH BOTANICAL GARDENS, 3330 Atwood Ave., Madison, WI 53704-5808. Tel.: 608-246-4550. Fax: 608-246-4719. TDD: 608-267-4980.
E-mail: rsladky@cityofmadison.com
Web Site: www.olbrich.org
Founded: 1952.
Congressional District: 2
Key Personnel: C.E.O., Roberta Sladky; Museum Shop Mgr., Shirley Homburg.
Personnel Profile: Full-Time Paid 23; Part-Time Paid 16; Part-Time Volunteers 600; Interns 7.
Governing Authority: municipal. Parent Institution: City of Madison, WI, Madison Parks Dept., County Bldg., 215 Martin Luther King Blvd. Tel. 608-266-4711. Tax-exempt: 501(c)(3).
Botanical Garden.
Collections: flower, herb, rose & rock gardens; tropical; perennials; horticultural library; tropical conservatory; Thai Garden; Thai Pavilion.
Facilities: 1,000-vol. library of horticultural books; botanical garden; classrooms; display atrium; tropical conservatory. Gift items for sale.
Activities: flower shows; art exhibits; concerts; children's activities; classes; horticulture & special interest groups meetings; tours; lectures.
Publications: newsletter, Olbrich Gardens Quarterly News.
Hours & Admission Prices: Garden: April-Sept. daily 8-8; Oct.-March daily 9-4. Conservatory: Mon.-Sat. 10-4, Sun. 10-5. Outdoor Gardens: no charge. Conservatory: $1; members, Wed. & Sat. mornings no charge. Closed New Year's Day; Thanksgiving; Christmas. ♿
Attendance: 250,000 (accurate)
Membership: Olbrich Botanical Society: Garden Friend $40; Garden Family $50; Garden Family & Guests $65; Garden Contributor $100; Garden Patron $250.

UNIVERSITY OF WISCONSIN-MADISON ARBORETUM, 1207 Seminole Hwy., Madison, WI 53711-3726. Tel.: 608-263-7888. Fax: 608-262-5209.
E-mail: info@uwarboretum.org
Web Site: www.uwarboretum.org
Founded: 1934.
Congressional District: 2
Key Personnel: Mgr. Friends of the Arboretum, Sara Minkoff; Dir., Dr. Kevin McSweeney; Museum Shop Mgr., Peggy Brown.
Personnel Profile: Full-Time Paid 12; Part-Time Paid 46; Part-Time Volunteers 610.
Governing Authority: university. Parent Institution: University of Wisconsin-Madison. Tax-exempt.
Arboretum.
Collections: natural groupings of plants and animals in ecological communities; horticultural collections.
Research Fields: landscape architecture; ecology; wildlife & restoration ecology; botany; natural history; herpetology; paleontology; entomology; geology; phenology; zoology; horticulture; soil science; plant pathology.
Facilities: information & public reception area in Visitor Center; research & teaching area for University of Wisconsin faculty & students; nurseries; greenhouses; outdoor classrooms for groups.
Activities: guided tours; restoration workshops & summer institutes for teachers & land managers.
Publications: maps; booklets; field guides; Newsleaf; quarterly, Ecological Restoration; prairie restoration materials for schools.
Hours & Admission Prices: Daily 7-10pm. No charge; donations accepted. ♿
Attendance: 650,000 (accurate)
Membership: Senior Citizen & Student $20; Single $25; Family $35; Business & Supporting $100; Patron $250 & up.

UNIVERSITY OF WISCONSIN ZOOLOGICAL MUSEUM, 250 North Mills St. Lowell E. Noland Zoology Building, Madison, WI 53706-1708. Tel.: 608-262-3766. Fax: 608-262-5395.
Web Site: www.zoology.wisc.edu/uwzm/index.html
Founded: 1887.
Congressional District: 2
Key Personnel: Dir., Distinguished Researcher & Cur. Osteology, E. Elizabeth Pillaert; Cur. Emeritus, Exhibits & Vertebrate Paleontology, Dr. John E. Dallman; Cur. Mammalogy & Ornithology, Paula M Holahan; Adjunct Cur. Fish, John D. Lyons; Adjunct Cur. Herpetology, Dr. Gregory C. Mayer; Registrar, Laura A. Halverson.
Personnel Profile: Full-Time Paid 3; Part-Time Paid 2; Part-Time Volunteers 2; Interns 1.
Governing Authority: university. Affiliated with the University of Wisconsin. Tax-exempt: 501(c)(3).
Zoology Museum.
Collections: 25,000 ornithology (including osteology); 26,000 mammology (including osteology); 13,000 ichthyology; 8,000 herpetology; 17,500 osteology (all vertebrate classes); 2,000 paleontology; 250,000 malacology; 110,000 histological slide preparations & tissue fragments; H. W. Mossman collection of mammalian reproductive organs, 3,100 specimens; W.B. Quay collection of fluid mammals, 2,600 specimens; 800 period artifacts.
Research Fields: herpetology; osteology; paleontology; mammalogy; ornithology; ichthyology; archaeology.
Facilities: 5,900-vol. library & 45,300 reprints of zoological materials available on premises; reading room.
Activities: lectures; formally organized education programs for undergraduate and graduate college students affiliated with the University of Wisconsin; permanent & temporary exhibitions.
Hours & Admission Prices: Sept.-June Mon.-Fri. 8:30-12 & 1-4:30 by appointment. No charge; donations accepted. Closed national holidays. ♿
Attendance: 3,500 (estimated)

WISCONSIN HISTORICAL MUSEUM, (M), 30 N. Carroll St., Madison, WI 53703-2707. Tel.: 608-264-6555. Fax: 608-264-6575.
E-mail: museum@wisconsinhistory.org
Web Site: www.wisconsinhistory.org
Formerly: State Historical Museum of Wisconsin
Founded: 1846.
Congressional District: 2
Key Personnel: C.E.O., Dr. Ellsworth Brown; Pres. (V), Judy Nagel; Dir., Jennifer Kolb; Deputy Dir., Jennifer Kolb; Dir. Museum Archaeology, Kelly Hamilton; Special Events & Public Programs, Kristina Clark; Chief Cur., Paul Bourcier; Cur. Costumes & Textiles, Leslie Bellais; Cur. Business & Technology, David Driscoll; Museum Shop Mgr., John Lemke; Volunteer Coord., Kristina Clark; Museum Educator, Beth Lemke; Cur. Domestic Life, Joe Kapler; Collections Mgr., Scott Roller.
Personnel Profile: Full-Time Paid 24; Part-Time Paid 40; Part-Time Volunteers 80; Interns 12.
Governing Authority: society. Parent Institution: Wisconsin Historical Society. Branch Museums: First Capitol, Belmont; The Villa Louis, Prairie du Chien; Old Wade House, Greenbush; Stonefield, Cassville; Madeline Island Historical Museum, LaPointe; Pendarvis, Mineral Point; Circus World Museum, Baraboo; Old World Wisconsin, Eagle; H.H. Bennett Studio & History Center, Wisconsin Dells; Reed School, Neillsville. See separate listings for hours & admissions. Tax-exempt: 170(b)(1)(A).
History Museum.
Collections: Wisconsin history from prehistoric to modern times; firearms; dolls; crafts; costumes; decorative arts; glass; ceramics; archives; photographs; toys.
Major Exhibits: Odd Wisconsin, 1/10-12/10.
Research Fields: Wisconsin history, anthropology & archaeology.

Facilities: library of North American history; archives; reading rooms; auditorium.
Activities: lectures; films; archives; gallery talks; workshops; formally organized education programs; inter-museum loan, permanent, temporary & traveling exhibitions.
Publications: Wisconsin Magazine of History; Columns.
Hours & Admission Prices: Tues.-Sat. 9-4. Donation: family $10, adults $4, children $3; discounts to AAM members; members no charge. Closed national holidays. ♿
Attendance: 72,500 (accurate)
Membership: Senior 65 & over $30; Individual & Senior Citizen Family $40; Family $50; Institutional $65; Supporting $100; Sustaining $250; Patron $500; Life $1,000.

THE WISCONSIN UNION GALLERIES, UNIVERSITY OF WISCONSIN-MADISON, (M), 800 Langdon St., Madison, WI 53706-1419. Mailing Address: 800 Langdon St., Rm. 507, Madison, WI 53706-1419. Tel.: 608-262-5969 & 7592. Fax: 608-262-8862.
E-mail: art@union.wisc.edu
Web Site: www.union.wisc.edu/art
Founded: 1928.
Congressional District: 2
Key Personnel: Gallery Dir., Cur. & Registrar, Robin Schmoldt; Committee Dir., Nicole Rodriguez; Union Dir., Mark Guthier.
Personnel Profile: Full-Time Paid 1; Part-Time Paid 2; Part-Time Volunteers 20.
Governing Authority: state; college. Affiliated with the University of Wisconsin, Madison, WI 53706. Parent Institution: Wisconsin Union. Tax-exempt.
Art Gallery.
Collections: 1,300 works of American, University of Wisconsin student or Wisconsin young professional, including photographs, prints, drawings, paintings, 3-D wood, fiber, metal & glass.
Major Exhibits: Lisa Koch, 12/4/09-1/19/10; Evan Baden, 12/4/09-1/19/10; Thomas Ferrella, 12/4/09-1/19/10; Student Curated, 12/4/09-1/19/10; Steven Poster, 1/29/10-3/9/10; Elisabeth Karpov, 1/29/10-3/9/10; Bobbette Rose & Katherine Steichen Rosing, 1/29/10-3/9/10; Logu Ramasamy, 1/29/10-3/9/10; Student Curated, 3/19/10-4/20/10; Masters of Fine Arts (MFA), 4/30/10-5/11/10.
Facilities: theater; indoor/outdoor music venues; craftshop; meeting rooms.
Activities: guided tours; lectures; films; gallery talks; concerts; dance recitals; arts festivals; drama; hobby workshops; formally organized education programs for children, adults undergraduate college students & graduate students affiliated with University of Wisconsin-Madison; loan, temporary & traveling exhibitions.
Publications: members newsletter, Terrace Views/Grapevine.
Hours & Admission Prices: Daily 10-8. No charge. Closed holidays & during school breaks. ♿
Attendance: 300,000 (estimated)
Membership: Union: Annual $50, Lifetime $250.

* **WISCONSIN VETERANS MUSEUM-MADISON, (M),** 30 W. Mifflin St., Suite 200, Madison, WI 53703-2589. Tel.: 608-267-7207. Fax: 608-264-7615.
Web Site: museum.dva.state.wi.us
Founded: 1901.
Congressional District: 2
Key Personnel: C.E.O., John Scocos; Acting Dir., Tony Cappozzo; Chm. WI Dept. of Veteran Affairs Bd., Mack E. Hughes; Museum Operations Mgr., Lynnette M. Wolfe; Chm. & Pres. (V), John Driscoll; Cur. Collections, William F. Brewster; Cur. Programs & Exhibitions, Jeffrey Kollath; Archivist, Gayle Martinson; Reference Archivist, Russell Horton; Visitor Svcs., Jennifer Carlson; Mktg. Specialist, Laura Kocum; Registrar, Kristine Zickuhr; Acting Museum Shop Mgr., Crystal Pierce.
Personnel Profile: Full-Time Paid 12; Part-Time Paid 15; Part-Time Volunteers 89; Interns 2.
Governing Authority: state. Parent Institution: State of Wisconsin. Subsidiary Institution: Wisconsin Dept. Veterans Affairs. Tax-exempt.
State Military History Museum: located downtown Madison.
Collections: State military & veterans' historical artifacts; aircraft; vehicles; arms; battle flag collection; uniformed figures in several major dioramas with equipment; archives & iconographic collections of Wisconsin's military & veterans organizations.
Major Exhibits: Faces in the Sand, 11/09-11/10.
Research Fields: Wisconsin military & veterans history 1861-present.
Facilities: research library & archives; education center. Books & museum-related items for sale.
Activities: permanent & temporary exhibitions; educational programs; lecture series; public tours; living history; research facility. Documentary: Wisconsin World War Two Stories; Wisconsin Korean War Series; Vietnam War stories & series; Iraq & Afghanistan programs.
Publications: museum brochure, A Tribute to Freedom; book, Old Abe the War Eagle; book, USS Wisconsin: The Story of Two Battleships; Flags of the Iron Brigade; Wisconsin in the Civil War; Flags of the Iron Brigade; Wisconsin At War; Wisconsin Grand Army of the Republic.
Hours & Admission Prices: April-Sept. Mon.-Sat. 9-4:30, Sun. 12-4; Oct.-March Mon.-Sat. 9-4:30. Research Center: Mon.-Fri. 9-4. No charge. Closed holidays. ♿
Attendance: 101,728 (accurate)

Manitowoc

LINCOLN PARK ZOO, North 8th St., Manitowoc, WI 54220. Mailing Address: 930 N. 18th St., Manitowoc, WI 54220-3133. Tel.: 920-683-4685 (Zoo); 4530 (Office). Fax: 920-683-4517.
E-mail: jmclafferty@manitowoc.org
Web Site: www.manitowoc.org
Founded: 1935.
Key Personnel: Dir. Parks & Recreation, Joseph McLafferty.
Personnel Profile: Full-Time Paid 2; Part-Time Paid 2; Part-Time Volunteers 25; Interns 1.
Governing Authority: municipal. Parent Institution: City of Manitowoc, Park & Recreation Dept. Affiliated with Parks Dept., 930 N. 18th St. Tax-exempt.
Zoo.
Collections: animals & birds chiefly native to Wisconsin; exotic birds.
Facilities: picnic area; playground; restrooms.
Activities: permanent exhibitions; fish rearing pond containing Coho & Chinook Salmon, Rainbow Trout; special events throughout the year.
Hours & Admission Prices: June-Aug. daily 7-7; Sept.-Oct. Mon.-Sat. 7-3, Sun. 11-3; Nov.-May Mon.-Sat. 7-3. No charge; donations accepted. ♿
Attendance: 55,584 (estimated)

MANITOWOC COUNTY HISTORICAL SOCIETY, 1701 Michigan Ave., Manitowoc, WI 54220-3137. Tel.: 920-684-4445. Fax: 920-684-0573.
E-mail: mchistsoc@lakefield.net
Web Site: www.mchistsoc.org
Formerly: Pinecrest Historical Village
Founded: 1906.
Congressional District: 6
Key Personnel: Pres. Bd., Kathy Kowalski; Exec. Dir., Mike Maher.
Personnel Profile: Full-Time Paid 2; Part-Time Paid 3; Part-Time Volunteers 250; Interns 1.
Governing Authority: board of directors. Subsidiary Institution: Heritage Center; Pinecrest Historical Village. Tax-exempt: 501(c)(3).
History Museum.
Collections: 28 19th & early 20th-century buildings from Manitowoc County; furnishings; household items; tools; agricultural machinery & equipment.
Research Fields: Manitowoc County.
Facilities: Heritage Center Museum & Library; Pinecrest Historical Village, 60 acre open air museum.
Activities: guided school & motorcoach tours; special events & programs; historical demonstrations.
Publications: newsletters; books; monographs; walking tour brochures.
Hours & Admission Prices: Heritage Center: Tues.-Fri. 9-4. Adults $5. Pinecrest Historical Village: May 1-Oct. 24 daily 9-4. Adults $6, children $4; discounts to MCHS members; members no charge.
Attendance: 6,444 (accurate)
Membership: Student $10; Senior $30; Individual $35; Senior Couple $40; Family $50; Friend $75; Contributing $90; Patron $150.

* **RAHR WEST ART MUSEUM, (M),** 610 N. 8th St., Manitowoc, WI 54220-3998. Tel.: 920-683-4501. Fax: 920-683-5047.
E-mail: rahrwest@manitowoc.org
Web Site: www.rahrwestartmuseum.org
Founded: 1950.
Congressional District: 6
Key Personnel: Dir., Barbara Bundy-Jost; Asst. Dir., Daniel Juchniewich; Chm. (V), Maureen Stokes; Pres. (V), Jennifer Hogan; Pres. Foundation, William Pohlmann.
Personnel Profile: Full-Time Paid 4; Part-Time Paid 5.
Governing Authority: municipal. Parent Institution: the City of Manitowoc, Manitowoc City Hall. Tax-exempt: 501(c)(3) & 170(b)(1)(A).
Art Museum.
Collections: 19th, 20th & 21st century American paintings; period rooms; 19th century American decorative arts & furnishings; dolls; Chinese ivory carvings. Historic House: 1891, Joseph Vilas House.
Research Fields: 20th century American art; historic buildings.
Facilities: 1,500-vol. library of history, archaeology, anthropology & art books available for use on premises; reading room; classrooms.
Activities: guided tours; opening receptions; artist workshops; docent program; traveling exhibitions; children's activity room.

Publications: special events program; catalogues; brochures, The Schwartz Collection of Chinese Ivories; The Ruth & John D. West Art Collection.
Hours & Admission Prices: Mon.-Tues. & Thurs.-Fri. 10-4, Wed. 10-8, Sat.-Sun. 11-4. Suggested Donation: $4; members no charge. Closed holidays.
Attendance: 22,000 (accurate)
Membership: Full-time Student $20; Teacher & Senior $35; Individual & Dual Senior $40; Family $50; Sustainer $100-$249; Contributor $250-$499; Sponsor $500; Patron $1,000; Benefactor $2,500.

* **WISCONSIN MARITIME MUSEUM, (M),** 75 Maritime Dr., Manitowoc, WI 54220-6823. Tel.: 920-684-0218. Fax: 920-684-0219.
E-mail: museum@wisconsinmaritime.org
Web Site: www.wisconsinmaritime.org
Founded: 1969.
Congressional District: 6
Key Personnel: Exec. Dir., Norma Bishop; Pres. (V), Thomas Jagemann; Cur., David Beard; Education Coord., Wendy Lutzke; Registrar & Collections Mgr., Cristin Waterbury; Financial Svcs. Mgr., Tom Smith; Maintenance Supvr., Paul Rutherford; Education & Submarine Program Coord., Karen Duvalle; Education Outreach, Kirsten Smith; Retail Supvr., Marlys Schwartz; Devel. Asst. & Member Svcs., Bobbie Novak; Receptionist, Toni Duvall; Visitor Svcs. Supvr., Cassi Adams.
Personnel Profile: Full-Time Paid 13; Part-Time Paid 40; Part-Time Volunteers 300.
Governing Authority: private; nonprofit. Tax-exempt: 501(c)(3).
Maritime Museum.
Collections: submarine artifacts; photos; documents; ship tools; salvage artifacts; models of Great Lakes ships; artifacts; furniture; house flags; manuscripts relating to history of Great Lakes; lake schooners; steamships; car ferries; bulk carriers; submarine; life boat. Historic Submarine: 1943 U.S.S. Cobia; full-scale reproduction of 19th century schooner midship section, Clipper City; former Coast Guard utility boat, Icelander; Wisconsin built recreational boats.
Research Fields: Great Lakes maritime history; WWII submarines; Wisconsin maritime history & culture.
Facilities: 8,000-vol. library & 40,000 photographs on Great Lakes maritime and Manitowoc submarine history & submarines available for use on the premises; reading room; classroom. Books, maritime gifts & other museum-related items for sale.
Activities: guided tours; films; permanent, temporary & traveling exhibitions; school loan service. Museum Sponsors: summer festival; picnic; Riverwalk Festival; Annual submariners Memorial Service; family series of Maritime related programs.
Publications: booklet, Manitowoc Submarines; quarterly newsletter, Anchor News; books Fresh Water Submarines: The Manitowoc Story; The Nau Tug Line.
Hours & Admission Prices: Museum & Submarine: May-Sept. daily 9-6; Oct.-April daily 9-5. Museum: adult $12, children $10; children 5 & under no charge. Museum & Submarine: adult $12, children $10; children 5 & under no charge. Discounts to family, veterans, senior citizens & AAA members. Council of American Maritime Museum & members no charge. Closed New Year's Day; Easter; Thanksgiving; Christmas. ♿
Attendance: 46,525 (accurate)
Membership: Student & Senior Citizen $25; Senior Couple $35; Individual $40; Family $60; Sustaining $100; Sponsor $250; Benefactor $500; Timothy J. Kelly Society $1,000; Edward Carus Society $2,500; Albert E. Goodrich Society $5,000; William W. Bates Society $10,000.

Marinette

MARINETTE COUNTY HISTORICAL MUSEUM, Stephenson Island, U.S. Hwy. 41, Marinette, WI 54143. Mailing Address: P.O. Box 262, Marinette, WI 54143-0262. Tel.: 715-732-0831.
Web Site: www.marinettecountyhistory.org
Founded: 1932.
Congressional District: 8
Key Personnel: Pres. (V), Frank Lauerman; Sec., Mary Falkenberg.
Personnel Profile: Part-Time Volunteers 30; Interns 1.
Governing Authority: society. Parent Institution: Marinette County Historical Society. Tax-exempt.
History Museum: housed in c.1895 log cabin.
Collections: logging & historical artifacts including miniature logging camp replica; copper culture; woodland Indian artifacts; manuscripts; fishing; agriculture; early social history; ice road rutter rig exhibit. Historic Building: 1897 homesteader's cabin.
Research Fields: logging; copper culture.
Facilities: 200-vol. library of books on logging & county history available on premises only.
Activities: guided tours; formally organized education programs; permanent & temporary exhibitions.
Publications: quarterly, Historian.
Hours & Admission Prices: Memorial Day to Labor Day Mon.-Fri. 10-4. Adults $3, students grades 7-12 $1; discounts to groups; members & children under 12 accompanied by parent no charge. Closed Independence Day. ♿
Attendance: 2,000 (estimated)
Membership: Individual $15; Couple $20.

Marshfield

NEW VISIONS GALLERY, INC., (M), 1000 N. Oak Ave., Marshfield, WI 54449-5703. Tel.: 715-387-5562.
E-mail: newvisions.gallery@verizon.net
Web Site: www.newvisionsgallery.org
Founded: 1975.
Congressional District: 7
Key Personnel: C.E.O. & Dir., Mary Peck; Pres. (V), Peggy Davis; Treas., Todd Diedrich.
Personnel Profile: Full-Time Paid 1; Part-Time Paid 2; Part-Time Volunteers 70.
Governing Authority: nonprofit organization. Tax-exempt: 501(c)(3).
Art Museum.
Collections: Japanese prints; West African masks & sculptures; Haitian paintings; Australian Aboriginal prints & paintings.
Major Exhibits: New Acquisitions, 1/17/10-3/5/10; Emerging Talents, 3/14/10-5/7/10; Martin Rowe & Julie Dierauer, 5/16/10-7/2/10; Culture & Agriculture, 7/11/10-9/4/10; Wisconsin Watercolor Society, 9/12/10-10/30/10; John Davenport, 11/7/10-12/10.
Activities: guided tours; lectures; films; arts festivals; hobby workshops; docent program; participatory & loan exhibitions.
Publications: monthly brochures; occasional exhibition catalogues.
Hours & Admission Prices: Mon.-Fri. 9-5:30. No charge; donations accepted. Closed legal holidays. ♿
Attendance: 20,000 (estimated)
Membership: Art Partners: Basic $50; Friend $75; Sponsor $125; Donor $250; Patron $500; Benefactor $1,000; Sustaining $5,000 & up.

UPHAM MANSION, 212 W. 3rd, Marshfield, WI 54449-2706. Mailing Address: P.O. Box 142, Marshfield, WI 54449-0142. Tel.: 715-387-3322. Fax: 715-387-3322.
E-mail: uphammansion@verizon.net
Web Site: www.uphamansion.com
Founded: 1952.
Congressional District: 7
Key Personnel: Pres., Richard Halle.
Personnel Profile: Part-Time Paid 1; Part-Time Volunteers 85.
Governing Authority: nonprofit. Parent Institution: North Wood County Historical Society. Tax-exempt: 170(b)(1)(A).
Historic Building/Site: Italianate-Victorian style home, built in 1880 by William Henry Upham, leading businessman of Marshfield till his death in 1924; governor of WI 1895-96.
Collections: pioneer artifacts & furnishings; clothing; household goods; utensils; toys; dolls; books; Pier mirror; Victorian furniture; curved glass curio cabinet; oval marble-topped table; Victorian cutter; horse-drawn fire hose cart; iron lung; scrap book collections; 32 varieties of roses in Heritage rose garden; photographs.
Research Fields: genealogy; early North Wood County history.
Facilities: 30-vol. library of books on early pioneers available on premises only; genealogical microfiche library; research center.
Activities: monthly meetings; four annual open houses; group tours; ice cream social. Museum Sponsors: Halloween party for preschool through grade 6; Mansion walk/run.
Publications: newsletter, Mansion News.
Hours & Admission Prices: Mansion: Wed. & Sun. 1:30-4; groups by special arrangements. Groups: $2 per person. Heritage Rose Garden: June-Sept. daily. No charge. Closed holidays. ♿
Attendance: 4,500 (estimated)
Membership: Individual $15; Family $25; Sustaining $35; Business $75; Life $200.

Mauston

THE BOORMAN HOUSE - THE JUNEAU COUNTY HISTORICAL SOCIETY, 211 N. Union St., Mauston, WI 53948-1418. Mailing Address: P.O. Box 321, Mauston, WI 53948-0321. Tel.: 608-847-4450 & 3294.
E-mail: rclarkjco@hotmail.com
Founded: 1963.
Congressional District: 6
Key Personnel: Pres. (V), Nancy McCullick; Historiographer, Rose Clark.
Personnel Profile: Full-Time Volunteers 2; Part-Time Volunteers 70.

Governing Authority: society. Parent Institution: Wisconsin State Historical Society. Tax-exempt.
Historical Site & Building. Listed on the National Register of Historic Places and on the Wisconsin Register of Historic Homes.
Collections: area history; photographs; Juneau County tax & country school records; Juneau County naturalization records; genealogy; historical documents c.1850; county officials from 1857; Native American artifacts.
Research Fields: Juneau County Native Americans.
Facilities: 1000-vol. library of books pertaining to state, local schools & war history available for use on premises.
Activities: guided tours; concerts; permanent & temporary exhibitions; research. Museum Sponsors: Christmas Open House; ice cream social; spring event; fall tea & fashion show.
Publications: quarterly newsletter, Juneau County History Notes.
Hours & Admission Prices: Memorial Day-Labor Day Sat.-Sun. 1-4 by appointment; Thanksgiving weekend & following weekend 1-8 by appointment; call historiographer Rose Clark at 608-847-4450. No charge; donations accepted.
Attendance: 2,080 (estimated)
Membership: Youth $1; Regular $5; Life $100.

Mayville

MAYVILLE HISTORICAL SOCIETY, INC., 1 N. German St., Mayville, WI 53050. Mailing Address: P.O. Box 82, Mayville, WI 53050-0082. Tel.: 920-387-2420 & 5787.
Web Site: mayvillehistoricalsociety.org
Founded: 1968.
Congressional District: 9
Key Personnel: Pres. & Membership Chm., Alyce Wurtz; Vice Pres., Ann Guse; Sec., Lois Gadow; Treas., Marcia Krieser.
Personnel Profile: Part-Time Volunteers 40.
Governing Authority: nonprofit organization. Affiliated with State Historical Society of Wisconsin, 816 State St., Madison, WI 53706. Tax-exempt: 170(b)(1)(A).
Historical Society Museum.
Collections: local historical items; wagons; agricultural materials; glassware; clothing; religious articles; pictures; manuscripts. Historic Buildings: 1874 fire station; 1888 Wagon & Carriage Factory with attached 1873 residence; 1885 Cigar Factory.
Research Fields: iron industry; local history.
Facilities: 500-vol. library of early school books, German language books, law books. Mayville history material & other museum-related items for sale.
Activities: guided tours; temporary exhibitions. Society Sponsors: Membership Dinner in April; Ice Cream Social in June.
Publications: quarterly newsletter.
Hours & Admission Prices: May-Oct. 2nd & 4th Sun. 1:30-4:30; tours by appointment only. Tour groups: $1 per person. ♿
Attendance: 427 (accurate)
Membership: Individual $10; Family $20; Business & Professional $20.

Mazomanie

MAZOMANIE HISTORICAL SOCIETY, 118 Brodhead St., Mazomanie, WI 53560. Mailing Address: Box 248, Mazomanie, WI 53560-0248. Tel.: 608-795-2992. Fax: 608-795-4576.
Founded: 1965.
Congressional District: 2
Key Personnel: Pres., Robert Dodsworth; Cur., Rita Frakes.
Personnel Profile: Part-Time Paid 1; Part-Time Volunteers 45.
Governing Authority: nonprofit organization. Affiliated with the State Historical Society, 816 State St., Madison, WI 53703. Tax-exempt: 501(3)(c).
General Museum.
Collections: artifacts relating to the history of the area; woodworking; cobbler; printing; automotive; blacksmith tool collection. Historic Building: 1857 train depot, wooden depot.
Research Fields: local history.
Facilities: research center. Gift items & stationery for sale.
Activities: guided tours; permanent & temporary exhibitions.
Publications: quarterly newsletter; local history pamphlets; books; annual research journal, Local Sheaves.
Hours & Admission Prices: May-Aug. Wed. & Sun. 1-4, call to confirm. Suggested Donation: adults $3. ♿
Attendance: 603 (estimated)
Membership: Individual $6; Family $10; Business $25; Life $100; Life Couple $175.

McFarland

MCFARLAND HISTORICAL SOCIETY, 5814 Main St., McFarland, WI 53558. Mailing Address: P.O. Box 94, McFarland, WI 53558-0094. Tel.: 608-838-3992.
E-mail: bluebee@madtown.net
Web Site: www.madison.com/communities/mhs/index.php
Founded: 1964.
Congressional District: 2
Key Personnel: Chm. (V) & Pres. (V), Dale Marsden; Treas., Carol Abernathy.
Personnel Profile: Part-Time Volunteers 25.
Governing Authority: nonprofit organization. Tax-exempt.
Historical Society Museum.
Collections: local artifacts.
Research Fields: local buildings; early citizens; artifacts.
Facilities: log cabin.
Activities: tours. Annual Events: Summer opening Bake Sale in May; Pioneer Day-Family Festival.
Publications: semi-annual newsletter.
Hours & Admission Prices: Memorial Day to late Sept. Sun. 1-4, Mon-Sat. by appointment. No charge; donations accepted.
Attendance: 2,000 (estimated)
Membership: Annual $5; Family $10; Supporting $20; Business & Professional $35; Life $100.

McNaughton

RIVERRUN CENTER FOR THE ARTS, 6938 Bridge Rd., McNaughton, WI 54543. Mailing Address: P.O. Box 95, McNaughton, MI 54543-0095. Tel.: 715-277-4224.
E-mail: riverrun@newnorth.net
Web Site: www.emill.com/riverrun/
Key Personnel: Dir. & Owner, Joan Molloy Slack
Art Gallery.
Collections: works by regional artists including sculpture, paintings, prints, & woodworking.
Activities: workshops; classes; demonstrations; performances. Annual Events: Summer Art Tour in July; Christmas Festival of the Arts in December.
Hours & Admission Prices: Call for hours.

Menasha

WEIS EARTH SCIENCE MUSEUM, University of Wisconsin-Fox Valley, 1478 Midway Rd., Menasha, WI 54952-1224. Tel.: 920-832-2925.
Earth Science Museum.
Collections: interactive & hands-on exhibits; video displays; colorful graphics; fossils; minerals & rocks.
Hours & Admission Prices: Wed.-Thurs. 12-4, Fri. 12-7, Sat. 10-5, Sun. 1-5. Adults 18-64 $2, seniors 65 & over and juniors 13-17 $1.50, children 3-12 $1; children under 3, UW Fox students, faculty & staff with ID no charge.

Menomonee Falls

OLD FALLS VILLAGE, N. 96 W. 15791 County Line Rd., Menomonee Falls, WI 53051-1537. Mailing Address: P.O. Box 91, Menomonee Falls, WI 53052-0091. Tel.: 262-250-5096. Fax: 262-250-5097.
E-mail: jsteliga@wi.rr.com
Web Site: www.menomonee-falls.org/index.aspx?NID=157
Founded: 1966.
Congressional District: 9
Key Personnel: Pres., Ruth Itzov; Museum Shop Mgr., Jean Armitage; Museum Devel. Dir., Deb Zindler.
Personnel Profile: Part-Time Volunteers 30; Interns 2.
Governing Authority: municipal; society. Affiliated with Menomonee Falls Historical Society, Inc. Tax-exempt: 501(c)(3).
Historic Houses.
Collections: primitive and country furniture 1800-1900; 18th & 19th-century decorative arts. Historic Houses: 1890 Railroad Depot; 1858 Miller Davidson House; 1845 Umhoefer log cabin; 1851 first schoolhouse; 1873 Farm House; 1842 log cabin; 1840 log cabin used as Catholic church.
Research Fields: local history.
Activities: guided tours. Museum Sponsors: Ice Cream Festival in June; Civil War Encampment in July; Quilt Show in August; Old Haunted Village in October; Silver Tea in December.
Publications: newsletter.
Hours & Admission Prices: Call for hours. Adults $3, children 6-16 $1.
Attendance: 6,000 (estimated)
Membership: Students & Seniors over 65 $7; Individuals $10; Family $20; Pioneer $25; Homesteader $50; Life $500.

Menomonie

DUNN COUNTY HISTORICAL SOCIETY, (M), 1820 Wakanda St., Menomonie, WI 54751-1631. Mailing Address: P.O. Box 437, Menomonie, WI 54751-0437. Tel.: 715-232-8685. Fax: 715-232-8687.
E-mail: info@dunnhistory.org
Web Site: www.dunnhistory.org
Founded: 1950.
Congressional District: 3
Key Personnel: Pres. (V), Roy S. Ostenso; Vice Pres., Rose Mary Stoll; Treas., Steve Cole; Education, Rich Sterry; Public Rels., Don Steffen; Registrar & Museum Supvr., Carol Thibado.
Personnel Profile: Full-Time Volunteers 8; Part-Time Paid 6; Part-Time Volunteers 30.
Governing Authority: private; nonprofit organization. Subsidiary Institutions: Russell J. Rassbach Heritage Museum & Hilkrest Rural School, 1820 Wakanda St., Menomonie, WI; Empire in Pine Museum, County Rd. C, Downsville, WI; Fulton & Edna Holtby Science & Technology Museum. Tax-exempt: 501(c)(3).
Historical Society Museum.
Collections: Wisconsin history from prehistoric to modern times with special emphasis on the history of the county of Dunn County & City of Menomonie. Historic Building: one-room school.
Facilities: library; 100-seat auditorium; 2,500 sq. ft. exhibit space; meeting room. Museum-related items for sale.
Activities: guided tours; lectures.
Publications: newsletter, The Dunn County Historian; pamphlet, Caddie Woodlawn: A Pioneer Girl on Wisconsin's Frontier; James Huff Stout - An Illustrated Timeline.
Hours & Admission Prices: Heritage Museum: Summer: Wed.-Sun. 10-5; Winter: Fri.-Sun. 12-4. Empire in Pine Museum: May-Sept. Sat.-Sun. 12-5. Adults $5, students $3; discount to AAM members; members no charge. Closed New Year's Day; Easter; Christmas. ♿
Attendance: 5,000 (accurate)
Membership: Senior $15; Individual & Senior Couple $25; Family $35; Supporting $100; Sustaining $250; Patron $500; Life $2,000.

JOHN FURLONG GALLERY, Micheels Hall, 415 13th Ave. E., Menomonie, WI 54751-3279. Tel.: 715-232-2261 & 1097. Fax: 715-232-1669.
E-mail: furlong@uwstout.edu
Web Site: www.furlonggallery.uwstout.edu
Founded: 1965.
Congressional District: 3
Key Personnel: Chm. & Cur., Susan Hunt; Cur., Geof Wheeler.
Governing Authority: university. Parent Institution: University of Wisconsin. Tax-exempt.
University Art Gallery.
Collections: 20th-century paintings, drawings, sculpture & prints.
Activities: guided tours; lectures; films; organized education programs for children; participatory, loan & temporary exhibitions.
Hours & Admission Prices: Mon.-Fri. 9-4 by appointment. No charge; donations accepted. Closed national holidays. ♿
Attendance: 7,000 (estimated)

WILSON PLACE MUSEUM, 101 Wilson Circle, Menomonie, WI 54751-1860. Tel.: 715-235-2283.
History Museum.
Collections: local history; period furnishings.
Hours & Admission Prices: April-May & Sept.-Oct. Sat.-Sun. 1-5; Memorial Day to Labor Day daily 1-5; mid-Nov. to early Jan. daily 1-8.

Mequon

CONCORDIA UNIVERSITY-WISCONSIN, ART GALLERY, 12800 N. Lake Shore Dr., Mequon, WI 53097-2418. Tel.: 262-243-4552. Fax: 262-243-4351.
Key Personnel: Dir., Jeff Shawhan.
Personnel Profile: Part-Time Paid 4.
Governing Authority: university; nonprofit organization. Parent Institution: Lutheran Church-Missouri Synod. Tax-exempt.
Art Gallery.
Collections: religious art; Russian bronzes; Chinese porcelain.
Activities: formal education programs for undergraduate & graduate college students; lectures; temporary exhibitions.
Hours & Admission Prices: Sun.-Wed. & Fri. 12-4, Thurs. 12-4 & 6-8. No charge. Closed major holidays. ♿
Attendance: 600 (estimated)

CRAFTS MUSEUM, 11458 N. Laguna Dr., 21W, Mequon, WI 53092-3118. Tel.: 262-242-1571.
Founded: 1972.
Congressional District: 9
Key Personnel: Dir. & C.E.O., Bob Siegel, Jr.
Personnel Profile: Full-Time Volunteers 1.
Governing Authority: individual operation.
Arts & Crafts Museum.
Collections: ice tools; ice harvesting history; wooden shoe carving skills; photographs; period prints & piano sheet music.
Research Fields: tools; wooden shoe carving; ice harvesting; sheet music.
Facilities: 600-vol. library of materials on tools for wood & ice available by written permission.
Activities: lectures; films; broadcast programs; formally organized education programs for children & adults; traveling exhibitions; mobile programs; school loan service.
Publications: pamphlets, ice harvesting & wooden shoe carving.
Hours & Admission Prices: Mobile programs only, call for information.
Attendance: 200,000 (estimated)

Merrill

MERRILL HISTORICAL SOCIETY, 102 E. Third St., Merrill, WI 54452-2321. Tel.: 715-536-5652.
E-mail: info@heritagehillgb.org
Founded: 1978.
Congressional District: 7
Key Personnel: Pres., David Finanger; Treas., Patricia Burg; Archivist, Mary Lagerbloom; Education, James Boettcher; Cur., Beverly King; Public Rels., Beatrice Lebal; Public Rels., Alice F. Krueger; Security & Museum Shop Mgr., Erin McCarthy.
Personnel Profile: Part-Time Paid 1; Part-Time Volunteers 8.
Governing Authority: private; nonprofit organization. Parent Institution: Merrill Historical Society, Inc., 804 E. Third St., Merrill, WI 54452. Subsidiary Institutions: Brickyard School Museum, Merrill, WI; Hermien Livingston Collections Building. Tax-exempt: 501(c)(3).
Historic Society Museum.
Collections: Wisconsin history from 1800 to present, special emphasis on Merrill Area, both rural & city; books; documents; early notebooks audio tapes, video tapes (transcribed from early movies).
Research Fields: materials to document village of Jenny 1847-1881, Merrill 1882-1998, Lincoln Co. Townships
Facilities: 975-vol. library; 360 sq. ft. exhibit space. Museum-related items for sale.
Activities: arts festivals; concerts; docent program; films; guided tours; lectures; participatory & traveling exhibitions.
Publications: bimonthly newsletter, Northwoods Historian.
Hours & Admission Prices: Library: Mon.-Fri. 1-4. Guided Tours: Wed. & Sun. 1-4; other tours by appointment. No charge. Closed New Year's Eve & Day; Martin Luther King Jr. Day; Good Friday; Easter; Memorial Day; Independence Day; Labor Day; Thanksgiving; Christmas. ♿
Attendance: 6,915 (accurate)
Membership: Senior Individual $13; Individual $16; Senior Family $18; Family $21; Business $25; Life Individual $200; Life Family $300.

Milton

MILTON HOUSE MUSEUM HISTORIC SITE, (M), 18 S. Janesville St., Hwys. 26 & 59, Milton, WI 53563-1527. Mailing Address: P.O. Box 245, Milton, WI 53563-0245. Tel.: 608-868-7772. Fax: 608-868-1698.
E-mail: miltonhouse@miltonhouse.org
Web Site: www.miltonhouse.org
Founded: 1948.
Congressional District: 1
Key Personnel: Pres., Guy Thomas; Exec. Dir., Cori Olson; Asst. Exec. Dir., Sue Schlueter.
Personnel Profile: Full-Time Paid 1; Part-Time Paid 1; Part-Time Volunteers 60.
Governing Authority: society. Parent Institution: Milton Historical Society. Tax-exempt: 501(c)(3).
History Museum: housed in a stagecoach inn used as a stop on the Underground Railroad.
Collections: mid-1800 pioneer items; Civil War artifacts; costumes; clocks; tools. Historic Buildings: 1844 Stage Coach Inn, first poured grout (lime mortar) building in U.S.; 1837 Log Cabin; 1867 Goodrich House; Livery stable; 1876 buggy shed; smoke house; country store; blacksmith shop.
Research Fields: local history; genealogy; underground railroad.
Facilities: 2,000-vol. research library of books & manuscripts.
Activities: guided tours; education programs for children; permanent & special exhibits. Museum Sponsors: annual arts & crafts show; annual Pioneer Dinner.

Publications: quarterly newsletter; pamphlets.
Hours & Admission Prices: May Sat.-Sun. 10-5; Memorial Day-Labor Day daily 10-5; other times by appointment. Adults 13 & over $6, seniors 62 & over $5, children 5-12 $3; discounts to groups, AAA & AAM members; children 5 & under and members no charge. Closed New Year's Eve & Day; Easter; Thanksgiving & weekend after; Christmas Eve, Day & week. ♿
Attendance: 8,027 (accurate)
Membership: Senior Citizen $10; Individual $12; Senior Family $15; Family $20; Conductor $30; Business $50; Station Master $100-$249; Abolitionist $250-$499; North Star Friend $500 & up.

Milwaukee

BETTY BRINN CHILDREN'S MUSEUM, 929 E. Wisconsin Ave., Milwaukee, WI 53202-5406. Tel.: 414-390-KIDS & 291-0888, ext. 200. Fax: 414-291-0906.
E-mail: questions@bbcmkids.org
Web Site: www.bbcmkids.org
Founded: 1995.
Key Personnel: C.E.O., Fern Shupeck; Pres. Bd. (V), Melissa Nelsen; Treas., Jane Frank; Exhibits, Jim Toth; Devel., Carrie Wettstein; Education, Carolyn Rydlewicz; Education, Lisa Balster; Public Rels., Kristen Adams; Museum Shop Mgr., Joel Cencius.
Personnel Profile: Full-Time Paid 17; Part-Time Paid 18; Part-Time Volunteers 12; Interns 3.
Governing Authority: private; nonprofit organization. Tax-exempt: 501(c)(3).
Children's Museum.
Collections: hands-on exhibits; Walt Disney cell art; Warner animation cells.
Research Fields: early childhood development.
Facilities: library; educational facilities; children's theater; 17,000 sq. ft. exhibit space. Museum-related items for sale.
Activities: guided tours; participatory & traveling exhibits; formal education programs for adults & children; birthday parties. Annual Events: July 3rd Event; Teacher of the Year Awards; Valentine's Day event in February; Halloween event in October; gala fundraiser.
Publications: member newsletter 3 times a year; brochure 3 times a year; monthy e-newsletter.
Hours & Admission Prices: June-Aug. Mon.-Sat. 9-5, Sun. 12-5; Sept.-May Tues.-Sat. 9-5, Sun. 12-5. Adults $6; discounts to Association of Children's museum members & groups; children under one & members no charge. Closed Memorial Day; Independence Day; Labor Day; Thanksgiving; Christmas Eve & Day. ♿
Attendance: 160,000 (estimated)
Membership: A $65; B $85; C $120; D $250; E $500; F $1,000; G $2,500.

THE CAPTAIN FREDERICK PABST MANSION, 2000 W. Wisconsin Ave., Milwaukee, WI 53233-2004. Tel.: 414-931-0808. Fax: 414-931-1005.
E-mail: info@pabstmansion.com
Key Personnel: Exec. Dir., Dawn M. Day Hourigan; Dir. Devel., John C. Eastberg; Dir. Visitor Svcs., Rikki Thompson; Cur., Jodi Rich-Bartz.
Personnel Profile: Full-Time Paid 4; Part-Time Paid 3; Part-Time Volunteers 50.
Governing Authority: Tax-exempt.
Historic House: former home of Captain Frederick Pabst, built in 1892.
Collections: local history & culture; period artifacts; furnishings; photographs.
Major Exhibits: Demolition Means Progress?, 1/22/10-6/6/10; The Cutting Edge, 6/11/10-10/10.
Activities: tours; temporary & permanent exhibitions; special events; educational programs; rental facilities.
Publications: Heritage Newsletter.
Hours & Admission Prices: mid-Jan. to Feb. Tues.-Sat. 10-4, Sun. 1-4; March to mid-Jan. Mon.-Sat. 10-4, Sun. 1-4. Adults $8, seniors & students $7, children 6-17 $4; children under 6 no charge. Closed New Year's Day; Easter; Thanksgiving; Christmas. ♿
Attendance: 25,000 (estimated)
Membership: First Mate $40; Sea Captain $60; Brewmaster $125; Gambrinus $250; Beer Baron $500; Blue Ribbon $1,500.

CHARLES ALLIS ART MUSEUM, (M), 1801 N. Prospect Ave., Milwaukee, WI 53202-1933. Tel.: 414-278-8295. Fax: 414-278-0335.
E-mail: ehaouchine@cavtmuseums.org
Web Site: www.cavtmuseums.org
Founded: 1945.
Congressional District: 5
Key Personnel: Exec. Dir., Maria Costello; Cur., Martha Monroe; Mgr. Mktg., Erica Haouchine; Events Mgr., Judith Hooks.
Personnel Profile: Full-Time Paid 4; Part-Time Paid 10; Part-Time Volunteers 40.
Governing Authority: Parent Institution: Milwaukee County War Memorial Corp., Inc., 750 N. Lincoln Memorial Dr., Milwaukee, WI 53202. Branch Museum: Villa Terrace Decorative Arts Museum, 2220 N. Terrace Ave., Milwaukee, WI 53202. Tax-exempt 501(c)(3).
Art Museum: housed in 1909 Tudor style mansion designed by Alexander Eschweiler.
Collections: Chinese porcelains from Han thru Ching Dynasties; 19th-century French Barbizon paintings; 19th-century American landscape paintings; 16th-19th century bronzes; English garden; ceramics.
Research Fields: Oriental & Asian decorative arts; Barbizon School & 19th-century American landscapes paintings; 16th-19th century bronzes; Wisconsin art.
Facilities: meeting rooms; lecture hall; reception area available for rent to the public.
Activities: guided tours; lectures; films; gallery talks; concerts; classes & workshops; teas; performances; permanent & temporary exhibitions; docent & educational programs.
Publications: exhibition catalogs; quarterly newsletter.
Hours & Admission Prices: Wed.-Sun. 1-5. Adults $5, seniors over 62 & students $3; children under 13 & members no charge. Closed major federal holidays. ♿
Attendance: 1,657 (accurate)
Membership: Student $25; Senior Citizen $35; Individual $45; Senior Couple $55; Family $60; Sustainer $75-$124; Patron $125-$249; Sponsor $250-$499; Benefactor $500-$999; Philanthropist $1,000 & up.

DISCOVERY WORLD, 500 N. Harbor Dr., Milwaukee, WI 53202-5601. Tel.: 414-765-9966. Fax: 414-765-0311.
E-mail: info@discoveryworld.org
Web Site: www.discoveryworld.org
Formerly: Discovery World - The James Lovell Museum of Science, Economics and Technology
Founded: 1984.
Key Personnel: Exec. Dir., Paul J. Krajniak; Pres., Joel Brennan; Dir. Mktg., Richard Cieslak; Dir. Exhibit Devel., Carl Schoettel; Museum Shop Mgr., Deena Thompson.
Personnel Profile: Full-Time Paid 75; Part-Time Paid 10; Part-Time Volunteers 100; Interns 3.
Governing Authority: nonprofit organization. Tax-exempt: 501(c)(3).
Science, Economics & Technology Museum.
Collections: interactive science & technology exhibits.
Facilities: Gift items for sale.
Activities: 140 hands-on exhibits; live theater productions; educational workshops; labs; progressive academic partnerships; fresh & salt water aquariums.
Publications: monthly newsletter; electronic newsletter.
Hours & Admission Prices: Tues.-Fri. 9-4, Sat.-Sun. 10-5. Adults $16.95, seniors $14.95, children 3-17 $12.95; discounts to AAA & ASTC members, Entertainment cardholders & groups; members & children under 2 no charge. Closed Independence Day; Thanksgiving; Christmas. ♿
Attendance: 400,000 (estimated)
Membership: College Student $15; Young Adult $25; Educator $35; Senior Citizen $40.50; Individual $45; Family & Senior Deluxe Family $65; Deluxe Family $100; Researcher $200; Explorer $350; Innovator $500; Discoverer's Society $1,000.

DRS. JOSEPH AND JAMES ENGLANDER SCHOOL OF DENTISTRY MUSEUM, Milwaukee, WI 53201. Mailing Address: Marquette University School of Dentistry, P.O. Box 1881, Milwaukee, WI 53201-1881. Tel.: 262-242-0931.
Key Personnel: Cur., Dr. Peter Jacobsohn
Dental Museum.
Collections: artifacts pertaining to the history of dental education & practice throughout the years.
Hours & Admission Prices: By appointment.

GREENE MEMORIAL MUSEUM, UNIVERSITY OF WISCONSIN-MILWAUKEE, 3209 N. Maryland Ave., Milwaukee, WI 53211-3102. Mailing Address: P.O. Box 413, Milwaukee, WI 53201. Tel.: 414-229-4561. Fax: 414-229-5452.
Web Site: www.geology.uwm.edu
Founded: 1913.
Congressional District: 5
Key Personnel: Chm., Tim Grundl; Sec., Lisa Alzalde; Cur., Stephen Dornbos.
Personnel Profile: Part-Time Paid 1.
Governing Authority: university. Parent Institution: University of Wisconsin, Milwaukee. Tax-exempt: 501(c)(3).
Geology Museum.
Collections: Devonian & Silurian fossils from Illinois & Wisconsin region; paleontology; mineralogy; conchology.
Research Fields: paleontology; mineralogy.
Activities: guided tours; lectures; formally organized education programs for children & college students; permanent exhibitions.

Publications: monographs.
Hours & Admission Prices: Fall Mon. & Wed.-Thurs. 10-2, Tues. 10-2 & 4-5. No charge; donations accepted. Closed major holidays.

HARLEY-DAVIDSON MUSEUM, 400 W. Canal St., Milwaukee, WI 53203-3208. Tel.: 414-343-4056; 877-HD MUSEUM.
Motorcycle Museum.
Collections: Harley-Davidson history, products & culture; riders, employees, dealers, & suppliers stories; photographs.
Facilities: Museum-related items for sale.
Hours & Admission Prices: Mon.-Wed. & Fri.-Sun. 10-6, Thurs. 10-8. Adults $16, senior citizens 65 & over, military and students with ID $12, children 5-17 $10; children under 5 no charge.

INSTITUTE OF VISUAL ARTS, UNIVERSITY OF WISCONSIN-MILWAUKEE, 2155 N. Prospect Ave., Milwaukee, WI 53202. Mailing Address: Box 413, Milwaukee, WI 53201. Tel.: 414-229-5070. Fax: 414-229-6785.
E-mail: inova@uwm.edu
Web Site: www.arts.uwm.edu/inova
Founded: 1982.
Congressional District: 5
Key Personnel: Dir., Bruce Knackert; Cur., Nicholas Frank.
Personnel Profile: Full-Time Paid 2; Part-Time Paid 11; Interns 1.
Governing Authority: state. Parent Institution: University of Wisconsin-Milwaukee. Tax-exempt.
Art Museum.
Collections: works by contemporary artists.
Major Exhibits: Spatial City: The Architecture of Idealism, 2/5/10-4/18/10.
Research Fields: studio art.
Facilities: offices; three art galleries.
Activities: lectures; gallery talks; symposia; changing contemporary art exhibits.
Publications: catalogs.
Hours & Admission Prices: Wed. & Fri.-Sun. 12-5, Thurs. 12-8. No charge; donations accepted. Closed holidays. ♿
Attendance: 18,000 (accurate)

THE INTERNATIONAL CLOWN HALL OF FAME & RESEARCH CENTER, INC., Tommy G. Thompson Youth Ctr., Wisconsin State Fair Park, 640 S. 84th St. #526, Milwaukee, WI 53214-1438. Tel.: 414-290-0105. Fax: 414-290-0106.
E-mail: contact@theclownmuseum.org
Web Site: www.theclownmuseum.org
Founded: 1986.
Congressional District: 1
Key Personnel: Pres., Chris K. Johnson; Pres. (V), Bertrand Berger, Ph.D.; Dir., Kathryn O'Dell; Financial Dir., Ron Zalben; Cur. & Archivist, Mark Renfro; Museum Shop Dir., Rachel Goers.
Personnel Profile: Full-Time Paid 2; Part-Time Volunteers 6.
Governing Authority: nonprofit. Tax-exempt: 501(c)(3).
Clown Museum.
Collections: history of clowns; 2,000 photographs; art.
Research Fields: history of clowns & healing power of humor.
Facilities: 1,000-vol. library of books; 2,500 sq. ft. exhibit area. Clown-related items for sale.
Activities: formal education programs for children & adults; guided tours; theatre; traveling exhibitions.
Publications: quarterly newsletter.
Hours & Admission Prices: Mon.-Fri. 10-3:30. Shows: $5. Museum: $2. Museum & Show: $8; members no charge. ♿
Attendance: 25,000 (estimated)
Membership: Clown/Supporter $35; Family $50; Joey/Patron $100; Jester/Advocate $500; Ringmaster/Founder $1,000.

* **MILWAUKEE ART MUSEUM,** 700 N. Art Museum Dr., Milwaukee, WI 53202-4098. Tel.: 414-224-3200 & 3220. Fax: 414-271-7588. TDD: 414-271-6678.
E-mail: mam@mam.org
Web Site: www.mam.org
Founded: 1888.
Congressional District: 5
Key Personnel: C.E.O. & Dir., Dan Keegan; Pres., W. Kent Velde; Cur. Earlier European Arts, Laurie Winters; Asst. Cur. Prints & Drawings, Mary Weaver Chapin; Assoc. Cur. Photographs, Lisa Hostetler; Sr. Dir. Devel., Mary Louise Mussoline; Registrar, Dawn Frank; Dir. Programs & Education, Brigid Globensky; Dir. Mktg. & Communications, Jonas Wittke; C.F.O., Jane Wochos; Librarian & Archivist, Heather Winter; Dir. Adult Programs & Tours, Fran Serlin; Sr. Dir. Business Enterprises, Gwen Benner; Dir. Human Resources, Jan Schmidt; Mgr. Retail Operations, Bambi Grajek-Specter.
Personnel Profile: Full-Time Paid 119; Part-Time Paid 83; Part-Time Volunteers 150; Interns 11.
Governing Authority: board of trustees, nonprofit organization. Tax-exempt: 501(c)(3).
Art Museum.
Collections: over 20,000 works; 19th- to 20th-century American & European art, contemporary art, American decorative arts, Old Master works, folk & self-taught art.
Major Exhibits: Andy Warhol: The Last Decade, 11/09-1/3/10; Green Furniture Design, 11/12/09-3/14/10; 50 Works for 50 States: The Dorothy & Herbert Vogel Collection, 12/17/09-2/28/10; Street Seen: The Psychological Gesture in Photography 1940-59, 1/30/10-4/25/10; Scholastic Art Awards: 2010 WI Regional Exhibition, 2/6/10-3/21/10; Raphael's La Donna Velata, 3/26/10-6/6/10; Theaster Gates: Resurrecting Dave the Potter, 4/15/10-8/1/10; Quilts in a Material World: Selections from the Winterthur Collection, 5/22/10-9/6/10; Out of Line: The Satirical Prints of Warrington Colescott, 6/17/10-9/26/10.
Research Fields: art in permanent collection, exhibitions & prospective acquisitions.
Facilities: Quadracci Pavilion; gardens; educational & public programming facilities.
Activities: guided tours; lectures; gallery talks; arts festival; education programs for children & adults; satellite specialization center for Milwaukee schools; docent program & council; inter-museum loan, permanent, temporary, & traveling exhibitions; school loan service; 10 special interest & support groups.
Publications: exhibition catalogs; calendar; collection handbook; annual report.
Hours & Admission Prices: Tues.-Wed. & Fri.-Sun. 10-5, Thurs. 10-8. Adults $9, senior citizens $7, students $5; discounts to AAM & ICOM members; members & children under 5 no charge. Closed Thanksgiving; Christmas. ♿
Attendance: 296,806 (accurate)
Membership: Student $25; Senior Citizen $50; Individual & Teacher $55; Family & Dual $70; Friends of Art $150; Donor $350; Patron $500; Partner $1,000; Benefactor $2,500; Philanthropist $5,000; Sustaining Philanthropist $10,000; Director's Patron $25,000; Calatrava Society $50,000; Peg Bradley Society $100,000.

MILWAUKEE COUNTY HISTORICAL SOCIETY, 910 N. Old World Third St., Milwaukee, WI 53203-1501. Tel.: 414-273-8288. Fax: 414-273-3268.
E-mail: info@milwaukeehistory.net
Web Site: www.milwaukeehistory.net
Founded: 1935.
Congressional District: 5
Key Personnel: C.E.O., Robert T. Teske; Pres., Randy Bryant; Cur. Research Collections, Steven L. Daily; Cur. Museum Collections, Michael Reuter.
Personnel Profile: Part-Time Paid 2; Part-Time Volunteers 30; Interns 6.
Governing Authority: nonprofit organization. Branch Museums: Kilbourntown House, Milwaukee; Lowell Damon House, Wauwatosa; Jeremiah Curtin House, Greendale; Trimborn Farm, Greendale. Tax-exempt: 501(c)(3).
History Museum: housed in 1913 bank.
Collections: county history; brewery materials; manuscripts; transportation artifacts; panorama paintings; early settlers materials; aeronautics; archives; paintings; costumes; decorative arts; marine; military; technology; theater. Historic Buildings: 1846 Jeremiah Curtin house; 1847 Lowell Damon House; 1844 Kilbourntown House; 1847 Trimborn Farm.
Research Fields: history of Milwaukee County.
Facilities: 10,000-vol. library of historical material available for use on premises; county archives & court records, including naturalization papers; reading room.
Activities: guided tours; lectures; films; gallery talks; radio programs; formally organized education programs for undergraduate students; permanent & temporary exhibitions; school loan service; home tours; ethnic dinners; wine & beer tasting; tours of historic public & private buildings in Milwaukee County.
Publications: quarterly magazine, Milwaukee History; newsletter; books.
Hours & Admission Prices: Mon.-Fri. 9:30-5, Sat. 10-5, Sun. 1-5. Adults $3, seniors 62 & over and children 6 & over $2; county residents on Mon. & members no charge. Closed national holidays. ♿
Attendance: 65,000 (estimated)
Membership: Student & Senior Citizen $30; Individual $35; Family $40; Contributing $75; Sustaining $125; Associate $250; Benefactor $500.

MILWAUKEE COUNTY ZOOLOGICAL GARDENS, 10001 W. Bluemound Rd., Milwaukee, WI 53226-4384. Tel.: 414-771-3040. Fax: 414-256-5410. TDD: 414-771-1180.
E-mail: jdilibertishea@milwcnty.com
Web Site: www.milwaukeezoo.org/
Founded: 1958.
Congressional District: 5
Key Personnel: Exec. Dir., Charles Wikenhauser; Deputy Dir. Animal, Bruce Beehler, D.V.M.; Public Affairs & Svcs. Dir., Laura Pedriani; Operations Mgr., Bldgs. & Grounds Mgr., Karl Hackbarth.
Personnel Profile: Full-Time Paid 125; Part-Time Paid 450; Part-Time Volunteers 580.
Governing Authority: county. Parent Institution: Milwaukee County Department of Zoological Gardens. Tax-exempt.
Zoo.
Collections: mammals; birds; fish; amphibians & reptiles of the world.
Research Fields: primate behavior; avian reptilian reproduction; elephant behavior; Humboldt penguin reproduction; snow leopard reproduction.
Facilities: approx. 500-vol. library of zoological reference books not available for outside use; education center; picnic area; restaurant. Museum-related items for sale.
Activities: formally organized education programs for children; permanent & temporary exhibitions; camel & pony rides; giraffe feeding; train; zoomobile; sea lion show.
Publications: quarterly newsletter, Alive (published by the Zoological Society of Milwaukee County).
Hours & Admission Prices: March to late May & early Sept.-Oct. daily 9-4:30; late May to early Sept. daily 9-5; Nov.-Feb. Mon.-Fri. 9:30-2:30, Sat.-Sun. 9:30-4:30. April-Oct. adults $12.25, seniors $11.25, children 3-12 $9.25; children 2 & under no charge. Nov.-Dec.: adults $10.75, seniors $7.75, children 3-12 $7.75. Parking: cars $10, buses $14; discount to Milwaukee County residents; members no charge. ♿
Attendance: 1,300,000 (accurate)
Membership: See Zoological Society of Milwaukee County: www.zoosociety-.org.

* **MILWAUKEE PUBLIC MUSEUM, (M),** 800 W. Wells St., Milwaukee, WI 53233-1478. Tel.: 414-278-2700. Fax: 414-278-6100.
E-mail: webmaster@mpm.edu
Web Site: www.mpm.edu
Founded: 1882.
Congressional District: 5
Key Personnel: Chm., Michael J. Falbo; Pres. & C.E.O., Daniel M. Finley; Sr. Vice Pres. Finance & C.F.O., Michael Bernatz; Sr. Vice Pres. Devel., Karen Spahn; Sr. Vice Pres. Museum Programs, Ellen Censky, Ph.D.; Dir. Mktg. & Communications, Mary Bridges; Exec. Dir. IMAX & Planetarium, Bob Bonadurer; Dir. Human Rels. & Labor Rels., Patricia Schneider; Dir. Exhibit Programs, James Kelly; Dir. Security, Ralph Jones; Dir. Facility Operations, Larry Bannister; Dir. Information Svcs., Linda Gruber; Dir. Corporate Rels., Karen Kancius; Dir. Admissions & Reservations, Laura Wake Wiesner; Gift Shops Operations Mgr., Katherine Pajewski.
Personnel Profile: Full-Time Paid 87; Part-Time Paid 53; Part-Time Volunteers 484; Interns 55.
Governing Authority: nonprofit. Tax-exempt: 501(c)(3).
Natural & Human History Museum.
Collections: anthropology, including all major sub-disciplines; botany; geology-paleontology; invertebrate zoology; vertebrate zoology; history-worldwide including local history; fine, decorative & folk arts; business machines; firearms; photos, film & specimen collection; sound recordings; bibliographic; archival collections & sound recordings.
Research Fields: American Indian; North American ethnology; New World archaeology; ethnobotany; metropolitan Milwaukee & Wisconsin flora; natural areas preservation; invertebrate paleontology; evolution & extinction of Paleozoic faunas; firearms; American technology; natural history, general ecology & population biology of insects; population biology & behavioral ecology of cocoa-pollinating midges; distributional studies of terrestrial gastropods & fairy shrimps in Wisconsin; ecology & conservation; behavior & ecology of West Indies reptiles; program development & evaluation; conservation of organic materials & causes of degradation; Egyptian mummies; U.S. military; local & Wisconsin history.
Facilities: 125,000-vol. library of natural & human history available for use on premises & inter-library loan; 148,178 sq. ft. exhibit space; 300-seat lecture hall; herbarium; IMAX Dome Theater; classrooms; restaurant; butterfly garden; planetarium. Museum-related items for sale.
Activities: guided tours; lecture series; educational programs; special events; special exhibits; IMAX films & planetarium shows; docent program; volunteer program; public programming; summer camps; after school programming; museum studies program for college students; private rental facilities.
Publications: membership newsletter & magazine; guides; pamphlets; annual report; teacher's guides; exhibition posters; postcards & notecards.
Hours & Admission Prices: Oct.-June 13 Mon.-Sat. 9-5, Sun. 12-5; June 14-Sept. Mon. & Wed.-Sat. 9-4, Sun. 10-4. Adults $11, senior citizens $8, children 4-17 $6; discounts to handicapped visitors & AAM members; ASTC reciprocal; Milwaukee County residents on Mon. & members no charge. Closed Independence Day; Thanksgiving; Christmas. ♿
Attendance: 611,379 (estimated)
Membership: Basic: Pathfinder $70; Trailblazer $130. Enrichment Club: Bronze $150-$249; Silver $250-$349; Gold $350-499; Platinum $500-$749; Diamond $750-$999.

MITCHELL GALLERY OF FLIGHT, (M), General Mitchell International Airport, c/o Milwaukee County Airport Div., 5300 S. Howell Ave., Milwaukee, WI 53207-6156. Tel.: 414-747-4503. Fax: 414-747-4525.
E-mail: flymitchell@mitchellgallery.org
Web Site: www.mitchellgallery.org
Founded: 1984.
Congressional District: 4
Key Personnel: Pres. (V) & Dir., Charles Boie; Financial Dir., Anthony Snieg; Devel. & Membership, Jackie Stueck.
Personnel Profile: Part-Time Paid 1; Part-Time Volunteers 15.
Governing Authority: nonprofit organization. Parent Institution: Mitchell International Airport. Tax-exempt.
Aviation Museum.
Collections: full size 1911 Curtiss Pusher aircraft; model airplanes; aviation art; miniature dioramas; photographs; aviation engines; medals & memorabilia on Gen. Billy Mitchell; historical archives; items relating to aviation in Wisconsin, Mitchell Airport, commercial & military aviation & lighter-than-air transportation.
Research Fields: history of local aviation; Gen. Mitchell.
Facilities: 1,400 sq. ft. exhibit space
Activities: self-guided tours. Museum Sponsors: Gen. Mitchell Open golf meet.
Publications: quarterly newsletter, Flightlines; General William Mitchell, Air Power Pioneer; General Mitchell International Airport - A Record of Progress.
Hours & Admission Prices: Daily 6am-10pm; airport open daily 24 hrs. No charge; donations accepted. ♿
Attendance: 200,000 (estimated)
Membership: Individual $10; Family $15; Contributing $25; Sustaining $100; Bronze Corporate Sponsor $250; Silver Corporate Sponsor $500; Gold Corporate Sponsor $1,000.

MITCHELL PARK HORTICULTURAL CONSERVATORY, 524 S. Layton Blvd., Milwaukee, WI 53215-1236. Tel.: 414-649-9830. Fax: 414-649-8616.
Web Site: www.countyparks.com/horticulture
Founded: 1959.
Congressional District: 4
Key Personnel: Dir., Sandy Folaron; Horticulturist II, Wayne Majerowski; Horticulturist I (Tropical), Patrick Kehoe; Horticulturist I (Arid), Lillian Torres; Horticulturist I (Display), Christopher Gaar; Operating Engineer, David Loosemore.
Personnel Profile: Full-Time Paid 9; Part-Time Paid 8.
Governing Authority: county. Parent Institution: Milwaukee County Park System, 9480 W. Watertown Plank Rd., Wauwatosa, WI 53226. Tel.: 414-257-5666. Tax-exempt.
Botanical Garden & Conservatory: housed on site of the Jacques Vieau settlement, one of the first permanent buildings built in the Milwaukee area.
Collections: tropical Bromeliads; 400 species/hybrid orchids; ferns; 550 species general tropicals; 75 species & forms of lithops; agaves; more than 1,000 cacti & succulents; Madagascar succulent collection; emphasis on tropical fruits; economic plants; birds; reptiles.
Research Fields: experiments on raising horticulture materials; conservation work; biological pest management.
Facilities: 250-vol. library of informational material for staff available for research; botanical garden. Plants & other museum-related items for sale.
Activities: guided tours; occasional concerts; hobby workshops. Museum Sponsors: seasonal shows; Holiday Shows; Ethnic Festivals.
Publications: various cultural brochures.
Hours & Admission Prices: Mon.-Fri. 9-5, Sat.-Sun. 9-4. Adults $6.50, Milwaukee senior citizens with ID, juniors 6-18 & handicapped $5; discounts to groups of 20 or more; members & Milwaukee County students & residents Mon. 9-12 no charge ♿
Attendance: 200,000 (accurate)
Membership: Friends of the Domes: Single $20; Family (1 & 3 guests) $40; Contributing $100; Corporate $250.

MOUNT MARY COLLEGE HISTORIC COSTUME COLLECTION, 2900 N. Menomonee River Pkwy., Milwaukee, WI 53222-4597. Tel.: 414-258-4810. Fax: 414-256-0172.
E-mail: gastone@mtmary.edu
Web Site: www.mtmary.edu
Founded: 1928.
Key Personnel: Cur., Elizabeth Gaston.
Personnel Profile: Part-Time Paid 2; Part-Time Volunteers 3; Interns 3.
Governing Authority: college; nonprofit organization. Parent Institution: Mount Mary College. Tax-exempt.
Costume Museum.
Collections: costume: 1750s-present; special emphasis on American & European designers.
Research Fields: historic pattern reproduction; Calvin Klein archival project site; Bonnie Cashin; Valentina; Lynn Fontanne; Hildegarde.
Facilities: library featuring fashion periodicals; educational facilities.
Activities: formal education programs for undergraduate & graduate college students; loan & temporary exhibitions.
Hours & Admission Prices: Sept. to mid-May Mon.-Fri. 10-4; call for summer hours. No charge; donations accepted. Closed Easter; Thanksgiving; Christmas. ♿
Membership: Trendsetter $35; Private Label $50; Pret-a-Porter $100; Haute Couture $500.

THE PATRICK & BEATRICE HAGGERTY MUSEUM OF ART, (M), Marquette University, 13th & Clybourn, Milwaukee, WI 53233. Mailing Address: P.O. Box 1881, Milwaukee, WI 53201-1881. Tel.: 414-288-7290. Fax: 414-288-5415.
Web Site: www.marquette.edu/haggerty
Founded: 1984.
Congressional District: 5
Key Personnel: Dir., Wally Mason; Assoc. Dir., Lee Coppernoll; Assoc. Cur., Dr. Annemarie Sawkins; Cur. Education, Lynne Shumow; Registrar, John Loscuito; Administrative Asst., Mary Wagner; Curatorial Asst., Jerome Fortier; Preparator, Dan Herro; Asst. Preparator, Ric Stultz; Communications Asst. & Admin. Sec., Mary Dornfeld; Chief Security Officer, Clayton Ray.
Personnel Profile: Full-Time Paid 8; Part-Time Paid 23; Part-Time Volunteers 50; Interns 2.
Governing Authority: university. Parent Institution: Marquette Univ., Milwaukee. Tax-exempt: 501(c)(3).
Art Museum.
Collections: European & American paintings from the 15th- to 20th-centuries; works by major international 20th-century artists; prints; photographs; sculpture; global arts.
Major Exhibits: Persian Visions (T), 11/09-1/10; 25th Anniversary Celebration, 11/09-1/10; Thomas Woodruff: Freak Parade (T), 1/10-4/10; Contemporary Views Lucinda Devlin, 1/10-4/10; Jennifer Steinkamp Recent Work, 1/10-4/10; Old Masters From the Haggerty, 1/10-4/10; Hollywood Icons, Local Demons (T), 9/10-1/11; Stained Glass From Oakbrook Esser Studio, 9/10-1/11; Stella Johnson Cameroon Images (T), 9/10-1/11; Old Masters Paintings, 9/10-1/11.
Research Fields: European painting & prints; aesthetics & contemporary art; photography.
Facilities: library; five galleries; 8,000 sq. ft. exhibit space. Museum-related gifts & books for sale.
Activities: participatory, loan, traveling & temporary exhibitions; guided tours; lectures; films; paintings & drawings; education programs for students & adults; performance art; concerts; docent training; Friends Assoc.; Old Master Collectors Group. Annual Events: spring gala in June; fall gala in October.
Publications: exhibition catalogs.
Hours & Admission Prices: Mon.-Wed. & Fri.-Sat. 10-4:30, Thurs. 10-8, Sun. 12-5; call to confirm. No charge; donations accepted. Closed some holidays. ♿
Attendance: 16,000
Membership: Student $15; Individual $40-$59; Family $60-$99; Sustaining $100-$249; Patron $250-$499; Benefactor $500-$999; Director's Circle $1,000-$2,499; Museum Partners $2,500-$4,999; Diamond Partners $5,000-$9,999; Platinum Partner $10,000 & up.

UWM UNION-ART GALLERY, 2200 E. Kenwood Blvd., Milwaukee, WI 53211-3361. Mailing Address: UWM Union P.O. Box 413, Milwaukee, WI 53201. Tel.: 414-229-6310. Fax: 414-229-6709.
E-mail: agallery@uwm.edu
Web Site: www.aux.uwm.edu/union/artgal.htm
Founded: 1972.
Congressional District: 5
Key Personnel: Mgr., Andrea Avery.
Personnel Profile: Part-Time Paid 3.
Governing Authority: university. Affiliated with University of Wisconsin-Milwaukee. Tax-exempt.
Art Gallery.
Collections: various art media by local, state, & national artists.
Activities: gallery lectures; concerts; poetry readings; multi-media exhibitions & performances; art & dance programs; temporary & traveling exhibitions; symposiums; special events.
Publications: flyers, posters & mailings.
Hours & Admission Prices: Sept.-May Mon.-Wed. & Fri-Sat. 12-5, Thurs. 12-7. No charge. Closed holidays; university vacation periods. ♿
Attendance: 13,000

VILLA TERRACE DECORATIVE ARTS MUSEUM, 2220 N. Terrace Ave., Milwaukee, WI 53202-1216. Tel.: 414-271-3656. Fax: 414-271-3986.
E-mail: ehaouchine@cavtmuseums.org
Web Site: www.cavtmuseums.org
Founded: 1967.
Congressional District: 5
Key Personnel: Exec. Dir., Marie Costello; Events Mgr., Judith Hooks; Mgr. Mktg., Erica Haouchine; Cur., Martha Monroe.
Personnel Profile: Full-Time Paid 4; Part-Time Paid 10; Part-Time Volunteers 35.
Governing Authority: Parent Institution: Milwaukee County War Memorial Corp. Branch Museum: Charles Allis Art Museum, 1801 N. Prospect Ave., Milwaukee, WI 53202. Tax-exempt: 501(c)(3).
European fine & decorative arts museum, housed in 1923 Italianate villa on shore of Lake Michigan designed by David Adler. The Museum features fine & decorative arts from the 15th-18th centuries.
Collections: European decorative arts from 15th-19th century; 16th-19th century European paintings; Renaissance garden redesigned by Dennis Buettner & Assoc.
Research Fields: Italian Renaissance art & architecture; European fine & decorative arts; garden design & history; David Adler.
Facilities: non-circulating library related to research fields; reception hall & terraced garden available to the public for private rental events.
Activities: guided tours; concerts; lectures; gallery talks; seminars; permanent & temporary exhibitions; docent program.
Publications: exhibition catalogues; quarterly newsletter.
Hours & Admission Prices: Wed.-Sun. 1-5. Adults $5, seniors & students $3; children under 13 & members no charge. Closed major federal holidays. ♿
Attendance: 4,465 (accurate)
Membership: Student $25; Senior Citizen $35; Individual $45; Senior Couple $55; Family $60; Sustainer $75-$124; Patron $125-$249; Sponsor $250-$499; Benefactor $500-$999; Philanthropist $1,000 & up.

WISCONSIN BLACK HISTORICAL SOCIETY/MUSEUM, 2620 W. Center St., Milwaukee, WI 53206-1155. Tel.: 414-372-7677.
Web Site: wbhsm.homestead.com
Key Personnel: Exec. Dir., Clayborn Benson
Historical Society Museum.
Collections: local history & culture pertaining to the historical heritage of African descent in Wisconsin.
Hours & Admission Prices: Mon.-Fri. 12-5, Sat. 9-2. Adults & college students with ID $5, seniors $4; children 12 & under $3; members no charge. Closed New Year's; Thanksgiving; Christmas.

WISCONSIN MARINE HISTORICAL SOCIETY, 814 W. Wisconsin Ave., Milwaukee, WI 53233-2385. Tel.: 414-286-3074.
E-mail: info@wmhs.org
Web Site: www.wmhs.org
Marine Historical Society.
Collections: artifacts relating to Great Lakes maritime history; photographs; period artifacts.
Hours & Admission Prices: Call for hours.

Mineral Point

PENDARVIS HISTORIC SITE, 114 Shake Rag St., Mineral Point, WI 53565-1063. Mailing Address: P.O. Box 270, Mineral Point, WI 53565-0270. Tel.: 608-987-2122. Fax: 608-987-3738.
E-mail: pendarvis@wisconsinhistory.org
Web Site: pendarvis.wisconsinhistory.org
Founded: 1971.
Congressional District: 2
Key Personnel: Dir., Allen Schroeder; Cur., Tamara Funk.
Personnel Profile: Full-Time Paid 3; Part-Time Paid 18.
Governing Authority: society. Parent Institution: State Historical Society of Wisconsin, 816 State St., Madison WI 53706. Tax-exempt.
Historic House: 1841-1848 miners' cottages built by immigrants from Cornwall, England.

Collections: 1840-1875 household furnishings; 19th-century mining tools & equipment; antiques; artifacts.
Research Fields: mining & smelting technology c.1825-1900; British immigration to mining frontiers c.1825-1900.
Facilities: Museum-related items for sale.
Activities: guided tours; special events.
Publications: site brochure; books, Mineral Point: A History, reprint 1986; On the Shake Rag: Mineral Point's Pendarvis House 1935-1970.
Hours & Admission Prices: mid May to Oct. daily 10-5. Adults $9, members & children 5-17 $4.50; discounts to senior citizens & groups; children under 5 no charge.
Attendance: 10,000 (accurate)

Mishicot

MISHICOT HISTORICAL MUSEUM, 411 Buchanan, Mishicot, WI 54228. Mailing Address: P.O. Box 237, Mishicot, WI 54228. Tel.: 920-755-2525 & 3317.
Web Site: www.mishicot.org
History Museum: housed in a former two-room schoolhouse, built in 1874.
Collections: artifacts of the Mishicot area history from pioneer days to the present; collections on rural schools & Potawatomie Indians; photographs.
Hours & Admission Prices: June-Aug. Sat.-Sun. 12-4; other times by appointment.

Mount Horeb

MT. HOREB AREA MUSEUM, 100 S. Second St., Mount Horeb, WI 53572-2106. Mailing Address: 138 E. Main St., Mt. Horeb, WI 53572-2138. Tel.: 608-437-6486.
E-mail: usemeum@mhtc.net
Web Site: www.mounthoreb.org
Founded: 1975.
Key Personnel: Pres. (V), Brian Bigler; Museum Shop Mgr., Laurie Boyden.
Governing Authority: Tax-exempt.
History Museum.
Collections: local cultural history; photographs; period artifacts.
Facilities: archives.
Publications: quarterly, Mt. Horeb Area Past Times.
Hours & Admission Prices: May-Dec. Fri.-Sat. 10-4, Sun. 12:30-4. No charge; donations accepted. ♿
Attendance: 2,000 (accurate)
Membership: Individual $15; Household $25; Lifetime $250; Benefactor $500.

MOUNT HOREB MUSTARD MUSEUM, 100 W. Main St., Mount Horeb, WI 53572-1913. Mailing Address: P.O. Box 468, Mount Horeb, WI 53572-0468. Tel.: 800-438-6878.
E-mail: curator@mustardmuseum.com
Web Site: www.mustardweb.com
Founded: 1986.
Congressional District: 2
Key Personnel: Cur., Barry Levenson; Dir. Mktg. & Tours, Patty Levenson
Food Museum.
Collections: over 6,000 jars, bottles, & tubes from all 50 states and over 60 countries; period mustard pots & tins; vintage mustard advertisements & memorabilia.
Facilities: Museum-related items for sale.
Activities: mustard samples.
Hours & Admission Prices: Daily 10-5. No charge; donations accepted. Closed New Year's Day; Easter; Thanksgiving; Christmas. ♿
Attendance: 30,000

Neenah

* **BERGSTROM-MAHLER MUSEUM, (M),** 165 N. Park Ave., Neenah, WI 54956-2956. Tel.: 920-751-4658. Fax: 920-751-4755. TDD: 920-751-4658.
E-mail: info@paperweightmuseum.com
Web Site: www.bergstrom-mahlermuseum.com
Founded: 1954.
Congressional District: 6
Key Personnel: Dir., Jan Smith; Education, Chelisa Behm; Mktg., Jen Bero; Museum Shop Mgr., Kathy Smits.
Personnel Profile: Full-Time Paid 5; Part-Time Paid 2; Part-Time Volunteers 70.
Governing Authority: nonprofit organization. Tax-exempt: 501(c)(3).
Art Museum.
Collections: glass paperweights; Germanic & contemporary glass; Victorian glass baskets.
Major Exhibits: The Italian Influence in Glass, 11/09-2/10.
Research Fields: European & American antique paperweights & related glass objects, contemporary paperweights, Germanic glass.
Facilities: Museum-related items for sale.
Activities: permanent & temporary art exhibits; guided tours; lectures; gallery talks; summer arts festival; films; art events; formally organized education programs for children & adults.
Publications: quarterly newsletter; exhibition catalogues; collection catalogues of paperweights & Germanic glass; annual report.
Hours & Admission Prices: Tues.-Sat. 10-4:30, Sun. 1-4:30. No charge; donations accepted. Closed legal holidays. ♿
Attendance: 23,711 (accurate)
Membership: Senior Citizen $25; Individual $35; Family $50; Associate $125; Apprentice $250; Partner $500.

NEENAH HISTORICAL SOCIETY, HIRAM SMITH, NEENAH'S HERITAGE PARK, OCTAGON HOUSE & WARD HOUSE, (M), 343 Smith St., Neenah, WI 54956-2434. Mailing Address: P.O. Box 343, Neenah, WI 54957-0343. Tel.: 920-729-0244.
E-mail: director@neenahhistoricalsociety.org
Web Site: www.neenahhistoricalsociety.org
Founded: 1948.
Congressional District: 6
Key Personnel: Pres., JoEllen Wollangk; Treas., Catherine Davis.
Personnel Profile: Full-Time Paid 1; Part-Time Volunteers 4.
Governing Authority: private; nonprofit organization. Tax-exempt: 501(c)(3).
General Museum: housed in 1850s octagon house.
Collections: period clothing & furnishings; personal artifacts; photographs; newspapers.
Facilities: library; archives; 3,000 sq. ft. exhibit space. Museum-related items for sale.
Activities: guided tours; lectures; loan & temporary exhibitions. Museum Sponsors: 4th & 5th grade students historical bike tour stop; annual meetings; Memorial Day Parade; Community Fest Parade; cemetery walk; Christmas open house.
Publications: bimonthly newsletter, The Society Times.
Hours & Admission Prices: By appointment. No charge; donations accepted. ♿
Membership: Individual $15; Family $35; Contributing $50; Supporting $100; Benefactor $500; Sponsor $1,000.

New Berlin

THE NEW BERLIN HISTORICAL SOCIETY, 19765 W. National Ave., New Berlin, WI 53146. Mailing Address: S46 W22212, Tansdale Rd., Waukesha, WI 53189-8036. Tel.: 262-542-4773.
E-mail: meidenbauer@juno.com
Founded: 1965.
Congressional District: 5
Key Personnel: Pres. (V) & Publicity, Dave Totten.
Personnel Profile: Part-Time Volunteers 30.
Governing Authority: municipal. Parent Institution: Wisconsin State Historical Society, 816 State St., Madison, WI 53706. Tax-exempt.
Historical Society Museum: housed in 1870 Winton-Sprengel House, Carriage House & 1840 log cabin.
Collections: area historical artifacts; farm implements & veterinary medicines from local farm; 1840 immigrant trunk; mid-19th century oil painting of New Berlin farmstead; general household items; accoutrements; organs; fainting couch; rope bed; toys; Murphy bed; general store; windmill; country store. Historic Buildings: 1863 schoolhouse; 1900 Carriage Barn; 1870 Winton-Sprengle Farm House; 1850 Pioneer Log House; 1847 Winton/Martin House.
Research Fields: genealogy & local history.
Activities: guided tours; slide show; permanent exhibitions; classes held in 1863 one-room schoolhouse. Museum Sponsors: Ice Cream Social in July; Historic Days in September; annual Apple Fest in October; open house & special entertainment.
Publications: annual magazine, The New Berlin Almanack; quarterly newsletter.
Hours & Admission Prices: May-Sept. call for hours; group tours by appointment. No charge; donations accepted.
Attendance: 1,200 (estimated)
Membership: Individual $10; Family $18; Lifetime $100.

New Glarus

CHALET OF THE GOLDEN FLEECE, 618 2nd Ave., New Glarus, WI 53574. Mailing Address: P.O. Box 564, New Glarus, WI 53574-0564. Tel.: 608-527-2095. Fax: 608-527-4991.
Founded: 1955.
Congressional District: 2
Key Personnel: Village Admin., Nicholas Owen; Mgr., Pete Etter.

Personnel Profile: Part-Time Paid 5.
Governing Authority: municipal. Parent Institution: Village of New Glarus, WI. Tax-exempt.
Historic House Museum: Swiss chalet.
Collections: period Swiss & early American furniture, glass & china; weapons; jewelry; Swiss carvings; period parchments; prints; French prints; Swiss doll collection.
Activities: guided tours.
Publications: brochures.
Hours & Admission Prices: May-Oct. by appointment. Adults $7, students $2; children under 6 no charge.
Attendance: 4,000 (estimated)

SWISS HISTORICAL VILLAGE, 612 7th Ave., New Glarus, WI 53574. Mailing Address: P.O. Box 745, New Glarus, WI 53574-0745. Tel.: 608-527-2317. Fax: 608-527-2302. TDD: 608-527-2317.
Web Site: www.swisshistoricalvillage.org
Founded: 1938.
Key Personnel: Pres., John F. Marty; Museum Shop Mgr., Gail Beal.
Personnel Profile: Part-Time Volunteers 18.
Governing Authority: society. Parent Institution: New Glarus Historical Society. Tax-exempt.
Historic Village.
Collections: tools, artifacts & replicas of buildings used by the early settlers; Hall of History; printshop; fire station; log church; log cabin; blacksmith shop; cheese factory; country store; school; bee house.
Activities: guided tours; permanent & temporary exhibitions.
Publications: membership newsletter.
Hours & Admission Prices: May-Oct. daily 10-4. Adults $9, children 6-13 $3; discounts to bus groups if paid in advance & AAA members. ♿
Attendance: 10,000 (estimated)
Membership: Single $20; Couple $30; Family $40.

New Holstein

TIMM HOUSE HISTORIC SITE, 1600 Wisconsin Ave., New Holstein, WI 53061-1340. Mailing Address: P.O. Box 144, New Holstein, WI 53061-0144. Tel.: 920-898-5900. Fax: 920-898-5879.
E-mail: tevents@dotnet.com
Formerly: Pioneer Corner Museum
Founded: 1961.
Congressional District: 6
Key Personnel: Pres., Terry Thiessen; Vice Pres., Jerry Hallstrom; Sec., Kay Nett.
Personnel Profile: Part-Time Volunteers 30.
Governing Authority: nonprofit organization. Parent Institution: New Holstein Historical Society. Branch Museums: The Timm House, 1600 Wisconsin Ave., New Holstein, WI 53061; The Pioneer Corner Museum, 2103 Main St., New Holstein, WI 53061. Tax-exempt.
Historical Society Museum: built in the 1870s with an addition added in 1892.
Collections: Victorian furnishings; farm machinery; furnished rooms; manuscripts; pictures; old tools; dolls; toys; clothing; guns; rocks; china; theme room displays & settings; general store; post office. Historic House: 1892 Timm house.
Facilities: library of books available for research in the public library of New Holstein.
Activities: guided tours; permanent & temporary exhibitions.
Publications: book, When I Was a Boy in New Holstein; Centennial Book; The New Holstein Story; Pioneers' Corner; Land of Peace and Plenty; Die Familie Thiel; Memories of the First Years of the Settlement of New Holstein.
Hours & Admission Prices: Pioneer Corner Museum: Memorial Day-Labor Day Sat.-Sun. 1-4; other times by appointment. Timm House Historic Site: Memorial Day to Labor Day Wed.-Fri. 1-3, Sat.-Sun. 1-4; Sept.-May Sat.-Sun. 1-4; other times by appointment. Pioneer Corner Museum: adults $7, children under 12 $3. Both Houses: adults $10; children under 12 $7. ♿
Attendance: 700 (estimated)
Membership: Individual $10; Family $15; Friend of the Society $50; Sustaining $250; Founder's Circle $500.

New London

NEW LONDON PUBLIC MUSEUM, (M), 406 S. Pearl St., New London, WI 54961-1441. Tel.: 920-982-8520. Fax: 920-982-8617.
Web Site: www.newlondonwi.org/museum
Founded: 1917.
Congressional District: 8
Key Personnel: Pres. Bd. (V), Ken Renning; Dir., Christine Cross.
Personnel Profile: Full-Time Paid 1; Part-Time Paid 2.
Governing Authority: municipal. Tax-exempt.
General Museum.
Collections: historical items; taxidermied specimens with emphasis on birds; Native American artifacts; geological specimens; world culture artifacts.
Facilities: 1,000-vol. library of bird & historical reference books available for use on the premises.
Activities: in-house & outreach educational programs; temporary & permanent exhibitions; historic home & cemetery walking tours.
Hours & Admission Prices: Memorial Day to Labor Day Tues. 10-8, Wed.-Fri. 10-5; Sept.-May Tues. 10-8, Wed.-Fri. 10-5, Sat. 10-1. No charge; donations accepted. ♿
Attendance: 6,800 (accurate)

New Richmond

NEW RICHMOND PRESERVATION SOCIETY, 1100 Heritage Dr., New Richmond, WI 54017-1741. Mailing Address: P.O. Box 96, New Richmond, WI 54017-0096. Tel.: 715-246-3276; 888-320-3276. Fax: 715-246-7215.
E-mail: nrpsinc@pressenter.com
Web Site: www.nrheritagecenter.org
Founded: 1982.
Congressional District: 3
Key Personnel: Dir., Irv Sather; Bd. Asst., Amy Lansing; Pres., Ken Cernohous; Treas., Mike Reiter; Cur., Mary Sather.
Personnel Profile: Full-Time Paid 1; Full-Time Volunteers 1; Part-Time Volunteers 2.
Governing Authority: private; nonprofit organization. Tax-exempt: 501(c)(3).
Heritage Center.
Collections: 1884 Marcus Sears Bell Farmstead; 1916 Barn & Granary; 1887 Norwegian Log Cabin; 1890 Northside House; 1902 Camp Nine School & Outhouse; 1933 Ubet Store; 1991 Agriculture Pavilion; 1875 Blacksmith Log Building; 1891 Heritage Church; 2004 Community Bandstand.
Facilities: Heritage Church farmhouse & pavilion available for rental; nature pathways. New Richmond related items for sale.
Activities: formal education programs for children; historical & cultural activities; guided tours; hobby workshops; temporary & traveling exhibitions; spring & fall programs. Annual Events: Heritage Days; Antique Show & Tell; Flea Market May to October; Farmer's Market July to October; Christmas Open House.
Publications: quarterly newsletter, Heritage Centerpieces.
Hours & Admission Prices: May-Oct. Mon.-Fri. 10-4, Sat. 7:30-2, Sun. 12-4; Nov.-April Mon.-Fri. 10-4. Adults $5, children $1; discounts to AAM & AAA members; members no charge. Closed New Year's Day; Memorial Day; Independence Day; Labor Day; Thanksgiving; Christmas. ♿
Attendance: 10,000 (estimated)
Membership: Student $5; Senior $10; Individual $15; Family $25; Contributing $30; Supporting $50; Benefactor $100; Patron $101-$999; Lifetime $1,000.

North Freedom

MID-CONTINENT RAILWAY MUSEUM, E8948 Diamond Hill Road, North Freedom, WI 53951-9699. Mailing Address: P.O. Box 358, North Freedom, WI 53951-0358. Tel.: 608-522-4261. Fax: 608-522-4490.
E-mail: jeff@midcontinent.org
Web Site: www.midcontinent.org
Founded: 1959.
Congressional District: 2
Key Personnel: C.E.O., Chm. (V) & Pres. (V), Jeffrey B. Bloohm; Museum Shop Mgr., Jeffrey Haertlien.
Personnel Profile: Full-Time Paid 1; Full-Time Volunteers 1; Part-Time Paid 15; Part-Time Volunteers 120.
Governing Authority: society; nonprofit organization. Parent Institution: Mid-Continent Railway Historical Society. Tax-exempt.
Railway Museum.
Collections: railway equipment: 1900 era steam locomotives, wood passenger and freight cars; artifacts; photos. Historic Building: c.1894 C & NW depot.
Research Fields: north central U.S. railroad history.
Facilities: library; displays in coach/track sheds and in depot. Railway-related items for sale.
Activities: train rides. Museum Sponsors: Snow Train in February; Railfest in May; Autumn Color in October; Pumpkin Special in October; Santa Express in November.
Publications: periodical magazine, Mid-Continent Railway Gazette; annual calendar, Whistle on the Wind; Rail Heritage Book series, Focus on Rails; guide, Tour of the Yards; Mid-Continent Compendium; Sauk County Mining; Louis W. Hill's Business Car, Great Northern A-22; Copper Range RR.
Hours & Admission Prices: mid-May to Labor Day daily 9:30-5; day after Labor Day to mid-Oct. Sat.-Sun. 9:30-5. Adults $11, senior citizens $10, children $6; discounts to groups & AAA members; members no charge. ♿
Attendance: 29,329 (accurate)

Membership: Associate $35; Regular $40; Life $1,000.

Oak Creek

OAK CREEK HISTORICAL SOCIETY-PIONEER VILLAGE, S. 15th Ave. & E. Forest Hill Ave., Oak Creek, WI 53154. Mailing Address: P.O. Box 243, Oak Creek, WI 53154-0243. Tel.: 414-529-0196.
Web Site: ochistorical.freeservers.com
Founded: 1964.
Congressional District: 1
Key Personnel: Pres., Elroy Honadel; Vice Pres., Henry Kohler; Sec., Joyce Willms; Treas., Dick Raatz; Cur., Marge Berres; Archivist & Genealogists, Judy Salchow.
Personnel Profile: Part-Time Volunteers 12.
Governing Authority: society; nonprofit organization. Parent Institution: State Historical Society of Wisconsin. Subsidiary Institution: Wisconsin Council for Local History, Oak Creek, WI. 53154. Tax-exempt.
History Museum.
Collections: hand sketches of the Village of Oak Creek of 1860 from the Henry E. Rile collections; china service set; farm shed; horse drawn equipment; 1924 McCormick tractor; hand operated farm field tools; period artifacts; genealogical resources. Historic Buildings: 1840 Hughes log house; 1874 Oak Creek Town Hall; 1886 Wohlust Blacksmith Shop; 1902 print shop & cobbler shop; 1900 Franke farm summer kitchen.
Research Fields: genealogical information; archives.
Facilities: meeting rooms; classrooms.
Activities: guided tours; lectures; permanent exhibitions; demonstrations.
Publications: cookbook of old recipes; brochures; pamphlets; booklet, Water Color Sketchings; book, Images of America - Oak Creek, Wisconsin.
Hours & Admission Prices: Memorial Day-Labor Day Sun. 2-4. No charge; donations accepted.
Attendance: 750 (estimated)
Membership: Single $8; Family $15; Business $50; Life $250.

Oconomowoc

OCONOMOWOC AREA HISTORICAL SOCIETY & MUSEUM, 103 W. Jefferson St., Oconomowoc, WI 53066-3633. Mailing Address: P.O. Box 969, Oconomowoc, WI 53066-0969. Tel.: 262-569-0740.
E-mail: oahs-m@sbcglobal.net
Web Site: www.oconomowochistoricalsociety.com
Key Personnel: Admin., Nancy Lins
Historical Society Museum.
Collections: local history & culture; period artifacts; photographs.
Hours & Admission Prices: Jan.-April by appointment; May-Dec. Fri.-Sun. 1-5.

Oconto

BEYER HOME, OCONTO COUNTY HISTORICAL SOCIETY MUSEUM, 917 Park Ave., Oconto, WI 54153-1641. Mailing Address: Box 272, Oconto, WI 54153-0272. Tel.: 920-835-5733.
E-mail: dscross@bayland.net
Web Site: ocontocountyhistsoc.org
Founded: 1940.
Congressional District: 8
Key Personnel: Pres., Peter Stark.
Personnel Profile: Part-Time Paid 5.
Governing Authority: society. Subsidiary Institutions: Holt & Balcom Logging Camp, Lakewood, WI; Copper Culture Park. Tax-exempt: 501(c)(3).
Historic House Museum: 1868 Beyer Home, Victorian brick mansion, carriage house & G.E. Hall Annex.
Collections: Native American artifacts; antique furnishings; fur trade; fishing & lumbering; period vehicle display; picture collection of Oconto County area; hand painted china; furnished 1800s log cabin.
Research Fields: Oconto county history.
Facilities: 50-vol. library of historical books available on premises.
Activities: guided tours; socials; ice cream social. Museum Sponsors: Area Art Show in August; Nighttime Open House in October.
Publications: quarterly newsletter, News from the Northwoods; pamphlets, Historic Oconto; Lumber Era Oconto; Holt & Balcom Logging Camp; Copper Culture People; Christian Science Church (first in world); books; Would You Believe It; Recollections of Oconto County; A History of Oconto, Bicentennial Recollections of Oconto County; John & Almira Volk; A Walking Tour of the Historic West; Main Street of Oconto.
Hours & Admission Prices: Beyer Home & Museum Annex: June-Labor Day Mon.-Fri. & Sun. 12-4. Family $10, adults $4, students 6-18 $2; discount to groups & AAA members; members & children under 6 no charge.
Attendance: 1,000 (estimated)
Membership: Senior Citizen $5; Adult $10; Family $15; Business & Sustaining $25.

COPPER CULTURE MUSEUM, Mill St., Oconto, WI 54153. Mailing Address: Oconto Historical Society, 917 Park Ave., Oconto, WI 54153-1641. Tel.: 920-834-6206.
Governing Authority: Parent Institution: Oconto Historical Society.
Historic Site: listed on the National Registry of Historic Places.
Collections: local history & culture; Native American artifacts; burial ground of North America's earliest metal users.
Hours & Admission Prices: June to Labor Day Thurs.-Sun. 11-4. No charge.

Oshkosh

* **EAA AIRVENTURE MUSEUM,** 3000 Poberezny Rd., Oshkosh, WI 54902-8900. Mailing Address: EAA Aviation Center, P.O. Box 3086, Oshkosh, WI 54903-3086. Tel.: 920-426-4818. Fax: 920-426-6765.
E-mail: museum@eaa.org
Web Site: www.airventuremuseum.org
Founded: 1963.
Congressional District: 4
Key Personnel: Dir., Alan Westby; Vice Pres. Membership, Adam Smith; Librarian, Susan Lurvey; Mgr. Visitor Svcs., Kathy Hanson; Cur. Collections, Ron Twellman; Supvr. Exhibits & Restoration, Mike Hertz; Coord. Group Tours, Mary McKeown; Museum Shop Mgr., Marge Woodfill.
Personnel Profile: Full-Time Paid 20; Part-Time Paid 1; Part-Time Volunteers 175; Interns 6.
Governing Authority: Parent Institution: Experimental Aircraft Association. Tax-exempt: 501(c)(3).
Aviation Museum.
Collections: over 250 aircrafts: Eagle hangar-all World War II aircraft & memorabilia; historical, military, civilian amateur built, rotor craft, gliders, engines, props; photo collection; paintings; prints; video presentations; hands-on displays; restoration shop.
Research Fields: aeronautics.
Facilities: 15,000-vol. library including collection of periodicals, magazines & pictures on aeronautics; restoration facility; field research station; 120-seat auditorium; educational facilities; nature center; Eagle Flight Leadership Center. Aviation publications, related material & models for sale.
Activities: seasonal flying program at Pioneer Airport on museum grounds; lectures; participatory, temporary & permanent exhibitions; docent program; formal education programs; guided tours; hobby workshops; forums; aircraft rides; theater. Museum Sponsors: EAA Air Academy for youth & adults; Young Eagles youth program. Annual Events: art competition; fly-in.
Publications: magazines.
Hours & Admission Prices: Mon.-Sat. 8:30-5, Sun. 10-5. Family $22, adults $8.75, senior citizens 62 & over $7.75, students 6-17 $6.75; discounts to groups & AAM members; children under 6 no charge. Closed New Year's Day; Easter; Thanksgiving; Christmas. ♿
Attendance: 126,342 (accurate)
Membership: Individual $40; Family $50.

MILITARY VETERANS MUSEUM, INC., 375 City Center, Ste. K, Oshkosh, WI 54901-4999. Mailing Address: P.O. Box 2194, Oshkosh, WI 54903-2194. Tel.: 920-426-8615.
E-mail: mvm@athenet.net
Web Site: www.mvmwisconsin.com
Founded: 1985.
Congressional District: 8
Key Personnel: Pres. & Special Projects, Ron Metz; Vice Pres., Mark Ropella; Sec., Lynn Beck; Treas., Displays & Special Events, Julie Nikolaus; Operations, Kate Robinson; Librarian, Luida Sanders; Shop Coord., Ralph Beck; Education, Donna Stammer; Education, John Pieper.
Personnel Profile: Full-Time Paid 1; Part-Time Volunteers 30.
Governing Authority: private; nonprofit. Tax-exempt: 501(c)(3).
Military Museum.
Collections: militaria with the emphasis on the role of the citizen soldier in the U.S. military; growing emphasis on education as it relates to patriotism; USS Wisconsin Recommissioning plaque; USS California's shiplog at Pearl Harbor on Dec. 7, 1941; a piece of the USS Arizona.
Publications: quarterly newsletter, News From Home.
Hours & Admission Prices: Temporarily closed.
Membership: Individual $25; Organization $100; Life $225-$325.

* **OSHKOSH PUBLIC MUSEUM, (M),** 1331 Algoma Blvd., Oshkosh, WI 54901-2799. Tel.: 920-236-5799. Fax: 920-424-4738.
E-mail: museum_info@ci.oshkosh.wi.us
Web Site: www.oshkoshmuseum.org
Founded: 1924.
Congressional District: 6
Key Personnel: Dir., Bradley Larson; Pres. (V), Carol Fenrich; Asst. Dir., Michael Breza; Cur., Debra Daubert; Registrar, Joan Lloyd; Mktg. & Membership, Megan Del Debbio; Archivist, Scott Cross.

Personnel Profile: Full-Time Paid 10; Part-Time Paid 4; Part-Time Volunteers 55; Interns 4.
Governing Authority: municipal. Parent Institution: City of Oshkosh. Tax-exempt.
General Museum.
Collections: decorative arts textiles; pressed glass; china; Wisconsin Indian archaeology & ethnology; collections related to local 19th-century social, military, cultural & industrial history; fur trade; horse-drawn firefighting vehicles, Tiffany stained glass windows & interior; military; manuscripts; natural history specimens.
Research Fields: military history; local history; decorative arts.
Facilities: 8,000-vol. library of books & pamphlets for reference use on premises & inter-library loan; reading room; photography studio; classroom. Books & other museum-related items for sale.
Activities: lectures; formally organized education programs for children & adults; internship for undergraduate college students affiliated with the University of Wisconsin, Oshkosh; inter-museum loan, permanent & temporary exhibitions.
Publications: newsletter; exhibit guides & catalogs; information leaflets; books, Like a Deer Chased by the Dogs: The Life of Chief Oshkosh; Voices of History, 1941-1945; Portraits in Glass: The Mayer Tiffany Windows of Trinity Episcopal Church, Oshkosh, Wisconsin; A Self-Guided Walking Tour of Riverside Cemetery: From the Newspapers: Graphic Stories of Death.
Hours & Admission Prices: Tues.-Sat. 10-4:30, Sun. 1-4:30. Adults $7, children 6 & over $4; children under 6 & members no charge. Closed national holidays. ♿
Attendance: 28,233 (accurate)
Membership: Senior Individual $15; Individual $20; Senior Couple $25; Family $30; Contributing $50; Sustaining $100; Business & Corporate $150.

* **PAINE ART CENTER AND GARDENS, (M),** 1410 Algoma Blvd., Oshkosh, WI 54901-7708. Tel.: 920-235-6903, ext. 21. Fax: 920-235-6303.
E-mail: info@thepaine.org
Web Site: www.thepaine.org
Founded: 1947.
Congressional District: 6
Key Personnel: Exec. Dir., Aaron Sherer; Public Rels., Connie Pirner.
Personnel Profile: Full-Time Paid 8; Part-Time Paid 11; Part-Time Volunteers 160; Interns 1.
Governing Authority: nonprofit organization. Tax-exempt: 101(6); 501(c)(3).
Art Museum & Arboretum: housed in 19th-century Tudor Revival Manor house.
Collections: 19th- & 20th-century American paintings, sculpture & prints; 18th- to 20th-century European paintings, sculpture & prints; decorative arts; botanical art; Oriental rugs; gardens including annuals, native & exotic trees, shrubs & herbaceous plants which grow in Wisconsin.
Research Fields: 18th-20th century painting, sculpture & prints; American & European decorative arts & architecture; English gardens; historic landscapes.
Facilities: reference library on art, art history, decorative arts, architecture & horticulture available for on premises research. Museum-related items for sale.
Activities: guided tours; lectures; films; gallery talks; concerts; formally organized education programs for children & adults; bus tours; docent training program; permanent, temporary & traveling exhibitions. Museum Sponsors: Nutcracker in the Castle from November to January.
Publications: bimonthly newsletter; exhibition catalogues; annual report.
Hours & Admission Prices: Tues.-Sun. 11-4. Adults $7, senior citizens $6, students $5, children 5-12 $4; discount to AAM members; children under 5 & members no charge. Closed national holidays. ♿
Attendance: 55,915 (accurate)
Membership: Individual $40; Family $60; Sustaining $100; Supporting $250; Benefactor $500. Patron: Director's Circle $1,200; President's Circle $2,500; Founder's Circle $5,000.

Peshtigo

PESHTIGO FIRE MUSEUM, 400 Oconto Ave., Peshtigo, WI 54157-1299. Mailing Address: 1100 French St., TRGR #72, Peshtigo, WI 54157-9783. Tel.: 715-582-3244.
E-mail: contact@peshtigo.info
Web Site: www.peshtigofire.info/museum.htm
Founded: 1962.
Key Personnel: Pres. & C.E.O., Don Hansen; Cur., Darlene Plump; Cur., Peggy Harrand; Cur., Linda Loser; Cur., Matt Wood; Cur., Marian Devory; Cur., Marilyn Olson; Cur., Jerry Devory.
Governing Authority: society. Parent Institution: State Historical. Tax-exempt.
History Museum: Housed in 1878 Old Church located on the 1871 site of the worst forest fire in U.S. history.
Collections: period furnishings; glass; agriculture; blacksmith shop; school room; old country store.
Activities: permanent exhibitions.
Publications: books, The Great Peshtigo Fire; Embers of October.
Hours & Admission Prices: May 17-Oct. 8 daily 10-4:30. No charge; donations accepted.
Attendance: 9,000 (accurate)
Membership: Individual $1; Life $25.

Platteville

PLATTEVILLE MINING MUSEUM, (M), 385 E. Main St., Platteville, WI 53818-3204. Mailing Address: P.O. Box 780, Platteville, WI 53818-0780. Tel.: 608-348-3301. Fax: 608-348-4640.
E-mail: museums@platteville.org
Web Site: www.mining.jamison.museum
Founded: 1965.
Congressional District: 3
Key Personnel: Dir., Stephen J. Kleefisch; Pres. (V), William Van Deest; Cur., Stephanie Saager-Bourret; Education Coord., Mary Huck.
Personnel Profile: Full-Time Paid 3; Part-Time Paid 12; Part-Time Volunteers 8.
Governing Authority: municipal. Parent Institution: City of Platteville. Tax-exempt.
Mining Museum: housed in 1863 schoolhouse & 1845 lead mine.
Collections: geology; mining; maps; archives; photographs; full-size replica head frame.
Research Fields: early European/American mining settlements in the southwest Wisconsin area.
Facilities: library of mining related materials; reopened 1840s lead mine.
Activities: guided tours; lectures; train ride; formally organized education programs for children & undergraduate college students; permanent exhibitions.
Hours & Admission Prices: May-Oct. daily 9-5; Nov.- April Mon.-Fri. 9-4; group tours by appointment. May-Oct. family $22, adults $8, senior citizens $7, children $4; discount to groups, AAM & ICOM members; members no charge. Nov.-April adults $3, children $1. Closed New Year's Day; Veterans Day; Thanksgiving & day after; Christmas. ♿
Attendance: 9,238 (accurate)
Membership: Individual $10; Family $25.

ROLLO JAMISON MUSEUM, 405 E. Main St., Platteville, WI 53818-2834. Mailing Address: P.O. Box 780, Platteville, WI 53818-0780. Tel.: 608-348-3301. Fax: 608-348-4640.
E-mail: museums@platteville.org
Web Site: www.mining.jamison.museum
Founded: 1981.
Congressional District: 3
Key Personnel: Dir., Stephen J. Kleefisch; Pres. (V), Nancy Daniels; Cur., Stephanie Saager-Bourret; Education Coord., Mary C. Huck.
Personnel Profile: Full-Time Paid 3; Part-Time Paid 12; Part-Time Volunteers 8.
Governing Authority: municipal. Parent Institution: City of Platteville. Tax-exempt.
History Museum.
Collections: historical artifacts of southwest Wisconsin; photographs; local history.
Research Fields: early European/American settlement in the southwest Wisconsin area; artifacts in the Rollo Jamison collection.
Facilities: workshop; meeting space. Gift items for sale.
Activities: guided tours; educational programs for children & adults.
Hours & Admission Prices: May-Oct. daily 9-5; Nov.-April Mon.-Fri. 9-4; group tours by appointment. May-Oct. family $22, adults $8, senior citizens $7, children $4; discount to groups, AAM & ICOM members; members no charge. Nov.-April adults $3, children $1. Closed New Year's Day; Thanksgiving & day after; Christmas. ♿
Attendance: 9,238 (accurate)
Membership: Individual $10; Family $25.

Plymouth

BRADLEY GALLERY OF ART, W. 3718 South Dr., Plymouth, WI 53073. Mailing Address: P.O. Box 359, Sheboygan, WI 53082-0359. Tel.: 920-565-2111 & 1280. Fax: 920-565-1206.
Web Site: www.lakeland.edu
Founded: 1988.
Key Personnel: Co-Dir., Denise Presnell-Weidner; Co-Dir., William Weidner.
Personnel Profile: Part-Time Paid 2; Interns 4.
Governing Authority: private college; nonprofit. Parent Institution: Lakeland College. Tax-exempt.
Art Gallery.

Collections: paintings & prints from the Bick collection.
Major Exhibits: Senior Art Exhibition I, 1/10-2/10; Senior Art Exhibition II, 3/10-4/10; Annual Student Art Exhibition, 4/10-5/10; Professional Exhibition, 9/10-10/10; Biennial Faculty Exhibit, 11/10-12/10.
Facilities: 265 sq. ft. exhibit space.
Activities: lectures.
Hours & Admission Prices: Sept.-May Mon.-Fri. 9-5. No charge. Closed school holidays; semester breaks. ♿
Attendance: 3,000 (estimated)

JOHN G. VOIGT HOUSE, W 5639 Anokijig Lane, Plymouth, WI 53073. Tel.: 920-893-0782. Fax: 920-893-0873.
Founded: 1850.
Congressional District: 6
Key Personnel: Camp Dir., Jim Scherer.
Governing Authority: non-profit organization. Affiliated with Friends of Camp Anokitig Inc.
Historic House: 1850 Log Cabin.
Collections: log cabin artifacts.
Activities: guided tours; wool-spinning demonstrations.
Hours & Admission Prices: By appointment only. No charge; donations accepted.

Port Edwards

ALEXANDER HOUSE, 1131 Wisconsin River Dr., Port Edwards, WI 54469-1039. Tel.: 715-887-3442.
Art & History Museum.
Collections: local history; Nekoosa-Edwards Paper Company artifacts; period furnishings; works by local & national artists; early lumbering; papermaking history.
Hours & Admission Prices: Tues., Thurs. & Sun. 1-4; other times by appointment. No charge.

Portage

FORT WINNEBAGO SURGEONS QUARTERS, W8687 St. Hwy. 33E, Portage, WI 53901-9703. Tel.: 608-742-2949.
Founded: 1938.
Congressional District: 2
Key Personnel: State Regent, Julie Stuhlmacher; Committee Chm., Beverly West; Museum Mgr. & Dir. Education, Mary Harding.
Personnel Profile: Full-Time Paid 1; Part-Time Paid 1; Part-Time Volunteers 7.
Governing Authority: restored & maintained by Wisconsin Society, National Society of the Daughters of the American Revolution. Tax-exempt.
History Museum: housed in 1819 surgeons quarters.
Collections: relics of Fort Winnebago; furniture of fort period and old country school; surgical instruments; archives; military. Historic Building: 1850 Garrison School.
Research Fields: pioneer history of the area & its significance; national & world history; pioneer/Indian relations.
Facilities: library of medical & school text books & general material.
Activities: guided tours; permanent exhibitions.
Publications: books, Early Days at the Fox-Wisconsin Portage; Fort Winnebago & The Surrender of Red Bird; Nicky's Bugle.
Hours & Admission Prices: May 15-Oct. 15 Mon.-Sat. 10-4, Sun. 11-4. Family $13, adults $5, senior citizens $4, children 7-17 $3; discounts for AAA members.
Attendance: 2,222 (accurate)

HISTORIC INDIAN AGENCY HOUSE, Agency House Rd., Portage, WI 53901-0084. Mailing Address: P.O. Box 84, Portage, WI 53901-0084. Tel.: 608-742-6362.
Web Site: www.nscda.org/museums/wisconsin.htm
Formerly: Old Indian Agency House
Founded: 1932.
Congressional District: 2
Key Personnel: Chm., Dr. Marilyn Baxter; Pres., Kathleen Seidel; Dir., Destinee Udelhoven.
Personnel Profile: Full-Time Paid 1; Part-Time Paid 6.
Governing Authority: society. Parent Institution: The National Society of The Colonial Dames in the State of Wisconsin. Tax-exempt: 501(c)(3).
Historic House: 1832 Historic Indian Agency House.
Collections: decorative arts of the American Empire period; period furnishings; Indian artifacts; Civil War memorabilia; early farm tools; objects from archaeological dig.
Major Exhibits: A Stitch in Time: Samplers and Other Fancy Work in Early America, 5/10-4/11.
Research Fields: local history; archaeology of area.
Facilities: Indian crafts & other museum-related items for sale.
Activities: guided tours; special events. Museum Sponsors: Hands-on History Days.
Publications: book, Wau-Bun, The Early Day in the North-West; biannual newsletter, Waubun Express.
Hours & Admission Prices: May 15 to Oct. 15 Mon.-Sat. 10-4, Sun. 11-4; other times by appointment. Family $15, adults $6, senior citizens $5, students 7-18 $3; discounts to groups, AAM, AAA, & National Trust for Historic Preservation members; members no charge.
Attendance: 2,492 (accurate)
Membership: Individual $15; Family $30; Silver Patron $100; Gold Patron $250; Platinum Patron $500; Benefactor $1,000.

Poynette

MACKENZIE ENVIRONMENTAL EDUCATION CENTER, Dept. of Natural Resources, W7303 County Rd. CS & Q, Poynette, WI 53955-9690. Tel.: 608-635-8105. Fax: 608-635-2743.
Web Site: www.wiwf.org/education/meec.php
Founded: 1961.
Congressional District: 2
Key Personnel: Dir., Derek Duane; Pres. Friends of Mackenzie (V), Berney Lohan; Resident Center Coord., Ruth Ann Lee; Customer Service, Linda Haddix; Asst. Service, Ruth Lindert; Animal Keeper, Dan Mautz; Maintenance Foreman, Dan Lee.
Personnel Profile: Full-Time Paid 7; Part-Time Paid 5; Part-Time Volunteers 60.
Governing Authority: state. Parent Institution: State of Wisconsin, Dept. of Natural Resources. Tax-exempt: 170(b)(1)(A).
Natural History Museum.
Collections: live native Wisconsin wildlife exhibit; Nelson cabin; logging history museum, pictures & tools from Wisconsin lumbering days; Alien & Oddities Museum, containing pictures & mounted specimens of alien plants & animals; conservation museum. Historic Building: c.1880 log cabin.
Facilities: 600-vol. library of teacher materials & resource related materials & specimens; classrooms; 80-bed resident center for environmental education programs; picnic grounds; hiking trails; ecology, wildlife, conifer & hardwood trails; trails to accommodate senior & disabled citizens; arboretum.
Activities: organized education programs for children & adults; workshops. Center Sponsors: Public Maple Fest in March.
Publications: brochures; trail guides.
Hours & Admission Prices: Exhibits & Zoo: May-Nov 1. daily 8-4; Nov.-April Mon.-Fri. 8-4; guided tours by reservation. Grounds: daily dawn-dusk; fee charged for use of overnight facility. No charge; donations accepted. ♿
Attendance: 46,000 (estimated)
Membership: Friends of MacKenzie Environmental Center: Individual $20; Family $30; Organization $25; Life $150.

Prairie du Chien

FORT CRAWFORD MUSEUM, c/o Prairie du Chien Historical Society Inc., 717 S. Beaumont Rd., Prairie du Chien, WI 53821. Mailing Address: P.O. Box 298, Prairie du Chien, WI 53821-0298. Tel.: 608-326-6960.
E-mail: ftcrawmu@mhtc.net
Web Site: www.fortcrawfordmuseum.com
Formerly: Prairie du Chien Museum at Fort Crawford
Founded: 1996.
Congressional District: 3
Key Personnel: Pres. Historical Society (V), Jim O'Meara; Sec. Historical Society, Janet Finn; Site Dir., Jenny Stevenson.
Personnel Profile: Part-Time Paid 4; Part-Time Volunteers 50.
Governing Authority: Parent Institution: Prairie du Chien Historical Society. Tax-exempt.
History Museum: a National Historical Landmark.
Collections: military, medical & Native American artifacts; Indian treaties; Dr. William Beaumont's experiments; cultural, economics, religious, & political history; regional late 19th-century; photographs; 19th & 20th-century medical books; early Crawford County Wisconsin manuscripts; dentist's office & pharmacy of the 1890s; electronic voice transparent twin exhibit; Mississippi River's history of employment opportunities; Dr. William Cannon; hospital ward of Dr. Beaumont's era; bridges of Prairie du Chien; Native American artifacts; Fort Crawford. Prairie du Chien Museum: local artifacts.
Research Fields: Fort Crawford 1829-1870 & the US military on the frontier; Indian Agency for Winnebago; Civil War; Dr. William Beaumont & early medicine; Prairie du Chien & Crawford County, WI.
Facilities: theater. Museum-related items for sale.
Activities: guided tours; special events; programs; inter-museum loan.
Publications: brochures, Fort Crawford Medical Museum & Local History Monographs; Prairie du Chien History; newsletter, The Union; book, Prairie

du Chien French, British & American Monographs on Fort Crawford; special historic editions of newsletters; Cook-Old Fort Crawford & The Frontier.
Hours & Admission Prices: May-Oct. daily 9-4. Family $12, adults $4, seniors & tour groups $3.25 per person, children 12 & under $2.25; members no charge. ♿
Attendance: 6,000 (accurate)
Membership: Senior & Student $15; Individual Adult $20; Senior Couple $30; Family $35; Sustaining $100; Founder's Club $250, $500, $1,000.

VILLA LOUIS HISTORIC SITE, 521 Villa Louis Rd., Prairie du Chien, WI 53821-1333. Mailing Address: P.O. Box 65, Prairie du Chien, WI 53821-0065. Tel.: 608-326-2721. Fax: 608-326-5507.
E-mail: villalouis@wisconsinhistory.org
Web Site: www.wisconsinhistory.org/villalouis
Founded: 1936.
Congressional District: 3
Key Personnel: Site Admin. & Site Dir., Michael Douglass; Cur., Susan Caya.
Personnel Profile: Full-Time Paid 3; Part-Time Paid 17; Part-Time Volunteers 35.
Governing Authority: state. Parent Institution: Wisconsin Historical Society, 816 State, Madison, WI 53706. Tax-exempt.
History Museum: housed in 1870 Villa Louis, home of family of fur trader Hercules Dousman, on the site of 1814 Fort Shelby & 1816-1829 Fort Crawford; recently restored interior shows influence of British Arts & crafts. esp. William Morris.
Collections: history; fur trade manuscripts; Victorian decorative arts; furnishings. Historic structure: 1851 general store adoptively used as Fur Trade Museum.
Research Fields: fur trade in old Northwest; Victorian life in upper Midwest.
Facilities: 2,000-vol. library of art history books & Dousman Family Collection available on premises. Wisconsin history books & museum-related items for sale.
Activities: guided tours; special events.
Publications: brochure, Wisconsin Historic Sites.
Hours & Admission Prices: Tours: early May-Oct. daily 9:30-5. Adults $9, seniors 65 and over & students $7.75, children 5-17 $4.50. ♿
Attendance: 16,000 (accurate)
Membership: Individual $10; Family $15.

Prairie du Sac

SAUK PRAIRIE AREA HISTORICAL SOCIETY, INC., 565 Water St., Prairie du Sac, WI 53578-1128. Tel.: 608-644-8444. Fax: 680-644-8444.
E-mail: spahs@verizon.net
Web Site: www.saukprairiehistory.org
Founded: 1961.
Congressional District: 2 & 3
Key Personnel: Pres., Jody Kapp; Cur., Rachel Seltzner; Sec., Daleen Heffron; Correspondence Sec., Phyllis France; Librarian, Jackie Murphy.
Personnel Profile: Part-Time Paid 1; Part-Time Volunteers 20.
Governing Authority: society. Subsidiary Institution: State Historical Society of Wisconsin, Office of Local History. Branch Museums: Firehouse Museum, 717 John Adams St.; Tripp Museum, 565 Water St., Prairie du Sac, WI 53578; Our Lady of Loretto Church Museum, Hwy. C, North Freedom, WI 53951; Salem Ragatz Church Museum, Hwy. PF, Prairie du Sac, WI 53578. Tax-exempt: 501(c)(3).
Historical Society Museum.
Collections: household items of the period, 1850-1900.
Research Fields: local history.
Facilities: library of local history books.
Activities: meetings; Indian & Pioneer Day open to all 4th graders. Museum Sponsors: Christmas Open House.
Publications: 4X-newsletter; book, Pictorial History of Sauk City & Prairie du Sac; Fire Department History book; Historic Houses of Prairie du Sac; Book on History of Milk Hauling & Creameries of the Past; Historical Book on Prairie du Sac Businesses; Lives Lived Here: History of Sauk City.
Hours & Admission Prices: June-Aug. Tues. & Thurs.-Sat. 9-1; other times by appointment. No charge; donations accepted.
Attendance: 3,500 (estimated)
Membership: Individual $25; Family $50; Friend $75; Sponsor $100; Patron $250; Benefactor $500; Historian $1,000 & up.

Racine

* **RACINE ART MUSEUM (RAM), (M),** 441 Main St., Racine, WI 53403-1030. Mailing Address: P.O. Box 187, Racine, WI 53401-0187. Tel.: 262-638-8300. Fax: 262-898-1045.
E-mail: raminfo@ramart.org
Web Site: www.ramart.org
Formerly: Charles A Wustum Museum of Fine Arts
Founded: 1941.
Congressional District: 1
Key Personnel: C.E.O., Bruce W. Pepich; Pres. (V), Tom Creecy; Facilities Mgr., Jim Sheppard; Receptionist Supvr., Heather A. Pugh; Business Mgr., Barb Namowicz; Dir. Devel., Laura D'Amato; Cur. Education, Tricia Blasko; Museum Shop Mgr., Lisa Englander; Devel. Coord., Susan K. Buhler-Maki; Bldg. Svcs. Asst., John Coley; Asst. Clerical Cur., David Zaleski; Education Asst., Susan Silver; Accounting Asst., Sharon Dickert; Assoc. Registrar, Susan Sorenson; Assoc. Registrar, Peg Lukow; Mktg. Specialist, Jessica N. Zalewski; Mktg. Asst., Laura Gillespie; Librarian, Nancy Elsmo.
Personnel Profile: Full-Time Paid 12; Part-Time Paid 20; Part-Time Volunteers 150; Interns 2.
Governing Authority: nonprofit organization. Parent Institution: The Racine Art Museum Assoc., Inc.; Branch Museum: Charles A. Wustum Museum of Fine Arts, 2519 Northwestern Ave., Racine, WI 53404-2299. Tel. 262-636-9177. Tax-exempt: 501(c)(3).
Arts Center.
Collections: contemporary American works on paper; 20th-century American crafts.
Major Exhibits: The Divine Schneier Collection Arrives at RAM: Art Jewelry of the 1980s and 1990s, 11/09-1/10; Therman Statom: Outside the Box, 11/09-7/10; Great Art for Tough Times: Wisconsin WPA Watercolors in RAM's Collection, 1/10-6/10; Collection Focus - Carol Eckert at RAM, 1/10-6/10; Catherine Chalmers: American Cockroach (T), 4/10-10/10; Creepie Crawlie: RAM's Students and Teachers Examine Insects - RAM's Wustum Museum, 6/10-8/10; The Miniature World of Bruce Metcalf, 9/10-1/11; Mariko Kusumoto: Metal Box Sculptures (T), 10/10-1/11; John McQueen: Collection Focus, 10/10-1/11; Watercolor Wisconsin 2010 - RAM's Wustum Museum, 12/10-4/11.
Research Fields: WPA art; regional, national & international artists; contemporary American crafts.
Facilities: 3,500-vol. library of art books and periodicals available for use upon request; classrooms; workshops; studios. Museum-related items for sale.
Activities: guided tours; lectures; gallery talks; art sales & rental gallery; study clubs; hobby workshops; formally organized educational programs; permanent, temporary & traveling exhibitions.
Publications: members newsletter; exhibition brochures & catalogues.
Hours & Admission Prices: RAM: Tues.-Sat. 10-5, Sun. 12-5. Wustum: Tues.-Sat. 10-5. Adults $5; discounts to AAM members; members no charge. NARM reciprocal membership over $100. Closed federal holidays; Easter. ♿
Attendance: 46,429 (accurate)
Membership: National Associate $30; Senior Citizen & Student $40; Individual $50; Family $70; Sustaining $125; Supporting $250; Benefactor $500; Master $1,000; Corporate Partner $1,500; RAM Society $1,000-$10,000.

RACINE HERITAGE MUSEUM, (M), 701 S. Main St., Racine, WI 53403-1211. Tel.: 262-636-3926. Fax: 262-636-3940.
E-mail: inquire@clmail.com
Web Site: www.racineheritagemuseum.org
Founded: 1960.
Congressional District: 1
Key Personnel: Exec. Dir., Christopher Paulson; Asst. Dir. & Cur., Karen Braun; Archivist, Richard Ammann, Ph.D.; Dir. Mktg. & Programs, Sally Orth; Cur. Education, Patty Wagner.
Personnel Profile: Full-Time Paid 3; Part-Time Paid 8; Part-Time Volunteers 139.
Governing Authority: private; nonprofit organization. Tax-exempt: 501(c)(3).
Southeast Wisconsin Industrial, Cultural, Invention & Product History: housed in 1904 Carnegie Library building.
Collections: 1840-present county, social & industrial history; archives; photographs; 1888 Bohemian schoolhouse.
Research Fields: county social & industrial history; genealogy.
Facilities: archives; schoolhouse.
Activities: permanent, temporary & traveling exhibitions; school loan service; regularly scheduled classes for school groups in 1888 Bohemian Schoolhouse & museum.
Publications: quarterly journal, The Outlook; Boat Manufacturing In Racine; book, Invention City: The Sesquicentennial History of Racine, Wisconsin; historical brochures.
Hours & Admission Prices: Tues.-Fri. 9-5, Sat. 10-3, Sun. 12-4. No charge; donations accepted. Closed national holidays.
Attendance: 30,000 (accurate)
Membership: Student $20; Senior $25; Individual & Senior Couple $40; Family $50; Supporting $100; Contributing $250; Sustaining $500; Benefactor $1,000.

RACINE ZOOLOGICAL SOCIETY, 2131 N. Main St., Racine, WI 53402-4795. Mailing Address: 200 Goold St., Racine, WI 53402-4795. Tel.: 262-636-9189. Fax: 262-636-9307.
E-mail: info@racinezoo.org
Web Site: www.racinezoo.org
Founded: 1923.
Congressional District: 1
Key Personnel: Pres. & C.E.O., Jay R. Christie; Chm. Bd., Chris Leberfing; Museum Shop Mgr., Sheri Halliday.
Personnel Profile: Full-Time Paid 19; Part-Time Paid 2; Part-Time Volunteers 185; Interns 11.
Governing Authority: municipal. Parent Institution: Racine Zoological Society. Tax-exempt.
Zoo.
Collections: 403 specimens; 85 species.
Activities: education programs; tours.
Publications: quarterly newsletter, Racine Zoocine.
Hours & Admission Prices: Memorial Day-Labor Day daily 9-7; Sept.-May daily 9-4:30. Adults $5; discounts to Association of Zoo & Aquarium members; reciprocating AZA institutions; members no charge. ♿
Attendance: 100,000 (estimated)
Membership: One Plus One Zoo Pass & Zoologist $50; Family Zoo Pass $60; Family Plus Zoo Pass & Curator $100; Conservationist $500; Safari Club $1,000.

Rhinelander

RHINELANDER LOGGING MUSEUM, Pioneer Park-Martin Lynch Dr., Rhinelander, WI 54501. Mailing Address: 1800 Englewood Rd. Lot 139, Englewood, FL 34223-1877. Tel.: 715-369-5004 & 5121.
Web Site: www.rhinelanderchamber.com
Founded: 1932.
Congressional District: 7
Key Personnel: Pres. (V), Walt Krause; Museum Shop Mgr., Thelma Swistak.
Personnel Profile: Part-Time Paid 1; Part-Time Volunteers 40.
Governing Authority: municipal. Tax-exempt.
Pioneer Logging Industry Museum.
Collections: items pertaining to logging; replica of 1870s lumber camp; history; printed materials; pictures; miniature saw mill; antique fire equipment; 1892 SOO Line restored depot; narrow gauge railroad, engine & rail cars; HO model railroad exhibit; one-room schoolhouse; Civilian Conservation Corps (CCC) barracks.
Research Fields: restored 1892 Soo Line Depot with HO scale model railroad.
Facilities: blacksmith shop; schoolhouse; bunk house dining room; Civilian Conservation Corps Building (CCC); antiques fire engines in barn. Gift items for sale.
Activities: self-guided tours.
Publications: tour guides; brochures.
Hours & Admission Prices: mid-May to Labor Day daily 10-5. No charge; donations accepted. ♿
Attendance: 14,378 (accurate)
Membership: $1 per member.

Ripon

LITTLE WHITE SCHOOLHOUSE, 303 Blackburn St., Ripon, WI 54971-1524. Mailing Address: P.O. Box 305, Ripon, WI 54971-0305. Tel.: 920-748-6764. Fax: 920-748-6784.
E-mail: birthplace@ripon.wi.com
Web Site: www.littlewhiteschoolhouse.org
Founded: 1951.
Congressional District: 6
Key Personnel: Exec. Dir., Paula T. Price; Pres. & Chm. (V), Kathy Schwandt; Museum Shop Mgr., Sue McConnell.
Personnel Profile: Part-Time Paid 5.
Governing Authority: Parent Institution: Ripon Area Chamber of Commerce. Tax-exempt.
Historic Building: c.1854 Little White Schoolhouse, birthplace of Republican Party.
Collections: Republican presidential memorabilia; political history; pioneer tools; furnished typical of 1800s schoolhouse. 1850 educational materials.
Facilities: Museum-related items for sale.
Activities: tours; docent presentations.
Publications: brochure, Little White Schoolhouse; booklet, A History of Ripon's Little White Schoolhouse, Birthplace of the Republican Party 1853-2005.
Hours & Admission Prices: May & Sept.-Oct. Sat.-Sun. 10-4; June to Labor Day daily 10-4; other times by appointment. Adults $1. ♿
Attendance: 14,000 (estimated)

River Falls

GALLERY 101, University of Wisconsin-River Falls, Fine Arts, 410 S. Third St., River Falls, WI 54022-5010. Tel.: 715-425-3266. Fax: 715-425-0657.
E-mail: susan.m.zimmeer@uwrf.edu
Web Site: www.uwrf.edu/art
Founded: 1973.
Key Personnel: Chm. Art Dept., Michael Padgett.
Governing Authority: Branch of University of Wisconsin. Tax-exempt.
Art Gallery.
Collections: W.P.A. graphics; contemporary prints; regional artists.
Activities: gallery talks.
Hours & Admission Prices: Sept.-May Mon.-Fri. 9-5 & 7-9, Sun. 2-4. No charge. ♿

Saint Croix Falls

ST. CROIX NATIONAL SCENIC RIVERWAY, 401 Hamilton St., Saint Croix Falls, WI 54024-9214. Tel.: 715-483-2274. Fax: 715-483-3288.
E-mail: jean_mschaeppi@nps.gov
Web Site: www.nps.gov/sacn
Founded: 1968.
Congressional District: 3
Key Personnel: Supt., Chris Stein; Chief of Interpretation, Julie Galonska; Interpretive Specialist, Jean Schaeppi.
Governing Authority: federal. National Park Service, Dept. of the Interior, Washington DC. Tax-exempt.
National Park & Museum.
Collections: aquarium; natural history concepts (riparian, floodplain forest & watershed).
Research Fields: history & natural history of the St. Croix & Namekagon Rivers.
Facilities: reference library. Books & museum-related items for sale.
Activities: group interpretive programs.
Hours & Admission Prices: May to mid-Oct. daily 8-4:30; mid-Oct. to April Mon.-Fri. 8-4:30. ♿
Attendance: 17,700 (accurate)

Saint Germain

SNOWMOBILE HALL OF FAME AND MUSEUM, 8481 W. Hwy. 70, Saint Germain, WI 54558. Mailing Address: P.O. Box 720, Saint Germain, WI 54558-0720. Tel.: 715-542-4488. Fax: 715-542-4477.
E-mail: loren@snowmobilehallofame.com
Web Site: www.snowmobilehalloffame.com
History Museum.
Collections: race sleds; trophies; clothing; photographs; racing videos.
Facilities: theater. Museum-related items for sale.
Activities: special events.
Hours & Admission Prices: Mon.-Fri. 10-5, Sat. 10-3; call to confirm.

Saukville

OZAUKEE COUNTY PIONEER VILLAGE, 4880 County Hwy. 1, Saukville, WI 53080. Mailing Address: P.O. Box 206, Cedarburg, WI 53012-0206. Tel.: 262-377-4510. Fax: 262-377-4568.
E-mail: mcsayner@yahoo.com
Web Site: www.co.ozaukee.wi.us/ochs
Formerly: Ozaukee County Historical Society Pioneer Village
Founded: 1960.
Congressional District: 9
Key Personnel: Pres. (V) & Gift Shop Mgr., Mary Sayner; Chm. (V), Lucy Kolb; 1st Vice Pres., Curt Gruenwald; 2nd Vice Pres., Allen Buohholz; Cur. Archives, Ruth Renz; Sec., Nina Look; Treas., Eleanor Prom.
Governing Authority: society. Affiliated with State Historical Society of Wisconsin. Parent Institution: Ozaukee Co. Historical Society. Tax-exempt: 501(c)(3).
Pioneer Village: over 20 buildings ranging from mid-1840 to 1907.
Collections: pioneer history; folklore; archives; agriculture; household equipment; photographs; railroad artifacts & memorabilia; 18th-century buildings & structures; newspapers; archives; tax records; school records; church histories; Ozaukee County history books. Historical Building: original one-room Stony Hill School, birthplace of National Flag Day.
Research Fields: genealogy.
Facilities: library.
Activities: guided tours; demonstrations; school tour program; quarterly programs; special events; research. Annual Events: National Flag Day ceremony & celebration; various special events during village open season.
Publications: quarterly newsletter, TimeLines.
Hours & Admission Prices: Memorial Day to 2nd Sun. in Oct. Sat.-Sun. 12-5; other times groups by appointment. Family $16, adults $6, senior citizens &

students 12-18 $4, children 6-12 $3; special pricing for special events; children 5 & under and members no charge. ♿
Attendance: 7,000 (accurate)
Membership: Individual $15; Family $30; Business & Professional $50; Life: Individual $200, Couple $350.

Seymour

SEYMOUR COMMUNITY MUSEUM, Depot St., Seymour, WI 54165. Mailing Address: P.O. Box 237, Seymour, WI 54165-1331. Tel.: 920-833-2868.
Founded: 1976.
Congressional District: 8
Key Personnel: Pres. (V), Bill Collar; Vice Pres., Lois Dalke; Historian, Marge Coenen; Business Officer, Janice Eick; Asst., Lucille Miller.
Personnel Profile: Part-Time Volunteers 8.
Governing Authority: municipal; nonprofit organization. Affiliated with the Wisconsin State Historical Society. Tax-exempt.
Historic Building & Site: housed in 1879 Lumber Sales Building.
Collections: local history items; 1914 Railroad Depot.
Research Fields: local history.
Activities: lectures. Museum Sponsors: Music in the Park June-August.
Publications: quarterly, Museum Muse.
Hours & Admission Prices: Memorial Day-Nov. Sat.-Sun. 1-5; open by appointment. No charge; donations accepted. ♿
Attendance: 1,432 (accurate)
Membership: Single $5; Family $7.

Shawano

SHAWANO COUNTY HISTORICAL SOCIETY, INC., 524 N. Franklin St., Shawano, WI 54166-1933. Mailing Address: P.O. Box 534, Shawano, WI 54166-0534. Tel.: 715-526-9033.
E-mail: schsociety@granitewave.com
Founded: 1940.
Congressional District: 8
Key Personnel: Pres., Richard Daniel Hoffman.
Personnel Profile: Part-Time Paid 1; Part-Time Volunteers 25.
Governing Authority: society. Branch Museum: Railroad Station Museum, Gresham, WI 54128. Tax-exempt.
General Museum: located in Heritage Park on the site where the first white man settled in 1848.
Collections: furniture; lamps; kitchen utensils; children's nursery; clothing; glassware and dishes; newspapers; books; 1895 one room country school; school-room artifacts; Indian artifacts; early judges stand; log cabin restoration; dairy exhibit; cheese-making display.
Activities: guided tours; permanent exhibitions. Society Sponsors: meetings for members and friends in April & Oct.
Hours & Admission Prices: Thurs. & Sat. 1:30-4:30; other times by appointment. No charge.
Attendance: 500 (estimated)
Membership: Active $2; Sustaining $5; Life $25.

Sheboygan

ABOVE & BEYOND CHILDREN'S MUSEUM, 902 N. 8th St., Sheboygan, WI 53081-4005. Tel.: 920-458-4263. Fax: 920-458-3402.
E-mail: melissa_n30@yahoo.com
Web Site: www.abkids.org
Founded: 1993.
Key Personnel: Exec. Dir., Melissa Nied Feldt
Children's Museum.
Collections: hands-on exhibits.
Facilities: 10,000 sq. ft. exhibit space.
Activities: birthday parties; school groups; educational programs; special events; fundraisers; sleepovers.
Hours & Admission Prices: Memorial Day to Labor Day Tues.-Sat. 10-5, Sun. 12-4; Sept.-May Tues.-Sat. 10-5. Admission $5; members & children under 2 no charge.
Attendance: 30,000 (estimated)
Membership: Grandparent $55; Family $65; Premier $100.

JOHN MICHAEL KOHLER ARTS CENTER, (M), 608 New York Ave., Sheboygan, WI 53081-4507. Tel.: 920-458-6144. Fax: 920-458-4473.
Web Site: www.jmkac.org
Founded: 1967.
Congressional District: 9
Key Personnel: Dir., Ruth DeYoung Kohler; Pres. Bd., Mary Lynne Donohue; Deputy Dir., Patti Sherman-Cisler; Deputy Dir., Joe Madeira; Senior Cur., Leslie Umberger; Registrar, Larry Donoval; Mktg. Mgr., Lisa Schultz; Librarian & Archivist, Jamie McFarlane; Human Resources Mgr., Anne Stauber Tritz; Arts Industry Coord., Beth Lipman; Accountant, Sally Bohenstengel; Museum Shop Mgr., Mary Kopp.
Personnel Profile: Full-Time Paid 50; Part-Time Paid 20; Part-Time Volunteers 500; Interns 8.
Governing Authority: nonprofit organization. Affiliated with Sheboygan Arts Foundation, Inc. Tax-exempt: 501(c)(3).
Visual & Performing Arts Center.
Collections: self-taught artists; contemporary ceramics; paintings; installations; American crafts; American furniture; artifacts from the J.M. Kohler home. Historic House: 1882 John Michael Kohler Home.
Major Exhibits: Language, 2/10-5/10; Humor, 6/10-9/10; Wild Kingdom, 7/10-2/11; Palmer Cox & Norman Pettingill, 7/10-2/11; Animal Instinct: Alle Gory; Allusion & Anthropomorphism, 10/10-1/11.
Research Fields: contemporary American art; crafts; decorative arts; photography; folk art; the art of natives & visionaries; self-taught Wisconsin artist.
Facilities: library of art books & periodicals; meeting rooms; 8 galleries; theater; studio-classrooms; Matrix performance space. Museum-related items for sale.
Activities: temporary & traveling exhibitions; guided tours; lectures; films; residencies for visual & performing artists; gallery talks; concerts; dance recitals; arts festivals; theater; formally organized education programs for children & adults; docent program; workshops for professional artists; inter-museum loan. Center Sponsors: Arts & Industry program with residencies & workshops for artists at manufacturing firms; readers theater groups; summer theater with professional guest directors; Arts Festival & Art Armada in July; Footlights Performing Art Series; Independent Lens Screenings; Flicks on Fridays; Family Festivals; Festive Fridays; Connecting Communities.
Publications: exhibitions catalogs; bimonthly newsletter; annual report;
Hours & Admission Prices: Mon., Wed. & Fri. 10-5, Tues. & Thurs. 10-8, Sat.-Sun. 10-4. No charge; donations accepted. Closed national holidays. ♿
Attendance: 200,000 (accurate)
Membership: Full-time Student $30; Senior Citizen Individual $40; Individual $48; Senior Citizen Couple $55; Family $60; Donor $100-$249; Supporter $250-$499; Sustainer $500-$999; Benefactor $1,000-$2,499; Silver Benefactor $2,500-$4,999; Gold Benefactor $5,000-$9,999; Platinum Benefactor $10,000 & up.

SHEBOYGAN COUNTY HISTORICAL MUSEUM, 3110 Erie Ave., Sheboygan, WI 53081-3660. Tel.: 920-458-1103. Fax: 920-458-5152.
Founded: 1954.
Congressional District: 9
Key Personnel: Exec. Dir. & C.E.O., Robert Harker.
Personnel Profile: Full-Time Paid 2; Part-Time Paid 7.
Governing Authority: society. Parent Institutions: Sheboygan County Historical Society. Tax-exempt.
History Museum.
Collections: artifacts of local history & local circus history; farm implements; household articles; medical aids. Historic House: Weinhold family homestead; 1864 log house; 1867 cheese factory; Schuchardt barn; Taylor House.
Research Fields: genealogy; history.
Activities: guided tours; permanent & temporary exhibitions.
Publications: quarterly newsletters; magazine; annual report; books: When Then Was Now; The Branded Hand-Struggles of an Abolitionist; Historic Sheboygan County; And That's The Way It Was; The Promise of Prosperity-The Story of Greenbush Wisconsin & its Waterpowered Sawmill; pamphlet, Brick House On A Hill; pamphlet, Touring Historical Sheboygan County; pamphlet, Reflections of a Sheboygan County Farmwife; pamphlet, Sheboygan Indian Mound Park; pamphlet, Baseball in Sheboygan 1886-1986; 1868-69 Sheboygan City Directory; Cheese Factories of Sheboygan County.
Hours & Admission Prices: April-Oct. Mon.-Fri. 10-5. Adults $4, children $2; members no charge. Closed Memorial Day; Independence Day; Labor Day. ♿
Attendance: 12,000 (estimated)
Membership: Individual $25; Family $35; Supporting $75; Sustaining $150; Sponsor & Corporate $300; Patron $500; Benefactor $1,000.

Shell Lake

MUSEUM OF WOODCARVING, 539 Hwy. 63, Shell Lake, WI 54871-4438. Mailing Address: P.O. Box 371, Shell Lake, WI 54871-0371. Tel.: 715-468-7100.
Web Site: www.roadsideamerica.com/attract/WISHEwood.html
Founded: 1950.
Congressional District: 7
Key Personnel: Owner, Cur. & Museum Shop Mgr., Maria McKay.
Personnel Profile: Part-Time Paid 2.
Governing Authority: private.
Woodcarving Museum.

Collections: over 100 life-sized carvings including one of The Last Supper; over 400 miniatures of animals, birds & historical events; Joseph Barta's tools.
Facilities: library; 10,000 sq. ft. exhibit space. Museum-related items for sale.
Activities: guided tours; lectures.
Hours & Admission Prices: May-Oct. daily 9-6. Adults $5.75, children under 12 $3.75; discounts to groups of 20 or more, AAA & AAM members. ♿
Attendance: 25,000 (estimated)

WASHBURN COUNTY HISTORICAL SOCIETY MUSEUM, 102 W. 2nd Ave., Shell Lake, WI 54871. Mailing Address: P.O. Box 366, Shell Lake, WI 54871-0366. Tel.: 715-468-2982.
Founded: 1954.
Congressional District: 7
Key Personnel: Pres. (V), Cathy Wahlstrom.
Personnel Profile: Part-Time Paid 1; Part-Time Volunteers 25.
Governing Authority: county. Affiliated with the State Historical Society of Wisconsin, 816 State St., Madison, WI 53706. Additional Location: Hwy. 63, Springbrook. Tax-exempt.
Historic Society Museum: housed in three buildings.
Collections: logging tools from county logging era; photographs; crafts; costumes; railroad & farming displays; household period artifacts; manuscripts; church period artifacts; old photographs & school books; furniture; items from the Civil War & World War I; bottles; 1888 clothing; music; button shoes; 70-year-old beaded Indian leather dress; teacher's desk with old schoolbooks; extensive Indian arrowhead display. Historic Buildings: 2 churches; one-room schoolhouse; sky watch building.
Research Fields: local memorabilia; vital statistics to 1940.
Facilities: 400-vol. library of mainly Wisconsin history material with specialties in Washburn County available for research on premises. History books & pamphlets for sale.
Activities: guided tours; permanent & temporary exhibitions.
Publications: books, Spooner 7 Vols.; Shell Lake Trego; Springbrook; Historical Collections of Washburn County; reprint booklet, 1915 Atlas of Washburn County; calendar, 1983 Historical Calendar; 4th Historical Collection out for sale.
Hours & Admission Prices: Memorial Day-Labor Day Fri.-Sat. 11-4. No charge; donations accepted. ♿
Attendance: 500 (estimated)
Membership: Individual $7; Couple $12; Family $15.

Sherwood

HIGH CLIFF HISTORICAL SOCIETY & GENERAL STORE MUSEUM, 7526 N. Lower Cliff Rd., Sherwood, WI 54169-0001. Mailing Address: N168W21700 Main St., Lot 171, Jackson, WI 53037-9647. Tel.: 920-989-1954.
Web Site: historical-sctyatwebtv.net
Founded: 1974.
Congressional District: 6
Key Personnel: Vice Pres., Marcal Head; Dir., Alice Bishop; Dir., Diane Goffard; Treas. & Sec., Karren Van Lyssel.
Personnel Profile: Part-Time Volunteers 10.
Governing Authority: society. Affiliated with The State Historical Society of Wisconsin, 816 State St., Madison, WI. 53706. Tel.: 608-262-3266. Tax-exempt: 501(c)(3).
Historical Society Museum: housed in 1850 General Store, original company store for lime kiln community.
Collections: wearing apparel; household utensils; machinery; tools; records of the lime kiln & store; payroll records; accounts; literature.
Research Fields: local history.
Facilities: snack bar. Museum-related items for sale.
Activities: permanent & temporary exhibitions.
Hours & Admission Prices: Memorial Day-Labor Day Fri.-Sun. & holidays 12-5, other times by appointment. No charge; donations accepted (state permit or park sticker is needed.) ♿
Attendance: 4,500 (estimated)
Membership: Individual $5; Couple & Family $10; Contributing $25; Business & Professional $50; Sustaining $75; Life $100.

Shullsburg

BADGER MINE AND MUSEUM, 279 W. Estey St., Shullsburg, WI 53586. Mailing Address: P.O. Box 580, Shullsburg, WI 53586. Tel.: 608-965-4860.
Founded: 1964.
Congressional District: 2
Personnel Profile: Full-Time Paid 1; Part-Time Paid 4.
Governing Authority: Parent Institution: Shullsburg Community Development Corporation.
General Museum.
Collections: early mining tools; farm equipment; Indian artifacts; toys; country store items; photographs. Historic Structure: 1827 lead mine.
Activities: guided tours; 1/4-mile mining tour; lectures.
Publications: brochure, Hidden Valley.
Hours & Admission Prices: Memorial Day-Labor Day Wed.-Thurs. 12-4, Fri.-Sun. 11-4. Museum: adults $4, seniors over 65 & children 6-15 $3; children under 5 no charge. Mine & Museum: adults $5, seniors over 65 & children 6-15 $4; children under 5 no charge. ♿
Attendance: 2,300 (accurate)
Membership: Lifetime Single $25; Lifetime Couple $45.

South Milwaukee

SOUTH MILWAUKEE HISTORICAL SOCIETY MUSEUM, 717 Milwaukee Ave., South Milwaukee, WI 53172-2113. Tel.: 414-762-5214.
Web Site: www.southmilwaukee.org
Founded: 1972.
Congressional District: 4
Key Personnel: C.E.O. & Pres., Robert M. Pfeiffer; Vice Pres., Lois L. Schreiter; Sec., Cur. & Historian, Dean Marlowe, Jr.; Treas., Richard Raatz.
Personnel Profile: Part-Time Volunteers 10.
Governing Authority: State of Wisconsin. Parent Institution: State Historical Society. Tax-exempt.
Historical Society Museum: housed in Victorian home.
Collections: pictures; genealogies; quilts; paintings; clothing; Lincoln Library; artifacts relating to South Milwaukee.
Research Fields: local history.
Facilities: library.
Activities: guided tours; slide program; talks to groups or school classes; temporary exhibitions. Museum Sponsors: Heritage Week in July.
Publications: quarterly, South Milwaukee Historical Society Newsletter; Images of America Series - South Milwaukee; South Milwaukee Then To Now.
Hours & Admission Prices: Memorial Day-Labor Day first Thurs. of the month 1-3; other times by appointment. No charge; donations accepted.
Attendance: 600 (estimated)
Membership: Senior Citizen $6; Individual $10; Family $15; Business & Sustaining $25; Life $100.

Sparta

MONROE COUNTY LOCAL HISTORY ROOM & LIBRARY, (M), 200 W. Main St., Sparta, WI 54656-2141. Tel.: 608-269-8680. Fax: 608-269-8921.
E-mail: mclhr@centurytel.net
Web Site: www.mclhr.org
Founded: 1976.
Congressional District: 3
Key Personnel: Chm. Bd. Trustees, Carolyn Habelman; Dir., Jarrod Roll.
Personnel Profile: Full-Time Paid 1; Part-Time Paid 1; Part-Time Volunteers 25.
Governing Authority: county government; nonprofit. Tax-exempt.
Historical Society Museum: located in the former Masonic Temple, Monroe County, Sparta, WI.
Collections: emphasis on genealogy of Monroe County people, 1850-present.
Facilities: 400-vol. library.
Hours & Admission Prices: Mon.-Fri. 9-4:30, Sat. 10-4:30. No charge; donations accepted. Closed Memorial Day; Independence Day; Labor Day; Thanksgiving; Christmas. ♿
Attendance: 7,000 (estimated)

Spring Green

THE HOUSE ON THE ROCK, 5754 State Rd. 23, Spring Green, WI 53588-8912. Tel.: 608-935-3639. Fax: 608-935-9472.
E-mail: information@thehouseontherock.com
Web Site: www.thehouseontherock.com
Founded: 1961.
Key Personnel: Owner, Art Donaldson; Pres., Susan Donaldson; Asst. Mgr., Paula Widdish; Mktg. Mgr., Betty Smith.
Governing Authority: privately owned.
Historical House Museum & Complex: original structure rests on a 60 foot chimney of rock jutting high above Wyoming Valley of Southwestern Wisconsin; multi-building complex on different levels & various outbuildings.
Collections: 13 rooms; gate house; walking ramp over treetops; mill house; streets of yesterday; music of yesterday; carousel; organ building; cannon building; dollhouse building; refreshments gardens; artist village; orchestrions & music machines; art objects; stained glass; bronzes; ceramics; ivory & porcelain; guns; mechanical banks; automatons; steam engines; scrimshaw; taxidermy; bisque dolls; wooden dollhouses; suits of armor;

carousel animals; theatre organ consoles; period artifacts; memorabilia; circus costumes; miniature circuses; entomology.
Facilities: concessions. Museum-related items for sale.
Publications: brochures; guide book; pictorial book; Alex Jodan biography; video and audio tapes.
Hours & Admission Prices: May-Aug. daily 9-6; Sept.-April daily 9-5. One Tour: adults $12.50, children $7.50. Additional tour packages available. ♿
Attendance: 500,000

Stevens Point

CENTRAL WISCONSIN CHILDREN'S MUSEUM, 1201 Third Court, Stevens Point, WI 54481-2805. Mailing Address: P.O. Box 474, Stevens Point, WI 54481-0474. Tel.: 715-344-2003.
Founded: 1997.
Personnel Profile: Full-Time Paid 1; Part-Time Paid 9; Part-Time Volunteers 20; Interns 2.
Children's Museum.
Collections: hands-on exhibits.
Hours & Admission Prices: Wed. & Fri.-Sat. 9-4, Thurs. 9-8, Sat. 10-4, Sun. 12-4. Adults $3; discounts to AAM members; children under one & members no charge.
Membership: Family $60; Enhanced $125.

PORTAGE COUNTY HISTORICAL SOCIETY, 1475 Water St., Stevens Point, WI 54481-2920. Mailing Address: P.O. Box 672, Stevens Point, WI 54481-0672.
Founded: 1952.
Congressional District: 7
Key Personnel: Pres., Tim Siebert; Treas., Jeanne Regnier; Cur., Anton Anday; Archivist, Ruth Nelson.
Personnel Profile: Part-Time Volunteers 15.
Governing Authority: private; nonprofit organization. Village located at Washington Ave., Plover, WI 54467; Grist Mill, Hwy. 161, Nelsonville, WI 54458; Synagogue Museum, 1475 Water St., Stevens Point, WI; Firehouse #2, 1800 Strongs Ave., Stevens Point, WI. Tax-exempt: 501(c)(3).
History Museum.
Collections: area domestic life; military; photographs; local Jewish heritage.
Research Fields: war veterans.
Facilities: 200-vol. library of local history books.
Activities: guided tours; lectures; temporary exhibitions. Museum sponsors: Plover Portage Rendevous; Civil War Re-enactment.
Publications: quarterly newsletter, Portage County Historical Society Newsletter; series of 25 local history booklets.
Hours & Admission Prices: June to early Sept. Sat.-Sun. 12-5. Admission $2; group rates available.
Attendance: 1,500 (estimated)
Membership: Annual $15; Business $25; Contributing $50; Life $100.

THE UWSP MUSEUM OF NATURAL HISTORY, 900 Reserve St., University of Wisconsin, Stevens Point, WI 54481-1962. Tel.: 715-346-2858 & 4888. Fax: 715-346-4213.
E-mail: rreser@uwsp.edu
Web Site: www.uwsp.edu/museum/
Founded: 1966.
Congressional District: 7
Key Personnel: Interim Dir., Ray P. Reser; Cur. Education & Museum Shop Mgr., Edward Marks.
Personnel Profile: Full-Time Paid 1; Part-Time Volunteers 3.
Governing Authority: university. Parent Institution: University of Wisconsin-Stevens Point. Tax-exempt.
Natural History Museum.
Collections: mammals; birds; Schoenebeck egg collection; reptiles; fossils; herbarium; Native American artifacts.
Facilities: Museum-related items for sale.
Activities: formally organized education programs for children, adults, undergraduate & graduate students.
Publications: reports of the UWSP Museum of Natural History.
Hours & Admission Prices: Mon. 9-5, Tues.-Fri. 9-4, Sat. 10-3, Sun, 1-4. No charge; donations accepted. ♿
Attendance: 12,000 (estimated)
Membership: Basic $25; Associate $50; Advocate $100; Sponsor $250; Patron $500; Benefactor $1,000.

Stoughton

STOUGHTON HISTORICAL SOCIETY, 324 S. Page St., Stoughton, WI 53589-2166. Mailing Address: 1547 Hwy. 51 N., Stoughton, WI 53589-3741. Tel.: 608-873-8005.
E-mail: shs@expressiveimage.com
Web Site: expressiveimage.com/historical.html
Founded: 1960.
Congressional District: 2
Key Personnel: Pres., Marilyn Granrud.
Governing Authority: nonprofit. Tax-exempt.
Historical Society Museum: housed in 1858 Universalist Church.
Collections: land grant papers; tools; surveying equipment; glass; costumes; musical instruments; Norwegian Rosemaling; military; portraits; wagon industry.
Activities: guided tours; lectures; formally organized education programs for children; permanent & traveling exhibitions; special events.
Publications: descriptive brochure.
Hours & Admission Prices: mid-May to Sept. Sun. 1-4. Requested Donation: $2.
Attendance: 1,500 (estimated)
Membership: Individual $7.50.

Sturgeon Bay

DOOR COUNTY HISTORICAL MUSEUM, 18 N. 4th Ave., Sturgeon Bay, WI 54235-2423. Tel.: 920-743-5809.
E-mail: dcmuseum@co.door.wi.us
Founded: 1939.
Congressional District: 9
Key Personnel: Cur., Margaret S. Weir; Asst. Cur., Ann Jinkins.
Personnel Profile: Part-Time Paid 4; Part-Time Volunteers 7.
Governing Authority: county. Tax-exempt: 501(c)(3).
Historical Museum.
Collections: farm & dairy; orchards; geology; blacksmith; turn-of-century storefronts; Belgian & Scandinavian settlers; replica fire department containing restored local fire trucks; schools' Door County wildlife; local history videos.
Hours & Admission Prices: May-Oct. daily 10-4:30. No charge; donations accepted. ♿
Attendance: 10,000 (estimated)

DOOR COUNTY MARITIME MUSEUM (AT STURGEON BAY), (M), 120 N. Madison Ave., Sturgeon Bay, WI 54235-3416. Tel.: 920-743-5958. Fax: 920-743-9483.
E-mail: info@dcmm.org
Web Site: www.dcmm.org
Founded: 1969.
Congressional District: 8
Key Personnel: Exec. Dir., Bob Desh; Pres., Dan Austad; Vice Pres., Jeff Weborg; Dir. Devel., Trudy Herbst; Treas., Pete Horton; Museum Shop Mgr., Jan Johnson; Cur., John Moga; Asst. Cur., June Larsen; Volunteer Coord., Kay Reiche.
Personnel Profile: Full-Time Paid 7; Part-Time Paid 35; Part-Time Volunteers 75.
Governing Authority: nonprofit organization. Door County Maritime Museums Inc., affiliated with Wisconsin State Historical Society, Madison, WI & the Door County Chamber of Commerce, Box 219, Sturgeon Bay, WI 54235. Tel. 414-743-4456. Branch Museum: Door County Marine Museum at Gills Rock (see separate listing). Tax-exempt.
Maritime Museum.
Collections: actual boats displayed from 1900; earliest shipping container; marine books; ship operating records; shipbuilding pictures; records; restored Great Lakes Pilothouse; fishery artifacts.
Facilities: library of miscellaneous papers, pictures, books from the shipyards & steamship operation & marine-oriented charts available for use on premises. Marine-related books for sale.
Activities: Museum Sponsors: Door County Lighthouse Walk in May; D.C. Maritime Museum Festival in August features antique wooden boat show, quick & dirty boat building contest & entertainment.
Publications: brochures; postcards; quarterly newsletter.
Hours & Admission Prices: Shipbuilding Museum: Labor Day-Memorial Day daily 10-5; May-Sept. daily 9-6. Cana Island Lighthouse: mid-May to Oct. grounds daily 10-5. Adults $7, children $4; members no charge. ♿
Attendance: 60,000 (estimated)
Membership: Individual $35; Family $45.

THE FARM, 4285 Hwy. 57, Sturgeon Bay, WI 54235. Mailing Address: P.O. Box 44, Sturgeon Bay, WI 54235-0044. Tel.: 920-743-6666. Fax: 920-743-2266.
E-mail: thetancks@aol.com
Web Site: www.thefarmindoorcounty.com
Founded: 1965.
Congressional District: 8
Key Personnel: Treas., David E. Tanck; Vice Pres., Jeff Tanck; Museum Shop Mgr., Jenny Tanck; Museum Shop Mgr., Shirley Tanck.
Personnel Profile: Part-Time Paid 11.

Governing Authority: Affiliated with the Door County Chamber of Commerce, P.O. Box 219, Sturgeon Bay, WI 54235.
Living Museum Complex: located on the Door County Peninsula.
Collections: farm tools; farm implements; gardens & crops. Historic Structures: c.1856 woodshed; granary; sugar shack; nature center; historical animals & poultry.
Facilities: Pioneer Farm Stead; nature trails; picnic area. Country gift items for sale.
Activities: visit farm animals in natural surroundings; feeding smaller animals; milk a nanny goat; watch chicks hatch.
Publications: tabloid, Down on the Farm; brochure.
Hours & Admission Prices: Memorial Day weekend to mid-Oct. daily 9-5. Adults $7, children 3-13 $3.50; discounts to AAA members, senior citizens & groups; children under 3 no charge. ♿
Attendance: 35,000 (estimated)

MILLER ART MUSEUM, (M), 107 S. 4th Ave., Sturgeon Bay, WI 54235-2203. Tel.: 920-746-0707 (Offices). Fax: 920-746-0865.
E-mail: bmam@dcwis.com
Web Site: millerartmuseum.org
Founded: 1975.
Congressional District: 8
Key Personnel: Dir., Bonnie Hartmann; Pres. (V), Kristi Roenning; Cur. Exhibits & Permanent Collections, Deborah Rosenthal.
Personnel Profile: Full-Time Paid 1; Part-Time Paid 3; Part-Time Volunteers 160.
Governing Authority: county. Miller Art Center Bd. of Directors by permission of the Door County Library, 107 S. 4th Ave., Sturgeon Bay, WI 54235. Tel. 920-746-0707. Subsidiary of: Miller Art Center Foundation. Tax-exempt.
Art Museum: housed in Door County Library.
Collections: 20th Century Wisconsin artists.
Major Exhibits: Barbara's Farm: Color Photos, 1/16/10-3/2/10; Midwest Printmakers Group Invitational, 3/6/10-4/20/10; 36th Annual Door County High School Art, 4/24/10-6/1/10; Gerhard C.F. Miller: Master Draughtsman, 6/5/10-8/24/10; Sturgeon Bay Past & Present, 8/28/10-11/9/10; 35th Juried Annual - NE WI, 11/13/10-12/28/10.
Facilities: classroom. Museum-related items for sale.
Activities: guided tours; lectures; gallery talks; docent program; music & performing arts programs; temporary exhibitions; classes.
Publications: catalogues for changing exhibits.
Hours & Admission Prices: Mon. 10-8, Tues.-Sat. 10-5. No charge; donations accepted. Closed major holidays & 3 days preceding each exhibit. ♿
Attendance: 19,000 (accurate)
Membership: Active I $10; Active II $20; Associate $30; Donor $50; Patron $100; Benefactor $250 & up.

POTAWATOMI STATE PARK, 3740 County PD, Sturgeon Bay, WI 54235. Tel.: 920-746-2890. Fax: 920-746-2896.
Web Site: www.wiparks.net
Key Personnel: Supt., Don McKinnon.
Governing Authority: state. Affiliated with the Wisconsin Dept. of Resources, P.O. Box 7921, Madison, WI 53707.
State Park: located on the Door County Peninsula.
Collections: wildlife & their habitats; natural science; geology.
Facilities: nature trails; tower; picnic areas; campsites.
Activities: hiking.
Hours & Admission Prices: Daily 6am-11pm. Entrance fee & camping fee. Reservations accepted.

WHITEFISH DUNES STATE PARK, 3725 Clark Lake Rd., Sturgeon Bay, WI 54235. Tel.: 920-823-2400. Fax: 920-823-2640.
E-mail: wiparks@dnr.state.wi.us
Web Site: www.dnr.state.wi.us
Founded: 1967.
Key Personnel: Park Mgr., Richard Ostrowski; Naturalist, Carolyn Rock; Pres. Friends Group (V), Dick Weidman.
Governing Authority: state. Parent Institution: Dept. of Natural Resources. Affiliated with Door County Chamber of Commerce, Sturgeon Bay, WI. Tax-exempt.
Nature Center.
Collections: local history & culture; ecology; geology; archaeology; Native American artifacts.
Facilities: beach area; cross-country ski trails. Limited use development in progress.
Activities: interpretive programs.
Publications: pamphlet, People of the Dunes; species lists; interpretive trail guide, Brachiopod Trail.
Hours & Admission Prices: Daily 8-8. State Park admission sticker required, fees apply. Closed winter holidays. ♿
Attendance: 250,000 (estimated)

Sun Prairie

SUN PRAIRIE HISTORICAL LIBRARY & MUSEUM, 115 E. Main St., Sun Prairie, WI 53590-2222. Tel.: 608-837-2511. Fax: 608-825-6879.
E-mail: pklein@cityofsunprairie.com
Web Site: www.sunprairie.com
Founded: 1967.
Congressional District: 2
Key Personnel: Pres. (V) & C.E.O., Frank Peot; Registrar, Mary O'Grady; Exhibit Cur., Peter Klein; Historian, Rev. Ardin Lapor; Asst., Shirley Thompson.
Personnel Profile: Full-Time Volunteers 1; Part-Time Volunteers 75; Interns 1.
Governing Authority: nonprofit organization. Parent Institution: City of Sun Prairie. Tax-exempt: 501(c)(3).
History Museum: housed on the site of the home of the first settlers, Charles Bird & family.
Collections: artifacts & manuscripts relating to Sun Prairie; photographs; obituary & cemetery records from Sun Prairie area.
Research Fields: genealogy; local history; city government.
Facilities: archives of local history; documents, city records, school records, organizational records relating to Sun Prairie available for research on premises under supervision.
Activities: guided tours; docent program; permanent, temporary & traveling exhibitions; speakers bureau; local history classes for members & tour guides; outreach programs; research; traveling children programs.
Publications: quarterly newsletter, Sun Prairie Historical Newsletter; pamphlets, Walking Tours; History Pamphlet of O'Keeffe Family; History of Sun Prairie 1830s-1940s; Death List: a compilation of 16,000 burials in area cemeteries available on website.
Hours & Admission Prices: May-Nov. Wed. & Fri.-Sat. 2-4, Sun.-Mon. 6:30-8:30; research by appointment. No charge. ♿
Attendance: 6,200 (accurate)
Membership: Society: Individual $10; Sustaining $50; Life $100.

Superior

DOUGLAS COUNTY HISTORICAL SOCIETY, (M), 1101 John Ave., Superior, WI 54880-1640. Tel.: 715-392-8449. Fax: 715-395-5639.
E-mail: dchs@douglashistory.org
Web Site: www.douglashistory.org
Founded: 1854.
Congressional District: 7
Key Personnel: C.E.O. & Pres. (V), Valerie Burke; Dir., Kathy Laakso.
Personnel Profile: Full-Time Paid 1; Part-Time Paid 1; Part-Time Volunteers 19.
Governing Authority: Parent Institution: Wisconsin State Historical Society. Tax-exempt.
County Historical Society Museum.
Collections: c.1890 furniture & furnishings; Ojibwa Chippewa Indian crafts; David F. Barry collection of Sioux Indian portraits; archives & manuscripts; photographs & clippings of local history; oral histories on audiotape; President Calvin Coolidge artifacts including a desk, scrapbook, pictures of Coolidge & a plaque from the Class of 1929 donated by the former Central High School.
Research Fields: local history of Douglas County.
Facilities: 600-vol. library of area history.
Activities: lectures; arts festivals; loan, permanent & temporary exhibitions; school loan service by request.
Publications: newsletter, History News.
Hours & Admission Prices: Tues.-Thurs. 11-5, Fri. 10-2. Adults $3.
Attendance: 590 (estimated)
Membership: Single $15; Family $30; Conserving $50; Preserving $100; Supporting $250; Maintaining $500; Sustaining $1,000.

FAIRLAWN MANSION & MUSEUM, 906 E. 2nd St., Superior, WI 54880-3245. Tel.: 715-394-5712. Fax: 715-394-2043.
E-mail: info@superiorpublicmuseums.org
Web Site: www.superiorpublicmuseums.org
Founded: 1999.
Key Personnel: C.E.O., Susan K. Anderson; Pres., Kelly Thimm; Museum Shop Mgr., Sara Jackson.
Personnel Profile: Full-Time Paid 4; Part-Time Paid 20; Part-Time Volunteers 30.
Governing Authority: Tax-exempt.
Historic House Museum: housed in 42 room Queen Anne Victorian style mansion, c.1891. Home of Martin & Grace Pattison until 1918 when it was donated to be used as a home & refuge for children and young women.
Collections: period furnishings; photographs, children's home exhibit.
Research Fields: orphanage; children's home; foster care.

Facilities: Victorian-inspired gardens. Museum-related items for sale.
Activities: special events; guided tours.
Publications: quarterly newsletter; Fairlawn, Restoring the Splendor.
Hours & Admission Prices: mid-May to Dec. Mon.-Sat. 9-5, Sun. 11-5. Winter: Thurs.-Sat. 10-4, Sun. 12-4. Adults $8, seniors & students 6-18 $6.50; children under 6 no charge. ♿
Attendance: 8,000 (accurate)
Membership: Member $20; Patron $50.

RICHARD I. BONG VETERANS HISTORICAL CENTER, (M), 305 Harbor View Pkwy., Superior, WI 54880-6845. Tel.: 715-392-7151. Fax: 715-395-5526.
E-mail: fuhrman@bvhcenter.org
Web Site: www.brhcenter.org
Formerly: Richard I. Bong WWII Heritage Center
Founded: 2002.
Key Personnel: Exec. Dir., Robert B. Fuhrman; Chm. (V), Terry Lunberg; Cur., Gina Sacchetti; Museum Shop Mgr., Sandy Harty.
Personnel Profile: Full-Time Paid 3; Part-Time Paid 2; Part-Time Volunteers 80.
Governing Authority: private; nonprofit organization. Parent Institution: Bong P-38 Fund, Inc. Tax-exempt: 501(c)(3).
History Museum.
Collections: military artifacts from WWII to present.
Research Fields: World War II to present conflicts.
Facilities: library; classrooms; 14,000 sq. ft. exhibit space; 62-seat theater. Museum-related items for sale.
Activities: formal education programs; internships; guided tours; lectures; study clubs; temporary & traveling exhibitions; book study club; public programs & lectures.
Publications: quarterly newsletter, The Bong Flyer.
Hours & Admission Prices: May-Oct. Mon.-Sat. 9-5, Sun. 12-5; Winter: Tues.-Sat. 9-5. Adults $9, senior citizens & students $8, children $7; discounts to groups; active military & members no charge. Closed New Year's Day; Easter; Thanksgiving; Christmas. ♿
Attendance: 9,979 (accurate)
Membership: Aviator $40; Aviator Plus $55; Squadron $75; Squadron Plus $100; Pilot $250; Command Pilot $500; Ace $1,000.

S.S. METEOR MARITIME MUSEUM, 300 Marina Dr., Barker's Island, Superior, WI 54880-3287. Mailing Address: 906 E. 2nd St., Superior, WI 54880-3245. Tel.: 715-394-5712. Fax: 715-394-2043.
E-mail: info@superiorpublicmuseums.org
Web Site: www.superiorpublicmuseums.org
Founded: 1999.
Congressional District: 7
Key Personnel: Dir., Susan K. Anderson; Bd. Pres., Kelly Thimm; Administrative Coord., Sara Jackson.
Personnel Profile: Full-Time Paid 4; Part-Time Paid 12; Part-Time Volunteers 40.
Governing Authority: nonprofit organization. Parent Institution: Superior Public Museums, Inc. Tax-exempt: 501(c)(3).
Historic Ship Museum: housed in the hull & quarters of the 1896 S.S. Meteor, last of the whalebacks.
Collections: whaleback artifacts; boat models; ship equipment; ship building history; gallery display; Seamen's Memorial Statue, in part dedicated to 29 hands aboard the Edmund Fitzgerald; ship models.
Facilities: Gift items for sale.
Activities: guided tours; formally organized education programs for children; loan, permanent & temporary exhibitions.
Publications: brochures; quarterly newsletter, Superior Public Museums; book, Pigboat: The Story of the Whalebacks; annual, The Whaleback Log.
Hours & Admission Prices: May-Sept. daily 10-5. Adults $6, students 6-18 & senior citizens 65 & over $5; discount to groups; children under 6 no charge. ♿
Attendance: 6,000 (estimated)
Membership: Member $20; Patron $50.

Two Rivers

HAMILTON WOOD TYPE PRINTING MUSEUM, 1619 Jefferson St., Two Rivers, WI 54241-3066. Tel.: 920-794-6272.
E-mail: hwt@woodtype.org
Web Site: www.woodtype.org
Key Personnel: Museum Coord., James Van Lanen, Sr.
Printing History Museum.
Collections: printing history; 1.5 million pieces of wood type including over 1,000 styles & sizes of patterns.
Activities: demonstrations; field trips; workshops.
Hours & Admission Prices: May-Oct. Mon.-Sat. 9-5, Sun. 1-5; Nov.-April daily 1-5.

Viroqua

VERNON COUNTY MUSEUM, 410 S. Center Ave., Viroqua, WI 54665-2001. Mailing Address: P.O. Box 444, Viroqua, WI 54665-0444. Tel.: 608-637-7396.
E-mail: vcmuseum@frontiernet.net
Web Site: www.frontiernet.net/~vcmuseum/
Founded: 1942.
Congressional District: 3
Key Personnel: Pres. (V), Mike Callan; Cur., Judy K. Mathison; Asst. Cur., Carol Krogan; Asst. Cur., Kristen Parrott.
Personnel Profile: Part-Time Paid 3; Part-Time Volunteers 100.
Governing Authority: county. Parent Institution: Vernon County Historical Society. Affiliated with Wisconsin State Historical Society. Tax-exempt.
Local History Museum: housed in Vernon County Normal School.
Collections: general store; professional room; Indian artifacts; Governor Rusk; genealogy & research room. Historic Buildings: c.1900 church; 1889 rural school; 1870 Sherry-Butt House; 1919-1972 Teacher's college/museum.
Research Fields: genealogy & Vernon County history.
Facilities: library of census records; local newspapers on microfilm; research room; local history books.
Activities: guided tours; Round Barn Driving tour; Black Hawk Trail.
Publications: Museum Notes; special features; brochures, Blackhawk Trail Brochure: Walking Tours of Viroqua; newsletter.
Hours & Admission Prices: Museum: mid-May to mid-Sept. Mon.-Sat.12-4; mid-Sept. to mid-May Tues.-Thurs. 12-4; other times by appointment. No charge; donations accepted. Sherry-Butt House: Sat.-Sun. 1-5. Adults $3; members no charge. Closed holidays. ♿
Attendance: 3,500 (estimated)
Membership: Individual $10; Family $15; Associate $25; Life $250.

Washburn

WASHBURN HISTORICAL MUSEUM & CULTURAL CENTER, INC. AKA WASHBURN CULTURAL CENTER, 1 E. Bayfield St., Washburn, WI 54891-4401. Mailing Address: P.O. Box 725, Washburn, WI 54891-0725. Tel.: 715-373-5591.
E-mail: washburnw@centurytel.net
Founded: 1991.
Congressional District: 7
Key Personnel: C.E.O. & Chm. (V), Richard Olson; Pres. (V), A.H. (Tony) Woiak; Treas., Lois Tetzner; Public Rels., Dora Kling; Museum Shop Mgr., Joanne Weister.
Personnel Profile: Part-Time Paid 3; Part-Time Volunteers 15.
Governing Authority: private; nonprofit organization. Tax-exempt: 501(c)(3).
Historical Museum & Cultural Arts Center.
Collections: Washburn area history, industries & people; paintings.
Facilities: 15-vol. library of historical books; 100 bound newspapers 1886-1989; 2,800 sq. ft. exhibit space.
Activities: concerts; films; formal education programs; guided tours; hobby workshops; lectures; loan & temporary exhibitions; rental gallery; classes; meetings; receptions.
Publications: annual, Brownstone Notes.
Hours & Admission Prices: Tues.-Sat. 10-4. No charge; donations accepted. Closed New Year's Day; Thanksgiving; Christmas. ♿
Attendance: 3,608 (accurate)
Membership: Individual $5; Family $10; Business $15.

Washington Island

ROCK ISLAND STATE PARK, 1924 Indian Point Rd., Washington Island, WI 54246-9078. Tel.: 920-847-2235.
Web Site: www.dnr.state.wi.us/parks/
Founded: 1965.
Congressional District: 8
Key Personnel: Supt., Kirby Foss.
Personnel Profile: Part-Time Paid 1.
Governing Authority: state. Parent Institution: State of WI, Dept. of Natural Resources. Tax-exempt.
State Park: located on the Door County Peninsula.
Collections: local history & culture; period furnishings; historic buildings.
Facilities: 900-acres state park; trails; 40 campsites; picnic area; sand beach; dock; backpacking only, motorized vehicles or horses not allowed. Accessible by boat only; public boat ramp at Jackson Harbor & ferry service from Washington Island.
Activities: nature programs & nature hikes.
Hours & Admission Prices: Memorial Day-Columbus Day daily. Park: No charge; donations accepted. Camping fee, camping reservations recommended, to reserve a campsite, call Reserve America at 888-947-2747.

Attendance: 30,000
Membership: Friends of Rock Island: Individual $10; Family $25; Lifetime $300.

Watertown

OCTAGON HOUSE-FIRST KINDERGARTEN IN AMERICA, 919 Charles St., Watertown, WI 53094-5001. Tel.: 920-261-2796.
Web Site: www.watertownhistory.org
Founded: 1933.
Congressional District: 9
Key Personnel: C.E.O. & Museum Shop Mgr., Linda Werth; Pres., William Jannke, III
Personnel Profile: Full-Time Paid 1; Part-Time Paid 4; Part-Time Volunteers 20; Interns 1.
Governing Authority: society; nonprofit organization. Parent Institution: Watertown Historical Society. Tax-exempt: 501(c)(3).
History Museum: housed in 1854 Victorian Octagon House belonging to John & Eliza Richards and family; 1856 first kindergarten building in America.
Collections: memorabilia of early Watertown; archives; folk art; Civil War materials; children's museum; decorative arts; folklore; manuscripts. Historic Structure: 1853 pioneer barn.
Research Fields: genealogies; kindergarten; octagon houses.
Facilities: 400-vol. library of historical, biographical and kindergarten materials available for inter-library loan and for use on premises. Museum-related items for sale.
Activities: guided tours; gallery talks; concerts; permanent & temporary exhibitions. Museum Sponsors: annual Ice Cream Social in August; Christmas Play in November & December; Christmas Open House.
Publications: books, Heritage of Homes; John Richards: The Hill and the Mill; Reprint of Margaret Schurz Biography; Handi & Pussy Go to Kindergarten; monograph on the Octagon House; monograph on first kindergarten; monograph, Froebel's gifts.
Hours & Admission Prices: May 1 to the day before Memorial Day & Sept.-Oct. daily 11-3; Memorial Day to Labor Day 10-4. Adults $7, senior citizens & AAA members & groups of 20 or more $6, children (6-17) $4; discounts to AAM & AAA members.
Attendance: 7,000 (accurate)
Membership: Individual $12; Couple$18; Family $25.

Waukesha

WAUKESHA COUNTY MUSEUM, 101 W. Main St., Waukesha, WI 53186-4811. Tel.: 262-521-2859. Fax: 262-521-2865.
Web Site: www.waukeshacountymuseum.org
Formerly: Waukesha County Historical Society & Museum
Founded: 1914.
Congressional District: 4
Key Personnel: Exec. Dir., Kirsten Lee Villegas; Pres. (V), Dave Frazer; Dir. Devel. & Mktg., Jim Hahn, CFRE; Dir. Education, Kristen Matlick; Cur., Elisabeth Engel; Archivist, Eric Vanden Heuvel; Dir. Visitor Svcs., Marjorie Mahler.
Personnel Profile: Full-Time Paid 6; Part-Time Paid 2; Part-Time Volunteers 100; Interns 4.
Governing Authority: Tax-exempt: 501(c)(3).
History Museum: housed in 1893 Waukesha County Courthouse.
Collections: county history including manuscripts & visual images; textiles; house & farm ware; Springs Era artifacts; military; Native American; stonework; Waukesha County history from Ice Age to the present.
Research Fields: local history; genealogy; historic preservation.
Facilities: research center.
Activities: permanent & temporary exhibits; spring & summer camps; scout days; guided tours; programs; events; school loan of Discovery Boxes.
Publications: magazines; quarterly publication, "Landmark"; books, From Farmland to Freeways: A History of Waukesha County, Discovering Waukesha County.
Hours & Admission Prices: Exhibits: Tues.-Sat. 10-4:30. Adults $3, seniors 62 & over $2, students $1; Waukesha County residents on Sat. & members no charge. Research Center: Tues. & Fri.-Sat. 10-12 & 12:30-4:30, Thurs. 12:30-4:30. Adults $3; members no charge. Closed major holidays. ♿
Attendance: 16,683 (accurate)
Membership: Institution & Preservationist $30; Builder $50; Educator $100; Visionary $250.

Waupaca

HOLLY HISTORY CENTER & HUTCHINSON HOUSE MUSEUM, 321 S. Main St., Waupaca, WI 54981-1745. Tel.: 715-258-5958 (museum) & 256-9980 (history center).
E-mail: wauphistsoc@waupacaonline.net
Web Site: www.waupacahistory.org
Founded: 1953.
Congressional District: 6
Key Personnel: Pres., Dick Bidwell; Vice Pres., Mike Kirk; Treas., Robert Kessler; Sec., Betty Stewart; Dir., Julie Hintz.
Personnel Profile: Part-Time Paid 1; Part-Time Volunteers 20.
Governing Authority: society. Hutchinson House Museum: S. Main St. at South Park, Waupaca, WI 54981. Parent Institution: Waupaca Historical Society, Waupaca 54981. Subsidiary Institution: Waupaca Train Depot. Branch Museum: Holly History & Genealogy Center. Tax-exempt: 501(c)(3).
Historic House & Preservation Project: 1854 Hutchinson House.
Collections: Victorian home furnishings & clothing; vintage china & glassware; early quilts, lace, linens, & samplers; magazines Victorian-1930s; photographs; manuscripts. Holly History & Genealogy Center: genealogy & history research section; Royal Doulton character jugs; historical photographs; history of Waupaca; Plat books; maps; family histories; Bibles; historical postcards; train depot.
Research Fields: genealogy; photography; Victorian Americana; Waupaca history; Wisconsin history.
Facilities: library.
Activities: guided tours; arts festivals; permanent & temporary exhibitions; genealogy assistance; history programs.
Publications: quarterly member newsletter.
Hours & Admission Prices: Museum: Memorial Day-Labor Day Sat.-Sun. & holidays 1-4; special group tours by appointment. No charge. History Center: Wed. & Fri. 12-3, Sat. 9-12. No charge.
Attendance: 1,000 (estimated)
Membership: Waupaca Historical Society: 1 Year: Single $10; Family $25; 5 Year: Single $45; Family $75. Lifetime: Single $75; Family $125.

Wausau

* **LEIGH YAWKEY WOODSON ART MUSEUM, (M),** 700 N. 12th St., Wausau, WI 54403-5007. Tel.: 715-845-7010. Fax: 715-845-7103.
E-mail: museum@lywam.org
Web Site: www.lywam.org
Founded: 1973.
Congressional District: 7
Key Personnel: Dir., Kathy Kelsey Foley; Assoc. Dir., Marcia Theel; Cur. Exhibitions, Andrew J. McGivern; Cur. Collections, Jane Weinke; Cur. Education, Jayna Hintz; Cur. Education, Erin Narloch; Office Mgr., Shari Schroeder; Facilities Mgr., Joe Ruelle.
Personnel Profile: Full-Time Paid 9; Part-Time Paid 21; Part-Time Volunteers 115.
Governing Authority: nonprofit organization. Tax-exempt: 501(c)(3).
Art Museum.
Collections: paintings, sculpture, drawings & graphics depicting the natural world, with an emphasis on avian life; porcelain; glass.
Major Exhibits: In Search of Norman Rockwell's America (T), 11/21/09-1/24/10; Las Artes de Mexico (T), 1/30/10-4/11/10; William Steig: The Man Who Never Grew Up (T), 4/17/10-6/20/10; Elliott Erwitt: Dog Dogs, 4/17/10-6/20/10; Birds in Art, 9/11/10-11/14/10; I Want Candy: The Sweet Stuff in American Art, 11/20/10-1/23/11.
Research Fields: artistic depictions of birds.
Facilities: 2,000-vol. library of art books available to staff & docents at all times & to the general public by appointment only.
Activities: sculpture garden; guided tours; docent & volunteer program; lectures; garden concerts; demonstrations; family programs; Art Park (family interactive area); videos; inter-museum loan, permanent, temporary & traveling exhibitions; audio tours.
Publications: exhibition catalogs; quarterly newsletter.
Hours & Admission Prices: Tues.-Fri. 9-4, Sat.-Sun. 12-5. No charge; donations accepted. Closed national holidays. ♿
Attendance: 55,000 (estimated)
Membership: Household $50; Partner $75; Associate $150; Patron $250; Friend $350; Connoisseur $500; Collector $1,000; Benefactor $2,500.

MARATHON COUNTY HISTORICAL SOCIETY, 410 McIndoe St., Wausau, WI 54403-4745. Tel.: 715-842-5750. Fax: 715-848-0576.
E-mail: director@marathoncountyhistory.org
Web Site: www.marathoncountyhistory.org
Founded: 1952.
Congressional District: 7
Key Personnel: Dir., Mary Forer; Pres., John Hattenhauer; Cur. & Public Rels., Shelley Green; Librarian, Gary Gisselman; Cur. Events, Kristine Johnson; Cur. Education, Anna Straub; Yawkey House Attendant, Gary Walters.
Personnel Profile: Part-Time Paid 6; Part-Time Volunteers 60.
Governing Authority: bd. of directors. Branch Museum: Yawkey House Museum, 403 McIndoe St., Wausaw, WI.
Historic House Museum: housed in the A.P. Woodson House; built in 1914.

Collections: Wisconsin history; lumbering artifacts; period furnishings; pioneer artifacts; memorabilia; writings & photographs; period documents. Historic House: Yawkey House, built in 1901.
Research Fields: logging; Native American; genealogy; photographs; history of Marathon County.
Facilities: research library of books on the history of Wausau, Marathon County, Wisconsin; meeting rooms.
Activities: tours; lectures; films; slides; programs for children & adults; permanent, temporary & traveling exhibitions; school programs; research. Annual Events: Victorian Valentine's Tea in February; Living History Festival; cemetery tours.
Publications: quarterly, Wanigan.
Hours & Admission Prices: Tues.-Thurs. 9-4:30, Sat.-Sun. 1-4:30. Woodson History Center: no charge. Yawkey House Museum: adults $7; members no charge. Closed national holidays.
Attendance: 20,000 (estimated)
Membership: Student $10; Individual $35-$49; Family $50-$99; Pinery $100-$249; Pioneer $250-$499; Lumberjack $500-$999; Lumber Baron $1,000 & up.

Wauwatosa

LOWELL DAMON HOUSE, 2107 Wauwatosa Ave., Wauwatosa, WI 53213-1730. Mailing Address: 910 N. Old World 3rd St., Milwaukee, WI 53203-1501. Tel.: 414-273-8288. Fax: 414-273-3268.
E-mail: info@milwaukeehistory.net
Web Site: www.milwaukeehistory.net
Founded: 1941.
Congressional District: 4
Key Personnel: Exec. Dir., Robert T. Teske; Pres. (V), Randy Bryant; Cur. Collections, Michael Reuter.
Personnel Profile: Full-Time Paid 9; Part-Time Paid 1.
Governing Authority: Milwaukee County Historical Society. Tax-exempt.
Historic House.
Collections: 1840-1880 furnishings.
Activities: guided tours.
Publications: brochure.
Hours & Admission Prices: Wed. 3-5, Sun. 1-5. No charge; donations accepted. Closed major holidays.
Membership: Senior Citizen & Student $20; Individual $30; Family $35.

West Allis

WEST ALLIS HISTORICAL SOCIETY MUSEUM, 8405 West National Ave., West Allis, WI 53227-1733. Tel.: 414-541-6970.
E-mail: wahs8405@gmail.com
Web Site: www.westallishistory.org
Founded: 1966.
Congressional District: 4
Key Personnel: Pres. (V), Devan Gracyalny, Jr.; 1st Vice Pres., Betty M. Hartwig; Treas., Helen Lundquist; Sec., Ed Wilkommen.
Personnel Profile: Part-Time Volunteers 20.
Governing Authority: nonprofit. Affiliated with State Historical Society, 816 State St., Madison 53706. Tax-exempt.
General Museum: housed in 1887 cream city brick Romanesque style school building.
Collections: toys; model steam engine; motors; 1900 dental office; 1835 pioneer room & workshop with pioneer implements; turn-of-the-century grocery & post office; clothing from Civil War to present; manuscripts.
Research Fields: cemetery; government; pioneer families; artifacts; churches.
Facilities: 1,000-vol. library on local history available on premises; reading room; classrooms.
Activities: guided tours; lectures. Museum Sponsors: annual picnic on museum grounds in June; annual banquet in October; Holiday Open House on Sundays in December.
Publications: quarterly bulletin, Historic Buzz.
Hours & Admission Prices: Tues. 7pm-9pm, Sun. 2-4; groups by appointment. No charge; donations accepted. Closed New Year's Eve & Day; Memorial Day; Independence Day; Thanksgiving; Christmas. ♿
Attendance: 831 (accurate)
Membership: Student $5; Individual $8; Patron $50 & up; Business, Civic, Professional, Organization $50; Life $100.

West Bend

MUSEUM OF WISCONSIN ART, (M), 300 S. 6th Ave., West Bend, WI 53095-0426. Tel.: 262-334-9638. Fax: 262-334-8080.
E-mail: greid@wisconsinart.org
Web Site: www.wisconsinart.org
Formerly: West Bend Art Museum
Founded: 1961.
Congressional District: 9
Key Personnel: Pres. (V), Dale Kent; Exec. Dir., Thomas D. Lidtke; Asst. Dir., Graeme Reid; Registrar, Andrea Waala; Dir. Operations, Rebecca Conde; Dir. Devel., Joan Rudnitzki; Cur. Education, Courtney Spousta.
Personnel Profile: Full-Time Paid 6; Part-Time Paid 5; Part-Time Volunteers 100; Interns 2.
Governing Authority: nonprofit organization. Tax-exempt.
Art Museum.
Collections: works of late 19th- & early 20th-century American expatriate artist Carl Von Marr consisting of more than 400 works of art; early Wisconsin art (from Euro-American settlement to 1950); photographs; books; video tapes; audio recordings.
Research Fields: Carl von Marr; Wisconsin art.
Facilities: Wisconsin art history archives.
Activities: guided tours; lectures; films; gallery talks; permanent & temporary exhibitions; tours; adult & children humanities classes; educational outreach programs for grade schools.
Publications: monthly newsletter; catalog, Carl von Marr: German American Artist; early Wisconsin art exhibition catalogues.
Hours & Admission Prices: Wed.-Sat. 10-4:30, Sun. 1-4:30. Adults $5, seniors & students $3; discounts to AAM & ICOM members; members & children under 12 no charge. Closed holidays. ♿
Attendance: 14,000 (accurate)
Membership: Student $15; Seniors & Teacher $25; Individual $30; Family $50; Friends of Art $125; Sustaining $300; Exceptional Friend $500; Carl von Marr Society $1,000.

WASHINGTON COUNTY HISTORICAL SOCIETY, (M), 320 S. 5th Ave., West Bend, WI 53095-3333. Tel.: 262-335-4678. Fax: 262-335-4612.
E-mail: info@historyisfun.com
Web Site: www.historyisfun.com
Founded: 1937.
Congressional District: 9
Key Personnel: Exec. Dir., M.Q. "Chip" Beckford; Pres. (V), Richard Becker; Dir. Mktg. & Devel., Lisa Rogers; Cur., Christopher Borchert; Cur. Education, Jessica Sawinski; Research Supvr., Jancan Moller Vanbeckum.
Personnel Profile: Full-Time Paid 6; Part-Time Paid 1; Part-Time Volunteers 130; Interns 3.
Governing Authority: nonprofit organization. Subsidiary Institution: St. Agnes Historic Site. Tax-exempt: 501(c)(3).
History Museum: housed in 1889 County Courthouse; 1886 Old County Jailhouse Museum.
Collections: period artifacts; photographs; maps; genealogies; manuscripts; death & burial records; Veterans records.
Research Fields: genealogy & history.
Facilities: 7,000-vol. archives; reading room. Gift items for sale.
Activities: guided tours; concerts; docent program; formal education programs for adults & children; hobby workshops; lectures; permanent & temporary exhibitions; bimonthly meetings; school tours; living history encampment. Annual Events: Old Settlers' Club Banquet; Pioneer Kids Day; Haunted Fun in October; Christmas Open House; Vintage Baseball Game.
Publications: quarterly newsletter, The Court Reporter; Annual Calendar of Events; catalogs; brochure
Hours & Admission Prices: Wed.-Fri. 11-5, Sat. 9-5, Sun. 1-4:30. Jailhouse Tour: $4. Closed New Year's Eve & Day; Easter; Mother's Day; Father's Day; Independence Day; Labor Day; Christmas Eve & Day. ♿
Attendance: 9,300 (estimated)
Membership: Student $12; Individual $15; Family $25; Patron $75; Sustaining $150; Benefactor $300; Sponsor $550; Corporate $1,000.

West Salem

HAMLIN GARLAND HOMESTEAD, 357 W. Garland St., West Salem, WI 54669-1146. Mailing Address: P.O. Box 884, West Salem, WI 54669-0884. Tel.: 608-786-1399.
Founded: 1976.
Congressional District: 3
Key Personnel: C.E.O. & Pres., Errol Kindschy.
Personnel Profile: Part-Time Volunteers 30.
Governing Authority: nonprofit organization. Owned and operated by West Salem Historical Society, Inc. Tax-exempt: 501(c)(3).
Historic House: 1857-60 Hamlin Garland Homestead.
Collections: local historical materials; musical items; fans. Historic House: 1856 Gullickson Octagonal Home.
Research Fields: Garland materials; history of West Salem area.
Facilities: 70-vol. library of books by Garland and about Garland; letters; magazines available by request. Museum-related items for sale.
Activities: guided tours; lectures; films; school loan service.
Publications: monthly newsletter.
Hours & Admission Prices: Memorial Day to Labor Day Mon.-Sat. 10-4:30,

Sun. 1-4:30; other times by appointment. Family $2.50, adults $1, students $.50; discounts to AAM members; members no charge.
Attendance: 641 (accurate)
Membership: Individual $3; Family $5; Individual Life $75; Couple Life $125.

PALMER/GULLICKSON OCTAGON HOME, 360 N. Leonard, West Salem, WI 54669-1238. Mailing Address: P.O. Box 884, West Salem, WI 54669-0884. Tel.: 608-786-1399.
Founded: 1976.
Congressional District: 3
Key Personnel: C.E.O. & Pres., Errol Kindschy.
Personnel Profile: Part-Time Volunteers 30.
Governing Authority: nonprofit organization. Owned & operated by West Salem Historical Society, Inc. Tax-exempt.
Historical Society Museum.
Collections: local historical items. Historic Building: Palmer/Gullickson Octagon Home.
Publications: monthly newsletter.
Hours & Admission Prices: Memorial Day-Labor Day Mon.-Sat. 10-5, Sun. 1-5; other times by appointment. Family $2.50, adults $1, students $.50.
Attendance: 369 (accurate)
Membership: Individual $3; Family $5; Individual Life $75; Couple Life $125.

Westfield

MARQUETTE COUNTY HISTORICAL SOCIETY, 125 Lawrence St., Westfield, WI 53964-9030. Mailing Address: Box 172, Westfield, WI 53964-0172. Tel.: 608-296-4700.
Formerly: Cochrane-Nelson House
Founded: 1962.
Congressional District: 6
Key Personnel: Pres., Ellen Martin; Vice Pres., Neil Kruger; Treas., Tim Martin; Cur., Mrs. Donald Sprain; Cur., Joannie Ingraham; Sec. & Publications Dir., Rosa Haskett.
Personnel Profile: Part-Time Volunteers 8.
Governing Authority: county. Tax-exempt: 170(b)(1)(A).
Historical Society Museum: housed in c.1903 Cochrane-Nelson House.
Collections: pictures; textiles; farm & shop tools; home, schoolroom, war, business & church artifacts pertaining to Marquette County; manuscripts; displays pertaining to granite quarrying; replica of first Ferris wheel; dental equipment c.1950; 19th-century dolls; railroad artifacts.
Research Fields: Fox River in Wisconsin; cemeteries; ethnic groups; county personages, businesses, schools, post offices & creameries; obituaries.
Facilities: files of catalogued manuscripts, library items, pictures & photographs, available for research at museum or by duplicate copy.
Activities: guided tours; temporary exhibitions.
Publications: brochure, Imprints On The Sands of Marquette County.
Hours & Admission Prices: Wed. 1-4; other times by appointment. Adults $1. ♿
Attendance: 1,000 (estimated)
Membership: Individual $10; Family & Sustaining $25; Life $200.

Weyauwega

LITTLE RED SCHOOL HOUSE MUSEUM, Weyauwega Community Park, 411 W. High St., Weyauwega, WI 54983. Mailing Address: P.O. Box 531, Weyauwega, WI 54983-0531. Tel.: 920-867-2500 & 2630.
E-mail: info@weyauwegachamber.com
Web Site: www.weyauwegachamber.com
Founded: 1970.
Congressional District: 7
Key Personnel: Caretaker, Suzanne Dyer.
Governing Authority: county. Tax-exempt.
Historic Building: housed in 1861 Old Wood School House.
Collections: old school desks; books; hand made toys; old wood heater; area maps from 1871.
Activities: tours; student demonstrations; senior citizen discussions.
Hours & Admission Prices: Memorial Day-Labor Day Mon.-Fri. 8-4:30, Sat.-Sun. 12:30-4:30; other times by appointment; special tour arrangements. No charge; donations accepted.

Whitewater

CROSSMAN GALLERY, UW-WHITEWATER, 950 W. Main St., Whitewater, WI 53190. Mailing Address: 800 W. Main Street, Whitewater, WI 53190-1705. Tel.: 262-472-5708. Fax: 262-472-2808.
E-mail: flanagam@uww.edu
Web Site: www.uww.edu
Founded: 1970.
Key Personnel: Dir., Michael Flanagan.
Personnel Profile: Part-Time Paid 1; Interns 2.
Governing Authority: university; nonprofit organization. Parent Institution: University of Wisconsin-Whitewater. Tax-exempt.
University Art Gallery.
Collections: student teaching collection; contemporary American & European; American outsider and folk art.
Research Fields: contemporary American art.
Facilities: 1,300-seat auditorium; educational facilities; 2,400 sq. ft. exhibit space; 400-seat theater.
Activities: temporary & traveling exhibitions. Museum Sponsors: biannual faculty show; 1-4 person & group invitationals. Museum Hosts: annual ceramics invitational; annual fiber show.
Publications: exhibit brochures & catalogs.
Hours & Admission Prices: Academic Year Mon.-Fri. 10-5, Sat. 1-4; Summer: call for hours. No charge. Closed Easter; Christmas. ♿
Attendance: 9,500 (accurate)

WHITEWATER HISTORICAL MUSEUM, 301 W. Whitewater St., Whitewater, WI 53190. Mailing Address: W7646 Hackett Rd., Whitewater, WI 53190-4354. Tel.: 262-473-6820.
E-mail: ccart@idcnet.com
Founded: 1974.
Congressional District: 1
Key Personnel: Pres., Ellen Penwell.
Personnel Profile: Part-Time Volunteers 1.
Governing Authority: society. Affiliated with the Whitewater Historical Society. Tax-exempt.
History Museum: housed in 1890 Chicago, Milwaukee & St. Paul Railroad depot.
Collections: china; glass; furniture; clothing & tools; books; genealogies; local artifacts.
Research Fields: local history; settlement of village; early industries; early homes; presidents.
Facilities: Museum-related items for sale.
Activities: guided tours; permanent exhibitions.
Publications: book, The Rile Collection; Sketches and Autobiography of Henry E. Rile's Whitewater Years 1856-1862.
Hours & Admission Prices: Memorial Day-Labor Day Thurs. 5:30pm-7:30pm, Sun. 1-4; other times by appointment. No charge; donations accepted. ♿
Attendance: 400 (estimated)
Membership: Annual $1; Life $25.

Wild Rose

PIONEER MUSEUM, Main St., Wild Rose, WI 54984. Mailing Address: P.O. Box 63, Wild Rose, WI 54984-0063.
Founded: 1964.
Congressional District: 6
Key Personnel: Pres. & Cur., Pam Anderson; Vice Pres., Rodney Radloff; Treas., Helen Coy; Museum Shop Mgr., Mary Ann Erdman.
Personnel Profile: Part-Time Volunteers 30.
Governing Authority: Wild Rose Historical Society. Parent Institution: State Historical Society of Wisconsin. Tax-exempt.
Pioneer Museum.
Collections: agriculture; costumes; medical; children's museum; textiles; manuscripts; Pioneer Hall & Carriage House. Historic Buildings: 1880 Elisha Stewart house; 1880 tool & buggy shed; 1860 smokehouse & blacksmith shop; 1860 cobblers shop & weaving room; 1860 drugstore-country store; one-room schoolhouse.
Research Fields: local history.
Facilities: tape recordings, manuscripts, pictures & newspapers available for use at Patterson Memorial Library. Museum-related items for sale.
Activities: guided tours; lectures; permanent & temporary exhibitions; demonstrations.
Publications: two centennial booklets; postcards.
Hours & Admission Prices: mid-June to Labor Day Wed. & Sat. 1-4. Adults $1, children 6-12 $.50; discounts to school groups; children under 6 no charge. Gift Shop: Wed. & Sat. 1-4. Closed Independence Day.
Attendance: 350 (estimated)
Membership: Annual $1.

Wisconsin Dells

BEAVER SPRINGS PUBLIC AQUARIUM, 600 Trout Rd., Wisconsin Dells, WI 53965-0001. Mailing Address: P.O. Box 1, Wisconsin Dells, WI 53965-0001. Tel.: 608-254-2735. Fax: 608-253-9446.
Aquarium.
Collections: over 1,000 fish & marine life.
Activities: hands-on exhibits; videos.
Hours & Admission Prices: April-May & Sept.-Oct. daily 10-5; June-Aug. daily 9-7; Nov.-March daily 10-4. Adults $7.99, children $5.99.

EXPLORATORY INTERACTIVE SCIENCE CENTER, 560 Wisconsin Dells Pkwy., Wisconsin Dells, WI 53965. Tel.: 608-254-2525.
Science Center.
Collections: science; technology; Mercury space capsule; Russian space station MIR; static electricity; hands-on exhibits.
Activities: hands-on exhibits.
Hours & Admission Prices: Summer: daily 9-9; Spring, Fall, & Winter: daily 10-4. Adults $12, seniors 65 & over $9.60, children 6-11 $9; discounts to groups of 20 or more; children 5 & under no charge.

H.H. BENNETT STUDIO, 215 Broadway, Wisconsin Dells, WI 53965. Mailing Address: P.O. Box 147, Wisconsin Dells, WI 53965. Tel.: 608-253-3523. Fax: 608-253-4635.
Key Personnel: Site Dir., Dale Williams; Admin. Asst. & Museum Store Mgr., Annie Kurtz
Photography Museum.
Collections: Bennett's life & family history; photographs; glass plate negatives; photography inventions; cameras & equipment.
Facilities: Museum-related items for sale.
Activities: tours.
Hours & Admission Prices: Adults $7, students and seniors 65 & over $6, children 5-17 $3.50; children under 5 no charge.

PARSON'S INDIAN TRADING POST & MUSEUM, 370 Wisconsin Dells Pkwy., Wisconsin Dells, WI 53965. Tel.: 608-254-8533; 866-281-8704.
E-mail: parsonitp@hotmail.com
Founded: 1918.
Native American History Museum.
Collections: Native American crafts; clothing weapons; household utensils; religious artifacts; jewelry.
Facilities: Museum-related items for sale.
Hours & Admission Prices: Summer: daily 9-9; Winter: daily 9-5. ♿

RIVERSIDE & GREAT NORTHERN RAILWAY, N115 County Rd. N., Wisconsin Dells, WI 53965-9124. Tel.: 608-254-6367. Fax: 608-254-5628.
Railway History Museum.
Collections: railway history, equipment, & artifacts; photographs; R&GN's locomotives & cars.
Facilities: Museum-related items for sale.
Activities: train rides.
Hours & Admission Prices: Call for hours.

TIMBAVATI WILDLIFE PARK AT STORYBOOK GARDENS, 1500 Wisconsin Dells Pkwy., (Hwy. 12), Wisconsin Dells, WI 53965. Mailing Address: P.O. Box 68, Wisconsin Dells, WI 53965-0068. Tel.: 608-253-2391.
Wildlife Park.
Collections: animals from around the world including giraffe, zebra, kangaroo, birds, & white lions.
Facilities: Museum-related items for sale.
Activities: wildlife show; camel rides; pet & feed.
Hours & Admission Prices: May to mid-Sept. daily 9-7; call for additional hours. Adults $11.95; children 2-12 $9.95; children under 2 no charge.

WISCONSIN DEER PARK, 583 Wisconsin Dells Pkwy., Wisconsin Dells, WI 53965. Tel.: 608-253-2041.
Nature Center.
Collections: wildlife including White-tail deer, American elk & bison, European Fallow deer, Japanese Silka deer, goats, birds, llamas, horses, emus, & pigs.
Facilities: nature trails.
Activities: hiking.
Hours & Admission Prices: May & Sept.-Oct. daily 10-4; Memorial Day to Labor Day daily 9-7. Adults 12 & over $10, children 3-11 $8; children 2 & under no charge. ♿

Wisconsin Rapids

SOUTH WOOD COUNTY HISTORICAL CORP., 540 Third St. S., Wisconsin Rapids, WI 54494-4352. Tel.: 715-423-1580. Fax: 715-423-6369.
E-mail: dave@swch-museum.com
Web Site: www.swch-museum.com
Founded: 1955.
Congressional District: 7
Key Personnel: Pres., Philip M. Brown; Dir., Dave Engel; Admin., Lori Brost.
Personnel Profile: Part-Time Paid 7; Part-Time Volunteers 6.
Governing Authority: nonprofit organization. Tax-exempt: 501(c)(3).
Historical Society Museum: housed in 1907 mansion.
Collections: railroad station; surveying equipment; lumbering & blacksmith items; toys; country kitchen; country school; tools, machinery, equipment & archives relating to the cranberry industry from 1870-present day.
Research Fields: local genealogy; cranberry industry; paper making.
Activities: guided tours; permanent & temporary exhibitions.
Publications: quarterly newsletter.
Hours & Admission Prices: Memorial Day to Labor Day Sun., Tues. & Thurs. 1-4. No charge; donations accepted.
Attendance: 1,883 (estimated)
Membership: Individual $15.

WYOMING

(129 listings)

Afton

STAR VALLEY DAUGHTERS OF UTAH PIONEERS HISTORICAL MUSEUM, Washington St., Afton, WY 83110. Mailing Address: P.O. Box 301, Thayne, WY 83127-0301.
Formerly: Lincoln County Daughters of Utah Pioneer Museum
Key Personnel: Pres., Carly Jensen
History Museum.
Collections: area history; Mormon history; period furnishings; photographs.
Hours & Admission Prices: June-Aug. Fri.-Sat. 11-3; other times by appointment. No charge; donations accepted.

Banner

FORT PHIL KEARNY, 528 Wagon Box Rd., Banner, WY 82832-9604. Tel.: 307-684-7629. Fax: 307-684-7967.
Web Site: www.philkearny.vcn.com
Founded: 1913.
Congressional District: 1
Key Personnel: Site Supt., Robert C. Wilson; Cur., Sonny Reisch; Dept. Dir., Milward Simpson; State Parks & Historic Sites Div. Head, Dominic Bravo.
Personnel Profile: Full-Time Paid 3; Part-Time Paid 3.
Governing Authority: state. Parent Institution: Wyoming State Parks & Cultural Resources Department. Subsidiary Institution: State Parks & Historic Sites Division. Tax-exempt.
Historic Site & Visitor Center: Fort Phil Kearny, the Wagon Box Fight site & the Fetterman Fight site.
Collections: Native American & military history.
Research Fields: Indian wars; military history.
Facilities: visitor center.
Activities: living history programs; tours.
Publications: information guide.
Hours & Admission Prices: April to mid-May & Oct.-Nov. Wed.-Sun. 12-4, weather permitting; mid-May to Sept. daily 8-6. Adults $4 (residents), $2 (non-residents). ♿
Attendance: 24,000 (accurate)

Big Horn

BRADFORD BRINTON MEMORIAL & MUSEUM, (M), 239 Brinton Rd., Big Horn, WY 82833. Mailing Address: P.O. Box 460, Big Horn, WY 82833-0460. Tel.: 307-672-3173. Fax: 307-672-3258.
E-mail: kls_bbm@vcn.com
Web Site: www.bbmandm.org
Founded: 1961.
Congressional District: 1
Key Personnel: Dir. & Chief Cur., Kenneth L. Schuster; Facility Mgr., Jon Teigland; Asst. Cur. & Registrar, Barbara Schuster; Curatorial Asst., Winifred Galloway.
Personnel Profile: Full-Time Paid 3; Part-Time Paid 10; Part-Time Volunteers 6.
Governing Authority: privately endowed. Parent Institution: The Northern Trust Company of Chicago. Tax-exempt.
Historic House and Art Museum: housed in a ranch, built 1892.
Collections: Western paintings, prints, drawings & sculpture by Frederic Remington, Charles M. Russell, Edward Borein, Frank Tenney Johnson, Winold Reiss, E. W. Gollings, Frank W. Benson & Hans Kleiber; display of Indian arts & crafts including Navajo rugs & blankets; American Indian ethnology; American West history. Historic House: 1892 Quarter Circle A ranch & ranchhouse; ranch hand quarters; Little Goose Creek Lodge.
Research Fields: American West artists; early ranching in Wyoming.
Facilities: 2,400-vol. library of art & history books available for use on-site by appointment. Books, reproductions & original art work for sale.
Activities: temporary & permanent exhibitions; gallery talks; lectures.
Publications: annual catalogs & monographs; newsletter.

Hours & Admission Prices: Memorial Day to Labor Day Mon.-Sat. 10-4, Sun. 12-4; other times by appointment. Adults $4, seniors & students over 13 $3; discounts to ICOM members; children 13 & under, members and AAM members no charge. ♿
Attendance: 10,000 (estimated)
Membership: Senior & Student 13 & over $15; Individual $20; Family $30; Contributor $55; Sponsor $100; Collector $350; Patron & Corporate Contributor $500; Benefactor & Corporate Sponsor $1,000; Little Goose Creek Lodge Club $3,000.

Big Piney

GREEN RIVER VALLEY MUSEUM, 206 N. Front St., Big Piney, WY 83113. Mailing Address: P.O. Box 12, Big Piney, WY 83113-0012. Tel.: 307-276-5343.
Web Site: www.grvm.com
Founded: 1991.
Key Personnel: Dir., Carrie Anderson; Bookkeeper, Karen Taylor.
Personnel Profile: Interns 2.
History Museum.
Collections: history & culture of Green River Valley; prehistoric Indian artifacts; early ranching & brands; ranch equipment; area oil & gas history; period oil field tools; oral histories; homesteader cabin.
Activities: tours.
Hours & Admission Prices: June 15-Oct. 15 Tues.-Sat. 10-4. No charge; donations accepted.
Membership: Member $25; Sponsor $50; Patron $100; Benefactor $500.

Buffalo

* **JIM GATCHELL MEMORIAL MUSEUM, (M),** 100 Fort St., Buffalo, WY 82834. Mailing Address: P.O. Box 596, Buffalo, WY 82834-0596. Tel.: 307-684-9331.
E-mail: jmuseum@vcn.com
Web Site: www.jimgatchell.com
Founded: 1957.
Key Personnel: C.E.O., John Gavin; Pres. (V), David Osmundsen; Museum Educator, Jennifer Romanoski; Registrar, Sylvia Bruner; Collections Asst., Charlie Brown.
Personnel Profile: Full-Time Paid 4; Part-Time Paid 12; Part-Time Volunteers 30.
Governing Authority: county. Tax-exempt.
History Museum.
Collections: military, pioneer, & Indian history in Wyoming & the West; Indian artifacts; archaeology; archives; mineralogy; military; paintings; period vehicles including chuck wagon, bed roll & supply wagon; sheep wagon; road wagon; buggies.
Research Fields: Bozeman Trail; Indian wars; Johnson County Cattle War.
Activities: guided tours; lectures; Bozeman trail map.
Publications: quarterly newsletter, The Sentry; book, Jim Gatchell the Man and the Museum.
Hours & Admission Prices: Museum: May-Sept. call for hours. Store: Mon.-Fri. 9-4. Family $12, adults $5, children 6-16 $3; discounts for AAM, ICOM, AASLH, MPMA & CWAM members; members & children under 6 no charge. ♿
Attendance: 7,500 (accurate)
Membership: Level 1 $35; Level 2 $65; Level 3 $150; Patron $2,500.

MUSEUM OF THE OCCIDENTAL, 10 N. Main St., Buffalo, WY 82834-1815. Mailing Address: P.O. Box 383, Buffalo, WY 82834-0383. Tel.: 307-684-0451. Fax: 307-684-5980.
E-mail: info@occidentalwyoming.com
Web Site: www.occidentalwyoming.com
Key Personnel: Dir., Dawn Wexo
History Museum.
Collections: photographs; documents; period artifacts.
Hours & Admission Prices: Daily 10-6. No charge.

Casper

CASPER PLANETARIUM, 904 N. Poplar St., Casper, WY 82601-1348. Tel.: 307-577-0310. Fax: 307-577-6750.
E-mail: michele_wistien@ncsd.k12.wy.us
Web Site: www.natronaschools.org/planetarium
Planetarium.
Collections: astronomy-related exhibits.
Activities: educational astronomy-related programs.
Hours & Admission Prices: Summer: Tues.-Sat. 8:30 am-9:30 pm; Winter: Sat. 6:30 am-8 pm. Closed major holidays.

FORT CASPAR MUSEUM, (M), 4001 Fort Caspar Rd., Casper, WY 82604-2923. Tel.: 307-235-8462. Fax: 307-235-8464.
E-mail: ryoung@cityofcasperwy.com
Web Site: www.fortcasparwyoming.com
Founded: 1936.
Congressional District: 1
Key Personnel: C.E.O., Richard L. Young; Cur., Michelle Bahe; Cur. Education, Erin Rose; Administrative Support Tech, Anne Holman.
Personnel Profile: Full-Time Paid 3; Part-Time Paid 3; Part-Time Volunteers 60; Interns 3.
Governing Authority: municipal. Parent Institution: City of Casper. Subsidiary Institution: Fort Caspar Museum Association. Affiliated with the Advisory Guidance of Leisure Services Board of Directors. Tax-exempt.
Social History Museum: Listed on the National Register of Historic Places.
Collections: Civil War, Indian wars, Indian & pioneer artifacts; central Wyoming materials; reconstructed c.1865 fort buildings.
Research Fields: Indian war periods; local & state history.
Facilities: interpretative center.
Activities: lectures; TV & radio programs; formally organized education programs for children; permanent & traveling exhibitions.
Publications: brochures; books, Fort Caspar; Bison Hunters to Black Gold; Frontier Crossroads: A History of Fort Caspar and the Upper Platte Crossing; The Life & Letters of Caspar W. Collins; Fort Caspar Activity Book.
Hours & Admission Prices: May & Sept. daily 8-5; June-Aug. daily 8-7; Oct.-April Tues.-Sat. 8-5. Adults $3, youth 13-18 $2; children 12 & under and members no charge. ♿
Attendance: 35,000 (estimated)
Membership: Student & Senior Citizen $10; Individual $15; Family $30; Business $250; Patron $500; Benefactor $1,000.

IDA GOODSTEIN VISUAL ARTS CENTER, Casper College, 125 College Dr., Casper, WY 82601-4612. Tel.: 307-268-2060. Fax: 307-268-3337.
E-mail: veggemeyer@caspercollege.edu
Web Site: www.caspercollege.edu
Key Personnel: Dir., Valerie Innella
Art Museum.
Collections: drawings; paintings; photography; ceramics; printmaking; graphic design; sculpture; jewelry.
Hours & Admission Prices: Mon.-Thurs. 9-4. No charge. Closed holidays.

NATIONAL HISTORIC TRAILS INTERPRETIVE CENTER, 1501 N. Poplar St., Casper, WY 82601-1375. Tel.: 307-261-7700.
History Museum.
Collections: local history & culture; period furnishings; personal artifacts; photographs; hands-on exhibits; Oregon Trail; Mormon Trail; California Trail; Pony Express Trail.
Activities: group tours; hands-on exhibits.
Hours & Admission Prices: late April to mid-Oct. daily 8-7; mid-Oct. to late April Tues.-Sat. 9-4:30. Adults $6, seniors 60 & over $5, students 16 & over $4; children 15 & under no charge. Closed New Year's Day; Easter; Thanksgiving; Christmas.

* **NICOLAYSEN ART MUSEUM AND DISCOVERY CENTER, (M),** 400 East Collins Dr., Casper, WY 82601-2815. Tel.: 307-235-5247. Fax: 307-235-0923.
E-mail: info@thenic.org
Web Site: www.thenic.org
Founded: 1967.
Congressional District: 1
Key Personnel: Bd. Chm. (V), Val Innella; Exec. Dir., Holly Turner; Registrar, Ingrid Burnett; Cur., Lisa Hatchodoorian; Museum Shop Mgr., TimAnn Day; Museum Shop Mgr., Jan DeBeer; Asst. Cur. Education, Jim Kopp; Dir. Operations, Val Kulhavy; Volunteer Svcs., Lori Klatt; Cur. Education, Linda Lyman; Asst. Cur. Education, Lisa Vlastos; Public Rels., Clay Anthony.
Personnel Profile: Full-Time Paid 11; Part-Time Paid 7; Part-Time Volunteers 50; Interns 3.
Governing Authority: private; nonprofit organization. Tax-exempt: 501(c)(3).
Art Museum.
Collections: regional contemporary art.
Major Exhibits: Artecoop: The Aesthetics of the New Energy Economy (T), 11/09-1/3/10; Karen Kitchel, 1/22/10-4/11/10; Kate Petley, 1/22/10-4/11/10.
Research Fields: contemporary art.
Facilities: discovery center.
Activities: traveling exhibitions; workshops; lectures; hands-on; self guided; art making; formally organized education programs for children & adults.
Publications: newsletters; catalogs.
Hours & Admission Prices: Tues.-Sat. 10-5, Sun. 12-4. Adults $5; discounts to AAM & ICOM members. Closed holidays. ♿

Attendance: 50,000 (accurate)
Membership: Individual $35; Family $60; Business $250.

THE SCIENCE ZONE, INC., (M), 3960 S. Poplar St., Sunrise Center, Casper, WY 82601-5921. Mailing Address: P.O. Box 2701, Mills, WY 82644-2701. Tel.: 307-473-9663. Fax: 307-261-6131.
Key Personnel: Exec. Dir., Kevin Jones
Science Center.
Collections: hands-on science exhibits.
Activities: educational programs.
Hours & Admission Prices: Mon.-Sat. 10-5. Adults $4, children $3; discounts to groups of 10 or more; children under 3 no charge.
Membership: Family $50.

TATE GEOLOGICAL MUSEUM, (M), Casper College, 125 College Dr., Casper, WY 82601-4612. Tel.: 307-268-2447. Fax: 307-268-3308.
E-mail: dschaff@caspercollege.edu
Web Site: www.caspercollege.edu/tate/webpage.htm
Founded: 1979.
Key Personnel: Dir., Deanna K. Schaff; Public Rels., Lisa Icenogle.
Personnel Profile: Full-Time Paid 3; Part-Time Volunteers 54.
Governing Authority: public college. Parent Institution: Casper College. Tax-exempt.
Geology Museum.
Collections: paleontological & mineralogical heritage of Wyoming.
Publications: bimonthly newsletter, Tate Museum Geological Times.
Hours & Admission Prices: Mon.-Fri. 9-5, Sat. 10-4. No charge; donations accepted.
Attendance: 9,000 (accurate)
Membership: Individual: Basic $10; Family $25; Supporting $50; Sustaining $100; Sponsor $250; Defender $500; Patron $1,000 & up. Business: Small Business $100; Company $250; Corporate $1,000 & up.

WERNER WILDLIFE MUSEUM, Casper College, 125 College Dr., Casper, WY 82601-4612. Tel.: 307-235-2108.
Founded: 1970.
Key Personnel: Dir., Thomas Clifford
Wildlife Museum.
Collections: wildlife from Wyoming & around the world.
Activities: tours.
Hours & Admission Prices: Mon., Wed. & Fri. 1-5, Tues. & Thurs. 8:30-5. No charge; donations accepted. Closed school holidays. ♿

WYOMING VETERANS' MEMORIAL MUSEUM, 3740 Jourgensen Ave., Casper, WY 82604. Mailing Address: P.O. Box 1677, Casper, WY 82602-1677. Tel.: 307-472-1857.
E-mail: jgoss@state.wy.us
Web Site: www.wvmm.org
Founded: 2001.
Key Personnel: Dir., John G. Goss; Founder, Joye Kading; Cur., Eric Wimmer.
Personnel Profile: Full-Time Paid 1; Part-Time Volunteers 7.
Governing Authority: Parent Institution: Wyoming Military Department.
Military History Museum.
Collections: Casper Army Air Base heritage; oral military history & equipment; photographs; veterans memorial; archives; photographs.
Research Fields: military history & personnel; Casper Army Air Base heritage.
Facilities: library; archives.
Activities: lectures; workshops; guided tours.
Hours & Admission Prices: Winter: Tues.-Sat. 9-4, Sun. 1-4. No charge. ♿
Attendance: 1,000 (accurate)

Centennial

NICI SELF MUSEUM, 2734 Hwy. 130, Centennial, WY 82055. Mailing Address: P.O. Box 201, Centennial, WY 82055-0201. Tel.: 307-742-7763.
E-mail: cagoldie@msn.com
Founded: 1974.
Congressional District: 1
Key Personnel: Chm. (V) & Pres. (V), Jim Chase; Vice Pres. (V), Dick Clifton; Sec., Nancy Taft; Treas., Cecily Goldie.
Personnel Profile: Part-Time Volunteers 30; Interns 1.
Governing Authority: nonprofit organization. Parent Institution: Centennial Valley Historical Association. Tax-exempt: 501(c)(3).
History Museum: housed in 1907 Railroad Depot located at the base of the Medicine Bow Mountains.
Collections: railroad equipment; 1944 Union Pacific caboose; gold & platinum mining; lumbering & ranching; Native American artifacts.
Research Fields: newspapers & books of the area.
Activities: educational & research activities; special tours. Annual Event: art show.
Publications: book, Centennial, Wyoming 1876-1976: The Real Centennial; annual letter to members.
Hours & Admission Prices: mid-June to Labor Day Thurs.-Mon. 12-4. No charge; donations accepted.
Attendance: 1,047 (estimated)
Membership: Individual $5; Family $10; Life $50.

Cheyenne

CHEYENNE BOTANIC GARDENS, (M), 710 S. Lions Park Dr., Cheyenne, WY 82001-7503. Tel.: 307-637-6458. Fax: 307-637-6453.
E-mail: info@botanic.org
Web Site: www.botanic.org
Founded: 1976.
Key Personnel: Dir., Shane Smith; Chm. (V), Joe Bonds; Asst. Dir., Claus Johnson; Dir. Devel., Riana Perez; Head Horticulture, Steve Scott; Horticulturist, Sue Whetten; Exec. Sec., Trudy Fox.
Personnel Profile: Full-Time Paid 6; Part-Time Volunteers 60; Interns 2.
Governing Authority: municipal government. Tax-exempt.
Botanical Garden.
Collections: plants; trees; flowers.
Facilities: library available to public; educational facilities.
Activities: guided tours; lectures; broadcast programs; passive solar energy demonstration; Wetland Discovery area; horticultural therapy for seniors & youth at risk. Annual Events: Stain Glass Show; Perennial Plant Exchange.
Publications: quarterly newsletter, The Cheyenne Garden Gazette.
Hours & Admission Prices: Grounds: daily dawn-dusk. Conservatory: Mon.-Fri. 8-4:30, Sat.-Sun. 11-3:30. No charge; donations accepted. Closed New Year's Day; Easter; Thanksgiving; Christmas. ♿
Attendance: 42,525 (accurate)
Membership: Individual $25; Family $35; Business Associate $65; Sustaining $100; Business Circle $250; Ponderosa Patron $500.

CHEYENNE DEPOT MUSEUM, Number One Depot Sq., 115 W. 15th, Cheyenne, WY 82001. Mailing Address: P.O. Box 2160, Cheyenne, WY 82003-2160. Tel.: 307-632-3905.
E-mail: waynehasenII@hotmail.com
Web Site: www.cheyennedepotmuseum.org
Formerly: Wyoming Transportation Museum
Founded: 2002.
Key Personnel: Dir., Wayne N. Hansen.
Personnel Profile: Full-Time Paid 2; Full-Time Volunteers 1; Part-Time Paid 9; Part-Time Volunteers 11.
Governing Authority: Tax-exempt.
History Museum.
Collections: period artifacts.
Hours & Admission Prices: Mon.-Fri. 9-7, Sat. 9-5, Sun. 11-5. ♿

CHEYENNE FRONTIER DAYS OLD WEST MUSEUM, (M), 4610 N. Carey Ave., Cheyenne, WY 82001-7505. Mailing Address: P.O. Box 2720, Cheyenne, WY 82003-2720. Tel.: 307-778-7290. Fax: 307-778-7288.
Web Site: oldwestmuseum.org
Founded: 1978.
Key Personnel: Dir., Wayne N. Hansen; Assoc. Dir., Chris Bird; Pres., Carol Farthing; Exhibits, Michael Kassel; Cur. Collections, Bob Gant; Facilities Mgr., Ron Duckworth; Public Programs Coord., Debbie Love; Devel., Tiffany Smith; Bookkeeper & Sec., Marcia Biedermann; Volunteer Coord., Janet Wampler; Weekend Security, Wil Madrid.
Personnel Profile: Full-Time Paid 7; Part-Time Paid 5; Part-Time Volunteers 394.
Governing Authority: nonprofit organization. Tax-exempt: 501(c)(3).
History Museum.
Collections: Cheyenne frontier days rodeo collection, horse-drawn vehicle collection, Western art collection, Cheyenne & Wyoming history.
Research Fields: Cheyenne Frontier Days; Cheyenne; Laramie County.
Facilities: 1,000-vol. library of books on Cheyenne Frontier Days, western history & Cheyenne-Wyoming history; educational facilities. Educational & souvenir items pertaining to western history, rodeo & Cheyenne Frontier Days for sale.
Activities: guided tours; school loan service; formally organized education programs. Museum Sponsors: Western Spirit Art Show & Sale; Western Invitational Art Show & Sale.
Publications: quarterly newsletter, The Stageline.
Hours & Admission Prices: Mon.-Fri. 9-5, Sat.-Sun. 10-5. Adults $7; discounts to AAM members & groups; children under 12 & members no charge. Closed New Year's Day; Presidents' Day; Easter; Thanksgiving; Christmas. ♿
Attendance: 45,000 (estimated)
Membership: Senior $20; Individual $35; Family $50; Phaeton $150; Brougham $500; Lifetime $2,000.

COWGIRLS OF THE WEST, 205 W. 17th St., Cheyenne, WY 82001-4411. Tel.: 307-638-4994.
Web Site: www.wyomingcowgirlsofthewest.com
Founded: 1994.
Key Personnel: Pres. (V), Carol Barnett; Dir., Chris Caltagirone.
Governing Authority: nonprofit organization.
History Museum.
Collections: history of the western cowgirl & pioneering women; western culture; photographs; personal artifacts.
Activities: special events. Museum Sponsors: Frontier Days in July.
Hours & Admission Prices: Jan. 16-Dec. Tues.-Fri. 11-4, Sat. 11-3. No charge.

THE ESTHER AND JOHN CLAY FINE ARTS GALLERY, Laramie County Community College, Fine Arts Bldg., 1400 E. College Dr., Cheyenne, WY 82007-3204. Tel.: 307-777-1158.
Web Site: www.lccc.wy.edu
Art Gallery.
Collections: paintings; sculpture; ceramics; drawings.
Hours & Admission Prices: Mon.-Fri. 8-5. No charge.

HISTORIC GOVERNORS' MANSION, 300 E. 21st. St., Cheyenne, WY 82001-3712. Mailing Address: Dept. of State Parks & Cultural Resources, Barrett Bldg., Cheyenne, WY 82002-0001. Tel.: 307-777-7878. Fax: 307-635-7077.
E-mail: sphs@state.wy.us
Web Site: www.artsparkhistory.com
Founded: 1904.
Key Personnel: Dir. Div. Parks, Domenic Bravo; Supt., Deborah Amend.
Personnel Profile: Full-Time Paid 1; Part-Time Volunteers 2; Interns 1.
Governing Authority: state. Parent Institution: Dept. of State Parks & Cultural Resources, Barrett Bldg., Cheyenne, WY 82002. Tax-exempt.
Historic Building: 1904 Colonial Revival Mansion & Carriage House.
Collections: turn-of-the-century art, photographs, quilts; 1937 Chicago Furniture Mart furnishings; furnishings belonging to the first families of Wyoming including Nellie Taylor Ross, the first elected woman governor of the US in 1925.
Major Exhibits: Christmas Tinsel Through Time, 12/09; Christmas Tinsel Through Time, 12/10.
Research Fields: political history of the state of Wyoming.
Facilities: limited on-site research materials.
Activities: guided tours; public programs; historic hospitality house; video tour; touch screen kiosks; audio tours; cell phone tours.
Publications: information guide; self-guided brochure.
Hours & Admission Prices: June-Aug. Mon.-Sat. 9-5, Sun. 1-5; Sept.-May Tues.-Sat. 9-5; groups by appointment. No charge; donations accepted. Closed most holidays. ♿
Attendance: 10,189 (accurate)

NELSON MUSEUM OF THE WEST, (M), 1714 Carey Ave., Cheyenne, WY 82001-4420. Tel.: 307-635-7670.
E-mail: director@nelsonmuseum.com
Web Site: www.nelsonmuseum.com
Founded: 1998.
Key Personnel: Dir., Robert Nelson; Pres. (V), Beth Nelson; Museum Shop Mgr., Dale Beard.
Governing Authority: Tax-exempt.
History Museum.
Collections: cowboy & American Indian artifacts; Western fine art; rodeo; paintings; sculpture; beadwork; pottery; weavings; spurs; baskets; chaps; saddles; period firearms; military; outlaws & lawmen; wildlife mounts from around the world; U.S. Cavalry artifacts including uniforms, saddles, & weapons; U.S. Army & Air Force officers uniforms.
Hours & Admission Prices: May-Aug. Mon.-Sat. 9-4:30; Sept.-Nov. 1 Mon.-Fri. 9-4:30; other times by appointment. Adults $4, seniors 65 & over $2; discounts to groups and AAM & ICOM members; children under 12 no charge. ♿
Attendance: 5,000 (accurate)

WYOMING ARTS COUNCIL GALLERY, 2320 Capitol Ave., Cheyenne, WY 82002-0001. Tel.: 307-777-7742. Fax: 307-777-5499. TDD: 307-777-5964.
E-mail: rbasom@state.wy.us
Web Site: www.wyomingartscouncil.org
Founded: 1976.
Congressional District: 7
Key Personnel: Program Mgr., Rita Basom.
Personnel Profile: Full-Time Paid 9.
Governing Authority: state. Subsidiary Institution: Commerce Department, Division of Cultural Resources, Cheyenne, WY. Tax-exempt: 501(c)(3).
Art Gallery: located in the historic Kendrick House.
Collections: concentration on Wyoming artists living & working in the state; the gallery does not maintain a permanent collection.
Facilities: library of periodicals including Art in America, Sculpture, Art Calendar, American Crafts, The Crafts Report; 700 sq. ft. exhibit space.
Activities: lectures.
Hours & Admission Prices: Mon.-Fri. 8-5. No charge; donations accepted. Closed major holidays. ♿
Attendance: 1,200 (estimated)

* **WYOMING STATE MUSEUM, (M),** 2301 Central Ave., Barrett Bldg., Cheyenne, WY 82001-3110. Tel.: 307-777-7022. Fax: 307-777-5375.
E-mail: mvigil@state.wy.us
Web Site: wyomuseum.state.wy.us
Founded: 1895.
Key Personnel: Museum Supvr., Manny Vigil; Pres. (V), Carolyn Turbiville; Supvr. Interpretation & Education, Heyward Schrock; Supvr. Collections, Jennifer Alexander; Supvr. Collections, Jim Allison; Education Cur., Sarah Ligocki; Cur. Collections, Mandy Langfald; Cur. Collections, Mariah Emmons; Cur. Education, Sarah Wigocki; Registrar, Dominique Schultes; Exhibits Designer, Larry Lujan; Museum Store Mgr., Beth Miller.
Personnel Profile: Full-Time Paid 10; Part-Time Volunteers 60; Interns 1.
Governing Authority: state. Parent Institution: State of Wyoming. Subsidiary Institution: Dept. of State Parks & Cultural Resources. Tax-exempt.
State History Museum.
Collections: over 100,000 artifacts related to Wyoming's heritage; textiles; firearms; household artifacts; Native American artifacts.
Research Fields: History Museum.
Facilities: meeting room. Museum-related items for sale.
Activities: guided tours; programs; monthly lecture series; monthly children's programs; temporary & traveling exhibitions; discovery trunks for schools statewide; demonstrations; workshops.
Publications: exhibition brochures & handouts.
Hours & Admission Prices: May-Oct. Mon.-Sat. 9-4:30; Nov.-April Mon.-Fri. 9-4:30, Sat. 10-2. No charge; donations accepted. Closed state & federal holidays. ♿
Attendance: 25,000 (estimated)
Membership: Active $12; Associate $25; Benefactor $50-$100, $100-$200, $200 & up.

Chugwater

CHUGWATER MUSEUM, Main St., Chugwater, WY 82210. Mailing Address: P.O. Box 33, Chugwater, WY 82210-0033. Tel.: 307-422-3227.
History Museum.
Collections: local history; period furnishings; tools; horsedrawn farm equipment; sheep wagon; caboose; early office & business equipment; maps.
Activities: research.
Hours & Admission Prices: Memorial Day to Labor Day Sat.-Sun. & holidays 1-4; other times by appointment. No charge; donations accepted.

Clearmont

UCROSS FOUNDATION ART GALLERY, 30 Big Red Lane, Clearmont, WY 82835-9723. Tel.: 307-737-2291. Fax: 307-737-2322.
E-mail: info@ucross.org
Art Gallery.
Collections: works by contemporary artists; local history. Historic House: 1880s ranch house.
Hours & Admission Prices: Mon.-Fri. 8:30-4, Sat. by appointment. No charge. Closed major holidays.

Cody

BIG HORN GALLERIES, 1167 Sheridan Ave., Cody, WY 82414-3627. Tel.: 307-527-7587. Fax: 307-527-7586.
Art Gallery.
Collections: western & wildlife art and landscapes.
Hours & Admission Prices: Call for hours.

BUFFALO BILL DAM VISITOR CENTER, 47 Lakeside Dr., Cody, WY 82414-8501. Tel.: 307-527-6076.
Governing Authority: nonprofit organization.
History Museum.
Collections: dam & Big Horn Basin history; photographs.
Facilities: Museum-related items for sale.
Hours & Admission Prices: May & Sept. Mon.-Sat. 8-6, Sun. 10-6; June-Aug. Mon.-Fri. 8-8, Sat. 8-6, Sun. 10-6. No charge; donations accepted.

* **BUFFALO BILL HISTORICAL CENTER, (M),** 720 Sheridan Ave., Cody, WY 82414-3428. Tel.: 307-587-4771, ext. 0. Fax: 307-578-4066.
E-mail: leeh@bbhc.org
Web Site: www.bbhc.org
Founded: 1917.
Congressional District: 1
Key Personnel: Exec. Dir., Bruce Eldredge; Chm. (V), Alan K. Simpson; Dir. Devel., Wendy K. Schneider; Cur. Whitney Gallery of Western Art, Mindy Besaw; Cur. Plains Indian Museum, Emma Hansen; Cur. Draper Museum of Natural History, Dr. Charles Preston; Cur. Research Library, Dr. Kurt Graham; Cur. Buffalo Bill Museum, John Rumm; Dir. Public Rels., Lee Haines; Accounting Mgr., Meg Kath; Facilities Mgr., Paul Brock; Museum Shop Mgr., Kelly Webber.
Personnel Profile: Full-Time Paid 86; Part-Time Paid 60; Part-Time Volunteers 150; Interns 9.
Governing Authority: nonprofit organization. Owned and operated by Buffalo Bill Memorial Association. Tax-exempt.
Art/History/Natural Museum Complex: consisting of five collections of the America West.
Collections: Western memorabilia including personal possessions of Buffalo Bill Cody & his Wild West show. Whitney Gallery of Western Art: paintings & sculpture. Plains Indian Museum: ethnological & archaeological materials. Cody Firearms Museum: 16th-century to present American-European firearms; study gallery of firearms; two sculpture gardens; Powwow garden. Draper Museum of Natural History: vertebrate zoology, geology & paleontology of the Yellowstone region. Historic Buildings: 1842 Buffalo Bill's boyhood home; 1905 Joseph Henry Sharp cabin.
Major Exhibits: Splendid Heritage, 4/10-9/10.
Research Fields: American firearms; Western art & history; Buffalo Bill; Native American studies; Yellowstone Sights & Sounds.
Facilities: 20,000-vol. library of books, manuscripts & 250,000 photographs pertaining to Western Americana available for research on premises; archives; 190,000 sq. ft. exhibit space; restaurant. Books & museum-related items for sale.
Activities: inter-museum loan exhibitions; permanent & loan exhibitions of Western art and Americana; public programs; seminars; symposiums; receptions & fund-raising events. Museum Sponsors: Larom Institute of Western American Studies; Plains Indian Seminar; Powwow. Traces of Tradition: How We Live, Work and Play in the West.
Publications: newsletter, Points West; catalogues; annual report; exhibition & gallery brochures.
Hours & Admission Prices: May-Sept. 15 daily 8-6; Sept. 16-Oct. daily 8-5; Nov.-March Thurs.-Sun. 10-5. Adults $15, senior $13, student 18 & over with ID $13, youth 6-17 $10; discounts to groups; children under 6 & members no charge. Closed New Year's Day; Thanksgiving; Christmas. ♿
Attendance: 200,000 (accurate)
Membership: Individual $35; Family $60; Centennial $100; Cody Firearms $150-$1,000; Sponsor $250; Sustaining $500; Benefactor $1,000; Pahaska League $2,000; Corporate membership available.

MUSEUM OF THE OLD WEST & OLD TRAIL TOWN, 1831 DeMaris Dr., Cody, WY 82414. Mailing Address: P.O. Box 546, Cody, WY 82414-0546. Tel.: 307-587-5302.
Historic Buildings: 26 buildings built 1879-1901.
Collections: local history & culture; guns; period furnishings & clothing; over 100 horse drawn vehicles; Native American artifacts. Historic Buildings: saloon; livery barn; blacksmith shop; general stores; post office; schools; Butch Cassidy and the Sundance Kid's cabin.
Hours & Admission Prices: mid-May to Sept.

SIMPSON GALLAGHER GALLERY, 1161 Sheridan Ave., Cody, WY 82414-3627. Tel.: 307-587-4022.
E-mail: sue@simpsongallaghergallery.com
Web Site: www.simpsongallaghergallery.com
Founded: 1994.
Art Gallery.
Collections: landscape paintings; wildlife sculpture; western intaglios.
Hours & Admission Prices: Call for hours. ♿

TECUMSAH'S OLD WEST MINIATURE VILLAGE & MUSEUM, 142 W. Yellowstone Ave., Cody, WY 82414. Mailing Address: 140 W. Yellowstone Ave., Cody, WY 82414-8735. Tel.: 307-587-5362.
Web Site: www.tecumsehs.com
Key Personnel: Owner, Jerry Fick
History Museum.
Collections: miniature village depicting 19th century frontier history in Wyoming; Geronimo's bow, arrows, & quiver; guns; Native American & cowboy artifacts.
Activities: school tours.
Hours & Admission Prices: June-Aug. 8am-9pm; Sept.-May 9-6; Winter: call for hours. Adults $5, seniors & students 13-18 $3, children 7-12 $2; children 6 & under no charge.

Colter Bay Village

GRAND TETON NATIONAL PARK, COLTER BAY INDIAN ARTS MUSEUM, Colter Bay Visitor Center, Grand Teton National Park, Colter Bay Village, WY 83012. Mailing Address: P.O. Drawer 170, Moose, WY 83012-0170. Tel.: 307-739-3494. Fax: 307-739-3504.
E-mail: alice_hart@nps.gov
Web Site: www.nps.gov/grte/
Founded: 1972.
Key Personnel: Cur., Alice Hart; Ranger Naturalist, Laine Thom.
Personnel Profile: Full-Time Paid 1; Part-Time Paid 18.
Governing Authority: federal. Parent Institution: National Park Service. Subsidiary Institution: Grand Teton National Park. Tax-exempt: 501(c)(3).
Indian Arts Museum.
Collections: Colter Bay Indian Art Museum: David T. Vernon Indian Art collection; 1875-1900 Native American reservation period pieces.
Facilities: theater-Colter Bay. Descriptive & interpretive items on natural & local history for sale.
Activities: guided walks; illustrated talks; films; Indian cultural demonstrations.
Publications: booklets; leaflets; paperbacks.
Hours & Admission Prices: May-June 1 & Sept. 2-Oct. 13 daily 8-5; June 2-Sept. 1 daily 8-7. No charge; donations accepted. ♿

Devils Tower

DEVILS TOWER VISITOR CENTER, Devils Tower National Monument, State Hwy. 110, Bldg. 170, Devils Tower, WY 82714. Mailing Address: P.O. Box 10, Devils Tower, WY 82714-0010. Tel.: 307-467-5283. Fax: 307-467-5350.
E-mail: christine_czazasty@nps.gov
Web Site: www.nps.gov/deto
Founded: 1906.
Congressional District: 1
Key Personnel: Chief Resources Mgmt. & Cur., Mark Biel; Supt., Dorothy Firecloud.
Personnel Profile: Full-Time Paid 9; Part-Time Paid 15; Part-Time Volunteers 5.
Governing Authority: federal. U.S. Dept. of the Interior, National Park Service. Tax-exempt.
National Monument Museum; 1930s CCC/WPA log building.
Collections: geology; history; botany; Indian artifacts.
Research Fields: history; geology; botany; local Indian artifacts.
Facilities: limited access library.
Activities: guided walks; talks in summer; cultural program series.
Publications: brochures on local rock climbing history, natural history & geology.
Hours & Admission Prices: April-Oct. Call for hours. Monument: $10 per vehicle. No charge for visitors center; donations accepted; discounts to Devils Tower Natural History Assoc. members. Visitors Center closed in winter. ♿
Attendance: 358,000
Membership: Devils Tower Natural History Association: Single $10; Family & Associate $25.

Diamondville

STOLEN BELL MUSEUM, 316 Diamondville Ave., Diamondville, WY 83116. Mailing Address: P.O. Box 281, Diamondville, WY 83116-0281. Tel.: 307-877-6676.
History Museum.
Collections: area history; photographs; personal artifacts.
Hours & Admission Prices: Temporarily closed.

Douglas

DOUGLAS RAILROAD INTERPRETIVE CENTER, 121 Brownfield Rd., Douglas, WY 82633-2558. Tel.: 307-358-2950. Fax: 307-358-2972.
Historic Building: housed in the former Fremont, Elkhorn and Missouri Valley Railroad depot; built in 1886.
Collections: railroad history & artifacts; photographs; period furnishings.
Hours & Admission Prices: Summer: Mon.-Fri. 8-8, Sat.-Sun. 10-5; Winter: Mon.-Fri. 8-5, Sat.-Sun. 11-4.

FORT FETTERMAN STATE HISTORIC SITE, 752 Hwy. 93, Douglas, WY 82633-9267. Mailing Address: P.O. Box 911, Douglas, WY 82633-0911. Tel.: 307-358-2864 & 9288. Fax: 307-358-2864 & 9293.
E-mail: aeklan@state.wy.us
Formerly: Fort Fetterman State Museum
Founded: 1963.
Key Personnel: C.E.O., Dominic Bravo; Site Supvr., Arlene Ekland-Earnst; Museum Shop Mgr., Peg Fetterman.
Personnel Profile: Full-Time Paid 1; Part-Time Paid 2; Part-Time Volunteers 1.
Governing Authority: state. Parent Institution: Wyoming Dept. of State Parks & Cultural Resources. Subsidiary Institution: Wyoming State Parks & Historic Sites. Tax-exempt: 170(b)(1)(A).
Military Museum: housed in 1867-1882 historic Fort Fetterman Officer's Quarters & ordnance building on original site.
Collections: military exhibits & artifacts; archaeology; early wagons. Historic Building: Ordnance Building.
Research Fields: history of Fort Fetterman.
Facilities: Publications & museum-related items for sale.
Activities: living history demonstrations & crafts. Museum Sponsors: Ft. Fetterman Days.
Publications: information guide; site brochure.
Hours & Admission Prices: Memorial Day to Labor Day daily 9-5. Non-residents $4, residents $2; children under 17 no charge. ♿
Attendance: 10,000 (accurate)

WYOMING PIONEER MEMORIAL MUSEUM, Wyoming State Fairgrounds, 400 W. Center St., Douglas, WY 82633. Mailing Address: P.O. Box 911, Douglas, WY 82633-0911. Tel.: 307-358-9288. Fax: 307-358-9293.
E-mail: aeklan@state.wy.us
Web Site: www.spacr.state.wy.us
Founded: 1956.
Key Personnel: Dir. & Cur., Arlene E. Earnst.
Personnel Profile: Full-Time Paid 2; Part-Time Paid 1; Part-Time Volunteers 2.
Governing Authority: state. Parent Institution: State of Wyoming. Tax-exempt.
General Museum.
Collections: Indian artifacts; pioneer relics; textiles; agriculture; pioneer costumes. Historic Houses: 1886 schoolhouse; 1896 first log cabin museum; original 1925 log cabin museum.
Activities: permanent & temporary exhibitions.
Hours & Admission Prices: Summer: Mon.-Fri. 8-5, Sat. 1-5; Winter: Mon.-Fri. 8-5. No charge. Closed national holidays. ♿
Attendance: 20,000

Dubois

DUBOIS MUSEUM, 909 West Ramshorn, Dubois, WY 82513. Mailing Address: P.O. Box 896, Dubois, WY 82513-0896. Tel.: 307-455-2284. Fax: 307-455-2912.
E-mail: dmuseum@dteworld.com
Web Site: duboismuseum.org
Formerly: Wind River Historical Center Dubois Museum
Founded: 1976.
Key Personnel: Dir., Norma Williamson.
Personnel Profile: Full-Time Paid 2; Part-Time Paid 4.
Governing Authority: county; nonprofit. Subsidiary Institution: Fremont County Museum, 450 N. Second St., Rm. 320, Lander, WY 82520. Tax-exempt.
Local History & Natural History Museum and Interpretive Center.
Collections: history of the Wind River Valley in northwest Wyoming; Scandinavian tie-hack history; Mountain Shoshone archaeology; Indian artifacts; timbering relics; wildlife mounts; ranch equipment; rocks; historical documents; photographs; saddles; historic buildings; oral history file; manuscripts; CM Guest Ranch collection.
Research Fields: local & natural history.
Facilities: library of local history, historical photographs, letters, newspapers, wild game available to writers, students & researchers upon request; reading room.
Activities: guided tours; formally organized education programs.
Hours & Admission Prices: Winter: Tues.-Sat. 10-4. Summer: daily 9-6. Adults $2, children $.50; members no charge.
Attendance: 10,500 (accurate)
Membership: Single $10; Family $15; Contributing $25; Century Club $100.

NATIONAL BIGHORN SHEEP INTERPRETIVE CENTER, (M), 907 W. Ramshorn St., Dubois, WY 82513. Mailing Address: P.O. Box 1435, Dubois, WY 82513-1435. Tel.: 307-455-3429.
E-mail: info@bighorn.org
Web Site: www.bighorn.org
Founded: 1993.
Congressional District: 1
Key Personnel: Exec. Dir., Suzan Moulton; Pres. (V), Robert Betts.
Personnel Profile: Full-Time Paid 1; Full-Time Volunteers 2; Part-Time Paid 1; Part-Time Volunteers 11.
Governing Authority: private; nonprofit organization. Tax-exempt: 501(c)(3).
Nature Center.
Collections: life-size dioramas; interactive exhibits; mounted specimens of wild sheep of the world.
Facilities: 4,000 sq. ft. exhibit space; nature center; 30-seat large screen theater. Museum-related items for sale.
Activities: guided wildlife tours; lectures; school loan service. Annual Events: birthday in July; fundraiser banquet in November.
Publications: quarterly newsletter, Sheep Tracks.
Hours & Admission Prices: Memorial Day to Labor Day daily 9-7; Sept.-May Mon.-Sat. 9-5. Adults $2.50, children $.75; members no charge. Closed New Year's Day; Easter; Thanksgiving; Christmas. ♿
Attendance: 10,000 (estimated)
Membership: Junior $5; Individual $25; Family $50; Business & Sponsor $100; Partner $250; Patron's Circle $500; Summit Club Member $1,000.

Encampment

GRAND ENCAMPMENT MUSEUM, INC., 807 Barnett Ave., Encampment, WY 82325. Mailing Address: P.O. Box 43, Encampment, WY 82325-0043. Tel.: 307-327-5308 & 5101 (off season). Fax: 307-327-5427.
E-mail: gemuseum@aol.com
Web Site: www.grandencampmentmuseum.org
Founded: 1965.
Key Personnel: Pres. (V), Kate Moon; Cur. & Museum Shop Mgr., Candy Moulton.
Personnel Profile: Part-Time Paid 4; Part-Time Volunteers 25.
Governing Authority: nonprofit organization. Tax-exempt: 501(c)(3).
Mining Museum.
Collections: transportation; local history; general items; costumes; uniforms; glass; Indian artifacts; mining; manuscript collections; U.S. Forest Service display; Andrikopolis hat cleaning shop; Civil War, World War I, World War II & Korean War display; Civil Conservation Corps display; schoolhouse; lookout tower; air force display; Mason's display.
Research Fields: local history; U.S. Forest Service; World War I & World War II; Civil Conservation Corps.
Facilities: 200-vol. library of history books, manuscripts, letters available for use on premises. Maps, brochures, books, bottles, rocks for sale.
Activities: guided tours; permanent exhibitions.
Publications: annual newsletter; brochure, Encampment Museum; maps: Map of Grand Encampment & Riverside; The Grand Encampment; Relief Map of the Grand Encampment Mining District 1903.
Hours & Admission Prices: Memorial Weekend-Labor Day Mon.-Sat. 10-5, Sun. 1-5. No charge; donations accepted.
Attendance: 4,013 (accurate)
Membership: Individual (1 year) $10; Life $100.

Evanston

CHINESE JOSS HOUSE MUSEUM, 920 Front St., Evanston, WY 82930-3464. Mailing Address: 1200 Main St., Evanston, WY 82930-3316. Tel.: 307-783-6320.
E-mail: museum@uintanet.com
Web Site: www.uintacounty.com/index.asp?NID=195
Founded: 1940.
Governing Authority: city.
Chinese History Museum: housed in a replica of the 19th century Chinese temple that stood in Evanston's Chinatown.
Collections: Chinese history; photographs; ceramic & metal artifacts; medicinal materials.
Activities: Annual Event: Chinese New Year in February.
Hours & Admission Prices: Mon.-Fri. 9-5, Sat. 10-4. No charge; donations accepted.

UINTA COUNTY MUSEUM, 1020 Front St., Evanston, WY 82930-3437. Tel.: 307-789-8248; 888-989-8248.
Founded: 1987.
Key Personnel: Dir., Barbara Allen Bogart; Cur., M. Kay Rossiter.
Governing Authority: county. Tax-exempt.
History Museum.
Collections: Uinta county history & culture; photographs.
Hours & Admission Prices: Mon.-Fri. 9-5, Sat. 10-4. No charge. ♿
Attendance: 4,000 (accurate)

Evansville

RESHAW EXHIBIT, 235 Curtis, Evansville Center, Evansville, WY 82636. Mailing Address: P.O. Drawer 158, Evansville, WY 82636-0158. Tel.: 307-234-6530. Fax: 307-266-5109.
E-mail: town_evansville@bresnan.net
Web Site: www.townofevansville.gov
Founded: 1963.
Key Personnel: Chm. (V), Caroline Buff; Financial Dir., Shirley Rogers; Clerk & Treas., Janelle Underwood.
Governing Authority: municipal. Tax-exempt.
History Museum.
Collections: Indian & pioneer artifacts.
Activities: permanent exhibitions.
Hours & Admission Prices: Mon.-Fri. 8-5. No charge. Closed holidays. ♿
Attendance: 225 (estimated)

Fort Bridger

FORT BRIDGER STATE MUSEUM, 37,000 Business Loop I-80, Fort Bridger, WY 82933. Mailing Address: P.O. Box 35, Fort Bridger, WY 82933-0035. Tel.: 307-782-3842. Fax: 307-782-7181.
E-mail: lnewma@state.wy.us
Web Site: www.artsparkshistory.com
Founded: 1843.
Key Personnel: Dir., Milward Simpson; Dept. Dir., Mr. Domenic Bravo; Cur., Cecil Sanderson; Pres. (V), Martin Lammers; Historic Site Supt., Linda N. Byers; Museum Shop Mgr., Martha Powers.
Personnel Profile: Full-Time Paid 4; Full-Time Volunteers 2; Part-Time Paid 15; Part-Time Volunteers 10; Interns 1.
Governing Authority: state. Parent Institution: State Parks and Cultural Resources. Subsidiary Institution: Fort Bridger Historical Association. Tax-exempt: 170(b)(1)(A).
General Museum: housed in 1888-1890 enlisted men's barracks located at historic Fort Bridger.
Collections: living history; military life; officers quarters; commanding officers life style & quarters; relating to historical Fort Bridger; westward expansion exhibits on Indian mountain men; emigrants; turn-of-the-century ranching; Mormon pioneers.
Research Fields: historic; pioneer lifestyle; military.
Facilities: Books, pamphlets, videos for viewing & for sale.
Activities: self-guided tours & guided tours at nominal cost; special summer events. Museum Sponsors: Mt. Man Rendezvous in September.
Hours & Admission Prices: April & Oct. Sat.-Sun. 9-4:30; May-Sept. daily 9-5:30. Non-residents $4, residents $2. ♿
Attendance: 97,000 (accurate)
Membership: Individual $9; Family $12.

Fort Laramie

FORT LARAMIE NATIONAL HISTORIC SITE, 965 Gray Rocks Rd., Fort Laramie, WY 82212-7625. Tel.: 307-837-2221. Fax: 307-837-2120.
Web Site: www.nps.gov/fola
Founded: 1938.
Key Personnel: Supt., Mitzi Frank; Museum Specialist, Baird Todd; Museum Tech., Sarah Allen.
Governing Authority: federal. Parent Institution: National Park Service.
Historic Site.
Collections: 19th-century military objects & accoutrements; plains Indian artifacts & cultural material; Victorian period furnishings; small arms, & ordnance vehicles & equipment; archeological materials. Historic Buildings: Bedlam 1855-1864; Post Trader's Store 1876; Surgeon's quarters 1880; Captain's quarters 1872; guardhouse 1866; enlisted men's bar, officer's club & post office 1883; Lieutenant Colonel's quarters 1888.
Research Fields: Trans-Mississippi Westward Expansion.
Facilities: 5,000-vol. library of books on the history of the Westward movement.
Activities: permanent & temporary exhibitions; tours; history talks; living history programs during the summer including military & civilian activities of a 19th-century frontier Army post.
Hours & Admission Prices: Labor Day to mid-June daily 8-4:30; mid-June to Labor Day daily 8-8. Adults $3; children no charge. Closed New Year's Day; Thanksgiving; Christmas. ♿
Attendance: 50,820 (accurate)
Membership: National Park Service: Single $3; Golden Age $10; Annual $15; NPS Pass $50; Golden Eagle $65.

Fort Washakie

SHOSHONE TRIBAL CULTURAL CENTER, 90 Ethete Rd., Fort Washakie, WY 82514-1008. Tel.: 307-332-9106. Fax: 307-332-3055.
E-mail: glendatrosper@washakie.net
Founded: 1988.
Key Personnel: C.E.O., Glenda Trosper; Museum Shop Mgr., Marsha Allen.
Personnel Profile: Full-Time Paid 1; Full-Time Volunteers 1.
Governing Authority: tribal government. Tax-exempt.
Cultural Center.
Collections: Shoshone tribal history from the reservation treaty establishment, emphasizing tribal art, historic tribal individuals, historic research for Shoshone prehistory, and contemporary times.
Activities: tours; cultural arts & crafts classes; Shoshone language classes; multimedia development.
Publications: brochures.
Hours & Admission Prices: Mon.-Fri. 8-4:45. No charge; donations accepted. Tours $15-$300. Closed all legal holidays; American Indian Day; holidays for annual tribal ceremonies in August.
Attendance: 1,500 (accurate)

Frances E. Warren Air Force Base

WARREN ICBM & HERITAGE MUSEUM, 7405 Marne Loop, 90th SW/MU, Bldg. 210, Frances E. Warren Air Force Base, WY 82005-2865. Mailing Address: 90 SW/MU, Francis E. Warren Air Force Base, WY 82005. Tel.: 307-773-2980. Fax: 307-773-2791.
E-mail: paula.taylor@warren.af.mil
Web Site: www.warrenmuseum.com
Founded: 1967.
Key Personnel: Dir., Paula Bauman Taylor; Cur., Larry Sprague.
Personnel Profile: Full-Time Paid 3.
Governing Authority: U.S. Air Force Museum, Wright Patterson Air Force Base, OH. Tax-exempt.
Military Museum: housed in c.1900 Military Post Headquarters Building located on the site of 1867 Fort D. A. Russell.
Collections: military uniforms; equipment dating from 1840-present; ICBM missile; period rooms of old army life; memorabilia & artifacts of the 90th Bomb Group-The Jolly Rogers of WWII.
Research Fields: Wyoming territory military history.
Activities: Modern ICBM exhibits.
Hours & Admission Prices: Mon.-Fri. 8-4; tours by appointment. No charge; donations accepted. Closed holidays. ♿
Attendance: 31,000 (estimated)

Gillette

CAMPBELL COUNTY ROCKPILE MUSEUM, (M), 900 W. 2nd St., Gillette, WY 82716-3405. Tel.: 307-682-5723 & 686-8551. Fax: 307-686-8528.
E-mail: rockpile@vcn.com
Founded: 1974.
Congressional District: 6
Key Personnel: Dir., Terry Girouard; Chm., Tommie Butler; Education Coord. & Museum Shop Mgr., Penny Schroder; Registrar, Robert Henning.
Personnel Profile: Full-Time Paid 4; Part-Time Paid 3; Part-Time Volunteers 12.
Governing Authority: county. Parent Institution: Campbell County; Wyoming government. Tax-exempt.
History Museum.
Collections: Native American weapons & tools; agricultural equipment; farming & ranching materials; saddles; rifles & guns; textiles & clothing; transportation materials including chuckwagon, sheepwagon, early automobiles; Burlington northern caboose; technological materials including phonographs; radios; printing press; linotype; blacksmith tools; local document & photographic archives; windmill exhibit & one-room rural schoolhouse all located on museum grounds; kitchen furnishings; homestead cabin.
Research Fields: local history; ranching, homesteading & American Indian artifacts.
Activities: lectures; guided tours; educational programs.
Publications: brochures; informational sheets; newsletter.
Hours & Admission Prices: Mon.-Sat. 9-5. No charge; donations accepted. Closed holidays. ♿
Attendance: 9,843 (estimated)
Membership: Students & Seniors $5; Individual $15; Family $20; Supporting $50-$99; Contributing $100-$199; Sustaining $200 & up; Corporate $500 & up.

Glendo

GLENDO HISTORICAL MUSEUM, Town Hall on Yellowstone Ave., Glendo, WY 82213. Mailing Address: P.O. Box 396, Glendo, WY 82213-0396. Tel.: 307-735-4242.
Founded: 1967.
History Museum.
Collections: paleontology; Native American artifacts; area history.
Hours & Admission Prices: Mon.-Fri. 8-12 & 1-4. No charge; donations accepted. Closed holidays. ♿

Glenrock

GLENROCK DEER CREEK MUSEUM, 935 W. Birch St., Glenrock, WY 82637. Mailing Address: P.O. Box 1674, Glenrock, WY 82637-1674. Tel.: 307-436-2810 & 9443.
Founded: 1998.
Personnel Profile: Part-Time Volunteers 12.
Governing Authority: Tax-exempt.
History Museum.
Collections: local history & culture; period voting records & building permits; early maps; Native American artifacts; photographs; clothing; hand tools; jewelry.
Hours & Admission Prices: Memorial Day to Labor Day Fri.-Tues. 10-4; other times by appointment. No charge; donations accepted. ♿
Attendance: 400 (accurate)

GLENROCK PALEONTOLOGICAL MUSEUM, 506 W. Birch St., Glenrock, WY 82637. Mailing Address: P.O. Box 1362, Glenrock, WY 82637-1362. Tel.: 307-436-2667. Fax: 307-436-5477.
Key Personnel: Dir., Stuart I. McCrary
Paleontology Museum.
Collections: prehistoric life; dinosaurs; period sea animals; Oligocene mammals; modern animals; scientific papers about prehistoric animals.
Research Fields: paleontology & geology of local area.
Facilities: library; children's education center. Museum-related items for sale.
Activities: movies; games.
Hours & Admission Prices: Tues.-Sat. 9-5. No charge; donations accepted.

Green River

SEEDSKADEE NATIONAL WILDLIFE REFUGE, Hwy. 372, Green River, WY 82935. Mailing Address: P.O. Box 700, Green River, WY 82935. Tel.: 307-875-2187. Fax: 307-875-4425.
Wildlife Refuge.
Collections: wildlife & their habitat; ecology; photographs.
Facilities: education center.
Activities: educational programs.
Hours & Admission Prices: Call for hours.

SWEETWATER COUNTY HISTORICAL MUSEUM, (M), 3 E. Flaming Gorge Way, Green River, WY 82935-4239. Tel.: 307-872-6435. Fax: 307-872-3234.
E-mail: swchm@sweetwater.net
Web Site: sweetwatermuseum.org
Founded: 1967.
Key Personnel: Dir., Ruth Lauritzen; Pres. (V), Donna Mundschenk; Cur., Mark Nelson; Exhibits Coord., Gary Perkins; Museum Shop Mgr., Cyndi McCullers.
Personnel Profile: Full-Time Paid 4; Part-Time Paid 2; Part-Time Volunteers 1; Interns 1.
Governing Authority: county. Parent Institution: Sweetwater County. Subsidiary Institution: Sweetwater County Museum Foundation. Tax-exempt: 170(b)(1)(A).
History Museum.
Collections: Indian & pioneer artifacts; industry, ranching & Chinese mementos; guns; photographs; items of historical significance to Sweetwater County & Southwestern Wyoming.
Research Fields: local history.
Facilities: 400-vol. library of local history books available for use on premises; 400 vertical files; 100-seat auditorium. Historic books, commemorative coins, gifts, & post cards for sale.
Activities: guided tours; lectures; formally organized education programs for children; permanent & temporary exhibitions.
Publications: quarterly newsletter, Overland & Underground.
Hours & Admission Prices: Mon.-Sat. 10-6. No charge; donations accepted. Closed holidays. ♿
Attendance: 4,550 (accurate)

Greybull

GREYBULL MUSEUM, 325 Greybull Ave., Greybull, WY 82426-2049. Mailing Address: Box 348, Greybull, WY 82426-0348. Tel.: 307-765-2444.
Founded: 1968.
Key Personnel: Dir., Wanda L. Bond.
Personnel Profile: Part-Time Paid 3; Part-Time Volunteers 2.
Governing Authority: municipal. Tax-exempt: 501(c)(3).
General Museum.
Collections: geology; history; Indian artifacts; fossils & minerals.
Facilities: auditorium. Books, minerals, rocks, fossil material, raw gem stone material & jewelry for sale.
Activities: guided tours; field trips; lectures; films; formally organized education programs for children; permanent & temporary exhibitions.
Publications: brochure.
Hours & Admission Prices: April-May & Sept.-Oct. Mon.-Fri. 1-5; June-Aug. Mon.-Fri. 10-8, Sat. 10-6; Nov.-March Mon., Wed. & Fri. 1-4. No charge; donations accepted. ♿
Attendance: 7,000 (estimated)

THE MUSEUM OF FLIGHT AND AERIAL FIREFIGHTING, South Big Horn County Airport, Greybull, WY 82426. Mailing Address: South Big Horn County Airport, P.O. Box 412, Greybull, WY 82426-0412. Tel.: 307-765-4322.
E-mail: flight@tctwest.net
Key Personnel: Dir., Bob Hawkins; Tour Dir. & Museum Shop Mgr., Lorraine Reiner.
Personnel Profile: Full-Time Volunteers 1.
Governing Authority: Tax-exempt.
Aviation Museum.
Collections: aviation history; aerial firefighting; aircraft; retardant systems.
Activities: walking tours; school group tours.
Hours & Admission Prices: mid-May to Sept. Wed. & Fri.-Sun. 10-4. No charge; donations accepted.
Attendance: 2,000 (estimated)

Guernsey

LAKE GUERNSEY MUSEUM-GUERNSEY STATE PARK, Interstate 25, exit 92 to US 26 to State Rte. 270, Guernsey, WY 82214. Mailing Address: P.O. Box 429, Guernsey, WY 82214-0429. Tel.: 307-836-2334 (office) & 2900 (museum). Fax: 307-836-3088.
Web Site: wyoparks.state.wy.us/parks/guernsey/index.asp
Founded: 1936.
Key Personnel: Dir. Wyoming Dept. of State Parks & Cultural Resources, Milward Simpson; Parks Supt., Todd Stevenson.
Personnel Profile: Part-Time Paid 1.
Governing Authority: Wyoming State Parks & Historic Sites, Barrett Bldg., 2301 Central Ave., Cheyenne, WY 82002. Tax-exempt.
Historical Museum: housed in 1930s building constructed by the CCC.
Collections: agriculture; anthropology; ethnology; industry; transportation; military; historical museum building & 1930s exhibits; botany; archaeology.
Research Fields: pertaining to collections & history of facility.
Facilities: picnic area with pavilion.
Activities: permanent exhibits by Dr. John C. Ewers; temporary exhibits from local area; art, photo display.
Hours & Admission Prices: May-Oct. daily 10-6. Nonresident $4, resident $2. ♿
Attendance: 5,000 (estimated)
Membership: Friends of Guersney Park.

Hanna

HANNA BASIN MUSEUM, Old Community Hall, Front St., Hanna, WY 82327. Mailing Address: P.O. Box 252, Hanna, WY 82327-0252. Tel.: 307-324-3915.
Key Personnel: Cur., Nancy Anderson
History Museum.
Collections: Hanna history; coal camps; railroad; homesteading; ranching.
Activities: special events.
Hours & Admission Prices: Summer: Fri.-Sun. 1-5; Winter: Fri. 1-5; other times by appointment. No charge; donations accepted.

Jackson

DI TOMMASO GALLERIES, 172 Center St., Jackson, WY 83001. Mailing Address: P.O. Box 1928, Scottsdale, AZ 85252-1928. Tel.: 307-734-9677.
Art Gallery.
Collections: 19th-20th century art; African art; furniture.
Hours & Admission Prices: Call for hours.

JACKSON HOLE HISTORICAL SOCIETY AND MUSEUM, (M), 105 Mercill Ave., Jackson, WY 83001. Mailing Address: P.O. Box 1005, Jackson, WY 83001-1005. Tel.: 307-733-2414 (Museum) & 9605 (Historical Society). Fax: 307-739-9019.
E-mail: jhhsm@wyom.net
Web Site: www.jacksonholehistory.org
Founded: 1958.
Congressional District: 1
Key Personnel: C.E.O. & Dir., Lokey Lytjen; Pres. Bd. Dirs., Jim Luebbers; Pres. (V), Joe Albright; Office Mgr., Melinda Barnett; Membership Asst., Liz Jacobson; Cur. Asst., Shannon Sullivan; Dir. Devel., Gary Hughes; Education & Outreach, Karen Reinhart; Museum Shop Mgr., Jean Hansen; Education & Research Asst., Rebecca Stephens; Asst. to Exec. Dir., Robin Allison.
Personnel Profile: Full-Time Paid 6; Part-Time Paid 3; Part-Time Volunteers 5.
Governing Authority: Jackson Hole Historical Society & Museum. Tax-exempt.
History Museum & Research Center: housed in 1906 building.
Collections: archaeology; regional prehistory; Plains Indians; historical photographs; fur trade memorabilia; big game heads; local pioneer history; maps; regional & local history; conservation history; tourism; oral history; western Americana.
Research Fields: archaeology; history; folklore; traditions.
Facilities: library; archives; photograph archives.
Activities: lectures; permanent & rotating exhibits; summer walking tours; summer field trips; school & youth programs; volunteer program; publications program; oral histories.
Publications: newsletter; books, Jackson Hole: Crossroads of the Western Fur Trade 1807-1840, David E. Jackson, Field Captain of the Rocky Mountain Fur Trade, Landmarks of the Rocky Mountain Fur Trade: Two One-day Self-guided Tours from Jackson, Wyoming; And That's The Way It Was in Jackson's Hole; Historic Downtown Jackson: Self-Guided Walking Tour; Windows to the Past: Early Settlers in Jackson Hole.
Hours & Admission Prices: Jackson Hole Museum: late May to early Oct. daily 10-6. Families $6, adults $3, senior citizens & tours $2, students 7-18 $1; members & children under 6 no charge. Walking Tours: Tues. & Thurs 10:30am. No charge. Jackson Hole Historical Society: Tues.-Fri. 10-5. No charge; donations accepted. ♿
Attendance: 16,000 (accurate)
Membership: Senior Citizen $25; Individual $35; Family $60; Contributing $100 & up; Donor $250 & up; Sustaining $500 & up; Patron $1,000 & up.

* **NATIONAL MUSEUM OF WILDLIFE ART, (M),** 2820 Rungius Rd., Jackson, WY 83001. Mailing Address: P.O. Box 6825, Jackson, WY 83002-6825. Tel.: 307-733-5771. Fax: 307-733-5787.
E-mail: info@wildlifeart.org
Web Site: www.wildlifeart.org
Formerly: Wildlife of the American West
Founded: 1987.
Key Personnel: Pres. & C.E.O., James C. McNutt, Ph.D.; C.F.O., Lisa Holms; Sugden Family Cur. Education, Jane Lavino; Cur. Art, Adam Duncan Harris, Ph.D.; Facilities & Security, Joe Bishop; Registrar, Fay Bisbee.
Personnel Profile: Full-Time Paid 28; Part-Time Paid 2; Part-Time Volunteers 67; Interns 2.
Governing Authority: nonprofit organization. Tax-exempt: 501(c)(3).
Art Museum.
Collections: 2500 B.C.-present fine art that depicts humanity's relationship to nature, focused on images of wildlife.
Research Fields: Fine wildlife art & artists; museum education research & program development.
Facilities: 1,500-vol. library of art history & artists' biography books available to the public; 15,000 sq. ft. exhibit space; 200-seat auditorium; 2 classrooms; 45-seat cafe. Museum-related items for sale.
Activities: guided tours; lectures; films; theatre; organized education programs for children, adults & college students; docent program; training programs for museum professionals; participatory, loan, temporary & traveling exhibitions; school loan service. Annual Event: Western Visions.
Publications: magazine, annual; calendar 2 times per year.
Hours & Admission Prices: Daily 9-5. Adults $10, senior citizens & students $9; discounts to AAM & Museum's West members; children & members no charge. Closed Columbus Day; Veterans Day; Thanksgiving; Christmas. ♿
Attendance: 64,069 (accurate)
Membership: Pika $35; Otter $65; Pronghorn $100; Caribou $250; Elk $500; Paintbox Society $1,000; Rungius Society $3,000.

WILD EXPOSURES GALLERY, 60 E. Broadway, Jackson, WY 83001. Mailing Address: P.O. Box 1889, Jackson, WY 83001-1889. Tel.: 307-739-1777. Fax: 307-739-2331.
Art Gallery.
Collections: photographs by Jeff Hogan, Scott McKinley & Andrew Weller.
Activities: workshops.
Hours & Admission Prices: Daily.

Kaycee

HOOFPRINTS OF THE PAST MUSEUM, 344 Nolan Ave., Kaycee, WY 82639. Mailing Address: P.O. Box 42, Kaycee, WY 82639-0042. Tel.: 307-738-2381.
History Museum.
Collections: Johnson County history; Dull Knife Battlefield; Fort Reno; Bozeman Trail; Johnson County Invasion.
Publications: newsletter.
Hours & Admission Prices: Mon.-Sat. 9-5, Sun. 1-5. No charge; donations accepted.

Kelly

THE MURIE MUSEUM, 1 Ditch Creek Rd., Kelly, WY 83011. Mailing Address: P.O. Box 68, Kelly, WY 83011-0068. Tel.: 307-734-5657, ext. 3106. Fax: 307-739-9388.
E-mail: info@tetonscience.org
Web Site: www.tetonscience.org
Founded: 1973.
Key Personnel: C.E.O., John Shea; Chm. (V), Dick Jones; Dir., April Landale; Museum Mgr. & Dir. Research, Dr. Dale Gentry.
Personnel Profile: Part-Time Paid 1; Interns 2.
Governing Authority: private; nonprofit organization. Parent Institution: Teton Science Schools. Tax-exempt.
Natural History Museum.
Collections: 9,000 mammals & birds.
Research Fields: ecology & conservation biology.
Facilities: 4,000-vol. library of journals & books on natural history; classrooms; laboratories; field research station; nature & conservation center.
Activities: formal education programs for adults & children; wildlife, ecology, ornithology & animal behavior programs; lectures.
Hours & Admission Prices: Mon.-Fri. 8-4:30 by appointment, Sat.-Sun. by appointment. No charge; donations accepted. Closed Christmas.
Attendance: 2,500 (estimated)

Kemmerer

FOSSIL BUTTE NATIONAL MONUMENT VISITOR CENTER, 864 Chicken Creek Rd., Kemmerer, WY 83101. Mailing Address: P.O. Box 592, Kemmerer, WY 83101. Tel.: 307-877-4455. Fax: 307-877-4457.
History Museum.
Collections: over 80 fossils including fish, crocodile, turtle, bats, & birds; geology; habitats; photographs.
Activities: educational programs; create a fossil; video programs; demonstrations; ranger programs.
Hours & Admission Prices: Monument: daily sunrise to sunset. Visitor Center: Memorial Day to Labor Day daily 8-7; Sept.-May daily 8-4:30. No charge; donations accepted. Closed winter holidays.

FOSSIL COUNTRY MUSEUM, (M), 400 Pine, Kemmerer, WY 83101. Mailing Address: P.O. Box 854, Kemmerer, WY 83101-0854. Tel.: 307-877-6551. Fax: 307-877-6552.
E-mail: museum@hamsfork.net
Founded: 1989.
Congressional District: 3
Key Personnel: Dir., Judy Julian; Pres., Mary Service; Vice Pres., Sue Giorgis.
Personnel Profile: Full-Time Paid 2; Part-Time Volunteers 10.
Governing Authority: private; nonprofit organization. Parent Institution: Fossil County Futures, Inc. Tax-exempt: 501(c)(3).
History Museum.
Collections: history of Kemmerer/Diamondville, Wyoming from late 1890s-present; replica of Kemmerer coal mine; genuine whiskey stills.
Research Fields: southwest Wyoming history; history of coal mining in southwest Wyoming.
Facilities: 50-vol. library of books on Wyoming history; Kemmerer newspapers; rooms available to rent for meetings & social activities; 175-seat auditorium; board room. Museum-related items for sale.
Activities: arts festivals; concerts; guided tours; hobby workshops; lectures; temporary & traveling exhibitions. Annual Event: Wyoming Heritage Auction.
Publications: Kemmerer History.
Hours & Admission Prices: Mon.-Sat. 10-4. No charge; donations accepted. Closed New Year's Day; Independence Day; Thanksgiving; Christmas. ♿
Attendance: 3,000 (accurate)
Membership: Individual $20.

J.C. PENNEY HOMESTEAD & HISTORICAL FOUNDATION, 107 J.C. Penney Dr., Kemmerer, WY 83101-2941. Tel.: 307-877-3164.
E-mail: swchm@sweetwater.net
History Museum: housed in the Penney's first home & the site of the first J.C. Penney store which is still in operation today. Cottage is a National Historic Landmark.
Collections: period furnishings; photographs; personal artifacts.
Hours & Admission Prices: May-Sept. Mon.-Sat. 9-6, Sun. 1-6. No charge; donations accepted.

ULRICH'S FOSSIL GALLERY, Fossil Station #308, Kemmerer, WY 83101. Mailing Address: 4400 Fossil Butte Bounty Rd. 300, Kemmerer, WY 83101. Tel.: 307-877-6466. Fax: 307-877-3289.
Fossil Gallery.
Collections: fish & plant fossils.
Activities: fossil digs; fossil preparation kits.
Hours & Admission Prices: Gallery: daily 8-5. Fossil Digs: by appointment.

Lander

EVANS/DAHL MEMORIAL MUSEUM, 545 Main St., Lander, WY 82520-3075. Tel.: 307-332-8190; 800-768-7743.
History Museum.
Collections: One Shot Antelope Hunt history; wildlife preservation; antelope habitats; photographs.
Facilities: Museum-related items for sale.
Hours & Admission Prices: Mon.-Fri. 10-5.

FREMONT COUNTY PIONEER MUSEUM, 1443 Main St., Lander, WY 82520-2649. Tel.: 307-332-4137. Fax: 307-332-6498.
E-mail: info@fcpm.org
Web Site: www.fcpm.org
Founded: 1908.
Congressional District: 1
Key Personnel: Dir., Carol Thiesse; Cur., Traci Foutz.
Personnel Profile: Full-Time Paid 1; Part-Time Paid 5; Part-Time Volunteers 4.
Governing Authority: county. Tax-exempt.
History Museum.
Collections: pioneer era artifacts from late 1840-1920; Indian artifacts; agricultural & transportation artifacts & implements; pioneer era artifacts.
Research Fields: local, regional & state history; Oregon Trail; Indians; women's suffrage.
Facilities: research library; picnic area. Books for sale.
Activities: permanent & temporary exhibitions; lectures; programs.
Publications: quarterly historical magazine, Wind River Mountaineer.
Hours & Admission Prices: Tues.-Sat. 10-6.
Attendance: 10,000 (estimated)
Membership: Individual $1; Life $25.

LANDER ART CENTER, 244 Main St., Lander, WY 82520. Tel.: 307-332-5772.
E-mail: brad@landerartcenter.com
Founded: 2002.
Governing Authority: nonprofit organization.
Art Gallery.
Collections: works by local, regional & national artists; paintings; photographs; sculpture.
Activities: temporary exhibits; classes; workshops; special events. Museum Sponsors: Summer of Arts Program.
Hours & Admission Prices: Call for hours. No charge; donations accepted.

LANDER CHILDREN'S MUSEUM, 465 Lincoln Ave., Lander, WY 82520-2831. Mailing Address: P.O. Box 533, Lander, WY 82520-0533. Tel.: 307-332-1341.
E-mail: info@landerchildrensmuseum.org
Web Site: www.landerchildrensmuseum.org
Founded: 1999.
Key Personnel: Mgr., Jennifer O'Connor.
Personnel Profile: Full-Time Paid 1; Part-Time Paid 1; Part-Time Volunteers 15.
Children's Museum.
Collections: hands-on exhibits.
Activities: special events; educational programs.
Hours & Admission Prices: Summer: Tues.-Fri. 10-3; Sept.-May Tues.-Fri. 10-1, Sat. 10-3. Adults $3; children under 2 & members no charge.
Attendance: 3,500
Membership: Family $50; Corporate $100.

Laramie

THE GEOLOGICAL MUSEUM, THE UNIVERSITY OF WYOMING, 1000 E. University Ave., Laramie, WY 82071-3006. Tel.: 307-766-2650. Fax: 307-766-2622.
E-mail: uwgeoms@uwyo.edu
Web Site: www.uwyo.edu.geomuseum
Founded: 1887.
Key Personnel: Dir. & Cur., Brent H. Breithaupt.
Personnel Profile: Full-Time Paid 1; Part-Time Paid 3; Part-Time Volunteers 2; Interns 2.
Governing Authority: university. Parent Institution: University of Wyoming. Tax-exempt: 501(c)(3).
Geology Museum.
Collections: vertebrate & invertebrate paleontology; rocks; minerals.
Research Fields: vertebrate & invertebrate paleontology.
Activities: guided tours; field trips: formally organized education programs for undergraduate & graduate college students; permanent & temporary exhibitions.
Publications: newsletter, Bronto.
Hours & Admission Prices: Mon.-Fri. 8-5, Sat.-Sun. 10-3. No charge; donations accepted. Closed university holidays. ♿
Attendance: 30,000 (estimated)
Membership: Individual $25; Family $30; Supporting $50; Contributing $100; Sponsor $200; Patron $500; Advanced Patron $1,000.

LARAMIE PLAINS MUSEUM, (M), 603 E. Ivinson Ave., Laramie, WY 82070-3243. Tel.: 307-742-4448.
E-mail: laramiemuseum@bresnan.net
Web Site: www.laramiemuseum.org/
Founded: 1966.
Key Personnel: C.E.O., Dir. & Museum Shop Mgr., Mary Mountain; Pres. (V), Janet Killian; Cur., Connie Lindmier; Admin. Asst., Gina Gibson.
Personnel Profile: Part-Time Paid 4; Part-Time Volunteers 100.
Governing Authority: nonprofit organization. Parent Institution: Board of Laramie Museum Association, Inc. Tax-exempt: 501(c)(3).
Historical House Museum: housed in 1892 Victorian Mansion built by early pioneer banker, Edward Ivinson.
Collections: dishes, cookware, buggies, harness, tools & furniture of early pioneer families; Indian artifacts; photographs & maps of area; Victorian furnishings & fixtures; business records of Laramie City.
Research Fields: early history of Albany County; pioneer family histories; cattle & sheep industries; Union Pacific Railroad history.
Facilities: 200-vol. library of Western books, pamphlets & newspaper articles available for use on premises; adjacent community center.
Activities: guided tours. Museum Sponsors: Victorian Teas; special summer & holiday programs.
Publications: brochure; newsletter, Ghost Towns of Albany County.
Hours & Admission Prices: Feb.-May & Sept.-Dec. 14 Tues.-Sat. 1-4; June-Aug. Tues.-Sat. 9-5, Sun. 1-4. Adults $7, senior citizens $5.50, students $4; discounts to AAM members; children under 6 & members no charge. Closed major holidays. ♿
Attendance: 3,968 (estimated)
Membership: Senior Citizen $25; Individual $45; Senior Citizen Family $50; Family $75.

ROCKY MOUNTAIN HERBARIUM, Aven Nelson Building-3rd Fl., 9th St., Laramie, WY 82071-3165. Mailing Address: University of Wyoming-Department of Botany, Dept. 3165, 1000 E. University Ave., Laramie, WY 82071-2000. Tel.: 307-766-2236 & 4393. Fax: 307-766-2851.
E-mail: rhartman@uwyo.edu
Web Site: www.rmh.uwyo.edu
Founded: 1893.
Key Personnel: Cur. Prof. Botany, Ronald L. Hartman; Herbarium Mgr., Burrell E. Nelson.
Personnel Profile: Full-Time Paid 2; Part-Time Paid 6.
Governing Authority: university. Parent Institution: University of Wyoming, Dept. of Botany. Tax-exempt.
Herbarium.
Collections: botany; 780,000 plant specimens, including United States Forest Service National Herbarium.
Research Fields: plant systematics.
Facilities: library of research journals & monographs related to plant systematics.
Activities: temporary exhibitions.
Hours & Admission Prices: Academic year Mon.-Fri. 8-5; summer Mon.-Fri. 7:30-4:30. No charge; donations accepted. ♿
Attendance: 200

UNION PACIFIC HISTORICAL SOCIETY (UPHS), American Heritage Center, University of Wyoming, Laramie, WY 82071. Mailing Address: P.O. Box 4006, Cheyenne, WY 82003-4006. Tel.: 307-635-5197.
E-mail: uphs@wyoming.com
Web Site: www.uphs.org
Founded: 1984.
Key Personnel: Pres. (V), Larry Hochhalter; Treas., Hilding Larson; Business Mgr., Robert Krieger.
Personnel Profile: Part-Time Paid 1.
Governing Authority: private; nonprofit organization. Tax-exempt: 501(c)(3).
Historical Society Museum.
Collections: Union Pacific Railroad drawings of locomotives & cars; historic records, films & photographs.
Activities: available for research.
Publications: quarterly magazine, Streamliner; book series (see website)
Hours & Admission Prices: Mon.-Fri. 8-5, Sat. 11-5. No charge.
Membership: Regular $30; International $45; Sustaining $50.

UNIVERSITY OF WYOMING, AMERICAN HERITAGE CENTER, 2111 Willett Dr., Centennial Complex, Laramie, WY 82071. Mailing Address: 1000 E. University Ave., Dept. 3924, Laramie, WY 82071-2000.
Web Site: ahc.uwyo.edu
Key Personnel: Dir., Mark Greene
History Museum.
Collections: archives; books; manuscripts; Wyoming & American west history; mining & petroleum industries; U.S. politics; world affairs.
Activities: research.
Hours & Admission Prices: Center: Mon. 8 am-9 pm, Tues.-Fri. 8-5. Reference Services: Mon. 10-9, Tues.-Fri. 8-5.

UNIVERSITY OF WYOMING ANTHROPOLOGY MUSEUM, 12th & Lewis, Laramie, WY 82071. Mailing Address: 1000 E. University Ave., Dept. 3431 - Anthropology, Laramie, WY 82071-2000. Tel.: 307-766-2208. Fax: 307-766-2473.
E-mail: arrow@uwyo.edu
Web Site: uwadmnweb.uwyo.edu/anthropology/museum
Founded: 1966.
Key Personnel: Dir., Dr. Charles A. Reher.
Personnel Profile: Part-Time Paid 2; Part-Time Volunteers 3.
Governing Authority: university. Affiliated with the University of Wyoming. Tax-exempt.
Anthropology Museum.
Collections: ethnology; American Indian emphasis; archaeology; faunal, human osteology, & archaeological collections.
Research Fields: pertaining to collections.
Facilities: human osteology & archaeological laboratories.
Activities: formally organized education programs for undergraduate & graduate college students; permanent & temporary exhibitions; guided tours; display internships.
Hours & Admission Prices: mid-May to Aug. Mon.-Fri. 9-4; Sept. to mid-May Mon.-Fri. 9-5. No charge. Closed school vacations & holidays.
Attendance: 10,000 (estimated)

* **UNIVERSITY OF WYOMING ART MUSEUM, (M),** 2111 Willett Dr., Laramie, WY 82071. Mailing Address: 1000 E. University Ave., Dept. 3807, Laramie, WY 82071-2000. Tel.: 307-766-6622. Fax: 307-766-3520.
E-mail: uwartmus@uwyo.edu
Web Site: www.uwyo.edu/artmuseum
Founded: 1968.
Congressional District: 1
Key Personnel: Dir., Susan Moldenhauer; Pres. Bd., James Pearce; Cur. Education, Wendy Bredehoft; Collection Mgr., E.K. Kim; Chief Preparator, Sterling Smith; Registrar, Sarah Gadd; Museum Shop Mgr., Rosanne Chapp.
Personnel Profile: Full-Time Paid 8; Part-Time Paid 12; Part-Time Volunteers 55; Interns 5.
Governing Authority: university. Parent Institution: University of Wyoming. Tax-exempt.
Art Museum.
Collections: American art; European art; art of Asia, Africa and the Americas; contemporary art; photography
Major Exhibits: Artists from France, 11/09-12/10; Peter Sarkisian (T), 1/10-5/10; Harold Garde Contemporaries, 1/10-8/10; Harold Garde - Painting 50 Years, 3/10-8/10; John Clymer, 9/10-11/10; Anne-Karin Furones, 9/10-12/10; Andy Warhol Photographs, 9/10-12/10.
Research Fields: 19th- & 20th-century American art.
Facilities: 20,000 sq. ft. outdoor sculpture terrace; 12,000 sq. ft. galleries; education studio. Museum-related items for sale.
Activities: loan, temporary & traveling exhibitions; lectures; gallery talks; workshops; symposia; films; formally organized education programs for adults, K-12 & college students; statewide outreach programs.
Publications: exhibition brochures & catalogs; quarterly newsletter.
Hours & Admission Prices: Feb.-April & Sept.-Nov. Mon. 10-9, Tues.-Sat. 10-5; May-Aug. & Dec. Mon.-Sat. 10-5. No charge; donations accepted. Closed Christmas Eve, Day & week after. ♿
Attendance: 177,415 (accurate)
Membership: Student $25; Individual $40; Family $60; Sustaining $250; Donor $500; Patron $1,000 & up.

UNIVERSITY OF WYOMING GEOLOGICAL MUSEUM, S.H. Knight Geology Bldg., 1000 E. University Ave., Laramie, WY 82071-2000. Tel.: 307-766-2646.
Geology Museum.
Collections: fossils; rocks; minerals.
Hours & Admission Prices: Mon.-Fri. 8-5, Sat.-Sun. 10-3. No charge. Closed university holidays.

UNIVERSITY OF WYOMING INSECT MUSEUM, Dept. of Renewable Resources, 100 E. University, Laramie, WY 82071-3354. Mailing Address: Department of Renewable Resources, P.O. Box 3354, Laramie, WY 82071-3354. Tel.: 307-766-1121.
Key Personnel: Dir., Scott Shaw
Insect Museum.
Collections: over 250,000 specimens; hymenoptera; diptera; lepidoptera; coleoptera.
Hours & Admission Prices: Call for hours.

WYOMING CHILDREN'S MUSEUM & NATURE CENTER, 968 N. 9th St., Laramie, WY 82072-2761. Mailing Address: P.O. Box 51, Laramie, WY 82073-0051. Tel.: 307-745-6332.
E-mail: info@wcmnc.org
Children's Museum.
Collections: hands-on exhibits; natural & physical sciences, the arts, and the humanities; live animals.
Facilities: nature center; discovery center.
Activities: youth pottery & ceramic classes; birthday parties; outreach exhibits & programs; special events.
Hours & Admission Prices: Wed.-Sat. 10-4

WYOMING TERRITORIAL PRISON STATE HISTORIC SITE, 975 Snowy Range Rd., Laramie, WY 82070-6719. Tel.: 307-745-6161. Fax: 307-745-8620.
E-mail: tbeyer@state.wy.us
Web Site: wyoparks.state.wy.us
Formerly: Wyoming Territorial Park
Founded: 1986.
Congressional District: 1
Key Personnel: C.E.O. & Exec. Dir., Tom Lindmier; Pres. (V), Connie Kercher; Cur., Teresa Beyer; Museum Shop Mgr., Lynette Nelson.
Personnel Profile: Full-Time Paid 4; Full-Time Volunteers 5; Part-Time Paid 2; Part-Time Volunteers 20; Interns 1.
Governing Authority: private; not-for-profit organization. Parent Institution: Wyoming State Parks & Cultural Resources. Tax-exempt: 501(c)(3).
Historic Site: 1872-1903 Wyoming Territorial Prison; only prison in North America to hold Butch Cassidy.
Collections: Historic Buildings: 1872-1903 Wyoming Territorial Prison; Wyoming Frontier Town; warden's house; Ranchland exhibit; horse barn dinner theatre; boxcar house; broom factory; country church.
Research Fields: archaeology; period folk arts & trades; historical personalities; historic ranches.
Facilities: 150-seat dinner theatre; nature trail. Museum-related items & Wyoming products for sale.
Activities: self-guided tours; concerts; theater; temporary exhibitions; educational programs for children. Annual Event: Ghost Tours.
Hours & Admission Prices: May-Oct. 9-6. Adults $5. ♿
Attendance: 47,000 (accurate)

Lingle

WESTERN HISTORY CENTER, 2308 U.S. Hwy. 26, Lingle, WY 82223-8527. Tel.: 307-837-3052. Fax: 307-837-2043.
History Museum.
Collections: historic, prehistoric, & paleontological artifacts; archaeology; mining; the Texas Trail; paleontology; oral histories.
Activities: research.
Publications: newsletter.
Hours & Admission Prices: Summer: Tues.-Sat. 9-4; Winter: Thurs.-Sat. 9-4 by appointment. Adults $2.

Lovell

BIGHORN CANYON NRA VISITOR CENTER, 20 Hwy. 14A E., Lovell, WY 82431. Tel.: 406-666-2412. Fax: 406-666-2415.
Visitor Center.
Collections: local history & culture; photographs; geology; life science.
Hours & Admission Prices: Memorial Day to Labor Day daily 8-6; Sept.-May daily 8:30-4:30. Closed New Year's Day; Thanksgiving; Christmas.

Lusk

CHEYENNE-BLACK HILLS STAGECOACH, 322 S. Main, Lusk, WY 82225. Mailing Address: P.O. Box 367, Lusk, WY 82225-0367. Tel.: 307-334-3444.
Web Site: www.luskmuseum.org
History Museum: stagecoach used on the Cheyenne-Black Hills Stage and Express Line; built in 1860s by Abbott & Downing at Concord, NH.
Collections: stagecoach; pioneer & trail history.
Hours & Admission Prices: Mon.-Sat. 10-5. Admission $2. Closed holidays. ♿

Lyman

BRIDGER VALLEY HERITAGE MUSEUM, 100 E. Sage-Lyman Town Hall 2 Fl., Lyman, WY 82937. Mailing Address: P.O. Box 184, Lyman, WY 82937-0184. Tel.: 307-787-3525.
E-mail: bvhmuseum@union-tel.com
Formerly: Trona Mining Museum of Bridger Valley
Founded: 2005.
Personnel Profile: Part-Time Paid 1.
Governing Authority: Parent Institution: Uinta County Museum. Tax-exempt.
History Museum.
Collections: Trona mining; personal artifacts; western trails history; Lincoln Highway; pioneer trails.
Hours & Admission Prices: Mon.-Thurs. 10-4; 2nd Tues. & 3rd Thurs 1-5; tours by appointment. No charge. Closed holidays. ♿
Attendance: 145 (estimated)

Medicine Bow

MEDICINE BOW MUSEUM, 405 Lincoln Hwy., Medicine Bow, WY 82329. Mailing Address: P.O. Box 187, Medicine Bow, WY 82329-0187. Tel.: 307-379-2383.
Web Site: www.medicinebow.org
History Museum: housed in the former old railroad depot, built in 1913. Listed on the National Register of Historical Places.
Collections: local history; cattle & sheep ranch brands; caboose; railroad history.
Hours & Admission Prices: Summer: daily; Winter: call for hours.

Meeteetse

MEETEETSE MUSEUM DISTRICT, 1947 State St., Meeteetse, WY 82433. Mailing Address: P.O. Box 248, Meeteetse, WY 82433-0248. Tel.: 307-868-2423. Fax: 307-868-2423.
E-mail: mmuseum@tctwest.net
Founded: 1974.
Congressional District: 1
Key Personnel: Pres. (V), Jim Allen; Vice Pres., Sharon Fech; Treas., Lili Turnell; Sec., Yvonne Renner; Cur. & Museum Shop Mgr., Paige Paisley.
Personnel Profile: Full-Time Paid 1; Part-Time Paid 3; Part-Time Volunteers 6.
Governing Authority: county; nonprofit organization. Branch Museum: Charles J. Beldon Museum of Western Photography, 1947 State, Meeteetse, WY. Tax-exempt: 501(c)(3).
History Museums: Bank Museum: on the National Register of Historic Buildings.
Collections: Meeteetse Museum: local history; wildlife; ranching; photographs; Harry Jackson sculptures. Belden Museum: photographs, Pitchfork Ranch collections.
Research Fields: local early families.
Facilities: Museum-related items for sale.
Activities: temporary & traveling exhibitions. Annual Events: Kirwin Excursion in August; Arland Townsite & Old Meeteetse Cemetery tour in September.
Publications: quarterly newsletter.
Hours & Admission Prices: May-Sept. Mon.-Sat. 9:30-4; Oct.-April Tues.-Sat. 10-3, Sun. 12-4. Bank Museum: Tues.-Sat. 11-3. No charge; donations accepted. ♿
Attendance: 7,000 (accurate)

Midwest

SALT CREEK MUSEUM, 531 Peake St., Midwest, WY 82643. Mailing Address: P.O. Box 190, Midwest, WY 82643-0190. Tel.: 307-437-6513.
Key Personnel: Cur., Sandra Schutte
History Museum.
Collections: Salt Creek oilfields from 1889 to present; area history; oilfield workers & their families; doctor's office; school room; kitchen; dining room; barber shop; household artifacts.
Activities: research.
Hours & Admission Prices: By appointment. No charge; donations accepted.

Newcastle

ANNA MILLER MUSEUM, 401 Delaware, Newcastle, WY 82701-2943. Mailing Address: P.O. Box 698, Newcastle, WY 82701-0698. Tel.: 307-746-4188. Fax: 307-746-4629.
E-mail: wcmd@rtconnect.net
Founded: 1966.
Key Personnel: Dir., Bobbie Jo Tysdal; Pres. (V) & Chm. (V), Mary Capps.
Personnel Profile: Full-Time Paid 3; Part-Time Paid 2; Interns 1.
Governing Authority: Tax-exempt.
Local History Museum: housed in 1930s cavalry barn, Troop F, 115th Cavalry, Wyoming National Guard.
Collections: local history; Indian artifacts; natural history; paleontology; archives. Historic Buildings: 1898 Green Mountain Country School; 1875 Jenney Stockade Cabin, turn-of-the-century women's homestead cabin.
Research Fields: local & Black Hills history; genealogy.
Facilities: 600-vol. library of Wyoming history & Congressman Frank Mondell; Weston County newspapers; incomplete set of Bits and Pieces Western History magazine; Godey's Lady; 10-vols. of American Heritage; numerous bound volumes Harpers magazine. Postcards, fossils & local books for sale.
Activities: lectures; films; organized education programs for children; permanent & temporary exhibitions; school loan service; exhibits taken to area schools; mini-museum loans to school. Museum Sponsors: Living History Days in September; Candle Light Living Christmas.
Hours & Admission Prices: Mon.-Fri. 9-5. No charge; donations accepted. Closed legal holidays.
Attendance: 2,800 (estimated)
Membership: Patrons of the Anna Miller Museum: Sustaining $25; Sponsor $100; Benefactor $250; Corporate $500; Champion $1,000.

Pine Bluffs

HIGH PLAINS ARCHAEOLOGY MUSEUM, 211 Elm St., Pine Bluffs, WY 82082. Mailing Address: P.O. Box 429, Pine Bluffs, WY 82082-0429. Tel.: 307-245-9372.
History Museum.
Collections: local history & culture; photographs; archaeological artifacts.
Hours & Admission Prices: June-Aug. by appointment.

TEXAS TRAIL MUSEUM, 3rd & Market Sts., Pine Bluffs, WY 82082. Mailing Address: P.O. Box 545, Pine Bluffs, WY 82082-0545. Tel.: 307-245-3713.
Web Site: www.texastrailmuseumoflaramiecounty.org
Founded: 1986.
Key Personnel: Pres., Anthony J. Sacco, Sr.
Personnel Profile: Part-Time Paid 2; Part-Time Volunteers 2.
Governing Authority: Tax-exempt.
History Museum.
Collections: Texas Trail history; early pioneer history & culture; 2 diesel fired generators; quilting; school house; U.P. Caboose; St. Mary's Catholic Church artifacts; homestead cabin.
Facilities: picnic area.
Activities: lectures. Museum Sponsors: Ice Cream Socials; Golf Tournament.
Publications: quarterly newsletter.
Hours & Admission Prices: Memorial Day to Labor Day Mon.-Sat. 11-4. No charge; donations accepted. ♿
Attendance: 600 (accurate)
Membership: Individual $10; Family $15; Silver Shield $50; Gold Shield $100; Life $500.

Pinedale

MUSEUM OF THE MOUNTAIN MAN, 700 E. Hennick, Pinedale, WY 82941. Mailing Address: P.O. Box 909, Pinedale, WY 82941-0909. Tel.: 307-367-4101. Fax: 307-367-6768.
E-mail: director@mmmuseum.com
Web Site: www.museumofthemountainman.com
Founded: 1990.

Key Personnel: C.E.O., Laurie Hartwig; Pres., Jay Fear; Museum Shop Mgr., Mildred Pape.
Personnel Profile: Full-Time Paid 2; Part-Time Paid 6; Part-Time Volunteers 200; Interns 1.
Governing Authority: society. Parent Institution: Sublette County Historical Society. Tax-exempt: 501(c)(3).
History Museum.
Collections: fur trade; Western exploration; Plains Indians; early settlement history of western Wyoming.
Research Fields: Rocky Mountain rendezvous; Alfred Jacob Miller art; fur trade bibliography; historic western sites.
Facilities: research library; 15,000 sq. ft. exhibit space; outdoor amphitheatre; picnic area. Museum-related items for sale.
Activities: education programs for children; guided tours; lectures; loan, traveling & temporary exhibitions; living history events; educational programs for adults & children; lectures; guided tours. Museum Sponsors: Green River Rendezvous weekend in July.
Publications: newsletter.
Hours & Admission Prices: May-Oct. 1 daily 9-5; Oct. 2-April by appointment. Adults $5, senior citizens $4, children $3; discounts to groups; members no charge. ♿
Attendance: 12,000 (accurate)
Membership: Astorian (Individual, Couple & Family) $35; Trapper (Patron) $100; Rocky Mountain Fur Trade Co. (Business) $150; The Rendezvous (Benefactor) $500; Jim Bridger League $1,000.

Powell

HOMESTEADER MUSEUM, (M), 324 E. 1st St., Powell, WY 82435. Mailing Address: P.O. Box 54, Powell, WY 82435-0054. Tel.: 307-754-9481.
E-mail: homesteader@bresnan.net
Founded: 1968.
Key Personnel: Dir., Rowene Weems; Museum Shop Mgr., Darleen Carroll; Museum Asst., Judith Skinner; Registrar Collections, Brandi Wright.
Personnel Profile: Full-Time Paid 1; Part-Time Paid 3; Part-Time Volunteers 12.
Governing Authority: Parent Institution: Park County Museum Board. Tax-exempt.
History Museum.
Collections: history of Powell and Shoshone Reclamation Project; homesteading; Heart Mountain Japanese Relocation Center memorabilia; early 20th century Big Horn Basin settlers' memorabilia; homesteader house.
Hours & Admission Prices: March-April & Oct.-Dec. Tues.-Fri. 10-4; May-Sept. Tues.-Fri. 10-5, Sat. 10-2. No charge; donations accepted. ♿
Attendance: 3,500
Membership: Senior $10; Single $15; Family $25; Business $50.

Ranchester

T-REX NATURAL HISTORY MUSEUM, 1116 Big Horn Dr., Ranchester, WY 82839. Mailing Address: P.O. Box 612, Ranchester, WY 82839-0612. Tel.: 307-655-3359.
History Museum.
Collections: local history; fossils; dinosaurs; minerals; crystals.
Facilities: Museum-related items for sale.
Activities: lectures.
Hours & Admission Prices: Call for hours.

Rawlins

CARBON COUNTY MUSEUM, (M), 904 W. Walnut St., Rawlins, WY 82301-6556. Mailing Address: P.O. Box 52, Rawlins, WY 82301-0052. Tel.: 307-328-2740. Fax: 307-328-2666.
E-mail: carbonc@wyoming.com
Web Site: www.carboncountymuseum.org
Founded: 1940.
Key Personnel: Dir., Denise Patton.
Personnel Profile: Full-Time Paid 1; Part-Time Paid 5.
Governing Authority: county; nonprofit. Parent Institution: Carbon County Commission. Tax-exempt.
History Museum.
Collections: local history.
Facilities: 25,000 sq. ft. exhibit space.
Hours & Admission Prices: June-Sept. Tues.-Fri. 10-6, Sat. 1-5; Oct.-May Tues.-Sat. 1-5; other times by appointment. ♿
Attendance: 2,434 (accurate)

WYOMING FRONTIER PRISON MUSEUM, (M), 500 W. Walnut St., Rawlins, WY 82301-4768. Tel.: 307-324-4422. Fax: 307-328-4004.
Key Personnel: Dir., Tina Hill
Prison Museum: housed in the Wyoming Frontier Prison which operated from 1901 to 1981. Site for the filming of the 1987 movie, Prison.
Collections: prison history; gas chamber.
Activities: Museum Sponsors: Special Halloween Night Tours in October; Christmas in the Big House Craft Bazaar in December.
Publications: cookbook, Savory Recipes by Unsavory Characters; The Sweet Smell of Sagebrush.
Hours & Admission Prices: Guided Tours: Memorial Day to Labor Day daily 8:30-4:30; Sept.-May call for hours. Guided Tours: family (parents & minor children) $30, adults $7, seniors 60 & over and children 12 & under $6.
Attendance: 15,000
Membership: Friends of the Old Pen: Student $5; Single $15; Family $20; Corporate & Club and Inmate $75; Trusty $100; Guard $250; Warden $500-$1,000.

Riverton

RIVERTON MUSEUM, 700 E. Park Ave., Riverton, WY 82501-3657. Tel.: 307-856-2665.
E-mail: lrnjost@yahoo.com
Founded: 1956.
Congressional District: 1
Key Personnel: Dir., Loren Jost.
Personnel Profile: Full-Time Paid 3; Part-Time Volunteers 12.
Governing Authority: county; nonprofit organization. Tax-exempt.
Local History Museum.
Collections: rotating exhibits; clothing; Indian artifacts; dentist material; saloon; mining; logging; books; trappers material; oil industry material; typewriters; musical instruments; beauty shop; nursery; library section; church; general store; shoes shop; flag display; sewing machines.
Research Fields: local & Wyoming history.
Facilities: 800-vol. library.
Activities: guided tours; school demonstrations; films; study clubs; work shops; tape interviews.
Publications: Wind River Mountaineer magazine.
Hours & Admission Prices: Tues.-Sat. 10-4. No charge; donations accepted. Closed holidays. ♿
Attendance: 7,500 (accurate)

ROBERT A. PECK ART CENTER, 2660 Peck Ave., Riverton, WY 82501-2215. Tel.: 307-855-2211; 800-735-8418, ext. 2211. Fax: 307-855-2090.
Art Center.
Collections: works by local, regional & national artists including paintings & contemporary sculpture.
Facilities: 6,000 sq. ft. exhibit space; 940-seat theater.
Activities: performances; theater & music productions; permanent & temporary exhibitions.
Hours & Admission Prices: Mon.-Fri. 8 am-10 pm, Sat. call for hours. No charge. Closed holidays.
Attendance: 5,000 (estimated)

WIND RIVER HERITAGE CENTER, 412 E. Freemont St., Riverton, WY 82501-4407. Mailing Address: P.O. Box 206, Riverton, WY 82501-0039. Tel.: 307-856-0706.
Key Personnel: Dir., Lew Diehl
Heritage Center.
Collections: Wyoming wildlife; period traps; Native American art.
Activities: Center Sponsors: Native American powwow dance program June to August.
Hours & Admission Prices: May-Dec. Tues.-Sat. 10-4. No charge.

Rock Springs

COMMUNITY FINE ARTS CENTER, 400 C St., Rock Springs, WY 82901-6225. Tel.: 307-362-6212. Fax: 307-352-6657.
E-mail: cfac@sweetwaterlibraries.com
Web Site: www.cfac4art.com
Founded: 1966.
Congressional District: 1
Key Personnel: Dir., Debora Thaxton Soule; Chm. (V), Kim Loppicolo; Asst. to Dir., Jennifer Messer.
Personnel Profile: Full-Time Paid 2; Part-Time Paid 1; Part-Time Volunteers 10.
Governing Authority: county; Fine Arts Center Board. Affiliated with School District #1. Parent Institution: Sweetwater County Library System. Tax-exempt.
Arts Center.
Collections: paintings; sculpture; drawing; graphics; photographs.
Facilities: meeting & workshop rooms.

Activities: guided tours; lectures; films; gallery talks; concerts; dance recitals; art festivals; formally organized education programs for adults & children; inter-museum loan & permanent exhibitions.
Publications: quarterly newsletter, CFAC; circulars on exhibits & demonstrations by recognized artists.
Hours & Admission Prices: Mon.-Thurs. 10-6, Fri.-Sat. 12-5. No charge; donations accepted. ♿
Attendance: 7,000 (estimated)

NATURAL HISTORY MUSEUM OF WESTERN WYOMING COLLEGE, 2500 College Dr., Rock Springs, WY 82901-5802. Mailing Address: P.O. Box 428, Rock Springs, WY 82902-0428. Tel.: 307-382-1600.
Web Site: wyshs.org/mus-wwcnathist.htm
Key Personnel: Dir., Kevin Thompson
History Museum.
Collections: archaeology; ethnography; natural history.
Hours & Admission Prices: Daily 9am-10pm. No charge.

ROCK SPRINGS HISTORICAL MUSEUM, (M), 201 "B" St., Rock Springs, WY 82901-6250. Tel.: 307-362-3138. Fax: 307-352-1516.
Founded: 1988.
Key Personnel: Pres. (V), Cindi Sullivan; Dir., Bob Nelson; Exhibits Coord., Norma Jean Robins.
Personnel Profile: Full-Time Paid 1; Part-Time Paid 3; Part-Time Volunteers 20; Interns 1.
Governing Authority: municipal government. Parent Institution: City of Rock Springs, Dept. of Parks & Recreation. Tax-exempt.
History Museum: 1894 Rock Springs City Hall, listed on the National Register of Historic Places, houses 1894 Rock Springs fire station & jail, stable & jail additions. A two-story sandstone structure, the building features two turreted bays, council chambers & mayor's balcony.
Collections: structure; furnishings; personal artifacts; tools & equipment.
Facilities: 2,500 sq. ft. exhibit space. Museum-related items for sale.
Activities: guided group tours on request; docent program; temporary exhibits. Annual Event: International Day.
Hours & Admission Prices: Summer: Mon.-Sat. 10-5; Winter: Wed.-Sat. 10-5. No charge; donations accepted. Closed Independence Day; major holidays. ♿
Attendance: 5,080 (accurate)

WEIDNER WILDLIFE MUSEUM, Western Wyoming Community College, 2500 College Dr., Rock Springs, WY 82901-5802. Tel.: 301-382-1600.
E-mail: emerrell@wwcc.wy.edu
Wildlife Museum.
Collections: over 125 species of wildlife from around the world.
Hours & Admission Prices: Mon. & Fri. 10-1, Tues. & Thurs. 1-4 & 7-9, Wed. 10-1 & 7-9. No charge.

WESTERN WYOMING COMMUNITY COLLEGE ART GALLERY, 2500 College Dr., Rock Springs, WY 82901-5802. Mailing Address: P.O. Box 428, Rock Springs, WY 82902-0428. Tel.: 307-382-1723.
Founded: 1989.
Key Personnel: Dir., Florence Alfano McEwin, Ph.D.
Governing Authority: Parent Institution: Western Wyoming College. Tax-exempt.
Art Gallery.
Collections: contemporary paintings; sculpture; photographs.
Hours & Admission Prices: Daily 8-10. No charge. ♿
Attendance: 2,000 (estimated)

Saratoga

SARATOGA MUSEUM, 104 Constitution Ave., Saratoga, WY 82331. Mailing Address: P.O. Box 1131, Saratoga, WY 82331-1131. Tel.: 307-326-5511.
E-mail: saratogamuseum@carbonpower.net
Web Site: www.saratoga-museum.com
Founded: 1978.
Key Personnel: Dir., Kathy Hennek.
Personnel Profile: Full-Time Paid 1; Part-Time Volunteers 18.
Governing Authority: nonprofit organization. Parent Institution: Saratoga Historical & Cultural Association. Tax-exempt: 170(b)(1)(A).
Historical Society Museum: housed in c.1890 Union Pacific Depot.
Collections: Union Pacific memorabilia; archaeology of Wyoming; items & artifacts of Carbon County. Historic Structures: renovated caboose; sheep wagon; blacksmith shop; geology exhibit.
Research Fields: history; archaeology.
Facilities: pavilion.
Activities: lectures; films; concerts; formally organized education programs for children; docent program; loan & permanent exhibitions. Annual Events: historical trips; architectural awards presentation.
Publications: Lewis Shutterly Diary; Saratoga & Encampment, an Album of Family Histories; Window in Time; Winchester Williams.
Hours & Admission Prices: Memorial Day-Labor Day Tues.-Sat. 1-4. No charge; donations accepted. ♿
Attendance: 1,800 (accurate)
Membership: Individual $15; Family $20; Sustaining $25; Business $50; Patron $100.

Savery

LITTLE SNAKE RIVER MUSEUM, Rte. 70, Savery, WY 82332. Mailing Address: P.O. Box 13, Savery, WY 82332-0013. Tel.: 307-383-7262.
Web Site: www.littlesnakerivermuseum.com
History Museum.
Collections: community history; personal artifacts; photographs.
Hours & Admission Prices: Memorial Day to Oct. daily 11-5. No charge; donations accepted. ♿

Sheridan

HISTORIC SHERIDAN INN/SHERIDAN HERITAGE CENTER, 856 Broadway St., Sheridan, WY 82801-3623. Mailing Address: P.O. Box 6393, Sheridan, WY 82801-1793. Tel.: 307-674-2178.
Web Site: www.sheridaninn.com
Governing Authority: nonprofit organization. Tax-exempt: 501(c)(3).
Historic Building: Sheridan Inn built c.1892.
Collections: Inn: period furnishings; photographs. Center: local history & culture.
Activities: rental facilities.
Hours & Admission Prices: Daily 10-8. Tours: daily 10-2. ♿

KING SADDLERY MUSEUM, 184 N. Main, Sheridan, WY 82801-3906. Tel.: 307-672-2702; 800-443-8919. Fax: 307-672-5235.
Key Personnel: Cur., Jean King
Western History Museum.
Collections: Western leather work; cowboy & Western history; saddles; Indian artifacts; guns; photographs; braidwork.
Activities: research.
Publications: catalogue, A King Saddlery.
Hours & Admission Prices: Mon.-Sat. 8-5. No charge; donations accepted.

SHERIDAN COUNTY MUSEUM, 850 Sibley Cir., Sheridan, WY 82801-9626. Tel.: 307-673-0644.
Key Personnel: Dir., Dana Prater; Pres. (V), Judy Musgrave; Museum Shop Mgr., Diana Oedekoven.
Personnel Profile: Full-Time Paid 2; Part-Time Paid 1; Part-Time Volunteers 20.
Governing Authority: Parent Institution: Sheridan County Historical Society. Tax-exempt.
History Museum.
Collections: Sheridan County history; photographs; personal artifacts.
Activities: special events; rental facilities. Museum Sponsors: monthly programs on the Porch; Tidbit Tuesdays for Kids.
Hours & Admission Prices: May & Sept.-Dec. 16 daily 1-5; June-Aug. daily 10-6. Adults $4, seniors over 60 $3, students $2; members and children 12 & under no charge. Closed Veterans Day; Thanksgiving. ♿
Attendance: 4,000 (accurate)
Membership: Senior $25; Single $30; Couple $50; Business $100; Corporate $1,000.

TRAIL END STATE HISTORIC SITE, 400 Clarendon Ave., Sheridan, WY 82801-4053. Tel.: 307-674-4589. Fax: 307-672-1720.
E-mail: trailend@state.wy.us
Web Site: www.trailend.org
Founded: 1982.
Key Personnel: Historic Program Mgr., Cynde Georgen; Cur., Sharie L. Mooney.
Personnel Profile: Full-Time Paid 2; Part-Time Paid 3; Part-Time Volunteers 15.
Governing Authority: state; nonprofit. Parent Institution: Wyoming Dept. of Parks & Cultural Resources, Division of State Parks & Historic Sites, Cheyenne, WY. Tax-exempt: 501(c)(3).
Historic House.
Collections: early 20th-century social history with emphasis on the Kendrick family; local history from 1913-1933.
Research Fields: Kendrick family; Northern Plains agriculture; 1913-1933 Social history; history of entertainment in the 20th century.
Facilities: 1,300-vol. library; 80-seat auditorium. Site-related items for sale.

Activities: docent program; self-guided tours; guided group tours by appointment; temporary exhibitions; theater. Annual Events: fundraiser in July; Holiday Open House in December.
Publications: quarterly newsletter, End Notes; One Cowboy's Dream: John B. Kendrick, His Family, Home and Ranching Empire.
Hours & Admission Prices: March-May & Sept.-Dec. 14 daily 1-4; June-Aug. daily 9-6. Adults $2; discounts to Wyoming residents; 17 & under no charge. Closed Veterans Day; Thanksgiving. ♿
Attendance: 14,000 (accurate)
Membership: Individual $5; Supporting $25; Sponsor $50; Patron $100; Benefactor $250; Cornerstone $500; Foundation $1,000.

Sinclair

PARCO SINCLAIR MUSEUM, 300 E. Lincoln Ave., Sinclair, WY 82334. Mailing Address: P.O. Box 247, Sinclair, WY 82334-0247. Tel.: 307-324-3058.
History Museum: housed in the former First National Bank; built in 1924.
Collections: local history & culture; photographs; period furnishings.
Hours & Admission Prices: Mon.-Fri. 9-12 & 1-4:30. No charge.

South Pass City

SOUTH PASS CITY STATE HISTORIC SITE, 125 South Pass Main, South Pass City, WY 82520-8703. Tel.: 307-777-6323. Fax: 307-332-3688.
E-mail: jellis@state.wy.us
Web Site: www.southpasscity.com
Founded: 1967.
Key Personnel: Cur. Public Programs, Jon Lane; Supt., Joe Ellis.
Personnel Profile: Full-Time Paid 4; Part-Time Paid 2.
Governing Authority: state. Parent Institution: Wyoming State Parks & Historic Sites, 2301 Central Ave., Cheyenne, WY 82002. Tax-exempt.
Historic Building & Site: c.1867-1910 gold-mining town consisting of 25 furnished buildings.
Collections: general store; hotel; school; bank; saloon; jail; dance hall; livery stable; gold mining memorabilia & artifacts; clothing; furnishings; bottles; photographs; guns; documents. Historic Buildings: 9 historic structures of the Carissa Mine including Mill house, hoist house, cook house, dorm, office, & residence.
Research Fields: history of mining; Oregon Trail history; community development; Woman Suffrage; 19th-century textiles; clothing; economic cycles.
Facilities: picnic grounds; concession desk.
Activities: guided tours; living history demonstrations; interpretive talks. Museum Sponsors: Gold Rush Days in July, Wyoming State Mining Championships & 1900 Vintage Baseball Tournament in July.
Publications: brochures, nature & historical.
Hours & Admission Prices: mid-May to Sept. daily 9-6. Adults: nonresident $4, resident $2; children 18 & under no charge. ♿
Attendance: 20,000 (accurate)
Membership: $5.

Sundance

CROOK COUNTY MUSEUM & ART GALLERY, (M), 309 Cleveland St., Sundance, WY 82729. Mailing Address: P.O. Box 63, Sundance, WY 82729-0063. Tel.: 307-283-3666. Fax: 307-283-1192.
E-mail: trudyw@crookcounty.wy.gov
Web Site: www.crookcountymuseum.com
Founded: 1971.
Key Personnel: Dir., Trudy Wadley; Chm., Rocky Courchaine.
Personnel Profile: Full-Time Paid 2.
Governing Authority: county. Parent Institution: Crook County. Tax-exempt.
History Museum.
Collections: furniture; pictures; western historical items; land records.
Facilities: library.
Activities: special tours for individual groups; special activities for school groups & senior citizens.
Publications: brochure.
Hours & Admission Prices: June-Aug. Mon.-Sat. 8-5; Sept.-May Mon.-Fri. 8-5. No charge; donations accepted. Closed holidays. ♿
Attendance: 7,000 (estimated)
Membership: Single $30; Couple $45; Family $80; Corporate $500.

Ten Sleep

TEN SLEEP PIONEER MUSEUM, 500 S. Second St., Ten Sleep, WY 82442. Mailing Address: P.O. Box 93, Ten Sleep, WY 82442-0093. Tel.: 307-366-2759.
Key Personnel: Dir., Gloria Cutt
History Museum.
Collections: pioneer life; tools; clothing; local family histories; books.
Activities: research.
Hours & Admission Prices: Daily 9-4; groups by appointment. No charge; donations accepted.

Thermopolis

DANCING BEAR FOLK CENTER, 119 S. 6th St., Thermopolis, WY 82443. Mailing Address: 110 Carter Ranch Rd., Thermopolis, WY 82443-2457. Tel.: 307-864-9396. Fax: 307-864-2657.
Folk Art Museum.
Collections: quilts; teddy bears; toys; marbles; model trains; planes.
Hours & Admission Prices: May 15-Sept. 29 daily 9-5; Sept. 30-May 14 daily 10-4. Closed New Year's Day; Thanksgiving; Christmas.

HOT SPRINGS COUNTY MUSEUM AND CULTURAL CENTER, (M), 700 Broadway, Thermopolis, WY 82443-2722. Tel.: 307-864-5183. Fax: 307-864-2974.
E-mail: hschistory@rtconnect.net
Web Site: hschistory.org
Founded: 1941.
Key Personnel: Dir. & Museum Shop Mgr., Ross R. Rhodes; Chm. (V), Doris Ann Ready.
Personnel Profile: Full-Time Paid 1; Part-Time Paid 4; Part-Time Volunteers 4.
Governing Authority: county; nonprofit. Tax-exempt.
History Museum.
Collections: county history from prehistoric to present times; 1880-1920s pioneering; arrowheads & related artifacts; ephemera & documentary archives; photographs.
Facilities: library; 80-seat auditorium; 18,000 sq. ft. exhibit space. Museum-related items for sale.
Activities: guided tours; lectures; temporary exhibitions.
Publications: brochure, Hot Springs County Historical Museum.
Hours & Admission Prices: Memorial Day-Labor Day Mon.-Sat. 9-5; Sept.-May Tues.-Sat. 9-4. Adults $4, senior citizens & children 6-12 $2; discounts to locals; children 5 & under no charge. ♿
Attendance: 4,983 (accurate)

OLD WEST WAX MUSEUM, 119 S. 6th St., Thermopolis, WY 82443. Mailing Address: 110 Carter Ranch Rd., Thermopolis, WY 82443-2457. Tel.: 307-864-9396. Fax: 307-864-2657.
E-mail: westwax@westwaxmuseum.com
Web Site: westwaxmuseum.com
Formerly: Dancing Bear Folk Center
Founded: 1999.
Congressional District: 20
Personnel Profile: Full-Time Paid 1; Part-Time Paid 3.
Wax Museum.
Collections: over 50 life-size wax figures in 20 Western frontier historical dioramas; historical newspapers; graphic arts; barbed wire & tools; period traps.
Facilities: 23,000 sq. ft. exhibit space.
Hours & Admission Prices: May 15-Sept. 14 daily 9-5; Sept. 15-May 14 Wed.-Sat. 10-2, Sun. 12-4. Adults $4.50, senior citizens, veterans & children 4-18 $3; discounts to groups; children under 4 no charge.

THE WYOMING DINOSAUR CENTER, 110 Carter Ranch Rd., Thermopolis, WY 82443-2457. Mailing Address: P.O. Box 868, Thermopolis, WY 82443-0868. Tel.: 307-864-2997; 800-455-3466. Fax: 307-864-5762.
E-mail: wdinoc@wyodino.org
Web Site: www.wyodino.org
Founded: 1995.
Congressional District: 20
Key Personnel: C.E.O., Burkhard Pohl; Treas., Patty Stegman; Dir. Science, Scott Hartman; Museum Shop Mgr., Judi Moore; Office Mgr., Angie Guyon.
Personnel Profile: Full-Time Paid 8; Part-Time Paid 12; Part-Time Volunteers 4; Interns 1.
Governing Authority: privately owned. Parent Institution: Big Horn Prospecting. Branch Museum: Old West Wax Museum.
Paleontology (Science) Museum.
Collections: 22 full size dinosaur mounts including Tyrannosaurus Rex, Triceratops & Camarasaurus; geology & prehistoric life on earth.
Research Fields: Paleontology-Jurassic, identification of primary dinosaur fossils, bone preparation and mounting.
Facilities: library; field research station; 18,000 sq. ft. exhibit area; bone preparation laboratory (viewable by visitors); bone storage; major dinosaur digsites comprising five acres on a 7,000-plus acre property (off-premises). Museum-related items for sale.
Activities: guided tours; Dig-for-a-day program for the public; kids' dinosaur dig; Elderhostel service programs.

Hours & Admission Prices: May 15-Sept. 14 daily 8-6; Sept. 15-May 14 Mon.-Sat. 10-5, Sun. 1-4. Adults $8, senior citizens 60 and over & children 4-13 $4.50; discounts to groups & families; children 3 & under no charge. Closed New Year's Day; Thanksgiving; Christmas. ♿
Attendance: 32,000 (estimated)

WYOMING PIONEER HOME, 141 Pioneer Home Dr., Thermopolis, WY 82443-2451. Tel.: 307-864-3151. Fax: 307-864-2934.
Founded: 1950.
Key Personnel: Facility Mgr., Sharon Skiver.
Governing Authority: state.
General Museum.
Collections: Indian artifacts; pioneer relics.
Hours & Admission Prices: Mon.-Fri. 8-5. No charge. ♿

Torrington

HOMESTEADERS MUSEUM, 495 Main St., Torrington, WY 82240. Mailing Address: P.O. Box 250, Torrington, WY 82240-0250. Tel.: 307-532-5612.
E-mail: museum@city-of-torrington.org
Founded: 1975.
Key Personnel: Dir., Dan Ringle; Pres. (V), Jean Dalton.
Personnel Profile: Full-Time Paid 1; Part-Time Paid 4; Interns 1.
Historic House: built in 1910 by Ben Trout.
Collections: period artifacts & records; photographs; land claims.
Hours & Admission Prices: Call for hours. No charge; donations accepted. Closed New Year's Day; Presidents' Day; Memorial Day; Independence Day; Thanksgiving & day after; Christmas.
Attendance: 2,800 (accurate)

Upton

UPTON RED ONION MUSEUM, 609 Pine St., Upton, WY 82730. Mailing Address: P.O. Box 543, Upton, WY 82730-0543. Tel.: 307-468-2672. Fax: 307-468-2672.
E-mail: urom@trib.com
History Museum.
Collections: Upton & Weston County history; photographs; paintings; period artifacts; documents.
Activities: school programs. Museum Sponsors: The Old Fashioned Christmas Celebration in December.
Hours & Admission Prices: Mon.-Fri. 9-5. No charge.

UPTON RED ONION MUSEUM, 203 Pine St., Upton, WY 82730. Mailing Address: P.O. Box 543, Upton, WY 82730-0543. Tel.: 307-468-2672. Fax: 307-468-2441.
History Museum.
Collections: local history & culture; photographs; period furnishings; personal artifacts; paintings.
Activities: research; school group tours. Museum Sponsors: The Old Fashioned Christmas Celebration in December.
Hours & Admission Prices: Mon.-Fri. 10-5. No charge.

Wheatland

LARAMIE PEAK MUSEUM, 1601 16th St., Wheatland, WY 82201. Mailing Address: P.O. Box 573, Wheatland, WY 82201-2609. Tel.: 307-322-2052, 2409 & 2309.
Founded: 1982.
Key Personnel: Dir., Judy Wilson; Chm. (V), Marlin Marshall
History Museum.
Collections: area history; photographs; personal artifacts.
Activities: research.
Hours & Admission Prices: mid-May to mid-Sept. Mon.-Fri. 10-5, Sat. 10-3. No charge; donations accepted. Closed holidays.

WYOMING TRAILS GALLERY, 1004 16th St., Wheatland, WY 82201-2530. Tel.: 307-322-3300.
Art Gallery.
Collections: paintings; bronze; pottery; jewelry; folk arts.
Hours & Admission Prices: Wed.-Sat. 9-4; other times by appointment.

Worland

WASHAKIE MUSEUM, 1115 Obie Sue, Worland, WY 82401-3527. Tel.: 307-347-4102. Fax: 307-347-4865.
Web Site: www.washakiemuseum.com
Founded: 1986.
Congressional District: 5
Key Personnel: C.E.O., Cheryl L. Reichelt; Chm. (V), Richard Dunne; Pres. (V), Martha Lawley; Treas., Kathy Koch; Education, Cheri Shelp.
Personnel Profile: Full-Time Paid 2; Part-Time Paid 6; Part-Time Volunteers 6.
Governing Authority: private; nonprofit organization. Tax-exempt: 501(c)(3).
General Museum.
Collections: history of Big Horn Basin, especially Washakie County; Paleo-Indian; paleontology; archaeology; geology; Native American; art; culture.
Facilities: 300-vol. library; 8,000 sq. ft. exhibit space; 120-seat auditorium; family discovery center. Museum-related items for sale.
Hours & Admission Prices: Call for hours. No charge; donations accepted. ♿
Attendance: 10,000 (accurate)

Wright

WRIGHT CENTENNIAL MUSEUM, 104 Ranch Court, Wright, WY 82732. Mailing Address: P.O. Box 354, Wright, WY 82732-0354. Tel.: 307-464-1222.
History Museum.
Collections: homestead; period dishes; World War I artifacts; mining tools; woodworking artifacts; present-day oil drilling & coal mining; windmills.
Publications: brochure.
Hours & Admission Prices: May 20 to Oct. 15 Mon.-Fri. 10-5, Sat. 10-3. No charge.

(U.S. TERRITORIES) AMERICAN SAMOA

(1 listings)

Pago Pago

JEAN P. HAYDON MUSEUM, Fagatogo, Pago Pago, AS 96799. Mailing Address: Fagatogo, P.O. Box 1540, Pago Pago, AS 96799-1540. Tel.: 684-633-4347. Fax: 684-633-2059.
E-mail: ascach07@gmail.com
Founded: 1969.
Key Personnel: Dir., Leala E. Pili; Chm. (V), Pagofie A. Fiaigoa; Program Coord., Rexx Yandall; Museum Shop Mgr., Johnston Yardall.
Personnel Profile: Full-Time Paid 3.
Governing Authority: territorial government; nonprofit organization. Affiliated with American Samoa Arts Council. Tax-exempt.
Historic Building & Site, General Museum & Art Museum: housed in 1900s old Post Office Building.
Collections: cultural, historical & environmental collections describing Samoan art & culture & its development to present times.
Research Fields: Samoan culture.
Facilities: classrooms; art gallery; herbarium. Books, tapes & other museum-related items for sale.
Activities: guided tours; lectures; films; formally organized education programs for children & adults.
Publications: Faasamoa PEA; Samoan Way.
Hours & Admission Prices: Mon.-Fri. 7:30-4. Special Programs: Sat. by appointment. No charge; donations accepted. ♿
Attendance: 30,000 (estimated)

COMMONWEALTH OF THE NORTH

(1 listings)

Saipan

COMMONWEALTH OF THE NORTHERN MARIANA ISLANDS MUSEUM OF HISTORY AND CULTURE, Caller Box 10007, Saipan, MP 96950. Mailing Address: P.O. Box 504570, Saipan, MP 96950-4305. Tel.: 670-664-2160. Fax: 670-664-2170.
Web Site: www.cnmimuseum.org
Founded: 1996.
Key Personnel: Exec. Dir., Mary Margaret Sablan; Admin. Officer, Gina Wesley; Exhibits Cur., Noel B. Quitugua; Museum Dir., Barbara G. Moir, Ph.D.; Physical Plant Mgr., James Macaranas.
Personnel Profile: Full-Time Paid 6; Full-Time Volunteers 1; Part-Time Volunteers 4.
Governing Authority: Parent Institute: CNMI Government. Tax-exempt.
History & Archaeology Museum: housed in historic Japanese hospital.
Collections: cultural & personal artifacts; folk culture; archaeology; decorative arts.
Activities: temporary exhibits; workshops; cultural events; educational outreach.
Hours & Admission Prices: Mon.-Fri. 9-4:30, Sat. 9-12. Adults $3, students with I.D. $1; discounts to groups; pre-scheduled school tours, children 11 & under and disabled individuals no charge. Closed holidays ♿

Attendance: 8,600 (estimated)

GUAM

(3 listings)

Hagatna

FANINADAHEN KOSAS GUAHAN-GUAM MUSEUM, (M), Rm. 408, PNB Bldg., Hagatna, GU 96910. Mailing Address: P.O. Box 2950, Hagatna, GU 96932-2950. Tel.: 671-475-4229 & 4230. Fax: 671-475-4227.
E-mail: am_palomo@yahoo.com
Web Site: www.guam.nex/gov/museum/
Founded: 1932.
Key Personnel: Dir. & Cur., Anthony Ramirez; Pres., J. Lawrence Cruz; Chm. (V), Doring Duenas.
Personnel Profile: Full-Time Paid 5; Part-Time Paid 1; Part-Time Volunteers 25.
Governing Authority: nonprofit; U.S. unincorporated territory. Parent Institution: Department of Chamorro Affairs. Subsidiary: Guam Museum. Tax-exempt.
General Museum: housed in 1776 Garden House.
Collections: artifacts from 1500 B.C.E.; Spanish Colonial historical artifacts from 17th-century to1899; historical artifacts from 1900-1945; Sgt. Shoichi Yokoi handmade survival gear.
Research Fields: pre-World War II Guam; prehistoric ceramics.
Facilities: 2,000-vol. library of Guam reference materials, available for use by public; 1,500 sq. ft. exhibit space. Postcard, books and posters for sale.
Activities: concerts; films; guided tours; lectures; participatory & temporary exhibits. Annual Events: Chamorro Week Feb.-March; Museum Week in May.
Publications: newsletter, Pappet.
Hours & Admission Prices: Daily 11-6. No charge; donations accepted. Closed holidays ♿
Attendance: 60,000 (accurate)

Mangilao

ISLA CENTER FOR THE ARTS AT THE UNIVERSITY OF GUAM, #15 Dean's Circle, Mangilao, GU 96923. Mailing Address: UOG Station, Mangilao, GU 96923. Tel.: 671-735-2965 & 2966. Fax: 671-735-2967.
E-mail: islacenter@gmail.com
Web Site: www.uog.edu/dynamicdata/classislacenterarts.aspx?siteid+l&p=191
Founded: 1980.
Key Personnel: Dir., Velma Yamashita; Extension Assoc., Gi Young Hwang; Extension Assoc., Liann Marie Castro.
Personnel Profile: Part-Time Paid 3.
Governing Authority: nonprofit. Parent Institution: Univ. of Guam.
Art Museum.
Collections: Pacific artifacts; prints; paintings; sculpture.
Facilities: 1,000 sq. ft. exhibit space. Books, postcards & exhibition catalogs for sale.
Activities: films; hobby workshops; lectures; temporary & traveling exhibitions.
Publications: quarterly exhibition catalogs.
Hours & Admission Prices: Mon.-Fri. 10-5, Sat. 10-2. No charge; donations accepted. Closed federal & government of Guam holidays. ♿
Attendance: 5,000 (estimated)
Membership: Student $15; Senior Citizen $25; Contributor $50; Patron $100; Benefactor $250; Key Member $500; Director's Club $1,000; President's Circle $2,500; Regent's Circle $5,000.

Piti

WAR IN THE PACIFIC NATIONAL HISTORICAL PARK, 460 N. Marine Dr., Piti, GU 96922. Mailing Address: 135 Murray Blvd., Ste. 100, Hagatna, GU 96910-5104. Tel.: 671-477-9362 & 472-7240, exts. 221 (Admin.), 233 (Cur.). Fax: 671-472-7241.
E-mail: WAPA_Administration@NPS.Gov
Web Site: www.nps.gov/wapa
Founded: 1982.
Key Personnel: Supt., Eric Brunnemann; Interpretive Specialist, Rose S.N. Manibusan; Museum Shop Mgr., Cindy Rapadas.
Personnel Profile: Full-Time Paid 11; Part-Time Paid 2; Part-Time Volunteers 3.
Governing Authority: federal. Dept. of the Interior. Parent Institution: National Park Service, Washington, DC. Tax-exempt.
World War II Military Museum: located on the site of the American recapture of Guam.
Collections: items & artifacts related to the War in the Pacific from 1939-1945.
Research Fields: military history of the War in the Pacific; 1939-1945 Pacific Island history; cause & effects of World War II 1939-1945; underwater archaeology of WW II sites in Micronesia.
Facilities: 150-vol. library of collection and 600-vols. of documentary material relating to the War in the Pacific from 1937-1945, in English & Japanese, available for research on premises only.
Activities: guided tours upon special request; formally organized educational programs for children; permanent exhibits; audiovisual program in Japanese & English.
Publications: park brochures; site bulletins.
Hours & Admission Prices: Mon.-Fri. 9-4:30, Sat.-Sun. & holidays 10-4:30. No charge. Closed New Year's Day; Thanksgiving; Christmas. ♿
Attendance: 45,000 (accurate)

PUERTO RICO

(23 listings)

Barranquitas

LUIS MUNOZ RIVERA LIBRARY AND MUSEUM, 10 Munoz Rivera St., Barranquitas, PR 00794-1607. Tel.: 787-857-0230. Fax: 787-857-0230.
Founded: 1916.
Key Personnel: C.E.O., Dr. Teresa Tio; Librarian & Cur., Maria L. Valencia.
Personnel Profile: Full-Time Paid 1; Part-Time Paid 1; Part-Time Volunteers 2.
Governing Authority: state. Parent Institution: Puerto Rican Culture Institute. Tax-exempt.
History Museum: housed in the birthplace of patriot, Luis Munoz Rivera.
Collections: mural representing the civic & political life of the patriot; articles, documents & photographs related to the life & death of Don Luis Munoz Rivera.
Research Fields: Puerto Rican literature, history & folklore.
Facilities: 3,000-vol. library of books & pamphlets of Puerto Rican literature, history & folklore; children's books; vertical files, three drawers.
Activities: guided tours; permanent exhibitions; expositions.
Publications: cultural bulletins.
Hours & Admission Prices: Wed.-Sun. 8-4. Admission charged. ♿
Attendance: 20,000 (accurate)

Bayamon

DR. JOSE CELSO BARBOSA MUSEUM & LIBRARY, Calle Barbosa No. 16, Bayamon, PR 00961-6346. Mailing Address: Instituto de Cultura Puertorriquena, Apartado 9024184, San Juan, PR 00902-4184. Tel.: 787-786-8115. Fax: 787-723-7837.
Web Site: www.icp.gobierno.pr
Founded: 1970.
Key Personnel: C.E.O., Dr. Jose Luis Vega; Dir., Jorge Rosado Santiago.
Personnel Profile: Full-Time Paid 1.
Governing Authority: state. Affiliated with Instituto de Cultura Puertorriquena; Tel. 787-786-8115. Tax-exempt.
Historic House.
Collections: furniture; personal objects; documents.
Hours & Admission Prices: Tues.-Sat. 8:30-12 & 1-4:30. No charge.
Attendance: 1,534 (accurate)

Cayey

DR. PIO LOPEZ MARTINEZ ART MUSEUM, (M), University of Puerto Rico, Cayey Campus, 205 Antonio R. Barcelo Ave., Cayey, PR 00736-4127. Tel.: 787-738-2161, ext. 2209 & 2191. Fax: 787-738-0650.
E-mail: museo@cayey.upr.edu
Founded: 1979.
Key Personnel: Dir., Prof. Humberto Figueroa.
Personnel Profile: Full-Time Paid 5; Part-Time Paid 3.
Governing Authority: Tax-exempt.
Art & History Museum.
Collections: paintings; drawings; prints; period artifacts.
Publications: exhibtions catalogs & brochures, Legado Frade; Homar Homo Humoris; Frade Arquitecto.
Hours & Admission Prices: Mon.-Fri. 8-4:30, Sat.-Sun. 11-5. No charge. ♿
Attendance: 4,360 (accurate)

Fajardo

LAS CABEZAS DE SAN JUAN NATURE RESERVE (EL FARO), Rte. 987, Km 5.9, Fajardo, PR 00738. Mailing Address: The Conservation Trust of Puerto Rico, P.O. Box 9023554, San Juan, PR 00902-3554. Tel.: 787-860-2560. Fax: 787-722-5872 & 860-1451.
E-mail: fideicomiso@fideicomiso.org

Web Site: www.fideicomiso.org
Founded: 1991.
Key Personnel: Exec. Dir., Fernando Lloveras San Miguel, Esq.; Chm., Jorge San Miguel, Esq.; Archivist, Rafael Lebron; Supt., Elizabeth Padilla.
Personnel Profile: Full-Time Paid 11; Part-Time Paid 3.
Governing Authority: private; nonprofit organization. Parent Institution: The Conservation Trust of Puerto Rico. Tax-exempt: 501(c)(3).
Nature Reserve: 316-acre reserve on northeastern tip of Puerto Rico includes 1880 lighthouse (El Faro), second oldest of Puerto Rico's 14 lighthouses.
Collections: aquarium collections (nonliving): crustaceans, echinoderms, sponges, shells, coral, insects, rocks; aquarium collections (living): iguanas, hermit crabs, sea marine invertebrates, fish. Environmental collections: mangroves, lagoons, rocky beaches, dry forests, offshore cays, reefs; endangered species; archaeological artifacts; herbarium.
Research Fields: archaeological excavations; migration of South American Indians; marine science; neurobiology; ornithology; environmental studies.
Facilities: 100-vol. library on natural science available to scholars and researchers; aquarium; nature center; field research station; theater; educational facilities. Museum-related items for sale.
Activities: guided tours; lectures; educational programs for adults & children; assistance with school projects & science fairs; training programs for professional museum workers.
Publications: quarterly newsletter, Boletin El Faro.
Hours & Admission Prices: mid-Sept. to Aug. Wed.-Sun. by reservation only. Tours: 9:30, 10, 10:30 & 2. Adults $8, senior citizens & students $5; discounts to groups of 20 or more; children under 4 no charge. Closed New Year's Day; Epiphany; Good Friday; Mother's Day; Father's Day; Independence Day; Thanksgiving; Christmas.
Attendance: 43,830 (accurate)
Membership: Student K-12 $7; University Student $15; Seniors 65 & over $25; Individual $30; Family $60; Company $300.

Guaynabo

CAPARRA MUSEUM AND HISTORIC PARK, Villa Caparra, 212 Carretera No. 2, Guaynabo, PR 00966-1718. Mailing Address: Instituto de Cultura Puertorriquena, Apartado 9024184, San Juan, PR 00902-4184. Tel.: 787-781-4795. Fax: 787-723-7837.
Web Site: www.icp.gobierno.pr
Founded: 1970.
Key Personnel: Dir. Museums & Parks, Nicole Pietri.
Personnel Profile: Full-Time Paid 2.
Governing Authority: state. Affiliated with Instituto de Cultura Puertorriquena; Tel. 787-724-0700. Tax-exempt.
Historic Site: ruins of Caparra was the first spot of colonization in Puerto Rico founded by Ponce de Leon in 1508.
Collections: memorial plaques; period artifacts.
Hours & Admission Prices: Mon.-Fri. 8-12 & 1-4:30, Sat.-Sun. by appointment. No charge. ♿
Attendance: 3,227 (accurate)

Gurabo

TURABO UNIVERSITY, Carr. 189, Km. 3.1, Gurabo, PR 00778. Mailing Address: P.O. Box 3030, Gurabo, PR 00778-3030. Tel.: 787-743-7979, ext. 4135. Fax: 787-743-7979, ext. 4149.
Founded: 1980.
Personnel Profile: Part-Time Paid 1.
Governing Authority: private university; nonprofit.
Archaeology Museum.
Collections: concentration on the archaeology of the eastern part of Puerto Rico; folkloric arts & crafts artifacts; ethnological representation of the region in the 19th-century.
Research Fields: archaeological studies of the region; urban development in 1940s; archaeological history in the 19th-century.
Facilities: 600-vol. library on art, history & archaeology available to the public; classroom; field research station.
Activities: temporary exhibitions. Annual Events: photography & art workshops.
Publications: annual bulletin, Center of Humanistic Studies.
Hours & Admission Prices: Aug.-May daily 8-12 & 1-5. No charge; donations accepted.
Attendance: 3,500

Hato Rey

* **MUSEO DE ARTE DE PONCE,** 525 FD. Roosevelt Ave. -3er Nivel #611, Hato Rey, PR 00918. Mailing Address: P.O. Box 9027, Ponce, PR 00732-9027. Tel.: 787-200-7090 & 7091; 787-848-0505 (Temporary location). Fax: 787-200-7094; 787-841-7309 (Temporary location).
E-mail: map@museoarteponce.org
Web Site: www.museoarteponce.org
Founded: 1959.
Key Personnel: C.E.O. & Dir., Dr. Agustin Arteaga; Volunteer Coord., Ms. Coral Cosals; Deputy Dir. Communications, Denise Berlingeri; Financial & Administration Dir., Miriam B. Quintero-Casanovas; Dir. Education, Ana Margarita Hernandez; Chief Cur., Cheryl Hartup; Registrar, Zorali De Feria; Dir. Conservation Laboratory, Lidia Aravena; Mgr. Human Resources, Nancy Colon; Facilities, Security & IT Mgr., Emilio Ruiz; Museum Shop Mgr., Mrs. Lourdes Vargas.
Personnel Profile: Full-Time Paid 36; Part-Time Paid 6; Part-Time Volunteers 100; Interns 1.
Governing Authority: nonprofit. Parent Institution: Luis A. Ferre Foundation, Inc. Tax-exempt: 501(c)(3).
Art Museum.
Collections: European art from 14th-19th centuries with emphasis on Victorian Italian & Spanish painting; Latin American art from 19th century to present; Puerto Rican art from 18th century to present; paintings; sculptures; archaeology; Oriental & pre-Columbian ceramics; glassware.
Major Exhibits: Masterpieces of European Painting from Museo de Arte de Ponce (T), 11/09-5/10; Sleeping Beauty: Victorian Painting from Museo de Arte de Ponce (T), 11/09-9/10; Julio Micheli: Beetles in P.R. Fall 2010-Spring 2011; Reinstallation of the Permanent Collection Fall 2010-Fall 2011.
Research Fields: Puerto Rican & Latin American art; European painting & sculpture.
Facilities: conservation laboratory; 5,000-vol. library of art books for research available for use on premises; reading room. Pamphlets, slides, postcards, reproductions & photographs of paintings for sale.
Activities: guided tours; lectures; films; gallery talks; concerts; workshops for students of all ages; formally organized education programs for children & undergraduate college students; inter-museum loan, permanent, temporary & traveling exhibitions; summer camps; collecting program; open houses.
Publications: book, Catalogues of Paintings & Sculptures; exhibition catalogues.
Hours & Admission Prices: Temporary location until 2010: 2325 Ave. Las Americas, Ponce, PR 00717-0076. Mon.-Fri. 11-7, Sat. 11-8, Sun. 11-5. Adults $5, children under 12 $2.50; discounts to groups, ICOM & AAM members; members no charge. Closed New Year's Day; Good Friday; Thanksgiving; Christmas. ♿
Attendance: 87,028 (accurate)
Membership: Students, Clergy, Senior Citizens & Handicapped $20; Individual $35; Family $50; Miguel Pou Category $100; Ramon Frade $250. Companies: Francisco Oller Category $500; Jesus Maria Sanroma Category $1,000; Jose Campeche Category $2,500; Mecenas Club $5,000; Gran Mecenas $10,000; Medici $20,000.

Mayaguez

UNIVERSITY OF PUERTO RICO DEPARTMENT OF MARINE SCIENCES MUSEUM, Dept. of Marine Sciences, Univ. of Puerto Rico, Mayaguez, PR 00681. Mailing Address: Call Box 9000, Mayaguez, PR 00681. Tel.: 787-832-4040, exts. 3443, 3447 & 3838. Fax: 787-899-5500 & 265-5408 & 832-3432.
E-mail: cimadiretor@uprm.edu
Web Site: cima.uprm.edu
Founded: 1954.
Key Personnel: Dir., Dr. Nilda Aponte; Cur. Marine Algae, Dr. David Ballantine; Cur. Marine Invertebrates, Dr. Nikolaos Schizas; Cur. Fish, Dr. Matthew Craig.
Governing Authority: state. Affiliated with University of Puerto Rico, Mayaguez Campus. Tax-exempt.
Marine Museum.
Collections: invertebrates; fishes; shells; tropical algae.
Research Fields: algae; fishes; invertebrates.
Facilities: research library of marine subjects; field research station; seawater systems; classrooms.
Publications: contributions of the Dept. of Marine Sciences.
Hours & Admission Prices: Call 787-899-2048 for appointment. No charge. ♿

Ponce

HACIENDA BUENA VISTA, Rte. 123, Km. 16.8, Ponce, PR 00731. Mailing Address: The Conservation Trust of Puerto Rico, P.O. Box 9023554, San Juan, PR 00902-3554. Tel.: 787-722-5882. Fax: 787-841-5997.
E-mail: fideicomiso@fideicomiso.org
Web Site: www.fideicomiso.org
Founded: 1987.
Key Personnel: Exec. Dir., Fernando Lloveras San Miguel, Esq.; Chm., Jorge San Miguel, Esq.; Visitor Svcs. Mgr., Sandra Franqui.
Personnel Profile: Full-Time Paid 14; Part-Time Paid 5.
Governing Authority: private; nonprofit organization. Parent Institution: The Conservation Trust of Puerto Rico. Tax-exempt: 501(c)(3).

Historic Site: reconstructed 1833 coffee plantation & corn mill in southern Puerto Rico.
Collections: Vives family records, documents, business papers & photographs; gardens; trails; reconstructed coffee processing machinery. Restored Buildings: manor house with period furniture, slave quarters; corn mill.
Research Fields: history of slavery in relation to Hacienda Buena Vista.
Facilities: 587-vol. library of Spanish & English catalogues, medical books, musical scores, accounting records, European & New World magazines, manuscripts & other documents; 350 sq. ft. exhibit space; gardens; trails. Museum-related items for sale.
Activities: guided tours; lectures; workshops; concerts; temporary & traveling exhibits; educational programs; docent program; training program for professional museum workers.
Publications: LaBuena Vista 1833-1904.
Hours & Admission Prices: Wed.-Sun. by appointment. Adults $8, senior citizens & students $5; discounts to groups of 20 or more; children 4 & under no charge. Closed New Year's Day; Epiphany; Good Friday; Independence Day; Thanksgiving; Christmas.
Attendance: 25,130 (accurate)
Membership: Student $7; University Student $15; Senior Citizen $25; Adult $30; Family $60.

San Juan

CASA BLANCA MUSEUM, Calle San Sebastian No. 1, San Juan, PR 00901-1156. Mailing Address: Instituto de Cultura Puertorriquena, Apartado 9024184, San Juan, PR 00902-4184. Tel.: 787-725-1454. Fax: 787-723-7837.
Web Site: www.icp.gobierno.pr
Founded: 1975.
Key Personnel: Dir., Nicole Pietri.
Personnel Profile: Full-Time Paid 2.
Governing Authority: state. Affiliated With Instituto de Cultura Puertorriquena; Tel.: 787-724-0700. Tax-exempt.
Historic House: c.1521 building constructed for the sons of Juan Ponce de Leon & inhabited by their descendants until mid-18th century.
Collections: domestic life in San Juan during the first three centuries of Spanish colonization; furniture; household decorations.
Publications: Casa Blanca, residence of the descendants of Juan Ponce de Leon colonizer of Puerto Rico.
Hours & Admission Prices: Wed.-Sun. 8:30-12 & 1-4:30. Adults $2, children $1; seniors no charge. ♿
Attendance: 12,300 (accurate)

LA CASA DEL LIBRO, (M), Calle Cristo 255, San Juan, PR 00901. Mailing Address: P.O. Box 9023544, San Juan, PR 00902-3544. Tel.: 787-723-0354. Fax: 787-723-0354.
E-mail: lcdl@prw.net
Web Site: www.lacasadellibro.org
Founded: 1955.
Key Personnel: Dir., Maria Teresa Arraras; Pres., Antonio J. Molina; Museum Shop Mgr., Sarah Massameno.
Personnel Profile: Full-Time Paid 3; Part-Time Paid 2; Part-Time Volunteers 3.
Governing Authority: Amigos Calle Del Cristo 255, Inc. Parent Institution: state. Subsidiary Institution: Instituto de Cultura Puertorriquena. Tax-exempt: 501(c)(3).
Rare Book/Book Arts Museum.
Collections: typography & other arts related to bookmaking, printing, calligraphy, lettering, design, illustration, papermaking, binding; manuscripts; rare books: manuscripts, incunabula, 20th-century masterpieces, 14th- to 15th-century Spanish books. Historic Building: 18th-century colonial townhouse.
Research Fields: early Spanish printed books; incunabula; bindings; fine printing; arts of the book 19th-century U.S. wooden types; Puerto Rican posters; maps.
Facilities: 7,000-vol. library.
Activities: lectures; temporary exhibitions; storytelling for children; book arts workshops.
Publications: Libros Espanoles Siglos XV-XVI; Coleccion La Casa del Libro, La Temprana Imprenta Sevillana; Repetitiones I, II & III; Libros Venecianos S.XV-XVI; Coleccion Quijote.
Hours & Admission Prices: Due to building renovations, please call before visiting.
Attendance: 30,000 (estimated)
Membership: Bernardo de Balbuena $35; Alonso Manso $100; Isabel la Catolica $500; El Quijote $1,000.

LUIS TORRES DIAZ PHARMACY MUSEUM, (M), Pharmacy and Deanship of Students Bldg., Medical Sciences Campus, University of Puerto Rico, San Juan, PR 00936. Mailing Address: P.O. Box 365067, San Juan, PR 00936-5067. Tel.: 787-758-2525. Fax: 787-751-5680.
E-mail: farma@rcm.upr.edu
Web Site: farmacia.rcm.upr.edu
Pharmacy Museum.
Collections: 210 porcelain apothecary jars; mortars; pestles; pharmaceutical artifacts from Spain, France & other countries.
Hours & Admission Prices: Tues.-Fri. 1-4.

MUSEO DE LAS AMERICAS, Cuartel de Ballaja, at the entrance of El Morro, 2nd Fl., San Juan, PR 00901. Mailing Address: P.O. Box 9023634, San Juan, PR 00902-3634. Tel.: 787-724-5052. Fax: 787-722-2848.
E-mail: museolasamericas@gmail.com
Web Site: www.prtc.net/~musame
Founded: 1992.
Key Personnel: Dir., Maria Angela Lopez-Vilella; Museum Shop Mgr., Walleska Rivera.
Personnel Profile: Full-Time Paid 8; Part-Time Paid 18; Part-Time Volunteers 2.
Governing Authority: private; nonprofit organization.
Folk Art Museum: housed in the 19th-century Ballaja Barracks.
Collections: folk art from the Americas; Native American artifacts from North, Central, & South America & the Caribbean; African anthropology.
Facilities: Museum-related items for sale.
Activities: children's workshops; arts & crafts; demonstrations; documentaries; lectures.
Publications: exhibition catalogues; biannual newsletter.
Hours & Admission Prices: Tues.-Fri. 10-4, Sat.-Sun. 11-5. American Indian Exhibit: adults $2. Closed New Year's Eve & Day; Good Friday; Mother's Day; Father's Day; Thanksgiving; Christmas Eve & Day. ♿
Attendance: 60,000 (estimated)

MUSEO DEL NINO, Calle Cristo 150, San Juan, PR 00901-1509. Mailing Address: P.O. Box 9022467, San Juan, PR 00902-2467. Tel.: 787-722-3791. Fax: 787-723-2058.
E-mail: info@museodelninopr.org
Founded: 1987.
Key Personnel: C.E.O., Ms. Carmen L. Vega; Bd. Member, Tere Bolivar.
Personnel Profile: Full-Time Paid 4; Part-Time Paid 1; Part-Time Volunteers 35; Interns 5.
Governing Authority: private; nonprofit organization. Tax-exempt: local exemption.
Children's Museum.
Collections: hands-on exhibits.
Research Fields: AIDS, with the purpose of developing an exhibit aimed at kids.
Facilities: 25-seat theater; 8,000 sq. ft. exhibit space. T-shirts, hats, bags, books & museum-related items for sale.
Activities: lectures; participatory exhibits; theater; broadcast programs. Annual Event: fundraiser.
Publications: biannual newsletter, Boletin del Museo del Nino.
Hours & Admission Prices: Tues.-Thurs. 9-3:30, Fri. 9-5, Sat.-Sun. 12:30-5. Adults $5, children 14 & under $4; discount to members. Closed major holidays. ♿
Attendance: 45,000 (accurate)
Membership: Kids $12; Family of six $100.

MUSEUM OF CONTEMPORARY ART OF PUERTO RICO, (M), Rafael M. Labra Bldg., Ponce de Leon Ave., Corner of Roberto H. Todd (Stop 18), San Juan, PR 00936. Mailing Address: P.O. Box 362377, San Juan, PR 00936-2377. Tel.: 787-977-4030. Fax: 787-977-4036.
E-mail: adm1@museocontemporaneopr.org
Web Site: www.museocontemporaneopr.org
Founded: 1984.
Key Personnel: Exec. Dir., Marianne Ramirez Aponte; Interim Pres. Bd. Dir., Mr. Frankie Vazquez; Pres. (V), Rafael J. Torrez Torrez; Accountant, Jose Padilla; Registrator, Anna Astor Blanco; Conservator, Mr. Ulrik Runeberg; Admin., Michelle Dilan; Education & Programming Officer, Evita Busa; Museum Shop Mgr., Jorge L. Pardo.
Personnel Profile: Full-Time Paid 12; Part-Time Paid 5; Part-Time Volunteers 2.
Governing Authority: private; nonprofit organization. Tax-exempt.
Art Museum.
Collections: contemporary art produced by artists from Latin America, Puerto Rico & the Caribbean since 1940 to the present; installations; conceptual art; mixed media; video art.

Major Exhibits: Careos/Relevos: 25 anos del Museo de Arte Contemporaneo de Puerto Rico, 12/3/09-5/3/10; FAS 2010 (Feria de Arte Sonoro), 5/21/10-8/30/10.
Research Fields: Puerto Rican, Caribbean & Latin American Art produced since 1940.
Facilities: 15,000-vol. library; 7,180 sq. ft. exhibit space; documentation center; conservation & restoration laboratory; digital workshop; education studio; administrative offices. Museum-related items for sale.
Activities: concerts; dance recitals; docent program; films; formal education programs for adults, school students & college students; guided tours; lectures; loan, participatory & traveling exhibitions; training programs for professional museum workers & Title I teachers; theater; summer camp. Annual Events: video art series.
Publications: members bulletin; exhibition catalogues; book series, Conversando con nuestros artistas (Talking With Our Artists); education brochures; multimedia productions (cd-roms), Contemporary Puerto Rican Art (1940-1999).
Hours & Admission Prices: Tues.-Sat. 10-4, Sun. 12-4. No charge; donations accepted. Closed New Year's Day; Three Kings Day; Good Friday; Constitution Day; Independence Day; Discovery of America Day; Discovery of Puerto Rico Day; Thanksgiving; Christmas. ♿
Attendance: 10,000 (estimated)
Membership: Students $25; Senior $35; Individual $50; Family $100; Associate $250; Benefactor $500; Sponsor $1,000; Honor $5,500; Patron $10,000.

MUSEUM OF HISTORY, ANTHROPOLOGY AND ART, (M), University of Puerto Rico, San Juan, PR 00931. Mailing Address: P.O. Box 21908 UPR, San Juan, PR 00931-1908. Tel.: 787-764-0000, ext. 2452 & 763-3939. Fax: 787-763-4799.
E-mail: fmarichal@uprrp.edu
Founded: 1940.
Key Personnel: Dir. & Cur. Art Collections, Flavia Marichal Lugo; Cur. Archaeological Collections, Ivan Mendez; Designer, Lionel Ortiz-Melendez; Educator, Lisa Ortega; Art Photographer, Jesus E. Marrero; Asst. Cur., Victor Gonzalez; Admin. Sec., Vilma de Jesus Ortega; Registrar, Chakira Santiago; Administrative Sec., Yolanda Vasquez; Admin., Maritza Rodriguez; Security, Gregorio Gonzalez.
Personnel Profile: Full-Time Paid 14; Part-Time Paid 2.
Governing Authority: university. Parent Institution: the University of Puerto Rico. Tax-exempt.
Art, History & Archaeology Museum.
Collections: 18th- to 21st-century Puerto Rican paintings, sculpture, prints & drawings; archaeology; ethnography; international graphics; Puerto Rican painters of the past & present; archaeology; history; popular arts; numismatics; documents & memorabilia.
Research Fields: Puerto Rican art, history & archaeology.
Facilities: library of Puerto Rican exhibition catalogs from 1950-present, artists archives & slides from art collection available for research on premises; 4,582 sq. ft. exhibit space.
Activities: guided tours; concerts; inter-museum loan, permanent, temporary & traveling exhibitions.
Publications: exhibition catalogues.
Hours & Admission Prices: Sun. 11-5, Mon.-Tues. & Fri. 9-4:30, Wed. 9-8:30. No charge. Closed holidays; university recesses. ♿
Attendance: 20,000

MUSEUM OF THE PUERTO RICAN FAMILY OF THE 19TH CENTURY, 319 Fortaleza St., San Juan, PR 00901-1715. Mailing Address: Instituto de Cultura Puertorriguena, P.O. Box 9024184, San Juan, PR 00902-4184. Tel.: 787-977-2700. Fax: 787-723-7837.
Web Site: www.icp.gobierno.pr
Founded: 1964.
Key Personnel: Dir., Nicole Pietri.
Personnel Profile: Full-Time Paid 2.
Governing Authority: state. Affiliated with Instituto de Cultura Puertorriquena; Tel. 787-724-0700. Tax-exempt.
Furniture Museum.
Collections: Puerto Rican 19th-century furniture.
Hours & Admission Prices: Wed.-Sun. 8:30-12 & 1-4:30. No charge.
Attendance: 2,024 (estimated)

PABLO CASALS MUSEUM, 101 San Sebastian St., San Juan, PR 00901. Mailing Address: P.O. Box 41227, San Juan, PR 00940-1227. Tel.: 787-723-9185. Fax: 787-722-3338 & 723-5843.
Founded: 1977.
Key Personnel: C.E.O. & Gen. Mgr., Evangelina Colon; Admin., Anibal Ramirez.
Personnel Profile: Full-Time Paid 1; Part-Time Paid 4.
Governing Authority: Theatrical Musical Arts Corp. Parent Institution: Corp. Artes Escenico Musicales. Institution subsidized by Puerto Rican government.
Classical Music Museum.
Collections: photographs & memorabilia of Pablo Casals; videos of past Casals concerts.
Research Fields: classical music history related to Pablo Casals.
Hours & Admission Prices: Tues.-Sat. 9:30-5. Adults $1, senior citizens & children $.50; discounts to AAM members.
Attendance: 15,000 (estimated)

POPULAR ARTS MUSEUM, Calle Cristo 253, San Juan, PR 00901-1518. Mailing Address: Instituto de Cultura Puertorriquena, Apartado 9024184, Division Artes Populares, San Juan, PR 00902-4184. Tel.: 787-722-0621. Fax: 787-723-2320.
Web Site: www.icp.gobierno.pr
Key Personnel: Interim Dir., Jorge Rosado.
Governing Authority: state. Parent Institution: Instituto Cultura Puertorriquena, Tel. 787-724-0700. Tax-exempt.
Folk Art Museum.
Collections: folk art by Puerto Rican artisans.
Hours & Admission Prices: Tues.-Fri. 10-5, Sat.-Sun. 12-5. No charge.

SAN JUAN NATIONAL HISTORIC SITE, 501 Norzagaray St., San Juan, PR 00901-1213. Tel.: 787-729-6777. Fax: 787-289-7972.
E-mail: doris_diaz@nps.gov
Web Site: www.nps.gov/saju/
Founded: 1949.
Key Personnel: Dir., Paul B. Hartwig; Supt., Walter Chavez; Eastern National Store Mgr., Bernice Velez.
Governing Authority: federal. Parent Institution: National Park Service. Tax-exempt.
Historic Buildings: 16th to 19th-century Spanish fort located in Old San Juan, 3 miles of city walls.
Collections: Old Spanish uniforms & artifacts; weapons; coins; ceramics; construction plans; rare books; period furnishings; troop quarters; military archives on the history of the forts of Old San Juan including: 5,000 maps & plans; 10,000 photos; 50,000 manuscripts; microfilms & documents.
Research Fields: Spanish-colonial military history; preservation of masonry structures.
Facilities: 2,000-vol. library pertaining to the history of Europe & Latin America, available for use by researchers or institutions under special circumstances; Fort San Cristobal.
Activities: guided tours; 30-min. video history of the forts of San Juan.
Hours & Admission Prices: Daily 9-6. Adults $3, seniors 65 & over and children 13-17 $2; children 15 & under no charge. Closed New Year's Day; Thanksgiving; Christmas. ♿
Attendance: 2,200,000 (accurate)

Santurce

MUSEO DE ARTE DE PUERTO RICO, 299 De Diego Ave., Stop 22, Santurce, PR 00909-1766. Mailing Address: P.O. Box 41209, San Juan, PR 00940-1209. Tel.: 787-977-6277. Fax: 787-977-4444.
Web Site: www.mapr.org
Founded: 2000.
Key Personnel: Exec. Dir., Ms. Lourdes Ramos Rivas, Ph.D.; Bd. Pres., Marcos Rodriguez Ema, Esq.; Devel., Myrna Z. Perez; Cur., Juan Carlos Lopez; Education, Doreen Colon; Treas., Sonia Dominguez, CPA; Registrar, Doris Diaz; Security Mgr., Carlos Ruiz; Mgr. Exhibitions, Jaquelina Rodriguez; Mgr. Public Rels., Yetzenia Alvarez; Dir. Sales & Mktg., Leslie Alvarado; Museum Shop Mgr., Salvatore Curreri.
Personnel Profile: Full-Time Paid 59; Part-Time Paid 10; Part-Time Volunteers 69; Interns 8.
Governing Authority: private; nonprofit organization. Tax-exempt: 501(c)(3).
Art Museum.
Collections: 18th to 21st century Puerto Rican paintings, sculpture, prints & drawings; installations.
Major Exhibits: Claudio Gallina, 11/09-1/10; Puerto Rico Human Geography, 11/09-2/10; Donation Angel Ramos and Tina Hills Collection, 11/09-11/2/10; Puerto Rican Context: From Colonial Rococo to Global Art, 11/09-12/10.
Research Fields: Puerto Rican art, painting & graphics from colonial art to present.
Facilities: library; botanical garden; 92-seat restaurant; 32-seat cafeteria; 41,962 sq. ft. exhibit space; 400-seat theater; classrooms; workshops; computer lab; seminar room. Museum-related items for sale.
Activities: arts festivals; concerts; docent program; films; formal education programs; guided tours; hobby workshops; lectures; loan, traveling &

temporary exhibitions; theater; training programs for professional museum workers. Annual Events: MAPR Annual Gala; MAPR Annual Auction.
Publications: annual report; exhibition catalogues; brochures.
Hours & Admission Prices: Tues. & Thurs.-Sat. 10-5, Wed. 10-8, Sun. 11-6. Adults $6, senior citizens, children & students $3; tax not included; Wed. 2-8 & members no charge. Closed New Year's Day; Good Friday; Election Day; Thanksgiving; Christmas. ♿
Attendance: 125,923 (accurate)
Membership: Students, Teachers, Seniors & Handicapped $25; Individual $50; Family $100; Friend $250; Collaborated $500; Executive $1,000.

Utuado

CAGUANA INDIAN CEREMONIAL PARK & MUSEUM, Rte. 111 km 12.3, Utuado, PR 00641. Tel.: 787-894-7325. Fax: 787-894-7310.
Founded: 1975.
Key Personnel: C.E.O., Milagros Castro; Museum Dir., Linda Gregory.
Personnel Profile: Full-Time Paid 9.
Governing Authority: state. Affiliated with Instituto de Cultura Puertorriquena; Tel. 809-724-5477. Tax-exempt.
Indian Park Museum.
Collections: petroglyphs; Indian objects; pre-hispanic artifacts, Tainos culture.
Hours & Admission Prices: Wed.-Sun. 9-4:30. Adults $2, children 6-12 $1; seniors over 60 & children under 6 no charge.
Attendance: 104,000 (accurate)

Vieques

MUSEO FUERTE CONDE DE MIRASOL DE VIEQUES, Apartado 71, Vieques, PR 00765-0071. Mailing Address: P.O. Box 71, Vieques, PR 00765-0071. Tel.: 787-741-1717.
E-mail: bieke@prdigital.com
Web Site: www.icp.gobierno.pr/
Founded: 1991.
Key Personnel: Dir., Roberto L. Rabin Siegal.
Personnel Profile: Full-Time Paid 7; Part-Time Volunteers 10; Interns 8.
Governing Authority: state government; nonprofit. Parent Institution: Instituto del Cultura Puertorriquena. Tax-exempt.
History Museum: housed in a two-story 19th-century Spanish fortress constructed of brick & local wood.
Collections: archeological material from pre-Hispanic groups indigenous to Vieques & main island of Puerto Rico; artifacts, photos & maps documenting Vieques' history, 1514-present; artifacts, photos & tools relative to Vieques' historic architecture, 1844-1940; itinerant plastic arts exhibits: photos, paintings; artisanry, sculpture, textiles.
Research Fields: Vieques' archaeology; African slavery in Vieques, 19th century; historic relations between Vieques & St. Croix, U.S. Virgin Islands; environmental & other impacts of the U.S. Navy presence on Vieques, 1940-present; Vieques' historic architecture.
Facilities: library of historical texts; local newspapers; microfilm archives of varied documents; programs/bulletins from local festivities & community organizations; 100-seat auditorium; classrooms. Museum-related items for sale.
Activities: cultural festival; concerts; docent program; films; formal education programs for undergraduate & graduate college students; guided tours; lectures; school loan service; study clubs; temporary & traveling exhibitions; theater.
Hours & Admission Prices: Museum: Wed.-Sun. 9-5:30. Historic Archives: Mon.-Fri. by appointment. Adults $3, seniors over 60 & children under 12 $1; discounts to AAM & ICOM members; children under 12 no charge. Closed Good Friday; Mother's Day; Father's Day.
Attendance: 15,000 (estimated)

VIRGIN ISLANDS

(4 listings)

Saint Croix

CHRISTIANSTED NATIONAL HISTORIC SITE, 2nd Fl., Danish Custom House, Kingswharf-Christiansted, Saint Croix, VI 00820. Mailing Address: 2100 Church St. #100, Danish Custom House, Christiansted, St. Croix, VI 00820-5402. Tel.: 340-773-1460. Fax: 340-773-5995.
E-mail: CHRI_superintendent@nps.gov
Web Site: www.nps.gov/chri
Founded: 1952.
Key Personnel: Interpretive Ranger, Anibal Colon, Jr.; Chief Resource Management, Zandy Hillis-Starr; Park Supt., Joel A. Tutein; Chief Interpretation, William Cissel.
Personnel Profile: Full-Time Paid 16; Part-Time Volunteers 8.
Governing Authority: federal. National Park Service, Southeast Region, 100 Alabama St., S.W., 1924 Bldg., Atlanta, GA. 30303. Tel. 404-562-3327. Tax-exempt.
Historic Site & Historic Houses: depicts Danish Colonial development in the West Indies.
Collections: Folmer Andersen collection of over 16,000 prehistoric artifacts; architectural specimens; Danish military uniforms; Colonial Bottle Collection. Historic Houses: 1753 Steeple Building; 1738 Fort Christiansvaern; 1855-56 Scale House; 1748-49 Danish West India & Guinea Company Ware House; 1751 Old Custom House.
Research Fields: pre-Columbian cultures in the Virgin Islands; Danish West Indian military history.
Facilities: microfilm library pertaining to Danish period.
Activities: guided tours.
Publications: brochures, Christiansted National Historic Site, Fort Christiansvaern; Folmer Andersen; Steeple Building; Government House; Buck Island Reef National Monument; Salt River Bay National Historic Park & Ecological Preserve.
Hours & Admission Prices: Mon.-Fri. 8-5, Sat.-Sun. 9-5. Adult $3; senior citizens with Golden Age Pass & youth under 16 no charge. Closed Thanksgiving; Christmas.
Attendance: 100,000 (accurate)
Membership: Golden Age Pass $10.

Saint John

VIRGIN ISLANDS NATIONAL PARK, 1300 Cruz Bay Creek, Saint John, VI 00830-6108. Tel.: 340-776-6201, ext. 238.
E-mail: susanna-pershern@nps.gov
Web Site: www.nps.gov/viis
Founded: 1956.
Key Personnel: Supt., Mark Hardgrove; Chief Interpretive Ranger, Paul Thomas.
Personnel Profile: Full-Time Paid 4; Part-Time Volunteers 10.
Governing Authority: federal. National Park Service, Southeast Field area, 75 Spring St., S.W. Atlanta, GA. 30303. Tel. 404-331-5187. Headquarters: Virgin Islands National Park No. 10 Estate Nazareth, St. Thomas, VI 00802. Tax-exempt.
National Park Museum & Visitor Center.
Collections: archaeological; history; marine. Historic Structures: c.1717-late 1800s, sugar mills & estate houses.
Research Fields: tropical, marine & terrestrial West Indian & Danish colonial history.
Facilities: 1,000-vol. library pertaining to Caribbean & natural history available for research on premises. Books & other museum-related items for sale.
Activities: guided tours; lectures; films; formally organized education programs for children; permanent & temporary exhibits.
Publications: Annaberg plantation self-guided tour brochures; safe boating brochure; trail guide.
Hours & Admission Prices: Visitor Center: daily 8-4:30. ♿
Attendance: 250,000 (estimated)

St. Croix

WHIM PLANTATION MUSEUM, 52 Estate Whim, Frederiksted, St. Croix, VI 00840-3744. Tel.: 340-772-0598. Fax: 340-772-9446.
E-mail: info@stcroixlandmarks.org
Web Site: www.stcroixlandmarks.com
History Museum: housed on an early 18th century sugar plantation.
Collections: sugar plantation life & history; restored windmill; sugar factory; gardens.
Facilities: library; 12 acre plantation.
Activities: special events; rental facilities.
Hours & Admission Prices: Mon.-Sat. 10-4. Adults $10, seniors $5, children 6-12 $4; VI residents on Sat. & children under 6 no charge. ♿

St. Thomas

SEVEN ARCHES MUSEUM, Off Kongens Gade, Government Hill, St. Thomas, VI 00802. Mailing Address: P.O. Box 6456, St. Thomas, VI 00804-6456. Tel.: 340-774-9295.
E-mail: sevenarchesmuseum@yahoo.com
Web Site: www.sevenarchesmuseum.com
Key Personnel: Cur., Barbara Demaras
History Museum: built in the late 1700s and named for the seven arches that support the main staircase.
Collections: local history & culture; "welcoming arms" staircase, gun turret slots in the walls, letters, photographs & postcards from the 1800s.
Hours & Admission Prices: Mon.-Sat. 10-4; other times by appointment.

Products & Services Suppliers

L—Continued

M

N

O

P

Q

R

S

T

U

V

W

X

Z

AUDIO & VIDEO-GENERAL

bpi
imagine. what we do.

BOSTON PRODUCTIONS, INC.
100 Morse St.
Norwood, MA 02062
Tel: 781-255-1555; FAX: 781-255-1556
E-mail: imagine@bostonproductions.com
Web Site: www.bostonproductions.com

Type of Business:
For twenty years, Boston Productions has been telling compelling stories to museum and visitor center audiences across the country through engaging and immersive media exhibits. Always putting the visitor experience first, we continue to surprise, enthrall and inform with uniquely diverse ideas and cutting-edge methods. Our signature AV presentations and interactive visitor experiences require multidisciplinary services and skill sets, such that we are equally expert in media design, content development, production services, software programming, exhibit prototyping and full AV hardware integration services. Knowing what works creatively with today's multigenerational audiences and being able to produce media, interactive exhibits and AV hardware systems with a strong value quotient is an organizational imperative. Boston Productions is truly a creative concept-to-installation business. - imagine. what we do.

Personnel:
Bob Noll (President & Creative Director)
Chet Kaplan (COO & Director AV Hardware Integration)
Mark Dorgan (Associate Creative Director)

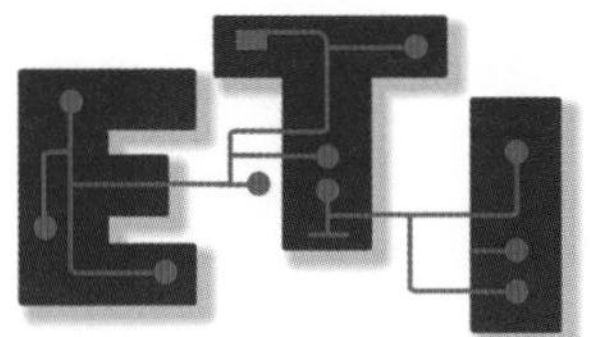

EDWARDS TECHNOLOGIES, INC.
139 Maryland St.
El Segundo, CA 90245
Tel: 310-536-7070; FAX: 310-322-1459
E-mail: roberta.perry@etiemail.com
Web Site: www.edwardstechnologies.com

Type of Business:
Founded in 1984, ETI specializes in the design, engineering, fabrication and installation of custom audio, visual displays, lighting, show control and digital HD 3D/4D theaters, Mobile Cinemas. Clients: Discovery Science Center, CA, Discovery Center, NC, Health Museum, El Trompo, Tijuana; Museum of Science & Industry, Chicago; Aquarium of the Pacific, CA, Riverbank Zoo, SC; Boston Museum of Science & Industry, Fort Worth Museum of Science and History; and the Franklin Institute.

Personnel:
Brian Edwards (President & CEO)
Roberta Perry (Vice President Business Development)
Ravi Shankar (Vice President Operations)
David Krueger (Midwest/East Coast Business Development)

RBH MULTIMEDIA, INC.
12 Hatch Ter.
Dobbs Ferry, NY 10522
Tel: 914-693-8755; FAX: 914-693-3539
E-mail: rbh@rbhmedia.com
Web Site: www.rbhmedia.com

Type of Business:
RBH Multimedia, Inc. is a media production company dedicated to developing and producing audiovisual experiences and exhibits. We bring imagination, skill, flair and years of experience to designing and producing audio, video and multiple media exhibits for museums, historic sites, visitor and interpretive centers, and cultural institutions. We also design and program websites and computer interactive exhibits. RBH is particularly known for producing signature multi-sensory, multimedia "experience" theater shows. Other services include hardware system design, engineering and installation, with expertise in videoconference technology. For more information about RBH Multimedia, Inc., please visit us online at www.rbhmedia.com.

Personnel:
Steve Brosnahan (Partner)
Nancy Haffner (Partner)
Edgardo J. Resto (Associate)

SUNRISE SYSTEM, INC.
720 Washington St.
Pembroke, MA 02359
Tel: 781-826-9706; FAX: 781-826-0061
E-mail: sales@sunrisesystems.com
Web Site: www.sunrisesystems.com

Type of Business:
Sunrise Systems, Inc. is a manufacturer of custom LED signage. Founded in 1976, Sunrise has been a lifelong producer of fascinating public art, first-in-the-industry technological advances and uniquely tailored information systems. Our LED displays are installed in countries all over the world and in industries across the map. Transit system integrators, stock tickers, retail applications and academic exhibits are just a few well-established areas of Sunrise's expertise. Past installments are prominently featured in many permanent exhibits at prestigious museums around the globe. Our ability to meet even the most complex architectural, electrical and mechanical requirements keeps us at the forefront of the industry. A dedication to innovative technology and customer support make us a good place to start planning your next LED display project.

Personnel:
Henry C. Appleton (President, Director Sales)
Eric Harrington (Director, Engineering)
Kaleb Christenson (Marketing Director & Project Manager)

TOUR-MATE SYSTEMS CANADA LTD
137 St. Regis Crescent
Toronto, ON, Canada M3J 1Y6
Tel: 800-216-0029 & 416-636-5654; FAX: 416-636-9541
E-mail: info@tourmate.com
Web Site: www.tourmate.com

Type of Business:
Tour-Mate Systems was established in 1988 to develop and market self-guided audio tours for the interpretive market. We have installed systems in the United States, Canada, United Kingdom, Puerto Rico, Barbados, Japan, Australia, Switzerland, China and Macao. Millions of visitors have experienced Tour-Mate audio tours in museums, art galleries, historic sites, zoos, aquariums, and botanical gardens. Our Traditional and Mobile Audio Tour Systems feature high quality sound, random access capability, and multiple language options. Tour-Mate's content creation coupled with its approach to client care ensures each visitor has a significantly enhanced tour experience. Tour-Mate has over 20 years of experience, including the provision of audio tours to attractions such as the Art Gallery of Ontario, Montreal Museum of Fine Arts, Vancouver Art Gallery, Mount Rushmore, the Walt Disney Concert Hall, and the Corning Museum of Glass. Our commitment to customer service is second to none.

Personnel:
Neil Poch (President)
David Hayes (Director, Technology)
Atul Garg (Sales & Marketing Manager)
Shahar Chudy (Support Services Manager)

3D

ARIUS3D, INC.
755 The Queensway E.
Mississauga, ON, Canada L4Y 4C5
Tel: 905-270-7999; FAX: 905-270-6888
E-mail: info@arius3d.com
Web Site: www.arius3d.com; www.pointstream.net

Type of Business:
Arius3D delivers scientific quality 3D models with true color and accurate geometry. The patented 'non-touch' 3D color laser is free of ambient light artifacts or UV rays. We bring alive the concept of Scan Once: Use Many Times. Models can be easily scaled for a myriad of different applications including: digital repatriation, disaster recovery, digital archiving, conservation, virtual museum exhibits, object replication for digital & physical learning objects. Arius3D models can be used on pc's, kiosks, mobile devices, in digital learning galleries, VR theatres and caves in digital (mono or stereo), print, holographic or physical formats. Call us when accurate high resolution models are necessary!

Personnel:
Susan Dineen (Vice President Business Development)

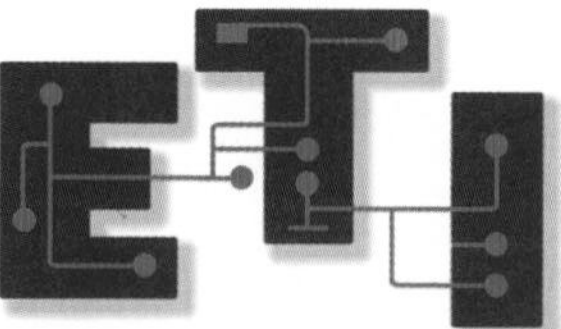

EDWARDS TECHNOLOGIES INC
139 Maryland St.
El Segundo, CA 90245
Tel: 310-536-7070; FAX: 310-322-1459
E-mail: roberta.perry@etiemail.com
Web Site: www.edwardstechnologies.com

Type of Business:
Founded in 1984, ETI specializes in the design, engineering, fabrication and installation of custom audio, visual displays, lighting, show control and digital HD 3D/4D theaters, Mobile Cinemas. Clients: Discovery Science Center, CA, Discovery Center, NC, Health Museum, El Trompo, Tijuana; Museum of Science & Industry, Chicago; Aquarium of the Pacific, CA, Riverbank Zoo, SC; Boston Museum of Science & Industry, Fort Worth Museum of Science and History; and the Franklin Institute. STIMULUS PACKAGE: All inclusive - Panasonic Digital Theater 3D/4D starting at $100,000.

Personnel:
Brian Edwards (President & CEO)
Roberta Perry (Vice President Business Development)
Ravi Shankar (Vice President Operations)
David Krueger (Midwest/East Coast Business Development)

OLSON VISUAL, INC.
13000 Weber Way
Hawthorne, CA 90250
Tel: 800-480-6643; FAX: 310-263-6980
E-mail: graphics@olsonvisual.com
Web Site: www.olsonvisual.com

Type of Business:
Olson Visual has been a supplier of large format graphics to museums for over 50 years and is committed to providing superior service from start to finish. We have dedicated an entire segment of the business to Museum and Fine Art projects and take pride in supplying our clientele with quality custom pieces. OV will evaluate your needs and give recommendations on a combination of output and display possibilities. Our team of Museum Consultants can also help you integrate green materials into your projects wherever possible, while still maintaining the integrity of your design concept. Call us and inquire about your next project.

Personnel:
Daniel Olson (Vice President)
Eder Cetina (Creative Director/ Museum Consultant)
Ashleigh Turner (Project Manager/Museum Consultant)

Audio Visual Equipment

AVITRA EXHIBIT TECHNOLOGIES
1567 S. Cora St.
Des Plaines, IL 60018
Tel: 847-803-4832; FAX: 847-699-3116
E-mail: sales@avitra.com
Web Site: www.avitra.com

Type of Business:
Full service supplier of audio, visual, lighting, control, and motion equipment to the museum, trade show, POP, and amusement industries. Equipment lines include solid-state A/V playback units, interactive touchscreens, directed sound speakers and handsets, walking tour repeaters, LED lighting, portable PA systems, custom controllers, etc. Services: A/V productions, programming, system design, exhibit design/consultation, fabrication, technical assistance. Complete custom packages available: audio walking tours, touchscreen kiosks, soundscapes, automated presentations, indoor and outdoor message repeaters.

Personnel:
Tom Schafer (President)
Jim Bebarski (Vice President)

bpi
imagine. what we do.

BOSTON PRODUCTIONS, INC.
100 Morse St.
Norwood, MA 02062
Tel: 781-255-1555; FAX: 781-255-1556
E-mail: imagine@bostonproductions.com
Web Site: www.bostonproductions.com

Type of Business:
For twenty years, Boston Productions has been telling compelling stories to museum and visitor center audiences across the country through engaging and immersive media exhibits. Always putting the visitor experience first, we continue to surprise, enthrall and inform with uniquely diverse ideas and cutting-edge methods. Our signature AV presentations and interactive visitor experiences require multidisciplinary services and skill sets, such that we are equally expert in media design, content development, production services, software programming, exhibit prototyping and full AV hardware integration services. Knowing what works creatively with today's multigenerational audiences and being able to produce media, interactive exhibits and AV hardware systems with a strong value quotient is an organizational imperative. Boston Productions is truly a creative concept-to-installation business. - imagine. what we do.

Personnel:
Bob Noll (President & Creative Director)
Chet Kaplan (COO & Director AV Hardware Integration)
Mark Dorgan (Associate Creative Director)

DESIGN AND PRODUCTION INCORPORATED
7110 Rainwater Place
Lorton, VA 22079
Tel: 703-550-8640; FAX: 703-339-0296
E-mail: dmoalli@d-and-p.com
Web Site: www.d-and-p.com

Type of Business:
In service to the museum community since 1949, our global portfolio is comprised of hundreds of high-profile projects, including interpretive history, interactive science, sports, children's museums, and immersive environments. D&P specializes in large-scale, multi-discipline exhibit projects, with a full complement of in-house production capabilities: Project development and management, custom fabrication, interactive exhibits, A/V hardware and software development, artifact mounting, graphic production, installation, and service. D&P is FSC-certified and a charter member of USGBC.

Personnel:
Jay Barnwell (President)
Dan Moalli (Vice President Business Development)
Donna Kuba (Project Director)
Rachel Childress (Marketing Associate)

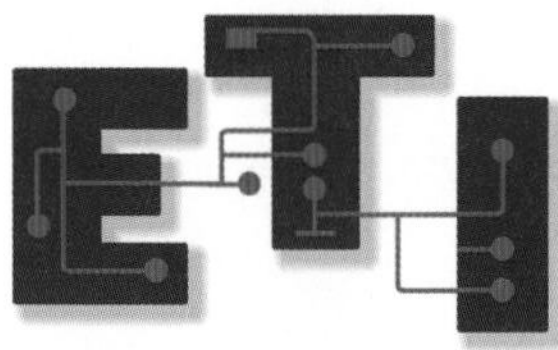

EDWARDS TECHNOLOGIES, INC.
139 Maryland St.
El Segundo, CA 90245
Tel: 310-536-7070; FAX: 310-322-1459
E-mail: roberta.perry@etiemail.com
Web Site: www.edwardstechnologies.com

Type of Business:
Founded in 1984, ETI specializes in the design, engineering, fabrication and installation of custom audio, visual displays, lighting, show control and digital HD 3D/4D theaters, Mobile Cinemas. Clients: Discovery Science Center, CA, Discovery Center, NC, Health Museum, El Trompo, Tijuana; Museum of Science & Industry, Chicago; Aquarium of the Pacific, CA, Riverbank Zoo, SC; Boston Museum of Science & Industry, Fort Worth Museum of Science and History; and the Franklin Institute.

(Continued on next page)

(Continued from previous page)

Personnel:
Brian Edwards (President & CEO)
Roberta Perry (Vice President Business Development)
Ravi Shankar (Vice President Operations)
David Krueger (Midwest/East Coast Business Development)

TOUR-MATE SYSTEMS CANADA LTD
137 St. Regis Crescent
Toronto, ON, Canada M3J 1Y6
Tel: 800-216-0029 & 416-636-5654; FAX: 416-636-9541
E-mail: info@tourmate.com
Web Site: www.tourmate.com

Type of Business:
Tour-Mate Systems was established in 1988 to develop and market self-guided audio tours for the interpretive market. We have installed systems in the United States, Canada, United Kingdom, Puerto Rico, Barbados, Japan, Australia, Switzerland, China and Macao. Millions of visitors have experienced Tour-Mate audio tours in museums, art galleries, historic sites, zoos, aquariums, and botanical gardens. Our Traditional and Mobile Audio Tour Systems feature high quality sound, random access capability, and multiple language options. Tour-Mate's content creation coupled with its approach to client care ensures each visitor has a significantly enhanced tour experience. Tour-Mate has over 20 years of experience, including the provision of audio tours to attractions such as the Art Gallery of Ontario, Montreal Museum of Fine Arts, Vancouver Art Gallery, Mount Rushmore, the Walt Disney Concert Hall, and the Corning Museum of Glass. Our commitment to customer service is second to none.

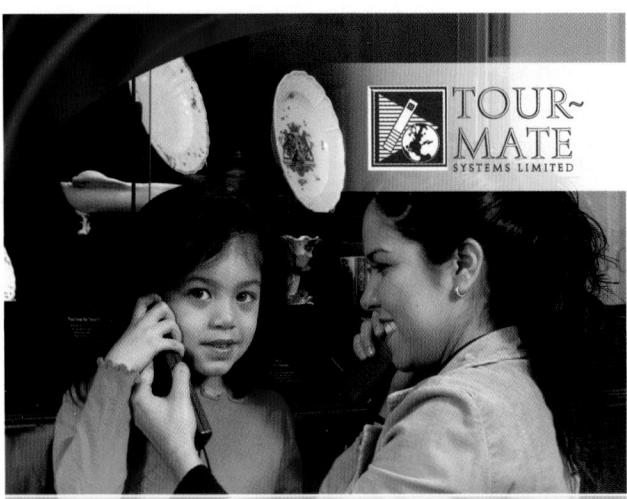

Personnel:
Neil Poch (President)
David Hayes (Director, Technology)
Atul Garg (Sales & Marketing Manager)
Shahar Chudy (Support Services Manager)

VISTA GROUP INTERNATIONAL, INC.
25 Van Zant St., Unit 8D
Norwalk, CT 06555
Tel: 203-852-5557; FAX: 203-852-5559
E-mail: info@VistaGroupInternational.com
Web Site: www.VistaGroupInternational.com

Type of Business:
Vista Group International offers innovative audio interpretation systems and services including audio tours, visitor-interactive systems, solar powered systems and SoundStik systems. Meeting the changing needs of the museum community for more than 25 years, Vista Group products are supported by a wide range of scripting, production and translation services. Vista Group works with museums, state parks, libraries, science centers, tourist attractions, tradeshows and other visitor oriented sites.

Personnel:
Noel A. Yaney (President)

Audio Visual Presentations

bpi
imagine. what we do.

BOSTON PRODUCTIONS, INC.
100 Morse St.
Norwood, MA 02062
Tel: 781-255-1555; FAX: 781-255-1556
E-mail: imagine@bostonproductions.com
Web Site: www.bostonproductions.com

Type of Business:
For twenty years, Boston Productions has been telling compelling stories to museum and visitor center audiences across the country through engaging and immersive media exhibits. Always putting the visitor experience first, we continue to surprise, enthrall and inform with uniquely diverse ideas and cutting-edge methods. Our signature AV presentations and interactive visitor experiences require multidisciplinary services and skill sets, such that we are equally expert in media design, content development, production services, software programming, exhibit prototyping and full AV hardware integration services. Knowing what works creatively with today's multigenerational audiences and being able to produce media, interactive exhibits and AV hardware systems with a strong value quotient is an organizational imperative. Boston Productions is truly a creative concept-to-installation business. - imagine. what we do.

Personnel:
Bob Noll (President & Creative Director)
Chet Kaplan (COO & Director AV Hardware Integration)
Mark Dorgan (Associate Creative Director)

ELECTROSONIC

ELECTROSONIC
3320 N. San Fernando Blvd.
Burbank, CA 91504
Tel: 888-343-3604; FAX: 818-566-4923
E-mail: information@electrosonic.com
Web Site: www.electrosonic.com

Type of Business:
Electrosonic was founded in 1964 to develop and manufacture specialized products for the presentation room and audiovisual industry. Electrosonic is a highly specialized provider of custom designed audiovisual and control systems for attractions, theme parks, museums and visitor centers. Electrosonic's primary strength is the collective experience of over 300 individuals, in five countries. Electrosonic offers the security of working with a stable, well organized operation, with global experience in system design and contracting.

Personnel:
Jim Bowie (CEO)
Scott Meyer (CFO)
Chris Conte (General Manager NA/Asia)

museum planning | exhibit design

HILFERTY
14240 State Rte. 550
Athens, OH 45701
Tel: 740-448-3821; FAX: 740-448-2331
E-mail: gha@hilferty.com
Web Site: www.hilferty.com

Type of Business:
For more than thirty years, Hilferty has provided a full range of interpretive services to museums, visitor centers, nature centers, botanical gardens, historic sites, zoos/aquariums, and halls of fame. We excel at interpretive and facility master planning; concept development; content research; label writing; exhibit and graphic design; and providing donor recognition and funding support materials. From social histories to natural sciences, football to physics, presidents to children's gardens, every Hilferty exhibit vividly captures the stories that engage visitors' minds and hearts. Each project is approached with a unique mix of techniques chosen to best bring the subject to life. Our innovative portfolio spans the spectrum of intimate displays of precious objects, captivating immersive environments, enthralling interactive components, and breathtaking theatrical presentations. In short, Hilferty creates memorable museum experiences.

Personnel:
Gerard Hilferty (President & Creative Director)
Dean Clouse (CEO)

MONADNOCK MEDIA, INC.

MONADNOCK MEDIA, INC.
112 Amherst Rd.
Sunderland, MA 01375
Tel: 413-665-1390; FAX: 413-665-1394
E-mail: steve@monadnock.org
Web Site: www.monadnock.org

Type of Business:
Audio visual/multi-media design, production and project management for museums, science centers, historic sites, visitor centers, zoos and cultural/educational organizations. Since 1980 Monadnock Media has been specializing in producing video, audio, soundscapes, computer interactive sound and light shows, design and production of orientation programs, video wall/multi-screen, multi-media exhibit interactive and immersive theater experiences. Design includes AV/multi-media exhibit integration, presentation technology specification and technical systems. Our services include full production capabilities from concept/design, research, scripting, to post production, installation, staffing training and consultation.

Personnel:
Steve Bressler (Director)

RBH MULTIMEDIA, INC.
12 Hatch Ter.
Dobbs Ferry, NY 10522
Tel: 914-693-8755; FAX: 914-693-3539
E-mail: rbh@rbhmedia.com
Web Site: www.rbhmedia.com

Type of Business:
RBH Multimedia, Inc. is a media production company dedicated to developing and producing audiovisual experiences and exhibits. We bring imagination, skill, flair and years of experience to designing and producing audio, video and multiple media exhibits for museums, historic sites, visitor and interpretive centers, and cultural institutions. We also design and program websites and computer interactive exhibits. RBH is particularly known for producing signature multi-sensory, multimedia "experience" theater shows. Other services include hardware system design, engineering and installation, with expertise in videoconference technology. For more information about RBH Multimedia, Inc., please visit us online at www.rbhmedia.com.

Personnel:
Steve Brosnahan (Partner)
Nancy Haffner (Partner)
Edgardo J. Resto (Associate)

TOUR-MATE SYSTEMS CANADA LTD
137 St. Regis Crescent
Toronto, ON, Canada M3J 1Y6
Tel: 800-216-0029 & 416-636-5654; FAX: 416-636-9541
E-mail: info@tourmate.com
Web Site: www.tourmate.com

Type of Business:
Tour-Mate Systems was established in 1988 to develop and market self-guided audio tours for the interpretive market. We have installed systems in the United States, Canada, United Kingdom, Puerto Rico, Barbados, Japan, Australia, Switzerland, China and Macao. Millions of visitors have experienced Tour-Mate audio tours in museums, art galleries, historic sites, zoos, aquariums, and botanical gardens. Our Traditional and Mobile Audio Tour Systems feature high quality sound, random access capability, and multiple language options. Tour-Mate's content creation coupled with its approach to client care ensures each visitor has a significantly enhanced tour experience. Tour-Mate has over 20 years of experience, including the provision of audio tours to attractions such as the Art Gallery of Ontario, Montreal Museum of Fine Arts, Vancouver Art Gallery, Mount Rushmore, the Walt Disney Concert Hall, and the Corning Museum of Glass. Our commitment to customer service is second to none.

Personnel:
Neil Poch (President)
David Hayes (Director, Technology)
Atul Garg (Sales & Marketing Manager)
Shahar Chudy (Support Services Manager)

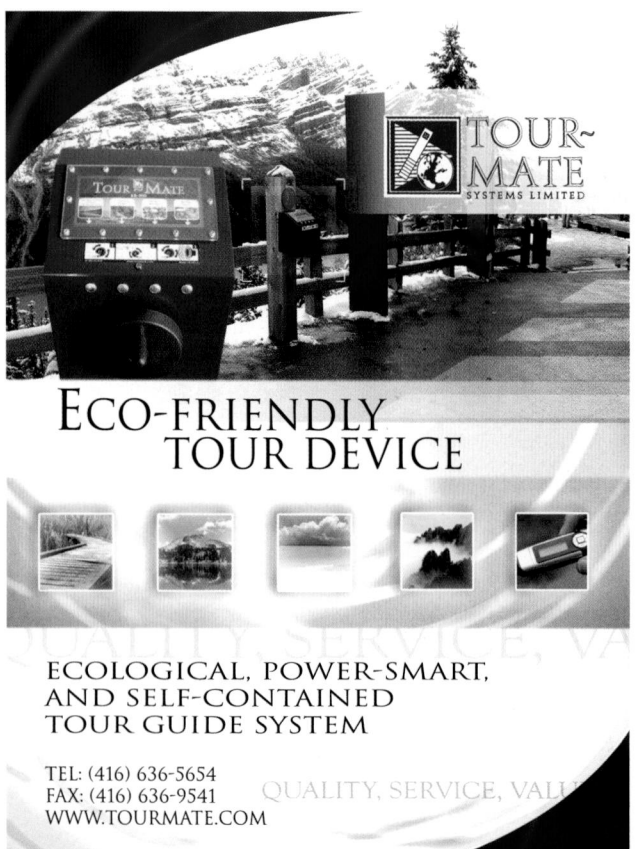

Digital Imaging Services

ARIUS3D, INC.
755 The Queensway E.
Mississauga, ON, Canada L4Y 4C5
Tel: 905-270-7999; FAX: 905-270-6888
E-mail: info@arius3d.com
Web Site: www.arius3d.com; www.pointstream.net

Type of Business:
Arius3D delivers scientific quality 3D models with true color and accurate geometry. The patented 'non-touch' 3D color laser is free of ambient light artifacts or UV rays. We bring alive the concept of Scan Once: Use Many Times. Models can be easily scaled for a myriad of different applications including: digital repatriation, disaster recovery, digital archiving, conservation, virtual museum exhibits, object replication for digital & physical learning objects. Arius3D models can be used on pc's, kiosks, mobile devices, in digital learning galleries, VR theatres and caves in digital (mono or stereo), print, holographic or physical formats. Call us when accurate high resolution models are necessary!

Personnel:
Susan Dineen (Vice President Business Development)

NORTHEAST DOCUMENT CONSERVATION CENTER
100 Brickstone Square
Andover, MA 01810
Tel: 978-470-1010; FAX: 978-475-6021
E-mail: nedcc@nedcc.org
Web Site: www.nedcc.org

Type of Business:
The nonprofit Northeast Document Conservation Center (NEDCC) performs paper conservation, book conservation, preservation microfilming, duplication of photographs and negatives, and digitization of visual materials. The Center specializes in the treatment of paper-based materials including works of art on paper, photographs, wallpaper, books, documents, maps, architectural drawings, and posters. It provides consulting services, performs assessments of preservation needs, presents workshops and conferences, and offers a 24-hour disaster assistance hotline.

Personnel:
Bill Veillette (Executive Director)

OLSON VISUAL, INC.
13000 Weber Way
Hawthorne, CA 90250
Tel: 800-480-6643; FAX: 310-263-6980
E-mail: graphics@olsonvisual.com
Web Site: www.olsonvisual.com

Type of Business:
Olson Visual has been a supplier of large format graphics to museums for over 50 years and is committed to providing superior service from start to finish. We have dedicated an entire segment of the business to Museum and Fine Art projects and take pride in supplying our clientele with quality custom pieces. OV will evaluate your needs and give recommendations on a combination of output and display possibilities. Our team of Museum Consultants can also help you

(Continued on next page)

(Continued from previous page)

integrate green materials into your projects wherever possible, while still maintaining the integrity of your design concept. Call us and inquire about your next project.

Personnel:
Daniel Olson (Vice President)
Eder Cetina (Creative Director/ Museum Consultant)
Ashleigh Turner (Project Manager/Museum Consultant)

Fiber Optics

Luxam Lighting for Museums

LUXAM, INC.
2246 Country Club Rd.
Appomattox, VA 24522
Tel: 434-352-0084; FAX: 434-352-0089
E-mail: Rick@luxam.com
Web Site: www.luxam.com

Type of Business:
Luxam manufactures specialty lighting products for museum showcases and exhibits. We manufacture fiber optic and hybrid fiber/LED lighting systems and software. We also offer a full range of on-site services including installation and focus. Our newest illuminator, LED/Max, has 24 channels of high wattage LEDs mated to our fiber delivery systems for stunning interactive and multimedia exhibits controlled via DMX, all within conservation norms. Custom solutions, on time and budget.

Personnel:
Rick Jellow (Principal)
Jean Francois Hocquard (Principal)

NOUVIR RESEARCH
20915 Sussex Hwy.
Seaford, DE 19973
Tel: 302-628-9933; FAX: 302-628-9932
Web Site: www.nouvir.com

Type of Business:
NoUVIR invented fiber optic, museum, preservation lighting. Fifty different miniature floodlights, spotlights, across-the-room pinspots, eyeballs, wall washers, pendants...all pure-white, stone-cold light with no UV and no IR...NoUVIR®. Our 24 U.S. patents guarantee superior performance. A 10-year warranty on optical hardware and fiber guarantees quality. Save energy, save money and save our art and heritage with NoUVIR. Call for conservation lighting textbooks, seminar information or for free product specifications, photometry and lighting design information.

Personnel:
Miss Ruth Ellen Miller (President)
Mr. Matthew S. Miller (Vice President Marketing)

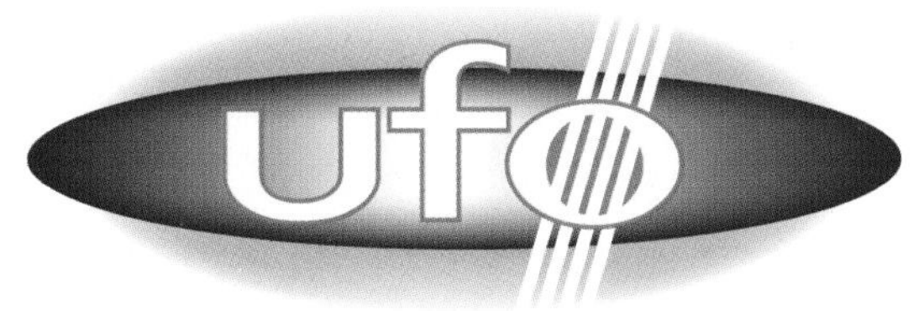

UNIVERSAL FIBRE OPTICS LTD.
Home Place
Coldstream
Berwickshire, U.K. TD12 4DT
Tel: 1-800-UFO-5554 (1-800-836-5554); FAX: 011-44-1890-883-062
E-mail: info@universal-fibre-optics.com
Web Site: www.lightingformuseums.com

Type of Business:
UFO is one of only three manufacturers in the world of raw fiber for lighting; and we are one of the world's largest manufacturers of complete fiber-optic lighting systems. All fiber, harnesses, fittings, and illuminators are designed and manufactured by us in our dedicated factory. Past projects include The Crown Jewels, Tutankhamun's tomb, Westminster Abbey, Art Gallery of Ontario, The Victoria and Albert Museum, Bob Bullock Texas State History Museum, and many more. USA & Canada Sales: 941-343-8454, jim@universal-fibre-optics.com; International Sales: konrad@universal-fibre-optics.com, ctait@universal-fibre-optics.com.

Personnel:
Jim Ashley-Down (USA & Canada Sales (USA & UK based))
Konrad Moller (International Sales (UK based))
Calum Tait (International Sales (UK based))
Rob Bowey (Managing Director (USA & UK based))

Presentations/Integration

AVITECTURE, INC.
1 Export Dr.
Sterling, VA 20164
Tel: 703-404-8900; FAX: 703-404-8940
E-mail: info@avitecture.com
Web Site: www.avitecture.com

Type of Business:
Avitecture® is the integration of audiovisual systems with information technology for museums. In our fourth decade, we have comprehensive experience integrating multimedia into exhibits that convey a museum's message. Our technical expertise and innovative designs facilitate the creation of versatile, high quality and high-impact facilities on time, within budget, and often, beyond our client's expectations. From design-build services, equipment sales, rentals, and ongoing technical support Avitecture partners with you for the long term.

Personnel:
Sidney Lissner (Chairman of the Board)
Greg Boyd (President)

bpi
imagine. what we do.

BOSTON PRODUCTIONS, INC.
100 Morse St.
Norwood, MA 02062
Tel: 781-255-1555; FAX: 781-255-1556
E-mail: imagine@bostonproductions.com
Web Site: www.bostonproductions.com

(Continued on next page)

(Continued from previous page)

Type of Business:
For twenty years, Boston Productions has been telling compelling stories to museum and visitor center audiences across the country through engaging and immersive media exhibits. Always putting the visitor experience first, we continue to surprise, enthrall and inform with uniquely diverse ideas and cutting-edge methods. Our signature AV presentations and interactive visitor experiences require multidisciplinary services and skill sets, such that we are equally expert in media design, content development, production services, software programming, exhibit prototyping and full AV hardware integration services. Knowing what works creatively with today's multigenerational audiences and being able to produce media, interactive exhibits and AV hardware systems with a strong value quotient is an organizational imperative. Boston Productions is truly a creative concept-to-installation business. - imagine. what we do.

Personnel:
Bob Noll (President & Creative Director)
Chet Kaplan (COO & Director AV Hardware Integration)
Mark Dorgan (Associate Creative Director)

DESIGN AND PRODUCTION INCORPORATED
7110 Rainwater Place
Lorton, VA 22079
Tel: 703-550-8640; FAX: 703-339-0296
E-mail: dmoalli@d-and-p.com
Web Site: www.d-and-p.com

Type of Business:
In service to the museum community since 1949, our global portfolio is comprised of hundreds of high-profile projects, including interpretive history, interactive science, sports, children's museums, and immersive environments. D&P specializes in large-scale, multi-discipline exhibit projects, with a full complement of in-house production capabilities: Project development and management, custom fabrication, interactive exhibits, A/V hardware and software development, artifact mounting, graphic production, installation, and service. D&P is FSC-certified and a charter member of USGBC.

Personnel:
Jay Barnwell (President)
Dan Moalli (Vice President Business Development)
Donna Kuba (Project Director)
Rachel Childress (Marketing Associate)

JACK ROUSE ASSOCIATES
600 Vine St., Ste. 1700
Cincinnati, OH 45202-1100
Tel: 513-381-0055; FAX: 513-381-2691
E-mail: s.mccoy@jackrouse.com
Web Site: www.jackrouse.com

Type of Business:
Jack Rouse Associates conceives, visualizes and realizes exceptional visitor experiences around the world. Specific services include master planning, exhibit design, media production and project management.

Personnel:
Jack Rouse (CEO)
Keith James (President)
Randy Vuksta (Creative Director)
Shawn McCoy (Vice President Marketing & Business Development)

Producers

BRC IMAGINATION ARTS
2711 Winona Ave.
Burbank, CA 91504
Tel: 818-841-8084; FAX: 818-841-4996
E-mail: brc@brcweb.com
Web Site: www.brcweb.com

Type of Business:
BRC is an award winning full service museum design and production company with a comprehensive range of skills from vision and master planning, to design, and production of exhibits and theatrical media experiences. Continental Europe Office: Science Park 5644, 5692 EN Eindhoven, P.O. Box 1245, 5602 BE Eindhoven, The Netherlands, Tel: +31.40.2676.871; Fax: +31.40.2676.895. United Kingdom Office: 8 Kimblesworth Grange, Potterhouse Lane, Durham DH1 5SL, United Kingdom, Tel: +44.7879.655950; Fax: +44.1913.719141. Shanghai Office: A405, Tomorrow Square, 399 West Nanjing Road, Shanghai 200003, People's Republic of China, Tel: +86.21.2308.1077.

Personnel:
Carmel Lewis (Vice President, Educational Experiences)
Matthew Solari (Director, Education Development)
Mark Hayward (Creative Director, Educational Experiences)
Bart Dohmen (Managing Director, Continental Europe)
Donna Davidson (Director, United Kingdom)

bpi
imagine. what we do.

BOSTON PRODUCTIONS, INC.
100 Morse St.
Norwood, MA 02062
Tel: 781-255-1555; FAX: 781-255-1556
E-mail: imagine@bostonproductions.com
Web Site: www.bostonproductions.com

Type of Business:
For twenty years, Boston Productions has been telling compelling stories to museum and visitor center audiences across the country through engaging and immersive media exhibits. Always putting the visitor experience first, we continue to surprise, enthrall and inform with uniquely diverse ideas and cutting-edge methods. Our signature AV presentations and interactive visitor experiences require multidisciplinary services and skill sets, such that we are equally expert in media design, content development, production services, software programming, exhibit prototyping and full AV hardware integration services. Knowing what works creatively with today's multigenerational audiences and being able to produce media, interactive exhibits and AV hardware systems with a strong value quotient is an organizational imperative. Boston Productions is truly a creative concept-to-installation business. - imagine. what we do.

Personnel:
Bob Noll (President & Creative Director)
Chet Kaplan (COO & Director AV Hardware Integration)
Mark Dorgan (Associate Creative Director)

CORTINA PRODUCTIONS

CORTINA PRODUCTIONS, INC.
6623-A Old Dominion Dr.
McLean, VA 22101
Tel: 703-556-8481; FAX: 703-847-9694
E-mail: jim@cortinaproductions.com
Web Site: www.cortinaproductions.com

Type of Business:
We are media designers and storytellers; crafters of image and light, sound and touch. From theater experiences, to large format multi-screen presentations, to engaging interactive exhibits and videos, we produce award-winning media exhibits that educate, entertain, and inspire. From initial concept development through final post-production, we collaborate with you to blend story and technology into a single artistic vision.

Personnel:
Joseph Cortina (President)
Amy Maddox (Vice President Production)

HILLMANN & CARR INCORPORATED
2233 Wisconsin Ave., N.W., Ste. 425
Washington, DC 20007
Tel: 202-342-0001; FAX: 202-342-0117
E-mail: michalcarr@hillmanncarr.com
Web Site: www.hillmanncarr.com

Type of Business:
Full-service creative producers of award winning media: film, HDTV, computer interactive, audio environments, video-tours, immersion and object theaters, graphic and multimedia presentations. Extensive expertise in science, history and art museums, visitor centers, corporate exhibit media, expositions and multi-language international projects, created in traditional, non-traditional and unique formats. Wide-ranging experience in concept development, content research, immersive experiences and audiovisual media master planning. Producers and project managers skilled in AV systems design, integration and installation. WOSB.

Personnel:
Alfred Hillmann (President)
Michal Brand Carr (Vice President)

JACK ROUSE ASSOCIATES
600 Vine St., Ste. 1700
Cincinnati, OH 45202-1100
Tel: 513-381-0055; FAX: 513-381-2691
E-mail: s.mccoy@jackrouse.com
Web Site: www.jackrouse.com

Type of Business:
Jack Rouse Associates conceives, visualizes and realizes exceptional visitor experiences around the world. Specific services include master planning, exhibit design, media production and project management.

Personnel:
Jack Rouse (CEO)
Keith James (President)
Randy Vuksta (Creative Director)
Shawn McCoy (Vice President Marketing & Business Development)

RBH MULTIMEDIA, INC.
12 Hatch Ter.
Dobbs Ferry, NY 10522
Tel: 914-693-8755; FAX: 914-693-3539
E-mail: rbh@rbhmedia.com
Web Site: www.rbhmedia.com

Type of Business:
RBH Multimedia, Inc. is a media production company dedicated to developing and producing audiovisual experiences and exhibits. We bring imagination, skill, flair and years of experience to designing and producing audio, video and multiple media exhibits for museums, historic sites, visitor and interpretive centers, and cultural institutions. We also design and program websites and computer interactive exhibits. RBH is particularly known for producing signature multi-sensory, multimedia "experience" theater shows. Other services include hardware system design, engineering and installation, with expertise in videoconference technology. For more information about RBH Multimedia, Inc., please visit us online at www.rbhmedia.com.

Personnel:
Steve Brosnahan (Partner)
Nancy Haffner (Partner)
Edgardo J. Resto (Associate)

TOUR-MATE SYSTEMS CANADA LTD
137 St. Regis Crescent
Toronto, ON, Canada M3J 1Y6
Tel: 800-216-0029 & 416-636-5654; FAX: 416-636-9541
E-mail: info@tourmate.com
Web Site: www.tourmate.com

Type of Business:
Tour-Mate Systems was established in 1988 to develop and market self-guided audio tours for the interpretive market. We have installed systems in the United States, Canada, United Kingdom, Puerto Rico, Barbados, Japan, Australia, Switzerland, China and Macao. Millions of visitors have experienced Tour-Mate audio tours in museums, art galleries, historic sites, zoos, aquariums, and botanical gardens. Our Traditional and Mobile Audio Tour Systems feature high quality sound, random access capability, and multiple language options. Tour-Mate's content creation coupled with its approach to client care ensures each visitor has a significantly enhanced tour experience. Tour-Mate has over 20 years of experience, including the provision of audio tours to attractions such as the Art Gallery of Ontario, Montreal Museum of Fine Arts, Vancouver Art Gallery, Mount Rushmore, the Walt Disney Concert Hall, and the Corning Museum of Glass. Our commitment to customer service is second to none.

(Continued on next page)

(Continued from previous page)

Personnel:
Neil Poch (President)
David Hayes (Director, Technology)
Atul Garg (Sales & Marketing Manager)
Shahar Chudy (Support Services Manager)

Special Effects

BRC IMAGINATION ARTS
2711 Winona Ave.
Burbank, CA 91504
Tel: 818-841-8084; FAX: 818-841-4996
E-mail: brc@brcweb.com
Web Site: www.brcweb.com

Type of Business:
BRC is an award winning full service museum design and production company with a comprehensive range of skills from vision and master planning, to design, and production of exhibits and theatrical media experiences. Continental Europe Office: Science Park 5644, 5692 EN Eindhoven, P.O. Box 1245, 5602 BE Eindhoven, The Netherlands, Tel: +31.40.2676.871; Fax: +31.40.2676.895. United Kingdom Office: 8 Kimblesworth Grange, Potterhouse Lane, Durham DH1 5SL, United Kingdom, Tel: +44.7879.655950; Fax: +44.1913.719141. Shanghai Office: A405, Tomorrow Square, 399 West Nanjing Road, Shanghai 200003, People's Republic of China, Tel: +86.21.2308.1077.

Personnel:
Carmel Lewis (Vice President, Educational Experiences)
Matthew Solari (Director, Education Development)
Mark Hayward (Creative Director, Educational Experiences)
Bart Dohmen (Managing Director, Continental Europe)
Donna Davidson (Director, United Kingdom)

Luxam Lighting for Museums

LUXAM, INC.
2246 Country Club Rd.
Appomattox, VA 24522
Tel: 434-352-0084; FAX: 434-352-0089
E-mail: Rick@luxam.com
Web Site: www.luxam.com

Type of Business:
Luxam manufactures specialty lighting products for museum showcases and exhibits. We manufacture fiber optic and hybrid fiber/LED lighting systems and software. We also offer a full range of on-site services including installation and focus. Our newest illuminator, LED/Max, has 24 channels of high wattage LEDs mated to our fiber delivery systems for stunning interactive and multimedia exhibits controlled via DMX, all within conservation norms. Custom solutions, on time and budget.

Personnel:
Rick Jellow (Principal)
Jean Francois Hocquard (Principal)

PEVNICK DESIGN
2301 W. Brantwood Ave.
Glendale, WI 53209
Tel: 414-540-0051; FAX: 414-540-0052
E-mail: info@pevnickdesign.com
Web Site: www.pevnickdesign.com

Type of Business:
Graphical Waterfalls® by Pevnick Design use state-of-the-art computer technology to produce a custom designed dazzling display of kinetic graphics, logos & words in falling water droplets. Graphical Waterfalls® have been shown in the trade exhibit industry since 1989 and a permanent installation was completed in 2008 in Guatemala City, Guatemala. Current innovations include entering words in real time, DMX control, color coordinated lighting and interactivity between viewers & the waterfall using switches. Temporary displays or permanent installations available. Non-computer waterfalls also available.

Personnel:
Stephen Pevnick (President/Creative Director)
Laurie Pevnick (Vice President)
John Benzinger (Marketing Manager)

RBH MULTIMEDIA, INC.
12 Hatch Ter.
Dobbs Ferry, NY 10522
Tel: 914-693-8755; FAX: 914-693-3539
E-mail: rbh@rbhmedia.com
Web Site: www.rbhmedia.com

Type of Business:
RBH Multimedia, Inc. is a media production company dedicated to developing and producing audiovisual experiences and exhibits. We bring imagination, skill, flair and years of experience to designing and producing audio, video and multiple media exhibits for museums, historic sites, visitor and interpretive centers, and cultural institutions. We also design and program websites and computer interactive exhibits. RBH is particularly known for producing signature multi-sensory, multimedia "experience" theater shows. Other services include hardware system design, engineering and installation, with expertise in videoconference technology. For more information about RBH Multimedia, Inc., please visit us online at www.rbhmedia.com.

Personnel:
Steve Brosnahan (Partner)
Nancy Haffner (Partner)
Edgardo J. Resto (Associate)

Videos

bpi
imagine. what we do.

BOSTON PRODUCTIONS, INC.
100 Morse St.
Norwood, MA 02062
Tel: 781-255-1555; FAX: 781-255-1556
E-mail: imagine@bostonproductions.com
Web Site: www.bostonproductions.com

Type of Business:
For twenty years, Boston Productions has been telling compelling stories to museum and visitor center audiences across the country through engaging and immersive media exhibits. Always putting the visitor experience first, we continue to surprise, enthrall and inform with uniquely diverse ideas and cutting-edge methods. Our signature AV presentations and interactive visitor experiences require multidisciplinary services and skill sets, such that we are equally expert in media design, content development, production services, software programming, exhibit prototyping and full AV hardware integration services. Knowing what works creatively with today's multigenerational audiences and being able to produce media, interactive exhibits and AV hardware systems with a strong value quotient is an organizational imperative. Boston Productions is truly a creative concept-to-installation business. - imagine. what we do.

Personnel:
Bob Noll (President & Creative Director)
Chet Kaplan (COO & Director AV Hardware Integration)
Mark Dorgan (Associate Creative Director)

CORTINA PRODUCTIONS, INC.
6623-A Old Dominion Dr.
McLean, VA 22101
Tel: 703-556-8481; FAX: 703-847-9694
E-mail: jim@cortinaproductions.com
Web Site: www.cortinaproductions.com

Type of Business:
We are media designers and storytellers; crafters of image and light, sound and touch. From theater experiences, to large format multi-screen presentations, to engaging interactive exhibits and videos, we produce award-winning media exhibits that educate, entertain, and inspire. From initial concept development through final post-production, we collaborate with you to blend story and technology into a single artistic vision.

Personnel:
Joseph Cortina (President)
Amy Maddox (Vice President Production)

RBH MULTIMEDIA, INC.
12 Hatch Ter.
Dobbs Ferry, NY 10522
Tel: 914-693-8755; FAX: 914-693-3539
E-mail: rbh@rbhmedia.com
Web Site: www.rbhmedia.com

Type of Business:
RBH Multimedia, Inc. is a media production company dedicated to developing and producing audiovisual experiences and exhibits. We bring imagination, skill, flair and years of experience to designing and producing audio, video and multiple media exhibits for museums, historic sites, visitor and interpretive centers, and cultural institutions. We also design and program websites and computer interactive exhibits. RBH is particularly known for producing signature multi-sensory, multimedia "experience" theater shows. Other services include hardware system design, engineering and installation, with expertise in videoconference technology. For more information about RBH Multimedia, Inc., please visit us online at www.rbhmedia.com.

Personnel:
Steve Brosnahan (Partner)
Nancy Haffner (Partner)
Edgardo J. Resto (Associate)

BUILDING & FACILITIES-GENERAL

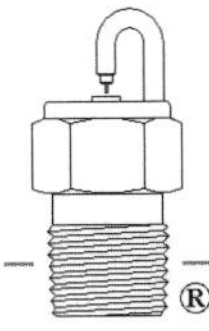

ATOMIZING SYSTEMS INC
Manufacturers of *COLD FOG®* Systems
®

ATOMIZING SYSTEMS INC.
One Hollywood Ave.
HoHoKus, NJ 07423
Tel: 201-447-1222; FAX: 201-447-6932
E-mail: info@coldfog.com
Web Site: www.coldfog.com

Type of Business:
Atomizing Systems Inc., a manufacturer of water fog equipment for humidity & special effects, uses the world's only laser-drilled, ruby orifice fog nozzle (recently granted a US patent). Nozzles create water fog evaporative cooling, special effects, cool zones, walkways, landscaping, entrances, waterfalls, rockwork, fountains, haze, smoke & cloud simulation. Systems utilized worldwide include major projects in Orlando, far east, middle east, Latin America. 20-year nozzle Warranty against orifice wear standard. Each fog Nozzles equipped with individual filter. Full engineering & design services available.

Personnel:
Michael Elkas (President & Owner)

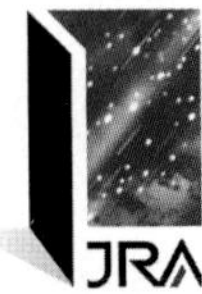

JRA
Jack Rouse
Associates

JACK ROUSE ASSOCIATES
600 Vine St., Ste. 1700
Cincinnati, OH 45202-1100
Tel: 513-381-0055; FAX: 513-381-2691
E-mail: s.mccoy@jackrouse.com
Web Site: www.jackrouse.com

Type of Business:
Jack Rouse Associates conceives, visualizes and realizes exceptional visitor experiences around the world. Specific services include master planning, exhibit design, media production and project management.

Personnel:
Jack Rouse (CEO)
Keith James (President)
Randy Vuksta (Creative Director)
Shawn McCoy (Vice President Marketing & Business Development)

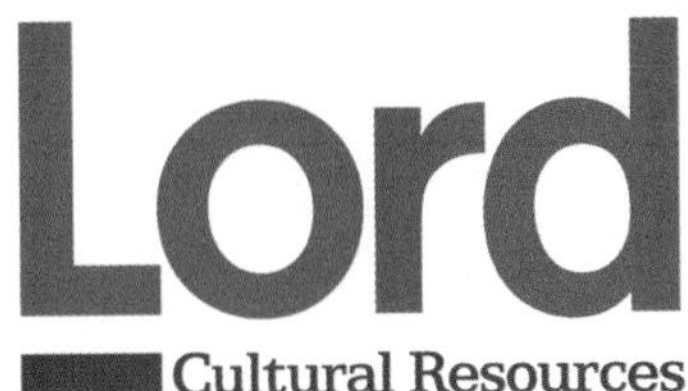

LORD CULTURAL RESOURCES
43 West 24th Street, 10th Fl.
New York, NY 10010
Tel: 646-375-2500; FAX: 212-675-4763
E-mail: info@lord.ca
Web Site: www.lord.ca

Type of Business:
Founded in 1981 in response to an emerging need for specialized planning services in the museum, cultural and heritage sector, Lord Cultural Resources is dedicated to creating cultural capital through visioning, planning and implementation. We work with museums, large and small, helping them to maximize their cultural capital by engaging with their communities, improving their buildings and inspiring collaboration and learning. We have benefited clients through the entire spectrum of cultural services including master plans, business plans, strategic plans, facility plans, functional programs, architect selection, exhibition design and development, project management, retail plans and cultural plans. In addition, Lord Cultural Resources has made a definitive contribution to the development of museum planning through its pioneering publications. The firm also has a San Francisco location.

Personnel:
Gail Dexter Lord (Co-President)
Barry Lord (Co-President)
Maria Piacente (Vice President, Exhibitions)
Catharine Tanner (Vice President, Facility Planning)
Paul Alezraa (Vice President, Europe)
Amy Kaufman (Managing Director, U.S.)
Brad King (Director, Management Consulting, Principal)
Margaret May (Senior Principal)
Ted Silberberg (Senior Principal)
Joy Bailey (Senior Consultant)
Lindsay Martin (Senior Consultant)
Andrea Ott (Director, Client Relations & Marketing)

Architectural Design Firms

BERGMEYER ASSOCIATES, INC.
51 Sleeper St.
Boston, MA 02210
Tel: 617-542-1025; FAX: 617-542-1026
E-mail: marketing@bergmeyer.com
Web Site: www.bergmeyer.com

Type of Business:
Bergmeyer is an award winning architecture and interior design firm. We have specialized expertise in the development of public spaces and visitor amenities including museum stores, exhibit shops, restaurants, and admissions and information centers. Our services include architecture and interior design, identity development, wayfinding and graphic design, merchandising, strategic planning, business plan development, and consumer/visitor research and analysis. We are committed to design excellence and we create architecture that supports our client's brand and business. With more than thirty years of experience in a culture that challenges us to think in new ways, clients know that Bergmeyer's design solutions will be unique and specific to their needs.

Personnel:
David Tubridy, AIA (President)
Amy Bernhardt (Vice President Marketing & Human Resources)
Joseph P. Nevin, Jr. (Senior Principal)
Michael R. Davis, AIA (Vice President)
Anne Johnson (Marketing Director)

BROWNING
DAY MULLINS
DIERDORF
ARCHITECTS

BROWNING DAY MULLINS DIERDORF ARCHITECTS
626 N. Illinois St.
Indianapolis, IN 46204
Tel: 317-635-5030; FAX: 317-634-5409
E-mail: cwmullins@bdmd.com
Web Site: www.bdmd.com

Type of Business:
The museum design practice of Browning Day Mullins Dierdorf Architects focuses on unique and creative design solutions for a variety of museum types. Our expertise has produced award-winning designs for the Indianapolis Museum of Art, Eiteljorg Museum, Herron School of Art & Design as well as for sports hall of fames, children's museums and other art museums. Professional services can be provided for master planning, programming, architectural and landscape architectural design and exhibit development. Visit us at www.bdmd.com.

Personnel:
Craig W. Mullins, AIA (Chairman of the Board)
Jonathan R. Hess, AIA (President)

CAMBRIDGE SEVEN ASSOCIATES, INC.
1050 Massachusetts Ave.
Cambridge, MA 02138
Tel: 617-492-7000; FAX: 617-492-7007
E-mail: joltman@c7a.com
Web Site: www.c7a.com

Type of Business:
Architects, exhibit and graphic designers providing specialized services for museums, visitor centers, aquaria, zoos, and traveling exhibits. Areas of expertise include science, children's, sports, and history museums, art galleries, large format film theaters, educational facilities, nature centers, aquaria and zoos. Services include architectural design, exhibit and habitat design, feasibility assessments, site analysis, master planning, space programming, institutional and operational planning, exhibit installation coordination, graphic design and signage programs, production of fund raising materials, and construction administration. Award-winning designs completed for existing and new facilities, internationally.

Personnel:
Peter Kuttner, FAIA (President)
John Stebbins, AIA, LEED AP (Principal)
Steven Imrich, AIA, LEED AP (Principal)
Penny Sander (Senior Associate Exhibit Planner)
David Perry (Associate Exhibit Designer)
Doug Simpson, LEED AP (Associate Exhibit Designer)
Douglas Flandro, LEED AP (Exhibit Designer)
Jo Oltman (Marketing Manager)

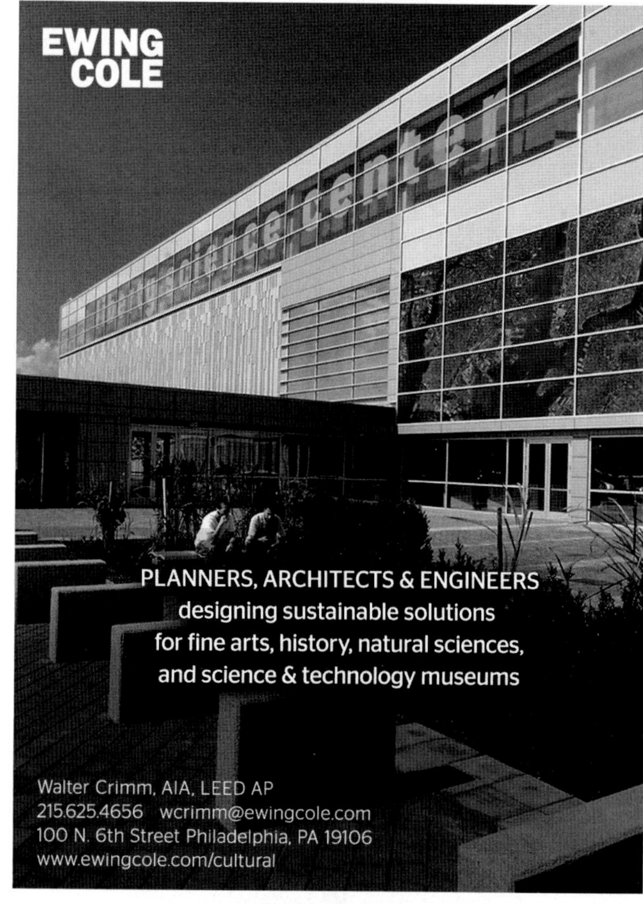

EWING
COLE

EWINGCOLE CULTURAL DESIGN GROUP
100 N. 6th St.
Philadelphia, PA 19106
Tel: 215-923-2020; FAX: 215-574-9163
E-mail: wcrimm@ewingcole.com
Web Site: www.ewingcole.com/cultural

Type of Business:
EwingCole is a multi-discipline architecture and engineering firm specializing in design for cultural institutions. We work with national and regional museums for the fine arts, history, natural sciences and science and technology. Our Cultural Practice experts apply deep industry knowledge to enhance the visitor experience and to develop a design closely aligned with the museum's strategic plan. Our process engages the board and staff at all levels to create solutions that are intellectually stimulating, fiscally responsible and environmentally sustainable.

Personnel:
Walter Crimm, AIA, LEED AP (Vice President, Cultural Design Group)

FENTRESS ARCHITECTS
421 Broadway
Denver, CO 80203
Tel: 303-722-5000; FAX: 303-722-5080
E-mail: studio@fentressarchitects.com
Web Site: www.fentressarchitects.com

(Continued on next page)

(Continued from previous page)

Type of Business:
Fentress Architects is an internatonal design studio that passionately pursues sustainable and iconic public architecture. Curtis Fentress, FAIA, RIBA, has designed over $22 billion of architectural landmarks worldwide, visited by 300 million people annually. Museums designed by Fentress speak eloquently to culture and geography, becoming cherished landmarks. Fentress projects, which include the National Museum of the Marine Corps, National Museum of Wildlife Art and the National Cowboy & Western Heritage Museum, have been honored with over 300 awards for design innovation and excellence.

Personnel:
Curtis Fentress (President & Principle-in-Charge of Design)
Karen Gilbert (Principal, Director Marketing)

GARY WOLF ARCHITECTS, INC.
7 Marshall St.
Boston, MA 02108-2404
Tel: 617-742-7557; FAX: 617-742-7656
E-mail: info@wolfarchitects.com
Web Site: www.wolfarchitects.com

Type of Business:
An award-winning architectural studio, Gary Wolf Architects provides services to museums, historical societies, educational institutions and public agencies, among other clients. Gary first worked with museum clients over twenty years ago. We develop masterplans, evaluate existing buildings, and design both new construction and renovations. Our preservation experience ranges from restoration to adaptive reuse. We can assist with new buildings, exhibition galleries, visitor services, assembly spaces, accessibility, and historic houses.

Personnel:
Gary Wolf, AIA (Principal)

GWWO, INC./ARCHITECTS
800 Wyman Park Dr., Ste. 300
Baltimore, MD 21211
Tel: 410-332-1009; FAX: 410-332-0038
E-mail: info@gwwoinc.com
Web Site: www.gwwoinc.com

Type of Business:
GWWO specializes in the planning and design of museum, visitor center and related facilities, with emphasis on quality design that is both inspirational and evocative. We work in partnership with our clients to develop individualized design solutions that respond to the unique mission, character and collections of each institution. Our services span all project stages, from site selection, master planning and programming through final design and construction administration. Clients include George Washington's Mount Vernon Estate & Gardens, the Museum of the Rockies, the Children's Museum & Theatre of Maine and the Brandywine River Museum.

Personnel:
Alan E. Reed, AIA, LEED AP (Principal)
David G. Wright, AIA, LEED AP (Principal)
Paul L. Hume, AIA, LEED AP (Principal)
Mark A. Lapointe, AIA (Principal)

GYROSCOPE, INC.
283 4th St., Suite 201
Oakland, CA 94607
Tel: 510-986-0111; FAX: 510-986-0222
E-mail: maeryta@gyroscopeinc.com
Web Site: www.gyroscopeinc.com

Type of Business:
Gyroscope is an award winning, museum planning, architecture and exhibit design company with offices in Oakland, CA, and Cambridge, MA. We are known for innovative strategies and design solutions grounded in a thorough understanding of the challenges museums face. We offer full-service planning and design for all phases of your project from earliest vision through opening.

Personnel:
Maeryta Medrano, AIA, LEED AP (President)
Chuck Howarth (Vice President)
Ron Davis, LEED AP (Principal)
Justine Roberts (Principal)

JACK ROUSE ASSOCIATES
600 Vine St., Ste. 1700
Cincinnati, OH 45202-1100
Tel: 513-381-0055; FAX: 513-381-2691
E-mail: s.mccoy@jackrouse.com
Web Site: www.jackrouse.com

Type of Business:
Jack Rouse Associates conceives, visualizes and realizes exceptional visitor experiences around the world. Specific services include master planning, exhibit design, media production and project management.

Personnel:
Jack Rouse (CEO)
Keith James (President)
Randy Vuksta (Creative Director)
Shawn McCoy (Vice President Marketing & Business Development)

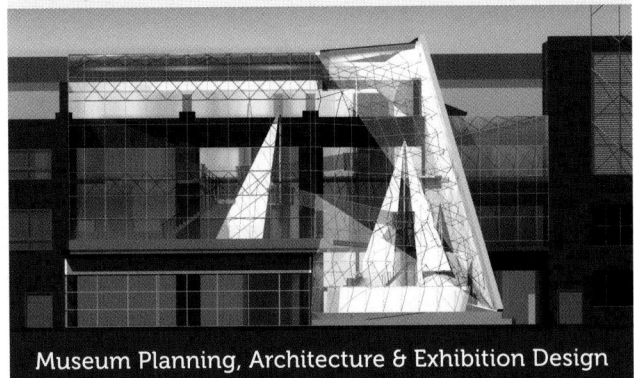

lscdesign
architects / engineers

LSC DESIGN, INC.
1110 E. Princess St.
York, PA 17403
Tel: 717-845-8383; FAX: 717-852-0916
E-mail: marketing@lscdesign.com
Web Site: www.lscdesign.com

Type of Business:
LSC plans and designs award winning museums and visitor centers with an emphasis on engaging experiences and regional designs. Our clients praise our ability to first listen then respond with solutions geared toward the mission and culture of each institution. We believe in reinventing the American museum through inspiration, education, and environmental responsibility. With four Mid-Atlantic offices, LSC is poised to continue pushing the limits of creative and functional design for museums and visitor centers throughout the region.

Personnel:
Robert A. Kinsley, II, AIA (President)
Elizabeth G. Paul (Marketing)

MARK CAVAGNERO ASSOCIATES
1045 Sansome St., Ste. 200
San Francisco, CA 94111
Tel: 415-398-6944; FAX: 415-398-6943
E-mail: info@cavagnero.com
Web Site: www.cavagnero.com

Type of Business:
Since its establishment in 1988, San Francisco-based Mark Cavagnero Associates has completed a wide range of architectural and master planning projects for museums of various scales, with local, regional, and national impact. The firm specializes in working with museums from programming through design and construction, bringing together staff, city officials, and the community to create projects that fulfill multiple goals. It has won local, state and national awards from the American Institute of Architects. Past and current projects include the Oakland Museum of California, the California Palace of the Legion of Honor Museum in San Francisco, the Judah L. Magnes Museum in Berkeley and the Park City Museum in Utah.

Personnel:
Mark Cavagnero, FAIA (Principal)
Laura Blake (Principal)
Kang Kiang, AIA (Senior Associate)
John Fung (Associate)
Goetz Frank (Associate)

THE
PORTICO
GROUP

THE PORTICO GROUP
1500 4th Ave., Third Fl.
Seattle, WA 98101-1670
Tel: 206-621-2196; FAX: 206-621-2199
E-mail: portico@porticogroup.com
Web Site: www.porticogroup.com

Type of Business:
Celebrating 25 years of design, The Portico Group creates informal learning opportunities in memorable settings—settings that include natural and cultural museums, zoos and aquaria, and botanic gardens and arboreta. We are a talented team of interpretive exhibit designers, architects, and landscape architects capable of guiding a project from concept to conclusion. We seek opportunities to touch lives in meaningful ways—to connect people with nature and culture. Recent projects include: Jilkaat Kwaan Cultural Heritage Center, San Francisco Conservatory of Flowers, KidsQuest Children's Museum, USS Arizona Memorial Visitor Center and the Chicago Botanic Garden.

Personnel:
Michael Hamm, ASLA (President & CEO)
Charles G. Mayes, AIA (Principal)
Keith McClintock, ASLA (Principal)
Dennis Meyer, ASLA (Principal)
Alissa Rupp, AIA (Principal)
Allison CraigSundine (Senior Associate)
Devin Lai, AAIA (Senior Associate)
Richard Larson (Senior Associate)

LEE H. SKOLNICK ARCHITECTURE + DESIGN PARTNERSHIP
7 W. 22nd St., 10th Fl.
New York, NY 10010
Tel: 212-989-2624; FAX: 212-727-1702
E-mail: skolnick@skolnick.com
Web Site: www.skolnick.com

Type of Business:
Established in 1980, Lee H. Skolnick Architecture + Design Partnership is an award-winning 30-person architectural and museum exhibit design firm. Museum facilities design services include: master planning, program development, conceptual and complete architectural services for new institutions, site planning, adaptive re-use of existing structures, historic preservation, renovative design, feasibility studies. Exhibition, programming and museum education services include: conceptual development, script and copy development, interpretive exhibition design, exhibition project management, evaluation of exhibits, educational programming, facility operations, and collections storage, audience assessments.

Personnel:
Jo Ann Secor (Principal & Director Museum Services)
Scott Briggs (Senior Associate Museum Services)

SOLOMON & BAUER ARCHITECTS INC.
63 Pleasant St.
Watertown, MA 02472
Tel: 617-924-8200; FAX: 617-924-6685
E-mail: info@solomonbauer.com
Web Site: www.solomonbauer.com

Type of Business:
Award-winning Architecture and Interior Design Firm with over forty projects for museums. Master-planning; programming; feasibility studies; design of new museums; renovation and adaptive reuse of existing and historic structures; and exhibit design support. Special expertise in collections storage analysis, planning, and design. Recent projects for Dallas Museum of Art, Harvard Art Museums, Sam Noble Oklahoma Museum of Natural History, Museum of Fine Arts Houston, Princeton Art Museum, New Bedford Whaling Museum, and Museum of Fine Arts Boston.

Personnel:
Stuart B. Solomon, FAIA (Principal)
Lawrence C. Bauer, AIA (Principal)

UJMN ARCHITECTS + DESIGNERS
718 Arch St., Ste. 5N
Philadelphia, PA 19106
Tel: 215-440-0190; FAX: 215-440-0197
E-mail: nicholson@ujmn.com; blankin@ujmn.com
Web Site: www.ujmn.com

Type of Business:
Founded in 1967, UJMN Architects + Designers offers architectural design, museum planning, and exhibit design within a single firm, maximizing the integration of exhibits with museum facilities; the effectiveness of cost, schedule, and project management; and ultimately, the quality of the visitor experience. Recent projects include: the Liberty Bell Center Exhibits; the President's House at

(Continued on next page)

(Continued from previous page)

Independence National Historical Park; the National Civil War Museum Exhibits (Harrisburg, PA); the Louisville Slugger Museum; the Stoogeum; the Joliet Area Historical Museum; Hagley Museum and Library; the National Civil Rights Museum in Mississippi; the Eagles Mere Museum Exhibits, and Historic Deerfield.

Personnel:
Joseph A. Nicholson, AIA, IDSA (Principal)
Stacey Blankin (Associate)

Engineering Design Firms

LANDMARK
FACILITIES
GROUP, INC.

LANDMARK FACILITIES GROUP, INC.
252 East Ave.
Norwalk, CT 06855
Tel: 203-866-4626; FAX: 203-866-8019
E-mail: info@lfginc.com

Type of Business:
Landmark is a professional engineering firm offering HVAC, mechanical, electrical, plumbing, and fire protection engineering design, focusing its services on the special needs of museums, libraries, archives, historic structures, and their collections. The staff has a special capability in environmental controls and is well acquainted with facilities where the needs of preservation and sensitivity to architectural features are governing priorities. Services include monitoring, testing, long-range planning, systems design, constructions support, operations training, and commissioning.

Personnel:
Thomas E. Newbold, P.E., LEED AP (Principal)
Gerard J. Rauth, P.E., LEED AP (Principal)
Ernest A. Conrad, P.E., LEED AP (Principal)

Landscaping

BROWNING
DAY MULLINS
DIERDORF
ARCHITECTS

BROWNING DAY MULLINS DIERDORF ARCHITECTS
626 N. Illinois St.
Indianapolis, IN 46204
Tel: 317-635-5030; FAX: 317-634-5409
E-mail: cwmullins@bdmd.com
Web Site: www.bdmd.com

Type of Business:
The museum design practice of Browning Day Mullins Dierdorf Architects focuses on unique and creative design solutions for a variety of museum types. Our expertise has produced award-winning designs for the Indianapolis Museum of Art, Eiteljorg Museum, Herron School of Art & Design as well as for sports hall of fames, children's museums and other art museums. Professional services can be provided for master planning, programming, architectural and landscape architectural design and exhibit development. Visit us at www.bdmd.com.

Personnel:
Craig W. Mullins, AIA (Chairman of the Board)
Jonathan R. Hess, AIA (President)

Security Equipment

SDC
3580 Willow Lane
Westlake Village, CA 91361
Tel: 800-413-8783 & 805-494-0622; FAX: 800-959-4732 & 805-494-8861
E-mail: Service@sdcsecurity.com
Web Site: www.SDCsecurity.com

Type of Business:
SDC is an ISO 9001 Certified manufacturer of premium grade access control hardware that practices an internationally recognized quality management system. Products include: Digital and Card Access Control Systems, Mechanical and Electromechanical Locks and Exit Devices; Magnetic Locks; Delayed Egress Systems; Electric Strikes, Battery Back-up Power Supplies and Custom System Engineering.

Personnel:
Brent Maynard (National Sales Manager)

Theater & Auditorium Design

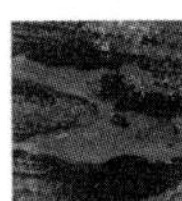

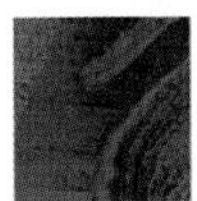
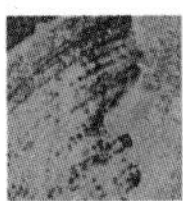

ADIRONDACK
■ STUDIOS ■

ADIRONDACK STUDIOS
439 County Rte. 45, Ste. 1
Argyle, NY 12809
Tel: 518-638-8000; FAX: 518-638-8238
E-mail: sales@adkstudios.com
Web Site: www.adkstudios.com

Type of Business:
Adirondack Studios is a full service company serving the museum and entertainment markets. For over thirty years, Adirondack has been providing custom environments and specialty exhibits to customers around the world. Adirondack is poised to participate in all phases and at all levels of project development, specialty fabrication and implementation.

Personnel:
Carl H. Zutz (Sales Manager)
Michael Blau (Creative Director)
Maurice O'Connell (Museum Sales)

BRC IMAGINATION ARTS
2711 Winona Ave.
Burbank, CA 91504
Tel: 818-841-8084; FAX: 818-841-4996
E-mail: brc@brcweb.com
Web Site: www.brcweb.com

Type of Business:
BRC is an award winning full service museum design and production company with a comprehensive range of skills from vision and master planning, to design, and production of exhibits and theatrical media experiences. Continental Europe Office: Science Park 5644, 5692 EN Eindhoven, P.O. Box 1245, 5602 BE Eindhoven, The Netherlands, Tel: +31.40.2676.871; Fax: +31.40.2676.895. United Kingdom Office: 8 Kimblesworth Grange, Potterhouse Lane, Durham DH1 5SL, United Kingdom, Tel: +44.7879.655950; Fax: +44.1913.719141. Shanghai Office: A405, Tomorrow Square, 399 West Nanjing Road, Shanghai 200003, People's Republic of China, Tel: +86.21.2308.1077.

Personnel:
Carmel Lewis (Vice President, Educational Experiences)
Matthew Solari (Director, Education Development)
Mark Hayward (Creative Director, Educational Experiences)
Bart Dohmen (Managing Director, Continental Europe)
Donna Davidson (Director, United Kingdom)

Theater Planning

BRC IMAGINATION ARTS
2711 Winona Ave.
Burbank, CA 91504
Tel: 818-841-8084; FAX: 818-841-4996
E-mail: brc@brcweb.com
Web Site: www.brcweb.com

Type of Business:
BRC is an award winning full service museum design and production company with a comprehensive range of skills from vision and master planning, to design, and production of exhibits and theatrical media experiences. Continental Europe Office: Science Park 5644, 5692 EN Eindhoven, P.O. Box 1245, 5602 BE Eindhoven, The Netherlands, Tel: +31.40.2676.871; Fax: +31.40.2676.895. United Kingdom Office: 8 Kimblesworth Grange, Potterhouse Lane, Durham DH1 5SL, United Kingdom, Tel: +44.7879.655950; Fax: +44.1913.719141. Shanghai Office: A405, Tomorrow Square, 399 West Nanjing Road, Shanghai 200003, People's Republic of China, Tel: +86.21.2308.1077.

Personnel:
Carmel Lewis (Vice President, Educational Experiences)
Matthew Solari (Director, Education Development)
Mark Hayward (Creative Director, Educational Experiences)
Bart Dohmen (Managing Director, Continental Europe)
Donna Davidson (Director, United Kingdom)

CHICAGO SCENIC STUDIOS, INC.
1315 N. North Branch St.
Chicago, IL 60642
Tel: 312-274-9900; FAX: 312-274-9901
E-mail: info@chicagoscenic.com
Web Site: www.chicagoscenic.com

Type of Business:
Chicago Scenic Studios provides museums, science & technology centers, zoos, aquariums and visitor centers more than 30 years of multi-disciplinary experience in themed environment engineering, design, fabrication, and installation. Our highly skilled staff of project managers, designers, carpenters, painters, electricians, and specialists in metals, plastics and fabrics partner with your team to provide safe, educational, immersive environments and exciting experiences through custom exhibits, retail, restaurant, and admission spaces. Chicago Scenic can serve as a general contractor, fabricator or project manager in support of your design or ours. Our background in exhibits, retail, theater, amusements, special events and corporate spaces provides us with the ability to cater to differing needs in unique spaces. We have enjoyed partnering with world-class institutions such as: The Chicago Museum of Science & Industry, The Notebaert Nature Museum, The Field Museum of Natural History, The Shedd Aquarium, Chicago History Museum, Kohl's Children's Museum and many more to bring numerous exciting, educational, and successful stories to life. We'd like to help tell your story as well.

Personnel:
Robert Doepel (President)
Jim Notarianni (Business Development)

WHITE OAK ASSOCIATES, INC.
17 Essex St.
Marblehead, MA 01945
Tel: 781-639-0722; FAX: 781-639-2491
E-mail: info@whiteoakassoc.com
Web Site: www.whiteoakassoc.com

Type of Business:
White Oak Associates is dedicated to high quality planning services for museums and special format theaters. Services include community needs assessments, concept development plans, strategic master plans, business plans, theater studies, architectural program planning, and staff and operating plans. White Oak also offers executive production services and implementation management from concept through post-opening for new museums and expansions. Our mission is to collaborate with museums to create sustainable institutions providing essential community services.

Personnel:
John W. Jacobsen (President)
Jeanie Stahl (Vice President)
Mark B. Peterson (Director, Theater Analysis & Planning)
Victor A. Becker (Director, Program Development)

BUSINESS/RETAIL SERVICES-GENERAL

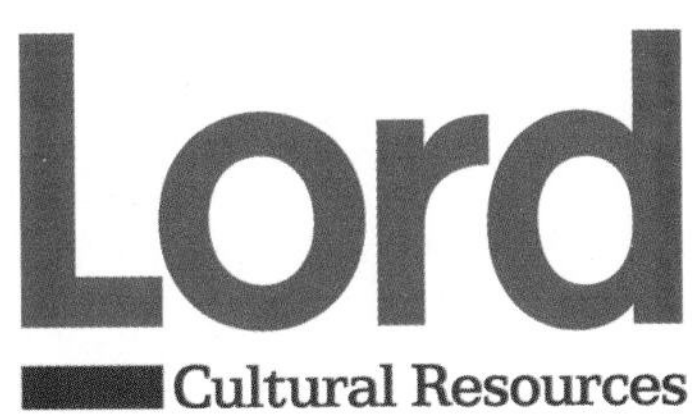

LORD CULTURAL RESOURCES
43 West 24th Street, 10th Fl.
New York, NY 10010
Tel: 646-375-2500; FAX: 212-675-4763
E-mail: info@lord.ca
Web Site: www.lord.ca

Type of Business:
Founded in 1981 in response to an emerging need for specialized planning services in the museum, cultural and heritage sector, Lord Cultural Resources is dedicated to creating cultural capital through visioning, planning and implementation. We work with museums, large and small, helping them to maximize their cultural capital by engaging with their communities, improving their buildings and inspiring collaboration and learning. We have benefited clients through the entire spectrum of cultural services including master plans, business plans, strategic plans, facility plans, functional programs, architect selection, exhibition design and development, project management, retail plans and cultural plans. In addition, Lord Cultural Resources has made a definitive contribution to the development of museum planning through its pioneering publications. The firm also has a San Francisco location.

Personnel:
Gail Dexter Lord (Co-President)
Barry Lord (Co-President)
Maria Piacente (Vice President, Exhibitions)
Catharine Tanner (Vice President, Facility Planning)
Paul Alezraa (Vice President, Europe)
Amy Kaufman (Managing Director, U.S.)
Brad King (Director, Management Consulting, Principal)
Margaret May (Senior Principal)
Ted Silberberg (Senior Principal)
Joy Bailey (Senior Consultant)
Lindsay Martin (Senior Consultant)
Andrea Ott (Director, Client Relations & Marketing)

Appraisers

AMERICAN SOCIETY OF APPRAISERS
555 Herndon Pkwy., #125
Herndon, VA 20170
Tel: 919-468-5557; FAX: 877-841-8270
E-mail: janella.smyth@gmail.com
Web Site: www.appraisers.org

Type of Business:
When you hire an ASA-accredited appraiser, you are ensured the best valuation expertise. The Personal Property accredited appraisers of ASA have the specialized knowledge achieved through academic study and practical experience to competently provide appraisals. Each ASA-accredited Personal Property appraiser has earned a professional designation in one or more appraisal specialties. Such accreditation is based on appraisal education, experience, written and verbal examinations and submission of acceptable appraisal reports.

Personnel:
Janella N. Smyth, FASA (Treasurer Personal Property Committee)

LH LESLIE HINDMAN AUCTIONEERS

LESLIE HINDMAN AUCTIONEERS
1338 W. Lake St.
Chicago, IL 60607
Tel: 312-280-1212; FAX: 312-280-1211
E-mail: alyssa@lesliehindman.com
Web Site: www.lesliehindman.com

Type of Business:
Leslie Hindman Auctioneers is one of the nation's leading fine art auctioneers and appraisers, holding regularly scheduled auctions of post-war and contemporary art, prints, American and European art, fine furniture, decorative arts, books and manuscripts, fine jewelry and timepieces, Asian works of art and vintage couture and textiles. All auctions attract an international audience through concentrated internet and print marketing efforts, resulting in exceptional prices realized. The auction house's longstanding reputation for excellent service has resulted in ongoing relationships with museums and institutions, who look to Leslie Hindman Auctioneers for a discreet and personalized approach tailored to meet their specific needs.

Personnel:
Leslie Hindman (CEO & President)
Alyssa Quinlan (Director, Museum Services)
Kate Pettenati (Museum Services)

SKINNER
Auctioneers and Appraisers of Antiques and Fine Art

SKINNER, INC.
63 Park Plaza
Boston, MA 02116
Tel: 617-350-5400; FAX: 617-350-5429
E-mail: info@skinnerinc.com
Web Site: www.skinnerinc.com

Type of Business:
Skinner, Inc. is one of the nation's leading auction houses for antiques and fine art and the only major auction house headquartered in New England. With expertise in over 20 specialty collecting areas, Skinner draws the interest of buyers from all over the world and its auctions regularly achieve world record prices. Skinner provides a broad range of auction, appraisal, and deaccession services for museums, educational institutions and nonprofit organizations worldwide. Skinner works one-on-one with museum curators and directors, helping to improve the quality and value of collections. Skinner's flexible, hands-on approach enables it to accept single items, groups, or entire collections — a factor that sets Skinner apart from most other national auction houses. Skinner is widely regarded as one of the most reputable names in the auction business — a factor that is increasingly important in today's highly competitive art and antiques market. Skinner's specialty departments include American Furniture & Decorative Arts, Paintings & Prints, English & Continental Furniture & Decorations, Fine Ceramics, Jewelry, Couture, 20th Century Furniture & Decorative Arts, Fine Musical Instruments, Asian Art,

(Continued on next page)

(Continued from previous page)

Fine Judaica & Silver, Toys, Dolls & Collectibles, Science & Technology, Oriental Rugs & Carpets, and American Indian & Ethnographic Art.

Personnel:
Karen Keane (CEO/Director, Museum Services)
Tish King (Director, Appraisals)
Catherine Riedel (Director, Marketing & Public Relations)

SWANN GALLERIES, INC.
104 E. 25th St., 6th Fl.
New York, NY 10010
Tel: 212-254-4710; FAX: 212-979-1017
E-mail: swann@swanngalleries.com
Web Site: www.swanngalleries.com

Type of Business:
Auctioneers and appraisers of rare books, autographs and manuscripts, maps, photographs, prints and drawings, vintage posters, and African-American Fine Art. We conduct 35 or more auctions each year. Catalogues and schedule online. Newsletter with full auction schedule on request. Member International Auctioneers.

Personnel:
George S. Lowry (Chairman)
Nicholas Lowry (President & Principal Auctioneer, Posters)
Caroline Birenbaum (Director, Communications)
Todd Weyman (Prints & Drawings)
Daile Kaplan (Photographs)
Christine Von der Linn (Art & Architecture Books)
Nigel Freeman (African-American Fine Art)

Fundraising/Membership Services

ALEXANDER HAAS: MUSEUM SERVICES
Piedmont Pl., 3520 Piedmont Rd., N.E., Ste. 300
Atlanta, GA 30305-1512
Tel: 404-525-7575; FAX: 404-524-2992
E-mail: info@fundraisingcounsel.com
Web Site: www.fundraisingcounsel.com

Type of Business:
Alexander Haas: Museum Services works with museums throughout the country. We specialize in your unique challenges and attributes. Alexander Haas is dedicated to helping museums build strong advancement programs to meet both immediate and long-term goals. The Alexander Haas: Museum Services consultants offers extensive knowledge ranging from how to build a strong case for support to how to organize a capital campaign and how to build a better board. We offer all the services that help you achieve the greatest RESULTS.

Personnel:
James R. Hackney, Jr., CFRE (Managing Partner for Museum Services)
David H. King, CFRE (President & CEO)
David T. Shufflebarger, CFRE (Managing Partner)

BENTZ GROUP
303 Washington St., N.W.
Warren, OH 44483-4736
Tel: 800-582-3493 & 330-399-9095; FAX: 330-399-9007
E-mail: info@bentzgroup.com
Web Site: www.bentzgroup.com

Type of Business:
A full-service fundraising firm, the Bentz Group provides counsel to non-profit organizations in all areas of philanthropy. Serving museums for more than 30 years, we work closely with our clients to provide right-sized solutions. Our services include planning and management of capital and endowment campaigns, development of fundraising plans, and expert counsel in annual giving and membership, board and volunteer training, grant writing, case statement preparation, major gift planning, and prospect research.

Personnel:
Charles H. Bentz (Chairman)
John T. Bentz (President)
Laura Lee Martin (Vice President)
Whitney F. Bohan (Consultant)
(Management Team)

Campbell
&Company

CAMPBELL & COMPANY
One E. Wacker Dr., Suite 3350
Chicago, IL 60601
Tel: 312-644-7100; FAX: 312-644-3559
E-mail: info@campbellcompany.com
Web Site: www.campbellcompany.com

Type of Business:
Campbell & Company is a full-service philanthropic consulting firm offering strategic planning, fundraising, communications and talent management services from offices in Chicago and across the country. Clients include The Adler Planetarium & Astronomy Museum (Chicago), Catalina Island Museum (Avalon, CA), Chicago Botanic Garden, Kohl Children's Museum (Chicago), Milwaukee Public Museum, Motorcycle Hall of Fame (Pickerington, OH), Mystic Seaport (CT), The National Railroad Hall of Fame (Galesburg, IL), Speed Art Museum (Louisville, KY) and the Zoological Society of San Diego.

Personnel:
Edith H. Falk, CFRE (President)
William R. Hausman (Senior Vice President)

Gateway
TICKETING SYSTEMS ™

GATEWAY TICKETING SYSTEMS, INC.
315 E. Second St.
Boyertown, PA 19512
Tel: 800-487-8587 & 610-987-4000; FAX: 610-987-4001
E-mail: info@gatewayticketing.com
Web Site: www.gatewayticketing.com

Type of Business:

Gateway Ticketing Systems, Inc. is the world leader in admission control and ticketing software for the cultural, leisure and transportation industries. In business for 21 years, Gateway provides sales, service, and support throughout North America and worldwide. Galaxy, Gateway's revenue management and admission control system, provides a comprehensive solution for museums to control data, revenue and security. They can manage and monitor admissions, events, guest services and retail from one central location, and track sales whenever and wherever they take place. Gateway provides the tools to improve operations efficiency, enhance the guest experience, cut costs and increase sales.

Personnel:

Michael Andre (President & CEO)
Michael A. Furman (Director, Sales & Marketing)

development, management, marketing

SCHULTZ & WILLIAMS, INC.
325 Chestnut St., Ste. 700
Philadelphia, PA 19106
Tel: 215-625-9955; FAX: 215-625-2701
E-mail: mail@schultzwilliams.com
Web Site: www.schultzwilliams.com

Type of Business:

Founded in 1987, Schultz & Williams is a national consulting firm specializing in development, marketing, management, and direct response services for nonprofit organizations. We consistently meet our clients' needs in traditional areas of development—capital campaign feasibility and planning studies, annual funds, major gifts and Board development—and with cost-effective direct response and multi-channel marketing campaigns that promote, build and sustain family membership and annual giving programs. Learn more at www.schultzwilliams.com or call 215-625-9955.

Personnel:

L. Scott Schultz (President)
M. Jane Williams (Partner)
Jessica Harrington (Vice President S & W Direct)
Dell Fascione (Vice President Marketing)
Shirley Trauger (Vice President)

Insurance

CHUBB GROUP OF INSURANCE COMPANIES
202 Hall's Mill Rd.
P.O. Box 1650
Whitehouse Station, NJ 08889
Tel: 908-572-4200
E-mail: csm@chubb.com
Web Site: www.chubb.com

Type of Business:

For more than 50 years, curators and directors from arboretums to zoos have turned to The Chubb Group of Insurance Companies (Chubb) for quality insurance protection. Chubb products and services can help museums and cultural institutions build a well-rounded insurance program. Chubb provides property, casualty, directors & officers, employment practices, crime, and fine arts insurance products and services to commercial customers worldwide through 8,000 independent agents and brokers.

Personnel:

Maureen Waterbury (Vice President)
Michael Schraer (Vice President)

HUNTINGTON T. BLOCK
INSURANCE AGENCY, INC.

HUNTINGTON T. BLOCK INSURANCE AGENCY, INC.
AN AON GROUP COMPANY
1120 20th St., N.W., Suite 600
Washington, DC 20036-3406
Tel: 800-424-8830 & 202-223-9853; FAX: 202-331-8409
Web Site: www.huntingtonblock.com

Type of Business:

HTB is a leading provider of insurance services for museums & exhibitions, universities, galleries and collectors. As a full service brokerage firm, we are the only agency with an in-house claims department, proprietary museum collection and temporary loans policy forms and have the largest underwriting authority available. Office locations include Washington DC, New York City, San Francisco, Houston and representation in London.

Personnel:

Jeff Minett (New York, Fine Art Insurance)
Lynn Marcin (Washington DC, Fine Art Insurance)
Adrienne Reid (Houston, Fine Art Insurance)
Sarah Barr (San Francisco, Fine Art Insurance)
Richard Mercado (Washington DC, Commercial Lines Insurance)

WELLS FARGO INSURANCE SERVICES, INC.
330 Madison Ave.
New York, NY 10017
Tel: 212-682-7500; FAX: 212-682-1043
E-mail: Ellen_Ross@wellsfargois.com
Web Site: www.wellsfargo.com

Type of Business:

The Wells Fargo Fine Arts Team with over 125 years of combined experience has been referred to as the "Masters in the Art of Insuring Art." We specialize in providing significant guidance and innovative solutions to meet the changing needs of the museum world. Our

(Continued on next page)

(Continued from previous page)

professional staff provides comprehensive insurance programs in all lines of business, including Fine Arts, Property & Casualty, Workers Compensation and Benefits.

Personnel:
Ellen Hoener Ross
Jeffrey A. Haber
Michael E. Fischman

Willis

WILLIS OF MARYLAND INC.
Washington DC Office, 6700 Rockledge Dr., 5th Fl.
Bethesda, MD 20817-1824
Tel: 301-581-4247 & 800-456-3162; FAX: 301-897-7302
E-mail: Robert.Salmon@willis.com
Web Site: www.willis.com

Type of Business:
The Willis Fine Art, Jewelry & Specie Division (FAJS) is one of the leading specialist art and collections insurance brokers in the world. With a team of very experienced professionals in Chicago, Los Angeles, New York, Washington DC, and London, clients include many prominent museums, institutions, universities, exhibitions and private collections. Willis FAJS provides a flexible, broad insurance program tailored specifically to suit the special needs of your museum at a competitive cost. We are an acknowledged authority to the extent that many other brokers in the USA come to Willis to use our services in placing coverage for this specialized class of business.

Personnel:
Robert F. Salmon, ACII (Mng. Dir. Willia Fine Art, Jewelry & Specie)

Management Consultants

development, management, marketing

SCHULTZ & WILLIAMS, INC.
325 Chestnut St., Ste. 700
Philadelphia, PA 19106
Tel: 215-625-9955; FAX: 215-625-2701
E-mail: mail@schultzwilliams.com
Web Site: www.schultzwilliams.com

Type of Business:
Founded in 1987, Schultz & Williams is a national consulting firm specializing in development, marketing, management, and direct response services for nonprofit organizations. We consistently meet our clients' needs in traditional areas of development—capital campaign feasibility and planning studies, annual funds, major gifts and Board development—and with cost-effective direct response and multi-channel marketing campaigns that promote, build and sustain family membership and annual giving programs. Learn more at www.schultzwilliams.com or call 215-625-9955.

Personnel:
L. Scott Schultz (President)
M. Jane Williams (Partner)
Jessica Harrington (Vice President S & W Direct)
Dell Fascione (Vice President Marketing)
Shirley Trauger (Vice President)

Museum Shop Merchandise

SAFARI LIMITED
1400 N.W. 159 St., Ste. 104
Miami Gardens, FL 33169
Tel: 800-554-5414; FAX: 305-621-6894
E-mail: sales@safariltd.com
Web Site: www.safariltd.com

Type of Business:
For over 25 years, Safari Ltd. has been a leading manufacturer of innovative, educational toys that are inspired by nature and fuel our children's imaginations. Our goal is to enrich the lives of children by providing enduring and captivating toys which are a great value for the money. One of Safari's strengths lies in our licenses with the Carnegie Museum of Natural History and the Monterey Bay Aquarium. These 2 licenses have helped to make the Safari brand known worldwide and have established us as a leading company in the manufacture of museum-quality replicas. Safari does not just sell plastic, we sell imagination, and because we care about our children and the environment, our replicas are phthalate-free. Phthalates are softening agents added to PVC plastics and have been banned in the U.S., Japan and Europe. We provide 5-language educational information with all our replicas to stimulate children's interest in the animal kingdom and the environment. Visit our website at www.safariltd.com to view all our replica collections. We guarantee you will not be disappointed.

Personnel:
Ramona Pariente (President)

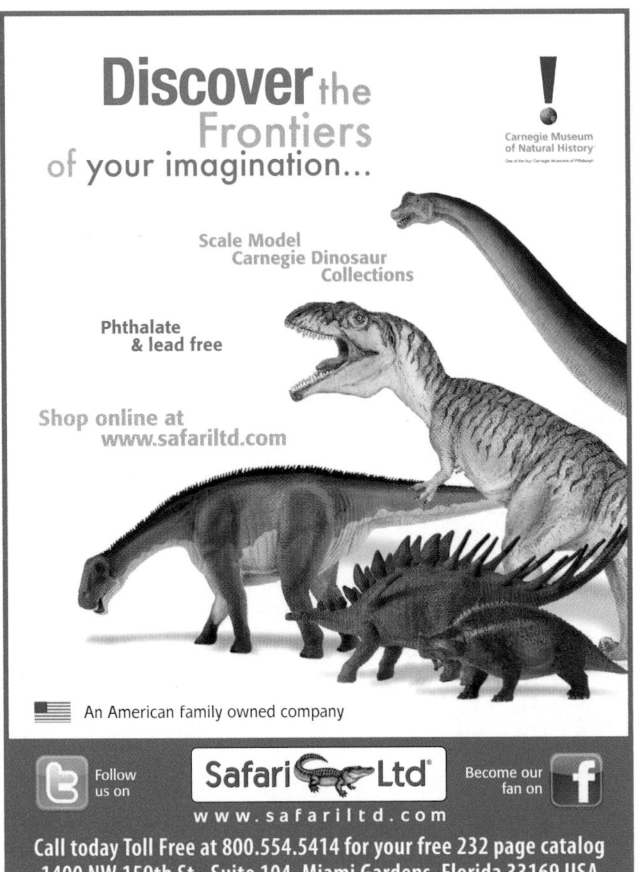

Professional Services

ConsultEcon, Inc.
Economic and Management Consultants

CONSULTECON, INC.
545 Concord Ave., Ste. 210
Cambridge, MA 02138
Tel: 617-547-0100; FAX: 617-547-0102
E-mail: info@consultecon.com
Web Site: www.consultecon.com

Type of Business:
ConsultEcon, Inc. provides services to clients in the areas of project and plan concept development, market and financial evaluation, visitor surveys, economic impact and project implementation. We are dedicated to serving museums of all sizes and types, and have worked over many years with clients responding to a broad spectrum of issues, ranging from the economics of operations to strategic planning.

Personnel:
Thomas J. Martin (President)
Robert E. Brais (Vice President)
Elena Kazlas (Principal)
Jason Drebitko (Senior Associate)

LORD CULTURAL RESOURCES
43 West 24th Street, 10th Fl.
New York, NY 10010
Tel: 646-375-2500; FAX: 212-675-4763
E-mail: info@lord.ca
Web Site: www.lord.ca

Type of Business:
Founded in 1981 in response to an emerging need for specialized planning services in the museum, cultural and heritage sector, Lord Cultural Resources is dedicated to creating cultural capital through visioning, planning and implementation. We work with museums, large and small, helping them to maximize their cultural capital by engaging with their communities, improving their buildings and inspiring collaboration and learning. We have benefited clients through the entire spectrum of cultural services including master plans, business plans, strategic plans, facility plans, functional programs, architect selection, exhibition design and development, project management, retail plans and cultural plans. In addition, Lord Cultural Resources

(Continued on next page)

(Continued from previous page)

has made a definitive contribution to the development of museum planning through its pioneering publications. The firm also has a San Francisco location.

Personnel:
Gail Dexter Lord (Co-President)
Barry Lord (Co-President)
Maria Piacente (Vice President, Exhibitions)
Catharine Tanner (Vice President, Facility Planning)
Paul Alezraa (Vice President, Europe)
Amy Kaufman (Managing Director, U.S.)
Brad King (Director, Management Consulting, Principal)
Margaret May (Senior Principal)
Ted Silberberg (Senior Principal)
Joy Bailey (Senior Consultant)
Lindsay Martin (Senior Consultant)
Andrea Ott (Director, Client Relations & Marketing)

WHITE OAK ASSOCIATES, INC.
17 Essex St.
Marblehead, MA 01945
Tel: 781-639-0722; FAX: 781-639-2491
E-mail: info@whiteoakassoc.com
Web Site: www.whiteoakassoc.com

Type of Business:
White Oak Associates is dedicated to high quality planning services for museums and special format theaters. Services include community needs assessments, concept development plans, strategic master plans, business plans, theater studies, architectural program planning, and staff and operating plans. White Oak also offers executive production services and implementation management from concept through post-opening for new museums and expansions. Our mission is to collaborate with museums to create sustainable institutions providing essential community services.

Personnel:
John W. Jacobsen (President)
Jeanie Stahl (Vice President)
Mark B. Peterson (Director, Theater Analysis & Planning)
Victor A. Becker (Director, Program Development)

Ticketing Services

GATEWAY TICKETING SYSTEMS, INC.
315 E. Second St.
Boyertown, PA 19512
Tel: 800-487-8587 & 610-987-4000; FAX: 610-987-4001
E-mail: info@gatewayticketing.com
Web Site: www.gatewayticketing.com

Type of Business:
Gateway Ticketing Systems, Inc. is the world leader in admission control and ticketing software for the cultural, leisure and transportation industries. In business for 21 years, Gateway provides sales, service, and support throughout North America and worldwide. Galaxy, Gateway's revenue management and admission control system, provides a comprehensive solution for museums to control data, revenue and security. They can manage and monitor admissions, events, guest services and retail from one central location, and track sales whenever and wherever they take place. Gateway provides the tools to improve operations efficiency, enhance the guest experience, cut costs and increase sales.

Personnel:
Michael Andre (President & CEO)
Michael A. Furman (Director, Sales & Marketing)

CONSERVATION/EDUCATION-GENERAL

ARIUS3D, INC.
755 The Queensway E.
Mississauga, ON, Canada L4Y 4C5
Tel: 905-270-7999; FAX: 905-270-6888
E-mail: info@arius3d.com
Web Site: www.arius3d.com; www.pointstream.net

Type of Business:
Arius3D delivers scientific quality 3D models with true color and accurate geometry. The patented 'non-touch' 3D color laser is free of ambient light artifacts or UV rays. We bring alive the concept of Scan Once: Use Many Times. Models can be easily scaled for a myriad of different applications including: digital repatriation, disaster recovery, digital archiving, conservation, virtual museum exhibits, object replication for digital & physical learning objects. Arius3D models can be used on pc's, kiosks, mobile devices, in digital learning galleries, VR theatres and caves in digital (mono or stereo), print, holographic or physical formats. Call us when accurate high resolution models are necessary!

Personnel:
Susan Dineen (Vice President Business Development)

NORTHEAST DOCUMENT CONSERVATION CENTER
100 Brickstone Square
Andover, MA 01810
Tel: 978-470-1010; FAX: 978-475-6021
E-mail: nedcc@nedcc.org
Web Site: www.nedcc.org

Type of Business:
The nonprofit Northeast Document Conservation Center (NEDCC) performs paper conservation, book conservation, preservation microfilming, duplication of photographs and negatives, and digitization of visual materials. The Center specializes in the treatment of paper-based materials including works of art on paper, photographs, wallpaper, books, documents, maps, architectural drawings, and posters. It provides consulting services, performs assessments of preservation needs, presents workshops and conferences, and offers a 24-hour disaster assistance hotline.

Personnel:
Bill Veillette (Executive Director)

Archival Products

MASTERPAK
145 E. 57th St., 5th Fl.
New York, NY 10022
Tel: 800-922-5522; FAX: 212-586-6961
E-mail: als@masterpak-usa.com
Web Site: www.masterpak-usa.com

Type of Business:
Unique & archival materials for the protection of fine art, artifacts and antiques in packing, shipping, storing and display. Hard-to-find materials for conservators, artists, museums, galleries, collectors, framers and art shippers. Products include: Archival Softwrap® Tyvek®, Nomex® and Archival Hardwrap® Tyvek® Liners by DuPont, Sealed Air's Ethafoam®/Cellu-Cushion® in planks and rolls, Sealed Air's BubbleWrap®, Voltek's Volara® Polyethylene Foam, Archival Rolling & Storage Tubes, Unbuffered & Buffered Tissue in rolls and sheets, Photo-Tex Tissue in rolls and sheets, Glassine Paper in rolls and sheets, Silicone Parchment Release Paper in rolls and sheets, Corrugated Multi-Use Board, Archival tapes, Glass Skin®, Strongboxes™ & Print Pads™, Oz Clips™ Link Lock® Latches, Steel Closure Plates, PEM2 Data Loggers and specialty preservation management software developed by The Image Permanence Institute especially for the collections of Museums, Libraries & Archives. All products are available in small or large quantities and can ship within 24 hours. Our website, located at www.masterpak-usa.com, is open 24 hours for easy online ordering.

Personnel:
E. William Judson (Chairman)
Andrew L. Smith (President)

Conservation Supplies

A Division Of Library Binding Service

ARCHIVAL PRODUCTS (A DIVISION OF LIBRARY BINDING SERVICE)
P.O. Box 1413
Des Moines, IA 50306-1413
Tel: 800-526-5640; FAX: 888-220-2397
E-mail: info@archival.com
Web Site: www.archival.com

Type of Business:
Committed to serving you with archival quality elegant solutions for preservation needs, Archival Products specializes in quality preservation enclosures and custom produced materials offering the New Eco Binder, custom four flap enclosures, academy folders, manuscript folders, pamphlet binders, Century boxes, archival boards, binder albums, polypropylene sheet and photo protectors. Mylar sheet protectors, newspaper and map folders, pamphlet and music binders, Archival Mist, Bookkeeper deacidification sprays, non-glare polypropylene book covers, Colibri Book Cover System.

DORFMAN
MUSEUM FIGURES, INC.

DORFMAN MUSEUM FIGURES, INC.
6224 Holabird Ave.
Baltimore, MD 21224
Tel: 800-634-4873 & 410-284-3248; FAX: 410-284-3249
E-mail: info@museumfigures.com
Web Site: www.museumfigures.com

Type of Business:
We've been standing still for 50 years! Dorfman is the leader in creating lifelike, life-size human figures, and ETHAFOAM™ Conservation Forms. Choose non-ident, generic realistic figures with rigid or flexible foam bodies, or recognizable historic characters for your exhibit needs. Or choose from our line of Conservation Forms, Dress or Suit Forms,

(Continued on next page)

(Continued from previous page)

and Hangers for your archival display and storage needs. Dorfman Museum Figures, Inc. has been in business since 1957. Our Museum Figures and Conservation Forms are used in museums internationally.

Personnel:
Robert Dorfman (President)
Penny Clifton (Project Manager)

MASTERPAK
145 E. 57th St., 5th Fl.
New York, NY 10022
Tel: 800-922-5522; FAX: 212-586-6961
E-mail: als@masterpak-usa.com
Web Site: www.masterpak-usa.com

Type of Business:
Unique & archival materials for the protection of fine art, artifacts and antiques in packing, shipping, storing and display. Hard-to-find materials for conservators, artists, museums, galleries, collectors, framers and art shippers. Products include: Archival Softwrap® Tyvek®, Nomex® and Archival Hardwrap® Tyvek® Liners by DuPont, Sealed Air's Ethafoam®/Cellu-Cushion® in planks and rolls, Sealed Air's BubbleWrap®, Voltek's Volara® Polyethylene Foam, Archival Rolling & Storage Tubes, Unbuffered & Buffered Tissue in rolls and sheets, Photo-Tex Tissue in rolls and sheets, Glassine Paper in rolls and sheets, Silicone Parchment Release Paper in rolls and sheets, Corrugated Multi-Use Board, Archival tapes, Glass Skin®, Strongboxes™ & Print Pads™, Oz Clips™ Link Lock® Latches, Steel Closure Plates, PEM2 Data Loggers and specialty preservation management software developed by The Image Permanence Institute especially for the collections of Museums, Libraries & Archives. All products are available in small or large quantities and can ship within 24 hours. Our website, located at www.masterpak-usa.com, is open 24 hours for easy online ordering.

Personnel:
E. William Judson (Chairman)
Andrew L. Smith (President)

MULTIFORM STUDIOS/EXHIBIT SOURCE
12012 Doane Rd.
South Lyon, MI 48178
Tel: 248-437-5964; FAX: 248-446-3197
E-mail: james@multiformstudios.com
Web Site: www.multiformstudios.com

Type of Business:
We provide design and fabrication of artifact mounts in brass, acrylic and steel, book/document mounts, textile strainers, and mannequins as well as museum exhibit services and consulting. Services include: on site fabrication, installation, exhibits and conservation consulting. Our web site includes details of services, products and contact information. Located in South Lyon, Michigan, USA. Member AAM, AIC. www.multiformstudios.com

Personnel:
James Leacock (Owner)

TRU VUE, INC.
9400 W. 55th St.
McCook, IL 60525-3636
Tel: 708-485-5080; FAX: 708-854-2660
E-mail: info@tru-vue.com
Web Site: www.tru-vue.com/museums

Type of Business:
Tru Vue is a leading manufacturer of high-performance glazing, including Optium® Acrylic Glazing. Optium combines the best of both worlds, anti-reflective safety glass and UV filtering acrylic, in one product for all your design and conservation needs. And now, Optium® Museum Display Acrylic™ is available for display cases, vitrines, and framed exhibits. Find out why museums around the world depend on Optium to protect, conserve, and display their most valuable and historic collections. For more information, visit www.tru-vue.com/museums.

Personnel:
Patti Dumbaugh (Vice President)
Julie Heath (Museum Market Manager)

Education Supplies/Toys

SAFARI LIMITED
1400 N.W. 159 St., Ste. 104
Miami Gardens, FL 33169
Tel: 800-554-5414; FAX: 305-621-6894
E-mail: sales@safariltd.com
Web Site: www.safariltd.com

Type of Business:
For over 25 years, Safari Ltd. has been a leading manufacturer of innovative, educational toys that are inspired by nature and fuel our children's imaginations. Our goal is to enrich the lives of children by providing enduring and captivating toys which are a great value for the money. One of Safari's strengths lies in our licenses with the Carnegie Museum of Natural History and the Monterey Bay Aquarium. These 2 licenses have helped to make the Safari brand known worldwide and have established us as a leading company in the manufacture of museum-quality replicas. Safari does not just sell plastic, we sell imagination, and because we care about our children and the environment, our replicas are phthalate-free. Phthalates are softening agents added to PVC plastics and have been banned in the U.S., Japan and Europe. We provide 5-language educational information with all our replicas to stimulate children's interest in the animal kingdom and the environment. Visit our website at www.safariltd.com to view all our replica collections. We guarantee you will not be disappointed.

Personnel:
Ramona Pariente (President)

EXHIBITS-GENERAL

2FLYPLANES
Barkly Wharf, Suites 340-345
Le Caudan, Port Louis, Mauritius
Tel: 27-83-2346582
E-mail: nikpatel@2flyplanes.com
Web Site: www.2flyplanes.com

Type of Business:
We manufacture full motion and highly realistic flight simulators based on commercial, military and space craft for the public entertainment and education markets.

LORD CULTURAL RESOURCES
43 West 24th Street, 10th Fl.
New York, NY 10010
Tel: 646-375-2500; FAX: 212-675-4763
E-mail: info@lord.ca
Web Site: www.lord.ca

Type of Business:
Founded in 1981 in response to an emerging need for specialized planning services in the museum, cultural and heritage sector, Lord Cultural Resources is dedicated to creating cultural capital through visioning, planning and implementation. We work with museums, large and small, helping them to maximize their cultural capital by engaging with their communities, improving their buildings and inspiring collaboration and learning. We have benefited clients through the entire spectrum of cultural services including master plans, business plans, strategic plans, facility plans, functional programs, architect selection, exhibition design and development, project management, retail plans and cultural plans. In addition, Lord Cultural Resources has made a definitive contribution to the development of museum planning through its pioneering publications. The firm also has a San Francisco location.

Personnel:
Gail Dexter Lord (Co-President)
Barry Lord (Co-President)
Maria Piacente (Vice President, Exhibitions)
Catharine Tanner (Vice President, Facility Planning)
Paul Alezraa (Vice President, Europe)
Amy Kaufman (Managing Director, U.S.)
Brad King (Director, Management Consulting, Principal)
Margaret May (Senior Principal)
Ted Silberberg (Senior Principal)
Joy Bailey (Senior Consultant)
Lindsay Martin (Senior Consultant)
Andrea Ott (Director, Client Relations & Marketing)

SPLIT ROCK STUDIOS
2071 Gateway Blvd.
Arden Hills, MN 55112
Tel: 651-631-2211 & 800-433-9599; FAX: 651-631-0707
E-mail: info@splitrockstudios.com
Web Site: www.splitrockstudios.com

Type of Business:
Split Rock Studios is a full-service firm specializing in designing and building interactive exhibits for interpretive centers, museums and related institutions. In addition to our exhibit design and development capabilities, we have the in-house capabilities to produce all facets of a major exhibition, including interactive components, themed environments, dioramas, interpretive murals, realistic animal and human sculpture, graphics, and custom exhibit furniture. Whatever your exhibit project needs, our staff will provide the ultimate in quality service and workmanship.

Personnel:
Craig Sommerville (President)
Lisa Friedlander (Sales & Marketing)

SUNRISE SYSTEM, INC.
720 Washington St.
Pembroke, MA 02359
Tel: 781-826-9706; FAX: 781-826-0061
E-mail: sales@sunrisesystems.com
Web Site: www.sunrisesystems.com

Type of Business:
Sunrise Systems, Inc. is a manufacturer of custom LED signage. Founded in 1976, Sunrise has been a lifelong producer of fascinating public art, first-in-the-industry technological advances and uniquely tailored information systems. Our LED displays are installed in countries all over the world and in industries across the map. Transit system integrators, stock tickers, retail applications and academic exhibits are just a few well-established areas of Sunrise's expertise. Past installments are prominently featured in many permanent exhibits at prestigious museums around the globe. Our ability to meet even the most complex architectural, electrical and mechanical requirements keeps us at the forefront of the industry. A dedication to innovative technology and customer support make us a good place to start planning your next LED display project.

Personnel:
Henry C. Appleton (President, Director Sales)
Eric Harrington (Director, Engineering)
Kaleb Christenson (Marketing Director & Project Manager)

Animation/Animatronics

BLUE TELESCOPE
236 W. 30th St., 7th Fl.
New York, NY 10001
Tel: 212-675-7702, ext. 12; FAX: 212-675-7703
E-mail: contact@blue-telescope.com
Web Site: www.blue-telescope.com

Type of Business:
Blue Telescope creates interactive media experiences that educate and communicate. We use rich media to dynamically illustrate complex concepts and data, to create fun, engaging experiences out of challenging content, and to immerse audiences in compelling stories and environments. Blue Telescope uses multi-user technology to facilitate communication among visitors and educators. From competitive and collaborative games, to group content exploration, to live surveys, we create shared experiences that get people talking and engaged.

GARNER HOLT PRODUCTIONS, INC.
825 E. Cooley Ave.
San Bernardino, CA 92408
Tel: 909-799-3030, ext. 229; FAX: 909-799-7351
E-mail: jvanmeter@garnerholt.com
Web Site: www.garnerholt.com

Type of Business:
Garner Holt Productions, Inc. creates custom, high quality animatronics figures, themed environments and special effects. We are a full service company, offering concept design through installation. The company maintains a large library of molds, which includes realistic, life-size animals and human figures. Garner Holt Productions also provides traveling exhibits, including Backyard Monsters which feature gigantic robot insects, interactive displays and an insect collection endorsed by the American Entomological Society.

Personnel:
Garner Holt (President)
Jody Van Meter (Vice President, Marketing & Sales)
Philip Previtire (Director, Scenic Production)
Michelle Berg (Vice President Administration)

RBH MULTIMEDIA, INC.
12 Hatch Ter.
Dobbs Ferry, NY 10522
Tel: 914-693-8755; FAX: 914-693-3539
E-mail: rbh@rbhmedia.com
Web Site: www.rbhmedia.com

Type of Business:
RBH Multimedia, Inc. is a media production company dedicated to developing and producing audiovisual experiences and exhibits. We bring imagination, skill, flair and years of experience to designing and producing audio, video and multiple media exhibits for museums, historic sites, visitor and interpretive centers, and cultural institutions. We also design and program websites and computer interactive exhibits. RBH is particularly known for producing signature multi-sensory, multimedia "experience" theater shows. Other services include hardware system design, engineering and installation, with expertise in videoconference technology. For more information about RBH Multimedia, Inc., please visit us online at www.rbhmedia.com.

Personnel:
Steve Brosnahan (Partner)
Nancy Haffner (Partner)
Edgardo J. Resto (Associate)

Artifact Mounting Supplies & Installation

MULTIFORM STUDIOS/EXHIBIT SOURCE
12012 Doane Rd.
South Lyon, MI 48178
Tel: 248-437-5964; FAX: 248-446-3197
E-mail: james@multiformstudios.com
Web Site: www.multiformstudios.com

Type of Business:
We provide design and fabrication of artifact mounts in brass, acrylic and steel, book/document mounts, textile strainers, and mannequins as well as museum exhibit services and consulting. Services include: on site fabrication, installation, exhibits and conservation consulting. Our web site includes details of services, products and contact information. Located in South Lyon, Michigan, USA. Member AAM, AIC. www.multiformstudios.com

Personnel:
James Leacock (Owner)

MUSEUM PROFESSIONALS
4875 Sunset Lane
Loretto, MN 55357
Tel: 763-479-7177
E-mail: museumpr@spacestar.net
Web Site: www.museumprofessionals.com

Type of Business:
EXHIBIT FABRICATION...combining science and aesthetics to create natural science and historical exhibits, artifact mounts and installation, dioramas, plant reproductions, field collecting, sculpture, murals model-making and consulting. Specialists in producing exhibits in the fields of zoology, botany, paleontology, geology and archaeology.

Personnel:
Terry Brown (President)

Dioramas

CHASE STUDIO, INC.

CHASE STUDIO, INC.
205 Wolf Creek Rd.
Cedar Creek, MO 65627
Tel: 417-794-3303; FAX: 417-794-3741
E-mail: chasestudio@chasestudio.com
Web Site: www.chasestudio.com

Type of Business:
Designers and builders of natural history and environmental science exhibits; paleontological reconstructions, zoological models, botanical reproductions, dioramas and habitat groups, illustration and mural painting, graphic design, photography, lighting design, fine cabinetwork, taxidermy, research, script writing, exhibit planning and consultation. Exhibits for over 200 museums worldwide since 1973.

Personnel:
Dr. Terry L. Chase (Director)
David F. Darby (Assistant Director Exhibits)
William L. Talbot (Assistant Director Business)
Greg L. Rogers (Assistant Director Operations)

MUSEUM PROFESSIONALS

MUSEUM PROFESSIONALS
4875 Sunset Lane
Loretto, MN 55357
Tel: 763-479-7177
E-mail: museumpr@spacestar.net
Web Site: www.museumprofessionals.com

Type of Business:
EXHIBIT FABRICATION...combining science and aesthetics to create natural science and historical exhibits, artifact mounts and installation, dioramas, plant reproductions, field collecting, sculpture, murals model-making and consulting. Specialists in producing exhibits in the fields of zoology, botany, paleontology, geology and archaeology.

Personnel:
Terry Brown (President)

SPLIT ROCK STUDIOS
2071 Gateway Blvd.
Arden Hills, MN 55112
Tel: 651-631-2211 & 800-433-9599; FAX: 651-631-0707
E-mail: info@splitrockstudios.com
Web Site: www.splitrockstudios.com

Type of Business:
Split Rock Studios is a full-service firm specializing in designing and building interactive exhibits for interpretive centers, museums and related institutions. In addition to our exhibit design and development capabilities, we have the in-house capabilities to produce all facets of a major exhibition, including interactive components, themed environments, dioramas, interpretive murals, realistic animal and human sculpture, graphics, and custom exhibit furniture. Whatever your exhibit project needs, our staff will provide the ultimate in quality service and workmanship.

Personnel:
Craig Sommerville (President)
Lisa Friedlander (Sales & Marketing)

TAYLOR STUDIOS, INC.
1320 Harmon Drive
Rantoul, IL 61866
Tel: 217-893-4874 & 800-707-2047; FAX: 217-893-1998
E-mail: sales@taylorstudios.com
Web Site: www.taylorstudios.com/omd

Type of Business:
"Taylor Studios, Inc. is an interpretive planning, exhibit design, and fabrication firm that assists museums and other clients in creating exhibits that are educational, creative, and enduring. We are committed to completing exhibits to the fulfillment of each client's unique needs, timelines, and goals. Our exhibit creativity is built on a firm interpretive foundation. Our team has the experience and talent to coordinate, communicate, research, plan, design, manage, and produce exhibits of the highest quality. We believe in excellent customer service and back our fabricated products with an unprecedented five-year warranty."

Personnel:
Betty Brennan (President)
Kara Vanskike (Marketing Coordinator)

Display Fixtures

CASE[WERKS], LLC
1501 Saint Paul St., Ste. 116
Baltimore, MD 21202
Tel: 410-332-4160 & 800-810-2852 (toll free); FAX: 410-332-4106
E-mail: info@casewerks.com
Web Site: www.casewerks.com

Type of Business:
Case[werks] is a sales and service firm offering a range of products uniquely designed to meet exhibit requirements for original art, artifacts and special collections in all types of interior environments. Providing consultative sales support for institutions large & small, Case[werks] is THE museum professional's source for archival display cases & exhibit furnishings, library furnishings, gallery accessories, art hanging hardware, signage & graphic display products as well as conservation equipment including miniClima Humidity Control Systems. Many of our best-selling gallery accessories are in stock, ready to ship; major credit cards are accepted. An extensive catalog is

(Continued on next page)

(Continued from previous page)

available and custom inquiries are always welcome. Ask about enrolling in our institutional "gift" registry. Case[werks] is the North American representative for Vitrinen- und Glasbau REIER (Germany).

Personnel:
Matt Malaquias (Principal)
Reinhard Nottrodt (Principal)

PANELOCK SYSTEMS LIMITED
129 Church St., Ste. 516
New Haven, CT 06510
Tel: 203-643-2060 & 877-315-1998 (toll free)
E-mail: sales@panelock.com
Web Site: www.panelock.com

Type of Business:
Designers and manufacturers of the Panelock patented range of movable display walls for permanent and temporary exhibition spaces.

Personnel:
Maureen Moreau

TECNO DISPLAY, INC.
2277 National Ave.
Hayward, CA 94545
Tel: 800-255-3536; FAX: 510-782-5003
E-mail: tecno@tecnodisplay.com
Web Site: www.tecnodisplay.com

Type of Business:
Manufacturers of pre-assembled tempered glass display showcases, wall units, free standing towers, and exhibit display stands and pedestals. Halogen, fluorescent, LED etc. lighting available. Standard & custom showcases available. Small runs of custom showcases can be manufactured. We work with all types of laminates and solid wood veneers, stains, moldings. We have built our reputation on our quality products, reliable delivery and excellent customer support.

Personnel:
Patrick Lowe (Sales Manager)
Cathie Harvey (Customer Service)
John Wyatt (Customer Service)

Display Stands

ART DISPLAY ESSENTIALS
2 W. Crisman Rd.
Columbia, NJ 07832
Tel: 800-862-9869; FAX: 908-496-4956
E-mail: cmidkiff@artdisplay.com
Web Site: www.artdisplay.com

Type of Business:
After many years of working with museums and dealers in the area of antiquities, ancient art and other fine collectibles, we have seen an increasing need for reliable, quality stock display materials. Using only top quality materials and applying our knowledge of art mounting for museums and collectors, we have designed and produced a catalog containing over 300 different cabinets and stands. If we do not have the item you're in search of, then we can design and build one specifically to suit your needs. BETTER BY DESIGN, BETTER BY CHOICE.

Personnel:
William Stender (President)
Chris Midkiff (General Manager)

PANELOCK SYSTEMS LIMITED
129 Church St., Ste. 516
New Haven, CT 06510
Tel: 203-643-2060 & 877-315-1998 (toll free)
E-mail: sales@panelock.com
Web Site: www.panelock.com

Type of Business:
Designers and manufacturers of the Panelock patented range of movable display walls for permanent and temporary exhibition spaces.

Personnel:
Maureen Moreau

Engineering Design & Consultation

EWING
COLE

EWINGCOLE CULTURAL DESIGN GROUP
100 N. 6th St.
Philadelphia, PA 19106
Tel: 215-923-2020; FAX: 215-574-9163
E-mail: wcrimm@ewingcole.com
Web Site: www.ewingcole.com/cultural

Type of Business:
EwingCole is a multi-discipline architecture and engineering firm specializing in design for cultural institutions. We work with national and regional museums for the fine arts, history, natural sciences and science and technology. Our Cultural Practice experts apply deep industry knowledge to enhance the visitor experience and to develop a design closely aligned with the museum's strategic plan. Our process engages the board and staff at all levels to create solutions that are intellectually stimulating, fiscally responsible and environmentally sustainable.

Personnel:
Walter Crimm, AIA, LEED AP (Vice President, Cultural Design Group)

GOPPION MUSEUM WORKSHOP, INC.
300 Linwood Ave.
Newton, MA 02460
Tel: 617-297-2546; FAX: 617-848-2641
E-mail: info@goppion-us.com
Web Site: www.goppion.com

Type of Business:

Established in 1952, Goppion SpA is one of the world's premier fabricators of high performance steel and glass display cases for museums, archives, libraries and other similar cultural institutions. Goppion does not offer a standard line of casework, nor do we have stock profiles and components from which to fabricate our work. Rather, we collaboratively develop the engineering and design in response to the performance, aesthetic, schedule, and budget requirements of your project.

Personnel:

Ted Paschkis (Director, Operations, U.S.)
Peter Hohenstatt (Commercial Manager, Goppion SpA (U.S.))

Environmental Equipment

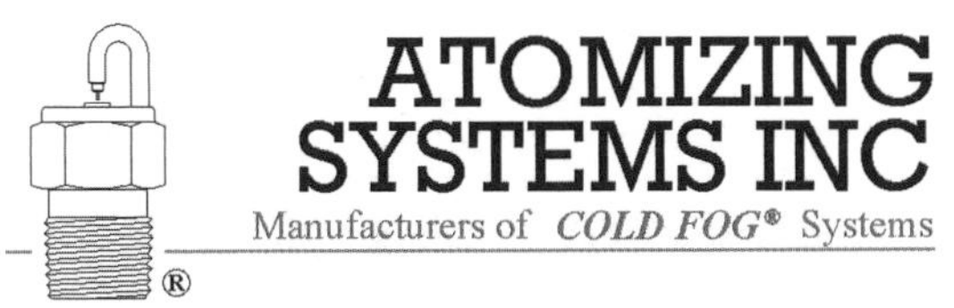

ATOMIZING SYSTEMS INC.
One Hollywood Ave.
HoHoKus, NJ 07423
Tel: 201-447-1222; FAX: 201-447-6932
E-mail: info@coldfog.com
Web Site: www.coldfog.com

Type of Business:

Atomizing Systems Inc., a manufacturer of water fog equipment for humidity & special effects, uses the world's only laser-drilled, ruby orifice fog nozzle (recently granted a US patent). Nozzles create water fog evaporative cooling, special effects, cool zones, walkways, landscaping, entrances, waterfalls, rockwork, fountains, haze, smoke & cloud simulation. Systems utilized worldwide include major projects in Orlando, far east, middle east, Latin America. 20-year nozzle Warranty against orifice wear standard. Each fog Nozzles equipped with individual filter. Full engineering & design services available.

Personnel:

Michael Elkas (President & Owner)

cāse[werks] SM

CASE[WERKS], LLC
1501 Saint Paul St., Ste. 116
Baltimore, MD 21202
Tel: 410-332-4160 & 800-810-2852 (toll free); FAX: 410-332-4106
E-mail: info@casewerks.com
Web Site: www.casewerks.com

Type of Business:

Case[werks] is a sales and service firm offering a range of products uniquely designed to meet exhibit requirements for original art, artifacts and special collections in all types of interior environments. Providing consultative sales support for institutions large & small, Case[werks] is THE museum professional's source for archival display cases & exhibit furnishings, library furnishings, gallery accessories, art hanging hardware, signage & graphic display products as well as conservation equipment including miniClima Humidity Control Systems. Many of our best-selling gallery accessories are in stock, ready to ship; major credit cards are accepted. An extensive catalog is available and custom inquiries are always welcome. Ask about enrolling in our institutional "gift" registry. Case[werks] is the North American representative for Vitrinen- und Glasbau REIER (Germany).

Personnel:

Matt Malaquias (Principal)
Reinhard Nottrodt (Principal)

Lighting Services Inc

LIGHTING SERVICES INC
2 Kay Fries Dr.
Stony Point, NY 10980
Tel: 800-999-9574 & 845-942-2800; FAX: 845-942-2177
E-mail: Sales@mailLSI.com
Web Site: www.LightingServicesInc.com

Type of Business:

Lighting Services Inc (LSI) is the leading independent manufacturer of track, accent, display and LED lighting systems for museum environments. Since 1958, LSI has been dedicated to designing, engineering and manufacturing lighting fixtures of the highest quality. Our reputation for creativity and innovative design, coupled with specification grade products and intelligent personalized service, has made us the manufacturer of choice amongst the most discriminating specifiers of lighting for museums and galleries.

Personnel:

Daniel Gelman (President)

MASTERPAK
145 E. 57th St., 5th Fl.
New York, NY 10022
Tel: 800-922-5522; FAX: 212-586-6961
E-mail: als@masterpak-usa.com
Web Site: www.masterpak-usa.com

Type of Business:
Unique & archival materials for the protection of fine art, artifacts and antiques in packing, shipping, storing and display. Hard-to-find materials for conservators, artists, museums, galleries, collectors, framers and art shippers. Products include: Archival Softwrap® Tyvek®, Nomex® and Archival Hardwrap® Tyvek® Liners by DuPont, Sealed Air's Ethafoam®/Cellu-Cushion® in planks and rolls, Sealed Air's BubbleWrap®, Voltek's Volara® Polyethylene Foam, Archival Rolling & Storage Tubes, Unbuffered & Buffered Tissue in rolls and sheets, Photo-Tex Tissue in rolls and sheets, Glassine Paper in rolls and sheets, Silicone Parchment Release Paper in rolls and sheets, Corrugated Multi-Use Board, Archival tapes, Glass Skin®, Strongboxes™ & Print Pads™, Oz Clips™ Link Lock® Latches, Steel Closure Plates, PEM2 Data Loggers and specialty preservation management software developed by The Image Permanence Institute especially for the collections of Museums, Libraries & Archives. All products are available in small or large quantities and can ship within 24 hours. Our website, located at www.masterpak-usa.com, is open 24 hours for easy online ordering.

Personnel:
E. William Judson (Chairman)
Andrew L. Smith (President)

Exhibit Cases

case[werks]℠

CASE[WERKS], LLC
1501 Saint Paul St., Ste. 116
Baltimore, MD 21202
Tel: 410-332-4160 & 800-810-2852 (toll free); FAX: 410-332-4106
E-mail: info@casewerks.com
Web Site: www.casewerks.com

Type of Business:
Case[werks] is a sales and service firm offering a range of products uniquely designed to meet exhibit requirements for original art, artifacts and special collections in all types of interior environments. Providing consultative sales support for institutions large & small, Case[werks] is THE museum professional's source for archival display cases & exhibit furnishings, library furnishings, gallery accessories, art hanging hardware, signage & graphic display products as well as conservation equipment including miniClima Humidity Control Systems. Many of our best-selling gallery accessories are in stock, ready to ship; major credit cards are accepted. An extensive catalog is available and custom inquiries are always welcome. Ask about enrolling in our institutional "gift" registry. Case[werks] is the North American representative for Vitrinen- und Glasbau REIER (Germany).

Personnel:
Matt Malaquias (Principal)
Reinhard Nottrodt (Principal)

CHICAGO SCENIC STUDIOS, INC.
1315 N. North Branch St.
Chicago, IL 60642
Tel: 312-274-9900; FAX: 312-274-9901
E-mail: info@chicagoscenic.com
Web Site: www.chicagoscenic.com

Type of Business:
Chicago Scenic Studios provides museums, science & technology centers, zoos, aquariums and visitor centers more than 30 years of multi-disciplinary experience in themed environment engineering, design, fabrication, and installation. Our highly skilled staff of project managers, designers, carpenters, painters, electricians, and specialists in metals, plastics and fabrics partner with your team to provide safe, educational, immersive environments and exciting experiences through custom exhibits, retail, restaurant, and admission spaces. Chicago Scenic can serve as a general contractor, fabricator or project manager in support of your design or ours. Our background in exhibits, retail, theater, amusements, special events and corporate spaces provides us with the ability to cater to differing needs in unique spaces. We have enjoyed partnering with world-class institutions such as: The Chicago Museum of Science & Industry, The Notebaert Nature Museum, The Field Museum of Natural History, The Shedd Aquarium, Chicago History Museum, Kohl's Children's Museum and many more to bring numerous exciting, educational, and successful stories to life. We'd like to help tell your story as well.

Personnel:
Robert Doepel (President)
Jim Notarianni (Business Development)

CLICK NETHERFIELD USA
708 Fellowship Rd.
Mount Laurel, NJ 08054
Tel: 856-234-3448; FAX: 856-234-0760
E-mail: r.skorch@clicknetherfieldusa.com
Web Site: www.clicknetherfield.com

Type of Business:
Click Netherfield design & manufacture museum showcases around the world. The global resources of Click Netherfield with Project Teams on six continents and production facilities in Scotland, Egypt, China and Australia stand ready for our next exciting and challenging project. Worldwide leaders in the industry, our reputation for creative design solutions, comprehensive project management, collaborative design development combined with state of the art manufacturing have become the benchmark standard for museum showcase manufacturing & design. Click Netherfield is committed to the professional development of museum expertise and seeks to work through collaborative projects to develop local skills and capabilities around the world. When you work with the Click Netherfield USA team, you have access to a unique range of showcase design, construction and manufacturing expertise embracing many different disciplines. We look forward to speaking with you about your project.

Designand**Production** Incorporated

DESIGN AND PRODUCTION INCORPORATED
7110 Rainwater Place
Lorton, VA 22079
Tel: 703-550-8640; FAX: 703-339-0296
E-mail: dmoalli@d-and-p.com
Web Site: www.d-and-p.com

(Continued on next page)

(Continued from previous page)

Type of Business:

In service to the museum community since 1949, our global portfolio is comprised of hundreds of high-profile projects, including interpretive history, interactive science, sports, children's museums, and immersive environments. D&P specializes in large-scale, multi-discipline exhibit projects, with a full complement of in-house production capabilities: Project development and management, custom fabrication, interactive exhibits, A/V hardware and software development, artifact mounting, graphic production, installation, and service. D&P is FSC-certified and a charter member of USGBC.

Personnel:

Jay Barnwell (President)
Dan Moalli (Vice President Business Development)
Donna Kuba (Project Director)
Rachel Childress (Marketing Associate)

GLASBAU HAHN AMERICA, LLC

15 Little Brook Lane
Newburgh, NY 12550
Tel: 845-566-3331 & 877-452-7228; FAX: 845-566-3176
E-mail: info@glasbau-hahn.com
Web Site: www.glasbau-hahn.com

Type of Business:

GLASBAU HAHN enjoys a worldwide reputation for its superbly crafted museum display cases, technical innovation and seismic technology development. In business since 1836, we set standards for security, micro-environmental control, fiber optic or LED lighting, conservation, accessibility and design. GLASBAU HAHN award-winning cases and installations are in over 300 Museums and Art Galleries around the world, including over 100 in the United States. The Allglass Display Case, pioneered in 1935, is one of many GLASBAU HAHN designs to receive international awards. Other technical advances include 3-Way Sliding Doors, Hinged Openings, the HAHN Swing-Door and the "Protector" Case, the ultimate safeguard for the display and transportation of hanging art. All display cases are either custom-built or modular for convenient exhibit installations. GLASBAU HAHN is well known for incorporating the vision of architects and designers while considering the need for functionality, low maintenance and ideal art conservation. Thirty-four full-time representatives around the world regularly networking to bring GLASBAU HAHN's standards and innovations to each exhibition requirement, whether working for a world-famous institution or a small local museum. In addition, GLASBAU HAHN offers a full range of museum services. GLASBAU HAHN: Trusted with the World's Treasures for over 170 years! Home Office: GLASBAU HAHN GmbH, Hanauer Landstrasse 211, D-60314 Frankfurt am Main, Germany. Tel: 011-49-69-944-1753, Fax: 011-49-69-944-1761.

Personnel:

Isabel Hahn (President GH GmbH)
Till Hahn (President GHA)
Jamie J. Ponton (Vice President GHA)
Norbert Leonhardt (Construction GH GmbH)
Cathy Lima (Office Manager GHA)

GOPPION MUSEUM WORKSHOP, INC.

300 Linwood Ave.
Newton, MA 02460
Tel: 617-297-2546; FAX: 617-848-2641
E-mail: info@goppion-us.com
Web Site: www.goppion.com

Type of Business:

Established in 1952, Goppion SpA is one of the world's premier fabricators of high performance steel and glass display cases for museums, archives, libraries and other similar cultural institutions. Goppion does not offer a standard line of casework, nor do we have stock profiles and components from which to fabricate our work. Rather, we collaboratively develop the engineering and design in response to the performance, aesthetic, schedule, and budget requirements of your project.

Personnel:

Ted Paschkis (Director, Operations, U.S.)
Peter Hohenstatt (Commercial Manager, Goppion SpA (U.S.))

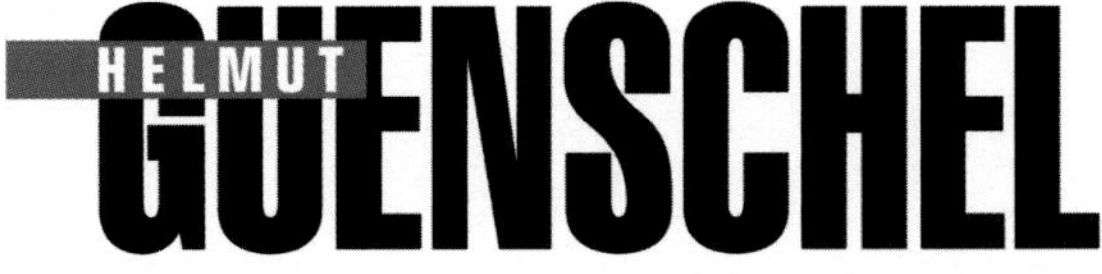

HELMUT GUENSCHEL, INC.

10 Emala Ave.
Baltimore, MD 21220
Tel: 410-686-5900 & 800-852-2525; FAX: 410-687-9342
E-mail: info@guenschel.com
Web Site: www.guenschel.com

Type of Business:

The highest quality museum exhibit cases available are custom designed, engineered, and manufactured exclusively by Helmut Guenschel, Inc. at our facility in Baltimore, MD. Used by many of the most prestigious museums in the world, our premier museum exhibit cases address the full range of technical requirements and collections issues including all facets of active and passive conservation, the use of proven environmentally safe materials, integrated security options, and effective seismic anchoring. For more than 40 years we have custom designed, fabricated and installed exhibit systems of the highest quality. Today our cases protect, preserve, and display some of the world's most valuable and important artwork, artifacts, and documents.

Personnel:

Helmut Guenschel (President)
Cynthia Shaffer (Vice President)

Luxam Lighting for Museums

LUXAM, INC.
2246 Country Club Rd.
Appomattox, VA 24522
Tel: 434-352-0084; FAX: 434-352-0089
E-mail: Rick@luxam.com
Web Site: www.luxam.com

Type of Business:
Luxam manufactures specialty lighting products for museum showcases and exhibits. We manufacture fiber optic and hybrid fiber/LED lighting systems and software. We also offer a full range of on-site services including installation and focus. Our newest illuminator, LED/Max, has 24 channels of high wattage LEDs mated to our fiber delivery systems for stunning interactive and multimedia exhibits controlled via DMX, all within conservation norms. Custom solutions, on time and budget.

Personnel:
Rick Jellow (Principal)
Jean Francois Hocquard (Principal)

MALONE DESIGN/FABRICATION
5403 Dividend Dr.
Decatur, GA 30035
Tel: 770-987-2538; FAX: 770-987-0326
E-mail: twright@maloneinc.com
Web Site: www.maloneinc.com

Type of Business:
From inspiration to installation, Malone Design/Fabrication provides complete exhibition development and production services to the museum community. These services include interpretive planning, design, project management, fabrication and installation. Our fabrication capabilities include graphics, display cases, interactives, multimedia, scenic and more. Malone has nearly 50 years of experience designing and fabricating exhibits and store fixtures for all types of museums and visitor centers.

Personnel:
Tom Wright (CEO)
Brad Parker (Account Executive)

NOUVIR® RESEARCH
20915 Sussex Hwy.
Seaford, DE 19973
Tel: 302-628-9933; FAX: 302-628-9932
Web Site: www.nouvir.com

Type of Business:
Ten years of research gives you practical, effective, case RH and pollution control for under $500.00. The perfect compliment to NoUVIR's perfect zero UV, zero IR fiber optic museum lighting. NoUVIR invented museum preservation lighting. NoUVIR developed Reflected Energy Matching, extending exhibit life 70 to 100 times. Now NoUVIR gives you safe, affordable RH control plus protection from all chemical and particulate pollutants. Technical support, seminars, textbooks and research materials are available. Call for details.

Personnel:
Miss Ruth Ellen Miller (President)
Mr. Matthew S. Miller (Vice President Marketing)

PROTO PRODUCTIONS, INC.
840 Fiene Dr.
Addison, IL 60101
Tel: 630-628-6626; FAX: 630-628-2232
E-mail: contact@protoproductions.com
Web Site: www.protoproductions.com; www.artifactcases.com

Type of Business:
Since the inception of Proto Productions in 1974, we have grown to be a prominent museum exhibit fabricator and a trusted resource to museum related professionals. Our clients span the museum specialties including art, history and science museums, aquariums, zoos, and visitor centers. Proto has completed hundreds of museum projects and in doing so has developed and maintained an approach to projects that nurtures solid working relationships with exhibit designers, museum planners, architects, curators, educators and the corporate community. Not only is Proto prepared to collaborate with the client's team, but our staff's creative spirit opens up solutions that have not previously been seen by others. Proto is always willing to discuss alternative options to provide your desired visitor experience within the boundaries of financial and scheduling concerns. Our continuing commitment is to provide you, the client and your team, with museum quality exhibit components that exceed all of your expectations. We achieve this ultimate goal by telling your story in such a way that meets your aesthetic and interpretive goals and takes your concept to our reality™.

Personnel:
Ken Hopkins (President)
Mike Slayton (Vice President)

STANDEX STRUCTURAL ALUMINUM DESIGNS
12935 Arroyo St.
Sylmar, CA 91342
Tel: 818-365-6464; FAX: 818-365-6465
E-mail: eclange@msn.com
Web Site: www.system-standex.dk; www.standexdesign.com

Type of Business:
Distribution and fabrication of museum exhibits and displays using System Standex, a square aluminum tubing system. Standex Designs has been meeting the exhibition needs of museums for over 20 years. Our lightweight, durable, and attractive material is perfect for showcases, exhibits, signage, and much more. Services provided include design, engineering, and fabrication of all projects. Tube sizes are 13/16 in., 1 in., & 1-3/16 in. square anodized aluminum with channels and flanges and are available in a variety of finishes. We offer three types of connectors: Permanent (glue-in or mechanical assembly), Semi-permanent (rap-in assembly), and Flexible (twist-lock for quick assembly/disassembly). Call or write for free catalog. eclange@msn.com www.system-standex.dk

Personnel:
Eric C. Lange (President)
Thelma Lyden (Office Manager)

TECNO DISPLAY, INC.
2277 National Ave.
Hayward, CA 94545
Tel: 800-255-3536; FAX: 510-782-5003
E-mail: tecno@tecnodisplay.com
Web Site: www.tecnodisplay.com

Type of Business:
Manufacturers of pre-assembled tempered glass display showcases, wall units, free standing towers, and exhibit display stands and pedestals. Halogen, fluorescent, LED etc. lighting available. Standard & custom showcases available. Small runs of custom showcases can be manufactured. We work with all types of laminates and solid wood veneers, stains, moldings. We have built our reputation on our quality products, reliable delivery and excellent customer support.

Personnel:
Patrick Lowe (Sales Manager)
Cathie Harvey (Customer Service)
John Wyatt (Customer Service)

TRU VUE
www.tru-vue.com

TRU VUE, INC.
9400 W. 55th St.
McCook, IL 60525-3636
Tel: 708-485-5080; FAX: 708-854-2660
E-mail: info@tru-vue.com
Web Site: www.tru-vue.com/museums

Type of Business:
Tru Vue is a leading manufacturer of high-performance glazing, including Optium® Acrylic Glazing. Optium combines the best of both worlds, anti-reflective safety glass and UV filtering acrylic, in one product for all your design and conservation needs. And now, Optium® Museum Display Acrylic™ is available for display cases, vitrines, and framed exhibits. Find out why museums around the world depend on Optium to protect, conserve, and display their most valuable and historic collections. For more information, visit www.tru-vue.com/museums.

Personnel:
Patti Dumbaugh (Vice President)
Julie Heath (Museum Market Manager)

ZONE DISPLAY CASES INC.
660, Rue de l'Argon
Charlesbourg, Quebec, Canada G2N 2G5
Tel: 418-841-4004; FAX: 418-841-2866
E-mail: info@zonedisplaycases.com
Web Site: www.zonedisplaycases.com

Type of Business:
Zone Display Cases is a sister company of Concetti Design Inc, a 20 year old company, specializing in the design, fabrication and installation of various exhibits, modular displays or complete turnkey exhibitions for museums. The Zone Display Cases company was created in 1999, after those many years working with the museology community. We developed our museum display cases using the latest software, in a cutting edge 3D environment renowned for its engineering and manufacturing. Zone Display Cases are offered in modular or regular construction, standard sizes or custom fabrication, and in a wide variety of finishes. Airtight and atmosphere-controlled to meet museum standards, Zone Display Cases feature an elegant yet discrete design that draws attention to the objects on display. They also offer numerous other features sought after by museum experts: compliance with standards, security, Optiwhite laminated glass, out-of-case premounting, LED or optic fiber lighting, total visibility, and much more. Our cases are designed and manufactured in Canada, offering fast turnover and delivery. Learn more about us, visit our web site, or call us...we will be happy to discuss your needs and projects.

Personnel:
Pierre Giguere (Vice President Sales)
Louis St-Gelais (President & Senior Designer)

Exhibit Design Firms

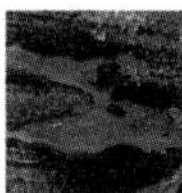

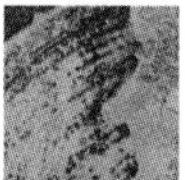

ADIRONDACK
STUDIOS

ADIRONDACK STUDIOS
439 County Rte. 45, Ste. 1
Argyle, NY 12809
Tel: 518-638-8000; FAX: 518-638-8238
E-mail: sales@adkstudios.com
Web Site: www.adkstudios.com

Type of Business:
Adirondack Studios is a full service company serving the museum and entertainment markets. For over thirty years, Adirondack has been providing custom environments and specialty exhibits to customers around the world. Adirondack is poised to participate in all phases and at all levels of project development, specialty fabrication and implementation.

Personnel:
Carl H. Zutz (Sales Manager)
Michael Blau (Creative Director)
Maurice O'Connell (Museum Sales)

museums
visitor attractions
retail experiences
digital environments
creative strategies & design

ANCONA + ASSOCIATES, INC.
2450 S.W. Sherwood Dr.
Portland, OR 97201
Tel: 503-274-4444; FAX: 503-961-7797
E-mail: portland@ancona-a.com
Web Site: www.ancona-a.com

Type of Business:
Creative strategies & design services for clients seeking multi-disciplinary creative services for museums, visitor attractions, retail experiences and digital environments. We are expert at creating engaging experiences at the intersection of culture and commerce, with a focus on themes that include Industry & Heritage, The Environment, Sports & Entertainment and Retail. Our work explores the graceful convergence of physical and digital realms. Clients include adidas, Boudin at the Wharf, British Waterways, Nike, NASA, Lucasfilm, Universal Studios, Rio Tinto Diamonds, Henry Ford Museum, California Academy of Sciences and the Art Institute of Chicago.

Personnel:
Tomas Ancona (President)

André & Associates
[Interpretation and Design Ltd.]

ANDRE & ASSOCIATES INTERPRETATION AND DESIGN LTD.
#302-560 Johnson St.
Victoria, BC, Canada V8W 3C6
Tel: 250-389-1677; FAX: 250-389-1515
E-mail: info@aaid.ca
Web Site: www.aaid.ca

Type of Business:
Community museums, special interest museums, interpretive centers...All offer challenges and rewards. All have stories and points of view. All are rich and complex, regardless of size. We consult, help fundraise, write master plans, interpret and design exhibits, create concepts, make models, build exhibits, write text, design and produce graphics, develop media, coordinate with architects, engineers, fabricators and exhibit specialists and manage projects. We work with the wisdom of the client, to weave a world of words, images, showcases, murals, recreated structures, icons, special effects and interactive media, that flows through time and captures and conveys moods and emotions.

Personnel:
Bianca Message (President)

ANDREW MERRIELL & ASSOCIATES, LLC
7198 Old Santa Fe Trail
Santa Fe, NM 87505
Tel: 505-982-3950; FAX: 505-820-6674
E-mail: andy@merriell.com
Web Site: www.merriell.com

Type of Business:
For over thirty years Andrew Merriell has assisted museums and interpretive centers with planning and designing visitor experiences. Working collaboratively with his clients, he identifies opportunities to advance beyond the usual and predictable museum offerings, finding innovative ways to immerse visitors in exhibit stories. Each project provides visitors with memorable, meaningful experiences they can find nowhere else. Services include feasibility studies, interpretive master plans, concept studies, exhibition development, and exhibit design.

Personnel:
Andrew Merriell (Principal)
Rebecca Shreckengast (Senior Designer)
Margaret Hennessey (Polymath First Class)

BRC IMAGINATION ARTS
2711 Winona Ave.
Burbank, CA 91504
Tel: 818-841-8084; FAX: 818-841-4996
E-mail: brc@brcweb.com
Web Site: www.brcweb.com

Type of Business:
BRC is an award winning full service museum design and production company with a comprehensive range of skills from vision and master planning, to design, and production of exhibits and theatrical media experiences. Continental Europe Office: Science Park 5644, 5692 EN Eindhoven, P.O. Box 1245, 5602 BE Eindhoven, The Netherlands, Tel: +31.40.2676.871; Fax: +31.40.2676.895. United Kingdom Office: 8 Kimblesworth Grange, Potterhouse Lane, Durham DH1 5SL, United Kingdom, Tel: +44.7879.655950; Fax: +44.1913.719141. Shanghai Office: A405, Tomorrow Square, 399 West Nanjing Road, Shanghai 200003, People's Republic of China, Tel: +86.21.2308.1077.

Personnel:
Carmel Lewis (Vice President, Educational Experiences)
Matthew Solari (Director, Education Development)
Mark Hayward (Creative Director, Educational Experiences)
Bart Dohmen (Managing Director, Continental Europe)
Donna Davidson (Director, United Kingdom)

CAMBRIDGE SEVEN ASSOCIATES, INC.
1050 Massachusetts Ave.
Cambridge, MA 02138
Tel: 617-492-7000; FAX: 617-492-7007
E-mail: joltman@c7a.com
Web Site: www.c7a.com

Type of Business:
Architects, exhibit and graphic designers providing specialized services for museums, visitor centers, aquaria, zoos, and traveling exhibits. Areas of expertise include science, children's, sports, and history museums, art galleries, large format film theaters, educational facilities, nature centers, aquaria and zoos. Services include architectural design, exhibit and habitat design, feasibility assessments, site analysis, master planning, space programming, institutional and operational planning, exhibit installation coordination, graphic design and signage programs, production of fund raising materials, and construction administration. Award-winning designs completed for existing and new facilities, internationally.

Personnel:
Peter Kuttner, FAIA (President)
John Stebbins, AIA, LEED AP (Principal)
Steven Imrich, AIA, LEED AP (Principal)
Penny Sander (Senior Associate Exhibit Planner)
David Perry (Associate Exhibit Designer)
Doug Simpson, LEED AP (Associate Exhibit Designer)
Douglas Flandro, LEED AP (Exhibit Designer)
Jo Oltman (Marketing Manager)

CHRISTOPHER CHADBOURNE & ASSOCIATES
129 Portland St.
Boston, MA 02114
Tel: 617-305-1000; FAX: 617-367-6222
E-mail: exhibits@ccadesign.com
Web Site: www.ccadesign.com

Type of Business:
CCA collaborates with clients to design memorable, story-driven visitor experiences that attract, educate and entertain. We are graphic, industrial, and stageset designers; educators and writers; architects, curators and media specialists. Together, we have created art, science, cultural and natural history, and children's exhibits, as well as educationally-based themed attractions. Our services range from

(Continued on page 44)

(Continued from page 42)

feasibility studies and master planning, to architectural and media coordination, to supervision of fabrication and installation, all with strict adherence to budget and schedule.

Personnel:
Christopher Chadbourne (President & Creative Director)
Michael Biddle (Director, Design)
Andrea Medalie (Director, Projects)
Mary Ruggieri Macfarlane (Director, Graphic Design)
David Whitemyer (Director, Production)
Valerie Taylor (Director, Exhibit Development)
Felicia O'Keefe (Director, Marketing)

CHASE STUDIO, INC.

CHASE STUDIO, INC.
205 Wolf Creek Rd.
Cedar Creek, MO 65627
Tel: 417-794-3303; FAX: 417-794-3741
E-mail: chasestudio@chasestudio.com
Web Site: www.chasestudio.com

Type of Business:
Designers and builders of natural history and environmental science exhibits; paleontological reconstructions, zoological models, botanical reproductions, dioramas and habitat groups, illustration and mural painting, graphic design, photography, lighting design, fine cabinetwork, taxidermy, research, script writing, exhibit planning and consultation. Exhibits for over 200 museums worldwide since 1973.

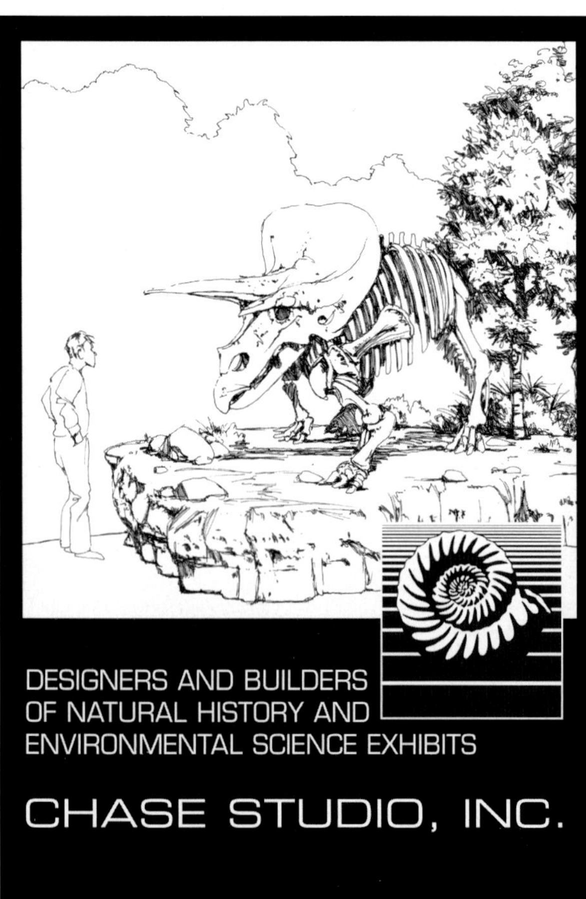

Personnel:
Dr. Terry L. Chase (Director)
David F. Darby (Assistant Director Exhibits)
William L. Talbot (Assistant Director Business)
Greg L. Rogers (Assistant Director Operations)

DESIGN BUILD MANAGE

CHICAGO SCENIC STUDIOS, INC.
1315 N. North Branch St.
Chicago, IL 60642
Tel: 312-274-9900; FAX: 312-274-9901
E-mail: info@chicagoscenic.com
Web Site: www.chicagoscenic.com

Type of Business:
Chicago Scenic Studios provides museums, science & technology centers, zoos, aquariums and visitor centers more than 30 years of multi-disciplinary experience in themed environment engineering, design, fabrication, and installation. Our highly skilled staff of project managers, designers, carpenters, painters, electricians, and specialists in metals, plastics and fabrics partner with your team to provide safe, educational, immersive environments and exciting experiences through custom exhibits, retail, restaurant, and admission spaces. Chicago Scenic can serve as a general contractor, fabricator or project manager in support of your design or ours. Our background in exhibits, retail, theater, amusements, special events and corporate spaces provides us with the ability to cater to differing needs in unique spaces. We have enjoyed partnering with world-class institutions such as: The Chicago Museum of Science & Industry, The Notebaert Nature Museum, The Field Museum of Natural History, The Shedd Aquarium, Chicago History Museum, Kohl's Children's Museum and many more to bring numerous exciting, educational, and successful stories to life. We'd like to help tell your story as well.

Personnel:
Robert Doepel (President)
Jim Notarianni (Business Development)

Vincent Ciulla Design

VINCENT CIULLA DESIGN ASSOCIATES, INC.
1269 First St., Studio 5
Sarasota, FL 34236
Tel: 941-917-0388 & 917-312-3951 (cell); FAX: 941-917-0386
E-mail: info@ciulladesign.com
Web Site: www.ciulladesign.com; www.umbrellahouse.com

Type of Business:
Your team will work directly with the Ciullas, who will create an individualized interpretive plan or design for your institution. Ciulla Design has created close to 300 museum, park and cultural experiences and new facilities, indoors and outdoors, on a vast range of topics. We are developing new educational experiences about the arts, society, history and the environment under our own auspices, that can become opportunities for partnership with you. We are also restoring Paul Rudolph's internationally renowned Umbrella House, which will soon become Ciulla Design's new studio.

Personnel:
Vincent A. Ciulla (President)
Julie Ciulla (Vice President & General Manager)

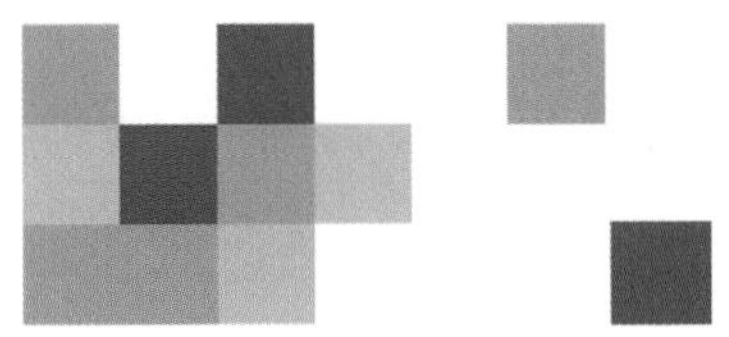

DIMENSIONAL COMMUNICATIONS INC.
173 Ludlow Ave.
Northvale, NJ 07647-2305
Tel: 201-767-1500; FAX: 201-767-9696
E-mail: info@dimcom.com
Web Site: www.dimcom.com

Type of Business:
Dimensional Communications Inc. creates customer and visitor experiences — from museum exhibits and multimedia to events, and from trade shows and corporate interiors to retail displays — that help our clients connect more productively with their customers. We not only work in 3 dimensions, but also in the 4th dimension: time. The time a person spends at an interactive exhibit, or gazing in wonder at the space they're in. These are moments that can only happen in immersive environments. Dimensional has been creating these experiences for nearly 50 years. We are a full-service custom builder and producer, offering everything from inspired design consultation and fine artisanship, to logistical management and enduring client-relationships.

Personnel:
Douglas Fixell (President)
Robert Sneed (Vice President Multimedia Technologies)

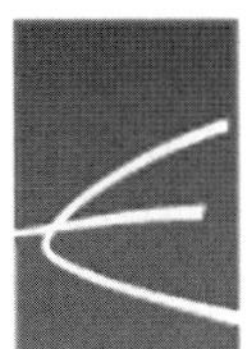

EISTERHOLD ASSOCIATES, INC.
19310 N.W. Farley Hampton Rd.
Kansas City, MO 64153
Tel: 816-330-3276; FAX: 816-330-3278
E-mail: eai@eisterhold.com
Web Site: www.eisterhold.com

Type of Business:
Museum planners and designers. Our creative mission: Create memorable, iconic experiences that are unique to their purpose and setting. Engage in fundamental, protean examination of the content, allowing exploration of solutions that go beyond founding notions. Create truly interdisciplinary exhibits that employ a variety of media and interpretive formats. Be relevant to current issues. Connect with audiences of all kinds, via all learning styles. Create projects that work logistically, as well as philosophically. Explore and be excited, so that visitors can can explore and be excited.

Personnel:
Gerard Eisterhold (President)
Benjamin Lawless (Vice President)

DESIGN®

ESI DESIGN
111 Fifth Ave., 12th Fl.
New York, NY 10003
Tel: 212-989-3993; FAX: 212-673-4061
E-mail: mmullineaux@esidesign.com
Web Site: www.esidesign.com

Type of Business:
ESI Design is an award-winning design company that combines exhibit design with interactive media and environmental graphic design to produce immersive, participatory, and sustainable museum experiences. Our multidisciplinary team creates original, compelling environments that inspires visitors to explore, participate and learn through repeated visits. Our range of services include: museum master planning, exhibit design, communication design and more. Current and recent projects include the Hall of Human Life at the Boston Museum of Science, the Shanghai Corporate Pavilion at the 2010 World Expo in Shanghai, The College Basketball Experience in Kansas City, MO, Infinity at NASA Stennis Space Center in Mississippi, the Pope John Paul II Cultural Center in Washington, DC, the Ellis Island National Immigration Museum, and the Brooklyn Children's Museum. For more information about ESI Design, visit us online at www.esidesign.com.

Personnel:
Edwin Schlossberg (President)
Michelle Mullineaux (Business Development)

EXPERIENCE DESIGN
(formerly KRENT/PAFFETT/CARNEY, INC.)
355 Congress St.
Boston, MA 02210-1806
Tel: 617-451-6301; FAX: 617-451-2983
E-mail: info@EXPdesign.com
Web Site: www.EXPdesign.com

Type of Business:
With a talented team of industrial designers, interpretive developers, graphic artists and multimedia producers and programmers, Experience Design has long been recognized for innovative design and unique multimedia installations. We are particularly cognizant of what works to capture a visitor's attention, and we collaborate with our clients to determine the best methods to express storylines and create engaging, educational environments. EXP is a full-service museum exhibit planning and design firm; we have been creating award-winning experiences, from concept through installation, for over 25 years.

Personnel:
John Carney (CEO\President)
Larissa Hansen (COO\Principal)
Michael Roper (Principal)

FORMATIONS INC.
621 S.E. 202nd Ave.
Portland, OR 97233
Tel: 503-665-7110; FAX: 503-665-7188
E-mail: formations@formationsinc.com
Web Site: www.formationsinc.com

Type of Business:
We're great storytellers! FORMATIONS is a full-service exhibit firm specializing in planning, design, and fabrication/installation of intrepretive exhibits and thematic interiors. We apply fresh, creative thinking to each project, designing exhibits with memorable imagery and regional identity. Our areas of expertise range from natural history to social, cultural, transportation, sports, and corporate history. We are an experienced team of interpretive planners/evaluators, exhibit and graphic designers, writers, detailers, multimedia specialists, estimators, fabricators, and project managers, working in a highly integrated facility in order to provide excellence to each project.

Personnel:
Craig Kerger (President, Design Principal)
Phil Buettner (Operations Manager)

Gallagher & Associates

GALLAGHER & ASSOCIATES
8665 Georgia Ave.
Silver Spring, MD 20910
Tel: 301-656-7575; FAX: 301-656-5455
E-mail: gc@gallagherdesign.com
Web Site: www.gallagherdesign.com

Type of Business:
Gallagher & Associates is a professional design firm practicing internationally. The firm specializes in museum master planning and exhibition design, environmental graphics, brand development, and media programming and development. Expertise includes a wide spectrum of visitor experiences such as public- and private-sector museums, visitor centers, hall of fame exhibits, science and learning centers, traveling exhibitions and corporate experiences.

Personnel:
Patrick Gallagher (Principal)
Gretchen Coss (Business Development)
Randy Anderson (Business Development)

GYROSCOPE, INC.
283 4th St., Suite 201
Oakland, CA 94607
Tel: 510-986-0111; FAX: 510-986-0222
E-mail: maeryta@gyroscopeinc.com
Web Site: www.gyroscopeinc.com

Type of Business:
Gyroscope is an award winning, museum planning, architecture and exhibit design company with offices in Oakland, CA, and Cambridge, MA. We are known for innovative strategies and design solutions grounded in a thorough understanding of the challenges museums face. We offer full-service planning and design for all phases of your project from earliest vision through opening.

Personnel:
Maeryta Medrano, AIA, LEED AP (President)
Chuck Howarth (Vice President)
Ron Davis, LEED AP (Principal)
Justine Roberts (Principal)

HADLEY EXHIBITS, INC.
1700 Elmwood Ave.
Buffalo, NY 14207
Tel: 716-874-3666, ext. 3018; FAX: 716-874-9994
E-mail: pwarner@hadleyexhibits.com
Web Site: www.hadleyexhibits.com

Type of Business:
Award-winning exhibit design, fabrication, and installation services for museums, visitor centers, zoos, historic sites, special events, and expositions. Additional skills and expertise in graphic design, graphics production, custom display cases, model making, and artifact mounting, to name a few. Significant experience with interactive environments and ADA compliance. In business over 60 years, Hadley Exhibits is housed in a well-equipped 180,000 square foot facility.

Personnel:
Ted Johnson (President)
Paul Warner (National Account Executive)

haleysharpedesign

HALEY SHARPE DESIGN
116 Spadina Ave., Ste. 201
Toronto, ON, Canada MSV 2K6
Tel: 416-361-3338; FAX: 416-361-3588
E-mail: info@haleysharpe.com
Web Site: www.haleysharpe.com

Type of Business:
Haley Sharpe Design brings expertise in masterplanning, design and implementation of dynamic projects for museums, galleries, heritage sites, and visitor centers. Our multidisciplinary team integrates concept development, interpretative planning, two- and three-dimensional design services. Our diverse portfolio or international projects, large and small speaks to our collective experience.

Personnel:
Jan Faulkner (Creative Director)
Nicole Mackereth (Business Development Consultant)

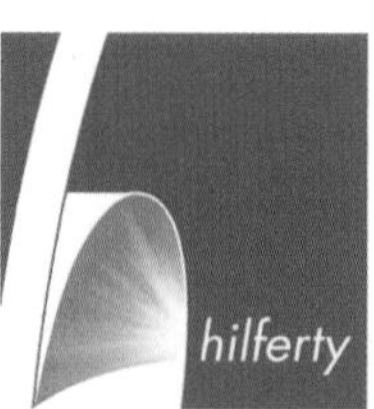

HILFERTY
14240 State Rte. 550
Athens, OH 45701
Tel: 740-448-3821; FAX: 740-448-2331
E-mail: gha@hilferty.com
Web Site: www.hilferty.com

Type of Business:
For more than thirty years, Hilferty has provided a full range of interpretive services to museums, visitor centers, nature centers, botanical gardens, historic sites, zoos/aquariums, and halls of fame. We excel at interpretive and facility master planning; concept

(Continued on next page)

(Continued from previous page)

development; content research; label writing; exhibit and graphic design; and providing donor recognition and funding support materials. From social histories to natural sciences, football to physics, presidents to children's gardens, every Hilferty exhibit vividly captures the stories that engage visitors' minds and hearts. Each project is approached with a unique mix of techniques chosen to best bring the subject to life. Our innovative portfolio spans the spectrum of intimate displays of precious objects, captivating immersive environments, enthralling interactive components, and breathtaking theatrical presentations. In short, Hilferty creates memorable museum experiences.

Personnel:
Gerard Hilferty (President & Creative Director)
Dean Clouse (CEO)

JACK ROUSE ASSOCIATES
600 Vine St., Ste. 1700
Cincinnati, OH 45202-1100
Tel: 513-381-0055; FAX: 513-381-2691
E-mail: s.mccoy@jackrouse.com
Web Site: www.jackrouse.com

Type of Business:
Jack Rouse Associates conceives, visualizes and realizes exceptional visitor experiences around the world. Specific services include master planning, exhibit design, media production and project management.

Personnel:
Jack Rouse (CEO)
Keith James (President)
Randy Vuksta (Creative Director)
Shawn McCoy (Vice President Marketing & Business Development)

LYONS/ZAREMBA INC.
4 Faneuil Hall Marketplace
Boston, MA 02109
Tel: 617-248-0970; FAX: 617-248-0994
E-mail: info@lyonszaremba.com
Web Site: www.lyonszaremba.com

Type of Business:
Lyons/Zaremba Inc. is an internationally recognized firm with extensive experience in planning, designing and managing exhibits for museums, visitor centers, nature centers, aquariums and zoos. Our services include: feasibility analysis; master planning; concept development; facility programming; content research and development; graphic design and production; exhibit design and documentation; media software design; and construction administration. Our goal is to create special places where people come to explore, discover and learn in exciting multi-sensorial ways through exhibits that are accessible, enjoyable, and meaningful for visitors of diverse ages, learning styles, and cultural backgrounds. We welcome your visit to our web site, or call us to learn more.

Personnel:
Frank Zaremba (Principal)
Steve Lenox (Principal)
Rosanne Gregory (Business Manager)
Michael Shackelford (Exhibit Designer)
James Wertheimer (Exhibit Designer)
Julia Misiewicz (Exhibit Designer)
Christina Yung (Graphic Designer)

MALONE DESIGN/FABRICATION
5403 Dividend Dr.
Decatur, GA 30035
Tel: 770-987-2538; FAX: 770-987-0326
E-mail: twright@maloneinc.com
Web Site: www.maloneinc.com

Type of Business:
From inspiration to installation, Malone Design/Fabrication provides complete exhibition development and production services to the museum community. These services include interpretive planning, design, project management, fabrication and installation. Our fabrication capabilities include graphics, display cases, interactives, multimedia, scenic and more. Malone has nearly 50 years of experience designing and fabricating exhibits and store fixtures for all types of museums and visitor centers.

Personnel:
Tom Wright (CEO)
Brad Parker (Account Executive)

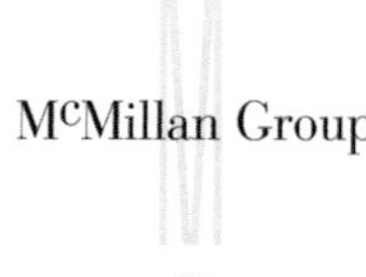

MCMILLAN GROUP, INC.
25 Otter Trail
Westport, CT 06880
Tel: 203-227-8696; FAX: 203-227-2898
E-mail: nancy@mcmillangroup.com
Web Site: www.mcmillangroup.com

Type of Business:

McMillan Group is an award winning design firm that specializes in museum exhibits, corporate visitor centers and entertainment venues. Our value is in: developing fresh, untapped creative ideas, extensive research of content and audience, uniqueness of interpretive vision, broad range of experience and talents, thoroughness of management and communication skills. McMillan Group combines multiple disciplines in creating visitor experiences including: Exhibition Design, Master Planning, Concept Development, Architectural and Interior Design, Environmental Graphics and Wayfinding, Interactive and Media Design, Fundraising Presentation Materials, Theatrical Production Design, Lighting Design, Construction Engineering and Documentation, Production Bid Packaging and Processing, Cost Estimating and Tracking, Project Management and Team Collaboration. McMillan Group creates effective educational and entertaining experiences.

Personnel:

Charlie McMillan (Principal)
Nancy McMillan (Principal)

MUSEUM ARTS, INC.
2639 Freewood
Dallas, TX 75220
Tel: 800-299-2787 & 214-357-5644; FAX: 214-357-2875
E-mail: terybrown@museumarts.net
Web Site: www.museumarts.net

Type of Business:

Museums seeking creative, high quality exhibit design and fabrication services may miss an opportunity if Museum Arts is not considered. With over 30 years of experience in delivering exhibits that effectively educate and entertain, we have become expert at operating within your budget without sacrificing quality or compromising your objectives.

Personnel:

Tery Brown (Vice President)
Lary Brown (Vice President)

MUSEUM DESIGN ASSOCIATES, INC.
24 Thorndike St.
Cambridge, MA 02141
Tel: 617-497-0215; FAX: 617-497-0222
E-mail: info@mda-design.com
Web Site: www.mda-design.com

Type of Business:
MDA has provided comprehensive planning and design services for museums, visitor centers, historic sites, and corporations since 1981. From DNA to dinosaurs to Duke Ellington, our experience covers social and cultural history, science and technology, decorative and fine arts. We value the client-designer relationship and strive to create unique installations that inspire, educate and entertain. Combined with strong museum management and collections experience, our services include interpretive planning, content development, text writing, 3D and graphic design, and contract administration of fabrication/installation.

Personnel:
David T. Seibert (President & Creative Director)

ONE + TWO, INC.
2244 N.W. Quimby St.
Portland, OR 97210
Tel: 503-227-7878; FAX: 503-227-8335
E-mail: tipw@oneplustwodesign.com
Web Site: www.oneplustwodesign.com

Type of Business:
One + Two, Inc. is a team of experienced professionals offering complete exhibit design services including master planning, writing services, concept design, design development, graphic design, illustration, detail design & specifications, and construction oversight. Our focus on content and visitor experience has allowed us to create award-winning designs for cultural institutions, science centers, government agencies, and zoological institutions.

Personnel:
Tip Wilson (President)

The PRD Group Ltd

THE PRD GROUP LTD.
14555 Avion Pkwy., Ste. 175
Chantilly, VA 20151
Tel: 703-352-2288; FAX: 703-352-2376
Web Site: www.theprdgroup.com

Type of Business:
The Planning, Research and Design Group Ltd. — specialists in museum planning and design. Services include master planning; programming and design through bid specifications for permanent and temporary exhibitions; interactive and video design; graphic design for exhibits and publications; project management.

Personnel:
Daniel B. Murphy (Principal)
William C. Lazenby

THE
PORTICO
GROUP

THE PORTICO GROUP
1500 4th Ave., Third Fl.
Seattle, WA 98101-1670
Tel: 206-621-2196; FAX: 206-621-2199
E-mail: portico@porticogroup.com
Web Site: www.porticogroup.com

Type of Business:
Celebrating 25 years of design, The Portico Group creates informal learning opportunities in memorable settings—settings that include natural and cultural museums, zoos and aquaria, and botanic gardens and arboreta. We are a talented team of interpretive exhibit designers, architects, and landscape architects capable of guiding a project from concept to conclusion. We seek opportunities to touch lives in meaningful ways—to connect people with nature and culture. Recent projects include: Jilkaat Kwaan Cultural Heritage Center, San Francisco Conservatory of Flowers, KidsQuest Children's Museum, USS Arizona Memorial Visitor Center and the Chicago Botanic Garden.

Personnel:
Michael Hamm, ASLA (President & CEO)
Charles G. Mayes, AIA (Principal)
Keith McClintock, ASLA (Principal)
Dennis Meyer, ASLA (Principal)
Alissa Rupp, AIA (Principal)
Allison CraigSundine (Senior Associate)
Devin Lai, AAIA (Senior Associate)
Richard Larson (Senior Associate)

QUATREFOIL ASSOCIATES, INC.
29 C St.
Laurel, MD 20707
Tel: 301-470-4748; FAX: 301-470-4749
E-mail: info@quatrefoil.com
Web Site: www.quatrefoil.com

Type of Business:
Quatrefoil creates engaging museum experiences that educate, inspire and amuse the visitor and reflect the essence of our client's vision and values. We deliver a full spectrum of expertise, applied with artistic and technical excellence - museum planning, exhibit design, content development, graphics, interactives, multimedia, custom electronics, fabrication and installation. West Coast Design Studio, 1524 Cloverfield Blvd., Ste. A, Santa Monica, CA 90404. Tel.: 310-829-9390.

Personnel:
Abbie Chessler (Design Director & Founding Partner)
Paula Schuman (Founding Partner & CFO)
Ernie Falcone (Founding Partner & Technical Director)
Paul DeCamp (COO & Partner)

RHODESWORKS LTD
1701 S. Prospect Ave., Ste. 204
Champaign, IL 61820
Tel: 217-398-4572; FAX: 217-398-4555
E-mail: rrhodes@rhodesworksltd.com

Type of Business:
Committed to translating visions into interpretive experiences that provoke visitors' thinking, arouse their senses and emotions, and cause them to have a new appreciation of their universe. Services include concept visioning, strategic and master planning, content development, experiential design, interpretive design, interactive design, theater design, media and publication design, graphic design, identity program creation, storytelling, copywriting, detailing and specification, project cost estimating, project management, architectural liaison and integration.

Personnel:
Ralph Skip Rhodes (Principal)
Catherine L. Rhodes (Principal)

RIGGS WARD DESIGN, L.C.
2315 W. Main St.
Richmond, VA 23220
Tel: 804-254-1740; FAX: 804-254-1742
E-mail: tfallen@riggsward.com
Web Site: www.riggsward.com

Type of Business:
Riggs Ward Design is an internationally recognized, award-winning team of design professionals who provide a holistic approach to exhibition development. While our focus is design, our services also include feasibility, interpretive, and master planning; content and storyline development; graphic, wayfinding, and retail design; and turnkey management of the fabrication and installation process. Our success is due to long-term client relationships that result in experiential, evocative, and effective solutions for every project, no matter the size.

Personnel:
Robert Riggs (Principal)
L. Brent Ward (Principal)

STEPHEN SAITAS DESIGNS
123 Fourth Ave., 3rd Fl.
New York, NY 10003
Tel: 212-388-0997; FAX: 212-388-0816
E-mail: ssaitas@aol.com

Type of Business:
Specializing in museum exhibition design, Stephen Saitas Designs provides services from schematic design through installation supervision for projects ranging from the design of a single pedestal through complete reinstallations of permanent collections. Clients have included museums, galleries, libraries, and historic houses. Since being established in 1982, SSD has planned, designed, and supervised over 200 permanent installations and temporary exhibitions, and provided related graphic design services to over forty institutions across the country.

Personnel:
Stephen Saitas (Principal)

LEE H. SKOLNICK ARCHITECTURE + DESIGN PARTNERSHIP
7 W. 22nd St., 10th Fl.
New York, NY 10010
Tel: 212-989-2624; FAX: 212-727-1702
E-mail: skolnick@skolnick.com
Web Site: www.skolnick.com

Type of Business:
Established in 1980, Lee H. Skolnick Architecture + Design Partnership is an award-winning 30-person architectural and museum exhibit design firm. Museum facilities design services include: master planning, program development, conceptual and complete architectural services for new institutions, site planning, adaptive re-use of existing structures, historic preservation, renovative design, feasibility studies. Exhibition, programming and museum education services include: conceptual development, script and copy development, interpretive exhibition design, exhibition project management, evaluation of exhibits, educational programming, facility operations, and collections storage, audience assessments.

Personnel:
Jo Ann Secor (Principal & Director Museum Services)
Scott Briggs (Senior Associate Museum Services)

SOUTHWEST MUSEUM SERVICES
6399 Windfern Rd.
Houston, TX 77040
Tel: 713-462-7754; FAX: 713-934-9930
E-mail: twebber@swmuseum.com
Web Site: www.swmuseum.com

Type of Business:
Founded in 1987, we provide museum feasibility analyses, interpretive and master planning, fund raising assistance, design, fabrication, and installation from start to finish. We have a 45,000 square foot facility and a staff of museum professionals degreed in fields from Museum Studies and History to Engineering, Graphic and Multimedia Design as well as teams of dedicated artists and artisans. We work with our clients to achieve a synthesis of culture, content and structure in each exhibit to engage and inspire every museum visitor.

Personnel:
Tony Webber (CEO)
Charles Fleming (Vice President)
Mark Fleming (Director, Projects)
Jana Reed (Director, Marketing)
Tracie Fleming (Graphic Design Manager)
Norman Lee (Senior Concept Developer)
Rudy Rocha (General Manager)

SPLIT ROCK STUDIOS
2071 Gateway Blvd.
Arden Hills, MN 55112
Tel: 651-631-2211 & 800-433-9599; FAX: 651-631-0707
E-mail: info@splitrockstudios.com
Web Site: www.splitrockstudios.com

Type of Business:
Split Rock Studios is a full-service firm specializing in designing and building interactive exhibits for interpretive centers, museums and related institutions. In addition to our exhibit design and development capabilities, we have the in-house capabilities to produce all facets of a major exhibition, including interactive components, themed environments, dioramas, interpretive murals, realistic animal and human sculpture, graphics, and custom exhibit furniture. Whatever your exhibit project needs, our staff will provide the ultimate in quality service and workmanship.

Personnel:
Craig Sommerville (President)
Lisa Friedlander (Sales & Marketing)

steve feldman design LLC

STEVE FELDMAN DESIGN, LLC
16 S. Third St.
Philadelphia, PA 19106
Tel: 215-873-0700; FAX: 215-873-0707
E-mail: stevef@stevefeldmandesign.com
Web Site: www.stevefeldmandesign.com

Type of Business:
Innovative planning, interpretation, design and implementation. Providing comprehensive services for the creation of engaging environments, exhibitions, and activities devoted to history, the humanities and natural sciences. Services include: Museum master planning, exhibition development, design and documentation, presentation renderings for fund-raising, fabrication and installation management. Clients include: Museums, history and visitor centers, corporate and government facilities, historic sites, historical societies and nature centers.

Personnel:
Steve Feldman (Principal)
Katy Blander (Associate)

TAYLOR STUDIOS, INC.
1320 Harmon Drive
Rantoul, IL 61866
Tel: 217-893-4874 & 800-707-2047; FAX: 217-893-1998
E-mail: sales@taylorstudios.com
Web Site: www.taylorstudios.com/omd

Type of Business:
"Taylor Studios, Inc. is an interpretive planning, exhibit design, and fabrication firm that assists museums and other clients in creating exhibits that are educational, creative, and enduring. We are committed to completing exhibits to the fulfillment of each client's unique needs, timelines, and goals. Our exhibit creativity is built on a firm interpretive foundation. Our team has the experience and talent to coordinate, communicate, research, plan, design, manage, and produce exhibits of the highest quality. We believe in excellent customer service and back our fabricated products with an unprecedented five-year warranty."

Personnel:
Betty Brennan (President)
Kara Vanskike (Marketing Coordinator)

UJMN ARCHITECTS + DESIGNERS
718 Arch St., Ste. 5N
Philadelphia, PA 19106
Tel: 215-440-0190; FAX: 215-440-0197
E-mail: nicholson@ujmn.com; blankin@ujmn.com
Web Site: www.ujmn.com

Type of Business:
Founded in 1967, UJMN Architects + Designers offers architectural design, museum planning, and exhibit design within a single firm, maximizing the integration of exhibits with museum facilities; the effectiveness of cost, schedule, and project management; and ultimately, the quality of the visitor experience. Recent projects include: the Liberty Bell Center Exhibits; the President's House at Independence National Historical Park; the National Civil War Museum Exhibits (Harrisburg, PA); the Louisville Slugger Museum; the Stoogeum; the Joliet Area Historical Museum; Hagley Museum and Library; the National Civil Rights Museum in Mississippi; the Eagles Mere Museum Exhibits, and Historic Deerfield.

Personnel:
Joseph A. Nicholson, AIA, IDSA (Principal)
Stacey Blankin (Associate)

UNIVERSAL EXHIBITS INC.
9517 E. Rush St.
South El Monte, CA 91733
Tel: 323-686-0562; FAX: 626-444-1535
E-mail: UEexhibits@worldnet.att.net
Web Site: www.UniversalExhibits.com

Type of Business:
We have over sixty-three (63) years of experience of providing full service to the museum industry worldwide. We can provide full turnkey service to team support delivering the following services: design, master plans, drafting, fabrication, graphic production, interactive exhibitry, engineering, audio/visual production, special effects, environments, project planning, transportation and installation. Among our projects include presidential libraries, George H.W. Bush (twice) (2007 and 1997), Ronald Reagan and Richard Nixon. Visitor centers, mini planetarium dome for the Griffith Observatory, Vista Del Lago and Lake Oroville. Museums, The J. Paul Getty, Museum of Tolerance (Los Angeles and New York), The Bowers Museum of Cultural Art (Terra Cotta Soldiers) tribute room on the George H.W. Bush Aircraft Carrier (CVN-77), The City of Highland (Environmental Learning Center) L.E.E.D. Gold Rating Facility with interactive children exhibitions. Mission San Juan Capistrano Interactive Interpretation Exhibitry (south wing).

Personnel:
M. Robert Bell (President & CEO)
John Hall (Project Manager)
Mike Salomone (Project Manager)

xibitz
Experiential Spaces for Work and Life

XIBITZ, INC.
7604 Harwood Ave., Ste. 202
Milwaukee, WI 53213
Tel: 414-727-4699 & 616-247-3500 (Home Office: Grand Rapids, MI); FAX: 414-727-4883
E-mail: ezuern@xibitz.com
Web Site: www.xibitz.com

Type of Business:
Xibitz offers museum planning, design, project management, fabrication, and installation services. Our work encompasses museums of history, art, science, and nature, as well as children's museums and visitor

(Continued on next page)

(Continued from previous page)

centers. We help your visitors to create greater meaning in their lives through a clearer understanding of the world around them. Our exhibit environments are engaging, interactive, accessible, and understandable.

Personnel:
Erich Zuern (Producer)
James Hungerford (CEO)

Exhibit Fabricators

1220 EXHIBITS, INC.
3801 Vulcan Dr.
Nashville, TN 37211
Tel: 615-333-1220; FAX: 615-331-7141
E-mail: cdunn@1220.com
Web Site: www.1220.com

Type of Business:
For 32 years, 1220 Exhibits has specialized in the project management, fabrication and installation of museum exhibits. Our 100,000 square foot production facility is equipped for wood, metal, paint, scenic and graphic production. 1220's expert staff of project managers, estimators, builders, artisans, and administrators is dedicated to producing state-of-the-art museum exhibits. From history museums to halls of fame, and visitor centers to sports museums, the final product is high quality craftsmanship, exceptional service and a lasting relationship.

Personnel:
Craig Dunn (Senior Vice President)

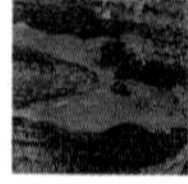

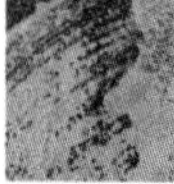

ADIRONDACK STUDIOS
439 County Rte. 45, Ste. 1
Argyle, NY 12809
Tel: 518-638-8000; FAX: 518-638-8238
E-mail: sales@adkstudios.com
Web Site: www.adkstudios.com

Type of Business:
Adirondack Studios is a full service company serving the museum and entertainment markets. For over thirty years, Adirondack has been providing custom environments and specialty exhibits to customers around the world. Adirondack is poised to participate in all phases and at all levels of project development, specialty fabrication and implementation.

Personnel:
Carl H. Zutz (Sales Manager)
Michael Blau (Creative Director)
Maurice O'Connell (Museum Sales)

ARTGUILD
the experience matters

ART GUILD, INC.
300 Wolf Dr.
West Deptford, NJ 08086
Tel: 973-701-1812; FAX: 973-701-1813
E-mail: jgunning@artguildinc.com
Web Site: www.artguildinc.com

Type of Business:
Art Guild's team of museum professionals works with design firms and museums nationwide building exceptional exhibit environments, which include casework, graphics, interactives, AV, and specialty fabrications. Working in two state of the art facilities, totaling over 400,000 square feet, we employ an expert project management team, experienced craftsmen, and utilize the latest technologies to transform your exhibit concepts into built reality. Art Guild, because the experience always matters.

Personnel:
John Gunning (Vice President Museum Services)
Geri Frankenstein (Director, Business Development)

BONE CLONES, INC.
21416 Chase St., Unit #1
Canoga Park, CA USA 91304
Tel: 818-709-7991 & 800-914-0091 (toll-free in USA); FAX: 818-709-7993
E-mail: museum@boneclones.com
Web Site: www.boneclones.com

Type of Business:
Manufacturer of Bone Clones®, we specialize in molding and casting of human and animal skulls and skeletons, ranging from fossils to modern. Our current catalog of over 1,500 specimens offers a wide selection to Museums and Universities for exhibits and display, including Neaderthal, human and primate skeletons. Our high quality resins capture the best original detail. Bone Clones® catalog can be ordered or found on our website.

Personnel:
David Kronen (R&D & Operations)
Gita Newman (Office & Public Relations)

CHASE STUDIO, INC.

CHASE STUDIO, INC.
205 Wolf Creek Rd.
Cedar Creek, MO 65627
Tel: 417-794-3303; FAX: 417-794-3741
E-mail: chasestudio@chasestudio.com
Web Site: www.chasestudio.com

(Continued on next page)

(Continued from previous page)

Type of Business:
Designers and builders of natural history and environmental science exhibits; paleontological reconstructions, zoological models, botanical reproductions, dioramas and habitat groups, illustration and mural painting, graphic design, photography, lighting design, fine cabinetwork, taxidermy, research, script writing, exhibit planning and consultation. Exhibits for over 200 museums worldwide since 1973.

Personnel:
Dr. Terry L. Chase (Director)
David F. Darby (Assistant Director Exhibits)
William L. Talbot (Assistant Director Business)
Greg L. Rogers (Assistant Director Operations)

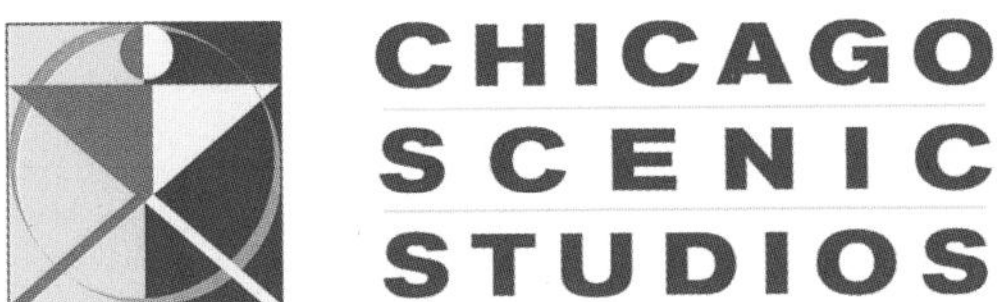

DESIGN BUILD MANAGE

CHICAGO SCENIC STUDIOS, INC.
1315 N. North Branch St.
Chicago, IL 60642
Tel: 312-274-9900; FAX: 312-274-9901
E-mail: info@chicagoscenic.com
Web Site: www.chicagoscenic.com

Type of Business:
Chicago Scenic Studios provides museums, science & technology centers, zoos, aquariums and visitor centers more than 30 years of multi-disciplinary experience in themed environment engineering, design, fabrication, and installation. Our highly skilled staff of project managers, designers, carpenters, painters, electricians, and specialists in metals, plastics and fabrics partner with your team to provide safe, educational, immersive environments and exciting experiences through custom exhibits, retail, restaurant, and admission spaces. Chicago Scenic can serve as a general contractor, fabricator or project manager in support of your design or ours. Our background in exhibits, retail, theater, amusements, special events and corporate spaces provides us with the ability to cater to differing needs in unique spaces. We have enjoyed partnering with world-class institutions such as: The Chicago Museum of Science & Industry, The Notebaert Nature Museum, The Field Museum of Natural History, The Shedd Aquarium, Chicago History Museum, Kohl's Children's Museum and many more to bring numerous exciting, educational, and successful stories to life. We'd like to help tell your story as well.

Personnel:
Robert Doepel (President)
Jim Notarianni (Business Development)

DESIGN AND PRODUCTION INCORPORATED
7110 Rainwater Place
Lorton, VA 22079
Tel: 703-550-8640; FAX: 703-339-0296
E-mail: dmoalli@d-and-p.com
Web Site: www.d-and-p.com

Type of Business:
In service to the museum community since 1949, our global portfolio is comprised of hundreds of high-profile projects, including interpretive history, interactive science, sports, children's museums, and immersive environments. D&P specializes in large-scale, multi-discipline exhibit projects, with a full complement of in-house production capabilities: Project development and management, custom fabrication, interactive exhibits, A/V hardware and software development, artifact mounting, graphic production, installation, and service. D&P is FSC-certified and a charter member of USGBC.

Personnel:
Jay Barnwell (President)
Dan Moalli (Vice President Business Development)
Donna Kuba (Project Director)
Rachel Childress (Marketing Associate)

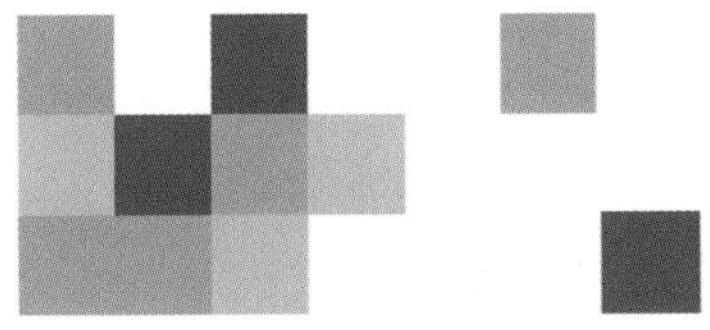

DIMENSIONAL COMMUNICATIONS INC.
173 Ludlow Ave.
Northvale, NJ 07647-2305
Tel: 201-767-1500; FAX: 201-767-9696
E-mail: info@dimcom.com
Web Site: www.dimcom.com

Type of Business:
Dimensional Communications Inc. creates customer and visitor experiences — from museum exhibits and multimedia to events, and from trade shows and corporate interiors to retail displays — that help our clients connect more productively with their customers. We not only work in 3 dimensions, but also in the 4th dimension: time. The time a person spends at an interactive exhibit, or gazing in wonder at the space they're in. These are moments that can only happen in immersive environments. Dimensional has been creating these experiences for nearly 50 years. We are a full-service custom builder and producer, offering everything from inspired design consultation and fine artisanship, to logistical management and enduring client-relationships.

Personnel:
Douglas Fixell (President)
Robert Sneed (Vice President Multimedia Technologies)

EXHIBIT CONCEPTS, INC.
700 Crossroads Ct.
Vandalia, OH 45377
Tel: 800-324-5063; FAX: 937-890-1750
E-mail: slowry@exhibitconcepts.com
Web Site: www.exhibitconcepts.com/museum

Type of Business:
Providing full-service contracting, engineering and exhibit fabrication for all categories of museums, visitor centers, halls of fame, science centers and nature centers. Services include: custom casework and millwork; graphic production; dioramas; scale models; animation; fiber optics; electro-mechanics and automated audio-visual presentations and equipment; artifact mounting; project management; and installation.

Personnel:
Kelli Glasser (President & COO)
Gerald T. Spangler (Vice President Special Environments)
Steven Lowry (Account Executive)

FORMATIONS INC.
621 S.E. 202nd Ave.
Portland, OR 97233
Tel: 503-665-7110; FAX: 503-665-7188
E-mail: formations@formationsinc.com
Web Site: www.formationsinc.com

Type of Business:
We're great storytellers! FORMATIONS is a full-service exhibit firm specializing in planning, design, and fabrication/installation of intrepretive exhibits and thematic interiors. We apply fresh, creative thinking to each project, designing exhibits with memorable imagery

(Continued on next page)

(Continued from previous page)

and regional identity. Our areas of expertise range from natural history to social, cultural, transportation, sports, and corporate history. We are an experienced team of interpretive planners/evaluators, exhibit and graphic designers, writers, detailers, multimedia specialists, estimators, fabricators, and project managers, working in a highly integrated facility in order to provide excellence to each project.

Personnel:
Craig Kerger (President, Design Principal)
Phil Buettner (Operations Manager)

HADLEY EXHIBITS, INC.
1700 Elmwood Ave.
Buffalo, NY 14207
Tel: 716-874-3666, ext. 3018; FAX: 716-874-9994
E-mail: pwarner@hadleyexhibits.com
Web Site: www.hadleyexhibits.com

Type of Business:
Award-winning exhibit design, fabrication, and installation services for museums, visitor centers, zoos, historic sites, special events, and expositions. Additional skills and expertise in graphic design, graphics production, custom display cases, model making, and artifact mounting, to name a few. Significant experience with interactive environments and ADA compliance. In business over 60 years, Hadley Exhibits is housed in a well-equipped 180,000 square foot facility.

Personnel:
Ted Johnson (President)
Paul Warner (National Account Executive)

KUBIK
1680 Mattawa Ave.
Mississauga, ON, Canada L4X 3A5
Tel: 877-252-2818; FAX: 905-272-2120
E-mail: info@thinkkubik.com
Web Site: www.thinkkubik.com

Type of Business:
For over 25 years, kubik has been a global company providing clients with the most extraordinary experience in the world. We offer a full range of museum services including project development, management, fabrication, interactive exhibit, media and software development, artifact mounting, custom showcase systems and graphic production of both permanent and temporary exhibits for museums, visitor centers and World's Fair Pavilions. Additional Locations: Europe, Plotterstraat 1, 1033 RX, Amsterdam, The Netherlands Tel.: +31 20 581 3030; Fax: +31 20 581 3031; New Jersey, 708 Fellowship Road, Mount Laurel, NJ 08054-1004 Tel.: 1.856.234.0052; Fax: 1.856.234.0760.

Personnel:
Sam Kohn (President & CEO)
Elliot Kohn (COO & Principal)

MALONE DESIGN/FABRICATION
5403 Dividend Dr.
Decatur, GA 30035
Tel: 770-987-2538; FAX: 770-987-0326
E-mail: twright@maloneinc.com
Web Site: www.maloneinc.com

Type of Business:
From inspiration to installation, Malone Design/Fabrication provides complete exhibition development and production services to the museum community. These services include interpretive planning, design, project management, fabrication and installation. Our fabrication capabilities include graphics, display cases, interactives, multimedia, scenic and more. Malone has nearly 50 years of experience designing and fabricating exhibits and store fixtures for all types of museums and visitor centers.

Personnel:
Tom Wright (CEO)
Brad Parker (Account Executive)

MALTBIE - A KUBIK COMPANY
708 Fellowship Rd.
Mount Laurel, NJ 08054
Tel: 856-234-0052; FAX: 856-234-0760
E-mail: info@maltbie.com
Web Site: www.maltbie.com

Type of Business:
For more than 45 years, Maltbie has focused on developing its ability to produce industry-leading permanent museum exhibitions and memorable visitor experiences. Our portfolio of over 290 international installations includes work in interpretive history, interactive science, and children's museums. Today we offer state-of-the-art facilities in the US and Canada, providing services that include project development, management, fabrication, interactive exhibit, media and software development, artifact mounting, custom showcase systems and graphic production. Additional Locations: Canada, 1680 Mattawa Avenue, Mississauga, Ontario L4X 3A5 Tel.: 1.877.252.2818; FAX: 1.905.272.2120. Europe: Plotterstraat 1, 1033 RX, Amsterdam, The Netherlands Tel.: +31 20 581 3030; Fax: +31 20 581 3031.

Personnel:
Charles M. Maltbie, Jr. (President)
Sam Kohn (CEO)
Gary Brooks (Executive Vice President)
Curt Cederquist (Vice President Museum Sales)

MUSEUM PROFESSIONALS

MUSEUM PROFESSIONALS
4875 Sunset Lane
Loretto, MN 55357
Tel: 763-479-7177
E-mail: museumpr@spacestar.net
Web Site: www.museumprofessionals.com

Type of Business:
EXHIBIT FABRICATION…combining science and aesthetics to create natural science and historical exhibits, artifact mounts and installation, dioramas, plant reproductions, field collecting, sculpture, murals model-making and consulting. Specialists in producing exhibits in the fields of zoology, botany, paleontology, geology and archaeology.

Personnel:
Terry Brown (President)

PACIFIC STUDIO
5311 Shilshole Ave., N.W.
Seattle, WA 98107-4021
Tel: 206-783-5226; FAX: 206-783-5409
E-mail: kadams@pacific-studio.com
Web Site: www.pacific-studio.com

Type of Business:
At Pacific Studio, we create interpretive and interactive exhibits for museums, interpretive centers, visitor centers, zoos and aquaria. Our artisans and craftspeople specialize in exhibit -grade cabinetry, custom metal fabrication, prototyping, interactive displays, hand painted murals, illustrations, sculpting and casting. As the exclusive American distributor for Armour Systems Ltd., we are also able to provide the latest case system technology for projects with critical environmental, security and access requirements.

Personnel:
Al Salm (General Manager)
Marc Burns (Sales & Marketing)
Norm Scrivner (Art Director)

PROTO PRODUCTIONS, INC.
840 Fiene Dr.
Addison, IL 60101
Tel: 630-628-6626; FAX: 630-628-2232
E-mail: contact@protoproductions.com
Web Site: www.protoproductions.com; www.artifactcases.com

Type of Business:
Since the inception of Proto Productions in 1974, we have grown to be a prominent museum exhibit fabricator and a trusted resource to museum related professionals. Our clients span the museum specialties including art, history and science museums, aquariums, zoos, and visitor centers. Proto has completed hundreds of museum projects and in doing so has developed and maintained an approach to projects that nurtures solid working relationships with exhibit designers, museum planners, architects, curators, educators and the corporate community. Not only is Proto prepared to collaborate with the client's team, but our staff's creative spirit opens up solutions that have not previously been seen by others. Proto is always willing to discuss alternative options to provide your desired visitor experience within the boundaries of financial and scheduling concerns. Our continuing commitment is to provide you, the client and your team, with museum quality exhibit components that exceed all of your expectations. We achieve this ultimate goal by telling your story in such a way that meets your aesthetic and interpretive goals and takes your concept to our reality™.

Personnel:
Ken Hopkins (President)
Mike Slayton (Vice President)

QUATREFOIL ASSOCIATES, INC.
29 C St.
Laurel, MD 20707
Tel: 301-470-4748; FAX: 301-470-4749
E-mail: info@quatrefoil.com
Web Site: www.quatrefoil.com

Type of Business:
Quatrefoil creates engaging museum experiences that educate, inspire and amuse the visitor and reflect the essence of our client's vision and values. We deliver a full spectrum of expertise, applied with artistic and technical excellence - museum planning, exhibit design, content development, graphics, interactives, multimedia, custom electronics, fabrication and installation. West Coast Design Studio, 1524 Cloverfield Blvd., Ste. A, Santa Monica, CA 90404. Tel.: 310-829-9390.

Personnel:
Abbie Chessler (Design Director & Founding Partner)
Paula Schuman (Founding Partner & CFO)
Ernie Falcone (Founding Partner & Technical Director)
Paul DeCamp (COO & Partner)

SPLIT ROCK STUDIOS
2071 Gateway Blvd.
Arden Hills, MN 55112
Tel: 651-631-2211 & 800-433-9599; FAX: 651-631-0707
E-mail: info@splitrockstudios.com
Web Site: www.splitrockstudios.com

Type of Business:
Split Rock Studios is a full-service firm specializing in designing and building interactive exhibits for interpretive centers, museums and related institutions. In addition to our exhibit design and development capabilities, we have the in-house capabilities to produce all facets of a major exhibition, including interactive components, themed environments, dioramas, interpretive murals, realistic animal and human sculpture, graphics, and custom exhibit furniture. Whatever your exhibit project needs, our staff will provide the ultimate in quality service and workmanship.

Personnel:
Craig Sommerville (President)
Lisa Friedlander (Sales & Marketing)

TAYLOR STUDIOS INC.
1320 Harmon Dr.
Rantoul, IL 61866
Tel: 217-893-4874 & 800-707-2047; FAX: 217-893-1998
E-mail: sales@taylorstudios.com
Web Site: www.taylorstudios.com/omd

Personnel:
Betty Brennan (President)
Kara Vanskike (Marketing Coordinator)

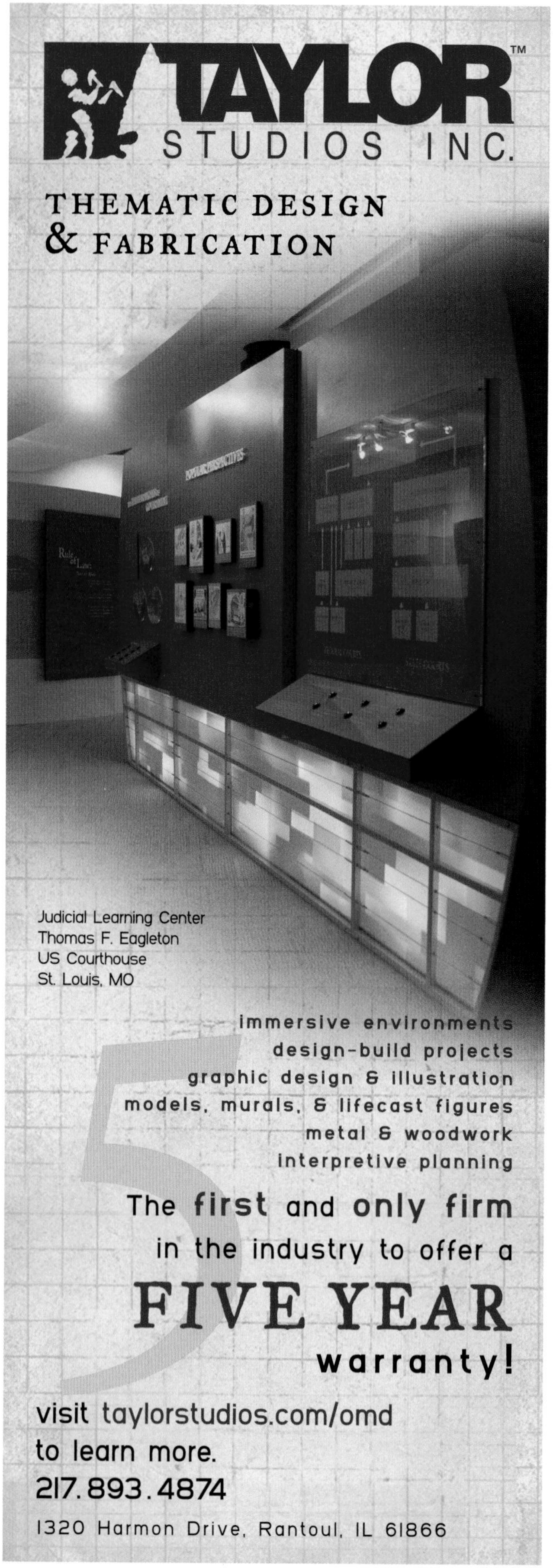

TRIEBOLD PALEONTOLOGY, INC.
201 S. Fairview
Woodland Park, CO 80863
Tel: 719-686-1820
Web Site: www.trieboldpaleontology.com

Type of Business:
Mounting and re-mounting any size skeleton from 8 inches to over 80 feet. Molding and casting for over 20 years the finest cast skeletons in the world including dinosaurs, marine and flying reptiles, prehistoric fish, mammals, trackways and more. Fossil specimens at www.dinosaursanctuary.com. Ask about out institutional collaborations. We can design and build your project from start to finish. Traveling Exhibitions include: Savage Ancient Seas, Bringing Dinosaurs to Life, Darwin & Dinosaurs. Visit www.embeddedexhibitions.com.

UNIVERSAL EXHIBITS INC.
9517 E. Rush St.
South El Monte, CA 91733
Tel: 323-686-0562; FAX: 626-444-1535
E-mail: UEexhibits@worldnet.att.net
Web Site: www.UniversalExhibits.com

Type of Business:
We have over sixty-three (63) years of experience of providing full service to the museum industry worldwide. We can provide full turnkey service to team support delivering the following services: design, master plans, drafting, fabrication, graphic production, interactive exhibitry, engineering, audio/visual production, special effects, environments, project planning, transportation and installation. Among our projects include presidential libraries, George H.W. Bush (twice) (2007 and 1997), Ronald Reagan and Richard Nixon. Visitor centers, mini planetarium dome for the Griffith Observatory, Vista Del Lago and Lake Oroville. Museums, The J. Paul Getty, Museum of Tolerance (Los Angeles and New York), The Bowers Museum of Cultural Art (Terra Cotta Soldiers) tribute room on the George H.W. Bush Aircraft Carrier (CVN-77), The City of Highland (Environmental Learning Center) L.E.E.D. Gold Rating Facility with interactive children exhibitions. Mission San Juan Capistrano Interactive Interpretation Exhibitry (south wing).

Personnel:
M. Robert Bell (President & CEO)
John Hall (Project Manager)
Mike Salomone (Project Manager)

xibitz
Experiential Spaces for Work and Life

XIBITZ, INC.
7604 Harwood Ave., Ste. 202
Milwaukee, WI 53213
Tel: 414-727-4699 & 616-247-3500 (Home Office: Grand Rapids, MI); FAX: 414-727-4883
E-mail: ezuern@xibitz.com
Web Site: www.xibitz.com

Type of Business:
Xibitz offers museum planning, design, project management, fabrication, and installation services. Our work encompasses museums of history, art, science, and nature, as well as children's museums and visitor

(Continued on next page)

(Continued from previous page)

centers. We help your visitors to create greater meaning in their lives through a clearer understanding of the world around them. Our exhibit environments are engaging, interactive, accessible, and understandable.

Personnel:
Erich Zuern (Producer)
James Hungerford (CEO)

ZONE DISPLAY CASES INC.
660, Rue de l'Argon
Charlesbourg, Quebec, Canada G2N 2G5
Tel: 418-841-4004; FAX: 418-841-2866
E-mail: info@zonedisplaycases.com
Web Site: www.zonedisplaycases.com

Type of Business:
Zone Display Cases is a sister company of Concetti Design Inc, a 20 year old company, specializing in the design, fabrication and installation of various exhibits, modular displays or complete turnkey exhibitions for museums. The Zone Display Cases company was created in 1999, after those many years working with the museology community. We developed our museum display cases using the latest software, in a cutting edge 3D environment renowned for its engineering and manufacturing. Zone Display Cases are offered in modular or regular construction, standard sizes or custom fabrication, and in a wide variety of finishes. Airtight and atmosphere-controlled to meet museum standards, Zone Display Cases feature an elegant yet discrete design that draws attention to the objects on display. They also offer numerous other features sought after by museum experts: compliance with standards, security, Optiwhite laminated glass, out-of-case premounting, LED or optic fiber lighting, total visibility, and much more. Our cases are designed and manufactured in Canada, offering fast turnover and delivery. Learn more about us, visit our web site, or call us...we will be happy to discuss your needs and projects.

Personnel:
Pierre Giguere (Vice President Sales)
Louis St-Gelais (President & Senior Designer)

Exhibition Equipment & Services

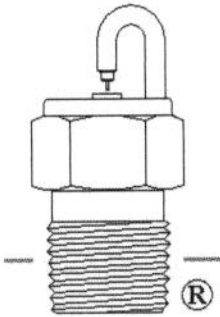

ATOMIZING SYSTEMS INC
Manufacturers of *COLD FOG*® Systems

ATOMIZING SYSTEMS INC.
One Hollywood Ave.
HoHoKus, NJ 07423
Tel: 201-447-1222; FAX: 201-447-6932
E-mail: info@coldfog.com
Web Site: www.coldfog.com

Type of Business:
Atomizing Systems Inc., a manufacturer of water fog equipment for humidity & special effects, uses the world's only laser-drilled, ruby orifice fog nozzle (recently granted a US patent). Nozzles create water fog evaporative cooling, special effects, cool zones, walkways, landscaping, entrances, waterfalls, rockwork, fountains, haze, smoke & cloud simulation. Systems utilized worldwide include major projects in Orlando, far east, middle east, Latin America. 20-year nozzle Warranty against orifice wear standard. Each fog Nozzles equipped with individual filter. Full engineering & design services available.

Personnel:
Michael Elkas (President & Owner)

case[werks]℠

CASE[WERKS], LLC
1501 Saint Paul St., Ste. 116
Baltimore, MD 21202
Tel: 410-332-4160 & 800-810-2852 (toll free); FAX: 410-332-4106
E-mail: info@casewerks.com
Web Site: www.casewerks.com

Type of Business:
Case[werks] is a sales and service firm offering a range of products uniquely designed to meet exhibit requirements for original art, artifacts and special collections in all types of interior environments. Providing consultative sales support for institutions large & small, Case[werks] is THE museum professional's source for archival display cases & exhibit furnishings, library furnishings, gallery accessories, art hanging hardware, signage & graphic display products as well as conservation equipment including miniClima Humidity Control Systems. Many of our best-selling gallery accessories are in stock, ready to ship; major credit cards are accepted. An extensive catalog is available and custom inquiries are always welcome. Ask about enrolling in our institutional "gift" registry. Case[werks] is the North American representative for Vitrinen- und Glasbau REIER (Germany).

Personnel:
Matt Malaquias (Principal)
Reinhard Nottrodt (Principal)

GLASBAU HAHN AMERICA, LLC
15 Little Brook Lane
Newburgh, NY 12550
Tel: 845-566-3331 & 877-452-7228; FAX: 845-566-3176
E-mail: info@glasbau-hahn.com
Web Site: www.glasbau-hahn.com

Type of Business:
GLASBAU HAHN enjoys a worldwide reputation for its superbly crafted museum display cases, technical innovation and seismic technology development. In business since 1836, we set standards for security, micro-environmental control, fiber optic or LED lighting, conservation, accessibility and design. GLASBAU HAHN award-winning cases and installations are in over 300 Museums and Art Galleries around the world, including over 100 in the United States. The Allglass Display Case, pioneered in 1935, is one of many GLASBAU HAHN designs to receive international awards. Other technical advances include 3-Way Sliding Doors, Hinged Openings, the HAHN Swing-Door and the "Protector" Case, the ultimate safeguard for the display and transportation of hanging art. All display cases are either custom-built or modular for convenient exhibit installations. GLASBAU HAHN is well known for incorporating the vision of architects and designers while considering the need for functionality, low maintenance and ideal art conservation. Thirty-four full-time representatives around the world regularly networking to bring GLASBAU HAHN's standards and innovations to each exhibition requirement, whether working for a world-famous institution or a small local museum. In addition, GLASBAU HAHN offers a full range of museum services.
GLASBAU HAHN: Trusted with the World's Treasures for over 170

(Continued on next page)

(Continued from previous page)

years! Home Office: GLASBAU HAHN GmbH, Hanauer Landstrasse 211, D-60314 Frankfurt am Main, Germany. Tel: 011-49-69-944-1753, Fax: 011-49-69-944-1761.

Personnel:
Isabel Hahn (President GH GmbH)
Till Hahn (President GHA)
Jamie J. Ponton (Vice President GHA)
Norbert Leonhardt (Construction GH GmbH)
Cathy Lima (Office Manager GHA)

HELMUT GUENSCHEL
THE FINE ART OF EXHIBITION

HELMUT GUENSCHEL, INC.
10 Emala Ave.
Baltimore, MD 21220
Tel: 410-686-5900 & 800-852-2525; FAX: 410-687-9342
E-mail: info@guenschel.com
Web Site: www.guenschel.com

Type of Business:
The highest quality museum exhibit cases available are custom designed, engineered, and manufactured exclusively by Helmut Guenschel, Inc. at our facility in Baltimore, MD. Used by many of the most prestigious museums in the world, our premier museum exhibit cases address the full range of technical requirements and collections issues including all facets of active and passive conservation, the use of proven environmentally safe materials, integrated security options, and effective seismic anchoring. For more than 40 years we have custom designed, fabricated and installed exhibit systems of the highest quality. Today our cases protect, preserve, and display some of the world's most valuable and important artwork, artifacts, and documents.

Personnel:
Helmut Guenschel (President)
Cynthia Shaffer (Vice President)

Hahn Bros.
FINE ART AND ANTIQUE SERVICES

HAHN BROS. FIREPROOF WAREHOUSES, INC.
622 Communipaw Ave.
Jersey City, NJ 07304
Tel: 212-926-1505; FAX: 201-432-9547
E-mail: info@hahnbros.com
Web Site: www.hahnbros.com

Type of Business:
Over 100 years of fine art services to the museum and art community. Full service specialists offering customized crating and traveling cases and freight forwarding for collections and shows. Packing, moving, relocation and installation. Registrar, photography and gallery services available. Secure, climate-controlled storage in two locations with the ability to set up to client specifications.

Personnel:
Karen O. Dowling (President)
Marianne Mikulka (Fine Art Director)

HIGHMARK TECHNOLOGIES
WALL PANEL SYSTEMS
8343 Clinton Park Dr.
Fort Wayne, IN 46825
Tel: 260-483-0012; FAX: 260-482-4877
E-mail: contact@highmarktech.com

Type of Business:
EXZACT is an attractively priced modular panel system constructed of patented aluminum frames that accept a wide variety of standard wall surfaces. Lightweight, strong, and extremely fast and easy to assemble without special tools. EXTTREME is an elegant seamless wall panel used for monolithic or linear structures. It is nailable, paintable or can be finished with an appropriate laminate. Both products are partition modules and are ideal for many museum applications; especially temporary or traveling exhibits.

Personnel:
Michael V. Parrott (President)
Chris Lake (Vice President)

Lighting Services Inc

LIGHTING SERVICES INC
2 Kay Fries Dr.
Stony Point, NY 10980
Tel: 800-999-9574 & 845-942-2800; FAX: 845-942-2177
E-mail: Sales@mailLSI.com
Web Site: www.LightingServicesInc.com

Type of Business:
Lighting Services Inc (LSI) is the leading independent manufacturer of track, accent, display and LED lighting systems for museum environments. Since 1958, LSI has been dedicated to designing, engineering and manufacturing lighting fixtures of the highest quality. Our reputation for creativity and innovative design, coupled with specification grade products and intelligent personalized service, has made us the manufacturer of choice amongst the most discriminating specifiers of lighting for museums and galleries.

Personnel:
Daniel Gelman (President)

THE ULSTER LINEN CO. INC.
383 Moffit Blvd.
Islip, NY 11751
Tel: 631-859-5244; FAX: 631-859-4990
Web Site: www.ulsterlinen.com

Type of Business:
The Ulster Linen Company has a great reputation for luxury European fine linens, kitchen textiles and piece goods. We provide the highest quality and largest selection of linen by the yard available in the USA. We import elegant Irish handkerchiefs, table linens, printed tea cozies and towels, and with our custom design team, we can also produce and print your unique designs in-house, including beautiful hemstitched table and bed linens in unique sizes and shapes.

Personnel:
J. Dever Larmor (President)
Yoselin Songco

ZONE DISPLAY CASES INC.
660, Rue de l'Argon
Charlesbourg, Quebec, Canada G2N 2G5
Tel: 418-841-4004; FAX: 418-841-2866
E-mail: info@zonedisplaycases.com
Web Site: www.zonedisplaycases.com

Type of Business:
Zone Display Cases is a sister company of Concetti Design Inc, a 20 year old company, specializing in the design, fabrication and installation of various exhibits, modular displays or complete turnkey

(Continued on next page)

(Continued from previous page)

exhibitions for museums. The Zone Display Cases company was created in 1999, after those many years working with the museology community. We developed our museum display cases using the latest software, in a cutting edge 3D environment renowned for its engineering and manufacturing. Zone Display Cases are offered in modular or regular construction, standard sizes or custom fabrication, and in a wide variety of finishes. Airtight and atmosphere-controlled to meet museum standards, Zone Display Cases feature an elegant yet discrete design that draws attention to the objects on display. They also offer numerous other features sought after by museum experts: compliance with standards, security, Optiwhite laminated glass, out-of-case premounting, LED or optic fiber lighting, total visibility, and much more. Our cases are designed and manufactured in Canada, offering fast turnover and delivery. Learn more about us, visit our web site, or call us...we will be happy to discuss your needs and projects.

Personnel:
Pierre Giguere (Vice President Sales)
Louis St-Gelais (President & Senior Designer)

Hanging & Fastening Devices

ARAKAWA HANGING SYSTEMS
2505 S.E. 11th Ave., Ste. 122
Portland, OR 97202
Tel: 503-236-0440 & 888-272-5292; FAX: 503-236-0427
E-mail: sales@arakawagrip.com
Web Site: www.arakawa-art.com

Type of Business:
The Arakawa Hanging System is the premier method for displaying framed art in a museum setting, used for over 20 years in museums worldwide. A superior product in both function and design, the Arakawa System integrates multiple rail designs with quick release cable Grippers, allowing maximum horizontal and vertical flexibility for adjusting displays. Multiple rail and Gripper designs and sizes help you meet your most demanding needs. Please call for a catalog and references.

Personnel:
Stan Pfeifer (Sales Manager)
Shane Carrico

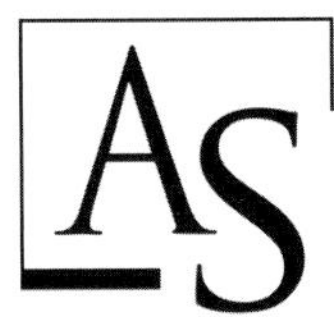

AS HANGING SYSTEMS
3600 Matte Blvd., Ste. L
Brossard, QC, Canada J4Y 2Z2
Tel: 866-935-6949 (toll free US/Canada only) & 450-619-7999; FAX: 450-619-1871
E-mail: info@ASHanging.com
Web Site: www.ASHanging.com

Type of Business:
AS Hanging Systems, your exhibition partner with over 8,500 installations, brings over 20 years of experience to the interior decor, museum and gallery markets. Solutions include tensioned cable and specific hardware for curved walls, permanent and temporary exhibits, OEM applications and construction build-out. AS Systems is versatile. Select from stand-offs or a selection of track designs, cables and/or rods and a wide variety of specialty fittings for infinite horizontal and vertical display flexibility. Systems support up to 600 lbs. We also manage a robust eCommerce site for your convenience. Login, research, plan, order and receive email status right up to your shipment arrival. Most all orders ship within 24 hours. Contact Laurent Venturi for your special projects. Installing, resetting or dismantling your next display is a breeze.

Personnel:
Walter Moncade (President, Managing Director)
Dave Veilleux (Vice President Business Development)
Laurent Venturi (Sales Manager)

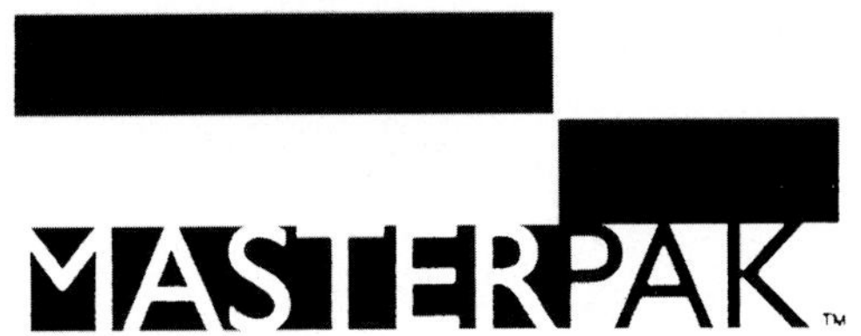

MASTERPAK
145 E. 57th St., 5th Fl.
New York, NY 10022
Tel: 800-922-5522; FAX: 212-586-6961
E-mail: als@masterpak-usa.com
Web Site: www.masterpak-usa.com

Type of Business:
Unique & archival materials for the protection of fine art, artifacts and antiques in packing, shipping, storing and display. Hard-to-find materials for conservators, artists, museums, galleries, collectors, framers and art shippers. Products include: Archival Softwrap® Tyvek®, Nomex® and Archival Hardwrap® Tyvek® Liners by DuPont, Sealed Air's Ethafoam®/Cellu-Cushion® in planks and rolls, Sealed Air's BubbleWrap®, Voltek's Volara® Polyethylene Foam, Archival Rolling & Storage Tubes, Unbuffered & Buffered Tissue in rolls and sheets, Photo-Tex Tissue in rolls and sheets, Glassine Paper in rolls and sheets, Silicone Parchment Release Paper in rolls and sheets, Corrugated Multi-Use Board, Archival tapes, Glass Skin®, Strongboxes™ & Print Pads™, Oz Clips™ Link Lock® Latches, Steel Closure Plates, PEM2 Data Loggers and specialty preservation management software developed by The Image Permanence Institute especially for the collections of Museums, Libraries & Archives. All products are available in small or large quantities and can ship within 24 hours. Our website, located at www.masterpak-usa.com, is open 24 hours for easy online ordering.

Personnel:
E. William Judson (Chairman)
Andrew L. Smith (President)

Instruments/Laboratory

2FLYPLANES
Barkly Wharf, Suites 340-345
Le Caudan, Port Louis, Mauritius
Tel: 27-83-2346582
E-mail: nikpatel@2flyplanes.com
Web Site: www.2flyplanes.com

Type of Business:
We manufacture full motion and highly realistic flight simulators based on commercial, military and space craft for the public entertainment and education markets.

Interactive Multimedia Programs & Exhibits

2FLYPLANES
Barkly Wharf, Suites 340-345
Le Caudan, Port Louis, Mauritius
Tel: 27-83-2346582
E-mail: nikpatel@2flyplanes.com
Web Site: www.2flyplanes.com

Type of Business:

We manufacture full motion and highly realistic flight simulators based on commercial, military and space craft for the public entertainment and education markets.

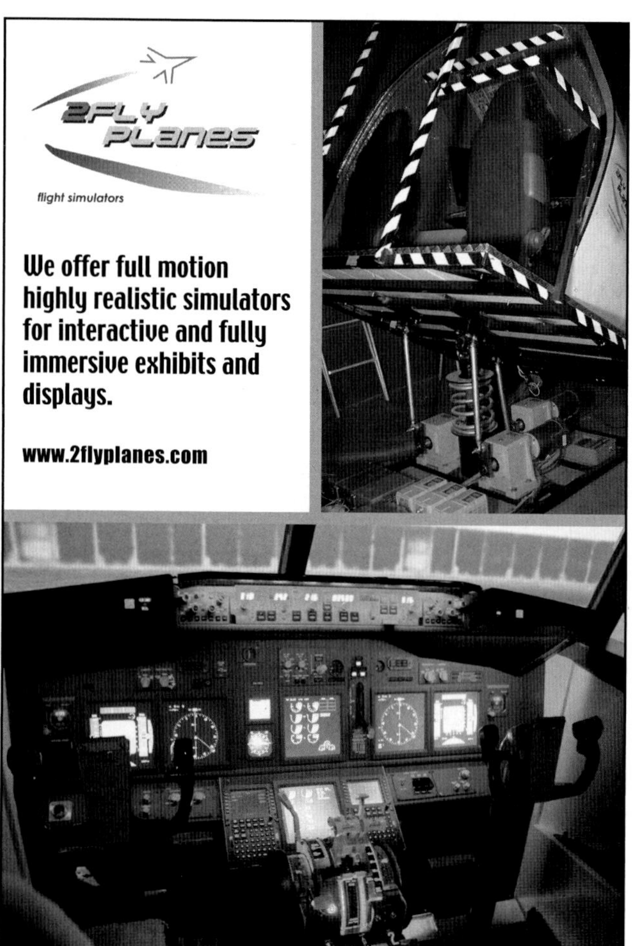

2FLY
PLANES
flight simulators
We offer full motion highly realistic simulators for interactive and fully immersive exhibits and displays.
www.2flyplanes.com

Blue Telescope

BLUE TELESCOPE
236 W. 30th St., 7th Fl.
New York, NY 10001
Tel: 212-675-7702, ext. 12; FAX: 212-675-7703
E-mail: contact@blue-telescope.com
Web Site: www.blue-telescope.com

Type of Business:

Blue Telescope creates interactive media experiences that educate and communicate. We use rich media to dynamically illustrate complex concepts and data, to create fun, engaging experiences out of challenging content, and to immerse audiences in compelling stories and environments. Blue Telescope uses multi-user technology to facilitate communication among visitors and educators. From competitive and collaborative games, to group content exploration, to live surveys, we create shared experiences that get people talking and engaged.

bpi
imagine. what we do.

BOSTON PRODUCTIONS, INC.
100 Morse St.
Norwood, MA 02062
Tel: 781-255-1555; FAX: 781-255-1556
E-mail: imagine@bostonproductions.com
Web Site: www.bostonproductions.com

Type of Business:

For twenty years, Boston Productions has been telling compelling stories to museum and visitor center audiences across the country through engaging and immersive media exhibits. Always putting the visitor experience first, we continue to surprise, enthrall and inform with uniquely diverse ideas and cutting-edge methods. Our signature AV presentations and interactive visitor experiences require multidisciplinary services and skill sets, such that we are equally expert in media design, content development, production services, software programming, exhibit prototyping and full AV hardware integration services. Knowing what works creatively with today's multigenerational audiences and being able to produce media, interactive exhibits and AV hardware systems with a strong value quotient is an organizational imperative. Boston Productions is truly a creative concept-to-installation business. - imagine. what we do.

Personnel:
Bob Noll (President & Creative Director)
Chet Kaplan (COO & Director AV Hardware Integration)
Mark Dorgan (Associate Creative Director)

CORTINA PRODUCTIONS, INC.
6623-A Old Dominion Dr.
McLean, VA 22101
Tel: 703-556-8481; FAX: 703-847-9694
E-mail: jim@cortinaproductions.com
Web Site: www.cortinaproductions.com

Type of Business:
We are media designers and storytellers; crafters of image and light, sound and touch. From theater experiences, to large format multi-screen presentations, to engaging interactive exhibits and videos, we produce award-winning media exhibits that educate, entertain, and inspire. From initial concept development through final post-production, we collaborate with you to blend story and technology into a single artistic vision.

Personnel:
Joseph Cortina (President)
Amy Maddox (Vice President Production)

ESI DESIGN
111 Fifth Ave., 12th Fl.
New York, NY 10003
Tel: 212-989-3993; FAX: 212-673-4061
E-mail: mmullineaux@esidesign.com
Web Site: www.esidesign.com

Type of Business:
ESI Design is an award-winning design company that combines exhibit design with interactive media and environmental graphic design to produce immersive, participatory, and sustainable museum experiences. Our multidisciplinary team creates original, compelling environments that inspires visitors to explore, participate and learn through repeated visits. Our range of services include: museum master planning, exhibit design, communication design and more. Current and recent projects include the Hall of Human Life at the Boston Museum of Science, the Shanghai Corporate Pavilion at the 2010 World Expo in Shanghai, The College Basketball Experience in Kansas City, MO, Infinity at NASA Stennis Space Center in Mississippi, the Pope John Paul II Cultural Center in Washington, DC, the Ellis Island National Immigration Museum, and the Brooklyn Children's Museum. For more information about ESI Design, visit us online at www.esidesign.com.

Personnel:
Edwin Schlossberg (President)
Michelle Mullineaux (Business Development)

EXHIBIT ENGINEERING, LLC
7220 Thor Lane
Pensacola, FL 32526
Tel: 850-941-1800; FAX: 850-944-2744
Web Site: www.exhibitengineering.com

Type of Business:
Exhibit Engineering designs and produces innovative interactive products. I-Viewer (IV), our proprietary sliding interactive touchscreen module will dramatically enhance any exhibit storyline or timeline. Glide the programmed module along its rails for hands-on interaction with specific data, in-depth information or images delivered instantly on screen via text, graphics, 3D animation, video or the Internet; and Augmented Reality (AR), where live video and 3D animation merge on the screen for real-time interaction with 3D objects. Sales Office: Greg Morrow, Director Sales/Marketing, Anniston, AL 36207. Tel: 850.941.1800; Email: gregm@exhibitengineering.com.

Personnel:
Greg Morrow (Director, Sales & Marketing)
Terry Murphy (Interactive Exhibit Development)

HILLMANN & CARR INCORPORATED
2233 Wisconsin Ave., N.W., Ste. 425
Washington, DC 20007
Tel: 202-342-0001; FAX: 202-342-0117
E-mail: michalcarr@hillmanncarr.com
Web Site: www.hillmanncarr.com

Type of Business:
Full-service creative producers of award winning media: film, HDTV, computer interactive, audio environments, video-tours, immersion and object theaters, graphic and multimedia presentations. Extensive expertise in science, history and art museums, visitor centers, corporate exhibit media, expositions and multi-language international projects, created in traditional, non-traditional and unique formats. Wide-ranging experience in concept development, content research, immersive experiences and audiovisual media master planning. Producers and project managers skilled in AV systems design, integration and installation. WOSB.

Personnel:
Alfred Hillmann (President)
Michal Brand Carr (Vice President)

JACK ROUSE ASSOCIATES
600 Vine St., Ste. 1700
Cincinnati, OH 45202-1100
Tel: 513-381-0055; FAX: 513-381-2691
E-mail: s.mccoy@jackrouse.com
Web Site: www.jackrouse.com

Type of Business:
Jack Rouse Associates conceives, visualizes and realizes exceptional visitor experiences around the world. Specific services include master planning, exhibit design, media production and project management.

Personnel:
Jack Rouse (CEO)
Keith James (President)
Randy Vuksta (Creative Director)
Shawn McCoy (Vice President Marketing & Business Development)

MONADNOCK MEDIA, INC.

MONADNOCK MEDIA, INC.
112 Amherst Rd.
Sunderland, MA 01375
Tel: 413-665-1390; FAX: 413-665-1394
E-mail: steve@monadnock.org
Web Site: www.monadnock.org

Type of Business:
Audio visual/multi-media design, production and project management for museums, science centers, historic sites, visitor centers, zoos and cultural/educational organizations. Since 1980 Monadnock Media has been specializing in producing video, audio, soundscapes, computer interactive sound and light shows, design and production of orientation programs, video wall/multi-screen, multi-media exhibit interactive and immersive theater experiences. Design includes AV/multi-media exhibit integration, presentation technology specification and technical systems. Our services include full production capabilities from concept/design, research, scripting, to post production, installation, staffing training and consultation.

Personnel:
Steve Bressler (Director)

QUATREFOIL ASSOCIATES, INC.
29 C St.
Laurel, MD 20707
Tel: 301-470-4748; FAX: 301-470-4749
E-mail: info@quatrefoil.com
Web Site: www.quatrefoil.com

Type of Business:
Quatrefoil creates engaging museum experiences that educate, inspire and amuse the visitor and reflect the essence of our client's vision and values. We deliver a full spectrum of expertise, applied with artistic and technical excellence - museum planning, exhibit design, content development, graphics, interactives, multimedia, custom electronics, fabrication and installation. West Coast Design Studio, 1524 Cloverfield Blvd., Ste. A, Santa Monica, CA 90404. Tel.: 310-829-9390.

Personnel:
Abbie Chessler (Design Director & Founding Partner)
Paula Schuman (Founding Partner & CFO)
Ernie Falcone (Founding Partner & Technical Director)
Paul DeCamp (COO & Partner)

RBH MULTIMEDIA, INC.
12 Hatch Ter.
Dobbs Ferry, NY 10522
Tel: 914-693-8755; FAX: 914-693-3539
E-mail: rbh@rbhmedia.com
Web Site: www.rbhmedia.com

Type of Business:
RBH Multimedia, Inc. is a media production company dedicated to developing and producing audiovisual experiences and exhibits. We bring imagination, skill, flair and years of experience to designing and producing audio, video and multiple media exhibits for museums, historic sites, visitor and interpretive centers, and cultural institutions. We also design and program websites and computer interactive exhibits. RBH is particularly known for producing signature multi-sensory, multimedia "experience" theater shows. Other services include hardware system design, engineering and installation, with expertise in videoconference technology. For more information about RBH Multimedia, Inc., please visit us online at www.rbhmedia.com.

Personnel:
Steve Brosnahan (Partner)
Nancy Haffner (Partner)
Edgardo J. Resto (Associate)

WEATHERHEAD EXPERIENCE DESIGN GROUP, INC.
3400 Harbor Ave., S.W.
Ste. 419, Box 319
Seattle, WA 98126
Tel: 206-447-0853
E-mail: contact@weatherhead-design.com
Web Site: www.weatherhead-design.com

Type of Business:
WEATHERHEAD Experience Design Group excels in supporting the multiple goals of institutions we work with by developing imaginative, clearly communicated and audience centered content development, design, and integrated media. We enjoy challenging projects which require imaginative problem solving to achieve a seamless convergence of the physical and the virtual. Our experience design services include: Exhibit design and development; Interactive development; Multimedia production; Multimedia installations; Media production (film, video, audio).

Personnel:
Andrea K. Weatherhead (Principal)

Lighting

EDISON PRICE LIGHTING
41-50 22nd St.
Long Island City, NY 11101
Tel: 718-685-0700; FAX: 718-786-8530
E-mail: info@epl.com
Web Site: www.epl.com

Type of Business:
Designers and manufacturers of architectural lighting products and systems. Our track lighting - at work in hundreds of museums and galleries worldwide - includes track shapes for a variety of installation requirements and elegantly durable fixtures for a wide range of lighting programs. Our recessed fixtures include optically precise

(Continued on next page)

(Continued from previous page)

wallwashers and accent lights. An array of lenses, filters, louvers and screens permits all fixtures to be 'fine-tuned' for the optimal display and conservation of art and artifacts.

Personnel:
Emma Price (President)
Joel R. Siegel (Executive Vice President Marketing & Sales)

Lighting Services Inc 

LIGHTING SERVICES INC
2 Kay Fries Dr.
Stony Point, NY 10980
Tel: 800-999-9574 & 845-942-2800; FAX: 845-942-2177
E-mail: Sales@mailLSI.com
Web Site: www.LightingServicesInc.com

Type of Business:
Lighting Services Inc (LSI) is the leading independent manufacturer of track, accent, display and LED lighting systems for museum environments. Since 1958, LSI has been dedicated to designing, engineering and manufacturing lighting fixtures of the highest quality. Our reputation for creativity and innovative design, coupled with specification grade products and intelligent personalized service, has made us the manufacturer of choice amongst the most discriminating specifiers of lighting for museums and galleries.

Personnel:
Daniel Gelman (President)

Luxam Lighting for Museums

LUXAM, INC.
2246 Country Club Rd.
Appomattox, VA 24522
Tel: 434-352-0084; FAX: 434-352-0089
E-mail: Rick@luxam.com
Web Site: www.luxam.com

Type of Business:
Luxam manufactures specialty lighting products for museum showcases and exhibits. We manufacture fiber optic and hybrid fiber/LED lighting systems and software. We also offer a full range of on-site services including installation and focus. Our newest illuminator, LED/Max, has 24 channels of high wattage LEDs mated to our fiber delivery systems for stunning interactive and multimedia exhibits controlled via DMX, all within conservation norms. Custom solutions, on time and budget.

Personnel:
Rick Jellow (Principal)
Jean Francois Hocquard (Principal)

NOUVIR RESEARCH®
20915 Sussex Hwy.
Seaford, DE 19973
Tel: 302-628-9933; FAX: 302-628-9932
Web Site: www.nouvir.com

Type of Business:
Pure-white, stone-cold, perfectly controlled lighting with no UV and no IR from NoUVIR Research radically reduces photochemical and photomechanical damage to exhibits and can give you documented 70% gallery energy savings. Fifty different miniature floodlights, spotlights, across-the-room pinspots, eyeballs, wall washers, pendants and more. Our 24 U.S. patents guarantee superior performance. A 10-year warranty on hardware and fiber guarantees quality. Call for conservation textbooks, seminar information or free product specifications, photometry and lighting design information.

Personnel:
Miss Ruth Ellen Miller (President)
Mr. Matthew S. Miller (Vice President Marketing)

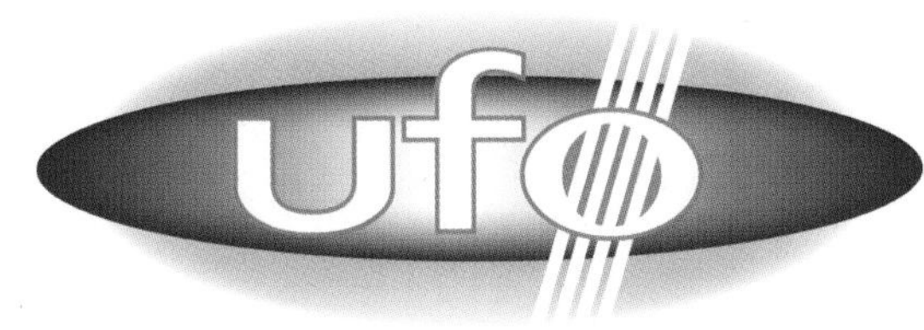

UNIVERSAL FIBRE OPTICS LTD.
Home Place
Coldstream
Berwickshire, U.K. TD12 4DT
Tel: 1-800-UFO-5554 (1-800-836-5554); FAX: 011-44-1890-883-062
E-mail: info@universal-fibre-optics.com
Web Site: www.lightingformuseums.com

Type of Business:
UFO is one of only three manufacturers in the world of raw fiber for lighting; and we are one of the world's largest manufacturers of complete fiber-optic lighting systems. All fiber, harnesses, fittings, and illuminators are designed and manufactured by us in our dedicated factory. Past projects include The Crown Jewels, Tutankhamun's tomb, Westminster Abbey, Art Gallery of Ontario, The Victoria and Albert Museum, Bob Bullock Texas State History Museum, and many more. USA & Canada Sales: 941-343-8454, jim@universal-fibre-optics.com; International Sales: konrad@universal-fibre-optics.com, ctait@universal-fibre-optics.com.

Personnel:
Jim Ashley-Down (USA & Canada Sales (USA & UK based))
Konrad Moller (International Sales (UK based))
Calum Tait (International Sales (UK based))
Rob Bowey (Managing Director (USA & UK based))

Modeling & Casting

BONE CLONES, INC.
21416 Chase St., Unit #1
Canoga Park, CA USA 91304
Tel: 818-709-7991 & 800-914-0091 (toll-free in USA); FAX: 818-709-7993
E-mail: museum@boneclones.com
Web Site: www.boneclones.com

Type of Business:
Manufacturer of Bone Clones®, we specialize in molding and casting of human and animal skulls and skeletons, ranging from fossils to modern. Our current catalog of over 1,500 specimens offers a wide selection to Museums and Universities for exhibits and display, including Neaderthal, human and primate skeletons. Our high quality resins capture the best original detail. Bone Clones® catalog can be ordered or found on our website.

Personnel:
David Kronen (R&D & Operations)
Gita Newman (Office & Public Relations)

DORFMAN
MUSEUM FIGURES, INC.

DORFMAN MUSEUM FIGURES, INC.
6224 Holabird Ave.
Baltimore, MD 21224
Tel: 800-634-4873 & 410-284-3248; FAX: 410-284-3249
E-mail: info@museumfigures.com
Web Site: www.museumfigures.com

Type of Business:
We've been standing still for 50 years! Dorfman is the leader in creating lifelike, life-size human figures, and ETHAFOAM™ Conservation Forms. Choose non-ident, generic realistic figures with rigid or flexible foam bodies, or recognizable historic characters for your exhibit needs. Or choose from our line of Conservation Forms, Dress or Suit Forms, and Hangers for your archival display and storage needs. Dorfman Museum Figures, Inc. has been in business since 1957. Our Museum Figures and Conservation Forms are used in museums internationally.

Personnel:
Robert Dorfman (President)
Penny Clifton (Project Manager)

TAYLOR STUDIOS, INC.
1320 Harmon Drive
Rantoul, IL 61866
Tel: 217-893-4874 & 800-707-2047; FAX: 217-893-1998
E-mail: sales@taylorstudios.com
Web Site: www.taylorstudios.com/omd

Type of Business:
"Taylor Studios, Inc. is an interpretive planning, exhibit design, and fabrication firm that assists museums and other clients in creating exhibits that are educational, creative, and enduring. We are committed to completing exhibits to the fulfillment of each client's unique needs, timelines, and goals. Our exhibit creativity is built on a firm interpretive foundation. Our team has the experience and talent to coordinate, communicate, research, plan, design, manage, and produce exhibits of the highest quality. We believe in excellent customer service and back our fabricated products with an unprecedented five-year warranty."

Personnel:
Betty Brennan (President)
Kara Vanskike (Marketing Coordinator)

Models & Mannequins

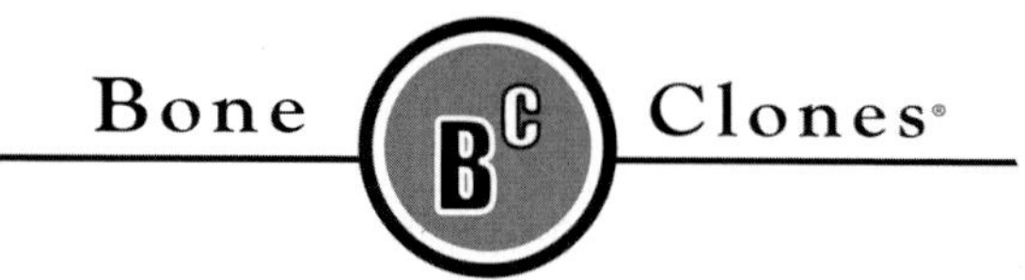

BONE CLONES, INC.
21416 Chase St., Unit #1
Canoga Park, CA USA 91304
Tel: 818-709-7991 & 800-914-0091 (toll-free in USA); FAX: 818-709-7993
E-mail: museum@boneclones.com
Web Site: www.boneclones.com

Type of Business:
Manufacturer of Bone Clones®, we specialize in molding and casting of human and animal skulls and skeletons, ranging from fossils to modern. Our current catalog of over 1,500 specimens offers a wide selection to Museums and Universities for exhibits and display, including Neaderthal, human and primate skeletons. Our high quality resins capture the best original detail. Bone Clones® catalog can be ordered or found on our website.

Personnel:
David Kronen (R&D & Operations)
Gita Newman (Office & Public Relations)

CHASE STUDIO, INC.

CHASE STUDIO, INC.
205 Wolf Creek Rd.
Cedar Creek, MO 65627
Tel: 417-794-3303; FAX: 417-794-3741
E-mail: chasestudio@chasestudio.com
Web Site: www.chasestudio.com

Type of Business:
Designers and builders of natural history and environmental science exhibits; paleontological reconstructions, zoological models, botanical reproductions, dioramas and habitat groups, illustration and mural painting, graphic design, photography, lighting design, fine cabinetwork, taxidermy, research, script writing, exhibit planning and consultation. Exhibits for over 200 museums worldwide since 1973.

Personnel:
Dr. Terry L. Chase (Director)
David F. Darby (Assistant Director Exhibits)
William L. Talbot (Assistant Director Business)
Greg L. Rogers (Assistant Director Operations)

DORFMAN
MUSEUM FIGURES, INC.

DORFMAN MUSEUM FIGURES, INC.
6224 Holabird Ave.
Baltimore, MD 21224
Tel: 800-634-4873 & 410-284-3248; FAX: 410-284-3249
E-mail: info@museumfigures.com
Web Site: www.museumfigures.com

Type of Business:

We've been standing still for 50 years! Dorfman is the leader in creating lifelike, life-size human figures, and ETHAFOAM™ Conservation Forms. Choose non-ident, generic realistic figures with rigid or flexible foam bodies, or recognizable historic characters for your exhibit needs. Or choose from our line of Conservation Forms, Dress or Suit Forms, and Hangers for your archival display and storage needs. Dorfman Museum Figures, Inc. has been in business since 1957. Our Museum Figures and Conservation Forms are used in museums internationally.

Personnel:
Robert Dorfman (President)
Penny Clifton (Project Manager)

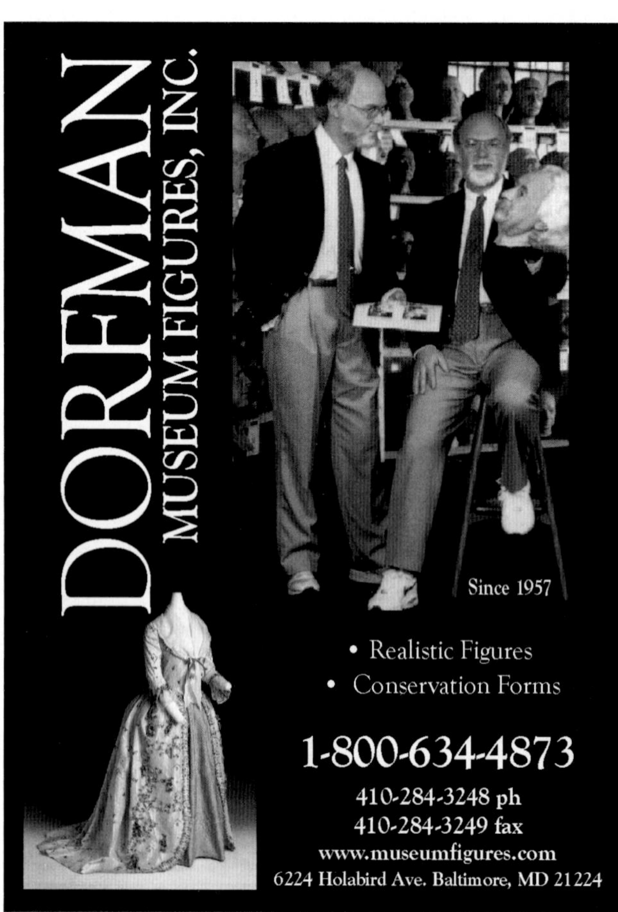

www.safariltd.com

SAFARI LIMITED
1400 N.W. 159 St., Ste. 104
Miami Gardens, FL 33169
Tel: 800-554-5414; FAX: 305-621-6894
E-mail: sales@safariltd.com
Web Site: www.safariltd.com

Type of Business:

For over 25 years, Safari Ltd. has been a leading manufacturer of innovative, educational toys that are inspired by nature and fuel our children's imaginations. Our goal is to enrich the lives of children by providing enduring and captivating toys which are a great value for the money. One of Safari's strengths lies in our licenses with the Carnegie Museum of Natural History and the Monterey Bay Aquarium. These 2 licenses have helped to make the Safari brand known worldwide and have established us as a leading company in the manufacture of museum-quality replicas. Safari does not just sell plastic, we sell imagination, and because we care about our children and the environment, our replicas are phthalate-free. Phthalates are softening agents added to PVC plastics and have been banned in the U.S., Japan and Europe. We provide 5-language educational information with all our replicas to stimulate children's interest in the animal kingdom and the environment. Visit our website at www.safariltd.com to view all our replica collections. We guarantee you will not be disappointed.

Personnel:
Ramona Pariente (President)

TAYLOR STUDIOS, INC.
1320 Harmon Drive
Rantoul, IL 61866
Tel: 217-893-4874 & 800-707-2047; FAX: 217-893-1998
E-mail: sales@taylorstudios.com
Web Site: www.taylorstudios.com/omd

Type of Business:

"Taylor Studios, Inc. is an interpretive planning, exhibit design, and fabrication firm that assists museums and other clients in creating exhibits that are educational, creative, and enduring. We are committed to completing exhibits to the fulfillment of each client's unique needs, timelines, and goals. Our exhibit creativity is built on a firm interpretive foundation. Our team has the experience and talent to coordinate, communicate, research, plan, design, manage, and produce exhibits of the highest quality. We believe in excellent customer service and back our fabricated products with an unprecedented five-year warranty."

Personnel:
Betty Brennan (President)
Kara Vanskike (Marketing Coordinator)

Murals

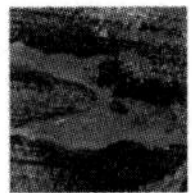
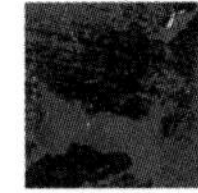
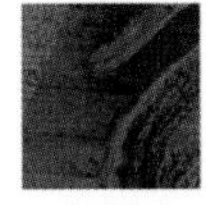
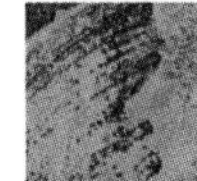

ADIRONDACK
STUDIOS

ADIRONDACK STUDIOS
439 County Rte. 45, Ste. 1
Argyle, NY 12809
Tel: 518-638-8000; FAX: 518-638-8238
E-mail: sales@adkstudios.com
Web Site: www.adkstudios.com

Type of Business:
Adirondack Studios is a full service company serving the museum and entertainment markets. For over thirty years, Adirondack has been providing custom environments and specialty exhibits to customers around the world. Adirondack is poised to participate in all phases and at all levels of project development, specialty fabrication and implementation.

Personnel:
Carl H. Zutz (Sales Manager)
Michael Blau (Creative Director)
Maurice O'Connell (Museum Sales)

CHASE STUDIO, INC.

CHASE STUDIO, INC.
205 Wolf Creek Rd.
Cedar Creek, MO 65627
Tel: 417-794-3303; FAX: 417-794-3741
E-mail: chasestudio@chasestudio.com
Web Site: www.chasestudio.com

Type of Business:
Designers and builders of natural history and environmental science exhibits; paleontological reconstructions, zoological models, botanical reproductions, dioramas and habitat groups, illustration and mural painting, graphic design, photography, lighting design, fine cabinetwork, taxidermy, research, script writing, exhibit planning and consultation. Exhibits for over 200 museums worldwide since 1973.

Personnel:
Dr. Terry L. Chase (Director)
David F. Darby (Assistant Director Exhibits)
William L. Talbot (Assistant Director Business)
Greg L. Rogers (Assistant Director Operations)

OLSON VISUAL, INC.
13000 Weber Way
Hawthorne, CA 90250
Tel: 800-480-6643; FAX: 310-263-6980
E-mail: graphics@olsonvisual.com
Web Site: www.olsonvisual.com

Type of Business:
Olson Visual has been a supplier of large format graphics to museums for over 50 years and is committed to providing superior service from start to finish. We have dedicated an entire segment of the business to Museum and Fine Art projects and take pride in supplying our clientele with quality custom pieces. OV will evaluate your needs and give recommendations on a combination of output and display possibilities. Our team of Museum Consultants can also help you integrate green materials into your projects wherever possible, while still maintaining the integrity of your design concept. Call us and inquire about your next project.

Personnel:
Daniel Olson (Vice President)
Eder Cetina (Creative Director/ Museum Consultant)
Ashleigh Turner (Project Manager/Museum Consultant)

Structural Panels

PANELOCK SYSTEMS LIMITED
129 Church St., Ste. 516
New Haven, CT 06510
Tel: 203-643-2060 & 877-315-1998 (toll free)
E-mail: sales@panelock.com
Web Site: www.panelock.com

Type of Business:
Designers and manufacturers of the Panelock patented range of movable display walls for permanent and temporary exhibition spaces.

Personnel:
Maureen Moreau

Theming

TAYLOR STUDIOS, INC.
1320 Harmon Drive
Rantoul, IL 61866
Tel: 217-893-4874 & 800-707-2047; FAX: 217-893-1998
E-mail: sales@taylorstudios.com
Web Site: www.taylorstudios.com/omd

Type of Business:
"Taylor Studios, Inc. is an interpretive planning, exhibit design, and fabrication firm that assists museums and other clients in creating exhibits that are educational, creative, and enduring. We are committed to completing exhibits to the fulfillment of each client's unique needs, timelines, and goals. Our exhibit creativity is built on a firm interpretive foundation. Our team has the experience and talent to coordinate, communicate, research, plan, design, manage, and produce

(Continued on next page)

(Continued from previous page)

exhibits of the highest quality. We believe in excellent customer service and back our fabricated products with an unprecedented five-year warranty."

Personnel:
Betty Brennan (President)
Kara Vanskike (Marketing Coordinator)

Traveling Exhibitions

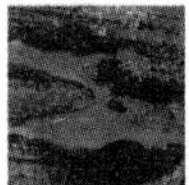

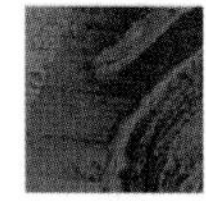
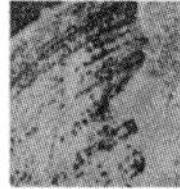

ADIRONDACK
▪ STUDIOS ▪

ADIRONDACK STUDIOS
439 County Rte. 45, Ste. 1
Argyle, NY 12809
Tel: 518-638-8000; FAX: 518-638-8238
E-mail: sales@adkstudios.com
Web Site: www.adkstudios.com

Type of Business:
Adirondack Studios is a full service company serving the museum and entertainment markets. For over thirty years, Adirondack has been providing custom environments and specialty exhibits to customers around the world. Adirondack is poised to participate in all phases and at all levels of project development, specialty fabrication and implementation.

Personnel:
Carl H. Zutz (Sales Manager)
Michael Blau (Creative Director)
Maurice O'Connell (Museum Sales)

ART SERVICES INTERNATIONAL
1319 Powhatan St.
Alexandria, VA 22314
Tel: 703-548-4554; FAX: 703-548-3305
E-mail: info@ASIexhibitions.org
Web Site: www.ASIexhibitions.org

Type of Business:
Art Services International is a nonprofit educational institution that organizes and circulates fine art exhibitions of the highest quality to museums in the United States and abroad. These exhibitions, drawn from sources throughout the world, cover a wide range of artistic topics and vary in scope from large, all-inclusive showings with popular appeal to small, intensive explorations of scholarly subjects. From the conception of an exhibition, ASI arranges the loans, schedules the tour, seeks funding to reduce participation fees, produces an all-color scholarly catalogue, administers insurance, supplies publicity and educational materials, and oversees packing, transportation, and safety of the works of art.

Personnel:
Lynn K. Rogerson (Director & CEO)
Douglas Shawn (Deputy Director, Exhibitions)
Liz Beirise (Manager, Publications & Public Relations)
Meredith Cain (Registrar)

DESIGN ▲ BUILD ▲ MANAGE

CHICAGO SCENIC STUDIOS, INC.
1315 N. North Branch St.
Chicago, IL 60642
Tel: 312-274-9900; FAX: 312-274-9901
E-mail: info@chicagoscenic.com
Web Site: www.chicagoscenic.com

Type of Business:
Chicago Scenic Studios provides museums, science & technology centers, zoos, aquariums and visitor centers more than 30 years of multi-disciplinary experience in themed environment engineering, design, fabrication, and installation. Our highly skilled staff of project managers, designers, carpenters, painters, electricians, and specialists in metals, plastics and fabrics partner with your team to provide safe, educational, immersive environments and exciting experiences through custom exhibits, retail, restaurant, and admission spaces. Chicago Scenic can serve as a general contractor, fabricator or project manager in support of your design or ours. Our background in exhibits, retail, theater, amusements, special events and corporate spaces provides us with the ability to cater to differing needs in unique spaces. We have enjoyed partnering with world-class institutions such as: The Chicago Museum of Science & Industry, The Notebaert Nature Museum, The Field Museum of Natural History, The Shedd Aquarium, Chicago History Museum, Kohl's Children's Museum and many more to bring numerous exciting, educational, and successful stories to life. We'd like to help tell your story as well.

Personnel:
Robert Doepel (President)
Jim Notarianni (Business Development)

EVERGREEN EXHIBITIONS
3737 Broadway, Ste. 100
San Antonio, TX 78209
Tel: 210-582-0015; FAX: 210-590-1071
E-mail: christi@evergreenexhibitions.com
Web Site: www.evergreenexhibitions.com

Type of Business:
Evergreen Exhibitions offers traveling exhibitions and services including comprehensive development, production, venue booking, installation and tour maintenance, serving more than 200 natural history museums, science centers and art museums worldwide. Traveling exhibitions include Leonardo da Vinci Machines in Motion; Brain; Extreme Deep; Genome; Inside Africa; Microbes; Robot Zoo; Space; Vatican Splendors; The Enemy Within (created by International Spy Museum), and PLAY!

Personnel:
Mark Greenberg (President)
Anne Kinsey (Vice President Exhibitions)
Christi Klingelhefer (Venue Sales Manager)

GARNER HOLT PRODUCTIONS, INC.
825 E. Cooley Ave.
San Bernardino, CA 92408
Tel: 909-799-3030, ext. 229; FAX: 909-799-7351
E-mail: jvanmeter@garnerholt.com
Web Site: www.garnerholt.com

Type of Business:
Garner Holt Productions, Inc. creates custom, high quality animatronics figures, themed environments and special effects. We are a full service company, offering concept design through installation. The company maintains a large library of molds, which includes realistic, life-size animals and human figures. Garner Holt Productions also provides traveling exhibits, including Backyard Monsters which feature gigantic robot insects, interactive displays and an insect collection endorsed by the American Entomological Society.

(Continued on next page)

(Continued from previous page)

Personnel:
Garner Holt (President)
Jody Van Meter (Vice President, Marketing & Sales)
Philip Previtire (Director, Scenic Production)
Michelle Berg (Vice President Administration)

GOPPION MUSEUM WORKSHOP, INC.
300 Linwood Ave.
Newton, MA 02460
Tel: 617-297-2546; FAX: 617-848-2641
E-mail: info@goppion-us.com
Web Site: www.goppion.com

Type of Business:
Established in 1952, Goppion SpA is one of the world's premier fabricators of high performance steel and glass display cases for museums, archives, libraries and other similar cultural institutions. Goppion does not offer a standard line of casework, nor do we have stock profiles and components from which to fabricate our work. Rather, we collaboratively develop the engineering and design in response to the performance, aesthetic, schedule, and budget requirements of your project.

Personnel:
Ted Paschkis (Director, Operations, U.S.)
Peter Hohenstatt (Commercial Manager, Goppion SpA (U.S.))

KUBIK
1680 Mattawa Ave.
Mississauga, ON, Canada L4X 3A5
Tel: 877-252-2818; FAX: 905-272-2120
E-mail: info@thinkubik.com
Web Site: www.thinkubik.com

Type of Business:
For over 25 years, kubik has been a global company providing clients with the most extraordinary experience in the world. We offer a full range of museum services including project development, management, fabrication, interactive exhibit, media and software development, artifact mounting, custom showcase systems and graphic production of both permanent and temporary exhibits for museums, visitor centers and World's Fair Pavilions. Additional Locations: Europe, Plotterstraat 1, 1033 RX, Amsterdam, The Netherlands Tel.: +31 20 581 3030; Fax: +31 20 581 3031; New Jersey, 708 Fellowship Road, Mount Laurel, NJ 08054-1004 Tel.: 1.856.234.0052; Fax: 1.856.234.0760.

Personnel:
Sam Kohn (President & CEO)
Elliot Kohn (COO & Principal)

LORD CULTURAL RESOURCES
43 West 24th Street, 10th Fl.
New York, NY 10010
Tel: 646-375-2500; FAX: 212-675-4763
E-mail: info@lord.ca
Web Site: www.lord.ca

Type of Business:
Founded in 1981 in response to an emerging need for specialized planning services in the museum, cultural and heritage sector, Lord Cultural Resources is dedicated to creating cultural capital through visioning, planning and implementation. We work with museums, large and small, helping them to maximize their cultural capital by engaging with their communities, improving their buildings and inspiring collaboration and learning. We have benefited clients through the entire spectrum of cultural services including master plans, business plans, strategic plans, facility plans, functional programs, architect selection, exhibition design and development, project management, retail plans and cultural plans. In addition, Lord Cultural Resources has made a definitive contribution to the development of museum planning through its pioneering publications. The firm also has a San Francisco location.

Personnel:
Gail Dexter Lord (Co-President)
Barry Lord (Co-President)
Maria Piacente (Vice President, Exhibitions)
Catharine Tanner (Vice President, Facility Planning)
Paul Alezraa (Vice President, Europe)
Amy Kaufman (Managing Director, U.S.)
Brad King (Director, Management Consulting, Principal)
Margaret May (Senior Principal)
Ted Silberberg (Senior Principal)
Joy Bailey (Senior Consultant)
Lindsay Martin (Senior Consultant)
Andrea Ott (Director, Client Relations & Marketing)

MALTBIE - A KUBIK COMPANY
708 Fellowship Rd.
Mount Laurel, NJ 08054
Tel: 856-234-0052; FAX: 856-234-0760
E-mail: info@maltbie.com
Web Site: www.maltbie.com

Type of Business:
For more than 45 years, Maltbie has focused on developing its ability to produce industry-leading permanent museum exhibitions and memorable visitor experiences. Our portfolio of over 290 international installations includes work in interpretive history, interactive science, and children's museums. Today we offer state-of-the-art facilities in the US and Canada, providing services that include project development, management, fabrication, interactive exhibit, media and software development, artifact mounting, custom showcase systems and graphic production. Additional Locations: Canada, 1680 Mattawa Avenue, Mississauga, Ontario L4X 3A5 Tel.: 1.877.252.2818; FAX: 1.905.272.2120. Europe: Plotterstraat 1, 1033 RX, Amsterdam, The Netherlands Tel.: +31 20 581 3030; Fax: +31 20 581 3031.

Personnel:
Charles M. Maltbie, Jr. (President)
Sam Kohn (CEO)
Gary Brooks (Executive Vice President)
Curt Cederquist (Vice President Museum Sales)

QUATREFOIL ASSOCIATES, INC.

29 C St.
Laurel, MD 20707
Tel: 301-470-4748; FAX: 301-470-4749
E-mail: info@quatrefoil.com
Web Site: www.quatrefoil.com

Type of Business:

Quatrefoil creates engaging museum experiences that educate, inspire and amuse the visitor and reflect the essence of our client's vision and values. We deliver a full spectrum of expertise, applied with artistic and technical excellence - museum planning, exhibit design, content development, graphics, interactives, multimedia, custom electronics, fabrication and installation. West Coast Design Studio, 1524 Cloverfield Blvd., Ste. A, Santa Monica, CA 90404. Tel.: 310-829-9390.

Personnel:

Abbie Chessler (Design Director & Founding Partner)
Paula Schuman (Founding Partner & CFO)
Ernie Falcone (Founding Partner & Technical Director)
Paul DeCamp (COO & Partner)

SMITH KRAMER TRAVELING EXHIBITIONS

1622 Westport Rd.
Kansas City, MO 64111
Tel: 800-222-7522; FAX: 816-756-3779
E-mail: skexhibit@smithkramer.com
Web Site: www.smithkramer.com

Type of Business:

Smith Kramer is a full service traveling exhibition company that partners with museums, curators, and private collectors to promote, budget, crate, insure, transport and manage all services of the exhibition from concept to completion. Since 1981 Smith Kramer has provided over 100 quality exhibitions to the national museum community. Smith Kramer also provides tour management services for fully curated and marketed exhibitions; we also design and construct crates for national and international travel. Please visit our website at www.smithkramer.com or contact us at 800-222-7522 if you have any questions or if you discover an exhibition that fits the needs of your museum schedule and audience.

Personnel:

Karen Grossi (President & CFO)
Becca Bruce (Registrar)
Kaci Schroeder (Graphics Designer)
Jorge Garcia (Preparator)
Jamie Sanders (Preparator)
Anne Chiarelli Jones (Director, Exhibition Development)

GRAPHIC DESIGN/PUBLISHING-GENERAL

THE CREATIVE COMPANY, INC.
1082 St. Moritz
Lawrenceburg, IN 47025
Tel: 812-537-5731; FAX: 800-762-1623
E-mail: creativebooks@comcast.net
Web Site: www.creativesitebooks.com

Type of Business:
Publisher of custom "site specific" guide books, souvenir books, Educational workbooks and children's discovery books for museums, aquariums, zoos, historical sites, national parks, conservatories and historic homes.

Personnel:
Richard L. Ruehrwein (Director, Product Development & Marketing)

LYONS/ZAREMBA INC.
4 Faneuil Hall Marketplace
Boston, MA 02109
Tel: 617-248-0970; FAX: 617-248-0994
E-mail: info@lyonszaremba.com
Web Site: www.lyonszaremba.com

Type of Business:
Lyons/Zaremba Inc. is an internationally recognized firm with extensive experience in planning, designing and managing exhibits for museums, visitor centers, nature centers, aquariums and zoos. Our services include: feasibility analysis; master planning; concept development; facility programming; content research and development; graphic design and production; exhibit design and documentation; media software design; and construction administration. Our goal is to create special places where people come to explore, discover and learn in exciting multi-sensorial ways through exhibits that are accessible, enjoyable, and meaningful for visitors of diverse ages, learning styles, and cultural backgrounds. We welcome your visit to our web site, or call us to learn more.

Personnel:
Frank Zaremba (Principal)
Steve Lenox (Principal)
Rosanne Gregory (Business Manager)
Michael Shackelford (Exhibit Designer)
James Wertheimer (Exhibit Designer)
Julia Misiewicz (Exhibit Designer)
Christina Yung (Graphic Designer)

SUNRISE SYSTEM, INC.
720 Washington St.
Pembroke, MA 02359
Tel: 781-826-9706; FAX: 781-826-0061
E-mail: sales@sunrisesystems.com
Web Site: www.sunrisesystems.com

Type of Business:
Sunrise Systems, Inc. is a manufacturer of custom LED signage. Founded in 1976, Sunrise has been a lifelong producer of fascinating public art, first-in-the-industry technological advances and uniquely tailored information systems. Our LED displays are installed in countries all over the world and in industries across the map. Transit system integrators, stock tickers, retail applications and academic exhibits are just a few well-established areas of Sunrise's expertise. Past installments are prominently featured in many permanent exhibits at prestigious museums around the globe. Our ability to meet even the most complex architectural, electrical and mechanical requirements keeps us at the forefront of the industry. A dedication to innovative technology and customer support make us a good place to start planning your next LED display project.

Personnel:
Henry C. Appleton (President, Director Sales)
Eric Harrington (Director, Engineering)
Kaleb Christenson (Marketing Director & Project Manager)

Exhibit Graphics

DESIGN AND PRODUCTION INCORPORATED
7110 Rainwater Place
Lorton, VA 22079
Tel: 703-550-8640; FAX: 703-339-0296
E-mail: dmoalli@d-and-p.com
Web Site: www.d-and-p.com

Type of Business:
In service to the museum community since 1949, our global portfolio is comprised of hundreds of high-profile projects, including interpretive history, interactive science, sports, children's museums, and immersive environments. D&P specializes in large-scale, multi-discipline exhibit projects, with a full complement of in-house production capabilities: Project development and management, custom fabrication, interactive exhibits, A/V hardware and software development, artifact mounting, graphic production, installation, and service. D&P is FSC-certified and a charter member of USGBC.

Personnel:
Jay Barnwell (President)
Dan Moalli (Vice President Business Development)
Donna Kuba (Project Director)
Rachel Childress (Marketing Associate)

haleysharpedesign

HALEY SHARPE DESIGN
116 Spadina Ave., Ste. 201
Toronto, ON, Canada M5V 2K6
Tel: 416-361-3338; FAX: 416-361-3588
E-mail: info@haleysharpe.com
Web Site: www.haleysharpe.com

Type of Business:
Haley Sharpe Design's graphic designers can provide a wide range of custom services in response to clients' needs. Specializing in branding, wayfinding, identification signage, and interpretive graphics, Haley Sharpe Design will oversee your graphic projects from conceptualization to installation.

Personnel:
Jan Faulkner (Creative Director)
Nicole Mackereth (Business Development Consultant)

OLSON VISUAL, INC.
13000 Weber Way
Hawthorne, CA 90250
Tel: 800-480-6643; FAX: 310-263-6980
E-mail: graphics@olsonvisual.com
Web Site: www.olsonvisual.com

Type of Business:

Olson Visual has been a supplier of large format graphics to museums for over 50 years and is committed to providing superior service from start to finish. We have dedicated an entire segment of the business to Museum and Fine Art projects and take pride in supplying our clientele with quality custom pieces. OV will evaluate your needs and give recommendations on a combination of output and display possibilities. Our team of Museum Consultants can also help you integrate green materials into your projects wherever possible, while still maintaining the integrity of your design concept. Call us and inquire about your next project.

Personnel:
Daniel Olson (Vice President)
Eder Cetina (Creative Director/ Museum Consultant)
Ashleigh Turner (Project Manager/Museum Consultant)

UJMN ARCHITECTS + DESIGNERS
718 Arch St., Ste. 5N
Philadelphia, PA 19106
Tel: 215-440-0190; FAX: 215-440-0197
E-mail: nicholson@ujmn.com; blankin@ujmn.com
Web Site: www.ujmn.com

Type of Business:

Founded in 1967, UJMN Architects + Designers offers architectural design, museum planning, and exhibit design within a single firm, maximizing the integration of exhibits with museum facilities; the effectiveness of cost, schedule, and project management; and ultimately, the quality of the visitor experience. Recent projects include: the Liberty Bell Center Exhibits; the President's House at Independence National Historical Park; the National Civil War Museum Exhibits (Harrisburg, PA); the Louisville Slugger Museum; the Stoogeum; the Joliet Area Historical Museum; Hagley Museum and Library; the National Civil Rights Museum in Mississippi; the Eagles Mere Museum Exhibits, and Historic Deerfield.

Personnel:
Joseph A. Nicholson, AIA, IDSA (Principal)
Stacey Blankin (Associate)

Graphic Design Firms

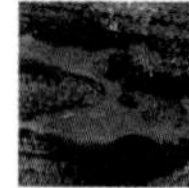  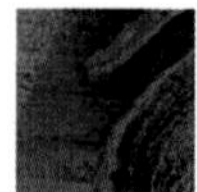 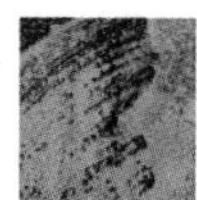

ADIRONDACK
▪ STUDIOS ▪

ADIRONDACK STUDIOS
439 County Rte. 45, Ste. 1
Argyle, NY 12809
Tel: 518-638-8000; FAX: 518-638-8238
E-mail: sales@adkstudios.com
Web Site: www.adkstudios.com

Type of Business:

Adirondack Studios is a full service company serving the museum and entertainment markets. For over thirty years, Adirondack has been providing custom environments and specialty exhibits to customers around the world. Adirondack is poised to participate in all phases and at all levels of project development, specialty fabrication and implementation.

Personnel:
Carl H. Zutz (Sales Manager)
Michael Blau (Creative Director)
Maurice O'Connell (Museum Sales)

museum planning | exhibit design

HILFERTY
14240 State Rte. 550
Athens, OH 45701
Tel: 740-448-3821; FAX: 740-448-2331
E-mail: gha@hilferty.com
Web Site: www.hilferty.com

Type of Business:

For more than thirty years, Hilferty has provided a full range of interpretive services to museums, visitor centers, nature centers, botanical gardens, historic sites, zoos/aquariums, and halls of fame. We excel at interpretive and facility master planning; concept development; content research; label writing; exhibit and graphic design; and providing donor recognition and funding support materials. From social histories to natural sciences, football to physics, presidents to children's gardens, every Hilferty exhibit vividly captures the stories that engage visitors' minds and hearts. Each project is approached with a unique mix of techniques chosen to best bring the subject to life. Our innovative portfolio spans the spectrum of intimate displays of precious objects, captivating immersive environments, enthralling interactive components, and breathtaking theatrical presentations. In short, Hilferty creates memorable museum experiences.

Personnel:
Gerard Hilferty (President & Creative Director)
Dean Clouse (CEO)

JACK ROUSE ASSOCIATES
600 Vine St., Ste. 1700
Cincinnati, OH 45202-1100
Tel: 513-381-0055; FAX: 513-381-2691
E-mail: s.mccoy@jackrouse.com
Web Site: www.jackrouse.com

Type of Business:
Jack Rouse Associates conceives, visualizes and realizes exceptional visitor experiences around the world. Specific services include master planning, exhibit design, media production and project management.

Personnel:
Jack Rouse (CEO)
Keith James (President)
Randy Vuksta (Creative Director)
Shawn McCoy (Vice President Marketing & Business Development)

Mapmaking

MAPCRAFT CUSTOM CARTOGRAPHY
731 Margaret Dr.
Woodstock, IL 60098
Tel: 815-337-7137; FAX: 815-337-7137
E-mail: tomw@mapcraft.com
Web Site: www.mapcraft.com

Type of Business:
High-quality maps, custom-designed by Mapcraft, are among the most attractive, accessible and cost-effective communications tools available to cultural institutions of all sizes. Mapcraft produces suberbly-detailed perspective views, illustrations, cutaway diagrams, and historical recreations for Orientation/Visitors Guides, Exhibits, and Publications. Clients include the Art Institute of Chicago, the National Gallery of Art, Philadelphia Zoo, Winterthur Country Estate, Audubon Society, Morton Arboretum, Illinois Historic Preservation Agency, Missouri Botanic Garden, St. Louis' Forest Park, and Chicago's Millennium Park.

Personnel:
Tom Willcockson (Owner)

Media Design

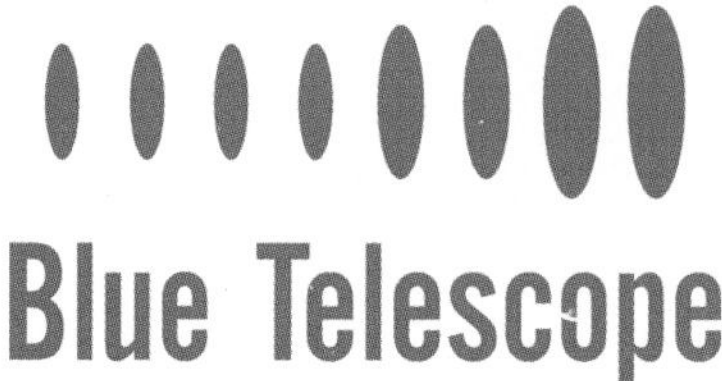

BLUE TELESCOPE
236 W. 30th St., 7th Fl.
New York, NY 10001
Tel: 212-675-7702, ext. 12; FAX: 212-675-7703
E-mail: contact@blue-telescope.com
Web Site: www.blue-telescope.com

Type of Business:
Blue Telescope creates interactive media experiences that educate and communicate. We use rich media to dynamically illustrate complex concepts and data, to create fun, engaging experiences out of challenging content, and to immerse audiences in compelling stories and environments. Blue Telescope uses multi-user technology to facilitate communication among visitors and educators. From competitive and collaborative games, to group content exploration, to live surveys, we create shared experiences that get people talking and engaged.

bpi
imagine. what we do.

BOSTON PRODUCTIONS, INC.
100 Morse St.
Norwood, MA 02062
Tel: 781-255-1555; FAX: 781-255-1556
E-mail: imagine@bostonproductions.com
Web Site: www.bostonproductions.com

Type of Business:
For twenty years, Boston Productions has been telling compelling stories to museum and visitor center audiences across the country through engaging and immersive media exhibits. Always putting the visitor experience first, we continue to surprise, enthrall and inform with uniquely diverse ideas and cutting-edge methods. Our signature AV presentations and interactive visitor experiences require multidisciplinary services and skill sets, such that we are equally expert in media design, content development, production services, software programming, exhibit prototyping and full AV hardware integration services. Knowing what works creatively with today's multigenerational audiences and being able to produce media, interactive exhibits and AV hardware systems with a strong value quotient is an organizational imperative. Boston Productions is truly a creative concept-to-installation business. - imagine. what we do.

Personnel:
Bob Noll (President & Creative Director)
Chet Kaplan (COO & Director AV Hardware Integration)
Mark Dorgan (Associate Creative Director)

CORTINA
PRODUCTIONS

CORTINA PRODUCTIONS, INC.
6623-A Old Dominion Dr.
McLean, VA 22101
Tel: 703-556-8481; FAX: 703-847-9694
E-mail: jim@cortinaproductions.com
Web Site: www.cortinaproductions.com

Type of Business:
We are media designers and storytellers; crafters of image and light, sound and touch. From theater experiences, to large format multi-screen presentations, to engaging interactive exhibits and videos, we produce award-winning media exhibits that educate, entertain, and inspire. From initial concept development through final post-production, we collaborate with you to blend story and technology into a single artistic vision.

Personnel:
Joseph Cortina (President)
Amy Maddox (Vice President Production)

Production

KUBIK
1680 Mattawa Ave.
Mississauga, ON, Canada L4X 3A5
Tel: 877-252-2818; FAX: 905-272-2120
E-mail: info@thinkubik.com
Web Site: www.thinkubik.com

Type of Business:
For over 25 years, kubik has been a global company providing clients with the most extraordinary experience in the world. We offer a full range of museum services including project development, management, fabrication, interactive exhibit, media and software development, artifact mounting, custom showcase systems and graphic production of both permanent and temporary exhibits for museums, visitor centers and World's Fair Pavilions. Additional Locations: Europe, Plotterstraat 1, 1033 RX, Amsterdam, The Netherlands Tel.: +31 20 581 3030; Fax: +31 20 581 3031; New Jersey, 708 Fellowship Road, Mount Laurel, NJ 08054-1004 Tel.: 1.856.234.0052; Fax: 1.856.234.0760.

Personnel:
Sam Kohn (President & CEO)
Elliot Kohn (COO & Principal)

LYONS/ZAREMBA INC.
4 Faneuil Hall Marketplace
Boston, MA 02109
Tel: 617-248-0970; FAX: 617-248-0994
E-mail: info@lyonszaremba.com
Web Site: www.lyonszaremba.com

Type of Business:
Lyons/Zaremba Inc. is an internationally recognized firm with extensive experience in planning, designing and managing exhibits for museums, visitor centers, nature centers, aquariums and zoos. Our services include: feasibility analysis; master planning; concept development; facility programming; content research and development; graphic design and production; exhibit design and documentation; media software design; and construction administration. Our goal is to create special places where people come to explore, discover and learn in exciting multi-sensorial ways through exhibits that are accessible, enjoyable, and meaningful for visitors of diverse ages, learning styles, and cultural backgrounds. We welcome your visit to our web site, or call us to learn more.

Personnel:
Frank Zaremba (Principal)
Steve Lenox (Principal)
Rosanne Gregory (Business Manager)
Michael Shackelford (Exhibit Designer)
James Wertheimer (Exhibit Designer)
Julia Misiewicz (Exhibit Designer)
Christina Yung (Graphic Designer)

MALTBIE - A KUBIK COMPANY
708 Fellowship Rd.
Mount Laurel, NJ 08054
Tel: 856-234-0052; FAX: 856-234-0760
E-mail: info@maltbie.com
Web Site: www.maltbie.com

Type of Business:
For more than 45 years, Maltbie has focused on developing its ability to produce industry-leading permanent museum exhibitions and memorable visitor experiences. Our portfolio of over 290 international installations includes work in interpretive history, interactive science, and children's museums. Today we offer state-of-the-art facilities in the US and Canada, providing services that include project development, management, fabrication, interactive exhibit, media and software development, artifact mounting, custom showcase systems and graphic production. Additional Locations: Canada, 1680 Mattawa Avenue, Mississauga, Ontario L4X 3A5 Tel.: 1.877.252.2818; FAX: 1.905.272.2120. Europe: Plotterstraat 1, 1033 RX, Amsterdam, The Netherlands Tel.: +31 20 581 3030; Fax: +31 20 581 3031.

Personnel:
Charles M. Maltbie, Jr. (President)
Sam Kohn (CEO)
Gary Brooks (Executive Vice President)
Curt Cederquist (Vice President Museum Sales)

Publishing & Distribution Services

AMERICAN ASSOCIATION OF MUSEUMS
1575 Eye St., N.W., Suite 400
Washington, DC 20005-1105
Tel: 202-289-1818; FAX: 202-289-6578
Web Site: www.aam-us.org

Type of Business:
The American Association of Museums (AAM) has been a leader of the museum community since 1906, developing and establishing standards and best practices, gathering and sharing knowledge and advocating on issues of concern to all museums. Dedicated to ensuring that museums remain a vital part of the American landscape, Moreover, AAM is the only organization serving the interests of the broad scope of the museum field, serving those who work for and with museums, representing some 20,000 museum professionals and volunteers, 3,000 institutions and 300 corporate members. AAM members span the range of museum vocations, from directors to volunteers and every profession in between.

Personnel:
John Strand (Editor & Publisher)

MARKETING-GENERAL

Marketing

ConsultEcon, Inc.

Economic and Management Consultants

CONSULTECON, INC.
545 Concord Ave., Ste. 210
Cambridge, MA 02138
Tel: 617-547-0100; FAX: 617-547-0102
E-mail: info@consultecon.com
Web Site: www.consultecon.com

Type of Business:
ConsultEcon, Inc. provides services to clients in the areas of project and plan concept development, market and financial evaluation, visitor surveys, economic impact and project implementation. We are dedicated to serving museums of all sizes and types, and have worked over many years with clients responding to a broad spectrum of issues, ranging from the economics of operations to strategic planning.

Personnel:
Thomas J. Martin (President)
Robert E. Brais (Vice President)
Elena Kazlas (Principal)
Jason Drebitko (Senior Associate)

development, management, marketing

SCHULTZ & WILLIAMS, INC.
325 Chestnut St., Ste. 700
Philadelphia, PA 19106
Tel: 215-625-9955; FAX: 215-625-2701
E-mail: mail@schultzwilliams.com
Web Site: www.schultzwilliams.com

Type of Business:
Founded in 1987, Schultz & Williams is a national consulting firm specializing in development, marketing, management, and direct response services for nonprofit organizations. We consistently meet our clients' needs in traditional areas of development—capital campaign feasibility and planning studies, annual funds, major gifts and Board development—and with cost-effective direct response and multi-channel marketing campaigns that promote, build and sustain family membership and annual giving programs. Learn more at www.schultzwilliams.com or call 215-625-9955.

Personnel:
L. Scott Schultz (President)
M. Jane Williams (Partner)
Jessica Harrington (Vice President S & W Direct)
Dell Fascione (Vice President Marketing)
Shirley Trauger (Vice President)

MUSEUM RESOURCES/TECHNICAL INFORMATION-GENERAL

AMERICAN ASSOCIATION OF MUSEUMS
1575 Eye St., N.W., Suite 400
Washington, DC 20005-1105
Tel: 202-289-1818; FAX: 202-289-6578
Web Site: www.aam-us.org

Type of Business:
The American Association of Museums (AAM) has been a leader of the museum community since 1906, developing and establishing standards and best practices, gathering and sharing knowledge and advocating on issues of concern to all museums. Dedicated to ensuring that museums remain a vital part of the American landscape, Moreover, AAM is the only organization serving the interests of the broad scope of the museum field, serving those who work for and with museums, representing some 20,000 museum professionals and volunteers, 3,000 institutions and 300 corporate members. AAM members span the range of museum vocations, from directors to volunteers and every profession in between.

Personnel:
John Strand (Editor & Publisher)

Lighting Services Inc 

LIGHTING SERVICES INC
2 Kay Fries Dr.
Stony Point, NY 10980
Tel: 800-999-9574 & 845-942-2800; FAX: 845-942-2177
E-mail: Sales@mailLSI.com
Web Site: www.LightingServicesInc.com

Type of Business:
Lighting Services Inc (LSI) is the leading independent manufacturer of track, accent, display and LED lighting systems for museum environments. Since 1958, LSI has been dedicated to designing, engineering and manufacturing lighting fixtures of the highest quality. Our reputation for creativity and innovative design, coupled with specification grade products and intelligent personalized service, has made us the manufacturer of choice amongst the most discriminating specifiers of lighting for museums and galleries.

Personnel:
Daniel Gelman (President)

Associations

AMERICAN ASSOCIATION OF MUSEUMS
1575 Eye St., N.W., Suite 400
Washington, DC 20005-1105
Tel: 202-289-1818; FAX: 202-289-6578
Web Site: www.aam-us.org

Type of Business:
The American Association of Museums (AAM) has been a leader of the museum community since 1906, developing and establishing standards and best practices, gathering and sharing knowledge and advocating on issues of concern to all museums. Dedicated to ensuring that museums remain a vital part of the American landscape, Moreover, AAM is the only organization serving the interests of the broad scope of the museum field, serving those who work for and with museums, representing some 20,000 museum professionals and volunteers, 3,000 institutions and 300 corporate members. AAM members span the range of museum vocations, from directors to volunteers and every profession in between.

Personnel:
John Strand (Editor & Publisher)

NEW ENGLAND MUSEUM ASSOCIATION
22 Mill St., #409
Arlington, MA 02476
Tel: 781-641-0013; FAX: 781-641-0053
E-mail: nema@tiac.net
Web Site: www.nemanet.org

Personnel:
Katheryn P. Viens (Executive Director)
BJ Larson (Deputy Director)
Jane Coughlin (Operations Manager & Membership Coordinator)
Heather Riggs (Publications Manager & Corporate Member Services)

Auctioneers & Liquidators

CHRISTIE'S
20 Rockefeller Plaza
New York, NY 10020
Tel: 212-636-2620; FAX: 212-636-2370
E-mail: awhiting@christies.com
Web Site: www.christies.com

Type of Business:
Christie's is available to assist museums in a variety of areas including: appraising collections, objects and bequests and establishing values for loans; managing sales of major objects and minor collections; and consulting on buying and selling at auction. We welcome collector circle visits, and our specialists are available for participation in lectures, symposia and scholarly talks.

Personnel:
Allison Whiting (Senior Vice President & Director Museum Services)

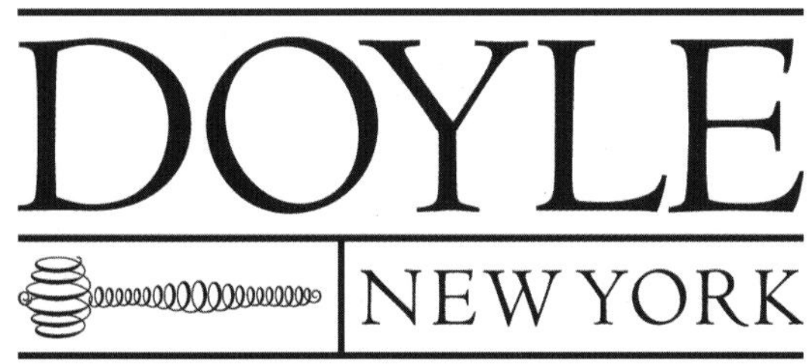

DOYLE NEW YORK
Auctioneers & Appraisers
175 E. 87th St.
New York, NY 10128
Tel: 212-427-2730; FAX: 212-369-0892
E-mail: info@DoyleNewYork.com
Web Site: www.DoyleNewYork.com

Type of Business:

Doyle New York is one of the world's foremost auctioneers and appraisers of fine art, jewelry, furniture, decorations, books, manuscripts, prints and a variety of other categories. Headquartered in New York City, the global capital of the auction market, Doyle offers approximately forty sales each year that attract a broad base of buyers and consignors from around the world. Doyle New York regularly works with prominent museums and distinguished institutions, providing individualized appraisal and auction services for collections of all sizes. Museums, universities, libraries and other institutions rely on Doyle New York's experience and expertise in handling all aspects of the auction process with discretion, from the initial call through the final settlement.

Personnel:

Kathleen M. Doyle (Chairman & CEO)
Joanne Porrino Mournet (Executive Vice President, Appraisals & Consignments)
David A. Gallager (Director, Museum Services)

LH LESLIE HINDMAN AUCTIONEERS

LESLIE HINDMAN AUCTIONEERS
1338 W. Lake St.
Chicago, IL 60607
Tel: 312-280-1212; FAX: 312-280-1211
E-mail: alyssa@lesliehindman.com
Web Site: www.lesliehindman.com

Type of Business:

Leslie Hindman Auctioneers is one of the nation's leading fine art auctioneers and appraisers, holding regularly scheduled auctions of post-war and contemporary art, prints, American and European art, fine furniture, decorative arts, books and manuscripts, fine jewelry and timepieces, Asian works of art and vintage couture and textiles. All auctions attract an international audience through concentrated internet and print marketing efforts, resulting in exceptional prices realized. The auction house's longstanding reputation for excellent service has resulted in ongoing relationships with museums and institutions, who look to Leslie Hindman Auctioneers for a discreet and personalized approach tailored to meet their specific needs.

Personnel:

Leslie Hindman (CEO & President)
Alyssa Quinlan (Director, Museum Services)
Kate Pettenati (Museum Services)

SKINNER

Auctioneers and Appraisers of Antiques and Fine Art

SKINNER, INC.
63 Park Plaza
Boston, MA 02116
Tel: 617-350-5400; FAX: 617-350-5429
E-mail: info@skinnerinc.com
Web Site: www.skinnerinc.com

Type of Business:

Skinner, Inc. is one of the nation's leading auction houses for antiques and fine art and the only major auction house headquartered in New England. With expertise in over 20 specialty collecting areas, Skinner draws the interest of buyers from all over the world and its auctions regularly achieve world record prices. Skinner provides a broad range of auction, appraisal, and deaccession services for museums, educational institutions and nonprofit organizations worldwide. Skinner works one-on-one with museum curators and directors, helping to improve the quality and value of collections. Skinner's flexible, hands-on approach enables it to accept single items, groups, or entire collections — a factor that sets Skinner apart from most other national auction houses. Skinner is widely regarded as one of the most reputable names in the auction business — a factor that is increasingly important in today's highly competitive art and antiques market. Skinner's specialty departments include American Furniture & Decorative Arts, Paintings & Prints, English & Continental Furniture & Decorations, Fine Ceramics, Jewelry, Couture, 20th Century Furniture & Decorative Arts, Fine Musical Instruments, Asian Art, Fine Judaica & Silver, Toys, Dolls & Collectibles, Science & Technology, Oriental Rugs & Carpets, and American Indian & Ethnographic Art.

Personnel:

Karen Keane (CEO/Director, Museum Services)
Tish King (Director, Appraisals)
Catherine Riedel (Director, Marketing & Public Relations)

Sotheby's EST. 1744

SOTHEBY'S
1334 York Ave.
New York, NY 10021
Tel: 212-894-1138; FAX: 212-606-7328
Web Site: www.sothebys.com

Type of Business:

Sotheby's Museum Services Department provides crucial support when selling works at auction. In addition to offering special services to museums regarding the deaccession of property, we also provide insurance evaluations, assistance with auction purchases, special programs for members and fund-raising and support for special projects.

Personnel:

Nina del Rio (Senior Vice President, Director, Museum Services)
Jason Herrick (Museum Services)

SWANN GALLERIES, INC.
104 E. 25th St., 6th Fl.
New York, NY 10010
Tel: 212-254-4710; FAX: 212-979-1017
E-mail: swann@swanngalleries.com
Web Site: www.swanngalleries.com

Type of Business:
Auctioneers and appraisers of rare books, autographs and manuscripts, maps, photographs, prints and drawings, vintage posters, and African-American Fine Art. We conduct 35 or more auctions each year. Catalogues and schedule online. Newsletter with full auction schedule on request. Member International Auctioneers.

Personnel:
George S. Lowry (Chairman)
Nicholas Lowry (President & Principal Auctioneer, Posters)
Caroline Birenbaum (Director, Communications)
Todd Weyman (Prints & Drawings)
Daile Kaplan (Photographs)
Christine Von der Linn (Art & Architecture Books)
Nigel Freeman (African-American Fine Art)

Computer Software

GATEWAY TICKETING SYSTEMS, INC.
315 E. Second St.
Boyertown, PA 19512
Tel: 800-487-8587 & 610-987-4000; FAX: 610-987-4001
E-mail: info@gatewayticketing.com
Web Site: www.gatewayticketing.com

Type of Business:
Gateway Ticketing Systems, Inc. is the world leader in admission control and ticketing software for the cultural, leisure and transportation industries. In business for 21 years, Gateway provides sales, service, and support throughout North America and worldwide. Galaxy, Gateway's revenue management and admission control system, provides a comprehensive solution for museums to control data, revenue and security. They can manage and monitor admissions, events, guest services and retail from one central location, and track sales whenever and wherever they take place. Gateway provides the tools to improve operations efficiency, enhance the guest experience, cut costs and increase sales.

Personnel:
Michael Andre (President & CEO)
Michael A. Furman (Director, Sales & Marketing)

Executive Search Organizations

LORD CULTURAL RECRUITMENT
66 Parker Ave.
San Francisco, CA 94118
Tel: 415-751-2005; FAX: 415-751-1840
E-mail: info@lordculturalrecruitment.com
Web Site: www.lordculturalrecruitment.com

Type of Business:
Lord Cultural Recruitment is your global recruitment partner dedicated exclusively to the museum, cultural and heritage sector. We offer a range of recruitment and human resources services which can be tailored specifically to meet your requirements. Our clients benefit from the years of experience that we bring to the field in recruitment, planning and management. With a highly trained specialist team that can fully understand your organization's critical requirements, we can provide quick, cost-effective and successful human resources, recruitment and training solutions including basic recruitment, executive recruitment, training, managed international advertising, vacancy response handling, HR consultancy, job description preparation, personnel planning, psychometric profiling and more.

Personnel:
Paul Alezraa (Operational Project Director)
Micah Styles (Project Director International Recruitment)
Christina Sjoberg (Recruitment Project Manager)
Ian Duckworth (Operational Project Manager)

MUSEUM MANAGEMENT CONSULTANTS, INC.
120 Green St., Ste. 200
San Francisco, CA 94111
Tel: 415-982-2288; FAX: 415-982-0504
E-mail: mmc@museum-management.com
Web Site: www.museum-management.com

Type of Business:
Museum Management Consultants, Inc. (MMC) specializes in organizational assessment, institutional planning, executive search, audience research, and professional coaching. Founded in 1987 and based in San Francisco, MMC has provided consulting services to over 250 museums and cultural organizations throughout the United States and abroad. MMC helps museums accentuate their strengths, address critical issues, and move strategically into the future. Services include: organizational assessments, strategic plans, business plans, staffing and governance plans, marketing plans, master plans, feasibility studies, executive search, audience research, program evaluation, and professional coaching.

Personnel:
Adrienne Horn (President)
Stephen Horn (Senior Vice President)
Emily Cohen (Senior Vice President)
Katie Sevier (Assistant Vice President)

Museum Planners

museums
visitor attractions
retail experiences
digital environments

creative strategies & design

ANCONA + ASSOCIATES, INC.
2450 S.W. Sherwood Dr.
Portland, OR 97201
Tel: 503-274-4444; FAX: 503-961-7797
E-mail: portland@ancona-a.com
Web Site: www.ancona-a.com

Type of Business:
Creative strategies & design services for clients seeking multi-disciplinary creative services for museums, visitor attractions, retail experiences and digital environments. We are expert at creating engaging experiences at the intersection of culture and commerce, with a focus on themes that include Industry & Heritage, The Environment, Sports & Entertainment and Retail. Our work explores the graceful convergence of physical and digital realms. Clients include adidas, Boudin at the Wharf, British Waterways, Nike, NASA, Lucasfilm, Universal Studios, Rio Tinto Diamonds, Henry Ford Museum, California Academy of Sciences and the Art Institute of Chicago.

Personnel:
Tomas Ancona (President)

ANDREW MERRIELL & ASSOCIATES, LLC
7198 Old Santa Fe Trail
Santa Fe, NM 87505
Tel: 505-982-3950; FAX: 505-820-6674
E-mail: andy@merriell.com
Web Site: www.merriell.com

Type of Business:
For over thirty years Andrew Merriell has assisted museums and interpretive centers with planning and designing visitor experiences. Working collaboratively with his clients, he identifies opportunities to advance beyond the usual and predictable museum offerings, finding innovative ways to immerse visitors in exhibit stories. Each project provides visitors with memorable, meaningful experiences they can find nowhere else. Services include feasibility studies, interpretive master plans, concept studies, exhibition development, and exhibit design.

Personnel:
Andrew Merriell (Principal)
Rebecca Shreckengast (Senior Designer)
Margaret Hennessey (Polymath First Class)

BRC IMAGINATION ARTS
2711 Winona Ave.
Burbank, CA 91504
Tel: 818-841-8084; FAX: 818-841-4996
E-mail: brc@brcweb.com
Web Site: www.brcweb.com

Type of Business:
BRC is an award winning full service museum design and production company with a comprehensive range of skills from vision and master planning, to design, and production of exhibits and theatrical media experiences. Continental Europe Office: Science Park 5644, 5692 EN Eindhoven, P.O. Box 1245, 5602 BE Eindhoven, The Netherlands, Tel: +31.40.2676.871; Fax: +31.40.2676.895. United Kingdom Office: 8 Kimblesworth Grange, Potterhouse Lane, Durham DH1 5SL, United Kingdom, Tel: +44.7879.655950; Fax: +44.1913.719141. Shanghai Office: A405, Tomorrow Square, 399 West Nanjing Road, Shanghai 200003, People's Republic of China, Tel: +86.21.2308.1077.

Personnel:
Carmel Lewis (Vice President, Educational Experiences)
Matthew Solari (Director, Education Development)
Mark Hayward (Creative Director, Educational Experiences)
Bart Dohmen (Managing Director, Continental Europe)
Donna Davidson (Director, United Kingdom)

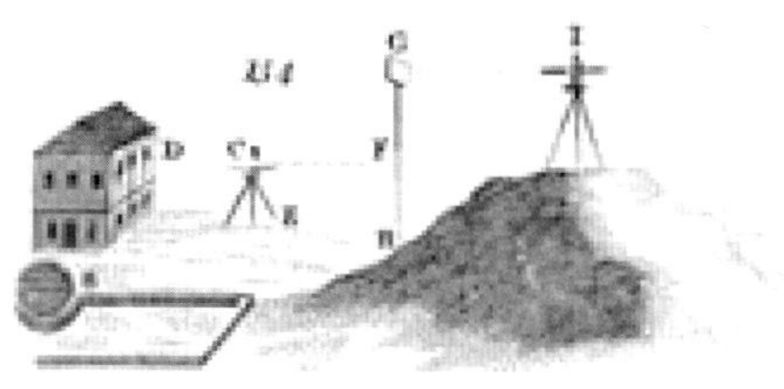

CHRISTOPHER CHADBOURNE & ASSOCIATES
129 Portland St.
Boston, MA 02114
Tel: 617-305-1000; FAX: 617-367-6222
E-mail: exhibits@ccadesign.com
Web Site: www.ccadesign.com

Type of Business:
CCA collaborates with clients to design memorable, story-driven visitor experiences that attract, educate and entertain. We are graphic, industrial, and stageset designers; educators and writers; architects, curators and media specialists. Together, we have created art, science, cultural and natural history, and children's exhibits, as well as educationally-based themed attractions. Our services range from feasibility studies and master planning, to architectural and media coordination, to supervision of fabrication and installation, all with strict adherence to budget and schedule.

Personnel:
Christopher Chadbourne (President & Creative Director)
Michael Biddle (Director, Design)
Andrea Medalie (Director, Projects)
Mary Ruggieri Macfarlane (Director, Graphic Design)
David Whitemyer (Director, Production)
Valerie Taylor (Director, Exhibit Development)
Felicia O'Keefe (Director, Marketing)

Vincent Ciulla Design

VINCENT CIULLA DESIGN ASSOCIATES, INC.
1269 First St., Studio 5
Sarasota, FL 34236
Tel: 941-917-0388 & 917-312-3951 (cell); FAX: 941-917-0386
E-mail: info@ciulladesign.com
Web Site: www.ciulladesign.com; www.umbrellahouse.com

Type of Business:
Your team will work directly with the Ciullas, who will create an individualized interpretive plan or design for your institution. Ciulla Design has created close to 300 museum, park and cultural experiences and new facilities, indoors and outdoors, on a vast range of topics. We are developing new educational experiences about the arts, society, history and the environment under our own auspices, that can become opportunities for partnership with you. We are also restoring Paul Rudolph's internationally renowned Umbrella House, which will soon become Ciulla Design's new studio.

Personnel:
Vincent A. Ciulla (President)
Julie Ciulla (Vice President & General Manager)

ConsultEcon, Inc.
Economic and Management Consultants

CONSULTECON, INC.
545 Concord Ave., Ste. 210
Cambridge, MA 02138
Tel: 617-547-0100; FAX: 617-547-0102
E-mail: info@consultecon.com
Web Site: www.consultecon.com

Type of Business:
ConsultEcon, Inc. provides services to clients in the areas of project and plan concept development, market and financial evaluation, visitor surveys, economic impact and project implementation. We are dedicated to serving museums of all sizes and types, and have worked over many years with clients responding to a broad spectrum of issues, ranging from the economics of operations to strategic planning.

Personnel:
Thomas J. Martin (President)
Robert E. Brais (Vice President)
Elena Kazlas (Principal)
Jason Drebitko (Senior Associate)

EWING COLE

EWINGCOLE CULTURAL DESIGN GROUP
100 N. 6th St.
Philadelphia, PA 19106
Tel: 215-923-2020; FAX: 215-574-9163
E-mail: wcrimm@ewingcole.com
Web Site: www.ewingcole.com/cultural

Type of Business:
EwingCole is a multi-discipline architecture and engineering firm specializing in design for cultural institutions. We work with national and regional museums for the fine arts, history, natural sciences and science and technology. Our Cultural Practice experts apply deep industry knowledge to enhance the visitor experience and to develop a design closely aligned with the museum's strategic plan. Our process engages the board and staff at all levels to create solutions that are intellectually stimulating, fiscally responsible and environmentally sustainable.

Personnel:
Walter Crimm, AIA, LEED AP (Vice President, Cultural Design Group)

GYROSCOPE, INC.
283 4th St., Suite 201
Oakland, CA 94607
Tel: 510-986-0111; FAX: 510-986-0222
E-mail: maeryta@gyroscopeinc.com
Web Site: www.gyroscopeinc.com

Type of Business:
Gyroscope is an award winning, museum planning, architecture and exhibit design company with offices in Oakland, CA, and Cambridge, MA. We are known for innovative strategies and design solutions grounded in a thorough understanding of the challenges museums face. We offer full-service planning and design for all phases of your project from earliest vision through opening.

Personnel:
Maeryta Medrano, AIA, LEED AP (President)
Chuck Howarth (Vice President)
Ron Davis, LEED AP (Principal)
Justine Roberts (Principal)

haleysharpedesign

HALEY SHARPE DESIGN
116 Spadina Ave., Ste. 201
Toronto, ON, Canada M5V 2K6
Tel: 416-361-3338; FAX: 416-361-3588
E-mail: info@haleysharpe.com
Web Site: www.haleysharpe.com

Type of Business:
Haley Sharpe Design brings expertise in masterplanning, design and implementation of interpretive projects for museums, galleries, heritage sites and visitor centers. We work collaboratively with clients to provide architectural briefings, learning and interpretative strategies, functional and business plans to inform funding applications and project development.

Personnel:
Jan Faulkner (Creative Director)
Nicole Mackereth (Business Development Consultant)

museum planning | exhibit design

HILFERTY
14240 State Rte. 550
Athens, OH 45701
Tel: 740-448-3821; FAX: 740-448-2331
E-mail: gha@hilferty.com
Web Site: www.hilferty.com

Type of Business:
For more than thirty years, Hilferty has provided a full range of interpretive services to museums, visitor centers, nature centers, botanical gardens, historic sites, zoos/aquariums, and halls of fame. We excel at interpretive and facility master planning; concept development; content research; label writing; exhibit and graphic design; and providing donor recognition and funding support materials. From social histories to natural sciences, football to physics, presidents to children's gardens, every Hilferty exhibit vividly captures the stories that engage visitors' minds and hearts. Each project is approached with a unique mix of techniques chosen to best bring the subject to life. Our innovative portfolio spans the spectrum of intimate displays of precious objects, captivating immersive environments, enthralling interactive components, and breathtaking theatrical presentations. In short, Hilferty creates memorable museum experiences.

Personnel:
Gerard Hilferty (President & Creative Director)
Dean Clouse (CEO)

LORD CULTURAL RESOURCES
43 West 24th Street, 10th Fl.
New York, NY 10010
Tel: 646-375-2500; FAX: 212-675-4763
E-mail: info@lord.ca
Web Site: www.lord.ca

Type of Business:
Founded in 1981 in response to an emerging need for specialized planning services in the museum, cultural and heritage sector, Lord Cultural Resources is dedicated to creating cultural capital through visioning, planning and implementation. We work with museums, large and small, helping them to maximize their cultural capital by engaging with their communities, improving their buildings and inspiring collaboration and learning. We have benefited clients through the entire spectrum of cultural services including master plans, business plans, strategic plans, facility plans, functional programs, architect selection, exhibition design and development, project management, retail plans and cultural plans. In addition, Lord Cultural Resources has made a definitive contribution to the development of museum planning through its pioneering publications. The firm also has a San Francisco location.

Personnel:
Gail Dexter Lord (Co-President)
Barry Lord (Co-President)
Maria Piacente (Vice President, Exhibitions)
Catharine Tanner (Vice President, Facility Planning)
Paul Alezraa (Vice President, Europe)
Amy Kaufman (Managing Director, U.S.)
Brad King (Director, Management Consulting, Principal)
Margaret May (Senior Principal)
Ted Silberberg (Senior Principal)
Joy Bailey (Senior Consultant)
Lindsay Martin (Senior Consultant)
Andrea Ott (Director, Client Relations & Marketing)

MMC
MUSEUM MANAGEMENT
CONSULTANTS, INC.

MUSEUM MANAGEMENT CONSULTANTS, INC.
120 Green St., Ste. 200
San Francisco, CA 94111
Tel: 415-982-2288; FAX: 415-982-0504
E-mail: mmc@museum-management.com
Web Site: www.museum-management.com

Type of Business:
Museum Management Consultants, Inc. (MMC) specializes in organizational assessment, institutional planning, executive search, audience research, and professional coaching. Founded in 1987 and based in San Francisco, MMC has provided consulting services to over 250 museums and cultural organizations throughout the United States and abroad. MMC helps museums accentuate their strengths, address critical issues, and move strategically into the future. Services include: organizational assessments, strategic plans, business plans, staffing and governance plans, marketing plans, master plans, feasibility studies, executive search, audience research, program evaluation, and professional coaching.

Personnel:
Adrienne Horn (President)
Stephen Horn (Senior Vice President)
Emily Cohen (Senior Vice President)
Katie Sevier (Assistant Vice President)

The PRD Group Ltd

THE PRD GROUP LTD.
14555 Avion Pkwy., Ste. 175
Chantilly, VA 20151
Tel: 703-352-2288; FAX: 703-352-2376
Web Site: www.theprdgroup.com

Type of Business:
The Planning, Research and Design Group Ltd. — specialists in museum planning and design. Services include master planning; programming and design through bid specifications for permanent and temporary exhibitions; interactive and video design; graphic design for exhibits and publications; project management.

Personnel:
Daniel B. Murphy (Principal)
William C. Lazenby

TAYLOR STUDIOS, INC.
1320 Harmon Drive
Rantoul, IL 61866
Tel: 217-893-4874 & 800-707-2047; FAX: 217-893-1998
E-mail: sales@taylorstudios.com
Web Site: www.taylorstudios.com/omd

(Continued on next page)

(Continued from previous page)

Type of Business:
"Taylor Studios, Inc. is an interpretive planning, exhibit design, and fabrication firm that assists museums and other clients in creating exhibits that are educational, creative, and enduring. We are committed to completing exhibits to the fulfillment of each client's unique needs, timelines, and goals. Our exhibit creativity is built on a firm interpretive foundation. Our team has the experience and talent to coordinate, communicate, research, plan, design, manage, and produce exhibits of the highest quality. We believe in excellent customer service and back our fabricated products with an unprecedented five-year warranty."

Personnel:
Betty Brennan (President)
Kara Vanskike (Marketing Coordinator)

UJMN ARCHITECTS + DESIGNERS
718 Arch St., Ste. 5N
Philadelphia, PA 19106
Tel: 215-440-0190; FAX: 215-440-0197
E-mail: nicholson@ujmn.com; blankin@ujmn.com
Web Site: www.ujmn.com

Type of Business:
Founded in 1967, UJMN Architects + Designers offers architectural design, museum planning, and exhibit design within a single firm, maximizing the integration of exhibits with museum facilities; the effectiveness of cost, schedule, and project management; and ultimately, the quality of the visitor experience. Recent projects include: the Liberty Bell Center Exhibits; the President's House at Independence National Historical Park; the National Civil War Museum Exhibits (Harrisburg, PA); the Louisville Slugger Museum; the Stoogeum; the Joliet Area Historical Museum; Hagley Museum and Library; the National Civil Rights Museum in Mississippi; the Eagles Mere Museum Exhibits, and Historic Deerfield.

Personnel:
Joseph A. Nicholson, AIA, IDSA (Principal)
Stacey Blankin (Associate)

White Oak Associates
Museum Planners and Producers

WHITE OAK ASSOCIATES, INC.
17 Essex St.
Marblehead, MA 01945
Tel: 781-639-0722; FAX: 781-639-2491
E-mail: info@whiteoakassoc.com
Web Site: www.whiteoakassoc.com

Type of Business:
White Oak Associates is dedicated to high quality planning services for museums and special format theaters. Services include community needs assessments, concept development plans, strategic master plans, business plans, theater studies, architectural program planning, and staff and operating plans. White Oak also offers executive production services and implementation management from concept through post-opening for new museums and expansions. Our mission is to collaborate with museums to create sustainable institutions providing essential community services.

Personnel:
John W. Jacobsen (President)
Jeanie Stahl (Vice President)
Mark B. Peterson (Director, Theater Analysis & Planning)
Victor A. Becker (Director, Program Development)

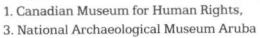

SHIPPING/STORAGE-GENERAL

LAWRENCE FINE ART SERVICES
375 Oyster Point Blvd., Unit 2
South San Francisco, CA 94080
Tel: 650-624-9882; FAX: 650-624-8437
E-mail: info@lawrencefinearts.com
Web Site: www.lawrenceFAS.com

Type of Business:
Caring for fine art & antiques since 1984. Climate and non-climate controlled, secure storage. Climate-controlled, air-ride trucks with regular runs throughout California and neighboring states. Domestic & international shipping. Crate construction & packing — from simple, one-way crates to museum-quality traveling crates. Expert installation and rigging in both simple and difficult situations. Coordination, packing & storage during remodeling & moving. Serving museums, galleries, private collectors, corporations, universities & artists.

Personnel:
Dick Drossler (President)

MASTERPAK
145 E. 57th St., 5th Fl.
New York, NY 10022
Tel: 800-922-5522; FAX: 212-586-6961
E-mail: als@masterpak-usa.com
Web Site: www.masterpak-usa.com

Type of Business:
Unique & archival materials for the protection of fine art, artifacts and antiques in packing, shipping, storing and display. Hard-to-find materials for conservators, artists, museums, galleries, collectors, framers and art shippers. Products include: Archival Softwrap® Tyvek®, Nomex® and Archival Hardwrap® Tyvek® Liners by DuPont, Sealed Air's Ethafoam®/Cellu-Cushion® in planks and rolls, Sealed Air's BubbleWrap®, Voltek's Volara® Polyethylene Foam, Archival Rolling & Storage Tubes, Unbuffered & Buffered Tissue in rolls and sheets, Photo-Tex Tissue in rolls and sheets, Glassine Paper in rolls and sheets, Silicone Parchment Release Paper in rolls and sheets, Corrugated Multi-Use Board, Archival tapes, Glass Skin®, Strongboxes™ & Print Pads™, Oz Clips™ Link Lock® Latches, Steel Closure Plates, PEM2 Data Loggers and specialty preservation management software developed by The Image Permanence Institute especially for the collections of Museums, Libraries & Archives. All products are available in small or large quantities and can ship within 24 hours. Our website, located at www.masterpak-usa.com, is open 24 hours for easy online ordering.

Personnel:
E. William Judson (Chairman)
Andrew L. Smith (President)

U.S. ART COMPANY, INC.
FINE ART HANDLERS
Corporate Headquarters, 66 Pacella Park Dr.
Randolph, MA 02368
Tel: 800-872-7826; FAX: 781-986-5595
E-mail: msilverman@usart.com
Web Site: www.usart.com

Type of Business:
U.S. Art Company, Inc. is worldwide, offers decades of experience, trained fine art handlers, museum quality packing, crating, shipping, installation, climate-controlled trucks & storage, international import/export & customs liaison services, offices in nine major cities & trucks continuously traversing nationwide. BOSTON - CORPORATE: 800-872-7826; DALLAS: 866-898-7278; LOS ANGELES: 877-528-7278; NEW YORK: 800-472-5784; ORLANDO: 888-802-4459; ST. LOUIS: 866-928-7278; WASHINGTON, DC: 877-508-7278.

Personnel:
Mark Lank (CEO)
Mark Silverman (COO)

Archival Storage Equipment

DELTA DESIGNS LTD.
P.O. Box 1733
Topeka, KS 66601
Tel: 785-234-2244 & 800-656-7426; FAX: 785-233-1021
E-mail: bdanielson@deltadesignsltd.com
Web Site: www.deltadesignsltd.com

Type of Business:
Custom and standard museum storage cabinets, free standing or mounted on high density mobile storage systems. Cabinets available for your collection: Natural History, Works on Paper, Textiles, Art Objects, Historical Artifacts. Design and Installation services provided. Quality through Incremental Change.

Personnel:
Bruce Danielson (President)

MASTERPAK
145 E. 57th St., 5th Fl.
New York, NY 10022
Tel: 800-922-5522; FAX: 212-586-6961
E-mail: als@masterpak-usa.com
Web Site: www.masterpak-usa.com

Type of Business:

Unique & archival materials for the protection of fine art, artifacts and antiques in packing, shipping, storing and display. Hard-to-find materials for conservators, artists, museums, galleries, collectors, framers and art shippers. Products include: Archival Softwrap® Tyvek®, Nomex® and Archival Hardwrap® Tyvek® Liners by DuPont, Sealed Air's Ethafoam®/Cellu-Cushion® in planks and rolls, Sealed Air's BubbleWrap®, Voltek's Volara® Polyethylene Foam, Archival Rolling & Storage Tubes, Unbuffered & Buffered Tissue in rolls and sheets, Photo-Tex Tissue in rolls and sheets, Glassine Paper in rolls and sheets, Silicone Parchment Release Paper in rolls and sheets, Corrugated Multi-Use Board, Archival tapes, Glass Skin®, Strongboxes™ & Print Pads™, Oz Clips™ Link Lock® Latches, Steel Closure Plates, PEM2 Data Loggers and specialty preservation management software developed by The Image Permanence Institute especially for the collections of Museums, Libraries & Archives. All products are available in small or large quantities and can ship within 24 hours. Our website, located at www.masterpak-usa.com, is open 24 hours for easy online ordering.

Personnel:
E. William Judson (Chairman)
Andrew L. Smith (President)

MONTEL INC.
225 4th Ave.
Montmagny, QC, Canada G5V 3S5
Tel: 877-935-0236; FAX: 418-248-7266
E-mail: system@montel.com
Web Site: www.montel.com

Type of Business:

The Art of Storage by Montel for Museums & Archival Collections: The Montel high density fixed and mobile storage systems allows each system to be custom-designed to the particular safety storage requirements for each type of collection. Montel has developed a line of efficient and safe products which respect the integrity and value of all types of art work regardless of their size & shape. Specializing in storage systems since 1924, Montel offers its expertise to insure planning solutions that maximize capacity, cost savings, security and accessibility. We offer our complete line for your particular collection requirement, including art racks, full line of cabinetry, textile racks, shelving, drawer cabinets and mobile storage systems.

Personnel:
Joey P. Boudreau (Marketing Director)

SPACESAVER CORPORATION
1450 Janesville Ave.
Fort Atkinson, WI 53538-2798
Tel: 920-563-6362 & 800-492-3434; FAX: 920-563-2702
E-mail: ssc@spacesaver.com
Web Site: www.spacesaver.com

Type of Business:

Collection storage - collection care. Arguably the single-most important undertaking for museums both large and small. As collections continue to grow, efficient artifact storage space and optimum convenience and control over artifacts have become primary needs in today's museum collection preservation strategies. Spacesaver offers innovative storage solutions that help museums better manage time, space and security. Spacesaver provides storage solutions that protect and preserve your valuable collections.

Personnel:
Brandy Thayer (Business Development)

VIKING METAL CABINET CO., INC.
5321 W. 65th St.
Chicago, IL 60638
Tel: 800-776-7767 & 708-594-1111; FAX: 708-594-1028
E-mail: sales@vikingmetal.com
Web Site: www.vikingmetal.com

Type of Business:

Viking manufactures a full line of museum cabinetry that meets the requirements for conservation, preservation, and archival storage for a wide variety of collections. Major institutions and universities throughout the world rely on Viking cabinets to protect their most precious specimens and artifacts. Additionally, Viking has been innovative in the design of custom storage solutions that meet the special needs of the museum community. Versatility is the hallmark of Viking's full and counter height conservation cabinets. A wide range of sizes and unique optional accessories make these cabinets the choice to house a multitude of diverse collections. We also provide specialized cabinets for botanical, geological, and entomological collections. Our archival flat file cabinets have stainless steel tracks and plated rollers that eliminate contamination from flaking paint. And if your storage application is unique, Viking is ready to adapt or design a custom cabinet that meets your particular needs. Attention to detail is important to you - and to Viking. Our state-of-the-art manufacturing processes, talented and capable engineering team, and unique skills of our experienced craftsmen deliver museum storage products of unparalleled quality. At Viking, our commitment to your satisfaction begins the moment you give us a call. Our first priority is your long-term satisfaction...because we know that our greatest asset is a satisfied customer. Viking cabinets provide the best value in preserving the objects, artifacts, and specimens that you value most. Trust our experience...over half a century of manufacturing quality metal cabinetry. Trust our reputation...earned and the world's most prestigious institutions. Trust Viking.

Personnel:
Jim Dolan (Vice President Sales)
Mark Roer (Western Region Sales Manager)

Art Storage Equipment

BIBLIO DESIGN LTD.
1240 Park Ave., Suite 1F
New York, NY 10128-1754
Tel: 212-876-1114; FAX: 212-369-1872
E-mail: pd1240@aol.com; ebrown1240@aol.com
Web Site: www.bibliodesignltd.com

Type of Business:
Designers and Manufacuturers of High Density Museum Storage Systems. Mobile Storage Systems; "ModuPanel" kits; lateral art storage panels; pull-out art storage panels; mobile wide-span racking systems; oversize flat cabinet storage; oversize painting storage; flat and rolled textile storage. Also distributors of MONTEL storage systems, and STEEL FIXTURE Mfg. Co. Museum quality cabinets and flat files. Consulting services available to Architects and Curators.

Personnel:
Peter Diemand (President)
Elaine Brown (Vice President)

BORROUGHS CORPORATION
3002 N. Burdick St.
Kalamazoo, MI 49004
Tel: 800-748-0227; FAX: 269-342-4161
E-mail: lindag@borroughs.com
Web Site: www.borroughs.com

Type of Business:
Museum Storage Solutions are part of the family of high-quality and durable storage products produced by Borroughs Corporation for nearly 70 years. Our storage professionals provide expert product knowledge, design capabilities, dependable service and responsive support, all on a local level and backed by the manufacturer's warranty. Borroughs knows how important the preservation of your valuable artifacts is to you and your organization. Our knowledge of the specialized requirements of museum storage will assure that your limited space is maximized while minimizing your investment. We can also provide design assistance so that flexibility can be maintained as your collection grows and changes. Rely on Borroughs to design and deliver all your museum and preservation storage needs: Vertebrate Cabinets, Herbarium Cabinets, Art and Textile Racks, High-Density Mobile Storage, Archival Record Storage, Open Shelf Filing, Heavy-Duty Steel Shelving, Library Bookstacks, Storage Cabinets and Drawer Units.

Personnel:
Joe Cascio (Vice President Sales)
Kris Macomber (Customer Service Manager)
Mike Proos (Technical Support Manager)

CRYSTALIZATIONS SYSTEMS, INC.
1401 Lincoln Avenue
Holbrook, NY 11741
Tel: 631-467-0090; FAX: 631-467-0061
E-mail: CSIstorage@aol.com
Web Site: www.CSIstorage.com

Type of Business:
Collection Storage Systems are safe, light-weight ALUMINUM. We design, manufacture and install. Our well known Moving Painting and Moving Rolled Textile Storage Systems are available in any size. Installation options include Ceiling or Floor supported plus Convertible or Free-Standing. Aisles are always Track-Free and full system can be relocated. The "Oversized Flat" and "Display /Storage" Cabinets are offered in both standard and custom sizes and can be assembled on-site. Full budgeting and grant support.

Personnel:
Patricia J. Ellenwood (President)
Carmine Billotto (Operations Manager)

DELTA DESIGNS LTD.
P.O. Box 1733
Topeka, KS 66601
Tel: 785-234-2244 & 800-656-7426; FAX: 785-233-1021
E-mail: bdanielson@deltadesignsltd.com
Web Site: www.deltadesignsltd.com

Type of Business:
Custom and standard museum storage cabinets, free standing or mounted on high density mobile storage systems. Cabinets available for your collection: Natural History, Works on Paper, Textiles, Art Objects, Historical Artifacts. Design and Installation services provided. Quality through Incremental Change.

Personnel:
Bruce Danielson (President)

CHARLES J. DICKGIESSER & CO. INC.
257 Roosevelt Dr.
Derby, CT 06418-0475
Tel: 203-734-2553; FAX: 203-734-9221
E-mail: nancy.dickgiesser@sbcglobal.net
Web Site: Portastoragesystems.com

Type of Business:
Designers and manufacturers of museum storage systems. Porta Storage™ is a versatile, cost-effective system for displaying and storing textiles, paintings, photos and other art objects. Our pull-out art

(Continued on next page)

(Continued from previous page)

storage panels are floor supported for greater stability, maintenance free and custom designed to your specific needs. Call us today for more information.

Personnel:
Nancy L. Dickgiesser (President)

MONTEL INC.
225 4th Ave.
Montmagny, QC, Canada G5V 3S5
Tel: 877-935-0236; FAX: 418-248-7266
E-mail: system@montel.com
Web Site: www.montel.com

Type of Business:
The Art of Storage by Montel for Museums & Archival Collections: The Montel high density fixed and mobile storage systems allows each system to be custom-designed to the particular safety storage requirements for each type of collection. Montel has developed a line of efficient and safe products which respect the integrity and value of all types of art work regardless of their size & shape. Specializing in storage systems since 1924, Montel offers its expertise to insure planning solutions that maximize capacity, cost savings, security and accessibility. We offer our complete line for your particular collection requirement, including art racks, full line of cabinetry, textile racks, shelving, drawer cabinets and mobile storage systems.

Personnel:
Joey P. Boudreau (Marketing Director)

SPACESAVER CORPORATION
1450 Janesville Ave.
Fort Atkinson, WI 53538-2798
Tel: 920-563-6362 & 800-492-3434; FAX: 920-563-2702
E-mail: ssc@spacesaver.com
Web Site: www.spacesaver.com

Type of Business:
Collection storage - collection care. Arguably the single-most important undertaking for museums both large and small. As collections continue to grow, efficient artifact storage space and optimum convenience and control over artifacts have become primary needs in today's museum collection preservation strategies. Spacesaver offers innovative storage solutions that help museums better manage time, space and security. Spacesaver provides storage solutions that protect and preserve your valuable collections.

Personnel:
Brandy Thayer (Business Development)

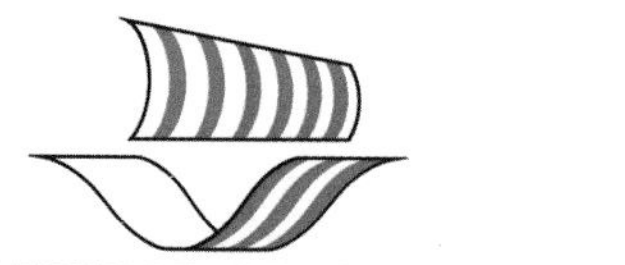

VIKING METAL CABINET COMPANY

VIKING METAL CABINET CO., INC.
5321 W. 65th St.
Chicago, IL 60638
Tel: 800-776-7767 & 708-594-1111; FAX: 708-594-1028
E-mail: sales@vikingmetal.com
Web Site: www.vikingmetal.com

Type of Business:
Viking manufactures a full line of museum cabinetry that meets the requirements for conservation, preservation, and archival storage for a wide variety of collections. Major institutions and universities throughout the world rely on Viking cabinets to protect their most precious specimens and artifacts. Additionally, Viking has been innovative in the design of custom storage solutions that meet the special needs of the museum community. Versatility is the hallmark of Viking's full and counter height conservation cabinets. A wide range of sizes and unique optional accessories make these cabinets the choice to house a multitude of diverse collections. We also provide specialized cabinets for botanical, geological, and entomological collections. Our archival flat file cabinets have stainless steel tracks and plated rollers that eliminate contamination from flaking paint. And if your storage application is unique, Viking is ready to adapt or design a custom cabinet that meets your particular needs. Attention to detail is important to you - and to Viking. Our state-of-the-art manufacturing processes, talented and capable engineering team, and unique skills of our experienced craftsmen deliver museum storage products of unparalleled quality. At Viking, our commitment to your satisfaction begins the moment you give us a call. Our first priority is your long-term satisfaction...because we know that our greatest asset is a satisfied customer. Viking cabinets provide the best value in preserving the objects, artifacts, and specimens that you value most. Trust our experience...over half a century of manufacturing quality metal cabinetry. Trust our reputation...earned and the world's most prestigious institutions. Trust Viking.

Personnel:
Jim Dolan (Vice President Sales)
Mark Roer (Western Region Sales Manager)

Crating

LAWRENCE
FINE ART SERVICES

LAWRENCE FINE ART SERVICES
375 Oyster Point Blvd., Unit 2
South San Francisco, CA 94080
Tel: 650-624-9882; FAX: 650-624-8437
E-mail: info@lawrencefinearts.com
Web Site: www.lawrenceFAS.com

Type of Business:
Caring for fine art & antiques since 1984. Climate and non-climate controlled, secure storage. Climate-controlled, air-ride trucks with regular runs throughout California and neighboring states. Domestic & international shipping. Crate construction & packing — from simple, one-way crates to museum-quality traveling crates. Expert installation

(Continued on next page)

(Continued from previous page)

and rigging in both simple and difficult situations. Coordination, packing & storage during remodeling & moving. Serving museums, galleries, private collectors, corporations, universities & artists.

Personnel:
Dick Drossler (President)

Packing Services/Materials

ARTPACK SERVICES INC. & A.I.R.

ARTPACK SERVICES
24650 Crestview Ct.
Farmington Hills, MI 48335
Tel: 240-478-8946; FAX: 248-478-9588
E-mail: wendy@artpack.com
Web Site: www.artpack.com

Type of Business:
Artpack was founded in 1981 to provide professional services to museums, auction houses, galleries, corporate and private collectors for fine arts and antiques. We specialize in fine arts storage, custom crating and packing, installation, local and long distance shipping including a monthly New York shuttle. Our operations are climate controlled and staff trained to museum standards. Artpack also offers collection/project management and courier services, mount and pedestal fabrication, rigging and conservation services.

Personnel:
Ted Lee Hadfield (President)
Wendy MacGaw (Vice President)

ARTWORKS OF KANSAS CITY FINE ART SERVICES
3017 Gillham Rd.
Kansas City, MO 64108
Tel: 816-753-4005 & 800-481-9856; FAX: 816-753-4007
E-mail: mike@artworkskc.com
Web Site: www.artworkskc.com

Type of Business:
Professional fine art packer and shipper providing museum-quality services nationwide. ARTworks' Midwest Regional Art Shuttle serves St. Louis, Chicago, Milwaukee, Minneapolis, Des Moines, Omaha, Lincoln, Kansas City - and all points in between. Air-ride, climate service with double drivers. AWKC offers custom EU-compliant crating, worldwide shipping, climate-controlled storage and installation. State-of-the-art facilities with professional staff.

Personnel:
Michael G. Otto (President)
Kris L. Luke (General Manager)

TERRY DOWD, INC.
2501 W. Armitage Ave.
Chicago, IL 60647-4324
Tel: 773-342-8686; FAX: 773-342-8650
E-mail: info@terrydowd.com
Web Site: www.terrydowd.com

Type of Business:
Providing museum quality fine art services in the Chicago and Denver areas. Professionals in packing, crating, transportation and storage of fine art and artifacts. Air ride, climate controlled transportation available in the Midwest and Mountain Plains areas and exclusive use nationally. Secure climate controlled storage provided in Chicago and Denver. Packing, installation, rigging and freight forwarding services provided by our experienced staff. Denver Tel.: 303-297-8686; Fax: 303-297-1919.

Personnel:
Terry Dowd (President)

FINE ART SERVICES & TRANSPORTATION

FINE ART SERVICES AND TRANSPORTATION
100 W. Forest
Detroit, MI 48201
Tel: 313-832-3278; FAX: 313-832-3293
E-mail: info@fineartsolutions.com
Web Site: www.fineartsolutions.com

Type of Business:
F.A.S.T. is a full service museum quality art handling company specializing in fine art crating, packing, installation and storage. F.A.S.T. also offers pickup and delivery service for the entire state of Michigan and Northern Ohio, Indiana and Illinois. Freight forwarding, Registrar, mount making and rigging services are also provided by our professional museum trained staff.

Personnel:
Paul Smith (President)
Chris McInnis (Office Coordinator)

Hahn Bros.

HAHN BROS. FIREPROOF WAREHOUSES, INC.
622 Communipaw Ave.
Jersey City, NJ 07304
Tel: 212-926-1505; FAX: 201-432-9547
E-mail: info@hahnbros.com
Web Site: www.hahnbros.com

Type of Business:
Over 100 years of fine art services to the museum and art community. Full service specialists offering customized crating and traveling cases and freight forwarding for collections and shows. Packing, moving,

(Continued on next page)

(Continued from previous page)

relocation and installation. Registrar, photography and gallery services available. Secure, climate-controlled storage in two locations with the ability to set up to client specifications.

Personnel:
Karen O. Dowling (President)
Marianne Mikulka (Fine Art Director)

MASTERPAK
145 E. 57th St., 5th Fl.
New York, NY 10022
Tel: 800-922-5522; FAX: 212-586-6961
E-mail: als@masterpak-usa.com
Web Site: www.masterpak-usa.com

Type of Business:
Unique & archival materials for the protection of fine art, artifacts and antiques in packing, shipping, storing and display. Hard-to-find materials for conservators, artists, museums, galleries, collectors, framers and art shippers. Products include: Archival Softwrap® Tyvek®, Nomex® and Archival Hardwrap® Tyvek® Liners by DuPont, Sealed Air's Ethafoam®/Cellu-Cushion® in planks and rolls, Sealed Air's BubbleWrap®, Voltek's Volara® Polyethylene Foam, Archival Rolling & Storage Tubes, Unbuffered & Buffered Tissue in rolls and sheets, Photo-Tex Tissue in rolls and sheets, Glassine Paper in rolls and sheets, Silicone Parchment Release Paper in rolls and sheets, Corrugated Multi-Use Board, Archival tapes, Glass Skin®, Strongboxes™ & Print Pads™, Oz Clips™ Link Lock® Latches, Steel Closure Plates, PEM2 Data Loggers and specialty preservation management software developed by The Image Permanence Institute especially for the collections of Museums, Libraries & Archives. All products are available in small or large quantities and can ship within 24 hours. Our website, located at www.masterpak-usa.com, is open 24 hours for easy online ordering.

Personnel:
E. William Judson (Chairman)
Andrew L. Smith (President)

U.S. ART COMPANY, INC.
FINE ART HANDLERS
Corporate Headquarters, 66 Pacella Park Dr.
Randolph, MA 02368
Tel: 800-872-7826; FAX: 781-986-5595
E-mail: msilverman@usart.com
Web Site: www.usart.com

Type of Business:
U.S. Art Company, Inc. is worldwide, offers decades of experience, trained fine art handlers, museum quality packing, crating, shipping, installation, climate-controlled trucks & storage, international import/export & customs liaison services, offices in nine major cities & trucks continuously traversing nationwide. BOSTON - CORPORATE: 800-872-7826; DALLAS: 866-898-7278; LOS ANGELES: 877-528-7278; NEW YORK: 800-472-5784; ORLANDO: 888-802-4459; ST. LOUIS: 866-928-7278; WASHINGTON, DC: 877-508-7278.

Personnel:
Mark Lank (CEO)
Mark Silverman (COO)

Shelving Storage Equipment

MONTEL INC.
225 4th Ave.
Montmagny, QC, Canada G5V 3S5
Tel: 877-935-0236; FAX: 418-248-7266
E-mail: system@montel.com
Web Site: www.montel.com

Type of Business:
The Art of Storage by Montel for Museums & Archival Collections: The Montel high density fixed and mobile storage systems allows each system to be custom-designed to the particular safety storage requirements for each type of collection. Montel has developed a line of efficient and safe products which respect the integrity and value of all types of art work regardless of their size & shape. Specializing in storage systems since 1924, Montel offers its expertise to insure planning solutions that maximize capacity, cost savings, security and accessibility. We offer our complete line for your particular collection requirement, including art racks, full line of cabinetry, textile racks, shelving, drawer cabinets and mobile storage systems.

Personnel:
Joey P. Boudreau (Marketing Director)

Shipping & Moving Services

ACTION MOVING SERVICES, INC.
12400 Washburn Ave., S.
Burnsville, MN 55337
Tel: 800-328-3803; FAX: 952-894-0020
E-mail: sales@actionmoving.com
Web Site: www.actionmoving.com

Type of Business:
Action Moving Services is an award winning interstate agent for Atlas Van Lines. Action has a great deal of experience with handling: Exhibits on Tour, Museum Works/Artifacts and High Value Products. Action has specialized equipment for the specialized needs of the museum industry including climate control units, 53 ft. flat floors with gates, etc.

Personnel:
Dave Doebler
Shirley Hillestad
Bill Everson

ARTPACK SERVICES INC. & A.I.R.

ARTPACK SERVICES
24650 Crestview Ct.
Farmington Hills, MI 48335
Tel: 240-478-8946; FAX: 248-478-9588
E-mail: wendy@artpack.com
Web Site: www.artpack.com

Type of Business:
Artpack was founded in 1981 to provide professional services to museums, auction houses, galleries, corporate and private collectors for fine arts and antiques. We specialize in fine arts storage, custom

(Continued on next page)

(Continued from previous page)

crating and packing, installation, local and long distance shipping including a monthly New York shuttle. Our operations are climate controlled and staff trained to museum standards. Artpack also offers collection/project management and courier services, mount and pedestal fabrication, rigging and conservation services.

Personnel:
Ted Lee Hadfield (President)
Wendy MacGaw (Vice President)

ARTWORKS OF KANSAS CITY FINE ART SERVICES
3017 Gillham Rd.
Kansas City, MO 64108
Tel: 816-753-4005 & 800-481-9856; FAX: 816-753-4007
E-mail: mike@artworkskc.com
Web Site: www.artworkskc.com

Type of Business:
Professional fine art packer and shipper providing museum-quality services nationwide. ARTworks' Midwest Regional Art Shuttle serves St. Louis, Chicago, Milwaukee, Minneapolis, Des Moines, Omaha, Lincoln, Kansas City - and all points in between. Air-ride, climate service with double drivers. AWKC offers custom EU-compliant crating, worldwide shipping, climate-controlled storage and installation. State-of-the-art facilities with professional staff.

Personnel:
Michael G. Otto (President)
Kris L. Luke (General Manager)

TERRY DOWD, INC.
2501 W. Armitage Ave.
Chicago, IL 60647-4324
Tel: 773-342-8686; FAX: 773-342-8650
E-mail: info@terrydowd.com
Web Site: www.terrydowd.com

Type of Business:
Providing museum quality fine art services in the Chicago and Denver areas. Professionals in packing, crating, transportation and storage of fine art and artifacts. Air ride, climate controlled transportation available in the Midwest and Mountain Plains areas and exclusive use nationally. Secure climate controlled storage provided in Chicago and Denver. Packing, installation, rigging and freight forwarding services provided by our experienced staff. Denver Tel.: 303-297-8686; Fax: 303-297-1919.

Personnel:
Terry Dowd (President)

FINE ART SERVICES AND TRANSPORTATION
100 W. Forest
Detroit, MI 48201
Tel: 313-832-3278; FAX: 313-832-3293
E-mail: info@fineartsolutions.com
Web Site: www.fineartsolutions.com

Type of Business:
F.A.S.T. is a full service museum quality art handling company specializing in fine art crating, packing, installation and storage. F.A.S.T. also offers pickup and delivery service for the entire state of Michigan and Northern Ohio, Indiana and Illinois. Freight forwarding, Registrar, mount making and rigging services are also provided by our professional museum trained staff.

Personnel:
Paul Smith (President)
Chris McInnis (Office Coordinator)

Hahn Bros.

FINE ART AND ANTIQUE SERVICES

HAHN BROS. FIREPROOF WAREHOUSES, INC.
622 Communipaw Ave.
Jersey City, NJ 07304
Tel: 212-926-1505; FAX: 201-432-9547
E-mail: info@hahnbros.com
Web Site: www.hahnbros.com

Type of Business:
Over 100 years of fine art services to the museum and art community. Full service specialists offering customized crating and traveling cases and freight forwarding for collections and shows. Packing, moving, relocation and installation. Registrar, photography and gallery services available. Secure, climate-controlled storage in two locations with the ability to set up to client specifications.

Personnel:
Karen O. Dowling (President)
Marianne Mikulka (Fine Art Director)

THE ICON GROUP, INC.
2747 W. Taylor St.
Chicago, IL 60612-4047
Tel: 773-533-1800; FAX: 733-533-1900
E-mail: info@icongroup.us
Web Site: www.icongroup.us

(Continued on next page)

(Continued from previous page)

Type of Business:
Museum Quality Fine Art Services to Museums, Galleries, Collectors and Auction Houses since 1980. Our Air-Ride Climate Control Transportation services the Chicago area as well as the Midwest and Northeast regions, along with exclusive use nationally. Climate Control Storage available as well as Collection Management, private viewing and photography services. Other services include Custom Crating and Packing as well as installation, rigging and freight forwarding.

Personnel:
Bruce MacGilpin (President)
Ingrid Fassbender (Collection Management/Storage)
Walt Solomon (Director, Long Distance Transportation)
Colby Starck (Long Distance Services)
Kevin Brosnan (Local Services)
Michael Gamis (Storage Services)
Eric Dimas (Crating Services)

NAGLEE FINE ARTS
1525 Grand Central Ave.
Elmira, NY 14901
Tel: 800-950-4533; FAX: 607-733-4850
E-mail: nfa@nagleegroup.com
Web Site: www.nagleegroup.com

Type of Business:
Conservation quality storage and transportation services for artistic and historic objects. High security, precision climate-controlled facility: 67% fahrenheit at 45% relative humidity. Professional, museum-trained staff offering quality art handling, installation and crating services for individual artists and institutions alike. Naglee Fine Arts is a division of Naglee Moving & Storage Inc., a full-service United Van Lines agent specializing in commercial moves for libraries and school systems.

Personnel:
Scott M. Hoose (Vice President)
Matthias H. Smith (Assistant Director)
Allen C. Smith (Consultant)

U.S. ART COMPANY, INC.
FINE ART HANDLERS
Corporate Headquarters, 66 Pacella Park Dr.
Randolph, MA 02368
Tel: 800-872-7826; FAX: 781-986-5595
E-mail: msilverman@usart.com
Web Site: www.usart.com

Type of Business:
U.S. Art Company, Inc. is worldwide, offers decades of experience, trained fine art handlers, museum quality packing, crating, shipping, installation, climate-controlled trucks & storage, international import/export & customs liaison services, offices in nine major cities & trucks continuously traversing nationwide. BOSTON - CORPORATE: 800-872-7826; DALLAS: 866-898-7278; LOS ANGELES: 877-528-7278; NEW YORK: 800-472-5784; ORLANDO: 888-802-4459; ST. LOUIS: 866-928-7278; WASHINGTON, DC: 877-508-7278.

Personnel:
Mark Lank (CEO)
Mark Silverman (COO)

ZAMPRELLI FINE ARTS
P.O. Box 9088
Bardonia, NY 10954-9088
Tel: 845-624-6430; FAX: 845-624-6431
E-mail: zamprellifineart@aol.com

Type of Business:
Zamprelli Fine Arts is a full-service art shipping and transportation firm. We specialize in transporting fine arts to and from museums and galleries both nationally and into Canada. Our experienced crews specialize in moving high-value cargo and provide high-quality services that include crating/packing and virtually any other requirements you may have. Our climate controlled transportation services are C.A.R.B. (California Air Resources Board) Compliant. Contact us at (845) 624-6430, or email us at zamprellifineart@aol.com.

Personnel:
Steve Zamprelli
Carolyn Zamprelli-Piranio
Laurel Zamprelli-Pasiuk
Michael Zamprelli

Specimen Storage Equipment

BORROUGHS CORPORATION
3002 N. Burdick St.
Kalamazoo, MI 49004
Tel: 800-748-0227; FAX: 269-342-4161
E-mail: lindag@borroughs.com
Web Site: www.borroughs.com

Type of Business:
Museum Storage Solutions are part of the family of high-quality and durable storage products produced by Borroughs Corporation for nearly 70 years. Our storage professionals provide expert product knowledge, design capabilities, dependable service and responsive support, all on a local level and backed by the manufacturer's warranty. Borroughs knows how important the preservation of your valuable artifacts is to you and your organization. Our knowledge of the specialized requirements of museum storage will assure that your limited space is maximized while minimizing your investment. We can also provide design assistance so that flexibility can be maintained as your collection grows and changes. Rely on Borroughs to design and deliver all your museum and preservation storage needs: Vertebrate Cabinets, Herbarium Cabinets, Art and Textile Racks, High-Density Mobile Storage, Archival Record Storage, Open Shelf Filing, Heavy-Duty Steel Shelving, Library Bookstacks, Storage Cabinets and Drawer Units.

Personnel:
Joe Cascio (Vice President Sales)
Kris Macomber (Customer Service Manager)
Mike Proos (Technical Support Manager)

DELTA DESIGNS LTD.
P.O. Box 1733
Topeka, KS 66601
Tel: 785-234-2244 & 800-656-7426; FAX: 785-233-1021
E-mail: bdanielson@deltadesignsltd.com
Web Site: www.deltadesignsltd.com

Type of Business:
Custom and standard museum storage cabinets, free standing or mounted on high density mobile storage systems. Cabinets available for your collection: Natural History, Works on Paper, Textiles, Art Objects, Historical Artifacts. Design and Installation services provided. Quality through Incremental Change.

Personnel:
Bruce Danielson (President)

MONTEL INC.
225 4th Ave.
Montmagny, QC, Canada G5V 3S5
Tel: 877-935-0236; FAX: 418-248-7266
E-mail: system@montel.com
Web Site: www.montel.com

Type of Business:
The Art of Storage by Montel for Museums & Archival Collections: The Montel high density fixed and mobile storage systems allows each system to be custom-designed to the particular safety storage requirements for each type of collection. Montel has developed a line of efficient and safe products which respect the integrity and value of all types of art work regardless of their size & shape. Specializing in storage systems since 1924, Montel offers its expertise to insure planning solutions that maximize capacity, cost savings, security and accessibility. We offer our complete line for your particular collection requirement, including art racks, full line of cabinetry, textile racks, shelving, drawer cabinets and mobile storage systems.

Personnel:
Joey P. Boudreau (Marketing Director)

VIKING METAL CABINET CO., INC.
5321 W. 65th St.
Chicago, IL 60638
Tel: 800-776-7767 & 708-594-1111; FAX: 708-594-1028
E-mail: sales@vikingmetal.com
Web Site: www.vikingmetal.com

Type of Business:
Viking manufactures a full line of museum cabinetry that meets the requirements for conservation, preservation, and archival storage for a wide variety of collections. Major institutions and universities throughout the world rely on Viking cabinets to protect their most precious specimens and artifacts. Additionally, Viking has been innovative in the design of custom storage solutions that meet the special needs of the museum community. Versatility is the hallmark of Viking's full and counter height conservation cabinets. A wide range of sizes and unique optional accessories make these cabinets the choice to house a multitude of diverse collections. We also provide specialized cabinets for botanical, geological, and entomological collections. Our archival flat file cabinets have stainless steel tracks and plated rollers that eliminate contamination from flaking paint. And if your storage application is unique, Viking is ready to adapt or design a custom cabinet that meets your particular needs. Attention to detail is important to you - and to Viking. Our state-of-the-art manufacturing processes, talented and capable engineering team, and unique skills of our experienced craftsmen deliver museum storage products of unparalleled quality. At Viking, our commitment to your satisfaction begins the moment you give us a call. Our first priority is your long-term satisfaction...because we know that our greatest asset is a satisfied customer. Viking cabinets provide the best value in preserving the objects, artifacts, and specimens that you value most. Trust our experience...over half a century of manufacturing quality metal cabinetry. Trust our reputation...earned and the world's most prestigious institutions. Trust Viking.

Personnel:
Jim Dolan (Vice President Sales)
Mark Roer (Western Region Sales Manager)

Storage Design Consultants

SOLOMON & BAUER ARCHITECTS INC.
63 Pleasant St.
Watertown, MA 02472
Tel: 617-924-8200; FAX: 617-924-6685
E-mail: info@solomonbauer.com
Web Site: www.solomonbauer.com

Type of Business:
Award-winning Architecture and Interior Design Firm with over forty projects for museums. Master-planning; programming; feasibility studies; design of new museums; renovation and adaptive reuse of existing and historic structures; and exhibit design support. Special expertise in collections storage analysis, planning, and design. Recent projects for Dallas Museum of Art, Harvard Art Museums, Sam Noble Oklahoma Museum of Natural History, Museum of Fine Arts Houston, Princeton Art Museum, New Bedford Whaling Museum, and Museum of Fine Arts Boston.

Personnel:
Stuart B. Solomon, FAIA (Principal)
Lawrence C. Bauer, AIA (Principal)

Storage Equipment

BORROUGHS CORPORATION
3002 N. Burdick St.
Kalamazoo, MI 49004
Tel: 800-748-0227; FAX: 269-342-4161
E-mail: lindag@borroughs.com
Web Site: www.borroughs.com

Type of Business:
Museum Storage Solutions are part of the family of high-quality and durable storage products produced by Borroughs Corporation for nearly 70 years. Our storage professionals provide expert product knowledge, design capabilities, dependable service and responsive

(Continued on next page)

(Continued from previous page)

support, all on a local level and backed by the manufacturer's warranty. Borroughs knows how important the preservation of your valuable artifacts is to you and your organization. Our knowledge of the specialized requirements of museum storage will assure that your limited space is maximized while minimizing your investment. We can also provide design assistance so that flexibility can be maintained as your collection grows and changes. Rely on Borroughs to design and deliver all your museum and preservation storage needs: Vertebrate Cabinets, Herbarium Cabinets, Art and Textile Racks, High-Density Mobile Storage, Archival Record Storage, Open Shelf Filing, Heavy-Duty Steel Shelving, Library Bookstacks, Storage Cabinets and Drawer Units.

Personnel:
Joe Cascio (Vice President Sales)
Kris Macomber (Customer Service Manager)
Mike Proos (Technical Support Manager)

Crystalizations Systems, Inc.

CRYSTALIZATIONS SYSTEMS, INC.
1401 Lincoln Avenue
Holbrook, NY 11741
Tel: 631-467-0090; FAX: 631-467-0061
E-mail: CSIstorage@aol.com
Web Site: www.CSIstorage.com

Type of Business:
Collection Storage Systems are safe, light-weight ALUMINUM. We design, manufacture and install. Our well known Moving Painting and Moving Rolled Textile Storage Systems are available in any size. Installation options include Ceiling or Floor supported plus Convertible or Free-Standing. Aisles are always Track-Free and full system can be relocated. The "Oversized Flat" and "Display /Storage" Cabinets are offered in both standard and custom sizes and can be assembled on-site. Full budgeting and grant support.

Personnel:
Patricia J. Ellenwood (President)
Carmine Billotto (Operations Manager)

DELTA DESIGNS LTD.
P.O. Box 1733
Topeka, KS 66601
Tel: 785-234-2244 & 800-656-7426; FAX: 785-233-1021
E-mail: bdanielson@deltadesignsltd.com
Web Site: www.deltadesignsltd.com

Type of Business:
Custom and standard museum storage cabinets, free standing or mounted on high density mobile storage systems. Cabinets available for your collection: Natural History, Works on Paper, Textiles, Art Objects, Historical Artifacts. Design and Installation services provided. Quality through Incremental Change.

Personnel:
Bruce Danielson (President)

Hahn Bros.
FINE ART AND ANTIQUE SERVICES

HAHN BROS. FIREPROOF WAREHOUSES, INC.
622 Communipaw Ave.
Jersey City, NJ 07304
Tel: 212-926-1505; FAX: 201-432-9547
E-mail: info@hahnbros.com
Web Site: www.hahnbros.com

Type of Business:
Over 100 years of fine art services to the museum and art community. Full service specialists offering customized crating and traveling cases and freight forwarding for collections and shows. Packing, moving, relocation and installation. Registrar, photography and gallery services available. Secure, climate-controlled storage in two locations with the ability to set up to client specifications.

Personnel:
Karen O. Dowling (President)
Marianne Mikulka (Fine Art Director)

MONTEL INC.
225 4th Ave.
Montmagny, QC, Canada G5V 3S5
Tel: 877-935-0236; FAX: 418-248-7266
E-mail: system@montel.com
Web Site: www.montel.com

Type of Business:
The Art of Storage by Montel for Museums & Archival Collections: The Montel high density fixed and mobile storage systems allows each system to be custom-designed to the particular safety storage requirements for each type of collection. Montel has developed a line of efficient and safe products which respect the integrity and value of all types of art work regardless of their size & shape. Specializing in storage systems since 1924, Montel offers its expertise to insure planning solutions that maximize capacity, cost savings, security and accessibility. We offer our complete line for your particular collection requirement, including art racks, full line of cabinetry, textile racks, shelving, drawer cabinets and mobile storage systems.

Personnel:
Joey P. Boudreau (Marketing Director)

SPACESAVER CORPORATION
1450 Janesville Ave.
Fort Atkinson, WI 53538-2798
Tel: 920-563-6362 & 800-492-3434; FAX: 920-563-2702
E-mail: ssc@spacesaver.com
Web Site: www.spacesaver.com

(Continued on page 96)

(Continued from page 94)

Type of Business:

Collection storage - collection care. Arguably the single-most important undertaking for museums both large and small. As collections continue to grow, efficient artifact storage space and optimum convenience and control over artifacts have become primary needs in today's museum collection preservation strategies. Spacesaver offers innovative storage solutions that help museums better manage time, space and security. Spacesaver provides storage solutions that protect and preserve your valuable collections.

Personnel:
Brandy Thayer (Business Development)

VIKING METAL CABINET CO., INC.
5321 W. 65th St.
Chicago, IL 60638
Tel: 800-776-7767 & 708-594-1111; FAX: 708-594-1028
E-mail: sales@vikingmetal.com
Web Site: www.vikingmetal.com

Type of Business:

Viking manufactures a full line of museum cabinetry that meets the requirements for conservation, preservation, and archival storage for a wide variety of collections. Major institutions and universities throughout the world rely on Viking cabinets to protect their most precious specimens and artifacts. Additionally, Viking has been innovative in the design of custom storage solutions that meet the special needs of the museum community. Versatility is the hallmark of Viking's full and counter height conservation cabinets. A wide range of sizes and unique optional accessories make these cabinets the choice to house a multitude of diverse collections. We also provide specialized cabinets for botanical, geological, and entomological collections. Our archival flat file cabinets have stainless steel tracks and plated rollers that eliminate contamination from flaking paint. And if your storage application is unique, Viking is ready to adapt or design a custom cabinet that meets your particular needs. Attention to detail is important to you - and to Viking. Our state-of-the-art manufacturing processes, talented and capable engineering team, and unique skills of our experienced craftsmen deliver museum storage products of unparalleled quality. At Viking, our commitment to your satisfaction begins the moment you give us a call. Our first priority is your long-term satisfaction...because we know that our greatest asset is a satisfied customer. Viking cabinets provide the best value in preserving the objects, artifacts, and specimens that you value most. Trust our experience...over half a century of manufacturing quality metal cabinetry. Trust our reputation...earned and the world's most prestigious institutions. Trust Viking.

Personnel:
Jim Dolan (Vice President Sales)
Mark Roer (Western Region Sales Manager)

Storage Services

ARTPACK SERVICES INC. & A.I.R.

ARTPACK SERVICES
24650 Crestview Ct.
Farmington Hills, MI 48335
Tel: 240-478-8946; FAX: 248-478-9588
E-mail: wendy@artpack.com
Web Site: www.artpack.com

Type of Business:
Artpack was founded in 1981 to provide professional services to museums, auction houses, galleries, corporate and private collectors for fine arts and antiques. We specialize in fine arts storage, custom crating and packing, installation, local and long distance shipping including a monthly New York shuttle. Our operations are climate controlled and staff trained to museum standards. Artpack also offers collection/project management and courier services, mount and pedestal fabrication, rigging and conservation services.

Personnel:
Ted Lee Hadfield (President)
Wendy MacGaw (Vice President)

ARTWORKS OF KANSAS CITY FINE ART SERVICES
3017 Gillham Rd.
Kansas City, MO 64108
Tel: 816-753-4005 & 800-481-9856; FAX: 816-753-4007
E-mail: mike@artworkskc.com
Web Site: www.artworkskc.com

Type of Business:
Professional fine art packer and shipper providing museum-quality services nationwide. ARTworks' Midwest Regional Art Shuttle serves St. Louis, Chicago, Milwaukee, Minneapolis, Des Moines, Omaha, Lincoln, Kansas City - and all points in between. Air-ride, climate service with double drivers. AWKC offers custom EU-compliant crating, worldwide shipping, climate-controlled storage and installation. State-of-the-art facilities with professional staff.

Personnel:
Michael G. Otto (President)
Kris L. Luke (General Manager)

TERRY DOWD, INC.
2501 W. Armitage Ave.
Chicago, IL 60647-4324
Tel: 773-342-8686; FAX: 773-342-8650
E-mail: info@terrydowd.com
Web Site: www.terrydowd.com

(Continued on page 98)

(Continued from page 96)

Type of Business:
Providing museum quality fine art services in the Chicago and Denver areas. Professionals in packing, crating, transportation and storage of fine art and artifacts. Air ride, climate controlled transportation available in the Midwest and Mountain Plains areas and exclusive use nationally. Secure climate controlled storage provided in Chicago and Denver. Packing, installation, rigging and freight forwarding services provided by our experienced staff. Denver Tel.: 303-297-8686; Fax: 303-297-1919.

Personnel:
Terry Dowd (President)

Hahn Bros.

FINE ART AND ANTIQUE SERVICES

HAHN BROS. FIREPROOF WAREHOUSES, INC.
622 Communipaw Ave.
Jersey City, NJ 07304
Tel: 212-926-1505; FAX: 201-432-9547
E-mail: info@hahnbros.com
Web Site: www.hahnbros.com

Type of Business:
Over 100 years of fine art services to the museum and art community. Full service specialists offering customized crating and traveling cases and freight forwarding for collections and shows. Packing, moving, relocation and installation. Registrar, photography and gallery services available. Secure, climate-controlled storage in two locations with the ability to set up to client specifications.

Personnel:
Karen O. Dowling (President)
Marianne Mikulka (Fine Art Director)

THE ICON GROUP, INC.
2747 W. Taylor St.
Chicago, IL 60612-4047
Tel: 773-533-1800; FAX: 733-533-1900
E-mail: info@icongroup.us
Web Site: www.icongroup.us

Type of Business:
Museum Quality Fine Art Services to Museums, Galleries, Collectors and Auction Houses since 1980. Our Air-Ride Climate Control Transportation services the Chicago area as well as the Midwest and Northeast regions, along with exclusive use nationally. Climate Control Storage available as well as Collection Management, private viewing and photography services. Other services include Custom Crating and Packing as well as installation, rigging and freight forwarding.

Personnel:
Bruce MacGilpin (President)
Ingrid Fassbender (Collection Management/Storage)
Walt Solomon (Director, Long Distance Transportation)
Colby Starck (Long Distance Services)
Kevin Brosnan (Local Services)
Michael Gamis (Storage Services)
Eric Dimas (Crating Services)

NAGLEE FINE ARTS
1525 Grand Central Ave.
Elmira, NY 14901
Tel: 800-950-4533; FAX: 607-733-4850
E-mail: nfa@nagleegroup.com
Web Site: www.nagleegroup.com

Type of Business:
Conservation quality storage and transportation services for artistic and historic objects. High security, precision climate-controlled facility: 67% fahrenheit at 45% relative humidity. Professional, museum-trained staff offering quality art handling, installation and crating services for individual artists and institutions alike. Naglee Fine Arts is a division of Naglee Moving & Storage Inc., a full-service United Van Lines agent specializing in commercial moves for libraries and school systems.

Personnel:
Scott M. Hoose (Vice President)
Matthias H. Smith (Assistant Director)
Allen C. Smith (Consultant)

SOFIA STORAGE CENTERS
SOFIA BROS., INC.

SOFIA BROS., INC.
475 Amsterdam Ave.
New York, NY 10024
Tel: 212-873-3600; FAX: 212-799-2233
Web Site: www.sofiastorage.com

Type of Business:
Since our inception in 1910, Sofia Brothers has been owned and managed by the same family. We have built our reputation on the quality, reliability, and integrity of the services we provide. Our customers rely on our reputation and experience to store their treasures. Whether you require storage for a few months or a few years, call Sofia Brothers. We have custom built warehouses conveniently located in and around the metropolitan area to serve you. We offer facilities equipped with vaulted, fire-resistant, private storage rooms. When you use one of our warehouses, you are assured of having your goods placed in clean, well maintained, secured buildings.

Personnel:
Leonard Sofia (Secretary & Treasurer)
John Sofia, Jr. (President)

U.S. ART COMPANY, INC.
FINE ART HANDLERS
Corporate Headquarters, 66 Pacella Park Dr.
Randolph, MA 02368
Tel: 800-872-7826; FAX: 781-986-5595
E-mail: msilverman@usart.com
Web Site: www.usart.com

Type of Business:
U.S. Art Company, Inc. is worldwide, offers decades of experience, trained fine art handlers, museum quality packing, crating, shipping, installation, climate-controlled trucks & storage, international import/export & customs liaison services, offices in nine major cities & trucks continuously traversing nationwide. BOSTON - CORPORATE: 800-872-7826; DALLAS: 866-898-7278; LOS ANGELES: 877-528-7278; NEW YORK: 800-472-5784; ORLANDO: 888-802-4459; ST. LOUIS: 866-928-7278; WASHINGTON, DC: 877-508-7278.

Personnel:
Mark Lank (CEO)
Mark Silverman (COO)

Textiles Storage Equipment

Crystalizations Systems, Inc.

CRYSTALIZATIONS SYSTEMS, INC.
1401 Lincoln Avenue
Holbrook, NY 11741
Tel: 631-467-0090; FAX: 631-467-0061
E-mail: CSIstorage@aol.com
Web Site: www.CSIstorage.com

Type of Business:
Collection Storage Systems are safe, light-weight ALUMINUM. We design, manufacture and install. Our well known Moving Painting and Moving Rolled Textile Storage Systems are available in any size. Installation options include Ceiling or Floor supported plus Convertible or Free-Standing. Aisles are always Track-Free and full system can be relocated. The "Oversized Flat" and "Display /Storage" Cabinets are offered in both standard and custom sizes and can be assembled on-site. Full budgeting and grant support.

Personnel:
Patricia J. Ellenwood (President)
Carmine Billotto (Operations Manager)

DELTA DESIGNS LTD.
P.O. Box 1733
Topeka, KS 66601
Tel: 785-234-2244 & 800-656-7426; FAX: 785-233-1021
E-mail: bdanielson@deltadesignsltd.com
Web Site: www.deltadesignsltd.com

Type of Business:
Custom and standard museum storage cabinets, free standing or mounted on high density mobile storage systems. Cabinets available for your collection: Natural History, Works on Paper, Textiles, Art Objects, Historical Artifacts. Design and Installation services provided. Quality through Incremental Change.

Personnel:
Bruce Danielson (President)

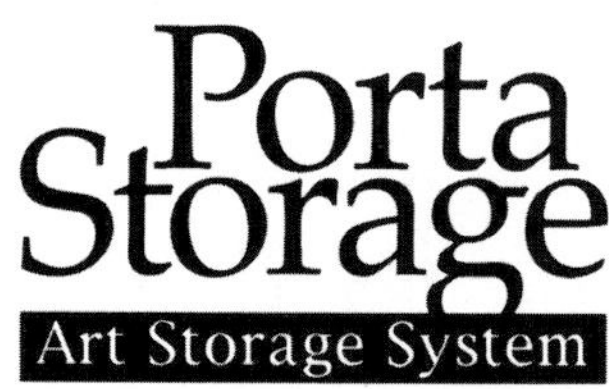

CHARLES J. DICKGIESSER & CO. INC.
257 Roosevelt Dr.
Derby, CT 06418-0475
Tel: 203-734-2553; FAX: 203-734-9221
E-mail: nancy.dickgiesser@sbcglobal.net
Web Site: Portastoragesystems.com

Type of Business:
Designers and manufacturers of museum storage systems. Porta Storage™ is a versatile, cost-effective system for displaying and storing textiles, paintings, photos and other art objects. Our pull-out art storage panels are floor supported for greater stability, maintenance free and custom designed to your specific needs. Call us today for more information.

Personnel:
Nancy L. Dickgiesser (President)

MASTERPAK
145 E. 57th St., 5th Fl.
New York, NY 10022
Tel: 800-922-5522; FAX: 212-586-6961
E-mail: als@masterpak-usa.com
Web Site: www.masterpak-usa.com

Type of Business:
Unique & archival materials for the protection of fine art, artifacts and antiques in packing, shipping, storing and display. Hard-to-find materials for conservators, artists, museums, galleries, collectors, framers and art shippers. Products include: Archival Softwrap® Tyvek®, Nomex® and Archival Hardwrap® Tyvek® Liners by DuPont, Sealed Air's Ethafoam®/Cellu-Cushion® in planks and rolls, Sealed Air's BubbleWrap®, Voltek's Volara® Polyethylene Foam, Archival Rolling & Storage Tubes, Unbuffered & Buffered Tissue in rolls and sheets, Photo-Tex Tissue in rolls and sheets, Glassine Paper in rolls and sheets, Silicone Parchment Release Paper in rolls and sheets, Corrugated Multi-Use Board, Archival tapes, Glass Skin®, Strongboxes™ & Print Pads™, Oz Clips™ Link Lock® Latches, Steel Closure Plates, PEM2 Data Loggers and specialty preservation management software developed by The Image Permanence Institute especially for the collections of Museums, Libraries & Archives. All products are available in small or large quantities and can ship within 24 hours. Our website, located at www.masterpak-usa.com, is open 24 hours for easy online ordering.

Personnel:
E. William Judson (Chairman)
Andrew L. Smith (President)

MONTEL INC.
225 4th Ave.
Montmagny, QC, Canada G5V 3S5
Tel: 877-935-0236; FAX: 418-248-7266
E-mail: system@montel.com
Web Site: www.montel.com

Type of Business:
The Art of Storage by Montel for Museums & Archival Collections: The Montel high density fixed and mobile storage systems allows each system to be custom-designed to the particular safety storage requirements for each type of collection. Montel has developed a line of efficient and safe products which respect the integrity and value of all types of art work regardless of their size & shape. Specializing in storage systems since 1924, Montel offers its expertise to insure planning solutions that maximize capacity, cost savings, security and accessibility. We offer our complete line for your particular collection requirement, including art racks, full line of cabinetry, textile racks, shelving, drawer cabinets and mobile storage systems.

Personnel:
Joey P. Boudreau (Marketing Director)

VIKING METAL CABINET CO., INC.
5321 W. 65th St.
Chicago, IL 60638
Tel: 800-776-7767 & 708-594-1111; FAX: 708-594-1028
E-mail: sales@vikingmetal.com
Web Site: www.vikingmetal.com

Type of Business:
Viking manufactures a full line of museum cabinetry that meets the requirements for conservation, preservation, and archival storage for a wide variety of collections. Major institutions and universities throughout the world rely on Viking cabinets to protect their most precious specimens and artifacts. Additionally, Viking has been innovative in the design of custom storage solutions that meet the special needs of the museum community. Versatility is the hallmark of Viking's full and counter height conservation cabinets. A wide range of sizes and unique optional accessories make these cabinets the choice to house a multitude of diverse collections. We also provide specialized cabinets for botanical, geological, and entomological collections. Our archival flat file cabinets have stainless steel tracks and plated rollers that eliminate contamination from flaking paint. And if your storage application is unique, Viking is ready to adapt or design a custom cabinet that meets your particular needs. Attention to detail is important to you - and to Viking. Our state-of-the-art manufacturing processes, talented and capable engineering team, and unique skills of our experienced craftsmen deliver museum storage products of unparalleled quality. At Viking, our commitment to your satisfaction begins the moment you give us a call. Our first priority is your long-term satisfaction…because we know that our greatest asset is a satisfied customer. Viking cabinets provide the best value in preserving the objects, artifacts, and specimens that you value most. Trust our experience…over half a century of manufacturing quality metal cabinetry. Trust our reputation…earned and the world's most prestigious institutions. Trust Viking.

Personnel:
Jim Dolan (Vice President Sales)
Mark Roer (Western Region Sales Manager)

Index to Advertisers

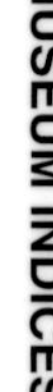
MUSEUM INDICES

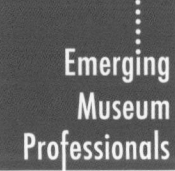

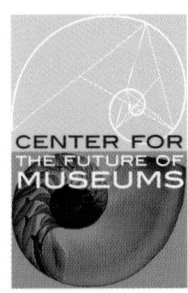

Index to Institutions

A

A–*Continued*

A–Continued

A–*Continued*

B

B–*Continued*

B–*Continued*

C

C–*Continued*

C–Continued

C–Continued

C–*Continued*

D

D–*Continued*

D–*Continued*

E

E–Continued

F

F–*Continued*

F–Continued

G

G–*Continued*

G–*Continued*

H

H–*Continued*

H–*Continued*

H–*Continued*

I

J

J–*Continued*

K

K–*Continued*

L

L–*Continued*

L–*Continued*

M

M–Continued

M–Continued

M–Continued

M–*Continued*

N

N–*Continued*

N–*Continued*

N–*Continued*

O

O–*Continued*

P

P–*Continued*

P–*Continued*

Q

R

R–*Continued*

R–*Continued*

S

S–*Continued*

S–*Continued*

S–*Continued*

T

T–*Continued*

T–*Continued*

U

U–*Continued*

V

W

W–*Continued*

W–*Continued*

W–*Continued*

X

Y

Z

Index to Personnel

A

A–*Continued*

A–*Continued*

A–*Continued*

Allen, Stacey, Naturalist (Garfield Park), Cleveland Metroparks Outdoor Education Division, Garfield Heights, OH....1322
Allen, Stacy D., Chief Interpretation & Resource Mgmt., Shiloh National Military Park & Cemetery, Shiloh, TN .1573
Allen, Susan, Mktg. Mgr., Cleveland Metroparks Zoo, Cleveland, OH....1307
Allen, Susan, Museum Shop Mgr., Sterling Historical Society and Little Red Schoolhouse Museum, Sterling Center, NY....1217
Allenick, Bob, Dir., The Temple Museum of Religious Art, Cleveland, OH....1311
Alley, Bill, Dir. & Cur., Pearson Air Museum, Vancouver, WA....1792
Alley, Ivy, Cur. Education, Mississippi Museum of Art, Jackson, MS....910
Allgaier, Joseph, Registrar, Bethlehem Historical Association, Selkirk, NY....1211
Allie, Stephen J., Dir., Frontier Army Museum, Fort Leavenworth, KS....612
Allison, Allen, Ph.D., Vice Pres. Science, Bishop Museum, Honolulu, HI....443
Allison, Brian, Cur., Travellers Rest Plantation & Museum, Nashville, TN...1570
Allison, Brooke, Dir., Buddy Holly Center, Lubbock, TX....1629
Allison, Brooke, Dir., Silent Wings Museum, Lubbock, TX....1629
Allison, David K., Assoc. Dir. Curatorial, National Museum of American History, Washington, DC....324
Allison, Jim, Supvr. Collections, Wyoming State Museum, Cheyenne, WY....1855
Allison, Kandi, Administrative Asst., Brucemore, Cedar Rapids, IA....577
Allison, Kris, Coord. Education, The Discovery Center of Idaho, Boise, ID....455
Allison, Laurie, Sr. Sec., Marshall M. Fredericks Sculpture Museum, University Center, MI....866
Allison, Nancy, Museum Shop Mgr., Milton J. Rubenstein Museum of Science & Technology, Syracuse, NY...1219
Allison, Robin, Asst. to Exec. Dir., Jackson Hole Historical Society and Museum, Jackson, WY....1860
Allman, Denny, Treas., Biedenharn Coca-Cola Museum, Vicksburg, MS....918
Allman, William G., Cur., The White House, Washington, DC....333
Allmon, Dr. Warren D., Dir., Paleontological Research Institution, Ithaca, NY....1147
Alloway, Mike, Sr., Dir., Forest County Potawatomi Cultural Center and Museum, Crandon, WI....1815
Allred, Kelley, Dir. Operations, Fort Worth Zoological Association, Inc., Fort Worth, TX....1610
Allsbrook, Robert, Museum Assn. Treas., Hampton History Museum, Hampton, VA....1716
Allshouse, Frances, Dir., The Old Jail Museum, Warrenton, VA....1753
Almand, Bob, Chm. (V), The Appalachian Trail Conservancy, Harpers Ferry, WV....1799
Almeda, Dr. Frank, Chm. Botany, California Academy of Sciences, San Francisco, CA....187
Almeida, Mary, Program Dir. & Early Childhood Coord., Cape Cod Children's Museum, Mashpee, MA....789
Almond, Jackie, Dir. Information Technology, Thomas Jefferson's Poplar Forest, Forest, VA....1710
Almy Gerry, Caroline, Co Vice Chm., Shelburne Museum, Inc., Shelburne, VT....1690
Alonso, Elisa, Administrative Asst. to Dir., Bass Museum of Art, Miami Beach, FL....367
Alowan, Zoe, Vice Pres. & Dir. Children's Art Academy, Museum of Ancient & Modern Art, Penn Valley, CA....163
Alpe, Carole, Museum Shop Mgr., The Masonic Library and Museum of Pennsylvania, Philadelphia, PA....1456
Alphonso, Christina, Mgr. Administration, The Cloisters, New York, NY....1166
Alsobrook, David, Dir., The Museum of Mobile, Mobile, AL....18
Alsobrook, David, Exec. Dir., Phoenix Fire Museum, Mobile, AL....18
Alsobrook, Gail, Dir. Devel., San Diego Museum of Man, San Diego, CA....184
Alstadt, Sgt. John, Cur., Delaware State Police Museum, Dover, DE....306
Alston, Leesha, Registrar, Phoenix Art Museum, Phoenix, AZ....51
Alston, Lisa, Financial & Administrative Officer, Marian Koshland Science Museum, Washington, DC....321
Alston, Samuel, Devel. & Cur., Museum of Great Christian Preachers & Ministries, Orange Park, FL....373
Alswang, Hope, Dir., Museum of Art, Rhode Island School of Design, Providence, RI....1495
Altadonna, Leigh, Chm. (V), John James Audubon Center at Mill Grove, Audubon, PA....1410
Altergott, Laura, Dir. Information Svcs., Chicago Botanic Garden, Glencoe, IL....497
Althaus, Richard, Pres., The Hicksville Gregory Museum, Hicksville, NY....1141
Althiser, Fran, Controller, National Baseball Hall of Fame and Museum, Inc., Cooperstown, NY....1123
Altieri Haslinger, Myriam, Pres. (V), Akron Art Museum, Akron, OH....1292
Altimus, Mandy, Archivist, The Massillon Museum, Massillon, OH....1331
Altis, Bethany, Museum Shop Mgr., The Magic House, St. Louis Children's Museum, Saint Louis, MO....948
Altman, Ellie, Dir., Adkins Arboretum, Ridgely, MD....743
Altman, Mary, Sr. Dir. Mktg., World Golf Hall of Fame, Saint Augustine, FL....383
Altobello, Maureen, Museum Shop Mgr., The Montgomery County Historical Society, Inc., Rockville, MD....744
Alvarado, Laura, Dir. Outreach, Indianapolis Art Center, Indianapolis, IN....549
Alvarado, Leslie, Dir. Sales & Mktg., Museo de Arte de Puerto Rico, Santurce, PR....1871
Alvarado, Dr. Tom, Staff Veterinarian, Dallas Zoo, Dallas, TX....1598
Alvare, Gigi, Dir. Education, Rockwell Museum of Western Art, Corning, NY..1124
Alvarez, Juan, Cur. Exhibits, The Michigan State University Museum, East Lansing, MI....838
Alvarez, Julio, Security Mgr., The Patricia & Phillip Frost Art Museum, Miami, FL....367
Alvarez, Raul, Asst. Gardener, Hakone Estate and Gardens, Saratoga, CA....209
Alvarez, Walter, Cur., Museum of Paleontology, Berkeley, CA....93
Alvarez, Yetzenia, Mgr. Public Rels., Museo de Arte de Puerto Rico, Santurce, PR....1871
Alves, C. Douglass, Jr., Dir., Calvert Marine Museum, Solomons, MD....748
Alvey, Christine, Librarian, Maryland State Archives, Annapolis, MD....718
Alvey, John, Museum Mgr., Dalton Defenders Museum, Coffeyville, KS....608
Alvey, Wendy, Museum Mgr., Dalton Defenders Museum, Coffeyville, KS....608
Alvord, Ellen, Andrew W. Mellon Coord. Academic Affairs, Mount Holyoke College Art Museum, South Hadley, MA....806
Alzalde, Lisa, Sec., Greene Memorial Museum, University of Wisconsin-Milwaukee, Milwaukee, WI.1833
Amack, Rex, Dir., Arbor Lodge State Historical Park, Nebraska City, NE....992
Amaducci, Thomas, Pres., American Truck Historical Society, Kansas City, MO....932
Amaker, Betty, Gift Shop Mgr. JFK Special Warfare Museum, Fort Bragg, NC....1246
Aman, Karen, Cur., Middlebury Historical Society, Wyoming, NY....1229
Amaro, Sophia, Dir. Devel, Cooper-Hewitt, National Design Museum, Smithsonian Institution, New York, NY....1167
Amash, Carissa, Cur., New York Transit Museum, Brooklyn Heights, NY....1113
Amason, Otis, Chm. & Pres. (V), Midway Museum, Inc., Midway, GA....427
Amatangelo, Marie Elena, Exhibition Coord., Smithsonian American Art Museum, Washington, DC....329
Amato, Carol, C.O.O., Virginia Museum of Fine Arts, Richmond, VA....1742
Amato, Helen C., Asst. to Dir., Lightner Museum, Saint Augustine, FL....381
Amato, Michael, Park Ranger, Theodore Roosevelt Birthplace National Historic Site, New York, NY....1183
Amato, Stephen G., Vice Chm., Lexington History Museum, Lexington, KY....652
Amaya Flynn, Tammi, Dir. Mktg., Florence Griswold Museum, Old Lyme, CT....291
Ambrose, Andy, Exec. Dir, Tubman African-American Museum, Macon, GA....426
Ambrose, John, Pres., Depot Park Museum, Sonoma, CA....212
Ambrose, Pamela E., Dir. Cultural Affairs, Loyola University Museum of Art, Chicago, IL....483
Ambrose, Steven, Chief Natural Resources, Hopewell Furnace National Historic Site, Elverson, PA....1423
Ambrosini, Kathy, Dir. Education, Mohonk Preserve, Inc., Gardiner, NY....1136
Ambrosini, Lynne D., Ph.D., Chief Cur., Taft Museum of Art, Cincinnati, OH....1306
Ambrosio, Jo, Rental Coord., National Museum of Dance & Hall of Fame, Saratoga Springs, NY....1207
Amburgey, Kendra, Interim Dir. & Business Mgr., West Valley Art Museum, Surprise, AZ....56
Amend, Deborah, Supt., Historic Governors' Mansion, Cheyenne, WY....1855
Amentas, Peter, Mgr. Security, Center for Curatorial Studies and the Hessel Museum of Art, Annandale-on-Hudson, NY....1099
Ameri, Dr. Anan, C.E.O. & Dir., Arab American National Museum, Dearborn, MI....831
America, Denise, Fiscal Officer, Jefferson Patterson Park & Museum, Saint Leonard, MD....744
Amerine Carter, Kristine, Mktg. & Membership, Hands On! Regional Museum, Johnson City, TN....1555

Amerski, Stan, Cur., The Jackson Barracks Military Museum, New Orleans, LA 681
Ames, Diane, Pres., Cortland County Historical Society, Cortland, NY 1125
Ames, Ruth, Treas., East Lyme Historical Society/Thomas Lee House, Niantic, CT 289
Ames Sheret, Mary, Cur. Collections, Battleship North Carolina, Wilmington, NC 1271
Amick, Alison, Assoc. Cur., Oklahoma City Museum of Art, Oklahoma City, OK 1371
Amiden, Cindy, Museum Dir., Hancock Historical Society, Hancock, NH 1019
Amidon, Catherine, Gallery Dir., Karl Drerup Art Gallery, Plymouth, NH 1026
Amie, Jennifer, Editor, Bell Museum of Natural History, Minneapolis, MN 884
Amiel, Jennifer, Dir. Education, Museum on Main, Pleasanton, CA 165
Amis, Anne, Dir. Finance & Operations, Zeum, San Francisco, CA 194
Ammann, Richard, Ph.D., Archivist, Racine Heritage Museum, Racine, WI ..1842
Amneus, Cindy, Cur. Fashion Arts & Textiles, Cincinnati Art Museum, Cincinnati, OH 1304
Amneus, Elizabeth, Public Rels., Mktg. Dir. & Retail Mgr., Audubon House & Tropical Gardens, Key West, FL 358
Amport, Caroline, Dir. Programs, The Pierce Manse/New Hampshire Political Library, Concord, NH 1015
Amrheim, Tom, Sec., Phoenix Trolley Museum/Arizona Street Railway Museum, Phoenix, AZ 51
Amrhein, Edward M., Admin. Vice Pres., Baltimore Streetcar Museum, Inc., Baltimore, MD 720
Amrhein, Rev. James, O.F.M.Conv., Assoc. Dir. & Museum Shop Mgr., Native American Exhibit, National Kateri Shrine, Fonda, NY 1134
Amrine, T.R., Mgr. Guest Rels., Cincinnati Zoo & Botanical Garden, Cincinnati, OH 1304
Amsler, Cory, Vice Pres. Collections & Interpretation, Mercer Museum of the Bucks County Historical Society, Doylestown, PA 1421
Amundson, Don, Treas., Upper Musselshell Historical Society, Harlowton, MT 966
Amundson, Jeff, Devel. Dir., Olmsted County Historical Society dba History Center of Olmsted County, Rochester, MN 891
Amussen, Laura, Dir. Exhibitions & Collection Coord., Rosenberg Gallery, Goucher College, Baltimore, MD 726
Anable, Susan, Dir. Educational Resources & Svcs., Dayton Art Institute, Dayton, OH 1316
Anathas, Thomas J., Treas., Nantucket Historical Association, Nantucket, MA ...792
Anawalt, Patricia, Dir. Center for Study Rgnl. Dress, Fowler Museum at UCLA, Los Angeles, CA 135
Ancheta, Brooke, Museum Shop Mgr., The Living Desert, Palm Desert, CA 160
Ancona, Stephanie, Dir. Devel., The Children's Museum of New Hampshire, Dover, NH 1016
Anday, Anton, Cur., Portage County Historical Society, Stevens Point, WI....1846
Ander, Greg, Dir. & Museum Shop Mgr., Los Nogales Museum, Seguin, TX....1648
Andera, Jo Ann, Dir. Texas Folklife Festival, Institute of Texan Cultures, San Antonio, TX 1643
Anderko, Robin, Registrar, Dearborn Historical Museum, Dearborn, MI 831
Anders, June, Dir., Black Range Museum, Hillsboro, NM 1079
Anders, Marguerite, Museum Shop Mgr. & Asst. Admin., The James Madison Museum, Orange, VA 1732
Anders, Roland, Pres., National Electronics Museum, Linthicum, MD 741
Andersen, Amy, Cur. Collections, Clarksville-Montgomery County Museum dba Customs House Museum & Cultural Center, Clarksville, TN 1549
Andersen, David, Designer & Preparator, Hallie Ford Museum of Art, Salem, OR 1403
Andersen, Jeffrey W., C.E.O. & Dir., Florence Griswold Museum, Old Lyme, CT 291
Andersen, Laura, Tourism & Visitor Rels. Coord., Hillwood Estate, Museum & Gardens, Washington, DC 318
Andersen, Marie, Devel. & Public Rels., San Diego Archaeological Center, Escondido, CA 111
Andersen, Nikki, Exec. Dir., Higgins Armory Museum, Worcester, MA 819
Andersen, Patricia, Librarian, The Montgomery County Historical Society, Inc., Rockville, MD 744
Anderson, Amber, Registrar, Maltz Museum of Jewish Heritage, Beachwood, OH 1296
Anderson, Andrea, Site Supvr. Zwaanendael Museum, Delaware Division of Historical & Cultural Affairs, Dover, DE 305
Anderson, Andy, Historian, Ezra Meeker Mansion, Puyallup, WA 1778
Anderson, Angela, Chm. (V), David Traylor Zoo of Emporia, Emporia, KS 611
Anderson, Annelle, C.E.O. & Pres. (V), National Museum of Roller Skating, Lincoln, NE 989
Anderson, August, Pres., Meeker County Historical Society Museum & G.A.R. Hall, Litchfield, MN 882
Anderson, Avis H., Exec. Dir., The Monmouth Museum, Lincroft, NJ 1045
Anderson, Beth, Dir. Devel., The Cornell Plantations, Ithaca, NY 1146
Anderson, Betsey, Administrative Asst., Belle Grove Plantation, Middletown, VA 1725
Anderson, Betty, Museum Shop Mgr., St. Albans Historical Museum, Saint Albans, VT 1689
Anderson, Bill, Museum Shop Mgr., General George Patton Museum, Fort Knox, KY 646
Anderson, Blue, Museum Shop Mgr., Columbia River Maritime Museum, Astoria, OR 1382
Anderson, Bradley, Dir. Children's Theatre, The Arkansas Arts Center, Little Rock, AR 76
Anderson, Brenda, Coord. & Cur., North Seattle Community College Art Gallery, Seattle, WA 1782
Anderson, Bruce, Sec., Clearwater Historical Museum, Orofino, ID 464
Anderson, Camille, Cur. Natural History, Maturango Museum of the Indian Wells Valley, Ridgecrest, CA 171
Anderson, Carl A., Supreme Knight & C.E.O., Knights of Columbus Museum, New Haven, CT 286
Anderson, Carol, Pres. (V), Minnesota Pioneer Park Museum, Annandale, MN 868
Anderson, Carrie, Dir., Green River Valley Museum, Big Piney, WY 1853
Anderson, Catherine, Accounting Mgr., Museum of Photographic Arts, San Diego, CA 181
Anderson, Catherine, Treas., Wentworth Gardner & Tobias Lear Houses Association, Portsmouth, NH 1028
Anderson, Charles E., Pres. Bd. Trustees, Sheehan Gallery at Whitman College, Walla Walla, WA 1793
Anderson, Chris, Business Mgr., Chippewa Nature Center, Midland, MI ...854
Anderson, Chris, Program Coord., Hartman Reserve Nature Center, Cedar Falls, IA 576
Anderson, Chris, Planetarium Production Specialist, Herrett Center for Arts & Science, Faulkner Planetarium and Centennial Observatory, Twin Falls, ID 467
Anderson, Christiane, Research Scientist, Herbarium of the University of Michigan, Ann Arbor, MI 822
Anderson, Christie, Registrar Univ. Exhibitions & Collections, Richard E. Peeler Art Center, Greencastle, IN 544
Anderson, Christie, Registrar University Exhibitions & Collections, William Weston Clarke Emison Museum of Art, Greencastle, IN 544
Anderson, Christine, Museum Shop Mgr., Denison Pequotsepos Nature Center, Mystic, CT 283
Anderson, Cindy, Mktg., Art Museum of South Texas, Corpus Christi, TX 1594
Anderson, Claudia, Asst . Site Mgr., Ford's Theatre National Historic Site (Lincoln Museum), Washington, DC 317
Anderson, Corinne, Devel. Officer of Foundations & Government Support, The High Museum of Art, Atlanta, GA...405
Anderson, Crystal, Pres. (V), Rifle Creek Museum, Rifle, CO 262
Anderson, Dale W., Dir., Wisconsin Automotive Museum, Hartford, WI 1822
Anderson, Daryl Anne, Pres., South County Museum Inc., Narragansett, RI.1489
Anderson, David, Dir., Creek Council House Museum, Okmulgee, OK 1374
Anderson, Debbie, Cur. Science, Alden B. Dow Museum of Science and Art of the Midland Center for the Arts, Midland, MI 854
Anderson, Deborah L., Exec. Dir. DSC, Inc., Danville Science Center, Danville, VA 1708
Anderson, Dennis, Cur., The Carter House, Franklin, TN 1551
Anderson, Donald B., C.E.O. & Pres., Anderson Museum of Contemporary Art, Roswell, NM 1086
Anderson, Donald R., Professor Emeritus, Allen R. Hite Art Institute, Louisville, KY 654
Anderson, Donna, Devel. Asst., The Health Adventure, Asheville, NC 1232
Anderson, Douglas, Cur. Res., Haffenreffer Museum of Anthropology, Brown University, Providence, RI 1494
Anderson, Douglas, Museum Shop Mgr., New York Museum of Transportation, West Henrietta, NY 1227
Anderson, Ed, Pres. (V), International Peace Garden, Dunseith, ND 1280
Anderson, Ellen, Dir., Oxford Museum, Inc., Oxford, MD 742
Anderson, Eric, 2nd Vice Pres., Norfolk Historical Museum, Norfolk, CT 289
Anderson, Erin, Cur., Western Heritage Museum Complex & Lea County Cowboy Hall of Fame, Hobbs, NM 1079
Anderson, Erin W., Dir., Helen E. Copeland Gallery, Bozeman, MT 958

A–*Continued*

A–*Continued*

A–*Continued*

Atwood, Leland, Pres. (V), Trainland U.S.A., Colfax, IA....579
Atwood, Shirley, Education Coord., Art Center Waco, Waco, TX....1653
Atwood, Ted, Pres. (V), Chatillon-DeMenil Mansion, Saint Louis, MO....946
Atzen, Scott, Horticulture Mgr., Des Moines Botanical Center, Des Moines, IA....583
Au Hoy, Fanny, Palace Admin., Hulihee Palace, Kailua-Kona, HI....449
Aubert, Ben, Cur., Grossmont College Hyde Art Gallery, El Cajon, CA....109
Aubert, Joseph, Mgr. Visitors Svcs., Norman Rockwell Museum, Stockbridge, MA....810
Aubrey, Sarah, Cur. Exhibitions & Programs, Fort Wayne Museum of Art, Fort Wayne, IN....542
Aubuchon, Kimberly, Archivist, Artpace San Antonio, San Antonio, TX....1643
Aucella, Frank J., Museum Dir., Woodrow Wilson House, Washington, DC....333
Auch, Steve, Cur., Jack Nicklaus Museum, Columbus, OH....1313
Aucoin, Brian, Dir. Animal Management, Oklahoma City Zoo, Oklahoma City, OK....1372
Audelo, Joe, Bd. Pres., Bakersfield Museum of Art, Bakersfield, CA....89
Auerbach, Amy, Sr. Vice Pres. & C.F.O., Boston Children's Museum, Boston, MA....758
Auerbach, Erik, Education Coord., San Francisco Camerawork, San Francisco, CA....192
Auermuller, Rob, Supt., Batsto Village, Hammonton, NJ....1042
Augelli, John, C.E.O. & Exec. Dir., Rosenberg Library, Galveston, TX....1615
Augenstein, Jan, Pres., The Marion County Historical Society Museum, Marion, OH....1330
Augura, Oscar, Registrar, The National Museum of Catholic Art & History, New York, NY....1177
Augustin, Trish, Gen. Mgr., The Old Church Society, Inc., Portland, OR....1399
Augustine, Sylvia, Dir., Independence Historical Museum, Independence, KS...618
Augustowski, Nancy, Tour Coord., Town of Yorktown Museum, Yorktown Heights, NY....1230
Auld, A. Michael, Co Chm. (Jamaica), Fondo Del Sol Visual Arts & Media Center/El Museo de Culturas y Herencias Americanas/MOCHA, Washington, DC....317
Auld, Marnie, Dir. Finance, The Farmers' Museum, Inc., Cooperstown, NY....1123
Auld, Marnie, Dir. Finance, New York State Historical Association/Fenimore Art Museum, Cooperstown, NY....1123
Aulisi, Joseph E., Dir., National Museum of Racing and Hall of Fame, Saratoga Springs, NY....1207
Aulisio, Terry, Museum Shop Mgr., Polk Museum of Art, Lakeland, FL....362
Aull, William E., Chm. (V), Hawaii Pacific University Gallery, Honolulu, HI....445
Ault, James A., Ph.D., Dir. Environmental Horticulture, Chicago Botanic Garden, Glencoe, IL....497
Aultz, Kathy, Dir. Devel., Omaha Children's Museum, Omaha, NE....995
Auping, Michael, Chief Cur., Modern Art Museum of Fort Worth, Fort Worth, TX....1611
Aurand, Karen L., Sec., McCoy House, Lewistown, PA....1442
Aurele Simons, Michael, Dir., National Electronics Museum, Linthicum, MD....741
Auriemma, Jamie, Education Coord., Mount Vernon Hotel Museum & Garden, New York, NY....1173
Ausein, Stephanie, Vice Pres., Fort Bissell Museum, Phillipsburg, KS....631
Ausfeld, Margaret Lynne, Cur. Art, Montgomery Museum of Fine Arts, Montgomery, AL....20
Ausich, Bill, Dir. & Professor, Orton Geological Museum, Ohio State University, Columbus, OH....1314
Austad, Dan, Pres. (V), Door County Maritime Museum (at Gills Rock), Gills Rock, WI....1820
Austad, Dan, Pres., Door County Maritime Museum (at Sturgeon Bay), Sturgeon Bay, WI....1846
Austerman, Carol, Businss Mgr., Alutiiq Museum and Archaeological Repository, Kodiak, AK....33
Austerman, Jack, Cur., Yukon's Best Railroad Museum, Yukon, OK....1381
Austin, Art, Park Mgr. Tombstone Courthouse State Historic Park, Arizona State Parks Board, Phoenix, AZ....49
Austin, Bethany, Registrar, Hampton History Museum, Hampton, VA....1716
Austin, Dr. Bob, Pres., Anderson County Arts Center, Anderson, SC....1499
Austin, Chris, Dir., Coolspring Power Museum, Coolspring, PA....1419
Austin, Dr. Christopher C., Cur. Herpetology, Museum of Natural Science, Baton Rouge, LA....668
Austin, Fran, Museum Shop Mgr., Limberlost State Historic Site, Geneva, IN....544
Austin, Gloria, Dir., Florida Carriage Museum and Resort, Weirsdale, FL....396
Austin, Gloria R., Exec. Dir., National Multicultural Western Heritage Museum, Fort Worth, TX....1611
Austin, Jen, Special Events Coord., Kalamazoo Valley Museum, Kalamazoo, MI....848
Austin, Jon N., Dir., Museum of Funeral Customs, Springfield, IL....522
Austin, Judy, Dir., Kentucky Down Under, Horse Cave, KY....650
Austin, Karen, Museum Shop Mgr., Columbia Gorge Discovery Center and Wasco County Museum, The Dalles, OR....1405
Austin, Megan, Gallery Office Asst., The Emerson Gallery, Clinton, NY....1122
Austin, Ramona, Cur., Baron & Ellin Gordon Art Galleries, Old Dominion University, Norfolk, VA....1729
Austin, Rebecca, Head Interpreter, Blue Ridge Institute and Museum, Ferrum, VA....1710
Austin, Rowe, Pres., Atlantic No. 1 Veterans Firemen's Association, Inc., Swampscott, MA....811
Austrain, Sarah, Chief Counsel, Solomon R. Guggenheim Museum, New York, NY....1181
Auter, Tye, Chm. (V), Fountain County War Museum, Inc., Veedersburg, IN....568
Auterson, Jenna, Membership, Swope Art Museum, Terre Haute, IN....567
Autry, Brick, Cur., Fort Davidson State Historic Site, Pilot Knob, MO....942
Autry, Jackie, Founding Chm., Autry National Center of the American West, Los Angeles, CA....133
Autry, Pamela, Dir. Human Resources, Dallas Museum of Art, Dallas, TX....1598
Auwarter, Tyler, Exhibitions Admin. SITE Santa Fe, Santa Fe, NM....1090
Avant, Joanne, Chief Cur., Texas Parks and Wildlife Department, Austin, TX....1584
Averett, Rhoda, Pres., Bedingfield Inn Museum, Lumpkin, GA....424
Averill, Tami, Education Mgr., Michigan Historical Museum, Michigan Historical Center, Lansing, MI....849
Avery, Andrea, Mgr. UWM Union-Art Gallery, Milwaukee, WI....1836
Avery, Dalton J., Treas., Shirley-Eustis House, Boston, MA....763
Avery, Deb, Exec. Dir., Cortez Cultural Center, Cortez, CO....235
Avery, Dorman, Chm. (V), Iron & Steel Museum of Alabama, Tannehill Ironworks Historical State Park, McCalla, AL....16
Avery, Dr. Julie, Extension Specialist & Cur. Education, The Michigan State University Museum, East Lansing, MI....838
Avery, Laura, Asst. Dir., Ringling College of Art and Design, Selby Gallery, Sarasota, FL....387
Avery, Lauren, Dir. Devel., Pacific Aviation Museum - Pearl Harbor, Honolulu, HI....447
Avery, Linda, Exhibit Mgr., Kaleidoscope, Kansas City, MO....933
Avery, Mary, Cur. & Clerk, South Bannock County Historical Center, Lava Hot Springs, ID....461
Avery, Pat, Pres. (V), Texas Energy Museum, Beaumont, TX....1587
Avery, Robert, Dir., Rome Historical Society Museum, Rome, NY....1204
Avery, Stan, Treas., A.W.A. Electronic-Communication Museum, Bloomfield, NY....1105
Avery, Susan, Dir., Woods Hole Oceanographic Institution, Ocean Science Exhibit Center, Woods Hole, MA....818
Avnet, John, Chm. Bd. Directors, The American Film Institute, Los Angeles, CA....133
Avoli, G. John, Exec. Dir., Frontier Culture Museum, Staunton, VA....1746
Avril, Ellen, Chief Cur. & Cur. Asian Art, Herbert F. Johnson Museum of Art, Ithaca, NY....1146
Awborg, Peabody, Chm. (V), Robert S. Peabody Museum of Archaeology, Andover, MA....754
Awsumb, Drew, Treas., St. Clair County Historical Society, Belleville, IL....470
Axsom, Richard H., Cur. Collections, Madison Museum of Contemporary Art, Madison, WI....1828
Axson, Richard, Senior Cur., Prints & Photographs, Grand Rapids Art Museum, Grand Rapids, MI....842
Axtman, Seb, Cur., South Dakota National Guard Museum, Pierre, SD....1538
Ayer, Dean, Cur. History, Riverside Metropolitan Museum, Riverside, CA....173
Ayers, Betsy, Asst. Dir. & Gift Shop Mgr., Oglethorpe University Museum of Art, Atlanta, GA....407
Ayers, Dena J., Administrative Dir., Mote Marine Laboratory/Aquarium, Sarasota, FL....387
Ayers, Marguerite, Museum Shop Mgr., Mount Clare Museum House, Baltimore, MD....725
Ayers, Marilyn L., Site Mgr., Bryant Cottage, Bement, IL....471
Ayers, Michael, Pres. (V), Aztalan Museum, Jefferson, WI....1824
Ayers, Stephen, Acting Dir., United States Botanic Garden, Washington, DC....331
Ayers, Steven T., AIA, Acting Architect of the Capitol, United States Capitol, Washington, DC....331

A–*Continued*

B

B–*Continued*

B–*Continued*

Barmore, Jim, Dir., Nevada State Museum, Carson City, NV....................1001
Barnany, Patrick, Pres. (V), Historical Society of the Tonawandas, Inc., Tonawanda, NY....................1221
Barnard, Cheryl, Pres. Historical Society, Troy Museum & Historic Village, Troy, MI....................866
Barnard, Katie, Dir. Education & Visitor Svcs., Westmoreland Museum of American Art, Greensburg, PA....................1429
Barnard, Melissa, Chm., Alden B. Dow Museum of Science and Art of the Midland Center for the Arts, Midland, MI....................854
Barneby, Mark, Chm. (V), Manatee Village Historical Park, Bradenton, FL....................336
Barnes, Althemese, Exec. Dir. & C.E.O., Riley House Museum of African American History & Culture, Tallahassee, FL....................391
Barnes, Bradford S., Pres. (V), Cattle Raisers Museum, Fort Worth, TX....................1609
Barnes, Florida, Treas., Frontier Times Museum, Bandera, TX....................1585
Barnes, Heather, Coord. Devel., Mingei International Museum, San Diego, CA....................180
Barnes, Iris, Public Rels., Havre de Grace Maritime Museum, Havre de Grace, MD....................739
Barnes, Janet, Sec., Ipswich River Wildlife Sanctuary (Massachusetts Audubon Society), Topsfield, MA....................812
Barnes, Jay, Dir., North Carolina Aquarium at Pine Knoll Shores, Pine Knoll Shores, NC....................1261
Barnes, Jill, Interim Exec. Dir. & Operations Mgr., Willard Arts Center/Carr Gallery, Idaho Falls, ID....................460
Barnes, Judy, Exec. Dir., Rogue Gallery & Art Center, Medford, OR....................1395
Barnes, Karin, Personnel Mgr., Kentucky Down Under, Horse Cave, KY....................650
Barnes, Katy, Asst. Dir. Conf. & Exhibitions, Savannah College of Art & Design-Atlanta Galleries, Atlanta, GA....................408
Barnes, Laurie, Cur. Chinese Art, Norton Museum of Art, West Palm Beach, FL....................397
Barnes, Lori, Dir. Education & Training, Marbles Kids Museum, Raleigh, NC....................1262
Barnes, Lucinda, Chief Cur. and Dir. Programs & Collections, University of California Berkeley Art Museum and Pacific Film Archive, Berkeley, CA....................94
Barnes, Nathan, Carr Gallery Cur., Willard Arts Center/Carr Gallery, Idaho Falls, ID....................460
Barnes, Reinaldo, Historic Site Mgr., Longfellow Evangeline State Historic Site, Saint Martinville, LA....................686
Barnes, Shirley, Historian, Narragansett Historical Society, Templeton, MA....................812
Barnes, Tamara C., Exec. Dir., Salem County Historical Society, Salem, NJ....................1060
Barnes, Taylor, Dir., The Arts Center, Jamestown, ND....................1285
Barnes, Toi, Park Guide, Mary McLeod Bethune Council House National Historic Site, Washington, DC....................321
Barnet, Peter, Cur. in Charge & Dept. Medieval Art & The Cloisters, The Cloisters, New York, NY....................1166
Barnet, Peter, Michel David-Weill Cur. in Charge Medieval Art & the Cloisters, The Metropolitan Museum of Art, New York, NY....................1172
Barnett, Alaina, Dir. Devel., The Columbus Museum, Columbus, GA....................414
Barnett, Bryan, Mayor, Rochester Hills Museum at Van Hoosen Farm, Rochester Hills, MI....................862
Barnett, Carol, Pres. (V), Cowgirls of the West, Cheyenne, WY....................1855
Barnett, Carolyn, Museum Shop Mgr., Oatlands, Leesburg, VA....................1720
Barnett, Carolyn, Treas, West Tennessee Regional Art Center, Humboldt, TN....................1555
Barnett, Dan, Studios Mgr., Craft Alliance, Saint Louis, MO....................946
Barnett, Eric B., Dir., The University Museum, Edwardsville, IL....................492
Barnett, Glenn, Dir. Interpretation & Exhibits, Fort Richardson State Historical Park, Jacksboro, TX....................1624
Barnett, James, Pres., Southern Forest Heritage Museum, Long Leaf, LA....................674
Barnett, James F., Jr., Dir., Grand Village of the Natchez Indians, Natchez, MS....................913
Barnett, Jenny, Dir. Wildlife Management, Binder Park Zoo, Battle Creek, MI....................825
Barnett, Joy, Office Mgr., Texas Association of Museums, Austin, TX....................1583
Barnett, Judy, Chm. (V), Craftsmen's Guild of Mississippi & Mississippi Craft Center, Ridgeland, MS....................916
Barnett, Julie, Dir. Devel., Chesapeake Bay Maritime Museum, Saint Michaels, MD....................745
Barnett, Lawrence, C.E.O., Chm. & Pres. (V), Brookings County Historical Society Museum, Volga, SD....................1544
Barnett, Mary, Museum Shop Mgr., High Point Museum & Historical Park, High Point, NC....................1252
Barnett, Melinda, Office Mgr., Jackson Hole Historical Society and Museum, Jackson, WY....................1860
Barnett, Redmond J., Head Exhibits, Washington State Historical Society, Tacoma, WA....................1790
Barnett, Rick, Owner, Thomas Kinkade Gallery, Monterey, CA....................149
Barnett, Roy, Treas., Missisquoi Valley Historical Society, North Troy, VT....................1685
Barney, Cheryl, Sr. Dir. Human Resources & Volunteer Svcs., Genesee Country Village & Museum, Mumford, NY....................1160
Barney, David, Cur. Exhibits, North Carolina Aquarium at Fort Fisher, Kure Beach, NC....................1255
Barney, Edres, Dir., Eastern Arizona Museum and Historical Society of Graham County Inc., Pima, AZ....................52
Barney, Jeff, Exhibition Design, Brigham Young University Museum of Art, Provo, UT....................1667
Barney, Ray, Museum Shop Mgr., Frederic Remington Art Museum, Ogdensburg, NY....................1187
Barney, Suzanne, Custodial Supvr., Brigham Young University Museum of Art, Provo, UT....................1667
Barnham, Katherine, Chm. (V), Governor Stephen Hopkins House Museum, Providence, RI....................1494
Barnhardt, Alan, Dir., Catawba Science Center, Hickory, NC....................1251
Barnhart, Alisa, Pres. Bd., West Overton Museums, Scottdale, PA....................1472
Barnhart, Audrey, Cur., Fort Union Trading Post National Historic Site, Williston, ND....................1291
Barnhart, Dale, Coord. Special Events, Pioneer Settlement for the Creative Arts, Barberville, FL....................334
Barnhill, Georgia, Andrew W. Mellon Cur. Graphic Arts, American Antiquarian Society, Worcester, MA....................818
Barnhill, Michael, Chm. (V), Edison Museum, Beaumont, TX....................1586
Barnidge, Tena, Museum Shop Mgr., Jacksonville Zoo and Gardens, Jacksonville, FL....................355
Barnidge-McIntyre, Marie, Horticulturist, Rancho Los Cerritos Historic Site, Long Beach, CA....................132
Barnow, Penny, Co Exec. Dir., Sr. Admin., Finance, Boulder Museum of Contemporary Art, Boulder, CO....................229
Barns, Joan, Public Rels. Mgr., Virginia Aquarium & Marine Science Center, Virginia Beach, VA....................1752
Barnwell, Andrea D., Dir., Spelman College Museum of Fine Art, Atlanta, GA....................409
Baroff, Deborah, Head Cur., Museum of the Great Plains, Lawton, OK....................1366
Baron, Donna K., Dir., Lebanon Historical Society, Lebanon, CT....................280
Baron, Eve, Dir. Planning Center, The Municipal Art Society of New York, New York, NY....................1173
Barone, Constance B., Site Mgr., Sackets Harbor Battlefield State Historic Site, Sackets Harbor, NY....................1205
Barone, Karen, Pres., National Association of Miniature Enthusiasts, Carmel, IN....................535
Barone, Nancy, Volunteer Coord., Nassau County Museum of Art, Roslyn Harbor, NY....................1204
Barongi, Rick, Dir., Houston Zoo, Inc., Houston, TX....................1621
Barons, Richard, Exec. Dir., Clinton Academy Museum, East Hampton, NY....................1128
Barons, Richard, Exec. Dir., East Hampton Historical Society, Inc., East Hampton, NY....................1128
Barons, Richard, Exec. Dir., East Hampton Town Marine Museum, Amagansett, NY....................1098
Barons, Richard, Exec. Dir., Mulford Farm Museum, East Hampton, NY....................1129
Barons, Richard, Exec. Dir., Osborn-Jackson House, East Hampton, NY....................1129
Barquist, David, Cur. American Decorative Arts, Philadelphia Museum of Art, Philadelphia, PA....................1459
Barr, Amie, Museum Shop Mgr., Museum of Contemporary Art Jacksonville, (MOCA Jacksonville), Jacksonville, FL....................355
Barr, Beverly, Mgr. Welcome Desk, The Nature Center at Shaker Lakes, Cleveland, OH....................1310
Barr, Brian, Dir. Horticulture, Hillwood Estate, Museum & Gardens, Washington, DC....................318
Barr, Cheryl B., Head Cur., Essig Museum of Entomology, University of California, Berkeley, Berkeley, CA....................92
Barr, Deb, Cur., Montrose County Historical Museum, Montrose, CO....................258
Barr, Janet, Commissioner Bd., The Downers Grove Park District Museum, Downers Grove, IL....................491
Barr, Matt, Dir. Camp, The Institute For American Indian Studies (IAIS), Washington, CT....................299
Barr, Peter J., Ph.D., Dir. Gallery, Klemm Gallery, Adrian, MI....................820
Barr, Robert, Pres. (V), Evanston Historical Center and Charles Gates Dawes House, Evanston, IL....................494
Barr, Ruth, Education Coord., The Institute For American Indian Studies (IAIS), Washington, CT....................299
Barrack, Antoinette, Pres. (V), Filoli Center, Woodside, CA....................225

B–*Continued*

B–*Continued*

B–*Continued*

B–*Continued*

B–*Continued*

B–*Continued*

B–*Continued*

B–*Continued*

B–*Continued*

Bolin, Liz, Administrative Asst., The General Douglas L. McBride Museum, New Mexico Military Institute, Roswell, NM....1086
Boling, Jean, Chm. (V), Schmidt House Museum & Research Library, Grants Pass, OR....1391
Bolinger, Brenda, Mgr. Volunteers, Rancho Santa Ana Botanic Garden, Claremont, CA....102
Bolivar, Tere, Bd. Member, Museo Del Nino, San Juan, PR....1870
Bollack, Marge, Museum Shop Mgr., Dakota Discovery Museum, Mitchell, SD....1536
Bollard, Jeff, C.E.O., Pella Historical Village, Pella, IA....597
Bollen, Norm, Chm., Fort Plain Museum, Fort Plain, NY....1134
Bollendorf, Jeanne, C.E.O., History Museum of Western Virginia, Roanoke, VA....1744
Bollendorf, Jeanne M., Exec. Dir., O. Winston Link Museum, Roanoke, VA...1744
Bolling, Jeff, Cur. Mammals, Disney's Animal Kingdom Theme Park, Bay Lake, FL....334
Bolling, Richard G., Cur. Naturalist, The Natural Science Center of Greensboro, Inc., Greensboro, NC....1249
Bolm, George C., Dir. & Cur., Old Court House Museum-Eva Whitaker Davis Memorial, Vicksburg, MS....918
Bolognani, Betty, Pres. (V), Readsboro Historical Society, Readsboro, VT....1688
Bolona, Shannon, Museum Shop Mgr., Anderson Ranch Arts Center & Museum, Snowmass Village, CO....263
Bolos, Julie, Administrative Svcs. Mgr., The St. Louis County Historical Society, Duluth, MN....875
Bolster, Jane, Literature & Richard Rodgers Awards, American Academy of Arts and Letters, New York, NY....1162
Bolt, Bud, Chm. (V), Bolt's Antique Tool Museum, Oroville, CA....158
Bolt, Ed L., Mill Site Mgr., Pickens County Museum of Art & History, Pickens, SC....1521
Bolt, Harold, Treas., Lynden Pioneer Museum, Lynden, WA....1771
Bolt, Liala, Museum Shop Mgr., Bolt's Antique Tool Museum, Oroville, CA....158
Bolt, Dr. Marvin, Dir. Astronomy History, Adler Planetarium & Astronomy Museum, Chicago, IL....476
Bolte, Ron, Carondelet Historic Center, Saint Louis, MO....946
Bolton, Todd P.H., Visitor Svcs., Harpers Ferry National Historical Park, Harpers Ferry, WV....1799
Bolyard, Ron, Pres., Kern River Valley Historical Society Museum, Kernville, CA....125
Bomar, Bill, Dir., Moundville Archaeological Park, Moundville, AL....21
Bombard, LuAnn, Dir., West Chicago City Museum, West Chicago, IL....527
Bomberger, Bruce, Cur., Landis Valley Museum, Lancaster, PA....1439
Bomford, David, Assoc. Dir. Collections, The J. Paul Getty Museum, Los Angeles, CA....137
Bommelyn, Loren, Pres. (V), Del Norte County Historical Society, Crescent City, CA....105
Bonacci, Robert, Dir., Butterfly Pavilion, Westminster, CO....265
Bonadies, Stephen, Chief Conservator & Deputy Dir. Collections Management, Virginia Museum of Fine Arts, Richmond, VA....1742
Bonadurer, Bob, Exec. Dir. IMAX & Planetarium, Milwaukee Public Museum, Milwaukee, WI....1835
Bonansinga, Kate, Dir., Stanlee & Gerald Rubin Center for the Visual Arts, University of Texas, El Paso, El Paso, TX....1605
Bonaparte, Sheree, Archivist, National Museum of the American Indian, Smithsonian Institution, New York, NY....1177
Bond, Birgitta, Librarian & Database Coord., James A. Michener Art Museum, Doylestown, PA....1420
Bond, Charles, Treas., Summit Historical Society, Breckenridge, CO....231
Bond, Dave, Bd. Member, Museum of Radio & Technology, Inc., Huntington, WV....1801
Bond, Gretchen, Dir., Miners Foundry Cultural Center, Nevada City, CA....151
Bond, Hallie, Cur., The Adirondack Museum, Blue Mountain Lake, NY....1105
Bond, John, Treas., South Shore Natural Science Center, Inc., Norwell, MA....797
Bond, Karen, Deputy Dir., Gateway to the Panhandle, Gate, OK....1362
Bond, Kaye, Cur., Cherokee Strip Museum and Rose Hill School, Perry, OK....1375
Bond, Margaret, C.E.O., Jesse Peter Museum, Santa Rosa, CA....208
Bond, Dr. Stanley, Park Supt., Kennesaw Mountain National Battlefield Park, Kennesaw, GA....422
Bond, Wanda L., Dir., Greybull Museum, Greybull, WY....1859
Bonde, Steve, Museum Shop Mgr., Idaho Military History Museum, Boise, ID....455
Bondi, Vickie, Admin., Centerville - Washington Township Historical Society & Asahel Wright Community Center, Centerville, OH....1301
Bondi, Vickie, Dir., Centerville - Washington Township Historical Society & Walton House Museum, Centerville, OH....1302
Bonds, Christy, Gift Shop Mgr., Cavanaugh Flight Museum, Addison, TX....1576
Bonds, Joe, Chm. (V), Cheyenne Botanic Gardens, Cheyenne, WY....1854
Bone, Anne J., Dir. Devel., Telfair Museum of Art, Savannah, GA....435
Bone, Jennifer, Museum Shop Mgr., Marshall County Historical Museum, Holly Springs, MS....909
Bone, Joe, Pres. & Treas. (V), David Crockett Cabin, Rutherford, TN....1573
Bone, Capt. Johnny, Security, Holocaust Museum Houston, Houston, TX....1620
Bone, Laurie, Cur. Programs, Robert T. Longway Planetarium, Flint, MI....840
Bonebakker, Odilia, Asst. Dir. & Cur., Muscarelle Museum of Art, Williamsburg, VA....1755
Bones, Marta, Exec. Dir., Pittock Mansion, Portland, OR....1400
Bonetas, Sarah, Dir. Devel., Blank Park Zoo, Des Moines, IA....582
Boney, Joe, Museum Shop Mgr., West End Hose Co. No. 3 Museum and Fire Educational Center, Biloxi, MS....904
Bongartz, Seth B., Exec. Dir., Hildene, The Lincoln Family Home, Manchester, VT....1683
Bonham, Jim, Bldg. & Grounds Supt., This Is The Place Heritage Park, Salt Lake City, UT....1671
Bonham, Rebecca, Exec. Dir., Studebaker National Museum, Inc., South Bend, IN....566
Bonica, Vince, Supt., Hancock House, Hancock's Bridge, NJ....1042
Bonilla, Danilo, Vice Pres. & Chm., Center on Contemporary Art, Seattle, WA....1780
Bonilla, Ileana, Asst. Cur., Wells Fargo History Museum, Los Angeles, CA....143
Bonito, Ruth, Dir., Noden-Reed Farm Museum, Windsor Locks, CT....303
Bonk, Erin, Coord. Devel., Utica Zoo, Utica, NY....1223
Bonk, Susan, Dir. Education, EdVenture, Inc., Columbia, SC....1508
Bonn, Claudia, Exec. Dir. & Pres., Wave Hill, Bronx, NY....1109
Bonn, Greg, Museum Dir., Oregon Electric Railway Historical Society, Inc., Salem, OR....1404
Bonnell, Tim, Sr., Pres. (V), Kansas Aviation Museum, Wichita, KS....638
Bonner, Charles, Chm., Keystone Gallery, Scott City, KS....633
Bonner Ganter, Deanna, Cur. Photography, Fine Arts & Archives, Maine State Museum, Augusta, ME....690
Bonner, Jeffrey P., Ph.D., Pres. & C.E.O., Saint Louis Zoo, Saint Louis, MO....951
Bonnett, Barb, Phelps House Chm., Phelps House, Burlington, IA....575
Bonneville, Ann, Cur., Guilford Historical Society, Guilford, VT....1681
Bonno, Gilbert, Pres. (V), Michigan Museum of Surveying, Lansing, MI....849
Bonny, Francesca Biella, Registrar, Nemours Mansion and Gardens, Wilmington, DE....313
Bonny, Jack, Chm., National Route 66 Museum and Old Town Complex, Elk City, OK....1361
Boo, Barbara, Museum Shop Mgr., Tweed Museum of Art, Duluth, MN....875
Boocher, Susan, Museum Shop Asst., Studebaker National Museum, Inc., South Bend, IN....566
Boogaert, John, Pres. (V), Kearney Mansion Museum, Fresno, CA....116
Booker, Robert, Chief of Security, Brandywine River Museum, Chadds Ford, PA....1417
Booker, William, Preparator, Siouxland Heritage Museums, Sioux Falls, SD....1542
Bookless, Mary Beth, Chief Cur., Salter Museum, Argonia, KS....604
Bookless, Troy, Pres. Argonia & Western Sumner Historical Society, Salter Museum, Argonia, KS....604
Boone, Allyn C., Dir. Devel., Lauren Rogers Museum of Art, Laurel, MS....912
Boone, Betty Ann, Exec. Sec., Sherman House Museum, Lancaster, OH....1327
Boone, Vicki, Deputy Dir., Harvard Museum of Natural History, Cambridge, MA....767
Boord, Charlotte, Museum Asst., Spanish Governor's Palace, San Antonio, TX....1646
Booream, Rick, Librarian, Newtown Historic Association, Newtown, PA....1447
Boorsch, Suzanne, Cur. Prints, Drawings & Photographs, Yale University Art Gallery, New Haven, CT....287
Booth, Bob, Chm. (V), Caldwell Heritage Museum, Lenoir, NC....1255
Booth, Carter, Pres., The Glebe House Museum and Gertrude Jekyll Garden, Woodbury, CT....303
Booth, Connie, Volunteer Coord., Civic Garden Center of Greater Cincinnati, Cincinnati, OH....1305

Booth, Gregory W., C.E.O. & Pres. Zippo Mfg. Co., Zippo/Case Visitors Center, Bradford, PA 1415

Booth, Larry, Guard, Spurlock Museum, University of Illinois at Urbana-Champaign, Urbana, IL 525

Booth, Peter, Exec. Dir., Mission Mill Museum Association, Salem, OR 1404

Booth Ricciardi, Cynthia, Ph.D., Pres. (V), Old Colony Historical Society, Taunton, MA 811

Boothby, Ron, Dir. Facilities, Kalamazoo Institute of Arts, Kalamazoo, MI 847

Bopp, Edward S., Pres. (V) & C.E.O., New Orleans Pharmacy Museum, New Orleans, LA 683

Bopp, Patricia S., Membership Sec., New Orleans Pharmacy Museum, New Orleans, LA 683

Boprey, Richard, Dir., Norwood Historical Association and Museum, Norwood, NY 1187

Boraggina, John, Museum Shop Mgr., Catalina Island Museum Society, Inc., Avalon, CA 89

Borba, Norene, Recreation Supvr., Applegate Park Zoo, Merced, CA 146

Borbee-Louvell, Wendy, Mgr. Visitor Svcs., Whitney Museum of American Art, New York, NY 1184

Borchardt, Ali, Dir. Education, Columbia Museum of Art, Columbia, SC 1508

Borchardt, Bill, Co Pres., Alaska Zoo, Anchorage, AK 27

Borchert Cadon, Carol, Assoc. Dir. Collections, Mount Vernon: George Washington's Estate & Gardens, Mount Vernon, VA 1727

Borchert, Christopher, Cur., Washington County Historical Society, West Bend, WI 1850

Bordeaux, Mary, Museum Shop Mgr., Boyhood Home of President Woodrow Wilson, Augusta, GA 410

Bordeaux, Sally, Museum Shop Mgr. & Bookstore Mgr., National Wildlife Visitor Center, Patuxent Research Refuge, Laurel, MD 740

Borden, Lee, Events & Communications Mgr., The Art Center, Grand Junction, CO 249

Borden, Michael, Chm., EdVenture, Inc., Columbia, SC 1508

Borders, Britt, Treas., EdVenture, Inc., Columbia, SC 1508

Bordner, Liz, Exhibits Mgr., KidZone Museum, Truckee, CA 218

Borecky, Dortha, Pres. (V), Van Buren County Historical Museum, Clinton, AR 68

Borg, Betty, Museum Shop Mgr., Eagle Historical Society & Museums, Eagle, AK 29

Borges, Kim, Museum Shop Mgr., Honolulu Zoo, Honolulu, HI 446

Borgeson, Jacqueline L., Cur., Martin and Osa Johnson Safari Museum, Chanute, KS 607

Borgman, Kathy, Admin., Friends of Arrow Rock, Inc., Arrow Rock, MO 920

Borgmann, James, Chm. (V), Muncie Children's Museum, Muncie, IN 558

Borgonovo, Roy, Treas., Presidio Historical Association, Presidio of San Francisco, CA 167

Borhlert, George, Chm. (V), Oregon Coast Aquarium, Newport, OR 1395

Borick, Carl P., Asst. Dir., The Charleston Museum, Charleston, SC 1503

Boris, Staci, Sr. Cur., Spertus Museum, Chicago, IL 486

Borkowski, Adrienne, Studio Asst., Society for Contemporary Craft, Pittsburgh, PA 1468

Borland, Pirkko, Treas., Nordic Heritage Museum, Seattle, WA 1782

Borlaug, David, Dir., The North Dakota Lewis & Clark Interpretive Center, Washburn, ND 1291

Borleske, Mark, Education, Depot Museum/Cascade Rail Foundation, South Cle Elum, WA 1786

Borleson, Ashley, Pres., Moss Mansion Historic House Museum, Billings, MT 956

Borlinghaus, Jennifer, Dir. Devel. & Public Rels. CAF Airpower Museum, Midland, TX 1632

Born, Carol, Pres. (V), Rocky Mountain Quilt Museum, Golden, CO 249

Born, Cathy, Museum Shop Mgr., Historic General Dodge House, Council Bluffs, IA 580

Born, Richard A., Senior Cur., Smart Museum of Art, Chicago, IL 486

Bornfriend, Carl, Exec. Dir., Frisco Native American Museum and Natural History Center, Frisco, NC 1247

Bornfriend, Joyce, Education & Public Rels., Frisco Native American Museum and Natural History Center, Frisco, NC 1247

Bornhorst, Dr. Theodore J., Dir. & Prof., A. E. Seaman Mineral Museum, Houghton, MI 846

Bornstein, Sara, Mgr. Visitor Svcs., Autry National Center of the American West, Los Angeles, CA 133

Borowski, Pete, Treas., McLean County Museum of History, Bloomington, IL 472

Borowsky, Gwen, C.E.O. & Vice Pres., National Liberty Museum, Philadelphia, PA 1458

Borowsky, Irvin J., Founder & Chm. (V), National Liberty Museum, Philadelphia, PA 1458

Borrego Pierce, Alicia, Deputy Dir., New Mexico Museum of Natural History & Science, Albuquerque, NM 1072

Borromeo, Gina, Cur. Ancient Art, Museum of Art, Rhode Island School of Design, Providence, RI 1495

Borrowdale-Cox, Deborah, Cur. Education, The Art Museum at the University of Kentucky, Lexington, KY 651

Borsanyi, Jackie, Cur. Art, Brevard Art Museum, Melbourne, FL 364

Borst, Lindsay, Museum Collections Mgr., The Society of the Cincinnati at Anderson House, Washington, DC 330

Bortner, Ray, Volunteer Coord., Cupertino Historical Society & Museum, Cupertino, CA 105

Bortoli, Natalie, Vice Pres. Educ. & Community Connections, Chicago Children's Museum, Chicago, IL 478

Boruff, Timothy, Exec. Dir., Price Tower Arts Center, Bartlesville, OK 1357

Bos, Peggy, Cur., Clovis Big Dry Creek Historical Museum, Clovis, CA 103

Bos, Saskia, Dean of Art School, Arthur A. Houghton Jr. Gallery & The Great Hall Gallery, New York, NY 1164

Bosarge, Johnette, Administrative Asst., J.L. Scott Marine Education Center and Aquarium, Gulf Coast Research Laboratory College of Marine Sciences, The U. of Southern Mississippi, Ocean Springs, MS 914

Boschan, Bobbie, Museum Shop. Mgr., Ojai Valley Historical Society and Museum, Ojai, CA 157

Boschult, Andrea, Administrative Asst., The Durham Museum, Omaha, NE 994

Bosco, Christine, Dir. Special Events & Rentals, Caramoor Center for Music & the Arts, Inc., Katonah, NY 1149

Bose, Julie, C.E.O., The New York City Police Museum, New York, NY 1178

Bosky, Edward R., Dir., Gamble House, Pasadena, CA 162

Bosle, David, Pres. Bd., Children's Museum of Central Nebraska, Hastings, NE 985

Bosley, Doug, Museum Shop Mgr., Allegheny Portage Railroad National Historic Site and Johnstown Flood National Memorial, Gallitzin, PA 1426

Bosse, David, Librarian, Memorial Hall Museum, Pocumtuck Valley Memorial Assoc., Deerfield, MA 774

Bosse, David C., Librarian, Historic Deerfield, Inc., Deerfield, MA 774

Bosskoff, Nancy, Dir., Finch Lane Gallery, Salt Lake City, UT 1670

Bost, Barbara M., Cur., House with the Eye Museum, Leadville, CO 256

Bostick, Virginia, Pres. (V), Union County Historical Museum, Liberty, IN 553

Bostock, Bret, Registrar & Collection Mgr., Glencairn Museum: Academy of the New Church, Bryn Athyn, PA 1415

Boston, Janet, Dir. Community Svcs., The Children's Museum of Indianapolis, Indianapolis, IN 547

Boston, Mike, Security, Elizabeth Myers Mitchell Art Gallery, St. John's College, Annapolis, MD 717

Bostrom, Antonia, Sr. Cur. Sculpture & Decorative Arts, The J. Paul Getty Museum, Los Angeles, CA 137

Bostrom, Don, Pres. (V), Sherburne History Center, Becker, MN 870

Bostwick, Todd, City Archaeologist, Pueblo Grande Museum and Archaeological Park, Phoenix, AZ 51

Boswell, Mary Rose, Dir., Enfield Shaker Museum, Enfield, NH 1017

Boswell, Peter, Asst. Dir. Programs & Sr. Cur., Miami Art Museum, Miami, FL 365

Boswell, Tom, Property Mgr., Enfield Shaker Museum, Enfield, NH 1017

Both, Peter, Mgr., James A. McFaul Environmental Center of Bergen County, Wyckoff, NJ 1068

Bothe, Jim, Membership Chm., Galloway House and Village - Blakely Museum, Fond du Lac, WI 1819

Bothma Ellerman, Trudi, Educator CDC/Global Health Odyssey, Atlanta, GA 403

Bothner, Vera, Chm., Exploration Place, Inc., Wichita, KS 637

Bothwell, Jay, Pres. (V), District of Columbia Arts Center, Washington, DC 316

Botros, Ceres, Mgr. Special Events, Pasadena Museum of California Art, Pasadena, CA 163

Botsch, Barbara, Pres. (V), Bonner County Historical Museum, Sandpoint, ID 466

Bott, James, Dir., Officer & Pres. (V), The Oyster and Maritime Museum of Chincoteague, Chincoteague, VA 1706

Bottger, Dee, Treas., Burt County Museum, Tekamah, NE 998

Bottinelli, Lora, Exec. Dir., The Ward Museum of Wildfowl Art, Salisbury University, Salisbury, MD 746

Bottler, Florence, Pres. (V), The Paterson Museum, Paterson, NJ 1056

Bottomley, Kristina, Registrar, Mary and Leigh Block Museum of Art, Northwestern University, Evanston, IL 494

B–*Continued*

B–*Continued*

Bradbury, Mary Jane, Coord. (V), Four Mile Historic Park, Denver, CO 240
Braddock, Daniel L., Chm. & C.E.O., White Pine Public Museum, Ely, NV....1003
Bradeen, Gwen, Cur., Milo Historical Society, Milo, ME 702
Braden, Geoff, Shipwright in Residence, Center for Wooden Boats, Seattle, WA .1779
Braden, Gerald, Research Biologist, San Bernardino County Museum, Redlands, CA...170
Braden, John, Dir., Seattle Aquarium, Seattle, WA 1783
Bradenburg, Lorraine, Library Asst., Woodford County Historical Society Museum, Versailles, KY..........................664
Bradfield, Gerald, Cur., Fort William Henry Museum, Lake George, NY........1152
Bradford, Dr. Bruce C., Cur., The Gillespie Museum - Stetson University, De Land, FL 343
Bradford, Dr. Carol, Veterinarian, Potawatomi Zoo, South Bend, IN............566
Bradford, Jolene, Dir., Museum Shop Mgr. & Membership Chm., Herington Historical Society & Museum, Inc. - SE Dickinson County, Herington, KS 616
Bradford, Marilyn, Black Pioneer Committee, Alton Museum of History and Art, Inc., Alton, IL...........................468
Bradford, Theodore, Chm. (V), Orlando Science Center, Inc., Orlando, FL 374
Bradham, J. Elizabeth, Pres., Gibbes Museum of Art, Charleston, SC.............1504
Bradham, Sharon, Exec. Dir., Cedarhurst Center for the Arts, Mount Vernon, IL....507
Bradley, Alisa, Museum Mgr., Mississippi River Museum at Mud Island River Park, Memphis, TN 1564
Bradley, Betsy, Dir., Mississippi Museum of Art, Jackson, MS.................................910
Bradley, Caroline L., Cur., Dir & Treas., Spotsylvania Historical Association and Museum, Spotsylvania, VA............1746
Bradley, Darlene, Public Rels., Ruth and Charles Gilb Arcadia Historical Museum, Arcadia, CA..................................88
Bradley, David B., Foundation Vice Pres. Finance & Admin., Virginia Museum of Fine Arts, Richmond, VA 1742
Bradley Dean, Kathy, Dir. Operations & Visitor Svcs., Young at Art Children's Museum, Davie, FL.................................342
Bradley, Douglas E., Cur. Ethnographic Arts, The Snite Museum of Art, University of Notre Dame, Notre Dame, IN 561
Bradley, Larry, Pres. Bd., W.H. Over Museum, Vermillion, SD.......................1544
Bradley, Laurel, Dir. & Cur., Carleton College Art Gallery, Northfield, MN 888
Bradley, M. Lynn, Chm. (V), The Children's Museum of Science and Technology, Troy, NY 1221
Bradley, Marie, Asst. to Dir., Academy Art Museum, Easton, MD.......................733
Bradley, Molly, Animal Exhibit Asst., Randall Museum, San Francisco, CA......191
Bradley, Naomi, Chm. (V), Shattuck Windmill Museum & Park, Shattuck, OK..1377
Bradley, Noreen, Vice Pres. Mktg., Brooklyn Botanic Garden, Brooklyn, NY...1110
Bradley, Pat, Museum Shop Mgr., The Franklin Pierce Homestead, Hillsborough, NH 1020
Bradley, Rudy, Trustee, Florida Agricultural Museum, Palm Coast, FL....376
Bradley, Stephanie, Treas., Weems-Botts Museum, Dumfries, VA........................1709
Bradley, Tom, Supt., Jefferson National Expansion Memorial, Saint Louis, MO...947
Bradshaw, Barbara, Administrative Asst., Piedmont Arts Association, Martinsville, VA 1724
Bradshaw, Jim, Office Staff & Archivist, Nita Stewart Haley Memorial Library & J. Evetts Haley History Center, Midland, TX 1633
Bradshaw, Linda, Museum Shop Mgr. & Front Desk Staffer, New England Ski Museum, Franconia, NH 1018
Bradshaw, Louise, Dir. Education, Saint Louis Zoo, Saint Louis, MO...................951
Bradshaw, Terri, Mgr. Special Events, Los Angeles County Museum of Art, Los Angeles, CA 138
Bradshaw, Victoria, Coord. Collections, Phoebe Apperson Hearst Museum of Anthropology, Berkeley, CA........................93
Bradshaw, William, C.E.O. & Dir., Roper Mountain Science Center, Greenville, SC...1514
Bradstreet, David A., C.E.O., Cutler Botanic Garden, Binghamton, NY........1104
Bradt, Kay, Dir., Quayle Rare Bible Collection, Baldwin City, KS..................606
Bradt, Rachelle, Education Cur., Yeshiva University Museum at the Center for Jewish History, New York, NY............1184
Brady, Ann, Dir., Atlantic Center for the Arts, Inc., New Smyrna Beach, FL 371
Brady, Dr. Charles A., Pres. & C.E.O., Memphis Zoo, Memphis, TN................1563
Brady, Christine, Pres., Mystic Arts Center, Mystic, CT 283
Brady, David, Vice Pres. Mktg., Houston Zoo, Inc., Houston, TX.........................1621
Brady, Doug, Pres. (V), Beaufort Historic Site, Beaufort, NC 1234
Brady, Edith, Dir., High Point Museum & Historical Park, High Point, NC...........1252
Brady, Elizabeth, Pres., The Toledo Museum of Art, Toledo, OH...................1345
Brady, Gerald, Cur., Potter Park Zoo, Lansing, MI 849
Brady, Heather, Head Education, Isamu Noguchi Garden Museum, Long Island City, NY...1154
Brady, Jana, Public Rels. Assoc., Mississippi Museum of Art, Jackson, MS..910
Brady, Kathleen, Public Affairs Officer, Blanton Museum of Art, Austin, TX.....1581
Brady, Kathleen D., Exec. Dir., Birdsong Nature Center, Thomasville, GA 436
Brady, Melissa, Museum Shop Mgr., Chihuahuan Desert Research Institute, Fort Davis, TX...1607
Brady, Mildred, Gen. Office Mgr., White County Historical Society, Cleveland, GA...414
Brady, Tess, Dir., Judith Basin County Museum, Stanford, MT.............................972
Brady, Travis, Cur., The Greenburgh Nature Center, Scarsdale, NY 1208
Brafford, C.J., C.E.O. & Museum Shop Mgr., Ute Indian Museum/Montrose Visitor Center, Montrose, CO 258
Bragalone, Ellen, Museum Shop Mgr., Museum of Fine Arts, Boston, MA 761
Bragaw, Catherine, Education Specialist, Harpers Ferry National Historical Park, Harpers Ferry, WV.......................1799
Bragdon, David, Council Pres., Oregon Zoo, Portland, OR 1400
Bragg, Cheryl, Dir., Berman Museum of World History, Anniston, AL 3
Bragg, Cheryl H., Exec. Dir., Anniston Museum of Natural History, Anniston, AL 3
Bragg, Donald, Chm. Bd. Trustees (V), Anderson/Abruzzo Albuquerque International Balloon Museum, Albuquerque, NM 1070
Bragg, Gary O., Pres., Wheels O' Time Museum, Peoria, IL..................................512
Bragg, Janice M., Museum Shop Mgr., Wheels O' Time Museum, Peoria, IL.......512
Bragg, Kim, Chm. Bd. (V), The National Museum of Communications, Richardson, TX...1640
Bragg, Sherry, Outreach Dir., The Curious Kids' Museum, Saint Joseph, MI...864
Bragg, Capt. Terry, Exec. Dir., Battleship North Carolina, Wilmington, NC...........1271
Bragg, William J., Founder & Exec. Cur., The National Museum of Communications, Richardson, TX 1640
Braginton, Linda, Asst. Librarian, Bixby Memorial Library, Vergennes, VT 1692
Braho, Alisa, Dir. Devel., Carnegie Museum of Natural History, Pittsburgh, PA 1464
Brahs, Stuart J., Chm. (V), Woodrow Wilson House, Washington, DC 333
Braide, Carol, Publications Mgr., The Museum for African Art, Long Island City, NY..1154
Brake, Dr. Donald L., Sr., Chm. (V), The Living Word National Bible Museum, Aledo, TX 1576
Brakefield, Peggy, Assoc. Archivist, Camden Archives & Museum, Camden, SC...1501
Brako, Jeanne, Cur., Center of Southwest Studies/Fort Lewis College, Durango, CO..243
Braman, Andrew, Controller, Rockwell Museum of Western Art, Corning, NY..1124
Bramley, Herb, Cur., Long Beach Fire Museum, Long Beach, CA.......................131
Branagan, Carmine, Exec. Dir., National Academy Museum and School of Fine Arts, New York, NY...................................1176
Branagin, Audrey, Bd. Member, Clinton County Museum, Frankfort, IN 543
Brancazio, Judy, Pres., The Jefferson County Historical Assoc., Steubenville, OH 1344
Branch, Joseph, Chm. Bd., International Crane Foundation, Baraboo, WI 1811
Branch, Paul R., Park Ranger, Fort Macon State Park, Atlantic Beach, NC .1233
Brand, Beth, Librarian, Desert Botanical Garden, Phoenix, AZ...................................50
Brand, Michael, Dir., The J. Paul Getty Museum, Los Angeles, CA 137
Brandeis, Ann, Bus. Mgr., Cora Hartshorn Arboretum and Bird Sanctuary, Short Hills, NJ 1061
Brandes, Paula, Exec. Dir., San Diego Automotive Museum, San Diego, CA.....183
Brandon, Lynnette, Acting Dir., Besh-Ba-Gowah Archaeological Park, Globe, AZ 44
Brandrup, Jessica, Head Mktg. & Public Rels., Kimbell Art Museum, Fort Worth, TX...1610
Brandt, Arlene, Dir., North Pinellas Historical Museum, Palm Harbor, FL 376
Brandt, Carl, Pres. (V), Clermont State Historic Site, Germantown, NY 1137
Brandt, Dorothy M., Chm. (V), San Luis Valley Museum, Alamosa, CO..................228
Brandt, Ken, Dir., Robeson Planetarium and Science Center, Lumberton, NC 1256
Brandt, Kevin, Supt., Chesapeake and Ohio Canal National Historical Park, Hagerstown, MD 737

Brandt, Robert, Pres. (V) Weston Historical Society, Farrar-Mansur House & Old Mill Museum, Weston, VT 1694
Brandt, Sarah, Administrative Asst., Alden B. Dow Museum of Science and Art of the Midland Center for the Arts, Midland, MI....854
Brandt, Terry, Pres. & Founder, Western Antique Aeroplane & Automobile Museum, Hood River, OR 1392
Brandt, Tova, Cur., Vesterheim Norwegian-American Museum, Decorah, IA 582
Brandt, Wayne, Supt., Rock Creek Station State Historic Park, Fairbury, NE 982
Brandt, William, Treas., Trolley Museum of New York, Kingston, NY 1151
Brandy, George, Cur. Aquarium, Houston Zoo, Inc., Houston, TX 1621
Brandyburg, Tyrone, District Supvr., Sugarlands Visitor Center, Gatlinburg, TN 1552
Branham, Howard, Dir., Camden Archives & Museum, Camden, SC 1501
Brannan, Rev. Emora, Pres. (V), Lovely Lane Museum and Archives, Baltimore, MD....723
Brannegan, Daniel, Treas., Denison Pequotsepos Nature Center, Mystic, CT 283
Brannock, Larry, Chm. (V), Schiele Museum of Natural History and Lynn Planetarium, Gastonia, NC....1247
Brannon, Sid, Farm Mgr., Alabama Agricultural Museum, Dothan, AL 10
Brannon, Sidney A., Historical Farm Mgr., Landmark Park, Dothan, AL....10
Bransford, Pamela, Registrar, Montgomery Museum of Fine Arts, Montgomery, AL 20
Branson, Janet, Plantation Store Mgr., Stratford Hall, Robert E. Lee Memorial Association, Inc., Stratford, VA 1748
Branson, Karen, Exec. Asst. & Office Mgr., Blue Star Contemporary Art Center, San Antonio, TX....1643
Branson, Victoria, Dir., Fort Laurens State Memorial, Bolivar, OH 1297
Brant, Nancy, Museum Shop Mgr., John Stark Edwards House, Warren, OH 1348
Brant, Robert L., Esq., Chm. Art Advisory Bd., Philip and Muriel Berman Museum of Art at Ursinus College, Collegeville, PA 1418
Brantley, Dr. Sandra, Collection Mgr. Arthropods (0.5), Museum of Southwestern Biology, Albuquerque, NM....1072
Brase, Gertrude, Pres., Garnavillo Historical Museum, Garnavillo, IA 587
Brasfield, Evans B., Pres. (V), Agecroft Hall, Richmond, VA....1736
Brasier, Robert, Deputy Dir. Education & Public Programs, Palm Springs Art Museum, Palm Springs, CA....161
Brasile, Jeanne, Dir., Walsh Gallery, Seton Hall University, South Orange, NJ....1061
Brass, Kathryn, Dir. Devel., The Contemporary Arts Center, Cincinnati, OH....1305
Braswell, Alvin L., Deputy Dir. Museum Operations, North Carolina Museum of Natural Sciences, Raleigh, NC....1263
Braswell, Tom, Dir., Wellington B. Gray Gallery, Greenville, NC....1250
Bratiotis, Alexia, Dir. Communications & Mktg., Nevada Museum of Art, Reno, NV....1009
Bratton, Chris, Pres., San Francisco Art Institute - Walter & McBean Galleries, San Francisco, CA....192
Bratton, Clara Ann, Naturalist, Carl G. Fenner Nature Center, Lansing, MI....848
Bratton, Karen, Research Librarian & Museum Shop Mgr., Douglas County Museum of History and Natural History, Roseburg, OR 1402
Brauer, Daniel, Dir. Publications, Fowler Museum at UCLA, Los Angeles, CA....135
Brauer, Gerald J., Dir., Ellwood House Museum, DeKalb, IL....489
Braun, Anne M., Sec., Louisville Visual Art Association, Louisville, KY....656
Braun, Dr. J.K., Asst. Cur. Mammals, Sam Noble Oklahoma Museum of Natural History, Norman, OK....1369
Braun, Julianne, Pres. (V), Arcade Historical Society, Arcade, NY....1099
Braun, Karen, Asst. Dir. & Cur., Racine Heritage Museum, Racine, WI....1842
Braun, Lon R., Business Mgr. & Museum Shop Mgr., Fort Wayne Museum of Art, Fort Wayne, IN 542
Braun, Mary E., Dir., The Dwight Frederic Boyden Gallery, Saint Mary's City, MD....745
Braun, Matthew, Exec. Dir., Samuel S. Fleisher Art Memorial, Philadelphia, PA....1461
Braund, Sue, Membership Coord., Middleton Place House Museum, Charleston, SC....1505
Braunlein, John H., Dir., Lyndhurst, Tarrytown, NY....1220
Braunstein, Arlene, Educator, Derfner Judaica Museum + The Art Collection at the Hebrew Home at Riverdale, Riverdale, NY....1200
Braunstein, Susan L., Cur. Archaeology & Judaica and Chm. Curatorial Affairs, The Jewish Museum, New York, NY....1171
Bravard, Janet, Education & Program Dir., Pennyroyal Area Museum, Hopkinsville, KY....650
Braverman, Marsha, Sr. Vice Pres. Mktg. & Communications, Pennsylvania Academy of the Fine Arts, Philadelphia, PA 1458
Bravo, Mr. Domenic, Dept. Dir., Fort Bridger State Museum, Fort Bridger, WY....1858
Bravo, Domenic, Dir. Div. Parks, Historic Governors' Mansion, Cheyenne, WY....1855
Bravo, Dominic, C.E.O., Fort Fetterman State Historic Site, Douglas, WY 1857
Bravo, Dominic, State Parks & Historic Sites Div. Head, Fort Phil Kearny, Banner, WY 1852
Bravo, John, C.E.O. & Pres. (V), The Houdini Museum & Theater, Scranton, PA....1472
Brawley, Rich, Dir., Le Sault de Sainte Marie Historical Sites, Inc., Sault Ste. Marie, MI....864
Braxton, Gail G., Dir., Hugh Mercer Apothecary Shop, Fredericksburg, VA ..1713
Braxton, Gail G., Dir. & C.E.O., Mary Washington House, Fredericksburg, VA....1713
Braxton, Gail G., Dir., Rising Sun Tavern, Fredericksburg, VA 1713
Braxton, Gail G., Dir., St. James' House, Fredericksburg, VA....1713
Braxton, Toni, Supervisory Park Ranger, Lincoln Memorial, Washington, DC....321
Bray, Alida, Pres. & C.E.O., History San Jose, San Jose, CA 195
Bray, Bill, Chm. & Pres. (V), Old St. Ferdinand's Shrine, Florissant, MO....927
Bray, Brian W., Mgr. Historic Sites, Durst-Taylor Historic House and Gardens, Nacogdoches, TX....1634
Bray, Brian W., Historic Sites Mgr., Sterne-Hoya House Museum and Library, Nacogdoches, TX 1634
Bray, Bridget, Mgr. Collections, Pacific Asia Museum, Pasadena, CA....162
Bray, Julie, Exec. Dir., Kearney Area Children's Museum, Kearney, NE 986
Bray, Tamara, Ph.D., Dir., Wayne State University Museum of Anthropology, Detroit, MI....836
Brayson, Albert A., II, Chm. (V), Long Island Museum of American Art, History & Carriages, Stony Brook, NY....1217
Brayton, Nathanel R., Treas., The Rotch-Jones-Duff House & Garden Museum, Inc., New Bedford, MA....793
Brazeal, Earl, Treas., Woodstock Historical Society, Inc., Woodstock, CT....304
Brazel, Chase, Museum Specialist, Indiana War Memorials, Indianapolis, IN 549
Brazel, Jennifer, Dir. Education, Hunterdon Museum of Art, Clinton, NJ....1036
Brazell, Gerald, Dir., The National Vietnam War Museum, Weatherford, TX....1656
Brazell, Julie, Naturalist, Custer State Park, Custer, SD 1529
Brazil, Terry, Exec. Dir., Tulare Historical Museum, Tulare, CA 219
Brearley, Marie, Pres. (V), Fort Washita, Durant, OK 1360
Breaux, Robbie, Pres. (V), The Art Center, Grand Junction, CO....249
Breceda, Susan, Pres. (V), Living Memorial Sculpture Garden, Weed, CA....223
Brech, Jeremy, Dir., Museum of Visual Materials, Sioux Falls, SD 1542
Brecht, Bill, Dir., Lewis & Clark Boat House and Nature Center, Saint Charles, MO....943
Brechter, Bart, Cur. Gardens, Bayou Bend Collection and Gardens, Houston, TX....1618
Brecker, Neil, Vice Pres., Archives Museum, Temple Mickve Israel, Savannah, GA....433
Breckner, Thomas W., Asst. Dir., Travel Town Transportation Museum, Los Angeles, CA....142
Bredbeck, Nancy P., Chm. (V), Whitehall Museum House, Middletown, RI....1489
Bredehoft, Wendy, Cur. Education, University of Wyoming Art Museum, Laramie, WY 1862
Bredhoff, Stacey, Cur., John F. Kennedy Presidential Library & Museum, Boston, MA 760
Bredt, Thomas, Pres. (V), Tahoe Maritime Museum, Homewood, CA 123
Breed, Nancy, Exec. Dir., Galena-Jo Daviess County Historical Society & Museum, Galena, IL....496
Breeden, Angela, Exec. Dir., Centre County Historical Society, State College, PA....1475
Breedlove, Craig, Financial Dir., Fayette County Museum, Washington Court House, OH 1348
Breedlove, Randall, Dir., Carolinas Historic Aviation Museum, Charlotte, NC....1238
Breen, F. Traynor, C.E.O., Fort Mifflin on the Delaware, Philadelphia, PA....1453

B–*Continued*

B–*Continued*

Brizins, Charles A., Pres. (V), The Institute of Contemporary Art/Boston, Boston, MA 760
Bro, Peter, Museum Shop Mgr., Future of Flight Aviation Center & Boeing Tour, Mukilteo, WA 1773
Broach, Barbara K., Dir., Frank Lloyd Wright Rosenbaum House, Florence, AL 11
Broach, Barbara K., Dir., Indian Mound & Museum, Florence, AL 11
Broach, Barbara K., Dir., Kennedy-Douglass Center for the Arts, Florence, AL 12
Broach, Barbara K., Dir., W.C. Handy Home Museum and Library, Florence, AL 12
Broadhurst, Jennifer, Vice Pres., Children's Museum of Pittsburgh, Pittsburgh, PA 1465
Broadrick, Tom, Dir. Planning, Zoning & Historical Preservation, Trayser Museum Group dba Coast Guard Heritage Museum, Barnstable, MA 756
Brock, Betsey, Assoc. Dir. Communications & Outreach, Henry Art Gallery, Seattle, WA 1781
Brock, Dale, Pres. (V), Wichita Falls Museum and Art Center, Wichita Falls, TX 1657
Brock, Daniel, Archaeologist, The Hermitage: Home of President Andrew Jackson, Hermitage, TN 1554
Brock, Lauren, Dir. Travel Program, Harvard Museum of Natural History, Cambridge, MA 767
Brock, Paris, Maintenance, Carnegie Center for Art & History, New Albany, IN 559
Brock, Paul, Facilities Mgr., Buffalo Bill Historical Center, Cody, WY 1856
Brock, Ron, Vice Pres., Northeast Oakland Historical Museum, Oxford, MI 859
Brockelman, Michael D., Trustees Chm., Old Sturbridge Village, Sturbridge, MA 811
Brockelsby, John, Public Rels., Black Hills Reptile Gardens, Inc., Rapid City, SD 1539
Brockett, Walter, Treas., North Haven Historical Society, North Haven, CT 290
Brockman, Anne, Public Information Officer, Gilcrease Museum, Tulsa, OK 1379
Brockmann, Paul, Sr. Vice Pres. Gen. Svcs., Missouri Botanical Garden, Saint Louis, MO 949
Brockmyer, Ron, Financial Dir., Fort Wayne Firefighters Museum, Fort Wayne, IN 541
Brock-Richmond, Renne, Volunteer Coord., Museum and Arts Center in the Sequim Dungeness Valley, Sequim, WA 1785
Brode, Joanna, Vice Pres. Institutional Advancement, Strawbery Banke Museum, Portsmouth, NH 1027
Broder, Deborah, Dir., Museum of Contemporary Art Jacksonville, (MOCA Jacksonville), Jacksonville, FL 355
Broder, Phil, Education, The Wetlands Institute, Stone Harbor, NJ 1062
Broderick, Clif, C.O.O., The U.S. Space & Rocket Center, Huntsville, AL 15
Broderick, Janice K., Pres. (V), Campbell House Museum, Saint Louis, MO 945
Brodeur, Jeanne, Vice Pres. Devel., Aquarium of the Pacific, Long Beach, CA 131
Brodeur, Stephen, Jr., Chm. (V), Plimoth Plantation Inc., Plymouth, MA 800
Brodhead, Richard H., C.E.O., Pres. & Pres. of Duke University, Nasher Museum of Art at Duke University, Durham, NC 1243
Brodie, Judith, Cur. & Head Modern Prints & Drawings, National Gallery of Art, Washington, DC 323
Brodie, Dr. Lee, Cur. Education, Museum of Texas Tech University, Lubbock, TX 1629
Brodnax, Kathy, Collections Mgr., Meadows Museum of Art of Centenary College, Shreveport, LA 686
Brodnicki, Chris, Exec. Dir., Midwest Museum of Natural History, Sycamore, IL 524
Brody, Aaron, Museum Dir., The Bade Museum of Biblical Archaeology, Berkeley, CA 92
Brody, Michael, Dir. & Cur., Marvin Samson Center for History of Pharmacy/USP Museum, Philadelphia, PA 1456
Brody, Roger, Pres., The Collectors Club, Inc., New York, NY 1166
Broege, Wallace W., Dir., Suffolk County Historical Society, Riverhead, NY 1201
Brogan, Annie, Librarian, Burlington County Historical Society, Burlington, NJ 1032
Brogan, Dawn, Exec. Asst., Drayton Hall, Charleston, SC 1504
Brogan, Sheila, Pres., Schoolhouse Museum of the Ridgewood Historical Society, Inc., Ridgewood, NJ 1059
Brogdon, Kathryn, Public Rels. & Facilities Supvr., Armstrong Browning Library, Waco, TX 1653
Brogiotti, Glenda, Cur., Northeast Texas Rural Heritage Museum, Pittsburg, TX 1638
Brohi, Charlotte, Vice Pres. IMAX Operations & Production, Houston Museum of Natural Science, Houston, TX 1620
Brok, Cindy, Administrative Asst., Mount Prospect Historical Society Museums, Mount Prospect, IL 507
Brokamp, Ken, Zoo Society, Charles Paddock Zoo, Atascadero, CA 89
Brokke, Harris, Dir., Maturango Museum of the Indian Wells Valley, Ridgecrest, CA 171
Brolsma, Allen, Pres. (V) & Cur., Polk County Historical Society, Crookston, MN 873
Brom, Jodi, Cur., Arches Museum of Pioneer Life, Winona, MN 902
Brom, Jodi, Cur. Collections, Winona County Historical Museum, Winona, MN 902
Broman, Dave, Pres., Howard County Historical Museum, Kokomo, IN 552
Bromberg, Francine, Preservation Archaeologist, Alexandria Archaeology Museum, Alexandria, VA 1696
Brome, Thomas R., 1st Vice Pres., The Hermitage, Ho-Ho-Kus, NJ 1042
Bromley, John, Dir. Historic Programs, Union Pacific Railroad Museum, Council Bluffs, IA 580
Bromley, Suzette, Cur. Collections, Port Huron Museum, Port Huron, MI 861
Bronander, Joni, Dir. Special Events, Yogi Berra Museum and Learning Center, Little Falls, NJ 1045
Bronder, Kenneth, Vice Pres. & Treas., Maridon Museum, Butler, PA 1415
Bronk, Diane, Pres., Rollingstone-Luxembourg Heritage Museum, Rollingstone, MN 892
Bronson, Dr. Ellen, Veterinarian, The Maryland Zoo in Baltimore, Baltimore, MD 724
Brook, Dr. David, Chief Division of Historical Resources, North Carolina Office of Archives and History, Raleigh, NC 1264
Brook, Monica, Archivist, Mel Fisher Maritime Heritage Society, Key West, FL 359
Brooke, Anna, Librarian, Hirshhorn Museum and Sculpture Garden, Smithsonian Institution, Washington, DC 319
Brooke, Charles, Exec. Dir., Iowa Transportation Museum, Grinnell, IA 588
Brooke, Debora, Dir. Security, Mount Vernon: George Washington's Estate & Gardens, Mount Vernon, VA 1727
Brooke, Jennifer, Dir. Museum Svcs., Figge Art Museum, Davenport, IA 581
Brooker, Peggy, Administrative Asst., Centerville - Washington Township Historical Society & Asahel Wright Community Center, Centerville, OH 1301
Brookover, Andrea, Dir. Operations, Decorative Arts Center of Ohio, Lancaster, OH 1326
Brooks, Aimee, Registrar, The Columbus Museum, Columbus, GA 414
Brooks, Anthony T.P., Exec. Dir., Luzerne County Historical Society, Wilkes-Barre, PA 1482
Brooks, Arthur S., Chm. (V), Fairbanks Museum and Planetarium, Saint Johnsbury, VT 1689
Brooks, Bradley, Dir. Lilly House IMA - Indianapolis Museum of Art, Indianapolis, IN 548
Brooks, Bradley, Chm. (V) Advisory Committee, Morris-Butler House Museum, Indianapolis, IN 550
Brooks, Carol, Cur., Arizona Historical Society Sanguinetti House Museum and Garden, Yuma, AZ 65
Brooks, Caroline, Asst. Dir., Roswell Museum and Art Center, Roswell, NM 1087
Brooks, Celia, Museum Shop Mgr., Lyndon House Arts Center, Athens, GA 401
Brooks, Charlotte, Dir. Events, The Antique Boat Museum, Clayton, NY 1121
Brooks, Dr. Dan, Cur. Vertebrate Zoology, Houston Museum of Natural Science, Houston, TX 1620
Brooks, Daniel F., Dir., Arlington, Birmingham, AL 5
Brooks, David, Conservation Svcs. Mgr., Spring Valley Nature Center & Heritage Farm, Schaumburg, IL 519
Brooks, Dick, Public Rels., The Houdini Museum & Theater, Scranton, PA 1472
Brooks, Dr. Earl D., II, C.E.O. & Cur., Trine University, General Lewis B. Hershey Museum, Angola, IN 531
Brooks, Elizabeth, Chm. (V), Charles H. Wright Museum of African American History, Detroit, MI 833
Brooks, Eric, Cur., Ashland, The Henry Clay Estate, Lexington, KY 651
Brooks, Erin, Mgr. Finance & Operations, Upper Peninsula Children's Museum, Marquette, MI 853
Brooks, Frank, Acting Horticulture Mgr., United States Botanic Garden, Washington, DC 331
Brooks, Grace, Campaign Coord., Aspen Art Museum, Aspen, CO 228
Brooks, James, Pres., School for Advanced Research, Indian Arts Research Center, Santa Fe, NM 1091
Brooks, Jonathan, C.E.O., Imagination Station Science Museum, Wilson, NC 1272
Brooks, Joslin A., Custodian, Daggett House, Pawtucket, RI 1492

B–*Continued*

B–*Continued*

Bruce, Roger, Dir. Interpretation, George Eastman House/International Museum of Photography and Film, Rochester, NY....1201
Bruch, Fred, Resource Mgmt., Great Sand Dunes National Monument and Preserve, Mosca, CO....259
Brucken, Carolyn, Dept. Dir. Inst. & Asst. Cur. Western Women's History, Autry National Center of the American West, Los Angeles, CA....133
Brucksch, John, Chief Historic Furnishing, Harpers Ferry Center, Harpers Ferry, WV....1799
Brue, Julie, Chm. (V), Pettigrew Home and Museum, Sioux Falls, SD....1542
Brueggen, John, Dir., St. Augustine Alligator Farm, Saint Augustine, FL....382
Bruemmer, Betsy, Mgr. Collections, Museum of History & Industry (MOHAI), Seattle, WA....1782
Bruff, Mike, Advisor, The Movie Museum, Owosso, MI....859
Brugger, Susan, Dir., Brookings Arts Council, Brookings, SD....1527
Bruhl, Win, Chm. Dept. of Art, University of Arkansas at Little Rock Art Department Gallery I & II & III, Little Rock, AR....78
Bruhn, Thomas P., Acting Dir. & Cur. Collections, The William Benton Museum of Art, Storrs, CT....296
Brukardt, David, Bd. Pres., Northwest Museum of Arts & Culture (Eastern Washington State Historical Society), Spokane, WA....1787
Brum, David, Volunteer Coord., Northwest Museum of Arts & Culture (Eastern Washington State Historical Society), Spokane, WA....1787
Brumback, William, Dir. Conservation, Garden in the Woods of the New England Wild Flower Society, Framingham, MA....778
Brumbaugh, Lee, Cur. Photography, Nevada Historical Society, Reno, NV....1009
Brumberg, Esther, Cur. Collections, Museum of Jewish Heritage-A Living Memorial to the Holocaust, New York, NY....1175
Brumfield, Dennis, Financial Dir. & Treas., West Virginia State Farm Museum, Point Pleasant, WV....1805
Brumfield, Jennifer, Naturalist & Artist, Cleveland Metroparks Outdoor Education Division, Garfield Heights, OH....1322
Brumfield, Dr Robb, Cur. Genetic Resource, Museum of Natural Science, Baton Rouge, LA....668
Brumgardt, Dr. John R., Dir. & C.E.O., The Charleston Museum, Charleston, SC....1503
Brumit, Joe, Chm. Bd., The Health Adventure, Asheville, NC....1232
Brumley, Jacqui, Museum Shop Mgr., Sci-Port Discovery Center, Shreveport, LA....687
Brumley, Tom, Operations Mgr., New Museum, New York, NY....1177
Brummett, Tina, Museum Shop Mgr., Living Desert Zoo and Gardens State Park, Carlsbad, NM....1076
Brummund, Fran, Exec. Dir., Fargo Air Museum, Fargo, ND....1281
Brundage, Melissa, Business Mgr., South Carolina Cotton Museum, Bishopville, SC....1501
Brundage, Ronald F., Jr., Pres. (V), & Museum Shop Mgr., Conneaut Railroad Museum, Conneaut, OH....1314
Brune, Eva, Dir. Devel., Museum at Eldridge Street, New York, NY....1174
Brunell, Mark, Cur., The Herbarium of the University of the Pacific, Stockton, CA....214
Bruner, Matt, Park Mgr., Kolomoki Mounds State Park Museum, Blakely, GA....411
Bruner, Sylvia, Registrar, Jim Gatchell Memorial Museum, Buffalo, WY....1853
Brunnemann, Eric, Supt., Pinnacles National Monument, Paicines, CA....160
Brunnemann, Eric, Supt., War in the Pacific National Historical Park, Piti, GU....1868
Brunner, Carol, Museum Shop Mgr., Graeme Park, Horsham, PA....1434
Brunner, Jeanette, Cur. Education, Aquarium of Niagara, Niagara Falls, NY....1185
Brunner, Theresa, Cur., Mission San Rafael Arcangel, San Rafael, CA....201
Bruno, Lesley, Dir. Public Rels., Valentine Richmond History Center, Richmond, VA....1741
Bruns, Beverly, Treas., Yorktown Historical Museum, Yorktown, TX....1658
Bruns, Craig, Cur., Independence Seaport Museum, Philadelphia, PA....1455
Brunschwyler, Greta, Vice Pres. Programs, High Desert Museum, Bend, OR....1384
Brunson, Dr. Jeana, Bureau Chief, Museum of Florida History, Tallahassee, FL....391
Brunson, Neal E., Dir. & Pres. (V), Afro-American Historical Society Museum, Jersey City, NJ....1043
Brunson, Theodore, Consultant, Afro-American Historical Society Museum, Jersey City, NJ....1043
Brunswick, Ken, Rgnl. Ecologist, Limberlost State Historic Site, Geneva, IN....544
Brusca, Maureen, Dir. Finance, National Museum of American Jewish History, Philadelphia, PA....1458
Brusca, Richard C., Ph.D., Exec. Program Dir., Arizona-Sonora Desert Museum, Tucson, AZ....59
Bruseth, Jim, Archaeology Div., Texas Historical Commission, Austin, TX....1583
Brush, Don, Treas., Living History Farms, Urbandale, IA....601
Brush, Maura M., Dir. Horticulture, Old Westbury Gardens, Old Westbury, NY....1188
Brust, Howard, Treas., Champaign County Historical Museum, Urbana, OH....1347
Brustman, Jeff, Mgr., Samoa Cookhouse & Logging Museum, Samoa, CA....178
Brutschy, Sarah, Dir. Visitor & Member Svcs., Flagler Museum, Palm Beach, FL....375
Brutvan, Cheryl, Cur. Contemporary Art, Norton Museum of Art, West Palm Beach, FL....397
Bruzelius, Ellen, Exec. Dir., Bartow-Pell Mansion Museum, Carriage House & Gardens, Bronx, NY....1107
Bryan, Ann, Museum Shop Mgr., Carry A. Nation Home Memorial, Medicine Lodge, KS....627
Bryan, Dr. Betsy, Dir. Dept. Near Eastern Studies, The Johns Hopkins University Archaeological Collection, Baltimore, MD....723
Bryan, Cheryl, Museum Shop Mgr., Rancho Los Cerritos Historic Site, Long Beach, CA....132
Bryan, Frank, Chm. Bd. (V), Kentucky Railway Museum, Inc., New Haven, KY....660
Bryan, Gail, Pres. Bd., Museum of Photographic Arts, San Diego, CA....181
Bryan, J. Stewart, III, Chm., Virginia Historical Society, Richmond, VA....1742
Bryan, John, Cur., Jonathan Hager House & Museum, Hagerstown, MD....738
Bryan, Paul, Security Supvr., Smart Museum of Art, Chicago, IL....486
Bryan, Robert L., Jr., Pres., Historical Society of Kent County, Inc., Chestertown, MD....730
Bryan, Suzan, Museum Shop Mgr., Thomas Jefferson's Poplar Forest, Forest, VA....1710
Bryan, Tracey, Mgr. Virginia House, Virginia Historical Society, Richmond, VA....1742
Bryant, Aaron, Cur., James E. Lewis Museum of Art, Morgan State University, Baltimore, MD....723
Bryant, Danny, Vice Pres., Fayetteville Lincoln County Museum and Civic Center, Fayetteville, TN....1551
Bryant, Elaine, Dir. Arts Education, Arts Council of Fayetteville/Cumberland County, Fayetteville, NC....1245
Bryant, James, Cur. Natural History, Riverside Metropolitan Museum, Riverside, CA....173
Bryant, Laura, Bd. Pres., Grayson Crossroads Museum and Cultural Exhibits, Independence, VA....1718
Bryant, Lori, Museum Shop Mgr., Corpus Christi Museum of Science and History, Corpus Christi, TX....1594
Bryant, Marti, Member Rels. Dir., Sanibel-Captiva Conservation Foundation, Inc., Sanibel, FL....386
Bryant, Megan, Dir. Collections, The Sixth Floor Museum at Dealey Plaza, Dallas, TX....1600
Bryant, Peter, C.O.O., Isabella Stewart Gardner Museum, Boston, MA....760
Bryant, Randy, Pres. (V), Lowell Damon House, Wauwatosa, WI....1850
Bryant, Randy, Pres., Milwaukee County Historical Society, Milwaukee, WI....1834
Bryant, Randy, Chm. Bd., Ten Chimneys Foundation, Genesee Depot, WI....1820
Bryant, Ron D., Park Mgr., Waveland State Historic Site, Lexington, KY....653
Bryant, Sara, Exec. Dir., Historic Carson House, Marion, NC....1257
Bryant, Sharon C., African American Outreach Coord., Tryon Palace Historic Sites & Gardens, New Bern, NC....1259
Bryant, Stephen, Editor & Publisher, Upper Room Chapel Museum, Nashville, TN....1570
Bryant, Susan, Admin. Tech., Humpback Rocks Mountain Farm & Visitor Center, Waynesboro, VA....1753
Bryant, Tammy, Museum Shop Mgr., National Corvette Museum, Bowling Green, KY....642
Bryant, Terry, Events Coord., North Carolina Aquarium at Fort Fisher, Kure Beach, NC....1255
Bryant Tinley, Eloise, Pres. (V), The Drake House Museum, Plainfield, NJ....1057
Bryant, Toph, Museum Shop Mgr., Louisville Science Center, Louisville, KY....655
Bryck, Jack, C.E.O. & Pres. (V), Baldwin Historical Society and Museum, Baldwin, NY....1101
Bryden, Amanda, Collections Asst., Historic New Harmony, New Harmony, IN....560
Bryer, Cornelia, Bd. Pres. SITE Santa Fe, Santa Fe, NM....1090

Bryerton, John B., Treas., Piper Aviation Museum Foundation, Lock Haven, PA..1442
Bryner, Kyle Elizabeth, Registrar & Collections Mgr., Museum of Anthropology, Winston-Salem, NC 1274
Bryson, Mary, Cur., Troutdale Historical Society, Troutdale, OR 1406
Bryson, Ralph, Exec. Vice Pres., The U.S. Space & Rocket Center, Huntsville, AL 15
Bryson, Terri, Registrar, Mingei International Museum, San Diego, CA ...180
Brzezinski, George, Dir. Visitor Svcs., Admissions & Museum Shop Mgr., Children's Museum of Pittsburgh, Pittsburgh, PA 1465
Brzezinski, Jackie, Museum Shop Mgr., Lilacia Park-Lombard Park District, Lombard, IL..504
Brzon, Narveen, Chm. (V), Pawnee Indian Village State Historic Site, Republic, KS..632
Bubac, David, Facility Mgr., Jefferson National Expansion Memorial, Saint Louis, MO..947
Bubp, Ken, C.O.O., Conner Prairie Interactive History Park, Fishers, IN.......540
Bucceri, Lou, Cur., Salisbury Cannon Museum, Lakeville, CT..........................280
Bucci, Jonathan, Cur. Collections, Hallie Ford Museum of Art, Salem, OR 1403
Bucco, Kate, Park Ranger, Kenilworth Park and Aquatic Gardens, Washington, DC.......................................320
Buchanan, Annette, Administrative Dir., Anderson County Arts Center, Anderson, SC..1499
Buchanan, Bill, Vice Pres. Finance & Operations, Minnetrista, Muncie, IN.......558
Buchanan, Bob, Public Rels., Old Timers Museum, Murphys, CA..........................150
Buchanan, Donna, Dir. Group Tours Sales, Edsel & Eleanor Ford House, Grosse Pointe Shores, MI 843
Buchanan, John E., Jr., Dir., The Fine Arts Museums of San Francisco, de Young Museum, San Francisco, CA........188
Buchanan, John E., Jr., Dir., The Fine Arts Museums of San Francisco, Legion of Honor, San Francisco, CA......189
Buchanan, Mandy, Cur. Education, Lauren Rogers Museum of Art, Laurel, MS..912
Buchanan, Richard, Treas., Historic Carson House, Marion, NC...................1257
Buchanan, Suzanne, Dir., Hingham Historical Society, Hingham, MA...........782
Buchannon, Teresa, Education, The Hyland House, Guilford, CT..................276
Bucher, Kristen, Registrar, Cummer Museum of Art & Gardens, Jacksonville, FL.......................................354
Bucher, Nancy, Dir. Horticulture & Maintenance, The Toledo Zoo, Toledo, OH..1346
Buchholz, Jane, Office Mgr. & Bookkeeper, Volcano Art Center Gallery, Volcano, HI.......................................453
Buchsen, Dolores, Historic Site Admin., Pennsylvania Lumber Museum, Galeton, PA...1426
Buchta, David, Dir., The Old Governor's Mansion, Frankfort, KY.........................647
Buchta, David, Dir. & Cur., Vest-Lindsey House, Frankfort, KY...........................647
Buchtel, John, Head Special Collections, Georgetown University Art Collection, Washington, DC..318
Buchter, Tom, C.E.O., The Marie Selby Botanical Gardens, Inc., Sarasota, FL 387
Bucino, Erika G., Museum Shop Mgr., Brandywine River Museum, Chadds Ford, PA..1417
Buck, Angela, Museum Dir., Wanapum Dam Heritage Center, Beverly, WA.......1760
Buck, Cleta, Office Asst. III, Fort Macon State Park, Atlantic Beach, NC.............1233
Buck, David, Pres., Frye Art Museum, Seattle, WA 1780
Buck, Dennis, Sr. Cur., Aurora Historical Society, Aurora, IL 469
Buck, Rebecca A., Deputy Dir. Collections, The Newark Museum, Newark, NJ 1053
Buck, Rose, Cur. & Museum Shop Mgr., Presque Isle County Historical Museum, Rogers City, MI.......................862
Buck, Dr. William R., Cur., The New York Botanical Garden, Bronx, NY.......1109
Buckaloo, Terence, Dir. & Cur., Sterling-Rock Falls Historical Society Museum, Sterling, IL 523
Buckel, Walter, Pres., Dal-Paso Museum, Lamesa, TX 1627
Buckellew, Shari Spaniol, Museum Mgr., Children's Discovery Museum, Normal, IL 509
Buckenmyer, Jim, Chm. & Pres. (V), Governor John Sevier Memorial Association, Knoxville, TN...................1558
Buckingham, Bethany, Cur., Dorothy G. Page Museum, Wasilla, AK 37
Buckingham, Bill, Exhibits Mgr. NASA Glenn Research Center's Visitor Center, Cleveland, OH 1310
Buckingham, Tom, Pres. (V), Surratt House Museum, Clinton, MD 730
Buckius, Christine, Dir. Aquarium, Oceanographic Teaching Station Inc. - Roundhouse Marine Studies Lab & Aquarium, Manhattan Beach, CA............144
Buckley, Annmarie, Museum Shop Mgr., The Accokeek Foundation, Inc., Accokeek, MD..716
Buckley, Gary, Treas., Greentown Glass Museum, Inc., Greentown, IN 545
Buckley, John, Dir. Institutional Advancement, Naper Settlement, Naperville, IL...508
Buckley, Kerry W., Dir., Historic Northampton, Northampton, MA.............796
Buckley, Laurene, Exec. Dir., Jersey City Museum, Jersey City, NJ 1043
Bucklin, Stacey, Public Programs Coord., Museum of Nature & Science, Dallas, TX 1599
Buckman, Jane, Dir., Longboat Key Center for the Arts, Longboat Key, FL ...363
Buckman, Pamela, Mgr. Sculpture Garden, New Orleans Museum of Art, New Orleans, LA.......................................683
Buckmaster, Pat, Museum Shop Mgr., Heritage Hill State Historical Park, Green Bay, WI...1821
Buck-Miser, Kathleen, Exhibits Cur., Tulsa Zoo & Living Museum, Tulsa, OK 1380
Buckner, Cindy, Asst. Cur., Grand Rapids Art Museum, Grand Rapids, MI............842
Buckner, Marlene, Deputy Dir., Mobile Museum of Art, Mobile, AL 17
Buckner-Webb, Cherie, Pres., Idaho Black History Museum, Boise, ID...........455
Bucuvalas, Tina, Cur., Safford House Historic House Museum, Tarpon Springs, FL 394
Bucuvalas, Tina, Ph.D., Cur., Tarpon Springs Cultural Center, Tarpon Springs, FL 394
Buczkowske, Bud, Pres., Sierra County Historical Society (Kentucky Mine Museum), Sierra City, CA......................211
Budas, Kathy, Dir. Mktg., Yerba Buena Center for the Arts, San Francisco, CA...194
Budd, Jerry, Horticulturist, Lilacia Park-Lombard Park District, Lombard, IL..504
Budde, Pamela, Visitor Svcs., The Lyceum, Alexandria's History Museum, Alexandria, VA 1698
Budde-Jones, K.T., Dir. Education, Pacific Aviation Museum - Pearl Harbor, Honolulu, HI 447
Budden, Cory, Coord., Viking Union Gallery, Bellingham, WA 1759
Buddenhagen, Jennifer, Mktg. & Public Programs Mgr., Rochester Art Center, Rochester, MN......................................891
Buddle, Ann, Sec., Interlaken Historical Society, Interlaken, NY 1146
Budeni, Michelle, Mgr. Collections, Betsy Ross House, Philadelphia, PA 1451
Budig, Otto M., Jr., Chm., The Contemporary Arts Center, Cincinnati, OH..1305
Budinger, Meghan, Asst. Dir. & Cur., James Monroe Museum and Memorial Library, Fredericksburg, VA...............1713
Budlong, Cynthia, Asst. Dir. Exhibitions, University of Oregon Museum of Natural and Cultural History, Eugene, OR 1389
Budrovich, Tony, Deputy Dir. Operations, California Science Center, Los Angeles, CA...134
Budrys, Milda, M.D., Dir. Medical Museum, The Lithuanian Museum, Chicago, IL 483
Budzynski, Jan, Business Officer, George L. Luthy Memorial Botanical Garden, Peoria, IL 512
Budzynski, Jim, Cur., The Coopersville Area Historical Society Museum, Coopersville, MI......................................831
Budzynski, Lillian, Dir., The Coopersville Area Historical Society Museum, Coopersville, MI......................................831
Bueche, Shirley S., Admin., Lynnhaven House, Virginia Beach, VA 1752
Buecker, Thomas R., Cur., Nebraska State Historical Society's Fort Robinson Museum, Crawford, NE.............980
Buehl, Gudrun, Dir. Museum, Dumbarton Oaks Research Library & Collections, Washington, DC...317
Buehler, Daniel, Pres., The Wilderness Center Inc., Wilmot, OH.......................1351
Buehler, Ken, Dir., Lake Superior Railroad Museum, Duluth, MN 874
Buehler, Lisa, Chm. Docent Council (V), Little Rock Zoological Gardens, Little Rock, AR 77
Buehrer, Carl, Pres. (V), Fulton County Historical Museum, Wauseon, OH 1349
Buell, Alex, Asst. Dir. Programs, Amelia Island Museum of History, Fernandina Beach, FL...346
Buenger, William, Trustee Pres., Ventura County Maritime Museum, Inc., Oxnard, CA...159
Buermeyer, Chris, C.E.O., New Jersey Naval Museum, Hackensack, NJ 1040
Bueschel, Tiffanie, Museum Dir., American Numismatic Association Money Museum, Colorado Springs, CO 233
Buescher, Al, Vice Pres., California Automobile Museum, Sacramento, CA...174
Buesing, Kay, Dir., World Kite Museum & Hall of Fame, Long Beach, WA.........1771
Buesing, Susan, Museum Shop Mgr., National Museum of Dance & Hall of Fame, Saratoga Springs, NY.................1207
Buettner, Jim, Security, Northern Gila County Historical Society, Inc. - Rim Country Museum, Payson, AZ.....................47

B–*Continued*

B–Continued

B–*Continued*

Bye, Joellen, Historic Site Cur., Culbertson Mansion State Historic Site, New Albany, IN 559
Byers, Bill, Dir., Spiers Gallery, Brevard, NC 1235
Byers, Kathleen, Administrative Asst., El Pueblo History Museum, Pueblo, CO 260
Byers, Linda N., Historic Site Supt., Fort Bridger State Museum, Fort Bridger, WY 1858
Byer-Tyre, David, African/American Cur., Nassau County, Division of Museum Services, Department of Recreation, Parks & Museums, East Meadow, NY ..1130
Bykowski, Jonathan, Museum Shop Mgr., Florida Museum of Photographic Arts, Tampa, FL 392
Byles, Richard, Dir. Education, Virginia Air & Space Center, Hampton, VA 1716
Bylin, Stephen, Park Supt., Fort Tejon State Historic Park, Lebec, CA 129
Bynum, Brant, Pres., Spartanburg Art Museum (SAM), Spartanburg, SC 1523
Bynum, Delois, Receptionist, Green Hill Center for North Carolina Art, Greensboro, NC 1248
Bynum, Ralph, Vice Pres., Moore County Art Association, Dumas, TX 1602
Bynum Robertson, Marci, Dir. Collections & Research and Grantwriter, Museum of Discovery: Arkansas Museum of Science and History, Little Rock, AR 78
Byram, Dr. Merith, Co-Chm., Bessemer Hall of History, Bessemer, AL 4
Byrd, A. Keene, Exec. Dir., Bath County Historical Society, Warm Springs, VA...1752
Byrd, Amy, Staff Dir., Lilian Fendig Art Gallery, Rensselaer, IN 563
Byrd, Betsy B., Docent, Bath County Historical Society, Warm Springs, VA...1752
Byrd, Cathy, Exec. Dir., Maryland Art Place, Baltimore, MD 724
Byrd, Cindy, Museum Shop Mgr., Reynolda House Museum of American Art, Winston-Salem, NC 1275
Byrd, Dr. Cynthia, Cur. & Folklorist, The Ward Museum of Wildfowl Art, Salisbury University, Salisbury, MD 746
Byrd, Jeffery, Head Dept. Art UNI Gallery of Art, University of Northern Iowa, Cedar Falls, IA 576
Byrd, Kathy, Museum Shop Mgr., Jackson Zoological Park, Inc., Jackson, MS 909
Byrd, Ken, Dir. Horticulture & Facilities, Tucson Botanical Gardens, Tucson, AZ 62
Byrd, Mary, Mgr., Dayton Historical Depot Society, Dayton, WA 1763
Byrd, Michelle, Dir. Public Rels., Memphis College of Art, Memphis, TN 1563
Byrd, Oliver W., Chm. (V), August Wilson Center for African American Culture, Pittsburgh, PA 1464
Byrn, Brian, Cur., Midwest Museum of American Art, Elkhart, IN 538
Byrne, Alison, Assoc. Cur. Education, Contemporary Art Center of Virginia, Virginia Beach, VA 1751
Byrne, Frank, Museum Shop Mgr., National Air and Space Museum, Washington, DC 322
Byrne, Jeffrey, Treas., Warrick County Museum, Inc., Boonville, IN 534
Byrne, Jessica, Pres., Aurora Historical Society, Aurora, IL 469
Byrne, John P., Dir. Devel., Callaway Gardens, Pine Mountain, GA 429
Byrne, Kathleen, Museum Registrar, National Park Service, Washington, DC 326
Byrne, Loraine, Administrative & Membership Mgr., Newport Historical Society & The Museum of Newport History, Newport, RI 1491
Byrne, Mary, Mktg. Mgr., The Canton Museum of Art, Canton, OH 1300
Byrne, Mary Jo, Pres., Honolulu House Museum, Marshall, MI 853
Byrne, Peter, Recording Sec., Queens Historical Society, Flushing, NY 1133
Byrne, Richard, 1st Vice Pres., Norfolk Historical Museum, Norfolk, CT 289
Byrne, Roger, Cur., Museum of Paleontology, Berkeley, CA 93
Byrnes, David, Pres., Midway Village Museum, Rockford, IL 517
Byrum, Ann T., Office Asst., Historic Edenton State Historic Site, Edenton, NC 1244
Bytnar, Bruce, District Ranger, Humpback Rocks Mountain Farm & Visitor Center, Waynesboro, VA 1753
Bytof, Cory, Public Programs & Public Rels., Falkirk Cultural Center, San Rafael, CA 200
Byzewski, Leah, Dir., Grand Forks County Historical Society, Grand Forks, ND 1283

C

Cabalce, Gail, Museum Shop Mgr., Waimea Arboretum and Botanical Garden in Waimea Valley, Haleiwa, HI...441
Cabarga, Paul, Exhibitions Mgr., Henry Art Gallery, Seattle, WA 1781
Cabiness, Rochelle, Dir. Human Resources, Brooklyn Botanic Garden, Brooklyn, NY 1110
Cable, Bob, Pres. (V), San Juan Bautista State Historic Park, San Juan Bautista, CA 197
Cable, Christopher B., Exec. Dir., The Imaginarium Science Discovery Center, Anchorage, AK 27
Cable, Janis, Dir. Devel., North Texas History Center, McKinney, TX 1632
Cabral, Wayne, Dir., Clouds Hill Victorian House Museum, Warwick, RI 1498
Cabrera, Eileen M., Asst. to Pres., Museum of Science and Industry, Chicago, IL 484
Cadby-Sorensen, Robin, Dir., Cur. & Museum Shop Mgr., Headwaters Heritage Museum, Three Forks, MT 972
Cadd, Maila, Pres. (V), Cowlitz County Historical Museum, Kelso, WA 1769
Caddick, Meghan, Education Coord., The Handweaving Museum & Thousand Islands Arts Center, Clayton, NY 1121
Caddick, William D., Assoc. Vice Pres. Physical Plant, The Art Institute of Chicago, Chicago, IL 476
Cade, Esther, Cashier, Paul W. Bryant Museum, Tuscaloosa, AL 24
Cade, Peter H., Registrar & Collections Mgr., African Art Museum of the S.M.A. Fathers, Tenafly, NJ 1063
Cadenbach, Terry, Pres. (V), Fort Davidson State Historic Site, Pilot Knob, MO 942
Cady, Cheryl, Collectors' Gallery Asst., Mingei International Museum, Escondido, CA 111
Cady, Don, Pres. (V), Burwell-Morgan Mill, Millwood, VA 1726
Cady, Nora, Office Mgr., Pioneer Farm Museum and Ohop Indian Village, Eatonville, WA 1764
Caesar, Dianne, Exec. Dir., Delta Arts Center, Winston-Salem, NC 1273
Cafferty, Jack, Dir., World Center for Birds of Prey, Boise, ID 456
Caffery, Beth, Cur., Liberty Hall Historic Site, Frankfort, KY 647
Caffey, Sheri-Lynn, Mktg. Mgr., Columbus Cultural Arts Center, Columbus, OH 1312
Caffrey, Jim, Supt., William Cullen Bryant Homestead, Cummington, MA 773
Cagan, Charlotte, Dir. Mktg., Mingei International Museum, San Diego, CA ...180
Cagenello, Cynthia, Mgr. Communications, Hill-Stead Museum, Farmington, CT 274
Cagle, Amanda, Dir., Lincoln County Historical Society and Museum of Pioneer History, Chandler, OK 1358
Cagle, Margaret, House Chm., Meadow Garden Museum, Augusta, GA 410
Cagno, Michael, Exec. Dir., The Noyes Museum of Art, Oceanville, NJ 1054
Cahail, Mary Jean, Pres., San Juan Historical Society, Friday Harbor, WA..1767
Cahill, Christopher P., Exec. Dir., American Irish Historical Society, New York, NY 1162
Cahill, Kevin M., M.D., Pres. Gen., American Irish Historical Society, New York, NY 1162
Cahn, Jennifer, Ph.D., Cur., Brownsville Museum of Fine Art, Brownsville, TX .1590
Caiazza, Katherine, Registrar, The Museum for African Art, Long Island City, NY 1154
Caijas, Idalia, Accountant, The Museum for African Art, Long Island City, NY ..1154
Cain, Ann, Pres., Historic Wolcott House, Wolcott, IN 571
Cain, Christina, Collection Mgr. Anthropolgy, University of Colorado Museum of Natural History, Boulder, CO 230
Cain, Dan, Pres. Bd. Trustees (V) & Chm. (V), Norman Rockwell Museum, Stockbridge, MA 810
Cain, Greg, Museum Shop Mgr., Zoo Atlanta, Atlanta, GA 409
Cain, John, Exec. Dir., South Shore Arts, Munster, IN 558
Cain, Joyce, Museum Shop Mgr., The George Bush Presidential Library and Museum, College Station, TX 1593
Cain, Lynn, Museum Shop Mgr., Lake Waccamaw Depot Museum, Lake Waccamaw, NC 1255
Cain, Rick, Deputy Dir., St. Augustine Lighthouse & Museum, Inc., Saint Augustine, FL 382
Cain, Roger, Maintenance & Groundskeeper, Rosemount Museum, Pueblo, CO 261
Caine, Shari, Mgr. Archives, Des Plaines History Center, Des Plaines, IL 490
Caine, Sheryl, Museum Shop Mgr., Lake Erie Nature & Science Center, Bay Village, OH 1295
Cairns, Dee, Museum Shop Mgr., Lewis County Historical Museum, Chehalis, WA 1761
Cairns, Stephen D., Chm. Dept. Invertebrate Zoology, National Museum of Natural History, Washington, DC 325
Caivano, Felice, Cur., Widener Gallery, Austin Arts Center, Trinity College, Hartford, CT 279
Calabrese, Lindsey, Public Rels., Hofstra University Museum, Hempstead, NY 1141
Calabrese, Patricia, Exec. Vice Pres. & C.F.O., Bronx Zoo, Bronx, NY 1107

C–*Continued*

C–Continued

C–*Continued*

C–*Continued*

C–*Continued*

C–*Continued*

C–*Continued*

C–*Continued*

Coggiola, Michael, Pres., Sunnyvale Historical Society and Museum Association, Sunnyvale, CA....................215
Coghill, Pamela, Asst. Dir., Alfred Starr Nenana Cultural Center, Nenana, AK........34
Cogswell, Michael, Dir., Louis Armstrong House & Archives, Corona, NY 1125
Cohalan, Mary Lou, Exec. Dir., Islip Art Museum, East Islip, NY 1129
Cohan Lange, Suzanne, Pres. (V), Lubeznik Center for the Arts, Michigan City, IN.....................................556
Cohan, Paul, Vice Pres., Herington Historical Society & Museum, Inc. - SE Dickinson County, Herington, KS 616
Cohan, Peter N., Cur., National Knife Museum, Inc., Sevierville, TN...............1573
Cohen, Arnold, 2nd Vice Pres., Beck Cultural Exchange Center, Inc., Knoxville, TN..1557
Cohen, David, Dir. Gallery, The New York Studio School of Drawing, Painting & Sculpture, New York, NY ...1179
Cohen, David A., Museum Shop Mgr., Shore Line Trolley Museum, East Haven, CT...271
Cohen, Evelyn, Gallery Staff, Boston University Art Gallery, Boston, MA........759
Cohen, Jack, Cur. & Library Coord., Philadelphia Mummers Museum, Philadelphia, PA 1459
Cohen, Janie, Dir., Robert Hull Fleming Museum, Burlington, VT 1678
Cohen, Jody, Mgr. Exhibitions, The High Museum of Art, Atlanta, GA 405
Cohen, Laura, Chief Interpretation, Prince William Forest Park Visitor Center, Triangle, VA...1750
Cohen, Lauren, Exec. Dir., Monterey County Youth Museum (MY Museum), Monterey, CA..........................148
Cohen, Lauren, Exec. Dir. MY Museum, Monterey, CA 149
Cohen, Marvin H., Pres. (V), C.E.O. & Cur., Historical Society of Middletown and the Wallkill Precinct, Inc., Middletown, NY 1158
Cohen, Sandor, Museum Cur., Lyndon Baines Johnson Library and Museum, Austin, TX 1582
Cohen, Saul, Pres. (V), Georgia O'Keeffe Museum, Santa Fe, NM 1088
Cohen, Stan, Museum of Mountain Flying, Missoula, MT..............................970
Cohen, Stephen, Bd. Chm., San Diego Natural History Museum, San Diego, CA 184
Cohen, Steve, Chm. (V), The Light Factory - Contemporary Museum of Photography & Film, Charlotte, NC......1239
Cohen-Baruch, Rosalind, Dir. Human Resources, The Walt Disney Family Museum, LLC, San Francisco, CA..........194
Cohen-Stratyner, Barbara, Head Exhibitions, The New York Public Library for the Performing Arts, New York, NY 1179
Cohern, Judith, Dir. Photographic Reference Collection, United States Holocaust Memorial Museum, Washington, DC...332
Cohn, Arthur B., Exec. Dir., The Lake Champlain Maritime Museum, Vergennes, VT 1692
Cohn, Hote, Dir. Exhibitions, Spruill Gallery, Atlanta, GA...............................409
Cohon, Dr. Robert, Cur. Art of Ancient World, The Nelson-Atkins Museum of Art, Kansas City, MO...............................934
Cohoon, Leila, Owner, Leila's Hair Museum, Independence, MO 930
Cohorst, Lois, Dir., Doll House Museum, Marysville, KS 626
Coit, Tom, Bldg. Supt., North Carolina Aquarium at Fort Fisher, Kure Beach, NC 1255
Coke, Bobbye Jo, Cur. Education, American Airlines C.R. Smith Museum, Fort Worth, TX.......................1608
Coker, Elizabeth, Cur. Collections, Pendleton District Historical, Recreational and Tourism Commission, Pendleton, SC...................1521
Coker, Jereme, Exec. Dir., Evergreen Aviation Museum, McMinnville, OR 1394
Coker, Jo An, Vice Pres., Light Crust Doughboys Hall of Fame & Museum - Governor Jim Hogg City Park, Quitman, TX 1639
Coker, Michael D., Dir. Zoo, Topeka Zoological Park, Topeka, KS 636
Colafrancesco, Mike, C.E.O., Firehouse Museum, San Diego, CA 179
Colahan, Hollie, Cur. Primates, Houston Zoo, Inc., Houston, TX 1621
Colaiacovo, Arlene, Museum Shop Mgr., Sturgis Motorcycle Museum and Hall of Fame, Sturgis, SD 1543
Colaizzi, Jeannie, Gen. Mgr. Food & Beverage, Disney's Animal Kingdom Theme Park, Bay Lake, FL......................334
Colato, Juan, Cur., Wells Fargo History Museum, Los Angeles, CA 143
Colberg, David C., Coord. Public Information, Connecticut State Museum of Natural History and Connecticut Archaeology Center, Storrs, CT..296
Colbert, Rani, Mgr. Communications, Middleton Place House Museum, Charleston, SC 1505
Colbert, Richard A., Exec. Dir., Tyler Arboretum, Media, PA 1444
Colbert, Mr. Virgis W., Chm. (V), The Fisk University Galleries, Nashville, TN 1568
Colborne, Allison, Librarian, Museum of Indian Arts & Culture/Laboratory of Anthropology, Santa Fe, NM 1089
Colburn, Bolton, Dir., Laguna Art Museum, Laguna Beach, CA 128
Colby, Clark, Dir., Coolspring Power Museum, Coolspring, PA 1419
Colby, Fran, Museum Shop Mgr., Coolspring Power Museum, Coolspring, PA...1419
Colby, James, Dir., The CCC Weeks Gallery, Jamestown, NY.........................1148
Colclasure, Kenn, Dir. Education, San Diego Automotive Museum, San Diego, CA 183
Colclough, Don, Coord. Special Group Tours, Truckee's Old Jail Museum, Truckee, CA..218
Coldren, Andrew, Cur., Civil War and Underground Railroad Museum of Philadelphia, Philadelphia, PA 1451
Cole, Ann, Sec., Clay County Historical Museum, Liberty, MO 939
Cole, Bruce, Pres. & C.E.O., The American Revolution Center, Wayne, PA..1481
Cole, Carol, Pres. (V), The Kansas African American Museum, Wichita, KS 638
Cole, Carolyn, Cur. Photographs, Los Angeles (Central) Public Library, Los Angeles, CA..138
Cole, Craig, Chm. (V), American Museum of Radio and Electricity, Bellingham, WA 1759
Cole, Deborah, Museum Shop Mgr., The Kentucky Library & Museum, Bowling Green, KY...............................642
Cole, Dianne, Museum Shop Mgr., Whittier Home Association, Amesbury, MA 751
Cole, Don, Dir. Photography, Fowler Museum at UCLA, Los Angeles, CA......135
Cole, Garret E., Chm. (V), Cole Land Transportation Museum, Bangor, ME 691
Cole, Glory, C.E.O., Akwesasne Museum, Hogansburg, NY 1142
Cole Holladay, Wilhelmina, Chm. (V), National Museum of Women in the Arts, Washington, DC 325
Cole, Janice, CRC Administrative Officer, National Museum of the American Indian, Smithsonian Institution, New York, NY..1177
Cole, Jennifer, Coord. Membership, Special Events & Volunteer Svcs., The Frances Lehman Loeb Art Center, Poughkeepsie, NY 1197
Cole, Joelene, Vice Pres., Sidney Historical Association, Sidney, NY 1212
Cole, John, Pres. & Dir., Brooke County Public Library Museum Branch, Wellsburg, WV 1807
Cole, Kathy, Language Teacher, Confederated Tribes of Grand Ronde Cultural Resources Department, Grand Ronde, OR 1390
Cole, Ken, Chm. & Pres. (V), Columbia Gorge Interpretive Center Museum, Stevenson, WA......................................1787
Cole, Dr. Kenneth, Cur. Fossil Middens, Colorado Plateau Biodiversity Center, Flagstaff, AZ 41
Cole, Lois M., Exec. Dir., Historic Deepwood Estate, Salem, OR 1403
Cole, Mark, Assoc. Cur. American Painting & Sculpture, The Cleveland Museum of Art, Cleveland, OH............1308
Cole, Mary, Site Supt., Vandalia Statehouse State Historic Site, Vandalia, IL 526
Cole, Matthew, Dir. Education, Denver Botanic Gardens, Inc., Denver, CO 238
Cole, Nancy, Education Dir., Martha's Vineyard Museum, Edgartown, MA........776
Cole, Nikki, Vice Pres. Devel., Lakeview Museum of Arts and Sciences, Peoria, IL..512
Cole, Nita, Cur., Louisiana State Exhibit Museum, Shreveport, LA........................686
Cole, Dr. Patricia, Asst. Dir. & Cur. Animals, Prospect Park Zoo, Brooklyn, NY..1112
Cole, Phyllis, Museum Retail Mgr., Kansas Cosmosphere and Space Center, Hutchinson, KS 617
Cole, Steve, Treas., Dunn County Historical Society, Menomonie, WI.......1832
Cole, Tom, Museum Shop Mgr., Cornish Colony Museum, Windsor, VT 1694
Cole-Cunningham, Ragan, Dir. Exhibitions & Education, Contemporary Art Center of Virginia, Virginia Beach, VA...............................1751
Colegrove, Jim, Computer Systems Mgr., Modern Art Museum of Fort Worth, Fort Worth, TX 1611
Colegrove, Susan, Curatorial Administrative Asst., Modern Art Museum of Fort Worth, Fort Worth, TX 1611
Coleman, Adrienne, Park Supt., National Park Service - Peirce Barn, Washington, DC..326
Coleman, C. Allen, Exec. Dir., Pickens County Museum of Art & History, Pickens, SC..1521
Coleman, Chris, Chm. & Pres. (V), Highlands Center for Natural History, Prescott, AZ 52
Coleman, Christopher, Museum Shop Mgr., Delta Blues Museum, Clarksdale, MS 905

C–*Continued*

Coleman, Christy S., Pres., The American Civil War Center at Historic Tredegar, Richmond, VA 1736
Coleman, David, Cur. Photography, Harry Ransom Center at The University of Texas at Austin, Austin, TX.................1582
Coleman, David, Park Mgr., Old Fort Harrod State Park Mansion Museum, Harrodsburg, KY 649
Coleman Dibella, Emily, Assoc. Dir. Public Affairs, Mount Vernon: George Washington's Estate & Gardens, Mount Vernon, VA................................1727
Coleman, Dr. Floyd, Co Chm., Fondo Del Sol Visual Arts & Media Center/El Museo de Culturas y Herencias Americanas/MOCHA, Washington, DC.....................................317
Coleman, Holly, Dir. Human Resources, Norman Rockwell Museum, Stockbridge, MA 810
Coleman, James S., Pres & C.E.O., American Textile History Museum, Lowell, MA 787
Coleman, John S., Treas., Hoiles-Davis Museum, Greenville, IL 499
Coleman, Kathleen, Cur., Saratoga County Historical Society, Brookside Museum, Ballston Spa, NY...................1102
Coleman, Larry, Pres., Hancock County Historical Society, Carthage, IL..............474
Coleman, Linda, Historical Supvr., Charlotte County Historical Center, Charlotte Harbor, FL...............................338
Coleman, Lonzo, Maintenance Supvr., Waterloo Center for the Arts, Waterloo, IA 601
Coleman, M. Louise, Dir., Harrison House, Fayette, MS 906
Coleman, Marcia, Museum Shop Mgr., Madeline Island Museum, La Pointe, WI 1826
Coleman, Margaret, Museum Shop Mgr., Mary McLeod Bethune Council House National Historic Site, Washington, DC...321
Coleman, Martha, Dir., Town Square Post Office & Museum, Pontotoc, MS 916
Coleman, Mary Sue, Pres., Kelsey Museum of Archaeology, Ann Arbor, MI..822
Coleman, Neil, Preparator, Rocky Mount Arts Center, Rocky Mount, NC 1265
Coleman, Pam, Chm. (V), Stamford Historical Society, Inc., Stamford, CT.....294
Coleman, Peggy, Museum Shop Mgr., Pioneers, Trail Drivers and Texas Rangers Memorial Museum, San Antonio, TX...1644
Coleman, Romaula, Museum Shop Mgr., Southern Illinois Art & Artisans Center, Whittington, IL 529
Coleman, Ronald, Dir. Library, United States Holocaust Memorial Museum, Washington, DC.......................................332
Coleman, Susan, Exhibitions Coord., McWethy Hall, Luce Gallery, Cornell College, Mount Vernon, IA.....................594
Coleman, Wayne, Head Archives, Birmingham Civil Rights Institute, Birmingham, AL..5
Colen, Jamie, C.E.O. & Dir., Fuller Gardens, North Hampton, NH 1025
Coles, John, Mktg. Asst., Avery Research Center for African American History & Culture, Charleston, SC 1503
Coley, Cheri, Library Asst., Shiloh Museum of Ozark History, Springdale, AR...84
Coley, Dwaine C., Exec. Dir., Hiddenite Center, Inc., Hiddenite, NC..................1252
Coley, John, Pres. (V), Lincoln County Historical Museum, Davenport, WA......1763
Coley, John, Bldg. Svcs. Asst., Racine Art Museum (RAM), Racine, WI..........1842
Colfax, Ralph, Museum Shop Mgr., Ringwood Manor, Ringwood, NJ 1059
Collar, Bill, Pres. (V), Seymour Community Museum, Seymour, WI......1844
Collatz, Eugene, Treas., Nantucket Lightship Basket Museum, Nantucket, MA 792
Collens, David R., Dir. & Cur., Storm King Art Center, Mountainville, NY 1159
Collerre, Carla, Cur. Education, Point Defiance Zoo & Aquarium, Tacoma, WA 1789
Collett, Morine, Chm. (V), Cur. & Museum Shop Mgr., Iraan Museum, Iraan, TX...1624
Collette, Alice, C.E.O. & Exec. Dir., The Heritage Society, Houston, TX 1620
Collette, John, Zoological & Gen. Cur., Dickerson Park Zoo, Springfield, MO.....953
Collette, William, Pres., Trayser Museum Group dba Coast Guard Heritage Museum, Barnstable, MA 756
Collier, Bonnie, Librarian, Fairfield Museum and History Center, Fairfield, CT 273
Collier, Chris, Mgr. Nature Center Programs, Vermont Institute of Natural Science, Quechee, VT 1688
Collier, Denise, Admin. Mgr., Cranbrook Art Museum, Bloomfield Hills, MI 828
Collier, Jean, Mgr. Collections, University of Virginia Art Museum, Charlottesville, VA 1705
Collier, John, Vice Pres., Abbe Museum, Bar Harbor, ME..................................692
Collier, Marcia, VMFA Fund Mgr., Virginia Museum of Fine Arts, Richmond, VA 1742
Collier, Margaret, M.B.A., MSISeC, Office Mgr., Arkansas State University Museum, Jonesboro, AR 75
Collignon, Joan, Docent Coord., Oakland Museum of California, Oakland, CA.......155
Collin, Richard E., Dir. Communications, State Historical Society of North Dakota, Bismarck, ND 1278
Collingsworth, Shawn M., Exec. Dir., The Endowment Fund of the Phi Kappa Psi Fraternity-Heritage Hall, Indianapolis, IN 547
Collingwood Blumenthal, Julie, Special Events Coord., Kemper Museum of Contemporary Art, Kansas City, MO 934
Collins, Betty, Exec. Dir. & Museum Shop Mgr., American Museum of Magic & Lund Memorial Library, Inc., Marshall, MI..................................853
Collins Blackmon, Mary, Dir. & Cur., Elisabet Ney Museum, Austin, TX........1581
Collins, Brian, Exec. Dir., Pejepscot Historical Society, Brunswick, ME..........695
Collins, Cheri, Coord. Programs, Connecticut State Museum of Natural History and Connecticut Archaeology Center, Storrs, CT...................................296
Collins, Chris, Guide, Henry Whitfield State Historical Museum, Guilford, CT...276
Collins, Cindy, Vice Pres. Operations, U.S. Navy Memorial Foundation and Naval Heritage Center, Washington, DC...332
Collins Coleman, Clara, Cur. Educational Interpretation, Laumeier Sculpture Park & Museum, Saint Louis, MO..........948
Collins, Cynthia C., Cur. Education, Miami University Art Museum, Oxford, OH 1338
Collins, D. Cheryl, Contact, Goodnow Museum State Historic Site, Manhattan, KS 624
Collins, D. Cheryl, Dir., Hartford House Museum, Manhattan, KS........................625
Collins, D. Cheryl, Dir., Pioneer Log Cabin, Manhattan, KS 625
Collins, D. Cheryl, Dir., Riley County Historical Museum, Manhattan, KS.........626
Collins, D. Cheryl, Dir., Wolf House Museum, Manhattan, KS.........................626
Collins, David, Sec., Colebrook Area Historical Museum, Colebrook, NH 1014
Collins, Donna, Admin. Asst. & Bookkeeper, Allen County Museum, Lima, OH 1328
Collins, Doris, Community Coord., Art Complex Museum, Duxbury, MA 775
Collins, Edward, C.E.O. & Chm. (V), Irish American Heritage Museum, Albany, NY..1096
Collins, George, Dir., Doak House Museum, Greeneville, TN 1553
Collins, George, Dir., President Andrew Johnson Museum and Library, Greeneville, TN 1553
Collins, Holly, Gallery Dir., University of West Florida Art Gallery, Pensacola, FL...378
Collins, J. Christopher, Pres., Worcester Art Museum, Worcester, MA..................819
Collins, J. Thomas, C.E.O., Pres. & Mgr., The Museum of Bus Transportation, Inc., Hershey, PA..................................1433
Collins, James H., Dir. Community Affairs, Deere & Company, Administrative Center, Moline, IL...........505
Collins, James H., Dir. & Pres., John Deere Historic Site, Dixon, IL...............490
Collins, Jennifer, Dir., Gwinnett History Museum, Lawrenceville, GA 423
Collins, Jennifer, Office Mgr., Indianapolis Art Center, Indianapolis, IN 549
Collins, Joe, Adjunct Cur. Herptiles, Sternberg Museum of Natural History, Hays, KS...616
Collins, John, Controller, Whitney Museum of American Art, New York, NY 1184
Collins, Kathleen, Asst. Dir., Columbia Gorge Discovery Center and Wasco County Museum, The Dalles, OR 1405
Collins, Kelley, Chief Interpretation & Resource Management, Fort Scott National Historic Site, Fort Scott, KS.....613
Collins, Laura, Museum Shop Mgr., Blithewold Mansion, Gardens & Arboretum, Bristol, RI 1485
Collins, Lauren, Dir. Talent & Mktg., Center on Contemporary Art, Seattle, WA 1780
Collins, Mary, Dir., Museum of Anthropology, Pullman, WA 1777
Collins, Michael, Chm. Bd. Dir., Museum of Contemporary Art (MOCA), North Miami, FL...371
Collins, Michele, Museum Shop Mgr., Maritime Museum at Historic Coast Guard Station, Saint Simons Island, GA...432
Collins, Michele, Museum Shop Mgr., St. Simons Island Lighthouse Museum, Saint Simons Island, GA.........................432
Collins, Paul W., Cur. Vertebrate Zoology, Santa Barbara Museum of Natural History, Santa Barbara, CA 204
Collins, Phillip, Cur., African American Museum, Dallas, TX 1596
Collins, Richard B., Chm. (V), Springfield Museums - Connecticut Valley Historical Museum, Springfield, MA 808

C–*Continued*

Conklin, Donnelle, Head Librarian, Lauren Rogers Museum of Art, Laurel, MS 912
Conklin, Dr. Janine, Dir., The Crosby Arboretum, Mississippi State University, Picayune, MS 915
Conklin, Jo-Ann, Dir., David Winton Bell Gallery, Providence, RI 1493
Conklin, Kelly, Officer, The Oyster and Maritime Museum of Chincoteague, Chincoteague, VA 1706
Conklin, Lois, Second Vice Pres., Ten Broeck Mansion - Albany County Historical Association, Albany, NY 1097
Conklin, Michelle, Exec. Dir., Tucson Botanical Gardens, Tucson, AZ 62
Conklin, Sewain, Pres. (V), Northeast Classic Car Museum, Norwich, NY 1187
Conklin, Tom, Park Mgr., Bennington Battlefield State Historic Site and Barnett Homestead Visitors' Center, Hoosick Falls, NY 1142
Conklin-Wingfield, Cara, Deputy Dir. Education, The Parrish Art Museum, Southampton, NY 1213
Conkright, Lance, Pres. (V), Kruse House Museum, West Chicago, IL 527
Conley, Dave, Vice Pres. Exhibits, Museum of Science and Industry, Tampa, FL 392
Conley, Lois D., Dir., Griot Museum of Black History, Saint Louis, MO 947
Conley, Marnie, Mgr. Mktg., Longwood Gardens, Kennett Square, PA 1437
Conley, Melinda, Cur. Exhibits, Lakeshore Museum Center, Muskegon, MI 857
Conlin, Bob, Museum Shop Mgr., Aztalan Museum, Jefferson, WI 1824
Conlin, Deb, Museum Shop Mgr., Aztalan Museum, Jefferson, WI 1824
Conlon, Jerry, Deputy Assoc. Dir & Special Projects, National Museum of Natural History, Washington, DC 325
Connally, Betty, Museum Shop Mgr., San Angelo Museum of Fine Arts, San Angelo, TX 1642
Connell, Anne, Dir. Silvermine School of Art, Silvermine Guild Arts Center, New Canaan, CT 285
Connell, Brendan, Dir. & Counsel Administration, Solomon R. Guggenheim Museum, New York, NY 1181
Connell, Casey, Park Mgr., Rose Hill Plantation State Historic Site, Union, SC 1525
Connell, Charlie, Chm. (V), Arizona Mining and Mineral Museum, Phoenix, AZ 48
Connell, Dixie, Sales & Mktg., Alabama Music Hall of Fame, Tuscumbia, AL 25
Connell, E. Jane, Senior Cur., Dir. Collections & Exhibitions, Muskegon Museum of Art, Muskegon, MI 857
Connell, Linda, Museum Shop Mgr., Coronado National Memorial, Hereford, AZ 45
Connelly, Chris, Gen. Mgr., Ripley's Believe It or Not! Museum, Atlantic City, NJ 1031
Connelly, David O., Dir. Public Rels., Museum of Fine Arts of St. Petersburg, Florida, Saint Petersburg, FL 384
Connelly, Donna M., Business Officer & Sales Mgr., Hunt Institute for Botanical Documentation, Pittsburgh, PA 1466
Connelly, Rob, Chm. (V), Dayton History at Carillon Park, Dayton, OH 1316
Conner, Carolyn O., Pres. (V), Allegheny Highlands Arts & Crafts Center, Inc., Clifton Forge, VA 1707
Conner, Cindy, Council Chm., Frank Lloyd Wright's Pope-Leighey House, Alexandria, VA 1697
Conner, Cindy, Chm. Property Council, Woodlawn, Alexandria, VA 1699
Conner, Doyle, Trustee, Florida Agricultural Museum, Palm Coast, FL 376
Conner, Judy, Dir. Mktg. & Communications, Dallas Museum of Art, Dallas, TX 1598
Conner, Laura, Coord. Public Education Programs, University of Alaska Museum of the North, Fairbanks, AK 30
Conner, Lisa, Acting Dir., Steffen Thomas Museum of Art, Buckhead, GA 412
Conner, Lisa, Arts Outreach Program Coord., Steffen Thomas Museum of Art, Buckhead, GA 412
Conner, Margie, Mktg. Mgr., Anniston Museum of Natural History, Anniston, AL 3
Conner, Dr. Michael, Assoc. Cur., Dickson Mounds Museum, Lewistown, IL 502
Conner, Dr. Michael, Assoc. Cur. Dickson Mounds Museum, Illinois State Museum, Springfield, IL 521
Conner, Neil, Vice Pres., Clinton County Museum, Frankfort, IN 543
Conner, Rebecca, Sr. Sales Asst., Historic New Harmony, New Harmony, IN 560
Conner, Roberta, C.E.O., Tamastslikt Cultural Institute, Pendleton, OR 1397
Connolly, Michael, Dir., New Castle Historical Society, New Castle, DE 309
Connolly, Paula, Treas., The Peekskill Museum, Peekskill, NY 1194
Connolly, Rachel, Dir., Gheens Science Hall and Rauch Planetarium, Louisville, KY 654
Connolly, Dr. Robert, Dir., C.H. Nash Museum at Chucalissa, Memphis, TN 1560
Connolly, Stacey, Administrative Asst., Virginia Zoological Park, Norfolk, VA 1731
Connolly, Thomas, Dir. Research, University of Oregon Museum of Natural and Cultural History, Eugene, OR 1389
Connor, Anne, Dir. Central Library, Los Angeles (Central) Public Library, Los Angeles, CA 138
Connor, Etain, Dir. Devel., The Patricia & Phillip Frost Art Museum, Miami, FL 367
Connor, Kathy, Cur. George Eastman Collection, George Eastman House/International Museum of Photography and Film, Rochester, NY 1201
Connor, Mike, Finance Chm., The Dennison Railroad Depot Museum, Dennison, OH 1318
Connor, Sara W., Dir. Education, Camp Five Museum Foundation, Inc., Laona, WI 1827
Connor, Tina, Exec. Vice Pres., Historic Landmarks Foundation of Indiana, Indianapolis, IN 548
Connors, Andrew, Cur. Art, Albuquerque Museum of Art & History, Albuquerque, NM 1070
Connors, Dennis, Cur. History, Onondaga Historical Association Museum & Research Center, Syracuse, NY 1219
Connors, Janice, Fin. Mgr., Rome Art and Community Center, Rome, NY 1204
Connors, Mary Ann, Co.-Dir., Keeler Tavern Museum, Ridgefield, CT 292
Connors McQuade, Margaret E., Asst. Dir. & Cur. Decorative Arts, The Hispanic Society of America, New York, NY 1169
Conod, Kevin, Astronomer, The Newark Museum, Newark, NJ 1053
Conod, Nancy, Treas., Minisink Valley Historical Society, Port Jervis, NY 1196
Conors, John, Research Asst., Historical Society of Saratoga Springs, Saratoga Springs, NY 1207
Conrad, Geoffrey, Dir., Mathers Museum of World Cultures, Bloomington, IN 533
Conrad, Gilda, Concessions Mgr., Baton Rouge Zoo, Baton Rouge, LA 666
Conrad, Maggie, Weekend Mgr., Decorative Arts Center of Ohio, Lancaster, OH 1326
Conrad, Nicole, Naturalist Teacher, Aullwood Audubon Center and Farm, Dayton, OH 1315
Conrad, Pam, Museum Shop Mgr., Folsom History Museum, Folsom, CA 113
Conrad, Sharron, Cur. Education, The Sixth Floor Museum at Dealey Plaza, Dallas, TX 1600
Conrado, Emily, Archive Mgr., Sacramento Valley Museum, Williams, CA 224
Conrads, Dr. Margaret C., Samuel Sosland Sr. Cur. American Art, The Nelson-Atkins Museum of Art, Kansas City, MO 934
Conradsen, David, Assoc. Cur. Decorative Arts & Design, Saint Louis Art Museum, Saint Louis, MO 950
Conricote, Martin, Aquarist, Children's Aquarium at Fair Park, Dallas, TX 1597
Conron, Linda, Admin., Sayville Historical Society, Sayville, NY 1208
Conroy, Bill, Exec. Dir., Ventura County Maritime Museum, Inc., Oxnard, CA 159
Conroy, Patrick, Dir. Finance, The Children's Museum of Cleveland, Cleveland, OH 1307
Considine, Brian, Sr. Conservator, Decorative Arts & Sculpture, The J. Paul Getty Museum, Los Angeles, CA 137
Considine, Caroline, Dir. Devel., The Preservation Society of Newport County/The Newport Mansions, Newport, RI 1492
Consino, Shannon, Dir. Education, Duluth Art Institute, Duluth, MN 874
Constable, William G., Pres., Old South Meeting House, Boston, MA 762
Constantino, John, Pres., Kauai Museum, Lihue, HI 452
Constantopoulos, Dr. Jim, Dir., Miles Mineral Museum, Portales, NM 1084
Conte, Christine, Dir. Center for Sonoran Desert Studies, Arizona-Sonora Desert Museum, Tucson, AZ 59
Conte, Cynthia, Cur., Michie Tavern ca. 1784, Charlottesville, VA 1704
Conte, George, Operations Mgr., Yale Center for British Art, New Haven, CT 287
Conte, Dr. Robert S., Cur., President's Cottage Museum-The Greenbrier, White Sulphur Springs, WV 1809
Conti, Cathy, Dir., Timexpo Museum, Waterbury, CT 299
Conti, Fred, Treas., Mystic Arts Center, Mystic, CT 283
Conti, Richard C., Dir. & C.E.O., Science Museum of Virginia, Richmond, VA 1740
Contini, Alexander F., Pres. (V), Klyne Esopus Museum, Ulster Park, NY 1222
Contompasis, Marion, Dir. Membership, Impression 5 Science Center, Lansing, MI 849

C–*Continued*

Corcoran, Christine, Assoc. Dir. Individual Giving, American Folk Art Museum, New York, NY....1162
Corcoran, Kathryn, Head Librarian, Munson-Williams-Proctor Arts Institute Museum of Art, Utica, NY....1222
Corcoran, Mr. Kim, Chm. Bd., Kansas Cosmosphere and Space Center, Hutchinson, KS....617
Corcoran, Mark, Security, Crawford Auto-Aviation Museum, Cleveland, OH....1309
Cordani-Stevenson, Lisa, Museum Shop Mgr., Southold Indian Museum, Southold, NY....1214
Cordell, Linda S., Prof. Emeritus Anthropology, University of Colorado Museum of Natural History, Boulder, CO....230
Cordes, Frank, Dir. Mktg. & Admin., National Archives Experience, Washington, DC....322
Cordish, Suzi, Chm. (V), Maryland Art Place, Baltimore, MD....724
Cordor, Rusty, Cur., Wapello County Historical Museum, Ottumwa, IA....597
Cordova, Bozo, Owner, Route 66 Auto Museum, Santa Rosa, NM....1092
Cordova, Elizabeth, Administrative Assoc., Arizona State Museum, Tucson, AZ....59
Cordry, Earvin, Park Ranger, Hamburg State Park Museum, Mitchell, GA....428
Cordulack, Jeff, Education Mgr., Audubon Greenwich, Greenwich, CT....275
Cordy-Collins, Dr. Alana, Dir., Anthropology Museum, University of San Diego, San Diego, CA....179
Corey, Catherine, Gift Shop Mgr., Audubon Society of Rhode Island, Smithfield, RI....1497
Corey, Cathy, Retail Svcs. Mgr. & Volunteer Coord., Audubon Society of Rhode Island Environmental Education Center, Bristol, RI....1485
Corey, Heather, Archives & Visual Resources Mgr., Hillwood Estate, Museum & Gardens, Washington, DC....318
Corillo, Nora Jean, Museum Educator II, Francis Land House Historic Site, Virginia Beach, VA....1751
Coriston, Anne, Deputy Dir. Administrative Svcs., The Branch Libraries, The New York Public Library, Astor, Lenox and Tilden Foundations, New York, NY....1178
Cork, Shelia, Librarian, New Orleans Museum of Art, New Orleans, LA....683
Corkern, Wilton C., Pres., The Accokeek Foundation, Inc., Accokeek, MD....716
Corkran, L.D. (Corky), Chm. Bd., Mgr. & C.E.O., Pioneer Air Museum, Fairbanks, AK....30
Corkum, Kate, Exec. Dir., The Rotch-Jones-Duff House & Garden Museum, Inc., New Bedford, MA....793
Corley, Kathleen, Interim Exec. Dir., Bloomington Art Center, Bloomington, MN....870
Cormier, Cynthia, Dir. Education & Curatorial Svcs., Hill-Stead Museum, Farmington, CT....274
Cormier, George Ann, Dir., Calhoun County Museum, Port Lavaca, TX....1639
Cormosino, Sal, Curatorial Asst., The Webb-Deane-Stevens Museum, Wethersfield, CT....301
Cornelisen, Erika, Advancement Coord., Corp. & Foundation Rels., Loyola University Museum of Art, Chicago, IL....483
Cornelius, Dr. Carol, Area Mgr., Oneida Nation Museum, De Pere, WI....1816
Cornelius, James, Cur. Lincoln, Abraham Lincoln Presidential Library & Museum, Springfield, IL....520
Cornell, Anne, Dir., Pomerene Center for the Arts, Coshocton, OH....1315
Cornell, Daniell, Sr. Cur. & Deputy Dir. Art, Palm Springs Art Museum, Palm Springs, CA....161
Cornell, Don, Pres. Museum Council (V), The Children's Museum of Rose Hill Manor Park, Frederick, MD....735
Cornell, Karon, Dir., Tucker Wildlife Sanctuary, Silverado, CA....211
Corner, R. George, Collection Mgr. Vertebrate Paleontology, University of Nebraska State Museum, Lincoln, NE....991
Cornett, Bonnie, Museum Shop Mgr., Railroad Museum of Long Island, Riverhead, NY....1200
Cornett, Peggy L., Dir. Center for Historic Plants, Monticello, Home of Thomas Jefferson, Thomas Jefferson Foundation, Inc., Charlottesville, VA....1705
Cornette, Dale, Chm., Port Tobacco One Room School, Port Tobacco, MD....743
Cornish, Jamie, Dir. Public Rels. & Public Outreach, Museum of the Rockies, Bozeman, MT....958
Cornish, Marilyn, Museum Shop Mgr., The Benjamin Banneker Park & Museum, Baltimore, MD....721
Cornwell, Dick, Chm. (V), Phippen Museum, Prescott, AZ....52
Cornwell, Gregory, Cur. Education, Roper Mountain Science Center, Greenville, SC....1514
Cornyn-Selby, Alyce, Dir., The Hat Museum, Portland, OR....1398
Corp, Steve, Vice Pres., Great Plains Transportation Museum, Wichita, KS....638
Corpuz, Paula, Sr. Dir. IHS Press, Indiana Historical Society, Indianapolis, IN....548
Corradini, Ellen, Dir. Human Resources, The Corning Museum of Glass, Corning, NY....1124
Correa, Luis, Deputy Dir. Finance & Administration, Vizcaya Museum and Gardens, Miami, FL....367
Correll, Emily, School Program Coord., The Montgomery County Historical Society, Inc., Rockville, MD....744
Correll, Phillip G., Pres., Salem County Historical Society, Salem, NJ....1060
Corridan, James, Pres., William Henry Harrison Mansion, Grouseland, Vincennes, IN....570
Corrigan, Caitlin, Chief Registrar, Museum of the City of New York, New York, NY....1176
Corrigan, David J., Cur. Collections, Museum of Connecticut History, Hartford, CT....278
Corrigan, Karina, H.A. Crosby Forbes Cur. Asian Export Art, Peabody Essex Museum, Salem, MA....804
Corrin, Lisa, Dir., Williams College Museum of Art, Williamstown, MA....817
Corriveau, Linda, Program Devel. & Cur. 19th- & 20th-Century Works on Paper, Museum of Ancient & Modern Art, Penn Valley, CA....163
Corry, Alan, Gift Shop Mgr., The Carter House, Franklin, TN....1551
Corry, Frank, Financial Dir., Mount Prospect Historical Society Museums, Mount Prospect, IL....507
Cort, Cynthia, Pres. (V) & Cur., Granville Historical Society Museum, Granville, OH....1323
Cort, Louise, Cur. Ceramics, Freer and Sackler Galleries of Art, Washington, DC....318
Cortello, Raphaella, Museum Shop Mgr., Texas Energy Museum, Beaumont, TX.1587
Cortes, Raziel, Membership Asst. & Special Events, Fresno Art Museum, Fresno, CA....115
Cortes, Rose Mary, Mktg. Mgr., El Museo del Barrio, New York, NY....1168
Cortes, Tess, Gallery Coord., Robert and Elaine Stein Galleries, Dayton, OH....1317
Cortese, Lucille, Museum Shop Mgr., Old St. Ferdinand's Shrine, Florissant, MO....927
Cortese, MaryAnn, Pres. (V) & Museum Shop Mgr., Bosque Redondo Memorial Fort Sumner State Monument, Fort Sumner, NM....1078
Cortez, Diego, Cur. Photography, New Orleans Museum of Art, New Orleans, LA....683
Cortez, Fernando, Museum Dir., History and Traditions Museum, Lackland Air Force Base, TX....1627
Cortez, Marti, Senior Vice Pres. Visitor Experience, St. Louis Science Center, Saint Louis, MO....950
Cortez, Mike, IT Specialist, Jule Collins Smith Museum of Fine Art, Auburn, AL....4
Cortiana, Bev, Pres. Bd., Tontitown Historical Museum, Tontitown, AR....85
Corum, Sharon, Exec. Sec., Korean War National Museum, Springfield, IL....521
Corwin, Linda, Site Mgr., Sanchez Adobe Historic Site, Pacifica, CA....160
Corwin, Sharon, Carolyn Muzzy Dir. & Chief Cur., Colby College Museum of Art, Waterville, ME....714
Cory, Claudia, Administrative Asst., Museum of Texas Tech University, Lubbock, TX....1629
Cory, Mary, Museum Admin., El Dorado County Historical Museum, Placerville, CA....165
Cory, Val, Museum Shop Mgr., New Mexico Museum of Space History, Alamogordo, NM....1069
Cosals, Ms. Coral, Volunteer Coord., Museo de Arte de Ponce, Hato Rey, PR....1869
Cosby, Lynne, Registrar, U.S. Army Aviation Museum, Fort Rucker, AL....12
Cosby, Sarah, Museum Shop Mgr., Chippokes Farm & Forestry Museum, Surry, VA....1748
Cosgriff, Judy, Sec., Crazy Mountain Museum, Big Timber, MT....956
Cosgrove, Patricia, C.E.O., White River Valley Museum, Auburn, WA....1758
Cosio, Christina, Asst. Cur. & Registrar, William & Florence Schmidt Art Center, Belleville, IL....470
Coski, Dr. John M., Historian, The Museum of the Confederacy, Richmond, VA....1739
Cossaboom, J.V., C.O.O., The New York Botanical Garden, Bronx, NY....1109
Cossalter, Cal, Pres., United States Hockey Hall of Fame Museum, Eveleth, MN....876
Costa, Alisha, Zookeeper, Applegate Park Zoo, Merced, CA....146
Costa, Ave, Dir. Corporate Rels., Adler Planetarium & Astronomy Museum, Chicago, IL....476
Costa, Gina, Mktg. & Public Affairs Specialist, The Snite Museum of Art, University of Notre Dame, Notre Dame, IN....561
Costa, Joseph, Photo Archivist, The Paterson Museum, Paterson, NJ....1056
Costa, Ken, Treas., Lincoln's New Salem State Historic Site, Petersburg, IL....513

C–*Continued*

C–Continued

C–*Continued*

Crouse, Michael, Exec. Dir. & Museum Shop Mgr., Yeiser Art Center, Paducah, KY....661
Crow, E.C., III, Cur. Exhibits, Wake Forest College Birthplace Society, Inc., Wake Forest, NC....1269
Crow, Heather, Dir. Devel., Rogue Gallery & Art Center, Medford, OR....1395
Crow, Dr. Jeffrey J., Deputy Sec., North Carolina Office of Archives and History, Raleigh, NC....1264
Crow, Jerry, Dir. Operations, Waikiki Aquarium, Honolulu, HI....448
Crow, Trammell S., Pres. (V), The Trammell & Margaret Crow Collection of Asian Art, Dallas, TX....1600
Crowder, Linda, Dir., Children's Museum of the Highlands, Sebring, FL....388
Crowder, Windy, Dir. Volunteers, The Florida International Museum at St. Petersburg College, Saint Petersburg, FL....383
Crowe, Dr. D., Cur. Economic Geology, Georgia Museum of Natural History, Athens, GA....400
Crowe, Lilah J., C.E.O., Itasca Historical Society & Itasca Genealogy, Grand Rapids, MN....879
Crowell, Eunice, Vice Pres., Readsboro Historical Society, Readsboro, VT....1688
Crowell, Kimberlyn, Cur., U.S. Navy Seabee Museum, Port Hueneme, CA....166
Crowell, Liz, Mgr. Cultural Resources Protection, Fairfax County Park Authority, Resource Management Division, Fairfax, VA....1709
Crowl, Cheryl, Pres., Keeler Tavern Museum, Ridgefield, CT....292
Crowl, Tom, Pres., Pittsburgh County Genealogical and Historical Society, Inc., McAlester, OK....1367
Crowley, Brenda, Administrative Asst., Mississippi Armed Forces Museum, Camp Shelby, MS....904
Crowley, Lynne, Archivist, Larchmont Historical Society, Mamaroneck, NY....1156
Crowser, Cathy, Dir. Special Events & Donor Rels., Autry National Center of the American West, Los Angeles, CA....133
Crowther, Michael I., C.E.O. & Pres., Indianapolis Zoo, Indianapolis, IN....550
Crowther, Otis C., Jr., Vice Pres. Advancement, The Museum of the Confederacy, Richmond, VA....1739
Croy, David, Pres., Chase County Historical Society, Inc., Cottonwood Falls, KS....608
Croy, David E., Pres. & Cur., Roniger Memorial Museum, Cottonwood Falls, KS....609
Croze, Mame, Dir. Public Rels. & Mktg., Decatur House Museum, Washington, DC....316
Crozier, Dr. George, Exec. Dir., Estuarium, Dauphin Island, AL....8
Cruise, Tim, Visitor Center Supvr., Sugarlands Visitor Center, Gatlinburg, TN....1552
Crum, David, Dir., Cherokee County Historical Museum, Centre, AL....7
Crumbley, Laura, Pres. (V) & Museum Shop Mgr., Lynchburg Museum System, Lynchburg, VA....1723
Crumbley, Laura, Museum Shop Mgr., Point of Honor, Lynchburg, VA....1723
Crumley, Todd, Archivist, Reynolda House Museum of American Art, Winston-Salem, NC....1275
Crump, Princess, Exec. Dir., George Washington Carver Museum and Cultural Center, Phoenix, AZ....50
Crumpton, Margaret, Business Officer, Iron & Steel Museum of Alabama, Tannehill Ironworks Historical State Park, McCalla, AL....16
Crumrin, Tim, Deputy Dir. Museum Experience, Conner Prairie Interactive History Park, Fishers, IN....540
Crupi, Tamara, Dir., Whitehouse Nature Center, Albion, MI....821
Crusan, Keith, Pres. (V), The Glynn Art Association, Inc., Saint Simons Island, GA....432
Crusan, Ron, Dir., Ogunquit Museum of American Art, Ogunquit, ME....705
Crutch, Minister Donald L., Dir., Museum of Great Christian Preachers & Ministries, Orange Park, FL....373
Crutch, Lisa A., Pres. (V), Museum of Great Christian Preachers & Ministries, Orange Park, FL....373
Crutcher, Nick, Chm. & Pres., Mississippi Sports Hall of Fame & Museum, Jackson, MS....910
Crutchfield, Margo, Sr. Cur., Museum of Contemporary Art Cleveland, Cleveland, OH....1309
Cruz, Aileen, Gallery Attendant, McNamara House Museum, Victoria, TX....1652
Cruz, Dena, Teacher & Mgr. School Programs, Arizona Museum For Youth, Mesa, AZ....46
Cruz, J. Lawrence, Pres., Faninadahen Kosas Guahan-Guam Museum, Hagatna, GU....1868
Cruz, Laura, Rental & Special Events Coord., Mission Mill Museum Association, Salem, OR....1404
Cruz, Michelle, Dir. Education, Mount Washington Museum and The Weather Discovery Center, North Conway, NH....1025
Cruz, Ramona, Administrative Asst., California Indian Museum & Cultural Center, Santa Rosa, CA....208
Cruzen, Dr. Shawn, Exec. Dir., Coca-Cola Space Science Center, Columbus, GA....414
Cryans, Cathy, Museum Shop Mgr., Fuller Gardens, North Hampton, NH....1025
Csage, Florence, Museum Shop Mgr., Ella Sharp Museum, Jackson, MI....847
Csaki, Jerry, Education Program Coord., National Football Museum, Inc., Canton, OH....1301
Csala, Margaret, Dir. Museum Shop, The New York Botanical Garden, Bronx, NY....1109
Csar, Mary, Dir., Boca Raton Historical Society, Boca Raton, FL....335
Csikesz, Julia, Asst. to Dir., Mary and Leigh Block Museum of Art, Northwestern University, Evanston, IL....494
Cubby, Tonya, Chairperson, West Milford Museum, West Milford, NJ....1067
Cuchine, Wally, Dir., Eureka Opera House, Eureka, NV....1003
Cuddy, Patricia A., Vice Pres., Rutland Area Art Association d/b/a Chaffee Art Center, Rutland, VT....1689
Cudiamat, Brian, Coord. Special Events, Spurlock Museum, University of Illinois at Urbana-Champaign, Urbana, IL....525
Cudlin, Jeffry, Dir. Exhibitions, Arlington Arts Center, Arlington, VA....1699
Cudnik, Carolyn M., Office Mgr., Old Barracks Museum, Trenton, NJ....1064
Cudworth, Keith R., Exec. Dir., White Memorial Conservation Center, Inc., Litchfield, CT....280
Cuenco, Joseph S., Dir., The Science Center of Pinellas County, Saint Petersburg, FL....385
Cuervo, Adriana, Asst. Archivist Music & Fine Arts, Sousa Archives and Center for American Music, Champaign, IL....475
Cueva, Arlie, Public Rels., Lynden Pioneer Museum, Lynden, WA....1771
Cueva, Cesar, Visitor Svcs. Coord., Wing Luke Asian Museum, Seattle, WA....1784
Cuff, Kathy, Museum Asst., President Andrew Johnson Museum and Library, Greeneville, TN....1553
Culbertson, Margaret, Librarian, The Museum of Fine Arts, Houston, Houston, TX....1622
Culbertson, Michael, Pres. Bd. (V), Maitland Historical Society and Museums, Maitland, FL....363
Culbertson, Thomas J., Exec. Dir., Rutherford B. Hayes Presidential Center, Fremont, OH....1320
Culbreath, Gray, Chm. (V), South Carolina State Museum, Columbia, SC....1510
Culek, Ann, Dir. Farm Program, Slate Run Living Historical Farm, Metro Parks, Canal Winchester, OH....1300
Culipher-Ross, Susan, Coord. Education Programs, J.L. Scott Marine Education Center and Aquarium, Gulf Coast Research Laboratory College of Marine Sciences, The U. of Southern Mississippi, Ocean Springs, MS....914
Cull, Anne C., Cur., Cape Coral Historical Museum, Cape Coral, FL....337
Cullen, Cecily, Asst. Dir. & Cur., Metropolitan State College of Denver/Center for Visual Art, Denver, CO....241
Cullen, Dana, Vice Pres. (V), Meriks Historical Society, Dover, AR....69
Cullen, Deborah, Chief Cur., El Museo del Barrio, New York, NY....1168
Cullen, Elizabeth, Office Mgr., Evanston Environmental Association/Evanston Ecology Center, Evanston, IL....493
Cullen, Kimbrie, Educator, The Minna Anthony Common Nature Center at Wellesley State Park, Fineview, NY....1132
Culler, Casey, Museum & Gift Shop Mgr., National Lacrosse Hall of Fame/US Lacrosse, Baltimore, MD....725
Culley, Delores, Exec. Dir., Kell House Museum, Wichita Falls, TX....1657
Culligan, Jenine, Sr. Cur., Huntington Museum of Art, Inc., Huntington, WV....1800
Cullins, Kimberly, Mktg. & Programs, St. Clements Island and Piney Point Museums, Colton's Point, MD....732
Culliton, Christie, Operations & Devel. Mgr., Duluth Art Institute, Duluth, MN....874
Cullivan, Lynn, Public Affairs Officer, San Francisco Maritime National Historical Park, San Francisco, CA....193
Cullum, Garrett, Information Systems Admin., Oklahoma City Museum of Art, Oklahoma City, OK....1371
Culmone, Margaret, Gallery Asst., Ben Shahn Galleries at William Paterson University of New Jersey, Wayne, NJ....1066
Culp, Brandy, Cur., Historic Charleston Foundation, Charleston, SC....1505
Culp, Patti, 2nd Vice Pres., Alton Museum of History and Art, Inc., Alton, IL....468
Culver, Dennis, Exhibitions Preparator, Museum of Indian Arts & Culture/Laboratory of Anthropology, Santa Fe, NM....1089
Culver, Jim, Miniature Train Owner & Operator, Seward County Historical Society Museum, Goehner, NE....983
Culver, Michael, Ph.D., Dir. & Chief Cur., Patty and Jay Baker Naples Museum of Art, Naples, FL....370

C–*Continued*

Curry, Richard, Park Science Coord., Biscayne National Park, Homestead, FL 353
Cursa, Dale, Business Mgr., The Antique Boat Museum, Clayton, NY 1121
Curtin, Donna D., Exec. Dir., Plymouth Antiquarian Society, Plymouth, MA 801
Curtis, Amanda, Education & Museum Shop Mgr., Intuit: The Center for Intuitive and Outsider Art, Chicago, IL...482
Curtis, Bonnie, Sec., Sidney Historical Association, Sidney, NY 1212
Curtis, David, Treas., Shaftsbury Historical Society, Shaftsbury, VT 1690
Curtis, Donna, Vice Pres. Human Rels. & Administration, Lincoln Park Zoological Gardens, Chicago, IL 483
Curtis, Donnie, Security, The Museum of Mobile, Mobile, AL 18
Curtis, Eleanor, Museum Shop Mgr., Nevada State Fire Museum & Comstock Firemen's Museum, Virginia City, NV 1011
Curtis, Jeff, Dir. Gardens & Grounds, The Preservation Society of Newport County/The Newport Mansions, Newport, RI 1492
Curtis, Joan, Cur., Steilacoom Historical Museum Association, Steilacoom, WA..1787
Curtis, John, Exec. Dir., Allaire Village Inc., Farmingdale, NJ 1038
Curtis, John, Pres., Martinez Museum, Martinez, CA 145
Curtis, Joseph L., Sec. & Treas., Nevada State Fire Museum & Comstock Firemen's Museum, Virginia City, NV..1011
Curtis, Lori, Program Asst., Tennessee Valley Art Center, Tuscumbia, AL 25
Curtis, Nan, Dir. MSC Forsyth Center Galleries, Texas A&M University, College Station, TX 1593
Curtis, Pat, Security, Fred Harman Art Museum, Pagosa Springs, CO 259
Curtis, Susan, Collections Asst. Anthropology & NAGPRA Asst., University of Nebraska State Museum, Lincoln, NE 991
Curtis, William D., Pres. (V), Maritime Museum of Monterey, Monterey, CA 148
Curtis, William D., Pres. (V), Monterey History and Art Association, Monterey, CA 149
Curwen, John, Supervisory Park Ranger, Channel Islands National Park, Robert J. Lagomarsino Visitor Center, Ventura, CA 221
Curzon, Mick, Head Facilities, Birch Aquarium at Scripps, Scripps Institution of Oceanography, University of California, San Diego, La Jolla, CA 126
Cusack-McVeigh, Holly, Cur. Exhibits, Pratt Museum, Homer, AK 31
Cushing, Catherine, Administrative Mgr., National Eagle Center, Wabasha, MN 900
Cushing Davis, Lisa, Exec. Dir., Mitchell Museum of the American Indian, Evanston, IL 494
Cushing, Margaret, Treas., Temecula Valley Museum, Temecula, CA 216
Cushing, Dr. Paula, Cur. Invertebrate Zoology & Dept. Chair, Denver Museum of Nature & Science, Denver, CO 239
Cushing, Robert, Pres., The Fishermen's Museum, New Harbor, ME 703
Cushing, Stanley E., Cur. Rare Books, The Boston Athenaeum, Boston, MA 758
Cushman, Brad, Dir., University of Arkansas at Little Rock Art Department Gallery I & II & III, Little Rock, AR 78
Cushman, Robin, Administrative Dir., Galveston Arts Center, Galveston, TX ..1613
Cusick, Ann E., Museum Educator, University of Nebraska State Museum, Lincoln, NE 991
Cusick, Bonnie A., Cur., Duluth Children's Museum, Duluth, MN 874
Custalow, Gertrude, Dir., Mattaponi Indian Museum, West Point, VA 1753
Custer, Katrina, Museum Shop Mgr., Garrett Historical Museum, Garrett, IN...543
Custer, Mandi, Dir. Devel. & External Affairs, Decorative Arts Center of Ohio, Lancaster, OH 1326
Custer, Dr. Stewart, Dir., Howell Memorial Planetarium, Greenville, SC..1514
Cuthrell, Carolyn, Dir. Devel., Virginia Living Museum, Newport News, VA 1729
Cutler, Alice D., Interim Dir., Macculloch Hall Historical Museum & Gardens, Morristown, NJ 1050
Cutler, Ann, Museum Shop Mgr., Swedish American Museum, Chicago, IL 487
Cutler, Jean H., Dir. Bureau for Historic Preservation, Pennsylvania Historical & Museum Commission, Harrisburg, PA 1431
Cutler, Judy Goffman, Dir. & Co-Founder, National Museum of American Illustration, Newport, RI 1490
Cutler, Laurence, Dir. Institutional Devel., National Museum of American Illustration, Newport, RI 1490
Cutler, Laurence S., Chm. & Co-Founder, National Museum of American Illustration, Newport, RI 1490
Cutler, Scott, Cur. Collections & Exhibits, Centennial Museum and Chihuahuan Desert Gardens, El Paso, TX 1603
Cutler, Zachary W.S., Asst. Dir., National Museum of American Illustration, Newport, RI 1490
Cutshaw, Steve, Park Mgr., Torreya State Park, Bristol, FL 337
Cutt, Gloria, Dir., Ten Sleep Pioneer Museum, Ten Sleep, WY 1866
Cuttler, David, Gift Shop, J.M. Davis Arms & Historical Museum, Claremore, OK 1358
Cutts, Kenneth, Pres., Albany Civil Rights Movement Museum at Old Mt. Zion Church, Albany, GA 399
Cvjeticanin, Sanja, Dir. Visitor Svcs., Harvard Art Museum, Cambridge, MA...767
Cynova, Kay, Historical Interpretation Mgr., Stuhr Museum of the Prairie Pioneer, Grand Island, NE 984
Cyphert, Rebecca, Bookstore & Office Mgr., The Wilderness Center Inc., Wilmot, OH 1351
Cyr, Mrs. Nowetah, Owner & Cur., Nowetah's American Indian Museum & Store, New Portland, ME 703
Cytacki, Joe, Dir. Programs & Exhibits, Museum of Discovery and Science, Fort Lauderdale, FL 348
Cytacki, Kristen, Dir. Education, Palm Beach Zoo, West Palm Beach, FL 397
Czaplewski, Dr. N.J., Cur. Vertebrate Paleontology, Sam Noble Oklahoma Museum of Natural History, Norman, OK 1369
Czaplewski, Russ, Collections Mgr., Johnson County Museum, Shawnee, KS 634
Czarnecki, Steven, Pres. (V), Aquarium of Niagara, Niagara Falls, NY 1185
Czarniecki, M.J., III, Museologist, American Museum of Asmat Art, Saint Paul, MN 893
Czarniecki, Steven, Cur., Fire Island National Seashore, Mastic Beach, NY ..1157
Czekanski, Thomas, Dir. Collections & Exhibitions, The National World War II Museum, New Orleans, LA 682
Czerwinski, Ginny, Historical Interpreter, Troy Museum & Historic Village, Troy, MI 866

D

Daas, Charles, Dir., Cambodian American Heritage Museum and Killing Fields Memorial, Chicago, IL 477
D'Abate, Richard, Dir., Maine Historical Society, Portland, ME 707
Dabbene, John, Pres. & C.E.O., Garibaldi-Meucci Museum, Staten Island, NY 1215
Dabek, Lisa, Dir. Conservation, Woodland Park Zoo, Seattle, WA 1785
Dabney, Walt, Dir. Parks, Fort Leaton State Historical Site, Presidio, TX 1639
Dabney, Walt, Dir. Public Lands, Fort Richardson State Historical Park, Jacksboro, TX 1624
Dabney, Walt, Dir. Parks, Goliad State Park, Goliad, TX 1616
Dabney, Walt, Dir. State Parks, Texas Parks and Wildlife Department, Austin, TX 1584
Dackerman, Susan M., Cur. Prints, Harvard Art Museum, Cambridge, MA...767
Dacko, Bill, Treas., Maitland Art Center, Maitland, FL 363
DaDa, Jamil, Pres. (V), March Field Air Museum, Riverside, CA 172
Daddis, Dick, C.E.O. & Pres. (V), Pike County Historical Society, Milford, PA.1445
Dadisman, Olive, Museum Shop Mgr., Anna Jarvis Birthplace Museum, Grafton, WV 1798
Dadisman, Tom, Pres. (V), Anna Jarvis Birthplace Museum, Grafton, WV 1798
Dadone, David, Operations Mgr., Museo de las Americas, Denver, CO 241
Dady, Lisa, Dir. Education & Public Programs, Newport Restoration Foundation, Newport, RI 1491
Daeschler, Edward, Ph.D., Vice Pres. Systematics & Library, The Academy of Natural Sciences, Philadelphia, PA ...1449
Daetwyler, Margie, Museum Shop Mgr., Helvetia Museum, Helvetia, WV 1799
Daffron, Cindy, Dir. Devel., Pony Express Museum, Saint Joseph, MO 944
Dage, Carol J., Cur. Museum, Harry S Truman National Historic Site - Truman Home, Independence, MO 930
Dagenais, Mike, Mgr. Guest Svcs., Las Vegas Springs Preserve, Las Vegas, NV 1006
Dagg, David, Security & Facilities Operations, Sam Noble Oklahoma Museum of Natural History, Norman, OK 1369
Daggett Dillenberger, Jane, Chm. (V), Museum of Contemporary Religious Art (MOCRA)-St. Louis University, Saint Louis, MO 949
Daggett, John E., Project Engineer, Fort Peck Interpretive Center, Fort Peck, MT 963
D'Agostino, Rachel, Cur. Printed Books, Library Company of Philadelphia, Philadelphia, PA 1456
Dague, Arlene, Treas., Washington County Historical Society, Washington, KS 637
Dahan, Amy, Dir., Heathcote Botanical Gardens, Inc., Fort Pierce, FL 349
Dahl, Deb, Chm., Arizona Museum For Youth, Mesa, AZ 46

D–*Continued*

D–*Continued*

D–*Continued*

D–*Continued*

D–*Continued*

Deveau, Linda, Acting Administrative Officer & Contractor, Statue of Liberty National Monument & Ellis Island Immigration Museum, New York, NY ..1182
Devendorf, Cathy, Dir. Volunteers & Outreach, Chippewa Nature Center, Midland, MI....854
Devereaux Ohara, Arlene, Sec., The Lackawanna Historical Society at the Catlin House, Scranton, PA....1472
Devereux, Dennis, Chm. (V), Mount Holly Community Historical Museum, Belmont, VT....1676
Devine, Jack, Pres. (V), The Montgomery County Historical Society, Inc., Rockville, MD....744
Devine, Jacqueline, Dir. Devel., Terrace Hill Historic Site and Governor's Mansion, Des Moines, IA....584
Devine, Mercedes, Bookkeeper, The Society of California Pioneers, San Francisco, CA....193
DeVine, Meta, Museum Shop Mgr., Minnesota Historical Society, Saint Paul, MN....895
Devine, Michael J., Dir., Harry S. Truman Library & Museum, Independence, MO....930
Devine, Steve, Vice Pres. Human Resources, The Maryland Zoo in Baltimore, Baltimore, MD....724
Devinney, Rosemary, Mgr., Coord. & Museum Shop Mgr., Shoshone-Bannock Tribal Museum, Fort Hall, ID....459
DeVito, Lindsay, Environmental Education Specialist, Audubon Greenwich, Greenwich, CT....275
Devlin, Christina, Dir. Retail, Pewabic Pottery, Detroit, MI....835
Devlin, Morgan, Dir. Mktg., Newport Restoration Foundation, Newport, RI....1491
Devlin, Teresa, Mgr. Mktg., The Historic New Orleans Collection, New Orleans, LA....680
DeVore, Susan, Education, Howell Living History Farm, Lambertville, NJ....1045
Devory, Jerry, Cur., Peshtigo Fire Museum, Peshtigo, WI....1840
Devory, Marian, Cur., Peshtigo Fire Museum, Peshtigo, WI....1840
DeVos, Brenda, Co.-Dir., Keeler Tavern Museum, Ridgefield, CT....292
Devries, Fred, Pres. (V), Old Lighthouse Museum, Michigan City, IN....556
DeVries, Mrs. H., Cur. South Canaan Meeting House, Falls Village-Canaan Historical Society, Falls Village, CT....274
DeVries, Karl, Asst. Dir., Ships of the Sea Maritime Museum/William Scarbrough House, Savannah, GA....435
DeVries, Lowell, Pres., Prairie Village, Madison, SD....1535
DeVries, Susan, Dir., Dyckman Farmhouse Museum and Park, New York, NY....1167
deVries, Terry, Exec. Dir., Kimberly Crest House & Gardens, Redlands, CA....170
Dewald, Ann L., Dir. & Museum Shop Mgr., Indian Museum of Lake County, Ohio, Willoughby, OH....1350
DeWald, Sarah, Dir. Education, Lincoln Children's Museum, Lincoln, NE....988
DeWall, Lynn, Maintenance & Housekeeping, Hearthstone Historic House Museum, Appleton, WI....1810
DeWalt, Dr. Billie, Dir., Musical Instrument Museum, Phoenix, AZ....50
DeWalt, Jim, Dept. Head, Free Library of Philadelphia Rare Book Department, Philadelphia, PA....1454
Dewan, Vikram, C.E.O. & Pres., The Philadelphia Zoo, Philadelphia, PA....1460
Dewey, David, Cur., Bolt's Antique Tool Museum, Oroville, CA....158
Dewey, David, Cur., Butte County Pioneer Memorial Museum, Oroville, CA....158
Dewey, David, Cur., C.F. Lott Historic Home, Oroville, CA....158
Dewey, David, Cur., Oroville Chinese Temple, Oroville, CA....158
Dewhirst, Barbara, Keeper, House of Refuge Museum, Stuart, FL....389
Dewhurst, Dr. C. Kurt, Cur. Folk Art., The Michigan State University Museum, East Lansing, MI....838
DeWitt, Chris, Restoration Supvr., Nevada State Railroad Museum, Carson City, NV....1001
DeWitt, Connie, Deputy Dir., San Jose Museum of Quilts & Textiles, San Jose, CA....196
DeWitt, David A., Ph.D., Dir., Museum of Earth and Life History, Lynchburg, VA....1723
Dewitz, Becky, Museum Shop Mgr., Roosevelt Park Zoo, Minot, ND....1287
Dexter, Linda, Dir., Fort Delaware Museum of Colonial History, Narrowsburg, NY....1160
Dexter, Sean, Dir. Public Rels., Golden State Model Railroad Museum, Point Richmond, CA....165
Deyle, Betty, Co-Pres., Dundy County Historical Society, Benkelman, NE....977
Deyoe, Sheryl, Pres. (V), Grant County Museum aka Historic Adobe Museum, Ulysses, KS....636
DeYoung, Jo, Cur., Marquette County History Museum, Marquette, MI....853
DeYoung, Sarah, Education Asst., High Point Museum & Historical Park, High Point, NC....1252
Dhody, Anna N., Cur., Mutter Museum, College of Physicians of Philadelphia, Philadelphia, PA....1457
d'Humieres, Ghislain, The Wylodean & Bill Saxon Dir., The Fred Jones Jr. Museum of Art, Norman, OK....1368
Di Candido, Joseph, Vice Pres., Military Museum of Southern New England, Danbury, CT....270
Di Tommaso, Francis, Dir., Visual Arts Museum, New York, NY....1183
Diachkoff, Nicholas, Cur., Museum of Russian Culture, San Francisco, CA....191
Dial, John, Pres. (V), American Saddlebred Horse Museum, Mexico, MO....940
Dial, John, Pres. (V), Audrain Historical Museum, Graceland, Mexico, MO....940
Dial, Julie, Exec. Dir., Western Heritage Center, Billings, MT....956
Diamantopoulos, Aella, Chief Conservator, Pennsylvania Academy of the Fine Arts, Philadelphia, PA....1458
Diamond, Charles M., Exec. Dir. & Pres., Harrimans Falls Educational Centre and Museum, Bath, NH....1012
Diamond, Hannah, Exec. Asst., Brigham Young University Museum of Art, Provo, UT....1667
Diamond, Dr. Judy, Cur., Professor & Informal Science Education, University of Nebraska State Museum, Lincoln, NE....991
Diamond, Julie, Dir. Communications, Long Island Museum of American Art, History & Carriages, Stony Brook, NY....1217
Dias-Reid, Cynthia, Dir., Willard House and Clock Museum, Inc., Grafton, MA...780
Diaz, Doris, Registrar, Museo de Arte de Puerto Rico, Santurce, PR....1871
Diaz, Josef, Cur., Palace of the Governors/New Mexico History Museum, Santa Fe, NM....1090
Diaz, Sonia, Registrar, Abrons Arts Center/Henry Street Settlement, New York, NY....1161
Diaz, Victor, Chm. (V), Maitland Art Center, Maitland, FL....363
DiCarlo, Douglas, Archivist, LaGuardia and Wagner Archives, Long Island City, NY....1154
DiChristina, Joan, Exec. Dir., Chittenango Landing Canal Boat Museum, Chittenango, NY....1121
DiCiurcio, John, Chm., Chicago Architecture Foundation, Chicago, IL....477
Dick, Alvin, Chm. Bd, Heritage Village, Mountain Lake, MN....888
Dick, Christopher, Cur., Herbarium of the University of Michigan, Ann Arbor, MI....822
Dick, James, Founder, Dir. & Pres., Festival-Institute, James Dick Foundation, Round Top, TX....1641
Dick, Ryan, Dir., International Game Fish Association - Fishing Hall of Fame and Museum, Dania Beach, FL....341
Dick, William G., II, Chm. (V), Columbia Gorge Discovery Center and Wasco County Museum, The Dalles, OR....1405
Dicke, James F., II, C.E.O., The Bicycle Museum of America, New Bremen, OH....1334
Dickens, Tameka, Educator, Imagination Station Science Museum, Wilson, NC...1272
Dickenson, Gary, Pres. (V), Coos County Logging Museum, Myrtle Point, OR....1395
Dickerson, C. D., Assoc. Cur. European Art, Kimbell Art Museum, Fort Worth, TX....1610
Dickerson, Nicole, Museum Dir., Angels Attic Museum, Santa Monica, CA....207
Dickerson, Patricia, Exec. Dir., The World Organization of China Painters, Oklahoma City, OK....1373
Dickert, Sharon, Accounting Asst., Racine Art Museum (RAM), Racine, WI....1842
Dickey, Dennis, Admissions, Canton Classic Car Museum, Canton, OH....1300
Dickey, Elizabeth, Educator, Idaho Botanical Garden, Boise, ID....455
Dickey, Michael, Dir., Arrow Rock State Historic Site, Arrow Rock, MO....920
Dickey, Michael, Dir., Boone's Lick State Historic Site, Boonesboro, MO....921
Dickey, Michael, Site Admin., Sappington Cemetery State Historic Site, Nelson, MO....941
Dickey, Rita, Museum Interpreter, Agua Caliente Cultural Museum, Palm Springs, CA....160
Dickinson, Bob, Chm. (V), Old Dominion Railway Museum, Richmond, VA....1739
Dickinson, Cindy, Dir. Interpretation & Programming, Emily Dickinson Museum: The Homestead and The Evergreens, Amherst, MA....752
Dickinson, James L., Pres. (V), Medina Railroad Museum, Medina, NY....1158
Dickinson, Roger, C.E.O., Indiana Basketball Hall of Fame, New Castle, IN....560
Dickinson, Rose, Mgr. Mktg. & Advertising, Wally Parks NHRA Motorsports Museum, Pomona, CA....166

D–*Continued*

D–*Continued*

D–*Continued*

D–*Continued*

Dugan, Anne, Dir., Carlton County Historical Society, Cloquet, MN..............872
Dugan, Jack, Deputy & Exhibit Specialist, 1st Cavalry Division Museum, Fort Hood, TX.......................1607
Dugan, Pamela, Management Asst. & Support Supvr., National Historic Oregon Trail Interpretive Center, Baker City, OR.......................................1384
Dugan, Steven, Volunteer Coord., Workman & Temple Family Homestead Museum, City of Industry, CA...102
Dugas, Tasha B., Dir., Bayou Teche Museum, New Iberia, LA.......................677
Dugdale, Pat, Chm., West Windsor Historical Society, Brownsville, VT......1677
Duggal, Elizabeth, Assoc. Dir. Public Programs, National Museum of Natural History, Washington, DC............325
Duggal, Elizabeth, Dir. External Affairs & Develop., National Museum of the American Indian, Smithsonian Institution, New York, NY.....................1177
Duggan, David, Business Officer, Swenson Memorial Museum of Stephens County, Breckenridge, TX.......1589
Duggan, Ervin S., Pres., The Society of the Four Arts, Palm Beach, FL...............375
Duggan, Gloria, Archivist, The Stratford Historical Society & Catherine B. Mitchell Museum, Stratford, CT.............297
Duggan, John K., Jr., Pres. (V), Southern Alleghenies Museum of Art at Loretto, Loretto, PA...1443
Duggar, Danna Kay, Dir., Jacksonville Museum of Military History, Jacksonville, AR...75
Dugger, Anne, Registration Asst., Mingei International Museum, San Diego, CA...180
Duggins, Stephen, Museum Preparator, University of Richmond Museums, Richmond, VA...1740
Dugus, Monica, Museum Shop Mgr., Louisiana Naval War Memorial/U.S.S. Kidd, Baton Rouge, LA..........................667
Duillio, Steven, Museum Shop Mgr., Discovery Center of Springfield, Springfield, MO..953
Dujin, Veljko, Cur. Collections, The Morikami Museum and Japanese Gardens, Delray Beach, FL.........................344
Duke, Amy, Registrar, Kemper Museum of Contemporary Art, Kansas City, MO...934
Duke, Ben, Vice Pres. Devel., Denver Zoological Gardens, Denver, CO.............239
Duke, Dana, Registrar, Mesker Park Zoo & Botanic Garden, Evansville, IN...........540
Duke, Jacqueline, Asst. Dir., Museum of International Folk Art, Santa Fe, NM....1089
Duke, Judy, C.E.O. & Museums Admin., Cookeville Depot Museum, Cookeville, TN.......................................1550
Duke, Laurie, Asst. to Deputy Dir., Grey Art Gallery, New York University Art Collection, New York, NY....................1169
Duke, Linda, Dir. Education IMA - Indianapolis Museum of Art, Indianapolis, IN..548
Dukes Edinberg, Lucinda, Art Educator, Elizabeth Myers Mitchell Art Gallery, St. John's College, Annapolis, MD.........717
Dulaban, Alta, Dir. & Chm. (V), Henry County Museum and Cultural Arts Center, Clinton, MO................................924
Dulaney, Dave, Pres. (V), Historical Society of Quincy and Adams County, Quincy, IL...514
Dulaney, H.G., Consultant & Dir. Emeritus, The Sam Rayburn Library and Museum, a Division of the Dolph Briscoe Center for American History, Bonham, TX..1589
Dulaney, Kathy, Chm. (V) & Museum Shop Mgr., Dorn Mill Center, McCormick, SC....................................1518
Dulcich, Tom, Chm. (V), Columbia River Maritime Museum, Astoria, OR.............1382
Dulen, Deanna, Park Mgr., Devils Postpile National Monument, Mammoth Lakes, CA..............................144
Duley, Elizabeth, Head Collection Management, Freer and Sackler Galleries of Art, Washington, DC............318
Dulin, Mark, Dir. Administrative Svcs., Mystic Seaport - The Museum of America and the Sea, Mystic, CT...........284
Duling, Lynne, Sec. & Treas., South Dakota Hall of Fame, Chamberlain, SD..1528
Dulisse, Kathy, Membership Coord., Elizabeth Myers Mitchell Art Gallery, St. John's College, Annapolis, MD..........717
Dull, Dawn, Pres., Carmel Heritage Society's First Murphy House, Carmel-by-the-Sea, CA...............................98
Dull, Tim, Pres. (V), Garden Grove Historical Society, Garden Grove, CA....118
Dumas, Cathy, Librarian & Cur., Rock Island Depot Museum, Waurika, OK....1380
Dumas, Gary, Museum Shop Mgr., National Route 66 Museum and Old Town Complex, Elk City, OK...............1361
Dumbacher, Dr. John, Chm. Ornithology & Mammalogy, California Academy of Sciences, San Francisco, CA..............187
Dumelin, Bruce, Pres., North Haven Historical Society, North Haven, CT.......290
Dumermuth, Derryl, Coord. Docent, Tulare Historical Museum, Tulare, CA...219
Dumlao, Kathy, Assoc. Cur. Education, Memphis Brooks Museum of Art, Memphis, TN..1563
Dumont, Elizabeth, Dir., Natural History Collections, Amherst, MA.......................753
Dumont, John, Pres., Historical Society of Princeton, Princeton, NJ...................1058
Dumville, Helen, Business Officer & Publications Dir., Royalton Historical Society, Royalton, VT........................1688
Dumville, John P., Historic Sites Operations Chief, Bennington Battle Monument, Old Bennington, VT...........1686
Dumville, John P., Historic Sites Operations Chief, Calvin Coolidge Historic Site, Plymouth Notch, VT.......1687
Dumville, John P., Historic Site Operations Chief, Chimney Point State Historic Site, Addison, VT....................1675
Dumville, John P., Historic Sites Operations Chief, Eureka School House, Springfield, VT..........................1691
Dumville, John P., Historic Sites Operations Chief, Hubbardton Battlefield Museum, Hubbardton, VT...1681
Dumville, John P., Historic Site Operations Chief, Justin Smith Morrill Homestead, Strafford, VT....................1692
Dumville, John P., Operations Chief, Mount Independence Historic Site, Orwell, VT...1686
Dumville, John P., Historic Sites Operations Chief, Old Constitution House, Windsor, VT..............................1694
Dumville, John P., Historic Sites Operations Chief, President Chester A. Arthur Historic Site, Fairfield, VT.........1680
Dumville, John P., Pres., Royalton Historical Society, Royalton, VT...........1688
Dun, George, Preparator, Wood Street Galleries, Pittsburgh, PA.......................1468
Dunagan, Casey, Museum Shop Mgr., Cedar Rapids Museum of Art, Cedar Rapids, IA...577
Dunagan, Rob L., Pres. (V), Chihuahuan Desert Research Institute, Fort Davis, TX...1607
Dunavant, William B., III, Bd. Pres., Memphis Botanic Garden, Goldsmith Civic Garden Center, Memphis, TN......1563
Dunaway, Bob, Librarian, Central Texas Area Museum, Inc., Salado, TX............1642
Dunaway, Joy, Librarian, Central Texas Area Museum, Inc., Salado, TX............1642
Dunbar, Betsy, Communications & Reader Svcs., American Baptist Historical Society, Atlanta, GA................401
Dunbar, Bonnie J., Ph.D., Pres. & C.E.O., The Museum of Flight, Seattle, WA...1781
Dunbar, Burton L., Dir. & Chm., University of Missouri-Kansas City Gallery of Art, Kansas City, MO............936
Dunbar, Elizabeth, Cur., Arthouse, Austin, TX...1579
Dunbeck, Helen, Dir. Admin., Museum of Contemporary Art, Chicago, IL...............483
Duncan, Anna, C.E.O., Moody County Museum, Flandreau, SD.......................1530
Duncan, Anne, Dir. Devel., Hartman Reserve Nature Center, Cedar Falls, IA...576
Duncan, Barbara, Treas., Wilderness Road Regional Museum, Newbern, VA...1727
Duncan, Beth M., Public Rels., Lake Superior Maritime Visitors Center, Duluth, MN...874
Duncan, Fred, Dir. Devel. IMA - Indianapolis Museum of Art, Indianapolis, IN...548
Duncan, J. Kelly, Chm. (V), Audubon Zoo, New Orleans, LA............................679
Duncan, James, Pres. (V), Historical Society of Stanton County Museums at Stanton and Pilger, Pilger, NE............996
Duncan, Jan, Pres., San Angelo Museum of Fine Arts, San Angelo, TX...............1642
Duncan, Janice, Tour Guide, Ernie Pyle State Historic Site, Dana, IN..................537
Duncan, Jean, Sec., Lars Noak Blacksmith Shop, Larsson/Ostlund Log Home & One-Room Capitol School, New Sweden, ME.......................704
Duncan, Karen, Registrar, Frederick R. Weisman Art Museum, Minneapolis, MN...885
Duncan, Larry, District Mgr., Old Dorchester State Historic Site, Summerville, SC...................................1524
Duncan, Sam, Dir. Library, Amon Carter Museum, Fort Worth, TX......................1609
Duncan, William, Pres. (V), Lars Noak Blacksmith Shop, Larsson/Ostlund Log Home & One-Room Capitol School, New Sweden, ME.......................704
Duncan-Huse, Ramona, Sr. Dir. Conservation, Indiana Historical Society, Indianapolis, IN..........................548
Duncanson, Heidi, Dir. Mktg., The Children's Museum of New Hampshire, Dover, NH..........................1016
Duncanson, Rev. Msgr. Richard F., Pastor, Mission San Diego de Alcala, San Diego, CA..181
Dunckel, Dr. Betty A., Assoc. Scientist & Program Dir. Center for Informal Science Education, Florida Museum of Natural History, Gainesville, FL..............351
Dunehoo, Andrew, Educator, Fort Morgan Museum, Fort Morgan, CO.....................246
Dunfey, Patrick, Exhibitions Designer, Hood Museum of Art, Hanover, NH.....1019

D–*Continued*

E

E–*Continued*

Egan Jones, Patricia, Chm., Battleship New Jersey Museum & Memorial, Camden, NJ 1033
Egan, Kathy, CFRE, Vice Pres. Devel., Atlanta Historical Society, Atlanta, GA...402
Egan, Laurie, Registrar, Agua Caliente Cultural Museum, Palm Springs, CA 160
Egan, Lisa, Dir. Education, Historic Southwest Ohio, Inc., Sharonville, OH .1343
Egan, Lynn, Dir. Programs, Southampton Historical Museums and Research Center, Southampton, NY 1213
Egan, Moira, Exec. Vice Pres., Heritage Preservation, Washington, DC 318
Egan, Natasha, Assoc. Dir., Museum of Contemporary Photography, Columbia College Chicago, Chicago, IL....484
Egan, Robert A., Pres., Egan Maritime Institute, Nantucket, MA....791
Egan, Shannon, Ph.D., Dir., Schmucker Art Gallery, Gettysburg, PA 1427
Egan Stalfort, Heather, Coord. Mktg., Evergreen Museum & Library, Johns Hopkins University Museums, Baltimore, MD....722
Egan Stalfort, Heather, Coord. Mktg. & Communications, Homewood Museum, Baltimore, MD 723
Egbert, Elizabeth, C.E.O., Staten Island Museum, Staten Island, NY 1216
Egelseer, Alan, Pres. (V), Wisconsin Automotive Museum, Hartford, WI.......1822
Eggert, Adm. Gus, USN (Ret.), Pres., Patuxent River Naval Air Museum, Lexington Park, MD....740
Egipciaco, Wanda, Administrative Asst., Abrons Arts Center/Henry Street Settlement, New York, NY....1161
Egram, Susan, Museum Shop Mgr., National Civil War Naval Museum at Port Columbus, Columbus, GA 414
Egy, Scott, Park Supvr., Old Las Vegas Mormon Fort State Historic Park, Las Vegas, NV....1006
Ehlers, Lyle, Lead Exhibit Technician, Kirby Science Discovery Center at the Washington Pavilion, Sioux Falls, SD...1542
Ehlmann, Dr. Arthur, Cur., Oscar E. Monnig Meteorite Gallery - Texas Christian University, Fort Worth, TX 1611
Ehlmann, Dr. Arthur, Cur., Oscar E. Monning Meteorite Gallery, Fort Worth, TX....1611
Ehmen, Linda, Registrar & Collection Mgr., The George D. and Harriet W. Cornell Fine Arts Museum, Winter Park, FL....398
Ehmke, Lee C., C.E.O., Minnesota Zoo, Apple Valley, MN....869
Ehrig-Burges, Kristi, Coord. Library Svcs. & Volunteer Coord., Mingei International Museum, San Diego, CA ...180
Ehringer, Martha, Dir. Public Rels., Mingei International Museum, San Diego, CA....180
Ehrke, Stan, Chm. (V) & Pres. (V), McLeod County Historical Society, Hutchinson, MN....881
Ehrler, Steve, Park Mgr., Fejervary Zoo, Davenport, IA 581
Ehrlich, Hedy, Grant Mgr., The Magic House, St. Louis Children's Museum, Saint Louis, MO....948
Ehry, Carl A., Pres. RV/MH Heritage Foundation, Inc., Elkhart, IN 539
Eichenaur, Pam, Dir. Devel., The Holden Arboretum, Kirtland, OH....1326
Eichenberg, Roberta, Dir., Norman R. Eppink Art Gallery, Emporia State University, Emporia, KS 611
Eichensehr, Kasey, Cur., Clark County Historical Society - Heritage Center of Clark County, Springfield, OH....1343
Eicher, Dee, Pres. (V), Lower Cape Fear Historical Society, Inc., Wilmington, NC....1272
Eichman, Shawn, Cur. Asian Art, Honolulu Academy of Arts, Honolulu, HI 445
Eichner, Steven, Assoc. Registrar, Utah Museum of Fine Arts, Salt Lake City, UT 1671
Eichold, Dr. Samuel, II, Founder & Advisor, Mobile Medical Museum, Mobile, AL....17
Eichten Albrecht, Shirley, Gallery Dir., Sedona Arts Center, Inc., Sedona, AZ.......55
Eick, Janice, Business Officer, Seymour Community Museum, Seymour, WI......1844
Eickmann, Margaret, Exec. Dir., The Berry Botanic Garden, Portland, OR.....1398
Eickmann, Theodore, Dir. Vehicle Collection Management, Shore Line Trolley Museum, East Haven, CT..........271
Eifel-Porter, Rhoda, Cur. Charles Engelhard & Head Dept. Drawings & Prints, The Morgan Library & Museum, New York, NY....1173
Eiken, Dr. Douglas, C.E.O., Locust Creek Covered Bridge State Historic Site, Laclede, MO 937
Eikenberry, Dan, Pres., Cass County Museum & Research Center, Walker, MN....900
Eikmeier, Linda, Asst. Site Mgr., Henrico County Historic Preservation & Museum Services, Richmond, VA 1738
Eiland, Chris, Cur., Bessemer Hall of History, Bessemer, AL....4
Eiland, William U., Dir., Georgia Museum of Art, University of Georgia, Athens, GA 400
Eilers, Alice A. "Alex", Mgr. Education, Pink Palace Family of Museums, Memphis, TN....1564
Eilertsen, John, Exec. Dir., Bridgehampton Historical Society, Bridgehampton, NY....1106
Eilertsen, Kate, Exec. Dir., Sonoma Valley Museum of Art, Sonoma, CA......213
Einreinhofer, Nancy, Ph.D., Dir. & Cur., Ben Shahn Galleries at William Paterson University of New Jersey, Wayne, NJ....1066
Einstein, Clifford J., Chm. Bd. Trustees (V), The Museum of Contemporary Art, Los Angeles, Los Angeles, CA 140
Eisbart, Ben, Vice Pres., Fort Wayne Museum of Art, Fort Wayne, IN....542
Eiseman, Susan, Advanced Coord., Mighty Eighth Air Force Museum, Pooler, GA....429
Eisenbeiss, William C., Pres., Norfolk Botanical Garden, Norfolk, VA....1731
Eisenberg, Elsa, Weekend Coord., Coe Hall, Oyster Bay, NY 1192
Eisenburg, Chris, Dir. Devel., Utah Museum of Natural History, Salt Lake City, UT 1672
Eisenhauer, Paul, Cur., Dir. Programs & Membership, The Wharton Esherick Museum, Malvern, PA....1443
Eisenman, Bonnie, Admin., Beth Ahabah Museum & Archives, Richmond, VA....1737
Eisenzimmer, Andy, Chancellor, Archives - Archdiocese of St. Paul and Minneapolis, Saint Paul, MN....893
Ekechi, Lawrence, Education Coord. & Security, The Museum for African Art, Long Island City, NY 1154
Ekland-Earnst, Arlene, Site Supvr., Fort Fetterman State Historic Site, Douglas, WY....1857
Eklund, John, 2nd Vice Pres., The Drake House Museum, Plainfield, NJ....1057
Eklund, Lori, C.O.O., Amon Carter Museum, Fort Worth, TX....1609
Ekstrum, Richard, Chm., South Dakota Hall of Fame, Chamberlain, SD 1528
Elan, Julie, Office Mgr., Lakewood's Heritage Center, Lakewood, CO....254
Elbo, Ofelia B., Museum Technician, Hampton Roads Naval Museum, Norfolk, VA 1730
Elder, Blair, Dir. Education, Historic Latta Plantation, Huntersville, NC.........1253
Elder, Sarah M., Cur. Collections, St. Joseph Museum Inc., Saint Joseph, MO....945
Elderfield, John, Chief Cur. Painting & Sculpture, The Museum of Modern Art, New York, NY 1176
Eldred, Tim, Supt. Bldgs. & Grounds, Madeline Island Museum, La Pointe, WI 1826
Eldred, Wayne A., Mgr. Collections & Programs, Newtown History Center, Stephens City, VA....1747
Eldredge, Bruce, Exec. Dir., Buffalo Bill Historical Center, Cody, WY 1856
Eldredge, Ward, Museum Technician, Sequoia and Kings Canyon National Parks, Three Rivers, CA 217
Eleazor, George, Sr., Security, Mashantucket Pequot Museum and Research Center, Mashantucket, CT........281
Elesh, James, Chm., Mary and Leigh Block Museum of Art, Northwestern University, Evanston, IL....494
Elgee, Michael, Co Pres. (V), Milford Historical Society, Milford, CT 282
Elgen, Fran, Dir., Crazy Mountain Museum, Big Timber, MT 956
Elgersman Lee, Dr. Maureen, Dir., Black History Museum & Cultural Center of Virginia, Richmond, VA....1737
Elhilow, Mark B., Chm., Historical Society of Palm Beach County, West Palm Beach, FL....396
Elias, Janet, Museum Shop Mgr., Arab American National Museum, Dearborn, MI 831
Elias, Pamela, Museum Shop Mgr., The Jewish Museum, New York, NY 1171
Elias, Dr. Thomas, Dir., U.S National Arboretum, Washington, DC....331
Elisens, Wayne J., Cur., Robert Bebb Herbarium, Norman, OK....1369
Elk, Sara Jane, Exec. Dir., Eastern State Penitentiary Historic Site, Philadelphia, PA 1452
Elkema, Harry, Museum Shop Mgr., Hall of Fame & Classic Car Museum, Weedsport, NY 1227
Elkin, Marge, Visitor Svcs. Mgr., Rochester Art Center, Rochester, MN 891
Elkins, David, Mgr. Events & Group Programs, Naismith Memorial Basketball Hall of Fame, Springfield, MA....807
Elkins, Vicki S., Dir., Zephyrhills Depot Museum, Zephyrhills, FL....398
Ellebracht, Mr. Pat, C.E.O., Pres. & Devel., Adair County Historical Society, Inc., Kirksville, MO 936
Ellenberg, Dolores F., Vice Pres. Devel., Carnegie Museum of Art, Pittsburgh, PA....1464
Ellenberg, Dolores F., Vice Pres. CMP Devel., Carnegie Museum of Natural History, Pittsburgh, PA....1464
Ellenberg, Dolores F., Vice Pres. Devel., Carnegie Museums of Pittsburgh (Carnegie Institute), Pittsburgh, PA 1465
Ellenberg, Dolores F., Vice Pres. Devel., Carnegie Science Center, Pittsburgh, PA....1465

E–*Continued*

Emerick, Emily W., C.E.O., Cur. House & Exec. Dir., Ladew Topiary Gardens, Monkton, MD....741
Emerson, Brad, Pres. (V), The Jonathan Fisher Memorial, Inc., Blue Hill, ME.....693
Emerson, Frances, Museum Dir., The Thomas J. Boyd, Wytheville, VA..........1756
Emerson, Francis, Museum Dir., Rock House Museum, Wytheville, VA............1756
Emerson, JoAnn, Exec. Dir., Lux Center for the Arts, Lincoln, NE.......................989
Emerson, Julie, The Ruth J. Nutt, Cur. Decorative Arts, Seattle Art Museum, Seattle, WA..1783
Emerson, Karen L., Museum Shop Mgr., Historical Society of Kent County, Inc., Chestertown, MD..............................730
Emerson, Noka, Financial Dir., Grant County Museum, Sheridan, AR................84
Emerson, Philip G., Exec. Dir., Jamestown Settlement, Yorktown Victory Center, The Jamestown-Yorktown Foundation, Williamsburg, VA..............................1754
Emerson, Rae, Site Mgr., Ford's Theatre National Historic Site (Lincoln Museum), Washington, DC......................317
Emerson, Robert L., C.E.O., Old Fort Niagara, Youngstown, NY......................1230
Emerson, W. Eric, Ph.D., Exec. Dir., Charleston Library Society, Charleston, SC...1503
Emert, Carol, Cur. Collections & Exhibitions, Mulvane Art Museum, Topeka, KS...636
Emert, Jerry, Park Mgr. Yuma Crossing State Historic Park, Arizona State Parks Board, Phoenix, AZ.........................49
Emert, Jerry, Park Mgr. & Museum Shop Mgr., Yuma Quartermaster Depot State Historic Park, Yuma, AZ...........................66
Emery, Dr. Katherine F., Assoc. Cur. Environmental Archaeology, Florida Museum of Natural History, Gainesville, FL..351
Emery, Kenneth, Dir., Museum of Aviation at Robins Air Force Base, GA, Warner Robins, GA........................439
Emery, Lea, Dir. Devel., Neuberger Museum of Art, Purchase College, State University of New York, Purchase, NY..1198
Emery, Mike, Museum Educator, Landis Valley Museum, Lancaster, PA.............1439
Emery, Robert, Mgr., Traveler's Rest State Historic Site, Toccoa, GA..............438
Emfinger, Henry, Owner, Aldrich Coal Mine Museum, Montevallo, AL...............19
Emfinger, Rose, Owner, Aldrich Coal Mine Museum, Montevallo, AL...............19
Emmans, Deb, Dir. School Svcs., Discovery Place, Inc., Charlotte, NC.....1238
Emmel, Dr. Thomas C., Dir. McGuire Center for Lepidoptera & Biodiversity, Florida Museum of Natural History, Gainesville, FL..351
Emmertt, Lou, Museum Shop Mgr., Madera County Museum, Madera, CA...143
Emmes, David, II, Chm. & Pres., Orange County Museum of Art, Newport Beach, CA..152
Emmett, Ryan, Preparator, Wood Street Galleries, Pittsburgh, PA.....................1468
Emmons, Gene, Budget Analyst BG John C.L. Scribner Texas Military Forces Museum, Austin, TX 1580
Emmons, Jasen, Dir. Curatorial Affairs, EMP, Experience Music Project/Science Fiction Museum, Seattle, WA..1780
Emmons, Jennifer, Cur., Fort Ontario State Historic Site, Oswego, NY 1191
Emmons, Mariah, Cur. Collections, Wyoming State Museum, Cheyenne, WY..1855
Emmons, Nicole, Editor, Oklahoma City Museum of Art, Oklahoma City, OK....1371
Emmons-Andarawis, Deborah, Cur., Historic Cherry Hill, Albany, NY..........1096
Emory, Margaret Anne, Dir., Hostess & Museum Shop Mgr., Lincoln Parish Museum & Historical Society, Ruston, LA...685
Emrich, Chris, Vice Pres. Public Rels., Dallas Arboretum & Botanical Garden, Dallas, TX..............................1597
Emrich, Dwight, Pres., Campbell Flannagan Murrell House, Hinton, WV..1800
Emrick, Shirley, Vice Pres., Meux Home Museum, Fresno, CA............................116
Emry, Howard, Cur. Paleontology, Orma J. Smith Museum of Natural History, Caldwell, ID..457
Emsley, Tara, Registrar, Museum of Art, Rhode Island School of Design, Providence, RI...1495
Encell, Arlene, Museum Shop Mgr., California Heritage Museum, Santa Monica, CA...207
Encina, Sebastian, Coord. Museum Collections, Kelsey Museum of Archaeology, Ann Arbor, MI..................822
Ende, Ellen, Pres. (V), Petersburg Area Art League, Petersburg, VA..................1733
Endelman, Judith, Dir. Benson Ford Research Center, The Henry Ford, Dearborn, MI...832
Enders, Don, Cur. Exhibits & Historic Sites, Brigham Young's Winter Home, Saint George, UT..................................1668
Enders, Don, Cur. Exhibits & Historic Sites, Jacob Hamblin Home, Santa Clara, UT 1673
Enders, Donald L., Senior Cur. Historic Sites, Museum of Church History and Art, Salt Lake City, UT..........................1670
Enders, John, Exec. Dir., Children's Museum, Jacksonville, OR...................1392
Enders, John, Exec. Dir., Southern Oregon Historical Society, Jacksonville, OR.................................1392
Endersby, Linda, Site Admin., Jefferson Landing State Historic Site, Jefferson City, MO 931
Endersby, Linda, Asst. Dir., Missouri State Museum, Jefferson City, MO..........931
Endslow, Ellen, Dir. Collections & Cur., Chester County Historical Society, West Chester, PA.....................................1481
Endzweig, Pamela, Dir. Collections, University of Oregon Museum of Natural and Cultural History, Eugene, OR...1389
Eng, David, Vice Pres. Public Affairs, Lower East Side Tenement Museum, New York, NY 1172
Eng, Robert, Museum Shop Mgr., The Paley Center for Media, New York, NY..1179
Engberg, Siri, Cur., Walker Art Center, Minneapolis, MN..886
Engel, Dave, Dir., South Wood County Historical Corp., Wisconsin Rapids, WI 1852
Engel, Elisabeth, Cur., Waukesha County Museum, Waukesha, WI........................1849
Engel, Michael, Cur. Entomology KU Biodiversity Institute - KU Natural History Museum, Lawrence, KS 621
Engel-Accettura, Katheryn, Sec. Bd. of Park Commissioners, The Downers Grove Park District Museum, Downers Grove, IL................................491
Engelkemier, Jennifer, Cur., Amana Heritage Museum, Amana, IA 572
Engen, Danielle, Devel. Dir., Kauai Children's Discovery Museum, Kapaa, HI 450
Enget, Orris, Museum Shop Mgr., Burke County Historical Powers Lake Complex, Powers Lake, ND 1289
Engh, Nina, Vice Pres., Renville County Historical Society, Mohall, ND.............1288
Engisch, Mary Grace, Sec., Holmes County Historical Society, Millersburg, OH...................................1333
England, Ann, Cur. Visual Resources, Georgia State University School of Art & Design Gallery, Atlanta, GA...............405
England, Cathy, Pres. Bd. Dir., Photographic Resource Center, Boston, MA 763
England, Lettie M., Admin., The Presidential Museum and Leadership Library, Odessa, TX 1636
England, Megan, Museum Shop Mgr., Kemper Museum of Contemporary Art, Kansas City, MO...............................934
England, Tawna, Museum Shop Mgr., The Works: Ohio Center for History, Art & Technology, Newark, OH............1335
England, Timothy, Mgr., Collier County Museum, Naples, FL..............................369
Englander, Caryl S., Chm. Bd. (V), International Center of Photography, New York, NY...1170
Englander, Lisa, Museum Shop Mgr., Racine Art Museum (RAM), Racine, WI 1842
Engle, Duane E., Pres. (V), Reading Railroad Heritage Museum, Hamburg, PA..1430
Englebright, Steven E., Cur. Geology, Museum of Long Island Natural Sciences, Stony Brook, NY 1218
Englehardt, Joann, Chm. (V), The Houdini Museum & Theater, Scranton, PA..1472
Engleman, Virginia M., Museum Shop Mgr., Woodrow Wilson Presidential Library, Staunton, VA..........................1746
Englert, Thad, Co-Chm. (V), Saguache County Museum, Saguache, CO.............262
English, Beth, Treas., Georgia State Cotton Museum, Vienna, GA.......................439
English, Beth, Treas., Walter F. George Law Office Museum, Vienna, GA 439
English, John, Mgr. Mktg., Fresno Metropolitan Museum of Art & Science, Fresno, CA 116
English, Louella F., Dir., Old Stone House Museum, Windsor, NY 1229
English, Marie, Cur., Northeast Oakland Historical Museum, Oxford, MI 859
Engmark, Deb, Gardener, Brucemore, Cedar Rapids, IA.......................................577
Engquist, Dale B., Supt., Indiana Dunes National Lakeshore, Porter, IN 562
Enkler, Meg, Dir., Dinosaur State Park, Rocky Hill, CT..293
Enlow, Sally, Program Coord., Heritage Hill State Historical Park, Green Bay, WI 1821
Ennes, Anne, Collections Conservator, The Textile Museum, Washington, DC ...330
Ennis, Betsy, Dir. Media & Public Rels., Solomon R. Guggenheim Museum, New York, NY 1181
Ennis, Dr. Lynn J., Interim Dir. & Cur. Collection, Gregg Museum of Art & Design at North Carolina State University, Raleigh, NC 1262
Enniss, Dr. Stephen, Librarian, Folger Shakespeare Library, Washington, DC 317
Enote, Jim, Exec. Dir., A:shiwi A:wan Museum and Heritage Center, Zuni, NM 1095

E–*Continued*

E–*Continued*

F

F–*Continued*

F–*Continued*

F–*Continued*

F–*Continued*

Fleetham, Daniel W., Sr., Pres. (V), Canaan Historical Society and Museum, Canaan, NH 1013
Fleets, Diane, Exec. Dir., Fairbanks Community Museum, Fairbanks, AK 30
Fleharty, Gene, Cur. Emeritus, Sternberg Museum of Natural History, Hays, KS ...616
Fleischman, Stephen, Dir., Madison Museum of Contemporary Art, Madison, WI 1828
Fleischmann, Laura, Registrar, Albright-Knox Art Gallery, Buffalo, NY 1114
Fleisher, Toni, Devel. Coord., Anderson/Abruzzo Albuquerque International Balloon Museum, Albuquerque, NM 1070
Fleming, Derek, Museum Shop Mgr., California Automobile Museum, Sacramento, CA 174
Fleming, Don, Public Rels., Rhinebeck Aerodrome Museum, Rhinebeck, NY....1199
Fleming, Elvis E., Librarian & Archivist, Historical Center for Southeast New Mexico, Roswell, NM 1086
Fleming, Geoffrey, Dir. & Museum Shop Mgr., Southold Historical Society and Museum, Southold, NY 1213
Fleming, Greg, D.V.M., Dipl. A.C.Z.M., Veterinarian, Disney's Animal Kingdom Theme Park, Bay Lake, FL 334
Fleming, Jeff, Dir., Des Moines Art Center, Des Moines, IA..........583
Fleming, Jennie, Asst. Dir., The Art Gallery at the University of Maryland, College Park, College Park, MD 731
Fleming, Karen, Vice Pres. Devel. & Mktg., Country Music Hall of Fame and Museum, Country Music Foundation, Nashville, TN 1567
Fleming, Kathleen, Museum Coord., Gloucester County Historical Society, Woodbury, NJ 1068
Fleming, Keith, Mgr., Georgia Veterans Memorial Museum, Cordele, GA 415
Fleming, Leslie, Cur. Conservation, Merritt Museum of Anthropology, Oakland, CA 155
Fleming, Marty, Mgr., Jarrell Plantation Georgia State Historic Site, Juliette, GA..........421
Fleming, Nan, Museum Shop Mgr., Smith College Museum of Art, Northampton, MA 797
Fleming, Nancy, Public Rels., Anderson Museum of Contemporary Art, Roswell, NM..........1086
Fleming, Rob, Chm. (V), Wyck, Philadelphia, PA 1463
Flemm, Corinne, Pres. (V), Lombard Historical Museum, Lombard, IL 504
Flemm, Corinne, Pres., Sheldon Peck Homestead, Lombard, IL 504
Flemmger, Susan, Deputy Dir. & Visual Arts Dir., Abrons Arts Center/Henry Street Settlement, New York, NY 1161
Flemming, Julie, Pres. (V), Seippel Homestead and Center for the Arts, Beaver Dam, WI..........1812
Flesch, Edward, Cur., Wings of Eagles Discovery Center, Horseheads, NY 1142
Flesher, Franklin A., Exec. Dir., National Military Heritage Museum, Saint Joseph, MO..........944
Flesher, Karen, Program Coord., Spurlock Museum, University of Illinois at Urbana-Champaign, Urbana, IL..........525
Fleshman, Jim, Zoo Dir., Cameron Park Zoo, Waco, TX 1654
Flessner, Sharon, Guide, Fort Sidney Museum & Post Commander's Home, Sidney, NE..........997
Fletcher, Carol, C.E.O., Harrison County Historical Museum, Marshall, TX 1630
Fletcher, Corinne, Park Supt., Hampson Archeological Museum State Park, Wilson, AR 86
Fletcher, Dorothy, Housekeeper, Belle Grove Plantation, Middletown, VA........1725
Fletcher, H. George, Brooke Russell Astor Librarian for Special Collections, The New York Public Library, Astor, Lenox and Tilden Foundations, New York, NY..........1178
Fletcher, Jean, Dir. Cultural Programs, Nicholas Roerich Museum, New York, NY..........1179
Fletcher, Laurel, Dir., Captain Salem Avery House Museum, Shady Side Rural Heritage Society, Inc., Shady Side, MD..........746
Fletcher, Louise, Dir. Museum Store, The National World War II Museum, New Orleans, LA 682
Fletcher, Scott, Pres., Central Texas Area Museum, Inc., Salado, TX 1642
Fletcher, Vicki B., Dir., Pendleton District Agricultural Museum, Pendleton, SC 1521
Fletcher, Vicki B., Dir., Pendleton District Historical, Recreational and Tourism Commission, Pendleton, SC..........1521
Flick, Lisa A., Dir., Rockingham, Kingston, NJ 1044
Flicker, John, Pres. & C.E.O., National Audubon Society, New York, NY..........1176
Fliegel, Stephen N., Cur. Medieval Art, The Cleveland Museum of Art, Cleveland, OH 1308
Flinn, Karen, Asst. Cur. Archaeology & Ethnology, New Jersey State Museum, Trenton, NJ 1064
Flint, Jody, Co-Pres. (V), Floyd County Historical Museum, Charles City, IA 578
Flint, Richard, Dir., Howard County Historical Society, Ellicott City, MD.......734
Flint, Steve, C.F.O., National Naval Aviation Museum, Pensacola, FL 378
Flitner, Jane V., Asst. Educator, Brandywine River Museum, Chadds Ford, PA..........1417
Flobeck, Mrs. Polly S., Chm. (V), Hotel de Paris Museum, Georgetown, CO 247
Flood, Jerry, Chief Ranger, Chamizal National Memorial, El Paso, TX 1604
Flood, Richard, Chief Cur., New Museum, New York, NY..........1177
Flook, Kimberly, Dir., Philipse Manor Hall State Historic Site, Yonkers, NY ...1230
Florence, Kelly, Coord. Education, Minnesota Discovery Center, Chisholm, MN..........872
Florer, Michael R., Museum Cur., Eisenhower National Historic Site, Gettysburg, PA..........1427
Flores, Amelia, Librarian & Archivist, Colorado River Indian Tribes Museum, Parker, AZ 47
Flores, Cindy, Office Mgr., Lower Rio Grande Valley Nature Center, Weslaco, TX 1656
Flores Garcia, Jessica, Cur. Contemporary Art, Cincinnati Art Museum, Cincinnati, OH..........1304
Flores, Luis, Security, Mingei International Museum, San Diego, CA ...180
Flores, Lulu, Pres. (V), Mexic-Arte Museum, Austin, TX 1582
Flores, Rick, Cur. Native Collection, Arboretum at UC Santa Cruz, Santa Cruz, CA..........205
Flores, Yolanda, Sec., Children's Museum at La Habra, La Habra, CA 126
Florez, Naomi, Registrar, Artesia Historical Museum & Art Center, Artesia, NM 1074
Flournoy, Keith, Park Mgr., Anna Scripps Whitcomb Conservatory, Detroit, MI......832
Flournoy, Paula, Dir., Mansfield Female College Museum, Mansfield, LA..........675
Flower, Paul, Pres. (V), Old Jefferson Town, Oskaloosa, KS 629
Flower, Rebecca, Chm. (V), Community Memorial Museum of Sutter County, Yuba City, CA 227
Flowers, George G., Bd. Chm., Historic Columbus Foundation, Inc., Columbus, GA..........414
Flowers, Richard, Cur., Beauvoir, The Jefferson Davis Home and Presidential Library, Biloxi, MS 903
Flowers, Susan L., Controller, Tryon Palace Historic Sites & Gardens, New Bern, NC..........1259
Flowers, Tom, Project Coord., Blanton Museum of Art, Austin, TX..........1581
Flowers, William, Pres. (V), Central Iowa Art Association, Marshalltown, IA 593
Floyd, Chris, Mgr., Wormsloe State Historic Site, Savannah, GA 436
Floyd, David, Exec. Dir., Rural Life Museum & Windrush Gardens, Baton Rouge, LA 668
Floyd, Joanne, Museum Shop Mgr., Belle Meade Plantation, Nashville, TN..........1566
Floyd, Rick, Registrar, Modern Art Museum of Fort Worth, Fort Worth, TX..........1611
Floyd, Roger, Chm. (V), Emmett Kelly Historical Museum, Sedan, KS..........633
Flynn, Duane, Cur. Life Sciences, Schiele Museum of Natural History and Lynn Planetarium, Gastonia, NC..........1247
Flynn, James, Environmental Education Specialist, Audubon Greenwich, Greenwich, CT..........275
Flynn, Jim, Chm., The U.S. Space & Rocket Center, Huntsville, AL..........15
Flynn, Dr. Lawrence, Asst. Dir. Security, Peabody Museum of Archaeology & Ethnology, Cambridge, MA 768
Flynn, Marcia, Dir. Visitor Svcs., Desert Botanical Garden, Phoenix, AZ..........50
Flynn, Patrick, Vice Pres. Devel., Museum of Discovery and Science, Fort Lauderdale, FL..........348
Flynn, Rich, Landscape Designer, New Jersey Botanical Garden at Skylands (NJBG), Ringwood, NJ 1059
Flynt, Suzanne, Cur., Memorial Hall Museum, Pocumtuck Valley Memorial Assoc., Deerfield, MA..........774
Flythe, Jimmy T., Bd. Chm., Sciworks, Winston-Salem, NC..........1275
Foat, Kathy, Vice Pres. Education, The Maryland Zoo in Baltimore, Baltimore, MD..........724
Fobbs, Archie, Collection Mgr., Neuroanatomical, National Museum of Health and Medicine, Washington, DC...324
Focht, Mark A., Exec. Dir., Fairmount Park Horticulture Center, Philadelphia, PA..........1453
Focke, Sarah, Sec., Kearney Area Children's Museum, Kearney, NE 986
Foe, Peter, Collections Cur., University of South Florida Contemporary Art Museum, Tampa, FL 393
Foerster, Tim, Dir. Exhibits, San Antonio Museum of Art, San Antonio, TX 1645
Fogarty, Lori, Exec. Dir., Oakland Museum of California, Oakland, CA.......155
Fogarty, Lori, Exec. Dir., Oakland Museum of California-Sculpture Court at City Center, Oakland, CA..........156
Fogarty, Steve, Business Mgr., The Natural Science Center of Greensboro, Inc., Greensboro, NC..........1249

F–*Continued*

Foreman, Eldon, Pres., Augusta Historical Museum & Genealogy, Augusta, KS.......605
Foreman, Hank T., Dir., Turchin Center for the Visual Arts, Boone, NC.............1235
Foreman, Karlene, Treas., Tama County Historical Museum, Toledo, IA...............600
Foreman, L. Ronald, C.E.O. & Pres., Audubon Aquarium of the Americas, New Orleans, LA.......................................678
Foreman, Melba, Cur., Czech Heritage Museum & Genealogy Center, Temple, TX..1650
Foreman, Regina, Museum Attendant, Tongass Historical Museum, Ketchikan, AK..33
Forer, Mary, Dir., Marathon County Historical Society, Wausau, WI 1850
Foresman, Dr. Kerry, Cur. Mammalogy, Philip L. Wright Zoological Museum and University of Montana Herbarium, Missoula, MT...970
Forestier, Leslie, C.F.O., Houston Zoo, Inc., Houston, TX.................................1621
Forgeng, Dr. Jeffrey, Paul S. Morgan Cur., Higgins Armory Museum, Worcester, MA.......................................819
Forgey, Melissa, Exec. Dir., DeKalb History Center Museum, Decatur, GA 416
Forman, L. Ronald, Pres. & C.E.O., Audubon Zoo, New Orleans, LA............679
Fornasiere, Gail, Coord. Membership, Catalina Island Museum Society, Inc., Avalon, CA 89
Fornes, Jeanne, Vice Pres., Concord Historical Society, Warner Museum, Springville, NY.....................................1214
Forney, Jack D., Pres. Bd., Forney Museum of Transportation, Denver, CO...240
Forno, Aimee Rose, Program Coord., Morris-Butler House Museum, Indianapolis, IN 550
Forrand, Kendra, Dir. Gift Shop, New England Aquarium Corporation, Boston, MA 762
Forrer, Douglas, Treas., The Lackawanna Historical Society at the Catlin House, Scranton, PA 1472
Forrester, Gillian, Assoc. Cur. Prints & Drawings, Yale Center for British Art, New Haven, CT.......................................287
Forry, Gerald, Security, Mechanicsburg Museum Association, Mechanicsburg, PA...1444
Forry, Sonia L., Library Coord., Cape May County Historical Museum and Genealogical Society, Cape May Court House, NJ...1035
Forsberg, Shawna, Dir. Community Rels., The Durham Museum, Omaha, NE.......994
Forschler-Tarrasch, Dr. Anne, Cur. Decorative Arts, Birmingham Museum of Art, Birmingham, AL..............................5
Forsell, Lynn, Pres., The Carter House, Summit, NJ 1062
Forsman, Leonard, Tribal Chm., Suquamish Museum, Poulsbo, WA........1777
Forster, Lisa, Office Mgr., Pratt Museum, Homer, AK...31
Forster, Michelle, Museum Shop Mgr., Tillamook Air Museum, Tillamook, OR 1405
Forsythe, Anne-Marie, Program Mgr., Hui No'eau Visual Arts Center, Makawao, Maui, HI 452
Forsythe, Christine A., Dir., M. Louise Aughinbaugh Gallery at Messiah College, Grantham, PA........................1429
Fort, Bill, Vice Pres. (V), Humboldt County Historical Association Museum, Dakota City, IA 581
Fort, Karen, Deputy Asst. Dir. Exhibitions & Public Spaces, National Museum of the American Indian, Smithsonian Institution, New York, NY..1177
Fort, Karen Gebhardt, Dir., McAllen Heritage Center, McAllen, TX..............1631
Fort, Tom A., Sr. Cur., Museum of South Texas History, Edinburg, TX 1603
Forte, Doris, Corresponding Sec., The Gardner Museum, Inc., Gardner, MA......779
Forte, Gloria, Treas., The Scarsdale Historical Society, Scarsdale, NY..........1209
Forte, Judy, Supt., Martin Luther King, Jr. National Historic Site and Preservation District, Atlanta, GA 406
Forte, Larry, Art Handler, Georgia Museum of Art, University of Georgia, Athens, GA 400
Forte, Maria, Registrar, U.S. Army Medical Department Museum, Fort Sam Houston, TX...................................1608
Forte, Richard V., Sr., Chm. (V), Beauvoir, The Jefferson Davis Home and Presidential Library, Biloxi, MS 903
Forte, Vince, C.F.O. & C.A.O., Oakland Zoo, Oakland, CA 156
Fortescue, Ann, Dir. Education & Visitor Svcs., Senator John Heinz History Center, Pittsburgh, PA 1468
Forti, John, Cur. Historic Landscapes, Strawbery Banke Museum, Portsmouth, NH.....................................1027
Fortier, Denise, Dir. Statewide Education, Audubon Society of Rhode Island, Smithfield, RI...1497
Fortier, Jerome, Curatorial Asst., The Patrick & Beatrice Haggerty Museum of Art, Milwaukee, WI.........................1836
Fortier, Rollin, Designer, University Art Museum, Santa Barbara, Santa Barbara, CA 204
Fortini, Derek, Cur. Collections & Exhibits, Estes Park Museum, Estes Park, CO 243
Fortmann, Carla, Museum Shop Mgr., Lexington Historical Society, Lexington, MA 785
Fortmann, Tracy, Park Supt., Fort Vancouver National Historic Site, Vancouver, WA 1792
Fortmueller, Shari, C.E.O., San Dieguito Heritage Museum, Encinitas, CA 110
Fortney, Kim, Pres. (V), Mid-Atlantic Association of Museums, Washington, DC...322
Fortney, Kimberly, Vice Pres., Heritage Center of Lancaster County, Inc., Lancaster, PA...1439
Fortson, Mrs. Ben J., Pres., Kimbell Art Museum, Fort Worth, TX.......................1610
Fortson, Dr. Lucy, Vice Pres. Research, Adler Planetarium & Astronomy Museum, Chicago, IL...............................476
Fortune, Diana, Dir. Devel., Natural History Museum of the Adirondacks/The Wild Center, Tupper Lake, NY 1221
Fosco, Maria, Devel., Italian American Museum, New York, NY.........................1171
Foshay, Bobbie, Honorary Chm. SITE Santa Fe, Santa Fe, NM 1090
Foss, Frith, Office Mgr., Museums of Old York, York, ME 716
Foss, John, Treas., Marilla Historical Society Museum, Marilla, NY 1157
Foss, Kirby, Supt., Rock Island State Park, Washington Island, WI 1848
Fossum, Marc, Pres., Groveland Yosemite Gateway Museum, Groveland, CA..........120
Foster, Amy, Devel. Assoc., Marin History Museum, San Rafael, CA 200
Foster, Anne, Chm. (V), Wickersham House Museum (Tanana-Yukon Historical Society), Fairbanks, AK 30
Foster, Barbara M., Pres. (V), The Fort Pitt Block House, Pittsburgh, PA...........1466
Foster, Bill, Dir. Northwest Film Center, Portland Art Museum, Portland, OR 1400
Foster, Billie, Chief Cur., Seminole Canyon State Park and Historic Site, Comstock, TX...1594
Foster, Bob, Dir., Hoboken Historical Museum, Hoboken, NJ 1042
Foster, Carmen F., Dir. Community Affairs, Virginia Museum of Fine Arts, Richmond, VA 1742
Foster, Carter, Cur. & Cur. Drawings, Whitney Museum of American Art, New York, NY...1184
Foster, Catherine P., Assoc. Cur., The Bade Museum of Biblical Archaeology, Berkeley, CA.............................92
Foster, Daniel, Exec. Dir., Riverside Art Museum, Riverside, CA 172
Foster, David, Park Mgr., Fort Zachary Taylor Historic State Park, Key West, FL...358
Foster, Dr. David, Cur. Botany & Entomology, The Oakes Museum at Messiah College, Grantham, PA 1429
Foster, David G., Exec. Dir., American Cave Museum & Hidden River Cave, Horse Cave, KY 650
Foster, David R., Dir. Harvard Forest, Fisher Museum of Forestry, Petersham, MA 799
Foster, Drew, Technical Coord., Gheens Science Hall and Rauch Planetarium, Louisville, KY 654
Foster, Gus, Vice Pres., The Harwood Museum of Art of the University of New Mexico, Taos, NM.............................1093
Foster, Rev. James, Immaculate Conception Catholic Church, Natchitoches, LA 677
Foster, James, Security Coord., Mary and Leigh Block Museum of Art, Northwestern University, Evanston, IL ...494
Foster, Jill, Dir. School Programs, The Discovery Museums, Acton, MA...............751
Foster, Jim, Pres. (V), Maryhill Museum of Art, Goldendale, WA 1768
Foster, John, Chm. Bd., Stepping Stones Museum for Children, Norwalk, CT 290
Foster, Dr. John R., Cur. Paleontology, Museum of Western Colorado, Grand Junction, CO 250
Foster, Kathleen, Cur. American Art, Philadelphia Museum of Art, Philadelphia, PA 1459
Foster, Kathy, Asst., Museum of World War II, Natick, MA.....................................793
Foster, Kenneth, Exec. Dir., Yerba Buena Center for the Arts, San Francisco, CA...194
Foster, Laura, Cur., Frederic Remington Art Museum, Ogdensburg, NY 1187
Foster, Laura, Exec. Dir., Please Touch Museum, Philadelphia, PA 1460
Foster, Linda, Museum Shop Mgr., Chrysler Museum of Art, Norfolk, VA..1729
Foster, Linda, Caretaker, Rancho La Patera - The Stow House G.V.H.S., Goleta, CA 119
Foster, Lisa, Registrar, Mississippi Armed Forces Museum, Camp Shelby, MS 904
Foster, Martha, Pres. (V), Arlington Arts Center, Arlington, VA.............................1699
Foster, Mike, Asst. Supt., Lost River State Park, Mathias, WV.........................1802
Foster, Phyllis, Museum Asst., Old Depot Museum, Ottawa, KS 630
Foster, Ray, C.E.O., Gates House, Machiasport Historical Society, Machiasport, ME 702

F–*Continued*

F–*Continued*

French, Marsha, Pres. (V), Dunham Tavern Museum, Cleveland, OH 1309
French, Ryan, Dir. Mktg. & Public Rels., Walker Art Center, Minneapolis, MN......886
French, Tim, Dir., Riverside Zoo, Scottsbluff, NE..........997
French, Tim, Deputy Dir. Animal Care, Roger Williams Park Zoo, Providence, RI..........1497
Frenz, Bonnie, Dir., Kinney Pioneer Museum and Historical Society of North Iowa, Clear Lake, IA..........579
Frerichs, Herbert, Jr., Chm. (V) USS Constellation Museum & Baltimore Maritime Museum, Baltimore, MD 727
Frerichs, Rebecca, Vice Pres., Historical Society of Stanton County Museums at Stanton and Pilger, Pilger, NE............996
Frerichs, Saundra, Museum Educator, University of Nebraska State Museum, Lincoln, NE..........991
Frese, Jeanette, Treas., Mario Lanza Institute/Museum, Philadelphia, PA.......1456
Fretz, Phelan R., Exec. Dir. ECHO Lake Aquarium and Science Center/Leahy Center for Lake Champlain, Burlington, VT..........1677
Freund, Barbara, Registrar, Hirshhorn Museum and Sculpture Garden, Smithsonian Institution, Washington, DC..........319
Freund, Leslie, Collections Mgr., Phoebe Apperson Hearst Museum of Anthropology, Berkeley, CA..........93
Frew, Ken, Librarian, The Historical Society of Dauphin County, Harrisburg, PA..........1430
Frew, Robert, Dir., Old Timers Museum, Murphys, CA..........150
Frew, William J., Jr., Pres., Staten Island Zoo, Staten Island, NY..........1217
Frey, Caroleen, Dir. Finance, Mystic Seaport - The Museum of America and the Sea, Mystic, CT..........284
Frey Gilboe, Roberta, Registrar, Cranbrook Art Museum, Bloomfield Hills, MI..........828
Frey, Julie, Cur., Litchfield Historical Society and Museum, Litchfield, CT.......280
Frey, Patricia, Business, Landis Valley Museum, Lancaster, PA..........1439
Freyer, Bryna, Cur., National Museum of African Art, Smithsonian Institution, Washington, DC..........324
Frick, Karen, Museum Shop Mgr., The Children's Museum in Easton, North Easton, MA..........795
Frick, Linda C., Cur., Jim Thorpe Home, Yale, OK..........1381
Frick, Tracy J., Interim Dir., Western Center for Archaeology and Paleontology, Hemet, CA..........122
Fricke, Verna, ArtQuest Operations Mgr., Green Hill Center for North Carolina Art, Greensboro, NC..........1248
Frickman, Linda, Dir., Colorado State University Art Museum, Fort Collins, CO..........245
Friday Lamb, Susan, Public Information Officer, North Carolina Museum of History, Raleigh, NC..........1263
Fridlington, Robert, Trustee, Cranford Historical Society, Cranford, NJ..........1037
Frie, Robert, Park Supt., Fort Richardson State Historical Park, Jacksboro, TX.....1624
Fried, Judith M., Pres. (V), Buckstop Junction, Bismarck, ND..........1276
Fried, Laura, Asst. Cur., Contemporary Art Museum St. Louis, Saint Louis, MO..........946
Friedberg, Erin H., Dir., Thomas Center Galleries, Gainesville, FL..........352
Friedeman, Amanda, Educator, Spertus Museum, Chicago, IL..........486
Friederichs, Terry, Pres., Calumet County Historical Society, Inc., Chilton, WI......1815
Friedlaender, Linda, Cur. Education, Yale Center for British Art, New Haven, CT..........287
Friedlander, Bee, Pres. (V), Plymouth Historical Museum, Plymouth, MI..........860
Friedle, Kathy, Education Coord., Sheldon Museum and Cultural Center, Inc., Haines, AK..........31
Friedle, Pat, Acting Chm., Wildwood Historic Center, Nebraska City, NE..........992
Friedman, Ann, Dir., Evergreen Gallery, Olympia, WA..........1773
Friedman, Ann, Mgr. Grants & Foundations, The Nelson-Atkins Museum of Art, Kansas City, MO..........934
Friedman, Barbara, Museum Shop Mgr., Alley Pond Environmental Center, Inc., Douglaston, NY..........1127
Friedman, Betty, Art Chm., The Wiegand Gallery, Belmont, CA..........91
Friedman, Gary, Pres. (V) Bd. Trustees, New Mexico Museum of Natural History & Science, Albuquerque, NM...1072
Friedman, Jane, Pres. (V), The Friends of Lucy Hayes Heritage Center, Chillicothe, OH..........1302
Friedman, John, Chm. & Pres. (V), Awbury Arboretum, Philadelphia, PA....1450
Friedman, Ken, 1st Vice Pres., Keeler Tavern Museum, Ridgefield, CT..........292
Friedman, Lynn, Pres. (V), Madison Historical Society, Madison, CT..........281
Friedman, Mark, Chm. (V), Ohef Sholom Temple Archives, Norfolk, VA..........1731
Friedman, Marsha, Administrative Asst., Dallas Holocaust Museum/Center for Education & Tolerance, Dallas, TX.......1598
Friedman, Matt, Pres. OTS Bd. (V), Oceanographic Teaching Station Inc. - Roundhouse Marine Studies Lab & Aquarium, Manhattan Beach, CA..........144
Friedman, Maxine, Chief Cur., Historic Richmond Town, Staten Island, NY......1215
Friedman, Maxine, Chief Cur., Staten Island Historical Society, Staten Island, NY..........1216
Friedman, Robert, Cur., Davis Art Gallery, Columbia, MO..........924
Friedman, Terry, Chm. (V), Oriental Institute Museum, University of Chicago, Chicago, IL..........485
Friedmann, Beth, Dir. Administration, Loudoun Museum, Inc., Leesburg, VA..1720
Friedmann, Nadine, Pres. (V), Historic Southwest Ohio, Inc., Sharonville, OH.1343
Friedrichs, Paul, Exec. Dir., Lilacia Park-Lombard Park District, Lombard, IL..........504
Friedricks, Larri, NAGPRA Scientist, Phoebe Apperson Hearst Museum of Anthropology, Berkeley, CA..........93
Friel, Mary Anne, Master Printer & Project Coord., The Fabric Workshop and Museum, Philadelphia, PA..........1453
Frieling, Rudolf, Cur. Media Arts, San Francisco Museum of Modern Art, San Francisco, CA..........193
Friend, Glenda, Cur., Old Washington Historic State Park, Washington, AR.........85
Friend, Jennifer, Dir. Human Resources, Science Museum Oklahoma, Oklahoma City, OK..........1373
Friend, Karen, Tech Asst., Cave Creek Museum, Cave Creek, AZ..........39
Friend, Michael, Pres., Timexpo Museum, Waterbury, CT..........299
Frierson, Amy H., C.E.O. & Museum Shop Mgr., Houston Museum of Decorative Arts, Chattanooga, TN.........1548
Fries, Dee, Co-Pres., Dundy County Historical Society, Benkelman, NE.........977
Fries, Dr. Jim, C.E.O., The Ray Drew Gallery-New Mexico Highlands University, Las Vegas, NM..........1081
Friese, Julia, Visitor Svcs. Mgr., Maine Lighthouse Museum, Rockland, ME.......710
Friesen, Leslie, Designer-in-Residence, Allen R. Hite Art Institute, Louisville, KY..........654
Friesen, Steve, Dir., Buffalo Bill Museum & Grave, Golden, CO..........248
Friess, Peter, C.E.O. & Pres., The Tech Museum, San Jose, CA..........196
Friesz, Kessie, Treas., General Sterling Price Museum, Keytesville, MO..........936
Friggens, Tom, Upper Peninsula Mgr., Michigan Historical Museum, Michigan Historical Center, Lansing, MI..........849
Frignoca, Jeffrey, Museum Mgr., The Museum of Flight, Seattle, WA..........1781
Friis-Hansen, Dana, Exec. Dir. & Chief Cur., Austin Museum of Art - Downtown, Austin, TX..........1580
Frilingos, Timothy, Mgr., Georgia Capitol Museum, Atlanta, GA..........405
Frins, Jennifer, Gallery Mgr., Sweeney Art Gallery, University of California, Riverside, CA..........173
Frinsko, Linda M., Guide, Chm. (V) & Pres. Bd. Library Trustees (V), Baxter House Museum, Gorham, ME..........699
Frischhertz, Janet, Chm. (V), New Orleans Museum of Art, New Orleans, LA..........683
Frischmeyer, Denis, Pres. (V), National Balloon Museum and Hall of Fame, Indianola, IA..........588
Frischmuth, Robert, Pres. (V), Pacific Grove Museum of Natural History, Pacific Grove, CA..........159
Frisell, Linda, Operations & Finance Mgr., International Wolf Center, Ely, MN..........876
Frisse, Carol, Archivist, Madison County Historical Museum & Archival Library, Edwardsville, IL..........491
Frist, Jennifer, Chm. (V), Nashville Zoo at Grassmere, Nashville, TN..........1568
Frist, William R., Chm. & Pres., Frist Center for the Visual Arts, Nashville, TN..........1568
Frith, Deidre, Dir. Community Rels., Wiregrass Museum of Art, Dothan, AL..........10
Fritz, Joanne, Treas. & Museum Shop Mgr., Puget Sound Coast Artillery Museum at Fort Worden, Port Townsend, WA..........1776
Fritz, Marsha, Education & Collections, Burnside Plantation, Inc., Bethlehem, PA..........1411
Fritz, Marsha, Collections & Education, Moravian Museum of Bethlehem, Inc., Bethlehem, PA..........1412
Fritz, Marsha L., Education & Collections, Colonial Industrial Quarter, Bethlehem, PA..........1412
Fritzinger, Jeff, Site Interpreter, Bentonville Battlefield State Historic Site, Four Oaks, NC..........1246
Froehlich, Conrad G., Dir., Martin and Osa Johnson Safari Museum, Chanute, KS..........607
Froelich Sims, Esther, Exec. Dir., Texas Civil War Museum, Fort Worth, TX......1611
Fromberg, Jeffrey, Sec., Heartland, The California Museum of the Heart, Rancho Mirage, CA..........168

F–*Continued*

G

G–Continued

Gammon, Sandra, Dir., Ramsey House Plantation, Knoxville, TN 1559
Gammons, Doris, Museum Shop Mgr., Richard Petty Museum, Randleman, NC 1264
Gampp, Ute, Administrative Mgr., San Joaquin County Historical Society & Museum, Lodi, CA 129
Gamson, Alice, Archivist, Holocaust Memorial Resource and Education Center of Florida, Inc., Maitland, FL 363
Gandall, Shelly, Museum Shop Mgr. USS Bowfin Submarine Museum & Park, Honolulu, HI 448
Gandee, Cynthia, C.E.O., Henry B. Plant Museum, Tampa, FL 392
Gandy, Doris, C.E.O. & Dir., Jacob Kelley House Museum, Hartsville, SC..1516
Gandy, Jim, Archivist, New York State Military Museum and Veterans Research Center, Saratoga Springs, NY 1208
Gane, Constance, Cur., Siegfried H. Horn Archaeological Museum, Berrien Springs, MI 827
Ganer, Fredda, Sec., Top of Oklahoma Historical Museum, Blackwell, OK.......1357
Gangarosa, Louis, Finance Officer, Morris Museum of Art, Augusta, GA 411
Ganger, Liz, Pres., Hawkins House, Bennington, VT 1676
Gangi, Joanne M., Visitor Svcs., Springfield Armory National Historic Site, Springfield, MA 807
Gangopadhyay, Paula, Dir. Historical Resources & Education, The Henry Ford, Dearborn, MI 832
Gangwere, Stanley K., Cur. Insects, The Wayne State University Museum of Natural History, Detroit, MI....................836
Ganje Dahlquist, Melissa, Cur., Elmhurst Art Museum, Elmhurst, IL....................493
Gann, Jim, Supt., Logoly State Park, McNeil, AR 79
Gannon, Chris, Asst. Registrar, Gregg Museum of Art & Design at North Carolina State University, Raleigh, NC.1262
Gannon, Tom, Cur., Lake Superior Railroad Museum, Duluth, MN 874
Ganpant, Iris, Dir. Horticultural, Queens County Farm Museum, Floral Park, NY 1133
Gans, Liz, Exec. Dir., Holter Museum of Art, Helena, MT 966
Gansz, Kevin, Cur. Education, Siouxland Heritage Museums, Sioux Falls, SD......1542
Gansziniec, Zen, Assoc. Conservator, Wadsworth Atheneum Museum of Art, Hartford, CT 279
Gant, Bob, Cur. Collections, Cheyenne Frontier Days Old West Museum, Cheyenne, WY....................1854
Gant, Dallas, Chm. (V), Desert Caballeros Western Museum, Wickenburg, AZ....................64
Gant, Sally, Dir. Education & Special Programs, Museum of Early Southern Decorative Arts (MESDA), Winston-Salem, NC 1274
Gant, Speed, Sec., Yankee Air Force, Inc. (Yankee Air Museum), Ypsilanti, MI.......867
Gantt, Judy M., Dir. CDC/Global Health Odyssey, Atlanta, GA 403
Gantt, Nancy, Co-Dir., Sturdivant Hall, Selma, AL 22
Ganz, Michelle, Museum Archivist, Abraham Lincoln Library & Museum, Lincoln Memorial University, Harrogate, TN 1554
Gapido, Irene, Gallery Attendant, Museum of History & Art, Ontario, Ontario, CA 157
Gara, James, C.O.O., The Museum of Modern Art, New York, NY....................1176
Garabrandt, Gary, Dir. Science & Stewardship, Fontenelle Nature Association, Bellevue, NE 977
Garbarino, Eileen, Museum Shop Mgr., Philadelphia Mummers Museum, Philadelphia, PA 1459
Garber, Patty, Center Rep., Hoover Historical Center, North Canton, OH 1336
Garcia, Alex, Chief Operations, Orlando Museum of Art, Orlando, FL....................374
Garcia, Anna, Office Mgr., Bisbee Mining & Historical Museum, Bisbee, AZ 38
Garcia, Anthony, NAGPRA Coord., Phoebe Apperson Hearst Museum of Anthropology, Berkeley, CA 93
Garcia, Christine, Museum Shop Mgr., Lindsay Wildlife Museum, Walnut Creek, CA 222
Garcia, Connie, Gen. Mgr., Sky City Cultural Center, Pueblo of Acoma, NM 1085
Garcia de Oreyza, Juan, Dir., Aperture Foundation, New York, NY 1163
Garcia, Deborah, Registrar, Museum of New Mexico, Santa Fe, NM 1089
Garcia, Edward, Exhibit Design Supvr., California African-American Museum, Los Angeles, CA 133
Garcia, Erica, Educator, Palace of the Governors, Museum of New Mexico, Santa Fe, NM....................1089
Garcia, Erica, Education, Palace of the Governors/New Mexico History Museum, Santa Fe, NM 1090
Garcia, Jesse, Museum Shop Mgr., National Steinbeck Center, Salinas, CA 178
Garcia, Kristen, Educator, Lake Pontchartrain Basin Maritime Museum, Madisonville, LA 674
Garcia, Magdalena A., Exec. Dir., El Museo Latino, Omaha, NE 994
Garcia, Marilyn G., Pres. (V), Fossil Museum, Fossil, OR....................1390
Garcia, Michael P., C.E.O., Duluth Children's Museum, Duluth, MN 874
Garcia, Mike, Dir. Facilities, Autry National Center of the American West, Los Angeles, CA 133
Garcia, Mike, Exec. Dir., Santa Barbara Contemporary Arts Forum, Santa Barbara, CA 203
Garcia, Pamela, Dir. Finance, California Historical Society, San Francisco, CA.....187
Garcia, Ron, Preparator, Triton Museum of Art, Santa Clara, CA....................205
Garcia, Rosemary, Exec. Admin., National Hispanic Cultural Center, Art Museum, Albuquerque, NM....................1072
Garcia, Sandi, Vice Pres. Devel., Denver Museum of Nature & Science, Denver, CO 239
Garcia, Stacey, Exhibit Preparator, The Morikami Museum and Japanese Gardens, Delray Beach, FL....................344
Garcia, Susan, Museum Shop Mgr., Historical Museum of Southern Florida, Miami, FL 365
Garcia, Terry, Exec. Vice Pres., National Geographic Museum, Washington, DC ...323
Garcia, Theresa, Admin., New Mexico Museum of Art, Santa Fe, NM 1090
Garcia, Yvonne, Dir. Devel., The Bronx Museum of the Arts, Bronx, NY 1107
Garcia-Anderson, Beverly, Chm. (V), Jacques Marchais Museum of Tibetan Art, Staten Island, NY....................1215
Garcia-Culler, Laura, Exec. Vice Pres., Georgia Historical Society, Savannah, GA 434
Gardella, Joyce, Dir. Mktg., The Exploratorium, San Francisco, CA 188
Gardiner, Margaret Halsey, Exec. Dir., Merchant's House Museum, New York, NY 1172
Gardiner, Shelly, Business Mgr., Arts Club of Washington, Washington, DC.....315
Gardinier, Paul, Exhibitions Designer, Alaska State Museum, Juneau, AK 32
Gardner, Alicia, Museum Shop Mgr. & Museum Educator, City of Fort Walton Beach Heritage Park & Cultural Center, Fort Walton Beach, FL 350
Gardner, Brandon, Printmaking & Design, The Art Galleries at UAH, Huntsville, AL 14
Gardner, Brandon, Membership & Adoption Coord., Loggerhead Marinelife Center, Juno Beach, FL..........357
Gardner Broske, Janet, Cur. Collections, University Museums, University of Delaware, Newark, DE....................310
Gardner, Carol, Cur., Catherine V. Yost Museum & Arts Center, Pontiac, IL........513
Gardner, Cindy, Cur. Collections, Museum of Mississippi History/Museum Division, Jackson, MS 911
Gardner, Debra, Cur., Huntington County Historical Society Museum, Huntington, IN....................546
Gardner, Erin, Educator, Wayne County Historical Society's Museum of Wayne County History, Lyons, NY 1155
Gardner Gates, Mimi, Dir. The Illsley Ball Nordstrom, Seattle Art Museum, Seattle, WA 1783
Gardner, Ida, Sec., Ischua Valley Historical Society, Inc., Franklinville, NY 1135
Gardner, Jennifer, Devel., Arthouse, Austin, TX 1579
Gardner, John, Cur. Exhibits, Museum of Mississippi History/Museum Division, Jackson, MS 911
Gardner, John L., Chm. (V), Isabella Stewart Gardner Museum, Boston, MA 760
Gardner, Judith, Garden Rentals & Visitor Svcs. Mgr., The South Carolina Botanical Garden, Clemson, SC....................1507
Gardner, Karleen, Cur. Education, Memphis Brooks Museum of Art, Memphis, TN....................1563
Gardner, Leah, Education & Vol. Coord., O. Winston Link Museum, Roanoke, VA 1744
Gardner, Robin, Business Mgr., Meadow Brook Hall, Rochester, MI 862
Gardner, Scott L., Cur. Parasitology, University of Nebraska State Museum, Lincoln, NE 991
Gardner, Terri, Coord. Period Clothing, Watkins Woolen Mill State Historic Site & Park, Lawson, MO 938
Gardner, Tony, Head Wood Dept., Worcester Center for Crafts, Worcester, MA....................819
Gardner, Tracy, Education Asst., Heritage Farmstead Museum, Plano, TX 1638
Gardner, William F., Jr., Dir., North Florida Community College Art Gallery, Madison, FL 363
Garelle, Dr. Della, Dir. Conservation, Animal Health & Staff Veterinarian, Cheyenne Mountain Zoological Park, Colorado Springs, CO 233
Gareri, Cathy, Dir. Operations, Danvers Historical Society, Danvers, MA 773

G–Continued

Gehring, Tonya, Volunteer Coord., Kansas Underground Salt Museum, Hutchinson, KS....618
Gehrke, Rick, Chief Preparator, Jordan Schnitzer Museum of Art, Eugene, OR.1388
Gehrt, John, Pres. (V), Wabaunsee County Historical Museum, Alma, KS....604
Geib, Barbara, Cur. Registration, San Francisco International Airport; San Francisco Airport Museums, San Francisco, CA....192
Geibel, Bill, Pres., Chanute Air Museum, Rantoul, IL....514
Geier, Marilyn, Museum Shop Mgr., Lincoln Children's Museum, Lincoln, NE....988
Geiger, Amy R., Visitor Service Mgr., University of Alaska Museum of the North, Fairbanks, AK....30
Geiger, Fred, IMAX Operations, National Naval Aviation Museum, Pensacola, FL....378
Geiger, Jenny, Dir. Retail IMA - Indianapolis Museum of Art, Indianapolis, IN....548
Geiger, Joe, Dir. Archives & History, West Virginia State Museum, Charleston, WV....1797
Geise, Gregory B., Pres. & C.E.O., Binder Park Zoo, Battle Creek, MI....825
Geiselman, Annette, Exec. Dir., Discovery Science Center, Fort Collins, CO....246
Geiser, Ray, Exhibits Mgr., Nevada State Museum, Carson City, NV....1001
Geiser, Sandra, Curatorial Asst. DAAP Galleries, Cincinnati, OH....1305
Geisler, Dave, C.E.O., Dir. & Cur., Pioneer Auto Museum, Murdo, SD....1537
Geisler, John, Deputy Dir. & Cur., Pioneer Auto Museum, Murdo, SD....1537
Geisler, Dr. Jonathan, Cur. Paleontology, Georgia Southern University Museum, Statesboro, GA....436
Geist, Aimee, Cur. Education, Ulrich Museum of Art, Wichita, KS....639
Geist, Joseph E., Ph.D., Chm. Bd. & Cur., The Ashby-Hodge Gallery of American Art, Central Methodist University, Fayette, MO....926
Gelardi Holmes, Meghan, Asst. Cur. Skinner Museum, Mount Holyoke College Art Museum, South Hadley, MA....806
Gelardi Holmes, Meghan, Asst. Cur., The Skinner Museum of Mount Holyoke College, South Hadley, MA....807
Gelbach, Helen, Treas., Gates Mills Historical Society, Gates Mills, OH....1322
Gelber, Irwin, Exec. Dir., St. Johnsbury Athenaeum, Saint Johnsbury, VT....1689
Geldin, Sherri, Dir., Wexner Center for the Arts, Columbus, OH....1314
Geller, Bruce, Dir., Colorado School of Mines Geology Museum, Golden, CO....249
Gelwicks, Robert, Pres. Bd. of Park Commissioners, The Downers Grove Park District Museum, Downers Grove, IL....491
Gemignani, Gino, Jr., Vice Pres., Baltimore & Ohio Railroad Museum, Baltimore, MD....719
Geminn, Kim, Dir. Mktg. & Devel., The Magic House, St. Louis Children's Museum, Saint Louis, MO....948
Gemmell, Sarah, Volunteer Coord. & Museum Shop Mgr., Shenandoah Valley Discovery Museum, Winchester, VA....1755
Generous, Diane, Vice Pres. Devel., Mystic Aquarium & Institute for Exploration, Mystic, CT....283
Genga, Curt, Properties Dir., The Preservation Society of Newport County/The Newport Mansions, Newport, RI....1492
Gengenbacher, Rick, Dir., All Wars Museum, Quincy, IL....514
Gengler, Tom, Asst. Registrar, Spertus Museum, Chicago, IL....486
Gennari, Flaminia, Deputy Dir. Collections & Curatorial Affairs, Vizcaya Museum and Gardens, Miami, FL....367
Gennaro, Judy, Cur., Buccleuch Mansion, New Brunswick, NJ....1051
Genovese, Patti, Dir. Devel., Johnstown Area Heritage Association, Johnstown, PA....1437
Genrich, Dan, Education, Oatland Island Wildlife Center, Savannah, GA....434
Genrich, Terry, Natural Resources Mgr., Pioneers Park Nature Center, Lincoln, NE....990
Genszler, Leslie, Dir. Retail Operations, Madison Museum of Contemporary Art, Madison, WI....1828
Gentele, Glen, C.E.O. & Pres., Oklahoma City Museum of Art, Oklahoma City, OK....1371
Genther, Marilyn, Pres. (V), Mount Prospect Historical Society Museums, Mount Prospect, IL....507
Gentile, Betsy, Pres. Bd, Brattleboro Museum & Art Center, Brattleboro, VT....1677
Gentile, Chris, Dir., Western North Carolina Nature Center, Asheville, NC.1233
Gentilini, David, Asst. to Dir., The Schumacher Gallery, Capital University, Columbus, OH....1314
Gentine, Muriel, Sec., Birger Sandzen Memorial Gallery, Lindsborg, KS....623
Gentis, Thierry, Assoc. Cur., Haffenreffer Museum of Anthropology, Brown University, Providence, RI....1494
Gentry, Chrystal, Office Asst., Yakima Area Arboretum & Botanical Garden, Yakima, WA....1795
Gentry, Dr. Dale, Museum Mgr. & Dir. Research, The Murie Museum, Kelly, WY....1860
Gentry, Erin, Education, Arthouse, Austin, TX....1579
Gentry, Linda R., Exec. Dir., Camden County Historical Society, Camden, NJ....1034
Gentry, Liz, Librarian & Archivist, Booth Western Art Museum, Cartersville, GA...412
Gentry, Mark, Dir., Pres. & Chm. (V), Warrick County Museum, Inc., Boonville, IN....534
Gentry, Martha, Pres. (V) & Administrative Officer, Fillmore Historical Museum, Inc., Fillmore, CA...113
Gentry, Terry, Co Chm., Black American West Museum & Heritage Center, Denver, CO....237
Georg, Raymond, Museum Mgr., Barbed Wire Museum, La Crosse, KS....620
Georgalan, Peter, Media, Publicity & Public Rels., Hellenic Museum & Cultural Center, Chicago, IL....481
George, Barbara, Exec. Dir., Snohomish County Museum of History, Everett, WA....1765
George, C. Michael, Chief Interpretive Svcs., Oakwoods Metropark Nature Center, Belleville, MI....826
George, Dave, Dir., Buckhorn Saloon & Museum, San Antonio, TX....1643
George, Diane, Sec., McCook House, Civil War Museum, Carrollton, OH....1301
George, Hardy, Ph.D., Chief Cur., Oklahoma City Museum of Art, Oklahoma City, OK....1371
George, Jean P., Museum Shop Mgr., Roy Historical Museum, Roy, UT....1668
George, Louise, Museum Shop Mgr., World Forestry Center Discovery Museum, Portland, OR....1401
George, Dr. Orlando, Pres., Treasures of the Sea Exhibit, Georgetown, DE....307
George, Sarah B., Dir., Utah Museum of Natural History, Salt Lake City, UT....1672
George, Susan, Mgr. Membership, Museum of Photographic Arts, San Diego, CA....181
George, Terri, Dir. & Museum Shop Mgr., Moore County Historical Museum, Dumas, TX....1603
Georgen, Cynde, Historic Program Mgr., Trail End State Historic Site, Sheridan, WY....1865
Georgeson, Melinda, Dir. Education, Norman Rockwell Museum, Stockbridge, MA....810
Georgick, Tamara, Info Tech Mgr., Washington State Historical Society, Tacoma, WA....1790
Gephart, Glenda, Journal Editor, Schuyler County Historical Society, Inc., Montour Falls, NY....1159
Geppner, G.B., D.P.M., Pres. Emeritus & College Historian, Feet First: The Scholl Story, Rosalind Franklin University, North Chicago, IL....509
Gerace, Gloria, Coord. Exhibits, Los Angeles (Central) Public Library, Los Angeles, CA....138
Gerarden, Sheldon, Pres. & Exec. Dir., Lockwood-Mathews Mansion Museum, Norwalk, CT....290
Gerardi, Dr. Pamela, Dir. External Rels., Peabody Museum of Archaeology & Ethnology, Cambridge, MA....768
Gerbauckas, Maryanne, Supt., Edison National Historic Site, West Orange, NJ....1067
Gerber, Craig, Museum Maintenance, Utah Field House of Natural History State Park, Vernal, UT....1674
Gerber, Emilie, C.E.O. & Coord., Littman & White Galleries, Portland, OR....1398
Gerber, Jan, Asst. Dir., Museum of Northwest Colorado, Craig, CO....236
Gerber, Linda, Museum Shop Mgr., Fernbank Museum of Natural History, Atlanta, GA....404
Gerber, Richard, C.F.O., California Museum of Ancient Art, Beverly Hills, CA....94
Gerdes, Paul, Cur., Virginia Institute of Marine Science, Gloucester Point, VA..1715
Gerdes Stoltz, Kirsten, Assoc. Cur., Boulder Museum of Contemporary Art, Boulder, CO....229
Gerdts, Elly, Coord. Public Rels., Family Museum, Bettendorf, IA....574
Gereck, Kathy, Museum Shop Mgr., Lynn Museum & Historical Society, Lynn, MA....788
Gereck, Tom, Museum Shop Mgr., Lynn Museum & Historical Society, Lynn, MA....788
Geremia, Amie, Registrar, Frist Center for the Visual Arts, Nashville, TN....1568
Gerhanser, William, Ph.D., Chm. (V), Allaire Village Inc., Farmingdale, NJ....1038
Gerhardt, Peg, Sec., Pioneers, Trail Drivers and Texas Rangers Memorial Museum, San Antonio, TX....1644
Gerhardt, Stephanie, Cur. Education, Evansville Museum of Arts History & Science, Evansville, IN....539

G–Continued

Gerhartz, Karen, Treas., Calumet County Historical Society, Inc., Chilton, WI......1815
Gerig, Barry, Pres., National Automotive & Truck Museum of the United States, Inc. (NATMUS), Auburn, IN.......531
Geritz, Kathy, Film Cur., University of California Berkeley Art Museum and Pacific Film Archive, Berkeley, CA..........94
Gerlach, Tom, Chm. (V), The Children's Museum, Seattle, Seattle, WA................1780
Gerling, Dr. John, Pres., International Museum of Art and Science, McAllen, TX........1631
Gerlough, Kate, Museum Shop Mgr., The Frick Collection, New York, NY..........1168
German, Andy, Dir. Publications, Mystic Seaport - The Museum of America and the Sea, Mystic, CT..........284
German, Todd, Chm. (V), Key West Tropical Forest & Botanical Garden, Key West, FL..........359
Germann, Roger, Dir. Public Rels., John G. Shedd Aquarium, Chicago, IL............482
Germick, Brian, Dive Coord., North Carolina Aquarium at Fort Fisher, Kure Beach, NC..........1255
Gerrard, Susan, Dir. Mktg., Museum of Ventura County, Ventura, CA..........221
Gerrie, Bruce, Archivist, City Museum, Saint Louis, MO..........946
Gerring, Todd E., Coord. Museum Visitor Programs, Kelsey Museum of Archaeology, Ann Arbor, MI..........822
Gerrish, Haden, Sec., Wentworth Gardner & Tobias Lear Houses Association, Portsmouth, NH..........1028
Gerry, Elbridge T., Jr., Pres., The Harness Racing Museum and Hall of Fame, Goshen, NY..........1139
Gerry, Rip, Conservation Asst., Storage Mgr. & Exhibit Preparator, Haffenreffer Museum of Anthropology, Brown University, Providence, RI.........1494
Gersch, Fred, Clerk, Log Cabin Village, Fort Worth, TX..........1610
Gershuny, Justin, Cur. Architecture, Heritage Square Museum, Los Angeles, CA..........136
Gerson, Denise M., Assoc. Dir., Lowe Art Museum, University of Miami, Coral Gables, FL..........340
Gersonde, William, Dir., Tautphaus Park Zoo, Idaho Falls, ID..........460
Gerstein, Stuart, Dir. Wholesale & Retail Operations, Philadelphia Museum of Art, Philadelphia, PA..........1459
Gerstein, Stuart, Museum Shop Mgr., Rodin Museum, Philadelphia, PA..........1460
Gersten, Jilian, Dir. Devel. Grants & Annual Giving, Museum of Jewish Heritage-A Living Memorial to the Holocaust, New York, NY..........1175
Gerstheimer, Christian, Cur., El Paso Museum of Art, El Paso, TX..........1604
Gerts, Richard, Cur., George Ade Memorial Association Inc., Brook, IN....534
Gertz, Faust, Technology Specialist, Vesterheim Norwegian-American Museum, Decorah, IA..........582
Gerulskis, Jeanne T., C.E.O., McAuliffe-Shepard Discovery Center, Concord, NH..........1015
Gervasi, Shelley, Cur., St. Francis County Museum, Forrest City, AR..........71
Gervis, Scott, Natural Science Program Mgr., Berkshire Museum, Pittsfield, MA..........799
Gerwin, John, Cur. Birds, North Carolina Museum of Natural Sciences, Raleigh, NC..........1263
Gessler, Thomas U., Photography & Installations, Museum of Fine Arts of St. Petersburg, Florida, Saint Petersburg, FL..........384
Gessner, Ben, Visitor Svcs. & Member Coord., Minnesota Museum of American Art, Saint Paul, MN..........895
Gessner, Nancy, Chm. (V), The Massillon Museum, Massillon, OH..........1331
Gestring, Ron, Pres. (V), Webster County Historical Museum, Red Cloud, NE........997
Getchell, Katherine, Deputy Dir., Museum of Fine Arts, Boston, MA.........761
Getek, Lauren Marie, Exec. Dir., Rome Art and Community Center, Rome, NY..........1204
Gett, Thomas, Dir., Marion County Museum, Marion, SC..........1517
Gette, Tim, Exec. Dir., Institute of Texan Cultures, San Antonio, TX..........1643
Getterman, Holt, Chm. (V), The Earle-Harrison House and Gardens on 5th Street, Waco, TX..........1654
Gettig, Roger, Dir. Horticulture & Conservation, The Holden Arboretum, Kirtland, OH..........1326
Getz, Bert A., Vice Pres., Hall of Flame Museum of Firefighting, Phoenix, AZ.......50
Getz, George F., Pres. (V), Hall of Flame Museum of Firefighting, Phoenix, AZ.......50
Getz, Lynn, Vice Pres., Hall of Flame Museum of Firefighting, Phoenix, AZ.......50
Getzels, Julia E., Exec. Vice Pres., The Art Institute of Chicago, Chicago, IL......476
Geurts, Chad, Interpreter, Kensington Metropark Nature Center, Milford, MI....855
Gevas, Sophia, Dir., The Gallery of Contemporary Art - Sacred Heart University, Fairfield, CT..........274
Geving, Renee, Dir., Cass County Museum & Research Center, Walker, MN..........900
Geyer, Henry, Pres., Briar Bush Nature Center, Abington, PA..........1407
Geyer, Jim, Dir., Dr. Increase Mathews House, Zanesville, OH..........1354
Geyer, Nancy, C.E.O., Boulder History Museum, Boulder, CO..........229
Gfeller, Irma E., Dir. & Sec., Adams County Historical Society Museum, Lind, WA..........1771
Ghapman, Melanie, Treas., Praters Mill Foundation, Dalton, GA..........415
Gharrity, Mary Lou, Dir., Milford Historical Museum, Milford, MI..........855
Ghelerter, Donna, Curatorial Assoc., The Museum for African Art, Long Island City, NY..........1154
Ghez, Susanne, Dir. & Cur., The Renaissance Society at The University of Chicago, Chicago, IL..........486
Ghiorsi Hart, Carl, Exec. Dir., Suffolk County Vanderbilt Museum, Centerport, NY..........1120
Ghirarduzzi, Aldo, Treas., Chancellor Robert R. Livingston Masonic Library & Museum, New York, NY..........1165
Gholson, Charlie, Chm. (V), Biedenharn Coca-Cola Museum, Vicksburg, MS.......918
Ghose, Madhuvanti, Cur. Indian & Islamic Art, The Art Institute of Chicago, Chicago, IL..........476
Ghose, Seve, Dir. Parks & Recreation, Fejervary Zoo, Davenport, IA..........581
Giacoletti, Larry, Registrar, Isamu Noguchi Garden Museum, Long Island City, NY..........1154
Giacopuzzi, Michelle, Exhibitions Coord., Art Galleries, California State University, Northridge, Northridge, CA..........152
Giaimo, Catherine L., Asst. Librarian, The Masonic Library and Museum of Pennsylvania, Philadelphia, PA..........1456
Giancola, Paul, Bd. Chm., Scottsdale Museum of Contemporary Art, Scottsdale, AZ..........54
Giandomenico, Jolene, Museum Shop Mgr., 1708 Gallery, Richmond, VA.......1740
Gianelloni, Marcelle, Education Cur., Louisville Zoological Garden, Louisville, KY..........656
Gianetti, Kim, Museum Shop Mgr., United States Golf Association Museum, Far Hills, NJ..........1038
Giangiuli, Gloria, Museum Shop Mgr., El Pueblo Historical Monument, Los Angeles, CA..........135
Giannasi, Dr. D., Cur. Botany, Georgia Museum of Natural History, Athens, GA..........400
Gianopulos, Christiana N., Chm., Harriet Beecher Stowe Center, Hartford, CT.......278
Giard, Elizabeth, Collections Mgr., Harriet Beecher Stowe Center, Hartford, CT..........278
Giattini, Cheryl, Legacy Funds Coord., Sanibel-Captiva Conservation Foundation, Inc., Sanibel, FL..........386
Gibb Roff, Samantha, Exec. Dir., Duluth Art Institute, Duluth, MN..........874
Gibb, Yvonne, Mgr. Volunteer Svcs., The von Liebig Art Center - The Naples Art Association, Naples, FL..........370
Gibbins, Kristen, Public Rels., Nasher Sculpture Center, Dallas, TX..........1600
Gibbons, Connie S., Exec. Dir., B.B. King Museum and Delta Interpretive Center, Indianola, MS..........909
Gibbons, Danny, Museum Lobby Mgr., Monongalia Arts Center, Morgantown, WV..........1803
Gibbons, Douglas F., Dir. Library & Information Svcs., The Paley Center for Media, New York, NY..........1179
Gibbons, Jan, Arts Supvr., Roswell Visual Arts Center & Gallery, Roswell, GA.......431
Gibbons, JoAnn, Dir., Hanford Carnegie Museum, Hanford, CA..........120
Gibbons, Michael, Cur., Yaquina River Museum of Art, Toledo, OR..........1406
Gibbons, Michael L., Exec. Dir., The Babe Ruth Museum and Sports Legends at Camden Yards, Baltimore, MD..........719
Gibbons, Molly, Mgr. Collections, The Morris Museum, Morristown, NJ..........1050
Gibbons, Tom, Treas. & Museum Shop Mgr., Huntington Beach International Surfing Museum, Huntington Beach, CA..........123
Gibbs, Craig, Asst. Cur. Animals, Wildlife Conservation Society, Queens Zoo, Flushing, NY..........1134
Gibbs, Daniel R., Dir., Eliza Cruce Hall Doll Collection, Ardmore, OK..........1356
Gibbs, Delia, Exec. Dir., The Long Island Science Center, Riverhead, NY..........1200
Gibbs, Dr. Elizabeth, Chair, Beaumont Botanical Gardens, Beaumont, TX........1586
Gibbs, Emily, Museum Shop Mgr., Amazement Square, The Rightmire Children's Museum, Lynchburg, VA.....1722
Gibbs, Judith, Deputy Dir. Devel., The Baltimore Museum of Art, Baltimore, MD..........720
Gibbs, Judy, Pres. (V), Waldport Heritage Museum, Waldport, OR..........1407
Gibbs, Lawrence, Chm. (V), Cimarron Valley Railroad Museum, Cushing, OK..........1359
Gibbs, Margaret, Dir., Adirondack History Center, Elizabethtown, NY.......1130

G–*Continued*

G–*Continued*

Glinz, Twilla, Pres. (V), Bottineau County Historical Museum, Bottineau, ND....1278
Glisson, Ed, Exec. Dir., Mid-Hudson Children's Museum, Poughkeepsie, NY....1198
Globensky, Brigid, Dir. Programs & Education, Milwaukee Art Museum, Milwaukee, WI....1834
Glock, Stephanie, Financial Mgr., Robert Hull Fleming Museum, Burlington, VT....1678
Glodbille, Lara, Dir., U.S. Navy Seabee Museum, Port Hueneme, CA....166
Glomski, Dan, Dir. Planetarium, Hastings Museum, Hastings, NE....985
Glosson, Enice, Registrar, DeWitt Wallace Decorative Arts Museum, Williamsburg, VA....1754
Glotzhober, Robert, Cur. Natural History, Ohio Historical Society, Columbus, OH....1313
Glouatsky, Elizabeth, Office Mgr., North Dakota Museum of Art, Grand Forks, ND....1283
Glover, Cherie, Co-Owner, Old West Museum, Wimberley, TX....1658
Glover, Jack N., Owner & Cur., Old West Museum, Wimberley, TX....1658
Glover, Jessica, Museum Shop Mgr., Bellevue Arts Museum, Bellevue, WA....1758
Glover, Kathleen, Asst. Dir., Loxahatchee River Historical Society - Jupiter Inlet Lighthouse & Museum, Jupiter, FL....357
Glover, Susan L., Keeper Special Collections, Boston Public Library, Boston, MA....758
Glover-Wilson, Mary Beth, Chm. (V), Grant County Museum, Sheridan, AR....84
Glueckert, Stephen, Cur. Exhibitions, Missoula Art Museum, Missoula, MT....969
Glutting, Keith, Assoc. Mgr. Visitor Svcs., The Cloisters, New York, NY....1166
Glynias, Lexi, Opers. Dir., Craft Alliance, Saint Louis, MO....946
Glynn, Gary, Chm. (V), Historical Museum at Fort Missoula, Missoula, MT....969
Gnegy, Brenda, Asst. Cur., Garrett County Historical Museum, Oakland, MD....742
Gneier, Nancy, Museum Shop Mgr., Travel Town Transportation Museum, Los Angeles, CA....142
Gnidovec, Dale, Collection Mgr. & Cur., Orton Geological Museum, Ohio State University, Columbus, OH....1314
Goar, Katherine, Education & Programs Coord. USC Fisher Museum of Art, Los Angeles, CA....142
Gobble, William C., Pres. (V), Wise County Historical Society, Wise, VA....1756
Gobel, Mary, Pres. & Chm. (V), Alamo Township Museum-John E. Gray Memorial Museum, Kalamazoo, MI....847
Goben, Carolyn, Museum Store Mgr., Maritime Museum of San Diego, San Diego, CA....180
Gobetz, Scott, Mgr. Human Resources, Disney's Animal Kingdom Theme Park, Bay Lake, FL....334
Goble, Renee, Chm. (V), Stuhr Museum of the Prairie Pioneer, Grand Island, NE....984
Gochnauer, Becky, Dir., 1719 Hans Herr House & Museum, Willow Street, PA....1482
Godbey, Martin, Pres., Sarasota Classic Car Museum, Sarasota, FL....388
Godbout, Jill, Office Coord., American Clock and Watch Museum, Inc., Bristol, CT....268
Goddard, Elizabeth, Acting Dir., Newport Art Museum & Art Association, Newport, RI....1491
Goddard, Elizabeth, Mgr. Expressive Arts Program, Urban Institute for Contemporary Arts, Grand Rapids, MI....843
Goddard, Janet, Museum Store Mgr., McNay Art Museum, San Antonio, TX....1644
Goddard, Stephen, Sr. Cur. Prints & Drawings, Spencer Museum of Art, The University of Kansas, Lawrence, KS....621
Godfrey, Anthony, Dir. & Pres., Georgia Aquarium, Atlanta, GA....404
Godfrey, Pam, Dir. Protection & Visitor Svcs. IMA - Indianapolis Museum of Art, Indianapolis, IN....548
Godfrey, Stephen J., Cur. Paleontology, Calvert Marine Museum, Solomons, MD....748
Godin, Kathy, Flight Dir., Challenger Center, Kalamazoo Valley Museum, Kalamazoo, MI....848
Godsey, Lisa, Administrative Asst. & Museum Shop Mgr., The Veterans' Museum, Halls, TN....1554
Godsey, William, Chm., The Art Gallery, John C. Calhoun State Community College, Decatur, AL....9
Godshall, Anne, Museum Shop Mgr., Asia Society Museum, New York, NY....1164
Godshall, Janice, Volunteer Coord. & Museum Shop Mgr., Mennonite Heritage Center, Harleysville, PA....1430
Godwin, Huston, Dir., Fort Bedford Museum, Bedford, PA....1411
Goebel, Patsy, Chm. (V), DeWitt County Historical Museum, Cuero, TX....1596
Goedert, Rick, Pres. (V), Saginaw Art Museum, Saginaw, MI....863
Goehring, Alicia L., Dir. Div. Historic Sites, Madeline Island Museum, La Pointe, WI....1826
Goel, A.B., Mgr. Facilities, Georgia Music Hall of Fame, Macon, GA....425
Goergen, Jude, Community Rels. Mgr., Museum of Contemporary Art Cleveland, Cleveland, OH....1309
Goering, Karen M., Mng. Dir. Operations, Missouri Historical Society, Saint Louis, MO....949
Goering, Loren, Chief Interpretation, Zane Grey Museum, Lackawaxen, PA....1438
Goers, Rachel, Museum Shop Dir., The International Clown Hall of Fame & Research Center, Inc., Milwaukee, WI....1834
Goes, James, Chm. & Pres., Frisco Native American Museum and Natural History Center, Frisco, NC....1247
Goetz, Megan, Exhibitions, Dallas Contemporary, Dallas, TX....1597
Goetz, Robert, Exhibits Preparator, Laumeier Sculpture Park & Museum, Saint Louis, MO....948
Goff, Allison, Dir. Education, Flagler Museum, Palm Beach, FL....375
Goff, Don, Dir. Animal Care & Operations, Connecticut's Beardsley Zoo, Bridgeport, CT....267
Goff, Jonathan, Exhibitions & Programs, Herreshoff Marine Museum/America's Cup Hall of Fame, Bristol, RI....1485
Goff, Mary, Information Asst., The Columbus Museum, Columbus, GA....414
Goff, Neill, Pres., St. John's Episcopal Church, Richmond, VA....1740
Goff, Phyllis, Hostess & Guide, Alexandre Mouton House/Lafayette Museum, Lafayette, LA....673
Goff, Robert, Sec., Scantic Academy Museum, East Windsor Historical Society, Inc., East Windsor, CT....272
Goffard, Diane, Dir., High Cliff Historical Society & General Store Museum, Sherwood, WI....1845
Goffe, Gwendolyn H., Assoc. Dir. Investment & Finance, The Museum of Fine Arts, Houston, Houston, TX....1622
Goganian, Susan, Dir., Beverly Historical Society and Museum, Beverly, MA....756
Goggin, Dorothy, Museum Shop Mgr., Art Galleries, California State University, Northridge, Northridge, CA....152
Gogolin, Gary, Dir. Leisure & Cultural Svcs., De Graaf Nature Center, Holland, MI....845
Gohring, Roger, Pres. (V), Great Valley Museum of Natural History, Modesto, CA....147
Goings, Drew, Business Mgr., San Jose Museum of Quilts & Textiles, San Jose, CA....196
Goings, Dr. Kenneth, Chm. (V), National Afro-American Museum & Cultural Center, Wilberforce, OH....1350
Goire, Eric, Operations Mgr., The Museum of Arts and Sciences, Inc. and Center for Florida History, Daytona Beach, FL....342
Golas, Theresa, Exec. Dir., Iredell Museums - Heritage Farmstead & Learning Center, Statesville, NC....1268
Golat, Henry, Pres., Rusk County Historical Society, Ladysmith, WI....1826
Golben, Pam, Cur. Living Exhibits, Hudson Highlands Nature Museum, Cornwall-on-Hudson, NY....1125
Gold, Brian, Business Mgr., Sciencenter, Ithaca, NY....1147
Gold, Jack, Exec. Dir., Haas-Lilienthal House, San Francisco, CA....189
Gold, Ruth C., Cur., Atlantic Heritage Center, Somers Point, NJ....1061
Gold, Susan, Exec. Dir., Westport Historical Society, Westport, CT....301
Gold, Wendy, Vice Chair, Neuberger Museum of Art, Purchase College, State University of New York, Purchase, NY....1198
Goldberg, Beth, Cur., Falkirk Cultural Center, San Rafael, CA....200
Goldberg, Dara, Dir. External Affairs, United States Holocaust Memorial Museum, Washington, DC....332
Goldberg, Dee, Dir., Robert A. Vines Environmental Science Center, Houston, TX....1623
Goldberg, Ellen, Curatorial Asst., The Webb-Deane-Stevens Museum, Wethersfield, CT....301
Goldberg, Elyse B., Historic Site Mgr., Washington's Headquarters State Historic Site, Newburgh, NY....1185
Goldberg, Gail, Mgr. Retail & MTA Products Devel., New York Transit Museum, Brooklyn Heights, NY....1113
Goldberg, Margaret, Chm. (V), The Greenburgh Nature Center, Scarsdale, NY....1208
Goldberg, Margery, Dir., Zenith Gallery, Washington, DC....333
Goldberg, Michael, Chm. (V), Holocaust Museum Houston, Houston, TX....1620
Goldberg, Phyllis, Museum Shop Mgr., Faust Park Foundation, Chesterfield, MO....923
Goldberger, Clem, Assoc. Vice Pres. Mktg., The National World War II Museum, New Orleans, LA....682
Golden, Ann, Museum Technician, Moses Lake Museum & Art Center, Moses Lake, WA....1772
Golden, Debbie, Events Coord., Grant-Humphreys Mansion, Denver, CO....240

G–*Continued*

G–Continued

Goyette, Barbara, Pres., Hammond-Harwood House Association, Annapolis, MD 717
Goyette, Betsy, Museum Shop Mgr., Storrowton Village Museum, West Springfield, MA 815
Goyette, Caroline E., Arts Quarterly Editor, New Orleans Museum of Art, New Orleans, LA 683
Goza, Linda, Museum Interpreter, Plantation Agriculture Museum, Scott, AR 83
Gozani, Tal, Assoc. Cur., Skirball Cultural Center, Los Angeles, CA 142
Grabau, Flora, Pres. (V), Fillmore County Historical Center, Fountain, MN 878
Grabenhorst, Coburn, Pres. (V), Marion County Historical Society, Salem, OR ..1403
Graber, Clifford C., II, C.E.O. & Dir., Graber Olive House Museum, Ontario, CA 157
Grabowski, John, Dir. Research, Western Reserve Historical Society, Cleveland, OH 1311
Grace, Anna, Exhibit Coord., Explorit Science Center, Davis, CA 106
Grace, Bill, Pres. (V), Koreshan State Historic Site, Estero, FL 346
Grace, Trisha, Collections Mgr., Shippensburg Historical Society Museum, Shippensburg, PA 1474
Grace, Trudie Alexis, Cur., Putnam County Historical Society & Foundry School Museum, Cold Spring, NY 1122
Gracey, Patty, Administrative Asst., Rose Center Museum, Morristown, TN 1565
Grachos, Louis, Dir., Albright-Knox Art Gallery, Buffalo, NY 1114
Gracyalny, Devan, Jr., Pres. (V), West Allis Historical Society Museum, West Allis, WI 1850
Gradwohl, Judith, Assoc. Dir., National Museum of American History, Washington, DC 324
Graefen, Barbara, Corresponding Sec., The Palette & Chisel, Chicago, IL 485
Graf, Lana, Library Volunteer, Dundee Township Historical Society, Inc., Dundee, IL 491
Graf, Marie, Dir. Communications & Mktg., The Cleveland Museum of Natural History, Cleveland, OH 1308
Graf, Ronni, C.E.O., Science Museum of Long Island, Manhasset, NY 1156
Grafe, Steve, Cur. Native American Collections, National Cowboy & Western Heritage Museum, Oklahoma City, OK 1371
Graff, John, Pres. (V), Freeport Art Museum, Freeport, IL 495
Graffam, Olive, Cur. Collections, Daughters of the American Revolution Museum, Washington, DC 316
Gragert, Steven K., Dir., Will Rogers Memorial Museum, Claremore, OK 1358
Graham, Angela, Mgr. Maintenance, The Nelson-Atkins Museum of Art, Kansas City, MO 934
Graham, Arthur, Pres. (V), Clinton Academy Museum, East Hampton, NY 1128
Graham, Arthur, Pres. (V), East Hampton Historical Society, Inc., East Hampton, NY 1128
Graham, Arthur, Pres. (V), East Hampton Town Marine Museum, Amagansett, NY 1098
Graham, Arthur, Pres. (V), Mulford Farm Museum, East Hampton, NY 1129
Graham, Arthur, Pres. (V), Osborn-Jackson House, East Hampton, NY 1129
Graham, Frances, Admin., Fayette County Helpers Club & Historical Society, West Union, IA 602
Graham, Gail, Museum Guide, Orange Beach Indian and Sea Museum, Orange Beach, AL 21
Graham, Gretchen, Vice Pres., Greene County Historical Museum, Waynesburg, PA 1481
Graham, Isis, Pres. (V) & Museum Shop Mgr., The Turner Museum and Thomas Moran Galleries, Sarasota, FL ...388
Graham, John R., Cur. Exhibits, Western Illinois University Art Gallery, Macomb, IL 504
Graham, Kenna, Park Ranger, Russell Cave National Monument, Bridgeport, AL 7
Graham, Dr. Kurt, Cur. Research Library, Buffalo Bill Historical Center, Cody, WY 1856
Graham, Linda, Sec., Lincoln Parish Museum & Historical Society, Ruston, LA 685
Graham, Mary E., Head Librarian, Arizona State Museum, Tucson, AZ 59
Graham, Michael S., Cur., Shaker Museum, New Gloucester, ME 703
Graham, Ray, Security, Fred Wolf, Jr. Gallery/Klein Branch Jewish Community Center, Philadelphia, PA 1453
Graham, Russell W., C.E.O. & Dir., Earth & Mineral Sciences Museum and Art Gallery, University Park, PA 1478
Graham, Sandi, Devel., Vista Historical Museum, Vista, CA 222
Graham, Shelby, Dir. & Cur., Mary Porter Sesnon Art Gallery, Santa Cruz, CA 206
Graham, Terry, Mgr. Programs APVA Preservation Virginia, Richmond, VA ...1736
Graham, Tom, Pres. (V), Mississippi County Historical Society, Charleston, MO 923
Graham Wade, Karen, Dir., Workman & Temple Family Homestead Museum, City of Industry, CA 102
Graham, Wendy, Pres., The Discovery Center of the Southern Tier, Binghamton, NY 1105
Graichen, Ernest, Pres. (V), Veterans Memorial Museum, Chehalis, WA 1761
Grainer, Elizabeth, Vice Pres., Auxiliary Operations, The Art Institute of Chicago, Chicago, IL 476
Grais, Betsey, Vice Pres. Mktg., Communications & Guest Svcs., Chicago Children's Museum, Chicago, IL 478
Grajal, Alejandro, Ph.D., Sr. Vice Pres. Conservation, Education, & Training, Chicago Zoological Society/Brookfield Zoo, Brookfield, IL 473
Grajek-Specter, Bambi, Mgr. Retail Operations, Milwaukee Art Museum, Milwaukee, WI 1834
Gralak, Joyce, Dir. Education, Children's Museum of Oak Ridge, Inc., Oak Ridge, TN 1571
Grallert, Matthew, Historic Commission, Kingman Tavern Historical Museum, Cummington, MA 772
Gramer, Kevin, Admin., Byers-Evans House Museum, Denver, CO 237
Gramer, Kevin, Admin., Grant-Humphreys Mansion, Denver, CO 240
Gramlich, Leisa, C.E.O., Fort Smith Museum of History, Fort Smith, AR 72
Grams, Greg, C.E.O. & Owner, Volvo Auto Museum Attraction, Volo, IL 526
Grams, Myra, Devel. & Museum Shop Mgr., Volvo Auto Museum Attraction, Volo, IL 526
Granbois, Judith, Pres. (V), Hilltop Garden and Nature Center, Bloomington, IN 532
Grand, Stanley I., Ph.D., Exec. Dir., Lancaster Museum of Art, Lancaster, PA 1439
Grande, Lance, Sr. Vice Pres. Collections & Research, Field Museum of Natural History, Chicago, IL 480
Grando, Constance, C.E.O., Pres. (V) & Public Rels. Dir., Baldwin Historical Society and Museum, Baldwin, NY 1101
Grandrud, Dr. Reba, Education & Historian, Slaughter Ranch Museum, Douglas, AZ 40
Grandy, Ann, Artifact & Inventory Mgr., Pope County Historical Society, Glenwood, MN 878
Grandy, Matt, Vice Pres., Lars Noak Blacksmith Shop, Larsson/Ostlund Log Home & One-Room Capitol School, New Sweden, ME 704
Grandy, Patrick, Dir., Zippo/Case Visitors Center, Bradford, PA 1415
Granere, Jim, Museum Shop Mgr., Western North Carolina Air Museum, Hendersonville, NC 1251
Granfield, Marian, Educ. Coord., Castellani Art Museum of Niagara University, Niagara University, NY 1186
Grange, Caroline, Dir. Devel., Santa Barbara Museum of Natural History, Santa Barbara, CA 204
Grange, Ileen, Vice Pres. Accounting, Middleton Place House Museum, Charleston, SC 1505
Granger, Brenda, Exec. Dir., Oklahoma Museums Association, Oklahoma City, OK 1372
Granger, Pat, Museum Shop Mgr., Pearce Collections Museum, Corsicana, TX 1595
Granger, Steven T., C.A., Archivist, Archives - Archdiocese of St. Paul and Minneapolis, Saint Paul, MN 893
Graning, Connie, Treas. & Sec., Furnas-Gosper Historical Society & Museum, Arapahoe, NE 975
Graning, David, Pres., Sherburne History Center, Becker, MN 870
Granitto, Andrew, Cur. Exhibits & Programs, Yakima Valley Museum and Historical Association, Yakima, WA......1795
Grannan, John, Pres. Historical Society, The Old Courthouse Heritage Museum, Inverness, FL 354
Grannan, Nancy, Human Resources Mgr., Strawbery Banke Museum, Portsmouth, NH 1027
Grannis, Sue Ellen, Cur. Books, Art & Artifacts, Kentucky Gateway Museum Center, Maysville, KY 658
Granof, Corinne, Assoc. Cur., Mary and Leigh Block Museum of Art, Northwestern University, Evanston, IL ...494
Granrud, Marilyn, Pres., Stoughton Historical Society, Stoughton, WI 1846
Grant, Betsy, C.E.O., Greensboro Children's Museum, Greensboro, NC 1248
Grant, Carolyn, Exec. Dir., Museum of Making Music, A Division of the NAMM Foundation, Carlsbad, CA 98
Grant, Chris, Assoc. Dir., Krannert Art Museum and Kinkead Pavilion, Champaign, IL 474
Grant, Gordon, Education Asst., Island County Historical Society Museum, Coupeville, WA 1763
Grant, Hugh, Dir., Kirkland Museum of Fine & Decorative Art, Denver, CO 241

Grant, Jacqueline, Exec. Dir., Hudson Highlands Nature Museum, Cornwall-on-Hudson, NY....1125
Grant, Jayne, Gallery Mgr., Santa Fe Gallery, Gainesville, FL....352
Grant, Jerry, Dir. Research, The Shaker Museum and Library, Old Chatham, NY....1188
Grant, John, Chm. Center for Earth & Planetary Studies, National Air and Space Museum, Washington, DC....322
Grant, Karen G., Pres. (V), Spellman Museum of Stamps and Postal History, Weston, MA....816
Grant, Kimberli, Dir. Exhibitions, MoCADA - The Museum of Contemporary African Diasporan Arts, Brooklyn, NY....1112
Grant, Lynn, Interim Head Conservator, University of Pennsylvania Museum of Archaeology and Anthropology, Philadelphia, PA....1462
Grant, Michael, Exhibition Preparator, Mingei International Museum, San Diego, CA....180
Grant, Richard A., Jr., Chm. Bd. Trustees, Rancho Santa Ana Botanic Garden, Claremont, CA....102
Grant, Stuart, Pres. (V), Dallas Firefighter's Museum, Inc., Dallas, TX.1597
Grant, Timothy, Public Rels. & Exhibits, U.S. Mint-Philadelphia, Philadelphia, PA....1463
Grantham, Cathy, Dir. Human Resources, Hillwood Estate, Museum & Gardens, Washington, DC....318
Grantham, Tom, Pres. (V), Glenn House/Historical Association of Greater Cape Girardeau, Cape Girardeau, MO....922
Granville, Lee, Cur., Skowhegan History House Inc., Skowhegan, ME....712
Granville, Mark F., Pres. (V), Connecticut Eastern Railroad Museum, Willimantic, CT....302
Granzow-De La Cerda, Inigo, Asst. Cur., Herbarium of the University of Michigan, Ann Arbor, MI....822
Graper, David F., Ph.D., Dir., McCrory Gardens at South Dakota State University, Brookings, SD....1527
Grasselli Brown, Jeanette, Chm. Bd., Great Lakes Science Center, Cleveland, OH....1309
Grasselli, Eleanor, Vice Pres., Historical Society of Washington County, Virginia, Abingdon, VA....1695
Grasselli, Eleanor, Bulletin Editor, Historical Society of Washington County, Virginia, Abingdon, VA....1695
Grasselli, Margaret Morgan, Cur. & Head Old Master Drawings, National Gallery of Art, Washington, DC....323
Grasso, Henry, M.A., Exhibits & Education, DeWitt Stetten, Jr., Museum of Medical Research, Bethesda, MD....727
Grasso, Linda, Interpreter, Queens County Farm Museum, Floral Park, NY....1133
Gratt, David, Mng. Dir., Coney Island Museum, Brooklyn, NY....1111
Graubman, Daniel, Research Assoc., Belz Museum of Asian & Judaic Art, Memphis, TN....1560
Grauer, Michael R., Cur. Art, Panhandle-Plains Historical Museum, Canyon, TX....1592
Graulich, Janie, Receptionist, Lowe Art Museum, University of Miami, Coral Gables, FL....340
Gravenhorst, Susan Loving, Chm., Lake County Discovery Museum, Wauconda, IL....526
Graves, Cheryl, Accountant, Lakeshore Museum Center, Muskegon, MI....857
Graves, Erin, Dir. Programs, Catawba Science Center, Hickory, NC....1251
Graves, Gordon, Pres. Bd., Oxford Museum, Inc., Oxford, MD....742
Graves, Jean, Assoc. Cur. Docent & School Svcs., Taft Museum of Art, Cincinnati, OH....1306
Graves, Jim, Sec., Heritage Square Museum, Ontario, NY....1190
Graves, Joseph R., Vice Pres. Operations, Rochester Museum & Science Center, Rochester, NY....1202
Graves, Judy, Dir. Education & Research, Portland Children's Museum, Portland, OR....1400
Graves, Paul, Museum Shop Mgr., Vonore Heritage Museum, Vonore, TN.1575
Graves, Sherry, Dir., Working Men's Institute, New Harmony, IN....560
Graves, Stan, Architecture Div., Texas Historical Commission, Austin, TX....1583
Graves, Tolley, Exec. Dir., American Saddlebred Museum, Lexington, KY....651
Graves, Vera, Pres., Heritage Square Museum, Ontario, NY....1190
Gravesen, Dianne, Pres., Forts Folle Avoine Historic Park, Danbury, WI....1816
Gravley, Kurt, Pres., Museum of Wildlife, Science & Industry, Webster, SD....1545
Gravois, Renee, Asst. Registrar, Lyndon Baines Johnson Library and Museum, Austin, TX....1582
Graw, Donald, Asst. Dir., My Jewish Discovery Place Children's Museum, Fort Lauderdale, FL....348
Gray, Alden, Pres. (V), Ashfield Historical Society, Ashfield, MA....754
Gray, Bill W., Chm. (V), Bulloch Hall, Roswell, GA....431
Gray, Bud, Supvr. Facilities, The Antique Boat Museum, Clayton, NY....1121
Gray, Dr. Campbell B., Dir., Brigham Young University Museum of Art, Provo, UT....1667
Gray, Catherine, Challenger Flight Dir., Discovery Museum, Sacramento Museum of History, Science and Technology, Sacramento, CA....176
Gray, Dan, Pres. (V), Logan County Museum, Paris, AR....81
Gray, Debra C., Dir., Contemporary Art Center of Virginia, Virginia Beach, VA.1751
Gray, Donovan, Public Rels., Depot Museum/Cascade Rail Foundation, South Cle Elum, WA....1786
Gray, Elinor, Historian & Genealogist, Historical Society of Brookfield-Marvin Newton House, Brookfield Center, VT....1677
Gray, Frances B., Archivist, Miles B. Carpenter Museum, Waverly, VA....1753
Gray, Gabrielle, C.E.O. & Exec. Dir., International Bluegrass Music Museum, Owensboro, KY....660
Gray, George A., Pres. (V), Fostoria Area Historical Museum, Fostoria, OH....1320
Gray, Harvey, Treas., Pacific Aviation Museum - Pearl Harbor, Honolulu, HI....447
Gray, Helen T., Pres. (V), Glenmore Mansion, Jefferson City, TN....1555
Gray, Jenny, Administrative Asst., Montana Natural History Center, Missoula, MT....969
Gray, John L., Pres. & C.E.O., Autry National Center of the American West, Los Angeles, CA....133
Gray, Karen C., Chm. (V), Stow West School Museum, Stow, MA....811
Gray, Kathy, Owner LARK Toys & Carousel, Kellogg, MN....881
Gray, Dr. Lee, Cur. Exhibitions & Collections, Paul and Lulu Hilliard University Art Museum, University of Louisiana at Lafayette, Lafayette, LA....673
Gray, Mary, Sec., H.G. Albee Memorial Museum, Estherville, IA....586
Gray, Michelle, Mng. Dir., Warren County Historical Society, Warren, PA..1479
Gray, Nancy, Exhibit Developer, Tryon Palace Historic Sites & Gardens, New Bern, NC....1259
Gray, Paige, World Show Pres., The World Organization of China Painters, Oklahoma City, OK....1373
Gray, Phil, Parks Mgr., Fort Boonesborough Museum, Richmond, KY....662
Gray, Ron, Owner LARK Toys & Carousel, Kellogg, MN....881
Gray, Roze, Museum Shop Mgr., Georgia Sports Hall of Fame, Macon, GA....425
Gray, Sam, C.E.O., Dir. & Cur., Mountain Gateway Museum, Old Fort, NC....1260
Gray, Sara, Mgr., Stremmel Gallery, Reno, NV....1009
Gray, Sara, Accountant, Texas Natural Science Center, Austin, TX....1584
Gray, Steve, Treas., Montrose County Historical Museum, Montrose, CO....258
Gray, Terry, Asst. Archivist, Sicangu Heritage Center, Mission, SD....1536
Gray, Xanthi, Exhibits Developer, The Children's Museum of New Hampshire, Dover, NH....1016
Graybeal, Jay, Dir. Army Heritage Museum, United States Army Heritage and Education Center - Army Heritage Museum, Carlisle, PA....1416
Gray-Burlingham, Miranda, Owner LARK Toys & Carousel, Kellogg, MN....881
Gray-Burlingham, Scott, Owner LARK Toys & Carousel, Kellogg, MN....881
Graydon Smith, John, Dir., The Children's Museum of Science and Technology, Troy, NY....1221
Grayson, John, Dir. Devel., Museum of Contemporary Art Cleveland, Cleveland, OH....1309
Grayson, Paul, Deputy Dir. & Senior Vice Pres., Indianapolis Zoo, Indianapolis, IN....550
Gray-Young, Rhonda, Collections Asst., Federal Reserve Board, Washington, DC....317
Graze, Sue, Exec. Dir., Arthouse, Austin, TX....1579
Graziotto, Ray, Chm. (V), Loggerhead Marinelife Center, Juno Beach, FL....357
Grazzini, Patricia J., Deputy Dir., Minneapolis Institute of Arts, Minneapolis, MN....886
Greaney, Loretta, Controller, The Morgan Library & Museum, New York, NY....1173
Greathouse, Joe, Animal Mgr., Oglebay's Good Zoo, Wheeling, WV....1808
Greathouse, Leisa, Assoc. Cur. Education, Museum of the Cape Fear Historical Complex, Fayetteville, NC....1245
Greaves, Ryan, Graphic Designer, Urban Institute for Contemporary Arts, Grand Rapids, MI....843
Grebl, James, Library Mgr., San Diego Museum of Art, San Diego, CA....183
Greco, Greg, Pres., Hartman Reserve Nature Center, Cedar Falls, IA....576
Greco, Maria, Museum Shop Mgr., Amherst Museum, Amherst, NY....1099
Greczanik, Vince, Dir. Facilities, National Inventors Hall of Fame, Akron, OH....1292
Gredo, Stanisliv, Cur., Ukrainian Institute of Modern Art, Chicago, IL....487

G–*Continued*

G–*Continued*

Griffin, Teresa, Museum Shop Mgr., Whitaker Center for Science and the Arts, Harrisburg, PA 1432
Griffin, Travis, Mgr., Stephen C. Foster State Park, Fargo, GA 418
Griffin-Underhill, Colleen, Museum Shop Mgr., Memorial Art Gallery of the University of Rochester, Rochester, NY 1202
Griffis, Larry L., Dir., Birger Sandzen Memorial Gallery, Lindsborg, KS....623
Griffith, Alan, Vice Chm., Chesapeake Bay Maritime Museum, Saint Michaels, MD 745
Griffith, Alison, Asst. Dir. Devel., The Children's Museum of Houston, Houston, TX 1619
Griffith, Bill, Education, Arrowmont School of Arts & Crafts, Gatlinburg, TN 1552
Griffith, Darlene, Museum Shop Mgr., Tunica Museum, Tunica, MS 917
Griffith, Janie, Dir., Breathitt County Museum, Inc., Jackson, KY 650
Griffith, John, Pres., Historic Shepherdstown Museum, Shepherdstown, WV 1806
Griffith, Karen, Cur., Howard County Historical Society, Ellicott City, MD....734
Griffith, Lee Ellen, Ph.D, Dir., Monmouth County Historical Association, Freehold, NJ....1039
Griffith, Les, Pres., Safety Harbor Museum of Regional History, Safety Harbor, FL 380
Griffith, Dr. Mark, Pres. Bd., Clinton County Museum, Frankfort, IN 543
Griffith, William, Collections Mgr., University Museum & Historic Houses, The University of Mississippi, Oxford, MS....915
Griffith, William D., Cur., Rowan Oak, Home of William Faulkner, Oxford, MS....915
Griffiths, Charles, Pres., Cumberland County Historical Society, Greenwich, NJ 1040
Griffiths, Happy, Herbalist, Enfield Shaker Museum, Enfield, NH 1017
Griffiths, Roy, Vice Pres. Exhibits & Planning, Museum of Life and Science, Durham, NC....1243
Griggs, David W., Dir. & Cur., Carpinteria Valley Historical Society & Museum of History, Carpinteria, CA....99
Griggs, Joe, Chm. (V), Cottage Grove Museum & Annex, Cottage Grove, OR 1387
Grigione, Dr. Melissa, Pres., Weinberg Nature Center, Scarsdale, NY 1209
Grignon, Dennis, Cur. Exhibits, Neville Public Museum of Brown County, Green Bay, WI....1821
Grigsby, Eddy, Asst. Dir., Silent Wings Museum, Lubbock, TX 1629
Grigsby, Martha, Visitor Svcs. Coord. & Museum Shop Mgr., Stuhr Museum of the Prairie Pioneer, Grand Island, NE....984
Grigsby, Thea, Exec. Dir., Cappon & Settlers House Museums, Holland, MI....845
Grigsby, Thea, Gallery Mgr., Hearst Art Gallery, St. Mary's College, Moraga, CA....150
Grill, Eli, Gift Shop Mgr., Pittsburgh Zoo and PPG Aquarium, Pittsburgh, PA....1467
Grillo, Barbara, Pres. (V), Caldwell Parsonage, Union, NJ 1065
Grills, Joe, Montpelier Foundation Chm. (V), James Madison's Montpelier - The Montpelier Foundation, Montpelier Station, VA....1726
Grim, Bruce, Pres., Tooele Valley Railroad Museum, Tooele, UT....1674
Grimaldi, Ann, Cur. Education, Weatherspoon Art Museum, Greensboro, NC....1249
Grimaldo, Sylvia, Weekend Supvr., San Angelo Museum of Fine Arts, San Angelo, TX 1642
Grimes, Carmen, Pres. Bd. Trustees (V), Fleming Castle Museum, Flemington, NJ 1038
Grimes, Chuck, Dir. Accounting, Central Florida Zoo & Botanical Gardens, Sanford, FL....385
Grimes, James, Treas., Ipswich Historical Society and Museum, Ipswich, MA 783
Grimes, Jan, Exec. Dir., Abraham Lincoln Presidential Library & Museum, Springfield, IL....520
Grimes, Jan, Dir., Pierre Menard Home State Historic Site, Ellis Grove, IL....492
Grimes, Jan, Dir., State of Illinois-Historic Preservation Agency, Historic Sites Division, Springfield, IL ...523
Grimes, Jan, Dir. IHPA, Vandalia Statehouse State Historic Site, Vandalia, IL 526
Grimes, Lee T., Dir., Veterans Memorial Museum, Chehalis, WA....1761
Grimes, Michael, Mgr. Maintenance, Delaware Agricultural Museum and Village, Dover, DE 305
Grimes Rand, Anne, Exec. Vice Pres. USS Constitution Museum, Boston, MA 763
Grimes, Sharon, Pres., Hoiles-Davis Museum, Greenville, IL 499
Grimes, Stan, Chm. (V), Tucson Rodeo Parade Museum, Tucson, AZ....63
Grimm, Daniel K, Pres., Washington State Historical Society, Tacoma, WA...1790
Grimm, Daniel K., Pres. (V), Washington State History Museum, Tacoma, WA.....1791
Grimm, Emily, Mgr. Visitor Svcs., Loyola University Museum of Art, Chicago, IL....483
Grimm, Dr. Eric, Botany Chair, Illinois State Museum, Springfield, IL....521
Grimm, Ron, Chm., Crescent Bend/The Armstrong-Lockett House and The William P. Toms Memorial Gardens, Knoxville, TN....1557
Grimmer, Jean H.M., Dir., Egan Maritime Institute, Nantucket, MA....791
Grimsley, Molly, Assoc. Registrar Exhibitions, National Portrait Gallery, Washington, DC....326
Grinage, Jeanine, Head Education, New York State Museum, Albany, NY 1096
Grindell, Beth, Ph.D., Dir., Arizona State Museum, Tucson, AZ 59
Grindle, Ira, Vice Pres., Cordova Historical Museum, Cordova, AK 28
Grindstaff, Linda, Coord. Events, Maidu Museum and Historic Site, Roseville, CA....174
Grinmer, Jean, Exec. Dir. Egan Foundation, Nantucket Life-Saving Museum, Nantucket, MA 792
Grinnell, Dave, Acquisitions Archivist, Senator John Heinz History Center, Pittsburgh, PA....1468
Grinnell, Debbie, Dir. Preservation Svcs., Naper Settlement, Naperville, IL....508
Grinolds, Dale, Park Supt., Sainte Marie among the Iroquois, Liverpool, NY.......1153
Grinolds, Dale, Park Supt., Salt Museum, Liverpool, NY....1153
Grinspoon, Dr. David, Cur. Astrobiology, Denver Museum of Nature & Science, Denver, CO 239
Grinstead, Steve, Mng. Editor, History Colorado, The Colorado Historical Society, Denver, CO 240
Gripekoven, Hilary, Pres. (V), Dumbarton House, Washington, DC 316
Grisell, Sid, Pres. (V), West Virginia Penitentiary, Moundsville, WV 1804
Grisham, Jack, Vice Pres. Animal Collection, Saint Louis Zoo, Saint Louis, MO....951
Grismer, Randy, Pres. (V), Dacotah Prairie Museum, Aberdeen, SD 1526
Grissom, Jackie, Pres. (V), Hayward Area Historical Society, Hayward, CA....121
Grissom, Jackie, Pres. (V), McConaghy House, Hayward, CA 121
Grissom Kiely, Kay, Collections Assoc., Montana Museum of Art & Culture, Missoula, MT....969
Grissom, Marlene M., Chm. (V), Kentucky Museum of Art and Craft, Louisville, KY 655
Grissom, Tom, Pres. (V), New Jersey Botanical Garden at Skylands (NJBG), Ringwood, NJ 1059
Griswold, Emily, Asst. Dir. Education UC Davis Arboretum, Davis, CA 108
Griswold, Gerri, Dir. Administration & Devel., White Memorial Conservation Center, Inc., Litchfield, CT 280
Griswold, Justin, Collections Registrar & Preparator, University Gallery, University of Massachusetts at Amherst, Amherst, MA 753
Griswold, William M., Dir., The Morgan Library & Museum, New York, NY......1173
Groce, Dr. W. Todd, Pres., Georgia Historical Society, Savannah, GA....434
Grochowski, Amy, Dir. Education, Maxwell Museum of Anthropology, Albuquerque, NM....1071
Grodek, Mary, Public Rels., Cleveland State University Art Gallery, Cleveland, OH 1308
Groehner, Tom, Cur. Education, The Textile Museum, Washington, DC....330
Groeneveld, Paul, Business Mgr., Washington Pavilion of Arts and Science, Sioux Falls, SD....1542
Groenewold, Rod, Dir., Antique Gas & Steam Engine Museum, Inc., Vista, CA 222
Groff, Amy, Dir. Operations Learning & Devel., Disney's Animal Kingdom Theme Park, Bay Lake, FL....334
Groff, Bethany, Site Mgr., Coffin House, Newbury, MA 794
Groff, Bethany, Site Mgr., Spencer-Peirce-Little Farm, Newbury, MA 794
Groft, Tammis K., Deputy Dir. Collections & Exhibitions, Albany Institute of History & Art, Albany, NY.1095
Grogan, Cynthia, Education, Louisiana State Exhibit Museum, Shreveport, LA...686
Grogan, John, Dir. Investments Management, The Children's Museum of Indianapolis, Indianapolis, IN 547
Grogan, Kevin, Exec. Dir., Morris Museum of Art, Augusta, GA 411
Grogg, Donald, Exec. Dir., National Automotive & Truck Museum of the United States, Inc. (NATMUS), Auburn, IN....531
Groh, Barton, C.F.O., Mount Vernon: George Washington's Estate & Gardens, Mount Vernon, VA....1727
Grohalski, James, Chm. (V), Binder Park Zoo, Battle Creek, MI 825
Grojean, Charles, Exec. Dir., National Museum of the Pacific War, Fredericksburg, TX....1612

G–*Continued*

Gustafsson, John, Pres. (V), Staten Island Historical Society, Staten Island, NY....1216
Gustavson, Carrie, Dir., Bisbee Mining & Historical Museum, Bisbee, AZ................38
Gustavson, Kjirsten, Education Dir., Clermont State Historic Site, Germantown, NY....................................1137
Gustavson, Radm Gus, Chm. (V) USS Bowfin Submarine Museum & Park, Honolulu, HI...448
Gustavson, Todd, Cur. Tech., George Eastman House/International Museum of Photography and Film, Rochester, NY..1201
Gustin, Karen, Supt., Olympic National Park Visitor Center, Port Angeles, WA..1775
Guston, Judith M., Cur. & Dir. Collections, Rosenbach Museum & Library, Philadelphia, PA 1461
Gutenkauf, Diane, Dir., Robert R. McCormick Museum at Cantigny, Wheaton, IL..529
Gutfreund, Owen, Treas., The Skyscraper Museum, New York, NY......................1181
Guthier, Mark, Union Dir., The Wisconsin Union Galleries, University of Wisconsin-Madison, Madison, WI....1829
Guthrie, Alyce N., C.E.O. & Treas., The P.T. Boat Museum & Library, Germantown, TN.................................1552
Guthrie, Jill, Mng. Editor, Princeton University Art Museum, Princeton, NJ .1058
Guthrie, Pam, Cur., Reitz Home Museum, Evansville, IN..540
Gutierrez, Braxton, Site Coord., Lee Hall Mansion, Newport News, VA 1728
Gutierrez, Fidel, Pres. (V) & Chm. Bd. (V), Santa Fe Children's Museum, Santa Fe, NM..1091
Gutierrez, Joseph A., Jr., Sr. Dir. Museum Operations & Education, Jamestown Settlement, Yorktown Victory Center, The Jamestown-Yorktown Foundation, Williamsburg, VA 1754
Gutierrez, Mario, Chm. (V), La Raza/Galeria Posada, Sacramento, CA....176
Gutierrez, Patti, Museum Shop Mgr., Lincoln Log Cabin State Historic Site, Lerna, IL 502
Gutierrez-Solana, Carlos, Deputy Dir., New York Transit Museum, Brooklyn Heights, NY 1113
Gutknecht, Eugene, Pres. (V), Jackson County Historical Society, Black River Falls, WI 1813
Gutman, Ilene, Dir. National Programs, National Museum of Women in the Arts, Washington, DC 325
Gutman, Richard J.S., Cur., Culinary Arts Museum, Providence, RI.......................1493
Gutowski, Arlene, Museum Shop Mgr., Iris & B. Gerald Cantor Center for Visual Arts at Stanford University, Stanford, CA...213
Gutowski, Robert, Dir. Public Programs, Morris Arboretum of the University of Pennsylvania, Philadelphia, PA.............1456
Gutterman, Carole, Assoc. Cur. Education, Norton Museum of Art, West Palm Beach, FL..............................397
Guttman, Dennis, Shop Mgr., San Francisco Botanical Garden at Strybing Arboretum, San Francisco, CA...192
Gutwein, Julie, Pres., White County Historical Society Museum, Monticello, IN 557
Guy, Charles, Chm. Bd., West Tennessee Regional Art Center, Humboldt, TN......1555
Guy, John, Pres. APVA Preservation Virginia, Richmond, VA 1736
Guy, John H., IV, Pres. (V), Bacon's Castle, Surry County, VA......................1749
Guy, John H., IV, Pres. (V), Cape Henry Lighthouse, Virginia Beach, VA 1751
Guy, John H., IV, Pres. (V), Isle of Wight Courthouse, Smithfield, VA...................1745
Guy, Leslie, Conservator & Cur. Collections, The African American Museum in Philadelphia, Philadelphia, PA...1449
Guy, Louis, Pres. (V), Norfolk Historical Society, Norfolk, VA 1731
Guyaux, Joseph, Bd. Chm., Carnegie Museum of Natural History, Pittsburgh, PA 1464
Guyon, Angie, Office Mgr., The Wyoming Dinosaur Center, Thermopolis, WY 1866
Guyton, Dick, Exec. Dir., Elvis Presley Birthplace and Museum, Tupelo, MS......917
Guzman, Aaron, Planetarium Coord., Don Harrington Discovery Center, Amarillo, TX 1578
Guzman, Antonio, Dir. Human Resources, United States Holocaust Memorial Museum, Washington, DC 332
Guzman, Juana, Vice Pres., National Museum of Mexican Art, Chicago, IL 484
Gwartney, Richard, Exec. Dir., Alexandria Museum of Art, Alexandria, LA 665
Gwyn, Brenda, Pres. (V), Smyth County Museum, Marion, VA...........................1724
Gwynne, Tom, Vice Pres. Programs, Cradle of Aviation Museum, Garden City, NY 1135
Gyllenhaal, C. Edward, Cur., Glencairn Museum: Academy of the New Church, Bryn Athyn, PA 1415
Gyorfy, Jim, Co Dir., Collectors' Corner Museum, Idaho Falls, ID 460
Gyorfy, Nida, Co Dir., Collectors' Corner Museum, Idaho Falls, ID 460
Gyuk, Dr. Geza, Dir. Astronomy, Adler Planetarium & Astronomy Museum, Chicago, IL 476

H

Ha, Nhan, Security, Mingei International Museum, Escondido, CA........................111
Ha, Nhan, Security, Mingei International Museum, San Diego, CA 180
Ha, Paul, Dir., Contemporary Art Museum St. Louis, Saint Louis, MO.......946
Haag, Angela, Researcher, Central Nevada Museum, Tonopah, NV............1010
Haag, Laurie B., Vice Pres. & C.O.O., The Museum of Flight, Seattle, WA......1781
Haag, Lewetta, Dir., Mulberry Phosphate Museum, Mulberry, FL 369
Haak, Dr. Bill, Museum Mgr., Gila County Historical Museum, Globe, AZ.....44
Haak, Charles G., Asst. Cur. & Archivist, World Erotic Art Museum, Miami Beach, FL...368
Haakanson, Sven, Jr., C.E.O., Alutiiq Museum and Archaeological Repository, Kodiak, AK............................33
Haake, Adrienne, Asst. Cur., National Silk Art Museum, Weston, MO 955
Haake, Susan M., Cur., Lincoln Home National Historic Site, Springfield, IL.....521
Haan, Ruth, Vice Pres., Butler County Historical Society, Allison, IA 572
Haarsager, Jim, Maintenance Supvr., Seattle Asian Art Museum, Seattle, WA 1783
Haas, Frank, Cur. Horticulture, Cheyenne Mountain Zoological Park, Colorado Springs, CO 233
Haas, Gordon, Cur. Ichthyology, University of Alaska Museum of the North, Fairbanks, AK 30
Haas, Jean, Pres. (V), Le Sueur Museum, Le Sueur, MN 881
Haas, JoAnna, C.E.O. & Dir., Louisville Science Center, Louisville, KY...............655
Haas, Julie, Dir. College Information, Nerman Museum of Contemporary Art, Overland Park, KS.........................630
Haas, Kara, Dir. Exhibits & Public Programs, Kalamazoo Nature Center, Inc., Kalamazoo, MI...............................847
Haas, Nicole, Mktg. Communications Mgr., Heard Museum, Phoenix, AZ...........50
Haas, Pat, Vice Pres., Westminster Historical Society, Westminster, VT 1694
Haas, Ruth, Dir., Cape Fear Museum of History and Science, Wilmington, NC ..1271
Haas, Steven, Pres., Gunn Memorial Library and Museum, Washington, CT ...298
Haase, Jennifer, Education Cur., Tulsa Zoo & Living Museum, Tulsa, OK 1380
Haase, Kris, Pres. (V), Museum of Religious Arts, Logan, IA 592
Haase, William, Sr. Vice Pres., National Baseball Hall of Fame and Museum, Inc., Cooperstown, NY 1123
Haase, Ynez, Research Librarian, Fillmore Historical Museum, Inc., Fillmore, CA 113
Habelman, Carolyn, Chm. Bd. Trustees, Monroe County Local History Room & Library, Sparta, WI 1845
Haberman, Lise, Office Mgr., The Renaissance Society at The University of Chicago, Chicago, IL...........................486
Haberman, Patty, Cur., Mesa Contemporary Arts, Mesa, AZ..................46
Habermann, Doug, State Parks Mgr. Region 5, Chief Plenty Coups Museum, Pryor, MT 971
Habes, Scott, Dir., The Picker Art Gallery, Hamilton, NY 1140
Habif, Gail, Coord. Patron Rels., Michael C. Carlos Museum, Atlanta, GA.............407
Haboush Plunkett, Stephanie, Deputy Dir. & Chief Cur., Norman Rockwell Museum, Stockbridge, MA 810
Hachmeister, John, Dir., Garden of Eden and Cabin Home, Lucas, KS 624
Hack, Francoise, Registrar, John and Mable Ringling Museum of Art, Sarasota, FL..387
Hack, Janice, Exec. Dir., Lake Forest-Lake Bluff Historical Society, Lake Forest, IL 502
Hack, Sheryl, Dir., Nathan Hale Homestead Museum, Coventry, CT.........270
Hack, Sheryl N., Exec. Dir., Connecticut Landmarks, Hartford, CT 278
Hack, Steve, Membership Coord., Museum of Fine Arts of St. Petersburg, Florida, Saint Petersburg, FL...384
Hackbarth, Karl, Operations Mgr., Bldgs. & Grounds Mgr., Milwaukee County Zoological Gardens, Milwaukee, WI.....1835
Hacker, Christine, Museum Shop Mgr., Princeton University Art Museum, Princeton, NJ 1058
Hackett, Fran, Public Rels. Mgr., New York Aquarium, Brooklyn, NY 1112
Hackett, Richard, C.E.O., The Children's Museum of Memphis, Memphis, TN 1561
Hackett, Richard C., Pres. & C.E.O., Wonders: Memphis International Cultural Series, Memphis, TN 1565
Hackett, Vera, Treas., Fox Island Historical Society, Fox Island, WA........1766
Hacking, Mary, Vice Pres. Visitor Experience, Denver Museum of Nature & Science, Denver, CO...............239
Hackney, Drew, Educator, Imagination Station Science Museum, Wilson, NC...1272

H–*Continued*

Hackney, Rod, Public Rels. Mgr., North Carolina Zoological Park, Asheboro, NC....1231
Hadaway, Sandra S., Admin., Telfair Museum of Art, Savannah, GA....435
Haddad Ikonomopoulos, Marcia, Dir., Kehila Kedosha Janina Synagogue & Museum, New York, NY....1171
Haddad, Tom, Asst. Dir. Facilities & Collections, Mayborn Museum Complex, Waco, TX....1655
Haddix, Linda, Customer Service, MacKenzie Environmental Education Center, Poynette, WI....1841
Hadfield, Roxanne, Administration Coord., Frye Art Museum, Seattle, WA....1780
Hadland, Curt, Exhibits Coord., Bell Museum of Natural History, Minneapolis, MN....884
Hadley, Craig, Collections Mgr., Wright Museum of Art, Beloit College, Beloit, WI....1813
Hadley, Diana, Dir. Ethnohistorical Research, Arizona State Museum, Tucson, AZ....59
Hadley, Jennifer, Registrar, Museum of Church History and Art, Salt Lake City, UT....1670
Hadley, Richard, Dir., Abby Aldrich Rockefeller Folk Art Museum, Williamsburg, VA....1753
Hadley, Richard, Dir. Exhibitions, Abby Aldrich Rockefeller Folk Art Museum, Williamsburg, VA....1753
Hadley, Richard, Dir., Bassett Hall, Williamsburg, VA....1754
Hadley, Richard, Dir., DeWitt Wallace Decorative Arts Museum, Williamsburg, VA....1754
Hadley, Richard J., Exhibition Design & Production, DeWitt Wallace Decorative Arts Museum, Williamsburg, VA....1754
Hadly, Joan, Sr. Vice Pres. Advancement, Museum of Science, Boston, MA....762
Haefner, Cathy, Treas., Lowell Area Historical Museum, Lowell, MI....850
Haeg, Frank, Bd. Chm. (V), Luther Burbank Home & Gardens, Santa Rosa, CA....208
Haertel, Paul F., Exec. Vice Pres., Wendell Gilley Museum, Southwest Harbor, ME....712
Haertlien, Jeffrey, Museum Shop Mgr., Mid-Continent Railway Museum, North Freedom, WI....1838
Hafen, Eric, Artistic Dir. Bickford Theatre, The Morris Museum, Morristown, NJ....1050
Hafen, Lyman, Museum Shop Mgr., Cedar Breaks National Monument, Cedar City, UT....1660
Hafen, Lyman, Zion Natural History Assoc., Zion Human History Museum, Springdale, UT....1673
Hafertepe, Dr. Ken, Assoc. Prof., Interim Chm. Museum Studies & Dir. Academic Programs, Mayborn Museum Complex, Waco, TX....1655
Haffar, Nadra E., Cur. Education, Nora Eccles Harrison Museum of Art, Logan, UT....1664
Haffenreffer Moran, Kristen, Special Events, Providence Children's Museum, Providence, RI....1495
Hafner, Dr. Mark, Cur. Animals, Museum of Natural Science, Baton Rouge, LA....668
Hagaman, Wally, Cur. Firehouse Museum, Nevada County Historical Society, Inc., Nevada City, CA....151
Hagan, Marylee, Exec. Dir., Paul Dresser Memorial Birthplace, Terre Haute, IN....567
Hagan, Marylee, C.E.O. & Exec. Dir., Vigo County Historical Museum, Terre Haute, IN....568
Hagan-Michel, Ann, Exec. Dir., Ashland, The Henry Clay Estate, Lexington, KY....651
Hagar Krusell, Cynthia, Pres. (V), Historic 1699 Winslow House, Marshfield, MA....789
Hagar, Mitzy, Pres. (V), Frontier Village Association, Inc., Jamestown, ND....1285
Hagarty, Sarah, Dir. Museum, Camden County Historical Society, Camden, NJ....1034
Hagberg, Betty S., Mgr. Library Svcs., Deere & Company, Administrative Center, Moline, IL....505
Hagedorn, Dan, Sr. Cur., The Museum of Flight, Seattle, WA....1781
Hageman, Ken, Park Mgr., Admiralty Head Lighthouse, Coupeville, WA....1763
Hagen, Charlie, Dir. Facilities, Colorado Springs Fine Arts Center (Taylor Museum), Colorado Springs, CO....233
Hagen, Corey, Education & Devel. Asst., The Chattanooga Nature Center, Chattanooga, TN....1547
Hagen, Harold, C.E.O., Steamtown National Historic Site, Scranton, PA....1473
Hagen, John, Art Dir., Alaska Indian Arts, Inc., Haines, AK....31
Hagen, Sue, Bookkeeping, Saginaw Art Museum, Saginaw, MI....863
Hagenah, William J., Chm. Bd. (V), Chicago Botanic Garden, Glencoe, IL....497
Hager, Jerri, Devel. & Public Rels., Maritime Museum at Historic Coast Guard Station, Saint Simons Island, GA....432
Hager, Louise, Staff, Lesueur County Historical Museum-Chapter 1, Elysian, MN....876
Hager, Michael, Preparator, Mulvane Art Museum, Topeka, KS....636
Hager, Dr. Michael W., Pres. & C.E.O., San Diego Natural History Museum, San Diego, CA....184
Hager, Tucker, Dir. Retail Operations, Please Touch Museum, Philadelphia, PA....1460
Hagerbaumer, Ruby, Curatorial Coord., Joslyn Art Museum, Omaha, NE....995
Hagerman, Kelly, Devel., Fort Wayne Children's Zoo, Fort Wayne, IN....541
Hagerman, Nancy, Museum Shop Mgr., Schiele Museum of Natural History and Lynn Planetarium, Gastonia, NC....1247
Hagerty, John B., Chm., Patriots Point Naval and Maritime Museum, Mount Pleasant, SC....1519
Hagge, Greg, Dir. & Cur., Fort Lewis Military Museum, Fort Lewis, WA....1766
Hagle, John, Vice Pres., Beaufort Historic Site, Beaufort, NC....1234
Hagle, Polly, Chm. (V), Beaufort Historic Site, Beaufort, NC....1234
Hagler, Jane, Volunteer Coord., The Quincy Museum, Quincy, IL....514
Haglich, Gary, Sands Pt. Preserve Supvr., Nassau County, Division of Museum Services, Department of Recreation, Parks & Museums, East Meadow, NY....1130
Haglund, Kris, Archivist & Dept. Chair, Denver Museum of Nature & Science, Denver, CO....239
Hagne, Martin, Exec. Dir., Lower Rio Grande Valley Nature Center, Weslaco, TX....1656
Hagood, Anne W., Chm., Barnwell County Museum, Barnwell, SC....1500
Hague, Cara, Horticulturist I, Civic Garden Center of Greater Cincinnati, Cincinnati, OH....1305
Hague, Ronn, Dir., Pearl River Community College Museum, Poplarville, MS....916
Hahn, Alex, Sec. & Office Coord. SUArt Galleries - Syracuse University, Syracuse, NY....1219
Hahn, Andrew, C.E.O., Campbell House Museum, Saint Louis, MO....945
Hahn, Cheryl H., Dir., Larson Museum and Gallery, Yakima, WA....1795
Hahn, Claudia, Museum Shop Mgr., Historic Oakland Cemetery, Atlanta, GA....405
Hahn, David, Asst. Dir. & Cur., Virginia Aviation Museum, Richmond International Airport, VA....1743
Hahn, Elizabeth, Librarian, American Numismatic Society, New York, NY....1163
Hahn, Jim, CFRE, Dir. Devel. & Mktg., Waukesha County Museum, Waukesha, WI....1849
Hahn, Mimi, Dir. Mktg., Monterey Bay Aquarium, Monterey, CA....148
Hahn, Patricia A., Chm. (V), Erlanger Historical Society, Erlanger, KY....645
Hahn, Richard, C.A.P., Dir., Catoctin Wildlife Preserve & Zoo, Thurmont, MD....748
Hahn, Tom, Pres., Arlington Heights Historical Museum, Arlington Heights, IL....468
Hahs, Ellen, Cur. Education, Rosemary Berkel and Harry L. Crisp II Museum, Cape Girardeau, MO....922
Hahscom, Eva, Admissions Asst., Mingei International Museum, Escondido, CA....111
Hai Chang, Willow, Dir., China Institute Gallery, China Institute In America, New York, NY....1166
Haidet, Mark, Devel. Officer, Minnesota Historical Society, Saint Paul, MN....895
Haifley, Julie, Registrar, National Museum of African Art, Smithsonian Institution, Washington, DC....324
Haigh, Abby, Museum Shop Mgr., James & Meryl Hearst Center for the Arts and Hearst Sculpture Garden, Cedar Falls, IA....576
Haigh, Donnie, Co Dir. & Park Naturalist, El Dorado Nature Center, Long Beach, CA....131
Haigh, Katie, Chief Registrar IMA - Indianapolis Museum of Art, Indianapolis, IN....548
Haight, Pete, Chm. (V), Winnebago Area Museum, Winnebago, MN....902
Haigler, Shunzyu, Dir. Devel., The Stickley Museum at Craftsman Farms, Morris Plains, NJ....1049
Hail, Barbara A., Cur. Emerita, Haffenreffer Museum of Anthropology, Brown University, Providence, RI....1494
Hail, Noah, Physical Plant, Seminole Nation Museum, Wewoka, OK....1381
Hailey, Dabney, Cur. Paintings, Sculpture & Photography, Davis Museum and Cultural Center, Wellesley, MA....814
Hailey, Denny, Building & Grounds Supt., North Carolina Maritime Museum, Beaufort, NC....1234
Haines, Ann, Operations Coord. & Museum Shop Mgr., Hoover Historical Center, North Canton, OH....1336
Haines, Carol, Public Rels., Concord Museum, Concord, MA....771
Haines, Jean, Museum Shop Mgr., American Clock and Watch Museum, Inc., Bristol, CT....268

H–*Continued*

Hall, Lisa, Vice Pres., Marcella Sembrich Opera Museum, Bolton Landing, NY....1106
Hall, Lisa J., C.E.O., Aiken Thoroughbred Racing Hall of Fame and Museum, Aiken, SC 1499
Hall, Marc, Museum Shop Mgr., The Los Angeles County Arboretum & Botanic Garden, Arcadia, CA 88
Hall, Marci, Dir. Mktg & Communications, Fort Ticonderoga, Ticonderoga, NY 1221
Hall, Marlene, Dir. & C.E.O., Conway Homestead and Cramer Museum, Camden, ME...696
Hall, Mary, Mgr. Education, Utica Zoo, Utica, NY..1223
Hall, Mary Anne, Museum Educator, The Slater Memorial Museum - Norwich Free Academy, Norwich, CT 291
Hall, Melissa, Coord. Education, Watkins Woolen Mill State Historic Site & Park, Lawson, MO 938
Hall, Michael D., C.E.O. & Exec. Dir., Gold Coast Railroad Museum, Inc., Miami, FL...365
Hall, Michael S., C.E.O. & Pres., Wings of Eagles Discovery Center, Horseheads, NY 1142
Hall, Mike, Pres., Pennsbury Manor, Morrisville, PA 1446
Hall, Mrs. Nancy, C.E.O., Pres. (V) Chm. Old Jail Museum Commission, Franklin County Old Jail Museum, Winchester, TN.....................................1575
Hall, Pamela, Chm. (V), Seacoast Science Center, Rye, NH.........................1028
Hall, Patti, Dir., Alabama Gulf Coast Zoo, Gulf Shores, AL...............................13
Hall, Perry, Volunteer Coord., University of California Botanical Garden, Berkeley, CA 94
Hall, Philip, Preparator, Grey Art Gallery, New York University Art Collection, New York, NY 1169
Hall, Richard, Exhibition Preparator, Palmer Museum of Art, The Pennsylvania State University, University Park, PA..............................1478
Hall, Robert, Asst. Dir. Education, Anacostia Community Museum, Washington, DC...314
Hall, Sarah, Dir. Curatorial Affairs, The Frick Art & Historical Center, Pittsburgh, PA 1466
Hall, Stan, C.E.O., Jacqueline Casey Hudgens Center for the Arts, Duluth, GA..417
Hall, Stan, Pres. (V), Oklahoma Railway Museum, Oklahoma City, OK 1373
Hall, Steve, Pres., Piedmont Environmental Center, High Point, NC.1252
Hall, Suzanne D., Chief Communications Officer, Virginia Museum of Fine Arts, Richmond, VA 1742
Hall, Taffey, Archivist, Southern Baptist Historical Library and Archives, Nashville, TN..1569
Hall, Thom, Registrar, The Arkansas Arts Center, Little Rock, AR...............................76
Hall, Dr. Thomas B., III, Pres. (V), Friends of Arrow Rock, Inc., Arrow Rock, MO 920
Hall, Wanda B., Asst. Archivist, Lovely Lane Museum and Archives, Baltimore, MD..723
Hall Weaver, Sarah, Coord. Grants & Exhibits, National Museum of Dance & Hall of Fame, Saratoga Springs, NY..1207
Halladay, Reed, Chm., Pasadena Museum of California Art, Pasadena, CA 163
Hallaran, Kevin, Archivist, Riverside Metropolitan Museum, Riverside, CA.....173
Hallatt, Kim, Asst. Dir. for Admin., Memorial Art Gallery of the University of Rochester, Rochester, NY..1202
Hallberg, Sara, Dir. Education, The Hyde Collection, Glens Falls, NY 1138
Halle, Cynthia Von, Supvr., Joshua Tree National Park, Oasis Visitor Center, Twentynine Palms, CA...........................219
Halle, Richard, Pres., Upham Mansion, Marshfield, WI..1830
Haller, Steve, Sr. Dir. Collections, Indiana Historical Society, Indianapolis, IN 548
Hallett, Dale, Interpretive Resource Tech., First Missouri State Capitol-State Historic Site, Saint Charles, MO 943
Hallett, Megan, Cur. Education, Utah Museum of Fine Arts, Salt Lake City, UT 1671
Hallett, Paul, Operations Mgr., Conway Scenic Railroad, Inc., North Conway, NH..1025
Hallick, Dr. Lesley M., Pres., Pacific University Museum, Forest Grove, OR.1390
Halliday, Betsy, Sales Shop Mgr., Brookfield Craft Center, Brookfield, CT 268
Halliday, Sheri, Museum Shop Mgr., Racine Zoological Society, Racine, WI.1843
Hallis, Jimmie, Archivist, 82nd Airborne Division War Memorial Museum, Fort Bragg, NC..1246
Hallman, Jane, Volunteer, Downieville Museum, Downieville, CA......................109
Hallman, Lee, Cur., Archivist & Registrar, Museum of Indian Culture, Allentown, PA.......................................1408
Hallman, Tim, Dir. Mktg. & Communications, Asian Art Museum of San Francisco, Chong-Moon Lee Center for Asian Art and Culture, San Francisco, CA 186
Hallock, Dale, Pres. (V), Gilbert Historical Museum, Gilbert, AZ 43
Hallock, Robert, C.E.O., Pres. (V) & Museum Shop Mgr., Bronck Museum, Coxsackie, NY 1126
Hallowell, John, Pres. Colonial Williamsburg Hospitality Group, Colonial Williamsburg, Williamsburg, VA 1754
Hall-Patton, Mark, Museum Admin., Clark County Museum, Henderson, NV..1004
Hall-Patton, Mark P., Admin., Howard W. Cannon Aviation Museum, Las Vegas, NV 1005
Hallquist, Carol, Chm., Kansas City Zoo, Kansas City, MO 933
Hallquist, Denise, Dir. Mktg., Joslyn Art Museum, Omaha, NE 995
Halls, Ray K., Mgr. Exhibits, Museum of Church History and Art, Salt Lake City, UT 1670
Hallstrom, David, Chm. (V), Goodhue County Historical Society, Red Wing, MN...890
Hallstrom, Jerry, Vice Pres., Timm House Historic Site, New Holstein, WI...........1838
Hallterberg, Peggy, Devel. & Community Outreach, Atomic Testing Museum, Las Vegas, NV 1004
Hally, Dr. D.J., Cur. Archaeology, Georgia Museum of Natural History, Athens, GA 400
Halman, Doug, Dir. Finance, Indianapolis Art Center, Indianapolis, IN......................549
Halpin, Jim, Pres., Northborough Historical Society, Inc., Northborough, MA 797
Halpin, Pat, Pres. (V), Pioneers, Trail Drivers and Texas Rangers Memorial Museum, San Antonio, TX 1644
Halpin, Pat, Chm. (V), Texas Transportation Museum, San Antonio, TX 1646
Halstead, Aiesha, Coord. Exhibitions Planning, Virginia Museum of Fine Arts, Richmond, VA 1742
Halstead, Jeff, Exhibit Specialist, Gulf Islands National Seashore, Gulf Breeze, FL 352
Halsted, Everett, Dir., Watson's Grocery Store Museum, State Center, IA 600
Halteman, Ellen L., Dir. Collections, California State Railroad Museum, Sacramento, CA...175
Halteman, Ellen L., Dir. Collections, Old Sacramento State Historic Park, Old Sacramento, CA...157
Halteman, Susan, Cur., The Harold F. Pitcairn Wings of Freedom Aviation Museum, Horsham, PA 1434
Halunen, Kristin, Registrar, Museum of History & Industry (MOHAI), Seattle, WA 1782
Halver, Karen, Asst. to Pres., The National Sporting Library, Middleburg, VA 1725
Halverson, Laura A., Registrar, University of Wisconsin Zoological Museum, Madison, WI..............................1828
Halvey, Kathie, Regent, The Madam Brett Homestead, Beacon, NY..............1103
Halvorson, Cleta, Chm. (V), Air Force Armament Museum, Eglin Air Force Base, FL...345
Haly, Marbella, Dir. Finance & Admin., The Trustees of Reservations, Beverly, MA 757
Ham, David, Pres. (V), The National Border Patrol Museum and Memorial Library, El Paso, TX 1605
Ham, Eugene, Dir., Fayetteville Lincoln County Museum and Civic Center, Fayetteville, TN...................................1551
Ham, Hal, Dir., John E. Conner Museum, Kingsville, TX 1626
Hambleton, Judy, Dir. Education, Newport Art Museum & Art Association, Newport, RI.......................1491
Hamblin, Diane, Education & Exhibits, Chenango County Historical Society Museum, Norwich, NY 1187
Hambourg, Maria Morris, Cur. in Charge, Photographs, The Metropolitan Museum of Art, New York, NY............1172
Hambrecht, Sarah, Pres. (V), Asian Art Museum of San Francisco, Chong-Moon Lee Center for Asian Art and Culture, San Francisco, CA 186
Hambrick, Kathe, Dir., River Road African American Museum, Donaldsonville, LA 670
Hambuechen, W. Garrett, C.O.O., Palm Beach Zoo, West Palm Beach, FL...........397
Hamby, Elaine, Cur., Mendocino County Museum, Willits, CA.............................224
Hamby, Thomas L., Chm., Birmingham Museum of Art, Birmingham, AL 5
Hamdan, Leila, Registrar, National Ornamental Metal Museum, Memphis, TN 1564
Hamer, Fritz, Cur. History, South Carolina State Museum, Columbia, SC.1510
Hamer, Gail, Dir. Business Operations, Dayton History at Carillon Park, Dayton, OH..1316
Hamil, Sherrie, Cur. Education, Alabama Department of Archives & History, Montgomery, AL 19
Hamilton, Amy, 3rd Vice Pres., Historic Mobile Preservation Society, Mobile, AL 17

H–*Continued*

H–*Continued*

Harrill, Norman, Vice Pres., The Southern Appalachian Radio Museum, Asheville, NC 1233
Harrill, Raymond, Pres. (V), The Museum of Automobiles, Morrilton, AR 79
Harrington, Charles, Pres. (V), Fort Ontario State Historic Site, Oswego, NY 1191
Harrington, Dennis, Trustee, Railroad Museum of Long Island, Riverhead, NY 1200
Harrington, Gary, Dir., Ironwood Area Historical Museum, Ironwood, MI 846
Harrington, Karen, Visitor Svcs., The Bennington Museum, Bennington, VT ..1676
Harrington, Katie, Dir., Delta Cultural Center, Helena, AR 73
Harrington, Page, Exec. Dir., Sewall-Belmont House and Museum, Washington, DC 329
Harrington, Rob, Chm., Levine Museum of the New South, Charlotte, NC 1239
Harris, Adam Duncan, Ph.D., Cur. Art, National Museum of Wildlife Art, Jackson, WY 1860
Harris, Amanda, Educator, Headley-Whitney Museum, Lexington, KY 652
Harris, Amy S., Dir., University of Michigan Exhibit Museum of Natural History, Ann Arbor, MI 823
Harris, Ann, Financial Dir., The Library of Virginia, Richmond, VA 1738
Harris, Dr. Art, Dir. Laboratory of Environmental Biology, Centennial Museum and Chihuahuan Desert Gardens, El Paso, TX 1603
Harris, Avaline, Treas., Christian County Historical Society and Museum, Ozark, MO 941
Harris, Bert, Pres. (V), The Museum of East Alabama, Opelika, AL 21
Harris, Beth, Cur. Education, Kemper Museum of Contemporary Art, Kansas City, MO 934
Harris, Brad, Pres. (V), Smithtown Historical Society, Smithtown, NY 1212
Harris, Bruce, Eastern National Bookstore, Castillo de San Marcos National Monument, Saint Augustine, FL 381
Harris, Bruce, Bookstore Mgr., Fort Matanzas National Monument, Saint Augustine, FL 381
Harris, Carol, Mgr. Historical Programs, Maymont, Richmond, VA 1739
Harris, Caroline, Cur. Education, Princeton University Art Museum, Princeton, NJ 1058
Harris, Carter, Cur., The National Watch & Clock Museum, Columbia, PA 1418
Harris, Celia, Pres. (V), Stone House Gallery, Fredonia, KS 613
Harris, Cindy, Park Mgr., Niagara Gorge Discovery Center, Niagara Falls, NY 1185
Harris, Don, City Seattle Liaison, Dept. Parks & Recreation, University of Washington Botanic Garden, Seattle, WA 1784
Harris, Donna, Dir., Ralls Historical Museum, Ralls, TX 1640
Harris, Dorothy, Park Specialist, Highlands Hammock State Park/Civilian Conservation Corps Museum, Sebring, FL 388
Harris, Ed, Pres., Belhaven Memorial Museum, Inc., Belhaven, NC 1235
Harris, Edward J., Vice Pres. Administration, American Antiquarian Society, Worcester, MA 818
Harris, Elizabeth, Mgr. Wine Auction, The High Museum of Art, Atlanta, GA...405
Harris, Florence E., Pres. (V) & Dir., Judith Basin County Museum, Stanford, MT 972
Harris, Frank, Pres., Collingwood Library and Museum on Americanism, Alexandria, VA 1696
Harris, Gina, Membership Coord. & Facility Rentals, Northwest Museum of Arts & Culture (Eastern Washington State Historical Society), Spokane, WA 1787
Harris, Gloria, Museum Shop Mgr., Pennsylvania Lumber Museum, Galeton, PA 1426
Harris, Gregory, Vice Pres. Devel., The Rock and Roll Hall of Fame and Museum, Cleveland, OH 1310
Harris, Hugh, Dir. Security, Lafayette College Art Galleries, Williams Center for the Arts, Easton, PA 1421
Harris, Dr. James, Chm. (V), Museum of Idaho, Idaho Falls, ID 460
Harris, J.C., Gen. Mgr. & Security, World Erotic Art Museum, Miami Beach, FL....368
Harris, Jenn, Asst. Dir. Devel. & Mktg., Danforth Museum of Art, Framingham, MA 778
Harris, Jessica, Dir. Exhibition & Collections, Dr Pepper Museum and Free Enterprise Institute, Waco, TX 1654
Harris, Jim, Dir., Lea County Museum, Lovington, NM 1083
Harris, Joe, Chm. (V), Black Hills Museum of Natural History, Hill City, SD 1532
Harris, Joe, Exec. Dir., National Society of the Sons of the American Revolution, Louisville, KY 657
Harris, Judith A., Assoc. Prof. Emeritus, Natural History, University of Colorado Museum of Natural History, Boulder, CO 230
Harris, Julie, Exec. Dir., River Discovery Center, Paducah, KY 661
Harris, Juliette, Editor International Review of African American Art, Hampton University Museum, Hampton, VA 1716
Harris, Julius, Weekend Coord., Nassau County Museum of Art, Roslyn Harbor, NY 1204
Harris, Kathryn M., Dir. Library Svcs., Abraham Lincoln Presidential Library & Museum, Springfield, IL 520
Harris, Lane, Interpretive Ranger, Wormsloe State Historic Site, Savannah, GA 436
Harris, Lani, Operations Mgr., Louisiana Art & Science Museum - Irene W. Pennington Planetarium, Baton Rouge, LA 667
Harris, Mac R., Dir., State Agricultural Heritage Museum, Brookings, SD 1527
Harris, Mark W., Assoc. Dir., University of Nebraska State Museum, Lincoln, NE 991
Harris, Marva H., Pres. & C.E.O., August Wilson Center for African American Culture, Pittsburgh, PA 1464
Harris, Michael, Consulting Cur. African American Art, The High Museum of Art, Atlanta, GA 405
Harris, Monte, Adult Programs Asst., Rogers Historical Museum, Rogers, AR 83
Harris, Nicole, Bulletin Editor, Whitley County Historical Museum, Columbia City, IN 536
Harris, Patti, Dir. Education, Lindsay Wildlife Museum, Walnut Creek, CA....222
Harris, Peggy, Chm. (V), Decorative Arts Collection, Inc. Museum of Decorative Painting, Atlanta, GA 404
Harris, Penny, Chm., Center For Maine Contemporary Art, Rockport, ME 710
Harris, Ralph, Pres., Railroad Museum of New England, Thomaston, CT 297
Harris, Rene, Asst. Dir., Palace of the Governors/New Mexico History Museum, Santa Fe, NM 1090
Harris, Richie, Chm. (V), H.E.A.R.T.S. Veterans Museum of Texas, Huntsville, TX 1623
Harris, Rick, Supt., Chamizal National Memorial, El Paso, TX 1604
Harris, Sandra, Deputy Dir., Phoebe Apperson Hearst Museum of Anthropology, Berkeley, CA 93
Harris, Scott H., Dir., New Market Battlefield State Historical Park, New Market, VA 1727
Harris, Shannon, Dir., Museum of the Gulf Coast, Port Arthur, TX 1639
Harris, Shawnya, Dir., North Carolina A&T State University Galleries, Greensboro, NC 1249
Harris, Sue, Dir. Education & Programs, Stark Museum of Art, Orange, TX 1636
Harris, Tammy, Coord. Special Events, Hershey Gardens, Hershey, PA 1433
Harris, Tom, Pres., Porter-Phelps-Huntington Foundation, Inc., Hadley, MA 780
Harris, William T., Sr. Vice Pres. Devel. & Mktg., California Science Center, Los Angeles, CA 134
Harris, Winona, Vice Pres., Frankfort Area Historical Museum, West Frankfort, IL 527
harrisburg, halley k., Co. Chm., Children's Museum of Manhattan, New York, NY 1165
Harris-Featherstone, LaNeysa, Asst. Mgr., Russell C. Davis Planetarium, Jackson, MS 911
Harris-Fernandez, Al, Dir., Sioux City Art Center, Sioux City, IA 599
Harrison, Al, Pres., National Oregon/California Trail Center, Montpelier, ID 462
Harrison, Ann, Volunteer Coord., Maine Maritime Museum, Bath, ME 693
Harrison, Arioth, Dir. Special Events, Decatur House Museum, Washington, DC 316
Harrison, Barbara, Museum Shop Mgr., Brookgreen Gardens, Murrells Inlet, SC 1519
Harrison, Cliff, Dir. Retail Sales, Saint Louis Art Museum, Saint Louis, MO 950
Harrison, Glenn, Chm. Trust (V), Linn County Historical Museum and Moyer House, Brownsville, OR 1385
Harrison, Jack, Security, Paul and Lulu Hilliard University Art Museum, University of Louisiana at Lafayette, Lafayette, LA 673
Harrison, Jefferson, Chief Cur. & Acting Cur. American and Contemporary Art, Chrysler Museum of Art, Norfolk, VA..1729
Harrison, Mr. John, Chm. (V), Mel Fisher Maritime Heritage Society, Key West, FL 359
Harrison, Keith, Chm. (V), Cincinnati Museum Center at Union Terminal, Cincinnati, OH 1304
Harrison, Ken, Dir. Finance, Museum of Discovery: Arkansas Museum of Science and History, Little Rock, AR 78
Harrison, Liz, Chm. (V), Bee Family Centennial Farm Museum, Fort Collins, CO 245
Harrison, Loretta, C.E.O., Oregon Coast History Center, Newport, OR 1396
Harrison, Lucy, Treas., Mabel Hartzell Historical Home, Alliance, OH 1293

H–*Continued*

Harrison, Megan, Dir. Corporate Giving, Museum of Nature & Science, Dallas, TX 1599
Harrison, Myra, Supt., Frederick Law Olmsted National Historic Site, Brookline, MA 765
Harrison, Myra, Supt., John Fitzgerald Kennedy National Historic Site, Brookline, MA 765
Harrison, Myra, Supt., Longfellow National Historic Site, Cambridge, MA 768
Harrison, Natasha, Asst. Exec. Dir., Norman Bird Sanctuary, Middletown, RI 1489
Harrison Reilly, Anthea, Acquisition Librarian, The Boston Athenaeum, Boston, MA 758
Harrison, Rob, Controller, Skirball Cultural Center, Los Angeles, CA 142
Harrison, Robert, Chm. (V), Abrons Arts Center/Henry Street Settlement, New York, NY 1161
Harrison, Shelia, Dir. Mktg. & Public Rels., Nauticus, Norfolk, VA 1730
Harrison, Simon, Chm. (V), Descanso Gardens Guild, Inc., La Canada Flintridge, CA 125
Harrison, Stephen A., Cur. Decorative Art & Design, The Cleveland Museum of Art, Cleveland, OH 1308
Harrison, Susan, Dir. Exhibits & Theaters, Adler Planetarium & Astronomy Museum, Chicago, IL 476
Harrison, Susan B., Pres., The Ebenezer Maxwell Mansion, Inc., Philadelphia, PA 1452
Harrison, Suzanne, Museum Shop Mgr., The Museum of Fine Arts, Houston, Houston, TX 1622
Harrison, Tommy, Chm. (V), Duncan Museum & Art Gallery, Greenville, KY 648
Harrity, Gail M., C.O.O. & Interim C.E.O., Philadelphia Museum of Art, Philadelphia, PA 1459
Harrold, Dr. Christopher, Dir. Conservation Research, Monterey Bay Aquarium, Monterey, CA 148
Harrower, David, Vice Chm., Richard Wall House Museum, Elkins Park, PA ..1422
Harry, Travis, Asst. Site Mgr., B&O Railroad Museum: Ellicott City Station, Ellicott City, MD 734
Harsanyi, Zsolt, Chm. (V), American Hungarian Foundation/Museum of the American Hungarian Foundation, New Brunswick, NJ 1051
Harsh, Del, Vice Pres., Museum of the High Plains, McCook, NE 991
Harsh, Joy, Cur. Education, Abilene Zoological Gardens, Abilene, TX 1576
Harshaw, Gail, Admin., Stone House Gallery, Fredonia, KS 613
Harshman, Meredith, Treas., National Museum of Civil War Medicine, Frederick, MD 735
Harsma, Becky, Registrar, Hamline University, Soeffker Gallery, Saint Paul, MN 894
Hart, Alice, Cur., Grand Teton National Park, Colter Bay Indian Arts Museum, Colter Bay Village, WY 1856
Hart, Ann, Pres., Wiregrass Museum of Art, Dothan, AL 10
Hart, Dee, Chm. (V) & Museum Shop Mgr., Douglas County Historical Society - Genoa Courthouse Museum, Genoa, NV 1003
Hart, Diane, Dir. Museum Registration, Williams College Museum of Art, Williamstown, MA 817
Hart, Donna, Cur., Thomas Downs House, Charlestown, IN 535
Hart, Freya K., Dir., Moses Lake Museum & Art Center, Moses Lake, WA 1772
Hart, Jane, Cur. Exhibitions, Art and Culture Center of Hollywood, Hollywood, FL 353
Hart, John, Dir. Research & Collections, New York State Museum, Albany, NY ..1096
Hart, Karen, C.E.O., Mary Ball Washington Museum & Library, Inc., Lancaster, VA 1719
Hart, Karen, Exec. Dir., Southdown Plantation House/The Terrebonne Museum, Houma, LA 672
Hart, Katherine, Assoc. Dir. & Cur. Academic Programming, Hood Museum of Art, Hanover, NH 1019
Hart, Katherine, Registrar & Collections Mgr., Hood Museum of Art, Hanover, NH 1019
Hart, Lisa, Administrative Asst., Phoebe Apperson Hearst Museum of Anthropology, Berkeley, CA 93
Hart, Lois, Pres. (V), Polson-Flathead Historical Museum, Polson, MT 970
Hart, Macy B., C.E.O. & Pres., Museum of the Southern Jewish Experience, Jackson, MS 911
Hart, Nancy, C.E.O. & Dir., Clinton County Museum, Frankfort, IN 543
Hart, Pat, Chm. (V), Ventura County Maritime Museum, Inc., Oxnard, CA 159
Hart, Paul, Exec. Dir., Tuckerton Seaport Museum, Tuckerton, NJ 1065
Hart, Redden, Financial Dir., Lowndes County Historical Society and Museum, Valdosta, GA 438
Hart, Robert L., Dir., Lane County Historical Society & Museum, Eugene, OR 1389
Hart, Shari, Museum Shop Mgr. & Dir. Mktg., Alaska Aviation Heritage Museum, Anchorage, AK 26
Hart, Sidney, Historian, National Portrait Gallery, Washington, DC 326
Hart Yellowman, Connie, Exec. Dir., Red Earth Museum, Oklahoma City, OK 1373
Harte, Larry, Chm. (V), Four Mile Historic Park, Denver, CO 240
Harte, Nancy, Museum Shop Mgr., William King Museum Center for Art and Cultural Heritage, Abingdon, VA 1695
Hartenburg, Vern J., C.E.O. & Exec. Dir., Cleveland Metroparks Outdoor Education Division, Garfield Heights, OH 1322
Harter, Christopher, Dir. Reference & Library Svcs., Amistad Research Center, Inc., New Orleans, LA 678
Harter, Dale, Cur., Reuel B. Pritchett Museum, Bridgewater, VA 1702
Hartfield, Libby, Dir., Mississippi Museum of Natural Science, Jackson, MS 910
Hartge, Ellen, Administrative Mgr., Sandy Spring Museum, Sandy Spring, MD 746
Hartge Solbert, Sharon, Dir. & Lead Teacher, Carrie Weedon Science Center, Galesville, MD 736
Harthorn, Sandy, Cur. Art, Boise Art Museum, Boise, ID 455
Harting-McChesney, Jan, Pres. (V), Bellport-Brookhaven Historical Society and Museum, Bellport, NY 1103
Hartje, Zelda, Admin., Pembina County Historical Society and Museum, Cavalier, ND 1279
Hartley, Barbara, Events Mgr., Jack Nicklaus Museum, Columbus, OH 1313
Hartley, Blair, Dir. Devel., American Folk Art Museum, New York, NY 1162
Hartley, Don, Historical Architect, Utah State Historical Society, Salt Lake City, UT 1672
Hartley, Kathryn A., Chm. (V), Friends of Hearthside, Inc., Lincoln, RI 1488
Hartley, Laura, Office Mgr., Kansas Sports Hall of Fame, Wichita, KS 638
Hartley, Pam, Vice Pres. Exhibits, Marbles Kids Museum, Raleigh, NC 1262
Hartley, Scott, Supt. & Naturalist, Weymouth Woods-Sandhills Nature Preserve Museum, Southern Pines, NC.1268
Hartline, Jane, Mktg. Mgr., Oregon Zoo, Portland, OR 1400
Hartman, Bruce, Dir., Nerman Museum of Contemporary Art, Overland Park, KS 630
Hartman, Daniel, Veterans' Memorial Hall Program Dir., The St. Louis County Historical Society, Duluth, MN 875
Hartman, Diane A., Deputy Dir. & Museum Shop Mgr., The University of Arizona Museum of Art and Archive of Visual Arts, Tucson, AZ 63
Hartman, Elizabeth, Dir. Human Resources, The Magic House, St. Louis Children's Museum, Saint Louis, MO 948
Hartman, Julia, Pres. (V), University of Alabama Arboretum, Tuscaloosa, AL 24
Hartman, Leslie, Museum Shop Mgr., Historic Sauder Village, Archbold, OH.1293
Hartman, Pat, Pres. Bd., Rawls Museum Arts, Courtland, VA 1707
Hartman, Ronald L., Cur. Prof. Botany, Rocky Mountain Herbarium, Laramie, WY 1861
Hartman, Scott, Dir. Science, The Wyoming Dinosaur Center, Thermopolis, WY 1866
Hartmann, Bonnie, Dir., Miller Art Museum, Sturgeon Bay, WI 1847
Hartmann, Brian, Membership Sec., American Jewish Historical Society, New York, NY 1162
Hartmann, Cynthia, Deputy Dir., The Bakken Library and Museum, Minneapolis, MN 884
Hartmann, Harold, Cur., Savin Rock Museum, West Haven, CT 300
Hartmann, Roger, Dir., Hartmann Model R.R. & Toy Museum, Intervale, NH 1020
Hartmond, Uli, Dir. Butterfly House & Insectarium, Museum of Life and Science, Durham, NC 1243
Hartness, Richard, Bd., Cross County Museum & Archives, Wynne, AR 86
Hartnett, Helena, Dir. Devel., Isabella Stewart Gardner Museum, Boston, MA 760
Hartnett, Patricia, Museum Shop Mgr., Fort Davis National Historic Site, Fort Davis, TX 1607
Harto, Brian E., Chm. (V), Eureka Fire Museum, Milltown, NJ 1047
Hartranft, Ellen, Supvr. Enterprise, Brookside Gardens, Wheaton, MD 750
Hartsell, Brandis, Cur. Marine & Earth, Roper Mountain Science Center, Greenville, SC 1514
Hartshorn, Gary, C.E.O. & Pres., World Forestry Center Discovery Museum, Portland, OR 1401
Hartshorn, Willis E., Dir., International Center of Photography, New York, NY.1170
Hartson, Sharman, Cur., Disciples of Christ Historical Society, Nashville, TN 1567

H–*Continued*

H–*Continued*

H–*Continued*

Heitzman, Jeff, Interpreter & V.I.P. Coord., Hot Springs National Park Visitor Center, Hot Springs, AR 74
Hejnar, Henry, Museum Shop Mgr., The Academy of Natural Sciences, Philadelphia, PA 1449
Hekkers, Jim, Mng. Dir., Monterey Bay Aquarium, Monterey, CA........................148
Helbert, Theresa, Sec., Frontier Times Museum, Bandera, TX 1585
Helbing, Michael, Chief Cur. & Head Art Committee, National Vietnam Veterans Art Museum, Chicago, IL 484
Helbling, Pat, Dir. Operations, Birch Aquarium at Scripps, Scripps Institution of Oceanography, University of California, San Diego, La Jolla, CA...126
Held, Joe, Public Rels., Winterset Art Center, Winterset, IA..............................603
Held, Michael, Chm., Center for Book Arts, New York, NY 1165
Held, Peter, Sr. Cur., Arizona State University Art Museum, Tempe, AZ 56
Held, Robin, Chief Cur., Frye Art Museum, Seattle, WA............................1780
Hele, Mary, Dir. Merchandising, Minneapolis Institute of Arts, Minneapolis, MN.....................................886
Helfant-Browning, Dorcas, Pres. Virginia Aquarium Foundation, Virginia Aquarium & Marine Science Center, Virginia Beach, VA................................1752
Helfenstein, Josef, Dir., The Menil Collection, Houston, TX 1621
Helfrich, Leonard, Pres., Fort Wayne Museum of Art, Fort Wayne, IN.............542
Helfstein, Josef, Dir., Cy Twombly Gallery, Houston, TX 1619
Helget, James, Operations Mgr., Sternberg Museum of Natural History, Hays, KS 616
Helgren, Heidi Holmes, Dir., Cannon Falls Area Historical Museum, Cannon Falls, MN 871
Heline, Frederick, Custodian, The Wilderness Center Inc., Wilmot, OH.....1351
Helland, Mary, Pres. (V) & Museum Shop Mgr., Valley County Pioneer Museum, Glasgow, MT.................................964
Helland, Rebecca A., Collections Mgr., Billings Farm & Museum, Woodstock, VT 1695
Hellenthal, Barbara J., Cur., Museum of Biodiversity and Greene-Nieuwland Herbarium, Notre Dame, IN 561
Hellenthal, Ronald A., Dir. Museum of Biodiversity, Museum of Biodiversity and Greene-Nieuwland Herbarium, Notre Dame, IN 561
Heller, Allison, Collections, Hellenic Museum & Cultural Center, Chicago, IL...481
Heller, Barbara, Head Conservator, Detroit Institute of Arts, Detroit, MI 834
Heller, Dr. Ena, Exec. Dir., Museum of Biblical Art, New York, NY..................1175
Heller, Dr. H. William, Pres. (V), Great Explorations Children's Museum, Saint Petersburg, FL................................384
Heller, Kevin, Asst. Dir. Education, The Newark Museum, Newark, NJ..............1053
Heller, Larry, Chief Exhibitions Designer, Wexner Center for the Arts, Columbus, OH 1314
Heller, Laura, Cur., Putney Historical Society, Putney, VT...........................1687
Heller, Mike, Senior Parks Specialist, Fort Christmas Historical Park, Christmas, FL 338
Hellerstein, Bruce S., Dir. & Pres., B's Ballpark Museum, Centennial, CO..........232
Hellige, Kristan, Coord. Communications, Cedar Rapids Museum of Art, Cedar Rapids, IA 577
Hellinger, Dean, Bd. Member & Vice Pres., Marias Museum of History and Art, Shelby, MT...972
Hellkamp, Dot, Bd. Member, Carnegie Historical Museum, Fairfield, IA 586
Hellman, Theodore W., Chm. Bd. of Commissioners, St. Louis Science Center, Saint Louis, MO 950
Hellstern, Jean, Museum Shop Mgr., The Living Word National Bible Museum, Aledo, TX 1576
Hellstern, Dr. John R., C.E.O., The Living Word National Bible Museum, Aledo, TX 1576
Helm, Charles, Dir. Performing Arts, Wexner Center for the Arts, Columbus, OH..1314
Helm, Cherie, Co Chm., The Lace Museum, Sunnyvale, CA 214
Helmer, Dave, C.E.O., Fosterfields Living Historical Farm, Morristown, NJ 1049
Helmer, David, C.E.O., The George G. Frelinghuysen Arboretum, Morris Township, NJ 1049
Helmer, David, Pres. (V), O. Winston Link Museum, Roanoke, VA.................1744
Helmer, Grace, Museum Shop Mgr., Virginia Museum of Transportation, Inc., Roanoke, VA 1745
Helmick, Kelly, D.V.M., Acting Dir. Animal Health, Woodland Park Zoo, Seattle, WA 1785
Helmke, Dick, Cur., Glenwood Railroad Museum, Glenwood Springs, CO 248
Helms, Cheryl V., Library Dir., Redwood Library and Athenaeum, Newport, RI ...1492
Helms, Sharon, MCHS Bd. Vice Pres., Madison County Historical Museum & Archival Library, Edwardsville, IL 491
Helou, Lora, Public Rels. Coord., The Michigan State University Museum, East Lansing, MI 838
Helsby, Kenneth M., Asst. Cur. Facilities & Educator, Cornelius Low House/Middlesex County Museum, Piscataway, NJ...1057
Helstrom, Linnea, Dir., Lars Noak Blacksmith Shop, Larsson/Ostlund Log Home & One-Room Capitol School, New Sweden, ME 704
Heltne, Dr. Paul G., Pres. Emeritus & Academy Counselor, The Peggy Notebaert Nature Museum, Chicago, IL..485
Helton, Christine, Devel., Museum of the Middle Appalachians, Saltville, VA.......1745
Helton, Debra M., Dir., Spring Street Historical Museum, Shreveport, LA........688
Helton, JoLynn, Business Mgr., Lauren Rogers Museum of Art, Laurel, MS........912
Helton, Kelly, Pres. (V), Churchill County Museum and Archives, Fallon, NV...1003
Helzel, Larry, Vice Pres., Sun Valley Center for the Arts, Ketchum, ID 461
Hembree, A.G., Site Mgr., Peter Conser House, Heavener, OK.............................1363
Hemdal, Jay F., Cur. Fishes, The Toledo Zoo, Toledo, OH...................................1346
Hemenway, Kevin, Treas., The Imaginarium Science Discovery Center, Anchorage, AK 27
Hemenway, Lori Ann, Corresponding Sec., Putnam County Historical Society Museum, Kalida, OH 1325
Hemer, Patricia, Dir., Page Farm & Home Museum - The University of Maine, Orono, ME 706
Hemm, Marsha, C.E.O., Vermont Marble Museum, Proctor, VT 1687
Hemmerlein, Tamara, Exec. Dir., Lane Place, Crawfordsville, IN 537
Hemmerlein, Tamara, Dir., The Rotary Jail Museum, Crawfordsville, IN............537
Hemphill, Hugh, Dir. & Museum Shop Mgr., Texas Transportation Museum, San Antonio, TX...................................1646
Henager, James G., Chm. (V), Henager "Memories and Nostalgia" Museum and National Veterans Memorial, Buckskin, IN 534
Hendershot, L, Site Mgr., Campus Martius Museum, Marietta, OH.............1329
Hendershot, Le Ann, Interim Mgr., Ohio River Museum, Marietta, OH 1330
Henderson, Anne, Education, Frist Center for the Visual Arts, Nashville, TN.........1568
Henderson, Bill, Pres. (V), Ark-La-Tex Antique & Classic Vehicle Museum, Shreveport, LA 686
Henderson, Bill, Asst. Supt., Crater of Diamonds State Park Museum, Murfreesboro, AR.......................................80
Henderson, Cherel, Dir., East Tennessee Historical Society, Knoxville, TN............1558
Henderson, Dr. Dee W., Dir., Fleischmann Planetarium, Reno, NV.....1008
Henderson, Della, Membership Mgr., The Morikami Museum and Japanese Gardens, Delray Beach, FL.....................344
Henderson Fahnestock, Andrea, Cur. Paintings & Sculpture, Museum of the City of New York, New York, NY 1176
Henderson, Howard, Historic Site Mgr., Burrowes Mansion Museum, Matawan, NJ 1046
Henderson, Jaime, Asst. Dir. Administration & Devel., Center for Curatorial Studies and the Hessel Museum of Art, Annandale-on-Hudson, NY...................1099
Henderson, Jake, Pres., P. Buckley Moss Museum, Waynesboro, VA..................1753
Henderson, Jan, Pres., Dakota Discovery Museum, Mitchell, SD 1536
Henderson, Justin, Cur., Colorado Ski & Snowboard Museum, Vail, CO 265
Henderson, Laura B., Registrar, Miami University Art Museum, Oxford, OH....1338
Henderson, Malia, Vice Pres., Hana Cultural Center, Hana, Maui, HI 441
Henderson, Mary, Dir., Lafayette Science Museum, Lafayette, LA 673
Henderson, Mary Alice, Chm., California Oil Museum, Santa Paula, CA................208
Henderson, Ray, Museum Shop Mgr. & Chief of Interpretation & Resources Mgmt., William Howard Taft National Historic Site, Cincinnati, OH 1307
Henderson, Richard, Chm. (V), Lyman Museum, Hilo, HI.......................................442
Henderson, Richard, Chm. Bd., Museum of Southern History, Jacksonville, FL 356
Henderson, Scott, Dir., Arkansas Game and Fish Commission, Little Rock, AR.....76
Henderson, Sherri, Dir. Personnel, Oklahoma Historical Society, Oklahoma City, OK 1372
Henderson, Tom, Chm., Bosque Museum, Clifton, TX...1593
Henderson, Vickie, Vice Pres. Human Resources, The U.S. Space & Rocket Center, Huntsville, AL...............................15
Hendley, Jeffrey, Security & Maintenance, Maitland Art Center, Maitland, FL...363
Hendren, Eileen, Asst. Dir., Pence Gallery, Davis, CA 107
Hendrick, AW2 (AW/NAC/IUSS) Erin, LPO/Educator, Hampton Roads Naval Museum, Norfolk, VA 1730

H–*Continued*

H–*Continued*

Hibbard, Jo-el, Business Mgr., The Granger Homestead Society, Inc., Canandaigua, NY....1117
Hibbard, Sally, Chief Registrar, The J. Paul Getty Museum, Los Angeles, CA...137
Hibel, Edna, Chief Cur. Artworks & Exhibitions, Hibel Museum of Art, Jupiter, FL....357
Hichwa, Bryant, Pres. Bd., Audubon Canyon Ranch, Stinson Beach, CA....213
Hicken, Elizabeth, Treas., Rowley Historical Society, Rowley, MA....803
Hickerson, Bill, Cur., West Tennessee Regional Art Center, Humboldt, TN....1555
Hickerson, Robert, Photographer, Spencer Museum of Art, The University of Kansas, Lawrence, KS....621
Hickey, Arthur, Vice Pres., The Friends of the Caleb Pusey House, Inc., Upland, PA....1479
Hickey, Donald, Physical Plant Dir., Indiana War Memorials, Indianapolis, IN....549
Hickey, Elizabeth, Dir. Waters House Site, The Montgomery County Historical Society, Inc., Rockville, MD...744
Hickey, Janet, Dir. & Membership, Schoolcraft County Historical Society, Manistique, MI....852
Hickey, Leo J., Cur. Paleobotany, Peabody Museum of Natural History, New Haven, CT....286
Hickman, Carole S., Cur., Museum of Paleontology, Berkeley, CA....93
Hickman, Ken, Dir., Penn State All-Sports Museum, University Park, PA....1478
Hickman, Marcus, Valentine-Varian House Mgr., The Bronx County Historical Society, Bronx, NY....1107
Hickman, Melvin, Cur., Richardson Maritime Museum, Cambridge, MD....729
Hickman, Pat, Flight Deck Museum Shop Mgr., National Naval Aviation Museum, Pensacola, FL....378
Hickok, Jim, Treas., Grant County Museum aka Historic Adobe Museum, Ulysses, KS....636
Hicks, Angela, Museum Shop Mgr., Mexic-Arte Museum, Austin, TX....1582
Hicks, Brian, Dir., DeSoto County Museum, Hernando, MS....908
Hicks, Christina, Asst. Registrar, Oklahoma City Museum of Art, Oklahoma City, OK....1371
Hicks, Colleen, C.E.O., Marin Museum of the American Indian, Novato, CA....153
Hicks, Erin, Registrar, The Haggin Museum, Stockton, CA....214
Hicks, Holly, Educator, Carson County Square House Museum, Panhandle, TX....1637
Hicks, J. Allen, Treas., Tennessee Central Railway Museum, Nashville, TN....1569
Hicks, Julie, Dir. Retail, Callaway Gardens, Pine Mountain, GA....429
Hicks, Linda, Asst. Dir. Special Events, National Air and Space Museum, Washington, DC....322
Hicks, Louis, Dir., Alexandria Black History Museum, Alexandria, VA....1696
Hicks, Louis, Dir. Black History Museum, Office of Historic Alexandria, Alexandria, VA....1698
Hicks, Patsy, Dir. Education, Santa Barbara Museum of Art, Santa Barbara, CA....203
Hicks, Robert, Dir., Mutter Museum, College of Physicians of Philadelphia, Philadelphia, PA....1457
Hicks, Sandra, Chm. Bd., Silver City Museum, Silver City, NM....1092
Hicks, Stephen M., Pres. (V), Santa Barbara Museum of Natural History, Santa Barbara, CA....204
Hicks, Steven, Refuge Mgr., Fort Niobrara National Wildlife Refuge, Valentine, NE....999
Hicks, Thomas H., CPA, Treas., Indiana Transportation Museum, Noblesville, IN....561
Hicks, Tina, Mgr. Visitor Svcs. COSI Toledo, Toledo, OH....1345
Hicks-Connors, Robin, C.E.O., Elliott Museum, Stuart, FL....389
Hidalga-Bartolomei, Ana, Coord. Membership, Maitland Art Center, Maitland, FL....363
Hidalgo, Denise, Exec. Asst. to Dir., New Mexico Museum of Natural History & Science, Albuquerque, NM....1072
Hidalgo, William, Customer Svc. & Education Asst., Institute of Contemporary Art, University of Pennsylvania, Philadelphia, PA....1455
Hiebel, Kaye, Exec. Dir., Marquette County History Museum, Marquette, MI....853
Hiebert, Debra, Dir., Harvey County Historical Society, Newton, KS....628
Hier, Marlene F., Dir. Membership Devel., Museum of Tolerance, Los Angeles, CA....140
Hier, Rabbi Marvin, Founder & Dean, Museum of Tolerance, Los Angeles, CA....140
Hiesinger, Kathryn B., Cur. European Decorative Arts After 1700, Philadelphia Museum of Art, Philadelphia, PA....1459
Hiester, Jan Z., Registrar, The Charleston Museum, Charleston, SC....1503
Hietala, Esther, Pres. (V), Itasca Historical Society & Itasca Genealogy, Grand Rapids, MN....879
Higa, Karin, Dir. Curatorial & Exhibitions, Japanese American National Museum, Los Angeles, CA....137
Higashino, Tommy, Asst. Dir., Honolulu Zoo, Honolulu, HI....446
Higbee, Brad, Technical Dir., Willard Arts Center/Carr Gallery, Idaho Falls, ID....460
Higby, Sue, Exec. Dir., Studio Place Arts, Barre, VT....1675
Higdon, Bernard M., Cur., The Veterans' Museum, Halls, TN....1554
Higdon, Debbie, C.F.O., Huntsville Museum of Art, Huntsville, AL....15
Higdon, Michael, Museum Shop Mgr., National Building Museum, Washington, DC....323
Higdon, Patricia M., Dir., Chm. & Pres. (V), The Veterans' Museum, Halls, TN.1554
Higginbotham, Mary Ellen, Cur., The Root House Museum, Marietta, GA....427
Higginbotham, Ron, Pres., Historical Center for Southeast New Mexico, Roswell, NM....1086
Higgingbotham, Scott, Pres., Moore County Historical Museum, Dumas, TX....1603
Higgins, Beth, Public Rels. & Devel. Coord., Fort Collins Museum, Fort Collins, CO....246
Higgins, C. Ed., Bd. Pres., The Museum of Culpeper History, Culpeper, VA....1708
Higgins, James, Dir., Agrirama, Georgia's Living History Museum & Village, Tifton, GA....437
Higgins, Lisa, Dir. Missouri Folk Arts Program, Museum of Art and Archaeology, University of Missouri, Columbia, MO....924
Higgins, Margaux, Dir. Finance, The Contemporary Arts Center, Cincinnati, OH....1305
Higgins, Melissa, Dir. Education, Akron Art Museum, Akron, OH....1292
Higgins, Sally, Chm. (V), The Stowitts Museum & Library, Pacific Grove, CA...159
Higgins, Sarah, Exec. Dir., Matagorda County Museum, Bay City, TX....1585
Higgins, William, Chm. (V), J.M. Davis Arms & Historical Museum, Claremore, OK....1358
High, Mardy, Chm., Enfield Shaker Museum, Enfield, NH....1017
High, Steven S., Dir., Telfair Museum of Art, Savannah, GA....435
Highley, Susan, Museum Shop Mgr., Florida Air Museum At Sun'n Fun, Lakeland, FL....362
Highsmith, Betty, Vice Pres., White County Historical Society, Cleveland, GA....414
Hight, Cliff, Archivist & Cur., Royal Gorge Regional Museum & History Center, Canon City, CO....232
Hightower, Jack, C.E.O., Masonic Grand Lodge Library and Museum of Texas, Waco, TX....1654
Higley, David, Teacher-in-Residence, The Bakken Library and Museum, Minneapolis, MN....884
Hiigel, Sharon, Cur. Collections & Education Coord., Kearney Mansion Museum, Fresno, CA....116
Hikade, Gale, Vice Pres., Fairmount Historical Museum & Gift Shop, Fairmount, IN....540
Hikiji, Patricia, Volunteer Coord., National Czech & Slovak Museum & Library, Marion, IA....593
Hilaman, Ann, Museum Shop Mgr., Lewes Historical Society, Lewes, DE....308
Hilarski, Thomas, Maintenance, The Granger Homestead Society, Inc., Canandaigua, NY....1117
Hilberg, Inge, Archivist, The Belknap Mill Society, Laconia, NH....1021
Hilberg, Thomas D., Cur., Medina County Historical Society, The John Smart House, Medina, OH....1331
Hilbert, Robert J., C.E.O., El Pomar Foundation Carriage Museum, Colorado Springs, CO....234
Hilborn, Jack, Vice Pres. (V), Ohio Railway Museum, Worthington, OH....1352
Hilburn, Bob, Pres., Mojave River Valley Museum, Barstow, CA....91
Hild, Edwin, Pres., The Parry Mansion Museum, New Hope, PA....1447
Hildebrand, Carla, Park Mgr., Wickliffe Mounds State Historic Site, Wickliffe, KY....664
Hildebrandt, A. Thomas, Chm., Genesee Country Village & Museum, Mumford, NY....1160
Hildebrandt, Patricia, Dir. Education, Society for the Preservation of Long Island Antiquities, Cold Spring Harbor, NY....1122
Hildebrandt, Paula, Specimen Preparator, The Michigan State University Museum, East Lansing, MI....838
Hildebrandt, Sandra, Dir., Stagecoach Inn Museum Complex, Newbury Park, CA...151
Hildreth, Ann, Museum Shop. Mgr., American Swedish Institute, Minneapolis, MN....884
Hile, Liz, Cur. Animals, The Living Desert, Palm Desert, CA....160

H–*Continued*

Hitt, Lloyd, Pres. (V) & Museum Shop Mgr., Bolton Hall Historical Museum, Tujunga, CA 218
Hitt, Dr. Robert J., C.E.O., Chesapeake Planetarium, Chesapeake, VA 1706
Hittle, Richard, Chm. (V) & Pres. (V), Dorset Historical Society, Dorset, VT 1679
Hixon, Karen, Chm. Bd., San Antonio Museum of Art, San Antonio, TX 1645
Hixson, Maiza, Curatorial Asst., The Contemporary Arts Center, Cincinnati, OH 1305
Hjalatin, Nellie, Museum Shop Mgr., The History Museum of Hood River County, Hood River, OR 1392
Hnedack, John, Deputy Supt., Statue of Liberty National Monument & Ellis Island Immigration Museum, New York, NY 1182
Hoag, Rebecca, Dir. Business Svcs., University of California Berkeley Art Museum and Pacific Film Archive, Berkeley, CA 94
Hoagland, Eleanor T.M., Pres., Wendell Gilley Museum, Southwest Harbor, ME 712
Hoagland, Glenn D., Exec. Dir., Mohonk Preserve, Inc., Gardiner, NY 1136
Hoaglund, Lyle, Property Chm, Mantorville Restoration, Mantorville, MN 883
Hoaglund, Theresa, Museum Shop Mgr., Mantorville Restoration, Mantorville, MN 883
Hoard, Constance G., Pres. (V) & Corresponding Sec., General Jacob Brown Historical Society, Brownville, NY 1114
Hoback, Thomas G., Chm. (V), Indiana Historical Society, Indianapolis, IN 548
Hoban, Chris, Chm., Aurora Public Art Commission, Aurora, IL 469
Hobart, Christine, Dir., McKee Botanical Garden, Vero Beach, FL 395
Hobart, Rebecca, Archivist & Editor, Dennys River Historical Society, Dennysville, ME 697
Hobart, Richard H., Treas., Dennys River Historical Society, Dennysville, ME 697
Hobbs, Kay, Finance Mgr., Hands On! Regional Museum, Johnson City, TN 1555
Hobbs, Marjorie, Vice Pres., Washington County Museum of Fine Arts, Hagerstown, MD 738
Hobbs, Mary Alice, Dir. Research, Brigham City Museum-Gallery, Brigham City, UT 1660
Hobby, Adele, Asst. Cur., Town of Yorktown Museum, Yorktown Heights, NY 1230
Hoberg, Shelly, Museum Shop Mgr., National Heisey Glass Museum, Newark, OH 1335
Hobson, Sarah, Dir., Mid-America Windmill Museum, Kendallville, IN 551
Hoch, Brad, Chm. (V), The David Wills House, Gettysburg, PA 1427
Hochberg, Dr. F. G., Cur. Invertebrate Zoology, Santa Barbara Museum of Natural History, Santa Barbara, CA 204
Hochhalter, Larry, Pres. (V), Union Pacific Historical Society (UPHS), Laramie, WY 1862
Hochman, Debbie, Dir., My Jewish Discovery Place Children's Museum, Fort Lauderdale, FL 348
Hochradel, Rebecca, Fiscal Mgr., Historic Arkansas Museum, Little Rock, AR 77
Hockett, Carol, Coord. School & Children's Programs, Herbert F. Johnson Museum of Art, Ithaca, NY 1146
Hockett, Esther, Gallery Coord., Memorial Union Gallery, Fargo, ND 1281
Hocking, Linda, Librarian & Archivist, Litchfield Historical Society and Museum, Litchfield, CT 280
Hockridge, Andrea, Financial Dir. MASS MoCA, North Adams, MA 795
Hockwelt, Helen, Cur., Pickens County Museum of Art & History, Pickens, SC 1521
Hodapp, Nita, Sec., Waterloo Center for the Arts, Waterloo, IA 601
Hodge, Andi, Museum Shop Mgr., Union Pacific Railroad Museum, Council Bluffs, IA 580
Hodge, Beth, Exec. Dir., Staunton Augusta Art Center, Staunton, VA 1746
Hodge, Kathy, Sec., Utica Museum, Utica, MT 973
Hodge, Rhonda, Asst., Fine Arts Center for New River Valley, Pulaski, VA 1735
Hodges, Adam, Dir. West Virginia State Museum, West Virginia State Museum, Charleston, WV 1797
Hodges, David, Cur., Duluth Art Institute, Duluth, MN 874
Hodges, Doreen, Attendant, The Valdez Museum & Historical Archive Association, Inc., Valdez, AK 36
Hodges, Rhoda, Co Dir., Coutts Memorial Museum of Art, Inc., El Dorado, KS 610
Hodges, Richard, Ph.D., Dir., University of Pennsylvania Museum of Archaeology and Anthropology, Philadelphia, PA 1462
Hodges, William B., Jr., Cur., Rocky Ford Historical Museum, Rocky Ford, CO 262
Hodgkins, Mary, Dir., Snyder Museum & Creative Arts Center, Bastrop, LA 666
Hodkin, Debra, Mgr. & Cur., Barstow Route 66 Mother Road Museum, Barstow, CA 91
Hodson, Joel, Dir. Education, Woodrow Wilson Presidential Library, Staunton, VA 1746
Hoefs, Brian, Financial Dir., Hearthstone Historic House Museum, Appleton, WI 1810
Hoehlen, Jack, Cur. Barn, Dover Historical Society - Sawin Museum, Dover, MA 775
Hoehne, Mary, Security & Maintenance, The Moody Mansion Museum, Galveston, TX 1614
Hoehne, Susan, Dir. Education Asst., Lower Rio Grande Valley Nature Center, Weslaco, TX 1656
Hoel, Randall, C.E.O., Cur. & Devel., Centerville Historical Museum, Centerville, MA 769
Hoel, Randall, Cur., The Sharon Arts Center, Inc., Sharon, NH 1029
Hoelscher, Jean, Dir. Mktg., Museum of the Southwest, Midland, TX 1633
Hoeltzel, Susan, Dir., Lehman College Art Gallery, Bronx, NY 1108
Hoelzeman, Buddy, Dir., The Museum of Automobiles, Morrilton, AR 79
Hoener, Ross, Vice Pres., Pratt County Historical Society Museum, Pratt, KS 631
Hoenig, Thomas M., C.E.O., The Money Museum-Federal Reserve Bank of Kansas City, Kansas City, MO 934
Hoepner, Leon, Cultural Resources Supvr., Wanapum Dam Heritage Center, Beverly, WA 1760
Hoerig, Dr. Karl, Dir., Nohwike Bagowa, The White Mountain Apache Cultural Center and Museum, Fort Apache, AZ 43
Hoernle, Kate, Editor, Telfair Museum of Art, Savannah, GA 435
Hoert, Jennifer, Dir. Klein Family Learning Center, Kentucky Derby Museum, Louisville, KY 655
Hoewing, VADM (Ret) G.L., USN (Ret), Found. Pres. & C.E.O., National Naval Aviation Museum, Pensacola, FL 378
Hoey, Carolyn, Education Dir., Sotterley Plantation, Hollywood, MD 739
Hoey, Kimberley, Treas., The Whalehead Club, Corolla, NC 1241
Hof, Liselotte, Publicity, Micanopy Historical Society Museum, Micanopy, FL 368
Hofbauer, John D., Pres., California Museum of Ancient Art, Beverly Hills, CA 94
Hofelich-Jack, Emily, Volunteer Coord., Tanglewood Nature Center and Museum, Elmira, NY 1131
Hofer, Amy, Project Mgr., American Labor Museum, Botto House National Landmark, Haledon, NJ 1041
Hofer, James, Pres. (V), Lincoln Memorial Shrine, Redlands, CA 170
Hoffberger, Bruce, Deputy Exec. Dir. Finance, C.F.O. & Administration, National Aquarium, Baltimore, MD 725
Hoffeditz, G. Richard, Cur., The Virginia War Museum, Newport News, VA 1729
Hoffer, Shayann, Education Coord., Maude I. Kerns Art Center, Eugene, OR 1389
Hoffius, Susan, Cur., Macaulay Museum of Dental History, Charleston, SC 1505
Hoffius, Susan, Cur., Waring Historical Library, Charleston, SC 1506
Hoffman, Amy Moe, Mgr. Collections, Dunn-Seiler Museum, Mississippi State University, MS 913
Hoffman, Angela, Dir. Education, Palos Verdes Art Center, Rancho Palos Verdes, CA 168
Hoffman, Arlene, Museum Shop Mgr., Heisey Museum, Clinton County Historical Society, Lock Haven, PA 1442
Hoffman, Barbara, Museum Shop Mgr., City Island Nautical Museum, Bronx, NY 1108
Hoffman, Betty, Treas., Old Prison Museums, Deer Lodge, MT 961
Hoffman, Dr. C., Cur. Education & Outreach, Georgia Museum of Natural History, Athens, GA 400
Hoffman, Carol, Museum Shop Mgr., Wenatchee Valley Museum and Cultural Center, Wenatchee, WA 1794
Hoffman, Claire, Devel. Assoc., The Museum for African Art, Long Island City, NY 1154
Hoffman, Daryl, Cur. Large Mammals, Houston Zoo, Inc., Houston, TX 1621
Hoffman, Edna Alice, Museum Shop Mgr., Middletown Valley Historical Society, Middletown, MD 741
Hoffman, Erick, Dir. Communications, Jordan Schnitzer Museum of Art, Eugene, OR 1388
Hoffman, Jean, Dir., Saratoga Automobile Museum, Saratoga Springs, NY 1208
Hoffman Jelin, Andrea, Vice Pres. Education & Community Svcs., Please Touch Museum, Philadelphia, PA 1460
Hoffman, Jill, Ph.D., Exec. Dir., Millicent Rogers Museum of Northern New Mexico, Taos, NM 1093
Hoffman, Jim, Dir. Mktg., Discovery Place, Inc., Charlotte, NC 1238
Hoffman, Jim, APR, Dir. Mktg. & Guest Svcs., Daniel Stowe Botanical Garden, Belmont, NC 1235

H–*Continued*

Hoffman, Joan, Vice Pres. Education, Strong National Museum of Play, Rochester, NY 1203

Hoffman, Joel M., Exec. Dir., Vizcaya Museum and Gardens, Miami, FL 367

Hoffman, John B., Pres., The Lebanon County Historical Society, Lebanon, PA 1441

Hoffman, Kenneth, Dir. Education, The National World War II Museum, New Orleans, LA 682

Hoffman, Lisa, Dir., Charlotte Nature Museum, Charlotte, NC 1238

Hoffman, Lyn, Education Coord., Trails & Rails Museum, Kearney, NE 987

Hoffman, Marlow, Dir. Communications, Salt Lake Art Center, Salt Lake City, UT 1671

Hoffman, Nicholas, Museum Dir., Elkhart County Historical Museum, Bristol, IN...534

Hoffman, Patricia A., Exec. Dir., Oneida Community Mansion House, Oneida, NY 1189

Hoffman, Peggy, Cur., Schoolcraft County Historical Society, Manistique, MI 852

Hoffman, Rich, Naturalist, Environmental Education Center, Somerset County Park Commission, Basking Ridge, NJ...1032

Hoffman, Richard, Treas., Adams County Historical Society Museum, Brighton, CO 231

Hoffman, Richard Daniel, Pres., Shawano County Historical Society, Inc., Shawano, WI 1844

Hoffman, Sheila, Cur. Collections, Rockwell Museum of Western Art, Corning, NY 1124

Hoffman, Steve, C.E.O., Kirby Science Discovery Center at the Washington Pavilion, Sioux Falls, SD 1542

Hoffman, Steven A., Dir., National Steinbeck Center, Salinas, CA 178

Hoffman, Thomas, Historian, Sandy Hook National Seashore, Fort Hancock, NJ 1039

Hoffmann, Amy, Coord. Education, Bowman's Hill Wildflower Preserve, New Hope, PA 1447

Hoffmann, David, Chm., Contemporary Art Museum St. Louis, Saint Louis, MO 946

Hoffmann, Kim, Cur. Collections & Exhibitions, South Bend Regional Museum of Art, South Bend, IN 566

Hoffpauer, Diane, C.E.O., Crystal Rice Heritage Farm, Crowley, LA 670

Hofland, Amy L., Dir., The Trammell & Margaret Crow Collection of Asian Art, Dallas, TX 1600

Hofmann, Bernard, Pres. (V), Boyertown Museum of Historic Vehicles, Boyertown, PA 1414

Hofmann, Irene, Exec. Dir., Contemporary Museum, Baltimore, MD 721

Hofmann, John, Sec., Merced County Courthouse Museum, Merced, CA 146

Hofreuter-Londini, Liz, Pres., Children's Museum of the Ohio Valley, Wheeling, WV 1807

Hofrichter, Rita, Documentation Dept. Coord., Holocaust Documentation & Education Center, Inc., Hollywood, FL...353

Hofstedt, Matthew, Assoc. Cur., The Supreme Court of the United States, Washington, DC 330

Hofwolt, Gerald, C.E.O. & Pres. USS Bowfin Submarine Museum & Park, Honolulu, HI 448

Hogan, Carrie, Cur., American Swedish Historical Foundation & Museum, Philadelphia, PA 1450

Hogan, Christopher, Chm. Bd., Arizona Zoological Society, dba the Phoenix Zoo, Phoenix, AZ 49

Hogan, Erin, Coord. Outreach, Grout Museum District: Grout Museum of History and Science, Bluedorn Science Imaginarium, Rensselaer Russell House Museum, Snowden House, Waterloo, IA 601

Hogan, Fran, Mgr. Customer Svc., Midway Village Museum, Rockford, IL 517

Hogan, Jacqueline, Dir. Asst., University Art Museum, Binghamton, NY 1105

Hogan, Jennifer, Pres. (V), Rahr West Art Museum, Manitowoc, WI 1829

Hogan, John, Operations Asst., Museum of Photographic Arts, San Diego, CA 181

Hogan, Johnnie, Vice Pres., Lincoln Parish Museum & Historical Society, Ruston, LA 685

Hogan, Margo, Pres. (V), Zelienople Historical Society, Zelienople, PA 1484

Hogan, Tim, Collections Mgr. Botany, University of Colorado Museum of Natural History, Boulder, CO 230

Hoge, Joan R., Exec. Dir., Delaware Historical Society, Wilmington, DE 312

Hoge, Robert, American Cur., American Numismatic Society, New York, NY 1163

Hoggan Groppel, Melissa, Mgr. Mktg. & Events, Dumbarton House, Washington, DC 316

Hoggson, Nancy, Pres., Norwich Historical Society, Norwich, VT 1686

Hogue, James M., Pres., Dallas Holocaust Museum/Center for Education & Tolerance, Dallas, TX 1598

Hogue, Kate, Cur., Bent's Old Fort National Historic Site, La Junta, CO 253

Hogue, Kate, Cur., Big Bend National Park, Big Bend National Park, TX 1588

Hoh, Josephine, Botanical Mgr., Waimea Arboretum and Botanical Garden in Waimea Valley, Haleiwa, HI 441

Hohberg, Tonian, Pres. FIDM Museum & Galleries, Los Angeles, CA 135

Hoheisel, Timothy M., Dir. Outreach & Communication, The Center for Western Studies, Sioux Falls, SD 1541

Hohman, Dana, Museum Shop Mgr., Lincoln Herdon Law Offices State Historic Site, Springfield, IL 521

Hohman, Ron, Museum Shop Mgr., Lincoln Herdon Law Offices State Historic Site, Springfield, IL 521

Hohne, Matt, Dir. Animal Operations, Disney's Animal Kingdom Theme Park, Bay Lake, FL 334

Hohstadt, Sharon, Pres. (V), Union County Museum, Union, OR 1406

Hoilman, Allen, Cur. & Dir. of Exhibits & Collections, Virginia Air & Space Center, Hampton, VA 1716

Hoisington, Susan, Gallery Dir., Cabrillo Gallery, Aptos, CA 87

Hokans, Gregory J., Chief Devel. & Mktg., Mackinac Island State Park Commission-Mackinac State Historic Parks, Mackinaw City, MI 851

Hokans, Gregory J., Chief Devel. & Mktg., Mackinac State Historic Parks-Colonial Michilimackinac & Old Mackinac Point Lighthouse, Mackinaw City, MI 852

Hokans, Gregory J., Chief Devel., Mackinac State Historic Parks-Fort Mackinac & Mackinac Island State Park, Mackinac Island, MI 851

Hokans, Gregory J., Chief Devel. & Mktg., Mackinac State Historic Parks-Historic Mill Creek Discovery Park, Mackinaw City, MI 852

Hokanson, Randee, Dir. & Museum Shop Mgr., Stevens County Historical Society Museum, Morris, MN 887

Hokanson, Stan, Dir. Research, Minnesota Landscape Arboretum, University of Minnesota, Chaska, MN....872

Hoke, Donald, Dir., Stanley Museum, Estes Park, CO 244

Holahan, Paula M, Cur. Mammalogy & Ornithology, University of Wisconsin Zoological Museum, Madison, WI 1828

Holaway, Laura, Museum Shop Mgr., College Football Hall of Fame, South Bend, IN 565

Holbach, Joseph, Chief Registrar, The Phillips Collection, Washington, DC 328

Holben Ellis, Margaret, Dir., Thaw Conservation Center, The Morgan Library & Museum, New York, NY 1173

Holben, Nanette, Devel., American Philosophical Society Museum (APS), Philadelphia, PA 1449

Holbert, Melissa, Outreach Education Technical Coord., Smart Museum of Art, Chicago, IL 486

Holbren, Roberta, Chm. (V), Palmer Museum, Jewell, KS 619

Holbrook, Jean Ann, Museum Shop Mgr., Santa Monica History Museum, Santa Monica, CA 207

Holcomb, Grant, III, Dir., Memorial Art Gallery of the University of Rochester, Rochester, NY 1202

Holcomb, Julie, Ed.D., C.E.O., Education & Cur., Pearce Collections Museum, Corsicana, TX 1595

Holcomb, Peggy, Dir. Tourism & Cur., Eagle Tavern Museum, Watkinsville, GA 440

Holcombe, Holly, Exec. Dir., Steamship William G. Mather Museum, Cleveland, OH 1311

Holdcraft, T. Rose, Head Conservator, Peabody Museum of Archaeology & Ethnology, Cambridge, MA 768

Holden, Abbie, Office Mgr., Mill Race Historical Village, Northville, MI 858

Holden, Huey, Exec. Dir., Memphis Botanic Garden, Goldsmith Civic Garden Center, Memphis, TN 1563

Holden, Jacque, Dir. Human Resources, Turtle Bay Exploration Park, Redding, CA 169

Holden, Thomas, Dir., Lake Superior Maritime Visitors Center, Duluth, MN....874

Holdengraber, Paul, Mgr. Public & Education Programs, The New York Public Library, Astor, Lenox and Tilden Foundations, New York, NY 1178

Holder, Gary, Cur. Education, Sangre de Cristo Arts Center & Conference Center, Pueblo, CO 261

Holder, Teresa, Gallery Dir., Gardiner Art Gallery, Stillwater, OK 1377

Holder, Tim, Pres., Aurora Historical Society, Aurora, OH 1294

Holderbaum, Linda, Exec. Dir., Art Center of Battle Creek, Battle Creek, MI 824

Holderman, Mae, Archivist, Territorial Capital-Lane Museum, Lecompton, KS 622

Holdridge, Emmy, Chm. Friends of Patuxent (V), National Wildlife Visitor Center, Patuxent Research Refuge, Laurel, MD 740

Holdsworth, David G., Pres., Morris County Historical Society (Acorn Hall House Museum), Morristown, NJ 1050

H–*Continued*

Holmes, Phil, Cultural Anthropologist, Santa Monica Mountains National Recreation Area, Thousand Oaks, CA.....216
Holmes, Robert, Bd. Chm., Birmingham Civil Rights Institute, Birmingham, AL.....5
Holmes, Willard, Assoc. Dir. Administration, The Museum of Fine Arts, Houston, Houston, TX.....1622
Holmgrain, Ardith, Music Programs, American Academy of Arts and Letters, New York, NY.....1162
Holmquist, Harlan, Exec. Dir., Farmamerica, The Minnesota Agricultural Interpretive Center, Waseca, MN.....901
Holmquist, Rebecca, Vice Pres. Visitor Experience, Minnetrista, Muncie, IN.....558
Holms, Lisa, C.F.O., National Museum of Wildlife Art, Jackson, WY.....1860
Holo, Dr. Selma, Dir. USC Fisher Museum of Art, Los Angeles, CA.....142
Holroyd, Pat, Museum Scientist, Museum of Paleontology, Berkeley, CA.....93
Holsclaw, Ali, Asst. Language Teacher, Confederated Tribes of Grand Ronde Cultural Resources Department, Grand Ronde, OR.....1390
Holsen, Kim, Education Specialist, Indiana Dunes National Lakeshore, Porter, IN.....562
Holster, Melanie, Collections Specialist, Historic Speedwell, Morristown, NJ.....1049
Holston, Douglas, Dir. Bldgs. & Grounds, DeCordova Sculpture Park & Museum, Lincoln, MA.....786
Holt, Bill, Owner, Holt Heritage Museum, Lolo, MT.....968
Holt, Eileen, Public Rels., Hatton-Eielson Museum & Historical Association, Hatton, ND.....1284
Holt, Eileen, Treas. & Museum Shop Mgr., Hatton-Eielson Museum & Historical Association, Hatton, ND.....1284
Holt, Frank, C.E.O., Mennello Museum of American Art, Orlando, FL.....373
Holt, Henry, Pres. (V), The Airborne & Special Operations Museum, Fayetteville, NC.....1244
Holt, K. Paul, Pres., Cameron Park Zoo, Waco, TX.....1654
Holt, Linda, Tribal Council Sec., Suquamish Museum, Poulsbo, WA.....1777
Holt, Loucinda, Cur., Steamship William G. Mather Museum, Cleveland, OH.....1311
Holt, Nancy, Pres. (V), Republic County Historical Society Museum, Belleville, KS.....606
Holt, Nici, Devel. & Membership Dir., Missoula Art Museum, Missoula, MT.....969
Holt, Peter, Chm. Commission, Goliad State Park, Goliad, TX.....1616
Holt, Peter M., Chm. Commission, Fort Leaton State Historical Site, Presidio, TX.....1639
Holt, Peter M., Chm. Commission, Seminole Canyon State Park and Historic Site, Comstock, TX.....1594
Holt, Ramona, Owner, Holt Heritage Museum, Lolo, MT.....968
Holt, Sharon Ann, Exec. Dir., Sandy Spring Museum, Sandy Spring, MD.....746
Holt, Steven, Pres. Bd. (V), Michigan Maritime Museum, South Haven, MI.....865
Holt, Townsend, C.E.O., Florence Museum of Art, Science & History and the Florence Railroad Museum, Florence, SC.....1512
Holte, Ellen, Museum Store Mgr., Museum of Fine Arts of St. Petersburg, Florida, Saint Petersburg, FL.....384
Holter, Cynthia S., CFRE, Vice Pres. External Rels., Saint Louis Zoo, Saint Louis, MO.....951
Holthausen, Erica, Dir. Devel., Museums of Old York, York, ME.....716
Holton, John, Asst. Collections Mgr., Spurlock Museum, University of Illinois at Urbana-Champaign, Urbana, IL.....525
Holton, Kerry, Pres., Delaware Nation Museum, Anadarko, OK.....1355
Holton, Linda, Dir., High Plains Museum, Goodland, KS.....614
Holtry, Cara, Librarian, Cumberland County Historical Society, The Hamilton Library and The Two Mile House, Carlisle, PA.....1415
Holtyapple, Terry, Pres., A.R. Bowman Memorial Museum, Prineville, OR.....1401
Holtz, Barb, Mgr. Look About Lodge, Cleveland Metroparks Outdoor Education Division, Garfield Heights, OH.....1322
Holtz, Gisela, Sec. & Treas., Morton House Museum, Benton Harbor, MI.....826
Holtzapple, John C., Dir., James K. Polk Ancestral Home, Columbia, TN.....1550
Holtzhauser, John, Vice Pres. Finance & Administration, Western Reserve Historical Society, Cleveland, OH.....1311
Holzapfel, Forrest, Pres., Marlboro Historical Society, Marlboro, VT.....1683
Holzer, Harold, Vice Pres. Communications & Mktg., The Metropolitan Museum of Art, New York, NY.....1172
Holzhouser, John, C.F.O., Crawford Auto-Aviation Museum, Cleveland, OH.....1309
Holzweiss, Dr. Robert, Supervisory Archivist, The George Bush Presidential Library and Museum, College Station, TX.....1593
Hom, Gayle, Exec. Dir., New Americans Museum, San Diego, CA.....182
Homan, Joyce, Administrative Mgr., The Genealogical Society of Pennsylvania, Philadelphia, PA.....1454
Homanick, Thomas, Finance, Colonial Industrial Quarter, Bethlehem, PA.....1412
Homanick, Thomas, Finance, Moravian Museum of Bethlehem, Inc., Bethlehem, PA.....1412
Homanick, Tom, Finance, Burnside Plantation, Inc., Bethlehem, PA.....1411
Homann, Dana, Museum Shop Mgr., Old State Capitol, Springfield, IL.....522
Homann, Joachim, Cur., The Picker Art Gallery, Hamilton, NY.....1140
Homann, Ron, Museum Shop Mgr., Old State Capitol, Springfield, IL.....522
Homburg, Shirley, Museum Shop Mgr., Olbrich Botanical Gardens, Madison, WI.....1828
Homer, Amy, Hospitality Supvr., Farmington Museum, Farmington, NM.1078
Homer, Michael, Chm. (V), Utah State Historical Society, Salt Lake City, UT..1672
Homer, Paul B., (CLMF), Pres., U.S. Naval Museum of Armament & Technology, China Lake, CA.....101
Homewood, Kay, Pres., Russell County Historical Society/Fossil Station Museum, Russell, KS.....632
Honadel, Elroy, Pres., Oak Creek Historical Society-Pioneer Village, Oak Creek, WI.....1839
Honaker, Cortney A., Cur., Historic Crab Orchard Museum & Pioneer Park, Inc., Tazewell, VA.....1750
Honan, Mary, Vice Pres., The Falmouth Historical Society, Falmouth, ME.....698
Hone, Dann W., Chm. (V), The Crandall Historical Printing Museum, Provo, UT.....1668
Honey, Margaret, Pres. & C.E.O., New York Hall of Science, Queens, NY.....1199
Honeycutt, David, Chm. (V), South Carolina Tennis Hall of Fame, Belton, SC.....1500
Honeyman, Mary, Historic Site Admin., Kaw Mission State Historic Site, Council Grove, KS.....609
Hong, Deborah, Vice Pres. LACE (Los Angeles Contemporary Exhibitions), Los Angeles, CA.....138
Hong, Irene, Program Coord., Korean American Museum, Los Angeles, CA.....138
Hong, Nancy, Gallery Monitor, Lentz Center for Asian Culture, Lincoln, NE.....988
Honick, Kennard, Treas., The Appalachian Trail Conservancy, Harpers Ferry, WV.....1799
Honious, Ann, Chief Museum Svcs. & Interpretation, Jefferson National Expansion Memorial, Saint Louis, MO...947
Honomichl, Marisa, Vice Pres. Devel., Kansas Cosmosphere and Space Center, Hutchinson, KS.....617
Hoober, David H., Dir., Arizona Capitol Museum, Phoenix, AZ.....48
Hood, Mrs. Betty, Cur., Bowers Mansion, Washoe Valley, NV.....1011
Hood, Bob, Exhibit Technician, Great Smoky Mountains Heritage Center, Townsend, TN.....1574
Hood, Dr. Craig, Adjunct Cur. Mammals, The Tulane University Museum of Natural History, Belle Chasse, LA.....669
Hood, Gary, Cur. Art, West Point Museum, West Point, NY.....1228
Hood, J. Edward, Vice Pres. Museum Program, Old Sturbridge Village, Sturbridge, MA.....811
Hood, Mary Bryan, C.E.O. & Dir., Owensboro Museum of Fine Art, Inc., Owensboro, KY.....661
Hood, Mary Jane, Pres. (V), Animas Museum, Durango, CO.....242
Hood, Michael, Dean College of Fine Arts, Kipp Gallery at Indiana University of Pennsylvania, Indiana, PA.....1435
Hood, Michael, Dean, The University Museum, Indiana, PA.....1436
Hood, Robert, Dir. Facilities & Museum Shop Mgr., Motown Historical Museum, Detroit, MI.....835
Hoogacker, Rachel, Information Svcs., Coca-Cola Space Science Center, Columbus, GA.....414
Hooghkirk, Sylvia, Pres. (V), Museum of Fife and Drum, Ivoryton, CT.....279
Hook, Beth, Dir. Mktg., Museum of Nature & Science, Dallas, TX.....1599
Hook, James, C.E.O. & Pres., International Crane Foundation, Baraboo, WI.....1811
Hook, Thomas, Mgr. Visitor Svcs., The J. Paul Getty Museum, Los Angeles, CA...137
Hooker, David S., Pres. & C.E.O., Frederik Meijer Gardens & Sculpture Park, Grand Rapids, MI.....842
Hooks, Dr. Benjamin, Chm. (V), National Civil Rights Museum at the Lorraine Motel, Memphis, TN.....1564
Hooks, Beth, Museum Shop Mgr., Arkansas Museum of Natural Resources, Smackover, AR.....84

H–*Continued*

H–*Continued*

H–*Continued*

Hussong, Carissa, Dir., National Ornamental Metal Museum, Memphis, TN....1564
Husted, MSG (Ret.) Glenn L., III, MSARNG, Arms & Military Vehicle Conservator, Mississippi Armed Forces Museum, Camp Shelby, MS....904
Huston, James, Dir., Railroad Museum of Minot, Minot, ND....1287
Hutchcroft, Sally, Cur., Knox County Museum, Knoxville, IL....501
Hutcherson, Mary Ann, Museum Shop Mgr., King Vintage Clothing Museum, Oakhurst, CA....154
Hutchings, David, Dir., Sonnenberg Gardens & Mansion State Historic Park, Canandaigua, NY....1118
Hutchins, Amy, Office of Public Affairs, Smithsonian American Art Museum, Washington, DC....329
Hutchins, Carma, Pres., Audubon County Historical Society, Exira, IA....586
Hutchins, Kathy, Health Cur., Roper Mountain Science Center, Greenville, SC....1514
Hutchins, Nancy, Chm. (V) & Treas., Marshall County Historical Museum, Holly Springs, MS....909
Hutchins, Patricia, Dir., Castine Scientific Society aka Wilson Museum, Castine, ME....696
Hutchins, Shirley, Dir., Bennington Center for the Natural & Cultural Arts, Bennington, VT....1676
Hutchinson, Alan, Museum Shop Mgr., The Antique Boat Museum, Clayton, NY....1121
Hutchinson, David, Museum Shop Mgr., Sloan Museum & Longway Planetarium, Flint, MI....840
Hutchinson, Diane, Pres. (V), Mid-Atlantic Center for the Arts/Emlen Physick Estate/Cape May Lighthouse/Fire Control Tower No. 23, Cape May, NJ....1034
Hutchinson, Donald, C.E.O. & Pres., The Maryland Zoo in Baltimore, Baltimore, MD....724
Hutchinson, Doug, Mayor, Fort Collins Museum, Fort Collins, CO....246
Hutchinson, John, Public Rels. Dir., The Museum of the Alphabet, Waxhaw, NC....1269
Hutchinson, Ken, Dir. Operations, Bronx Zoo, Bronx, NY....1107
Hutchinson, Roni, Interpreter, Oakwoods Metropark Nature Center, Belleville, MI....826
Hutchison, Senator Kay Bailey, Chm., Frontiers of Flight Museum, Dallas, TX....1598
Hutfles, Lori, Friends of Dole Institute, The Robert J. Dole Institute of Politics, Lawrence, KS....621
Huth, Paul C., Dir. Research, Mohonk Preserve, Inc., Gardiner, NY....1136
Hutin, Toni, Museum Shop Mgr., New Castle Historical Society - Horace Greeley House, Chappaqua, NY....1120
Hutlova-Foy, Zora, Mgr. Exhibitions & Cur. Publications, Seattle Art Museum, Seattle, WA....1783
Hutsell, Diane, Exec. Dir., McMinn County Living Heritage Museum, Athens, TN....1546
Hutson, Alex, Administrative Assoc., C.H. Nash Museum at Chucalissa, Memphis, TN....1560
Hutt, Cindy, Museum Shop Mgr., Blank Park Zoo, Des Moines, IA....582
Hutt, Marilyn, Asst., Overland Trail Museum, Sterling, CO....264
Hutter, Rachel, Dir. Engineering Svcs., Disney's Animal Kingdom Theme Park, Bay Lake, FL....334
Hutterer, Dr. Karl L., Exec. Dir., Santa Barbara Museum of Natural History, Santa Barbara, CA....204
Huttinger, Peter, Coord. Neighborhood Gardens, Civic Garden Center of Greater Cincinnati, Cincinnati, OH....1305
Huttlinger, John B., Jr., Treas., The History Museum, Lake Placid-North Elba Historical Society, Lake Placid, NY....1152
Hutto, Dr. Richard, Cur. Ornithology, Philip L. Wright Zoological Museum and University of Montana Herbarium, Missoula, MT....970
Hutto, Stan, Recreation Mgr. & Biology Cur., South Carolina Department of Parks, Recreation and Tourism, Columbia, SC....1509
Hutton, Kathleen F.G., Cur. Education, Reynolda House Museum of American Art, Winston-Salem, NC....1275
Hutton, Kim, Coord. Special Events, University of South Florida Botanical Garden, Tampa, FL....393
Hutton, Susan, C.E.O., Silver Cliff Museum, Silver Cliff, CO....263
Hutton, Trudy, Pres., Gillespie County Historical Society, Fredericksburg, TX....1612
Huxley, Geralyn H., Cur. Film & Video, The Andy Warhol Museum, Pittsburgh, PA....1464
Hviding, Ken, Vice Pres. (V), Polk County Historical Society, Crookston, MN....873
Hyde, Alice, Pres. (V), Panhandle-Plains Historical Museum, Canyon, TX....1592
Hyde, Colleen, Museum Technician, Grand Canyon National Park Museum Collection, Grand Canyon National Park, AZ....44
Hyde, Mr. J.R., Chm. Exec. Committee, National Civil Rights Museum at the Lorraine Motel, Memphis, TN....1564
Hyde, Kay, Museum Shop Mgr., Union Station Kansas City, Inc., Kansas City, MO....936
Hyde, Larry, Park Supt., Crowders Mountain State Park, Kings Mountain, NC....1254
Hyde, Robb, Exec. Dir., Wayne Center for the Arts, Wooster, OH....1351
Hyde-Holmes, Susan, Graphic Designer, Museum of New Mexico, Santa Fe, NM....1089
Hydorn, Lorene, Chm. (V), John Brown Museum State Historic Site, Osawatomie, KS....629
Hykes, David, Chm. (V), Renfrew Museum & Park, Waynesboro, PA....1481
Hyland, Alice, Consulting Cur., Art Complex Museum, Duxbury, MA....775
Hyland, Douglas, Dir., New Britain Museum of American Art, Inc., New Britain, CT....284
Hylton, Dave, Treas., San Juan Historical Society, Friday Harbor, WA....1767
Hyma, Deana, Financial Dir. & Museum Shop Mgr., Holocaust Museum Houston, Houston, TX....1620
Hyman, Paulyn, Vice Pres. & Membership, National Museum of Ceramic Art and Glass, Baltimore, MD....725
Hyman, Ryan, F.M. Kirby Cur. Collections, Macculloch Hall Historical Museum & Gardens, Morristown, NJ....1050
Hynes, Bob, Public Rels., Yankee Air Force, Inc. (Yankee Air Museum), Ypsilanti, MI....867
Hynes, Patricia, Deputy Dir. Institutional Advancement, Cincinnati Art Museum, Cincinnati, OH....1304
Hynes, Dr. Roger, Education, Palmer Museum of Chiropractic History, Davenport, IA....581
Hynson, Judith S., Dir. Research & Library Collections, Stratford Hall, Robert E. Lee Memorial Association, Inc., Stratford, VA....1748
Hyppolite, Dr. Joanne, Chief Cur., Historical Museum of Southern Florida, Miami, FL....365
Hyre, Kim, Ranger & Naturalist, Weymouth Woods-Sandhills Nature Preserve Museum, Southern Pines, NC.1268

I

Iacono, Domenic J., Dir. SUArt Galleries - Syracuse University, Syracuse, NY....1219
Iacono, Nello, Dir. Parks, Recreation & Community Svcs., Casa Adobe de San Rafael, Glendale, CA....119
Iams, Linda, Admin., Hardin County Historical Museums, Inc., Kenton, OH.1326
Iandoli, Michael, Exec. Dir., Larz Anderson Auto Museum, Brookline, MA....766
Iannucci, Heather, C.E.O. & Historic Site Mgr., John Jay Homestead State Historic Site, Katonah, NY....1149
Ibarra, Bobbie, Human Resources, Jungle Island, Miami, FL....365
Ice, Dr. Joyce, Dir. Museum of International Folk Art, Museum of New Mexico, Santa Fe, NM....1089
Icenogle, Lisa, Public Rels., Tate Geological Museum, Casper, WY....1854
Ickert-Bond, Stefanie, Cur. Herbarium, University of Alaska Museum of the North, Fairbanks, AK....30
Ickes, Jennifer, Registrar, New Orleans Museum of Art, New Orleans, LA....683
Ide, Evan, Cur., Larz Anderson Auto Museum, Brookline, MA....766
Idelson, Jeffrey, Pres., National Baseball Hall of Fame and Museum, Inc., Cooperstown, NY....1123
Ifert, Ray, Chm. (V), Tampa Museum of Art, Tampa, FL....393
Ifuku, Glenn, Treas., Hawaii's Plantation Village, Waipahu, HI....454
Igna, Mary Ann, Interim Dir., Desert Caballeros Western Museum, Wickenburg, AZ....64
Ignatowich, William, C.F.O., Dahesh Museum of Art, New York, NY....1167
Ihnen, Lorraine, Mgr. Collections, Grout Museum District: Grout Museum of History and Science, Bluedorn Science Imaginarium, Rensselaer Russell House Museum, Snowden House, Waterloo, IA....601
Ihran, Lois, Museum Shop Mgr., Douglas County Historical Society - Genoa Courthouse Museum, Genoa, NV....1003
Ihrig, Elizabeth, Librarian, The Bakken Library and Museum, Minneapolis, MN....884
Iles, Chrissie, Anne and Joel Ehrenkranz Cur., Whitney Museum of American Art, New York, NY....1184
Iler, Janice M., Sec., Parsonsfield-Porter Historical Society, Porter, ME....707
Iles, Sarah, Collection Mgr., Renton Historical Society and Museum, Renton, WA....1778
Iliff, Lori, Registrar, Denver Art Museum, Denver, CO....238
Illari, Jason D., Cur., City of Bowie Museums, Bowie, MD....729

I–*Continued*

J

J–*Continued*

J–*Continued*

Jensen, Jennifer R., Owner, The Agricultural Memories Museum, Penn Yan, NY 1195
Jensen, Joy, Museum Shop Mgr., Millicent Rogers Museum of Northern New Mexico, Taos, NM 1093
Jensen, Karla R., Exec. Dir., Seippel Homestead and Center for the Arts, Beaver Dam, WI 1812
Jensen, Kirsten, Cur. Parasitology KU Biodiversity Institute - KU Natural History Museum, Lawrence, KS 621
Jensen, Kristen, GIS Mgr., Utah State Historical Society, Salt Lake City, UT ..1672
Jensen, Leslie D., Cur. Arms, West Point Museum, West Point, NY 1228
Jensen, Mary, Museum Shop Mgr., Lacey Historical Society, Forked River, NJ 1038
Jensen, Mike, Security, Nasher Sculpture Center, Dallas, TX 1600
Jensen, Ove, Park Ranger-Interpreter, Horseshoe Bend National Military Park, Daviston, AL 9
Jensen, Pam, Dir. Operations, Daniel Boone Home and Boonesfield Village, Lindenwood University, Defiance, MO ...925
Jensen, Pat, Exhibit Specialist, Portsmouth Museums, Portsmouth, VA .1734
Jensen, Richard J., Guest Dir. Herbarium, Museum of Biodiversity and Greene-Nieuwland Herbarium, Notre Dame, IN 561
Jensen, Rusty, Chief Ranger, White Sands National Monument, Alamogordo, NM .1070
Jensen, Virgine, Treas., Historical Society of Stanton County Museums at Stanton and Pilger, Pilger, NE 996
Jensen, William, Pres. (V), McKinley Birthplace Home, Niles, OH 1336
Jensen, Dr. William, Dir., Richard H. Schmidt Museum of Natural History, Emporia, KS 611
Jentzsch, Keith, Program Coord., Colorado State University Art Museum, Fort Collins, CO 245
Jeppson, Sally, Gallery Dir., The Arts Center, Jamestown, ND 1285
Jergenson, Glenn, Vice Chm., South Dakota Hall of Fame, Chamberlain, SD 1528
Jerin, Suzanne, Public Rels., Croatian Heritage Museum & Library, Eastlake, OH 1319
Jerolmon, Linda, Membership Mgr., Yale Center for British Art, New Haven, CT 287
Jerome, Jeff, Cur., Edgar Allan Poe House and Museum, Baltimore, MD 721
Jerred, George, Pres., Banner County Historical Society, Harrisburg, NE 985
Jerris, Rand, Ph.D., Dir., United States Golf Association Museum, Far Hills, NJ 1038
Jeschke, Tannis, Dir. Visitors Information Center & Sec., Lincoln County Historical Museum, Davenport, WA 1763
Jesselson, Michael, Vice Chair., Yeshiva University Museum at the Center for Jewish History, New York, NY 1184
Jessen, Mark, Maintenance & Security, Blanden Memorial Art Museum, Fort Dodge, IA 587
Jeter, Niki, Public Rels., Tunica-Biloxi Native American Museum, Marksville, LA 675
Jeter, Verona Middleton, C.E.O. & Dir., Abrons Arts Center/Henry Street Settlement, New York, NY 1161
Jett, Susan, Dir. Horticulture, Rancho Santa Ana Botanic Garden, Claremont, CA 102
Jette, Carol, Chief Exec. Dir. & Dir. Community Affairs, Copper Village Museum & Arts Center of Deer Lodge County, Anaconda, MT 955
Jette, David, Museum Shop Mgr., Trinity Museum of the Parish of Trinity Church, New York, NY 1183
Jewell, Alice, Dir., McKenna Children's Museum, New Braunfels, TX 1635
Jewell, Anne, Exec. Dir., Louisville Slugger Museum & Factory, Louisville, KY 656
Jewell, Christine, Dir. Education, Fairfield Museum and History Center, Fairfield, CT 273
Jewell, Jeff, Photo Research, Whatcom Museum of History and Art, Bellingham, WA 1760
Jewell, Robert, C.E.O. & Pres., Brookgreen Gardens, Murrells Inlet, SC 1519
Jezioro, Frank, Dir. WV Div. Natural Resources, West Virginia State Wildlife Center, French Creek, WV 1798
Jian, Li, E. Rhodes and Leona B. Carpenter Cur. East Asian Art, Virginia Museum of Fine Arts, Richmond, VA 1742
Jilovec, Andrea, Education Coord., Cedar Rapids Museum of Art, Cedar Rapids, IA 577
Jimenez, Eva, Asst. to Exec. Dir., The Mexican Museum, San Francisco, CA 190
Jimenez, Paloma, Dir. Programs, The Spanish Institute, New York, NY 1182
Jimenez-Torres, Maria, Dir. Education, Plaza de La Raza, Inc. & Boathouse Gallery, Los Angeles, CA 141
Jimison, Tom, Cur., Baldwin Photographic Gallery, Murfreesboro, TN 1565
Jimmie, Charles, Sr., Trustee & Cultural Dir., Alaska Indian Arts, Inc., Haines, AK 31
Jines, Alysia, Museum Coord., Children's Museum of Tacoma, Tacoma, WA 1788
Jinkins, Ann, Asst. Cur., Door County Historical Museum, Sturgeon Bay, WI ..1846
Jirges, Barbara, Dir., The Else Forde Gallery at Bismarck State College, Bismarck, ND 1277
Jividen, Thomas C., Chm. (V), Amazement Square, The Rightmire Children's Museum, Lynchburg, VA 1722
Joans, Dr. Barbara, Dir., Merritt Museum of Anthropology, Oakland, CA 155
Joassin, Odile V., Cur. Textiles, The Art Institute of Chicago, Chicago, IL 476
Jobe, Peggy, Museum Shop Mgr., Hackley & Hume Historic Site, Muskegon, MI 857
Jobe, Peggy, Museum Shop Mgr., Lakeshore Museum Center, Muskegon, MI 857
Joerg, Rita, Sec., Fillmore County Historical Center, Fountain, MN 878
Johann, Barbara, Museum Shop Mgr., Osterville Historical Museum, Osterville, MA 798
Johannes, Janet, Archivist & Dir., Ellis County Historical Society, Hays, KS 616
Johanowicz, Steve, Preparator, Chazen Museum of Art, Madison, WI 1827
Johanson, Bert, Pres. (V), Connecticut Fire Museum, East Windsor, CT 272
Johanson, Bruce, Pres. (V), Ontonagon County Historical Society Museum, Ontonagon, MI 858
Johansson, Capt. Eric J., Dir., Maritime Industry Museum at Fort Schuyler, Bronx, NY 1108
Johansson, Vanessa, Museum Shop Mgr., Frederick R. Weisman Art Museum, Minneapolis, MN 885
John, Tammy, Museum Shop Mgr., Warhawk Air Museum, Nampa, ID 463
Johns, Bob, Coord. Educational Resource Room, Virginia Museum of Fine Arts, Richmond, VA 1742
Johns, Daniel, C.E.O., U.S. Vice Presidential Museum at the Dan Quayle Center, Huntington, IN 546
Johns, David E., Cur., Thomas Warne Historical Museum & Library, Old Bridge, NJ 1055
Johns, Diane, Treas., Spring Grove Hospital Center, Alumni Museum, Catonsville, MD 730
Johns, Eileen, Cur. & Archivist, Amos Herr House Foundation and Historic Society, Landisville, PA 1440
Johns, Jean, Experience Works Receptionist, Upper Peninsula Children's Museum, Marquette, MI 853
Johns, Jeffrey D., Assoc. Dir. & Chief Cur., American Airlines C.R. Smith Museum, Fort Worth, TX 1608
Johns, Jennifer, Registrar, Copshaholm House Museum & Historic Oliver Gardens, South Bend, IN 565
Johns, Jennifer, Registrar, Northern Indiana Center for History, South Bend, IN 565
Johns, Matt, Membership, Artpace San Antonio, San Antonio, TX 1643
Johns, Ronald N., Park Mgr., McLarty Treasure Museum, Vero Beach, FL 396
Johns, Sharleen, Assoc. Dir., Stephens County Historical Society and Museum, Duncan, OK 1360
Johns, Tim, C.E.O., Hawaii Maritime Center, Honolulu, HI 444
Johns, Timothy, C.E.O. & Pres., Bishop Museum, Honolulu, HI 443
Johnsen, Brandee, Outreach Coord., Weber State University Art Gallery, Ogden, UT 1666
Johnsen, Frederick A., Dir. & Cur., Air Force Flight Test Center Museum, Edwards AFB, CA 109
Johnsen, Leigh, Archivist, San Joaquin County Historical Society & Museum, Lodi, CA 129
Johnson, Alan, Vice Pres., Octagon Center for the Arts, Ames, IA 573
Johnson, Alice, Administrative Officer, Horseshoe Bend National Military Park, Daviston, AL 9
Johnson, Allen S., Pres., Lincoln County Pioneer Museum, Hendricks, MN 880
Johnson, Amy, Collections Management Specialist, Indian Pueblo Cultural Center, Albuquerque, NM 1071
Johnson, Andrew B., Collection Mgr. Birds, Museum of Southwestern Biology, Albuquerque, NM 1072
Johnson, Ann, Museum Shop Mgr., Historic Town of Salem, Winston-Salem, NC 1274
Johnson, Ann Marie, Collections Mgr., Charles A. Weyerhaeuser Memorial Museum, Little Falls, MN 882
Johnson, Annie, Treas. FIDM Museum & Galleries, Los Angeles, CA 135
Johnson Austin, Saundra, C.E.O., San Miguel Mission Church, Santa Fe, NM 1091
Johnson, Barbara, Dir. Flagship Niagara League, Erie Maritime Museum & Flagship Niagara, Erie, PA 1424
Johnson, Barbara, Dir. Operations, History San Jose, San Jose, CA 195
Johnson, Betty, Sec., Renville County Historical Society, Mohall, ND 1288

J–*Continued*

Johnson, Bill, Exec. Dir., American Truck Historical Society, Kansas City, MO.......932
Johnson, Bill, Horticulture Volunteer Coord., Hillwood Estate, Museum & Gardens, Washington, DC.......................318
Johnson, Brooks, Cur. Photography, Chrysler Museum of Art, Norfolk, VA..1729
Johnson, Bruce, Security & Operations, Mighty Eighth Air Force Museum, Pooler, GA...429
Johnson, Byron A., Dir., Texas Ranger Hall of Fame and Museum, Waco, TX .1655
Johnson, Carl, House & Night Mgr., Abrons Arts Center/Henry Street Settlement, New York, NY....................1161
Johnson, Carol K., Museum Shop Mgr., Lyndon Baines Johnson Library and Museum, Austin, TX............................1582
Johnson, Carrie, Customer Svc. Coord., Rockford Art Museum, Rockford, IL......517
Johnson, Charlene, Pres. Emeritus & Office Mgr., Alton Museum of History and Art, Inc., Alton, IL............................468
Johnson, Charles, Librarian, Museum of Ventura County, Ventura, CA..................221
Johnson, Cheri, Dir. Admin., Crocker Art Museum, Sacramento, CA......................175
Johnson, Cherry, Cur., Rome Area History Museum, Rome, GA..................430
Johnson, Chris, Biologist, Loggerhead Marinelife Center, Juno Beach, FL..........357
Johnson, Chris K., Pres., The International Clown Hall of Fame & Research Center, Inc., Milwaukee, WI..1834
Johnson, Christina, Collections Mgr. FIDM Museum & Galleries, Los Angeles, CA...135
Johnson, Christy, Dir. & Cur., American Museum of Ceramic Art, Pomona, CA...165
Johnson, Christyl, Volunteer Coord., Krohn Conservatory, Cincinnati, OH.....1305
Johnson, Cindy, Dir., Chestnut Square - Heritage Guild of Collin County, McKinney, TX..1631
Johnson, Claus, Asst. Dir., Cheyenne Botanic Gardens, Cheyenne, WY..........1854
Johnson, Craig, Site Mgr., James J. Hill House, Saint Paul, MN...........................894
Johnson, Craig L., Pres., Monterey Museum of Art, Monterey, CA...............149
Johnson, Curt, Pres., Bureau County Historical Society Museum, Princeton, IL...513
Johnson, Cynthia, Sec., Carlton County Historical Society, Cloquet, MN.............872
Johnson, Dale A., Pres. (V), Moody County Museum, Flandreau, SD...........1530
Johnson, David A., Exec. Dir., Alabama Music Hall of Fame, Tuscumbia, AL........25
Johnson, David J., Museum Technician, Casemate Museum, Fort Monroe, VA...1711
Johnson, Dawn, Deputy Dir. Programming, Tampa Museum of Art, Tampa, FL...393
Johnson, DeLena, Dir., Palmer Museum of History and Art, Palmer, AK................34
Johnson, Denise J.H., Registrar, Addison Gallery of American Art, Andover, MA..753
Johnson, Derek, Operations Mgr., Holland Area Arts Council, Holland, MI..845
Johnson, Diane, Dir. Parks & Recreation, George Washington's Headquarters, Cumberland, MD...733
Johnson, Diane, Chm., Lake Tahoe Historical Society & Museum, South Lake Tahoe, CA.......................................213
Johnson, Donna, Museum Shop Mgr., Mashantucket Pequot Museum and Research Center, Mashantucket, CT.......281
Johnson, Donna, Museum Shop Mgr., Seacoast Science Center, Rye, NH........1028
Johnson, Dorothy, Animal Cur. Alum Rock, Youth Science Institute, San Jose, CA..197
Johnson, Douglas, C.E.O. & Exec. Dir., McLean County Arts Center, Bloomington, IL.......................................472
Johnson, Doyle "Doye" G., Exec. Vice Pres. & Dir., Elberton Granite Museum & Exhibit, Elberton, GA..........417
Johnson, Drew, Cur. Art Photography, Oakland Museum of California, Oakland, CA..155
Johnson, Earl F., Vice Pres. Finance & Operations, Strong National Museum of Play, Rochester, NY..........................1203
Johnson, Edward, Dir. Science, Staten Island Museum, Staten Island, NY........1216
Johnson, Edward C., Pres. (V), Goschenhoppen Folklife Library and Museum, Green Lane, PA.....................1429
Johnson, Dr. Eileen, Cur. Anthropology, Museum of Texas Tech University, Lubbock, TX..1629
Johnson, Elizabeth, Educator, Fort Hunter Mansion & Park, Harrisburg, PA..........1430
Johnson, Elizabeth, Cur. Collections, Pendleton District Agricultural Museum, Pendleton, SC..........................1521
Johnson, Elizabeth M., Dir. Historical Svcs., South Carolina Department of Archives & History, Columbia, SC.......1509
Johnson, Eric, Treas., Dayton Historical Depot Society, Dayton, WA..................1763
Johnson, Evelyn, Dir., Cave Creek Museum, Cave Creek, AZ..........................39
Johnson, Everett, Cur., Big Sandy Heritage Center, Pikeville, KY...............662
Johnson, F.C., III, Historian, Legacy Museum on Main: A History Museum for West Georgia, LaGrange, GA...........423
Johnson, Felicia, Cur. Education, Baton Rouge Zoo, Baton Rouge, LA................666
Johnson, Fred, Dir. Exhibition Design, Peabody Essex Museum, Salem, MA......804
Johnson, Frederic P., Pres. Historical Society (V), Redington Museum, Waterville, ME..714
Johnson, Gary T., Pres., Chicago History Museum, Chicago, IL.................................478
Johnson, Genea, Museum Shop Mgr., Merchant and Drovers Tavern Museum, Rahway, NJ............................1059
Johnson, Gil, Museum Shop Mgr., San Diego Hall of Champions Sports Museum, San Diego, CA.........................183
Johnson, Gina, Program Dir., Saratoga National Historical Park, Stillwater, NY...1217
Johnson, Glen D., Chm. (V), Gaylord-Pickens Oklahoma Heritage Museum, Oklahoma City, OK..............1370
Johnson, Glenn, Pres., Fort Sidney Museum & Post Commander's Home, Sidney, NE..997
Johnson, Gloria, Security Chief, West Point Museum, West Point, NY............1228
Johnson, Greg, Pres. Bd., Kidspace Children's Museum, Pasadena, CA.........162
Johnson, H. Reed, Supt., Appomattox Court House National Historical Park, Appomattox, VA.................................1699
Johnson, Harold, Pres. (V), Andrew County Museum & Historical Society, Savannah, MO...952
Johnson, Heather, Acting Exec. Dir. & Cur., Octagon Center for the Arts, Ames, IA...573
Johnson, Heather, Dir. Education, Santa Barbara Zoological Gardens, Santa Barbara, CA..204
Johnson, Heidi, Public Rels., Queen Emma Summer Palace, Honolulu, HI.....447
Johnson, Jacquie, Pres., Krasl Art Center, Saint Joseph, MI.......................................864
Johnson, James, Pres. (V), Cherry Valley Museum, Cherry Valley, NY................1120
Johnson, Jan, Museum Shop Mgr., Door County Maritime Museum (at Gills Rock), Gills Rock, WI.........................1820
Johnson, Jan, Museum Shop Mgr., Door County Maritime Museum (at Sturgeon Bay), Sturgeon Bay, WI.........1846
Johnson, Jason, Railroad Restoration, The Dennison Railroad Depot Museum, Dennison, OH...1318
Johnson, Jean, Pres., Carlton County Historical Society, Cloquet, MN.............872
Johnson, Jennifer, Public Rels., Denison Pequotsepos Nature Center, Mystic, CT..283
Johnson, Jennifer L., Arts Admin., Columbus Cultural Arts Center, Columbus, OH...1312
Johnson, Jerome Martin, Dir., Garfield Farm Museum, LaFox, IL.......................502
Johnson, Jerry, Vice Pres., Jackson County Historical Society, Black River Falls, WI..1813
Johnson, Jerry L., Vice Pres., The Lyons Redstone Museum, Lyons, CO...............257
Johnson, Jessica A., Senior Cur., Amherst Museum, Amherst, NY..........................1099
Johnson, Jill, Chm. Bd. Dir., The Sixth Floor Museum at Dealey Plaza, Dallas, TX...1600
Johnson, Jimmy, Maintenance, Wilderness Road Regional Museum, Newbern, VA...1727
Johnson, Joe, Chm. (V), Discovery Center (East Tennessee Discovery Center), Knoxville, TN..........................1557
Johnson, Joedi, Volunteer & Tour Coord., Moss Mansion Historic House Museum, Billings, MT...............................956
Johnson, John, Cur., Agrirama, Georgia's Living History Museum & Village, Tifton, GA..437
Johnson, John, Devel., American Sign Museum, Cincinnati, OH.......................1303
Johnson, Dr. John R., Cur. Anthropology, Santa Barbara Museum of Natural History, Santa Barbara, CA....................204
Johnson, Joia, Bd. Advisory Chm., Southeastern Center for Contemporary Art, Winston-Salem, NC.......................1275
Johnson, Joseph, Cur., Georgia Music Hall of Fame, Macon, GA......................425
Johnson, Judy, Pres. (V), Hawkeye Log Cabin, Burlington, IA.............................575
Johnson, Judy, Pres. (V), Phelps House, Burlington, IA...575
Johnson, Julie, Sec., Eastern Oregon Museum, Haines, OR..........................1391
Johnson, Julie, Aquarist, North Carolina Aquarium at Fort Fisher, Kure Beach, NC..1255
Johnson, Karen, Dir., Charles M. Schulz Museum and Research Center, Santa Rosa, CA...208
Johnson, Karen, Treas., Harlow Gallery, Kennebec Valley Art Association, Hallowell, ME...699
Johnson, Kate, Chm. Education Div., Minneapolis Institute of Arts, Minneapolis, MN...886
Johnson, Katheryne, Pres. (V), Red River Valley Museum, Vernon, TX.................1652
Johnson, Kathleen E., Cur., Historic Hudson Valley, Tarrytown, NY.............1220
Johnson, Kathryn Jill, Painting, The Art Galleries at UAH, Huntsville, AL.............14

J–*Continued*

J–*Continued*

Joyce, Julie, Cur. Contemporary Art, Santa Barbara Museum of Art, Santa Barbara, CA 203
Joyce, Larry, Chm. & Pres., Iroquois Indian Museum, Howes Cave, NY 1142
Joyce, Leah, C.E.O. Cahokia Mounds Museum Society, Cahokia Mounds State Historic Site, Collinsville, IL 488
Joyce, Lillian, Art History, The Art Galleries at UAH, Huntsville, AL 14
Joyce, Tari-Lynn, Education Coord., The Webb-Deane-Stevens Museum, Wethersfield, CT 301
Joyner, Elizabeth, Museum Cur., National Park Service Vicksburg National Military Park-Cairo Museum, Vicksburg, MS 918
Joyner, Gary T., Sr. Retail Operations Mgr., Jamestown Settlement, Yorktown Victory Center, The Jamestown-Yorktown Foundation, Williamsburg, VA 1754
Joyner, J. Brooks, Dir., Joslyn Art Museum, Omaha, NE 995
Joyner, Joy L., Mgr., Providence Canyon State Park, Lumpkin, GA 424
Joyner, Roger D., Cur. Planetarium, The Natural Science Center of Greensboro, Inc., Greensboro, NC 1249
Juaire, Ray, Exhibitions Mgr., Museum of Contemporary Art Cleveland, Cleveland, OH 1309
Juarez, Brenda, Museum Shop Mgr., Staatsburgh State Historic Site, Staatsburg, NY 1214
Jucha, Paul, Controller, Johnstown Area Heritage Association, Johnstown, PA 1437
Juchniewich, Daniel, Asst. Dir., Rahr West Art Museum, Manitowoc, WI 1829
Juday, Nicole, Horticulturist, Wyck, Philadelphia, PA 1463
Judd, Ernest, Dir., Holland Historical Society Museum, Inc., Holland, VT 1681
Judd, Martha, Dir., Holland Historical Society Museum, Inc., Holland, VT 1681
Judge, Joseph M., Cur., Hampton Roads Naval Museum, Norfolk, VA 1730
Judge McCalpin, Sara, Pres., China Institute Gallery, China Institute In America, New York, NY 1166
Judis, Sue, Ranger, Perry's Victory & International Peace Memorial, Put-in-Bay, OH 1341
Judkin, Brandon, Pres., Indianapolis Museum of Contemporary Art, Indianapolis, IN 550
Judkins, Barbara, Tour Mgr. & Museum Shop Mgr., Dallas Heritage Village at Old City Park, Dallas, TX 1597
Judkins, Barbara, Museum Educator, Farmers Branch Historical Park, Farmers Branch, TX 1606
Judson, Jack, C.E.O. & Cur., The Magic Lantern Castle Museum, San Antonio, TX 1644
Judy, Dave, Communications Mgr., Kohl Children's Museum of Greater Chicago, Glenview, IL 498
Juechter, Clare, Museum Shop Mgr., Historic Cold Spring Village, Cape May, NJ 1034
Juelich, Clarence, Pres., Traverse County Historical Society, Wheaton, MN 901
Juergens, Jackie, Museum Shop Mgr., West Valley Art Museum, Surprise, AZ 56
Juergens, Karyn, Museum Shop Mgr., Kalamazoo Institute of Arts, Kalamazoo, MI 847
Juhasz, Monica, Naturalist, Environmental Education Center, Somerset County Park Commission, Basking Ridge, NJ 1032
Julian, Judy, Dir., Fossil Country Museum, Kemmerer, WY 1860
Julian, Kitty, Dir. Mktg., Carnegie Museum of Art, Pittsburgh, PA 1464
Julian, Kitty, Dir. Mktg., Carnegie Museum of Natural History, Pittsburgh, PA 1464
Julian, Randy Lee, Museum Committee Chm., Excelsior-Lake Minnetonka Historical Society, Excelsior, MN 877
Julich, Gordon, Supt. Heritage Museums & Programs, Fort Osage National Historic Landmark, Sibley, MO 952
Julich, Gordon, Supt. Heritage Programs & Museums, Harry S. Truman Office & Courtroom, Independence, MO 930
Julich, Gordon, Supt. Heritage Museums & Programs, Missouri Town 1855, Lee's Summit, MO 938
Julis, Judy, Controller, Delaware Museum of Natural History, Wilmington, DE 312
Julius, Eric, Aquarist, Children's Aquarium at Fair Park, Dallas, TX 1597
Julo, Tony, Admin. Asst., Toy & Miniature Museum of Kansas City, Kansas City, MO 935
Junak, Steve, Cur. Herbarium, Santa Barbara Botanic Garden, Santa Barbara, CA 203
Juneau, Kathy, Chm. (V), Corpus Christi Museum of Science and History, Corpus Christi, TX 1594
Jung, Alice, Museum Education Asst., Arizona Museum of Natural History, Mesa, AZ 46
Jung, Jim, Pres., Robbins Hunter Museum, Avery-Downer House, Granville, OH 1323
Jung, Theresa Flynn, Asst. Supt., Edison National Historic Site, West Orange, NJ 1067
Junge, Randy, D.V.M., Dir. Animal Health, Saint Louis Zoo, Saint Louis, MO 951
Jungi, Mary, Dir. & Chm. (V), Downieville Museum, Downieville, CA 109
Jungman, Jodi, Public Program Coord., Star of the Republic Museum, Washington, TX 1655
Junior, Pamela D., Mgr. & Museum Shop Mgr., Smith Robertson Museum & Cultural Center, Jackson, MS 912
Junkins, J.T., Pres., Aliceville Museum, Aliceville, AL 3
Junor, Maggi, Database & Office Mgr., Mizel Museum, Denver, CO 241
Juras, Jackie, Volunteer Coord., Missouri Botanical Garden, Saint Louis, MO 949
Jurcsek, Stephen, Admin., Meriks Zoo, Graysville, AL 13
Jurcsek, Thomas, Collections Mgmt., Meriks Historical Society, Dover, AR 69
Jurgemeyer, Marne, Dir., Fort Morgan Museum, Fort Morgan, CO 246
Jurgens, Allison, Cur., Kent Historical Society Museum, Kent, WA 1769
Jurgensen, Patricia M., Second Vice Pres., Columbus Museum of Art, Columbus, OH 1312
Jurgonski, Marilyn, Finance Mgr., Copshaholm House Museum & Historic Oliver Gardens, South Bend, IN 565
Jurgonski, Marilyn, Finance Mgr., Northern Indiana Center for History, South Bend, IN 565
Jurkiewicz, Mary, Dir., Montpelier Mansion, Laurel, MD 740
Jurovics, Toby, Cur. Photography, Smithsonian American Art Museum, Washington, DC 329
Jurus, Julian S., 1st Vice Pres., Polish American Museum, Port Washington, NY 1196
Just, Bryan, Peter J. Sharp Cur. & Lecturer, Art of Ancient America, Princeton University Art Museum, Princeton, NJ 1058
Justice, Adam, Cur. Fine Art, William King Museum Center for Art and Cultural Heritage, Abingdon, VA 1695
Justice, Bill, Interpretation Chief, Chesapeake and Ohio Canal National Historical Park, Hagerstown, MD 737
Justice, Brenda, Supt., Goliad State Park, Goliad, TX 1616
Justice, Caitlin, Museum Shop Mgr., Justice Brothers Racing Museum, Duarte, CA 109
Justice, Ed, Jr., C.E.O. & Pres., Justice Brothers Racing Museum, Duarte, CA 109
Justice, Eddie, Museum Shop Mgr., Tennessee Central Railway Museum, Nashville, TN 1569
Justus, Sherry, Public Affairs Specialist, Lyndon B. Johnson National Historical Park, Johnson City, TX 1625
Jutilla, Thomas M., Dir., The Karpeles Manuscript Museum, Tacoma, WA 1790
Jutzi, Alan, Cur. Rare Books, Huntington Library, Art Collections, and Botanical Gardens, San Marino, CA 198
Juull, Allison, Collections Mgmt. & Communications Coord., Brunnier Art Museum, Ames, IA 572
Juull, Allison, Collections Mgmt. & Communications Coord., Christian Petersen Art Museum, Ames, IA 572
Juull, Allison, Collections Mgmt. & Communications Coord., Farm House Museum, Ames, IA 573
Juveland, Omar, Exhibits Designer, Bradbury Science Museum, Los Alamos, NM 1082
Juzaitis, Ms. Barbara, Pres. (V), Avalon Historical Society, Avalon, NJ 1031
Juzaitis, Jennifer, Vice Pres. Devel., Museum of the City of New York, New York, NY 1176
Juzaitis, Jennifer, Dir. Devel., The Paley Center for Media, New York, NY 1179

K

Ka'aihue, Garry, Facility Mgr., The Contemporary Museum, Honolulu, HI 443
Ka'aihue, Garry, Bldg. & Grounds Mgr., The Contemporary Museum at First Hawaiian Center, Honolulu, HI 443
Kaat, Linda, Pres., Brandywine Battlefield Park, Chadds Ford, PA 1416
Kabler, Christine, Cur., Chase County Historical Society, Inc., Cottonwood Falls, KS 608
Kabrud, Jack, Cur., Hennepin History Museum, Minneapolis, MN 885
Kading, Joye, Founder, Wyoming Veterans' Memorial Museum, Casper, WY 1854
Kaduk, Ken, Sr. Vice Pres. Finance & Administration, Chicago Zoological Society/Brookfield Zoo, Brookfield, IL 473
Kaeb, Luanne, Education, Lowell Area Historical Museum, Lowell, MI 850
Kaeding, Marlene, Co-Pres., Burt County Museum, Tekamah, NE 998
Kaemmerer, Ken, Cur. Mammals, Dallas Zoo, Dallas, TX 1598
Kafel, Diane, Vice Pres., Morris County Historical Society (Acorn Hall House Museum), Morristown, NJ 1050
Kaffenberger, Schorsch, Collectors' Gallery Asst., Mingei International Museum, San Diego, CA 180

K–*Continued*

Kaffenberger, Vicki, Mng. Dir. Institutional Advancement, Missouri Historical Society, Saint Louis, MO........949

Kaftner, Lois, Museum Shop Mgr., Fort Leavenworth Historical Society, Fort Leavenworth, KS........612

Kaftner, Lois, Museum Shop Mgr., Frontier Army Museum, Fort Leavenworth, KS........612

Kagan, Ron L., C.E.O., Belle Isle Nature Zoo, Detroit, MI........833

Kagan-Moore, Lori, Cur., The Great American Doll House Museum, Danville, KY........645

Kageyama, Mariko, Collections Mgr. Zoology, University of Colorado Museum of Natural History, Boulder, CO........230

Kahan, Mitchell, Ph.D., Dir. & C.E.O., Akron Art Museum, Akron, OH........1292

Kahle, David, Dir., Bede Art Gallery, Yankton, SD........1545

Kahle, Jan, Education Coord., Historic New Harmony, New Harmony, IN........560

Kahle, Patricia, Dir., The Shadows-on-the-Teche, New Iberia, LA........678

Kahler, Christina, Dir. Mktg., Omaha Children's Museum, Omaha, NE........995

Kahler, John, Chm. (V), Minnesota Air National Guard Historical Foundation, Inc., Saint Paul, MN........894

Kahn, David, Dir., The Marston House/San Diego Historical Society, San Diego, CA........180

Kahn, David, Dir., Museum of San Diego History and Research Library, San Diego, CA........181

Kahn, David, Dir., Serra Museum/San Diego Historical Society, San Diego, CA........185

Kahn, Eunice, Archivist, Navajo Nation Museum, Window Rock, AZ........65

Kahn, Gilbert S., Chm. (V), A.K.C. Museum of The Dog, Saint Louis, MO........945

Kahn, Tammie, Exec. Dir., The Children's Museum of Houston, Houston, TX........1619

Kahng, Dr. Eik, Cur. 18th & 19th Century Art, Walters Art Museum, Baltimore, MD........727

Kaholokula, Robbie, Exec. Dir., Kauai Museum, Lihue, HI........452

Kahula, Jackie, Chm. (V), Hana Cultural Center, Hana, Maui, HI........441

Kaiser, Adrienne, Dir. Events, Vizcaya Museum and Gardens, Miami, FL........367

Kaiser, Arlene R., Treas., Waterloo Area Historical Society, Grass Lake, MI........843

Kaiser, Ellie, Asst. Mgr. Photograph Archives, United States Golf Association Museum, Far Hills, NJ........1038

Kaiser, Karen, Asst. Cur. Education, Jundt Art Museum, Spokane, WA........1786

Kaiser, Lynn, Vice Pres., Rusk County Historical Society, Ladysmith, WI........1826

Kajer, Andrea, Deputy Dir. External Rels., Minnesota Historical Society, Saint Paul, MN........895

Kaji, Neeta, Officer Mgr. & Internal Accountant, Meadows Museum of Art of Centenary College, Shreveport, LA....686

Kakouris, George, Chm. (V), Coral Gables Museum, Coral Gables, FL........340

Kalani, Lyn, Dir., Fort Ross State Historic Park Visitor Center and Museum, Jenner, CA........125

Kaldahl, Dr. Eric, Cur., The Amerind Foundation, Inc., Dragoon, AZ........40

Kalen, Kim, Asst. Dir., Charles River Museum of Industry & Innovation, Waltham, MA........812

Kalinoski, Eileen, Museum Shop Mgr., Hampton National Historic Site, Towson, MD........748

Kalinovska, Milena, Program Dir., Hirshhorn Museum and Sculpture Garden, Smithsonian Institution, Washington, DC........319

Kalisperis, Rachel, Cur., South Carolina Aquarium, Charleston, SC........1506

Kalla, Joe, Vice Pres. Operations, Houston Zoo, Inc., Houston, TX........1621

Kallas, Nick, Exec. Dir., Illinois Railway Museum, Union, IL........524

Kallenberger, Christine Knop, Dir. Exhibitions & Collections, The Philbrook Museum of Art, Inc., Tulsa, OK........1379

Kallhoff, Traci, Dir. Exhibits & Technical Svcs., Exploration Place, Inc., Wichita, KS........637

Kallmeyer, Carol, Sec., Historic Hermann Museum, Hermann, MO........929

Kallmeyer, Joy, Pres. (V), Historic Hermann Museum, Hermann, MO........929

Kalmar, Stefan, Exec. Dir., Artists Space, New York, NY........1164

Kalmes, Jean, Chm. (V) & Museum Shop Mgr., Rollingstone-Luxembourg Heritage Museum, Rollingstone, MN......892

Kalnins, Indulis, Cur., Wells Fargo History Museum, Sacramento, CA........177

Kaltenbach, Ryan, Asst. Cur., Saginaw Art Museum, Saginaw, MI........863

Kaltved, David, Pres., H.G. Albee Memorial Museum, Estherville, IA........586

Kaluahine, Chacha, Volunteer Coord., Kauai Museum, Lihue, HI........452

Kaluzniacki, Sophia, D.V.M., Chm. Bd. Trustees, Arizona-Sonora Desert Museum, Tucson, AZ........59

Kam, Betty Lou, Vice Pres. Cultural Resources, Bishop Museum, Honolulu, HI........443

Kama-Drake, Lyah, Education & Art Mezzanine Gallery, Kauai Museum, Lihue, HI........452

Kamen, Brian, Preparator, University Museums, University of Delaware, Newark, DE........310

Kamerer, Tracy, Chief Cur., Flagler Museum, Palm Beach, FL........375

Kamerling, Leonard J., Dir. Alaska Center for Documentary Film, University of Alaska Museum of the North, Fairbanks, AK........30

Kamin, Sophie, Mgr. Exhibitions & Collections, Children's Museum of the Arts, New York, NY........1166

Kaminitz, Marian, Head of Conservation, National Museum of the American Indian, Smithsonian Institution, New York, NY........1177

Kaminsky, Joy, Dir., Bayard Cutting Arboretum, Great River, NY........1139

Kamm, David, Gallery Coord., Fine Arts Collection, Luther College, Decorah, IA........582

Kamm, Mary Fae, C.E.O., International Museum of Cultures, Dallas, TX........1599

Kammer, Carol, Pres., Telluride Historical Museum, Telluride, CO........264

Kamp, Dr. Diane D., Dir., Lake County Historical Museum, Tavares, FL........394

Kampe, Allen, Dir., Lars Noak Blacksmith Shop, Larsson/Ostlund Log Home & One-Room Capitol School, New Sweden, ME........704

Kamperman, Christy, Media & Membership Coord., McDonough Museum of Art, Youngstown, OH........1353

Kamps, Lisa, Museum Shop Mgr., Eisenhower National Historic Site, Gettysburg, PA........1427

Kamps, Sylvia, Correspondence Sec., Lars Noak Blacksmith Shop, Larsson/Ostlund Log Home & One-Room Capitol School, New Sweden, ME........704

Kamps, Toby, Sr. Cur., The Contemporary Arts Center, Cincinnati, OH........1305

Kamps, Toby, Sr. Cur., Contemporary Arts Museum Houston, Houston, TX....1619

Kamsky, Virginia A., Chm., China Institute Gallery, China Institute In America, New York, NY........1166

Kamsler, Brigette, Archivist, The Historical Society of Frederick County, Inc., Frederick, MD........735

Kanaga, Marian, Cur. Education, The Monmouth Museum, Lincroft, NJ........1045

Kanatani, Kim, Dir. Education, Solomon R. Guggenheim Museum, New York, NY........1181

Kancher, Pam, Exec. Dir., Holocaust Memorial Resource and Education Center of Florida, Inc., Maitland, FL......363

Kancius, Karen, Dir. Corporate Rels., Milwaukee Public Museum, Milwaukee, WI........1835

Kancler, Audrey, Pres., Twinsburg Historical Society, Twinsburg, OH........1346

Kandebo, Joshua, Program Specialist, Historic Speedwell, Morristown, NJ......1049

Kandel, Herb, Pres. (V), Dana Adobe, Nipomo, CA........152

Kandianis, Patricia, Editor, Lehigh University Art Galleries/Museum Operations, Bethlehem, PA........1412

Kandoll, Kari, Cur., Wahkiakum County Historical Museum, Cathlamet, WA......1761

Kane, Adam, Basin Harbor Site Mgr. & Nautical Archaeologist, The Lake Champlain Maritime Museum, Vergennes, VT........1692

Kane, Allen, Dir., National Postal Museum, Smithsonian Institution, Washington, DC........326

Kane, George, Historic Sites & Facilities, Ohio Historical Society, Columbus, OH........1313

Kane, Joseph, Pres. (V), Historic Speedwell, Morristown, NJ........1049

Kane, Katherine, Exec. Dir. & C.E.O., Harriet Beecher Stowe Center, Hartford, CT........278

Kane, Kathleen, Visitor & Membership Svcs., The Corcoran Gallery of Art, Washington, DC........315

Kane, Kevin, Preparator, Derfner Judaica Museum + The Art Collection at the Hebrew Home at Riverdale, Riverdale, NY........1200

Kane, Kevin, Chm. (V), Memphis Rock 'n' Soul Museum, Memphis, TN........1563

Kane, Martin, Pres., Lake Hopatcong Historical Museum, Landing, NJ........1045

Kane, Patricia, Cur. American Decorative Arts, Yale University Art Gallery, New Haven, CT........287

Kane, Randy, Historian, Fort Union Trading Post National Historic Site, Williston, ND........1291

Kanjo, Kathryn, Dir., University Art Museum, Santa Barbara, Santa Barbara, CA........204

Kanno, Brenda, Chm. (V), Cal State Northridge Botanic Garden, Northridge, CA........153

Kanofsky, Joe, Pres. (V), Highland Community College Arboretum, Freeport, IL........495

K–*Continued*

K–*Continued*

K–*Continued*

K–Continued

K–Continued

K–*Continued*

Kopczak, Dr. Chuck, Cur. World Ecology, California Science Center, Los Angeles, CA....134
Kopecky, Carle J., C.E.O. & Dir., Old Stone Fort Museum Complex, Schoharie, NY....1210
Kopelke, Harold, Restoration & Conservation, James S. Copley Library, La Jolla, CA....126
Koperski, Kate, Dir., Castellani Art Museum of Niagara University, Niagara University, NY....1186
Kopielski, Camille, Treas., Polish Museum of America, Chicago, IL....485
Kopis, Mildred, Cur., Miami County Museum, Peru, IN....562
Koplin, Nancy, Dir., Cambridge Historic Museum, Cambridge, WI....1814
Kopp, Donald, Chm. & Pres. (V), 19th Century Willowbrook Village, Newfield, ME....704
Kopp, Jim, Asst. Cur. Education, Nicolaysen Art Museum and Discovery Center, Casper, WY....1853
Kopp, Mary, Museum Shop Mgr., John Michael Kohler Arts Center, Sheboygan, WI....1844
Kopp, Sandra, Dir. Mktg., The California Museum For History, Women and the Arts, Sacramento, CA....174
Koppert, Mike, Dir., Abbie Gardner State Site, Arnolds Park, IA....573
Koppes, Linda, Photo Technician, Harvey County Historical Society, Newton, KS....628
Koproski, Patricia, Chm. (V), The American Center of Polish Culture, Washington, DC....314
Kopylczak, Vicki, Chm. (V), Narcissa Prentiss House, Prattsburgh, NY....1198
Korch, Chris, Preparator, Wood Street Galleries, Pittsburgh, PA....1468
Kordish, Heike, Dir. Humanities & Social Sciences, The New York Public Library, Astor, Lenox and Tilden Foundations, New York, NY....1178
Korenblat, Ellen, Dir. Communications, Historic Arkansas Museum, Little Rock, AR....77
Koretsky, Nicholas, Pres., Museum of Russian Culture, San Francisco, CA....191
Korhammer, Richard, Pres., International Swimming Hall of Fame, Inc., Fort Lauderdale, FL....347
Korman, Jaymie, Site Supvr., Minnesota State Capitol Historic Site, Saint Paul, MN....895
Kormos, Andrea, Administrative Asst., Museum of Contemporary Art Cleveland, Cleveland, OH....1309
Kornak, Andi, Cur. Collections, Binder Park Zoo, Battle Creek, MI....825
Kornegay, Karen, Mktg. Mgr., Morehead Planetarium and Science Center, Chapel Hill, NC....1237
Kornhauser, Stephen, Chief Paintings Conservator, Wadsworth Atheneum Museum of Art, Hartford, CT....279
Kornick, Brenda, Collections Mgr., C.M. Russell Museum, Great Falls, MT....964
Kors, David, Planetarium Mgr. & Technical Dir., Louisiana Art & Science Museum - Irene W. Pennington Planetarium, Baton Rouge, LA....667
Korsmo-Kennon, Peggy, Head Public Programs, Bell Museum of Natural History, Minneapolis, MN....884
Korte, Maureen, Museum Theater, State Historical Museum of Iowa, Des Moines, IA....584
Korth, Tony, Dir., Ak-Sar-Ben Aquarium Outdoor Education Center, Gretna, NE....985
Kortlander, Christopher, C.E.O., Custer Battlefield Museum, Garryowen, MT....963
Korzec, Patricia, C.E.O., March Field Air Museum, Riverside, CA....172
Korzelius, Carol, Museum Shop Mgr., Hildene, The Lincoln Family Home, Manchester, VT....1683
Kosaka, Denise H., Gallery Dir., Hawaii State Foundation on Culture & the Arts and Hawaii State Art Museum, Honolulu, HI....445
Kosakowski, Kate, Volunteer Coord., Discovery Science Center, Fort Collins, CO....246
Kosch, Brad, Rgnl. Mgr., Mormon Station State Historic Park, Genoa, NV....1004
Koschmeder, Krista, Pres. (V), Mitchell County Historical Museum, Osage, IA....596
Koshalek, Richard, Exec. Dir., Hirshhorn Museum and Sculpture Garden, Smithsonian Institution, Washington, DC....319
Kosharek, Daniel, Photo Archivist, Palace of the Governors/New Mexico History Museum, Santa Fe, NM....1090
Kosier, Hope E., Project Coord., Diplomatic Reception Rooms, Department of State, Washington, DC....316
Kosier, Marilyn, Devel., Bradford Ohio Railroad Museum, Bradford, OH....1298
Kosinski, Dorothy, Dir., The Phillips Collection, Washington, DC....328
Koski, Carl, Photographer, The History Center in Tompkins County, Ithaca, NY....1146
Koski, Elizabeth, Exec. Dir., Ashtabula Arts Center, Ashtabula, OH....1294
Koslow, Alan, Esq., Chm. (V), Art and Culture Center of Hollywood, Hollywood, FL....353
Kostelny, Elizabeth, Exec. Dir. APVA Preservation Virginia, Richmond, VA....1736
Kostelny, Elizabeth, Exec. Dir., Bacon's Castle, Surry County, VA....1749
Kostelny, Elizabeth, Exec. Dir. APVA, Cape Henry Lighthouse, Virginia Beach, VA....1751
Kostelny, Elizabeth, Exec. Dir. Preservation Virginia, Historic Jamestowne, Jamestown, VA....1718
Kostelny, Elizabeth, Exec. Dir., Isle of Wight Courthouse, Smithfield, VA....1745
Kostelny, Elizabeth, Exec. Dir. APVA, The John Marshall House, Richmond, VA....1738
Kostelny, Elizabeth, C.E.O. (APVA), Lynnhaven House, Virginia Beach, VA.1752
Kostelny, Elizabeth, C.E.O., Smith's Fort Plantation, Surry, VA....1749
Kostelny, Elizabeth, Exec. Dir., Warner Hall Graveyard, Gloucester, VA....1714
Kostenbader, Tracy, Designer, Spertus Museum, Chicago, IL....486
Koster, Emlyn H., Ph.D., Pres. & C.E.O., Liberty Science Center, Jersey City, NJ....1044
Koster, John, Conservator, National Music Museum, Vermillion, SD....1544
Koster, Julia, Museum Shop Mgr., Naval War College Museum, Newport, RI....1491
Kosty, Pam, Asst. Dir. Public Information, University of Pennsylvania Museum of Archaeology and Anthropology, Philadelphia, PA....1462
Kot, Malgorzata, Librarian, Polish Museum of America, Chicago, IL....485
Kotarba, Kathleen, Dir., Edgar Allan Poe House and Museum, Baltimore, MD....721
Kotch, Ammiee, Administrative Asst., Frankenmuth Historical Museum, Frankenmuth, MI....841
Kotei, Ebenezer, Objects Conservator, Hagley Museum and Library, Wilmington, DE....313
Kotik, Charlotta, Cur. Contemporary Art, Brooklyn Museum, Brooklyn, NY....1111
Kouba, Jess, Chm. (V), Hettinger County Historical Society, Regent, ND....1289
Kouzmanoff, Derek, Sec., Monticello Railway Museum, Monticello, IL....506
Kovalcik, Anne, Dir., The Great Passion Play Bible Museum, Eureka Springs, AR....70
Kovalcik, Paul, Dir., Walkersville Southern Railroad Museum, Walkersville, MD....749
Kovalenko, Donna, Collections Mgr. & Registrar, Frye Art Museum, Seattle, WA....1780
Kovaleski, Kerrie, Dir. Volunteers, The Maryland Zoo in Baltimore, Baltimore, MD....724
Kovaleski, Theresa, Membership Sec., Lock Museum of America, Inc., Terryville, CT....297
Kovatch, Ann, Sec., Wayne County Historical Society, Honesdale, PA....1434
Koverman, Jill, Cur. Collections, The University of South Carolina McKissick Museum, Columbia, SC....1510
Kovry, Michelle, Administrative Asst., Humboldt State University Natural History Museum, Arcata, CA....88
Kowalczyk, Susan, Collections Mgr., The Schein-Joseph International Museum of Ceramic Art, Alfred, NY....1098
Kowaliw, Robert, Custodian, South Bannock County Historical Center, Lava Hot Springs, ID....461
Kowalski, Very Rev. Dr. James A., C.E.O., The Cathedral of St. John the Divine, New York, NY....1165
Kowalski, Kathy, Pres. Bd., Manitowoc County Historical Society, Manitowoc, WI....1829
Kowalski, Michael J., Chm. (V), Bd. Overseers, University of Pennsylvania Museum of Archaeology and Anthropology, Philadelphia, PA....1462
Koy, Gary, Mktg., National Historic Oregon Trail Interpretive Center, Baker City, OR....1384
Kozel, Jennifer, School & Outreach Programs Mgr., Children's Museum of Manhattan, New York, NY....1165
Kozik, Jennifer, Collections & Programs Mgr., Washington County Historical Society, Portland, OR....1401
Kozikowski, Lance, Museum Asst., Old New-Gate Prison and Copper Mine, East Granby, CT....271
Kozikowski, Linda, Museum Shop Mgr., The New England Carousel Museum, Bristol, CT....268
Kozlowski, Kazimiera, Cur. II, Prudence Crandall Museum, Canterbury, CT....269
Kozma, LuAnne, Asst. Cur. Folk Arts, The Michigan State University Museum, East Lansing, MI....838
Krabill, Donna, Dir. Education, Norfolk Botanical Garden, Norfolk, VA....1731
Kraczon, Kate, Curatorial Asst., Institute of Contemporary Art, University of Pennsylvania, Philadelphia, PA....1455
Krafchik, Jennifer, Collection Mgr., Sewall-Belmont House and Museum, Washington, DC....329
Krafft, Robert E., Exec. Dir., National Military History Center, Auburn, IN....531
Kraft, Brian, Head Registration, Minneapolis Institute of Arts, Minneapolis, MN....886
Kraft, Doreen, Exec. Dir., The Firehouse Gallery, Burlington, VT....1678

K–*Continued*

Kraft, Dottie, Volunteer Coord., Davenport House Museum, Savannah, GA....433
Kraft, Joe C., C.E.O. & Chm., Bushwhacker Museum, Nevada, MO....941
Kraft, Susan, Pres. & Museum Shop Mgr., Yellowstone Gateway Museum of Park County, Livingston, MT....968
Kragliak, Amanda, Gallery Dir., Ann Arbor Art Center, Ann Arbor, MI....822
Kragness, Kurt K., Exec. Dir., Sherburne History Center, Becker, MN....870
Krah, Pat, Pres., Menominee County Heritage Museum, Menominee, MI....854
Krahmer, Fred W., C.E.O., Pioneer Museum - Martin County Historical Society, Fairmont, MN....877
Krahoviak, Carla, Asst. Dir. Education, The Magic House, St. Louis Children's Museum, Saint Louis, MO....948
Kraina, Jane, Archivist, Brooke County Public Library Museum Branch, Wellsburg, WV....1807
Krainik, Paul, Chm., West Virginia University-Mesaros Galleries, Morgantown, WV....1803
Krajniak, Paul J., Exec. Dir., Discovery World, Milwaukee, WI....1833
Krakora, Joseph J., Exec. Officer, Devel. & External Affairs, National Gallery of Art, Washington, DC....323
Kralickova, Petra, Cur., Kennedy Museum of Art, Athens, OH....1294
Kralickova, Petra, Dir. Exhibition, Ohio University Art Gallery, Athens, OH....1294
Kramer, Andrea T., Exec. Dir. BGCI-US, Chicago Botanic Garden, Glencoe, IL....497
Kramer, Bethany, Museum Shop Mgr., Brigham Young University Museum of Art, Provo, UT....1667
Kramer, Cheryl, Dir. & Asst. Prof., Handwerker Gallery, Ithaca, NY....1146
Kramer DeBalko, Brittany, Dir., Sordoni Art Gallery, Wilkes-Barre, PA....1482
Kramer, Julie, Dir., North Shore Arts Association, Gloucester, MA....779
Kramer, Lovetta, Museum Dir., Queen Mary, Long Beach, CA....132
Kramer, Lovetta, Pres. Foundation (V), Rancho Los Cerritos Historic Site, Long Beach, CA....132
Kramer, Nancy, Pres. (V), Schweinfurth Memorial Art Center, Auburn, NY....1101
Kramer, Rob, Pres., International Game Fish Association - Fishing Hall of Fame and Museum, Dania Beach, FL....341
Kramer Russell, Karen, Assoc. Cur. Native American Art, Peabody Essex Museum, Salem, MA....804
Kramer, Sheryl, Volunteer & Special Events Coord., The Contemporary Museum, Honolulu, HI....443
Kramer, Sheryl, Volunteer & Special Events Coord., The Contemporary Museum at First Hawaiian Center, Honolulu, HI....443
Kramme, Dr. Mike, Cur. Theatre, Midwest Old Settlers & Threshers Association, Inc., Mount Pleasant, IA....594
Krane, Susan, Exec. Dir., San Jose Museum of Art, San Jose, CA....196
Krantz, Joan, Pres. (V), The North Castle Historical Society, Armonk, NY....1100
Krantz, Kevin, Exhibit Cur., Lafayette Science Museum, Lafayette, LA....673
Krantz, Palmer E., III, Exec. Dir., Riverbanks Zoo & Garden, Columbia, SC....1509
Kranyik, Jay, Horticulture Chm., Botanical Gardens at Asheville, Asheville, NC....1232
Kranz, Karl, C.O.O., The Maryland Zoo in Baltimore, Baltimore, MD....724
Kraskin, Sandra, Ph.D., Dir., Sidney Mishkin Gallery of Baruch College, New York, NY....1180
Krasser, Alta, Chm. Exhibits, Seward County Historical Society Museum, Goehner, NE....983
Krassner, Lisa, Dir. Membership & Visitor Svcs., Museum of Fine Arts, Boston, MA....761
Kratsas, James R., Deputy Dir., Gerald R. Ford Presidential Museum, Grand Rapids, MI....842
Kratt, Kevin, Chm., Cheyenne Mountain Zoological Park, Colorado Springs, CO....233
Kratz, Scott, Vice Pres. Education, National Building Museum, Washington, DC....323
Kratzman, Carol, Dir. Education, Connecticut Audubon Center at Fairfield, Fairfield, CT....273
Kraus, Aniza, Cur., Ukrainian Museum-Archives, Inc., Cleveland, OH....1311
Kraus, Scott, Vice Pres. Research, New England Aquarium Corporation, Boston, MA....762
Kraus, William, Exec. Dir., Tahoe Maritime Museum, Homewood, CA....123
Krause, Emily, Registrar, Fresno Art Museum, Fresno, CA....115
Krause, Glenn, Group Coord., North American Bear Center, Ely, MN....876
Krause, Irv, Volunteer Service League Pres. (V), Museum of Science, Boston, MA....762
Krause, Joanne, Dir. Johnson Heritage Post, Cook County Historical Museum, Grand Marais, MN....878
Krause, Martin F., Jr., Cur. Prints, Drawings & Photographs IMA - Indianapolis Museum of Art, Indianapolis, IN....548
Krause, Nancy, Membership Dir., North American Bear Center, Ely, MN....876
Krause, Troy, Pres. (V), Redwood County Museum, Redwood, MN....891
Krause, Walt, Pres. (V), Rhinelander Logging Museum, Rhinelander, WI....1843
Krauskopf, John, Sec., The Western Railway Museum, Suisun City, CA....214
Krauskopf, Kurt, Pres. & Vice Pres. Bldg. & Property, Circus City Festival Museum, Peru, IN....561
Krauss, A., Sec., Shelter Island Historical Society, Shelter Island, NY....1212
Krauss, David, Chm. (V), Railroad and Heritage Museum Inc., Temple, TX....1650
Krauss, Jeff, Dir. Finance, Museum of the Rockies, Bozeman, MT....958
Krauss, John, Vice Chm. IMA - Indianapolis Museum of Art, Indianapolis, IN....548
Kravec, Steven, Art Handler, Patty and Jay Baker Naples Museum of Art, Naples, FL....370
Kravis, Marie-Josee, Pres., The Museum of Modern Art, New York, NY....1176
Krawczak, Anne, Sec., Empire Area Heritage Group, Empire, MI....839
Krawiec Faubert, Alison, Dir., Passaic County Historical Society & Lambert Castle Museum, Paterson, NJ....1056
Kray, Debbie, Dir. Education, Children's Museum of Tacoma, Tacoma, WA....1788
Kray, Hazel, Dir., The Bartlett Museum, Amesbury, MA....751
Krazmien, Mindy, Exec. Dir., Putnam County Historical Society & Foundry School Museum, Cold Spring, NY....1122
Kreager, Marina, Dir. Human Resources COPIA: The American Center for Wine, Food & the Arts, Napa, CA....150
Kreamer, Christine Mullen, Cur., National Museum of African Art, Smithsonian Institution, Washington, DC....324
Kreamer, Connie, Chm. (V), Sunnyslope Historical Society Museum, Phoenix, AZ....52
Kreamer, Todd A., Cur. History, The Museum of Mobile, Mobile, AL....18
Krecek, Elizabeth, Registrar, General Crook House Museum and Library/Archives Center, Omaha, NE....995
Krech, Shepard, III, Dir., Haffenreffer Museum of Anthropology, Brown University, Providence, RI....1494
Kreider, David, Museum Technician, Kauffman Museum, North Newton, KS....628
Kreider, Lisa, Vice Pres. Operations, Whitaker Center for Science and the Arts, Harrisburg, PA....1432
Kreider, Louisa, Interpretive Technology Specialist, Cleveland Metroparks Outdoor Education Division, Garfield Heights, OH....1322
Kreipe de Montano, Marty, Resource Center Mgr., National Museum of the American Indian, Smithsonian Institution, New York, NY....1177
Krell-Salgado, June, Dir. Cultural Affairs, Salisbury State University Galleries, Salisbury, MD....745
Kremer, Gary R., Exec. Dir., State Historical Society of Missouri, Columbia, MO....924
Kremer, Randall, Public Affairs Mgr., National Museum of Natural History, Washington, DC....325
Kren, Thomas, Sr. Cur. Manuscripts, The J. Paul Getty Museum, Los Angeles, CA....137
Kreps, Dr. Christina, Dir., Museum of Anthropology, University of Denver, Denver, CO....241
Kreps, Dennis, Librarian, Kalamazoo Institute of Arts, Kalamazoo, MI....847
Kress, Brady, Pres. & C.E.O., Dayton History at Carillon Park, Dayton, OH....1316
Kress, Katherine, Museum Shop Mgr., Norton Museum of Art, West Palm Beach, FL....397
Kress, Stephanie, Media Coord., Pensacola Museum of Art, Pensacola, FL....378
Kret, Robert A., Dir., Hunter Museum of American Art, Chattanooga, TN....1548
Kretser, Jennifer, Dir. Programs, Natural History Museum of the Adirondacks/The Wild Center, Tupper Lake, NY....1221
Kretzer, Jayson, Exhibits & Education, Visual Arts Center of Northwest Florida, Panama City, FL....376
Kretzschmar, Sabine, Exec. Dir., The Shaker Historical Society, Shaker Heights, OH....1343
Kreuger, William R., Asst. Librarian, Iowa Masonic Library and Museum, Cedar Rapids, IA....578
Kreutzer-Hodson, Teresa, Cur., Hastings Museum, Hastings, NE....985
Krick, Robert K., Chief Historian, Fredericksburg & Spotsylvania National Military Park, Fredericksburg, VA....1712
Kridel, Dr. Craig, Cur., The Museum of Education, Columbia, SC....1509
Krider, Patricia, Exec. Dir., National First Ladies' Library, Canton, OH....1301
Krieg, Justin, Dir. Planning & Devel., Historic Columbus Foundation, Inc., Columbus, GA....414

Krieg, Linda, Museum Shop Mgr. Cahokia Mounds Museum Society, Cahokia Mounds State Historic Site, Collinsville, IL....488
Krieger, Kim, Dir. Public Rels., Historic Sauder Village, Archbold, OH....1293
Krieger, Robert, Business Mgr., Union Pacific Historical Society (UPHS), Laramie, WY....1862
Krieger, Stella, Museum Shop Mgr., Fowler Museum at UCLA, Los Angeles, CA....135
Krier, Patricia, Dir. Prog., University of Oregon Museum of Natural and Cultural History, Eugene, OR....1389
Krieser, Marcia, Treas., Mayville Historical Society, Inc., Mayville, WI....1831
Kriff, Leslie, Registrar, Jane Voorhees Zimmerli Art Museum, New Brunswick, NJ....1052
Krigsten, Ray, Chm. (V), Sioux City Public Museum, Sioux City, IA....599
Krigsvold, Joyce, Mgr., Pamunkey Indian Museum, King William, VA....1719
Krill, Philip, Pres., Franconia Heritage Museum, Franconia, NH....1018
Krimmel, Elizabeth, Exec. Dir., Wellesley Historical Society, Inc., Wellesley, MA....814
Kriner, Lisa, MFA, Chm. Art Dept., Berea College, Doris Ulmann Galleries, Berea, KY....641
Kring, Kelly, Lead Interpreter, 1860s Living Farmstead, Dallas Heritage Village at Old City Park, Dallas, TX....1597
Kring, Kelly, Facilities Mgr., Heritage Farmstead Museum, Plano, TX....1638
Kring, Sara, Chm. (V) & Cur., Hampton County Historical Society Museum, Hampton, SC....1515
Krinsky, Linda, Dir. Tours, Valentine Richmond History Center, Richmond, VA....1741
Krippene, Carolyn, Museum Technician, Yellowstone National Park, Gardiner, MT....963
Krische-Dee, Helen, Archivist, Watkins Community Museum of History, Lawrence, KS....622
Krishnan, Sarada, Dir. Horticulture, Denver Botanic Gardens, Inc., Denver, CO....238
Krishtalka, Dr. Leonard, Dir. KU Biodiversity Institute - KU Natural History Museum, Lawrence, KS....621
Krissinger, Jack, Chm. (V), National Canal Museum, Hugh Moore Historical Park and Museums, Easton, PA....1421
Kristl, Tim, Chm. Bd. Governors, National World War I Museum at Liberty Memorial, Kansas City, MO....934
Kristoff, Marianne, Supvr. Gardeners, Queens Botanical Garden, Flushing, NY....1133
Krivak, Andrea, Coord. Publications, Erie Art Museum, Erie, PA....1424
Krizek, Barb, Pres. Friends of the Art Center (V), Waterloo Center for the Arts, Waterloo, IA....601
Krody, Sumru, Cur. Eastern Hemisphere, The Textile Museum, Washington, DC....330
Kroeck, L. John, Pres., Sewickley Valley Historical Society, Sewickley, PA....1474
Kroeger, Debby, Education & Volunteer Svcs., California Living Museum CALM, Bakersfield, CA....90
Kroeger, Laura, Museum Shop Mgr., Tennessee Aquarium, Chattanooga, TN....1548
Kroeger, Nancy, Museum Shop Mgr., Poplar Grove Historic Plantation, Wilmington, NC....1272
Kroes, Ronald, Controller, National Liberty Museum, Philadelphia, PA....1458
Krogan, Carol, Asst. Cur., Vernon County Museum, Viroqua, WI....1848
Krogedal, Allison, Sec., Northeastern Montana Threshers and Antique Association, Culbertson, MT....961
Krogedal, David, Pres. (V), Northeastern Montana Threshers and Antique Association, Culbertson, MT....961
Krogman, Mary, Dir., Four Mile Old West Town, Custer, SD....1529
Krohlow, Mary, Museum Shop Mgr., Hawkeye Log Cabin, Burlington, IA....575
Krohlow, Mary, Museum Shop Mgr., Phelps House, Burlington, IA....575
Krohn-Andros, Laurie, Cafe Mgr., Worcester Art Museum, Worcester, MA....819
Krohn-David, Robin, Exec. Dir., Maritime & Seafood Industry Museum, Biloxi, MS....904
Kroll, Amanda, Asst. Dir., Quinlan Visual Arts Center, Gainesville, GA....420
Kromer, Lindsay, Photographer, Frank H. McClung Museum, Knoxville, TN....1558
Kronberg, David A., Exhibit Designer, Mackinac Island State Park Commission-Mackinac State Historic Parks, Mackinaw City, MI....851
Kronberg, David A., Exhibit Designer, Mackinac State Historic Parks-Colonial Michilimackinac & Old Mackinac Point Lighthouse, Mackinaw City, MI....852
Kronberg, David A., Exhibit Designer, Mackinac State Historic Parks-Fort Mackinac & Mackinac Island State Park, Mackinac Island, MI....851
Kronhofman, Mary, Sec. & Cataloging, Tobias Community Historical Society, Tobias, NE....998
Kroning, Melissa, Registrar, Smithsonian American Art Museum, Washington, DC....329
Kronman, George, Chm. Bd., The Museum of Printing History, Houston, TX....1622
Kropf, Joan R., Deputy Dir. Collections, Salvador Dali Museum, Saint Petersburg, FL....385
Kropp, Shari, Pres., Owatonna Arts Center, Owatonna, MN....889
Krossman, Cindy, Exec. Dir., The Scarsdale Historical Society, Scarsdale, NY....1209
Krotky, Gene, Head Cur., Lisbon Historical Society, Lisbon, OH....1328
Krout, Joe, Supvr., Brookside Gardens, Wheaton, MD....750
Krucoff, Carole, Head Museum Education & Pub. Programs, Oriental Institute Museum, University of Chicago, Chicago, IL....485
Krueger, Alice F., Public Rels., Merrill Historical Society, Merrill, WI....1832
Krueger, Catherine M., Dir., Jacksonville Maritime Museum Society, Jacksonville, FL....355
Krueger, Charity, Exec. Dir., Aullwood Audubon Center and Farm, Dayton, OH....1315
Krueger, Dana, Registrar, The Emerson Gallery, Clinton, NY....1122
Krueger, John, Dir., Kent-Delord House Museum, Plattsburgh, NY....1195
Krueger, Markus, Coord. Visitor Svcs., Historical and Cultural Society of Clay County, Moorhead, MN....887
Krueger, Royal, Museum Shop Mgr., Shawnee Town, Shawnee, KS....634
Kruelle, Michael, Head Visitor Svcs., Hillwood Estate, Museum & Gardens, Washington, DC....318
Krueper, Ron, District Supt., Antelope Valley California Poppy Natural Reserve, Lancaster, CA....128
Krug, Andre, Dir. Klein Branch, Fred Wolf, Jr. Gallery/Klein Branch Jewish Community Center, Philadelphia, PA....1453
Kruger, Neil, Vice Pres., Marquette County Historical Society, Westfield, WI....1851
Krugger, Dorothy, Financial Dir., The Houdini Museum & Theater, Scranton, PA....1472
Kruk, Joann, Museum Shop Mgr., West Virginia State Wildlife Center, French Creek, WV....1798
Krul, Jim, Exec. Dir., Catskill Fly Fishing Center & Museum, Livingston Manor, NY....1153
Krulewitch, Deborah, Co Chm., Historic House Trust of New York City, New York, NY....1170
Krulewitch, Peter, Acting Treas., The New York Studio School of Drawing, Painting & Sculpture, New York, NY....1179
Krum, Greg, Dir. Shop, Cooper-Hewitt, National Design Museum, Smithsonian Institution, New York, NY....1167
Krumenaker, Robert J., Supt., Apostles Islands National Lakeshore, Bayfield, WI....1812
Krumm, Debra, Dir. & Museum Shop Mgr., Arthur Roy Mitchell Memorial Museum, Trinidad, CO....264
Krummel, Teresa, Interpretive Ranger, Dahlonega Gold Museum State Historic Site, Dahlonega, GA....415
Krumwiede, Vivian, Sec., Traverse County Historical Society, Wheaton, MN....901
Krupkin, Sid, Education, Jewish Museum of Florida, Miami Beach, FL....368
Krupp, Dr. Edwin C., Dir., Griffith Observatory, Los Angeles, CA....136
Krupp, Susan C., Office Mgr. & Museum Shop Mgr., Catskill Fly Fishing Center & Museum, Livingston Manor, NY....1153
Kruppa, Gail, Cur., Torrington Historical Society, Inc., Torrington, CT....298
Kruppner, Keith, 1st Vice Pres., Middlebury Historical Society, Wyoming, NY....1229
Kruse, Carol, Asst. Dir., Miami Metrozoo, Miami, FL....366
Kruse, Dave, Supt., Lava Beds National Monument, Tulelake, CA....219
Kruse, Dean V., Pres. (V), National Military History Center, Auburn, IN....531
Kruse, Robert, Head Technical Svcs., The Boston Athenaeum, Boston, MA....758
Kruse-Buckingham, Pamela, Dir. & Museum Shop Mgr., Oakland Aviation Museum, Oakland, CA....155
Krusi, Beth, Dir. Mktg. & Communications, Montshire Museum of Science, Inc., Norwich, VT....1686
Kruzich, Judy, Sec., World Museum of Mining, Butte, MT....959
Krynak, Timothy, Naturalist (North Chagrin), Cleveland Metroparks Outdoor Education Division, Garfield Heights, OH....1322
Krzyzanowski, Virginia, Museum Shop Mgr., Howell Historical Society & Committee Museum, Howell, NJ....1043
Kuasnicka, Nadine, Tour Guide, Fick Fossil & History Museum, Oakley, KS....628
Kub, Candis, Sec., J.W. Parmley Historical Home Society, Ipswich, SD....1533
Kub, Ray, Treas., J.W. Parmley Historical Home Society, Ipswich, SD....1533

K–*Continued*

L–*Continued*

Lammi, Jennifer, Business Mgr., Marquette County History Museum, Marquette, MI....853
Lamonaca, Marianne, Assoc. Dir. Curatorial Affairs & Education, The Wolfsonian - Florida International University, Miami Beach, FL....368
Lamond, Joe, C.E.O. & Pres., Museum of Making Music, A Division of the NAMM Foundation, Carlsbad, CA....98
Lamont, Bruce, Pres. (V), Oregon Air & Space Museum, Eugene, OR....1389
Lamont, Doris, Archivist, Historical Society of Saratoga Springs, Saratoga Springs, NY....1207
Lamontagne, Richard, C.F.O., Plimoth Plantation Inc., Plymouth, MA....800
LaMothe, Laurie J., Dir. External Affairs, DeCordova Sculpture Park & Museum, Lincoln, MA....786
LaMountain, Amanda, Dir. Education, The Children's Museum of Memphis, Memphis, TN....1561
Lamp, Frederick, Cur. African Art, Yale University Art Gallery, New Haven, CT....287
Lamp, Mary, Library Volunteer, Dundee Township Historical Society, Inc., Dundee, IL....491
Lampe, Anne M., Dir., Demuth Museum, Lancaster, PA....1438
Lampert, Andrew, Archivist, Anthology Film Archives, New York, NY....1163
Lampert, Stephen P., Vice Pres., Spotsylvania Historical Association and Museum, Spotsylvania, VA....1746
Lampi, Patrick S., Dir., Alaska Zoo, Anchorage, AK....27
Lampkin, Sheilla, Dir., Drew County Historical Museum, Monticello, AR....79
Lampman, D.B., Dir. Programs, The Noble Maritime Collection, Staten Island, NY....1215
Lampo, Joseph, Deputy Dir. Programs, The Arkansas Arts Center, Little Rock, AR....76
Lancaster, Ivan, Pres. (V), Brown County Historical Society Pioneer Museum, Nashville, IN....559
Lancaster, Jean, Chm. (V), Belair Mansion, Bowie, MD....728
Lancaster, Pete, Dir. Facilities, The Children's Museum of Houston, Houston, TX....1619
Lance, Kipper, Dir. Mktg. & Public Rels., Norton Museum of Art, West Palm Beach, FL....397
Lancefield, Robert, Registrar Collections & Mgr. Museum Information Svcs., Davison Art Center, Wesleyan University, Middletown, CT....282
Land, Chris, Art Handler, The Columbus Museum, Columbus, GA....414
Landale, April, Dir., The Murie Museum, Kelly, WY....1860
Landau, Andrea, Project Coord., The Fabric Workshop and Museum, Philadelphia, PA....1453
Landauer, Susan, Sr. Scholar, San Jose Museum of Art, San Jose, CA....196
Landavazo, Jamin, Chief Cur., Reno County Museum, Hutchinson, KS....618
Landavazo, Shawntel, Interim Vice Pres. Education, Museum of Life and Science, Durham, NC....1243
Landen, Jill, Cur., The Whalehead Club, Corolla, NC....1241
Landeros, Abelardo, Dir. Facilities & Horticulture, Santa Barbara Zoological Gardens, Santa Barbara, CA....204
Landeros, Alexandra M., Dir. Public Rels., Mexic-Arte Museum, Austin, TX....1582
Landers, Bridget, Volunteer Coord., Sedgwick County Zoo, Wichita, KS....639
Landers, Helen, County Historian, Broward County Historical Commission, Fort Lauderdale, FL....347
Landes, Carolyn, Museum Cur., Mesa Verde National Park Museum, Mesa Verde National Park, CO....258
Landes, Dorothy, Accounting Mgr., James A. Michener Art Museum, Doylestown, PA....1420
Landfried, Maxine, Sec., Jackson County Historical Society, Washington's Lands Museum & Sayre Log House, Ravenswood, WV....1806
Landgraf, Gerald, Foundation Pres. (V), Anderson/Abruzzo Albuquerque International Balloon Museum, Albuquerque, NM....1070
Landis, Ellen, Cur., Grounds For Sculpture, Hamilton, NJ....1041
Landis, Mary Ann, Site Dir., Old Economy Village, Ambridge, PA....1409
Landis, Sandy, Exec. Dir., Community Council for the Arts, Kinston, NC....1254
Landkamer, Mary, Researcher, Custer County Historical Society, Inc., Broken Bow, NE....978
Landon, Bill, Vice Pres., Old Jail Museum, Albion, IN....530
Landry, Craig, Lead Interpreter, Grevemberg House Museum, Franklin, LA....671
Landry, Drew, Pres., Mount Washington Museum and The Weather Discovery Center, North Conway, NH....1025
Landry, Karin, Pres. (V), Thompson-Ames Historical Society, Gilford, NH....1019
Landry, Linda, Conservator, Missouri Historical Society, Saint Louis, MO....949
Landry, Martha, Mgr. Special Events, New Mexico Museum of Art, Santa Fe, NM....1090
Landshof, Suzanne H., Treas. & Museum Shop Mgr., The Museum of Miniature Houses and Other Collections, Inc., Carmel, IN....535
Landsman, Blythe, Office Mgr., Vesterheim Norwegian-American Museum, Decorah, IA....582
Landy, John, Bd. Trustees Pres. (V), T.W. Wood Gallery & Arts Center, Montpelier, VT....1684
Landy, Mort, 1st Vice Pres., Clearfield County Historical Society, Clearfield, PA....1418
Lane, Alexandra, Asst. Dir. Devel. & Admin., Sculpture Center, Long Island City, NY....1155
Lane, Christina, Public Rels. & Mktg. Dir., The Museum of Arts and Sciences, Inc. and Center for Florida History, Daytona Beach, FL....342
Lane, Corky, Pres., James W. Dillon House Museum, Dillon, SC....1511
Lane, Dick, Vice Pres., Watermen's Museum, Yorktown, VA....1757
Lane, Doug, Dir. Operations, National Cowboy & Western Heritage Museum, Oklahoma City, OK....1371
Lane, Eliza, Tourism Mgr., Pearson Air Museum, Vancouver, WA....1792
Lane, Jacqueline, Pres. (V), Thornton W. Burgess Museum, Sandwich, MA....805
Lane, Janet, Education, Schmidt House Museum & Research Library, Grants Pass, OR....1391
Lane, Jeff, Dir., Lane Motor Museum, Nashville, TN....1568
Lane, Jenny, Communications Mgr., Huntsville Museum of Art, Huntsville, AL....15
Lane, Jessica, Dir. Volunteers & Events, The Health Adventure, Asheville, NC....1232
Lane, Jon, Cur. Public Programs, South Pass City State Historic Site, South Pass City, WY....1866
Lane, Joshua W., Cur. Academic Programs, Historic Deerfield, Inc., Deerfield, MA....774
Lane, Lisa, Museum Shop Mgr., Country Music Hall of Fame and Museum, Country Music Foundation, Nashville, TN....1567
Lane, Michael, C.E.O., Norman R. Eppink Art Gallery, Emporia State University, Emporia, KS....611
Lane, Mikki, Bookstore & Receptionist Coord., Middlebury College Museum of Art, Middlebury, VT....1684
Lane, Skip, Pres., St. Helena Historical Society, Saint Helena, CA....177
Laney, Brad, Mgr. Visitor Svcs., The Children's Museum of Memphis, Memphis, TN....1561
Laney, Renee, Dir. & Museum Shop Mgr., Lake Meredith Aquatic and Wildlife Museum, Fritch, TX....1613
Lanford, Kathleen, Pres. (V), Arizona Doll and Toy Museum, Phoenix, AZ....48
Lang, Deborah, Exec. Dir., The Parry Mansion Museum, New Hope, PA....1447
Lang, Edward, Chm. (V), Adventure Science Center, Nashville, TN....1566
Lang, Edward P., Cur., Stanton House, Clinton, CT....269
Lang, Ruth, Oral History Coord., Kearney Mansion Museum, Fresno, CA....116
Lang, Sherry, Cur., Juliette Gordon Low Birthplace, Savannah, GA....434
Lang, Tom, Gen. Mgr. & Vice Pres., Black Hills Reptile Gardens, Inc., Rapid City, SD....1539
Langager, Tyrone, Vice Pres., International Peace Garden, Dunseith, ND....1280
Langdon, Donald D., C.E.O., Fleming Historical Society, Fleming, CO....244
Lange, Allynne, Cur., Hudson River Maritime Museum, Kingston, NY....1151
Lange, Amanda E., Chm. Curatorial Dept., Historic Deerfield, Inc., Deerfield, MA....774
Lange, Connie G., Exec. Dir., Ronald Reagan Boyhood Home, Dixon, IL....490
Lange, Gerard, Dir., Barton Art Galleries, Wilson, NC....1272
Lange, Jane, Dir., Falkirk Cultural Center, San Rafael, CA....200
Lange, Janet, Pres. Members Bd., Missouri Botanical Garden, Saint Louis, MO....949
Lange, Karen, Dir. & Cur., Campbell Historical Museum & Ainsley House, Campbell, CA....97
Lange, Pam, Dir., Bureau County Historical Society Museum, Princeton, IL....513
Lange, Russell, Exec. Dir., Hudson River Maritime Museum, Kingston, NY....1151
Langellier, John, Ph.D., Dir., Sharlot Hall Museum, Prescott, AZ....53
Langenfeld, Heidi, Museum Shop Mgr., Dakota County Historical Society, South Saint Paul, MN....898
Langer, James, Gallery Dir., Irene Cullis Gallery, Greensboro College, Greensboro, NC....1249
Langer, Yonina, Admin., Derfner Judaica Museum + The Art Collection at the Hebrew Home at Riverdale, Riverdale, NY....1200

L–*Continued*

L–*Continued*

Lawrimore, Katrina P., Dir., Reedville Fishermen's Museum, Reedville, VA 1735
Laws, Marianne, Museum Shop Mgr., Aerospace Museum of California, McClellan, CA 145
Lawson, Colleen, Retail Sales Mgr., Utah Field House of Natural History State Park, Vernal, UT 1674
Lawson, Dwight, Sr. Vice Pres. Animal Programs & Science, Zoo Atlanta, Atlanta, GA 409
Lawson, Gayla, Chm., The French Legation Museum, Austin, TX 1581
Lawson, H. William, Dir., The Arms Family Museum of Local History, Youngstown, OH 1353
Lawson, Jodi, Pres., Northfield Historical Society Museum, Northfield, MN 889
Lawson, John R., II, Chm., The Mariners' Museum, Newport News, VA 1728
Lawson, Karol A., Ph.D., Dir., Sweet Briar College Art Collection and Galleries, Sweet Briar, VA 1749
Lawson, Leanne, Guild Mgr., Creative Arts Guild, Dalton, GA 415
Lawson, Mark, Gallery Mgr., Shenandoah Valley Discovery Museum, Winchester, VA 1755
Lawson, Mary, Devel. Officer & Museum Shop Mgr., Greenville County Museum of Art, Greenville, SC 1514
Lawson, Monica, Dir., Schminck Memorial Museum, Lakeview, OR 1394
Lawson, Robert, Exec. Dir., Kentucky Music Hall of Fame and Museum, Renfro Valley, KY 662
Lawson, Scott J., Dir., Plumas County Museum, Quincy, CA 167
Lawson, Stacey, C.O.O., Binder Park Zoo, Battle Creek, MI 825
Lawton, Christine J., Programs & Education, New Britain Youth Museum, New Britain, CT 285
Lawton, Gary, Dir., Corbin Art Center, Spokane, WA 1786
Lawton, Gregory, C.E.O. & Pres. (V), Hurricane Valley Heritage Park Museum, Hurricane, UT 1663
Lawton, Phyllis, Cur., Hurricane Valley Heritage Park Museum, Hurricane, UT.1663
Lawton, Rebecca, Cur. Paintings & Sculpture, Amon Carter Museum, Fort Worth, TX 1609
Lawton, Robert, Chm. (V), Lake Winnipesaukee Museum & Historical Society, Laconia, NH 1022
Lawton, Sheryl, Unit Ranger, Jack London State Historic Park, Glen Ellen, CA 118
Lawtor, Rev. Philip, Conference Historian, Barratt's Chapel and Museum, Frederica, DE 307
Laxer-Limmer, Beth, Education, Suffolk County Vanderbilt Museum, Centerport, NY 1120
Lay, Allen, Pres. (V), Palos Verdes Art Center, Rancho Palos Verdes, CA 168
Lay, Robert, Asst. Archivist, The Robert J. Dole Institute of Politics, Lawrence, KS 621
Laylin, Leora, Museum Shop Buyer, Carl G. Fenner Nature Center, Lansing, MI....848
Layman, Donna, Treas. & Museum Shop Mgr., Historic Hermann Museum, Hermann, MO 929
Layman, Sandra, Membership Coord. & Education, Tennessee Museum of Aviation, Sevierville, TN......................1573
Layne, Brenda, Trustee, Morton House Museum, Benton Harbor, MI 826
Layne, Margaret Mary, Exec. Dir., Huntington Museum of Art, Inc., Huntington, WV 1800
Layton, Dr. Thomas N., Guest Cur. Archaeology, Mendocino County Museum, Willits, CA.................................224
Lazarus, Fred, IV, Pres., The Maryland Institute, College of Art: Decker, Meyerhoff and Pinkard Galleries, Baltimore, MD..724
Lazarus, Phyllis, Public Rels. & Mktg., The Breman Jewish Heritage & Holocaust Museum, Atlanta, GA 403
Lazin, Rachel, Institutional Advancement Dir., Yeshiva University Museum at the Center for Jewish History, New York, NY..1184
Lazo, Maria, Education Coord., Assoc. Dir. & Museum Shop Mgr., Brazos Valley Museum of Natural History, Bryan, TX 1590
Le Duc, M. Vonciel, Pres. (V), Schoolcraft County Historical Society, Manistique, MI 852
Le Fevre, Elizabeth, Education, Eustis Historical Museum & Preservation Society, Inc., Eustis, FL 346
Lea, Allen, Cur. Collections, McFaddin-Ward House, Beaumont, TX 1587
Lea, Maya, Cur., Helen Louise Allen Textile Collection, Madison, WI............1827
Leach, Gregory M., Dir., Aitkin County Historical Society, Aitkin, MN................868
Leach, Jerry, Treas. & Security, Arkansas Country Doctor Museum, Lincoln, AR 76
Leach, Mark R., Dir., Southeastern Center for Contemporary Art, Winston-Salem, NC 1275
Leach, Patricia, Dir., Whatcom Museum of History and Art, Bellingham, WA.....1760
Leach, Stephanie, Dir. Education & Gallery, Lux Center for the Arts, Lincoln, NE 989
Leacock, Kathy, Cur. Collections, Buffalo Museum of Science, Buffalo, NY 1115
Leadabrand, Elaine, Museum Shop Mgr., Bent's Old Fort National Historic Site, La Junta, CO..253
Leader, Jonathan M., State Archaeologist, South Carolina Institute of Archaeology & Anthropology, Columbia, SC 1510
Leader, Simon, Dir. Security, Mingei International Museum, San Diego, CA ...180
Leaf, Jamie, Visitor Svcs., Jordan Schnitzer Museum of Art, Eugene, OR.1388
Leafdale, Judy, C.E.O. & Cur., Banner County Historical Society, Harrisburg, NE 985
League, Alice, C.E.O. & Museum Shop Mgr., Dakota Dinosaur Museum, Dickinson, ND..1280
Leahy, Andy, Security, The University of Arizona Museum of Art and Archive of Visual Arts, Tucson, AZ 63
Leahy, Eileen, C.E.O. & Pres. (V), Children's Museum at Holyoke, Inc., Holyoke, MA 782
Leahy, Marie, Dir. Mktg., Brooklyn Botanic Garden, Brooklyn, NY.............1110
Leahy, Maureen, Asst. Cur. Primates, Lincoln Park Zoological Gardens, Chicago, IL 483
Leahy, Patrick, Pres. (V), The 100th Meridian Museum, Cozad, NE 980
Leak, Laurie, Business Asst., Center for Wooden Boats, Seattle, WA 1779
Leal, Jose H., Ph.D., Dir., The Bailey-Matthews Shell Museum, Sanibel, FL..386
Leamy, Kristina, Dir. Special Events, Katonah Museum of Art, Katonah, NY.1150
Lean, Bryan, Cur., Collin County Farm Museum, McKinney, TX........................1631
Lean, Bryan, Cur. Collections, North Texas History Center, McKinney, TX ...1632
Lear, Julie, Technician, Muscatine Art Center, Muscatine, IA 595
Lear, Kathy, Exec. Dir., Paris Gibson Square Museum of Art, Great Falls, MT..965
Lear, Paul, Site Mgr., Fort Ontario State Historic Site, Oswego, NY....................1191
Learmonth, Stephanie, Registrar & Assoc. Cur., Triton Museum of Art, Santa Clara, CA 205
Learned, Bob, Museum Shop Mgr., Lewis & Clark Boat House and Nature Center, Saint Charles, MO 943
Leary, Fay, Processing Asst., Museum of the Albemarle, Elizabeth City, NC 1244
Leary, Nadine A., Admin., Captain Forbes House Museum, Milton, MA.......791
Lease, Michael, Gallery Assoc., Anderson Gallery, School of the Arts, Virginia Commonwealth University, Richmond, VA 1736
Leath, Robert, Vice Pres. & Chief Cur., Museum of Early Southern Decorative Arts (MESDA), Winston-Salem, NC.....1274
Leathem, Dr. Karen, Museum Historian, Louisiana State Museum, New Orleans, LA 681
Leatherman, Larry R., Pres., Milton J. Rubenstein Museum of Science & Technology, Syracuse, NY 1219
Leavell, Heather, Co Chm., Cyrus E. Dallin Art Museum, Inc., Arlington, MA 754
Leavell, Heather, Cur., Peabody Historical Society, Peabody, MA 798
Leavengood, Pam, Dir., Cherokee Strip Regional Heritage Center, Enid, OK 1361
Leavenworth, Gregg, Facilities Caretaker, Arnot Art Museum, Elmira, NY 1130
Leavey, Jane, Dir., The Breman Jewish Heritage & Holocaust Museum, Atlanta, GA..403
Leavitt, Christie, Cur. Education, Clark County Museum, Henderson, NV..........1004
Leback, Capt. Warren, Chm. (V), American Merchant Marine Museum, Kings Point, NY 1150
Lebal, Beatrice, Public Rels., Merrill Historical Society, Merrill, WI...............1832
LeBaron, Kathy, Pres. (V), Sheldon Museum of Art and Sculpture Garden/University of Nebraska-Lincoln, Lincoln, NE 990
Leberfing, Chris, Chm. Bd., Racine Zoological Society, Racine, WI 1843
LeBlanc, Anna Mary, Acting Collections Mgr., Fashion Columbia Study Collection, Chicago, IL 479
LeBlanc, Denise, Dir. Education Science Discovery Museum, The Discovery Museums, Acton, MA 751
LeBlanc, Guy R., Museum Svcs. Mgr., Longfellow's Wayside Inn, Sudbury, MA 811
LeBlanc, Rick, Chm. (V), Art Association of Harrisburg, Harrisburg, PA 1430
LeBlanc, Dr. Steven, Dir. Collections, Peabody Museum of Archaeology & Ethnology, Cambridge, MA 768
LeBlanc, Suzanne, Exec. Dir., Long Island Children's Museum, Garden City, NY 1135
Leblanc, Yvonne, Curatorial Technician, The Shadows-on-the-Teche, New Iberia, LA..678
LeBlue, Virgie, Vice Pres., Crowley Art Association & Gallery, Crowley, LA.......669

L–*Continued*

L–*Continued*

Lett, Amanda, Registrar, Gilcrease Museum, Tulsa, OK 1379
Lettenberger, Bob, Mgr. Operations, National Railroad Museum, Green Bay, WI 1821
Letton, Laura, Dir. Planned Gifts & Membership Coord., Dayton Art Institute, Dayton, OH 1316
Leu, Marcia, Chm. (V) & Pres. (V), Pocahontas County Iowa Historical Society Museum, Laurens, IA 591
Leung, Corinne, Dir. Museum, Hull Lifesaving Museum Inc., the Museum of Boston Harbor Heritage, Hull, MA....783
Leusch, Kelly, Devel., Cedar Rapids Museum of Art, Cedar Rapids, IA....577
Leva, Shannon, Cur. Asst., International Museum of the Horse, Lexington, KY....652
LeVan, Steve, Dir. Education, Fine Arts Center of Kershaw County, Inc., Camden, SC 1501
Levander, James A., Chm. (V), America's Presidency Museum and Gallery of American History, Branson, MO 921
Levandoski, Patricia, Dir. Finance, New Britain Museum of American Art, Inc., New Britain, CT 284
Levchuck, Michael, Treas., Polish American Museum, Port Washington, NY 1196
LeVeck, Thomas, Pres., Tarble Arts Center, Eastern Illinois University, Charleston, IL 475
Levee, Catherine, Pres. (V), Johnstown Historical Society, Johnstown, NY 1149
LeVeille, Fayn, Dir., Halifax Historical Museum, Daytona Beach, FL 342
Leveille, Susan, Dir. Education, The Zoo, Gulf Breeze, FL....352
Levengood, Dr. Paul A., Pres. & C.E.O., Virginia Historical Society, Richmond, VA 1742
Levens, Dwight R., Dir., Children's Museum/Detroit Public Schools, Detroit, MI 833
Levenson, Barry, Cur., Mount Horeb Mustard Museum, Mount Horeb, WI....1837
Levenson, Patty, Dir. Mktg. & Tours, Mount Horeb Mustard Museum, Mount Horeb, WI....1837
Leventhal, James G., Dir. Devel. & Mktg., Judah L. Magnes Museum, Berkeley, CA 92
Leverant, Louise, Pres. (V), Arizona Jewish Historical Society, Phoenix, AZ....48
Levering, Carol D., Regent DAR-Hervey Ely House, Rochester, NY 1201
Levesque, Kristen, Dir. Mktg. & Public Rels., Portland Museum of Art, Portland, ME....708
Levey, Jodie, Dir. Guest Svcs., Woodland Park Zoo, Seattle, WA....1785
Levey, Larry, Pres. (V), Highlands Hammock State Park/Civilian Conservation Corps Museum, Sebring, FL....388
Levi, Vicki Gold, Exhibit Dir., Atlantic City Historical Museum, Atlantic City, NJ 1031
Levin, Carie, Education Coord., Morris County Historical Society (Acorn Hall House Museum), Morristown, NJ....1050
Levin, Jhanna, Pres. (V), The Laurel Museum, Laurel, MD....740
Levin, Robert, Education Project Coord., National Museum of American Jewish History, Philadelphia, PA 1458
Levin, Ruth, Sec., Shaftsbury Historical Society, Shaftsbury, VT....1690
Levine, Dr. Bern M., Pres., Jungle Island, Miami, FL....365
Levine, Brandi, Exec. Dir., Philadelphia Society for the Preservation of Landmarks, Philadelphia, PA 1459
Levine, Dr. Frances, Dir. Palace of the Governors, Museum of New Mexico, Santa Fe, NM....1089
Levine, Frances, Ph.D., Dir., Palace of the Governors/New Mexico History Museum, Santa Fe, NM 1090
Levine, Hope, Volunteer & Tour Coord., Dallas Holocaust Museum/Center for Education & Tolerance, Dallas, TX....1598
Levine, Jeffrey, Chief Mktg. & Communications Officer, Whitney Museum of American Art, New York, NY 1184
Levine, Jennifer, Pres. (V), The Renaissance Society at The University of Chicago, Chicago, IL....486
Levine, Mark, Treas., LongHouse Reserve, East Hampton, NY 1129
Levine, Phyllis, Dir. Communications, International Center of Photography, New York, NY 1170
Levine, Sarah, Dir. Community Rels., Mayborn Museum Complex, Waco, TX 1655
Levine, Tom, Foundation Dir., Anderson/Abruzzo Albuquerque International Balloon Museum, Albuquerque, NM....1070
Levinsky, Annie, Exec. Dir. Historic Denver, Molly Brown House Museum, Denver, CO 241
Levinson, Louis, Chm. (V), Shore Line Trolley Museum, East Haven, CT 271
Levinthal, Beth E., Exec. Dir., Hofstra University Museum, Hempstead, NY....1141
Leviticus, Lou, Cur., Larsen Tractor Museum, Lincoln, NE 988
Leviton, Dr. Alan, Chm. Herpetology, California Academy of Sciences, San Francisco, CA 187
Levitski, Vlad, Maintenance Worker, Environmental Education Center, Somerset County Park Commission, Basking Ridge, NJ....1032
Levitt, Howard, Chief Interpretation, Golden Gate National Recreation Area, San Francisco, CA....189
Levkoff, Mary, Cur. & Head Dept., Sculpture & Decorative Arts, National Gallery of Art, Washington, DC 323
Levy, Annyce, Chm. (V), Glencoe Museum, Radford, VA....1735
Levy, Beth, Dir. Publications, Solomon R. Guggenheim Museum, New York, NY 1181
Levy Dolovacky, Carol, Pres. Bd., Washington County Historical Society, Washington, PA 1480
Levy, Elliott, Dir., Aiken County Historical Museum, Aiken, SC....1499
Levy, Faye, Accounting, San Diego Automotive Museum, San Diego, CA....183
Levy, Harry A. (Hap), Pres. (V), Holocaust Documentation & Education Center, Inc., Hollywood, FL...353
Levy, Tom, Supt., Starved Rock State Park, Oglesby, IL....510
Levy, Tracey, Museum Shop Mgr., Albright-Knox Art Gallery, Buffalo, NY 1114
Levy-Weston, Julie, Special Projects Coord., The Michigan State University Museum, East Lansing, MI....838
Lewallen, Sanders E., Dir., Calusa Nature Center and Planetarium, Fort Myers, FL....348
Lewandoski, Jan, Pres., Stannard Historical Society, Stannard, VT....1691
Lewandowski, Sue, C.E.O., Pres. & Dir. (V), Ethnic Heritage Museum, Rockford, IL 516
Lewark, Lalena, Registrar, Permanent Collections, Autry National Center of the American West, Los Angeles, CA 133
Lewars, James, Historic Site Admin., Daniel Boone Homestead, Birdsboro, PA....1413
Lewellen, Amy, Registrar, Clarksville-Montgomery County Museum dba Customs House Museum & Cultural Center, Clarksville, TN....1549
Lewellen, Anne, Museum Cur., Kingsley Plantation, Jacksonville, FL 355
Lewellen, Anne R., Museum Cur., Timucuan Ecological and Historic Preserve and Fort Caroline National Memorial, Jacksonville, FL....356
Lewin, Jacqueline A., Exec. Dir., St. Joseph Museum Inc., Saint Joseph, MO 945
Lewin, Sarah, Dir. Institutional Advancement, The Adirondack Museum, Blue Mountain Lake, NY 1105
Lewinson, Shawn, Dir. Human Resources, Wadsworth Atheneum Museum of Art, Hartford, CT....279
Lewis, Andrea, Dir., The Dairy Barn Arts Center, Athens, OH 1294
Lewis, Angela, Curatorial Asst., Kemper Museum of Contemporary Art, Kansas City, MO 934
Lewis, Anne, Cur. & Archivist, Bay View Historical Museum, Bay View, MI....825
Lewis, Anne, Special Programs, South Dakota Discovery Center, Pierre, SD....1538
Lewis, Ann-Eliza, Exec. Dir., Columbia County Historical Society, Inc., Kinderhook, NY 1150
Lewis, Audrey, Assoc. Cur., Brandywine River Museum, Chadds Ford, PA....1417
Lewis, Bob, Finance Mgr., Craft Alliance, Saint Louis, MO 946
Lewis Butler, Maggie, Program Coord., Riley House Museum of African American History & Culture, Tallahassee, FL 391
Lewis, Carl E., Ph.D., Dir., Fairchild Tropical Botanic Garden, Coral Gables, FL 340
Lewis, Cary, Grounds Maintenance, Hildene, The Lincoln Family Home, Manchester, VT 1683
Lewis, Casey, Cur., Chemung Valley History Museum, Elmira, NY....1131
Lewis, Catharin, Dir., West Bay Common School Children's Museum, League City, TX 1628
Lewis, Charla, Coord. Education, Camden County Historical Society, Camden, NJ 1034
Lewis, Cheryl L., Pres. (V), Oswego Historical Museum, Inc., Oswego, KS....630
Lewis, Chris, Dir. Education, Virginia Living Museum, Newport News, VA....1729
Lewis, Christy, Education Facilitator & Museum Shop Mgr., Discovery Center (East Tennessee Discovery Center), Knoxville, TN....1557
Lewis, Dallas, Sec., Lemhi County Historical Museum, Salmon, ID 466
Lewis, Dan, Pres., The New Hampshire Snowmobile Museum, Allenstown, NH....1012
Lewis, Darnella, Museum Shop Mgr., The Skyscraper Museum, New York, NY....1181
Lewis, David, Cur., Aurora Regional Fire Museum, Aurora, IL....469
Lewis, David, Cultural Resource Mgr., Confederated Tribes of Grand Ronde Cultural Resources Department, Grand Ronde, OR 1390
Lewis, Debra J., Dir. Devel., Virginia Museum of Natural History, Martinsville, VA 1724

L–*Continued*

L–Continued

Lipsky, Jill, Gift Shop Mgr., Berkshire Botanical Garden, Stockbridge, MA.......809
Liptak, Jessica, Volunteers & Outreach, Harpers Ferry National Historical Park, Harpers Ferry, WV.......1799
Liptak, Laura, Museum Shop Mgr., Blue Hills Trailside Museum, Milton, MA......791
Lipton, Charlotte, Treas., Tex Ark Antique Auto Museum, Texarkana, AR.....85
Lipton, Elaine, Visitor Svcs., The New England Carousel Museum, Bristol, CT.......268
Lipton, Ivan, C.O.O., Plimoth Plantation Inc., Plymouth, MA.......800
Liput, Peg, Dir. Finance & Admin., Smart Museum of Art, Chicago, IL.......486
Lipzin, Janice, Dir., Banana Factory, Bethlehem, PA.......1411
Lis, Jennifer, Conservator, Mackinac Island State Park Commission-Mackinac State Historic Parks, Mackinaw City, MI.......851
Lis, Jennifer, Conservator, Mackinac State Historic Parks-Colonial Michilimackinac & Old Mackinac Point Lighthouse, Mackinaw City, MI....852
Lis, Jennifer, Conservator, Mackinac State Historic Parks-Fort Mackinac & Mackinac Island State Park, Mackinac Island, MI.......851
Lis, Jennifer, Conservator, Mackinac State Historic Parks-Historic Mill Creek Discovery Park, Mackinaw City, MI.......852
Lisai, Virginia, C.E.O. & Pres. (V), Westminster Historical Society, Westminster, VT.......1694
Lisemby, Betty, Dir., Pioneer Village, Rison, AR.......82
Lisenby, Jimmy, Dir. Concessions, Mann Wildlife Learning Museum, Montgomery, AL.......20
Lish, Floyd, Exhibits, The Quincy Museum, Quincy, IL.......514
Lisiecki, Denise, School Dir., Kalamazoo Institute of Arts, Kalamazoo, MI.......847
Lisinicchia, Lisa, Dir. Operations, Ocean Star Offshore Drilling Rig & Museum, Galveston, TX.......1615
Lisk, Susan J., Dir. & C.E.O., Porter-Phelps-Huntington Foundation, Inc., Hadley, MA.......780
Lisk Wyckoff, E., Jr., Chm. (V), The Wyckoff Farmhouse Museum, Brooklyn, NY.......1113
Lisowsky, Bill, Gen. Mgr. USDA Forest Service - Land Between the Lakes, Golden Pond, KY.......648
Liss, Ken, Pres., Brookline Historical Society, Brookline, MA.......765
Liss, Laurence A., Pres. (V), The Wharton Esherick Museum, Malvern, PA.......1443
Lissauer, Linda, Pres. (V), The Shaker Historical Society, Shaker Heights, OH.......1343
Lissoway, Brenna, Asst. Archivist, The Yosemite Museum, National Park Service, Yosemite National Park, CA......226
List, Myrna, Pres., Bergen Museum of Local History, Bergen, NY.......1104
Lister, Kristin, Conservator, Paintings, The Art Institute of Chicago, Chicago, IL.......476
Liston, Theodore, Treas., Denison Pequotsepos Nature Center, Mystic, CT.......283
Litchfield, Bekah, Museum Shop Mgr., The David Davis Mansion, Bloomington, IL.......471
Litteral, Steve, Visitor Svcs., Tinker Swiss Cottage Museum, Rockford, IL.....518
Litterst, Michael, Information Officer, CNHP, Historic Jamestowne, Jamestown, VA.......1718
Little, Beverly, Mgr. Visitor Svcs., Forney Museum of Transportation, Denver, CO.......240
Little, Billie, Exec. Dir., Discovery Center at Murfree Spring, Murfreesboro, TN.......1565
Little, Carol, Public Rels., Worthington Historical Society, Worthington, OH.....1352
Little, Clay, Preparator, The Fred Jones Jr. Museum of Art, Norman, OK.......1368
Little, Clay, Preparator, Mabee-Gerrer Museum of Art, Shawnee, OK.......1377
Little, Cynthia, Historian, Atwater Kent Museum of Philadelphia dba Philadelphia History Museum, Philadelphia, PA.......1450
Little, Janea, Naturalist, Chippewa Nature Center, Midland, MI.......854
Little, Jennifer, Dir. Devel., Lewis Ginter Botanical Garden, Richmond, VA.......1738
Little, Kate, Asst. Cur., Wood Street Galleries, Pittsburgh, PA.......1468
Little, Kay, Education Coord., Bartlesville Area History Museum, Bartlesville, OK.......1356
Little, Nancy, Dir. School, National Academy Museum and School of Fine Arts, New York, NY.......1176
Little, Ruth, Sec., Beaverhead County Museum, Dillon, MT.......962
Little, Stephen, Dir., Honolulu Academy of Arts, Honolulu, HI.......445
Little, Tricia, Asst. Dir., Catawba Science Center, Hickory, NC.......1251
Littlefield, Sarah, Teamster, Billings Farm & Museum, Woodstock, VT.......1695
Littlejohn, Sharon, Administrative Mgr. & Museum Shop Mgr., Museum of the Cherokee Indian, Cherokee, NC.......1240
Littlejohn, Susan, Pres., Dunedin Historical Society & Museum, Dunedin, FL.......345
Littlepage, Wendy, Dir., Denver Museum of Miniatures, Dolls and Toys, Denver, CO.......239
Littman, Brett, Exec. Dir., The Drawing Center, New York, NY.......1167
Litton, Lana J., Office Asst., Natchitoches National Fish Hatchery, Natchitoches, LA.......677
Littrell, Dawn, Museum Shop Mgr., Fort William Henry Museum, Lake George, NY.......1152
Littrell, Gail A., Sec. Research & Publications, University of Nebraska State Museum, Lincoln, NE.......991
Littrell, Ginger, Cur., Lake Waccamaw Depot Museum, Lake Waccamaw, NC..1255
Litts, Niki, Dir. Gallery, Community Council for the Arts, Kinston, NC.......1254
Litzelman, Jenny, Dir. Education & Outreach, Raleigh City Museum, Raleigh, NC.......1264
Litzenbauer, Joan, Treas., Wayne County Historical Society, Honesdale, PA.......1434
Litzinger, Jim, Dir. Mktg., Fine Arts Center of Kershaw County, Inc., Camden, SC.......1501
Liu, Cary Y., Cur. Asian Art, Princeton University Art Museum, Princeton, NJ .1058
Lively, Amy, Dir. Devel., Tyler Museum of Art, Tyler, TX.......1652
Lively, Ann, Registrar, Orangetown Historical Museum and Archives - Salyer House and DePew House, Orangeburg, NY.......1190
Lively, Mr. Carter C., Exec. Dir., Hammond-Harwood House Association, Annapolis, MD.......717
Livenstein, Barbara, Dir. Communications, Museum of the City of New York, New York, NY.......1176
Liverman, Jeff, Exec. Dir., Danville Science Center, Danville, VA.......1708
Livermore, Garet, Vice Pres. Education, The Farmers' Museum, Inc., Cooperstown, NY.......1123
Livermore, Garet, Vice Pres. Education, New York State Historical Association/Fenimore Art Museum, Cooperstown, NY.......1123
Liverpool, B'journ, Museum Shop Mgr., U.S. Navy Memorial Foundation and Naval Heritage Center, Washington, DC.......332
Livesay, Thomas A., Exec. Dir., Louisiana State University Museum of Art, Baton Rouge, LA.......667
Livezey, Dr. Bradley C., Cur. Birds, Carnegie Museum of Natural History, Pittsburgh, PA.......1464
Livingston, Bob, Admin., Paul H. Karshner Memorial Museum, Puyallup, WA.......1778
Livingston, Mandy, Mktg. & Public Rels., Mighty Eighth Air Force Museum, Pooler, GA.......429
Livingston, Tracey L., Dir., Huntley Project Museum of Irrigated Agriculture, Huntley, MT.......966
Livingston, William, Trustee, Florida Agricultural Museum, Palm Coast, FL....376
Livsey, Karen E., Librarian & Archivist, Fenton History Center-Museum & Research Center, Jamestown, NY.......1148
Lizarraga, Darlene, Mktg. Coord., Arizona State Museum, Tucson, AZ.......59
Lizotte, Bill, Pres. (V), Noyes House Museum, Morrisville, VT.......1685
Lizzadro, John S., Exec. Dir., Lizzadro Museum of Lapidary Art, Elmhurst, IL...493
Llanes, William, Museum Shop Mgr., Bass Museum of Art, Miami Beach, FL.......367
Llewellyn, John, Chm. (V), Forest Lawn Museum, Glendale, CA.......119
Lloveras San Miguel, Fernando, Esq., Exec. Dir., Hacienda Buena Vista, Ponce, PR.......1870
Lloveras San Miguel, Fernando, Esq., Exec. Dir., Las Cabezas de San Juan Nature Reserve (El Faro), Fajardo, PR .1869
Lloyd, Col. (Ret.) Albert, Pres. BG John C.L. Scribner Texas Military Forces Museum, Austin, TX.......1580
Lloyd, Arlo P., Pres. (V), Minidoka County Historical Museum, Rupert, ID...465
Lloyd, Caroline, Museum Shop Mgr., Falmouth Historical Society, Falmouth, MA.......777
Lloyd, Connie, Museum Shop Mgr., Zane Grey Museum, Lackawaxen, PA.......1438
Lloyd, Jim, Cur., Bramble Park Zoo, Watertown, SD.......1544
Lloyd, Joan, Registrar, Oshkosh Public Museum, Oshkosh, WI.......1840
Lloyd, Karen, Dir. Devel. Oregon Zoo Foundation, Oregon Zoo, Portland, OR.......1400
Lloyd, Kenita, Deputy Dir., The Museum for African Art, Long Island City, NY ..1154
Lloyd, Kristin B., Asst. Dir., The Lyceum, Alexandria's History Museum, Alexandria, VA.......1698
Lloyd, Lynette, Administrative Sec., Utah State Historical Society, Salt Lake City, UT.......1672
Lloyd, Peggy S., Archival Mgr., Southwest Arkansas Regional Archives (SARA), Washington, AR.......85

L–*Continued*

L–*Continued*

Lord, Richard, Pres., Durham Historic Association Museum, Durham, NH.......1016
Lord, Richard, Treas., Macartney House Museum, Oakland, ME 705
Lord, Shelley, Dir., Cando Arts Center, Cando, ND 1278
Loren, Dr. Diana, Assoc. Cur., Peabody Museum of Archaeology & Ethnology, Cambridge, MA 768
Lorenz, Marianne, Exec. Dir., Fort Collins Museum of Contemporary Art, Fort Collins, CO 246
Lorenz, Rich, Pres., J.J. Jackson Memorial Museum, Weaverville, CA 223
Lorenzen, Dan, Security Mgr., Oregon Zoo, Portland, OR 1400
Loret, John, Ph.D., Dir., Science Museum of Long Island, Manhasset, NY 1156
Lorge, Lucille, Museum Shop Mgr., McConaghy House, Hayward, CA 121
Lorigan, Marty, Technical Asst., Main Art Gallery, California State University, Fullerton, Fullerton, CA 118
Lorin, Elisabeth, Chm., Lehman College Art Gallery, Bronx, NY 1108
Loring, Karla, Dir. Media, Museum of Contemporary Art, Chicago, IL 483
Lormand, Paul, Dir., Fine Arts Museum - Western Carolina University Fine & Performing Arts Center, Cullowhee, NC 1241
Lorrain, Michelle, Receptionist, Wenatchee Valley Museum and Cultural Center, Wenatchee, WA 1794
Lorys, Mr. Jan M., Dir., Polish Museum of America, Chicago, IL.........................485
Losavio, Sam, Asst. Dir., Louisiana Art & Science Museum - Irene W. Pennington Planetarium, Baton Rouge, LA 667
Loschen, Diane, Dir. Mktg., Cheyenne Mountain Zoological Park, Colorado Springs, CO 233
Loscher, Tricia, Assoc. Cur. Heard Museum North, Heard Museum, Phoenix, AZ..50
LoSchiavo, Joseph A., Exec. Dir., The Regina A. Quick Center for the Arts, Saint Bonaventure, NY 1206
Loscuito, John, Registrar, The Patrick & Beatrice Haggerty Museum of Art, Milwaukee, WI...1836
Losekamp, Linda, Treas., Village Historical Society of Harrison, Inc., Harrison, OH 1324
Loser, Linda, Cur., Peshtigo Fire Museum, Peshtigo, WI.........................1840
Loshaw, Ann, Deputy Dir. Learning, Vizcaya Museum and Gardens, Miami, FL...367
Losher, Cathy, Admin. Officer, Gulf Islands National Seashore, Gulf Breeze, FL 352
Losito, Lisa, Vice Pres., The Laurel Museum, Laurel, MD 740
Lotspeich, Charlie, Supvr., Holyoke Heritage State Park, Holyoke, MA..........782
Lott, Louis, Information Center, Utah State Historical Society, Salt Lake City, UT 1672
Lott, Robin, Dir. Retail & Visitor Svcs., Genesee Country Village & Museum, Mumford, NY 1160
Lott, Mrs. Terry, Museum Shop Mgr., North Alabama Railroad Museum, Huntsville, AL 15
Lotz, Rick, Chm. (V), Ava Gardner Museum, Smithfield, NC.......................1267
Lotz, Theo, Dir., University of Central Florida Art Gallery, Orlando, FL............374
Lou, Julie, Dir. Finance, Queens Museum of Art, Queens, NY 1199
Loud, Patricia C., Cur. Architecture & Archivist, Kimbell Art Museum, Fort Worth, TX 1610
Louden, Elizabeth, Chm. (V) & Education Cur., University of Washington Botanic Garden, Seattle, WA 1784
Loudon, Michelle, Education, Wenatchee Valley Museum and Cultural Center, Wenatchee, WA.......................................1794
Loughan, Patricia, Pres., Kent-Delord House Museum, Plattsburgh, NY..........1195
Loughney, Patrick, Chief, Packard Campus of the Natl. Audiovisual Conservation Center, Library of Congress, Washington, DC 320
Loughran, Francis J., Park Ranger, Olustee Battlefield Historic State Park, Olustee, FL 373
Loughry, Jean, Pres. (V), Bushy Run Battlefield, Jeannette, PA.......................1436
Louise, Helen B., Dir. Museums, South Dakota State Historical Society, Pierre, SD 1538
Lounsbury, Kathryn, Exec. Asst., Greyhound Hall of Fame, Abilene, KS ...603
Lourens, Celia, Mgr. Mktg., The National Aquarium in Washington DC, Washington, DC...322
Lourie, Alexander "Sasha", Cur. Artistic Property, Maryland State Archives, Annapolis, MD 718
Lourie, Peg, Editor, Kelsey Museum of Archaeology, Ann Arbor, MI 822
Love, Camille R., Dir., The Atlanta Cyclorama, Atlanta, GA 402
Love, Debbie, Public Programs Coord., Cheyenne Frontier Days Old West Museum, Cheyenne, WY 1854
Love, Fran, Chm. (V), Ojai Valley Historical Society and Museum, Ojai, CA 157
Love, Lisa, Dir., Georgia Music Hall of Fame, Macon, GA 425
Love, Mick, Treas., Eugene V. Debs Home, Terre Haute, IN...........................567
Love, Mindi C., Pres., Johnson County Museum, Shawnee, KS 634
Love, Reeve, Dir. Performing Arts, National Hispanic Cultural Center, Art Museum, Albuquerque, NM.................1072
Love, Robert, Dir., O.K. Corral, Tombstone, AZ 57
Love, Sue, Interpretive Resource Tech., First Missouri State Capitol-State Historic Site, Saint Charles, MO 943
Love, Susan, Treas. Assoc., Depreciation Lands Museum, Allison Park, PA.........1409
Love, Tim, Dir. Operations, Oakland Zoo, Oakland, CA 156
Love, Victoria, Site Admin., First Missouri State Capitol-State Historic Site, Saint Charles, MO 943
Loveall, Don, Vice Pres., Bishop Hill Heritage Museum, Bishop Hill, IL 471
Loveday, Joan, Pres. (V), Fulton County Museum, Gloversville, NY 1138
Loveday, Linda, Cur. Education, Litchfield Historical Society and Museum, Litchfield, CT 280
Lovejoy, Barbara, Registrar, The Art Museum at the University of Kentucky, Lexington, KY 651
Lovejoy, Claudine, Administrative Asst., The Museum of East Texas, Lufkin, TX 1630
Lovejoy, Diane, Dir. Publications, The Museum of Fine Arts, Houston, Houston, TX 1622
Lovejoy, Kim, Exec. Dir., Military Heritage Museum, Punta Gorda, FL.........380
Lovejoy-May, Laura, Special Events Coord., Museum of International Folk Art, Santa Fe, NM.....................................1089
Lovelace, Joan, Admininstrative Operations Dir., Rochester Art Center, Rochester, MN...891
Lovelace, Patricia, Dir., The Thomas Griswold House and Museum, Guilford, CT 277
Lovelady, Tracy, Controller, Monticello, Home of Thomas Jefferson, Thomas Jefferson Foundation, Inc., Charlottesville, VA 1705
Loveland, Barry, Chief Div. Architecture & Preservation, Pennsylvania Historical & Museum Commission, Harrisburg, PA 1431
Lovell, Carol, Cur., The Stratford Historical Society & Catherine B. Mitchell Museum, Stratford, CT.............297
Lovell, Charles M., Dir., The Harwood Museum of Art of the University of New Mexico, Taos, NM.......................1093
Lovell, Charles M., Dir., Newcomb Art Gallery, New Orleans, LA 683
Lovell, Dr. Cindy, Exec. Dir., Mark Twain Boyhood Home & Museum, Hannibal, MO 928
Lovell, John, Acting Dir., New York State Bureau of Historic Sites, Waterford, NY...1225
Lovell, John, Asst. Dir. Bureau Historic Sites, New York State Office of Parks, Recreation & Historic Preservation, Albany, NY 1097
Lovell, Montgomery, Horticulturist, Terrace Hill Historic Site and Governor's Mansion, Des Moines, IA.....584
Lovelock, Liz, Paleobotanist, John Day Fossil Beds National Monument, Kimberly, OR..1393
Loven, Mike, Pres. (V), The Arboretum at Flagstaff, Flagstaff, AZ..........................41
Loven, Patricia, Museum Shop Mgr. & Office Coord., Enfield Shaker Museum, Enfield, NH...........................1017
Loverin, Jan, Cur. Clothing & Textiles, Nevada State Museum, Carson City, NV..1001
Lovern, Liz, Chm. Tours, The Anne Spencer Memorial Foundation, Inc., Lynchburg, VA...1722
Lovett, Beverly, Parks Specialist, Red Rock Museum, Church Rock, NM 1076
Lovett, Chris, Asst. Registrar, Museum of the Southwest, Midland, TX 1633
Lovett, James, Cur. Collections & Exhibitions, Museum of the Southwest, Midland, TX 1633
Lovett, Keith, Dir. Living Collections, Palm Beach Zoo, West Palm Beach, FL...397
Lovick, Emily, Museum Technician, Fort Smith National Historic Site, Fort Smith, AR 72
Loving, Charles R., Dir., The Snite Museum of Art, University of Notre Dame, Notre Dame, IN 561
Loving, Sharon, Head Horticulture Dept., Longwood Gardens, Kennett Square, PA...1437
Lovis, Dr. William, Cur. Anthropology, The Michigan State University Museum, East Lansing, MI.....................838
Lovold, Anne, Exec. Dir., Putnam County Museum, Greencastle, IN.........................544
Low, Cynthia, Registrar, Exhibitions, Honolulu Academy of Arts, Honolulu, HI 445
Low, Ellen, Exec. Dir., Columbia River Exhibition of History, Science and Technology, Richland, WA....................1779
Low, William, Cur., Bates College Museum of Art, Lewiston, ME................701

Lowden, Nancy, Special Program Coord., Maymont, Richmond, VA 1739
Lowdermilk, Kathy, Deputy Dir., William King Museum Center for Art and Cultural Heritage, Abingdon, VA..........1695
Lowdon, Ray, Pres., City of Burlington Historical Society, Burlington, NJ 1033
Lowe, Bill, Pres. (V), Grants Pass Museum of Art, Grants Pass, OR 1391
Lowe, Carole, Exec. Dir., American Water Ski Educational Foundation, Polk City, FL..380
Lowe, Damon, Cur. Biology, Indiana State Museum, Indianapolis, IN..............549
Lowe, David B., Pres. (V), Sterling-Rock Falls Historical Society Museum, Sterling, IL..523
Lowe, Donna, Museum Shop Mgr., Historical Museum of Bay County, Bay City, MI..825
Lowe, Gail, Historian, Anacostia Community Museum, Washington, DC...314
Lowe, Martha, Treas., Lake Waccamaw Depot Museum, Lake Waccamaw, NC..1255
Lowe, Sarah, Tour Guide, Civil War Museum at the Exchange Hotel, Gordonsville, VA.................................1715
Lowe, Susan, Business Mgr., South Carolina Institute of Archaeology & Anthropology, Columbia, SC 1510
Lowe, Todd, Chm. Bd. Dirs., Southern Arts Federation, Atlanta, GA 408
Lowe, Todd P., Chm., The Speed Art Museum, Louisville, KY.........................658
Lowe, Tom, Pres. (V), The Polk County Historical Society, Cedartown, GA..........413
Lowe, Vivian, Pres. (V), Limon Heritage Museum, Limon, CO..............................256
Lowell, A. Lee, Treas., Franklin Mineral Museum, Franklin, NJ..........................1039
Lowell, Molly W., Exec. Vice Pres., Mercer Museum of the Bucks County Historical Society, Doylestown, PA.......1421
Lowell Putnam, William, Trustee, Lowell Observatory, Flagstaff, AZ 41
Lowell, Sheryl, Dir. Mktg. & Public Rels., Don F. Pratt Memorial Museum, Fort Campbell, KY..................................646
Lowenberg, Nancy, Devel. Officer, Strawbery Banke Museum, Portsmouth, NH...................................1027
Lowenthal, Robert, Chm., Sonnenberg Gardens & Mansion State Historic Park, Canandaigua, NY.........................1118
Lowerre, Robert, Pres., Woodstock Museum of Shenandoah County, Inc., Woodstock, VA.....................................1756
Lowman, Don, Pres. (V), Cur. & Public Rels., Otero Museum Association, La Junta, CO 254
Lowrance, Liz, Exec. Dir., MacCallum More Museum and Gardens, Chase City, VA 1705
Lowrey, Dr. Carol, Cur. National Arts Club Permanent Collection, National Arts Club, New York, NY....................1176
Lowrey, Dr. Timothy K., Cur. Herbarium, Museum of Southwestern Biology, Albuquerque, NM..................................1072
Lowrie, Angie, Public Rels., Crawford Auto-Aviation Museum, Cleveland, OH..1309
Lowrie, Angie, Dir. Sales & Mktg., Western Reserve Historical Society, Cleveland, OH 1311
Lowry, Glenn, Dir., The Museum of Modern Art, New York, NY..................1176
Lowry, Joe Dan, Pres. & Cur., Turquoise Museum, Albuquerque, NM................1073
Lowry, Katy, Museum Shop Mgr., Turquoise Museum, Albuquerque, NM .1073
Lowry Straz, Catherine, Chm. (V), Tampa's Lowry Park Zoo, Tampa, FL 393
Lowsley-Williams, Elizabeth, Corp. Gifts Mgr., Virginia Museum of Fine Arts, Richmond, VA 1742
Loy, Sallie, Archivist, The Southern Museum of Civil War and Locomotive History, Kennesaw, GA..........................422
Loya, Ron, Pres. (V), Mariposa Museum and History Center Inc., Mariposa, CA...145
Loyd, Darla, Museum Shop Mgr., Emmett Kelly Historical Museum, Sedan, KS 633
Loyd, Kathy, Pres., Browntown Museum, Lake City, SC 1517
Loyd, Lynn, Vice Pres., National Quilt Museum, Museum of the American Quilter's Society, Paducah, KY 661
Loynd, Chris, Mktg., The Maritime Aquarium at Norwalk, Norwalk, CT.......290
Lozo, Mark, Education Dir., Theodore Roosevelt Inaugural National Historic Site, Buffalo, NY 1116
Lu Chen, Louise, Public Rels. & Cur., T.F. Chen Cultural Center, New York, NY 1182
Lubar, Steven, Dir., John Nicholas Brown Center for Public Humanities and Cultural Heritage, Providence, RI..........1494
Lubarsky, Kate, Administrator, Museum of the Southern Jewish Experience, Jackson, MS 911
Lubeck, Patricia, Cur. & Museum Shop Mgr., Redwood County Museum, Redwood, MN 891
Luberda, Janet, Museum Shop Mng., Sheldon Peck Homestead, Lombard, IL..504
Lubic, James E., Exec. Dir., American Watchmakers-Clockmakers Institute, Harrison, OH 1324
Lubin, Adam, Security Supvr., Oriental Institute Museum, University of Chicago, Chicago, IL 485
Lubowsky Talbott, Susan, Dir., Wadsworth Atheneum Museum of Art, Hartford, CT 279
Luca, Francis X., Chief Librarian, The Wolfsonian - Florida International University, Miami Beach, FL..................368
Lucas, Bertie, Park Mgr., Big Bone Lick State Park Museum, Union, KY 663
Lucas, Beverly, Cur., Connecticut Landmarks, Hartford, CT 278
Lucas, Bruce, Exhibit Designer, Southern Museum of Flight, Birmingham, AL..........6
Lucas, Charles C., Jr., M.D., Chm. (V), Fraunces Tavern Museum, New York, NY..1168
Lucas, Cindy, Asst. to Dir., Muscarelle Museum of Art, Williamsburg, VA........1755
Lucas, Cindy L., Assoc. Dir. & Cur., Doak House Museum, Greeneville, TN 1553
Lucas, Ed, Dir., Crossroads Museum, Corinth, MS 906
Lucas, June, Dir. Research, Museum of Early Southern Decorative Arts (MESDA), Winston-Salem, NC 1274
Lucas, Laura, Coord. Patron Svcs., Locust Lawn and Terwilliger House, Gardiner, NY 1136
Lucas, Laurie, Chm. (V), Arches Museum of Pioneer Life, Winona, MN...902
Lucas, Laurie, Pres. (V), Winona County Historical Museum, Winona, MN...........902
Lucas, Lynne, Sec., University of Tennessee Arboretum, Oak Ridge, TN ..1571
Lucas, Mary Lea, Dir. & Cur., Clarion County Historical Society, Sutton-Ditz House Museum, Clarion, PA.................1417
Lucas, Palma B., Exec. Dir., Philadelphia Mummers Museum, Philadelphia, PA ...1459
Lucas, Pat, Magazine Editor, Grant County Museum, Sheridan, AR 84
Lucas, Raymond, Historical Interpreter, Troy Museum & Historic Village, Troy, MI 866
Lucas, Robb, Mgr. Case Trading Post, The Wheelwright Museum of the American Indian, Santa Fe, NM............1091
Lucas, Scott, Greenhouse Supvr., Old Westbury Gardens, Old Westbury, NY ..1188
Luce, Donald T., Cur. Exhibits, Bell Museum of Natural History, Minneapolis, MN.....................................884
Luce, Russell, Treas., Sidney Historical Association, Sidney, NY 1212
Lucero, Carolina, Gallery Asst. Cur., Mission Cultural Center for Latino Arts, San Francisco, CA...............................190
Lucero, Donella, Cur., Fort Columbia House Museum, Chinook, WA 1762
Lucero-Criswell, Amber, Dir. Education & Public Programs, Museum of Photographic Arts, San Diego, CA..........181
Lucewicz Golding, Cher, Exec. Dir., Harn Homestead and 1889er Museum, Oklahoma City, OK..............................1370
Lucey, Patrick, Pres. (V), Amherst Museum, Amherst, NY.............................1099
Lucey, Thomas J., Pres. (V), Cape Cod Museum of Art, Dennis, MA 774
Luchans, Miriam, Registrar, The Yosemite Museum, National Park Service, Yosemite National Park, CA......226
Luchs, Alison, Cur. Early European Sculpture, National Gallery of Art, Washington, DC..323
Luchsinger, Dave, Supt., Statue of Liberty National Monument & Ellis Island Immigration Museum, New York, NY...1182
Lucia, Daniel S., Pres. (V), National Temple Hill Association, Inc., New Windsor, NY 1161
Lucier, Julie, Dir. Sales & Guest Svcs., Museum of Life and Science, Durham, NC...1243
Luck, Barbara, Cur., Abby Aldrich Rockefeller Folk Art Museum, Williamsburg, VA 1753
Luck, Johnna, Museum Shop Mgr., Cripple Creek District Museum, Inc., Cripple Creek, CO..................................236
Lucke, Susan, Registrar, University Art Museum, Santa Barbara, Santa Barbara, CA 204
Luckert, Steven, Cur. Permanent Exhibition, United States Holocaust Memorial Museum, Washington, DC 332
Luckett, Jeannie, Education Cur., West Baton Rouge Museum, Port Allen, LA ...685
Luckett, Mildred, Museum Shop Mgr., Society for the Preservation of Long Island Antiquities, Cold Spring Harbor, NY 1122
Luckhurst, Ailene, Historian, Beauvais Heritage Center, Clark, SD 1528
Luckow, Melissa, Assoc. Professor, L.H. Bailey Hortorium, Ithaca, NY...............1147
Lucky, Rosemary, Pres. (V), Sarpy County Historical Museum, Bellevue, NE 977
Ludden, Andrea, Owner, Salt and Pepper Shaker Museum, Gatlinburg, TN...........1552
Ludden, Rolf, Owner, Salt and Pepper Shaker Museum, Gatlinburg, TN...........1552
Luderowski, Barbara, C.E.O. & Pres. (V), Mattress Factory, Ltd., Pittsburgh, PA...1466
Ludvik, Dana, Friends Liaison, University of Nebraska State Museum, Lincoln, NE 991
Ludwig, David, Dir. Boat Shed, Michigan Maritime Museum, South Haven, MI......865

L–*Continued*

L–*Continued*

M

M–*Continued*

Magee, Eileen M., Asst. Dir. Programs, The Athenaeum of Philadelphia, Philadelphia, PA 1450
Magee, Henry J., Museum Shop Mgr., Fireman's Hall Museum, Philadelphia, PA 1453
Magee, Karen, Public Rels., Cheboygan County Historical Museum Complex, Cheboygan, MI 830
Magee, Michael, Planetarium Mgr., Flandrau Science Center and Planetarium, Tucson, AZ 60
Magee, Sandra, Mgr. Community Rels., The World of Energy, Seneca, SC 1523
Magee, Vern, Pres. (V), Geneva Lake Museum, Lake Geneva, WI 1826
Magelky, Brian, Pres. (V), McConnell Mansion, Moscow, ID 462
Maggar, Shawn, Museum Shop Mgr., Four Rivers Cultural Center & Museum, Ontario, OR 1396
Maggard, David, Gen. Mgr., Cumberland Inn & Museum, Williamsburg, KY 664
Maggard, Jane, Exec. Asst. & Membership, The Hermitage: Home of President Andrew Jackson, Hermitage, TN 1554
Maghakyan, Simon, Asst. Visitor Svcs. Mgr., Colorado State Capitol, Denver, CO 238
Magid, Barbara H., Asst. Dir., Alexandria Archaeology Museum, Alexandria, VA .1696
Magidson, David L., Pres. (V), National Museum of American Jewish Military History, Washington, DC 324
Magidson, Phyllis, Cur. Costumes, Museum of the City of New York, New York, NY 1176
Magill, Robert, Ph.D., Sr. Vice Pres. Research, Missouri Botanical Garden, Saint Louis, MO 949
Magill, Tina M., Dir., Margaret Harwell Art Museum, Poplar Bluff, MO 942
Maginnis, Margaret, Ph.D., Co-Editor, American Catholic Historical Society, Philadelphia, PA 1449
Magnani, Patricia, Registrar, Neuberger Museum of Art, Purchase College, State University of New York, Purchase, NY 1198
Magneson, Lyle, 2nd Vice Pres., Phelps House, Burlington, IA 575
Magnus, Lawrence, Public Rels., Blackhawk Museum (Behring-Hofmann Educational Institute, Inc.), Danville, CA 106
Magnuson, Lynnea, Ph.D., Museum & Collections Exec., Soldiers Memorial Military Museum, Saint Louis, MO 951
Magnuson, Rosalind, Archivist, Brick Store Museum, Kennebunk, ME 700
Magnusson, Mishell, Pres. (V), Madison County Historical Society-Cottage Lawn, Oneida, NY 1188
Magowan, Merrill L., Chm., National Tropical Botanical Garden, Kalaheo, HI 449
Magruder, Blue, Dir. Communications, Harvard Museum of Natural History, Cambridge, MA 767
Magruder, Marge, Shelter Mgr., Gathland State Park, Burretsville, MD 729
Magsamen, Sandra, Chairperson, American Visionary Art Museum, Baltimore, MD 719
Maguire, Carol A., Exec. Dir., Huntington Sewing & Trade School, Huntington, NY 1144
Maguire, Cathy, Asst. Dir. & Membership, National Museum of Racing and Hall of Fame, Saratoga Springs, NY 1207
Maguire, JoAnn, Museum Shop Mgr., Calhoun County Museum, Rockwell City, IA 598
Maguire Murphy, Patricia, Dir., Historical Resources and Museum Services, Little Rock, AR 77
Maguire, Nancy, Deputy Dir. & Gallery Cur., Stedman Gallery, Camden, NJ 1034
Maguire, Sharmon, Administrative Asst., Nordic Heritage Museum, Seattle, WA .1782
Maguire, Sharon, Dir., Palm Springs Air Museum, Palm Springs, CA 161
Magurany, J. D., Site Mgr., Laumeier Sculpture Park & Museum, Saint Louis, MO 948
Mahadevan, Dr. Kumar, Pres., Mote Marine Laboratory/Aquarium, Sarasota, FL 387
Mahaffay, Suzie, Financial Dir., Lindsay Wildlife Museum, Walnut Creek, CA 222
Mahaffey, Barbara "Bobbie", Museum Shop Mgr., Museum of the Islands, Pine Island Center, FL 379
Mahan, John, Pres., Gilmer Arts and Heritage Association, Ellijay, GA 418
Mahan, Kim, Deputy Dir., Amarillo Museum of Art, Amarillo, TX 1577
Mahanes, Pat, Exec. Sec., James Madison's Montpelier - The Montpelier Foundation, Montpelier Station, VA 1726
Mahaney, Nancy, Cur. Arts & Cultures of the Americas, Africa, & Oceania, Spencer Museum of Art, The University of Kansas, Lawrence, KS 621
Mahaney, Timothy, Vice Pres. Facilities, Planning & Operations, Carnegie Museums of Pittsburgh (Carnegie Institute), Pittsburgh, PA 1465
Maharg, Chrissy, Financial Officer, The Nature Center at Shaker Lakes, Cleveland, OH 1310
Maher, Christine, Museum Store Asst., Williams College Museum of Art, Williamstown, MA 817
Maher, Kathleen, Exec. Dir. & Cur., The Barnum Museum, Bridgeport, CT 267
Maher, Kristie, C.E.O., South Dakota Discovery Center, Pierre, SD 1538
Maher, Michael, Research Librarian, Nevada Historical Society, Reno, NV ...1009
Maher, Mike, Exec. Dir., Manitowoc County Historical Society, Manitowoc, WI 1829
Mahla, Susan, Dir. Visitor Svcs., Cummer Museum of Art & Gardens, Jacksonville, FL 354
Mahler, Marjorie, Dir. Visitor Svcs., Waukesha County Museum, Waukesha, WI 1849
Mahnken, Cecelia, Accounting, Fraunces Tavern Museum, New York, NY 1168
Mahon, Harry E., Pres., The Northern Virginia Fine Arts Association at the Athenaeum, Alexandria, VA 1698
Mahon, Todd, Exec. Dir., Anoka County Historical Society, Anoka, MN 869
Mahoney, Cathy, Treas. Bd. of Park Commissioners, The Downers Grove Park District Museum, Downers Grove, IL 491
Mahoney, Janet C., Chm. Bd. (V), Julian H. Sleeper House, Saint Paul, MN 894
Mahoney, Linda, Supvr. Store, Cracker Country, Tampa, FL 391
Mahoney, Maggie, Asst. to Dir., The Robert J. Dole Institute of Politics, Lawrence, KS 621
Mahoney, Marc F., Pres. (V), Audubon Society of Rhode Island, Smithfield, RI 1497
Mahoney, Marc F., Pres., Audubon Society of Rhode Island Environmental Education Center, Bristol, RI 1485
Mahoney, Martin, Mgr. Collections & Registration, Norman Rockwell Museum, Stockbridge, MA 810
Mahoney, Dr. Meredith, Asst. Cur. Zoology, Illinois State Museum, Springfield, IL 521
Mahoney, Olivia, Chief Cur., Chicago History Museum, Chicago, IL 478
Mahoney, Ryan, Collections Asst., The Antique Boat Museum, Clayton, NY 1121
Mahony, Archbishop Roger, Chm., San Fernando Mission, Mission Hills, CA 147
Mahovlic, Joe, Chm. Bd. (V), The Holden Arboretum, Kirtland, OH 1326
Maicki, Richard J., Pres. Bd. (V), The Children's Museum of Cleveland, Cleveland, OH 1307
Maida, Cardinal Adam, Pres. (V), Pope John Paul II Cultural Center, Washington, DC 328
Maier, Cheryl, Museum Shop Mgr., Genesee Country Village & Museum, Mumford, NY 1160
Maier, James, Pres., Historic Langhorne Association, Langhorne, PA 1440
Maierhauser, Joe, C.E.O., Pres. & Dir., Black Hills Reptile Gardens, Inc., Rapid City, SD 1539
Maifield, Liz, Aide & Gift Shop Mgr., The Nylander Museum of Natural History, Caribou, ME 696
Maijala, Kevin, Dir. & Security, Alexander Ramsey House, Minnesota Historical Society, Saint Paul, MN 893
Mailander, Chris, Dir. Exhibits, The Museum of Flight, Seattle, WA 1781
Mailloux, Eleanor F., Mgr., Helvetia Museum, Helvetia, WV 1799
Mailloux, Thomas, Asst. Treas., The Gardner Museum, Inc., Gardner, MA 779
Main, Don, Vice Pres. Institutional Advancement USS Constitution Museum, Boston, MA 763
Main, Sally, Senior Cur., Newcomb Art Gallery, New Orleans, LA 683
Mainer, Ben, Service Asst., John Brown Museum State Historic Site, Osawatomie, KS 629
Maines, Renee, Bookkeeper, Belle Grove Plantation, Middletown, VA 1725
Mainwaring, Leigh, Dir. & C.E.O., Mabel Hartzell Historical Home, Alliance, OH 1293
Maiocco, Frank, Archivist, Petrified Creatures Museum of Natural History, Richfield Springs, NY 1200
Maioho, William, Cur., Royal Mausoleum State Monument, Honolulu, HI 447
Maisano, John, Artist, Texas Natural Science Center, Austin, TX 1584
Maisel, Andrew, Pres. (Pomo), California Indian Museum & Cultural Center, Santa Rosa, CA 208
Maitinsky, Jean Paul, Asst. Dir. Exhibitions & Programs, Hudson River Museum, Yonkers, NY 1229
Maitland, Douglas, Acting Treas., Swampscott Historical Society (Sir John Humphrey House), Swampscott, MA 811
Maitland, Douglas B., Treas., Atlantic No. 1 Veterans Firemen's Association, Inc., Swampscott, MA 811
Maitland, Edna, Sec., Atlantic No. 1 Veterans Firemen's Association, Inc., Swampscott, MA 811
Maitland, Richard, Dir., Atlantic No. 1 Veterans Firemen's Association, Inc., Swampscott, MA 811

M–*Continued*

Maltz, Milton, Chm. Bd., Maltz Museum of Jewish Heritage, Beachwood, OH.....1296
Maltz, Tamar, Pres., Maltz Museum of Jewish Heritage, Beachwood, OH 1296
Malvin, Fred, Treas., Watermen's Museum, Yorktown, VA........................1757
Malys Wilson, Ann, Naturalist, Myrtle Beach State Park Nature Center, Myrtle Beach, SC 1519
Mamalakis, Helen, Archives Specialist, Dearborn Historical Museum, Dearborn, MI 831
Mamatt, Mary, Pres. Terrace Hill Commission, Terrace Hill Historic Site and Governor's Mansion, Des Moines, IA 584
Mammel, Jim, Pres. (V), El Museo Latino, Omaha, NE..............................994
Manachelli, Linda, Dir., Camp Gordon Johnston Museum, Carrabelle, FL..........337
Mancebo-Ingram, Kary, Cur., Tulare Historical Museum, Tulare, CA..............219
Manchester, Carri L., Dir. Education, Olana State Historic Site, Hudson, NY .1143
Manchester, Karen, Cur. Ancient Art, The Art Institute of Chicago, Chicago, IL......476
Manchester, Robert C., Cur., Yellowstone Art Museum, Billings, MT.....................957
Manchester, Dr. Steven R., Cur. Paleobotony, Florida Museum of Natural History, Gainesville, FL.............351
Mancusi-Ungaro, Carol, Dir. Center for the Technical Study of Modern Art, Harvard Art Museum, Cambridge, MA...767
Mancusi-Ungaro, Carol, Assoc. Dir. Conservation & Research, Whitney Museum of American Art, New York, NY 1184
Mancuso, Brian, Dir. Exhibits, John P. McGovern Museum of Health & Medical Science, Houston, TX 1621
Mancuso, John, Education, The Greenburgh Nature Center, Scarsdale, NY 1208
Mandel, David, Cur. Exhibits, The Hubbard Museum of the American West, Ruidoso Downs, NM...................1087
Mandelker, Carolyn, Public Rels., Neuberger Museum of Art, Purchase College, State University of New York, Purchase, NY 1198
Mandell, Linda, Treas., Queens Historical Society, Flushing, NY 1133
Mander, Phyllis, Pres. (V), Monona County Historical Museum, Onawa, IA 596
Mandevile, Joyce, C.E.O., T.W. Wood Gallery & Arts Center, Montpelier, VT.1684
Mandeville, Jeffrey, Pres., Richland County Museum, Lexington, OH...........1327
Mandeville, Lynn, Dir. Devel. & Community Affairs, Museum of Art/Fort Lauderdale, Fort Lauderdale, FL..347
Mandic, Teri, Vice Pres. Operations, The Pearl S. Buck House, Perkasie, PA 1449
Mandracchia, Mrs. James, Cur., Gunnison Museum of Natural History, Pawling, NY..1194
Maneely, Larry, Pres., World Sports Humanitarian Hall of Fame, Boise, ID ...456
Manella, Mary Alice, Budget & Finance Mgr., The Patricia & Phillip Frost Art Museum, Miami, FL...............................367
Maner, Anne, Temple Admin., Archives Museum, Temple Mickve Israel, Savannah, GA...433
Manes, John, Exhibit Specialist, The Old Guard Museum, Fort Myer, VA............1711
Maney, Pat, Treas., Musical Instrument Museum, Phoenix, AZ..............................50
Manfrey Vogelstein, Barbara, Vice Chm., Brooklyn Museum, Brooklyn, NY..........1111
Manfrina, Debbie, Recording Sec., Lompoc Valley Historical Society, Inc., Lompoc, CA.....................................130
Mangan, Lenore, Museum Shop Mgr., Trailside Nature and Science Center, Mountainside, NJ.................................1051
Manganaro, Doris, Vice Pres., South County Museum Inc., Narragansett, RI.1489
Mangels, Joanne, Treas. & Museum Shop Mgr., Miracle of America Museum Inc., Polson, MT 970
Mangels, W. Gilbert, C.E.O., Miracle of America Museum Inc., Polson, MT 970
Mangione, JoAnn, C.O.O., Mid-America Science Museum, Hot Springs, AR 74
Mangum, David, Pres. (V), Delta County Museum, Delta, CO...............................237
Mangus, Patrick T., Exec. Dir., National Aviary in Pittsburgh, Inc., Pittsburgh, PA...1467
Manguso, John M., Dir., Fort Sam Houston Museum, Fort Sam Houston, TX 1608
Manhart, Patty, Cur. & Museum Shop Mgr., Louis E. May Museum, Fremont, NE 982
Maniatis, John, Registrar, The First Division Museum at Cantigny, Wheaton, IL 529
Manibusan, Rose S.N., Interpretive Specialist, War in the Pacific National Historical Park, Piti, GU 1868
Maniez, Erica S., Dir., Issaquah History Museum, Issaquah, WA.......................1769
Manini, Paula, Dir., Trinidad History Museum - Colorado Historical Society, Trinidad, CO 264
Manion, Lucibel, C.E.O., Callahan County Pioneer Museum, Baird, TX 1585
Manion, Sheila, Dir. Devel. & Campaign, Saint Louis Art Museum, Saint Louis, MO 950
Manipella, Addy, Dir. Education, Staten Island Children's Museum, Staten Island, NY..1216
Mankin Kornhauser, Elizabeth, Chief Cur. & Cur. Krieble American Painting & Sculpture, Wadsworth Atheneum Museum of Art, Hartford, CT 279
Manley, Jill, Dir. Public Rels. & Mktg., Hershey Gardens, Hershey, PA..........1433
Manley, Rebecca, Cur., Historical Society of the Phoenixville Area, Phoenixville, PA..1463
Manly, Nancy, Museum Shop Mgr., Heritage Museum & Gallery, Leadville, CO...255
Mann, Ben, Pres. (V), 1859 Jail, Marshal's Home & Museum, Independence, MO.................................929
Mann, C. Griffith, Chief Cur., The Cleveland Museum of Art, Cleveland, OH..1308
Mann, Dr. James, Cur., Las Vegas Art Museum, Las Vegas, NV 1005
Mann, Judith, Cur. European Art to 1800, Saint Louis Art Museum, Saint Louis, MO 950
Mann, Kerry, Museum Shop Buyer, The John Marshall House, Richmond, VA ...1738
Mann, LaDonna, Dir., The Museum of the Alphabet, Waxhaw, NC 1269
Mann, Stephen, Pres. (V), Dutchess County Historical Society, Poughkeepsie, NY 1197
Mann-Cherry, Julie, Museum Shop Mgr., Golden Spike National Historic Site, Brigham City, UT 1660
Mannell, Terry, Pres. (V), Fort Hays State Historic Site, Hays, KS 616
Mannen, Frank, 1st Vice Chm., San Diego Botanic Garden, Encinitas, CA.....110
Mannes, Mary Ann, Museum Shop Mgr., Herzstein Memorial Museum, Clayton, NM 1076
Manning, Altha, Pres. (V), Gadsden Arts Center, Quincy, FL 380
Manning, Angie, Monument Mgr., Bosque Redondo Memorial Fort Sumner State Monument, Fort Sumner, NM 1078
Manning, Angie, Mgr., Coronado State Monument, Bernalillo, NM...................1075
Manning, Anne, Deputy Dir. Education & Interpretation, The Baltimore Museum of Art, Baltimore, MD..............................720
Manning, Archie, Chm. (V), College Football Hall of Fame, South Bend, IN 565
Manning, Catherine, Chm. (V), Atlanta Historical Society, Atlanta, GA...............402
Manning, Catreva, Archivist, Grout Museum District: Grout Museum of History and Science, Bluedorn Science Imaginarium, Rensselaer Russell House Museum, Snowden House, Waterloo, IA 601
Manning, Elisabeth, Cur. Collections & Exhibits, Brazos Valley Museum of Natural History, Bryan, TX...................1590
Manning, James W., Jr., Exec. Dir., Oaklands Historic House Museum, Murfreesboro, TN 1565
Manning, Loni, Educational Program Asst., Museum of Contemporary Native Arts, Santa Fe, NM...................1088
Manning, Lynne, Mktg. Coord., SullivanMunce Cultural Center, Zionsville, IN...571
Manning, Michael, Chief Interpreter & Resource Mgr., Fort Donelson National Battlefield, Dover, TN 1551
Manning, Patrick, Sec., Sierra County Historical Society (Kentucky Mine Museum), Sierra City, CA....................211
Manning, Robert J., Bd. Pres. (V), John Brown House Museum, Providence, RI..1494
Manning, Robert J., Pres., Rhode Island Historical Society, Providence, RI 1496
Mannix, Anne, Dir. Communications, The Baltimore Museum of Art, Baltimore, MD 720
Mano, Charlene, Senior Program Mgr., Wing Luke Asian Museum, Seattle, WA 1784
Manoguerra, Paul, Cur. American Art, Georgia Museum of Art, University of Georgia, Athens, GA 400
Manoogian, Daron, Dir. Communications, Harvard Art Museum, Cambridge, MA...767
Manor, Kathy, Dir., Sacramento Valley Museum, Williams, CA...........................224
Manoux, Christine, Education Coord., University of California Botanical Garden, Berkeley, CA 94
Manring, Lynne, Dir. Youth Programs, Memorial Hall Museum, Pocumtuck Valley Memorial Assoc., Deerfield, MA 774
Mansell, JoAnne, Exec. Dir., Seward County Historical Museum, Liberal, KS 623
Mansfield, Dr. Bernard M., Acting Dir., Galion Historical Museum, Galion, OH..1321
Mansfield, Doug, Dir., G.I. Museum, Ocean Springs, MS.................................914
Mansfield, Kelly, Administrative Officer, Oregon Trail Museum, Gering, NE 983
Mansfield, Terrye, C.E.O., Great Lakes Museum of Military History, Michigan City, IN 556

M–*Continued*

M–*Continued*

Martin, Lisa, Deputy Dir. Museum Affairs, Taubman Museum of Art, Roanoke, VA....1744
Martin, Lolly, Museum Shop Mgr., El Rancho de Las Golondrinas Museum, Santa Fe, NM....1088
Martin, Loretta, Dir., Louden-Henritze Archaeology Museum, Trinidad, CO....264
Martin, Louise, Chm. (V), Benicia Historical Museum, Benicia, CA....91
Martin, Margery, C.E.O. & Pres. (V), Bernard Historical Society and Museum, Delton, MI....832
Martin, Mary Jo, Chm. (V), Museum of Geneva History, Geneva, FL....352
Martin McKinney, Janet, Chm. (V) KU Biodiversity Institute - KU Natural History Museum, Lawrence, KS....621
Martin, Melissa, Education, Flint River Quarium, Albany, GA....399
Martin, Melissa, Exec. Dir., Texas Discovery Gardens, Dallas, TX....1600
Martin, Meredith, Museum Store Mgr., Air Zoo, Kalamazoo, MI....847
Martin, Michael, Cur. Collections & Exhibitions, Flint Institute of Arts, Flint, MI....840
Martin, Mike, Treas., The Museum of East Alabama, Opelika, AL....21
Martin Mintz, Deborah, Exec. Dir., Arts Council of Fayetteville/Cumberland County, Fayetteville, NC....1245
Martin, Nancy, Bd. Sec., Rocky Ford Historical Museum, Rocky Ford, CO....262
Martin, Paul, Vice Pres. Exhibits, The Science Museum of Minnesota, Saint Paul, MN....896
Martin, Paula, Asst. Dir. Public Rels., Special Events & Retail, Historical Society of Palm Beach County, West Palm Beach, FL....396
Martin, Peggy, Museum Shop Mgr., Hiddenite Center, Inc., Hiddenite, NC..1252
Martin, Peter, Co Vice Chm., Shelburne Museum, Inc., Shelburne, VT....1690
Martin, R. Brad, Chm., Dixon Gallery and Gardens, Memphis, TN....1561
Martin, Rebecca, Dir. Education Outreach, Sid Richardson Museum, Fort Worth, TX....1611
Martin, Rebecca J., Asst. Dir., Kansas Museum of History, Topeka, KS....636
Martin, Rex Paul, Exec. Dir., Westport Maritime Museum, Westport, WA....1794
Martin, Rick, Chief Operations, National Park Service Vicksburg National Military Park-Cairo Museum, Vicksburg, MS....918
Martin, LTC (Ret.) Robert, Pres. Foundation (V), Casemate Museum, Fort Monroe, VA....1711
Martin, Robert, Pres., Oldham County History Center, La Grange, KY....651
Martin, Rosalind, Assoc. Cur. Education K-12, Knoxville Museum of Art, Knoxville, TN....1558
Martin, Rose M., Exec. Dir., Chattanooga African Museum/Bessie Smith Hall, Chattanooga, TN....1547
Martin, Roy, Chm. Bd., Kentucky Music Hall of Fame and Museum, Renfro Valley, KY....662
Martin, Sandra W., Dir., Pres. & Founder, The Little Nature Museum, Contoocook, NH....1015
Martin, Sean, Archivist, Maltz Museum of Jewish Heritage, Beachwood, OH....1296
Martin, Shannon, Dir., Ziibiwing Center of Anishinabe Culture & Lifeways, Mount Pleasant, MI....856
Martin, Sharon, Events Coord., Carroll County Farm Museum, Westminster, MD....750
Martin, Sheryl, Pres., Framingham History Center, Framingham, MA....778
Martin, Shiela, Museum Shop Mgr., Gravette Historical Museum, Gravette, AR....73
Martin, Shirley, Tours, Jekyll Island Museum, Jekyll Island, GA....421
Martin, Staci R., District Program Specialist, First Landing State Park, Virginia Beach, VA....1751
Martin, Stephen, Dir., Moore-Lindsay House Historical Museum, Norman, OK....1369
Martin, Steve, Supt., Grand Canyon National Park Museum Collection, Grand Canyon National Park, AZ....44
Martin, Dr. Terry, Anthropology Chair, Illinois State Museum, Springfield, IL....521
Martin, Tim, Treas., Marquette County Historical Society, Westfield, WI....1851
Martin, Tim, M.D., Pres. (V), Historic Arkansas Museum, Little Rock, AR....77
Martin, Wendell, Pres., Bessemer Hall of History, Bessemer, AL....4
Martin, Wendy, Municipal Clerk, Carter-Coile Country Doctors Museum, Winterville, GA....440
Martin, William J., Dir., Valentine Richmond History Center, Richmond, VA....1741
Martin, Wilson, State Historic Preservation Officer, Utah State Historical Society, Salt Lake City, UT..1672
Martina, Amy, Registrar, Hagley Museum and Library, Wilmington, DE....313
Martinek, Doreen, Events, Idaho Botanical Garden, Boise, ID....455
Martinelli, Susan, Vice Pres. Business Affairs, Historic Deerfield, Inc., Deerfield, MA....774
Martinez, Carla, Registrar, Carson County Square House Museum, Panhandle, TX....1637
Martinez, Carlos, C.E.O., D.C. Booth Historic National Fish Hatchery and Archive, Spearfish, SD....1543
Martinez, Cipriano, Lead Guard, Spurlock Museum, University of Illinois at Urbana-Champaign, Urbana, IL....525
Martinez, Connie, Exec. Dir., Children's Discovery Museum of San Jose, San Jose, CA....195
Martinez, Daniel, Historian USS Arizona Memorial, Honolulu, HI....448
Martinez, George, Bd. Pres., Museo de las Americas, Denver, CO....241
Martinez, Joe, Park Mgr. Tubac Presidio State Historic Park, Arizona State Parks Board, Phoenix, AZ....49
Martinez, Joe, Park Mgr., Tubac Presidio State Historic Park, Tubac, AZ....58
Martinez, Johnny, Zoo Dir., Washington Park Zoological Gardens, Michigan City, IN....556
Martinez, Patricia, Business Mgr., The Wheelwright Museum of the American Indian, Santa Fe, NM....1091
Martinez, Robert, Pres., Connecticut Audubon Birdcraft Museum, Fairfield, CT....273
Martinez, Robert, Pres., Connecticut Audubon Society, Fairfield, CT....273
Martinez, Shannon, Pres. (V), A.C. Gilbert's Discovery Village, Salem, OR....1403
Martinez, Vidal, Supt., Zane Grey Museum, Lackawaxen, PA....1438
Martin-Mathewson, Nancy, Museum Shop Mgr., The Yager Museum of Art & Culture, Oneonta, NY....1189
Martino, Mike, Pres. (V), Academy Hall Museum of the Rocky Hill Historical Society, Inc., Rocky Hill, CT....292
Martino, Dr. Ronald L., Geology Dept., Geology Museum, Huntington, WV....1800
Martins, Michael, Cur., Fall River Historical Society Museum, Fall River, MA....777
Martinson, Betsy, Educational Programs Coord., Buffalo Bill Museum & Grave, Golden, CO....248
Martinson, Gayle, Archivist, Wisconsin Veterans Museum-Madison, Madison, WI....1829
Martinson, Gordon, C.E.O. & Pres., Wilkin County Historical Society, Breckenridge, MN....871
Martinson, Susan, Treas., Lauder Museum - Amityville Historical Society, Amityville, NY....1099
Martin-Wicoff, Jenny, Registrar Fine Art & Cultural History, New Jersey State Museum, Trenton, NJ....1064
Martiny, Sandy, Cur. Education, National Academy Museum and School of Fine Arts, New York, NY....1176
Martis, Ingrid, Library Asst., Museum of Photographic Arts, San Diego, CA....181
Martoia, Ronald J., Treas., Automotive Hall of Fame, Inc., Dearborn, MI....831
Marton, Florence, Owner, Hawaii Loves Barbie Dolls Museum, Kailua, HI....449
Martonis, Stephen, Exhibitions Mgr. CU Art Galleries, Boulder, CO....229
Martucci, Patty, Program Dir., Warwick Museum of Art, Warwick, RI....1498
Martus, Ginger, Devel., Presidential Pet Museum, Williamsburg, VA....1755
Martus, Marilyn, Pres. (V), Wayne County Historical Museum, Richmond, IN....564
Marty, John F., Pres., Swiss Historical Village, New Glarus, WI....1838
Maruicsin, Yami, Chm. (V), Cherokee Strip Regional Heritage Center, Enid, OK....1361
Maruna, Joyce, Archivist, Bedford Historical Society Museum and Library, Bedford, OH....1296
Marushin, James, Cur., Pioneer Museum - Martin County Historical Society, Fairmont, MN....877
Marvin, Amy, Vice Pres. Institutional Advancement, Bishop Museum, Honolulu, HI....443
Marwell, David, Dir., Museum of Jewish Heritage-A Living Memorial to the Holocaust, New York, NY....1175
Marx, Anthony W., Pres. Amherst College, Mead Art Museum, Amherst, MA....752
Marx, Bridget, Collections Mgr. & Cur. of Exhibitions, Meadows Museum, Dallas, TX....1599
Marx, Stephen F., Pres., Wabash Frisco and Pacific Association, Inc. "The Uncommon Carrier", Glencoe, MO....928
Maryniak, Gregg, Vice Pres. Aerospace Science, St. Louis Science Center, Saint Louis, MO....950
Marz, Steve, Deputy Dir., Delaware Division of Historical & Cultural Affairs, Dover, DE....305
Marzio, Frances, Cur. The Glassell Collections, The Museum of Fine Arts, Houston, Houston, TX....1622
Marzio, Peter C., Dir., The Museum of Fine Arts, Houston, Houston, TX....1622

M–*Continued*

Matheson, Mary Pat, Exec. Dir., Atlanta Botanical Garden, Atlanta, GA 402
Matheson, Susan B., Cur. Ancient Art, Yale University Art Gallery, New Haven, CT..287
Mathew, Mike, 1st Vice Pres., Moss Mansion Historic House Museum, Billings, MT 956
Mathewes, Melanie L., Exec. Dir., Hermitage Museum and Gardens, Norfolk, VA 1730
Mathews, Bill, Exec. Sec., Alabama Women's Hall of Fame, Marion, AL.........16
Mathews, Elaine, Treas., Malki Museum, Banning, CA 90
Mathews, George K., Jr., Curatorial Dir., Virginia Living Museum, Newport News, VA..1729
Mathews, Greg, Exec. Dir. & Pres., Kentucky Railway Museum, Inc., New Haven, KY..660
Mathews, Prof. Heather, Pacific Lutheran University Gallery, Tacoma, WA 1789
Mathews, Lloyd, Dir. Public Rels., Wilderness Road Regional Museum, Newbern, VA 1727
Mathews, M. Marguerite, Sec., John Paul Jones House Museum, Portsmouth, NH..1026
Mathews, Nancy, Sr. Cur. Education, Dinosaur Discovery Museum, Kenosha, WI 1824
Mathews, Nancy, Sr. Cur. Education, Kenosha Public Museum, Kenosha, WI 1824
Mathews, Wayne, Facilities Mgr., Museum of the Albemarle, Elizabeth City, NC...1244
Mathews, William, Vice Pres. Mktg. & Communications, Wilton Historical Museums, Wilton, CT 303
Mathewson, Barbara, Museum Shop Mgr., Montshire Museum of Science, Inc., Norwich, VT 1686
Mathewson, Dave, Pres. (V), Academy of Model Aeronautics/National Model Aviation Museum, Muncie, IN 557
Mathey, Carole, Asst. Dir., St. Lawrence University - Richard F. Brush Art Gallery and Permanent Collection, Canton, NY 1118
Mathias, Katy, Business Mgr., Center for Wooden Boats, Seattle, WA 1779
Mathies, Linda, Tour Coord., Old Barracks Museum, Trenton, NJ 1064
Mathieu, James, Chief of Staff, University of Pennsylvania Museum of Archaeology and Anthropology, Philadelphia, PA 1462
Mathis, Connie, Health Programmer, Roper Mountain Science Center, Greenville, SC 1514
Mathis, Frances, Museum Shop Mgr., Old Independence Regional Museum, Batesville, AR..66
Mathis, Joseph, Pres. (V), Mote Marine Laboratory/Aquarium, Sarasota, FL.........387
Mathis, Natalie N., Mgr. Devel., Taft Museum of Art, Cincinnati, OH 1306
Mathis, Rae, Outreach Coord., Oren Dunn City Museum, Tupelo, MS............917
Mathis, Sharon, Program Asst., DeWitt Stetten, Jr., Museum of Medical Research, Bethesda, MD.........................727
Mathisen, Jennie, Museum Shop Mgr. & Dir. Guest Svcs., Omaha Children's Museum, Omaha, NE..............................995
Mathison, Judy K., Cur., Vernon County Museum, Viroqua, WI..........................1848
Matias, Chris, Museum Shop Mgr., Dragon Dreams Museum & Gift Shop, Chattanooga, TN...................................1548
Matijcio, Steven, Cur. Art, Southeastern Center for Contemporary Art, Winston-Salem, NC 1275
Matin, Marty, Exhibits, Fort Huachuca Museum, Fort Huachuca, AZ....................43
Matis, Kelly E., Dir. Education & Public Conservation Programs, Mystic Aquarium & Institute for Exploration, Mystic, CT..283
Matis, Walter, Prog. & Volunteer Coord., Fairfield Museum and History Center, Fairfield, CT..273
Matlick, Kristen, Dir. Education, Waukesha County Museum, Waukesha, WI...1849
Matney, Matt, Dir. Facilities, Huntington Museum of Art, Inc., Huntington, WV.1800
Matos, Jennifer, Dir. Education, Noah Webster House/West Hartford Historical Society, West Hartford, CT 300
Matrisciano, John, Sec., California Museum of Ancient Art, Beverly Hills, CA..94
Matson, Jim, Historic Site Admin., Alexander Ramsey House, Minnesota Historical Society, Saint Paul, MN.........893
Matson, Dr. Timothy, Cur. Vertebrate Zoology, The Cleveland Museum of Natural History, Cleveland, OH............1308
Matsuoka, Jeff, Vice Pres. Business & Operations, Indiana Historical Society, Indianapolis, IN..548
Matt, Lawrence, Vice Pres., Air Classic Inc. Museum of Aviation, Sugar Grove, IL 524
Matt, Uncle, Museum Shop Mgr., South Dakota Discovery Center, Pierre, SD....1538
Matte, Eileen, Coord. Devel. & Membership, Hofstra University Museum, Hempstead, NY 1141
Mattei, Theresa, Mng. Dir. Visitor Experiences, Louisville Science Center, Louisville, KY 655
Matteis, Justine, Museum Shop Mgr., Bruce Museum, Greenwich, CT 276
Mattelin, Ruth, Treas., Culbertson Museum, Culbertson, MT 961
Matterson, Melissa, Dir. Foundation & Government Rels., Chicago Botanic Garden, Glencoe, IL...............................497
Matteson, Judith, Dir., U.S. Army Women's Museum, Fort Lee, VA 1711
Mattheusen, John, Immediate Past Chm., Battleship New Jersey Museum & Memorial, Camden, NJ 1033
Matthew, Kathryn, Dir. Devel., Historic Charleston Foundation, Charleston, SC.1505
Matthews, Henry, Dir., Grand Valley State University Art Gallery, Allendale, MI...821
Matthews Hoffmann, Catherine, Cur., Davidson County Historical Museum, Lexington, NC 1256
Matthews, Keri, Communications & Collections Mgr., Albemarle Charlottesville Historical Society, Charlottesville, VA 1704
Matthews, Louise, Dir., The Lion and Lamb Peace Arts Center, Bluffton, OH.1297
Matthews, Marsha, Dir. Artifact Collections & Exhibits, Oregon Historical Society, Portland, OR............1399
Matthews, Pat, Education, Plymouth Historical Society, Inc., Plymouth, PA ..1468
Matthews, Paula, Acting Dir. & Librarian, The Boston Athenaeum, Boston, MA 758
Matthews, Ronald, Pres. (V) & Treas., Volunteer Firemen's Mall and Museum of Kingston, Kingston, NY 1151
Matthews, Sarah, Educator, Museum of Natural History and Planetarium, Providence, RI 1495
Matthews, Tonya M., Ph.D., Vice Pres. Museums, Cincinnati Museum Center at Union Terminal, Cincinnati, OH........1304
Matthias, Diana, Cur. Education, Academic Programs, The Snite Museum of Art, University of Notre Dame, Notre Dame, IN 561
Matthiessen, Joy A., Dir., Des Plaines History Center, Des Plaines, IL 490
Mattia, Mark, Vice Pres. Mktg. & Communications, Liberty Science Center, Jersey City, NJ 1044
Mattice, Fia, Gallery Mgr., Volcano Art Center Gallery, Volcano, HI....................453
Mattice, Genevieve, Public Rels. & Museum Shop Mgr., Chico Creek Nature Center, Chico, CA......................100
Mattice, Matt, Exec. Dir., King Kamehameha V-Judiciary History Center, Honolulu, HI 446
Mattice, Shelby, Site Mgr., Bronck Museum, Coxsackie, NY.......................1126
Mattice, Steve, Vice Pres., Eastern Arizona Museum and Historical Society of Graham County Inc., Pima, AZ 52
Matticks, Rebecca, C.E.O. & Dir., Hastings Museum, Hastings, NE 985
Mattingley, Aida, Chm. (V), Bountiful/Davis Art Center, Bountiful, UT 1659
Mattioli, Bill, Park Supvr., Gillette Castle State Park, East Haddam, CT 271
Mattocks, Bob, Pres. (V), Tryon Palace Historic Sites & Gardens, New Bern, NC 1259
Mattox, Angela, Asst. Cur. Performing Arts, Yerba Buena Center for the Arts, San Francisco, CA.......................................194
Mattson, Andrea, Sec. & Treas., National Oregon/California Trail Center, Montpelier, ID 462
Mattson, Cheryl, Dir. Devel. & Membership, Mystic Seaport - The Museum of America and the Sea, Mystic, CT...284
Mattson, Jack, Site Supvr. & Museum Store Mgr., Fort Totten State Historic Site, Fort Totten, ND.................................1282
Mattson, John, Preparator, San Angelo Museum of Fine Arts, San Angelo, TX.1642
Mattson, Karen, Cur. Education, Placer County Museums, Auburn, CA..................89
Matus, Julie, Cur. Education, Tampa Bay History Center, Inc., Tampa, FL..............393
Matuscak, Melissa, Dir. & Cur., The DeVos Art Museum at Northern Michigan University, Marquette, MI 852
Matyniak, Margaret, Pres. & Museum Shop Mgr., Old Bohemia Historical Society, Warwick, MD 749
Matyseck, Christine, Education Coord., Portsmouth Museums, Portsmouth, VA.1734
Matz, Chris, Staff, Lesueur County Historical Museum-Chapter 1, Elysian, MN 876
Matz, Darrell, Asst. Dir. Management Svcs., Tacoma Public Library/Thomas Handforth Gallery, Tacoma, WA............1790
Matz, Tom, Treas., Yankee Air Force, Inc. (Yankee Air Museum), Ypsilanti, MI..867
Matzek Davis, Eileen, C.E.O. & Pres. (V), Osage County Historical Society Research Center, Lyndon, KS 624
Mauch, Jamie, Museum Shop Mgr., Culbertson Mansion State Historic Site, New Albany, IN 559
Mauch, Timothy, Chief Ranger, Richmond National Battlefield Park, Richmond, VA 1740
Maue, Bonnie, Pres. (V), Rockford Area Historical Society, Rockford, MN 891

M–*Continued*

McBride, Heather, Mktg. & Communications Div., Texas Historical Commission, Austin, TX.......1583
McBride, Jeff, Cur, Hyrum City Museum, Hyrum, UT..1663
McBride, Joe, Jr., C.E.O. (V), National Hall of Fame for Famous American Indians, Anadarko, OK..........................1355
McBride, John, C.F.O., Nasher Sculpture Center, Dallas, TX................................1600
McBride, Dr. Michael, Veterinarian, Roger Williams Park Zoo, Providence, RI..1497
McBride, Michael A., Cur., Henry Whitfield State Historical Museum, Guilford, CT 276
McBride, Pennie, Asst. Collections Mgr., Palace of the Governors/New Mexico History Museum, Santa Fe, NM...........1090
McBride, Dr. Susan, Pres. College, Thomas E. McMillan Museum, Brewton, AL 7
McBride, Virginia, Museum Shop Mgr., Kitsap County Historical Society Museum, Bremerton, WA......................1760
McBrien, Kate, Cur. Historical Collections, Maine State Museum, Augusta, ME...690
McCabe, Chris, Dir. Facilities, Desert Botanical Garden, Phoenix, AZ 50
McCabe, Donna, Treas., Schoharie Colonial Heritage Association, Schoharie, NY 1210
McCabe, Edward P., Dir. Maritime Program, Hull Lifesaving Museum Inc., the Museum of Boston Harbor Heritage, Hull, MA.................................783
McCabe, Jennifer, Dir., Museum of Craft and Folk Art, San Francisco, CA............190
McCabe, John R., Registrar, Springfield Armory National Historic Site, Springfield, MA.......................................807
McCabe, Prudence, Exec. Asst., Kitsap County Historical Society Museum, Bremerton, WA...1760
McCabe, Scott, Dir., Dr. William Robinson Plantation & Museum, Clark, NJ..1035
McCabe, Stephen, Dir. Education, Arboretum at UC Santa Cruz, Santa Cruz, CA...205
McCabe Thompson, Elsie, Pres., The Museum for African Art, Long Island City, NY...1154
McCabe, Tom, Museum Shop Mgr., Johnson County Museum, Shawnee, KS 634
McCafferty, Janet, Museum Shop Mgr., The Georgian Museum, Lancaster, OH.1327
McCafferty, Janet, Museum Shop Mgr., Sherman House Museum, Lancaster, OH..1327
McCafferty, Michael, Dir. Exhibition Design & Museum Svcs., Seattle Art Museum, Seattle, WA..............................1783
McCain, Christy, Cur. Vvertebrate Zoology & Asst. Prof. Biology, University of Colorado Museum of Natural History, Boulder, CO 230
McCain, Tom, Mgr. Information, Phippen Museum, Prescott, AZ...................................52
McCain, Wanda, Sec., Immaculate Conception Catholic Church, Natchitoches, LA 677
McCall, Janet L., Exec. Dir., Society for Contemporary Craft, Pittsburgh, PA 1468
McCall, Kris, Dir. Planetarium, Adventure Science Center, Nashville, TN 1566
McCall, Laura, Museum Shop Mgr., Lizzadro Museum of Lapidary Art, Elmhurst, IL...493
McCallie, Ellen, Deputy Dir., Carnegie Museum of Natural History, Pittsburgh, PA...1464
McCallister, Angella, Receptionist, Confederated Tribes of Grand Ronde Cultural Resources Department, Grand Ronde, OR 1390
McCallister Clark, Ellen, Dir. Library, The Society of the Cincinnati at Anderson House, Washington, DC 330
McCallister, Colleen, Visitor Svcs. Coord., Kansas Underground Salt Museum, Hutchinson, KS 618
McCallister, Doug, Museum Shop Mgr., University of California Berkeley Art Museum and Pacific Film Archive, Berkeley, CA 94
McCallum, Cheryl, Dir. Education, The Children's Museum of Houston, Houston, TX 1619
McCallum, Sue, C.E.O. & Museum Shop Mgr., Clausen Memorial Museum, Petersburg, AK...34
McCalment, Tina, Dir., Berea College, Doris Ulmann Galleries, Berea, KY........641
McCammon, Robert, C.E.O. & Pres., Historical Museum of Southern Florida, Miami, FL...................................365
McCandless, Leonard, Dir., Ozark Military Museum, Fayetteville, AR 71
McCanless, George, Bd. Vice Chm., Tubman African-American Museum, Macon, GA 426
McCann, Linda, Museum Shop Mgr., Shell Rock Community Historical Museum, Shell Rock, IA.........................599
McCann, Mac, Head of Kiwanis Committee, Kiwanis Van Slyke Museum Foundation Inc., Caldwell, ID 457
McCann, Pat, Supvr. Everglades Exhibits, Zooamerica North American Wildlife Park, Hershey, PA.................................1434
McCarden, Kimberly, Publicist, El Paso Museum of Art, El Paso, TX 1604
McCargo, Jamie, Exhibit Designer, Museum of the Albemarle, Elizabeth City, NC 1244
McCarney, David, Treas., Allison-Antrim Museum, Inc., Greencastle, PA.............1429
McCarroll, Glenda, Business Mgr., Southern Museum of Flight, Birmingham, AL...6
McCarry, Jane, Education Coord., Laughing Brook Education Center & Wildlife Sanctuary, Hampden, MA..........781
McCarter, John W., Jr., C.E.O. & Pres., Field Museum of Natural History, Chicago, IL 480
McCarthy, Angela, Museum Asst., Frisco Historic Park & Museum, Frisco, CO 247
McCarthy, Christine, C.E.O., Provincetown Art Association and Museum, Provincetown, MA 801
McCarthy, Cliff, Archivist, The Stone House Museum, Belchertown, MA 756
McCarthy, Dave, Exec. Dir., Ted Williams Museum and Hitters Hall of Fame, Saint Petersburg, FL....................385
McCarthy, Erin, Security & Museum Shop Mgr., Merrill Historical Society, Merrill, WI..1832
McCarthy, John, Deputy Dir. NM History Museum, Museum of New Mexico, Santa Fe, NM...1089
McCarthy, John J., Deputy Dir., Palace of the Governors/New Mexico History Museum, Santa Fe, NM 1090
McCarthy, Margaret, Treas., Franklin County Historical & Museum Society, Malone, NY 1156
McCarthy, Mary, Public Rels., Greenville County Museum of Art, Greenville, SC..1514
McCarthy, Tom, Video Production, Museum of New Mexico, Santa Fe, NM 1089
McCarthy, Wayne, Co-Pres., Waltham Historical Society, Waltham, MA 813
McCarthy, Wayne T., Communications, Waltham Historical Society, Waltham, MA 813
McCartney, Allison, Public Rels., The Newark Museum, Newark, NJ..............1053
McCartney, Jack, Retail Mgr., Preservation Virginia, Historic Jamestowne, Jamestown, VA 1718
McCartney, Kelly, Cur., The Historical Society of Frederick County, Inc., Frederick, MD 735
McCartney, Dr. Kevin, Dir., The Northern Maine Museum of Science, University of Maine, Presque Isle, ME..................709
McCartney, Dr. Nancy G., Cur. Zoology, The University Museum Collections, Fayetteville, AR..71
McCarty, Cara, Cur. Dir., Cooper-Hewitt, National Design Museum, Smithsonian Institution, New York, NY...1167
McCarty, Kimberly, Cur., Pennsbury Manor, Morrisville, PA...........................1446
McCarty, R. Paul, C.E.O. & Historian, Old Fort House Museum, Fort Edward, NY 1134
McCarty, Ronnie, Horticulturist, Memphis Botanic Garden, Goldsmith Civic Garden Center, Memphis, TN......1563
McCarty, Steve, Interpretive Ranger, Etowah Indian Mounds Historical Site, Cartersville, GA..413
McCary, Wayne, C.E.O., Storrowton Village Museum, West Springfield, MA 815
McCashey, Bob, Devel., American Museum of Straw Art, Long Beach, CA 130
McCaskill, Horace, Chm. (V), Civil War Life - The Soldier's Museum, Fredericksburg, VA.....................................1712
McCauley, Anne, Prof, Albion College Department of Art and Art History, Albion, MI 820
McCauley, Anne H., Exec. Dir., Longyear Museum, Chestnut Hill, MA...................770
McCauley, Frank, Asst. Dir. & Cur., Sumter County Gallery of Art, Sumter, SC..1524
McCauley, Gerri, Treas., Tappantown Historical Society, Tappan, NY.............1220
McCauley, Lt. John F., Cur., Ancient and Honorable Artillery Company of Massachusetts, Boston, MA 757
McCauley Lee, Eric, Dir., Kimbell Art Museum, Fort Worth, TX.......................1610
McCausland, Beth, Pres. (V), Graeme Park, Horsham, PA 1434
McCausland, Gwen, Cur. Collections, The Hubbard Museum of the American West, Ruidoso Downs, NM ..1087
McCausland, Peter, Chm. (V), Independence Seaport Museum, Philadelphia, PA 1455
McCaw, Sharlene, Museum Shop Mgr., Luther Burbank Home & Gardens, Santa Rosa, CA 208
McCawley, Paul, Pres. (V), Fort Lauderdale Historical Society, Fort Lauderdale, FL...347
McCay, Patrick, Academic Dean, New Hampshire Institute of Art, Manchester, NH.....................................1023
McClaflin, Karen, Dir., California Automobile Museum, Sacramento, CA...174
McClain, Daniel, Cur., Junior Center of Art and Science, Oakland, CA................155

M–*Continued*

McClain, Heather, Museum Shop Mgr., Kingwood Center, Mansfield, OH 1329
McClain, Jenny, Naturalist-Brecksville, Cleveland Metroparks Outdoor Education Division, Garfield Heights, OH........1322
McClain, Ron, Pres., Conklin Reed Organ & History Museum, Hanover, MI........844
McClamroch, Susan, Dir., Pitot House Museum, New Orleans, LA 683
McClanahan, Russell, Archivist, Rome Area History Museum, Rome, GA 430
McClancy, Carl, Pres. (V), Pioneer Settlement for the Creative Arts, Barberville, FL........334
McClatchey, Glenda, Museum Admin., Art Museum of Greater Lafayette, Lafayette, IN 552
McClatchy, J.D., Pres., American Academy of Arts and Letters, New York, NY 1162
McClave, Kate, Cur. Animal Hospital, New York Aquarium, Brooklyn, NY 1112
McCleaf, Angela, Cur., Battleship Texas State Historic Site, La Porte, TX........1627
McCleary, Pattie, Museum Shop Mgr., Noah Webster House/West Hartford Historical Society, West Hartford, CT 300
McClellan, Betty, Pres., Eustis Historical Museum & Preservation Society, Inc., Eustis, FL........346
McClellan, Faith, Registrar, Grounds For Sculpture, Hamilton, NJ 1041
McClellan, Hillary, Museum Shop Mgr., Utah's Hogle Zoo, Salt Lake City, UT..1672
McClellan, Zelda, Devel. & Membership, McLean-Alanreed Area Museum, McLean, TX........1632
McClelland, Judy, Coord. Education, Museum of South Texas History, Edinburg, TX 1603
McClelland, Kelley, Mgr. Guest Svcs. & Coord. Volunteers, The Children's Museum of Cleveland, Cleveland, OH..1307
McClelland, Mary, Gallery Mgr., South Shore Arts, Munster, IN 558
McClenahan, Heather, Website Admin., Los Alamos Historical Museum, Los Alamos, NM 1082
McClenney-Brooker, Cheryl, Dir. External Affairs, Philadelphia Museum of Art, Philadelphia, PA 1459
McClenny, Bart, Dir., Museum of the Western Prairie, Altus, OK........1354
McCloskey, Anne M., Exec. Dir., Heisey Museum, Clinton County Historical Society, Lock Haven, PA 1442
McCloskey, Karen, Bd. Pres. (V), Tucson Botanical Gardens, Tucson, AZ 62
McCloskey, Martha, Bookkeeper, San Angelo Museum of Fine Arts, San Angelo, TX 1642
McCloskey, Peg, Registrar, Piper Aviation Museum Foundation, Lock Haven, PA..1442
McCloud, Alex, Cur., Shaw Island Library & Historical Society, Shaw Island, WA 1785
McClow, Keith R., Supvr., Kline Creek Farm, West Chicago, IL 527
McClung, Elizabeth, Exec. Dir., Belle Grove Plantation, Middletown, VA........1725
McClung, Franceen, Admin. Sec., Los Angeles Maritime Museum, San Pedro, CA 200
McClure, Donna, Pres. (V), Monticello Railway Museum, Monticello, IL........506
McClure, Ian, Chief Conservator, Yale University Art Gallery, New Haven, CT 287
McClure, Judy, Museum Shop Mgr., Mississippi Agriculture & Forestry/National Agricultural Aviation Museum, Jackson, MS 910
McClure, Kent, Supt. Locomotives, Monticello Railway Museum, Monticello, IL........506
McClure, Maggie, Dir., Lake George Historical Association Museum, Lake George, NY........1152
McClure, Mike, Gen. Cur., The Maryland Zoo in Baltimore, Baltimore, MD 724
McClure, Robert, Dir. Wild Animal Park, San Diego Zoo's Wild Animal Park, Escondido, CA........112
McClure, Rod, Dir., Western Pacific Railroad Museum, Portola, CA........167
McCluskey, Holly, Cur. Glass, The Museums of Oglebay Institute - Mansion Museum & Glass Museum, Wheeling, WV 1808
McClusky, Pamela, Cur. Art of Africa & Oceania, Seattle Art Museum, Seattle, WA........1783
McCoig Cupit, Kim, Cur. Collections, Courthouse-on-the-Square Museum, Denton, TX 1601
McColl, Marvin, Sec., Bannock County Historical Museum, Pocatello, ID........464
McColley, Selena, Cur. Education, The United States Army Quartermaster Museum, Fort Lee, VA........1711
McCollister, Traci, Dir. Devel., Randall Museum, San Francisco, CA 191
McCollough, Pam, Pres., Casa Amesti, Monterey, CA 148
McCollum, Jay, C.E.O., Chm. & Pres., Heart of West Texas Museum, Colorado City, TX........1594
McCollum, Randy, C.E.O. & Pres. Historical Society, Old Court House Museum-Eva Whitaker Davis Memorial, Vicksburg, MS 918
McCollum, Suzanne, Museum Shop Mgr., Alaska Indian Arts, Inc., Haines, AK........31
McColman, Richard, Dir. Star Theater, Morehead Planetarium and Science Center, Chapel Hill, NC 1237
McComb, Joseph H. "Choppo", Past Pres. & Historian, Moriarty Historical Society & Museum, Moriarty, NM........1083
McCombie, LaVonne, Sec., The Octagon House, Hudson, WI 1823
McConaghy, Dr. Lorraine, Historian, Museum of History & Industry (MOHAI), Seattle, WA........1782
McConal, Leslie, Dir., Treas. & Museum Shop Mgr., Seagraves-Loop Museum and Art Center Inc., Seagraves, TX........1647
McConathy, Steve, Security, The Menil Collection, Houston, TX 1621
McConnachie, Peter, Sec., Indiana Transportation Museum, Noblesville, IN 561
McConnell, Ed, Treas., Wilbur Wright Birthplace & Interpretive Center, Hagerstown, IN........545
McConnell, Jo, Coord. Events & Tours, Pendleton District Agricultural Museum, Pendleton, SC 1521
McConnell, Jo, Events & Tours Coord., Pendleton District Historical, Recreational and Tourism Commission, Pendleton, SC........1521
McConnell, John, Vice Pres., Griffin Museum of Photography, Winchester, MA........818
McConnell, Michelle, Artist & Illustrator, North Carolina Maritime Museum, Beaufort, NC........1234
McConnell, Pamela Violante, Registrar, United States Capitol, Washington, DC........331
McConnell, Rich, Dir., Territorial Capital-Lane Museum, Lecompton, KS 622
McConnell, Sue, Museum Shop Mgr., Little White Schoolhouse, Ripon, WI....1843
McConville, Shayna V., Interim Dir., Temple Gallery, Tyler School of Art of Temple University, Philadelphia, PA 1462
McCool, Marilyn, Museum Shop Mgr., Buffalo Bill Cody Homestead, Princeton, IA........598
McCord, Deborah, Pres., Lee County Historical Society, Loachapoka, AL 16
McCord, Lisa R., Asst. Dir. Art, New Orleans Museum of Art, New Orleans, LA 683
McCord, Dr. Robert, Cur. Natural History, Arizona Museum of Natural History, Mesa, AZ 46
McCorkle, Kathryn W., Exec. Dir., The Historical Society of Dauphin County, Harrisburg, PA 1430
McCormack, Daniel, Archivist, Burlington Historical Museum, Burlington, MA 766
McCormack, Larry, Exec. Dir., Pro Rodeo Hall of Fame & Museum of the American Cowboy, Colorado Springs, CO 235
McCormack, Lynne, Museum Store Mgr., Palmer Museum of Art, The Pennsylvania State University, University Park, PA........1478
McCormally, Erin, Mgr. Adult Audiences, Hillwood Estate, Museum & Gardens, Washington, DC........318
McCormick, Amy, Foundation & Corp. Rels. Mgr., The Appalachian Trail Conservancy, Harpers Ferry, WV 1799
McCormick, Daniel Y., Mgr. Operations & Finance, George Eastman House/International Museum of Photography and Film, Rochester, NY..1201
McCormick, Elizabeth, Dir., The Institute For American Indian Studies (IAIS), Washington, CT 299
McCormick, Ken, Chm. Bd. Overseers, Huntington Library, Art Collections, and Botanical Gardens, San Marino, CA........198
McCormick, Lynn, Chm. (V), Archivist, Education & Museum Shop Mgr., Out of This World Museum, Las Vegas, NV........1007
McCormick, Maureen, Chief Registrar, Princeton University Art Museum, Princeton, NJ 1058
McCormick, Mike, Dir. Reference Svcs., Maryland State Archives, Annapolis, MD........718
McCormick, Todd, Dir. & Cur., Logan County Historical Society Museum, Bellefontaine, OH........1296
McCorriston, John, Pres., Shippensburg Historical Society Museum, Shippensburg, PA........1474
McCosker, Dr. John, Chm. Aquatic Biology, California Academy of Sciences, San Francisco, CA 187
McCourt, Bonnie, Coord. Publicity, Garibaldi-Meucci Museum, Staten Island, NY........1215
McCourt, Frank A., II, Owner, Dinosaur Gardens, LLC, Ossineke, MI........859
McCourt, Helen, Museum Shop Mgr., Tulare Historical Museum, Tulare, CA ...219
McCowan, Kurt, Cur. & Museum Shop Mgr., Central Texas Museum of Automotive History, Rosanky, TX........1641
McCown, Robert, Business Mgr., The Victorian Society in America, Philadelphia, PA 1463

McCoy, Rev. Msgr. James P., Exec. Dir., American Catholic Historical Society, Philadelphia, PA 1449
McCoy, Joann, Museum Asst., Longmont Museum, Longmont, CO....................257
McCoy, John, Industrial Exhibits Specialist, Hagley Museum and Library, Wilmington, DE....................313
McCoy, John, Admin. & Collections, McMullen Museum of Art, Boston College, Chestnut Hill, MA 770
McCoy, Josh, Dir. Devel., Florida Museum of Natural History, Gainesville, FL 351
McCoy, Mary, Treas., Tomball Community Museum Center, Tomball, TX 1651
McCoy, Nancy, Education, John F. Kennedy Presidential Library & Museum, Boston, MA 760
McCoy, Riley, Vice Pres., Beatty Museum and Historical Society, Beatty, NV 1000
McCoy, Sandy, Museum Shop Mgr., Boca Raton Historical Society, Boca Raton, FL....................335
McCoy, Steven A., Supt., Fort Donelson National Battlefield, Dover, TN....................1551
McCoy, Suzy, Treas., Beatty Museum and Historical Society, Beatty, NV....................1000
McCracken, Sally, Human Resources Mgr., Modern Art Museum of Fort Worth, Fort Worth, TX 1611
McCrary, Stuart I., Dir., Glenrock Paleontological Museum, Glenrock, WY....................1859
McCray, Harry, Chm. Bd. Trustees, The Nelson-Atkins Museum of Art, Kansas City, MO 934
McCray, Kim, Dir. Interpretation, Nantucket Historical Association, Nantucket, MA 792
McCrea, Bill, Assoc. Dir., North Carolina Museum of History, Raleigh, NC....................1263
McCrea, Margaret, Acting Cur., Thomaston Historical Society, Thomaston, ME 713
McCreary, Bradley D., Exec. Dir., SoDus Bay Historical Society, Sodus Point, NY....................1212
McCreary, Kathleen, Bookkeeper, Children's Museum at Holyoke, Inc., Holyoke, MA....................782
McCree, Timothy, Park Supt., Morrow Mountain State Park, Albemarle, NC....1230
McCreedy, Michael, Exec. Dir., Scott & Zelda Fitzgerald Museum, Montgomery, AL 20
McCreery, Cindy, Chm. (V), Creative Arts Guild, Dalton, GA....................415
McCretz, George, Pres. (V), Catawba Science Center, Hickory, NC 1251
McCrickard, Nancy, Exec. Dir., Science Museum of Western Virginia, Roanoke, VA....................1744
McCrimmon, Ed, Maintenance Mechanic, Weymouth Woods-Sandhills Nature Preserve Museum, Southern Pines, NC.1268
McCrossin, Dr. Monte, Dir., University Museum, New Mexico State University, Las Cruces, NM....................1081
McCudden, Anne, Museum Dir., Ah-Tah-Thi-Ki Museum at Okalee, Hollywood, FL....................353
McCue, Donald, Cur. & Archivist, Lincoln Memorial Shrine, Redlands, CA 170
McCuistion, Mary Ann, Exec. Dir., Red River Valley Museum, Vernon, TX 1652
McCullagh, Suzanne, Cur. Prints & Drawings, The Art Institute of Chicago, Chicago, IL 476
McCullah, Carole, Museum Shop Mgr., Ashtabula Historic House, Pendleton, SC....................1521
McCullan, Carole, Museum Shop Mgr., Woodburn Historic House, Pendleton, SC....................1521
McCullar, Sharon, Registrar, Lakeshore Museum Center, Muskegon, MI 857
McCullers, Cyndi, Museum Shop Mgr., Sweetwater County Historical Museum, Green River, WY 1859
McCulley, Sharla, Museum Shop Mgr., Houston Zoo, Inc., Houston, TX 1621
McCulley, Mayor Tom, Fort Jones Museum, Fort Jones, CA....................114
McCullick, Nancy, Pres. (V), The Boorman House - The Juneau County Historical Society, Mauston, WI....................1831
McCullough, Gavin, Collections Specialist, Arizona Museum of Natural History, Mesa, AZ 46
McCullough, Gloria, Librarian, Wayne County Historical Society, Honesdale, PA....................1434
McCullough, Hollis K., Cur. Fine Arts & Exhibitions, Telfair Museum of Art, Savannah, GA....................435
McCullough, Janice, Sec., Humboldt Historical Museum, Humboldt, KS 617
McCullough, Kathryn, Dir., Manitoga/The Russel Wright Design Center, Garrison, NY....................1136
McCullough, Rayo, Collection Mgr. NHNM, Museum of Southwestern Biology, Albuquerque, NM....................1072
McCully, Kathleen J., C.E.O. & Dir., Isanti County Historical Society, Cambridge, MN....................871
McCumsey, Greg, Cur. Primates & Carnivores, Baton Rouge Zoo, Baton Rouge, LA 666
McCune, Fred, Vice Pres., Beaufort Historic Site, Beaufort, NC....................1234
McCune, Stephanie, Dir. Public Programs, Copshaholm House Museum & Historic Oliver Gardens, South Bend, IN....................565
McCune, Stephanie, Dir. Public Programs, Northern Indiana Center for History, South Bend, IN....................565
McCurdy, Cindy, Assoc. Vice Pres. Operations, The National World War II Museum, New Orleans, LA 682
McCurdy, David, Exec. Dir., Rose Island Lighthouse, Rose Island, RI....................1497
McCurtis, Barbara S., Dir., Command Museum, Marine Corps Recruit Depot, San Diego, San Diego, CA 179
McCusker, Carol, Cur. Photography, Museum of Photographic Arts, San Diego, CA....................181
McCusker, J. Stephen, Exec. Dir., San Antonio Zoological Society, San Antonio, TX....................1645
McCutchen, Brian, Supt., Knife River Indian Villages National Historic Site, Stanton, ND 1290
McDade, John, Museum Cur., Islesford Historical Museum, Islesford, ME....................700
McDade, John, Museum Cur., Sieur de Monts Springs Nature Center, Bar Harbor, ME 692
McDade, John, Museum Cur., William Otis Sawtelle Collections and Research Center, Bar Harbor, ME 693
McDade, Lucinda, Dir. Research, Rancho Santa Ana Botanic Garden, Claremont, CA....................102
McDaniel, Allen, Cur., Tupelo Automobile Museum, Tupelo, MS 917
McDaniel, Anita, Collections, Taos Historic Museums, Taos, NM 1094
McDaniel, George W., Exec. Dir., Drayton Hall, Charleston, SC 1504
McDaniel, Laurie, Treas., Korner's Folly, Kernersville, NC....................1254
McDaniel, Lesley, Site Admin., Bollinger Mill State Historic Site, Burfordville, MO 922
McDaniel, Lisa, Sec., Bloomington Art Center, Bloomington, MN....................870
McDaniel, Noel, Dir. Mktg., Rosenbruch Wildlife Museum, Saint George, UT.....1669
McDaniel, Pat, Dir., Nita Stewart Haley Memorial Library & J. Evetts Haley History Center, Midland, TX 1633
McDaniel, Patrick, Exec. Dir., Macon County History Museum, Decatur, IL 490
McDaniel, Reginald, Dir., S.C. Tobacco Museum, Mullins, SC....................1519
McDaniel, Robert, Dir. & Museum Shop Mgr., Animas Museum, Durango, CO.....242
McDaniel, Shawn, Dir. Devel., The Robert J. Dole Institute of Politics, Lawrence, KS 621
McDaniel, Sue Lynn, Special Collections, The Kentucky Library & Museum, Bowling Green, KY....................642
McDaniel Williams, Amy, Pres. (V), Maymont, Richmond, VA 1739
McDaniels, Chief Warren E., C.E.O., New Orleans Fire Dept. Museum & Educational Center, New Orleans, LA 682
McDavid, Joseph, Pres., Florissant Valley Historical Society, Florissant, MO....................926
McDavis, Wendy, Cur. FASNY Museum of Fire Fighting, Hudson, NY 1143
McDearmon, Nancy, Registrarial Asst., Sweet Briar College Art Collection and Galleries, Sweet Briar, VA 1749
McDermott, Dona, Cur., Valley Forge National Historical Park, King of Prussia, PA....................1437
McDermott, Georgia, Museum Store Mgr. & Visitor Svcs. Mgr., Santa Barbara Museum of Art, Santa Barbara, CA 203
McDermott, Hugh, Gardener, Randall Museum, San Francisco, CA 191
McDermott, Jameson, Educator, Cape Fear Museum of History and Science, Wilmington, NC 1271
McDermott, Kathleen, Pres., The Museums of Oglebay Institute - Mansion Museum & Glass Museum, Wheeling, WV 1808
McDermott, Marise, Pres., Witte Museum, San Antonio, TX 1646
McDermott, Maura, Public Rels., Overstreet-Kerr Historical Farm, Keota, OK....................1365
McDermott, Wayne, Exhibit Design, National Mississippi River Museum & Aquarium, Dubuque, IA....................585
McDermott-Lewis, Melora, Dir. Education, Denver Art Museum, Denver, CO 238
McDevitt, Jim, Pres. Bd. Trustees (V), Hunterdon Museum of Art, Clinton, NJ 1036
McDevitt, John, Vice Pres. Operations, Please Touch Museum, Philadelphia, PA....................1460
McDonagh, John, C.E.O. & Exec. Dir., Plimoth Plantation Inc., Plymouth, MA 800
McDonald, A J, Dir., St. Albans Historical Museum, Saint Albans, VT...1689
McDonald, Amy, Public Rels. & Mktg. Mgr., Yale Center for British Art, New Haven, CT....................287
McDonald, David, M.Ed., Dir. Education, McAuliffe-Shepard Discovery Center, Concord, NH....................1015

M–*Continued*

M–Continued

McIntosh, Nancy, Business Mgr., Midway Village Museum, Rockford, IL....517
McIntosh, Patricia, Pres., La Puente Valley Historical Society, Inc., La Puente, CA....127
McIntosh, Roderick, Cur. Anthropology, Peabody Museum of Natural History, New Haven, CT....286
McIntyre, Ida C., Business Mgr., Chester County Historical Society, West Chester, PA....1481
McIntyre, Joyce, Chm. (V), Clawson Historical Museum, Clawson, MI....830
McIntyre, Lloyd E., II, Pres. (V) & Registrar, Museum of Radio & Technology, Inc., Huntington, WV....1801
McIntyre, Nancy, Dir. Devel., Woodrow Wilson Presidential Library, Staunton, VA....1746
McIntyre, Patrick, Exec. Dir., Tennessee Historical Commission, Nashville, TN..1569
McIntyre, Randy L., Vice Pres., General Jacob Brown Historical Society, Brownville, NY....1114
McIvor, Ross, Bd. Pres., Eastside Heritage Center, Bellevue, WA....1758
McKain, David L., Dir., Oil & Gas Museum, Parkersburg, WV....1804
McKain, Martha, Museum Site Dir., Liberty Hall Historic Center, Lamoni, IA....591
McKale, William, C.E.O., U.S. Cavalry Museum, Fort Riley, KS....612
McKamey, Sheldon, Dean & Dir., Museum of the Rockies, Bozeman, MT....958
McKay, Gayle, Business Mgr., Kentucky Gateway Museum Center, Maysville, KY....658
McKay, Greg, Museum Shop Mgr., Denver Art Museum, Denver, CO....238
McKay, James A., Chief Interpretation, Martin Van Buren National Historic Site, Kinderhook, NY....1150
McKay, Jodi, Chm., Huntington Beach International Surfing Museum, Huntington Beach, CA....123
McKay, Kathy, Chief Ranger, Cowpens National Battlefield, Gaffney, SC....1513
McKay, Maria, Owner, Cur. & Museum Shop Mgr., Museum of Woodcarving, Shell Lake, WI....1845
McKay, Michael, Controller, National Academy Museum and School of Fine Arts, New York, NY....1176
McKay, Patrick J., Supvr. Interpretive Services, Rochester Hills Museum at Van Hoosen Farm, Rochester Hills, MI....862
McKay, Sally, Pres., Lowell's Boat Shop, Amesbury, MA....751
McKay, Sally, Library Mgr., Pacific Asia Museum, Pasadena, CA....162
McKechnie, Michael, Exec. Dir., San Francisco Botanical Garden at Strybing Arboretum, San Francisco, CA....192
McKee, Alexis, Mgr. AV Svcs., San Diego Natural History Museum, San Diego, CA....184
McKee, Becky, Pres. NPM Foundation, Neville Public Museum of Brown County, Green Bay, WI....1821
McKee, Bonnie, Gallery Mgr., Honeywell Center, Wabash, IN....570
McKee, Christopher, Asst. Cur., New Mexico Bureau of Geology Mineral Museum, Socorro, NM....1093
McKee, Dorothy, Cur., McLean-Alanreed Area Museum, McLean, TX....1632
McKee, E. Marie, Pres. (V), The Corning Museum of Glass, Corning, NY....1124
McKee, Jan, Cur. & Registrar, Springfield Museum, Springfield, OR....1404
McKee, Kristi, Mktg., Neuberger Museum of Art, Purchase College, State University of New York, Purchase, NY....1198
McKee, Leona, Cur. Ho Chunk Artifacts, Jackson County Historical Society, Black River Falls, WI....1813
McKee, Linda, Head Librarian, John and Mable Ringling Museum of Art, Sarasota, FL....387
McKee, Margaret, Exec. Dir., Shenandoah Valley Discovery Museum, Winchester, VA....1755
McKee, Nancy, C.F.O., Miami Science Museum, Miami, FL....366
McKeel, Randy, Dir. Public Rels. & Mktg., The Children's Museum of Memphis, Memphis, TN....1561
McKeel, Rick, Dir. Mktg. & Public Affairs, Virginia Aviation Museum, Richmond International Airport, VA....1743
McKeen, Erin, Registrar, United States Department of the Interior Museum, Washington, DC....331
McKeever, Christine, Dir., 6th Cavalry Museum, Fort Oglethorpe, GA....419
McKeigney, Norton, Exhibits Supvr., Mississippi Museum of Natural Science, Jackson, MS....910
McKeil, Richard, Vice Pres., Moosehead Marine Museum, Greenville, ME....699
McKeithen, Peggy, Museum Shop Mgr., Fort Morgan Museum, Gulf Shores, AL....13
McKellar, Susan, Admin. Mgr., The Charleston Museum, Charleston, SC....1503
McKelvain, Burrell, Chm. Bd., Swenson Memorial Museum of Stephens County, Breckenridge, TX....1589
McKelvey, Don, Treas., Ohio Railway Museum, Worthington, OH....1352
McKelvey, Marcia, Exec. Asst., Vesterheim Norwegian-American Museum, Decorah, IA....582
McKelvey, Max, Education, Oatland Island Wildlife Center, Savannah, GA....434
McKelvy, Dr. Marianne, Pres., Chippewa Nature Center, Midland, MI....854
McKemey, Sarah, Mktg. & Public Rels. Mgr., Mann Wildlife Learning Museum, Montgomery, AL....20
McKendrick, Mark, Dir., Benson Grist Mill, Stansbury Park, UT....1674
McKenna, James, Site Dir., Old Bethpage Village Restoration, Old Bethpage, NY....1188
McKenna, Jim, Old Bethpage Village Restoration Supvr., Nassau County, Division of Museum Services, Department of Recreation, Parks & Museums, East Meadow, NY....1130
McKenna, Marylynn, Pres. (V), Copper Village Museum & Arts Center of Deer Lodge County, Anaconda, MT....955
McKenna, Tom, Pres. (V), Lisbon Historical Society, Lisbon, OH....1328
McKenna, Yuri, Asst. Mgr. Retail Operations, New York Transit Museum, Brooklyn Heights, NY....1113
McKenney, Kimberly, Mgr. Research & Assessment, Children's Museum of Tacoma, Tacoma, WA....1788
McKenny, Cathy, Dir., George Washington's Headquarters, Cumberland, MD....733
McKenrick, Fremont, C.E.O. & Pres. (V), Cambria County Historical Society, Ebensburg, PA....1422
McKenzie, Catherine, Publications Mng. & Editor, Louisiana Art & Science Museum - Irene W. Pennington Planetarium, Baton Rouge, LA....667
McKenzie, Debbie, Devel. & Membership Mgr., Children's Discovery Museum of San Jose, San Jose, CA....195
Mckenzie, Michelle, Museum Store Mgr., Crocker Art Museum, Sacramento, CA...175
McKenzie, Molly, Site Supt., Cahokia Courthouse State Historic Site, Cahokia, IL....473
McKenzie, Raymond, Museum Shop Mgr., San Francisco Museum of Craft+Design, San Francisco, CA....193
McKenzie, Sharon, Dir., Boca Grand Lighthouse Museum and Visitor's Center, Boca Grande, FL....334
McKenzie, Stephen J., Mgr. Arts Workshop, The Newark Museum, Newark, NJ....1053
McKeown, Kim, Vice Pres., Historic General Dodge House, Council Bluffs, IA....580
McKeown, Mary, Coord. Group Tours EAA AirVenture Museum, Oshkosh, WI....1839
McKernan, Pat, Cur., Botanica, The Wichita Gardens, Wichita, KS....637
McKernan, Robert, Dir., Agua Mansa Pioneer Memorial Cemetery, Colton, CA....104
McKernan, Robert, Dir., Asistencia: San Gabriel Mission Outpost, Redlands, CA....169
McKernan, Robert, Dir., John Rains House, Rancho Cucamonga, CA....168
McKernan, Robert, Dir., Yorba and Slaughter Families Adobe, Chino, CA....101
McKernan, Robert, Dir., Yucaipa Adobe, Yucaipa, CA....227
McKernan, Robert L., Dir., San Bernardino County Museum, Redlands, CA....170
McKerrow, Toni B., Chm. (V), Maria Mitchell Association Natural History Museum, Nantucket, MA....792
McKerrow, Toni B., Pres. (V), Nantucket Maria Mitchell Association, Nantucket, MA....792
McKiernan, Hank, Facility Mgr., Mint Museum of Art, Charlotte, NC....1239
McKiernan, Hank, Facility Mgr., Mint Museum of Craft + Design, Charlotte, NC....1239
McKim, Matt, Gen. Cur., Micke Grove Zoo, Lodi, CA....129
McKinley Forbes, Marla, Museum Shop Mgr., Liberty Village Arts Center & Gallery, Chester, MT....959
McKinley, Mrs. John P., Pres. Midland County Hist. Society, Z. Taylor Brown-Sarah Dorsey House, Midland, TX....1634
McKinley, Kimberly, Education Coord., South Shore Arts, Munster, IN....558
McKinley, Mary, Dir., Ogden Nature Center, Ogden, UT....1665
McKinley, Mrs. Nancy R., Pres. Midland County Historical Society (V), Midland County Historical Museum, Midland, TX....1633
McKinney, David, Pres., The Metropolitan Museum of Art, New York, NY....1172
McKinney, Dr. David, C.E.O., United States Department of the Interior Museum, Washington, DC....331
McKinney, Heyward, C.O.O., North Carolina Museum of History, Raleigh, NC....1263

McKinney, Jack N., Dir., Dr Pepper Museum and Free Enterprise Institute, Waco, TX....1654
McKinney, Ruth, Pres. (V), Mem-Erie Historical Museum, Erie, KS....611
McKinney, Shirley, Supt., Castle Clinton National Monument, New York, NY....1165
Mckinney, Shirley, Supt., General Grant National Memorial, New York, NY....1168
McKinnon, Don, Supt., Potawatomi State Park, Sturgeon Bay, WI....1847
McKinnon, E. Luanne, Dir., University Art Museum, The University of New Mexico, Albuquerque, NM....1074
McKinnon, Karl, Asst. Dir., Schiele Museum of Natural History and Lynn Planetarium, Gastonia, NC....1247
McKinsey, Kristan H., Vice Pres. Collections, Lakeview Museum of Arts and Sciences, Peoria, IL....512
McKinstry, Margaret, Pres. (V), Richardson-Bates House Museum, Oswego, NY....1191
McKnight, Chris, Lighthouse Mgr., Loxahatchee River Historical Society - Jupiter Inlet Lighthouse & Museum, Jupiter, FL....357
McKnight, Donna, Operations Mgr. & Museum Shop Mgr., New Jersey Meadowlands Environment Center, Lyndhurst, NJ....1046
McKoy, Jerry, Dir. Facilities, The Discovery Museum, Inc., Bridgeport, CT....267
McKoy, Johnnie, Property Mgr., Cameron Art Museum, Wilmington, NC....1271
McKoy, Kyle, Education & Outreach Division Dir., Arizona Historical Society/Arizona History Museum, Tucson, AZ....58
McKoy, Kyle, Education & Outreach Div. Dir., Arizona Historical Society Museum at Papago Park, Tempe, AZ....56
McKune, Amy, Dir. Collections, Eiteljorg Museum of American Indians and Western Art, Indianapolis, IN....547
McLachlan, Michael, Dir. Public Rels., Fred Harman Art Museum, Pagosa Springs, CO....259
McLafferty, Joseph, Dir. Parks & Recreation, Lincoln Park Zoo, Manitowoc, WI....1829
McLain, Brenda, Cur., Arizona Capitol Museum, Phoenix, AZ....48
McLain, Christopher M., Chm., Oakland Museum of California, Oakland, CA....155
McLain, Guy, Dir., Springfield Museums - Connecticut Valley Historical Museum, Springfield, MA....808
McLain, Guy, Dir., Springfield Museums - Museum of Springfield History, Springfield, MA....808
McLain, Kathryn, Sec. & Treas., Jefferson County Historical Museum, Rigby, ID....465
McLain, Nancy A., Business Mgr., Hood Museum of Art, Hanover, NH....1019
McLain, Robert, Exec. Dir., Landmarks Foundation/Old Alabama Town, Montgomery, AL....19
McLain, Sandra, C.E.O., Chm. Bd. & Museum Shop Mgr., Big Thunder Gold Mine, Keystone, SD....1534
McLain, Sandra, Pres., Keystone Area Historical Society, Keystone, SD....1534
McLane, D. Mike, Business Mgr., Birmingham Museum of Art, Birmingham, AL....5
McLaren, Theresa, Museum Shop Mgr., Humboldt State University Natural History Museum, Arcata, CA....88
McLary, Kathleen, Vice Pres. State Historic Sites, Indiana State Museum, Indianapolis, IN....549
McLatchy, Patricia, Exhibitions Coord., The Hoyt Institute of Fine Arts, New Castle, PA....1447
McLaughlin, Angela, Museum Shop Mgr., Old Washington Historic State Park, Washington, AR....85
McLaughlin, Brian, Chm., Nita Stewart Haley Memorial Library & J. Evetts Haley History Center, Midland, TX....1633
McLaughlin, Dr. Castle, Assoc. Cur., Peabody Museum of Archaeology & Ethnology, Cambridge, MA....768
McLaughlin, David, Cur. Fungi & Lichens, Bell Museum of Natural History, Minneapolis, MN....884
McLaughlin, Dorothy, Dir. & Devel., Museum of Women's History, Billings, MT....956
McLaughlin, Gail, Event Mktg. Specialist, National Football Museum, Inc., Canton, OH....1301
McLaughlin, Joseph, Dir. Properties, Norman Bird Sanctuary, Middletown, RI....1489
Mclaughlin, Kelly, Dir. Limited Edition Prints, Aperture Foundation, New York, NY....1163
McLaughlin, Mac, Pres. USS Midway Museum, San Diego, CA....185
McLaughlin, Pam, Cur. Education, Everson Museum of Art, Syracuse, NY....1218
McLaughlin, Penny, C.E.O., Tipton-Haynes State Historic Site, Johnson City, TN....1556
McLaughlin, Scott A., Dir., Noyes House Museum, Morrisville, VT....1685
McLaughlin, Stacy B., C.E.O., Douglas County Museum of History and Natural History, Roseburg, OR....1402
McLaughlin, Timothy, Museum Shop Mgr., Erie Maritime Museum & Flagship Niagara, Erie, PA....1424
McLaughlin, William F., C.E.O. & Pres., Michigan Sports Hall of Fame, Detroit, MI....835
McLaughlin-Miller, Ursula, Special Projects Admin., Muscarelle Museum of Art, Williamsburg, VA....1755
McLaurin, Genette, Head Reference, The Schomburg Center for Research in Black Culture, New York, NY....1180
McLea, Mr., Dir., Beehive House, Salt Lake City, UT....1669
McLean, Charles D., Sr. Vice Pres. Communications & Mktg., American Museum of Natural History, New York, NY....1163
McLean, Deborah, Pres., The Harwood Museum of Art of the University of New Mexico, Taos, NM....1093
McLean, John, Treas., Gold Coast Railroad Museum, Inc., Miami, FL....365
McLean, Linda E., Dir. Olana State Historic Site, Olana State Historic Site, Hudson, NY....1143
McLean, Mac, Exec. Dir., Strategic Air & Space Museum, Ashland, NE....975
McLean, Pat, Chm. (V), Lauren Rogers Museum of Art, Laurel, MS....912
McLean, Shea, Cur. Collections, The Museum of Mobile, Mobile, AL....18
McLean Ward, Dr. Barbara, Dir. & Cur., Moffatt-Ladd House and Garden, Portsmouth, NH....1026
McLelland, Darlene, Cur., Edmonds Art Festival Museum, Edmonds, WA....1764
McLendon, Dr. Matthew, Cur. Academic Initiatives, The George D. and Harriet W. Cornell Fine Arts Museum, Winter Park, FL....398
McLenton, Andre, Dir., Confederate Museum, Crawfordville, GA....415
McLeod, Dr. Alisea, Educator, Museum at Southwestern Michigan College, Dowagiac, MI....836
McLeod, Barbara, Vice Pres., Abbe Museum, Bar Harbor, ME....692
McLeod, Brian, Chm., Fonthill Museum of the Bucks County Historical Society, Doylestown, PA....1420
McLeod, Brian, Chm., Mercer Museum of the Bucks County Historical Society, Doylestown, PA....1421
McLeod, Nicole, Mktg. & Public Rels. Coord., Morris Museum of Art, Augusta, GA....411
McLeod, Patricia, Deputy Dir. External Affairs, San Jose Museum of Art, San Jose, CA....196
McLeod, Susan M., C.E.O. & Dir., Chippewa Valley Museum, Inc., Eau Claire, WI....1817
McLerran, Dr. Jennifer, Cur. Museum, Museum of Northern Arizona, Flagstaff, AZ....41
McLerran, Jennifer, Dir. NAU Art Museum, Flagstaff, AZ....42
McLoud, Melissa, Dir., Center for Chesapeake Studies, Chesapeake Bay Maritime Museum, Saint Michaels, MD....745
McLoughlin, Boo, Exec. Dir., Craft Alliance, Saint Louis, MO....946
McLoughlin, Mark, C.O.O., Asian Art Museum of San Francisco, Chong-Moon Lee Center for Asian Art and Culture, San Francisco, CA....186
McMahon, Cynthia, Past Pres. (V), Historic Pullman Foundation, Chicago, IL....481
McMahon, James E., C.E.O., Parker-O'Malley Air Museum, Hudson, NY....1143
McMahon, James P., Dir. Devel., Monmouth County Historical Association, Freehold, NJ....1039
McMahon, Joanna, Museum Shop Mgr., San Juan Bautista State Historic Park, San Juan Bautista, CA....197
McMahon, John, Assoc. Registrar Collections, National Portrait Gallery, Washington, DC....326
McMahon, Kathy, Treas., Meriden Historical Society, Inc., Meriden, CT....282
McMahon, Laurel, Pres. (V), Historical Society of Oak Park & River Forest, Oak Park, IL....510
McMahon, Patrick, Dir. Exhibitions & Design, Museum of Fine Arts, Boston, MA....761
McMahon, Sean, Ph.D., Sec., Lake City Columbia County Historical Museum, Inc., Lake City, FL....361
McMahon, Stephen, Western Rgnl. Dir., The Mission House, Stockbridge, MA....809
McMahon, Stephen, Rgnl. Dir., Naumkeag, Stockbridge, MA....810
McManaman, Robert, Chm. (V), Fairmount Historical Museum & Gift Shop, Fairmount, IN....540
McManners, Katie, Dir. Mktg., Museum of Discovery: Arkansas Museum of Science and History, Little Rock, AR....78
McManus, Amy, Public Rels. & Publications Dir., Louisburg College Art Gallery, Louisburg, NC....1256
McManus, Laura, Cur. Education, Museum of Biblical Art, New York, NY....1175
McManus, Marcia, Dir. & Cur., U.S. Army Chaplain Museum, Fort Jackson, SC....1512
McManus, Tina, Gift Shop Mgr., Watermen's Museum, Yorktown, VA....1757

M–*Continued*

McManus Zurko, Kitty, Dir., The College of Wooster Art Museum, Wooster, OH .1351

McMaster, Gerald, Deputy Asst. Dir. Cultural Resources, National Museum of the American Indian, Smithsonian Institution, New York, NY 1177

McMaster, Michael, Education Coord., Wood County Historical Center and Museum, Bowling Green, OH 1298

McMaster, Steve, Multimedia Production Specialist, Stedman Gallery, Camden, NJ 1034

McMasters, Thomas O., (Ret.), Dir., U.S. Army Medical Department Museum, Fort Sam Houston, TX..........................1608

McMath, Hope, Dir., Cummer Museum of Art & Gardens, Jacksonville, FL.........354

McMath, Lavita, Government & Community Rels. Officer, Brooklyn Museum, Brooklyn, NY 1111

McMath, Robert, Cur. Farm & Railroad Museum, C.H. Moore Homestead, Clinton, IL 487

McMeekin, Joy, Mgr. Devel. Technology, Dayton History at Carillon Park, Dayton, OH...1316

McMichael, Sindy, Cur. & Sec., Great Basin Historical Society & Museum, Delta, UT 1661

McMillan, Bobbie, Dir. Museum School, Brevard Art Museum, Melbourne, FL.....364

McMillan, David, Mgr. Security, Kimbell Art Museum, Fort Worth, TX 1610

McMillan, Edward, Ph.D., C.E.O. (V), Mississippi Baptist Historical Commission, Clinton, MS.......................905

McMillan, Francis W., II, Chm. (V), Detroit Historical Society, Detroit, MI 834

McMillan, Dr. Lex, Pres., Freedman Gallery-Albright College, Reading, PA .1470

McMillan, Mary Ann, Volunteer Coord., The Rutgers Gardens, New Brunswick, NJ 1052

McMillan, Maurine, C.E.O. & Dir., Valencia County Historical Society's Harvey House Museum, Belen, NM 1074

McMillan, Morgan, Cur., Peter Wentz Farmstead, Worcester, PA.....................1483

McMillan, Patsy H., Dir., Favell Museum Inc., Klamath Falls, OR 1393

McMillan, Whit, Education, South Carolina Aquarium, Charleston, SC.......1506

McMillen, Jim, Living History Program, Historic Pensacola Village, Pensacola, FL...377

McMillen, Jim, Living History Program, West Florida Historic Preservation, Inc., Pensacola, FL 379

McMillian, Greg, Newsletter Editor, Historical Society of Washington County, Virginia, Abingdon, VA 1695

McMillian Lowe, Gwen, Dir., A.C. McMillan African American Museum, Emory, TX 1606

McMillian, Robert, Mgr. Rikard's Mill Museum, Monroe County Heritage Museum, Monroeville, AL.......................18

McMorris, Lillian, Public Rels., The Walker African American Museum & Research Center, Las Vegas, NV..........1007

McMullen, Ann, Head Cur. Research, National Museum of the American Indian, Smithsonian Institution, New York, NY 1177

McMullen, Dennis, Admin. Reference & Museum Svcs., Sandusky Library Follett House Museum, Sandusky, OH .1342

McMullen, Molly, Head Mktg., The Kreeger Museum, Washington, DC 320

McMullen, Nicole, Exec. Dir., Bailey House Museum - Maui Historical Society, Wailuku, HI 453

McMurray, Rebecca, Chm. (V), National Center for Children's Illustrated Literature, Abilene, TX 1576

McMurry, Kevin, Supt., Fort Larned National Historic Site, Larned, KS..........620

McMurtrey, J.K. Keith, Administrative Asst., Tennessee Valley Art Center, Tuscumbia, AL 25

McNab, Cheryl, C.E.O., The Art Center, Grand Junction, CO.................................249

McNabb, Kirby, Pres., Oaklands Historic House Museum, Murfreesboro, TN.......1565

McNair, Cynthia, Sec., Middleborough Historical Association, Inc., Middleborough, MA................................790

McNair, Jim, C.E.O. & Pres., American Royal Museum & Visitors Center, Kansas City, MO 932

McNair, John, Chm. Bd. Trustees, Cape Cod Museum of Natural History, Inc., Brewster, MA 765

McNair, Willie, Ranger, John Gorrie Museum State Park, Apalachicola, FL 333

McNair-Lewis, Gareth, Conservation Tech, Jefferson Patterson Park & Museum, Saint Leonard, MD..................744

McNally, Christopher M., Exec. Vice Pres., Baltimore Streetcar Museum, Inc., Baltimore, MD 720

McNamara, C. J., Dir. & Owner, Mississippi Petrified Forest, Flora, MS ...906

McNamara, Carole, Sr. Cur. Western Art, The University of Michigan Museum of Art, Ann Arbor, MI 824

McNamara, Eric, Dir. Physical Plant, Binder Park Zoo, Battle Creek, MI 825

McNamara, Capt. James J., Chm., Maritime Industry Museum at Fort Schuyler, Bronx, NY 1108

McNamara, Sarah, Community Rels. Coord., Rockford Art Museum, Rockford, IL 517

McNamee Bower, Mary, Cur. Collections, Evansville Museum of Arts History & Science, Evansville, IN 539

McNames, Kris, Treas., Silvercreek Museum, Freeport, IL..............................495

Mcnary, Jean, Pres. (V), Dade Battlefield Historic State Park, Bushnell, FL............337

McNaughton, Cindy, Head History Dept., Los Angeles (Central) Public Library, Los Angeles, CA 138

McNaughton, John William, Pres., National Heritage Museum, Lexington, MA 785

McNay, Linda, Dir. Museum Advancement, The High Museum of Art, Atlanta, GA 405

McNealy, Terry, Archivist, The Parry Mansion Museum, New Hope, PA 1447

McNeece, David, Rights & Reproductions, Museum of Indian Arts & Culture/Laboratory of Anthropology, Santa Fe, NM 1089

McNeel, William P., Librarian & Historian, Pocahontas County Museum, Marlinton, WV 1802

McNeil, Dan, Dir. Devel., Figge Art Museum, Davenport, IA...........................581

McNeil, Dwayne, Dir. Mktg., Six Flags Discovery Kingdom, Vallejo, CA 220

McNeil, Jan, Co-Chm., Chief Vann House Historic Site, Chatsworth, GA......413

McNeil, Kay, Historian, Historic Jefferson College, Washington, MS 919

McNeil, Rebecca, Dir. Finance, Children's Museum of Pittsburgh, Pittsburgh, PA 1465

McNeil Wyner, Jean, Chm. (V), Santa Monica History Museum, Santa Monica, CA 207

McNeill, Cathy, Office Mgr., Century Village Museum, Burton, OH 1299

McNerney, Michael J., Pres. (V), General John A. Logan Museum, Murphysboro, IL...508

McNett, Nancy, Sec., Chisholm Trail Museum, Wellington, KS 637

McNew, Glenda, Gift Shop Mgr., Archives Museum, Temple Mickve Israel, Savannah, GA.................................433

McNorton, Sandi, Public Rels. USS Lexington Museum on the Bay, Corpus Christi, TX 1595

McNully, Kristin, Ground Mgr., Oak Hill and The Martha Berry Museum, Rome, GA 430

McNulty, Cheryl, Site Mgr. & Museum Shop Mgr., Century Village Museum, Burton, OH 1299

McNulty, E.C., Asst. Dir., Tintic Mining Museum, Eureka, UT 1661

McNulty, J. L., C.E.O., Dir. & Registrar, Tintic Mining Museum, Eureka, UT 1661

McNulty, John, Museum Shop Mgr., Tucson Museum of Art & Historic Block, Tucson, AZ...63

McNulty, Neely, School & Family Programs Coord., Hood Museum of Art, Hanover, NH 1019

McNutt, Ann, Sec., Historic Carson House, Marion, NC 1257

McNutt, James C., Ph.D., Pres. & C.E.O., National Museum of Wildlife Art, Jackson, WY...1860

McNutt, Mrs. Ruth, Hostess, Franklin County Old Jail Museum, Winchester, TN 1575

McPherson, Benjamin, Financial Dir., Harry S. Truman Little White House Museum, Key West, FL 359

McPherson, Ernie, Deputy Dir. Special Projects, The California State Military Museum, Sacramento, CA 175

McPherson, Penny, Pres. (V), Kit Carson Historical Society, Kit Carson, CO..........253

McPherson, Tommy, Dir., Mobile Museum of Art, Mobile, AL 17

McQuaid, Chyrl, Sec., Beltrami County History Center, Bemidji, MN..................870

McQuaid, Matilda, Cur. Textiles, Cooper-Hewitt, National Design Museum, Smithsonian Institution, New York, NY 1167

McQuaid, Mike, Dir., World Sports Humanitarian Hall of Fame, Boise, ID ...456

McQueary, Kathy, Pres., Colfax County Society of Art, History and Archaeology, Raton, NM 1086

McQueary, Kathy, Pres. (V), Raton Museum, Raton, NM...............................1086

McQueen, Jack, Vice Pres., Old Mill Museum, El Molino Viejo - Old Mill Foundation, San Marino, CA 198

McQueeny, Betty, Museum Shop Mgr., Suffolk County Vanderbilt Museum, Centerport, NY 1120

McQuigg, Jackson, Vice Pres. Capital Projects, Atlanta Historical Society, Atlanta, GA...402

McQuilkin, JoAnne, Chm., Historical and Genealogical Society of Indiana County, Indiana, PA...............................1435

McRae, Annetta, Administrative Officer, National Portrait Gallery, Washington, DC 326

McRae, Misha D., Dir. Client Svcs., Key West Tropical Forest & Botanical Garden, Key West, FL...........................359

McRainey, D. Lynn, Dir. Education, The Elizabeth F. Cheney, Chicago History Museum, Chicago, IL..............................478

McRay, Sara, Registrar, Nevada Museum of Art, Reno, NV 1009

McRay, Wendy, Financial, Museum of the Cherokee Indian, Cherokee, NC......1240

M–*Continued*

M–*Continued*

Meyers, Sarah, Dir., Furnace Town Living Heritage Museum, Snow Hill, MD.....747
Meyersburg, David, Exhibit Specialist, New York State Bureau of Historic Sites, Waterford, NY.....1225
Meyerson, Randi, Cur. Mammals, The Toledo Zoo, Toledo, OH.....1346
Meyr, Evelyn, Museum Shop Mgr., Lutheran Heritage Center & Museum of the Perry County Lutheran Historical Society, Altenburg, MO.....920
Mhiripiri, John, Financial Dir., Anthology Film Archives, New York, NY.....1163
Miao, Desui, Collection Mgr. Vertebrate Paleontology KU Biodiversity Institute - KU Natural History Museum, Lawrence, KS.....621
Miaoulis, Dr. Ioannis, Dir. & Pres., Museum of Science, Boston, MA.....762
Micciche, Tracy, Mktg., Harry P. Leu Gardens, Orlando, FL.....373
Michael, Edward A., Chm. Bd., Vero Beach Museum of Art, Inc., Vero Beach, FL.....396
Michael, Martha, Payroll Specialist, Saint Louis Zoo, Saint Louis, MO.....951
Michael, Ron, Cur., Birger Sandzen Memorial Gallery, Lindsborg, KS.....623
Michaelis, Peter T., Pres. (V), Museum of the Bedford Historical Society, Bedford, NY.....1103
Michaelree, Jennifer, Dir. Education, Dumbarton House, Washington, DC.....316
Michaels, Bonni-Dara, Collection Cur., Yeshiva University Museum at the Center for Jewish History, New York, NY.....1184
Michaels, Deborah, Exec. Dir., Hui No'eau Visual Arts Center, Makawao, Maui, HI.....452
Michaels, Gary J., Treas., Michigan Transit Museum, Inc., Mount Clemens, MI.....856
Michaels, Jane, Recording Sec., Brooks Academy Museum, Harwich, MA.....781
Michaels, Dr. Tom, Head, Dept. Horticultural Science, Minnesota Landscape Arboretum, University of Minnesota, Chaska, MN.....872
Michalek, Martha, Museum Shop Mgr., Cape Cod Museum of Art, Dennis, MA.....774
Michaletz, Jan, Chm. (V), American Swedish Institute, Minneapolis, MN.....884
Michalka, Justin, Dir. Devel., Lady Bird Johnson Wildflower Center, Austin, TX.....1582
Michaud, Bruce P., C.E.O. & Public Rels., Salem Witch Museum, Salem, MA.....804
Michaud, Peter, Sec., Warner House, Portsmouth, NH.....1027
Michel, Barb, Gallery Dir., Robert E. Wilson Gallery, Huntington, IN.....546
Michel, James, C.E.O., Clearwater County Historical Society, Shevlin, MN.....898
Michel, John, Bd. Vice Pres., Crowley Museum & Nature Center, Sarasota, FL.....386
Michelena, Barbara, Museum Shop Mgr., Center For Maine Contemporary Art, Rockport, ME.....710
Michelin, Rosemary, Research Librarian, Marquette County History Museum, Marquette, MI.....853
Michels, Bob, Chm. Bd., The Dennison Railroad Depot Museum, Dennison, OH.....1318
Michels, Lance, Pres. Bd., Miramont Castle Museum, Manitou Springs, CO.....258
Michels, Lara, Ph.D., Archivist, Western Jewish History Center, Judah L. Magnes Museum, Berkeley, CA.....92
Michelson, Molly, Production Coord., Alexander F. Morrison Planetarium, San Francisco, CA.....186
Michener, Kathryn, Astronomer, McAuliffe-Shepard Discovery Center, Concord, NH.....1015
Michener, Sandt, Producer, McAuliffe-Shepard Discovery Center, Concord, NH.....1015
Michener, Sandt, Producer, McAuliffe-Shepard Discovery Center, Concord, NH.....1015
Micikas, Jenifer, Museum Shop Mgr., Grounds For Sculpture, Hamilton, NJ.....1041
Mick, Dolores, Museum Shop Mgr., Galloway House and Village - Blakely Museum, Fond du Lac, WI.....1819
Mickelson, Judith, Dir., The Fluvanna County Historical Society Old Stone Jail Museum, Palmyra, VA.....1732
Mickenberg, David, Exec. Dir., Taubman Museum of Art, Roanoke, VA.....1744
Mickey, Greta, Administrative Asst., Yates County Genealogical and Historical Society and Oliver House Museum and L. Caroline Underwood Museum, Penn Yan, NY.....1195
Mickle Smaczny, Lynne, Exec. Dir., Will County Historical Society, Lockport, IL.....504
Micklich, Judy, Pres., Salida Museum, Salida, CO.....262
Middag, Lisa, Design & Publicatons Dir., Walker Art Center, Minneapolis, MN.....886
Middendorf, Dwight, Sr. Dir. Finance, Arizona Science Center, Phoenix, AZ.....49
Middendorf, Mike, Site Tech, Nauvoo Historical Society Museum, Nauvoo, IL.....508
Middents, Paul, Pres. (V), Kitsap County Historical Society Museum, Bremerton, WA.....1760
Middlebrook Herron, Ellen, Dir., City of Fort Walton Beach Heritage Park & Cultural Center, Fort Walton Beach, FL.....350
Middlekauff, W.W., Assoc. Cur. Emeritus, Essig Museum of Entomology, University of California, Berkeley, Berkeley, CA.....92
Middleton, John, Vice Pres. Business Administration, Seashore Trolley Museum, Kennebunkport, ME.....701
Middleton, Ross, Dir., American Quarter Horse Hall of Fame & Museum, Amarillo, TX.....1578
Midgett, Corinne, Registrar, High Point Museum & Historical Park, High Point, NC.....1252
Midgette, Darroll, Registrar, Museum of the Albemarle, Elizabeth City, NC.....1244
Midthun, Betsy, Exec. Dir., Minnesota Marine Art Museum, Winona, MN.....902
Miedema, Laurie, Museum Shop Mgr., The Children's Museum of Science and Technology, Troy, NY.....1221
Miel, Karen, Dir. Education, Palo Alto Junior Museum and Zoo, Palo Alto, CA.....161
Mielke, Mary, Bd. Member, Marias Museum of History and Art, Shelby, MT.....972
Miers, Della, Membership & Exhibits, Seward County Historical Society Museum, Goehner, NE.....983
Miers, Dick, Treas., Seward County Historical Society Museum, Goehner, NE.....983
Miessner, Elizabeth, Chm. (V), Scituate Historical Society, Scituate, MA.....805
Miessner, Elizabeth, Chm. (V), Scituate Maritime and Irish Mossing Museum, Scituate, MA.....806
Migalla, Matt, Asst. Site Mgr., Cahokia Mounds State Historic Site, Collinsville, IL.....488
Migdal, Michele, Museum Shop Mgr., Williams College Museum of Art, Williamstown, MA.....817
Might-Dyer, Dorene, Dir. Education, Historical Museum at Fort Missoula, Missoula, MT.....969
Miglinas, Skirmante, Dir., The Lithuanian Museum, Chicago, IL.....483
Miglinas, Thomas R., Dir. Technical Svcs., The Lithuanian Museum, Chicago, IL.....483
Miglorle, Cathy, Museum Shop Mgr., Vermont Marble Museum, Proctor, VT.....1687
Miguel, Kathleen, Mgr., Gallery West, Waimea, HI.....453
Migui, Rita, Pres. (V), Yuma Art Center Museum - Yuma Fine Arts, Yuma, AZ.....65
Mihalko, Judy, Dir. Finance, Wadsworth Atheneum Museum of Art, Hartford, CT.....279
Mihm, Judy, Museum Shop Mgr., Hutchinson County Museum, Borger, TX.....1589
Mijo, Darin, Head Finance, Honolulu Academy of Arts, Honolulu, HI.....445
Miklas, Lois, Mgr. Public Programs, The Hershey Story, Hershey, PA.....1433
Mikolaj, Heather, Dir., Memorial Union Art Gallery, Davis, CA.....107
Miksch, Heidi, Decorative Arts Conservator, New York State Bureau of Historic Sites, Waterford, NY.....1225
Miksula, Jennifer, Ranger, Jemez State Monument, Jemez Springs, NM.....1079
Milad, Jackie, Program Coord., Union Gallery, College Park, MD.....732
Milam, Chuck, Treas., Oceanographic Teaching Station Inc. - Roundhouse Marine Studies Lab & Aquarium, Manhattan Beach, CA.....144
Milan, James, Dir., Meeker County Historical Society Museum & G.A.R. Hall, Litchfield, MN.....882
Milan, Jerry B., Chm. (V), Czech Heritage Museum & Genealogy Center, Temple, TX.....1650
Milani, Arch, Vice Pres., Palmer House, Historical Society of Olde Northfield, Northfield, OH.....1336
Milani, Mark, Chief Preparator, The Nelson-Atkins Museum of Art, Kansas City, MO.....934
Milarcik, Laura, Dir. Mktg., The Dennison Railroad Depot Museum, Dennison, OH.....1318
Milbourne, John, Dir., Florida Institute of Technology Botanical Gardens, Melbourne, FL.....364
Milbrandt, Dr. Eric, Research Scientist, Sanibel-Captiva Conservation Foundation, Inc., Sanibel, FL.....386
Milbrath, Dr. Susan, Cur. Latin American Art & Archaeology, Florida Museum of Natural History, Gainesville, FL.....351
Milburn, David, Pres., Museum of the Berkeley Springs, Berkeley Springs, WV.....1796
Miles, Carolyn P., C.E.O. & Dir., Atrium Gallery Ltd., Saint Louis, MO.....945
Miles, Christine M., Dir. & C.E.O., Albany Institute of History & Art, Albany, NY.....1095
Miles, David A., Dir. Education & Interpretation, Billings Farm & Museum, Woodstock, VT.....1695

M–*Continued*

Miles, Ellen, Cur. of Painting & Sculpture, National Portrait Gallery, Washington, DC.....326
Miles, Elly, Museum Store Mgr., The Nelson-Atkins Museum of Art, Kansas City, MO.....934
Miles, Yvonne, Dir. Corporate Merchandising & Museum Shop Mgr., San Diego Zoo, San Diego, CA.....184
Miles, Yvonne, Corporate Dir. Merchandising, San Diego Zoo's Wild Animal Park, Escondido, CA.....112
Milestone, Jim F., Supt., Whiskeytown Unit, Whiskeytown-Shasta-Trinity National Recreation Area, Whiskeytown, CA.....224
Milewski, Melody, Mgr., Erie Canal Village, Rome, NY.....1203
Miley, Sherry, Mktg., Agrirama, Georgia's Living History Museum & Village, Tifton, GA.....437
Milford, Amy, Deputy Dir., Museum at Eldridge Street, New York, NY.....1174
Milhomme, Maria, Head Security, Lowe Art Museum, University of Miami, Coral Gables, FL.....340
Milkova, Liliana, Cur. Academic Programs, Allen Memorial Art Museum - Oberlin College, Oberlin, OH.....1337
Mill, Dennis J., C.E.O. & Pres., Orchard Park Historical Society, Orchard Park, NY.....1190
Millan, Dorinda, Cur., West of the Pecos Museum, Pecos, TX.....1638
Millard, Betsy, Exec. Dir., Columbia Pacific Heritage Museum, Ilwaco, WA.....1769
Millard, Beverly, Librarian, Waukegan History Museum, Waukegan Historical Society, Waukegan, IL.....527
Millard, Blake, Preparator, Patty and Jay Baker Naples Museum of Art, Naples, FL.....370
Millard, J.K., Pres. & C.E.O., Lexington History Museum, Lexington, KY.....652
Millard, Lee S., Gallery Assoc., Haas Gallery of Art - Bloomsburg University, Bloomsburg, PA.....1413
Millard, Pat, Museum Shop Mgr., Fontenelle Nature Association, Bellevue, NE.....977
Millard, Wil, Chief Preparator, Herbert F. Johnson Museum of Art, Ithaca, NY.....1146
Millaway, John, Pres., Philadelphia Mummers Museum, Philadelphia, PA.....1459
Milledge, Vashion, Imagination Theater Mgr., Flint River Quarium, Albany, GA.....399
Millegan, Roy, Sec., Jefferson Valley Museum, Whitehall, MT.....974
Millenbruch, Gary L., Pres. (V), Allentown Art Museum, Allentown, PA.....1408
Miller, Adrienne, Registrar, Audubon Zoo, New Orleans, LA.....679
Miller, Alexa, Cur. Education, Davis Museum and Cultural Center, Wellesley, MA.....814
Miller, Alice, Office Asst., Tarpon Springs Cultural Center, Tarpon Springs, FL.....394
Miller, Alinder, Chm. & Pres. (V), Civil War Museum of Lone Jack, Jackson County, Lone Jack, MO.....939
Miller, Allan R., C.E.O., Pres. & Cur., Kruger Street Toy & Train Museum, Wheeling, WV.....1808
Miller, Alvin, Chief of Security, Herbert F. Johnson Museum of Art, Ithaca, NY.....1146
Miller, Amy, Museum Shop Mgr., Abraham Lincoln Presidential Library & Museum, Springfield, IL.....520
Miller, Amy, Museum Shop Mgr., Georgia Museum of Art, University of Georgia, Athens, GA.....400
Miller, Andrea, Admin., Lakewood's Heritage Center, Lakewood, CO.....254
Miller, Andrea, Asst. Museum Shop Mgr., South Shore Arts, Munster, IN.....558
Miller, Anelle, Dir., The Museum of American Illustration at the Society of Illustrators, New York, NY.....1174
Miller, April, Museum Shop Mgr., The Museum, Greenwood, SC.....1515
Miller, Barbara, Membership Sec., Louisiana Art & Science Museum - Irene W. Pennington Planetarium, Baton Rouge, LA.....667
Miller, Beth, Asst. to Dir., The Carl & Mary Koehler History Center, Cedar Rapids, IA.....577
Miller, Beth, Museum Store Mgr., Wyoming State Museum, Cheyenne, WY.....1855
Miller, Beth, Assoc. Dir. Devel. & External Affairs, Yale Center for British Art, New Haven, CT.....287
Miller, Beulah, Treas., Garden Grove Historical Society, Garden Grove, CA.....118
Miller, Bev, Gift Shop Supvr., Bois Forte Heritage Center, Tower, MN.....899
Miller, Bo, Dir., Amory Regional Museum, Amory, MS.....903
Miller, Bobby, Park Ranger, Peaks of Otter Visitor Center, Bedford, VA.....1701
Miller, Brad, Dir., Coolspring Power Museum, Coolspring, PA.....1419
Miller, Bridgit, Accountant, Longue Vue House & Gardens, New Orleans, LA.....681
Miller, Bryan, Visitor Svcs. & Museum Shop Mgr., Fresno Metropolitan Museum of Art & Science, Fresno, CA.....116
Miller, Rev. Byron, C.SS.R., Dir., National Shrine of Blessed Francis Xavier Seelos, New Orleans, LA.....682
Miller, Candace, Dir., Louis H. & Lena Firn Grover Museum, Shelbyville, IN.....565
Miller, Carin, Dir. Education, The Cleveland Museum of Natural History, Cleveland, OH.....1308
Miller, Dr. Carl, C.E.O. & Dir., Swarthout Memorial Museum, La Crosse, WI.....1826
Miller, Dr. Carl R., C.E.O., Hixon House, La Crosse, WI.....1825
Miller, Carl R., C.E.O. & Dir., Riverside Museum, La Crosse, WI.....1825
Miller, Carol, Business. Mgr., Louisville Zoological Garden, Louisville, KY.....656
Miller, Chad A., Dir. Facilities, Roscoe Village Foundation, Coshocton, OH.....1315
Miller, Charles, C.E.O. & Dir. Parks, Oroville Chinese Temple, Oroville, CA.....158
Miller, Chasity, Donor Rels. Mgr., Virginia Museum of Fine Arts, Richmond, VA.....1742
Miller, Mrs. Cherry, Chm. (V), Dr. John Harris Dental Museum, Bainbridge, OH.....1295
Miller, Chris, Ph.D., CPA, Dir. Finance ECHO Lake Aquarium and Science Center/Leahy Center for Lake Champlain, Burlington, VT.....1677
Miller, Christine, Asst. to Dir., Taft Museum of Art, Cincinnati, OH.....1306
Miller, Christopher, Vice Pres., Lewis County Historical Society Museum, Lowville, NY.....1155
Miller, Christopher, Cur., Musical Instrument Museum, Phoenix, AZ.....50
Miller, Chuck, Vice Pres. Information Technology & Chief Information Officer, Missouri Botanical Garden, Saint Louis, MO.....949
Miller, C.J., C.E.O. & Pres., Gunnison County Pioneer and Historical Society, Gunnison, CO.....251
Miller, Clark, Dir. Facilities, The Museum of Flight, Seattle, WA.....1781
Miller, Cledus, Maintenance Mechanic, Weymouth Woods-Sandhills Nature Preserve Museum, Southern Pines, NC.1268
Miller, Connie, Dir. Landscaping, Roscoe Village Foundation, Coshocton, OH.....1315
Miller, Craig, Folk Arts Coord., Chase Home Museum of Utah Folk Arts, Salt Lake City, UT.....1669
Miller, Cyrus, Exhibits Officer, Impression 5 Science Center, Lansing, MI.....849
Miller, Dan, Exhibits Coord., Tempe Historical Museum, Tempe, AZ.....57
Miller, Dan D., C.E.O. & Dir., Bramble Park Zoo, Watertown, SD.....1544
Miller, Dana, Cur. Permanent Collection, Whitney Museum of American Art, New York, NY.....1184
Miller, Daniel, Cur., The Antique Boat Museum, Clayton, NY.....1121
Miller, Darren, Dir., Allegheny College Art Galleries (Bowman, Penelec & Megahan Galleries), Meadville, PA.....1443
Miller, David, Museum Shop Mgr., Reuben H. Fleet Science Center, San Diego, CA.....182
Miller, David, Show Productions, Six Flags Discovery Kingdom, Vallejo, CA.....220
Miller, David M., Pres. & C.E.O., Mercer County Historical Society, Mercer, PA..1444
Miller, Deborah, Pres. (V), Devel. & Membership, Malibu Lagoon Museum, Malibu, CA.....144
Miller, Delores, Museum Shop Mgr., Rocky Mount Museum, Piney Flats, TN.....1572
Miller, Diane, Dir. Education, Interpreter & Museum Shop Mgr., Queens County Farm Museum, Floral Park, NY.....1133
Miller, Diane, Senior Vice Pres. Community, St. Louis Science Center, Saint Louis, MO.....950
Miller, Dick, Pres., Historic General Dodge House, Council Bluffs, IA.....580
Miller, Don, Chm. Bd., The Bennington Museum, Bennington, VT.....1676
Miller, Donna, Admin., St. George's United Methodist Church, Philadelphia, PA.....1461
Miller, Douglas, Dir., Pennsbury Manor, Morrisville, PA.....1446
Miller, Douglas, Acting Historic Site Admin., Washington Crossing Historic Park, Washington Crossing, PA.....1480
Miller, Duane, Cur., Monona County Veteran's Memorial Museum, Onawa, IA.....596
Miller, Elliott L., Pres. (V), Highland Park Historical Society, Highland Park, IL.....499
Miller, Eric, Cur. & Owner, Cimarron Valley Railroad Museum, Cushing, OK.....1359
Miller, Ethelbert, Chm. (V), Provisions Library, Washington, DC.....328
Miller, Florence, Dir., Columbia Museum of History, Columbia, PA.....1418
Miller, Francene, C.E.O. & Devel., Ark-La-Tex Antique & Classic Vehicle Museum, Shreveport, LA.....686

M–Continued

Miller, Stephen, Dir. Bureau of Historic Sites & Museums, Pennsylvania Historical & Museum Commission, Harrisburg, PA 1431
Miller, Stephen, Chm., Pithole Visitor Center, Pleasantville, PA 1468
Miller, Steve, Chm. (V), Robert C. Williams Paper Museum, Atlanta, GA 408
Miller, Steven, Exec. Vice Pres., Biltmore Estate, Asheville, NC 1231
Miller, Steven H., Pres., C.E.O. & Chief Cur., The Morris Museum, Morristown, NJ 1050
Miller, Sue, Site Mgr., Varner-Hogg Plantation State Historic Site, West Columbia, TX 1656
Miller, Susan, Chm. City Hall, Kiwanis Van Slyke Museum Foundation Inc., Caldwell, ID....457
Miller, Susan, Archivist, Scholte House Museum, Pella, IA....597
Miller, Susan B., Chm., Rosenbach Museum & Library, Philadelphia, PA....1461
Miller, Sylvia, Pres. Circus & Recording Sec., Circus City Festival Museum, Peru, IN....561
Miller, Terry J., Site Mgr., Old Market House State Historic Site, Galena, IL 496
Miller, Terry J., Site Mgr., U.S. Grant's Home State Historic Site, Galena, IL....496
Miller, Tobias, Site Interpreter, Starved Rock State Park, Oglesby, IL....510
Miller, Vivian, Treas., Bowdon Centennial Museum, Bowdon, ND....1278
Miller, Walter, C.E.O., Museum of Automobile Art and Design, Syracuse, NY....1219
Miller, Walter R., Chief Administrative Officer & Pres. (V), New Haven Museum, New Haven, CT 286
Miller, Wendy, Environmental Education Specialist, Sharon Audubon Center, Sharon, CT....293
Miller, Wendy W., Dir., Canyon County Historical Society & Museum, Nampa, ID 463
Miller Wynne, Jeannette, Treas., Lompoc Valley Historical Society, Inc., Lompoc, CA 130
Miller Zohn, Kristen, Cur. Collections & Exhibitions, The Columbus Museum, Columbus, GA....414
Miller-Betts, Christine, Exec. Dir., Lucy Craft Laney Museum of Black History and Conference Center, Augusta, GA....410
Millet, Tony, Operations Mgr. & Museum Shop Mgr., Utah Museum of Natural History, Salt Lake City, UT 1672
Millhouse, Barbara B., Founding Dir., Reynolda House Museum of American Art, Winston-Salem, NC 1275
Millican, Rhonda, Exhibit Specialist, Arkansas Museum of Natural Resources, Smackover, AR 84
Millick, Sally, Cur., Macedon Historical Society, Inc., Macedon, NY 1156
Milligan, Dr. Frank D., Dir., President Lincoln's Cottage, Washington, DC 328
Milligan, Marshall C., Chm. Bd. Trustees (V), Santa Barbara Museum of Art, Santa Barbara, CA....203
Milligan, Robert B., Jr., Dir., Astors' Beechwood Mansion - Living History Museum, Newport, RI....1489
Milliken, Margueritte, Museum Shop Mgr., The John Wornall House Museum, Kansas City, MO....933
Milliman, Patrick, Dir. Communications & Mktg., The Morgan Library & Museum, New York, NY....1173
Millin, Laura J., Exec. Dir., Missoula Art Museum, Missoula, MT 969
Millington, Kevin, Pres. (V), Empire State Aerosciences Museum, Glenville, NY....1138
Millington, Robert, Vice Pres., Shaftsbury Historical Society, Shaftsbury, VT....1690
Millis, Lisa, Pres., Historical Society of Saratoga Springs, Saratoga Springs, NY....1207
Millis, Robert L., Dir., Lowell Observatory, Flagstaff, AZ 41
Millman, David, Exec. Dir., Nevada State Museum, Las Vegas, Las Vegas, NV....1006
Millmann, Betsy, Museum Shop Mgr., Fairbanks Museum and Planetarium, Saint Johnsbury, VT 1689
Millmore, Mark, Dir. Retail Operations, Museum of Contemporary Art, Chicago, IL 483
Millon, Henry A., Chm. (V), American Philosophical Society Museum (APS), Philadelphia, PA 1449
Mills, Alane, Sec., North Carolina Transportation Museum, Spencer, NC...1268
Mills, Allison, Mgr., Biltmore Homespun Shops - Grovewood Gallery, Asheville, NC 1231
Mills, Allison, Mgr., Estes-Winn Antique Automobile Museum, Asheville, NC....1232
Mills, Amy, Pres. (V), Des Moines Botanical Center, Des Moines, IA....583
Mills, Audrey S., Museum Shop Mgr., Mount Desert Oceanarium, Bar Harbor, ME....692
Mills, Barbara B., Business Mgr., Golden Pioneer Museum, Golden, CO 249
Mills, Brendan, Historic Site Asst., John Brown Farm State Historic Site, Lake Placid, NY....1152
Mills, Carrie, Museum Shop Mgr., Hills and Dales Estate, LaGrange, GA....422
Mills, Cynthia, Vice Pres. Programs, Birmingham Bloomfield Art Center, Birmingham, MI 828
Mills, Dan, Dir., Samek Art Gallery, Lewisburg, PA 1441
Mills, David, Assoc. Dir. Finance & Administration, Yale Center for British Art, New Haven, CT 287
Mills, David K., C.E.O. & Dir., Mount Desert Oceanarium, Bar Harbor, ME 692
Mills, Diana, Administrative Officer, Casa Grande Ruins National Monument, Coolidge, AZ 40
Mills, Dianne N., Museum Dir., World Methodist Museum, Lake Junaluska, NC....1255
Mills, Eminor, Business & Operations Mgr., Alden B. Dow Museum of Science and Art of the Midland Center for the Arts, Midland, MI....854
Mills, Geoff, Chm. (V), Texas Seaport Museum, Galveston, TX 1615
Mills, Gregory, Exhibits Specialist, Polk Museum of Art, Lakeland, FL 362
Mills, Herbert, Dir. Museum Svcs. Div., Nassau County, Division of Museum Services, Department of Recreation, Parks & Museums, East Meadow, NY..1130
Mills, Holly, Dir., Amherst County Museum & Historical Society, Amherst, VA 1699
Mills, John K., Cur., Thomas Clarke House/Princeton Battlefield State Park, Princeton, NJ 1059
Mills, Judy, Pres., Harvey House Museum, Florence, KS....612
Mills, Karen, Dir., The Sevier County Historical Museum, De Queen, AR....69
Mills, Mary, Chm. (V), Pendleton District Historical, Recreational and Tourism Commission, Pendleton, SC....1521
Millsap, Gina, C.E.O., Alice C. Sabatini Gallery-Topeka and Shawnee County Public Library, Topeka, KS....635
Milnarik, Elizabeth, Assoc. Architect, National Trust for Historic Preservation, Washington, DC 327
Milne, Chris, Chm. (V), The Eric Carle Museum of Picture Book Art, Amherst, MA....752
Milne, David, Treas., Union County Historical Society, Lewisburg, PA 1441
Milne, Debbie, Museum Shop Mgr., Santa Fe Trail Museum, Ingalls, KS 618
Milne, George M., Jr., Ph.D., Chm. Bd. (V), Mystic Aquarium & Institute for Exploration, Mystic, CT....283
Milne, Gordon, Dir. Facilities & Security, Great Lakes Science Center, Cleveland, OH 1309
Milne, Victoria, DVM, Veterinarian, El Paso Zoo, El Paso, TX....1605
Milner, Andrew R. C., Cur., St. George Dinosaur Discovery Site at Johnson Farm, Saint George, UT....1669
Milnes, Dr. Robert, Dean School Visual Arts, University of North Texas Art Gallery, Denton, TX 1602
Milnor, Arthur S., Exec. Dir., Flanders Nature Center, Woodbury, CT....303
Milone, Joe, Park Ranger, West Rock Nature Center, New Haven, CT....287
Milosch, Jane, Cur., Renwick Gallery of the Smithsonian American Art Museum, Washington, DC 328
Milosevich, Joe, Gallery Dir., Laura A. Sprague Art Gallery, Joliet, IL....500
Milotich, Jane, Bd. Pres., Sonoma Valley Museum of Art, Sonoma, CA 213
Miltner, Richard, Exhibition Designer, The Wolfsonian - Florida International University, Miami Beach, FL....368
Milts, Anna, Museum Shop Mgr., Wildlife World Zoo & Aquarium, Litchfield Park, AZ....46
Mims, Michael, Museum Shop Mgr., Atlanta Historical Society, Atlanta, GA...402
Min Chung, Young, Registrar, Blaffer Gallery, The Art Museum of the University of Houston, Houston, TX....1619
Mina, Virginia, Museum Shop Mgr., Museum Village, Monroe, NY....1158
Minaga, Akiko, Education Specialist, Phoebe Apperson Hearst Museum of Anthropology, Berkeley, CA....93
Minard, Barbara, Collections Mgr., Columbia Pacific Heritage Museum, Ilwaco, WA 1769
Minch, Ardyce, Pres. (V), Miners Foundry Cultural Center, Nevada City, CA....151
Minch, Timothy, Greenhouse Mgr., Tryon Palace Historic Sites & Gardens, New Bern, NC....1259
Minchew, Kaye L., Exec. Dir., Legacy Museum on Main: A History Museum for West Georgia, LaGrange, GA 423
Miner, Curt, Sr. Cur. Popular Culture, The State Museum of Pennsylvania, Harrisburg, PA 1432
Miner, Douglas P., Pres. (V), Children's Discovery Museum, Grand Rapids, MN....879
Miner, Douglas P., Pres. (V), Judy Garland Museum, Grand Rapids, MN....879
Minerva, Michael, Dir. Operations, Museum of Jewish Heritage-A Living Memorial to the Holocaust, New York, NY....1175
Mingalone, Maria, Dir. Education & Programs, Berkshire Museum, Pittsfield, MA....799
Minish, Mrs. Marveen, Pres. (V), Sibley House Historic Site, Mendota, MN 884

M–*Continued*

Molgaard, John, Treas., The Danish Immigrant Museum, Elk Horn, IA 586
Molin, Elaine, Museum Shop Mgr., Conner Prairie Interactive History Park, Fishers, IN 540
Molina, Antonio J., Pres., La Casa Del Libro, San Juan, PR 1870
Molina, Bill, Dir. Exhibits, The Discovery Center of Idaho, Boise, ID 455
Molina, Mario, Chm. (V), Aquarium of the Pacific, Long Beach, CA 131
Moline, Brian, Chm. (V), Kansas Museum of History, Topeka, KS 636
Moline, Lisa, Museum Operations Coord., Appleton Museum of Art, Ocala, FL 371
Molineaux, Sharon Vanessa, Park Mgr., Oxon Cove Park, Oxon Hill, MD 743
Molinelli, Marla, Museum Shop Mgr., Lincoln Park Zoological Gardens, Chicago, IL 483
Molineux, Ann, Collection Coord., Non-Vertebrate Paleontology Collection, Texas Natural Science Center, Austin, TX 1584
Molinski, Chris, Assoc. Cur. Education & Adult Programs, Knoxville Museum of Art, Knoxville, TN 1558
Moll, Richard, Conservator, Autry National Center of the American West, Los Angeles, CA 133
Moll, Ruth, Vice Pres., The Friends of the Caleb Pusey House, Inc., Upland, PA 1479
Moller, Ellyn, Chm. (V), Milton Art Museum, Canton, MA 769
Moller Vanbeckum, Jancan, Research Supvr., Washington County Historical Society, West Bend, WI 1850
Molleson, Toni, Interim Dir. Harris Arts Center, Roland Hayes Museum, Calhoun, GA 412
Mollick, Lois J., Pres. (V), Portage Community Historical Society, Portage, IN 562
Mollitt, Mary, Program Mgr., Children's Museum of Winston-Salem, Winston-Salem, NC 1273
Mollman, T. Lea, Registrar, The Arms Family Museum of Local History, Youngstown, OH 1353
Molloy, James, Cur., Old Orchard Beach Historical Society, Old Orchard Beach, ME 705
Molloy, Dr. Peter M., Exec. Dir., Hall of Flame Museum of Firefighting, Phoenix, AZ 50
Molloy Slack, Joan, Dir. & Owner, Riverrun Center for the Arts, McNaughton, WI 1831
Molnar, August J., Pres. & Acting Dir., American Hungarian Foundation/Museum of the American Hungarian Foundation, New Brunswick, NJ 1051
Molnar, Cindy Lou, Conservator, National Portrait Gallery, Washington, DC 326
Moloney, Jim, Pres. (V), Corpus Christi Museum of Science and History, Corpus Christi, TX 1594
Moloney, Kate, Exec. Asst. & Coord. Membership, Pensacola Museum of Art, Pensacola, FL 378
Molter, Ted, Mktg. Dir., San Diego Zoo, San Diego, CA 184
Molter, Ted, Dir. Mktg., San Diego Zoo's Wild Animal Park, Escondido, CA 112
Molzberger, Deborah, Museum Shop Mgr., Cincinnati Art Museum, Cincinnati, OH 1304
Moman, Orthello, Head Librarian, Tougaloo College, Tougaloo, MS 917
Momberger, Lynn, Dir. Devel., Discovery Center Museum, Rockford, IL 516
Momsen, Joan, Pres. (V) & Devel., Schmidt House Museum & Research Library, Grants Pass, OR 1391
Monacelli, Bob, Pres., Van Riper-Hopper House Museum and Mead-Van Duyne House Museum, Wayne, NJ 1066
Monahan, Dr. Kathleen, Dir., Tarpon Springs Cultural Center, Tarpon Springs, FL 394
Monahan, Dr. Kathleen, Dir., Tarpon Springs Heritage Museum, Tarpon Springs, FL 394
Monahan, Kitty, Docent Coord., New Almaden Quicksilver Mining Museum, San Jose, CA 195
Monck, Margherita, Business Mgr., Staten Island Children's Museum, Staten Island, NY 1216
Monck, Maureen, Pres., Oyster Bay Historical Society, Oyster Bay, NY 1192
Moncrief, Mrs. Charles, Co-Chm., Fort Worth Zoological Association, Inc., Fort Worth, TX 1610
Moncrief, Nancy D., Ph.D., Cur. Mammalogy, Virginia Museum of Natural History, Martinsville, VA 1724
Monday, Tanis, Asst. Dir., Putnam County Museum, Greencastle, IN 544
Mondi, Annelies, Deputy Dir., Georgia Museum of Art, University of Georgia, Athens, GA 400
Monds, Kathryn M., Exec. Dir., Clallam County Historical Society, Port Angeles, WA 1775
Monenerkit, Marcus, Assoc. Registrar, Heard Museum, Phoenix, AZ 50
Money, Johanna, Pres. (V), Fernwood Botanical Garden & Nature Preserve, Niles, MI 858
Money, Ted, Vice Pres., Holmes County Historical Society, Millersburg, OH 1333
Moneyhun, Cheryl, Dir. Collections, Longyear Museum, Chestnut Hill, MA 770
Mong, S. Alice, Exec. Dir., Museum of Chinese in the Americas, New York, NY 1175
Monger, Janice, Museum Shop Mgr., The Brooklyn Historical Society, Brooklyn, NY 1110
Mongo, Jonella, Friends Contact, Children's Museum/Detroit Public Schools, Detroit, MI 833
Monjar, A., Paid Staff, Downieville Museum, Downieville, CA 109
Monje, Scott, Pres., The Historical Society, serving Sleepy Hollow and Tarrytown, Tarrytown, NY 1220
Monk, Elsie, Membership & Business Mgr. Special Events, Madison-Morgan Cultural Center, Madison, GA 426
Monk, Robert, Dir. Facilities & Security, Peabody Essex Museum, Salem, MA 804
Monkhouse, Christopher P., Chm. European Decorative Arts, The Art Institute of Chicago, Chicago, IL 476
Monnette, Lyn, Museum Shop Mgr., Palm Beach Zoo, West Palm Beach, FL 397
Monroe, Alexandra, Sr. Cur. Asian Art, Solomon R. Guggenheim Museum, New York, NY 1181
Monroe, Arthur, Registrar Art, Oakland Museum of California, Oakland, CA 155
Monroe, Beth, Mgr. Public Rels., Lewis Ginter Botanical Garden, Richmond, VA 1738
Monroe, Dan L., Exec. Dir. & C.E.O., Peabody Essex Museum, Salem, MA 804
Monroe, Eleanor, Treas., Oswego Historical Museum, Inc., Oswego, KS 630
Monroe, Martha, Cur., Charles Allis Art Museum, Milwaukee, WI 1833
Monroe, Martha, Cur., Villa Terrace Decorative Arts Museum, Milwaukee, WI 1836
Monroe, Mary, Bd. Pres., Baranov Museum, Kodiak, AK 33
Monroe, Michael, Dir. Curatorial Affairs, Bellevue Arts Museum, Bellevue, WA 1758
Monroe, Murray, Jr., Pres. (V), Betts House Research Center, Cincinnati, OH 1303
Monroe, Dr. Sam, Pres. (V), Museum of the Gulf Coast, Port Arthur, TX 1639
Monroe, Virginia, Chief Docent, The Ashby-Hodge Gallery of American Art, Central Methodist University, Fayette, MO 926
Monsberger, Audrey, Museum Shop Mgr. USS Constellation Museum & Baltimore Maritime Museum, Baltimore, MD 727
Monson, Gene, Treas., Grand Forks County Historical Society, Grand Forks, ND 1283
Monson, Todd, Lead Gardener, Des Moines Botanical Center, Des Moines, IA 583
Montague, Amy, Dir., Visual Arts Center and Mildred Morse Allen Wildlife Sanctuary, Canton, MA 769
Montano, Luz, Tour Coord., New York Transit Museum, Brooklyn Heights, NY 1113
Montanti, Deborah, Museum Dir., Jonesborough-Washington County History Museum, Jonesborough, TN 1556
Montcalmo, Anthony, Pres. (V), Asian Arts & Culture Center, Towson University, Towson, MD 748
Montegomery, Don, C.E.O. & Dir., Virgin Valley Heritage Museum, Mesquite, NV 1008
Monteiro, Antonia, Cur. Entomology, Peabody Museum of Natural History, New Haven, CT 286
Monteleone, Sue Ann, Registrar, Nevada State Museum, Carson City, NV 1001
Montes, Peggy A., Pres., Bronzeville Children's Museum, Chicago, IL 477
Montesano, Frank, Exec. Dir. USS Lexington Museum on the Bay, Corpus Christi, TX 1595
Montez, Roqua, Mktg. & Public Rels., The Tech Museum, San Jose, CA 196
Montfort, Dr. Steven, Acting Dir. & Assoc. Dir. Conservation and Science, National Zoological Park, Smithsonian Institution, Washington, DC 327
Montgomery, Annette, Asst. Dir., African Art Gallery, Norfolk, VA 1729
Montgomery, Betty, Treas., Rittman Historical Society, Rittman, OH 1341
Montgomery, Charlotte A., CPA, Dir. Resource Allocation, C.F.O. & Human Resources Dir., Illinois State Museum, Springfield, IL 521
Montgomery, David, Librarian, The History Place, Morehead City, NC 1258
Montgomery, Denise, Dir. Communications, Museum of Contemporary Art San Diego, La Jolla, CA 127
Montgomery, Denise, Dir. Communications, Museum of Contemporary Art San Diego - Downtown, San Diego, CA 181
Montgomery, Erick D., Exec. Dir., Boyhood Home of President Woodrow Wilson, Augusta, GA 410
Montgomery, Florence, Pres. (V), Bromfield Art Gallery, Boston, MA 759

M–*Continued*

M–*Continued*

M–*Continued*

M–Continued

M–*Continued*

N

N–Continued

N–*Continued*

N–Continued

N–*Continued*

O

O–Continued

Odim, Onuoha, Bd. Co-Chm. (V), The Museum for African Art, Long Island City, NY 1154
Odle, Wesley, Dir., Mammoth Cave Wax Museum, Cave City, KY 643
Odom, Don, Maintenance Supvr., Thomas E. McMillan Museum, Brewton, AL 7
Odom, Donna, Interpretation Coord., Kalamazoo Valley Museum, Kalamazoo, MI 848
Odom, George, Pres., Center for Visual Artists - Greensboro, Greensboro, NC ..1248
O'Donnell, Eleanor, Treas., Nobleboro Historical Society, Nobleboro, ME 704
O'Donnell, Janice, Exec. Dir., Providence Children's Museum, Providence, RI 1495
O'Donnell, John, Dir., Old Prison Museums, Deer Lodge, MT 961
O'Donnell, John, Dir., Powell County Museum, Deer Lodge, MT 961
O'Donnell, Rev. John, O.S.B., Dir., Ave Maria Grotto, Cullman, AL 8
O'Donnell, Kate, Asst. Cur. Education, North Texas History Center, McKinney, TX 1632
O'Donnell, Sean, Chm. (V) & Public Rels., Zoo Montana, Billings, MT 957
O'Donnell, Tim, C.E.O. & City Mgr., City of Brea Art Gallery, Brea, CA 96
O'Dougherty, Peter, Chief Maintenance, Statue of Liberty National Monument & Ellis Island Immigration Museum, New York, NY 1182
Odum, Andy, Cur. Herpetology, The Toledo Zoo, Toledo, OH 1346
Oechler, Kathy, Docent Chm. (V), Princeton University Art Museum, Princeton, NJ 1058
Oedekoven, Diana, Museum Shop Mgr., Sheridan County Museum, Sheridan, WY 1865
Oehlschlaeger, Clay, Membership Coord., Dallas Heritage Village at Old City Park, Dallas, TX 1597
Oehlschlaeger-Garvey, Barbara, Cur. History, Early American Museum, Mahomet, IL 505
Oehring, Joanne, Pres. (V) & Museum Shop Mgr., Pioneer Museum & The Big Stampede, Fairbanks, AK 30
Oelkers, Karl, Facilities Mgr., New Orleans Museum of Art, New Orleans, LA 683
Oerichbauer, Edgar S., C.E.O., Koochiching County Historical Museum, International Falls, MN 881
Oesch, Eric, Dir. Communications, Red Earth Museum, Oklahoma City, OK 1373
Oestreich, JoBeth, Treas., New Braunfels Conservation Society, New Braunfels, TX 1635
Oestreicher, Tom, Pres. (V), Sycamore Historical Society & Museum, Sycamore, IL 524
Oettinger, Dr. Marion, Jr., Dir. & Cur. Latin American Art, San Antonio Museum of Art, San Antonio, TX 1645
Ofe, Don, Site Supvr., Nebraska State Historical Society's Neligh Mill State Historic Site, Neligh, NE 993
Offenbach, Jane, Devel., Nasher Sculpture Center, Dallas, TX 1600
Offensend, David, Sr. Vice Pres. & Administrative Officer, The New York Public Library, Astor, Lenox and Tilden Foundations, New York, NY 1178
Offutt, Cathy, Chm. (V) & Coord., Vaile Mansion-Dewitt Museum, Independence, MO 931
Ofiesh, Lucy, Mktg. Mgr., Children's Museum of the Arts, New York, NY 1166
Oftelie, Jessica, Librarian, Minnesota Discovery Center, Chisholm, MN 872
Oganich, Tony, Treas., Houghton County Historical Museum Society, Lake Linden, MI 848
Ogburn, Peggy, Pres., Kershaw County Historical Society, Camden, SC 1502
Ogden, Dale, Chief Cur. Cultural History, Indiana State Museum, Indianapolis, IN 549
Ogden, Elizabeth, Museum Shop Mgr., Historical Society of Ocean Grove, New Jersey, Ocean Grove, NJ 1054
Ogden, Jacqueline J., Ph.D., Vice Pres., Disney's Animal Kingdom Theme Park, Bay Lake, FL 334
Ogden, O.J., Museum Shop Mgr., The Museum of Bus Transportation, Inc., Hershey, PA 1433
Ogden, Sharon, Sec., Grand Village of the Natchez Indians, Natchez, MS 913
Ogger, Judy, Museum Shop Mgr., Ashland, The Henry Clay Estate, Lexington, KY 651
Ogilvie, Sarah, Dir. NIHE, United States Holocaust Memorial Museum, Washington, DC 332
Ogle, Harlan, Dir. & Cur., William Crenshaw Kennedy, Jr. Memorial Museum, Monticello, KY 659
Ogle, Susan, Dir., Drum Barracks Civil War Museum, Wilmington, CA 225
Oglesbee, Brent, Dept. Head, Western Kentucky University Gallery, Bowling Green, KY 643
Oglesbee, Ruth, Recording Sec., Putnam County Historical Society Museum, Kalida, OH 1325
Oglesby, Bill, Pres. (V), West of the Pecos Museum, Pecos, TX 1638
Oglesby, Mary, Dir. Education & Outreach, Thomasville Cultural Center, Inc., Thomasville, GA 437
O'Gorman, Dr. Jodie, Asst. Cur. Great Lakes Archaeology, The Michigan State University Museum, East Lansing, MI 838
O'Gorman, Tim, Dir., The United States Army Quartermaster Museum, Fort Lee, VA 1711
O'Grady, Caitlin, Conservator, Virginia Department of Historic Resources, Richmond, VA 1741
O'Grady, Mary, Registrar, Sun Prairie Historical Library & Museum, Sun Prairie, WI 1847
O'Grady, Tom, Pres. (V), Athens County Historical Society and Museum, Athens, OH 1294
O'Grody, Dr. Jeannine, Chief Cur. & Cur. European Art, Birmingham Museum of Art, Birmingham, AL 5
Ogurcak, Janice L., Dir., Peter J. McGovern Little League Museum, South Williamsport, PA 1475
Oguss, Valerie R., Dir. Education, Kidspace Children's Museum, Pasadena, CA 162
O'Hanian, Hunter, Pres., Anderson Ranch Arts Center & Museum, Snowmass Village, CO 263
O'Hanley, Roderick, Pres., Newport Art Museum & Art Association, Newport, RI 1491
O'Hara, Ann Marie, Museum Asst., The Lackawanna Historical Society at the Catlin House, Scranton, PA 1472
O'Hara, Bruce, Assoc. Professor Art, Tougaloo College, Tougaloo, MS 917
O'Hara, Catherine, Assoc. Cur. Public Programs & Publications, Taft Museum of Art, Cincinnati, OH 1306
O'Hara, Lois, Pres. (V), Northport Historical Society, Northport, NY 1187
O'Hara, Michael, Chm. (V), Museum of Contemporary Science, Trenton, NJ 1064
O'Hara, Randy, Head Security, Brigham Young University Museum of Art, Provo, UT 1667
O'Hara, Susan, Chm., Humboldt Redwoods State Park Visitor Center, Weott, CA 223
O'Hara, Virginia H., Cur. Collections, Brandywine River Museum, Chadds Ford, PA 1417
O'Hare, Mary Kate, Asst. Cur. American Art, The Newark Museum, Newark, NJ 1053
O'Harrow, Dr. Sean, Exec. Dir., Figge Art Museum, Davenport, IA 581
O'Hear, John, Cur. Artifacts, Cobb Institute of Archaeology, Mississippi State University, MS 913
O'Hearn, Lisa, Bookkeeper, Haverhill Historical Society, Haverhill, MA 781
O'Herron, Sean, Supvr., Longstreet Farm, Holmdel, NJ 1042
Ohles, Fred, Pres., Elder Art Gallery, Nebraska Wesleyan University, Lincoln, NE 988
Ohlhorst, Sharon, Dir., Museum of Natural Science, Ogden, UT 1665
Ohlin, Charlie, Devel., National Packard Museum, Warren, OH 1348
Ohlschwager, Brenda, Exec. Dir., Rocky Mountain Quilt Museum, Golden, CO 249
Ohlsen, Stephanie, Discovery Days Coord., Longmont Museum, Longmont, CO 257
Ohnesorgen, Maggie, Museum Shop Mgr., Museum of Contemporary Native Arts, Santa Fe, NM 1088
O'Hore, Richard, Chm. (V), 82nd Airborne Division War Memorial Museum, Fort Bragg, NC 1246
Ohrenstein, Manfred, Vice Chm. (V), Museum of Jewish Heritage-A Living Memorial to the Holocaust, New York, NY 1175
Oic, Jacki, Dir., Daniels County Museum and Pioneer Town, Scobey, MT 971
Ojard, Bruce, Studio Mgr., Duluth Art Institute, Duluth, MN 874
Oka, Sara, Mgr. Textiles, Honolulu Academy of Arts, Honolulu, HI 445
Okada, Wataru, Registrar, George Eastman House/International Museum of Photography and Film, Rochester, NY 1201
Okamoto, Charissa, Sec., Ruth Chandler Williamson Gallery, Scripps College, Claremont, CA 103
Okamura, Hideyo, Chief Preparator & Exhibition Designer, Williams College Museum of Art, Williamstown, MA 817
Okamura, Ivy, Mgr. Museum Events, The J. Paul Getty Museum, Los Angeles, CA 137
Okaya, Michiko, Dir. Lafayette Art Galleries, Lafayette College Art Galleries, Williams Center for the Arts, Easton, PA 1421
Okazaki, Nicole, Chm. (V), Ogden Nature Center, Ogden, UT 1665
O'Keefe, Anne, Museum Shop Mgr., Spellman Museum of Stamps and Postal History, Weston, MA 816
O'Keefe, Barbara, Exec. Dir., Coral Springs Museum of Art, Coral Springs, FL 340
O'Keefe, Dean, Sr. Dir. Mktg., Naismith Memorial Basketball Hall of Fame, Springfield, MA 807
O'Keefe, Kelly, Educator, The Georgia Sea Turtle Center, Jekyll Island, GA 421

O–*Continued*

Olson, Karen, Museum Shop Mgr., Franklin G. Burroughs-Simeon B. Chapin Art Museum, Myrtle Beach, SC....1519
Olson, Kathleen, Exec. Dir. Zoo Society, Point Defiance Zoo & Aquarium, Tacoma, WA....1789
Olson, Kathryne, Dir., Lost City Museum, Overton, NV....1008
Olson, Kathy, Exec. Dir., Owensboro Area Museum of Science & History, Owensboro, KY....660
Olson, Kelly, Dir. Mktg., Jacqueline Casey Hudgens Center for the Arts, Duluth, GA....417
Olson, Kyle, IT Specialist, Blue Star Contemporary Art Center, San Antonio, TX....1643
Olson, Leonard, Head Kaleidoscope Maker, The Kaleidoscope Factory, Pomeroy, IA....598
Olson, Letha, Financial Dir., Miles B. Carpenter Museum, Waverly, VA....1753
Olson, Linda A., Dir., North Dakota Art Gallery Association, Minot, ND....1287
Olson, Link E., Cur. Mammalogy, University of Alaska Museum of the North, Fairbanks, AK....30
Olson, Marilyn, Cur., Peshtigo Fire Museum, Peshtigo, WI....1840
Olson, Michael, Vice Pres. Financial Svcs. & Controller, Missouri Botanical Garden, Saint Louis, MO....949
Olson, Nicky, Dir. & Cur., Dallam-Hartley XIT Museum, Dalhart, TX....1596
Olson, Oliver, Dir., Judith Basin County Museum, Stanford, MT....972
Olson, Peter, Asst. Dir. NIU Art Museum, DeKalb, IL....489
Olson, Richard, C.E.O. & Chm. (V), Washburn Historical Museum & Cultural Center, Inc. aka Washburn Cultural Center, Washburn, WI....1848
Olson, Ruth Ann, Dir., South Bannock County Historical Center, Lava Hot Springs, ID....461
Olson, Sarah, Supt., Home of Franklin D. Roosevelt National Historic Site, Hyde Park, NY....1145
Olson, Sarah, Supt., Vanderbilt Mansion National Historic Site, Hyde Park, NY....1145
Olson, Shawn, Dir., Mt. Kearsarge Indian Museum, Warner, NH....1029
Olson, Sue, Devel. Sec., Brunnier Art Museum, Ames, IA....572
Olson, Sue, Devel. Sec., Christian Petersen Art Museum, Ames, IA....572
Olson, Sue, Devel Sec., Farm House Museum, Ames, IA....573
Olson, Suzanne, C.E.O. & Exec. Dir., Children's Museum & Theatre of Maine, Portland, ME....707
Olson, Thomas H., Pres., New England Maple Museum, Pittsford, VT....1686
Olsson, Susan, Cur., Hinsdale Historical Society, Hinsdale, IL....500
Oltmans, Kay, Dir. CU Heritage Center, Boulder, CO....230
Oltrogge, Sarah, Public Rels., State Historical Museum of Iowa, Des Moines, IA....584
O'Malley, Cynthia, Dir. Retail Sales, The Preservation Society of Newport County/The Newport Mansions, Newport, RI....1492
O'Malley, Jeannette, Exec. Dir., Pasadena Museum of History, Pasadena, CA....163
O'Malley, Kathleen, Pres., Captain John Wilson House, Cohasset, MA....770
O'Malley, Kathleen, Assoc. Registrar, Hood Museum of Art, Hanover, NH....1019
O'Malley, Kathleen, Pres., Maritime Museum - Cohasset Historical Society, Cohasset, MA....770
O'Malley, Kathleen, Pres., Pratt Building - Cohasset Historical Society, Cohasset, MA....771
O'Malley, Sue, Business Mgr., Figge Art Museum, Davenport, IA....581
O'Malley, Teresa, Exec. Asst., Burritt on the Mountain - A Living Museum, Huntsville, AL....14
O'Malley, Thomas, Chm. (V), Fire Museum of Memphis, Memphis, TN....1562
O'Malley, Tom, Head Ceramics Dept., Worcester Center for Crafts, Worcester, MA....819
Oman, Richard G., Cur. Art & Artifacts, Brigham Young's Winter Home, Saint George, UT....1668
Oman, Richard G., Cur. Art & Artifacts, Jacob Hamblin Home, Santa Clara, UT....1673
Oman, Richard G., Senior Cur. Art, Museum of Church History and Art, Salt Lake City, UT....1670
O'Meara, Jim, Pres. Historical Society (V), Fort Crawford Museum, Prairie du Chien, WI....1841
O'Meara, John, C.E.O., Slate Run Living Historical Farm, Metro Parks, Canal Winchester, OH....1300
O'Meara, Sean, Volunteer Coord., Klondike Gold Rush National Historical Park, Seattle, WA....1781
Omoqbai, Meme, Deputy Dir. Finance & Administration, The Newark Museum, Newark, NJ....1053
Oncay, Carla, Gen. Cur., Alexandria Zoological Park, Alexandria, LA....665
Ondercho, Judith, Chm. (V), Ford County Historical Society, Paxton, IL....511
Ondish, Andrea, Cur. Education, Marshall M. Fredericks Sculpture Museum, University Center, MI....866
O'Neal, Michael, Protection Svc. Dir., Des Moines Art Center, Des Moines, IA....583
O'Neal, Susan, Dir. Devel., Thomasville Cultural Center, Inc., Thomasville, GA....437
O'Neil, Brian, Dir. Horticulture, Norfolk Botanical Garden, Norfolk, VA....1731
O'Neil, Brianne, Administrative Asst., Fuller Craft Museum, Brockton, MA....765
O'Neil, Christy, Museum Shop Mgr., Monterey History and Art Association, Monterey, CA....149
O'Neil, Daniel, Exec. Dir., Ethan Allen Homestead Museum & Historic Site, Burlington, VT....1678
O'Neil, Francis, Archivist, Maryland Historical Society, Baltimore, MD....724
O'Neil, Kelly, Mgr., Escondido Children's Museum, Escondido, CA....111
O'Neill, Audrey, Museum Shop Mgr., West Pasco Historical Society Museum and Library, New Port Richey, FL....370
O'Neill, Betty, Museum Shop Mgr., The Friends of Peace Church, Camp Hill, PA....1415
O'Neill, Brian, Gen. Supt., Alcatraz Island, San Francisco, CA....186
O'Neill, Brian, Supt., Fort Point National Historic Site, San Francisco, CA....189
O'Neill, Brian, Supt., Golden Gate National Recreation Area, San Francisco, CA....189
O'Neill, Brian, Supt., Muir Woods National Monument, Mill Valley, CA....146
O'Neill, Carla, Dir., Conoco Museum, Ponca City, OK....1375
O'Neill, Cheryl, Librarian, Art Complex Museum, Duxbury, MA....775
O'Neill, Daniel, Chm. (V), Boston Fire Museum, Boston, MA....758
O'Neill, Deborah, Dir. Education, Mount Vernon Hotel Museum & Garden, New York, NY....1173
O'Neill, Heidi, Registrar, The Eric Carle Museum of Picture Book Art, Amherst, MA....752
O'Neill, Jim, Sec., Santa Maria Valley Historical Museum, Santa Maria, CA....207
O'Neill, John, Cur. Manuscripts & Rare Books, The Hispanic Society of America, New York, NY....1169
O'Neill, John J., Pres., Baltimore Streetcar Museum, Inc., Baltimore, MD....720
O'Neill, John P., Editor-in-Chief & Gen. Mgr. Publications, The Metropolitan Museum of Art, New York, NY....1172
O'Neill, Karen, Museum Mgr., Mingei International Museum, Escondido, CA....111
O'Neill, Kevin, Dir., Chatillon-DeMenil Mansion, Saint Louis, MO....946
O'Neill, Meaghan, Co Dir. & Park Naturalist, El Dorado Nature Center, Long Beach, CA....131
O'Neill, Richard J., Exec. Dir., Liberty Hall Museum at Kean University, Union, NJ....1066
O'Neill, Sara, Chm., Kearney Area Children's Museum, Kearney, NE....986
O'Neill, Stephen C., Assoc. Dir. & Cur., Pilgrim Hall Museum, Plymouth, MA....800
O'Neil-Teer, Kelly, Acting Dir., Fort Ticonderoga, Ticonderoga, NY....1221
Onkey, Lauren, Vice Pres. Education & Public Programs, The Rock and Roll Hall of Fame and Museum, Cleveland, OH....1310
Onnfer, Judy, Coord. Education, Hudson Highlands Nature Museum, Cornwall-on-Hudson, NY....1125
Onysko, Mike, Asst. Vice Pres. Mktg., Intrepid Sea, Air & Space Museum, New York, NY....1171
Oosterom, Lisa, Comptroller, Nassau County Museum of Art, Roslyn Harbor, NY....1204
Ooton, Susan, Dir., Royal Gorge Regional Museum & History Center, Canon City, CO....232
O'Pecko, Paul J., Librarian, Mystic Seaport - The Museum of America and the Sea, Mystic, CT....284
Ophime, Jeffery, Exec. Dir., Colquitt County Arts Center, Moultrie, GA....428
Opicka, Allison, Administrative & Mktg. Mgr., U.S National Arboretum, Washington, DC....331
Opitz, Cindy, Mgr. Collections, University of Iowa Museum of Natural History, Iowa City, IA....590
Opp, Charles W., Chm. (V), North Star Museum of Boy Scouting and Girl Scouting, North Saint Paul, MN....888
Opp, Edmund, Dir., Cur. & Museum Shop Mgr., Eureka Pioneer Museum of McPherson County, Inc., Eureka, SD....1530
Opp, Hulda, Chm. (V), Asst. Dir. & Cur., Eureka Pioneer Museum of McPherson County, Inc., Eureka, SD....1530
Oppenheim, Phyllis, Collections Mgr., Herrett Center for Arts & Science, Faulkner Planetarium and Centennial Observatory, Twin Falls, ID....467
Oppenheimer, Esther, Pres. Bd. of Trustees, Boise Art Museum, Boise, ID....455
Oppenhimer, Ann, Pres. (V), Folk Art Society of America, Richmond, VA....1737

Oppenhimer, William, Financial Dir., Folk Art Society of America, Richmond, VA 1737
Opphile, Gayle, Museum Shop Mgr. USS Radford National Naval Museum, Newcomerstown, OH 1336
Oppio, Amy, Deputy Dir., Nevada Museum of Art, Reno, NV 1009
Opsina, Adriana, Coord. Education, Art Museum of the Americas, OAS, Washington, DC 315
Oram, Fern, Cur., Mechanicsburg Museum Association, Mechanicsburg, PA 1444
Oram, Dr. Richard W., Librarian, Harry Ransom Center at The University of Texas at Austin, Austin, TX 1582
O'Rangers, Kevin, Dir. Programs, National Liberty Museum, Philadelphia, PA 1458
Orcutt, Jeanne, Dir., California Oil Museum, Santa Paula, CA 208
Ordonel, Maria, Cur., Jewish Museum of Florida, Miami Beach, FL 368
O'Rear, Regina, Gallery Asst., Elder Art Gallery, Nebraska Wesleyan University, Lincoln, NE 988
O'Reilly, Jane, Dir. Human Resources, Museum of Fine Arts, Boston, MA 761
O'Reilly, Margaret M., Cur. Fine Art, New Jersey State Museum, Trenton, NJ 1064
O'Reilly-Lawrence, Priscilla, Exec. Dir., The Historic New Orleans Collection, New Orleans, LA 680
Orescan, Sara, Reservations, Estuarium, Dauphin Island, AL 8
Oresman, Enid, Pres., Bates-Scofield Homestead, The Darien Historical Society, Darien, CT 271
Oresman, Janice, Chm. (V), International Print Center New York (IPCNY), New York, NY 1170
Oresman, Stephen B., Chm. (V), Connecticut Audubon Birdcraft Museum, Fairfield, CT 273
Oresman, Stephen B., Chm. (V), Connecticut Audubon Society, Fairfield, CT 273
Orlandini, Donna, Museum Shop Mgr., Kruse House Museum, West Chicago, IL 527
Orlando, Fran, Exec. Dir., Hicks Art Center Gallery - Bucks County Community College, Newtown, PA 1447
Orleans, Sarah, Exec. Dir., Portland Children's Museum, Portland, OR 1400
Orloff, Doug, Vice Pres. Mktg., Retail & Sales, Oregon Museum of Science and Industry, Portland, OR 1399
Orlyk, Kerry M., Exec. Dir., Schenectady Museum and Suits-Bueche Planetarium, Schenectady, NY 1210
Ormasen, Debbie, Account Clerk, Frederic Remington Art Museum, Ogdensburg, NY 1187
Orme, Joyce, Staff Asst. III, Appleton Museum of Art, Ocala, FL 371
Ormenyi, Steven, Cur. Grounds & Gardens, Heritage Square Museum, Los Angeles, CA 136
Ormsby, Susan, Chm. (V), Nathan Manilow Sculpture Park, Governors State University, University Park, IL 525
Ornay, Gregory, Exhibits Asst. KU Biodiversity Institute - KU Natural History Museum, Lawrence, KS 621
Orosco, Juanishi V., Gallery Coord., La Raza/Galeria Posada, Sacramento, CA 176
O'Rourke, John, State Park Liaison, Humboldt Redwoods State Park Visitor Center, Weott, CA 223
Orozco, Sylvia, C.E.O., Mexic-Arte Museum, Austin, TX 1582
Orr, Charlene, Exec. Dir., Florence Ranch Homestead, Mesquite, TX 1632
Orr, James, Program Assoc., Huddleston Farmhouse Inn Museum, Cambridge City, IN 535
Orr, Janice, Coord., Museum of the Middle Appalachians, Saltville, VA 1745
Orr, John, Pres. Bd. Dir. (V), Museum of Ventura County, Ventura, CA 221
Orr, Dr. Lynn Federle, Cur. European Paintings, The Fine Arts Museums of San Francisco, de Young Museum, San Francisco, CA 188
Orr, Dr. Lynn Federle, Cur. European Art, The Fine Arts Museums of San Francisco, Legion of Honor, San Francisco, CA 189
Orr, Mary Beth, Volunteer & Public Program Coord., Kirkland Museum of Fine & Decorative Art, Denver, CO 241
Orr, Peter, Pres. (V), Museum of Art and History at the McPherson Center, Santa Cruz, CA 206
Orr, Sara, Asst. Dir. Mktg. & Devel., Springfield Museums - Connecticut Valley Historical Museum, Springfield, MA 808
Orr, Sara, Asst. Dir. Mktg. & Devel., Springfield Museums - George Walter Vincent Smith Art Museum, Springfield, MA 808
Orr, Sara, Asst. Dir. Mktg. & Devel., Springfield Museums - Michele & Donald D'Amour Museum of Fine Arts, Springfield, MA 808
Orr, Sara, Asst. Dir. Mktg. & Devel., Springfield Museums - Museum of Springfield History, Springfield, MA 808
Orr, Sara, Asst. Dir. Mktg. & Devel., Springfield Museums - Springfield Science Museum, Springfield, MA 808
Orr, Tom, Chm., Clearwater Marine Aquarium, Clearwater, FL 338
Orr-Cahall, Christina, C.E.O. & Dir., Experience Music Project/Science Fiction Museum, Seattle, WA 1780
Ortega, Adela, Dir., Mission Historical Museum, Mission, TX 1634
Ortega, Ernesto, Dir. State Monuments, Fort Selden State Monument, Radium Springs, NM 1085
Ortega, Ernesto, Dir. NM State Monuments, Museum of New Mexico, Santa Fe, NM 1089
Ortega, Jean, Asst. Dir. Operations, Bass Museum of Art, Miami Beach, FL 367
Ortega, Lee, Dir. Mktg. & Public Rels., Bass Museum of Art, Miami Beach, FL 367
Ortega, Lisa, Educator, Museum of History, Anthropology and Art, San Juan, PR 1871
Ortega, M. Therese, Head Human Resources, Seattle Art Museum, Seattle, WA 1783
Ortega, Tina, Vice Pres., Moriarty Historical Society & Museum, Moriarty, NM 1083
Orth, Sally, Dir. Mktg. & Programs, Racine Heritage Museum, Racine, WI 1842
Orthwein, Stephen, C.E.O. & Chm. (V), National Museum of Polo and Hall of Fame, Inc., Lake Worth, FL 361
Ortiz, Gustavo, Theater Mgr., Art and Culture Center of Hollywood, Hollywood, FL 353
Ortiz, Jose, Deputy Dir., Harvard Art Museum, Cambridge, MA 767
Ortiz, Juventino, Supt. Coastal Sector, Hearst Castle, San Simeon, CA 201
Ortiz, Maria, Archivist, Kearney Mansion Museum, Fresno, CA 116
Ortiz, Mary Ellen, Community Programs Coord., Bradbury Science Museum, Los Alamos, NM 1082
Ortiz, Patty, Exec. Dir., Museo de las Americas, Denver, CO 241
Ortiz-Melendez, Lionel, Designer, Museum of History, Anthropology and Art, San Juan, PR 1871
Ortner, Becky, Coord. Group Svcs., Family Museum, Bettendorf, IA 574
Orton, Donald, Pres., Concord Historical Society, Warner Museum, Springville, NY 1214
Orton, Lois, Vice Pres., Cass County Museum & Research Center, Walker, MN 900
Orwoll, Christopher D., C.E.O. & Pres., Kansas Cosmosphere and Space Center, Hutchinson, KS 617
Orzel, Robyn P., Dir. Devel., Vero Beach Museum of Art, Inc., Vero Beach, FL 396
Osada, Louise, Library Volunteer, Dundee Township Historical Society, Inc., Dundee, IL 491
Osberg, Allan, Pres., Nordic Heritage Museum, Seattle, WA 1782
Osborn, Dr. Alan, Cur. Anthropology, University of Nebraska State Museum, Lincoln, NE 991
Osborn, Mark, Cur., Don Laughlin's Classic Car Collection, Laughlin, NV 1007
Osborn, Marti, Education, Pueblo Zoo, Pueblo, CO 261
Osborn, Ruth, Treas., Life on the Ohio River History Museum, Vevay, IN 569
Osborn, Teresa, Interim Dir., Jacqueline Casey Hudgens Center for the Arts, Duluth, GA 417
Osborn, Toby, Public Rels. Mgr., Mktg. & Sales Officer, Turtle Bay Exploration Park, Redding, CA 169
Osborne, Andrew, Visitor Svcs. Mgr., Lake County Discovery Museum, Wauconda, IL 526
Osborne, Christie, Digital Projects, Mountain Heritage Center, Cullowhee, NC 1241
Osborne, Dawn, Museum Shop Mgr. & Office Mgr., Sharon Audubon Center, Sharon, CT 293
Osborne, Denver J., Vice Pres., Wise County Historical Society, Wise, VA 1756
Osborne, Doug, Vice Pres., Brownella Cottage, Galion, OH 1321
Osborne, Ethel Lee, Sec., Winterset Art Center, Winterset, IA 603
Osborne, Frances, Pres., New Castle Historical Society - Horace Greeley House, Chappaqua, NY 1120
Osborne, Jen, Asst. Dir., Pratt Manhattan Gallery, New York, NY 1179
Osborne, Jen, Asst. Dir., The Rubelle & Norman Schafler Gallery, Brooklyn, NY 1112
Osborne, Jim R., Dir., Indiana Military Museum Inc., Vincennes, IN 569
Osborne, Linda, Pres. (V), Alden House Historic Site, Duxbury, MA 775
Osborne, Peter, III, Exec. Dir., Minisink Valley Historical Society, Port Jervis, NY 1196
Osborne, Veronica, Museum Shop Mgr., Pope John Paul II Cultural Center, Washington, DC 328
Osburn, Karen D., Archivist, Geneva History Museum, Geneva, NY 1137
O'Scannlain, Brendan, Pres. Bd., Portland Children's Museum, Portland, OR 1400
Osceola, Louise, Museum Shop Mgr., Ah-Tah-Thi-Ki Museum, Big Cypress Seminole Indian Reservation, FL 334

O–*Continued*

Osceola, Louise, Museum Shop Mgr., Ah-Tah-Thi-Ki Museum at Okalee, Hollywood, FL....353
Osceola, Tina M., Exec. Dir., Ah-Tah-Thi-Ki Museum, Big Cypress Seminole Indian Reservation, FL....334
Osceola, Tina M., Exec. Dir., Ah-Tah-Thi-Ki Museum at Okalee, Hollywood, FL....353
Osgood, Bill, Pres. (V), Siloam Springs Museum, Siloam Springs, AR....84
Osgood, Sarah, Business Mgr., The Children's Museum of New Hampshire, Dover, NH....1016
O'Shaughnessy, Margaret, Admin., Fraunces Tavern Museum, New York, NY....1168
O'Shaughnessy, William, Park Mgr., Historic Walnford, Allentown, NJ....1031
O'Shea, Eileen, Acquisitions, Miller-Cory House Museum, Westfield, NJ....1067
O'Shea, John, Cur. Great Lakes Archaeology, University of Michigan Museum of Anthropology, Ann Arbor, MI....823
O'Shea, Maura, Deputy Dir. & Cur. Education, New Britain Museum of American Art, Inc., New Britain, CT....284
Oshel, Laurie, Asst. Dir., Finney County Kansas Historical Society, Inc., Garden City, KS....613
Oshiro, Richard, 3rd Vice Pres., Hawaii's Plantation Village, Waipahu, HI....454
Osier, Cristine, Dir. Devel., Marquette County History Museum, Marquette, MI....853
Oskam, Alice, Pres., Historic Schaefferstown, Inc., Schaefferstown, PA....1471
Osler, John, Dir., Chase County Historical Museum, Champion, NE....979
Osman, Dave, Dir. Finance & I.T., Virginia Living Museum, Newport News, VA....1729
Osman, Don, Pres. (V), Steppingstone Museum, Havre de Grace, MD....739
Osment, Tim, Exec. Dir., Zachary-Tolbert House, Cashiers, NC....1236
Osmer, Patty, Museum Shop Mgr., Danbury Railway Museum, Danbury, CT....270
Osmond, Lynn, Pres. & C.E.O., Chicago Architecture Foundation, Chicago, IL....477
Osmundsen, David, Pres. (V), Jim Gatchell Memorial Museum, Buffalo, WY....1853
Osmundson, Margaret, Historian, Greenwood County Historical Society & Museum, Eureka, KS....612
Osona, Rafael, Vice Pres., Nantucket Lightship Basket Museum, Nantucket, MA....792
Ossman, Laurie, Exec. Dir., Frank Lloyd Wright's Pope-Leighey House, Alexandria, VA....1697
Ossman, Dr. Laurie, Exec. Dir., Woodlawn, Alexandria, VA....1699
Ostapow, Peter Paul, Pres. (V), Three Village Historical Society, Setauket, NY....1212
Ostenso, Roy S., Pres. (V), Dunn County Historical Society, Menomonie, WI....1832
Oster, Barbara, Museum Shop & Business Office, Suffolk County Vanderbilt Museum, Centerport, NY....1120
Osterbuhr, Connie, Dir., Franklin County Museum, Franklin, NE....982
Ostfeld, Keith, Dir. Exhibits Devel., The Children's Museum of Houston, Houston, TX....1619
Ostgarden, Alison, Cur., Cass County Historical Society at Bonanzaville, West Fargo, ND....1291
Ostlund, Ralph, Dir., Lars Noak Blacksmith Shop, Larsson/Ostlund Log Home & One-Room Capitol School, New Sweden, ME....704
Ostman, Rae, Dir. Education, Sciencenter, Ithaca, NY....1147
Ostrand, Don, Dir., Museum of Communications, Seattle, WA....1781
Ostrem, Delmer, Vice Pres., Geographical Center Historical Museum, Rugby, ND....1289
Ostrenko, Wit, Pres., Museum of Science and Industry, Tampa, FL....392
Ostrowski, Richard, Park Mgr., Whitefish Dunes State Park, Sturgeon Bay, WI....1847
Ostwald, Don, Pres., Fort Morgan Museum, Fort Morgan, CO....246
Osugi, Frances, Asst. to Dir., Joslyn Art Museum, Omaha, NE....995
Oswald, April, Museum Educator, Munson-Williams-Proctor Arts Institute Museum of Art, Utica, NY....1222
Oswald, Bonnie, Business Mgr., Studebaker National Museum, Inc., South Bend, IN....566
Oswald, Charles, Dir. & Sec., Kit Carson Historical Society, Kit Carson, CO....253
Otake, Akiki, Consultant Asian Design & History, The Great American Doll House Museum, Danville, KY....645
Otocka, Mary, Pres. (V), New Canaan Nature Center, New Canaan, CT....285
O'Toole, Brian, Nature Shop Mgr., Audubon Greenwich, Greenwich, CT....275
O'Toole, Judith H., Dir. & C.E.O., Westmoreland Museum of American Art, Greensburg, PA....1429
O'Toole, Marjory, Mng. Dir., Little Compton Historical Society, Little Compton, RI....1488
Otsuji, Dennis, Pres., Japanese Friendship Garden Society of San Diego, San Diego, CA....180
Otsuka, Ronald, Cur. Asian, Denver Art Museum, Denver, CO....238
Ott, Edwina, Regent (V), Beauchamp Newman Museum, Elizabeth, WV....1798
Ott, Lili, Exec. Dir., Concord Art Association, Concord, MA....771
Ott, Margaret, Dir. & Museum Shop Mgr., Old Jail Museum, Albion, IN....530
Ott, Pete, Registrar, Flint Institute of Arts, Flint, MI....840
Ott, Steve, Museum Shop Mgr., Banana Factory, Bethlehem, PA....1411
Ott, Tom, Pres., Smithsonian Institution, Washington, DC....329
Ott, Wendell, Museum Svcs. Mgr., Temecula Valley Museum, Temecula, CA....216
Ottaviano, Bev, School Scout Coord., Arlington Heights Historical Museum, Arlington Heights, IL....468
Ottaway, Terri, Cur., Gemological Institute of America Museum, Carlsbad, CA....98
Otte, Stacey A., Exec. Dir., Catalina Island Museum Society, Inc., Avalon, CA....89
Otten, Rebecca, Museum Shop Mgr., The Glebe House Museum and Gertrude Jekyll Garden, Woodbury, CT....303
Otterbein, Claire, Dir., Julia A. Purnell Museum, Snow Hill, MD....747
Ottinger, Matthew, Facilities Mgr., Old State House-The Bostonian Society, Boston, MA....763
Ottmann, Klaus, Robert Lehman Cur., The Parrish Art Museum, Southampton, NY....1213
Otto, Don, Pres., Science Museum Oklahoma, Oklahoma City, OK....1373
Otto, John, Pres. (V), Cannon Falls Area Historical Museum, Cannon Falls, MN....871
Otto, Rick, Supt. Ashfall Fossil Beds State Historical Park, University of Nebraska State Museum, Lincoln, NE....991
Otto-Diniz, Sara, Cur. Academic Initiatives, University Art Museum, The University of New Mexico, Albuquerque, NM....1074
Otto-Miller, Jackie, Dir., Anita S. Wooten Gallery at Valencia Community College East Campus, Orlando, FL....373
Ottoson, Jack, Pres., Morrison's Heritage Museum, Morrison, IL....507
Otts, Dylan, Site Mgr., Stone Quarry Hill Art Park, Inc., Cazenovia, NY....1119
Ouellette, Stefanie, Marine Field Programs Coord., The Georgia Sea Turtle Center, Jekyll Island, GA....421
Ouimette, Nicole, Museum Shop, St. Photios Greek Orthodox National Shrine, Saint Augustine, FL....382
Oulianov, Konstantine, Museum Shop Mgr., Wings Over Miami Air Museum, Inc., Miami, FL....367
Outlaw, Billy, Finance & Operations Mgr., Alexandria Museum of Art, Alexandria, LA....665
Outten, Leslie, Vice Pres., The Palette & Chisel, Chicago, IL....485
Overby, Charles, C.E.O., Newseum, Washington, DC....327
Overby, Connie, Dir., Humboldt County Historical Association Museum, Dakota City, IA....581
Overby, Eddie, Dir. Operations & Maintenance, The Texas Zoo, Victoria, TX....1653
Overland, Christian W., Vice Pres. Museums & Collections, The Henry Ford, Dearborn, MI....832
Overlie, Jill, Cur. Education, Longmont Museum, Longmont, CO....257
Overton, Irvin, Pres. (V), Chattanooga African Museum/Bessie Smith Hall, Chattanooga, TN....1547
Overton, Robert, Assoc. Dir., Historic Pensacola Village, Pensacola, FL....377
Overton, Robert, Assoc. Dir., Pensacola Historical Society, Pensacola, FL....378
Overton, Robert, Assoc. Dir., T.T. Wentworth, Jr. Florida State Museum, Pensacola, FL....378
Overton, Robert, Assoc. Dir., West Florida Historic Preservation, Inc., Pensacola, FL....379
Owczarski, Marian, Dir. & Artist-in-Residence, Galeria, Orchard Lake, MI....859
Owen, Conni, Chm. (V), Heritage Hall Museum, Dubois, ID....459
Owen, Donovan, Business Mgr., Flagler Museum, Palm Beach, FL....375
Owen, Janet, Asst. Programs Coord. MAK Center for Art and Architecture at the Schindler House, West Hollywood, CA....223
Owen, Nicholas, Village Admin., Chalet of the Golden Fleece, New Glarus, WI....1838
Owen, Pamela, Sr. Paleontology Educator, Texas Natural Science Center, Austin, TX....1584
Owen, Paula, Dir., Southwest School of Art & Craft, San Antonio, TX....1646
Owen, Pittman, Pres., Heart of Dixie Railroad Museum, Calera, AL....7
Owen, Robert, Facility Mgr., Tyler Museum of Art, Tyler, TX....1652
Owen, Sammye, Chm. (V), The Arts & Science Center for Southeast Arkansas, Pine Bluff, AR....81

P

P–*Continued*

Papageorge, Kent, Pres. (V), National Ceramic Museum and Heritage Center, Roseville, OH 1341

Papai, Margaret, Librarian, American Hungarian Foundation/Museum of the American Hungarian Foundation, New Brunswick, NJ 1051

Papanikolas, Theresa, Cur. European & American Art, Honolulu Academy of Arts, Honolulu, HI 445

Papasan, Larry, Pres. (V), Biblical Resource Center & Museum, Collierville, TN 1550

Papavero, Emily, Store Contact UCR/California Museum of Photography, Riverside, CA 173

Papayanopulos, Rose Marie, Garden Librarian, Coe Hall, Oyster Bay, NY 1192

Papazian, Aline, Asst. Dir., Passaic County Community College, Paterson, NJ 1056

Pape, Linda, Gift Shop Mgr., Abilene Zoological Gardens, Abilene, TX 1576

Pape, Mildred, Museum Shop Mgr., Museum of the Mountain Man, Pinedale, WY 1864

Papelbon, John, Deputy Dir., Ted Williams Museum and Hitters Hall of Fame, Saint Petersburg, FL 385

Papenfuse, Edward C., State Archivist, Maryland State Archives, Annapolis, MD 718

Papierniak, Anna, Coord. Special Events, Evergreen Museum & Library, Johns Hopkins University Museums, Baltimore, MD 722

Papin, Mary Jo, Chm., LaGrange Plantation, Cambridge, MD 729

Papini, Rita, Museum Asst., Toy & Miniature Museum of Kansas City, Kansas City, MO 935

Papola, Mary Galanti, Pres., Mario Lanza Institute/Museum, Philadelphia, PA 1456

Pappas, Emilia, Asst. for Leadership Support, Smart Museum of Art, Chicago, IL 486

Pappathan, Jessica, Asst. Cur., Alva deMars Megan Chapel Art Center, Manchester, NH 1022

Papson, Don, Interim Dir., The Hershey Story, Hershey, PA 1433

Paquelet, Judy, Museum Shop Mgr., The Massillon Museum, Massillon, OH 1331

Paquet, Kristen, Dir., Heritage Hill State Historical Park, Green Bay, WI 1821

Paquette, Andrian, Cur., Slater Mill, Pawtucket, RI 1492

Paquette, Nancy, Visitor Svcs. Specialist, The Belknap Mill Society, Laconia, NH 1021

Paquin, Lester W., Sec., Barre Historical Society, Inc., Barre, MA 756

Parcel, Carole, Sec., Wapello County Historical Museum, Ottumwa, IA 597

Parcells, Kathryn H., Pres. (V), Huron City Museums, Port Austin, MI 861

Parchman, Bryn, C.E.O. & Pres., Port Discover Children's Museum, Baltimore, MD 726

Pardee, Carol, Controller, Cape Cod Children's Museum, Mashpee, MA 789

Pardee, Pattie, Asst. to Exec. Dir., The Museum of Arts and Sciences, Inc. and Center for Florida History, Daytona Beach, FL 342

Pardo, Jorge L., Museum Shop Mgr., Museum of Contemporary Art of Puerto Rico, San Juan, PR 1870

Pardue, Diana, Cur. Collections, Heard Museum, Phoenix, AZ 50

Pardue, Diana, Chief Museum Svcs. Div., Statue of Liberty National Monument & Ellis Island Immigration Museum, New York, NY 1182

Pardue, Scott, Supt., DeSoto National Memorial, Bradenton, FL 336

Pare, George, Exec. Dir., Coggeshall Farm Museum Inc., Bristol, RI 1485

Paredes, Liana, Acting Dir. Collections, Chief Cur. & Sr. Cur. Western European Art, Hillwood Estate, Museum & Gardens, Washington, DC 318

Parelli, Mary, Museum Shop Mgr., Landis Valley Museum, Lancaster, PA ..1439

Parent, Brenda, Administrative Asst., Children's Museum at Holyoke, Inc., Holyoke, MA 782

Parent, Marcel, Education & Volunteerism Mgr., Las Vegas Springs Preserve, Las Vegas, NV 1006

Parent, William, Dir. Facilities Management, Mystic Seaport - The Museum of America and the Sea, Mystic, CT 284

Parente, Kathleen, Museum Clerk, Ocean County Historical Society, Toms River, NJ 1063

Parham, Kathy, Exec. Dir., The Children's Playhouse, Boone, NC 1235

Paridon, Seth, Mgr. Research, The National World War II Museum, New Orleans, LA 682

Parikh, Setul, Pres., Fort Bissell Museum, Phillipsburg, KS 631

Parillo, James D., Dir., Historical Society of Saratoga Springs, Saratoga Springs, NY 1207

Paris, Roger, Exec. Dir., Tall Grass Arts Association, Park Forest, IL 511

Paris, Tiara L., Mgr. Exhibitions, North Carolina Museum of Art, Raleigh, NC ..1263

Parish, Karen, Pres. (V), Museum Admin., & Museum Shop Mgr., Randolph County Heritage Museum, Pocahontas, AR 82

Parish, Preston S., Chm. Bd., Air Zoo, Kalamazoo, MI 847

Parish, Suzanne D., Pres., Air Zoo, Kalamazoo, MI 847

Parizek, Wilma, Exec. Sec., Tama County Historical Museum, Toledo, IA 600

Park, Barley, Interpretive Naturalist, Logoly State Park, McNeil, AR 79

Park Curry, David, Cur. Decorative Arts and American Painting & Sculpture, The Baltimore Museum of Art, Baltimore, MD 720

Park, Donna, Collections Mgr., Arkansas Tech University Museum, Russellville, AR 83

Park, Joann, Museum Shop Mgr., Allen County Museum, Lima, OH 1328

Park, John, Treas., Bay Area Discovery Museum, Sausalito, CA 210

Park Leggett, Barbara, C.E.O. & Dir., Explore & More...A Children's Museum, East Aurora, NY 1127

Park, Lena, Dir. Fund Devel., Wing Luke Asian Museum, Seattle, WA 1784

Park, Myoungsook, Gallery Coord., China Institute Gallery, China Institute In America, New York, NY 1166

Parke, Julia C., C.E.O., Decorative Arts Center of Ohio, Lancaster, OH 1326

Parker, Arthur, Chm. (V), Blithewold Mansion, Gardens & Arboretum, Bristol, RI 1485

Parker, Barbara, Museum Dir., Columbia County Historical and Genealogical Society, Bloomsburg, PA 1413

Parker, Barbara, Sec., Marlboro Historical Society, Marlboro, VT 1683

Parker, Barbara, Dir. Programs, Piedmont Arts Association, Martinsville, VA 1724

Parker, Candace, Dir. Human Resources, Shaker Village of Pleasant Hill, Harrodsburg, KY 649

Parker, Chase, Seasonal, Chief Vann House Historic Site, Chatsworth, GA 413

Parker, Connie, Pres., 103rd Ohio Volunteer Infantry Civil War Museum, Sheffield Lake, OH 1343

Parker, Deanie, Interim C.E.O. STAX Museum of American Soul Music, Memphis, TN 1564

Parker, Donna, Cur. Exhibits, The Kentucky Library & Museum, Bowling Green, KY 642

Parker, Duane, Treas., Historical Society of the Phoenixville Area, Phoenixville, PA 1463

Parker, Etta, Museum Shop Mgr., The Scarsdale Historical Society, Scarsdale, NY 1209

Parker Farris, Teresa, Coord. Mktg. & Membership, Newcomb Art Gallery, New Orleans, LA 683

Parker, Gertrud, Honorary Chm. (V), Museum of Craft and Folk Art, San Francisco, CA 190

Parker, H. Wayne, Dir., St. Francis County Museum, Forrest City, AR 71

Parker, Herschell, Exhibits & Collections Mgr., Adventure Science Center, Nashville, TN 1566

Parker, Horry, Pres. (V), Hampton Plantation State Historic Site, McClellanville, SC 1518

Parker, Jane, Pres. (V), Muckenthaler Cultural Center and Mansion Museum, Fullerton, CA 118

Parker, Jeff, Dir. Operations, Rolling Hills Wildlife Adventure, Salina, KS 633

Parker, Jennifer, Asst. Dir., The Trammell & Margaret Crow Collection of Asian Art, Dallas, TX 1600

Parker, Jim, Park Dir., Fort Toulouse/Jackson Park, Wetumpka, AL 26

Parker, John, Exhibits Mgr., Anniston Museum of Natural History, Anniston, AL 3

Parker, John J., Exec. Dir., Berkshire Botanical Garden, Stockbridge, MA 809

Parker, Josephine S., Pres. (V), The Hill Country Museum, Kerrville, TX 1625

Parker, Joyce Ann, Sales Mgr., Wonders: Memphis International Cultural Series, Memphis, TN 1565

Parker, Kari, Mgr. Mktg., Binder Park Zoo, Battle Creek, MI 825

Parker, Kate, Education & Museum Shop Mgr., The Cape Cod Maritime Museum, Hyannis, MA 783

Parker, Katie O., Dir., Baranov Museum, Kodiak, AK 33

Parker, Kimberly, Dir., O. Winston Link Museum, Roanoke, VA 1744

Parker, Larry, Supvr. Mt. Airy, Mount Airy Arboretum, Cincinnati, OH 1305

Parker, Dr. Lorann, D.Sc., Ph.D., Pres. & Chm., Mountain Skies Astronomical Society & Science Center, Lake Arrowhead, CA 128

Parker, Margaret, Pres., Meigs County Museum, Pomeroy, OH 1339

Parker, Martha, Public Rels., Historical Society of the Phoenixville Area, Phoenixville, PA 1463

Parker, Melanie, Dir. Mktg., Birmingham Museum of Art, Birmingham, AL 5

Parker, Mike, Pres. (V), Whitehead Memorial Museum, Del Rio, TX 1601

Parker, Nancy, Exec. Dir., Children's Zoo at Celebration Square, Saginaw, MI 863

P–Continued

P–*Continued*

Pedersen, Jennifer, Registrar, Herbert Hoover Presidential Library-Museum, West Branch, IA 602
Pedersen, Vegor, Graphic Designer, Woodbury Art Museum, Orem, UT 1666
Pederson, Curt, Cur. Collections, American Swedish Institute, Minneapolis, MN 884
Pederson, Cyndi, Dir. Iowa Dept. Cultural Affairs, State Historical Museum of Iowa, Des Moines, IA 584
Pederson, Jerry, Vice Pres., Hatton-Eielson Museum & Historical Association, Hatton, ND 1284
Pederson, Steve, Membership, Patty and Jay Baker Naples Museum of Art, Naples, FL 370
Pederson, Vonnie, Vice Pres., Meagher County Historical Association Castle Museum, White Sulphur Springs, MT 974
Pedone, Francis, Dir. Operations, Worcester Art Museum, Worcester, MA 819
Pedriani, Laura, Public Affairs & Svcs. Dir., Milwaukee County Zoological Gardens, Milwaukee, WI 1835
Pedroza, Melissa, C.E.O. & Dir., Folsom History Museum, Folsom, CA 113
Peebles, Richard, Pres. (V), National Museum of Nuclear Science and History, Albuquerque, NM 1072
Peebles, Tricia, C.F.O., Artpace San Antonio, San Antonio, TX 1643
Peek, Lisa, Animal Care Mgr., Mann Wildlife Learning Museum, Montgomery, AL 20
Peele, Grace, Museum Shop Mgr., Frisco Native American Museum and Natural History Center, Frisco, NC 1247
Peeler, Dierdre, Receptionist & Museum Shop Mgr., Maitland Art Center, Maitland, FL 363
Peeler, Jackie, Asst. Dir. & Cur., Henson Robinson Zoo, Springfield, IL 520
Peeling, Chad, Cur., Clyde Peeling's Reptiland, Allenwood, PA 1409
Peeling, Chris, Office Mgr. & Museum Shop Mgr., Clyde Peeling's Reptiland, Allenwood, PA 1409
Peeling, Clyde, C.E.O., Clyde Peeling's Reptiland, Allenwood, PA 1409
Peeling, Elliot, Exhibit Designer, Clyde Peeling's Reptiland, Allenwood, PA 1409
Peeples, Christine, Treas., Hampton County Historical Society Museum, Hampton, SC 1515
Peerbolte, Greg, Exec. Dir., Mount Prospect Historical Society Museums, Mount Prospect, IL 507
Peete, Heather, Science Center Educator, Children's Science Explorium at Sugar Sand Park, Boca Raton, FL 335
Pegues, Jutta C., Pres. Worthington Historical Society (V), Worthington Historical Society, Worthington, OH 1352
Pegues, Sally, Sec. & Trustee, Wise County Heritage Museum, Decatur, TX 1601
Peiffer, Georganna, Bd. Member, Cripple Creek District Museum, Inc., Cripple Creek, CO 236
Peihl, Mark, Archivist, Historical and Cultural Society of Clay County, Moorhead, MN 887
Peimer, Jordan, Dir. Programs, Skirball Cultural Center, Los Angeles, CA 142
Peitsmeyer, Karen, Public Rels., The Amerind Foundation, Inc., Dragoon, AZ 40
Pekala, Bob, Preparator, University Museum & Historic Houses, The University of Mississippi, Oxford, MS 915
Pekar, Rachel, Dir. Library, Camden County Historical Society, Camden, NJ 1034
Pekor, Renee, Dir. Devel., Carnegie Museum of Art, Pittsburgh, PA 1464
Pekrul, Sharon L., Cur., South Carolina Institute of Archaeology & Anthropology, Columbia, SC 1510
Pelger, Gary, Operations Mgr., Canton Classic Car Museum, Canton, OH 1300
Pelham, Terri, Retail Shop Mgr., Oregon Zoo, Portland, OR 1400
Pelke, Craig, Asst. Supvr. Animal Svcs., Virginia Zoological Park, Norfolk, VA 1731
Pelkey, Anne, Cur., Pittsford Historical Society Museum, Pittsford, VT 1687
Pelkey, Philip, Museum Shop Mgr., Music House Museum, Acme, MI 820
Pell, Dallas, Public Rels., National Museum of American Illustration, Newport, RI 1490
Pell, Edward W., Pres. (V), Fort Ticonderoga, Ticonderoga, NY 1221
Pellegrini, Rodrigo, Natural History Registrar, New Jersey State Museum, Trenton, NJ 1064
Pellet, Aimee, Rental & Special Events Dir., Four Mile Historic Park, Denver, CO 240
Pelleteri, Sara, Dir. Education, Waikiki Aquarium, Honolulu, HI 448
Pelletier, Betty, Museum Shop Mgr., Pembina State Museum, Pembina, ND 1288
Pelletier, Karen, Dir. Settlement, The House of the Seven Gables, Salem, MA 803
Pelletier, Philip F., Dir. Special Events, The Preservation Society of Newport County/The Newport Mansions, Newport, RI 1492
Pelligrini, Elena, Public Programs, Neuberger Museum of Art, Purchase College, State University of New York, Purchase, NY 1198
Pelligrino, Rosann, Sec., Bergen County Historical Society, River Edge, NJ 1060
Pellnat, Allan, Deputy Dir., A.W.A. Electronic-Communication Museum, Bloomfield, NY 1105
Pelrine, Diane, Assoc. Dir. Curatorial Svcs., Indiana University Art Museum, Bloomington, IN 533
Peltier, Cynthia, Operations Mgr., Samek Art Gallery, Lewisburg, PA 1441
Pelzer, Mary Ellen, Pres. & C.E.O., South Street Seaport Museum, New York, NY 1181
Pelzman Liscio, Fran, Pres. (V), The Presby Memorial Iris Gardens, Upper Montclair, NJ 1066
Pemberton, Christi, Cur., North Carolina A&T State University Galleries, Greensboro, NC 1249
Pemberton, Fraser, Pres. (V), Rancho Santa Ana Botanic Garden, Claremont, CA 102
Pemberton, Gregory, Chm. Bd., Indiana State Museum, Indianapolis, IN 549
Pemberton, Jean, Pres. (V), Copper Range Historical Museum, South Range, MI 865
Pence, Debra L., Dir., St. Clements Island and Piney Point Museums, Colton's Point, MD 732
Pence, Noel, Chm. (V), Choctaw County Historical Society, Hugo, OK 1364
Pence, Norman, Treas. & Museum Shop Mgr., Choctaw County Historical Society, Hugo, OK 1364
Pendergast, David, Chm. (V), Children's Museum of History, Natural History and Science at Utica, New York, Utica, NY 1222
Pendergraft, Don, Exhibits Chief, Museum of the Albemarle, Elizabeth City, NC 1244
Pendergrass, Bob, Nature Center Dir., Dan Nicholas Park Nature Center, Salisbury, NC 1266
Pendergrass, Candice, Dir. Membership & Mktg., Fresno Metropolitan Museum of Art & Science, Fresno, CA 116
Pendergrass, Gayle, Gallery Committee, Arkansas State University Art Gallery, Jonesboro, AR 75
Pendleton, Carmen, Mgr. Community & Artist Programs, Stedman Gallery, Camden, NJ 1034
Pendleton, Chris, C.E.O. & Pres., Edison & Ford Winter Estates, Fort Myers, FL 349
Pendleton, Debbie, Asst. Dir. Public Svcs., Alabama Department of Archives & History, Montgomery, AL 19
Penfield, Carolyn, Dir., Petrified Wood Park & Museum, Lemmon, SD 1535
Penfield, John, Exec. Dir. & Pres., Bluegrass Railroad Museum, Versailles, KY 664
Peng, Synderela, Bd. Member LACE (Los Angeles Contemporary Exhibitions), Los Angeles, CA 138
Penhall, Michele, Cur. Photographs & Prints, University Art Museum, The University of New Mexico, Albuquerque, NM 1074
Penick, Steven, Cur., Stearns History Museum, Saint Cloud, MN 892
Peninger, Kay, Exec. Dir., St. John's Episcopal Church, Richmond, VA 1740
Penisi, Matt, Pres., Colonial Burlington Foundation, Inc., Burlington, NJ 1033
Peniston, Dr. William A., Librarian, The Newark Museum, Newark, NJ 1053
Penka, Brad, Mgr. Visitor Svcs., Sternberg Museum of Natural History, Hays, KS 616
Penka, Bradley R., C.E.O. & Pres. (V), Barbed Wire Museum, La Crosse, KS 620
Penman-Morgan, Ann, Dir. Security, Utah Museum of Fine Arts, Salt Lake City, UT 1671
Penn, David, Exec. Dir., Great Explorations Children's Museum, Saint Petersburg, FL 384
Penn, Joyce, Registrar, Paul and Lulu Hilliard University Art Museum, University of Louisiana at Lafayette, Lafayette, LA 673
Penner, Liisa, Cur. & Archivist, Flavel House Museum, Astoria, OR 1383
Penner, Liisa, Archivist, The Heritage Museum, Astoria, OR 1383
Penner, Liisa, Archivist, Uppertown Firefighters Museum, Astoria, OR 1383
Penney, David, Native American Art & Vice Pres. Exhibitions & Collection Strategies, Detroit Institute of Arts, Detroit, MI 834
Penniman, Eleanor, Chm., Lemon Hill Mansion, Philadelphia, PA 1456
Pennington, Billy, Dir., Cherokee County History and Arts Museum, Gaffney, SC 1513
Pennington, Claudia L., C.E.O. & Exec. Dir., East Martello Museum, Key West, FL 358
Pennington, Claudia L., C.E.O. & Dir., Key West Lighthouse Museum, Key West, FL 359
Pennington, Claudia L., Exec. Dir., Key West Museum of Art and History, Key West, FL 359
Pennington, James, City Mgr., Hartsville Museum, Hartsville, SC 1516

P–*Continued*

Perron, Michelle M., Dir., Center Galleries, College for Creative Studies, Detroit, MI....833
Perrone, Andrea, Sec., Cass County Historical Society, Logansport, IN....554
Perrone, Rena, Event Planner, Grounds For Sculpture, Hamilton, NJ....1041
Perrot, Mollie, C.E.O., Cur. & Public Rels., Ottawa Scouting Museum, Ottawa, IL....511
Perrot, Steve, Security, Ottawa Scouting Museum, Ottawa, IL....511
Perrotta, Lorraine, Head Technical Svcs., Huntington Library, Art Collections, and Botanical Gardens, San Marino, CA....198
Perry, A. Michael, Chm. (V), Heritage Farm Museum & Village, Huntington, WV....1800
Perry, Candace K., Cur. Collections, Schwenkfelder Library & Heritage Center, Pennsburg, PA....1448
Perry, Carole, Exec. Dir., Edward Hopper Landmark Preservation Foundation, Nyack, NY....1187
Perry, Carolyn, Pres. (V), South Dakota Discovery Center, Pierre, SD....1538
Perry, Darlene, Collections Mgr., North Carolina Maritime Museum, Beaufort, NC....1234
Perry, Ed, Dir., McLarty Treasure Museum, Vero Beach, FL....396
Perry, Fred, Grounds Mgr., Blithewold Mansion, Gardens & Arboretum, Bristol, RI....1485
Perry, Henriella, Pres. (V), Heritage Farm Museum & Village, Huntington, WV....1800
Perry, Ira D., Public Rels., Holocaust Museum Houston, Houston, TX....1620
Perry, James, Cur. Jamestown, Colonial National Historical Park: Jamestown & Yorktown, Yorktown, VA....1756
Perry, James, Site Mgr., CNHP, Historic Jamestowne, Jamestown, VA....1718
Perry, Jesse P., III, Dir. Public Programs, North Carolina Museum of Natural Sciences, Raleigh, NC....1263
Perry, John, Pres., Spirit of '76 Museum, Wellington, OH....1349
Perry, Lake, Museum Shop Mgr., Fort Ross State Historic Park Visitor Center and Museum, Jenner, CA....125
Perry, Mark, Exec. Dir., Florida Oceanographic Coastal Center, Stuart, FL....389
Perry, Mary, Assoc. Dir. Devel., Agua Caliente Cultural Museum, Palm Springs, CA....160
Perry, Megan, Education Assoc., Indianapolis Art Center, Indianapolis, IN....549
Perry, Michael L., Exec. Dir., Museum of Western Colorado, Grand Junction, CO....250
Perry, Nancy, Dir., Portsmouth Museums, Portsmouth, VA....1734
Perry, Patricia, Museum Shop Mgr., Fort Plain Museum, Fort Plain, NY....1134
Perry, Patricia, Facilities & Retail Mgr., Maryhill Museum of Art, Goldendale, WA....1768
Perry, Paul, Dir. Education & Public Programs, Anchorage Museum, Anchorage, AK....27
Perry, Penny, Dir., Garst Museum, Greenville, OH....1323
Perry, Rachel, Cur. Fine Arts, Indiana State Museum, Indianapolis, IN....549
Perry, Robert, Vice Chm., Fort Plain Museum, Fort Plain, NY....1134
Perry, Rosalind, Devel., The Quilters Hall of Fame, Inc., Marion, IN....555
Perry, Sherry, Cur., Porterville Historical Museum, Porterville, CA....166
Perry, Stephen, Pres. & Exec. Dir., National Football Museum, Inc., Canton, OH....1301
Perry, Wendy, Deputy Dir. External Affairs, Heritage Museums & Gardens, Sandwich, MA....805
Perry, Wynn, Dir. & Cur., Owens Community College/Walter E. Terhune Gallery, Perrysburg, OH....1339
Perry-Lube, Linda, Sr. Vice Pres. & Chief Digital Officer, American Museum of Natural History, New York, NY....1163
Perryman, Christina, Dir. Public Rels., Kearney Mansion Museum, Fresno, CA....116
Perry-Uhlman, Anne, Dir. & Cur., Fayette Art Museum, Fayette, AL....11
Pershey, Ed, Vice Pres. Museums & Historical Properties, Western Reserve Historical Society, Cleveland, OH....1311
Pershey, Dr. Edward Jay, Vice Pres. Museums, Crawford Auto-Aviation Museum, Cleveland, OH....1309
Person, Marilu, Cur., Traill County Historical Society, Hillsboro, ND....1284
Persons, Leah, Museum Shop Mgr., Albuquerque Museum of Art & History, Albuquerque, NM....1070
Persson, Ann, Cur., Havre de Grace Maritime Museum, Havre de Grace, MD....739
Persun, Anne, Museum Store Mgr., The Thomas T. Taber Museum of the Lycoming County Historical Society, Williamsport, PA....1482
Perusi, Richard, Chm., Connecticut's Beardsley Zoo, Bridgeport, CT....267
Peruzzi, Geno, Museum Shop Mgr., Newtown Historic Association, Newtown, PA....1447
Pesaresi, Vera, Treas., Museum of Chicot County Arkansas, Lake Village, AR....76
Peschel, Christine, Museum Shop Mgr., The Institute For American Indian Studies (IAIS), Washington, CT....299
Pesenti, Allegra, Assoc. Cur., Grunwald Center for the Graphic Arts, Hammer Museum, Los Angeles, CA....136
Pesesky, Jill, Cur. Education, Agecroft Hall, Richmond, VA....1736
Pesikoff, David, Pres. Bd., Houston Center for Contemporary Craft, Houston, TX....1620
Pesola, Barbara, Cur., Menominee County Heritage Museum, Menominee, MI....854
Peszka, Kristin, Interpretations & Visitor Svcs. Dir., Paul Revere House/Paul Revere Memorial Association, Boston, MA....763
Pete, C. Gideon, Pres. (V), Historic Fort Steilacoom, Lakewood, WA....1770
Petellat, Michael, Park Ranger & Museum Shop Mgr., Crystal River Archaeological State Park, Crystal River, FL....341
Peter, Carolyn, Dir. & Cur., Laband Art Gallery, Loyola Marymount University, Los Angeles, CA....138
Peter, George, Chm. & Pres., East End Seaport Museum and Marine Foundation, Greenport, NY....1140
Peter, Jack, Sr. Vice Pres. & C.O.O., World Golf Hall of Fame, Saint Augustine, FL....383
Peter, Michael E., Sec., Grand Army of the Republic Museum & Library, Philadelphia, PA....1454
Peterman, Eugenia, Lead Interpreter Vereins Kirche, Pioneer Museum and Vereins Kirche, Fredericksburg, TX....1612
Petermann Jamison, Virginia, Pres. (V), Keweenaw County Historical Society, Eagle Harbor, MI....837
Peters, Anita, Pres., Stoddard County Museum, Bloomfield, MO....921
Peters, Ben, Exhibit Preparator, Phoebe Apperson Hearst Museum of Anthropology, Berkeley, CA....93
Peters, Betsy, Cur. Education, The Charles Hosmer Morse Museum of American Art, Winter Park, FL....398
Peters Bowron, Edgar, Audrey Jones Beck Cur. European Art, The Museum of Fine Arts, Houston, Houston, TX....1622
Peters, Christine, Exec. Dir., Copper Shop Gallery, East Aurora, NY....1127
Peters, Cindy, Exec. Dir., Avery County Museum, Newland, NC....1259
Peters, Dana, Program Dir., Landmark Park, Dothan, AL....10
Peters, Deborah, Exhibits Mgr., Whitaker Center for Science and the Arts, Harrisburg, PA....1432
Peters, Douglas, Archivist, Rockhill Trolley Museum, Rockhill Furnace, PA....1471
Peters, Douglas E., Librarian, Railways to Yesterday, Inc., Rockhill Furnace, PA....1471
Peters, Elaine, C.E.O. & Dir., Ak-Chin Him-Dak Eco-Museum, Maricopa, AZ....46
Peters, Gabrielle, Admissions Clerk, Bass Museum of Art, Miami Beach, FL....367
Peters, Glenn, Chm. (V), Museum of Art and History at the McPherson Center, Santa Cruz, CA....206
Peters, Helene, Mgr. Educational Loan Collections, The Newark Museum, Newark, NJ....1053
Peters, Ingrid, Dir. of Education, Newport Historical Society & The Museum of Newport History, Newport, RI....1491
Peters, Kenton, Coord. Education, Myriad Botanical Gardens, Oklahoma City, OK....1371
Peters, Kim, Women's Society, The Dennison Railroad Depot Museum, Dennison, OH....1318
Peters, Marge, Pres. (V) & Museum Shop Mgr., Washington County Rural Heritage Museum, Boonsboro, MD....728
Peters, Marybeth, Register of Copyrights, Copyright Office, Library of Congress, Washington, DC....320
Peters, Rick, Dir. Grounds & Gardens, Shelburne Museum, Inc., Shelburne, VT....1690
Peters, Ruth Olson, Dir., Santa Fe Trail Center, Larned, KS....621
Peters, Stephanie, Events Coord., Longview Museum of Fine Arts, Longview, TX....1628
Peters, Trina, Pres., Sun Valley Center for the Arts, Ketchum, ID....461
Petersen, Gary, MIS, National Naval Aviation Museum, Pensacola, FL....378
Petersen, Gerrit, Devel., Old State House-The Bostonian Society, Boston, MA....763
Petersen, James, Dir. Operations, Timken Museum of Art, San Diego, CA....185
Petersen, Jerome, Chm. (V), Sibley County Historical Museum, Henderson, MN....880
Petersen, Laurie, Pres., Winnetka Historical Society, Winnetka, IL....529
Petersen, Marc, Pres. (V), The Danish Immigrant Museum, Elk Horn, IA....586
Petersen, Natalie, Assoc. Dir., Springville Museum of Art, Springville, UT....1673
Petersen, Stacie, Registrar, Roswell Museum and Art Center, Roswell, NM....1087

P–Continued

P–*Continued*

P–*Continued*

P–*Continued*

P–Continued

P–*Continued*

Purkey Levine, Anne Marie, Registrar, Museum of Contemporary Art San Diego - Downtown, San Diego, CA........181
Purkey, Nancy, Financial Dir., Northern Gila County Historical Society, Inc. - Rim Country Museum, Payson, AZ..........47
Purmal, Kathie, Exec. Dir., Lake County Historical Society, Painesville, OH.......1338
Purnell, Dr. Brian, Bronx African American Project, The Bronx County Historical Society, Bronx, NY 1107
Purpura, Allyson, Cur., Krannert Art Museum and Kinkead Pavilion, Champaign, IL..474
Purtill, John, Treas., Military Museum of Southern New England, Danbury, CT.....270
Purvis, Amy, Assoc. Dir. Devel., The Museum of Fine Arts, Houston, Houston, TX 1622
Purvis, JoAnn, Administrative Asst., Sam Houston Memorial Museum, Huntsville, TX 1623
Purvis, William, Interim Dir., Yale University Collection of Musical Instruments, New Haven, CT..................288
Pusey, Sandy, Cultural Resources Program Mgr., Charles Pinckney National Historic Site, Mount Pleasant, SC..1518
Puterbaugh, Travis, Mgr. Collections, Tampa Bay History Center, Inc., Tampa, FL..393
Putman, Kevin, Pres. Bd. Trustees (V), James A. Michener Art Museum, Doylestown, PA 1420
Putman, Polly, Museum Shop Mgr., Obion County Museum, Union City, TN 1575
Putnam, Andrea, Sr. Naturalist, River Hills Visitor Center, Wildwood, MO.......955
Putnam, Catherine, Deputy Dir. SITE Santa Fe, Santa Fe, NM 1090
Putnam, Christy, Assoc. Dir. Collections & Exhibitions Management, Whitney Museum of American Art, New York, NY...1184
Putnam, Kelly, Aquarist, Flint River Quarium, Albany, GA..............................399
Putnam, Tom, Dir. Library & Museum, John F. Kennedy Presidential Library & Museum, Boston, MA..........................760
Putney, Carolyn, Chief Cur., The Toledo Museum of Art, Toledo, OH.................1345
Putzel, Michelle, Administrative Asst., United States Hockey Hall of Fame Museum, Eveleth, MN 876
Pyatt, Sherman, Archivist, Avery Research Center for African American History & Culture, Charleston, SC..........1503
Pye, Jennifer, Cur., The Monhegan Museum, Monhegan, ME..........................702
Pye, Robert, Mgr., Vermont Marble Museum, Proctor, VT...........................1687
Pygin, Cynthia, Sr. Vice Pres. & Chief Financial Officer, California Science Center, Los Angeles, CA.........................134
Pyhrr, Stuart, Arthur Ochs Sulzberger Cur. in Charge, Arms & Armor, The Metropolitan Museum of Art, New York, NY 1172
Pyle, Aaron, Museum Technician, University of Maine Museum of Art, Bangor, ME...691
Pyle, Christine, Mgr. Historical Resources, Lake County Discovery Museum, Wauconda, IL 526
Pyle, Julie, Museum Shop Mgr., Myriad Botanical Gardens, Oklahoma City, OK...1371
Pyle, Scott, Gen. Mgr., Iowa Great Lakes Maritime Museum, Arnolds Park, IA......573
Pyle-Vowles, Devon, Collections Mgr., Adler Planetarium & Astronomy Museum, Chicago, IL.............................476
Pyne Connor, Dr. Holly, Assoc. Cur. American Art, The Newark Museum, Newark, NJ 1053
Pyne, Elaine, Dir. Advancement, Albright-Knox Art Gallery, Buffalo, NY 1114
Pyrek, Geri, Pres., Satterlee Clark House, Horicon, WI 1823
Pytel, Margaret, Administrative Asst., Maitland Art Center, Maitland, FL..........363

Q

Qian, Dr. Hong, Assoc. Cur. Botany, Illinois State Museum, Springfield, IL 521
Qing, Dr. Chang, Assoc. Cur. Asian Art, John and Mable Ringling Museum of Art, Sarasota, FL 387
Quackenbush, Molly, Exec. Dir. & Site Supt., Theodore Roosevelt Inaugural National Historic Site, Buffalo, NY.......1116
Quainton, Andrew, Asst. to Dir., University of Alaska Museum of the North, Fairbanks, AK 30
Quam, Curtis, Museum Technician, A:shiwi A:wan Museum and Heritage Center, Zuni, NM 1095
Quan, Jean, Chm., Chabot Space & Science Center, Oakland, CA 154
Quandt, Kendra, Dir. Devel., Birmingham Museum of Art, Birmingham, AL 5
Quarcoopome, Nii, Cur. Africa, Oceanic, Detroit Institute of Arts, Detroit, MI 834
Quarless, Anthony, Dir. Security, Brooklyn Botanic Garden, Brooklyn, NY 1110
Quast, Bruce, Exhibits Coord., Discovery Center Museum, Rockford, IL 516
Quave, Elaine, Cur., The Living Arts and Science Center, Inc., Lexington, KY.......653
Quayle, Sen. Frederick M., Pres. (V), Chippokes Farm & Forestry Museum, Surry, VA 1748
Quayle-Hauck, Cindy, Preparator, Springfield Art Museum, Springfield, MO 953
Queen, Bill, Asst. to Cur., Montana Museum of Art & Culture, Missoula, MT..969
Querio, Robert, Dir. Finance, Carnegie Museum of Natural History, Pittsburgh, PA 1464
Quibuyen, George, Exhibits Coord., Wing Luke Asian Museum, Seattle, WA..........1784
Quick, Betsy D., Dir. Education, Fowler Museum at UCLA, Los Angeles, CA......135
Quick, Edward R., Staff Cur., Nixon Presidential Materials Staff, College Park, MD 731
Quick, James, Public Rels., Mechanicsburg Museum Association, Mechanicsburg, PA..........................1444
Quick, Richard, Museum Store Mgr., Ten Chimneys Foundation, Genesee Depot, WI 1820
Quigley, John, Financial Dir., John Jay French House, Beaumont Heritage Society, Beaumont, TX 1587
Quigley, Samuel, Vice Pres. Collection Management & Technology, The Art Institute of Chicago, Chicago, IL 476
Quijano-West, Richard, Supt., Springfield Armory National Historic Site, Springfield, MA.......................................807
Quill, Timothy J., Dir. & Museum Shop Mgr., Ward W. O'Hara Agricultural Museum, Auburn, NY 1101
Quillen Thomas, Beth, Bd. Pres., National Women's Hall of Fame, Seneca Falls, NY 1211
Quillin, J.D., III, Pres. (V), Ocean City Life-Saving Station Museum, Ocean City, MD 742
Quillin, Patty, Pres. Bd. (V), Santa Cruz Museum of Natural History, Santa Cruz, CA..206
Quilnan, William, Treas., Rebecca Nurse Homestead, Danvers, MA.......................773
Quilter, Dr. Jeffrey, Deputy Dir. Curatorial Affairs, Peabody Museum of Archaeology & Ethnology, Cambridge, MA 768
Quimby, Tracy, Dir. Education, Victoria Mansion, Portland, ME 709
Quinlan, Maria, Membership & Communications Mgr., Contemporary Art Museum St. Louis, Saint Louis, MO 946
Quinlan-Brown, Susan, Museum Shop Mgr., Cahoon Museum of American Art, Cotuit, MA 772
Quinn, Ms. Alana, Sr. Program Assoc., National Academy of Sciences, Washington, DC..322
Quinn, Diane, Dir. Education, Burke Museum of Natural History and Culture, Seattle, WA...............................1779
Quinn, Erin, Museum Mgr., Centennial Village Museum, Greeley, CO 250
Quinn, Erin, Cur. Collections, Greeley History Museum, Greeley, CO.................250
Quinn, Erin, Cur. Collections, Meeker Home Museum, Greeley, CO 251
Quinn, Erin, Coord. Collections, Plumb Farm Learning Center, Greeley, CO........251
Quinn, Jeanette, Co Dir. USS Montpelier Museum, Montpelier, VT 1684
Quinn, Jim, Dir., Marshall Point Lighthouse Museum, Saint George, ME..711
Quinn, Kate, Head Exhibits & Lead Exhibit Designer, University of Pennsylvania Museum of Archaeology and Anthropology, Philadelphia, PA......1462
Quinn, Linda, Sr. Vice Pres. Operations & C.F.O., Charlotte Nature Museum, Charlotte, NC 1238
Quinn, Linda, Sr. Vice Pres. Operations & C.F.O., Discovery Place, Inc., Charlotte, NC..1238
Quinn, Linda, Exec. Dir., Lied Discovery Children's Museum, Las Vegas, NV 1006
Quinn, Mark, Park Supvr., Highland Botanical Park, Rochester, NY..............1201
Quinn, Michael C., Pres. & Exec. Dir., James Madison's Montpelier - The Montpelier Foundation, Montpelier Station, VA..1726
Quinn, Todd, Museum Shop Mgr., California Surf Museum, Oceanside, CA 156
Quinones, Victor, Controller, International Center of Photography, New York, NY.1170
Quintana, Mary, Museum Shop Mgr., Mesalands Community College's Dinosaur Museum, Tucumcari, NM 1094
Quintanilla, Mr. Faustino, Dir. QCC Art Gallery/CUNY, Bayside, NY 1102
Quintanilla, Mimi, Dir., Witte Museum, San Antonio, TX...................................1646
Quintanilla, Sonya, Ph.D., Cur. Asian Art, San Diego Museum of Art, San Diego, CA 183
Quintero, Adam, Animal Caretaker, Fort Sam Houston Museum, Fort Sam Houston, TX 1608
Quintero-Casanovas, Miriam B., Financial & Administration Dir., Museo de Arte de Ponce, Hato Rey, PR..1869
Quinting, Annie, Education, Oatland Island Wildlife Center, Savannah, GA 434

Q–*Continued*

R

Rainey, Robert, Preparator, Vertebrate Paleontology Lab, Texas Natural Science Center, Austin, TX....1584
Rains, C. Jay, Chm. (V), United States Golf Association Museum, Far Hills, NJ....1038
Raintree, Shawn, Interim Pres. & C.E.O., Colorado Springs Fine Arts Center (Taylor Museum), Colorado Springs, CO....233
Raisor, Jerry, Cur., Fort Boonesborough Museum, Richmond, KY....662
Rait, Eleanor, Cur. Collections, Hofstra University Museum, Hempstead, NY....1141
Rajala, Reuben, Pres., Gorham Historical Society and Rail Museum, Gorham, NH....1019
Rakers, Tim, Mgr. Comp & Benefits, Saint Louis Zoo, Saint Louis, MO....951
Rakes, Susan, Asst. Dir. & Dir. Education, Art and Culture Center of Hollywood, Hollywood, FL....353
Rakestraw, Gerald, Gen. Mgr., Georgia's Stone Mountain Park, Stone Mountain, GA....436
Rakita, Martha, Museum Shop Mgr., Historical Society of Ocean Grove, New Jersey, Ocean Grove, NJ....1054
Rakow, Catherine, Curatorial Asst., Boise Art Museum, Boise, ID....455
Rakow, Donald A., Dir., The Cornell Plantations, Ithaca, NY....1146
Raleigh, Elaine, Finance & Museum Shop Mgr., Living History Farms, Urbandale, IA....601
Raley, Diane M., Vice Pres., The Money Museum-Federal Reserve Bank of Kansas City, Kansas City, MO....934
Raley, Gwendolen, Admin. Morris-Butler House, Historic Landmarks Foundation of Indiana, Indianapolis, IN....548
Raley, Gwendolen, Museum Admin., Morris-Butler House Museum, Indianapolis, IN....550
Ralkonen, Dan, Pres. (V), Future of Flight Aviation Center & Boeing Tour, Mukilteo, WA....1773
Ralph, Fran, Dir. Mktg. & Devel., Kateri Galleries, Shrine of Our Lady of Martyrs aka The National Shrine of the North American Martyrs, Auriesville, NY....1101
Ralph, Mr. Thomas F., Dir. Operations, Kateri Galleries, Shrine of Our Lady of Martyrs aka The National Shrine of the North American Martyrs, Auriesville, NY....1101
Ralston, Kathy, Museum Shop Mgr., Drum Barracks Civil War Museum, Wilmington, CA....225
Ralston, Sally, Co-Pres., Copper Village Museum & Arts Center of Deer Lodge County, Anaconda, MT....955
Ramadan, Diane, Ranch & Facility Mgr., Leonis Adobe Museum, Calabasas, CA....97
Rambo, Robert, C.F.O., Philadelphia Museum of Art, Philadelphia, PA....1459
Rambo, Susan, Museum Asst., Klamath County Museum, Klamath Falls, OR....1393
Rambow, Charles, Dir. & Museum Shop Mgr., Old Fort Meade Museum and Historic Research Association, Fort Meade, SD....1531
Ramer, Randy, Collections Mgr., Gilcrease Museum, Tulsa, OK....1379
Ramer, Wayne, Museum Shop Mgr., Creek Council House Museum, Okmulgee, OK....1374
Rametta, Fran, Mgr. Visitor Center, Congaree National Park, Hopkins, SC....1516
Ramey, Bruce, Mgr. Hall of Fame, International Motorsports Hall of Fame and Museum, Lincoln, AL....16
Ramey, Marilyn, Asst. Dir., Art Museum of South Texas, Corpus Christi, TX....1594
Ramey, Paul, Dir. Mktg. & Public Rels., Florida Museum of Natural History, Gainesville, FL....351
Ramian, Randall, Dir. USS Hornet Museum, Alameda, CA....86
Ramin, Robert A., C.E.O., The National Aquarium in Washington DC, Washington, DC....322
Ramirez, Anibal, Admin., Pablo Casals Museum, San Juan, PR....1871
Ramirez, Anthony, Dir. & Cur., Faninadahen Kosas Guahan-Guam Museum, Hagatna, GU....1868
Ramirez Aponte, Marianne, Exec. Dir., Museum of Contemporary Art of Puerto Rico, San Juan, PR....1870
Ramirez, Armando G., Chm. (V), Plaza de La Raza, Inc. & Boathouse Gallery, Los Angeles, CA....141
Ramirez, Deyanira, Accountant, Brownsville Museum of Fine Art, Brownsville, TX....1590
Ramirez, Florentino, Chm.-Elect, International Museum of Cultures, Dallas, TX....1599
Ramirez, Gus, Supvr. Security, Nerman Museum of Contemporary Art, Overland Park, KS....630
Ramirez, Ken, Exec. Vice Pres. Animal Collections & Training, John G. Shedd Aquarium, Chicago, IL....482
Ramirez, Mari Carmen, The Wortham Cur. of Latin American Art & Dir. Intl. Center for the Arts of the Americas (ICAA), The Museum of Fine Arts, Houston, Houston, TX....1622
Ramirez, Dr. Rey, C.E.O., Frontera Audubon Society, Weslaco, TX....1656
Ramirez-Ortiz, Gabriel, Cur. Collections, The Santa Barbara Historical Museum, Santa Barbara, CA....203
Ramjoue, Bryn, Mktg. & Public Rels., Red Butte Garden & Arboretum, Salt Lake City, UT....1670
Ramming, Nita, Museum Shop Mgr., Carson County Square House Museum, Panhandle, TX....1637
Ramoran, Edwin, Dir. Exhibitions & Programs, Aljira, a Center for Contemporary Art, Newark, NJ....1052
Ramos, Bahia, Dir. Government & Community Affairs, Brooklyn Botanic Garden, Brooklyn, NY....1110
Ramos, Flori, Dir. Resource Management, Lawrence Hall of Science, Berkeley, CA....93
Ramos, Michael, Exhibits Technician, Arizona Museum of Natural History, Mesa, AZ....46
Ramos, Paula, Events, March Field Air Museum, Riverside, CA....172
Ramos, Pedro, Supt., Big Cypress National Preserve, Ochopee, FL....372
Ramos Rivas, Ms. Lourdes, Ph.D., Exec. Dir., Museo de Arte de Puerto Rico, Santurce, PR....1871
Ramotnik, Cindy A., USGS Collection Mgr., Museum of Southwestern Biology, Albuquerque, NM....1072
Rampton, Tony, Chm. (V), Red Butte Garden & Arboretum, Salt Lake City, UT....1670
Ramsay, Jeanne, Historic Preservation Asst., Aurora History Museum, Aurora, CO....229
Ramsay, Stewart, Curatorial Asst., The Belknap Mill Society, Laconia, NH....1021
Ramsburg, Laura Jane, Exhibition & Program Coord., Eleanor D. Wilson Museum, Hollins University, Roanoke, VA....1743
Ramsell, Roberta, Museum Shop Mgr., Ruth and Charles Gilb Arcadia Historical Museum, Arcadia, CA....88
Ramsey, Barbara, Dir. Special Events, Birch Aquarium at Scripps, Scripps Institution of Oceanography, University of California, San Diego, La Jolla, CA....126
Ramsey, Betty, Dir., Two Rivers Heritage Museum, Washougal, WA....1793
Ramsey Cid, Christina, Museum Educator, Texas Natural Science Center, Austin, TX....1584
Ramsey, Diana, Pres. (V), MacCallum More Museum and Gardens, Chase City, VA....1705
Ramsey, Lori, Sec. & Treas., Pioneer Farm Museum and Ohop Indian Village, Eatonville, WA....1764
Ramsey, Maryclaire, C.E.O., The Textile Museum, Washington, DC....330
Ramsey, Regan, Site Supt., Nauvoo Historical Society Museum, Nauvoo, IL....508
Ramsey, Robert, Chm. Bd., New Britain Youth Museum, New Britain, CT....285
Ramsey, Robert, Chm. (V), New Britain Youth Museum at Hungerford Park, Kensington, CT....279
Ramsey, Steve, Chm. (V), Audie Murphy/American Cotton Museum, Inc, Greenville, TX....1617
Ramsey, Steve, Dir., Lansing Manor House Museum, North Blenheim, NY....1186
Ramsey, Terry, Museum Shop Mgr., Bushwhacker Museum, Nevada, MO....941
Ramspott, Becca, Mktg. & Communications Assoc., Kemper Museum of Contemporary Art, Kansas City, MO....934
Rand, Chuck, Dir. Research Center, National Cowboy & Western Heritage Museum, Oklahoma City, OK....1371
Rand, Ian, Asst. Dir. Mktg., Member Rels. & New Media, The Wolfsonian - Florida International University, Miami Beach, FL....368
Rand, Richard, Maintenance, Gaineswood, Demopolis, AL....9
Rand, Richard, Sr. Cur., Sterling and Francine Clark Art Institute, Williamstown, MA....817
Randall, Brad, Chm. (V), National Music Museum, Vermillion, SD....1544
Randall, Cara, Librarian, California State Railroad Museum, Sacramento, CA....175
Randall, Debra, Dir., Rowayton Arts Center, Rowayton, CT....293
Randall, Dennis, Dir. (V), Old Brutus Historical Society, Inc., Weedsport, NY....1227
Randall, Earle, Pres., Crystal Lake Falls Historical Association, Barton, VT....1675
Randall, Jean, Pres., Rialto Historical Society, Rialto, CA....171
Randall, John L., Asst. Dir. Conservation, North Carolina Botanical Garden, Chapel Hill, NC....1237
Randall, Kathleen, Museum Shop Mgr., Delta Cultural Center, Helena, AR....73
Randall, Lindsay, Educator, Robert S. Peabody Museum of Archaeology, Andover, MA....754
Randall, Marilyn, Sec., Chickasaw County Historical Society Bradford Pioneer Village Museum, Nashua, IA....595
Randall, Sean, Chm. (V), National Marine Life Center, Buzzards Bay, MA....766

R–*Continued*

Rauch, Wanda, Museum Shop Mgr., Hope Lodge and Mather Mill, Fort Washington, PA 1426
Raudibaugh, Dawn, Mill Operations Foreman, Hanford Mills Museum, East Meredith, NY....1130
Rauhauser, Barry, Cur., Lancaster County Historical Society, Lancaster, PA....1439
Rauhoff, Christopher, Dir. Exhibitions, Carnegie Museum of Art, Pittsburgh, PA....1464
Rausch, Lian, Museum Shop Mgr., Children's Museum of the Sierra, Oakhurst, CA....154
Rausch, Mike, Pres., McPherson Museum & Arts Foundation, McPherson, KS....627
Rauscher, Carol, Dir. Institutional Advancement, South Street Seaport Museum, New York, NY....1181
Ravel Abarbanel, Stacey, Dir. Communications, Fowler Museum at UCLA, Los Angeles, CA....135
Raven, Alexandra, Visitor Svcs., Michigan Historical Museum, Michigan Historical Center, Lansing, MI....849
Raven, Erica, Dir. Institutional Giving, Lower East Side Tenement Museum, New York, NY....1172
Raven, Peter H., Ph.D., Pres., Missouri Botanical Garden, Saint Louis, MO....949
Ravenal, John, Sydney and Frances Lewis Family Cur. Modern & Contemporary Art, Virginia Museum of Fine Arts, Richmond, VA....1742
Raves, Pat, Cur. Education, North Carolina Aquarium on Roanoke Island, Manteo, NC....1256
Ravet, John, Museum Shop Mgr., National Academy Museum and School of Fine Arts, New York, NY....1176
Rawles, Dr. Susan J., Asst. Cur. American Decorative Art, Virginia Museum of Fine Arts, Richmond, VA...1742
Rawlings, Sheila, Dir. Education, Burpee Museum of Natural History, Rockford, IL....516
Rawlings, William, Chm., San Diego Botanic Garden, Encinitas, CA....110
Rawlins, Cybil, Chm. (V), Waimea Arboretum and Botanical Garden in Waimea Valley, Haleiwa, HI....441
Rawlins, Dr. John E., Assoc. Cur., Invertebrate Zoology, Carnegie Museum of Natural History, Pittsburgh, PA....1464
Rawls, S. Waite, III, Pres. & C.E.O., The Museum of the Confederacy, Richmond, VA....1739
Rawls, Susan, Dir. Membership, Museum of Science and Industry, Chicago, IL....484
Rawson, Gale, Sr. Registrar, Pennsylvania Academy of the Fine Arts, Philadelphia, PA....1458
Rawstern, Sherri, Cur. Education, Dacotah Prairie Museum, Aberdeen, SD....1526
Raxworthy, Dr. Christopher, Assoc. Dean Science Education and Exhibition, & Assoc. Cur. Div. Vertebrate Zoology, American Museum of Natural History, New York, NY....1163
Ray, Allen, Financial Dir., Mary G. Hardin Center for Cultural Arts, Gadsden, AL....12
Ray, Cassandra, Controller, Saint Louis Zoo, Saint Louis, MO....951
Ray, Clara, Security, Gregg Museum of Art & Design at North Carolina State University, Raleigh, NC....1262
Ray, Clayton, Chief Security Officer, The Patrick & Beatrice Haggerty Museum of Art, Milwaukee, WI....1836
Ray, Codie, Chm. (V), Hermione Museum, Tallulah, LA....689
Ray, Debra, Supt., Graham Cave State Park, Montgomery City, MO....941
Ray, Ernestine, Dir., Old Dillard Museum, Fort Lauderdale, FL....348
Ray, Holly, Exec. Asst., Cheyenne Mountain Zoological Park, Colorado Springs, CO....233
Ray, Ivette, Museum Cur., Log Cabin Village, Fort Worth, TX....1610
Ray, James, Main Tech, Oklahoma Territorial Museum, Guthrie, OK....1363
Ray, Jeff, Dir., Barber Vintage Motorsports Museum, Leeds, AL....16
Ray, Jeffrey R., Senior Cur., Atwater Kent Museum of Philadelphia dba Philadelphia History Museum, Philadelphia, PA....1450
Ray, Judy, Accounting Clerk, University of Nebraska State Museum, Lincoln, NE....991
Ray, Larry, Vice Pres., Seward County Historical Society Museum, Goehner, NE....983
Ray, Mary Lou Ryan, Chm. (V), Gladys Porter Zoo, Brownsville, TX....1590
Ray, Randy, C.F.O., Amon Carter Museum, Fort Worth, TX....1609
Ray, Randy W., C.E.O., Copshaholm House Museum & Historic Oliver Gardens, South Bend, IN....565
Ray, Randy W., C.E.O. & Exec. Dir., Northern Indiana Center for History, South Bend, IN....565
Ray, Rebekah, Mgr. Operations, The Arts & Science Center for Southeast Arkansas, Pine Bluff, AR....81
Ray, Richard, Treas., Heritage House Museum of Montgomery County, Mount Ida, AR....80
Ray, Robert, Vice Pres. (V), John S. Barry Historical Society, Constantine, MI....831
Ray, Roy L., Vice Pres. Finance, Cleveland State University Art Gallery, Cleveland, OH....1308
Ray, Sandra, Cur., Whipple House Museum, Ashland Historical Society, Ashland, NH....1012
Rayburn, Heather, Administrative Asst., Botanical Gardens at Asheville, Asheville, NC....1232
Rayca, Brian, Collection Analyst, West Point Museum, West Point, NY....1228
Raye, Frances, Pres., Border Historical Society, Eastport, ME....697
Raymond, Chris, Cur., Shores Memorial Museum, Lyndon Center, VT....1682
Raymond, Glenn, Museum Shop Mgr., Hydroplane & Raceboat Museum, Kent, WA....1769
Raymond, Larry R., Dir., Walter B. Jacobs Memorial Nature Park, Shreveport, LA....688
Raymond, Renate, Deputy Dir., Bellevue Arts Museum, Bellevue, WA....1758
Raymond, Ronald, Chm. (V), Heritage of the Americas Museum, El Cajon, CA....109
Raynard, Shirley, Treas., Middleton Historical Society - Lura Woodside Watkins Museum, Middleton, MA....790
Rayne, Angela, Exec. Dir. & Museum Shop Mgr., Denver Firefighters Museum, Denver, CO....239
Rayne, Angela, Dir., Houston Fire Museum, Houston, TX....1620
Rayner, Margaret, Museum Shop Mgr., Tarpon Springs Area Historical Society - Depot Museum, Tarpon Springs, FL....394
Raynor, Bill, Security, Railroad Museum of Long Island, Riverhead, NY....1200
Raynor, Rachel, Collections Mgr., Fowler Museum at UCLA, Los Angeles, CA....135
Razor, Ann, Supt., Tumacacori National Historical Park, Tumacacori, AZ....64
Rdzanek, Christopher, Facilities Mgr., Natural History Museum of the Adirondacks/The Wild Center, Tupper Lake, NY....1221
Re, Michael, Dir. Visitor Svcs., The Walt Disney Family Museum, LLC, San Francisco, CA....194
Rea, Debbie, Mgr. Zoology, Maymont, Richmond, VA....1739
Rea, Kimberly G., Dir., National Great Rivers Museum, East Alton, IL....491
Rea, Liz, Dir. Education & Public Programs, General Crook House Museum and Library/Archives Center, Omaha, NE....995
Read, Bob, Dir., The Ray Drew Gallery-New Mexico Highlands University, Las Vegas, NM....1081
Read, Ellen, Admin., Texas Governor's Mansion, Austin, TX....1583
Read, Krystal, Education Coord., The Trammell & Margaret Crow Collection of Asian Art, Dallas, TX....1600
Read, Robert W., Pres. (V), Nantucket Life-Saving Museum, Nantucket, MA....792
Reade-Hale, Corrie, Museum Shop Mgr., The Railway Exposition Co., Inc., Covington, KY....644
Reading, Wayne, Dir. Finance, San Francisco Zoological Gardens, San Francisco, CA....193
Ready, Doris Ann, Chm. (V), Hot Springs County Museum and Cultural Center, Thermopolis, WY....1866
Ready, Tim, Dir. Opers., Six Flags Discovery Kingdom, Vallejo, CA....220
Reagan, Bobbi, Dir. & Cur., Stockton Heritage Museum, Stockton, IL....523
Reagan, Charles, Pres. (V), Marianna Kistler Beach Museum of Art at Kansas State University, Manhattan, KS....625
Real, Will, Dir. Technology Initiatives, Carnegie Museum of Art, Pittsburgh, PA....1464
Realie, A. C., Pres., Glenview Area Historical Society, Glenview, IL....498
Ream, Heidi, Chm. (V), Hay House Museum, Macon, GA....425
Ream, Jason, Treas., North House Museum, Lewisburg, WV....1801
Ream, Jay, Asst. Dir., Arizona State Parks Board, Phoenix, AZ....49
Ream, Nancy, Cur. Animals, Wildlife Prairie State Park, Hanna City, IL....499
Reames, Marvin, Museum Shop Mgr., Chisholm Trail Museum, Kingfisher, OK....1365
Reames, Marvin, Museum Shop Mgr., Governor Seay Mansion, Kingfisher, OK....1365
Reams, Sarah, Museum Shop Mgr., Paul W. Bryant Museum, Tuscaloosa, AL....24
Reardon, Bridget, Controller, Maui Ocean Center, Maalaea, HI....452
Reardon, Matt, Exec. Dir., New England Civil War Museum, Vernon, CT....298
Reaske, Chris, Chief Philanthropy Officer, Peabody Essex Museum, Salem, MA....804
Reason, Bruce, Pres. (V), Depot Museum/Cascade Rail Foundation, South Cle Elum, WA....1786
Reaume, Lynn, Education Coord., Monroe County Historical Museum, Monroe, MI....855
Reaves, Abbie, Pres., Folsom Museum, Inc., Folsom, NM....1078

R–*Continued*

Reaves, James E., C.E.O. & Dir., Lovely Lane Museum and Archives, Baltimore, MD....723
Reaves, Sharon, Dir. Human Resources, The Cleveland Museum of Art, Cleveland, OH....1308
Reaves, Dr. Stacy, C.E.O., Dir. & Museum Shop Mgr., Sand Springs Cultural & Historical Museum, Sand Springs, OK....1376
Reaves, Wendy Wick, Cur. Prints & Drawings, National Portrait Gallery, Washington, DC....326
Reavis, Ken, Operations Mgr., Museum of World Treasures, Wichita, KS....638
Rebbert, Carolyn, Cur. Science, Bruce Museum, Greenwich, CT....276
Reber, Paul C., Exec. Dir., Stratford Hall, Robert E. Lee Memorial Association, Inc., Stratford, VA....1748
Reber, Paul G., Pres., Historic Town of Salem, Winston-Salem, NC....1274
Rebman, Dr. Jon, Cur. Botany, San Diego Natural History Museum, San Diego, CA....184
Rebori, Lisa, Vice Pres. Collections, Houston Museum of Natural Science, Houston, TX....1620
Rechler, Scott, Co Chm. (V), Long Island Children's Museum, Garden City, NY....1135
Recht, Howard, Pres. (V), Daly Museum, Hamilton, MT....965
Rechtman, Janet, Chm. (V), The Foxfire Museum & Heritage Center, Mountain City, GA....429
Reckard, Jim, Pres. (V), Rhinebeck Aerodrome Museum, Rhinebeck, NY....1199
Reckas, Melanie, Museum Shop Mgr., Indianapolis Art Center, Indianapolis, IN....549
Recker, Richard, Dir., Old Jail Museum, Albion, IN....530
Reckon, Lisa, Exhibits Coord., Children's Museum at La Habra, La Habra, CA....126
Record, Mary, Dir. Communications, New York Hall of Science, Queens, NY....1199
Recore, John, Dir. Devel., Ravalli County Museum/Bitter Root Valley Historical Society, Hamilton, MT....965
Rector, Ron, Exec. Dir., Northwest Museum of Arts & Culture (Eastern Washington State Historical Society), Spokane, WA....1787
Recuparo, Joan, Administrative Asst. SUArt Galleries - Syracuse University, Syracuse, NY....1219
Red Corn, Kathryn, Dir., Osage Tribal Museum, Library, and Archives, Pawhuska, OK....1374
Redd, Beth, Dir., South Boston-Halifax County Museum of Fine Arts & History, South Boston, VA....1745
Reddell, James R., Cur. Arthropods, Texas Natural Science Center, Austin, TX....1584
Redden, David N., Chm. (V), Hudson Highlands Nature Museum, Cornwall-on-Hudson, NY....1125
Redder-Lacey, Joan, Chm. (V) & Museum Shop Mgr., Little Village Farm Museum, Dell Rapids, SD....1530
Reddic, Bryan, Pres., Chemung Valley History Museum, Elmira, NY....1131
Reddick Carey, Tricia, Exec. Dir., The Granger Homestead Society, Inc., Canandaigua, NY....1117
Reddick, Terry, Dir. Devel., Johnson-Humrickhouse Museum, Coshocton, OH....1314
Redding, Mary Anne, Cur. Historical Photography, Palace of the Governors/New Mexico History Museum, Santa Fe, NM....1090
Reddy, James, Pres. (V), Rutland Area Art Association d/b/a Chaffee Art Center, Rutland, VT....1689
Redford, James, Staff Historian, Carnton Plantation, Franklin, TN....1551
Redhair, Adrienne, Museum Shop Mgr. & Visitor Svcs. Mgr., Abbe Museum, Bar Harbor, ME....692
Reding, Nicholas L., Chm. Bd. Trustees, Missouri Botanical Garden, Saint Louis, MO....949
Reding, Sarah, Exec. Asst., Edison & Ford Winter Estates, Fort Myers, FL....349
Reding, Sarah, Vice Pres. Offsite Programs, Kalamazoo Nature Center, Inc., Kalamazoo, MI....847
Redman, Johnna, Administrative Asst., Hemingway-Pfeiffer Museum and Educational Center, Piggott, AR....81
Redman, Ken, Dir., Honolulu Zoo, Honolulu, HI....446
Redman, Paul, Dir., Longwood Gardens, Kennett Square, PA....1437
Redmon, Maggie, C.O.O., Turtle Bay Exploration Park, Redding, CA....169
Redmon, Michael, Dir. Research, The Santa Barbara Historical Museum, Santa Barbara, CA....203
Redmond, Dr. Brian, Cur. Archaeology, The Cleveland Museum of Natural History, Cleveland, OH....1308
Redmond, Leo, Dir., Cayce Historical Museum, Cayce, SC....1502
Redvale, Jolene, Cur. Education, San Bernardino County Museum, Redlands, CA....170
Redwine, Tom, Admin., Newnan-Coweta Historical Society - Male Academy Museum, Newnan, GA....429
Reece, Evelyn, Dir., Church-Waddel-Brumby House Museum & Athens Welcome Center, Athens, GA....400
Reece Hardy, Saralyn, Dir., Spencer Museum of Art, The University of Kansas, Lawrence, KS....621
Reece-Hughes, Shirley, Asst. Cur. Paintings & Sculpture, Amon Carter Museum, Fort Worth, TX....1609
Reed, Anita, Museum Shop Mgr., Solanco Historical Society, Quarryville, PA....1469
Reed, Bruce, Dir. Nursery, Santa Barbara Botanic Garden, Santa Barbara, CA....203
Reed, Burton, Pres., Cass County Historical Society, Logansport, IN....554
Reed Campbell, Janice, Regulation Assistance, Utah State Historical Society, Salt Lake City, UT....1672
Reed, Cindy, Museum Shop Mgr., Big Thicket National Preserve, Kountze, TX....1626
Reed, Cynthia, Museum Shop Mgr., San Antonio Botanical Garden, San Antonio, TX....1644
Reed, Darla, Sec., Sapulpa Historical Museum, Sapulpa, OK....1376
Reed, Dr. David L., Assoc. Cur. Mammals, Florida Museum of Natural History, Gainesville, FL....351
Reed, Dorothy, C.E.O. & Treas., Carry A. Nation Home Memorial, Medicine Lodge, KS....627
Reed, Douglas, Pres. (V), Sandwich Glass Museum, Sandwich, MA....805
Reed, Ed, Vice Pres., Union County Historical Society Museum, Blairsville, GA....411
Reed, Elmer, Chm. (V), Punxsutawney Area Historical & Genealogical Society, Punxsutawney, PA....1469
Reed, Fran, Museum Coord., Southeastern Colorado Heritage Center, Pueblo, CO....261
Reed, Greg, Pres., Historic Rugby, Rugby, TN....1572
Reed, Henry, Chm. (V), Shoreline Historical Museum, Seattle, WA....1784
Reed, Dr. Holly, Veterinarian, Point Defiance Zoo & Aquarium, Tacoma, WA....1789
Reed, James, Archivist, History San Jose, San Jose, CA....195
Reed, James, Pres., Meagher County Historical Association Castle Museum, White Sulphur Springs, MT....974
Reed, Janell, Pres., Iosco County Historical Museum, East Tawas, MI....838
Reed, Jimmie, Security Officer, The Columbus Museum, Columbus, GA....414
Reed, Julia, Chm. (V), The Ogden Museum of Southern Art, New Orleans, LA....683
Reed, Karla, Exec. Dir., Station 15, Norton, KS....628
Reed, Kathleen, Volunteer Resources Mgr., Virginia Aquarium & Marine Science Center, Virginia Beach, VA....1752
Reed, Kathy, Asst. to Dir., The Hyde Collection, Glens Falls, NY....1138
Reed, Kenyon, Collections Specialist, Museum of Art and Archaeology, University of Missouri, Columbia, MO....924
Reed, Leon B., Pres., Potter County Historical Society, Coudersport, PA....1419
Reed, Mark, Exec. Dir., Des Moines Botanical Center, Des Moines, IA....583
Reed, Mark, Chm. (V) Admin., Francis Land House Historic Site, Virginia Beach, VA....1751
Reed, Mark, Dir., International Museum of Carousel Art, Parkdale, OR....1397
Reed, Mark, Operations Dir., World Forestry Center Discovery Museum, Portland, OR....1401
Reed, Mark A., Admin., Adam Thoroughgood House, Virginia Beach, VA....1750
Reed, Mark C., Dir., Sedgwick County Zoo, Wichita, KS....639
Reed, Mary, Chm. & Pres. (V), Nauvoo Historical Society Museum, Nauvoo, IL....508
Reed, Michael, Asst. Dir., Contemporary Arts Museum Houston, Houston, TX....1619
Reed, Michelle, Museum Shop Mgr., Robert T. Longway Planetarium, Flint, MI....840
Reed, Mike, Mgr., Belle Isle Nature Zoo, Detroit, MI....833
Reed, Mike, Museum Shop Mgr., Good Old Days Vintage Motorcar Museum, Inc., Hardy, AR....73
Reed Mitchell, Charles, Pres. (V), Knox Historical Museum, Barbourville, KY....641
Reed, Patrick, Supt., Mammoth Cave National Park, Mammoth Cave, KY....658
Reed, Paula, Pres. (V), Oldest Stone House Museum, Lakewood, OH....1326
Reed, Phylis, Librarian, Historical Society of Glastonbury, Glastonbury, CT....275
Reed, Robert, Pres., Smith County Historical Society, Tyler, TX....1652
Reed Sanchez, Pamela, Dir. Devel., George Eastman House/International Museum of Photography and Film, Rochester, NY....1201
Reed, Scott, Chm. Zoological Park Council, North Carolina Zoological Park, Asheboro, NC....1231

R–*Continued*

R–*Continued*

R–*Continued*

R–*Continued*

R–*Continued*

R–*Continued*

R–*Continued*

Rossi, Michelle, Chm. (V), Itasca Historical Society & Itasca Genealogy, Grand Rapids, MN 879
Rossi, Robert, Pres. (V), Fitchburg Art Museum, Fitchburg, MA 778
Rossi, Ronald, Pres. (V), Southold Historical Society and Museum, Southold, NY 1213
Rossing, Chris, Dir., Kirby Science Discovery Center at the Washington Pavilion, Sioux Falls, SD 1542
Rossing, Chris, Dir., Washington Pavilion of Arts and Science, Sioux Falls, SD 1542
Rossino, Sharon, Exec. Dir., Hamill House Museum, Georgetown, CO 247
Rossiter, Dr. Andrew, Dir., Waikiki Aquarium, Honolulu, HI 448
Rossiter, M. Kay, Cur., Uinta County Museum, Evanston, WY 1857
Rossiter, Shannon, Dir. & C.E.O., Mohave Museum of History and Arts, Kingman, AZ 45
Rossman, James, Chm. (V), The Brooklyn Historical Society, Brooklyn, NY 1110
Rossotti, Lynn, Head Communications & Media Rels., Hillwood Estate, Museum & Gardens, Washington, DC 318
Rossy, Caroline, Membership & Visitor Svcs., American Swedish Historical Foundation & Museum, Philadelphia, PA 1450
Rotblatt, Marty, Exec. Dir., Farmington Valley Arts Center (FVAC), Avon, CT 266
Rotegard, Laura, Supt., Grant-Kohrs Ranch National Historic Site, Deer Lodge, MT 961
Rotenberg, Judi, Pres. (V), Rockport Art Association, Rockport, MA 802
Rotenizer, David E., Mgr., Grave Creek Mound Archaeological Complex, Moundsville, WV 1803
Roth, Allison, Pres., Reverend Dan Foster House, Museum of the Weathersfield Historical Society, Weathersfield, VT 1693
Roth, Amy, Dir. Corporate Partnerships, Whitney Museum of American Art, New York, NY 1184
Roth, Dave, Mgr. Operations, Golden Gate Railroad Museum, Sunol, CA 215
Roth, Dennis, Chm. & Pres., Grant County Museum, Carson, ND 1279
Roth, Eric J., Exec. Dir., The Huguenot Historical Society, New Paltz, NY 1161
Roth, Eric J., Exec. Dir., Locust Lawn and Terwilliger House, Gardiner, NY 1136
Roth, Gary G., Pres. & C.E.O., Mordecai Historic Park, Raleigh, NC 1263
Roth, James, Deputy Dir., John F. Kennedy Presidential Library & Museum, Boston, MA 760
Roth, Jeffrey, Vice Pres. Budget & Planning, The New York Public Library, Astor, Lenox and Tilden Foundations, New York, NY 1178
Roth, Jennifer, Mgr., The David Wills House, Gettysburg, PA 1427
Roth, Linda H., Senior Cur. and Charles C. & Eleanor Lamont Cunningham Cur. European Decorative Arts, Wadsworth Atheneum Museum of Art, Hartford, CT 279
Roth, Paige, Admin. Asst., Martha's Vineyard Museum, Edgartown, MA 776
Roth, Ronald C., C.E.O. & Dir., Planetarium at the Reading Public Museum, Reading, PA 1470
Roth, Ronald C., Dir. & C.E.O., Reading Public Museum, Reading, PA 1470
Roth, William, Vice Chm. (V), Audubon County Historical Society, Exira, IA 586
Roth Williams, Jane, Cur., Kitsap County Historical Society Museum, Bremerton, WA 1760
Rothenberg, Peter, Cur., Museum of Early Trades & Crafts, Madison, NJ 1046
Rothermel, Barbara, Dir., Daura Gallery, Lynchburg, VA 1722
Rothkopf, Katherine, Cur. Painting & Sculpture, The Baltimore Museum of Art, Baltimore, MD 720
Rothlein, Anne, C.E.O., The Kearny Cottage, Perth Amboy, NJ 1057
Rothman, Mark, Dir., Los Angeles Museum of the Holocaust, Los Angeles, CA 139
Rothschild, Alan, Owner, Rothschild Petersen Patent Model Museum, Cazenovia, NY 1119
Rotsart, John A., Exec. Dir., San Diego Model Railroad Museum, Inc., San Diego, CA 183
Rotsart, Veronique, Gift Shop Mgr., San Diego Model Railroad Museum, Inc., San Diego, CA 183
Rottenberg, Fran, Cur. Education, Robert C. Williams Paper Museum, Atlanta, GA 408
Rotterman, John, Pres. (V), Jesse James Home Museum, Saint Joseph, MO 944
Rotterman, John, Pres. (V), Patee House Museum, Saint Joseph, MO 944
Rouge, John, Dir. Visitor Svcs. & Facilities, Museum of Science & History of Jacksonville, Jacksonville, FL 356
Roulston, Dr. T'ai H., Cur., Orland E. White Arboretum, Boyce, VA 1702
Round, Nancy, Assoc. Cur. Education, Youth, Family & Community, Joslyn Art Museum, Omaha, NE 995
Rounds, Jon, Chm. Bd., Boston Children's Museum, Boston, MA 758
Rounds, Kathleen, Visitor Center Coord., Harriet Beecher Stowe Center, Hartford, CT 278
Rounds, Leslie, Exec. Dir., Saco Museum, Saco, ME 711
Rouse, Cheli, Mgr. Operations & Museum Shop Mgr., Oak Hill and The Martha Berry Museum, Rome, GA 430
Rouse, John, Dir. Operations, Aquarium of the Pacific, Long Beach, CA 131
Rouse, Marcia, Coord. Education, Centerville - Washington Township Historical Society & Asahel Wright Community Center, Centerville, OH 1301
Rousey Murdock, Jodean, Cur. Education, Rock Island Arsenal Museum, Rock Island, IL 516
Rousey, Robert, Guide, Rogers Historical Museum, Rogers, AR 83
Roush, David H., Chm. (V), Historical Society of Carroll County, Westminster, MD 750
Roush, Ruth, Editor, The Snyder County Historical Society, Middleburg, PA 1445
Roussel, Denise, Exec. Dir., McNamara House Museum, Victoria, TX 1652
Routhier, Jessica, Dir., Saco Museum, Saco, ME 711
Routley, Keith, Cur., Fort Stanwix National Monument, Rome, NY 1203
Routt, Brooke, Museum Store Mgr., Kentucky Railway Museum, Inc., New Haven, KY 660
Rouvier, Helene, Cultural Dir., Wiyot Heritage Center, Loleta, CA 130
Rowan, Bruce, Treas., Roger Tory Peterson Institute of Natural History, Jamestown, NY 1148
Rowan, Jackie, Pres. (V), Harbour House Museum, Crystal Falls, MI 831
Rowan, Jo, Pres. (V), University of Virginia Art Museum, Charlottesville, VA 1705
Rowars, Lorelei, Museum Shop Mgr., The Newark Museum, Newark, NJ 1053
Rowbottom, Debra, Dir. Visitor Svcs., Minnesota Discovery Center, Chisholm, MN 872
Rowe, Ann, Research Assoc. Western Hemisphere, The Textile Museum, Washington, DC 330
Rowe, Barbara L., Cur., Cape Fear Museum of History and Science, Wilmington, NC 1271
Rowe Berry, Victoria, C.E.O. & Dir., Nora Eccles Harrison Museum of Art, Logan, UT 1664
Rowe, Bruce, Program Mgr., Indiana Dunes National Lakeshore, Porter, IN 562
Rowe, Carol, Pres., Boone County Historical Museum, Belvidere, IL 471
Rowe, Dale, Vice Pres., Junction City Historical Society, Junction City, OR 1393
Rowe, Elizabeth, Dir. Operations, Squam Lakes Natural Science Center, Holderness, NH 1020
Rowe, Janis, Mktg. & Graphics, The Hubbard Museum of the American West, Ruidoso Downs, NM 1087
Rowe, Joni, Museum Specialist, Morristown National Historical Park, Morristown, NJ 1050
Rowe, Timothy, Dir. Vertebrate Paleontology Lab, Texas Natural Science Center, Austin, TX 1584
Rowell, Olivia, Cur., Alabama River Museum, Finchburg, AL 11
Rowell, Olivia, Mgr. Alabama River Museum, Monroe County Heritage Museum, Monroeville, AL 18
Rowland, Ann, C.F.O., Los Angeles County Museum of Art, Los Angeles, CA 138
Rowland, David B., Pres. (V), Old York Road Historical Society, Jenkintown, PA 1436
Rowland, Mike, Cur., Museum of Aviation at Robins Air Force Base, GA, Warner Robins, GA 439
Rowland, Rodney, Collections Mgr., Strawbery Banke Museum, Portsmouth, NH 1027
Rowland, Tari, Garden Historian, Midway Village Museum, Rockford, IL 517
Rowland, William, Maintenance & Repair Tech., Heavener Runestone State Park, Heavener, OK 1363
Rowlands, Chris, Outreach Naturalist, Aullwood Audubon Center and Farm, Dayton, OH 1315
Rowley, Dean, Historian, Martin Luther King, Jr. National Historic Site and Preservation District, Atlanta, GA 406
Rowley, Doug, Gardener Foreman, Kenilworth Park and Aquatic Gardens, Washington, DC 320
Rowley, Ina, Treas., Westport Maritime Museum, Westport, WA 1794
Rowley, Linda, Unit Business Mgr., Allen R. Hite Art Institute, Louisville, KY 654
Rowley, Londi, Budget & Accounting Officer, Utah State Historical Society, Salt Lake City, UT 1672
Rowold, Kathleen L., Cur., Elizabeth Sage Historic Costume Collection, Bloomington, IN 532
Rowsom, Christopher, Exec. Dir. USS Constellation Museum & Baltimore Maritime Museum, Baltimore, MD 727
Roxburgh, Karen, Mgr. Collections & Exhibits, Rocky Mountain Quilt Museum, Golden, CO 249

R–*Continued*

Russo, Walter, Sec., Children's Discovery Museum of the Desert, Rancho Mirage, CA 168
Russomano, Raymond, C.E.O. & Pres. (V), Historical Society of Ocean Grove, New Jersey, Ocean Grove, NJ ...1054
Rusterholtz, Pauline, Dir. Retail Sales, Bowers Museum, Santa Ana, CA 201
Rustin, Jim, Maintenance Supvr., Vizcaya Museum and Gardens, Miami, FL 367
Rustuhaltz, Don, Chm. (V), Saunders Memorial Museum, Berryville, AR 67
Ruta, Anne, Collections Mgr., Daughters of the American Revolution Museum, Washington, DC 316
Ruta, Paula, Office Mgr., Danvers Historical Society, Danvers, MA 773
Rutberg, Carl, Exec. Dir., Alice Austen House Museum, Staten Island, NY 1214
Ruth, Darryl, Pres., West Virginia Northern Community College Alumni Association Museum, Wheeling, WV 1808
Ruth, Dave, Supt., Richmond National Battlefield Park, Richmond, VA 1740
Ruth, David R., Supt., Maggie L. Walker National Historic Site, Richmond, VA ..1739
Rutherford, E. Howard, Pres., The Pier Aquarium, Saint Petersburg, FL 384
Rutherford, J.J., Dir. Education, History Colorado, The Colorado Historical Society, Denver, CO 240
Rutherford, Mary Jane, Community Rels. Officer, The Fred Jones Jr. Museum of Art, Norman, OK 1368
Rutherford, Nichole, Dir. Devel., Seacoast Science Center, Rye, NH 1028
Rutherford, Paul, Maintenance Supvr., Wisconsin Maritime Museum, Manitowoc, WI 1830
Ruthford, Rich, Vice Chm., Newell Museum, Newell, SD 1537
Ruthruff, Middy, Archivist, Blackman House Museum, Snohomish, WA 1785
Rutka, Sofia, Registry Coord., Maryland Art Place, Baltimore, MD 724
Rutkin, Lynne, Mgr. Devel., The Frick Collection, New York, NY 1168
Rutkowski, Henry W., Bldg. Chm., Rebecca Nurse Homestead, Danvers, MA 773
Rutkowski, Kathryn P., Cur., Rebecca Nurse Homestead, Danvers, MA 773
Rutland, Harriet, Owner & C.E.O., Harbor Ranch, Dripping Springs, TX 1602
Rutland, Jan, Dir., National Bottle Museum, Ballston Spa, NY 1101
Rutledge, David, Business Mgr., Concordia Historical Institute, Saint Louis, MO 946
Rutledge, Heather, Asst. Dir., Abington Art Center, Jenkintown, PA 1436
Rutter, Kim, Pres. Bd. Trustees, Martin and Osa Johnson Safari Museum, Chanute, KS 607
Ruud, Brandon K., Asst. Cur. American Art, The Art Institute of Chicago, Chicago, IL 476
Rux, Sandra, Dir., John Paul Jones House Museum, Portsmouth, NH 1026
Ruxin, Paul T., Chm. (V), Folger Shakespeare Library, Washington, DC 317
Ruyter, Mia, Dir. Mktg., The Renaissance Society at The University of Chicago, Chicago, IL 486
Ruzbarsky, Erica, Administrative Asst., Knights of Columbus Museum, New Haven, CT 286
Ruzzamenti, LeAnne, Dir. Mktg., Crocker Art Museum, Sacramento, CA 175
Ryan, Charles E., Supvr. Maintenance, Virginia Zoological Park, Norfolk, VA ..1731
Ryan Cook, Joelle, Deputy Dir., Columbia Museum of Art, Columbia, SC 1508
Ryan, Darlene, Chm. (V), Port Angeles Fine Arts Center & Webster's Woods Art Park, Port Angeles, WA 1775
Ryan, David, Cur. & Registrar, Colorado Springs Museum, Colorado Springs, CO 234
Ryan, Debora, Sr. Cur., Everson Museum of Art, Syracuse, NY 1218
Ryan, Donna, Sec., Almond Historical Society/Hagadorn House Museum, Almond, NY 1098
Ryan, Elizabeth G., Dir. Museums, The Beaufort Arsenal, Beaufort, SC 1500
Ryan, Elizabeth G., Dir. Museums, The Verdier House, Beaufort, SC 1500
Ryan, Ethel I., Public Rels., Eustis Historical Museum & Preservation Society, Inc., Eustis, FL 346
Ryan, Evelyne H., Exec. Dir., Museum of the Bedford Historical Society, Bedford, NY 1103
Ryan, Jack, Gallery Dir., Watkins Institute - Brownlee O. Curry Jr. Gallery, Nashville, TN 1570
Ryan, Dr. James K., Cur. Entomology, Orma J. Smith Museum of Natural History, Caldwell, ID 457
Ryan, Jane, Education Asst., Grout Museum District: Grout Museum of History and Science, Bluedorn Science Imaginarium, Rensselaer Russell House Museum, Snowden House, Waterloo, IA 601
Ryan, Jay, Asst. Farm Mgr., Peter Wentz Farmstead, Worcester, PA 1483
Ryan, Jennifer, Asst. Dir. & Museum Shop Mgr., Niabi Zoo, Coal Valley, IL ...488
Ryan, Joleen, Asst. Cur. Children's Museum, Sangre de Cristo Arts Center & Conference Center, Pueblo, CO 261
Ryan, Kellyn, Museum Shop Mgr., Elmhurst Art Museum, Elmhurst, IL 493
Ryan, Lee A., Pres., Almond Historical Society/Hagadorn House Museum, Almond, NY 1098
Ryan, Mark, Vice Pres. Registration & Collections, Plains Art Museum, Fargo, ND 1281
Ryan, Dr. Michael, Cur. Vertebrate Paleontology, The Cleveland Museum of Natural History, Cleveland, OH 1308
Ryan, Paul, Dir., Mary Baldwin College/Hunt Gallery, Staunton, VA 1746
Ryan, Raymund, Cur. Architecture, Carnegie Museum of Art, Pittsburgh, PA 1464
Ryan, Richard, Cur., Walt Whitman House Museum and Library, Camden, NJ 1034
Ryan, Richard A., Archivist, Walt Whitman Birthplace State Historic Site and Interpretive Center, Huntington Station, NY 1144
Ryan, Robert, Dir., Boothbay Railway Village, Boothbay, ME 694
Ryan, Rose, Museum Shop Mgr., Connecticut's Beardsley Zoo, Bridgeport, CT 267
Ryan, Thomas R., Pres. & C.E.O., Lancaster County Historical Society, Lancaster, PA 1439
Ryan, Zoe J., Cur. Architecture & Design, The Art Institute of Chicago, Chicago, IL 476
Rybka, Walter, Site Admin. & Sr. Captain, Erie Maritime Museum & Flagship Niagara, Erie, PA 1424
Rychlak, Bonnie, Dir. Collections Cur., Isamu Noguchi Garden Museum, Long Island City, NY 1154
Rychtarik, John, Cur. Exhibits, South Dakota Art Museum, Brookings, SD 1527
Ryckbosch, Bart, Archivist, The Art Institute of Chicago, Chicago, IL 476
Ryczek, William, Pres., Middlesex County Historical Society, Middletown, CT 282
Rydberg, Marsha, Chm., Tampa Bay History Center, Inc., Tampa, FL 393
Rydell, Rebecca, Business Mgr., Burpee Museum of Natural History, Rockford, IL 516
Ryder, Debra, Dir. Education, Kansas City Zoo, Kansas City, MO 933
Ryder, Elizabeth, Pres. (V), Southeast Museum Association, Inc., Brewster, NY 1106
Ryder, Oliver, Ph.D., Geneticist, San Diego Zoo, San Diego, CA 184
Ryder, Timothy, Museum Technician, Southern Ute Cultural Center and Museum, Ignacio, CO 252
Rydlewicz, Carolyn, Education, Betty Brinn Children's Museum, Milwaukee, WI 1833
Rye, Leigh, Asst. Sec., Reading Public Museum, Reading, PA 1470
Ryen, Jim, Pres., Frontier Museum, Williston, ND 1292
Rykels, Sam, Exec. Dir., Louisiana State Museum, New Orleans, LA 681
Rylaarsdam, Tammi, Volunteer & Membership Mgr., Lynden Pioneer Museum, Lynden, WA 1771
Ryland, James, Cur. Collections, Monroe County Historical Museum, Monroe, MI 855
Rynd, Chase, Exec. Dir., National Building Museum, Washington, DC 323
Rynkewitz, Stephen J., Jr., Pres., McCoy House, Lewistown, PA 1442
Ryon, Sandy, Chm. (V), Bowman's Hill Wildflower Preserve, New Hope, PA 1447
Ryser, Alice, Archivist, Baranov Museum, Kodiak, AK 33

S

Saage, Wallace, Cur. Collections, The Heritage Society, Houston, TX 1620
Saager, Laurie, Asst. Gallery Shop Mgr., Madison Museum of Contemporary Art, Madison, WI 1828
Saager-Bourret, Stephanie, Cur., Platteville Mining Museum, Platteville, WI 1840
Saager-Bourret, Stephanie, Cur., Rollo Jamison Museum, Platteville, WI 1840
Saarnio, Robert, Deputy Dir., Honolulu Academy of Arts, Honolulu, HI 445
Saavadra, Kari, Museum Mgr., The Children's Museum of Rose Hill Manor Park, Frederick, MD 735
Saavedra, Lon, Exec. Dir., Hakone Estate and Gardens, Saratoga, CA 209
Saba, Khaleel, Archivist, Western Archeological & Conservation Center, Tucson, AZ 64
Sabel, Kris, Vice Pres. Cultural Programming, The May Gallery, Patron's Lounge, Beaver Creek, CO 229
Sabick, Chris, Dir. Conservation, The Lake Champlain Maritime Museum, Vergennes, VT 1692
Sabin, Carleen, Dir. Operations, Historic Bowens Mills & Pioneer Park, Middleville, MI 854
Sabin, Owen, Dir. Operations, Historic Bowens Mills & Pioneer Park, Middleville, MI 854
Sabine, J. David, Pres., The Arms Family Museum of Local History, Youngstown, OH 1353

S–*Continued*

Sablan, Mary Margaret, Exec. Dir., Commonwealth of the Northern Mariana Islands Museum of History and Culture, Saipan, MP 1867

Sable, Donald, II, C.E.O. & Pres. (V), Horseless Carriage Foundation & Automotive Research Library, La Mesa, CA 127

Sacca, Michael, Chm., Long Island Maritime Museum, West Sayville, NY..1228

Sacchetti, Gina, Cur., Richard I. Bong Veterans Historical Center, Superior, WI 1848

Sacco, Anthony J., Sr., Pres., Texas Trail Museum, Pine Bluffs, WY 1863

Sacco, Janis, Dir. Exhibitions, Harvard Museum of Natural History, Cambridge, MA 767

Sacco, Joan, Sec., Greater Hazleton Historical Society, Hazleton, PA 1433

Sacco, Joseph, Assoc. Dir. Education, National Zoological Park, Smithsonian Institution, Washington, DC 327

Sacco, Louise R., Exec. Dir., Museum of Bad Art, Dedham, MA 774

Sachnik, Stephen, C.F.O., Houston Museum of Natural Science, Houston, TX 1620

Sachs, Charles L., Sr. Cur., New York Transit Museum, Brooklyn Heights, NY 1113

Sachs, Jon, Web Designer, The Great American Doll House Museum, Danville, KY 645

Sachs, Samuel, II, Chm., Isamu Noguchi Garden Museum, Long Island City, NY 1154

Sachs, Sid, Dir., The University of the Arts - Rosenwald-Wolf Gallery, Philadelphia, PA 1462

Sack, Donna, Dir. Visitor Svcs., Naper Settlement, Naperville, IL 508

Sack, Jessica, Assoc. Cur. Public Education, Yale University Art Gallery, New Haven, CT 287

Sackey, James, Museum Shop Mgr., Northwest Railway Museum, Snoqualmie, WA 1786

Sackman, K.C., Mgr. Collection, Old Prison Museums, Deer Lodge, MT 961

Sackner, Sara, Dir. Devel., University of California Berkeley Art Museum and Pacific Film Archive, Berkeley, CA 94

Sacran, Jason, Programs Dir., Fort Smith Art Center, Fort Smith, AR 71

Sacrey, Dennis E., Pres. (V), Virginia Baptist Historical Society, Richmond, VA 1741

Sadeghi, John, Dir. Finance, The Sixth Floor Museum at Dealey Plaza, Dallas, TX 1600

Sadler, Bob, Public Rels. Dir., Dossin Great Lakes Museum, Detroit, MI 834

Sadler, David, Town Historian, Fryer Memorial Museum, Munnsville, NY 1160

Sadler, Dr. Donna, Chm., Dalton Galleries, Decatur, GA 416

Sadler, Edward, Pres., City Island Nautical Museum, Bronx, NY 1108

Sadler, Elizabeth, Librarian, Historical Society of Fort Washington, Fort Washington, PA 1426

Sadler, Eric, Maintenance, Somerset Historical Center, Somerset, PA 1474

Sadler, Ivan, Pres. (V), Children's Museum of Southeastern Connecticut, Niantic, CT 289

Sadler, Laura M., Sr. Vice Pres. Museum Enterprises, Field Museum of Natural History, Chicago, IL 480

Sadler, Patsy, Dir., Pella Historical Village, Pella, IA 597

Sadler, Wendy, Dir., Shalom Street, West Bloomfield, MI 867

Sadongei, Alyce, Asst. Cur. American Indian Rels., Arizona State Museum, Tucson, AZ 59

Sadowski, Laura J., Vice Pres. Institutional Advancement, Strong National Museum of Play, Rochester, NY 1203

Safanda, Elizabeth, Dir., Beith House Museum, Saint Charles, IL 519

Saferstein, Merle, Dir. Educational Outreach, Holocaust Documentation & Education Center, Inc., Hollywood, FL...353

Saffiotti Dale, Maria, Cur. Paintings, Sculpture & Decorative Arts, Chazen Museum of Art, Madison, WI 1827

Saffos, Mitzi, Dir. Special Events, Fredericksburg Area Museum & Cultural Center, Inc., Fredericksburg, VA 1712

Safir, Carol, Pres. & Chm. (V), The New York City Police Museum, New York, NY 1178

Safirt, Lynn Scott, Pres., The Cannon Village Visitor Center, Kannapolis, NC.1253

Sagar, Scott, Cur., The Thomas T. Taber Museum of the Lycoming County Historical Society, Williamsport, PA 1482

Sage, Jon, Park Ranger, Grand Portage National Monument, Grand Portage, MN 879

Sage, Sandy, Program Assoc., Texas Association of Museums, Austin, TX....1583

Sager, Susan Joy, Coord. Visitor Svcs. & Museum Shop Mgr., Ogunquit Museum of American Art, Ogunquit, ME 705

Sago, Janice, Sales Shop Mgr., Grand Village of the Natchez Indians, Natchez, MS 913

Sahagen, Gary, Business Admin., Huntington Beach International Surfing Museum, Huntington Beach, CA 123

Sahramaa, Arja, Museum Shop Mgr., Reston Museum, Reston, VA 1736

Said, Tania, Cur. Education, Ball State University Museum of Art, Muncie, IN 557

Saidpour, Massoud, Dir. Performing Arts, Music & Film, The Cleveland Museum of Art, Cleveland, OH 1308

Saieed, Dan, Chm. (V), National Medal of Honor Museum of Military History, Chattanooga, TN 1548

Saiki, Donna W., Dir., Pacific Tsunami Museum, Hilo, HI 442

Saily, John, Pres. (V), Talkeetna Historical Society and Museum, Talkeetna, AK 36

Sain, Annette J., Dir. & Museum Shop Mgr., The Ralph Foster Museum, Point Lookout, MO 942

Saint-Pierre, Adrienne, Cur., Fairfield Museum and History Center, Fairfield, CT 273

Saitta, Dr. Dean, Dept. of Anthropology Faculty Member, Museum of Anthropology, University of Denver, Denver, CO 241

Saivetz, Aliza, Dir. Education, Old South Meeting House, Boston, MA 762

Saja, Dr. David, Cur. Mineralogy, The Cleveland Museum of Natural History, Cleveland, OH 1308

Sajadian, Mort, Ph.D., Pres. & C.E.O., Amazement Square, The Rightmire Children's Museum, Lynchburg, VA 1722

Sajet, Kim, Pres., Historical Society of Pennsylvania, Philadelphia, PA 1454

Sakaguchi, Misa, Business Mgr., San Mateo County Historical Association and Museum, Redwood City, CA 170

Sakaguchi, Scott, Mgr. Cafe Kitchen, The Contemporary Museum at First Hawaiian Center, Honolulu, HI 443

Sakagucui, Scott, Exec. Chef, The Contemporary Museum, Honolulu, HI....443

Sakas, Ginger, Program & Membership, Mathias Ham House Historic Site, Dubuque, IA 585

Sakas, Ginger, Devel. Dir., National Mississippi River Museum & Aquarium, Dubuque, IA 585

Sakow, Neil, Owner & Cur., Neil's American Dream Museum, West Hartford, CT 300

Sakurai, Motoatsu, Pres., Japan Society Gallery, New York, NY 1171

Salafia, Marlaine, Dir. Operations, Newport Restoration Foundation, Newport, RI 1491

Salam, Halide, Cur., Radford University Art Museum, Radford, VA 1735

Salatino, Kevin, Dir., Bowdoin College Museum of Art, Brunswick, ME 694

Salcedo, Zinnia, Exhibitions & Program Mgr., Blue Star Contemporary Art Center, San Antonio, TX 1643

Salchow, Judy, Archivist & Genealogists, Oak Creek Historical Society-Pioneer Village, Oak Creek, WI 1839

Saldana-Lopez, Norma, Exec. Dir., Laredo Center for the Arts, Laredo, TX 1628

Salerno, Victor E., Chm. Bd. (V), Rochester Museum & Science Center, Rochester, NY 1202

Salesses, John, Pres. Emeritus (V), Newport Historical Society & The Museum of Newport History, Newport, RI 1491

Salgado, Jesus, Operations Supvr., El Paso Museum of Art, El Paso, TX 1604

Salgo, Christina, Trustee, The Salgo Trust for Education, Port Washington, NY.....1197

Salgo, Miklos, Trustee, The Salgo Trust for Education, Port Washington, NY.....1197

Saliga, Pauline, C.E.O., Charnley-Persky House Museum, Chicago, IL 477

Salinas, Andrew, Archives & Library Asst., Amistad Research Center, Inc., New Orleans, LA 678

Saling, Wally, Chief Docent & Museum Shop Mgr., The Crandall Historical Printing Museum, Provo, UT 1668

Salisbury, Richard A., Assoc. Cur. Mollusca, Orma J. Smith Museum of Natural History, Caldwell, ID 457

Sall, Candace A., Assoc. Cur., Museum of Anthropology, University of Missouri, Columbia, MO 924

Sall, Joan C., Dir., Philadelphia Museum of Jewish Art/Congregation Rodeph Shalom, Philadelphia, PA 1459

Sallee, Margaret, Financial Admin., Benjamin Harrison Presidential Site, Indianapolis, IN 546

Salley, Ron, Supt., Pinnacle Mountain State Park, Little Rock, AR 78

Sallie, Eddie, Dir. Security, Museum of Contemporary Art, Chicago, IL 483

Sallot, John, Mgr. Mktg., Desert Botanical Garden, Phoenix, AZ 50

Salmen, Nora, Cur. & Historian, The Log House Museum of the Historical Society of Columbiana-Fairfield Township, Columbiana, OH 1312

Salmeron, Peter, Pres. (V), Botanica, The Wichita Gardens, Wichita, KS 637

Salmi, Lyle J., Asst. Dir., Perkinson Gallery, Decatur, IL 490

S–*Continued*

S–*Continued*

Sawicki, Christine K., Exec. Dir., Stuart Heritage Museum, Stuart, FL....389
Sawinski, Jessica, Cur. Education, Washington County Historical Society, West Bend, WI....1850
Sawkins, Dr. Annemarie, Assoc. Cur., The Patrick & Beatrice Haggerty Museum of Art, Milwaukee, WI....1836
Sawyer, Andrew, Sun Water Indian Village/Archaeological Park Site Mgr. & Site Anthropologist, Boonshoft Museum of Discovery, Dayton, OH....1315
Sawyer, Andrew, Site Mgr., SunWatch Indian Village/Archaeological Park, Dayton, OH....1317
Sawyer, Carol, Conservator Paintings, Virginia Museum of Fine Arts, Richmond, VA....1742
Sawyer, Christian, Museum Coord., Billy Graham Center Museum, Wheaton, IL....528
Sawyer, Dorothy, Owner, Sawyer's Sandhills Museum, Valentine, NE....999
Sawyer, Jane, Vice Pres., Whipple House Museum, Ashland Historical Society, Ashland, NH....1012
Sawyer, Julia, Pres. Bd., Society for Contemporary Craft, Pittsburgh, PA....1468
Sawyer, Kim, Acting Exec. Dir., Roanoke Island Festival Park, Manteo, NC....1257
Sawyer, Lynette, Lighting, Electronics & Interactive Technician, Museum of the Albemarle, Elizabeth City, NC....1244
Sawyer, Millie, Vice Pres., Rifle Creek Museum, Rifle, CO....262
Sawyer, Robert, IV, Vice Pres., Ashland Logging Museum, Inc., Ashland, ME....690
Sawyer, Robert, V, Pres. (V), Ashland Logging Museum, Inc., Ashland, ME....690
Sawyer, Tom, C.E.O. & Pres. (V), Nordica Homestead, Farmington, ME....698
Sawyers, Claire, Dir., Scott Arboretum of Swarthmore College, Swarthmore, PA....1477
Saxon, Jeffrey, Dir., The Children's Museum of Cleveland, Cleveland, OH....1307
Saxton, Carolyn, Exec. Dir. & Museum Shop Mgr., Lubeznik Center for the Arts, Michigan City, IN....556
Saxton, Natalie, Museum Shop Mgr., Sonnenberg Gardens & Mansion State Historic Park, Canandaigua, NY....1118
Sayger, Bill, Dir., Central Delta Depot Museum, Brinkley, AR....68
Sayles, Mary, C.E.O. & Pres. (V), Texana Museum and Library Association, Edna, TX....1603
Saylor, Brenda, Business Office Mgr., Mid Atlantic Air Museum, Reading, PA....1470
Sayner, Mary, Pres. (V) & Gift Shop Mgr., Ozaukee County Pioneer Village, Saukville, WI....1843
Saywell, Edward, Chm. Contemporary Art & MFA Programs, Museum of Fine Arts, Boston, MA....761
Sazonoff, Dayle, Pres. (V), The Palette & Chisel, Chicago, IL....485
Sbuttoni, Lisa, Public Rels. & Mktg. Mgr., Edison & Ford Winter Estates, Fort Myers, FL....349
Scaduto, Adria, Museum Shop Mgr., Historic Richmond Town, Staten Island, NY....1215
Scaduto, Adria, Museum Shop Mgr., Staten Island Historical Society, Staten Island, NY....1216
Scaggs, Tom, Complex Mgr., Barrington Living History Farm, Washington, TX....1655
Scaife, Chad, Superintendent Botanical Garden, Washington Park Botanical Garden, Springfield, IL....523
Scala, Joseph A., Exec. Dir., Stone Quarry Hill Art Park, Inc., Cazenovia, NY....1119
Scala, Mark, Cur., Frist Center for the Visual Arts, Nashville, TN....1568
Scala, Nadine, Devel. Assoc., National Museum of Nuclear Science and History, Albuquerque, NM....1072
Scalco, Peter, Park Mgr., Fort Clinch State Park, Fernandina Beach, FL....346
Scalera, Michelle, Chief Conservator, John and Mable Ringling Museum of Art, Sarasota, FL....387
Scalf, Daniel R., Pres. & Gen. Mgr., The Lexington Cemetery, Lexington, KY....652
Scalf, Michael, Sr., Exec. Dir., International Photography Hall of Fame & Museum, Oklahoma City, OK....1370
Scalise, Bob, Registrar & Collections Mgr., University at Buffalo Art Galleries, Buffalo, NY....1116
Scalise, Charles, Pres. (V), The Battles Museums of Rural Life, Girard, PA....1428
Scalise, Charles, Pres. (V), Erie County History Center & Cashier's House, Erie, PA....1424
Scalzo, William C., Chm., Arizona State Parks Board, Phoenix, AZ....49
Scanlan, Mary, Chm. (V), Anderson Ranch Arts Center & Museum, Snowmass Village, CO....263
Scanlen, Jean, Administrative Asst., Boca Raton Historical Society, Boca Raton, FL....335
Scanlin, Ann, Pres. (V), Ojai Valley Historical Society and Museum, Ojai, CA....157
Scanlon, Tom, Dir. Public Programs, Harvard Museum of Natural History, Cambridge, MA....767
Scarbrough, Dennis, Maintenance Mechanic, Natchitoches National Fish Hatchery, Natchitoches, LA....677
Scarduzio, Linda, Cur., Historical Society of Glastonbury, Glastonbury, CT....275
Scarpuzzi, Michael, Vice Pres. Zoological Operations, SeaWorld San Diego, San Diego, CA....184
Scataloni, Gini, Museum Shop Mgr., New Jersey State Museum, Trenton, NJ....1064
Scearce, Gerry, Office Mgr., Danville Museum of Fine Arts & History, Danville, VA....1708
Scearce, Kenneth, Dir., The George D. and Harriet W. Cornell Fine Arts Museum, Winter Park, FL....398
Scelsa, Dr. Joseph V., C.E.O., Chm. (V), Pres. (V) & Cur., Italian American Museum, New York, NY....1171
Schaack, Megan, Cur., Wells Fargo History Museum, Minneapolis, MN....886
Schaad, Gerrianne, Cur. Image Collections & Fieldwork Archives, Dumbarton Oaks Research Library & Collections, Washington, DC....317
Schaadt, Mike, Dir. CMA, Cabrillo Marine Aquarium, San Pedro, CA....199
Schaadt, Robert L., Dir., Sam Houston Regional Library & Research Center, Liberty, TX....1628
Schaar, Raja, Dir. Programs & Operations, Museum of Design Atlanta, Atlanta, GA....407
Schack, Ralph, Pres. (V), Musical Box Society International, Houston, TX....1623
Schacknow, Max, Founder & Dir., Schacknow Museum of Fine Arts, Plantation, FL....379
Schaechner, Ann, Pres. (V), El Paso Holocaust Museum & Study Center, El Paso, TX....1604
Schaede, Chris, Dept. Sec., Krannert Art Museum and Kinkead Pavilion, Champaign, IL....474
Schaedler, Prof. Barbara, Bd. Chm., Bayard Cutting Arboretum, Great River, NY....1139
Schaedlich, Paula, Dept. Exec. Dir. Programs & Operations, and C.O.O., National Aquarium, Baltimore, MD....725
Schaefer, Beth, Cur. Natural Encounters, Houston Zoo, Inc., Houston, TX....1621
Schaefer, Carl, Pres. (V), Heritage Museum & Gallery, Leadville, CO....255
Schaefer, Elizabeth Meg, Cur., Wright's Ferry Mansion, Columbia, PA....1418
Schaefer, John-Paul, Asst. Dir. External Affairs, Aspen Art Museum, Aspen, CO....228
Schaefer, Mary, Financial Mgr., Boise Art Museum, Boise, ID....455
Schaefer, Matthew, Outreach Archivist, Herbert Hoover Presidential Library-Museum, West Branch, IA....602
Schaefer, Scott, Sr. Cur. Paintings, The J. Paul Getty Museum, Los Angeles, CA....137
Schaeffer, Astrida, Asst. Dir., Museum of Art, UNH, Durham, NH....1017
Schaeppi, Jean, Interpretive Specialist, St. Croix National Scenic Riverway, Saint Croix Falls, WI....1843
Schaeufele, James P., Dir. Operations, Dia: Beacon, Beacon, NY....1102
Schafer, Brian, Dir., The Memorial Opera House, Valparaiso, IN....568
Schafer, Carl, Assoc. Dir., Ball State University Museum of Art, Muncie, IN....557
Schafer, David, Exec. Dir., Florida Holocaust Museum, Saint Petersburg, FL....383
Schafer, Richard L., Chm. (V), Clark Center for Japanese Art and Culture, Hanford, CA....120
Schafer, Ron, District Supt., Will Rogers State Historic Park, Pacific Palisades, CA....159
Schafer, Rosemary, Office Mgr., Plantation Historical Museum, Plantation, FL....379
Schafer, Shelby, Buffet Mgr., Kimbell Art Museum, Fort Worth, TX....1610
Schafer, Sheldon, Vice Pres. Education, Lakeview Museum of Arts and Sciences, Peoria, IL....512
Schafer, Stacy, Co-Dir., Museum of Anthropology, Chico, CA....100
Schaff, Deanna K., Dir., Tate Geological Museum, Casper, WY....1854
Schaffenburg, Karen, Dir. Dance, Sangre de Cristo Arts Center & Conference Center, Pueblo, CO....261
Schaffer, Dale, C.E.O. & Owner, National Museum of Woodcarving, Custer, SD....1529
Schaffer, Gloria, Co-Owner, National Museum of Woodcarving, Custer, SD....1529
Schaffer, Stephen A., Dir., Argus Planetarium, Ann Arbor, MI....822
Schaffner, Bill, Vice Pres., Interlaken Historical Society, Interlaken, NY....1146
Schaffner, Ingrid, Senior Cur., Institute of Contemporary Art, University of Pennsylvania, Philadelphia, PA....1455
Schafroth, Colleen, C.E.O. & Dir., Maryhill Museum of Art, Goldendale, WA....1768
Schalch, Chuck, Vice Pres., American Helicopter Museum & Education Center, West Chester, PA....1481
Schalkwyk, Dr. David, Dir. Research, Folger Shakespeare Library, Washington, DC....317

Schall, Dr. Jan, Sanders Sosland Cur. Modern & Contemporary Art, The Nelson-Atkins Museum of Art, Kansas City, MO 934
Schaller, Anne K., Cur., Natick Historical Society, South Natick, MA 807
Schaller, Hydee, Dir., Elizabeth Myers Mitchell Art Gallery, St. John's College, Annapolis, MD 717
Schaller, Linda, Dir. Education & Tour Coord., Bonnet House Museum & Gardens, Fort Lauderdale, FL 347
Schaller, Russell, Sec., City Island Nautical Museum, Bronx, NY 1108
Schalliol, Garry, Dir. Outreach Svcs., Washington State Historical Society, Tacoma, WA 1790
Schallom, Jim, Membership Mgr., St. Louis Science Center, Saint Louis, MO 950
Schambach, Gayle, Museum Shop Mgr., Sharlot Hall Museum, Prescott, AZ....53
Schaming, Mark, Dir. Exhibits, New York State Museum, Albany, NY 1096
Schandel, Tim, Dir. Railroad Operations & Museum Shop Mgr., Lake Superior Railroad Museum, Duluth, MN 874
Schano, Ned, Dir. Mktg. & Communications, Senator John Heinz History Center, Pittsburgh, PA 1468
Schantz, James D., Chm. (V), Seashore Trolley Museum, Kennebunkport, ME....701
Schantz, Jennifer, Gen. Counsel & Chief Administrative Officer, New-York Historical Society, New York, NY 1178
Schantz, Michael W., Ph.D., C.E.O., Dir. & Cur., Woodmere Art Museum, Philadelphia, PA 1463
Schapp, Rebecca M., Dir., de Saisset Museum, Santa Clara, CA 205
Schar, Beverly, Chm. Acquisitions Committee, Libertyville-Mundelein Historical Society, Inc., Libertyville, IL 502
Scharf, Patricia, Dir. Admin. & Finance, Santa Monica Museum of Art, Santa Monica, CA 208
Scharfenberg, Jackie, Forest Naturalist, Henry S. Reuss Ice Age Visitor Center, Campbellsport, WI 1814
Schatz, Dennis, Sr. Vice Pres. Strategic Programs, Pacific Science Center, Seattle, WA 1783
Schatz, Nancy, Chm. (V), New Britain Industrial Museum, New Britain, CT 284
Schatzberg, Kathleen, Pres., Higgins Art Gallery - Cape Cod Community College, West Barnstable, MA 815
Schaub, Becca, Mgr. Youth Programs, Urban Institute for Contemporary Arts, Grand Rapids, MI 843
Schaub, Diane, Garden Cur., The Conservatory Garden, New York, NY 1166
Schaub, William, C.E.O., Evergreen Aviation Museum, McMinnville, OR 1394
Schaunaman, Lora, Cur. Exhibits, Dacotah Prairie Museum, Aberdeen, SD 1526
Schaunanman, Laura, Dir., Granary Memorial Gallery, Groton, SD 1532
Schaut, Robin, Museum Mgr. & Museum Shop Mgr., New Almaden Quicksilver Mining Museum, San Jose, CA 195
Scheben, John, Pres. (V), Erlanger Historical Society, Erlanger, KY 645
Scheeder, Donna, Acting Law Librarian, Library of Congress, Washington, DC 320
Scheel, Charnelle, Dir., Dakotaland Museum, Huron, SD 1533
Scheele, Edward, Dir., Greyhound Hall of Fame, Abilene, KS 603
Scheer, Randy, Gen. Cur., Lincoln Children's Zoo, Lincoln, NE 989
Scheets, Jeanne, Vice Pres. Mktg. & Public Rels., Indiana Historical Society, Indianapolis, IN 548
Scheetz, Jennifer E., Archivist, The Charleston Museum, Charleston, SC 1503
Scheetz, Rod, Ph.D., Cur., Brigham Young University Museum of Paleontology, Provo, UT 1668
Schefcik, Jerry A., Dir., Donna Beam Fine Art Gallery, UNLV, Las Vegas, NV 1005
Scheiblauer, Kim, Dir. Operations, Santa Cruz Art League, Inc., Santa Cruz, CA...206
Scheible, Ellen, Treas., Tarpon Springs Area Historical Society - Depot Museum, Tarpon Springs, FL 394
Scheicher, Judith, Pres. Park Comm., Fosterfields Living Historical Farm, Morristown, NJ 1049
Scheid, Irene V., Exec. Dir., Alley Pond Environmental Center, Inc., Douglaston, NY 1127
Scheider, Karen, Museum Shop Mgr., Idaho State Historical Museum, Boise, ID 456
Scheidt, Diana, Dir., Big Horn County Historical Museum, Hardin, MT 965
Schein, Elissa, Dir. Public Programs, Museum of Jewish Heritage-A Living Memorial to the Holocaust, New York, NY 1175
Schein, Jason, Asst. Cur. Natural History, New Jersey State Museum, Trenton, NJ 1064
Scheirbeck, Helen, Asst. Dir. Public Programs, National Museum of the American Indian, Smithsonian Institution, New York, NY 1177
Scheirman, Mary Anne, Volunteer Coord., McLean County Museum of History, Bloomington, IL 472
Scheldberg, Robin, Pres. (V), South Holland Historical Society, South Holland, IL 520
Schell, Rev. Edwin, Exec. Sec. (V), Lovely Lane Museum and Archives, Baltimore, MD 723
Schell, Kent, Dir. Devel., Rancho Santa Ana Botanic Garden, Claremont, CA 102
Schell, Ralph, Dir., Hiwan Homestead Museum, Evergreen, CO 244
Schelle, Leslie, Dir. Devel., Tucson Museum of Art & Historic Block, Tucson, AZ 63
Schelske, Dan, Park Mgr, Fort Abraham Lincoln State Park, Mandan, ND 1286
Schember, George R., Pres. & Dir., Winchester-Frederick County Historical Society, Inc., Winchester, VA 1756
Schenck, Kimberly, Head Paper Conservation, National Gallery of Art, Washington, DC 323
Schenck, Marc, Owner, Butterfly Zoo, Tiverton, RI 1497
Schenck, Marvin, Cur., Grace Hudson Museum & Sun House, Ukiah, CA 219
Schenk, Anne, Museum Shop Mgr., Minidoka County Historical Museum, Rupert, ID 465
Schenk, Joseph B., Dir., Art Museum of South Texas, Corpus Christi, TX 1594
Schenkel, Hunt, Archivist, Schwenkfelder Library & Heritage Center, Pennsburg, PA 1448
Schepmann, Andrea, Dir. & Museum Shop Mgr., Krohn Conservatory, Cincinnati, OH 1305
Schepmoes, Jim, Dir. Mktg., Stratford Hall, Robert E. Lee Memorial Association, Inc., Stratford, VA 1748
Scher, Adam, Vice Pres. Operations, The American Civil War Center at Historic Tredegar, Richmond, VA 1736
Scher, Anne, Dir. Communications, The Jewish Museum, New York, NY 1171
Scher, Herb, Dir. Public Rels., The New York Public Library, Astor, Lenox and Tilden Foundations, New York, NY 1178
Scherer, Jim, Camp Dir., John G. Voigt House, Plymouth, WI 1841
Scherer, Katherine, Deputy Dir., Robert A. Bogan Fire Museum, Baton Rouge, LA 668
Scherer, Scott, Dir., The University of Texas at San Antonio, Art Gallery, San Antonio, TX 1646
Schermesser, Jeanie, Admin. & Docent, The Hallmark Museum of Contemporary Photography, Turners Falls, MA 812
Scherting, Bruce, Dir. Exhibits KU Biodiversity Institute - KU Natural History Museum, Lawrence, KS 621
Schertz, Dr. Peter, Cur. Ancient Art, Virginia Museum of Fine Arts, Richmond, VA 1742
Schesny, Alex (Buck), Aquarium Supvr. & Facilities Coord., J.L. Scott Marine Education Center and Aquarium, Gulf Coast Research Laboratory College of Marine Sciences, The U. of Southern Mississippi, Ocean Springs, MS 914
Scheu, Molly, Gallery Staff, Boston University Art Gallery, Boston, MA 759
Scheuer, Cindy, Cur. Education, Air Zoo, Kalamazoo, MI 847
Scheunemann, Terri, Museum Shop Mgr., Marjorie McNeely Conservatory, Saint Paul, MN 894
Scheutz, Nancy J., Treas., The Museum of Nursing History, Inc., Philadelphia, PA 1457
Schexnayder, Charlotte, Bd. Dir., Desha County Museum, Dumas, AR 69
Schexnayder, Paul, Public Rels., Bayou Teche Museum, New Iberia, LA 677
Schiavo, Pasco, Esq., Pres., Eckley Miners' Village, Eckley, PA 1422
Schick, Al, Treas., Railroad Museum of Long Island, Riverhead, NY 1200
Schiebout, Dr. Judith A., Cur. Paleontology, Museum of Natural Science, Baton Rouge, LA 668
Schiefelbein, Arlene, Sec., Hillsboro Area Historical Society, Hillsboro, WI 1822
Schiefer, Carl, Dir., Don Garlits Museum of Drag Racing Inc., Ocala, FL 372
Schiefer, Chris, Museum Shop Mgr., Fresno Chaffee Zoo, Fresno, CA 116
Schiefer, Terence L., Cur., Mississippi Entomological Museum, Mississippi State University, MS 913
Schiele, Jim, Cur., Lake Region Heritage Center, Devils Lake, ND 1279
Schierkolk, Andrea, Public Programs Mgr., National Museum of Health and Medicine, Washington, DC 324
Schierup, Chris, Cur., John Day Fossil Beds National Monument, Kimberly, OR 1393
Schietinger, James, Dir., Perkinson Gallery, Decatur, IL 490
Schiffer, Lois, Sec., Audubon Naturalist Society, Chevy Chase, MD 730
Schiffer, Tim, C.E.O., Museum of Ventura County, Ventura, CA 221
Schifferdecker, Patrick, Site Mgr., Minnesota Historical Society's North West Company Fur Post, Pine City, MN 890
Schiffke, Robert, Vice Pres., Buffalo Bill Museum of Le Claire, Iowa, Inc., Le Claire, IA 591
Schiffner, Amanda, Student Registrar, Meadows Museum of Art of Centenary College, Shreveport, LA 686

S–*Continued*

Schmidt, Donna, Pres., Cramer-Kenyon Heritage Home, Yankton, SD....1545
Schmidt, Elaine, Vice Pres., Brooklyn Historical Society, Brooklyn, OH....1298
Schmidt, Freida, Cur. & Archivist, The Houdini Museum & Theater, Scranton, PA....1472
Schmidt, Gary, Pres. (V), Nicollet County Historical Society, Saint Peter, MN....897
Schmidt, Jan, Dir. Human Resources, Milwaukee Art Museum, Milwaukee, WI....1834
Schmidt, Jan, Cur. Dance, The New York Public Library for the Performing Arts, New York, NY....1179
Schmidt, Kathleen, Naturalist (Rocky River), Cleveland Metroparks Outdoor Education Division, Garfield Heights, OH....1322
Schmidt, Kristen, Asst. Registrar, Tucson Museum of Art & Historic Block, Tucson, AZ....63
Schmidt, Kristen, Registrar, The University of Arizona Museum of Art and Archive of Visual Arts, Tucson, AZ....63
Schmidt, Lois, Sr. National Pres., National Society of the Children of the American Revolution Museum, Washington, DC....326
Schmidt, Lori, Wolf Cur., International Wolf Center, Ely, MN....876
Schmidt, Lori, Treas., Scotland Heritage Chapel & Museum, Scotland, SD....1541
Schmidt, Mark A., Exec. Dir., Historic 1699 Winslow House, Marshfield, MA....789
Schmidt, Muriel H., Owner & Cur., Family Heritage Museum, Eureka Springs, AR....70
Schmidt, Peggy, Sales Shop Mgr., Sherman Gardens, Corona del Mar, CA....104
Schmidt, Phyllis, Dir. & Museum Shop Mgr., Grand River Museum, Lemmon, SD....1535
Schmidt, Robert, Pres. (V), Lutheran Heritage Center & Museum of the Perry County Lutheran Historical Society, Altenburg, MO....920
Schmidt, Rod, Advisor, The Movie Museum, Owosso, MI....859
Schmidt, Rolf, Chm., Reading Public Museum, Reading, PA....1470
Schmidt, Rolf D., Chm. (V), Planetarium at the Reading Public Museum, Reading, PA....1470
Schmidt, Sarah, Tour Program Educator, New Jersey State House, Trenton, NJ....1064
Schmidt, Saskia, Dir. Education & Community Programs, The Noyes Museum of Art, Oceanville, NJ....1054
Schmidt, Steve, Pres. Bd., Lincoln Children's Museum, Lincoln, NE....988
Schmidt, Steve, Space Science Educator, Rocky Mount Children's Museum and Science Center, Inc., Rocky Mount, NC....1265
Schmidt, Stuart T., Pres., Grand River Museum, Lemmon, SD....1535
Schmidt, Susan, Dir. Food Service, The Henry Ford, Dearborn, MI....832
Schmidt, Terry, Museum Shop Mgr., Batsto Village, Hammonton, NJ....1042
Schmidt, William H., Chm. (V), Calkins Nature Area/Field Museum, Iowa Falls, IA....590
Schmink, Donna M., Museum Specialist Collections, Indiana War Memorials, Indianapolis, IN....549
Schmit Nason, Dr. Marilee, Cur. Collections, Anderson/Abruzzo Albuquerque International Balloon Museum, Albuquerque, NM....1070
Schmitt, Ann, Dir. Education, Lakeview Museum of Arts and Sciences, Peoria, IL....512
Schmitt, Beth Ann, Education Coord., Strawbery Banke Museum, Portsmouth, NH....1027
Schmitt, Larry, Dir. Properties, Chicago History Museum, Chicago, IL....478
Schmitt, Lila, Vice Pres., Russell County Historical Society/Fossil Station Museum, Russell, KS....632
Schmitt, Linda, Exec. Dir., Reno County Museum, Hutchinson, KS....618
Schmitt, Pam, Dir., Prairie Village Museum, Rugby, ND....1289
Schmitt, Pamela, Museum Shop Mgr., Geographical Center Historical Museum, Rugby, ND....1289
Schmitz, Chris, Cur. Education, Utah's Hogle Zoo, Salt Lake City, UT....1672
Schmoeckel, Carolyn, Pres. (V), Great Plains Dinosaur Museum and Field Station, Malta, MT....968
Schmoker, William C., Chm. (V), Minnesota Children's Museum, Saint Paul, MN....895
Schmoldt, Robin, Gallery Dir., Cur. & Registrar, The Wisconsin Union Galleries, University of Wisconsin-Madison, Madison, WI....1829
Schmucker, Kris, Cur., Harvey County Historical Society, Newton, KS....628
Schneck, Sue, Exec. Asst., National Soaring Museum, Elmira, NY....1131
Schneider, Claire, Sr. Cur., Scottsdale Museum of Contemporary Art, Scottsdale, AZ....54
Schneider, Don, C.E.O. (V), The Movie Museum, Owosso, MI....859
Schneider, Edward L., Ph.D., Pres. & C.E.O., Santa Barbara Botanic Garden, Santa Barbara, CA....203
Schneider, Elizabeth, Chm. (V), Colton Hall Museum, Monterey, CA....148
Schneider, Gary, Dir. Education, Montclair Art Museum, Montclair, NJ....1048
Schneider, Jack, Education, The Maritime Aquarium at Norwalk, Norwalk, CT....290
Schneider, Judge James F., Dir., Museum of Baltimore Legal History, Baltimore, MD....725
Schneider, Karen, Librarian, The Phillips Collection, Washington, DC....328
Schneider, Kenny, Exhibits Supervisor, Panhandle-Plains Historical Museum, Canyon, TX....1592
Schneider, Kerry, Devel. & Membership, Intuit: The Center for Intuitive and Outsider Art, Chicago, IL....482
Schneider, Linda, Museum Shop Mgr., Lawrence Hall of Science, Berkeley, CA....93
Schneider, Lynn, Mgr., Garden of Eden and Cabin Home, Lucas, KS....624
Schneider, Mark, Horticulture Cur., Virginia Zoological Park, Norfolk, VA....1731
Schneider, Mary Etta, Pres. (V), The Huguenot Historical Society, New Paltz, NY....1161
Schneider, Melissa, Museum Asst., Albany Regional Museum, Albany, OR....1382
Schneider, Patricia, Dir. Human Rels. & Labor Rels., Milwaukee Public Museum, Milwaukee, WI....1835
Schneider, Paul, Dir., County of Los Angeles Fire Museum, Los Angeles, CA....134
Schneider, Rhonda, Finance Mgr., Rocky Mountain Quilt Museum, Golden, CO....249
Schneider, Vince, Cur. Paleontology, North Carolina Museum of Natural Sciences, Raleigh, NC....1263
Schneider, Wendy K., Dir. Devel., Buffalo Bill Historical Center, Cody, WY....1856
Schneiderman, Kara, Asst. Dir., Lowe Art Museum, University of Miami, Coral Gables, FL....340
Schneiderman, Lisa, Museum Shop Mgr., Cobb County Youth Museum, Marietta, GA....426
Schneidmiller, Ken, Cur. Collections, The Natural Science Center of Greensboro, Inc., Greensboro, NC....1249
Schnell, Dr. G., Cur. Ornithology, Sam Noble Oklahoma Museum of Natural History, Norman, OK....1369
Schnelle, Dr. Mike, Cur., Oklahoma State University Botanical Garden, Stillwater, OK....1378
Schnepp, Suzanne, Conservator, Objects, The Art Institute of Chicago, Chicago, IL....476
Schneyer, Rosemary, C.E.O., Stockbridge Library Historical Collection, Stockbridge, MA....810
Schnitzler, John, Restoration, Strawbery Banke Museum, Portsmouth, NH....1027
Schnormeier, Jim, Cur., Sacramento Zoo, Sacramento, CA....176
Schnuck, Mark J., Chm. Zoological Park Commission, Saint Louis Zoo, Saint Louis, MO....951
Schnupp, Connie, Retail Operations Mgr., The Children's Museum of Houston, Houston, TX....1619
Schnur, Melissa, Devel. & Mktg., Sherwin Miller Museum of Jewish Art, Tulsa, OK....1379
Schnurr, Marie, Cur. Millard Fillmore House, Aurora Historical Society, Inc., East Aurora, NY....1127
Schnurr, Marie, Cur., Millard Fillmore House, East Aurora, NY....1128
Schober, Kirsten R., Kirkman House Museum, Walla Walla, WA....1793
Schoeberlein, Rob, Dir. Special Collections, Maryland State Archives, Annapolis, MD....718
Schoelwer, Dr. Susan P., Florence S. Marcy Crofut Dir. Collections, Connecticut Historical Society, Hartford, CT....277
Schoen, Darlene, Vice Chm. (V), Trenton Historical Museum, Trenton, MI....866
Schoen, Gina, Librarian, The Textile Museum, Washington, DC....330
Schoenberg, E. Randol, Chm., Los Angeles Museum of the Holocaust, Los Angeles, CA....139
Schoenberger, Lori, Gallery Attendant, Appleton Art Center, Appleton, WI....1809
Schoenewaldt, Karen, Registrar, Rosenbach Museum & Library, Philadelphia, PA....1461
Schoenfeld, Judy, Chm., Mason County Museum, Mason, TX....1631
Schoenhals, Roberta, Aide, Crockett County Museum, Ozona, TX....1636
Schoening, Damon, Dir. NCAA Hall of Champions, Indianapolis, IN....551
Schoenke, Marilyn, Exec. Dir., Moanalua Gardens Foundation, Honolulu, HI....447
Schoensee, Suzi, Chm. Membership, Sierra County Historical Society (Kentucky Mine Museum), Sierra City, CA....211
Schoenthal, Rebecca K., Exec. Dir., Second Street Gallery, Charlottesville, VA....1705
Schoepske, Carol, Vol. (V), Glassboro Heritage Glass Museum, Glassboro, NJ....1040
Schoettel, Carl, Dir. Exhibit Devel., Discovery World, Milwaukee, WI....1833

S–*Continued*

S–*Continued*

Schwarz, Mr. Jim, Horticulturist, Dubuque Arboretum & Botanical Gardens, Dubuque, IA.....585
Schwarz, Melanie, Public Rels., Moss Mansion Historic House Museum, Billings, MT.....956
Schwarzer, Joe, Dir., North Carolina Maritime Museum, Beaufort, NC.....1234
Schwarzer, Dr. Joseph, Chief North Carolina Maritime Museum, North Carolina Office of Archives and History, Raleigh, NC.....1264
Schwarzer, Joseph K., Dir. NC Maritime Museums & The Graveyard of the Atlantic Museum, North Carolina Museum of History, Raleigh, NC.....1263
Schweitzer, Rob, Dir. Public Rels., Historic Hudson Valley, Tarrytown, NY.....1220
Schweitzer, Robert, Museum Shop Mgr., Historical Society of the Tonawandas, Inc., Tonawanda, NY.....1221
Schweitzer, Susan, Dir. Devel., Akron Art Museum, Akron, OH.....1292
Schweizer, Al, Site Mgr. Children's Museum of Virginia, Portsmouth Museums, Portsmouth, VA.....1734
Schweizer, Dr. Paul D., Dir. Museum of Art, Munson-Williams-Proctor Arts Institute Museum of Art, Utica, NY.....1222
Schwender, Judith, Registrar & Cur. Collections, National Quilt Museum, Museum of the American Quilter's Society, Paducah, KY.....661
Schwickerath, Judy, Accountant, Madison Museum of Contemporary Art, Madison, WI.....1828
Schwiekert, Willy, Chm., The Science Center of Pinellas County, Saint Petersburg, FL.....385
Schwing, Beverly, Pres. (V), Elkton Community Museum and Historical Society, Elkton, SD.....1530
Schwitz, Fred, Pres., Grevemberg House Museum, Franklin, LA.....671
Sciacca, Jane, Pres., Wayland Historical Society, Wayland, MA.....814
Sciame, Frank J., Jr., Chm. Bd. (V), South Street Seaport Museum, New York, NY.....1181
Scibetta, Peter, Museum Shop Mgr., Isamu Noguchi Garden Museum, Long Island City, NY.....1154
Scime, Toniann, Cur. Library & Archives, Amherst Museum, Amherst, NY.....1099
Scinto, David, C.P.A., Pres. (V), Underground Gold Miners Museum, Alleghany, CA.....86
Scism, Doris, Cur., Brown Mansion, Coffeyville, KS.....608
Sciutto, John, Chm. (V), Monticello Railway Museum, Monticello, IL.....506
Scoates, Chris, Dir., California State University, Long Beach, University Art Museum, Long Beach, CA.....131
Scocos, John, C.E.O., Wisconsin Veterans Museum-King, King, WI.....1825
Scocos, John, C.E.O., Wisconsin Veterans Museum-Madison, Madison, WI.....1829
Scofield, David, Dir. Meadowcroft Rockshelter & Museum of Rural Life, Senator John Heinz History Center, Pittsburgh, PA.....1468
Scofield, David R., Dir., Meadowcroft Rockshelter and Museum of Rural Life, Avella, PA.....1410
Scofield, Oscar, Chm., Motorcycle Hall of Fame Museum, Pickerington, OH.....1339
Scofield-Swanson, Mary, Dir., Silvercreek Museum, Freeport, IL.....495
Scoggins, Anthony, Photographer, Mingei International Museum, San Diego, CA.....180
Scoggins, Wilma, Bookstore Mgr., Kings Mountain National Military Park, Blacksburg, SC.....1501
Scoles, Jon, Dir. Strategic Mktg., Robert Crown Center for Health Education, Hinsdale, IL.....500
Sconyers, Pam, Dir. Finance, Mighty Eighth Air Force Museum, Pooler, GA.....429
Scopes, Nadia, Museum Shop Mgr., Catawba Science Center, Hickory, NC.....1251
Scopinich, Kris, Program Specialist, Drumlin Farm Education Center, Lincoln, MA.....786
Scotchmoor, Judy, Museum Rels., Museum of Paleontology, Berkeley, CA.....93
Scott, Adrienne, Cur., Museum of Anthropology, Chico, CA.....100
Scott, Amy, Cur. Visual Arts, Autry National Center of the American West, Los Angeles, CA.....133
Scott, Andreese, Archivist Staff, Hampton University Museum, Hampton, VA.....1716
Scott, April, Facilities Operational Dir., Mid-America All Indian Center, Wichita, KS.....638
Scott, Arvid T., Chm. (V) & Museum Shop Mgr., Petrified Forest of the Black Hills, Piedmont, SD.....1538
Scott, Barbara L., Dir., Howard Weeden House Museum, Huntsville, AL.....14
Scott, Bob, Vice Pres. Philanthropy, Minnetrista, Muncie, IN.....558
Scott, Brian, Chm. (V) & Pres. Flagship Niagara League, Erie Maritime Museum & Flagship Niagara, Erie, PA.....1424
Scott, Ms. Carol, 1st Vice Pres., Beck Cultural Exchange Center, Inc., Knoxville, TN.....1557
Scott Clement, Anne, Exec. Dir., Waterworks Visual Arts Center, Salisbury, NC.....1266
Scott, David, Chm., Colorado Ski & Snowboard Museum, Vail, CO.....265
Scott, David, Pres., Old Stone House Museum, Pennsboro, WV.....1805
Scott, David E., C.E.O., Baltimore Public Works Museum, Inc., Baltimore, MD.....720
Scott, Donna A., Asst. Dir. Admin., National Museum of the American Indian, Smithsonian Institution, New York, NY.....1177
Scott, Dwight, C.E.O. & Exec. Dir., Oklahoma City Zoo, Oklahoma City, OK.....1372
Scott, Earl, Visitor Information Asst., National Historic Oregon Trail Interpretive Center, Baker City, OR.....1384
Scott, Eileen M., Pres. (V), Cambridge Historic Museum, Cambridge, WI.....1814
Scott, Elva, C.E.O. & Pres. (V), Eagle Historical Society & Museums, Eagle, AK.....29
Scott, Frachele, Site Mgr., Historic Stagville, Durham, NC.....1242
Scott, Garland, Head External Rels., Folger Shakespeare Library, Washington, DC.....317
Scott, Giles F., Jr., Devel., Old Dominion Railway Museum, Richmond, VA.....1739
Scott, Gordon, Pres., Pahrump Valley Museum, Pahrump, NV.....1008
Scott Hackman, Mary, Early Childhood, Providence Children's Museum, Providence, RI.....1495
Scott, Heron, Lead Boatwright, Center for Wooden Boats, Seattle, WA.....1779
Scott, James, Vice Pres., Conneaut Railroad Museum, Conneaut, OH.....1314
Scott, Jan, Dir., Sid Richardson Museum, Fort Worth, TX.....1611
Scott, Jason, Assoc. Dir., Santa Fe Children's Museum, Santa Fe, NM.....1091
Scott, Jeanne, Mgr., Albinger Archeological Museum, Ventura, CA.....220
Scott, Jeanne, Operations Mgr., Museum of Ventura County, Ventura, CA.....221
Scott, John, Supt., Pea Ridge National Military Park, Garfield, AR.....72
Scott, Joshua, Pres., John Paul Jones House Museum, Portsmouth, NH.....1026
Scott, Julie, Dir., Rosicrucian Egyptian Museum, San Jose, CA.....196
Scott, Jutta, Pres. (V), Peacham Historical Association, Peacham, VT.....1686
Scott, Karen, Pres., East Brunswick Museum Corporation, East Brunswick, NJ.....1037
Scott, Kathy, Memberships, Botanica, The Wichita Gardens, Wichita, KS.....637
Scott, Kristen, Pres., The Chesapeake Beach Railway Museum, Chesapeake Beach, MD.....730
Scott, Marge, Cur., Pulaski County Courthouse Museum, Waynesville, MO.....955
Scott, Marjorie T., Cur., Jefferson County Historical Museum, Rigby, ID.....465
Scott, Martha, Mgr. Business & Mktg., Marianna Kistler Beach Museum of Art at Kansas State University, Manhattan, KS.....625
Scott, Mary, Pres., Issaquah History Museum, Issaquah, WA.....1769
Scott, Melissa, Aquarist, Flint River Quarium, Albany, GA.....399
Scott, Meredith, Dir. & Cur., Vermont Ski Museum, Stowe, VT.....1691
Scott, Mitch, Museum Shop Mgr. & Exhibits Designer, National Inventors Hall of Fame, Akron, OH.....1292
Scott, Monica, Office Asst., Diggs Gallery at Winston-Salem State University, Winston-Salem, NC.....1273
Scott, Myra, Registrar, Nasher Museum of Art at Duke University, Durham, NC.....1243
Scott, Dr. Randall, Cur. Botany, Colorado Plateau Biodiversity Center, Flagstaff, AZ.....41
Scott, Richard, Cur. Collections, Gallier House, New Orleans, LA.....680
Scott, Richard, Cur. Collections, Hermann-Grima, New Orleans, LA.....680
Scott, Robert H., Pres. (V), DeCordova Sculpture Park & Museum, Lincoln, MA.....786
Scott, Dr. Roger L., Dir., Hardin Planetarium, Bowling Green, KY.....642
Scott, Rose, C.E.O. & Museum Shop Mgr., Schmidt House Museum & Research Library, Grants Pass, OR.....1391
Scott Rummage, Kathy, Public Rels. & Media, Spirit Square Center for Arts and Education, Charlotte, NC.....1240
Scott, RyAnn, Mgr. Library, American Numismatic Association Money Museum, Colorado Springs, CO.....233
Scott, Sandy, Cur., Cracker Trail Museum, Zolfo Springs, FL.....399
Scott, Sharyl, Sec., Newell Museum, Newell, SD.....1537
Scott, Shirley, Pres. & Webmaster, Christian County Historical Society and Museum, Ozark, MO.....941
Scott, Shirley, Dir., Heart of West Texas Museum, Colorado City, TX.....1594
Scott, Steve, Head Horticulture, Cheyenne Botanic Gardens, Cheyenne, WY.....1854
Scott, Terri, Co Dir., Coutts Memorial Museum of Art, Inc., El Dorado, KS.....610
Scott, Tim, Gen. Mgr., Petrified Forest of the Black Hills, Piedmont, SD.....1538

S–Continued

S–*Continued*

Shaffer, Glendora, Bd. Chm., Longmont Museum, Longmont, CO.....257
Shaffer, Mark, Dir., Carnegie Historical Museum, Fairfield, IA.....586
Shaffer, Mike, Treas., Historical Society of Washington County, Virginia, Abingdon, VA.....1695
Shaffer, Randy, Pres. (V), Ehrhart Museum, Antwerp, OH.....1293
Shaffer, Robert L., Cur. Emeritus, Herbarium of the University of Michigan, Ann Arbor, MI.....822
Shaffer, Todd, Facilities Mgr., History San Jose, San Jose, CA.....195
Shaffner, Denny, Pres., Clearfield County Historical Society, Clearfield, PA.....1418
Shagley, Rick, Pres. Bd. Mgrs. (V), Swope Art Museum, Terre Haute, IN.....567
Shagonaby, Joyce, Mgr., Andrew J. Blackbird Museum, Harbor Springs, MI.....844
Shagonaby, Robert, Pres. (V), Andrew J. Blackbird Museum, Harbor Springs, MI.....844
Shaheen, Diane, Museum Coord., Patty and Jay Baker Naples Museum of Art, Naples, FL.....370
Shaheen, Yvonne, Chm. Trustees (V), The Children's Museum of Indianapolis, Indianapolis, IN.....547
Shahid, Sy, Dir., Heard Natural Science Museum & Wildlife Sanctuary, McKinney, TX.....1631
Shaiman, Jason, Chief Cur. Exhibitions, The University of South Carolina McKissick Museum, Columbia, SC.....1510
Shain Schloss, Karen, Chm. (V), The Temple Judea Museum of Reform Congregation Keneseth Israel, Elkins Park, PA.....1422
Shainin, Christopher, Exec. Dir., Kirkland Arts Center, Kirkland, WA.....1770
Shakespear, Janie, Admin. Asst., Lost City Museum, Overton, NV.....1008
Shakespeare, Lain, Interim Bd. Pres., Wren's Nest, Atlanta, GA.....409
Shalberg, Jackie, Archivist, Academy of Model Aeronautics/National Model Aviation Museum, Muncie, IN.....557
Shalewitz, Warren, Museum Shop Mgr., Museum of Jewish Heritage-A Living Memorial to the Holocaust, New York, NY.....1175
Shalikashvili, Joan, Past Pres. (V), Steilacoom Historical Museum Association, Steilacoom, WA.....1787
Shaller, Rolla, Asst. Archaeologist, Panhandle-Plains Historical Museum, Canyon, TX.....1592
Shambarger, Sara, Dir. Art Fair, Krasl Art Center, Saint Joseph, MI.....864
Shambaugh, T.J., IV, Pres. (V), Piatt County Museum, Monticello, IL.....506
Shamblin, Sydney, Receptionist, Hana Cultural Center, Hana, Maui, HI.....441
Shamo, Stella, Education, Hurricane Valley Heritage Park Museum, Hurricane, UT.....1663
Shanahan, Jacqueline, Museum Shop Mgr., Aurora Historical Society, Aurora, IL.....469
Shanahan, Michael, Dir. Education, Bishop Museum, Honolulu, HI.....443
Shanahan, Patricia M., Sr. Advancement Officer, Chicago Botanic Garden, Glencoe, IL.....497
Shanan, Michele, Museum Shop Mgr., America's Presidency Museum and Gallery of American History, Branson, MO.....921
Shanberg, Ariel, Exec. Dir., Center for Photography at Woodstock, Woodstock, NY.....1229
Shaner, Gregory, Dir., The Arthur & Kriebel Herbaria, Purdue University, West Lafayette, IN.....571
Shanis, Carole, Pres. (V), The Philadelphia Art Alliance, Philadelphia, PA.....1458
Shank, Nicholas B., Dir., Katherine Nash Gallery, Minneapolis, MN.....885
Shankland, Debra, Naturalist-Brecksville, Cleveland Metroparks Outdoor Education Division, Garfield Heights, OH.....1322
Shankle, Kent, Cur., Waterloo Center for the Arts, Waterloo, IA.....601
Shanklin, Michael, ED, C.E.O., Discovery Science Place, Tyler, TX.....1651
Shankman, Marsha, Dir. Publications, Maude I. Kerns Art Center, Eugene, OR.....1389
Shanley, Michael, Exhibits Mgr., Staten Island Children's Museum, Staten Island, NY.....1216
Shanley-Koeber, Mary, Sanctuary Dir., Laughing Brook Education Center & Wildlife Sanctuary, Hampden, MA.....781
Shanley-Koeber, Mary, Dir., Massachusetts Audubon at Connecticut River Valley Sanctuaries, Easthampton, MA.....776
Shannon, Anna-Maria, Asst. Dir., Museum of Art, Pullman, WA.....1777
Shannon, Brooke, Exec. Dir., Windham Textile and History Museum (The Mill Museum), Willimantic, CT.....302
Shannon, Christie, Museum Coord., Gulf Shores Museum, Gulf Shores, AL.....13
Shannon, Denny, Business Officer, Historic Sauder Village, Archbold, OH.1293
Shannon, Don, P.T. Boat Cur., The P.T. Boat Museum & Library, Germantown, TN.....1552
Shannon, Donna, Pres. Calaveras Historical Society, Calaveras County Historical Society Museum, San Andreas, CA.....178
Shannon, Jenkins, Exec. Dir., Pasadena Museum of California Art, Pasadena, CA.....163
Shannon, Kathy, Exec. Dir., The Petroleum Museum, Midland, TX.....1633
Shannon, Mary Kay, Cur. Education, The Branigan Cultural Center, Las Cruces, NM.....1080
Shannon, Nancy, Dir. Devel. & Mktg., Jersey City Museum, Jersey City, NJ....1043
Shannon, Patrice, Coord. Mktg., Oak Hill and The Martha Berry Museum, Rome, GA.....430
Shannon, Peggy, Dir. Mktg., The Contemporary Arts Center, Cincinnati, OH.....1305
Shannon, William, Pres., Chatham Railroad Museum, Chatham, IL.....475
Shannon-Miller, Joan, Dir., Mariani Gallery, University of Northern Colorado, Greeley, CO.....250
Shapiro, Avra, Dir. Public Rels, Museum of Tolerance, Los Angeles, CA.....140
Shapiro, Deborah D., Dir., Middlesex County Historical Society, Middletown, CT.....282
Shapiro, Elizabeth G., Exec. Dir., Sharon Historical Society, Sharon, CT.....293
Shapiro, Esther, Dir., Zimmer Children's Museum, Los Angeles, CA.....143
Shapiro, Jim, Second Vice Pres., Holocaust Memorial Resource and Education Center of Florida, Inc., Maitland, FL.....363
Shapiro, Jodi, Exec. Sec., Los Angeles Museum of the Holocaust, Los Angeles, CA.....139
Shapiro, Michael E., Dir., The High Museum of Art, Atlanta, GA.....405
Shapiro, Paul, Dir. Center for Advanced Holocaust Studies, United States Holocaust Memorial Museum, Washington, DC.....332
Shapiro, Robert N., Pres. (V), Peabody Essex Museum, Salem, MA.....804
Shapiro, Samuel, Chm. (V), Queens County Farm Museum, Floral Park, NY.....1133
Sharbaugh, Kathryn, Asst. Dir. Devel., Flint Institute of Arts, Flint, MI.....840
Sharik, Lisa, Deputy Dir. & Registrar BG John C.L. Scribner Texas Military Forces Museum, Austin, TX.....1580
Sharkey, Carolann, Dir., Key West Tropical Forest & Botanical Garden, Key West, FL.....359
Sharkey, Marilyn, Cur., Old Jefferson Town, Oskaloosa, KS.....629
Sharley, Marvin F., Vice Pres., Sutton County Historical Society - Miers Home Museum, Cauthorn Memorial Depot, Sonora, TX.....1649
Sharman, George, Vice Pres., Frontier Times Museum, Bandera, TX.....1585
Sharon, Dr. John, Pres. (V), Sarett Nature Center, Benton Harbor, MI.....826
Sharp, Avery T., Research Librarian & Museum Coord., Armstrong Browning Library, Waco, TX.....1653
Sharp, Cary, Horticulturist, San Diego Zoo's Wild Animal Park, Escondido, CA.....112
Sharp, Corwin, Dir. Program Devel., Billings Farm & Museum, Woodstock, VT.....1695
Sharp, G. Thomas, Pres. & Founder, Museum of Earth History, Eureka Springs, AR.....70
Sharp, Greg, Cur., Wally Parks NHRA Motorsports Museum, Pomona, CA.....166
Sharp, Holly, Pres. Bd. (V), Preservation Resource Center, New Orleans, LA.....684
Sharp, Jane, Research Cur., Dodge Collection, Jane Voorhees Zimmerli Art Museum, New Brunswick, NJ.....1052
Sharp, Jane P., Museum Shop Mgr., Pocahontas County Museum, Marlinton, WV.....1802
Sharp, Kevin, Dir., Dixon Gallery and Gardens, Memphis, TN.....1561
Sharp, Lewis I., Dir., Denver Art Museum, Denver, CO.....238
Sharp, Llyn, Coord., Museum of Geosciences, Blacksburg, VA.....1702
Sharp, Megan, Dir. & Cur., Plainsman Museum, Aurora, NE.....976
Sharp, Michelle, Gift Shop Mgr., The National Great Blacks in Wax Museum, Inc., Baltimore, MD.....725
Sharp, Pender, Chm. (V), Tobacco Farm Life Museum, Inc., Kenly, NC.....1253
Sharp, Robert V., Exec. Dir. Publications, The Art Institute of Chicago, Chicago, IL.....476
Sharp, Roger, Exec. Dir., Tioga County Historical Society Museum, Owego, NY.....1192
Sharp, Steve, Dir. Devel., Agua Caliente Cultural Museum, Palm Springs, CA.....160
Sharpe, Amory, Dir. Devel., Asian Art Museum of San Francisco, Chong-Moon Lee Center for Asian Art and Culture, San Francisco, CA.....186
Sharpe, Ed, Archivist, Southwest Museum of Engineering, Communications and Computation, Glendale, AZ.....44

S–*Continued*

Shelley, Majorie, Sherman Fairchild Conservator in Charge, Sherman Fairchild Center for Works on Paper and Photographs Conservation, The Metropolitan Museum of Art, New York, NY 1172
Shelley, Dr. Rowland, Cur. Terrestrial Invertebrates, North Carolina Museum of Natural Sciences, Raleigh, NC 1263
Shellow, Barbara, Chm. (V), The Japanese Garden, Van Nuys, CA 220
Shelly, Diane, Dir., ArtCenter Manatee, Bradenton, FL 336
Shelly, Ruth G., Exec. Dir., Madison Children's Museum, Madison, WI 1827
Shelp, Cheri, Education, Washakie Museum, Worland, WY 1867
Shelton, Barbara, Dir., Keystone Gallery, Scott City, KS 633
Shelton, Candice L., Education Specialist, Virginia War Memorial, Richmond, VA 1743
Shelton, Cully, Naturalist, Cable Natural History Museum, Cable, WI 1813
Shelton, Deborah, Southern Arizona Division Dir., Arizona Historical Society/Arizona History Museum, Tucson, AZ 58
Shelton, Deborah, Southern Arizona Division Dir., Arizona Historical Society Downtown History Museum, Tucson, AZ 58
Shelton, Deborah, Southern Arizona Division Dir., Arizona Historical Society Fort Lowell Museum, Tucson, AZ 59
Shelton, Deborah, Southern Arizona Division Dir., Arizona Historical Society Sosa-Carrillo-Frémont House Museum, Tucson, AZ 59
Shelton, Edwin, Dir. Exhibits & Education, Lubeznik Center for the Arts, Michigan City, IN 556
Shelton, George, Exec. Dir., Attleboro Area Industrial Museum, Inc., Attleboro, MA 755
Shelton, Sally, Mgr. Collections, Museum of Geology and Paleontology, South Dakota School of Mines and Technology, Rapid City, SD 1540
Shenk, Anne, Dir. Education, The State Botanical Garden of Georgia, Athens, GA 401
Shenk, Deborah, Dir. Devel., Shelburne Museum, Inc., Shelburne, VT 1690
Shenkman, Arlen, Chm. (V), Abington Art Center, Jenkintown, PA 1436
Sheoships, Susan, Education, Tamastslikt Cultural Institute, Pendleton, OR 1397
Shepard, Alma Jane, Sr. Vice Pres. Institutional Advancement, The National World War II Museum, New Orleans, LA 682
Shepard, Betty J., Dir. & Cur., Holyland Exhibition, Los Angeles, CA 137
Shepard, Charles A., III, Dir., Fort Wayne Museum of Art, Fort Wayne, IN 542
Shepard, Cher, Pres., Ashtabula County Historical Society, Geneva-on-the-Lake, OH 1322
Shepard, Dan, Dir. Program, BGCI (US), Brooklyn Botanic Garden, Brooklyn, NY 1110
Shepard, Don, Dir. Operations & Museum Shop Mgr., Kenosha County Historical Society and Museum, Inc., Kenosha, WI 1824
Shepard, E. Lee, Dir. Manuscripts & Archives, Virginia Historical Society, Richmond, VA 1742
Shepard, Joel, Film Video Cur., Yerba Buena Center for the Arts, San Francisco, CA 194
Shepard, Randall T., Honorary Chm., Historic Landmarks Foundation of Indiana, Indianapolis, IN 548
Shepard, Rebecca, Curatorial Asst., Fresno Art Museum, Fresno, CA 115
Shephard, Dr. Steven J., Asst. Dir., Alexandria Archaeology Museum, Alexandria, VA 1696
Shepheard, Ann, Archivist, Old Depot Museum, Ottawa, KS 630
Shepherd, Al, Chm. (V), Wyman Museum, Craig, CO 236
Shepherd, Barry, Exec. Dir., American Police Hall of Fame and Museum, Titusville, FL 395
Shepherd, Carolyn, Bd. Pres., Maturango Museum of the Indian Wells Valley, Ridgecrest, CA 171
Shepherd, Danielle, Volunteer Coord., Krasl Art Center, Saint Joseph, MI 864
Shepherd, Donna, C.E.O., American Police Hall of Fame and Museum, Titusville, FL 395
Shepherd, Joyce, Dir. Library, Lawrence County Historical and Genealogical Society, Bedford, IN 532
Shepherd, Larry, Exec. Dir., American Numismatic Association Money Museum, Colorado Springs, CO 233
Shepherd, Mary L., Dir. Operations, B.B. King Museum and Delta Interpretive Center, Indianola, MS 909
Shepherd, Terry, Resident Artist - Ceramics, The Art Center, Grand Junction, CO 249
Shepley, Joan, Pres. (V), History San Jose, San Jose, CA 195
Sheppard, Jennie, Communication Coord., Dr Pepper Museum and Free Enterprise Institute, Waco, TX 1654
Sheppard, Jim, Facilities Mgr., Racine Art Museum (RAM), Racine, WI 1842
Sheppard, Jude, Cur., Blaine County Museum, Chinook, MT 960
Sheppard, Lisa, Educator Museum of Indian Arts & Culture, Museum of New Mexico, Santa Fe, NM 1089
Sheppard, Louise, Sec., South Boston-Halifax County Museum of Fine Arts & History, South Boston, VA 1745
Sheppard, Mitch, Dir., Foellinger-Freimann Botanical Conservatory, Fort Wayne, IN 541
Sher, Kathy, Deputy Exec. Dir. External Affairs, National Aquarium, Baltimore, MD 725
Sheraw, Harry F., Chm. (V), Museum of Science and Industry, Tampa, FL 392
Sherbin, Joshua, Chm. Bd., Birmingham Bloomfield Art Center, Birmingham, MI 828
Sherburne, Jessie, Community Programs Coord., Montana Natural History Center, Missoula, MT 969
Sherefkin, Donald, Vice Pres., Marlboro Historical Society, Marlboro, VT 1683
Sherer, Aaron, Exec. Dir., Paine Art Center and Gardens, Oshkosh, WI 1840
Sherer, Jim, Financial Dir., Home of Stone (The Mueller-Schmidt House 1881), a Ford County Museum, curated by Ford County Historic Society, Dodge City, KS 609
Sherfey, Sharman, Devel., Creative Discovery Museum, Chattanooga, TN 1547
Sherfey, Sharman, CFRE, Public Rels., Creative Discovery Museum, Chattanooga, TN 1547
Sheridan, Brian, Dir. Devel., Heritage Square Museum, Los Angeles, CA 136
Sheridan, Clare, Librarian, American Textile History Museum, Lowell, MA 787
Sheridan, Terri, Librarian, Santa Barbara Museum of Natural History, Santa Barbara, CA 204
Sherk, Lea C., Chm. (V), The Athenaeum of Philadelphia, Philadelphia, PA 1450
Sherlund, Janet L., Pres., Nantucket Historical Association, Nantucket, MA 792
Sherma, Elizabeth, C.E.O. & Museum Shop Mgr., Berkshire County Historical Society, Inc. - Arrowhead, Pittsfield, MA 799
Sherman, Cathy R., Dir., Cordova Historical Museum, Cordova, AK 28
Sherman, George F., Cur. & Archivist, Museum of Women's History, Billings, MT 956
Sherman, James, Recording Sec., Gates House, Machiasport Historical Society, Machiasport, ME 702
Sherman, Jean, Pres., General Wait House, Waitsfield, VT 1692
Sherman, John, Chief Ranger, San Juan Island National Historical Park, Friday Harbor, WA 1767
Sherman, Rita, Pres. (V), Alley Pond Environmental Center, Inc., Douglaston, NY 1127
Sherman, Sarah, C.E.O., Schoharie Colonial Heritage Association, Schoharie, NY 1210
Sherman, Tom, Chm. Bd., Thomas Edison House, Louisville, KY 658
Sherman-Cisler, Patti, Deputy Dir., John Michael Kohler Arts Center, Sheboygan, WI 1844
Shermantine, Ray, Facilities Supt., The Haggin Museum, Stockton, CA 214
Sherrer, John, III, Dir. Cultural Resources, Historic Columbia Foundation, Columbia, SC 1508
Sherretts, Joshua F., Cur., Baldwin-Reynolds House Museum, Meadville, PA 1443
Sherrick, Rebecca, Aurora Univ. Pres., Schingoethe Center for Native American Cultures, Aurora, IL 469
Sherrill, Russell, Chm., Blaffer Gallery, The Art Museum of the University of Houston, Houston, TX 1619
Sherring, Jim, Vice Pres., Susquehanna Museum of Havre de Grace Inc. at the Lock House, Havre de Grace, MD 739
Sherritt, Brooke, Museum Shop Mgr. & Visitor Svcs., Taft Museum of Art, Cincinnati, OH 1306
Sherrock, Roger, C.E.O., Clark County Historical Society - Heritage Center of Clark County, Springfield, OH 1343
Sherry, Daniel, Dir. Shop Operations, The Art Institute of Chicago, Chicago, IL 476
Shertz, Brian, Chm. (V), Iron Hill Museum, Newark, DE 310
Sherwood, Amy, Events & Facilities Rental Mgr., Strawbery Banke Museum, Portsmouth, NH 1027
Sherwood, Frederick, Dir. Exhibits, Shore Line Trolley Museum, East Haven, CT 271
Sherwood Parker, Lynne, Exec. Dir., American Museum of Radio and Electricity, Bellingham, WA 1759
Sherwood, Robert, Vice Pres. Finance & Administration, Santa Barbara Botanic Garden, Santa Barbara, CA 203
Sheth, Hela, Mktg. Mgr., Gulf Coast Exploreum Science Center, Mobile, AL 17
Shevenell, Tom, Pres. (V), Sandwich Historical Society, Center Sandwich, NH 1013

Shewchuk, Diane, Cur., Columbia County Historical Society, Inc., Kinderhook, NY 1150
Shick, Richard, Ph.D., Pres. (V), Old Fort Niagara, Youngstown, NY 1230
Shickler, Roger, Ways & Means, Fresno Flats Historical Park, Oakhurst, CA 154
Shickles, Tim, Dir., Robert T. Longway Planetarium, Flint, MI 840
Shickles, Tim, Dir., Sloan Museum & Longway Planetarium, Flint, MI 840
Shieh, Mrs. Suewhei, Dir., Asian Arts & Culture Center, Towson University, Towson, MD 748
Shields, Kathleen, Admin., Dia Center for the Arts, Quemado, NM 1085
Shields, Lloyd, Treas., The Ogden Museum of Southern Art, New Orleans, LA 683
Shields, Scott, Cur., Crocker Art Museum, Sacramento, CA 175
Shields, Van, Dir., Historic Brattonsville, McConnells, SC 1518
Shields, Van W., Dir., Museum of York County, Rock Hill, SC 1522
Shiffer, Jamie, Ground Mgr., Hershey Gardens, Hershey, PA 1433
Shiffermiller, Laura, Dir. Devel., Fontenelle Nature Association, Bellevue, NE 977
Shifflett, Tammy, C.E.O., North House Museum, Lewisburg, WV 1801
Shifke, Sally, Museum Rels., Henry B. Plant Museum, Tampa, FL 392
Shifman, Barry, Sydney and Frances Lewis Family Cur. Decorative Arts from 1890 to Present, Virginia Museum of Fine Arts, Richmond, VA 1742
Shifrin, Susan, Assoc. Dir. Education, Philip and Muriel Berman Museum of Art at Ursinus College, Collegeville, PA 1418
Shigaki, Joy, Capital Campaign Mgr., Wing Luke Asian Museum, Seattle, WA 1784
Shigematsu, Karen, Research Assoc. II, Harold L. Lyon Arboretum, Honolulu, HI 444
Shih, Chia-Chun, Librarian, Kimbell Art Museum, Fort Worth, TX 1610
Shillieto, Sadie, Art Advisory Bd. Fellow, Mount Holyoke College Art Museum, South Hadley, MA 806
Shilling, Amanda, Devel., Ten Chimneys Foundation, Genesee Depot, WI 1820
Shilling, Sam, Education Coord., National Naval Aviation Museum, Pensacola, FL 378
Shils, Jon, Chm. (V), Atlanta Contemporary Art Center, Atlanta, GA 402
Shimada, K., Adjunct Cur. Vert Paleontology, Sternberg Museum of Natural History, Hays, KS 616
Shimerdla, Anne, Dir. Operations, Blank Park Zoo, Des Moines, IA 582
Shimizu, Holly H., Exec. Dir., United States Botanic Garden, Washington, DC 331
Shin, Roberta, Exec. Asst., Hood Museum of Art, Hanover, NH 1019
Shinaberry, Curt, Dir. Finance & Operations, Austin Museum of Art - Downtown, Austin, TX 1580
Shine, Greg, Chief Ranger, Fort Vancouver National Historic Site, Vancouver, WA 1792
Shine, Jenna, Financial Dir., Kellogg Historical Society, Kellogg, IA 590
Shinkle, Bradford, IV, Pres., The Museum of Russian Art, Minneapolis, MN 886
Shinkle, Kathy, Dir. Publicity, Palos Verdes Art Center, Rancho Palos Verdes, CA 168
Shinlever, Donna, Vice Pres., Thompson-Ames Historical Society, Gilford, NH 1019
Shin-tsu Tai, Susan, Cur. Asian Art, Santa Barbara Museum of Art, Santa Barbara, CA 203
Shipka, Susan, Controller, Desert Botanical Garden, Phoenix, AZ 50
Shiplet, Kevin, Operations Mgr., National Football Museum, Inc., Canton, OH 1301
Shipley, Alex, Dir. Museum Operations, Merchant and Drovers Tavern Museum, Rahway, NJ 1059
Shipley, Ben, Housekeeper, Museum of the Albemarle, Elizabeth City, NC 1244
Shipley, Sandra, Vice Pres. Exhibits & Museum Planning, Cincinnati Museum Center at Union Terminal, Cincinnati, OH 1304
Shipman, Adams K., Jr., Pres. (V), Natick Historical Society, South Natick, MA 807
Shipman, John, Dir., The Art Gallery at the University of Maryland, College Park, College Park, MD 731
Shipman, Margaret, Gallery Mgr., Brattleboro Museum & Art Center, Brattleboro, VT 1677
Shipp, Linda, Cur., Salisbury State University Galleries, Salisbury, MD 745
Shippy, Angela, Administrative Specialist & Museum Shop Mgr., Brunnier Art Museum, Ames, IA 572
Shippy, Angela, Administrative Specialist & Museum Shop Mgr., Christian Petersen Art Museum, Ames, IA 572
Shippy, Angela, Administrative Specialist & Museum Shop Mgr., Farm House Museum, Ames, IA 573
Shipstead, Kristi, Dir., Daniels County Museum and Pioneer Town, Scobey, MT 971
Shirakawa, Tessy, Chief, Interpretation, Mesa Verde National Park Museum, Mesa Verde National Park, CO 258
Shireman, Joyce A., Ph.D., C.E.O., Joseph Smith Historic Site, Nauvoo, IL 508
Shirer, Martha Emily, Chm. & Pres. (V), Calhoun County Museum & Cultural Center, Saint Matthews, SC 1522
Shires, Christopher, Dir. Education, Edsel & Eleanor Ford House, Grosse Pointe Shores, MI 843
Shires, James, Ph.D., Cur. Education, Kentucky Gateway Museum Center, Maysville, KY 658
Shires, Jeanette, Assoc. Dir., The Arts Center, Mattie Kelly Arts Center Galleries at Northwest Florida State College, Niceville, FL 371
Shirey, Carroll, Souvenir Shop Mgr., Baton Rouge Zoo, Baton Rouge, LA 666
Shirk, Karen, Dir. Devel., Copshaholm House Museum & Historic Oliver Gardens, South Bend, IN 565
Shirley, Jon, Chm. Bd., Seattle Asian Art Museum, Seattle, WA 1783
Shiroki, Kathy Gaye, Cur. Education, Burchfield-Penney Art Center, Buffalo, NY 1115
Shisler, Thomas, Site Mgr., Wahkeena Nature Preserve, Sugar Grove, OH 1344
Shive, Sonny, Chm. (V), Glasgow Museum, Glasgow, MO 927
Shivers, David J., Pres. (V), Salem Historical Society and Museum, Salem, OH 1342
Shives, Tracy L., Park Ranger & Collateral Curator, Monocacy National Battlefield, Frederick, MD 735
Shmeis, Beverly, Museum Shop Mgr., Isabella Stewart Gardner Museum, Boston, MA 760
Shoaf, Chrystal, State Park Ranger, Sonoma State Historic Park, Sonoma, CA 212
Shoaf, Crystal, Ranger, Petaluma Adobe State Historic Park, Petaluma, CA 164
Shoaff, Roger, Gen. Mgr., Boulder City/Hoover Dam Museum, Boulder City, NV 1001
Shoaff, Roseanne, Mgr., Boulder City/Hoover Dam Museum, Boulder City, NV 1001
Shoap, Toni, Annual Fund Mgr., Motorcycle Hall of Fame Museum, Pickerington, OH 1339
Shobe, Don, Accountant KU Biodiversity Institute - KU Natural History Museum, Lawrence, KS 621
Shober, Susan, Museum Shop Mgr., Ephrata Cloister, Ephrata, PA 1423
Shock, L. Jacob, Collections Cur., Biblical Resource Center & Museum, Collierville, TN 1550
Shockey, Bonnie A., Pres., Allison-Antrim Museum, Inc., Greencastle, PA 1429
Shoemaker, Chuck, Administrative Officer, Fort Smith National Historic Site, Fort Smith, AR 72
Shoemaker, Deborah, Museum Shop Mgr., Mississippi Petrified Forest, Flora, MS 906
Shoemaker, Doug, Park Mgr.-Outdoor Museum, Mississippi Petrified Forest, Flora, MS 906
Shoemaker, Innis H., Sr. Cur. Prints, Drawings & Photographs, Philadelphia Museum of Art, Philadelphia, PA 1459
Shoemaker, Marjorie J., Dir., Cur. & Museum Shop Mgr., Mennonite Heritage & Agricultural Museum, Goessel, KS 614
Shoemaker, Marla, Cur. Education, Philadelphia Museum of Art, Philadelphia, PA 1459
Shoemaker, Mary, Coop. Assoc. & Museum Shop Mgr., Antelope Valley Indian Museum, Lancaster, CA 128
Shoemaker, Rene D., C.E.O., Circle Gallery/College of Environment & Design - University of Georgia, Athens, GA 400
Shoemaker, Scott, C.E.O., Sunset Zoological Park, Manhattan, KS 626
Shogren, Samuel, Exec. Dir., Washington County Historical Society, Portland, OR 1401
Sholly, Cameron H., Supt., Natchez Trace Parkway, Tupelo, MS 917
Shomate, Lu, Exec. Dir., Schoolhouse History & Art Center, Colstrip, MT 960
Shomer, Dan, Dir. Facilities, Kentucky Derby Museum, Louisville, KY 655
Shonek, Gita, Curatorial Asst., Lowe Art Museum, University of Miami, Coral Gables, FL 340
Shonyo, David, Archaeologist, Gunston Hall Plantation, Mason Neck, VA 1725
Shook, Ray, Cur., Patterson Homestead, Dayton, OH 1317
Shook, Valarie, Coord. Membership, Flint Institute of Arts, Flint, MI 840
Shope, Erin, Mgr. School & Family Programs, Asheville Art Museum, Asheville, NC 1231
Shopsis, Mari, Dir. Education, Rensselaer County Historical Society, Troy, NY 1221
Shor, Cynthia, Exec. Dir. & Public Rels., Walt Whitman Birthplace State Historic Site and Interpretive Center, Huntington Station, NY 1144

S–*Continued*

S–*Continued*

Simmons, Byron, Facilities Mgr./Security, Hammonds House Museum, Atlanta, GA....405
Simmons, Christina, Assoc. Dir. Public Rels., San Diego Zoo's Wild Animal Park, Escondido, CA....112
Simmons, David, Timeline Editor, Ohio Historical Society, Columbus, OH....1313
Simmons, David, Dir., Wade House Historic Site, Greenbush, WI....1821
Simmons, Diane, Museum Shop Mgr., Los Altos History Museum aka Association of the Los Altos Historical Museum, Los Altos, CA....132
Simmons, Emily, Grant Coord., The Schuylkill Center for Environmental Education, Philadelphia, PA....1461
Simmons, Gerianne, Administrative Sec., Pajaro Valley Historical Association, Watsonville, CA....223
Simmons, Jamie, Cur., Ace of Clubs House, Texarkana, TX....1650
Simmons, Jamie, Cur., Texarkana Museums System, Texarkana, TX....1650
Simmons, Jerry, Museum Coord., Thomas E. McMillan Museum, Brewton, AL....7
Simmons, L. Patricia, Pres. & C.E.O., Akron Zoological Park, Akron, OH....1292
Simmons, Dr. Lee G., D.V.M., Dir., Henry Doorly Zoo, Omaha, NE....995
Simmons, LeRoy, Operations Mgr., Birmingham Civil Rights Institute, Birmingham, AL....5
Simmons, Lisa, Education, Monroe County Historical Society, Bloomington, IN....533
Simmons, Lloyd, Nature Park Programmer, Moccasin Lake Nature Park, An Environmental & Energy Education Center, Clearwater, FL....339
Simmons, Merrill, Dir. Whitehall House, Historic Homes Foundation, Inc., Louisville, KY....655
Simmons, Dr. Nancy B., Chm. & Cur. Division Vertebrate Zoology, American Museum of Natural History, New York, NY....1163
Simmons, Nikki, Accountant, Colorado Springs Fine Arts Center (Taylor Museum), Colorado Springs, CO....233
Simmons, Rich, Pres. (V), Ybor City Museum State Park, Tampa, FL....393
Simmons, Sharyl, Asst. Cur., Community Memorial Museum of Sutter County, Yuba City, CA....227
Simmons, Susan, Financial Dir., Membership & Public Rels., Islip Art Museum, East Islip, NY....1129
Simmons, William, Ph.D., Vice Pres., Rhode Island Historical Society, Providence, RI....1496
Simms, Carl, Visitor Center Mgr., Tryon Palace Historic Sites & Gardens, New Bern, NC....1259
Simms, Jenny, Interim Dir., Columbus Museum of Art and Design, Columbus, IN....536
Simms, Shelley, Cur. Asst., Jonson Gallery of the University of New Mexico Art Museum, Albuquerque, NM....1071
Simon, Arleyn, Archaeology & Ethography Collections, Arizona State University Museum of Anthropology, Tempe, AZ....57
Simon, Chloe, Museum Shop Mgr., The J. Paul Getty Museum, Los Angeles, CA....137
Simon, Dan, Vice Pres. Operations, Great Plains Zoo & Delbridge Museum of Natural History, Sioux Falls, SD....1541
Simon, David, C.E.O. New Mexico State Parks, Living Desert Zoo and Gardens State Park, Carlsbad, NM....1076
Simon, Elena Pinto, Dean Academic Admin. & Student Affairs, Bard Graduate Center: Decorative Arts, Design History, & Material Culture, New York, NY....1164
Simon, Hal, Chief Cur., Dallas Heritage Village at Old City Park, Dallas, TX....1597
Simon, Hal, Exec. Dir., Heritage Farmstead Museum, Plano, TX....1638
Simon, Harry, Treas., Rangeley Lakes Region Logging Museum, Rangeley, ME....709
Simon, Jane, Cur. Exhibitions, Madison Museum of Contemporary Art, Madison, WI....1828
Simon, Joyce, Exec. Vice Pres. & C.F.O., John G. Shedd Aquarium, Chicago, IL....482
Simon, Leslie, Rgnl. Archives Dir., National Archives and Records Administration - Mid-Atlantic Region, Philadelphia, PA....1457
Simon, Lou Anna, C.E.O., Kresge Art Museum, East Lansing, MI....837
Simon, Nancy, Dir., Poplar Grove Historic Plantation, Wilmington, NC....1272
Simon, Rochelle, Dir. Communications & Mktg., Connecticut Landmarks, Hartford, CT....278
Simon, Ronald, Cur., The Paley Center for Media, New York, NY....1179
Simoncini, Jacinta, Dir. Mktg., Mystic Aquarium & Institute for Exploration, Mystic, CT....283
Simonelli, Lynn, Vice Pres. Collections & Research, Boonshoft Museum of Discovery, Dayton, OH....1315
Simonian, Heidi, Dir. Mktg. & Public Rels., Bowers Museum, Santa Ana, CA....201
Simonian, Karen, Dir. Public Rels. & Media Rels., Wexner Center for the Arts, Columbus, OH....1314
Simons, Andrew, Cur. Ichthyology, Bell Museum of Natural History, Minneapolis, MN....884
Simons, Ben, Chief Cur., Nantucket Historical Association, Nantucket, MA....792
Simons, Jan, Vice Pres. Retail Operations & Museum Shop Mgr., Missouri Botanical Garden, Saint Louis, MO....949
Simons, Sherry, Museum Shop Mgr., Gulfcoast Wonder and Imagination Zone, dba G.WIZ, Sarasota, FL....387
Simons, Tom, Dir. Education, Omaha Children's Museum, Omaha, NE....995
Simonsen, Oliver, Pres. (V), Canajoharie Library and Art Gallery, Canajoharie, NY....1117
Simonson, Karen, Dir. Finance & Admin., Queens Botanical Garden, Flushing, NY....1133
Simonson, Mike, Chm. (V), Salisbury House & Gardens, Des Moines, IA....584
Simonton, Cindy, Pres. (V), Museum of Geneva History, Geneva, FL....352
Simpson, Alan K., Chm. (V), Buffalo Bill Historical Center, Cody, WY....1856
Simpson, Carolyn, Pres. (V), Johnson-Humrickhouse Museum, Coshocton, OH....1314
Simpson, Erion, Exec. Dir., Taos Art Museum, Taos, NM....1093
Simpson, John I., Pres. (V), Cole Land Transportation Museum, Bangor, ME....691
Simpson, Katherine, Sec., Stevens Museum, Salem, IN....564
Simpson, Kathleen, Dir. Institutional Advancement & Education, Springfield Museums - Connecticut Valley Historical Museum, Springfield, MA....808
Simpson, Kathleen, Dir. Institutional Advancement & Education, Springfield Museums - George Walter Vincent Smith Art Museum, Springfield, MA....808
Simpson, Kathleen, Dir. Institutional Advancement & Education, Springfield Museums - Michele & Donald D'Amour Museum of Fine Arts, Springfield, MA....808
Simpson, Kathleen, Dir. Institutional Advancement & Education, Springfield Museums - Museum of Springfield History, Springfield, MA....808
Simpson, Kathleen, Dir. Institutional Advancement & Education, Springfield Museums - Springfield Science Museum, Springfield, MA....808
Simpson Lutts, Lisa, Exec. Dir., Museum Center at 5ive Points, Cleveland, TN....1549
Simpson, Milward, Dir., Fort Bridger State Museum, Fort Bridger, WY....1858
Simpson, Milward, Dept. Dir., Fort Phil Kearny, Banner, WY....1852
Simpson, Milward, Dir. Wyoming Dept. of State Parks & Cultural Resources, Lake Guernsey Museum-Guernsey State Park, Guernsey, WY....1859
Simpson, Monica, Registrar Permanent Collection, Memorial Art Gallery of the University of Rochester, Rochester, NY....1202
Simpson, Ron, Pres. (V), Thronateeska Heritage Foundation, Inc., Albany, GA....399
Simpson, Roy, Cur., Tumacacori National Historical Park, Tumacacori, AZ....64
Simpson, Shannon, Dir. & Cur., Ellis County Museum, Inc., Waxahachie, TX....1655
Simpson, Shayla, Dir. Public Rels. & Museum Events, National Cowboy & Western Heritage Museum, Oklahoma City, OK....1371
Simpson, Vicki, Devel. Coord., James & Meryl Hearst Center for the Arts and Hearst Sculpture Garden, Cedar Falls, IA....576
Sims, Ben, Park Ranger, DeSoto National Memorial, Bradenton, FL....336
Sims, Bill, Chm., The Museum of Western Art, Kerrville, TX....1625
Sims, Elizabeth, Public Rels. Mgr., Biltmore Estate, Asheville, NC....1231
Sims, Jo Ann, Chief External Affairs, Smithsonian American Art Museum, Washington, DC....329
Sims, Judith, Sr. Dir. Education, Austin Museum of Art - Downtown, Austin, TX....1580
Sims, Lee, Dir., Greenville Zoo, Greenville, SC....1514
Sims, Merle, Treas., Korean War National Museum, Springfield, IL....521
Sims, Patti, Head Fiber Arts, Worcester Center for Crafts, Worcester, MA....819
Sims, Richard, Dir., Montana Historical Society, Helena, MT....966
Sims, Timothy, Volunteer Coord., Booker T. Washington National Monument, Hardy, VA....1717
Sims-Burch, Wylene, Dir., Howard County Center of African American Culture, Columbia, MD....732
Sinchak, Cindy, Pres. (V), Fort Klock Historic Restoration, Saint Johnsville, NY....1206
Sinclair, David, Admin., Jefferson Historical Society and Museum, Jefferson, TX....1625

S–*Continued*

S–Continued

Smith, David, C.E.O., Cheney Homestead, Manchester, CT 281
Smith, David, Pres. (V), Ellis County Museum, Inc., Waxahachie, TX............1655
Smith, Dr. David, Chancellor, Museum of Texas Tech University, Lubbock, TX....1629
Smith, David, Exec. Dir., National Bird Dog Museum, Grand Junction, TN 1553
Smith, Dr. David A., Dir. Powdermill Nature Reserve, Carnegie Museum of Natural History, Pittsburgh, PA..............1464
Smith, David Abner, Dir., Wilkinson County Museum, Woodville, MS 919
Smith, David K., Museum Rels., Museum of Paleontology, Berkeley, CA..................93
Smith, Debbie, Sec., Buffalo Bill Museum of Le Claire, Iowa, Inc., Le Claire, IA 591
Smith, Debbie, Special Events Coord., Historic Charlton Park Village and Museum, Hastings, MI 844
Smith, Debbie, Area Mgr., Memorial Art Gallery of the University of Rochester, Rochester, NY.......................................1202
Smith, Debbie, Museum Shop Mgr., Missouri Town 1855, Lee's Summit, MO 938
Smith, Delford M., Chm. (V), Evergreen Aviation Museum, McMinnville, OR 1394
Smith, Dena, Cur. Invertebrate Paleontology & Assoc. Prof. Geological Sciences, University of Colorado Museum of Natural History, Boulder, CO...230
Smith, Denise A., Co Dir. WCIV, Wolf Creek Indian Village & Museum, Bastian, VA 1701
Smith, Dennis, Vice Pres. Operations, Denver Zoological Gardens, Denver, CO 239
Smith, Denny, Pres. (V), Evergreen Aviation Museum, McMinnville, OR 1394
Smith DeTarnowsky, Andrea, Historic Site Mgr., T.C. Steele State Historic Site, Nashville, IN 559
Smith, Diane, Mgr., Dir. & Cur., Depot Park Museum, Sonoma, CA.....................212
Smith, Diane, Administrative Asst., Stearns History Museum, Saint Cloud, MN 892
Smith, Dianne, Pres. (V), Washington Area Museum Foundation/Varnado Store Museum, Franklinton, LA 671
Smith, Don, Dir., Historical Society of Millersburg & Upper Paxton Township Museum, Millersburg, PA 1445
Smith, Don, Bd. Pres., Isabel Anderson Comer Museum & Arts Center, Sylacauga, AL..22
Smith, Donald, Chm. (V), Veterans Tribute and Museum of Osceola County, Inc., Kissimmee, FL 360
Smith, Donna, Coord. Volunteers, Fort Davis National Historic Site, Fort Davis, TX..1607
Smith, Donna, Librarian, Lauren Rogers Museum of Art, Laurel, MS...................912
Smith, Dorothea, Museum Shop Mgr., Kateri Galleries, Shrine of Our Lady of Martyrs aka The National Shrine of the North American Martyrs, Auriesville, NY...1101
Smith, Edward, Dir., Art Gallery Marist College, Poughkeepsie, NY...................1197
Smith, Edward, Acting Cur., South Holland Historical Society, South Holland, IL...520
Smith, Elizabeth, Senior Cur., Museum of Contemporary Art, Chicago, IL 483
Smith, Elizabeth, Exec. Dir., North Carolina Transportation Museum, Spencer, NC 1268
Smith, Elizabeth, Pres., The Sharon Arts Center, Inc., Sharon, NH...................1029
Smith, Elizabeth A., Dir., Manlius Historical Society and Museum, Manlius, NY 1157
Smith, Elizabeth A., Cur., Susquehanna County Historical Society & Free Library Association, Montrose, PA........1446
Smith, Emily, Curatorial Fellow Modern & Contemporary Art, Virginia Museum of Fine Arts, Richmond, VA...1742
Smith, Eric, Acting Park Supt., Cravens House, Lookout Mountain, TN.............1559
Smith, Erica, Admin. Asst., Arkansas River Valley Arts Center, Russellville, AR 83
Smith, Ernie, Security Chief, Detroit Institute of Arts, Detroit, MI..................834
Smith, Florence C., Museum Shop Mgr., Howard County Center of African American Culture, Columbia, MD..........732
Smith, Dr. Frank, Jr., Exec. Dir., African American Civil War Memorial Freedom Foundation and Museum, Washington, DC....................................314
Smith, Gail, Asst. Cur., Historical and Genealogical Society of Somerset County, Somerset, PA............................1474
Smith, Garry, Cimarron Valley Railroad Museum, Cushing, OK.........................1359
Smith, Gary, BLM State Archaeologist, Billings Curation Center, Billings, MT ...956
Smith, Gary, Facility Mgr., Fort Smith National Historic Site, Fort Smith, AR 72
Smith, Gary, Chief Security, Georgia O'Keeffe Museum, Santa Fe, NM.........1088
Smith, Gary, C.E.O. & Pres., Har-Ber Village, Grove, OK...............................1362
Smith, Gary, Pres., The Toledo Zoo, Toledo, OH 1346
Smith, Gary N., Exec. Dir. & Pres., Dallas Heritage Village at Old City Park, Dallas, TX 1597
Smith, Gary N., Pres., The Highlands, Fort Washington, PA 1426
Smith, Dr. Gene, Cur. History, Fort Worth Museum of Science and History, Fort Worth, TX 1609
Smith, Georgia, C.E.O., Dir. & Museum Shop Mgr., Fort Harker Museum Complex, Kanopolis, KS.......................619
Smith, Georgia, Museum Shop Mgr., Hodgden House Museum Complex, Ellsworth, KS..610
Smith, Dr. Gerald R., Cur. Fossil Fishes, Orma J. Smith Museum of Natural History, Caldwell, ID 457
Smith, Gerard V., Pres. (V), The Science Center, Carbondale, IL 473
Smith, Grayce, Museum Shop Mgr., Calusa Nature Center and Planetarium, Fort Myers, FL 348
Smith, Greg, Pres. (V), Fort Smith Museum of History, Fort Smith, AR.........72
Smith, Gregory Jay, Preparator, Williams College Museum of Art, Williamstown, MA 817
Smith, Gretchen M., C.E.O. & Dir., Edisto Island Historic Preservation Society Museum, Edisto Island, SC 1512
Smith Grindberg, Michelle, Dir. Art Collections & Registrar, The Mary Brogan Museum of Art and Science, Tallahassee, FL...390
Smith, Dr. G.T., C.E.O., Historic Bethany - Alexander Campbell Mansion, Bethany, WV..1796
Smith, Guy, Historic Site Mgr. CSS Neuse State Historic Site and Gov. Richard Caswell Memorial, Kinston, NC 1254
Smith, H. Brooks, Pres. (V), Nassau County Museum of Art, Roslyn Harbor, NY 1204
Smith, Heather, Dir. Cinema, Salina Art Center, Salina, KS 633
Smith, Helen, Cur., Holmes County Historical Society, Millersburg, OH 1333
Smith, Henry L., Park Ranger & Chm. (V), Crystal River Archaeological State Park, Crystal River, FL 341
Smith, Howard, Gen. Mgr., Pioneer Tunnel Coal Mine & Steam Train, Ashland, PA 1410
Smith, Jamie, Pres. Bd. Dirs. FASNY Museum of Fire Fighting, Hudson, NY 1143
Smith, Jan, Dir., Bergstrom-Mahler Museum, Neenah, WI...........................1837
Smith, Jan, Museum Shop Mgr., Marshall Point Lighthouse Museum, Saint George, ME...711
Smith, Janele, Museum Shop Mgr., Naples Botanical Garden, Naples, FL 370
Smith, Jay, Museum Dir., The Hubbard Museum of the American West, Ruidoso Downs, NM...........................1087
Smith, Jay, Dir. Historic Site, Union Station Kansas City, Inc., Kansas City, MO 936
Smith, Jayleane, Chm. (V), Morton Museum of Cooke County, Gainesville, TX.....................................1613
Smith, Mrs. J.B., C.E.O., Dir. & Cur., Osage County Historical Society Museum, Pawhuska, OK......................1374
Smith, Jeanette, Museum Shop Mgr., Cape Ann Historical Association dba Cape Ann Museum, Gloucester, MA.......779
Smith, Jeff, Cur., Columbia River Maritime Museum, Astoria, OR..............1382
Smith, Jeff, Assoc. Archivist, Lincoln Memorial Shrine, Redlands, CA 170
Smith, Jeff, Site Mgr., Walter E. Heller Nature Center, Highland Park, IL............500
Smith, Jen, Pres. Bd., Old Independence Regional Museum, Batesville, AR............66
Smith, Jennifer, Asst. Cur., Washington County Museum of Fine Arts, Hagerstown, MD 738
Smith, Jerry, Cur. American Art, Phoenix Art Museum, Phoenix, AZ........................51
Smith, Jill, Dir., Union County Heritage Museum, New Albany, MS 914
Smith, Jim, Education Coord., The Hickories Museum of the Lorain County Historical Society, Elyria, OH ..1319
Smith, Jim, Sec., Watermen's Museum, Yorktown, VA 1757
Smith, Joe, Veterinarian, Fort Wayne Children's Zoo, Fort Wayne, IN 541
Smith, Joel, Cur. Photography, Princeton University Art Museum, Princeton, NJ .1058
Smith, John, Pres., Little Traverse Regional Historical Society, Petoskey, MI..860
Smith, John W., Dir., Archives of American Art, Smithsonian Institution, Washington, DC..315
Smith, Joseph, Pres., Stranahan House, Inc., Fort Lauderdale, FL 348
Smith, Joshua, Chm., Humboldt Bay Maritime Museum, Samoa, CA 178
Smith, Joshua M., Interim Coord., American Merchant Marine Museum, Kings Point, NY 1150
Smith, Joy, Museum Shop Mgr., Lyndhurst, Tarrytown, NY 1220
Smith, Judith C., Registrar & Collections Mgr., Georgia O'Keeffe Museum, Santa Fe, NM...1088
Smith, Julia, Business Mgr., Old Prison Museums, Deer Lodge, MT 961

Smith, Julia, Business Mgr., Powell County Museum, Deer Lodge, MT 961
Smith, Karen, Volunteer Coord. & Museum Shop Mgr., Cape Fear Museum of History and Science, Wilmington, NC 1271
Smith, Karen, Registrar, Seminole Nation Museum, Wewoka, OK 1381
Smith, Karen S., Office Mgr., The Georgian Museum, Lancaster, OH.........1327
Smith, Karen S., Office Mgr., Sherman House Museum, Lancaster, OH 1327
Smith, Katherine K., Dir. Operations, Hellenic Museum & Cultural Center, Chicago, IL 481
Smith, K.C., Cur. Historic Sites & Education, Museum of Florida History, Tallahassee, FL 391
Smith, Kell, Museum Shop Mgr., Oregon Historical Society, Portland, OR 1399
Smith, Kelly, Dir., Charley Creek Gardens, Wabash, IN 570
Smith, Kelly, Cur., Overfield Tavern Museum, Troy, OH 1346
Smith, Kendall, II, Exec. Dir., Art Museum of Greater Lafayette, Lafayette, IN 552
Smith, Kent, Dir. Art, Illinois State Museum, Springfield, IL 521
Smith, Kent, Dir., Illinois State Museum, Chicago Gallery, Chicago, IL 481
Smith, Kevin P., Deputy Dir. & Chief Cur., Haffenreffer Museum of Anthropology, Brown University, Providence, RI 1494
Smith, Kim, Assoc. Dir., Cattle Raisers Museum, Fort Worth, TX 1609
Smith, Kim, Assoc. Dir., National Cowgirl Museum and Hall of Fame, Fort Worth, TX 1611
Smith, Kirsten, Education Outreach, Wisconsin Maritime Museum, Manitowoc, WI 1830
Smith Lake, Kendal, Public Rels. Mgr., Modern Art Museum of Fort Worth, Fort Worth, TX 1611
Smith, Lamar, Vice Pres. Exhibits & Creative Svcs., McWane Science Center, Birmingham, AL 6
Smith, Larry, Pres. (V), West End Hose Co. No. 3 Museum and Fire Educational Center, Biloxi, MS 904
Smith, Larry D., Pres., Ruggles House Society, Columbia Falls, ME 696
Smith, Laura, Museum Academy Dir., Huntsville Museum of Art, Huntsville, AL 15
Smith, LaWanda, Dir. Collections, Museum of World Treasures, Wichita, KS 638
Smith, Lee Roy, C.E.O., National Wrestling Hall of Fame & Museum, Stillwater, OK 1378
Smith, Leon, Pres. (V), Allen County Historical Society, Iola, KS 618
Smith, Leon, Pres. (V), The Major General Frederick Funston Boyhood Home and Museum, Iola, KS 618
Smith, Leslie, Dir., Historical Society of Millersburg & Upper Paxton Township Museum, Millersburg, PA 1445
Smith, Lester, Cur., The King House Museum, Suffield, CT 297
Smith, Letitia, Admin. Graduate Program, Center for Curatorial Studies and the Hessel Museum of Art, Annandale-on-Hudson, NY 1099
Smith, Linda, Pres., Eastern Oregon Museum, Haines, OR 1391
Smith, Lindsay, Exhibitions Designer, Marianna Kistler Beach Museum of Art at Kansas State University, Manhattan, KS 625
Smith, Lindsie, Dir. Mktg. & Communications, Discovery Gateway Children's Museum, Salt Lake City, UT 1670
Smith, Lon, Dir., Kansas Aviation Museum, Wichita, KS 638
Smith, Lucy, Exec. Dir., Hockaday Museum of Art, Kalispell, MT 967
Smith, Lynn, Photo Archivist, Herbert Hoover Presidential Library-Museum, West Branch, IA 602
Smith, Lynnea, Museum Shop Mgr., International Museum of Surgical Science, Chicago, IL 481
Smith, M. Carmen, Dir. Education, Meadows Museum, Dallas, TX 1599
Smith, M. Catherine, Pres. (V), The Mattatuck Museum Arts and History Center, Waterbury, CT 299
Smith, Maggie, Mktg. & Events Dir., Atomic Testing Museum, Las Vegas, NV 1004
Smith, Marcia, Treas., Sisson Museum, Mount Shasta, CA 150
Smith, Margery, Pres. Bd., Denver Museum of Miniatures, Dolls and Toys, Denver, CO 239
Smith, Margo, Dir. & Cur., Kluge-Ruhe Aboriginal Art Collection, UVA, Charlottesville, VA 1704
Smith, Mariann, Cur. Education, Albright-Knox Art Gallery, Buffalo, NY 1114
Smith, Marilyn, Dir. Children & Family Programs, Brooklyn Botanic Garden, Brooklyn, NY 1110
Smith, Marion, Vice Pres. & Publicity Dir., Nordica Homestead, Farmington, ME 698
Smith, Mark, Volunteer Coord., Lakewood's Heritage Center, Lakewood, CO 254
Smith, Mark, Asst. Dir. Promotions & Events, Mayborn Museum Complex, Waco, TX 1655
Smith, Marsha, Pres., Henryetta Territorial Museum, Henryetta, OK 1364
Smith, Marty, Mgr. Riverbend, Fairfax County Park Authority, Resource Management Division, Fairfax, VA 1709
Smith, Mary A., Accountant, The Ozark Folk Center, Mountain View, AR 80
Smith, Mary Ellen, Dir. Volunteer Programs, Institute of Texan Cultures, San Antonio, TX 1643
Smith, Mary Lou, Pres., Village Historical Society of Harrison, Inc., Harrison, OH 1324
Smith, Mary R., Pres. (V), Old Fort House Museum, Fort Edward, NY 1134
Smith, Maureen, Dir. Finance & Operations, Southern Oregon Historical Society, Jacksonville, OR 1392
Smith, Maurine P., 1st Vice Pres., Daughters of Utah Pioneers Pioneer Memorial Museum & International Society Daughters of Utah Pioneers, Salt Lake City, UT 1670
Smith, Melinda K., Assoc. Cur., United States Senate Commission on Art, Washington, DC 332
Smith, Melissa, Dir. Devel., Museum of the American Railroad, Dallas, TX 1600
Smith, Melissa, C.O.O., University of Pennsylvania Museum of Archaeology and Anthropology, Philadelphia, PA 1462
Smith, Melody, Sec., The Friends of Lucy Hayes Heritage Center, Chillicothe, OH 1302
Smith, Merlin, Pres. (V), Maine Art Gallery, Wiscasset, ME 715
Smith, Michael, Museum Dir., Academy of Model Aeronautics/National Model Aviation Museum, Muncie, IN 557
Smith, Michael, Trax Diner Inc., The Dennison Railroad Depot Museum, Dennison, OH 1318
Smith, Michael J., C.E.O. & Exec. Dir., Nebraska History Museum, Lincoln, NE 990
Smith, Michael J., C.E.O. & Exec. Dir., Nebraska State Historical Society's Fort Robinson Museum, Crawford, NE...980
Smith, Michael J., C.E.O. & Exec. Dir., Nebraska State Historical Society's George Norris State Historic Site, McCook, NE 991
Smith, Michael J., C.E.O. & Exec. Dir., Nebraska State Historical Society's Neligh Mill State Historic Site, Neligh, NE 993
Smith, Michael J., C.E.O. & Dir., Nebraska State Historical Society's Thomas P. Kennard House, Lincoln, NE 990
Smith, Michael O., Interim Museum Dir. & Chief Cur., State Historical Museum of Iowa, Des Moines, IA 584
Smith, Mike, C.F.O., Mint Museum of Art, Charlotte, NC 1239
Smith, Mitchel, Dir. Finance, The Adirondack Museum, Blue Mountain Lake, NY 1105
Smith, Nancy, Cur., Allegheny Portage Railroad National Historic Site and Johnstown Flood National Memorial, Gallitzin, PA 1426
Smith, Nancy, Dir., Hopewell Museum, Paris, KY 662
Smith, Nancy, Cur., Johnstown Flood National Memorial, South Fork, PA 1475
Smith, Nancy, Education Mgr., Naper Settlement, Naperville, IL 508
Smith, Nathaniel T., Pres. (V), The Cleveland Museum of Natural History, Cleveland, OH 1308
Smith, Neal, Events & Communications Mgr., Kansas Sports Hall of Fame, Wichita, KS 638
Smith, Ned, Interim Dir., Alaska SeaLife Center, Seward, AK 34
Smith, Norma, Pres., Western Rhode Island Civic Historical Society, Coventry, RI 1486
Smith, Norma Lee, Cur. & Museum Shop Mgr., Hamilton Van Wagoner Museum, Clifton, NJ 1036
Smith, Norman, Dir., Blue Hills Trailside Museum, Milton, MA 791
Smith, Norman C., Dir. Education & Mktg., National Soaring Museum, Elmira, NY 1131
Smith, Orris, Exec. Dir., Sauk County Historical Society and Museum, Baraboo, WI 1811
Smith, P. Daniel, Supt., Colonial National Historical Park: Jamestown & Yorktown, Yorktown, VA 1756
Smith, Pat, Dir., Oklahoma Route 66 Museum, Clinton, OK 1359
Smith, Patricia, Dir., Allen County Museum, Lima, OH 1328
Smith, Patricia, Dir. Retail Operations, The Museum of Fine Arts, Houston, Houston, TX 1622
Smith, Patricia F., Dir., Libby Museum, Wolfeboro, NH 1030
Smith, Patricia F., Chm. (V), Sea Cliff Village Museum, Sea Cliff, NY 1210
Smith, Patrick, Cur. Education, Museum of Connecticut History, Hartford, CT 278
Smith, Paula, Mgr. Membership, Birch Aquarium at Scripps, Scripps Institution of Oceanography, University of California, San Diego, La Jolla, CA 126
Smith, Perry, Security, Louisiana State Exhibit Museum, Shreveport, LA 686

S–*Continued*

S–Continued

S–Continued

S–Continued

Stafford, John, Museum Shop Mgr., New Mexico Museum of Art, Santa Fe, NM.1090
Stafford, Jon, Pres. Bd., Mount Pisgah Arboretum, Eugene, OR.........................1389
Stafford, Margo, Sec., Wayne County Historical Society, Wooster, OH 1351
Stafford, Michael, Pres. (V), Sea Isle City Historical Museum, Sea Isle City, NJ ...1060
Stafford, Dr. Michael D., Dir., Cranbrook Institute of Science, Bloomfield Hills, MI...828
Stafford, Susan, Dir., Bicentennial Art Center & Museum, Paris, IL...................511
Stafford, Suzanne, Treas., Granville Museum, Inc., Granville, TN 1553
Stafford, Tamra, Human Resources & Volunteer Coord., Air Zoo, Kalamazoo, MI..847
Stage, Dr. Elizabeth K., Dir., Lawrence Hall of Science, Berkeley, CA..................93
Stage, Heidi, Bookkeeper, Pratt Museum, Homer, AK...31
Stager, Claudette, Historic Preservation Specialist, Tennessee Historical Commission, Nashville, TN 1569
Stager, Prof. Lawrence E., Dir. & Cur., Harvard University Semitic Museum, Cambridge, MA.......................................767
Stager-Snow, Dania, Pres., Franklin Historical Society, Franklin, ME 698
Staggs, Angela, Sec., Tennessee Historical Commission, Nashville, TN ..1569
Staggs, Tonya, Dir. Education, Travellers Rest Plantation & Museum, Nashville, TN...1570
Stahl, Jennifer, Exec. Dir., Huntingdon County Historical Society, Huntingdon, PA 1435
Stahl, Joan, Librarian, Mount Vernon: George Washington's Estate & Gardens, Mount Vernon, VA.................1727
Stahl, Kathleen P., Dir., Kershaw County Historical Society, Camden, SC............1502
Stahl, Michelle M., Exec. Dir., Peterborough Historical Society, Peterborough, NH..................................1025
Stahl, Patti, Treas., Grand Lake Area Historical Society, Grand Lake, CO 250
Stahl, Sarah, Operations Mgr., Vermont Folklife Center, Middlebury, VT 1684
Staicer, John M., Exec. Dir., Historic Madison, Inc., Madison, IN 554
Stainback, Charlie, Cur. Photography, Norton Museum of Art, West Palm Beach, FL..397
Stakenas, Carol, Exec. Dir. LACE (Los Angeles Contemporary Exhibitions), Los Angeles, CA 138
Staker, Mark L., Senior Historic Sites Researcher, Museum of Church History and Art, Salt Lake City, UT 1670
Staker, Ron, Dir., Fairview Museum of History & Art, Fairview, UT.................1661
Stalcup, Wanda, Dir. & Museum Shop Mgr., Cherokee County Historical Museum, Inc., Murphy, NC 1259
Staley, Bill, Head Preparator, The Speed Art Museum, Louisville, KY 658
Staley, Cheryl, Museum Shop Mgr., Illinois State Museum, Springfield, IL 521
Staley, Jennifer, Membership, Rudolph E. Lee Gallery, Clemson, SC.....................1507
Staley, Meg, Vice Pres., Garrison Art Center, Garrison, NY...............................1136
Staley, Dr. Thomas F., Dir., Harry Ransom Center at The University of Texas at Austin, Austin, TX..................1582
Stalf, Colleen, Cur., Niabi Zoo, Coal Valley, IL 488
Stalf, Tom, Dir., Niabi Zoo, Coal Valley, IL..488
Stalker, Laura, Readers' Svcs. Librarian, Huntington Library, Art Collections, and Botanical Gardens, San Marino, CA 198
Stallcup, Paula X., Dir. Downtown Operations, Spanish Governor's Palace, San Antonio, TX........................1646
Staller, Ellen, Dir. Devel. & Communications, Socrates Sculpture Park, Long Island City, NY 1155
Stalling, Steve, Pres., Martin County Historical Museum, Stanton, TX 1649
Stallings, Ridley, Dir. Cultural Outreach, Historic Columbus Foundation, Inc., Columbus, GA 414
Stallings, W. Doris, Vice Pres. & Dir., Collingsworth County Museum, Wellington, TX 1656
Stallwitz, Carolyn, C.E.O. Procurement & Pres., Moore County Art Association, Dumas, TX...1602
Stallwitz, Kurt, C.E.O. Procurement & Pres., Moore County Historical Museum, Dumas, TX 1603
Stalvey, Nathan, Cur. Temporary Exhibitions, The University of South Carolina McKissick Museum, Columbia, SC 1510
Stalvey, Rip, Dir., Cracker Country, Tampa, FL...391
Stambler Neaberger, Helen, Chm., Neuberger Museum of Art, Purchase College, State University of New York, Purchase, NY 1198
Stamey, Emily, Cur. Modern & Contemporary Art, Ulrich Museum of Art, Wichita, KS 639
Stamey, Jean, Museum Shop Mgr., Environmental Education Center, Somerset County Park Commission, Basking Ridge, NJ.................................1032
Stammer, Donna, Education, Military Veterans Museum, Inc., Oshkosh, WI ...1839
Stamps, Ray, C.E.O., Heritage Museum & Gallery, Leadville, CO 255
Stancil, Jeff, Museum Shop Mgr. & Site Supvr., Chief Vann House Historic Site, Chatsworth, GA 413
Standera, Ashley, Curatorial Assoc., Cameron Art Museum, Wilmington, NC...1271
Standerford, Judy, Vice Pres., Monroe Historical Society, Monroe, CT 283
Standish, John, CRC Bldg. Mgr., National Museum of the American Indian, Smithsonian Institution, New York, NY..1177
Standish, Leann, Asst. Dir. External Affairs, Minneapolis Institute of Arts, Minneapolis, MN.......................................886
Standish, Stephanie, Mgr. Collection, Swope Art Museum, Terre Haute, IN......567
Standring, Timothy J., Gates Cur. Paintings & Sculpture, Denver Art Museum, Denver, CO..................................238
Stanek, Dale, Museum Shop Mgr., South Dakota Tractor Museum, Kimball, SD..1534
Stanfield, Margie, Education, Lake City Columbia County Historical Museum, Inc., Lake City, FL 361
Stanford, Charles, Vice Pres. Devel., Chicago Architecture Foundation, Chicago, IL..477
Stanford, Jeff, Dir. Public Rels., Orlando Science Center, Inc., Orlando, FL 374
Stanford, Virginia, Cur., Jim Thorpe Home, Yale, OK 1381
Stanforth, Rick, Park Mgr., Cox Arboretum MetroPark, Dayton, OH 1316
Stanga, Ginger, Dir., Madisonville Museum, Madisonville, LA 675
Stangenberger, Alan, Treas., The Western Railway Museum, Suisun City, CA.........214
Stanger, Alexa, Dir. Education, The Art Museum of Eastern Idaho, Idaho Falls, ID 460
Stanger, Donna, Museum Asst., Eastern California Museum, Independence, CA...124
Stanger, Tom, Exhibits Mgr., Family Museum, Bettendorf, IA.........................574
Stangl, Denise, Asst. Dir., Lehigh University Art Galleries/Museum Operations, Bethlehem, PA 1412
Stanhope, Carolyn, Pres., The Rufus Porter Museum and Cultural Heritage Center, Bridgton, ME 694
Stanhope, David, Deputy Dir., Jimmy Carter Library and Museum, Atlanta, GA...406
Stanis, Suzanne, Dir. Library & Education, Historic Landmarks Foundation of Indiana, Indianapolis, IN 548
Stanish, Loretta, Dir. Devel., Pittsburgh Filmmakers/Pittsburgh Center for the Arts, Pittsburgh, PA 1467
Stanislau, Richard, Cur., Eckley Miners' Village, Eckley, PA...............................1422
Stanislaus, Richard, Cur., Pennsylvania Anthracite Heritage Museum, Scranton, PA 1473
Stankaitis, Janet, Recording Sec., The Gardner Museum, Inc., Gardner, MA......779
Stankowski, Cindy, Dir., San Diego Archaeological Center, Escondido, CA ...111
Stanley, B., Dir., District of Columbia Arts Center, Washington, DC...................316
Stanley, B. Dean, Chm., Owensboro Museum of Fine Art, Inc., Owensboro, KY 661
Stanley, Beverly, Library Staff, Salem County Historical Society, Salem, NJ ...1060
Stanley, Cindy, Office Mgr., Hill-Stead Museum, Farmington, CT 274
Stanley Coleman, Judith, Pres., Monmouth County Historical Association, Freehold, NJ 1039
Stanley, Darlene, Pres. (V), U.S. Vice Presidential Museum at the Dan Quayle Center, Huntington, IN 546
Stanley, Eric, Cur. Exhibitions, Sonoma County Museum, Santa Rosa, CA 209
Stanley, Janet, Librarian, National Museum of African Art, Smithsonian Institution, Washington, DC.....................324
Stanley, Janie, Dir. Devel., Florence Griswold Museum, Old Lyme, CT 291
Stanley, John, Deputy Dir., Whitney Museum of American Art, New York, NY...1184
Stanley, Linda, Archivist, Old York Road Historical Society, Jenkintown, PA........1436
Stanley, Lynn, Education Coord., Provincetown Art Association and Museum, Provincetown, MA 801
Stanley, Marguerite, C.F.O., Bellevue Arts Museum, Bellevue, WA 1758
Stanley, Tamar, Exec. Dir., Ravalli County Museum/Bitter Root Valley Historical Society, Hamilton, MT...........965
Stanley, Tom, Dir., Winthrop University Galleries, Rock Hill, SC......................1522
Stansberry, Lucy, Cur., National Route 66 Museum and Old Town Complex, Elk City, OK..1361
Stansberry, Tammy, Museum Shop Mgr., The Amerind Foundation, Inc., Dragoon, AZ 40
Stansbury, Henry, Chm., Baltimore Civil War Museum, Baltimore, MD..................719
Stansbury, Henry, Chm., Maryland Historical Society, Baltimore, MD............724
Stansbury, Pat, Exec. Dir., National Museum of Patriotism, Atlanta, GA 407

Stansbury-O'Donnell, Mark, Chm. Art Historian, University Saint Thomas Art History, Saint Paul, MN 896
Stansfield, Mary, Visitor Svcs. Mgr., Georgia Music Hall of Fame, Macon, GA....425
Stanton, Carole, Dir., Sam Rayburn House Museum, Bonham, TX 1589
Stanton, Crysta, Exec. Dir., Highland County Museum and Heritage Center, McDowell, VA....1725
Stanton, Joseph, Pres. (V), Anna Scripps Whitcomb Conservatory, Detroit, MI 832
Stanton, Katie, Dir. Mktg. & Communications, Missoula Art Museum, Missoula, MT 969
Stanton, Meridith, Dir., Indian Arts and Crafts Board, Washington, DC 319
Stanton, Dr. Paul, Pres. ETSU, Carroll Reece Museum, Johnson City, TN 1555
Stanton, Steve, Museum Shop Mgr., Western Museum of Mining & Industry, Colorado Springs, CO....235
Stanton, Todd, Security, Monocacy National Battlefield, Frederick, MD 735
Stanton, William L., Bd. Chm. (V), Bonnet House Museum & Gardens, Fort Lauderdale, FL....347
Stanuga, Ted, Cur. & Project Devel., National Vietnam Veterans Art Museum, Chicago, IL....484
Stanzel, Robert, Pres., Stanzel Model Aircraft Museum, Schulenburg, TX 1647
Stanzel, Theodore, Vice Pres., Stanzel Model Aircraft Museum, Schulenburg, TX 1647
Staples, Amy, Cur. Photographic Archives, National Museum of African Art, Smithsonian Institution, Washington, DC....324
Staples, Don, Account Mgr., Ocean Star Offshore Drilling Rig & Museum, Galveston, TX....1615
Staples, Dr. George, III, Research Affiliate, Harold L. Lyon Arboretum, Honolulu, HI....444
Stapleton, Douglas, Asst. Cur., Illinois State Museum, Chicago Gallery, Chicago, IL 481
Stapleton, Wes, Pres., Korean War National Museum, Springfield, IL 521
Stapp, Callie, Cur. Collections, Gadsby's Tavern Museum, Alexandria, VA....1697
Starace, Maureen, Coord. Membership, The Monmouth Museum, Lincroft, NJ..1045
Starbuck, Marilyn, Deputy Dir. Grants, The California State Military Museum, Sacramento, CA....175
Starbuck, Octavia, Dir. Interpretation, Thomas Jefferson's Poplar Forest, Forest, VA....1710
Starck, Milt, Pres. (V), Antelope Valley California Poppy Natural Reserve, Lancaster, CA 128
Stardridge, Tracey, Park Mgr., Dade Battlefield Historic State Park, Bushnell, FL 337
Stark, Andrea, Exec. Dir., Maine Discovery Museum, Bangor, ME 691
Stark, Barbara, Asst. to the Dir., National Music Museum, Vermillion, SD 1544
Stark, Bonnie, Museum Asst., Big Horn County Historical Museum, Hardin, MT....965
Stark, David, Dir. Administration & Interpretive Media Museum Education, The Art Institute of Chicago, Chicago, IL 476
Stark, Douglas, Dir., International Tennis Hall of Fame & Museum, Newport, RI....1490
Stark, Dr. Frank, Pres., The Grand River Historical Society & Museum, Chillicothe, MO 923
Stark, Gail, Museum Shop Mgr., National Packard Museum, Warren, OH 1348
Stark, Jane, Exec. Dir., The Sam Azeez Museum of Woodbine Heritage, Woodbine, NJ 1068
Stark, Jennifer, Membership, Dallas Contemporary, Dallas, TX....1597
Stark, John, Mgr. Facilities, The Eric Carle Museum of Picture Book Art, Amherst, MA 752
Stark, Julie, Dir., Community Memorial Museum of Sutter County, Yuba City, CA 227
Stark, Mike, Chm. (V), Akron Zoological Park, Akron, OH....1292
Stark, Patsy, Archivist & Registrar, Frontier Historical Society and Museum, Glenwood Springs, CO 248
Stark, Peter, Pres., Beyer Home, Oconto County Historical Society Museum, Oconto, WI 1839
Stark, Sharon, Administrative Asst., Owatonna Arts Center, Owatonna, MN...889
Stark, W., Asst. Cur. Fishes, Sternberg Museum of Natural History, Hays, KS ...616
Stark, William, Dir. Museum Branch, Louisiana State Museum, New Orleans, LA 681
Starkey, James H., Chm., Science Museum of Virginia, Richmond, VA 1740
Starkman, Christine, Cur. Asian Art, The Museum of Fine Arts, Houston, Houston, TX 1622
Starling, John, Site Coord., Cape Henry Lighthouse, Virginia Beach, VA 1751
Starling, Steven P., Vice Pres., Gwinnett Historical Society, Lawrenceville, GA 423
Starling, Zoe, Cur. Education & Resources, Gregg Museum of Art & Design at North Carolina State University, Raleigh, NC 1262
Starnes, Vicki, Administrative Mgr., Crawford W. Long Museum, Jefferson, GA....421
Starnes, Dr. Wayne, Cur. Fishes, North Carolina Museum of Natural Sciences, Raleigh, NC 1263
Starr, Anne, Asst. Cur. Exhibitions, National Heritage Museum, Lexington, MA 785
Starr, Emily, Women's Committee Chair, University of Pennsylvania Museum of Archaeology and Anthropology, Philadelphia, PA 1462
Starr, Hanley, Vice Pres., Guernsey County Museum, Cambridge, OH 1299
Starr, John, Vice Pres., Missisquoi Valley Historical Society, North Troy, VT....1685
Starr, Lisa, Friends Sec., Jefferson Patterson Park & Museum, Saint Leonard, MD 744
Starrett, Margaret, Museum Shop Mgr., Doll & Miniature Museum of High Point, High Point, NC....1252
Starring, Bona, Art Shop Mgr., Munson-Williams-Proctor Arts Institute Museum of Art, Utica, NY....1222
Startzell, David N., Exec. Dir., The Appalachian Trail Conservancy, Harpers Ferry, WV 1799
Stasiak, Marilyn, Cur. Art, Neville Public Museum of Brown County, Green Bay, WI....1821
Stasko, Gary, Financial Dir., Iowa Railroad Historical Society, Boone, IA ...574
Stassun, Lorraine, Museum Shop Mgr., Lowe Art Museum, University of Miami, Coral Gables, FL 340
Staten, Phillip, Dir. Retail & Volunteers, Virginia Museum of Transportation, Inc., Roanoke, VA 1745
Statia, Barry, Visitor Svcs. Mgr., The National World War II Museum, New Orleans, LA 682
Staton, Christine, Mgr. Retail Operations, Price Tower Arts Center, Bartlesville, OK....1357
Staton, David, Dir., Springfield Museum, Springfield, OR....1404
Stats, Dan, Museum Shop Mgr., Ezra Meeker Mansion, Puyallup, WA....1778
Stauber Tritz, Anne, Human Resources Mgr., John Michael Kohler Arts Center, Sheboygan, WI....1844
Stauder, Sarah, Exec. Dir., Rochester Art Center, Rochester, MN 891
Staudt, Brandi, Dir. Devel., Boise Art Museum, Boise, ID....455
Stauffer, Terry, Pres. Friends of Hopewell Furnace NHS, Hopewell Furnace National Historic Site, Elverson, PA 1423
Stavast, Paul, Interim Dir., Museum of Peoples and Cultures, Provo, UT....1668
Stavitsky, Gail, Ph.D., Chief Cur., Montclair Art Museum, Montclair, NJ ..1048
Stayton, Kevin, Cur. Decorative Arts, Brooklyn Museum, Brooklyn, NY 1111
Steadman, Casey, C.O.O., Atlanta Historical Society, Atlanta, GA....402
Steadman, Dr. David W., Assoc. Dir. Collections & Research and Cur. Ornithology, Florida Museum of Natural History, Gainesville, FL....351
Steadman, Todd, Dir., Bob Campbell Geology Museum, Clemson, SC....1507
Stearn, R. Gwenn, State Archivist, Rhode Island State Archives, Providence, RI ...1496
Stearns, Louise J., Dir., Oakland Museum, Oakland, OR....1396
Stebbing, Larry, Preparator, Museum of Art and Archaeology, University of Missouri, Columbia, MO 924
Stebbins, Theodore E., Cur. American Art, Harvard Art Museum, Cambridge, MA 767
Stebich, Stephanie A., Dir., Tacoma Art Museum, Tacoma, WA 1789
Steblecki, Edith, Cur., Paul Revere House/Paul Revere Memorial Association, Boston, MA 763
Steck, Ardyce Elaine, Museum Shop Mgr., Brooklyn Historical Society, Brooklyn, OH 1298
Steckler, Jenny, Pres. (V), Roosevelt Park Zoo, Minot, ND....1287
Stedman, John, Farm Mgr., Aullwood Audubon Center and Farm, Dayton, OH....1315
Steeber, Mark, Treas., Eureka Fire Museum, Milltown, NJ....1047
Steed, Martha J., Dir. Mktg., The Discovery Center of the Southern Tier, Binghamton, NY....1105
Steedman, Charles, Pres., Museums of Old York, York, ME 716
Steel, David H., Cur. Ancient Art, North Carolina Museum of Art, Raleigh, NC..1263
Steel, Latanne, Membership & Advertising, American Airlines C.R. Smith Museum, Fort Worth, TX....1608
Steel, Virginia Oberlin, Dir., Stedman Gallery, Camden, NJ 1034
Steele, Bruce, Treas., LaGrange Plantation, Cambridge, MD 729
Steele, Debby, Mktg. Dir., The Marie Selby Botanical Gardens, Inc., Sarasota, FL....387
Steele, Fannie, Archivist, Wise County Historical Society, Wise, VA....1756
Steele, George, Science Educator, George Landis Arboretum, Esperance, NY 1132

S–Continued

Steele, Gil, Pres., Pennsylvania Military Museum and 28th Division Shrine, Boalsburg, PA 1414
Steele, Jack, Exec. Dir., The Museum of Western Art, Kerrville, TX 1625
Steele, Jeff, Pres. (V), Herkimer County Historical Society, Herkimer, NY 1141
Steele, Jeremy, Museum Devel. Assoc., Larsen Tractor Museum, Lincoln, NE 988
Steele, Kelly, Historic Preservation Officer, United States Senate Commission on Art, Washington, DC 332
Steele, Marcia, Paintings Conservator, The Cleveland Museum of Art, Cleveland, OH 1308
Steele, Norma B., Dir., Paris-Henry County Heritage Center, Paris, TN 1571
Steele, Robert, Zoo Cur., Palo Alto Junior Museum and Zoo, Palo Alto, CA 161
Steele, Sheldon, Master Teacher, Larz Anderson Auto Museum, Brookline, MA 766
Steele, Sheridan, Supt., Islesford Historical Museum, Islesford, ME 700
Steele, Sheridan, Supt., Sieur de Monts Springs Nature Center, Bar Harbor, ME 692
Steele, Sheridan, Supt., William Otis Sawtelle Collections and Research Center, Bar Harbor, ME 693
Steele, Stasia, Volunteer Coord., Denver Museum of Miniatures, Dolls and Toys, Denver, CO 239
Steele, Steven, C.E.O., Rocky Mountain College of Art + Design Galleries, Lakewood, CO 255
Steele, Sue, Pres., San Dieguito Heritage Museum, Encinitas, CA 110
Steele, Terra, Dir. Interpretive Programs, Everhart Museum: Natural History, Science and Art, Scranton, PA 1472
Steele, Dr. Valerie, Dir. & Chief Cur., The Museum at FIT, New York, NY 1174
Steeler, Chip, Exhibition Designer, The Patricia & Phillip Frost Art Museum, Miami, FL 367
Steen, Barbara, Corresponding Sec., Vashon Maury Island Heritage Association, Vashon, WA 1792
Steen, Morris, Pres., North Florida Community College Art Gallery, Madison, FL 363
Steen, Ron, Chm. (V), St. Johnsbury Athenaeum, Saint Johnsbury, VT 1689
Steenburgh, Ruth Ann, Dir. Retail Operations, Virginia Aquarium & Marine Science Center, Virginia Beach, VA 1752
Steenhoek, Bill, Pres. (V), Kellogg Historical Society, Kellogg, IA 590
Steer, Louise N., Museum Shop Mgr., May Natural History Museum and Museum of Space Exploration, Colorado Springs, CO 234
Stefani, Minerva, Treas., Iron County Historical Museum, Hurley, WI 1823
Stefanski, George, Collections, The Airborne & Special Operations Museum, Fayetteville, NC 1244
Steffan, Kristen, Pres. (V), Dickinson Museum Center, Dickinson, ND 1280
Steffanoff, Nick, Pres. (V), The Living Desert, Palm Desert, CA 160
Steffen, Don, Public Rels., Dunn County Historical Society, Menomonie, WI 1832
Steffen, Genevieve, Cur. Elbert Hubbard Museum, Aurora Historical Society, Inc., East Aurora, NY 1127
Steffen, Genevieve, Co-Cur., Elbert Hubbard-Roycroft Museum, East Aurora, NY 1127
Steffen, Joe, Cur., Miamisburg Historical Society, Miamisburg, OH 1332
Steffens, Charlotte, Treas., Fort Sidney Museum & Post Commander's Home, Sidney, NE 997
Steffes, Colleen, Pres. (V) & Dir., Sinclair Lewis Boyhood Home & Interpretive Center/Museum, Sauk Centre, MN 897
Steffian, Amy, Deputy Dir., Alutiiq Museum and Archaeological Repository, Kodiak, AK 33
Steger, Carolyn, Business Mgr., Drake Planetarium, Norwood, OH 1337
Steger, Carolyn, Business Mgr., Drake Science Center, Norwood, OH 1337
Steglitz, Marc, C.O.O. Solomon R. Guggenheim Museum, Solomon R. Guggenheim Museum, New York, NY 1181
Stegman, Patty, Treas., The Wyoming Dinosaur Center, Thermopolis, WY 1866
Stehle, Emily, Museum Shop Mgr., The Pier Aquarium, Saint Petersburg, FL 384
Steichen, Kathy, Chief Park Interpreter, Olympic National Park Visitor Center, Port Angeles, WA 1775
Steidley, Dr. David, Club. Sec., The Collectors Club, Inc., New York, NY 1166
Steigelman, Herb, Exec. Dir. & Cur., Military Museum of North Florida, Green Cove Springs, FL 352
Steiger, Dia, Exec. Dir., Wing Haven Gardens and Bird Sanctuary, Charlotte, NC 1240
Steigerwald, Mark, Dir. Archives & Admin., International Motor Racing Research Center at Watkins Glen, Watkins Glen, NY 1227
Steigerwald, Paula, Dir., Huntsville/Madison County Botanical Garden, Huntsville, AL 14
Steigerwald, Steve, Cur., Aztalan Museum, Jefferson, WI 1824
Steijlen, Maria, Accountant, Tampa Bay History Center, Inc., Tampa, FL 393
Steil, Capt. Peter, Vice Pres., Delaware State Police Museum, Dover, DE 306
Stein, Arthur, Pres. (V), Berkshire County Historical Society, Inc. - Arrowhead, Pittsfield, MA 799
Stein, Chris, Supt., St. Croix National Scenic Riverway, Saint Croix Falls, WI 1843
Stein, Christin L., Dir., The Museums of Oglebay Institute - Mansion Museum & Glass Museum, Wheeling, WV 1808
Stein, Gil, Dir., Oriental Institute Museum, University of Chicago, Chicago, IL 485
Stein, Ira, Head Visitor Svcs., Lyndhurst, Tarrytown, NY 1220
Stein, Dr. Julie K., Exec. Dir., Burke Museum of Natural History and Culture, Seattle, WA 1779
Stein, Karen, Program Specialist, Drumlin Farm Education Center, Lincoln, MA 786
Stein, Karen, Dir. Education, Katonah Museum of Art, Katonah, NY 1150
Stein, Kathleen F., Visitor Svcs., Meriks Gallery, Anchorage, AK 27
Stein, Laurie, Cur., Lake Forest-Lake Bluff Historical Society, Lake Forest, IL 502
Stein, Margaret, Chm. (V), Riverview at Hobson Grove, Bowling Green, KY 642
Stein, Maria, Vice Pres., Meriks Gallery, Anchorage, AK 27
Stein, Mark R., Jr., Conservation, Meriks Gallery, Anchorage, AK 27
Stein, Marty, Photographic Svcs. Mgr., The Museum of Fine Arts, Houston, Houston, TX 1622
Stein, Paul, Pres., Meriks Zoo, Graysville, AL 13
Stein, Renee, Conservator, Michael C. Carlos Museum, Atlanta, GA 407
Stein, Robert, Chief Information Officer IMA - Indianapolis Museum of Art, Indianapolis, IN 548
Stein, Susan R., Vice Pres. Museum Programs & Cur., Monticello, Home of Thomas Jefferson, Thomas Jefferson Foundation, Inc., Charlottesville, VA 1705
Steinberg, Dr. David, Pres., Hillwood Art Museum, Brookville, NY 1113
Steinbrink, Nathaniel, Cur. Exhibits, University Museum, Carbondale, IL 473
Steinecke, Brad, Collections Mgr., Spartanburg Regional Museum of History, Spartanburg, SC 1524
Steiner, Charles K., Dir., Wichita Art Museum, Wichita, KS 639
Steiner, Edwin, Asst. Operations Admin., Glencairn Museum: Academy of the New Church, Bryn Athyn, PA 1415
Steiner, Jack, Pres. (V), Hastings Museum, Hastings, NE 985
Steiner, Julie, Museum Shop Mgr., Barnes Foundation, Merion, PA 1444
Steinert, Chris, Treas., Galloway House and Village - Blakely Museum, Fond du Lac, WI 1819
Steinkeller, Prof. Piotr, Cur. Cuneiform Collections, Harvard University Semitic Museum, Cambridge, MA 767
Steinle, John, Admin., Hiwan Homestead Museum, Evergreen, CO 244
Steinmetz, Nadine, Div. Chief Historic Sites & Museums, Pennsylvania Historical & Museum Commission, Harrisburg, PA 1431
Steinmetz, Nadine, Acting Dir., Railroad Museum of Pennsylvania, Strasburg, PA 1476
Steinway, Kate, Exec. Dir., Connecticut Historical Society, Hartford, CT 277
Steinzor, Nadia, Dir. Communications, Mohonk Preserve, Inc., Gardiner, NY 1136
Steitz, Ken, Mgr. Finance, Birch Aquarium at Scripps, Scripps Institution of Oceanography, University of California, San Diego, La Jolla, CA 126
Stell, Cortney, Cur., Rocky Mountain College of Art + Design Galleries, Lakewood, CO 255
Stella, Robert, Cur., Bare Cove Fire Museum, Hingham, MA 782
Steller, Tom, Chief Cur. Natural Sciences, Oakland Museum of California-Sculpture Court at City Center, Oakland, CA 156
Stelljes, Felice, Museum Store Mgr., Mighty Eighth Air Force Museum, Pooler, GA 429
Stello, Alan, Dir., The Powder Magazine, Charleston, SC 1506
Stelzer, Doug, C.F.O., The Cleveland Museum of Natural History, Cleveland, OH 1308
Stemm, James, Asst. Cur., Pima Air & Space Museum, Tucson, AZ 61
Stenberg, Denise, Museum Shop Mgr., The Guest House Museum, Fort Bragg, CA 114
Stengel, Eva, Sec., First Consolidated School in Minnesota, Saum, MN 897
Stengel, Regina, Cur. Education, Ormond Memorial Art Museum & Garden, Ormond Beach, FL 375
Steninger, Kim, C.E.O., Northeastern Nevada Museum, Elko, NV 1002
Stenke, Colton, Asst. Cur., Torrance Art Museum, Torrance, CA 217

Stenning, Mark, C.E.O., International Tennis Hall of Fame & Museum, Newport, RI 1490
Stepanov, Leonid, Exhibit Fabricator, The Iowa Children's Museum, Coralville, IA 580
Stepanyan, Mariam, Exec. Dir., Armenian Library and Museum of America (ALMA), Watertown, MA....814
Stephen, Iris, Museum Shop Mgr., The New York City Police Museum, New York, NY 1178
Stephens, Claude, Dir. Education, Bernheim Arboretum and Research Forest, Clermont, KY 644
Stephens, Danielle, Mgr. Docent Program, The Museum of Fine Arts, Houston, Houston, TX 1622
Stephens, Dawn, Cur., State Agricultural Heritage Museum, Brookings, SD....1527
Stephens, Eric, Dir., Miami Metrozoo, Miami, FL....366
Stephens, Harold, Dir. Finance & Admin., Walters Art Museum, Baltimore, MD....727
Stephens, Jane, Auxiliary Chm., Panhandle-Plains Historical Museum, Canyon, TX 1592
Stephens, Joanna, Museum Shop Mgr. & Collections, Carnton Plantation, Franklin, TN 1551
Stephens, John, Security Officer, The Columbus Museum, Columbus, GA....414
Stephens, John D., Pres. (V), Bellingham Railway Museum, Bellingham, WA 1759
Stephens, Kent, Collections Mgr., College Football Hall of Fame, South Bend, IN 565
Stephens Kruize, Priscilla G., Pres., Black Heritage Museum, Miami, FL....364
Stephens, Mary, Docent Coord., Michigan Maritime Museum, South Haven, MI....865
Stephens, Phil, Naturalist, Chippewa Nature Center, Midland, MI....854
Stephens, Phyllis, Cultural Administrator, Lanier Mansion State Historic Site, Madison, IN....555
Stephens, Rebecca, Education & Research Asst., Jackson Hole Historical Society and Museum, Jackson, WY....1860
Stephens, Retha, Cur., Kennesaw Mountain National Battlefield Park, Kennesaw, GA 422
Stephens, Sherry, Interpreter, Providence Canyon State Park, Lumpkin, GA 424
Stephens, Spencer, C.E.O., Chm. (V) & Pres. (V), Stephens African-American Museum, Shreveport, LA....688
Stephenson, Dr. Bruce, Cur., Adler Planetarium & Astronomy Museum, Chicago, IL 476
Stephenson, Carol Ann, Office Mgr., Harriet Beecher Stowe Center, Hartford, CT 278
Stephenson, Ed, Pres. (V), Anderson Island Historical Society, Anderson Island, WA 1757
Stephenson, Jessica, Assoc. Cur. African Art, Michael C. Carlos Museum, Atlanta, GA....407
Stephenson, Jill, Museum Shop Mgr., Fort Nisqually Living History Museum, Tacoma, WA 1788
Stephenson, Kay, Museum Shop Mgr., Wayne County Historical Society, Honesdale, PA....1434
Stephenson, Rich, Museum Shop Mgr., Big Well, Greensburg, KS....615
Stephenson, Toby, Dir., Bar Harbor Whale Museum, Bar Harbor, ME....692
Stephenson-Marbury, Ina, Corresponding Sec., Historical Society of Washington County, Virginia, Abingdon, VA 1695
Stepic, Barbara, Pres. (V), Brooklyn Historical Society, Brooklyn, OH 1298
Stepleton, Ellen, Preparator Vertebrate Paleontology, University of Nebraska State Museum, Lincoln, NE....991
Stepp, Heather, Bd. Pres., Greenville Museum of Art, Inc., Greenville, NC....1250
Stepp, Ms. Sharon, Museum Shop Mgr., Carl Sandburg Home National Historic Site, Flat Rock, NC 1245
Sterbenk, Yvette, Communications Mgr., The Corning Museum of Glass, Corning, NY 1124
Sterkx Gasperecz, Mamie, Exec. Dir., Gallier House, New Orleans, LA....680
Sterkx Gasperecz, Mamie, Exec. Dir., Hermann-Grima, New Orleans, LA....680
Sterling, Christopher, Pres., Radio & Television Museum, Bowie, MD 729
Sterling, Drew, Dir. IT, New-York Historical Society, New York, NY 1178
Sterling, Dr. Eleanor J., Dir. Center for Biodiversity & Conservation, American Museum of Natural History, New York, NY 1163
Sterman, Chris, Tours, Jefferson Landing State Historic Site, Jefferson City, MO ...931
Sterman, Chris, Tour & Museum Shop Mgr., Missouri State Museum, Jefferson City, MO 931
Stermer, Jenifer, Cur. Collections, International Museum of the Horse, Lexington, KY 652
Stern, Dan, Cur., Coker Arboretum of the North Carolina Botanical Garden, Chapel Hill, NC....1237
Stern, H. Peter, Chm., Storm King Art Center, Mountainville, NY 1159
Stern, Herbert B., Vice Chm., Atlantic City Historical Museum, Atlantic City, NJ 1031
Stern, Ilene, Vice Pres. Advancement, Frontiers of Flight Museum, Dallas, TX 1598
Stern, Mr. Jean, Exec. Dir., The Irvine Museum, Irvine, CA....124
Stern, John P., Pres., Storm King Art Center, Mountainville, NY 1159
Stern, Rachel, Vice Chair, Neuberger Museum of Art, Purchase College, State University of New York, Purchase, NY 1198
Sternberg, Edie, Owner, Starhill Forest Arboretum, Petersburg, IL 513
Sternberg, Guy, Owner, Starhill Forest Arboretum, Petersburg, IL 513
Sternberg, Joy, Museum Shop Mgr., Fort Smith Museum of History, Fort Smith, AR....72
Sternberg, Dr. Paul, Jr., Chm. (V), Cheekwood Botanical Garden & Museum of Art, Nashville, TN 1567
Sterner, Katherine, Volunteer Coord. & Museum Shop Mgr., Coe Hall, Oyster Bay, NY 1192
Sterner, Katherine, Volunteer Coord., Planting Fields Arboretum State Historic Park, Oyster Bay, NY 1192
Sterner, Nelson, Public Rels. & Admin. Olana Partnership, Olana State Historic Site, Hudson, NY 1143
Sternleib, Jack J., M.D., Chm. (V), Heartland, The California Museum of the Heart, Rancho Mirage, CA 168
Sterrett, Jill, Dir. Collections & Conservation, San Francisco Museum of Modern Art, San Francisco, CA....193
Sterrett, Peter, Dir. Devel., Herreshoff Marine Museum/America's Cup Hall of Fame, Bristol, RI 1485
Sterrett, Tom, Pres. (V), Franklin Gem & Mineral Museum, Franklin, NC....1246
Sterry, Rich, Education, Dunn County Historical Society, Menomonie, WI....1832
Stertz, Dr. Stephen, Researcher, The Bronx County Historical Society, Bronx, NY....1107
Stertzbach, Marcia, Vice Pres., McCook House, Civil War Museum, Carrollton, OH....1301
Stervier, Lorene, Gift Mgmt. & Graphic Artist, Kelsey Museum of Archaeology, Ann Arbor, MI 822
Stets, Mary Anne, Cur. Photography & Dir. Intellectual Property, Mystic Seaport - The Museum of America and the Sea, Mystic, CT....284
Stetson, Daniel E., Exec. Dir., Polk Museum of Art, Lakeland, FL 362
Stetter, Mark, D.V.M., Dipl. A.C.Z.M., Dir. Dept. of Animal Health, Disney's Animal Kingdom Theme Park, Bay Lake, FL....334
Stetzenbach, Dr. Klaus, Dir. UNLV Marjorie Barrick Museum, Las Vegas, NV....1007
Steuer, Joseph, C.F.O., The Philadelphia Zoo, Philadelphia, PA....1460
Steve, Wendy, Dir. Finance, Cummer Museum of Art & Gardens, Jacksonville, FL....354
Stevens, Andrew, Cur., Prints & Drawings, Chazen Museum of Art, Madison, WI....1827
Stevens Appelhof, Ruth, Ph.D., Exec. Dir., Guild Hall Museum, East Hampton, NY....1128
Stevens, Brad, Preparator, The Fred Jones Jr. Museum of Art, Norman, OK....1368
Stevens, Christopher, Chief Finance & Devel., Walker Art Center, Minneapolis, MN....886
Stevens, Cynthia, Interpretive Resource Technician, Van Meter State Park, Miami, MO....940
Stevens, Daniel E., Pres., Barre Historical Society, Inc., Barre, MA 756
Stevens, David W., Pres., Cooper Regional History Museum, Upland, CA....220
Stevens, Doreen, Museum Admin., The Arlington Historical Society, Arlington, MA 754
Stevens, Ernest, Dir., Louisiana Military Museum, Ruston, LA 685
Stevens, Jane, Illinois State Museum Chicago Gallery Asst. Gallery Admin., Illinois State Museum, Springfield, IL 521
Stevens, Jane, Assoc. Cur., Illinois State Museum, Chicago Gallery, Chicago, IL....481
Stevens, Jeanette, C.E.O., Antique Gas & Steam Engine Museum, Inc., Vista, CA 222
Stevens, Joe, Pres., Kodiak Military History Museum, Kodiak, AK 33
Stevens, Karen D., Archivist, Independence National Historical Park, Philadelphia, PA....1455
Stevens, Kathy C., Pres. (V), North Andover Historical Society, North Andover, MA 795
Stevens, Kris, Dir. & Devel., Maidu Museum and Historic Site, Roseville, CA 174
Stevens, Kristen, Exec. Asst., American Academy of Arts and Letters, New York, NY....1162
Stevens, Dr. Lawrence E., Cur. Ecology & Conservation, Museum of Northern Arizona, Flagstaff, AZ....41
Stevens, Linda, Office Mgr., Kankakee County Museum, Kankakee, IL....501

S–*Continued*

S–Continued

S–Continued

S–*Continued*

Swader, Fred N., Ph.D., Pres. (V), Mifflinburg Buggy Museum Association, Inc., Mifflinburg, PA 1445
Swadley, Ben H., Dir., Plantation Agriculture Museum, Scott, AR................83
Swaford, Toby, Education Coord., Fort Collins Museum, Fort Collins, CO..........246
Swagman, Rhonda, Office Coord., Faust Park-Thornhill Historic Site & Faust Historic Village, Chesterfield, MO 923
Swaim, Shirley, Museum Shop Mgr., The Children's Museum of Rose Hill Manor Park, Frederick, MD....................735
Swain, Adrian, Cur., The Kentucky Folk Art Center, Morehead, KY......................659
Swain, Colleen, Asst Dir. Downtown Operations, Spanish Governor's Palace, San Antonio, TX.....................1646
Swain, Donna, Administrative Coord., Virginia Sports Hall of Fame, Portsmouth, VA....................................1735
Swain, Kristin, Exec. Dir., Rockwell Museum of Western Art, Corning, NY..1124
Swallow, Nancy, Registrar, The Corcoran Gallery of Art, Washington, DC 315
Swalwell, Max, Vice Pres., Community Historical Museum, Maxwell, IA 593
Swan, Amanda, Museum Shop Mgr., The Airborne & Special Operations Museum, Fayetteville, NC 1244
Swan, Kelly, Dir. Finance, Thomasville Cultural Center, Inc., Thomasville, GA...437
Swanagan, Jeffery S., Dir., Columbus Zoo and Aquarium, Powell, OH 1340
Swanberg, Kristen, Sr. Dir. Education Programs, Audubon Society of Rhode Island, Smithfield, RI 1497
Swanberg, Kristen, Sr. Dir. Education, Audubon Society of Rhode Island Environmental Education Center, Bristol, RI 1485
Swanda, Danny, Chm. & Pres. (V), Apache Historical Society Museum, Apache, OK 1356
Swanda, Mary Joyce, Museum Shop Mgr., Apache Historical Society Museum, Apache, OK 1356
Swane, Leigh, Site Mgr., Historic Bath State Historic Site, Bath, NC 1234
Swanee Shipp, Lois, Dir., Marshall County Historical Museum, Holly Springs, MS 909
Swaney, Sally, Exec. Admin., Norton Simon Museum, Pasadena, CA...............162
Swanick, Lindsey, Dir. Parks, Faust Park-Thornhill Historic Site & Faust Historic Village, Chesterfield, MO 923
Swank, Alison, Dir. Mktg., Knoxville Zoological Gardens, Knoxville, TN.......1559
Swank, Dr. Scott D., Cur., Dr. Samuel D. Harris National Museum of Dentistry, Baltimore, MD...721
Swank, Dr. Scott T., Exec. Dir., Heritage Museums & Gardens, Sandwich, MA.....805
Swann, Carinda, Exec. Dir., Garrison Art Center, Garrison, NY............................1136
Swann, Patty, Chm. (V) & Pres.(V), Sanford Museum, Sanford, FL................385
Swanson, Ann, Cur., Rome Historical Society Museum, Rome, NY 1204
Swanson, B. Jean, Treas., Larimore Community Museum, Larimore, ND.....1285
Swanson, Catherine, Archivist, National Heritage Museum, Lexington, MA..........785
Swanson, Cynthia, Chm. (V), Ford County Historical Society, Paxton, IL 511
Swanson, Donald, Treas. C.H.A.L. Inc., Garfield Farm Museum, LaFox, IL 502
Swanson, Edward N., Chm., Gertrude Smith House, Mount Airy, NC 1258
Swanson, Harry, Ph.D., Dean, Discovery Park Campus, Safford, AZ.........................53
Swanson, Jennie, Mgr. Membership & Museum Svcs., Laumeier Sculpture Park & Museum, Saint Louis, MO..........948
Swanson, Jennifer, Pres., Shaw Island Library & Historical Society, Shaw Island, WA 1785
Swanson, John, Exec. Dir., Science Station, Cedar Rapids, IA 578
Swanson, John, Bd. Pres., Springfield Art & Historical Society - Miller Art Center, Springfield, VT 1691
Swanson, Kevin J., Dir. Acquisition & Preservation, Maryland State Archives, Annapolis, MD 718
Swanson, Larry, Museum Shop Mgr., Manassas National Battlefield Park, Manassas, VA 1724
Swanson, Lynne, Collections Mgr., Cultural Collections, The Michigan State University Museum, East Lansing, MI 838
Swanson, Robert, Pres. & Cur., Community Historical Museum, Maxwell, IA...593
Swanson, Stephan, Dir., The Grove, Glenview, IL 498
Swanson, Dr. Vern G., Dir., Springville Museum of Art, Springville, UT...........1673
Swanton, Wendy, Consulting Cur., The Gibson Society, Inc. dba Gibson House Museum, Boston, MA.................759
Swark, Sandy, Museum Shop Mgr., Cliveden of the National Trust, Philadelphia, PA 1451
Swart, Ian, Cur., Plains Indians and Pioneers Museum, Woodward, OK........1381
Swartout, Dawn, Dir. Devel., Delaware Museum of Natural History, Wilmington, DE...312
Swartout, Dennis W., Dir., Tri-Cities Historical Museum, Grand Haven, MI....841
Swartout, Tracy, Supt., Congaree National Park, Hopkins, SC....................1516
Swarts, Nicole, Mgr. Guest Svcs. & Museum Shop Mgr., High Desert Museum, Bend, OR...............................1384
Swartz, Betsy, Museum Shop Mgr., National Aviary in Pittsburgh, Inc., Pittsburgh, PA 1467
Swartz, Jack, Pres. (V), Vilna Shul Boston's Center for Jewish Culture, Boston, MA 764
Swartz, Kate, Membership Coord., Public Rels. & Mktg. Dir., C.M. Russell Museum, Great Falls, MT.......................964
Swartz, Leslie, Sr. Vice Pres. Research & Program Planning, Boston Children's Museum, Boston, MA 758
Swearingen, John D., Jr., Dir., Fulton County Historical Museum, Wauseon, OH...1349
Swearingen, Pat, Museum Shop Mgr., Logoly State Park, McNeil, AR.................79
Sweedler, Sarah, Pres. (V), Fort Ross State Historic Park Visitor Center and Museum, Jenner, CA 125
Sweeney, Alan, Imaginarium Mgr., Grout Museum District: Grout Museum of History and Science, Bluedorn Science Imaginarium, Rensselaer Russell House Museum, Snowden House, Waterloo, IA 601
Sweeney, Barbara, Sec., National Bird Dog Museum, Grand Junction, TN 1553
Sweeney, Caitlin, Coord. Capital Campaign, Arthouse, Austin, TX..........1579
Sweeney, Chris, Museum Shop Mgr., Figge Art Museum, Davenport, IA..........581
Sweeney, David, Historic Site Asst., Schoharie Crossing State Historic Site, Fort Hunter, NY.......................................1134
Sweeney, Dennis F., Mgr. Operations, The Frick Collection, New York, NY....1168
Sweeney, Jim, Treas., Larchmont Historical Society, Mamaroneck, NY 1156
Sweeney, Julie, Center Mgr., J. Robert Donnelly Husky Heritage Sports Museum, Storrs, CT 296
Sweeney, Kathy, Dir. Education, Wichita Center for the Arts, Wichita, KS 640
Sweeney, Paggy, Devel., National Liberty Museum, Philadelphia, PA 1458
Sweeney, Pauline, Sec., Wenatchee Valley Museum and Cultural Center, Wenatchee, WA..................................1794
Sweeney, P.R., Pres., Michel Brouillet House & Museum, Vincennes, IN 569
Sweeney, Robert, FOSH, Pres. MAK Center for Art and Architecture at the Schindler House, West Hollywood, CA 223
Sweeney, Thomas W., Dir. Public Affairs, National Museum of the American Indian, Smithsonian Institution, New York, NY 1177
Sweeney, Dr. Tom, Dir., General Sweeny's Museum, Republic, MO 942
Sweet, Christina, Cur., Kam Wah Chung State Heritage Site, John Day, OR 1393
Sweet, David, Pres. VMNH Foundation, Virginia Museum of Natural History, Martinsville, VA 1724
Sweet, Donald E., Owner, Billy the Kid Museum, Fort Sumner, NM 1078
Sweet Espinosa, Nancy, Dir. Education, San Juan County Archaeological Research Center and Library at the Salmon Ruin/San Juan County Museum Association, Bloomfield, NM .1075
Sweet, Jennifer, Collections Asst., Rogers Historical Museum, Rogers, AR 83
Sweet, Joseph C., Historian, New Canaan Historical Society, New Canaan, CT 285
Sweet, Lula, Museum Shop Mgr., Billy the Kid Museum, Fort Sumner, NM......1078
Sweet, Pati, Chm. (V), Canyon County Historical Society & Museum, Nampa, ID 463
Sweet, Sam, C.O.O., The Corcoran Gallery of Art, Washington, DC 315
Sweet, Tim, Museum Shop Mgr., Billy the Kid Museum, Fort Sumner, NM......1078
Sweeten, David, Dir. Conference Svcs. DAR Museum First Ladies of Texas Historic Costumes Collection, Denton, TX 1602
Sweeten, Elvin R., Dir., Gene Autry Oklahoma Museum, Gene Autry, OK ...1362
Sweeten, Flora R., Museum Shop Mgr., Gene Autry Oklahoma Museum, Gene Autry, OK 1362
Sweeters, Jim, Interim Dir., Art Galleries, California State University, Northridge, Northridge, CA 152
Sweeting, Robert, Museum Shop Mgr., Maritime & Seafood Industry Museum, Biloxi, MS 904
Sweetman, Dr. Harold E., Dir., Jenkins Arboretum, Devon, PA..........................1420
Sweetman, Sherry, Archivist, Olmsted County Historical Society dba History Center of Olmsted County, Rochester, MN 891
Sweets, Henry, Cur., Mark Twain Boyhood Home & Museum, Hannibal, MO 928
Sweets, Judy, Media & Exhibits Archivist, The Robert J. Dole Institute of Politics, Lawrence, KS 621
Sweier, Cathy, Museum Shop Mgr., Detroit Institute of Arts, Detroit, MI 834
Swenson, Andrea, Treas., Lyon County Historical Society Museum, Marshall, MN 883
Swenson, Anne, Mgr., Hinsdale Historical Society, Hinsdale, IL...............................500

S–*Continued*

T

T–*Continued*

Taylor, Laura, Museum Shop Mgr., Fox River Trolley Museum/Fox River Trolley Association, South Elgin, IL.......520
Taylor, Laura, Museum Educator, Toy & Miniature Museum of Kansas City, Kansas City, MO.......935
Taylor, Lillian, Pres., The Wine Museum of Greyton H. Taylor, Hammondsport, NY.......1140
Taylor, Lorraine, Chm. Bd., Irving Arts Center, Irving, TX.......1624
Taylor, Marla, Asst. Collection Mgr., Robert S. Peabody Museum of Archaeology, Andover, MA.......754
Taylor, Michael, Cur. Modern Art, Philadelphia Museum of Art, Philadelphia, PA.......1459
Taylor, Michael V., Architectural Historian, Hampton Roads Naval Museum, Norfolk, VA.......1730
Taylor, Monecia, Dir. Devel., National Air and Space Museum, Washington, DC.......322
Taylor, N.J., Museum Shop Mgr., Pacific Grove Museum of Natural History, Pacific Grove, CA.......159
Taylor, Norma, Historian, Casey Jones Home and Railroad Museum, Jackson, TN.......1555
Taylor, Pam, Registrar, Aspen Art Museum, Aspen, CO.......228
Taylor, Pam, Naturalist-Brecksville, Cleveland Metroparks Outdoor Education Division, Garfield Heights, OH.......1322
Taylor, Paula, Museum Shop Mgr., Louisiana Art & Science Museum - Irene W. Pennington Planetarium, Baton Rouge, LA.......667
Taylor, Paula Bauman, Dir., Warren ICBM & Heritage Museum, Frances E. Warren Air Force Base, WY.......1858
Taylor, Peggy, Bd. Member, Marias Museum of History and Art, Shelby, MT.......972
Taylor, Raquel, Museum Shop Mgr., Southern Ute Cultural Center and Museum, Ignacio, CO.......252
Taylor, Ree, Dir., Eureka Sentinel Museum, Eureka, NV.......1003
Taylor, Regina, Volunteer Coord., Torrance Art Museum, Torrance, CA.......217
Taylor, Rich, Society Pres., Finnup Park and Lee Richardson Zoo, Garden City, KS.......613
Taylor, Richard, Pres. (V), National Museum of Ceramic Art and Glass, Baltimore, MD.......725
Taylor, Richard, Dir., Tunica Museum, Tunica, MS.......917
Taylor, Robert, Sr. Vice Pres., Colonial Williamsburg, Williamsburg, VA.......1754
Taylor, Robert L., Chm. & C.E.O., Airpower Museum Inc., Ottumwa, IA.......597
Taylor, Robert T., Chm. (V), Nauticus, Norfolk, VA.......1730
Taylor, Robin, Librarian, Philmont Museums, Cimarron, NM.......1076
Taylor, Roi, Dir. History Center, Cranbury Historical & Preservation Society, Cranbury, NJ.......1036
Taylor, Rose, Membership & Mktg., The Ward Museum of Wildfowl Art, Salisbury University, Salisbury, MD.......746
Taylor, Ruth, Exec. Dir., Newport Historical Society & The Museum of Newport History, Newport, RI.......1491
Taylor, Saddler, Chief Cur. Research & Folklife, The University of South Carolina McKissick Museum, Columbia, SC.......1510
Taylor, Samuel M., Dir. Carnegie Museum of Natural History, Carnegie Museums of Pittsburgh (Carnegie Institute), Pittsburgh, PA.......1465
Taylor, Samuel M., Ph.D., Dir., Carnegie Museum of Natural History, Pittsburgh, PA.......1464
Taylor, Shar, Vice Pres. Devel., National Building Museum, Washington, DC.......323
Taylor, Sidney, Registrar, Los Angeles Municipal Art Gallery - Barnsdall Art Park, Los Angeles, CA.......139
Taylor, Steve, Chm., Second Street Gallery, Charlottesville, VA.......1705
Taylor, Steve H., Dir., Cleveland Metroparks Zoo, Cleveland, OH.......1307
Taylor, Sue Ellen, Dir., The Prairie Museum of Art & History, Colby, KS.......608
Taylor, Ted, Cur., Edwards County Historical Museum, Kinsley, KS.......620
Taylor, Tim, Cur. Natural Science, Roper Mountain Science Center, Greenville, SC.......1514
Taylor, Tim, Museum Technician, U.S. Army Chaplain Museum, Fort Jackson, SC.......1512
Taylor, Tom, Cur. Paleobotany KU Biodiversity Institute - KU Natural History Museum, Lawrence, KS.......621
Taylor, Tom, Coord. Festivals, The von Liebig Art Center - The Naples Art Association, Naples, FL.......370
Taylor, Trent, Treas., American Quarter Horse Hall of Fame & Museum, Amarillo, TX.......1578
Taylor, Vicki, Museum Shop Mgr., Oklahoma Forest Heritage Center, Broken Bow, OK.......1358
Taylor, W.A. "Lex", III, C.E.O., The American Heritage "Big Red" Fire Museum, Louisville, MS.......912
Taylor, Wendy, Dir. Tour Svcs., Arnot Art Museum, Elmira, NY.......1130
Taylor, Winston J., Teaching Artist, Arkansas River Valley Arts Center, Russellville, AR.......83
Taylor-Godwin, Christina, Museum Retail Mgr. COPIA: The American Center for Wine, Food & the Arts, Napa, CA.......150
Taylor-Schran, Susan, Museum Shop Mgr., Gari Melchers Home and Studio, Fredericksburg, VA.......1712
Teagle, Rachel, Exec. Dir., The New Children's Museum, San Diego, CA.......182
Teague, Anita, Exec. Dir., Sam Davis Home, Smyrna, TN.......1574
Teague, Russell, Park Maintenance II, Watkins Woolen Mill State Historic Site & Park, Lawson, MO.......938
Teague, William, Art Handler, Patty and Jay Baker Naples Museum of Art, Naples, FL.......370
Teahan, John, Librarian & Cur. Special Book Collection, Wadsworth Atheneum Museum of Art, Hartford, CT.......279
Teal, Parke, Pres. (V), Museum of Florida Art, DeLand, FL.......343
Team, Ben, Dir., Autrey Mill Nature Preserve & Heritage Center, Johns Creek, GA.......421
Teasley, Andy, Park Mgr., Dr. Thomas Walker State Historic Site, Barbourville, KY.......641
Tebbenhoff, Karen, Public Rels., Currier Museum of Art, Manchester, NH.......1022
Tecco, James, Museum Shop Mgr., National Underground Railroad Freedom Center, Cincinnati, OH.......1306
Tedder, Ron, Cur., First Territorial Capitol of Kansas, Fort Riley, KS.......612
Tederick, Lydia S., Asst. Cur., The White House, Washington, DC.......333
Teders, Mark, Park Naturalist, Tucker Tower Nature Center, Ardmore, OK.......1356
Tedeschi, Martha, Cur. Prints & Drawings, The Art Institute of Chicago, Chicago, IL.......476
Tedford, Catherine L., Dir., St. Lawrence University - Richard F. Brush Art Gallery and Permanent Collection, Canton, NY.......1118
Tedrow, Gerald, C.E.O., Liberty Jail Historic Site, Liberty, MO.......939
Tedrow, Gerald W., Dir., Mormon Visitors Center, Independence, MO.......930
Tee, Dr. Kim K., Pres. (V), Chinese-American Museum of Chicago, Chicago, IL.......479
Teel, Cierra, Curatorial Asst., Agua Caliente Cultural Museum, Palm Springs, CA.......160
Teer, Janet, Pres. (V), The Kentuck Museum Association/Art Center/Festival of the Arts, Northport, AL.......21
Teese, Paul, Ph.D., Cur., Bowman's Hill Wildflower Preserve, New Hope, PA.......1447
Teeter, Charles, Pres. (V), New Braunfels Museum of Art & Music, New Braunfels, TX.......1635
Teeter, Wendy, Cur. Archaeology, Fowler Museum at UCLA, Los Angeles, CA.......135
Teeters, Claire, Pres., Yucaipa Valley Historical Society Museum, Yucaipa, CA.......227
Teeters-Eichacker, Mary Jane, Cur. Social History, Indiana State Museum, Indianapolis, IN.......549
Tefft, Anna, Treas., Connecticut Fire Museum, East Windsor, CT.......272
Tefft, Carvel, Pres., Portsmouth Athenaeum, Portsmouth, NH.......1027
Tefft, Fred, Membership, Great Plains Transportation Museum, Wichita, KS.......638
Teichart, Joan, Museum Shop Mgr., Zelienople Historical Society, Zelienople, PA.......1484
Teigland, Jon, Facility Mgr., Bradford Brinton Memorial & Museum, Big Horn, WY.......1852
Teixeira, Joaquina, Dir., Rhode Island Black Heritage Society, Providence, RI.......1496
Tejada, Susan, Dir., Grier Musser Museum, Los Angeles, CA.......136
Tejada, Susana, Librarian, Albright-Knox Art Gallery, Buffalo, NY.......1114
Telepchak, Beverly, Business Mgr., The Dawes Arboretum, Newark, OH.......1334
Telewski, Dr. Frank W., Cur., W.J. Beal Botanical Garden, East Lansing, MI.......838
Tella, Michele, Account Clerk, Lincoln's New Salem State Historic Site, Petersburg, IL.......513
Teller, Betty, Dir. Visitor Svcs. COPIA: The American Center for Wine, Food & the Arts, Napa, CA.......150
Tellford, Suzanne, Museum Educator, Mt. Kearsarge Indian Museum, Warner, NH.......1029
Tellier, Dr. Cassandra, Dir., The Schumacher Gallery, Capital University, Columbus, OH.......1314
Tellyer, Donna, Sec., Kerbyville Museum, Kerby, OR.......1393
Telonidis, Julia, Cur. Manuscripts & Acting Dir. Library, The New Jersey Historical Society, Newark, NJ.......1052
Telzrow, Michael E., Exec. Dir., National Railroad Museum, Green Bay, WI.......1821
Tempel, Denison, C.E.O., Donkey Milk House, Historic Home, Key West, FL.......358
Temple, Bill, Pres. (V), Rome Area History Museum, Rome, GA.......430

T–*Continued*

T–*Continued*

T–*Continued*

Thornton, Talon J., Dir., Henson Robinson Zoo, Springfield, IL 520
Thornton, Terri, Cur. Education, Modern Art Museum of Fort Worth, Fort Worth, TX 1611
Thornton, Tom, Chm. (V), Fort Inglish, Bonham, TX 1589
Thorpe, Clare, Dir. Guest Svcs., Abraham Lincoln Presidential Library & Museum, Springfield, IL 520
Thorpe, Dana L., Exec. Dir., Fresno Metropolitan Museum of Art & Science, Fresno, CA 116
Thorsen, Sue, Cur., Sitka National Historical Park, Sitka, AK.........................35
Thorsgard, Eirik, Cultural Resources Specialist, Confederated Tribes of Grand Ronde Cultural Resources Department, Grand Ronde, OR.............1390
Thorson, Ellan, Dir., Rising Sun Inn, Crownsville, MD 732
Thorson, Harold, Pres. (V), Barron County Historical Society's Pioneer Village Museum, Cameron, WI 1814
Thrash, Mary F., Asst. Mgr., Roosevelt's Little White House State Historic Site, Warm Springs, GA 439
Thrash, Troy A., Exec. Dir., Da Vinci Science Center, Allentown, PA 1408
Thrasher, B. Holt, Chm., National Audubon Society, New York, NY..........1176
Threadwell, Kathy, Mgr., Quanah Parker Star House/Eagle Park Ghost Town, Cache, OK 1358
Threet, Tonya, Vice Pres., Kosciusko Museum and Visitors Center, Kosciusko, MS...912
Thrift, Linda, Keeper, Center for Electronic & Outreach Svcs., National Portrait Gallery, Washington, DC 326
Throckmorton, Jodi, Curatorial Asst., San Jose Museum of Art, San Jose, CA.........196
Throne, Walter, Treas., Greater Hazleton Historical Society, Hazleton, PA...........1433
Thrush, Brad, Museum Shop Mgr., Fort Collins Museum, Fort Collins, CO..........246
Thumberg, Carol, Treas., Laura Ingalls Wilder Park & Museum, Inc., Burr Oak, IA 575
Thuotte, G. F., Dir., Port Townsend Aero Museum, Port Townsend, WA 1776
Thurber, Jim, Pres. (V), Los Altos History Museum aka Association of the Los Altos Historical Museum, Los Altos, CA...132
Thurber, T. Barton, Cur. European Art, Hood Museum of Art, Hanover, NH 1019
Thurman Heisch, Melvena, Deputy State Historic Preservation Officer, Oklahoma Historical Society, Oklahoma City, OK..............................1372
Thurman, Rev. Michael F., Pres. (V), Dexter Parsonage Museum, Montgomery, AL 19
Thurman, Tony, Exhibits Technician, The Kentucky Library & Museum, Bowling Green, KY...............................642
Thurmer, Robert, Dir. & Cur., Cleveland State University Art Gallery, Cleveland, OH 1308
Thurow, Chuck, Exec. Dir., Hyde Park Art Center, Chicago, IL..........................481
Thurston, Deborah, Museum Shop Mgr., Phippen Museum, Prescott, AZ 52
Thurston, Karla, Business Mgr. & Museum Shop Mgr., Pennsylvania Military Museum and 28th Division Shrine, Boalsburg, PA 1414
Tiano, Patty, Museum Shop Mgr., Brandywine Zoo, Wilmington, DE 311
Tibbits, Cory, Dir. Exhibitions, Lakeview Museum of Arts and Sciences, Peoria, IL...512
Tibbits, Rena, Museum Shop Mgr., Greater Southwest Historical Museum, Ardmore, OK 1356
Tibbitts, Norma, Chm. (V), The Heritage Center, Pine Ridge, SD 1539
Tibbs Copeland, Jacqueline, Dir. Education, Walters Art Museum, Baltimore, MD..727
Tibbs, Pam, Gen. Mgr., Cafe Sebastienne, Kemper Museum of Contemporary Art, Kansas City, MO.............................934
Tice, Lisa, Dir., Suzanne H. Arnold Art Gallery, Lebanon Valley College, Annville, PA 1410
Tice, Penelope, Pres., Holland Historical Society Museum, Inc., Holland, VT......1681
Tichenor, Daryl L., C.E.O. & Dir., Virginia City J. Spencer Watkins Memorial Museum, Virginia City, MT....973
Ticknor, Will, Dir., City of Las Cruces Museum System, Las Cruces, NM 1080
Tidwell, Eric, Acting Mng. Dir., Martin Luther King, Jr. Center for Nonviolent Social Change, Inc., Atlanta, GA............406
Tiede, Mary Lou, Museum Shop Mgr., Nez Perce National Historical Park, Spalding, ID...466
Tiede, Saralee, Dir. Communications, Lady Bird Johnson Wildflower Center, Austin, TX 1582
Tiedgen, Mary Jane, Vice Pres., Isle La Motte Historical Society, Isle La Motte, VT...1681
Tiegel, Connie, Bd. Pres., San Jose Museum of Quilts & Textiles, San Jose, CA...196
Tierney, Caroline, Financial Dir., Audubon Zoo, New Orleans, LA............679
Tierney, Lennox, Asian Art Cur., Mingei International Museum, San Diego, CA ...180
Tierney, Paul, Park Naturalist & Cur., Blue Licks Pioneer Museum, Mount Olivet, KY 659
Tieszen, Pam, C.E.O., Heritage Hall Museum & Archives, Freeman, SD.......1531
Tiff, Keith, Farm Worker, Billings Farm & Museum, Woodstock, VT 1695
Tiffany, Sharon, Dir., Columbia Gorge Interpretive Center Museum, Stevenson, WA...1787
Tijerina, Melissa, Programming Officer, Museum of South Texas History, Edinburg, TX 1603
Tikjoeb, Sanne, Dir. Communications & Publications, Fondo Del Sol Visual Arts & Media Center/El Museo de Culturas y Herencias Americanas/MOCHA, Washington, DC 317
Tilghman, Richard, Pres., Historical Society of Talbot County, Easton, MD....733
Tiller, Reggie, Supt., William Howard Taft National Historic Site, Cincinnati, OH...1307
Tiller, Reginald, Supt., George Washington Carver National Monument, Diamond, MO......................925
Tilley, Alisha, Clerk, National Heisey Glass Museum, Newark, OH 1335
Tilley, Carey, Exec. Dir., Cherokee National Museum, Park Hill, OK 1374
Tilley, Libby, Grant Writer, Blue Star Contemporary Art Center, San Antonio, TX...1643
Tilley, Melissa, Public Rels., Art Museum of Southeast Texas, Beaumont, TX 1585
Tillman, Patricia, Dir. Studio Arts & Chm. Fine Arts Dept., Widener Gallery, Austin Arts Center, Trinity College, Hartford, CT..............................279
Tilly, Stephen, Interim Chm. Bd., Lyndhurst, Tarrytown, NY 1220
Tilton, Diane E., Asst. to Exec. Dir., Vero Beach Museum of Art, Inc., Vero Beach, FL...396
Tilton, Doug, Dir. Visitor Svcs., The Children's Museum of New Hampshire, Dover, NH..........................1016
Tim, Ty, Museum Archivist, Cambodian American Heritage Museum and Killing Fields Memorial, Chicago, IL 477
Timberlake, Stephanie, Cur. & Historic Park Coord., Burritt on the Mountain - A Living Museum, Huntsville, AL 14
Timken, Melissa, Public Rels., White 1 Foundation - WWII Aircraft Museum, Kissimmee, FL...360
Timken, Dr. M.J., Dir. & Cur., White 1 Foundation - WWII Aircraft Museum, Kissimmee, FL...360
Timm, Jean, Treas., Osage County Historical Society Research Center, Lyndon, KS 624
Timm, Peggi, Chm. (V), Baker Heritage Museum, Baker City, OR......................1384
Timm, Robert, Cur. Mammalogy KU Biodiversity Institute - KU Natural History Museum, Lawrence, KS 621
Timmerman, John, Exhibits Designer, Cape Fear Museum of History and Science, Wilmington, NC.....................1271
Timmerman, Lynn A., Site Mgr., John Deere Historic Site, Dixon, IL................490
Timmermann, Dale, Dir., The Little Brick House, Vandalia, IL 525
Timmermeister, William C., Pres., Allen County Museum, Lima, OH..................1328
Timmons, Chuck, Chm. (V), Museum at Southwestern Michigan College, Dowagiac, MI 836
Timmons, Mary Lou, House Mgr., Alden B. Dow Home & Studio, Midland, MI ...854
Timmons, Traci, Librarian, Seattle Art Museum, Seattle, WA...........................1783
Timmons, Traci, Librarian, Seattle Asian Art Museum, Seattle, WA 1783
Timms, Gary, Museum Coord., Linn County Historical Museum and Moyer House, Brownsville, OR.......................1385
Timms, Peter, Dir., Fitchburg Art Museum, Fitchburg, MA 778
Timms, Rufus, Museum Shop Mgr., The South Carolina Railroad Museum, Winnsboro, SC..1526
Timney, Matthew, Business Mgr., Penobscot Marine Museum, Searsport, ME..711
Timoshuk, Walter W., Pres., Norton Simon Museum, Pasadena, CA...............162
Timothy, John, Museum Dir., Ataloa Lodge Museum, Muskogee, OK...........1367
Timpano, Anne, Dir. DAAP Galleries, Cincinnati, OH...1305
Timpano, Anne, Dir., University of Mary Washington Galleries, Fredericksburg, VA 1714
Timpone, Andrea, Pres. & C.E.O., Elachee Nature Science Center, Gainesville, GA 420
Timpson, Richard, Dir. Facilities & Exhibitions Production, The Textile Museum, Washington, DC 330
Tinaiero Dowdle, Maria, Bilingual Programs Mgr., Children's Museum at La Habra, La Habra, CA.........................126
Tingle, Jackson, Vice Pres., Rebecca Nurse Homestead, Danvers, MA 773
Tingley, Austin, Treas., West Valley Art Museum, Surprise, AZ 56
Tingley, Karen, Cur. Education, Prospect Park Zoo, Brooklyn, NY 1112

T–*Continued*

T–*Continued*

T–*Continued*

Turner, Steve, Historic Preservation & Deputy SHPO, History Colorado, The Colorado Historical Society, Denver, CO 240
Turner, Sue, Dir., Telephone Museum of New Mexico, Albuquerque, NM....1073
Turner, Dr. Thomas F., C.E.O. & Dir., Museum of Southwestern Biology, Albuquerque, NM....1072
Turner, Walter, Historian, North Carolina Transportation Museum, Spencer, NC...1268
Turner, Willie, Vice Pres. Mktg., Hiller Aviation Institute, San Carlos, CA 179
Turner-Lowe, Susan, Vice Pres. Communications, Huntington Library, Art Collections, and Botanical Gardens, San Marino, CA....198
Turnham, Stephanie, Dir., Bell County Museum, Belton, TX....1587
Turnock, Prof. Jack, Dir. & Cur., Alexander Brest Museum and Gallery, Jacksonville, FL....354
Turnquist, Jan, Exec. Dir., Orchard House, Concord, MA 772
Turnquist, Noreen, Treas., Frontier Gateway Museum, Glendive, MT....964
Turo, Sharon, Librarian, New Canaan Historical Society, New Canaan, CT....285
Turpin, Mark, Site Mgr., Asistencia: San Gabriel Mission Outpost, Redlands, CA 169
Turtell, Neal T., Exec. Librarian, National Gallery of Art, Washington, DC 323
Turton, Ray, Pres., Centerville - Washington Township Historical Society & Asahel Wright Community Center, Centerville, OH....1301
Turton, Roy, Pres. (V), Centerville - Washington Township Historical Society & Walton House Museum, Centerville, OH....1302
Tusim, Pearl J., Pres. (V), Mansfield Township Historical Society (1849 Georgetown School/Museum), Columbus, NJ 1036
Tutein, Joel A., Park Supt., Christiansted National Historic Site, Saint Croix, VI .1872
Tutino, Judy, Pres. (V), Depreciation Lands Museum, Allison Park, PA....1409
Tuttle, Art, Pres. (V), West Florida Railroad Museum, Milton, FL 369
Tuttle, Dick, Pres. (V), Stone Quarry Hill Art Park, Inc., Cazenovia, NY 1119
Tvedten, Lenny, Exec. Dir., Pioneer Museum - Martin County Historical Society, Fairmont, MN....877
Twedt, Jane, Dir. Devel., The Living Desert, Palm Desert, CA....160
Tweedy, Jeffrey C., Chm. (V), Museum of the Bedford Historical Society, Bedford, NY 1103
Tweedy, Sheila, Museum Shop Mgr., Academy of Model Aeronautics/National Model Aviation Museum, Muncie, IN 557
Tweet, David, Museum Shop Mgr., Columbus Museum of Art, Columbus, OH....1312
Twellman, Ron, Cur. Collections EAA AirVenture Museum, Oshkosh, WI 1839
Tweten, Donene, Sec., Alutiiq Museum and Archaeological Repository, Kodiak, AK....33
Twiford, Barbara, Treas., Utica Museum, Utica, MT....973
Twigg, Martha B., Exec. Dir. & Devel. Officer, South Shore Natural Science Center, Inc., Norwell, MA 797
Twiss Hooting, Beth, Dir. Education & Public Programs, Chester County Historical Society, West Chester, PA....1481
Twitchell, Mike, Exhibit Builder, The Discovery Center of Idaho, Boise, ID....455
Twitchey, Orvin, Pres. (V), Mud Lake Historical Society, Terreton, ID 466
Twomey, Susan, Dir., Buchanan Center for the Arts, Monmouth, IL 506
Ty, Marychris, Mgr. Exhibition Programs, Socrates Sculpture Park, Long Island City, NY....1155
Tyler Doub, Mary, Chm., International Bluegrass Music Museum, Owensboro, KY 660
Tyler, Fielding L., Exec. Dir., Virginia Beach Maritime Museum, Inc./The Old Coast Guard Station, Virginia Beach, VA....1752
Tyler, Frances P.B., Pres. (V), Sherwood Forest Plantation, Charles City, VA....1703
Tyler, Gregory, Cur., Historic Hope Foundation, Inc., Windsor, NC 1273
Tyler, Harrison R., Dir., Sherwood Forest Plantation, Charles City, VA 1703
Tyler, John Ann, Dir., Louisiana State Cotton Museum, Lake Providence, LA...674
Tyler, Lori, Pres. (V), City Arts Center, Oklahoma City, OK....1370
Tyler, Nora Mae, Treas., Brush Country Museum, Cotulla, TX....1595
Tyler, Ron, Dir., Amon Carter Museum, Fort Worth, TX 1609
Tyler, Ronald, Dir. & Pres. (V), Enumclaw Plateau Historical Society, Enumclaw, WA 1765
Tyler, Sundi, Interim Dir. Art, New Mexico State Fair Fine Arts Gallery, Albuquerque, NM....1073
Tynch, David, Chm., Virginia Sports Hall of Fame, Portsmouth, VA....1735
Tyor, Peter, Treas., The Kenilworth Historical Society, Kenilworth, IL....501
Tyre, William, Exec. Dir., Glessner House Museum, Chicago, IL 480
Tysdal, Bobbie Jo, Dir., Anna Miller Museum, Newcastle, WY....1863
Tyson, Ed, Librarian, Searls Historic Library, Nevada County Historical Society, Inc., Nevada City, CA 151
Tyson, Dr. Neil deGrasse, Frederick P. Rose Dir., Hayden Planetarium, American Museum of Natural History, New York, NY....1163
Tystad Koupal, Nancy, Dir. Research & Publications, South Dakota State Historical Society, Pierre, SD 1538
TzeHuey, Chiou-Peng, Cur. Asia, Spurlock Museum, University of Illinois at Urbana-Champaign, Urbana, IL....525
Tzouras, Tom, Mgr. Oral History, Hellenic Museum & Cultural Center, Chicago, IL 481

U

Ubben, Dolores, Corresponding Sec., The Peekskill Museum, Peekskill, NY....1194
Uber, Judith, Treas., Cumberland County Historical Society, Greenwich, NJ 1040
Uberuaga, Dave, Supt., Mt. Rainier National Park, Ashford, WA 1758
Uchin, Andrew, Museum Shop Mgr., Norton Simon Museum, Pasadena, CA...162
Uddin, Bibi, Museum Shop Mgr., The Schomburg Center for Research in Black Culture, New York, NY 1180
Udelhoven, Destinee, Dir., Historic Indian Agency House, Portage, WI 1841
Udolph, Greg, Roundhouse Foreman, Steam Railroading Institute, Owosso, MI....859
Udris, Andi, Pres. & C.E.O., Union Station Kansas City, Inc., Kansas City, MO 936
Udris, Cindy, Chm. (V), Shoal Creek Living History Museum, Kansas City, MO 935
Uebelhor, Christopher, Asst. Cur., Fredericksburg Area Museum & Cultural Center, Inc., Fredericksburg, VA 1712
Uetz, Katherine, Dir., Xavier University Art Gallery, Cincinnati, OH 1307
Ugrinov, Mirjana, Treas. ARC Gallery (Artists, Residents of Chicago), Chicago, IL 476
Uhlenbrock, Dr. Jaimee, Assoc. Cur. Collections, Samuel Dorsky Museum of Art, State University of New York at New Paltz, New Paltz, NY 1161
Uhrich, Jeffery, Supt., Ash Hollow State Historical Park, Lewellen, NE 987
Uithol, Ruthann, Asst. Dir. Collections & Collections Mgr., Hillwood Estate, Museum & Gardens, Washington, DC 318
Ulak, Dr. James, Deputy Dir., Freer and Sackler Galleries of Art, Washington, DC....318
Ulbrich, Marjorie, C.E.O., Gardner House Museum, Albion, MI 820
Ulerick, Lois, Pres., Fulton County Historical Society Museum, Rochester, IN 564
Ullman, Jonathan, Vice Pres. Business Devel. & Operations, The National Soccer Hall of Fame, Oneonta, NY....1189
Ullmann, Katya, Receptionist, American Folk Art Museum, New York, NY....1162
Ullrich, Suzanne, Volunteer Coord., Hillforest House Museum, Aurora, IN 531
Ulman, Patty, Asst. Dir., Badlands Petrified Gardens, Kadoka, SD 1533
Ulmann, Charles E., Cur., The Christian C. Sanderson Museum, Chadds Ford, PA....1417
Ulmen, Patti, Financial Officer, Kadoka Depot Museum, Kadoka, SD 1533
Ulmer, Sean, Cur., Cedar Rapids Museum of Art, Cedar Rapids, IA....577
Ulrich, Alan, Pres. (V), Parker Tavern, Reading, MA 802
Ultan, Prof. Lloyd, Historian, The Bronx County Historical Society, Bronx, NY..1107
Umar, Mirriam A., Program Dir., Freetown Village Living History Museum, Indianapolis, IN....547
Umbach, Joyce, Park Ranger Interpretation, Capulin Volcano National Monument, Capulin, NM....1075
Umberger, Eugene, Dir., Neville Public Museum of Brown County, Green Bay, WI 1821
Umberger, Leslie, Senior Cur., John Michael Kohler Arts Center, Sheboygan, WI 1844
Umlauf, Sarah, Community Resource Coord., Historic Hanley House, Clayton, MO 923
Umphrey, Cathy, Horticulturist, Historic London Town and Gardens, Edgewater, MD....733
Uncil, Kathy, C.F.O., Fort William Henry Museum, Lake George, NY 1152
Underdahl, Hans, Chm. (V), Portland Museum of Art, Portland, ME 708
Underwood, Charlene, Receptionist, Children's Museum at La Habra, La Habra, CA....126
Underwood, Dorothy, Receptionist, Nassau County Museum of Art, Roslyn Harbor, NY....1204
Underwood, Janelle, Clerk & Treas., Reshaw Exhibit, Evansville, WY....1858
Underwood, Jonathan A., Dir., Stanly County Historic Preservation Commission and Museum, Albemarle, NC....1230

V

V–Continued

V–*Continued*

V–*Continued*

Vincent, Frantz, Vice Dir. Operations, Brooklyn Museum, Brooklyn, NY........1111
Vincent, Gary, Mgr., Collier County Museum, Naples, FL............................369
Vincent, George, Past Pres., Cincinnati Museum Center at Union Terminal, Cincinnati, OH...1304
Vincent, Jacob, Head Glass Dept., Worcester Center for Crafts, Worcester, MA...819
Vincent, Karen, Dir. Collections, Minnetrista, Muncie, IN.........................558
Vincent, Marcus Alan, Dir., Woodbury Art Museum, Orem, UT.......................1666
Vincent, Roberta, Pres., Alden Historical Society, Inc., Alden, NY....................1098
Vincent, Todd, Pres. (V), Sci-Tech Center of Northern New York, Watertown, NY...1226
Vincent, William, Ph.D., C.E.O. & Dir., Alamance County Historical Museum, Burlington, NC...................................1236
Vincenti, Patrick, Vice Pres., Havre de Grace Decoy Museum, Havre de Grace, MD...738
Vinci, Anna M., Pres. (V) & Dir., Wildwood Historical Society, Inc., Wildwood, NJ.......................................1068
Vinci, Sarah G., Dir. Publications & Public Rels., California State University, Long Beach, University Art Museum, Long Beach, CA..............131
Vines, Faye, Administrative Asst., Kennedy-Douglass Center for the Arts, Florence, AL..12
Vines, Jason, Chm., Automotive Hall of Fame, Inc., Dearborn, MI.......................831
Vines, Martha, Art History, The Art Galleries at UAH, Huntsville, AL............14
Viney, Lt. Col. Mark A., Dir. Operations, United States Army Heritage and Education Center - Army Heritage Museum, Carlisle, PA...........................1416
Vinnedge, Gardiner, Treas., Snoqualmie Valley Historical Museum, North Bend, WA...1773
Vinovich, Jennifer, Special Projects Mgr., South Shore Arts, Munster, IN...............558
Vinson, Paul, Dir. Exhibits, Museum of Nature & Science, Dallas, TX..............1599
Vinson, Roger, Pres., A.L. Fetterman Educational Museum, Fort Valley, GA....419
Vinson, Judge Roger, Pres., Massee Lane Gardens, Home of American Camellia Society, Fort Valley, GA.........................419
Viola, Elise, Front Desk Asst., Art and Culture Center of Hollywood, Hollywood, FL.....................................353
Violette, Alderico "Dick", Chm. (V), New Hampshire Telephone Museum, Warner, NH...1030
Violette, Paul E., Pres. (V), New Hampshire Telephone Museum, Warner, NH...1030
Violette, Patricia A., Cur. Education, Old Fort Western, Augusta, ME....................691
Virden, Walter, Pres. & Chm. (V), Arlington Museum of Art, Arlington, TX...1579
Virgilio, Barry, Environmental Educator 2, Niagara Gorge Discovery Center, Niagara Falls, NY................................1185
Virgin, Louise, Cur. Asian Art, Worcester Art Museum, Worcester, MA.................819
Virgint, Dwayne, C.O.O., Indian Pueblo Cultural Center, Albuquerque, NM.......1071
Visante, Mika, Museum Shop Mgr., The California Museum For History, Women and the Arts, Sacramento, CA....174
Viso, Olga, Dir., Walker Art Center, Minneapolis, MN...................................886
Visser, Susan R., Exec. Dir., South Bend Regional Museum of Art, South Bend, IN...566
Vissia, Larry, Chm., Newell Museum, Newell, SD...1537
Vitagliano, Christine, Administrative Sec., Museum of International Folk Art, Santa Fe, NM...1089
Vitas, Robert, Ph.D., Financial Dir., The Lithuanian Museum, Chicago, IL...........483
Vitelli, Margo, Educ. Dir., Manoa Heritage Center, Honolulu, HI....................446
Vitez, Cheri, Asst. Registrar, Spurlock Museum, University of Illinois at Urbana-Champaign, Urbana, IL..................525
Vitiello, Erie, Dir., Davis Art Center, Davis, CA...106
Vititoe, Sue, Chm. (V), Marshall M. Fredericks Sculpture Museum, University Center, MI.................................866
Vitt, Dr. L.J., Cur. Reptiles, Sam Noble Oklahoma Museum of Natural History, Norman, OK..............................1369
Vittitow, Dorothy J., Mktg., Gheens Science Hall and Rauch Planetarium, Louisville, KY.......................................654
Vitullo, Don, Vice Pres., Price Pioneer Museum, Florence, CO...........................244
Vitullo, Goldie, Sec., Price Pioneer Museum, Florence, CO...........................244
Vivian, C.T., Chm. (V), National Voting Rights Museum and Institute, Selma, AL..22
Vivian, Octavia, Cur., National Voting Rights Museum and Institute, Selma, AL..22
Vivilecchia, Joe, Shop Mgr., New Hampshire Institute of Art, Manchester, NH.................................1023
Vivirito, Jackie, Cur. Asst., Lorenzo State Historic Site, Cazenovia, NY................1119
Vizard, Joseph, Corresponding Sec., Waltham Historical Society, Waltham, MA...813
Vlack, Donald J., Sr. Designer, The New York Public Library for the Performing Arts, New York, NY...........1179
Vlahakis, Stephanie A., Exec. Dir., Hellenic Museum & Cultural Center, Chicago, IL...481
Vlasic, James J., Chm. Bd. Trustees, Cranbrook Institute of Science, Bloomfield Hills, MI...............................828
Vlastos, Lisa, Asst. Cur. Education, Nicolaysen Art Museum and Discovery Center, Casper, WY.............1853
Vlcek, Deborah, Museum Shop Mgr., Yakima Valley Museum and Historical Association, Yakima, WA......................1795
Vliek, Erik, Business Mgr., Museum of Western Colorado, Grand Junction, CO..250
Vliet, Marni, Chm. Bd. & Pres., Wichita Art Museum, Wichita, KS.......................639
Vlna, Jennifer, Museum Shop Mgr., Chicago History Museum, Chicago, IL...478
Vlna, Jim, Exec. Dir., Knoxville Zoological Gardens, Knoxville, TN.......1559
Vlna, Marie, Dir. Guest Svcs., Knoxville Zoological Gardens, Knoxville, TN.......1559
Vocasek, Joe E., Sec. & City Delegate, Wilson Czech Opera House Corporation, Foundation, Inc. & House of Memories Museum, Wilson, KS..640
Vodrey, Jackman, Treas., Lou Holtz/Upper Ohio Valley Hall of Fame, East Liverpool, OH......................1318
Vodrey, S.W., Dir. & Museum Shop Mgr., Museum of Ceramics, East Liverpool, OH...1319
Voelkel, David B., Consultant, Ash Lawn-Highland, Charlottesville, VA......1704
Voelker, Dr. Judy, Dir., Museum of Anthropology, Highland Heights, KY.....649
Voelkle, William M., Cur. & Dept. Medieval & Renaissance Manuscripts, The Morgan Library & Museum, New York, NY...1173
Vogel, Craig, Treas., Pacific Northwest Truck Museum, Brooks, OR................1385
Vogel, Dwight, Pres. (V), Petterson Museum of Intercultural Art, Claremont, CA...102
Vogel, Grace, Volunteer Coord., Imagine Nation Museum, Bristol, CT...................268
Vogel, Jerome, Sr. Advisor to Pres., The Museum for African Art, Long Island City, NY..1154
Vogel, Jim, Cur., Museum of New Jersey Maritime History, Beach Haven, NJ......1032
Vogel, Julie, Museum Shop Mgr., Imagine Children's Museum, Everett, WA..1765
Vogel, Morris, Pres., Lower East Side Tenement Museum, New York, NY.......1172
Vogt, Brian, C.E.O., Denver Botanic Gardens, Inc., Denver, CO.....................238
Vogt, Elizabeth, Treas. (V), Ashtabula Historic House, Pendleton, SC..............1521
Vogt, Elizabeth, Treas. (V), Woodburn Historic House, Pendleton, SC..............1521
Vogt, George, Exec. Dir., Oregon Historical Society, Portland, OR............1399
Vogt, Jay D., Exec. Dir., South Dakota State Historical Society, Pierre, SD.......1538
Vogt, Michael J., Cur., Basque Museum & Cultural Center, Boise, ID..................455
Vogt, William, Bd. Trustees Chm., Hancock Shaker Village, Inc., Pittsfield, MA...799
Voight, Ralph, Dir. Guest Rels., Witte Museum, San Antonio, TX..................1646
Voigt, Bradford, Dir. Institutional Advancement, Harvard Art Museum, Cambridge, MA.......................................767
Voigt, John, Chm. Bd., Young at Art Children's Museum, Davie, FL..............342
Voigt, Lois, Treas., The Oakes Museum at Messiah College, Grantham, PA........1429
Voigt, Susan L., Business Mgr., Peabody Museum of Natural History, New Haven, CT...286
Voirol, Shannon, Exec. Dir., Astor House Museum, Golden, CO...........................248
Voirol, Shannon, Exec. Dir., Clear Creek History Park, Golden, CO.......................248
Volentine, Linda, Project Dir., The Herbert S. Ford Memorial Museum, Homer, LA..671
Volk, Steven B., C.E.O., Shelby American Collection, Boulder, CO..........230
Volkert, James, Assoc. Dir. Mall Museum Transition, National Museum of the American Indian, Smithsonian Institution, New York, NY....................1177
Vollbach, Paula, C.E.O. & Pres. (V), East Jordan Portside Art & Historical Museum, East Jordan, MI.........................837
Vollenweider, Katherine, Exec. Dir. & Registrar, Museum and Arts Center in the Sequim Dungeness Valley, Sequim, WA..1785
Vollmer, David L., Acting Dir. & Deputy Dir., Blaffer Gallery, The Art Museum of the University of Houston, Houston, TX...1619
Vollmer, Janis, Pres., Call of the Wild Museum, Gaylord, MI...............................841
Vollnogle, Leslie, Collections Mgr., Stuhr Museum of the Prairie Pioneer, Grand Island, NE...984
Voloshin, Delaine, Pres. (V), Museum of Northwest Colorado, Craig, CO..............236
Volpe, Ralph, Exec. Dir., Walter E. Heller Nature Center, Highland Park, IL............500

W

W–*Continued*

Walker, David, Progrma Mgr., Merchant and Drovers Tavern Museum, Rahway, NJ....1059
Walker, David B., Exec. Dir., Nevada Museum of Art, Reno, NV....1009
Walker, Dorothy, Office Mgr., The Old Jail Art Center, Albany, TX....1576
Walker, Douglas, Cur., Walter Anderson Museum of Art, Ocean Springs, MS....914
Walker, Ed, Cur., Birks Museum, Decatur, IL....489
Walker, RADM Edward K., SC, USN (Ret.), C.E.O. & Pres., U.S. Navy Memorial Foundation and Naval Heritage Center, Washington, DC....332
Walker, Edward, USN, (Ret.), Treas., U.S. Navy Memorial Foundation and Naval Heritage Center, Washington, DC....332
Walker, Frank, Security, Yesteryear Village, West Palm Beach, FL....397
Walker, George, Shop Foreman, Tennessee Valley Railroad Museum Inc., Chattanooga, TN....1549
Walker, George, Co Dir. USS Montpelier Museum, Montpelier, VT....1684
Walker, Gwen, Site Mgr., Confederate Memorial Museum, Atoka, OK....1356
Walker, Gwendolyn, Pres. (V), Dir. & Cur., The Walker African American Museum & Research Center, Las Vegas, NV....1007
Walker, Hamza, Dir. Education & Assoc. Cur., The Renaissance Society at The University of Chicago, Chicago, IL....486
Walker, Hobert, Chm. (V), David Crockett Cabin, Rutherford, TN....1573
Walker, Jan B., Dir., Bowie Arts Center, Due West, SC....1511
Walker, Janet, Mgr. Visitor Svcs., Smithsonian American Art Museum, Washington, DC....329
Walker, Jeanne, Volunteer Coord., Poplar Grove Historic Plantation, Wilmington, NC....1272
Walker, Jeff, Exec. Dir., Automobile Driving Museum, El Segundo, CA....110
Walker, Jeffrey, C.F.O., National World War I Museum at Liberty Memorial, Kansas City, MO....934
Walker, Jessica, Collectors' Gallery Asst., Mingei International Museum, San Diego, CA....180
Walker, Joel B., Chm. (V), Space Center Houston, Houston, TX....1623
Walker, John, Museum Store Mgr., Nevada State Railroad Museum, Carson City, NV....1001
Walker, Juanita, Treas., The Walker African American Museum & Research Center, Las Vegas, NV....1007
Walker, Judy, Summer Festival Gen. Mgr., Ash Lawn-Highland, Charlottesville, VA....1704
Walker, Kandice, Dir., The John Wornall House Museum, Kansas City, MO....933
Walker, Karen, Chm. (V), Historic New Harmony, New Harmony, IN....560
Walker, Karen B., Administrative Asst. & Public Rels., Hiddenite Center, Inc., Hiddenite, NC....1252
Walker, Dr. Karen J., Asst. Scientist FL Archaeology, Florida Museum of Natural History, Gainesville, FL....351
Walker, Kathie, Chm. (V), Colorado Springs Museum, Colorado Springs, CO....234
Walker, Kristina, Dir. Education, Spencer Museum of Art, The University of Kansas, Lawrence, KS....621
Walker, Laurie, Dir., University of South Florida Botanical Garden, Tampa, FL....393
Walker, LuLen, Cur. Art, Georgetown University Art Collection, Washington, DC....318
Walker, Maggie, Co Pres. Bd., Museum of History & Industry (MOHAI), Seattle, WA....1782
Walker, Mallory, Chm., National Portrait Gallery, Washington, DC....326
Walker, Mary Ellen, Public Rels., Descanso Gardens Guild, Inc., La Canada Flintridge, CA....125
Walker, Matt, C.E.O. & Park Admin., Iron & Steel Museum of Alabama, Tannehill Ironworks Historical State Park, McCalla, AL....16
Walker, Natalie, Coord. Art Education, Alexandria Museum of Art, Alexandria, LA....665
Walker, Norma, Museum Shop Mgr., St. Clair County Historical Society, Belleville, IL....470
Walker, Pat, Dir. Education, Danforth Museum of Art, Framingham, MA....778
Walker, Richard A., Lecturer & Instructor, Robert T. Longway Planetarium, Flint, MI....840
Walker, Robert, Custodial & Security, Hiddenite Center, Inc., Hiddenite, NC....1252
Walker, Ronald, Preparator, Boise Art Museum, Boise, ID....455
Walker, Dr. Roslyn A., Sr. Cur. Arts of Africa, the Pacific & the Americas, Dallas Museum of Art, Dallas, TX....1598
Walker, Sam, Security, National Voting Rights Museum and Institute, Selma, AL....22
Walker, Sandy, Pres. (V), Crossroads Museum, Corinth, MS....906
Walker, Sandy, Cur., Rolling Hills Wildlife Adventure, Salina, KS....633
Walker Schlageck, Katherine, Sr. Educator, Marianna Kistler Beach Museum of Art at Kansas State University, Manhattan, KS....625
Walker, Sharon, Pres. (V), Major James McLaughlin Heritage Center, McLaughlin, SD....1536
Walker, Sharon H., Ph.D., Admin., J.L. Scott Marine Education Center and Aquarium, Gulf Coast Research Laboratory College of Marine Sciences, The U. of Southern Mississippi, Ocean Springs, MS....914
Walker, Sonia, Cur., Callahan County Pioneer Museum, Baird, TX....1585
Walker, Stephen, Dir., Tulsa Zoo & Living Museum, Tulsa, OK....1380
Walker, Steve, Museum Shop Mgr. STAX Museum of American Soul Music, Memphis, TN....1564
Walker, Sue, Museum Shop Mgr., Gadsby's Tavern Museum, Alexandria, VA....1697
Walker, Susan, Assoc. Cur., New York State Bureau of Historic Sites, Waterford, NY....1225
Walker, Tina, Dir. & Museum Shop Mgr., Ben E. Clement Mineral Museum, Marion, KY....658
Walker, Tom, Exec. Dir., The American Village, Montevallo, AL....19
Walker, Tom, Cur. & Archivist, Tennessee Museum of Aviation, Sevierville, TN....1573
Walker, Wendell, Deputy Dir. Collections, Exhibitions & Operations, Museum of the Moving Image, Astoria, NY....1100
Walker, William H., Chm. (V), Wings Over Miami Air Museum, Inc., Miami, FL....367
Walkowich, Russell, Chief of Police, National Zoological Park, Smithsonian Institution, Washington, DC....327
Walks Over Ice, Loreen, Business Mgr., Little Bighorn Battlefield National Monument, Crow Agency, MT....960
Wall, Charlotte, Museum Shop Mgr., Louisiana's Old State Capitol, Baton Rouge, LA....668
Wall, Donna, Asst. Dir., Platt R. Spencer Memorial Archives and Special Collections Area, Geneva, OH....1322
Wall, Gordon, Pres., Paul Bunyan Logging Camp Museum, Eau Claire, WI....1818
Wall, Jed, Museum Shop Mgr., Pebble Hill Plantation, Thomasville, GA....437
Wall McGee, Paula, Corresponding Sec., Gwinnett Historical Society, Lawrenceville, GA....423
Wall, Michael, Seed Cur., Rancho Santa Ana Botanic Garden, Claremont, CA....102
Wall, Michael, Dir. Biodiversity Research Center of the Californias, San Diego Natural History Museum, San Diego, CA....184
Wall, Sarah, Museum Shop Mgr., Audubon Society of New Hampshire, Concord, NH....1014
Wall, Susan, Dir. Devel., Bard Graduate Center: Decorative Arts, Design History, & Material Culture, New York, NY....1164
Wall, Virginia, Cur. Horticulture, North Carolina Zoological Park, Asheboro, NC....1231
Wall, William J., Pres., Shore Line Trolley Museum, East Haven, CT....271
Wallace, Andrew, Registrar, Figge Art Museum, Davenport, IA....581
Wallace, Angell, Office Mgr., The Carter House, Franklin, TN....1551
Wallace, Beth, Information Technology Mgr., John and Mable Ringling Museum of Art, Sarasota, FL....387
Wallace, Brian, Cur., Samuel Dorsky Museum of Art, State University of New York at New Paltz, New Paltz, NY....1161
Wallace, Cindy, Assoc. Dir. Education, San Diego Zoo's Wild Animal Park, Escondido, CA....112
Wallace, Danielle, Dir. Programs, Battleship North Carolina, Wilmington, NC....1271
Wallace, Danny, Vice Pres., Tucumcari Historical Research Institute, Tucumcari, NM....1094
Wallace, D.J., Dir., Grant County Museum, Sheridan, AR....84
Wallace, Ellen, Mktg. & Public Rels., Southeastern Center for Contemporary Art, Winston-Salem, NC....1275
Wallace, Eva, Museum Shop Mgr., Bee Family Centennial Farm Museum, Fort Collins, CO....245
Wallace, Frankie, Cur., Benton County Historical Museum, Prosser, WA....1777
Wallace, Frederic A., Research, Framingham History Center, Framingham, MA....778
Wallace, George, Devel. & Public Rels., Brooke County Public Library Museum Branch, Wellsburg, WV....1807
Wallace, Heather, Administrative Asst., Orcas Island Historical Museum, Orcas Island, WA....1774
Wallace, J. Don, Dir., McCormick Gallery, Midland, TX....1633
Wallace, Karen, Dir. Center for Science Learning, Buffalo Museum of Science, Buffalo, NY....1115
Wallace, Kristi, Dir. Devel., Santa Barbara Museum of Art, Santa Barbara, CA....203

W–*Continued*

Wallace, Louise, Recording Sec., Gwinnett Historical Society, Lawrenceville, GA....423
Wallace, Margaret, Registrar, Middlebury College Museum of Art, Middlebury, VT....1684
Wallace, Mary Kay, Cur., Brooke County Public Library Museum Branch, Wellsburg, WV....1807
Wallace, Matthew, Dir. Rural Art, North Dakota Museum of Art, Grand Forks, ND....1283
Wallace, Mike, C.E.O., Forest Park Museum and Arboretum, Perry, IA....597
Wallace, Mike, C.E.O., The Voas Nature Area/Voas Museum, Minburn, IA....594
Wallace, Pam, Tearoom Mgr., Minnesota Landscape Arboretum, University of Minnesota, Chaska, MN....872
Wallace, Paula S., Pres., Savannah College of Art & Design-Atlanta Galleries, Atlanta, GA....408
Wallace, Scott, Deputy Dir. & Dir. Finance, The Durham Museum, Omaha, NE....994
Wallace, Stephen, Interpretive Programs Asst., Sackets Harbor Battlefield State Historic Site, Sackets Harbor, NY....1205
Wallace, Teresa, Cur., Minute Man National Historical Park, Concord, MA....771
Wallace, William, Exec. Dir., Worcester Historical Museum, Worcester, MA....819
Walldroff, Lenka, Cur. Collections, Jefferson County Historical Society, Watertown, NY....1226
Waller, Barbara, Dir. MIS, New England Aquarium Corporation, Boston, MA....762
Waller, Richard, Exec. Dir., University of Richmond Museums, Richmond, VA....1740
Waller, Roger, Chm. (V), Seaside Museum & Historical Society, Seaside, OR....1404
Waller, Steve, Treas., The Old Jail Art Center, Albany, TX....1576
Waller, Valerie, Vice Pres. Mktg. & Public Rels., Museum of Science and Industry, Chicago, IL....484
Wallerstein, Nancy, Chm. Advisory Council (V), Johnson County Museum, Shawnee, KS....634
Wall-Gilmore, Alexandra, Mgr., Dallas Arboretum & Botanical Garden, Dallas, TX....1597
Wallin, Scott, Designer, Whatcom Museum of History and Art, Bellingham, WA....1760
Walling, Gay, Exec. Dir., The Philadelphia Art Alliance, Philadelphia, PA....1458
Walling, Mary A., C.O.O., The Jewish Museum, New York, NY....1171
Wallis, Brian, Deputy Dir. Exhibitions & Collections and Chief Cur., International Center of Photography, New York, NY....1170
Wallis, Bruce, Chm. (V), Western Center for Archaeology and Paleontology, Hemet, CA....122
Wallis, Cindy, Museum Dir., Confederate Memorial Museum, Atoka, OK....1356
Wallisch, Kristy, Publications Coord., Barataria Preserve, Jean Lafitte National Historical Park and Preserve, Marrero, LA....675
Wallner, Peter A., Library Dir., New Hampshire Historical Society, Concord, NH....1015
Walls, Nancy, Dir., Hibel Museum of Art, Jupiter, FL....357
Wallsmith, Dr. Debbie, Interpretation, Parks, Recreation & Historic Sites Division, Georgia Dept. of Natural Resources, Atlanta, GA....408
Wallsmith, Matt, Treas., Yesteryear Village, West Palm Beach, FL....397
Wall-Wild, James, Archives, National Mississippi River Museum & Aquarium, Dubuque, IA....585
Walmsley, Beth, 2nd Vice Pres., Historic Mobile Preservation Society, Mobile, AL....17
Walmsley, Faye, Chief Interpretation, Martin Luther King, Jr. National Historic Site and Preservation District, Atlanta, GA....406
Walrath, Gary, C.E.O. & Exec. Dir., Rocky Mount Museum, Piney Flats, TN....1572
Walrig, Steve, Science Educator, The Bakken Library and Museum, Minneapolis, MN....884
Walser, Dr. Chris, Asst. Prof. Biology, Assoc. Cur. Fishes & Bd. Member, Orma J. Smith Museum of Natural History, Caldwell, ID....457
Walsh, Anne, Dir. Finance, Henry Art Gallery, Seattle, WA....1781
Walsh, Bud, Chief Ranger, Manassas National Battlefield Park, Manassas, VA....1724
Walsh, Cindy, Div. Dir., Fairfax County Park Authority, Resource Management Division, Fairfax, VA....1709
Walsh, Dave, Chm., The American Museum of Fly Fishing, Manchester, VT....1682
Walsh, J.O.K., Pres. Historical Society, Museum of Rural Life, Denton, MD....733
Walsh, Larry, Treas. ECHO Lake Aquarium and Science Center/Leahy Center for Lake Champlain, Burlington, VT....1677
Walsh, Mike, Asst., Ward W. O'Hara Agricultural Museum, Auburn, NY....1101
Walsh, Molly, Dir. Devel., The Nature Center at Shaker Lakes, Cleveland, OH....1310
Walsh, Patrick, Pres., Salisbury Historical Society, Salisbury, NH....1028
Walsh, Stacey, Collections Mgr., Sheldon Museum of Art and Sculpture Garden/University of Nebraska-Lincoln, Lincoln, NE....990
Walsh, Steven, Registrar, Acquisitions, Autry National Center of the American West, Los Angeles, CA....133
Walsh, Dr. Timothy, Head Pathologist, National Zoological Park, Smithsonian Institution, Washington, DC....327
Walsh, Tom, Pres. (V), White Pillars Museum, De Pere Historical Society, De Pere, WI....1816
Walsh-Piper, Kathleen, Dir., The Art Museum at the University of Kentucky, Lexington, KY....651
Walter, Charlie, C.O.O., Fort Worth Museum of Science and History, Fort Worth, TX....1609
Walter, Matt, Cur., Museum of the Big Bend, Alpine, TX....1577
Walter, Peggy, Registrar & Data Management Specialist, Gemological Institute of America Museum, Carlsbad, CA....98
Walter, Thomas, Pres. (V), Ontario County Historical Society, Canandaigua, NY....1118
Walters, Andra, Dir. Devel., Historic Landmarks Foundation of Indiana, Indianapolis, IN....548
Walters, Cheryl, C.E.O. & Cur., Lapham-Patterson House, Thomasville, GA....437
Walters, G., Exhibits Dir., Sternberg Museum of Natural History, Hays, KS....616
Walters, Gary, Yawkey House Attendant, Marathon County Historical Society, Wausau, WI....1850
Walters, Joan, Pres., Lincoln Memorial Garden and Nature Center, Springfield, IL....522
Walters, Jorie, Research Asst., Kankakee County Museum, Kankakee, IL....501
Walters, Mary, Dir. Finance & Administration, Contemporary Art Museum St. Louis, Saint Louis, MO....946
Walters, Norman, Security, Great Plains Transportation Museum, Wichita, KS....638
Walters, Tim, Coord. Exhibits, Arizona Museum of Natural History, Mesa, AZ....46
Walterscheid, Chelsea, Cur., Truckee's Old Jail Museum, Truckee, CA....218
Walthall, Nina, Asst. Cur. Education, Illinois State Museum, Springfield, IL....521
Walther, Jim, Dir., National Museum of Nuclear Science and History, Albuquerque, NM....1072
Walther, Nancy, Chief Resource Education, Chattahoochee River National Recreation Area, Atlanta, GA....403
Walti, Rick, Pres. (V), Island County Historical Society Museum, Coupeville, WA....1763
Waltner, Jeremy, Vice Pres., Heritage Hall Museum & Archives, Freeman, SD....1531
Waltner, Russel, Cur. & Museum Shop Mgr., Heritage Hall Museum & Archives, Freeman, SD....1531
Walton, Amy, Dir. Devel., Contemporary Art Center of Virginia, Virginia Beach, VA....1751
Walton, Connie, Pres. Bd., Coutts Memorial Museum of Art, Inc., El Dorado, KS....610
Walton, Dan, Dir. Operations, San Antonio Museum of Art, San Antonio, TX....1645
Walton, Dori, Chm., Museum of Science & History of Jacksonville, Jacksonville, FL....356
Walton, Jeff, Dir. Human Resources, Cincinnati Zoo & Botanical Garden, Cincinnati, OH....1304
Walton, Linda, Pres. Volunteers' Assoc., New Mexico Museum of Natural History & Science, Albuquerque, NM....1072
Walton, Patricia, Heritage Interpreter, Kline Creek Farm, West Chicago, IL....527
Walton, Paula, Dir., The New Milford Historical Society, New Milford, CT....289
Walton, Peter, C.F.O., Museum of Contemporary Art, Chicago, IL....483
Walton, Steve, Exhibit Technician, Augusta Museum of History, Augusta, GA....410
Walton, Zachary, Bd. Pres., Museum of Craft and Folk Art, San Francisco, CA....190
Waltz, James, Pres. Historical Society, Cape May County Historical Museum and Genealogical Society, Cape May Court House, NJ....1035
Waltz, Scott, Curatorial Asst., Henry B. Plant Museum, Tampa, FL....392
Walz, Carol, Dir., John Woolman Memorial, Mount Holly, NJ....1051
Walz, Greg, Information Svcs., Utah State Historical Society, Salt Lake City, UT....1672
Walz, Jack, Dir., John Woolman Memorial, Mount Holly, NJ....1051
Wamboldt, Ian, Experience Coord., The Dennison Railroad Depot Museum, Dennison, OH....1318
Wamelink, Garrit, Treas., Dunham Tavern Museum, Cleveland, OH....1309

W–*Continued*

W–*Continued*

W–*Continued*

W–*Continued*

W–*Continued*

W–*Continued*

W–*Continued*

Williams, Kevin, Cur. Education, Bell Museum of Natural History, Minneapolis, MN....884
Williams, Kevin, Supervising Ranger, Big Basin Redwoods State Park, Boulder Creek, CA....96
Williams, Kiersten, Education & Facilities Coord., Helen Day Art Center, Stowe, VT....1691
Williams, Leslie, Coord. Community Outreach, Children's Museum/Detroit Public Schools, Detroit, MI....833
Williams, Linda, Tour Coord. & Sec., Submarine Force Museum and Historic Ship Nautilus, Groton, CT....276
Williams, Liz, Museum Educator, Kentucky Derby Museum, Louisville, KY....655
Williams, Lizabeth, Asst. Dir., Gadsby's Tavern Museum, Alexandria, VA....1697
Williams, Lyle, Cur. Prints & Drawings, McNay Art Museum, San Antonio, TX.1644
Williams, Lynda, Business Mgr., Arnot Art Museum, Elmira, NY....1130
Williams, Lynn, Membership Coord., Harry P. Leu Gardens, Orlando, FL....373
Williams, Ms. Macon, 2nd Vice Pres., Portsmouth Historical Association, Portsmouth, VA....1734
Williams, Maggie, Finance Mgr., History San Jose, San Jose, CA....195
Williams, Marjorie, Dir. Education & Public Programs, The Cleveland Museum of Art, Cleveland, OH....1308
Williams, Marshall, Sec., Old Fort Meade Museum and Historic Research Association, Fort Meade, SD....1531
Williams, Mary Agnes, Dir. Devel., Woodmere Art Museum, Philadelphia, PA....1463
Williams, Mary Beth, Programs, Locust Grove, Louisville, KY....655
Williams, Mary C., Administrative Asst., Wilderness Road Regional Museum, Newbern, VA....1727
Williams, Mary L., Historian, Fort Davis National Historic Site, Fort Davis, TX..1607
Williams, Megan, Mktg. & Devel. Coord., Jefferson Patterson Park & Museum, Saint Leonard, MD....744
Williams, Melanie, Mgr., Healdton Oil Museum, Healdton, OK....1363
Williams, Michael, Cur., Archivist & Museum Shop Mgr., New Orleans Fire Dept. Museum & Educational Center, New Orleans, LA....682
Williams, Michelle D., Research Asst., Belz Museum of Asian & Judaic Art, Memphis, TN....1560
Williams, Mike, Pres. (V), Koochiching County Historical Museum, International Falls, MN....881
Williams, Mildred, Museum Dir., Fort Croghan Museum, Burnet, TX....1591
Williams, Nancy, Dir. Mktg., Great Smoky Mountains Heritage Center, Townsend, TN....1574
Williams, Nicholas L., Photographer, The Corning Museum of Glass, Corning, NY....1124
Williams, Dr. Norris H., Cur. Botany & Keeper of the Herbarium, Florida Museum of Natural History, Gainesville, FL....351
Williams, Pam, Sec., The Museum of Prints and Printmaking, Albany, NY....1096
Williams, Pamela, Dir., Belair Mansion, Bowie, MD....728
Williams, Pamela, Dir., Belair Stable Museum, Bowie, MD....728
Williams, Pamela, Dir., Bowie Heritage Welcome Center, Bowie, MD....728
Williams, Pamela, Dir., Bowie Railroad Station Museum, Bowie, MD....728
Williams, Pamela, Dir., City of Bowie Museums, Bowie, MD....729
Williams, Pat, Museum Shop Mgr., J.J. Jackson Memorial Museum, Weaverville, CA....223
Williams, Pat, Vice Pres. Devel., St. Louis Science Center, Saint Louis, MO....950
Williams, Patricia, Museum Shop Mgr., Shaker Heritage Society, Albany, NY...1097
Williams, Patricia E., Chm., The Accokeek Foundation, Inc., Accokeek, MD....716
Williams, Paul, Security, Deer Park Escondido Winery & Auto Museum, Escondido, CA....111
Williams, Paul, C.E.O. & Pres., This Is The Place Heritage Park, Salt Lake City, UT....1671
Williams, Peggy, Pres. (V), Arboretum at UC Santa Cruz, Santa Cruz, CA....205
Williams, Peter, Assoc. Vice Pres. Exhibit & Bldg. Operations, Chicago Children's Museum, Chicago, IL....478
Williams, Phil, Dir, Cur, Clovis Depot Model Train Museum, Clovis, NM....1077
Williams, Ragan, Security Guard, The Patricia & Phillip Frost Art Museum, Miami, FL....367
Williams, Ray, Dir. Education, Harvard Art Museum, Cambridge, MA....767
Williams, Rhys, Chm. Bd., South Florida Science Museum, West Palm Beach, FL....397
Williams, Richard, Administrative Asst., Children's Museum at La Habra, La Habra, CA....126
Williams, Richmond, Sec., Delaware Nature Society, Hockessin, DE....307
Williams, Dr. Rick, Life Sciences Cur., Idaho Museum of Natural History, Pocatello, ID....464
Williams, Rick, Dir., Lane Community College Art Gallery, Eugene, OR....1388
Williams, Roger, Pres., New Hampshire Institute of Art, Manchester, NH....1023
Williams, Ruby, Dir. Technology, National Hispanic Cultural Center, Art Museum, Albuquerque, NM....1072
Williams, Sally, Public Information Officer, Brooklyn Museum, Brooklyn, NY....1111
Williams, Sandra, Museum Shop Mgr., Museum of Transportation, Saint Louis, MO....949
Williams, Sarah, Volunteer & Intern Resources Coord., Chicago Children's Museum, Chicago, IL....478
Williams, Scott, Collection Mgr., Burpee Museum of Natural History, Rockford, IL....516
Williams, Sharon R., Head Guard, Museum of Texas Tech University, Lubbock, TX....1629
Williams, Shawna, Cur. Mammals & Birds, Meriks Zoo, Graysville, AL....13
Williams, Sheldon, Exec. Dir., Turtle Mountain Chippewa Historical Society, Belcourt, ND....1276
Williams, Sherda, Site Mgr., James A. Garfield National Historic Site, Mentor, OH....1332
Williams, Stacy, C.E.O., Classic Cars International, Salt Lake City, UT....1669
Williams, Steve, Pres. (V), Beaches Museum & History Center, Jacksonville Beach, FL....356
Williams, Sue, Vice Pres., Galloway House and Village - Blakely Museum, Fond du Lac, WI....1819
Williams, Sue, Treas., Greenwood County Historical Society & Museum, Eureka, KS....612
Williams, Tabitha, Administrative Asst., The Fisk University Galleries, Nashville, TN....1568
Williams, Teri, Cur., Robert C. Williams Paper Museum, Atlanta, GA....408
Williams, Theresa, Public Rels., Maidu Museum and Historic Site, Roseville, CA....174
Williams, Theresa, Sec., Wildwood Crest Historical Society, Wildwood Crest, NJ....1068
Williams, Thomas, Treas., The Thomas Griswold House and Museum, Guilford, CT....277
Williams, Tim, Sanctuary Mgr., Clyde E. Buckley Wildlife Sanctuary, Frankfort, KY....646
Williams, Tina, Administrative Asst., Historical Center for Southeast New Mexico, Roswell, NM....1086
Williams, Tod, Chief Resources, Great Basin National Park, Baker, NV....1000
Williams, Tracey, Facility Rental Mgr., Dusable Museum of African-American History, Inc., Chicago, IL....479
Williams, Traci, Naturalist (North Chagrin), Cleveland Metroparks Outdoor Education Division, Garfield Heights, OH....1322
Williams, Twilah, Treas., Harvey House Museum, Florence, KS....612
Williams Vaughn, Renee, Pres. Trustee (V), Henry B. Plant Museum, Tampa, FL....392
Williams, Virginia, Pres. (V), Museum of Primitive Art and Culture, Peace Dale, RI....1493
Williams, Wes, Park Ranger, Pinson Mounds State Archaeological Area, Pinson, TN....1572
Williams, Willard, Dir. & Pres. (V), Fountain County War Museum, Inc., Veedersburg, IN....568
Williams, Wray, Park Ranger, West Rock Nature Center, New Haven, CT....287
Williams, Yvonne, Resource Gallery Attendant, Birmingham Civil Rights Institute, Birmingham, AL....5
Williamson, Bill, Treas., Collingwood Library and Museum on Americanism, Alexandria, VA....1696
Williamson III, John B., Pres. Bd. Trustees, Taubman Museum of Art, Roanoke, VA....1744
Williamson, Jane, Dir., Rokeby Museum, Ferrisburgh, VT....1680
Williamson, Jay, Cur., Historical Society of Old Newbury, Cushing House Museum, Newburyport, MA....794
Williamson, Kate, Museum Coord., Museum of Biblical Art, New York, NY....1175
Williamson, Kathy, Administrative Asst. & Museum Shop Mgr., Awbury Arboretum, Philadelphia, PA....1450
Williamson, Mark, Vice. Pres., Kitsap County Historical Society Museum, Bremerton, WA....1760
Williamson, Mary Ellen, Site Mgr., Bartow-Pell Mansion Museum, Carriage House & Gardens, Bronx, NY....1107
Williamson, Norma, Dir., Dubois Museum, Dubois, WY....1857
Williamson, Patrick, Dir. Purchasing & Distribution, Saint Louis Zoo, Saint Louis, MO....951

W–*Continued*

Wilson, John, Naturalist Teacher, Aullwood Audubon Center and Farm, Dayton, OH....1315
Wilson, John, Ph.D., Exec. Dir., Timken Museum of Art, San Diego, CA....185
Wilson, Jon, Deputy Dir. Operations, The National Great Blacks in Wax Museum, Inc., Baltimore, MD....725
Wilson, Judy, Dir., Laramie Peak Museum, Wheatland, WY....1867
Wilson, Karen, Museum Shop Mgr., Chickasaw County Historical Society Bradford Pioneer Village Museum, Nashua, IA....595
Wilson, Karen, Exec. Dir., WildCare, San Rafael, CA....201
Wilson, Kathleen A., Vice Pres. External Rels., The Science Museum of Minnesota, Saint Paul, MN....896
Wilson, Kay, Cur. Collections, Faulconer Gallery at Grinnell College, Grinnell, IA....588
Wilson, Keith, Assoc. Dir. & Cur. Ancient China, Freer and Sackler Galleries of Art, Washington, DC....318
Wilson, Kelly E., Audience Devel., Miami University Art Museum, Oxford, OH....1338
Wilson, Kevin, Supt. Bldgs. & Grounds, Santa Fe Trail Center, Larned, KS....621
Wilson, Kevin, Vice Pres. Operations & Finance, Science Museum Oklahoma, Oklahoma City, OK....1373
Wilson, Kirk, Press Sec., The State Museum of Pennsylvania, Harrisburg, PA....1432
Wilson, Lamar, Dir. & Cur., Cleveland County Historical Museum, Shelby, NC....1267
Wilson, Lawrence, Vice Pres. Devel., Japanese American National Museum, Los Angeles, CA....137
Wilson, Lewis, Coord., The MOOseum, Montgomery, AL....20
Wilson, Marc F., Dir. & C.E.O., The Nelson-Atkins Museum of Art, Kansas City, MO....934
Wilson, Marc L., Head Minerals, Carnegie Museum of Natural History, Pittsburgh, PA....1464
Wilson, Marcelle R., Ph.D, Dir., Aurora Historical Society, Aurora, OH....1294
Wilson, Martha, C.E.O. & Dir., Franklin Furnace Archive, Inc., Brooklyn, NY....1111
Wilson, Martha, 1st Vice Pres., Phelps House, Burlington, IA....575
Wilson, Mary Alice, Pres. (V), Museum of the Waxhaws & Andrew Jackson Memorial, Waxhaw, NC....1270
Wilson, Molly, Art Education, The Living Arts and Science Center, Inc., Lexington, KY....653
Wilson, Nancy, Cur. Collections, Elmhurst Historical Museum, Elmhurst, IL....493
Wilson, Niki, Dir. Mktg. & Devel., Shenandoah Valley Discovery Museum, Winchester, VA....1755
Wilson, Orme, III, Pres. (V), The Filson Historical Society, Inc., Louisville, KY...654
Wilson, Patricia, Pres., San Antonio Children's Museum, San Antonio, TX..1645
Wilson, Patsy, Science Specialist & Dir. Planetarium, Horizons Unlimited Supplementary Educational Center, Salisbury, NC....1266
Wilson, Phil, Chief, Science & Resource Management, Big Bend National Park, Big Bend National Park, TX....1588
Wilson, Randon, Chm. (V), This Is The Place Heritage Park, Salt Lake City, UT....1671
Wilson, Reba, Mgr., Museum of Apopkans, Apopka, FL....333
Wilson, Richard T., III, Pres. (V), Steamboat Era Museum, Irvington, VA.1718
Wilson, Rick, Chief Interpretation & Resources Mgmt. & Visitor Protection, Florissant Fossil Beds National Monument, Florissant, CO....245
Wilson, Robert, Chm. (V), La Purisima Mission State Historic Park, Lompoc, CA....130
Wilson, Dr. Robert, Pres. (V), New Hampshire Antiquarian Society, Hopkinton, NH....1020
Wilson, Robert C., Site Supt., Fort Phil Kearny, Banner, WY....1852
Wilson, Ronald C., Chief Cur., National Park Service, Washington, DC....326
Wilson, Rosalie, Pres., Triton Museum of Art, Santa Clara, CA....205
Wilson, Rosemary, Chm. (V), Lynnhaven House, Virginia Beach, VA....1752
Wilson, Roy E., Dir., Fort Nashborough, Nashville, TN....1568
Wilson, Rudy, Pres., Governor Ross Plantation, Seaford, DE....311
Wilson, Sandy, Registrar, Myriad Botanical Gardens, Oklahoma City, OK....1371
Wilson, Scott, Pres., Children's Discovery Museum of the Desert, Rancho Mirage, CA....168
Wilson, Shalla, Cur., Old Capitol Museum, Iowa City, IA....589
Wilson, Shalla, Asst. Dir., University of Iowa Museum of Natural History, Iowa City, IA....590
Wilson, Shannon, Vice Pres., Pembroke Historical Society, Inc., Pembroke, MA....798
Wilson, Sharon, C.E.O. & Pres. (V), Kelly-Griggs House Museum, Red Bluff, CA....169
Wilson, Shirley, Public Rels. FIDM Museum & Galleries, Los Angeles, CA....135
Wilson, Stan, Cur., Shafter Depot Museum, Shafter, CA....211
Wilson, Steve, Interpretive Specialist, Fort Osage National Historic Landmark, Sibley, MO....952
Wilson, Steven, Cur. & Asst. Dir., Abraham Lincoln Library & Museum, Lincoln Memorial University, Harrogate, TN....1554
Wilson, Susan, Devel. Coord., Martha's Vineyard Museum, Edgartown, MA....776
Wilson, Sylvia P., Co-Pres., Parsonsfield-Porter Historical Society, Porter, ME....707
Wilson, Ted, Security Supvr., Kemper Museum of Contemporary Art, Kansas City, MO....934
Wilson, Terri, Pres., The Avon Historical Society, Inc., Avon, CT....266
Wilson, Thomas, Interpreter, Providence Canyon State Park, Lumpkin, GA....424
Wilson, Dr. Thomas H., Dir., Arizona Museum of Natural History, Mesa, AZ....46
Wilson, Tina, Dir. Education, Desert Botanical Garden, Phoenix, AZ....50
Wilson, Tom, Vice Pres. Exhibits, Sciworks, Winston-Salem, NC....1275
Wilson, Walter, Exhibition Designer, Krannert Art Museum and Kinkead Pavilion, Champaign, IL....474
Wilson, Wayne W., Chm., The Endowment Fund of the Phi Kappa Psi Fraternity-Heritage Hall, Indianapolis, IN....547
Wilsterman, Jim, Art Dept. Chm., Grossmont College Hyde Art Gallery, El Cajon, CA....109
Wiltgen, Cathy, Museum Store Mgr., Carbon County Historical Society and Museum, Red Lodge, MT....971
Wiltsher, Harris, Dir., Foster-Tanner Fine Arts Gallery, Tallahassee, FL....390
Wiltshire, Ayeshah, Asst. Dir. Education & Public Programs, The Studio Museum in Harlem, New York, NY....1182
Wilusz, Mike, Mgr., Fort Knox State Historic Site and Penobscot Narrows Observatory, Prospect, ME....709
Wilzig, Naomi, Dir., Pres. (V) & Cur., World Erotic Art Museum, Miami Beach, FL....368
Wiman, Al, Vice Pres. Public Understanding of Science, St. Louis Science Center, Saint Louis, MO....950
Wimberg, Virginia, Vice Pres., Reverend Dan Foster House, Museum of the Weathersfield Historical Society, Weathersfield, VT....1693
Wimberger, Dr. Peter, Dir., James R. Slater Museum of Natural History, Tacoma, WA....1788
Wimbley, Jessica, Museum Coord., Pomona College Museum of Art, Claremont, CA....102
Wimett, E.L., Cur. Museum Collections, Patriots Point Naval and Maritime Museum, Mount Pleasant, SC....1519
Wimikates, Margaret, Assoc. Dir. Education Science Discovery Museum, The Discovery Museums, Acton, MA....751
Wimmer, Eric, Cur., Wyoming Veterans' Memorial Museum, Casper, WY....1854
Wimpfheimer, Lisa, Horticulture Branch Head, Tryon Palace Historic Sites & Gardens, New Bern, NC....1259
Winans, Melissa, LAN Mgr., Texas Natural Science Center, Austin, TX....1584
Winans, Sam, Pres. Bd. (V), Parkersburg Art Center, Parkersburg, WV....1804
Winans-Bagnall, Trena, Educational Coord., Midland County Historical Society, Midland, MI....855
Winberg, Amy, Mgr., Sheppard Fine Arts Gallery, Reno, NV....1009
Winborne, Belinda, Administrative Asst., Historic Hope Foundation, Inc., Windsor, NC....1273
Winch, Barbara, Chm. (V), Cur. & Pres. (V), South Hero Bicentennial Museum, South Hero, VT....1690
Winch, Terence, Head of Publications, National Museum of the American Indian, Smithsonian Institution, New York, NY....1177
Winchell, Jane, Sarah Frasier Robbins Dir. Art & Nature Center and Cur. Natural History, Peabody Essex Museum, Salem, MA....804
Wincik, Stephanie, Pres., Hazel Kibler Memorial Museum, Girard, PA....1428
Winckler, Paul, Park Mgr., Fort Sisseton Historic State Park, Lake City, SD....1534
Winders, Dr. Bruce, Historian & Cur., The Alamo, San Antonio, TX....1643
Windhager, Steve, Ph.D., Dir. Landscape Restoration, Lady Bird Johnson Wildflower Center, Austin, TX....1582
Windhorst, Colin J.C., Dir. Programs & Devel., Dennys River Historical Society, Dennysville, ME....697
Windhorst, Ronald A., Pres., Dennys River Historical Society, Dennysville, ME....697
Windish, Richard, Pres. (V), Green Mountain Club, Inc., Waterbury Center, VT....1693
Windley, Debbie, Dir. Advancement, Schiele Museum of Natural History and Lynn Planetarium, Gastonia, NC....1247

W–*Continued*

W–*Continued*

W–Continued

Wright, Shawn, Pres., Eastern Arizona Museum and Historical Society of Graham County Inc., Pima, AZ.................52
Wright, Suzanne, Dir. of Education, The Phillips Collection, Washington, DC.......328
Wright, Tim, Vice Pres., Hahns Peak Area Historical Society and School House, Clark, CO.....................................233
Wright, Tony, Head Design & Installation, Modern Art Museum of Fort Worth, Fort Worth, TX..................1611
Wright, Trish, Museum Shop Mgr., U.S. Army Transportation Museum, Fort Eustis, VA...1711
Wright, Twyla, Cur., Old Independence Regional Museum, Batesville, AR............66
Wright, Valerie M., Collections Mgr., The Rose Art Museum of Brandeis University, Waltham, MA.......................813
Wright-Gidley, Jodi, Dir., Galveston County Historical Museum, Galveston, TX...1614
Wright-Parsons, Ann, MA, Dir., The Anthropology Museum, DeKalb, IL........488
Wright-Sedam, Jeffrey, Preparator, University Art Museum, University at Albany, Albany, NY..............................1097
Wrightstone, Ruth N., Ph.D., Pres. (V), Mechanicsburg Museum Association, Mechanicsburg, PA.............................1444
Wrinkle, Anne, Dir. External Affairs SITE Santa Fe, Santa Fe, NM.....................1090
Wroath, Tami, Dir. Mktg. & Public Rels., Samuel P. Harn Museum of Art, Gainesville, FL..351
Wroblewski, Charles, Pres., Seaford Historical Museum, Seaford, NY..........1211
Wrubel, Faye, Conservator, Paintings, The Art Institute of Chicago, Chicago, IL...476
Wu, David, Vice Pres. Devel., Woodland Park Zoo, Seattle, WA..........................1785
Wu, Eva, Interim Exec. Dir., Children's Museum of Winston-Salem, Winston-Salem, NC..............................1273
Wu, Nancy, Museum Educator, The Cloisters, New York, NY.......................1166
Wu, Shi-Kuei, Cur. Zoology Emeritus, University of Colorado Museum of Natural History, Boulder, CO.................230
Wu, Xiaojin, Asst. Cur. Asian Art, Princeton University Art Museum, Princeton, NJ...1058
Wuerl, Archbishop Donald, Chm. (V), Pope John Paul II Cultural Center, Washington, DC.......................................328
Wuest, John, Chm. Bd., Laumeier Sculpture Park & Museum, Saint Louis, MO...948
Wulf, Irene, Pres., Yorktown Historical Museum, Yorktown, TX........................1658
Wulffleff, Andrea, Cur., Wilton Historical Museums, Wilton, CT.............................303
Wulkan, Reba, Cur. Contemporary Exhibitions, Yeshiva University Museum at the Center for Jewish History, New York, NY.......................1184
Wullner-Faiss Cloak, Janet, Pres. (V), The History Museum at the Castle, Appleton, WI...1810
Wunderlich, George, Exec. Dir., National Museum of Civil War Medicine, Frederick, MD...735
Wunderly, Kathleen, Cur., Centre County Library and Historical Museum, Bellefonte, PA...1411
Wurf, Sabrina, Mgr. Membership, Skirball Cultural Center, Los Angeles, CA...142
Wurl, Phyllis, Dir., Museum of Overbeck Art Pottery, Cambridge City, IN.............535
Wurm, Joe, Museum Shop Mgr., U.S. Army Ordnance Museum, Aberdeen Proving Ground, MD.............................716
Wurm, Sharleen, Cur., Decatur County Last Indian Raid Museum, Oberlin, KS...629
Wurster, Denise, Museum Shop Mgr., Central Florida Railroad Museum, Winter Garden, FL.................................398
Wurtele, Gail, Museum Shop Mgr., Wildwood Historic Center, Nebraska City, NE...992
Wurtman, Richard, Pres. (V), Provincetown Art Association and Museum, Provincetown, MA..................801
Wurtz, Alyce, Pres. & Membership Chm., Mayville Historical Society, Inc., Mayville, WI..1831
Wurtz, Michael, Archivist, Holt-Atherton Special Collections, Stockton, CA...........214
Wurtz, Sally, Pres. (V), Lanier Mansion State Historic Site, Madison, IN.............555
Wyakoop, David, Pres. (V), The Wagnalls Memorial Foundation, Lithopolis, OH...................................1328
Wyatt, Andrew, Dir. Horticulture, Santa Barbara Botanic Garden, Santa Barbara, CA..203
Wyatt, Becky, Sec., Fort Sidney Museum & Post Commander's Home, Sidney, NE...997
Wyatt, Connie, Bookkeeper, Four Mile Historic Park, Denver, CO.......................240
Wyatt, Frederica, Cur., Kimble County Historical Museum, Junction, TX..........1625
Wyatt, Jeffrey, D.V.M., Veterinarian, Seneca Park Zoo, Rochester, NY..........1203
Wyatt, Kyle K., Cur. History & Technology, California State Railroad Museum, Sacramento, CA.......................175
Wyatt, Roma, Asst. to Gen. Sec., World Methodist Museum, Lake Junaluska, NC...1255
Wyatt, Sherry, Pres., Montgomery Museum & Lewis Miller Regional Art Center, Christiansburg, VA...................1706
Wyatt, Steve, Cur. Collections & Exhibits, Children's Museum, Jacksonville, OR...................................1392
Wyatt, Thelma, Devel. & Mktg., Miles B. Carpenter Museum, Waverly, VA..........1753
Wyatt, William, Maintenance Asst., Jefferson Patterson Park & Museum, Saint Leonard, MD..744
Wyckoff, Dr. D., Cur. Archeology, Sam Noble Oklahoma Museum of Natural History, Norman, OK...........................1369
Wyckoff, Elizabeth, Asst. Dir. Curatorial & Education and Cur. Prints & Drawings, Davis Museum and Cultural Center, Wellesley, MA..............814
Wyckoff, Virginia, Museum Shop Mgr., Children's Museum at La Habra, La Habra, CA...126
Wye, Deborah, Chief Cur. Prints & Illustrated Books, The Museum of Modern Art, New York, NY..................1176
Wygant, Shelley D., Pres. (V), Howard County Historical Society, Ellicott City, MD...734
Wyka, Betty, Visitor Svcs. Coord., The Stickley Museum at Craftsman Farms, Morris Plains, NJ.................................1049
Wykert, Lillian, Dir. Grounds, Bayard Cutting Arboretum, Great River, NY.....1139
Wykes, Paul D., Vice Pres. Finance & Info Systems, Old Sturbridge Village, Sturbridge, MA...811
Wykoff, Kim, Dir. Mktg., Apple Farm Mill House, San Luis Obispo, CA...........197
Wylde, Kim, Museum Shop Mgr., Pratt Museum, Homer, AK...............................31
Wylie, Charles, Cur. Contemporary Art, Dallas Museum of Art, Dallas, TX........1598
Wylong, Dawn, Pres. Bd., U.S. Bicycling Hall of Fame, Davis, CA........................108
Wyman, Lou, Co Dir., Wyman Museum, Craig, CO...236
Wyman, Paula, Co Dir., Wyman Museum, Craig, CO...............................236
Wyman, Rick, Dir., Lucille Ball-Desi Arnaz Center, Jamestown, NY..............1148
Wynn, Linda T., Asst. Dir. State Programs, Tennessee Historical Commission, Nashville, TN..................1569
Wynn, Nan L., Site Mgr., Lincoln Tomb State Historic Site, Springfield, IL...........522
Wynn, Steve, Security, Tamastslikt Cultural Institute, Pendleton, OR...........1397
Wynne, Debra, Museum Shop Mgr., Florida Historical Society, Cocoa, FL.....339
Wynne, Michael, Cur. Emeritus, Herbarium of the University of Michigan, Ann Arbor, MI.......................822
Wynnemer, Donald, Pres. (V), Waseca County Historical Society, Museum and Research Library, Waseca, MN.........901
Wyrick, David, Chief Interpretation, Grant-Kohrs Ranch National Historic Site, Deer Lodge, MT.............................961
Wysk, Susan C., Dir., Randall Library, Stow, MA..810
Wysocki, Jack, Exec. Dir., Ira G. Ross Aerospace Museum, Buffalo, NY..........1116
Wyss, Tim, Vice Pres., Clear Lake Area Historical Museum, Clear Lake, WI......1815

X

Xenick, Cindy, Pres. Volunteer Council (V), Henry B. Plant Museum, Tampa, FL...392
Xiong, Sua, Museum Shop Mgr., Providence Children's Museum, Providence, RI.......................................1495
Xu, Jay, Dir., Asian Art Museum of San Francisco, Chong-Moon Lee Center for Asian Art and Culture, San Francisco, CA...186

Y

Yablon, Nancy A., Devel. & Membership, Heartland, The California Museum of the Heart, Rancho Mirage, CA..................................168
Yaconiello, Lisa, Dir. Devel. & External Affairs, Intrepid Sea, Air & Space Museum, New York, NY.....................1171
Yaeger, Dan, Dir. & Exec. Dir., Charles River Museum of Industry & Innovation, Waltham, MA...........................812
Yaffe Lottes, Karen, Education & Program Coord., The Montgomery County Historical Society, Inc., Rockville, MD..744
Yager, Jessica, Dir., Springfield Art & Historical Society - Miller Art Center, Springfield, VT......................................1691
Yager, Lisa, Research Coord., Mississippi Museum of Natural Science, Jackson, MS...910
Yager, Peggie, Treas. & Museum Shop Mgr., Miramont Castle Museum, Manitou Springs, CO...............................258
Yagoda, Marvin, Owner, Marvin's Marvelous Mechanical Museum, Farmington Hills, MI.................................840
Yahyavi, Margie, Dir. Operations, Santa Barbara Contemporary Arts Forum, Santa Barbara, CA...203
Yajima Andrew, Lenny, Pres. & Exec. Dir., Japanese Cultural Center of Hawaii, Honolulu, HI...............................446

Y–*Continued*

Z–Continued

Index to Institutions by Category

List of Categories

ART

Art Associations, Councils and Commissions, Foundations and Institutes

Art Museums and Galleries

Art Museums and Galleries–Continued

Art Museums and Galleries–Continued

Art Museums and Galleries–Continued

Art Museums and Galleries–Continued

Art Museums and Galleries–Continued

Art Museums and Galleries–Continued

Art Museums and Galleries–Continued

Art Museums and Galleries–Continued

Arts and Crafts Museums

Arts and Crafts Museums–Continued

China, Glass and Silver Museums

Civic Art and Cultural Centers

Civic Art and Cultural Centers–Continued

Decorative Arts Museums

Folk Art Museums

Folk Art Museums–Continued

Textile Museums

CHILDREN'S MUSEUMS

CHILDREN'S MUSEUMS–Continued

CHILDREN'S MUSEUMS–Continued

COLLEGE AND UNIVERSITY MUSEUMS

COLLEGE AND UNIVERSITY MUSEUMS–Continued

COLLEGE AND UNIVERSITY MUSEUMS–Continued

COLLEGE AND UNIVERSITY MUSEUMS–Continued

COMPANY MUSEUMS

EXHIBIT AREAS

EXHIBIT AREAS–Continued

GENERAL MUSEUMS

GENERAL MUSEUMS–Continued

GENERAL MUSEUMS–Continued

GENERAL MUSEUMS–Continued

GENERAL MUSEUMS–Continued

HISTORY

Historic Agencies, Councils, Commissions, Foundations and Research Institutes

Historic Agencies, Councils, Commissions, Foundations and Research Institutes–Continued

Historic Houses and Historic Buildings

Historic Houses and Historic Buildings–Continued

Historic Houses and Historic Buildings–Continued

Historic Houses and Historic Buildings–Continued

Historic Houses and Historic Buildings–Continued

Historic Houses and Historic Buildings–Continued

Historic Houses and Historic Buildings–Continued

Historic Houses and Historic Buildings–Continued

Historic Houses and Historic Buildings–Continued

Historic Houses and Historic Buildings–Continued

Historic Houses and Historic Buildings–Continued

Historic Houses and Historic Buildings–Continued

Historic Houses and Historic Buildings–Continued

Historic Houses and Historic Buildings–Continued

Historic Houses and Historic Buildings–Continued

Historic Sites

Historic Sites–Continued

Historic Sites–Continued

Historic Sites–Continued

Historic Sites–Continued

Historic Sites–Continued

Historic Sites–Continued

Historic Sites–Continued

Historical and Preservation Societies

Historical and Preservation Societies–Continued

Historical Society Museums

Historical Society Museums–Continued

Historical Society Museums–Continued

Historical Society Museums–Continued

Historical Society Museums–Continued

Historical Society Museums–Continued

Historical Society Museums–Continued

Historical Society Museums–Continued

History Museums

History Museums–Continued

History Museums–Continued

History Museums–Continued

History Museums–Continued

History Museums–Continued

History Museums–Continued

History Museums–Continued

History Museums–Continued

History Museums–Continued

History Museums–Continued

History Museums–Continued

History Museums–Continued

History Museums–Continued

History Museums–Continued

History Museums–Continued

History Museums–Continued

History Museums–Continued

History Museums–Continued

History Museums–Continued

Maritime, Naval Museums and Historic Ships

Maritime, Naval Museums and Historic Ships–Continued

Military Museums

Military Museums–Continued

Military Museums–Continued

Preservation Projects

Preservation Projects–Continued

LIBRARIES HAVING COLLECTIONS OF BOOKS

LIBRARIES HAVING COLLECTIONS OF BOOKS–Continued

LIBRARIES HAVING COLLECTIONS OTHER THAN BOOKS

LIBRARIES HAVING COLLECTIONS OTHER THAN BOOKS–Continued

NATIONAL AND STATE AGENCIES, COUNCILS AND COMMISSIONS

NATURE CENTERS

NATURE CENTERS–Continued

NATURE CENTERS–Continued

PARK MUSEUMS AND VISITOR CENTERS

PARK MUSEUMS AND VISITOR CENTERS–Continued

PARK MUSEUMS AND VISITOR CENTERS–Continued

SCIENCE

Academies, Associations, Institutes and Foundations

Aeronautics and Space Museums

Aeronautics and Space Museums–Continued

Anthropology and Ethnology Museums

Anthropology and Ethnology Museums–Continued

Aquariums, Marine Museums and Oceanariums

Aquariums, Marine Museums and Oceanariums–Continued

Arboretums

Arboretums–Continued

Archaeology Museums and Archaeological Sites

Archaeology Museums and Archaeological Sites–Continued

Aviaries and Ornithology Museums

Botanical and Aquatic Gardens, Conservatories, and Horticulture Societies

Botanical and Aquatic Gardens, Conservatories, and Horticulture Societies–Continued

Entomology Museums

Geology, Mineralogy and Paleontology Museums

Geology, Mineralogy and Paleontology Museums–Continued

Herbariums

Herpetology Museums

Medical, Dental, Health, Pharmacology, Apothecary and Psychiatry Museums

Natural History and Natural Science Museums

Natural History and Natural Science Museums–Continued

Natural History and Natural Science Museums–Continued

Natural History and Natural Science Museums–Continued

Planetariums, Observatories and Astronomy Museums

Planetariums, Observatories and Astronomy Museums–Continued

Science Museums and Centers

Science Museums and Centers–Continued

Wildlife Refuges and Bird Sanctuaries

Wildlife Refuges and Bird Sanctuaries–Continued

Zoos

SPECIALIZED

Agriculture Museums

Agriculture Museums–Continued

Antiques Museums

Antiques Museums–Continued

Architecture Museums

Architecture Museums–Continued

Audiovisual and Film Museums

Circus Museums

Comedy Museums

Communications Museums

Costume Museums

Crime Museums

Culturally Specific

Culturally Specific–Continued

Culturally Specific–Continued

Culturally Specific–Continued

Electricity Museums

Fire-Fighting Museums

Fire-Fighting Museums–Continued

Forestry Museums

Furniture Museums

Gun Museums

Hobby Museums

Horological Museums

Industrial Museums

Musical Instruments Museums–Continued

Philatelic Museums

Photography Museums

Religious Museums

Religious Museums–Continued

Scouting Museums

Sports Museums

Technology Museums

Technology Museums–Continued

Theatre Museums

Toy and Doll Museums

Transportation Museums

Transportation Museums–Continued

Transportation Museums–Continued

Typography Museums

Village Museums

Wax Museums

Wax Museums–Continued

Whaling Museums

Woodcarving Museums

Index to Institutions by Collection

List of Collections

ANTHROPOLOGY AND ARCHAEOLOGICAL COLLECTIONS

Archaeological

Archaeological–Continued

Archaeological–Continued

Archaeological–Continued

Archaeological–Continued

Archaeological–Continued

Archaeological–Continued

Archaeological–Continued

Ethnological/Ethnographical

Ethnological/Ethnographical–Continued

Ethnological/Ethnographical–Continued

Ethnological/Ethnographical–Continued

Ethnological/Ethnographical–Continued

Folk Culture

Folk Culture–Continued

Folk Culture–Continued

Folk Culture–Continued

Folk Culture–Continued

Physical Anthropology

Physical Anthropology–Continued

ART COLLECTIONS

Archaeological/Ethnographical

Archaeological/Ethnographical–Continued

Archaeological/Ethnographical–Continued

Archaeological/Ethnographical–Continued

Audiovisual and Film

Audiovisual and Film–Continued

Audiovisual and Film–Continued

Audiovisual and Film–Continued

Audiovisual and Film–Continued

Audiovisual and Film–Continued

Audiovisual and Film–Continued

Costumes and Textiles

Costumes and Textiles–Continued

Costumes and Textiles–Continued

Costumes and Textiles–Continued

Costumes and Textiles–Continued

Costumes and Textiles–Continued

Costumes and Textiles–Continued

Costumes and Textiles–Continued

Costumes and Textiles–Continued

Costumes and Textiles–Continued

Costumes and Textiles–Continued

Costumes and Textiles–Continued

Costumes and Textiles–Continued

Decorative Arts

Decorative Arts–Continued

Decorative Arts–Continued

Decorative Arts–Continued

Decorative Arts–Continued

Decorative Arts–Continued

Decorative Arts–Continued

Decorative Arts–Continued

Decorative Arts–Continued

Paintings

Paintings–Continued

Paintings–Continued

Paintings–Continued

Paintings–Continued

Paintings–Continued

Paintings–Continued

Paintings–Continued

Paintings–Continued

Paintings–Continued

Paintings–Continued

Paintings–Continued

Paintings–Continued

Paintings–Continued

Paintings–Continued

Paintings–Continued

Paintings–Continued

Paintings–Continued

Photographs

Photographs–Continued

Photographs–Continued

Photographs–Continued

Photographs–Continued

Photographs–Continued

Photographs–Continued

Photographs–Continued

Photographs–Continued

Photographs–Continued

Photographs–Continued

Photographs–Continued

Photographs–Continued

Photographs–Continued

Photographs–Continued

Photographs–Continued

Photographs–Continued

Photographs–Continued

Photographs–Continued

Photographs–Continued

Photographs–Continued

Photographs–Continued

Photographs–Continued

Photographs–Continued

Photographs–Continued

Photographs–Continued

Prints, Drawings, Graphic Arts

Prints, Drawings, Graphic Arts–Continued

Prints, Drawings, Graphic Arts–Continued

Prints, Drawings, Graphic Arts–Continued

Prints, Drawings, Graphic Arts–Continued

Prints, Drawings, Graphic Arts–Continued

Prints, Drawings, Graphic Arts–Continued

Prints, Drawings, Graphic Arts–Continued

Prints, Drawings, Graphic Arts–Continued

Prints, Drawings, Graphic Arts–Continued

Prints, Drawings, Graphic Arts–Continued

Prints, Drawings, Graphic Arts–Continued

Prints, Drawings, Graphic Arts–Continued

Sculpture

Sculpture–Continued

Sculpture–Continued

Sculpture–Continued

Sculpture–Continued

Sculpture–Continued

Sculpture–Continued

Sculpture–Continued

Sculpture–Continued

HISTORICAL COLLECTIONS

Communication Artifacts

Communication Artifacts–Continued

Communication Artifacts–Continued

Communication Artifacts–Continued

Communication Artifacts–Continued

Communication Artifacts–Continued

Communication Artifacts–Continued

Communication Artifacts–Continued

Communication Artifacts–Continued

Communication Artifacts–Continued

Communication Artifacts–Continued

Distribution and Transportation Artifacts

Distribution and Transportation Artifacts–Continued

Distribution and Transportation Artifacts–Continued

Distribution and Transportation Artifacts–Continued

Distribution and Transportation Artifacts–Continued

Distribution and Transportation Artifacts–Continued

Distribution and Transportation Artifacts–Continued

Distribution and Transportation Artifacts–Continued

Distribution and Transportation Artifacts–Continued

Furnishings

Furnishings–Continued

Furnishings–Continued

Furnishings–Continued

Furnishings–Continued

Furnishings–Continued

Furnishings–Continued

Furnishings–Continued

Furnishings–Continued

Furnishings–Continued

Furnishings–Continued

Furnishings–Continued

Furnishings–Continued

Furnishings–Continued

Furnishings–Continued

Furnishings–Continued

Furnishings–Continued

Furnishings–Continued

Furnishings–Continued

Furnishings–Continued

Personal Artifacts

Personal Artifacts–Continued

Personal Artifacts–Continued

Personal Artifacts–Continued

Personal Artifacts–Continued

Personal Artifacts–Continued

Personal Artifacts–Continued

Personal Artifacts–Continued

Personal Artifacts–Continued

Personal Artifacts–Continued

Personal Artifacts–Continued

Personal Artifacts–Continued

Personal Artifacts–Continued

Personal Artifacts–Continued

Personal Artifacts–Continued

Personal Artifacts–Continued

Personal Artifacts–Continued

Personal Artifacts–Continued

Personal Artifacts–Continued

Personal Artifacts–Continued

Personal Artifacts–Continued

Personal Artifacts–Continued

Personal Artifacts–Continued

Recreational Artifacts

Recreational Artifacts–Continued

Recreational Artifacts–Continued

Recreational Artifacts–Continued

Recreational Artifacts–Continued

Recreational Artifacts–Continued

Recreational Artifacts–Continued

Recreational Artifacts–Continued

Recreational Artifacts–Continued

Recreational Artifacts–Continued

Recreational Artifacts–Continued

Structures

Structures–Continued

Structures–Continued

Structures–Continued

Structures–Continued

Structures–Continued

Structures–Continued

Structures–Continued

Structures–Continued

Structures–Continued

Structures–Continued

Structures–Continued

Structures–Continued

Structures–Continued

Tools and Equipment for Communication

Tools and Equipment for Communication–Continued

Tools and Equipment for Communication–Continued

Tools and Equipment for Communication–Continued

Tools and Equipment for Communication–Continued

Tools and Equipment for Communication–Continued

Tools and Equipment for Communication–Continued

Tools and Equipment for Communication–Continued

Tools and Equipment for Communication–Continued

Tools and Equipment for Communication–Continued

Tools and Equipment for Materials

Tools and Equipment for Materials–Continued

Tools and Equipment for Materials–Continued

Tools and Equipment for Materials–Continued

Tools and Equipment for Materials–Continued

Tools and Equipment for Materials–Continued

Tools and Equipment for Materials–Continued

Tools and Equipment for Materials–Continued

Tools and Equipment for Materials–Continued

Tools and Equipment for Materials–Continued

Tools and Equipment for Materials–Continued

Tools and Equipment for Materials–Continued

Tools and Equipment for Materials–Continued

Tools and Equipment for Materials–Continued

Tools and Equipment for Science and Technology

Tools and Equipment for Science and Technology–Continued

Tools and Equipment for Science and Technology–Continued

Tools and Equipment for Science and Technology–Continued

Tools and Equipment for Science and Technology–Continued

Tools and Equipment for Science and Technology–Continued

Tools and Equipment for Science and Technology–Continued

Tools and Equipment for Science and Technology–Continued

NATURAL COLLECTIONS

Botanical (Living)

Botanical (Living)–Continued

Botanical (Living)–Continued

Botanical (Living)–Continued

Botanical (Living)–Continued

Botanical (Nonliving)

Botanical (Nonliving)–Continued

Botanical (Nonliving)–Continued

Geological

Geological–Continued

Geological–Continued

Geological–Continued

Geological–Continued

Paleontological

Paleontological–Continued

Paleontological–Continued

Zoological (Living)

Zoological (Living)–Continued

Zoological (Living)–Continued

Zoological (Living)–Continued

Zoological (Nonliving)

Zoological (Nonliving)–Continued

Zoological (Nonliving)–Continued

Zoological (Nonliving)–Continued